THE SCHOTTENSTEIN DAF YOMI EDITION

מהדורת דף היומי

The ArtScroll Series®

THE HORN EDITION OF SEDER MOED

מסכת שבת
TRACTATE SHABBOS

THE HORN EDITION OF SEDER MOED

מסכת שבת
TRACTATE SHABBOS

VOLUME IV

Elucidated by
Rabbis Michoel Weiner and Henoch Moshe Levin (chapter 16)
Rabbi Eliezer Herzka (chapter 17)
Rabbi Avrohom Neuberger (chapter 18)
Rabbi Nesanel Kasnett (chapter 19)
Rabbi Asher Dicker (chapters 20,21)
Rabbi Shlomo Fox-Ashrei (chapter 22)
Rabbi Dovid Katz (chapter 23)
Rabbi Henoch Moshe Levin (chapter 24)

R' Hersh Goldwurm זצ"ל
General Editor
תש"נ-תשנ"ג / 1990-1993

under the General Editorship of
Rabbi Yisroel Simcha Schorr
and Rabbi Chaim Malinowitz
in collaboration with a team of Torah Scholars

The Schottenstein Daf Yomi Edition

THE GEMARA: THE CLASSIC VILNA EDITION,
WITH AN ANNOTATED, INTERPRETIVE ELUCIDATION,
AS AN AID TO TALMUD STUDY

The Hebrew folios are reproduced from
the newly typeset and enhanced
Oz Vehadar Edition of the Classic Vilna Talmud

Published by
Mesorah Publications, ltd

We gratefully acknowledge the outstanding
Torah scholars who contributed to this volume:

Rabbi Yisroel Simcha Schorr, Rabbi Chaim Malinowitz,
Rabbi Yitzchok Meir Schorr, and **Rabbi Mordechai Marcus**
who reviewed and commented on the manuscript,
Rabbis Hillel Danziger, Yosef Davis, David Fohrman,
Eliezer Herzka, Nesanel Kasnett, Zev Meisels, Eli Schulman,
Feivel Wahl, Yosaif Asher Weiss, Yirmiyahu Benyowitz, Eliyahu Cohen,
Avi Goldstein, Henoch Moshe Levin, and **Moshe Rosenblum**
who edited, and assisted in the production of this volume.
Rabbi Yehezkel Danziger, Editorial Director

We are also grateful to our proofreaders: Mrs. Judi Dick, Mrs. Mindy Stern, and Mrs. Faigie Weinbaum,
and our typesetters: Mr. Yehuda Gordon, Mrs. Dvory Bick, Miss Toby Brander, Mrs. Estie Dicker, Mrs. Esther Feierstein,
Mrs. Bassie Guttman, Miss Toby Heilbrun, Miss Udi Hershkowitz, Mrs. Chaya Gitty Loevy, and Mrs. Miryam Stavsky

FULL-SIZE EDITION
First Impression . . . January 1997

DAF YOMI EDITION
First Impression . . . March 2004
Second Impression . . . April 2005

Published and Distributed by
MESORAH PUBLICATIONS, Ltd.
4401 Second Avenue
Brooklyn, New York 11232

Distributed in Europe by
LEHMANNS
Unit E, Viking Business Park
Rolling Mill Road
Jarrow, Tyne & Wear NE32 3DP
England

Distributed in Israel by
SIFRIATI / A. GITLER — BOOKS
6 Hayarkon Street
Bnei Brak 51127

Distributed in Australia & New Zealand by
GOLDS WORLD OF JUDAICA
3-13 William Street
Balaclava, Melbourne 3183
Victoria Australia

Distributed in South Africa by
KOLLEL BOOKSHOP
Shop 8A Norwood Hypermarket
Norwood 2196, Johannesburg, South Africa

THE ARTSCROLL SERIES® / SCHOTTENSTEIN DAF YOMI EDITION
TALMUD BAVLI / TRACTATE SHABBOS VOL. IV

ISBN: 1-57819-618-3

Typography by CompuScribe at ArtScroll Studios, Ltd.
Custom bound by **Sefercraft, Inc.,** Brooklyn, N.Y.

A PROJECT OF THE

Mesorah Heritage Foundation

Dedication of the FULL-SIZE EDITION

לעילוי נשמות הורינו היקרים

ר׳ לוי ב״ר יהודה הלוי ע״ה – כ״ג שבט

וצירל בת ר׳ מרדכי ע״ה לוינגר – כ״ז אדר א

ולעילוי נשמות זקנינו היקרים

ר׳ יהודה ב״ר אליעזר צבי הלוי ע״ה – י״ז אלול וטלצא בת פרומט ע״ה לוינגר – ג׳ תשרי

ר׳ מרדכי ב״ר שמואל ע״ה – כ״ד אדר ב׳ ומלכה בת ר׳ נתן ע״ה אדלר – א׳ מרחשון

ולעילוי נשמות אחינו

שמואל ב״ר לוי הלוי ע״ה – ה׳ סיון

יהודה ב״ר לוי הלוי ע״ה – כ״ד אלול

יהונתן ב״ר לוי הלוי הי״ד – ח׳ אדר

ולעילוי נשמת אחותנו

לאה בת ר׳ לוי סג״ל ע״ה – כ״א אייר ובעלה ר׳ טוביה ב״ר שמעון ע״ה

ולעילוי נשמות גיסינו

ר׳ מיכאל ב״ר ברוך שמואל ע״ה שווייצר – כ״ב טבת

והוריו ויוצאי חלוציהם שנהרגו על קידוש השם הי״ד

ר׳ שמואל ב״ר יעקב ע״ה מיכל – כ״ט סיון

ולעילוי נשמות דודינו ודודותינו שנפטרו ושנהרגו על קידוש השם הי״ד

ר׳ יעקב משה ב״ר יהודה ע״ה – י״ט שבט וזוגתו חנה ע״ה – ב׳ אלול

ר׳ בן ציון ב״ר יהודה ע״ה – י״ד כסלו וזוגתו מלכה בת ר׳ מאיר הי״ד – כ״ו סיון

ר׳ גרשון ב״ר יהודה ע״ה – כ׳ אדר וזוגתו בלומה ע״ה – י״ב ניסן ובתם לאה ע״ה ובעלה דוד משולם ע״ה

הב׳ אשר לעמל ב״ר יהודה ע״ה – כ״ה אב

האשה פרומעט בת ר׳ יהודה ע״ה – י״ג מרחשון

האשה לאה בת ר׳ יהודה ובעלה אברהם ב״ר שבתי שטיינהערץ ויוצ״ח הי״ד – י׳ תמוז

ר׳ אליעזר צבי ב״ר אברהם ע״ה – כ״ג אדר וזוגתו ובנם שבתי ובתם הי״ד – י׳ תמוז

ר׳ יצחק ב״ר אברהם הי״ד – כ״ד אדר וזוגתו מלכה ובנם ישראל מנחם ובתם הי״ד – י׳ תמוז

הב׳ אהרן ב״ר אברהם הי״ד – י״ז מרחשון הב׳ מנחם ב״ר אברהם ע״ה – י״ד מרחשון

ר׳ יהודה ב״ר אברהם ע״ה – י״ג מרחשון

ר׳ אברהם ב״ר מרדכי וזוגתו מטל וילדיהם מרדכי, יהודה, יענטל, חוה, ורחל שנהרגו עקה״ש הי״ד – ז׳ ניסן

ונכדם אליעזר ב״ר שמואל – כ״ח כסלו אברהם ב״ר שלמה – ט״ו אייר

ר׳ שמואל נתן ב״ר מרדכי – י״ד מרחשון וזוגתו ייטל – י״ט ניסן ובנם מרדכי שנהרגו עקה״ש הי״ד – י״ד מרחשון

ובנם ר׳ פינחס ע״ה – כ״ב אלול ובנו נתנאל ב״ר פינחס ע״ה – כ״ז טבת

ר׳ יעקב ב״ר מרדכי וזוגתו גאלדע בת חנה הי״ד – י״ג תשרי וילדיהם שנהרגו עקה״ש הי״ד

ר׳ יוסף ב״ר מרדכי הי״ד – י״ג תשרי וזוגתו וילדיהם שנהרגו עקה״ש הי״ד

הב׳ יצחק ב״ר מרדכי ע״ה – ב׳ כסלו

האשה גאלדה בת ר׳ מרדכי הי״ד – כ״א ניסן ובעלה יעקב מיכל – כ״ח אב וילדיהם שנהרגו עקה״ש הי״ד

האשה ביילא בת ר׳ מרדכי ובעלה ר׳ יעקב קליין וילדיהם רחל, יצחק, לאה, רייזל, אליז, מרדכי, יוסף, ואפרים

שנהרגו עקה״ש הי״ד – כ׳ ניסן

האשה חיה שרה בת ר׳ מרדכי – כ׳ ניסן ובעלה עמרם געשטעטנער ע״ה, ובתם עמרה הי״ד – י״א ניסן

הב׳ יהודה ב״ר יעקב ע״ה – י״ז תשרי

נתנדב ע״י

אליעזר צבי הלוי לוינגר

משה יצחק הלוי לוינגר

טלצא שווייצער

גאלדא מיכל

פרומט באלדינגער

בלומעלע לוינגר

Dedication of the DAF YOMI EDITION

This volume is dedicated
in loving memory to our father

Sidney Friedlander ע״ה
סיני בן אריה לייב ע״ה
נפ׳ כ״ח אייר תשס״ג

Integrity and principle were his emblems. There was no such thing as walking away from an obligation or a friend, or standing aside when Jews in Israel were in danger, when Jews in Europe needed sponsors to bring them to freedom and safety, or when people here needed help. When Shabbos was in danger in America, he was its fearless, uncompromising champion.

. . . and to our grandparents

Joseph David and Jennie Trattner ע״ה
יוסף דוד בן משה ע״ה
נפ׳ כ״ו אייר תשי״ח

זיסל בת ישעיהו ע״ה
נפ׳ ר״ח שבט תש״נ

They lived in America at a time when the standard refrain was *"Es iz shver tzu zein a Yid* (It's hard to be a Jew)." To them it wasn't hard. It was good and sweet — the only conceivable way to live. It is impossible to do justice in mere words to their dedication to Shabbos; he commuted for hours every day to a job where he would not be pressured to work on Shabbos.
Paying yeshivah tuition was as important as paying the grocer.
Guests and suffering relatives had first call on food, beds, time, and concern.
But their children never lacked for love and attention.
Their memories and example are as fresh and inspiring as ever.

We pay tribute to our mother

Gussie Friedlander שתחי׳ לאוי״ט

American born and public school-educated, she remained — and remains — uncompromisingly devoted to Torah and mitzvos. She was a living *Shulchan Aruch* of *Kibud Av Va'eim,* in the care she gave her beloved parents. She did the same for her husband. Warm, giving, generous, competent, dedicated — she answers every call for help, and there are many. Like her husband ע״ה, she is devoted to our brothers and sisters in Israel; they are family. May she be blessed with long life, good health, and boundless nachas.

Leonard and Cassia Friedlander
Malkie and Nachum Silberman
Elkie Friedlander

The publishers pay tribute to
the memory of the unforgettable

Jerome Schottenstein ז״ל

whose wisdom, warmth, vision, and generosity wrote new chapters
of Jewish life and learning in America and around the world.
Generations from now, he will be remembered as the one
whose enlightened support made the Talmud accessible
to English-speaking Jews everywhere;

Geraldine Schottenstein תחי׳

who wears her mantle with unusual grace
and firm adherence to the values with which she set
the strong foundation of her family.
She sets a powerful and principled example
for her children and grandchildren.
We are grateful for her support and that of her children:

Jay and Jeanie Schottenstein,
Ann and Ari Deshe,
Susan and Jon Diamond,
and **Lori Schottenstein,**

friends from the start,
as staunch supporters who have been instrumental
in the ten years of the Talmud's success.
They bring energy, devotion, magnanimity, and graciousness
to a host of vital causes
in their native Columbus and throughout the world.

This edition — in a convenient new size
to serve the growing number of people
who are making the Talmud an indispensable part of their lives —
is dedicated by

Jay and Jeanie Schottenstein

and their children

Joseph Aaron, Jonathan Richard, and Jeffrey Adam

They dedicate it in honor of their cherished loved ones
who have left indelible marks on their own lives
and the lives of countless others,
as models of inspiration, generosity, integrity,
and devotion to the noblest causes of Jewish life.

They are:
his parents

Jerome ע"ה and Geraldine Schottenstein

her parents

Leonard and Heddy Rabe

and their uncle and aunt

Saul and Sonia Schottenstein

❧ ❧ ❧

Jay and Jeanie Schottenstein

have a perspective that transcends time and community.
Their names have become synonymous with
imaginative and effective initiatives
to bring Torah study and Jewish tradition to the masses of our people.

Through their magnanimous support of the various editions of

The Schottenstein Talmud

— this Daf Yomi Edition, the Hebrew Edition,
and the original full-size English Edition —
they spread Torah study around the globe and across generations.
Few people have ever had such a positive impact on Jewish life.
Myriads yet unborn will be indebted to them
for their vision and generosity.

PATRONS OF THE TALMUD • DAF YOMI EDITION

With generosity, vision, and devotion to the perpetuation of Torah study,
the following patrons have dedicated individual volumes
of the Daf Yomi Edition of the Talmud

BERACHOS I: In memory of
Jerome Schottenstein ע״ה
יעקב מאיר חיים בן אפרים אליעזר הכהן ע״ה

BERACHOS II: **Zvi and Betty Ryzman**
and their children
Mickey and Shelly Fenig, Aliza, Yissachar David, and Batsheva
Elie and Adina Ryzman, Leora and Yonatan Zev
Avi and Rafi
In memory of
Hagaon Harav Meir Shapiro זצ״ל, the unforgettable Rav of Lublin,
and in honor of
Hagaon Harav Yisrael Meir Lau שליט״א, Chief Rabbi of Israel

SHABBOS I: **Dr. Paul and Esther Rosenstock** **Jake and Dr. Helaine Harman**
Mrs. Faigy Harman
and their children and grandchildren
Nechama Mordechai Binyamin **Michelle Marc**
Yonina and Dov Wisnicki, Avi and Leora
Shira and Shlomie Rosenberg
in memory of our father, husband, and grandfather
מרדכי ב״ר אברהם ע״ה — Mordechai (Mottel) Harman

SHABBOS II: **Stanley and Ellen Wasserman**
and their children
Alan and Svetlana Wasserman Mark and Anne Wasserman
Neil and Yael Wasserman Stuart and Rivka Berger
and families
In loving memory of
בילא בת יעקב ע״ה יוסף בן דוב בער ע״ה — Joseph and Bess Wasserman ע״ה, and
רבקה בת הרב יוסף הכהן ע״ה שמריהו בן משה ע״ה — Sascha and Regina (Czaczkes) Charles ע״ה

SHABBOS III: **Stanley and Ellen Wasserman**
and their children
Alan and Svetlana Wasserman Mark and Anne Wasserman
Neil and Yael Wasserman Stuart and Rivka Berger
and families
in loving memory of
בילא בת יעקב ע״ה יוסף בן דוב בער ע״ה — Joseph and Bess Wasserman ע״ה, and
רבקה בת הרב יוסף הכהן ע״ה שמריהו בן משה ע״ה — Sascha and Regina (Czaczkes) Charles ע״ה

SHABBOS IV: **Malkie and Nachum Silberman**
Leonard and Cassia Friedlander
Elkie Friedlander
in honor of their mother
Gussie Friedlander שתחי׳ לאוי״ט
in memory of their father
ר׳ סיני ב״ר אריה לייב ז״ל — Sidney Friedlander ז״ל
and in memory of their grandparents
ר׳ יוסף דוד ב״ר משה ז״ל וזיסל בת ר׳ ישעיהו ע״ה — Joseph and Jennie Trattner ז״ל

ERUVIN: [two volumes] **Jerome and Geraldine Schottenstein Saul and Sonia Schottenstein**
Jay and Jeanie Schottenstein Ann and Ari Deshe
Susan and Jon Diamond Lori Schottenstein
in memory of
אפרים אליעזר בן יהושע הכהן ע״ה — Ephraim Schottenstein ע״ה
חנה בת צבי הירש ע״ה — Anna Schottenstein ע״ה

PATRONS OF THE TALMUD ◆ DAF YOMI EDITION

PESACHIM I: **Tommy and Judy Rosenthal**
Yitzchok and Tamar **Dani and Michali** **Michal**
in memory of his father
ר׳ יצחק ב״ר יעקב קאפיל ז״ל — Yitzchok Rosenthal
and יבלח״ט in honor of their parents עמו״ש
Magda Rosenthal שתחי׳
and her children שיחי׳
Moshe Yaakov and Beila Jakabovits שיחי׳
and their children שיחי׳

PESACHIM II: **Yisroel and Rochi Zlotowitz**
Gitty, Aaron and Sori
in memory of their beloved grandparents and great grandparents
הרב אהרן ב״ר מאיר יעקב זצ״ל והרבנית פרומא בת ר׳ חיים צבי ע״ה — Zlotowitz
ר׳ חיים חייקל ב״ר שמואל ז״ל וחיה בת הרב ישראל יהודה ע״ה — Schulman
הרב משה יהודה ב״ר יצחק צבי ז״ל ושרה בת הרב שבתי ע״ה — Maybloom
החבר שלום בן שבתי ז״ל וגיטל בת החבר פינחס צבי ע״ה — Goldman

PESACHIM III: **Lorraine and Mordy Sohn** **Ann and Pinky Sohn**
in memory of
ר׳ צבי ב״ר אלעזר ע״ה — Dr. Harry Sohn ע״ה
מרת הענדיל דבורה ב״ר אברהם שלמה ע״ה — Dora F. Sohn ע״ה
ר׳ יחזקאל ב״ר אליקים חנוך הלוי ע״ה — Harold Levine ע״ה
רבקה הענא בת שמעון הלוי ע״ה — Ruth Levine ע״ה
רייזל ב״ר שמשון ע״ה — Rosalie Sohn ע״ה

BEITZAH: **Eric and Joyce Austein**
and their children
Ilana and Avi Lyons **Michael**
Jonathan and Ilana Miriam **Adam and Sara** **Eytan**
in honor of their parents and grandparents שיחי׳
Morris and Susi Austein
Leo and Shirley Schachter

ROSH HASHANAH: **Steve and Genie Savitsky**
and their children and families
Julie and Shabsi Schreier **Avi and Cheryl Savitsky**
Penina and Zvi Wiener **Yehuda and Estie Berman**
In honor of their mothers and grandmothers
Mrs. Hilda Savitsky שתחי׳ Mrs. Amelia Seif שתחי׳
And in honor of their grandparents
Mrs. Faye Raitzik שתחי׳ Max and Edith Grunfeld שתחי׳
לעילוי נשמות — And in loving memory of their grandparents
ר׳ שבתי בן ר׳ מיכאל הלוי ע״ה — Shabsi Raitzik ע״ה
ר׳ אשר זעליג בן ר׳ יהושע הלוי ע״ה רבקה בת ר׳ משה נתן ע״ה — Sigmund and Regina Schreier ע״ה
ר׳ ישראל יצחק בן ר׳ אלימלך הכהן ע״ה גולדה בת ר׳ דוד לייב ע״ה — Irving and Goldie Stein ע״ה
ר׳ שמואל סנדר בן ר׳ אליעזר ליפא ע״ה ריזל זלדה בת ר׳ שלום קלמן ע״ה — Sam and Rose Gottlieb ע״ה
ר׳ צבי הירש בן ר׳ נחום ע״ה חיה שרה גאלדא בת ר׳ יוסף ע״ה — Harry and Goldie Wiener ע״ה
And in loving memory of Cheryl Savitsky's father
ר׳ שמעון פייביש בן ר׳ ישראל יצחק הכהן ע״ה — Dr. Steven F. Stein ע״ה

YOMA I: **Mrs. Ann Makovsky**
Shmulie and Daryle Spero and children
Reuven and Dvora Makovsky and children
Leslie and Linda Spero and children
in memory of
משה דוד בן אברהם אשר ז״ל — Morris Makovsky ז״ל
אברהם אשר בן משה דוד ז״ל ופרומא דבורה בת אלחנן דוב ע״ה — Abraham Osher and Fanny Makovsky ז״ל
גמליאל בן שלמה ז״ל ורבקה בת אברהם חיים ע״ה — Meyer and Riva Nissen ז״ל

PATRONS OF THE TALMUD ◆ DAF YOMI EDITION

YOMA II: **Trudy and David Justin**
and their children
Daniel, Brandel, Nina, Adam and Ayala Justin
in honor of their parents and grandparents
Malka Karp תחי׳
Kitty and Zoltan Justin שיחיו
and in loving memory of
Hersh Karp ז״ל — צבי בן דוב ז״ל

SUCCAH II: **Reuven and Ruth Fasman and Family**
Rudolph and Esther Lowy and Family
Allan and Ettie Lowy and Family
in memory of their parents
Marcus Lowy ז״ל — מרדכי אריה בן ר׳ רפאל הלוי ז״ל
Mina Lowy ע״ה — מינדל בת ר׳ שלמה זלמן ע״ה

TAANIS: **The Bernstein Family**
David and Jean
Matthew Peter
Scott and Andrea Samara Jonah
in memory of
Anna and Harry Bernstein ע״ה
Sarah and Joseph Furman ע״ה

MEGILLAH: In memory of
Jerome Schottenstein ע״ה
יעקב מאיר חיים בן אפרים אליעזר הכהן ע״ה

MOED KATAN: In honor of our beloved parents
Jochanan and Barbara Klein שיחי׳ לאוי״ט (Sao Paulo, Brazil)
by their children
Leon and Olga Klein Allen and Sylvia Klein Daniel and Esther Ollech and Families

CHAGIGAH: **Benzi and Esther Dunner**
in memory of their grandparents
Reb Uri Cohen ז״ל — החבר ר׳ אורי יהודה ז״ל ב״ר אברהם אריה הכהן הי״ד
נפ׳ באמשטרדם כג כסלו תשס״א
Mrs. Rivka Cohen ע״ה — מרת רבקה ע״ה בת ר׳ יצחק הי״ד
נפ׳ באמשטרדם יב מרחשון תשס״א
Reb Moshe Stempel הי״ד — הרה״צ ר׳ משה ב״ר שרגא פייבעל הי״ד
נהרג על קדה״ש ד׳ מנחם אב תש״ב

YEVAMOS I: **Phillip and Ruth Wojdyslawski and Family**
In memory of his beloved parents
Abraham Michel and Ora Wojdyslawski ע״ה
ר׳ אברהם מיכאל ב״ר פינחס ע״ה
אורה בת ר׳ צבי הירש ע״ה

YEVAMOS II: **Phillip and Ruth Wojdyslawski and Family**
In memory of her beloved mother
Chaya (Cytryn) Valt ע״ה
חיה צירל בת ר׳ שלמה זלמן ע״ה

YEVAMOS III: **Phillip and Ruth Wojdyslawski and Family**
In honor of
Benjamin C. Fishoff לאוי״ט
To the public he is a leader with vision and dedication.
To us he has always been a role model, a father,
and a constant inspiration.

KESUBOS I: **The Fishoff Families**
in memory of their beloved mother
מינדל בת ר' ישראל ע"ה – Mrs. Marilyn Fishoff ע"ה
נפ' כד תשרי תשמ"ט
and in memory of their dear grandparents
ר' דוב ב"ר מנחם אשר ע"ה מרת מירל בת ר' מנחם מענדל ע"ה – Fishoff
ר' ישראל ב"ר אברהם ע"ה מרת חיה זיסא בת ר' שרגא פייוועל ע"ה – Neider

KESUBOS II: **Moise Hendeles Hayim and Miriam Hendeles Jerry and Cecille Cohen**
and their families
in memory of their beloved father and grandfather
אליעזר ב"ר משה ז"ל – Lazare Hendeles ז"ל
נפ' כ' ניסן ד' חוה"מ פסח תשס"א
and in honor of their loving mother and grandmother
Mrs. Moselle Hendeles שתחי'

KESUBOS III: **Brenda and Isaac Gozdzik**
Tova Chava Tzeryl Leah
in memory of their beloved parents and grandparents
שרגא פייוועל בן משה הענדעלעס ז"ל – Fred Hendeles ז"ל
נפ' ה' אלול תשס"ג
ביילע בת אליהו הלוי פערשלייסער ע"ה – Betty Hendeles ע"ה
נפ' כ"ו בניסן תשנ"ט

NEDARIM I: **Fradie Rapp**
Raizy, Menachem, Shimshon, Bashie, Tzvi
in memory of their beloved husband and father
הרב ישראל בן יעקב ז"ל – David Rapp ז"ל
נפ' כ' מרחשון תשס"ד

NEDARIM II: In memory of
Laurence A. Tisch
לייבל בן אברהם ע"ה

NAZIR I: **Andrew and Nancy Neff**
Abigail, Esther, Barnet and Philip
in honor of our parents and grandparents
Alan and Joyce Neff
Sidney and Lucy Rabin

NAZIR II: **Andrew and Nancy Neff**
Abigail, Esther, Barnet and Philip
in honor of our brothers and sisters
Garth and Valerie Heald
Lauren Neff
Douglas and Vivian Rabin
Andrew and Liat Rabin

SOTAH: **Motty and Malka Klein and Family**
In memory of
ר' ישעי' נפתלי הירץ ב"ר אהרן ז"ל – Norman Newman

GITTIN I: **Mrs. Kate Tannenbaum**
Elliot and Debra Tannenbaum Edward and Linda Zizmor
and Families
in memory of beloved husband, father and grandfather
ר' נפתלי ב"ר יהודה אריה ע"ה – Fred Tannenbaum ע"ה
נפטר ח' ניסן תשנ"ב

PATRONS OF THE TALMUD ❖ DAF YOMI EDITION

GITTIN II: **Mrs. Kate Tannenbaum**
Elliot and Debra Tannenbaum **Edward and Linda Zizmor and Families**
in memory of beloved husband, father and grandfather
ר׳ נפתלי ב״ר יהודה אריה ע״ה — Fred Tannenbaum ע״ה
נפטר ח׳ ניסן תשנ״ב

KIDDUSHIN I: **Ellis A. and Altoon Safdeye**
in memory of their beloved parents
המנוח יהודה אצלאן ומרת צלחה ויקטוריא ע״ה — Aslan and Victoria Safdeye ע״ה
המנוח יהודה ומרת מרגלית ע״ה — Judah and Margie Sultan ע״ה
and in memory of his brother יוסף ע״ה — Joseph Safdeye ע״ה

KIDDUSHIN II: **Malcolm and Joy Lyons**
in loving memory of her father
זיסל בן אברהם דוד ז״ל — Cecil Jacobs ז״ל
and in honour of their parents שיחי׳
Leo and Eve Lyons
Mona Jacobs

BAVA KAMMA I: **Yitzchok and Shoshana Ganger**
in honor of their children and grandchildren
Aviva and Moshe Sigler
Aliza Saul Chani
Ilana and Menachem Ostreicher
Dov Ber Miriam Binyomin Paltiel Daniella
Dovid and Penina Ganger
Yosef Yaakov Gavriel Moshe Ettie
and in memory of their fathers
ר׳ יוסף יעקב ב״ר יצחק ישעיהו ע״ה — Joseph Ganger ע״ה
נפטר טז כסלו תשנ״ו
הרב אריה ליב ב״ר מתתיהו ע״ה — Rabbi Aria Leib Newman ע״ה
נפטר כח ניסן תשס״ד

BAVA KAMMA II: **The Magid Families** (Sao Paulo, Brazil)
לעילוי נשמת — in memory of their dear husband and father
ר׳ אברהם יהודה אביר בן ר׳ יהושע ז״ל — R' Abir Magid ז״ל
נלב״ע כ״ו אדר תשמ״ב
ולעילוי נשמות — and in memory of
ר׳ יהושע ב״ר צבי חיים ז״ל וזוגתו מרת שרה פייגא בת ר׳ ישׂשכר דוב ע״ה
ר׳ יעקב ישראל ב״ר מרדכי ז״ל וזוגתו מרת אסתר פרומה בת ר׳ חיים ע״ה

BAVA KAMMA III: **Robert and Malka Friedlander** (Sao Paulo, Brazil)
Debby, David and Daniel
in memory of their fathers and grandfathers
הרב ישראל יעקב ב״ר יצחק מאיר ז״ל — Rabbi Israel Jacob Weisberger ז״ל
הרב נפתלי צבי נח ב״ר יהודה לייביש ז״ל — Rabbi Bela Friedlander ז״ל

BAVA METZIA I: **Drs. Robert and Susan Schulman** **Howard and Tzila Schulman**
Fred and Cindy Schulman
in honor of our beloved parents
Molly Schulman
Stanley and Ruth Beck
Mrs. Sylvia Kuhr
Naftali and Berta Rendel

BAVA METZIA II: **Suzy and Yussie Ostreicher and Ricki** **Ilana and Menachem Ostreicher**
Miriam and Dovid Ostreicher **Shayna and Yitzchok Steg**
in honor of our parents and grandparents
Michael and Rose Pollack
Hershi and Helly Ostreicher

PATRONS OF THE TALMUD ❖ DAF YOMI EDITION

BAVA METZIA III: **Stephanie and George Saks**
in memory of
The Gluck Family
זאב בן דוד צבי ע״ה ואסתר בת אשר זעליג ע״ה – Zev and Esther Gluck ע״ה
ליבא, אשר זעליג, דוד צבי, שמואל, מנשה, יחזקאל שרגא ע״ה –
Lee, George, David H., Samuel C., Emanuel M., Henry ע״ה, and
in memory of their parents and grandparents
פייוועל בן אליה ע״ה ומלכה בת אברהם ע״ה – Philip and Mildred Pines ע״ה
יעקב יצחק בן זאב ע״ה ומיימי בת זאב ע״ה – Dr. Jack I. and Mrs. Mae Saks ע״ה
זאב בן חיים דוד ע״ה וחיה ביילע בת יצחק יעקב ע״ה – Wolf and Chaye Beilah Saks ע״ה
and in memory of
יחיאל בן משה ע״ה – Elie Neustadter ע״ה

BAVA BASRA I: **Nachum and Malkie Silberman**
in memory of his parents
ר׳ צבי ב״ר זאב הלוי ז״ל דבורה אסתר בת ר׳ ישראל ע״ה – Silberman
his paternal grandparents and their children who perished על קידוש השם in the Holocaust
ר׳ זאב ב״ר משה הלוי ז״ל הי״ד גיטל בת ר׳ אפרים אלימלך הכהן ע״ה הי״ד – Silberman
ובנותיהם רחל, לאה, ומרים ע״ה הי״ד
and his maternal grandparents
ר׳ ישראל ב״ר לוי משה ז״ל שיינדל רחל בת ר׳ יעקב ע״ה – Weitman

BAVA BASRA II: **Roger and Caroline Markfield**
and their children
Eric and **Maxine**
in memory of his parents
מרדכי ב״ר נתנאל ואודל בת ר׳ מאיר דוד ז״ל – Max and Eileen Markfield ז״ל
and his sister
זיסל ע״ה – Lynn Herzel ע״ה

BAVA BASRA III: **Jaime and Marilyn Sohacheski**
in honor of their children
Jasmine and David Brafman and their baby **Shlomo Zalman**
Melisa and her chatan Jonathan Beck
Lindsay and Bennett

SANHEDRIN I: **Martin and Rivka Rapaport**
and their children
Mordechai Ezriel Yehuda Aryeh Miriam Dreizel Shimshon
Leah Penina Eliyahu Meir Bracha
in memory of
ר׳ יהודה אריה ב״ר מרדכי הכהן ז״ל – Leo Rapaport ז״ל

SANHEDRIN II: **Martin and Rivka Rapaport**
and their children
Mordechai Ezriel Yehuda Aryeh Miriam Dreizel Shimshon
Leah Penina Eliyahu Meir Bracha
in memory of
ר׳ ישראל דוב ב״ר מרדכי ז״ל – Albert Berger ז״ל
חנה גיטל בת ר׳ עזריאל ע״ה – Chana Gittel Berger ע״ה

SANHEDRIN III: **Marvin and Roz Samuels**
in memory of
ר׳ צבי יוסף ב״ר יצחק ז״ל – Joseph Samuels ז״ל
רחל בת ר׳ זכריה מנחם ע״ה – Rose Samuels ע״ה
of Scranton, PA
בנימין נח ב״ר ישראל הלוי ז״ל – Norman Newman ז״ל
אלטא ביילא ראשקה בת נחמן הלוי ע״ה – Ruth Newman ע״ה

PATRONS OF THE TALMUD • DAF YOMI EDITION

SHEVUOS: **Michael and Danielle Gross** (Herzlia and London)
in loving memory of their fathers
Paul Gross — פסח בן צבי הלוי ע״ה
David Beissah — דוד בן נתן ע״ה

MAKKOS: **The Tepper Families**
Beth and Yisroel Rabinowitz **Jay and Sari Tepper**
Hope and Moshe Abramson **Neil and Leah Tepper**
and children
in honor of their parents
David and Joan Tepper
and in memory of their grandparents
Tepper — ר׳ מנחם מענדל ב״ר יעקב ז״ל ומרת מינדל בת ר׳ אריה ליב ע״ה
Gralla — ר׳ ראובן ב״ר נחמיה ז״ל ומרת עטיל בת ר׳ ישראל נתן נטע ע״ה

AVODAH ZARAH I: **The Kuhl Family**
in memory of
Dr. Julius Kuhl ע״ה יחיאל ב״ר יצחק אייזיק ע״ה
Mrs. Yvonne Kuhl ע״ה פרומט בת ר׳ שמואל הלוי ע״ה
Sydney Kuhl ע״ה שמואל ב״ר יחיאל ע״ה

AVODAH ZARAH II: In memory of
Jerome Schottenstein ע״ה
יעקב מאיר חיים בן אפרים אליעזר הכהן ע״ה

HORAYOS-EDUYOS: **Woli and Chaja Stern** (Sao Paulo, Brazil)
in honor of their children
Jacques and Ariane Stern Jaime and Ariela Landau Michäel and Annete Kierszenbaum

ZEVACHIM I: **Robin and Warren Shimoff**
in memory of his parents
Irving Shimoff ז״ל — ישראל דוב ב״ר אהרן יעקב ז״ל
Lynn Shimoff ע״ה — חיה רבקה לאה בת ר׳ אליעזר יהודה ע״ה
and יבלח״ט in honor of their children שיחיו
Lael Atara Alexander Ariana

ZEVACHIM II: **Abbie Spetner**
Ari and Chaya **Sara and Dovi Nussbaum** **Chanoch** **Moshe**
Rivkah Dinah **Moshe Yosef**
in honor of their father and grandfather
Kenneth Spetner שיחיי לאוי״ט
and in memory of their mother and grandmother
Rita Spetner ע״ה — רבקה דינה בת ר׳ משה יעקב ע״ה
נפ׳ ד׳ ניסן תשס״ב

ZEVACHIM III: **Yaakov and Yona Spinner**
Dovi **Elisheva** **Yitzy** **Shiri** **Leora**
in memory of their father and grandfather
Ephraim Spinner ז״ל — אפרים יצחק ב״ר אברהם ז״ל
נפ׳ י״ז שבט תשנ״ז
and in memory of their grandparents and great-grandparents
משה יודה בן דוד ע״ה רחל בת חיים דוד יהודה הכהן ע״ה
אברהם בן יוסף משה ע״ה צירל בת אברהם אליהו ע״ה
משה שלמה בן יעקב ע״ה רבקה בת משה ע״ה

MENACHOS I: **Terumah Foundation**

MENACHOS II: **Terumah Foundation**

MENACHOS III: **Terumah Foundation**

PATRONS OF THE TALMUD ❖ DAF YOMI EDITION

CHULLIN I: **Rabbi Heshie and Rookie Billet**

in honor of their mothers Mrs. Pearl Billet and Mrs. Phyllis Katz

their children Daniel and Hadassa Jacobson David Billet

Avraham and Chana Billet Moshe Billet Shira Billet Nava Billet

their grandchildren Tehila, Aharon, and Yehuda Jacobson

and in memory of their fathers

Arthur Katz ז״ל — ר׳ אהרן ב״ר יצחק הכהן כ״ץ ז״ל

Jack Billet ז״ל — ר׳ יהודה יעקב ב״ר אברהם ז״ל

their daughter Miriam Rus ע״ה — מרים רות ע״ה

their granddaughter Eliana Sara ע״ה — אליענה שרה ע״ה

CHULLIN II: **Elly and Brochie Kleinman**

and their children **Deenie and Yitzy Schuss** **Yossie and Blimi Kleinman**

Aliza and Lavey Freedman and families

לעילוי נשמות their fathers

Avrohom Kleinman ז״ל — ר׳ אברהם אייזיק ב״ר אלכסנדר ז״ל

Mendel Indig ז״ל — ר׳ מנחם דוד ב״ר מרדכי שמואל ז״ל

his grandparents שנהרגו על קידוש השם

Kleinman (Weiss) — ר׳ אלכסנדר ב״ר צבי אריה ז״ל ומרת סימא לאה בת ר׳ אברהם ע״ה – הי״ד

Fischman — הרב אלימלך ב״ר ישראל ז״ל ומרת יוטא ברכה בת ר׳ אברהם ע״ה – הי״ד

her grandparents

Indig — ר׳ מרדכי שמואל ב״ר יוסף יעקב ז״ל שנהרג על קדה״ש הי״ד ומרת פרידה בת ר׳ מרדכי אריה ע״ה

Solomon — ר׳ יעקב ב״ר שאול ז״ל ומרת חיה בת ר׳ יעקב ע״ה

and יבלח״ט in honor of their mothers

Mrs. Ethel Kleinman שתחי׳ Mrs. Rose Indig שתחי׳

CHULLIN III: **Members of the International Board of Governors of the Mesorah Heritage Foundation**

as a source of merit for all our brethren wherever they are

CHULLIN IV: **Terumah Foundation**

BECHOROS I: **Jeff and Leslie Gould** **Jody and Sheldon Hirst**

Rachel Jacob **Marci Tracy**

in memory of their father

Rubin Gould ע״ה — ראובן בן יוסף ע״ה

BECHOROS II: **Hilda and Yitz Applbaum**

in honor of their children

Aaron Jacob Ariel Tsvi Miriam Gabriella Zahava

and in memory of their deceased parents

Aaron and Miriam Goetz ע״ה — אהרן ב״ר יהודה לייב ז״ל ומרים בת ר׳ מנחם מענדל ע״ה

Tova Gertrude Applbaum ע״ה — טובה גיטל בת ר׳ אברהם יהושע העשיל ע״ה

ARACHIN: **The Brown Family**

in memory of

Bernard and Tillie Tublin ז״ל — בעריש דוב בן מרדכי אליהו ז״ל וטובא בת אברהם ע״ה

Abraham and Mae Tublin ז״ל — אברהם בן בעריש דוב ז״ל ומייטא בת ישראל ע״ה

Neil Tublin ז״ל — נחום בן אברהם ז״ל

Harry and Molly Brown ז״ל

Beatrice Geller ע״ה

Sophie Noble Scherr ע״ה

PATRONS OF THE TALMUD • DAF YOMI EDITION

TEMURAH: **Dr. Thomas and Anne Kohn** and their children

Dennis and Chayie Kohn **Yitzy and Dina Gunsburg** **Yaakov and Aviva Eisenberger**

Dr. Allan and Susan Seidenfeld and their children

Mordechai and Shaindy **Aaron and Dassi** **Dov and Chanala**

Yosef and Ahuva **Ahuva Libe** **Eliezer Chaim Yitzchok**

in honour of Eugene and Eva Kohn

in memory of מינדל בת חיים ע״ה (נפ׳ כ״ה אדר ב׳ תשס״ג) — Vera Rubinstein ע״ה

in honour of Daniel Rubinstein

in memory of חיה מירל בת אברהם ע״ה (נפ׳ כ״ה מרחשון תש״ס) — Margit Seidenfeld ע״ה

in honour of Salomon Seidenfeld

KEREISOS: לעילוי נשמת

מיסד ורוח החיים של רעיון הדף יומי

הגאון הרב ר׳ מאיר ב״ר יעקב שמשון שפירא זצ״ל

נפ׳ ז׳ חשון תרצ״ד

In memory of

Rabbi Meir Shapiro זצ״ל, the Lubliner Rav

whose revolutionary Daf Yomi initiative grows day by day.

ME'ILAH, TAMID, MIDDOS, KINNIM: **Steven and Renée Adelsberg**

Sarita and Rubin Gober **David** **Sammy** **Avi**

in loving memory of

שמואל שמעלקא ב״ר גדליה ז״ל — Samuel Adelsberg ז״ל

and יבלח״ט in honor of

Helen Adelsberg Weinberg שתחי׳

and

Chaim and Rose Fraiman שיחי׳

NIDDAH I: In memory of

Joseph and Eva Hurwitz ע״ה

יוסף ב״ר מרדכי הלוי וחוה פיגא ב״ר אליעזר הלוי ע״ה

and

Lorraine Hurwitz Greenblott — לאה בילא חיה בת ר׳ יוסף ע״ה

by

Marc and Rachel Hurwitz,
Elisheva Ruchama, Michal, and Nechama Leah;

Martin and Geraldine Schottenstein Hoffman,
Jay and Jeanie Schottenstein, Ann and Ari Deshe,
Susan and Jon Diamond, and Lori Schottenstein;

and Pam and Neil Lazaroff, Frank Millman, and Dawn and Avi Petel

NIDDAH II: In memory of

Jerome Schottenstein ע״ה

יעקב מאיר חיים בן אפרים אליעזר הכהן ע״ה

The Schottenstein Edition of the Talmud

This pioneering elucidation of the entire Talmud was named THE SCHOTTENSTEIN EDITION in memory of EPHRAIM AND ANNA SCHOTTENSTEIN ז״ל, of Columbus, Ohio. Mr. and Mrs. Schottenstein came to the United States as children, but they never surrendered the principles of Judaism or the love of Torah that they had absorbed in their native Lithuania. Tenacious was their devotion to the Sabbath, kashruth, and halachah; their support of needy Jews in a private, sensitive manner; their generosity to Torah institutions; and their refusal to speak ill of others.

They never surrendered the principles of Judaism or the love of Torah that they had absorbed in Lithuania.

This noble and historic gesture of dedication was made by their sons and daughters-in-law JEROME ז״ל AND GERALDINE SCHOTTENSTEIN and SAUL AND SONIA SCHOTTENSTEIN.

With the untimely passing of JEROME SCHOTTENSTEIN ז״ל, it became our sad privilege to rededicate THE SCHOTTENSTEIN EDITION to his memory, in addition to that of his parents.

Jerome left numerous memorials of accomplishment and generosity, but surely the Schottenstein Edition of the Talmud — spanning centuries — will be the most enduring.

Jerome Schottenstein ז״ל was a dear friend and inspirational patron. He saw the world through the lens of eternity, and devoted his mind, heart and resources to the task of assuring that the Torah would never be forgotten by its people. He left numerous memorials of accomplishment and generosity, but surely the SCHOTTENSTEIN EDITION OF THE TALMUD — spanning centuries — will be the most enduring.

The Schottensteins are worthy heirs to the traditions and principles of Jerome and his parents. Gracious and generous, kind and caring, they have opened their hearts to countless causes and people.

The Schottensteins are worthy heirs to the traditions and principles of Jerome and his parents. Gracious and generous, kind and caring, they have opened their hearts to countless causes and people. Quietly and considerately, they elevate the dignity and self-respect of those they help; they make their beneficiaries feel like benefactors; they imbue institutions with a new sense of mission to be worthy of the trust placed in them.

THE MESORAH HERITAGE FOUNDATION is proud and grateful to be joined with the Schottenstein family as partners in this monumental endeavor.

We pray that this great undertaking will be a source of merit for the continued health and success of the entire Schottenstein family, including the children and grandchildren:

JAY and JEANIE SCHOTTENSTEIN and their children, Joseph Aaron, Jonathan Richard, and Jeffrey Adam; ANN and ARI DESHE and their children, Elie Michael, David Scott, Dara Lauren, and Daniel Matthew; SUSAN and JON DIAMOND and their children, Jillian Leigh, Joshua Louis, and Jacob Meyer; and LORI SCHOTTENSTEIN.

The Schottensteins will be remembered with gratitude for as long as English-speaking Jews are nourished by the eternity of the Talmud's wisdom, for, thanks to them, millions of Jews over the generations will become closer to their heritage.

A Jew can accomplish nothing more meaningful or lasting in his sojourn on earth.

is reverently dedicated to the memory of
the patron of this Talmud
and of countless other noble causes in Jewish life

יעקב מאיר חיים בן אפרים אליעזר הכהן ע״ה

נפטר ה׳ אדר ב׳ תשנ״ב

Jerome Schottenstein ע״ה

and to the memory of his parents

אפרים אליעזר בן יהושע הכהן ע״ה

נפטר ב׳ אייר תשט״ז

חנה בת צבי הירש ע״ה

נפטרה ט״ו מנחם אב תשט״ו

Ephraim and Anna Schottenstein ע״ה

by

Geraldine Schottenstein

Saul and Sonia Schottenstein

and

Jay and Jeanie Schottenstein

and their children
Joseph Aaron, Jonathan Richard, Jeffrey Adam

Ann and Ari Deshe

and their children
Elie Michael, David Scott, Dara Lauren, Daniel Matthew

Susan and Jon Diamond

and their children
Jillian Leigh, Joshua Louis, Jacob Meyer

and

Lori Schottenstein

PATRONS OF THE SEDARIM

Recognizing the need for the holy legacy of the Talmud
to be available to its heirs in their own language,
these generous and visionary patrons have each dedicated
one of the six Sedarim/Orders of the Talmud.

THE FORMAN EDITION OF SEDER ZERAIM

is lovingly dedicated by

Mr. and Mrs. Sam Forman, Brett and Wendy

in memory of their beloved parents and grandparents

Mr. and Mrs. George Forman ע״ה **Dr. and Mrs. Morey Chapman ע״ה**

THE HORN EDITION OF SEDER MOED

is lovingly dedicated to the memory of

ר׳ משה מניס ב״ר יעקב יצחק ע״ה — Moishe Horn ע״ה

נפטר ב׳ מנחם אב תשנ״ד

by his wife **Malkie**

his parents **Jacob ע״ה and Genia Horn שתחי׳**

and her children

Shimmie and Alissa
Ari Shana Michal Tali

Devorah and Dov Elias
Moishe Ariella Eli Chaviva

Shandi and Sruli Glaser
Ruthi Jack Miri

THE ELLIS A. SAFDEYE EDITION OF SEDER NASHIM

is reverently dedicated to the memory of

המנוח יהודה אצלאן ומרת צלחה ויקטוריא ע״ה

Aslan and Victoria Safdeye ע״ה

and

המנוח יהודה ומרת מרגלית ע״ה

Judah and Margie Sultan ע״ה

by their children

Ellis A. and Altoon Safdeye

and grandchildren

Alan Judah and Rachel Safdeye
Ezra and Victoria Esses

Joseph and Rochelle Safdeye
Michael and Bobbi Safdeye

PATRONS OF THE SEDARIM

THE DAVIDOWITZ FAMILY
RENOV STAHLER ROSENWALD PERLYSKY EDITION OF SEDER NEZIKIN

is lovingly dedicated to

Rozi and Morty Davis-Davidowitz

builders of this dynasty

by their children and grandchildren

Esti and Ushi Stahler

Jamie, Danny, Duvi, Lisi, Avi, Eli, Malka and Loni

Rivki and Lindsay Rosenwald

Doni, Joshy, Demi, Davey and Tamar Rina

Ruki and Kal Renov

Tova, Tani, Eli, Ari, Yoni, Yael, Emi and Benji

Laya and Dov Perlysky

Ayala Malka, Tova Batsheva, Naftali Yonatan, Atara Yael, Eitan Moshe, Shira Avital and Akiva Yair

and is lovingly dedicated to the memory of our grandparents

Emily and Nathan Selengut ע״ה

נפתלי ב״ר יעקב ע״ה ומלכה בת ר׳ אלתר חיים ע״ה

THE SCHWARTZ EDITION OF SEDER KODASHIM

is lovingly dedicated by

Avrohom Yeshaya and Sally Schwartz

and their children

Ari, Moshe, Dani, and Dovi

in memory of their beloved parents and grandparents

ר׳ יצחק ב״ר אשר ז״ל וחיה רבקה בת הרב בצלאל הירש ז״ל — Isaac and Rebecca Jarnicki ז״ל

נפ׳ יג׳ תמוז תשנ״ז   נפ׳ ג׳ אדר תשס״ד

and their beloved grandmother

פערל בת ר׳ מרדכי ע״ה — Mrs. Pearl Septytor ע״ה

and in honor of יבלח״ט their parents and grandparents

Rabbi and Mrs. Gedalia Dov Schwartz שליט״א

and in memory of our grandparents

Rabbi Eliezer and Pesha Chaya Poupko ז״ל   **Abraham Schwartz ז״ל**

Betzalel Hersh and Hendel Berliner ז״ל   **Asher and Gittel Jarnicki ז״ל**

PATRONS OF THE TALMUD • FULL-SIZE EDITION

With generosity, vision, and devotion to the perpetuation of Torah study, the following patrons have dedicated individual volumes of the Talmud

Reference/ Introduction: **George and Vita Kolber**
In loving memory of
Joseph and Frieda Hirschfeld ע״ה

BERACHOS I: In memory of
Jerome Schottenstein ע״ה
יעקב מאיר חיים בן אפרים אליעזר הכהן ע״ה

BERACHOS II: **Zvi and Betty Ryzman**
in honor of their children שיחיו
Mickey and Shelly Fenig — Aliza, Yissachar David, Batsheva and Aharon Yakov
Elie and Adina Ryzman — Leora and Yonatan Zev
Avi Rafi

Malcolm and Joy Lyons
in honour of their parents שיחיו
Eve Lyons
Cecil and Mona Jacobs
and in memory of his father
Leopold Lyons ע״ה — יהודה בן גרשון ע״ה נפ׳ כ״ב שבט תשס״ג

SHABBOS I: **Nachshon and Bruria Minucha [Nuchi] Draiman and Family**
in memory of
הר״ר יהודה ליב מנדלקורן זצ״ל בן הר״ר צבי הי״ו
Rabbi Yehuda Leib Mandelcorn זצ״ל — נפטר כ׳ תמוז, תשנ״ג

SHABBOS II: **David and Bonnie Anfang** **Chaim and Ruthie Anfang**
Rachel, Julie and Elliot **Ariella Hope** **Michael Brett**
In loving memory of
Leib Anfang ע״ה — ר׳ אריה ליב ב״ר דוד אביגדור ע״ה
Barbara Anfang ע״ה — בשה לאה בת ר׳ אלימלך דוב ע״ה

Mimi and Steven Rosenbaum **Joseph and Sharon Prawer** **Alan and Louisa Prawer**
Stacey and Danny **Dena, Dovid, Alana, Naomi** **Ruben Pinchas**
In loving memory of
Pinkus and Genia Prawer ע״ה, and — ר׳ פנחס ב״ר יוסף ברוך הלוי ע״ה גילה בת אשר יונה ע״ה
Sarah Cukierman ע״ה — שרה בת שמעון ליב ע״ה

A Hebrew edition of the Talmud Bavli is now in progress.
The Hebrew edition is dedicated by

Jay and Jeanie Schottenstein

and their children

Joseph Aaron, Jonathan Richard, and Jeffrey Adam

— in honor of their cherished loved ones who have left indelible marks on their own lives and the lives of countless others, as models of inspiration, generosity, integrity, and devotion to the noblest causes in Jewish life:
his parents **JEROME ז״ל AND GERALDINE SCHOTTENSTEIN**,
her parents **LEONARD AND HEDDY RABE**
and **SAUL AND SONIA SCHOTTENSTEIN**

❦ ❦ ❦

JAY AND JEANIE SCHOTTENSTEIN
have a perspective that transcends time and community.
Through their dedication of these editions of the Talmud, they spread Torah study around the globe and across generations.
Multitudes yet unborn will be indebted to them for their vision and generosity.

PATRONS OF THE TALMUD ❖ FULL-SIZE EDITION

SHABBOS II: [continued]
Rabbi Eliyahu and Yehudit Fishman
Rivka and Zvi Silberstein and Leah **Akiva Yitzchak Fishman**
Rabbi Yechiel Meir and Chagit Fishman **Rabbi Yosef and Aliza Fishman**
Talia Chanah, Ariel Yishai and Daniel
In loving memory of
ר׳ יוסף ב״ר טוביה ע״ה רודע רבקה בת ר׳ הירש מאיר ע״ה — Yosef and Rude Rivka Fishman ע״ה
and their children Yechiel Meir, Leah and Chanah הי״ד who perished in the Holocaust

SHABBOS III: **Stanley and Ellen Wasserman**
and their children
Alan and Svetlana Wasserman **Mark and Anne Wasserman**
Neil and Yael Wasserman **Stuart and Rivka Berger**
and families
In loving memory of
יוסף בן דוב בער ע״ה בילא בת יעקב ע״ה — Joseph and Bess Wasserman ע״ה, and
שמריהו בן משה ע״ה רבקה בת הרב יוסף הכהן ע״ה — Sascha and Regina (Czaczkes) Charles ע״ה

SHABBOS IV: לעילוי נשמות
הורינו היקרים **ר׳ לוי ב״ר יהודה הלוי ע״ה וצירל בת ר׳ מרדכי ע״ה לוינגר**
זקנינו היקרים **ר׳ יהודה ב״ר אליעזר צבי הלוי ע״ה וטלצא בת פרומט ע״ה לוינגר**
ר׳ מרדכי ב״ר שמואל ע״ה ומלכה בת ר׳ נתן ע״ה אדלר
אחינו **שמואל הלוי ע״ה יהודה הלוי ע״ה יהונתן הלוי הי״ד**
אחותנו **לאה בת ר׳ לוי סג״ל ע״ה ובעלה ר׳ טוביה ע״ה**
גיסינו **ר׳ מיכאל ב״ר ברוך שמואל ע״ה שוויצר ר׳ שמואל ב״ר יעקב ע״ה מיכל**
ולעילוי נשמות דודינו ודודותינו ויוצאי חלוציהם שנפטרו ושנהרגו על קידוש השם הי״ד
Dedicated by **Louis and Morris Lowinger**
Teri Schweitzer **Kato Michel** **Margit Baldinger** **Eva Lowinger**

ERUVIN: [two volumes]
Jerome and Geraldine Schottenstein **Saul and Sonia Schottenstein**
Jay and Jeanie Schottenstein **Ann and Ari Deshe**
Susan and Jon Diamond **Lori Schottenstein**
in memory of
אפרים אליעזר בן יהושע הכהן ע״ה — Ephraim Schottenstein ע״ה
חנה בת צבי הירש ע״ה — Anna Schottenstein ע״ה

PESACHIM I: **Vera and Soli Spira and Family**
in memory of
ברוך בן חיים ע״ה — Baruch Spira ע״ה
בילה בת נתן שלום ע״ה — Bella Spira ע״ה
שמואל בן אברהם ע״ה — Shmuel Lebovits ע״ה
and their respective families הי״ד who perished in the Holocaust
and in honor of
שפרה בת משה — Caroline Lebovits תחי׳

The Edmond J. Safra Edition of the Talmud Bavli in French,
adapted from the Schottenstein Edition, is now in progress.

The Edmond J. Safra Edition
is dedicated by
Lily Safra
in memory of her beloved husband
Edmond J. Safra רפאל אדמון עזרא בן אסתר ע״ה

His desire is in the Torah of HASHEM, and in His Torah he meditates day and night.
He shall be like a tree deeply rooted alongside brooks of water;
that yields its fruit in due season, and whose leaf never withers,
and everything that he does will succeed (Psalms 1:2-3).

PATRONS OF THE TALMUD ❖ FULL-SIZE EDITION

PESACHIM II: **Vera and Soli Spira and Family**
in memory of an uncle who was like a father
and a cousin who was like a brother
ישראל בן נתן שלום ע״ה — Israel Stern ע״ה
נתן שלום בן ישראל ע״ה — Noussi Stern ע״ה

PESACHIM III: **Lorraine and Mordy Sohn** **Ann and Pinky Sohn**
in memory of
ר׳ צבי ב״ר אלעזר ע״ה — Dr. Harry Sohn ע״ה
מרת הענדיל דבורה ב״ר אברהם שלמה ע״ה — Dora F. Sohn ע״ה
ר׳ יחזקאל ב״ר אליקים חנוך הלוי ע״ה — Harold Levine ע״ה
רבקה הענא בת שמעון הלוי ע״ה — Ruth Levine ע״ה
רייזל ב״ר שמשון ע״ה — Rosalie Sohn ע״ה

SHEKALIM: In loving memory of
Mr. Maurice Lowinger ז״ל
ר׳ מאיר משה ב״ר בן ציון הלוי ז״ל
נפ׳ כ״ז אדר תשס״א

YOMA I: **A. Joseph and Rochelle Stern**
Moshe Dov, Zev, Shani, Esty, and Shaye
in honor of their parents and grandparents
Eli and Frieda Stern שיחיו
Frida Weiss שתחי׳
and in memory of
ר׳ ישעי׳ בן ר׳ ישראל שמואל ווייס ז״ל

YOMA II: **A. Leibish and Edith Elbogen and Family**
לזכר נשמות
מוה״ר אהרן בן מוה״ר יעקב קאפל עלבוגן ז״ל
וזו׳ אלטע חנה חיה מלכה בת מוה״ר חיים יצחק מאיר ע״ה
אחותי פערל עם בעלה ושבע בנים ובנות
ושלשה אחי: חיים יצחק מאיר, משה יוסף, יעקב קאפל הי״ד
בני אהרן עלבוגן שנהרגו עקד״ה
מוה״ר נתן פייטל בן מוה״ר אברהם וואלד ז״ל
וזו׳ ברכה בת מוה״ר דוד יהודה הי״ד שנאספה עקד״ה באושוויץ

SUCCAH I: **Howard and Roslyn Zuckerman** **Steven and Shellie Zuckerman**
Leo and Rochelle Goldberg
in memory of their parents
ר׳ פסח יהודה ב״ר יצחק אייזיק ע״ה וחוה בת ר׳ יהודה לייב ע״ה — Philip and Evelyn Zuckerman ע״ה

in honor of their children
Yisroel and Shoshana Pesi Zuckerman שיחי׳
Pesach Yehudah and Asher Anshel שיחי׳
Michael (Ezra) and Lauren Zuckerman שיחי׳
Adrianne & Shawn Meller, Elliot, & Joshua Goldberg שיחי׳

in honor of their children
Glenn and Heidi, Jamie Elle, Benjamin,
Brett and Robin, Brandon Noah, Ross and T.J. שיחי׳
and in honor of their parents
Marilyn and Aaron Feinerman שיחי׳

in memory of
ר׳ ישראל צבי ב״ר ברוך ע״ה ושיינדל בת ר׳ ישראל ע״ה — Israel and Shaindel Ray ע״ה
and in memory of Mrs. Rose Ray (Glass) ע״ה

Arthur and Randi Luxenberg
in honor of their parents
Irwin and Joan Luxenberg שיחי׳ Bernard and Evelyn Beeber שיחי׳
their children Elizabeth Jewel and Jacqueline Paige שיחי׳
in memory of his grandparents
ר׳ אברהם בן אהרן מרדכי ז״ל ורחל בת ר׳ משה ע״ה — Abraham and Rose Luxenberg ע״ה
ישעיהו צבי בן הרב טוביה ז״ל ושרה צירל בת ר׳ יעקב ע״ה — Jesse and Celia Aronson ע״ה

PATRONS OF THE TALMUD ❖ FULL-SIZE EDITION

SUCCAH II: **Thomas and Lea Schottenstein** **William and Amy Schottenstein**
in memory of
אריה ליב בן אפרים אליעזר הכהן ע״ה — Leon Schottenstein ע״ה
מאיר אבנר בן דוד הלוי ע״ה — Meir Avner Levy ע״ה
and in honor of
Mrs. Jean S. Schottenstein שתחי׳ Bertram and Corinne Natelson שיחי׳
Mrs. Flory Levy שתחי׳

BEITZAH: **Paul and Suzanne Peyser** **Irwin and Bea Peyser**
in memory of
פריידע רייזעל בת יהושע ע״ה דוד בן פינחס ע״ה — David and Rose Peyser ע״ה

ROSH HASHANAH: **Steve and Genie Savitsky** **David and Roslyn Savitsky**
In memory of
יואל בן אברהם ע״ה — Jerry J. Savitsky ע״ה
ישראל בן מנחם מאנעס ע״ה — Irving Tennenbaum ע״ה
שמואל בן יצחק ע״ה — George Hillelsohn ע״ה
רחל בת דוד הלוי ע״ה — Ruth Hillelsohn ע״ה
אהרן בן יהודה אריה ע״ה — Aaron Seif ע״ה

TAANIS: **David and Jean Bernstein, and Scott**
Matthew Bernstein
Albert and Gail Nassi, **Jessica and Garrett**
in memory of
Mr. and Mrs. Harry Bernstein ע״ה Mr. and Mrs. Joseph Furman ע״ה
Mr. Samuel Nassi ע״ה

MEGILLAH: Special Commemorative Edition published in conjunction
with the *Sh'loshim* of the patron of this edition of the Talmud
Jerome Schottenstein ע״ה
יעקב מאיר חיים בן אפרים אליעזר הכהן ע״ה

MOED KATAN: **Solomon T. and Leah Scharf**
and their children
David and Tzipi Diamond **Alexander and Naomi Scharf**
Joseph Scharf **Dovid and Chani Scharf**
לזכרון עולם
ר׳ אליהו בן משה יעקב ע״ה — R' Eliyahu Scharf ע״ה
שרה בת אלכסנדר זיסקינד ע״ה — Sara Scharf ע״ה
ר׳ יוסף בן צבי הירש ע״ה — R' Joseph Felder ע״ה

CHAGIGAH: **The Alvin E. Schottenstein Family**
In memory of
חיים אברהם יונה בן אפרים אליעזר הכהן ז״ל — Alvin E. Schottenstein ז״ל
יצחק אייזיק בן עקיבא הכהן ז״ל — Irving Altman ז״ל
הדס בת אברהם אביש ע״ה — Helen Altman ע״ה
שרגא פייוול בן יצחק אייזיק הכהן ז״ל — Frank Altman ז״ל

YEVAMOS I: **Phillip and Ruth Wojdyslawski and Family**
In memory of his beloved parents
Abraham Michel and Ora Wojdyslawski ע״ה
ר׳ אברהם מיכאל ב״ר פינחס ע״ה
אורה בת ר׳ צבי הירש ע״ה

YEVAMOS II: **Phillip and Ruth Wojdyslawski and Family**
In memory of her beloved mother
Chaya (Cytryn) Valt ע״ה
חיה צירל בת ר׳ שלמה זלמן ע״ה

PATRONS OF THE TALMUD • FULL-SIZE EDITION

YEVAMOS III: **Phillip and Ruth Wojdyslawski and Family**
In honor of
Benjamin C. Fishoff לאוי"ט
To the public he is a leader with vision and dedication.
To us he has always been a role model, a father,
and a constant inspiration.

KESUBOS I: **The Fishoff Families**
in memory of their beloved mother
מינדל בת ר׳ ישראל ע"ה — Mrs. Marilyn Fishoff ע"ה
נפ׳ כד תשרי תשמ"ט
and in memory of their dear grandparents
ר׳ דוב ב"ר מנחם אשר ע"ה   מרת מירל בת ר׳ מנחם מענדל ע"ה — Fishoff
ר׳ ישראל ב"ר אברהם ע"ה   מרת חיה זיסא בת ר׳ שרגא פייוועל ע"ה — Neider

KESUBOS II **Arthur A. and Carla Rand**
in memory of their parents
ר׳ ישראל ב"ר צבי Rand ומרת ליבא מלכה ב"ר יהודה Marcus ע"ה
ר׳ שלמה ב"ר מרדכי יהודה Ratzersdorfer ומרת חוה ב"ר חיים Finkelstein ע"ה
and in honor of their children
ר׳ אריה יהושע ב"ר אליהו דוב ומרת ליבא מלכה שיחי׳ — Lydia M. and Lionel S. Zuckier
ר׳ יואל אשר ב"ר חיים שלמה ומרת גנענדל חנה שיחי׳ — Gigi A. and Joel A. Baum
ר׳ ישראל יהודה ומרת צפורה געלא ב"ר יצחק חיים שיחי׳ — Jay J. and Cyndi G. Finkel-Rand
and grandchildren
דניאל יעקב, נפתלי צבי, חוה, בנימין, צפורה מרים, רחל, בתשבע Baum שיחי׳
שלמה יצחק, שירה חיה, צבי, שפרה לאה, בן ציון Zuckier שיחי׳
אליהו אריה לייב, יעקב שלמה, צבי, חסיה ליבא, מתתיהו דוד Rand שיחי׳

KESUBOS III **ישימך אלהים כשרה רבקה רחל ולאה**
May God make you like Sarah, Rebecca, Rachel and Leah

NEDARIM I: **Mrs. Goldy Golombeck**
Hyman P. and Elaine Golombeck   **Blanche B. Lerer**
Moishe Zvi and Sara Leifer   **Avrohom Chaim and Renee Fruchthandler**
In memory of
ר׳ משה יוסף ב"ר חיים פנחס ע"ה — Morris J. Golombeck ע"ה
and by Moishe Zvi and Sara Leifer in memory of
הרב ברוך יוסף ב"ר משה צבי ע"ה — האשה הצנועה מרים יוטא בת ר׳ לוי יצחק ע"ה
Mr. and Mrs. Baruch Leifer ע"ה

NEDARIM II: **The Rothstein Family**
In loving memory of
וועלוועל ב"ר יוסף ע"ה — Warren Rothstein ע"ה
David and Esther Rothstein ע"ה   Max and Gussie Gottlieb ע"ה
and in honor of
Howard and Beatrice Rothstein

NAZIR I: **Albert and Gail Nassi**
Garrett A. Nassi
Jessica Lea Nassi
in memory of
Samuel Nassi ע"ה
Albert and Leona Nassi ע"ה
Benjamin and Adell Eisenberg ע"ה
Arthur and Sarah Dector ע"ה

Daniel and Susan Kane
Jessica, Adam and Stacey
in memory of
Abraham and Rose Kanofsky ע"ה
Benjamin and Sophie Gornstein ע"ה
Elie and Irma Darsa ע"ה
Mack and Naomi Mann ע"ה

NAZIR II: **Alan and Myrna Cohen, Alison and Matthew**
in memory of
Harry and Kate Cohen ע"ה   Harry and Pauline Katkin ע"ה

SOTAH: **Motty and Malka Klein**
for the merit of their children שיחי׳
Esther and Chaim Baruch Fogel Dovid and Chavie Binyomin Zvi
Elana Leah Moshe Yosef Yaakov Eliyahu
In honor of his mother שתחי׳
Mrs. Suri Klein לאוי״ט
In memory of his father
ר׳ יהודה ב״ר דוד הלוי ז״ל נפ׳ כ״ז אדר ב׳ תשס״ג – Yidel Klein
In memory of her parents
ר׳ אשר אנשיל ב״ר משה יוסף ז״ל נפ׳ ג׳ שבט תשנ״ט – Anchel Gross
שרה בת ר׳ חיים אליהו ע״ה נפ׳ כ״ד סיון תשס״א – Suri Gross
And in memory of their grandparents who perished על קידוש השם in the Holocaust
ר׳ דוד ב״ר יעקב הלוי ע״ה ופערל בת ר׳ צבי ע״ה הי״ד – Klein
ר׳ מרדכי ב״ר דוד הלוי ע״ה ולאה בת ר׳ יעקב הלוי ע״ה הי״ד – Klein
ר׳ משה יוסף ב״ר בנימין צבי ע״ה ומלכה בת ר׳ יחיאל מיכל ע״ה הי״ד – Gross
ר׳ חיים אליהו ב״ר מרדכי ע״ה ויוטא בת ר׳ שלמה אליעזר ע״ה הי״ד – Gartenberg

GITTIN I: **Mrs. Kate Tannenbaum**
Elliot and Debra Tannenbaum Edward and Linda Zizmor and Families
commemorating the first *yahrzeit* of beloved husband, father and grandfather
ר׳ נפתלי ב״ר יהודה אריה ע״ה – Fred Tannenbaum ע״ה
נפטר ח׳ ניסן תשנ״ב

GITTIN II: **Richard and Bonnie Golding**
in honor of Julian and Frances Golding Lawrence Cohen and Helen Lee Cohen
and in memory of Vivian Cohen ע״ה
Irving and Ethel Tromberg Clarence and Jean Permut
in memory of
Benjamin and Sara Tromberg ע״ה Harry and Lena Brown ע״ה
Molly and Julius Permut ע״ה Lizzie and Meyer Moscovitz ע״ה

KIDDUSHIN I: **Ellis A. and Altoon Safdeye**
in memory of their beloved parents
המנוח יהודה אצלאן ומרת צלחה ויקטוריא ע״ה – Aslan and Victoria Safdeye ע״ה
המנוח יהודה ומרת מרגלית ע״ה – Judah and Margie Sultan ע״ה
and in memory of his brother יוסף ע״ה – Joseph Safdeye ע״ה

KIDDUSHIN II: **Mr. and Mrs. Ben Heller**
in memory of his father
יואל נתן ב״ר חיים הלוי ע״ה – Joseph Heller ע״ה
and in honor of his mother
צפורה שתחי׳ לאוי״ט בת ר׳ בנימין ע״ה – Fanya Gottesfeld-Heller שתחי׳

BAVA KAMMA I: **Yitzchok and Shoshana Ganger and Children**
in memory of
ר׳ יצחק ישעיהו ב״ר שלמה זלמן ע״ה–רויזא גיטל בת ר׳ משה ע״ה – Ganger
מיכאל ב״ר אברהם מרדכי ע״ה–מרים יוכבד בת ר׳ בנימין ע״ה – Ferber
ר׳ משה דוד ב״ר יצחק זעליג מקוצק ע״ה–פיגא בת ר׳ אברהם מרדכי ע״ה – Morgenstern
ר׳ מתתיהו ב״ר שמואל דוב ע״ה–אסתר מלכה בת ר׳ אריה ליב ע״ה – Newman

BAVA KAMMA II: **William and Esther Bein, and**
Joseph Hillel, Abraham Chaim Zev, and Bella Leah
In memory of parents and grandparents
מנחם מענדל ב״ר שמואל יצחק הכהן ע״ה – Edward (Mendus) Bein ע״ה
לאה בת חיים זאב הכהן ע״ה – Ilus Hartstein Bein ע״ה
מרדכי בן יוסף ע״ה – Mordochej Szer ע״ה
בילה בת אברהם ע״ה – Baila Silber Szer ע״ה
שמואל יצחק הכהן ושרה ביין ע״ה – חיים זאב הכהן ושרה הרטשטיין ע״ה
יוסף ויענטה שער ע״ה – אברהם ואסתר זילבר ע״ה

PATRONS OF THE TALMUD • FULL-SIZE EDITION

BAVA KAMMA III: **Dedicated to Klal Yisrael,**
and particularly to the Six Million.
הקב״ה שוכן בתוך בני ישראל והוא חד עם כנסת ישראל
"The Holy One Blessed is He dwells among the children of Israel;
He and the congregation of Israel are one."
— *Tzidkas Hatzaddik* 179

BAVA METZIA I: **Drs. Robert and Susan Schulman**
Howard and Tzila Schulman **Fred and Cindy Schulman**
and Families
in memory of
מיכאל בן צבי הירש ע״ה ומלכה בת ר׳ יוסף ע״ה — Milton and Molly Schulman ע״ה

BAVA METZIA II: **Donald E. and Eydie R. Garlikov, and Jennifer**
in memory of beloved son and brother
צבי שלמה בן דן ע״ה — Kenneth Scott Garlikov ע״ה
and in memory of parents and grandparents
עזריאל וועלוויל ב״ר אנשיל ע״ה טשארנא בת ר׳ אריה לייב ע״ה
Irve W. and Cecelia (Kiki) Garlikov ע״ה
and in honor of parents and grandparents, brother and uncle
מרדכי ואסתר פריידל ריטטער — Marcus and Elfrieda Ritter
נפתלי חיים ריטטער — Dr. Nathaniel Ritter

BAVA METZIA III: **The David H. Gluck Foundation**
in memory of
The Gluck Family
זאב בן דוד צבי ע״ה ואסתר בת אשר זעליג ע״ה — Zev and Esther Gluck ע״ה
ליבא, אשר זעליג, דוד צבי, שמואל, מנשה, יחזקאל שרגא ע״ה —
Lee, George, David H., Samuel C., Emanuel M., Henry ע״ה, and
יעקב יצחק בן זאב ע״ה ומיימי בת זאב ע״ה — Dr. Jack I. and Mrs. Mae Saks ע״ה
and in memory of
זאב בן חיים דוד וחיה ביילע בת יצחק יעקב ע״ה — Wolf and Chaye Beilah Saks ע״ה
יחיאל בן משה ע״ה — Elie Neustadter ע״ה

BAVA BASRA I: In memory of
מנחם מענדל בן אלימלך יהושע העשל ע״ה
חיה בת יהושע הכהן ע״ה

BAVA BASRA II: **Paul and Beth Guez and Family**
in memory of
Felix (Mazal) Guez ע״ה

BAVA BASRA III: **Irving and Frances Schottenstein**
in honor of their beloved parents
מאיר בן יהושע הכהן ע״ה ליבא בת הרב יצחק משה ע״ה — Meyer and Libbie Schottenstein
טוביה ע״ה ויבדל״ח שיינדל תחי׳ — Tobias ע״ה and Jennie Polster תחי׳
Melvin ע״ה and Lenore תחי׳ Schottenstein
in honor of their beloved parents
אברהם יוסף בן יהושע הכהן ע״ה ויבדל״ח בליה זילפה בת יצחק תחי׳
Abe J. ע״ה and Bessie (Stone) תחי׳ Schottenstein
יצחק ע״ה ויבדל״ח שרה תחי׳ — Isadore J. ע״ה and Sophie תחי׳ Green

PATRONS OF THE TALMUD ◆ FULL-SIZE EDITION

SANHEDRIN I: **Mortimer and Barbara Klaus** **Lester and Esther Klaus**
Arthur and Vivian Klaus
in memory of their beloved parents
ר׳ שמשון ב״ר יעקב ע״ה באשא בת ר׳ מרדכי נתן ע״ה
Samuel and Bessie Klaus ע״ה
and in memory of their sister
רייזל בת ר׳ שמשון ע״ה — **Rosalie Klaus Sohn**

SANHEDRIN II: Dedicated by a fellowship of people who revere the Talmud, its sanctity and wisdom, who foster its study, and who join in helping bring its treasures to future generations, the world over.

SANHEDRIN III: **Joseph and Adina Russak**
Dr. Leonard and Bobbee Feiner
Larry and Rochelle Russak
in memory of
צבי הירש ורחל רוסק ע״ה — Mr. and Mrs. Harry Russak ע״ה
אליעזר ובריינדל דייטש ע״ה — Mr. and Mrs. Eliezer Deutsch ע״ה
יעקב ורבקה לאה פיינר ע״ה — Mr. and Mrs. Jacob Feiner ע״ה

MAKKOS: **Mr. and Mrs. Marcos Katz**
in honor of הרב אפרים לייבוש בן הרב מרדכי דוד הכהן כ״ץ שליט״א
Rabbi Ephraim Leibush Katz שליט״א

SHEVUOS: Dedicated by
Michael and Danielle Gross
(London)

AVODAH ZARAH I: **The Kuhl Family**
in memory of
יחיאל ב״ר יצחק אייזיק ע״ה Dr. Julius Kuhl ע״ה
פרומט בת ר׳ שמואל הלוי ע״ה Mrs. Yvonne Kuhl ע״ה
שמואל ב״ר יחיאל ע״ה Sydney Kuhl ע״ה

AVODAH ZARAH II: In memory of
Jerome Schottenstein ע״ה
יעקב מאיר חיים בן אפרים אליעזר הכהן ע״ה

HORAYOS-EDUYOS: **Woli and Chaja Stern** (Sao Paulo, Brazil)
in memory of his parents
ר׳ צבי בן ר׳ חיים הלוי ומרת מרים ז״ל – Stern
מרת דאכא בת ר׳ פרץ ומרת ברכה ע״ה — Tager
and in memory of her parents
ר׳ דוד אריה בן ר׳ יעקב ומרת שיינדל ז״ל – Brenner
מרת איטלה בת ר׳ חיים ומרת מדל ע״ה — Stern
and in memory of their mechutanim
ר׳ ישראל מרדכי ב״ר צבי יוסף סג״ל ז״ל – Landau
ר׳ יששכר טוביה ב״ר יוסף ז״ל — Weitman
ר׳ שמואל עקיבא ב״ר שלמה צבי ז״ל — Kierszenbaum
and in memory of their sister-in-law
מרת זלטה פסל בת ר׳ אברהם יעקב ומרת חנה גיטל ע״ה – Stern
and in honor of their children
Jacques and Ariane Stern Jaime and Ariela Landau Michäel and Annete Kierszenbaum

ZEVACHIM I: **Mr. and Mrs. Samson Bitensky**

ZEVACHIM II: **Victor Posner**

PATRONS OF THE TALMUD ✧ FULL-SIZE EDITION

ZEVACHIM III: **Friends of Value City Department Stores**
In memory of
יעקב מאיר חיים בן אפרים אליעזר הכהן ע״ה — Jerome Schottenstein ע״ה

MENACHOS I: **Terumah Foundation**

MENACHOS II: **Terumah Foundation**

MENACHOS III: **Terumah Foundation**

CHULLIN I: **The Kassin Family**
in memory of
הרב יעקב שאול קצין זצ״ל — Rabbi Dr. Jacob Saul Kassin זצ״ל
The late Chief Rabbi of the Syrian-Sephardic Community
and in honor of
הרב שאול יעקב קצין שליט״א — Rabbi Saul Jacob Kassin שליט״א
Chief Rabbi of the Syrian-Sephardic Community

CHULLIN II: **Marty Silverman**
in memory of
Joseph and Fannie Silverman ע״ה and Dorothy Silverman ע״ה

CHULLIN III: **Harold and Ann Platt**
in memory of their beloved parents
אליעזר ושרה פיגא ע״ה — Eliezer and Sarah Feiga (Olshak) Platkowski ע״ה of Malkinia, Poland
ברוך ולאה ע״ה — Baruch and Laura Bienstock ע״ה of Lwow, Poland
and in memory of their entire families who perished in the Holocaust

CHULLIN IV: **Terumah Foundation**

BECHOROS I: **Howard Tzvi and Chaya Friedman**
Gabrielle Aryeh Yerachmiel Alexander and Daniella
in memory of their father and grandfather
הרב ירחמיאל ברוך בן הרה׳׳ח ר׳ אלעזר ז׳׳ל — Yerachmiel Friedman ז׳׳ל

BECHOROS II: **Howard and Chaya Balter**
Nachum and Perri Augenbaum Naftali Aryeh Akiva
in memory of his mother and their grandmother
רחל בת ר׳ חיים ע״ה, נפ׳ ז׳ שבט תשנ״ט — **Ruth Balter** ע״ה
and in honor of their parents and grandparents שיחי׳
David Balter
Noah and Shirley Schall
and in beloved memory of their grandparents and great grandparents
ר׳ שלמה ב״ר דוד זאב ז״ל אדי בת ר׳ זאב ע״ה — Balter
ר׳ חיים ב״ר לייב ז״ל פערל בת ר׳ ביניש ע״ה — Lelling
ר׳ דוב בער ב״ר אליעזר ז״ל ליבה בת ר׳ ישראל ע״ה — Zabrowsky
ר׳ נפתלי ב״ר יעקב שלמה ז״ל שרה בת ר׳ רפאל ע״ה — Schall

ARACHIN: **Chanoch and Hadassah Weisz and Family**
in memory of his father:
לעי״נ אביו ר׳ צבי ב״ר שמחה הלוי ע״ה, נפ׳ כ״ז מנחם אב תשמ״ה — Weisz
his maternal grandfather:
לעי״נ ר׳ שלמה ב״ר יצחק ע״ה, נפ׳ ה׳ סיון תש״א — Grunwald
his maternal grandmother and their children who perished in the Holocaust:
לעי״נ מרת גננדל בת ר׳ חנוך העניך ע״ה, שנהרגה עקה״ש כ״ז סיון תש״ד הי״ד — Grunwald
ולעי״נ בניהם משה ב״ר שלמה, יעקב ב״ר שלמה, יצחק ב״ר שלמה, בנימין ב״ר שלמה,
שנהרגו עקה״ש כ״ז סיון תש״ד הי״ד
and in memory of her grandparents:
לעי״נ ר׳ חייא בן חכם ר׳ רפאל ע״ה, נפ׳ כ״ד מנחם אב תשל״ה — Aryeh
וזוגתו מרת מלכה בת ר׳ אליהו ע״ה, נפ׳ י״ח טבת תשל״ד

TEMURAH: **Dr. and Mrs. Walter Silver**
Shlomo, Chani, and Avi Cohen
Sheri, Terri, Jennifer and Michelle Kraut
Evan and Alison Silver
in memory of our parents, and great grandparents
צבי יצחק ב״ר שמואל ע״ה — Harry Silver ע״ה
שרה פיגא בת מענדל ע״ה — Sarah Silver ע״ה
אברהם משה בן הרב שלמה זאלי ע״ה — Morris Bienenfeld ע״ה
גוטקה טובה בת אברהם דוד ע״ה — Gertrude Bienenfeld ע״ה

KEREISOS: **Mouky and Charlotte Landau** (Antwerp)
in honor of their children
Natalie and Chemi Friedman **Yanky and Miriam Landau**
Steve and Nechama Landau
and in beloved memory of their parents
חיים יעקב ב״ר יהושע ז״ל — Chaim Yaakov Landau ז״ל
אסתר בת ר׳ יעקב קאפל הכהן ע״ה — Esther Landau ע״ה
בן ציון ב״ר יצחק צבי ז״ל — Benzion Gottlob ז״ל
צילה בת ר׳ שמואל יהודה לייב ע״ה — Cila Herskovic ע״ה
and in beloved memory of our partner
מורנו הרב ר׳ יוסף יצחק בן מורנו ורבנו הרה״ג ר׳ מרדכי רוטנברג זצ״ל אבדק״ק אנטווערפן

ME'ILAH, TAMID, MIDDOS, KINNIM: **Steven and Renée Adelsberg**
Sarita and Rubin Gober **David** **Sammy** **Avi**
in loving memory of
שמואל שמעלקא ב״ר גדליה ז״ל — Samuel Adelsberg ז״ל
and in honor of
Helen Adelsberg Weinberg שתחי׳
and
Chaim and Rose Fraiman שיחי׳

NIDDAH I: In memory of
Joseph and Eva Hurwitz ע״ה
יוסף ב״ר מרדכי הלוי וחוה פיגא ב״ר אליעזר הלוי ע״ה
and
Lorraine Hurwitz Greenblott — לאה בילא חיה בת ר׳ יוסף ע״ה
by
Marc and Rachel Hurwitz,
Elisheva Ruchama, Michal, and Nechama Leah;
Martin and Geraldine Schottenstein Hoffman,
Jay and Jeanie Schottenstein, Ann and Ari Deshe,
Susan and Jon Diamond, and Lori Schottenstein;
and Pam and Neil Lazaroff, Frank Millman, and Dawn Petel

NIDDAH II: In memory of
Jerome Schottenstein ע״ה
יעקב מאיר חיים בן אפרים אליעזר הכהן ע״ה

Guardians of the Talmud*

A society of visionary people who recognize the primacy of the Jewish people's commitment to intellect, ethics, integrity, law, and religion — and pursue it by presenting the treasures of the eternal Talmud in the language of today . . . for the generations of tomorrow.

❦ ❦ ❦

David and Jean Bernstein
Matthew Bernstein
Scott and Andrea Bernstein

in memory of
Mr. and Mrs. Harry Bernstein ע״ה
Mr. and Mrs. Joseph Furman ע״ה

❦ ❦ ❦

The publishers pay tribute to the memory of a couple that embodied Torah knowledge and service to our people

הרב יצחק בן ר׳ שמואל ז״ל – Rabbi Yitzchok Filler ז״ל
נפטר ל״ג בעומר תש״ל
הרבנית דבורה בת ר׳ אברהם בצלאל ע״ה – Mrs. Dorothy Filler ע״ה
נפטרה כ״א מרחשון תשס״ג

and the memory of a man of integrity and sensitivity

ר׳ יוסף בן הרב יהודה אריה ז״ל – George May ז״ל
נפטר כ״ז שבט תש״ס
תנצב״ה

We also honor a matriarch and role model
Mrs. Sylvia May תחי׳

❦ ❦ ❦

Stephen L. and Terri Geifman and children
Leonard and Linda Comess and children
Alan and Cherie Weiss and children

in loving memory of
משה מרדכי בן יחיאל מיכאל ז״ל – Morris M. Geifman
and in honor of
Geraldine G. Geifman

❦ ❦ ❦

Elliot and Debbie Gibber
Daniel and Amy Gibber and family, Jacob and Jennifer Gibber and family,
Marc, Michael, Mindy, and David

in memory of our parents and grandparents
אלימלך חיים בן ירמיה הלוי ז״ל – Charles Goldner ז״ל
נפ׳ כ׳ חשון תשס״ב
who completed Shas many times
מינדל בת משולם ע״ה – Kate Ettlinger Goldner ע״ה
נפ׳ כ״א תמוז תשכ״ח

*In formation

The Written Word is Forever

*Guardians of the Talmud**

A society of visionary people who recognize the primacy of the Jewish people's commitment to intellect, ethics, integrity, law, and religion — and pursue it by presenting the treasures of the eternal Talmud in the language of today . . . for the generations of tomorrow.

❦ ❦ ❦

Milton and Rita Kramer

in honor of their 50th wedding anniversary and Milton's 80th birthday (April 1999),
in honor of the marriage of Ellen to George Gross (September 18, 2000),
and in honor of their children and grandchildren

Daniel and Gina Kramer and Children **Jonathan and Marian Kramer and Children**
Ellen K. and George Gross and their Children

and in everlasting memory of their beloved parents and grandparents
Hyman S. and Fannie D. Kramer ע״ה — חיים שניאור זלמן הלוי (חזק) ופייגע דינה ע״ה
Adolph H. and Sadie A. Gross ע״ה — חיים אלטער ושרה חנה ע״ה
Morris L. and Rachel E. Kramer ע״ה — משה אליעזר הלוי ורחל עלקא ע״ה
Barney and Dvorah Cohen ע״ה — דוב בער הכהן ודבורה ע״ה
Herman M. and Leah Gross ע״ה — משולם צבי ולאה ע״ה
Peisach and Hannah Neustadter ע״ה — פסח אלכסנדר וחנה ע״ה

❦ ❦ ❦

Helene and Moshe Talansky **Ida Bobrowsky** **Irene and Kalman Talansky** **Shoshana Silbert**

in honor of
Rebecca Talansky's 100th birthday עמו״ש
and in memory of
Rabbi David Talansky ז״ל — הרב דוד בן הרב אברהם חיים ז״ל
Blanche Moshel ע״ה — בלומא בת ר׳ שלמה הלוי ע״ה
Abraham R. Talansky ז״ל — ר׳ אברהם חיים בן הרב דוד ז״ל
Rabbi Jacob Bobrowsky ז״ל — הרב יעקב בן ר׳ אברהם ז״ל
Tema Bobrowsky ע״ה — תמר בת הרב יעקב ע״ה
Rebecca and Morris Weisinger ז״ל — ר׳ משה בן ר׳ לייב ז״ל – בריינה בת ר׳ זלמן ע״ה
Rabbi Avraham Silbert ז״ל — הרב אברהם בן ר׳ נחמיה ז״ל
Ruth and Marek Stromer ז״ל — ר׳ מרדכי בן ר׳ שאול ז״ל – שפרה רייזל בת ר׳ צבי ע״ה
Rose and Aaron Lerer ז״ל — ר׳ אהרון בן ר׳ שלמה אריה ז״ל – רחל בת ר׳ יהושע אהרון ע״ה

❦ ❦ ❦

Thomas R. and Janet F. Ketteler

in memory of his mentor

Jerome Schottenstein ע״ה

❦ ❦ ❦

Alan and Myrna Cohen

in honor of

their children

Alison and Matthew

*In formation

Guardians of the Talmud*

A society of visionary people who recognize the primacy of the Jewish people's commitment to intellect, ethics, integrity, law, and religion — and pursue it by presenting the treasures of the eternal Talmud in the language of today . . . for the generations of tomorrow.

❦ ❦ ❦

Rona and Edward Jutkowitz

In honor of our family's continuing commitment to Torah learning and Klal Yisrael.
We dedicate this volume to our daughters, **Rebecca and Mollie,**
who are the light of our lives and our blessings, and always fill our hearts with nachas;
and to their zeide, **Mr. Herman Jutkowitz,** who is a constant source of guidance and inspiration;
and in memory of our beloved parents
משה בן מאניס ז״ל ורחל בת אברהם הכהן ע״ה — Martin W. and Ruth Trencher ז״ל
ברכה בת שניאור זלמן ע״ה — Bernice Jutkowitz ע״ה
May our daughters have the honor to teach the value of Torah to their own children,
and may Torah be the guiding light for all of Klal Yisrael.

❦ ❦ ❦

לעילוי נשמת

הבחור מרדכי גדליהו ז״ל בן משה ואסתר שיחי׳ — Franky Ehrenberg

June 22, 2003 / נפ׳ כ״ג סיון תשס״ג

With a life of Torah study and service to Klal Yisrael ahead of him,
our beloved son, brother, and uncle was plucked from this life at only twenty-three.

כי מרדכי . . . דרש טוב לעמו ודבר שלום לכל זרעו

Dr. Martin and Esther Ehrenberg

Scott Leon **Dr. Judy and Hillel Olshin**

Yonatan Eliezer **Sara Elisheva** **Shmuel Abba**

❦ ❦ ❦

Richard Bookstaber and Janice Horowitz

In memory of his son

May his memory be a blessing
to all those whose lives he touched.

❦ ❦ ❦

Michael and Patricia Schiff

Sophia, Juliette and Stefan

in memory and appreciation of

Jerome Schottenstein ז״ל

and in honor of beloved parents and grandparents

Shirlie and Milton Levitin **Solange and Joseph Fretas** **Judy and Robert Schiff**

and Torah scholars

Rabbi Mordechai Schiff ז״ל and **Rabbi Ephraim Schiff ז״ל**

May we all bring honor to Hashem

*In formation

The Written Word is Forever

Community Guardians of the Talmud

A community is more than a collection of individuals. It is a new entity that is a living expression of support of Torah and dedication to the heritage of Klal Yisrael.

In honor of
Rabbi Reuven Fink and the *maggidei shiur* of **Young Israel of New Rochelle**

Dr. Joey and Lisa Bernstein
in memory of
שרה אלטע בת אברהם ע"ה
Mrs. Sondra Goldman ע"ה

Meyer and Ellen Koplow
in honor of their children
Tovah and Michael Koplow,
Jonathan, and Aliza

Stanley and Sheri Raskas
in memory of his parents
ראובן ב"ר חיים שבתי לייב ע"ה וחנה בת הרב טוביה ע"ה
Ralph and Annette Raskas ז"ל

Stanley and Ellen Wasserman
in memory of
חיה פיגא בת שמריהו — Viola Charles ע"ה
רות גולדה בת שמריהו — Ruth Schreiber ע"ה
לאה בת יוסף — Lee Salzberg ע"ה

Stanley and Vivian Bernstein and children
in honor of their parents and grandparents
Jules and Adele Bernstein
Andrew and Renee Weiss

Dr. Ronald and Susan Moskovich
in honor of their children
Adam Moshe, Leah Rivka, and David
"עשה תורתך קבע"

Drs. Arthur and Rochelle Turetsky
in honor of their children and grandson
Avi and Melissa, Jonathan and Nili, Yehuda
Shmuel Chaim

Gerald and Judith Ziering
in memory of
יחיאל מיכל בן אפרים פישל ז"ל וזלטא בת נחמן ע"ה
Jesse and Laurette Ziering ז"ל

Aaron and Carol Greenwald
in honor of their children and grandchildren
Ira and Jamie Gurvitch and children
Shlomo and Tobi Greenwald and children

Karen and Michael Raskas and Family

Mark and Anne Wasserman
in honor of their children
Joseph, Bailey, Erin, Rebeccah
and Jordyn

Daf Yomi shiur
in honor of their wives

Lakewood Links
in honor of
Rabbi Abish Zelishovsky

The Community of Great Neck, New York

YOUNG ISRAEL OF GREAT NECK
Rabbi Yaacov Lerner
Rabbi Eric Goldstein
Dr. Leeber Cohen
Professor Lawrence Schiffman

GREAT NECK SYNAGOGUE
Rabbi Ephraim R. Wolf ז"ל
Rabbi Dale Polakoff
Rabbi Shalom Axelrod
Rabbi Yoel Aryeh
Rabbi Yossi Singer

In Memoriam
Rabbi Ephraim R. Wolf ז"ל,
a pioneer of *harbotzas Torah,* a *kiruv* visionary, and a gifted spiritual leader. His legacy is the flourishing Torah community of Great Neck, New York.

The Community of Columbus, Ohio

In memory of **Jerome Schottenstein** Of Blessed Memory
and in honor of **Geraldine Schottenstein and Family**

Jay And Jeanie Schottenstein
Joseph, Jonathan, Jeffrey
Ann And Ari Deshe
Elie, David, Dara, Daniel
Susie And Jon Diamond
Jillian, Joshua, Jacob
Lori Schottenstein
Saul And Sonia Schottenstein

Sarah and Edward Arndt & Family
Irwin and Beverly Bain
Daniela & Yoram Benary
Liron & Alexandra, Oron, Doreen
Deborah & Michael Broidy
Michelle & Daniel
Families of Columbus Kollel
Naomi & Reuven Dessler
Sylvia & Murray Ebner & Family

Tod and Cherie Friedman
Rachel, Ross & Kara
Jim & Angie Gesler
Gerald & Karon Greenfield
Ben & Tracy Kraner & Family
Mike, Heidi, Brian, Deena & Leah Levey
Helene & Michael Lehv
Gary Narin
Ira & Laura Nutis & Family

Lea & Thomas Schottenstein & Family
Jeff & Amy Swanson
Jon
Marcy, Mark, Sam, & Adam Ungar
Drs. Philip & Julia Weinerman
Michael & Channa Weisz & Family
Dr. Daniel & Chaya Wuensch & Family
Main Street Synagogue
Howard Zack, Rabbi

The Talmud Associates*

A fellowship of benefactors dedicated to
the dissemination of the Talmud

❖

Audrey and Sargent Aborn and Family

Dr. Mark and Dr. Barbara Bell,
Bentzion Yosef and Mordechai Yehudah

The Belz Family

Richard Bookstaber and Janice Horowitz
In memory of his son

Michael and Bettina Bradfield
Gabrielle and Matthew
(London)

Nachi and Zippi Brown,
Jessica, Daniella, Shachar and Mindy
in honor of their parents and grandparents

Columbus Jewish Foundation

Milton Cooper and Family

Dr. and Mrs. David Diamond

Nahum and Feige Hinde Dicker and Family

Sophia, Alberto and Rose Djmal

Dr. Richard Dubin

Kenneth and Cochava Dubin

Dr. Martin and Esther Ehrenberg

David and Simone Eshaghian

Louis, Reuben and Larry Feder and Family

Rabbi Judah and Ruth Feinerman

In honor of
Mr. and Mrs. Yehoshua Chaim Fischman
by their children

Mayer and Ruthy Friedman
Ari, Yitzy, Suri, Dovi

Dr. Michael and Susan Friedman
לזכות בניהם, כלתם, ונכדם; בנותיהם, וחתניהם שיחי׳

Yeshaya and Perel Friedman

Julius Frishman

David and Sally Frenkel
לזכות בניהם וכלתם היקרים שיחיו:
דניאל שמואל ומאשה שושנה, אורי גבריאל, רונית פרימיט

The Furmanovich Family

Sander and Tracy Gerber
לזכות בניהם היקרים יעקב עקיבא, אסתר פערל, טליה גולדה,
חנה טובה, ורותי רבקה שיחי׳ שיתעלו בתורה ויראת שמים

Leon and Agi Goldenberg
in honor of the marriage of their children
Mendy and Estie Blau

Robert and Rita Gluck
לרפו״ש טויבא רחל בת פריידא שתחי׳

Shari and Jay Gold and Family

Dr. Martin and Shera Goldman and Family

Esther Henzel

Hirtz, Adler and Zupnick Families

Hashi and Miriam Herzka

Norman and Sandy Nissel Horowitz

Mrs. Farokh Imanuel, Kamram Imanuel
Dr. Mehran and Sepideh Imanuel
Eli and Fariba Maghen

David and Trudy Justin and Family
in honor of their parents
Zoltan and Kitty Justin

Nosson Shmuel and Ann Kahn and Family
ולזכות בניהם היקרים שיחיו:
חיים דוד, צבי מנחם, אברהם יצחק, ומשפחתם
ולכבוד אמו מרת גיטל שתחי׳ לאויוש״ט

David J. and Dora Kleinbart

In honor of
Mr. and Mrs. Label Kutoff
by their children

The Landowne Family

Ezriel and Miriam Langer

Mr. and Mrs. Chaim Leibel

Yehuda and Rasie Levi

Donald Light

Rudolph and Esther Lowy

Raphael and Blimie Manela
לזכות בניהם היקרים שיחיו:
מתתיהו, ישראל, ישעיהו, חיים משה, ושמעון

Howard and Debra Margolin and Family

Mendy and Phyllis Mendlowitz

*In formation

The Written Word is Forever

The Talmud Associates*

A fellowship of benefactors dedicated to
the dissemination of the Talmud

Robby and Judy Neuman and Family
לזכות בניהם היקרים שיחיו:
אברהם לייב, שרה מאטיל, מרדכי שרגא, זיסל,
שמואל שמעלקא, רחל ברכה, ישראל זכריהו ומנשה ברוך

RoAnna and Moshe Pascher
לזכות בניהם היקרים שיחיו:
נח צבי, דוד ישראל

Naftali Binyomin and Zypora Perlman
In honor of
Mr. and Mrs. Yosef Perlman עמו״ש

Kenneth Ephraim and Julie Pinczower
לרפו״ש ישראל חיים בן פייגלא שיחי׳

Dr. Douglas and Vivian Rabin

Michael G. Reiff

Ingeborg and Ira Leon Rennert

Alan Jay and Hindy Rosenberg

Aviva and Oscar Rosenberg

John and Sue Rossler Family

Mr. and Mrs. David Rubin and Family

Dinah Rubinoff and Family

Ms. Ruth Russ

Mr. and Mrs. Alexander Scharf

Mark and Chani Scheiner

Avi and Michou Schnur

Rubin and Marta Schron

Rivie and Leba Schwebel and Family

Shlomo Segev (Smouha)

Bernard and Chaya Shafran
לזכות בניהם היקרים שיחיו:
דבורה, יעקב חיים, דוד זאב, אסתר מנוחה

Jeffrey and Catherine Shachat
in honor of Rabbeim Howard Zack and Judah Dardik

Steven J. Shaer

Joel and Malka Shafran
לזכות בניהם היקרים שיחיו:
אשר נחמן, טובה חיה, תמר פעסיל, שרה חוה

Robin and Warren Shimoff

Nathan B. and Malka Silberman

The Soclof Family

Dr. Edward L. and Judith Steinberg

Avrohom Chaim and Elisa Taub
Hadassah, Yaakov Yehuda Aryeh, Shifra, Faige,
Devorah Raizel, and Golda Leah

Max Taub
and his son Yitzchak

Jay and Sari Tepper

Walter and Adele Wasser

Melvin, Armond and Larry Waxman

William and Noémie Wealcatch

The Wegbreit Family

Robert and Rachel Weinstein and Family

Dr. Zelig and Evelyn (Gutwein) Weinstein
Yaakov, Daniella, Aliza and Zev

Erwin and Myra Weiss

Morry and Judy Weiss

Shlomo and Esther Werdiger

Leslie M. and Shira Westreich

Willie and Blimie Wiesner

The Yad Velvel Foundation

Moshe and Venezia Zakheim

Dr. Harry and Holly Zinn

Mrs. Edith Zukor and Family

*In formation

In Memoriam — לזכרון עולם

Dedicated by the Talmud Associates
to those who forged eternal links

Abraham — שמחה בן ר׳ יהודה לייב הכהן ע״ה
דוד חי ב״ר שלום הכהן ע״ה וחנה בת ר׳ עזרא ע״ה
אהרן בן חיים זאב ע״ה גאלדע בת ר׳ דוד ע״ה
Ashkenazy – ר׳ שלמה ב״ר יצחק זצ״ל ורעיתו עלי׳ מינדעל בת ר׳ יעקב ע״ה
Sarah T. Belz — שרה בת אהרן צבי הלוי ע״ה
Ben-Ari — אליעזר בן מרדכי ע״ה ושרה בת ר׳ אברהם ע״ה
Ben-Ari — מרדכי בן אליעזר ע״ה
Berber — משה ורחל
Bernath – מנשה ב״ר שמואל שמעלקא ע״ה Meizner – מרדכי חיים ב״ר זבולן יצחק חייא ע״ה
Biegeleisen — שמעון דוד ז״ל ב״ר יעקב שלמה שיחי׳ לאוי״ט
Blitz — דוב מאיר ב״ר דוד הכהן ע״ה
Freddy Bradfield — יעקב בן צבי ע״ה
אהרן ב״ר דוד הכהן ז״ל
Elihu Brodsky — אליהו ב״ר חיים ע״ה
Vera (Greif) Brodsky — יונה בת ר׳ פינחס ע״ה
Cooperberg — שימה רייזל בת ר׳ אהרן שלמה ע״ה
Cooperberg — אברהם אשר בן ר׳ מאיר ע״ה
Cumsky – דוב בער בן אברהם יששכר ע״ה ופעשא מאטלא בת יוסף ע״ה
צבי טעביל בן ישראל ע״ה וליבע בת דוד ע״ה
Diamant — אשר ב״ר יהושע מרדכי הכהן ע״ה
Diamant — שרה בת ר׳ אריה ע״ה
Diamant — ר׳ דוב ב״ר משה ע״ה ורייזל בת ר׳ אברהם ע״ה
Diamond — דר. ר׳ יצחק ב״ר ברוך בענדיט ע״ה
Dicker — מרדכי צבי ב״ר יעקב ע״ה
Dicker — קיילא בת ר׳ משה ע״ה
Djmal — טופיק טוביה בן משה ושושנה ע״ה
Paul and Jeannette Dubin ע״ה
Mollie Dubinsky ע״ה
Abram B. Efroymson ע״ה
Sylvia Spira Efroymson ע״ה
Ehrenberg — אברהם בן עמנואל ע״ה ויוכבד בת ר׳ אלימלך ע״ה
Einhorn — משה בן ברוך ז״ל ורבקה נעכא בת חיים צבי ע״ה
Eshaghian — אברהם בן דוד ע״ה
Esrig — דוד בן שלמה ע״ה וחיה אייגא בת שלום ע״ה
Feder — מלכה בת ירחמיאל הכהן ע״ה
Feiden — ישראל בן אהרן ע״ה
Feinerman — אליעזר בן יוסף ע״ה ולאה בת ישראל יצחק ע״ה
יוסף בן צבי יחזקאל ע״ה ושרה בת ר׳ משה ע״ה
Freier — ישעיה צבי ב״ר חיים אלכסנדר יוסף ע״ה
Freier — שיינדל בת ר׳ משה הלוי ע״ה
Freilich — הרב יצחק דוב ב״ר אברהם יעקב ז״ל
Frenkel – גרשון בן יחיאל דוד ע״ה Rottenstreich – דוד בן עקיבא ע״ה
Friedman — ר׳ אהרן ב״ר יעקב מאיר ע״ה
Friedman — ר׳ אברהם ב״ר אלטר יצחק אייזיק ע״ה
Frishman — מרים בת ר׳ יוסף מרדכי ע״ה

Frishman — יצחק אריה ב״ר יהודה ע״ה ומרים לאה בת ר׳ יצחק ע״ה
Furmanovich — לע״נ שרה הניה בת פסח הלוי ע״ה
Furmanovich — לע״נ גדליה דב בן אברהם יואל ז״ל
Goldman — אמו, שפרה בת ר׳ קלונימוס קלמן ע״ה
Gugenheim — החבר אפרים בן רפאל ע״ה
Gugenheim — בריינדל בת החבר נתן הכהן ע״ה
Hanz — חיים בן מרדכי הי״ד
Henzel — אברהם בן ר׳ מנחם זאב ע״ה
Hirtz — אליעזר בן ישעיה ז״ל ולאה בת יוסף הלוי ע״ה
Horowitz – שלמה יהודה ב״ר זלמן יוסף הלוי ז״ל ומרים בת אברהם הכהן ע״ה
Imanuel — מרדכי בן רחמים ז״ל
Kahn — ר׳ ישראל אריה ב״ר שמואל הכהן ז״ל
Katzef — פרומה באדענה בת אלחנן ע״ה
Kleinbart — משה ב״ר אריה לייב ע״ה
Kleinbart — בתיה בת ר׳ משה אברהם ע״ה
Kriegel — רויזא מינצא בת הרב ישראל יהודה ע״ה
Kulefsky — הילד יהודה לייב ע״ה בן נתן נטע לאוי״ט
Langer — משה בן יצחק הי״ד
Landowne — שלמה בן יוסף ע״ה
Lasry — שאול ב״ר אברהם ע״ה וזהרה אסתר בת משה ע״ה
Lazar — אליעזר שאול בן זאב מאיר ע״ה
Lefkovich — ר׳ זאב וועלוול ב״ר יצחק אייזיק ע״ה
Lemberger — יצחק בן אריה ע״ה
Leibel — יחזקאל שרגא ב״ר חיים ע״ה
Leibel — רויזא בת ר׳ אברהם משה ע״ה
Levi — הרב חיים מאיר בן ר׳ מנחם ע״ה
Levi — שושנה טייבא רייזל בת ר׳ יחזקאל גרשון ע״ה
Light — משה גבריאל בן אברהם אליהו ז״ל וחנה בת נתן ע״ה
Lowy – מרדכי אריה ב״ר רפאל הלוי ז״ל ומינדל בת ר׳ שלמה זלמן ע״ה
May — ר׳ יוסף בן הרב יהודה אריה ע״ה
Miller — אלטער משה יוסף ב״ר צבי אריה ז״ל
Moskowitz — אליעזר ב״ר אברהם ברוך ז״ל וזהבה בת ר׳ משה ע״ה
Neuman — יצחק אייזיק ב״ר אהרן ע״ה
Nissel — שלמה מאיר בן הרב חיים לייב עזריאל ז״ל
Paneth — אלטע חיה שרה ע״ה בת ר׳ פנחס שיחי׳ לאוי״ט
Parnes — אריה לייבש בן יוסף יצחק ועטיא בת אשר ראובן ע״ה
Parnes — הרב אברהם זאב ב״ר ישכר ע״ה
Parsons — משה זלמן בן אהרן דוב ע״ה
Perlowitz — הרב משה ב״ר אליעזר הלל ע״ה
Pinczower — אפרים ב״ר ישראל חיים ופייגלא בת ר׳ יעקב ע״ה
Rabin — ישראל בן נחום ע״ה
Reiff — לוי יצחק ב״ר עזריאל ז״ל ויהודית בת ר׳ יצחק אייזיק ע״ה
Rennert — שרה בת יצחק יעקב ע״ה
Rennert — יונה מנחם בן אהרן ע״ה

תנצב״ה

In Memoriam — לזכרון עולם

Dedicated by the Talmud Associates
to those who forged eternal links

Rosenberg — חיים נחמן ב״ר דוד ולאה בת יוסף ע״ה
Sam and Leah Rosenbloom ע״ה
Roth — ר׳ צבי יהודה ז״ל ב״ר אברהם יצחק שיחי׳ לאוי״ט
Roth — משה ב״ר יעקב הכהן ע״ה Weisner — יצחק ב״ר זאב ע״ה
In memory of the Sanz-Klausenburger Rebbe זצוק״ל
כ״ק אדמו״ר אבדק״ק צאנז-קלויזענבורג זי״ע
מרן הרהגה״צ ר׳ יקותיאל יהודה בהרהגה״צ ר׳ צבי זצוק״ל
נלב״ע ש״ק פ׳ חקת, ט׳ תמוז תשנ״ד
William Shachat ע״ה and Israel Ira Shachat ע״ה
Scharf — אליהו ב״ר משה יעקב ושרה בת אלכסנדר זיסקינד ע״ה
Scherman — ר׳ אברהם דוב ב״ר שמואל נטע ע״ה
Scherman — ליבא בת ר׳ זאב וואלף ע״ה
Schnur — אברהם יצחק בן אהרן הי״ד וחנה בת חיים יעקב ע״ה
Schoenbrun — שרגא פייבל ב״ר יעקב הכהן ומאטל אסתר בת מרדכי הלוי ע״ה
Schron — אליעזר דוב בן חיים משה ע״ה
Schron — חוה בת שמעון ע״ה
Schulman — חיים חייקל בן ר׳ שמואל ע״ה
Schulman — חיה בת הרב ישראל יהודה ע״ה
Schwebel — אברהם זכריה מנחם בן יוסף ומחלה בת ישראל מרדכי ע״ה
Scherman — חיים שמואל ב״ר אברהם דוב ע״ה
Scherman — הילד אברהם דוב ע״ה ב״ר זאב יוסף שיחי׳
Sol Scheiner — שלמה טוביה בן יהושע מנחם הלוי ע״ה
Rose Schwartz — רייזל בת הרה״ג ר׳ אברהם יצחק ע״ה
Shafran — ר׳ יהושע ב״ר אברהם ע״ה
Shayovich — משה יעקב ב״ר נחום ועטיא פייגא בת מרדכי ע״ה
Shimoff — ר׳ ישראל דוב ב״ר אהרן יעקב ז״ל
Shimoff — חיה רבקה לאה בת ר׳ אליעזר יהודה ע״ה
Shubow — יוסף שלום בן משה ע״ה
Silberman — ר׳ צבי ב״ר זאב הלוי ע״ה
Silberman — דבורה אסתר בת ישראל ע״ה
Silbermintz — יהושע ב״ר יוסף שמריהו ע״ה
Singer — צבי בן ר׳ חיים ע״ה
Singer — הינדי בת ר׳ שלמה ע״ה

Soclof — אברהם אבא ב״ר שמריהו ע״ה
Soclof — חיה ברכה בת צבי הירש הלוי ע״ה
Smouha — הרב אליהו בן מאיר הלוי ע״ה
Steir — משה בן מיכאל ע״ה
Steinberg — יצחק גדליה בן יהודה לייב ע״ה
Steinberg — מלכה בת מאיר לוי ע״ה
Stern — ר׳ חיים מאיר ב״ר שמחה ז״ל ובינה בת ר׳ יוסף מרדכי ע״ה
Tabak — שיינא רחל בת יוסף מרדכי ע״ה
Taub — ר׳ יעקב ב״ר יהודה אריה ע״ה נפ׳ ד׳ מנחם אב תשל״ט
Taub — אליעזר יוסף בן מענדל ע״ה
Taub — מענדל בן אליעזר יוסף חיה בת הירש ע״ה
Taub — רויזא בת ר׳ משה ע״ה
Wealcatch — חיים דוב ב״ר זאב ואסתר בת ר׳ יוסף אייזיק ע״ה
Weiss — צבי בן יואל ע״ה
Weiss — גיטל בת ישראל ע״ה
Werdiger — ר׳ שלמה אלימלך ב״ר ישראל יצחק ע״ה
Westreich — הרב יהושע בן הרב יוסף יאסקא ז״ל
Leo Werter ע״ה
Wiesner — הרב שמעיה בן הרב זאב ע״ה
Wiesner — שרה לאה בת ר׳ צבי אריה ע״ה
Zakheim-Brecher — בתיה רחל ע״ה בת ר׳ משה יוסף שיחי׳ לאוי״ט
Zalstain — שמעון בן מרדכי יוסף הלוי ע״ה
Zimmer — ר׳ אברהם יעקב בן אהרן אליעזר ע״ה
הרב אהרן ב״ר מאיר יעקב ע״ה
הרבנית פרומא בת ר׳ חיים צבי ע״ה
Zinn — צבי יהודה בן שמעון ע״ה
Zinn — דבורה בת יחיאל מרדכי ע״ה
Leslie Zukor — ר׳ יצחק חיים ב״ר יוסף ע״ה
Zlatow — ר׳ שמואל דוד ב״ר מאיר יעקב ז״ל
הרב אהרן ב״ר מאיר יעקב זצ״ל
הרבנית פרומא בת ר׳ חיים צבי ע״ה
צבי יהודה ז״ל בן אברהם יצחק לאוי״ט
חיים מאיר בן שמחה ז״ל ובינה בת יוסף מרדכי הכהן ע״ה
אליעזר ב״ר אברהם ברוך ז״ל וגולדה זהבה בת משה הלוי ע״ה

תנצב״ה

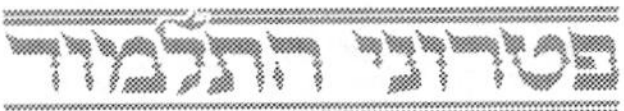

We express our appreciation to the distinguished patrons
who have dedicated volumes in the

HEBREW ELUCIDATION OF THE SCHOTTENSTEIN EDITION OF THE TALMUD

Dedicated by
JAY AND JEANIE SCHOTTENSTEIN
and their children
Joseph Aaron, Jonathan Richard, and Jeffrey Adam

SEDER ZERA'IM:	**Mrs. Margot Guez and Family** **Paul Vivianne Michelle Hubert Monique Gerard Aline Yves**
SEDER NASHIM:	**Ellis A. and Altoon Safdeye and Family**
SEDER NEZIKIN:	**Yisrael and Gittie Ury and Family** (Los Angeles)
BERACHOS I:	**Jay and Jeanie Schottenstein** (Columbus, Ohio)
BERACHOS II:	**Zvi and Betty Ryzman** (Los Angeles)
SHABBOS I:	**Moshe and Hessie Neiman** (New York)
SHABBOS II:	**David and Elky Retter and Family** (New York)
SHABBOS III:	**Mendy and Itta Klein** (Cleveland)
SHABBOS IV:	**Mayer and Shavy Gross** (New York)
ERUVIN I:	**The Schottenstein Family** (Columbus, Ohio)
ERUVIN II:	**The Schottenstein Family** (Columbus, Ohio)
PESACHIM I:	**Serge and Nina Muller** (Antwerp)
PESACHIM III:	**Morris and Devora Smith** (New York / Jerusalem)
YOMA I:	**Peretz and Frieda Friedberg** (Toronto)
YOMA II:	**Avi Klein and Family** (New York)
SUCCAH I:	**The Pruwer Family** (Jerusalem)
SUCCAH II:	**The Pruwer Family** (Jerusalem)
BEITZAH:	**Chaim and Chava Fink** (Tel Aviv)
ROSH HASHANAH:	**Avi and Meira Schnur** (Savyon)
TAANIS:	**Mendy and Itta Klein** (Cleveland)
MEGILLAH:	**In memory of Jerome Schottenstein ז״ל**
MOED KATTAN:	**Yisroel and Shoshana Lefkowitz** (New York)
CHAGIGAH:	**Steven and Hadassah Weisz** (New York)
YEVAMOS I:	**Phillip and Ruth Wojdyslawski** (Sao Paulo, Brazil)
YEVAMOS II:	**Phillip and Ruth Wojdyslawski** (Sao Paulo, Brazil)
YEVAMOS III:	**Phillip and Ruth Wojdyslawski** (Sao Paulo, Brazil)
KESUBOS I:	**Ben Fishoff and Family** (New York)
KESUBOS II:	**Jacob and Esther Gold** (New York)
KESUBOS III:	**David and Roslyn Lowy** (Forest Hills)
NEDARIM I:	**Soli and Vera Spira** (New York / Jerusalem)
NAZIR:	**Shlomo and Esther Ben Arosh** (Jerusalem)
SOTAH:	**Motty and Malka Klein** (New York)

פטרוני התלמוד

GITTIN I:	**Mrs. Kate Tannenbaum;** **Elliot and Debra Tannenbaum; Edward and Linda Zizmor**
KIDDUSHIN I:	**Ellis A. and Altoon Safdeye** (New York)
KIDDUSHIN II:	**Jacqui and Patty Oltuski** (Savyon)
BAVA KAMMA I:	**Lloyd and Hadassah Keilson** (New York)
BAVA KAMMA II:	**Faivel and Roiza Weinreich** (New York)
BAVA METZIA I:	**Joseph and Rachel Leah Neumann** (Monsey)
BAVA METZIA II:	**Shlomo and Tirzah Eisenberg** (Bnei Brak)
BAVA METZIA III:	**A. George and Stephanie Saks** (New York)
SANHEDRIN I:	**Martin and Rivka Rapaport** (Jerusalem)
SANHEDRIN III:	In honor of **Joseph and Anita Wolf** (Tel Aviv)
MAKKOS:	**Hirsch and Raquel Wolf** (New York)
SHEVUOS:	**Jacques and Miriam Monderer** (Antwerp)
HORAYOS-EDUYOS:	**Woli and Chaja Stern** (Sao Paulo, Brazil)
ZEVACHIM I:	**Mr. and Mrs. Eli Kaufman** (Petach Tikva)
ZEVACHIM II:	**Mr. and Mrs. Eli Kaufman** (Petach Tikva)
CHULLIN I:	**The Pluczenik Families** (Antwerp)
CHULLIN II:	**Avrohom David and Chaya Baila Klein** (Monsey)
CHULLIN III:	**Avrohom David and Chaya Baila Klein** (Monsey)
CHULLIN IV:	**The Frankel Family** (New York)
BECHOROS II:	**Howard and Chaya Balter** (New York)
ARACHIN:	**Mr. and Mrs. Eli Kaufman** (Petach Tikva)
NIDDAH I:	**Daniel and Margaret, Allan and Brocha, and David and Elky Retter and Families**

ACKNOWLEDGMENTS

We are grateful to the distinguished *roshei hayeshivah* and rabbinic leaders שליט״א in Israel and the United States whose guidance and encouragement have been indispensable to the success of this Talmud, from its inception. Their letters of approbation appear in volume 1 of Tractate Berachos.

A huge investment of time and resources was required to make this edition of the Talmud a reality. Only through the generous support of many people is it possible not only to undertake and sustain such a huge and ambitious undertaking, but to keep the price of the volumes within reach of the average family and student. We are grateful to them all.

The Trustees and Governors of the MESORAH HERITAGE FOUNDATION saw the need to support the scholarship and production of this and other outstanding works of Torah literature. Their names are listed on an earlier page.

JAY SCHOTTENSTEIN is chairman of the Board of Governors and has enlisted many others in support of this monumental project. In addition, he and his wife JEANIE have dedicated the HEBREW ELUCIDATION OF THE SCHOTTENSTEIN EDITION OF THE TALMUD and the DAF YOMI EDITION OF THE TALMUD in honor of their parents. But those are only formal identifications. The Schottensteins are deeply involved in a host of causes and their generosity is beyond description. Most recently they have undertaken sponsorship of the SCHOTTENSTEIN INTERLINEAR SERIES, which is bringing a new and innovative dimension of understanding to tefillah. Nevertheless, this Talmud is their *liebling*. They surpass every commitment to assure its continuity and it has justly become synonymous with their name.

HAGAON RAV DAVID FEINSTEIN שליט״א has been a guide, mentor, and friend since the first day of the ArtScroll Series. We are honored that, though complex halachic matters come to the Rosh Yeshivah from across the world, he regards our work as an important contribution to *harbatzas haTorah* and that he has graciously consented to be a trustee of the Foundation.

We join in mourning the recent passing of LAURENCE A. TISCH, who was more than gracious on numerous occasions.

We are grateful to JAMES S. TISCH and THOMAS J. TISCH, who are a credit to their family tradition of community service; JOEL L. FLEISHMAN, Founding Trustee of the Foundation, whose sage advice and active intervention was a turning point in our work; ELLIS A. SAFDEYE, the dedicator of the SAFDEYE EDITION OF SEDER NASHIM, a legendary supporter of worthy causes and a warm, treasured friend; BENJAMIN C. FISHOFF, patron of several volumes of the Talmud, and a sensitive, visionary friend who has brought many people under the banner of this project; ZVI RYZMAN, patron of the HEBREW RYZMAN EDITION OF THE MISHNAH and of tractates in this Talmud edition, a dynamic and imaginative force for Torah life and scholarship, and a loyal, devoted friend; SOLI SPIRA, patron of Talmud volumes, who is respected on three continents for his learning and magnanimity; RABBI MEYER H. MAY, a man who devotes his considerable acumen and prestige to the service of Torah. He has been a proven and invaluable friend at many junctures; ABRAHAM BIDERMAN, a Trustee, whose achievement for Torah and community, here and abroad, are astounding; JUDAH SEPTIMUS, a Trustee, whose acumen and resources are devoted to numerous Torah causes; and RABBI SHLOMO GERTZULIN, whose competence and vision are invaluable assets to Klal Yisrael.

Loyal friends who have been instrumental in the success of our work and to whom we owe a debt of gratitude are, in alphabetical order:

Our very dear friends: RABBI RAPAHEL B. BUTLER, founder of the Afikim Foundation, a laboratory to create innovative Torah programs; RABBI ALAN CINER, whose warmth and erudition will draw Jews closer to Judaism in his new position in Palm Beach, Florida. RABBIS BUTLER and CINER were instrumental in moving this edition of the Talmud from dream to reality in its formative stage; REUVEN DESSLER, a good friend and respected leader who adds luster to a distinguished family lineage; ABRAHAM FRUCHTHANDLER, who has placed support for Torah institutions on a new plateau; LOUIS GLICK, who sponsored the ArtScroll Mishnah Series with the *Yad Avraham* commentary; SHIMMIE HORN, patron of the HORN EDITION OF SEDER MOED, a self-effacing gentleman to whom support of Torah is a priority; MOSHE REICHMANN, whose name is synonymous with visionary magnanimity for Torah study; DAVID RUBIN, dedicator of the RUBIN EDITION OF THE PROPHETS, whose visionary generosity is a vital force in his community and beyond; SHLOMO SEGEV of Bank Leumi, who has been a responsible and effective friend; HESHE SEIF, patron of the SEIF EDITION TRANSLITERATED PRAYER BOOKS, who has added our work to his long list of important causes; NATHAN SILBERMAN, who makes his skills and judgment available in too many ways to mention; A. JOSEPH STERN, patron of the SEFARD ARTSCROLL MACHZORIM and of tractates in this Talmud edition, whose warmth and concern for people and causes are justly legendary; ELLIOT TANNENBAUM, a warm and gracious patron of several volumes, whose example has motivated many others; STEVEN WEISZ, whose infectious zeal for our work has brought many others under its banner; and HIRSCH WOLF, a valued friend from our very beginning, and an energetic, effective leader in many causes.

We are grateful, as well, to many other friends who have come forward when their help was needed most: DR. YISRAEL BLUMENFRUCHT, YERUCHAM LAX, YEHUDAH LEVI, RABBI ARTHUR SCHICK, FRED SCHULMAN, and MENDY YARMISH.

We thank RABBI YEHOSHUA LEIFER, head of KOLLEL OZ VEHADAR, for permission to reproduce the folios from their new edition of the classic Vilna Talmud. Newly typeset and with many additions and enhancements, it establishes a new standard in Talmud publishing.

We conclude with gratitude to *Hashem Yisbarach* for His infinite blessings and for the privilege of being the vehicle to disseminate His word. May this work continue so that all who thirst for His word may find what they seek in the refreshing words of the Torah.

Rabbi Nosson Scherman / Rabbi Meir Zlotowitz

Adar 5764
March, 2004

מסכת שבת
TRACTATE SHABBOS

Chapter Sixteen

Mishnah כָּל כִּתְבֵי הַקֹּדֶשׁ מַצִּילִין אוֹתָן מִפְּנֵי הַדְּלֵיקָה – **All Holy Scriptures** – whether they are Torah scrolls or scrolls of the other books of the Bible – **may be saved from a fire** on the Sabbath,[1] בֵּין שֶׁקּוֹרִין בָּהֶן – **whether we read from them** publicly in the synagogue on the Sabbath, such as *Neviim* scrolls, from which the *haftarah* is read, וּבֵין שֶׁאֵין קוֹרִין בָּהֶן – **or whether we do not read from them,** such as *Kesuvim* scrolls,[2] אַף עַל פִּי שֶׁכְּתוּבִים בְּכָל לָשׁוֹן – **and even though they are written in any language** other than Hebrew.[3] טְעוּנִים גְּנִיזָה – **They** [the abovementioned foreign-language translations] **warrant being hidden away,** i.e. they may not be discarded in an unprotected area where they may come to disgrace.[4]

The Mishnah returns to explain its statement that *Kesuvim* are not read on the Sabbath:

וּמִפְּנֵי מָה אֵין קוֹרִין בָּהֶם – **And why do we not read from them?** מִפְּנֵי בִּיטּוּל בֵּית הַמִּדְרָשׁ – **Because of neglect of the *beis hamidrash*.**[5]

Gemara The Gemara cites a dispute regarding foreign-language translations:

אִיתְּמַר – **It was stated:** הָיוּ כְּתוּבִים תַּרְגּוּם אוֹ בְּכָל לָשׁוֹן – **If they** [scrolls of Scriptures] **were written in Aramaic**[6] **or in any** other **language** besides Hebrew, רַב הוּנָא אָמַר – **Rav Huna says:** אֵין מַצִּילִין אוֹתָן מִפְּנֵי הַדְּלֵיקָה – **We may not save them from a fire** on the Sabbath, וְרַב חִסְדָּא אָמַר – **and Rav Chisda says:** מַצִּילִין אוֹתָן מִפְּנֵי הַדְּלֵיקָה – **We may save them from a fire.**[7]

The Gemara explains the disagreement:

אַלִּיבָּא דְּמַאן דְּאָמַר נִיתְּנוּ לִקְרוֹת בָּהֶן דְּכוּלֵּי עָלְמָא לָא פְּלִיגִי דְּמַצִּילִין – **According to the one** (i.e. the Tanna) **who says** that **we may read from them** [translations], **no one argues that they may be saved.** כִּי פְּלִיגִי אַלִּיבָּא דְּמַאן דְּאָמַר לֹא נִיתְּנוּ לִקְרוֹת בָּהֶן – **When do they argue? According to the one who says we may not read from them.**[8] רַב הוּנָא אָמַר אֵין מַצִּילִין – **Rav Huna says:**

NOTES

1. [Torah scrolls are more sacred than scrolls of the other books of Scripture. Nevertheless,] the Mishnah teaches that *all* Holy Scriptures may be rescued, even scrolls of *Neviim* (the Prophets) and *Kesuvim* (the Hagiographa).

In granting permission for these scrolls to be rescued, the Mishnah means to allow them to be carried from the burning house or courtyard into an adjacent alleyway, or *mavoi* (see Mishnah below, 116b). Although in general the Rabbis forbade the efforts that one would expend to save his belongings from a fire on the Sabbath (see below, 117b, for the reason for this decree), an exception was made for, among other things, the sake of the Holy Scriptures. Furthermore, while carrying into a *mavoi* normally requires a *shituf mevo'os* to have been established in the *mavoi* before the Sabbath (see below, 117a note 10, for an explanation of what a *shituf mevo'os* is), scrolls of the Scriptures may be rescued by carrying them even into a *mavoi* lacking a *shituf* (see below, 117b note 2). It is only these two details of the Sabbath restrictions (the limitation on saving things from a fire and the prohibition on carrying things into a *mavoi* lacking a *shituf*) that the Rabbis relaxed to save Holy Scriptures. All other Sabbath laws remain in force (see *Rashi*).

2. The weekly *haftarah* selection is never read from *Kesuvim* (*Rashi*). Furthermore, and as the Mishnah will go on to explain, the Rabbis forbade even private individuals to read *Kesuvim* on the Sabbath. Nevertheless, even *Kesuvim* scrolls may be rescued from a fire (*Rashi* in the name of *Rabbeinu HaLevi*).

3. We will learn in the Gemara of a Tannaic dispute as to whether scrolls of the Scriptures written in a language other than Hebrew may be read at all. Our Mishnah follows the stringent view which forbids this. Nevertheless, the Mishnah teaches that if such outlawed scrolls are endangered by fire on the Sabbath, they may be rescued, just like Hebrew scrolls (*Rashi,* following the Gemara's initial understanding of this phrase).

[*Rashi* cites his teachers as having explained the phrase "and even though they are written in any other language" as referring specifically to scrolls of *Kesuvim,* not to *Neviim* scrolls. *Rashi* conjectures that his teachers felt compelled to interpret the Mishnah thus because of the well-known fact that Yonasan ben Uziel, an early Tanna and disciple of Hillel, composed an Aramaic *Targum* of *Neviim.* This would seem to prove that even those opinions in the Gemara who forbid translating the Scriptures were referring only to *Kesuvim* (which, the Gemara in *Megillah* 3a relates, Yonasan ben Uziel did not translate).

Rashi, however, rejects this proof, arguing that when the Gemara in *Megillah* (ibid.) states that Yonasan ben Uziel composed the *Targum,* it means merely that he did so orally. He did not commit it to writing. Only years later, when the prohibition against translating the Scriptures was relaxed (see below, 115b note 3), was his *Targum* written down.]

4. [Although these translations may not be read,] they may not simply be abandoned in an unguarded place [where they can come to degradation]. Rather, one must hide them away, e.g. bury them (*Rashi*).

5. In Talmudic times it was customary to lecture in the *beis hamidrash* (study hall) for the general population on the Sabbath. In these lectures were included discourses on various practical aspects of the halachah. [This could not be done during the week, when most people were occupied with earning a livelihood.] In order to maximize attendance, the Rabbis prohibited the reading of *Kesuvim* on the Sabbath, since people might become engrossed in them and fail to attend the lecture. [*Kesuvim* were regarded as the most engaging part of Scriptures, as evidenced by the fact that these books were read to the Kohen Gadol on the night of Yom Kippur to keep him from falling asleep (*Yoma* 18b).] Since the lecture pertained to daily observances, it was considered more beneficial to the public to attend the lectures than to study the *Kesuvim* (see *Rashi*).

[From *Rashi's* words (see note 2) it might appear that he is setting forth two distinct explanations of the words אֵין קוֹרִין בָּהֶן: a) his own, that *Kesuvim* are not read publicly in the synagogue for the *haftarah* reading, and b) *Rabbeinu HaLevi's,* that even private individuals are forbidden to read *Kesuvim.* If so, however, it is difficult to see how *Rashi* would interpret according to his own explanation the Mishnah's closing line that the reason *Kesuvim* are not read is because of neglect of the *beis hamidrash.* What neglect of the *beis hamidrash* would be caused by having a public *haftarah* reading from *Kesuvim*? (see *Hagahos Chavos Yair* to *Rashi* on *Rif*). We have therefore assumed that even *Rashi* agrees to *Rabbeinu HaLevi's* explanation that אֵין קוֹרִין בָּהֶן refers also to individuals. The Mishnah means that since there is no public *haftarah* reading of *Kesuvim* in the synagogue, the Rabbis were able to decree that private individuals should also not read from them, because of neglect of the *beis hamidrash.* Had *Kesuvim* been used for the *haftarah* reading, however, the Rabbis could not have outlawed their reading by individuals. See also Meiri where such an explanation is indicated. Cf. *Chidushei R' Moshe Kazis* ד״ה כתב הר״ן who offers a novel explanation of *Rashi* according to which *Rashi* is indeed giving two distinct explanations of this phrase. See also *Rabbeinu Perachyah.*]

6. *Targum.* [*Targum* literally means translation. Aramaic was called *Targum* because in Talmudic times Aramaic was the translation most frequently used.]

7. Rav Huna maintains that the leniencies granted by the Rabbis for saving scrolls of the Scriptures from a fire do not apply to translations. Rav Chisda, however, holds that they are treated in this respect like Hebrew scrolls.

[Obviously, according to Rav Chisda not only *may* we save these holy scrolls but we *must* save them.]

8. The Mishnah in *Megillah* 8b records a Tannaic dispute as to whether scrolls of the Scriptures may be written in a foreign language: The Tanna Kamma permits this while Rabban Shimon ben Gamliel allows only Greek translations [see there, 9b, for why Greek is an exception to the

[א] מותר בקניבת ירק (א) [ב] ואמר רבי חייא בר אבא אמר רבי יוחנן יום כיפורים שחל להיות בחול [ג] מפצעין באגוזים ומפרכסין ברימונים מן המנחה ולמעלה מפני ב) עגמת נפש דבי רב יהודה מקנבי כרבא דבי רבה גרדי קארי כיון דחזא דהוו קא מחרפי אמר להו אתא איגרתא ממערבא משמיה דר' יוחנן דאסיר:

הדרן עלך ואלו קשרים

כל כתבי הקדש מצילין אותן מפני הדליקה בין שקורין בהן ובין שאין קורין בהן (א) אע"פ שכתובים בכל לשון א) טעונים גניזה ומפני מה אין קורין בהם מפני ביטול בית המדרש: **גמ'** איתמר ב) היו כתובים תרגום או בכל לשון רב הונא אמר אין מצילין אותן מפני הדליקה ורב חסדא אמר מצילין אותן מפני הדליקה אליבא דמאן דאמר ניתנו לקרות בהן דכולי עלמא לא פליגי דמצילין כי פליגי אליבא דמאן דאמר לא ניתנו לקרות בהן רב הונא אמר אין מצילין דהא לא ניתנו לקרות בהן רב חסדא אמר מצילין משום בזיון כתבי הקדש תנן כל כתבי הקדש מצילין אותן מפני הדליקה בין שקורין בהן בין שאין קורין בהן (ב) אע"פ שכתובין בכל לשון מאי לאו שקורין בהן נביאים ושאין קורין בהן כתובים אע"פ שכתובין בכל לשון דלא ניתנו לקרות בהן וקתני מצילין ותיובתא דרב הונא אמר לך רב הונא ותסברא אימא סיפא טעונין גניזה השתא אצולי מצילינן גניזה מיבעי אלא רב הונא מתרץ לטעמיה ורב חסדא מתרץ לטעמיה רב הונא מתרץ לטעמיה בין שקורין בהם נביאים ובין שאין קורין בהם כתובים במה דברים אמורים שכתובים בלשון הקדש אבל בכל לשון לא מצילין ואפילו הכי גניזה בעו רב חסדא מתרץ לטעמיה בין שקורין בהן נביאים ובין שאין קורין בהן כתובים אע"פ שכתובין בכל לשון נמי מצילין והכי קאמר ומקק שלהן טעונין גניזה מיתיבי היו כתובים תרגום (ג) וכל לשון מצילין אותן מפני הדליקה תיובתא דרב הונא אמר לך רב הונא האי תנא סבר ניתנו לקרות בהן ת"ש היו כתובין גיפטית מדית עיברית עילמית יוונית אע"פ שלא ניתנו לקרות בהן מצילין אותן מפני הדליקה תיובתא דרב הונא אמר לך רב הונא תנאי היא דתניא ג) היו כתובין תרגום ובכל לשון מצילין אותן מפני הדליקה ר' יוסי אומר אין מצילין אותן מפני הדליקה אמר ר' יוסי ד) מעשה באבא חלפתא שהלך אצל רבן גמליאל בריבי לטבריא ומצאו שהי' יושב על שלחנו של (ה) יוחנן הנזוף) ובידו ספר איוב תרגום והוא קורא בו אמר לו זכור אני ברבן גמליאל אבי אביך שהיה עומד ע"ג מעלה בהר הבית והביאו לפניו ספר איוב תרגום ואמר לבנאי שקעהו תחת הנדבך אף הוא צוה עליו וגנזו ר' יוסי ברבי יהודה אומר עריבה של טיט כפו עליו אמר רבי שתי תשובות בדבר חדא וכי טיט בהר הבית מנין ועוד וכי מותר לאבדן ביד אלא מניחן במקום התורפה והן ו) מרקיבין מאליהן מאן תנאי אילימא

רש"י

מותר בקניבת ירק. דשבות לאו איסורא דאורייתא הוא אלא דרבנן והכא משום עגמת נפש שמתקן ואינו אוכל והרי קרוב לעינוי שרי ודווקא מן המנחה ולמעלה שהוא שואף ומצפה לעת אכילה ואיכא עגמת נפש טפי: כיון דחזי דהוי קא מחרפי. מקדימין לפני המנחה דהשתא לאו עגמת נפש הוא: אמר להו. לאינשי ביתיה: אתא איגרתא ממערבא כו'. כי היכי דלקבלו מיניה:

הדרן עלך ואלו קשרים

כל כתבי הקדש. כגון תורה נביאים וכתובים ולא תימא תורה לחוד הוא דשרי למיטרח ולאצולי ולא שאר ספרים: מצילין אותן. כדקתני לקמן למבוי שאינו מפולש וטירחא בעלמא הוא דשרי (ד) בה וחסרון עירוב כדמפרש בגמרא: בין שקורין בהן. כגון נביאים שמפטירין בהן בשבת בבית הכנסת: בין שאין קורין בהן. כגון כתובים ורבינו הלוי אמר דאפי' יחידים אין קורין בהן כדקתני טעמא משום ביטול בית המדרש דמשכי לגא ובשבת היו דורשין דרשה לבעלי בתים שעסוקין במלאכה כל ימות החול ובתוך הדרשה היו מורין להן הלכות איסור והיתר וטוב להן לשמוע מלקרות בכתובים: ואע"פ שכתובין בכל לשון. ואיכא למאן דאמר לקמן לא ניתנו לקרות בהן מצילין אותן: טעונין גניזה. אסור להניחן במקום הפקר ובגמרא מתרץ לה ורבותי פירשו דהאי בכל לשון דקאמר אכתובים קאי ולא אנביאים ומדומה אני מפני שמצינו ביונתן בן עוזיאל שאמרו תרגום הן מפרשין כך ואני אומר אף בנביאים אם אמר יונתן לא כתבו ולא ניתנו ליכתב והכי מפרש במסכת מגילה (דף ט.) ומאן דאסר בכולהו אסר בר מס"ת יוונית משום מעשה דתלמי המלך ולא מפליג התם בין נביאים לכתובים: מפני בטול בית המדרש. שהיה קבוע בשבת כדפרישית לעיל: גמ' איתמר היו כתובין תרגום. אכתובים קאמר ול"נ אכל כתבי הקדש קאי: אליבא דמאן דאמר ניתנו לקרות בהן. מותר לקרות בכתבי הקדש הכתובין בכל לשון במסכת מגילה (דף ח:) ואין בין ספרי' ותפילין ומזוזות אלא שהספרים נכתבין בכל לשון: לא ניתנו. (ז) רבן גמליאל) פליג עלה ואמר אף ספרים לא התירו שיכתבו אלא יוונית: ואע"פ שכתובין בכל לשון. ולא ניתנו לקרות למדקאמר אף על פי מכלל דלא ניתנו לקרות בהן דאי ניתנו מאי גריעותייהו: אימא סיפא. לדידך דאמרת אע"פ שכתובין בכל לשון אמצילין קאי אימא סיפא על כרחיך מילתא באנפיה נפשיה הוא וטעונין גניזה בחול פשיטא השתא בשבת מצילין להו גניזה בחול מיבעיא: ואפילו הכי בעו גניזה. ודקתני ואע"פ שכתובין בכל לשון לאו אהצלה קאי אלא אטעונין גניזה והכי קאמר אף על פי שכתובים בכל לשון ובשבת אין מצילין אותן בחול מיהא טעונין גניזה: ומקק שלהם. אם בלו ונעשו רקבון אף המקק רקבובית (ה) של אכילת התולעים טעונין גניזה: עברית. כתב של עבר הנהר: אבא חלפתא. אבא של רבי יוסי חלפתא שמו: רבן גמליאל בריבי. לא שהיה בנו של רבי אלא אדם גדול קרי בריבי: רבן גמליאל אבי אביך. הוא רבן גמליאל הזקן ורבן גמליאל שהיה בדורו של חלפתא הוא אבי אביו של רבינו הקדוש: גב מעלה בהר הבית. שבהר הבית היו מעלות כשהוא הולך וגבוה כדתנן במסכת מדות (פ"ב מ"ג): נדבך. שורת אבני הבנין: טיט בהר הבית מנין. וכי בטיט היו בונין והלא בטרכסיד היו בונים סול וסיד מעורבין וטיט לא הוי אלא עפר ומים: התורפה. גלוי והפקר: מאן תנאי. דקאמר רב הונא לעיל תנאי היא מאן מהני תנאי קאי כרב חסדא ומאן כרב הונא: אילימא

תוספות

כל כתבי הקדש מצילין אותן מפני הדליקה כו'. אומר ר"ת דכולא האי פירקא איירי כשנפלה דליקה באותו בית או באותו חצר דכיון שהאש שם ודאי בהול הוא ואי שרית ליה אתי לכבויי כדמפרש בגמרא אבל נפלה דליקה בבית אחר מותר להציל הכל:

אליבא דמ"ד ניתנו לקרות בהן כ"ע לא פליגי דמצילין. והשתא ספרים שלנו מצילין דנתנו לקרות בהן משום עת לעשות לה' הפרו תורתך כדאמרינן בהניזקין (גיטין ס.): **לא** ניתנו לקרות בהן. פירש רש"י דהיינו רבן שמעון בן גמליאל דפליג במתניתין בפ"ק דמגילה (דף ח:) דאף ספרים לא התירו שיכתבו אלא יוונית ופירש הרב פור"ת דהיינו טעמא כיון דלא ניתנו ליכתב אסור לקרות בהן משום דדברים שבכתב אסור לאומרן בעל פה וקשה דאין זה אי אתה רשאי לאומרו בעל פה כיון שאינו אומרו בלשון הקדש אלא באותו לשון כשהן כתובין דהא שרי למימר בעל פה תרגום ° כדמתרגם רב יוסף:

עילמית יוונית. אומר ר"י דאתיא כרבי יהודה דאסר שאר ספרים לכתוב יוונית ולא התיר אלא בס"ת בלבד אבל רבנן שרו אף בשאר ספרים כדאמר בפ"ק דמגילה (דף ט.):

ובידו ספר איוב תרגום. משמע שבימי התנאים כבר נעשה תרגום כתובים וכן תניא במגילה (דף כא:) (ו) במגילה וההלל אפילו עשרה קורין ועשרה מתרגמין מה שאין כן בתורה אע"פ שיונתן לא עשאו מ"מ שוב נעשה בימי התנאים ודלא (ז) כאומרים דתרגום של כתובים רב יוסף עשאו ח):

עין משפט נר מצוה

א א מיי' פ"ו מהלכות ס"ת הלכה ג טוש"ע יו"ד סימן רפב סעיף ה:
ב ב מיי' פכ"ג מהלכות שבת הלכה כו סמג לאוין סה טוש"ע או"ח סימן שלד סעיף יב:

רבינו חננאל

מהתם. דגרסי' התם א"ר ישמעאל אחוי דר' ברכיה ויבדיל שכן הוא מותר להדיח כבשים ושלקות. כלומר דברים שאסורי' בשבת ומותרי' ביוה"כ ומשני לא מן המנחה ולמעלה מותר להדיח דאלמא שבת דחוקה היא ויבדיל מן המנחה ולמעלה. ושנינן מה נפשך כוס אין כאן נר אין כאן במה מבדילין א"ר אבין בתפלה: וראינו שפירש בה רבינו האיי הגאון נר ישראל יחיה ויפרה לעד. האי קושטא קושטיא היא מיהו מחוריא מילתא דבערב יוה"כ נמי הות תקיעה להבטיל העם מן המלאכה ולהבדיל בין קודש לחול ולערבי יו"ט נמי איכא טובא אלא מיהו כד הוי ערב יוה"כ ועיו"ט חול. אלא כד הוי קודש לא תקעינן. ואע"ג דלא מיפרשא בתקיעות שהיו במקדש. דייקינן מהא דתנן בפ' קמא דשחיטת חולין (דף כו:) כל מקום שיש הבדלה אין תוקעין וכל מקום שיש תקיעה אין הבדלה כיצד יו"ט שחל להיות ערב שבת תוקעין אבל לא מבדילין מכלל דביו"ט שאינו ע"ש היו מבדילין אבל לא תוקעין א) מכלל דאי הוה יו"ט בתר חול היו תוקעין וראוי לדעת דהני כולהו שמעתתא אליבא דאחרים. אבל לדילן לא מיתרמי לן יוה"כ סמוך לשבת לא מלפניה ולא מאחריה. ומפרש בגמרא דחליל. דכד מיקלע כפורים בחד בשבא מדחינן ליה. ומקשינן ומי דחינן והתנן חלבי שבת קריבין ביוה"כ. וא"ר זירא כי הוינא בבבל אמרי' הא דתניא יוה"כ שחל להיות ע"ש לא היו תוקעין ובמוצ"ש לא היו מבדילין דברי הכל היא. ופרקי' ההיא מתניתא אחרים היא דתניא אחרים אומרים אין בין עצרת לעצרת אין בין ר"ה לר"ה אלא ד' ימים. ואם היתה שנה מעוברת חמשה. וגרסינן בירושל' בתחלת מגילה. א"ר יוסי לית כאן חל להיות בשני חל להיות בשבת דאם חל להיות י"ד בשני צומא רבא בחד בשבא. ואם חל בשבת צומא רבא בעירובתא שמעינן מינה דאע"ג דסתם משנה היא דחויה היא ומשנת יחיד היא ולאו דסמכא היא. וכן כל משנה והלכה שהיא כיוצא בה. וכולן בדן ואודן בה תלוין שהלכה למשה מסיני שלא לקבוע יוה"כ סמוך לשבת בין מלפניה בין מאחריה ולענין קניבת ירק הלכתא יוה"כ שחל להיות בשבת אסור

מסורת הש"ס

א) רש"ל מ"ז, ב) [פי' שלא יהא עורם במוצאי יום בקניבה והכא נפשו עגומה עליו וכן מפצעין באגוזים ומפרכין ברמונים ודוקא מן המנחה ולמעלה שמאחר שהוא קרוב לעת האוכל דומה למי שיש לו פת בסלו ולא אתי למיכל מיניהו אבל קודם המנחה אסור גזרינן דילמא אתי למיכל מיניה ורש"י פי' בזה שאמרו משום עגמת נפש כענין אחר ולא ישר בעיני עכ"ל בעל המאור], ג) [תוספ' פי"ד], ד) [מס' סופרים פ"ה הט"ו], ה) [בתוספתא אי' ר' יוחנן בן נזוף], ו) [נ"ל מתאבדין], ז) [צ"ל רשב"ג], ח) [וע"ע תוס' מגילה כא: ד"ה ובמגילה ותוס' ב"ק ג: ד"ה כדמתרגם].

הגהות הב"ח

(א) במשנה ואע"פ שכתובין: (ב) גמ' ואע"פ כו' ואע"פ כו' לא ניתנו: (ג) שם תרגום ובכל לשון: (ד) רש"י ד"ה מצילין וכו' דשרי בהו ומסרון: (ה) ד"ה ומקק שלהן וכו' רקבובית. נ"ב עי' לעיל דף צ ע"א: (ו) תוס' ד"ה ובידו וכו' במגילה וההלל אפילו עשרה: (ז) בא"ד ולא כאומרים. נ"ב כלומר אבל קודם זה לא נעשה בימי התנאים. ולא גרסי' ועשרה מתרגמין וכמו שפירש"י במגילה אלא ככר נעשה בימי התנאים כמו שמוכח הכא:

גליון הש"ס

תוס' ד"ה לא ניתנו. כדמתרגם ר"י. עיין בב"ק דף ג ע"ב תוס' ד"ה כדמתרגם.

הגהות הגר"א

[א] גמ' מותר. נ"ל אסור: [ב] שם ואמר רחב"א אר"י. מא"מ: [ג] שם בחול. נ"ב מותר כן הוא גירסת הרמב"ם ז"ל והמ"מ ושמ"מ רבינו בא"ח סימן תר"ד סק"ד).

ליקוטי רש"י

ומקק שלהן. אכילת תולעת אוכלת הספרים ומקקן ומשו מקק [לעיל צ.]. בריבי. אדם גדול בדורו וכל היכא דקרי ליה בריבי אדם גדול בדורו היה וכל היכא דקרי ליה בריבי לשון חשיבות הוא [קידושין כא:]. כלומר אדם גדול ובן קורין לו כינוי [ע"ז מג.].

חשק שלמה על רבינו חננאל

א) ספר וצ"ל ומדתנן יו"ט שחל מבדילין ולא תוקעין.

בקניבת ירק ואפילו מן המנחה ולמעלה. ואם חל להיות בחול מפצעין באגוזים ומפרכין ברמונים ומותר בקניבת ירק מן המנחה ולמעלה אבל [משום] מיגדר [מילתא אסרוה]: **הדרן עלך ואלו קשרים**

פרק טז כל כתבי הקודש מצילין אותן מפני הדליקה בין שקורין בהן בין שאין קורין בהן. פירוש קורין בהן בצבור. תורה הפרשה בתורה ואפטרתא בנביאים ושאין קורין בהן בצבור כתובים. איתמר היו כתובין תרגום ובכל לשון רב הונא אמר אין מצילין אותן ורב חסדא אמר מצילין ובכתבי הקדש שמתורגמין בלשון אחר בין בכתב עברי בין בכתב אחר. ר' יוסי אמר לא ניתנו לקרות בהן דא"ר יוסי מעשה באבא חלפתא שהלך אצל רבן גמליאל לטבריא ומצאו יושב על שולחנו של יוחנן בן הנזוף ובידו ספר איוב תרגום א"ל זכור אני את רבן גמליאל אבי אביך שהיה עומד ע"ג מעלה בהר הבית והביאו לפניו ספר איוב תרגום ואמר לבנאי שקעהו תחת הנדבך. אף הוא צוה עליו וגנזו ור' נמי הכי קאמר מניחן במקום התורפה והן כלין מאליהן. ולפום הכי תנא ר' יוסי אין מצילין אותן.

We may not save them, דְּהָא לֹא נִיתְּנוּ לִקְרוֹת בָּהֶן – **since they may not be read.**[9] רַב חִסְדָּא אָמַר מַצִּילִין – **Rav Chisda,** however, **says: We may save** them, מִשּׁוּם בִּזְיוֹן כִּתְבֵי הַקֹּדֶשׁ – **on account of the disgrace to the Holy Scriptures.**[10]

The Gemara challenges Rav Huna:

תְּנַן – **We have learned in the Mishnah:** כָּל כִּתְבֵי הַקֹּדֶשׁ מַצִּילִין אוֹתָן מִפְּנֵי הַדְּלֵיקָה – ALL HOLY SCRIPTURES MAY BE SAVED FROM A FIRE, בֵּין שֶׁקּוֹרִין בָּהֶן בֵּין שֶׁאֵין קוֹרִין בָּהֶן – WHETHER WE READ FROM THEM OR WHETHER WE DO NOT READ FROM THEM, אַף עַל פִּי שֶׁכְּתוּבִין בְּכָל לָשׁוֹן – and EVEN THOUGH THEY ARE WRITTEN IN ANY other LANGUAGE. מַאי לָאו – Now, **is not** the meaning of the Mishnah as follows: שֶׁקּוֹרִין בָּהֶן נְבִיאִים – WE READ FROM THEM – this refers to *Neviim* scrolls, וְשֶׁאֵין קוֹרִין בָּהֶן כְּתוּבִים – and WE DO NOT READ FROM THEM on the Sabbath – this refers to *Kesuvim* scrolls; אַף עַל פִּי שֶׁכְּתוּבִין בְּכָל לָשׁוֹן – EVEN THOUGH THEY ARE WRITTEN IN ANY LANGUAGE – דְּלֹא נִיתְּנוּ לִקְרוֹת בָּהֶן – this implies **that they may not be read** at all?[11] וְקָתָנֵי מַצִּילִין – **And** still **the Mishnah teaches:** WE MAY SAVE them. וּתְיוּבְתָּא דְּרַב הוּנָא – **Thus,** we have **a refutation of Rav Huna's** view.[12] – ? –

The Gemara rejects the proof:

אָמַר לָךְ רַב הוּנָא – **Rav Huna would say to you:** וְתִסְבְּרָא – **Now do you** really **think this** explanation of the Mishnah **reasonable?** אֵימָא סֵיפָא – But **consider the end** of the Mishnah: טְעוּנִין גְּנִיזָה – THEY WARRANT BEING HIDDEN AWAY. הַשְׁתָּא אַצּוֹלֵי מַצִּילִינַן – **Now, if** the Mishnah teaches that **we may** disregard certain of the Sabbath restrictions to **save** these translations, גְּנִיזָה מִיבַּעְיָא – **is it necessary** to state that on a weekday they warrant **hiding away?**[13]

In view of this question, the Mishnah is difficult according to *both* Amoraim. The Gemara answers:

אֶלָּא רַב הוּנָא מְתָרֵץ לְטַעֲמֵיהּ – **Rather, Rav Huna interprets** the Mishnah **according to his reasoning,** וְרַב חִסְדָּא מְתָרֵץ לְטַעֲמֵיהּ – **and Rav Chisda interprets** the Mishnah **according to his reasoning.**

The Gemara first clarifies how Rav Huna would interpret the Mishnah, explaining that in his view some words must be added to the Mishnah:

רַב הוּנָא מְתָרֵץ לְטַעֲמֵיהּ – **Rav Huna interprets** the Mishnah **according to his reasoning,** as follows: בֵּין שֶׁקּוֹרִין בָּהֶם נְבִיאִים – WHETHER WE READ FROM THEM – this refers to *Neviim* – וּבֵין שֶׁאֵין קוֹרִין בָּהֶם כְּתוּבִים – OR WHETHER WE DO NOT READ FROM THEM – this refers to ***Kesuvim.*** Both of these scrolls may be saved. (The Mishnah's first sentence ends here.) At this point the Mishnah is missing words and this is how it should read: בַּמֶּה דְּבָרִים אֲמוּרִים – **In what** case **are these words said?** שֶׁכְּתוּבִין בִּלְשׁוֹן הַקֹּדֶשׁ – **Where [the scrolls] are written in the Holy Tongue** [i.e. Hebrew], אֲבָל בְּכָל לָשׁוֹן – **but** if they are written **in any** other **language,** אֵין מַצִּילִין – **they may not be saved.** וַאֲפִילּוּ הָכִי גְּנִיזָה בָּעוּ – **But nevertheless they require being hidden away.**[14]

The Gemara explains how Rav Chisda would interpret our Mishnah:

רַב חִסְדָּא מְתָרֵץ לְטַעֲמֵיהּ – **Rav Chisda interprets** the Mishnah **according to his reasoning,** as follows: בֵּין שֶׁקּוֹרִין בָּהֶן נְבִיאִים – WHETHER WE READ FROM THEM – this refers to ***Neviim,*** וּבֵין שֶׁאֵין קוֹרִין בָּהֶן כְּתוּבִים – OR WHETHER WE DO NOT READ FROM THEM – this refers to ***Kesuvim.*** אַף עַל פִּי שֶׁכְּתוּבִין בְּכָל לָשׁוֹן נַמִּי מַצִּילִין – The Mishnah teaches that EVEN THOUGH [THESE BOOKS] ARE WRITTEN IN ANY LANGUAGE, THEY MAY BE SAVED as well. וְהָכִי קָאָמַר – **And this is what [the Mishnah] is saying** with the phrase *they warrant being hidden away*: וּמֶקֶק שֶׁלָּהֶן טְעוּנִין גְּנִיזָה – It means to add: **And their decay,** i.e. the decayed particles of these scrolls, also WARRANT BEING HIDDEN AWAY.[15]

The Gemara again challenges Rav Huna:

מֵיתִיבֵי – **They challenged** Rav Huna from a Baraisa: הָיוּ כְּתוּבִים תַּרְגּוּם וְכָל לָשׁוֹן מַצִּילִין אוֹתָן מִפְּנֵי הַדְּלֵיקָה – If THEY [books of the Scripture] WERE WRITTEN IN ARAMAIC OR IN ANY other LANGUAGE, WE MAY SAVE THEM FROM A FIRE on the Sabbath. תְּיוּבְתָּא דְּרַב הוּנָא – This is **a refutation of Rav Huna.** – ? –

The Gemara rejects this proof:

אָמַר לָךְ רַב הוּנָא – **Rav Huna would say to you:** הַאי תַּנָּא סָבַר נִיתְּנוּ לִקְרוֹת בָּהֶן – **This Tanna maintains** that **[translations]**

NOTES

rule] (see *Rashi*). Our Gemara states that according to the Tanna Kamma there can be no question that these translations may be rescued. Since they may be written, they may surely be read; accordingly, they have the full status of Hebrew scrolls, which may be saved. It is only according to Rabban Shimon ben Gamliel that the dispute applies.

9. Since Rabban Shimon ben Gamliel forbids writing these scrolls, he presumably forbids reading them as well (see *Maginei Shlomo* and *Leshon HaZahav*; cf. *Tosafos* ד״ה לא). It stands to reason, therefore, that they may not be rescued.

10. The fact that these books are, despite their illegal status, renditions of the Holy Scriptures is sufficient reason to permit rescuing them. To allow them to burn like secular objects would be a disgrace to the Holy Scriptures.

11. The wording *even though* implies that there is a problem with the fact that they were written in a language other than Hebrew. This indicates that our Mishnah follows the opinion of Rabban Shimon ben Gamliel, who forbids translations (*Rashi*).

12. [The Rishonim ask: The Gemara's question is from the words "even though they are written in any language." Why, then, does the Gemara preface its question with the seemingly extraneous explanation that the phrase "we read from them" refers to *Neviim* and the phrase "we do not read from them" refers to *Kesuvim*?

Rashba answers that the Gemara wishes to preclude a possible challenge to Rav Huna's view from the Mishnah's *earlier* statement. That is, one might have thought to explain that the phrase "whether we read from them" refers to Hebrew copies of Scripture, which may be read, while the phrase "whether we do not read from them" refers to translations, which one may not read. Were this interpretation correct, the latter phrase would pose a difficulty to Rav Huna, for the Mishnah would be stating that translations may be saved from a fire. The Gemara therefore states that this is not the correct interpretation of these phrases, and no challenge to Rav Huna may be mounted from them. Nevertheless, Rav Huna's view may be refuted from the Mishnah's *next* phrase. Cf. *Ran MHK* ed.]

13. According to the questioner, the phrase "even though they are written in any language" refers back to the phrase "All Holy Scriptures may be saved"; i.e. the Mishnah states that even though these translations may not be read, we may save them from a fire. Accordingly, the phrase "they warrant being hidden away" is an independent clause which teaches that these books must be protected from degradation during the week by placing them in a safe place rather than abandoning them in an unguarded area. But if they possess sufficient sanctity to allow them to be rescued on the Sabbath, is it not obvious they may not simply be put away in an unprotected manner on the weekdays? (*Rashi*).

14. According to this interpretation, the phrase *even though they are written in any language* does not refer back to the subject of saving books of the Scriptures from a fire on the Sabbath. Rather, it refers to the *following* phrase: *they warrant being hidden away.* The intent of the Mishnah is to say that even though these scrolls are written in languages other than Hebrew, and on the Sabbath they may not be saved from a fire, nevertheless they must be kept in a safe place to protect them from degradation (*Rashi*).

15. It is indeed unnecessary to state that translations need to be hidden away. By adding *they warrant being hidden away,* however, the Mishnah teaches that even after these books have decayed due to old age or worm infestation, their *remains* must be treated with respect and hidden away in a repository for holy objects (*Rashi*).

[א] מותר בקניבת ירק (א) [ב] ואמר רבי חייא בר אבא אמר רבי יוחנן יום כיפורים שחל להיות בחול [ג] מפצעין באגוזים ומפרכסין ברימונים מן המנחה ולמעלה מפני (ב) עגמת נפש דבי רב יהודה מקנבי כרבא דבי רבה גרדי קארי כיון דחזא דהוו קא מחרפי אמר להו אתא איגרתא ממערבא משמיה דר' יוחנן דאסיר:

הדרן עלך ואלו קשרים

כל כתבי הקדש מצילין אותן מפני הדליקה בין שקורין בהן ובין שאין קורין בהן (א) אע"פ שכתובים בכל לשון (א) טעונים גניזה ומפני מה אין קורין בהם מפני ביטול בית המדרש: גמ' איתמר (ב) היו כתובים תרגום או בכל לשון רב הונא אמר אין מצילין אותן מפני הדליקה ורב חסדא אמר מצילין אותן מפני הדליקה אליבא דמאן דאמר ניתנו לקרות בהן דכולי עלמא לא פליגי דמצילין כי פליגי אליבא דמאן דאמר לא ניתנו לקרות בהן רב הונא אמר אין מצילין דהא לא ניתנו לקרות בהן רב חסדא אמר מצילין משום בזיון כתבי הקדש תנן כל כתבי הקדש מצילין אותן מפני הדליקה בין שקורין בהן בין שאין קורין בהן (ג) אע"פ שכתובין בכל לשון מאי לאו שקורין בהן נביאים ושאין קורין בהן כתובים אע"פ שכתובין בכל לשון דלא ניתנו לקרות בהן וקתני מצילין ותיובתא דרב הונא אמר לך רב הונא ותסברא אימא סיפא טעונין גניזה השתא אצולי מצילינן גניזה מיבעי אלא רב הונא מתרץ לטעמיה ורב חסדא מתרץ לטעמיה רב הונא מתרץ לטעמיה בין שקורין בהם נביאים ובין שאין קורין בהם כתובים במה דברים אמורים שכתובין בלשון הקודש אבל בכל לשון אין מצילין ואפילו הכי גניזה בעו רב חסדא מתרץ לטעמיה בין שקורין בהן נביאים ובין שאין קורין בהן כתובים אע"פ שכתובין בכל לשון נמי מצילין והכי קאמר ומקק שלהן טעונין גניזה מיתיבי היו כתובים תרגום (ג) וכל לשון מצילין אותן מפני הדליקה תיובתא דרב הונא אמר לך רב הונא האי תנא סבר ניתנו לקרות בהן ת"ש היו כתובין גיפטית מדית עיברית עילמית יוונית אע"פ שלא ניתנו לקרות בהן מצילין אותן מפני הדליקה תיובתא דרב הונא אמר לך רב הונא תנאי היא דתניא (ג) היו כתובין תרגום ובכל לשון מצילין אותן מפני הדליקה ר' יוסי אומר אין מצילין אותן מפני הדליקה אמר ר' יוסי (ד) מעשה באבא חלפתא שהלך אצל רבן גמליאל בריבי לטבריא ומצאו שהי' יושב על שלחנו של (ה) יוחנן הנזוף ובידו ספר איוב תרגום והוא קורא בו אמר לו זכור אני ברבן גמליאל אבי אביך שהיה עומד ע"ג מעלה בהר הבית והביאו לפניו ספר איוב תרגום ואמר לבנאי שקעהו תחת הנדבך אף הוא צוה עליו וגנזו ר' יוסי ברבי יהודה אומר עריבה של טיט כפו עליו אמר רבי שתי תשובות בדבר חדא וכי טיט בהר הבית מנין ועוד וכי מותר לאבדן ביד אלא מניחן במקום התורפה והן (ו) מרקיבין מאליהן מאן תנאי אילימא

רש"י

מותר בקניבת ירק. דשבות לאו איסורא דאורייתא הוא אלא דרבנן והכא משום עגמת נפש שמתקן ואינו אוכל והרי קרוב לעינוי שרי ודווקא מן המנחה ולמעלה שהוא סואף ומצפה לעת אכילה ואיכא עגמת נפש טפי: כיון דחזי דהוי קא מחרפי. מקדימין לפני המנחה דהשתא לאו עגמת נפש הוא: אמר להו. לאינשי ביתיה: אתא איגרתא ממערבא כו'. כי היכי דלקבלו מיניה:

הדרן עלך ואלו קשרים

כל כתבי הקדש. כגון תורה נביאים וכתובים ולא תימא תורה לחוד הוא דשרי לטרוח ולאצולי ולא שאר ספרים: מצילין אותן. כדקתני לקמן למבוי שאינו מפולש וטירחא בעלמא הוא דשרי (ד) בה וחסרון עירוב כדמפרש בגמרא: בין שקורין בהן. כגון נביאים שמפטירין בהן בשבת בבית הכנסת: בין שאין קורין בהן. כגון כתובים ורבינו הלוי אמר דאפי' יחידים אין קורין בהן כדקתני טעמא משום ביטול בית המדרש דמשכי לבא ובשבת היו דורשין דרשה לבעלי בתים שעסוקין במלאכה כל ימות החול ובתוך הדרשה היו מורין להן הלכות איסור והיתר וטוב להן לשמוע מלקרות בכתובים: ואע"פ שכתובין בכל לשון. ואיכא למאן דאמר לקמן לא ניתנו לקרות בהן מצילין אותן: טעונין גניזה. אסור להניחן במקום הפקר ובגמרא מתרץ לה ורבותי פירשו דהאי בכל לשון דקאמר אכתובים קאי ולא אנביאים ומדומה אני מפני שמצינו ביונתן בן עוזיאל שאמרו תרגום הן מפרשין כך ואני אומר אף בנביאים אם אמר יונתן לא כתבו ולא ניתנו ליכתב והכי מפרש במסכת מגילה (דף ט.) ומאן דאסר בכולהו אסר בר מס"ת יוונית משום מעשה דתלמי המלך ולא מפליג התם בין נביאים לכתובים: מפני בטול בית המדרש. שהיה קבוע בשבת כדפרישית לעיל: גמ' איתמר היו כתובין תרגום. אכתובים קאמר ול"נ אכל כתבי הקדש קאי: אליבא דמאן דאמר ניתנו לקרות בהן. מותר לקרות בכתבי הקדש הכתובין בכל לשון במסכת מגילה (דף ח:) ואין בין ספרי' ותפילין ומזוזות אלא שהספרים נכתבין בכל לשון: לא ניתנו. (") רבן גמליאל) פליג עלה ואמר אף ספרים לא התירו שיכתבו אלא יוונית: ואע"פ שכתובין בכל לשון. ולא ניתנו לקרות דמדקאמר אף על פי מכלל דלא ניתנו לקרות בהן דאי ניתנו מאי גריעותייהו: אימא סיפא. לדידך דאמרת אע"פ שכתובין בכל לשון אמצילין קאי אימא סיפא על כרחיך מילתא באנפיה נפשיה הוא וטעונין גניזה בחול פשיטא השתא בשבת מצילין להו גניזה בחול מיבעיא: ואפילו הכי בעו גניזה. ודקתני ואע"פ שכתובין בכל לשון לאו אהצלה קאי אלא אטעונין גניזה והכי קאמר אף על פי שכתובים בכל לשון ובשבת אין מצילין אותן בחול מיהא טעונין גניזה: ומקק שלהם. אם בלו ונעשו רקבון אף המקק רקבובית (ה) של אכילת התולעים טעון גניזה: עברית. כתב של עבר הנהר: אבא חלפתא. אבא של רבי יוסי חלפתא שמו: רבן גמליאל בריבי. לא שהיה בנו של רבי אלא אדם גדול קרי בריבי: רבן גמליאל אבי אביך. הוא רבן גמליאל הזקן ורבן גמליאל שהיה בדורו של חלפתא הוא אבי אביו של רבינו הקדוש: גב מעלה בהר הבית. שבהר הבית היו מעלות וגבוה לדוכן במסכת מדות (פ"ב מ"ג): נדבך. שורת אבני הבנין: טיט בהר הבית מנין. וכי בטיט היו בונין והלא בטרכסית היו בונים הוא וסיד ועורכין וטיט לא הוי אלא עפר ומים: התורפה. גלוי והפקר: מאן תנאי. דקאמר רב הונא לעיל תנאי היא מאן מהני תנאי קאי כרב חסדא ומאן כרב הונא: אילימא

תוספות

כל כתבי הקדש מצילין אותן מפני הדליקה כו'. אומר ר"ת דכולה האי פירקא איירי כשנפלה דליקה באותו בית או באותו חצר דכיון שהאש שם ודאי בהול הוא ואי שרית ליה אתי לכבויי כדמפרש בגמרא אבל נפלה דליקה בבית אחר מותר להציל הכל:

אליבא דמ"ד ניתנו לקרות בהן כ"ע לא פליגי דמצילין. והשתא ספרים שלנו מצילין דנתנו לקרות בהן משום עת לעשות לה' הפרו תורתך כדאמרינן בהניזקין (גיטין ס.): לא ניתנו לקרות בהן. פירש רש"י דהיינו רבן שמעון בן גמליאל דפליג במתניתין בפ"ק דמגילה (דף ח:) דאף ספרים לא התירו שיכתבו אלא יוונית ופירש הרב פור"ת דהיינו טעמא כיון דלא ניתנו ליכתב אסור לקרות בהן משום דדברים שבכתב אסור לאומרן בעל פה וקשה דאין זה אי אתה רשאי לאומרו בעל פה כיון שאינו אומרו בלשון הקדש אלא באותו לשון כשהן כתובין דהא שרי למימר בעל פה תרגום ° כדמתרגם רב יוסף:

עילמית יוונית. אומר ר"י דאתיא כרבי יהודה דאסר שאר ספרים לכתוב יוונית ולא התיר אלא בס"ת בלבד אבל רבנן שרו אף בשאר ספרים כדאמר בפ"ק דמגילה (דף ט.):

ובידו ספר איוב תרגום. משמע שבימי התנאים כבר נעשה תרגום כתובים וכן תניא במגילה (דף כא:) (ו) במגילה ובהלל אפילו עשרה קורין ועשרה מתרגמין מה שאין כן בתורה אע"פ שיונתן לא עשאו מ"מ שוב נעשה בימי התנאים ולא (ז) כאומרים דתרגום של כתובים רב יוסף עשאו (ח):

מסורת הש"ס

א) רש"ל מ"ז, ב) [פי' אלא יהא טורח במוצאי יום כפורים והוא נכנס מעונה עליו וכן מפצעין באגוזים ומפרכסין ברמונים דוקא מן המנחה ולמעלה שמאחר שהוא קרוב לעת האוכל דומה למי שיש לו פת בסלו ולא אתי למיכל מינייהו אבל קודם המנחה אסור גזרינן דילמא אתי למיכל מיניה ורש"י פי' שם שאמרו משום עגמת נפש בענין אחר ולא אסר בעניי עכ"ל בעל המאור], ג) [תוספ' פי"ד], ד) [מס' סופרים פ"ה הט"ו], ה) [בתוספתא אי' ר' יוחנן בן ניזוף], ו) [ס"א מתאבדין], ז) [צ"ל רשב"ג], ח) [וע"ע תוס' מגילה כא: ד"ה ולמגילה ותוס' ב"ק ג: ד"ה כדמתרגם].

עין משפט נר מצוה

א א מיי' פ"י מהלכות ס"ת הלכה ג טוש"ע יו"ד סימן רפב סעיף ה:
ב ב מיי' פכ"ג מהלכות שבת הלכה כו סמג לאוין סה טוש"ע או"ח סימן שלד סעיף יב:

הגהות הב"ח

(א) במשנה ואע"פ שכתובין: (ב) גמ' ואע"פ כו' ואע"פ כו' ואע"פ לא ניתנו: (ג) שם תרגום ובכל לשון: (ד) רש"י ד"ה מצילין וכו' דשרי בהו וחסרון: (ה) ד"ה ומקק שלהן וכו' רקבובית. נ"ב עי' לעיל דף צ ע"ב: (ו) תוס' ד"ה ובידו וכו' ובהלל ובמגילה אפילו עשרה: (ז) בא"ד ולא כאומרים. נ"ב כלומר אבל קודם זה לא נעשה בימי התנאים. ולא גרסי' ועשרה מתרגמין וכמו שפירש"י במגילה אלא כבר נעשה בימי התנאים כמו שמוכח הכא:

גליון הש"ס

תוס' ד"ה לא ניתנו. כדמתרגם ר"י. עיין בב"ק דף ג ע"ב בתוס' ד"ה כדמתרגם.

הגהות הגר"א

[א] גמ' מותר. נ"ל אסור: [ב] שם (ואמר רחב"א א"ר). תא"מ: [ג] שם בחול. נ"ב מותר כן הוא גירסת הרמב"ם ומ"מ (ומגמ"ה) רבינו בא"ח סימן תרי"א סק"ד:

ליקוטי רש"י

ומקק שלהן. אכילת תולעת אוכלת הספרים ומקקין ושמו מקק [לעיל צ.]. בריבי. אדם גדול בדורו וכל היכא דקרי בריבי אדם גדול [עירובין נג.]. גדול בדורו היה וכל היכא דקרי ליה בריבי לשון חכמה ומריפות הוא [קידושין כא:]. כלומר אדם גדול הוא ואין קורין לו בכינוי [ע"ז מג.].

חשק שלמה על רבינו חננאל

א) ספר ונ"ל ומדמסן יו"ט שחל בשבת אין מבדילין ולא תוקעין.

רבינו חננאל

מהתם. דגרסי' התם א"ר ישמעאל אחוי דר' ברכיה ויבדיל שכן הוא מותר להדיח כבשים ושלקות. כלומר דברים שאסורי' בשבת ומותרי' ביוה"כ ומשני לא מן המנחה ולמעלה מותר להדיח דאלמא שבת דחוקה היא ויבדיל מן המנחה ולמעלה. ושנינן מה נפשך כוס אין כאן נר אין כאן במה מבדילין א"ר אבין בתפלה: ודאינו שפירש בה רבינו האיי הגאון נר ישראל יחיה ויפרה לעד. האי קושיא קושיא היא מיהו מחוורא מילתא דבערב יוה"כ נמי הות תקיעה להבטיל העם מן המלאכה ולהבדיל בין קודש לחול ולערבי יו"ט נמי איכא תקיעה אלא מיהו כד הוי ערב יוה"כ ועיו"ט חול. אלא כד הוי קודש לא תקעינן. ואע"ג דלא מיפרשא בתקיעות שהיו במקדש. דייקינן מהא דתנן בפ' קמא דשחיטת חולין (דף כו:) כל מקום שיש הבדלה אין תוקעין וכל מקום שיש תקיעה אין הבדלה כיצד ערב שבת שחל להיות יו"ט תוקעין אבל לא מבדילין מכלל דביו"ט שאינו ע"ש היו מבדילין אבל לא תוקעין (א) מכלל דאי הוה יו"ט בתר חול היו תוקעין ודאי לדעת דהני כולהו שמעתתא אליבא דאחרים. אבל לדילן לא מיתרמי לן יוה"כ סמוך לשבת לא מלפניה ולא מאחריה. ומפרש בגמרא דחליל. דכד מיקלע כפורים בחד בשבא מדחינן ליה. ומקשינן ומי דחינן והתנן חלבי שבת קריבין ביוה"כ. וא"ר זירא כי הוינא בבבל אמרי' הא דתניא יוה"כ שחל להיות ע"ש לא היו תוקעין ובמוצ"ש לא היו מבדילין דברי הכל היא. ופרקי' ההיא מתניתא אחרים היא דתניא אחרים אומרים אין בין עצרת לעצרת אלא ד' ימים. בין ר"ה לר"ה אלא ד' ימים. ואם היתה שנה מעוברת חמשה. וגרסינן בירושל' בתחלת מגילה. א"ר יוסי לית כאן חל להיות בשני חל להיות בשבת דהא חל להיות י"ד בשני צומא רבא בחד בשבא. ואם חל בשבת צומא רבא בעירובתא שמעינן מינה דאע"ג דסתם משנה היא דחויה היא ומשנת יחיד היא ולאו דסמכא היא. וכן כל משנה והלכה שהיא כיוצא בה. וכולן בין ואורן בה תלוין שהלכה למשה מסיני שלא לקבוע יוה"כ סמוך לשבת בין מלפניה בין מאחריה ולענין קניבת ירק הלכתא ביוה"כ שחל להיות בשבת אסור בקניבת ירק ואפילו מן המנחה ולמעלה. ואם חל להיות בחול מפצעין באגוזים ומפרכין ברמונים ומותר בקניבת ירק מן המנחה ולמעלה אבל [משום] מיגדר [מילתא אסרוה]: הדרן עלך ואלו קשרים

פרק טז כל כתבי הקודש מצילין אותן מפני הדליקה בין שקורין בהן בין שאין קורין בהן. פירוש קורין בהן בצבור. תורה הפרשה בתורה והפטרתא בנביאים ושאין קורין בהן בצבור כתובים. איתמר היו כתובין תרגום ובכל לשון רב הונא אמר אין מצילין ורב חסדא אמר מצילין ובכתבי הקדש שמתרגמין בלשון אחר כגון עברי בין בכתב אחד. א"ר יוסי אמר לא ניתנו לקרות בהן דא"ר זכור אני ברבן גמליאל אבי אביך שהיה עומד ע"ג מעלה בהר הבית והביאו לפניו ספר איוב תרגום ואמר לבנאי שקעהו תחת הנדבך. אף הוא צוה עליו וגנזו ור' נמי הכי קאמר מניחן במקום התורפה והן כלין מאליהן. ולפום הכי תנא ר' יוסי אין מצילין אותן.

may be read. Therefore, he holds that they may be saved. When I expressed my view that these books may not be saved, however, it was according to the Tanna who says that they may not be read.

Again the Gemara challenges Rav Huna:

תָּא שְׁמַע – **Come, learn** a proof for Rav Chisda: הָיוּ כְּתוּבִין גִּיפְּטִית מָדִית עִיבְרִית עֵילָמִית יְוָונִית – If THEY WERE WRITTEN IN COPTIC,[16] MEDIAN, IVRIS,[17] EILAMEAN or GREEK, אַף עַל פִּי שֶׁלֹּא נִיתְּנוּ לִקְרוֹת בָּהֶן – EVEN THOUGH THEY MAY NOT BE READ, מַצִּילִין אוֹתָן מִפְּנֵי הַדְּלֵיקָה – WE MAY SAVE THEM FROM A FIRE on the Sabbath. תְּיוּבְתָּא דְּרַב הוּנָא – This is **a refutation of Rav Huna.**[18] – ? –

The Gemara answers:

אָמַר לָךְ רַב הוּנָא – **Rav Huna would say to you:** תַּנָּאֵי הִיא – **[This matter] is** the subject of **a dispute of Tannaim,** i.e. I take the position of the Tanna cited below, who disagrees with the ruling in the Baraisa just quoted. דְּתַנְיָא – **For it was taught in a Baraisa:** הָיוּ כְּתוּבִין תַּרְגּוּם וּבְכָל לָשׁוֹן מַצִּילִין אוֹתָן מִפְּנֵי הַדְּלֵיקָה – If THEY WERE WRITTEN IN ARAMAIC OR IN ANY other foreign LANGUAGE, WE MAY SAVE THEM FROM A FIRE. רַבִּי יוֹסֵי אוֹמֵר – R' YOSE SAYS: אֵין מַצִּילִין אוֹתָן מִפְּנֵי הַדְּלֵיקָה – WE MAY NOT SAVE THEM FROM A FIRE.

אָמַר רַבִּי יוֹסֵי – R' YOSE SAID: מַעֲשֶׂה בְּאַבָּא חֲלַפְתָּא שֶׁהָלַךְ אֵצֶל רַבָּן גַּמְלִיאֵל בְּרִיבִּי לְטְבֶרְיָא – There was AN INCIDENT INVOLVING my FATHER CHALAFTA[19] WHO WENT TO RABBAN GAMLIEL B'RIBBI[20] IN TIBERIAS, וּמְצָאוֹ שֶׁהָיָה יוֹשֵׁב עַל שֻׁלְחָנוֹ שֶׁל יוֹחָנָן הַנָּזוּף – AND FOUND HIM SITTING AT THE TABLE OF YOCHANAN HANAZUF וּבְיָדוֹ סֵפֶר אִיּוֹב תַּרְגּוּם וְהוּא קוֹרֵא בּוֹ – WITH AN ARAMAIC translation of the BOOK OF *JOB* IN HIS HAND, WHICH HE WAS READING.[21] אָמַר לוֹ – [FATHER] SAID TO [RABBAN GAMLIEL]: זָכוּר אֲנִי בְּרַבָּן גַּמְלִיאֵל אֲבִי אָבִיךָ שֶׁהָיָה עוֹמֵד עַל גַּב מַעֲלָה בְּהַר הַבַּיִת – I RECALL THAT RABBAN GAMLIEL, YOUR PATERNAL GRANDFATHER,[22] WAS once STANDING ON A STEP ON THE TEMPLE MOUNT[23] וְהֵבִיאוּ לְפָנָיו סֵפֶר אִיּוֹב תַּרְגּוּם – WHEN THEY BROUGHT BEFORE HIM AN ARAMAIC BOOK OF *JOB*, וְאָמַר לַבַּנַּאי שַׁקְּעֵהוּ תַּחַת הַנִּדְבָּךְ – AND HE INSTRUCTED A BUILDER who was working nearby: BURY IT UNDER THE ROW OF BRICKS! אַף הוּא צִוָּה עָלָיו וּגְנָזוֹ – Upon hearing this, [RABBAN GAMLIEL B'RIBBI] ALSO ORDERED CONCERNING IT [the translation of *Job* that *he* was holding] AND THEY HID IT AWAY. רַבִּי יוֹסֵי בְּרַבִּי יְהוּדָה אוֹמֵר – R' YOSE THE SON OF R' YEHUDAH SAYS: עֲרֵיבָה שֶׁל טִיט כָּפוּ עָלָיו – A TROUGH OF CLAY THEY OVERTURNED UPON IT.[24]

The veracity of the version of R' Yose the son of R' Yehudah is challenged:

אָמַר רַבִּי – REBBI SAID: שְׁתֵּי תְשׁוּבוֹת בַּדָּבָר – There are TWO REBUTTALS TO THIS MATTER (i.e. account) of R' Yose the son of R' Yehudah. חֲדָא וְכִי טִיט בְּהַר הַבַּיִת מִנַּיִן – FIRSTLY, HOW DOES CLAY COME to be ON THE TEMPLE MOUNT?[25] וְעוֹד וְכִי מוּתָּר לְאַבְּדָן בַּיָּד – AND FURTHERMORE, IS IT PERMITTED TO DESTROY THEM [translations] WITH THE HAND, i.e. directly?[26] אֶלָּא מַנִּיחָן בְּמָקוֹם הַתּוּרְפָּה וְהֵן מַרְקִיבִין מֵאֲלֵיהֶן – RATHER, ONE LEAVES THEM IN AN UNGUARDED PLACE AND THEY DECAY OF THEIR OWN ACCORD.[27]

Rav Huna cited the foregoing Baraisa to show that the dispute between himself and Rav Chisda parallels an earlier Tannaic disagreement. The Gemara asks:

מַאן תַּנָּאֵי – **Which** of the **Tannaim** cited in this Baraisa sides with Rav Chisda and which with Rav Huna?

NOTES

16. I.e. ancient Egyptian (the word גִּיפְּטִית comes from the Greek *Aigyptios*).

17. The script of עֵבֶר הַנָּהָר, *the other side of the River* [Euphrates] (*Rashi*). [This was an ancient form of Hebrew script used up until the times of Ezra (see *Sanhedrin* 21b-22a). It differs dramatically from the present-day script, which is known as כְּתָב אַשּׁוּרִית.]

18. From the Baraisa's statement, "even though they may not be read," it is clear that the Baraisa follows the view of Rabban Shimon ben Gamliel who forbids translations. Yet, the Baraisa states that translations may not be saved. This contradicts Rav Huna.

Although even Rabban Shimon ben Gamliel permits writing in Greek (as mentioned in note 8), and this Baraisa states that even Greek translations may not be read, the Baraisa follows the opinion of R' Yehudah who [states in *Megillah* 9a that Rabban Shimon ben Gamliel] permits only a Torah scroll in Greek, but not *Neviim* and *Kesuvim* (*Tosafos*). [The Baraisa, then, refers specifically to *Neviim* and *Kesuvim*.]

19. [Although it is forbidden to call one's father by his name, this is permitted if he precedes the name with a title, e.g. "*Father* Chalafta" (*Rabbi Akiva Eiger,* based on *Rashi* to *Sanhedrin* 100a ד״ה בשמו; see *Beur HaGra, Yoreh Deah* 242:36; cf. *Menachem Meishiv Nefesh*).]

20. *B'Ribbi* was a title of distinction accorded to great men (*Rashi*).

21. [This translation was not authored by Yonasan ben Uziel, because, as mentioned in note 3, Yonasan ben Uziel did not compose a *Targum* to *Kesuvim*. Rather, it was a later translation (*Tosafos* here and to *Megillah* 21b ד״ה ובמגילה).]

22. This Rabban Gamliel, who lived during the time of the Temple, was known as Rabban Gamliel the Elder. He was the grandfather of the Rabban Gamliel who lived in the time of R' Chalafta; this Rabban Gamliel, in turn, was the grandfather of R' Yehudah HaNasi, redactor of the Mishnah (*Rashi*).

23. There were steps on the slope of the Temple Mount (*Rashi*; see *Middos* 2:3,5).

24. Rabban Gamliel the Elder did not order that the Aramaic copy of *Job* be buried under a row of bricks, but rather that a trough full of clay be spilled on top of it.

25. Clay, i.e. a mixture of earth and water, was not employed for building on the Temple Mount; rather, a mixture of lime and sand was used (*Rashi*). It is therefore highly unlikely that a worker would have clay handy to pour onto the scroll.

26. Pouring clay over the scrolls hastens their decay and is considered like destroying them directly (see *Chazon Ish, Yoreh Deah* 164:12 and *Iggros Moshe*, *Yoreh Deah* 1:6).

27. [This reflects an opposing view to that of the Mishnah, which, as interpreted by Rav Huna, states that while foreign translations may not be rescued, they may not be left in an unguarded area but must be hidden away (see *Shaar HaTziyun* 334:30; see also *Leshon HaZahav*).]

[א] מותר בקניבת ירק א) ([ב] ואמר רבי חייא בר אבא אמר רבי יוחנן יום כיפורים שחל להיות בחול [ג]) מפצעין באגוזים ומפרכסין ברימונים מן המנחה ולמעלה מפני ב) עגמת נפש דבי רב יהודה מקנבי כרבא דבי רבה גרדי קארי כיון דחזא דהוו קא מחרפי אמר להו אתא איגרתא ממערבא משמיה דר' יוחנן דאסיר:

הדרן עלך ואלו קשרים

כל כתבי הקדש מצילין אותן מפני הדליקה בין שקורין בהן ובין שאין קורין בהן (א) אע"פ שכתובים בכל לשון א טעונים גניזה ומפני מה אין קורין בהם מפני ביטול בית המדרש: גמ' איתמר ב היו כתובים תרגום או בכל לשון רב הונא אמר אין מצילין אותן מפני הדליקה ורב חסדא אמר מצילין אותן מפני הדליקה אליבא דמאן דאמר ניתנו לקרות בהן דכולי עלמא לא פליגי דמצילין כי פליגי אליבא דמאן דאמר לא ניתנו לקרות בהן רב הונא אמר אין מצילין דהא לא ניתנו לקרות בהן רב חסדא אמר מצילין משום בזיון כתבי הקדש תנן כל כתבי הקדש מצילין אותן מפני הדליקה בין שקורין בהן בין שאין קורין בהן (ב) אע"פ שכתובין בכל לשון מאי לאו שקורין בהן נביאים ושאין קורין בהן כתובים אע"פ שכתובין בכל לשון דלא ניתנו לקרות בהן וקתני מצילין ותיובתא דרב הונא אמר לך רב הונא ותסברא אימא סיפא טעונין גניזה השתא אצולי מצילינן גניזה מיבעי אלא רב הונא מתרץ לטעמיה ורב חסדא מתרץ לטעמיה רב הונא מתרץ לטעמיה בין שקורין בהן נביאים ובין שאין קורין בהם כתובים במה דברים אמורים שכתובין בלשון הקדש אבל בכל לשון אין מצילין ואפילו הכי גניזה בעו רב חסדא מתרץ לטעמיה בין שקורין בהן נביאים ובין שאין קורין בהן כתובים אע"פ שכתובין בכל לשון נמי מצילין והכי קאמר ומקק שלהן טעונין גניזה מיתיבי היו כתובים תרגום (ג) ובכל לשון מצילין אותן מפני הדליקה תיובתא דרב הונא אמר לך רב הונא האי תנא סבר ניתנו לקרות בהן ת"ש היו כתובין גיפטית מדית עיברית עילמית יוונית אע"פ שלא ניתנו לקרות בהן מצילין אותן מפני הדליקה תיובתא דרב הונא אמר לך רב הונא תנאי היא דתניא ג היו כתובין תרגום ובכל לשון מצילין אותן מפני הדליקה ר' יוסי אומר אין מצילין אותן מפני הדליקה אמר ר' יוסי ד מעשה באבא חלפתא שהלך אצל רבן גמליאל בריבי לטבריא ומצאו שהי' יושב על שלחנו של (ה יוחנן הנזוף) ובידו ספר איוב תרגום והוא קורא בו אמר לו זכור אני ברבן גמליאל אבי אביך שהיה עומד ע"ג מעלה בהר הבית והביאו לפניו ספר איוב תרגום ואמר לבנאי שקעהו תחת הנדבך אף הוא צוה עליו וגנזו ר' יוסי ברבי יהודה אומר עריבה של טיט כפו עליו אמר רבי שתי תשובות בדבר חדא וכי טיט בהר הבית מנין ועוד וכי מותר לאבדן ביד אלא מניחן במקום התורפה והן ו מרקיבין מאליהן מאן תנאי אילימא

רש"י

מותר בקניבת ירק. דשבות לאו איסורא דאורייתא הוא אלא דרבנן והכא משום עגמת נפש שמתקן ואינו אוכל והרי קרוב לעינוי שרי ודווקא מן המנחה ולמעלה שהוא שואף ומצפה לעת אכילה ואיכא עגמת נפש טפי: כיון דחזו דהוו קא מחרפי. מקדימין לפני המנחה דהשתא לאו עגמת נפש הוא. לאינשי ביתיה: אתא איגרתא ממערבא כו'. כי היכי דלקבלו מיניה:

הדרן עלך ואלו קשרים

כל כתבי הקדש. כגון תורה נביאים וכתובים ולא תימא תורה לחוד הוא דשרי למיטרח ולאצולי ולא שאר ספרים: מצילין אותן. כדקתני לקמן למבוי שאינו מפולש וטירחא בעלמא הוא דשרי (ד) בה וחסרון עירוב כדמפרש בגמרא: בין שקורין בהן. כגון נביאים שמפטירין בהן בשבת בבית הכנסת: בין שאין קורין בהן. כגון כתובים ורבינו הלוי אמר דאפי' יחידים אין קורין בהן דקתני טעמא משום ביטול בית המדרש דמשכי לגא ובשבת היו דורשין דרשה לבעלי בתים שעסוקין במלאכה כל ימות החול ובתוך הדרשה היו מורין להן הלכות איסור והיתר וטוב להן לשמוע מלקרות בכתובים: ואע"פ שכתובין בכל לשון. ואיכא למאן דאמר לקמן לא ניתנו לקרות בהן מצילין אותן: טעונין גניזה. אסור להניחן במקום הפקר ובגמרא מתרץ לה ורבותי פירשו דהאי בכל לשון דקאמר אכתובים קאי ולא אנביאים ומדומה אני מפני שמצינו ביונתן בן עוזיאל שאמרו תרגום הן מפרשין כך ואני אומר אף בנביאים אם אמר יונתן לא כתבו ולא ניתנו ליכתב והכי מפרש במסכת מגילה (דף ט.) ומאן דאסר בכולהו אסר בר מס"ת יוונית משום מעשה דתלמי המלך ולא מפליג התם בין נביאים לכתובים: מפני בטול בית המדרש. שהיה קבוע בשבת כדפרישית לעיל: גמ' איתמר היו כתובין תרגום. אכתובים קאמר ול"נ אכל כתבי הקדש קאי: אליבא דמאן דאמר ניתנו לקרות בהן. מותר לקרות בכתבי הקדש הכתובין בכל לשון במסכת מגילה (דף ח:) ואין בין ספרי' ותפילין ומזוזות אלא שהספרים נכתבין בכל לשון: לא ניתנו. (רבן גמליאל) פליג עלה ואמר אף ספרים לא התירו שיכתבו אלא יוונית: ואע"פ שכתובין בכל לשון. ולא ניתנו לקרות דמדקאמר אף על פי מכלל דלא ניתנו לקרות בהן דאי ניתנו מאי גריעותייהו: אימא סיפא. לדידך דאמרת אע"פ שכתובין בכל לשון אמצילין קאי אימא סיפא על כרחיך מילתא באנפיה נפשיה הוא וטעונין גניזה בחול פשיטא השתא בשבת מצילין להו גניזה בחול מיבעיא: ואפילו הכי בעו גניזה. ודקתני ואע"פ שכתובין בכל לשון לאו אהצלה קאי אלא אטעונין גניזה והכי קאמר אף על פי שכתובים בכל לשון ובשבת אין מצילין אותן בחול מיהא טעונין גניזה: ומקק שלהם. אם בלו ונעשו רקבון אף המקק רקבובית (ה) של אכילת התולעים טעונין גניזה: עברית. כתב של עבר הנהר: אבא חלפתא. אבא של רבי יוסי חלפתא שמו: רבן גמליאל בריבי. לא שהיה בנו של רבי אלא אדם גדול קרי בריבי: רבן גמליאל אבי אביך. הוא רבן גמליאל הזקן ורבן גמליאל שהיה בדורו של חלפתא הוא אבי אביו של רבינו הקדוש: גב מעלה בהר הבית. שבהר הבית היו מעלות כשהוא הולך וגבוה כדתנן במסכת מדות (פ"ב מ"ג): נדבך. שורת אבני הבנין: טיט בהר הבית מנין. וכי בטיט היו בונין והלא בטרכסיד היו בונים סיד וסיד מעורבין וטיט לא הוי אלא עפר ומים: התורפה. גלוי והפקר: מאן תנאי. דקאמר רב הונא לעיל תנאי היא מאן מהני תנאי קאי כרב חסדא ומאן כרב הונא: אילימא

תוספות

כל כתבי הקדש מצילין אותן מפני הדליקה כו'. אומר ר"ת דכולה האי פירקא איירי כשנפלה דליקה באותו בית או באותו חצר דכיון שהאש שם ודאי בהול הוא ואי שרית ליה אתי לכבויי כדמפרש בגמרא אבל נפלה דליקה בבית אחר מותר להציל הכל:

אליבא דמ"ד ניתנו לקרות בהן כ"ע לא פליגי דמצילין. והשתא ספרים שלנו מצילין דנתנו לקרות בהן משום עת לעשות לה' הפרו תורתך כדאמרינן בהניזקין (גיטין ס.): לא ניתנו לקרות בהן. פירש רש"י דהיינו רבן שמעון בן גמליאל דפליג במתניתין בפ"ק דמגילה (דף ח:) דאף ספרים לא התירו שיכתבו אלא יוונית ופירש הרב פור"ת דהיינו טעמא כיון דלא ניתנו ליכתב אסור לקרות בהן משום דדברים שבכתב אסור לאומרן בעל פה וקשה דאין זה אי אתה רשאי לאומרו בעל פה כיון שאינו אומרו בלשון הקדש אלא באותו לשון כשהן כתובין דהא שרי למימר בעל פה תרגום ° כדמתרגם רב יוסף:

עילמית יוונית. אומר ר"י דאתיא כרבי יהודה דאסר שאר ספרים לכתוב יוונית ולא התיר אלא בס"ת בלבד אבל רבנן שרו אף בשאר ספרים כדאמר בפ"ק דמגילה (דף ט.):

ובידו ספר איוב תרגום. משמע שבימי התנאים כבר נעשה תרגום כתובים וכן תניא במגילה (דף כא:) (ו) במגילה ובהלל אפילו עשרה קורין ועשרה מתרגמין מה שאין כן בתורה אע"פ שיונתן לא עשאו מ"מ שוב נעשה בימי התנאים ודלא (ז) כאומרים דתרגום של כתובים רב יוסף עשאו ח):

עין משפט נר מצוה

א א מיי' פ"י מהלכות ס"ת הלכה ג טוש"ע יו"ד סימן רפג סעיף ס:
ב ב מיי' פכ"ג מהלכות שבת הלכה כו סמג לאוין סה טוש"ע או"ח סימן שלד סעיף יב:

רבינו חננאל

מהחם. דגרסי' התם א"ר ישמעאל אחוי דר' ברכיה ויבדיל שכן הוא מותר להדיח כבשים ושלקות. כלומר דברים שאסורי' בשבת ומותרי' ביוה"כ ומשני לא מן המנחה ולמעלה מותר להדיח דאלמא שבת דחוקה היא ויבדיל מן המנחה ולמעלה. ושנינן מה נפשך כוס אין כאן נר אין כאן במה מבדילין א"ר אבין בתפלה: וראינו שפירש בה רבינו האיי הגאון נר ישראל יחיה ויפרה לעד. האי קושטא קושטיא היא מיהו מחויא מילתא דבערב יוה"כ נמי הות תקיעה להבטיל העם מן המלאכה ולהבדיל בין קודש לחול ולערבי יו"ט נמי איכא טובא אלא מיהו כד הוי ערב יוה"כ ועיו"ט חול. אלא כד הוי קודש לא תקעינן. ואע"ג דלא מיפרשא בתקיעות שהיו במקדש. דייקינן מהא דתנן בפ' קמא דשחיטת חולין (דף כו:) כל מקום שיש הבדלה אין תוקעין וכל מקום שיש תקיעה אין הבדלה כיצד יו"ט שחל להיות ערב שבת תוקעין אבל לא מבדילין מכלל דביו"ט שאינו ע"ש היו מבדילין אבל לא תוקעין א) מכלל דאי הוה יו"ט בתר חול היו תוקעין וראוי לדעת דהני כולהו שמעתתא אליבא דאחרים. אבל לדילן לא מיתרמי לן יוה"כ סמוך לשבת לא מלפניה ולא מאחריה. ומפרש בגמרא דחליל. דכד מיקלע כפורים בחד בשבא מרחינן ליה. ומקשינן ומי דחינן והתנן חלבי שבת קריבין ביוה"כ. וא"ר זירא כי הוינא בבבל אמרי' הא דתניא יוה"כ שחל להיות ע"ש לא היו תוקעין ובמוצ"ש לא היו מבדילין מפני דברי הכל היא. ופרקי' ההיא מתניתא אחרים היא דתניא אחרים אומרים אין בין עצרת לעצרת ואין בין ר"ה לר"ה אלא ד' ימים. ואם היתה שנה מעוברת חמשה. וגרסינן בירושל' בתחלת מגילה. א"ר יוסי לית כאן חל להיות בשני חל להיות בשבת דאם חל להיות י"ד בשני צומא רבא בחד בשבא. ואם חל בשבת צומא רבא בעירובתא שמעינן מינה דאע"ג דסתם משנה היא דחויה היא ומשנת יחיד היא ולאו דסמכא היא. וכן כל משנה הלכה שהיא כיוצא בה. וכולן בדן ודאין בה תלוין שהלכה למשה מסיני שלא לקבוע יוה"כ סמוך לשבת בין מלפניה בין מאחריה ולענין קניבת ירק הלכתא יוה"כ שחל להיות בשבת אסור

מסורת הש"ס

א) רש"ל מ"ז, ב) [פי' שלא יהא עורם כמולאי היום בקניבה ותהא נפשו עגומה עליו וכן מפצעין באגוזים ומפרכסין ברמונים דוקא מן המנחה ולמעלה שמאמר שהוא קרוב לעת האוכל דומה למי שיש לו פת בסלו ולא אמר לו מיכול מיניהו אבל קודם המנחה אסור גזרינן דילמא אתי למיכל ועיין רש"י פי' בזה שאמרו משום עגמת נפש בענין אחר ולא ישר בעיני ע"כ בעל המאור], ג) [תוספ' פי"ד], ד) [מס' סופרים פ"ה הט"ו], ה) [בתוספתא אי' ר' יוחנן בן גיזוף], ו) ס"א מתאבדין, ז) [נ"ל רשב"ג], ח) [וע"ע תוס' מגילה כא: ד"ה ובמגילה ותוס' ב"ק ג: ד"ה כדמתרגם].

הגהות הב"ח

(א) במשנה ואע"פ שכתובין: (ב) גמ' ואע"פ כו' ואע"פ כו' ואע"פ כו' לא ניתנו: (ג) שם תרגום ובכל לשון: (ד) רש"י ד"ה מצילין וכו' דשרי בהו וחסרון: (ה) ד"ה ומקק שלהן וכו' רקבובית. נ"ב ע"י לעיל דף ל ע"ב: (ו) תוס' ד"ה ובידו וכו' והלל ובמגילה אפילו עשרה: (ז) באו"ד ודלא כאומרים. נ"ב כלומר אבל קודם זה לא נעשה בימי התנאים. ולא גרסי' ועשרה מתרגמין וכמו שפירש"י במגילה אלא כבר נעשה בימי התנאים כמו שמוכח הכא:

גליון הש"ס

תוס' ד"ה לא ניתנו. כדמתרגם רי"י. עיין בב"ק דף ג ע"ב תוס' ד"ה כדמתרגם.

הגהות הגר"א

[א] גמ' מותר. נ"ל אסור: [ב] שם ואמר רחב"א אריו"ח. מה"מ: [ג] שם בחול. נ"ב מותר כן הוא גירסת הרמב"ם וכ"ה (ועמ"ש) רבינו בא"ח סימן תרי"א סק"ד):

ליקוטי רש"י

ומקק שלהן. אכילת תולעת אוכלת הספרים ומרקבן וכמו מקק [לעיל צ.]. בריבי. אדם גדול בדורו וכל היכא דקרי בריבי לשון חכמה ומריפוס הוא [עירובין נג.]. גדול בדורו היה וכל היכא דקרי ליה בריבי לשון חכמה ומריפוס הוא [קידושין כא.]. כלומר אדם גדול וכן קורין לו ברבי [ע"ז מג.].

חשק שלמה על רבינו חננאל

א) חסר וצ"ל ולמחזן יו"ט שחל כמו"ש מבדילין ולא תוקעין.

בקניבת ירק ואפילו מן המנחה ולמעלה. ואם חל להיות בחול מפצעין באגוזים ומפרכין ברמונים ומותר בקניבת ירק מן המנחה ולמעלה אבל [משום] מיגדר [מילתא אסרוהו]: הדרן עלך ואלו קשרים
פרק טז כל כתבי הקודש מצילין אותן מפני הדליקה בין שקורין בהן בין שאין קורין בהן. פירוש קורין בהן בצבור. תורה הפרשה בתורה ואפטרתא בנביאים ושאין קורין בהן בצבור כתובים. איתמר היו כתובין תרגום ובכל לשון רב הונא אמר אין מצילין אותן מפני הדליקה. רב חסדא אמר מצילין ובכתבי הקדש שמתורגמין בלשון אחר בין בכתב עברי בין בכתב אחר. ר' יוסי אמר לא ניתנו לקרות בהן דא"ר יוסי מעשה באבא חלפתא שהלך אצל רבן גמליאל לטבריא ומצאו יושב על שולחנו של יוחנן בן הנזוף ובידו ספר איוב תרגום א"ל רבי זכור אני את רבן גמליאל אבי אביך שהיה עומד ע"ג מעלה בהר הבית והביאו לפניו ספר איוב תרגום ואמר לבנאי שקעהו תחת הנדבך. אף הוא צוה עליו וגנזו ור' נמי הכי קאמר מניחו במקום התורפה והן כלין מאליהן. ולפום הכי תנא ר' יוסי אין מצילין אותן.

אילימא תנא קמא [א] דרבי יוסי ודילמא בהא קמיפלגי מר סבר ניתנו לקרות בהן ומר סבר לא ניתנו לקרות בהן אלא רבי יוסי ותנא דגיפטית [ג] ת"ר [א] הברכות [ב] והקמיעין אע"פ שיש בהן אותיות של שם ומעניינות הרבה שבתורה אין מצילין אותן מפני הדליקה אלא נשרפים במקומן [הן ואזכרותיהן] מכאן אמרו כותבי ברכות כשורפי תורה מעשה באחד שהיה כותב בצידן באו והודיעו את רבי ישמעאל והלך רבי ישמעאל לבודקו כשהיה עולה בסולם הרגיש בו נטל טומוס של ברכות ושקען בספל של מים ובלשון הזה אמר לו רבי ישמעאל גדול עונש האחרון מן הראשון בעא מיניה ריש גלותא מרבה בר רב הונא [ג] היו כתובין בסם ובסיקרא בקומוס ובקנקנתום בלשון הקדש מצילין אותן מפני הדליקה או אין מצילין תיבעי למ"ד מצילין תיבעי למ"ד אין מצילין תיבעי למ"ד אין מצילין הני מילי היכא דכתיבי תרגום ובכל לשון אבל הכא דכתיבי בלשון הקדש מצילין או דילמא אפי' למ"ד מצילין ה"מ היכא דכתיבי בדיו דמיקיים אבל הכא כיון דלא מיקיים לא א"ל אין מצילין והא רב המנונא תנא מצילין א"ל [ג] אי תניא תניא מאי תניא אמר רב אשי כדתניא [ד] אין בין ספרים למגילה אלא שהספרים נכתבים בכל לשון [ד] ומגילה עד שתהא כתובה אשורית על הספר ובדיו בעא מיניה רב הונא בר חלוב מרב נחמן ס"ת שאין בו ללקט שמונים וחמש אותיות כגון פרשת ויהי בנסוע הארון מצילין אותה מפני הדליקה או אין מצילין א"ל ותיבעי לך פרשת ויהי בנסוע הארון גופה [ה] היכא דחסר פרשת ויהי בנסוע לא קמיבעיא לי דכיון דאית ביה הזכרות אע"ג דלית ביה שמונים וחמש אותיות מצילין כי קא מיבעיא לי ס"ת שאין בו ללקט מאי א"ל [ו] אין מצילין איתיביה [ז] תרגום שכתבו מקרא ומקרא שכתבו תרגום וכתב עברית מצילין מפני הדליקה ואצ"ל תרגום שבעזרא ושבדניאל ושבתורה תרגום שבתורה מאי ניהו [א] יגר שהדותא ואף על גב דלית בה שמונים וחמש אותיות כי תניא ההיא להשלים איבעיא להו הני שמונים וחמש אותיות מכונסות או מפוזרות רב הונא אמר מכונסות רב חסדא אמר אפילו מפוזרות מיתיבי ס"ת שבלה אם יש בו ללקט שמונים וחמש אותיות כגון פרשת ויהי בנסוע הארון מצילין ואם לאו אין מצילין תיובתא דרב הונא [ה] תרגמה רב חסדא אליבא דרב הונא [ח] בתיבות ת"ר [ב] ויהי בנסוע הארון ויאמר משה פרשה זו עשה לה הקב"ה סימניות מלמעלה ולמטה לומר שאין

רש"י

אילימא ת"ק. כרב חסדא ור' יוסי כרב הונא: דילמא. טעמא דת"ק משום דקסבר ניתנו לקרות בהן ונהי דר' יוסי קאי כרב הונא מיהו כרב חסדא לא קאי ולא חד דהא רב חסדא אפי' למ"ד לא ניתנו קאמר מצילין: הברכות. מטבע ברכות שטבעו חכמים כגון י"ח ושאר ברכות: ומעניינות הרבה. מפרשיות שהיו כותבין בקמיעין פסוקים ללחש כגון כל המחלה וכגון לא תירא מפחד לילה: נשרפין במקומן. אם נפלה דליקה בשבת: כשורפי תורה. שהרי לא יצילם בשבת: לבודקו. אם אמת היה הדבר: טומוס. קבוצות קונטריסים: היו כתובין. תורה נביאים וכתובים: תיבעי למ"ד. בנכתבים בכל לשון מצילין תיבעי למ"ד אין מצילין: דלא מיקיים. אין מתקיים כדיו: הא רב המנונא תנא. מצילין: מאי תניא. היכא תניא: מדקאמר מגילה בדיו. וקתני דהוא מן הדברים שבין ספרים למגילה ש"מ שאר ספרים נכתבים בסם ובסיקרא: בר חלוב. שם אדם: פ"ה אותיות. זהו שיעור לספר תורה שנמחק או בלה להיות עומד בקדושתו: כגון פרשת ויהי בנסוע הארון. שהוא ספר לעצמו כדלקמן ויש בה פ"ה אותיות: ללקט. שנשארת כאן תיבה ובמקום אחר תיבה: מהו. להצילן: ותיבעי לך לפרשת ויהי בנסוע הארון גופה. שנכתבה לבדה וחסרה אות מהו להצילה: שאין בו כדי ללקט. ובאותו ליקוט עצמו ליכא אזכרות: תרגום שבתורה. יגר שהדותא ושבנביאים כגון כדנה תימרון להום (ירמיה י) שכתבו מקרא: [א"נ] התרגום שבעזרא כתבו מקרא: כתב עברית. אותיות גדולות הן ואין דומות לכתב אשורית אף ע"פ שכתובין בלשון הקדש אלא שכתב האותיות משונות: ואין צריך לומר תרגום שבעזרא ושבדניאל ושבתורה. שכתבו תרגום כהלכתו: להשלים. אם היה בו כדי ללקט ותרגום זו משלימתו מצטרף ומצילין בשבילו: תיובתא דרב הונא. דמדקתני ללקט מכלל דמפוזרות ניהו: בתיבות. הא דקתני ללקט משמע מפוזרות לא ללקט אות ואות לבד אלא ללקט תיבה שלימה תיבה כאן ותיבה כאן עד פ"ה אותיות וכי פליגי באותיות המפוזרות: עשה לה סימניות מלמעלה ולמטה. להבדילה מן הסמוכות לה: למעלה ולמטה. בתחלה ובסוף ויהי בנסוע הארון: שאין

תוספות

היו כתובים בסם ובסיקרא כו'. משמע דפשיטא ליה שאין קורין בהן דאי קורין בהן פשיטא דמצילין כדאמר לעיל וקשה לרשב"א דבסמוך משמע דפשיטא ליה לריש גלותא גופיה דקורין בהן דקאמר והתניא מצילין והיינו ההוא ברייתא דמייתי שהספרים נכתבים בכל לשון ומגילה עד שתהא כתובה אשורית על הספר ובדיו אבל שאר ספרים נכתבין שלא בדיו ולפי מה שאפרש בסמוך דהך ברייתא איירי לענין הלכה אתי שפיר ולעולם אין קורין בהן:

אבל הכא כיון דלא מקיים לא. אע"ג דבפ"ב דגיטין (דף יט.) קרי להו דבר שמתקיים דתנן בכל כותבין בסם ובדיו ובסקרא ובקומוס ובקנקנתוס ובכל דבר שמתקיים אומר ר"י דהתם קרי ליה מתקיים טפי ממשקין ומי פירות דקתני התם בסיפא דאין כותבין בהן אבל אין מתקיימין כמו דיו אבל קשה לר"י דתנן בפ"ב דסוטה (דף יז:) גבי מגילת סוטה אין כותבין לא בקומוס ולא בקנקנתוס שנאמר ומחה כתב שיכול למחוק אלמא קומוס וקנקנתוס מתקיימין יותר מדיו ואומר ר"י דלעולם אין מתקיימין כמו דיו ואין יכול למחות כמו דיו לפי שנבלעין בקלף: מגילה עד שתהא כתובה אשורית על הספר ובדיו. משמע דשאר ספרים לא בעי ספר ודיו וקשה דבפ' המוציא יין (לעיל דף עט:) משמע דספר תורה בעי ספר דתני' על הנייר ועל המטלית פסולה ומוקי לה בס"ת וה"ה על הדיפתרא אע"ג דלא חשיב ליה לענין פסול ה"נ לא חשיב ליה לענין כשרות דקתני על הקלף ועל הדוכסוסטוס כשירה ולא קתני דיפתרא ועוד תנן במסכת סופרים (פ"א) אין כותבין לא ע"ג דיפתרא ולא ע"ג נייר מחוק ועוד דמגילה פסולה אדיפתרא כדתנן בפ"ב דמגילה (דף יז.) וכן מגילת סוטה פסולה אדיפתרא כדאמר בפ"ב דסוטה (דף יז:) משום דבעיא ספר וכ"ש ס"ת דנקראת כמה פעמים ספר ודיו נמי צריך כדאמר בפרק הבונה (לעיל קג:) כתבה שלא בדיו או שכתב האזכרות בזהב הרי אלו יגנזו ותירץ הרב יוסף דס"ת ודאי בעי ספר ודיו והכא איירי דווקא בשאר ספרים והא דלא קתני אין בין ספרים לס"ת ומגילה משום דס"ת נכתבים בכל לשון להכי לא עריב לה ואכתי קשה לר"י דתנן בפ"ק דמגילה (דף ח:) אין בין ספרים לתפילין ומזוזות אלא שהספרים נכתבין בכל לשון כו' ופריך בגמרא וספרים נכתבין בכל לשון ורמינהו מקרא שכתבו תרגום ותרגום שכתבו מקרא וכתב עברי אינו מטמא את הידים עד שיכתבנו בכתב אשורית על הספר ובדיו ומשני כאן בספרים כאן במגילה ורב אשי משני כי תניא ההיא בשאר ספרים ורבי יהודה היא אלמא בשאר ספרים נמי בעי רבי יהודה ספר ודיו והוא הדין לרבנן דלא אשכחן דפליגי רבנן עליה אלא בכתב אשורית אבל בספר ודיו לא אשכחן דפליגי ועוד קשה דשביק רב אשי התם שינויא קמא דמוקי לה במגילה ומקשיא ליה ברייתא דהכא דקתני בהדיא דמגילה בעי שתהא כתובה אשורית וספר ודיו ורב אשי גופיה מייתי לה הכא ונראה לר"י דדוקא לענין הלכה מיתניא הך ברייתא דאין בין ספרים למגילה אלא שהספרים נכתבין בכל לשון ואפי' בלא ספר ודיו חשיבו לענין דמצילין אותו מפני הדליקה אע"ג דלא חזו לקריאה משום דיש בהו אזכרות אבל במגילה אין מצילין אלא א"כ ראויה לקריאה שתהא כתובה אשורית על הספר ובדיו לפי שאין בה אזכרה ולא"ה א"כ תקשה מברייתא דהכא דאמר לעיל כל היכא דלא ניתנו לקרות בהן אין מצילין וי"ל דהא מסיק לעיל תנאי היא:

מיתיבי ס"ת שבלה אם יש בה כדי ללקט כו'. השתא משמע דמלשון ללקט קא פריך דמשמע אפי' מפוזרות ותימה א"כ אמאי קא בעי מעיקרא מכונסות או אפי' מפוזרות פשיטא דאפי' מפוזרות מדבעא רב הונא ס"ת שאין בו ללקט משמע הא יש בו ללקט מצילין אע"פ שהן מפוזרות:

עין משפט נר מצוה

ג א מיי' שם הלכה כו סמג שם טוש"ע שם:
ד ב מיי' שם וסמג שם טור שו"ע שם סעיף יד:
ה ג מיי' שם טוש"ע שם סעיף יג:
ו ד מיי' פ"ב מהלכות מגילה הלכה ט סמג עשין ד טוש"ע א"ח סימן תרצא סעיף ט:
ז ה ו ז ח מיי' פרק כג מהלכות שבת הלכה כח סמג לאוין סה טור שו"ע א"ח סימן שלד סעיף יב:

רבינו חננאל

ושאר תנאי לא (דתנן) [דאמרי'] מצילין לא מסיים מן מינהון סבר ניתנו לקרות בהן. ומאן מנהון סבר לא ניתנו לקרות בהן אלא האי תנא דגפטית. דתני אע"פ שלא ניתנו לקרות בהן מצילין אותן. ות"ק דר' יוסי בניתנו לקרות בהן פליג. וקי"ל כרב הונא דרב חסדא לגביה תלמיד הוא. והא דתנינן כל כתבי הקדש מוקים לה רב הונא בתרי בבי. כל כתבי הקדש מצילין אותן מפני הדליקה בין בנביאי' בין כתובים שקורין בהן ובין כתובים שאין קורין בהן. בד"א בכתבי הקדש הכתובים בלשה"ק [אבל אי הוו] אינן כתבי הקדש כתובי' בכל לשון אין מצילין אותן מפני הדליקה ואפי' הכי טעונין גניזה והא ברייתא דתניא הברכות והקמיעות אע"פ שיש בהן של שם ומעניינות של תורה הרבה אין מצילין אותן מפני הדליקה ונגנזין במקומן הלכה היא. והלכה כדתנא רב המנונא שאם היו כתובים בסם ובסיקרא מצילין אותן אע"פ שאינו דבר של קיימא. ולענין בעיא דרב הונא בר חלוב מרב נחמן סוגיא דשמעתא. כל ס"ת דאית ביה פיסקא דאית ביה שם אע"ג דאין בו ללקט פ"ה אותיות מצילין אותו. והאי דתניא יגר שהדותא מצילין אותו להשלים דאי אית ביה פ"ה אותיות אע"ג שמהן יגר שהדותא מצילין אותו. והלכתא כרב הונא דהני פ"ה אותיות מכונסות ולא מפוזרות. ופי' מכונסות כדתרגמא רב חסדא אליבא דרב הונא בתיבו' אי יכול ללקט פ"ה אותיות מס"ת מתוך תיבות שלימות מצילין אותו כגון דמשכחת בראשית והיא תיבה שלימה דאית בה לשש. ויצא מנויה לארבע. ואלה מנויה לארבע. ויקרא מנויה לחמשה כולן תיבות שלימות עשרים (וא"ו) [או] פחות או יתר שמנין אותיותיהן פ"ה. אבל אותיות שמתוך תיבות שאינן שלימות אין מצילין כגון ויאמ ויאמר. אבר מכלל אברם ואברהם וכיוצא בהן. כל שנמצאת תיבה שלימה מונין אותיותיה להעלות לפ"ה אותיות ואם מקצתה מטושטשת אין אותיותיה המוגהות עולות למנין פ"ה. ומשו"ה אמרו ללקט ואע"פ שהתיבות מפוזרו' במקומו' רחוקין זה מזה: גליונים של ס"ת. איבעיא אם מצילין אותן או לא איפשטא. ס"ת שנמחק מקום המחק אין בו קדושה דאמרינן כי קדוש היכא דאיכא כתב. ליכא כתב לא קדוש. ומשום דאית טעותא בנוסחאות בהא שמעתא כתבנוה כולה. ת"ש ס"ת שבלה אם יש בו ללקט פ"ה אותיות מצילין אותו ואם לאו אין מצילין אותו. וליפרוק ליה משום גליון. בלה שאני כלומר אם מצילין מפני הגליונים לא הוה צריך לדקדוקי בתר פ"ה אותיות. ושנינן בלה שאני מכלל כי אם לא בלה מצילין אותו מפני הגליונים אע"פ שאין בו ללקט פ"ה אותיות. [illegible] ספרי תורה שכתבן מין אינו מינין דקי"ל כר"ג דאמר נקיטינן ס"ת שכתבו מין ישרף. כתבו נכרי יגנז. [illegible] אבל הספרים שחיברו אותן המינין דברי הבל ישרפו. דהא כתבי קדש שכתובין תרגום אפילו בהן אם

מסורת הש"ס

א) נ"ל ור' יוסי, ב) לעיל סא: ע"ש [תוספתא פי"ד מ"ש פ' טו הלכה כ], ג) [מגילה יט: מו"ק ד. יומא לח. יבמות קיד. נדרים יט: זבחים נד: מנחות קז: בכורות לו. חולין כג. תמורה לא. נדה כב: וע"ש פרש"י], ד) [מגילה ח:], ה) [לעיל כב: וש"נ].

תורה אור השלם

א) וַיִּקְרָא לוֹ לָבָן יְגַר שָׂהֲדוּתָא וְיַעֲקֹב קָרָא לוֹ גַּלְעֵד: [בראשית לא, מז]
ב) וַיְהִי בִּנְסֹעַ הָאָרֹן וַיֹּאמֶר מֹשֶׁה קוּמָה יְיָ וְיָפֻצוּ אֹיְבֶיךָ וְיָנֻסוּ מְשַׂנְאֶיךָ מִפָּנֶיךָ: [במדבר י, לה]

ליקוטי רש"י

הברכות. שתקנו חכמים כגון משנה של לאה שנה שיש בהם מלשון הכתובים ושופרות. ומעניינות. מפרשיות הרבה שכותבין בהן את הפסוקים של רפואה [לעיל סא:]. סם. זרניך בלשון קודש אורפימנט"א בלע"ז [מגילה יח.]. סיקרא. מיני"א בלע"ז אדום שצובעין בו הכיסוין. קומוס. גומ"א בלע"ז. קנקנתום. וויטריאול"ו. יגר שהדותא. תרגומו של גלעד [בראשית לא, מז]. אליבא דרב הונא. סימנים. סימנין פוסקין [ראש השנה יז:].

פורענות

חשק שלמה על רבינו חננאל א) נראה מזה דלרבינו לא היה גורס אילימא ת"ק דר"י ודילמא בהא קמיפלגי. רק היה לו גי' אחרת בזה וצ"ע:

[1]אִילֵימָא תַּנָּא קַמָּא (ד)וְרַבִּי יוֹסֵי – **If you will say the Tanna Kamma,** who permits saving translations, holds like Rav Chisda, **and R' Yose,** who prohibits rescuing translations, sides with Rav Huna, this is not compelling. וְדִילְמָא בְּהָא קָמִיפְלְגֵי – For **perhaps they dispute regarding the following,** מַר סָבַר נִיתְּנוּ לִקְרוֹת בָּהֶן – that one **master** [the Tanna Kamma] **maintains** that **[translations] may be read,** וּמַר סָבַר לֹא נִיתְּנוּ לִקְרוֹת בָּהֶן – **while** the other **master** [R' Yose] **maintains** that **[translations] may not be read.** But neither Tanna maintains, as Rav Chisda does, that even if translations may not be read, they may, nevertheless, be saved.[2] – ? –

The Gemara answers:

אֶלָּא רַבִּי יוֹסֵי וְתַנָּא דְגִיפְּטִית – **Rather,** the Tannaim in question are **R' Yose and the Tanna of** the Baraisa of **"Coptic."**[3]

The Gemara continues its discussion of what writings may be saved from a fire on the Sabbath:

תָּנוּ רַבָּנָן – **The Rabbis taught:** הַבְּרָכוֹת וְהַקְּמֵיעִין – BLESSINGS[4] AND AMULETS, אַף עַל פִּי שֶׁיֵּשׁ בָּהֶן אוֹתִיּוֹת שֶׁל שֵׁם וּמֵעִנְיָנוֹת הַרְבֵּה שֶׁבַּתּוֹרָה – ALTHOUGH THEY CONTAIN LETTERS OF God's NAME[5] AND verses FROM MANY SECTIONS OF THE TORAH,[6] אֵין מַצִּילִין אוֹתָן מִפְּנֵי הַדְּלֵיקָה – WE DO NOT SAVE THEM FROM A FIRE on the Sabbath. אֶלָּא נִשְׂרָפִים בִּמְקוֹמָן – RATHER THEY are allowed to BURN IN THEIR PLACE, [הֵן וְאַזְכָּרוֹתֵיהֶן] – [THEY TOGETHER WITH THEIR DIVINE NAMES]. מִכָּאן אָמְרוּ – FROM HERE THEY SAID: כּוֹתְבֵי בְרָכוֹת כְּשׂוֹרְפֵי תוֹרָה – THOSE WHO WRITE DOWN BLESSINGS ARE COMPARABLE TO THOSE WHO BURN A TORAH.[7] מַעֲשֶׂה בְּאֶחָד שֶׁהָיָה כּוֹתֵב בְּצַיְדָּן – There was AN INCIDENT IN WHICH ONE man WAS WRITING blessings IN SIDON. בָּאוּ וְהוֹדִיעוּ אֶת רַבִּי יִשְׁמָעֵאל – THEY CAME AND INFORMED R' YISHMAEL, וְהָלַךְ רַבִּי יִשְׁמָעֵאל לְבוֹדְקוֹ – WHEREUPON R' YISHMAEL WENT TO INTERROGATE HIM to determine if the report was true. כְּשֶׁהָיָה עוֹלֶה בַּסּוּלָּם – WHILE [R' YISHMAEL] WAS ASCENDING THE LADDER to the man's dwelling, הִרְגִּישׁ בּוֹ – [THE MAN] SENSED [R' YISHMAEL'S] presence. נָטַל טוֹמוֹס שֶׁל בְּרָכוֹת וְשִׁקְעָן בְּסֵפֶל שֶׁל מַיִם – HE TOOK A PACKET OF BLESSINGS AND PLUNGED IT INTO A BOWL OF WATER. וּבַלָּשׁוֹן הַזֶּה אָמַר לוֹ רַבִּי יִשְׁמָעֵאל – THEREUPON R' YISHMAEL SPOKE TO HIM THESE WORDS: גָּדוֹל עוֹנֶשׁ הָאַחֲרוֹן מִן הָרִאשׁוֹן – GREATER IS THE PUNISHMENT FOR THE LATTER deed, i.e. destroying the blessings with your own hands, THAN FOR THE FORMER, i.e. writing them down.[8]

Thus far the Gemara had considered whether the Mishnah's permission to save the Holy Scriptures applies to translations. The Gemara now considers whether this permission applies to scrolls written in Hebrew but with inferior ink:

בְּעָא מִינֵּיהּ רֵישׁ גָּלוּתָא מֵרַבָּה בַּר רַב הוּנָא – **The Exilarch inquired of Rabbah bar Rav Huna:** הָיוּ כְּתוּבִין בְּסַם וּבְסִיקְרָא בְּקוֹמוֹס וּבְקַנְקַנְתּוֹם – If **they** [the Holy Scriptures] **were written with paint, with red pigment, with gum, or with copper sulfate,** בִּלְשׁוֹן הַקֹּדֶשׁ – but **in the Holy Tongue,** מַצִּילִין אוֹתָן מִפְּנֵי הַדְּלֵיקָה – **may we save them from a fire** on the Sabbath אוֹ אֵין מַצִּילִין – **or may we not save** them?

The Exilarch continued:

תִּיבָּעֵי לְמַאן דְּאָמַר מַצִּילִין – **You may inquire according to the one who says we may save** translations, תִּיבָּעֵי לְמַאן דְּאָמַר אֵין מַצִּילִין – and **you may inquire according to the one who says we may not save** them. תִּיבָּעֵי לְמַאן דְּאָמַר אֵין מַצִּילִין – **You may inquire according to the one who says we may not save** translations, הָנֵי מִילֵּי הֵיכָא דִּכְתִיבֵי תַּרְגּוּם וּבְכָל לָשׁוֹן – for perhaps **this ruling applies** only **where [the scrolls] are written in Aramaic or in any** other foreign **language.** אֲבָל הָכָא דִּכְתִיבֵי בִּלְשׁוֹן הַקֹּדֶשׁ מַצִּילִין – **But here, where they are written in the Holy Tongue, we may save** them.[9] אוֹ דִילְמָא אֲפִילוּ לְמַאן דְּאָמַר מַצִּילִין – **Or, perhaps, even according to the one who says we may save** translations, הָנֵי מִילֵּי הֵיכָא דִּכְתִיבֵי בִּדְיוֹ דְּמִיקַּיֵּים – **this applies only to where [the scrolls] are written in black ink, which lasts.** אֲבָל הָכָא כֵּיוָן דְּלֹא מִיקַּיֵּים לֹא – **But here, since**

NOTES

1. Emendation follows *Mesoras HaShas*.

2. Above it was explained that all agree according to the Tanna who says that translations may be read, that they may be saved, and that the dispute applies only according to the Tanna who maintains that translations may not be read. Accordingly, what compels us to say that the Tanna Kamma of this Baraisa, who permits saving translations, follows Rav Chisda? Perhaps he maintains that translations may be read (*Rashi*). [R' Yose certainly holds that translations may *not* be read, and thus may not be saved, as Rav Huna holds.]

The halachah follows Rav Huna (*Rif, Rambam, Hil. Shabbos* 23:26). Nevertheless, due to a general decline in the level of scholarship and the fact that many Jews had become unfamiliar with the Holy Tongue, the Rabbis subsequently permitted writing the Scriptures in other languages. Accordingly, translations may be saved from the fire nowadays (see *Maseches Soferim* 17:1, *Tosafos* to 115a ד״ה אליבא, *Shulchan Aruch, Orach Chaim* 334:12).

3. I.e. the Baraisa which begins: "If they were written in Coptic . . ."

In asking its question, the Gemara did not mean that Rav Huna's position was per se difficult. Certainly it is a sufficient defense of Rav Huna that his view is supported by the Tanna R' Yose. However, from the fact that Rav Huna answered that his dispute with Rav Chisda parallels a dispute of Tannaim, and he then proceeded to cite the Baraisa which delineates the dispute between R' Yose and the Tanna Kamma, it was implied that both his own view and that of Rav Chisda were reflected in that Baraisa. The Gemara answers that Rav Huna did not mean that Rav Chisda's view was reflected in that Baraisa. Rather, it is the Baraisa of Coptic, which was cited previously by the Gemara, that supports Rav Chisda's view (*Chidushei HaRan* in explanation of *Rashi* on 115a ד״ה מאן; cf. *Ritva MHK* ed.).

4. I.e. blessings that the Sages instituted, such as the eighteen blessings of the *Amidah* prayer and blessings that are recited on various occasions (*Rashi*).

Blessings are classified as part of the Oral Law, and as such were not permitted to be written down. This Baraisa was taught at a time when it was still forbidden to put the Oral Law into writing (see *Ritva MHK* ed.; see below, note 8).

5. See *Ritva MHK* ed. to 61b.

6. Amulets often contain verses of the Torah which speak of healing and protection, such as *Exodus* 15:26: *Any of the diseases that I placed upon Egypt, I will not place upon you, for I am Hashem, your Healer,* or *Psalms* 91:5: *You shall not fear the terror of night* (*Rashi*).

7. For if a fire should break out on the Sabbath, one would not be permitted to rescue these blessings (*Rashi*; see *Iggros Moshe, Yoreh Deah* 1:4,6).

8. Even though is it not permitted to write down blessings, destroying them is tantamount to destroying books of the Scriptures (*Meiri*), which is a much more severe sin. [This is true even if the blessings have marks in place of God's Name, so that no erasure of God's Name is involved (*Teshuvos Tashbetz* §2; *Iggros Moshe, Yoreh Deah* II §135 בא״ד ועוד נראה).]

As explained above, this Baraisa's ruling applied during the times in which writing down the Oral Torah was still forbidden. Subsequently, however, the many calamities that befell the Jews brought about a decline in the intensity of Torah study, and the Oral Law, which had until then been studied by heart, was in danger of being forgotten (see *Rambam,* Introduction to *Mishneh Torah*). The Rabbis therefore permitted writing down the Oral Torah, and, consequently, nowadays all Torah works, including Talmud, commentaries, and *siddurim* may be saved from the fire on the Sabbath (see *Orach Chaim* 334:12 with commentaries). [Whether or not this permission extends to amulets as well, which do not aid in the study of Torah, is the subject of a dispute; see ibid. 334:14.]

9. As explained above, Rav Huna's reason for maintaining that translations may not be saved was the fact that translations may not be read. But perhaps scrolls written in Hebrew but in inferior ink *may* be read. Hence, they may be saved (*Maginei Shlomo,* in accordance with *Rashi's* approach; cf. *Tosafos* ד״ה היו).

אילימא תנא קמא [א] דרבי יוסי ודילמא בהא קמיפלגי מר סבר ניתנו לקרות בהן ומר סבר לא ניתנו לקרות בהן אלא רבי יוסי ותנא דגיפטית: [ג] ת"ר [א] הברכות [ב] והקמיעין אע"פ שיש בהן אותיות של שם ומעניינות הרבה שבתורה אין מצילין אותן מפני הדליקה אלא נשרפים במקומן [הן ואזכרותיהן] מכאן אמרו כותבי ברכות כשורפי תורה מעשה באחד שהיה כותב בצידן באו והודיעו את רבי ישמעאל והלך רבי ישמעאל לבודקו כשהיה עולה בסולם הרגיש בו נטל טומוס של ברכות ושקען בספל של מים ובלשון הזה אמר לו רבי ישמעאל גדול עונש האחרון מן הראשון בעא מיניה ריש גלותא מרבה בר רב הונא [ג] היו כתובין בסם ובסיקרא בקומוס ובקנקנתום בלשון הקדש מצילין אותן מפני הדליקה או אין מצילין תיבעי למ"ד מצילין תיבעי למ"ד אין מצילין תיבעי למ"ד אין מצילין הני מילי היכא דכתיבי תרגום ובכל לשון אבל הכא דכתיבי בלשון הקדש מצילין או דילמא אפי' למ"ד מצילין ה"מ היכא דכתיבי בדיו דמיקיים אבל הכא כיון דלא מיקיים לא א"ל אין מצילין והא רב המנונא תנא מצילין א"ל [ג] אי תניא תניא מאי תניא אמר רב אשי כדתניא [ד] אין בין ספרים למגילה אלא שהספרים נכתבים בכל לשון [ד] ומגילה עד שתהא כתובה אשורית על הספר ובדיו בעא מיניה רב הונא בר חלוב מרב נחמן ס"ת שאין בו ללקט שמונים וחמש אותיות כגון פרשת ויהי בנסוע הארון מצילין אותה מפני הדליקה או אין מצילין א"ל ותיבעי לך פרשת ויהי בנסוע הארון גופה [ה] היכא דחסר פרשת ויהי בנסוע לא קמיבעיא לי דכיון דאית ביה הזכרות אע"ג דלית ביה שמונים וחמש אותיות מצילין כי קא מיבעיא לי ס"ת שאין בו ללקט מאי א"ל [ו] אין מצילין איתיביה [ז] תרגום שכתבו מקרא ומקרא שכתבו תרגום וכתב עברית מצילין מפני הדליקה ואצ"ל תרגום שבעזרא ושבדניאל ושבתורה תרגום שבתורה מאי ניהו [א] יגר שהדותא ואף על גב דלית בה שמונים וחמש אותיות כי תניא ההיא איבעיא להו להשלים הני שמונים וחמש אותיות מכונסות או מפוזרות רב הונא אמר מכונסות רב חסדא אמר אפילו מפוזרות מיתיבי ס"ת שבלה אם יש בו ללקט שמונים וחמש אותיות כגון פרשת ויהי בנסוע הארון מצילין ואם לאו אין מצילין תיובתא דרב הונא [ט] תרגמה רב חסדא אליבא דרב הונא [ח] בתיבות ת"ר [ב] ויהי בנסוע הארון ויאמר משה פרשה זו עשה לה הקב"ה סימניות מלמעלה ולמטה לומר שאין

רש"י

אילימא ת"ק. כרב חסדא ור' יוסי כרב הונא: **דילמא.** טעמא דת"ק משום דקסבר ניתנו לקרות בהן ונהי דר' יוסי קאי כרב הונא מיהו כרב חסדא לא קאי ולא חד דהוא רב חסדא אפי' למ"ד לא ניתנו לקרות קאמר מצילין: **הברכות.** מטבע ברכות שטבעו חכמים כגון י"ח ושאר ברכות: **ומעניינות הרבה.** מפרשיות שהיו כותבין בקמיעין פסוקים ללחש כגון כל המחלה וכגון לא תירא מפחד לילה: **נשרפין במקומן.** אם נפלה דליקה בשבת: **כשורפי תורה.** שהרי לא יצילם בשבת: **לבודקו.** אם אמת היה הדבר: **טומוס.** קבוצת קונטריסים: **היו כתובין.** תורה נביאים וכתובים: **תיבעי למ"ד.** בנכתבים בכל לשון מצילין תיבעי למ"ד אין מצילין: **דלא מיקיים.** אין מתקיים כדיו: **הא רב המנונא תנא.** מצילין: **מאי תניא.** היכא תניא: **מדקאמר מגילה בדיו.** וקתני דהוא מן הדברים שבין ספרים למגילה ש"מ שאר ספרים נכתבים בסם ובסיקרא: **בר חלוב.** שם אדם: **פ"ה אותיות.** זהו שיעור לספר תורה שנמחק או בלה להיות עומד בקדושתו: **כגון פרשת ויהי בנסוע הארון.** שהוא ספר לעצמו כדלקמן ויש בה פ"ה אותיות: **ללקט.** שנשארו כאן תיבה ובמקום אחר תיבה: **מהו.** להצילן: **ותיבעי לך פרשת ויהי בנסוע הארון גופה.** שנכתבה לבדה וחסרה אות מהו להצילה: שאין בו כדי ללקט. ובאותו ליקוט עצמו ליכא אזכרות: **תרגום שבתורה.** יגר שהדותא ושבנביאים כגון כדנא תימרון להום (ירמיה י) שכתבו מקרא [א"נ] התרגום שבעזרא כתבו מקרא: **כתב עברית.** אותיות גדולות הן ואין דומות לכתב אשורית אף ע"פ שכתובין בלשון הקדש אלא שכתב האותיות משונות: **ואין צריך לומר תרגום שבעזרא ושבדניאל ושבתורה.** שכתבו תרגום כהלכתו: **להשלים.** אם היה בו כדי ללקט ותרגום זו משלימו מצטרף ומצילין בשבילו: **תיובתא דרב הונא.** דמדקתני ללקט מכלל דמפוזרות נינהו: **בתיבות.** הא דקתני ללקט דמשמע מפוזרות לא ללקט אות ואות לבד אלא ללקט תיבה שלימה תיבה כאן ותיבה כאן עד פ"ה אותיות וכי פליגינן באותיות המפוזרות: **עשה לה סימניות מלמעלה ולמטה.** להבדילה מן הסמוכות לה: **למעלה ולמטה.** בתחלה ובסוף ויהי בנסוע הארון: שאין

תוספות

היו כתובים בסם ובסיקרא כו'. משמע דפשיטא ליה שאין קורין בהן דלאי קורין בהן פשיטא דמצילין כדאמר לעיל וקשה לרשב"א דבסמוך משמע דפשיטא ליה לריש גלותא גופיה דקורין בהן דקאמר והתניא מצילין והיינו ההיא ברייתא דמייתי שהספרים נכתבים בכל לשון ומגילה עד שתהא כתובה אשורית על הספר ובדיו אבל שאר ספרים נכתבין שלא בדיו ולפי מה שאפרש בסמוך דהך ברייתא איירי לענין הלכה אתי שפיר ולעולם אין קורין בהן:

אבל הכא כיון דלא מקיים לא. אע"ג דבפ"ב דגיטין (דף יט.) קרי להו דבר שמתקיים דתנן בכל כותבין בסם ובדיו ובסקרא ובקומוס ובקנקנתוס ובכל דבר שמתקיים אומר ר"י דהתם קרי ליה מתקיים טפי ממשקין ומי פירות דקתני התם בסיפא דאין כותבין בהן אבל אין מתקיימין כמו דיו אבל קשה לר"י דתנן בפ"ב דסוטה (דף יז:) גבי מגילת סוטה אין כותבין לא בקומוס ולא בקנקנתוס שנאמר ומחה כתב שיכול למחוק אלמא קומוס וקנקנתוס מתקיימין יותר מדיו ואומר ר"י דלעולם אין מתקיימין כמו דיו ואין יכול למחות כמו דיו לפי שנבלעין בקלף: **מגילה** עד שתהא כתובה אשורית על הספר ובדיו. משמע דשאר ספרים לא בעי ספר ודיו וקשה דבפ' המוציא יין (לעיל דף עט:) משמע דספר תורה בעי ספר דתני' על הנייר ועל המטלית פסולה ומוקי לה בס"ת וה"ה על הדיפתרא אע"ג דלא חשיב ליה לענין פסול ה"נ לא חשיב ליה לענין כשרות דקתני על הקלף ועל הדוכסוסטוס כשירה ולא קתני דיפתרא ועוד תנן במסכת סופרים (פ"א) אין כותבין לא ע"ג דיפתרא ולא ע"ג נייר מחוק ועוד דמגילה פסולה אדיפתרא כדתנן בפ"ב דמגילה (דף יז.) וכן מגילת סוטה פסולה אדיפתרא כדאמר בפ"ב דסוטה (דף יז:) משום דבעיא ספר וכ"ש ס"ת דנקראת כמה פעמים ספר ודיו נמי צריך כדאמר בפרק הבונה (לעיל קג:) כתבה שלא בדיו או שכתב האזכרות בזהב הרי אלו יגנזו ותירץ הרב יוסף דס"ת ודאי בעי ספר ודיו והכא איירי דווקא בשאר ספרים והא דלא קתני אין בין ספרים לס"ת ומגילה משום דס"ת נכתבים בכל לשון להכי לא עריב לה ואכתי קשה לר"י דתנן בפ"ק דמגילה (דף ח:) אין בין ספרים לתפילין ומזוזות אלא שהספרים נכתבין בכל לשון כו' ופריך בגמרא וספרים נכתבין בכל לשון ורמינהו מקרא שכתבו תרגום ותרגום שכתבו מקרא וכתב עברי אינו מטמא את הידים עד שיכתבנו בכתב אשורית על הספר ובדיו ומשני כאן בספרים כאן במגילה ורב אשי משני כי תניא ההיא בשאר ספרים ורבי יהודה היא אלמא בשאר ספרים נמי בעי רבי יהודה ספר ודיו והוא הדין לרבנן דלא אשכחן דפליגי רבנן עליה אלא בכתב אשורית אבל בספר ודיו לא אשכחן דפליגי ועוד קשה דשביק רב אשי התם שינויא קמא דמוקי לה במגילה ומסייע ליה ברייתא דהכא דקתני בהדיא דמגילה בעי שתהא כתובה אשורית וספר ודיו ורב אשי גופיה מייתי לה הכא ונראה לר"י דדוקא לענין הלכה מיתניא הך ברייתא דאין בין ספרים למגילה אלא שהספרים נכתבין בכל לשון ואפי' בלא ספר ודיו חשיבו לענין דמצילין אותו מפני הדליקה אע"ג דלא חזו לקריאה משום דיש בהו אזכרות אבל במגילה אין מצילין אלא א"כ ראויה לקריאה שתהא כתובה אשורית על הספר ובדיו לפי שאין בה הזכרה וא"ת א"כ תקשה מברייתא דהכא דאמר לעיל כל היכא דלא ניתנו לקרות בהן אין מצילין וי"ל דהא מסיק לעיל תנאי היא:

מיתיבי ס"ת שבלה אם יש בה כדי ללקט כו'. השתא משמע דמלשון ללקט קא פריך דמשמע אפי' מפוזרות ותימה א"כ אמאי קא בעי מעיקרא מכונסות או אפי' מפוזרות פשיטא דאפי' מפוזרות מדבעא רב הונא ס"ת שאין בו ללקט משמע הא יש בו ללקט מצילין אע"פ שהן מפוזרות:

פורענות

עין משפט נר מצוה

ג א מיי' שם הלכה כו סמג שם טוש"ע שם:
ד ב מיי' וסמג שם טור שו"ע שם סעיף יד:
ה ג מיי' שם טוש"ע שם סעיף יב:
ו ד מיי' פ"ב מהלכות מגילה הלכה ט סמג עשין ד טוש"ע או"ח סימן תרצא סעיף א:
ז ה ו ז ח מיי' פרק כג מהלכות שבת הלכה כח סמג לאוין סה טור שו"ע או"ח סימן שלד סעיף יב:

רבינו חננאל

ושאר תנאי א) (דתנן) [דאמרי] מצילין לא מסיים מן מינהון סבר ניתנו לקרות בהן. ומאן מנהון סבר לא ניתנו לקרות בהן אלא האי תנא דגפטית. דתני אע"פ שלא ניתנו לקרות בהן מצילין אותן. ות"ק דר' יוסי בניתנו לקרות בהן פליג. וקי"ל כרב הונא דרב חסדא לגביה תלמיד הוא. והא דתנינן כל כתבי הקדש מוקים לה רב הונא בתרי בבי. כל כתבי הקדש מצילין אותן מפני הדליקה בין נביאי' שקורין בהן בין כתובים שאין קורין בהן. בד"א בכתבי הקדש הכתובים בלשה"ק [אבל אי הוי] אינון כתבי הקדש כתובי' בכל לשון אין מצילין אותן מפני הדליקה ואפי' הכי טעונין גניזה והא ברייתא דתניא הברכות והקמיעות אע"פ שיש בהן של שם ומעניינות של תורה הרבה אין מצילין אותן מפני הדליקה ונגנזין במקומן הלכה היא. והלכה כדתנא רב המנונא שאם היו כתובים בסם ובסיקרא מצילין אותן אע"פ שאינו דבר של קיימא. ולענין בעיא דרב הונא בר חלוב מרב נחמן סוגיא דשמעתא. כל ס"ת דאית ביה פיסקא דאית ביה שם אע"ג דאין בו ללקט פ"ה אותיות מצילין אותו. והאי דתניא יגר שהדותא מצילין אותו להשלים דאי איכא פ"ה אותיות אע"ג שמהן יגר שהדותא מצילין אותו. והלכתא כרב הונא דהני פ"ה אותיות מכונסות ולא מפוזרות. ופי' מכונסות כדתרגמא רב חסדא אליבא דרב הונא בתיבו' אי יכול ללקט פ"ה אותיות מס"ת מתוך תיבות שלימות מצילין אותו כגון דמשכחת בראשית והיא מנויה לשש. ויצא מנויה לארבע. ואלה מנויה לארבע. ויקרא מנויה לחמש כולן תיבות שלימות עשרים (וא"ו) [או] פחות או יתר שמנין אותיותיהן פ"ה. אבל אותיות שמתוך תיבות שאינן שלימות אין מצילין כגון ויאמ מכלל ויאמר. אבר מכלל אברם או אברהם וכיוצא בהן. כל שנמצאת תיבה שלימה מונין אותיותיה להעלות לפ"ה אותיות וכל תיבה מקצתה מטושטשת אין אותיותיה המוגהות עולות למנין פ"ה. ומשו"ה אמרן ללקט ואע"פ שהתיבות מפוזרו' במקומו' רחוקין זה מזה: **גליונים** של ס"ת. איבעיא אם מצילין אותן ולא איפשיטא. ס"ת שנמחק מקום המחק אין בו קדושה דאמרינן כי קדוש היכא דאיכא כתב. ליכא כתב לא קדוש. ומשום דאית טעותא בנוסחאות בהא שמעתא כתבנא כולה. ת"ש ס"ת שבלה אם יש בו ללקט פ"ה אותיות מצילין אותו ואם לאו אין מצילין אותו. וליפוק ליה משום גליון. בלה שאני כלומר אם מצילין מפני הגליונים לא הוה צריך לדקדוקי בתר פ"ה אותיות. ושנינן בלה שאני מכלל כי אם לא בלה מצילין אותו מפני הגליונין אע"פ שאין בו ללקט פ"ה אותיות. ת"ש ס"ת שנמחק אם יש בו כדי ללקט פ"ה אותיות מצילין אותו ואם לאו אין מצילין אותו. ושנינן נמחק לא קא מיבעיא לן דכי קדוש כי איכא כתב. כי ליכא כתב לא קדוש. כי קא מיבעיא לי גליונות של מעלה ושל מטה ושבין דף לדף ושבין פרשה לפרשה שבתחלת הספר ושבסופו (מ"ט) [מאי]. ת"ש גליונין של מעלה ושל מטה שבין דף לדף שבין פרשה לפרשה שבתחלת הספר ושבסופו מטמאין את הידים. ומשנינן דילמא כי חשיבי אגב ס"ת. אבל גליונים דלא מטמא את הידים לאו כוותיה אינון. וכיון דבעיא זו לא איפשיטא מחמרינן בזכרון כתבי קדש. ומצילין אותן הגליונין מפני הדליקה בשבת ורוב מהא דתניא הגליונים וספרי המינין אין מצילין אותן מפני הדליקה. מיגו דדחינן ומוקמינן לה לגליונין מכלל דספרי מינין הרי הן כספרי קדש. כלומר כשם שגליונים שאין כתובה עליהם אין להן כבוד ואין קורין בהן כך ספרי מינין אין מצילין אותן. והני ספרי מינין ספרי תורה שכתבן מין אינון דקי"ל כר"נ דאמר נקיטנן ס"ת שכתבו מין ישרף. ביד נכרי יגנז. נמצא ביד מין יגנז. ביד כותי נכרי קורין בו. אבל הספרים שחיברו המינין מדעתם ודבריהם אין בהם קדושה כלל. ומה שכתוב בהן אזכרות אלו ודאי נשרפין. דהא כתבי קדש שכתובין אותן תרגום אפילו בהן אם

חשק שלמה על רבינו חננאל א) נראה מזה דרבינו לא היה גורס אלימא ת"ק דר"י ודילמא בהא קמיפלגי. רק היה לו גי' אחרת בזה וצ"ע:

מסורת הש"ס

א) ל"ל ור' יוסי, ב) לעיל סא: ע"ש [תוספתא פי"ד מ"ס פ' טו הלכה ד], ג) [חגיגה יט: מו"ק ז. יומא לא: יבמות קיג: נדרים יט: זבחים טו: לא: לו: מנחות קז. בכורות ז. חולין גג. תמורה לא. נדה כג: וע"ש פרש"י], ד) [מגילה ח:], ה) [לעיל נג: וש"נ].

תורה אור השלם

א) וַיִּקְרָא לוֹ לָבָן יְגַר שָׂהֲדוּתָא וְיַעֲקֹב קָרָא לוֹ גַּלְעֵד: [בראשית לא, מז]

ב) וַיְהִי בִּנְסֹעַ הָאָרֹן וַיֹּאמֶר מֹשֶׁה קוּמָה יְיָ וְיָפֻצוּ אֹיְבֶיךָ וְיָנֻסוּ מְשַׂנְאֶיךָ מִפָּנֶיךָ: [במדבר י, לה]

ליקוטי רש"י

הברכות. שתקנו חכמים כגון תשעה של ראש השנה שיש בהן מלכיות זכרונות ושופרות. **ומעניינות.** מפרשיות הרבה שכותבין בהן את מקראות של רפואה [לעיל סא:]. **סם.** זרניך בלשון קודש אורפימנט"ו בלע"ז [מגילה יח:]. **סיקרא.** מיני"א לצבע אדום שצובעין בה תריסין. **קומוס.** קומא. גומ"א שרף אילן [שבת קד:]. שרף האילן ומתיכו במים וכותב הימנו. **קנקנתום.** וויטריאול"ו או אורדימנ"ט קורין אותו [סוטה יז:]. סם שצובעין בו מנעלים שחורין [מגילה יט.]. **בדיו.** עלנו של שרף [סוטה שם]. **אי תניא תניא.** אי תניא בהדיא תניא ונלך אחריה ותחזר אני בי [חגיגה יט:]. אי משנת ברייתא תניא [נדרים יט:]. **אין בין ספרים.** תורה נביאים וכתובים. **עד שתהא כתובה אשורית.** כתב אשורית הוא כתב שלנו [מגילה ח:]. כתב שלנו אשורית שבא מאשור כדאמר באלהך פירקין (סנהדרין כב.) [סנהדרין צז:]. **על הספר.** קלף [מגילה ז.]. **תרגום.** שהיה ראוי ליכתוב בו תרגום כגון יגר שהדותא (בראשית לא). **שכתבו מקרא.** גלעד וכגון תרגום (כתב) של דניאל ועזרא. **ומקרא שכתבו תרגום.** ספר שכתוב בלשון הקודש הראוי לכתוב בו מקרא כתבו לשון ארמי. **וכתב עברית.** או שלא שינה את הלשון אבל שינה את הכתב שכתבו בכתב של עבר הנהר ובמסכת סנהדרין (כא:) קרי ליה כתבא ליבונאה [שם ח:]. ליבונאה, אותיות גדולות כעין אותן שכותבין בקמיעות ומזוזות [סנהדרין כא:]. **יגר שהדותא.** תרגומו של גלעד [בראשית לא, מז]. **אליבא דרב הונא.** במקום (אביי) ובשבילו שתהא (משנה) זו מתורגמת לפי דבריו [סוכה יט. בסוגיין רב הונא]. **סימניות.** סימנין הפוכין [ראש השנה יז:].

[the paint, pigment, etc.] does not last as long as black ink, **no,** we may not save the scrolls.[10] – ? –

Rabbah bar Rav Huna responded:

אָמַר לֵיהּ – He said to [the Exilarch]: אֵין מַצִּילִין – We may not save them.

The Exilarch questions this ruling:

וְהָא רַב הַמְנוּנָא תָּנָא מַצִּילִין – But Rav Humnuna taught a Baraisa which states **that we may save** such scrolls! – ? –

Rabbah bar Rav Huna responded:

אָמַר לֵיהּ – He said to [the Exilarch]: אִי תַּנְיָא תַּנְיָא – If it was taught in a Baraisa, it was taught, and I retract my ruling.[11]

The Gemara elaborates:

מַאי תַּנְיָא – What is the Baraisa that teaches this? **אָמַר רַב אַשִׁי כִּדְתַנְיָא – Rav Ashi said: As was taught in a Baraisa: אֵין בֵּין סְפָרִים לִמְגִילָּה –** THERE IS NO DIFFERENCE BETWEEN the laws pertaining to the BOOKS of the Scriptures AND those pertaining to A MEGILLAH (Book of Esther), **אֶלָּא שֶׁהַסְּפָרִים נִכְתָּבִים בְּכָל לָשׁוֹן –** EXCEPT THAT THE BOOKS of the Scriptures MAY BE WRITTEN IN ANY LANGUAGE **וּמְגִילָּה עַד שֶׁתְּהֵא כְּתוּבָה אַשּׁוּרִית עַל הַסֵּפֶר וּבִדְיוֹ –** WHEREAS A MEGILLAH is not valid UNLESS IT IS WRITTEN in *ASHURIS* script,[12] ON PARCHMENT, AND WITH BLACK INK. From the fact that the Baraisa lists black ink as one of the differences between a Megillah and other books of the Scriptures, we may infer that other books of the Scriptures may be written even with paint, red pigment, gum or ferrous sulfate. And since it is legal to write other books with these inferior-type inks, it is also permissible to save them from a fire on the Sabbath.[13]

The Gemara considers the permissibility of saving another type of deficient scroll:

בְּעָא מִינֵּיהּ רַב הוּנָא בַּר חָלוּב מֵרַב נַחְמָן – Rav Huna bar Chaluv inquired of Rav Nachman: סֵפֶר תּוֹרָה שֶׁאֵין בּוֹ לְלַקֵּט שְׁמוֹנִים וְחָמֵשׁ אוֹתִיּוֹת – A Torah scroll in which there is not sufficient writing **to gather eighty-five letters,** i.e. most of the writing in the scroll is erased, and the number of intact letters in words scattered throughout the scroll does not total eighty-five, **כְּגוֹן פָּרָשַׁת ,,וַיְהִי בִּנְסֹעַ הָאָרֹן'' – similar to** the number of letters in **the section** that begins: ***And when the Ark would journey,*** **מַצִּילִין אוֹתָהּ מִפְּנֵי הַדְּלֵיקָה אוֹ אֵין מַצִּילִין – may we save it from a fire** on the Sabbath **or may we not save** it?[14]

Rav Nachman questions the phrasing of the inquiry:

אָמַר לוֹ – He said to [Rav Huna bar Chaluv]: וְתִיבָּעֵי לָךְ פָּרָשַׁת ,,וַיְהִי בִּנְסֹעַ הָאָרֹן'' גּוּפָהּ – Why do you inquire about a complete Torah scroll? **Inquire about the section of *And when the Ark would journey* itself,** i.e. whether we may save a parchment containing this section alone, in a case in which this section is missing a letter. – ? –

Rav Huna bar Chaluv replies:

הֵיכָא דְּחָסֵר פָּרָשַׁת ,,וַיְהִי בִּנְסֹעַ'' לֹא קָמִיבַּעְיָא לִי – Where the section *And when [the Ark] would journey* itself **is missing** a letter, **I have no question, דְּכֵיוָן דְּאִית בֵּיהּ הַזְכָּרוֹת – for since it contains Divine Names, אַף עַל גַּב דְּלֵית בֵּיהּ שְׁמוֹנִים וְחָמֵשׁ אוֹתִיּוֹת מַצִּילִין – even though it does not contain eighty-five letters, it may** certainly **be saved.**[15] **כִּי קָא מִיבַּעְיָא לִי – When do I have a question? סֵפֶר תּוֹרָה שֶׁאֵין בּוֹ לְלַקֵּט –** In the case of **a Torah scroll in which there is not** sufficient writing **to gather** eighty-five letters, and there are *no* Divine Names among the remaining words. **מַאי – What** is the law in that case? May the scroll be saved from the fire, or not?

Rav Nachman responded:

אָמַר לֵיהּ אֵין מַצִּילִין – He said to [Rav Huna bar Chaluv]: We may not save it.

This ruling is questioned:

אֵיתִיבֵיהּ – [Rav Huna bar Chaluv] challenged [Rav Nachman] from a Baraisa: **תַּרְגּוּם שֶׁכְּתָבוֹ מִקְרָא –** An ARAMAIC passage from Scriptures THAT ONE WROTE IN HEBREW,[16] **וּמִקְרָא שֶׁכְּתָבוֹ תַּרְגּוּם –** OR a HEBREW passage THAT ONE WROTE IN ARAMAIC, **וּכְתָב עִבְרִית –** OR a passage that was written in the correct language but in *IVRI* SCRIPT,[17] **מַצִּילִין מִפְּנֵי הַדְּלֵיקָה –** WE MAY SAVE FROM A FIRE on the Sabbath, **וְאֵין צָרִיךְ לוֹמַר תַּרְגּוּם שֶׁבְּעֶזְרָא וְשֶׁבְּדָנִיֵּאל וְשֶׁבַּתּוֹרָה –** AND IT GOES WITHOUT SAYING that this is true for THE ARAMAIC parts OF *EZRA, DANIEL* AND THE PENTATEUCH which were written in Aramaic.

Rav Huna bar Chaluv develops the challenge:

תַּרְגּוּם שֶׁבַּתּוֹרָה מַאי נִיהוּ – Now, **what is** the only case of an **Aramaic** passage **in the Pentateuch?**[18] **,,יְגַר שָׂהֲדוּתָא'' –** It is ***yegar sahadusa.***[19] **וְאַף עַל גַּב דְּלֵית בָּהּ שְׁמוֹנִים וְחָמֵשׁ אוֹתִיּוֹת – And** the

NOTES

10. The Gemara explained above that Rav Chisda permits saving translations, despite the fact that they may not be read, on account of the resultant disgrace to the Holy Scriptures. But perhaps where they are written in a type of ink that fades, the disgrace of their being burnt is not that great. Thus, they may not be saved (ibid.).

11. [Although the Exilarch apparently knew of the existence of this Baraisa all along, he still posed his question. When Rabbah bar Rav Huna resolved the matter one way, the Exilarch brought up the Baraisa, to see if Rabbah bar Rav Huna might interpret it in a manner consistent with his own ruling (*Maginei Shlomo*), or might respond that the Baraisa, having been cited by Rav Hamnuna rather than by the Baraisa authorities R' Chiya and R' Oshaya, was erroneous (the Gemara states elsewhere that any Baraisa not taught in the academies of R' Chiya and R' Oshaya was prone to be erroneous) (*Leshon HaZahav*).

12. [See 115a note 17.] See *Maharshal*; see also *Tosafos* here and *Megillah* 8b-9a for a discussion of which Tannaic views are reflected here.

13. *Rashi,* as explained by *Maginei Shlomo;* cf. *Tosafos.*

14. [The Torah scroll in question was written according to law and acquired the same sanctity as any other Torah scroll. Subsequently, however,] most of it letters became erased or faded. For a Torah scroll to retain its sanctity it must possess at least eighty-five still-legible letters, equivalent to the number of letters in the section of the Torah which begins with the words: וַיְהִי בִּנְסֹעַ הָאָרֹן, *And when the Ark would journey* (*Numbers* 10:35-36). As we will learn below, Rebbi maintains that this small, two-verse section is considered a separate "Book" of the Torah in its own right. Since it contains eighty-five letters, this number was chosen as the minimum number of intact letters necessary for a Torah scroll to retain its sanctity (*Rashi*). Rav Huna bar Chaluv inquires whether a scroll lacking this number of letters may be saved from a fire on the Sabbath. [There is no question that such a scroll requires being placed in a repository for old sacred writings, for it is surely no less holy than the worm-eaten remains of a scroll which, we learned above, require such care. The question is only whether it retains sufficient sanctity to merit being saved from a fire on the Sabbath (*Mishneh Berurah* 334:37 with *Shaar HaTziyun*).]

15. The section of וַיְהִי בִּנְסֹעַ contains the Name of God two times. On this strength alone the parchment must be saved, even if, by itself, a scroll containing fewer than eighty-five letters does not merit saving, for even one Name of God may not be allowed to burn (*Ritva MHK* ed.).

16. [*Mikra,* literally: reading.] Practically all of Scripture is written in Hebrew. However, a few isolated phrases in *Chumash* and *Neviim,* and some entire chapters in *Kesuvim,* are written in Aramaic. The sole case of this in *Chumash* is *Genesis* 31:47: יְגַר שָׂהֲדוּתָא. Examples of such passages in *Neviim* and *Kesuvim* are *Jeremiah* 10:11 and *Ezra* 4:8-6:18 respectively. The Baraisa discusses a case in which one of these Aramaic verses, rather than being written in its original form, was translated into Hebrew.

17. See above, 115a note 17.

18. [I.e. to what verse does the Baraisa refer when it states in its concluding line that an Aramaic part of the Pentateuch (i.e. *Chumash*) written in Aramaic may be saved?]

19. See note 16.

ג א מיי' שם הלכה כו סמג שם טוש"ע שם:
ד ב מיי' ומוש"ע שם טור שו"ע שם סעיף יד:
ה ג מיי' שם טוש"ע שם סעיף יב:
ו ד מיי' פ"א מהלכות מגילה הלכה ט סמג עשין ד טוש"ע או"ח סימן תרלא סעיף א:
ז ה ו ז ח מיי' פרק כג מהלכות שבת הלכה כט סמג לאוין סה טוש"ע או"ח סימן שלד סעיף יב:

א) נ"ל ור' יוסי, ב) לעיל קא: ע"ש [תוספתא פי"ד מ"ם פ' טו הלכה ד], ג) [מגילה יט: מו"ק ח. יומא לא: יבמות קיג: נדרים יט: זבחים טו: לה: לו: מנחות קז. בכורות כג: חולין כג. תמורה לא. נדה כב: וע"ש פרש"י], ד) [מגילה ח:], ה) [לעיל נב: ופ"ג].

אילימא תנא קמא [א] דרבי יוסי ודילמא בהא קמיפלגי מר סבר ניתנו לקרות בהן ומר סבר לא ניתנו לקרות בהן אלא רבי יוסי ותנא דגיפטית [ב] ת"ר [א] הברכות [ב] והקמיעין אע"פ שיש בהן אותיות של שם ומעניינות הרבה שבתורה אין מצילין אותן מפני הדליקה אלא נשרפים במקומן [הן ואזכרותיהן] מכאן אמרו כותבי ברכות כשורפי תורה מעשה באחד שהיה כותב בצידן באו והודיעו את רבי ישמעאל והלך רבי ישמעאל לבודקו כשהיה עולה בסולם הרגיש בו נטל טומוס של ברכות ושקען בספל של מים ובלשון הזה אמר לו רבי ישמעאל גדול עונש האחרון מן הראשון בעא מיניה ריש גלותא מרבה בר רב הונא [ג] היו כתובין בסם ובסיקרא בקומוס ובקנקנתום בלשון הקדש מצילין אותן מפני הדליקה או אין מצילין תיבעי למ"ד מצילין תיבעי למ"ד אין מצילין הני מילי היכא דכתיבי תרגום ובכל לשון אבל הכא דכתיבי בלשון הקדש מצילין או דילמא אפי' למ"ד מצילין ה"מ היכא דכתיבי בדיו דמיקיים אבל הכא כיון דלא מיקיים לא א"ל אין מצילין והא רב המנונא תנא מצילין א"ל [ג] אי תניא תניא מאי תניא אמר רב אשי דתניא [ד] אין בין ספרים למגילה אלא שהספרים נכתבים בכל לשון [ד] ומגילה עד שתהא כתובה אשורית על הספר ובדיו בעא מיניה רב הונא בר חלוב מרב נחמן ס"ת שאין בו ללקט שמונים וחמש אותיות כגון פרשת ויהי בנסוע הארון מצילין אותו מפני הדליקה או אין מצילין א"ל ותיבעי לך פרשת ויהי בנסוע הארון גופה [ה] היכא דחסר פרשת ויהי בנסוע לא קמיבעיא לי דכיון דאית ביה הזכרות אע"ג דלית ביה שמונים וחמש אותיות מצילין כי קא מיבעיא לי ס"ת שאין בו ללקט מאי א"ל [ו] אין מצילין איתיביה [ז] תרגום שכתבו מקרא ומקרא שכתבו תרגום וכתב עברית מצילין מפני הדליקה ואצ"ל תרגום שבעזרא ושבדניאל ושבתורה תרגום שבתורה מאי ניהו [א] יגר שהדותא ואף על גב דלית בה שמונים וחמש אותיות כי תניא ההיא איבעיא להו להשלים הני שמונים וחמש אותיות מכונסות או מפוזרות רב הונא אמר מכונסות רב חסדא אמר אפילו מפוזרות מיתיבי ס"ת שבלה אם יש בו ללקט שמונים וחמש אותיות כגון פרשת ויהי בנסוע הארון מצילין ואם לאו אין מצילין תיובתא דרב הונא [ט] תרגמה רב חסדא אליבא דרב הונא [ח] בתיבות ת"ר [ב] ויהי בנסוע הארון ויאמר משה פרשה זו עשה לה הקב"ה סימניות מלמעלה ולמטה לומר שאין

אילימא ת"ק. כרב חסדא ור' יוסי כרב הונא: דילמא. טעמא דת"ק משום דקסבר ניתנו לקרות בהן ונהי דר' יוסי קאי כרב הונא מיהו כרב חסדא לא קאי ולא חד דהא רב חסדא אפי' למ"ד לא ניתנו קאמר מצילין: הברכות. מטבע ברכות שטבעו חכמים כגון י"ח ושאר ברכות: ומעניינות הרבה. מפרשיות שהיו כותבין בקמיעין פסוקים ללחש כגון כל המחלה וכגון לא תירא מפחד לילה: נשרפין במקומן. אם נפלה דליקה בשבת: כשורפי תורה. שהרי לא יצילם בשבת: לבודקו. אם אמת היה הדבר: טומוס. קבולות קונטריסים: היו כתובין. תורה נביאים וכתובים: תיבעי למ"ד. בנכתבים בכל לשון מצילין תיבעי למ"ד אין מצילין: דלא מיקיים. אין מתקיים כדיו: הא רב המנונא תנא. מצילין: מאי תניא. היכא תניא: מדקאמר מגילה בדיו. וקתני דהוא מן הדברים שבין ספרים למגילה ש"מ שאר ספרים נכתבים בסם ובסיקרא: בר חלוב. שם אדם: פ"ה אותיות. זהו שיעור לספר תורה שנמחק או בלה להיות עומד בקדושתו: כגון פרשת ויהי בנסוע הארון. שהוא ספר לעצמו כדלקמן ויש בה פ"ה אותיות: ללקט. שנשארת כאן תיבה ובמקום אחר תיבה: מהו. להצילן: ותיבעי לך לפרשת ויהי בנסוע הארון גופה. שנכתבה לבדה וחסרה אות מהו להצילה: שאין בו כדי ללקוט. ובאותו ליקוט עצמו ליכא אזכרות: תרגום שבתורה. יגר שהדותא ושבנביאים כגון כדנא תימרון להום (ירמיה י) שכתבו מקרא [א"נ] התרגום שבעזרא כתבו מקרא: כתב עברית. אותיות גדולות הן ואין דומות לכתב אשורית אף ע"פ שכתובין בלשון הקדש אלא שכתב האותיות משונות: ואין צריך לומר תרגום שבעזרא ושבדניאל ושבתורה. שכתבו תרגום כהלכתו: להשלים. אם היה בו כדי ללקט ותרגום זו משלימו מצטרף ומצילין בשבילו: תיובתא דרב הונא. דמדקתני ללקט מכלל דמפוזרות נינהו: בתיבות. הא דקתני ללקט דמשמע מפוזרות לא ללקט אות ואות לבד אלא ללקט תיבה שלימה תיבה כאן ותיבה כאן עד פ"ה אותיות וכי פלגינן באותיות המפוזרות: עשה לה סימניות מלמעלה ומלמטה. להבדילה מן הסמוכות לה: למעלה ולמטה. בתחלה ובסוף ויהי בנסוע הארון: שאין

היו כתובים בסם ובסיקרא כו'. משמע דפשיטא ליה שאין קורין בהן דלאי קורין בהן פשיטא דמצילין כדאמר לעיל וקשה לרשב"א דבסמוך משמע דפשיטא ליה לריש גלותא גופיה דקורין בהן דקאמר והתניא מצילין והיינו ההוא ברייתא דמייתי שהספרים נכתבים בכל לשון ומגילה עד שתהא כתובה אשורית על הספר ובדיו אבל שאר ספרים נכתבין שלא בדיו ולפי מה שאפרש בסמוך דהך ברייתא איירי לענין הלכה אתי שפיר ולעולם אין קורין בהן: אבל הכא כיון דלא מקיים לא. אע"ג דבפ"ב דגיטין (דף יט.) קרי להו דבר שמתקיים דתנן בכל כותבין בסם ובדיו ובסקרא ובקומוס ובקנקנתום ובכל דבר שמתקיים אומר ר"י דהתם קרי ליה מתקיים טפי ממשקין ומי פירות דקתני התם בסיפא דאין כותבין בהן אבל אין מתקיימין כמו דיו אבל קשה לר"י דתנן בפ"ב דסוטה (דף יז:) גבי מגילת סוטה אין כותבין לא בקומוס ולא בקנקנתום שנאמר ומחה כתב שיכול למחוק אלמא קומוס וקנקנתום מתקיימין יותר מדיו ואומר ר"י דלעולם אין מתקיימין כמו דיו ואין יכול למחות כמו דיו לפי שנבלעין בקלף: מגילה עד שתהא כתובה אשורית על הספר ובדיו. משמע דשאר ספרים לא בעי ספר ודיו וקשה דבפ' המוציא יין (לעיל דף עט:) משמע דספר תורה בעי ספר דתני' על הנייר ועל המטלית פסולה ומוקי לה בס"ת וה"ה על הדיפתרא אע"ג דלא חשיב ליה לענין פסול ה"נ לא חשיב ליה לענין כשרות דקתני על הקלף ועל הדוכסוסטוס כשירה ולא קתני דיפתרא ועוד תנן במסכת סופרים (פ"א) אין כותבין לא ע"ג דיפתרא ולא ע"ג נייר מחוק ועוד דמגילה פסולה אדיפתרא כדתנן בפ"ב דמגילה (דף יז.) וכן מגילת סוטה פסולה אדיפתרא כדאמר בפ"ב דסוטה (דף יז:) משום דבעיא ספר וכ"ש ס"ת דנקראת כמה פעמים ספר ודיו נמי צריך כדאמר בפרק הבונה (לעיל קג:) כתבה שלא בדיו או שכתב האזכרות בזהב הרי אלו יגנזו ותירץ הרב יוסף דס"ת ודאי בעי ספר ודיו והכא איירי דווקא בשאר ספרים והא דלא קתני אין בין ספרים לס"ת ומגילה משום דס"ת נכתבים בכל לשון להכי לא עריב לה ואכתי קשה לר"י דתנן בפ"ק דמגילה (דף ח:) אין בין ספרים לתפילין ומזוזות אלא שהספרים נכתבין בכל לשון כו' ופריך בגמרא וספרים נכתבין בכל לשון ורמינהו מקרא שכתבו תרגום ותרגום שכתבו מקרא וכתב עברי אינו מטמא את הידים עד שיכתבנו בכתב אשורית על הספר ובדיו ומשני כאן בספרים כאן במגילה ורב אשי משני כי תניא ההיא בשאר ספרים ורבי יהודה היא אלמא בשאר ספרים נמי בעי רבי יהודה ספר ודיו והוא הדין לרבנן דלא אשכחן דפליגי רבנן עליה אלא בכתב אשורית אבל בספר ודיו לא אשכחן דפליגי ועוד קשה דשביק רב אשי התם שינויא קמא דמוקי לה במגילה ומסייע ליה ברייתא דהכא דקתני בהדיא דמגילה בעי שתהא כתובה אשורית וספר ודיו ורב אשי גופיה מייתי לה הכא ונראה לר"י דדווקא לענין הלכה מיתניא הך ברייתא דאין בין ספרים למגילה אלא שהספרים נכתבין בכל לשון ולפי' בלא ספר ודיו ראויה לקריאה שאין בהן שום הזכרה משום דיש בהו אזכרות אבל במגילה אין מצילין אלא א"כ ראויה לקריאה שתהא כתובה אשורית על הספר ובדיו לפי שאין בה הזכרה וא"ת תקשה מברייתא דהכא דקאמר לעיל כל היכא דלא ניתנו לקרות בהן אין מצילין ור"י דהא מסיק לעיל תנאי היא:

מיתיבי ס"ת שבלה אם יש בו כדי ללקט כו'. הכא משמע דמלשון ללקט קא פריך דמשמע אפי' מפוזרות ותימה לר"י א"כ אמאי קא בעי מעיקרא מכונסות או אפי' מפוזרות פשיטא דאפי' מפוזרות מדבעא רב הונא שאין בו ללקט מאי משמע הא יש בו ללקט מצילין אע"פ שהן מפוזרות:

רבינו חננאל

ושאר תנאי (א) [דתנן] [דאמרי] מצילין לא מסיים מן מינהון סבר ניתנו לקרות בהן. ומאן מנהון סבר לא ניתנו לקרות בהן אלא האי תנא דגפטית. דתני אע"פ שלא ניתנו לקרות בהן מצילין אותן. ות"ק דר' יוסי בניתנו לקרות בהן פליג. וקי"ל כרב הונא דרב חסדא לגביה תלמיד הוא. והא דתנינן כל כתבי הקדש מצילין אותן מפני הדליקה בין בנביא' שקורין בהן בין כתובים שאין קורין בהן. בד"א בכתבי הקדש הכתובים בלשה"ק [אבל אי הוו] אינהו כתבי הקדש כתובי' בשאר לשון אין מצילין אותן מפני הדליקה ואפי' הכי טעונין גניזה והא ברייתא דתניא הברכות והקמיעות אע"פ שיש בהן של שם ומעניינות של תורה הרבה אין מצילין אותן מפני הדליקה ונגנזין במקומן הלכה היא. הלכה כדתנא רב המנונא שאם היו כתובין בסם ובסיקרא מצילין אותן אע"פ שאינו דבר של קיימא. ולענין בעיא דרב הונא בר חלוב מרב נחמן סוגיא דשמעתא. כל ס"ת דאית ביה פסוקא דאית ביה שם אע"ג דאין בו ללקט פ"ה אותיות מצילין אותו. והאי דתניא יגר שהדותא מצילין אותו להשלים דאי איכא פ"ה אותיות אע"ג שמהן יגר שהדותא מצילין אותו. והלכתא כרב הונא דהני פ"ה אותיות מכונסות ולא מפוזרות. ופי' מכונסות כדתרגמא רב חסדא אליבא דרב הונא בתיבות אי יכול ללקט פ"ה אותיות מס"ת מתוך תיבות שלימות מצילין אותו כגון דמשכחת בראשית והיא מנויה לשש. ויצא מנויה לארבע. ואלה מנויה לארבע. ויקרא מנויה לחמש כולן תיבות שלימות עשרים (וא"ו) [און פחות או יתר] שמנין אותיותיהן פ"ה. אבל אותיות שמתוך תיבות שאינן שלימות אין מצילין כגון ויאמ מכלל ויאמר. אבר מכלל אברם או אברהם וכיוצא בהן. כל שנמצאת תיבה שלימה מונין אותיותיה להעלות לפ"ה אותיות וכל תיבה מקצתה מטושטשת אין אותיותיה המגונות עולות למנין פ"ה. משו"ה אמרן דאע"פ שהתיבות מפוזרה' במקומו' רחוקין זה מזה: גליונים של ס"ת. איבעיא אם מצילין אותן ולא איפשיטא. ס"ת שנמחק מקום המחק אין קדוש דאמרינן כי ליכא היכא דאיכא כתב. ליכא כתב לא קדוש. ומשום דאית טעותא בנוסחאות בהא שמעתא כתבנא כולה.

תורה אור השלם

א) וַיִּקְרָא לוֹ לָבָן יְגַר שָׂהֲדוּתָא וְיַעֲקֹב קָרָא לוֹ גַּלְעֵד: [בראשית לא, מז]

ב) וַיְהִי בִּנְסֹעַ הָאָרֹן וַיֹּאמֶר מֹשֶׁה קוּמָה יְיָ וְיָפֻצוּ אֹיְבֶיךָ וְיָנֻסוּ מְשַׂנְאֶיךָ מִפָּנֶיךָ: [במדבר י, לה]

ליקוטי רש"י

הברכות. שתקנו חכמים כגון תפלה של שמונה עשרה שיש בהן מלכיות וזכרונות ושופרות. ומעניינות. מפרשיות הרבה שכותבין בהן את מקראות של רפואה [לעיל סא.]. סם. זרניך בלשון קודש אורפימנ"ט בלע"ז [מגילה יח.]. סיקרא. אדמוני"א בלע"ז אדום שצובעין בה תריסין. קומוס. קומא. גומ"א שרף אילן [שבת קד:]. שרף האילן ומחיו במים וכותב. קנקנתום. וויטריולו"ו אורדימנ"ט קורין אותו [סוטה יז:]. סם שצובעין בו מנעלים שחורין [מגילה יט.]. בדיו. שלנו של שרף [סוטה שם]. אי תניא תניא. אי תניא הדתנא ותדר אני כי [חגיגה יג.]. אי מסכת בריתא תנינא [נדרים יז.]. אין בין ספרים. תורה נביאים וכתובים. עד שתהא כתובה אשורית. כתב אשורית שלנו [מגילה ח:]. כתב שלנו אשורית שבא מאשור כדאמר בפרק [סנהדרין כב.]. על הספר. קלף [מגילה ז.]. תרגום. שהיה ראוי ליכתוב בו תרגום כגון יגר שהדותא [בראשית לא]. שכתבו מקרא. גלעד. וכגון (כתב) של דניאל ועזרא. ומקרא שכתבו תרגום. ספר שכתוב בלשון הקודש הראוי לכתוב בו מקרא כתבו לשון ארמי. וכתב עברית. כל שפה שינה את הלשון אבל שינה את הכתב שכתבו בכתב של עבר הנהר [סנהדרין כא:]. קרי ליה ליבונאה. אותיות גדולות כעין אותן שכותבין בקמיעות ומזוזות [סנהדרין כא:]. יגר שהדותא. תרגומו של גלעד [בראשית לא, מז]. אליבא דרב הונא. במקום [אחר] ונסיבין שאמה (משנה) [סוכה יט. בסוגיין רב הונא]. סימניות. סימנין הפוכין [ראש השנה יז:].

פורענות

כתבנא כולה. ת"ש ס"ת שבלה אם יש בו ללקט פ"ה אותיות מצילין אותו ואם לאו אין מצילין אותו. [illegible]

חשק שלמה על רבינו חננאל א) נראה מזה דרבינו לא היה גורס אילימא ת"ק דר"י ודילמא בהא קמיפלגי. רק היה לו גי' אחרת בזה וצ"ע:

Baraisa states that this phrase may be saved **even though it lacks eighty-five letters.** This contradicts the ruling of Rav Nachman that a passage which contains fewer than eighty-five letters may not be saved. – ? –

Rav Nachman replied:

כִּי תַּנְיָא הַהִיא לְהַשְׁלִים – When that Baraisa was taught, it was taught in regard **to completing** the quota of eighty-five.[20]

The Gemara continues:

אִיבַּעְיָא לְהוּ – They inquired: הָנֵי שְׁמוֹנִים וְחָמֵשׁ אוֹתִיּוֹת **– These eighty-five letters** that are necessary to maintain the sanctity of a Torah scroll, מְכוּנָּסוֹת אוֹ מְפוּזָּרוֹת – must they be **together, or** may they even be **scattered** throughout the scroll? **רַב הוּנָא אָמַר מְכוּנָּסוֹת – Rav Huna said:** They must be **together.** **רַב חִסְדָּא אָמַר אֲפִילּוּ מְפוּזָּרוֹת – Rav Chisda said: Even scattered.**

The Gemara attempts to disprove one opinion:

מֵיתִיבֵי – They challenged Rav Huna **from a Baraisa:** סֵפֶר תּוֹרָה שֶׁבָּלָה – In regard to A TORAH SCROLL THAT BECAME WORN, אִם יֵשׁ בּוֹ לְלַקֵּט שְׁמוֹנִים וְחָמֵשׁ אוֹתִיּוֹת – IF THERE IS WITHIN IT sufficient writing TO GATHER EIGHTY-FIVE LETTERS, i.e. eighty-five letters are still intact, כְּגוֹן פָּרָשַׁת ,,וַיְהִי בִּנְסֹעַ הָאָרֹן״ – SIMILAR TO THE SECTION which begins: *AND WHEN THE ARK WOULD JOURNEY,* מַצִּילִין – WE MAY SAVE it from a fire on the Sabbath, וְאִם לָאו אֵין מַצִּילִין – BUT IF NOT, WE MAY NOT SAVE it. From the fact that the Baraisa uses the words "*to gather,*" it is implied that the letters are scattered throughout the scroll. Yet the Baraisa rules that if a total of eighty-five letters can be found, the scroll may be saved. **תְּיוּבְתָּא דְּרַב הוּנָא – This is a refutation of Rav Huna. – ? –**

Rav Huna's view is defended:

תַּרְגְּמָהּ רַב חִסְדָּא אַלִּיבָּא דְּרַב הוּנָא בְּתֵיבוֹת – Rav Chisda explained [the Baraisa] according to Rav Huna as referring to the gathering of whole **words.**[21]

Having mentioned the section *And when the Ark would journey* etc., the Gemara digresses to comment on it:

תָּנוּ רַבָּנָן – The Rabbis taught in a Baraisa: ,,וַיְהִי בִּנְסֹעַ הָאָרֹן וַיֹּאמֶר מֹשֶׁה״ – *AND WHEN THE ARK WOULD JOURNEY, MOSES SAID* etc. פָּרָשָׁה זוֹ עָשָׂה לָהּ הַקָּדוֹשׁ בָּרוּךְ הוּא סִימָנִיּוֹת מִלְמַעְלָה וּלְמַטָּה – THIS SECTION THE HOLY ONE, BLESSED IS HE, MADE SIGNS ABOVE AND BELOW IT, i.e. He placed markings immediately preceding and following this section to enclose and separate it from the rest of the Torah,[22] לוֹמַר – TO TEACH

NOTES

20. The Baraisa does not mean that the scroll contained only the words *yegar sahadusa;* rather, it contained other words as well. The Baraisa teaches that although the words *yegar sahadusa* are Aramaic, their letters may be counted to complete the total of eighty-five letters needed to save a scroll (*Rashi*).

21. The phrase "to gather," which implies that the letters are scattered throughout the scroll, does not mean that individual *letters* are scattered. Rather, whole *words* are scattered, one here and one there, with the sum of their letters totaling eighty-five. The dispute between Rav Huna and Rav Chisda, on the other hand, pertains specifically to where individual *letters* are scattered (*Rashi*).

The question arises: Above, Rav Huna bar Chaluv inquired of Rav Nachman whether a Torah scroll containing fewer than eighty-five letters merits saving. But why did the Gemara not resolve this question by citing the present Baraisa, which addresses this very point and rules that the scroll may not be saved?

Rashba answers that Rav Huna bar Chaluv himself was aware of this Baraisa. However, he inquired whether this Baraisa reflects the accepted halachah, since he was also aware of the Baraisa cited previously by the Gemara (regarding *yegar sahadusa*) from which the reverse ruling may be inferred. This is why when Rav Nachman responded that the scroll may not be saved, Rav Huna immediately challenged him from the previously cited Baraisa.

22. The Gemara does not identify the nature of these "signs." For many centuries, however, the custom has been, no doubt based on tradition, for these signs to take the form of inverted *nuns*, one immediately preceding this section and one following it [see diagram]. See *Noda BiYehudah, Mahadura Kamma, Yoreh Deah* §74 who cites a ruling dating back to *Rav Hai Gaon* which supports this custom (see also following note in the name of *Rabbeinu Bachya*). *Maharshal*, however, [*Chochmas Shlomo* and *She'eilos U'Teshuvos* §73], vehemently opposed the use of inverted *nuns* and explained these "signs" in other ways. See also *Minchas Shai* to *Numbers* 10:35.

המחנה ׆ ויהי בנסע הארן
ויאמר משה קומה ה׳ ויפצו איביך וינסו
משנאיך מפניך ובנחה יאמר שובה ה׳
רבבות אלפי ישראל ׆

שֶׁאֵין זֶה מְקוֹמָהּ – THAT THIS IS NOT ITS proper PLACE.[1] רַבִּי אוֹמֵר – REBBI SAYS: לֹא מִן הַשֵּׁם הוּא זֶה – IT IS NOT FOR THIS REASON that the signs appear, אֶלָּא מִפְּנֵי שֶׁסֵּפֶר חָשׁוּב הוּא בִּפְנֵי עַצְמוֹ – BUT RATHER BECAUSE [THIS SECTION] RANKS AS a significant BOOK UNTO ITSELF.[2]

The Gemara comments:

כְּמַאן אַזְלָא הָא דְּאָמַר רַבִּי שְׁמוּאֵל בַּר נַחְמָנִי אָמַר רַבִּי יוֹנָתָן – **With whom does the following statement made by R' Shmuel bar Nachmani in the name of R' Yonasan agree?** Scripture states:[3] "חָצְבָה עַמּוּדֶיהָ שִׁבְעָה" – *Wisdom has built her house, **she has hewn out her seven pillars*** – אֵלּוּ שִׁבְעָה סִפְרֵי תוֹרָה – **these represent the seven books of the Torah.** כְּמַאן – **In accordance with whom** was this statement made? כְּרַבִּי – **In accordance with Rebbi.**[4]

The Gemara seeks to identify the Tanna Kamma of the Baraisa:

מַאן תַּנָּא דִּפְלִיג עֲלֵיהּ דְּרַבִּי – **Who is the Tanna that disagrees with Rebbi?** רַבָּן שִׁמְעוֹן בֶּן גַּמְלִיאֵל הוּא – **It is Rabban Shimon ben Gamliel.** דְּתַנְיָא – **For it was taught in a Baraisa:** רַבָּן שִׁמְעוֹן בֶּן גַּמְלִיאֵל אוֹמֵר – RABBAN SHIMON BEN GAMLIEL SAYS: עֲתִידָה פָּרָשָׁה זוֹ שֶׁתֵּיעָקֵר מִכָּאן וְתִכָּתֵב בִּמְקוֹמָהּ – THIS SECTION IS DESTINED TO BE UPROOTED FROM HERE AND BE WRITTEN IN ITS proper PLACE. וְלָמָּה כְּתָבָהּ כָּאן – AND WHY WAS IT WRITTEN HERE? כְּדֵי לְהַפְסִיק בֵּין פּוּרְעָנוּת רִאשׁוֹנָה לְפוּרְעָנוּת שְׁנִיָּה – IN ORDER TO SEPARATE BETWEEN the narrative of THE FIRST PUNISHMENT AND the narrative of THE SECOND PUNISHMENT.[5]

The Gemara elucidates the Baraisa:

פּוּרְעָנוּת שְׁנִיָּה מַאי הִיא – **What is** the narrative of **the second punishment?** "וַיְהִי הָעָם כְּמִתְאֹנְנִים" – ***And the people took to seeking complaints.***[6] פּוּרְעָנוּת רִאשׁוֹנָה – What is the narrative **of the first punishment?** "וַיִּסְעוּ מֵהַר ה׳" – ***And they traveled from the mountain of Hashem** a journey of three days*;[7] וְאָמַר רַבִּי חָמָא בְּרַבִּי חֲנִינָא – **and** regarding this verse **R' Chama the son of R' Chanina commented:** שֶׁסָּרוּ מֵאַחֲרֵי ה׳ – Within three days of their setting out from Mount Sinai **they turned away from God.**[8] וְהֵיכָן מְקוֹמָהּ – **And where is [this section's]** proper **place?** אָמַר רַב אַשִׁי – **Rav Ashi said:** בִּדְגָלִים – **With** the topic of **the banners.**[9]

The Gemara returns to the Mishnah's ruling that books of the Scriptures may be saved from a fire on the Sabbath:

אִיבַּעְיָא לְהוּ – **They inquired:** הַגִּלְיוֹנִין שֶׁל סֵפֶר תּוֹרָה – Regarding **the blank portions of a Torah scroll,** מַצִּילִין אוֹתָן מִפְּנֵי הַדְּלֵיקָה אוֹ אֵין מַצִּילִין אוֹתָן מִפְּנֵי הַדְּלֵיקָה – **may we save them from a fire** on the Sabbath **or may we not save them from a fire?**[10]

The Gemara attempts a resolution:

תָּא שְׁמַע – **Come, learn** a proof from a Baraisa: סֵפֶר תּוֹרָה שֶׁבָּלָה – In regard to A TORAH SCROLL THAT BECAME WORN, אִם יֵשׁ בּוֹ לְלַקֵּט שְׁמוֹנִים וְחָמֵשׁ אוֹתִיּוֹת – IF THERE IS WITHIN IT sufficient writing TO GATHER EIGHTY-FIVE LETTERS, כְּגוֹן פָּרָשַׁת "וַיְהִי בִּנְסֹעַ

NOTES

1. This is because these verses properly belong in *Numbers* ch. 2, where the Torah describes how each tribe camped under its banner (*Rashi,* from Gemara below; cf. *Chizkuni* ad loc.). After stating there that the banner of Yehudah would travel first and the banner of Reuben second, the Torah relates, in v.17, that the Tabernacle would travel next. Since the Tabernacle contained the Ark, *this* is the proper place for the Torah to state: *And when the Ark would journey* etc. (*Rabbeinu Bachya* ad loc.).

[*Rabbeinu Bachya* adds that the Torah "chose reversed *nuns*" to indicate these verses' misplacement because the numerical value of the letter *nun* is fifty, and *Numbers* 2:17, where these verses belong, is written fifty sections before ("in *reverse* of") this section.]

(It has been observed that even counting both end sections, these sections are in fact only forty-nine sections apart — see note by *R' C.D. Chavel* to the *Mossad HaRav Kook* edition of *Rabbeinu Bachya.* However, this discrepancy may be attributed to the fact, noted by *Minchas Shai* to *Numbers* 10:22, that ancient Torah scrolls contain a paragraph break between *Numbers* 10:21 and 10:22 which does not appear in our scrolls.)

2. The signs before and after this section indicate that these verses are to be regarded as a separate "Book" of the Torah.

Rebbi maintains that this section does indeed belong in its place, because it follows on the heels of the narrative describing the first time the Jews traveled [according to their commanded formations, which was] when they departed from Mount Sinai (*Rashi*). [That is, although the *commandment* to observe the banner formations is recorded in *Numbers* ch. 2, the first *account* of how the Jews traveled according to these configurations appears in *Numbers* ch. 10. Thus, this is an appropriate place for the verse: *And when the Ark would journey* etc.]

3. *Proverbs* 9:1.

4. According to Rebbi, the section which begins: *And when the Ark would journey* etc. is in its proper place, and it was set off from the rest of the Torah to teach that it is to be reckoned as a separate book of the Torah. Consequently, the portions of *Numbers* that precede and follow this section are also to be viewed as separate "books." Thus, the Book of *Numbers* is actually made up of three "books," the portion from the beginning of *Numbers* until this section, this section itself, and the portion after this section until the end of *Numbers* (*Rashi*). When we add these to the books of *Genesis, Exodus, Leviticus* and *Deuteronomy,* we get a total of seven books.

5. As the Gemara will soon explain, the Israelites acted sinfully two times, one following the other. The Torah did not want to record in succession two Jewish sins deserving of Divine retribution, and therefore inserted the portion of *And when the Ark would journey* . . . as an interlude. In the future, however [i.e. after the Messiah comes (*Rabbeinu Bachya* loc. cit.)], when Divine retribution will cease and the Evil Inclination will no longer hold sway, this section will be returned to its rightful place (*Rashi*).

6. *Numbers* 11:1. Immediately after the section which begins *And when the Ark would journey* etc., the Torah relates that the people took to complaining [about the rigors of their travels (*Rashi* ad loc.)], and that, as a result, a Divine fire broke out and consumed some of them.

7. Ibid. 10:33.

8. R' Chama means: אַל תִּקְרֵי מֵהַר ה׳ אֶלָּא מֵאַחַר ה׳, *do not read "from the mountain of Hashem" but "from behind Hashem"* (*Amar Nekei* by *R' Ovadiah MiBartenura,* ad loc.; cf. commentary attributed to *Rashi* to *Taanis* 29a ד״ה אמר רבי חמא; *Maharsha*).

Following the narrative of the complainers, the Torah relates the story of the אֲסַפְסֻף, *the rabble,* i.e. the mixed multitude of converts who accompanied the Jews when they left Egypt. This group incited other Jews to complain about their diet of manna and clamor for meat, in order to foment a general rebellion against God. In response to this complaint, God caused flocks of quail to descend upon the camp, but many of those who had complained were struck down by God even as they began to eat (see *Numbers* 11:33 with *Rashi*).

The Gemara states that although this incident is recorded after the sin of the complainers, the rabble actually began cultivating the desire for meat among the people beforehand, within three days of the nation's departure from Mount Sinai, as hinted to by R' Chama's interpretation of the verse וַיִּסְעוּ מֵהַר ה׳. The Torah interrupts with the section of *And when the Ark would journey* before mentioning the second sin of the complainers so as to separate the accounts of the two sins (see *Rashi;* see also *Leshon HaZahav* here and *Ramban* to *Numbers* 10:35 in explanation of *Rashi*). According to this explanation, when the Torah states in verse 4: *And the rabble that was among them cultivated a craving,* it actually means: "the rabble *had previously* cultivated a craving" (*Mizrachi* ad loc.).

Alternatively, in stating that the Jews "turned away from God," R' Chama alludes to the Midrash that the Children of Israel "fled from the mountain of God, at which they had learned much Torah, with glee, like a child running away from school" (*Tosafos,* see also *Ramban* ad loc.). According to this explanation, the Gemara refers to this sin as a "punishment" imprecisely, for no punishment befell them as a result of this sin (see *Ramban* ibid.).

9. See note 1.

10. At this point the Gemara assumes the query to pertain to any blank portion, whether the [cut-off] margin of a Torah scroll, or the parchment of a scroll from which the writing became erased (*Rashi*).

שאין זה מקומה ר' אומר לא מן השם הוא זה אלא מפני שספר חשוב הוא בפני עצמו כמאן אזלא הא דא"ר שמואל בר נחמן א"ר יונתן חצבה עמודיה שבעה אלו שבעה ספרי תורה כמאן כרבי מאן תנא דפליג עליה דר' רשב"ג הוא דתניא רשב"ג אומר עתידה פרשה זו שתיעקר מכאן ותכתב במקומה ולמה כתבה כאן כדי להפסיק בין פורענות ראשונה לפורענות שנייה פורענות שנייה מאי היא ויהי העם כמתאוננים פורענות ראשונה ויסעו מהר ה' וא"ר חמא בר' חנינא שסרו מאחרי ה' והיכן מקומה אמר רב אשי ברגלים • איבעיא להו הגליונין של ס"ת מצילין אותן מפני הדליקה או אין מצילין אותן מפני הדליקה ת"ש ס"ת שבלה אם יש בו ללקט שמונים וחמש אותיות כגון פרשת ויהי בנסוע הארון מצילין ואם לאו אין מצילין ואמאי תיפוק ליה משום גיליון דידיה בלה שאני ת"ש ס"ת שנמחק אם יש בו ללקט שמונים וחמש אותיות כגון פרשת ויהי בנסוע הארון מצילין ואם לאו אין מצילין ואמאי תיפוק ליה משום גיליון דידיה מקום הכתב לא קמיבעיא לי דכי קדוש אגב כתב הוא דקדוש אזל כתב אזלא לה קדושתיה כי קמיבעיא לי של מעלה ושל מטה שבין פרשה לפרשה שבין דף לדף שבתחלת הספר שבסוף הספר ותיפוק ליה משום ההוא • דגייז ושדי ת"ש הגליונין של מעלה ושל מטה שבין פרשה לפרשה שבין דף לדף שבתחלת הספר שבסוף הספר מטמאין את הידים דילמא אגב ס"ת שאני ת"ש הגליונין וספרי מינין אין מצילין אותן מפני הדליקה אלא נשרפין במקומן הן ואזכרותיהן מאי לאו גליונין דספר תורה לא גליונין דספרי מינין (א) השתא ספרי מינין גופייהו אין מצילין גליונין מבעיא הכי קאמר וספרי מינין הרי הן כגליונים גופא הגליונים וספרי מינין אין מצילין אותם מפני הדליקה רבי יוסי אומר בחול קודר את האזכרות שבהן וגונזן והשאר שורפן א"ר טרפון • אקפח את בני שאם יבאו לידי שאני אשרוף אותם ואת האזכרות שבהן שאפי' אדם רודף אחריו להורגו ונחש רץ להכישו נכנס לבית ע"ז ואין נכנס לבתיהן של אלו שהללו מכירין וכופרין והללו אין מכירין וכופרין ועליהן הכתוב אומר [ו]אחר הדלת והמזוזה שמת זכרונך א"ר ישמעאל ק"ו ומה לעשות שלום בין איש לאשתו אמרה תורה שמי שנכתב בקדושה ימחה על המים הללו שמטילין קנאה ואיבה ותחרות בין ישראל לאביהן שבשמים על אחת כמה וכמה ועליהם אמר דוד הלא משנאיך ה' אשנא ובתקוממיך אתקוטט תכלית שנאה שנאתים לאויבים היו לי וכשם שאין מצילין אותן מפני הדליקה כך אין מצילין אותן לא מן המפולת ולא מן המים ולא מדבר המאבדן בעי מיניה (ב) יוסף בר חנין מר' אבהו הני ספרי דבי אבידן מצילין אותן מפני הדליקה או אין מצילין אין ולאו ורפיא בידיה רב • לא אזיל לבי אבידן וכ"ש לבי נצרפי שמואל לבי נצרפי לא אזיל לבי אבידן אזיל אמרו ליה לרבא מ"ט לא אתית לבי אבידן אמר להו דיקלא פלניא איכא באורחא וקשי לי ניעקריה דוכתיה קשי לי מר בר יוסף אמר אנא מינייהו אנא ולא מסתפינא מינייהו זימנא חדא אזיל בעו לסכוניה אימא שלום דביתהו דרבי אליעזר אחתיה דרבן גמליאל הואי הוה ההוא פילוסופא בשבבותיה
דהוה

רש"י

שאין זה מקומה. שאינה ראויה לכאן דלאו בהליכות מסעות משתעי לעיל מיניה אלא בדגלים היתה ראויה ליכתב בפרשת במדבר סיני: **לא מן השם הוא זה.** לא זה הטעם של טעמי הסימניות למקומה הוא דפרשה זו בתחלת מסע שנסעו מהר סיני איירי כדכתיב לעיל מיניה (ג) ויהי בחדש השני בשנה השנית בעשרים לחדש נעלה הענן וגו': **ז' ספרי תורה.** דפרשה זו ספר לעצמו נמצא שלמעלה ספר לעצמו [ושלמטה ספר לעצמו] הואיל וזה מקומה נמצא ספר וידבר נחלק לג' ספרים: **עתידה פרשה זו.** לעתיד שיהו כל הפורעניות בטלין ולא ידאגו לפורענות ויצר הרע בטל: **מאחרי ה'.** בתוך ג' ימים למסעם התאוו האספסוף תאוה להתרעם על הבשר כדי למרוד בהקב"ה: **הגליונין.** קלפים חלקים וקס"ד השתא דבכל לדדין שיהו חלקים קמיבעיא ליה כגון חלק שלמעלה ושלמטה ושנמחק כתבו ונעשה חלק: **בלה שאני.** דכיון שבלה אף הגליון בטל וכי מיבעיא ליה שהגליונין קיימים אלא שהכתב הלך: **ותיפוק ליה משום גליון דידיה.** דהיינו כל הספר תורה: **מקום הכתב.** שנמחק: **לא מבעיא לי.** דודאי מיגרע גרע דכי קדיש לאו לשם גליון חלק קדיש אלא אדעתא דכתב וכיון דאזל ליה כתב פקע קדושתיה: **של מעלה ומטה.** דמתחלה לשם חלק קדיש והשתא כשנמחק כתב הספר נמי חלק הוא: ה"ג **ותיפוק ליה משום ההוא דגייז ושדי.** והכי פירושא ותיפוק לי' דאע"ג דאין בו כדי ללקט פ"ה אותיות הוה ליה למיתני בברייתא מצילין משום ההוא ריוח של מעלה ומטה אלא לאו פשוט מיניה דאין מצילין. ומשני דגייז ושדי שנחתכו הגליונים ולא נשייר בו אלא מקום הכתב: **שבתחלת הספר ושבסוף הספר.** שכולן היו כתובין כמגילה כס"ת ואמרי' בב"ב בפ"ק (דף יג:) ראשו כדי לגול עמוד סופו כדי לגול היקף להקיף כל הכרך: **מטמא את הידים.** אם נגע בו ונגע בתרומה פוסלה דמגזירת י"ח דבר היא (לעיל דף יד.): **דילמא אגב ס"ת.** שלא נמחק כתב הספר אלא כולו קיים וזה נגע בגליונים וכי מבעיא לן בנמחק הספר ואין כאן קדושה אלא משום גליון ששמשו בעודו קיים: **ספרי מינין.** משרתים לע"ז וכתבו להן תורה נביאים כתובים כתב אשורית ולשון הקודש: **וספרי המינין גופייהו מצילין.** בתמיה: **ספרי המינין הרי הן כגליונים.** כקלפים חלקים שלא נכתב בהם מעולם: **קודר.** חותך חתיכות הקלף מקום השם: **שאפי' רודף אדם להורגו.** על עצמו קאמר: **שהללו.** נכרים העובדים ע"ז אין אינן מכירין שהרי בכך גדלו וכך למדום אבותם: **ואחר הדלת והמזוזה שמת זכרונך.** זכרון הוא בידך ואינה שכחה לך אלא שהשלכת אותי אחרי הדלת: **כך אין מצילין אותן.** אפי' בחול: **דבי אבידן.** ספרים שכתבו להם המינין להתווכח עם ישראל ומקום שמתווכחים שם קרי ליה בי אבידן: **אין ולא.** זימנין אמר ליה אין זימנין א"ל לא: **לבי נצרפי.** ע"ז וכך שמה: **וקשה לי.** שורשן נעשו גבשושית ולדחוס בקש בא: **אמרי ליה ניעקריה קשה לי דוכתיה.** שתהא שם גומא אי נמי נסיתיו וקשה לי ריחו וכל זה שהיו מתיראין רב ורבא מלכת לבי אבידן שמא מתוך שיתווכחו יעמדו עליהם ויהרגום: **מינייהו אנא.** מכירי הם: **פילוסופא.** מין:
דהוה

תוספות

פורענות ראשונה ויסעו וא"ר חנינא שסרו מאחרי השם. פי' בקונטרס שמאז התחילו לשאול בשר ואומר ר"י דאין נ"ל כן אלא פורענות ראשונה כדאמר במדרש (ילמדנו) ויסעו שנסעו מהר סיני דרך שלשת ימים כתינוק היוצא מבית הספר שבורח לו והולך לו כך היו בורחים מהר סיני דרך שלשת ימים לפי שלמדו הרבה תורה בסיני ועוד אמר הקב"ה (ד) נסמוך פורענות לפורענות לאו אלא נפסוק פרשת ויהי בנסוע הארון:

ספרי מינין כו' א"ר טרפון כו'. אומר ר"י דמיירי בנמצא ביד מינין דאי כתבן מין הא אמר בפרק השולח (גיטין דף מה:) נמצא ביד מין יגנז כתבו מין ישרף ודוחק לומר דאתי כר"ט ודלא כרבנן ורבי יוסי:

כך אין מצילין אותן לא מן המים כו'. דלא תימא דוקא מן הדליקה אין מצילין משום דאי שרית ליה אתי לכבויי אלא אפילו היכא דליכא למיגזר מידי אסור לטלטלן ולהוציאן והך סיפא כרבנן דלרבי טרפון לא איצטריך:

פילוסופא. מין כדפי' בקונטרס ורבינו שמע [מיהודי אחד שבא מארץ יון ואמר] דבלשון יון פלוספוס הוא דוד החכמה ואית דגרסי פילא סבא והוא לשון לצון שחוק כדאמר באיכה רבתי דפלי ביהודאי פירוש שחק ונתלוצץ:
ושמואל

עין משפט נר מצוה

ח א מיי' פכ"ג מהלכות שבת הלכה כו טוש"ע או"ח סימן שלד סעיף כ:
ט ב מיי' פ"ט מהלכות שאר אבות הטומאות הלכה ו:
י ג ד מיי' פ"ו מהלכות יסודי התורה הלכה ח ופ"א מהלכות תפילין הלכה יג טור שו"ע או"ח סימן שלד סעיף כא וטור שו"ע יו"ד סימן רפא סעיף א:
יא ה טוש"ע יו"ד סימן קנז סעיף ג:

רבינו חננאל

אם מצילין אותן מפני הדליקה אי לא. ספרי מינין מיבעיא. ולא פ"ה אותיו' כנגד פרשת ויהי בנסוע הארון. ופרשת ויהי בנסוע הארון ספר בפני עצמו הוא. ומקומו בדגלים ולמה נכתב כאן. להפסיק בין פורענו' ראשונה שהיא ויסעו מהר ה' וגו' לפורענות שנייה. שהיא ויהי העם כמתאוננים וגו': ספרי דבי אבידן. חצר ידועה ויש בה ספרי חכמות מכל אומה ויש בה ספרי תורה קדש נביאים וכתובי' כתובי' בלשה"ק. ומפני שאינו ידוע מי כתבו אם ישראל או זולתן. אמרו על ר' אבהו שהיה הדבר רפוי בידיה להורות עליהן להציל או לא. וכן [בי] אבידן היו מתקבצין שם חכמי' ונבונים מכל אומה ונושאין ונותנין בדברי חכמה. וכן בי נצרפי. מהו בבי נצרפי היתה שם ע"ז. דגרסי' בע"ז איזו היא אשירה סתם. אמר שמואל כגון דאמרי הני תמרי נהורין לשכרא דבי נצרפי ושתו ליה ביום אידם. אמימר אמרו לי סבי (דשם בריתא) [דפומבדיתא] הלכתא כשמואל והני מילי אלה שהיו באותו זמן (הן) שעד אותה שעה לא טוכסין להן הטורכסטין שהן עכשיו בידיהן אלא כתובין היו יש מהן שומרין התורה ויש מהן שאינן שומרין וכולן קוראין אותה ויש מי שהיה קוראה בלשה"ק כיון דאסיקנא קוראין בהן בתורה ובנביאים. אבל בכתובים אין קוראין בהן.

רב נסים גאון

פט"ז כמאן אזלא הא דא"ר שמואל בר נחמני חצבה עמודיה שבעה אלו ז' חומשי תורה כמאן כר'. דר' סבר ויהי בנסוע הארון ספר בפני עצמו א"ב לא דעת ר' מתחילת ספר וידבר עד ויהי בנסוע הארון ספר בפני עצמו ויהי בנסוע הארון ספר בפני עצמו ומן שם עד סוף ספר וידבר ספר בפני עצמו נחלק ספר וידבר לג' ספרים הרי ג' ספרי וידבר עם ד' ספרים הנשארים יהיו הכל ז' ובבראשי' דר' אושעיא בפרשת אלה תולדות יצחק (פרשה סד) תניא כוותיה ויקרא אותה שבעה כנגד ספר וידבר שהוא משלים ז' ספרי תורה והלא ה' הם אלא בר קפרא עבד מן ספר וידבר עד ויהי בנסוע הארון ספר בפני עצמו מן תמן ועד סיפיה דספרא ספר בפני עצמו: בי נצרפי מן בתי ע"ז ומשכחת לה בפרק חלון (דף פ) ובמסכת ע"ז בפרק כל הצלמין (דף מח) אי זו היא אשירה סתם אמר רב אותה שאין טועמין מפירותיה ושמואל אמר כגון דאמרי הני תמרי נינהו לשיכרא דבי נצרפי דשתו ליה ביום אידם.

מסורת הש"ס

א) [נ"ל נחמני], ב) [תענית כט.], ג) ידים פרק ג' מ"ד עי"ש, ד) [תוספתא פרק י"ד], ה) [לעיל יג.] [זבחים יג.], ו) [סוכה נג: נדרים סו. מכות יא. חולין קמא.], ז) [לעיל קיג. וש"נ], ח) [פירוש מחוז כוכבים ערוך], ט) בס"י דלמיי' לעיל מיניה, י) [ובע"ז דף מד: פירש רש"י פילוסופין חכמי האומות], כ) [עי' תוי"ט פ"ה דאבות משנה ז].

הגהות הב"ח

(א) גמ' דספרי מינין השתא ספרי וכו' מנא מצי"ל דמ"מ ונ"ב ג' רש"י וספרי מינין גופייהו מצילין: (ב) שם בעי מיניה רב יוסף: (ג) רש"י ד"ה לא מן השם וכו' כדכתיב לעיל מיניה ויהי בחדש השני בעשרים בחדש: (ד) תוס' ד"ה פורענות וכו' ועוד אמר הקב"ה לא נסמוך פורענות לפורענות אלא:

גליון הש"ס

גמ' איבעיא להו הגליונין. עי' מגילה דף לב ע"ב תוס' ד"ה שם: דגייז ושדי. עי' תשובות זכרון יוסף סימן יא ויב: שם אקפח את בני. עיין לעיל דף יג ע"ב. זבחים דף יג ע"ב: שם לא אזיל לבי אבידן. עי' ע"ז דף יז ע"א תוס' ד"ה הרחק: רש"י בד"ה פילוסופא מין. עי' מס' ד"א רבה: תוס' ד"ה פורענות פי' בקונטרס. עי' תוי"ט פ"ה מ"ד דאבות.

תורה אור השלם

א) חָכְמוֹת בָּנְתָה בֵיתָהּ חָצְבָה עַמּוּדֶיהָ שִׁבְעָה: [משלי ט, א]
ב) וַיְהִי הָעָם כְּמִתְאֹנְנִים רַע בְּאָזְנֵי יְיָ וַיִּשְׁמַע יְיָ וַיִּחַר אַפּוֹ וַתִּבְעַר בָּם אֵשׁ יְיָ וַתֹּאכַל בִּקְצֵה הַמַּחֲנֶה: [במדבר יא, א]
ג) וַיִּסְעוּ מֵהַר יְיָ דֶּרֶךְ שְׁלֹשֶׁת יָמִים וַאֲרוֹן בְּרִית יְיָ נֹסֵעַ לִפְנֵיהֶם דֶּרֶךְ שְׁלֹשֶׁת יָמִים לָתוּר לָהֶם מְנוּחָה: [במדבר י, לג]
ד) וְאַחַר הַדֶּלֶת וְהַמְּזוּזָה שַׂמְתְּ זִכְרוֹנֵךְ כִּי מֵאִתִּי גִּלִּית וַתַּעֲלִי הִרְחַבְתְּ מִשְׁכָּבֵךְ וַתִּכְרָת לָךְ מֵהֶם אָהַבְתְּ מִשְׁכָּבָם יָד חָזִית: [ישעיה נז, ח]
ה) הֲלוֹא מְשַׂנְאֶיךָ יְיָ אֶשְׂנָא וּבִתְקוֹמְמֶיךָ אֶתְקוֹטָט: תַּכְלִית שִׂנְאָה שְׂנֵאתִים לְאוֹיְבִים הָיוּ לִי: [תהלים קלט, כא-כב]

ליקוטי רש"י

חצבה עמודיה שבעה. ז' ספרים יש בתורה ויהי בנסוע הארון ספר לעצמו במסכת שבת [משלי ט, א]. שבתחלת הספר. מניח חלק כדי לגול לגולל על גבי עמוד של עץ שהספר נגלל עליו. שבסוף הספר. בסופו מניח חלק גדול כדי לגול בו כל היקפו שאין עושה שני עמודים לגוללו לאמצעו כמו שאנו עושין לספר תורה אלא גוללו מתחלתו לסופו וכורך החלק על כל היקפו [ב"ב יג:]. אקפח את בני. שבועה היא שהיה רגיל לומר אקפח את בני [כתובות נב.] [ב"מ פה. ע"ש]. לעשות שלום בין איש לאשתו. [לעיל יג. ע"ש]. ימחה על המים. [סוכה נג:]. שמי שנכתב בקדושה. דכתיב וכתב את האלות האלה וגו' (במדבר ה) ומחה אל מי המרים. אין ולאו. מתחלה אמר אין וחזר ואמר לאו ולא היה פוסק בדבר. ורפיא בידיה. רפויה היתה השמועה בידו ולא היה מתוקן בה. לבי אבידן. לבי נצרפי. פילוסופין, חכמי האומות [ע"ז נד:].

הָאָרֶץ'' – SIMILAR TO THE SECTION which begins: *AND WHEN THE ARK WOULD JOURNEY,* מַצִּילִין – WE MAY SAVE it from a fire on the Sabbath, וְאִם לַאו אֵין מַצִּילִין – BUT IF NOT, WE MAY NOT SAVE it. וְאַמַּאי – **But why?** תֵּיפּוּק לֵיהּ מִשּׁוּם גִּילָּיוֹן דִּידֵיהּ – **Derive** that **it** may be saved **on account of its blank portion!**[11] Apparently blank portions do not merit saving.

The Gemara responds:

בָּלָה שַׁאנִי – A **worn** scroll **is different.**[12]

The Gemara again attempts a resolution:

תָּא שְׁמַע – **Come, learn** a proof from a Baraisa: סֵפֶר תּוֹרָה שֶׁנִּמְחַק – In regard to A TORAH SCROLL [WHOSE WRITING] BECAME ERASED, אִם יֵשׁ בּוֹ לְלַקֵּט שְׁמוֹנִים וְחָמֵשׁ אוֹתִיּוֹת – IF THERE IS WITHIN IT sufficient writing TO GATHER EIGHTY-FIVE LETTERS, כְּגוֹן פָּרָשַׁת ,,וַיְהִי בִּנְסֹעַ הָאָרֹן'' – SIMILAR TO THE SECTION which begins: *AND WHEN THE ARK WOULD JOURNEY,* מַצִּילִין – WE MAY SAVE it from a fire on the Sabbath, וְאִם לַאו אֵין מַצִּילִין – BUT IF NOT, WE MAY NOT SAVE it. וְאַמַּאי – **But why?** תֵּיפּוּק לֵיהּ מִשּׁוּם גִּילָּיוֹן דִּידֵיהּ – **Derive** that it may be saved **on account of its blank portion!**[13]

The Gemara replies:

מְקוֹם הַכְּתָב לֹא קָמִיבַּעְיָא לִי – In regard to **the place on which there once was writing, I have no doubt** that it loses its sanctity, דְּכִי קָדוֹשׁ – **because when [this portion]** originally **received** its **sanctity,** אַגַּב כְּתָב הוּא דְּקָדוֹשׁ – **it received** its **sanctity only on account of the writing** on it. אָזַל כְּתָב אַזְלָא לָהּ קְדוּשָּׁתֵיהּ – Thus, when **the writing departs, the sanctity of [this portion] departs** as well.[14] כִּי קָמִיבַּעְיָא לִי – **When am I in doubt?** שֶׁל מַעְלָה וְשֶׁל מַטָּה שֶׁבֵּין פָּרָשָׁה לְפָרָשָׁה שֶׁבֵּין דַּף לְדַף שֶׁבִּתְחִלַּת הַסֵּפֶר שֶׁבְּסוֹף הַסֵּפֶר – In regard to the blank portions, i.e. margins, **above and below** the writing, **between one section and the next, between one column and the next,** and **at the beginning and end of the scroll.**[15] These portions were always intended to remain blank. Therefore, it may be argued that the fact that the whole Torah is now blank is no reason for them to lose their sanctity.

The Gemara counters:

וְתֵיפּוּק לֵיהּ מִשּׁוּם הַהוּא – **But derive** that the scroll should be saved **on account of that,** i.e. the very margins just mentioned! Since the Baraisa requires that the scroll possess eighty-five letters, we may derive that the margins do not merit saving.

The Gemara replies:

דְּגַיְיז וּשְׁדֵי – The Baraisa is speaking about a case **where [the margins] were cut off and thrown away.** The sanctity of the parchment is thus dependent solely on the portion upon which the writing had been.[16]

The Gemara again attempts to resolve the inquiry:

תָּא שְׁמַע – **Come, learn** a proof:[17] הַגִּלְיוֹנִין שֶׁל מַעְלָה וְשֶׁל מַטָּה שֶׁבֵּין פָּרָשָׁה לְפָרָשָׁה שֶׁבֵּין דַּף לְדַף שֶׁבִּתְחִלַּת הַסֵּפֶר שֶׁבְּסוֹף הַסֵּפֶר מְטַמְּאִין אֶת הַיָּדַיִם – THE BLANK PORTIONS, i.e. margins, ABOVE AND BELOW the writing, BETWEEN ONE SECTION AND THE NEXT, BETWEEN ONE COLUMN AND THE NEXT, and AT THE BEGINNING AND END OF THE SCROLL, RENDER HANDS *TAMEI.*[18] Thus, we see that the margins of a scroll have the same sanctity as the scroll itself.

The Gemara dismisses the proof:

דִּילְמָא אַגַּב סֵפֶר תּוֹרָה שַׁאנִי – **Perhaps** when the margins are **together with an** unerased **Torah scroll, it is different.**[19]

The Gemara's final attempt to resolve the inquiry:

תָּא שְׁמַע – **Come, learn** a proof from a Baraisa: הַגִּילְיוֹנִין וְסִפְרֵי מִינִין – In regard to BLANK PORTIONS AND BOOKS OF SECTARIANS,[20] אֵין מַצִּילִין אוֹתָן מִפְּנֵי הַדְּלֵיקָה – WE MAY NOT SAVE THEM FROM A FIRE on the Sabbath, אֶלָּא נִשְׂרָפִין בִּמְקוֹמָן הֵן וְאַזְכָּרוֹתֵיהֶן – BUT THEY are allowed to BURN IN THEIR PLACE, THEY AND THEIR DIVINE NAMES. מַאי לַאו גִּלְיוֹנִין דְּסֵפֶר תּוֹרָה – **Now,** by "blank portions," does the Baraisa **not** mean **the blank portions of a Torah scroll?** Thus, we see that blank portions of Torah scrolls may not be saved.

The Gemara refutes this proof:

לֹא גִּלְיוֹנִין דְּסִפְרֵי מִינִין – **No,** it means **blank portions of books of sectarians.**

The Gemara questions this interpretation:

הַשְׁתָּא סִפְרֵי מִינִין גּוּפַיְיהוּ אֵין מַצִּילִין – **Now, if** the Baraisa teaches that **books of sectarians themselves may not be saved,** גִּלְיוֹנִין מִבַּעְיָא – **is it necessary** to state this for the **blank portions** of these books?

The Gemara accepts this refutation and offers another interpretation of the Baraisa:

הָכִי קָאָמַר – **This is what it is saying:** וְסִפְרֵי מִינִין הֲרֵי הֵן כְּגִלְיוֹנִים – **And books of** Scriptures written by **sectarians are like blank portions** of parchment.[21]

NOTES

11. If it is true that even the blank portion of a Torah scroll merits being saved, why is the number of intact letters important? Let the scroll be saved on account of its blank portions.

12. When a Torah scroll loses its sanctity because it is worn, everyone concurs that even the blank portions lose their sanctity, since these portions also are presumably in that state. Our inquiry relates specifically to a Torah scroll whose letters were erased but whose parchment is still in good condition (*Rashi*).

13. I.e. the parchment beneath the writing, which is now blank (*Rashi*). [Here the Gemara cannot answer, as it did before, that the parchment lost its sanctity because it is worn, since in this Baraisa we are dealing with parchment that is in good condition with only its script missing.]

14. Since these portions of parchment were never intended to remain blank, when they lose their writing their holiness departs as well (*Rashi*).

15. All books of Scripture in Mishnaic times were written on scrolls [wound around a pole]. The Gemara in *Bava Basra* 13b explains that in the beginning of a scroll, one must leave enough blank parchment to wind around its pole, while at the end of the scroll one must leave enough parchment to wind around the circumference of the entire scroll. These are "the blank portions at the beginning and end of the book" to which the Gemara refers (*Rashi* below ד״ה שבתחלת).

16. The questions arises: Granted that the margins were removed, but let the scroll merit to be saved on account of the blank spaces between the lines [and letters]. These surely could not have been cut off, else the Baraisa could not refer to the parchment as a "Torah scroll."

Rashba answers that the spaces between the lines [and letters] are considered on a par with the place on which the writing appears. This is because these spaces are essential for the writing to remain legible. The margins, by contrast, are intended merely to lend aesthetic beauty to the scroll. Accordingly, their sanctity is independent of that of the writing.

17. The following is essentially a Mishnah in *Yadaim* 3:4.

18. The Rabbis enacted that hands which touch the parchment of a scroll of Scripture are *tamei,* and render *terumah* unfit on contact until they are ritually washed [נְטִילַת יָדַיִם]. (The Gemara above, 14a, explains the reason for this law.) This is one of "the Eighteen Enactments" mentioned by the Mishnah on 13b (*Rashi;* see *Tos. Yom Tov* to *Yadaim* 3:2 ד״ה מטמאים; cf. *Tosafos* to 14a ד״ה אף ידים).

19. The scroll is unerased and fully intact, and the person touched its margins. Since the scroll is sacred, it stands to reason that the margins are sacred as well, and render the hands *tamei.* Our inquiry, however, pertains to where the scroll's writing is erased. Do we say that the sanctity of the margin is independent of the written portion and remains even after the writing has been erased, or not? (*Rashi*).

20. I.e. books of Scripture written in Hebrew and with kosher ink, but by Jews who have adopted idolatrous beliefs (*Rashi,* as emended by *Dikdukei Soferim;* see also *Ritva MHK* ed. in the name of *Rashi,* and *Hagahos Yavetz*).

21. I.e. they are like blank pieces of parchment on which no words of the Torah were ever written (*Rashi*). By grouping these books together with never-written-on, blank pieces of parchment, the Baraisa indicates the utter lack of sanctity of these books.

שאין זה מקומה ר' אומר לא מן השם הוא זה אלא מפני שספר חשוב הוא בפני עצמו כמאן אזלא הא דא"ר שמואל בר [א] נחמן א"ר יונתן [א] חצבה עמודיה שבעה אלו שבעה ספרי תורה כמאן כרבי מאן תנא דפליג עליה דר' רשב"ג הוא דתניא רשב"ג אומר עתידה פרשה זו שתיעקר מכאן ותכתב במקומה ולמה כתבה כאן כדי להפסיק בין פורענות ראשונה לפורענות שנייה פורענות שנייה מאי היא [ב] ויהי העם כמתאוננים פורענות ראשונה [ג] ויסעו מהר ה' וא"ר חמא בר' חנינא שסרו מאחרי ה' והיכן מקומה אמר רב אשי בדגלים • איבעיא להו הגליונין של ס"ת מצילין אותן מפני הדליקה או אין מצילין אותן מפני הדליקה ת"ש ס"ת שבלה אם יש בו ללקט שמונים וחמש אותיות כגון פרשת ויהי בנסוע הארון מצילין ואם לאו אין מצילין ואמאי תיפוק ליה משום גיליון דידיה בלה שאני ת"ש ס"ת שנמחק אם יש בו ללקט שמונים וחמש אותיות כגון פרשת ויהי בנסוע הארון מצילין ואם לאו אין מצילין ואמאי תיפוק ליה משום גיליון דידיה מקום הכתב לא קמיבעיא לי דכי קדוש אגב כתב הוא דקדוש אזל כתב אזלא לה קדושתיה כי קמיבעיא לי של מעלה ושל מטה שבין פרשה לפרשה שבין דף לדף שבתחלת הספר שבסוף הספר ותיפוק ליה משום ההוא • דגויז ושדי ת"ש הגליונין של מעלה ושל מטה שבין פרשה לפרשה שבין דף לדף שבתחלת הספר שבסוף הספר מטמאין את הידים דילמא אגב ס"ת שאני ת"ש הגליונין וספרי מינין אין מצילין אותן מפני הדליקה אלא נשרפין במקומן הן ואזכרותיהן מאי לאו גליונין דספר תורה לא גליונין דספרי מינין (א) השתא ספרי מינין גופייהו אין מצילין גליונין מבעיא הכי קאמר וספרי מינין הרי הן כגליונים גופא הגליונים וספרי מינין אין מצילין אותם מפני הדליקה רבי יוסי אומר בחול קודר את האזכרות שבהן וגונזן והשאר שורפן א"ר טרפון • אקפח את בני שאם יבאו לידי שאני אשרוף אותם ואת האזכרות שבהן שאפי' אדם רודף אחריו להורגו ונחש רץ להכישו נכנס לבית ע"ז ואין נכנס לבתיהן של אלו שהללו מכירין וכופרין והללו אין מכירין וכופרין ועליהן הכתוב אומר [ד] [ו]אחר הדלת והמזוזה שמת זכרונך א"ר ישמעאל ק"ו ומה לעשות שלום בין איש לאשתו אמרה תורה שמי שנכתב בקדושה ימחה על המים הללו שמטילין קנאה ואיבה ותחרות בין ישראל לאביהן שבשמים על אחת כמה וכמה ועליהם אמר דוד [ה] הלא משנאיך ה' אשנא ובתקוממיך אתקוטט תכלית שנאה שנאתים לאויבים היו לי וכשם שאין מצילין אותן מפני הדליקה כך אין מצילין אותן לא מן המפולת ולא מן המים ולא מדבר המאבדן בעי מיניה (ב) יוסף בר חנין מר' אבהו הני ספרי דבי אבידן מצילין אותן מפני הדליקה או אין מצילין אין ולאו ורפיא בידיה רב • לא אזיל לבי אבידן וכ"ש לבי נצרפי שמואל לבי נצרפי לא אזיל לבי אבידן אזיל אמרו ליה לרבא מ"ט לא אתית לבי אבידן אמר להו דיקלא פלניא איכא באורחא וקשי לי ניעקריה דוכתיה קשי לי מר בר יוסף אמר אנא מינייהו אנא ולא מסתפינא מינייהו זימנא חדא אזיל בעו לסכוניה אימא שלום דביתהו דרבי אליעזר אחתיה דרבן גמליאל הואי הוה ההוא פילוסופא בשבבותיה דהוה

רש"י

שאין זה מקומה. שאינה ראויה לכאן דלאו בהליכות מסעות משתעי לעיל מינה אלא בדגלים היתה ראויה ליכתב בפרשת במדבר סיני: לא מן השם הוא זה. לא זה הטעם של טעמי הסימניות למקומה הוא לפרשה זו בתחלת מסע שנסעו מהר סיני איירי כדכתיב לעיל מיניה (ג) ויהי בחדש השני בשנה השנית בעשרים לחדש נעלה הענן וגו': ז' ספרי תורה. דפרשה זו ספר לעצמו נמצא שלמעלה ספר לעצמו [ושלמטה ספר לעצמו] הואיל וזה מקומה נמצא ספר וידבר נחלק לג' ספרים: עתידה פרשה זו. לעתיד שיהו כל הפורעניות בטלין ולא ידאגו לפורענות ויצר הרע בטל: מאחרי ה'. בתוך ג' ימים למסעם התאוו התאוה להתרעם על הבשר כדי למרוד בהקב"ה: הגליונין. קלפים חלקים וקס"ד השתא דבכל לדדין שיהו חלקים קמיבעיא ליה כגון חלק שלמעלה ושלמטה ושנמחק כתבו ונעשה חלק: בלה שאני. דכיון שבלה אף הגליון בטל וכי מיבעיא ליה שהגליונין קיימים אלא שהכתב הלך: ותיפוק ליה משום גליון דידיה. דהיינו כל הספר תורה: מקום הכתב. שנמחק: לא מבעיא לי. דודאי מיגרע גרע דכי קדיש מעיקרא לאו לשם גליון חלק קדיש אלא אדעתא דכתב וכיון דאזל ליה כתב פקע מקדושתיה: של מעלה ומטה. דמתחלה לשם חלק קדיש והשתא כשנמחק כתב הספר נמי חלק הוא: ה"ג ותיפוק ליה משום ההוא דגויז ושדי. והכי פירושו ותיפוק לי' לאפע"ג דאין בו כדי ללקט פ"ה אותיות הוה ליה למיתני בברייתא מצילין משום הגליון ריוח של מעלה ומטה אלא לאו פשוט מיניה דאין מצילין. ומשני דגויז ושדי שנמחקו הגליונים ולא נשתייר בו אלא מקום הכתב: שבתחלת הספר ושבסוף הספר. שכך היו כותבין כמגילה כס"ת ואמרי' בב"ב בפ"ק (דף יג:) ראשו כדי לגול עמוד וסופו כדי לגול היקף להקיף כל הכרך: מטמא את הידים. אם נגע בו ונגע בתרומה פוסלה דמגזירת י"ח דבר היא (לעיל דף יד.): דילמא אגב ס"ת. שלא נמחק כתב הספר אלא כולו קיים וזה נגע בגליונים וכי מבעיא לן בנמחק הספר ואין כאן קדושה אלא משום גליון שמשמשו בעודו קיים: ספרי מינין. מפרשים לע"ז וכתבו להן תורה נביאים כתובים כתב אשורית ולשון הקודש: וספרי המינין גופייהו מצילין. בתמיה: ספרי המינין הרי הן כגליונים. כקלפים חלקים שלא נכתב בהם מעולם: קודר. חותך חתיכות הקלף מקום השם: שאפי' רודף אדם להורגו. על עצמו קאמר: שהללו. נכרים העובדים ע"ז אין מכירין שהרי בכך גדלו וכך למדום אבותם: ואחר הדלת והמזוזה שמת זכרונך. זכרון הוא בידך ואינה שכחה לך אלא שהשלכת אותי אחרי הדלת: כך אין מצילין אותן. אפי' בחול: דבי אבידן. ספרים שכתבו להם המינין להתווכח עם ישראל ומקום שמתווכחים שם קרי ליה בי אבידן: אין ולא. זימנין אמר ליה אין זימנין א"ל לא: לבי נצרפי. ע"ז וכך שמה: וקשה לי. שסורשן נעשו גבשושית ולדוחם בקש בא: אמרי ליה ניעקריה קשה לי דוכתיה. שתהא שם גומא אי נמי נסיתיו וקשה לי ריחו וכל זה שהיו מתיראין רב ורבא מלכת לבי אבידן שמא מתוך שיתווכחו יעמדו עליהם ויהרגום: מינייהו אנא. מכירי הם: פילוסופא. מין:

תוספות

פורענות ראשונה ויסעו וא"ר חנינא שסרו מאחרי השם. פי' בקונטרס שמאז התחילו לשאול בשר ואומר ר"י דאין נ"ל כן אלא פורענות ראשונה כדאמר במדרש (ילמדנו) ויסעו שנסעו מהר סיני דרך שלשת ימים כתינוק היוצא מבית הספר שבורח לו והולך לו כך היו בורחים מהר סיני דרך שלשת ימים לפי שלמדו הרבה תורה בסיני אמר הקב"ה (ד) נסמוך פורענות לפורענות לאו אלא נפסוק פרשת ויהי בנסוע הארון: ספרי מינין כו' א"ר טרפון כו'. אומר ר"י דמיירי בנמצאו ביד מינין דאי כתבן מין הא אמר בפרק השולח (גיטין דף מה:) נמצא ביד מין יגנז כתבו מין ישרף ודוחק לומר דאתי כר"ט ודלא כרבנן ורבי יוסי: כך אין מצילין אותן לא מן המים כו'. דלא תימא דוקא מן הדליקה אין מצילין משום דאי שרית ליה אתי לכבויי אלא אפילו היכא דליכא למיגזר מידי אסור לטלטלן ולהוציאן והך סיפא כרבנן דלרבי טרפון לא איצטריך: פילוסופא. מין כדפי' בקונטרס ורבינו שמע [מיהודי אחד שבא מארץ יון ואמר] דבלשון יון פלוספוס הוא דוד החכמה ואית דגרסי פילא סבא והוא לשון לגון שחוק כדאמר באיכה רבתי דפלי ביהודאי פירוש ששחק ונתלוצץ:

עין משפט נר מצוה

ח א מיי' פכ"ו מהלכות שבת הלכה ט טוש"ע או"ח סימן של"ד סעיף כ:
ט ב מיי' פ"ט מהלכות שאר אבות הטומאות הלכה ו:
י ג ד מיי' פ"ו מהלכות יסודי התורה הלכה ח ופ"א מהלכות תפילין הלכה יג טור שו"ע או"ח סימן שלד סעיף כא וטור שו"ע יו"ד סימן רפא סעיף א:
יא ה טוש"ע יו"ד סימן קנ סעיף ג:

רבינו חננאל

אם מצילין אותן מפני הדליקה אי לא. ספרי מינין מיבעיא. ואלו פ"ה אותיו' כנגד פרשת ויהי בנסוע הארון. ופרשת ויהי בנסוע הארון ספר בפני עצמו הוא. ומקומו בדגלים ולמה נכתב כאן. להפסיק בין פורענ' ראשונה שהיא ויסעו מהר ה' וגו' לפורענות שנייה. שהיא ויהי העם כמתאוננים וגו': ספרי דבי אבידן. חצר ידועה ויש בה ספרי חכמות מכל אומה ויש בה ספרי תור' קדש ונביאים וכתובי' כתובי' בלשה"ק. ומפני שאינו ידוע מי כתבו או ישראל או זולתן. אמרו על ר' אבהו שהיה הדבר רפיא בידיה להורות עליהן להצילן או לא. וזה [בי] אבידן היו מתקבצין שם חכמי' ונבונים מכל אומה ונושאין ונותנין בדברי חכמה. וכן בי נצרפי. מהו בבי נצרפי היתה שם ע"ז. דגרסי' בע"ז איזו היא אשירה סתם. אמר שמואל כגון דאמרי הני תמרי נהורינן לשכרא דבי נצרפי ושתו ליה ביום אידם. אמר אמימר אמרו לי סבי (דשם בריתא) [דפומבדיתא] הלכתא כשמואל והני מילי אלה שהיו באותו זמן (הן) שעד אותה שעה לא טוכסין להן הטוכסוסין שהן עכשיו בידיהן אלא כתועין היו יש מהן שומרין התורה ויש מהן שאינן שומרין וכולן קוראין אותה ויש מי שהיה קוראה בלשה"ק כיון דאסיקנא קוראין בהן בתורה ובנביאים. אבל בכתובים אין קוראין בהן.

רב נסים גאון

פט"ז כמאן אזל הא דא"ר שמואל בר נחמני חצבה עמודיה שבעה אלו ד' חומשי תורה כמאן כר'. דר' סבר ויהי בנסוע הארון ספר בפני עצמו א"כ לא דעת ר' מתחלת ספר וידבר עד ויהי בנסוע הארון ספר בפני עצמו ופרשה ויהי בנסוע הארון ספר בפני עצמו ומן שם עד סוף ספר וידבר ספר בפני עצמו נחלק ספר וידבר לג' ספרים הרי ג' ספרי וידבר עם ד' ספרים הנשארים יהיו הכל ז' ובבראשי' דר' אושעיא בפרשת אלה תולדות יצחק (פרשה סד) תניא כוותיה ויקרא אותה שבעה כנגד ספר וידבר שהוא משלים ז' ספרי תורה והלא ה' הם אלא בר קפרא עבד מן ספר וידבר עד ויהי בנסוע הארן ספר בפני עצמו ויהי בנסוע הארן ספר בפני עצמו מן תמן ועד סיפיה דספרא ספר בפני עצמו: בי נצרפי מן בתי ע"ז ומשכחת במסכת עירובין בפרק חלון (דף פ) ובמסכת ע"ז בפרק כל הצלמין (דף מח) אי זו היא אשירה סתם אמר רב כל שכומרין משמרין אותה ואין טועמין מפירותיה ושמואל אמר כגון דאמרי הני תמרי ניניהו לשיכרא דבי ניצרופי ושתו ליה ביום אידם:

מסורת הש"ס

א) [נ"ל נחמני], ב) [תענית כט.], ג) יומא פרק ג מ"ד ע"ש, ד) [תוספתא פרק י"ד], ה) [לעיל יג.] [זבחים יג.], ו) [סוטה כו: נדרים סו: ערכין טו. חולין קמא.], ז) [לעיל קיג. וש"נ], ח) [פירוש מחה בכוכבים ערוך], ט) בס"י דלאייר לעיל מיניה, י) [ובע"י דף נד: פירש רש"י פילוסופין חכמי האומות], כ) [עי' תוס' פ"ה דלאכות משנה ד].

הגהות הב"ח

(א) גמ' דספרי מינין (השתא ספרי וכו' מבעיא תא"מ) ונ"ב גי' רש"ל וספרי מינין גופייהו מצילין: (ב) שם בעי מיניה רב יוסף: (ג) רש"י ד"ה לא מן השם וכו' כדכתיב לעיל מיניה ויהי בשנה השני בחדש השני בעשרים בחדש: (ד) תוס' ד"ה פורענות וכו' אמר הקב"ה לא נסמוך פורענות לפורענות אלא:

גליון הש"ס

גמ' איבעיא להו הגליונין. עי' מגילה דף לב ע"א תוס' ד"ה הגוללות: שם דגויז ושדי. עי' תשובות וזכרון יוסף סימן יא ויב: שם אקפח את בני. לעיל דף יז ע"א, זבחים דף יג ע"א: שם לא אזיל לבי אבידן. עי' ע"ז דף יז ע"א תוס' ד"ה הרלקא: רש"י בד"ה פילוסופא מין. עי' מס' ד"א רבה פ"ה: תוס' ד"ה פורענות פי' בקונטרס. עי' תוי"ט פ"ט מ"ד דלאכות.

תורה אור השלם

א) חָכְמוֹת בָּנְתָה בֵיתָהּ חָצְבָה עַמּוּדֶיהָ שִׁבְעָה: [משלי ט, א]

ב) וַיְהִי הָעָם כְּמִתְאֹנְנִים רַע בְּאָזְנֵי יְיָ וַיִּשְׁמַע יְיָ וַיִּחַר אַפּוֹ וַתִּבְעַר בָּם אֵשׁ יְיָ וַתֹּאכַל בִּקְצֵה הַמַּחֲנֶה: [במדבר יא, א]

ג) וַיִּסְעוּ מֵהַר יְיָ דֶּרֶךְ שְׁלֹשֶׁת יָמִים וַאֲרוֹן בְּרִית יְיָ נֹסֵעַ לִפְנֵיהֶם דֶּרֶךְ שְׁלֹשֶׁת יָמִים לָתוּר לָהֶם מְנוּחָה: [במדבר י, לג]

ד) וְאַחַר הַדֶּלֶת וְהַמְּזוּזָה שַׂמְתְּ זִכְרוֹנֵךְ כִּי מֵאִתִּי גִּלִּית וַתַּעֲלִי הִרְחַבְתְּ מִשְׁכָּבֵךְ וַתִּכְרָת לָךְ מֵהֶם אָהַבְתְּ מִשְׁכָּבָם יָד חָזִית: [ישעיה נז, ח]

ה) הֲלוֹא מְשַׂנְאֶיךָ יְיָ אֶשְׂנָא וּבִתְקוֹמְמֶיךָ אֶתְקוֹטָט: תַּכְלִית שִׂנְאָה שְׂנֵאתִים לְאוֹיְבִים הָיוּ לִי: [תהלים קלט, כא-כב]

ליקוטי רש"י

חצבה עמודיה שבעה. ז' ספרים יש בתורה ויהי בנסוע הארון ספר לעצמו במסכת שבת [משלי ט, א]. שבתחלת הספר. מניח חלק לגלול על גבי עמוד של עץ שהספר נגלל עליו. שבסוף הספר. בסופו מניח חלק גדול כדי לגול בו כדי להקיף שהוא עושה שני עמודים לגוללו לאמצעו כמו שאנו עושין לספר תורה אלא גוללו מתחלתו לסופו וכורך המלך על כל היקף [ב"ב יג:]. אקפח את בני. שהיה רגיל לומר אקפח את בני [כשהיה נשבע] [ב"מ פה. ע"ש]. אקפח. אקברם לשון סיתוך וקילור [לעיל יז. ע"ש]. לעשות שלום בין איש לאשתו. לבדוק את הסוטה ואם טהורה היא יהא שלום ביניהם. שמי שנכתב בקדושה. שכתב במגילה יתן ה' אותך וגו' כדכתיב וכתב את האלות האלו וגו' (במדבר ה) כתיב ומחה וכו' [מכות יא.]. אין ולאו. תחילה אמר אין וחזר ואמר לאו רפוי היה הדבר בידו [ב"מ יד:]. לא היה מחזיק בדבריו [קידושין סה.]. ורפיא בידיה. רפויה היתה התשובה בפיו אם לאסור אם להתיר [לעיל קיג.]. לבי אבידן. מקום הנעשה להתווכח שם לצדוקים ובייתוסים עם ישראל במקראות [לקמן קנב.]. פילוסופא. פילוסופין, חכמי האומות [ע"ז נד:].

Thus, no proof can be adduced as to our question, and the inquiry remains unresolved.

The Gemara quotes the above-cited Baraisa in its entirety: גּוּפָא – **The text itself** stated: הַגִּלְיוֹנִים וְסִפְרֵי מִינִין – BLANK PORTIONS AND BOOKS OF SECTARIANS אֵין מַצִּילִין אוֹתָם מִפְּנֵי הַדְּלֵיקָה – MAY NOT BE SAVED FROM A FIRE on the Sabbath. רַבִּי יוֹסֵי אוֹמֵר – R' YOSE SAYS: בְּחוֹל קוֹדֵר אֶת הָאַזְכָּרוֹת שֶׁבָּהֶן וְגוֹנְזָן וְהַשְּׁאָר שׂוֹרְפָן – ON WEEKDAYS ONE CUTS OUT THE DIVINE NAMES THEY CONTAIN, i.e. the pieces of parchment on which the Divine Names appear, AND HIDES THEM, i.e. places them in a repository for holy objects, AND THE REST HE BURNS. אָמַר רַבִּי טַרְפוֹן – R' TARFON SAID: אֲקַפֵּחַ אֶת בָּנַי שֶׁאִם יָבֹאוּ לְיָדִי שֶׁאֲנִי אֶשְׂרוֹף אוֹתָם וְאֶת הָאַזְכָּרוֹת שֶׁבָּהֶן – I WILL BURY MY SONS if, WERE [SUCH BOOKS] TO COME TO MY HAND, I WOULD not BURN THEM TOGETHER WITH THE DIVINE NAMES THEY CONTAIN![22] שֶׁאֲפִילּוּ אָדָם רוֹדֵף אַחֲרָיו לְהוֹרְגוֹ – FOR, R' Tarfon said about himself, EVEN IF A PERSON WERE PURSUING HIM TO KILL HIM, וְנָחָשׁ רָץ לְהַכִּישׁוֹ – OR A SNAKE WERE RUNNING after him TO BITE HIM, נִכְנָס לְבֵית עֲבוֹדָה זָרָה – HE WOULD ENTER A gentile HOUSE OF IDOLATRY to save himself, וְאֵין נִכְנָס לְבָתֵּיהֶן שֶׁל אֵלוּ – BUT HE WOULD NOT ENTER THE HOUSES OF THESE [Jewish sectarians]. שֶׁהַלָּלוּ מַכִּירִין וְכוֹפְרִין – BECAUSE THESE [Jewish sectarians] ARE AWARE of God YET DENY Him, וְהַלָּלוּ אֵין מַכִּירִין וְכוֹפְרִין – WHEREAS THESE [gentile idolaters] ARE UNAWARE of God AND DENY Him.[23] וַעֲלֵיהֶן הַכָּתוּב אוֹמֵר – AND CONCERNING THEM SCRIPTURE STATES: "וְאַחַר הַדֶּלֶת וְהַמְּזוּזָה שַׂמְתְּ זִכְרוֹנֵךְ" – *AND BEHIND THE DOOR AND THE DOORPOST YOU HAVE SET YOUR MEMORY.*[24]

Another Tanna concurs with R' Tarfon: אָמַר רַבִּי יִשְׁמָעֵאל – R' YISHMAEL SAID: קַל וָחוֹמֶר – We can derive from A *KAL VACHOMER* argument that these scrolls and the Divine Names they contain should be burned, as follows: וּמָה לַעֲשׂוֹת שָׁלוֹם בֵּין אִישׁ לְאִשְׁתּוֹ – NOW IF EVEN TO MAKE PEACE BETWEEN A HUSBAND AND HIS WIFE, אָמְרָה תּוֹרָה שְׁמִי שֶׁנִּכְתַּב בִּקְדוּשָּׁה יִמָּחֶה עַל הַמַּיִם – THE TORAH STATES that MY [God's] NAME, WHICH WAS WRITTEN IN HOLINESS, SHOULD BE ERASED INTO THE WATER,[25] הַלָּלוּ שֶׁמַּטִּילִין קִנְאָה וְאֵיבָה וְתַחֲרוּת בֵּין יִשְׂרָאֵל לַאֲבִיהֶן שֶׁבַּשָּׁמַיִם עַל אַחַת כַּמָּה וְכַמָּה – THESE people, WHO AROUSE JEALOUSY, ENMITY AND DISSENSION BETWEEN ISRAEL AND THEIR FATHER IN HEAVEN,[26] HOW MUCH MORE SO should the Divine Names they write be erased! וַעֲלֵיהֶם אָמַר דָּוִד – AND CONCERNING THEM DAVID SAID:[27] "הֲלוֹא־מְשַׂנְאֶיךָ ה׳ אֶשְׂנָא וּבִתְקוֹמְמֶיךָ אֶתְקוֹטָט תַּכְלִית שִׂנְאָה שְׂנֵאתִים לְאוֹיְבִים הָיוּ לִי" – *FOR INDEED THOSE WHO HATE YOU, HASHEM, I HATE, AND WITH THOSE WHO RISE UP AGAINST YOU I QUARREL. WITH THE UTMOST HATRED I HATE THEM; I REGARD THEM AS MY OWN ENEMIES.*

The Baraisa continues: וּכְשֵׁם שֶׁאֵין מַצִּילִין אוֹתָן מִפְּנֵי הַדְּלֵיקָה – AND JUST AS WE MAY NOT SAVE [THESE SCROLLS] FROM THE FIRE on the Sabbath, כָּךְ אֵין מַצִּילִין אוֹתָן לֹא מִן הַמַּפּוֹלֶת וְלֹא מִן הַמַּיִם וְלֹא מִדָּבָר הַמְאַבְּדָן – SO TOO, even on a weekday, WE DO NOT SAVE THEM FROM THE debris of a COLLAPSED BUILDING, OR FROM THE WATER, OR FROM ANY other THING THAT IS DESTROYING THEM.[28]

The Gemara continues: בָּעֵי מִינֵּיהּ יוֹסֵף בַּר חָנִין מֵרַבִּי אַבָּהוּ – **Yosef bar Chanin inquired of R' Abahu:** הָנֵי סִפְרֵי דְּבֵי אֲבִידָן – **These books of *Bei Avidan*,** מַצִּילִין אוֹתָן מִפְּנֵי הַדְּלֵיקָה אוֹ אֵין מַצִּילִין – **may we save them from a fire** on the Sabbath **or may we not save** them?[29]

R' Abahu's response: אֵין וְלָאו וְרַפְיָא בִּידֵיהּ – Sometimes he would say **yes, and** at other times he would say **no; he was uncertain about the matter.**[30]

The Gemara continues its discussion of *Bei Avidan*: רַב לֹא אָזִיל לְבֵי אֲבִידָן – **Rav would not go to** the debates at ***Bei Avidan,***[31] וְכָל שֶׁכֵּן לְבֵי נִצְרְפֵי – **and certainly not to** those at ***Bei Nitzrefei,*** which was an idolatrous shrine. שְׁמוּאֵל לְבֵי נִצְרְפֵי לֹא אָזִיל – **Shmuel,** however, **while he would not go to *Bei Nitzrefei,*** לְבֵי אֲבִידָן אָזִיל – **to *Bei Avidan* he would go.**[32]

Another Amora, who conducted himself like Rav, was forced to defend his position: אָמְרוּ לֵיהּ לְרָבָא – **They said to Rava:** מַאי טַעְמָא לֹא אָתֵית לְבֵי אֲבִידָן – **Why do you not come to** debate with us at ***Bei Avidan?*** אָמַר לְהוּ – **He said to them:** דִּיקְלָא פְּלַנְיָא אִיכָּא בְּאוֹרְחָא וְקָשֵׁי לִי – **There is a certain palm tree on the way, and it is difficult for me** to go past it because its roots make the road uneven.

NOTES

22. For the sectarian has in mind his deity when writing these Names (see *Rashi* to *Gittin* 45b ד״ה ישרף). Alternatively, since the sectarian does not believe in the holiness of the Name but considers it like any other mundane word, the Names he writes are not invested with sanctity. Moreover it is a *mitzvah* to burn them, in order not to leave any memorial to heretics and their deeds (*Rambam, Hil. Yesodei HaTorah* 6:8). [R' Yose and the Tanna Kamma, however, maintain that since the heretic did intend to write the Name which loyal Jews revere, it is improper to burn it (*Chazon Ish, Hil. Shabbos* 60:4).]

23. I.e. they were raised in ignorance of God by their parents (*Rashi*).

24. *Isaiah* 57:8. You are well aware of Me, only you have cast Me "behind the door," i.e. you deliberately deny Me (*Rashi*). [*Maharsha* suggests that the Baraisa means to interpret the word זִכְרוֹנֵךְ, *your memory,* as a euphemism for זִכְרוֹנִי, *the memory of Me.*]

25. In the case of the סוטה, *sotah* [*a married woman accused of adultery*], the Torah (*Numbers* 5:23) prescribes that the curses written in that chapter be inscribed on a scroll and erased into the bitter water for her to drink. The water miraculously tests the truth of her claim of innocence, and if she drinks the water and does not die, she is permitted to return to her husband. God's Name is mentioned several times in that passage, and yet He permitted It to be erased so that the woman could prove her innocence and return to her husband (*Rashi* to *Makkos* 11a ד״ה ימחה).

26. [I.e. they mislead Jews with their beliefs, thereby creating a rift, as it were, between God and His people. Alternatively,] they claim that God has become angry with His people and rejected them in favor of another (see *Maharsha*).

27. *Psalms* 139:21-22.

28. [This ruling of the Baraisa is necessary only according to R' Yose, who says that when scrolls written by heretics come into our possession we must cut out their Divine Names before burning them. The Baraisa explains that this is so only in regard to actively destroying the scrolls with our own hands. But if the scrolls are threatened by an external peril, such as a flood, R' Yose agrees that we do not intervene to save them, but rather allow them to be destroyed together with their Divine Names. According to R' Tarfon, however, this ruling would be superfluous, because if we are commanded to destroy such a scroll together with its Divine Names when it comes into our possession, obviously we should not go out of our way to rescue it from an external peril (*Tosafos*).]

29. These were books of the Holy Scriptures written by sectarians to be used to debate philosophical issues with [loyal] Jews. The place where these debates were held was called *Bei Avidan* (*Rashi*; cf. *Rabbeinu Chananel*). The questioner inquired whether the people who wrote these books were considered out-and-out heretics, or whether they were classified merely as "philosophers" (*R' Yaakov Emden*). [The foregoing follows our texts of *Rashi*. Old prints of the Talmud, however, cite *Rashi* as explaining these books as having been written by priests (see *Dikdukei Soferim*).]

30. Literally: it was loose in his hand.

31. See *Rabbeinu Chananel* and *Tosafos* to *Avodah Zarah* 17a ד״ה הרחק.

32. *Bei Avidan* was not a religious building per se, but rather served as a hall to which scholars of various persuasions would gather to debate philosophical issues. As such, it was permissible to enter there. Those Sages who avoided doing so acted thus because they feared that their opponents in the debates might rise up against them and kill them (see *Rashi* here and *Tosafos* to *Avodah Zarah* ibid.).

מסורת הש"ס

א) [נ"ל נחמני], ב) [תענית כט.], ג) ידים פרק ג מ"ד ע"ש, ד) [תוספתא פרק י"ד], ה) [לעיל יז.] [זבחים יג.], ו) [סוכה נג: נדרים סו: סוטה יא. חולין קמא.], ז) [לעיל קיג. וש"נ], ח) [פירוש מוחה בכוכבים ערוך], ט) בס"י דאיירי לעיל מיניה, י) [וכע"ז דף מד: פירש רש"י פילוסופין חכמי האומות], כ) [עי' תוי"ט פ"ה דאבות משנה ד].

הגהות הב"ח

(א) גמ' דספרי מינין (השתא ספרי וכו' מבעיא תא"מ) ונ"ב גי' רש"י וספרי מינין גופייהו מצילין: (ב) שם בעי מיניה רב יוסף: (ג) רש"י ד"ה לא מן השם וכו' כדכתיב לעיל מיניה ויהי בשנה השנית בחדש השני בעשרים בחדש: (ד) תוס' ד"ה פורענות וכו' אמר הקב"ה לא נסמוך פורענות לפורענות אלא:

גליון הש"ס

גמ' איבעיא להו הגליונין. עי' מגילה דף לב ע"א תוס' ד"ה הגוללו: שם דגייז ושדי. עי' תשובות זכרון יוסף סימן יא ויב: שם אקפח את בני. לעיל דף יז ע"א. זבחים דף יג ע"א: שם לא אזיל לבי אבידן. עי' ע"ז דף יז ע"א תוס' ד"ה הרחק: רש"י בד"ה פילוסופא מין. עי' תמ' ד"א רבה פ"ה: תוס' ד"ה פורענות פי' בקונטרס. עי' תוי"ט פ"ה מ"ד דאבות:

תורה אור השלם

א) חָכְמוֹת בָּנְתָה בֵיתָהּ חָצְבָה עַמּוּדֶיהָ שִׁבְעָה: [משלי ט, א]

ב) וַיְהִי הָעָם כְּמִתְאֹנְנִים רַע בְּאָזְנֵי יְיָ וַיִּשְׁמַע יְיָ וַיִּחַר אַפּוֹ וַתִּבְעַר בָּם אֵשׁ יְיָ וַתֹּאכַל בִּקְצֵה הַמַּחֲנֶה: [במדבר יא, א]

ג) וַיִּסְעוּ מֵהַר יְיָ דֶּרֶךְ שְׁלֹשֶׁת יָמִים וַאֲרוֹן בְּרִית יְיָ נֹסֵעַ לִפְנֵיהֶם דֶּרֶךְ שְׁלֹשֶׁת יָמִים לָתוּר לָהֶם מְנוּחָה: [במדבר י, לג]

ד) וְאַחַר הַדֶּלֶת וְהַמְּזוּזָה שַׂמְתְּ זִכְרוֹנֵךְ כִּי מֵאִתִּי גִּלִּית וַתַּעֲלִי הִרְחַבְתְּ מִשְׁכָּבֵךְ וַתִּכְרָת לָךְ מֵהֶם אָהַבְתְּ מִשְׁכָּבָם יָד חָזִית: [ישעיה נז, ח]

ה) הֲלוֹא מְשַׂנְאֶיךָ יְיָ אֶשְׂנָא וּבִתְקוֹמְמֶיךָ אֶתְקוֹטָט: תַּכְלִית שִׂנְאָה שְׂנֵאתִים לְאוֹיְבִים הָיוּ לִי: [תהלים קלט, כא-כב]

עין משפט נר מצוה

ח א מיי' פכ"ג מהלכות שבת הלכה כ טוש"ע או"ח סימן שלד סעיף כ:
ט ב מיי' פ"ט מהלכות שאר אבות הטומאות הלכה ו:
י ג ד מיי' פ"ו מהלכות יסודי התורה הלכה ח ופ"א מהלכות תפילין הלכה יג טור שו"ע או"ח סימן שלד סעיף כא וטור שו"ע יו"ד סימן רפא סעיף א:
יא ה טוש"ע יו"ד סימן קמ סעיף ג:

שאין זה מקומה ר' אומר לא מן השם הוא זה אלא מפני שספר חשוב הוא בפני עצמו כמאן אזלא הא דא"ר שמואל בר א) נחמן א"ר יונתן א) חצבה עמודיה שבעה אלו שבעה ספרי תורה כמאן כרבי מאן תנא דפליג עליה דר' רשב"ג הוא דתניא רשב"ג אומר עתידה פרשה זו שתיעקר מכאן ותכתב במקומה ולמה כתבה כאן כדי להפסיק בין פורענות ראשונה לפורענות שנייה פורענות שנייה מאי היא ב) ויהי העם כמתאוננים פורענות ראשונה ג) ויסעו מהר ה' וא"ר ב) חמא בר' חנינא שסרו מאחרי ה' והיכן מקומה אמר רב אשי בדגלים • איבעיא להו הגליונין של ס"ת מצילין אותן מפני הדליקה או ג) אין מצילין אותן מפני הדליקה ת"ש ס"ת שבלה אם יש בו ללקט שמונים וחמש אותיות כגון פרשת ויהי בנסוע הארון מצילין ואם לאו אין מצילין ואמאי תיפוק ליה משום גיליון דידיה בלה שאני ת"ש ס"ת שנמחק אם יש בו ללקט שמונים וחמש אותיות כגון פרשת ויהי בנסוע הארון מצילין ואם לאו אין מצילין ואמאי תיפוק ליה משום גיליון דידיה מקום הכתב לא קמיבעיא לי דכי קדוש אגב כתב הוא דקדוש אזל כתב אזלא לה קדושתיה כי קמיבעיא לי של מעלה ושל מטה שבין פרשה לפרשה שבין דף לדף שבתחלת הספר שבסוף הספר ותיפוק ליה משום ההוא • דגייז ושדי ת"ש ג) ב) הגליונין של מעלה ושל מטה שבין פרשה לפרשה שבין דף לדף שבתחלת הספר שבסוף הספר מטמאין את הידים דילמא אגב ס"ת שאני ת"ש ג) הגיליונין וספרי מינין אין מצילין אותן מפני הדליקה אלא נשרפין במקומן הן ואזכרותיהן מאי לאו גליונין דספר תורה לא גליונין דספרי מינין (א) השתא ספרי מינין גופייהו אין מצילין גליונין מבעיא הכי קאמר וספרי מינין הרי הן כגליונים גופא ד) הגליונים וספרי מינין אין מצילין אותם מפני הדליקה רבי יוסי אומר בחול קודר את האזכרות שבהן וגונזן והשאר שורפן א"ר טרפון ה) • אקפח את בני ד) שאם יבאו לידי שאני אשרוף אותם ואת האזכרות שבהן ה) שאפי' אדם רודף אחריו להורגו ונחש רץ להכישו נכנס לבית ע"ז ואין נכנס לבתיהן של אלו שהללו מכירין וכופרין והללו אין מכירין וכופרין ועליהן הכתוב אומר ד) [ו]אחר הדלת והמזוזה שמת זכרונך א"ר ישמעאל ק"ו ו) ומה לעשות שלום בין איש לאשתו אמרה תורה שמי שנכתב בקדושה ימחה על המים הללו שמטילין קנאה ואיבה ותחרות בין ישראל לאביהן שבשמים על אחת כמה וכמה ועליהם אמר דוד ה) הלא משנאיך ה' אשנא ובתקוממיך אתקוטט תכלית שנאה שנאתים לאויבים היו לי וכשם שאין מצילין אותן מפני הדליקה כך אין מצילין אותן לא מן המפולת ולא מן המים ולא מדבר המאבדן בעי מיניה (ב) יוסף בר חנין מר' אבהו הני ספרי דבי אבידן מצילין אותן מפני הדליקה או אין מצילין ז) אין ולאו ורפיא בידיה רב • לא אזיל לבי אבידן וכ"ש לבי נצרפי שמואל לבי נצרפי לא אזיל לבי אבידן אזיל אמרו ליה לרבא מ"ט לא אתית לבי אבידן אמר להו דיקלא פלניא איכא באורחא וקשי לי ניעקריה דוכתיה קשי לי מר בר יוסף אמר אנא מינייהו אנא ולא מסתפינא מינייהו זימנא חדא אזיל בעו לסכוניה אימא שלום דביתהו דרבי אליעזר אחתיה דרבן גמליאל הואי הוה ההוא ט) פילוסופא בשבבותיה דהוה

דהוה

פורענות ראשונה ויסעו וא"ר חנינא שסרו מאחרי השם. פי' בקונטרס שמאז התחילו לשאול בשר ואומר ר"י דאין נ"ל כן אלא פורענות ראשונה כדאמר במדרש (ילמדנו) ויסעו שנסעו מהר סיני דרך שלשת ימים כתינוק היוצא מבית הספר שבורח לו והולך לו כך היו בורחים מהר סיני דרך שלשת ימים לפי שלמדו הרבה תורה בסיני אמר הקב"ה (ד) נסמוך פורענות לפורענות לאו אלא נפסוק פרשת ויהי בנסוע הארון: **ספרי** מינין כו' א"ר טרפון כו'. אומר ר"י דמיירי בנמצאו ביד מינין דלאי כתבו מין הא אמר בפרק השולח (גיטין דף מה:) נמצא ביד מין יגנז כתבו מין ישרף ודוחק לומר דלאי כר"ט ולא כרבנן ורבי יוסי:

כך אין מצילין אותן לא מן המים כו'. דלא תימא דוקא מן הדליקה אין מצילין משום דלאי שריא ליה אתי לכבויי אלא אפילו היכא דליכא למיגזר מידי אסור לטלטלן ולהוליכן והכן סיפא כרבנן דלרבי טרפון לא אצטריך:

פילוסופא. מין כדפי' בקונטרס ורבינו שמע [מיהודי] אחד שבא מארץ יון ואמר דבלשון יון פילוסופוס הוא דוד החכמה ואית דגרסי פילא סבא והוא לשון לגון שמוק כדאמר באיכה רבתי דפלי ביהודאי פירוש שמחק ונתלוצץ: ושמואל

שאין זה מקומה. שאינה ראויה לכאן דלאו בהלכות מסעות משתעי לעיל מינה אלא בדגלים היתה ראויה ליכתב בפרשת במדבר סיני: לא מן השם הוא זה. לא זה הטעם של טעמי הסימניות למקומה הוא לפרשה זו בתחלת מסע שנסעו מהר סיני ט) איירי כדכתיב לעיל מיניה (ג) ויהי בחדש השני בשנה השנית בעשרים לחדש נעלה הענן וגו': ז' ספרי תורה. דפרשה זו ספר לעצמו נמצא שלמעלה ספר לעצמו [ושלמטה ספר לעצמו] הואיל וזה מקומה נמצא ספר וידבר נחלק לג' ספרים: עתידה פרשה זו. לעתיד שיהו כל הפורעניות בטלין ולא ידאגו לפורענות ויצר הרע בטל: מאחרי ה'. בתוך ג' ימים למסעם התאוו האספסוף תאוה להתרעם על הבשר כדי למרוד בהקב"ה: הגליונין. קלפים חלקים וקס"ד השתא דבכל לדדין שיהו חלקים קמיבעיא ליה כגון חלק שלמעלה ושלמטה ושנמחק כתבו ונעשה חלק: בלה שאני. דכיון שבלה אף הגליון בטל וכי מיבעיא ליה שהגליונין קיימים אלא שהכתב הלך: ותיפוק ליה משום גליון דידיה. דהיינו כל הספר תורה: מקום הכתב. שנמחק: לא מבעיא לי. דודאי מיגרע גרע דכי קדיש מעיקרא לאו לשם גליון חלק קדיש אלא אדעתא דכתב וכיון דאזל ליה כתב פקע מקדושתיה: של מעלה ומטה. דמתחלה לשם חלק קדיש והשתא כשנמחק כתב הספר נמי חלק הוא: ה"ג ותיפוק ליה משום ההוא דגייז ושדי. והכי פירושא ותיפוק לי' דאע"ג דאין בו כדי ללקט פ"ה אותיות הוה ליה למיתני בברייתא מצילין משום ההוא ריוח של מעלה ומטה אלא לאו פשוט מיניה דאין מצילין. ומשני דגייז ושדי שנחתכו הגליונים ולא נשתייר בו אלא מקום הכתב: שבתחלת הספר ושבסוף הספר. שכולן היו כתובין כמגילה כס"ת ואמרי' בב"ב בפ"ק (דף יג:) ראשו כדי לגול עמוד סופו כדי לגול היקף להקיף כל הכרך: מטמא את הידים. אם נגע בו ונגע בתרומה פוסלה דמגזירת י"ח דבר היא (לעיל דף יד.): דילמא אגב ס"ת. שלא נמחק כתב הספר אלא כולו קיים וזה נגע בגליונים וכי מבעיא לן בנמחק הספר ואין כאן קדושה אלא משום גליון שמשמש בעודו קיים: ספרי מינין. משרתים לע"ז וכתבו להן תורה נביאים כתובים כתב אשורית ולשון הקודש: וספרי המינין גופייהו מצילין. בתמיה: ספרי המינין הרי הן כגליונים. כקלפים חלקים שלא נכתב בהם מעולם: קודר. חותך חתיכות הקלף מקום השם: שאפי' רודף אדם להורגו. על עצמו קאמר: שהללו. נכרים העובדים ע"ז אין מכירין שהרי בכך גדלו וכך למדום אבותם: ואחר הדלת והמזוזה שמת זכרונך. זכרון הוא בידך ואינה שכחה לך אלא שהשלכת אותי אחרי הדלת: כך אין מצילין אותן. אפי' בחול: דבי אבידן. ספרים שכתבו להם המינין להתווכח עם ישראל ומקום שמתווכחים שם קרי ליה בי אבידן: אין ולאו. זימנין אמר ליה אין זימנין אמר ל"א: לבי נצרפי. ע"ז וכך שמה: וקשה לי. שעורשן נעשו גבשושית ולדחותם בקש בלא: אמרי ליה ניעקריה קשה לי דוכתיה. שתהא שם גומא אי נמי נסיתיו וקשה לי רימו וכל זה שהיו מתייראין רב ורבא מלכת לבי אבידן שמא מתוך שמתווכחו יעמדו עליהם ויהרגום: מינייהו אנא. מכירי הם: פילוסופא. מין. ° דהוה

רבינו חננאל

אם מצילין אותן מפני הדליקה אי לא. ספרי מינין מיבעיא. ואלו פ"ה אותי' כנגד פרשת ויהי בנסוע הארון. ופרשת ויהי בנסוע הארון ספר בפני עצמו הוא. ומקומו בדגלים ולמה נכתב כאן. להפסיק בין פורענו' ראשונה שהיא ויסעו מהר ה' וגו' לפורענות שנייה. שהיא ויהי העם כמתאוננים וגו': ספרי דבי אבידן. חצר ידועה ויש בה ספרי חכמות מכל אומה ויש בה ספרי תור' קדש ונביאים וכתובי' כתובי' בלשה"ק. ומפני שאינו ידוע מי כתבו או ישראל או זולתן. אמרו על ר' אבהו שהיה הדבר רפיא בידיה להורות עליהן להצילן או לא. וזה [בין] אבידן היו מתקבצין שם חכמי' ונבונים מכל אומה ונושאין ונותנין בדברי חכמה. וכן בי נצרפי. מהו בבי נצרפי היתה שם ע"ז. דגרסי' בע"ז איזו היא אשירה סתם. אמר שמואל כגון דאמרי הני תמרי נהוינן לשכרא דבי נצרפי ושתו ליה ביום אידם. אמר אמימר אמרו לי סבי (דשם בריתא) [דפומבדיתא] הלכתא כשמואל והני מילי אלה שהיו באותו זמן (הן) שעד אותה שעה לא טוכסין להן הטוכסוסין שהן עכשיו בידיהן אלא כתועין היו יש מהן שומרין התורה ויש מהן שאינן שומרין וכולן קוראין אותה ויש מי שהיה קוראה בלשה"ק כיון דאסיקנא קוראין בהן בתורה ובנביאים. אבל בכתובים אין קוראין בהן.

רב נסים גאון

פט"ז כמאן אזל הא דא"ר שמואל בר נחמני חצבה עמודיה שבעה אלו ז' חומשי תורה כמאן כר'. דר' סבר ויהי בנסוע הארון ספר בפני עצמו א"כ על דעת ר' מתחילת ספר וידבר עד ויהי בנסוע הארון ספר בפני עצמו ופרש' ויהי בנסוע הארון ספר בפני עצמו ומן שם עד סוף ספר וידבר ספר בפני עצמו נחלק ספר וידבר לג' ספרים הרי ג' ספרי וידבר עם ד' ספרים הנשארים יהיו הכל ז' ובבראשי' דר' אושעיא בפרשת אלה תולדות יצחק (פרשה סד) תניא כוותיה ויקרא אותה שבעה כנגד ספר וידבר שהוא משלים ז' ספרי תורה והלא ה' הם אלא בר קפרא עבד מן ספר וידבר עד ויהי בנסוע הארון ספר בפני עצמו ויהי בנסוע הארון ספר בפני עצמו מן תמן ועד סיפיה דספרא ספר בפני עצמו: בי נצרפי מן בתי ע"ז ומשכחת במסכת עירובין בפרק חלון (דף מח) ובמסכת ע"ז בפרק כל הצלמים (דף מח) [illegible] אמר רב כל שכומרין משמרין אותה ואין טועמין מפירותיה ושמואל אמר כגון דאמרי הני תמרי ניתהו לשיכרא דבי ניצרופי ושתו ליה ביום אידם:

ליקוטי רש"י

חצבה עמודיה שבעה. ז' ספרים יש בתורה ויהי בנסוע הארון ספר לעצמו כמסכת שבת [משלי ט, א]. שבתחלת הספר. מניח קלף חלק לגלול על גבי עמוד של עץ שהספר נגלל עליו. שבסוף הספר. כשמו מניח חלק גדול כדי לגלול בו כל הקיפו שאין עושה שני עמודים לס"ת שלנו עושים לספר תורה אלא גוללו מתחלתו לסופו וכורך החלק על כל הסיקף [ב"ב יג:]. אקפח את בני. שהיה רגיל לומר אקפח את בני [ב"מ פה. ע"ש]. אקפח. אקברם לשון סימוך וקיפול [לעיל יז. ע"ש]. לעשות שלום בין איש לאשתו. לבדוק את הסוטה ואם טהורה היא יהא שלום ביניהם. שמי שנכתב בקדושה. שכתב במגילה [במדבר ה]. ימחה על המים. דכתיב ומחה אל מי המרים והכהנה הזכרות בפרשה ולפ"ה כתיב ומחה כו' [מכות יא.]. אין ולאו. [illegible] ורפיא בידיה. רפויה היתה השמועה בפיו ולא היתה מוחזקת הולכה זו בידו [קידושין סה.]. לבי אבידן. מקום העשוי להתוכח [לקמן קנב.]. בי נצרפי. שם עבודת כוכבים שלהם [ע"ז מח.]. פילוסופא. פילוסופין, חכמי האומות [ע"ז נד:].

נִיעַקְרֵיהּ – They volunteered: **We will uproot it!** דּוּכְתֵּיהּ קָשֵׁי לִי – Then, Rava replied, **its spot,** i.e. the place where it had stood, **will be difficult for me** to bypass because of the hole that will be created thereby.[33]

Another Amora's approach:
מַר בַּר יוֹסֵף אָמַר – **Mar bar Yosef said:** אֲנָא מִינַּיְיהוּ אֲנָא וְלָא מִסְתְּפִינָא מִינַּיְיהוּ – **I am one of them,** i.e. on good terms with them, **and I do not fear them.** זִימְנָא חֲדָא אֲזִיל בָּעוּ לְסַכּוּנֵיהּ – **One time,** however, **he went** to debate with them and **they attempted to endanger [his life].**

The Gemara relates an episode concerning a sectarian:
אִימָּא שָׁלוֹם דְּבֵיתְהוּ דְּרַבִּי אֱלִיעֶזֶר אֲחָתֵיהּ דְּרַבָּן גַּמְלִיאֵל הֲוַאי – **Imma Shalom, the wife of R' Eliezer, was the sister of Rabban Gamliel.** הֲוָה הָהוּא פִילוֹסוֹפָא בְּשַׁבְבוּתֵיהּ – **There was in their vicinity a certain philosopher**[34]

NOTES

33. Alternatively, Rava meant: I have tried traveling that road, but the smell there disturbs me (*Rashi*).

These were, of course, diplomatic excuses, because in truth Rava never intended to go. He feared that doing so could cost him his life (*Rashi*).

34. Who was a sectarian (*Rashi;* cf. *Rashi* to *Avodah Zarah* 54b ד״ה פילוסופין; *Tosafos* here ד״ה פילוסופא).

שאין זה מקומה ר' אומר לא מן השם הוא זה אלא מפני שספר חשוב הוא בפני עצמו כמאן אזלא הא דא"ר שמואל בר נחמן א"ר יונתן חצבה עמודיה שבעה אלו שבעה ספרי תורה כמאן כרבי מאן תנא דפליג עליה דר' רשב"ג הוא דתניא רשב"ג אומר עתידה פרשה זו שתיעקר מכאן ותכתב במקומה ולמה כתבה כאן כדי להפסיק בין פורענות ראשונה לפורענות שנייה פורענות שנייה מאי היא ויהי העם כמתאוננים פורענות ראשונה ויסעו מהר ה' וא"ר חמא בר' חנינא שסרו מאחרי ה' והיכן מקומה אמר רב אשי בדגלים • איבעיא להו הגליונין של ס"ת מצילין אותן מפני הדליקה או אין מצילין אותן מפני הדליקה ת"ש ס"ת שבלה אם יש בו ללקט שמונים וחמש אותיות כגון פרשת ויהי בנסוע הארון מצילין ואם לאו אין מצילין ואמאי תיפוק ליה משום גיליון דידיה בלה שאני ת"ש שנמחק אם יש בו ללקט שמונים וחמש אותיות כגון פרשת ויהי בנסוע הארון מצילין ואם לאו אין מצילין ואמאי תיפוק ליה משום גיליון דידיה מקום הכתב לא קמיבעיא לי דכי קדוש אגב כתב הוא דקדוש אזל כתב אזלא לה קדושתיה כי קמיבעיא לי של מעלה ושל מטה שבין פרשה לפרשה שבין דף לדף שבתחלת הספר שבסוף הספר ותיפוק ליה משום ההוא • דגייז ושדי ת"ש הגליונין של מעלה ושל מטה שבין פרשה לפרשה שבין דף לדף שבתחלת הספר שבסוף הספר מטמאין את הידים דילמא אגב ס"ת שאני ת"ש הגליונין וספרי מינין אין מצילין אותן מפני הדליקה אלא נשרפין במקומן הן ואזכרותיהן מאי לאו גליונין דספר תורה לא גליונין דספר מינין השתא ספרי מינין גופייהו אין מצילין גליונין מבעיא הכי קאמר וספרי מינין הרי הן כגליונים גופא הגליונים וספרי מינין אין מצילין אותם מפני הדליקה רבי יוסי אומר בחול קודר את האזכרות שבהן וגונזן והשאר שורפן א"ר טרפון אקפח את בני שאם יבאו לידי שאני אשרוף אותם ואת האזכרות שבהן שאפי' אדם רודף אחריו להורגו ונחש רץ להכישו נכנס לבית ע"ז ואין נכנס לבתיהן של אלו שהללו מכירין וכופרין והללו אין מכירין וכופרין ועליהן הכתוב אומר [ו]אחר הדלת והמזוזה שמת זכרונך א"ר ישמעאל ק"ו ומה לעשות שלום בין איש לאשתו אמרה תורה שמי שנכתב בקדושה ימחה על המים הללו שמטילין קנאה ואיבה ותחרות בין ישראל לאביהן שבשמים על אחת כמה וכמה ועליהם אמר דוד הלא משנאיך ה' אשנא ובתקוממיך אתקוטט תכלית שנאה שנאתים לאויבים היו לי וכשם שאין מצילין אותן מפני הדליקה כך אין מצילין אותן לא מן המפולת ולא מן המים ולא מדבר המאבדן בעי מיניה יוסף בר חנין מר' אבהו הני ספרי דבי אבידן מצילין אותן מפני הדליקה או אין מצילין אין ולאו ורפיא בידיה רב • לא אזיל לבי אבידן וכ"ש לבי נצרפי שמואל לבי נצרפי לא אזיל לבי אבידן אזיל אמרו ליה לרבא מ"ט לא אתית לבי אבידן אמר להו דיקלא פלניא איכא באורחא וקשי לי ניעקריה דוכתיה קשי לי מר בר יוסף אמר אנא מינייהו אנא ולא מסתפינא מינייהו זימנא חדא אזיל בעו לסכוניה אימא שלום דביתהו דרבי אליעזר אחתיה דרבן גמליאל הואי הוה ההוא פילוסופא בשבבותיה דהוה

רש"י

שאין זה מקומה. שאינה ראויה לכתוב דלאו בהליכות מסעות משתעי לעיל מיניה אלא בדגלים היתה ראויה ליכתב בפרשת במדבר סיני: לא מן השם הוא זה. לא זה הטעם של טעמי הסימניות דמקומה הוא דפרשה זו בתחלת מסע שנסעו מהר סיני לעיל מיניה ויהי בחדש השני בשנה השנית בעשרים לחדש נעלה הענן וגו': ז' ספרי תורה. דפרשה זו ספר לעצמו נמצא שלמעלה ספר לעצמו [ושלמטה ספר לעצמו] הואיל וזה מקומה נמצא ספר וידבר נחלק לג' ספרים: עתידה פרשה זו. לעתיד שיהו כל הפורעניות בטלין ולא יהא נקראו לפורענות ויהי הרע בטל: מאחרי ה'. בתוך ג' ימים למסעם התאוו האספסוף תאוה להתרעם על הבשר כדי למרוד בהקב"ה: הגליונין. קלפים חלקים וקס"ד השתא דככל לדין שיהו חלקים קמיבעיא ליה כגון חלק שלמעלה ושלמטה ושנמחק כתבו ונעשה חלק: בלה שאני. דכיון שבלה אף הגליון בטל וכי מיבעיא ליה שהגליון קיימים אלא שהכתב הלך: ותיפוק ליה משום גליון דידיה. דהיינו כל הספר תורה: מקום הכתב. שנמחק: לא מבעיא לי. דודאי מיגרע גרע דכי קדיש מעיקרא לאו לשם גליון חלק קדיש אלא אדעתא דכתב וכיון דאזל ליה כתב פקע מקדושתיה: של מעלה ושלמטה. דמתחלה לשם חלק קדיש והשתא כשנמחק כתב הספר נמי חלק הוא: ה"ג ותיפוק ליה משום ההוא דגייז ושדי. והכי פירושה ותיפוק לי' דאע"ג דאין בו כדי ללקט פ"ה אותיות הוה ליה למיתני בברייתא מצילין משום ההוא ריוח של מעלה ומטה אלא לאו פשוט מיניה דאין מצילין. ומשני דגייז ושדי שנחתכו הגליונים ולא נשתייר בו אלא מקום הכתב: שבתחלת הספר ושבסוף הספר. שכולן היו כתובין כמגילה כס"ת ואמרי' בב"ב בפ"ק (דף יג:) ראשו כדי לגול עמוד סופו כדי לגול היקף להקיף כל הכרך: מטמא את הידים. אם נגע בו ונגע בתרומה פוסלה דמגזירת י"ח דבר היא (לעיל דף יד.): דילמא אגב ס"ת. שלא נמחק כתב הספר אלא כולו קיים וזה נגע בגליונים וכי מבעיא לן בנמחק הספר ואין כאן קדושה אלא משום גליון שמשו בעודו קיים: ספרי מינין. משרתים לע"ז וכתבו להן תורה נביאים כתובים כתב אשורית ולשון הקודש: וספרי המינין גופייהו מצילין. בתמיה: ספרי המינין הרי הן כגליונים. כקלפים חלקים שלא נכתב בהם מעולם: קודר. חותך חתיכות הקלף מקום השם: שאפי' רודף אדם להורגו. על עצמו קאמר: שהללו. נכרים העובדים ע"ז אין אינן מכירין שהרי בכך גדלו וכך למדום אבותם: ואחר הדלת והמזוזה שמת זכרונך. זכרון הוא בידך ואינה שכחה לך אלא שהשלכת אותי אחרי הדלת: כך אין מצילין אותן. אפי' בחול: דבי אבידן. ספרים שכתבו להם המינין להתווכח עם ישראל ומקום שמתווכחים שם קרי ליה בי אבידן: אין ולאו. זימנין אמר ליה אין זימנין א"ל לא: לבי נצרפי. ע"ז וכך שמה: וקשה לי. שורשן נעשו גבשושית ולדחותם בקש בלא: אמרי ליה ניעקריה קשה לי דוכתיה. שתהא שם גומא אי נמי נסיתיו וקשה לי ריחו וכל זה שהיו מתיראין רב ורבא מלכת לבי אבידן שמא מתוך שיתווכחו יעמדו עליהם ויהרגום: מינייהו אנא. מכירי הם: פילוסופא. מין:

תוספות

פורענות ראשונה ויסעו וא"ר חנינא שסרו מאחרי השם. פי' בקונטרס שמזה התחילו לשאול בשר ואומר ר"י דאין נ"ל כן אלא פורענות ראשונה כדאמר במדרש (ילמדנו) ויסעו שנסעו מהר סיני דרך שלשת ימים כתינוק היוצא מבית הספר שבורח לו והולך לו כך היו בורחים מהר סיני דרך שלשת ימים לפי שלמדו הרבה תורה בסיני ואמר הקב"ה (ד) נסמוך פורענות לפורענות לאו אלא נפסוק פרשה ויהי בנסוע הארון: ספרי מינין כו' א"ר טרפון כו'. אומר ר"י דמיירי כשנכתבו ביד מינין דאי כתבן מין הא אמר בפרק השולח (גיטין דף מה:) נמצא ביד מין יגנז כתבו מין ישרף ודוחק לומר דאתי כר"ט ודלא כרבנן ורבי יוסי:

כך אין מצילין אותן לא מן המים כו'. דלא תימא דוקא מן הדליקה אין מצילין משום דאי שרית ליה אתי לכבויי אלא אפילו היכא דליכא למיגזר מידי אסור לטלטלן ולהוציאן והך סיפא כרבנן דלרבי טרפון לא איצטריך:

פילוסופא. מין כדפי' בקונטרס ורבינו שמע [מיהודי אחד שבא מארץ יון ואמר] דבלשון יון פלוספוס הוא דוד החכמה ואית דגרסי פילא סבא והוא לשון לגון שחוק כדאמר באיכה רבתי דפלי ביהודאי פירוש שחק ונתלוצץ:

ושמואל

עין משפט נר מצוה

ח א מיי' פכ"ג מהלכות שבת הלכה כו טוש"ע או"ח סימן שלד סעיף כ:
ט ב מיי' פ"ט מהלכות שאר אבות הטומאות הלכה ו:
י ג ד מיי' פ"ו מהלכות יסודי התורה הלכה ח ופ"א מהלכות תפילין הלכה יג טור שו"ע או"ח סימן שלד סעיף כא וטור שו"ע יו"ד סימן רפא סעיף א:
יא ה טוש"ע יו"ד סימן קנז סעיף ג:

רבינו חננאל

אם מצילין אותן מפני הדליקה אי לא. ספרי מינין מיבעיא. ואלו פ"ה אותיו' כנגד פרשת ויהי בנסוע הארון. ופרשת ויהי בנסוע הארון ספר בפני עצמו הוא. ומקומו בדגלים ולמה נכתב כאן. להפסיק בין פורענו' ראשונה שהיא ויסעו מהר ה' וגו' לפורענות שנייה. שהיא ויהי העם כמתאוננים וגו': ספרי דבי אבידן. חצר ידועה ויש בה ספרי חכמות מכל אומה ויש בה ספרי תור' קדש ונביאים וכתובי' כתובי' בלשה"ק. ומפני שאינו ידוע מי כתבו או ישראל או זולתן. אמרו על ר' אבהו שהיה הדבר רפיא בידיה להורות עליהן להצילן או לא. וזה [בי] אבידן היו מתקבצין שם חכמי' ונבונים מכל אומה ונושאין ונותנין בדברי חכמה. וכן בי נצרפי. מהו בבי נצרפי היתה שם ע"ז. דגרסי' בע"ז איזו היא אשירה סתם. אמר שמואל כגון דאמרי הני תמרי נהוינן לשכרא דבי נצרפי ושתו ליה ביום אידם. אמר אמימר אמרו לי סבי (דשם בריתא) [דפומבדיתא] הלכתא כשמואל והני מילי אלה שהיו באותו זמן (הן) שעד אותה שעה לא טוכסין להן הטוכסוסין שהן עכשיו בידיהן אלא כתועין היו יש מהן שומרין התורה ויש מהן שאינן שומרין וכולן קוראין אותה ויש מי שהיה קוראה בלשה"ק כיון דאסיקנא קוראין בהן בתורה ובנביאים. אבל בכתובים אין קוראין בהן.

רב נסים גאון

פט"ז כמאן אזל הא דא"ר שמואל בר נחמני חצבה עמודיה שבעה אלו ז' חומשי תורה כמאן כר'. דר' סבר ויהי בנסוע הארון ספר בפני עצמו א"כ על דעת ר' מתחילת ספר וידבר עד ויהי בנסוע הארון ספר בפני עצמו ופרש' ויהי בנסוע הארון ספר בפני עצמו ומן שם עד סוף ספר וידבר ספר בפני עצמו נחלק ספר וידבר לג' ספרים הרי ג' ספרי וידבר עם ד' ספרים הנשארים יהיו הכל ז' ובבראשי' דר' אושעיא בפרשת אלה תולדות יצחק (פרשה סד) תניא כוותיה ויקרא אותה שבעה כנגד ספר וידבר שהוא משלים ז' ספרי תורה והלא ה' הם אלא בר קפרא עבד מן ספר וידבר עד ויהי בנסוע הארון ספר בפני עצמו מן תמן ועד סיפיה דספרא ספר בפני עצמו: בי נצרפי מן בתי ע"ז ומשכחת במסכת עירובין בפרק חלון (דף פ) ובמסכת ע"ז בפרק כל הצלמין (דף מח) אי זו היא אשירה סתם אמר רב כל שכומרין משמרין אותה ואין טועמין מפירותיה ושמואל אמר כגון דאמרי הני תמרי ניהוו לשיכרא דבי ניצרופי ושתו ליה ביום אידם:

מסורת הש"ס

א) [ל"ל נחמני], ב) [תענית כז.], ג) ידים פרק ג מ"ד ע"ש, ד) [תוספתא פרק י"ד], ה) [לעיל יח.] [זבחים יג.], ו) [סוטה נג: נדרים סו: מכות יא. חולין קמא.], ז) [לעיל קיג. וש"נ], ח) [פירוש חוה בכוכבים ערוך], ט) בס"י לאיירי לעיל מיניה, י) [וע"ע"ז דף נד: פירש רש"י פילוסופין חכמי האומות], כ) [עי' תוי"ט פ"ה דאבות משנה ז].

הגהות הב"ח

(א) גמ' דספרי מינין (השתא ספרי וכו' מבעיא תא"מ) ונ"ב ג"י רש"י וספרי מינין גופייהו מצילין: (ב) שם בעי מיניה רב יוסף: (ג) רש"י ד"ה לא מן השם וכו' דכתיב לעיל מיניה ויהי בשנה השנית בחדש השני בעשרים בחדש: (ד) תוס' ד"ה פורענות וכו' אמר הקב"ה לא נסמוך פורענות לפורענות אלא:

גליון הש"ס

גמ' איבעיא להו הגליונין. עי' מגילה דף לב ע"א תוס' ד"ה הלוחות: שם דגייז ושדי. עי' תשובות זכרון יוסף סימן יא ויב: שם אקפח את בני. לעיל דף יז ע"א. זבחים דף יג ע"א: שם לא אזיל לבי אבידן. עי' ע"ז דף יז ע"א תוס' ד"ה הרחק: רש"י בד"ה פילוסופא מין. עי' מס' ד"א רבה פ"ה: תוס' ד"ה פורענות פי' בקונטרס. עי' תוי"ט פ"ה מ"ד דאבות:

תורה אור השלם

א) חָכְמוֹת בָּנְתָה בֵיתָהּ חָצְבָה עַמּוּדֶיהָ שִׁבְעָה: [משלי ט, א]

ב) וַיְהִי הָעָם כְּמִתְאֹנְנִים רַע בְּאָזְנֵי יְיָ וַיִּשְׁמַע יְיָ וַיִּחַר אַפּוֹ וַתִּבְעַר בָּם אֵשׁ יְיָ וַתֹּאכַל בִּקְצֵה הַמַּחֲנֶה: [במדבר יא, א]

ג) וַיִּסְעוּ מֵהַר יְיָ דֶּרֶךְ שְׁלֹשֶׁת יָמִים וַאֲרוֹן בְּרִית יְיָ נֹסֵעַ לִפְנֵיהֶם דֶּרֶךְ שְׁלֹשֶׁת יָמִים לָתוּר לָהֶם מְנוּחָה: [במדבר י, לג]

ד) וְאַחַר הַדֶּלֶת וְהַמְּזוּזָה שַׂמְתְּ זִכְרוֹנֵךְ כִּי מֵאִתִּי גִּלִּית וַתַּעֲלִי הִרְחַבְתְּ מִשְׁכָּבֵךְ וַתִּכְרָת לָךְ מֵהֶם אָהַבְתְּ מִשְׁכָּבָם יָד חָזִית: [ישעיה נז, ח]

ה) הֲלוֹא מְשַׂנְאֶיךָ יְיָ אֶשְׂנָא וּבִתְקוֹמְמֶיךָ אֶתְקוֹטָט: תַּכְלִית שִׂנְאָה שְׂנֵאתִים לְאוֹיְבִים הָיוּ לִי: [תהלים קלט, כא-כב]

ליקוטי רש"י

חצבה עמודיה שבעה. ז' ספרים יש בתורה ויהי בנסוע הארון ספר לעצמו במסכת שבת [משלי ט, א]. שבתחלת הספר. מניח קלף חלק לגלול על גבי עמוד של עץ שהספר נגלל עליו. שבסוף הספר. בסופו מניח חלק גדול כדי לגול בו כל הקיפו שאין עושה שני עמודים לגוללו לאמצעו כמו שאנו עושין לספר תורה אלא גוללו מתחלתו לסופו וכורך החלק על כל הסיקף [ב"ב יג:]. אקפח את בני. שהיה רגיל לומר אקפח את בני [כשהיה נשבע] [ב"מ פה. ע"ש]. אקפח. אקברם לשון סיתוך וקילול [לעיל יז. ע"ש]. לעשות שלום בין איש לאשתו. לבדוק את הסוטה ואם טהורה היא יהא שלום ביניהם. שמי שנכתב בקדושה. שכתב במגילה יתן ה' אותך וגו' כדכתיב וכתב את האלות האלו וגו' (במדבר ה) [סוטה נג:]. ימחה על המים. דכתיב בסוטה (במדבר ה) ומחה אל מי המרים והרבה אזכרות בפרשה ואפ"ה כתיב ומחה כו' [מכות יא.]. אין ולאו. תמילה אמר אין וחזר ואמר לאו רפוי היה הדבר בידו [ב"מ יד:]. לא היה מחזיק בדבריו לא לאיסור ולא להיתר פעמים שאמר הן ופעמים שאמר לאו ורפיא בידיה ולא היתה מוחזקת הוראה זו בידו [קידושין סה.]. ורפיא בידיה. רפויה היתה התשובה בפיו אם לאסור אם להתיר [לעיל קיג.]. לבי אבידן. מקום העשוי להתווכח שם לדוקים וביימוסים עם ישראל במקראות [לקמן קנב.]. בי נצרפי. שם עבודת כוכבים שלהם [ע"ז מח.]. פילוסופא. פילוסופין, חכמי האומות [ע"ז נד:].

עין משפט
נר מצוה

יב א מיי' פכ"ג מהל' שבת הלכה יט סמג לאוין סה:
יג ב מיי' שם הלכה כח סמג שם טוש"ע או"ח סימן שלד סעיף טו טז:
יד ג מיי' שם הלכה כו טור שו"ע שם סעיף יז יח:
טו ד מיי' פ"א מהלכות ק"פ הלכה טז:

ושמואל דאמר כר' נחמיה. ולא פליג אדרב דשפיר מודה דלמתני' דמפרש טעמא מפני ביטול בית המדרש קורין שלא בזמן בית המדרש אלא בא לומר דר' נחמיה פליג עלה דמתני':

וכ"ש בשטרי הדיוטות. פירש בקונטרס איגרות ותימה דנהגו העולם לקרות בכתב ואיגרות השלוחים ממקום למקום ובטלטול ודאי שרי דהא ראוין לצור ע"פ צלוחית ונראה לר"י דלא קרי שטרי הדיוטות אלא שטרי חובות וכיוצא בהן אבל איגרות שרי דפעמים שיש בהן פקוח נפש ואפי' יודע שאין בו פקוח נפש מתיר ר"ת דלא הוי שטרי הדיוטות כיון שאין צריך למה שכתוב בה לפי שיודע מה שבאיגרות ואם אינו יודע שמא יש בו צורך גדול או פקוח נפש ושרי וכ"מ בירושלמי דקאמר מפני מה אין קורין בכתבי הקדש מפני שטרי הדיוטות שאם אתה אומר לו שהוא מותר אף הוא אומר מה בכך אם אתעסק בשטרותי משמע דווקא כעין חובות ושטרות קאמר וכן פי' רש"י לקמן ט) גבי גזירה שלא יקרא בשטרי הדיוטות דבשטרי מקח וממכר קאמר וכן הגיה בפי' כתב ידו ומיהו אותן מלחמות הכתובין בלע"ז נראה לרבינו יהודה דאסור לעיין בהן דלא גרע מהא דתניא בפ' שואל (לקמן קמט.) כתב שתחת הצורה והדיוקנאות אסור לקרות בהן בשבת ואפי' בחול לא ידע ר"י מי התיר דהוי כמושב לצים:

פליגי בטלטול כו'. פי' אחר שנפשט כל העור פליגי דרבנן שרו לטלטל שעדיין צריך לבשר שלא יתלכלך ור' ישמעאל אסר אבל כשאינו מופשט אלא עד החזה שרי לכ"ע לטלטל כדמוכח בסמוך ואע"ג דר' ישמעאל לא שרי להפשיט אלא עד החזה מ"מ פליגי במופשט כולו כגון שעבר והפשיט אי נמי בתמידים ומוספים דמותר להפשיטן:
הכא

דהוה שקיל שמא דלא מקבל שוחדא. היה מוליא עליו שם שאינו מקבל שוחד מבעלי דינין הבאין לפניו והיה מקבלו בסתר: א"ל. פילוסופא לר"ג מיומא דגליתון כו': שפילית. כל סוף הדבר הוא תחתית שלו ושייך למימר שפילית לסיפיה: נהור נהוריך כשרגא. הנהר אורך כשרגא רמזה שנתנה לו מנורה בשוחד: אמר לו ר"ג אתא חמרא ובטשא. לדפתו לארך כלומר אני נלחתי בשוחד ז) [והכל כדי שישמעו המתפלספים שם שנלוותו ומי הוא]: בזמן בית המדרש. קודם אכילה היו דורשים: שלא בזמן בית המדרש. לאחר אכילה לא דרשו משום שכרות: פסקי סדרא בכתובים. ח) [היו רגילים לקרא בבהמ"ד פרשה בכתובים]: במקום בהמ"ד. שהכנס דורש היינו בבהמ"ד אבל בעלמא קורין: בין במקום בהמ"ד כו' בזמן בהמ"ד אין קורין. לפי שמבטלו מלילך אצל הדורש אבל שלא בזמן בהמ"ד כגון לאחר אכילה קורין: ושמואל. דאמר לעיל אפילו לאחר אכילה אין קורין כר' נחמיה. אמרה למילתיה דלית ליה טעמא דאין קורין משום בטול אלא כדי שיאמרו קל וחומר לשטרי הדיוטות ומיהו שמואל הנהיג במקומו כדברי חכמים דמתני' דאמרי טעמא (דמתני') משום ביטול תורה הלכך לאחר אכילה דליכא דרשה קורין: שונין בהן. כגון מדרש שה"ש וקהלת: שטרי הדיוטות. כגון של חשבונות או איגרות השלוחות למלא חפץ: גמ' עד החזה. מתחיל מרגליו האחרונים עד החזה שיוכל להוציא אימורים שהקטר חלבין דוחין שבת ותו לא מפשיט מידי עד אורתא דלורך הדיוט הוא: למענהו. לכבודו: שלא יסריח. שהעור מחממו ומסריחו ואין זה כבודו להיות פרש אוכלי שולחנו מגואל: אפתורא דדהבא. שאינו מוטל בבזיון אבל לשמא יסריח חייש רב יוסף ורבא לא חייש עד אורתא: יומא דאסתנא. רוח צפונית שהיא צינונית לא חמה ולא צנה כדאמרינן ביבמות בפרק הערל (דף עב.) ולאו רוח המסרחת רוח מזרחית בשעת החום כדאמרינן בגיטין (דף לא:) אפילו שכבת זרע שבמעי אשה מסרחת בו דכתיב (הושע יג) יבא קדים רוח ה' ממדבר עולה וגו' יש מפרשין יומא דאסתנא רוח דרומית שהיא צוננת אמת שרוח דרומית צוננת אבל אסתנא על כרחיך צפונית היא ונוחה כדאמר בעלמא (עירובין ד' סה.) צריכא שמעתא צילותא כיומא דאסתנא ורוח דרומית היא בלשון ארמי יומא דשותא: קודם הפשטת העור. עד החזה: מ"ט. עור לאימורין מאי קא עביד: משום נימין. של צמר הנדבקין באימורין: חברייא. בני מחלוקתו: אם מצילין. בשבת: תיק עם הספר. ואע"פ שיש בתוכו מעות ומשום כבוד הספר שהוא צורך גבוה עבדינן בהדיה הצלת מעות שהן צורך הדיוט: לא נפשיט את הפסח. בתמיה משום צורך גבוה לא שרי צורך הדיוט בהדיה: התם. תיק ומעות דקמייתי ראיה מיניה טלטול בעלמא הוא: הכא. גבי פלוגתייהו דפסח דאיירי בה השתא מלאכה גמורה דהפשטה מאבות מלאכות היא: בתרתי פליגי. גבי פסח פליגי בטלטולו דאסר רבי ישמעאל לטלטל [הפסח] אחר שהוציא אימוריו אפי' מחמה לצל משום עור דלאו בר טלטול הוא (א) ולא דמי לשלחין דאמרן בבמה טומנין (לעיל מט.) שמטלטלין אותן דהתם עור בהמה גסה דחזי למישטחיה ולמיזגא עליה: והכי קאמרי ליה. תשובה לענין טלטול: לא נטלטל עור אגב בשר. דהוי נמי כבוד שמים דבשר דומיא דספר ומותר לטלטלו מחמה לצל ואגב בשר יטלטלו עור המחובר בו:
מי

דהוה שקיל שמא דלא מקבל שוחדא בעו לאחוכי ביה אעיילא ליה שרגא דדהבא ואזול לקמיה אמרה ליה בעינא דניפלגי לי בנכסי דבי נשי אמר להו פלוגו א"ל כתיב לן במקום ברא ברתא לא תירות א"ל מן יומא דגליתון מארעכון איתנטלית אורייתא דמשה ואיתיהיבת ספרא אחריתי וכתיב ביה ברא וברתא כחדא ירתון למחר הדר עייל ליה איהו חמרא לובא אמר להו שפילית לסיפיה דספרא וכתב ביה אנא לא למיפחת מן אורייתא דמשה אתיתי [א] ולא לאוספי על אורייתא דמשה אתיתי וכתיב ביה במקום ברא ברתא לא תירות אמרה ליה נהור נהוריך כשרגא א"ל רבן גמליאל אתא חמרא ובטש לשרגא: ומפני מה אין קורין כו': אמר רב לא שנו א אלא בזמן בית המדרש אבל שלא בזמן בהמ"ד קורין ושמואל אמר אפילו שלא בזמן בית המדרש אין קורין איני והא נהרדעא אתריה דשמואל הוה ובנהרדעא ג פסקי סידרא בכתובים במנחתא דשבתא אלא אי איתמר הכי איתמר רב לא שנו אלא במקום בהמ"ד אבל שלא במקום בהמ"ד קורין ושמואל אמר בין במקום בהמ"ד בין שלא במקום בהמ"ד בזמן בהמ"ד אין קורין שלא בזמן בית המדרש קורין ואזדא שמואל לטעמיה ° דבנהרדעא פסקי סידרא דכתובים במנחתא דשבתא רב אשי אמר לעולם כדאמרן מעיקרא ושמואל כרבי נחמיה דתניא ד אע"פ שאמרו כתבי הקדש אין קורין בהן אבל שונין בהן ודורשין בהן נצרך לפסוק מביא ורואה בו א"ר נחמיה מפני מה אמרו כתבי הקדש אין קורין בהן כדי שיאמרו בכתבי הקדש אין קורין וכ"ש בשטרי הדיוטות: **מתני'** ב מצילין תיק הספר עם הספר ותיק התפילין עם התפילין ואע"פ שיש בתוכן מעות ג ולהיכן מצילין אותן למבוי שאינו מפולש בן בתירא אומר אף למפולש: **גמ'** ת"ר ארבעה עשר שחל להיות בשבת מפשיטין את הפסח עד החזה דברי רבי ישמעאל בנו של רבי יוחנן בן ברוקה וחכ"א ד מפשיטין את כולו בשלמא לרבי ישמעאל בנו של ר' יוחנן בן ברוקה דהא איתעביד ליה צורך גבוה אלא לרבנן מ"ט אמר רבה בר בר חנה א"ר יוחנן דאמר קרא א כל פעל ה' למענהו איכא רב יוסף אמר שלא יסריח רבא אמר ז שלא יהו קדשי שמים מוטלין כנבלה מאי בינייהו איכא בינייהו דמנח אפתורא דדהבא אי נמי יומא דאסתנא ורבי ישמעאל בנו של רבי יוחנן בן ברוקה האי ח פעל ה' למענהו מאי עביד ליה שלא יוציא את האימורין קודם הפשטת העור מ"ט אמר רב הונא בריה דרב נתן משום נימין אמר מר עוקבא מאי אהדרו ליה חברייא לרבי ישמעאל בנו של רבי יוחנן בן ברוקה הכי קאמרי ליה אם מצילין תיק הספר עם הספר לא נפשיט את הפסח מעורו מי דמי התם טלטול הכא מלאכה אמר רב אשי בתרתי פליגי בטלטול ופליגי במלאכה והכי קאמרי ליה אם מצילין תיק הספר עם הספר לא נטלטל עור אגב בשר
מי

רבינו חננאל

חזר ופירש מפני מה אין קוראין בכתובים מפני ביטול בהמ"ד ומסייעא לה הא דתני העוסק במקרא מדה שאינה מדה כו'. ובית תלמוד טפי עדיף [מהעוסק] במקרא. אמר רב לא שנו שאין קורין בהן אלא בזמן בית המדרש. פי' בשעה שהחכמים יושבי' במדר' ומתעסקין בתלמוד. אבל שלא בזמן בהמ"ד כגון שכבר עמדו בעלי מדרש ונכנסו לבתיהן קורין. ושמואל [אמר] במקום שיש מדרש קבוע כו'. ואסקה רב אשי הכי לעולם כדקאמרינן מעיקרא. אמר רב אין קורין בזמן בהמ"ד כדאמרן אבל בזמן שלא בהמ"ד קורין. ושמואל אמר בין בזמן בהמ"ד בין שלא בזמן בהמ"ד אין קורין. דסבירא ליה כר' נחמיה וגזירה היא משום שטרי הדיוטות והלכתא כלישנא קמא בזמן בית המדרש אין קורין שלא בזמן בית המדרש קורין: **ירושלמי** (ה"א) אמר ר' יהושע בן לוי הדא אגדתא הכותבה אין לו חלק. הדורשה מתחרך. השומעה אינו מקבל שכר. מיומי לא איסתכלית בה אלא חד זמן. ואשכחית כתוב בה קע"ה פרשיר' דיבור אמירה צווי שכתוב בתורה כנגד שנות [של] אהע"ה. שנא' לקחת מתנות באדם. וכתיב האדם הגדול בענקים. קמ"ז מזמורי' שכתוב בתילים כנגד שנות יעקב אבינו ללמד שכל קילוסין שישראל (עושין הללויה) מקלסין להקב"ה כנגד שנותיו של יעקב שנא' ואתה קדוש יושב תהלות ישראל קכ"ג פעמים שישראל עונין הללויה כנגד שני אהרן שנאמר הללויה הללו אל בקדשו לקדושו לאהרן קדוש ה' אפילו כן הוינא מיבעיא בליליא: **מצילין** תיק הספר עם הספר. אמרי רבנן דהאי תיק קאי לחודיה. ונוטלין ממקו' שהוא עם הספר וכן תיק [של] תפילין: **י"ד** שחל להיות בשבת ר' ישמעאל בנו של ר' יוחנן בן ברוקא אומר מפשיטין את הפסח עד החזה. סבר כיון דאיתעביד ליה צורך גבוה שיכול להוציא החלבים לא יפשוט יותר מזה. ורבנן סברי מפשיט כולו. וטעמא כל פעל ה' למענהו. מאי למענהו לעשות כבוד לקדשים: **פי'** יומא דאסתנא יום שמנשבת רוח צפון שאין הבשר מסריח בו. רבא אמר שלא יהו קדשים מוטלין בעורותיהן כנבילה. אבל אם הוא מוטל בשלחן של זהב שהוא דרך כבוד לא יפשיט יותר למטה מן החזה וכו'. וגרסי' בפסחים בפרק תמיד [נשחט] שהיו מפשיטין. דתנן י"ד שחל להיות בשבת מניח ידו על כתף חבירו כו'. ואמרינן עלה. תנא כל אחד נוטל פסחו בעורו ומפשילו לאחוריו. אמר רב עיליש טיית. פי' שהערביים מפשילין כליהן לאחוריהן. ור' ישמעאל בנו של ר' יוחנן בן ברוקא מוקים למענהו שלא יוצא האמורין קודם הפשטת העור כדי שלא ידבק שיער העור בחלבים: אמרו ליה רבנן (אין) [אי] מצילין תיק הספר עם הספר לא נפשוט (עור עם החזה) [את הפסח מעורן]. אמר להן מי דמי. הצלת תיק טלטול בעלמא הפשטת עור מלאכה דקא בעי ליה לעור. אמר רב אשי בתרי פליגי עליה במלאכה ובטלטול. והכי קאמרי ליה תינח הפשטה שהיא מלאכה טלטול מאי
דאינון

מסורת הש"ס

א) בספרים ישנים איתא אלא, ב) [היינו הפטרה עי' תוס' לעיל כד. ד"ה שאלמלא וכו' וכ"כ תוספות להדיא במגילה כא. ד"ה ואין מפטירין], ג) [תוספ' פי"ד מ"ס פט"ו הלכה ג ע"ש], ד) לקמן קלג: מנחות סג: [תוספ' דפסחי' פ"ד], ה) [זבחים פה:], ו) [צ"ל כל פעל], ז) גי' רש"ל, ח) גי' רש"ל, ט) [דף קמט.].

הגהות הב"ח

(א) רש"י ד"ה בתרתי פליגי וכו' דלאו בר טלטול הוא הס"ד ואחר כך מ"ה והכי קאמרי ואח"כ ד"ה לא נטלטל וכו' המחובר בו ולא דמי לשלחין וכו'. נ"ב כך קושיה היא אף למכריא וע"ל בתוס' פ' במה טומנין דף מט בד"ה טומנין בשלחין:

גליון הש"ס

גמ' דבנהרדעא פסקי סדרי. ע"ל דף כד ע"א תוס' ד"ה שאלמלא:

תורה אור השלם

א) כֹּל פָּעַל יְיָ לַמַּעֲנֵהוּ וְגַם רָשָׁע לְיוֹם רָעָה: [משלי טז, ד]

ליקוטי רש"י

שפילית לסיפא. כל דבר שהוא בסוף קרוי שפילו של דבר [ברכות י.]. **פסקי סידרא.** פרשיות של מקרא [ע"ז יט.]. **בשטרי הדיוטות.** של מקח וממכר [לקמן קמט. ועי' בתוס' כאן ושם]. **מפשיטין את הפסח עד החזה.** דתנן במסכת תמיד (פ"ד מ"ב) גבי הפשיטו שהיה מתחיל מן הרגלים והיה מפשיט ויורד עד שמגיע לחזה הגיע לחזה חתך את הראש ונתנו למי שזכה בו ואחר כך הכרעיים ומירק והפשיטו כו' שמעינן מינייה משהגיע לחזה הוא מתחיל ידיו מן הפשטו והתחיל להתעסק בניתוח וגבי עולה דכולה כליל מירק והפשיטו ומנתח חידים תחילה ואחר כך הפשיטו וגבי פסח נמי משהפשיטו עד החזה דיכול להוציא אימורין בלא נימין קודשו ומוליכן מיד והיה ליה פירש מן הפשטו וקאמר רבי ישמעאל שוב אינו גומר והפשיטו משום עשיה דפירש הוא חזרה מילתא דאמתחלא לנפשה ושלא לצורך גבוה [שם קלג:]. [וע"ש, וכאן ברש"י החדש]. **כל פעל ה' למענהו.** כל עשה בשביל קילוסו כמו עונו לה' בתודה (תהלים קמז) [משלי טז, ד]. **אפתורא דדהבא.** שולחן של זהב [תמיד לב.]. **יומא דאסתנא.** כשמנשבת רוח צפונית יום אורה הוא ונוח לכל כדאמר ביבמות בפרק הערל (עב.) מפני מה לא נשבה רוח צפונית [illegible] [עירובין סה.]. רוח צפונית נוחה היא לא חמה ולא צוננת וממתקת את שאר הרוחות [גיטין לא:].

דַהֲוָה שָׁקִיל שְׁמָא דְלֹא מְקַבֵּל שׁוֹחֲדָא – **who assumed the reputation that he would not accept bribes** from litigants who came before **him.**[1] בָּעוּ לְאַחוּכֵי בֵּיהּ – **They** [Rabban Gamliel and Imma Shalom] **wished to ridicule** and expose **him,** אַעֲיִילָא לֵיהּ שְׁרָגָא דְדַהֲבָא וַאֲזוּל לְקַמֵּיהּ – so **she** [Imma Shalom] secretly **brought him a golden lamp** as a bribe, **and went before him** for litigation.

The case opens:

אָמְרָה לֵיהּ – **She said to [the judge]:** בָּעֵינָא דְנִיפְלְגֵי לִי בְּנִכְסֵי דְבֵי נָשֵׁי – **I desire that a share be allotted me in** my deceased **father's estate.**[2] אָמַר לְהוּ – **Said he to them:** פְּלוּגוּ – **Divide** the inheritance! אָמַר לֵיהּ – **[Rabban Gamliel] said to him:** כְּתִיב לָן בִּמְקוֹם בְּרָא בְּרַתָּא לֹא תֵּירוֹת – But **it is written for us** in our Torah: **When there is a son, a daughter does not inherit.**[3] אָמַר לֵיהּ – **[The judge] said to [Rabban Gamliel]:** מִן יוֹמָא דִגְלֵיתוּן מֵאַרְעֲכוֹן אִיתְנְטִלַת אוֹרַיְיתָא דְמֹשֶׁה וְאִיתְיְהִיבַת סִפְרָא אַחֲרִיתִי – **From the day you** people **were exiled from your land, the Law of Moses has been taken away,** i.e. superseded, **and a different book given** in its place, וּכְתִיב בֵּיהּ – **and in [that book] it is written:** בְּרָא וּבְרַתָּא כַּחֲדָא יִרְתוּן – **"A son and a daughter inherit equally."**[4]

A new development in the case:

לְמָחָר הֲדַר עַיֵּיל לֵיהּ אִיהוּ חֲמָרָא לוּבָא – **The next day, [Rabban Gamliel] brought him a Luvian donkey.**[5] אָמַר לְהוּ – Reconvening the court, **[the judge] said to them:** שְׁפֵילִית לְסֵיפֵיהּ דְסִפְרָא וּכְתַב בֵּיהּ – **Proceed**[6] **to the end of the book, wherein it is written:** אֲנָא לֹא לְמִיפְחַת מִן אוֹרַיְיתָא דְמֹשֶׁה אֲתֵיתִי [וְלֹא] לְאוֹסֹפֵי עַל אוֹרַיְיתָא דְמֹשֶׁה אֲתֵיתִי – **"I come not to detract from the Law of Moses [nor] to add to the Law of Moses,"**[7] וּכְתִיב בֵּיהּ – **and in [the Law of Moses] is written:** בִּמְקוֹם בְּרָא בְּרַתָּא לֹא תֵּירוֹת – **"Where there is a son, a daughter does not inherit."** אָמְרָה לֵיהּ – **She said to him:** נְהוֹר נְהוֹרָיךְ כְּשְׁרָגָא – **Let your light shine forth like a lamp!**[8] אָמַר לֵיהּ רַבָּן גַּמְלִיאֵל – **Said Rabban Gamliel to him:** אֲתָא חֲמָרָא וּבְטַשׁ לִשְׁרָגָא – **A donkey has come and kicked over the lamp.**[9]

The Gemara cites and discusses the last segment of the Mishnah: וּמִפְּנֵי מָה אֵין קוֹרִין כו׳ – AND WHY DO WE NOT READ etc. from them? Because of the neglect of the *beis hamidrash.*

The Mishnah explained that the reason the Rabbis enacted a prohibition against reading *Kesuvim* on the Sabbath was to prevent people from becoming too engrossed in them and fail to attend the rabbi's lecture. The Gemara discusses the extent of this enactment:

אָמַר רַב – **Rav said:** לֹא שָׁנוּ אֶלָּא בִּזְמַן בֵּית הַמִּדְרָשׁ – **They did not teach** that it is forbidden to read *Kesuvim* on the Sabbath **except during the time of the** ***beis hamidrash,*** i.e. before the daytime meal, during which time the lecture is held, אֲבָל שֶׁלֹּא בִּזְמַן בֵּית הַמִּדְרָשׁ קוֹרִין – **but not during the time of the** ***beis hamidrash,*** i.e. after the meal, **we may read** them.[10] וּשְׁמוּאֵל אָמַר – **But Shmuel said:** אֲפִילּוּ שֶׁלֹּא בִּזְמַן בֵּית הַמִּדְרָשׁ אֵין קוֹרִין – **Even not during the time of the** ***beis hamidrash*** **we may not read** them.

The Gemara asks:

אִינִי – **Is this so?** וְהָא נְהַרְדְּעָא אַתְרֵיהּ דִּשְׁמוּאֵל הֲוָה – **Why, Nehardea was the place of Shmuel,** i.e. he was the dean there, וּבִנְהַרְדְּעָא פָּסְקֵי סִידְרָא בִּכְתוּבִים בְּמִנְחָתָא דְשַׁבְּתָא – **and in Nehardea they would recite a chapter from** ***Kesuvim*** **during the Sabbath Minchah service.** Apparently, Shmuel permitted reading *Kesuvim* at this time! – ? –

The Gemara accepts this objection and revises its account of the dispute:

אֶלָּא אִי אִיתְּמַר הָכִי אִיתְּמַר – **Rather, if [the dispute] was stated** at all, **this is how it was stated:** אָמַר רַב – **Rav said:** לֹא שָׁנוּ אֶלָּא בִּמְקוֹם בֵּית הַמִּדְרָשׁ – **They did not teach** that it is forbidden to read *Kesuvim* **except in the place of the** ***beis hamidrash,*** the site where the rabbi delivers his lecture, אֲבָל שֶׁלֹּא בִּמְקוֹם בֵּית הַמִּדְרָשׁ קוֹרִין – **but not in the place of the** ***beis hamidrash,*** **we may read** them. וּשְׁמוּאֵל אָמַר – **But Shmuel said:** בֵּין בִּמְקוֹם בֵּית הַמִּדְרָשׁ בֵּין שֶׁלֹּא בִּמְקוֹם בֵּית הַמִּדְרָשׁ – **Whether in the place of the** ***beis hamidrash*** **or not in the place of the** ***beis hamidrash,*** it depends solely on the following: בִּזְמַן בֵּית הַמִּדְרָשׁ אֵין קוֹרִין – **During the time of the** ***beis hamidrash,*** **we may not read** them,[11] שֶׁלֹּא בִּזְמַן בֵּית הַמִּדְרָשׁ קוֹרִין – but **not during the time of the** ***beis hamidrash,*** **we may read** them.

The Gemara observes that the custom of Nehardea in this matter is now consistent with the view of Shmuel:

וְאַזְדָא שְׁמוּאֵל לְטַעְמֵיהּ – **And Shmuel followed his own** line of **reasoning,** דִּבְנְהַרְדְּעָא פָּסְקֵי סִידְרָא דִכְתוּבִים בְּמִנְחָתָא דְשַׁבְּתָא – **for in Nehardea they would recite a chapter of** ***Kesuvim*** **during the Sabbath Minchah service.**[12]

An Amora defends the Gemara's initial understanding of Shmuel's view:

רַב אַשִׁי אָמַר לְעוֹלָם כִּדְאָמְרָן מֵעִיקָּרָא – **Rav Ashi said: Actually, it is as we said originally,** that Shmuel maintains that the prohibition is in force the entire day. וּשְׁמוּאֵל כְּרַבִּי נְחֶמְיָה – **And** as for the objection from the custom of Nehardea, **Shmuel** made his statement **in accordance with R' Nechemyah,** who disputes the Tanna of our Mishnah as to the reason for the prohibition against reading *Kesuvim.* דְּתַנְיָא – **For it was**

NOTES

1. In truth, however, he did so secretly (*Rashi*).

2. This was a concocted dispute staged by Rabban Gamliel and Imma Shalom to unmask the judge as a fraud (*Maharsha; She'eilos U'Teshuvos Chasam Sofer, Likkutim siman* 14, printed in the back of the volume on *Choshen Mishpat*).

[For an enlightening explanation of the term בֵּי נָשֵׁי, see *Rabbeinu Bachya* to *Genesis* 41:51.]

3. *Numbers* 27:8 states: *If a man dies and has no son, you shall cause his inheritance to pass over to his daughter.* The implication is that if he has a son, the daughter receives no share (see *Bava Basra* 110a).

4. [Interestingly, *Yerushalmi Bava Basra* 8:1 records that gentile scholars would dispute the Sages even in regard to the verse in *Numbers* cited in the previous note. They asserted that the words *and has no son* imply that if the deceased has a son, then the son and daughter share equally. *Yerushalmi* goes on to relate how the Sages demonstrated the absurdity of this interpretation. Cf. *Bava Basra* 110a-b.]

5. [This breed of donkey was apparently very strong and valuable (see above, 51b).]

6. Literally: descend.

7. [Old prints read: אֶלָּא לְאוֹסוֹפֵי, *rather to add* (see *Mesoras HaShas* and *Dikdukei Soferim*); i.e. my intent is not to alter any of the existing laws but only to add new ones.]

8. Alluding to the lamp she had given him the previous day (*Rashi*).

9. I.e. I won the case because I gave the bigger bribe.

[The onlookers understood the allusions.] Rabban Gamliel and his sister thus achieved their goal of exposing the judge as a scoundrel (*Rashi,* as emended by *Maharshal*).

10. After the Sabbath morning meal the rabbi did not lecture, because it is common to drink wine during this meal and one is forbidden to render legal decisions (which the lecture contained) after drinking wine (see *Rashi*).

11. Because this would prevent people from going to the *beis hamidrash* to hear the lecture (*Rashi*).

12. [The Gemara does not mean to imply that Rav would forbid this practice. Rather, the Gemara means that according to the present explanation, the custom in Nehardea no longer *contradicts* Shmuel's ruling. Cf. *Sfas Emes.*]

עין משפט נר מצוה

יב א מיי' פכ"ג מהל' שבת הלכה כה יט סמג לאוין סה:
יג ב מיי' שם הלכה כח סמג שם טוש"ע או"ח סימן שלד סעיף טו טז:
יד ג מיי' שם הלכה כו טור שו"ע שם סעיף יז יח:
טו ד מיי' פ"א מהלכות ק"פ הלכה טז:

גמרא

דהוה שקיל שמא דלא מקבל שוחדא בעו לאחוכי ביה אעיילא ליה שרגא דדהבא ואזול לקמיה אמרה ליה בעינא דניפלגי לי בנכסי דבי נשי אמר להו פלוגו א"ל כתיב לן במקום ברא ברתא לא תירות א"ל מן יומא דגליתון מארעכון איתנטלית אורייתא דמשה ואיתיהיבת ספרא אחריתי וכתיב ביה ברא וברתא כחדא ירתון למחר הדר עייל ליה איהו חמרא לובא אמר להו שפילית לסיפיה דספרא וכתב ביה אנא לא למיפחת מן אורייתא דמשה אתיתי [א] ולא לאוספי על אורייתא דמשה אתיתי וכתיב ביה במקום ברא ברתא לא תירות אמרה ליה נהור נהוריך כשרגא א"ל רבן גמליאל אתא חמרא ובטש לשרגא: ומפני מה אין קורין כו': אמר רב לא שנו א אלא בזמן בית המדרש אבל שלא בזמן בהמ"ד קורין ושמואל אמר אפילו שלא בזמן בית המדרש אין קורין איני והא נהרדעא אתריה דשמואל הוה ובנהרדעא ג פסקי סידרא בכתובים במנחתא דשבתא אלא אי איתמר הכי איתמר אמר רב לא שנו אלא במקום בהמ"ד אבל שלא במקום בהמ"ד קורין ושמואל אמר בין במקום בהמ"ד בין שלא במקום בהמ"ד בין בזמן בהמ"ד אין קורין בין שלא בזמן בית המדרש קורין ואזדא שמואל לטעמיה ° דבנהרדעא פסקי סידרא דכתובים במנחתא דשבתא רב אשי אמר לעולם כדאמרן מעיקרא ושמואל כרבי נחמיה דתניא ג אע"פ שאמרו כתבי הקדש אין קורין בהן אבל שונין בהן ודורשין בהן ונצרך לפסוק מביא ורואה בו א"ר נחמיה מפני מה אמרו כתבי הקדש אין קורין בהן כדי שיאמרו בכתבי הקדש אין קורין וכ"ש בשטרי הדיוטות: **מתני'** ב מצילין תיק הספר עם הספר ותיק התפילין עם התפילין ואע"פ שיש בתוכן מעות ולהיכן מצילין אותן למבוי שאינו מפולש בן בתירא אומר אף למפולש: **גמ'** ד ת"ר ארבעה עשר שחל להיות בשבת מפשיטין את הפסח עד החזה דברי רבי ישמעאל בנו של רבי יוחנן בן ברוקה וחכ"א ד מפשיטין את כולו בשלמא לרבי ישמעאל בנו של ר' יוחנן בן ברוקה דהא איתעביד ליה צורך גבוה אלא לרבנן מ"ט אמר רבה בר בר חנה א"ר יוחנן דאמר קרא א כל פעל ה' למענהו והכא מאי למענהו איכא רב יוסף אמר שלא יסריח רבא אמר ה שלא יהו קדשי שמים מוטלין כנבלה מאי בינייהו איכא בינייהו דמנח אפתורא דדהבא אי נמי יומא דאסתנא ורבי ישמעאל בנו של רבי יוחנן בן ברוקה האי ו פעל ה' למענהו מאי עביד ליה שלא יוציא את האימורין קודם הפשטת העור מ"ט אמר רב הונא בריה דרב נתן משום נימין אמר רב חסדא אמר מר עוקבא מאי אהדרו ליה חברייא לרבי ישמעאל בנו של רבי יוחנן בן ברוקה הכי קאמרי ליה אם מצילין תיק הספר עם הספר לא נפשיט את הפסח מעורו מי דמי התם טלטול הכא מלאכה אמר רב אשי בתרתי פליגי פליגי בטלטול ופליגי במלאכה והכי קאמרי ליה אם מצילין תיק הספר עם הספר לא נטלטל עור אגב בשר
מי

תוספות

ושמואל דאמר כר' נחמיה. ולא פליג אדרב דספיר מודה דלמתני' דמפרש טעמא מפני ביטול בית המדרש קורין שלא בזמן בית המדרש אלא בא לומר דר' נחמיה פליג עלה דמתני':

וכ"ש בשטרי הדיוטות. פירש בקונטרס איגרות ותימה דנהגו העולם לקרות בכתב ואיגרות השלומים ממקום למקום ולטלטלן ולאי שרי דהא ראוין לצור ע"פ צלוחית ונראה לר"י דלא קרי שטרי הדיוטות אלא שטרי חובות וכיוצא בהן אבל איגרות שרי דפעמים שיש בהן פקוח נפש ואפי' יודע שאין בו פקוח נפש מתיר ר"י דלא הוי שטרי הדיוטות כיון שאין צריך למה שכתוב בה לפי שיודע מה שבאיגרות ואם אינו יודע שמא יש בו צורך גדול או פקוח נפש ושרי וכ"מ בירושלמי דקאמר מפני מה אין קורין בכתבי הקדש מפני שטרי הדיוטות שאם אתה אומר לו שהוא מותר אף הוא אומר מה בכך אם אתעסק בשטרותי משמע דווקא כעין חובות ושטרות קאמר וכן פי' רש"י לקמן ט) גבי גזירה שלא יקרא בשטרי הדיוטות דבשטרי מקח וממכר קאמר וכן הגיה בפי' כתב ידו ומיהו אותן מלחמות הכתובין בלע"ז נראה לרבינו יהודה דאסור לעיין בהן דלא גרע מהא דתניא בפ' שואל (לקמן קמט.) כתב שתחת הצורה והדיוקנאות אסור לקרות בהן בשבת ואפי' בחול לא ידע ר"י מי התיר דהוי כמושב לצים:

פליגי בטלטול כו'. פי' אחר שנפשטו כל העור פליגי דרבנן שרו טלטול שעדיין צריך לבשר שלא יתלכלך ור' ישמעאל אסר אבל כשאינו מופשט אלא עד החזה שרי לכ"ע לטלטל כדמוכח בסמוך ואע"ג דר' ישמעאל לא שרי להפשיט אלא עד החזה מ"מ פליגי במופשט כולו כגון שעבר והפשיט אי נמי בתמידים ומוספים דמותר להפשיטן:
הכל

רש"י

דהוה שקיל שמא דלא מקבל שוחדא. היה מוליא עליו שם שאינו מקבל שוחד מבעלי דינין הבאין לפניו והיה מקבלו בסתר: **א"ל.** פילוסופא לר"ג מיומא דגליתון כו': **שפילית.** כל סוף הדבר הוא תחתית שלו ושייך למימר שפילית לסיפיה: **נהור נהורך כשרגא.** הגהר אורך כשרגא רמזה שנתנה לו מנורה בשוחד: **אמר לו ר"ג אתא חמרא ובטשא.** דחפתו לאחך כלומר אני נלחתי בשוחד ז) [והכל כדי שישמעו המתפספסים שם נבלותו ומי הוא]: **בזמן בית המדרש.** קודם אכילה היו דורשים: **שלא בזמן בית המדרש.** לאחר אכילה לא דרשו משום שכרות: **פסקי סדרא בכתובים.** ח) [היו רגילים לקרא בבהמ"ד פרשה בכתובים]: **במקום בהמ"ד.** שהכנס דורש להיינו בבהמ"ד אבל בעלמא קורין: **בין במקום בהמ"ד כו' בזמן בהמ"ד אין קורין.** לפי שמבטלו מלילך אצל הדורש אבל שלא בזמן בהמ"ד כגון לאחר אכילה קורין: **ושמואל.** דאמר לעיל אפילו לאחר אכילה אין קורין: **כר' נחמיה.** אמרה למילתיה דלית ליה טעמא דאין קורין משום בטול אלא כדי שיאמרו קל וחומר לשטרי הדיוטות ומיהו שמואל הנהיג במקומו כדברי חכמים דמתניתי' דאמרי טעמא (דמתני') משום ביטול תורה הלכך לאחר אכילה דליכא דרשה קורין: **שונין בהן.** כגון מדרש שס"ש וקהלת: **שטרי הדיוטות.** כגון של חשבונות או איגרות השלוחות למלא חפץ: **גמ' עד החזה.** מתחיל מרגליו האחרונים עד החזה שיוכל להוציא אימורים שהקטר חלבים דוחין שבת ותו לא מפשיט מידי עד אורתא דלורך הדיוט הוא: **למענהו.** לכבודו: **שלא יסריח.** שהעור מחממו ומסריחו ואין זה כבודו להיות פרס אוכלי שולחנו מגואל: **אפתורא דדהבא.** שאינו מוטל בבזיון אבל לשמא יסריח חייש רב יוסף ורבא לא חייש עד אורתא: **יומא דאסתנא.** רוח צפונית שהיא בינונית לא חמה ולא צנה כדאמרינן ביבמות בפרק הערל (דף עב.) ואיזו רוח המסרחת רוח מזרחית בשעת החום כדאמרינן בגיטין (דף לא:) אפילו שכבת זרע שבמעי אשה מסרחת בו דכתיב (הושע יג) יבא קדים רוח ה' ממדבר עולה וגו' יש מפרשין יומא דאסתנא רוח דרומית שהיא צוננת אמת שרוח דרומית צוננת אבל אסתנא על כרחיך צפונית היא ונוחה כדאמר בעלמא (עירובין ד' סה.) צריכא שמעתא צילותא כיומא דאסתנא ורוח דרומית היא בלשון ארמי יומא דשותא: **קודם הפשטת העור. עד החזה:** **מ"ט.** עור לאימורין מאי קא עביד: **משום נימין.** של צמר הנדבקין באימורין: **חברייא.** בני מחלוקתו: **אם מצילין.** בשבת: **תיק עם הספר.** ואע"פ שיש בתוכו מעות ומשום כבוד הספר שהוא צורך גבוה עבדינן בהדיה הצלת מעות שהן צורך הדיוט: **לא נפשיט את הפסח.** בתמיה משום צורך גבוה לא שרי צורך הדיוט בהדיה: **התם.** תיק ומעות דקמייתי ראיה מיניה טלטול בעלמא הוא: **הכא.** גבי פלוגתייהו דפסח דאיירי בה השתא מלאכה גמורה דהפשטה מאבות מלאכות היא: **בתרתי פליגי.** גבי פסח פליגי בטלטולו דאסר רבי ישמעאל לטלטל [הפסק] אחר שהוציא אימוריו אפי' מחמה לצל משום עור דלאו בר טלטול הוא (א) ולא דמי לשלחין דאמרן בבמה טומנין (לעיל מט.) שמטלטלין אותן דהתם עור בהמה גסה דחזי למישטחיה ולמיזגא עליה: **והכי קאמרי ליה.** תשובה לענין טלטול: **לא נטלטל עור אגב בשר.** דהוי נמי כבוד שמים דבשר דומיא דספר ומותר לטלטלו מחמה לצל ואגב בשר יטלטלו עור המחובר בו:
מי

רבינו חננאל

חזר ופירש מפני מה אין קוראין בכתובים מפני ביטול בהמ"ד ומסייעא לה הא דתני העוסק במקרא מדה שאינה מדה כו'. ובית תלמוד טפי עדיף [מהעוסק] במקרא. אמר רב לא שנו שאין קורין בהן אלא בזמן בית המדרש. פי' בשעה שהחכמים יושבי' במדר' ומתעסקין בתלמוד. אבל שלא בזמן בהמ"ד כגון שכבר עמדו בעלי מדרש ונכנסו לבתיהן קורין. ושמואל [אמר] במקום שיש מדרש קבוע כו'. ואסקה רב אשי הכי לעולם כדקאמרינן מעיקרא. אמר רב אין קורין בזמן בהמ"ד כדאמרן אבל בזמן שלא בהמ"ד קורין. ושמואל אמר בין בזמן בהמ"ד בין שלא בזמן בהמ"ד אין קורין. דסבירא ליה כר' נחמיה וגזירה היא משום שטרי הדיוטות והלכתא כלישנא קמא בזמן בית המדרש אין קורין שלא בזמן בית המדרש קורין: **ירושלמי** (ה"א) אמר ר' יהושע בן לוי הדא אגדתא הכותבה אין לו חלק. הדורשה מתחרך. השומעה אינו מקבל שכר. מיומוי לא איסתכלית בה אלא חד זמן. ואשכחית כתוב בה קע"ה פרשיי' דיבור אמירה צווי שכתוב בתורה כנגד שנות [של] אהע"ה. שנא' לקחת מתנות באדם. וכתיב האדם הגדול בענקים. קמ"ז מזמורי' שכתוב בתילים כנגד שנות יעקב אבינו ללמד שכל קילוסין שישראל (עושין הללויה) מקלסין להקב"ה כנגד שנותיו של יעקב שנא' ואתה קדוש יושב תהלות ישראל קכ"ג פעמים שישראל עונין הללויה כנגד שני אהרן שנאמר הללויה הללו אל בקדשו לקדושו לאהרן קדוש ה' אפילו כן הוינא מיבעיא בליליא: **מצילין** תיק הספר עם הספר. אמרי רבנן דהאי תיק קאי לחודיה. ונוטלין ממקו' שהוא עם הספר וכן תיק [של] תפילין: **י"ד** שחל להיות בשבת ר' ישמעאל בנו של ר' יוחנן בן ברוקא אומר מפשיטין את הפסח עד החזה. סבר כיון דאיתעביד ליה צורך גבוה שיכול להוציא החלבים לא יפשוט יותר מזה. ורבנן סברי מפשיט כולו. וטעמא כל פעל ה' למענהו. מאי למענהו לעשות כבוד לקדשים: **פי'** יומא דאסתנא יום שמנשבת רוח צפון שאין הבשר מסריח בו. רבא אמר שלא יהו קדשים מוטלין בעורותיהן כנבילה. אבל אם הוא מוטל בשלחן של זהב שהוא דרך כבוד לא יפשיט יותר למטה מן החזה וכו'. וגרסי' בפסחים בפרק תמיד [נשחט] שהיו מפשיטין. דתנן י"ד שחל להיות בשבת מניח ידו על כתף חבירו כו'. ואמרינן עלה. תנא כל אחד נוטל פסחו בעורו ומפשילו לאחוריו. אמר רב עיליש טיית. פי' שהערביים מפשילין כליהן לאחוריהן. ור' ישמעאל בנו של ר' יוחנן בן ברוקא מוקים למענהו שלא יוצא האמורין קודם הפשטת העור כדי שלא ידבק שיער העור בחלבים: אמרו ליה רבנן (אין) [אי] מצילין תיק הספר עם הספר לא נפשוט (עור עם החזה) [את הפסח מעורו]. אמר להן מי דמי. הצלת תיק טלטול בעלמא הפשטת עור מלאכה דקא בעי ליה לעור. אמר רב אשי בתרי פליגי עליה במלאכה ובטלטול. והכי קאמרי ליה תינח הפשטה שהיא מלאכה טלטול מאי
דאינון

מסורת הש"ס

א) בספרים ישנים ליתא אלא, ב) [היינו הספטרה עי' תוס' לעיל כד. ד"ה שאלמלא וכו' וכ"כ תוספות להדיא במגילה כא. ד"ה ואין מפטירין], ג) [תוספ' פי"ד מ"ס פט"ו הלכה ג ע"ש], ד) לקמן קנג: מנחות סג: [תוספ' דפסחי' פ"ד], ה) [זבחים פה:], ו) [נ"ל כל פעל], ז) גי' רש"ל, ח) גי' רש"ל, ט) [דף קמט.].

הגהות הב"ח

(א) רש"י ד"ה בתרתי פליגי וכו' דלאו בר טלטול הוא הס"ד ואח"כ מ"ה והכי קאמרי ואח"כ ד"ה לא נטלטל וכו' המחובר בו ולא דמי לשלחין וכו'. נ"ב הך קושיא היא אף למהרש"א ועי"ל בתוס' פ' במה טומנין דף מט בד"ה טומנין בשלחין:

גליון הש"ס

גמ' דבנהרדעא פסקי סדרי. ע"ל דף כד ע"א תוס' ד"ה שאלמלא:

תורה אור השלם

א) כֹּל פָּעַל יְיָ לַמַּעֲנֵהוּ וְגַם רָשָׁע לְיוֹם רָעָה: [משלי טז, ד]

ליקוטי רש"י

שפילית לסיפא. כל דבר שהוא בסוף קרוי שפילו של דבר [ברכות י.]. **פסקי סידרא.** פרשיות של מקרא [ע"ז יט.]. **בשטרי הדיוטות.** של מקח וממכר [לקמן קמט. ועי' בתוס' כאן ושם]. **מפשיטין את הפסח עד החזה.** דתנן במסכת תמיד (פ"ד מ"ב) גבי הפשטו שהיה מתחיל מן הרגלים והיה מפשיט ויורד עד שמגיע לחזה הגיע לחזה חתך את הראש ונתנו למי שזכה בו ואחר כך הכרעים ומירק והפשיט כו' שמעינן מיניה משהגיע לחזה סילק ידיו מן ההפשט והתחיל להתעסק בניתוח קלת וגבי עולה דכולה כליל מירק והפשיט ומנתח הידים תחילה אחר הראש וגבי פסח נמי משהפשיט עד החזה דיכול להוציא אימוריו בלא ימין קורעו ומוליכן מיד והוה ליה פירש מן ההפשט וקאמר רבי ישמעאל שוב אינו גומר ומפשיט משום דכיון דפירש הוא חזרה מילתא דאמתאתא לנפשה ושלא לצורך גבוה [שם קלג: וע"ש, וכאן בריטב"א החדש]. **כל פעל ה' למענהו.** הכל עשה בשביל קילוסו כמו עני לה' בתודה (תהלים קמז) [משלי טז, ד]. **אפתורא דדהבא.** שולחן של זהב [תמיד לב.]. **יומא דאסתנא.** כשמנשבת רוח צפונית יום אורה הוא ונוח לכל כדאמר ביבמות בפרק הערל (עב.) מפני מה לא נשבה בהן רוח צפונית אבל ביומא דשותא אמר התם שלא מלינן ביה ולא מסוכרין ביה [עירובין סה.]. רוח צפונית נוחה היא לא חמה ולא צוננת וממתקת את שאר הרוחות [גיטין לא:].

taught in a Baraisa: אַף עַל פִּי שֶׁאָמְרוּ כִּתְבֵי הַקֹּדֶשׁ אֵין קוֹרִין בָּהֶן – EVEN THOUGH THEY SAID THAT THE HOLY WRITINGS, i.e. *Kesuvim,* MAY NOT BE READ on the Sabbath, אֲבָל שׁוֹנִין בָּהֶן וְדוֹרְשִׁין בָּהֶן – HOWEVER, WE MAY STUDY the Oral Torah pertaining to THEM,[13] AND WE MAY EXPOUND THEM in lectures. נִצְרַךְ לְפָסוּק מֵבִיא וְרוֹאֶה בּוֹ – Furthermore, IF ONE NEEDS to look up A VERSE from them as a reference, HE MAY BRING a scroll AND LOOK INTO IT. אָמַר רַבִּי נְחֶמְיָה – R' NECHEMYAH SAID: מִפְּנֵי מָה אָמְרוּ כִּתְבֵי הַקֹּדֶשׁ אֵין קוֹרִין בָּהֶן – WHY DID THEY SAY THAT THE HOLY WRITINGS MAY NOT BE READ on the Sabbath? כְּדֵי שֶׁיֹּאמְרוּ – SO THAT [PEOPLE] SHOULD SAY: בִּכְתְבֵי הַקֹּדֶשׁ אֵין קוֹרִין – If WE MAY NOT READ THE HOLY WRITINGS on the Sabbath, וְכָל שֶׁכֵּן בִּשְׁטָרֵי הֶדְיוֹטוֹת – HOW MUCH MORE SO ORDINARY DOCUMENTS![14] R' Nechemyah disputes the reason given above that the enactment against reading *Kesuvim* was for the purpose of bolstering attendance at the lecture; rather, it was so that people would draw a *kal vachomer* to reading ordinary documents. According to this reason, reading *Kesuvim* is forbidden any time, even after the lecture. It was according to this reason of R' Nechemyah that Shmuel stated his ruling above. In actual practice, however, Shmuel instructed his townspeople to follow the majority opinion of our Mishnah that the reason is because of neglect of the *beis hamidrash.* Hence, he allowed them to read *Kesuvim* in the afternoon.[15]

Mishnah The Mishnah continues discussing the permission to save sacred writings from the fire: מַצִּילִין תִּיק הַסֵּפֶר עִם הַסֵּפֶר – **We may save the container of a scroll together with the scroll,** וְתִיק הַתְּפִילִין עִם הַתְּפִילִין – **and the container of tefillin together with the tefillin,** i.e. when saving a scroll of the Scriptures or a pair of tefillin from a fire on the Sabbath, their containers may be saved along with them, וְאַף עַל פִּי שֶׁיֵּשׁ בְּתוֹכָן מָעוֹת – **and even though there is money in them,** i.e. even though in addition to the scroll of the Scripture or tefillin these containers also hold money, which is *muktzeh,* they may still be rescued.[16] וּלְהֵיכָן מַצִּילִין אוֹתָן – **And to where may we** take them to **save them?** לְמָבוֹי שֶׁאֵינוֹ מְפוּלָּשׁ – **To a *mavoi* that is not open.** בֶּן בְּתֵירָא אוֹמֵר – **Ben Beseira says:** אַף לִמְפוּלָּשׁ – **Even to an open one.**[17]

Gemara The Gemara cites a Baraisa and then draws an analogy to our Mishnah: תָּנוּ רַבָּנָן – **The Rabbis taught in a Baraisa:** אַרְבָּעָה עָשָׂר שֶׁחָל לִהְיוֹת בְּשַׁבָּת – IF THE FOURTEENTH of Nissan FELL ON THE SABBATH, מַפְשִׁיטִין אֶת הַפֶּסַח עַד הֶחָזֶה – WE FLAY THE PESACH OFFERING AS FAR AS THE BREAST. דִּבְרֵי רַבִּי יִשְׁמָעֵאל בְּנוֹ שֶׁל רַבִּי יוֹחָנָן בֶּן בְּרוֹקָה – These are THE WORDS OF R' YISHMAEL THE SON OF R' YOCHANAN BEN BEROKAH. וַחֲכָמִים אוֹמְרִים מַפְשִׁיטִין אֶת כּוּלּוֹ – BUT THE SAGES SAY: WE FLAY ALL OF IT.[18]

The Gemara asks: בִּשְׁלָמָא לְרַבִּי יִשְׁמָעֵאל בְּנוֹ שֶׁל רַבִּי יוֹחָנָן בֶּן בְּרוֹקָה – Now **it is well according to R' Yishmael the son of R' Yochanan ben Berokah** that the *pesach* offering may be flayed only up until the breast, דְּהָא אִיתְעֲבִיד לֵיהּ צוֹרֶךְ גָּבוֹהַּ – **because the need of the Most High has** already **been fulfilled.** I.e. since to remove the sacrificial parts it is necessary to flay the animal only until the breast, further flaying is considered a personal need and is forbidden. אֶלָּא לְרַבָּנָן מַאי טַעְמָא – **But as for the**

NOTES

13. I.e. the *midrashim* on them, such as *Midrash Shir HaShirim* and *Midrash Koheles* (*Rashi*). [See however *Meromei Sadeh,* who asserts that this comment of *Rashi* belongs on the words וְדוֹרְשִׁין בָּהֶן.]

14. It is prohibited on the Sabbath to read documents containing calculations or letters of correspondence [''ordinary documents''] (see *Rashi*). By forbidding reading the *Kesuvim,* the Rabbis strove to strengthen observance of this prohibition. People would say: If we cannot read even holy *Kesuvim,* how much more so should we refrain from reading ordinary documents! [The Rishonim to 149a and *Tosafos* here understand our *Rashi* as forbidding the reading of even non-business related letters. However, *Tosafos* testify that *Rashi* later changed his mind and emended his commentary to state that only materials of a business nature are forbidden.] See also *Hagahos R' Elazar Moshe Horowitz.*

15. *Rif* rules that this is in fact the *halachah.* Reading *kesuvim* should thus be forbidden at least on the Sabbath morning. Nevertheless, since nowadays it is no longer the practice for the rabbi to deliver a halachic discourse every Sabbath, one may read *Kesuvim* at any time during the Sabbath (*Baal HaMaor,* as cited by *Beis Yosef* 307 ד"ה כתב שתחת).

[It has been suggested that the practice of reciting מִגְדּוֹל in *Bircas HaMazon* of the Sabbath rather than מַגְדִּיל as on the weekdays stems from the ancient prohibition to read *Kesuvim* on the Sabbath. מִגְדּוֹל appears in *II Samuel* 22:51 [*Neviim*] while מַגְדִּיל is found in *Psalms* 18:51 [*Kesuvim*] (*Tzafnas Pane'ach* [Dvinsk] 2:5).]

16. We learned in the previous Mishnah that the Rabbis relaxed certain prohibitions for the sake of saving scrolls of the Holy Scriptures (and, as our Mishnah adds, tefillin). Our Mishnah now states that in addition to the scrolls or the tefillin themselves, we may also save the containers in which these holy items are lying. Moreover, if there is money in the container together with the scroll or tefillin, it is not necessary to throw out the money from the container before rescuing them. For further elaboration, see Gemara below, 117a. See also *Ramban* and *Ran MHK* ed. here. Rather, the money may be saved together with the scroll or tefillin.

[Actually, it is forbidden to keep money or any other non-sacred object in a container designated for a Torah scroll or tefillin. Presumably, therefore, we discuss a case in which the money was placed there unlawfully. Alternatively, at the time the person made the container, he stated that he intended to use it for money as well, in which case he may legally do so (see *Orach Chaim* 42:3).]

17. The Gemara will define the terms ''unopen *mavoi*'' and ''open *mavoi.*''

18. As set forth in the Torah, every Jew is required to sacrifice a sheep or goat as a *pesach* offering on the afternoon of the fourteenth of Nissan, the eve of the Pesach holiday, and to partake of its flesh after nightfall. Although personal sacrifices may not be offered on the Sabbath, the *pesach* offering may be brought even when the fourteenth of Nissan falls on the Sabbath, even though this involves performing several ordinarily forbidden *melachos.* This law is derived from Scripture (see *Pesachim* 65b-66a).

However, not everything involving the *pesach* offering is permitted on the Sabbath. Only those procedures that are critical to the animal's sacrifice, and thus serve a ''Divine need,'' may be performed. As taught by the Mishnah in *Pesachim* 65b, this includes slaughtering the animal and burning its sacrificial parts on the Altar. In addition, flaying the animal's skin is also permitted, since one must flay the animal in order to remove its sacrificial parts (see Gemara below; see also *Tosafos* to *Pesachim* 65b ד"ה אלו).

The discussion in the Baraisa revolves around the extent of the permission for flaying. In ordinary years, the pilgrims would hang their slaughtered sacrifices from iron hooks attached either to the walls of the Temple Courtyard or to posts situated therein (Mishnah, *Pesachim* 64a), hind legs up and head down, and flay them in their entirety. R' Yishmael maintains that when the fourteenth of Nissan falls on the Sabbath, the sacrifice may be flayed only as far as the breast. This is enough to allow the sacrificial parts comprising the fats and the internal organs specified in *Leviticus* (3:9-10, 14-15) to be removed cleanly and burned on the Altar. The stripping of the remainder of the skin from the offering must wait until evening because, in the view of R' Yishmael, this serves to facilitate a personal need of the owner of the offering to eat the meat of the sacrifice, and as such does not merit overriding the Sabbath (*Rashi*). The Rabbis, however, permit flaying the entire animal.

עין משפט נר מצוה

יב א מיי' פכ"ג מהל' שבת הלכה יט סמג לאוין סה:
יג ב מיי' שם הלכה כו סמג שם טוש"ע או"ח סימן שלז סעיף טו טז:
יד ג מיי' שם הלכה כו טור ש"ע שם סעיף יז יח:
טו ד מיי' פ"א מהלכות ק"פ הלכה טו:

רבינו חננאל

חזר ופירש מפני מה אין קורין בכתובים מפני ביטול בהמ"ד ומסייעא לה הא דתני העוסק במקרא מדה שאינה מדה כו'. ובית תלמוד שטף עדיף [מהעוסק] במקרא. אמר רב לא שנו שאין קורין בהן אלא בזמן בית המדרש. פי' בשעה שהחכמים יושבי' במדר' ומתעסקין בתלמוד. אבל שלא בזמן בהמ"ד כגון שכבר עמדו בעלי מדרש ונכנסו לבתיהן קורין. ושמואל [אמר] במקום שיש מדרש קבוע כו'. ואסקה רב אשי לעולם כדקאמרינן מעיקרא. אמר רב אין קורין בזמן בהמ"ד כדאמרן אבל שלא בזמן בהמ"ד קורין. ושמואל אמר בין בזמן בהמ"ד בין שלא בזמן בהמ"ד אין קורין. דסבירא ליה כר' נחמיה וגזירה היא משום שטרי הדיוטות והלכתא כלישנא קמא דאמר רב בזמן בית המדרש אין קורין שלא בזמן בית המדרש קורין. ירושלמי (ה"א) אמר ר' יהושע בן לוי הדא אגדתא הכותבה אין לו חלק. הדורשה מתחרף. השומעה אינו מקבל שכר. מימרי לא הוה מסתכלית בה אלא חד זמן. ואשכחית כתוב בה קע"ה פרשי' דיבור אמירה צווי שכתוב בתורה כנגד שנות [של] אהע"ה. שנא' לקחת מתנות באדם. וכתיב האדם הגדול בענקים. קמ"ז מזמורי שכתוב בתילים כנגד שנות יעקב אבינו ללמד שכל קילוסין שישראל [עושין הללויה] מקלסין להקב"ה כנגד שנותיו של יעקב שנא' ואתה קדוש יושב תהלות ישראל קכ"ג פעמים שישראל עונין הללויה כנגד שני אהרן שנאמר הללויה הללו אל בקדשו לקדשו לאהרן קדוש ה'. אפילו בן הרינא מיבעיא בליליא: מצילין תיק הספר עם הספר. אמרי רבנן דהאי תיק קאי לחודיה. ונוטלין ממקו' שהוא עם הספר וכן תיק [של] תפילין: י"ד שחל להיות בשבת ר' ישמעאל בנו של ר' יוחנן בן ברוקא אומר מפשיטין את הפסח עד החזה. סבר כיון דאיתעביד ליה צורך גבוה שיכול להוציא החלבים לא יפשוט יותר מזה. ורבנן סברי מפשיט כולו. וטעמא כל פעל ה' למענהו. מאי למענהו לעשות כבוד לקדשים: פי' יומא דאסתנא יום שמנשבת רוח צפון שאין הבשר מסריח בו. רבא אמר שלא יהו קדשים מוטלין כנבילה. אבל אם הוא מונח בשלחן של זהב שהוא דרך כבוד לא יפשיט יותר למטה מן החזה וכו'. וגרסי' בפסחים פרק תמיד [נשחט] שהיו מפשיטין. דתנן י"ד שחל להיות בשבת מניח ידו על כתף חבירו כו'. ואמרינן עלה. תנא כל אחד נוטל פסחו בעורו ומפשילו לאחוריו. אמר רב עיליש טיית. פי' שהערביים מפשילין כליהן לאחוריהן. ור' ישמעאל בנו של ר' יוחנן בן ברוקא מוקים למענהו שלא יוצא האמורין קודם הפשטת העור כדי שלא ידבק שיער העור בחלבים: אמרו ליה רבנן (אין) [אין] מצילין תיק הספר עם הספר לא נפשוט (עור עם החזה) [את הפסח מעורו]. אמר להן מי דמי. הצלת תיק טלטול בעלמא הפשטת עור מלאכה דקא בעי ליה לעור. אמר רב אשי בתרי פליגי עליה במלאכה ובטלטול. והכי קאמרי ליה תינח הפשטה שהיא מלאכה טלטול מאי
דאינון

תוספות

ושמואל דאמר כר' נחמיה. ולא פליג אדרב דספיר מודה למתני' דמפרש טעמא מפני ביטול בית המדרש הקורין שלא בזמן בית המדרש אלא בא לומר דר' נחמיה פליג עלה דמתני': **וכ"ש** בשטרי הדיוטות. פירש בקונטרס איגרות ותימה דנהגו העולם לקרות בכתב ואיגרות השלוחים ממקום למקום ולטלטלן ולאו שרי דהא ראויין לצור ע"פ צלוחית ונראה לר"י דלא קרי שטרי הדיוטות אלא שטרי חובות וכיוצא בהן אבל איגרות שרי דפעמים שיש בהן פקוח נפש ואפי' יודע שאין בו פקוח נפש מתיר ר"ת דלא הוי שטרי הדיוטות כיון שאין צריך למה שכתוב בה לפי שיודע מה שבאיגרות ואם אינו יודע שמא יש בו צורך גדול או פקוח נפש ושרי וכ"מ בירושלמי דקאמר מפני מה אין קורין בכתבי הקדש מפני שטרי הדיוטות שאם אתה אומר לו שהוא מותר אף הוא אומר מה בכך אם אתעסק בשטרותי משמע דווקא כעין חובות ושטרות קאמר וכן פי' רש"י לקמן [ט] גבי גזירה שלא יקרא בשטרי הדיוטות דבשטרי מקח וממכר קאמר וכן הגיה בפי' כתב ידו ומיהו אותן מלחמות הכתובין בלע"ז נראה לרבינו יהודה דאסור לעיין בהן דלא גרע מהא דתניא בפ' שואל (לקמן קמט.) כתב שתחת הצורה והדיוקנאות אסור לקרות בהן בשבת ואפי' בחול לא ידע ר"י מי התיר דהו"ל כמושב לצים:

פליגי בטלטול כו'. פי' אחר שנפשט כל העור פליגי דרבנן שרו לטלטל שעדיין צריך לבשר שלא יתלכלך ור' ישמעאל אסר אבל כשאינו מופשט אלא עד החזה שרי לכ"ע לטלטל כדמוכח בסמוך ואע"ג דר' ישמעאל לא שרי להפשיט אלא עד החזה מ"מ פליגי במופשט כולו כגון שעבר והפשיט אי נמי בתמידים ומוספים דמותר להפשיטן:
הכא

גמרא

דהוה שקיל שמא דלא מקבל שוחדא בעו לאחוכי ביה עיילא ליה שרגא דדהבא ואזול לקמיה אמרה ליה בעינא דניפלגי לי בנכסי דבי נשי אמר להו פלוגו א"ל כתיב לן במקום ברא ברתא לא תירות א"ל מן יומא דגליתון מארעכון איתנטלית אורייתא דמשה ואיתיהיבת ספרא אחריתי וכתיב ביה ברא וברתא כחדא ירתון למחר הדר עייל ליה איהו חמרא לובא אמר להו שפילית לסיפיה דספרא וכתב ביה אנא לא למיפחת מן אורייתא דמשה אתיתי [א) ולא] לאוספי על אורייתא דמשה אתיתי וכתיב ביה במקום ברא ברתא לא תירות אמרה ליה נהור נהוריך כשרגא א"ל רבן גמליאל אתא חמרא ובטש לשרגא: ומפני מה אין קורין כו': אמר רב לא שנו א אלא בזמן בית המדרש אבל שלא בזמן בהמ"ד קורין ושמואל אמר אפילו שלא בזמן בית המדרש אין קורין איני והא נהרדעא אתריה דשמואל הוה ובנהרדעא ב פסקי סידרא בכתובים במנחתא דשבתא אלא אי איתמר הכי איתמר אמר רב לא שנו אלא במקום בהמ"ד אבל שלא במקום בהמ"ד קורין ושמואל אמר בין במקום בהמ"ד בין שלא במקום בהמ"ד בזמן בהמ"ד אין קורין שלא בזמן בית המדרש קורין ואזדא שמואל לטעמיה • דבנהרדעא פסקי סידרא דכתובים במנחתא דשבתא רב אשי אמר לעולם כדאמרן מעיקרא ושמואל כרבי נחמיה דתניא ג אע"פ שאמרו כתבי הקדש אין קורין בהן אבל שונין בהן ודורשין בהן נצרך לפסוק מביא ורואה בו א"ר נחמיה מפני מה אמרו כתבי הקדש אין קורין בהן כדי שיאמרו בכתבי הקדש אין קורין בהן וכ"ש בשטרי הדיוטות:

מתני' ד מצילין תיק הספר עם הספר ותיק התפילין עם התפילין ואע"פ שיש בתוכן מעות ולהיכן מצילין אותן למבוי שאינו מפולש בן בתירא אומר אף למפולש: **גמ'** ה ת"ר ארבעה עשר שחל להיות בשבת מפשיטין את הפסח עד החזה דברי רבי ישמעאל בנו של רבי יוחנן בן ברוקה וחכ"א ו מפשיטין את כולו בשלמא לרבי ישמעאל בנו של ר' יוחנן בן ברוקה דהא איתעביד ליה צורך גבוה אלא לרבנן מ"ט אמר רבה בר בר חנה א"ר יוחנן דאמר קרא א כל פעל ה' למענהו איכא רב יוסף אמר שלא יסריח רבא אמר ז שלא יהו קדשי שמים מוטלין כנבלה מאי בינייהו איכא בינייהו דמנח אפתורא דדהבא אי נמי יומא דאסתנא ורבי ישמעאל בנו של רבי יוחנן בן ברוקה האי ח פעל ה' למענהו מאי עביד ליה שלא יוציא את האימורין קודם הפשטת העור מ"ט אמר רב הונא בריה דרב נתן משום נימין אמר רב חסדא אמר מר עוקבא מאי אהדרו ליה חברייא לרבי ישמעאל בנו של רבי יוחנן בן ברוקה הכי קאמרי ליה אם מצילין תיק הספר עם הספר לא נפשיט את הפסח מעורו מי דמי התם טלטול הכא מלאכה אמר רב אשי בתרתי פליגי פליגי בטלטול ופליגי במלאכה והכי קאמרי ליה אם מצילין תיק הספר עם הספר לא נטלטל עור אגב בשר
מי

רש"י

דהוה שקיל שמא דלא מקבל שוחדא. היה מוליא עליו שם שאינו מקבל שוחד מבעלי דינין הבאין לפניו והיה מקבלו בסתר: א"ל. פילוספא לר"ג מיומא דגליתון כו': שפילית. כל סוף הדבר הוא תחתית שלו ושייך למימר שפילית לסיפיה: נהור נהורך כשרגא. הנהר אורך כשרגא רמזה שנתנה לו מנורה בשוחד: אמר לו ר"ג אתא חמרא ובטשא. דחפתו לארץ כלומר אני נלחתי בשוחד [ז) והכל כדי שישמעו המתאספים שם נבלותו ומי הוא]: בזמן בית המדרש. קודם אכילה היו דורשים: שלא בזמן בית המדרש. לאחר אכילה לא דרשו משום שכרות: פסקי סדרא בכתובים. [ח) והיו רגילים לקרא בבהמ"ד פרשה בכתובים]: במקום בהמ"ד. שהחכם דורש דהיינו בבהמ"ד אבל בעלמא קורין: בין במקום בהמ"ד כו' בזמן בהמ"ד אין קורין. לפי שמבטלו מלילך אבל הדורש אבל שלא בזמן בהמ"ד כגון לאחר אכילה קורין: ושמואל. דאמר לעיל אפילו לאחר אכילה אין קורין: כר' נחמיה. אמרה למילתיה דלית ליה טעמא דאין קורין משום בטול אלא כדי שיאמרו קל וחומר לשטרי הדיוטות ומיהו שמואל הנהיג במקומו כדברי חכמים דמתניתי' דאמרי טעמא (דמתני') משום ביטול תורה הלכך לאחר אכילה דליכא דרשה קורין: שונין בהן. כגון מדרש שה"ש וקהלת: שטרי הדיוטות. כגון של חשבונות או איגרות השלוחות למלא חפץ: גמ' עד החזה. מתחיל מרגליו האחרונים עד החזה שיוכל להוציא אימורים שהקטר חלביו דוחין שבת ותו לא מפשיט מידי עד אורתא דצורך הדיוט הוא: למענהו. לכבודו: שלא יסריח. שהעור מחממו ומסריחו ואין זה כבודו להיות פרש אוכלי שולחנו מגואל: אפתורא דדהבא. שאינו מוטל בבזיון אבל לשמא יסריח חייש רב יוסף ורבא לא חייש עד אורתא: יומא דאסתנא. רוח לפונית שהיא בינונית לא חמה ולא צנה כדאמרינן ביבמות בפרק הערל (דף עב.) ואיזו רוח המסרחת רוח מזרחית בשעת החום כדאמרינן בגיטין (דף לא:) אפילו שכבת זרע שבמעי אשה מסרחת בו דכתיב (הושע יג) יבא קדים רוח ה' ממדבר עולה וגו' יש מפרשין יומא דאסתנא רוח דרומית שהיא צוננת אמת שרוח דרומית צוננת אבל אסתנא על כרחיך לפונית היא ונוחה כדאמר בעלמא (עירובין ד' סה.) לריכא שמעתא צילותא כיומא דאסתנא ורוח דרומית היא בלשון ארמי יומא דשותא: קודם הפשטת העור. עד החזה: מ"ט. עור לאימורין מאי קא עביד: משום נימין. של צמר הנדבקין באימורין: חברייא. בני מחלוקתו: אם מצילין. בשבת: תיק עם הספר. ואע"פ שיש בתוכו מעות ומשום כבוד הספר שהוא צורך גבוה עבדינן בהדיה הצלת מעות שהן צורך הדיוט: לא נפשיט את הפסח. בתמיה משום צורך גבוה לא שרי צורך הדיוט בהדיה: התם. תיק ומעות דקמייתי ראיה מיניה טלטול בעלמא הוא: הכא. גבי פלוגתייהו דפסח דאיירי בה השתא מלאכה גמורה דהפשטה מאבות מלאכות היא: בתרתי פליגי. גבי פסח פליגי בטלטולו דאסר רבי ישמעאל לטלטל [הפסח] אחר שהוציא אימוריו אפי' מחמה לצל משום עור דלאו בר טלטול הוא (א) ולא דמי לשלחין דאמרן בבמה טומנין (לעיל מט.) שמטלטלין אותן דהתם עור בהמה גסה דחזי למישטחיה ולמיזגא עליה: והכי קאמרי ליה. תשובה לענין טלטול: לא נטלטל עור אגב בשר. דהוי נמי כבוד שמים דבשר דומיא דספר ומותר לטלטלו מחמה לצל ואגב בשר יטלטלו עור המחובר בו:
מי

מסורת הש"ס

א) בספרים ישנים ליתא אלא, ב) [עיין הספורה שלמלגלם וכו' ועי' תוס' עב. ד"ה שלמלגלת וכו' וכ"כ תוספות להדיא במגילה כב. ד"ה ואין מפטירין], ג) [תוספ' פי"ד מ"ש הלכה ג ע"ש], ד) לקמן קלג. מנחות סג: [תוספ' דפסחים פ"ד], ה) [זבחים פה.], ו) [ג"ל כל פעל], ז) גי' רש"ל, ח) גי' רש"ל, ט) [דף קמט.].

הגהות הב"ח

(א) רש"י ד"ה בתרתי פליגי וכו' ולאו בר טלטול הוא הס"ד ואחר כך מ"ה והכי קאמרי ואח"כ ד"ה לא נטלטל וכו' והמחובר בו ולא דמי לשלחין וכו'. נ"ב קן קושית היא אף למבריא ונ"ל כמוך פי' במה טומנין דף מט ע"ש:

גליון הש"ס

גמ' דבנהרדעא פסקי סדרי. ע"ל דף כד ע"א תוס' ד"ה שלמלגלת:

תורה אור השלם

א) כל פָּעַל יְיָ לַמַּעֲנֵהוּ וְגַם רָשָׁע לְיוֹם רָעָה: [משלי טז, ד]

ליקוטי רש"י

שפילית לסיפא. כל דבר שהוא בסוף קרוי שפילו של דבר [ברכות י.]. פסקי סידרא. פרשיות של מקרא [ע"ז יט.]. בשטרי הדיוטות. של מקח וממכר [לקמן קמט.]. מפשיטין את הפסח עד החזה. דתנן במסכת תמיד (פ"ד מ"ג) גבי הפשטו מתחיל מן הרגלים ויורד עד שמגיע לחזה הגיע לחזה חתך את הראש ונתנו לזה שזכה בו וחוזר ומפשיט עד שמגיע לחזה. יומא דאסתנא. רוח לפונית היא ונוחה. כל פעל ה' למענהו. לשם כבודו. אפתורא דדהבא. שלחן של זהב. יומא דאסתנא. כשמנשבת רוח לפונית שהיא נוחה ולא צוננת ולא חמה [גיטין לא:].

Rabbis, what is the reason they permit the flaying of the entire animal?

The Gemara answers:

אָמַר רַבָּה בַּר בַּר חָנָה אָמַר רַבִּי יוֹחָנָן – Rabbah bar bar Chanah said in the name of R' Yochanan: דְּאָמַר קְרָא ,,כֹּל פָּעַל ה׳ לַמַּעֲנֵהוּ״ – For the verse states: *All has Hashem wrought for His sake,* i.e. His honor.[19]

The Gemara inquires:

וְהָכָא מַאי ,,לַמַּעֲנֵהוּ״ אִיכָּא – And here, what fulfillment of ***for His sake* is there,** i.e. how does flaying the entire animal bring honor to God?

The Gemara replies:

רַב יוֹסֵף אָמַר שֶׁלֹּא יַסְרִיחַ – Rav Yosef said: So that [the meat of the Divine offering] should not putrefy.[20] **רָבָא אָמַר – Rava said: שֶׁלֹּא יְהוּ קָדְשֵׁי שָׁמַיִם מוּטָּלִין כִּנְבֵלָה – So that the Divine holies should not lie around like** worthless **carrion.**

The Gemara continues:

מַאי בֵּינַיְיהוּ – What is the practical difference **between [these two opinions]? אִיכָּא בֵּינַיְיהוּ דְּמַנַּח אַפְּתוֹרָא דְּדַהֲבָא – The** difference **between them is** in regard to a case **where [the carcass] is lying on a golden table;**[21] **אִי נַמִּי יוֹמָא דְּאַסְתָּנָא – alternatively,** if it is **a day of the northern wind,** i.e. a day on which the northern wind is blowing.[22]

The Gemara asks:

וְרַבִּי יִשְׁמָעֵאל בְּנוֹ שֶׁל רַבִּי יוֹחָנָן בֶּן בְּרוֹקָה הַאי ,,פָּעַל ה׳ לַמַּעֲנֵהוּ״ מַאי עָבֵיד לֵיהּ – And R' Yishmael the son of R' Yochanan ben Berokah, what does he do with this verse: *All has* ***Hashem wrought for His sake***? What interpretation does he derive therefrom?[23]

The Gemara answers:

שֶׁלֹּא יוֹצִיא אֶת הָאֵימוּרִין קוֹדֶם הַפְשָׁטַת הָעוֹר – He derives from it **that one should not remove the sacrificial parts** from the *pesach* offering **before flaying the hide** as far as the breast.

The Gemara asks:

מַאי טַעְמָא – But **what** indeed **is the reason** for this? Why cannot an incision simply be made in the hide of the offering, thereby allowing the sacrificial parts to be drawn out without the need to flay the animal at all?

The Gemara answers:

אָמַר רַב הוּנָא בְּרֵיהּ דְּרַב נָתָן – Rav Huna the son of Rav Nassan said: מִשּׁוּם נִימִין – Because of the **strands** of hair or wool that would otherwise get caught onto the sacrificial parts as they are being drawn out of the body cavity.[24]

The Gemara delves deeper into the reasoning of R' Yishmael the son of R' Yochanan ben Berokah's disputants:

אָמַר רַב חִסְדָּא אָמַר מַר עוּקְבָא – Rav Chisda said in the name of Mar Ukva: מַאי אַהֲדַרוּ לֵיהּ חַבְרַיָּיא לְרַבִּי יִשְׁמָעֵאל בְּנוֹ שֶׁל רַבִּי יוֹחָנָן בֶּן בְּרוֹקָה – What did the colleagues of R' Yishmael the son of R' Yochanan ben Berokah answer him? I.e. what argument did they advance in support of their view?[25]

The Gemara replies:

הָכִי קָאָמְרֵי לֵיהּ – This is what they told him: אִם מַצִּילִין תִּיק הַסֵּפֶר עִם הַסֵּפֶר – If we may save the container of the scroll together with the scroll even though there is money in it, **לֹא נַפְשִׁיט אֶת הַפֶּסַח מֵעוֹרוֹ – should we not** be permitted to **flay the *pesach* offering of its hide?**[26]

NOTES

19. *Proverbs* 16:4. This teaches that all that one does should have as its goal the glorification of God's Name. As a corollary to this principle, it is presumed that the Torah intended regarding the mitzvos it commanded that they be performed in the manner that brings the greatest honor to God. Accordingly, when the Torah commanded that the *pesach* offering be brought on the Sabbath, thereby giving permission for various *melachos* to be performed in the process, it included in that permission any act which, though technically not essential for the actual offering of the animal, serves a "Divine need" in that it enhances the honor of the service. The flaying of the animal beyond its breast is, in the Rabbis' view, an example of such an act (see *Ritva MHK* ed.). The Gemara will presently explain how this is so.

[It should be noted that in citing the verse *All has Hashem wrought for His sake,* the Gemara does not mean that this is the actual *source* for the permission to flay the skin beyond the breast. To be sure, a verse from *Tanach* cannot serve as a source for relaxing a prohibition. Rather, the Rabbis maintain that since such flaying enhances the mitzvah, it stands to reason by *logic* that the Torah wishes it to be done. They cited the verse from *Proverbs* as a mere *asmachta,* a Scriptural support, to this piece of logic (*Ritva MHK* ed.).]

20. If the entire hide is not removed from the animal, no cool air will be able to reach the meat. This added warmth will cause the flesh to decompose rapidly and give off a foul odor. It is dishonorable to God that the portions of meat eaten from His sacrifice, which are analogous to the portions served by the king to his servants at the royal table, be repulsive (*Rashi*).

21. If after the *pesach* offering is flayed up to the breast and its sacrificial parts are removed, it is placed with great respect on a golden table, Rava asserts that the Rabbis would agree with R' Yishmael that the meat may remain until nightfall without further flaying. This is because the meat is no longer lying around in a degrading manner. [Rava is never concerned that the meat will spoil before nightfall.] According to Rav Yosef, however, that the concern of the Rabbis is that the meat not become putrid, the sacrifice must still be flayed in its entirety, for placing the meat on a golden table does not preserve the meat's freshness (*Rashi*).

22. The northern wind is temperate, neither overly cold nor overly warm (cf. *Hagahos Yavetz*). When it prevails, even unskinned meat will keep for some time without spoiling. Under these circumstances Rav Yosef maintains that the Rabbis will agree to R' Yishmael that there is no need for the flaying to be completed on the Sabbath. According to Rava, however, that the concern is that the offering should not be allowed to appear as worthless carrion, the Rabbis will still require that the flaying be completed before nightfall (*Rashi*).

23. This verse teaches us that we must be particular not to handle the holies of God in a degrading manner. Since R' Yishmael does not utilize this verse to teach that we may complete the flaying of the *pesach* offering even on the Sabbath, what does he derive therefrom?

[As explained in note 19, this verse is only an *asmachta.* Therefore, the inquiry of the Gemara as to what R' Yishmael will derive from this verse is not meant in the usual sense, that if in fact we cannot find any exposition from this verse for R' Yishmael it would present a difficulty. Rather, the Gemara was aware that R' Yishmael also utilized this verse as an *asmachta* for a different teaching, and presented this information to us in question-and-answer form commonly employed by the Gemara (*Ritva MHK* ed.).]

24. If one does not remove the hide from the area above the sacrificial parts, it is inevitable that some hairs of the hide will get stuck onto the sacrificial parts. It is unseemly to offer such parts to God as a sacrifice.

25. [The Gemara apparently had a tradition that the Rabbis buttressed their position by citing an additional argument. What was this argument?]

26. The Rabbis had argued that flaying the *pesach* offering beyond its breast qualifies as a "Divine need" to be permitted on the Sabbath in that the meat of God's sacrifice is thereby rendered fresher or more presentable. Although the owner of the animal benefits from this flaying as well (i.e. the meat that he wishes to eat is uncovered), this does not diminish the honor to God that results from the flaying.

R' Yishmael, however, disputes this conclusion. In his view, only an act whose "beneficiary" is God alone can be included in the verse *for His sake.* An act which fills both a Divine need and a need of man simultaneously, such as flaying the skin from the portion of the sacrifice that will be eaten (God "benefits" as explained above, while man benefits in that the meat is made accessible), does not result in sufficient honor to God to merit performing a Biblical *melachah.*

The Rabbis now attempt to refute R' Yishmael's reasoning from our Mishnah. The Mishnah rules that one may rescue a scroll together with its container, even though the container holds money, for the sake of the honor of the Holy Scriptures. In this situation as well there is a dual

ושמואל דאמר כר' נחמיה. ולא פליג אדרב דשפיר מודה דלמתני' דמפרש טעמא מפני ביטול בית המדרש קורין שלא בזמן בית המדרש אלא בא לומר דר' נחמיה פליג עלה דמתני': **וכ"ש** בשטרי הדיוטות. פירש בקונטרס איגרות ותימה דנהגו העולם לקרות בכתב ואיגרות השלוחים ממקום למקום ולטלטלן ואמי שרי דהא לאוין לגור ע"פ אלוהים ונראה לר"י דלא קרי שטרי הדיוטות אלא שטרי חובות וכיוצא בהן אבל איגרות שרי דפעמים שיש בהן פקוח נפש ואפי' יודע שאין בו פקוח נפש מתיר ר"ת דלא הוי שטרי הדיוטות כיון שאין צריך למה שכתוב בה לפי שיודע מה שבאיגרות ואם אינו יודע שמא יש בו צורך גדול או פקוח נפש ושרי וכ"מ בירושלמי דקאמר מפני מה אין קורין בכתבי הקדש מפני שטרי הדיוטות שאם אתה אומר לו שהוא מותר אף הוא אומר מה בכך אם אתעסק בשטרותי משמע דווקא כעין חובות ושטרות קאמר וכן פי' רש"י לקמן [ו] גבי גזירה שלא יקרא בשטרי הדיוטות דבשטרי מקח וממכר קאמר וכן הגיה בפי' כתב ידו ומיהו אותן מלחמות הכתובין בלע"ז נראה לרבינו יהודה דאסור לעיין בהן דלא גרע מהא דמייתי בפ' שואל (לקמן קמט.) כתב שתחת הצורה והדיוקנאות אסור לקרות בהן בשבת ואפי' בחול לא ידע ר"י מי התיר דהוי כמושב לצים:

פליגי בטלטול כו'. פי' אחר שנפשטו כל העור פליגי דרבנן שרו לטלטל שעדיין צריך לבשר שלא יתלכלך ור' ישמעאל אסר אבל כשאינו מופשט אלא עד החזה שרי לכ"ע לטלטל כדמוכח בסמוך ואע"ג דר' ישמעאל לא שרי להפשיט אלא עד החזה מ"מ פליגי במופשט כולו כגון שעבר והפשיט אי נמי במתמידים ומוספים דמותר להפשיטן הכל:

דהוה שקיל שמא דלא מקבל שוחדא. היה מוליך עליו שם שאינו מקבל שוחד מבעלי דינין הבאין לפניו והיה מקבלו בסתר: א"ל. פילוסופא לר"ג מיומא דגליתון כו': שפילית. כל סוף הדבר הוא תחתית שלו ושייך למימר שפילית לסיפיה: נהור נהורך כשרגא. הנהר אורך כשרגא רמזה שנתנה לו מנורה בשוחד: אמר לו ר"ג אתא חמרא ובטשא. דחפתו לארץ כלומר אני נלחתי בשוחד [ז] והכל כדי שיתעו המתפלספים שם נגלותו ומי הוא]: בזמן בית המדרש. קודם אכילה היו דורשים: שלא בזמן בית המדרש. לאחר אכילה לא דרשו משום שכרות: פסקי סדרא בכתובים. [ח] [היו רגילים לקרות בבהמ"ד פרשה בכתובים]: במקום בהמ"ד. שהכסם דורש דהיינו בבהמ"ד אבל בעלמא קורין: בין במקום בהמ"ד כו' בזמן בהמ"ד אין קורין. לפי שמבטלו מליך אבל הדורש אבל שלא בזמן בהמ"ד כגון לאחר אכילה קורין: ושמואל. דאמר לעיל אפילו לאחר אכילה אין קורין: כר' נחמיה. אמרה למילתיה דלית ליה טעמא דאין קורין משום בטול אלא כדי שיאמרו קל וחומר לשטרי הדיוטות ומיהו שמואל הנהיג במקומו כדברי חכמים דמתניתי' דאמרי טעמא (דמתני') משום ביטול תורה הלכך לאחר אכילה דליכא דרשה קורין: שונין בהן. כגון מדרש שה"ש וקהלת: שטרי הדיוטות. כגון של חשבונות או איגרות השלוחות לאלה ספק: גמ' עד החזה. מתחיל מרגליו האחרונים עד החזה שיוכל להוציא אימורים שהקטר חלביו דוחין שבת ותו לא מפשיט מידי עד אורתא לצורך הדיוט הוא: למענהו. לכבודו: שלא יסריח. שהעור מחממו ומסריחו ואין זה כבודו להיות פרש אוכלי שולחנו מגואל: אפתורא דדהבא. שאינו מוטל בבזיון אבל לשמא יסריח חייש רב יוסף ורבא לא חייש עד אורתא: יומא דאסתנא. רוח צפונית שהיא בינונית לא חמה ולא צנה כדאמרינן ביבמות בפרק הערל (דף עב.) ואיזו רוח המסרחת רוח מזרחית בשעת החום כדאמרינן בגיטין (דף לא:) אפילו שכבת זרע שבמעי אשה מסרחת בו דכתיב (הושע יג) יבא קדים רוח ה' ממדבר עולה וגו' יש מפרשין יומא דאסתנא רוח דרומית שהיא צוננת אמת שרוח דרומית צוננת אבל אסתנא על כרחיך צפונית היא ונוחה כדאמר בעלמא (עירובין ד' סה.) צריכא שמעתא צילותא כיומא דאסתנא ורוח דרומית היא בלשון ארמי יומא דשותא: קודם הפשטת העור. עד החזה: מ"ט. עור לאימורין מאי קא עביד: משום נימין. של נמר הנדבקין באימורין: חברייא. בני מחלוקתו: אם מצילין. בשבת: תיק עם הספר. ואע"פ שיש בתוכו מעות ומשום כבוד הספר שהוא צורך גבוה עבדינן בהדיה הצלת מעות שהן צורך הדיוט: לא נפשיט את הפסח. בתמיה משום צורך גבוה לא שרי צורך הדיוט בהדיה: התם. תיק ומעות דקמייתי ראיה מיניה טלטול בעלמא הוא: הכא. גבי פלוגתייהו דפסח דאיירי בה השתא מלאכה גמורה דהפשטה מאבות מלאכות היא: בתרתי פליגי. גבי פסח פליגי בטלטולו דאסר רבי ישמעאל לטלטל [הפסח] אחר שהוציא אימוריו אפי' מחמה לצל משום עור דלאו בר טלטול הוא (א) ולא דמי לשלחין דאמרן בבמה טומנין (לעיל מט.) שמטלטלין אותן דהתם עור בהמה גסה דחזי למיטמיה ולמיזגא עליה: והכי קאמרי ליה. תשובה לענין טלטול: לא נטלטל עור אגב בשר. דהוי נמי כבוד שמים דבשר דומיא דספר ומותר לטלטלו מחמה לצל ואגב בשר יטלטלו עור המחובר בו:

דהוה שקיל שמא דלא מקבל שוחדא בעו לאחוכי ביה אעיילא ליה שרגא דדהבא ואזול לקמיה אמרה ליה בעינא דניפלגי לי בנכסי דבי נשי אמר להו פלוגו א"ל כתיב לן במקום ברא ברתא לא תירות א"ל מן יומא דגליתון מארעכון איתנטלית אורייתא דמשה ואיתיהיבת ספרא אחריתי וכתיב ביה ברא וברתא כחדא ירתון למחר הדר עייל ליה איהו חמרא לובא אמר להו שפילית לסיפיה דספרא וכתב ביה אנא לא למיפחת מן אורייתא דמשה אתיתי [ולא] לאוספי על אורייתא דמשה אתיתי וכתיב ביה במקום ברא ברתא לא תירות אמרה ליה נהור נהוריך כשרגא א"ל רבן גמליאל אתא חמרא ובטש לשרגא: ומפני מה אין קורין כו': אמר רב לא שנו אלא בזמן בית המדרש אבל שלא בזמן בהמ"ד קורין ושמואל אמר אפילו שלא בזמן בית המדרש אין קורין איני והא נהרדעא אתריה דשמואל הוה ובנהרדעא פסקי סידרא בכתובים במנחתא דשבתא אלא אי איתמר הכי איתמר אמר רב לא שנו אלא במקום בהמ"ד אבל שלא במקום בהמ"ד קורין ושמואל אמר בין במקום בהמ"ד בין שלא במקום בהמ"ד בזמן בהמ"ד אין קורין שלא בזמן בית המדרש קורין ואזדא שמואל לטעמיה דבנהרדעא פסקי סידרא דכתובים במנחתא דשבתא רב אשי אמר לעולם כדאמרן מעיקרא ושמואל כרבי נחמיה דתניא אע"פ שאמרו כתבי הקדש אין קורין בהן אבל שונין בהן ודורשין בהן נצרך לפסוק מביא ורואה בו א"ר נחמיה מפני מה אמרו כתבי הקדש אין קורין בהן כדי שיאמרו בכתבי הקדש אין קורין וכ"ש בשטרי הדיוטות: **מתני'** מצילין תיק הספר עם הספר ותיק התפילין עם התפילין ואע"פ שיש בתוכן מעות ולהיכן מצילין אותן למבוי שאינו מפולש בן בתירא אומר אף למפולש: **גמ'** ת"ר ארבעה עשר שחל להיות בשבת מפשיטין את הפסח עד החזה דברי רבי ישמעאל בנו של רבי יוחנן בן ברוקה וחכ"א מפשיטין את כולו בשלמא לרבי ישמעאל בנו של ר' יוחנן בן ברוקה דהא איתעביד ליה צורך גבוה אלא לרבנן מ"ט אמר רבה בר בר חנה א"ר יוחנן דאמר קרא כל פעל ה' למענהו איכא רב יוסף אמר שלא יסריח רבא אמר שלא יהו קדשי שמים מוטלין כנבלה מאי בינייהו איכא בינייהו דמנח אפתורא דדהבא אי נמי יומא דאסתנא ורבי ישמעאל בנו של רבי יוחנן בן ברוקה האי פעל ה' למענהו מאי עביד ליה שלא יוציא את האימורין קודם הפשטת העור מ"ט אמר רב הונא בריה דרב נתן משום נימין אמר רב חסדא אמר מר עוקבא מאי אהדרו ליה חברייא לרבי ישמעאל בנו של רבי יוחנן בן ברוקה הכי קאמרי ליה אם מצילין תיק הספר עם הספר לא נפשיט את הפסח מעורו מי דמי התם טלטול הכא מלאכה אמר רב אשי בתרתי פליגי פליגי בטלטול ופליגי במלאכה והכי קאמרי ליה אם מצילין תיק הספר עם הספר לא נטלטל עור אגב בשר

מי

יב א מיי' פכ"ג מהל' שבת הלכה יט סמג לאוין סה:
יג ב מיי' שם הלכה כח סמג שם טוש"ע או"ח סימן שלז סעיף טו:
יד ג מיי' שם הלכה כו טור שו"ע שם סעיף ח:
טו ד מיי' פ"א מהלכות ק"פ הלכה טז:

רבינו חננאל

חזר ופירש מפני מה אין קוראין בכתובים מפני ביטול בהמ"ד ומסייעא לה הא דתני העוסק במקרא מדה שאינה מדה כו'. ובית תלמוד טפי עדיף [מהעוסק] במקרא. אמר רב לא שנו שאין קורין בהן אלא בזמן בית המדרש. פי' בשעה שהחכמים יושבי במדר' ומתעסקין בתלמוד. אבל שלא בזמן בהמ"ד כגון שכבר עמדו בעלי מדרש ונכנסו לבתיהן קורין. ושמואל [אמר] במקום שיש מדרש קבוע כו'. ואסקה רב אשי הכי לעולם כדקאמרינן מעיקרא. אמר רב אין קורין בזמן בהמ"ד כדאמרן אבל בזמן שלא בהמ"ד קורין. ושמואל אמר בין בזמן בהמ"ד בין שלא בזמן בהמ"ד אין קורין. דסבירא ליה כר' נחמיה וגזרה היא משום שטרי הדיוטות והלכתא כלישנא קמא בזמן בית המדרש אין קורין שלא בזמן בית המדרש קורין: ירושלמי (ה"א) אמר ר' יהושע בן לוי הדא אגדה הכותבה אין לו חלק. הדורשה מתחרך. השומעה אינו מקבל שכר. מימרי לא איסתכלית בה אלא חד זמן. ואשכחית כתוב בה קע"ה פרשיי' דיבור אמירה צווי שכתוב בתורה כנגד שנות [של] אברהם. שנא' לקחת מתנות באדם. וכתיב האדם הגדול בענקים. קמ"ז מזמורי' שכתוב בתילים כנגד שנות יעקב אבינו ללמד שכל קילוסין שישראל [עושין הללויה] מקלסין להקב"ה כנגד שנותיו של יעקב שנא' ואתה קדוש יושב תהלות ישראל קכ"ג פעמים שישראל עונין הללויה כנגד שני אהרן שנאמר הללויה הללו אל בקדשו לקדושו לאהרן קדוש ה': אפילו כן הוינא מיבעיא בלילא. מצילין תיק הספר עם הספר. אמרי רבנן דהאי תיק קאי לחודיה. ונטולין מקמי שהוא עם הספר וכן תיק [של] תפילין: י"ד שחל להיות בשבת ר' ישמעאל בנו של ר' יוחנן בן ברוקה אומר מפשיטין את הפסח עד החזה. סבר כיון דאיתעביד ליה צורך גבוה שיכול להוציא החלבים לא יפשוט יותר מזה. ורבנן סברי מפשיטו כולו. וטעמא כל פעל ה' למענהו. מאי למענהו לעשות כבוד לקדשים: פי' יומא דאסתנא יום שמנשבת רוח צפון שאין הבשר מסריח בו. רבא אמר שלא יהו קדשים מוטלין בעזרותיהן כנבלה. אבל אם הוא מוטל בשלחן של זהב שהוא דרך כבוד לא יפשיט יותר למטה מן החזה וכו'. וגרסי' בפסחים בפרק תמיד [נשחט] שהיו מפשיטין כליהן לאחוריהן. ור' ישמעאל בנו של ר' יוחנן בן ברוקא מוקים לה למענהו שלא יוציא האמורין קודם הפשטת העור כדי שלא ידבק שיער העור בחלבים: אמרו ליה רבנן (אין) [אין] מצילין תיק הספר עם הספר לא נפשוט (עור עם החזה) [את הפסח מעורו]. אמר להן מי דמי. הצלת תיק טלטול בעלמא הפשטה עור מלאכה דקא בעי ליה לעור. אמר רב אשי בתרי פליגי עליה במלאכה ובטלטול. והכי קאמרי ליה תינח הפשטה שהיא מלאכה טלטול מאי דאיכא

א) בספרים ישנים איתא אלא, ב) [עי' הספרים], ג) [עי' תוס' לעיל צג: ד"ה שלמלך וכו'] וכ"י תוספות להדיא במגילה כה. ד"ה ואין מפטירין], ג) [תוספ' פי"ד מ"ש הלכה ג ע"ש], ד) לקמן קנב: מנחות סג: [תוספ' דפסחי' פ"ד], ה) [זבחים סה.], ו) [ע"ל כל פעל], ז) גי' רש"ל, ח) גי' רש"ל, ט) [דף קמט.].

הגהות הב"ח

(א) רש"י ד"ה בתרתי פליגי וכו' דלאו בר טלטול הוא הס"ד ואח"כ מ"ה והכי קאמרי ואח"כ ד"ה לא נטלטל וכו' המחובר בו ולא דמי לשלחין וכו'. נ"ב הך קושיא היא אף למכריע וע"ל בתוס' פ' במה טומנין דף מט ד"ה שמטלטלין.

גליון הש"ס

גמ' דבנהרדעא פסקי סדרי. ע"ל דף כד ע"א תוס' ד"ה שלמלך.

תורה אור השלם

א) כֹּל פָּעַל יְיָ לַמַּעֲנֵהוּ וְגַם רָשָׁע לְיוֹם רָעָה: [משלי טז, ד]

ליקוטי רש"י

שפילית לסיפא. כל דבר שהוא בסוף קרוי שפילו של דבר [ברכות י.]. פסקי סידרא. פרשיות של מקרא [ע"ז יט.]. בשטרי הדיוטות. של מקח וממכר [לקמן קמט. ועי' תוס' כאן ושם]. מפשיטין את הפסח עד החזה. דקתני במסכת תמיד (פ"ד מ"ב) גבי הפשטה שהיה מתחיל מן הרגלים שהיה מפשיט ויורד עד שמגיע לחזה הגיע לחזה חתך את הראש ונתנו לשני ולאחר כך הכרעיים וחותך והפשיט כו' שמעינן מיניה משהגיע לחזה פורק ידיו מן ההפשט והתחיל להתעסק בניתוח הלכך וגבי פסח נמי עד החזה דיכול להוציא אימורים בלא נימין קורעו ומוציא מיד והוא הדין ליה פירש מן הפשטו וקאמר רבי ישמעאל שוב אינו גומר ומפשיט משום דכיון דפירש הוא חוזר מלאכה דלאמתלא לנפשה ולאו לצורך גבוה [שם קלג. רע"ש, וכאן ברש"ש החדש]. כל פעל ה' למענהו. הכל עשה בשביל קילוסו כמו (ה') לפנהו בתודי [תהלים קמז] [משלי טז, ד]. אפתורא דדהבא. שולחן של זהב [תמיד לב:]. יומא דאסתנא. כשמנשבת רוח צפונית שאין בה לא חמה ולא צנה כדאמר בפרק הערל (עב.) מפני מה לא נשפו ישראל במדבר מפני שלא נשבה בהן רוח צפונית אבל ביומא דאסתנא נוחה היא לא חמה ולא צונה וממתקת את הפירות [גיטין לא:].

The Gemara rejects this reasoning:

מִי דָּמֵי – Is [the case of the Mishnah] similar to ours? **הָתָם טַלְטוּל – There,** in regard to saving the container, it is a question of **moving** *muktzeh,* **הָכָא מְלָאכָה** – whereas **here,** in regard to flaying the *pesach* offering, it is a question of performing a ***melachah.***[27]

The Gemara offers instead a different version of the Rabbis' argument:

אָמַר רַב אַשִׁי – Rather **Rav Ashi said: בְּתַרְתֵּי פְּלִיגֵי – [R' Yishmael and the Rabbis] disagree in regard to two** points. **פְּלִיגֵי בְּטַלְטוּל – They disagree concerning moving** *muktzeh,* **וּפְלִיגֵי בִּמְלָאכָה – and they disagree concerning** performing **a** forbidden ***melachah.***[28] **וְהָכִי קָאָמְרֵי לֵיהּ – And this is what [the Rabbis] said to [R' Yishmael the son of R' Yochanan ben Berokah]** to substantiate their opinion in the *muktzeh* part of the dispute:[29] **אִם מַצִּילִין תִּיק הַסֵּפֶר עִם הַסֵּפֶר – If we may save the container of the scroll together with the scroll, לֹא נְטַלְטֵל עוֹר אַגַּב בָּשָׂר – should we not** be permitted to **move the hide on account of the meat?**[30]

NOTES

benefit: God "benefits" in that the sacred writings are preserved, and the owner benefits because his money is salvaged. Yet the Mishnah permits rescuing the container with all its contents. This proves that we set aside a prohibition to perform a Divine need even though a need of man will be performed at the same time (*Rashi*).

27. Moving the [*muktzeh*] money is only a Rabbinic prohibition, while flaying an animal on the Sabbath constitutes one of the thirty-nine Biblically prohibited *melachos* (מַפְשִׁיט, *skinning*). The fact that we are lenient in regard to the former does not prove that the law is the same for the latter (*Rashi*).

28. There are two separate and distinct points of dispute between R' Yishmael the son of R' Yochanan ben Berokah and the Rabbis. One point is in regard to the Biblical labor of flaying, i.e. whether or not it is permissible to flay a *pesach* offering on the Sabbath beyond the breast: R' Yishmael forbids this while the Rabbis permit it. This is the dispute that we have discussed thus far, and in regard to this point, the Rabbis never cited a proof from our Mishnah.

Rav Ashi, asserts, however, that there is also a second dispute between these Tannaim that has hitherto not been discussed. This is whether one is permitted to move the *pesach* offering after it has been flayed up to the breast. According to R' Yishmael, once the sacrificial parts have been removed from the offering, the remainder of the offering may not be moved from the sun to the shade, because the hide of the animal, which is still attached to the meat, is *muktzeh* (*Rashi*). The Sages, however, permit moving the half-flayed *pesach,* and it was in regard to this point that the Rabbis adduced their proof from our Mishnah. [Although the Rabbis permit flaying the entire *pesach,* the case of a half-flayed *pesach* could occur according to them in a situation in which the *pesach* was lying on a golden table, or if the flaying was performed on a day on which the northern wind was blowing (*Ritva MHK* ed.).]

29. The Sages argued: Personally, we maintain that even the Biblical *melachah* of flaying is permitted for the sake of preventing degradation to the offering. Accordingly, it is obvious that the Rabbinic prohibition of *muktzeh* will also be lifted in this case, to move the offering from the hot sun to a cooler place, where the meat will not rot and be degraded. However, even you, who disagree in regard to the Biblical prohibition of flaying, should at least concur that the Rabbinic prohibition of *muktzeh* is not applicable in this case for the following reason (*Ritva MHK* ed.).

30. As explained above (115a note 1), one is permitted to rescue the scroll even by carrying it out into a *mavoi* lacking a *shituf mevo'os,* and even though one is ordinarily forbidden to rescue his possessions from a fire on the Sabbath. This was allowed for the sake of the honor of God, to prevent damage to His holy writings. Although this goal could be achieved by saving the scroll without its container, the Rabbis permitted saving the container as well, as taught in the Mishnah, since removing the scroll from the container could cost precious time and might result in the scroll being burned. Thus the container may be saved on account of the scroll. Similarly, it should be permitted to move the *muktzeh* hide, which is attached to the meat, on account of the meat, to save it from rotting in the sun (*Rashi*).

The Gemara rejects this reasoning also:

מִי דָּמֵי – Is [the case of the Mishnah] similar to ours? **הָתָם נַעֲשָׂה בָּסִיס לְדָבָר הַמּוּתָּר – There,** in regard to the scroll container, **[the container] serves as a base to something that** it is **permitted** to move, viz. the scroll of the Scriptures, **הָכָא נַעֲשָׂה בָּסִיס לְדָבָר הָאָסוּר** – whereas **here,** in regard to moving the *pesach* offering, **[the hide] serves as a base to something that** it is **forbidden** to move, viz. the meat of the offering.[1]

The Gemara rephrases the analogy drawn by the Rabbis: **אֶלָּא הָכִי קָאָמְרֵי לֵיהּ – Rather, this is what [the Rabbis] said to [R' Yishmael the son of R' Yochanan ben Berokah]: אִם מַצִּילִין תִּיק שֶׁל סֵפֶר עִם הַסֵּפֶר וְאַף עַל פִּי שֶׁיֵּשׁ בְּתוֹכוֹ מָעוֹת – If we may save the container of a scroll together with the scroll even though there is money in it, לֹא נְטַלְטֵל עוֹר אַגַּב בָּשָׂר – should we not** be permitted to **move the hide on account of the meat?**[2]

The Gemara rejects this reasoning also:

מִי דָּמֵי – Is [that case] similar to ours? **הָתָם נַעֲשָׂה בָּסִיס לְדָבָר הָאָסוּר וּלְדָבָר הַמּוּתָּר – There, [the scroll container] serves as a base** both **to something that is forbidden,** viz. the money, **and to something that is permitted,** viz. the scroll. **הָכָא כּוּלוֹ נַעֲשָׂה בָּסִיס לְדָבָר הָאָסוּר – Here, the entire [hide] serves as a base to something that is forbidden,** viz. the meat of the *pesach.*[3]

The Gemara again attempts to rephrase the analogy: **אֶלָּא הָכִי קָאָמְרֵי לֵיהּ – Rather, this is what [the Rabbis] said to [R' Yishmael the son of R' Yochanan ben Berokah]: אִם מְבִיאִין תִּיק שֶׁיֵּשׁ בְּתוֹכוֹ מָעוֹת מֵעָלְמָא לְהַצִּיל בּוֹ סֵפֶר תּוֹרָה – If we may bring a container containing** only **money from elsewhere** in the house **to save in it a Torah scroll,** i.e. the Torah scroll is lying unencased, and we bring a receptacle containing only money over to the scroll to place it inside the receptacle and carry it to safety, **לֹא נְטַלְטֵל עוֹר אַגַּב בָּשָׂר – should we not** be permitted to **move the hide on account of the meat?**[4]

The Gemara questions the premise of this analogy:

וְהִיא גּוּפָהּ מְנָלַן – But this very point (viz. that it is permitted to bring a container containing money over to the scroll), **from where do we know it? אִילֵימָא דְּמִדְּהֵיכָא דְּאִית בֵּיהּ לֹא שָׁדֵי לְהוּ – If you will say that since where there is [money] in [the container]** together with the scroll the Mishnah permits the person to move the container and **he need not** first **throw out [the money], אִיתּוּיֵי נַמֵּי מַיְיתִינַן** – it follows that **we may also bring** a container containing only money in it over to the scroll, **מִי דָּמֵי** – but **is [that case] similar** to the Mishnah's? **הָתָם אַדְּהָכִי וְהָכִי נָפְלָה דְּלֵיקָה – There,** in the Mishnah's case, if we obligate him to first throw out the money, there is the danger that **in the meantime the fire will catch** onto the scroll, **הָכָא אַדְּהָכָא וְהָכִי לִישְׁדִּינַן** – whereas **here,** in the case of bringing a container containing only money over to the scroll, **in the meantime,** i.e. as he is running with the container, **let him throw out** the money![5] Therefore, there is no basis for the assumption that it is permissible to carry a container with money in it over to the scroll.[6]

NOTES

1. The flesh of the *pesach* offering is *muktzeh,* since it may not be eaten until nighttime when it will be roasted. And, the fact that this holy flesh will spoil if left in the sun is insufficient reason according to R' Yishmael to permit moving it to the shade as a Divine need, since a human being will benefit from this action as well (see 116b note 26).

Accordingly, the comparison to the case of rescuing the scroll container together with the scroll is flawed. For whereas rescuing the scroll container by itself is not considered a Divine need, the scroll container serves as an ancillary base to the scroll, whose rescue does qualify as a Divine need. Hence, the container may be rescued along with the scroll. This cannot be compared to the case of moving the hide of the *pesach* together with the flesh, where the flesh itself is *muktzeh,* and moving it is not considered a Divine need according to R' Yishmael. Thus even if the hide per se were not *muktzeh,* it would be forbidden to be moved because it is a *base to muktzeh,* all the more so that the hide is *muktzeh* in its own right [and has nothing along with which it may be moved] (*Rashi,* as emended by *Hagahos HaBach*).

2. At this point the Gemara again introduces into the Rabbis' analogy the fact that the Mishnah permits moving the scroll container even if it has money in it. In this scenario, the scroll container is a base to *muktzeh* (the money). Nevertheless the Mishnah permits moving the container to save the scroll. Similarly, it should be permitted to move the hide, although it is a base to *muktzeh,* to preserve the meat.

The Rishonim ask: How can the Gemara speak of moving the hide "on account of the meat"? Why, we just finished saying that the meat itself cannot be moved according to R' Yishmael!

The Rishonim answer that at this point the Gemara understands that when something is a base to both a *muktzeh* and a non-*muktzeh* item, both the base and the non-*muktzeh* item take on the status of the *muktzeh* item. Consequently, if the Mishnah still permits moving the container with the money, we see that *muktzeh* may be moved for the sake of the honor of God (i.e. to save the scroll). It follows, therefore, that the hide and meat should be able to be moved as well, for the sake of the honor of the Divine meat (*Ritva MHK* ed.). According to this explanation, when the Gemara in its question speaks of moving the hide "on account of the meat," it does not mean on account of the meat *which is permissible to be moved.* Rather, it means on account of the meat *which is a Divine offering* (*Ramban,* in explanation of *Rashi;* cf. alternative explanations of *Rashi* advanced by *Maginei Shlomo* and *Leshon HaZahav*).

3. This reflects an altered understanding of the status of a base to a *muktzeh* item and a non-*muktzeh* item. Previously, the Gemara had understood that the base and the non-*muktzeh* item take on the status of the *muktzeh* item. The Gemara now states that the non-*muktzeh* item retains its permissible status. Moreover, assuming that the non-*muktzeh* item is more valuable than the *muktzeh* item (such as in this case, where presumably the scroll is more valuable than the money), the base itself does not become *muktzeh* either. Accordingly, it follows that in the case of the scroll container and the money, the container may be moved, for the container is a base to both a *muktzeh* item (the money) and a more valuable non-*muktzeh* item (the scroll). No analogy can be drawn to the case of the hide and the meat, where the hide is a base only to a *muktzeh* item (the meat).

4. In this situation the container is a base purely to something *muktzeh,* yet it may be brought to the scroll without first tilting out the money, for the sake of the honor of the scroll. [We speak of a situation in which we cannot save the scroll unless it is inserted into a container.] Similarly, it should be permitted to move the hide of the offering [to preserve the meat] (*Rashi*).

5. [Although it might be possible to shake the money out of the container while on the run without the scroll falling out at the same time, this is not an easy feat, and attempting to do so would consume precious time. We therefore do not obligate the person to do so. This cannot be compared to where the container contains only money. Perhaps in this case the person is obligated to dump out the money as he runs (cf. *Rabbeinu Chananel*).]

6. The question arises: Why did the Gemara have to differentiate between the two situations by speaking of the person's ability or inability to shake out the money? Why not simply say, as we did above, that in the situation where there is money and a scroll in the container, the container is a base to both a *muktzeh* item and a non-*muktzeh* item, whereas in the situation in which there is only money in the case, the container is a base to *muktzeh* alone?

Tosafos answer as follows: The law is that when something is a base to both a *muktzeh* and a non-*muktzeh* item, one must, if possible, first tilt off the *muktzeh* item before moving the base. Only if the *muktzeh* object cannot be tilted off may one move the base with the *muktzeh* item on it (see Gemara below, 142a). Accordingly, since the Mishnah does not require the person to shake the money out of the case, we can only conclude that the laws of *muktzeh* are suspended for the sake of saving a Torah scroll. Hence, the Gemara assumes, even bringing a container containing only money over to the scroll to save it would be permitted.

טז א מיי' פי"ז מהלכות שבת הל' ב סמג עשין א טוש"ע או"ח סימן שכג סעיף ג וסעיף יד:

מי דמי התם נעשה בסיס לדבר המותר הכא נעשה בסיס לדבר האסור אלא הכי קאמרי ליה אם מצילין תיק של ספר עם הספר ואע"פ שיש בתוכו מעות לא נטלטל עור אגב בשר מי דמי התם נעשה בסיס לדבר האסור ולדבר המותר הכא כולו נעשה בסיס לדבר האסור אלא הכי קאמרי ליה אם מביאין תיק שיש בתוכו מעות מעלמא להציל בו ספר תורה לא נטלטל עור אגב בשר והיא גופה מנלן אילימא מדהיכא דאית ביה לא שדי להו איתויי נמי מייתינן מי דמי התם אדהכי והכי נפלה דליקה הכא אדהכי והכי לישדינן אלא אמר מר בר רב אשי לעולם כדאמרינן מעיקרא ודקא קשיא לך (א) הכא טלטול והכא מלאכה כגון דלא קבעי ליה לעור והא (ב) אביי ורבא דאמרי תרווייהו מודה ר"ש בפסיק רישיה ולא ימות דשקיל ליה (ג) בברזי: ולהיכן מצילין אותן וכו': היכי דמי מפולש היכי דמי שאינו מפולש אמר רב חסדא שלש מחיצות ושני לחיין זהו מבוי שאינו מפולש ג' מחיצות ולחי אחד זהו מבוי המפולש ותרווייהו אליבא דרבי אליעזר דתנן (ד) הכשר מבוי ב"ש אומרים לחי וקורה וב"ה (א) אומרים או לחי או קורה ר' אליעזר אומר שני לחיים א"ל רבה ג' מחיצות ולחי אחד מפולש קרית ליה ועוד לרבנן נציל לתוכו אוכלין ומשקין אלא אמר רבה שתי מחיצות ושני לחיין זהו מבוי שאינו מפולש שתי מחיצות ולחי אחד זהו מבוי המפולש ותרווייהו אליבא דרבי יהודה (ה) דתניא יתר על כן אמר ר' יהודה מי שיש לו שני בתים בשני צדי ר"ה עושה לחי מיכן ולחי מיכן או קורה מיכן וקורה מיכן ונושא ונותן באמצע אמרו לו אין מערבין רה"ר בכך א"ל אביי לדידך נמי לרבנן נציל לתוכו אוכלין ומשקין אלא

רש"י

(א) מי דמי. תיק הספר נעשה בסיס לדבר המותר לטלטלו בלא שום דליקה דספר בר טלטול הוא ולדבר האסור כגון מעות: הכא. האי עור נעשה בסיס לדבר שכולו אסור בטלטול שהבשר אסור לטלטלו דלא חזי לאכילה עד אורתא דפסח שאינו נאכל אלא בלילה ולגו ורבי ישמעאל לית ליה כבוד שמים בנאכל להדיוט ואפילו הוי עור תורת כלי עליו מיתסר משום דהוי בסיס לאיסור וכ"ש דהוא גופיה לאו בר טלטול הוא: אם מביאין תיק שבתוכו מעות. דהוי בסיס לדבר שכולו אסור ומניח בו ספר להצילו ואינו צריך להשליך המעות כדמפרש והזיל לא נטלטל עור אגב בשר: אי נימא דמדהיכא דאית ביה. מעות עם הספר לא שדי להו לא מצריך ליה תנא דידן למשדינהו כדקתני ואע"פ שיש בתוכו מעות: איתויי נמי מייתינן. מעלמא מאחת זוית הבית תיק ובתוכו מעות להניח בתוכו ספר ולהציל: מי דמי. היכא דהספר מונח עם המעות להיכא דהוא בא עכשיו להביאו עם המעות ולתת בו ספר: התם. דספר ומעות בתוכו להכי לא מצרכינן ליה למישדינהו: דילמא אדהכי והכי נפלה דליקה. על הספר: הכא. אדמייתי ליה נישדינהו דרך ביאתו: כדאמרינן מעיקרא. דלא פליגי אלא בהפשטה ומייתי רבנן ראיה מתיק הספר דמתני' דמצילין מעות אגב ספר לצרכי הדיוט אגב לצרכי גבוה הואיל וליכא שהות למשדינהו וה"נ אגב לצרכי גבוה דכל פעל ה' למענהו יפשיט: ודקשיא לך כו' דלא בעי ליה לעור. אינו צריך לו לעור ואינו מתכוין להפשטו משום עור ולא דמי להפשט אילים ותחשים למשכן: והא ר"ש מודה בפסיק רישיה ולא ימות. והכא אע"ג דלא מיכוין מיפשיט הוא: דשקיל ליה בברזי. בחתיכות דקות מפשיט והולך דאין דרך הפשטה בכך ולאו מלאכה הוא אלא שבות: שני לחיים. לפתח שאין לו מחילה: זהו מבוי שאינו מפולש. כלומר מבוי הניתר בכל הלכותיו בין בעירוב בין בשאר דברים וכל היתר שאר מבואות יש לו כגון שיתופי מבואות: ותרווייהו. רבנן ובן בתירה סבירא להו כר"א דאמר אין מבוי ואפילו סתום ניתר בלחי אחד ואשמעינן בן בתירה דהצלת כתבי הקדש לא בעינן לחיים כרבי אליעזר: מפולש קרית ליה. נהי נמי דבעי ר' אליעזר לחיים מיהו מפולש לא מיקרי: ועוד לרבנן. דאמרי לשאינו מפולש וקאמרת דהיינו מבוי הניתר בכל לתוכו נציל אף אוכלין ומשקין. כמו לחצר המעורבת ואמאי פלגינהו מהדדי דגבי ספר קתני למבוי שאינו מפולש וגבי אוכלין קתני להיכן מצילין אותן לחצר המעורבת דמשמע אבל למבוי לא: שתי מחיצות. מכאן ומכאן: שני לחיין. לחי לכל פתח ופתח: אליבא דרבי יהודה. דאמר בשתי מחילות סגי ושני לחיים ואתא בן בתירה למימר דלגבי ספר מודה ר' יהודה דסגי בחד דכג' מחילות הוו: לדידך נמי. איכא למיפרך כאתקפתא דלעיל: לרבנן. כיון דאמרת דתרווייהו כר' יהודה לרבנן דאמרי לשאינו מפולש ומפרשי ליה לשאינו חסר כלום כר' יהודה דלא בעי אלא שתי מחילות ושני לחיים אי הכי לרבנן יציל לתוכו אוכלין ומשקין כמו לחצר המעורבת:

אלא

תוספות

הכא נעשה בסיס לדבר האסור. פי' בקונטרס שהבשר אסור לטלטל שהרי אינו ראוי לאכילה עד הלילה ואינו נראה דא"כ היכי קאמר לא נטלטל עור אגב בשר כיון דבשר אסור לטלטל ונראה דלכ"ע בשר מותר לטלטל אע"ג דמאן דשרי (ו) בשר תפל בעלמא לטלטל היינו משום דחזי לכלבים והכא לא חזי לכלבים מ"מ משום בזיון קדשי שמים שרי לכ"ע ובטלטול עור אגב בשר הוא דפליגי והא דקאמר הכא דהוי בסיס לדבר האסור היינו קודם שנשחטה היה בסיס לדבר האסור שכל הבהמה מוקצה היא מטלטול:

מי דמי התם אדהכי והכי נפלה דליקה. וא"ת אמאי לא קאמר התם נעשה בסיס לדבר המותר ולדבר האסור הכא נעשה בסיס לדבר האסור גרידא וי"ל דלאו נראה לו לחלק כיון דהשתא סבור שיכול לנער מעות מן הכיס ואפילו הכי א"צ לנער ושרי כל שהוא עושה להצלת ס"ת ה"ה דשרי להביא תיק שיש בו מעות גרידא:

אדהכי והכי לשדינהו. משמע דאי לא מצי למשדי המעות הוה מצי להביא התיק עם המעות להביא בו ס"ת וא"כ כשאינו מופשט אלא עד החזה מותר לכ"ע לטלטל הואיל ולא מצי שדי ליה ולא פליגי אלא כשהופשט לגמרי כדפי' לעיל:

דשקיל ליה בברזי. פירש בקונט' דליכא שבות בכה"ג וקשה דהוה ליה למיתני בפסחים בפרק אלו דברים (דף סה:) הפשט דלחי שבת בהדי הנהו שבות דקתני התם דדחו שבת ונראה לר"י דליכא אפילו שבות דאינו מפשיט כשיעור חשיבות עור יחד ולא דמי למפים מורסא דהתם פתח קעביד אך שא"צ לו וכן צד מזיקין מ"מ צד הוא אבל הכא דלא קא עביד הפשט אפי' שבות ליכא:

(ז) דשקיל ליה בברזי. וא"ת דתני' בסוף תמיד נשחט (פסחים סה:) תנא חשכה(ח) כל אחד ואחד נוטל פסחו בעורו אם כן לאו בברזי היה מופשט ומשמע דבשבת איירי דאמתני' דהתם קאי דקתני ארבעה עשר שחל בשבת ואיכא למימר דלא קאי אשבת א"נ נוטלו בעורו שנפשט עד החזה ועוד אומר ר"י דאיכא למימר דרבנן לדברי רבי ישמעאל קאמרי לדידן מותר להפשיט לגמרי לדידך אודי לן מיהא דמותר להפשיט בברזי וא"ת לפי זה ה"ל למיחשב התם דחיית הפשט וי"ל דפלוגתא לא קא מיירי דלר' ישמעאל לא דחי ליה הפשט כלל ואע"ג דחשיב הרכבתו והבאתו מחוץ לתחום דפליגי בה ר"ע ור' אליעזר לא חשיב לה פלוגתא דר"א דשמותי הוא ועוד דמההיא פלוגתא ילפינן דהזאה אינה דוחה להכי קתני לה:

שלש מחיצות ושני לחיים כו'. השתא האי דמפרש לה הכי ומוקי תרווייהו אליבא דר"א ולא בעי למימר שלש מחילות ולחי א' אינו מפולש ובלא לחי זהו מפולש והוה מפרש אליבא דהלכתא היינו משום דסבר דבלא לחי כלל לא הוה שרי בן בתירה דהוי כרמלית ולא דמי לחצר שאינה מעורבת דסיפא:

ועוד לרבנן נציל לתוכו אוכלין ומשקין. (ט) ואמאי נקט חצר מעורבת) ולאדמפלגי בין חצר מעורבת למבוי הוה לן לפלוגי בין מבוי משותף למבוי שאינו משותף דבמשותף יהא מותר להציל לתוכו אוכלין ומשקין ואמאי נקט חצר מעורבת:

אלא אמר רבה כו'. תימה מה תירץ רבה מקושיא דנציל לתוכו אוכלין ומשקין ואומר ר"י דרבה רוצה לומר דרבנן סברי כרבי יהודה דוקא לצורך הצלת כתבי הקדש ולא לצורך אחר ואביי פריך משום דאינו נראה לו סברא שיסברו כר' יהודה לחצאין ומשני אביי ג' מחילות כו' ולאביי לא סברי רבנן כר"א לחצאין דר"א להצלת כתבי הקדש סגי בלחי אחד כדמסיים ואזיל ואפילו לרבי אליעזר כו':

הא

רבינו חננאל

דאינון סברי מטלטלין העור ע"ג בשר מקום שחיטה כל חד לדוכתיה והוא אסר. ואהדרו ליה אם מטלטלין להציל תיק של ספר אנו לא נטלטל עור אגב בשר ואהדר להו מי דמי תיק נעשה בסיס לס"ת שמותר לטלטלו. עור נעשה בסיס לבשר אסור לטלטלו. קאמרו ליה כו' ודחה ר' ישמעאל מי דמי. התם תיק נעשה בסיס לס"ת שהוא מותר. ולמעות שהן אסורין הכא בבשר כולן אסור. והדר רב אשי ואמר הכי קאמרו ליה אם מביאין מעלמא תיק שיש בו מעות להציל בו ס"ת אנו לא נטלטל עור אגב בשר. והא מנ"ל אי נימא דדייקית מינה מה התיק שיש בו מעות וס"ת אינך מסיר המעות מתוך התיק ומציל הס"ת לבדו אלא אתה מציל אפי' המעות כך אם יש מעות בתיק והצרכת להביאו להציל ס"ת אינך מסיר המעות מתוכו דילמא שני התם במקום שכבר הגיעה הדליקה עד הספר ואם יתעסק בהשלכת המעות תאכלם הלהבה. אבל במקום שהדליקה לא הגיעה [עדיין] והולכין להביא תיק להציל הספר. אם יש בתיק מעות אסור לטלטלו עד שישליכם. ושני רב אשי לעולם כדאמרינן מעיקרא. ודקא אמרת התם בעור טלטול הכא בעור מלאכה כגון דמתכוין לגלות הבשר ואין כוונתו לעור. ואקשינן והא אביי ורבא דאמרי תרווייהו מודה ר"ש דסבר דבר שאינו מתכוין שרי בפסיק רישיה ולא ימות כגון זה אמרינן באומר המפשיט דאינו מתכוין לעור דומה לאומר הנני מחתך ראש זה העוף ואין כוונתי לשוחטו כגון זה אפי' ר' שמעון שוחט הוא. ואסקי' דשקיל ליה בברזי. פי' ברזי נקבים והכי קאמר מאן דמבעי ליה כשהוא מפשיטו מוכחא מילתא דלא בעי ליה לעור ולא הוי כפסיק רישיה ולא ימות. ולהיכן מצילין אותו למבוי שאינו מפולש וכו' ולית הלכתא כבן בתירא דאמר אפילו למבוי המפולש והיכי דמי מבוי שאינו מפולש. שמצילין בו כתבי הקדש:

אסקה

מסורת הש"ס

א) [נ"ל התם], ב) לעיל עה. קג. קיח: לקמן קכ: קמג. סוכה לג: [בילה לו.] כתובות ו. בכורות כה., ג) [ערוך פי' ברזא נקבים והכי קאמר מאן דבעי לי' לעור כשהוא מפשיטו מוכחא מילתא דלא בעי לעור ואין לו הנאה ממנו ולא דמי לפסיק רישא עכ"ל ולפי זה יתיישב קושית התוס' ד"ה דשקיל הא דתנא בתמיד נשחט תנא חשכה וכו'], ד) עירובין יא., ה) לעיל ו. עירובין ו: יב. כב. נג: כה., ו) לקמן קכח., ז) רש"ל מ"ז, ח) [תנא חשכה ליתא שם ע"ש], ט) רש"ל מ"ז.

הגהות הב"ח

(א) רש"י ד"ה (מי דמי) וכו' כגון מעות הכא האי וכו' אסור בטלטול. תא"מ ונ"ב ס"א ועיקר מי דמי תיק הספר נעשה בסיס לדבר המותר לטלטלו בלא שום דליקה דספר בר טלטול הוא הכא האי עור נעשה בסיס לדבר האסור בטלטול כו':

ליקוטי רש"י

מודה ר"ש. דאמר במסכת שבת (מא:) דבר שאין מתכוין מותר [בכורות כה.]. בפסיק רישיה ולא ימות. כאומר אחתוך ראש בהמה זו בשבת ואיני רוצה שתמות [illegible] [סוכה לג:]. הכשר מבוי. [illegible] [עירובין ב.] [illegible]

ומלירות פתוחות לו ויולאות ובאות לרשות הרבים הרי הוא רשות היחיד לבני חלירות ואסרו חכמים להוליא מרשותו לרשות חבירו בלא עירוב שהחלירות כל אחת רשות לעלמה והמבוי רשות לכולן והלריכו בו שיתוף להשתתף כל החלירות בפת או ביין ולהניח השיתוף באחת מן החלירות ולפי שאין לו מחילה רביעית וקרוב הוא להיות דומה לרשות הרבים הלריכו היכר בראשו הפתוח לרשות הרבים או לחי זקוף או קורה מוטלת לרוחב [סוכה ג:]. לחי. [illegible] אחד בראשו [עירובין שם:]. יתר על כן. רישא דברייתא אחד חלון שבין שני בתים ואחד חלון שבין שתי חלירות [illegible] רשות הרבים גמורה ואין שם תקרה למימר יורד וסותם שרי בשתי מחילות של שני לידי רשות הרבים [שם [illegible] [illegible] בשני צדי רה"ר. זו כנגד זו [לעיל ו.]. [illegible] לחי מכאן ולחי מכאן. [illegible] [עירובין שם]. [illegible]

The Gemara accepts this argument and reverts to its original suggestion:

אֶלָּא אָמַר מַר בַּר רַב אַשִׁי – **Rather said Mar bar Rav Ashi:** לְעוֹלָם כִּדְאָמְרִינַן מֵעִיקָּרָא – **After all, it is as we said originally,** that R' Yishmael the son of R' Yochanan ben Berokah and the Rabbis disagree only in regard to one point, whether it is permissible to flay the *pesach* in its entirety. The Rabbis brought proof that this is permissible from the fact that it is permitted to save the money along with the scroll, which benefits the owner at the same time as fulfilling a Divine need. Similarly, we should be permitted to complete the flaying of the *pesach* beyond the breast for the honor of God, despite the fact that there will be a peripheral benefit to the owner. וּדְקָא קַשְׁיָא לָךְ הָכָא טִלְטוּל וְהָכָא מְלָאכָה – **And as for your difficulty** that **here,** in regard to the scroll container, it is a question of **moving** *muktzeh,* which is forbidden only Rabbinically, **whereas here,** in regard to the *pesach* offering, it is a question of performing **a** Biblical ***melachah,*** the answer is כְּגוֹן דְּלָא קָבָעֵי לֵיהּ לְעוֹר – that we are discussing **a case in which [the person] does not need the hide.**[7]

The Gemara asks:

וְהָא אַבָּיֵי וְרָבָא דְּאָמְרֵי תַּרְוַיְיהוּ – **But Abaye and Rava have both said:** מוֹדֶה רַבִּי שִׁמְעוֹן בִּפְסִיק רֵישֵׁיהּ וְלֹא יָמוּת – **R' Shimon concedes** that one is liable **in** the case of **an inevitable consequence.**[8] – ? –

The Gemara answers:

דְּשָׁקִיל לֵיהּ בִּבְרָזֵי – We are dealing with a case **where he removes [the hide] in thin strips.**[9]

The next segment of the Mishnah discusses the place to which the scrolls may be carried when rescuing them:[10]

וּלְהֵיכָן מַצִּילִין אוֹתָן וכו׳ – AND TO WHERE MAY WE TAKE THEM TO SAVE THEM **etc.?** To an unopen *mavoi.* Ben Beseira says: Even to an open one.

The Gemara asks:

הֵיכִי דָּמֵי מְפוּלָּשׁ הֵיכִי דָּמֵי שֶׁאֵינוֹ מְפוּלָּשׁ – **What is** the meaning of the term **"open"** in our Mishnah and **what is** the meaning of the term **"unopen"?**[11]

The Gemara answers:

אָמַר רַב חִסְדָּא – **Rav Chisda said:** שָׁלֹשׁ מְחִיצוֹת וּשְׁנֵי לְחָיַיִן וְזֶהוּ מָבוֹי שֶׁאֵינוֹ מְפוּלָּשׁ – If the *mavoi* possesses **three walls and two** ***lechis*** (posts), one on each side of the entrance, **it is** considered **an unopen** ***mavoi;*** שָׁלֹשׁ מְחִיצוֹת וְלֶחִי אֶחָד וְזֶהוּ מָבוֹי הַמְפוּלָּשׁ – if it possesses **three walls and one** ***lechi,*** i.e. a *lechi* on only one side of the entrance, **it is** considered **an open** ***mavoi.***[12]

NOTES

7. His sole intent in flaying the animal is to uncover the sacrificial parts, not to gain the hide. Since the *melachah* of skinning is violated only when the goal is to obtain the hide, [the act is classified as a דָּבָר שֶׁאֵינוֹ מִתְכַּוֵּן, *unintentional act,* i.e. a forbidden labor performed unintentionally while one is engaged in a permitted activity. Such an act is not Biblically prohibited] (see *Rashi*; see also below, note 9).

8. [Literally: its head is cut off and it should not die?] As we have encountered numerous times in this tractate, a Tannaic dispute exists as to the status of an unintentional act; that is, may one perform a particular permitted act when he knows that another, forbidden act may unintentionally result? R' Yehudah forbids it while R' Shimon holds that it is permitted. Nevertheless, R' Shimon concedes that liability does occur when the forbidden labor is an *inevitable* consequence of the permitted action. Hence, if someone cuts off the head of a living creature on the Sabbath, he has violated the prohibition against taking a life on the Sabbath – even if he declares that he does not intend the creature to die. Since its death is inevitable, he is considered to have taken the creature's life intentionally, and he has transgressed even according to R' Shimon (*Rashi* to *Succah* 33b; *Rambam, Hil. Shabbos* 1:6). Here, too, when the hide is flayed from the *pesach* offering to get at the meat, it is inevitable that the hide will be obtained, and the person should be considered to have violated the Biblical prohibition of skinning on the Sabbath.

9. Since this is not the normal way of stripping hide, no Biblical *melachah* is transgressed thereby, and the act is only Rabbinically prohibited (*Rashi*).

The commentators are troubled by the give-and-take of the foregoing Gemara. Why, they ask, does the Gemara regard this case as an example of an unintentional act, to which the principle of פְּסִיק רֵישֵׁיהּ, *the inevitable consequence,* applies? Typically, an unintentional act is one in which one act is performed and another, intrinsically unrelated, result emerges. To use the Talmud's example, if one drags a chair across a lawn in such a manner that he may make a furrow in the ground (a violation of the *melachah* of חוֹרֵשׁ, *plowing*), the making of the furrow is an unintentional act. Dragging a bench and making a furrow are not in and of themselves connected; it just happens that in this case one results from the other. Accordingly, if the bench is so heavy that a furrow will inevitably be made, it is as if the person intended to make the furrow, and he is liable.

In the present case, however, flaying the hide to uncover the meat and flaying the hide to obtain the hide are one and the same act. There is no question that the person *intends* to flay the animal; the issue is only what his *purpose* in doing so is: Does he intend only to get at the meat below, or does he, as a secondary intent, also wish to obtain the hide? This touches on the issue of מְלָאכָה שֶׁאֵינָהּ צְרִיכָה לְגוּפָהּ, *a labor not needed for its defined purpose,* which is a separate question, and has nothing to do with the principle of פְּסִיק רֵישֵׁיהּ (*R' Akiva Eiger*).

For several different approaches to this problem, see *Ritva MHK* ed. and *Meiri.* See also *Chasam Sofer* to *Kesubos* 6a ד״ה ומה.

10. To understand the coming Gemara, certain information basic to Tractate *Eruvin* is necessary.

The layout of streets and houses in Mishnaic times was such that several houses would open into a *chatzeir,* courtyard, and several courtyards would, in turn, lead into a *mavoi,* alleyway, through which people would pass to get to the street. Typically, such an alley was a dead-end alley, closed on three sides by walls and open only on the fourth side where it met the street.

On a Biblical level, one is permitted to carry in such a *mavoi.* The Sages, however, were apprehensive that people might confuse the street with a *mavoi* and extend the practice of carrying there to the street. Consequently, they decreed that in order to carry in a *mavoi* the open side must be adjusted.

To adjust an alley it is not necessary to erect a full partition. Rather, only a relatively modest adjustment is required. The Gemara will soon cite three different opinions as to exactly what form this adjustment must take.

In addition to adjusting the open side, another problem must be dealt with before carrying freely in a *chatzeir* or *mavoi* is permitted. Since these areas are the joint property of all the houses or courtyards opening to them, they resemble *reshus harabims.* To permit carrying from the obvious *reshus hayachids* (e.g. the houses) into them, therefore, the Rabbis decreed that the houses or courtyards involved must all incorporate into one unit. This is done by collecting bread (or, in the case of a *mavoi,* any food) from each of the residents and placing it in one of the houses (or, in the case of a *mavoi,* even in one of the courtyards). This symbolizes that all the residents legally reside in one place. When performed to permit carrying into a courtyard, this procedure is known as *eruv chatzeiros.* In the case of an alleyway, it is known as *shituf mevo'os.*

The Gemara now proceeds to analyze our Mishnah.

11. Ordinarily, in Tractate *Eruvin* and elsewhere, the term "unopen *mavoi*" (or "closed *mavoi*") refers to an alley enclosed on three sides and open to the public domain only on its fourth side, while the term "open *mavoi*" refers to an alley enclosed on only two sides and open on the other two. The Gemara assumes, however, that these definitions do not hold true in our Mishnah, for no one would allow rescuing things into an alley that is open on two sides. Such an alley too closely resembles, and therefore can be confused with, a true *reshus harabim.* These terms must therefore have different definitions here. What, the Gemara asks, are these definitions? (*R' Moshe Kazis;* see also *Rambam, Commentary to Mishnah*).

12. Rav Chisda asserts that both *mavois* referred to by our Mishnah are walled on three sides. By the term "unopen *mavoi*" the Mishnah refers to a *mavoi* whose fourth side possesses the entire required adjustment, i.e. two *lechis* (posts), one on either side of the entrance, while by the term "open *mavoi*" the Mishnah means a *mavoi* possessing only half the necessary adjustment, i.e. one *lechi* at one of the entrances.

מי דמי התם נעשה בסיס לדבר המותר הכא נעשה בסיס לדבר האסור אלא הכי קאמרי ליה אם מצילין תיק של ספר עם הספר ואע"פ שיש בתוכו מעות לא נטלטל עור אגב בשר מי דמי התם נעשה בסיס לדבר האסור ולדבר המותר הכא כולו נעשה בסיס לדבר האסור אלא הכי קאמרי ליה אם מביאין תיק שיש בתוכו מעות מעלמא להציל בו ספר תורה לא נטלטל עור אגב בשר והיא גופה מנלן אילימא מדהיכא דאית ביה לא שדי להו איתויי נמי מייתינן מי דמי התם אדהכי והכי נפלה דליקה הכא אדהכי והכי לישדינהו אלא אמר מר בר רב אשי לעולם כדאמרינן מעיקרא ודקא קשיא לך [א] הכא טלטול והכא מלאכה כגון דלא קבעי ליה לעור והא [ב] אביי ורבא דאמרי תרוייהו מודה ר"ש בפסיק רישיה ולא ימות דשקיל ליה [ג] בברזי: ולהיכן מצילין אותן וכו': היכי דמי מפולש היכי דמי שאינו מפולש אמר רב חסדא שלש מחיצות ושני לחיין זהו מבוי שאינו מפולש ג' מחיצות ולחי אחד זהו מבוי המפולש ותרוייהו אליבא דרבי אליעזר דתנן [ד] הכשר מבוי ב"ש אומרים לחי וקורה וב"ה [א] אומרים או לחי או קורה ר' אליעזר אומר שני לחיים א"ל רבה ג' מחיצות ולחי אחד מפולש קרית ליה ועוד לרבנן נציל לתוכו אוכלין ומשקין אלא אמר רבה שתי מחיצות ושני לחיין זהו מבוי שאינו מפולש שתי מחיצות ולחי אחד זהו מבוי המפולש ותרוייהו אליבא דרבי יהודה [ה] דתניא יתר על כן אמר ר' יהודה מי שיש לו שני בתים בשני צדי ר"ה עושה לחי מיכן ולחי מיכן או קורה מיכן וקורה מיכן ונושא ונותן באמצע אמרו לו אין מערבין רה"ר בכך א"ל אביי לדידך נמי לרבנן נציל לתוכו אוכלין ומשקין אלא

רש"י

(א) מי דמי. תיק הספר נעשה בסיס לדבר המותר לטלטלו בלא שום דליקה דספר בר טלטול הוא ולדבר האסור כגון מעות: הכא. האי עור נעשה בסיס לדבר שכולו אסור בטילטול שהבשר אסור לטלטלו דלא חזי לאכילה עד אורתא דפסח אינו נאכל אלא בלילה ולאו ורבי ישמעאל לית ליה כבוד שמים בנצלא להדיוט ואפילו הוי עור תורת כלי עליו מיתסר משום דהוי בסיס לאיסור וכ"ש דהוא גופיה לאו בר טלטול הוא: אם מביאין תיק שבתוכו מעות. דהוי בסיס לדבר שכולו אסור ומניח בו ספר להצילו ואינו צריך להשליך המעות כדמפרש ואזיל לא נטלטל עור אגב הבשר: אי נימא דמדהיכא דאית ביה. מעות עם הספר לא שדי להו לא מצריך ליה תנא דידן למשדינהו כדקתני ואע"פ שיש בתוכו מעות: איתויי נמי מייתינן. מעלמא מאחת זווית הבית תיק ובתוכו מעות להניח בתוכו ספר ולהציל: מי דמי. היכא דהספר מונח עם המעות להציל דהוא לא עכשיו להביאו עם המעות ולתת בו ספר: התם. דספר ומעות בתוכו להכי לא מצרכינן ליה למשדינהו: דילמא אדהכי והכי נפלה דליקה. על הספר: הכא. אדמייתי ליה נישדינהו דרך ביאתו: כדאמרינן מעיקרא. דלא פליגי אלא בהפשטה ומייתי רבנן ראיה מתיק הספר דמתני' דמצילין מעות אגב ספר לרבי הדיוט אגב לרבי גבוה הואיל וליכא שהות למשדינהו וה"נ אגב לרבי גבוה דכל פעל ה' למענהו יפשטו: ודקשיא לך כו' דלא בעי ליה לעור. אינו צריך לו לעור ואינו מתכוין להפשט משום עור ולא דמי להפשט אילים ותחשים למשכן: והא ר"ש מודה בפסיק רישיה ולא ימות. והכא אע"ג דלא מיכוין מיפשיט הוא: דשקיל ליה בברזי. בחתיכות דקות מפשיט וחותך דאין דרך הפשטה בכך ולאו מלאכה הוא אלא שבות: שני לחיים. לפתח שאין לו מחיצה: זהו מבוי שאינו מפולש. כלומר מבוי הניתר בכל הלכותיו בין בעירוב בין בשאר דברים וכל היתר שאר מבואות יש לו כגון שיתופי מבואות: ותרוייהו. רבנן ובן בתירא סבירא להו כר"א דאמר אין מבוי ואפילו סתום ניתר בלחי א' ואשמעינן בן בתירא דהצלת כתבי הקדש לא בעינן לחיים כרבי אליעזר: מפולש קרית ליה. נהי נמי דבעי ר' אליעזר לחיים מיהו מפולש לא מיקרי: ועוד לרבנן. דאמרי לשאינו מפולש וקאמרת דהיינו מבוי הניתר בכל הלכותיו: נציל לתוכן אף אוכלין ומשקין. כמו לחצר המעורבת ואמאי פלגינהו מהדדי דגבי ספר קתני למבוי שאינו מפולש וגבי אוכלין קתני להיכן מצילין אותן לחצר המעורבת דמשמע אבל למבוי לא: שתי מחיצות. מכאן ומכאן: שני לחיין. לחי לכל פתח ופתח: אליבא דרבי יהודה. דאמר בשתי מחיצות סגי ושני לחיים ואתא בן בתירא למימר דלגבי ספר מודה ר' יהודה דסגי בחד דג' מחיצות הוו: לדידך נמי. איכא למיפרך כאתקפתא דלעיל: לרבנן. כיון דאמרת דתרוייהו כר' יהודה לרבנן דאמרי לשאינו מפולש ומפרשי ליה לשאינו חסר כלום כר' יהודה דלא בעי אלא שתי מחיצות ושני לחיים אי הכי לרבנן יציל לתוכו אוכלין ומשקין כמו לחצר המעורבת: אלא

תוספות

הכא נעשה בסיס לדבר האסור. פי' בקונטרס שהבשר אסור לטלטל שהרי אינו ראוי לאכילה עד הלילה ואינו נראה דא"כ היכי קאמר לא נטלטל עור אגב בשר כיון דבשר אסור לטלטל ונראה דלכ"ע בשר מותר לטלטל אע"ג דמאן דשרי [י] בשר תפל בעלמא לטלטל היינו משום דחזי לכלבים והכא לא חזי לכלבים מ"מ משום בזיון קדשי שמים שרי לכ"ע וטלטול עור אגב בשר הוא דפליגי והא דקאמר הכא דהוי בסיס לדבר האסור היינו קודם שנשחטה היה בסיס לדבר האסור שכל הבהמה מוקצה היא מטלטול:

מי דמי התם אדהכי והכי נפלה דליקה. וא"ת אמאי לא קאמר התם נעשה בסיס לדבר המותר ולדבר האסור הכא נעשה בסיס לדבר האסור גרידא וי"ל דאין נראה לו לחלק כיון דהשתא סבור שיכול לנער מעות מן הכיס ואפילו הכי א"צ לנער ושרי כל שהוא עושה להצלת ס"ת ה"ה דשרי להביא תיק שיש בו מעות גרידא:

אדהכי והכי לשדינהו. משמע דאי לא מצי למשדי המעות הוה מצי להביא התיק עם המעות להביא בו ס"ת וא"כ כשאינו מופשט אלא עד החזה מותר לכ"ע לטלטל הואיל ולא מצי שדי ליה ולא פליגי אלא כשהופשט לגמרי כדפי' לעיל:

דשקיל ליה בברזי. פירש בקונט' דליכא שבות בכה"ג וקשה דהוה ליה למיתני בפסחים בפרק אלו דברים (דף סה:) הפשט דדחי שבת בהדי הנהו שבות דקתני התם דדחו שבת ונראה לר"י דליכא אפילו שבות דאינו מפשיט כשיעור חשיבות עור יחד ולא דמי למפיס מורסא דהתם פתח קעביד אך שא"צ לו וכן צד מזיקין מ"מ צד הוא אבל הכא דלא קא עביד הפשט אפי' שבות ליכא:

(ז) דשקיל ליה בברזי). וא"ת דתני' בסוף תמיד נשחט (פסחים סה:) תנא חשכה[ח] כל אחד ואחד נוטל פסחו בעורו אם כן לאו בברזי היה מופשט ומשמע דבשבת איירי דאמתני' דהתם קאי דקתני ארבעה עשר שחל בשבת ואיכא למימר דלא קאי אשבת א"נ נוטלו בעורו שנפשט עד החזה ועוד אומר ר"י דאיכא למימר דרבנן לדברי רבי ישמעאל קאמרי לדידן מותר להפשיט לגמרי לדידך אודי לן מיהא דמותר להפשיט בברזי וא"ת לפי זה ה"ל למיחשב התם דחיית הפשט וי"ל דפלוגתא לא קא מיירי דלר' ישמעאל לא דחי ליה הפשט כלל ואע"ג דחשיב הרכבתו והבאתו מחוץ לתחום דפליגי בה ר"ע ור' אליעזר לא חשיב לה פלוגתא דר"א דשמותי הוא ועוד דמההיא פלוגתא ילפינן דהזאה אינה דוחה להכי קתני לה:

שלש מחיצות ושני לחיים כו'. השתא האי דמפרש לה הכי ומוקי תרוייהו אליבא דר"א ולא בעי למימר שלש מחיצות ולחי א' אינו מפולש ובלא לחי זהו מפולש והוה מפרש אליבא דהלכתא היינו משום דסבר דבלא לחי כלל לא הוה שרי בן בתירא דהוי כרמלית ולא דמי לחצר שאינה מעורבת דסיפא:

ועוד לרבנן נציל לתוכו אוכלין ומשקין. (ט) ואמאי נקט חצר מעורבת) ולאדמפלגי בין חצר מעורבת למבוי הוה לן לפלוגי בין מבוי משותף למבוי שאינו משותף דבמשותף יהא מותר להציל לתוכו אוכלין ומשקין ואמאי נקט חצר מעורבת:

אלא אמר רבה כו'. תימה מה תירץ רבה מקושיא דנציל לתוכו אוכלין ומשקין ואומר ר"י דרבה רוצה לומר דרבנן סברי כרבי יהודה דוקא לצורך הצלת כתבי הקדש ולא לצורך אחר ואביי פריך משום דאינו נראה לו סברא שיסברו כר' יהודה לחצאין ומשני אביי ג' מחיצות כו' ולאביי לא סברי רבנן כר"א לחצאין דר"א להצלת כתבי הקדש סגי בלחי אחד כדמסיים ואזיל ואפילו לרבי אליעזר כו': הא

עין משפט נר מצוה

טז א מיי' פי"ז מהלכות שבת הל' ב סמג עשין א טוש"ע או"ח סימן שסג סעיף ג וסעיף יד:

רבינו חננאל

דאינון סברי מטלטלין העור ע"ג בשר מקום שחיטה כל חד לדוכתיה והוא אסר. ואהדרו ליה אם מטלטלין להציל תיק של ספר אנו לא נטלטל עור אגב בשר ואהדר להו מי דמי תיק נעשה בסיס לס"ת שמותר לטלטלו. עור נעשה בסיס לבשר אסור לטלטלו. אלא הכי קאמרו ליה כו' ודחה ר' ישמעאל מי דמי. התם תיק נעשה בסיס לס"ת שהוא מותר. ולמעות שהן אסורין הכא בבשר כולן אסור. והדר רב אשי ואמר הכי אהדרו ליה אם מביאין מעלמא תיק שיש בו מעות להציל לו ס"ת אנו לא נטלטל עור אגב בשר. והא מנ"ל אי נימא דדייקית מינה מה התיק שיש בו מעות וס"ת אינך מסיר המעות מתוך התיק ומציל הס"ת לבדו אלא אתה מציל אפי' המעות כך אם יש מעות בתיק והצרכת להביאו להציל ס"ת אינך מסיר המעות מתוכו דילמא שני התם במקום שכבר הגיעה הדליקה עד הספר ואם יתעסק בהשלכת המעות תאכלם הלהבה. אבל במקום דהדליקה לא הגיעה [עדיין] והולכין להביא תיק להציל הספר. אם יש בתיק מעות אסור לטלטלן עד שישליכם. ושני רב אשי לעולם כדאמרינן מעיקרא. ודקא אמרת התם בתיק טלטול הכא בעור מלאכה כגון דמתכוין לגלות הבשר ואין כוונתו לעור. ואקשינן והא אביי ורבא דאמרי תרוייהו מודה ר"ש דסבר דבר שאינו מתכוין שרי בפסיק רישיה ולא ימות כגון זה אמרינן באומר המפשיט דאינו מתכוין לעור דומה לאומר הנני מחתך ראש זה העוף ואין כוונתי לשוחטו כגון זה אפי' לר' שמעון שוחט הוא. ואסקי' דשקיל ליה בברזי. פי' ברזי נקבים והכי קאמר מאן דמבזע ליה כשהוא מפשיטו מוכחא מילתא דלא בעי ליה לעור ולא דמי לפסיק רישיה ולא ימות. ולהיכן מצילין אותו למבוי שאינו מפולש וכן הלכה. ולית הלכתא כבן בתירא דאמר אפילו למבוי המפולש והיכי דמי מבוי שאינו מפולש. שמצילין בו כתבי הקדש:

אסקה

מסורת הש"ס

א) [נ"ל התם], ב) לעיל עה: קג. קיא: לקמן קכ: קלג. קמג. סוכה לג: [בילה לו.] כתובות ו. בכורות כה., ג) [ערוך פי' ברזא נקבים והכי קאמר מאן דבזע לי' לעור כשהוא מפשיטו מוכחא מילתא דלא בעי לעור ואין לו הנאה ממנו ולא דמי לפסיק רישא עכ"ל ולפי פי' זה יתיישב קושית התוס' ד"ה דשקיל הא דתניא בתמיד נשחט תנא חשכה וכו'], ד) עירובין יא:, ה) לעיל ו. עירובין ו. יב: כב. נט: לה., ו) לקמן קכח., ז) רש"ל מ"ז, ח) [מלת חשכה ליתא שם ע"ש], ט) רש"ל מ"ז.

הגהות הב"ח

(א) רש"י ד"ה (מי דמי וכו' כגון מעות הכא האי וכו' אסור בטלטול) תא"מ ונ"ב ס"א ועיקר מי דמי תיק הספר נעשה בסיס לדבר המותר לטלטלו בלא שום דליקה דספר בר טלטול הוא הכא האי עור נעשה בסיס לדבר האסור בטלטול כו':

ליקוטי רש"י

מודה ר"ש. דאמר במסכת שבת (מא:) דבר שאין מתכוין מותר [בכורות כה.]. בפסיק רישיה ולא ימות. באומר אחתוך ראש בהמה זו בשבת ואיני רוצה שתמות דכיון דאי אפשר שלא תמות כמתכוין חשיב ליה וכי אמרינן דבר שאין מתכוין מותר כגון היכא דאפשר ליה בלא איסור כגון גורר אדם מטה כסא וספסל ובלבד שלא יתכוין לעשות חריץ ואף על גב דאיכא למיחש דלמא עביד חריץ כיון דלא מתכוין להכי ואפשר לגרירה בלא חריץ כי עביד נמי חריץ דהוי מלאכה גמורה לא מיחייב אבל היכא דודאי עביד מודי [סוכה לג:]. הכשר מבוי. להתיר לטלטל לתוכה דמדאורייתא איתסר הואיל ורשות הרבים בשבת ומה היא רשות הרבים סרטיא ופלטיא גדולה כדאמרן בפרק יציאות השבת (שבת ו:) שדומין לדגלי מדבר דכל מילי דשבת ממשכן גמרינן ועגלות של לוים ברוחב שש עשרה אמה אזלי כדאמרן בהזורק (שבת צט.) הלכך לא הוי רשות הרבים בציר משש עשרה אמה רוחב ומפולש משני ראשין אבל מבוי קצר הוא ואינו רחב שש עשרה אמה ואי נמי רחב הוא אינו מפולש אלא ראשו אחד פתוח לרשות הרבים וראשו אחד סתום דאי הוה מפולש לא הוי משתרי בקורה כדאמרינן בגמרא (עירובין ו:) וכיון דלאו רשות הרבים הוא שרי לטלטולי ביה מן התורה בלי שום תיקון ורבנן גזור עליה משום דאתי לאיחלופי ברשות הרבים ושריוה בתקנתא דלחי או קורה דליהוי היכירא דלא ליתי למישרי רשות הרבים גמורה [עירובין ב.]. מבוי שהוא סתום משלש לצדדין וראשו פתוח לרשות הרבים וחצירות פתוחות לו ויוצאות ובאות לרשות הרבים הרי הוא רשות היחיד לבני חצירות ואסרו חכמים להוציא מרשותו לרשות חבירו בלא עירוב שהחצירות כל אחת רשות לעצמה והמבוי רשות לכולן והצריכו בו שיתוף להשתתף כל החצירות בפת או ביין ולהניח השיתוף באחת מן החצירות ולפי שאין לו מחיצה רביעית וקרוב הוא להיות דומה לרשות הרבים הצריכו היכר בראשו הפתוח לרשות הרבים או לחי זקוף או קורה מכותל לכותל [סוכה ב.]. לחי. קנה או לוח נעוץ אצל כותל האחד בראשו [עירובין שם:]. יתר על כן. רישא דברייתא אחד חלון שבין שני בתים ואחד חלון שבין שתי חצירות וגשרים ונפשות ורשות הרבים המקורה מטלטלין תחתיהן בשבת דברי ר' יהודה יתר על כן אמר ר' יהודה דאפילו רשות הרבים גמורה ואין שם תקרה למימר יורד וסותם שרי בשתי מחיצות של שני לידי רשות הרבים [שם צה.]. לעיל מיניה איירי בבונה עלייה מבית לבית שבשני לידי רשות הרבים וכן גשרים המפולשין לרשות הרבים דשרי ר' יהודה לטלטולי תותיה משום פי תקרה יורד וסותם בפרק כל גגות העיר וקאמר בברייתא יתר על כן אפילו היכא דליכא פי תקרה הואיל ואיכא שתי מחיצות מעלייתא מחיצת הבית מכאן ומחיצת בית השני מכאן סגי בתקנתא פורתא [שם ו.]. בשני צדי רה"ר. זו כנגד זו [לעיל ו.]. לחי מיכן. אצל פאת הבית האחד. ולחי מיכן. אצל פאת הבית השני לאותו בית עצמו והוא סתימה לשני ראשי רשות הרבים ומותר לטלטל מבית לבית [עירובין שם:]. לחי מכאן ולחי מכאן. בשתי פאות של אחד מן הבתים להיכר בעלמא דקסבר רבי יהודה שתי מחיצות הוו רשות היחיד מדאורייתא והא איכא שתי מחיצות מעלייתא מחיצות של שני בתים [לעיל שם:].

וְתַרְוַויְיהוּ אַלִּיבָּא דְּרַבִּי אֱלִיעֶזֶר – **And both of them** [the Rabbis and Ben Beseira] stated their views **in accordance with R' Eliezer.** דִּתְנַן – **For it was taught in a Mishnah:** הֶכְשֵׁר מָבוֹי – How is AN ADJUSTMENT OF A *MAVOI* effected to permit carrying within the *mavoi*? בֵּית שַׁמַּאי אוֹמְרִים לֶחִי וְקוֹרָה – BEIS SHAMMAI SAY: A *LECHI* AND A *KORAH* (crossbeam) must both be erected at the entrance.[13] וּבֵית הִלֵּל אוֹמְרִים אוֹ לֶחִי אוֹ קוֹרָה – BUT BEIS HILLEL SAY: EITHER A *LECHI* OR A *KORAH* is sufficient. רַבִּי אֱלִיעֶזֶר אוֹמֵר שְׁנֵי לְחָיַיִם – R' ELIEZER SAYS: TWO *LECHIS* are required, one on each side of the entrance.[14]

This explanation is questioned:

אָמַר לֵיהּ רַבָּה – **Rabbah said to [Rav Chisda]:** שָׁלֹשׁ מְחִיצוֹת וְלֶחִי אֶחָד מְפוּלָּשׁ קָרֵית לֵיהּ – **Do you call** a *mavoi* with **three walls and one** *lechi* **"open"?**[15] וְעוֹד לְרַבָּנָן נַצִּיל לְתוֹכוֹ אוֹכָלִין וּמַשְׁקִין – **And furthermore, according to the Rabbis** who permit saving scrolls only into a fully adjusted *mavoi*, **let us** be permitted to **save thereto foodstuffs and beverages** as well.[16] – ? –

On the strength of this objection, Rabbah abandons Rav Chisda's explanation of what is called an open (and unopen) *mavoi* and advances his own interpretation:

אֶלָּא אָמַר רַבָּה – **Rather, Rabbah said:** שְׁתֵּי מְחִיצוֹת וּשְׁנֵי לְחָיַיִן וְזֶהוּ מָבוֹי שֶׁאֵינוֹ מְפוּלָּשׁ – If the *mavoi* has **two** facing **walls and two** *lechis*, one at each entrance, **it is** considered **an unopen** *mavoi;* שְׁתֵּי מְחִיצוֹת וְלֶחִי אֶחָד וְזֶהוּ מָבוֹי הַמְפוּלָּשׁ – if it has **two walls and one** *lechi*, i.e. a *lechi* at one of the two entrances, **it is** considered **an open** *mavoi*.[17] וְתַרְוַויְיהוּ אַלִּיבָּא דְּרַבִּי יְהוּדָה – **And both [Tannaim]** stated their views **in accordance with R' Yehudah.** דְּתַנְיָא – **For it was taught in a Baraisa:** יָתֵר עַל כֵּן אָמַר רַבִּי יְהוּדָה מִי שֶׁיֵּשׁ לוֹ שְׁנֵי בָתִּים בִּשְׁנֵי צִדֵּי רְשׁוּת הָרַבִּים – MOREOVER, R' YEHUDAH SAID: If SOMEONE HAS TWO HOUSES ON TWO opposite SIDES OF THE PUBLIC DOMAIN, עוֹשֶׂה לֶחִי מִיכָּן וְלֶחִי מִיכָּן – HE MAY CONSTRUCT A *LECHI* HERE, at one end of the houses, AND A *LECHI* HERE, at the other end of the houses, אוֹ קוֹרָה מִיכָּן וְקוֹרָה מִיכָּן – OR A *KORAH* HERE AND A *KORAH* HERE, וְנוֹשֵׂא וְנוֹתֵן בָּאֶמְצַע – AND HE MAY then PICK things UP AND PLACE them down IN the street BETWEEN.[18] אָמְרוּ לוֹ – [THE SAGES] SAID TO [R' YEHUDAH]: אֵין מְעָרְבִין רְשׁוּת הָרַבִּים בְּכָךְ – ONE CANNOT ADJUST A PUBLIC DOMAIN IN THIS MANNER, i.e. with *lechis* or *korahs* to enclose the street between the houses.[19]

This explanation too is questioned:

אָמַר לֵיהּ אַבָּיֵי – **Abaye said to [Rabbah]:** לְדִידָךְ נַמִּי לְרַבָּנָן נַצִּיל לְתוֹכוֹ אוֹכָלִין וּמַשְׁקִין – Why, **according to you as well, let us** be permitted **according to the Rabbis to save into [this** *mavoi***] foodstuffs and beverages!**[20] – ? –

NOTES

13. A *lechi* must be placed vertically on one side of the entrance and a *korah*, crossbeam, must be laid horizontally above the entrance. Only when these two adjustments have been made may one carry in the *mavoi*.

14. Rav Chisda explains that both the Rabbis and Ben Beseira agree with R' Eliezer that a *mavoi* ordinarily requires two *lechis*. Additionally, the Rabbis maintain that this is true also of a *mavoi* into which one wishes to save sacred scrolls. No leniencies were allowed for saving scrolls. Ben Beseira, however, holds that we are lenient in regard to saving scrolls and allow the *mavoi* to possess only one *lechi* (*Rashi*).

The question is asked: As in almost all cases in which Beis Hillel are one of the parties in a dispute, the halachah here follows Beis Hillel. Why, then, did Rav Chisda choose to explain our Mishnah in accordance with the minority opinion of R' Eliezer? Why not explain, in accordance with Beis Hillel, that the term "unopen *mavoi*" refers to a *mavoi* possessing one *lechi*, while the term "open *mavoi*" means a *mavoi* without any *lechi* at all?

Chidushei HaRan (*MHK* ed.) answers that Rav Chisda deemed it unreasonable that anyone would permit rescuing into a *mavoi* whose fourth side possesses no adjustment at all, for such a *mavoi* is too easily confused with a *reshus harabim*. Cf. *Tosafos*.

15. True, R' Eliezer regards such a *mavoi* as insufficiently adjusted to permit carrying therein under normal circumstances, but it cannot be properly termed "open" (*Rashi*), since it is closed on three sides and even the fourth side has at least one *lechi*.

16. Rav Chisda has explained the Rabbis as maintaining that the *mavoi* into which sacred scrolls may be saved must possess the same two *lechis* as any other *mavoi*, for we are no more lenient with the *mavoi* in this case than for ordinary cases. It follows, therefore, that the Rabbis would require the *mavoi* to possess a *shituf mevo'os* as well, just as is required for any other *mavoi* (*Rashi;* see also *Rashi* ד״ה והו; see *Leshon HaZahav* to *Rashi* 115a ד״ה מצילין; cf. *Maharsha* here). Since the *mavoi* is fully rectified (i.e. it possesses both the required adjustment on its open end and a *shituf*), there seems to be no reason why the Rabbis should not permit saving even non-sacred items, such as food and drink, into it.

Yet from the Mishnah on 120a this appears not to be the case. There a dispute is cited between the Rabbis and Ben Beseira as to where one may carry foodstuffs when saving them from a fire on the Sabbath. The Rabbis state that they may be brought only into a *chatzeir* whose houses are joined by an *eruv*, while Ben Beseira permits this even into a *chatzeir* for which no *eruv* was made. From the fact that the Rabbis speak specifically of a "*chatzeir,*" switching from the case of "*mavoi*" used in the previous Mishnah, it is implied that foodstuffs may *not* be saved into the *mavoi* of the previous Mishnah. But why is this so, seeing that according to Rav Chisda the *mavoi* has been rectified in every required way? (*Rashi;* cf. *Tosafos*).

17. [Rabbah thus asserts that the term "open *mavoi*" means an alleyway open at both ends.]

18. According to most Tannaim a *lechi* or *korah* is effective only for the fourth side of a *mavoi* (alley or street) that is properly enclosed on its other three sides (see Mishnah, *Eruvin* 11b). R' Yehudah teaches that even a street open at *both* ends can be rendered permissible for carrying by means of a *lechi* or *korah* at each end.

19. According to R' Yehudah, two walls are enough to render the area between them a private domain under Biblical law. Thus, it is Biblically permitted to carry in the street between the two houses even without a *lechi* or *korah*. Therefore, to permit carrying on the Rabbinical level, R' Yehudah requires that a *lechi* or *korah* be placed at each end of the open street, not to complete the enclosure (since two walls suffice to enclose the area) but simply to serve as the Rabbinic marker required for the open end of a *mavoi*. The Sages, however, dispute R' Yehudah's contention that two walls are enough to remove *reshus harabim* status from the area in between them. Rather they require three complete walls.

Rabbah explains that both the Rabbis and Ben Beseira agree with R' Yehudah that a *lechi* on either end of a two-walled *mavoi* suffices to permit carrying therein. The Rabbis maintain that this holds true even for a *mavoi* into which one wishes to save sacred scrolls. [It is to such a two-walled *mavoi* with *lechis* at each end that the Rabbis refer by the term "unopen mavoi."] Ben Beseira, on the other hand, states that for the sake of saving the scrolls, R' Yehudah permits the *mavoi* to have only one *lechi* (*Rashi*).

20. Abaye argues that the same objection that Rabbah raised with the interpretation of Rav Chisda can be raised against his own. Rabbah stated that the Rabbis and Ben Beseira both follow R' Yehudah, with the Rabbis requiring, even in our case of rescuing sacred scrolls, the same adjustments for the two-walled *mavoi* as are ordinarily required. It follows, therefore, that they should require a *shituf mevo'os* as well. Why, then, should we not be able to save into this *mavoi* foodstuffs, just as we may to a *chatzeir* possessing an *eruv*? (*Rashi*).

To explain why Rabbah felt that this difficulty did not apply to his own explanation, *Ramban* offers the following rationale: According to Rav Chisda's interpretation that the *mavoi* is fully enclosed on three sides and is thus fully rectified, there is indeed no reason to forbid saving anything into it. But according to Rabbah's explanation that we are dealing with a *mavoi* possessing only two walls, it is conceivable that the Rabbis were concerned that in the panic of a fire one could come to carry from such a *mavoi* into the *reshus harabim*. Thus, although the *mavoi* is fully rectified, they forbade saving anything but sacred items into it.

Abaye, however, did not accept this reasoning. (Cf. *Tosafos.*)

טז א מיי' פ"ו מהלכות שבת הל' כ סמג עשין א טוש"ע או"ח סימן שלד סעיף ג וסעיף יד:

מי דמי התם נעשה בסים לדבר המותר הכא נעשה בסים לדבר האסור אלא הכי קאמרי ליה אם מצילין תיק של ספר עם הספר ואע"פ שיש בתוכו מעות לא נטלטל עור אגב בשר מי דמי התם נעשה בסים לדבר האסור ולדבר המותר הכא כולו נעשה בסים לדבר האסור אלא הכי קאמרי ליה אם מביאין תיק שיש בתוכו מעות מעלמא להציל בו ספר תורה לא נטלטל עור אגב בשר והיא גופה מנלן אילימא דמדהיכא דאית ביה לא שדי להו איתויי נמי מייתינן מי דמי התם אדהכי והכי נפלה דליקה הכא אדהכי והכי לישדינהו אלא אמר מר בר רב אשי לעולם כדאמרינן מעיקרא ודקא קשיא לך [א] הכא טלטול והכא מלאכה כגון דלא קבעי ליה לעור והא [ג] אביי ורבא דאמרי תרוייהו מודה ר"ש בפסיק רישיה ולא ימות דשקיל ליה [ג] בברזי: ולהיכן מצילין אותן וכו': היכי דמי מפולש היכי דמי שאינו מפולש אמר רב חסדא שלש מחיצות ושני לחיין זהו מבוי שאינו מפולש ג' מחיצות ולחי אחד זהו מבוי המפולש ותרוייהו אליבא דרבי אליעזר דתנן [ד] הכשר מבוי ב"ש אומרים לחי וקורה וב"ה [א] אומרים או לחי או קורה ר' אליעזר אומר שני לחיים א"ל רבה ג' מחיצות ולחי אחד מפולש קרית ליה ועוד לרבנן נציל לתוכו אוכלין ומשקין אלא אמר רבה שתי מחיצות ושני לחיין זהו מבוי שאינו מפולש שתי מחיצות ולחי אחד זהו מבוי המפולש ותרוייהו אליבא דרבי יהודה [ה] דתניא יתר על כן אמר ר' יהודה מי שיש לו שני בתים בשני צדי ר"ה עושה לחי מיכן ולחי מיכן או קורה מיכן וקורה מיכן ונושא ונותן באמצע אמרו לו אין מערבין רה"ר בכך א"ל אביי לדידך נמי לרבנן נציל לתוכו אוכלין ומשקין אלא

(א) מי דמי. תיק הספר נעשה בסים לדבר המותר לטלטלו בלא שום דליקה דספר בר טלטול הוא ולדבר האסור כגון מעות: הכא. האי עור נעשה בסים לדבר שכולו אסור בטלטול שהבשר אסור לטלטלו דלא חזי לאכילה עד אורתא דפסח אינו נאכל אלא בלילה ולאי ורבי ישמעאל לית ליה כבוד שמים בנאכל להדיוט ואפילו הוי עור תורת כלי עליו מיתסר משום דהוי בסים לאיסור וכ"ש דהוא גופיה לאו בר טלטול הוא: אם מביאין תיק שבתוכו מעות. דהוי בסים לדבר שכולו אסור ומניח בו ספר להצילו ואינו צריך להשליך המעות כדמפרש ואזיל לא נטלטל עור אגב הבשר: אי נימא דמדהיכא דאית ביה. מעות עם הספר לא שדי להו לא מצריך ליה תנא דידן למשדינהו כדקתני ואע"פ שיש בתוכו מעות: איתויי נמי מייתינן. מעלמא מאחת זויות הבית תיק ובתוכו מעות להניח בתוכו ספר ולהציל: מי דמי. היכא דהספר מונח עם המעות להיכא דהוא בא עכשיו להביאו עם המעות ולתת בו ספר: התם. דספר ומעות בתוכו להכי לא מצרכינן ליה למישדינהו: דילמא אדהכי והכי נפלה דליקה. על הספר: הכא. אדמייתי ליה נישדינהו דרך ביאתו: כדאמרינן מעיקרא. דלא פליגי אלא בהפשטה ומייתי רבנן ראיה מתיק הספר דמתני' דמצילין מעות אגב ספר לרכי הדיוט אגב לרכי גבוה הואיל וליכא שהות למשדינהו וה"נ אגב לרכי גבוה דכל פעל ה' למענהו יפשיט: ודקשיא לך כו' דלא בעי ליה לעור. אינו צריך לו לעור ואינו מתכוין להפשיט משום עור ולא דמי להפשט אילים ותחשים דמשכן: והא ר"ש מודה בפסיק רישיה ולא ימות. והכא אע"ג דלא מיכוין מיפשיט הוא: דשקיל ליה בברזי. בחתיכות דקות מפשיט וחותך דאין דרך הפשטה בכך ולאו מלאכה הוא אלא שבות: שני לחיים. לפתח שאין לו מחילה: זהו מבוי שאינו מפולש. כלומר מבוי הניתר בכל הלכותיו בין בעירוב בין בשאר דברים וכל היתר שאר מבואות יש לו כגון שיתופי מבואות: ותרוייהו. רבנן ובן בתירא סבירא להו כר"א דאמר אין מבוי ואפילו סתום ניתר בלאחי א' ואשמעינן בן בתירא דהצלת כתבי הקדש לא בעינן לחיים כרבי אליעזר: מפולש קרית ליה. נהי נמי דבעי ר' אליעזר לחיים מיהו מפולש לא מיקרי: ועוד לרבנן. דאמרי לשאינו מפולש וקאמרת דהיינו מבוי הניתר בכל הלכותיו: נציל לתוכן אף אוכלין ומשקין. כמו לחצר המעורבת ואמאי פלגינהו מהדדי דגבי ספר קתני למבוי שאינו מפולש וגבי אוכלין קתני להיכן מצילין אותן לחצר המעורבת דמשמע אבל למבוי לא: שתי מחיצות. מכאן ומכאן: שני לחיין. לחי לכל פתח ופתח: אליבא דרבי יהודה. דאמר בשתי מחילות סגי ושני לחיים ואתא בן בתירא למימר דלגבי ספר מודה ר' יהודה דסגי בחד דג' מחילות הוו: לדידך נמי. איכא למיפרך כאתקפתא דלעיל: לרבנן. כיון דאמרת דתרוייהו כר' יהודה לרבנן דאמרי לשאינו מפולש ומפרשי ליה לשאינו חסר כלום כר' יהודה דלא בעי אלא שתי מחילות ושני לחיים אי הכי לרבנן יציל לתוכו אוכלין ומשקין כמו לחצר המעורבת:
אלא

הכא נעשה בסים לדבר האסור. פי' בקונטרס שהבשר אסור לטלטל שהרי אינו ראוי לאכילה עד הלילה ואינו נראה דא"כ היכי קאמר לא נטלטל עור אגב בשר כיון דבשר אסור לטלטל ונראה דלכ"ע בשר מותר לטלטל אע"ג דמאן דשרי [י] בשר תפל בעלמא לטלטל היינו משום דחזי לכלבים והכא לא חזי לכלבים מ"מ משום בזיון קדשי שמים שרי לכ"ע ובטלטול עור אגב בשר הוא דפליגי והא דקאמר הכא דהוי בסים לדבר האסור היינו קודם שנשחטה היה בסים לדבר האסור שכל הבהמה מוקצה היא מטלטול:

מי דמי התם אדהכי והכי נפלה דליקה. וא"ת אמאי לא קאמר התם נעשה בסים לדבר המותר ולדבר האסור הכא נעשה בסים לדבר האסור גרידא וי"ל דאין נראה לו לחלק כיון דהשתא סבור שיכול לנער מעות מן הכיס ואפילו הכי א"צ לנער ושרי כל שהוא עושה להצלת ס"ת ה"ה דשרי להביא תיק שיש בו מעות גרידא:

אדהכי והכי לשדינהו. משמע דאי לא מצי למשדי המעות הוה מצי להביא התיק עם המעות להביא בו ס"ת וא"כ כשאינו מופשט אלא עד החזה מותר לכ"ע לטלטל הואיל ולא מצי שדי ליה ולא פליגי אלא כשהופשט לגמרי כדפי' לעיל:

דשקיל ליה בברזי. פירש בקונט' דאיכא שבות בכה"ג וקשה דהוה ליה למיתני בפסחים בפרק אלו דברים (דף סה:) הפשט דדחי שבת בהדי הנהו שבות דקתני התם דדחו שבת ונראה לר"י דליכא אפילו שבות דאינו מפשיט כשיעור חשיבות עור יחד ולא דמי למפיס מורסא דהתם פתח קעביד אך שא"צ לו וכן צד מזיקין מ"מ צד הוא אבל הכא דלא קא עביד הפשט אפי' שבות ליכא:

(ז) דשקיל ליה בברזי). וא"ת דתני' בסוף תמיד נשחט (פסחים סה:) תנא משכה[ח] כל אחד ואחד נוטל פסחו בעורו אם כן לאו בברזי היה מופשט ומשמע דבשבת איירי דאמתני' דהתם קאי דקתני ארבעה עשר שחל בשבת ואיכא למימר דלא קאי אשבת א"נ נוטלו בעורו שנפשט עד החזה ועוד אומר ר"י דאיכא למימר דרבנן לדברי רבי ישמעאל קאמרי לדידן מותר להפשיט לגמרי לדידך אודי לן מיהא דמותר להפשיט בברזי וא"ת לפי זה ה"ל למיחשב התם דחיית הפשט וי"ל דבפלוגתא לא קא מיירי דלר' ישמעאל לא דחי ליה הפשט כלל ואע"ג דחשיב הרכבתו והבאתו מחוץ לתחום דפליגי בה ר"ע ור' אליעזר לא חשיב לה פלוגתא דר"א דשמותי הוא ועוד דמההיא פלוגתא ילפינן דהזאה אינה דוחה להכי קתני לה:

שלש מחיצות ושני לחיים כו'. השתא האי דמפרש לה הכי ומוקי תרוייהו אליבא דר"א ולא בעי למימר שלש מחילות ולחי א' אינו מפולש ובלא לחי זהו מפולש והוה מפרש אליבא דהלכתא היינו משום דסבר דבלא לחי כלל לא הוה שרי בן בתירא דהוי כרמלית ולא דמי לחצר שאינה מעורבת דסיפא:

ועוד לרבנן נציל לתוכו אוכלין ומשקין. (ט) ואמאי נקט חצר מעורבת) ולאמפלגי בין חצר מעורבת למבוי הוה לן לפלוגי בין מבוי משותף למבוי שאינו משותף דבמשותף יהא מותר להציל לתוכו אוכלין ומשקין ואמאי נקט חצר מעורבת:

אלא אמר רבה כו'. תימה מה תירץ רבה מקושיא דנציל לתוכו אוכלין ומשקין ואומר ר"י דרבה רוצה לומר דרבנן סברי כרבי יהודה דוקא לצורך הצלת כתבי הקדש ולא לצורך אחר ואביי פריך משום דאינו נראה לו סברא שיסברו כר' יהודה לחלאין ומשני אביי ג' מחיצות כו' ולאביי לא סברי רבנן כר"א לחלאין דר"א להצלת כתבי הקדש סגי בלחי אחד כדמסיים ואזיל ואפילו לרבי אליעזר כו':
הא

רבינו חננאל

דאינון סברי מטלטלין העור ע"ג בשר מקום שחיטה כל חד לדוכתיה והוא אסר. והאהדור ליה אם מטלטלין להציל תיק של ספר אנו לא נטלטל עור אגב בשר והאהדר להו מי דמי תיק נעשה בסיס לס"ת שמותר לטלטל. עור נעשה בסיס לבשר אסור לטלטל. אלא הכי קאמרו ליה כו' ודחה ר' ישמעאל מי דמי. התם תיק נעשה בסיס לס"ת שהוא מותר. ולמעות שהן אסורין הכא בבשר כולו אסור. והדר רב אשי ואמר הכי אהדרו ליה אם מביאין מעלמא תיק שיש בו מעות להציל בו ס"ת אנו לא נטלטל עור אגב בשר. והא מנ"ל אי נימא דדייקינן מינה מה התיק שיש בו מעות וס"ת אינך מסיר המעות מתוך התיק ומציל הס"ת לבדו אלא אתה מציל אפי' המעות כך אם יש בתיק מעות והצרכת להביאו להציל ס"ת אינך מסיר המעות מתוכו דילמא שאני התם במקום שכבר הגיעה הדליקה עד הספר ואם יתעסק בהשלכת המעות תאכלם להבה. אבל במקום דהדליקה לא הגיעה [עדיין] והולכין להביא תיק להציל הספר. אם יש בתיק מעות אסור לטלטלן עד שישליכם. ושני רב אשי לעולם כדאמרינן מעיקרא. ודקא אמרת התם בתיק טלטול הכא מלאכה כגון דמתכוין לגלות הבשר ואין כוונתו לעור. ואקשינן והא אביי ורבא דאמרי תרוייהו מודה ר"ש דסבר דבר שאינו מתכוין שרי בפסיק רישיה ולא ימות כגון זה אמרינן באומר המפשיט דאינו מתכוין לעור דומה לאומר הנני מחתך ראש זה העוף ואין כוונתי לשוחטו כגון זה אפי' לר' שמעון שוחט הוא. ואסקי' דשקיל ליה בברזי. פי' ברזי נקבים והכי קאמר מאן דמבזע ליה כשהוא מפשיטו מוכחא מילתא דלא בעי ליה לעור ולא דמי לפסיק רישיה ולא ימות. ולהיכן מצילין אותו למבוי שאינו מפולש וכן הלכה. ולית הלכתא כבן בתירא דאמר אפילו למבוי המפולש והיכי דמי מבוי שאינו מפולש שמצילין בו כתבי הקדש:
אסקה

מסורת הש"ס

א) [נ"ל התם], ב) לעיל עה. קב. קיא: לקמן קמג. קנג. קמא. סוכה לג: [ביצה לו.] כתובות ו. בכורות כה., ג) [ערוך פי' ברזא נקבים והכי קאמר מאן דבזע ליה לעור כשהוא מפשיטו מוכחא מילתא דלא בעי לעור ואין בו הנאה ממנו ולא דמי לפסיק רישא עכ"ל ולפי פי' זה יתיישב קושית התוס' ד"ה דשקיל הא דתניא בתמיד נשחט תנא משכה וכו'], ד) עירובין יא:, ה) לעיל ו. עירובין ו: יב: כב. נט: לב., ו) לקמן קכח., ז) רש"ל מ"ז, ח) [תנא משכה ליתא שם ע"ש], ט) רש"ל מ"ז.

הגהות הב"ח

(א) רש"י ד"ה (מי דמי וכו' כגון מעות הכא האי וכו' אסור בטלטול) תא"מ ונ"ב ס"א ועיקר מי דמי תיק הספר נעשה בסיס לדבר המותר לטלטלו בלא שום דליקה דספר בר טלטול הוא הכא האי עור נעשה בסיס לדבר האסור בטלטול כו':

ליקוטי רש"י

מודה ר"ש. דאמר במסכת שבת (מא:) דבר שאין מתכוין מותר [בכורות כה.]. בפסיק רישיה ולא ימות. באומר אחתוך ראש בהמה זו בשבת ואיני רוצה שתמות...

אלא אמר רב אשי שלש מחיצות ולחי אחד זה מבוי שאינו מפולש ג' מחיצות בלא לחי זהו מבוי המפולש ואפילו לרבי אליעזר דאמר בעינן לחיים הני מילי לאוכלין ומשקין אבל לספר תורה בחד לחי סגי:

מתני' מצילין מזון ג' סעודות הראוי לאדם לאדם הראוי לבהמה לבהמה כיצד נפלה דליקה בלילי שבת מצילין מזון ג' סעודות בשחרית מצילין מזון ב' סעודות במנחה מזון סעודה אחת ר' יוסי אומר לעולם מצילין מזון שלש סעודות:

גמ' מכדי בהיתרא קטרח נציל טפי אמר רבא מתוך שאדם בהול על ממונו אי שרית ליה אתי לכבויי א"ל אביי אלא הא דתניא נשברה לו חבית בראש גגו מביא כלי ומניח תחתיה ובלבד שלא יביא כלי אחר ויקלוט כלי אחר ויצרף התם מאי גזירה איכא ה"נ גזירה שמא יביא כלי דרך רה"ר גופא נשברה לו חבית בראש גגו מביא כלי ומניח תחתיה ובלבד שלא יביא כלי אחר ויקלוט כלי אחר ויצרף נזדמן לו אורחין מביא כלי אחר וקולט כלי אחר ומצרף ולא יקלוט ואחר כך יזמין אלא יזמין ואח"כ יקלוט ואין מערימין בכך משום רבי יוסי בר יהודה אמרו מערימין לימא בפלוגתא דרבי אליעזר ור' יהושע קמיפלגי דתניא אותו ואת בנו שנפלו לבור רבי אליעזר אומר מעלה את הראשון על מנת לשוחטו והשני עושה לו פרנסה במקומו בשביל שלא ימות רבי יהושע אומר מעלין את הראשון על מנת לשוחטו ואינו שוחטו ומערים ומעלה את השני רצה זה שוחט רצה זה שוחט ממאי דילמא עד כאן לא קאמר רבי אליעזר התם דאפשר בפרנסה אבל הכא דלא אפשר לא ועד כאן לא קאמר רבי יהושע התם משום דאיכא צער בעלי חיים אבל הכא דליכא צער בעלי חיים לא ת"ר הציל פת נקיה אין מציל פת הדראה פת הדראה מציל פת נקיה ומצילין מיום הכפורים לשבת אבל לא משבת ליום הכפורים ואין צריך לומר משבת ליום טוב ולא משבת לשבת הבאה ת"ר שכח פת בתנור וקידש עליו היום מצילין מזון שלש סעודות ואומר לאחרים בואו והצילו לכם וכשהוא רודה לא ירדה במרדה אלא בסכין איני והא תנא דבי רבי ישמעאל (א) לא תעשה כל מלאכה יצא תקיעת שופר ורדיית הפת שהיא חכמה ואינה מלאכה כמה דאפשר לשנויי משנינן א"ר חסדא לעולם ישכים אדם להוצאת שבת שנאמר והיה ביום הששי והכינו את אשר יביאו לאלתר אמר ר' אבא בשבת חייב אדם לבצוע על שתי ככרות דכתיב לחם משנה אמר רב אשי חזינא ליה לרב כהנא דנקט תרתי ובצע חדא אמר לקטו כתיב רבי זירא הוה בצע אכולה שירותיה אמר ליה רבינא לרב אשי והא מיחזי כרעבתנותא אמר ליה כיון דכל יומא לא עביד והאידנא הוא דקעביד לא מיחזי כרעבתנותא רבי אמי ורבי אסי כי מיקלע להו ריפתא דעירובא שרו עילויה אמרי הואיל ואיתעביד בה חדא מצוה ליתעביד בה מצוה אחרינא: כיצד נפלה דליקה כו': ת"ר כמה סעודות חייב אדם לאכול בשבת שלש רבי חידקא אומר ארבע א"ר יוחנן ושניהם מקרא אחד דרשו ויאמר משה אכלוהו היום כי שבת היום לה' היום לא תמצאהו בשדה רבי חידקא סבר הני תלתא היום לבר מאורתא ורבנן סברי בהדי דאורתא תנן נפלה דליקה בלילי שבת מצילין

רש"י

אלא אמר רב אשי כו'. בין רבנן ובין בן בתירא כר' אליעזר סבירא להו דבעי ג' מחיצות וב' לחיים בעלמא והכא לגבי ספר אמרי רבנן מודה ר' אליעזר בלחי אחד ובן בתירא אמר דמודה ר' אליעזר אף בלא לחי: **בחד לחי סגי ליה.** מילתא דרבנן קא מפרשי: **מתני' נפלה דליקה בלילי שבת.** קודם אכילה: **שחרית.** קודם סעודה: **לעולם הוא מציל.** הואיל ויומא בר הכי הוא ובהיתרא טרח דהא בני טלטול נינהו ולחצר המעורבת ואפי' טובא הוה שרי ליה אי לאו משום גזירה וכדמפרש בגמרא: **גמ' מכדי בהיתרא קטרח.** חזו לטלטול ולחצר המעורבת: **ואי שרית ליה.** לאתחולי בהצלה כולי האי מתוך שהוא בהול מינשי ליה שבת ואתי נמי לכבויי: **ויקלוט.** קילוח הנופל מן האויר: **ויצרף.** סמוך לגג כעין שאיבה אלא שאינו ראוי לשאוב שהגג חלק והיין אינו בגומא מצרף כלי לגג שיזוב מן הגג לכלי והוא אוחז הכלי בידו: **התם מאי גזירה איכא.** כיון דמידי דהתירא הוא אמאי לא יקלוט ויצרף: **שמא יביא כלי כו'.** מתוך שהוא מחזר על כלים הרבה ישכח ויביא: **ולא יקלוט ואח"כ יזמין.** אורחים דבשעת קליטה לא מיבעיא ליה: **אין מערימין בכך.** לזמן אורחים שאינן צריכין לאכול ויותירו: **שנפלו לבור.** בי"ט ואין שניהם ראוים לשחיטה ביום אחד: **ואינו שוחטו.** שמוצא לו עלילה שמא חברו שמן ממנו: **עד כאן לא קאמר ר' אליעזר.** דאין מערימין: **הציל פת נקיה.** לשלש סעודות: **לא יציל פת הדראה.** פת קיבר שניטל הדרה לפי שאין ערמה כשרה לומר פת הדראה נוחה לי: **אבל לא משבת ליום הכפורים.** כגון אם חל יוה"כ באחד בשבת דהא לא אכיל עד לאורתא ולאורתא ליטרח ולייתי: **ואין צריך לומר משבת לי"ט.** דיכול להכין בו ביום: **מרדה.** כלי שרודין בו הפת ומפרידין אותו מכותל התנור שנדבק בה לא ירדה אותו במרדה שהוא דרך חול: **ישכים אדם.** בע"ש לטרוח ולזמן הוצאת שבת: **והכינו את אשר יביאו לאלתר.** בשעת הבאה הכנה והבאה בהשכמה היא דכתיב וילקטו אותו בבקר בבקר (שמות טז): **לבצוע.** ברכת המוציא: **נקיט תרתי.** אוחזן בידו: **לקטו כתיב.** דמשמע אחיזה אבל בליעה לא כתיב משנה: **בצע לכוליה שירותיה.** פרוסה גדולה ודי לו בה לאותה סעודה ולכבוד שבת ונראה כמחבב סעודת שבת להתחזק ולאכול הרבה: **כי מקלע להו.** פעמים שהעירוב בביתם ופעמים בבית אחד משאר בני אדם: **שרו ביה.** היינו ברכת המוציא שהיא התחלת אכילה. שרו מתחילין: **תלתא היום.** למנין שלש סעודות בא: לעולם

תוספות

הא דתניא נשברה לו חבית בראש גגו. הקשה הרב פורת אמאי לא פריך ממתניתין דריש חבית (לקמן קמג:) דתנן חבית שנשברה מצילין ממנה מזון שלש סעודות ואומר לאחרים בואו והצילו לכם ובלבד שלא יספוג ותירץ דההיא איכא למימר כגון שהחבית בכרמלית דחיישינן שמא יעביר כלי ד' אמות בכרמלית אבל בהך ברייתא קתני בהדיא בראש גגו ור"י תירץ דהתם מיירי כשנשפך היין לארץ דחיישינן שמא יספוג אומר ה"ר שמואל בשם ר"ת דדוקא נשברה לו חבית אבל נסדקה ועושה טיף טיף מותר להביא כלים לקלוט ולצרף דאינו בהול כל כך להביא כלים דרך רה"ר כמו כשנשברה:

כלי אחר ויקלוט כלי אחר ויצרף. אומר ר"י דזו אף זו קתני לא מבעי לקלוט דמינכר שמציל דאסור אלא אפילו לצרף דלא מינכר כולי האי שהוא מציל אסור: **הציל פת נקיה לא יציל פת הדראה.** אומר ר"י כשאפו בי"ט של פסח מצות מסולת נקיה שיש לו די לצורך י"ט אין אופין אחריהן פת של הדראה אלא מתחילה יעשה של הדראה ואחרי כן יעשה הנקיה:

אבל לא משבת ליום הכפורים. פירש בקונטרס למוצאי יוה"כ וא"ת פשיטא דחול גמור הוא ומ"ש משבת למוצאי שבת וי"ל דמצוה לאכול במוצאי יוה"כ כדפי' לעיל (ב) (דף קיד:) ועוד לפי שהתענו מותר יותר אי נמי ליום הכפורים עצמו קאמר ולהאכיל התינוקות:

והתנא דבי רבי ישמעאל כל מלאכת עבודה לא תעשו. וא"ת ואמאי מייתי קרא דכל מלאכת עבודה דכתיב גבי י"ט הא אפי' בשבת דכתיב לא תעשה מלאכה סתם ולא כתיב עבודה שרי לתקוע ולרדות מן התורה כדמשמע הכא דאשבת מייתי לה ופירש רבינו שמואל דגרס כל מלאכה לא תעשו ורשב"א מפרש דלעולם מכל מלאכת עבודה אימעיט תקיעה ורדייה ושבת ילפינן מי"ט דאין בין י"ט לשבת אלא אוכל נפש בלבד דכתיב אך אשר יאכל לכל נפש (שמות יב):

שהיא חכמה ואינה מלאכה. וכיון דמדאורייתא שריא אע"ג דמדרבנן אסירא כדאמר בר"ה השנה (דף לג.) אין מעכבין את התינוקות מלתקוע הא נשים מעכבין הכא הוה לן למישרי משום ג' סעודות:

עין משפט נר מצוה

יז א מיי' פט"ו מהל' שבת הלכה ג ופכ"ג הלכ"ו סמג לאוין סה ועשין ל טוש"ע או"ח סימן שלד סעיף יז וסימן שבה סעיף ה ג יד:
יח ב מיי' פכ"ג הלכ"א ומכ"ג שם טוש"ע או"ח סימן שלד סעיף א:
יט ג מיי' פרק כ"ג שם הלכה טז סמג שם טוש"ע או"ח סימן שלה סעיף ג:
כ ד מיי' שם טור שו"ע שם סעיף ג:
כא ה מיי' פ"א מהלכות יו"ט הלכה ד טור שו"ע או"ח סימן תקח סעיף י:
כב ו מיי' פכ"ג מהלכות שבת הלכה כא טור שו"ע או"ח סימן שלד סעיף ג:
כג ז מיי' שם טור שו"ע שם סעיף ד:
כד ח מיי' פכ"ג שם הלכה טז סמג שם טור שו"ע או"ח סימן רנד סעיף ה:
כה ט טוש"ע או"ח סי' רנ סעיף א:
כו י כ מיי' פ"ל שם הלכה ט סמג עשין ל טור שו"ע או"ח סימן רעד סעיף א ג וסימן רפט סעיף א:
כז ל טוש"ע או"ח סימן שלב סעיף ב בהג"ה:
כח מ מיי' וסמג שם טוש"ע או"ח סימן רצא סעיף א:

רבינו חננאל

אסקה רב אשי ג' מחיצות ולחי א' זהו מבוי שאינו מפולש שאין בו שיתוף ולא עירוב ודבר זה להציל כתבי הקדש אבל אוכלין ומשקין אין מצילין אלא לחצר המעורבת הלכה כת"ק. והא דאמר רבה ב' מחיצות ולחי אחד זהו מפולש. ב' מחיצות וב' לחיים זהו שאינו מפולש. ואליבא דר' יהודה דאמר מי שיש לו ב' בתים בב' צדי רה"ר עושה לחי מכאן ולחי מכאן או קורה מכאן וקורה מכאן ונושא ונותן באמצע והכי פי' דכך פסיק לה לרחבה מב' צדיה ב' בתים עושה לחי מכאן ולחי מכאן ומערב ונושא ונותן באמצע. והתם איכא פלוגתא דת"ק (וחנינא) [וחנניה] ורב אמר הלכה כת"ק. ושמואל אמר הלכה (כחנינא) [כחנניה]. וקאי במבוי שיש בו ב' מחיצי' בלבד כנגד זו ב' פתחים יש לו זה כנגד זה והאי איכא עליה לחי או קורה מכאן ולחי או קורה מכאן. לר' יהודה דלא מצריך דלת יכול לערב נמי. א"ל אביי לא למר נמי כיון שמתערבי יצילו לתוכן אוכלין ומשקין. ורב אשי ופריק. וסלקא כותיה: מצילין מזון ג' סעודות. ואקשינן מכדי בהיתרא קא טרח דקתני להיכן מצילין לחצר המעורבת נציל טפי. ופרקי אמר רבה מתוך שאדם בהול על ממונו דאי שרית ליה להציל כל מאי דבעי אתי לכבויי. א"ל אביי ואלא הא דתניא נשברה לו חבית בראש גגו מביא כלי ומניח תחתיה ובלבד שלא יביא כלי אחר ויקלוט כלי אחר ויצרף. התם מ"ט לא יביא כלי אחר ויקלוט כלי אחר ויצרף והא בהיתרא קא טרח. אהדר ליה רבה התם נמי גזרו עליה דאי שרית לאתויי כלי [אחר יביא כלין] דרך רה"ר וכיון שנאסר מלהביא כלי אחר הרי זה מייאש ולא פשיט באיסורא. והא דמי שנשברה לו חבית בראש גגו. סלקא דלאו בפלוגתא דר' אליעזר ור' יהושע היא. ולענין פת בתנור הלכתא כי הא דתניא שכח פת בתנור וקדש עליה היום מציל מזון ג' סעודות. ואומר לאחרים בואו והצילו לכם. ולא ירדה במרדה אלא בסכין. ואע"ג דתנא דבי שמואל כל מלאכת עבודה לא תעשו. יצא תקיעת שופר ורדיית הפת שהיא חכמה ואינה מלאכה. כמה שאפשר לשנויי משנינן: **אמר** רב חסדא לעולם ישכים אדם להוצאת שבת שנאמר והיה ביום הששי והכינו לאלתר. והלכתא כר' אבא דאמר חייב אדם לבצוע על ב' ככרות בשבת.
ואיתא

מסורת הש"ס

א) [לקמן קכ.], ב) [לקמן קמג:], ג) לעיל מב. ע"ש, ד) [לקמן קמג:], ה) ביצה לז. [תוספתא דביצה פ"ג], ו) [תוס' פ"ה], ז) [גי' הערוך בערך רד הדראה פי' לחם עב ובלע"ז מרי"ן], ח) [סוכה כ: ושם], ט) [לקמן קנב. ע"ש], י) [ברכות לט:], כ) [ברכות לט: ע"ש], ל) [לקמן קמג:], מ) כתובות סד:, נ) [ויקרא כג], ס) [ג"כ לא מעשה של מלאכה שמות כ].

הגהות הב"ח

(א) גמ' והא תנא דבי ר' ישמעאל לא תעשו. נ"ב עי' בפ' ר"ה דמילה דף קלא ע"ב דגורס קרא דכל מלאכת עבודה לא תעשו: (ב) תוס' ד"ה אבל וכו' כדפי' לעיל. נ"ב בס"פ אלו קשרים ממש. וכ"כ הסוף סוף יומא דף פא בד"ה והאמר רב:

גליון הש"ס

גמ' ואין מערימין בכך. מו"ק דף יב ע"ב:

תורה אור השלם

א) וְיוֹם הַשְּׁבִיעִי שַׁבָּת לַיי אֱלֹהֶיךָ לֹא תַעֲשֶׂה כָל מְלָאכָה אַתָּה וּבִנְךָ וּבִתֶּךָ עַבְדְּךָ וַאֲמָתְךָ וּבְהֶמְתֶּךָ וְגֵרְךָ אֲשֶׁר בִּשְׁעָרֶיךָ: [שמות כ, י]
ב) וְהָיָה בַּיּוֹם הַשִּׁשִּׁי וְהֵכִינוּ אֵת אֲשֶׁר יָבִיאוּ וְהָיָה מִשְׁנֶה עַל אֲשֶׁר יִלְקְטוּ יוֹם יוֹם: [שמות טז, ה]
ג) וַיְהִי בַּיּוֹם הַשִּׁשִּׁי לָקְטוּ לֶחֶם מִשְׁנֶה שְׁנֵי הָעֹמֶר לָאֶחָד וַיָּבֹאוּ כָּל נְשִׂיאֵי הָעֵדָה וַיַּגִּידוּ לְמֹשֶׁה: [שמות טז, כב]
ד) וַיֹּאמֶר מֹשֶׁה אִכְלֻהוּ הַיּוֹם כִּי שַׁבָּת הַיּוֹם לַיי הַיּוֹם לֹא תִמְצָאֻהוּ בַּשָּׂדֶה: [שמות טז, כה]

ליקוטי רש"י

אותו ואת בנו. שאינו מותרין לשחוט שניהן ביום [ביצה לז.]. **עושה לו פרנסה.** כל לשון פרנסה לשון פרנסה ולשון פרנסה הוא קונדריי"ר בלע"ז כמו לפרנסה שמין בתר (כתובות סח). וכמו מוליכין לפרנסה ואין מוליכין למזונות (שם סט.) [גיטין סה:]. כל צורך סיפוק ברכי פרנסה קונדוריי"ר בלע"ז [ב"מ מו.]. **הדראה.** סובין לכל הדרה דסיים פת קיבר [פסחים לו:]. **יצא תקיעת שופר.** דאפילו הרגום לית בה איסורא דאורייתא [לקמן קלא:]. **ורדיית הפת.** לרדות הפת שבתוך התנור שהיא חכמה ואינה מלאכה [לעיל ג:]. **ריפתא דעירובא.** שערבו בו לסמוך עירובי חלירות [ברכות לט:].

On the strength of Abaye's objection, the Gemara rejects Rabbah's explanation and offers a different interpretation: אֶלָּא אָמַר רַב אַשִׁי – **Rather, said Rav Ashi:** שָׁלֹשׁ מְחִיצוֹת וְלֶחִי אֶחָד זֶה מָבוֹי שֶׁאֵינוֹ מְפוּלָּשׁ – If the *mavoi* has **three walls and one** *lechi,* **it is** called **an unopen** *mavoi;* שָׁלֹשׁ מְחִיצוֹת בְּלֹא לֶחִי זֶהוּ מָבוֹי הַמְפוּלָּשׁ – if it has **three walls and no** *lechi,* **it is** called **an open** *mavoi.*[1] וַאֲפִילּוּ לְרַבִּי אֱלִיעֶזֶר דְּאָמַר בְּעִינָן לְחָיַיִם – **And even according to R' Eliezer who says** that **we need two** *lechis,* הָנֵי מִילֵּי לְאוֹכָלִין וּמַשְׁקִין – **this holds true in regard to** saving **foodstuffs and beverages,** אֲבָל לְסֵפֶר תּוֹרָה בְּחַד לֶחִי סַגִּי – **but in regard to** saving **a Torah scroll,** a *mavoi* **with one** *lechi* **suffices.**[2]

Mishnah The Mishnah discusses the Rabbinically decreed limitations on rescuing items from a fire on the Sabbath:

מַצִּילִין מְזוֹן שָׁלֹשׁ סְעוּדוֹת – **One may save** enough **food for three meals,** i.e. for the three meals that one is obligated to eat on the Sabbath; הָרָאוּי לְאָדָם לְאָדָם – **what is fit for people** may be saved **for people** הָרָאוּי לִבְהֵמָה לִבְהֵמָה – and **what is fit for animals** may be saved **for animals.**[3]

The Mishnah elaborates on the three-meals rule:

כֵּיצַד – **How so,** i.e. under what circumstances may one save enough food for three meals? נָפְלָה דְלֵיקָה בְּלֵילֵי שַׁבָּת – If **fire broke out on the Sabbath Eve** (i.e. Friday night) before the person ate, מַצִּילִין מְזוֹן שָׁלֹשׁ סְעוּדוֹת – **he may save** enough **food for three meals,** since three meals remain to be eaten that Sabbath; בְּשַׁחֲרִית – if it broke out **in the morning** before the meal, מַצִּילִין מְזוֹן שְׁתֵּי סְעוּדוֹת – **he may save** enough **food for two meals,** since only two meals remain; בְּמִנְחָה מְזוֹן סְעוּדָה אַחַת – if it broke out **in the afternoon** before the final meal, he may save enough **food for one meal,** since only one meal remains.[4]

A dissenting view:

רַבִּי יוֹסֵי אוֹמֵר – **R' Yose says:** לְעוֹלָם מַצִּילִין מְזוֹן שָׁלֹשׁ סְעוּדוֹת – **One may always save** enough **food for three meals.**[5]

Gemara The Gemara questions the ruling of the Mishnah that only enough food for three meals may be saved:

מִכְּדִי – **Now,** let us see: בְּהֶיתֵּרָא קָטָרַח – When one saves food from a burning building on the Sabbath, **he is busy with that which is permissible,** i.e. the food is not *muktzeh,* and he carries it out only to a courtyard whose houses are joined by an *eruv.* נַצִּיל טְפֵי – Hence, **let us** be permitted to **save** even **more** than this amount! – ? –

The Gemara answers:

אָמַר רָבָא – **Rava said:** מִתּוֹךְ שֶׁאָדָם בָּהוּל עַל מָמוֹנוֹ – **Because a person is in a turmoil over** the threatened loss of **his property,** i.e. he becomes panicky at the prospect of losing his possessions, אִי שָׁרֵית לֵיהּ אָתֵי לְכַבּוּיֵי – **if you permit him** to save more, **he may come to extinguish** the fire.[6]

Rava's explanation accounts for a Rabbinic decree specifically in a case in which the threat to the person's property is due to fire. The Gemara challenges this point:

אָמַר לֵיהּ אַבַּיֵי – **Abaye said to [Rava]:** אֶלָּא הָא דְּתַנְיָא – **But** how

NOTES

1. Both the Rabbis and Ben Beseira follow the opinion of R' Eliezer that ordinarily a *mavoi* requires three walls and two *lechis.* Furthermore, they both agree that R' Eliezer is lenient in regard to saving scrolls and relaxes the requirements for the *mavoi's* adjustment. The dispute between them pertains to how far R' Eliezer goes with his leniency. The Rabbis hold that R' Eliezer dispenses with the need for two *lechis* but still requires one, whereas Ben Beseira maintains that R' Eliezer requires no *lechis* at all (*Rashi*). [According to this explanation, the *mavoi* according to Ben Beseira is termed "open" because it is totally unenclosed on its fourth side.]

2. This statement is made according to the Rabbis (*Rashi*). Since the *mavoi* does not possess its normal adjustment of two *lechis,* only sacred scrolls may be salvaged into it, but not food and beverages.

According to the previous two explanations given by Rav Chisda and Rabbah that the Rabbis required the *mavoi* to be fully adjusted, the assumption was that the *mavoi* required a *shituf mevo'os* as well. Now, however, that Rav Ashi has explained that even the Rabbis do not require the *mavoi* to be fully adjusted, no *shituf* is required either, for a *shituf* is effective only for a fully adjusted *mavoi* (*Rashi* to the Mishnah on 115a ד״ה מצילין with explanation of *Leshon HaZahav* there; cf. *Rashash* to *Rashi* 61b ד״ה לאצולינהו).

Note that while Rav Ashi has explained both Tannaim of our Mishnah as holding with R' Eliezer that a *mavoi* ordinarily requires two *lechis,* this is not the *halachah.* Rather, we follow Beis Hillel that one *lechi* suffices. It emerges, therefore, that the Rabbis' ruling in our Mishnah, which the halachah follows, that the *mavoi* into which scrolls of the Scriptures may be saved requires one *lechi,* does not reflect a leniency for the Holy Scriptures, because a *mavoi* requires only one *lechi* in any case. The only leniency with respect to a *mavoi* when saving sacred scrolls into it is the fact that it does not require a *shituf* (see *Rashi* to Mishnah ibid.; cf. *Baal HaMaor*).

3. I.e. three meals' worth of food fit for human consumption may be saved for every person who requires it, and a supply of animal food may be saved for one's cattle.

The words "for three meals" refer only to people, not to animals [for obviously there is no obligation to feed one's cattle three meals on the Sabbath] (*Ritva MHK* ed., *Meiri*). Alternatively, since the Gemara [*Berachos* 40a] requires a person to feed his animals before he himself sits down to eat, in order to partake of the three Sabbath meals he must have sufficient fodder for three feedings of his livestock (*Tiferes Yisrael; Beur Halachah* to 334:1 ד״ה והראוי in the name of *Tos. Shabbos*).

4. [Peculiarly, in the case of the fire breaking out at night, *Rashi* states, "before he ate," whereas concerning the fire breaking out in the morning, he states, "before the meal." *Bach* (334) suggests that the reason for this change is as follows: Since the evening meal may be eaten anytime during the night, even though the usual suppertime has passed, one may save food for three meals as long as he has not yet eaten. In the daytime, however, if one has not eaten until the afternoon, he can no longer fulfill his obligation to eat the morning meal. *Rashi,* therefore, states, "before the meal," to intimate that he may save food for two meals only if the usual mealtime has not yet passed. If it has, even though he himself has not yet eaten, he may save only enough food for one meal. See *Mishbetzos Zahav* 334:1 for an alternative explanation of *Rashi.*]

5. R' Yose's reasoning runs as follows: Food is not *muktzeh,* nor, in contrast to scrolls of the Holy Scriptures, may it be saved into a courtyard whose houses are not properly joined by an *eruv* (see next Mishnah, 120a). Thus, in allowing food to be saved from a fire, the Rabbis were not relaxing any Sabbath laws; in fact we will learn in the Gemara that they would have permitted saving even more than three meals if not for a preventive measure. Accordingly, the Rabbis saw no reason to vary their limitations on how much food could be saved according to the time of day at which the blaze breaks out. Since three meals' worth may be saved if fire breaks out on Friday night, this same amount may be saved no matter when the blaze occurs (*Rashi*).

6. In his haste to save everything, he is likely to forget that it is the Sabbath and may come to extinguish the fire (*Rashi*). By limiting the amount he can remove to that needed for the Sabbath, the Rabbis removed the element of haste from his salvage efforts.

אלא אמר רב אשי שלש מחיצות ולחי אחד זה מבוי שאינו מפולש ג' מחיצות בלא לחי זהו מבוי המפולש ואפילו לרבי אליעזר דאמר בעינן לחיים הני מילי לאוכלין ומשקין אבל לספר תורה בחד לחי סגי:

מתני' מצילין מזון ג' סעודות הראוי לאדם לאדם הראוי לבהמה לבהמה כיצד נפלה דליקה בלילי שבת מצילין מזון ג' סעודות בשחרית מצילין מזון ב' סעודות במנחה מזון סעודה אחת ר' יוסי אומר לעולם מצילין מזון שלש סעודות:

גמ' מכדי בהיתרא קטרח נציל טפי אמר רבא מתוך שאדם בהול על ממונו אי שרית ליה אתי לכבויי א"ל אביי אלא הא דתניא נשברה לו חבית בראש גגו מביא כלי ומניח תחתיה ובלבד שלא יביא כלי אחר ויקלוט כלי אחר ויצרף התם מאי גזירה איכא ה"נ גזירה שמא יביא כלי דרך רה"ר גופא נשברה לו חבית בראש גגו מביא כלי ומניח תחתיה ובלבד שלא יביא כלי אחר ויקלוט כלי אחר ויצרף נזדמן לו אורחין מביא כלי אחר וקולט כלי אחר ומצרף ולא יקלוט ואחר כך יזמין אלא יזמין ואח"כ יקלוט ואין מערימין בכך משום רבי יוסי בר יהודה אמרו מערימין לימא בפלוגתא דרבי אליעזר ור' יהושע קמיפלגי דתניא אותו ואת בנו שנפלו לבור רבי אליעזר אומר מעלה את הראשון על מנת לשוחטו והשני עושה לו פרנסה במקומו בשביל שלא ימות רבי יהושע אומר מעלין את הראשון על מנת לשוחטו ואינו שוחטו ומערים ומעלה את השני רצה זה שוחט רצה זה שוחט ממאי דילמא עד כאן לא קאמר רבי אליעזר התם דאפשר בפרנסה אבל הכא דלא אפשר לא ועד כאן לא קאמר רבי יהושע התם משום דאיכא צער בעלי חיים אבל הכא דליכא צער בעלי חיים לא ת"ר הציל פת נקיה אין מציל פת הדראה פת הדראה מציל פת נקיה ומצילין מיום הכפורים לשבת אבל לא משבת ליום הכפורים ואין צריך לומר משבת ליום טוב ולא משבת לשבת הבאה ת"ר שכח פת בתנור וקידש עליו היום מצילין מזון שלש סעודות ואומר לאחרים בואו והצילו לכם וכשהוא רודה לא ירדה במרדה אלא בסכין איני והא תנא דבי רבי ישמעאל (א) לא תעשה כל מלאכה יצא תקיעת שופר ורדיית הפת שהיא חכמה ואינה מלאכה כמה דאפשר לשנויי משנינן א"ר חסדא לעולם ישכים אדם להוצאת שבת שנאמר והיה ביום הששי והכינו את אשר יביאו לאלתר אמר ר' אבא בשבת חייב אדם לבצוע על שתי ככרות דכתיב לחם משנה אמר רב אשי חזינא ליה לרב כהנא דנקט תרתי ובצע חדא אמר לקטו כתיב רבי זירא הוה בצע אכולה שירותיה אמר ליה רבינא לרב אשי והא מיחזי כרעבתנותא אמר ליה כיון דכל יומא לא עביד והאידנא הוא דקעביד לא מיחזי כרעבתנותא רבי אמי ורבי אסי כי מיקלע להו ריפתא דעירובא שרו עילויה אמרי הואיל ואיתעביד בה חדא מצוה ליתעביד בה מצוה אחרינא: כיצד נפלה דליקה כו': ת"ר כמה סעודות חייב אדם לאכול בשבת שלש רבי חידקא אומר ארבע א"ר יוחנן ושניהם מקרא אחד דרשו ויאמר משה אכלוהו היום כי שבת היום לה' היום לא תמצאהו בשדה רבי חידקא סבר הני תלתא היום לבר מאורתא ורבנן סברי בהדי דאורתא תנן נפלה דליקה בלילי שבת מצילין

רש"י

אלא אמר רב אשי כו'. בין רבנן ובין בן בתירא כר' אליעזר סבירא להו דבעי ג' מחיצות וב' לחיים בעלמא והכא לגבי ספר אמרי רבנן מודה ר' אליעזר בלחי אחד ובן בתירא אמר דמודה ר' אליעזר אף בלא לחי: בחד לחי סגי ליה. מילתא דרבנן קא מפרשי:

מתני' נפלה דליקה בלילי שבת. קודם אכילה: שחרית. קודם סעודה: לעולם הוא מציל. הואיל ויומא בר הכי הוא ובהיתרא טרח דהא בני טלטול נינהו ולחצר המעורבת ואפי' טובא הוה שרי ליה אי לאו משום גזירה וכדמפרש בגמרא: גמ' מכדי בהיתרא קטרח. חזו לטלטול ולחצר המעורבת: ואי שרית ליה. לאתחולי בהצלה כולי האי מתוך שהוא בהול מינשי ליה שבת ואתי נמי לכבויי: ויקלוט. קילוח הנופל מן האויר: ויצרף. סמוך לגג כעין שאיבה אלא שאינו ראוי לשאוב שהגג חלק ואין אינו בגומא מצרף כלי לגג שיזוב מן הגג לכלי והוא אוחז הכלי בידו: התם מאי גזירה איכא. כיון דמידי דהתירא הוא אמאי לא יקלוט ויצרף: שמא יביא כלי כו'. מתוך שהוא מחזר על כלים הרבה ישכח ויביא: ולא יקלוט ואח"כ יזמין. אורחים דבשעת קליטה לא מיבעיא ליה: אין מערימין בכך. לזמן אורחים שאינן צריכין לאכול ויותירו: שנפלו לבור. בי"ט ואין שניהם ראוים לשחיטה ביום אחד: ואינו שוחטו. שמואל לו עלילה שמא חברו שמן ממנו: עד כאן לא קאמר ר' אליעזר. דאין מערימין: הציל פת נקיה. לשלש סעודות: לא יציל פת הדראה. פת קיבר שניטל הדרה לפי שאין ערמה כשרה לומר פת הדראה נוחה לי: אבל לא משבת ליום הכפורים. כגון אם חל יוה"כ באחד בשבת דהא לא אכיל עד לאורתא ולאורתא ליטרח ולייתי: ואין צריך לומר משבת לי"ט. דיכול להכין בו ביום: מרדה. כלי שרודין בו הפת ומפרידין אותו מכותל התנור שנדבק בה לא ירדה אותו במרדה שהוא דרך חול: ישכים אדם. בע"ש לטרוח ולזמן הוצאת שבת: והכינו את אשר יביאו לאלתר. בשעת הבאה הכנה והבאה בהשכמה היא דכתיב וילקטו אותו בבקר בבקר (שמות טז): לבצוע. ברכת המוציא: נקיט תרתי. אוחזן בידו: לקטו כתיב. דמשמע אחיזה אבל בליעה לא כתיב משנה: בצע לכוליה שירותיה. פרוסה גדולה ודי לו בה לאותה סעודה ולכבוד שבת ונראה כמחבב סעודת שבת להתחזק ולאכול הרבה: כי מקלע להו. פעמים שהעירוב בביתם ופעמים בבית אחד משאר בני אדם: שרו ביה. היינו ברכת המוציא שהיא התחלת אכילה. שרו מתחילין: תלתא היום. למנין שלש סעודות בלא:

לעולם

תוספות

הא דתניא נשברה לו חבית בראש גגו. הקשה הרב פורת אמאי לא פריך ממתניתין דריש חבית (לקמן קמג:) דתנן חבית שנשברה מצילין ממנה מזון שלש סעודות ואומר לאחרים בואו והצילו לכם ובלבד שלא יספוג ותירץ דההיא איכא למימר כגון שהחבית בכרמלית דחיישינן שמא יעביר כלי ד' אמות בכרמלית אבל בהך ברייתא קתני בהדיא בראש גגו ור"י תירץ דהתם מיירי כשנשפך היין לארץ דחיישינן שמא יספוג אומר ה"ר שמואל בשם ר"ת דדוקא נשברה לו חבית אבל נסדקה ועושה טיף טיף מותר להביא כלים לקלוט ולצרף דאינו בהול כל כך להביא כלים דרך רה"ר כמו כשנשברה:

כלי אחר ויקלוט כלי אחר ויצרף. אומר ר"י דזו אף זו קתני לא מבעי לקלוט דמינכר שמציל דאסור אלא אפילו לצרף דלא מינכר כולי האי שהוא מציל אסור:

הציל פת נקיה לא יציל פת הדראה. אומר ר"י כשאפו בי"ט של פסח מצות מסולת נקיה שיש לו די לצורך י"ט אין אופין אחריהן פת של הדראה אלא מתחילה יעשה של הדראה ואחרי כן יעשה הנקיה:

אבל לא משבת ליום הכפורים. פירש בקונטרס למוצאי יוה"כ ואה"ת פשיטא דחול גמור הוא ומ"ש משבת למוצאי שבת וי"ל דמצוה לאכול במוצאי יוה"כ כדפי' לעיל (ג) (דף קיד:) ועוד לפי שהתענו מותר יותר אי נמי ליום הכפורים עצמו קאמר ולהאכיל התינוקות:

והתנא דבי רבי ישמעאל כל מלאכת עבודה לא תעשו. וא"ת ואמאי מייתי קרא דכל מלאכת עבודה דכתיב גבי י"ט הא אפי' בשבת דכתיב לא תעשה מלאכה סתם ולא כתיב עבודה שרי לתקוע ולרדות מן התורה כדמשמע הכא דלשבת מייתי לה ופירש רבינו שמואל דגרס (ב) כל מלאכה לא תעשו ורשב"א מפרש דלעולם מכל מלאכת עבודה איממעיט תקיעה ורדייה ושבת ילפינן מי"ט דאין בין י"ט לשבת אלא אוכל נפש בלבד כדכתיב אך אשר יאכל לכל נפש (שמות יב):

שהיא חכמה ואינה מלאכה. וכיון דמדאורייתא שריא אע"ג דמדרבנן אסירא כדאמר בראש השנה (דף לג.) אין מעכבין את התינוקות מלתקוע הא נשים מעכבין הכא הוה לן למישרי משום ג' סעודות:

במנחה

עין משפט נר מצוה

יז א מיי' פי"ו מהל' שבת הלכה ב ופכ"ג הלכ"ו סמג לאוין סה ועשין א טור שו"ע או"ח סימן שלד סעיף ח וסימן שמג סעיף א ג יד:

יח ב מיי' פכ"ג שם הלכ"א וסמג שם טור ושו"ע או"ח סימן שלד סעיף א:

יט ג מיי' פרק כ"ב שם הלכה ט סמג שם טוש"ע או"ח סימן שלה סעיף ב:

כ ד מיי' שם טור שו"ע שם סעיף ג:

כא ה מיי' פ"ב מהלכות יו"ט הלכה ד טור שו"ע או"ח סימן תלא סעיף י:

כב ו מיי' פכ"ג מהלכות שבת הלכה כה טור שו"ע או"ח סימן שלד סעיף ג:

כג ז מיי' שם טור שו"ע שם סעיף ד:

כד ח מיי' פכ"ב שם הל"א סמג שם טור ושו"ע או"ח סימן רנד סעיף ה:

כה ט טוש"ע או"ח סי' רנ סעיף א:

כו י כ מיי' פ"ל שם הלכה ט סמג עשין ל טור שו"ע או"ח סימן רעד סעיף א ב וסימן רפט סעיף א:

כז ל טוש"ע או"ח סימן שלד סעיף ב בהג"ה:

כח מ מיי' וסמג שם טוש"ע או"ח סימן רצא סעיף א:

רבינו חננאל

אסקה רב אשי ג' מחיצות ולחי א' והוא מבוי שאינו מפולש שאין בו שיתוף ולא עירוב וזה להציל כתבי הקדש אבל אוכלין ומשקין אין מצילין אלא לחצר המעורבת דהלכת' כת"ק. והא דאמר רבה ב' מחיצות ולחי אחד זהו מפולש. ב' מחיצות וב' לחיים זהו שאינו מפולש. ואליבא דר' יהודה דאמר מי שיש לו ב' בתים בב' צדי רה"ר עושה לחי מכאן ולחי מכאן או קורה מיכן וקורה מיכן ונושא ונותן באמצע והכי פי' דכד פסיק לה לרה"ר לרחבה מב' צדיה ב' בתים עושה לחי מיכן ולחי מיכן ומערב ונושא ונותן באמצע. והתם איכא פלוגתא דת"ק (וחנינא) [וחנניה] ורב אמר הלכה כת"ק. ושמואל אמר הלכה (כחנינא) [כחנניה]. וקאי במבוי שיש בו ב' מחיצו' בלבד כנגד זו וב' פתחים יש לו זה כנגד זה והאי איכא עליה לחי או קורה מיכן ולחי או קורה מיכן. לר' יהודה דלא מצריך דלת יכול לערב אותו. א"ל אביי א"כ למר נמי כיון שמתערב יצילו לתוכן אוכלין ומשקין. ובא רב אשי ופירק. וסלקא כותיה: מצילין מזון ג' סעודות. ואקשינן מכדי בהיתרא קא טרח דקתני להיכן מצילין לחצר המעורבת נציל טפי. ופרקי אמר רבה מתוך שאדם בהול על ממונו דאי שרית ליה להציל כל מאי דבעי אתי לכבויי. א"ל אביי ואלא הא דתניא נשברה לו חבית בראש גגו מביא כלי ומניח תחתיה ובלבד שלא יביא כלי אחר ויקלוט כלי אחר ויצרף. התם מ"ט לא יביא כלי אחר ויקלוט כלי אחר ויצרף והא בהיתרא קא טרח. אהדר ליה רבה התם נמי גזרו עליה דאי שרית לאתויי כלי [אחר יביא כלין] דרך רה"ר וכיון שנאסר מלהביא כלי אחר הרי זה מייאש ולא פשט באיסורא. והא דמי שנשברה לו חבית בראש גגו. סלקא דלאו בפלוגתא דר' אליעזר ור' יהושע היא. ולענין פת בתנור הלכתא כי הא דתניא שכח פת בתנור וקדש עליה היום מציל מזון ג' סעודות. ואומר לאחרים בואו והצילו לכם. ולא ירדה במרדה אלא בסכין. ואע"ג דתנא דבי שמואל כל מלאכת עבודה לא תעשו. יצא תקיעת שופר ורדיית הפת שהיא חכמה ואינה מלאכה. כמה שאפשר לשנויי משנינן: אמר רב חסדא לעולם ישכים אדם להוצאת שבת שנאמר והיה ביום הששי והכינו לאלתר. והלכתא כר' אבא דאמר חייב אדם לבצוע על ב' ככרות בשבת. ואיתא

מסורת הש"ס

א) [לקמן קכ.], ב) לקמן קכ:, ג) לעיל מב. ע"ש, ד) [לקמן קכ.], ה) ביצה לז. [תוספתא דביצה פ"ג], ו) לקמן קכד., ז) [תוס' פי"ד], ח) [גי' הערוך בערך רד הדראה פי' לחם עב ובלע"ז אורדי"ן], ט) [שם], י) לקמן קלא: ע"ש ר"ה כט: ע"ש, כ) [לקמן קכט: וש"נ], ל) [ברכות לט:], מ) ברכות לט:, נ) כתובות סד:, ס) (ויקרא כג), ע) [צ"ל לא תעשה כל מלאכה שמות כ].

הגהות הב"ח

(א) גמ' והא תנא דבי ר' ישמעאל לא תעשו. נ"ב עי' בפי' ר"ח דמילה דף קלא ע"ב דגורס קרא דכל מלאכת עבודה לא תעשו: (ב) תוס' ד"ה אבל וכו' כדפי' לעיל. נ"ב בס"פ אלו קשרים ממש. וכ"כ התוס' סוף יומא דף פח בד"ה והאמר רב:

גליון הש"ס

גמ' ואין מערימין בכך. מו"ק דף יב ע"ב:

תורה אור השלם

א) וְיוֹם הַשְּׁבִיעִי שַׁבָּת לַייָ אֱלֹהֶיךָ לֹא תַעֲשֶׂה כָל מְלָאכָה אַתָּה וּבִנְךָ וּבִתֶּךָ עַבְדְּךָ וַאֲמָתְךָ וּבְהֶמְתֶּךָ וְגֵרְךָ אֲשֶׁר בִּשְׁעָרֶיךָ: [שמות כ, י]

ב) וְהָיָה בַּיּוֹם הַשִּׁשִּׁי וְהֵכִינוּ אֵת אֲשֶׁר יָבִיאוּ וְהָיָה מִשְׁנֶה עַל אֲשֶׁר יִלְקְטוּ יוֹם יוֹם: [שמות טז, ה]

ג) וַיְהִי בַּיּוֹם הַשִּׁשִּׁי לָקְטוּ לֶחֶם מִשְׁנֶה שְׁנֵי הָעֹמֶר לָאֶחָד וַיָּבֹאוּ כָּל נְשִׂיאֵי הָעֵדָה וַיַּגִּידוּ לְמֹשֶׁה: [שמות טז, כב]

ד) וַיֹּאמֶר מֹשֶׁה אִכְלֻהוּ הַיּוֹם כִּי שַׁבָּת הַיּוֹם לַייָ הַיּוֹם לֹא תִמְצָאֻהוּ בַּשָּׂדֶה: [שמות טז, כה]

ליקוטי רש"י

אותו ואת בנו. שאין מותרין לשחוט שניהן היום [ביצה לז.]. עושה לו פרנסה. כל לשון פרנסה לשון עסיית צרכיה הוא קונדי"ר בלע"ז כמו לפרנסה שמן באב (כתובות סח.) וכמו מוליכין לפרנסה ואין מוליכין למזונות (שם סט.) [גיטין סה:]. כל צורך סיפוק קרי פרנסה קונדרי"ר בלע"ז [ב"מ מו.]. הדראה. שניטל כל הדרה דהיינו פת קיבר [פסחים לו:]. יצא תקיעת שופר. דאפילו תקיעת הרשות ליח בה איסורא דאורייתא [לקמן קלא:]. ורדיית הפת. לרדיית הפת שבות היא שהיא חכמה ואינה מלאכה [לעיל ג:]. ריפתא דעירובא. שערבו בו אמשול ערובי חצירות [ברכות לט:].

do you account for **that which was taught in a Baraisa,** where the threat is due to another source? For it was taught in a Baraisa: נִשְׁבְּרָה לוֹ חָבִית בְּרֹאשׁ גַּגּוֹ – If A BARREL filled with wine BROKE ON ONE'S ROOFTOP, מֵבִיא כְּלִי וּמַנִּיחַ תַּחְתֶּיהָ – HE MAY BRING A VESSEL AND PLACE IT BENEATH [THE BARREL] in the courtyard below in order to save the wine, וּבִלְבַד שֶׁלֹּא יָבִיא כְּלִי אַחֵר וִיקַלּוֹט – PROVIDED HE DOES NOT BRING ANOTHER VESSEL AND CATCH the wine in midair as it falls from the roof, כְּלִי אַחֵר וִיצָרֵף – or ANOTHER VESSEL AND HOLD IT LEVEL with the roof to collect the wine as it runs over the edge.[7] הָתָם מַאי גְּזֵירָה אִיכָּא – **There, what** reason for a **decree is there?** Why did the Rabbis limit saving the wine, since no forbidden acts are involved?

The Gemara answers:

הָכִי נַמִּי גְּזֵירָה שֶׁמָּא יָבִיא כְּלִי דֶּרֶךְ רְשׁוּת הָרַבִּים – **Here too** there is **a decree, lest** in his haste **[the person]** forget the Sabbath and **carry a vessel through the public domain.**[8]

The Gemara quotes the aforementioned Baraisa more fully and analyzes it:

גּוּפָא – **The text itself** stated: נִשְׁבְּרָה לוֹ חָבִית בְּרֹאשׁ גַּגּוֹ – If A BARREL filled with wine BROKE ON ONE'S ROOFTOP, מֵבִיא כְּלִי וּמַנִּיחַ תַּחְתֶּיהָ – HE MAY BRING A VESSEL AND PLACE IT BENEATH [THE BARREL] in the courtyard below in order to save the wine, וּבִלְבַד שֶׁלֹּא יָבִיא כְּלִי אַחֵר וִיקַלּוֹט – PROVIDED HE DOES NOT BRING ANOTHER VESSEL AND CATCH the wine in midair as it falls from the roof, כְּלִי אַחֵר וִיצָרֵף – or ANOTHER VESSEL AND HOLD IT LEVEL with the roof. נִזְדַּמֵּן לוֹ אוֹרְחִין – If GUESTS CHANCE TO VISIT HIM and he needs the wine to serve them, מֵבִיא כְּלִי אַחֵר וְקוֹלֵט – HE MAY BRING ANOTHER VESSEL AND CATCH the wine in midair, כְּלִי אַחֵר וּמְצָרֵף – or ANOTHER VESSEL AND HOLD IT LEVEL with the roof. וְלֹא יְקַלּוֹט וְאַחַר כָּךְ יַזְמִין – BUT HE MAY NOT CATCH the wine AND AFTERWARDS INVITE guests.[9] אֶלָּא יַזְמִין וְאַחַר כָּךְ יְקַלּוֹט – RATHER, HE SHOULD first INVITE guests AND AFTERWARDS CATCH the wine. וְאֵין מַעֲרִימִין בְּכָךְ – AND ONE MUST NOT EMPLOY A SUBTERFUGE IN THIS MATTER, i.e. he may not, as a pretext, invite guests whom he knows have already dined and will leave over most of the wine they are served. מִשּׁוּם רַבִּי יוֹסֵי בַּר יְהוּדָה אָמְרוּ מַעֲרִימִין – IN THE NAME OF R' YOSE BAR YEHUDAH THEY SAID: ONE MAY EMPLOY A SUBTERFUGE.

The Gemara attempts to connect the above dispute to an earlier dispute of Tannaim:

לֵימָא בִּפְלוּגְתָּא דְּרַבִּי אֱלִיעֶזֶר וְרַבִּי יְהוֹשֻׁעַ קָמִיפַּלְגֵי – **Let us say** that **[the Tanna Kamma and R' Yose bar Yehudah] dispute concerning** the same principle that underlies **a dispute between R' Eliezer and R' Yehoshua.** דְּתַנְיָא – **For it was taught in a Baraisa:** אוֹתוֹ וְאֶת בְּנוֹ שֶׁנָּפְלוּ לְבוֹר – [AN ANIMAL] AND ITS OFFSPRING THAT FELL INTO A PIT on Yom Tov,[10] רַבִּי אֱלִיעֶזֶר אוֹמֵר – R' ELIEZER SAYS: מַעֲלֶה אֶת הָרִאשׁוֹן עַל מְנָת לְשׁוֹחֲטוֹ – ONE MAY RAISE THE FIRST animal IN ORDER TO SLAUGHTER IT and he must then slaughter it; וְהַשֵּׁנִי עוֹשֶׂה לוֹ פַּרְנָסָה בִּמְקוֹמוֹ בִּשְׁבִיל שֶׁלֹּא יָמוּת – AND FOR THE SECOND ANIMAL HE PROVIDES SUSTENANCE IN ITS PLACE in the pit SO THAT IT NOT DIE. רַבִּי יְהוֹשֻׁעַ אוֹמֵר – R' YEHOSHUA SAYS: מַעֲלִין אֶת הָרִאשׁוֹן עַל מְנָת לְשׁוֹחֲטוֹ וְאֵינוֹ שׁוֹחֲטוֹ – ONE MAY RAISE THE FIRST animal ostensibly IN ORDER TO SLAUGHTER IT, BUT HE NEED NOT SLAUGHTER IT, וּמַעֲרִים וּמַעֲלֶה אֶת הַשֵּׁנִי – AND he may then EMPLOY A SUBTERFUGE TO RAISE THE SECOND animal.[11] רָצָה זֶה שׁוֹחֵט רָצָה זֶה שׁוֹחֵט – Subsequently, if HE WISHES HE MAY SLAUGHTER THIS ONE, and if HE WISHES HE MAY SLAUGHTER THAT ONE.[12] Thus, R' Yehoshua rules leniently in a case of financial loss and permits one to employ a subterfuge, while R' Eliezer rules stringently. Similarly, it would seem that R' Yehoshua would permit inviting guests who have no desire to drink as a subterfuge in order to be permitted to use more utensils to save the wine, while R' Eliezer would forbid this.

The Gemara responds that the two disputes are not necessarily interdependent:

מִמַּאי – **On what** basis do you conclude this? דִּילְמָא עַד כָּאן לָא קָאָמַר רַבִּי אֱלִיעֶזֶר הָתָם דְּאֶפְשָׁר בְּפַרְנָסָה – **Perhaps R' Eliezer ruled** stringently only **there, because it is possible** to avoid financial loss **by providing sustenance** for the animal in the pit; אֲבָל הָכָא דְּלָא אֶפְשָׁר לָא – **but here, where it is not possible** to avoid a financial loss without resorting to a subterfuge, he would **not** forbid a subterfuge. Rather, he might accept the lenient view of R' Yose bar Yehudah and allow the owner to save the wine by inviting guests whom he knows will not drink. וְעַד כָּאן לָא קָאָמַר רַבִּי יְהוֹשֻׁעַ הָתָם מִשּׁוּם דְּאִיכָּא צַעַר בַּעֲלֵי חַיִּים – **And perhaps R' Yehoshua ruled** leniently only **there, because there is suffering to a living creature** if we have to leave the animal in the pit until the conclusion of Yom Tov; אֲבָל הָכָא דְּלֵיכָּא צַעַר בַּעֲלֵי חַיִּים לָא – **but here, where there is no suffering to a living creature,** he would **not** permit the use of a subterfuge.

We therefore cannot say with certainty that the dispute between R' Eliezer and R' Yehoshua is analogous to the present dispute.

More rules that apply when saving food from a fire:

תָּנוּ רַבָּנַן – **The Rabbis taught in a Baraisa:** הִצִּיל פַּת נְקִיָּה אֵין מַצִּיל פַּת הַדְּרָאָה – If HE SAVED BREAD made OF FINE FLOUR enough for three meals, HE MAY NOT subsequently SAVE BREAD made OF INFERIOR FLOUR;[13] פַּת הַדְּרָאָה מַצִּיל פַּת נְקִיָּה – however, if he saved BREAD made OF INFERIOR FLOUR, HE MAY

NOTES

7. He positions the vessel directly next to the roof and catches the wine as it overspills the edge (*Rashi*).

8. If we allow him to bring an unlimited number of vessels to catch the liquid, he may become so involved in his search for containers that he will forget the Sabbath and carry them through the public domain (*Rashi*).

According to this explanation, the point is not *how* he uses the vessel to collect the wine (i.e. by placing a vessel on the ground of the courtyard as opposed to holding a vessel in his hand and catching the runoff in midair and/or next to the roof) but rather *the number* of vessels he employs to do this. If he uses only one vessel, he may even catch the wine in midair or place the vessel next to the roof (*Smag* and *Sefer HaTerumah,* cited by *Beis Yosef, Orach Chaim* 335 ד״ה ואם נשברה; see *Mishnah Berurah* 335:8,9).

9. For at the time of the saving he does not yet need the wine (*Rashi*).

10. According to Biblical law (see *Leviticus* 22:28) an animal and its offspring (i.e. a mother and her young) may not be slaughtered on the same day (see *Rashi*). Since an animal may be hauled out of a pit on Yom Tov only if it will be slaughtered and used on that day (*Beitzah* 25b-26a), it is forbidden to remove both animals from the pit on Yom Tov, since only one can be slaughtered.

11. I.e. he may claim that the first animal did not meet his expectations, e.g. it was too thin, and that the animal which is still in the pit might be more desirable for the Yom Tov meal (*Rashi*). [The owner prefers to have both animals removed from the pit as soon as possible because there is a danger that they may die there.]

12. He may choose to slaughter whichever he pleases. [Some authorities say that this includes the option of slaughtering *neither* of them. Others assert that he must in fact slaughter one (*Mishnah Berurah* 498:59).]

13. [פַּת הַדְּרָאָה is a euphemistic expression for bread whose beauty (הָדָר) has been removed (*Rashi;* cf. *Ran* to *Pesachim* fol. 10b).]

Even those who permit the employment of a subterfuge do so only when the subterfuge is credible. Since no one would desire bread made of coarse flour if he has bread made of fine flour, the person's claim that he prefers bread made of coarse flour is not a legally acceptable subterfuge (see *Rashi*).

עין משפט
נר מצוה

יז א מיי' פי"ז מהל' שבת הלכה ג ופכ"ג הלכ"ו סמג לאוין סה ועשין א טור שו"ע או"ח סימן שלד סעיף יז וסימן שמג סעיף א ג יד:
יח ב מיי' פכ"ג שם הלכ"א וסמג שם טור ושו"ע או"ח סימן שלד סעיף א:
יט ג מיי' פרק כ"ג שם הלכה טו סמג שם טוש"ע או"ח סימן שלה סעיף ג:
כ ד מיי' שם טור שו"ע שם סעיף ג:
כא ה מיי' פ"ג מהלכות יו"ט הלכה ד טור שו"ע או"ח סימן תקא סעיף י:
כב ו מיי' פכ"ג מהלכות שבת הלכה כה טור שו"ע או"ח סימן שלד סעיף ג:
כג ז מיי' שם טור שו"ע שם סעיף ד:
כד ח מיי' פכ"ג שם הל"א סמג שם טור ושו"ע או"ח סימן רנד סעיף ה:
כה ט טוש"ע או"ח סי' רנ סעיף א:
כו י כ מיי' פ"ל שם הלכה ט סמג עשין ל טור שו"ע או"ח סימן רעד סעיף א ג וסימן רפט סעיף א:
כז ל טוש"ע או"ח סימן שלד סעיף ג בהג"ה:
כח מ מיי' וסמג שם טוש"ע או"ח סימן רצא סעיף א:

מסורת הש"ס

א) [לקמן קכ.], ב) לקמן קכ:, ג) לעיל מג. ע"ש, ד) [לקמן קכ.], ה) ביצה לז. [תוספתא דביצה פ"ג לקמן קכד., ו) [תוס' פי"ד], ז) [גי' הערוך בערך רד הרדאה פי' לחם עב ובלע"ז אורד"ו], ח) [שם], ט) לקמן קלא: ע"ש ר"ה כט: ע"ש, י) [לקמן קכח: וש"נ], כ) [ברכות לט:], ל) ברכות לט:, מ) כתובות קד:, נ) (ויקרא כג), ס) [נ"ל לא תעשה כל מלאכה שמות כ].

אלא אמר רב אשי שלש מחיצות ולחי אחד זה מבוי שאינו מפולש ג' מחיצות בלא לחי זהו מבוי המפולש ואפילו לרבי אליעזר דאמר בעינן לחיים הני מילי לאוכלין ומשקין אבל לספר תורה בחד לחי סגי:

מתני' מצילין מזון ג' סעודות הראוי לאדם לאדם הראוי לבהמה לבהמה כיצד נפלה דליקה בלילי שבת מצילין מזון ג' סעודות בשחרית מצילין מזון ב' סעודות במנחה מזון סעודה אחת ר' יוסי אומר לעולם מצילין מזון שלש סעודות:

גמ' מכדי בהיתרא קטרח נציל טפי אמר רבא מתוך שאדם בהול על ממונו אי שרית ליה אתי לכבויי א"ל אביי אלא הא דתניא נשברה לו חבית בראש גגו מביא כלי ומניח תחתיה ובלבד שלא יביא כלי אחר ויקלוט כלי אחר ויצרף התם מאי גזירה איכא ה"נ גזירה שמא יביא כלי דרך רה"ר גופא נשברה לו חבית בראש גגו מביא כלי ומניח תחתיה ובלבד שלא יביא כלי אחר ויקלוט כלי אחר ויצרף נזדמנו לו אורחין מביא כלי אחר וקולט כלי אחר ומצרף ולא יקלוט ואחר כך יזמין אלא יזמין ואח"כ יקלוט ואין מערימין בכך משום רבי יוסי בר יהודה אמרו מערימין לימא בפלוגתא דרבי אליעזר ור' יהושע קמיפלגי דתניא אותו ואת בנו שנפלו לבור רבי אליעזר אומר מעלה את הראשון על מנת לשוחטו והשני עושה לו פרנסה במקומו בשביל שלא ימות רבי יהושע אומר מעלין את הראשון על מנת לשוחטו ואינו שוחטו ומערים ומעלה את השני רצה זה שוחט רצה זה שוחט ממאי דילמא עד כאן לא קאמר רבי אליעזר התם דאפשר בפרנסה אבל הכא דלא אפשר לא ועד כאן לא קאמר רבי יהושע התם משום דאיכא צער בעלי חיים אבל הכא דליכא צער בעלי חיים לא ת"ר הציל פת נקיה אין מציל פת הדראה פת הדראה מציל פת נקיה ומצילין מיום הכפורים לשבת אבל לא משבת ליום הכפורים ואין צריך לומר משבת ליום טוב ולא משבת לשבת הבאה ת"ר שכח פת בתנור וקידש עליו היום מצילין מזון שלש סעודות ואומר לאחרים בואו והצילו לכם וכשהוא רודה לא ירדה במרדה אלא בסכין איני והא תנא דבי רבי ישמעאל לא תעשה כל מלאכה יצא תקיעת שופר ורדיית הפת שהיא חכמה ואינה מלאכה כמה דאפשר לשנויי משנינן א"ר חסדא לעולם ישכים אדם להוצאת שבת שנאמר והיה ביום הששי והכינו את אשר יביאו לאלתר אמר ר' אבא בשבת חייב אדם לבצוע על שתי ככרות דכתיב לחם משנה אמר רב אשי חזינא ליה לרב כהנא דנקט תרתי ובצע חדא אמר לקטו כתיב רבי זירא הוה בצע אכולה שירותיה אמר ליה רבינא לרב אשי והא מיחזי כרעבתנותא אמר ליה כיון דכל יומא לא עביד והאידנא הוא דקעביד לא מיחזי כרעבתנותא רבי אמי ורבי אסי כי מיקלע להו ריפתא דעירובא שרו עילויה אמרי הואיל ואיתעביד בה חדא מצוה ליתעביד בה מצוה אחרינא: כיצד נפלה דליקה כו': ת"ר כמה סעודות חייב אדם לאכול בשבת שלש רבי חידקא אומר ארבע א"ר יוחנן ושניהם מקרא אחד דרשו ויאמר משה אכלוהו היום כי שבת היום לה' היום לא תמצאהו בשדה רבי חידקא סבר הני תלתא היום לבר מאורתא ורבנן סברי בהדי דאורתא תנן נפלה דליקה בלילי שבת מצילין

רש"י

אלא אמר רב אשי כו'. בין רבנן ובין בן בתירא כר' אליעזר סבירא להו דבעי ג' מחיצות וב' לחיים בעלמא והכא לגבי ספר אמרי רבנן מודה ר' אליעזר בלחי אחד ובן בתירא אמר למודה ר' אליעזר אף בלא לחי: בחד לחי סגי ליה. מילתא דרבנן קא מפרשי:
מתני' נפלה דליקה בלילי שבת. קודם אכילה: שחרית. קודם סעודה: לעולם הוא מציל. הואיל ויומא בר הכי הוא ובהיתרא טרח דהא בני טלטול נינהו ולחצר המעורבת ואפי' טובא נמי שרי ליה אי לאו משום גזירה ולדמפרש בגמרא: גמ' מכדי בהיתרא קטרח. חזו לטלטול ולחצר המעורבת: ואי שרית ליה. לאצולי בהלה כולי האי מתוך שהוא בהול מינשי ליה שבת ואתי נמי לכבויי: ויקלוט. קילוח הטופל מן האויר: ויצרף. סמוך לגג כעין שאיכא אלא שאינו רואי לשאוב שהגג חלק והיין אינו בגומא מצרף כלי לגג שיזוב מן הגג לכלי והוא אוחז הכלי בידו: התם מאי גזירה איכא. כיון דמידי דהתירה הוא אמאי לא יקלוט ויצרף: שמא יביא כלי כו'. מתוך שהוא מחזר על כלים הרבה ישכח ויביא: ולא יקלוט ואח"כ יזמין. אורחים דבשעת קליטה לא מיבעיא ליה: אין מערימין בכך. לזמן אורחים שאין צריכין לאכול ויומירו: שנפלו לבור. בי"ט ואין שניהם ראוים לשחיטה ביום אחד: ואינו שוחטו. שמעלה לו עלילה שמא חברו שמן ממנו: עד כאן לא קאמר ר' אליעזר. דאין מערימין: הציל פת נקיה. לשלש סעודות: לא יציל פת הדראה. פת קיבר שניטל הדרה לפי שאין ערמה כשרה לומר פת הדראה נוחה לי: אבל לא משבת ליום הכפורים. כגון אם חל יוה"כ באחד בשבת דהא לא אכיל עד לאורתא ולאורתא ליטרח ולייתי: ואין צריך לומר משבת לי"ט. דיכול להכין בו ביום: מרדה. כלי שרודין בו הפת ומפרידין אותו מכותל התנור שנדבק בה לא ירדה אותו במרדה שהוא דרך חול: ישכים אדם. בע"ש לטרוח ולזמן הוצאת שבת: והכינו את אשר יביאו לאלתר. בשעת הבאה הכנה והבאה בהשכמה היא דכתיב וילקטו אותו בבקר בבקר (שמות טז): לבצוע. ברכת המוציא: נקיט תרתי. אוחזן בידו: לקטו כתיב. דמשמע אחיזה אבל בציעה לא כתיב משנה: בצע אכולה שירותיה. פרוסה גדולה ודי לו בה לאותה סעודה ולכבוד שבת ונראה כמתכבד סעודת שבת להתחזק ולאכול הרבה: כי מקלע להו. פעמים שהעירוב בביתם ופעמים בבית אחד משאר בני אדם: שרו ביה. היינו ברכת המוציא שהיא התחלת אכילה. שרו מתחילין: תלתא היום. למנין שלש סעודות לא:
לעולם

תוספות

הא דתניא נשברה לו חבית בראש גגו. הקשה הרב פורת אמאי לא פריך ממתניתין דריש חבית (לקמן קמג:) דתנן חבית שנשברה מצילין ממנה מזון שלש סעודות ואומר לאחרים בואו והצילו לכם ובלבד שלא יספוג ותירץ דההיא איכא למימר כגון שהחבית בכרמלית דחיישינן שמא יעביר כלי ד' אמות בכרמלית אבל בהך ברייתא קתני בהדיא בראש גגו ור"י תירץ דהתם מיירי כשנשפך היין לארץ דחיישינן שמא יספוג אומר ה"ר שמואל בשם ר"ת דדוקא נשברה לו חבית אבל נסדקה ועושה טיף טיף מותר להביא כלים לקלוט ולצרף דאינו בהול כל כך להביא כלים דרך רה"ר כמו כשנשברה:

כלי אחר ויקלוט כלי אחר ויצרף. אומר ר"י דזו אף זו קתני לא מבעי לקלוט דמינכר שמציל דאסור אלא אפילו לצרף דלא מינכר כולי האי שהוא מציל אסור: **הציל** פת נקיה לא יציל פת הדראה. אומר ר"י כשאפו בי"ט של פסח מצות מסולת נקיה שיש לו די לצורך י"ט אין אופין אחריהן פת של הדראה אלא מתחילה יעשה של הדראה ואחרי כן יעשה הנקיה:

אבל לא משבת ליום הכפורים. פירש בקונטרס למוצאי יוה"כ וא"ת פשיטא דחול גמור הוא ומ"ש משבת למוצאי שבת וי"ל דמצוה לאכול במוצאי יוה"כ כדפי' לעיל (ב) (דף קיד:) ועוד לפי שהתענו מותר יותר אי נמי ליום הכפורים עצמו קאמר ולהאכיל התינוקות:

והתנא דבי רבי ישמעאל כל מלאכת עבודה לא תעשו. וא"ת ואמאי מייתי קרא דכל מלאכת עבודה דכתיב גבי י"ט הא אפי' בשבת דכתיב לא תעשה מלאכה סתם ולא כתיב עבודה שרי לתקוע ולרדות מן התורה כדמשמע הכא דאשבת מייתי לה ופירש רבינו שמואל דגרס כל מלאכה לא תעשו ורשב"א מפרש דלעולם מכל מלאכת עבודה אימעיט תקיעה ורדייה ושבת ילפינן מי"ט דאין בין י"ט לשבת אלא אוכל נפש בלבד כדכתיב אך אשר יאכל לכל נפש (שמות יב):

שהיא חכמה ואינה מלאכה. וכיון דמדאורייתא שריא אע"ג דמדרבנן אסירא כדאמר בראש השנה (דף לג.) אין מעכבין את התינוקות מלתקוע הא נשים מעכבין הכא הוה לן למישרי משום ג' סעודות:
במנחה

הגהות הב"ח

(א) גמ' והא תנא דבי ר' ישמעאל לא תעשו. נ"ב עי' בפ' ר"א דמילה דף קלא ע"ב דגורס קרא דכל מלאכת עבודה לא תעשו: (ב) תוס' ד"ה אבל וכו' כדפי' לעיל. נ"ב בס"פ אלו קשרים ממש. וכ"כ התוס' סוף יומא דף פח בד"ה והאמר רב:

גליון הש"ס

גמ' ואין מערימין בכך. מו"ק דף יב ע"ב:

תורה אור השלם

א) וְיוֹם הַשְּׁבִיעִי שַׁבָּת לַייָ אֱלֹהֶיךָ לֹא תַעֲשֶׂה כָל מְלָאכָה אַתָּה וּבִנְךָ וּבִתֶּךָ עַבְדְּךָ וַאֲמָתְךָ וּבְהֶמְתֶּךָ וְגֵרְךָ אֲשֶׁר בִּשְׁעָרֶיךָ: [שמות כ, י]
ב) וְהָיָה בַּיּוֹם הַשִּׁשִּׁי וְהֵכִינוּ אֵת אֲשֶׁר יָבִיאוּ וְהָיָה מִשְׁנֶה עַל אֲשֶׁר יִלְקְטוּ יוֹם יוֹם: [שמות טז, ה]
ג) וַיְהִי בַּיּוֹם הַשִּׁשִּׁי לָקְטוּ לֶחֶם מִשְׁנֶה שְׁנֵי הָעֹמֶר לָאֶחָד וַיָּבֹאוּ כָּל נְשִׂיאֵי הָעֵדָה וַיַּגִּידוּ לְמֹשֶׁה: [שמות טז, כב]
ד) וַיֹּאמֶר מֹשֶׁה אִכְלֻהוּ הַיּוֹם כִּי שַׁבָּת הַיּוֹם לַייָ הַיּוֹם לֹא תִמְצָאֻהוּ בַּשָּׂדֶה: [שמות טז, כה]

ליקוטי רש"י

אותו ואת בנו. שאין מותרין לשחוט שניהן היום [ביצה לז.]. עושה לו פרנסה. כל לשון פרנסה לשון עשיית צרכיו קונדוי"ר בלע"ז כמו לפרנסה שמן באש (כתובות סח.) וכמו מוליכין לפרנסה ואין מוליכין למותם (שם סב.) [גיטין סה:]. כל צורך סיפוק קרי פרנסה קונדוי"ר בלע"ז [ב"מ סו.]. הדראה. שניטל כל הדרה דהיינו פת קיבר [פסחים לז:]. יצא תקיעת שופר. דאפילו תקיעת הרשות ליכא בה איסורא דאורייתא [ר"ה כט:]. ורדיית הפת. לרדות הפת מן התנור היא שבות היא שהיא חכמה ואינה מלאכה [לעיל ג:]. ריפתא דעירובא. שעירבו בו לאמצע ערובי חצרות [ברכות לט:].

רבינו חננאל

אסקה רב אשי ג' מחיצות ולחי א' והוא מבוי שאינו מפולש שאין בו שיתוף ולא עירוב וזה להציל כתבי הקדש אבל אוכלין ומשקין אין מצילין אלא לחצר המעורבת דהלכת' כת"ק. והא דאמר רבה ב' מחיצות ולחי אחד זהו מפולש. ב' מחיצות וב' לחיים זהו שאינו מפולש. ואליבא דר' יהודה דאמר מי שיש לו ב' בתים בב' צדי רה"ר עושה לחי מכאן ולחי מכאן או קורה מיכן וקורה מיכן ונושא ונותן באמצע והכי פי' דכד פסיק לה לרה"ר לרחבה מב' צדיה ב' בתים עושה לחי מיכן ולחי מיכן ומערב ונושא ונותן באמצע. והתם איכא פלוגתא דת"ק (וחנינא) [וחנניה] ורב אמר הלכה כת"ק. ושמואל אמר הלכה (כחנינא) [כחנניה]. וקאי במבוי שיש בו ב' מחיצו' בלבד כנגד זו וב' פתחים יש לו זה כנגד זה והאי איכא עליה לחי או קורה מיכן ולחי או קורה מיכן. לר' יהודה דלא מצריך דלת יכול לערב אותו. א"ל אביי א"כ למר נמי כיון שמתערב יצילו לתוכן אוכלין ומשקין. ובא רב אשי ופירק. וסלקא כותיה: מצילין מזון ג' סעודות. ואקשינן מכדי בהיתרא קא טרח דקתני להיכן מצילין לחצר המעורבת נציל טפי. ופרקי' אמר רבה מתוך שאדם בהול על ממונו דאי שרית ליה להציל כל מאי דבעי אתי לכבויי. א"ל אביי ואלא הא דתניא נשברה לו חבית בראש גגו מביא כלי ומניח תחתיה ובלבד שלא יביא כלי אחר ויקלוט כלי אחר ויצרף. התם מ"ט לא יביא כלי אחר ויקלוט כלי אחר ויצרף והא בהיתרא קא טרח. אהדר ליה רבה התם נמי גזרו עליה דאי שרית לאחרי כלי [אחר יביא כלי] דרך רה"ר וכיון שנאסר מלהביא כלי אחר הרי זה מייאש ולא פשיט באיסורא. והא דמי שנשברה לו חבית בראש גגו. סלקא דלאו בפלוגתא דר' אליעזר ור' יהושע היא. ולענין פת בתנור הלכתא כי הא דתניא שכח פת בתנור וקדש עליה היום מציל מזון ג' סעודות. ואומר לאחרים בואו והצילו לכם. ולא ירדה במרדה אלא בסכין. ואע"ג דתנא דבי שמואל כל מלאכת עבודה לא תעשו. יצא תקיעת שופר ורדיית הפת שהיא חכמה ואינה מלאכה. כמה שאפשר לשנויי משנינן: אמר רב חסדא לעולם ישכים אדם להוצאת שבת שנאמר והיה ביום הששי והכינו לאלתר. והלכתא כר' אבא דאמר חייב אדם לבצוע על ב' ככרות בשבת.
ואיתא

subsequently SAVE BREAD made OF FINE FLOUR.[14] וּמַצִּילִין מִיּוֹם הַכִּפּוּרִים לְשַׁבָּת – AND WE MAY SAVE food ON YOM KIPPUR FOR THE SABBATH, i.e. if a fire breaks out on Yom Kippur which falls on a Friday, one may salvage food for the Sabbath, אֲבָל לֹא מִשַּׁבָּת לְיוֹם הַכִּפּוּרִים – BUT NOT ON THE SABBATH FOR YOM KIPPUR, i.e. if Yom Kippur falls on a Sunday, one may not save food from a fire that breaks out on the Sabbath, in order to have food with which to break the fast on Sunday night;[15] וְאֵין צָרִיךְ לוֹמַר מִשַּׁבָּת לְיוֹם טוֹב – AND, NEEDLESS TO SAY, NOT ON THE SABBATH FOR YOM TOV[16] וְלֹא מִשַּׁבָּת לְשַׁבָּת הַבָּאָה – OR ON THIS SABBATH FOR THE COMING ONE.[17]

The Gemara shifts to discuss saving food from a different type of "peril."

תָּנוּ רַבָּנַן – The Rabbis taught in a Baraisa: שָׁכַח פַּת בַּתַּנּוּר – If ONE FORGOT BREAD baking IN AN OVEN וְקִידֵּשׁ עָלָיו הַיּוֹם – AND THE DAY BECAME HOLY ON HIM, i.e. night fell and the Sabbath began without his having removed the bread, מַצִּילִין מְזוֹן שָׁלֹשׁ סְעוּדוֹת – HE MAY SAVE FOOD (i.e. bread) FOR THREE MEALS.[18] וְאוֹמֵר לַאֲחֵרִים בּוֹאוּ וְהַצִּילוּ לָכֶם – AND HE MAY TELL OTHERS, "COME AND SAVE FOR YOURSELVES."[19] וּכְשֶׁהוּא רוֹדֶה לֹא יִרְדֶּה בְּמַרְדֶּה אֶלָּא בְּסַכִּין – AND WHEN HE REMOVES the bread, HE MUST NOT REMOVE it WITH A baker's PADDLE in the normal manner, BUT WITH A KNIFE.[20]

The Gemara asks:

אֵינִי – **Is this** indeed **so?** וְהָא תָּנָא דְּבֵי רַבִּי יִשְׁמָעֵאל – **But it was taught in the academy of R' Yishmael:** The Torah states:[21] "לֹא־תַעֲשֶׂה כָל־מְלָאכָה" – *YOU SHALL NOT DO ANY LABOR* – יָצָא תְּקִיעַת שׁוֹפָר וּרְדִיַּית הַפַּת שֶׁהִיא חָכְמָה וְאֵינָהּ מְלָאכָה – EXCLUDED IS THE BLOWING OF THE SHOFAR OR THE REMOVAL OF BREAD from an oven, BECAUSE IT IS AN ART, NOT A LABOR, i.e. the Rabbis did not decree against performing these acts since they are not similar to *melachos* but are rather skills.[22] Since the removal of bread from an oven is not Biblically prohibited, why does the Baraisa require that it be performed in an unusual manner?

The Gemara answers:

כַּמָּה דְּאֶפְשָׁר לְשַׁנּוּיֵי מְשַׁנִּינַן – **As much as it is possible to deviate** from the norm, **we must deviate.**[23]

The Gemara discusses the Sabbath meals:

אָמַר רַב חִסְדָּא – **Rav Chisda said:** לְעוֹלָם יַשְׁכִּים אָדָם לְהוֹצָאַת שַׁבָּת – **A man should always arise early** on Friday morning to tend **to the expenditures of the Sabbath,** i.e. to do his Sabbath shopping, שֶׁנֶּאֱמַר – **as it is stated:**[24] "וְהָיָה בַּיּוֹם הַשִּׁשִּׁי וְהֵכִינוּ אֵת אֲשֶׁר־יָבִיאוּ" – ***And it shall be on the sixth day that they shall prepare that which they bring.*** לְאַלְתַּר – This implies: **immediately.**[25]

The Gemara derives another mitzvah pertaining to the Sabbath meals from this section of the Torah:

אָמַר רַבִּי אַבָּא – **R' Abba said:** בְּשַׁבָּת חַיָּיב אָדָם לִבְצוֹעַ עַל שְׁתֵּי כִּכָּרוֹת – **On the Sabbath a person is obligated to break** bread, i.e. to recite the *hamotzi* blessing, **over two loaves,** דִּכְתִיב "לֶחֶם מִשְׁנֶה" – **for it is written:** ***a double portion.***[26] אָמַר רַב אַשִׁי – **Rav Ashi said:** חֲזֵינָא לֵיהּ לְרַב כַּהֲנָא דְּנָקֵט תַּרְתֵּי וּבָצַע חֲדָא – **I saw that Rav Kahana would hold two** loaves when he made the *hamotzi* blessing, **but he would break,** i.e. cut, only **one.** אָמַר – **He said** in explanation of his actions: "לָקְטוּ" כְּתִיב – ***They "gathered"*** *a double portion* **is written,** not *they "broke" a double portion.*[27]

Another practice of an Amora at the Sabbath meals:

רַבִּי זֵירָא הֲוָה בָּצַע אַכּוּלָּה שֵׁירוּתֵיהּ – **R' Zeira would break** a piece of bread after he made the *hamotzi* blessing large enough **to last the entire meal.**[28]

This practice is questioned:

אָמַר לֵיהּ רָבִינָא לְרַב אַשִׁי – **Ravina said to Rav Ashi:** וְהָא מֶיחֱזֵי כְּרַעַבְתָנוּתָא – **Why, this appears like voraciousness!**[29]

Rav Ashi defends the practice:

אָמַר לֵיהּ – **He said to [Ravina]:** כֵּיוָן דְּכָל יוֹמָא לָא עָבִיד וְהָאִידְנָא

NOTES

14. He can say that he prefers bread made of fine flour over bread made of coarse flour. (See *Sfas Emes* who cites evidence to prove that this is true even according to the Rabbis who in the case of the barrel forbid using a subterfuge.)

15. Since he can obtain other food after the fast (*Rashi*).

16. If the Sabbath is immediately followed by Yom Tov, one may not save food on the Sabbath for the Yom Tov meals, since it is permissible to prepare new food on Yom Tov (*Rashi*).

17. Since it is possible to prepare during the upcoming week (*Rashi*).

[The occurrence of Yom Kippur on a Friday or Sunday was possible in former times when Rosh Chodesh was determined by the court according to witnesses' sighting of the new moon. Our present fixed calendar precludes such a possibility.]

18. Bread was commonly baked in Talmudic times by attaching the dough to the inside walls of the oven. As we will learn below, removing bread from the walls of an oven is forbidden on the Sabbath. The Baraisa teaches that if one forgot to remove bread which he placed into an oven before the Sabbath, he may salvage only three meals' worth on the Sabbath. The remainder of the bread must be allowed to burn.

19. He may urge others to save three meals' worth for themselves as well.

20. A special paddle was normally used to remove the bread from the oven walls. When removing the three meals' worth on the Sabbath, one should not use this tool, for this is the manner in which bread is removed on the weekdays. Rather, he should use a knife (*Rashi*).

21. *Exodus* 20:10.

22. It goes without saying that these acts are not Biblically forbidden, for they were not performed in the Mishkan [nor are they *toldos* of any of the other *avos melachos*]. The Baraisa teaches, however, that since in discussing the Sabbath prohibitions the Torah spoke of "labor," even the Sages, when formulating their own Rabbinical injunctions, did not decree against these acts, for they are considered skills rather than labors (*Ran* בדפי הרי"ף fol. 1b; cf. *Tosafos* and *Ritva MHK* ed.).

23. True, the Sages did not prohibit removing bread as a Rabbinical injunction unto itself. However, since this act is a weekday type of activity (עוּבְדָא דְחוֹל), where possible it should be performed in an unusual manner. Hence, a knife should be employed rather than a baker's paddle (*Ran* ibid.). [If this is not feasible, for example if no knife is available, a baker's paddle may in fact be used (*Ran* ibid., see also *Baal HaMaor* and *Milchamos* there; *Shulchan Aruch, Orach Chaim* 254:5).]

24. *Exodus* 16:5.

25. A double ration of manna fell on Friday, half for Friday and half for the Sabbath. God instructed the Jews to "prepare that which they bring," i.e. to cook or bake the Sabbath portion of the manna on Friday. Since the verse juxtaposes "preparing" and "bringing," we learn that the preparing should be performed immediately after the bringing, i.e. the collecting. And since the collecting was done early in the morning, as it is written (ibid. 16:21): *and they collected it each morning* (see *Berachos* 27a where it is explained that this means *early* in the morning), the preparation as well should be done early in the morning (*Rashi*).

26. Ibid. v. 22. A double ration of manna would fall on Friday in honor of the Sabbath. To commemorate this miracle, we recite the *hamotzi* blessing at the Sabbath meals over two loaves.

27. By taking up the two loaves into his hand, one commemorates the "gathering." It is not necessary to slice and eat both loaves (see *Rashi*).

28. He sliced off a large portion of bread to show that he was preparing himself to eat a great deal. By doing so, he demonstrated how dear the Sabbath meal was to him (*Rashi;* cf. *Rashba*).

29. The person's good intentions notwithstanding, he gives the impression of being a glutton, a major character flaw.

אלא אמר רב אשי א שלש מחיצות ולחי אחד זה מבוי שאינו מפולש ג' מחיצות בלא לחי זהו מבוי המפולש ואפילו לרבי אליעזר דאמר בעינן לחיים הני מילי לאוכלין ומשקין אבל לספר תורה בחד לחי סגי:

מתני' ב מצילין מזון ג' סעודות הראוי לאדם לאדם הראוי לבהמה לבהמה כיצד נפלה דליקה בלילי שבת מצילין מזון ג' סעודות בשחרית מצילין מזון ב' סעודות במנחה מזון סעודה אחת ר' יוסי אומר לעולם מצילין מזון שלש סעודות:

גמ' מכדי בהיתרא קטרח נציל טפי אמר רבא ג מתוך שאדם בהול על ממונו אי שרית ליה אתי לכבויי א"ל אביי אלא הא דתניא נשברה לו חבית בראש גגו מביא כלי ומניח תחתיה ובלבד שלא יביא כלי אחר ויקלוט כלי אחר ויצרף התם מאי גזירה איכא ה"נ גזירה שמא יביא כלי דרך רה"ר גופא נשברה לו חבית בראש גגו מביא כלי ומניח תחתיה ובלבד שלא יביא כלי אחר ויקלוט כלי אחר ויצרף נזדמן לו אורחין מביא כלי אחר וקולט כלי אחר ומצרף ולא יקלוט ואח"כ יזמין אלא יזמין ואח"כ יקלוט ואין מערימין בכך משום רבי יוסי בר יהודה אמרו מערימין לימא בפלוגתא דרבי אליעזר ור' יהושע קמיפלגי דתניא אותו ואת בנו שנפלו לבור רבי אליעזר אומר מעלה את הראשון על מנת לשוחטו והשני עושה לו פרנסה במקומו בשביל שלא ימות רבי יהושע אומר מעלין את הראשון על מנת לשוחטו ואינו שוחטו ומערים ומעלה את השני רצה זה שוחט רצה זה שוחט ממאי דילמא עד כאן לא קאמר רבי אליעזר התם דאפשר בפרנסה אבל הכא דלא אפשר לא ועד כאן לא קאמר רבי יהושע התם משום דאיכא צער בעלי חיים אבל הכא דליכא צער בעלי חיים לא ת"ר הציל פת נקיה אין מציל פת הדראה פת הדראה מציל פת נקיה ומצילין מיום הכפורים לשבת אבל לא משבת ליום הכפורים ואין צריך לומר משבת ליום טוב ולא משבת לשבת הבאה ת"ר שכח פת בתנור וקידש עליו היום מצילין מזון שלש סעודות ואומר לאחרים בואו והצילו לכם וכשהוא רודה לא ירדה במרדה אלא בסכין איני והא תנא דבי רבי ישמעאל (א) לא תעשה כל מלאכה יצא תקיעת שופר ורדיית הפת שהיא חכמה ואינה מלאכה כמה דאפשר לשנויי משנינן א"ר חסדא לעולם ישכים אדם להוצאת שבת שנאמר והיה ביום הששי והכינו את אשר יביאו לאלתר אמר ר' אבא בשבת חייב אדם לבצוע על שתי ככרות דכתיב לחם משנה אמר רב אשי חזינא ליה לרב כהנא דנקט תרתי ובצע חדא אמר לקטו כתיב רבי זירא הוה בצע אכולה שירותיה אמר ליה רבינא לרב אשי והא מיחזי כרעבתנותא אמר ליה כיון דכל יומא לא עביד והאידנא הוא דקעביד לא מיחזי כרעבתנותא רבי אמי ורבי אסי כי מיקלע להו ריפתא דעירובא שרו עלויה אמרי הואיל ואיתעביד בה חדא מצוה ליתעביד בה מצוה אחריתא: כיצד נפלה דליקה כו': ת"ר כמה סעודות חייב אדם לאכול בשבת שלש רבי חידקא אומר ארבע א"ר יוחנן ושניהם מקרא אחד דרשו ויאמר משה אכלוהו היום כי שבת היום לה' היום לא תמצאהו בשדה רבי חידקא סבר הני תלתא היום לבר מאורתא ורבנן סברי בהדי דאורתא תנן נפלה דליקה בלילי שבת מצילין

רש"י

אלא אמר רב אשי כו'. בין רבנן ובין בן בתירא כר' אליעזר סבירא להו דבעי ג' מחיצות וכו' לחיים בעלמא והכא לגבי ספר אמרי רבנן מודה ר' אליעזר בלחי אחד ובן בתירא אמר דמודה ר' אליעזר אף בלא לחי: בחד לחי סגי ליה. מילתא דרבנן קא מפרשי:

מתני' נפלה דליקה בלילי שבת. קודם אכילה: שחרית. קודם סעודה: לעולם הוא מציל. הואיל ויומא בר הכי הוא והשימור טורח דהא בני טלטול נינהו ולחצר המעורבת ואפי' טובא הוה שרי ליה אי לאו משום גזירה וכדמפרש בגמרא: גמ' מכדי בהיתרא קטרח. מזון לטלטול ולחצר המעורבת: ואי שרית ליה. לאצולי בהלכה כולי האי מתוך שהוא בהול מינשי ליה שבת ואתי נמי לכבויי: ויקלוט. קילוח הנופל מן האויר: ויצרף. סמוך לגג כעין שאיבה אלא שאינו ראוי לשאוב שהגג חלק והיין אינו בגומא מצרף כלי לגג שיזוב מן הגג לכלי והוא אוחז הכלי בידו: התם מאי גזירה איכא. כיון דמידי דהצילה הוא אמאי לא יקלוט ויצרף: שמא יביא כלי כו'. מתוך שהוא מחזר על כלים הרבה ישכח ויביא: ולא יקלוט ואח"כ יזמין. אורחים דבשעת קליטה לא מיבעיא ליה: אין מערימין בכך. לזמן אורחים שאין צריכין לאכול ויותירו: שנפלו לבור. בי"ט ואין שניהם ראוים לשחיטה ביום אחד: ואינו שוחטו. שמואל לו עלילה שמא חברו שמן ממנו: עד כאן לא קאמר ר' אליעזר. דאין מערימין: הציל פת נקיה. לשלש סעודות: לא יציל פת הדראה. פת קיבר שניטל הדרה לפי שאין ערמה כשרה לומר פת הדראה נוחה לי: אבל לא משבת ליום הכפורים. כגון אם חל יוה"כ באחד בשבת דהא לא אכיל עד לאורתא ולאורתא ליטרח ולייתי: ואין צריך לומר משבת לי"ט. דיכול להכין בו ביום: מרדה. כלי שרודין בו הפת ומפרידין אותו מכותל התנור שנדבק בה לא ירדה אותו במרדה שהוא דרך חול: ישכים אדם. בע"ש לטרוח ולזמן הוצאת שבת: והכינו את אשר יביאו לאלתר. בשעת הבאה הכנה והבאה בהשכמה היא דכתיב וילקטו אותו בבקר בבקר (שמות טז): לבצוע. ברכת המוציא: נקיט תרתי. אוחזן בידו: לקטו כתיב. דמשמע אחיזה אבל בליעה לא כתיב משנה: בצע אכוליה שירותיה. פרוסה גדולה ודי לו בה לאותה סעודה ולכבוד שבת ונראה כמחבב סעודת שבת להתחזק ולאכול הרבה: כי מקלע להו. פעמים שהעירוב בביתם ופעמים בבית אחד משאר בני אדם: שרו ביה. היינו ברכת המוציא שהיא התחלת אכילה. שרו מתחילין: תלתא היום. למנין שלש סעודות בא: לעולם

תוספות

הא דתניא נשברה לו חבית בראש גגו. הקשה הר"ר פורת אמאי לא פריך ממתניתין דריש חבית (לקמן קמג.) דתנן חבית שנשברה מצילין ממנה מזון שלש סעודות ואומר לאחרים בואו והצילו לכם ובלבד שלא יספוג ותירץ דהתם איכא למימר כגון שהחבית בכרמלית דחיישינן שמא יעביר כלי ד' אמות בכרמלית אבל בהך ברייתא קתני בהדיא בראש גגו ור"י מפרש דהתם מיירי כשנשפך היין לארץ דחיישינן שמא יספוג. אומר ה"ר שמואל דהאי ר"ש דדוקא נשברה לו חבית אבל נסדקה ועושה טיף טיף מותר להביא כלים לקלוט ולצרף דאינו בהול כל כך להביא כלים דרך רה"ר כמו כשנשברה:

כלי אחר ויקלוט כלי אחר ויצרף. אומר ר"י דזו אף זו קתני לא מבעי לקלוט דמינכר שמציל דאסור אלא אפילו לצרף דלא מינכר כולי האי שהוא מציל אסור: הציל פת נקיה לא יציל פת הדראה. אומר ר"י כשאפו בי"ט של פסח מצות מסולת נקיה שיש לו די לצורך י"ט אין אופין אחריהן פת של הדראה אלא מתחילה יעשה של הדראה ואחרי כן יעשה הנקיה:

אבל לא משבת ליום הכפורים. פירש בקונטרס למוצאי יוה"כ וא"ת פשיטא דחול גמור הוא ומ"ש משבת למוצאי שבת וי"ל דמצוה לאכול במוצאי יוה"כ כדפי' לעיל (נ) (דף קיד:) ועוד לפי שהתענו מותר יותר אי נמי ליום הכפורים עצמו קאמר ולהאכיל התינוקות:

והתנא דבי רבי ישמעאל כל מלאכת עבודה לא תעשו. וא"ת ואמאי מייתי קרא (י) דכל מלאכת עבודה דכתיב גבי י"ט הא אפי' בשבת דכתיב לא תעשה מלאכה סתם ולא כתיב עבודה שרי לתקוע ולרדות מן התורה כדמשמע הכא דאשבת מייתי לה ופירש רבינו שמואל דגרס (פ) כל מלאכה לא תעשו ורשב"א מפרש דלעולם מכל מלאכת עבודה אימעיט תקיעה ורדייה ושבת ילפינן מי"ט דאין בין י"ט לשבת אלא אוכל נפש בלבד כדכתיב אך אשר יאכל לכל נפש (שמות יב):

שהיא חכמה ואינה מלאכה. וכיון דמדאורייתא שריא אע"ג דמדרבנן אסירא כדאמר בראש השנה (דף לג.) אין מעכבין את התינוקות מלתקוע הא נשים מעכבין הכא הוה לן למישרי משום ג' סעודות:

במנחה

עין משפט נר מצוה

יז א מיי' פי"ח מהל' שבת הלכה ג וספ"ג מהל' עירובין סמג לאוין סה ועשין א טור שו"ע או"ח סימן שלב סעיף א וסימן שמב סעיף א ג ד:

יח ב מיי' פכ"ג שם הל"ח וסמג שם טור ושו"ע או"ח סימן שלד סעיף א:

יט ג מיי' פרק כ"ג שם הלכה כו סמג שם טוש"ע או"ח סימן שלה סעיף ב:

כ ד מיי' שם טור שו"ע שם סעיף ג:

כא ה מיי' פ"א מהלכות יו"ט הלכה ד טור שו"ע או"ח סימן תקו סעיף י:

כב ו מיי' פכ"ג מהלכות שבת הלכה כה טור שו"ע או"ח סימן שלד סעיף ג:

כג ז מיי' שם טור שו"ע שם סעיף ד:

כד ח מיי' פכ"ג שם הל"א סמג שם טור ושו"ע או"ח סימן רנד סעיף ו:

כה ט טוש"ע או"ח סי' רנ סעיף א:

כו י כ מיי' פ"ל שם הלכה ט סמג עשין ל טור שו"ע או"ח סימן רעד סעיף א ב וסימן רפט סעיף א:

כז ל טוש"ע או"ח סימן שלד סעיף א:

כח מ מיי' שם סמג שם טוש"ע או"ח סימן רצא סעיף א:

רבינו חננאל

אסקה רב אשי ג' מחיצות ולחי א' והוא מבוי שאינו מפולש שאין בו שיתוף ולא עירוב הוא להציל כתבי הקדש אבל אוכלין ומשקין אין מצילין אלא לחצר המעורבת הלכת' כת"ק. והא דאמר רבה ב' מחיצות ולחי אחד זהו מפולש. ב' מחיצות וב' לחיים זהו שאינו מפולש. ואליבא דר' יהודה דאמר מי שיש לו ב' בתים בב' צדי רה"ר עושה לחי מכאן ולחי מכאן או קורה מכאן וקורה מכאן ונושא ונותן באמצע. והכי פי' דכך פסיק לה להה"ר לרחבה מב' צדיה וב' בתים עושה לחי מכאן ולחי מכאן ומערב ונושא ונותן באמצע. והתם איכא פלוגתא דת"ק (וחנינא) [וחנניא] ורב אמר הלכה כת"ק. ושמואל אמר הלכה (כחנינא) [כחנניה]. וקאי במבוי שיש בו ב' מחיצ' בלבד כנגד זה וב' כנגד זה והאי איכא עליה לחי או קורה מיכן ולחי או קורה מיכן. לר' יהודה דלא מצריך דלת יכול לערב אותו. א"ל אביי א"כ לאמר נמי כל שכן שמתערב יצילו לתוכו אוכלין ומשקין. וכא רב אשי ופירק. וסלקא כותיה: מצילין מזון ג' סעודות. ואקשינן מכדי בהיתרא קא טרח מצילין לחצר המעורבת נציל טפי. ופרקי' אמר רבה מתוך שאדם בהול על ממונו דאי שרית ליה להציל כל מאי דבעי אתי לכבויי. א"ל אביי ואלא הא דתניא נשברה לו חבית בראש גגו מביא כלי ומניח תחתיה ובלבד שלא יביא כלי אחר ויקלוט כלי אחר ויצרף. התם מ"ט לא יביא כלי אחר ויקלוט כלי אחר ויצרף והא בהיתרא קא טרח. אהדר ליה רבה

מסורת הש"ס

[illegible]

הגהות הב"ח

(א) גמ' והא תנא דבי ר' ישמעאל לא תעשו. [illegible]

גליון הש"ס

גמ' ואין מערימין בכך. מו"ק דף יב ע"ב:

תורה אור השלם

א) וְיוֹם הַשְּׁבִיעִי שַׁבָּת לַיי אֱלֹהֶיךָ לֹא תַעֲשֶׂה כָל מְלָאכָה אַתָּה וּבִנְךָ וּבִתֶּךָ עַבְדְּךָ וַאֲמָתְךָ וּבְהֶמְתֶּךָ וְגֵרְךָ אֲשֶׁר בִּשְׁעָרֶיךָ: [שמות כ, י]

ב) וְהָיָה בַּיּוֹם הַשִּׁשִּׁי וְהֵכִינוּ אֵת אֲשֶׁר יָבִיאוּ וְהָיָה מִשְׁנֶה עַל אֲשֶׁר יִלְקְטוּ יוֹם יוֹם: [שמות טז, ה]

ג) וַיְהִי בַּיּוֹם הַשִּׁשִּׁי לָקְטוּ לֶחֶם מִשְׁנֶה שְׁנֵי הָעֹמֶר לָאֶחָד וַיָּבֹאוּ כָּל נְשִׂיאֵי הָעֵדָה וַיַּגִּידוּ לְמֹשֶׁה: [שמות טז, כב]

ד) וַיֹּאמֶר מֹשֶׁה אִכְלֻהוּ הַיּוֹם כִּי שַׁבָּת הַיּוֹם לַיי הַיּוֹם לֹא תִמְצָאֻהוּ בַּשָּׂדֶה: [שמות טז, כה]

ליקוטי רש"י

אותו ואת בנו. שאין מותרין לשחוט שניהם היום [ביצה לז.]. עושה לו פרנסה. כל לשון פרנסה לשון עשיית לרכיו הוא קונדריי"ר בלע"ז כמו לפרנסה שמן באלה (כתובות סה.) וכמו מוליכין לפרנסה ואין מוליכין למזונות (שם סט.) [גיטין סה:]. לו לורך פרנסה קרי פיפוס קונדריי"ר בלע"ז [ב"מ סו.]. הדראה. שניטל כל הדרה דהיינו פת קיבר [פסחים לו:]. יצא תקיעת שופר. דאפילו מקיעת הרשות לית בה איסורא דאורייתא [לקמן קלא.]. ורדיית הפת. דרדיית הפת שנות היא שהיא חכמה ואינה מלאכה [לעיל ג:]. ריפתא דעירובא. שערבו בו לאכול ערובי חצרות [ברכות לט:].

התחם נמי גזרו עליה דאי שרית ליה לאתויי כלי [אחר יביא כלין] דרך רה"ר וכיון שנאסר מלהביא כלי אחר הרי זה מייאש ולא פשיט באיסורא. והא דמי שנשברה לו חבית בראש גגו. סלקא דלאו בפלוגתא דר' אליעזר ור' יהושע היא. ולענין פת בתנור הלכתא כי הא דתניא שכח פת בתנור וקדש עליה היום מציל מזון ג' סעודות. ואומר לאחרים בואו והצילו לכם. ולא ירדה במרדה אלא בסכין. ואע"ג דתנא דבי שמואל כל מלאכת עבודה לא תעשו. יצא תקיעת שופר ורדיית הפת שהיא חכמה ואינה מלאכה. כמה שאפשר לשנויי משנינן: אמר רב חסדא לעולם ישכים אדם להוצאת שבת שנאמר והיה ביום הששי והכינו את אשר יביאו לאלתר. הלכתא כר' אבא דאמר חייב אדם לבצוע על ב' ככרות בשבת. ואיתא

הוּא דְּקָעָבִיד לֹא מֵיחֲזֵי כִּרְעַבְתָּנוּתָא – **Since he does not do** this **every day, and it is** only **today that he does** so, **it does not seem like voraciousness.**

Yet another Amoraic practice:

רַבִּי אַמִּי וְרַבִּי אַסִּי כִּי מִיקְּלַע לְהוּ רִיפְתָּא דְעֵירוּבָא – **R' Ami and R' Assi, when the bread of the** ***eruv chatzeiros*** **happened to be** deposited **with them,** שָׁרוּ עִילָּוֵיהּ – **would commence** the Sabbath meal **with it,** i.e. they would pronounce the *hamotzi* blessing over it.[30] אָמְרֵי – **They said:** הוֹאִיל וְאִיתְעֲבִיד בָּהּ חֲדָא מִצְוָה – **Since one mitzvah was performed with it,** i.e. the *mitzvah* of *eruv chatzeiros,* לִיתְעֲבִיד בָּהּ מִצְוָה אַחֲרִינָא – **let another mitzvah be performed with it.**

The Mishnah stated:

כֵּיצַד נָפְלָה דְלֵיקָה כו׳ – HOW SO? If A FIRE BROKE OUT etc.

The Mishnah rules that we may save enough food for three meals. The Gemara discusses the source for this law:

תָּנוּ רַבָּנָן – **The Rabbis taught in a Baraisa:** כַּמָּה סְעוּדוֹת חַיָּיב אָדָם לֶאֱכוֹל בְּשַׁבָּת – HOW MANY MEALS IS A PERSON OBLIGATED TO EAT ON THE SABBATH? שָׁלֹשׁ – THREE, i.e. one at night and two during the day. רַבִּי חִידְקָא אוֹמֵר – R' CHIDKA SAYS: אַרְבַּע – FOUR, i.e. one at night and three during the day.

The Gemara analyzes these two views:

אָמַר רַבִּי יוֹחָנָן – **R' Yochanan said:** וּשְׁנֵיהֶם מִקְרָא אֶחָד דָּרְשׁוּ – **Both of them** [R' Chidka and the Tanna Kamma] **expounded the same verse.** ,,וַיֹּאמֶר מֹשֶׁה אִכְלֻהוּ הַיּוֹם כִּי־שַׁבָּת הַיּוֹם לַה׳ הַיּוֹם לֹא תִמְצָאֻהוּ בַּשָּׂדֶה" – Scripture states in regard to the manna: ***Moses said:***[31] ***Eat it "today," for "today" is a Sabbath to Hashem, "today" you shall not find it in the field.*** רַבִּי חִידְקָא סָבַר הָנֵי תְּלָתָא ,,הַיּוֹם" לְבַר מֵאוּרְתָּא – **R' Chidka maintains** that **these three** mentions of ***"today,"*** each of which alludes to a separate meal, **are** reckoned **apart from the evening** meal. Thus, one must eat three meals during the daytime in addition to one on Friday night.[32] וְרַבָּנָן סָבְרֵי בַּהֲדֵי דְאוּרְתָּא – **But the Rabbis maintain** that these three words *"today"* are **inclusive of the evening** meal.

The Gemara attempts to show that our Mishnah is not in accord with the view of R' Chidka:

תְּנַן – **We learned in our Mishnah:** נָפְלָה דְלֵיקָה בְּלֵילֵי שַׁבָּת – If A FIRE BROKE OUT ON THE SABBATH EVE,

NOTES

30. [As explained previously, the *eruv chatzeiros* is made by placing bread collected from all the residents of the courtyard in one of the houses. Once the Sabbath has commenced, the bread may be consumed without negating the effect of the *eruv* for the duration of that Sabbath (*Orach Chaim* 368:4; see *Mishnah Berurah* there §16).] The custom in R' Ami and R' Assi's courtyard was that the members of the courtyard took turns keeping the *eruv* bread in their homes [and the person who had the *eruv* bread that week was allowed to eat it] (*Rashi*; see *Magen Avraham* to *Orach Chaim* 394:2 with *Mishnah Berurah.*). [R' Ami and R' Assi would follow this practice when the *eruv* was in their homes.]

31. *Exodus* 16:25.

32. See *Shabbos Shel Mi,* who discusses R' Chidka's source for the Friday night meal.

מַצִּילִין מְזוֹן שָׁלֹשׁ סְעוּדוֹת – WE MAY SAVE only enough FOOD FOR THREE MEALS. מַאי לָאו דְּלֹא אָכַל – Now, is the Mishnah **not** discussing a case **where he has not** yet **eaten** the Friday night meal? This proves that the Mishnah maintains that there is an obligation to eat only three meals on the Sabbath.

The Gemara refutes the proof:

לֹא דְּאָכַל – **No,** the Mishnah refers to **where he has** already **eaten** the Friday night meal. Therefore we permit him to save food for three *more* meals, for a total of four meals.

The Gemara again attempts to show, from the next part of the Mishnah, that the Mishnah does not accord with R' Chidka:

שַׁחֲרִית מַצִּילִין מְזוֹן שְׁתֵּי סְעוּדוֹת – If fire broke out in the MORNING, HE MAY SAVE FOOD FOR only TWO MEALS. מַאי לָאו דְּלֹא אָכַל – **Now,** is the Mishnah **not** discussing a case **where he has not** yet **eaten** the second meal? Nevertheless, the Mishnah allows him to save only two meals. This proves that the Mishnah maintains that there is an obligation to eat only two meals during the daytime hours, for a total of three Sabbath meals.

The Gemara refutes this proof as well:

לֹא דְּאָכַל – **No,** the Mishnah refers to **where he has** already **eaten** the second meal. We permit him to save enough food for two more meals, for a total of four meals.

The Gemara attempts another proof from the next part of the Mishnah:

בְּמִנְחָה מַצִּילִין מְזוֹן סְעוּדָה אַחַת – If fire broke out IN THE AFTERNOON, HE MAY SAVE FOOD FOR only ONE MEAL. מַאי לָאו דְּלֹא אָכַל – **Now,** is the Mishnah **not** discussing a case **where he has not** yet **eaten** the third meal? Thus, we see that the obligation is to eat only three meals.

This proof too is rejected:

לֹא דְּאָכַל – **No,** the Mishnah refers to **where he has** already **eaten** the third meal. We permit him to save enough food for one more meal, for a total of four Sabbath meals.

The Gemara attempts one final proof:

וְהָא מִדְּקָתָנֵי סֵיפָא – **But from the fact that the latter part of the Mishnah teaches:** רַבִּי יוֹסֵי אוֹמֵר לְעוֹלָם מַצִּילִין מְזוֹן שָׁלֹשׁ סְעוּדוֹת – R' YOSE SAYS: ONE MAY ALWAYS SAVE enough FOOD FOR THREE MEALS, מִכְּלָל דְּתַנָּא קַמָּא שָׁלֹשׁ סְבִירָא לֵיהּ – **it is implied that the Tanna Kamma maintains** that only **three** meals are required.[1]

The Gemara accepts this proof and concludes:

אֶלָּא מְחַוַּורְתָּא מַתְנִיתִין דְּלֹא כְּרַבִּי חִידְקָא – **Rather, it is clear that our Mishnah is not in accordance with** the view of **R' Chidka.**

In any event, all Tannaim agree that the number of meals on the Sabbath is greater than on the weekdays. This being so, the Gemara questions the position of another Mishnah, which establishes the criteria for determining eligibility for different forms of public assistance:

וְהָא דִּתְנַן – **And** how do we explain **that which we learned in the** following **Mishnah?**[2] מִי שֶׁיֵּשׁ לוֹ מְזוֹן שְׁתֵּי סְעוּדוֹת לֹא יִטּוֹל מִן הַתַּמְחוּי – ONE WHO HAS enough FOOD FOR TWO MEALS MAY NOT TAKE FROM THE communal PLATTER;[3] מְזוֹן אַרְבַּע עֶשְׂרֵה לֹא יִטּוֹל מִן הַקּוּפָּה – if he has enough FOOD FOR FOURTEEN MEALS, HE MAY NOT TAKE FROM THE charity BOX.[4] מַנִּי – **Who** is the Tanna of this Mishnah? לֹא רַבָּנָן וְלֹא רַבִּי חִידְקָא – Seemingly it is **neither the Rabbis nor R' Chidka.** אִי רַבָּנָן חֲמֵיסְרֵי הָוְיָין – For **if** it is **the Rabbis,** why, **there are fifteen** meals a week, אִי רַבִּי חִידְקָא שִׁית סְרֵי הָוְיָין – and **if** it is **R' Chidka, there are sixteen!**[5] – ? –

A resolution is advanced:

לְעוֹלָם רַבָּנָן – **Actually,** the Mishnah follows **the Rabbis,** and as for the argument that even a person who lacks fifteen meals should be eligible for assistance from the charity box, this is not a difficulty, דְּאָמְרִינַן לֵיהּ – **for we say to [the applicant]:** מַאי דְּבָעֵית לְמֵיכַל בְּאַפּוּקֵי שַׁבְּתָא אַכְלֵיהּ בְּשַׁבְּתָא – **What you were planning to eat** for your nighttime meal **after the conclusion of the Sabbath, eat** instead **on the Sabbath** close to sundown for your third, Sabbath meal.[6]

The Gemara asks:

לֵימָא רַבָּנָן הִיא וְלֹא רַבִּי חִידְקָא – **Shall we say** then that we have established that the Mishnah follows **the Rabbis and not R' Chidka?**

The Gemara replies:

אֲפִילּוּ תֵּימָא רַבִּי חִידְקָא – **You can even say** that it follows **R' Chidka.** דְּאָמְרִינַן לֵיהּ – **For we say to [the applicant]:**

NOTES

1. Since R' Yose did not say that one may always save enough for *four* meals, it is clear that he does not agree with R' Chidka. And since the Tanna Kamma and R' Yose do not dispute the number of meals one must eat on the Sabbath, only whether one may save food even corresponding to the meals that have already passed, it is clear that even the Tanna Kamma disagrees with R' Chidka (*Rashi*).

2. *Pe'ah* 8:7.

3. The "platter" was an institution that functioned as a sort of soup kitchen. Appointed officials would circulate among the householders of the community with a large plate and collect food contributions, which were then distributed to the poor. [Since it was the custom in Mishnaic times to eat two meals a day,] each eligible poor person would receive enough food for two meals.

The distribution from the platter took place before mealtimes. A poor person who possessed enough food for two meals was not eligible for this form of assistance [since he had enough food to tide him over to the next day when a new distribution would take place]. One who had enough for two meals yet took from the platter was guilty of stealing from the poor (*Rashi*).

4. This was a charity fund called *kuppah,* box, because of the container in which the money was kept (*Rambam, Commentary* to *Pe'ah* 8:7), which functioned as a separate institution from the "platter." It was a distribution of funds made weekly rather than daily. During the course of a week a person in Mishnaic times would normally eat fourteen meals, two each day, one at night and one in the morning. (How the Sabbath meals fit into this reckoning will be discussed in the Gemara.) The *kuppah* provided funds for these fourteen meals to poor people of high birth for whom taking from the platter might be demeaning (*Rashi;* cf. *Rambam, Hil. Matnos Aniyim* 9:6; see also *Bava Basra* 8b).

The allocation from this fund was distributed as a lump sum each Friday. A poor person who had enough for a week's worth of meals was not entitled to this form of assistance that week since he could wait until the next distribution on the following Friday. But if on a particular Friday he had only enough for, say, twelve meals, he was entitled to take from the charity fund, because the next distribution of funds would not be until the next Friday, by which time he would have run out of money (*Rashi;* see *Igros Moshe, Yoreh Deah* 1:146 for a discussion of why *Rashi* gives the example of one who has *twelve* meals when seemingly even one who owns *thirteen* meals should be entitled to take from the *kuppah*).

5. A person requires two meals for each day of the week from Sunday through Friday, for a total of twelve meals. On the Sabbath, the Rabbis require a person to eat three meals, and R' Chidka requires four. This should bring the total number of meals for the week to fifteen according to the Rabbis and sixteen according to R' Chidka. Yet the Mishnah states that the cutoff point for receiving money from the *kuppah* is *fourteen* meals!

6. [The evening meal is usually eaten after dark. On the Sabbath, however, we advise the person to eat this meal before sundown, so it can serve as the third Sabbath meal.] Since he will have eaten late in the day, he will not be hungry at night. Thus, the person needs only two meals on Saturday as well, and the fourteen-meal cutoff point for the *kuppah* is justified (*Rashi*).

[Actually, we will learn on 119b that there is a mitzvah to eat a separate meal, known colloquially as *melaveh malkah,* on Saturday night, to "escort" the Sabbath out. However, this applies only to one who can afford it. Public assistance is not provided for such a meal (*Rashi*).]

מצילין מזון ג' סעודות מאי לאו דלא אכל
לא דאכל שחרית מצילין מזון שתי סעודות
מאי לאו דלא אכל לא דאכל במנחה מצילין
מזון סעודה אחת מאי לאו דלא אכל לא
דאכל והא מדקתני סיפא רבי יוסי אומר
לעולם מצילין מזון ג' סעודות מכלל דתנא
קמא ג' סבירא ליה אלא מחוורתא מתני'
דלא כרבי חידקא והא [א] דתנן מי שיש לו
מזון שתי סעודות לא יטול מן התמחוי מזון
ארבע עשרה לא יטול מן הקופה מני לא
רבנן ולא רבי חידקא אי רבנן חמסרי הויין
אי רבי חידקא שית סרי הויין לעולם רבנן
דאמרינן ליה מאי דבעית למיכל באפוקי
שבתא אכליה בשבתא לימא רבנן היא ולא
ר' חידקא אפי' תימא ר' חידקא דאמרינן
ליה מאי דבעית למיכל במעלי שבתא
אכליה לאורתא וכולי יומא דמעלי שבתא
בתעניתא מותבינן ליה אלא הא מני רבי
עקיבא היא דאמר [ב] עשה שבתך חול ואל
תצטרך לבריות [ג] והא דתנן אין פוחתין
לעני העובר ממקום למקום מככר בפונדיון
מד' סאין בסלע לן נותנין לו פרנסת לינה
ואם שבת נותנין לו מזון ג' סעודות לימא
רבנן היא ולא ר' חידקא לעולם ר' חידקא
כגון דאיכא סעודה בהדיה דאמרינן ליה הא
דאיכא בהדך אכליה וכי אזיל בריקן אזיל
דמלווינן ליה סעודה בהדיה מאי פרנסת
לינה אמר רב פפא פוריא ובי סדיא: ת"ר
[ד] קערות שאכל בהן ערבית מדיחן לאכול
בהן שחרית שחרית מדיחן לאכול בהן
בצהרים בצהרים מדיחן לאכול בהן במנחה
מן המנחה ואילך שוב אינו מדיח אבל כוסות
וקיתוניות וצלוחיות מדיח והולך כל היום
כולו לפי שאין קבע לשתיה א"ר שמעון בן
פזי א"ר יהושע בן לוי משום בר קפרא [ה] כל
המקיים שלש סעודות בשבת ניצול משלש
פורעניות מחבלו של משיח ומדינה של גיהנם
וממלחמת גוג ומגוג מחבלו של משיח כתיב
הכא [א] יום וכתיב התם [ב] הנה אנכי שולח
לכם את אליה הנביא לפני בוא יום וגו' מדינה של גיהנם כתיב הכא יום וכתיב
התם [ג] יום עברה היום ההוא ממלחמת גוג ומגוג כתיב הכא יום וכתיב התם
[ד] ביום בא גוג א"ר יוחנן משום רבי יוסי כל המענג את השבת נותנין לו נחלה
בלי מצרים שנאמר [ה] אז תתענג על ה' והרכבתיך על במתי ארץ והאכלתיך
נחלת

רש"י

לעולם מצילין מזון ג' סעודות. מדלא אמר ארבע לית ליה דרבי חידקא: מכלל דתנא קמא שלש סעודות סבירא ליה. דבהאי לא איפליגו אלא דת"ק סבר מה שעבר כבר לא יציל ולרבי יוסי יציל: תמחוי. קערה גדולה היא וגובין בה גבאים מאכל מבעלי בתים ומחלקין לעניים ב' סעודות ליום מיום ליום: לא יטול. כיון דיש לו נמצא גוזל לעניים: קופה. מעות הן לפרנס עניים בני טובים דזיל להו מילתא דתמחוי ומתחלקין מע"ש לע"ש: י"ד סעודות לא יטול מן הקופה. שהרי יכול להמתין לע"ש הבאה אבל כשיש לו מזון י"ב יטול שהרי לא תחלק עוד עד שיגיע ע"ש והרי לשבעה ימי שבת צריכין י"ד סעודות: אכליה בשבתא. שהרי תאכלנה סמוך לערב ולא תצטרך לאכול בלילה ואף על גב דאמרינן לקמן לעולם יסדר אדם שלחנו במוצאי שבת ה"מ למאן דאפשר ליה: בתעניתא מותבינן ליה. בתמיה: אלא הא מני ר' עקיבא היא. ולענין סעודת שבת במאן דאפשר ליה איכא למימר כרבנן ואיכא למימר כרבי חידקא ומיהו האי דצריך לבריות יעשה שבתו חול ולא יטיל על אחרים כבוד שבתותיו: אין פוחתין לעני העובר ממקום למקום. שאינו לן בלילה אצלם: מככר. הלקוח בפונדיון כשהשער ד' סאין בסלע והפונדיון אחד מי"ב בדינר דהוא אחד ממ"ח בסלע ושיערו לו חכמים ככר זו לשתי סעודות היום והלילה: לן נותנין לו פרנסת לינה. לקמן מפרש מאי היא שהרי סעודה של לילה בכלל ככר היא וככר זו משערינן בעירובין (דף פב:) למזון שתי סעודות לעירובי תחומין: ואם שבת. אצלם בשבת: מאי פרנסת לינה. הא קבל ליה סעודת הלילה: בי סדיא. לבדין פולטר"א להניח תחת מראשותיו: שוב אינו מדיחן. דאין הדחה זו אלא לחול: חבלו של משיח. כדאמרי' בכתובות (דף קיא:) דור שבן דוד בא בו קטיגוריא בתלמידי חכמים שנאמר ועוד בה עשיריה וגו'. חבלי לשון חבלי יולדה (הושע יג): בלי מצרים. כלומר אין לה קץ: אז תתענג. בתר וקראת לשבת עונג כתיב:
נחלת

תוספות

במנחה מצילין מזון סעודה אחת. מכאן משמע דזמן אכילה שלישית בשבת היא מן המנחה ולמעלה דלא כאותם שמחלקין סעודת שחרית ומברכין בינתים ומיהו מהא דאמרינן בפסחים בפ"ק (דף יג.) י"ד שחל להיות בשבת משייר מזון שתי סעודות אין ראיה מדאין משיירין מזון ג' סעודות שאין לעשות ב' סעודות שחרית דהא כיון שאוכל הכל שחרית חשיב כסעודה אחת ועוד אומר ר"י שיש כאן איסור ברכה שאינה צריכה כדאי' בפ' בא לו (יומא דף ע.) גבי ובעשור שבחומש הפקודים דקאמר וניתי ס"ת אחרינא ונקרי א"ר שמעון בן לקיש מפני ברכה שאינה צריכה: מככר בפונדיון כו'. היינו כר' יוחנן בן ברוקא דחשיב ככר בפונדיון מד' סאין בסלע שתי סעודות לעירוב ופליג התם (עירובין דף פב:) ארבי מאיר ורבי יהודה שאומרים התם שיעור אחר:

והא דתנן אין פוחתין כו' נימא רבנן היא ולא רבי חידקא. אומר ר"י דאין לפרש שבת נותנין לו מזון ג' סעודות דהיינו כשבא שם בע"ש לעת האוכל דמסתמא ישבות שם שאין רגילות כל כך ללכת ערב שבת ובשביל שבת נותנים לו סעודה אחת יותר ממה שנותנין לו בשאר ימים דא"כ היכי ניחא לרבנן והלא מן הכל אין לו כי אם ד' סעודות אחת שהביא עמו דמלוינן בהדיה ושלשה שנתנו לו וכשיאכל אחת בערב שבת לא ישארו בידו רק ג' סעודות ואותן יאכל בשבת וא"כ תיקשי נמי לרבנן וכי אזיל ריקן אזיל כדפריך בסמוך ומיהו איכא למימר דבסמוך לרבנן נמי פריך אבל קשה דכי משני דמלוינן ליה סעודה בהדיה לא תירץ כלום לר' חידקא דאין לו לשבת כ"א שלש סעודות ולר' חידקא צריך ד' ונראה לר"י דכשבא בע"ש לעת האוכל נותנין לו מזון ב' סעודות כמו בשאר ימים ואם בא לשבות שם מוסיפין לו עוד ג' סעודות וקאמר לימא רבנן היא ולא רבי חידקא דלרבנן ניחא שיש בידו ה' סעודות בתחילת שבת ואותה שהביא עמו יאכל בע"ש ומאותן ה' סעודות יאכל ג' בשבת ואחת במוצאי שבת ואחת יוליך עמו אלא לרבי חידקא כשיאכל ד' בשבת ואחת להוליך עמו למחר א"כ מה יאכל במוצאי שבת וליכא למימר דאמרינן ליה מה דהוה לך למיכל באפוקי שבתא אכול בשבתא כדאמרי' לעיל דהתם אמרינן ליה כדי שלא יהא ניזון מן הצדקה אבל הכא כבר הוא ניזון ולהכי נוטל כל צרכו ומשני דאיכא סעודה בהדיה המתרץ היה סבור שהיה פשוט למקשה שהסעודה שיוליך עמו נותנין לו באחד בשבת אע"פ שבשאר ימים נותנין לו סעודה שיוליך עמו עם אחרות בע"ש אין נותנין לו אותה עד שילך לפי שאינו הולך מיד עד אחר השבת ולכך היה סבור שהמקשה לא היה יודע שהביא סעודה עמו ואין לו בתחלת השבת אלא ד' להכי משני ליה דאיכא סעודה בהדיה והמקשה משיב דפשיטא ליה דאיכא סעודה בהדיה אך קשה ליה כיון דמתרצת דאכיל לכולהו וכי אזיל בריקן אזיל שכמו שהביא עמו לכאן כן ישאנה עמו בלאתו מכאן ומשני דמלוינן ליה כו':

דמלוינן סעודה בהדיה. וא"ת א"כ אמאי נותנים לו ג' סעודות כיון שמביא אחת עמו יתנו לו אחת ויאכל אחת והאחת יוליך עמו וי"ל דאין מחלקין תמחוי בלילה אלא ביום בזמן הסעודה ולכך נותנין לו שנים שיאכל אחת מיד ואחת בלילה במקום שיהיה ואחת להוליך עמו למחר: לפי שאין קבע לשתיה. מכאן יש ללמוד בלילה כשרוצה להתענות למחר לאחר אכילה אע"פ שאינו יכול לאכול אם לא התנה לפי שמסתמא כשבירך סילק דעתו מלאכול מלשתות ודאי לא סילק דעתו כדאמר הכא דאין קבע לשתיה והיכא דלא שכיח יין אע"ג דסילק דעתו מן היין מ"מ ממים לא סילק דעתו ומיהו אומר ר"י דשמא דוקא בימיהם שהיו קובעין עצמן לשתיה אחר אכילה אמרו דאין קבע לשתיה אבל לדידן לא וריב"א פירש במסכת תענית (דף יב.) שאף לאחר שישן מותר לשתות על פי הירושלמי ואין ר"י רוצה להקל כל כך כיון שלא נזכר בהדיא בש"ס שלנו [עיין תוספות תענית יב: ד"ה נים]:
רובס

עין משפט נר מצוה

ל א מיי' פ"ט מהלכות מתנות עניים הלכה יג סמג עשין קסב טור שו"ע יו"ד סימן רנג סעיף א ב:
לא ב מיי' פ"ל מהלכות שבת הלכה ז סמג עשין ל טוש"ע או"ח סי' רמב:
לב ג מיי' פ"ז מהלכות מ"ע הלכה ח סמג עשין קסב טוש"ע יו"ד סימן רנ סעיף ד:
לג ד מיי' פכ"ג מהלכות שבת הלכה ז סמג לאוין סה טוש"ע או"ח סימן שכג סעיף ו:
לד ה מיי' פ"ל שם הלכה ט סמג עשין ל טוש"ע או"ח סימן רצא סעיף א:

רבינו חננאל

ואיתא בפ' כיצד מברכין: ת"ר כמה סעודות חייב אדם לוכל בשבת ג'. פי' א' בלילה וב' ביום. וכן הלכה. ולפיכך שנינו שמציל מזון ג' סעודו' ומתני' מחוורתא דלא כר' חידקא: כלי מאכל אינו מדיח אלא מה שצריך לוכל בו בשבת. לפי זמן סעודותיו אבל כלי שתיה כל היום. שאין קבע לשתיה:

מסורת הש"ס

א) פאה פרק ח מ"ז, ב) פסחים דף קיב. קיג., ג) פאה פ"ח מ"ז ב"ב ט ע"א.

תורה אור השלם

א) ויאמר משה אכלהו היום כי שבת היום לה' היום לא תמצאהו בשדה: [שמות טז, כה]
ב) הנה אנכי שלח לכם את אליה הנביא לפני בוא יום ה' הגדול והנורא: [מלאכי ג, כג]
ג) יום עברה היום ההוא יום צרה ומצוקה יום שאה ומשואה יום חשך ואפלה יום ענן וערפל: [צפניה א, טו]
ד) והיה ביום ההוא ביום בוא גוג על אדמת ישראל נאם אדני אלהים תעלה חמתי באפי: [יחזקאל לח, יח]
ה) אז תתענג על ה' והרכבתיך על במתי ארץ והאכלתיך נחלת יעקב אביך כי פי ה' דבר: [ישעיה נח, יד]

ליקוטי רש"י

תמחוי. מאכל לאם ומיני מאכל שגובין לחלק [פסחים יג.]. מאכל שגובין מבעלי בתים לחלק לעניים בכל יום [ב"מ לח.]. מככר בפונדיון. ככר הלקוח בפונדיון כשלוקחין ארבע סאין בסלע ומגיע לפונדיון אלו קב שהסלע מ"ח פונדיונין וארבע סאין מ"ח חצאי קבין והחנוני שהוא טוחן ואופה ומוכר בשוק משתכר מחצה הלכך ככר של רובע הקב בפונדיון. לן. בלילה. פרנסת לינה. צרכי לינה. בי סדיא. כר לתת מראשותיו [ב"ב ט.]. לבדין קשורין פלטר"ש ועשוין לתקנן להניח במקום הכר [לקמן קמ:]. חבלו של משיח. גורלו לישנא אחרינא חבלו פחדים וחבלים שיהיו בימיו מחיל העובדי כוכבים [סנהדרין צח:]. לפני בוא יום וגו'. לפני ביאת בן דוד יבא אליהו לבשר [עירובין מג:].

מַאי דְּבָעִית לְמֵיכַל בְּמַעֲלֵי שַׁבְּתָא אַכְלֵיהּ לְאוּרְתָּא – **What you were planning to eat on Friday** morning, **eat** instead **at night** for the Sabbath meal.[7]

The Gemara wonders:

וְכוּלֵּי יוֹמָא דְּמַעֲלֵי שַׁבְּתָא בְּתַעֲנִיתָא מוֹתְבִינַן לֵיהּ – **And the entire day of Friday we make him fast?** This is certainly not humanitarian! – ? –

The Gemara accepts this refutation and reconciles the Mishnah according to both the Rabbis and R' Chidka in a different way: אֶלָּא הָא מַנִּי רַבִּי עֲקִיבָא הִיא דְּאָמַר – **Rather, who is** the Tanna of **this** Mishnah? **It is R' Akiva, who said:** עֲשֵׂה שַׁבַּתְּךָ חוֹל וְאַל תִּצְטָרֵךְ לַבְּרִיּוֹת – **Treat your Sabbath as a weekday, but do not be dependent on people** for aid. Thus, the Mishnah could agree with the Rabbis or R' Chidka that the Sages enacted that a person should eat three or four meals on the Sabbath, but the enactment was only made for a person who can afford it. The Mishnah, on the other hand, speaks of a poor person who cannot afford any extra meals for the Sabbath. To him we tell, in accordance with the principle of R' Akiva, that it is better not to accept charity and to only eat two meals on the Sabbath, just as he would do on a weekday.[8]

The Gemara now considers whether the ruling of the first segment of the above-cited Mishnah can also be made consistent with the view of R' Chidka:

וְהָא דִּתְנַן – **And** in regard to **that which we learned in the** first segment of that **Mishnah:** אֵין פּוֹחֲתִין לֶעָנִי הָעוֹבֵר מִמָּקוֹם לְמָקוֹם – WE DO NOT GIVE A POOR MAN WHO TRAVELS FROM PLACE TO PLACE [i.e. one who is passing through the city and will depart before nightfall] LESS מִכִּכָּר בְּפוּנְדְיוֹן מֵאַרְבַּע סְאִין בְּסֶלַע – THAN A LOAF of bread THAT COSTS A *PUNDYON* WHEN FOUR *SE'AHS* OF FLOUR COST A *SELA*;[9] לָן – IF HE STAYS OVERNIGHT, נוֹתְנִין לוֹ פַּרְנָסַת לִינָה – WE GIVE HIM PROVISIONS FOR NIGHT-LODGING;[10] וְאִם שָׁבַת – IF HE SPENDS THE SABBATH in the city, נוֹתְנִין לוֹ מְזוֹן שָׁלֹשׁ סְעוּדוֹת – WE GIVE HIM FOOD FOR THREE MEALS; לֵימָא רַבָּנַן הִיא וְלֹא רַבִּי חִידְקָא – **shall we say** that this Mishnah follows **the Rabbis and not R' Chidka?**

The Gemara replies:

לְעוֹלָם רַבִּי חִידְקָא – **Actually,** the Mishnah can also follow **R' Chidka,** כְּגוֹן דְּאִיכָּא סְעוּדָה בַּהֲדֵיהּ – and it is discussing **a case in which he has** one **meal with him,** דְּאָמְרִינַן לֵיהּ הָא דְּאִיכָּא בַּהֲדָךְ אַכְלֵיהּ – **so that we say to him: That** meal **which you have with you eat** on the Sabbath, and, together with the three meals we have given you, you will be able to fulfill the commandment of eating four meals on the Sabbath.

The Gemara asks:

וְכִי אָזִיל בְּרֵיקָן אָזִיל – **But when he departs** on Sunday morning, **does he depart empty-handed?** By forcing him to eat on the Sabbath the only meal that he has in reserve, the result will be that when he leaves town on Sunday morning, he will leave without any food in his possession. Surely this is not reasonable! – ? –

The Gemara answers:

דִּמְלַוִּינַן לֵיהּ סְעוּדָה בַּהֲדֵיהּ – **We provide him with a meal to accompany him** when he is ready to leave on Sunday.[11] In the meantime, however, he must use his reserve meal for the Sabbath.[12]

The Gemara asks:

מַאי פַּרְנָסַת לִינָה – **What are "provisions for night-lodging"** to which the Mishnah refers?[13]

The Gemara answers:

אָמַר רַב פָּפָּא – **Rav Pappa said:** פּוּרְיָא וּבֵי סַדְיָא – **A bed and a pillow.**

תָּנוּ רַבָּנַן – **The Rabbis taught in a Baraisa:** קְעָרוֹת שֶׁאָכַל בָּהֶן עַרְבִית מְדִיחָן לֶאֱכוֹל בָּהֶן שַׁחֲרִית – PLATES IN WHICH ONE ATE Friday EVENING MAY BE WASHED TO EAT IN THEM IN THE MORNING; שַׁחֲרִית מְדִיחָן לֶאֱכוֹל בָּהֶן בַּצָּהֳרַיִם – those in which he ate in the MORNING MAY BE WASHED TO EAT IN THEM IN THE AFTERNOON; בַּצָּהֳרַיִם מְדִיחָן לֶאֱכוֹל בָּהֶן בַּמִּנְחָה – those in which he ate IN THE AFTERNOON MAY BE WASHED TO EAT IN THEM AT MINCHAH. מִן הַמִּנְחָה וְאֵילָךְ שׁוּב אֵינוֹ מֵדִיחַ – FROM MINCHAH AND ONWARDS, however, HE MAY NO LONGER WASH the plates, because they will no longer be needed that Sabbath.[14] אֲבָל כּוֹסוֹת וְקִיתוֹנִיּוֹת וּצְלוֹחִיּוֹת

NOTES

7. Skip the Friday morning meal and eat the food you would have eaten then on Friday night. The remaining Friday meal can then be shifted to Sabbath morning and eaten then as the second meal, and Saturday's two meals can be eaten one at midday and one just before sundown, just as we said according to the Rabbis.

8. It should be noted, however, that R' Akiva's principle is applicable only to a poor person who is otherwise self-sufficient and can sustain himself without the need to take any charity funds at all. R' Akiva agrees, however, that someone who has already reached the stage where he must accept charity from others, because he does not possess even two meals for each day of the week, is given by the trustees of the charity fund sufficient funds to allow him to fulfill three meals on the Sabbath according to the Rabbis or four meals according to R' Chidka (*Tosafos* ד"ה והא). See *Orach Chaim* §242 with commentaries for the parameters and applications of R' Akiva's ruling.

9. If a poor person who is traveling from place to place passes through a community, that community's official charity organization must see to it that he has enough food for the day – i.e. two meals' worth. Thus, he must receive at the very minimum the amount of bread that a *pundyon* will buy when a *sela* buys four *se'ahs* of wheat. When wheat is at this price, a *pundyon* will buy a loaf of bread containing a quarter-*kav* [or the volume of six eggs] of flour, and it is a loaf of bread this size that a poor person must be provided with daily (*Rav, Rashi* and *Rash* to Mishnah; see also *Rashi* here). A loaf this size is sufficient for two meals (*Rashi*). The recipient eats one meal now, in the morning, and takes the other meal along with him on his journey. If he should decide to spend the night in town, he eats that second meal at night and again receive two meals in the morning, one for now and one for his journey (*Ramban*).

That a loaf costing a *pundyon* contains a quarter-*kav* of flour is ascertained in the following way: A *se'ah* is a unit of volume equal to six *kavs,* so that four *se'ahs* are equal to 24 *kavs.* [A *sela* is a coin equal in value to 24 silver *ma'os;* a *ma'ah* (singular of *ma'os*) is equal to two *pundyons,* so that there are 48 *pundyons* in a *sela*.] Thus, when four *se'ahs* [24 *kavs*] of wheat sell for a *sela* [48 *pundyons*], two *pundyons* will buy a *kav* of wheat, and one *pundyon* will buy a half-*kav* (*Rashi*). A finished loaf of bread, however, costs twice as much as the wheat content, since the loaf's price reflects the additional cost of the baker's labor. Therefore, when a *pundyon* buys a half-*kav* of wheat, it will buy a loaf of bread containing a quarter-*kav* of flour (*Rav, Rashi* and *Rash* to Mishnah; *Rashi* to *Bava Basra* 9a).

10. The Gemara will explain this phrase.

11. I.e. we give him the regular two-meal allotment on Sunday morning before he leaves, one of which he will eat immediately and one which he will take with him on his journey (*Ramban*). Thus, he will not leave empty-handed.

12. For he may not take unless he is presently in need (*Ramban*).

13. The Mishnah stated that if the itinerant pauper wishes to spend the night in the community, we give him "provisions for night-lodging." What does this mean? It cannot refer to food, because we have already provided for his food needs by giving him one meal for the day and one meal for the night (*Rashi;* see end of first paragraph of note 9).

14. Washing plates at this time when there are no remaining Sabbath meals to be eaten constitutes טוֹרַחַ לְחוֹל, *exerting oneself for the weekdays,* which is forbidden (*Hasagos HaRaavad* to *Rambam, Hil. Shabbos* 23:7; see also *Maggid Mishneh* there).

This Baraisa follows R' Chidka, and holds that four meals are eaten on the Sabbath (*Rashbam* in a gloss to an old manuscript of *Rif* cited by *Dikdukei Soferim* §20; *Meiri; Maharam Kazis;* cf. *Tos. Rid, Mishbetzos Zahav* 334:1; *Korban Nesanel* §300).

מצילין מזון ג' סעודות מאי לאו דלא אכל לא דאכל שחרית מצילין מזון שתי סעודות מאי לאו דלא אכל לא דאכל במנחה מצילין מזון סעודה אחת מאי לאו דלא אכל לא דאכל והא מדקתני סיפא רבי יוסי אומר לעולם מצילין מזון ג' סעודות מכלל דתנא קמא ג' סבירא ליה אלא מחוורתא מתני' דלא כרבי חידקא והא [א] דתנן מי [א] שיש לו מזון שתי סעודות לא יטול מן התמחוי מזון ארבע עשרה לא יטול מן הקופה מני לא רבנן ולא רבי חידקא אי רבנן חמסרי הויין אי רבי חידקא שית סרי הויין לעולם רבנן דאמרינן ליה מאי דבעית למיכל באפוקי שבתא אכליה בשבתא לימא רבנן היא ולא ר' חידקא אפי' תימא ר' חידקא דאמרינן ליה מאי דבעית למיכל במעלי שבתא אכליה לאורתא וכולי יומא דמעלי שבתא בתעניתא מותבינן ליה אלא הא מני רבי עקיבא היא דאמר [ב] עשה שבתך חול ואל תצטרך לבריות [ג] והא דתנן [ג] אין פוחתין לעני העובר ממקום למקום מככר בפונדיון מד' סאין בסלע לן נותנין לו פרנסת לינה ואם שבת נותנין לו מזון ג' סעודות לימא רבנן היא ולא ר' חידקא לעולם ר' חידקא כגון דאיכא סעודה בהדיה דאמרינן ליה הא דאיכא בהדך אכליה וכי אזיל בריקן אזיל דמלווינן ליה סעודה בהדיה מאי פרנסת לינה אמר רב פפא פוריא ובי סדיא: ת"ר [ד] קערות שאכל בהן ערבית מדיחן לאכול בהן שחרית שחרית מדיחן לאכול בהן בצהרים בצהרים מדיחן לאכול בהן במנחה מן המנחה ואילך שוב אינו מדיח אבל כוסות וקיתוניות וצלוחיות מדיח והולך כל היום כולו לפי שאין קבע לשתיה א"ר שמעון בן פזי א"ר יהושע בן לוי משום בר קפרא [ה] כל המקיים שלש סעודות בשבת ניצול משלש פורעניות מחבלו של משיח ומדינה של גיהנם וממלחמת גוג ומגוג מחבלו של משיח כתיב הכא [א] יום וכתיב התם [ב] הנה אנכי שולח לכם את אליה הנביא לפני בוא יום וגו' מדינה של גיהנם כתיב הכא יום וכתיב התם [ג] יום עברה היום ההוא ממלחמת גוג ומגוג כתיב הכא יום וכתיב התם [ד] ביום בא גוג א"ר יוחנן משום רבי יוסי כל המענג את השבת נותנין לו נחלה בלי מצרים שנאמר [ה] אז תתענג על ה' והרכבתיך על במתי ארץ והאכלתיך
נחלת

רש"י

לעולם מצילין מזון ג' סעודות. מדלא אמר ארבע לית ליה דרבי חידקא: מכלל דתנא קמא שלש סעודות סבירא ליה. דבהאי לא איפליגו אלא דת"ק סבר מה שעבר כבר לא יציל ולרבי יוסי יציל: תמחוי. קערה גדולה היא וגובין בה גבאים מאכל מבעלי בתים ומחלקין לעניים ב' סעודות ליום מיום ליום: לא יטול. כיון דיש לו נמצא גוזל לעניים: קופה. מעות הן לפרנס עניים בני טובים דזיל להו מילתא דתמחוי ומחלקין מע"ש לע"ש: י"ד סעודות לא יטול מן הקופה. שהרי יכול להמתין לע"ש הבאה אבל כשיש לו מזון י"ג יטול שהרי לא תחלק עוד עד שיגיע ע"ש והרי לשבעה ימי שבת צריכין י"ד סעודות: אכליה בשבתא. שהרי תאכלנה סמוך לערב ולא תצטרך לאכול בלילה ואף על גב דאמרינן לקמן לעולם יסדר אדם שלחנו במוצאי שבת ה"מ למאן דאפשר ליה: בתעניתא מותבינן ליה. בתמיה: אלא הא מני ר' עקיבא היא. ולענין סעודת שבת במאן דאפשר ליה איכא למימר כרבנן ואיכא למימר כרבי חידקא ומיהו האי דצריך לבריות יעשה שבתו חול ולא יטיל על אחרים כבוד שבתותיו: אין פוחתין לעני העובר ממקום למקום. שאינו לן בלילה אצלם: מככר. הלקוח בפונדיון כשהשער ד' סאין בסלע והפונדיון אחד מי"ב בדינר דהוא אחד ממ"ח בסלע ושיערו לו חכמים ככר זו לשתי סעודות היום והלילה: לן נותנין לו פרנסת לינה. לקמן מפרש מאי היא שהרי סעודה של לילה בכלל ככר היא וככר זו משערין בעירובין (דף פב:) למזון שתי סעודות לעירובי תחומין: ואם שבת. אצלם בשבת: מאי פרנסת לינה. הא קבל ליה סעודת הלילה: בי סדיא. לבדין פולטר"א להניח תחת מראשותיו: שוב אינו מדיחן. דאין הדחה זו אלא לחול: חבלו של משיח. כדאמרי' בכתובות (דף קיב:) דור שבן דוד בא בו קטיגוריא בתלמידי חכמים שנאמר ועוד בה עשיריה וגו'. חבלי לשון חבלי יולדה (הושע יג): בלי מצרים. כלומר אין לה קץ: אז תתענג. בתר וקראת לשבת עונג כתיב: נחלת

תוספות

במנחה מצילין מזון סעודה אחת. מכאן משמע דזמן אכילה שלישית בשבת היא מן המנחה ולמעלה דלא כאותם שמחלקין סעודת שחרית ומברכין בינתים ומיהו מהא דאמרינן בפסחים בפ"ק (דף יג.) י"ד שחל להיות בשבת משייר מזון שתי סעודות אין ראיה מדאין משיירין מזון ג' סעודות שאין לעשות ג' סעודות שחרית דהא כיון שאוכל הכל שחרית חשיב כסעודה אחת ועוד אומר ר"י שיש כאן איסור ברכה שאינה צריכה כדאמ' בפ' בא לו (יומא דף ע.) גבי ועשור שבחומש הפקודים דקאמר ומיתי ס"ת אחרינא ונקרי א"ר שמעון בן לקיש מפני ברכה שאינה צריכה: **מככר** בפונדיון כו'. היינו כר' יוחנן בן ברוקא דחשיב ככר בפונדיון מד' סאין בסלע שתי סעודות לעירוב ופליג התם (עירובין דף פב:) ארבי מאיר ורבי יהודה שאומרים התם שיעור אחר: **והא** דתנן אין פוחתין כו' לימא רבנן היא ולא רבי חידקא. אומר ר"י דאין לפרש שבת נותנין לו מזון ג' סעודות דהיינו בשבת שם בע"ש לעת האוכל דמסתמא ישבות שם שאין רגילות כל כך ללכת ערב שבת ובשביל שבת נותנים לו סעודה אחת יותר ממה שנותנין לו בשאר ימים דא"כ היכי ניחא לרבנן והלא מן הכל אין לו כי אם ד' סעודות אחת שהביא עמו דמלוינן בהדיה ושלשה שנתנו לו וכשיאכל אחת בערב שבת לא ישארו בידו רק ג' סעודות ואותן יאכל בשבת וא"כ מיקשי נמי לרבנן וכי אזיל ריקן אזיל כדפריך בסמוך ומיהו איכא למימר דבסמוך לרבנן נמי פריך אבל קשה דהכי משני דמלווינן ליה סעודה בהדיה לא תירץ כלום לר' חידקא דאין לו לשבת כ"א שלש סעודות ולר' חידקא צריך ד' ונראה לר"י דבשבת בע"ש לעת האוכל נותנין לו מזון ב' סעודות כמו בשאר ימים ואם בא לשבות שם מוסיפין לו עוד ג' סעודות וקאמר לימא רבנן היא ולא רבי חידקא דלרבנן ניחא שיש בידו ה' סעודות בתחלת שבת ואותה שהביא עמו יאכל בע"ש ומאותן ה' סעודות יאכל ג' בשבת ואחת במוצאי שבת ואחת יוליך עמו אלא לרבי חידקא כשיאכל ד' בשבת ואחת להוליך עמו למחר א"כ מה יאכל במוצאי שבת וליכא למימר דאמרינן ליה מה דהוה לך למיכל באפוקי שבתא אכול בשבתא כדאמרי' לעיל דהתם אמרינן ליה כדי שלא יהא ניזון מן הצדקה אבל הכא כבר הוא ניזון ולהכי נוטל כל צרכו ומשני דאיכא סעודה בהדיה המתרץ היה סבור שהיה פשוט למקשה שהסעודה שיוליך עמו נותנין לו באחד בשבת אע"פ שבשאר ימים נותנין לו סעודה שיוליך עמו עם אחרות בע"ש אין נותנין לו אותה עד שילך לפי שאינו הולך מיד עד אחר השבת ולכך היה סבור שהמקשה לא היה יודע שהביא סעודה עמו ואין לו בתחלת השבת אלא ד' להכי משני ליה דאיכא סעודה בהדיה והמקשה משיב דפשיטא ליה דאיכא סעודה בהדיה אך קשה ליה כיון דמתרלת דאכיל לכולהו וכי אזיל בריקן אזיל שכמו שהביא עמו לכאן כן ישאנה עמו בצאתו מכאן ומשני דמלוינן ליה כו': **דמלוינן** סעודה בהדיה. וא"ת א"כ אמאי נותנים לו ג' סעודות כיון שמביא אחת עמו יתנו לו אחת ויאכל אחת והאחת יוליך עמו וי"ל דאין מחלקין תמחוי בלילה אלא ביום בזמן הסעודה ולכך נותנין לו שנים שיאכל אחת מיד ואחת בלילה במקום שיהיה ואחת להוליך עמו למחר: **לפי** שאין קבע לשתיה. מכאן יש ללמוד בלילה כשרוצה להתענות למחר לאחר אכילה אע"פ שאינו יכול לאכול אם לא התנה לפי שמסתמא כשבירך סילק דעתו מלאכול מלשתות ודאי לא סילק דעתו כדאמר הכא דאין קבע לשתיה והיכא דלא שכיח יין אע"ג דסילק דעתו מן היין מ"מ ממים לא סילק דעתו ומיהו אומר ר"י דשמא דוקא בימיהם שהיו קובעין עצמן לשתיה אחר אכילה אמרו דאין קבע לשתיה אבל לדידן לא וריב"א פירש במסכת תענית (דף יב.) שאף לאחר שישן מותר לשתות על פי הירושלמי ואין ר"י רוצה להקל כל כך כיון שלא נזכר בהדיא בש"ס שלנו [עיין תוספות תענית יב: ד"ה נים]:

רוגס

עין משפט נר מצוה

ל א מיי' פ"ט מהלכות מתנות עניים הלכה יג סמג עשין קסב טור שו"ע יו"ד סימן רנג סעיף א ב:
לא ב מיי' פ"ל מהלכות שבת הלכה ז סמג עשין ל טוש"ע או"ח סי' רמב:
לב ג מיי' פ"ז מהלכות מ"ע הלכה ח סמג עשין קסב טוש"ע יו"ד סימן רנ סעיף ד:
לג ד מיי' פכ"ג מהלכות שבת הלכה ז סמג לאוין סה טוש"ע או"ח סימן שכג סעיף ו:
לד ה מיי' פ"ל שם הלכה ט סמג עשין ל טוש"ע או"ח סימן רלא סעיף א:

רבינו חננאל

ואיתא בפ' כיצד מברכין: ת"ר כמה סעודות חייב אדם לוכל בשבת ג'. פי' א' בלילה וב' ביום. וכן הלכה. ולפיכך שנינו שמציל מזון ג' סעודו' ומתני' מחוורתא דלא כר' חידקא: כלי מאכל אינו מדיח אלא מה שצריך לוכל בו בשבת. לפי זמן סעודותיו אבל כלי שתיה כל היום. שאין קבע לשתיה:

מסורת הש"ס

א) פאה פרק ח מ"ז, ב) פסחים דף קיב. קיג., ג) פאה פ"ח מ"ז ב"ב ט ע"א.

תורה אור השלם

א) וַיֹּאמֶר מֹשֶׁה אִכְלֻהוּ הַיּוֹם כִּי שַׁבָּת הַיּוֹם לַייָ הַיּוֹם לֹא תִמְצָאֻהוּ בַּשָּׂדֶה: [שמות טז, כה]
ב) הִנֵּה אָנֹכִי שֹׁלֵחַ לָכֶם אֵת אֵלִיָּה הַנָּבִיא לִפְנֵי בּוֹא יוֹם יְיָ הַגָּדוֹל וְהַנּוֹרָא: [מלאכי ג, כג]
ג) יוֹם עֶבְרָה הַיּוֹם הַהוּא יוֹם צָרָה וּמְצוּקָה יוֹם שֹׁאָה וּמְשׁוֹאָה יוֹם חֹשֶׁךְ וַאֲפֵלָה יוֹם עָנָן וַעֲרָפֶל: [צפניה א, טו]
ד) וְהָיָה בַּיּוֹם הַהוּא בְּיוֹם בּוֹא גוֹג עַל אַדְמַת יִשְׂרָאֵל נְאֻם אֲדֹנָי אֱלֹהִים תַּעֲלֶה חֲמָתִי בְּאַפִּי: [יחזקאל לח, יח]
ה) אָז תִּתְעַנַּג עַל יְיָ וְהִרְכַּבְתִּיךָ עַל בָּמֳתֵי אָרֶץ וְהַאֲכַלְתִּיךָ נַחֲלַת יַעֲקֹב אָבִיךָ כִּי פִּי יְיָ דִּבֵּר: [ישעיה נח, יד]

ליקוטי רש"י

תמחוי. מאכל לאם ומיני מאכל שגובין לחלק [פסחים יג.]. מאכל שגובין מבעלי בתים לחלק לעניים בכל יום [ב"מ לח.]. מככר בפונדיון. ככר הלקוח בפונדיון כשלוקחין ארבע סאין חטין בסלע ומגיע לפונדיון חלי קב שהסלע מ"ח פונדיונין וארבע סאין מ"ח חצאי קבין והחנוני שהוא טוחן ואופה ומוכר בשוק משתכר מחצה אחד שנותן ככר של רובע הקב בפונדיון. לן. בלילה. פרנסת לינה. צרכי לינה. בי סדיא. כר לתת מראשותיו [ב"ב ט.]. לבדין קטורין פלטר"א ועושין לקטנן תחתיו במקום כר או הכסת [לקמן קמ.]. חבלו של משיח. גורלו לישנא אחרינא אבלו פחדים וחבלים שיהיו בימיו מחיל העובדי כוכבים [סנהדרין צח:]. לפני בוא יום וגו'. לפני ביאת בן דוד יבא אליהו לבשר [עירובין מג:].

מְדִיחַ וְהוֹלֵךְ כָּל הַיּוֹם כּוּלּוֹ – BUT CUPS, DRINKING LADLES AND PITCHERS MAY BE WASHED ALL DAY LONG, i.e. even after Minchah time, לְפִי שֶׁאֵין קֶבַע לִשְׁתִיָּה – BECAUSE THERE IS NO FIXED TIME FOR DRINKING, i.e. people are prone to drink anytime, even outside of mealtimes.

The Gemara digresses to discuss the reward for observing the three Sabbath meals:

אָמַר רַבִּי שִׁמְעוֹן בֶּן פָּזִי אָמַר רַבִּי יְהוֹשֻׁעַ בֶּן לֵוִי מִשּׁוּם בַּר קַפָּרָא – **R' Shimon ben Pazi said in the name of R' Yehoshua ben Levi who reported in the name of Bar Kappara:** כֹּל הַמְקַיֵּים שָׁלֹשׁ סְעוּדוֹת בְּשַׁבָּת נִיצּוֹל מִשָּׁלֹשׁ פּוּרְעָנִיּוֹת – **Whoever fulfills** the precept of eating **three meals on the Sabbath is spared from three misfortunes:** מֵחֶבְלוֹ שֶׁל מָשִׁיחַ – **from the travails of the Messiah,**[15] וּמִדִּינָהּ שֶׁל גֵּיהִנֹּם – **from the judgment of Gehinnom**[16] וּמִמִּלְחֶמֶת גּוֹג וּמָגוֹג – **and from the war of Gog and Magog.**[17]

The Gemara adduces Scriptural proof for each of these things:

מֵחֶבְלוֹ שֶׁל מָשִׁיחַ – That he is spared **from the travails of the Messiah** is deduced as follows: כְּתִיב הָכָא ,,יוֹם" – **It is written here** in regard to the Sabbath meals: ***"day,"***[18] וּכְתִיב הָתָם – **and it is written there,** in regard to the advent of Messiah: ,,הִנֵּה אָנֹכִי שֹׁלֵחַ לָכֶם אֵת אֵלִיָּה הַנָּבִיא לִפְנֵי בּוֹא יוֹם וגו׳ " – ***Behold! I send you Elijah the prophet before there arrives the "day"*** etc. *of Hashem, great and awesome.*[19] מִדִּינָהּ שֶׁל גֵּיהִנֹּם – That he is spared **from the judgment of Gehinnom** is derived as follows: כְּתִיב הָכָא ,,יוֹם" – **It is written here: *"day,"*** וּכְתִיב הָתָם ,,יוֹם עֶבְרָה הַיּוֹם הַהוּא" – **and it is written there,** in regard to Gehinnom: ***A "day" of anger is that day.***[20] מִמִּלְחֶמֶת גּוֹג וּמָגוֹג – That he is spared **from the war of Gog and Magog** is deduced as follows: כְּתִיב הָכָא ,,יוֹם" – **It is written here: *"day,"*** וּכְתִיב הָתָם ,,בְּיוֹם בּוֹא גוֹג" – **and it is written there: *on the "day" Gog comes.***[21]

A teaching regarding the reward for feasting on the Sabbath:

אָמַר רַבִּי יוֹחָנָן מִשּׁוּם רַבִּי יוֹסֵי – **R' Yochanan reported in the name of R' Yose:** כֹּל הַמְעַנֵּג אֶת הַשַּׁבָּת נוֹתְנִין לוֹ נַחֲלָה בְּלִי מְצָרִים שֶׁנֶּאֱמַר – **Whoever delights in the Sabbath**[22] **is granted a boundless heritage, as it says:**[23] ,,אָז תִּתְעַנַּג עַל־ה׳ וְהִרְכַּבְתִּיךָ עַל־בָּמֳתֵי אָרֶץ וְהַאֲכַלְתִּיךָ – *If you proclaim the Sabbath "a delight"*. . . ***then you shall be granted pleasure with Hashem, and I shall mount you astride the heights of the world; and I will provide you***

NOTES

15. The Messianic Era will be preceded by extremely difficult times. These are referred to in various places by the Talmud as "the travails of the Messiah" (see *Rashi*).

16. Upon death, the souls of sinners are punished in Gehinnom (hell).

17. Prior to the Final Redemption, Gog, king of Magog, will lead the nations in a cataclysmic war against the Jews in Eretz Yisrael, as described in *Ezekiel* chs. 38-39.

18. [See above, end of 117b, that the obligation to eat three meals on the Sabbath is derived from the verse's use of the word "day" three times in regard to the manna.]

19. *Malachi* 3:23. Elijah will appear in the midst of the travails preceding the Messiah to announce the Messiah's arrival. The word "day" appears in both contexts (cf. *Maharsha*).

20. *Zephaniah* 1:15. See *Rashash*.

21. *Ezekiel* 38:18.

For suggestions as to why being spared these specific misfortunes is an appropriate reward for fulfilling the precept of eating the three Sabbath meals, see *Maharam Kazis; Maharsha; Bach* to *Orach Chaim* 291.

22. The Gemara will explain below what this means.

23. *Isaiah* 58:14.

מצילין מזון ג' סעודות מאי לאו דלא אכל לא דאכל שחרית מצילין מזון שתי סעודות מאי לאו דלא אכל לא דאכל במנחה מצילין מזון סעודה אחת מאי לאו דלא אכל לא דאכל והא מדקתני סיפא רבי יוסי אומר לעולם מצילין מזון ג' סעודות מכלל דתנא קמא ג' סבירא ליה אלא מחוורתא מתני' דלא כרבי חידקא והא [א] דתנן מי [א] שיש לו מזון שתי סעודות לא יטול מן התמחוי מזון ארבע עשרה לא יטול מן הקופה מני לא רבנן ולא רבי חידקא אי רבנן חמסרי הויין אי רבי חידקא שית סרי הויין לעולם רבנן דאמרינן ליה מאי דבעית למיכל באפוקי שבתא אכליה בשבתא לימא רבנן היא ולא ר' חידקא אפי' תימא ר' חידקא דאמרינן ליה מאי דבעית למיכל במעלי שבתא אכליה לאורתא וכולי יומא דמעלי שבתא בתעניתא מותבינן ליה אלא הא מני רבי עקיבא היא דאמר [ב] עשה שבתך חול ואל תצטרך לבריות [ג] והא דתנן [ג] אין פוחתין לעני העובר ממקום למקום מככר בפונדיון מד' סאין בסלע לן נותנין לו פרנסת לינה ואם שבת נותנין לו מזון ג' סעודות לימא רבנן היא ולא ר' חידקא לעולם ר' חידקא כגון דאיכא סעודה בהדיה דאמרינן ליה הא דאיכא בהדך אכליה וכי אזיל בריקן אזיל דמלווינן ליה סעודה בהדיה מאי פרנסת לינה אמר רב פפא פוריא ובי סדיא: ת"ר [ד] קערות שאכל בהן ערבית מדיחן לאכול בהן שחרית שחרית מדיחן לאכול בהן בצהרים בצהרים מדיחן לאכול בהן במנחה מן המנחה ואילך שוב אינו מדיח אבל כוסות וקיתוניות וצלוחיות מדיח והולך כל היום כולו לפי שאין קבע לשתיה א"ר שמעון בן פזי א"ר יהושע בן לוי משום בר קפרא [ה] כל המקיים שלש סעודות בשבת ניצול משלש פורעניות מחבלו של משיח ומדינה של גיהנם וממלחמת גוג ומגוג מחבלו של משיח כתיב הכא [א] יום וכתיב התם [ב] הנה אנכי שולח לכם את אליה הנביא לפני בוא יום וגו' מדינה של גיהנם כתיב הכא יום וכתיב התם [ג] יום עברה היום ההוא ממלחמת גוג ומגוג כתיב הכא יום וכתיב התם [ד] ביום בא גוג א"ר יוחנן משום רבי יוסי כל המענג את השבת נותנין לו נחלה בלי מצרים שנאמר [ה] אז תתענג על ה' והרכבתיך על במתי ארץ והאכלתיך נחלת

נחלת

לעולם מצילין מזון ג' סעודות. מדלא אמר ארבע לית ליה דרבי חידקא: מכלל דתנא קמא שלש סעודות סבירא ליה. דהכאי לא איפליגו אלא דת"ק סבר מה שעבר כבר לא יציל ורבי יוסי יציל: תמחוי. קערה גדולה היא וגובין בה גבאים מאכל מבעלי בתים ומחלקין לעניים ב' סעודות ליום מיום ליום: לא יטול. כיון דיש לו נמצא גוזל עניים: קופה. מעות הן לפרנס עניים בני טובים דזיל להו מילתא דתמחוי ומחלקין מע"ש לע"ש: י"ד סעודות לא יטול מן הקופה. שהרי יכול להמתין לע"ש הבאה אבל כשיש לו מזון י"ג יטול שהרי לא תחלק עוד עד שיגיע ע"ש והרי לשבעה ימי שבת צריכין י"ד סעודות: אכליה בשבתא. שהרי מאכלנה סמוך לערב ולא תצטרך לאכול בלילה ואף על גב דאמרינן לקמן לעולם יסדר אדם שלחנו במוצאי שבת ה"מ למאן דאפשר ליה: בתעניתא מותבינן ליה. בתמיה: אלא הא מני ר' עקיבא היא. ולענין סעודת שבת במאן דלא אפשר ליה איכא למימר כרבנן ואיכא למימר כרבי חידקא ומיהו האי דצריך לבריות יעשה שבתו חול ולא יטיל על אחרים כבוד שבתותיו: אין פוחתין לעני העובר ממקום למקום. שאינו לן בלילה אלא: מככר. הלקוח בפונדיון כשהשער ד' סאין בסלע והפונדיון אחד מי"ב בדינר דהוא אחד ממ"ח בסלע ושיערו לו חכמים ככר זו לשתי סעודות היום והלילה: לן נותנין לו פרנסת לינה. לקמן מפרש מאי היא שהרי סעודה של לילה בכלל ככר היא וככר זו משערינן בעירובין (דף פב:) למזון שתי סעודות לעירובי תחומין: ואם שבת. אצלם בשבת: מאי פרנסת לינה. הא קבל ליה סעודת הלילה: בי סדיא. לבדין פולטר"ש להניח תחת מראשותיו: שוב אינו מדיחן. דאין הדחה זו אלא לחול: חבלו של משיח. כדאמרי' בכתובות (דף קיב:) דור שבן דוד בא בו קטיגוריא בתלמידי חכמים שנאמר ועוד בה עשיריה וגו'. חבלי לשון חבלי יולדה (הושע יג): בלי מצרים. כלומר אין לה קץ: אז תתענג. בתר וקראת לשבת עונג כתיב:

נחלת

במנחה מצילין מזון סעודה אחת. מכאן משמע דזמן אכילה שלישית בשבת היא מן המנחה ולמעלה דלא כאותם שמחלקין סעודת שחרית ומברכין בינתים ומיהו מהא דאמרינן בפסחים בפ"ק (דף יג.) י"ד שחל להיות בשבת משייר מזון שתי סעודות אין ראיה מדאין משיירין מזון ג' סעודות שאין לעשות ב' סעודות שחרית דהא כיון שאוכל הכל שחרית חשיב כסעודה אחת ועוד אומר ר"י שיש כאן איסור ברכה שאינה צריכה כדאמרי' בפ' בא לו (יומא דף ע.) גבי ובעשור שבחומש הפקודים דקאמר וליתי ס"ת אחרינא ונקרי א"ר שמעון בן לקיש מפני ברכה שאינה צריכה: מככר בפונדיון כו'. היינו כר' יוחנן בן ברוקא דחשיב ככר בפונדיון מד' סאין בסלע שתי סעודות דעירוב ופליג התם (עירובין דף פב:) ארבי מאיר ורבי יהודה שאומרים התם שיעור אחר: והא דתנן אין פוחתין כו' נימא רבנן היא ולא רבי חידקא. אומר ר"י דאין לפרש שבת נותנין לו מזון ג' סעודות דהיינו כשבא שם בע"ש לעת האוכל דמסתמא ישבות שם שאין רגילות כל כך ללכת ערב שבת ובשביל שבת נותנים לו סעודה אחת יותר ממה שנותנין לו בשאר ימים דא"כ היכי ניחא לרבנן והלא מן הכל אין לו כי אם ד' סעודות אחת שהביא עמו דמלוין בהדיה ושלשה שנתנו לו וכשיאכל אחת בערב שבת לא ישארו בידו רק ג' סעודות ואותן יאכל בשבת וא"כ תיקשי נמי לרבנן וכי אזיל ריקן אזיל כדפריך בסמוך ומיהו איכא למימר דבסמוך לרבנן נמי פריך אבל קשה דכי משני דמלוין ליה סעודה בהדיה לא תירץ כלום לר' חידקא דאין לו לשבת כ"א שלש סעודות ולר' חידקא צריך ד' ונראה לר"י דכשבא בע"ש לעת האוכל נותנין לו מזון ב' סעודות כמו בשאר ימים ואם בא לשבות שם מוסיפין לו עוד ג' סעודות וקאמר לימא רבנן היא ולא רבי חידקא דלרבנן ניחא שיש בידו ה' סעודות בתחילת שבת ואותה שהביא עמו יאכל בע"ש ומאותן ה' סעודות יאכל ג' בשבת ואחת במוצאי שבת ואחת יוליך עמו אלא לרבי חידקא כשיאכל ד' בשבת ואחת להוליך עמו למחר א"כ מה יאכל במוצאי שבת וליכא למימר דאמרינן ליה מה דהוה לך למיכל באפוקי שבתא אכול בשבתא כדאמרי' לעיל דהתם אמרינן ליה כדי שלא יהא ניזון מן הצדקה אבל הכא ככר הוא ניזון ולהכי נוטל כל צרכו ומשני דאיכא סעודה בהדיה המתרץ היה סבור שהיה פשוט למקשה שהסעודה שיוליך עמו נותנין לו באחד בשבת אע"פ שבשאר ימים נותנין לו סעודה שיוליך עמו עם אחרות בע"ש אין נותנין לו אותה עד שילך לפי שאינו הולך מיד עד אחר השבת ולכך היה סבור שהמקשה לא היה יודע שהביא סעודה עמו ואין לו בתחלת השבת אלא ד' להכי משני ליה דאיכא סעודה בהדיה והמקשה משיב דפשיטא ליה דאיכא סעודה בהדיה אך קשה ליה כיון דמתרלת דאכיל לכולהו וכי אזיל בריקן אזיל שכמו שהביא עמו לכאן כן ישאנה עמו בלאתו מכאן ומשני דמלוין ליה כו':

דמלוין סעודה בהדיה. וא"ת א"כ אמאי נותנים לו ג' סעודות כיון שמביא אחת עמו יתנו לו אחת ויאכל אחת והאחת יוליך עמו וי"ל דאין מחלקין תמחוי בלילה אלא ביום בזמן הסעודה ולכך נותנין לו שנים שיאכל אחת מיד ואחת בלילה במקום שיהיה ואחת להוליך עמו למחר: לפי שאין קבע לשתיה. מכאן יש ללמוד בלילה כשרוצה להתענות למחר לאחר אכילה אע"פ שאינו יכול לאכול אם לא התנה לפי שמסתמא כשבירך סילק דעתו מלאכול מלשתות ודאי לא סילק דעתו כדאמר הכא דאין קבע לשתיה והיכא דלא שכיח יין אע"ג דסילק דעתו מן היין מ"מ ממים לא סילק דעתו ומיהו אומר ר"י דשמא דוקא בימיהם שהיו קובעין עצמן לשתיה אחר אכילה אמרו דאין קבע לשתיה אבל לדידן לא וריב"א פירש במסכת תענית (דף יב.) שאף לאחר שישן מותר לשתות על פי הירושלמי ואין ר"י רוצה להקל כל כך כיון שלא נזכר בהדיא בש"ס שלנו [עיין תוספות תענית יב: ד"ה נים]:

רונס

עין משפט נר מצוה

ל א מיי' פ"ט מהלכות מתנות עניים הלכה יג סמג עשין קסב טור שו"ע יו"ד סימן רנג סעיף א ב:

לא ב מיי' פ"ל מהלכות שבת הלכה ז סמג עשין ל טוש"ע או"ח סי' רמב:

לב ג מיי' פ"ז מהלכות מ"ע הלכה ח סמג עשין קסב טוש"ע יו"ד סימן רנ סעיף ד:

לג ד מיי' פכ"ג מהלכות שבת הלכה ז סמג לאוין סה טוש"ע או"ח סימן שכג סעיף ו:

לד ה מיי' פ"ל שם הלכה ט סמג עשין ל טוש"ע או"ח סימן רלא סעיף א:

רבינו חננאל

ואיתא בפ' כיצד מברכין: ת"ר כמה סעודות חייב אדם לוכל בשבת ג'. פי' א' בלילה וב' ביום. וכן הלכה. ולפיכך שנינו שמציל מזון ג' סעודו' ומתני' מחוורתא דלא כר' חידקא: כלי מאכל אינו מדיח אלא מה שצריך לוכל בו בשבת. לפי זמן סעודותיו אבל כלי שתיה כל היום. שאין קבע לשתיה:

מסורת הש"ס

א) פאה פרק ח מ"ז, ב) פסחים דף קיב. קיג., ג) פאה פ"ח מ"ז ב"ב ט ע"א.

תורה אור השלם

א) וַיֹּאמֶר מֹשֶׁה אִכְלֻהוּ הַיּוֹם כִּי שַׁבָּת הַיּוֹם לַיְיָ הַיּוֹם לֹא תִמְצָאֻהוּ בַּשָּׂדֶה: [שמות טז, כה]

ב) הִנֵּה אָנֹכִי שֹׁלֵחַ לָכֶם אֵת אֵלִיָּה הַנָּבִיא לִפְנֵי בּוֹא יוֹם יְיָ הַגָּדוֹל וְהַנּוֹרָא: [מלאכי ג, כג]

ג) יוֹם עֶבְרָה הַיּוֹם הַהוּא יוֹם צָרָה וּמְצוּקָה יוֹם שֹׁאָה וּמְשׁוֹאָה יוֹם חֹשֶׁךְ וַאֲפֵלָה יוֹם עָנָן וַעֲרָפֶל: [צפניה א, טו]

ד) וְהָיָה בַּיּוֹם הַהוּא בְּיוֹם בּוֹא גוֹג עַל אַדְמַת יִשְׂרָאֵל נְאֻם אֲדֹנָי אֱלֹהִים תַּעֲלֶה חֲמָתִי בְּאַפִּי: [יחזקאל לח, יח]

ה) אָז תִּתְעַנַּג עַל יְיָ וְהִרְכַּבְתִּיךָ עַל בָּמֳתֵי אָרֶץ וְהַאֲכַלְתִּיךָ נַחֲלַת יַעֲקֹב אָבִיךָ כִּי פִּי יְיָ דִּבֵּר: [ישעיה נח, יד]

ליקוטי רש"י

תמחוי. מאכל לחם ומיני מאכל שגובין לחלק [פסחים יג.]. מאכל שגובין מבעלי בתים לחלק לעניים בכל יום [ב"מ לח.]. מככר בפונדיון. ככר הלקוח בפונדיון כשלוקחין ארבע סאין חטין בסלע ומגיע לפונדיון חצי קב שהסלע מ"ח פונדיונין וארבע סאין מ"ח חצאי קבין והחנוני שהוא טוחן ואופה ומוכר בשוק משתכר מחצה הרי שנותן ככר של רובע הקב בפונדיון. לן. בלילה. פרנסת לינה. צרכי לינה. בי סדיא. כר לתת מראשותיו [ב"ב ט.]. לבדין שקורין פלטר"ש ועשוין לקפלן תחתיו במקום הכר או הכסת [לקמן קמו:]. חבלו של משיח. גורלו לישנא אחרינא חבלו פחדים ומכאובים שיהיו בימיו מפני העובדי כוכבים [סנהדרין צח:]. לפני בוא יום וגו'. לפני ביאת בן דוד יבא אליהו [עירובין מג:].

נחלת יעקב אביך וגו' לא כאברהם שכתוב בו א) קום התהלך בארץ לארכה וגו' ולא כיצחק שכתוב בו ב) כי לך ולזרעך אתן את כל הארצות האל אלא כיעקב שכתוב בו ג) ופרצת ימה וקדמה וצפונה ונגבה ר"נ בר יצחק אמר ניצול משעבוד גליות כתיב הכא והרכבתיך על במתי ארץ וכתיב התם ד) ואתה על במותימו תדרוך אמר רב יהודה אמר רב כל המענג את השבת נותנין לו משאלות לבו שנאמר ה) והתענג על ה' ויתן לך משאלות לבך עונג זה איני יודע מהו כשהוא אומר ו) וקראת לשבת עונג *הוי אומר זה עונג שבת במה מענגו רב יהודה בריה דרב שמואל בר שילת משמי' דרב אמר בתבשיל של תרדין (א) ודגים גדולים וראשי שומין רב חייא בר אשי אמר רב אפי' דבר מועט ולכבוד שבת עשאו הרי זה עונג מאי היא א"ר פפא כסא דהרסנא אמר ר' חייא בר אבא א"ר יוחנן כל המשמר שבת כהלכתו אפי' עובד ע"ז [כדור] אנוש מוחלין לו שנאמר ז) אשרי אנוש יעשה זאת וגו' מחללו אל תקרי מחללו אלא מחול לו אמר רב יהודה אמר רב אלמלי שמרו ישראל שבת ראשונה לא שלטה בהן אומה ולשון שנאמר ח) ויהי ביום השביעי יצאו מן העם ללקוט וכתיב בתריה ט) ויבא עמלק אמר רבי יוחנן משום רבי שמעון בן יוחי אלמלי משמרין ישראל שתי שבתות כהלכתן מיד נגאלים שנא' י) כה אמר ה' לסריסים אשר ישמרו את שבתותי וכתיב בתריה כ) והביאותים אל הר קדשי וגו' אמר ר' יוסי יהא חלקי מאוכלי שלש סעודות בשבת א"ר יוסי יהא חלקי מגומרי הלל בכל יום איני והאמר מר הקורא הלל בכל יום הרי זה מחרף ומגדף כי קאמרינן בפסוקי דזמרא א"ר יוסי יהא חלקי ממתפללים עם דמדומי חמה א"ר חייא בר אבא א"ר יוחנן מצוה להתפלל עם דמדומי חמה א"ר זירא מאי קרא ל) ייראוך עם שמש ולפני ירח דור דורים וא"ר יוסי יהא חלקי ממתי בחולי מעיים דאמר מר רובן של צדיקים מתים בחולי מעיים וא"ר יוסי יהא חלקי ממתי בדרך מצוה וא"ר יוסי יהא חלקי ממכניסי שבת בטבריא וממוציאי שבת בצפורי וא"ר יוסי יהא חלקי ממושיבי בהמ"ד ולא ממעמידי בהמ"ד וא"ר יוסי יהא חלקי מגבאי צדקה ולא ממחלקי צדקה וא"ר יוסי יהא חלקי ממי שחושדין אותו ואין בו אמר רב פפא לדידי חשדן ולא הוה בי א"ר יוסי חמש בעילות בעלתי ונטעתי חמשה ארזים בישראל ומאן אינון ר' ישמעאל ברבי יוסי ור' אלעזר בר"י ור' חלפתא בר"י ור' אבטילס בר"י ורבי מנחם בר' יוסי והאיכא ורדימס היינו מנחם ואמאי קרי ליה ורדימס שפניו דומין לוורד למימרא דרבי יוסי מצות עונה לא קיים אלא אימא חמש בעילות בעלתי ושניתי אמר רבי יוסי מימי לא קריתי לאשתי אשתי ולשורי שורי אלא לאשתי ביתי ולשורי שדי אמר ר' יוסי מימי לא נסתכלתי במילה שלי איני והאמרו ליה לרבי מאי טעמא קראו לך רבינו הקדוש אמר להו מימי לא נסתכלתי במילה שלי ביה הוה מילתא אחריתי שלא הכניס ידו תחת אבנטו וא"ר יוסי מימי לא ראו קורות ביתי אימרי חלוקי וא"ר יוסי מימי לא עברתי על דברי חברי יודע אני בעצמי שאיני כהן אם אומרים לי חבירי עלה לדוכן אני עולה וא"ר יוסי מימי לא אמרתי דבר וחזרתי לאחורי אמר רב נחמן תיתי לי דקיימית ג' סעודות בשבת אמר רב יהודה תיתי לי דקיימית עיון תפלה אמר רב הונא בריה דרב יהושע תיתי לי דלא סגינא ד' אמות בגילוי הראש אמר רב ששת תיתי לי דקיימית מצות תפילין ואמר ר"נ תיתי לי דקיימית מצות ציצית אמר ליה רב יוסף לרב יוסף בריה דרבה אבוך במאי זהיר טפי אמר ליה בציצית יומא חד הוה קא סליק בדרגא איפסיק ליה חוטא ולא נחית ולא סליק עד דרמיה ואמר אביי תיתי לי דכי חזינא צורבא מרבנן דשלים מסכתיה עבידנא

תוספות

רובם של צדיקים מתים בחולי מעיים. פי' בקונטרס למרק עונותיהם ור"י אומר כי יש במדרש ל) למרק אכילה מן המעיים להיות נקיים וטהורים כמלאכי השרת: אימא ה' בעילות בעלתי ושניתי. ובירושלמי משני דיבמות היו ולא רצה לקיים מצות עונה אלא רק כדי לקיים מצות יבום דהיינו ביאה ראשונה: אילו היו אומרים לי חברי עלה לדוכן. ° לא ידע ר"י מה איסור יש בזר העולה לדוכן אם לא משום ברכה לבטלה שלכהנים אמרה תורה לברך את ישראל: עיון תפלה. פי' בכוונת הלב וכן ההיא דאלו דברים שאוכל מפירותיהן בעולם הזה (לקמן דף קכז.) דחשיב עיון תפלה אבל הא דאמר בברכות (דף לב: ונה.) המעיין בתפלתו סוף בא לידי כאב לב ההוא עיון דמצפה מתי יעשה הקב"ה בקשתו שסבור שתפלתו מקובלת כדמייתי עלה תוחלת ממושכה מחלה לב וכן ההיא מ) דאמר ר"י שלשה דברים מזכירין עונותיו של אדם קיר נטוי ועיון תפלה [ומוסר דין לשמים על חבירו] והא דאמר בפרק גט פשוט (ב"ב קסד:) שלשה דברים אין אדם ניצול מהם בכל יום לשון הרע והרהור עבירה ועיון תפלה אין לפרש שמצפה מתי תיעשה בקשתו שהרבה בני אדם ניצולים מזה אלא הוה כי הסוגיא דשמעתין כלומר שאינו מתכוין בתפלה שאי אפשר ליזהר כדאמרינן בירושלמי נ) מחזיקנא טיבו לרישא דכי מטא למודים מנפשיה כרע ס):

בתליסר

רש"י

נחלת יעקב. ולא נחלת אברהם ויצחק: לארכה ולרחבה. ארץ זו ולא יותר: הארצות האל. ותו לא: תבשיל של תרדין. חשוב הוא: ראשי שומין. חשובים היו להן: כסא דהרסנא. דגים קטנים מטוגנים בשמן קרביהן ובקמח: דור אנוש. התחילו לעבוד ע"ז דכתיב (בראשית ד) אז הוחל לקרוא וגו': בתריה. בתר ההיא פרשתא: הרי זה מחרף ומגדף. שנביאים הראשונים תיקנו לומר בפרקים לשבח והודיה כדאמרינן בערבי פסחים (דף קיז.) וזה הקוראה תמיד בלא עתה אינו אלא כמזמר שיר ומתלוצץ: פסוקי דזמרא. שני מזמורים של הילולים הללו את ה' מן השמים הללו אל בקדשו: דמדומי חמה. כשהיא אדומה שחרית אחרי הנץ מיד היא אדומה וערבית סמוך לשקיעתה: עם שמש. עם זריחתה: ולפני ירח. קודם אור הירח בעוד השמש לא שקעה: ממתי מחולי בני מעיים. שמתייסרין ביסורין ומתמרקין עונותיהן: ממכניסי שבת בטבריא. מפני שהיא עמוקה ומחשכת מבעוד יום וסבורין שחשכה וממוציאי שבת בצפורי שיושבת בראש ההר ובעוד כשהחמה שוקעת נראית שם אור גדול ומאחרין לצאת: ממושיבי בית המדרש. חזנים מאספי תלמידים בכל יום לבא: ממעמידי. ממונים לעת האוכל לומר הגיע עת לעמוד ולאכול: ממחלקי. לעניים צדקה דאמרינן בבבא בתרא פ"ק (דף ח:) צדקה נגבית בשנים ומתחלקת בשלשה והמחלקים אותה עליהם לבדוק לפי הצריך לכל אחד ואחד ופעמים שקרובין דעתם לרחם על זה ולחלוק יותר מן הצורך שאומדין אותו בהרווחה ואומדין את חברו בצמצום: בעלתי ושניתי. כדי שיהיו זכרים דאמר מר הרוצה שיהיו בניו זכרים יבעול וישנה (עירובין דף ק:): לא קריתי לאשתי אשתי. שאף שיחת חולין שלי יש ללמוד הימנה חכמה: אשתי ביתי. שהיא עיקר של בית: ולשורי שדי. שהוא עיקר של שדה דכתיב ורב תבואות בכח שור (משלי יד): לא נסתכלתי כו'. מרוב צניעות: והא אמרו לו כו'. וא"כ לרבי יוסי נמי הוה ליה למיקרייה רבינו הקדוש: תחת אבנטו. מן האבנט ולמטה: לא ראו קורות כו'. (ג) כשפושט חלוקו [פושטו] כמו שהוא לובשו דרך ראשו ומכסה את עצמו תחלה משום צניעות בסדינו מתחת ויושב במטתו: לא אמרתי דבר וחזרתי לאחורי. שאם בא מי שאמרתי עליו דבר ושאל אם אמרתי כן עליו לא חזרתי בי לאמר אינו כדבריו לפי שמתחלה אמת אמרתי וקסבר כל מילתא דמתאמרא באפי מרה לית בה משום לישנא בישא וכן מפרש במסכת ערכין (דף טו:): דקיימתי מצות תפילין. שלא הלך ארבע אמות בלא תפילין וכן לענין ציצית: עד דרמיה. שתקנה וזה לשון תליית ציצית כדאמרינן בעלמא (תענית ד' כב.) לא רמי חוטי: דשלים מסכתיה. שגרסה:

עבידנא

עין משפט נר מצוה

לה א מיי' פ"ל מהל' שבת הלכה ז סמג עשין ל טור שו"ע או"ח סימן רמב:

לו ב מיי' פ"ז מהלכות תפלה הלכה יב טור שו"ע או"ח סימן נא סעיף ט:

לז ג מיי' פ"ג מהלכות תפלה הלכה א' סמג עשין יט טוש"ע או"ח סימן פט סעיף א וסימן רלג סעיף א [ברי"ף לקמן ובפ"ק דברכות דף כו. וכן ברא"ש שם סי' ה']:

לח ד טור שו"ע או"ח סימן רסא סעיף ב וסימן רלג סעיף א:

לט ה מיי' פ"ט מהל' איסורי ביאה הלכה כג טוש"ע אה"ע סימן כג סעיף ו בהגה:

מ ו ז טוש"ע או"ח סימן ח סעיף א ו:

מא ח טוש"ע יו"ד סי' רמו סעיף כו בהג"ה:

רב נסים גאון

אמר ר' יוסי יהא חלקי עם מכניסי שבת בטבריא ועם מוציאי שבתות בציפורי. לפי שטבריא היתה נמוכה והחמה שוקעת שם בעוד יומם והיו יושביה מקבלין עליהן השבת משקיעת החמה אצלם ושקיעתה לשם קודם שקיעתה במקומות הגבוהין ומי שמקבל עליו הכנסת השבת מאותה השעה הרי עשה סייג לעצמו והוא משובח ומעולה מן היושבים במקומות הגבוהין וההרים וכנגדן מוציאי שבת בציפורי שהיא גבוהה שופי ומאחרין לשם פני המזרח להכסיף ושוהין ומאדימין והיו מקבלין עליהן שימור השבת עד שמכספין פני המזרח התחתון והעליון ולפיכך הן משובחים בזה הענין יותר מאנשי טבריא ובמסכת ראש השנה בפרק יו"ט (דף לא) משכחת וטבריא עמוקה מכולן שנאמר (ישעיה כט) ושפלת מארץ תדברי ובמסכת מגילה בפרק מגילה נקראת (דף ו) ולמה נקראת שמה ציפורי שיושבת בראש ההר כצפור והרי נתברר לך מיכן כי טבריא נמוכה וציפורי גבוהה:

ליקוטי רש"י

נחלת יעקב אביך. נחלה בלא מצרים [ישעיה נח, יד]. האל. כמו האלה [בראשית כו, ג]. אלא כיעקב וכו'. ויעקב שמר את השבת שנא' (בראשית לג) ויחן את פני העיר שקבע תחומין עם דמדומי חמה כך פי' ר' שמעון [ישעיה שם]. ואתה על במותימו תדרוך. כענין שנאמר (יהושע י, כד) שימו את רגליכם על צוארי המלכים האלה [דברים לג, כט]. [המשך בדף קיט.]

מסורת הש"ס

א) [ע"ל פ"ז ע"ב תוס' ד"ה כאשר], ב) [עי' תוס' נדה יג: ד"ה עד שיכלו], ג) [עי' תוס' בכורות ב: ד"ה שמא וכו'], ד) ברכות כט:, ה) [כתובות קג:], ו) מו"ק יח:, ז) בדפו"י אליעזר, ח) [סוטה לו:], ט) גיטין נב:, י) ערכין טו: [ע"ש ברש"י], כ) [לקמן ריש קיט. ז"ל רש"י תיתי לי ישולם שכרי ובבכורות ל. ז"ל רש"י תיתי לי שכר טוב ועי' תוס' בבכורות ב: ד"ה שמא], ל) [בראשית רבה פרשה פב], מ) [ברכות נה.], נ) [פרק היה קורא הלכה ין], ס) [ועי' תוס' ברכות לב: ד"ה כל].

הגהות הב"ח

(א) גמ' בתבשיל של תרדין. נ"ב בעירובין ראש ד' כ"ט אמר רב חסדא תבשיל של תרדין יפה ללב וטוב לעינים וכל שכן לבני מעים ואמר אביי והוא דיתיב אבי תפי וכו'. ובס"פ מרובה דף פ"ב ע"א חמשה דברים נאמרו בשום משביע ומשחין ומצהיל פנים ומרבה הזרע והורג כנים שבבני מעים ומכניס אהבה ומוציא קנאה. ובפ' כילד מעברין ריש דף נ"ו פירש"י לשבת ולא לגנאי וע"ש: (ב) רש"י ד"ה לא ראו קורות כו' כשפושט חלוקו. נ"ב ס"א לא היה הופכו מרוב צניעות שכשפושטו כו':

גליון הש"ס

גמרא יהא חלקי ממכניסי שבת בטבריא. ברבינו יונה פ"ח דברכות דף מג ע"א כתב די"מ שבטבריא היו מגמרים הכלים בע"ש מפני כבוד שבת שיריחו ריח טוב ובציפורי היו מגמרים במ"ש והיו עושין כן לכבוד שבת שהיו מראין הצער שיש להם מהנפש יתירה שהיה להם בשבת ועתה בפרידת השבת צריכין למוגמר להריח ריח טוב עיין שם. וכעין זה כ' בלבוש. והרא"ש כתב במשנה סימן מ"ה כ' יהא חלקי וכו' והיינו עם אותם שבתחלה שבת בטבריא ובמוצאי יומא בציפורי כי צפורא וטבריא תוך תחום אחד והקדמי ומאחרי שבת: תוס' ד"ה אילו וכו' לא ידע ר"י. וכמו לקמן קנא ע"ב תוס' ד"ה קמ"ל. וקלא ע"ב תוס' ד"ה מי שכרם. ובכתובות דף כד ע"ב תוס' ד"ה מימא:

תורה אור השלם

א) קוּם הִתְהַלֵּךְ בָּאָרֶץ לְאָרְכָּהּ וּלְרָחְבָּהּ כִּי לְךָ אֶתְּנֶנָּה: [בראשית יג, יז]

ב) גּוּר בָּאָרֶץ הַזֹּאת וְאֶהְיֶה עִמְּךָ וַאֲבָרְכֶךָּ כִּי לְךָ וּלְזַרְעֲךָ אֶתֵּן אֶת כָּל הָאֲרָצֹת הָאֵל וַהֲקִמֹתִי אֶת הַשְּׁבֻעָה אֲשֶׁר נִשְׁבַּעְתִּי לְאַבְרָהָם אָבִיךָ: [בראשית כו, ג]

ג) וְהָיָה זַרְעֲךָ כַּעֲפַר הָאָרֶץ וּפָרַצְתָּ יָמָּה וָקֵדְמָה וְצָפֹנָה וָנֶגְבָּה וְנִבְרְכוּ בְךָ כָּל מִשְׁפְּחֹת הָאֲדָמָה וּבְזַרְעֶךָ: [בראשית כח, יד]

ד) אַשְׁרֶיךָ יִשְׂרָאֵל מִי כָמוֹךָ עַם נוֹשַׁע בַּי"י מָגֵן עֶזְרֶךָ וַאֲשֶׁר חֶרֶב גַּאֲוָתֶךָ וְיִכָּחֲשׁוּ אֹיְבֶיךָ לָךְ וְאַתָּה עַל בָּמוֹתֵימוֹ תִדְרֹךְ: [דברים לג, כט]

ה) וְהִתְעַנַּג עַל יְיָ וְיִתֶּן לְךָ מִשְׁאֲלֹת לִבֶּךָ: [תהלים לז, ד]

ו) אִם תָּשִׁיב מִשַּׁבָּת רַגְלֶךָ עֲשׂוֹת חֲפָצֶךָ בְּיוֹם קָדְשִׁי וְקָרָאתָ לַשַּׁבָּת עֹנֶג לִקְדוֹשׁ יְיָ מְכֻבָּד וְכִבַּדְתּוֹ מֵעֲשׂוֹת דְּרָכֶיךָ מִמְּצוֹא חֶפְצְךָ וְדַבֵּר דָּבָר: [ישעיה נח, יג]

ז) אַשְׁרֵי אֱנוֹשׁ יַעֲשֶׂה זֹּאת וּבֶן אָדָם יַחֲזִיק בָּהּ שֹׁמֵר שַׁבָּת מֵחַלְּלוֹ וְשֹׁמֵר יָדוֹ מֵעֲשׂוֹת כָּל רָע: [ישעיה נו, ב]

ח) וַיְהִי בַּיּוֹם הַשְּׁבִיעִי יָצְאוּ מִן הָעָם לִלְקֹט וְלֹא מָצָאוּ: [שמות טז, כז]

ט) וַיָּבֹא עֲמָלֵק וַיִּלָּחֶם עִם יִשְׂרָאֵל בִּרְפִידִם: [שמות יז, ח]

י) כִּי כֹה אָמַר יְיָ לַסָּרִיסִים אֲשֶׁר יִשְׁמְרוּ אֶת שַׁבְּתוֹתַי וּבָחֲרוּ בַּאֲשֶׁר חָפָצְתִּי וּמַחֲזִיקִים בִּבְרִיתִי: [ישעיה נו, ד]

כ) וַהֲבִיאוֹתִים אֶל הַר קָדְשִׁי וְשִׂמַּחְתִּים בְּבֵית תְּפִלָּתִי עוֹלֹתֵיהֶם וְזִבְחֵיהֶם לְרָצוֹן עַל מִזְבְּחִי כִּי בֵיתִי בֵּית תְּפִלָּה יִקָּרֵא לְכָל הָעַמִּים: [ישעיה נו, ז]

ל) יִירָאוּךָ עִם שָׁמֶשׁ וְלִפְנֵי יָרֵחַ דּוֹר דּוֹרִים: [תהלים עב, ה]

"נַחֲלַת יַעֲקֹב אָבִיךָ וגו׳" – *the heritage of your forefather Jacob,* **etc.** "לֹא כְּאַבְרָהָם שֶׁכָּתוּב בּוֹ ,,קוּם הִתְהַלֵּךְ בָּאָרֶץ לְאָרְכָּהּ וגו׳" – Your heritage will **not** be **like** that of **Abraham, regarding whom it is written,**[1] ***Arise, walk about the land through its length,* etc.** *and its breadth, for to you will I give it.*[2] וְלֹא כְּיִצְחָק שֶׁכָּתוּב בּוֹ ,,כִּי־לְךָ וּלְזַרְעֲךָ אֶתֵּן אֶת־כָּל־הָאֲרָצֹת הָאֵל" – **And not like** that of **Isaac, regarding whom it is written,**[3] ***for to you and your offspring will I give all these lands.***[4] אֶלָּא כְּיַעֲקֹב שֶׁכָּתוּב בּוֹ ,,וּפָרַצְתָּ יָמָּה וָקֵדְמָה וְצָפֹנָה וָנֶגְבָּה" – **Rather,** your heritage will be **like** that of **Jacob, regarding whom it is written,**[5] ***and you shall burst out westward, eastward, northward and southward,*** i.e. without any limit or border.[6]

Another benefit:

רַב נַחְמָן בַּר יִצְחָק אָמַר: ניצול – **Rav Nachman bar Yitzchak said:** מִשִּׁעְבּוּד גָּלֻיּוֹת – **He is spared from the oppression of the exiles.** כְּתִיב הָכָא ,,וְהִרְכַּבְתִּיךָ עַל־בָּמֳתֵי אָרֶץ" – **It is written here,**[7] concerning one who delights in the Sabbath, ***and I shall mount you astride the heights of the world*** (*bamasei*), וּכְתִיב הָתָם ,,וְאַתָּה עַל־בָּמוֹתֵימוֹ תִדְרֹךְ" – **and it is written there,**[8] *your foes will try to deceive you,* ***but you will trample upon their haughty ones*** (*bamoseimo*). The similar wording relates the two passages to each other. Thus, one who calls the Sabbath a delight will be spared from the oppression of his adversaries.[9]

Another benefit:

אָמַר רַב יְהוּדָה אָמַר רַב – **Rav Yehudah said in the name of Rav:** כָּל הַמְעַנֵּג אֶת הַשַּׁבָּת נוֹתְנִין לוֹ מִשְׁאֲלוֹת לִבּוֹ – **Whoever delights in the Sabbath is granted his heart's wishes,** שֶׁנֶּאֱמַר ,,וְהִתְעַנַּג עַל־ה׳ וְיִתֶּן־לְךָ מִשְׁאֲלֹת לִבֶּךָ" – **as it says,** ***And take delight in Hashem and He will grant you your heart's wishes.***[10] עוֹנֶג זֶה אֵינִי יוֹדֵעַ מַהוּ – Now, **I do not know what is meant by** ***delight;***[11] כְּשֶׁהוּא אוֹמֵר ,,וְקָרָאתָ לַשַּׁבָּת עֹנֶג" – however, **when it says,**[12] ***and you shall proclaim the Sabbath a delight,*** הֱוֵי אוֹמֵר זֶה עֹנֶג שַׁבָּת – **I would say that it refers to the delight of the Sabbath** (*oneg Shabbos*).[13]

The Gemara defines this requirement:

בַּמֶּה מְעַנְּגוֹ – **With what** foods **should one delight in [the Sabbath]?** רַב יְהוּדָה בְּרֵיהּ דְּרַב שְׁמוּאֵל בַּר שִׁילַת מִשְּׁמֵיהּ דְּרַב אָמַר – **Rav Yehudah the son of Rav Shmuel bar Shilas said in the name of Rav:** בְּתַבְשִׁיל שֶׁל תְּרָדִין וְדָגִים גְּדוֹלִים וְרָאשֵׁי שׁוּמִין – **With a dish of cooked beets, large fish and cloves of garlic.**[14] רַב חִיָּיא בַּר אַשִׁי אָמַר רַב – **Rav Chiya bar Ashi said in the name of Rav:** אֲפִילוּ דָּבָר מוּעָט וְלִכְבוֹד שַׁבָּת עֲשָׂאוֹ – If one's funds are scarce,[15] then **even if he prepares something small, but he does it in honor of the Sabbath,** הֲרֵי זֶה עוֹנֶג – **that is** considered **an** ***oneg.*** מַאי הִיא – **What is** an example **of this?** אָמַר רַב פָּפָּא – **Rav Pappa said:** כָּסָא דְּהַרְסָנָא – ***casa deharsena.***[16]

The Gemara extols the benefits of Sabbath observance:

אָמַר רַבִּי חִיָּיא בַּר אַבָּא אָמַר רַבִּי יוֹחָנָן – **R' Chiya bar Abba said in the name of R' Yochanan:** כָּל הַמְשַׁמֵּר שַׁבָּת כְּהִלְכָתוֹ – **Whoever observes the Sabbath according to its law,** אֲפִילוּ עוֹבֵד עֲבוֹדָה זָרָה [כְּדוֹר] אֱנוֹשׁ מוֹחֲלִין לוֹ – **even if he worships idols like the generation of Enosh, he is forgiven.** שֶׁנֶּאֱמַר ,,אַשְׁרֵי אֱנוֹשׁ יַעֲשֶׂה־זֹּאת וגו׳ מֵחַלְּלוֹ" – **As it says,**[17] ***Happy is the man*** (*enosh*) ***who does this,* etc.** *who safeguards the Sabbath* ***from desecrating it*** (*meichallilo*). אַל תִּקְרֵי ,,מֵחַלְּלוֹ" – **Do not pronounce it** ***meichallilo,*** אֶלָּא ,,מָחוּל לוֹ" – **but rather,** ***machul lo,*** *it is forgiven him.*[18] אָמַר רַב יְהוּדָה אָמַר רַב – **Rav Yehudah said in the name of Rav:** אִלְמָלֵי שָׁמְרוּ יִשְׂרָאֵל שַׁבָּת רִאשׁוֹנָה – **If the Jewish people had only observed the first Sabbath,** לֹא שָׁלְטָה בָּהֶן אוּמָּה וְלָשׁוֹן – **no race or nation could have assailed them,** שֶׁנֶּאֱמַר ,,וַיְהִי בַּיּוֹם הַשְּׁבִיעִי יָצְאוּ מִן־הָעָם לִלְקֹט" – **as it says,**[19] ***It happened on the seventh day that some of the people went out to gather,***[20] וּכְתִיב בַּתְרֵיהּ ,,וַיָּבֹא עֲמָלֵק" – **and it is written after [this passage]:** ***And***

NOTES

1. *Genesis* 13:17.

2. Here, Abraham is promised only this land and nothing more (*Rashi*).

3. Ibid. 26:3.

4. [Although this is more than was promised Abraham (for the verse used the plural "lands"), still Isaac's inheritance is limited to these lands] and nothing more (*Rashi*).

5. Ibid. 28:14.

6. See *Sfas Emes.* One who delights in the Sabbath is paid back measure for measure: Just as he spends his funds for the Sabbath without restraint, so too he is granted an inheritance without restriction (*Beis Yosef* citing *Mahari Abuhav, Orach Chaim* 242 ד״ה גרסינן). One who delights in the Sabbath is likely to be one who sees God as the source of his sustenance, for one who believes that it is his labors and efforts alone that generate his income tends to view the Sabbath as an intrusion upon his money-making activities. Such a person's confidence is placed in his own finite abilities, and thus the portion given him is finite. On the other hand, a person who labors because that is God's will is overjoyed at the arrival of the Sabbath. His confidence is placed in the Infinite, and so his portion is infinite as well (*Anaf Yosef* citing *Iyei HaYam*).

7. *Isaiah* 58:14.

8. *Deuteronomy* 33:29.

9. Here too, he is rewarded measure for measure: Since he willingly accepted the weighty yoke of Sabbath observance upon himself, the yoke of the nations is lifted from him (*Beis Yosef* loc. cit. citing *Mahari Abuhav*).

10. *Psalms* 37:4. *Eitz Yosef* explains: Although it is permitted to merely think about one's business affairs on the Sabbath, *Smak* (§280) and *Reishis Chochmah* state that it is in keeping with *oneg Shabbos* not to think about these matters. Rather, he should proceed as if all his weekday pursuits had achieved their ends and as if all the concerns troubling his mind had been resolved happily. Measure for measure, he will be granted his heart's desire (see also *Ben Yehoyada*).

11. In what case would Scripture recommend the pursuit of pleasure? (see *Maharsha*).

12. *Isaiah* 58:13.

13. Some authorities rule that *oneg Shabbos* is a Torah requirement (*Rambam* cited by *Chasam Sofer* [Mechon Chasam Sofer ed.]; *Teshuvos Chasam Sofer* §168; *Ramban,* cited by *Mishnah Berurah* 242:1; Responsa of *Rivash* §513). Other authorities maintain that it is an enactment of the Prophets or the Rabbis (see *Mishnah Berurah* loc. cit.). See also *Pesichah Koleles* to *Pri Megadim,* section I, §18,19; and *Mishbetzos Zahav* to *Pri Megadim* §262; and *Shulchan Aruch HaRav* 242:1.

14. These particular foods were highly regarded in Talmudic times; in other times and places, any similarly esteemed dishes [in addition to the required bread eaten for the Sabbath meals (see *Rashba* to *Berachos* 49b and *Rambam, Hil. Shabbos* 30:9) fulfill the requirement of *oneg Shabbos* (*Levush,* cited by *Mishnah Berurah* 242:1). Therefore, in *Orach Chaim* 250:2, the *Shulchan Aruch* rules that one increase his consumption of meat, wine and dainties on the Sabbath (*Mishnah Berurah* loc. cit.). [*Hagahos HaBach* notes that cooked beets and garlic cloves are also described as healthful foods elsewhere in the Talmud.]

15. See *Pesachim* 112a; *Tur, Orach Chaim* 242 and *Mishnah Berurah* 242:1 (see also *Meiri*).

16. Small fish fried in their own oils and flour (*Rashi*).

17. *Isaiah* 56:2.

18. It was in Enosh's time that people began to worship idols, as it says (*Genesis* 4:26): *And to Seth also was a son born, and he named him Enosh: Then to call in God's Name became profaned,* i.e. that generation introduced idolatry (*Rashi; see Rambam, Hil. Avodas Kochavim* 1:1-2). One who worships idols is as if he had rejected the Torah in its entirety and one who observes the Sabbath is as if he had observed the entire Torah. Thus, in this sense, Sabbath observance atones for idolatry (*HaRif* in *Ein Yaakov;* see also *Cheifetz Hashem;* cf. *Beis Yosef, Orach Chaim* 242 ד״ה ומ״ש).

19. *Exodus* 16:27.

20. Even though Moses had told them that no manna would appear on the Sabbath, they nevertheless went out to gather it. They took their

עין משפט נר מצוה

לה א מיי' פ"ל מהל' שבת הלכה ז סמג עשין ל טור שו"ע או"ח סימן רמב:
לו ב מיי' פ"ז מהלכות תפלה הלכה יג טור שו"ע או"ח סימן נא סעיף ח:
לז ג מיי' פ"ג מהלכות תפילה הלכה א' סמג עשין יט טוש"ע או"ח סימן פט סעיף א וסימן רלג סעיף א [בר"ף כאן ובפ"ה דברכות דף כו. וכן ברא"ש כאן ושם סי' ה']:
לח ד טור שו"ע או"ח סימן רפא סעיף ב וסימן רלג סעיף א:
לט ה מיי' פכ"א מהל' איסורי ביאה הלכה כג טוש"ע אה"ע סימן כג סעיף ז בהגה:
מ ו ז טוש"ע או"ח סימן ב סעיף א ו:
מא ח טוש"ע יו"ד סי' רמו סעיף כו בהג"ה:

רב נסים גאון

אמר ר' יוסי יהא חלקי עם מכניסי שבת בטבריא ועם מוציאי שבתות בציפורי. לפי שטבריא היתה נמוכה והחמה שוקעת שם בעוד יומם והיו יושביה מקבלין עליהן השבת משקיעת החמה אצלם ושקיעתה לשם קודם שקיעתה במקומות הגבוהין ומי שמקבל עליו הכנסת השבת מאותה השעה הרי עשה סייג לעצמו והוא משובח ומעולה מן היושבים במקומות הגבוהין ובהרים וכנגדן מוציאי שבת בציפורי שהיא גבוהה טפי ומאחרין לשם פני המזרח להכסיף ושוהין ומאדימין והיו מקבלין עליהן שימור השבת עד שמכסיפין פני המזרח התחתון והעליון ולפיכך הן משובחים בזה הענין יותר מאנשי טבריא ובמסכת ראש השנה בפרק יו"ט של ראש השנה (דף לא) משכחת וטבריא עמוקה מכולן שנאמר (ישעיה כט) ושפלת מארץ תדברי ובמסכת מגילה בפרק מגילה נקראת (דף ו) ולמה נקראת שמה ציפורי אמר רב פפא שיושבת בראש ההר כצפור והרי נתברר לך מיכן כי טבריא נמוכה וציפורי גבוהה:

ליקוטי רש"י

נחלת יעקב אביך. נחלה בלא מצרים [ישעיה נח, יד]. **האל.** כמו האלה [בראשית כו, ג]. **אלא כיעקב וכו'.** ויעקב שמר את השבת שנא' (בראשית לג) ויחן את פני העיר שקבע תחומין עם דמדומי חמה כך פי' ר' שמעון [ישעיה שם]. **ואתה על במותימו תדרוך.** כענין שנאמר (יהושע י, כד) שימו את רגליכם על צוארי המלכים האלה [דברים לג, כט].
[המשך בדף קיט.]

תוספות

רובם של צדיקים מתים בחולי מעיים. פי' בקונטרס למרק עונותיהם ור"י אומר כי יש במדרש [ל] למרק אכילה מן המעיים להיות נקיים וטהורים כמלאכי השרת: **אימא** ה' בעילות בעלתי ושניתי. ובירושלמי משני דיבמות היו ולא רצה לקיים בהן מצות עונה אלא רק כדי לקיים מצות יבום דהיינו ביאה ראשונה: **אילו** היו אומרים לי חברי עלה לדוכן. [°] לא ידע ר"י מה איסור יש בזר העולה לדוכן אם לא משום ברכה לבטלה שלכהנים אמרה תורה לברך את ישראל: **עיון** תפלה. פי' בכוונת הלב וכן ההיא דאלו דברים שאוכל מפירותיהן בעולם הזה (לקמן דף קכז.) דחשיב עיון תפלה אבל הא דאמר בברכות (דף לב: ונה.) המעיין בתפלתו סוף בא לידי כאב לב ההוא עיון דמצפה מתי יעשה הקב"ה בקשתו שסבור שתפלתו מקובלת כדמייתי עלה תוחלת ממושכה מחלה לב וכן ההיא [מ] דאמר ר"י שלשה דברים מזכירין עוונותיו של אדם קיר נטוי ועיון תפלה [ומוסר דין לשמים על חבירו] והא דאמר בפרק גט פשוט (ב"ב קסד:) שלשה דברים אין אדם ניצול מהם בכל יום לשון הרע והרהור עבירה ועיון תפלה אין לפרש שמצפה מתי תיעשה בקשתו שהרבה בני אדם ניצולים מזה אלא הוה כי ההוא דשמעתין כלומר שאינו מתכוין בתפלה שאי אפשר ליזהר כדאמרינן בירושלמי [נ] מחזיקנא טיבו לרישא דכי מטא למודים מנפשיה כרע [ס]:
בתליסר

רש"י

נחלת יעקב. ולא נחלת אברהם ויצחק: **לארכה ולרחבה.** ארץ זו ולא יותר: **הארצות האל.** ותו לא: **תבשיל של תרדין.** חשוב הוא: **ראשי שומין.** חשובים היו להן: **כסא דהרסנא.** דגים קטנים מטוגנים בשמן קרביהן ובקמח: **דור אנוש.** התחילו לעבוד ע"ז דכתיב (בראשית ד) אז הוחל לקרוא וגו': **בתריה.** בתר ההיא פרשתא: **הרי זה מחרף ומגדף.** שנביאים הראשונים תיקנו לומר בפרקים לשבח והודיה כדאמרינן בערבי פסחים (דף קיז.) וזה הקוראה תמיד בלא עתה אינו אלא כמזמר שיר ומתלוצץ: **פסוקי דזמרא.** שני מזמורים של הילולים הללו את ה' מן השמים הללו אל בקדשו: **דמדומי חמה.** כשהיא אדומה שחרית אחרי הנץ מיד היא אדומה וערבית סמוך לשקיעתה: **עם שמש.** עם זריחתה: **ולפני ירח.** קודם אור הירח בעוד השמש לא שקעה: **ממתי מחולי בני מעיים.** שמתייסרין ביסורין ומתמרקין עונותיהן: **ממכניסי שבת בטבריא.** מפני שהיא עמוקה ומחשכת מבעוד יום וסבורין שחשכה וממוציאי שבת בצפורי שיושבת בראש ההר ובעוד כשהחמה שוקעת נראית שם אור גדול ומאחרין לצאת: **ממושיבי בית המדרש.** חזנים מאספי תלמידים בכל יום לבא: **ממעמידי.** ממונים לעת האוכל לומר הגיע עת לעמוד ולאכול: **ממחלקי.** לעניים לדקה דאמרינן בבבא בתרא פ"ק (דף ח:) לדקה נגבית בשנים ומתחלקת בשלשה והמחלקים אותה עליהם לבדוק לפי הצריך לכל אחד ואחד ופעמים שקרובין דעתם לרחם על זה ולחלוק יותר מן הצורך שאומדין אותו בהרווחה ואומדין את חברו בצמצום: **בעלתי ושניתי.** כדי שיהיו זכרים דאמר מר הרוצה שיהיו בניו זכרים יבעול וישנה (עירובין דף ק:): **לא קריתי לאשתי אשתי.** שאף שיחת חולין שלי יש ללמוד הימנה חכמה: **אשתי ביתי.** שהיא עיקר של בית: **ולשורי שדי.** שהוא עיקר של שדה דכתיב ורב תבואות בכח שור (משלי יד): **לא נסתכלתי כו'.** מרוב צניעות: **והא אמרו לו כו'.** וא"כ לרבי יוסי נמי הוה ליה למיקרייה רבינו הקדוש: **תחת אבנטו.** מן האבנט ולמטה: **לא ראו קורות כו'.** (ג) כשפושט חלוקו [פושטו] כמו שהוא לובשו דרך ראשו ומכסה את עצמו תחלה משום צניעות בסדינו מתחת ויושב במטתו: **לא אמרתי דבר וחזרתי לאחורי.** שאם לא מי שאמרתי עליו דבר ושאל אם אמרתי כן עליו לא חזרתי בי לאמר אינו כדבריו לפי שמתחלה אמת אמרתי וקסבר כל מילתא דמתאמרא באפי מרה לית בה משום לישנא בישא וכן מפרש במסכת ערכין (דף טו:): **דקיימית מצות תפילין.** שלא הלך ארבע אמות בלא תפילין וכן לענין ציצית: **עד דרמיה.** שתקנה וזה לשון תליית ציצית כדאמרינן בעלמא (תענית ד' כב.) לא רמי חוטי: **דשלים מסכתיה.** שגרסה:
עבידנא

גמרא

נחלת יעקב אביך וגו' לא כאברהם שכתוב בו [א] קום התהלך בארץ לארכה וגו' ולא כיצחק שכתוב בו [ב] כי לך ולזרעך אתן את כל הארצות האל אלא כיעקב שכתוב בו [ג] ופרצת ימה וקדמה וצפונה ונגבה ר"נ בר יצחק אמר ניצול משעבוד גליות כתיב הכא והרכבתיך על במתי ארץ וכתיב התם [ד] ואתה על במותימו תדרוך אמר רב יהודה אמר רב כל המענג את השבת נותנין לו משאלות לבו שנאמר [ה] והתענג על ה' ויתן לך משאלות לבך עונג זה איני יודע מהו כשהוא אומר [ו] וקראת לשבת עונג [א] הוי אומר זה עונג שבת במה מענגו רב יהודה בריה דרב שמואל בר שילת משמי' דרב אמר בתבשיל של תרדין (א) ודגים גדולים וראשי שומין רב חייא בר אשי אמר רב אפי' דבר מועט ולכבוד שבת עשאו הרי זה עונג מאי היא א"ר פפא כסא דהרסנא אמר ר' חייא בר אבא א"ר יוחנן כל המשמר שבת כהלכתו אפי' עובד ע"ז [כדור] אנוש מוחלין לו שנאמר [ז] אשרי אנוש יעשה זאת וגו' מחללו אל תקרי מחללו אלא מחול לו אמר רב יהודה אמר רב אלמלי שמרו ישראל שבת [ב] ראשונה לא שלטה בהן אומה ולשון שנאמר [ח] ויהי ביום השביעי יצאו מן העם ללקוט וכתיב בתריה [ט] ויבא עמלק אמר רבי יוחנן משום רבי שמעון בן יוחי [ג] אלמלי משמרין ישראל שתי שבתות כהלכתן מיד נגאלים שנא' [י] כה אמר ה' לסריסים אשר ישמרו את שבתותי וכתיב בתריה [כ] והביאותים אל הר קדשי וגו' אמר ר' יוסי [ג] יהא חלקי מאוכלי שלש סעודות בשבת א"ר יוסי [ד] יהא חלקי מגומרי הלל בכל יום איני והאמר מר הקורא הלל בכל יום הרי זה מחרף ומגדף כי קאמרינן בפסוקי דזמרא א"ר יוסי יהא חלקי ממתפללים עם דמדומי חמה [ה] א"ר חייא בר אבא א"ר יוחנן [ו] מצוה להתפלל עם דמדומי חמה א"ר זירא מאי קרא [ל] ייראוך עם שמש ולפני ירח דור דורים וא"ר יוסי יהא חלקי ממתי בחולי מעיים דאמר מר [ז] רובן של צדיקים מתים בחולי מעיים וא"ר יוסי יהא חלקי ממתי בדרך מצוה וא"ר יוסי [°] [ח] יהא חלקי ממכניסי שבת בטבריא ומממוציאי שבת בצפורי וא"ר יוסי יהא חלקי ממושיבי בהמ"ד ולא ממעמידי בהמ"ד וא"ר יוסי יהא חלקי מגבאי צדקה ולא ממחלקי צדקה [ט] וא"ר יוסי יהא חלקי ממי שחושדין אותו ואין בו אמר רב פפא לדידי חשדון ולא הוה בי א"ר יוסי חמש בעילות בעלתי ונטעתי חמשה ארזים בישראל ומאן אינון ר' ישמעאל ברבי יוסי ור' [י] אלעזר בר"י ור' חלפתא בר"י ור' אבטילס בר"י ורבי מנחם בר' יוסי והאיכא ורדימס היינו ורדימס היינו מנחם ואמאי קרי ליה ורדימס [כ] שפניו דומין לוורד למימרא דרבי יוסי מצות עונה לא קיים אלא אימא חמש בעילות בעלתי ושניתי [ל] אמר רבי יוסי מימי לא קריתי לאשתי אשתי ולשורי שורי אלא לאשתי ביתי ולשורי שדי אמר ר' יוסי [°] מימי לא נסתכלתי במילה שלי איני והאמרו ליה לרבי מאי טעמא קראו לך רבינו הקדוש אמר להו מימי לא נסתכלתי במילה שלי ברבי מילתא אחריתי הוה ביה שלא הכניס ידו תחת אבנטו וא"ר יוסי [מ] מימי לא ראו קורות ביתי אימרי חלוקי וא"ר יוסי מימי לא עברתי על דברי חברי יודע אני בעצמי שאיני כהן אם אומרים לי חבירי עלה לדוכן אני עולה [נ] וא"ר יוסי מימי לא אמרתי דבר וחזרתי לאחורי אמר רב נחמן [ס] תיתי לי דקיימית ג' סעודות בשבת אמר רב יהודה תיתי לי דקיימית עיון תפלה אמר רב הונא בריה דרב יהושע [ע] תיתי לי דלא סגינא ד' אמות בגילוי הראש אמר רב ששת תיתי לי דקיימית מצות תפילין ואמר ר"נ תיתי לי דקיימית מצות ציצית אמר ליה רב יוסף לרב יוסף בריה דרבה אבוך במאי זהיר טפי אמר ליה בציצית יומא חד הוה קא סליק בדרגא איפסיק ליה חוטא ולא נחית ואתא כמה דלא רמיה ואמר אביי תיתי לי דכי [פ] חזינא צורבא מרבנן דשלים מסכתיה
עבידנא

מסורת הש"ס

א) [ע"ל פ"ו ע"ב תוס' ד"ה כאשר], ב) [עי' תוס' נדה יג: ד"ה עד שיכלו], ג) [עי' תוס' בכורות ג: ד"ה שמא וכו'], ד) ברכות כט:, ה) [כתובות קג:], ו) מו"ק יח:, ז) בדפו"י אליעזר, ח) [סוטה לו:], ט) גיטין נב:, י) ערכין טו: [ע"ש ברש"י], כ) [לקמן ריש קיט. ז"ל רש"י תיתי לי ישולם שכרי ובבכורות ל: ז"ל רש"י תיתי לי שכר טוב ועי' תוס' בבכורות ל: ד"ה שמא], ל) [בראשית רבה פרשה פב], מ) [ברכות נה.], נ) [פרק היה קורא הלכה ה], ס) [ועי' תוס' ברכות לג: ד"ה כלן].

הגהות הב"ח

(א) גמ' בתבשיל של תרדין. נ"ב בעירובין ראש ד' כ"ט אמר רב חסדא תבשיל של תרדין יפה ללב וטוב לעינים וכל שכן לבני מעים ואמר אביי והוא דיתיב אבי ספי וכו'. ובס"פ מרובה דף פ"ב ע"א חמשה דברים נאמרו בשום משביע ומשחין ומצהיל פנים ומרבה הזרע והורג כנים שבבני מעיים ומכניס אהבה ומוציא קנאה. ובפ' כיצד מעברין ריש דף נ"ו פירש"י לשבח ולא לגנאי וע"ש: (ב) רש"י ד"ה לא ראו קורות כו' כשפושט חלוקו. נ"ב ס"א לא היה הופכו מרוב צניעות שכשפושטו כו':

גליון הש"ס

גמרא יהא חלקי ממכניסי שבת בטבריא. ברבינו יונה פ"ה דברכות דף מג ע"א כתב דר"י שבטבריה היו מגמרים הכלים בע"ש מפני כבוד שבת שיריחו ריח טוב ובציפורי היו מגמרים במ"ש והיו עושין כן לכבוד שבת שהיו מרמזין לצער שיש להם מהפסק ימירה שהיה להם בשבת ועתה בפרידת השבת לריכין למוגמר להריח ריח טוב עיין שם. וכענין זה כ' באגודה. והר"י מיגאש בתשובה סימן מ"ה כ' יהא חלקי וכו' היינו עם אותם שבתחלת שבת המה בטבריה ובמוצאי יומא הם בציפורי כי טבריא וציפורי תוך תחום אחד ומקדמי ומאחרי שבת: **תוס' ד"ה אילו וכו' לא ידע ר"י.** וכזה לקמן קלא ע"ב תוס' ד"ה קמ"ל. וקלח ע"א תוס' ד"ה מי סברת. ובכתובות דף לג ע"א תוס' ד"ה מיתה:

תורה אור השלם

א) קוּם הִתְהַלֵּךְ בָּאָרֶץ לְאָרְכָּהּ וּלְרָחְבָּהּ כִּי לְךָ אֶתְּנֶנָּה: [בראשית יג, יז]
ב) גּוּר בָּאָרֶץ הַזֹּאת וְאֶהְיֶה עִמְּךָ וַאֲבָרְכֶךָּ כִּי לְךָ וּלְזַרְעֲךָ אֶתֵּן אֶת כָּל הָאֲרָצֹת הָאֵל וַהֲקִמֹתִי אֶת הַשְּׁבֻעָה אֲשֶׁר נִשְׁבַּעְתִּי לְאַבְרָהָם אָבִיךָ: [בראשית כו, ג]
ג) וְהָיָה זַרְעֲךָ כַּעֲפַר הָאָרֶץ וּפָרַצְתָּ יָמָּה וָקֵדְמָה וְצָפֹנָה וָנֶגְבָּה וְנִבְרְכוּ בְךָ כָּל מִשְׁפְּחֹת הָאֲדָמָה וּבְזַרְעֶךָ: [בראשית כח, יד]
ד) אַשְׁרֶיךָ יִשְׂרָאֵל מִי כָמוֹךָ עַם נוֹשַׁע בַּייָ מָגֵן עֶזְרֶךָ וַאֲשֶׁר חֶרֶב גַּאֲוָתֶךָ וְיִכָּחֲשׁוּ אֹיְבֶיךָ לָךְ וְאַתָּה עַל בָּמוֹתֵימוֹ תִדְרֹךְ: [דברים לג, כט]
ה) וְהִתְעַנַּג עַל יְיָ וְיִתֶּן לְךָ מִשְׁאֲלֹת לִבֶּךָ: [תהלים לז, ד]
ו) אִם תָּשִׁיב מִשַּׁבָּת רַגְלֶךָ עֲשׂוֹת חֲפָצֶיךָ בְּיוֹם קָדְשִׁי וְקָרָאתָ לַשַּׁבָּת עֹנֶג לִקְדוֹשׁ יְיָ מְכֻבָּד וְכִבַּדְתּוֹ מֵעֲשׂוֹת דְּרָכֶיךָ מִמְּצוֹא חֶפְצְךָ וְדַבֵּר דָּבָר: [ישעיה נח, יג]
ז) אַשְׁרֵי אֱנוֹשׁ יַעֲשֶׂה זֹּאת וּבֶן אָדָם יַחֲזִיק בָּהּ שֹׁמֵר שַׁבָּת מֵחַלְּלוֹ וְשֹׁמֵר יָדוֹ מֵעֲשׂוֹת כָּל רָע: [ישעיה נו, ב]
ח) וַיְהִי בַּיּוֹם הַשְּׁבִיעִי יָצְאוּ מִן הָעָם לִלְקֹט וְלֹא מָצָאוּ: [שמות טז, כז]
ט) וַיָּבֹא עֲמָלֵק וַיִּלָּחֶם עִם יִשְׂרָאֵל בִּרְפִידִם: [שמות יז, ח]
י) כִּי כֹה אָמַר יְיָ לַסָּרִיסִים אֲשֶׁר יִשְׁמְרוּ אֶת שַׁבְּתוֹתַי וּבָחֲרוּ בַּאֲשֶׁר חָפָצְתִּי וּמַחֲזִיקִים בִּבְרִיתִי: [ישעיה נו, ד]
כ) וַהֲבִיאוֹתִים אֶל הַר קָדְשִׁי וְשִׂמַּחְתִּים בְּבֵית תְּפִלָּתִי עוֹלֹתֵיהֶם וְזִבְחֵיהֶם לְרָצוֹן עַל מִזְבְּחִי כִּי בֵיתִי בֵּית תְּפִלָּה יִקָּרֵא לְכָל הָעַמִּים: [ישעיה נו, ז]
ל) יִירָאוּךָ עִם שָׁמֶשׁ וְלִפְנֵי יָרֵחַ דּוֹר דּוֹרִים: [תהלים עב, ה]

Amalek came.[21] אָמַר רַבִּי יוֹחָנָן מִשּׁוּם רַבִּי שִׁמְעוֹן בֶּן יוֹחַי – **R' Yochanan said in the name of R' Shimon ben Yochai:** אִלְמָלֵי מְשַׁמְּרִין יִשְׂרָאֵל שְׁתֵּי שַׁבָּתוֹת כְּהִלְכָתָן מִיָּד נִגְאָלִים – **If the Jewish people would only observe two Sabbaths according to their law, they would be redeemed immediately,** שֶׁנֶּאֱמַר ,,כֹּה אָמַר ה' לַסָּרִיסִים אֲשֶׁר יִשְׁמְרוּ אֶת־שַׁבְּתוֹתַי'' – **as it says,**[22] ***So says Hashem: Regarding the eunuchs who observe My Sabbaths . . .*** וּכְתִיב בַּתְרֵיהּ ,,וַהֲבִיאוֹתִים אֶל־הַר קָדְשִׁי וגו' '' – **and it is written afterwards,**[23] ***And I will bring them to My holy mountain,* etc.** *and make them joyful in My house of prayer. Their burnt offerings and their sacrifices shall be accepted upon My altar.*[24]

The Gemara records a series of statements in which R' Yose says, "May my portion be among those who" do such-and-such: אָמַר רַבִּי יוֹסֵי – **R' Yose said:** יְהֵא חֶלְקִי מֵאוֹכְלֵי שָׁלֹשׁ סְעוּדוֹת בְּשַׁבָּת – **May my portion be among those who eat three meals on the Sabbath.**[25] אָמַר רַבִּי יוֹסֵי – **and R' Yose said:** יְהֵא חֶלְקִי מִגּוֹמְרֵי הַלֵּל בְּכָל יוֹם – **May my portion be among those who complete the Hallel every day.**[26]

The Gemara questions whether this is an acceptable practice: אִינִי – **Is this so?** וְהָאָמַר מַר – **But the master has said:** הַקּוֹרֵא הַלֵּל בְּכָל יוֹם הֲרֵי זֶה מְחָרֵף וּמְגַדֵּף – **One who recites the Hallel every day is thereby belittling and blaspheming God.**[27] How then could R' Yose have considered its daily recital a worthy practice?

The Gemara answers:

כִּי קָאָמְרִינַן – **In regard to what do we say** that one should complete the Hallel every day? בִּפְסוּקֵי דְּזִמְרָא – **In regard to** the two Psalms that begin *"hallel"* in ***Pesukei D'Zimra.***[28]

R' Yose's next statement:

וְאָמַר רַבִּי יוֹסֵי – **And R' Yose said:** יְהֵא חֶלְקִי מִמִּתְפַּלְּלִים עִם דִּמְדּוּמֵי חַמָּה – **May my portion be among those who pray during the redness of the sun.**[29]

Related statements:

אָמַר רַבִּי חִיָּיא בַּר אַבָּא אָמַר רַבִּי יוֹחָנָן – **R' Chiya bar Abba said in the name of R' Yochanan:** מִצְוָה לְהִתְפַּלֵּל עִם דִּמְדּוּמֵי חַמָּה – **It is a mitzvah to pray during the redness of the sun.** אָמַר רַבִּי זֵירָא – **R' Zeira said:** מַאי קְרָא – **What is the** source in **Scripture?** ,,יִירָאוּךָ עִם־שָׁמֶשׁ וְלִפְנֵי יָרֵחַ דּוֹר דּוֹרִים'' – ***May they revere you with** [the shining of] **the sun and before the moon** [shines] **throughout all generations.***[30]

The Gemara continues with R' Yose's statements:

וְאָמַר רַבִּי יוֹסֵי – **And R' Yose said:** יְהֵא חֶלְקִי מִמֵּתֵי בְּחוֹלֵי מֵעַיִים – **May my portion be among those who die of intestinal disease.** דְּאָמַר מַר – **For the master said:** רוּבָּן שֶׁל צַדִּיקִים מֵתִים בְּחוֹלֵי מֵעַיִים – **The majority of the righteous die from intestinal disease.**[31] וְאָמַר רַבִּי יוֹסֵי – **And R' Yose said:** יְהֵא חֶלְקִי מִמֵּתֵי בְּדֶרֶךְ מִצְוָה – **May my portion be among those who die** while **on the way to** perform **a mitzvah.**[32] וְאָמַר רַבִּי יוֹסֵי –

NOTES

vessels with them and thereby transgressed the *melachah* of *carrying* (*Chizkuni* ad loc.). Alternatively, they went beyond the Sabbath *techum* (*Moshav Zekeinim* there).

21. *Exodus* 17:8. Before Amalek launched out against them, the Jews bore an aura of invincibility: No other nation had the courage to attack them. Then Amalek came and led the way for all subsequent assailants. The Sages describe this historical turning point with a parable: A cauldron was full of boiling water that was too hot for any person to enter. Along came a cretin and jumped inside it. Even though he was burned, he nevertheless cooled it off for others (*Rashi* to *Deuteronomy* 25:18).

[The passage describing Amalek's attack does not directly follow the passage of the persons who went to find manna; verses 17:1-7 are interposed between them. See *Maharsha* and *HaRif,* who discuss this issue.]

22. *Isaiah* 56:4.

23. Ibid. 56:7.

24. [The first verse spoke of those who observe the *Sabbaths,* in the plural: The second verse relates that these Sabbath observers will be taken to God's house of prayer, i.e. the Beis HaMikdash which will be rebuilt amidst the final redemption.]

Two Sabbaths are required because every Sabbath influences the weekdays that follow and those weekdays influence the Sabbath that follows them. Therefore, if a single Sabbath is observed punctiliously, it is not yet in its perfect state, since it is missing the benefit of the previous Sabbath. Where two consecutive Sabbaths are carefully observed, the second Sabbath attains perfection and the Jews merit redemption (*Pri Tzaddik, Bamidbar* p. 78; see also at greater length, *Sfas Emes Vayikra,* p. 30 and *Pachad Yitzchak, Shabbos, Kuntreis HaReshimos* 2).

[*Yerushalmi Taanis* 1:1 and *Shemos Rabbah* 25:12 state that if even one Sabbath is observed "properly," the Jews will merit redemption.]

25. [The consumption of three meals on the Sabbath is a requirement.] However, in R' Yose's era, it was not a requirement that was well kept (*Tosafos* to *Bechoros* 2b ד״ה שמא) and thus its observance suffered. R' Yose therefore made this remark (and the following ones) in order to inspire others to comply with the halachah (*Maharsha*).

26. [At this point, the Gemara assumes that R' Yose refers to the Hallel said on festivals, comprising *Psalms* 113-118.]

27. The early Prophets ordained the recital of these words on special occasions as an expression of praise and gratitude to God (see *Pesachim* 117a). Someone who recites them constantly, outside of their appropriate times, reduces them to a musical song and a farce (*Rashi*). Furthermore, the Psalms of Hallel focus on God's ability to overrule the laws of nature and perform miraculous feats of salvation. Its recital is confined to a few days in the year so as not to diminish the impact of this message. One who says Hallel daily is guilty of diminishing God's reputation in this way and his utterances are thus a form of blasphemy (*Maharsha;* cf. *Maadanei Yom Tov* to *Rosh, Berachos* 5:5 אות ס׳).

Meshech Chochmah points out that nature is the handiwork of God and is a sequence of constant miracles. A person, however, may forget this and think that nature functions independently of God and His Providence. God will therefore override the laws of nature on occasion and thereby awaken people to His active participation in the world. Thus, one who says Hallel every day indicates that God is to be thanked only for the out-of-the-ordinary miracles, but not for the workings of nature post-Creation. Such a person is therefore a blasphemer (*Meshech Chochmah* to *Leviticus* 26:4).

28. I.e. *Psalms* 148 and 150, both of which begin, *Halleluyah, hallelu . . .* (*Rashi*; see *Beis Yosef* §52 ד״ה ואם בא and *Sfas Emes* here). These Psalms do not dote on the subject of miraculous intervention, but rather concern matters that warrant praise every day (*Maharsha*).

29. [דִּמְדּוּמֵי is cognate to אָדוֹם, *red.*] The sun is red in the morning immediately after dawn (הָנֵץ הַחַמָּה) and in the evening prior to sunset (*Rashi; see Yad David Mahadura Basra;* cf. *Ritva MHK* ed. who states that דִּמְדּוּמֵי is related to the phrase [*Joshua* 10:13]: וַיִּדֹּם הַשֶּׁמֶשׁ, *then the sun stood still*).

The Gemara in *Bava Basra* (84a) suggests [homiletically] that the sun appears red in the morning because it passes near the roses in Gan Eden and it appears red in the evening because it passes by the fires of Gehinnom. When one prays at dawn, one will thus recall [the promise of] Gan Eden and the reverence of Heaven will enter his heart. When one prays before dark, he will recall [the threat of] Gehinnom and will be overcome by thoughts of repentance. In each case, his prayers will be sublime prayers which shall be accepted favorably (*Ben Yehoyada*).

30. *Psalms* 72:5. *Before the moon* means before the light of the moon shines, i.e. while the sun has not yet set (*Rashi*).

31. This is a very painful form of death. However, those who suffer through it are cleansed of their sins (*Rashi; cf. Tosafos*).

32. There is a special spiritual quality associated with those who end their lives while attempting to fulfill a mitzvah. R' Yehoshua ben Levi once surveyed Gan Eden and found seven houses there: The sixth one was dedicated for those who die on the way to a mitzvah (*Megadim Chadashim,* citing *Kol Bo* 120).

R' Yose's statement does not conflict with the principle that "persons sent to perform a mitzvah will come to no harm" (*Pesachim* 8b). That principle means that they will come to no harm resulting from the *mitzvah* itself or the trip to perform it. It is entirely possible that they may suffer some harm while engaged in the mitzvah from a completely unrelated source (see *Maharsha;* cf. *Maharsha* to *Chullin* 7b ד״ה לדבר מצוה).

עין משפט
נר מצוה

לה א מיי' פ"ל מהל' שבת הלכה ז סמג עשין ל טור שו"ע או"ח סימן רמב:
לו ב מיי' פ"ו מהלכות תפלה הלכה יב טור שו"ע או"ח סימן נא סעיף ח:
לז ג מיי' פ"ג מהלכות תפילה הלכה א' סמג עשין יט טוש"ע או"ח סימן פט סעיף א וסימן רלג סעיף א [ברי"ף כאן ובפ"ה דברכות דף כו. וכן ברא"ש כאן ושם סי' ה']:
לח ד טור שו"ע או"ח סימן רפא סעיף ב וסימן רלג סעיף א:
לט ה מיי' פכ"א מהל' איסורי ביאה הלכה כג טוש"ע אה"ע סימן כג סעיף ז בהגה:
מ ו ז טוש"ע או"ח סימן ב סעיף א ו:
מא ח טוש"ע יו"ד סי' רמו סעיף כו בהג"ה:

רב נסים גאון

אמר ר' יוסי יהא חלקי עם מכניסי שבת בטבריא ועם מוציאי שבתות בציפורי. לפי שטבריא היתה נמוכה והחמה שוקעת שם בעוד יומם והיו יושביה מקבלין עליהן השבת משקיעת החמה אצלם ושקיעתה לשם קודם שקיעתה במקומות הגבוהין ומי שמקבל עליו הכנסת השבת מאותה השעה הרי עשה סייג לעצמו והוא משובח ומעולה מן היושבים במקומות הגבוהין ובהרים וכנגדן מוציאי שבת בציפורי שהיא גבוהה טפי ומאחרין לשם פני המזרח להכסיף ושוהין ומאדימין והיו מקבלין עליהן שימור השבת עד שמכסיפין פני המזרח התחתון והעליון ולפיכך הן משובחים בזה הענין יותר מאנשי טבריא ובמסכת ראש השנה בפרק יו"ט של ראש השנה (דף לא) משכחת וטבריא עמוקה מכולן שנאמר (ישעיה כט) ושפלת מארץ תדברי ובמסכת מגילה בפרק מגילה נקראת (דף ו) ולמה נקראת שמה ציפורי אמר רב פפא שיושבת בראש ההר כצפור והרי נתברר לך מיכן כי טבריא נמוכה וציפורי גבוהה:

ליקוטי רש"י

נחלת יעקב אביך. נחלה בלא מצרים [ישעיה נח, יד]. האל. כמו האלה [בראשית כו, ג]. אלא כיעקב וכו'. ויעקב שמר את השבת שנא' (בראשית לג) ויחן את פני העיר שקבע תחומין עם דמדומי חמה כך פי' ר' שמשון [ישעיה שם]. ואתה על במותימו תדרוך. כענין שנאמר (יהושע י, כד) שימו את רגליכם על צוארי המלכים האלה [דברים לג, כט].

[המשך בדף קיט.]

רובם של צדיקים מתים בחולי מעיים. פי' בקונטרס למרק עונותיהם ור"י אומר כי יש במדרש למרק אכילה מן המעיים להיות נקיים וטהורים כמלאכי השרת: אימא ה' בעילות בעלתי ושניתי. ובירושלמי משני דיבמות היו ולא רצה לקיים בהן מצות עונה אלא רק כדי לקיים מצות יבום דהיינו ביאה ראשונה: אילו היו אומרים לי חברי עלה לדוכן. * לא ידע ר"י מה איסור יש בזר העולה לדוכן אם לא משום ברכה לבטלה שלכהנים אמרה תורה לברך את ישראל: עיון תפלה. פי' בכוונת הלב וכן הוא דאלו דברים שאוכל מפירותיהן בעולם הזה (לקמן דף קכז.) דחשיב עיון תפלה אבל הא דאמר בברכות (דף לב: ושם) המעיין בתפלתו סוף בא לידי כאב לב היינו עיון דמצפה מתי יעשה הקב"ה בקשתו שסבור שתפלתו מקובלת כדמייתי עלה תוחלת ממושכה מחלה לב וכן הוא דאמר ר"י שלשה דברים מזכירין עוונותיו של אדם קיר נטוי ועיון תפלה [ומוסר דין לשמים על חבירו] והא דאמר בפרק גט פשוט (ב"ב דף קסד:) שלשה דברים אין אדם ניצול מהם בכל יום לשון הרע ועיון תפלה והרהור עבירה ועיון תפלה אין לפרש שמצפה מתי תיעשה בקשתו שהרבה בני אדם ניצולים מזה אלא הוה כי ההוא דשמעתין כלומר שאינו מתכוין בתפלה שאי אפשר ליזהר כדאמרינן בירושלמי מחזיקנא טיבו לרישא דכי מטא למודים מנפשיה כרע:
בתליסר

נחלת יעקב אביך וגו' לא כאברהם שכתוב בו א) קום התהלך בארץ לארכה וגו' ולא כיצחק שכתוב בו ב) כי לך ולזרעך אתן את כל הארצות האל אלא כיעקב שכתוב בו ג) ופרצת ימה וקדמה וצפונה ונגבה ר"נ בר יצחק אמר ניצול משעבוד גליות כתיב הכא והרכבתיך על במתי ארץ וכתיב התם ד) ואתה על במותימו תדרוך אמר רב יהודה אמר רב כל המענג את השבת נותנין לו משאלות לבו שנאמר ה) והתענג על ה' ויתן לך משאלות לבך עונג זה איני יודע מהו כשהוא אומר ו) וקראת לשבת עונג הוי אומר זה עונג שבת במה מענגו רב יהודה בריה דרב שמואל בר שילת משמי' דרב אמר בתבשיל של תרדין (א) ודגים גדולים וראשי שומין רב חייא בר אשי אמר רב אפי' דבר מועט ולכבוד שבת עשאו הרי זה עונג מאי היא א"ר פפא כסא דהרסנא אמר ר' חייא בר אבא א"ר יוחנן כל המשמר שבת כהלכתו אפי' עובד ע"ז [כדור] אנוש מוחלין לו שנאמר ז) אשרי אנוש יעשה זאת וגו' מחללו אל תקרי מחללו אלא מחול לו אמר רב יהודה אמר רב אלמלי שמרו ישראל שבת ראשונה לא שלטה בהן אומה ולשון שנאמר ח) ויהי ביום השביעי יצאו מן העם ללקוט וכתיב בתריה ט) ויבא עמלק אמר רבי יוחנן משום רבי שמעון בן יוחי אלמלי משמרין ישראל שתי שבתות כהלכתן מיד נגאלים שנא' י) כה אמר ה' לסריסים אשר ישמרו את שבתותי וכתיב בתריה כ) והביאותים אל הר קדשי וגו' אמר ר' יוסי יהא חלקי מאוכלי שלש סעודות בשבת א"ר יוסי יהא חלקי מגומרי הלל בכל יום איני והאמר מר הקורא הלל בכל יום הרי זה מחרף ומגדף כי קאמרינן בפסוקי דזמרא א"ר יוסי יהא חלקי ממתפללים עם דמדומי חמה א"ר חייא בר אבא א"ר יוחנן מצוה להתפלל עם דמדומי חמה א"ר זירא מאי קרא ל) ייראוך עם שמש ולפני ירח דור דורים וא"ר יוסי יהא חלקי ממתי בחולי מעיים דאמר מר רובן של צדיקים מתים בחולי מעיים וא"ר יוסי יהא חלקי ממתי בדרך מצוה וא"ר יוסי יהא חלקי ממכניסי שבת בטבריא וממוציאי שבת בצפורי וא"ר יוסי יהא חלקי ממושיבי בהמ"ד ולא ממעמידי בהמ"ד וא"ר יוסי יהא חלקי מגבאי צדקה ולא ממחלקי צדקה וא"ר יוסי יהא חלקי ממי שחושדין אותו ואין בו אמר רב פפא לדידי חשדן ולא הוה בי א"ר יוסי חמש בעילות בעלתי ונטעתי חמשה ארזים בישראל ומאן אינון ר' ישמעאל ברבי יוסי ור' אלעזר בר"י ור' חלפתא בר"י ור' אבטילס בר"י ורבי מנחם בר' יוסי והאיכא ורדימס היינו ורדימס היינו מנחם ואמאי קרי ליה ורדימס שפניו דומין לוורד למימרא דרבי יוסי מצות עונה לא קיים אלא אימא חמש בעילות בעלתי ושניתי אמר רבי יוסי מימי לא קריתי לאשתי אשתי ולשורי שורי אלא לאשתי ביתי ולשורי שדי אמר ר' יוסי מימי לא נסתכלתי במילה שלי איני והאמרו ליה לרבי מאי טעמא קראו לך רבינו הקדוש אמר להו מימי לא נסתכלתי במילה שלי ברבי מילתא אחריתי הוה ביה שלא הכניס ידו תחת אבנטו וא"ר יוסי מימי לא ראו קורות ביתי אימרי חלוקי וא"ר יוסי מימי לא עברתי על דברי חברי יודע אני בעצמי שאיני כהן אם אומרים לי חבירי עלה לדוכן אני עולה וא"ר יוסי מימי לא אמרתי דבר וחזרתי לאחורי אמר רב נחמן תיתי לי דקיימית ג' סעודות בשבת אמר רב יהודה תיתי לי דקיימית עיון תפלה אמר רב הונא בריה דרב יהושע תיתי לי דלא סגינא ד' אמות בגילוי הראש אמר רב ששת תיתי לי דקיימית מצות תפילין ואמר ר"נ תיתי לי דקיימית מצות ציצית אמר ליה רב יוסף לרב יוסף בריה דרבה אבוך במאי זהיר טפי אמר ליה בציצית יומא חד הוה קא סליק בדרגא איפסיק ליה חוטא ולא נחית ואתא כמה דלא רמיה ואמר אביי תיתי לי דכי חזינא צורבא מרבנן דשלים מסכתיה עבידנא

נחלת יעקב. ולא נחלת אברהם ולא יותר: הארצות האל. ותו לא: תבשיל של תרדין: ראשי שומין. חשובים היו להן: כסא דהרסנא. דגים קטנים מטוגנים בשמן קרביהן וקמחן: דור אנוש. התחילו לעבוד ע"ז דכתיב (בראשית ד) אז הוחל לקרוא וגו': בתריה. בתר ההיא פרשתא: הרי זה מחרף ומגדף. שהנביאים הראשונים תיקנו לומר בפרקים לשבח ולהודות כדאמרינן בערבי פסחים (דף קיז.) וזה הקורא תמיד בלא עתה אינו אלא כמזמר שיר ומתלוצץ: פסוקי דזמרא. שני מזמורים של הילולים הללו את ה' מן השמים הללו אל בקדשו: דמדומי חמה. כשהיא אדומה שחרית אחרי הנץ מיד היא אדומה וערבית סמוך לשקיעתה: עם שמש. עם זריחתה: ולפני ירח. קודם אור הירח בעוד השמש לא שקעה: ממתי מחולי בני מעיים. שמתייסרין ביסורין וממרקין עונותיהן: ממכניסי שבת בטבריא. מפני שהיא עמוקה וממשכת מבעוד יום וסבורין שחשכה וממוצאי שבת בצפורי שיושבת בראש ההר ובעוד שהחמה שוקעת נראית שם אור גדול ומאחרין לצאת: ממושיבי בית המדרש. חזנים מאספי תלמידים בכל יום לצאת: ממעמידי. ממונים לעת האוכל לומר הגיע עת לעמוד ולאכול: ממחלקי. לעניים צדקה דאמרינן בבבא בתרא פ"ק (דף ח:) צדקה נגבית בשנים ומתחלקת בשלשה והמחלקים אותה עליהם לדקדק לפי הצריך לכל אחד ואחד ופעמים שקרובין דעתם לרחם על זה ולחלוק יותר מן הצורך שאומדין אותו בהרווחה ואומדין את חברו בצמצום: בעלתי ושניתי. כדי שיהיו זכרים דאמר מר הרוצה שיהיו בניו זכרים יבעול וישנה (עירובין דף ק:): לא קריתי לאשתי אשתי. שאף שיחת חולין שלי יש ללמוד הימנה חכמה: אשתי ביתי. שהיא עיקר של בית: ולשורי שדי. שהוא עיקר של שדה דכתיב ורב תבואות בכח שור (משלי יד): לא נסתכלתי כו'. מרוב צניעות: והא אמרו לו כו'. ואע"ג דרבי יוסי נמי הוה ליה למיקרייה רבינו הקדוש: תחת אבנטו. מן האבנט ולמטה: לא ראו קורות כו'. (ג) כשפושט חלוקו [פושטו] כמו שהוא לובשו דרך ראשו ומכסה את עצמו תחלה משום צניעות בסדינו ממטתו ויושב במטתו: לא אמרתי דבר וחזרתי לאחורי. שאם בא מי שאמרתי עליו דבר ושאל אם אמרתי כן עליו לא חזרתי בי לאמר איני כדבריו לפי שמתחלה אמת אמרתי וקסבר כל מילתא דמתאמרא באפי מרה לית בה משום לישנא בישא וכן מפרש במסכת ערכין (דף טו:): דקיימתי מצות תפילין. שלא הלך ארבע אמות בלא תפילין וכן לענין ציצית: עד דרמיה. שתקנה וזה לשון תליית ציצית כדאמרינן בעלמא (מנחות ד' מ.) לא רמי חוטי: דשלים מסכתיה. שגרסה:
עבידנא

מסורת הש"ס

א) [ע"ל פ"ז ע"ב תוס' ד"ה כאשר], ב) [עי' תוס' נדה יג: ד"ה עד שיכלו], ג) [עי' תוס' בכורות ב: ד"ה שמא וכו'], ד) ברכות כט:, ה) [כתובות קג:], ו) מו"ק יח:, ז) בדפו"י אליעזר, ח) [סוטה לו:], ט) גיטין נב:, י) ערכין טו: [ע"ש ברש"י], כ) [לקמן ריש קיט. ז"ל רש"י תיתי לי ישולם שכרי ובבכורות ל. ז"ל רש"י תיתי לי שכר טוב ועי' תוס' בבכורות ב: ד"ה שמא], ל) [בראשית רבה פרשה פב], מ) [ברכות נה.], נ) [פרק היה קורא הלכה י], ס) [ועי' תוס' ברכות לג: ד"ה כל].

הגהות הב"ח

(א) גמ' בתבשיל של תרדין. נ"ב בעירובין ראש ד' כ"ט אמר רב חסדא תבשיל של תרדין יפה ללב וטוב לעינים וכל שכן לבני מעים ואמר אביי והוא דיתיב אבי תפי וכו'. ובס"פ מרובה דף פ"ב ע"א חמשה דברים נאמרו בשום משביע ומשחין ומצהיל פנים ומרבה הזרע והורג כנים שבבני מעים ומכניס אהבה ומוציא קנאה. ובפ' כילד מעברין ריש דף נ"ו פירש"י לשבח ולא לגנאי וע"ש: (ב) רש"י ד"ה לא ראו קורות כו' כשפושט חלוקו. נ"ב ס"א לא היה הופכו מרוב צניעות שכשפושטו כו':

גליון הש"ס

גמרא יהא חלקי ממכניסי שבת בטבריא. ברבינו יונה פ"ח דברכות דף מג ע"א כתב די"מ שבטבריא היו מגמרים הכלים בע"ש מפני כבוד שבת שיריחו ריח טוב ובציפורי היו מגמרים במ"ש והיו עושין כן לכבוד שבת שהיו מראין הצער שיש להם מהנפש יתירה שהיה להם בשבת ועתה בפרידת השבת צריכין למוגמר להריח ריח טוב עיין שם. וכענין זה כ' באגודה. והר"י מיגאש בתשובה סימן מ"ה כ' יהא חלקי וכו' היינו עם אותם שבתחלת שבת המה בטבריא ובמפוקי יומא הם בציפורי כי טבריא וציפורי תוך תחום אחד ומקדמי ומאחרי שבת: תוס' ד"ה אילו וכו' לא ידע ר"י. וכזה לקמן קלא ע"ב תוס' ד"ה קמ"ל. וקלח ע"א תוס' ד"ה מי סברת. ובכתובות דף כג ע"א תוס' ד"ה תימא:

תורה אור השלם

א) קוּם הִתְהַלֵּךְ בָּאָרֶץ לְאָרְכָּהּ וּלְרָחְבָּהּ כִּי לְךָ אֶתְּנֶנָּה: [בראשית יג, יז]

ב) גּוּר בָּאָרֶץ הַזֹּאת וְאֶהְיֶה עִמְּךָ וַאֲבָרְכֶךָּ כִּי לְךָ וּלְזַרְעֲךָ אֶתֵּן אֶת כָּל הָאֲרָצֹת הָאֵל וַהֲקִמֹתִי אֶת הַשְּׁבֻעָה אֲשֶׁר נִשְׁבַּעְתִּי לְאַבְרָהָם אָבִיךָ: [בראשית כו, ג]

ג) וְהָיָה זַרְעֲךָ כַּעֲפַר הָאָרֶץ וּפָרַצְתָּ יָמָּה וָקֵדְמָה וְצָפֹנָה וָנֶגְבָּה וְנִבְרְכוּ בְךָ כָּל מִשְׁפְּחֹת הָאֲדָמָה וּבְזַרְעֶךָ: [בראשית כח, יד] ד) אַשְׁרֶיךָ יִשְׂרָאֵל מִי כָמוֹךָ עַם נוֹשַׁע בַּיְיָ מָגֵן עֶזְרֶךָ וַאֲשֶׁר חֶרֶב גַּאֲוָתֶךָ וְיִכָּחֲשׁוּ אֹיְבֶיךָ לָךְ וְאַתָּה עַל בָּמוֹתֵימוֹ תִדְרֹךְ: [דברים לג, כט] ה) וְהִתְעַנַּג עַל יְיָ וְיִתֶּן לְךָ מִשְׁאֲלֹת לִבֶּךָ: [תהלים לז, ד] ו) אִם תָּשִׁיב מִשַּׁבָּת רַגְלֶךָ עֲשׂוֹת חֲפָצֶךָ בְּיוֹם קָדְשִׁי וְקָרָאתָ לַשַּׁבָּת עֹנֶג לִקְדוֹשׁ יְיָ מְכֻבָּד וְכִבַּדְתּוֹ מֵעֲשׂוֹת דְּרָכֶיךָ מִמְּצוֹא חֶפְצְךָ וְדַבֵּר דָּבָר: [ישעיה נח, יג] ז) אַשְׁרֵי אֱנוֹשׁ יַעֲשֶׂה זֹּאת וּבֶן אָדָם יַחֲזִיק בָּהּ שֹׁמֵר שַׁבָּת מֵחַלְּלוֹ וְשֹׁמֵר יָדוֹ מֵעֲשׂוֹת כָּל רָע: [ישעיה נו, ב] ח) וַיְהִי בַּיּוֹם הַשְּׁבִיעִי יָצְאוּ מִן הָעָם לִלְקֹט וְלֹא מָצָאוּ: [שמות טז, כז] ט) וַיָּבֹא עֲמָלֵק וַיִּלָּחֶם עִם יִשְׂרָאֵל בִּרְפִידִם: [שמות יז, ח] י) כִּי כֹה אָמַר יְיָ לַסָּרִיסִים אֲשֶׁר יִשְׁמְרוּ אֶת שַׁבְּתוֹתַי וּבָחֲרוּ בַּאֲשֶׁר חָפָצְתִּי וּמַחֲזִיקִים בִּבְרִיתִי: [ישעיה נו, ד] כ) וַהֲבִיאוֹתִים אֶל הַר קָדְשִׁי וְשִׂמַּחְתִּים בְּבֵית תְּפִלָּתִי עוֹלֹתֵיהֶם וְזִבְחֵיהֶם לְרָצוֹן עַל מִזְבְּחִי כִּי בֵיתִי בֵּית תְּפִלָּה יִקָּרֵא לְכָל הָעַמִּים: [ישעיה נו, ז] ל) יִירָאוּךָ עִם שָׁמֶשׁ וְלִפְנֵי יָרֵחַ דּוֹר דּוֹרִים: [תהלים עב, ה]

And R' Yose said: יְהֵא חֶלְקִי מִמַּכְנִיסֵי שַׁבָּת בִּטְבֶרְיָא וּמִמּוֹצִיאֵי שַׁבָּת בְּצִפּוֹרִי – **May my portion be among those who begin the Sabbath in Tiberias and who end the Sabbath in Sepphoris.**[33] וְאָמַר רַבִּי יוֹסֵי – **And R' Yose said:** יְהֵא חֶלְקִי מִמּוֹשִׁיבֵי בֵית הַמִּדְרָשׁ וְלֹא מִמַּעֲמִידֵי בֵּית הַמִּדְרָשׁ – **May my portion be among those appointed to seat the** students in the **house of study and not among those appointed to stand** them on their feet in **the house of study.**[34] וְאָמַר רַבִּי יוֹסֵי – **And R' Yose said:** יְהֵא חֶלְקִי מִגַּבָּאֵי צְדָקָה וְלֹא מִמְּחַלְּקֵי צְדָקָה – **May my portion be among charity collectors and not among charity distributors.**[35] וְאָמַר רַבִּי יוֹסֵי – **And R' Yose said:** יְהֵא חֶלְקִי מִמִּי שֶׁחוֹשְׁדִין אוֹתוֹ וְאֵין בּוֹ – **May my portion be among those who are suspected but are free** of guilt.[36]

A related statement:

אָמַר רַב פַּפָּא – **Rav Pappa said:** לְדִידִי חַשְׁדָן וְלֹא הֲוָה בִּי – **I myself was suspected but [the fault] was not mine.**[37]

The Gemara cites other personal statements of R' Yose:

אָמַר רַבִּי יוֹסֵי – **R' Yose said:** חָמֵשׁ בְּעִילוֹת בָּעַלְתִּי – **I performed five marital acts** וְנָטַעְתִּי חֲמִשָּׁה אֲרָזִים בְּיִשְׂרָאֵל – **and I sowed** the seeds for **five cedars within the Jewish people.**[38]

The Gemara identifies R' Yose's sons:

וּמַאן אִינּוּן – **And who are they?** רַבִּי יִשְׁמָעֵאל בְּרַבִּי יוֹסֵי וְרַבִּי אֶלְעָזָר בְּרַבִּי יוֹסֵי וְרַבִּי חֲלַפְתָּא בְּרַבִּי יוֹסֵי וְרַבִּי אַבְטִילַס בְּרַבִּי יוֹסֵי וְרַבִּי מְנַחֵם בְּרַבִּי יוֹסֵי – **R' Yishmael the son of R' Yose; and R' Elazar the son of R' Yose; and R' Chalafta the son of R' Yose; and R' Avtilas the son of R' Yose; and R' Menachem the son of R' Yose.**

The Gemara asks:

וְהָאִיכָּא וַרְדִּימַס – **But there is** yet another son of R' Yose: **Vardimas?!**

The Gemara answers:

הַיְינוּ וַרְדִּימַס הַיְינוּ מְנַחֵם – **Vardimas and Menachem are the same** person. His true name was Menachem; וְאַמַּאי קָרֵי לֵיהּ וַרְדִּימַס – **so why did they call him "Vardimas"?** שֶׁפָּנָיו דּוֹמִין לְוֶרֶד – **Because** the cast of **his face resembled a rose.**[39]

The Gemara expresses surprise at R' Yose's statement that he performed only five marital acts:

לְמֵימְרָא דְּרַבִּי יוֹסֵי מִצְוַת עוֹנָה לֹא קַיֵּים – Is that **to say that R' Yose did not observe the *onah* requirement?**[40]

The Gemara explains:

אֶלָּא אֵימָא – **Rather, say** R' Yose meant this: חָמֵשׁ בְּעִילוֹת בָּעַלְתִּי וְשָׁנִיתִי – **On five occasions I performed a marital act and** then **repeated it.** This led to the birth of five males.[41]

R' Yose's next statement:

אָמַר רַבִּי יוֹסֵי – **And R' Yose said:** מִיָּמַי לֹא קָרִיתִי לְאִשְׁתִּי אִשְׁתִּי וּלְשׁוֹרִי שׁוֹרִי – **In all my days I have never called my wife "my wife"** or **my ox "my ox."** אֶלָּא לְאִשְׁתִּי בֵּיתִי – **Rather,** I call **my wife "my house"** because she is the mainstay of my house, the one who is responsible for its proper functioning. וּלְשׁוֹרִי שָׂדִי – **And** I call **my ox "my field"** because it is the mainstay of my field.[42] אָמַר רַבִּי יוֹסֵי – **And R' Yose said:** מִיָּמַי לֹא נִסְתַּכַּלְתִּי בְּמִילָה שֶׁלִּי – **In all my days I have never gazed at my circumcised member.**[43]

The Gemara asks:

אֵינִי – **Could this be so?** וְהָאָמְרוּ לֵיהּ לְרַבִּי – **But they said to Rebbi,** מַאי טַעְמָא קָרְאוּ לָךְ רַבֵּינוּ הַקָּדוֹשׁ – **"Why do they call you, 'Our Holy Teacher'? "** אָמַר לְהוּ – **and he said to them,** מִיָּמַי לֹא נִסְתַּכַּלְתִּי בְּמִילָה שֶׁלִּי – **"In all my days I have never gazed at my circumcised member."** Now, if this was true of R' Yose as well, then R' Yose should have also been called, "Our Holy Teacher." – ? –

The Gemara explains:

בְּרַבִּי מִילְּתָא אַחֲרִיתִי הֲוָה בֵּיהּ – **There was another** modest **habit practiced by Rebbi** שֶׁלֹּא הִכְנִיס יָדוֹ תַּחַת אַבְנֵטוֹ – **in that he did**

NOTES

33. Tiberias was located in a valley and Sepphoris [Tzippori] was situated on a mountain. In Tiberias when the sun disappeared behind the mountains, it became dark and the residents thought that the sun had already set. On the other hand, in Sepphoris, the sky was still quite light after the sun had actually set. A Tiberian might typically begin the Sabbath early, and a Sepphorian would end it late. R' Yose thus recommended that one begin the Sabbath early and end it late (see *Rashi*). *Rav Nissim Gaon* explains that both the Tiberians and the Sepphorians were well aware of the right time for the beginning and ending of the Sabbath. Nevertheless, the Tiberians, as a preventive measure (סְיָג) against any possible error, adopted a custom to begin the Sabbath earlier, since it appeared as if the sun were already setting. Along the same lines, the Sepphorians adopted a custom to wait and not end the Sabbath until later in the evening, when all light had disappeared. R' Yose thus commends the residents of Tiberias and Sepphoris for their piety, wishing that he himself were one of them (see also *Gilyon HaShas* who cites alternative explanations). See *Igros Moshe* to *Orach Chaim* vol. 1 §97.

34. Some officials were charged with the task of rounding up the students each day to come to the study hall. Others were appointed to come at mealtime and announce that the session was over and it was time to eat (*Rashi*). [R' Yose preferred bringing people to the study of the Torah rather than removing them from it.]

35. Charity for the poor is collected by two people and distributed by three. It is the responsibility of the three distributors to examine the needs of each person who comes before them and to disburse funds accordingly. Sometimes, however, the judgment of the distributors is unfairly biased in favor of one person, to whom they give more liberally, while another person with similar needs is dealt with more stingily (*Rashi*).

36. If a person can tolerate the baseless suspicions against him that float in other people's minds, it is a great atonement for him (*Ritva MHK* ed.). However, R' Yose's statement does not apply to one who brings suspicions upon himself (*Maharsha* to 127b).

37. *Maharshal* suggests that Rav Pappa may be referring to an incident recorded in *Bava Basra* 10a. As Rav Pappa was climbing a ladder, his foot slipped on one of the rungs and he nearly fell to his death. Rav Pappa did not understand why he deserved this particular brush with death (which is akin to the capital punishment of stoning). Another Amora suggested that perhaps a pauper had come to him (Rav Pappa was the administrator of a charity fund) and he had neglected to assist him. Here Rav Pappa states that this was an undeserved reproach (cf. *Rashash* to 140b and *Maharsha* to *Bava Basra* 10a).

Alternatively, the reference may be to the incident cited by *Rashi* and *Rashbam* to *Pesachim* 112b: A certain gentile woman owed Rav Pappa some money. One day, before Rav Pappa came to collect the debt, she strangled her child and laid him on the bed. When Rav Pappa entered, she told him to sit on the bed while she would go and fetch the money. He did so. When she returned, she said, "You have killed my son!" [This generated a short-lived rumor regarding Rav Pappa (see *Moed Katan* 18b)] and he had to flee the country (*Zeicher Yehosef, Haamek She'eilah* 40:7, cited by *Megadim Chadashim*).

38. All of his five sons were ordained as rabbis and all were prominent men: R' Yose therefore refers to them as "cedars" using a common Scriptural metaphor (*Maharsha*).

39. I.e. he had a rosy complexion.

40. The Torah requires a husband to have relations with his wife periodically. Could it be that R' Yose would ignore this precept?

41. The Gemara in *Eruvin* (100b) states: If one wishes to have male children, he should perform the marital act and then repeat it (*Rashi;* see *Rashi* ad loc.).

42. *Rashi* cites the verse (*Proverbs* 14:4): *And manifold crops [come into being] through the strength of an ox.*

R' Yose discusses his private terminology because he wishes to demonstrate that one can gain wisdom from even his mundane remarks (*Rashi;* cf. *Maharsha*).

43. Out of extreme modesty (*Rashi*).

עין משפט נר מצוה

לה א מיי' פ"ל מהל' שבת הלכה ז סמג עשין ל טור שו"ע או"ח סימן רמב:

לו ב מיי' פ"ג מהלכות תפלה הלכה ז סמג עשין יט טור שו"ע או"ח סימן רמג:

לז ג מיי' פ"ג מהלכות תפלה הלכה ד' סמג עשין יט טוש"ע או"ח סימן פט סעיף א [ברי"ף כאן ובפ"ה דברכות דף כו. וכן ברא"ש כאן ושם סי' ה']:

לח ד טור שו"ע או"ח סימן רסא סעיף ב וסימן רצג סעיף א:

לט ה מיי' פכ"א מהל' איסורי ביאה הלכה כב טוש"ע אה"ע סימן כג סעיף ז בהגה:

מ ו טוש"ע או"ח סימן ב סעיף א:

מא ח טוש"ע יו"ד סי' רמו סעיף כו בהג"ה:

גמרא

נחלת יעקב אביך וגו' לא כאברהם שכתוב בו א) קום התהלך בארץ לארכה וגו' ולא כיצחק שכתוב בו ב) כי לך ולזרעך אתן את כל הארצות האל אלא כיעקב שכתוב בו ג) ופרצת ימה וקדמה וצפונה ונגבה ר"נ בר יצחק אמר ניצול משעבוד גליות כתיב הכא והרכבתיך על במתי ארץ וכתיב התם ד) ואתה על במותימו תדרוך אמר רב יהודה אמר רב כל המענג את השבת נותנין לו משאלות לבו שנאמר ה) והתענג על ה' ויתן לך משאלות לבך עונג זה איני יודע מהו כשהוא אומר ו) וקראת לשבת עונג הוי אומר זה עונג שבת במה מענגו רב יהודה בריה דרב שמואל בר שילת משמי' דרב אמר בתבשיל של תרדין (א) ודגים גדולים וראשי שומין רב חייא בר אשי אמר רב אפי' דבר מועט ולכבוד שבת עשאו הרי זה עונג מאי היא א"ר פפא כסא דהרסנא אמר ר' חייא בר אבא א"ר יוחנן כל המשמר שבת כהלכתו אפי' עובד ע"ז [כדור] אנוש מוחלין לו שנאמר ז) אשרי אנוש יעשה זאת וגו' מחללו אל תקרי מחללו אלא מחול לו אמר רב יהודה אמר רב אלמלי שמרו ישראל שבת ראשונה לא שלטה בהן אומה ולשון שנאמר ח) ויהי ביום השביעי יצאו מן העם ללקוט וכתיב בתריה ט) ויבא עמלק אמר רבי יוחנן משום רבי שמעון בן יוחי אלמלי משמרין ישראל שתי שבתות כהלכתן מיד נגאלים שנא' י) כה אמר ה' לסריסים אשר ישמרו את שבתותי וכתיב בתריה כ) והביאותים אל הר קדשי וגו' אמר ר' יוסי יהא חלקי מאוכלי שלש סעודות בשבת א"ר יוסי יהא חלקי מגומרי הלל בכל יום איני והאמר מר הקורא הלל בכל יום הרי זה מחרף ומגדף כי קאמרינן בפסוקי דזמרא א"ר יוסי יהא חלקי ממתפללים עם דמדומי חמה א"ר חייא בר אבא א"ר יוחנן מצוה להתפלל עם דמדומי חמה א"ר זירא מאי קרא ל) ייראוך עם שמש ולפני ירח דור דורים וא"ר יוסי יהא חלקי ממתי בחולי מעיים דאמר מר רובן של צדיקים מתים בחולי מעיים וא"ר יוסי יהא חלקי ממתי בדרך מצוה וא"ר יוסי יהא חלקי ממכניסי שבת בטבריא וממוציאי שבת בצפורי וא"ר יוסי יהא חלקי ממושיבי בהמ"ד ולא ממעמידי בהמ"ד וא"ר יוסי יהא חלקי מגבאי צדקה ולא ממחלקי צדקה וא"ר יוסי יהא חלקי ממי שחושדין אותו ואין בו אמר רב פפא לדידי חשדון ולא הוה בי א"ר יוסי חמש בעילות בעלתי ונטעתי חמשה ארזים בישראל ומאן אינון ר' ישמעאל ברבי יוסי ור' אלעזר בר"י ור' חלפתא בר"י ור' אבטילס בר"י ורבי מנחם בר' יוסי והאיכא ורדימס היינו מנחם ואמאי קרי ליה ורדימס שפניו דומין לוורד למימרא דרבי יוסי מצות עונה לא קיים אלא אימא חמש בעילות בעלתי ושניתי אמר רבי יוסי מימי לא קריתי לאשתי אשתי ולשורי שורי אלא לאשתי ביתי ולשורי שדי אמר ר' יוסי מימי לא נסתכלתי במילה שלי איני והאמרו ליה לרבי מאי טעמא קראו לך רבינו הקדוש אמר להו מימי לא נסתכלתי במילה שלי ברבי מילתא אחריתי הוה ביה שלא הכניס ידו תחת אבנטו וא"ר יוסי מימי לא ראו קורות ביתי אימרי חלוקי וא"ר יוסי מימי לא עברתי על דברי חברי יודע אני בעצמי שאיני כהן אם אומרים לי חבירי עלה לדוכן אני עולה וא"ר יוסי מימי לא אמרתי דבר וחזרתי לאחורי אמר רב נחמן תיתי לי דקיימית ג' סעודות בשבת אמר רב יהודה תיתי לי דקיימית עיון תפלה אמר רב הונא בריה דרב יהושע תיתי לי דלא סגינא ד' אמות בגילוי הראש אמר רב ששת תיתי לי דקיימית מצות תפילין ואמר ר"נ תיתי לי דקיימית מצות ציצית אמר ליה רב יוסף לרב יוסף בריה דרבה אבוך במאי זהיר טפי אמר ליה בציצית יומא חד הוה קא סליק בדרגא איפסיק ליה חוטא ולא נחית ואתא כמה דלא רמיה ואמר אביי תיתי לי דכי חזינא צורבא מרבנן דשלים מסכתיה עבידנא

רש"י

נחלת יעקב. ולא נחלת אברהם ויצחק: לארכה ולרחבה. ארץ זו ולא יותר: הארצות האל. ותו לא: תבשיל של תרדין. חשוב הוא: ראשי שומין. חשובים היו להן: כסא דהרסנא. דגים קטנים מטוגנים בשמן קרביהן ובקמח: דור אנוש. התחילו לעבוד ע"ז דכתיב (בראשית ד) אז הוחל לקרוא וגו': בתריה. בתר ההיא פרשתא: הרי זה מחרף ומגדף. שנביאים הראשונים תיקנו לומר בפרקים לשבח והודיה כדאמרינן בערבי פסחים (דף קיז.) וזה הקוראה תמיד בלא עתה אינו אלא כמזמר שיר ומתלוצץ: פסוקי דזמרא. שני מזמורים של הילולים הללו את ה' מן השמים הללו אל בקדשו: דמדומי חמה. כשהיא אדומה שחרית אחרי הנץ מיד היא אדומה וערבית סמוך לשקיעתה: עם שמש. עם זריחתה: ולפני ירח. קודם אור הירח בעוד השמש לא שקעה: ממתי מחולי בני מעיים. שמתייסרין ביסורין ומתמרקין עונותיהן: ממכניסי שבת בטבריא. מפני שהיא עמוקה ומחשכת מבעוד יום וסבורין שחשכה וממוציאי שבת בצפורי שיושבת בראש ההר ובעוד כשהחמה שוקעת נראית שם אור גדול ומאחרין לצאת: ממושיבי בית המדרש. חזנים מאספי תלמידים בכל יום לבא: ממעמידי. ממונים לעת האוכל לומר הגיע עת לעמוד ולאכול: ממחלקי. לעניים לדקה דאמרינן בבבא בתרא פ"ק (דף ח:) לדקה נגבית בשנים ומתחלקת בשלשה והמחלקים אותה עליהם לבדוק לפי הצריך לכל אחד ואחד ופעמים שקרובין דעתם לרחם על זה ולחלוק יותר מן הצורך שאומדין אותו בהרווחה ואומדין את חברו בצמצום: בעלתי ושניתי. כדי שיהיו זכרים דאמר מר הרוצה שיהיו בניו זכרים יבעול וישנה (עירובין דף ק:): לא קריתי לאשתי אשתי. שאף שיחת חולין שלי יש ללמוד הימנה חכמה: אשתי ביתי. שהיא עיקר של בית: ולשורי שדי. שהוא עיקר של שדה דכתיב ורב תבואות בכח שור (משלי יד): לא נסתכלתי כו'. מרוב צניעות: והא אמרו לו כו'. וא"כ לרבי יוסי נמי הוה ליה למיקרייה רבינו הקדוש: תחת אבנטו. מן האבנט ולמטה: לא ראו קורות כו'. (ג) כשפושט חלוקו [פושטו] כמו שהוא לובשו דרך ראשו ומכסה את עצמו תחלה משום צניעות בסדינו מתחת ויושב במטתו: לא אמרתי דבר וחזרתי לאחורי. שאם בא מי שאמרתי עליו דבר ושאל אם אמרתי כן עליו לא חזרתי בי לאמר איני כדבריו לפי שמתחלה אמת אמרתי וקסבר כל מילתא דמתאמרא באפי מרה לית בה משום לישנא בישא וכן מפרש במסכת ערכין (דף טו:): דקיימתי מצות תפילין. שלא הלך ארבע אמות בלא תפילין וכן לענין ציצית: עד דרמיה. שתקנה וזה לשון תליית ציצית כדאמרינן בעלמא (תענית ד' כב.) לא רמי חוטי: דשלים מסכתיה. שגרסה: עבידנא

תוספות

רובם של צדיקים מתים בחולי מעיים. פי' בקונטרס למרק עונותיהם ור"י אומר כי יש במדרש למרק אכילה מן המעיים להיות נקיים וטהורים כמלאכי השרת: אימא ה' בעילות בעלתי ושניתי. ובירושלמי משני דיבמות היו ולא רצה לקיים בהן מצות עונה אלא רק כדי לקיים מצות יבום דהיינו ביאה ראשונה: אילן היו אומרים לי חברי עלה לדוכן. לא ידע ר"י מה איסור יש בזר העולה לדוכן אם לא משום ברכה לבטלה שלכהנים אמרה תורה לברך את ישראל: עיון תפלה. פי' בכוונת הלב וכן ההיא דאלו דברים שאוכל מפירותיהן בעולם הזה (לקמן דף קכז.) דחשיב עיון תפלה אבל הא דאמר בברכות (דף לב: ונה.) המעיין בתפלתו סוף בא לידי כאב לב ההוא עיון דמצפה מתי יעשה הקב"ה בקשתו שסבור שתפלתו מקובלת כדמייתי עלה תוחלת ממושכה מחלה לב וכן ההיא דאמר ר"י שלשה דברים מזכירין עוונותיו של אדם קיר נטוי ועיון תפלה [ומוסר דין לשמים על חבירו] והא דאמר בפרק גט פשוט (ב"ב קסד:) שלשה דברים אין אדם ניצול מהם בכל יום לשון הרע והרהור עבירה ועיון תפלה אין לפרש שמצפה מתי תיעשה בקשתו שהרבה בני אדם ניצולים מזה אלא הוה כי ההוא דשמעתין כלומר שאינו מתכוין בתפלה שאי אפשר ליזהר כדאמרינן בירושלמי מחזיקנא טיבו לרישא דכי מטא למודים מנפשיה כרע: בתליסר

רב נסים גאון

אמר ר' יוסי יהא חלקי עם מכניסי שבת בטבריא ועם מוציאי שבתות בציפורי. לפי שטבריא היתה נמוכה והחמה שוקעת שם בעוד יומם והיו יושביה מקבלין עליהן השבת משקיעת החמה אצלם ושקיעתה לשם קודם שקיעתה במקומות הגבוהין ומי שמקבל עליו הכנסת השבת מאותה השעה הרי עשה סייג לעצמו והוא משובח ומעולה מן היושבים במקומות הגבוהין ובהרים וכנגדן מוצאי שבת בציפורי שהיא גבוהה טפי ומאחרין לשם פני המזרח להכסיף ושותין ומאדימין והיו מקבלין את שימור השבת עד שמכסיפין פני המזרח התחתון והעליון ולפיכך הן משובחים בזה הענין יותר מאנשי טבריא ובמסכת ראש השנה בפרק יו"ט של ראש השנה משכחת וטבריא עמוקה מכולן שנאמר (ישעיה כט) ושפלת מארץ תדברי ובמסכת מגילה בפרק מגילה נקראת (דף ו) ולמה נקראת שמה ציפורי אמר רב פפא שיושבת בראש ההר כצפור והרי נתברר לך מכאן שטבריא נמוכה וציפורי גבוהה:

ליקוטי רש"י

נחלת יעקב אביך. נחלה בלא מצרים [ישעיה נח, יד]. האל. כמו האלה [בראשית כו, ג]. אלא כיעקב וכו'. ויעקב שמר את השבת שנא' (בראשית לג) ויחן את פני העיר שקבע תחומין עם דמדומי חמה כך פי' ר' שמשון [ישעיה שם]. ואתה על במותימו תדרוך. כענין שנאמר (יהושע י, כד) שימו את רגליכם על צוארי המלכים האלה [דברים לג, כט].

[המשך בדף קיט.]

מסורת הש"ס

א) [ע"ל פ"ו ע"ב תוס' ד"ה לאשר], ב) [ער' תוס' נדה יג. ד"ה עד שיכלו], ג) [ער' תוס' בכורות ג. ד"ה שמא וכו'], ד) ברכות כט:, ה) [כתובות קג:], ו) מו"ק יח:, ז) כדפי' אליעזר, ח) [סוטה לו:], ט) גיטין נג:, י) ערכין טו:, כ) [לקמן ריש קיט.], ל) [ע"ש ברש"י], מ) [ע"ש ברש"י ז"ל], נ) [בראשית רבה פרשה פב], ס) [ברכות נה.], ע) [פרק היה קורא הלכה ז], פ) [ועי' תוס' ברכות לג: ד"ה כלן].

הגהות הב"ח

(א) גמ' בתבשיל של תרדין. נ"ב בעירובין ראש ד' כ"ע אמר רב חסדא תבשיל של תרדין יפה ללב וטוב לעינים וכל שכן לבני מעים ואמר אביי והוא דיתיב אבי תפי וכו'. (ב) שם מרובה הוא לי ע"ש חמשה דברים נאמרו בשום משביע ומחמם ומצהיל פנים ומרבה הזרע והורג כינים שבבני מעיים ומכניס אהבה ומוציא קנאה. (ג) רש"י ד"ה לא ראו קורות כו' כשפושט נ"ב כ"ה לא היה הופכו מרוב צניעות שכשפושטו כו':

גליון הש"ס

גמרא יהא חלקי ממכניסי שבת בטבריא. ברבינו יונה פ"ק דברכות כתב דר"ת שבצבורא היו מגמרים הכלים בע"ש.

תורה אור השלם

א) קוּם הִתְהַלֵּךְ בָּאָרֶץ לְאָרְכָּהּ וּלְרָחְבָּהּ כִּי לְךָ אֶתְּנֶנָּה: [בראשית יג, יז]

ב) גּוּר בָּאָרֶץ הַזֹּאת וְאֶהְיֶה עִמְּךָ וַאֲבָרְכֶךָּ כִּי לְךָ וּלְזַרְעֲךָ אֶתֵּן אֶת כָּל הָאֲרָצֹת הָאֵל וַהֲקִמֹתִי אֶת הַשְּׁבֻעָה אֲשֶׁר נִשְׁבַּעְתִּי לְאַבְרָהָם אָבִיךָ: [בראשית כו, ג]

ג) וְהָיָה זַרְעֲךָ כַּעֲפַר הָאָרֶץ וּפָרַצְתָּ יָמָּה וָקֵדְמָה וְצָפֹנָה וָנֶגְבָּה וְנִבְרְכוּ בְךָ כָּל מִשְׁפְּחֹת הָאֲדָמָה וּבְזַרְעֶךָ: [בראשית כח, יד]

ד) אַשְׁרֶיךָ יִשְׂרָאֵל מִי כָמוֹךָ עַם נוֹשַׁע בַּיי מָגֵן עֶזְרֶךָ וַאֲשֶׁר חֶרֶב גַּאֲוָתֶךָ וְיִכָּחֲשׁוּ אֹיְבֶיךָ לָךְ וְאַתָּה עַל בָּמוֹתֵימוֹ תִדְרֹךְ: [דברים לג, כט]

ה) וְהִתְעַנַּג עַל יי וְיִתֶּן לְךָ מִשְׁאֲלֹת לִבֶּךָ: [תהלים לז, ד]

ו) אִם תָּשִׁיב מִשַּׁבָּת רַגְלֶךָ עֲשׂוֹת חֲפָצֶךָ בְּיוֹם קָדְשִׁי וְקָרָאתָ לַשַּׁבָּת עֹנֶג לִקְדוֹשׁ יי מְכֻבָּד וְכִבַּדְתּוֹ מֵעֲשׂוֹת דְּרָכֶיךָ מִמְּצוֹא חֶפְצְךָ וְדַבֵּר דָּבָר: [ישעיה נח, יג]

ז) אַשְׁרֵי אֱנוֹשׁ יַעֲשֶׂה זֹּאת וּבֶן אָדָם יַחֲזִיק בָּהּ שֹׁמֵר שַׁבָּת מֵחַלְּלוֹ וְשֹׁמֵר יָדוֹ מֵעֲשׂוֹת כָּל רָע: [ישעיה נו, ב]

ח) וַיְהִי בַּיּוֹם הַשְּׁבִיעִי יָצְאוּ מִן הָעָם לִלְקֹט וְלֹא מָצָאוּ: [שמות טז, כז]

ט) וַיָּבֹא עֲמָלֵק וַיִּלָּחֶם עִם יִשְׂרָאֵל בִּרְפִידִם: [שמות יז, ח]

י) כִּי כֹה אָמַר יי לַסָּרִיסִים אֲשֶׁר יִשְׁמְרוּ אֶת שַׁבְּתוֹתַי וּבָחֲרוּ בַּאֲשֶׁר חָפָצְתִּי וּמַחֲזִיקִים בִּבְרִיתִי: [ישעיה נו, ד]

כ) וַהֲבִיאוֹתִים אֶל הַר קָדְשִׁי וְשִׂמַּחְתִּים בְּבֵית תְּפִלָּתִי עוֹלֹתֵיהֶם וְזִבְחֵיהֶם לְרָצוֹן עַל מִזְבְּחִי כִּי בֵיתִי בֵּית תְּפִלָּה יִקָּרֵא לְכָל הָעַמִּים: [ישעיה נו, ז]

ל) יִירָאוּךָ עִם שָׁמֶשׁ וְלִפְנֵי יָרֵחַ דּוֹר דּוֹרִים: [תהלים עב, ה]

not place his hand below the level of **his belt.** For this reason, Rebbi was known as "Our Holy Teacher."[44]

The Gemara continues R' Yose's statements:

וְאָמַר רַבִּי יוֹסֵי – And R' Yose said: מִיָּמַי לֹא רָאוּ קוֹרוֹת בֵּיתִי אִימְרֵי חֲלוּקִי – In all my days the beams of my house have never seen the seams of my tunic.[45] **וְאָמַר רַבִּי יוֹסֵי – And R' Yose said: מִיָּמַי לֹא עָבַרְתִּי עַל דִּבְרֵי חֲבֵרַי – In all my days I have never disobeyed the words of my colleagues. יוֹדֵעַ אֲנִי בְּעַצְמִי שֶׁאֵינִי כֹּהֵן** – For example, **I know about myself that I am not a Kohen. אִם אוֹמְרִים לִי חֲבֵירַי עֲלֵה לַדּוּכָן – But if my colleagues would tell me, "go up to the platform** where the Kohanim recite the Priestly Blessings," **אֲנִי עוֹלֶה – I would go up.**[46] **וְאָמַר רַבִּי יוֹסֵי – And R' Yose said: מִיָּמַי לֹא אָמַרְתִּי דָּבָר וְחָזַרְתִּי לַאֲחוֹרַי – In all my days I Have never said something** about someone **and had to retreat** when he confronted me.[47]

The Gemara records a series of statements from different Amoraim who were exceedingly careful in the observance of a particular mitzvah:[48]

אָמַר רַב נַחְמָן – Rav Nachman said: תֵּיתֵי לִי דְּקַיֵּימִית שָׁלֹשׁ סְעוּדוֹת בְּשַׁבָּת – May [a reward] come my way for having faithfully **discharged** the requirement to eat **three meals on the Sabbath. אָמַר רַב יְהוּדָה – Rav Yehudah said: תֵּיתֵי לִי דְּקַיֵּימִית עִיּוּן תְּפִלָּה – May [a reward] come my way for having practiced contemplation of** my **prayer.**[49] **אָמַר רַב הוּנָא בְּרֵיהּ דְּרַב יְהוֹשֻׁעַ – Rav Huna the son of Rav Yehoshua said: תֵּיתֵי לִי דְּלָא סָגִינָא אַרְבַּע אַמּוֹת בְּגִילּוּי הָרֹאשׁ – May [a reward] come my way for never having gone four *amos* with my head uncovered.**[50] **אָמַר רַב שֵׁשֶׁת – Rav Sheishess said: תֵּיתֵי לִי דְּקַיֵּימִית מִצְוַת תְּפִילִּין – May [a reward] come my way because I observed the mitzvah of tefillin.**[51] **וְאָמַר רַב נַחְמָן – And Rav Nachman said: תֵּיתֵי לִי דְּקַיֵּימִית מִצְוַת צִיצִית – May [a reward] come my way for having observed the mitzvah of *tzitzis*.**[52]

The Gemara relates a dialogue relevant to the previous statement:

אָמַר לֵיהּ רַב יוֹסֵף לְרַב יוֹסֵף בְּרֵיהּ דְּרַבָּה – Rav Yosef said to Rav Yosef the son of Rabbah, אָבוּךְ בְּמַאי זָהִיר טְפֵי – "In which mitzvah **was your father** (Rabbah) **especially careful?" אָמַר לֵיהּ – He replied to him, בְּצִיצִית – "In** the mitzvah of ***tzitzis*: יוֹמָא חַד הֲוָה קָא סָלִיק בְּדַרְגָּא –** It happened **one day** that as **he was going up a ladder, אִיפְּסִיק לֵיהּ חוּטָא – one of his strands was cut short, וְלָא נָחֵית וְאָתָא כַּמָּה דְּלָא רַמְיֵהּ – and he did not come back down until he had hung [another thread]** in its place."

A similar statement from another Amora:

וְאָמַר אַבַּיֵי – And Abaye said: תֵּיתֵי לִי דְּכִי חָזֵינָא צוּרְבָא מֵרַבָּנָן דִּשְׁלִים מַסֶּכְתֵּיהּ – May [a reward] come my way because whenever I see a young Talmudic scholar whose tractate has been completed,

NOTES

44. *Maharsha* applies here the principle: Wherever one finds a precaution against indecency, there one finds holiness (*Vayikra Rabbah* 24:6).

45. One normally removes a tunic by grabbing the bottom edge and lifting it up over one's head. In this way, the inside seams are visible to the ceiling as the tunic is being turned inside out. However, one is then left bare for several moments until one enters under the covers. R' Yose's approach was more modest: He would first sit in bed with his tunic on and cover himself partially. He would then slide the tunic up over his head without turning it inside out. In this way, he would not have to expose himself as he disrobed (see *Rashi*).

46. *Tosafos* cite *Ri,* who wonders what prohibition may be incurred by doing this. *Rama* (in *Darchei Moshe, Orach Chaim* 128:1) points out that a non-Kohen who performs the procedure of *Bircas Kohanim* transgresses a positive commandment, as the Gemara states in *Kesubos* 24b (see also *Tos. HaRosh*). Numerous Acharonim discuss this issue. See e.g. *Magen Avraham* 128:1; Responsa of *Noda BiYehudah, Orach Chaim, Mahadura Kamma* §6; Responsa of *Oneg Yom Tov* §15; *Dvar Abraham* I 31:3. See also *Be'er Sheva,* Responsa §7.

47. If I said something [negative] about someone and then he came and asked me if I indeed said that, I never had to deny my earlier words; rather, I stood by them.

R' Yose held that any negative remark that the speaker would be willing to say before the subject is not included in the prohibition of *lashon hara,* evil speech (*Rashi*; see also *Rashi's* second explanation in *Arachin* 15b ד״ה וחזרתי לאחורי; cf. *Rashi's* first explanation). The halachah does not follow this view as stated. (See *Chafetz Chaim, Hilchos Lashon Hara, Be'er Mayim Chaim* 3:1 for a lengthy discussion of R' Yose's opinion.)

48. Every one of these Amoraim observed all the commandments incumbent upon him. However, it is proper for a Torah scholar to pick one mitzvah that he will observe according to all its minutiae (*Ritva MHK* ed.), and so the Gemara relates the specialties of these Rabbis (see *HaEmunos VeHaDei'os* by *R' Saadiah Gaon* 5:4; see also *Tzidkas HaTzaddik* §49).

These Amoraim were disciples of Rav. Various sources state that there were ten saintly habits that Rav practiced and that each of his disciples attempted to adopt one of these habits.

The Amoraim listed here express their gratitude for successfully emulating Rav in their chosen aspects (*Megadim Chadashim* citing *Pesach Einayim* to *Menachos* 110a who in turn cites *Rashi's Sefer HaPardes, Teshuvos HaGeonim Shaarei Teshuvah* 178, *Sefer HaYuchsin HaShalem* p. 180, *Seder HaDoros* ערך אבא אריכא).

49. [*Tosafos* note that the term עִיּוּן תְּפִלָּה means significantly different things depending on the context. In our Gemara (and below, 127a), it is a praiseworthy practice: paying attention to the meaning of one's prayers. By contrast, in *Berachos* 55a, the term denotes an expectation that one's prayers will be fulfilled. This is not a good practice.]

50. [See *Magen Avraham* 2:6; *Beur HaGra* to *Orach Chaim* 8:2; *Iggros Moshe, Orach Chaim* I:1.]

51. That is, he never walked four *amos* without tefillin. This is also the explanation of the upcoming sentence: Rav Nachman never walked four *amos* without *tzitzis* (*Rashi*).

52. See previous note.

עָבִידְנָא יוֹמָא טָבָא לְרַבָּנָן – I make a holiday for the rabbis.[1]

The Gemara cites two statements by Amoraim concerning their love for rabbinical students:

אָמַר רָבָא – Rava said: תֵּיתֵי לִי – May [a reward] come my way, דְּכִי אָתָא צוּרְבָא מֵרַבָּנָן לְקַמַּאי לְדִינָא – for when a rabbinical student comes before me in a lawsuit, לֹא מָזִיגְנָא רֵישִׁי אַבֵּי סַדְיָא כַּמָּה דְּלָא מְהַפִּיכְנָא בִּזְכוּתֵיהּ – I do not lean my head on a pillow until I have turned the matter **over to** uncover **the merits of his** case.[2]

אָמַר מַר בַּר רַב אַשִׁי – Mar bar Rav Ashi said: פְּסִילְנָא לֵיהּ לְצוּרְבָא מֵרַבָּנָן לְדִינָא – I am disqualified to judge **a lawsuit involving a rabbinical student. מַאי טַעְמָא דַּחֲבִיב עָלַי כְּגוּפַאי – What is the reason? Because he is as dear to me as my own body, וְאֵין אָדָם רוֹאֶה חוֹבָה לְעַצְמוֹ – and a person does not** ordinarily **see a liability in regard to himself.**[3]

The Gemara returns to the topic of honoring the Sabbath:

רַבִּי חֲנִינָא מִיעֲטַף וְקָאֵי אַפַּנְיָא דְּמַעֲלֵי שַׁבְּתָא – R' Chanina would wrap himself in finery[4] **and stand towards evening on Friday, אָמַר בּוֹאוּ וְנֵצֵא לִקְרַאת שַׁבָּת הַמַּלְכָּה – and say, "Come, let us go out to greet Sabbath the queen." רַבִּי יַנַּאי לָבִישׁ מָאנֵיהּ מַעֲלֵי שַׁבָּת וְאָמַר – R' Yannai would put on his** Sabbath **clothes on Friday and say, בּוֹאִי כַלָּה בּוֹאִי כַלָּה – "Come, O bride, come O bride."**[5]

The Gemara tells of the special foods prepared by one Amora for the Sabbath:

רַבָּה בַּר רַב הוּנָא אִיקְלַע לְבֵי רַבָּה בַּר רַב נַחְמָן – Rabbah bar Rav Huna visited the home of Rabbah bar Rav Nachman. קָרִיבוּ לֵיהּ תְּלָת סָאוֵי טַחְיֵי – They brought before him three *se'ah* of oiled wafers.[6] **אָמַר לְהוּ מִי הֲוָה יַדְעִיתוּן דְּאָתֵינָא** – Surprised by this lavishness, **[Rabbah bar Rav Huna] said to them** [the members of the household], **"Did you know** then **that I was coming?"**[7] **אָמְרוּ לֵיהּ מִי עֲדִיפַתְּ לָן מִינָּהּ – They said to him, "Are you any more important to us than it** [the Sabbath]? The loaves were prepared in honor of the Sabbath and you just happened to arrive to join us on that day."

The Gemara recounts how various sages used to honor the Sabbath with their preparations for it:

רַבִּי אַבָּא זְבַן בִּתְלֵיסַר אַסְתִּירֵי פְּשִׁיטֵי בִּישְׂרָא מִתְּלֵיסַר טַבָּחֵי – R' Abba would buy meat from thirteen butchers for thirteen common *astiras*,[8] **וּמַשְׁלִים לְהוּ אַצִּינוֹרָא דְּדָשָׁא – and deliver it to the pivot of** his **door** to his kitchen staff, **וְאָמַר לְהוּ אַשּׁוּר הַיְיָא אַשּׁוּר הַיְיָא – and he would say to them, "Be energetic and hurry, be energetic and hurry**[9] to cook this meat before more arrives."[10]

R' Abahu's custom:

רַבִּי אַבָּהוּ הֲוָה יָתִיב אַתַּכְתְּקָא דְּשִׁינָּא וּמוֹשִׁיף נוּרָא – R' Abahu would sit on a stool of ivory and and fan the fire used to cook for the Sabbath.[11]

NOTES

1. Abaye was the dean of the yeshivah and made a party for all the students of the yeshivah when one of them had studied an entire tractate (*Rashi*). For even those who did not themselves study the tractate together with the celebrant are also rightful participants in his feast if they are his friends and colleagues (*Magen Avraham* 551:35 quoting *Yam Shel Shlomo* to *Bava Kamma* ch. 7). [This teaching has ramifications in regard to the custom of not eating meat from Rosh Chodesh Av until after Tishah B'Av, where an exception is made for someone celebrating a *siyum;* see *Magen Avraham* ibid. and *Rama* 551:10.]

2. Because of his great love for Torah scholars, when a case involving one came before Rava he would not rest until he thoroughly explored the Torah scholar's claims to see if they had any merit (*Rashi*). [This does not mean that Rava necessarily ruled in favor of the scholar; clearly, a judge must rule according to the evidence and the dictates of justice. Rava's point is that he did not put off his consideration of the case until morning but immediately set about seeing if there were proper grounds to uphold the scholar's claim.] From *Maharsha* it seems that Rava exerted himself beyond the ordinary to discover the merits of a Torah scholar's claim because he did not suspect a Torah scholar of acting in violation of the law (*Maharsha; Beis Yosef, Choshen Mishpat* 15:1; *Sma* 15:4; see *Bach* there).

3. [Thus, just as a person's reluctance to see wrongdoing in himself makes it impossible for him to judge himself impartially, so too Mar bar Rav Ashi felt that his great love for Torah scholars made it impossible for him to judge them impartially.]

Meiri suggests that Mar bar Rav Ashi did not actually consider himself disqualified to judge a case involving a rabbinical student. Rather, he wished to portray the deep love one should feel for a Torah scholar – so much, that a judge should wonder whether he was actually qualified to try the case.

4. *Rashi; Rambam* (*Hil. Shabbos* 30:2) understands this to refer to a garment fringed with *tzitzis* (see above, 25b, in regard to the practice of R' Yehudah bar Il'ai). Cf. *Maharshal.*

5. Out of his great love for this day of rest, he referred to the approaching Sabbath as a "bride" (*Rashi*).

Alternatively, this description reflects the Midrashic teaching that the Sabbath is Israel's "mate" (*Bereishis Rabbah* 11:8). Thus, at the arrival of the Sabbath, when Israel is united with its mate, R' Yannai would go out to greet the "bride." In a similar vein, R' Chanina called the Sabbath "queen" because Israel is considered like royalty [see above, 67a, and *Bava Metzia* 113b] and its "mate" is therefore a "queen" (*Maharsha* to *Bava Kamma* 32b).

6. Wafers smeared with oil or fat (*Rashi;* cf. *Rashi, Chullin* 111a ד״ה תלת סאוי טחאי). [Although it is generally forbidden to bake bread with animal fat for fear that someone will eat it with dairy, Sabbath breads may be baked this way because their appearance differs from that of ordinary breads and people will therefore be reminded that they were baked with fat (*Rama, Yoreh Deah* 97:1; see *Megadim Chadashim* for a lengthy discussion of this point).]

7. [Rabbah bar Rav Huna assumed that the large quantity of special loaves had been prepared in his honor but he was surprised because his visit had not been expected (cf. *Hagahos R' Yehudah Bachrach*).]

8. [I.e. one *astira's* worth of meat from each of thirteen butchers,] so that he would be sure to dine on the Sabbath from the choicest meat available (*Rashi;* see note 22 below).

An *astira* is a *sela.* A common *astira* is a provincial *sela* [סֶלַע מְדִינָה], which is worth one-eighth of a Tyrian *sela* [סֶלַע צֹרִי] (see *Kiddushin* 11a-b). Since a Tyrian *sela* is equal to four *dinars,* an ordinary *astira* is worth half a *dinar* (*Rashi*). [The Tyrian standard is the one referred to by the Torah when it speaks of coins such as *shekels;* see Gemara ibid.]

9. Literally: strengthen yourselves quickly.

10. R' Abba, after buying meat from one butcher, would return home with it and proceed no further than his front door, where he would hand it over to his cooks with the command that they hurry to prepare it. He would then immediately return to market to purchase more meat (*Rashi's* preferred explanation).

Alternatively, R' Abba would have his meat delivered to his doorstep and would leave the money for it next to the pivot of his door [so that the butchers would not have to tarry until he paid them]. When they arrived R' Abba would call out to them to make haste with their deliveries and hurry back to their shops to prepare more items for sale for the Sabbath (*Rashi's* first explanation, as emended by *Rashash*).

[According to both explanations, the sense of urgency that accompanied the purchase and preparation of the food were intended to demonstrate R' Abba's esteem for the Sabbath. For the grander the occasion, the more people are in a frenzy to prepare for it.]

11. [To light a wood fire, one places small thin pieces of wood (which catch fire easily) next to the larger logs and then ignites the small pieces and fans their flame until the fire spreads to the logs and takes hold of them (see *Taanis* 7a and *Rashi* there ד״ה תורה כעץ).] To show his honor for the Sabbath, R' Abahu – who was a prominent and wealthy person, as evidenced by the fact that he sat on an ivory stool – would perform this lowly task himself (*Rashi; Chidushei HaRan;* cf. *Hagahos R' Elazar Moshe Horowitz*).

עבידנא יומא טבא לרבנן אמר רבא תיתי לי דכי אתא צורבא מרבנן לקמאי לדינא לא מזיגנא (א) רישי אבי סדיא כמה דלא מהפיכנא בזכותיה אמר מר בר רב אשי פסילנא ליה לצורבא מרבנן לדינא מ"ט דחביב עלי כגופאי ואין אדם רואה חובה לעצמו רבי חנינא מיעטף וקאי אפניא דמעלי שבתא אמר בואו ונצא לקראת שבת המלכה רבי ינאי לביש מאניה (ב) מעלי שבת ואמר בואי כלה בואי כלה רבה בר רב הונא איקלע לבי רבה בר רב נחמן קריבו ליה תלת סאוי טחיי א"ל מי הוה ידעיתון דאתינא אמרו ליה מי עדיפת לן מינה רבי אבא זבן בתליסר אסתירי פשיטי בישרא מתליסר טבחי ומשלים להו אצינורא דדשא ואמר להו אשור הייא אשור הייא ר' אבהו הוה יתיב אתכתקא דשינא ומושיף נורא רב ענן לביש גונדא דתנא דבי רבי ישמעאל בגדים שבישל בהן קדירה לרבו אל ימזוג בהן כוס לרבו רב ספרא מחריך רישא רבא מלח שיבוטא רב הונא מדליק שרגי רב פפא גדיל פתילתא רב חסדא פרים סילקא רבה ורב יוסף מצלחי ציבי ר' זירא מצתת צתותי רב נחמן בר יצחק מכתף ועייל מכתף ונפיק אמר אילו מקלעין לי ר' אמי ור' אסי מי לא מכתיפנא קמייהו ואיכא דאמרי ר' אמי ורבי אסי מכתפי ועיילי מכתפי ונפקי אמרי אילו איקלע לן רבי יוחנן מי לא מכתפינן קמיה יוסף מוקיר שבי הוה ההוא נכרי בשבבותיה דהוה נפישי נכסיה טובא אמרי ליה כלדאי כולהו נכסי יוסף מוקר שבי אכיל להו אזל זבנינהו לכולהו ניכסי זבן בהו מרגניתא אותבה בסייניה בהדי דקא עבר מברא אפרחיה זיקא שדייה במיא בלעיה כוורא אסקוה אייתוה אפניא דמעלי שבתא אמרי מאן זבין כי השתא אמרי להו זילו אמטיוהו לגבי יוסף מוקר שבי דרגיל דזבין אמטיוה ניהליה זבניה קרעיה אשכח ביה מרגניתא זבניה בתליסר עיליתא דדינרי דדהבא פגע ביה ההוא סבא אמר מאן דיזיף שבתא פרעיה שבתא בעא מיניה רבי מר' ישמעאל ברבי יוסי עשירים שבא"י במה הן זוכין א"ל בשביל שמעשרין שנאמר עשר תעשר עשר בשביל שתתעשר שבבבל במה הן זוכין א"ל בשביל שמכבדין את התורה ושבשאר ארצות במה הן זוכין א"ל בשביל שמכבדין את השבת דאמר רבי חייא בר אבא פעם אחת נתארחתי אצל בעל הבית בלודקיא והביאו לפניו שלחן של זהב משוי ששה עשר בני אדם וששה עשר שלשלאות של כסף קבועות בו וקערות וכוסות וקיתוניות וצלוחיות קבועות בו ועליו כל מיני מאכל וכל מיני מגדים ובשמים וכשמניחים אותו אומרים לה' הארץ ומלואה וגו' וכשמסלקין אותו אומרים השמים שמים לה' והארץ נתן לבני אדם אמרתי לו בני במה זכית לכך אמר לי קצב הייתי ומכל בהמה שהיתה נאה אמרתי זו תהא לשבת אמרתי לו [אשריך שזכית] וברוך המקום שזיכך לכך א"ל קיסר לרבי יהושע בן חנניא מפני מה תבשיל של שבת ריחו נודף אמר לו תבלין אחד יש לנו ושבת שמו שאנו מטילין לתוכו וריחו נודף אמר לו תן לנו הימנו אמר לו כל המשמר את השבת מועיל לו ושאינו משמר את השבת אינו מועיל לו א"ל ריש גלותא לרב המנונא מאי דכתיב ולקדוש ה' מכובד א"ל זה יוה"כ שאין בו לא אכילה ולא שתיה אמרה תורה כבדהו בכסות נקיה וכבדתו רב אמר להקדים ושמואל אמר לאחר אמרו ליה בני רב פפא בר אבא לרב פפא כגון אנן דשכיח לן בישרא וחמרא כל יומא במאי נשנייה אמר להו אי רגיליתו לאקדומי אחרוה אי רגיליתו לאחרוה אקדמוה רב ששת בקיטא מותיב להו לרבנן היכא דמטיא שימשא בסיתווא מותיב להו לרבנן היכא דמטיא טולא כי היכי דליקומו ר' זירא
מהדר

בתליסר עיליתא דדינרי. אומר ר"ת דעיליתא שם כלי הוא כדאמרינן בריש כילד מעברין (עירובין דף נג:) עלת נקפת בכדה: **רב** אמר להקדים ושמואל אמר לאחר. ולא פליגי אלא רב איירי בדרכו לאחר ושמואל איירי בדרכו להקדים כדאמרינן בסמוך: ומלא

עבידנא יומא טבא לרבנן. לתלמידים ראש ישיבה היה: **תיתי לי.** ישולם שכרי: **דכי אתי צורבא מרבנן כו'.** שחיבת תלמידי חכמים עלי: **דלא מזיגנא רישא אבי סדיא.** איני מניח ראשי על הכר: **כמה דלא מהפיכנא ליה בזכותיה.** עד שארצה אם יש בדבריו לזכותו: **מתעטף.** בבגדים נאים: **בואי כלה.** הכי קרי ליה לשבת מתוך חביבות: **טחיי.** רקיקין טחין פניהן בשומן אליה או בשמן: **מי עדיפת לן מינה.** כלום אתה חשוב לנו מן השבת לכבוד שבת הכנוס ולא היינו יודעים שתבא: **מתליסר טבחי.** לטעום בשבת מן המובחר: **איסתירי.** סלעים איסתירי פשיטי סלעים מדינ' והן א' מח' בסלע צורי והיינו חצי דינר: **ומשלים להו אצינורא דדשא.** לפני בואם להביא לו הבשר היה מזמן להן מעותיהן על פתחן ואומר להן אשור הייא התאשרו והתחזקו מהר באומנותיכם למהר ולחזור ולמכור ולהתעסק בצרכי שבת ולי נראה ומשלים להו אצינורא דדשא כשהיה מביא ראשונה היה נותנה לשמשין המכינים סעודתו על פתח ביתו ולא היה נכנס אלא ממהר לחזור ולהביא אחרת ואמר להן לשמשין אשור הייא התאשרו מהר להכין את זו בעוד שאלך להביא את זו: **אתכתקא דשינא.** פסטודי"ל של שן שחשוב היה ועשיר: **ומושיף נורא.** נופח מפח אש לכבוד השבת ורבינו לוי גרס אתכתקא דשאגא מדסר: **לביש גונדא.** כלי שחור להודיע שהיום אינו כדי להתנהג בחשיבות מלהתעסק בתבשילי שבת ולא יטנף בגדיו בבישול קדירות: **דתנא דבי רבי ישמעאל כו'.** דבישול קדירה מטנף בגדים: **מחריך רישא.** אם היה שם ראש בהמה לחרוך מחרכו הוא בעצמו: **פרים.** לשון פרומים מחתך: **מצתת צתותי.** מלית האור בעצים דקים: **מכתף ועייל מכתף ונפיק.** בע"ש יוצא ונכנס להביא תמיד משואות כלי תשמיש ובגדי חופש ומגדים כאדם שמקבל את רבו בביתו ומראה לו שהוא חשוב עליו וחרד לכבודו לטרוח ולהרבות בשבילו: **מוקר שבי.** מכבד שבתות: **אמרי ליה כלדאי.** לההוא נכרי: **כלדאי.** חוזים בכוכבים: **אכיל להו.** סופן ליפול בידו: **אותבה בסייניה.** עשה לו כובע של לבד ושכלו במשבצות של זהב וקבע בו מרגליות וקבע את זו עמהם: **סייניה.** כובע. ורבינו הלוי גרס בסדיניה בסודרו ולשון הגון לי והוא לשון ר' יצחק ב"ר יהודה: **תריסר עיליתי דדינרי.** עליות מלאות דינרי זהב ° וגוזמא בעלמא הוא כלומר הון עתק מאד כך פירש רבינו הלוי וכן בכל מקום כגון תליסר גמלי ספיקי טריפתא (חולין דף נה:) וכן תליסר טבחי דלעיל: **במה הן זוכין.** לעושר גדול כזה: **לה' הארץ.** דאין אנו רשאין ליהנות עד שנברך שמו בברכת הלחם: **והארץ נתן לבני אדם.** ע"י מתנתו נהנינו הטובה הזאת: **מאי דכתיב ולקדוש ה' מכובד.** מדכתיב וקראת לשבת עונג מכלל דלקדוש ה' לאו אשבת קאי: **וכבדתו.** אשבת מהדר דאי ביוה"כ הא כתיב ביה מכובד: **להקדים.** זמן סעודת שבת לזמן סעודת חול וזהו כבודו: **לאחר.** וזהו כבודו שהוא מתאוה לאכול: **במאי נשנייה.** במאי נשניוהו משאר ימים: **אי רגיליתו לאקדומי.** סעודתכם בבקר אחרוה: **רב ששת.** סגי נהור היה ואינו רואה עת האכילה וכשהיה דורש בשבת מושיב התלמידים במקום שתגיע שם החמה לעת האוכל כדי שילטערו וימהרו לקום: **דמטי טולא.** שילטננו: **הייא.** מהר:
מהדר

מסורת הש"ס

א) [כתובות קה:], ב) ב"ק לב. ע"ש, ג) נ"א מעלי ולמכבי, ד) [חולין קיא.], ה) [נ"א דכתיב וקראת לשבת ענג רבי אבא וכו' וכ"ה בחולין קיא.], ו) פי' מכר וכ"כ בסוף עמוד זה, ז) לעיל קיז. [יומא כג.], ח) קדושין מא., ט) תענית ט., י) [עי' תוס' ברכות לה: ד"ה כאן], כ) עי' תוס' שם, ל) [וע"ע תוס' ב"ב קנג: ד"ה עיליתא].

ליקוטי רש"י

כסא דהרסנא. דגים המטוגנים בשמן בקמח [לעיל לז:]. סעודה מוטעמת דגים קטנים מטוגנין בקמח בשומן שלהן [סוכה מד:]. דגים מטוגנים עם הקמח בשמן שלהן [יומא פד:]. מטוגן בשומן קרוי דגים ובקמח [ביצה כג.]. טיגון במורייס שומן דגים עם קמח [ע"ז לח:]. קערה קטנה מלאה דגים מטוגנין בשמן בכולם [רשב"ם ב"ב ס:]. דג שטיגנהו בשומן היוצא ממנו עם קמח [ע"ז כח.]. [כ]דור אנוש. אז הוחל. לשון חולין לקרא את שמות האדם ואת שמות העצבים בשמו של הקב"ה לעשותן עבודה זרה ולקרותן אלהות [בראשית ד, כו]. עם דמדומי חמה. תפלת יוצר עם הנץ החמה ותפלת המנחה עם שקיעת החמה [ברכות כט:]. מאי קרא. דמצוה להתפלל עם הנץ החמה. ייראוך עם שמש וגו'. ממי מתיראין ממך כשמולך מקבלים עליהם דאין מלכות שמים שמקבלין עליהם בקריאת שמע [שם ט:]. זו תפלה יוצר [שם כט: ע"ש בב"ח]. עם שמש. כלומר כשהשמש יוצא היינו עם הנץ החמה. ולפני ירח. זו מנחה [שם כט:]. אף תפלת המנחה מצוה עם דמדומי חמה [שם ט:]. בעלתי ושניתי. שממתמת ביאה ראשונה נתאוה לאשה והולבשה תאוה ובשכלא ביאה שניה היא מוצעת תחלה והכלה היא מוצעת תחלה יולדת זכר [עירובין ק:]. לאשתי ביתי. של גרמי כך שהיא על ידה נבנית ושהיא עיקר הבית וכן שור עיקרו של שדה [גיטין נב.]. מימי לא אמרתי דבר ואחזרתי. לראות מי יעמוד אחורי אומרים וכו' ... ולא הוזל מרבנן קרי ליה [תענית ד.].

[ע"כ שייך לדף קיח:]

בי סדיא. לבדין שקורין פלטר"ש ועשוין לקפלן תחתיו במקום הכר או הכסת [לקמן קמו:]. אין אדם רואה חובה לעצמו. אין דעתו מתקרב לצד החובה לחייב את עצמו ואפילו מתכוין לדין אמת [כתובות קה:]. אפניא. לפנות ערב [תענית כג:]. בואו ונצא. כאדם המקבל פני מלך [ב"ק לב:]. תלת סאוי טחיי. שלש סאין פת נקיה פניה טוחין בשמן ודבש [חולין קיא.]. מין טיגון הוא שעושין מלחם וטשין התנור באליה ואופין את הלחם אחר שטחוהו וכמש' שבת נמי אמרינן תלתא סאוי טחיי [זבחים צה:]. מי עדיפת לן מינה. יום השבת היה [חולין שם]. בתליסר אסתירי פשיטי. איסתרא סלעי מדינה שהם פשוטים וקלים איסתרי סתם היינו סלעין צורי שהסלע ארבע דינרים ואיסתרי פשיטי הוא סלע מדינה שמינית שבסלע צורי דהיינו חצי דינר כדאמרינן בהחובל את חבירו (ב"ק לו:) איסתרא פלגא דזוזא וקרי ליה התם סלע מדינה [שם מד:]. צינורא דדשא. ציר שבמפתן הבית שהדלת סובב בו [ברכות יח:]. ציר שבמפתן וציר הדלת סובב בו [כתובות סז:]. אשור. כמו אשרתא דדייני (גיטין כו.) וכמו אשרו חמוץ (ישעיה א) לשון חיזוק [גיטין לד.]. אל ימזוג בהן כוס לרבו. לפי שנתעשו ונתלכלכו בבישול קדירה [יומא כג:]. מחריך רישא. לכבוד שבת. שיבוטא. דג [קידושין מא.]. סילקא. תרדין [שבועות כג.]. ציבי. עצים [עירובין סב.]. כוורא. דג [רשב"ם ב"ב עג:].

עין משפט נר מצוה

מב א טוש"ע או"ח סי' רנ סעיף א:
מג ב מיי' פ"ל מהלכות שבת הלכה ב סמג עשין ל טוש"ע או"ח סי' רסב סעיף ג:
מד ג מיי' שם הלכה ו סמג שם טור שו"ע או"ח סימן ר"נ סעיף א:
מה ד טוש"ע או"ח סי' רמב סעיף ד:
מו ה מיי' פ"ל שם הל"ט וסמג שם טוש"ע או"ח סימן רפח סעיף ז:

הגהות הב"ח

(א) גמ' לא מזיגנא רישא אבי: (ב) שם לביש מאניה במעלי:

גליון הש"ס

גמ' אשור הייא. גיטין דף לד ע"ב: רש"י ד"ה תליסר עיליתא דדינרי וכו' וגוזמא בעלמא. עי' ברכות דף כ ע"א תוס' ד"ה תליסר מתיבתא:

רבינו חננאל

ורבנן הני דעבדי צרכי שבת בנפשייהו. כגון ר' אבהו דהוה [יתיב] (הציב) אתכתקא דשינא ומשיף נורא. ורב חנן דשגר תנורא. ורב הונא מדליק שרגי. ורב פפא גדיל פתילתא. ורב חסדא פרים סילקי. רבה ורב יוסף צלחי ציבי כולהו כדמפרש בגמרא בריש האיש מקדש. שקיום המצוה באדם עצמו טפי עדיף יותר מבשלוחו. וכבדתו שמשנה זמן סעודתו בהקדמה או באיחור. ויחיד המתפלל בעצמו אומר ויכולו:

תורה אור השלם

א) עַשֵּׂר תְּעַשֵּׂר אֵת כָּל תְּבוּאַת זַרְעֶךָ הַיֹּצֵא הַשָּׂדֶה שָׁנָה שָׁנָה: [דברים יד, כב]
ב) לְדָוִד מִזְמוֹר לַיהוָה הָאָרֶץ וּמְלוֹאָהּ תֵּבֵל וְיֹשְׁבֵי בָהּ: [תהלים כד, א]
ג) הַשָּׁמַיִם שָׁמַיִם לַיהוָה וְהָאָרֶץ נָתַן לִבְנֵי אָדָם: [תהלים קטו, טז]
ד) אִם תָּשִׁיב מִשַּׁבָּת רַגְלֶךָ עֲשׂוֹת חֲפָצֶךָ בְּיוֹם קָדְשִׁי וְקָרָאתָ לַשַּׁבָּת עֹנֶג לִקְדוֹשׁ יְהוָה מְכֻבָּד וְכִבַּדְתּוֹ מֵעֲשׂוֹת דְּרָכֶיךָ מִמְּצוֹא חֶפְצְךָ וְדַבֵּר דָּבָר: [ישעיה נח, יג]

Rav Anan's custom:

רַב עָנָן לָבִישׁ גּוּנְדָּא – **Rav Anan would put on a black smock** on Fridays to demonstrate that this was not a day for keeping clean and neat but rather for cooking food for the Sabbath, which often causes one's clothes to become soiled, as we see from the following Baraisa: דְּתָנָא דְּבֵי רַבִּי יִשְׁמָעֵאל – **For a Baraisa of the academy of R' Yishmael has taught:** בְּגָדִים שֶׁבִּישֵּׁל בָּהֶן קְדֵירָה לְרַבּוֹ – **THE GARMENTS IN WHICH** one was dressed when **HE COOKED A POT** of food **FOR HIS MASTER,** אַל יִמְזוֹג בָּהֶן כּוֹס לְרַבּוֹ – **HE SHOULD NOT WEAR TO** stand before him and **POUR A CUP OF WINE FOR HIS MASTER,** for they have become soiled.[12]

The Gemara lists the Sabbath preparations of several other Amoraim:

רַב סַפְרָא מַחֲרִיךְ רֵישָׁא – **Rav Safra would singe the head** of the animal being prepared for the Sabbath meal.[13] רָבָא מָלַח שִׁיבּוּטָא – **Rava would salt the *shibbuta*** fish for the Sabbath meal.[14] רַב הוּנָא מַדְלִיק שְׁרָגֵי – **Rav Huna would light lamps** for the Sabbath.[15] רַב פָּפָּא גָּדִיל פְּתִילָתָא – **Rav Pappa would twine the wicks** for the lamps. רַב חִסְדָּא פָּרִים סִילְקָא – **Rav Chisda would mince the beets.**[16] רַבָּה וְרַב יוֹסֵף מְצַלְּחֵי צִיבֵי – **Rabbah and Rav Yosef would split wood.**[17] רַבִּי זֵירָא מְצַתַּת צִתּוּתֵי – **R' Zeira would kindle** the fire.[18]

Rav Nachman bar Yitzchak's practice:

רַב נַחְמָן בַּר יִצְחָק מְכַתֵּף וְעָיֵיל מְכַתֵּף וְנָפִיק – **Rav Nachman bar Yitzchak would lift up** bundles of Sabbath goods **and bring** them **in, and lift up** bundles **and take** them **out;** i.e. he would carry bundles of supplies in and out of the house to ready things for the Sabbath. אָמַר – **He said:** אִילּוּ מִקַּלְעִין לִי רַבִּי אַמִּי וְרַבִּי אַסִּי מִי לֹא מְכַתֵּיפְנָא קַמַּיְיהוּ – **If R' Ami and R' Assi were to visit me, would I not lift up bundles** and carry them in and out **in front of them?** I should do no less for the Sabbath.[19]

Another version of this story:

וְאִיכָּא דְּאָמְרֵי – **And there are those who say** that the story and statement went as follows: רַבִּי אַמִּי וְרַבִּי אַסִּי מְכַתְּפֵי וְעָיְילֵי מְכַתְּפֵי וְנָפְקֵי – **R' Ami and R' Assi would lift up** bundles of Sabbath goods **and bring** them **in and lift up** bundles **and take** them **out.** אָמְרֵי – **They said:** אִילּוּ אִיקְלַע לָן רַבִּי יוֹחָנָן מִי לֹא מְכַתְּפִינַן קַמֵּיהּ – **If R' Yochanan were to visit us, would we not lift up bundles** and carry them in and out **in front of him?** We should do no less for the Sabbath.

The Gemara tells the story of the great reward that came the way of one man who honored the Sabbath:

יוֹסֵף מוֹקִיר שַׁבֵּי הֲוָה הַהוּא נָכְרִי בְּשִׁבָבוּתֵיהּ – **There was a certain gentile in the neighborhood of Yosef Who Honors the Sabbaths**[20] דַּהֲוָה נְפִישֵׁי נִכְסֵיהּ טוּבָא – **whose possessions were very great.** אָמְרֵי לֵיהּ כַּלְדָּאֵי – **The astrologers said to him,** כּוּלְהוּ נִכְסֵי יוֹסֵף מוֹקֵר שַׁבֵּי אָכֵיל לְהוּ – **"All** your **possessions, Yosef Who Honors the Sabbaths will consume them,"** i.e. they will all eventually pass to him. אֲזַל זַבְנִינְהוּ לְכוּלְהוּ נִיכְסֵי זָבַן בְּהוּ מַרְגָּנִיתָא – Fearing their prediction and hoping to foil it, **he went and sold all** his **possessions** and **bought with [the proceeds] an** extremely valuable **pearl,** אוֹתְבָהּ בְּסַיְינֵיהּ – and **he placed it in his hat.**[21] בַּהֲדֵי דְּקָא עָבַר מַבְרָא – **As he was passing over a river crossing,** אַפְרְחֵיהּ זִיקָא שַׁדְיֵיהּ בְּמַיָּא – **a gust of wind sent [his hat] flying and cast** it **into the water,** בְּלָעֵיהּ כַּוְורָא – where **a fish** came and **swallowed [the pearl].** אַסְקוּהָ אַיְיתוּהָ אַפַּנְיָא דְּמַעֲלֵי שַׁבְּתָא – Some time later, **[fishermen] hauled up [the fish] and brought it** ashore **late in the day on Friday,** by which time everyone had already completed their purchases for the Sabbath. אָמְרֵי מַאן זָבֵין כִּי הַשְׁתָּא – Disappointed, **they said, "Who will buy** it **now,** at this late hour?" אָמְרֵי לְהוּ זִילוּ אַמְטְיוּהוּ לְגַבֵּי יוֹסֵף מוֹקֵר שַׁבֵּי דְּרָגִיל דְּזָבִין – **They said to them, "Go, bring it to Yosef Who Honors the Sabbaths – for he has the habit of buying** any delicacy that comes his way for the honor of the Sabbath, so he may still buy it." אַמְטְיוּהָ נִיהֲלֵיהּ וּזְבְנֵיהּ – **They brought it to him,** and indeed **he bought it.** קַרְעֵיהּ אַשְׁכַּח בֵּיהּ מַרְגָּנִיתָא – When **he cut it open, he found the pearl in it.** זַבְנֵיהּ בִּתְלֵיסַר עִילִיָּתָא דְּדִינָרֵי דְּדַהֲבָא – **He** then **sold [the pearl] for thirteen attics full of gold *dinars.***[22] פְּגַע בֵּיהּ הַהוּא סָבָא – **A certain**

NOTES

12. *Rashi.* [See Gemara above, 114a, for the context in which this was said.]

Hagahos R' Elazar Moshe Horowitz, however, suggests that Rav Anan cited this Baraisa to repudiate R' Abahu's approach. In Rav Anan's view it was not right to use finery (e.g. an ivory chair) to prepare for the Sabbath, for the finery should be saved for the Sabbath itself and, as this Baraisa has just stated, it is not fit to serve the Master with the articles one used to cook for Him.

13. I.e. if an animal had been slaughtered for the Sabbath and its head needed to be singed, Rav Safra would perform that task himself (*Rashi*). [Animal heads are singed to remove the hair from them before cooking (see *Avodah Zarah* 38a).]

14. A type of large fish (*Aruch*) eaten in Babylonia; see also *Tosafos* to *Avodah Zarah* 39a ד״ה סימנך.

15. Although it is generally the women who light the Sabbath candles, Rav Huna's home was illuminated with many lamps, and he made it a point to light some of them himself (see *Maharshal;* see also *Hagahos Yavetz*). Indeed, it was Rav Huna who lauded those who are especially diligent in lighting Sabbath candles, stating (above, 23b) that it would merit for them sons who were Torah scholars (*Maharsha;* see *Tosafos* there ד״ה הג).

16. *Rashi* here and above, 74b ד״ה דפרים סילקא; cf. *Rosh* there 7:5.

17. *Rashi* to *Rif.*

18. R' Zeira would light the small pieces of kindling used to start a wood fire (*Rashi;* see note 11 above).

19. When honored guests, such as one's teachers, come to visit, one displays his respect to them by personally carrying out or bringing in the items that need to be moved [e.g. furniture, bedding, extra food]. So too Rav Nachman bar Yitzchak would go in and out of the house many times on Friday to bring in furniture and bundles of special clothing and food for the Sabbath (*Rashi*).

[The language of the Gemara indicates that he would carry packages out as well. *Tur* and *Shulchan Aruch* (*Orach Chaim* 250:1) explain that he carried out weekday items (to make room for the Sabbath items); see also *Rashash.* However, from *Rashi* it seems that this may be merely a figure of speech and the Gemara means only to say that he ran in and out of the house to bring in things for the Sabbath.]

20. This was how he was known.

21. That is, he made for himself a felt hat with gold settings studded with pearls and he placed this extremely valuable pearl in among them (*Rashi*). In this manner he hoped to be able to guard his wealth at all times.

22. This is actually an exaggeration intended to convey that he sold it for a huge sum of money. Indeed, wherever the Gemara uses the number thirteen to describe a great quantity of something (as in *Chullin* 95b, where Shmuel is said to have sent to R' Yochanan thirteen camel-loads of answers to questions regarding *treifos*), it should not be taken literally but as hyperbole. Similarly, the reference above to the purchase of meat from thirteen different butchers should be understood merely to mean that he bought meat from many different shops, not necessarily thirteen (*Rashi*).

[The translation of עִילִיָּתָא as "attics" follows *Rashi. Tosafos* translate this as a kind of container. This explanation removes the element of hyperbole from the Gemara, since it is quite possible that the pearl was worth thirteen small containers of gold coins (*HaKosev* in *Ein Yaakov*).]

Maharsha questions *Rashi's* view that the number thirteen is used merely to indicate a multitude, since it is not a round number. Rather, *Maharsha* sees this number as an allusion to holiness, for we find this number often used in this context: There are thirteen Divine attributes of Mercy [י״ג מִדּוֹת הָרַחֲמִים], thirteen rules by which the Torah is expounded [י״ג מִדּוֹת שֶׁהַתּוֹרָה נִדְרֶשֶׁת בָּהֶן], the numerical value of the word אֶחָד is thirteen and the age at which a boy is considered sufficiently

עבידנא יומא טבא לרבנן אמר רבא תיתי לי דכי אתא צורבא מרבנן לקמאי לדינא לא מזיגנא רישי אבי סדיא כמה דלא מהפיכנא בזכותיה אמר מר בר רב אשי פסילנא ליה לצורבא מרבנן לדינא מ"ט דחביב עלי כגופאי ואין אדם רואה חובה לעצמו רבי חנינא מיעטף וקאי אפניא דמעלי שבתא אמר בואו ונצא לקראת שבת המלכה רבי ינאי לביש מאניה (ג) מעלי שבת ואמר בואי כלה בואי כלה רבה בר רב הונא איקלע לבי רבה בר רב נחמן קריבו ליה תלת סאוי טחיי א"ל מי הוה ידעיתון דאתינא אמרו ליה מי עדיפת לן מינה רבי אבא זבן בתליסר אסתירי פשיטי בישרא מתליסר טבחי ומשלים להו אצינורא דדשא ואמר להו אשור הייא אשור הייא ר' אבהו הוה יתיב אתכתקא דשינא ומושיף נורא רב ענן לביש גונדא דתנא דבי רבי ישמעאל בגדים שבישל בהן קדירה לרבו אל ימזוג בהן כוס לרבו רב ספרא מחריך רישא רבא מלח שיבוטא רב הונא מדליק שרגי רב פפא גדיל פתילתא רב חסדא פרים סילקא רבה ורב יוסף מצלחי ציבי ר' זירא מצתת צתותי רב נחמן בר יצחק מכתף ועייל מכתף ונפיק אמר אילו מקלעין לי ר' אמי ור' אסי מי לא מכתיפנא קמייהו ואיכא דאמרי ר' אמי ורבי אסי מכתפי ועיילי מכתפי ונפקי אמרי אילו איקלע לן רבי יוחנן מי לא מכתפינן קמיה יוסף מוקיר שבי הוה ההוא נכרי בשבבותיה דהוה נפישי נכסיה טובא אמרי ליה כלדאי כולהו נכסי יוסף מוקר שבי אכיל להו אזל זבנינהו לכולהו ניכסי זבן בהו מרגניתא אותבה בסייניה בהדי דקא עבר מברא אפרחיה זיקא שדייה במיא בלעיה כוורא אסקוה אייתוה אפניא דמעלי שבתא אמרי מאן זבין כי השתא אמרי להו זילו אמטיוהו לגבי יוסף מוקר שבי דרגיל דזבין אמטיוה ניהליה זבניה קרעיה אשכח ביה מרגניתא זבניה בתליסר עיליתא דדינרי דדהבא פגע ביה ההוא סבא אמר מאן דיזיף שבתא פרעיה שבתא בעא מיניה רבי מר' ישמעאל ברבי יוסי עשירים שבא"י במה הן זוכין א"ל בשביל שמעשרין שנאמר א) עשר תעשר עשר בשביל שתתעשר שבבבל במה הן זוכין א"ל בשביל שמכבדין את התורה ושבשאר ארצות במה הן זוכין א"ל בשביל שמכבדין את השבת דאמר רבי חייא בר אבא פעם אחת נתארחתי אצל בעל הבית בלודקיא והביאו לפניו שלחן של זהב משוי ששה עשר בני אדם וששה עשרה שלשלאות של כסף קבועות בו וקערות וכוסות וקיתוניות וצלוחיות קבועות בו ועליו כל מיני מאכל וכל מיני מגדים ובשמים וכשמניחים אותו אומרים ב) לה' הארץ ומלואה וגו' וכשמסלקין אותו אומרים ג) השמים שמים לה' והארץ נתן לבני אדם אמרתי לו בני במה זכית לכך אמר לי קצב הייתי ומכל בהמה שהיתה נאה אמרתי זו תהא לשבת אמרתי לו [אשריך שזכית] וברוך המקום שזיכך לכך א"ל קיסר לרבי יהושע בן חנניא מפני מה תבשיל של שבת ריחו נודף אמר לו תבלין אחד יש לנו ושבת שמו שאנו מטילין לתוכו וריחו נודף אמר לו תן לנו הימנו אמר לו כל המשמר את השבת מועיל לו ושאינו משמר את השבת אינו מועיל לו א"ל ריש גלותא לרב המנונא מאי דכתיב ד) ולקדוש ה' מכובד א"ל זה יוה"כ שאין בו לא אכילה ולא שתיה אמרה תורה כבדהו בכסות נקיה ה) וכבדתו רב אמר להקדים ושמואל אמר לאחר אמרו ליה בני רב פפא בר אבא לרב פפא כגון אנן דשכיח לן בישרא וחמרא כל יומא במאי נישנייה אמר להו אי רגיליתו לאקדומי אחרוה אי רגיליתו לאחרוה אקדמוה רב ששת בקיטא מותיב להו לרבנן היכא דמטיא שימשא בסיתוא מותיב להו לרבנן היכא דמטיא טולא כי היכי דליקומו הייא ר' זירא מהדר

תוספות

בתליסר עיליתא דדינרי. אומר ר"ת דעיליתא שם כלי הוא כדאמרינן בריש כילד מעברין (עירובין דף נג:) עלת נקפת בכדה[ו]:

רב אמר להקדים ושמואל אמר לאחר. ולא פליגי אלא רב איירי בדרכו לאחר ושמואל איירי בדרכו להקדים כדאמרינן בסמוך: ומלא

רש"י

עבידנא יומא טבא לרבנן. לתלמידים כשם ישיבה היה: תיתי לי. ישולם שכרי: דכי אתי צורבא מרבנן כו'. שחיבת תלמידי חכמים עלי: דלא מזיגנא רישא אבי סדיא. איני מניח ראשי על הכר: כמה דלא מהפיכנא ליה בזכותיה. עד שאראה אם יש בדבריו לזכותו: מתעטף. בבגדים נאים: בואי כלה. הכי קרי ליה לשבת מתוך חביבות: טחיי. רקיקין טמון פניהן בשומן אליה או בשמן: מי עדיפת לן מינה. כלום אתה חשוב לנו מן השבת לכבוד שבת הכנוס ולא היינו יודעים שתבא: מתליסר טבחי. לטעום בשבת מן המובחר: איסתירי. סלעים איסתירי פשיטי סלעים מדינ' והן א' ממ' בסלע צורי והיינו חצי דינר: ומשלים להו אצינורא דדשא. לפני בואם להביא לו הבשר היה מזמן להן מעותיהן על פתחן ואומר להן אשור הייא התאשרו והתחזקו מהר באומנותכם למהר ולחזור ולמכור ולהתעסק בצרכי שבת ולי נראה ומשלים להו אצינורא דדשא כשהיה מביא לאשתו היה נותנה לשמשין המכינים סעודתו על פתח ביתו ולא היה נכנס אלא ממהר לחזור ולהביא אחרת ואמר להן לשמשין אשור הייא התאשרו מהר להכין את זו בעוד שאלך להביא את זו: אתכתקא דשינא. פסטו"ל של שן שחשוב היה ועשיר: ומושיף נורא. נופח תחת האש לכבוד השבת והיינו לוי גרם אתכתקא דשגא מדכר: לביש גונדא. כלי שחור להודיע שהיום אינו כדי להתנאות בחשיבות מלהתעסק בתבשילי שבת ולא יטנף בגדיו בבישול קדירות: דתנא דבי רבי ישמעאל כו'. דבישול קדירה מטנף בגדים: מחריך רישא. אם היה שם ראש בהמה לחרוך מחרכו הוא בעצמו: פרים. לשון פרומים מחתך: מצתת צתותי. מלית האור בעצים דקים: מכתף ועייל מכתף ונפיק. בע"ש יוצא ונכנס להביא תמיד משואות כלי תשמיש ובגדי חופש ומגדים כאדם שמקבל את רבו בביתו ומראה לו שהוא חשוב עליו וחרד לכבודו לטרוח ולהרבות בשבילו: מוקר שבי. מכבד שבתות: אמרי ליה כלדאי. להאי נכרי: כלדאי. חוזים בכוכבים: אכיל להו. סופן ליפול בידו: אותבה בסייניה. עשה לו כובע של לבד ושבצו במשבצות של זהב וקבע בו מרגליות וקבע את זו עמהם: סייניה. כובע. ורבינו הלוי גרס בסדיניה בסודרו ולשון הגון לי והוא לשון ר' יצחק ב"ר יהודה: תריסר עיליתי דדינרי. עליות מלאות דינרי זהב ° וגוזמא בעלמא הוא כלומר הון עתק מאד כך פירש רבינו הלוי וכן בכל מקום כגון תליסר גמלי ספיקי טריפתא (חולין דף נה:) וכן תליסר טבחי דלעיל: במה הן זוכין. לעושר גדול כזה: לה' הארץ. לאין אנו רשאין ליהנות עד שנברך שמו בברכת הלחם: והארץ נתן לבני אדם. ע"י מתנתו נהנינו הטובה הזאת: מאי דכתיב ולקדוש ה' מכובד. מדכתיב וקראת לשבת עונג מכלל דלקדוש ה' לאו אשבת קאי: וכבדתו. אשבת מהדר דאי ביוה"כ הא כתיב ביה מכובד: להקדים. זמן סעודת שבת לזמן סעודת חול וזהו כבודו: לאחר. וזהו כבודו שהוא מתאוה לאכול: במאי נשנייה. במאי נשניוהו משאר ימים: אי רגיליתו לאקדומי. סעודתכם בבקר אחרוה: רב ששת סגי נהור היה ואינו רואה עת האכילה וכשהיה דורש בשבת מושיב התלמידים במקום שתגיע שם החמה לעת האוכל כדי שיצטערו וימהרו לקום: דמטי טולא. שילטננו: הייא. מהר: מהדר

מסורת הש"ס

א) [כתובות קה:], ב) ב"ק לב., ג) נ"א מעייל ומכפי, ד) [חולין קיא.], ה) [נ"ל דכתיב וקראת לשבת ענג רבי אבא וכו' וכ"ה בחולין קיא.], ו) פי' מכר וכ"כ בסוף עמוד זה, ז) לעיל קיד. [יומא כב.], ח) קדושין מא., ט) תענית ט., י) [עי' תוספות ברכות כ. ד"ה כאן], כ) עי' תוס' שם, ל) [וע"ע תוס' ב"ב קלג. ד"ה עיליתא].

ליקוטי רש"י

כפא דהרסנא. דגים המטוגנים בשמן בקמח [לעיל לז:]. סעודה מועטת דגים קטנים מטוגנים בקמח בשמן שלהן [סוכה מד:]. דגים מטוגנים עם הקמח בשמן שלהן [יומא פד.]. מטוגן בשמן ובקרבי דגים וקמח [ביצה טז:]. טיגון מבושלים שומן דגים עם קמח [ע"ז לח:]. קערה של מאכל דגים מטוגנים בשמן בקולא [רשב"ם ב"ב ס:]. לג טיגונהו בשומן דגים וקמח מעט עם הקמח [עי' כח.]. [כ]דיור אינש. לא הוכל. לשון מולין לקרא את שמות האדם ואת שמות הצלמים בשמו של הקב"ה לעשותן אלהות ... עם דמדומי חמה. תפלת יוצר עם הנץ החמה ותפלת המנחה עם שקיעת החמה [ברכות כט:]. מאי קרא. עם הנץ החמה. ייראוך עם שמש וגו'. ממי ממהלכין ממך כשמולכין מקבלים עליהם עול מלכות שמים שמקבלין עליהם תפלת יוצר [שם כט:]. עם שמש. כלומר כשהחמה יוצא היינו עם הנץ החמה ולפני ירח. זו תפלת המנחה [שם כט:]. אף תפלת המנחה מצוה עם דמדומי חמה [שם ט:]. בעלתי ושינתי. שממעת ביתה ... לאשתי ביתי. ... מימי לא אמרתי דבר והחזרתי לאחורי. ... תתי לי. ישולם שכרי [לקמן קכח.] ... צורבא מרבנן. כמור מריך כמו ביתי ... בי סדיא. לבדין שקורין פלטר"ש ועושין לקפלן ממיני ...

עין משפט נר מצוה

מב א טוש"ע או"ח סי' ער סעיף א:
מג ב מיי' פ"ל מהלכות שבת הלכה ב סמג עשין ל טוש"ע או"ח סי' רנ סעיף ב:
מד ג מיי' שם הלכה ו סמג שם טור ש"ע או"ח סימן ר"נ סעיף א:
מה ד טוש"ע או"ח סי' תרי סעיף ד:
מו ה מיי' פ"ל הל"ח וסמג שם טוש"ע או"ח סימן רפח סעיף ו:

הגהות הב"ח

(א) גמ' לא מזיגנא רישא אבי: (ב) שם לביש מאניה במעלי:

גליון הש"ס

גמ' אשור הייא. גיטין דף לד ע"ב: רש"י ד"ה תליסר עיליתא דדינרי וכו' וגוזמא בעלמא. עי' ברכות דף כ ע"ב תוס' ד"ה תליסר מחיכתא:

רבינו חננאל

ורבנן הני דעבדי צרכי שבת בגופייהו. כגון ר' אבהו דהוה [יתיב] (הציבי) אתכתקא דשינא ומשייף נורא. ורב ענן דשגר תנורא ורב הונא גדיל פתילתא. ורב חסדא מדליק שרגי ורב פפא פרים סילקי. רבה ורב יוסף צלחי ציבי כולהו כדמפרש בגמרא בריש האיש מקדש. שקיום המצוה באדם עצמו טפי עדיף יותר מבשלוחו וכבדתו שמשנה זמן סעודתו בהקדמה או באיחור. ויחיד המתפלל בעצמו אומר ויכולו:

תורה אור השלם

א) עַשֵּׂר תְּעַשֵּׂר אֵת כָּל תְּבוּאַת זַרְעֶךָ הַיֹּצֵא הַשָּׂדֶה שָׁנָה שָׁנָה: [דברים יד, כב]

ב) לְדָוִד מִזְמוֹר לַיְיָ הָאָרֶץ וּמְלוֹאָהּ תֵּבֵל וְיֹשְׁבֵי בָהּ: [תהלים כד, א]

ג) הַשָּׁמַיִם שָׁמַיִם לַייָ וְהָאָרֶץ נָתַן לִבְנֵי אָדָם: [תהלים קטו, טז]

ד) אִם תָּשִׁיב מִשַּׁבָּת רַגְלֶךָ עֲשׂוֹת חֲפָצֶךָ בְּיוֹם קָדְשִׁי וְקָרָאתָ לַשַּׁבָּת עֹנֶג לִקְדוֹשׁ יְיָ מְכֻבָּד וְכִבַּדְתּוֹ מֵעֲשׂוֹת דְּרָכֶיךָ מִמְּצוֹא חֶפְצְךָ וְדַבֵּר דָּבָר: [ישעיה נח, יג]

הכסא [לקמן קמ:]. אין אדם רואה חובה לעצמו. אין דעתו מתקרב לצד החובה לחייב את עצמו ואפילו מתכוין לדין אמת [כתובות קה:]. אפניא. לפנות ערב [תענית כג:]. בואו ונצא. כאדם המקבל פני מלך [ב"ק לב:]. תלת סאוי טחיי. פניה טוחין בשמן ודבש [חולין קיא:]. מין טיגון הוא שעושין מלחם ... מי עדיפת לן מינה. יום השבת היה ... בתליסר אסתירי פשיטי. איסתרי סלעי מדינה ... אל ימזוג בהן כוס לרבו. לפי שנתטנפו ונתלכלכו בבישול קדירה [יומא כג.]. מחריך רישא. לכבוד שבת. שיבוטא. ... צינורא דדשא. ... סילקא. ... ציבי. עצים [עירובין פב:]. כוורא. דג [רשב"ם ב"ב עג:].

elder[23] **encountered him** אָמַר מַאן דְּיָזִיף שַׁבְּתָא פָּרְעֵיהּ שַׁבְּתָא – and **said, "He who borrows for** the sake of **the Sabbath, the Sabbath repays him."**[24]

The Gemara presents a related discussion about the mitzvos for which people are rewarded with wealth:

בְּעָא מִינֵּיהּ רַבִּי מֵרַבִּי יִשְׁמָעֵאל בְּרַבִּי יוֹסֵי – **Rebbi inquired of R' Yishmael the son of R' Yose:** עֲשִׁירִים שֶׁבְּאֶרֶץ יִשְׂרָאֵל בַּמֶּה הֵן זוֹכִין – **The rich of Eretz Yisrael, through what** good deed **do they merit** their great wealth? אָמַר לוֹ בִּשְׁבִיל שֶׁמְּעַשְּׂרִין – **He said to him: Because they** faithfully **tithe** their crops, שֶׁנֶּאֱמַר – **as the verse says:** ,,עַשֵּׂר תְּעַשֵּׂר'' – ***Tithe, you shall tithe.***[25] The double use of this word teaches: עַשֵּׂר בִּשְׁבִיל שֶׁתִּתְעַשֵּׁר – **Tithe, so that you shall become wealthy.**[26] שֶׁבְּבָבֶל בַּמֶּה הֵן זוֹכִין – Rebbi asked further: **Those in Babylonia, through what** good deed **do they merit** their great wealth?[27] אָמַר לוֹ בִּשְׁבִיל שֶׁמְּכַבְּדִין אֶת הַתּוֹרָה – **He said to him: Because they honor the Torah.** וְשֶׁבִּשְׁאָר אֲרָצוֹת בַּמֶּה הֵן זוֹכִין – **And those in other lands, through what** good deed **do they merit** their great wealth? אָמַר לוֹ בִּשְׁבִיל שֶׁמְּכַבְּדִין אֶת הַשַּׁבָּת – **[R' Yishmael the son of R' Yose] said to him: Because they honor the Sabbath.**

The Gemara cites a story to support this last explanation:

דְּאָמַר רַבִּי חִיָּיא בַּר אַבָּא – **For R' Chiya bar Abba said:** פַּעַם אַחַת נִתְאָרַחְתִּי אֵצֶל בַּעַל הַבַּיִת בְּלוּדְקִיָּא – **I was once a guest at** the home of **a certain householder in Ludkaya,** וְהֵבִיאוּ לְפָנָיו שֻׁלְחָן שֶׁל זָהָב מַשּׂוֹי שִׁשָּׁה עָשָׂר בְּנֵי אָדָם – **and,** when it came time to eat, **they brought before him a gold table that required sixteen people to carry it.** וְשֵׁשׁ עֶשְׂרֵה שַׁלְשְׁלָאוֹת שֶׁל כֶּסֶף קְבוּעוֹת בּוֹ – **And there were sixteen silver chains set in it,**[28] וּקְעָרוֹת וְכוֹסוֹת וְקִיתוֹנִיּוֹת וּצְלוֹחִיּוֹת קְבוּעוֹת בּוֹ – **and there were plates and cups and drinking ladles and bottles set in it;** וְעָלָיו כָּל מִינֵי מַאֲכָל וְכָל מִינֵי מְגָדִים וּבְשָׂמִים – **and on [the table] were all kinds of foods and all kinds of delicacies and spices.** וּכְשֶׁמַּנִּיחִים אוֹתוֹ אוֹמְרִים ,,לַה' הָאָרֶץ וּמְלוֹאָהּ וגו' '' – **When they put the table down** before him **they said:** ***To Hashem is the earth and its fullness, etc.***[29] וּכְשֶׁמְּסַלְּקִין אוֹתוֹ אוֹמְרִים ,,הַשָּׁמַיִם שָׁמַיִם לַה' וְהָאָרֶץ נָתַן לִבְנֵי־אָדָם'' – **And when they removed it they said:** ***As for the heavens – the heavens are Hashem's, but the earth He has given to mankind.***[30] אָמַרְתִּי לוֹ בְּנִי בַּמֶּה זָכִיתָ לְכָךְ – **I said to him, "My son, through what did you merit** to have all **this?"** אָמַר לִי קַצָּב הָיִיתִי – **He said to me, "I was a butcher,** וּמִכָּל בְּהֵמָה שֶׁהָיְתָה נָאָה אָמַרְתִּי זוֹ תְּהֵא לְשַׁבָּת – **and from every animal that was nice** [i.e. of high quality], **I would say, 'Let a** piece of **this be for the Sabbath.'** ''[31] אָמַרְתִּי לוֹ [אַשְׁרֶיךָ שֶׁזָּכִיתָ] וּבָרוּךְ הַמָּקוֹם שֶׁזִּיכְּךָ לְכָךְ – **I said to him, "Fortunate are you that you merited this, and Blessed is God Who has granted you** all **this."**

We see from this incident that the extraordinary wealth of a rich man outside of Eretz Yisrael came to him in the merit of his honoring the Sabbath.

NOTES

developed to observe the mitzvos is thirteen. Accordingly, *Maharsha* asserts, when the Gemara stated above that R' Abba bought meat from thirteen butchers for the Sabbath, it meant this literally. To indicate his attachment to the *holiness* of the Sabbath, R' Abba made it his practice to make purchases for the Sabbath in groups of thirteen. In the same way, *Maharsha* suggests, Yosef *Mokir Shabbos* also made it his practice to make his purchases for the Sabbath in groups of thirteen. Therefore, he was rewarded with thirteen measures of gold coins. For other explanations of the symbolism of this Gemara see *Maharal* and *Olelos Ephraim* §88 (cited in *Chidushei Geonim* in the margin of *Ein Yaakov*).

23. See *Tosafos* to *Chullin* 6a, who cite an opinion that the phrase הַהוּא סָבָא, *a certain elder,* refers to the prophet Elijah.

24. [It is not clear why the elder spoke of "borrowing" for the Sabbath when there is no indication in this story that Yosef had to borrow to pay for his purchases. Perhaps the elder's comment was based on the teaching of the Gemara in *Beitzah* (16a): "All of a person's food (i.e. income) is fixed (each year) between Rosh Hashanah and Yom Kippur, with the exception of his expenditures for the Sabbaths and festivals and his expenditures for the Torah education of his children. For in regard to these, if . . . one spends more, he receives more." I.e. the amount a person spends to honor the Sabbath and festivals is not included in the total income decreed for him each year between Rosh Hashanah and Yom Kippur and he is repaid for these expenditures above and beyond that allocation. Nevertheless, a person must lay out the money for these expenditures as they arise and it is not until later that he is reimbursed. To this end he may even borrow money on the expectation of being reimbursed by God, as the Gemara there says (15b). Thus, when a person spends money for the Sabbath, he is in effect "borrowing" from his income for the year to make purchases for the Sabbath. The Sabbath in turn "repays" him, as this story so vividly demonstrates.]

25. *Deuteronomy* 14:22.

26. The homiletic interpretation of this verse takes the second word – תְּעַשֵּׂר (*you shall tithe*) – as if it were written with a *shin* – תְּעַשֵּׁר (*you shall become wealthy*). Alternatively, the exposition retains the original reading of תְּעַשֵּׂר (*you shall tithe*) but explains the double use of the word to mean: Tithe so that you shall tithe further – for you will be blessed with added crops necessitating even larger tithes. Thus you will become wealthy (*Maharsha* to *Taanis* 9a).

27. It cannot be in the merit of tithing because there is no [Biblical] obligation to tithe crops in Babylonia (*Hagahos Yavetz*).

[It would seem from this that although it is proper for one to give a tenth of his income to charity, the blessing of wealth is not promised for this kind of tithing because there is no strict *obligation* to do so; the Torah's blessing is promised specifically in return for tithing crops, which are subject (in the Land of Israel) to the obligation of *maaser* (*Hagahos Yavetz;* see also *She'eilas Yavetz* 1:3 and *Pischei Teshuvah, Yoreh Deah* 247:2). However, from *Tur* (*Yoreh Deah* 247) it is evident that the blessing for tithing goes even for one who tithes his money and gives it to charity (see *Beis Yosef* there ד״ה ומ״ש ואמרו חכמים and *Rama* 247:4). *Korban Nesanel* here (§8) therefore explains that Rebbi's question concerned only those who had merited unusual wealth (see *Rashi* ד״ה במה הן זוכין) and Rebbi did not believe that unusual wealth could be merited solely for tithing that is not Biblically mandated.

[As to whether there is an actual obligation to tithe one's earnings or it is merely the recommended level of charity, see (in addition to the sources already cited) *Tosafos* to *Taanis* 9a (ד״ה עשר תעשר) who quote *Sifrei* as deriving from this verse an obligation to tithe even one's business profits. This derivation, however, is only in the nature of an *asmachta,* a Scriptural allusion to support a Rabbinic enactment (see *Chavos Yair* §224). Indeed, *Bach* (at the end of *Yoreh Deah* 331) rules that it is not an absolute requirement even on the Rabbinic level, though he is disputed on this by *Taz* there §32. See *Shevus Yaakov* §85 who discusses the matter at length.]

28. Four chains were set in each side of the table to serve as handles for the sixteen porters (*Iyun Yaakov;* cf. *Maharsha*).

29. *Psalms* 24:1. [I.e. everything – even the food we have just put down – is God's, not ours,] because before we bless God's Name by reciting the blessing over the bread, we are forbidden to partake of it (*Rashi*). [The Gemara in *Berachos* (35a-b) derives from this verse that one who enjoys the pleasures of this world without blessing God for them is akin to one who misuses sacred property – since everything belongs to God.]

30. *Psalms* 115:16. It is only because God has given it to us that we are able to enjoy all the bounty (*Rashi*). [None of it is really ours, despite the illusion of our great wealth.]

[*Maharsha,* based on the Gemara's use of this verse in *Berachos* (ibid.), understands the statement here to mean that they removed this gold table immediately after reciting the blessing over the food and they did not eat the meal on it. The gold table was used only as a serving table; cf. *Chidushei HaRan.*]

31. I.e. he would set aside a piece to use for himself on the Sabbath (*Ohr Zarua* cited by *Bach* and *Taz* at the end of *Orach Chaim* 242; cf. *Ben Yehoyada* and *Megadim Chadashim*). [This accords with the custom of Shammai, who set aside for the Sabbath any choice food he obtained during the week (see *Beitzah* 16a).]

כל כתבי פרק ששה עשר שבת קיט.

עבידנא יומא טבא לרבנן אמר רבא א תיתי לי דכי אתא צורבא מרבנן לקמאי לדינא לא מזיגנא (א) רישי אבי סדיא כמה דלא מהפיכנא בזכותי' אמר מר בר רב אשי פסילנא ליה לצורבא מרבנן לדינא מ"ט דחביב עלי כגופאי ואין אדם רואה חובה לעצמו ב רבי חנינא מיעטף וקאי אפניא דמעלי שבתא אמר בואו ונצא לקראת שבת המלכה רבי ינאי לביש מאניה ג (ב) מעלי שבת ואמר בואי כלה בואי כלה רבה ד בר רב הונא איקלע לבי רבה בר רב נחמן קריבו ליה תלת סאוי טחיי א"ל מי הוה ידעיתון דאתינא אמרו ליה מי עדיפת לן מינה ה רבי אבא זבן בתליסר אסתירי פשיטי בישרא מתליסר טבחי ומשלים להו אצינורא דדשא ואמר להו ו אשור הייא אשור הייא ז ר' אבהו הוה יתיב אתכתקא דשינא ומושיף נורא רב ענן לביש גונדא ח דתנא דבי רבי ישמעאל בגדים שבישל בהן קדירה לרבו אל ימזוג בהן כוס לרבו ט רב ספרא מחריך רישא רבא מלח שיבוטא רב הונא מדליק שרגי רב פפא גדיל פתילתא רב חסדא פרים סילקא רבה ורב יוסף מצלחי ציבי ר' זירא מצתת צתותי רב נחמן בר יצחק מכתף ועייל מכתף ונפיק אמר אילו מקלעין לי ר' אמי ור' אסי מי לא מכתיפנא קמייהו ואיכא דאמרי ר' אמי ורבי אסי מכתפי ועיילי מכתפי ונפקי אמרי אילו איקלע לן רבי יוחנן מי לא מכתפינן קמיה יוסף מוקיר שבי הוה ההוא נכרי בשבבותיה דהוה נפישי נכסיה טובא אמרי ליה כלדאי כולהו נכסי יוסף מוקר שבי אכיל להו אזל זבנינהו לכולהו ניכסי זבן בהו מרגניתא אותבה בסייניה בהדי דקא עבר מברא אפרחיה זיקא שדייה במיא בלעיה כוורא אסקוה אייתוה אפניא דמעלי שבתא אמרי מאן זבן כי השתא אמרי להו זילו אמטיוהו לגבי יוסף מוקר שבי דרגיל דזבין אמטיוה ניהליה זבניה קרעיה אשכח ביה מרגניתא זבניה בתליסר עיליתא דדינרי דדהבא פגע ביה ההוא סבא אמר מאן דיזיף שבתא פרעיה שבתא בעא מיניה רבי מר' ישמעאל ברבי יוסי עשירים שבא"י במה הן זוכין א"ל בשביל שמעשרין שנאמר א עשר תעשר ט עשר בשביל שתתעשר שבבבל במה הן זוכין א"ל בשביל שמכבדין את התורה ושבשאר ארצות במה הן זוכין א"ל בשביל שמכבדין את השבת דאמר רבי חייא בר אבא פעם אחת נתארחתי אצל בעל הבית בלודקיא והביאו לפניו שלחן של זהב משוי ששה עשר בני אדם וששה עשרה שלשלאות של כסף קבועות בו וקערות וכוסות וקיתוניות וצלוחיות קבועות בו ועליו כל מיני מאכל וכל מיני מגדים ובשמים י וכשמניחים אותו אומרים ב) לה' הארץ ומלואה וגו' כ וכשמסלקין אותו אומרים ג) השמים שמים לה' והארץ נתן לבני אדם אמרתי לו בני במה זכית לכך אמר לי קצב הייתי ומכל בהמה שהיתה נאה אמרתי זו תהא לשבת אמרתי לו [אשריך שזכית] וברוך המקום שזיכך לכך א"ל קיסר לרבי יהושע בן חנניא מפני מה תבשיל של שבת ריחו נודף אמר לו תבלין אחד יש לנו ושבת שמו שאנו מטילין לתוכו וריחו נודף אמר לו תן לנו הימנו אמר לו כל המשמר את השבת מועיל לו ושאינו משמר את השבת אינו מועיל לו א"ל ריש גלותא לרב המנונא מאי דכתיב ד) ולקדוש ה' מכובד א"ל ל זה יוה"כ שאין בו לא אכילה ולא שתיה אמרה תורה כבדהו בכסות נקיה ד) מ וכבדתו רב אמר להקדים ושמואל אמר לאחר אמרו ליה בני רב פפא בר אבא לרב פפא כגון אנן דשכיח לן בישרא וחמרא כל יומא במאי נישנייה אמר להו אי רגיליתו לאקדומי אחרוה אי רגיליתו לאחרוה אקדמוה רב ששת בקיטא מותיב להו לרבנן היכא דמטיא שימשא בסיתוא מותיב להו לרבנן היכא דמטיא טולא כי היכי דליקומו הייא ר' זירא מהדר

תוספות

בתליסר עיליתא דדינרי. אומר ר"ת דעיליתא שם כלי הוא כדאמרינן בריש כילד מעברין (עירובין דף נג:) עלת נקפת בכדה (א): **רב** אמר להקדים ושמואל אמר לאחר. ולא פליגי אלא רב איירי בדרכו לאחר ושמואל איירי בדרכו להקדים כדאמרינן בסמוך: ומלא

רש"י

עבידנא יומא טבא לרבנן. לתלמידים ראש ישיבה היה: **תיתי לי.** ישולם שכרי: **דכי אתי צורבא מרבנן כו'.** שחיבת תלמידי חכמים עלי: **דלא מזיגנא רישא אבי סדיא.** איני מניח ראשי על הכר: **כמה דלא מהפיכנא ליה בזכותיה.** עד שאראה אם יש בדבריו לזכותו: **מתעטף.** בבגדים נאים: **בואי כלה.** הכי קרי ליה לשביתת שבת מתוך חביבות: **טחיי.** רקיקין טחין פניהן בשומן אליה או בשמן: **מי עדיפת לן מינה.** כלום אתה חשוב לנו מן השבת לכבוד שבת הכנוס ולא היינו יודעים שתבא: **מתליסר טבחי.** לטעום בשבת מן המובחר: **איסתירי.** סלעים איסתירי פשיטי סלעים מדינ' והן א' מח' בסלע צורי והיינו חצי דינר: **ומשלים להו אצינורא דדשא.** לפני בואם להביא לו הבשר היה מזמן להן מעותיהן על פתחו ואומר להן אשור הייא התאשרו והתחזקו מהר באמונותיכם למהר ולחזור ולמכור ולהתעסק בצרכי שבת ולי נראה ומשלים להו אצינורא דדשא כשהיה מביא ראשונה היה נותנה לשמשין המכינים סעודתו על פתח ביתו ולא היה נכנס אלא ממהר לחזור ולהביא אחרת ואמר להן לשמשין אשור הייא התאשרו מהר להכין את זו בעוד שאלך להביא את זו: **אתכתקא דשינא.** פסטו"ל של שן שחשוב היה ועשיר: ומושיף נורא. נופח משם נורא לכבוד השבת והיינו לוי גרס אתכתקא דשאגא מדסר: **לביש גונדא.** כלי שחור להודיע שהיום אינו כדי להתנהג בחשיבות מלהתעסק בתבשילי שבת ולא יטנף בגדיו בבישול קדירות: **דתנא דבי רבי ישמעאל כו'.** דבישול קדירה מטנף בגדים: **מחריך רישא.** אם היה שם ראש בהמה לחרוך מחרכו הוא בעצמו: **פרים.** לשון פרומים מחתך: **מצתת צתותי.** מצית האור בעצים דקים: **מכתף** ועייל מכתף ונפיק. בע"ש יוצא ונכנס להביא תמיד משואות כלי תשמיש ובגדי חופש ומגדים כאדם שמקבל את רבו בביתו ומראה לו שהוא חשוב עליו וחרד לכבודו לטרוח ולהרבות בשבילו: **מוקר שבי.** מכבד שבתות: **אמרי ליה כלדאי.** להאי נכרי: **כלדאי.** חוזים בכוכבים: **אכיל להו.** סופך ליפול בידו: **אותבה בסייניה.** עשה לו כובע של לבד ושבלו במשבצות של זהב וקבע בו מרגליות וקבע את זו עמהם: **סייניה.** כובע. ורבינו הלוי גרס בסדיניה בסודרו ולשון הגון לי והוא לשון ר' יצחק ב"ר יהודה: **תריסר עיליתי דדינרי.** עליות מלאות דינרי זהב ° וגוזמא בעלמא הוא כלומר הון עתק מאד כך פירש רבינו הלוי וכן בכל מקום כגון תליסר גמלי ספיקי טריפתא (חולין דף נה:) וכן תליסר טבחי דלעיל: **במה הן זוכין.** לעושר גדול כזה: **לה' הארץ.** דאין אנו רשאין ליהנות עד שנברך שמו בברכת הלחם: **והארץ נתן לבני אדם.** ע"י מתנתו נהנינו הטובה הזאת: **מאי דכתיב ולקדוש ה' מכובד.** מדכתיב וקראת לשבת עונג מכלל דלקדוש ה' לאו אשבת קאי: **וכבדתו.** אשבת מהדר דאי ביוה"כ הא כתיב ביה מכובד: **להקדים.** זמן סעודת שבת לזמן סעודת חול וזהו כבודו: **לאחר.** וזהו כבודו שהוא מתאוה לאכול: **במאי נשנייה.** במאי נשניוהו משאר ימים: **אי רגיליתו לאקדומי.** סעודתכם בבקר אחרוה: **רב ששת** סגי נהור היה ואינו רואה עת האכילה וכשהיה דורש בשבת מושיב התלמידים במקום שמגיע שם החמה לעת האוכל כדי שילטערו וימהרו לקום: **דמטי טולא.** שילטנו: **הייא.** מהר: מהדר

עין משפט נר מצוה

מב א טוש"ע חו"מ סי' טו סעיף א:
מג ב מיי' פ"ל מהלכות שבת הלכה ב סמג עשין ל טוש"ע או"ח סי' רסב סעיף ג:
מד ג מיי' שם הלכה ו סמג שם טור שו"ע או"ח סימן ר"נ סעיף א:
מה ד טוש"ע או"ח סי' תרי סעיף ד:
מו ה מיי' פ"ל שם הל"ח וסמג שם טוש"ע או"ח סימן רפח סעיף ז:

הגהות הב"ח

(א) גמ' לא מזיגנא רישא אבי: (ב) שם לביש מאניה במעלי:

גליון הש"ס

גמ' אשור הייא. גיטין דף לד ע"א: רש"י ד"ה תליסר עיליתא דדינרי וכו' וגוזמא בעלמא. עי' ברכות דף כ ע"א בסוף ד"ה תליסר מתיבתא:

רבינו חננאל

ורבנן הני דעבדי צרכי שבת בנפשייהו. כגון ר' אבהו דהוה [יתיב] (הציבי) אתכתקא דשינא ומשייף נורא. ורב חנן דשגר תנורא ורב הונא גדיל פתילתא. ורב חסדא מדליק שרגי ורב פפא פרים סילקי. רבה ורב יוסף צלחי ציבי כולהו כדמפרש בגמרא בריש האיש מקדש. שקיום המצוה באדם עצמו טפי עדיף יותר מבשלוחו: וכבדתו שמשנה זמן סעודתו בהקדמה או באיחור. ויחיד המתפלל בעצמו אומר ויכולו:

תורה אור השלם

א) עַשֵּׂר תְּעַשֵּׂר אֵת כָּל תְּבוּאַת זַרְעֶךָ הַיֹּצֵא הַשָּׂדֶה שָׁנָה שָׁנָה: [דברים יד, כב]
ב) לְדָוִד מִזְמוֹר לַיְיָ הָאָרֶץ וּמְלוֹאָהּ תֵּבֵל וְיֹשְׁבֵי בָהּ: [תהלים כד, א]
ג) הַשָּׁמַיִם שָׁמַיִם לַיְיָ וְהָאָרֶץ נָתַן לִבְנֵי אָדָם: [תהלים קטו, טז]
ד) אִם תָּשִׁיב מִשַּׁבָּת רַגְלֶךָ עֲשׂוֹת חֲפָצֶיךָ בְּיוֹם קָדְשִׁי וְקָרָאתָ לַשַּׁבָּת עֹנֶג לִקְדוֹשׁ יְיָ מְכֻבָּד וְכִבַּדְתּוֹ מֵעֲשׂוֹת דְּרָכֶיךָ מִמְּצוֹא חֶפְצְךָ וְדַבֵּר דָּבָר: [ישעיה נח, יג]

מסורת הש"ס

א) [כתובות קה:], ב) ב"ק לב. ע"ש, ג) ב"ק מעלי ולמכסי, ד) [חולין קיא.], ה) [נ"ל דכתיב וקראת לשבת עונג רבי אבא וכו' וכ"ה בחולין קיא.], ו) פי' מהר וכ"כ בסוף עמוד זה, ז) לעיל קיז. [יומא כג.], ח) קדושין מא. ט) תענית ט. י) [ע' תוספות ברכות לה: ד"ה כאן], כ) ע' תוס' שם, ל) [וע"ע תוס' ב"ב קמב: ד"ה עיליתא].

ליקוטי רש"י

כסא דהרסנא. דגים המטוגנים בשמן בקמח [לעיל לז:]. סעודה מוטעמת דגים קטנים מטוגנין בשמן שלהן [סוכה מד:]. דגים מטוגנים עם הקמח בשמן שלהן [יומא פד.]. מטוגן בשומן קרבי דגים ובקמח [ביצה טז.]. טיגון במורייס שומן דגים שעל מאכל דגים מטוגנין בשמן בכולם [פסחים ב"ב מ.]. דג שמיגונו בשמן היוצא ממנו עם הקמח [ע"ז כח.]. **[כ]דרור אנוש.** לא הוציא. לשון חולין לקרא את שמות הלוים ולא שמות העצבים לאמון של הקב"ה לעצמון עבודה זרה ולקרוון אלהים [בראשית ה, כז]. **עם דמדומי חמה.** תפלת יוצר עם הנץ החמה ותפלת המנחה עם שקיעת החמה [ברכות כט:]. **מאי קרא.** דמלוה להתפלל עם הנץ החמה. **ייראוך עם שמש וגו'.** מתי מתיראין ממך כשמרולאין מקבלים עליהם דייתנו מלכות שמים מקבלים עליהם בקריאת שמע [שם ט:]. זו תפלת יוצר [שם כט: ע"ש בב"ח]. **עם שמש.** כלומר כשהחמה יוצא היינו עם הנץ החמה [שם ט:]. **ולפני ירח.** זו מנחה [שם ט:]. אף תפלת המנחה מלוה עם דמדומי חמה [שם ט:]. **בעלתי ושניתי.** שמתמת ביאה ראשונה נתמלא האשה והולכבה תאוה והכשבא ביאה שניה היא מזרעת תחילה והילד היא מזרעת תחילה יולדת זכר [עירובין ק:]. **לאשתי ביתי.** שכל צרכי הבית על ידה נעשים והיא עיקר הבית וכן שור עיקרו של שדה [גיטין נב.]. **מימי לא אמרתי דבר וחזרתי לאחורי.** כלומר מי עומד אחורי אלף כפני הבעלים אני אומרים וכו' כ"ל שאם בא לבעלים ואמרו אשה אמרת כן לא חזרתי בי לאמר לא אמרתי אלא בפניהם הודיתי [ערכין טו:]. **תיתי לי.** ישולם שכרי [לקמן קיט.]. שכר טוב [בכורות ל.]. **עיון תפלה.** לכוין בתפלתו [לקמן קכז.]. **צורבא מרבנן.** בחור חריף כמו ביעי דלריבן במסכת ביצה (ז.) תלמיד חכם זקן לא קרי צורבא אלא הסוא מרבנן קרי ליה [תענית ד.].

[ע"כ שייך לדף קיח:]

אבי סדיא. לגדין שקורין פלטר"ש ועשויין לקפלן תחתיו במקום הכר או הכסת [לקמן קמו:]. **אין אדם רואה חובה לעצמו.** אין דעתו מתקרב לצד החובה לחייב את עצמו ואפילו מתכוין לדין אמת [כתובות קה:]. **אפניא.** לפנות ערב [תענית כג:]. **בואו ונצא.** כאדם המקבל פני מלך [ב"ק לב:]. **תלת סאוי טחיי.** לא סאין פת נקיה פניה טוחין בשמן ודבש [חולין קיא:]. מין טיגון הוא שעושין מלחם ועושין התנור באליה ואופין את הלחם אחר שטחוהו וכמס' שבת נמי אמרינן תלתא סאוי טחיי [זבחים צה:]. **מי עדיפת לן מינה.** יום השבת היה [חולין שם]. **בתליסר אסתירי פשיטי.** איסתרי סלעי מדינה שהם פשוטים וקלים איסתרי סתם היינו סלעין צורי שהסלע ארבע דינרים ואיסתרי פשיטי הוא סלע מדינה שמינית שבסלע צורי דהיינו חצי דינר כדאמרינן בהמוכר את הבירו (ב"ק ל:) איסתרא פלגא דזוזא וקרי ליה הכא סלע מדינה [שם מד:]. **צינורא דדשא.** חור מפתן הבית שהדלת סובב בו [ברכות יח:]. חור שבמפתן וציר הדלת סובב בו [כתובות סז:]. **אשור.** כמו אשרתא דדייני (גיטין כו.) וכמו אשרו חמוץ (ישעיה א) לשון חיזוק [גיטין לד.]. **אל ימזוג בהן כוס לרבו.** לפי שנתעשנו ונתלכלכו בבישול קדירה [יומא כג:]. **מחריך רישא.** לכבוד שבת. **שיבוטא.** דג [קידושין מא.]. **סילקא.** תרדין [שבועות כג.]. **ציבי.** עצים [עירובין פב:]. **כוורא.** דג [רשב"ם ב"ב עג:].

A story about the special quality of Sabbath foods:

אָמַר לוֹ קֵיסָר לְרַבִּי יְהוֹשֻׁעַ בֶּן חֲנַנְיָא – Caesar once said to R' Yehoshua ben Chananya: מִפְּנֵי מָה תַּבְשִׁיל שֶׁל שַׁבָּת רֵיחוֹ נוֹדֵף – "Why is it that the food cooked for the Sabbath has such a penetrating aroma?" אָמַר לוֹ תַּבְלִין אֶחָד יֵשׁ לָנוּ וְשַׁבָּת שְׁמוֹ – [R' Yehoshua] answered him: "We have this one spice, it is called Sabbath, שֶׁאָנוּ מַטִּילִין לְתוֹכוֹ וְרֵיחוֹ נוֹדֵף – which we throw into [the Sabbath food], and its aroma is very penetrating." אָמַר לוֹ תֵּן לָנוּ הֵימֶנּוּ – [Caesar] said to him: "Give us some of it." אָמַר לוֹ כֹּל הַמְשַׁמֵּר אֶת הַשַּׁבָּת מוֹעִיל לוֹ – [R' Yehoshua] said to him: "Whoever observes the Sabbath, for him [the spice] is effective; וְשֶׁאֵינוֹ מְשַׁמֵּר אֶת הַשַּׁבָּת אֵינוֹ מוֹעִיל לוֹ – but for one who does not observe the Sabbath it is not effective."

Other forms of honoring the Sabbath:

אָמַר לֵיהּ רֵישׁ גָּלוּתָא לְרַב הַמְנוּנָא – The Exilarch[32] **said to Rav Hamnuna: מַאי דִּכְתִיב "(ו)לִקְדוֹשׁ ה' מְכֻבָּד" – What is** the meaning of **that which is written:** *If you proclaim the Sabbath a delight, the holy one of Hashem "honored"...?*[33] **אָמַר לֵיהּ זֶה יוֹם הַכִּפּוּרִים שֶׁאֵין בּוֹ לֹא אֲכִילָה וְלֹא שְׁתִיָּה – [Rav Hamnuna] said to him: This** phrase **refers to Yom Kippur,** a day **on which there is no eating or drinking,** and it is thus impossible to honor that holy day with special food and beverage.[34] **אָמְרָה תּוֹרָה כַּבְּדֵהוּ בִּכְסוּת נְקִיָּה – The Torah** therefore **said: Honor it** nonetheless. How so? **With a clean garment.**[35]

The verse just cited continues:

"וְכִבַּדְתּוֹ", – ***And you honor it*** (the Sabbath) *by not engaging in your* [customary] *ways.* This further injunction to honor the day is now expounded: **רַב אָמַר לְהַקְדִּים – Rav says: To advance** the time of the meal, i.e. to eat earlier than usual. **וּשְׁמוּאֵל אָמַר לְאַחֵר – And Shmuel says: To postpone** the time of the meal, i.e. to eat later than usual.[36]

The Gemara cites a related ruling:

אָמְרוּ לֵיהּ בְּנֵי רַב פָּפָּא בַּר אַבָּא לְרַב פָּפָּא – The sons of Rav Pappa bar Abba said to Rav Pappa: כְּגוֹן אֲנַן דִּשְׁכִיחַ לָן בִּישְׂרָא וְחַמְרָא כָּל יוֹמָא – For people **such as ourselves, for whom it is common to have meat and wine every day, בְּמַאי נִישַׁנְּיֵיהּ – how should we make [the Sabbath] different? אָמַר לְהוּ אִי רְגִילִיתוּ לְאַקְדּוּמֵי אַחֲרוּהַ – He said to them: If you are accustomed to make** your meal **early, make it later. אִי רְגִילִיתוּ לְאַחֲרוּהַ אַקְדְּמוּהַ – If you are accustomed to make it late, make it earlier.**

The Gemara cites a story to demonstrate the importance of eating the Sabbath meal:

רַב שֵׁשֶׁת בְּקַיְטָא מוֹתִיב לְהוּ לְרַבָּנָן הֵיכָא דְּמָטְיָא שִׁימְשָׁא – Rav Sheishess, when he said his lecture on the Sabbath, **would, in the summer, seat the rabbis** in a place **where the sun would reach** as the day wore on, **בְּסִיתְוָא מוֹתִיב לְהוּ לְרַבָּנָן הֵיכָא דְּמָטְיָא טוּלָּא – and in the autumn he would seat the rabbis** in a place **where the shade would reach** as the day wore on, **כִּי הֵיכִי דְּלֵיקוּמוּ הַיְיָא – in order that they should rise quickly** when it became too warm or too cold and thereby alert him that it was time to conclude the lecture and send people home to eat their Sabbath meal. Rav Sheishess was blind and could not see for himself what time it was.[37]

The Gemara cites the practice of another Amora in this regard:

רַבִּי זֵירָא – R' Zeira

NOTES

32. The Exilarch [*Reish Galusa*] was the officially recognized civil authority of the Jewish people in Babylonia. He was a descendant of the royal house of David.

33. *Isaiah* 58:13. [This verse teaches the obligation to honor the Sabbath.] Since the previous phrase speaks of the Sabbath (*If you proclaim the Sabbath a delight*), the reference to *the holy one of Hashem* must be to some other holy day (*Rashi*).

34. This portion of the verse cannot be referring to any other holiday for it speaks of a day that is *the holy one of Hashem,* which implies a day whose holiness is directed *entirely* to Hashem and not, as in the previous phrase, a day that is *a delight* to people (an expression that denotes eating and drinking; see *Pesachim* 68b). Thus, it can only refer to Yom Kippur – a day on which there is no eating and drinking (*Maharsha*).

35. Although the verse does not specify clean clothing as the way of honoring the day, the Sages deduced this by process of elimination. Since there is no eating and drinking on this day, special attire is the only practical way left to honor the holy day (*Maharsha*).

[Above (113a), the Gemara explained this phrase to be teaching that one's garments should be different on the Sabbath than they are during the week. Clearly, Rav Hamnuna disputes that understanding of the verse (see *Maharsha* who explains this point at greater length). Nonetheless, it is instructive that the Gemara there speaks merely of altering one's attire on the Sabbath but it does not emphasize that it be *clean* as it does here in regard to Yom Kippur. This added requirement for Yom Kippur is the basis for the custom to wear white garments on Yom Kippur, in line with the Midrash's statement that we stand on Yom Kippur like angels before God (*Maharsha;* see *Pirkei DeRabbi Eliezer* 46; see also *Rama, Orach Chaim* 610:4).]

36. This honors the Sabbath by making the person hungrier and thus more appreciative of his meal (*Rashi*; see also *Tosafos*).

37. *Rashi.* When Rav Sheishess heard the students beginning to move from one side of him to the other, he realized what time of day it was and concluded his lecture (*Megadim Chadashim;* see also *Ben Yehoyada;* cf. *Maharsha*).

עבידנא יומא טבא לרבנן אמר רבא א תיתי לי דכי אתא צורבא מרבנן לקמאי לדינא לא מזיגנא (א) רישי אבי סדיא כמה דלא מהפיכנא בזכותי' אמר מר בר רב אשי פסילנא ליה לצורבא מרבנן לדינא מ"ט ב דחביב עלי כגופאי ואין אדם רואה חובה לעצמו ג רבי חנינא מיעטף וקאי אפניא דמעלי שבתא אמר בואו ונצא לקראת שבת המלכה רבי ינאי לביש מאניה ג (ב) מעלי שבת ואמר בואי כלה בואי כלה רבה ד בר רב הונא איקלע לבי רבה בר רב נחמן קריבו ליה תלת סאוי טחיי א"ל מי הוה ידעיתון דאתינא אמרו ליה מי עדיפת לן מינה ה רבי אבא זבן בתליסר אסתירי פשיטי בישרא מתליסר טבחי ומשלים להו אצינורא דדשא ואמר להו ו אשור הייא אשור הייא ר' אבהו הוה יתיב אתכתקא דשינא ומושיף נורא רב ענן לביש גונדא ז דתנא דבי רבי ישמעאל בגדים שבישל בהן קדירה לרבו אל ימזוג בהן כוס לרבו ח רב ספרא מחריך רישא רבא מלח שיבוטא רב הונא מדליק שרגי רב פפא גדיל פתילתא רב חסדא פרים סילקא רבה ורב יוסף מצלחי ציבי ר' זירא מצתת צתותי רב נחמן בר יצחק מכתף ועייל מכתף ונפיק אמר אילו מקלען לי ר' אמי ור' אסי מי לא מכתיפנא קמייהו ואיכא דאמרי ר' אמי ורבי אסי מכתפי ועיילי מכתפי ונפקי אמרי אילו איקלע לן רבי יוחנן מי לא מכתפינן קמיה יוסף מוקיר שבי הוה ההוא נכרי בשבבותיה דהוה נפישי נכסיה טובא אמרי ליה כלדאי כולהו נכסי יוסף מוקר שבי אכיל להו אזל זבנינהו לכולהו ניכסי זבן בהו מרגניתא אותבה בסייניה בהדי דקא עבר מברא אפרחיה זיקא שדייה במיא בלעיה כוורא אסקוה אייתוה אפניא דמעלי שבתא אמרי מאן זבין כי השתא אמרי להו זילו אמטיוהו לגבי יוסף מוקר שבי דרגיל דזבין אמטיוה ניהליה זבניה קרעיה אשכח ביה מרגניתא זבניה בתליסר עיליתא דדינרי דדהבא פגע ביה ההוא סבא אמר מאן דיזיף שבתא פרעיה שבתא בעא מיניה רבי מר' ישמעאל ברבי יוסי עשירים שבא"י במה הן זוכין א"ל בשביל שמעשרין שנאמר א עשר תעשר ט עשר בשביל שתתעשר שבבבל במה הן זוכין א"ל בשביל שמכבדין את התורה ושבשאר ארצות במה הן זוכין א"ל בשביל שמכבדין את השבת דאמר רבי חייא בר אבא פעם אחת נתארחתי אצל בעל הבית בלודקיא והביאו לפניו שלחן של זהב משוי ששה עשר בני אדם וששה עשרה שלשלאות של כסף קבועות בו וקערות וכוסות וקיתוניות וצלוחיות קבועות בו ועליו כל מיני מאכל וכל מיני מגדים ובשמים י וכשמניחים אותו אומרים ב לה' הארץ ומלואה וגו' י וכשמסלקין אותו אומרים ג השמים שמים לה' והארץ נתן לבני אדם אמרתי לו בני במה זכית לכך אמר לי קצב הייתי ומכל בהמה שהיתה נאה אמרתי זו תהא לשבת אמרתי לו [אשריך שזכית] וברוך המקום שזיכך לכך א"ל קיסר לרבי יהושע בן חנניא מפני מה תבשיל של שבת ריחו נודף אמר לו תבלין אחד יש לנו ושבת שמו שאנו מטילין לתוכו וריחו נודף אמר לו תן לנו הימנו אמר לו כל המשמר את השבת מועיל לו ושאינו משמר את השבת אינו מועיל לו א"ל ריש גלותא לרב המנונא מאי דכתיב ד ולקדוש ה' מכובד א"ל ד זה יוה"כ שאין בו לא אכילה ולא שתיה אמרה תורה כבדהו בכסות נקיה ה) ה וכבדתו רב אמר להקדים ושמואל אמר לאחר אמרו ליה בני רב פפא בר אבא לרב פפא כגון אנן דשכיח לן בישרא וחמרא כל יומא במאי נישנייה אמר להו אי רגיליתו לאקדומי אחרוה אי רגיליתו לאחרוה אקדמוה רב ששת בקיטא מותיב להו לרבנן היכא דמטיא שימשא בסיתוא מותיב להו לרבנן היכא דמטיא טולא כי היכי דליקומו הייא ר' זירא

מהדר

תוספות

בתליסר עיליתא דדינרי. אומר ר"ת דעיליתא שם כלי הוא כדאמרינן בריש כילד מעברין (עירובין דף נג:) עלת נקפת בכדה ל:

רב אמר להקדים ושמואל אמר לאחר. ולא פליגי אלא רב איירי בדרכו לאחר ושמואל איירי בדרכו להקדים כדאמרינן בסמוך

ומלא

רש"י

עבידנא יומא טבא לרבנן. לתלמידים ראש ישיבה היה: **תיתי לי.** ישולם שכרי: **דכי אתי צורבא מרבנן כו'.** שחיבת תלמידי חכמים עלי: **דלא מזיגנא רישא אבי סדיא.** איני מניח ראשי על הכר: **כמה דלא מהפיכנא ליה בזכותיה.** עד שאראה אם יש בדבריו לזכותו: **מתעטף.** בבגדים נאים: **בואי כלה.** הכי קרי ליה לשביתת שבת מתוך חביבות: **טחיי.** רקיקין טחין פניהן בשומן אליה או בשמן: **מי עדיפת לן מינה.** כלום אתה חשוב לנו מן השבת לכבוד שבת הכנוס ולא היינו יודעים שתבא: **מתליסר טבחי.** לטעום בשבת מן המובחר: **איסתירי.** סלעים איסתירי פשיטי סלעים מדינ' והן א' מח' בסלע צורי והיינו חצי דינר: **ומשלים להו אצינורא דדשא.** לפני בואם להביא לו הבשר היה מזמן להן מעותיהן על פתחן ואומר להן אשור הייא התאשרו והתחזקו מהר באומנותיכם למהר ולחזור ולמכור ולהתעסק בצרכי שבת ולי נראה ומשלים להו אצינורא דדשא כשהיה מביא ראשונה היה נותנה לשמשין המכינים סעודתו על פתח ביתו ולא היה נכנס אלא ממהר לחזור ולהביא אחרת ואמר להן לשמשין אשור הייא התאשרו מהר להכין את זו בעוד שאלך להביא את זו: **אתכתקא דשינא.** פסטדו"ל של שן שחשוב היה ועשיר: **ומושיף נורא.** נופח משם נורא לכבוד השבת ורבינו לוי גרס אתכתקא דשאגא תדהר: **לביש גונדא.** כלי שחור להודיע שהיום אינו כדי להתנהג בחשיבות מלהתעסק בתבשילי שבת ולא יטנף בגדיו בבישול קדירות: **דתנא דבי רבי ישמעאל כו'.** דבישול קדירה מטנף בגדים: **מחריך רישא.** אם היה שם ראש בהמה לחרוך מחרכו הוא בעצמו: **פרים.** לשון פרומים מחתך: **מצתת צתותי.** מצית האור בעצים דקים: **מכתף ועייל מכתף ונפיק.** בע"ש יוצא ונכנס להביא תמיד משואות כלי תשמיש ובגדי חופש ומגדים כאדם שמקבל את רבו בביתו ומראה לו שהוא חשוב עליו וחרד לכבודו לטרוח ולהרבות בשבילו: **מוקר שבי.** מכבד שבתות: **אמרי ליה כלדאי.** להאי נכרי: **כלדאי.** חוזים בכוכבים: **אכיל להו.** סופן ליפול בידו: **אותבה בסייניה.** עשה לו כובע של לבד ושבצו במשבצות של זהב וקבע בו מרגליות וקבע את זו עמהם: **סייניה.** כובע. ורבינו הלוי גרס בסדיניה בסודרו ולשון הגון לי והוא לשון ר' יצחק ב"ר יהודה: **תריסר עיליתי דדינרי.** עליות מלאות דינרי זהב ° וגוזמא בעלמא הוא כלומר הון עתק מאד כך פירש רבינו הלוי וכן בכל מקום כגון תליסר גמלי ספיקי טריפתא (חולין דף נה:) וכן תליסר טבחי דלעיל: **במה הן זוכין.** לעושר גדול כזה: **לה' הארץ.** דאין אנו רשאין ליהנות עד שנברך שמו בברכת הלחם: **והארץ נתן לבני אדם.** ע"י מתנתו נהנינו הטובה הזאת: **מאי דכתיב ולקדוש ה' מכובד.** מדכתיב וקראת לשבת עונג מכלל דלקדוש ה' לאו אשבת קאי: **וכבדתו.** אשבת מהדר דאי ביוה"כ הא כתיב ביה מכובד: **להקדים.** זמן סעודת שבת לזמן סעודת חול וזהו כבודו: **לאחר.** וזהו כבודו שהוא מתאוה לאכול: **במאי נשנייה.** במאי נשניוהו משאר ימים: **אי רגיליתו לאקדומי.** סעודתכם בבקר אחרוה: **רב ששת** סגי נהור היה ואינו רואה עת האכילה וכשהיה דורש בשבת מושיב התלמידים במקום שמגיע שם החמה לעת האוכל כדי שיצטערו וימהרו לקום: **דמטי טולא.** שיצטננו: **הייא.** מהר:

מהדר

מסורת הש"ס

א) [כתובות קה:], ב) כ"ק לב. ע"ש, ג) נ"א מעיילי ולמבסבי, ד) [חולין קיא.], ה) [נ"א דכתיב וקראת לשבת עונג רבי אבא וכו' וכ"ה בחולין קיא.], ו) פי' מהר וכ"כ בסוף עמוד זה, ז) לעיל קיד. [יומא כג:], ח) קדושין מא., ט) תענית ט., י) [עי' תוספות ברכות לה: ד"ה כאן], כ) עי' תוס' שם, ל) [וע"ע תוס' ב"ב קלג: ד"ה עיליתא].

ליקוטי רש"י

... **צורבא מרבנן.** בחור חריף כמו ביעי דצריכן במסכת ביצה (ז.) תלמיד חכם זקן לא קרי צורבא אלא בחור הוא דמיקרי צורבא מרבנן [תענית ד.]. [ע"כ שייך לדף קיח:]. **בי סדיא.** לבדין שקורין פלטר"ש ועשוין לקפלן ממתיו במקום הכר או הכסת [לקמן קמו:]. **אין אדם רואה חובה לעצמו.** אין דעתו ממקרב לצד החובה לחייב את עצמו ואפילו מתכוין לדין אמת [כתובות קה:]. **אפניא.** לפנות ערב [תענית כג:]. **בואו ונצא.** כאדם המקבל פני מלך [ב"ק לב:]. **תלת סאוי טחיי.** שלש סאין פת נקיה פניה טוחין בשמן ודבש [חולין קיא:]. מין עיגון הוא שעושין מלחם וטשין התנור באליה ואופין את הלחם אחר שטחוהו וכמס' שבת נמי אמרינן תלת סאוי טחיי [זבחים צה:]. **מי עדיפת לן מינה.** יום השבת היה [חולין שם]. **בתליסר אסתירי פשיטי.** איסתרי סלעי מדינה שהם פשוטים וקלים איסתרי קמו היינו סלעין צורי שהסלע ארבע דינרים ואיסתרי פשיטי הוא סלע מדינה שמינית שבסלע צורי דהיינו חצי דינר כדאמרינן בהחובל את חבירו (ב"ק לו:) איסתרא פלגא זוזא וקרי ליה התם סלע מדינה [שם מד:]. **צינורא דדשא.** חור שבמפתן וציר הדלת סובב בו [ברכות יח:]. חור מפתן הבית שהדלת סובב בו [כתובות סז:]. **אשור.** כמו אשרתא דדייני (גיטין כו.) וכמו אשרו חמוץ (ישעיה א) לשון חיזוק [גיטין לד.]. **אל ימזוג בהן כוס לרבו.** לפי שנתעטפו ונתלכלכו בבישול קדירה [יומא כג:]. **מחריך רישא.** לכבוד שבת. **שיבוטא.** דג [קידושין מא.]. **סילקא.** תרדין [שבועות כג.]. **ציבי.** עצים [עירובין פב:]. **כוורא.** דג [רשב"ם ב"ב עג:].

עין משפט נר מצוה

מב א טוש"ע או"ח סי' רנ סעיף א:

מג ב מיי' פ"ל מהלכות שבת הלכה ב סמג עשין ל טוש"ע או"ח סי' רנ סעיף ב:

מד ג מיי' שם הלכה ו סמג שם טור ושו"ע או"ח סימן ר"ן סעיף א:

מה ד טוש"ע או"ח סי' רמב סעיף ד:

מו ה מיי' פ"ל שם הל"ה וסמג שם טוש"ע או"ח סימן רפח סעיף ז:

הגהות הב"ח

(א) גמ' לא מזיגנא רישא אבי: (ב) שם לביש מאניה במעלי:

גליון הש"ס

גמ' אשור הייא. גיטין דף לד ע"א: רש"י ד"ה תליסר עיליתא דדינרי וכו' וגוזמא בעלמא. עי' ברכות דף כ ע"א תוס' ד"ה תליסר מתיבתא:

רבינו חננאל

ורבנן הני דעבדי צרכי שבת בנפשייהו. כגון ר' אבהו דהוה [יתיב] (הציב) אתכתקא דשינא ומשייף נורא. ורב חנן דשגר תנורא ורב הונא גדיל פתילתא. ורב חסדא מדליק שרגי ורב פפא פרים סילקי. רבה ורב יוסף צלחי ציבי כולהו כדמפרש בגמרא בריש האיש מקדש. שקיום המצוה באדם עצמו טפי עדיף יותר מבשלוחו: וכבדתו שמשנה זמן סעודתו בהקדמה או באיחור. ויחיד המתפלל בעצמו אומר ויכולו:

תורה אור השלם

א) עַשֵּׂר תְּעַשֵּׂר אֵת כָּל תְּבוּאַת זַרְעֶךָ הַיֹּצֵא הַשָּׂדֶה שָׁנָה שָׁנָה: [דברים יד, כב]

ב) לְדָוִד מִזְמוֹר לַיְיָ הָאָרֶץ וּמְלוֹאָהּ תֵּבֵל וְיֹשְׁבֵי בָהּ: [תהלים כד, א]

ג) הַשָּׁמַיִם שָׁמַיִם לַייָ וְהָאָרֶץ נָתַן לִבְנֵי אָדָם: [תהלים קטו, טז]

ד) אִם תָּשִׁיב מִשַּׁבָּת רַגְלֶךָ עֲשׂוֹת חֲפָצֶךָ בְּיוֹם קָדְשִׁי וְקָרָאתָ לַשַּׁבָּת עֹנֶג לִקְדוֹשׁ יְיָ מְכֻבָּד וְכִבַּדְתּוֹ מֵעֲשׂוֹת דְּרָכֶיךָ מִמְּצוֹא חֶפְצְךָ וְדַבֵּר דָּבָר: [ישעיה נח, יג]

מהדר אזוזי זוזי דרבנן. כשהיה רואה אותן זוגות זוגות ומדברין בתורה מחזר אחריהם ואומר להם במטותא מנכון לכו והתעסקו בעונג שבת ולא תחללוניה לבטל תענוגים: ויכלו. הקב"ה והם שמספר בשבחו של מקום ובשבח של שבת: יסדר אדם שלחנו בע"ש. ללילי שבת: במוצ"ש. נמי כבוד שבת ללוות ביציאתו דרך כבוד כאדם המלוה את המלך בצאתו מן העיר: חמין. לשתות ולרחוץ: מלוגמא. רפואה: אכליה אריא. לעגל הראוי לשחוט: בכל כחו. בכל כוונתו: בפרוע פרעות. ביטול פורעניות כגון פרוע דמתרגמינן בטל: בהתנדב עם ברכו. כשמתנדבין ישראל לברך את בוראן: כי פרוע. כי פרעו אהרן ע"ז והכי קאמר בהבטל פריעות ע"ז שמשתקע ומשתכח שלא יזכר עונש משום התנדב עם הוא: אל מלך נאמן. קן מעיד על בוראו שהוא אל מלך נאמן: שאין בני אדם מצויין לכבותה. בשבת: בבקר. בזמן ק"ש וכן מאחרי בנשף: והיה כנור ונבל. בסיפיה דקרא ואת פועל ה' לא יביטו לא שמו לב ליתן שמו על בריותיו: שפוך על עולל. רישא דקרא ואת חמת ה' נלאיתי הכיל שפוך וגו' שפוך החמה בנקמה בשביל שעולל לחוץ ובטלין מבית רבן: הובישו כי תועבה עשו וגו'. סיפיה דקרא גם בוש לא יבושו וגם הכלם לא כו': במשיחי אלו תינוקות של בית רבן. שלרך תינוקות למושחן בשמן (ט): ובנביאי אלו תלמידי חכמים. שנאמר ונביא לבב חכמה (תהלים צ): מחריבין. מחרימין. ליכא שיור: מתכסין בהן כשמלה. כששואלין אותן טעמי תורה הללו עושין עצמן כמעלימין את דבריהם מפני שאין יודעים להשיב: ישנן בידיך. אתה בקי לפיכך קלין תהיה לנו ותלמדנו חכמה:

ומצא נר דלוק ושלחן ערוך. ול"ה לאמר כריש ערבי פסחים (דף ק:) ושוין שאין מביאין את השלחן אא"כ קידש וי"ל דערוך הוא במקום אחר אלא שאין מביאין אותו עד אחר הקידוש כי היכי דליתי סעודתא ביקרא דשבת כדאיתא בשאלתות דרב אחאי (ג) ודוקא בימיהם שהיו להם שלחנות קטנים לפני כל אחד ואחד אבל שלנו גדולים הם וקשה לטלטלם (ג): כל העונה אמן יהא שמיה רבא בכל כחו. פי' בכל כוונתו וכן פירש ר"י ור"י אומר דיש בפסיקתא במעשה דר' ישמעאל בן אלישע דקאמר השם כשישראל נכנסים לבתי כנסיות ואומרים יהא שמיה רבא מברך בקול רם מבטלים גזירות קשות:

א"ר חנינא אל מלך נאמן. לריך להרהר בו בשעה שאומר אמן:

אידי

מהדר אזוזי זוזי דרבנן א"ל במטותא מינייכו לא תחללוניה אמר (א) רבא ואיתימא ר' יהושע בן לוי אפי' יחיד המתפלל בע"ש צריך לומר ויכולו דאמר רב המנונא כל המתפלל בע"ש ואומר ויכולו מעלה עליו הכתוב כאילו נעשה שותף להקב"ה במעשה בראשית שנאמר א) ויכולו אל תקרי ויכולו (א) אלא ויכלו אמר רבי אלעזר מנין שהדיבור כמעשה שנאמר ב) בדבר ה' שמים נעשו אמר רב חסדא אמר מר עוקבא כל המתפלל בע"ש ואומר ויכולו שני מלאכי השרת המלוין לו לאדם מניחין ידיהן על ראשו ואומרים לו ג) וסר עונך וחטאתך תכופר תניא ר' יוסי בר יהודה אומר שני מלאכי השרת מלוין לו לאדם בע"ש מבית הכנסת לביתו אחד טוב ואחד רע וכשבא לביתו ומצא נר דלוק ושלחן ערוך ומטתו מוצעת מלאך טוב אומר יהי רצון שתהא לשבת אחרת כך ומלאך רע עונה אמן בעל כרחו ואם לאו מלאך רע אומר יהי רצון שתהא לשבת אחרת כך ומלאך טוב עונה אמן בעל כרחו אמר ר' אלעזר לעולם יסדר אדם שלחנו בע"ש אע"פ שאינו צריך אלא לכזית ואמר ר' חנינא לעולם יסדר אדם שלחנו במוצאי שבת אע"פ שאינו צריך אלא לכזית חמין במוצאי שבת מלוגמא פת חמה במוצאי שבת מלוגמא ר' אבהו הוה עבדין ליה באפוקי שבתא עיגלא תילתא הוה אכיל מיניה כולייתא כי גדל אבימי בריה א"ל למה לך לאפסודי כולי האי נשבוק כולייתא ממעלי שבתא שבקוהו ואתא אריא אכליה אריב"ל כל העונה אמן יהא שמיה רבא מברך בכל כחו קורעין לו גזר דינו שנאמר ד) בפרוע פרעות בישראל בהתנדב עם ברכו ה' מ"ט בפרוע פרעות משום דברכו ה' רבי חייא בר אבא א"ר יוחנן אפילו יש בו שמץ של עבודה זרה מוחלין לו כתיב הכא בפרוע פרעות וכתיב התם ה) כי פרוע הוא (ב) אמר ריש לקיש כל העונה אמן בכל כחו פותחין לו שערי ג"ע שנאמר ו) פתחו שערים ויבא גוי צדיק שומר אמונים אל תיקרי שומר אמונים אלא שאומרים אמן מאי אמן א"ר חנינא אל מלך נאמן א"ר יהודה בריה דרב שמואל משמיה דרב אין הדליקה מצויה אלא במקום שיש חילול שבת שנאמר ז) ואם לא תשמעו אלי לקדש את יום השבת ולבלתי שאת משא וגו' והצתי אש בשעריה ואכלה ארמנות ירושלים ולא תכבה מאי ולא תכבה אמר רב נחמן בר יצחק בשעה שאין בני אדם מצויין לכבותה אמר אביי לא חרבה ירושלים אלא בשביל שחללו בה את השבת שנאמר ח) ומשבתותי העלימו עיניהם ואחל בתוכם אמר ר' אבהו לא חרבה ירושלים אלא בשביל שביטלו ק"ש שחרית וערבית שנאמר ט) הוי משכימי בבקר שכר ירדפו וגו' וכתיב י) והיה כנור ונבל תוף וחליל ויין משתיהם ואת פועל ה' לא יביטו וכתיב כ) לכן גלה עמי מבלי דעת אמר רב המנונא לא חרבה ירושלים אלא בשביל שביטלו בה תינוקות של בית רבן שנאמר ל) שפוך על עולל בחוץ וגו' מה טעם שפוך משום דעולל בחוץ אמר עולא לא חרבה ירושלים אלא מפני שלא היה להם בושת פנים זה מזה שנאמר מ) הובישו כי תועבה עשו גם בוש לא יבושו וגו' אמר ר' יצחק לא חרבה ירושלים אלא בשביל שהושוו קטן וגדול שנאמר נ) והיה כעם ככהן וכתיב בתריה ס) הבוק תבוק הארץ אמר רב עמרם בריה דר"ש בר אבא א"ר שמעון בר אבא א"ר חנינא לא חרבה ירושלים אלא בשביל שלא הוכיחו זה את זה שנאמר ע) היו שריה כאילים לא מצאו מרעה מה איל זה ראשו של זה בצד זנבו של זה אף ישראל שבאותו הדור כבשו פניהם בקרקע ולא הוכיחו זה את זה א"ר יהודה לא חרבה ירושלים אלא בשביל שביזו בה ת"ח שנאמר פ) ויהיו מלעיבים במלאכי האלהים ובוזים דבריו ומתעתעים בנביאיו עד עלות חמת ה' בעמו עד [ל]אין מרפא מאי עד לאין מרפא אמר רב יהודה אמר רב כל המבזה ת"ח אין לו רפואה למכתו אמר רב יהודה אמר רב מאי דכתיב צ) אל תגעו במשיחי ובנביאי אל תרעו אל תגעו במשיחי אלו תינוקות של בית רבן ובנביאי אל תרעו אלו ת"ח אמר ריש לקיש משום רבי יהודה נשיאה אין העולם מתקיים אלא בשביל הבל תינוקות של בית רבן א"ל רב פפא לאביי דידי ודידך מאי א"ל אינו דומה הבל שיש בו חטא להבל שאין בו חטא ואמר ריש לקיש משום ר"י נשיאה אין מבטלין תינוקות של בית רבן אפי' לבנין בית המקדש ואמר ר"ל לר"י נשיאה כך מקובלני מאבותי ואמרי לה מאבותיך כל עיר שאין בה תינוקות של בית רבן מחריבין אותה רבינא אמר מחרימין אותה ואמר רבא לא חרבה ירושלים אלא בשביל שפסקו ממנה אנשי אמנה שנאמר ק) שוטטו בחוצות ירושלים וראו נא [ודעו ובקשו ברחובותיה אם תמצאו איש] (אם יש איש) עושה משפט מבקש אמונה ואסלח לה איני והאמר רב קטינא אפי' בשעת כשלונה של ירושלים לא פסקו ממנה אנשי אמנה שנאמר ר) כי יתפש איש באחיו בית אביו (לאמר) שמלה לכה קצין תהיה לנו דברים שבני אדם מתכסין בהן כשמלה ישנן בידיך והמכשלה הזאת תחת ידך

דברים

עין משפט נר מצוה

מז א מיי' פכ"ט מהל' שבת הלכה ז סמג עשין ל טוש"ע או"ח סי' רסח סעיף א:

מח ב מיי' פ"ל שם הל' ה סמג שם טור שו"ע או"ח סימן רצב סעיף א:

מט ג מיי' שם הלכה ה וסמג שם:

נ ד מיי' וסמג שם טור שו"ע או"ח סימן נו:

נא ה מיי' פ"ט מהלכות תפלה הלכה א טוש"ע או"ח סימן נו סעיף א [וברב אלפס ברכות פ"ג דף ט"ו: וברא"ש שם סימן יט]:

נב ו מיי' פ"ו מהלכות ת"ת הלכה יא טור שו"ע יו"ד סימן רמג סעיף ז:

נג ז מיי' פ"ב שם הל"ב טוש"ע יו"ד סי' רמה סעיף יג [וברב אלפס פ"ב דב"ב דף קסג: וברא"ש פ"ג דמו"ק סי' פ"א]:

נד ח מיי' שם הלכה א טוש"ע שם סעיף ז [וברב אלפס שם]:

ליקוטי רש"י

עיגלא תילתא. שליטי לבטן שהוא משובח מפני שהבהמה בקטנותה אינה עדיין בכחה והולד ראשון ושני אינו בריא [לעיל יא.]. גדל שליש ואז הוא עומד בעיקר טעם בשרו כדתנן (ב"מ סח.) ומגדלין אותן עד שיהו משולשין ואמרינן נמי (שם סט.) מותר שליש בשכרך אלמא אורחיה עד שליש לישנא אחרינא שליטי לבטן וקשה לי הא דאמר בעלמא (סנהדרין סה:) רב חנינא ורב אושעיא הוו עסקי בספר יצירה וכל מעלי שבתא איברי להו עגלא תילתא דהתם מאי שליטי לבטן איכא הא לא היה בבטן מעולם [עירובין סג.]. שליטי לבטן ומובחר הוא [פסחים סח: ע"ש במסוה"ש]. הגיע לשליש שניו וגמרה גדילתו דהכי שכיחי ומעלי למיכל כמו (ב"מ סח.) ומגדלין אותן עד שיהו משולשין לישנא אחרינא שהיה טוב ובעל טעם [שליטי] לבטן [סנהדרין סה: ע"ש]. שומר אמונים. ששמר ולפה בגלותו ימים רבים לאמונתו של הקב"ה שיקיים הבטחתו שהבטיח ע"פ נביאיו לגאלם. שומר. ממתין וכן (בראשית לז) ואביו שמר את הדבר וכן (דברים ז) ושמר ה' אלהיך לך [ישעיה כו, ב]. מאי אמן. כשעונין על כל ברכה וברכה אמן היאך משמע קבלת יראת שמים. אל מלך נאמן. בנוטריקון שמאמין עליו הקב"ה [סנהדרין קיא.]. כנור ונבל. נימין יתרות יש בנבל מן הכנור ולמה נקרא שמו נבל שמנבל כל מיני כלי זמר במדרש תהלים. תוף. של עור הוא. וחליל. אבוב של קנה (בלעז"ל בלע"ז) [ישעיה ה, יב]. מבלי דעת. לפי שהיה לנס בלי דעת [שם, יג]. הובישו. עליהן למיכתם. גם בוש לא יבושו. אינם מתביישין ממעשיהם הרעים [ירמיה ו, טו]. הבוק תבוק. תתרוקן [ישעיה כד, ג]. כי יתפש איש באחיו. כאשר יתפוש איש באחיו בבית אביו לאמר עשיר אתה בתורה [ישעיה ג, ו]. באנשי ירושלים שפסקה תורה מהם והיו שואלין לחבריהם שמלה לך קלין היה לנו והמכשלה הזאת תחת ידיך [גיטין מג.]. הכתוב היה מגנן לומר שלא היו יודעין להשיב לשואלים הלכה. שבני אדם מתכסין בהן. נמכאין שלא ישאלו להן לפי שאין בקיאין בהן. ישנן בידך. כלומר אתה בקי בהן [חגיגה יד.].

מסורת הש"ס

א) [בהרא"ש וטור סי' רסח איתא אמר רב וכו' ואמר רב המנונא כל המתפלל וכו' וכ"א בשאלתות בראשית סי' א], ב) סנהדרין דף קי., ג) [סנהדרין דף קיא:], ד) [פי' מתרוקן], ה) חגיגה יד., ו) [חגיגה שם. גיטין מג.], ז) [חגיגה דף יד.], ח) [כדאיתא לעיל דף י:], ט) [פרשת יתרו סימן נד], י) [וע"ע תוס' פסחים ק: ד"ה שאין].

הגהות הב"ח

(א) גמ' אל תיקרי ויכלו אלא ויכלו: (ב) שם כי פרוע הוא כי פרעו אהרן אמר ריש לקיש: (ג) תוס' ד"ה ומלא וכו' וקשה לטלטלם. נ"ב פי' אחר קידוש שלא להפסיק כל כך בין קידוש לסעודה אנו רגילין לפרוס מפה ולקדש:

גליון הש"ס

גמ' שנאמר ויהיו מלעיבים במלאכי האלהים. ע"ד שאמו"ל נדרים דף כ ע"ב מאן מה"ש רבנן: שם כך מקובלני מאבותי. עיין ב"מ דף פד ע"א ד"ה אי הדרת:

תורה אור השלם

א) וַיְכֻלּוּ הַשָּׁמַיִם וְהָאָרֶץ וְכָל צְבָאָם: [בראשית ב, א]

ב) בִּדְבַר יְיָ שָׁמַיִם נַעֲשׂוּ וּבְרוּחַ פִּיו כָּל צְבָאָם: [תהלים לג, ו]

ג) וַיַּגַּע עַל פִּי וַיֹּאמֶר הִנֵּה נָגַע זֶה עַל שְׂפָתֶיךָ וְסָר עֲוֹנֶךָ וְחַטָּאתְךָ תְּכֻפָּר: [ישעיה ו, ז]

ד) בִּפְרֹעַ פְּרָעוֹת בְּיִשְׂרָאֵל בְּהִתְנַדֵּב עָם בָּרְכוּ יְיָ: [שופטים ה, ב]

ה) וַיַּרְא מֹשֶׁה אֶת הָעָם כִּי פָרֻעַ הוּא כִּי פְרָעֹה אַהֲרֹן לְשִׁמְצָה בְּקָמֵיהֶם: [שמות לב, כה]

ו) פִּתְחוּ שְׁעָרִים וְיָבֹא גוֹי צַדִּיק שֹׁמֵר אֱמֻנִים: [ישעיה כו, ב]

ז) וְאִם לֹא תִשְׁמְעוּ אֵלַי לְקַדֵּשׁ אֶת יוֹם הַשַּׁבָּת וּלְבִלְתִּי שְׂאֵת מַשָּׂא וּבֹא בְּשַׁעֲרֵי יְרוּשָׁלָיִם בְּיוֹם הַשַּׁבָּת וְהִצַּתִּי אֵשׁ בִּשְׁעָרֶיהָ וְאָכְלָה אַרְמְנוֹת יְרוּשָׁלַיִם וְלֹא תִכְבֶּה: [ירמיה יז, כז]

ח) כֹּהֲנֶיהָ חָמְסוּ תוֹרָתִי וַיְחַלְּלוּ קָדָשַׁי בֵּין קֹדֶשׁ לְחֹל לֹא הִבְדִּילוּ וּבֵין הַטָּמֵא לְטָהוֹר לֹא הוֹדִיעוּ וּמִשַּׁבְּתוֹתַי הֶעְלִימוּ עֵינֵיהֶם וָאֵחַל בְּתוֹכָם: [יחזקאל כב, כו]

ט) הוֹי מַשְׁכִּימֵי בַבֹּקֶר שֵׁכָר יִרְדֹּפוּ מְאַחֲרֵי בַנֶּשֶׁף יַיִן יַדְלִיקֵם: [ישעיה ה, יא]

י) וְהָיָה כִנּוֹר וָנֶבֶל תֹּף וְחָלִיל וָיַיִן מִשְׁתֵּיהֶם וְאֵת פֹּעַל יְיָ לֹא יַבִּיטוּ וּמַעֲשֵׂה יָדָיו לֹא רָאוּ: [ישעיה ה, יב]

כ) לָכֵן גָּלָה עַמִּי מִבְּלִי דָעַת וּכְבוֹדוֹ מְתֵי רָעָב וַהֲמוֹנוֹ צִחֵה צָמָא: [ישעיה ה, יג] ל) וְאֶת חֲמַת יְיָ מָלֵאתִי נִלְאֵיתִי הָכִיל שְׁפֹךְ עַל עוֹלָל בַּחוּץ וְעַל סוֹד בַּחוּרִים יַחְדָּו כִּי גַם אִישׁ עִם אִשָּׁה יִלָּכֵדוּ זָקֵן עִם מְלֵא יָמִים: [ירמיה ו, יא] מ) הֹבִישׁוּ כִּי תוֹעֵבָה עָשׂוּ גַּם בּוֹשׁ לֹא יֵבוֹשׁוּ גַּם הַכְלִים לֹא יָדָעוּ לָכֵן יִפְּלוּ בַנֹּפְלִים בְּעֵת פְּקַדְתִּים יִכָּשְׁלוּ אָמַר יְיָ: [ירמיה ו, טו] נ) וְהָיָה כָעָם כַּכֹּהֵן כַּעֶבֶד כַּאדֹנָיו כַּשִּׁפְחָה כַּגְּבִרְתָּהּ כַּקּוֹנֶה כַּמּוֹכֵר כַּמַּלְוֶה כַּלֹּוֶה כַּנֹּשֶׁה כַּאֲשֶׁר נֹשֵׁא בוֹ: [ישעיה כד, ב] ס) הִבּוֹק תִּבּוֹק הָאָרֶץ וְהִבּוֹז תִּבּוֹז כִּי יְיָ דִּבֶּר אֶת הַדָּבָר הַזֶּה: [ישעיה כד, ג] ע) וַיֵּצֵא מִבַּת צִיּוֹן כָּל הֲדָרָהּ הָיוּ שָׂרֶיהָ כְּאַיָּלִים לֹא מָצְאוּ מִרְעֶה וַיֵּלְכוּ בְלֹא כֹחַ לִפְנֵי רוֹדֵף: [איכה א, ו] פ) וַיִּהְיוּ מַלְעִבִים בְּמַלְאֲכֵי הָאֱלֹהִים וּבוֹזִים דְּבָרָיו וּמִתַּעְתְּעִים בִּנְבִאָיו עַד עֲלוֹת חֲמַת יְיָ בְּעַמּוֹ עַד לְאֵין מַרְפֵּא: [דברי הימים ב' לו, טז] צ) אַל תִּגְּעוּ בִּמְשִׁיחָי וּבִנְבִיאַי אַל תָּרֵעוּ: [דברי הימים א' טז, כב] ק) שׁוֹטְטוּ בְּחוּצוֹת יְרוּשָׁלַיִם וּרְאוּ נָא וּדְעוּ וּבַקְשׁוּ בִרְחוֹבוֹתֶיהָ אִם תִּמְצְאוּ אִישׁ אִם יֵשׁ עֹשֶׂה מִשְׁפָּט מְבַקֵּשׁ אֱמוּנָה וְאֶסְלַח לָהּ: [ירמיה ה, א] ר) כִּי יִתְפֹּשׂ אִישׁ בְּאָחִיו בֵּית אָבִיו שִׂמְלָה לְכָה קָצִין תִּהְיֶה לָּנוּ וְהַמַּכְשֵׁלָה הַזֹּאת תַּחַת יָדֶךָ: [ישעיה ג, ו]

מְהַדַּר אַזּוּזֵי זוּזֵי דְּרַבָּנָן – would go after the pairs of rabbis standing together on the Sabbath day engrossed in Torah discussions אָמַר לְהוּ בְּמָטוּתָא מִינַּיְיכוּ לֹא תְחַלְּלוּנֵיהּ – and say to them, "Please, do not desecrate [the Sabbath] by abstaining from its delights."[1]

The Gemara proceeds to a discussion of the Friday night prayers:

אָמַר רָבָא וְאִיתֵימָא רַבִּי יְהוֹשֻׁעַ בֶּן לֵוִי – Rava said, and some say it was R' Yehoshua ben Levi who said this: אֲפִילוּ יָחִיד הַמִּתְפַּלֵּל בְּעֶרֶב שַׁבָּת צָרִיךְ לוֹמַר ,,וַיְכֻלּוּ" – Even an individual who prays on the eve of the Sabbath must say *Vayechulu;*[2] דְּאָמַר רַב הַמְנוּנָא – for Rav Hamnuna said: כֹּל הַמִּתְפַּלֵּל בְּעֶרֶב שַׁבָּת וְאוֹמֵר ,,וַיְכֻלּוּ" – Whoever prays on the eve of the Sabbath and says *Vayechulu,* מַעֲלֶה עָלָיו הַכָּתוּב כְּאִילוּ נַעֲשָׂה שׁוּתָּף לְהַקָּדוֹשׁ בָּרוּךְ הוּא בְּמַעֲשֵׂה בְרֵאשִׁית – Scripture treats him as if he had become a partner to the Holy One, Blessed is He, in the act of Creation, שֶׁנֶּאֱמַר ,,וַיְכֻלּוּ" – as [the verse] states: *Vayechulu* (*and they* – the heaven and the earth – *were finished*). אַל תִּקְרֵי ,,וַיְכֻלּוּ" אֶלָּא וַיְכַלּוּ – Do not read this as *Vayechulu* (*and they were finished*) but as *Vayechalu* (*and they* – the Creator and the reciter – *finished*).[3]

Although the reciter has not performed any physical deed, his declaration of *Vayechulu* is considered tantamount to an *act* of creation, as the Gemara now teaches:[4]

אָמַר רַבִּי אֶלְעָזָר – R' Elazar said: מִנַּיִין שֶׁהַדִּיבּוּר כְּמַעֲשֶׂה – From where do we know that speech is considered like action? שֶׁנֶּאֱמַר ,,בִּדְבַר ה' שָׁמַיִם נַעֲשׂוּ" – For [the verse] states: ***By the word of Hashem the heavens were made,*** *and by the breath of His mouth all their legions.*[5]

Another statement concerning the importance of saying *Vayechulu* Friday night:

אָמַר רַב חִסְדָּא אָמַר מָר עוּקְבָא – Rav Chisda said in the name of Mar Ukva: כֹּל הַמִּתְפַּלֵּל בְּעֶרֶב שַׁבָּת וְאוֹמֵר ,,וַיְכֻלּוּ" – Whoever prays on the eve of the Sabbath and says *Vayechulu,* שְׁנֵי מַלְאֲכֵי הַשָּׁרֵת הַמְלַוִּין לוֹ לָאָדָם – the two ministering angels that escort a person home on the Sabbath eve[6] מַנִּיחִין יְדֵיהֶן עַל רֹאשׁוֹ וְאוֹמְרִים לוֹ – place their hands on his head and say to him: ,,וְסָר עֲוֹנֶךָ וְחַטָּאתְךָ תְּכֻפָּר" – ***And your iniquity will depart and your sin will be atoned.***[7]

The importance of having one's home properly prepared for the Sabbath:

תַּנְיָא – A Baraisa has taught: רַבִּי יוֹסֵי בַּר יְהוּדָה אוֹמֵר – R' YOSE BAR YEHUDAH SAYS: שְׁנֵי מַלְאֲכֵי הַשָּׁרֵת מְלַוִּין לוֹ לָאָדָם בְּעֶרֶב שַׁבָּת מִבֵּית הַכְּנֶסֶת לְבֵיתוֹ – TWO MINISTERING ANGELS ESCORT A PERSON FROM THE SYNAGOGUE TO HIS HOME ON THE EVE OF THE SABBATH, אֶחָד טוֹב וְאֶחָד רַע – ONE a GOOD angel AND ONE a BAD angel. וּכְשֶׁבָּא לְבֵיתוֹ וּמָצָא נֵר דָּלוּק וְשֻׁלְחָן עָרוּךְ וּמִטָּתוֹ מוּצַּעַת – AND WHEN HE COMES TO HIS HOME AND FINDS THE LAMP BURNING, THE TABLE SET AND HIS BED MADE, מַלְאָךְ טוֹב אוֹמֵר יְהִי רָצוֹן שֶׁתְּהֵא לְשַׁבָּת אַחֶרֶת כָּךְ – THE GOOD ANGEL SAYS, "MAY IT BE THE WILL of God THAT IT SHOULD BE THIS WAY THE NEXT SABBATH as well," וּמַלְאָךְ רַע עוֹנֶה אָמֵן בְּעַל כָּרְחוֹ – AND THE BAD ANGEL is forced to ANSWER "AMEN" AGAINST HIS WILL. וְאִם לָאו – BUT IF one comes home and the house is NOT set for the Sabbath, מַלְאָךְ רַע אוֹמֵר יְהִי רָצוֹן שֶׁתְּהֵא לְשַׁבָּת אַחֶרֶת כָּךְ – THE BAD ANGEL SAYS, "MAY IT BE THE WILL of God THAT IT SHOULD BE THIS WAY THE NEXT SABBATH as well," וּמַלְאָךְ טוֹב עוֹנֶה אָמֵן בְּעַל כָּרְחוֹ – AND THE GOOD ANGEL is forced to ANSWER "AMEN" AGAINST HIS WILL.[8]

NOTES

1. [Since there is a requirement to enjoy the Sabbath with special foods, one who abstains from these enjoyments – even for the purpose of engaging in Torah discussions – has desecrated this aspect of the Sabbath law. Naturally, this does not mean that one should engage all day in feasting. Rather, R' Zeira, like Rav Sheishess in the previous story, wished to ensure that when the time came to eat the Sabbath meal, the rabbis would not tarry in the study hall but return home to enjoy the meal.]

Rif (above, fol. 5a) and *Rosh* (1:24) cite the *Yerushalmi* that rules that one may not delay eating on the Sabbath past noon – even for the purpose of studying Torah or praying (see also *Shulchan Aruch, Orach Chaim* 288:1). *Beis Yosef* (ibid.) also cites (from *Yerushalmi* and *Midrash Tanchuma*) that Torah scholars, who devote their entire week to the intensive study of Torah, should spend proportionally more of their Sabbath eating and enjoying the day. Those who work a whole week, however, should devote most of their Sabbath day to the study of Torah. *Bach* there (ד"ה ר' זירא הוה מהדר) disputes this and rules that it is proper even for Torah scholars to spend most of their day studying Torah (see *Derishah* there §2). [It is certainly improper for people to arrange to have their Sabbath meal during the time set for the Torah lecture. Indeed, doing so is one of the things that causes people to lose their wealth, as the Gemara states in *Gittin* (38b).]

2. The Biblical passage that begins: ,,וַיְכֻלּוּ הַשָּׁמַיִם וְהָאָרֶץ וְכָל־צְבָאָם, *And the heavens and the earth were finished, and all their legions* (*Genesis* 2:1-3). Even when one prays alone he should say this passage in the *Amidah* of Friday night (*Tur, Orach Chaim* 268; see next note). [Although it is also the custom to repeat *Vayechulu* after the conclusion of the *Amidah,* this was instituted to provide for the recitation of *Vayechulu* on a Sabbath that coincides with Yom Tov, when *Vayechulu* is not said in the *Amidah* (*Tur* ibid. from *Tosafos, Pesachim* 106a ד"ה זוכרהו על היין). This is not the recitation to which Rav Hamnuna refers (cf. *Ritva MHK* ed.; *Meiri*).]

3. He who tells the praises of the Creator and the praises of the Sabbath is likened to one who contributed to the Creation of the world (*Rashi*). The purpose of the Sabbath is to attest to God's Creation of the world. But testimony requires witnesses, and until there are people to stand up and proclaim the testimony to the world, the purpose of the Sabbath, and indeed of Creation itself, have not been fulfilled. Therefore, one who recites *Vayechulu* and testifies aloud that God is the Creator is deemed a "partner" in Creation (*Maharsha*).

Rava adds that even when a person prays alone on Friday night, he should still recite *Vayechulu.* Although the testimony of an individual is not generally effective (since Torah law requires the testimony of two witnesses for most matters), he should still say *Vayechulu,* because even his incomplete testimony suffices to qualify him as a partner in the purpose of Creation (*Maharsha*).

[The expression אַל תִּקְרֵי, *do not read,* is not intended as an emendation of the text but simply as a homiletic device. Since the word is written in the Torah without vowels, it can be expounded homiletically according to a vowelization that differs from the traditional reading.]

4. See *Maharsha.*

5. *Psalms* 33:6. [For the heavens were *made* (an action) by the *word* (speech) of Hashem.] Since God Himself created the world simply through speech, an individual's declaration is also considered significant enough to accord him the status of a "partner" in Creation.

6. See Baraisa below.

7. *Isaiah* 6:7. The Torah states concerning one who withholds testimony that he has been called upon to give (*Leviticus* 5:1): *And he shall bear his sin.* Thus, when a person fulfills his obligation to attest to God's Creation of the world, the angel tells him, *And your iniquity will depart,* etc. (*Ritva MHK* ed. quoting *R' Yechiel*).

8. Two angels are assigned to a person for every mitzvah that comes his way, one to become his defender ("good angel") in the Heavenly Court should he perform the mitzvah, and one to serve as his prosecutor ("bad angel") should he fail to perform it (*Maharsha*).

The performance or non-performance of the mitzvah, however, has ramifications beyond the tally of the particular deed. Performing the mitzvah properly strengthens a person's hand to continue performing the mitzvah and weakens the *yetzer hara's* resistance to future performances of this mitzvah. Thus, the "good angel" blesses the person that his home be suitably prepared to greet the Sabbath the following week and even the "bad angel" is forced to answer "Amen." By the same token, failure to perform the mitzvah properly weakens the person's resolve to perform it properly the next time and strengthens the *yetzer hara's* resistance to it. Thus, if he fails to prepare

עין משפט
נר מצוה

מז א מיי' פכ"ט מהל' שבת הלכה ז סמג עשין ל טוש"ע או"ח סי' רסח סעיף א:
מח ב מיי' פ"ל שם הל' ה סמג שם טור שו"ע או"ח סימן רסב סעיף א:
מט ג מיי' שם הלכה ה וסמג שם:
נ ד מיי' וסמג שם טור שו"ע או"ח סימן ש:
נא ה מיי' פ"ט מהלכות תפלה הלכה א טוש"ע או"ח סימן נו סעיף א [וברב אלפס ברכות פ"ג דף ט"ו: וברא"ש שם סימן יט]:
נב ו מיי' פ"ו מהלכות ת"ת הלכה יא טור שו"ע יו"ד סימן רמג סעיף ז:
נג ז מיי' פ"ב שם הל"ב טוש"ע יו"ד סי' רמה סעיף יג [וברב אלפס פ"ב דב"ב דף קסג: וברא"ש פ"ג דמו"ק סי' פ"א]:
נד ח מיי' שם הלכה א טוש"ע שם סעיף ז [וברב אלפס שם]:

מסורת הש"ס

א) [בה"ג ובטור סי' רסח איתא אמר רב וכו' ואמר רב המנונא כל המתפלל וכו' וכ"ה בשאלתות פרשת בראשית סי' א], ב) סנהדרין דף קי:, ג) [סנהדרין דף קיא.], ד) [פי' פתרונות], ה) חגיגה יד., ו) [חגיגה דף יד., גיטין מג.], ז) [חגיגה דף יד.], ח) [כתובות לעיל דף י:], ט) [פרשת יתרו סימן נד], י) [וע"ע תוס' פסחים ק: ד"ה שאין].

מהדר אזוזי זוזי דרבנן א"ל במטותא מינייכו לא תחללוניה אמר [א] רבא ואיתימא ר' יהושע בן לוי [א]אפי' יחיד המתפלל בע"ש צריך לומר ויכולו דאמר רב המנונא כל המתפלל בע"ש ואומר ויכולו מעלה עליו הכתוב כאילו נעשה שותף להקב"ה במעשה בראשית שנאמר [א] ויכולו אל תקרי ויכולו (א) אלא ויכלו אמר רבי אלעזר מניין שהדיבור כמעשה שנאמר [ב] בדבר ה' שמים נעשו אמר רב חסדא אמר מר עוקבא כל המתפלל בע"ש ואומר ויכולו שני מלאכי השרת המלוין לו לאדם מניחין ידיהן על ראשו ואומרים לו [ג] וסר עונך וחטאתך תכופר תניא ר' יוסי בר יהודה אומר שני מלאכי השרת מלוין לו לאדם בע"ש מבית הכנסת לביתו אחד טוב ואחד רע [ב]וכשבא לביתו ומצא נר דלוק ושלחן ערוך ומטתו מוצעת מלאך טוב אומר יהי רצון שתהא לשבת אחרת כך ומלאך רע עונה אמן בעל כרחו ואם לאו מלאך רע אומר יהי רצון שתהא לשבת אחרת כך ומלאך טוב עונה אמן בעל כרחו אמר ר' אלעזר [ג]לעולם יסדר אדם שלחנו בע"ש אע"פ שאינו צריך אלא לכזית ואמר ר' חנינא [ד]לעולם יסדר אדם שלחנו במוצאי שבת אע"פ שאינו צריך אלא לכזית חמין במוצאי שבת מלוגמא פת חמה במוצאי שבת מלוגמא ר' אבהו הוה עבדין ליה באפוקי שבתא עיגלא תילתא הוה אכיל מיניה כוליתא כי גדל אבימי בריה א"ל למה לך לאפסודי כולי האי נשבוק כוליתא ממעלי שבתא שבקוהו ואתא אריא אכליה אריב"ל [ה]כל העונה אמן יהא שמיה רבא מברך בכל כחו קורעין לו גזר דינו שנאמר [ד] בפרוע פרעות בישראל בהתנדב עם ברכו ה' מ"ט בפרוע פרעות משום דברכו ה' רבי חייא בר אבא א"ר יוחנן אפילו יש בו שמץ של עבודה זרה מוחלין לו כתיב הכא בפרוע פרעות וכתיב התם [ה] כי פרוע הוא (ב) אמר ריש לקיש כל העונה אמן בכל כחו פותחין לו שערי ג"ע שנאמר [ו] פתחו שערים ויבא גוי צדיק שומר אמונים [ו]אל תיקרי שומר אמונים אלא שאומרים אמן [ז]מאי אמן א"ר חנינא אל מלך נאמן א"ר יהודה בריה דרב שמואל משמיה דרב אין הדליקה מצויה אלא במקום שיש חילול שבת שנאמר [ז] ואם לא תשמעו אלי לקדש את יום השבת ולבלתי שאת משא וגו' והצתי אש בשעריה ואכלה ארמנות ירושלים ולא תכבה מאי ולא תכבה אמר רב נחמן בר יצחק בשעה שאין בני אדם מצויין לכבותה אמר אביי לא חרבה ירושלים אלא בשביל שחללו בה את השבת שנאמר [ח] ומשבתותי העלימו עיניהם ואחל בתוכם אמר ר' אבהו לא חרבה ירושלים אלא בשביל שביטלו ק"ש שחרית וערבית שנאמר [ט] הוי משכימי בבקר שכר ירדפו וגו' וכתיב [י] והיה כנור ונבל תוף וחליל ויין משתיהם ואת פועל ה' לא יביטו וכתיב [כ] לכן גלה עמי מבלי דעת אמר רב המנונא לא חרבה ירושלים אלא בשביל שביטלו בה תינוקות של בית רבן שנאמר [ל] שפוך על עולל בחוץ וגו' מה טעם שפוך משום דעולל בחוץ אמר עולא לא חרבה ירושלים אלא מפני שלא היה להם בושת פנים זה מזה שנאמר [מ] הובישו כי תועבה עשו גם בוש לא יבושו וגו' אמר ר' יצחק לא חרבה ירושלים אלא בשביל שהושוו קטן וגדול שנאמר [נ] והיה כעם ככהן וכתיב בתריה [ס] [ד]הבוק תבוק הארץ אמר רב עמרם בריה דר"ש בר אבא א"ר שמעון בר אבא א"ר חנינא לא חרבה ירושלים אלא בשביל שלא הוכיחו זה את זה שנאמר [ע] היו שריה כאילים לא מצאו מרעה מה איל זה ראשו של זה בצד זנבו של זה אף ישראל שבאותו הדור כבשו פניהם בקרקע ולא הוכיחו זה את זה א"ר יהודה לא חרבה ירושלים אלא בשביל שביזו בה ת"ח [ה] שנאמר [פ] ויהיו מלעיבים במלאכי האלהים ובוזים דבריו ומתעתעים בנביאיו עד עלות חמת ה' בעמו עד [ל]אין מרפא מאי עד לאין מרפא אמר רב יהודה אמר רב [ט]כל המבזה ת"ח אין לו רפואה למכתו אמר רב יהודה אמר רב מאי דכתיב [צ] אל תגעו במשיחי ובנביאי אל תרעו אל תגעו במשיחי אלו תינוקות של בית רבן ובנביאי אל תרעו אלו ת"ח אמר ריש לקיש משום רבי יהודה נשיאה אין העולם מתקיים אלא בשביל הבל תינוקות של בית רבן א"ל רב פפא לאביי דידי ודידך מאי א"ל אינו דומה הבל שיש בו חטא להבל שאין בו חטא ואמר ריש לקיש משום ר"י נשיאה [י]אין מבטלין תינוקות של בית רבן אפי' לבנין בית המקדש ואמר ר"ל לר"י נשיאה כך מקובלני מאבותי ואמרי לה מאבותיך [כ]כל עיר שאין בה תינוקות של בית רבן מחריבין אותה רבינא אמר מחרימין אותה [ח] ואמר רבא לא חרבה ירושלים אלא בשביל שפסקו ממנה אנשי אמנה שנאמר [ק] שוטטו בחוצות ירושלים וראו נא [ודעו ובקשו ברחובותיה אם תמצאו איש] (אם יש איש) עושה משפט מבקש אמונה ואסלח לה איני והאמר רב קטינא [י] אפי' בשעת כשלונה של ירושלים לא פסקו ממנה אנשי אמנה שנאמר [ר] כי יתפש איש באחיו בית אביו (לאמר) שמלה לכה קצין תהיה לנו דברים שבני אדם מתכסין בהן כשמלה ישנן בידיך [י] [ר] והמכשלה הזאת תחת ידך
דברים

ומצא נר דלוק ושולחן ערוך. וא"ת דאמר בריש ערבי פסחים (דף ק:) ושוין שאין מביאין את השולחן אא"כ קידש וי"ל דערוך הוא במקום אחר אלא שאין מביאין אותו עד אחר הקידוש כי היכי דתיתי סעודתא ביקרא דשבת כדאיתא בשאלתות דרב אחאי [ט] ודוקא בימיהם שהיו להם שלחנות קטנים לפני כל אחד ואחד אבל שלנו גדולים הם וקשה לטלטלם [י] (ג): **כל** העונה אמן יהא שמיה רבא בכל כחו. פי' בכל כוונתו וכן פירש רש"י ור"י אומר דיש בפסיקתא במעשה דר' ישמעאל בן אלישע דקאמר התם כשישראל נכנסים לבתי כנסיות ואומרים יהא שמיה רבא מברך בקול רם מבטלים גזירות קשות: **א"ר** חנינא אל מלך נאמן. צריך להפסיק בו בשעה שאומר אמן. אידי

מהדר אזוזי זוזי דרבנן. כשהיה רואה אותן זוגות זוגות ומדברין בתורה מחזר אחריהם ואומר להם במטותא מנכון לכו והתעסקו בעונג שבת ולא תחללוניה לבטל תענוגים: ויכלו. הקב"ה וזה שמספר בשבחו של מקום ובשבח של שבת: יסדר אדם שלחנו בע"ש. ללילי שבת: במוצ"ש. נמי כבוד שבת ללוות ביציאתו דרך כבוד כאדם המלוה את המלך בצאתו מן העיר: חמין. לשתות ולרחוץ: מלוגמא. רפואה: אכליה אריא. לעגל הראוי לשחוט: בכל כחו. בכל כוונתו: בפרוע פרעות. ביטול פורעניות כגון פרוע דמתרגמין בטל: בהתנדב עם ברכו. כשמתנדבין ישראל לברך את בוראן: כי פרוע. כי פרעו אהרן ע"ז והכי קאמר בהבטל פריעות ע"ז שנשתקע ותשתכח שלא יזכר עונש משום התנדב עם הוא: אל מלך נאמן. כך מעיד על בוראו שהוא אל מלך נאמן: שאין בני אדם מצויין לכבותה. בשבת: בבקר. בזמן ק"ש וכן מאחרי בנשף: והיה כנור ונבל. בסיפיה דקרא ואת פועל ה' לא יביטו לא שמו לב ליחד שמו על בריותיו: שפוך על עולל. רישא דקרא ואת חמת ה' נלאיתי הכיל שפוך וגו' שפוך החמה בנקמה בשביל שעולל לחוץ ובטלין מבית רבן: הובישו כי תועבה עשו וגו'. סיפיה דקרא גם בוש לא יבושו וגם הכלם לא כו': במשיחי אלו תינוקות של בית רבן. שדרך תינוקות למושחן בשמן [ח]: ובנביאי אלו תלמידי חכמים. שנאמר ונביא לבב חכמה (תהלים צ): מחריבין. איכא שיור: מחרימין. ליכא שיור: מתכסין בהן בשמלה. כששואלין אותן טעמי תורה הללו עושין עצמן כמעלימין את דבריהם מפני שאינן יודעים להשיב: ישנן בידך. אתה בקי לפיכך קצין תהיה לנו ותלמדנו חכמה:
דברים

הגהות הב"ח

(א) גמ' אל תיקרי ויכלו אלא ויכלו: (ב) שם כי פרוע הוא כי פרעו אהרן אמר ריש לקיש: (ג) תוס' ד"ה ומצא וכו' וקשה לטלטלם. נ"ב פי' אחר קידוש שלא להפסיק כל כך בין קידוש לסעודה אנו רגילין לפרוס מפה ולקדש:

גליון הש"ס

גמ' שנאמר ויהיו מלעיבים במלאכי האלהים. ע"ד שאמה"ל נדרים דף כ ע"א מאן מה"ש רבנן: שם כך מקובלני מאבותי. עיין ב"מ דף פד ע"א ד"ה אי הדרת:

ליקוטי רש"י

עיגלא תילתא. שלישי לבטן שהוא משובח מפני שהבהמה בקטנותה אינה עדיין בכחה והולד ראשון ושני אינו בריא [לעיל יא.]. גדל שליש ואז הוא עומד בעיקר טעם בשרו כדתנן (ב"מ סח.) ומגדלין אותן עד שיהו משולשין ואמרינן נמי (שם סט.) מותר שליש בשכרך אלמא אורחיה עד שליש לישנא אחרינא שלישי לבטן וקשה לי הא דאמר בעלמא (סנהדרין סה:) רב חנינא ורב אושעיא הוו עסקי בספר יצירה וכל מעלי שבתא איברי להו עגלא תילתא דהתם מאי שלישי לבטן איכא הא לא היה בבטן מעולם [עירובין סג.]. שלישי לבטן ומובחר הוא [פסחים סח: ע"ש במסוה"ש]. הגיע לשליש שניו וגמרה גדילתו דהכי שביחי ומעלי למיכל כמו (ב"מ סח.) ומגדלין אותן עד שיהו משולשין לישנא אחרינא שהיה טוב ובעל טעם [שלישי] לבטן [סנהדרין סה: ע"ש]. שומר אמונים. שמר ולפה בגלותו ימים רבים לאמונתו של הקב"ה שיקיים הבטחתו שהבטיח ע"פ נביאיו לגאלם. שומר. ממתין וכן (בראשית לז) ואביו שמר את הדבר וכן (דברים ז) ושמר ה' אלהיך לך [ישעיה כו, ב]. מאי אמן. כשעונין על כל ברכה וברכה אמן היאך משמע קבלת יראת שמים. אל מלך נאמן. בנוטריקון שמאמין עליו הקב"ה [סנהדרין קיא.]. בכנור ונבל. נימין יתרות יש בנבל מן הכנור ולמה נקרא שמו נבל שמנבל כל מיני כלי זמר במדרש תהלים. תוף. של עור הוא. וחליל. אבוב של קנה (גלמיי"ל בלע"ז) [ישעיה ה, יב]. מבלי דעת. לפי שהיה לבם בלי דעת [שם, יג]. הובישו. עליהון למיבהת. גם בוש לא יבושו. אינם מתביישין ממעשיהם הרעים [ירמיה ו, טו]. הבוק תבוק. תתרוקן [ישעיה כד, ג]. כי יתפש איש באחיו. כאשר יתפוש איש באחיו בבית אביו לאמר עשיר אתה בתורה [ישעיה ג, ו]. באנשי ירושלים שפסקה תורה מהם והיו שואלין לחבריהם שמלה לך קצין תהיה לנו והמכשלה הזאת תחת ידיך [גיטין מג.]. הכשול היה מגנן לומר שלא היו יודעין להשיב לשואלים הלכה. שבני אדם מתכסין בהן. נמנעין שלא ישאלו להן לפי שאין בקיאין בהן. ישנן בידך. כלומר אתה בקי בהן [חגיגה יד.].

תורה אור השלם

א) וַיְכֻלּוּ הַשָּׁמַיִם וְהָאָרֶץ וְכָל צְבָאָם: [בראשית ב, א]
ב) בִּדְבַר יְיָ שָׁמַיִם נַעֲשׂוּ וּבְרוּחַ פִּיו כָּל צְבָאָם: [תהלים לג, ו]
ג) וַיַּגַּע עַל פִּי וַיֹּאמֶר הִנֵּה נָגַע זֶה עַל שְׂפָתֶיךָ וְסָר עֲוֺנֶךָ וְחַטָּאתְךָ תְּכֻפָּר: [ישעיה ו, ז]
ד) בִּפְרֹעַ פְּרָעוֹת בְּיִשְׂרָאֵל בְּהִתְנַדֵּב עָם בָּרְכוּ יְיָ: [שופטים ה, ב]
ה) וַיַּרְא מֹשֶׁה אֶת הָעָם כִּי פָרֻעַ הוּא כִּי פְרָעֹה אַהֲרֹן לְשִׁמְצָה בְּקָמֵיהֶם: [שמות לב, כה]
ו) פִּתְחוּ שְׁעָרִים וְיָבֹא גוֹי צַדִּיק שֹׁמֵר אֱמֻנִים: [ישעיה כו, ב]
ז) וְאִם לֹא תִשְׁמְעוּ אֵלַי לְקַדֵּשׁ אֶת יוֹם הַשַּׁבָּת וּלְבִלְתִּי שְׂאֵת מַשָּׂא וּבֹא בְּשַׁעֲרֵי יְרוּשָׁלָיִם בְּיוֹם הַשַּׁבָּת וְהִצַּתִּי אֵשׁ בִּשְׁעָרֶיהָ וְאָכְלָה אַרְמְנוֹת יְרוּשָׁלַיִם וְלֹא תִכְבֶּה: [ירמיה יז, כז]
ח) כֹּהֲנֶיהָ חָמְסוּ תוֹרָתִי וַיְחַלְּלוּ קָדָשַׁי בֵּין קֹדֶשׁ לְחֹל לֹא הִבְדִּילוּ וּבֵין הַטָּמֵא לְטָהוֹר לֹא הוֹדִיעוּ וּמִשַּׁבְּתוֹתַי הֶעְלִימוּ עֵינֵיהֶם וָאֵחַל בְּתוֹכָם: [יחזקאל כב, כו]
ט) הוֹי מַשְׁכִּימֵי בַבֹּקֶר שֵׁכָר יִרְדֹּפוּ מְאַחֲרֵי בַנֶּשֶׁף יַיִן יַדְלִיקֵם: [ישעיה ה, יא]
י) וְהָיָה כִנּוֹר וָנֶבֶל תֹּף וְחָלִיל וָיַיִן מִשְׁתֵּיהֶם וְאֵת פֹּעַל יְיָ לֹא יַבִּיטוּ וּמַעֲשֵׂה יָדָיו לֹא רָאוּ: [ישעיה ה, יב]
כ) לָכֵן גָּלָה עַמִּי מִבְּלִי דָעַת וּכְבוֹדוֹ מְתֵי רָעָב וַהֲמוֹנוֹ צִחֵה צָמָא: [ישעיה ה, יג]
ל) וְאֵת חֲמַת יְיָ מָלֵאתִי נִלְאֵיתִי הָכִיל שְׁפֹךְ עַל עוֹלָל בַּחוּץ וְעַל סוֹד בַּחוּרִים יַחְדָּו כִּי גַם אִישׁ עִם אִשָּׁה יִלָּכֵדוּ זָקֵן עִם מְלֵא יָמִים: [ירמיה ו, יא]
מ) הֹבִשׁוּ כִּי תוֹעֵבָה עָשׂוּ גַּם בּוֹשׁ לֹא יֵבוֹשׁוּ גַּם הַכְלִים לֹא יָדָעוּ לָכֵן יִפְּלוּ בַנֹּפְלִים בְּעֵת פְּקַדְתִּים יִכָּשְׁלוּ אָמַר יְיָ: [ירמיה ו, טו]
נ) וְהָיָה כָעָם כַּכֹּהֵן כַּעֶבֶד כַּאדֹנָיו כַּשִּׁפְחָה כַּגְּבִרְתָּהּ כַּקּוֹנֶה כַּמּוֹכֵר כַּמַּלְוֶה כַּלֹּוֶה כַּנֹּשֶׁה כַּאֲשֶׁר נֹשֶׁא בוֹ: [ישעיה כד, ב]
ס) הִבּוֹק תִּבּוֹק הָאָרֶץ וְהִבּוֹז תִּבּוֹז כִּי יְיָ דִּבֶּר אֶת הַדָּבָר הַזֶּה: [ישעיה כד, ג]
ע) וַיֵּצֵא מִבַּת צִיּוֹן כָּל הֲדָרָהּ הָיוּ שָׂרֶיהָ כְּאַיָּלִים לֹא מָצְאוּ מִרְעֶה וַיֵּלְכוּ בְלֹא כֹחַ לִפְנֵי רוֹדֵף: [איכה א, ו]
פ) וַיִּהְיוּ מַלְעִבִים בְּמַלְאֲכֵי הָאֱלֹהִים וּבוֹזִים דְּבָרָיו וּמִתַּעְתְּעִים בִּנְבִאָיו עַד עֲלוֹת חֲמַת יְיָ בְּעַמּוֹ עַד לְאֵין מַרְפֵּא: [דברי הימים ב' לו, טז]
צ) אַל תִּגְּעוּ בִּמְשִׁיחָי וּבִנְבִיאַי אַל תָּרֵעוּ: [דברי הימים א' טז, כב]
ק) שׁוֹטְטוּ בְּחוּצוֹת יְרוּשָׁלַיִם וּרְאוּ נָא וּדְעוּ וּבַקְשׁוּ בִרְחוֹבוֹתֶיהָ אִם תִּמְצְאוּ אִישׁ אִם יֵשׁ עֹשֶׂה מִשְׁפָּט מְבַקֵּשׁ אֱמוּנָה וְאֶסְלַח לָהּ: [ירמיה ה, א]
ר) כִּי יִתְפֹּשׂ אִישׁ בְּאָחִיו בֵּית אָבִיו שִׂמְלָה לְכָה קָצִין תִּהְיֶה לָּנוּ וְהַמַּכְשֵׁלָה הַזֹּאת תַּחַת יָדֶךָ: [ישעיה ג, ו]

Another teaching concerning the importance of setting one's table for the Sabbath:

אָמַר רַבִּי אֶלְעָזָר – **R' Elazar said:** לְעוֹלָם יְסַדֵּר אָדָם שֻׁלְחָנוֹ בְּעֶרֶב שַׁבָּת אַף עַל פִּי שֶׁאֵינוֹ צָרִיךְ אֶלָּא לִכְזַיִת – **A person should always** be sure to **set his table on the eve of the Sabbath,**[9] **even though he needs** to eat **only the amount of an olive.**[10]

A similar teaching regarding the departure of the Sabbath:

וְאָמַר רַבִּי חֲנִינָא – **And R' Chanina said:** לְעוֹלָם יְסַדֵּר אָדָם שֻׁלְחָנוֹ בְּמוֹצָאֵי שַׁבָּת אַף עַל פִּי שֶׁאֵינוֹ צָרִיךְ אֶלָּא לִכְזַיִת – **A person should always** be sure to **set his table on the night following the Sabbath, even though he needs** to eat **only the amount of an olive.**[11]

Having mentioned the importance of honoring the Sabbath with a meal at its departure as well, the Gemara expands on this topic:

חַמִּין בְּמוֹצָאֵי שַׁבָּת מְלוּגְמָא – **Hot water**[12] **on the night after the Sabbath is a remedy;** פַּת חַמָּה בְּמוֹצָאֵי שַׁבָּת מְלוּגְמָא – **hot** (i.e. freshly baked) **bread on the night after the Sabbath is a remedy.**[13]

The Gemara relates an incident:

רַבִּי אַבָּהוּ הֲוָה עָבְדִין לֵיהּ בְּאַפּוּקֵי שַׁבְּתָא עִיגְלָא תִּילְתָּא – **R' Abahu would have a third-born calf**[14] **prepared for him on the night after the Sabbath** הֲוָה אָכִיל מִינֵּיהּ כּוּלְיְיתָא – **and he would eat from it** just **the kidney.** כִּי גְּדַל אֲבִימִי בְּרֵיהּ אָמַר לֵיהּ – **When his son Avimi grew up, he said to [his father],** לָמָּה לָךְ לְאַפְסוּדֵי כּוּלֵּי הַאי – **"Why should you waste so much** meat? נִשְׁבּוֹק כּוּלְיְיתָא מִמַּעֲלֵי שַׁבְּתָא – **Leave over a kidney from** the animal slaughtered on **Friday** for the Sabbath meals, and eat that after the Sabbath." שַׁבְקוּהוּ וְאָתָא אַרְיָא אַכְלֵיהּ – So the next week **they left over [a kidney]** on Friday for the post-Sabbath meal, **and a lion came and ate [the calf].**[15]

The Gemara moves on to a new topic:

אָמַר רַבִּי יְהוֹשֻׁעַ בֶּן לֵוִי – **R' Yehoshua ben Levi said:** כׇּל הָעוֹנֶה אָמֵן יְהֵא שְׁמֵיהּ רַבָּא מְבָרַךְ בְּכׇל כֹּחוֹ – **Whoever responds** to the Kaddish by saying, **"Amen; may His great Name be blessed** forever and ever" **with all his might,**[16] קוֹרְעִין לוֹ גְּזַר דִּינוֹ – **the** evil **decree** made **in judgment against him is torn up;**[17] שֶׁנֶּאֱמַר – **as it states:** "בִּפְרֹעַ פְּרָעוֹת בְּיִשְׂרָאֵל בְּהִתְנַדֵּב עָם בָּרְכוּ ה'" – ***When calamities are averted in Israel, when the people dedicate themselves, bless Hashem.***[18] מַאי טַעְמָא "בִּפְרֹעַ פְּרָעוֹת" – **What is the reason that** ***calamities are averted?*** מִשּׁוּם דְּ"בָרְכוּ ה'" – **Because** *the people dedicate themselves* **to** ***bless Hashem.***

Another exposition along the same lines:

רַבִּי חִיָּיא בַּר אַבָּא אָמַר רַבִּי יוֹחָנָן – **R' Chiya bar Abba said in the name of R' Yochanan:** אֲפִילּוּ יֵשׁ בּוֹ שֶׁמֶץ שֶׁל עֲבוֹדָה זָרָה מוֹחֲלִין לוֹ – **Even if there is a trace of idolatry in him, he is forgiven** as a result of this response. כְּתִיב הָכָא "בִּפְרֹעַ פְּרָעוֹת" – **For it is written here:** ***When "peraos" are nullified,*** וּכְתִיב הָתָם "כִּי פָרֻעַ הוּא" – **and it is written there** in regard to the sin of the Golden Calf: *And Moses saw the people,* ***that they were "pharua"*** (uncovered).[19]

NOTES

his house properly, the "bad angel" wishes this failure on him for the following week and the "good angel" is forced to answer "Amen" (*Iyei HaYam,* cited in *Anaf Yosef;* see also *Milchemes Chovah,* quoted by *Chidushei Geonim* in *Ein Yaakov;* cf. *Abudraham* cited in *Anaf Yosef*).

9. I.e. on Friday afternoon in preparation for the Friday night meal (*Rashi;* see also *Tosafos, Pesachim* 102b ד״ה שאין מביאין את השלחן and *Ritva MHK* ed. here).

10. Even if a person is satiated when the Sabbath begins (for example, from having earlier eaten a meal to honor a mitzvah), and he does not intend to eat more than the bare minimum of food required for the Friday evening meal, he should still set his table properly to honor the Sabbath (*Maharsha*). [In general, however, one should not eat an unusually large meal on Friday that would cause him to be too satiated to eat the Sabbath meal that night; see *Orach Chaim* 249:2.]

[It would seem from the Gemara's statement here that the minimum amount required for a Sabbath meal is a *kezayis* (*Eliyahu Rabbah* 291:1). *Shulchan Aruch* (*Orach Chaim* 291:1) rules that it is a כְּבֵיצָה, *the volume of an egg,* or slightly more (*Magen Avraham* there). See *Machatzis HaShekel* there for further discussion of this.]

11. Just as people come out to escort the king both on his arrival and his departure from the city, so too it is proper to honor the Sabbath at both its arrival and departure (*Rashi*). Since it is important to honor the Sabbath with a meal on this occasion, one should set his table for it properly, with a tablecloth and the other utensils one uses on such occasions (*Taz, Orach Chaim* 300:1; cf. *Bach*). [This teaching is the source for the meal known as *melaveh malkah,* literally: escorting the queen. Indeed, the author of this ruling, R' Chanina, is the one who made it his practice to greet the arrival of the Sabbath by going out to welcome "Sabbath, the queen" (above, 119a).]

Although the Gemara states that it is proper to eat a meal after the Sabbath, it is not an absolute requirement to do so (*Ritva, MHK* ed.). Thus, if one does not have enough food for both the Sabbath meals and *melaveh malkah,* he should use the food for the Sabbath meals (*Mishnah Berurah* 300:2).

12. To drink and wash with (*Rashi*).

13. [Since it is forbidden to cook on the Sabbath, one generally does not have hot water to drink that day. Nor can one wash on the Sabbath with warm water (see above, 39b). Thus, a hot drink and washing with warm water after the Sabbath serve as a restorative for a chilled body. Similarly, bread straight out of the oven rejuvenates the body after a whole day of cold food.]

Maharsha adds that it is appropriate to honor the Sabbath at its departure with things that were unavailable on the Sabbath itself [for a person's appetite is improved by the anticipation of something new]. Thus, hot food and freshly baked bread are especially fitting for this meal since these were unavailable during the Sabbath day. See there.

14. The meat of such a calf was considered superior. The first two calves of a cow, produced when the cow has not yet reached its full maturity, are generally not as robust as the third one. The choicest meat is therefore assumed to come from the cow's third offspring (*Rashi* above, 11a ד״ה עיגלא תילתא). Alternatively, this term refers to a calf that has grown to one-third its adult size, when its meat is tastiest (*Rashi, Eruvin* 63a ד״ה עיגלא תילתא).

15. That is, the lion ate the calf that would have been slaughtered for that meal but due to Avimi's protest was not. [Thus the calf was "wasted" anyway.] (*Rashi*). Since this meal is to honor the departing Sabbath, it is proper to honor it with something newly prepared, not with leftovers (*Maharsha;* see *Shaarei Teshuvah, Orach Chaim* 300:1; cf. *Taz* who states that it is not necessary to cook new foods for this meal; see also *Mishnah Berurah* 300:1).

Magen Avraham (300:1) derives from this incident that it is preferable (for one who can afford it) to have meat for the *melaveh malkah* meal (see *Pri Megadim* there; see also *Eitz Yosef* in *Ein Yaakov*).

16. I.e. with his utmost concentration (*Rashi*). Alternatively, in a loud voice (*Tosafos,* based on a story in the *Pesikta*). To declare this blessing of Hashem very loudly arouses one's concentration and devotion (*Ritva MHK* ed. citing *Rabbeinu Yonah* in *Berachos; Orach Chaim* 56:1). Nevertheless, one should not say it so loudly as to cause people to laugh at him (*Mishnah Berurah* ibid.).

17. I.e. if a judgment has been made against him in Heaven that he should suffer some misfortune, the decree is nullified in the merit of this mitzvah.

18. *Judges* 5:2. This is from the Song of Deborah on the occasion of her victory over Sisera. The word בִּפְרֹעַ is taken by the Gemara to mean nullify [i.e. avert] (*Rashi;* see commentators to the verse).

19. According to R' Yochanan, the use of the root פרע in connection with the idolatry of the Golden Calf (*Exodus* 32:25) indicates that the word פְּרָעוֹת in the verse in *Judges* is a reference to the sin of idolatry. R' Yochanan therefore interprets the verse as follows: "When *peraos* – idolatry – is nullified (that is, made to be forgotten, so that the sin is no longer held against them), it is because the people bless Hashem's Name" (*Rashi*).

[It is not clear why the Gemara should cite the teachings of R'

עין משפט נר מצוה

מז א מיי' פכ"ט מהל' שבת הלכה ז סמג עשין ל טוש"ע א"ח סי' רסב סעיף א:
מח ב מיי' פ"ל שם הל' ה סמג שם טור ש"ע או"ח סימן רסב סעיף א:
מט ג מיי' שם הלכה ה וסמג שם:
נ ד מיי' שם וסמג שם טור ש"ע או"ח סימן ש:
נא ה מיי' פ"ט מהלכות תפלה הלכה א טוש"ע או"ח סימן נו סעיף א [וכרב אלפס ברכות פ"ג דף ש"ו: וברא"ש שם סימן יט]:
נב ו מיי' פ"ב מהל' ת"ת הלכה יא טור ש"ע יו"ד סימן רמה סעיף יג:
נג ז מיי' שם הל' ה טוש"ע יו"ד סי' רמה סעיף יא [וכרב אלפס שם דכ"ב דף קכב: וברא"ש פ"ג דמו"ק סי' מ"ח]:
נד ח מיי' שם הלכה ו טוש"ע שם סעיף ח [וכרב אלפס שם]:

מסורת הש"ס

א) [נהלכה"ס וטור סי' רסח איתא אמר רב וכו' ואמר רב המנונא כל המתפלל וכו' וכ"ה בשאלתות פרשת בראשית א], ב) סנהדרין דף קי:, ג) [סנהדרין דף קיא:], ד) [פי' תמרוקין], ה) מגילה יז., ו) [מגילה כו. גיטין מג.], ז) [מגילה דף יז.], ח) [כדאיתא לעיל דף י:], ט) [פרשת יתרו סימן נד], י) [וע"ע תוס' פסחים ק: ד"ה שאין].

מהדר אזווי זוזי דרבנן. כשהיה רואה אותן זוגות זוגות ומדברין בתורה מחזר אחריהם ואומר להם במטותא מנכון לכו והתעסקו בעונג שבת ולא תחללוניה לבטל תענוגים: ויכלו. הקב"ה וזה שמספר בשבחו של מקום ובשבח של שבת: יסדר אדם שלחנו בע"ש. ללילי שבת: במוצ"ש. נמי כבוד שבת ללוות ביציאתו דרך כבוד כאדם המלוה את המלך בצאתו מן העיר: חמין. לשתות ולרחוץ: מלוגמא. רפואה: אכליה אריא. לעגל הראוי לשחוט: בכל כחו. בכל כוונתו: בפרוע פרעות. ביטול פורעניות כגון פרוע דמתרגמין בטל: בהתנדב עם ברכו. כשמתנדבין ישראל לברך את בוראן: כי פרוע. כי פרעו אהרן ע"ז והכי קאמר בהבטל פריעות ע"ז שתשתקע ותשתכח שלא יזכר עונש משום התנדב עם הוא: אל מלך נאמן. כך מעיד על בוראו שהוא אל מלך נאמן: שאין בני אדם מצויין לכבותה. בשבת. בבקר. בזמן ק"ש וכן מאחרי בנשף: והיה כנור ונבל. בסיפיה דקרא ואת פועל ה' לא יביטו את שמו לא ליחד שמו על בריותיו: שפוך על עולל. רישא דקרא ואת חמת ה' נלאיתי הכיל שפוך וגו' שפוך החמה בנקמה בשביל שעולל לחוץ ובטלין מבית רבן: הובישו כי תועבה עשו וגו'. סיפיה דקרא גם בוש לא יבושו וגם הכלם לא כו': במשיחי אלו תינוקות של בית רבן. שדרך תינוקות למושחן בשמן ט): ובנביאי אלו תלמידי חכמים. שנאמר ונביא לבב חכמה (תהלים צ): מחריבין. איכא שיור: מחרימין. ליכא שיור: מתכסין בהן כשמלה. כששואלין אותן טעמי תורה הללו עושין עצמן כמעלימין את דבריהם מפני שאין יודעים להשיב: ישנן בידך. אתה בקי לפיכך קצין תהיה לנו ותלמדנו חכמה: דברים

ומצא נר דלוק ושולחן ערוך. וא"ת דאמר בריש ערבי פסחים (דף ק:) ושוין שאין מביאין את השולחן אא"כ קידש וי"ל דערוך הוא במקום אחר אלא שאין מביאין אותו עד אחר הקידוש כי היכי דתיתי סעודתא ביקרא דשבת כדאיתא בשאלתות דרב אחאי ט) ודוקא בימיהם שהיו להם שלחנות קטנים לפני כל אחד ואחד אבל שלנו גדולים הם וקשה לטלטלם י) (ג): **כל** העונה אמן יהא שמיה רבא בכל כחו. פי' בכל כוונתו וכן פירש רש"י ור"י אומר דיש בפסיקתא במעשה דר' ישמעאל בן אלישע דקאמר התם כשישראל נכנסים לבתי כנסיות ואומרים יהא שמיה רבא מברך בקול רם מבטלים גזירות קשות:

א"ר חנינא אל מלך נאמן. צריך להרהר בו בשעה שאומר אמן:

אידי

מהדר אזווי זוזי דרבנן א"ל במטותא מינייכו לא תחללוניה אמר א) רבא ואיתימא ר' יהושע בן לוי א אפי' יחיד המתפלל בע"ש צריך לומר ויכולו דאמר רב המנונא כל המתפלל בע"ש ואומר ויכולו מעלה עליו הכתוב כאילו נעשה שותף להקב"ה במעשה בראשית שנאמר א) ויכולו אל תקרי ויכולו (א) אלא ויכלו אמר רבי אלעזר מניין שהדיבור כמעשה שנאמר ב) בדבר ה' שמים נעשו אמר רב חסדא אמר מר עוקבא כל המתפלל בע"ש ואומר ויכולו שני מלאכי השרת המלוין לו לאדם מניחין ידיהן על ראשו ואומרים לו ג) וסר עונך וחטאתך תכופר תניא ר' יוסי בר יהודה אומר שני מלאכי השרת מלוין לו לאדם בע"ש מבית הכנסת לביתו אחד טוב ואחד רע ב וכשבא לביתו ומצא נר דלוק ושלחן ערוך ומטתו מוצעת מלאך טוב אומר יהי רצון שתהא לשבת אחרת כך ומלאך רע עונה אמן בעל כרחו ואם לאו מלאך רע אומר יהי רצון שתהא לשבת אחרת כך ומלאך טוב עונה אמן בעל כרחו אמר ר' אלעזר ג לעולם יסדר אדם שלחנו בע"ש אע"פ שאינו צריך אלא לכזית ואמר ר' חנינא ד לעולם יסדר אדם שלחנו במוצאי שבת אע"פ שאינו צריך אלא לכזית חמין במוצאי שבת מלוגמא פת חמה במוצאי שבת מלוגמא ר' אבהו הוה עבדין ליה באפוקי שבתא עיגלא תילתא הוה אכיל מיניה כוליתא כי גדל אבימי בריה א"ל למה לך לאפסודי כולי האי נשבוק כוליתא ממעלי שבתא שבקוהו ואתא אריא אכליה אריב"ל ה כל העונה אמן יהא שמיה רבא מברך בכל כחו קורעין לו גזר דינו שנאמר ד) בפרוע פרעות בישראל בהתנדב עם ברכו ה' מ"ט בפרוע פרעות משום דברכו ה' רבי חייא בר אבא א"ר יוחנן אפילו יש בו שמץ של עבודה זרה מוחלין לו כתיב הכא בפרוע פרעות וכתיב התם ה) כי פרוע הוא (ב) אמר ריש לקיש כל העונה אמן בכל כחו פותחין לו שערי ג"ע שנאמר ו) פתחו שערים ויבא גוי צדיק שומר אמונים ו אל תיקרי שומר אמונים אלא שאומרים אמן ו) מאי אמן א"ר חנינא אל מלך נאמן א"ר יהודה בריה דרב שמואל משמיה דרב אין הדליקה מצויה אלא במקום שיש חילול שבת שנאמר ז) ואם לא תשמעו אלי לקדש את יום השבת ולבלתי שאת משא וגו' והצתי אש בשעריה ואכלה ארמנות ירושלים ולא תכבה מאי ולא תכבה אמר רב נחמן בר יצחק בשעה שאין בני אדם מצויין לכבותה אמר אביי לא חרבה ירושלים אלא בשביל שחללו בה את השבת שנאמר ח) ומשבתותי העלימו עיניהם ואחל בתוכם אמר ר' אבהו לא חרבה ירושלים אלא בשביל שביטלו ק"ש שחרית וערבית שנאמר ט) הוי משכימי בבקר שכר ירדפו וגו' וכתיב י) והיה כנור ונבל תוף וחליל ויין משתיהם ואת פועל ה' לא יביטו וכתיב כ) לכן גלה עמי מבלי דעת אמר רב המנונא לא חרבה ירושלים אלא בשביל שביטלו בה תינוקות של בית רבן שנאמר ל) שפוך על עולל בחוץ וגו' מה טעם שפוך משום דעולל בחוץ אמר עולא לא חרבה ירושלים אלא מפני שלא היה להם בושת פנים זה מזה שנאמר מ) הובישו כי תועבה עשו גם בוש לא יבושו וגו' אמר ר' יצחק לא חרבה ירושלים אלא בשביל שהושוו קטן וגדול שנאמר נ) והיה כעם ככהן וכתיב בתריה ס) ז הבוק תבוק הארץ אמר רב עמרם בריה דר"ש בר אבא א"ר שמעון בר אבא א"ר חנינא לא חרבה ירושלים אלא בשביל שלא הוכיחו זה את זה שנאמר ע) היו שריה כאילים לא מצאו מרעה מה איל זה ראשו של זה בצד זנבו של זה אף ישראל שבאותו הדור כבשו פניהם בקרקע ולא הוכיחו זה את זה א"ר יהודה לא חרבה ירושלים אלא בשביל שביזו בה ת"ח ° שנאמר פ) ויהיו מלעיבים במלאכי האלהים ובוזים דבריו ומתעתעים בנביאיו עד עלות חמת ה' בעמו עד [ל]אין מרפא מאי עד לאין מרפא אמר רב יהודה אמר רב י כל המבזה ת"ח אין לו רפואה למכתו אמר רב יהודה אמר רב מאי דכתיב צ) אל תגעו במשיחי ובנביאי אל תרעו אל תגעו במשיחי אלו תינוקות של בית רבן ובנביאי אל תרעו אלו ת"ח אמר ריש לקיש משום רבי יהודה נשיאה אין העולם מתקיים אלא בשביל הבל תינוקות של בית רבן א"ל רב פפא לאביי דידי ודידך מאי א"ל אינו דומה הבל שיש בו חטא להבל שאין בו חטא ואמר ריש לקיש משום ר"י נשיאה ז אין מבטלין תינוקות של בית רבן אפי' לבנין בית המקדש ואמר ר"ל לר"י נשיאה כך מקובלני ° מאבותי ואמרי לה מאבותיך ח כל עיר שאין בה תינוקות של בית רבן מחריבין אותה רבינא אמר מחרימין אותה ח) ואמר רבא לא חרבה ירושלים אלא בשביל שפסקו ממנה אנשי אמנה שנאמר ק) שוטטו בחוצות ירושלים וראו נא [ודעו ובקשו ברחובותיה אם תמצאו איש] (אם יש איש) עושה משפט מבקש אמונה ואסלח לה איני והאמר רב קטינא ט אפי' בשעת כשלונה של ירושלים לא פסקו ממנה אנשי אמנה שנאמר ר) כי יתפש איש באחיו בית אביו (לאמר) שמלה לכה קצין תהיה לנו דברים שבני אדם מתכסין בהן כשמלה ישנן בידיך י) ר) והמכשלה הזאת תחת ידך

דברים

הגהות הב"ח

(א) גמ' אל תיקרי ויכולו אלא ויכלו: (ב) שם כי פרוע הוא כי פרעו אהרן כצ"ל ותיבת לקיש נמחק: (ג) תוס' ד"ה ומצא וכו' וקשה לטלטלם. נ"ב פי' אחר קידוש שלא להפסיק לכך בין קידוש לסעודה אנו רגילין לפרוס מפה ולקדש:

גליון הש"ס

גמ' שנאמר ויהיו מלעיבים במלאכי האלהים. ע"ד שאמה"ל נדרים דף כ ע"ב מאן מה"ש רבנן. שם כך מקובלני מאבותי. עיין ב"מ דף פה ע"א ד"ה אי הדרת:

ליקוטי רש"י

עיגלא תילתא. שליש לבטן שהוא משובח מפני שכשהוא בקטנותה אינה עדיין בכחה והולד ראשון ושני אינו בריא [לעיל יא.]. גדל שליש ואז הוא עומד בעיקר טעם בשרו כתקנו (ב"מ סח.) ומגדלין אותן עד שיהו משולשין ולמריך נמי (שם סט.). שלישי לבטן וקשה לי זה לא שמעתי בעולמה (סנהדרין סה:). ... כל העונה אמן בכל כחו. בכל כוונתו. שומר אמונים. ... אל מלך נאמן. ... הבוק תבוק. ... כי יתפש איש באחיו. ... [illegible]

תורה אור השלם

א) וַיְכֻלּוּ הַשָּׁמַיִם וְהָאָרֶץ וְכָל צְבָאָם: [בראשית ב, א]
ב) בִּדְבַר יְיָ שָׁמַיִם נַעֲשׂוּ וּבְרוּחַ פִּיו כָּל צְבָאָם: [תהלים לג, ו]
ג) וַיַּגַּע עַל פִּי וַיֹּאמֶר הִנֵּה נָגַע זֶה עַל שְׂפָתֶיךָ וְסָר עֲוֹנֶךָ וְחַטָּאתְךָ תְּכֻפָּר: [ישעיה ו, ז]
ד) בִּפְרֹעַ פְּרָעוֹת בְּיִשְׂרָאֵל בְּהִתְנַדֵּב עָם בָּרְכוּ יְיָ: [שופטים ה, ב]
ה) וַיַּרְא מֹשֶׁה אֶת הָעָם כִּי פָרֻעַ הוּא כִּי פְרָעֹה אַהֲרֹן לְשִׁמְצָה בְּקָמֵיהֶם: [שמות לב, כה]
ו) פִּתְחוּ שְׁעָרִים וְיָבֹא גוֹי צַדִּיק שֹׁמֵר אֱמֻנִים: [ישעיה כו, ב]
ז) וְאִם לֹא תִשְׁמְעוּ אֵלַי לְקַדֵּשׁ אֶת יוֹם הַשַּׁבָּת וּלְבִלְתִּי שְׂאֵת מַשָּׂא וּבֹא בְּשַׁעֲרֵי יְרוּשָׁלָיִם בְּיוֹם הַשַּׁבָּת וְהִצַּתִּי אֵשׁ בִּשְׁעָרֶיהָ וְאָכְלָה אַרְמְנוֹת יְרוּשָׁלַיִם וְלֹא תִכְבֶּה: [ירמיה יז, כז]
ח) כֹּהֲנֶיהָ חָמְסוּ תוֹרָתִי וַיְחַלְּלוּ קָדָשַׁי בֵּין קֹדֶשׁ לְחֹל לֹא הִבְדִּילוּ וּבֵין הַטָּמֵא לְטָהוֹר לֹא הוֹדִיעוּ וּמִשַּׁבְּתוֹתַי הֶעְלִימוּ עֵינֵיהֶם וָאֵחַל בְּתוֹכָם: [יחזקאל כב, כו]
ט) הוֹי מַשְׁכִּימֵי בַבֹּקֶר שֵׁכָר יִרְדֹּפוּ מְאַחֲרֵי בַנֶּשֶׁף יַיִן יַדְלִיקֵם: [ישעיה ה, יא]
י) וְהָיָה כִנּוֹר וָנֶבֶל תֹּף וְחָלִיל וָיַיִן מִשְׁתֵּיהֶם וְאֵת פֹּעַל יְיָ לֹא יַבִּיטוּ וּמַעֲשֵׂה יָדָיו לֹא רָאוּ: [ישעיה ה, יב]
כ) לָכֵן גָּלָה עַמִּי מִבְּלִי דָעַת וּכְבוֹדוֹ מְתֵי רָעָב וַהֲמוֹנוֹ צִחֵה צָמָא: [ישעיה ה, יג]
ל) וְאֵת חֲמַת יְיָ מָלֵאתִי נִלְאֵיתִי הָכִיל שְׁפֹךְ עַל עוֹלָל בַּחוּץ וְעַל סוֹד בַּחוּרִים יַחְדָּו כִּי גַם אִישׁ עִם אִשָּׁה יִלָּכֵדוּ זָקֵן עִם מְלֵא יָמִים: [ירמיה ו, יא]
מ) הֹבִשׁוּ כִּי תוֹעֵבָה עָשׂוּ גַּם בּוֹשׁ לֹא יֵבֹשׁוּ גַּם הַכְלִים לֹא יָדָעוּ לָכֵן יִפְּלוּ בַנֹּפְלִים בְּעֵת פְּקֻדָּתָם יִכָּשְׁלוּ אָמַר יְיָ: [ירמיה ו, טו]
נ) וְהָיָה כָעָם כַּכֹּהֵן כַּעֶבֶד כַּאדֹנָיו כַּשִּׁפְחָה כַּגְּבִרְתָּהּ כַּקּוֹנֶה כַּמּוֹכֵר כַּמַּלְוֶה כַּלֹּוֶה כַּנֹּשֶׁה כַּאֲשֶׁר נֹשֶׁא בוֹ: [ישעיה כד, ב]
ס) הִבּוֹק תִּבּוֹק הָאָרֶץ וְהִבּוֹז תִּבּוֹז כִּי יְיָ דִּבֶּר אֶת הַדָּבָר הַזֶּה: [ישעיה כד, ג]
ע) וַיֵּצֵא מִבַּת צִיּוֹן כָּל הֲדָרָהּ הָיוּ שָׂרֶיהָ כְּאַיָּלִים לֹא מָצְאוּ מִרְעֶה וַיֵּלְכוּ בְלֹא כֹחַ לִפְנֵי רוֹדֵף: [איכה א, ו]
פ) וַיִּהְיוּ מַלְעִבִים בְּמַלְאֲכֵי הָאֱלֹהִים וּבוֹזִים דְּבָרָיו וּמִתַּעְתְּעִים בִּנְבִאָיו עַד עֲלוֹת חֲמַת יְיָ בְּעַמּוֹ עַד לְאֵין מַרְפֵּא: [דברי הימים ב' לו, טז]
צ) אַל תִּגְּעוּ בִּמְשִׁיחָי וּבִנְבִיאַי אַל תָּרֵעוּ: [דברי הימים א' טז, כב]
ק) שׁוֹטְטוּ בְּחוּצוֹת יְרוּשָׁלַיִם וּרְאוּ נָא וּדְעוּ וּבַקְשׁוּ בִרְחוֹבוֹתֶיהָ אִם תִּמְצְאוּ אִישׁ אִם יֵשׁ עֹשֶׂה מִשְׁפָּט מְבַקֵּשׁ אֱמוּנָה וְאֶסְלַח לָהּ: [ירמיה ה, א]
ר) כִּי יִתְפֹּשׂ אִישׁ בְּאָחִיו בֵּית אָבִיו שִׂמְלָה לְכָה קָצִין תִּהְיֶה לָּנוּ וְהַמַּכְשֵׁלָה הַזֹּאת תַּחַת יָדֶךָ: [ישעיה ג, ו]

The Gemara now describes the merit of answering just "Amen":

אָמַר רֵישׁ לָקִישׁ – **Reish Lakish said:** כׇּל הָעוֹנֶה אָמֵן בְּכׇל כֹּחוֹ – **Whoever responds** to a blessing by answering **"Amen" with all his might,** פּוֹתְחִין לוֹ שַׁעֲרֵי גַן עֵדֶן – **the gates of the Garden of Eden**[20] **are opened for him;** שֶׁנֶּאֱמַר ,,פִּתְחוּ שְׁעָרִים וְיָבֹא גוֹי־צַדִּיק שֹׁמֵר אֱמֻנִים" – **as [the verse] states:**[21] ***Open O gates, and let enter the righteous nation that keeps faith*** (*shomer emunim*). אַל תִּיקְרִי ,,שֹׁמֵר אֱמֻנִים" אֶלָּא שֶׁאוֹמְרִים אָמֵן – **Do not read:** ***shomer emunim*** (*that keeps faith*), **but rather: *she'omerim Amen*** (*that say "Amen"*).[22]

The Gemara expounds the meaning of the word Amen:

מַאי אָמֵן – **What is** the meaning of the word **Amen?** אָמַר רַבִּי חֲנִינָא – **R' Chanina said:** אֵל מֶלֶךְ נֶאֱמָן – It means: **God, trustworthy King.**[23] By responding "Amen" a person affirms his belief in God's sovereignty and trustworthiness. For this reason, he deserves to have the gates of the Garden of Eden open for him.

The Gemara returns to the subject of the Sabbath:

אָמַר רַב יְהוּדָה בְּרֵיהּ דְּרַב שְׁמוּאֵל מִשְּׁמֵיהּ דְּרַב – **Rav Yehudah the son of Rav Shmuel said in the name of Rav:** אֵין הַדְּלֵיקָה מְצוּיָה אֶלָּא בְּמָקוֹם שֶׁיֵּשׁ חִילּוּל שַׁבָּת – **Fires are not common except in a place where there is Sabbath desecration;** שֶׁנֶּאֱמַר – **for [the verse] states:**[24] ,,וְאִם־לֹא תִשְׁמְעוּ אֵלַי לְקַדֵּשׁ אֶת יוֹם הַשַּׁבָּת וּלְבִלְתִּי שְׂאֵת מַשָּׂא וגו׳ – ***But if you will not listen to Me to sanctify the Sabbath day and not to carry any burden, etc.*** וְהִצַּתִּי אֵשׁ בִּשְׁעָרֶיהָ וְאָכְלָה אַרְמְנוֹת יְרוּשָׁלַםִ וְלֹא תִכְבֶּה" – ***then I will ignite a fire in its gates and it will consume the palaces of Jerusalem and it will not be extinguished.***

The Gemara asks:

מַאי ,,וְלֹא תִכְבֶּה" – **What** does the verse mean when it says ***it will not be extinguished?*** Why would it not be extinguished?

The Gemara answers:

אָמַר רַב נַחְמָן בַּר יִצְחָק – **Rav Nachman bar Yitzchak said:** בְּשָׁעָה שֶׁאֵין בְּנֵי אָדָם מְצוּיִין לְכַבּוֹתָהּ – The fire will break out **at a time when there are no people around to extinguish it.**[25]

The Gemara cites a related teaching in regard to the destruction of Jerusalem:

אָמַר אַבַּיֵּי – **Abaye said:** לֹא חָרְבָה יְרוּשָׁלַיִם אֶלָּא בִּשְׁבִיל שֶׁחִלְּלוּ בָּהּ אֶת הַשַּׁבָּת – **Jerusalem was destroyed only because they desecrated the Sabbath in it;** שֶׁנֶּאֱמַר – **as [the verse] states:** ,,וּמִשַּׁבְּתוֹתַי הֶעְלִימוּ עֵינֵיהֶם וָאֵחַל בְּתוֹכָם" – *Her Kohanim have done violence to my Torah ...* ***and from My Sabbaths they averted their eyes and I became profaned in their midst.***[26]

Having cited Abaye's teaching concerning the cause of Jerusalem's destruction, the Gemara digresses to cite other statements concerning this matter:[27]

אָמַר רַבִּי אַבָּהוּ – **R' Abahu said:** לֹא חָרְבָה יְרוּשָׁלַיִם אֶלָּא בִּשְׁבִיל שֶׁבִּיטְּלוּ קְרִיאַת שְׁמַע שַׁחֲרִית וְעַרְבִית – **Jerusalem was destroyed only because they neglected to recite the Shema mornings and evenings;** שֶׁנֶּאֱמַר – **for [the verse] states:** ,,הוֹי מַשְׁכִּימֵי בַבֹּקֶר שֵׁכָר יִרְדֹּפוּ וגו׳" – ***Woe [to] those that rise early in the morning [and] pursue old wine,*** *that linger late into the night [till] wine inflames them.*[28] וּכְתִיב – **And it is written** in the next verse there: ,,וְהָיָה כִנּוֹר וָנֶבֶל תֹּף וְחָלִיל וָיַיִן מִשְׁתֵּיהֶם וְאֵת פֹּעַל ה׳ לֹא יַבִּיטוּ" – ***And the harp and the lyre, the drum and the flute and the wine, are their parties; but to the works of***

NOTES

Yehoshua ben Levi and R' Yochanan concerning אָמֵן יְהֵא שְׁמֵיהּ רַבָּא here, in the midst of its discussions of the Sabbath. *Megadim Chadashim* notes that *Kol Bo* (§7) and *Baal HaTurim* (to *Genesis* 1:1, Reinitz edition) quote a statement of the Sages that cannot be found anywhere in the existing texts of the Talmud or Midrashim. This is: כׇּל הָעוֹנֶה אָמֵן יְהֵא שְׁמֵיהּ רַבָּא מְבָרַךְ כְּאִילּוּ נַעֲשָׂה שׁוּתָּף לְהַקָּדוֹשׁ בָּרוּךְ הוּא בְּמַעֲשֵׂה בְרֵאשִׁית, *Who responds, "Amen; may His great Name be blessed . . ." is treated as if he had became a partner to the Holy One, Blessed is He, in the act of Creation.* Now, this statement clearly echoes the Gemara's statement above concerning the recitation of *Vayechulu. Megadim Chadashim* therefore conjectures that these Rishonim had this statement in their texts of the Gemara here, and that the Gemara included it here precisely because it echoed the previous statement concerning *Vayechulu.* This statement in turn served as the bridge to R' Yehoshua ben Levi's teaching that we have just learned.]

20. I.e. the gates of Paradise in the World to Come.

21. *Isaiah* 26:2.

22. The word שֹׁמֵר is assumed to have an unarticulated *aleph* in it and is expounded as if were spelled שֶׁאֹמֵר, *who says.* Alternatively, the word שֹׁמֵר is expounded exactly as it is spelled and is understood in the sense of waiting for something (see for example *Rashi* to *Genesis* 37:11). The verse thus means: . . . *the righteous nation that takes the time* at the end of each blessing to respond *"Amen."* Although this is not, strictly speaking, a different reading of the verse, the Gemara will occasionally use the expression "do not read" to introduce an exposition based on a completely altered interpretation of the verse's words (*Maharsha*). [See note 3 regarding the meaning of this expression.]

23. The three letters of the word אָמֵן form an acronym for the words אֵל מֶלֶךְ נֶאֱמָן (*Rashi* to *Sanhedrin* 111a). [The plain meaning of the word "Amen" is an affirmation or acceptance of whatever has just been said; see for example *Numbers* 5:22 (see *Orach Chaim* 124:6).]

Tosafos maintain on the basis of this Gemara that it is proper for a person to have these three words in mind when he responds "Amen" (see *Orach Chaim* 124:8 and *Mishnah Berurah* there §36).

24. *Jeremiah* 17:27.

25. That is, on the Sabbath [when Jews are forbidden to extinguish a fire] (*Rashi;* see *Maharsha*).

[It would seem from *Rashi's* comment that though the verse criticizes the people for failing to observe the Sabbath, most people were still observant and would not extinguish a fire on the Sabbath. Since firefighting requires a large number of people (particularly before the invention of modern equipment, when the entire population of the town would have to turn out to fight it), a fire that broke out on the Sabbath would not be extinguished.]

The Gemara does not say that fires never come for other sins but rather that they are not common for other sins. There is a strong measure of justice in this. Since the worst fires occur on the Sabbath, when people are not available to put them out, the Sabbath desecrator's property is in effect destroyed by the Sabbath itself, a fitting retribution (*Rif* in *Ein Yaakov*).

It is also noteworthy that the only specific *melachah* expressly banned by the Torah is the kindling of fire: *You shall not kindle fire in any of your dwellings on the Sabbath day* (*Exodus* 35:3). This verse hints that if the Sabbath is observed in all its details, fire will not be kindled in the dwellings (*Maharsha*).

26. *Ezekiel* 22:26. Although Israel is called to task for many sins in that passage, the chapter concludes with the verse: *Therefore, I have poured out my anger against them, with the fire of My wrath I have consumed them.* Since the destruction described is by fire, which we have just learned comes primarily for the sin of desecrating the Sabbath, Abaye concludes that this was the primary sin for which Jerusalem was destroyed (*Maharsha*).

The sin is laid at the feet of the Kohanim because they were the primary Torah teachers of the people. It was therefore they who should have taken the lead in educating the masses in the difficult and complex laws of the Sabbath. Instead, "they averted their eyes from it" and are therefore blamed for the destruction (*Maharsha*).

27. *Maharsha* deduces from the fact that the Gemara does not quote this next statement as ר׳ אַבָּהוּ אָמַר but rather as אָמַר ר׳ אַבָּהוּ (and similarly those that follow), that the other opinions cited here do not dispute Abaye or each other. Each comments on a different aspect of the destruction, but all are in fact true (see there).

28. *Isaiah* 5:11. That is, who spend their mornings and evenings – when they should be reciting the Shema – drinking and partying instead (*Rashi*).

מהדר אזוזי זוזי דרבנן א"ל במטותא מינייכו לא תחללוניה אמר (א) רבא ואיתימא ר' יהושע בן לוי א אפי' יחיד המתפלל בע"ש צריך לומר ויכולו דאמר רב המנונא כל המתפלל בע"ש ואומר ויכולו מעלה עליו הכתוב כאילו נעשה שותף להקב"ה במעשה בראשית שנאמר א) ויכולו אל תקרי ויכולו (א) אלא ויכלו אמר רבי אלעזר מניין שהדיבור כמעשה שנאמר ב) בדבר ה' שמים נעשו אמר רב חסדא אמר מר עוקבא כל המתפלל בע"ש ואומר ויכולו שני מלאכי השרת המלוין לו לאדם מניחין ידיהן על ראשו ואומרים לו ג) וסר עונך וחטאתך תכופר תניא ר' יוסי בר יהודה אומר שני מלאכי השרת מלוין לו לאדם בע"ש מבית הכנסת לביתו אחד טוב ואחד רע ב וכשבא לביתו ומצא נר דלוק ושלחן ערוך ומטתו מוצעת מלאך טוב אומר יהי רצון שתהא לשבת אחרת כך ומלאך רע עונה אמן בעל כרחו ואם לאו מלאך רע אומר יהי רצון שתהא לשבת אחרת כך ומלאך טוב עונה אמן בעל כרחו אמר ר' אלעזר ג לעולם יסדר אדם שלחנו בע"ש אע"פ שאינו צריך אלא לכזית ואמר ר' חנינא ד לעולם יסדר אדם שלחנו במוצאי שבת אע"פ שאינו צריך אלא לכזית חמין במוצאי שבת מלוגמא פת חמה במוצאי שבת מלוגמא ר' אבהו הוה עבדין ליה באפוקי שבתא עיגלא תילתא הוה אכיל מיניה כולייתא כי גדל אבימי בריה א"ל למה לך לאפסודי כולי האי נשבוק כולייתא ממעלי שבתא שבקוהו ואתא אריא אכליה אריב"ל ה כל העונה אמן יהא שמיה רבא מברך בכל כחו קורעין לו גזר דינו שנאמר ד) בפרוע פרעות בישראל בהתנדב עם ברכו ה' מ"ט בפרוע פרעות משום דברכו ה' רבי חייא בר אבא א"ר יוחנן אפילו יש בו שמץ של עבודה זרה מוחלין לו כתיב הכא בפרוע פרעות וכתיב התם ה) כי פרוע הוא (ב) אמר ריש לקיש כל העונה אמן בכל כחו פותחין לו שערי ג"ע שנאמר ו) פתחו שערים ויבא גוי צדיק שומר אמונים ו אל תיקרי שומר אמונים אלא שאומרים אמן ג מאי אמן א"ר חנינא אל מלך נאמן א"ר יהודה בריה דרב שמואל משמיה דרב אין הדליקה מצויה אלא במקום שיש חילול שבת שנאמר ז) ואם לא תשמעו אלי לקדש את יום השבת ולבלתי שאת משא וגו' והצתי אש בשעריה ואכלה ארמנות ירושלים ולא תכבה מאי ולא תכבה אמר רב נחמן בר יצחק בשעה שאין בני אדם מצויין לכבותה אמר אביי לא חרבה ירושלים אלא בשביל שחללו בה את השבת שנאמר ח) ומשבתותי העלימו עיניהם ואחל בתוכם אמר ר' אבהו לא חרבה ירושלים אלא בשביל שביטלו ק"ש שחרית וערבית שנאמר ט) הוי משכימי בבקר שכר ירדפו וגו' וכתיב י) והיה כנור ונבל תוף וחליל ויין משתיהם ואת פועל ה' לא יביטו וכתיב כ) לכן גלה עמי מבלי דעת אמר רב המנונא לא חרבה ירושלים אלא בשביל שביטלו בה תינוקות של בית רבן שנאמר ל) שפוך על עולל בחוץ וגו' מה טעם שפוך משום דעולל בחוץ אמר עולא לא חרבה ירושלים אלא מפני שלא היה להם בושת פנים זה מזה שנאמר מ) הובישו כי תועבה עשו גם בוש לא יבושו וגו' אמר ר' יצחק לא חרבה ירושלים אלא בשביל שהושוו קטן וגדול שנאמר נ) והיה כעם ככהן וכתיב בתריה ס) ד הבוק תבוק הארץ אמר רב עמרם בריה דר"ש בר אבא א"ר שמעון בר אבא א"ר חנינא לא חרבה ירושלים אלא בשביל שלא הוכיחו זה את זה שנאמר ע) היו שריה כאילים לא מצאו מרעה מה איל זה ראשו של זה בצד זנבו של זה אף ישראל שבאותו הדור כבשו פניהם בקרקע ולא הוכיחו זה את זה א"ר יהודה לא חרבה ירושלים אלא בשביל שביזו בה ת"ח * שנאמר פ) ויהיו מלעיבים במלאכי האלהים ובוזים דבריו ומתעתעים בנביאיו עד עלות חמת ה' בעמו עד [ל]אין מרפא מאי עד לאין מרפא אמר רב יהודה אמר רב ו כל המבזה ת"ח אין לו רפואה למכתו אמר רב מאי דכתיב צ) אל תגעו במשיחי ובנביאי אל תרעו אל תגעו במשיחי אלו תינוקות של בית רבן ובנביאי אל תרעו אלו ת"ח אמר ריש לקיש משום רבי יהודה נשיאה אין העולם מתקיים אלא בשביל הבל תינוקות של בית רבן א"ל רב פפא לאביי דידי ודידך מאי א"ל אינו דומה הבל שיש בו חטא להבל שאין בו חטא ואמר ריש לקיש משום ר"י נשיאה ז אין מבטלין תינוקות של בית רבן אפי' לבנין בית המקדש ואמר ר"ל לר"י נשיאה כך מקובלני * מאבותי ואמרי לה מאבותיך ח כל עיר שאין בה תינוקות של בית רבן מחריבין אותה רבינא אמר מחרימין אותה ט) ואמר רבא לא חרבה ירושלים אלא בשביל שפסקו ממנה אנשי אמנה שנאמר ק) שוטטו בחוצות ירושלים וראו נא [ודעו ובקשו ברחובותיה אם תמצאו איש] (אם יש איש) עושה משפט מבקש אמונה ואסלח לה איני והאמר רב קטינא י) אפי' בשעת כשלונה של ירושלים לא פסקו ממנה אנשי אמנה שנאמר ר) כי יתפש איש באחיו בית אביו (לאמר) שמלה לכה קצין תהיה לנו דברים שבני אדם מתכסין בהן כשמלה ישנן בידיך ר) והמכשלה הזאת תחת ידך

דברים

רש"י

מהדר אזוזי זוזי דרבנן. כשהיה רואה אותן זוגות זוגות ומדברין בתורה מחזר אחריהם ואומר להם במטותא מנכון לכו והתעסקו בעונג שבת ולא תתבטלו לבטל תענוגים: ויכלו. הקב"ה וזה שמספר בשבחו של מקום ובשבח של שבת: יסדר אדם שלחנו בע"ש. ללילי שבת: במוצ"ש. נמי כבוד שבת ללוות ביציאתו דרך כבוד כאדם המלוה את המלך בצאתו מן העיר: חמין. לשתות ולרחוץ: מלוגמא. רפואה: אכליה אריא. לעגל הראוי לשחוט: בכל כחו. בכל כוונתו: בפרוע פרעות. ביטול פורעניות כגון פרוע דמתרגמינן בטל: בהתנדב עם ברכו. כשמתנדבין ישראל לברך את בוראן: כי פרוע. כי פרעו אהרן ע"ז והכי קאמר בהבטל פריעות ע"ז שתשתקע ותשתכח שלא יזכר עונש משום המתנדב עם הוא: אל מלך נאמן. כן מעיד על בוראו שהוא אל מלך נאמן: שאין בני אדם מצויין לכבותה. בשבת: בבקר. בזמן ק"ש וכן מאחרי בנשף: והיה כנור ונבל. בסיפיה דקרא ואת פועל ה' לא יביטו לא שמו לב ליחד שמו על בריותיו: שפוך על עולל. רישא דקרא ואת חמת ה' נלאיתי הכיל שפוך וגו' שפוך החמה בנקמה בשביל שעולל לחוץ ובטלין מבית רבן: הובישו כי תועבה עשו וגו'. סיפיה דקרא גם בוש לא יבושו וגם הכלם לא כו': במשיחי אלו תינוקות של בית רבן. שדרך תינוקות למושחן בשמן: ובנביאי אלו תלמידי חכמים. שנאמר ונביא לבב חכמה (תהלים צ): מחריבין. איכא שיור: מחרימין. ליכא שיור: מתכסין בהן כשמלה. כששואלין אותן טעמי תורה הללו עושין עצמן כמעלימין את דבריהם מפני שאינן יודעים להשיב: ישנן בידך. אתה בקי לפיכך קצין תהיה לנו ותלמדנו חכמה:

דברים

תוספות

ומצא נר דלוק ושולחן ערוך. וא"ת דאמר בריש ערבי פסחים (דף ק:) ושוין שאין מביאין את השולחן אא"כ קידש וי"ל דערוך הוא במקום אחר אלא שאין מביאין אותו עד אחר הקידוש כי היכי דמיתי סעודתא ביקרא דשבת כדאיתא בשאלתות דרב אחאי י) ודוקא כשמיסב שהיו להם שלחנות קטנים לפני כל אחד ואחד אבל שלנו גדולים הם וקשה לטלטלם (ג): כל העונה אמן יהא שמיה רבא בכל כחו. פי' בכל כוונתו וכן פירש ר"ש ור"י אומר דיש בפסיקתא במעשה דר' ישמעאל בן אלישע דקאמר התם כשישראל נכנסים לבתי כנסיות ואומרים יהא שמיה רבא מברך בקול רם מבטלים גזירות קשות: א"ר חנינא אל מלך נאמן. צריך להרהר בו בשעה שאומר אמן:

אידי

עין משפט נר מצוה

מז א מיי' פ"ל מהל' שבת הלכה ב סמג עשין ל טוש"ע או"ח סי' רסח סעיף א:
מח ב מיי' פ"ל שם הל' ה סמג שם טור שו"ע או"ח סימן רסב סעיף א:
מט ג מיי' שם הלכה ה וסמג שם:
נ ד מיי' שם וסמג שם טור שו"ע או"ח סימן ש:
נא ה מיי' פ"ט מהלכות תפלה הלכה א טוש"ע או"ח סימן נו סעיף א [וברב אלפס ברכות פ"ג דף ע"ו: וברא"ש שם סימן יג]:
נב ו מיי' פ"ו מהלכות ת"ת הלכה יא טור שו"ע יו"ד סימן רמג:
נג ז מיי' פ"ב שם הל"ב טוש"ע יו"ד סי' רמה סעיף יג [וברב אלפס פ"ב דב"ב דף קטב.: וברא"ש פ"ב דמו"ק]:
נד ח מיי' שם הלכה א טוש"ע שם סעיף ז [וברב אלפס שם]:

מסורת הש"ס

א) [בה"ג ש"ס וטור סי' רסח איתא אמר רב וכו' ואמר רב המנונא כל המתפלל וכו' וכ"ה בשאלתות בראשית סי' א], ב) סנהדרין דף קי:, ג) סנהדרין דף קיח:, ד) [פי' מתרוקן], ה) חגיגה יד., ו) [חגיגה שם. גיטין מג.], ז) [חגיגה דף יד.], ח) [כתובות לעיל דף י:], ט) [פרשת יתרו סימן נד], י) [וע"ע תוס' פסחים ק: ד"ה שאין].

הגהות הב"ח

(א) גמ' אל תיקרי ויכלו אלא ויכלו: (ב) שם כי פרוע הוא כי פרעו אהרן אמר ריש לקיש: (ג) תוס' ד"ה ומצא וכו' וקשה לטלטלם. נ"ב פי' אחר קידוש שלא להפסיק כל כך בין קידוש לסעודה אנו רגילין לפרוס מפה ולקדש:

גליון הש"ס

גמ' שנאמר ויהיו מלעיבים במלאכי האלהים. ע"ד שאמרו נדרים דף כ ע"ב מאן מה"ש רבנן: שם כך מקובלני מאבותי. עיין ב"מ דף פה ע"א ד"ה אי הדרה.

תורה אור השלם

א) וַיְכֻלּוּ הַשָּׁמַיִם וְהָאָרֶץ וְכָל צְבָאָם: [בראשית ב, א]
ב) בִּדְבַר יְיָ שָׁמַיִם נַעֲשׂוּ וּבְרוּחַ פִּיו כָּל צְבָאָם: [תהלים לג, ו]
ג) וַיַּגַּע עַל פִּי וַיֹּאמֶר הִנֵּה נָגַע זֶה עַל שְׂפָתֶיךָ וְסָר עֲוֺנֶךָ וְחַטָּאתְךָ תְּכֻפָּר: [ישעיה ו, ז]
ד) בִּפְרֹעַ פְּרָעוֹת בְּיִשְׂרָאֵל בְּהִתְנַדֵּב עָם בָּרְכוּ יְיָ: [שופטים ה, ב]
ה) וַיַּרְא מֹשֶׁה אֶת הָעָם כִּי פָרֻעַ הוּא כִּי פְרָעֹה אַהֲרֹן לְשִׁמְצָה בְּקָמֵיהֶם: [שמות לב, כה]
ו) פִּתְחוּ שְׁעָרִים וְיָבֹא גוֹי צַדִּיק שֹׁמֵר אֱמֻנִים: [ישעיה כו, ב]
ז) וְאִם לֹא תִשְׁמְעוּ אֵלַי לְקַדֵּשׁ אֶת יוֹם הַשַּׁבָּת וּלְבִלְתִּי שְׂאֵת מַשָּׂא וּבֹא בְּשַׁעֲרֵי יְרוּשָׁלָיִם בְּיוֹם הַשַּׁבָּת וְהִצַּתִּי אֵשׁ בִּשְׁעָרֶיהָ וְאָכְלָה אַרְמְנוֹת יְרוּשָׁלַיִם וְלֹא תִכְבֶּה: [ירמיה יז, כז]
ח) כֹּהֲנֶיהָ חָמְסוּ תוֹרָתִי וַיְחַלְּלוּ קָדָשַׁי בֵּין קֹדֶשׁ לְחֹל לֹא הִבְדִּילוּ וּבֵין הַטָּמֵא לְטָהוֹר לֹא הוֹדִיעוּ וּמִשַּׁבְּתוֹתַי הֶעְלִימוּ עֵינֵיהֶם וָאֵחַל בְּתוֹכָם: [יחזקאל כב, כו]
ט) הוֹי מַשְׁכִּימֵי בַבֹּקֶר שֵׁכָר יִרְדֹּפוּ מְאַחֲרֵי בַנֶּשֶׁף יַיִן יַדְלִיקֵם: [ישעיה ה, יא]
י) וְהָיָה כִנּוֹר וָנֶבֶל תֹּף וְחָלִיל וָיַיִן מִשְׁתֵּיהֶם וְאֵת פֹּעַל יְיָ לֹא יַבִּיטוּ וּמַעֲשֵׂה יָדָיו לֹא רָאוּ: [ישעיה ה, יב]
כ) לָכֵן גָּלָה עַמִּי מִבְּלִי דָעַת וּכְבוֹדוֹ מְתֵי רָעָב וַהֲמוֹנוֹ צִחֵה צָמָא: [ישעיה ה, יג]
ל) וְאֶת חֲמַת יְיָ מָלֵאתִי נִלְאֵיתִי הָכִיל שְׁפֹךְ עַל עוֹלָל בַּחוּץ וְעַל סוֹד בַּחוּרִים יַחְדָּו כִּי גַם אִישׁ עִם אִשָּׁה יִלָּכֵדוּ זָקֵן עִם מְלֵא יָמִים: [ירמיה ו, יא]
מ) הֹבִשׁוּ כִּי תוֹעֵבָה עָשׂוּ גַּם בּוֹשׁ לֹא יֵבוֹשׁוּ גַּם הַכְלִים לֹא יָדָעוּ לָכֵן יִפְּלוּ בַנֹּפְלִים בְּעֵת פְּקַדְתִּים יִכָּשְׁלוּ אָמַר יְיָ: [ירמיה ו, טו]
נ) וְהָיָה כָעָם כַּכֹּהֵן כַּעֶבֶד כַּאדֹנָיו כַּשִּׁפְחָה כַּגְּבִרְתָּהּ כַּקּוֹנֶה כַּמּוֹכֵר כַּמַּלְוֶה כַּלֹּוֶה כַּנֹּשֶׁה כַּאֲשֶׁר נֹשֶׁא בוֹ: [ישעיה כד, ב]
ס) הִבּוֹק תִּבּוֹק הָאָרֶץ וְהִבּוֹז תִּבּוֹז כִּי יְיָ דִּבֶּר אֶת הַדָּבָר הַזֶּה: [ישעיה כד, ג]
ע) וַיֵּצֵא מִבַּת צִיּוֹן כָּל הֲדָרָהּ הָיוּ שָׂרֶיהָ כְּאַיָּלִים לֹא מָצְאוּ מִרְעֶה וַיֵּלְכוּ בְלֹא כֹחַ לִפְנֵי רוֹדֵף: [איכה א, ו]
פ) וַיִּהְיוּ מַלְעִבִים בְּמַלְאֲכֵי הָאֱלֹהִים וּבוֹזִים דְּבָרָיו וּמִתַּעְתְּעִים בִּנְבִאָיו עַד עֲלוֹת חֲמַת יְיָ בְּעַמּוֹ עַד לְאֵין מַרְפֵּא: [דברי הימים ב' לו, טז]
צ) אַל תִּגְּעוּ בִּמְשִׁיחָי וּבִנְבִיאַי אַל תָּרֵעוּ: [דברי הימים א' טז, כב]
ק) שׁוֹטְטוּ בְּחוּצוֹת יְרוּשָׁלַיִם וּרְאוּ נָא וּדְעוּ וּבַקְשׁוּ בִרְחוֹבוֹתֶיהָ אִם תִּמְצְאוּ אִישׁ אִם יֵשׁ עֹשֶׂה מִשְׁפָּט מְבַקֵּשׁ אֱמוּנָה וְאֶסְלַח לָהּ: [ירמיה ה, א]
ר) כִּי יִתְפֹּשׂ אִישׁ בְּאָחִיו בֵּית אָבִיו שִׂמְלָה לְכָה קָצִין תִּהְיֶה לָּנוּ וְהַמַּכְשֵׁלָה הַזֹּאת תַּחַת יָדֶךָ: [ישעיה ג, ו]

ליקוטי רש"י

עיגלא תילתא. שליש לבנין שהוא משובח מפני שהבהמה בקטנותה אינה עדיין בכחה והולד לראשון ושני אינו בריא [לעיל יא.]. ... מבלי דעת. לפי שהיה להם בלי דעת [שם, יג]. הובישו. עליהן למיבהת. גם בוש לא יבושו. אינם מתביישין ממעשיהם הרעים [ירמיה ו, טו]. הבוק תבוק. מתרוקן [ישעיה כד, ג]. כי יתפש איש באחיו. כאשר יתפוש איש באחיו בבית אביו לאמר עשיר אתה בתורה [ישעיה ג, ו]. כאנשי ירושלים שפסקה תורה מהם והיו שואלין לחבריהם שמלה לך קצין תהיה לנו והמכשלה הזאת תחת ידיך [גיטין מג.]. הכתוב היה מגנן לומר שלא היו יודעין להשיב לשואלים הלכה. שבני אדם מתכסין בהן. נתכסין שלא ישאלו להן לפי שאין בקיאין בהן. ישנן בידך. כלומר אתה בקי בהן [חגיגה יד.].

Hashem they do not look.[29] וּכְתִיב ,,לָכֵן גָּלָה עַמִּי מִבְּלִי־דָעַת'' – **And in the next verse it is written: *Therefore, My people have gone into exile for want of knowledge.***[30]

Another cause for the destruction:
אָמַר רַב הַמְנוּנָא – **Rav Hamnuna said:** לֹא חָרְבָה יְרוּשָׁלַיִם אֶלָּא בִּשְׁבִיל שֶׁבִּיטְּלוּ בָהּ תִּינוֹקוֹת שֶׁל בֵּית רַבָּן – **Jerusalem was destroyed only because they diverted the schoolchildren in it** from their Torah studies; שֶׁנֶּאֱמַר – **as [the verse] states:** ,,שְׁפֹךְ עַל־עוֹלָל בַּחוּץ וגו' '' – ***[to] pour [fury] on little children in the streets,*** **etc.**[31] מַה טַּעַם ,,שְׁפֹךְ'' – **What is the reason that** *fury will* ***pour out?*** מִשּׁוּם דְּ,,עוֹלָל בַּחוּץ'' – **Because *little children are in the street*** instead of in the classroom where they belong.[32]

Another cause:
אָמַר עוּלָּא – **Ulla said:** לֹא חָרְבָה יְרוּשָׁלַיִם אֶלָּא מִפְּנֵי שֶׁלֹּא הָיָה לָהֶם בּוֹשֶׁת פָּנִים זֶה מִזֶּה – **Jerusalem was destroyed only because they had no shame for each other;** שֶׁנֶּאֱמַר – **as [the verse] states:** ,,הֹבִישׁוּ כִּי תוֹעֵבָה עָשׂוּ גַּם־בּוֹשׁ לֹא־יֵבוֹשׁוּ וגו' '' – ***They should have been ashamed, for they committed an abomination; yet they are not at all ashamed* etc.**[33]

Another cause for the destruction of Jerusalem:
אָמַר רַבִּי יִצְחָק – **R' Yitzchak said:** לֹא חָרְבָה יְרוּשָׁלַיִם אֶלָּא בִּשְׁבִיל שֶׁהוּשְׁווּ קָטָן וְגָדוֹל – **Jerusalem was destroyed only because the great and the small were considered equal;** שֶׁנֶּאֱמַר – **as [the verse] states:** ,,וְהָיָה כָעָם כַּכֹּהֵן'' – ***And it shall be as with the people so with the Kohen . . .***[34] וּכְתִיב בָּתְרֵיהּ – **and** immediately **afterwards it is written:** ,,הִבּוֹק תִּבּוֹק הָאָרֶץ'' – ***The land will be utterly emptied.***[35]

Another cause:
אָמַר רַב עַמְרָם בְּרֵיהּ דְּרַבִּי שִׁמְעוֹן בַּר אַבָּא אָמַר רַבִּי שִׁמְעוֹן בַּר אַבָּא אָמַר רַבִּי חֲנִינָא – **Rav Amram the son of R' Shimon bar Abba said in the name of R' Shimon bar Abba** who **said in the name of R' Chanina:** לֹא חָרְבָה יְרוּשָׁלַיִם אֶלָּא בִּשְׁבִיל שֶׁלֹּא הוֹכִיחוּ זֶה אֶת זֶה – **Jerusalem was destroyed only because they did not admonish one another;** שֶׁנֶּאֱמַר – **as [the verse] states:** ,,הָיוּ שָׂרֶיהָ כְּאַיָּלִים לֹא־מָצְאוּ מִרְעֶה'' – ***Its leaders were like harts that found no pasture.***[36] מָה אַיָּל זֶה רֹאשׁוֹ שֶׁל זֶה בְּצַד זְנָבוֹ שֶׁל זֶה – **Just as this hart** walks in a herd with **the head of this one next to the tail of that one,** אַף יִשְׂרָאֵל שֶׁבְּאוֹתוֹ הַדּוֹר כָּבְשׁוּ פְּנֵיהֶם בַּקַּרְקַע – **so too did the Israelites of that generation bury their faces in the ground** to avoid seeing the wrongdoing around them, וְלֹא הוֹכִיחוּ זֶה אֶת זֶה – **and they did not admonish one another.**[37]

Another cause:
אָמַר רַב יְהוּדָה – **Rav Yehudah said:** לֹא חָרְבָה יְרוּשָׁלַיִם אֶלָּא בִּשְׁבִיל שֶׁבִּיזּוּ בָהּ תַּלְמִידֵי חֲכָמִים – **Jerusalem was destroyed only because they demeaned Torah scholars in it;** שֶׁנֶּאֱמַר – **as [the verse] states:** ,,וַיִּהְיוּ מַלְעִבִים בְּמַלְאֲכֵי הָאֱלֹהִים וּבוֹזִים דְּבָרָיו וּמִתַּעְתְּעִים בִּנְבִאָיו עַד עֲלוֹת חֲמַת־ה' בְּעַמּוֹ עַד־לְ[אֵין מַרְפֵּא'' – ***But they mocked the messengers of God, despised His words and scoffed at His prophets, until the wrath of God rose up against His people, until there was no remedy.***[38]

The Gemara elaborates on the last part of this verse:
מַאי ,,עַד־אֵין מַרְפֵּא'' – **What** does it mean when it says ***until there was no remedy?*** אָמַר רַב יְהוּדָה אָמַר רַב – **Rav Yehudah said in the name of Rav:** כׇּל הַמְבַזֶּה תַּלְמִידֵי חֲכָמִים אֵין לוֹ רְפוּאָה לְמַכָּתוֹ – **Whoever demeans Torah scholars – there is no remedy for his wound.**[39]

NOTES

29. They pay no attention to their obligation to proclaim God's unity to His creations [for they are too busy pursuing their pleasures] (*Rashi*). Alternatively, drinking and singing late into the night cause people to forget to say the Shema at night and then to sleep late the following morning, so that they miss the time for saying that Shema as well (*Maharsha,* based on *Sotah* 48a).

[The כִּנּוֹר and נֶבֶל are both stringed instruments except that the נֶבֶל has a greater number of strings than the כִּנּוֹר (*Rashi* to *Isaiah* 5:12).]

30. [I.e. for their failure to recognize the importance of saying the Shema.]

The commentators to the verse (*Targum, Rashi* and *Radak*) explain the phrase וְאֵת פֹּעַל ה' לֹא יַבִּיטוּ, *but to the works of Hashem they do not look,* to refer to the failure to spend time studying Torah. Had the people studied Torah in place of pursuing good times, they would have learned what Hashem expected of them and would have been able to avert destruction. Instead, their indulgence in wine and song blinded them to the doom that awaited them; the exile came upon them for lack of knowledge.

[Although our Gemara interprets the verse to refer to the failure to recite the Shema, these two explanations are not mutually exclusive.] For as the Gemara says in *Menachos* (99b), reciting the Shema in the mornings and evenings is at least a partial fulfillment of the mitzvah to study Torah day and night. Thus, R' Abahu is saying that so little were the people of that time concerned with the study of Torah that they failed even to recite the Shema every day and night (see *Maharal*).

31. *Jeremiah* 6:11. The full text of the verse is: *I am filled with [prophecies of] the fury of Hashem, I am weary of bearing them; [to] pour out [this fury] onto little children in the streets and onto the gatherings of youths together.*

32. When the young are not educated in the Torah, it is the beginning of the end for a Torah society (*Maharal*). The destruction of the future soul of the society therefore brings about its physical destruction.

Similarly, when young men gather together in the streets instead of in the study hall, Hashem's wrath is aroused, as the conclusion of the verse makes clear [*"and onto the gatherings of the youths together"*] (*Maharsha*).

33. Ibid. v. 15. In the previous two verses the prophet castigates the leaders of the people for taking bribes, for not criticizing the people or each other, and even worse, for assuring them that all was well. So mired in corruption were they that even when some were caught committing a crime, they did not have the decency to show shame for their actions (*Rashi, Metzudos* to verse); nor did the others feel shame for not having done anything to halt the wrongdoing of their colleagues (*Maharsha*). Had a sense of shame at least been preserved, many would have held back from committing various offenses for fear of being caught and humiliated (*Maharsha*).

34. *Isaiah* 24:2.

35. A society that does not esteem greatness will cease to produce truly great people. Soon, even its Torah teachers will be flawed and devoid of true Torah greatness (*Maharsha;* see also *Anaf Yosef*).

36. *Lamentations* 1:6.

37. When harts walk in a group, one hart walks with its face right behind the tail of the next animal in line [and with its head hanging down]. Hence, it sees no more than the tail and is oblivious to what may be happening to any other part of the lead animal. In the same way, the leaders of the generation of the Destruction made it a point not to look too closely at what their colleagues were doing [so as not to have to criticize them] (*Maharsha*).

38. *II Chronicles* 36:16. The last chapter of *Chronicles* recounts the last years of the monarchy and Israel's destruction at the hands of the Babylonians. In it the prophet gives God's reasons for destroying the Land and the Temple. The verse just before the one quoted by our Gemara states: *And Hashem, the God of their fathers, sent to them at the hands of His messengers, early and repeatedly, because He had compassion on His people and on His dwelling place.* The verse cited here then continues: *But they mocked the messengers . . .* This was the last straw, the final sin that caused God's anger to pour out against His people.

The phrase, *the messengers of God,* which normally refers to prophets, is understood by Rav here to refer to Torah scholars, because the verse then goes on to mention prophets separately. Indeed, we find the sages sometimes referred to as "angels" [see above, 112b, and *Chagigah* 15b] (*Maharsha*); see also *Nedarim* 20b (*Gilyon HaShas*).

39. As explained in the previous note, the final sin of the people was that they mocked the sages and prophets that God, in His mercy, had sent to lead them back to the true and proper path. The last hope for a confirmed

מהדר אזוזי זוזי דרבנן. כשהיה רואה אומן זוגות זוגות ומדברין בתורה מחזר אחריהם ואומר להם במטותא מנכון לכו והתעסקו בעונג שבת ולא תחללוניה לבטל תענוגים: ויכלו. הקב"ה וזה שמספר בשבחו של מקום ובשבח של שבת: יסדר אדם שלחנו בע"ש. ללילי שבת: במוצ"ש. נמי כבוד שבת ללוות ביציאתו דרך כבוד כאדם המלוה את המלך בצאתו מן העיר: חמין. לשתות ולרחוץ: מלוגמא. רפואה: אכליה אריא. לעגל הראוי לשחוט: בכל כחו. בכל כוונתו: בפרוע פרעות. ביטול פורעניות כגון פרוע למתרגמין בטל: בהתנדב עם ברכו. כשמתנדבין ישראל לברך את בוראן: כי פרוע. כי פרעו אהרן ע"ז והכי קאמר בהבטל פריעות ע"ז שמשתקע ומשתכח שלא יזכר עונש משום התנדב עם הוא: אל מלך נאמן. כך מעיד על בוראו שהוא אל מלך נאמן: שאין בני אדם מצויין לכבותה. בשבת: בבקר. בזמן ק"ש וכן מאחרי בנשף: והיה כנור ונבל. בסיפיה דקרא ואת פועל ה' לא יביטו לא שמו לב ליחד שמו על בריותיו: שפוך על עולל. רישא דקרא ואת חמת ה' נלאיתי הכיל שפוך וגו' שפוך החמה בנקמה בשביל שעולל לחוץ ובטלין מבית רבן: הובישו כי תועבה עשו וגו'. סיפיה דקרא גם בוש לא יבושו וגם הכלם לא כו': במשיחי אלו תינוקות של בית רבן. שדרך תינוקות למושחן בשמן[ף]: ובנביאי אלו תלמידי חכמים. שנאמר ונביא לבב חכמה (תהלים צ): מחריבין. איכא שיור: מחרימין. ליכא שיור: מתכסין בהן כשמלה. כששואלין אותן טעמי תורה הללו עושין עצמן כמעלימין את דבריהם מפני שאין יודעים להשיב: ישנן בידך. אתה בקי לפיכך קצין תהיה לנו ותלמדנו חכמה: דברים

מהדר אזוזי זוזי דרבנן א"ל במטותא מינייכו לא תחללוניה אמר [א] רבא ואיתימא ר' יהושע בן לוי [א]אפי' יחיד המתפלל בע"ש צריך לומר ויכולו דאמר רב המנונא כל המתפלל בע"ש ואומר ויכולו מעלה עליו הכתוב כאילו נעשה שותף להקב"ה במעשה בראשית שנאמר א) ויכולו אל תקרי ויכולו (א) אלא ויכלו אמר רבי אלעזר מניין שהדיבור כמעשה שנאמר ב) בדבר ה' שמים נעשו אמר רב חסדא אמר מר עוקבא כל המתפלל בע"ש ואומר ויכולו שני מלאכי השרת המלוין לו לאדם מניחין ידיהן על ראשו ואומרים לו ג) וסר עונך וחטאתך תכופר תניא ר' יוסי בר יהודה אומר שני מלאכי השרת מלוין לו לאדם בע"ש מבית הכנסת לביתו אחד טוב ואחד רע [ב]וכשבא לביתו ומצא נר דלוק ושלחן ערוך ומטתו מוצעת מלאך טוב אומר יהי רצון שתהא לשבת אחרת כך ומלאך רע עונה אמן בעל כרחו ואם לאו מלאך רע אומר יהי רצון שתהא לשבת אחרת כך ומלאך טוב עונה אמן בעל כרחו אמר ר' אלעזר [ג]לעולם יסדר אדם שלחנו בע"ש אע"פ שאינו צריך אלא לכזית ואמר ר' חנינא [ד]לעולם יסדר אדם שלחנו במוצאי שבת אע"פ שאינו צריך אלא לכזית חמין במוצאי שבת מלוגמא פת חמה במוצאי שבת מלוגמא ר' אבהו הוה עבדין ליה באפוקי שבתא עיגלא תילתא הוה אכיל מיניה כולייתא כי גדל אבימי בריה א"ל למה לך לאפסודי כולי האי נשבוק כולייתא ממעלי שבתא שבקוהו ואתא אריא אכליה אריב"ל [ה]כל העונה אמן יהא שמיה רבא מברך בכל כחו קורעין לו גזר דינו שנאמר ד) בפרוע פרעות בישראל בהתנדב עם ברכו ה' מ"ט בפרוע פרעות משום דברכו ה' רבי חייא בר אבא א"ר יוחנן אפילו יש בו שמץ של עבודה זרה מוחלין לו כתיב הכא בפרוע פרעות וכתיב התם ה) כי פרוע הוא (ב) אמר ריש לקיש כל העונה אמן בכל כחו פותחין לו שערי ג"ע שנאמר ו) פתחו שערים ויבא גוי צדיק שומר אמונים [ו]אל תיקרי שומר אמונים אלא שאומרים אמן [ז]מאי אמן א"ר חנינא אל מלך נאמן א"ר יהודה בריה דרב שמואל משמיה דרב אין הדליקה מצויה אלא במקום שיש חילול שבת שנאמר ז) ואם לא תשמעו אלי לקדש את יום השבת ולבלתי שאת משא וגו' והצתי אש בשעריה ואכלה ארמנות ירושלים ולא תכבה מאי ולא תכבה אמר רב נחמן בר יצחק בשעה שאין בני אדם מצויין לכבותה אמר אביי לא חרבה ירושלים אלא בשביל שחללו בה את השבת שנאמר ח) ומשבתותי העלימו עיניהם ואחל בתוכם אמר ר' אבהו לא חרבה ירושלים אלא בשביל שביטלו ק"ש שחרית וערבית שנאמר ט) הוי משכימי בבקר שכר ירדפו וגו' וכתיב י) והיה כנור ונבל תוף וחליל ויין משתיהם ואת פועל ה' לא יביטו וכתיב כ) לכן גלה עמי מבלי דעת אמר רב המנונא לא חרבה ירושלים אלא בשביל שביטלו בה תינוקות של בית רבן שנאמר ל) שפוך על עולל בחוץ וגו' מה טעם שפוך משום דעולל בחוץ אמר עולא לא חרבה ירושלים אלא מפני שלא היה להם בושת פנים זה מזה שנאמר מ) הובישו כי תועבה עשו גם בוש לא יבושו וגו' אמר ר' יצחק לא חרבה ירושלים אלא בשביל שהושוו קטן וגדול שנאמר נ) והיה כעם ככהן וכתיב בתריה ס) [ח]הבוק תבוק הארץ אמר רב עמרם בריה דר"ש בר אבא א"ר שמעון בר אבא א"ר חנינא לא חרבה ירושלים אלא בשביל שלא הוכיחו זה את זה שנאמר ע) היו שריה כאילים לא מצאו מרעה מה איל זה ראשו של זה בצד זנבו של זה אף ישראל שבאותו הדור כבשו פניהם בקרקע ולא הוכיחו זה את זה א"ר יהודה לא חרבה ירושלים אלא בשביל שביזו בה ת"ח [ט] שנאמר פ) ויהיו מלעיבים במלאכי האלהים ובוזים דבריו ומתעתעים בנביאיו עד עלות חמת ה' בעמו עד [ל]אין מרפא מאי עד לאין מרפא אמר רב יהודה אמר רב [י]כל המבזה ת"ח אין לו רפואה למכתו אמר רב יהודה אמר רב מאי דכתיב צ) אל תגעו במשיחי ובנביאי אל תרעו אל תגעו במשיחי אלו תינוקות של בית רבן ובנביאי אל תרעו אלו ת"ח אמר ריש לקיש משום רבי יהודה נשיאה אין העולם מתקיים אלא בשביל הבל תינוקות של בית רבן א"ל רב פפא לאביי דידי ודידך מאי א"ל אינו דומה הבל שיש בו חטא להבל שאין בו חטא ואמר ריש לקיש משום ר"י נשיאה [כ]אין מבטלין תינוקות של בית רבן אפי' לבנין בית המקדש ואמר ר"ל לר"י נשיאה כך מקובלני מאבותי ואמרי לה מאבותיך [ל]כל עיר שאין בה תינוקות של בית רבן מחריבין אותה רבינא אמר מחרימין אותה ואמר רבא לא חרבה ירושלים אלא בשביל שפסקו ממנה אנשי אמנה שנאמר ק) שוטטו בחוצות ירושלים וראו נא ודעו ובקשו ברחובותיה אם תמצאו איש] [אם יש איש] עושה משפט מבקש אמונה ואסלח לה איני והאמר רב קטינא [מ]אפי' בשעת כשלונה של ירושלים לא פסקו ממנה אנשי אמנה שנאמר ר) כי יתפש איש באחיו בית אביו (לאמר) שמלה לכה קצין תהיה לנו דברים שבני אדם מתכסין בהן כשמלה ישנן בידיך והמכשלה הזאת תחת ידך

דברים

תוספות

ומצא נר דלוק ושולחן ערוך. וא"ת דאמר בריש ערבי פסחים (דף ק:) ושוין שאין מביאין את השולחן אא"כ קידש וי"ל דערוך הוא במקום אחר אלא שאין מביאין אותו עד אחר הקידוש כי היכי דמיתי סעודתא ביקרא דשבת כדאיתא בשאלתות דרב אחאי [ט] ודוקא בימיהם שהיו להם שלחנות קטנים לפני כל אחד ואחד אבל שלנו גדולים הם וקשה לטלטלם [י] (ג): כל העונה אמן יהא שמיה רבא בכל כחו. פי' בכל כוונתו וכן פירש רש"י ור"י אומר דיש בפסיקתא במעשה דר' ישמעאל בן אלישע דקאמר התם כשישראל נכנסים לבתי כנסיות ואומרים יהא שמיה רבא מברך בקול רם מבטלים גזירות קשות: א"ר חנינא אל מלך נאמן. צריך להרהר בו בשעה שאומר אמן: אידי

עין משפט נר מצוה

מז א מיי' פכ"ט מהל' שבת הלכה ז סמג עשין ל טוש"ע או"ח סי' רסח סעיף א:
מח ב מיי' פ"ל שם הל' ה סמג שם טור שו"ע או"ח סימן רסב סעיף א:
מט ג מיי' שם הלכה ה וסמג שם:
נ ד מיי' פ"ל שם טור שו"ע או"ח סימן ש:
נא ה מיי' פ"ט מהלכות תפלה הלכה ב טוש"ע או"ח סימן נו סעיף א [וברב אלפס ברכות דף ט: וברא"ש שם סימן יב]:
נב ו מיי' פ"ב מהלכות ת"ת הלכה יא טור שו"ע יו"ד סימן רמה סעיף ז:
נג ז מיי' פ"ב שם הל' ב טוש"ע יו"ד סי' רמה סעיף ד [וברב אלפס ב"ב פ"ב דף קסב: ...]
נד ח מיי' שם הלכה ב טוש"ע שם סעיף ג [וברב אלפס שם]:

ליקוטי רש"י

עיגלא תילתא. שליש לבטן שהוא משובח מפני שהבהמה בקטנותה אינה עדיין בכחה והולד ראשון ושני אינו בריא [לעיל יא.]. גדל שליש ולא הוא עומד בעיקר טעם בשרו כתמען [ב"מ סח.]. ומגדלין אותן עד שיהו משולשין ומוכרין נמי [שם סט.]. ... [עירובין סג.]. ... [פסחים סח: ע"ש במסורש"ש]. ... [סנהדרין סה: ע"ש]. שומר אמונים. שאמר ופשה כבגלותו ימים רבים לאמונתו של הקב"ה שמקיים הבטחתו שהבטיחם ע"פ נביאיו לגאלם. שומר. ממתין וכן (בראשית לז) ואביו שמר את הדבר וכן (דברים ז) ושמר ה' אלהיך לך [ישעיה כו, ב]. מאי אמן. כשעונין על כל ברכה וברכה אמן מאיך משמע קבלת יחוד שמים. אל מלך נאמן. נוטריקון שמאמין עליו הקב"ה [סנהדרין קיא.]. כנור ונבל. מיני זמרות יש בכנור ... נבל שמנבל כל מיני כלי זמר במדרש תהלים. תוף. של עור הוא. וחליל. אבוב של קנה [בלע"ז] [ישעיה ה, יב]. מבלי דעת. ... הובישו. ... גם בוש לא יבושו. אינם מתביישין ממעשיהם הרעים [ירמיה ו, טו]. הבוק תבוק. תתרוקן [ישעיה כד, ג]. כי יתפש איש באחיו. ... [ישעיה ג, ו].

מסורת הש"ס

א) [בהלכ"ש וטור סי' רסח איתא אמר רב וכו' ואמר רב המנונא כל המתפלל וכו' וכ"ה בשאלתות], ב) סנהדרין דף קי:, ג) [סנהדרין דף קיא.], ד) [פי' מתמרקין], ה) מגילה יז., ו) [מגילה שם. גיטין מג.], ז) [מגילה דף יז.], ח) [...], ט) [פרשת יתרו סימן נד], י) [וע"ע תוס' פסחים ק: ד"ה שאין].

הגהות הב"ח

(א) גמ' אל תיקרי ויכולו אלא ויכלו: (ב) שם כי פרוע הוא כי פרעו אהרן אמר ריש לקיש: (ג) תוס' ד"ה ומצא וכו' וקשה לטלטלם. נ"ב פי' אחר קידוש שלא להפסיק כל כך בין קידוש לסעודה אנו רגילין לפרוס מפה ולקדש:

גליון הש"ס

גמ' שנאמר ויהיו מלעיבים במלאכי האלהים. ע"ד שאמז"ל נדרים דף כ ע"ב ...: שם כך מקובלני מאבותי. עיין ...

תורה אור השלם

א) ויכלו השמים והארץ וכל צבאם: [בראשית ב, א]
ב) בדבר יי שמים נעשו וברוח פיו כל צבאם: [תהלים לג, ו]
ג) ויגע על פי ויאמר הנה נגע זה על שפתיך וסר עונך וחטאתך תכפר: [ישעיה ו, ז]
ד) בפרע פרעות בישראל בהתנדב עם ברכו יי: [שופטים ה, ב]
ה) וירא משה את העם כי פרע הוא כי פרעה אהרן לשמצה בקמיהם: [שמות לב, כה]
ו) פתחו שערים ויבא גוי צדיק שמר אמנים: [ישעיה כו, ב]
ז) ואם לא תשמעו אלי לקדש את יום השבת ולבלתי שאת משא ובא בשערי ירושלים ביום השבת והצתי אש בשעריה ואכלה ארמנות ירושלים ולא תכבה: [ירמיה יז, כז]
ח) כהניה חמסו תורתי ויחללו קדשי בין קדש לחל לא הבדילו ובין הטמא לטהור לא הודיעו ומשבתותי העלימו עיניהם ואחל בתוכם: [יחזקאל כב, כו]
ט) הוי משכימי בבקר שכר ירדפו מאחרי בנשף יין ידליקם: [ישעיה ה, יא]
י) והיה כנור ונבל תף וחליל ויין משתיהם ואת פעל יי לא יביטו ומעשה ידיו לא ראו: [ישעיה ה, יב]
כ) לכן גלה עמי מבלי דעת וכבודו מתי רעב והמונו צחה צמא: [ישעיה ה, יג]
ל) ואת חמת יי מלאתי נלאיתי הכיל שפך על עולל בחוץ ועל סוד בחורים יחדו כי גם איש עם אשה ילכדו זקן עם מלא ימים: [ירמיה ו, יא]
מ) הבישו כי תועבה עשו גם בוש לא יבשו גם הכלים לא ידעו לכן יפלו בנפלים בעת פקדתים יכשלו אמר יי: [ירמיה ו, טו]
נ) והיה כעם ככהן כעבד כאדניו כשפחה כגברתה כקונה כמוכר כמלוה כלוה כנשה כאשר נשא בו: [ישעיה כד, ב]
ס) הבוק תבוק הארץ והבוז תבוז כי יי דבר את הדבר הזה: [ישעיה כד, ג]
ע) ויצא מבת ציון כל הדרה היו שריה כאילים לא מצאו מרעה וילכו בלא כח לפני רודף: [איכה א, ו]
פ) ויהיו מלעבים במלאכי האלהים ובוזים דבריו ומתעתעים בנבאיו עד עלות חמת יי בעמו עד לאין מרפא: [דברי הימים ב לו, טז]
צ) אל תגעו במשיחי ובנביאי אל תרעו: [דברי הימים א טז, כב]
ק) שוטטו בחוצות ירושלים וראו נא ודעו ובקשו ברחובותיה אם תמצאו איש אם יש עשה משפט מבקש אמונה ואסלח לה: [ירמיה ה, א]
ר) כי יתפש איש באחיו בית אביו שמלה לכה קצין תהיה לנו והמכשלה הזאת תחת ידך: [ישעיה ג, ו]

הכתוב היה מגנן לומר שלא היו יודעין להשיב לשואלים הלכה. שבני אדם מתכסין בהן. ... ישנן בידך. ...

The Gemara cites a related teaching:

אָמַר רַב יְהוּדָה אָמַר רַב – Rav Yehudah said in the name of Rav: מַאי דִּכְתִיב ,,אַל־תִּגְּעוּ בִּמְשִׁיחָי וּבִנְבִיאַי אַל־תָּרֵעוּ" – **What is** the meaning of **that which is written:** ***Do not touch My anointed ones, and to My prophets do no harm?***[40] ,,אַל־תִּגְּעוּ בִּמְשִׁיחָי" אֵלּוּ תִּינוֹקוֹת שֶׁל בֵּית רַבָּן – ***Do not touch My anointed ones,*** **this refers to schoolchildren** who study Torah; ,,וּבִנְבִיאַי אַל־תָּרֵעוּ" אֵלּוּ תַּלְמִידֵי חֲכָמִים – ***and to My prophets do no harm,*** **this refers to Torah scholars.**[41]

The previous exposition makes clear that Hashem attaches *special* importance to the Torah studied by schoolchildren. This point is now elaborated:

אָמַר רֵישׁ לָקִישׁ מִשּׁוּם רַבִּי יְהוּדָה נְשִׂיאָה – **Reish Lakish said in the name of R' Yehudah Nesiah:**[42] אֵין הָעוֹלָם מִתְקַיֵּים אֶלָּא בִּשְׁבִיל הֶבֶל תִּינוֹקוֹת שֶׁל בֵּית רַבָּן – **The world continues to exist only in the merit of the breath** that comes from the mouths **of schoolchildren,** i.e. the words of Torah they utter as they study. אָמַר לֵיהּ רַב פָּפָּא לְאַבַּיֵי – **Rav Pappa said to Abaye:** דִּידִי וְדִידָךְ מַאי – **My breath and your breath, what** of them? Is our Torah study not at least as significant? אָמַר לֵיהּ – **[Abaye] said to him:** אֵינוֹ דוֹמֶה הֶבֶל שֶׁיֵּשׁ בּוֹ חֵטְא לְהֶבֶל שֶׁאֵין בּוֹ חֵטְא – **Breath that contains** the taint of **sin cannot be compared to breath that does not contain** the taint of **sin.**[43]

A further statement on the great importance attached to the Torah study of schoolchildren:

וְאָמַר רֵישׁ לָקִישׁ מִשּׁוּם רַבִּי יְהוּדָה נְשִׂיאָה – **And Reish Lakish said in the name of R' Yehudah Nesiah:** אֵין מְבַטְּלִין תִּינוֹקוֹת שֶׁל בֵּית רַבָּן אֲפִילּוּ לְבִנְיַן בֵּית הַמִּקְדָּשׁ – **We do not divert schoolchildren** from their Torah studies **even for** the sake of **building the Holy Temple.**

Reish Lakish adds to this teaching:

וְאָמַר רֵישׁ לָקִישׁ לְרַבִּי יְהוּדָה נְשִׂיאָה – **And Reish Lakish said to R' Yehudah Nesiah:** כָּךְ מְקוּבְּלַנִי מֵאֲבוֹתַי – **"I have received the following tradition from my fathers,"** וְאָמְרִי לָהּ מֵאֲבוֹתֶיךָ – **and some say** Reish Lakish said, **"from your fathers,"** i.e. from Rebbi and the *Nesiim* who preceded him: כָּל עִיר שֶׁאֵין בָּהּ תִּינוֹקוֹת שֶׁל בֵּית רַבָּן מַחֲרִיבִין אוֹתָהּ – **Any town in which there are no schoolchildren** studying Torah **is eventually destroyed.** רָבִינָא אָמַר מַחֲרִימִין אוֹתָהּ – **Ravina said: It is eventually annihilated.**[44]

Another teaching concerning the cause for Jerusalem's destruction:

וְאָמַר רָבָא – **And Rava said:** לֹא חָרְבָה יְרוּשָׁלַיִם אֶלָּא בִּשְׁבִיל שֶׁפָּסְקוּ מִמֶּנָּה אַנְשֵׁי אֲמָנָה – **Jerusalem was destroyed only because people of truth had disappeared from it;** שֶׁנֶּאֱמַר – **as it says:**[45] ,,שׁוֹטְטוּ בְּחוּצוֹת יְרוּשָׁלַםִ וּרְאוּ־נָא וּדְעוּ וּבַקְשׁוּ בִרְחוֹבוֹתֶיהָ – ***Search in the open places of Jerusalem and see now and know, and seek in its streets,*** אִם־תִּמְצְאוּ אִישׁ אִם־יֵשׁ (אִישׁ) עֹשֶׂה מִשְׁפָּט מְבַקֵּשׁ אֱמוּנָה וְאֶסְלַח לָהּ" – ***if you will find a man, if there is one who dispenses justice, who seeks the truth – and I will forgive her.***

Rava's assertion is challenged:

אִינִי – **Is this indeed so?** וְהָאָמַר רַב קְטִינָא – **But Rav Ketina has said:** אֲפִילוּ בִּשְׁעַת כִּשְׁלוֹנָהּ שֶׁל יְרוּשָׁלַיִם לֹא פָּסְקוּ מִמֶּנָּה אַנְשֵׁי אֲמָנָה – **Even in the hour of Jerusalem's downfall people of truth did not disappear from it;** שֶׁנֶּאֱמַר – **for it says** concerning the period before the destruction of the First Temple:[46] ,,כִּי יִתְפֹּשׂ אִישׁ בְּאָחִיו בֵּית אָבִיו (לאמר) שִׂמְלָה לְכָה קָצִין תִּהְיֶה־לָּנוּ" – ***When a man will grab hold of his brother of the house of his father***[47] ***[and say:] You have a garment, be a chief for us.***

The Gemara interrupts its citation of the verse to expound the metaphor of the garment.

דְּבָרִים שֶׁבְּנֵי אָדָם מִתְכַּסִּין בָּהֶן כְּשִׂמְלָה יֶשְׁנָן בְּיָדֶיךָ – **Matters** of Torah, **concerning which people cover themselves up, as with a garment,** pretending to withhold the answer from the questioner because they cannot answer it, **are** to be found **in your hand.**[48]

The verse continues:

,,וְהַמַּכְשֵׁלָה הַזֹּאת תַּחַת יָדֶךָ" – ***and [let] this stumbling block be under your hand.*** That is, since you are knowledgeable, let the teaching of Torah be under your hand. The Gemara now explains how the term "stumbling block" is a metaphor for Torah:

NOTES

sinner is that someone will show him the error of his ways and inspire him to repent. But once the sinner has fallen to the level of mocking those who are sent to save him, there is no longer any hope for him. His wound is too severe to be healed (*Maharsha*).

40. *I Chronicles* 16:22.

41. The phrase, *My anointed ones,* is appropriate for schoolchildren because it was the practice to anoint young children with oil (see Gemara above, 10b; *Yoma* 78b; *Chullin* 24b). The term *prophets* is applicable to scholars and sages in line with the verse (*Psalms* 90:12): וְנָבִא לְבַב חָכְמָה, *and a prophet is the heart of wisdom* (*Rashi*).

42. [The word *Nesiah* is Aramaic for *Nasi* (prince). R' Yehudah Nesiah was the grandson of R' Yehudah HaNasi (who is generally known simply as "Rebbi"). Like his grandfather, he served as the leader of the Sanhedrin and of the Jewish people in the Land of Israel. To distinguish him from his famous grandfather, he was referred to by the Aramaic name for his position.]

43. [Since children below the age of bar mitzvah (thirteen) are not held accountable for their deeds, their words of Torah are pure and untainted by sin. By contrast, the Torah of adults is tainted by their sins.] Since the world as a whole is assured of continued existence only in the merit of pure Torah, it must therefore rely on the untainted Torah of schoolchildren for its continued existence (*Maharal*).

44. According to Ravina, it is so utterly destroyed that nothing is left of it (*Rashi*). See *Shulchan Aruch, Yoreh Deah* 245:7.

45. *Jeremiah* 5:1.

46. *Isaiah* 3:6. The Gemara will intersperse its citation of the verse with explanatory remarks. Rav Ketina's proof does not emerge until the next verse is quoted and explained on 120a.

47. I.e. of a member of his extended family, not necessarily his brother (*Radak* to verse).

48. The verse discusses the period preceding the destruction of the Temple, when the men of Jerusalem had become lax in the study of Torah and people capable of answering questions of Torah were scarce. When confronted with a questioner, they would cover their ignorance by pretending not to hear the question. When they would find someone who knew some Torah, they would seize hold of him and beg him to be their "chief," i.e. teacher of Torah (*Rashi*).

דְּבָרִים שֶׁאֵין בְּנֵי אָדָם עוֹמְדִין עֲלֵיהֶם אֶלָּא אִם כֵּן נִכְשָׁלִים בָּהֶן יֶשְׁנָן תַּחַת יָדֶיךָ – **Matters that people do not fully grasp unless they** first **stumble over them,**[1] **these are** to be found **in your hands.** Therefore, we implore you: "קָצִין תִּהְיֶה־לָּנוּ" – ***Be a chief for us.*** The next verse continues: "יִשָּׂא בַיּוֹם הַהוּא לֵאמֹר לֹא־אֶהְיֶה חֹבֵשׁ וגו'" – ***He shall raise up*** *an oath* ***that day saying: I will not be a ruler,***[2] **etc.** *and in my house there is no bread and no garment; do not install me as a chief of the people.*[3] The Gemara explains: אֵין "יִשָּׂא" אֶלָּא לְשׁוֹן שְׁבוּעָה – **The word** ***raise up*** [*yisa*] **is nothing but an expression of oath;** וְכֵן הוּא אוֹמֵר "לֹא תִשָּׂא אֶת־שֵׁם־ה' " – **and so it says** in the Ten Commandments:[4] ***You shall not raise up the Name of Hashem,*** *your God, in vain.* "לֹא־אֶהְיֶה חֹבֵשׁ" – The phrase ***I will not be a ruler*** (*choveish*) means: לֹא אֶהְיֶה מְחוֹבְשֵׁי עַצְמָן בְּבֵית הַמִּדְרָשׁ – **I was not accustomed to be from those that shut** (*chovshei*) **themselves in the house of study,** i.e. I have not been diligent in my studies, "וּבְבֵיתִי אֵין לֶחֶם וְאֵין שִׂמְלָה" – ***and in my house there is no bread and no garment;*** שֶׁאֵין בְּיָדִי לֹא מִקְרָא וְלֹא מִשְׁנָה וְלֹא גְמָרָא – **that is, I have in my hand neither** knowledge of **Scripture nor** of **Mishnah nor** of **Talmud,** and therefore, despite appearances, I am not qualified to be your "chief" – instructor of Torah.

We see from this that even in the hour of Jerusalem's downfall, when it lacked true scholars, the people thought to be scholars who were offered positions of authority on that account were honest enough to admit that they lacked the necessary knowledge to fill the position. Thus, it is evident that down to the very end Jerusalem possessed men of truth, as Rav Ketina said. – ? –

The Gemara questions this proof:

וּמִמַּאי – **And from what** do you conclude that their admission was due to their integrity? דִּילְמָא שָׁאנֵי הָתָם – **Perhaps it was different in that** case, דְּאִי אָמַר לְהוּ גְּמִירְנָא אָמְרוּ לֵיהּ אֵימָא לָן – **since if one** of them **would have said to [the people], "I am learned," they would say to him, "Tell us** the principles of the Torah that we wish to know," and he would have been forced to admit his ignorance. Thus, he had no choice but to be truthful!

The Gemara answers:

הֲוָה לֵיהּ לְמֵימַר גָּמַר וְשָׁכַח – **He should** nonetheless **have responded** that **he had** once **learned but had forgotten.** מַאי "לֹא־אֶהְיֶה חֹבֵשׁ" – **What** did he mean when he said, **"I am not accustomed to shut myself in** the house of study"? כְּלָל – He meant, "I am not **at all** knowledgeable."[5] To be able to admit this to those who think otherwise is a mark of integrity and regard for the truth. How then could Rava have said that Jerusalem was destroyed only because men of truth had disappeared from its midst. – ? –

The Gemara answers in defense of Rava:

לָא קַשְׁיָא – **This is not a difficulty.** כָּאן בְּדִבְרֵי תוֹרָה כָּאן בְּמַשָּׂא וּמַתָּן – **Here** (in Rav Ketina's statement) we speak **in regard to matters of Torah,** concerning which people were indeed truthful and did not allow themselves to be lauded for what was not in fact true. Whereas **here** (in Rava's statement) we speak **in regard to business dealings;** in this respect there were no longer any people of truth left in Jerusalem.[6]

Mishnah

The Mishnah continues to list the things that can be saved from a fire on the Sabbath: מַצִּילִין סַל מָלֵא כִּכָּרוֹת – **One may save** from his burning house **a basket full of loaves** אַף עַל פִּי שֶׁיֵּשׁ בּוֹ מֵאָה סְעוּדוֹת – **even though it has** enough **in it** for **a hundred meals,** וְעִיגּוּל שֶׁל דְּבֵילָה – **and a round** cake **of pressed figs** וְחָבִית שֶׁל יַיִן – **and a barrel of wine,** even though these contain much more than needed for three meals. וְאוֹמֵר לַאֲחֵרִים – **And he may tell others,** בּוֹאוּ וְהַצִּילוּ לָכֶם – **"Come and save** food **for yourselves";** וְאִם הָיוּ פִּיקְחִין – **and if they were wise,** עוֹשִׂין עִמּוֹ חֶשְׁבּוֹן אַחַר הַשַּׁבָּת – **they make a reckoning with him after the Sabbath** for their wages as laborers.[7]

NOTES

1. The underlying principles of Torah law are not easily comprehended and a person does not usually fully grasp them until he "stumbles over them," i.e. misstates them two or three times [and is challenged and forced to retract and modify his previous understanding of them] (*Rashi*). *Rashi* to *Chagigah* 14a explains this to refer to the habit of students not to pay close attention to their lessons until they have been corrected several times.

2. Literally: an imprisoner. A ruler is known by this term because he imposes his will on the people by imprisoning those who do not follow his commands (*Radak* to verse).

3. This is the conclusion of the verse (*Isaiah* 3:7), which the Gemara will expound.

4. *Exodus* 20:7.

5. Although he would indeed be forced to concede the truth that he did not know the answer to their question, he would not be forced to concede that he *never* knew. He could simply have said that he had forgotten the answer – a response that would better have preserved his stature in the eyes of the people. To embarrass himself by admitting that he did not know because he had not studied diligently is a mark of true honesty.

6. For this reason, in the verse cited by Rava (119b) Jeremiah says to "search in *the open places* of Jerusalem . . . and seek in its *streets* [for an honest man]," for the dishonesty to which he referred was the dishonesty of the marketplace, not of the study halls (*Maharsha*).

In a very moving summation, *Maharsha* notes that almost all the sins listed by the Gemara here as causes for the destruction of Jerusalem were still prevalent in his time. *Maharsha* writes that few people in his time observe the Sabbath as carefully as they should, for they are not sufficiently knowledgeable of the many intricate laws of the Sabbath, nor are these laws taught by the rabbis as widely as they should be. Many people party [late into the evening] on Saturday night and thereby sleep late the next morning and miss saying the Shema in its proper time. The diversion of schoolchildren from their Torah studies is commonplace, and even among older students much time is wasted with vacations and excursions. The distinction between people of lesser and greater stature is blurred by the many lesser scholars who seek appointments to the highest rabbinical positions even though they lack the proper level of scholarship. And the common people seek to live up to the standards of the wealthy in their manner of dress and the lavishness of their homes, which often leads them to steal from one another. In the main communities, criticism of misdeeds is no longer heard and it is thought a greater virtue to be concerned for people's honor than to criticize their wrongdoing. The shaming of *talmidei chachamim* and the refusal to accept their criticism are everyday occurrences. And financial dealings are not conducted with honesty, with all manner of cheating, charging of interest (*ribbis*), and theft taking place. So widespread is this problem, *Maharsha* states, that people no longer even think it prohibited to withhold money that belongs to others. *Maharsha* concludes: "It is proper for every person who fears God to take these points to heart, and whoever has it within his power to protest these matters should certainly do so."

[It is perhaps worth concluding this discussion with the comment of the Sages (*Yerushalmi Yoma* 1:1) that "any generation in whose days the Temple is not rebuilt is considered a generation in whose days the Temple has been destroyed." When the sins that brought about the Temple's destruction will finally be rectified, we may expect to witness its long anticipated rebuilding.]

7. [I.e. if they decide not to keep the items for themselves (which, strictly speaking, they are entitled to do),] they may ask for wages instead (*Rashi*). The Gemara will explain this further.

[How much food may other people save? *Rambam* (*Hil. Shabbos* 23:24) and *Tur* (*Orach Chaim* 334) state that they too may each save only three meals' worth of food. *Ran,* however, cites the view of *R' Yeshayah of Trani* who states that since it is not their property being threatened by the flames, we are not concerned that they will forget and extinguish the fire. Thus, they may save as much as they wish.]

דברים שאין אדם עומד בהן. על בוריין לאומרן כהלכתן: אלא אם כן נכשל בהן. עד שאומרן ב' וג' פעמים בשיבוש דהיינו טעמי תורה המסותרין: לא אהיה חובש. איני רגיל להיות חובש חבוש בבהמ"ד. אהיה הורגלתי כמו שחוק לרעהו אהיה (איוב יב) אני הווה: וממאי. דמשום דיש בהן אמנה הוא דילמא על כרחך צריכים שישיבו האמת: דאי אמר להו גמירנא. אותן טעמי תורה: אמרי ליה. שואלים אימא לן: ומשני הוה ליה למימר גמר ושכח מאי לא אהיה חובש. מודה הוא על האמת שלא יגע בתורה: בדברי תורה. היו נאמנין ואין מתהללים על שקר:

דברים שאין בני אדם עומדין עליהם אלא אם כן נכשלים בהן ישנן תחת ידיך קצין תהיה לנו (א) ישא ביום ההוא לאמר לא אהיה חובש וגו' אין ישא אלא לשון שבועה וכן הוא אומר (ב) לא תשא את שם ה' לא אהיה חובש לא אהיה מחובשי עצמן בבית המדרש (א) ובביתי אין לחם ואין שמלה שאין בידי לא (ו) מקרא ולא משנה ולא גמרא וממאי דילמא שאני התם דאי אמר להו גמירנא אמרו ליה אימא לן הוה ליה למימר גמר ושכח מאי לא אהיה חובש כלל לא קשיא כאן בדברי תורה כאן במשא ומתן: מתני' (א) מצילין סל מלא ככרות אע"פ שיש בו מאה סעודות ועיגול של דבילה וחבית של יין ואומר לאחרים בואו והצילו לכם ואם היו פיקחין עושין עמו חשבון אחר השבת להיכן מצילין אותן (ב) לחצר המעורבת בן בתירא אומר אף לשאינה מעורבת (ג) ולשם מוציא כל כלי תשמישו (ד) ולובש כל מה שיכול ללבוש ועוטף כל מה שיכול לעטוף ר' יוסי אומר י"ח כלים (ה) וחוזר ולובש ומוציא ואומר לאחרים בואו והצילו עמי: גמ' והא תנא ליה (ג) רישא ג' סעודות ותו לא אמר רב הונא לא קשיא כאן בבא להציל כאן בבא לקפל (ו) בא להציל מציל את כולן בא לקפל אינו מקפל אלא מזון ג' סעודות (ז) ר' אבא בר זבדא אמר רב אידי ואידי בבא לקפל ולא קשיא כאן לאותה חצר כאן לחצר אחרת בעי רב הונא בריה דרב יהושע פירש טליתו וקיפל והניח וקיפל והניח מאי כבא להציל דמי או כבא לקפל דמי (א) מדאמר רבא אטעיה רב שיזבי לרב חסדא ודרש ובלבד שלא יביא כלי שהוא מחזיק יותר מג' סעודות ש"מ (ז) כבא להציל דמי ושפיר דמי א"ל רב נחמן בר יצחק לרבא מאי טעותא אמר ליה דקתני (ח) ובלבד שלא יביא כלי אחר ויקלוט כלי אחר ויצרף כלי אחר הוא דלא אבל בההוא מנא כמה דבעי מציל: ועיגול של דבילה כו': (ח) חשבון מאי עבידתיה מהפקירא קזכו אמר רב חסדא מדת חסידות שנו כאן אמר רבא חסידי אגרא דשבתא שקלי אלא אמר רבא הכא בירא שמים עסקינן (ב) (ט) ולא ניחא ליה דליתהני מאחרים ובחנם נמי לא ניחא ליה דליטרח והכי קאמר ואם היו פיקחין דידעי דכה"ג לאו שכר שבת הוא עושין עמו חשבון לאחר השבת: ולהיכן מצילין כו': מ"ש הכא דקתני לכם ומ"ש הכא דקתני עמי אמרי גבי מזונות קתני לכם משום דלא קא חזו (ג) אלא מזון ג' סעודות אבל גבי לבושים קתני עמי משום דקחזי ליה לכולי יומא: ת"ר לובש (ד) מוציא ופושט וחוזר ולובש ומוציא ופושט ואפילו כל היום כולו דברי רבי מאיר רבי יוסי אומר שמנה עשר כלים ואלו הם שמנה עשר כלים מקטורן (י) אונקלי ופונדא וקלבוס של פשתן וחלוק (י) ואפיליות ומעפורת (כ) ושני ספרקין ושני מנעלים ושני אנפילאות וב' פרגד וחגור שבמתניו וכובע שבראשו וסודר שבצוארו: מתני' ר' שמעון בן ננס אומר (ל) פורסין עור של גדי על גבי שידה תיבה ומגדל שאחז בהן את האור מפני שהוא מחרך (מ) ועושין מחיצה בכל הכלים בין מלאין בין ריקנים בשביל שלא תעבור הדליקה רבי יוסי אוסר בכלי חרס חדשים מלאין מים לפי שאין יכולין לקבל את האור והן מתבקעין ומכבין את הדליקה: גמ' אמר רב יהודה אמר רב טלית שאחז בה האור מצד אחד נותנין עליה מים מצד אחר ואם כבתה כבתה מיתיבי (פ) טלית שאחז בה האור מצד אחד פושטה ומתכסה בה ואם כבתה כבתה וכן ספר תורה שאחז בו האור פושטו וקורא בו ואם כבה כבה הוא

מתני' ועיגול של דבילה. שהוא גדול ויש בו סעודות הרבה: ואם היו פקחין. לישאל שכרן כפועלים: כל כלי תשמישו. שצריכין לו לאותו היום כגון כוסות וקיתוניות: י"ח כלים. מפרש להו בגמרא שכן דרך ללובשן בחול יחד אבל טפי מהכי לא ואינו פושטן לחזור וללבוש ולהציל אחרים: גמ' בבא להציל. [שהציל] בסל [אחד] כדקתני סל מלא ככרות ואינו טורח אלא להצילן מתוך הדליקה בבת אחת מציל כל מה שבסל דהא חדא זימנא הוא מה לי פורתא מה לי טובא: בבא לקפל. סלים הרבה זה עם זה לטרוח [ולאוספם] ולחזור ולהוציא מזון ג' סעודות הוא דיכול להציל בסלים הרבה ותו לא שכל א' טורח בעצמו הוא: פירש טליתו וקיפל והניח. הביא אוכלין והניח וחזר והביא והניח מהו: כבא להציל דמי. הואיל ואין כאן אלא כלי אחד ובפעם אחת הוא מוציאם: או כבא לקפל דמי. הואיל וטורח לאסוף ולכנוס: אטעייה רב שיזבי לרב חסדא (ט) [עד]. שדרש לפניו והודה לו רב חסדא והא מתני' דאמרן לעיל (דף קיז:) נשברה לו חבית בראש גגו מביא כלי ומניח תחתיה ודרש רב שיזבי לרב חסדא ובלבד שלא (ה) יתן כלי המחזיק יותר משלש סעודות והודה לו רב חסדא ומדאמר רבא אטעייה שמע מינה טעותא הוא דאפילו מחזיק סעודות הרבה מותר כיון דחד מנא הוא והאי כמקפל ונותן בכלי אחד דמי דהא מעט מעט הוא נופל (י) ומטפטף בו ש"מ בחד מנא כבא להציל דמי: מאי טעותא. מנא לך דטעותא הוא בידיה: אמר ליה. מדקתני בה בברייתא: ובלבד שלא יביא כלי אחר כו'. ש"מ כלים טובא הוא דאסירי אבל בחד שפיר דמי: מהפקירא וכו'. דהא הצילו לכם קאמר להו לצרכיהם ואם פקחים הם יעכבו הכל הוה ליה למיתני: מדת חסידות. שמחזירין לו: חסידי אגרא דשבתא שקלי. בתמיה אם חסידים הם יש להם לוותר משלהם בכל דבר שיש בו נדנוד עבירה ואע"ג דלאו שכר שבת גמור הוא שהרי לא התנה ומהפקירא קא זכו מיהו חסיד לא מיקרי אא"כ מוותר משלו: הכא בירא שמים עסקינן. המציל הזה ירא שמים הוא ולא חסיד לוותר משלו: דלא ניחא ליה דליתהני מאחריני. בזכייה דהפקירא דידע דלא מרצונו הפקירו: ובחנם נמי לא ניחא ליה דליטרח. דלאו חסיד הוא (ו) ולמחול על שלו: והכי קאמר כו'. כלומר דהאי אם היו פקחין דמתני' לאו פקחין בדין קאמר ליטול את הראוי להם דאם כן יעכבו הכל הוה ליה למתני אלא לאו הכי קאמר הני יראי שמים אם פקחין הן בהלכות שבת דידעי דכה"ג לאו שכר שבת הוא דמעיקרא לאו אדעתא דשכר פעולה נחית עושין עמו חשבון והכי קאמר אדרב חסדא נמי קאי אלא לא שבקיניה לרב חסדא לסיימיה למילתיה: (כ) לחצר המעורבת. ואפי' הכי טובא לא ליציל כדאמר לעיל (דף קיז:) מתוך שבהול אי שרי לאיעסוקי בהצלה כולי האי אתי לכבויי: מקטורן. מנטו"ל: אונקלי. לבוש רחב כעין סרבל"א ובלשון ערבי מחשיא"ה: פונדא. אזור חלול מעל למדיו: קלבוס. נביי"ש: חלוק. קמיש"א על בשרו: ואפליון. סדין להתעטף בו כולו: מעפורת. לעטוף ראשו: ושני ספרקין. פייסול"ש: אנפילייאות. קלצונ"ש של למר: פרגוד. גנליי"ש ובלשון אשכנז קני הוז"ן: חגור. על חלוקו מבפנים: וסודר שבצוארו. ותלויין ראשיו לפניו לקנח בו פיו ועיניו: מתני' עור של גדי. לח: מפני שהוא מחרך. מן האור ובלע"ז רטריי"ט ואינו נשרף ומתוך כך הוא מגין על התיבה: בין מלאים. מים: שאינן יכולין לקבל כח האור. מפני שחדשים הם:

אידי ואידי בבא לקפל. פירש הר"ב פורת דלקפל היינו אפי' בא לקפל דלר' אבא אין חילוק בין לקפל בין להציל דאפילו להציל בחצר אחרת לא שרי אלא מזון ג' סעודות אבל אין נראה לומר דלהציל שרי אפילו מאה סעודות בחצר אחרת גם לרבי אבא דאם כן הוה ליה לאוקומי מתני' אידי ואידי בחצר אחרת וכאן בבא לקפל וכאן בבא להציל: נותן מים מצד זה. פירש רשב"ם לאו דוקא על הטלית דהא קי"ל בפ' דם חטאת (זבחים צד:) דבבגד שרייתו זהו כיבוסו ולעיל בסוף פרק שמנה שרצים (דף קיא.) פירשתי:

גרס

גמ'

רבינו חננאל

מצילין סל מלא ככרות ואע"ג שיש בו ק' סעודות. אקשינן איני והא תני רישא מצילין מזון ג' סעודות ותו לא ושני רב הונא לא קשיא רישא בבא לקפל. פי' כגון שמקבץ מתוך הבית המקומות [הרבה] ונותן בכמה כלים שאין לו להציל אלא מזון של ג' סעודות בלבד. סיפא במציל כולו בכלי אחד כמות שהוא. ואע"פ שאין זה הטעם כאשר פירשנו. כי רישא במקפל ונותן בכלים שנים ושלשה. וסיפא במציל סל אחד כמות שהוא מפורש (היבננוהו מז'). בעי רב הונא בריה דרב יהושע פירש טליתו וקיפל והניח וקיפל והניח מהו. כבא לקפל דמי או כבא להציל דמי. דמגלי לן שאם קיפל בכלי אחד ונטלו. וחזר וקיפל בכלי אחר ונטלו זהו לקפל פשיטא שאינו מציל אלא מזון ג' סעודות. וכי קא מבעיא שקיפל והניח בתוך טליתו וחזר וקיפל והניח בתוך טליתו מי אמרינן כיון שמקפל ומביא כמקפל דמי ואסור. או דילמא כיון שהוא מניחן בתוך טלית אחד ונוטלן כאחד כבא להציל דמי ושרי. ומיפרשא נמי הא בגמ' בסוף יציאות השבת. הנהו תרי תלמידי. מר מציל בחד מנא ומר מציל בתרי מאני וקמפלגי בפלוגתא דר' אבא בר זבדא ורב הונא. הכין גמרא ומיגמר מינה דלקפל בתרי תלתא מני כדפרישנא לעיל דאסיר לרב הונא ושרי לר' אבא בר זבדא ומסתייע נמי בתלמוד א"י דאמרי על מצילין סל מלא ככרות מכיון שכלו גוף אחד כמין שכולה סעודה אחת היא והאי במימרא דרב הונא והא ר' אבא בר זבדא ופליק פירוק אחר. ואמר רישא דמתני' במציל לחצר אחרת שאין לו להציל אלא מזון ג' סעודות לבלבד בין בכלי א' בין בב' בג' כלים. וסיפא במציל באותו חצר שיש לו להציל אפילו ק' סעודות בין בכלי אחד בין בכמה כלים. ולענין בעיא דרב הונא בריה דר' יהושע פשיט מדאמר רבא הא מילתא אטעיה רב שיזבי ודרש ובלבד שלא יבא כלי אחר מחזיק יותר מג' סעודות. ש"מ כבא להציל דמי ש"מ. והכי קא גמרין מדקאמר רבא דבטעותא דרש רב חסדא שלא יביא כלי מחזיק יתר מג' סעודות. שמעינן מינה כי אפילו אם יביא כלי שמחזיק כל מה שהוא חפץ ויקפל ויניח בו ויטלנו כולו בבת אחת שפיר דמי. א"ל רב נחמן בר יצחק מאי טעותא. פירוש מנ"ל דטעותא היא דילמא דוקא אמר רב שיזבי. אהדר ליה רבא לא ס"ד מדקתני לענין מי שנשברה לו חבית בראש גגו מביא כלי ומניח תחתיה ובלבד שלא יביא כלי אחר ויקלוט כלי אחר ויצרף. כלי אחר לא יביא. הא בכלי אחד כמה דבעי נהוי וכן הלכה. וכיון שדרך בני אדם להזמין אורחים בשבת אומרים לאחרים בואו והצילו לכם. אבל להציל הוא ואח"כ להזמין אסור: ואם היו פקחין עושין עמו חשבון לאחר השבת. אף לשאינה מעורבת. ולובש כל מה שהוא יכול ללבוש ועוטף כל מה שהוא יכול להתעטף. ואפי' יתר מי"ח כלים. וכן הלכתא. וקי"ל שמותר להערים: ירושלמי תני אין מערימין. ר' יוסי בר אבין אמר מערימין. ועל זו

נה א מיי' פכ"ג מהל' שבת הל' כו כב סמג לאוין סה טוש"ע או"ח סימן שלג סעיף ו [וסימן שלד סעיף מז]:
נו ב מיי' שם הלכה כ טוש"ע שם סעיף יז:
נז ג מיי' שם טור שו"ע שם סעיף ז:
נח ד ה מיי' שם הלכה כה טור שו"ע שם סעיף ח:
נט ו ז מיי' שם הלכה כב טור שו"ע שם סעיף י:
ס ח ט מיי' שם הלכה כד טור שו"ע שם סעיף ט:
סא י כ מיי' פרק יב מהל' שבת הלכה ד ה סמג שם טוש"ע שם סעיף כג:
סב ל מיי' שם הלכה ו טור שו"ע שם סעיף כב כד:

א) ס"א מעם, ב) עירובין לט:, ג) לעיל קיז:, ד) [לעיל יט:], ה) לעיל קיז:, ו) עירובין נג:, ז) [פי' בגד רקיק שלובש אדם על בשרו ערוך], ח) [פי' מסוה], ט) [תוספתא פי"ד], ט) ס"י, י) [נ"ל ומטלטל ער' רש"א], כ) [שייך לעיל במשנה].

הגהות הב"ח
(א) גמ' לקפל דמי תא שמע מדאמר רבא: (ב) שם בירא שמים עסקינן דלא: (ג) שם לא קא חזו אלא: (ד) שם תנו רבנן לובש ומוציא: (ה) רש"י ד"ה אטעייה וכו' ובלבד שלא יביא כלי: (ו) ד"ה ובחנם וכו' דלמחול:

גליון הש"ס
מתני' ולובש כל מה שיכול ללבוש. ע"ל דף סה ע"ב: גמ' מקטורן אונקלי ופונדא. עי' לעיל דף נט ע"ב תוס' ד"ה תרי המיני: שם ושני ספרקין. נזכר במתני' פרק כ"ט משנה ב דכלים: מתני' עור של גדי. עיין לעיל דף מז ע"א תוס' ד"ה טומנין:

תורה אור השלם
א) יִשָּׂא בַיּוֹם הַהוּא לֵאמֹר לֹא אֶהְיֶה חֹבֵשׁ וּבְבֵיתִי אֵין לֶחֶם וְאֵין שִׂמְלָה לֹא תְשִׂימֻנִי קְצִין עָם: [ישעיה ג, ז]
ב) לֹא תִשָּׂא אֶת שֵׁם יְיָ אֱלֹהֶיךָ לַשָּׁוְא כִּי לֹא יְנַקֶּה יְיָ אֵת אֲשֶׁר יִשָּׂא אֶת שְׁמוֹ לַשָּׁוְא: [שמות כ, ז]

ליקוטי רש"י
אלא אם כן נכשלים בהן. כשהתלמיד נכשל בשמועתו פעם ראשונה ושניה הוא נותן לב לעמוד על שמועתו [חגיגה יד.]. דברי תורה שאין אדם עומד על אמיתתן עד שיכשל בהן להורות טעות ויכלימוהו והוא נותן לב ומבין תחת ידיך הן [גיטין מג.]. דילמא. האי נמי לאו משום דליכא אמנה ביה אלא לפי דאי הוה אמר גמירנא הוו אמרי ליה אימא לן ולא הוה ידע [חגיגה שם]. לחצר. שמתוקנה לבלטיק [עירובין צה:]. ולובש כל מה שיכול ללבוש. ואפילו עשרה חלוקים זה על זה [לעיל סה:]. בבא לקפל.

לְהֵיכָן מַצִּילִין אוֹתָן – **To where may they** remove these items to **save them?** לְחָצֵר הַמְעוֹרֶבֶת – **To a courtyard** whose houses were **joined by** means of **an *eruv*.**[8] בֶּן בְּתֵירָא אוֹמֵר – **Ben Beseira says:** אַף לְשֶׁאֵינָהּ מְעוֹרֶבֶת – **Even to [a courtyard]** whose houses were **not joined by an *eruv*.**[9] וּלְשָׁם מוֹצִיא כָּל כְּלֵי תַשְׁמִישׁוֹ – **And to there he may take out all the utensils that he** needs to **use** for his meals.[10] וְלוֹבֵשׁ כָּל מַה שֶּׁיָּכוֹל לִלְבּוֹשׁ – **And he may put on all** the clothing **that he can wear** וְעוֹטֵף כָּל מַה שֶּׁיָּכוֹל לַעֲטוֹף – **and wrap** himself in **all** the garments in **which he can wrap** himself and walk out of the house with them.[11] רַבִּי יוֹסֵי אוֹמֵר – **R' Yose says:** שְׁמוֹנָה עָשָׂר כֵּלִים – He is permitted to put on and remove from the house only **eighteen garments.**[12] וְחוֹזֵר וְלוֹבֵשׁ וּמוֹצִיא – **And he may return** to the house **and put on** more **clothing and take** that **out** of the house as well.[13] וְאוֹמֵר לַאֲחֵרִים בּוֹאוּ וְהַצִּילוּ עִמִּי – **And he may tell others, "Come and save with me."**[14]

Gemara The Gemara notes a contradiction between our Mishnah and the previous Mishnah:

וְהָא תָּנָא לֵיהּ רֵישָׁא שָׁלֹשׁ סְעוּדוֹת – **But the first part of the Mishnah** (i.e. the previous Mishnah) **taught** that one is permitted to save only THREE MEALS' worth of food from a burning house וְתוּ לֹא – **and not more!** How then can our Mishnah say that one may save a basket containing bread for a hundred meals?

The Gemara answers:

אָמַר רַב הוּנָא – **Rav Huna said:** לֹא קַשְׁיָא – **This is not a difficulty.** כָּאן בְּבָא לְהַצִּיל – **Here** in our Mishnah we are discussing a case **where one comes** simply **to save** (i.e. remove) a basket of food from a burning house; כָּאן בְּבָא לְקַפֵּל – whereas **here,** in the previous Mishnah, we are discussing a case **where one comes to bundle**[15] together several baskets and remove them. בָּא לְהַצִּיל מַצִּיל אֶת כּוּלָּן – **If one comes** simply **to save** a basket of food, **he may save all of [the loaves]** in it.[16] בָּא לְקַפֵּל אֵינוֹ מְקַפֵּל אֶלָּא מְזוֹן שָׁלֹשׁ סְעוּדוֹת – **But if one comes to bundle** together baskets of food and remove them, **he may bundle** and remove **only** enough **food for three meals.**[17]

The Gemara presents another resolution:

רַב אַבָּא בַּר זַבְדָּא אָמַר רַב – **Rav Abba bar Zavda in the name of Rav said:** אִידִי וְאִידִי בְּבָא לְקַפֵּל – **Both** our Mishnah and the previous Mishnah are discussing a case **where one comes to bundle** together containers before removing them, וְלֹא קַשְׁיָא – **and** nevertheless **there is no difficulty.** כָּאן לְאוֹתָהּ חָצֵר – **Here** in our Mishnah we are discussing a case where the items are being removed **to that courtyard,** כָּאן לְחָצֵר אַחֶרֶת – whereas **here,** in the previous Mishnah, we are discussing a case where the items are being removed **to another courtyard.**[18]

An inquiry:

בָּעֵי רַב הוּנָא בְּרֵיהּ דְּרַב יְהוֹשֻׁעַ – **Rav Huna the son of Rav**

NOTES

8. [I.e. one may carry the food out only to a place into which carrying is permitted even on the Rabbinic level. Since the Rabbis prohibited carrying from a privately owned house into a communally owned courtyard unless all the houses sharing the yard have joined in an *eruvei chatzeiros,* the food may be carried out only in such a yard. Similarly,] one may take out food from one courtyard to another only if the two courtyards have merged together in a single *eruv* (*Rambam, Hil. Shabbos* 23:20; see *Tosafos* 115a ד״ה כל כתבי).

Even so, the Rabbis limited the amount one may save because they were afraid that if one were permitted to try and save all his property, he might, in his haste to save it, forget that it is the Sabbath and extinguish the fire (*Rashi* [erroneously printed in his commentary to the Gemara], from Gemara above, 117b).

9. [I.e. a courtyard properly enclosed on all sides but which lacks an *eruvei chatzeiros.* Carrying into such a courtyard from its houses is only Rabbinically forbidden. In Ben Beseira's view, the Rabbis were lenient and relaxed their prohibition in such a case to allow one to save his property.]

10. For example, cups and jars (*Rashi*) and other table utensils (*Magen Avraham* 334:9).

11. I.e. he may put on even more articles than one would normally wear (see *Ran* ד״ה וטעמיה דר׳ יוסי), and even one garment on top of another (*Magen Avraham* 334:14; *Mishnah Berurah* 334:17). [Robes and turbans and the like were not tailored to fit the body but were simply wrapped around it. The Mishnah therefore speaks both of putting on and wrapping oneself in clothing.]

From *Rambam* (*Hil. Shabbos* 23:20) it seems that clothing, like food, may only be removed to a courtyard whose houses have been joined by an *eruv.* Others say that since one is wearing the excess clothing and not carrying it, he may remove it even to a courtyard lacking an *eruv* (*Smag* and *Hagahos Mordechai* cited by *Rama, Orach Chaim* 334:10). According to this view, the ruling concerning clothing should not be read as a continuation of the previous ruling concerning the removal of utensils but as a new and independent ruling (*Magen Avraham* 334:14).

12. The Gemara below will enumerate the eighteen garments. R' Yose permits wearing and removing only those garments that people customarily wear together during the week, not more (*Rashi*), because he views the excess garments as a מַשּׂוֹי, *burden,* rather than as clothing. He forbids wearing the excess garments out even to a courtyard joined by an *eruv* because of the possibility that, in his anxiety to save them from the fire, he might wear them out to the *reshus harabim* and be guilty of a Biblically forbidden transfer (*Ran*).

[The Tanna Kamma, though, permits wearing any number of garments together. *Ran* is uncertain whether his reason is that he does not consider excess garments a מַשּׂוֹי, *burden* (since they are being worn), or because he is not concerned that they will be worn into a *reshus harabim. Magen Avraham* 334:14 (cited in previous note) seems to follow the first explanation; see *Pri Megadim* there.]

13. This is a continuation of the Tanna Kamma's view. R' Yose, however, disagrees with this and permits removing clothing from the house only once (*Rashi;* see Baraisa below). *Rashba, Ritva MHK* ed. and *Ran MHK* ed., however, understand this ruling to be true according to both opinions (see *Kesef Mishneh* to *Hil. Shabbos* 23:25 concerning *Rambam's* view).

14. [The Gemara will explain why the Mishnah states here, "Come and save *with me,*" whereas the Mishnah previously stated that he tells them, "Come and save *for yourselves.*"]

15. Literally: to fold; i.e. to gather together several baskets of food and place them inside a single container for removal (*Rashi* here and on 19b ד״ה וחד מציל בארבע וחמש מאני, as explained here by *Ramban* and *Ritva MHK* ed.). [The use of the word לְקַפֵּל to mean *bundle* presumably derives from the fact that bundles were made by dropping items onto a cloth and then *folding* the cloth together to make a bundle. Indeed, *Ramban, Rashba* and *Ran* (*MHK* ed.) translate the term לְקַפֵּל here as *to fold* a garment around the several baskets. From *Rashi,* however, it seems that the word is used idiomatically to mean simply bringing together different items.]

16. Since his effort is limited to a single act (removing a basket of bread), what difference does it make how much he removes in that basket? (*Rashi*). [The three-meal limit enacted by the Rabbis was for the purpose of curtailing his *efforts* on behalf of his property, since additional efforts might lead him to extinguish the fire. But within the single act permitted to him by the Rabbis, there was no reason to limit how much he could remove at one time.]

17. Since collecting each basket requires a separate effort, the Rabbis did not permit one to remove more than three meals' worth of food (*Rashi*), even by placing all the baskets in a single large container and removing them together (*Rashi* 19b ד״ה וחד מציל בארבע וחמש מאני; see *Ramban*).

18. [Removing items to a second courtyard (beyond the one immediately in front of the area on fire) involves more effort. The Rabbis did not permit making this more extensive effort for more than three meals' worth of food.]

דברים שאין אדם עומד בהן. על בוריין לאומרן כהלכתן: אלא אם כן נכשל בהן. עד שאומרן ב' וג' פעמים בשיבוש דהיינו טעמי תורה המסותרין: לא אהיה חובש. איני רגיל להיות חובש חבוש בבהמ"ד. אהיה הורגלתי כמו שחוק לרעהו אהיה (איוב יב) אני הווה: וממאי. דמשום דיש בהן אמנה הוא דילמא על כרחך לריכים שישיבו האמת: דאי אמר להו גמירנא. אותן טעמי תורה: אמרי ליה. שואלים אימא לן: ומשני הוה ליה למימר גמר ושכח מאי לא אהיה חובש. מודה הוא על האמת שלא יגע בתורה: בדברי תורה. היו נאמנין ואין מתהללים על שקר:

דברים שאין בני אדם עומדין עליהם אלא אם כן נכשלים בהן ישנן תחת ידיך קצין תהיה לנו [א] ישא ביום ההוא לאמר לא אהיה חובש וגו' אין ישא אלא לשון שבועה וכן הוא אומר [ב] לא תשא את שם ה' לא אהיה חובש לא אהיה מחובשי עצמן בבית המדרש [א] ובביתי אין לחם ואין שמלה שאין בידי לא [ה] מקרא ולא משנה ולא גמרא וממאי דילמא שאני התם דאי אמר להו גמירנא אמרו ליה אימא לן הוה ליה למימר גמר ושכח מאי לא אהיה חובש כלל לא קשיא כאן בדברי תורה כאן במשא ומתן:

מתני' [א] מצילין סל מלא ככרות אע"פ שיש בו מאה סעודות ועיגול של דבילה וחבית של יין ואומר לאחרים בואו והצילו לכם ואם היו פיקחין עושין עמו חשבון אחר השבת להיכן מצילין אותן [ב] לחצר המעורבת בן בתירא אומר אף לשאינה מעורבת [ג] ולשם מוציא כל כלי תשמישו [ד] ולובש כל מה שיכול ללבוש ועוטף כל מה שיכול לעטוף ר' יוסי אומר י"ח כלים [ה] וחוזר ולובש ומוציא ואומר לאחרים בואו והצילו עמי:

גמ' [ג] והא תנא ליה רישא ג' סעודות ותו לא אמר רב הונא לא קשיא כאן בבא להציל כאן בבא לקפל [ו] בא להציל מציל את כולו בא לקפל אינו מקפל אלא מזון ג' סעודות [ז] ר' אבא בר זבדא אמר רב אידי ואידי בבא לקפל ולא קשיא כאן לאותה חצר כאן לחצר אחרת בעי רב הונא בריה דרב יהושע פירש טליתו וקיפל והניח וקיפל והניח מאי כבא להציל דמי או כבא לקפל דמי (א) מדאמר רבא אטעיה רב שיזבי לרב חסדא ודרש ובלבד שלא יביא כלי שהוא מחזיק יותר מג' סעודות ש"מ [ח] כבא להציל דמי ושפיר דמי א"ל רב נחמן בר יצחק לרבא מאי טעותא אמר ליה דקתני [ט] ובלבד שלא יביא כלי אחר ויקלוט כלי אחר ויצרף כלי אחר הוא דלא אבל בההוא מנא כמה דבעי מציל: ועיגול של דבילה כו': [י] חשבון מאי עבידתיה מהפקירא קזכו אמר רב חסדא מדת חסידות שנו כאן אמר רבא חסידי אגרא דשבתא שקלי אלא אמר רבא הכא בירא שמים עסקינן (ב) [ט] ולא ניחא ליה דליתהני מאחרים ובחנם נמי לא ניחא ליה דליטרח והכי קאמר ואם היו פיקחין דידעי דכה"ג לאו שכר שבת הוא עושין עמו חשבון לאחר השבת: ולהיכן מצילין כו': מ"ש הכא דקתני לכם ומ"ש הכא דקתני עמי אמרי גבי מזונות קתני לכם משום דלא קא חזו (ג) אלא מזון ג' סעודות אבל גבי לבושים קתני עמי משום דקחזי ליה לכולי יומא: ת"ר לובש (ד) ומוציא ופושט וחוזר ולובש ומוציא ופושט ואפילו כל היום כולו דברי רבי מאיר רבי יוסי אומר שמנה עשר כלים ואלו הם שמנה עשר כלים [ס] מקטורן [י] אונקלי ופונדא קלבוס של פשתן וחלוק [ז] ואפיליות ומעפורת [ס] ושני ספרקין ושני מנעלים ושני אנפילאות וב' פרגד וחגור שבמתניו וכובע שבראשו וסודר שבצוארו:

מתני' ר' שמעון בן ננס אומר [י] פורסין [ס] עור של גדי על גבי שידה תיבה ומגדל שאחז בהן את האור מפני שהוא מחרך [כ] ועושין מחיצה בכל הכלים בין מלאין בין ריקנים בשביל שלא תעבור הדליקה רבי יוסי אוסר בכלי חרס חדשים מלאין מים לפי שאין יכולין לקבל את האור והן מתבקעין ומכבין את הדליקה:

גמ' אמר רב יהודה אמר רב טלית שאחז בה האור מצד אחד נותנין עליה מים מצד אחר ואם כבתה כבתה מיתיבי [ל] טלית שאחז בה האור מצד אחד פושטה ומתכסה בה ואם כבתה כבתה וכן ספר תורה שאחז בו האור פושטו וקורא בו ואם כבה כבה הוא

רש"י

מתני' ועיגול של דבילה. שהוא גדול ויש בו סעודות הרבה: ואם היו פקחין. לישאל שכרן כפועלים: כל כלי תשמישו. שלריכין לו לאותו היום כגון כוסות וקיתוניות: י"ח כלים. מפרש להו בגמרא שכן דרך ללובשן בחול יחד אבל טפי מהכי לא ואינו פושטן לחזור וללבוש ולהציל אחרים: גמ' בבא להציל. [שהציל] בסל [אחד] כדקתני סל מלא ככרות ואינו טורח אלא להצילן מתוך הדליקה בבת אחת מציל כל מה שבסל דהא חדא זימנא הוא מה לי פורתא מה לי טובא: בבא לקפל. סלים הרבה זה עם זה לטרוח [ולאוספם] ולחזור ולהוציא מזון ג' סעודות הוא דיכול להציל בסלים הרבה ותו לא שכל א' טורח בעלמו הוא: פירש טליתו וקיפל והניח. הביא אוכלין והניח וחזר והביא והניח מהו: כבא להציל דמי. הואיל ואין כאן אלא כלי אחד ובפעם אחת הוא מוליאם: או כבא לקפל דמי. הואיל וטורח לאסוף ולכנוס: אטעייה רב שיזבי לרב חסדא [עדן]. שדרש לפניו והודה לו רב חסדא ואהא מתני' דאמרן לעיל (דף קיז:) נשברה לו חבית בראש גגו מביא כלי ומניח תחתיה ודרש רב שיזבי לרב חסדא ובלבד שלא (ה) יתן כלי המחזיק יותר משלש סעודות והודה לו רב חסדא ומדאמר רבא אטעייה שמע מינה טעותא הוא דאפילו מחזיק סעודות הרבה מותר כיון דחד מנא הוא והאי כמקפל ונותן בכלי אחד דמי דהא מעט מעט הוא נופל ומטפטף בו ש"מ בחד מנא כבא להציל דמי: מאי טעותא. מנא לך דטעותא הוא בידיה: אמר ליה. מדקתני בה בברייתא: ובלבד שלא יביא כלי אחר כו'. ש"מ כלים טובא הוא דאסירי אבל בחד שפיר דמי: מהפקירא זכו. דהא הצילו לכם קאמר להו ללרכיהם ואם פקחים הם יעכבו הכל הוה ליה למיתני: מדת חסידות. שמחזירין לו: חסידי אגרא דשבתא שקלי. בתמיה אם חסידים הם יש להם לוותר משלהם בכל דבר שיש בו נדנוד עבירה ואע"ג דלאו שכר שבת גמור הוא שהרי לא התנה והפקירא קא זכו מיהו חסיד לא מיקרי אלא א"כ מוותר משלו: הכא בירא שמים עסקינן. המציל הזה ירא שמים הוא ולא חסיד לוותר משלו: דלא ניחא ליה דליתהני מאחריני. בזכייה דהפקירא דידע דלא מרלונו הפקירו: ובחנם נמי לא ניחא ליה דליטרח. דלאו חסיד הוא (ו) ולמחול על שלו: והכי קאמר כו'. כלומר דהאי אם היו פקחין דקאמר לאו פקחין דמתני' לאו פקחין דדין קאמר ליטול את הראוי להם דאם כן יעכבו הכל הוה ליה למתני אלא לאו הכי קאמר הני ירא שמים אם פקחין הן בהלכות שבת דידעי דכה"ג לאו שכר שבת הוא דמעיקרא לאו לדעתא דשכר פעולה נחית עושין עמו חשבון והכי קאמר אדרב חסדא נמי קאי אלא לא שבקיה לרב חסדא לסיימיה למילתיה: לחצר המעורבת. ואפי' הכי טובא לא ליזיל כדאמר לעיל (דף קיז:) מתוך שבהול אי שרי ליה לאיעסוקי בהצלה כולי האי אתי לכבויי: מקטורן. מנטו"ל: אונקלי. לבוש רחב כעין סריבל"א ולשון ערבי מקטיל"ה: פונדא. אזור חלול מעל למדיו: קלבוס. ננב"ש: חלוק. קמינ"א על בשרו: ואפליון. סדין להתעטף בו כולו: מעפורת. לעטוף ראשו: ושני ספרקין. פייסול"ש: אנפילאות. קלצונ"ש של למר: פרגוד. גנגיל"ש ולשון אשכנז קני הו"ן: חגור. על חלוקו מכפניס: וסודר שבצוארו. ותלוין לפניו לקנח בו פיו ועיניו: מתני' עור של גדי. לח: מפני שהוא מחרך. מן האור ובלע"ז לטרלי"ט ואינו נשרף ומתוך כך הוא מגין על התיבה: בין מלאים. מים: שאינן יכולין לקבל כח האור. מפני שחדשים הם: גמ'

תוספות

אידי ואידי בבא לקפל. פירש הרב פורת דלקפל היינו אפי' בא לקפל דלר' אבא אין חילוק בין לקפל בין להציל דאפילו להציל בחצר אחרת לא שרי אלא מזון ג' סעודות אבל אין נראה לומר דלהציל שרי אפילו מאה סעודות בחצר אחרת גם לרבי אבא דאם כן הוה ליה לאוקומי מתני' אידי ואידי בחצר אחרת והכא בבא לקפל וכאן בבא להציל: **נותן** מים מצד זה. פירש רשב"ם דלאו דוקא על הטלית דהא קי"ל בפ' דם חטאת (זבחים לד:) דכבגד שריתו זהו כיבוסו ולעיל בסוף פרק שמנה שרצים (דף קיא.) פירשתי: גרס

עין משפט נר מצוה

נה א מיי' פכ"ג מהל' שבת הל' כב כג סמג לאוין סה טור שו"ע או"ח סימן שלד סעיף ו [וסימן שא סעיף מד]:
נו ב מיי' שם הלכה כ טוש"ע שם סעיף יז:
נז ג מיי' שם טור שו"ע שם סעיף ז:
נח ד ה מיי' שם הלכה כה טור שו"ע שם סעיף ח:
נט ו ז מיי' שם הלכה כב כג טור שו"ע שם סעיף ו:
ס ח ט מיי' שם הלכה כד טור שו"ע שם סעיף ט:
סא י כ מיי' פרק יב שם הלכה ד ה סמג שם טוש"ע שם סעיף כב:
סב ל מיי' שם הלכה ו טור שו"ע שם סעיף כג כד:

רבינו חננאל

מצילין סל מלא ככרות ואע"ג שיש בו ק' סעודות. אקשינן איני והא תני רישא מצילין מזון ג' סעודות ותו לא ושני רב הונא לא קשיא רישא בבא לקפל. פי' כגון שמקבץ מתוך הבית ממקומות [הרבה] ונותן בכמה כלים שאין לו להציל אלא מזון של ג' סעודות בלבד. סיפא במציל כולו בכלי אחד כמות שהוא. ואע"פ שאין זה הטעם כאשר פירשנו. כי רישא במקפל ונותן בכלים שנים ושלשה. וסיפא במציל סל אחד כמות שהוא מפורש (היבנגוהו מד). בעי רב הונא בריה דר' יהושע פירש טליתו וקיפל והניח וקיפל והניח מהו. כבא לקפל דמי או כבא להציל דמי. דמגלי לן שאם קיפל בכלי אחד ונטלו. וחוזר וקיפל בכלי אחר ונטלו זהו לקפל שאינו מציל אלא מזון ג' סעודות. וכי קא מבעיא שקיפל והניח בתוך טליתו וחוזר וקיפל והניח בתוך טליתו מי אמרינן כיון שמקפל ומביא כמקפל דמי ואסור. או דילמא כיון שהוא מניחן בתוך טלית אחד אחד ונוטלן כאחד כבא להציל דמי ושרי. ומפרשא נמי הא בגמ' בסוף יציאות השבת. הנהו תרי תלמידי. חד מציל בחד מנא וחד מציל בתרי מני קמפלגי בפלוגתא דר' אבא בר זבדא ורב הונא. הכין גמרא ומיגמר מינה דלקפל בתרי תלתא מני כדפרשינא לעיל דאסיר לרב הונא ושרי לר' אבא בר זבדא ומסתייע נמי בתלמוד א"י דאמרי על מצילין סל מלא ככרות מכיון שכולו גוף אחד כמין שכולה סעודה אחת היא והאי במימרא דרב הונא ובא ר' אבא בר זבדא ופירק פירוק אחר. ואמר רישא דמתני' במציל לחצר אחרת שאין לו להציל אלא מזון ג' סעודות בלבד בין בכלי א' בין בב' בין בג' כלים. וסיפא במציל באותו חצר שיש לו להציל אפילו ק' סעודות בין בכלי אחד בין בכמה כלים. ולענין בעיא דרב הונא בריה דר' יהושע פשיט פשיטא מדאמר רבא הא מילתא אטעייה רב שיזבי ודרש ובלבד שלא יבא כלי אחד מחזיק יותר מג' סעודות. ש"מ כבא להציל דמי ש"מ. והכי קא גמרין מדקאמר רבא דבטעותא דרש רב חסדא שלא יביא כלי מחזיק יותר מג' סעודות. שמעינן מינה כי אפילו אם יביא כלי שמחזיק כל מה שהוא חפץ ויקפל ויניח בו ויטלנו כולו בבת אחת שפיר דמי. א"ל רב נחמן בר יצחק לרבא מאי טעותא. פירוש מנ"ל דטעותא היא דילמא דוקא אמר רב שיזבי. אהדר ליה רבא לא ס"ד מדקתני לענין מי שנשברה לו חבית בראש גגו מביא כלי ומניח תחתיה ובלבד שלא יביא כלי אחר ויקלוט כלי אחר ויצרף. כלי אחר לא יביא. הא בכלי אחד כמה דבעי נהוי וכן הלכה. וכיון שדרך בני אדם להזמין אורחים בשבת אומרים לאחרים בואו והצילו לכם. אבל להציל הוא ואח"כ להזמין אסור: ואם היו פקחין עושין עמו חשבון לאחר השבת. אוקימנא בירא שמים ולא ניחא ליה לאיתהנויי מאחריני ובחנם [נמי לא ניחא ליה למטרח]. והכי פירושא דמתני' אם היו פקחין שיודעין דכי האי גוונא לאו שכר שבת הוא הואיל ומהפקירא קא זכו ליה לבעה"ב כגון מתנה מדידהו הוא עושין חשבון כשיעור שכרן ושקלי ליה. ושארא שבקי ליה לבעה"ב. סוגיא דשמעתא שהחסיד גדול הוא מירא שמים. ולשם מוציא כל כלי תשמישו. לרבנן בחצר המעורבת ולבן בתירא אף לשאינה מעורבת. ולובש כל מה שהוא יכול ללבוש ועוטף כל מה שהוא יכול להתעטף. ואפי' יתר מי"ח כלים. וכן הלכתא. וקי"ל שמותר להערים: ירושלמי תני אין מערימין. ר' יוסי בר אבין

מסורת הש"ס

א) ס"א טעם, ב) עירובין לה:, ג) לעיל קיז:, ד) [לעיל יט:], ה) לעיל קיח: עירובין לט:, ו) [פי' בגד רקיק שלובש אדם על בשרו ערוך], ז) [פי' מסוה], ח) [תוספתא פי"ד], ט) ס"א, י) [נ"ל ומטלטל עי' רש"א], כ) [שייך לעיל במשנה].

הגהות הב"ח

(א) גמ' לקפל דמי תא שמע מדאמר רבא: (ב) שם בירא שמים עסקינן דלא: (ג) שם דלא קא חזי ליה אלא: (ד) שם תנו רבנן לובש ומוליא: (ה) רש"י ד"ה אטעייה וכו' ובלבד שלא יביא כלי: (ו) ד"ה ובחנם וכו' דלמחול:

גליון הש"ס

מתני' ולובש כל מה שיכול ללבוש. ע"ל דף סה ע"ב: גמ' מקטורן אונקלי ופונדא. עי' לעיל דף נט ע"ב תוס' ד"ה תרי המייני: שם ושני ספרקין. נזכר במתני' פרק כ"ט משנה ב דכלים: מתני' עור של גדי. עיין לעיל דף מט ע"א תוס' ד"ה טומנין:

תורה אור השלם

א) יִשָּׂא בַיּוֹם הַהוּא לֵאמֹר לֹא אֶהְיֶה חֹבֵשׁ וּבְבֵיתִי אֵין לֶחֶם וְאֵין שִׂמְלָה לֹא תְשִׂימֻנִי קְצִין עָם: [ישעיה ג, ז]
ב) לֹא תִשָּׂא אֶת שֵׁם יְיָ אֱלֹהֶיךָ לַשָּׁוְא כִּי לֹא יְנַקֶּה יְיָ אֵת אֲשֶׁר יִשָּׂא אֶת שְׁמוֹ לַשָּׁוְא: [שמות כ, ז]

ליקוטי רש"י

אלא אם כן נכשלים בהן. כשהתלמיד נכשל בשמועתו פעם ראשונה ושניה הוא נותן לב לעמוד על שמועתו [חגיגה יד.]. דברי תורה שאין אדם עומד על אמיתתן עד שיכשל בהן להורות טעות ויכלימוהו והוא נותן לב ומבין תחת ידיך הן [גיטין מג.]. דילמא. האי נמי לאו משום דאנשי אמנה היו אלא דאי הוה אמר גמירנא הוו אמרי ליה אימא לן והוא לא הוה ידע [חגיגה שם]. לחצר. שסמוכה לדליקה [עירובין צה:]. ולובש כל מה שיכול ללבוש. ואפילו עשרה חלוקים זה על זה [לעיל סה:]. בבא לקפל. מציל בארבע וחמש מאני אלא שמקפלן כולן לתוך כלי גדול ונושאן בפעם אחת [שם יט: ע"ש בתוס']. ויקלוט. קילוח הנופל מן האויר. ויצרף. סמוך לגג כעין שאיבה אלא שאינו ראוי לשאוב שהגג חלק והיין אינו בגומא מצרף כלי לגג שיזוב מן הגג לכלי והוא אוחז הכלי בידו [שם קיז:]. שכר שבת. גזרה משום מקח וממכר ושכירות [כתובות סד.]. מקטורן. שמתכסה בו על כל בגדים שהוא לובש [רשב"ם ב"ב נז:]. אונקלי. מלבוש של עור [מנחות קט:]. שייפינ"ש חלוק [מו"ק כד.]. מעפורת. סודר ויתעטף באפר דכתיב [במלכים] גבי מיכה (מלכים א, כ) מתרגמינן ואישתני [במעפרתא] [חולין קכג:].

Yehoshua inquired: פֵּירֵשׂ טַלִּיתוֹ – If one spread his cloak on the ground וְקִיפֵּל וְהִנִּיחַ – and bundled food and placed it on the cloak,[19] וְקִיפֵּל וְהִנִּיחַ – and then bundled more food and placed it on the cloak, מַאי – what is the law? May he take out the cloak with all the food bundled in it or not? כְּבָא לְהַצִּיל דָּמֵי – Is this case similar to the case of one who comes to save, since he takes all the food out at one time and in a single container (the bundled cloak), and it is therefore permitted for him to remove even more than three meals' worth? אוֹ כְּבָא לְקַפֵּל דָּמֵי – Or is this case similar to that of one who comes to bundle together several baskets, since he exerts himself separately to bring each of the baskets and empty them into the cloak? Thus, he would not be permitted to take out more food than needed for three meals.[20]

The Gemara answers:

מִדְּאָמַר רָבָא – From the fact that Rava said that אַטְעְיֵיהּ רַב שֵׁיזְבִי לְרַב חִסְדָּא וְדָרֵשׁ – Rav Shizbi misled Rav Chisda and expounded before him[21] regarding a Baraisa that states that one may place a utensil in the courtyard to catch wine leaking from a barrel that broke on the roof[22] – וּבִלְבַד שֶׁלֹּא יָבִיא כְּלִי שֶׁהוּא מַחֲזִיק יוֹתֵר מִשָּׁלֹשׁ סְעוּדוֹת – "Provided he does not bring a utensil that holds more than three meals' worth of wine" – שְׁמַע מִינָּהּ כְּבָא לְהַצִּיל דָּמֵי – you may learn from this that one who collects a large amount of food in one utensil is indeed like one who comes to save a basket previously full of bread, וְשַׁפִּיר דָּמֵי – and it is proper (i.e. permissible) to remove even more than three meals' worth.[23]

Having resolved the inquiry, the Gemara records the question asked to Rava when he made this statement:

אָמַר לֵיהּ רַב נַחְמָן בַּר יִצְחָק לְרָבָא – Rav Nachman bar Yitzchak said to Rava: מַאי טְעוּתָא – What is the mistake; how do you know that Rav Shizbi's teaching is in error?

Rava responded:

אָמַר לֵיהּ – [Rava] said to him: דְּקָתָנֵי – For that Baraisa teaches: וּבִלְבַד שֶׁלֹּא יָבִיא כְּלִי אַחֵר וְיִקְלוֹט – One is permitted to place a utensil under the barrel PROVIDED HE DOES NOT BRING ANOTHER UTENSIL AND CATCH wine with it, כְּלִי אַחֵר וִיצָרֵף – or bring ANOTHER UTENSIL AND HOLD IT LEVEL with the roof wall to collect the dripping wine.[24] כְּלִי אַחֵר הוּא דְּלָא – This implies that it is only another utensil that one may not use to collect more wine, אֲבָל בְּהַהוּא מָנָא כַּמָּה דְּבָעֵי מַצִּיל – but in that single utensil that he is permitted to use, he may save as much wine as he wants. This disproves Rav Shizbi's contention that one is restricted to saving three meals' worth even in a single utensil.

The Gemara quotes the next part of the Mishnah:

וְעִיגּוּל שֶׁל דְּבֵילָה כו' – AND A ROUND cake OF PRESSED FIGS etc. . . . The Mishnah continues: And one may tell others, "Come and save for yourselves"; and if they were wise they make a reckoning with him after the Sabbath for their wages as laborers.

The Gemara questions the reason for such a reckoning:

חֶשְׁבּוֹן מַאי עֲבִידְתֵּיהּ – This reckoning of wages, what is its purpose? מֵהֶפְקֵירָא קָזָכוּ – They have acquired [the food] from a state of ownerlessness, and they should be permitted to keep whatever they saved![25] – ? –

NOTES

19. I.e. he brought food from different places in the house and deposited it in the cloak (*Rashi*). He then tied together the cloak to form a single bundle.

20. *Rashi*. As Rav Huna explained above, the Sages prohibited taking out more than three meals' worth of food only when the food is contained in several baskets but not when it is in a single basket. They extended this decree even to placing several baskets together inside a single large container, as explained in note 17. Rav Huna the son of Rav Yehoshua inquires, however, what the law would be if he did not place the separate *baskets* inside the single large container but rather emptied their *contents* into a single container, such as a cloak (*Ramban*, in explanation of *Rashi*; see also *Rashba*, *Ritva* and *Ran MHK* ed.). For this case is comparable in one respect to saving a single basket full of bread – since all the food is now in a single container (the cloak) – but is in another respect comparable to several baskets bundled together – since the person exerted himself separately to bring and empty each of the containers into the cloak (*Rashba*, in explanation of *Rashi*). [Although the reason the Sages prohibited removing extra food in separate containers was because of the excess effort involved (which might lead one to forget the Sabbath), the fact is that they did not forbid a person to *gather* food inside a burning house, rather they prohibited him to *remove* excess food from the house in more than one container. Thus, as long as the actual removal occurs in just a single utensil, it can be argued that the Rabbinic decree is not violated – despite the exertions made to gather the food into the container. See further in note 23.]

21. I.e. Rav Shizbi misled Rav Chisda to the point that when Rav Shizbi expounded his remark [in the public lecture,] Rav Chisda accepted it as correct (*Rashi*). [The expression דָּרֵשׁ, *expounded*, generally refers to a public teaching – in this case, in the yeshivah over which Rav Chisda presided (Sura). Rava asserts that Rav Chisda's acceptance of the following statement of Rav Shizbi was an error.]

22. This Baraisa was quoted and explained above, 117b. There too the Rabbis prohibited saving the wine in more than one utensil.

23. Since Rava said that Rav Shizbi's teaching was in error, it is clear that Rava holds that one may catch the wine even in a utensil that holds more than three meals' worth because it is nonetheless just a single utensil. Now this case is similar to the one of our question, for wine dripping slowly from the roof into the utensil is like food being gathered in small amounts into one cloak. We therefore see that food deliberately gathered into a single cloak is treated the same as food previously present in a utensil, and its removal is permitted (*Rashi*).

Maharsha notes the obvious difficulty in this comparison. In the case of the wine, only a single effort was needed to collect all the wine drippings in the barrel. The fact that Rava ruled leniently in this case does not prove that he would also rule leniently in the case of the cloak, where a number of separate efforts were needed to collect the food in the cloak. *Maharsha* does not offer an answer.

Ritva (*MHK* ed.), however, explains the comparison as follows: The reason to permit emptying the contents of several utensils into a cloak and then removing it is because the Sages only prohibited removal in multiple utensils, not in a single utensil. [Although their *concern* was for the extra effort involved, their *decree* was directed at the removal of multiple utensils, as explained in note 20.] The reason to forbid this, *Ritva* explains, is that [since the person exerted himself separately to collect each of the baskets and empty them into the cloak (see *Rashi*),] we should continue to classify their contents as the foods of several utensils despite their being mixed together in a single container. It is this position that the Gemara disproves from Rava's ruling. For the wine that slowly drips into the barrel is in effect like small batches of wine collected separately in different utensils and subsequently mixed together. [Indeed, it is presumably for this reason that Rav Shizbi and Rav Chisda prohibited catching the wine in a utensil that holds more than three meals' worth – for it is prohibited to save more than three meals' worth in multiple utensils.] Rava's ruling therefore demonstrates that once they mix together in a *single* utensil, we no longer view their separate origins as a factor.

24. I.e. he may use only one utensil to catch the dripping wine, not more. See 117b note 8.

25. The Mishnah states that "if they are wise, they make a reckoning for their wages" [i.e. they return the food to the owner and accept payment for their efforts in saving it]. But, in truth, they may do even more than this: They may keep everything they saved, since it was ownerless when they took it. For the homeowner said to them, "Come and save for *yourselves*" [implying that he was abandoning his rights to it]. Thus, the Mishnah should have said, "If they are wise [in matters of monetary law and realize that the food is ownerless], they keep it for themselves" (*Rashi*).

[Seemingly, the food should be considered *hefker* (ownerless) even without his declaration, since what he was forbidden to save would have been destroyed by the fire and was thus lost to him in any case. It was therefore like an item lost at sea (זוטו שֶׁל יָם), which is automatically

דברים שאין אדם עומד בהן. על בורין לאומרן כהלכתן: אלא אם כן נכשל בהן. עד שאומרן ב' וג' פעמים בשיבוש דהיינו טעמי תורה המסותרין: לא אהיה חובש. איני רגיל להיות חובש חבוש בבהמ"ד. אהיה הורגלתי כמו שחוק לרעהו אהיה (איוב יב) אני הווה: וממאי. דמשום דיש בהן אמנה הוא דילמא על כרחך לריכים שיחיו האמת: דאי אמר להו גמירנא. אותן טעמי תורה: אמרי ליה. שולים אימא לן: ומשני הוה ליה למימר גמר ושכח מאי לא אהיה חובש. מודה הוא על האמת שלא יגע בתורה: בדברי תורה. היו נאמנין ואין מהללים על שקר:

דברים שאין בני אדם עומדין עליהם אלא אם כן נכשלים בהן ישנן תחת ידיך קצין תהיה לנו [א] ישא ביום ההוא לאמר לא אהיה חובש וגו' אין ישא אלא לשון שבועה וכן הוא אומר [ב] לא תשא את שם ה' לא אהיה חובש לא אהיה מחובשי עצמן בבית המדרש [א] ובביתי אין לחם ואין שמלה שאין בידי לא [ו] מקרא ולא משנה ולא גמרא וממאי דילמא שאני התם דאי אמר להו גמירנא אמרו ליה אימא לן הוה ליה למימר גמר ושכח מאי לא אהיה חובש כלל לא קשיא כאן בדברי תורה כאן במשא ומתן:

מתני' [א] מצילין סל מלא ככרות אע"פ שיש בו מאה סעודות ועיגול של דבילה וחבית של יין ואומר לאחרים בואו והצילו לכם ואם היו פיקחין עושין עמו חשבון אחר השבת להיכן מצילין אותן [ב] לחצר המעורבת בן בתירא אומר אף לשאינה מעורבת [ג] ולשם מוציא כל כלי תשמישו [ד] ולובש כל מה שיכול ללבוש ועוטף כל מה שיכול לעטוף ר' יוסי אומר י"ח כלים [ה] וחוזר ולובש ומוציא ואומר לאחרים בואו והצילו עמי:

גמ' והא תנא ליה [ו] רישא ג' סעודות ותו לא אמר רב הונא לא קשיא כאן בבא להציל כאן בבא לקפל [ז] בא להציל מציל את כולן בא לקפל אינו מקפל אלא מזון ג' סעודות [ח] ר' אבא בר זבדא אמר רב אידי ואידי בבא לקפל ולא קשיא כאן לאותה חצר כאן לחצר אחרת בעי רב הונא בריה דרב יהושע פירש טליתו וקיפל והניח וקיפל והניח מאי כבא להציל דמי או כבא לקפל דמי (א) מדאמר רבא אטעיה רב שיזבי לרב חסדא ודרש ובלבד שלא יביא כלי שהוא מחזיק יותר מג' סעודות ש"מ [כ]כבא להציל דמי ושפיר דמי א"ל רב נחמן בר יצחק לרבא מאי טעותא אמר ליה דקתני [ט] ובלבד שלא יביא כלי אחר ויקלוט כלי אחר ויצרף כלי אחר הוא דלא אבל בההוא מנא כמה דבעי מציל: ועיגול של דבילה כו': [ח] חשבון מאי עבידתיה מהפקירא קזכו אמר רב חסדא מדת חסידות שנו כאן אמר רבא חסידי אגרא דשבתא שקלי אלא אמר רבא הכא בירא שמים עסקינן (ב) [ט] ולא ניחא ליה דליתהני מאחרים ובחנם נמי לא ניחא ליה דליטרחו והכי קאמר ואם היו פיקחין דידעי דכה"ג לאו שכר שבת הוא עושין עמו חשבון לאחר השבת: ולהיכן מצילין כו': מ"ש הכא דקתני לכם ומ"ש הכא דקתני עמי אמרי גבי מזונות קתני לכם משום דלא קא חזו (ג) אלא מזון ג' סעודות אבל גבי לבושים קתני עמי משום דקחזי ליה לכולי יומא: ת"ר לובש (ד) מוציא ופושט וחוזר ולובש ומוציא ופושט ואפילו כל היום כולו דברי רבי מאיר רבי יוסי אומר שמנה עשר כלים ואלו הם שמנה עשר כלים [ס] מקטורן [י] אונקלי ופונדא וקלבוס של פשתן וחלוק [י] ואפליות ומעפורת [ס] ושני ספרקין ושני מנעלים ושני אנפילאות וב' פרגד וחגור שבמתניו וכובע שבראשו וסודר שבצוארו:

מתני' ר' שמעון בן ננס אומר [ע] פורסין עור של גדי על גבי שידה תיבה ומגדל שאחז בהן את האור מפני שהוא מחרך [פ] ועושין מחיצה בכל הכלים בין מלאין בין ריקנים בשביל שלא תעבור הדליקה רבי יוסי אוסר בכלי חרס חדשים מלאין מים לפי שאין יכולין לקבל את האור והן מתבקעין ומכבין את הדליקה: **גמ'** אמר רב יהודה אמר רב טלית שאחז בה האור מצד אחד נותנין עליה מים מצד אחר ואם כבתה כבתה מיתיבי [צ] טלית שאחז בה האור מצד אחד פושטה ומתכסה בה ואם כבתה כבתה וכן ספר תורה שאחז בו האור פושטו וקורא בו ואם כבה כבה הוא

רש"י

היו נאמנין ואין מהללים על שקר:

מתני' ועיגול של דבילה. שהוא גדול ויש בו סעודות הרבה: ואם היו פקחין. ליטול שכר כפועלים: כל כלי תשמישו. שלריכין לו לאותו היום כגון כוסות וקיתוניות: י"ח כלים. מפרש להו בגמרא שכן דרך ללובשן בחול יחד אבל טפי מהכי לא ואינו פושטן לחזור וללבוש ולהציל אחרים: גמ' בבא להציל. [שהציל] בסל [אחד] כדקתני סל מלא ככרות ואינו טורח אלא להצילן מתוך הדליקה בבת אחת מציל כל מה שבסל דהא חדא זימנא הוא מה לי פורתא מה לי טובא: בבא לקפל. קליס הרבה זה עם זה לטרוח [ולאוספם] ולחזור ולהוליא מזון ג' סעודות הוא דיכול להציל בקליס הרבה ותו לא שכל א' טורח בעלמו הוא: פירש טליתו וקיפל והניח. הביא אוכלין והניח וחזר והביא והניח מהו: כבא להציל דמי. הואיל ואין כאן אלא כלי אחד ובפעם אחת הוא מוליאס: או כבא לקפל דמי. הואיל וטורח לאסוף ולכנוס: אטעייה רב שיזבי לרב חסדא (עד) [עדן]. שדרש לפניו והודה לו רב חסדא והאה מתני' דאמרן לעיל (דף קיז:) נשברה לו חבית בראש גגו מביא כלי ומניח תחתיה ודרש רב שיזבי לרב חסדא ובלבד שלא (ה) יתן כלי המחזיק יותר משלש סעודות והודה לו רב חסדא ומדאמר רבא אטעייה שמע מינה טעותא הוא דאפילו מחזיק סעודות הרבה מותר כיון דחד מנא הוא והאי כמקפל ונותן בכלי אחד דמי דהא מעט מעט הוא נופל ומטפטף בו ש"מ כחד מנא כבא להציל דמי: מאי טעותא. מנא לך דטעותא הוא בידיה: אמר ליה. מדקתני בה בברייתא: ובלבד שלא יביא כלי אחר כו'. ש"מ כלים טובא הוא דאסירי אבל בחד שפיר דמי: מהפקירא וכו'. דהא הצילו לכם קאמר להו ללרכיכם ואם פקחים הם יעכבו הכל הוה ליה למיתני: מדת חסידות. שמחזירין לו: חסידי אגרא דשבתא שקלי. בתמיה אם חסידים הם יש להם לוותר משלהם בכל דבר שיש בו נדנוד עבירה ואע"ג דלאו שכר שבת גמור הוא שהרי לא התנה והפקירא קא זכו מיהו חסיד לא מיקרי אא"כ מוותר משלו: הכא בירא שמים עסקינן. המציל הזה ירא שמים הוא ולא חסיד לוותר משלו: דלא ניחא ליה דליתהני מאחריני: בזכייה דהפקירא דידע דלא מרלונו הפקירו: ובחנם נמי לא ניחא ליה דליטרחו. דלאו חסיד הוא (ו) ולמחול על שלו: והכי קאמר כו'. כלומר דהאי אם היו פקחין דמתני' לאו פקחין בדין קאמר להם דהרשות בידן ליטול את הכל דאם כן יעכבו הכל הוה ליה למתני אלא לאו הכי קאמר הני יראי שמים אם פקחין הן בהלכות שבת דידעי דכה"ג לאו שכר שבת הוא דמעיקרא לאו אדעתא דשכר פעולה נחית עושין עמו חשבון והכי קאמר אדרב חסדא נמי קאי אלא לא שבקיניה לרב חסדא לסיימיה למילתיה: [ס] לחצר המעורבת. ואפי' הכי טובא לא ליזול כדאמר לעיל (דף קיז:) מתוך שבהול אי שרי לאיעסוקי בהצלה כולי האי אתי לכבויי: מקטורן. מנטו"ל: אונקלי. לבוש רחב כעין שרינ"א ובלשון ערבי מחשיל"ה: פונדא. אזור חלול מעל למדיו: קלבוס. נבי"ש: חלוק. קמיש"א על בשרו: ואפליון. סדין להתעטף בו כולו: מעפורת. לעטוף ראשו: ושני ספרקין. פיישול"ש: אנפילייאות. קלצו"ש של למר: פרגוד. גנילי"ש ובלשון אשכנז קני הוז"ן: חגור. על חלוקו מבפנים: וסודר שבצוארו. ותלויין ראשיו לפניו לקנח בו פיו ועיניו: מתני' עור של גדי. לח: מפני שהוא מחרך. מן האור ובלע"ז רטריי"ט ואינו נשרף ומתוך כך הוא מגין על התיבה: בין מלאים. מים: שאינן יכולין לקבל כח האור. מפני שחדשים הם:

גמ'

תוספות

אידי ואידי בבא לקפל. פירש הר"ב פורת דלקפל היינו אפי' בא לקפל דלר' אבא אין חילוק בין לקפל בין להציל דאפילו להציל בחצר אחרת לא שרי אלא מזון ג' סעודות אבל אין נראה לומר דלהציל שרי אפילו מאה סעודות בחצר אחרת גם לרבי אבא דאם כן הוה ליה לאוקומי מתני' אידי ואידי בחצר אחרת וכאן בבא לקפל וכאן בבא להציל: נותן מים מצד זה. פירש רשב"ס לאו דוקא על הטלית דהא קי"ל בפ' דם חטאת (זבחים לד:) דכנגד שרייתו זהו כיבוסו ולעיל בסוף פרק שמנה שרצים (דף קיא.) פירשתי: גרס

רבינו חננאל

מצילין סל מלא ככרות ואע"ג שיש בו ק' סעודות. אקשינן איני והא תני רישא מצילין מזון ג' סעודות ותו לא ושני רב הונא לא קשיא רישא בבא לקפל. פי' כגון שמקבץ מתוך הבית ממקומות [הרבה] ונותן בכמה כלים שאין לו להציל אלא מזון של ג' סעודות בלבד. סיפא במציל כולו בכלי אחד כמות שהוא. ואע"פ שאין זה הטעם כאשר פירשנו. כי רישא במקפל ונותן בכלים שנים ושלשה. וסיפא במציל סל אחד כמות שהוא מפורש (היבננוהו מז'). בעי רב הונא בריה דר' יהושע פירש טליתו וקיפל והניח וקיפל והניח מהו. כבא לקפל דמי או כבא להציל דמי. דמגלי לן שאם קיפל בכלי אחד ונטלו. וחזר וקיפל בכלי אחר ונטלו זהו לקפל פשיטא שאינו מציל אלא מזון ג' סעודות. וכי קא מבעיא שקיפל והניח בתוך טליתו וחזר וקיפל והניח בתוך טליתו מי אמרינן כיון שמקפל ומביא כמקפל דמי ואסור. או דילמא כיון שהוא מניחן בתוך טלית אחד אחד ונוטלן כאחד כבא להציל דמי ושרי. ומיפרשא נמי הא בגמ' בסוף יציאות השבת. הנהו תרי תלמידי. מר מציל בחד מנא ומר מציל בתרי מני קמפלגי בפלוגתא דר' אבא בר זבדא ורב הונא. הכין גמרא ומיגמר מינה דלקפל בתרי תלתא מני כדפרישנא לעילא דאסיר לרב הונא ושרי לר' אבא בר זבדא ומסתייע נמי בתלמוד א"י דאמרי על מצילין סל מלא ככרות מכיון שכולו גוף אחד כמין שכולה סעודה אחת היא והאי במימרא דרב הונא ובא ר' אבא בר זבדא ופירק פירוק אחר. ואמר רישא דמתני' במציל לחצר אחרת שאין לו להציל אלא מזון ג' סעודות בלבד בין בכלי א' בין בב' ג' כלים. וסיפא במציל באותו חצר שיש לו להציל אפילו ק' סעודות בין בכלי אחד בין בכמה כלים. ולענין בעיא דרב הונא בריה דר' יהושע פשיט מדאמר רבא הא מילתא אטעייה רב שיזבי ודרש ובלבד שלא יבא כלי אחד מחזיק יותר מג' סעודות. ש"מ כבא להציל דמי ש"מ. והכי קא גמרין מדקאמר רבא דבטעותא דרש רב חסדא שלא יביא כלי מחזיק יותר מג' סעודות. שמעינן מינה כי אפילו אם יביא כלי שמחזיק כל מה שהוא חפץ ויקפל ויניח בו ויטלנו כולו בבת אחת שפיר דמי. א"ל רב נחמן בר יצחק מאי טעותא. פירוש מנ"ל דטעותא היא דילמא דוקא אמר רב שיזבי. אהדר ליה רבא לא ס"ד מדקתני לענין מי שנשברה לו חבית בראש גגו מביא כלי ומניח תחתיה ובלבד שלא יביא כלי אחר ויקלוט כלי אחר ויצרף. כלי אחר לא יביא. הא בכלי אחד כמה דבעי נהוי וכן הלכה. וכיון שדרך בני אדם להזמין אורחים בשבת אומרים לאחרים בואו והצילו לכם. אבל להציל הוא ואח"כ להזמין אסור: ואם היו פקחין עושין עמו חשבון. אוקימנא בירא שמים ולא ניחא ליה לאיתהנויי מאחריני ובחנם [נמי לא ניחא ליה למטרח]. והכי פירושא דמתני' אם היו פקחין שיודעין דכי האי גוונא לאו שכר שבת הוא הואיל ומהפקירא קא זכו ליה לבעה"ב כגון מתנה מדידהו הוא עושין חשבון כשיעור שכרן ושקלי ליה. ושארא שבקי ליה לבעה"ב. סוגיא דשמעתא שהחסיד גדול הוא מירא שמים. ולשם מוציא כל כלי תשמישו. לרבנן בחצר אף לשאינה מעורבת. ולובש כל מה שהוא יכול ללבוש ועוטף כל מה שהוא יכול להתעטף. ואפי' יתר מי"ח כלים. וכן הלכתא. וקי"ל שמותר להערים: ירושלמי תני אין מערימין. ר' יוסי בר אבין ועל זו

עין משפט נר מצוה

נה א מיי' פכ"ג מהל' שבת הל' כג סמג לאוין סה טוש"ע או"ח סימן שלד סעיף ו [וסימן שא סעיף מד]:
נו ב מיי' שם הלכה כ טוש"ע שם סעיף יז:
נז ג מיי' שם טור שו"ע שם סעיף ז:
נח ד ה מיי' שם הלכה כה טור שו"ע שם סעיף ח:
נט ו ז מיי' שם הלכה כב כג טור שו"ע שם סעיף י:
ס ח ט מיי' שם הלכה כד טור שו"ע שם סעיף ט:
סא י כ מיי' שם הלכה יט טור שו"ע שם סעיף כב:
סב ל מיי' שם הלכה ו טור שו"ע שם סעיף כג כד:

מסורת הש"ס

א) ס"א טעם, ב) עירובין לה:, ג) [לעיל קיז:], ד) [לעיל יט:], ה) לעיל קיז: עירובין לג:, ו) [פי' בגד רקיק שלובש אדם על בשרו ערוך], ז) [פי' מסוה], ח) [תוספתא פי"ד], ט) ס"י, י) [ל"ל וממלכל ער' רס"א], כ) [שייך לעיל במשנה].

הגהות הב"ח

(א) גמ' לקפל דמי אם שמע מדאמר רבא: (ב) שם בירא שמים עסקינן דלא: (ג) שם דלא קא חזי ליה אלא: (ד) שם תנו רבנן לובש ומוציא: (ה) רש"י ד"ה אטעייה וכו' ובלבד שלא יביא כלי: (ו) ד"ה ובחנם וכו' למחול:

גליון הש"ס

מתני' ולובש כל מה שיכול ללבוש. ע"ל דף קמז ע"ב: גמ' מקטורן אונקלי ופונדא. ע' לעיל דף קג ע"ב תוס' ד"ה מרי המיני: שם ושני ספרקין. מכר בסוף חגיגה: מתני' עור של גדי. עיין לעיל דף מ"ז ע"ב תוס' ד"ה טומנין:

תורה אור השלם

א) יִשָּׂא בַיּוֹם הַהוּא לֵאמֹר לֹא אֶהְיֶה חֹבֵשׁ וּבְבֵיתִי אֵין לֶחֶם וְאֵין שִׂמְלָה לֹא תְשִׂימֻנִי קְצִין עָם: [ישעיה ג, ז]
ב) לֹא תִשָּׂא אֶת שֵׁם יְיָ אֱלֹהֶיךָ לַשָּׁוְא כִּי לֹא יְנַקֶּה יְיָ אֵת אֲשֶׁר יִשָּׂא אֶת שְׁמוֹ לַשָּׁוְא: [שמות כ, ז]

ליקוטי רש"י

אלא אם כן נכשלים בהן. כשהתלמיד נכשל בשמועתו ואינו יודע לאמתה ושונה אותה בשיבוש ושואל לרבו ועל ידי שנכשל בה עומד על אמתתה [חגיגה יד.]. ישא. לשון שבועה. לא אהיה חובש. לא אהיה מאותן המחבשים ומלמדים עד שיהו בקיאים בה לשון רבותינו ומבין מתוך ידיך הן [גיטין מג.]. דילמא. האי טעמא לאו משום דאמר להו גמירנא כפרו אמר שהוא משבע להודות על שעורו דאמר ליה [חגיגה שם]. לחצר. שמוכנה לדליקה [עירובין צה:]. ולובש כל מה שיכול ללבוש. ואפילו עשרה חלוקים זה על זה [לעיל סה:]. בבא לקפל. מציל מכרעם ומדחק נמי אלא שמקפלין כולן לתוך כלי גדול ונוטלן בפעם אחת [שם יט:] ויקלוט. קולט הנופל מן האויר. ויצרף. תמוך לגג כעין שאלה שאינו ראוי לאשר שבגג חלק והיין לאו בגמגמא מלרף כלי שם שהוא מן הגג בכלי והוא אוחז הכלי בידו [שם קיז:]. שכר שבת. גזרה משום מקח וממכר ושכירות [כתובות סד.]. מקטורן. שמתכסה בו על כל בגדים שהוא לובש [רש"ב ב"ב נז:]. אונקלי. מלבוש של עור [מנחות קט.] פייפינ"ש. חלוק [מו"ק כד.]. מעפורת. סודר ויתעטף במלבוש דלמיב [במלבים גגי משכר (מלבים ה, כ) מתרגמינן ואישתני [במעפרתא] [חולין קכג:].

The Gemara answers:

אָמַר רַב חִסְדָּא – **Rav Chisda said:** מִדַּת חֲסִידוּת שָׁנוּ כָּאן – **[The Sages] taught here** how one should act according to **the characteristic of piety.**[26]

The Gemara objects:

אָמַר רָבָא – **Rava asked:** חֲסִידֵי אַגְרָא דְשַׁבְּתָא שָׁקְלֵי – Do **pious people** then **take wages for** working on **the Sabbath?**[27]

Rava therefore offers a different answer:

אֶלָּא אָמַר רָבָא – **Rather, Rava said:** הָכָא בִּירֵא שָׁמַיִם עָסְקִינַן – **Here we are dealing with a person who fears Heaven,** וְלָא נִיחָא לֵיהּ דְּלִיתְהֲנֵי מֵאֲחֵרִים – **and it is** therefore **not agreeable to him to benefit from others,** וּבְחִנָּם נַמִּי לָא נִיחָא לֵיהּ דְּלִיטְרַח – **but** at the same time **it is also not agreeable to him to exert** himself **without compensation.**[28] וְהָכִי קָאָמַר – **And this is what [the Mishnah] is** really **saying:** וְאִם הָיוּ פִּיקְחִין – AND IF THEY ARE WISE דְּיָדְעֵי דִּכְהַאי גַּוְונָא לָאו שְׂכַר שַׁבָּת הוּא – **in that they know that in such a situation [the wages]** they take **are not** considered **Sabbath wages,** עוֹשִׂין עִמּוֹ חֶשְׁבּוֹן לְאַחַר הַשַּׁבָּת – THEY MAKE A RECKONING WITH HIM AFTER THE SABBATH for wages.[29]

The Gemara now discusses the next section of the Mishnah:

וּלְהֵיכָן מַצִּילִין כו׳ – **And to where may one** remove these items to **save etc.** [The Mishnah continues: And he may put on all that he can wear . . . And he may tell others, "Come and save things with me"].

The Gemara asks:

מַאי שְׁנָא הָכָא – **What is different here,** in the case of telling others to save food, דְּקָתָנֵי לָכֶם – **that the Mishnah teaches** that he may say, "Come and save FOR YOURSELVES," וּמַאי שְׁנָא הָכָא – **and what is different here,** in the case of telling others to save clothing, דְּקָתָנֵי עִמִּי – **that the Mishnah teaches** that he may say, "Come and save WITH ME?"

The Gemara answers:

אָמְרֵי – **They said:** גַּבֵּי מְזוֹנוֹת קָתָנֵי לָכֶם – **In the case of food the Mishnah teaches** that he says, "Come and save for YOURSELVES," מִשּׁוּם דְּלָא קָא חֲזוּ אֶלָּא מְזוֹן שָׁלֹשׁ סְעוּדוֹת – **because no more than three meals' worth** of food **are fit** for him, since the Rabbis prohibited a person to save more than this amount. Therefore, he cannot tell the neighbors to save it for him.[30] אֲבָל גַּבֵּי לְבוּשִׁים קָתָנֵי עִמִּי – **But in the case of clothes the Mishnah teaches** that he says, "Come and save **with me,**" מִשּׁוּם דְּקַחֲזוּ לֵיהּ לְכוּלֵּי יוֹמָא – **because [the clothes] are fit for him all day,** i.e. he may change many times in the course of a single day. Therefore, he may tell the neighbors to save for him.[31]

The Gemara cites a Baraisa that elaborates our Mishnah:

תָּנוּ רַבָּנַן – **The Rabbis taught in a Baraisa** regarding saving clothes from a fire: לוֹבֵשׁ מוֹצִיא וּפוֹשֵׁט – ONE may PUT ON clothes, TAKE THEM OUT, TAKE THEM OFF, וְחוֹזֵר וְלוֹבֵשׁ וּמוֹצִיא וּפוֹשֵׁט – AND then RETURN AND PUT ON other clothes, AND TAKE THEM OUT AND TAKE THEM OFF, וַאֲפִילּוּ כָּל הַיּוֹם כּוּלּוֹ – AND continue doing so EVEN THE ENTIRE DAY; דִּבְרֵי רַבִּי מֵאִיר – these are THE WORDS OF R' MEIR. רַבִּי יוֹסֵי אוֹמֵר – R' YOSE SAYS: שְׁמוֹנָה עָשָׂר כֵּלִים – One may put on and take out just EIGHTEEN GARMENTS. וְאֵלּוּ הֵם שְׁמוֹנָה עָשָׂר כֵּלִים – AND THESE ARE THE EIGHTEEN GARMENTS:[32] מִקְטוֹרֶן אוּנְקְלֵי וּפוּנְדָּא – A CLOAK, AN OUTER COAT,[33] AND AN OUTER BELT,[34] קַלְבּוּס שֶׁל פִּשְׁתָּן וְחָלוּק –

NOTES

deemed *hefker* (see *Bava Metzia* 24a). Indeed, *Ran* explains the Gemara to mean this.

Bach (*Orach Chaim* 334), however, answers that *Rashi* did not consider the excess food to be automatically *hefker* because the owner could still possibly get non-Jews to save it for him (see Gemara below, 121a, which teaches that one is permitted to tell non-Jews, when his property is on fire, "He who saves will not lose." *Magen Avraham* (334:11) adds that he may be able to find even Jewish friends who will save the items and return them to him. Thus, the items are not deemed ownerless unless he explicitly abandons them by declaring, "Save for yourselves."]

26. [The Mishnah teaches that although one has a right to keep what he saves, since the owner declared his abandonment of it,] a pious person should return it to its original owner (*Rashi*), because he did not abandon it willingly (see *Rashi* below ד״ה דלא ניחא ליה and note 29; see also *Rashash*). Instead, he should accept wages for his exertions (cf. *Ritva MHK* ed.).

27. A pious person is one who is willing to give up what is rightfully his to avoid even the hint of wrongdoing. Although it is true that such a person would certainly not keep what he had saved from the fire, as Rav Chisda said, his piety would not be limited to monetary concerns. Rather, he would be equally concerned to avoid the hint of forbidden Sabbath wages. Therefore, even though taking money from the owner in this case would, technically speaking, not violate the prohibition against taking wages for Sabbath work – because there was no stipulation in advance that he would be paid for saving the food and because he really has the right to keep everything [thus he is not taking wages from the owner for his work, he is simply making him a gift of the food minus the value of his salvage efforts] – nonetheless, he would not be considered a חָסִיד, *pious person,* unless he were willing to waive this money too and return *everything* to the original owner (*Rashi*). [The Mishnah, therefore, cannot be teaching that the proper procedure for a חָסִיד, *pious person,* is to return the food and take wages.]

28. A God-fearing person does not want to benefit at the expense of another person by acquiring property that he was forced to abandon against his will. At the same time he is not so pious as to forgo what is rightfully his [in order to avoid the hint of Sabbath wages]. He would therefore not give up his time and energy without compensation (*Rashi*).

29. Thus, when the Mishnah speaks of their being "wise," it does not mean wise in matters of monetary law, as was originally thought (see note 25). Rather, it means wise in matters of Sabbath law – i.e. they are knowledgeable enough to know that they are permitted to accept wages in such a case because it had not been stipulated in advance that they would be compensated for their salvage work (*Rashi;* see also *Rashi* ד״ה חסידי).

[The Gemara's new explanation of the phrase, "If they were wise," is said not only according to Rava but according to Rav Chisda as well. The Gemara, however, had previously interrupted Rav Chisda's answer with Rava's question. It now explains the Mishnah's wording according to both (*Rashi*).]

30. *Mishnah Berurah* 334:20.

31. I.e. since he is permitted to save all his clothing himself [by putting it on, taking it out, and returning to put on and remove more,] he is permitted to ask others to assist him in saving it. Thus, whatever they save remains his (*Mishnah Berurah* 334:20,21; cf. *Hagahos R' Elazar Moshe Horowitz*).

The reason the Sages were more lenient in regard to clothing than food (allowing him to save as much clothing as he can and not just what he needs for that day) is because they only allowed a person to remove extra clothing by wearing it. This alone serves to remind him of the Sabbath (*Rashba, Ritva MHK* ed., *Ran*). However, if one *carries* out clothing by hand, he can only remove that which he actually needs for that day (*Mishnah Berurah* 334:18, from *Eliyahu Rabbah* and *Pri Megadim*).

32. [These eighteen garments are an example of a set of clothes in which the function of one did not overlap the other, and which people actually wore together (in R' Yose's time). R' Yose does not mean to exclude wearing and removing other types of clothing. He merely requires that they be articles of clothing that would ordinarily be worn together. In his time, the maximum number was eighteen, which he now enumerates (see *Rav* to this Mishnah and note 12 above).]

33. An *unkali* was a wide garment similar to a top coat (*Rashi,* as translated by *Targum HaLaaz*).

34. A hollow belt worn over the outer garments (*Rashi*). *Rambam* (*Commentary to the Mishnah, Keilim* 29:1) renders this a type of undershirt.

דברים שאין אדם עומד בהן. על בוריין לאומרן כהלכתן: אלא אם כן נכשל בהן. עד שאומרן ב' וג' פעמים בשיבוש דהיינו טעמי תורה המסותרין: לא אהיה חובש. איני רגיל להיות חובש תבוש בבהמ"ד. אהיה הורגלתי כמו שחוק לרעהו אהיה (איוב יב) אני הווה: וממאי. דמשום דיש בהן אמנה הוא דילמא על כרחיך לריכים שיש בו האמת: דאי אמר להו גמירנא. אותן טעמי תורה: אמרי ליה. שואלים אימא לן: ומשני הוה ליה למימר גמר ושכח מאי לא אהיה חובש. מודה הוא על האמת שלא יגע בתורה: בדברי תורה. היו נאמנין ואין מתהללים על שקר:

דברים שאין בני אדם עומדין עליהם אלא אם כן נכשלים בהן ישנן תחת ידיך קצין תהיה לנו א) ישא ביום ההוא לאמר לא אהיה חובש וגו' אין ישא אלא לשון שבועה וכן הוא אומר ב) לא תשא את שם ה' לא אהיה חובש לא אהיה מחובשי עצמן בבית המדרש א) ובביתי אין לחם ואין שמלה שאין בידי לא ב) מקרא ולא משנה ולא גמרא וממאי דילמא שאני התם דאי אמר להו גמירנא אמרו ליה אימא לן הוה ליה למימר גמר ושכח מאי לא אהיה חובש כלל לא קשיא כאן בדברי תורה כאן במשא ומתן: **מתני'** א מצילין סל מלא ככרות אע"פ שיש בו מאה סעודות ועיגול של דבילה וחבית של יין ואומר לאחרים בואו והצילו לכם ואם היו פיקחין עושין עמו חשבון אחר השבת להיכן מצילין אותן ב לחצר המעורבת בן בתירא אומר אף לשאינה מעורבת ג) ולשם מוציא כל כלי תשמישו ד ולובש כל מה שיכול ללבוש ועוטף כל מה שיכול לעטוף ר' יוסי אומר י"ח כלים ה וחוזר ולובש ומוציא ואומר לאחרים בואו והצילו עמי: **גמ'** והא תנא ליה ג) רישא ג' סעודות ותו לא אמר רב הונא לא קשיא כאן בבא להציל כאן בבא לקפל ו בא להציל מציל את כולן בא לקפל אינו מקפל אלא מזון ג' סעודות ז) ר' אבא בר זבדא אמר רב אידי ואידי בבא לקפל ולא קשיא כאן לאותה חצר כאן לחצר אחרת בעי רב הונא בריה דרב יהושע פירש טליתו וקיפל והניח וקיפל והניח מאי כבא להציל דמי או כבא לקפל דמי (ה) מדאמר רבא אטעיה רב שיזבי לרב חסדא ודרש ובלבד שלא יביא כלי שהוא מחזיק יותר מג' סעודות ש"מ ז כבא להציל ושפיר דמי א"ל רב נחמן בר יצחק לרבא מאי טעותא אמר ליה דקתני י) ובלבד שלא יביא כלי אחר ויקלוט כלי אחר ויצרף כלי אחר הוא דלא אבל בההוא מנא כמה דבעי מציל: ועיגול של דבילה כו': ח חשבון מאי עבידתיה מהפקירא קזכו אמר רב חסדא מדת חסידות שנו כאן אמר רבא חסידי אגרא דשבתא שקלי אלא אמר רבא הכא בירא שמים עסקינן (ג) ט ולא ניחא ליה דליתהני מאחרים ובחנם נמי לא ניחא ליה דליטרח והכי קאמר ואם היו פיקחין דידעי דכה"ג לאו שכר שבת הוא עושין עמו חשבון לאחר השבת: ולהיכן מצילין כו': מ"ש הכא דקתני לכם ומ"ש הכא דקתני עמי אמרי גבי מזונות קתני לכם משום דלא קא חזו (ג) אלא מזון ג' סעודות אבל גבי לבושים קתני עמי משום דקחזי ליה לכולי יומא: ת"ר לובש (ד) מוציא ופושט וחוזר ולובש ומוציא ופושט ואפילו כל היום כולו דברי רבי מאיר רבי יוסי אומר שמנה עשר כלים ואלו הם שמנה עשר כלים מקטורן י אונקלי ופונדא קלבוס של פשתן וחלוק י) ואפיליות ומעפורת ושני ספרקין ושני מנעלים ושני אנפלאות וב' פרגוד וחגור שבמתניו וכובע שבראשו וסודר שבצוארו: **מתני'** ר' שמעון בן ננס אומר פורסין עור של גדי על גבי שידה תיבה ומגדל שאחז בהן את האור מפני שהוא מחרך כ ועושין מחיצה בכל הכלים בין מלאין בין ריקנים בשביל שלא תעבור הדליקה רבי יוסי אוסר בכלי חרס חדשים מלאין מים לפי שאין יכולין לקבל את האור והן מתבקעין ומכבין את הדליקה: **גמ'** אמר רב יהודה אמר רב טלית שאחז בה האור מצד אחד נותנין עליה מים מצד אחר ואם כבתה כבתה מיתיבי מ) ל טלית שאחז בה האור מצד אחד פושטה ומתכסה בה ואם כבתה כבתה וכן ספר תורה שאחז בו האור פושטו וקורא בו ואם כבה כבה הוא

רש"י

מתני' ועיגול של דבילה. שהוא גדול ויש בו סעודות הרבה: ואם היו פקחין. לישאל שכרן כפועלים: כל כלי תשמישו. שצריכין לו לאותו היום כגון כוסות וקיתוניות: י"ח כלים. מפרש להו בגמרא שכן דרך ללובשן בחול יחד אבל טפי מהכי לא ואינו פושטן לחזור וללבוש ולהציל אחרים: גמ' בבא להציל. [שהציל] בסל [אחד] כדקתני סל מלא ככרות ואינו טורח אלא להצילן מתוך הדליקה בבת אחת מציל כל מה שבסל דהא חדא זימנא הוא מה לי פורתא מה לי טובא: בבא לקפל. סלים הרבה זה עם זה לטרוח [ולאוספם] ולחזור ולהוציא מזון ג' סעודות הוא דיכול להציל בסלים הרבה ותו לא שכל א' טורח בעצמו הוא: פירש טליתו וקיפל והניח. הביא אוכלין והניח וחזר והביא והניח מהו: כבא להציל דמי. הואיל ואין כאן אלא כלי אחד ובפעם אחת הוא מוציאם: או כבא לקפל דמי. הואיל וטורח לאסוף ולכנוס: אטעייה רב שיזבי לרב חסדא ט) [עדן]. שדרש לפניו והודה לו רב חסדא והא מתני' דאמרן לעיל (דף קיז:) נשברה לו חבית בראש גגו מביא כלי ומניח תחתיה ודרש רב שיזבי לרב חסדא ובלבד שלא (ה) יתן כלי המחזיק יותר משלש סעודות והודה לו רב חסדא ומדאמר רבא אטעייה שמע מינה טעותא הוא דאפילו מחזיק סעודות הרבה מותר כיון דחד מנא הוא והאי כמקפל ונותן בכלי אחד דמי דהא מעט מעט הוא נופל י) ומטפטף בו ש"מ בחד מנא כבא להציל דמי: מאי טעותא. מנא לך דטעותא הוא בידיה: אמר ליה. מדקתני בה בברייתא: ובלבד שלא יביא כלי אחר כו'. ש"מ כלים טובא הוא דאסירי אבל בחד שפיר דמי: מהפקירא וכו'. דהא הצילו לכם קאמר להו לצרכיהם ואם פקחים הם יעכבו הכל הוה ליה למיתני: מדת חסידות. שמחזירין לו: חסידי אגרא דשבתא שקלי. בתמיה אם חסידים הם יש להם לוותר משלהם בכל דבר שיש בו נדנוד עבירה ואע"ג דלאו שכר שבת גמור הוא שהרי לא התנה ומהפקירא קא זכו מיהו חסיד לא מיקרי אא"כ מוותר משלו: הכא בירא שמים עסקינן. המציל הזה ירא שמים הוא ולא חסיד לוותר משלו: דלא ניחא ליה דליתהני מאחריני. בזכייה דהפקירא דידע דלא מרצונו הפקירו: ובחנם נמי לא ניחא ליה דליטרח. דלאו חסיד הוא (ו) ולמחול על שלו: והכי קאמר כו'. כלומר דהאי אם היו פקחין דמתני' לאו פקחין בדין קאמר ליטול את הראוי להם דאם כן יעכבו הכל הוה ליה למתני אלא לאו הכי קאמר הני יראי שמים אם פקחין הן בהלכות שבת דידעי דכה"ג לאו שכר שבת הוא דמעיקרא לאו אדעתא דשכר פעולה נחית עושין עמו חשבון והכי קאמר אדרב חסדא נמי קאי אלא לא שבקיה לרב חסדא לסיימיה למילתיה: כ) לחצר המעורבת. ואפי' הכי טובא לא ליזיל כדאמר לעיל (דף קיז:) מתוך שבהול אי שרי לאיעסוקי בהצלה כולי האי אתי לכבויי: מקטורן. מנטי"ל: אונקלי. לבוש רחב כעין שרבי"א ובלשון ערבי מקשי"ה: פונדא. אזור חלול מעל למדיו: קלבוס. פיישי"ל: חלוק. קמיס"א על בשרו: ואפליון. סדין להתעטף בו כולו: מעפורת. לעטוף ראשו: ושני ספרקין. פיסול"ש: אנפלאות. קלצו"ש של בגד: פרגוד. גנליי"ש ובלשון אשכנז קני הוזי"ן: חגור. על חלוקו מבפנים: וסודר שבצוארו. ותולין ראשיו לפניו לקנח בו פיו ועיניו: מתני' עור של גדי. לח: מפני שהוא מחרך. מן האור ונכוה ובלע"ז רטרי"ט ואינו נשרף ומתוך כך הוא מגין על התיבה: בין מלאים. מים: שאין יכולין לקבל כח האור. מפני שחדשים הם: גמ'

תוספות

אידי ואידי בבא לקפל. פירש הרב פורת דלקפל היינו אפי' בא לקפל דלר' אבא אין חילוק בין לקפל בין להציל דאפילו להציל בחצר אחרת לא שרי אלא מזון ג' סעודות אבל אין נראה לומר דלהציל שרי אפילו מאה סעודות בחצר אחרת גם לרבי אבא דאם כן הוה ליה לאוקומי מתני' אידי ואידי בחצר אחרת וכאן בבא לקפל וכאן בבא להציל: נותן מים מצד זה. פירש רשב"ם לאו דוקא על הטלית דהא קי"ל בפ' דם חטאת (זבחים לד:) דבבגד שרייתו זהו כיבוסו ולעיל בסוף פרק שמנה שרצים (דף קיא.) פירשתי:

גרס

מסורת הש"ס

א) ס"א טעם, ב) עירובין נה:, ג) לעיל קיז:, ד) לעיל יט:, ה) לעיל קיח:, ו) עירובין נג:, ז) פי' בגד דקיק שלובש אדם על בשרו ערוך, ח) [פי' מסוה], ט) [תוספתא פי"ד], י) ס"א, כ) [צ"ל ומתעטף ער' רש"א], ל) [שייך לעיל במשנה].

הגהות הב"ח

(א) גמ' לקפל דמי מאי שמע מדאמר רבא: (ב) שם בירא שמים עסקינן דלא: (ג) שם דלא קא חזי ליה אלא: (ד) שם תנו רבנן לובש ומוציא: (ה) רש"י ד"ה אטעייה וכו' ובלבד שלא יתן כלי: (ו) ד"ה ובחנם וכו' למחול:

גליון הש"ס

מתני' ולובש כל מה שיכול ללבוש. ע"ל דף קמז ע"ב: גמ' מקטורן אונקלי ופונדא. עי' לעיל דף נט ע"ב תוס' ד"ה אלא: ושני ספרקין. מנחות ... מתני' עור של גדי. עיין לעיל דף מז ע"ב תוס' ד"ה טומנין:

תורה אור השלם

א) יִשָּׂא בַיּוֹם הַהוּא לֵאמֹר לֹא אֶהְיֶה חֹבֵשׁ וּבְבֵיתִי אֵין לֶחֶם וְאֵין שִׂמְלָה לֹא תְשִׂימֻנִי קְצִין עָם: [ישעיה ג, ז]

ב) לֹא תִשָּׂא אֶת שֵׁם יְיָ אֱלֹהֶיךָ לַשָּׁוְא כִּי לֹא יְנַקֶּה יְיָ אֵת אֲשֶׁר יִשָּׂא אֶת שְׁמוֹ לַשָּׁוְא: [שמות כ, ז]

עין משפט נר מצוה

נה א מיי' פכ"ג מהל' שבת הל' כב סמג לאוין סה טוש"ע או"ח סימן שלד סעיף ו [וסימן שלה סעיף מה]:

נו ב מיי' שם הלכה כג טוש"ע שם סעיף יז:

נז ג מיי' שם טוש"ע שם סעיף ז:

נח ד ה מיי' שם הלכה כה טור שו"ע שם סעיף ח:

נט ו ז מיי' שם הלכה כב טור שו"ע שם סעיף ו:

ס ח ט מיי' שם הלכה כד טור שו"ע שם סעיף ט:

סא י כ מיי' פרק יב שם הלכה ד סמג שם טוש"ע שם סעיף כב:

סב ל מיי' שם הלכה ו טור שו"ע שם סעיף כג כד:

רבינו חננאל

מצילין סל מלא ככרות ואע"ג שיש בו ק' סעודות. אקשינן איני והא תני רישא מצילין מזון ג' סעודות ותו לא ושני רב הונא לא קשיא רישא בבא לקפל. פי' כגון שמקבץ מתוך הבית המקומות [הרבה] ונותן בכמה כלים שאין לו להציל אלא מזון של ג' סעודות בלבד. סיפא במציל כולו בבא בכלי אחד כמות שהוא. ואע"פ שאין זה הטעם כאשר פירשנו. כי רישא במקפל ונותן בכלים שנים ושלשה. וסיפא במציל של אחד כמות שהוא מפורש (היבנונהו מז'). בעי רב הונא בריה דרב יהושע פירש טליתו וקיפל והניח קיפל והניח מהו. כבא לקפל דמי או כבא להציל דמי. דמגלי לן שאם קיפל בכלי אחד ונטלו. וחזר וקיפל בכלי אחר ונטלו זהו לקפל פשיטא שאינו מציל אלא מזון ג' סעודות. וכי קא מבעיא שקיפל והניח בתוך טליתו וחזר וקיפל והניח בתוך טליתו מי אמרינן כיון שמקפל ומביא כמקפל דמי ואסור. או דילמא כיון שהוא מניחן בתוך טלית אחד ונוטלן כאחד כבא להציל דמי ושרי. ומיפרשא נמי הא בגמ' בסוף יציאות השבת. הנהו תרי תלמידי. מר מציל בחד מנא ומר מציל בתרי מני כפלוגתא דר' אבא בר זבדא ורב הונא. הכין גמרא ומיגמר מינה דלקפל בתרי תלתא מני כדפרישנא לעילא דאסיר לרב הונא ושרי לר' יוסי בר זבדא ומסתייע נמי בתלמוד א"י דאמרי על מצילין סל מלא ככרות מכיון שכולו גוף אחד כמין שכולה סעודה אחת היא והאי במימרא דרב הונא ובא ר' אבא בר זבדא ופליג פירוק אחר. ואמר רישא דמתני' במציל לחצר אחרת שאין לו להציל אלא מזון ג' סעודות בלבד בין בכלי א' בין בב' ג' כלים. וסיפא במציל באותו חצר שיש לו להציל אפילו ק' סעודות בין בכלי אחד בין בכמה כלים. ולענין בעיא דרב הונא בריה דר' יהושע פשיט מדאמר רבא הא מילתא אטעיה רב שיזבי ודרש ובלבד שלא יבא כלי אחר המחזיק יותר מג' סעודות. ש"מ כבא להציל דמי ש"מ. והכי קא גמרין מדקאמר רבא דבטעותא דרש רב חסדא שלא יביא כלי מחזיק יותר מג' סעודות. שמעינן מינה שאם אפילו אם יביא כלי שמחזיק כל מה שהוא חפץ ויקפל ויניח בו ויטלנו כולו בבת אחת שפיר דמי. א"ל רב נחמן בר יצחק מאי טעותא. פירוש מנ"ל דטעותא היא דילמא דוקא אמר רב שיזבי. אהדר ליה רבא לא לא ס"ד מדקתני בברייתא ובלבד שלא יביא כלי אחר ויקלוט כלי אחר ויצרף. כלי אחר לא יביא. אבל בההוא מנא כמה דבעי מציל. אוקימנא בירא שמים ולא ניחא ליה דליתהני מאחריני ובחנם [נמי לא ניחא ליה למטרח] אם היו פקחין שידעין דכי האי גוונא לאו שכר שבת הוא הואיל ומהפקירא קא זכו ואינון הוא דמהדרו ליה לבעה"ב כגון מתנה מדידהו הוא עושין חשבון לאחר השבת. ושארא שבקי ליה לבעה"ב. סוגיא דשמעתא שהחסיד גדול הוא מירא שמים. ולשם מוציא כל כלי תשמישו. לרבנן בחצר המעורבת. אף לשאינה מעורבת. ולובש כל מה שהוא יכול ללבוש ועוטף כל מה שהוא יכול להתעטף. ואפי' יותר מי"ח כלים. וכן הלכתא. וקי"ל שמותר להערים: ירושלמי תני אין מערימין. ר' יוסי בר אבין אמר מערימין. ועל זו

ליקוטי רש"י

אלא אם כן נכשלים בהן. כשמתלמידי נכשל בשמועתו פעם ראשונה ושניה הוא נותן לב לעמוד על שמועתו [חגיגה יד.]. דברי תורה שאין אדם עומד על אמיתתן עד שיכשל בהן להורות טעות וכלימותיו והוא נותן לב ומכוין אותן ... דילמא. האי נמי לאו משום דאיכא אמונה היא אלא לאי הוה אמרי גמירנא הוו אמרי ליה אימא לן והוא לא הוה ידע [חגיגה שם]. לחצר. שסמוכה לדליקה [עירובין צה:]. ולובש כל מה שיכול ללבוש. ואפילו עשרה חלוקים זה על זה [לעיל סה:]. בבא לקפל. מציל בארבע וחמש מאני אלא שמקפלן כולן למוך כלי גדול ושואלן בפעם אחת [שם שם: ע"ש בתוס']. ויקלוט. קילוט הטוטל מן הגולף. ויצרף. סמוך לגג כעין שפופרת אלא שלינו ראוי לשאוב שהגג משוך והזין אינו בגומא כלל מארץ כלי הגג שיזוב מן הגג לכלי והוא אוחז הכלי בידו [שם קיז:]. שכר שבת. גורה משום מקח וממכר ושכירות [כתובות סד.]. מקטורן. מתמפסס בו על בגדים שהוא לובש [רשב"ם ב"ב נז:]. אונקלי. מלבוש של עור [מנחות לט:]. שיפויי"ש מלוך [מו"ק כב.]. מעפורת. סודר ומתפסס באחר לכתיב [במלכים] גבי מיכה (מלכים א, כ) מתרגמינן ואיסתפי [במעפרתא] [חולין קכב.].

A LINEN DOUBLET,[35] A TUNIC, וְאַפִּילְיוֹת – A ROBE,[36] וּמַעֲפוֹרֶת – A KERCHIEF to wrap around the head, וּשְׁנֵי סַפְרְקִין – TWO LEG BANDS,[37] וּשְׁנֵי מִנְעָלִים – TWO SHOES, וּשְׁנֵי אַנְפִּילָאוֹת – TWO SOCKS, וּשְׁנֵי פַּרְגּוֹד – TWO GAITERS,[38] וַחֲגוֹר שֶׁבְּמָתְנָיו – THE BELT ON HIS LOINS,[39] וְכוֹבַע שֶׁבְּרֹאשׁוֹ – THE HAT ON HIS HEAD, וְסוּדָר שֶׁבְּצַוָּארוֹ – AND THE SCARF AROUND HIS NECK.[40]

Mishnah The previous Mishnahs have discussed what items may be rescued from a fire on the Sabbath. The following Mishnah discusses what may be done to contain a fire:

רַבִּי שִׁמְעוֹן בֶּן נַנָּס אוֹמֵר – R' Shimon ben Nannas says: פּוֹרְסִין עוֹר שֶׁל גְּדִי – **One may spread a kid's hide** עַל גַּבֵּי שִׁידָּה תֵּיבָה וּמִגְדָּל שֶׁאָחַז בָּהֶן אֶת הָאוּר – **over a carriage, trunk or closet in which a fire has taken hold,**[41] מִפְּנֵי שֶׁהוּא מְחָרֵךְ – **because [the hide] singes** but does not burn.[42] וְעוֹשִׂין מְחִיצָּה בְּכָל הַכֵּלִים בֵּין מְלֵאִין בֵּין רֵיקָנִים – **And we may make a partition** in the path of the fire **with all** kinds of **vessels, whether full or empty,** בִּשְׁבִיל שֶׁלֹּא תַּעֲבוֹר הַדְּלֵיקָה – **so that the fire should not** be able to **pass** beyond. רַבִּי יוֹסֵי אוֹסֵר בִּכְלֵי חֶרֶס חֲדָשִׁים מְלֵאִין מַיִם – **R' Yose prohibits** doing so with **new earthenware vessels filled with water,** לְפִי שֶׁאֵין יְכוֹלִין לְקַבֵּל אֶת הָאוּר – **because they cannot withstand the fire,**[43] וְהֵן מִתְבַּקְּעִין וּמְכַבִּין אֶת הַדְּלֵיקָה – **and they burst and** thereby **extinguish the fire.**

Gemara The Gemara presents a ruling:

אָמַר רַב יְהוּדָה אָמַר רַב – **Rav Yehudah said in the name of Rav:** טַלִּית שֶׁאָחַז בָּהּ הָאוּר מִצַּד אֶחָד – **A cloak in which a fire has taken hold** (i.e. which has begun to smolder) **on one side,** נוֹתְנִין עָלֶיהָ מַיִם מִצַּד אַחֵר – **we may place water on it on the other side,** וְאִם כָּבְתָה כָּבְתָה – **and if [the fire] is** thereby **extinguished, it is extinguished,** and one has not violated any prohibition.[44]

Rav Yehudah's ruling is questioned:

מֵיתִיבֵי – **They challenged this** ruling **from a Baraisa:** טַלִּית שֶׁאָחַז בָּהּ הָאוּר מִצַּד אֶחָד – A CLOAK IN WHICH A FIRE HAS TAKEN HOLD ON ONE SIDE, פּוֹשְׁטָהּ וּמִתְכַּסֶּה בָּהּ – ONE MAY UNFOLD IT[45] AND COVER HIMSELF WITH IT, וְאִם כָּבְתָה כָּבְתָה – AND IF [THE FIRE] IS thereby EXTINGUISHED, IT IS EXTINGUISHED. וְכֵן סֵפֶר תּוֹרָה שֶׁאָחַז בּוֹ הָאוּר – LIKEWISE, A TORAH SCROLL IN WHICH A FIRE HAS TAKEN HOLD, פּוֹשְׁטוֹ וְקוֹרֵא בּוֹ וְאִם כָּבָה כָּבָה – ONE MAY UNROLL IT AND READ IT, AND IF [THE FIRE] IS thereby EXTINGUISHED, IT IS EXTINGUISHED.[46] Now, the Baraisa permits dealing with the fire only in this more indirect manner but not by placing water on the other side of the cloak.[47] How then can Rav Yehudah permit this?

NOTES

35. A tight-fitting, vestlike garment with or without sleeves (*Rashi,* as translated by *Targum HaLaaz*).

36. A [togalike] garment wrapped around the entire body (*Rashi,* who has the reading אַפִּלְיוֹן [singular] rather than אַפִּילְיוֹת [plural]).

37. *Rashi,* as translated by *Targum HaLaaz.* Perhaps they were bands that held up the gaiters (see below).

Rash (*Keilim* 29:2) is of the opinion that the סוּבְרִיקִין mentioned there is the same as the סַפְרְקִין here. He cites two opinions as to what it means. *Aruch* renders it *trousers,* while *Rav Hai Gaon* renders it *gloves* that reach up to the elbows.

38. That is, leg coverings that extended from the knee to the instep (*Rashi,* according to *Targum HaLaaz*).

39. This was worn around the tunic (*Rashi*). [Two belts could not be worn one on top of the other unless there was a layer of clothing between them; otherwise the outer belt would not be serving any purpose. Thus, this belt must have been for the tunic, the inner garment (*Tosafos* 59b ד״ה תרי).]

40. The ends of this scarf hung in front of the person and could be used to wipe the mouth or eyes (*Rashi*).

41. I.e. he may spread it over the part of the object that has not yet caught fire to prevent the fire from damaging it (*Rambam, Hil. Shabbos* 12:5; *Tur* and *Shulchan Aruch, Orach Chaim* 334:22). [This is permitted because one is not extinguishing the fire but merely preventing the fire from spreading to the area covered by the hide.]

42. [The Gemara (120b) initially assumes this to be the reason that R' Shimon ben Nannas permits this – i.e. because the hide does not extinguish the fire, it merely prevents the fire from spreading because it itself does not burn. The Gemara, however, will conclude otherwise; see 120b note 3.]

The Mishnah speaks of a [raw] hide that is still moist (*Rashi;* cf. *Rabbeinu Tam* cited by *Tosafos* in 49a ד״ה טומנין בשלחין). [This, however, presents a problem, for the Gemara above (116b) said that a raw hide may only be carried when there is still meat attached to it; otherwise, it is considered *muktzeh.* How then does our Mishnah permit carrying such a hide to cover a burning carriage, trunk or closet? *Tosafos* (49a ד״ה טומנין בשלמין) answer that our Mishnah is speaking of a case where the hide had been designated for use in its raw condition, thereby removing it from the category of *muktzeh. Mishnah Berurah* (334:53) adds that according to those who hold that even *muktzeh* may be moved when it is threatened by fire (see *Orach Chaim* 334:2), our Mishnah can be discussing any kind of hide.]

43. Since they are new [they have not yet hardened sufficiently to endure the heat] (*Rashi*).

44. Although if the smolder continues to spread across the cloak it will reach the water-soaked part of the garment and be extinguished, the person has not *directly* extinguished the fire since he did not pour the water on the part that was already burning. Rather, he merely causes the fire to burn itself out when it reaches the wet part. According to Rav, *causing* a fire to be extinguished [גְּרַם כִּיבּוּי] is permitted (see Gemara below; *Beis Yosef, Orach Chaim,* end of 334 ד״ה וטלית שאחז בו האור).

[Seemingly, it should be forbidden to wet the other side of the garment because of the rule taught by the Gemara in *Zevachim* (94b): בֶּגֶד שְׁרִיָּיתוֹ זֶהוּ כִּיבּוּסוֹ, *in the case of a cloth, its wetting is its laundering,* and laundering (מְלַבֵּן) is forbidden on the Sabbath (Mishnah 73a). Because of this question, *Rashbam* (cited by *Tosafos*) explains that Rav does not mean that the water is actually poured onto the cloak. *Tosafos* are also of the opinion that the rule that wetting a cloth is equivalent to laundering it applies only to a cloth that is spotted or stained, as *Tosafos* explained at length on 111a,b (end of ד״ה האי מסוכרייתא). Therefore, pouring water on the unaffected portion of the cloak does not violate the *melachah* of laundering (*Beis Yosef* ibid. ד״ה ומ״ש רבינו; *Taz* 334:18; the differences between these two answers have important ramifications in halachah; see *Rama, Orach Chaim* 302:9 and *Beur Halachah* there).]

45. To keep the smolder from spreading through the folds (*Mishnah Berurah* 334:54 from *Taz*).

46. Opening up the cloak and putting it on, and unrolling the scroll, do not directly extinguish the fire but merely inhibit its ability to spread. This is considered a גְּרַם כִּיבּוּי, *causing extinguishment,* not direct extinguishment (*Bach* ibid.; *Magen Avraham* 334:25; see next note).

47. Unfolding a cloak and unrolling a scroll are even more indirect methods of extinguishing the fire than putting water on part of the garment. Water actually extinguishes the fire when it comes in contact with it, whereas opening up the cloak or unrolling the scroll merely localizes the fire by reducing the material in contact with it, and thereby [often] causes it to burn itself out in place and not spread (*Taz* 334:17; see also *Ritva MHK* ed.; cf. *Beis Yosef* end of 334 ד״ה וטלית and *Tur* there as explained by *Beis Yosef*).

[Although the Baraisa speaks of unfolding the cloak and *putting it on,* and similarly, unrolling the scroll and *reading from it,* it is not actually necessary to do so. The Baraisa means only to say that one may open the items as he does when he uses the items normally, and they may even be used, but he may not flap them around in order to put out the fire (*Bach;* see *Taz* for a slightly different explanation; cf. *Beis Yosef*).

דברים שאין אדם עומד בהן. על בוריין לאומרן כהלכתן: **אלא אם כן נכשל בהן.** עד שאומרן ג' וד' פעמים בשיבוש דהיינו טעמי תורה המסותרין: **לא אהיה חובש.** איני רגיל להיות חובש חבוש בבהמ"ד. אהיה הורגלתי כמו שחוק לרעהו אהיה (איוב יב) אני הווה: וממאי. דמשום דיש בהן אמנה הוא דילמא על כרחך לרגיס שישינו האמת: **דאי אמר להו גמירנא.** אותן טעמי תורה: **אמרי ליה.** שואלים אימא לן: ומשני הוה ליה למימר גמר ושכח מאי לא אהיה חובש. מודה הוא על האמת שלא יגע בתורה: **בדברי תורה.** היו נאמנין ואין מתהללים על שקר:

דברים שאין בני אדם עומדין עליהם אלא אם כן נכשלים בהן ישנן תחת ידיך קצין תהיה לנו [א] ישא ביום ההוא לאמר לא אהיה חובש וגו' אין ישא אלא לשון שבועה וכן הוא אומר [ב] לא תשא את שם ה' לא אהיה חובש לא אהיה מחובשי עצמן בבית המדרש [א] ובביתי אין לחם ואין שמלה שאין בידי לא [א] מקרא ולא משנה ולא גמרא וממאי דילמא שאני התם דאי אמר להו גמירנא אמרו ליה אימא לן הוה ליה למימר גמר ושכח מאי לא אהיה חובש כלל לא קשיא כאן בדברי תורה כאן במשא ומתן:

מתני' [א] מצילין סל מלא ככרות אע"פ שיש בו מאה סעודות ועיגול של דבילה וחבית של יין ואומר לאחרים בואו והצילו לכם ואם היו פיקחין עושין עמו חשבון אחר השבת להיכן מצילין אותן [ב] לחצר המעורבת בן בתירא אומר אף לשאינה מעורבת [ג] ולשם מוציא כל כלי תשמישו [ד] ולובש כל מה שיכול ללבוש ועוטף כל מה שיכול לעטוף ר' יוסי אומר י"ח כלים [ה] וחוזר ולובש ומוציא ואומר לאחרים בואו והצילו עמי: **גמ'** והא תנא ליה [ו] רישא ג' סעודות ותו לא אמר רב הונא לא קשיא כאן בבא להציל כאן בבא לקפל [ז] בא להציל מציל את כולן בא לקפל אינו מקפל אלא מזון ג' סעודות [ח] ר' אבא בר זבדא אמר רב אידי ואידי בבא לקפל ולא קשיא כאן לאותה חצר כאן לחצר אחרת בעי רב הונא בריה דרב יהושע פירש טליתו וקיפל והניח והניח מאי כבא להציל דמי או כבא לקפל דמי [א] מדאמר רבא אטעיה רב שיזבי לרב חסדא ודרש ובלבד שלא יביא כלי שהוא מחזיק יותר מג' סעודות ש"מ [ט] כבא להציל דמי ושפיר דמי א"ל רב נחמן בר יצחק לרבא מאי טעותא אמר ליה דקתני [ט] ובלבד שלא יביא כלי אחר ויקלוט כלי אחר ויצרף כלי אחר הוא דלא אבל בההוא מנא כמה דבעי מציל: ועיגול של דבילה כו': [ח] חשבון מאי עבידתיה מהפקירא קזכו אמר רב חסדא מדת חסידות שנו כאן אמר רבא חסידי אגרא דשבתא שקלי אלא אמר רבא הכא בירא שמים עסקינן [ג] [ט] ולא ניחא ליה דליתהני מאחרים ובחנם נמי לא ניחא ליה דליטרח והכי קאמר ואם היו פיקחין דידעי דכה"ג לאו שכר שבת הוא עושין עמו חשבון לאחר השבת: ולהיכן מצילין כו': מ"ש הכא דקתני לכם ומ"ש הכא דקתני עמי אמרי גבי מזונות קתני לכם משום דלא קא חזו [ג] אלא מזון ג' סעודות אבל גבי לבושים קתני עמי משום דקחזי ליה לכולי יומא: ת"ר לובש [ד] מוציא ופושט וחוזר ולובש ומוציא ופושט ואפילו כל היום כולו דברי רבי מאיר רבי יוסי אומר שמנה עשר כלים ואלו הם שמנה עשר כלים [ס] מקטורן [י] אונקלי ופונדא קלבוס של פשתן וחלוק [י] ואפיליות ומעפורת [ס] ושני ספרקין ושני מנעלים ושני אנפילאות וב' פרגד והגור שבמתניו וכובע שבראשו וסודר שבצוארו:

מתני' ר' שמעון בן ננס אומר [ס] פורסין [ס] עור של גדי על גבי שידה תיבה ומגדל שאחז בהן את האור מפני שהוא מחרך [כ] ועושין מחיצה בכל הכלים בין מלאין בין ריקנים בשביל שלא תעבור הדליקה רבי יוסי אוסר בכלי חרס חדשים מלאין מים לפי שאין יכולין לקבל את האור והן מתבקעין ומכבין את הדליקה: **גמ'** אמר רב יהודה אמר רב טלית שאחז בה האור מצד אחד נותנין עליה מים מצד אחר ואם כבתה כבתה מיתיבי [ס] [ל] טלית שאחז בה האור מצד אחד פושטה ומתכסה בה ואם כבתה כבתה וכן ספר תורה שאחז בו האור פושטו וקורא בו ואם כבה כבה

הוא

מתני' ועיגול של דבילה. שהוא גדול ויש בו סעודות הרבה: **ואם היו פקחין.** לישאל שכרן כפועלים: כל כלי תשמישו. שצריכין לו לאותו היום כגון כוסות וקיתוניות: י"ח כלים. מפרש להו בגמרא שכן דרך ללובשן בחול יחד אבל טפי מהכי לא ואינו פושטן לחזור וללבוש ולהציל אחרים: **גמ' בבא להציל.** [שהציל] בסל [אחד] כדקתני סל מלא ככרות ואינו טורח אלא להצילן מתוך הדליקה בבת אחת מציל כל מה שבסל דהא חדא זימנא הוא מה לי פורתא מה לי טובא: **בבא לקפל.** סלים הרבה זה עם זה לטרוח [ולאוספם] ולחזור ולהוציא מזון ג' סעודות הוא דיכול להציל בסלים הרבה ותו לא שכל א' טורח בעצמו הוא: **פירש טליתו וקיפל והניח.** הביא אוכלין והניח וחזר והביא והניח מהו: **כבא להציל דמי.** הואיל ואין כאן אלא כלי אחד ובפעם אחת הוא מוליכם: **או כבא לקפל דמי.** הואיל וטורח לאסוף ולכנוס: **אטעייה רב שיזבי לרב חסדא [עדן].** שדרש לפניו והודה לו רב חסדא והאי מתני' דאמרן לעיל (דף קיז:) נשברה לו חבית בראש גגו מביא כלי ומניח תחתיה ודרש רב שיזבי לרב חסדא ובלבד שלא (ה) יתן כלי המחזיק יותר משלש סעודות והודה לו רב חסדא ומדאמר רבא אטעייה שמע מינה טעותא הוא דאפילו מחזיק סעודות הרבה מותר כיון דחד מנא הוא והאי כמקפל ונותן בכלי אחד דמי דהא מעט מעט הוא נופל [י] ומטפטף בו ש"מ בחד מנא כבא להציל דמי: **מאי טעותא.** מנא לך לטעותא הוא בידיה: **אמר ליה.** מדקתני בה בברייתא: **ובלבד שלא יביא כלי אחר כו'.** ש"מ כלים טובא הוא דאסירי אבל בחד שפיר דמי: **מהפקירא וכו'.** דהא הצילו לכם קאמר להו לצרכיהם ואם פקחים הם יעכבו הכל הוה ליה למיתני: **מדת חסידות.** שמחזירין לו: **חסידי אגרא דשבתא שקלי.** בתמיה אם חסידים הם יש להם לוותר משלהם בכל דבר שיש בו נדנוד עבירה ואע"ג דלאו שכר שבת גמור הוא שהרי לא התנה ומהפקירא קא זכו מיהו חסיד לא מיקרי אא"כ מוותר משלו: **הכא בירא שמים עסקינן.** המציל הזה ירא שמים הוא ולא חסיד לוותר משלו: **דלא ניחא ליה דליתהני מאחריני.** בזכייה דהפקירא דידע דלא מרצונו הפקירו: **ובחנם נמי לא ניחא ליה דליטרח.** דלאו חסיד הוא (ו) ולמחול על שלו: **והכי קאמר כו'.** כלומר דהאי אם היו פקחין דמתני' לאו פקחין בדין קאמר ליטול את הראוי להם דאם כן יעכבו הכל הוה ליה למתני אלא לאו הכי קאמר הני יראי שמים אם פקחין הן בהלכות שבת דידעי דכה"ג לאו שכר שבת הוא דמעיקרא לאו אדעתא דשכר פעולה נחית עושין עמו חשבון והכי קאמר אדרב חסדא נמי קאי אלא לא שבקיניה לרב חסדא לסיימיה למילתיה: [י] **לחצר המעורבת.** ואפי' הכי טובא לא ליצול כדאמר לעיל (דף קיז:) מתוך שבהול אי שרי לאיעסוקי בהצלה כולי האי אתי לכבויי: **מקטורן.** מנטי"ל: **אונקלי.** לבוש רחב כעין שריגיש"א ובלשון ערבי מחסיא"ה: **פונדא.** אזור חלול מעל למדיו: **קלבוס.** נביי"ש: **חלוק.** קמיש"א על בשרו: **ואפליון.** סדין להתעטף בו כולו: **מעפורת.** לעטוף ראשו: **ושני ספרקין.** פיישול"ש: **אנפילייאות.** קלצנ"ש של למר: **פרגוד.** גנולי"ש ובלשון אחרינו קני הוז"ן: **חגור.** על חלוקו מבפנים: **וסודר שבצוארו.** ותלויין לפניו לקנח בו פיו ועיניו: **מתני' עור של גדי.** לח: **מפני שהוא מחרך.** מן האור ובלע"ז רטריי"ט ואינו נשרף ומתוך כך הוא מגין על התיבה: **בין מלאים.** מים: **שאינן יכולין לקבל כח האור.** מפני שמקדשים הם:

גמ'

אידי ואידי בבא לקפל. פירש הרב פורת דלקפל היינו אפי' בא לקפל דלר' אבא אין חילוק בין לקפל בין להציל דאפילו להציל בחצר אחרת לא שרי אלא מזון ג' סעודות אבל אין נראה לומר דלהציל שרי אפילו מאה סעודות בחצר אחרת גם לרבי אבא דאם כן הוה ליה לאוקומי מתני' אידי ואידי בחצר אחרת וכאן בבא לקפל וכאן בבא להציל: **נותן** מים מצד זה. פירש רשב"ם לאו דוקא על הטלית דהא קי"ל בפ' דם חטאת (זבחים לד:) דבבגד שרייתו זהו כיבוסו ולעיל בסוף פרק שמנה שרצים (דף קח.) פירשתי: גרס

רבינו חננאל

מצילין סל מלא ככרות ואע"ג שיש בו ק' סעודות. אקשינן איני והא תני רישא מצילין מזון ג' סעודות ותו לא ושני רב הונא לא קשיא רישא בבא לקפל. פי' כגון שמקבץ כל מה מתוך הבית ממקומות [הרבה] ונותן בכמה כלים שאין לו להציל אלא מזון של ג' סעודות בלבד. סיפא במציל כולו בכלי אחד כמות שהוא. ואע"פ שאין זה הטעם כאשר פירשנו. כי רישא במקפל ונותן בכלים שנים ושלשה. וסיפא במציל כל אחד כמות שהוא מפורש (היבנונהו מז:). **בעי רב** הונא בריה דר' יהושע פירש טליתו וקיפל והניח וקיפל והניח מהו. כבא לקפל דמי או כבא להציל דמי. דמגלי לן שאם קיפל בכלי אחד ונטלו. וחוזר וקיפל בכלי אחר ונטלו זהו לקפל פשיטא שאינו מציל אלא מזון ג' סעודות. וכי קא מבעיא שקיפל והניח בתוך טליתו וחזר וקיפל והניח בתוך טליתו מי אמרינן כיון שמקפל ומביא כמקפל דמי ואסור. או דילמא כיון שהוא מניחן בתוך טלית אחד אחד ונוטלן כאחד כבא להציל דמי ושרי. ומיפרשא נמי הא בגמ' בסוף יציאות השבת. הנהו תרי תלמידי. מר מציל בחד מנא ומר מציל בתרי מני קמפלגי בפלוגתא דר' אבא בר זבדא ורב הונא. הכין גמרא ומיגמר מינה דלקפל בתרי תלתא מני כדפרישנא לעילא דאסיר לרב הונא ושרי לר' אבא בר זבדא ומסתייע נמי בתלמוד א"י דאמרי על מצילין סל מלא ככרות מכיון שכולו גוף אחד כמין שכולה סעודה אחת היא והאי במימרא דרב הונא ובא ר' אבא בר זבדא ופירק פירוק אחר. ואמר רישא דמתני' במציל לחצר אחרת שאין לו להציל אלא מזון ג' סעודות בלבד בין בכלי א' בין בב' ג' כלים. וסיפא במציל באותו חצר שיש לו להציל אפילו ק' סעודות בין בכלי אחד בין בכמה כלים. ולענין בעיא דרב הונא בריה דר' יהושע פשיט מדאמר רבא הא מילתא אטעיה רב שיזבי ודרש ובלבד שלא יביא כלי אחד מחזיק יותר מג' סעודות. ש"מ כבא להציל דמי ש"מ. דהכי קא גמרין מדקאמר רבא

תורה אור השלם

א) יִשָּׂא בַיּוֹם הַהוּא לֵאמֹר לֹא אֶהְיֶה חֹבֵשׁ וּבְבֵיתִי אֵין לֶחֶם וְאֵין שִׂמְלָה לֹא תְשִׂימֻנִי קְצִין עָם: [ישעיה ג, ז]

ב) לֹא תִשָּׂא אֶת שֵׁם יְיָ אֱלֹהֶיךָ לַשָּׁוְא כִּי לֹא יְנַקֶּה יְיָ אֵת אֲשֶׁר יִשָּׂא אֶת שְׁמוֹ לַשָּׁוְא: [שמות כ, ז]

הגהות הב"ח

(א) גמ' לקפל דמי מה שמע מדאמר רבא: (ב) שם בירא שמים עסקינן דלא: (ג) שם דלא קא חזי ליה אלא: (ד) שם תנו רבנן לובש ומוציא: (ה) רש"י ד"ה אטעייה וכו' ובלבד שלא יביא כלי: (ו) ד"ה ובחנם וכו' לאמחול:

גליון הש"ס

מתני' ולובש כל מה שיכול ללבוש. ע"ל דף קמ ע"ב: גמ' מקטורן אונקלי ופונדא. ע' לעיל דף קנ ע"ב תוס' ד"ה חרי תחיי: שם ושני ספרקין. מכר במתני' פרק ב"ט משנה ג דכלים: מתני' עור של גדי. עיין לעיל דף מז ע"א תוס' ד"ה טומנין:

ליקוטי רש"י

אלא אם כן נכשלים בהן. כשהתלמיד נכשל בשמועתו פעם ראשונה ושניה הוא נותן לב לעמוד על שמועתו [חגיגה יד.]. דברי תורה שאין אדם עומד על אמיתתן עד שיכשל בהן להורות טעות וכלימותו והוא נותן לב ומבין אמת מה ידין [גיטין מג.]. **דילמא.** האי נמי לאו משום דלאמני אמנה היו אלא לאו דאי הוו אמרי ליה אימא לן והוא לא הוה ידע [חגיגה שם]. **לחצר.** שסמוכה לדליקה [עירובין צה.]. **ולובש כל מה שיכול ללבוש.** ואפילו עשרה חלוקים זה על גב זה [לעיל סה:]. **בבא לקפל.** אלא לאלצע ומתמו מאני מלו מתקמלן כולן לתוך כלי גדול ונוטלן בפעם אחת [שם יט: ע"ש בתוס']. **ויקלוט.** קילוט הנוטל מן האויר. **ויצרף.** סמוך לגג כעין שאינה אלא שאינו ראוי לשלוט בסכגג חלק וכיון שאינו בנוגמא מצרף כלי לגג אילו שיוב מן הגג לכלי [שם קיז:]. **שכר שבת.** גזרה משום מקח וממכר ושכירות [כתובות סד.]. **מקטורן.** מכולו ומקפח בו על כל בגדים שהוא לובש [רשב"ם ב"ב נז:]. **אונקלי.** מלבוש של שער [מנחות קח:]. **ספרקין.** שיפיש"ש פלוגי [מו"ק כד.]. **מעפורת.** סודר ומתעטף במצר דלמיק [במלכים גבי מיכה (מלכים א, כ) מתרגמינן ולמעפרתא] [חולין קכב.]

עין משפט נר מצוה

נה א מיי' פכ"ג מהל' שבת הל' כל כב סמג לאוין סה טור שו"ע או"ח סימן שלג סעיף ו וסימן שא סעיף מג:

נו ב מיי' שם הלכה כ טוש"ע שם סעיף יז:

נז ג מיי' שם טור שו"ע שם סעיף ז:

נח ד ה מיי' שם הלכה כה טור שו"ע שם סעיף ח:

נט ו ז מיי' שם הלכה כב טור שו"ע שם סעיף ו:

ס ח ט מיי' שם הלכה כד טור שו"ע שם סעיף ט:

סא י כ מיי' פרק יב מה הלכה ד ה סמג שם טוש"ע שם סעיף כב:

סב ל מיי' שם הלכה ו טור שו"ע שם סעיף כג כד:

מסורת הש"ס

א) ס"א מעם, ב) עירובין לה:, ג) לעיל קיז:, ד) [לעיל יז:], ה) לעיל קיז: עירובין לט:, ו) [פי' בגד רקיק שלובש אדם על בשרו ערוך], ז) [פי' מפוה], ח) [תוספתא פי"ד], ט) ס"י, י) [נ"ל ומטפטף ערי רש"א], כ) [שייך לעיל במשנה].

דבטעותא דרש רב חסדא שלא יביא כלי מחזיק יותר מג' סעודות. שמעינן מינה כי אפילו אם יביא כלי שמחזיק כל מה שהוא חפץ ויקפל ויניח בו ויטלנו כולו בבת אחת שפיר דמי. א"ל רב נחמן בר יצחק מאי טעותא. פירוש מנ"ל דטעותא היא דלמא הכי קאמר רב שיזבי. אהדר ליה רבא לא ס"ד מדקתני לענין מי שנשברה לו חבית בראש גגו מביא כלי ומניח תחתיה ובלבד שלא יביא כלי אחר ויקלוט כלי אחר ויצרף. לא יביא. הא בכלי אחד כמה דבעי מציל ורב חסדא דבעי טפי הא [טעות] בידו. וכיון שדרך בני אדם להזמין אורחים בשבת אומרים לאחרים בואו והצילו לכם. אבל להציל הוא ואח"כ להזמין אסור: **ואם** היו פקחין עושין עמו חשבון לאחר השבת. אוקימנא בירא שמים ולא ניחא ליה דליתהנו מאחריני ובחנם [נמי לא ניחא ליה למטרח]. והכי פירושא דמתני' אם היו פקחין שידעין דכי האי גוונא לאו שכר שבת הוא הואיל ומהפקירא קא זכו ואיתנן האי דמהדרו ליה לבעה"ב כגון מתנה מדידהו הוא ועושין חשבון כשיעור שכרן ושקלי ליה. ושארא שבקי ליה לבעה"ב. סוגיא דשמעתא שהחשבון אחר השבת כל מה שמציל לנפשיה משום שכבר מקבלין ליה כי להתעטף. ואפי' יותר מי"ח כלים. וכן הלכתא. וקי"ל שמותר להערים: **ירושלמי** תני ר' יוסי בר אבין אמר מערימין. ועל זו אף לשאינה מעורבת. ולובש כל מה שהוא יכול ללבוש ועוטף כל מה שהוא יכול להתעטף. ואפי' יותר מי"ח כלים. וכן הלכתא. וקי"ל שמותר להערים: **ירושלמי** תני ר' יוסי בר אבין אמר מערימין. ועל זו

עין משפט נר מצוה

סג א ב מיי' פ"ה מהל' שבת הלכה ו סמג לאוין סה טוש"ע או"ח סימן רעז סעיף ג:
סד ג מיי' שם פ"ה הל' יח טוש"ע שם ס"א:
סה ד מיי' שם טוש"ע שם סעיף ג:
סו ה ו מיי' פ"ו מהל' יסודי התורה הלכה ו סמג עשין ג:
סז ז מיי' פ"ב מהלכות מקוואות הלכה ב סמג לאוין קיא טוש"ע יו"ד סימן קצח סעיף טו:
סח ח מיי' פ"ו מהל' יסודי התורה הל"ו:

גמרא

הוא דאמר כר' שמעון בן ננס איתמר דאמר רבי שמעון בן ננס מפני שהוא מחרך גרם כיבוי מי אמר אין מדקתני סיפא רבי יוסי אוסר בכלי חרס חדשים מלאים מים שאינן יכולים לקבל את האור והן מתבקעין ומכבין את הדליקה מכלל דתנא קמא שרי ת"ר א) נר שעל גבי טבלא מנער את הטבלא והיא נופלת ואם כבתה כבתה אמרי דבי רבי ינאי ב) לא שנו אלא בשוכח אבל במניח נעשה בסים לדבר האסור תנא נר שאחורי הדלת פותח ונועל כדרכו ואם כבתה כבתה ג) לייט עלה רב אמר ליה רבינא לרב אחא בריה דרבא ואמרי לה רב אחא בריה דרבא לרב אשי מאי טעמא לייט עלה רב ג) אילימא משום דרב סבר לה כרבי יהודה ותנא קתני לה כר' שמעון משום דרב סבר לה כר' יהודה כל דתני כר' שמעון מילט לייט ליה אמר ליה בהא אפילו ר' שמעון מודה ג) דהא אביי ורבא דאמרי תרוייהו מודה רבי שמעון בפסיק רישיה ולא ימות אמר רב יהודה פותח אדם דלת כנגד (א) מדורה בשבת ד) לייט עלה אביי במאי עסקינן אילימא ברוח מצויה מאי טעמיה דמאן דאסר אי ברוח שאינה מצויה מאי טעמא דמאן דשרי לעולם ברוח מצויה מר סבר גזרינן ומר סבר לא גזרינן: עושין מחיצה כו': למימרא דרבנן סברי גרם כבוי מותר ור' יוסי סבר גרם כבוי אסור והא איפכא שמעינן להו דתניא עושין מחיצה בכלים ריקנין ובמלאין שאין דרכן להשתבר ואלו מלאין שאין דרכן להשתבר כלי מתכות רבי יוסי אומר אף כלי כפר שיחין וכלי כפר חנניה אין דרכן להשתבר וכי תימא איפוך מתני' ורבי יוסי דברייתא לדבריהם קאמר ומי מצית אפכת לה והאמר רבה בר תחליפא משמיה דרב מאן תנא גרם כבוי אסור ר' יוסי אלא לעולם לא תיפוך וברייתא כולה ר' יוסי היא וחסורי מחסרא והכי קתני עושין מחיצה בכלים ריקנין ובמלאים שאין דרכן להשתבר ואלו הן כלים שאין דרכן להשתבר כלי מתכות וכלי כפר חנניה נמי אין דרכן להשתבר שר' יוסי אומר אף כלי כפר שיחין וכלי כפר חנניה נמי אין דרכן להשתבר ורמי דרבנן אדרבנן ורמי דרבי יוסי אדרבי יוסי ה) דתניא ה) הרי שהיה שם כתוב לו על בשרו ° הרי זה לא ירחוץ ולא יסוך ולא יעמוד במקום הטינופת ו) נזדמנה לו טבילה של מצוה כורך עליה גמי ויורד וטובל רבי יוסי אומר לעולם יורד וטובל כדרכו ובלבד שלא ישפשף שאני התם דאמר קרא א) ואבדתם את שמם מן המקום ההוא לא תעשון כן לה' אלהיכם עשייה הוא דאסור גרמא שרי אי הכי הכא נמי כתיב ב) לא תעשה [כל] מלאכה עשייה הוא דאסור גרמא שרי ו) מתוך שאדם בהול על ממונו אי שרית ליה אתי לכבויי אי הכי קשיא דרבנן אדרבנן ומה התם דאדם בהול על ממונו שרי הכא לא כל שכן ותסברא האי גמי היכי דמי אי דמיהדק קא הוי חציצה אי לא מיהדק עיילי ביה מיא חציצה תיפוק ליה משום דיו בלחה ו) דתניא ז) הדם והדיו הדבש והחלב יבשין חוצצין לחים אין חוצצין מכל מקום קשיא אלא אמר רבא בר רב שילא ח) היינו טעמייהו דרבנן דקסברי אסור לעמוד בפני השם ערום מכלל דר"י סבר מותר לעמוד בפני השם ערום דמנח ידיה עילויה לרבנן נמי ° דמנח ידיה עילויה זימנין דמשתלי ושקיל ליה לר' יוסי נמי זימנין דמשתלי ושקיל ליה אלא אי דאיכא גמי ה"נ הב"ע לאהדורי אגמי רבנן סברי

טבילה

רש"י

גמ' הוא דאמר כר"ש. דשרי לעכובי דליקה בעור גדי: גרם כיבוי. כי האי גוונא כשמגיע למים הוא כבה: מי אמר. דילמא הא דקתני במתני' ועושין מחיצה בכל הכלים לאו בחדשים המתבקעים קאמר: נר. דולק קרוסיי"ל: אלא בשכח. דשכחו מבעוד יום על הטבלא שלא מדעת: אבל מניח נעשית. טבלא בסים לדבר האסור ואסור לטלטלה כדי לנערה: לייט עליה. על כל המורין כן: כר' יהודה. דאמר דבר שאין מתכוין אסור: בפסיק רישיה. והכא נמי הרוח מכבהו: כנגד המדורה. ואע"פ שרוח מנשבת ומבעיר האור: מאי טעמא דמאן דאסר. אין דרך להבעיר ברוח מצויה ולא פסיק רישיה ולא ימות הוא: אף כלי כפר שיחין. חרס העשוי מאותו עפר חזק הוא ואין משתבר אלמא לר' יוסי בגרם כבוי טפי מיקל מדרבנן: וכי תימא איפוך מתני'. ותני ברישא דברי ר' יוסי וחכמים אוסרין בכלי חרס חדשים כו': ור' יוסי דברייתא. דמשמע דבהנהו דפקעי מודה דהא כפר שיחין וכפר חנניה הוא דקשרי: לדבריהם קאמר להו. לדידי כל הכלים שרו דגרם כבוי מותר אלא לדידכו נהי דאסריתו גרם כבוי אודו לי מיהת דבהני אפילו גרם ליכא: כורך עליו גמי. קס"ד השתא כדי שלא ימחק את השם במים אלמא לרבנן גרם מחק אסור ולר' יוסי שרי: ובלבד שלא ישפשף. דהוי מוחק בידים: ותסברא. דהכא נמי דאצרכוה רבנן משום שלא ימחק הוא: האי גמי היכי דמי. להגין עליו: אי דמיהדק. שלא יכנסו בו מים וימחק הוי חציצה: ואי דלא מיהדק. לבשרו: עיילי ביה מיא. ואינו מגין מלמחוק: תיפוק ליה דמשום דיו. בלא גמי נמי חייץ דיו ומשני בלחה: מכל מקום קשיא. גמי לרבנן למה להו: מכלל דלר' יוסי כו'. בתמיה והא כתיב לא יראה בך ערות דבר (דברים כג): אלא אי איכא גמי הכי נמי. דמודה ר' יוסי דצריך לכרוך עליו גמי ולא סגי ליה לאנוחי ידיו עליו דילמא מישתלי ושקיל ידיה:

טבילה

תוספות

גרם כיבוי מי אמר. וא"ת הא קתני מתני' בין מלאים בין ריקנים ומאי רבותא איכא טפי במלאים מבריקנים אי לאו דמיירי בדרכן להשתבר וי"ל דס"ד דמיירי בכלים שאין דרכן להשתבר וקמ"ל דלא גזרינן אטו כלים שדרכן להשתבר:

מנער את הטבלא והיא נופלת ואם כבתה כבתה. אומר ר"י דמיירי דליכא שמן בנר דאי איכא שמן בנר חייב שהרי שופך ממנו והוי כמסתפק ממנו דחייב משום מכבה כדאמר בפ"ב דביצה (דף כב:) ובירושלמי מוקי לה בנר שכבה ולא קתני בהך ברייתא ואם כבתה כבתה ואתא לאשמעינן היתר טלטול ע"י ניעור לר' יהודה דאסר טלטול בנר שכבה אי נמי אפילו לר"ש ובנר גדול כגון קערה ועששית דמודה ר"ש כדאמר בפרק [כירה] (דף מד.) או כשיש אפר וגחלת אלא שכבה השלהבת: פותח ונועל כדרכו. אע"פ שע"י כן מתנדנד הנר ומתרחק השמן מן השלהבת או מתקרב והוי מכבה או מבעיר אבל אין לפרש משום כיבוי דרוח דאחורי הדלת ליכא רוח ועוד דא"כ הוה ליה למימר פותח אדם דלת כנגד הנר כדקאמר בסמוך כנגד המדורה ועוד דתינח פותח נועל מאי איסורא איכא אלא כדפרישית ואי לאו משום כיבוי והבערה משום טלטול אין לאסור דבנעילת דלת לא חשיב טלטול וגם לא הוי בסיס לדבר האסור דבית חשוב הוא ובטל אגב בית אי נמי בשכח דלא הוי בסיס: מר סבר גזרינן. הלכך צריך ליזהר שלא לפתוח הדלת לפני המדורה אפילו ברוח מצויה דהא לייט עלה אביי דהוי בתרא והני מילי כשהמדורה קצת קרובה אצל הדלת: והא איפכא שמעינן להו. לאו דווקא איפכא דר' יוסי דברייתא הוי כמו מתני' דאסר דרכו להשתבר אלא היינו איפכא דבמתניתין מחמיר ר' יוסי טפי מדרבנן ובברייתא מיקל טפי: וכי תימא איפוך מתני' כו'. וא"ת מ"מ תקשה דבמתני' לא אסרי רבנן אלא חרס חדש ובברייתא אסרי אפי' ישן מדנקט כלי מתכות וי"ל דנקט בברייתא כלי מתכות משום דאין חילוק בהם בין חדשים לישנים וה"ה כלי חרס ישן: והאמר רבה כו'. ואם תאמר ואמאי לא מפיך ברייתא דטפי אית לן לאפוכה ממתני' והוי אתי נמי שפיר הא דרבה בר תחליפא ונימא דרבנן לדברי ר' יוסי קאמרי ואינהו שרי אף בכלי חרס חדש וי"ל דהתלמוד לא קאמר אלא דאפילו מפיך מתני' לא אתי שפיר אלא על כרחיך ברייתא אית לן לתרוצי וכיון דאתינא להכי לא צריך להפוכה אלא למימר חסורי מיחסרא: אי הכי קשה דרבנן אדרבנן. בלאו הכי הוה קשיא דרבנן אדרבנן אלא משום דהשתא פריך מכ"ש קאמר אי הכי ה):

ליקוטי רש"י

דתנא קמא שרי. דהתם כי מטי דליקה לכלים דליקה הוא דפקע להו וגרמא בעלמא הוא [לעיל מז:]. בסים. מושב את כנו מתרגמינן בסיסיה [שם.]. לייט עלה. כל מאן דלית ליה [קידושין לג:]. כל שיסמוך על זה [שם עא:]. כר' שמעון. דאמר דבר שאין מתכוין מותר [בכורות כה.]. מודה ר' שמעון בפסיק רישיה ולא ימות. כלומר אפשר שלא יעשה זו הא המותר ולא רוצה שתמות בדיון ודאי אפשר שלא תמות כמתכוין חשיב ליה. וכי אמרינן דבר שאין מתכוין מותר כגון היכא דאפשר לאפשר איסור כגון גורר אדם מטה כסא וספסל ובלבד שלא יתכוין לעשות חריץ ואף על גב דאיכא למיחש דלמא עביד חריץ כיון דלא מתכוין להכי ואפשר לגרירה בלא חריץ כי עביד נמי חריץ דהוי מלאכה גמורה היכא דלא מיכוין אבל היכא דודאי עביד מודי [סוכה לג.]. לא ירחוץ. שלא יימחקו ואזהרה למוחק את השם ואבדתם את השם (דברים יב) וסמיך ליה לא תעשון כן וגו'. טבילה של מצוה. טבילת טהרה שטבילה הכתוב עליו. כורך עליה גמי. להגין עליו [מפני] חוזק שטף המים [יומא ח.]. לא תעשון כן. אזהרה למוחק את השם [דברים יב, ד]. מתוך שאדם בהול על ממונו. אי שריא ליה לאטרוחי בהצלה כולי האי מתוך שהוא בהול מינשי ליה שבת ואתי לכבויי [לעיל קיז:]. אי שרי לאישתמוטי בהצלה כולי האי אתי לכבויי [לעיל ע"א].

רבינו חננאל

אמרינן בגמרא דפורפת על האבן ועל האגוז כו' תיבעי למאן דאמר מערימין תיבעי למ"ד אין מערימין. ואמר לאחרים בואו והצילו עמי שכן דרך בני אדם להשאיל כליו בשבת. פי' י"ח כלים דקא"ר יוסי [מקטורין] כמו מעיל. ובלשון ישמעאל כרכום שיש לו בית ראש ועוטה לו הלובשו ויש לו לולאות וקרסים (שהוא הווה) [שמחברין והוא] כמו מלבוש. אונקלי. בגד דקיקי שנקרא מערקה שלובש אדם על בשרו ההולם כל גופו וכן שנינו (מגילה כ"ד) בענין תפלין של יד ציפהו זהב ונתנו על בית יד של אונקלי שלו הרי זה דרך החיצונים: פונדא. גם היא מגעת עד למטה מטבורו של אדם וקורין לו בלשון פרסי פַשְׁת. ונקשר כחשב אפודה והיא אפוד האמורה בתורה ויש בה כסים כסים כנגד הלב ותחת הידים: קנבוס של פשתן. חלוק התחתון שלובשין אותו ונקרא גלאלה. חלוק הוא המלובש העליון וקורין לו ורבנין: שני. ספרקים א) ויש שגורס סובריקין והם בלשון יון המכנסים ושמענו שאמר הגאון נט' דח' דם תפנקי שמלבישין בהן הידים עד האציל ויש בהן בתי אצבעות. שני מנעלים כמשמען: שני פרגוד. בלשון ישמעאל גודאבי: אנפליאות. גם הם מנעלים לשוקים עליון האניך שעל השוקים מן העור. ומעפורת וחגור שבמתנים וכובע הרי י"ח כלים: ר' שמעון בן ננס אומר פורשין עור של גדי כו'. אמר רב יהודה טלית שאחז בה האור מצד אחד נותן עליה מים מצד אחר ואם כבתה כבתה. והא ודאי גרם כיבוי הוא. ואקשינן עליה ממתנית' דקתני פושטה ומתכסה בה אבל מים שהן גרם כיבוי לא קתני ואתנינן לאוקמיה לרב יהודה כר' שמעון בן ננס ולא קם. דר' שמעון בן ננס לא קאמר אלא מפני שהוא מחרך הא גרמא בידים לא קאמר אלא קם רב יהודה כרבנן. דתנן עושין מחיצה בכל הכלים בין מלאים בין ריקנין דשרו גרם כיבוי ור' יוסי אוסר גרם כיבוי והלכה כרבנן וכרב יהודה: נר שעל גבי טבלא איתא דאוקמה דבי ר' ינאי בשכח נר שעל גבי טבלא. אבל המניח נר על טבלא נעשה טבלא בסיס לנר שהיא מוקצה מחמת איסור ואסור לטלטוליה. ודתנא תנא קמיה דרב ולייט עלה רב. היכא דידע שבודאי כשפותח ונועל יכבה הנר מפני שהדלת נוגעת בו ומכבתו שאסור דבהא אפי' ר"ש מודה דהוי פסיק רישיה ולא ימות. אבל אי גרם בעלמא שרי: אמר רב יהודה אמר שמואל פותח אדם דלת כנגד המדורה בשבת ואינו חושש. ואע"פ שהרוח מלבה את האש. לייט עלה אביי דחשיב ליה כמבעיר את האש ואי רוח שאינה מצויה היא והוא שמניף ומושבה לא פליגי דאסיר. כי פליגי ברוח מצויה. (רב) [אביי] סבר גזרינן ברוח מצויה אטו רוח שאינה מצויה. ומר סבר לא גזרינן והלכתא כאביי וקאמרינן בגמרא דהכונס צאן לדיר בנזיקין המלבה ואין בליבויו כדי ללבותה פטור. ואקשינן אמאי פטור. ליהוי כי זורה ורוח מסייעתו. ואמרינן בה כמה טעמי. סימן ברו"ש. אמר אביי כגון שליבה מצד זה וליבתה הרוח מצד אחר רבא אמר כגון שליבה ברוח מצויה וליבתו הרוח שאינה מצויה. רב זירא אמר דצמדא צמידי. רב אשי אמר היכא אמרינן זורה ורוח מסייעתו לענין שבת דמלאכת מחשבת אסרה תורה. אבל הכא גרמא בעלמא היא וגרמא בנזקין פטור. ש"מ דכיון דמשרי אורחא אפי' לרוח מצויה ללבות ומחשב לכן אסור בשבת דהיינו מלאכת מחשבת: סוגיא דשמעתא דר' יוסי מתיר בכלים מלאין מים כגון כלי מתכות וכלי כפר חנניה וכפר שיחין שחרש שלהן חזק ואינן מתבקעין באור. ואע"פ שאין גרם כיבוי אסור כגון הני שקי. ור' יוסי דשרי

מסורת הש"ס

א) לקמן קכה: ודף קמב:, ב) [חולין טו:], ג) לעיל עה. קג. קיא: קמג. [קמא.] ביצה לו. סוכה לג: כתובות ו. בכורות כה., ד) [קידושין לג. וש"נ], ה) יומא ח. כה. [מס' סופרים פ"ה הל"ג], ו) לעיל קיז:, ז) פסחים סה: מנחות כא. זבחים לה., ח) [ועי' תוס' עירובין כג. ובכלה ד: ובכתובות ג: וב"מ נג. שבועות מה: ד"ה אי הכי].

הגהות הב"ח

(א) גמ' כנגד המדורה:

גליון הש"ס

גמ' הרי זה לא ירחוץ. עי' נדה דף סו ע"ב תוס' ד"ה אם סמוך: שם דמנח ידיה עלויה. עי' בתרומת הדשן סימן י':

תורה אור השלם

א) וְנִתַּצְתֶּם אֶת מִזְבְּחֹתָם וְשִׁבַּרְתֶּם אֶת מַצֵּבֹתָם וַאֲשֵׁרֵיהֶם תִּשְׂרְפוּן בָּאֵשׁ וּפְסִילֵי אֱלֹהֵיהֶם תְּגַדֵּעוּן וְאִבַּדְתֶּם אֶת שְׁמָם מִן הַמָּקוֹם הַהוּא: לֹא תַעֲשׂוּן כֵּן לַייָ אֱלֹהֵיכֶם: [דברים יב, ג-ד]

ב) וְיוֹם הַשְּׁבִיעִי שַׁבָּת לַייָ אֱלֹהֶיךָ לֹא תַעֲשֶׂה כָל מְלָאכָה אַתָּה וּבִנְךָ וּבִתֶּךָ עַבְדְּךָ וַאֲמָתְךָ וּבְהֶמְתֶּךָ וְגֵרְךָ אֲשֶׁר בִּשְׁעָרֶיךָ: [שמות כ, י]

רב נסים גאון

מאי טעמא לייט עלה רב אי נימא דרב סבר לה כר' יהודה תמצא בירורו בפ' במה מדליקין (לעיל דף כב) רב אמר אין הלכה כר' שמעון בגרירה מכלל דכר' יהודה סבירא ליה דפליג על ר' שמעון ואסר דבר שאינו מתכוין ובסוף פ' שמונה שרצים (לעיל דף קיא) ובפרק הבתולה נשאת (כתובות דף ו) הלכה אמרו אמר רב הלכה כר' יהודה ורב חייא בר אבין אמר שמואל הלכה כר' שמעון ולא כגבורי רב אמר הלכה כר' יהודה ושמואל אמר הלכה כר' שמעון ותניא כוותיה בבכורות בפרק כל פסולי המוקדשין (דף לד) הרי מיכן למדנו שרב סבר דבר שאין מתכוין אסור כר' יהודה ההיא

חשק שלמה על רבינו חננאל

א) עיין ערוך ערך ספרק:

The Gemara answers:

הוּא דְּאָמַר כְּרַבִּי שִׁמְעוֹן בֶּן נַנָּס – **[Rav Yehudah] stated** his ruling **in accordance with R' Shimon ben Nannas** of our Mishnah, who permits covering an object with a kid's hide to prevent the fire from spreading over it.[1]

The Gemara protests that the cases are not analogous:

אֵימַר דְּאָמַר רַבִּי שִׁמְעוֹן בֶּן נַנָּס – But one could **say that R' Shimon ben Nannas** only **says** that one may cover the object with a kid's hide מִפְּנֵי שֶׁהוּא מְחָרֵךְ – **because it singes** and prevents the fire from spreading further. גְּרַם כִּיבּוּי מִי אָמַר – **Did he** ever **say** that it is permitted to actually **cause** the **extinguishment** of the fire, as Rav Yehudah says in the name of Rav?[2]

The Gemara answers:

אִין מִדְּקָתָנֵי סֵיפָא – **Yes,** R' Shimon ben Nannas does indeed permit causing extinguishment, **for the end of the Mishnah teaches:** רַבִּי יוֹסֵי אוֹסֵר בִּכְלֵי חֶרֶס חֲדָשִׁים מְלֵאִים מַיִם – **R' YOSE PROHIBITS** making a partition with **NEW EARTHENWARE VESSELS FILLED WITH WATER,** שֶׁאֵינָן יְכוֹלִים לְקַבֵּל אֶת הָאוּר וְהֵן מִתְבַּקְּעִין וּמְכַבִּין אֶת הַדְּלֵיקָה – because **THEY CANNOT WITHSTAND THE FIRE AND THEY BURST** open **AND** thereby **EXTINGUISH THE FIRE.** מִכְּלָל דְּתַנָּא קַמָּא שָׁרֵי – **We may infer** from this **that the Tanna Kamma** (R' Shimon ben Nannas), who disputes R' Yose, **permits** even the use of new earthenware filled with water, though they may burst and extinguish the fire.[3]

The Gemara cites a Baraisa:

תָּנוּ רַבָּנָן – **The Rabbis taught in a Baraisa:** נֵר שֶׁעַל גַּבֵּי טַבְלָא – **IF A** lit **LAMP IS ON TOP OF A BOARD** that one wishes to move, מְנַעֵר אֶת הַטַּבְלָא וְהִיא נוֹפֶלֶת – **ONE MAY SHAKE THE BOARD AND** let **[THE LAMP] FALL DOWN,** וְאִם כָּבְתָה כָּבְתָה – **AND IF [THE LAMP] IS** thereby **EXTINGUISHED, IT IS EXTINGUISHED.**[4]

The Gemara qualifies this law:

אָמְרֵי דְּבֵי רַבִּי יַנַּאי – **Those of the academy of R' Yannai said:** לֹא שָׁנוּ אֶלָּא בְּשׁוֹכֵחַ – **[The Rabbis] taught** that one may shake off the lamp and carry the board **only** in a case **where one forgets** and unintentionally leaves the lamp on the board before the Sabbath; אֲבָל בְּמַנִּיחַ נַעֲשָׂה בָּסִיס לְדָבָר הָאָסוּר – **but where one** intentionally **leaves** the lamp on top of the board to be there for the Sabbath, **[the board] has become a base to a forbidden object** (i.e. to *muktzeh*) and thus forbidden itself. Consequently, one would not be allowed to move or shake the board.

The Gemara cites another Baraisa:

תַּנְיָא – **It was taught in a Baraisa:** נֵר שֶׁאֲחוֹרֵי הַדֶּלֶת – **IF A LAMP** stands **BEHIND A DOOR,**[5] פּוֹתֵחַ וְנוֹעֵל כְּדַרְכּוֹ – **ONE MAY OPEN AND SHUT** the door **IN THE ORDINARY WAY,** וְאִם כָּבְתָה כָּבְתָה – **AND IF [THE FLAME] IS** thereby **EXTINGUISHED, IT IS EXTINGUISHED.**[6]

The Gemara records a negative reaction to this ruling:

לָיֵיט עֲלָהּ רַב – **Rav condemned this** ruling.[7]

The Gemara explores the reason for Rav's reaction:

אָמַר לֵיהּ רָבִינָא לְרַב אַחָא בְּרֵיהּ דְּרָבָא – **Ravina said to Rav Acha the son of Rava,** וְאָמְרֵי לָהּ רַב אַחָא בְּרֵיהּ דְּרָבָא לְרַב אַשִׁי – **and some say,** it was **Rav Acha the son of Rava** who **said** this **to Rav Ashi:** מַאי טַעְמָא לָיֵיט עֲלָהּ רַב – **Why did Rav condemn this** ruling? אִילֵימָא מִשּׁוּם דְּרַב סָבַר לָהּ כְּרַבִּי יְהוּדָה – **If you will say** it is **because Rav holds** in accord **with R' Yehudah,** who says that an "unintentional act" is prohibited,[8] וְתַנָּא קָתָנֵי לָהּ כְּרַבִּי שִׁמְעוֹן – **whereas the Tanna taught this Baraisa in accordance with R' Shimon** who maintains that an "unintentional act" is permitted – how can this be? מִשּׁוּם דְּרַב סָבַר לָהּ כְּרַבִּי יְהוּדָה – Just **because Rav sides with R' Yehudah,** כָּל דְּתָנֵי כְּר׳ שִׁמְעוֹן מֵילַט לָיֵיט לֵיהּ – is that a reason for **him** to **condemn anyone who teaches** a Baraisa **in accordance with R' Shimon?!**

The Gemara responds:

אָמַר לֵיהּ – **He said to him:** בְּהָא אֲפִילּוּ רַבִּי שִׁמְעוֹן מוֹדֶה – **In this** instance, **even R' Shimon concedes** that one may not open and shut the door דְּהָא אַבַּיֵי וְרָבָא דְּאָמְרֵי תַּרְוַיְיהוּ – **because Abaye and Rava both said:** מוֹדֶה רַבִּי שִׁמְעוֹן בִּפְסִיק רֵישֵׁיהּ וְלֹא יָמוּת – **R' Shimon concedes** that one is liable **in the case of an inevitable consequence.**[9] Thus, the Baraisa is at odds with both R' Yehudah's and R' Shimon's opinions, and Rav therefore condemned anyone who follows its ruling.[10]

NOTES

1. *Rashi.* Thus, he permits גְּרַם כִּיבּוּי, *causing extinguishment,* as well; see below.

2. For the water will actually extinguish the fire once the fire reaches it (*Rashi*).

Although R' Shimon ben Nannas also says that one may form a partition with all kinds of vessels – even those that are filled with water – he may be referring specifically to old vessels, which do not burst (*Rashi;* see *Tosafos* who explain why, if so, the Mishnah should find it necessary to permit the use of water-filled vessels).

3. [Accordingly, when R' Shimon ben Nannas said that one may spread a hide over the box "because it singes," he did not mean to say that it is permitted because it merely singes and *prevents* the spread of the fire, for in truth he permits even causing the fire to be extinguished. Rather,] R' Shimon ben Nannas gives this reason to explain the benefit of spreading a hide over the unburned part – because the hide itself does not burn and thus prevents the covered area from burning (*Rambam, Commentary to Mishnah*).

4. [Since the lamp is *muktzeh* and may not be carried, someone who wishes to carry the board must first endeavor to remove the lamp from it. He cannot simply remove it by hand, since it is *muktzeh.* Therefore, he must remove it indirectly, by shaking the board and allowing it to fall off. (Indirect movement of *muktzeh* is permitted in such a case; see Mishnah below, 142b.) Although this may result in extinguishing the fire of the lamp, since it is not his intention to extinguish it, nor is it inevitable (פְּסִיק רֵישֵׁיהּ) that he will do so, it is permitted.]

Tosafos ask how one is allowed to shake off the lamp when some of its oil is sure to be spilled as a result, and removing oil from a burning lamp is in itself a *melachah* of extinguishing (see *Beitzah* 22a). *Tosafos* therefore explain that the Baraisa is speaking of a lamp that has no more oil in it. Alternatively, we are dealing with a wax candle (*Rashba;* see also *Meiri*).

5. *Rashi,* as explained by *Rashba* and *Ritva MHK* ed. [See *Tosafos,* who understand the case to be where the lamp hangs on the back of the door.]

6. I.e. we are not concerned that the wind that comes in when the door is opened will extinguish the flame (*Rashi* ד״ה בפסיק רישיה). [Although the Baraisa speaks of opening *and closing* the door, the possible concern would only be for opening it; closing is mentioned incidentally. The Baraisa means to say that one may use the door without concern, opening and closing it as usual (*Rashba, Ritva* in explanation of *Rashi;* see *Rivash* §394, who explains *Rashi's* concern to be that the wind created by the movement of the door might extinguish the flame; cf. *Tosafos*).

7. I.e. anyone who ruled in accordance with this Baraisa (*Rashi*).

8. [R' Yehudah forbids performing a permitted act if, as an unintended consequence, a forbidden act may result from it (דָּבָר שֶׁאֵינוֹ מִתְכַּוֵּן אָסוּר). Thus, in our case, R' Yehudah would forbid opening the door because it might result in the extinguishment of the lamp's flame.] Rav indeed holds like R' Yehudah in this matter (see above, 22a and 111b, and *Kesubos* 6a).

9. [Literally: cut off its head and it will not die?] Since in the Baraisa's case, the wind will [certainly] extinguish the flame when the door is opened, even R' Shimon agrees that one may not open it (*Rashi*).

10. This raises the question of what the Tanna of the Baraisa held. *Maharsha* suggests that the flame's extinguishment is not actually inevitable, but is close to being so. Rav therefore prohibits this practice, but the Tanna of the Baraisa permits it. *Ritva* (*MHK* ed.) offers a similar explanation but suggests another one as well. Extinguishing the flame in this case does not violate a Biblical prohibition according to R' Shimon because it is a מְלָאכָה שֶׁאֵינָהּ צְרִיכָה לְגוּפָהּ, *a labor not needed for its defined*

עין משפט נר מצוה

סג א ב מיי' פי"ג מהל' שבת הלכה ו סמג לאוין סה טוש"ע או"ח סימן רעז סעיף ג:

סד ג מיי' שם פי"ב הל' ח טוש"ע שם ס"א:

סה ד מיי' שם טוש"ע שם סעיף ג:

סו ה ו מיי' פ"ו מהל' יסודי התורה הל' ו סמג עשין ג:

סז ז מיי' פ"ב מהלכות מקוואות הלכה ב סמג לאוין קיא טוש"ע יו"ד סימן קלח סעיף טו:

סח ח מיי' פ"ו מהל' יסודי התורה הל"ט:

מסורת הש"ס

א) לקמן קכה:, ב) [חולין עה.], ג) לעיל עה. קכ. קיז: קל. קמג. [קמג.] ביצה לו. סוכה לג. כתובות ו. בכורות כה., ד) [קידושין לג. ושם], ה) יומא ח. כח. [מס' סופרים פ"ה הל"ג], ו) לעיל קח: ז) פסחים סה: מנחות כא. זבחים לה., ח) [ועי' תוס' עירובין כג: ובכ"ב כג: וכתובות ג: וכ"מ כג. שבועות מה: ד"ה אי הכי].

הוא דאמר כר' שמעון בן ננס אימר דאמר רבי שמעון בן ננס מפני שהוא מחרך גרם כיבוי מי אמר אין מדקתני סיפא רבי יוסי אוסר בכלי חרס חדשים מלאים מים שאינן יכולים לקבל את האור והן מתבקעין ומכבין את הדליקה מכלל דתנא קמא שרי ת"ר [א] נר שעל גבי טבלא מנער את הטבלא והיא נופלת ואם כבתה כבתה אמרי דבי רבי ינאי [ב] לא (א) שנו אלא בשוכחה אבל במניח נעשה בסיס לדבר האסור תנא נר שאחורי הדלת פותח ונועל כדרכו ואם כבתה כבתה [ג] לייט עלה רב אמר ליה רבינא לרב אחא בריה דרבא ואמרי לה רב אחא בריה דרבא לרב אשי מאי טעמא לייט עלה רב [ד] אילימא משום דרב סבר לה כרבי יהודה ותנא קתני לה כר' שמעון משום דרב סבר לה כר' יהודה כל דתני כר' שמעון מילט לייט ליה אמר ליה בהא אפילו ר' שמעון מודה [ה] דהא אביי ורבא דאמרי תרוייהו מודה רבי שמעון בפסיק רישיה ולא ימות אמר רב יהודה פותח אדם דלת כנגד (א) מדורה בשבת [ו] לייט עלה אביי במאי עסקינן אילימא ברוח מצויה מאי טעמיה דמאן דאסר אי ברוח שאינה מצויה מאי טעמא דמאן דשרי לעולם ברוח מצויה מר סבר גזרינן ומר סבר לא גזרינן: עושין מחיצה כו': למימרא דרבנן סברי גרם כבוי מותר ור' יוסי סבר גרם כבוי אסור והא איפכא שמעינן להו דתניא עושין מחיצה בכלים ריקנין ובמלאין שאין דרכן להשתבר ואלו מלאין שאין דרכן להשתבר כלי מתכות רבי יוסי אומר אף כלי כפר שיחין וכלי כפר חנניה אין דרכן להשתבר וכי תימא איפוך מתני' ורבי יוסי דברייתא לדבריהם קאמר ומי מצית אפכת לה והאמר רבה בר תחליפא משמיה דרב מאן תנא גרם כבוי אסור ר' יוסי אלא לעולם לא תיפוך וברייתא כולה ר' יוסי היא וחסורי מחסרא והכי קתני עושין מחיצה בכלים ריקנין ובמלאים שאין דרכן להשתבר ואלו הן כלים שאין דרכן להשתבר כלי מתכות וכלי כפר חנניה נמי אין דרכן להשתבר שר' יוסי אומר אף כלי כפר שיחין וכלי כפר חנניה אין דרכן להשתבר ורמי דרבנן אדרבנן ורמי דרבי יוסי אדרבי יוסי [ט] דתניא [ה] הרי שהיה שם כתוב לו על בשרו • הרי זה לא ירחוץ ולא יסוך ולא יעמוד במקום הטינופת [ו] נזדמנה לו טבילה של מצוה כורך עליה גמי ויורד וטובל רבי יוסי אומר לעולם יורד וטובל כדרכו ובלבד שלא ישפשף שאני התם דאמר קרא א) ואבדתם את שמם מן המקום ההוא לא תעשון כן לה' אלהיכם עשייה הוא דאסור גרמא שרי אי הכי הכא נמי כתיב ב) לא תעשה [כל] מלאכה עשייה הוא דאסור גרמא שרי [י] מתוך שאדם בהול על ממונו אי שרית ליה אתי לכבויי אי הכי קשיא דרבנן אדרבנן ומה התם דאדם בהול על ממונו שרי הכא לא כל שכן ותסברא האי גמי היכי דמי אי דמיהדק קא הוי חציצה אי לא מיהדק עיילי ביה מיא חציצה תיפוק ליה משום דיו בלחה [י] דתניא [ז] הדם והדיו והדבש והחלב יבשין חוצצין לחים אין חוצצין מכל מקום קשיא אלא אמר רבא בר רב שילא [ח] היינו טעמייהו דרבנן דקסברי אסור לעמוד בפני השם ערום מכלל דר"י סבר מותר לעמוד בפני השם ערום דמנח ידיה עילויה לרבנן נמי • דמנח ידיה עילויה זימנין דמשתלי ושקיל ליה לר' יוסי נמי זימנין דמשתלי ושקיל ליה אלא אי דאיכא גמי ה"נ הב"ע לאהדורי אגמי רבנן סברי טבילה

רש"י

גמ' הוא דאמר כר"ש. דשרי לעכובי דליקה בעור גדי: גרם כיבוי. כי האי גוונא כשמגיע למים הוא כבה: מי אמר. דילמא הא דקתני במתני' ועושין מחיצה בכל הכלים לאו בחדשים המתבקעים קאמר: נר. דולק קרוסיי"ל: אלא בשכח. דשכחו מבעוד יום על הטבלא שלא מדעת: אבל מניח נעשית. טבלא בסיס לדבר האסור ואסור לטלטלה כדי לנערה: לייט עליה. על כל המורין כן: כר' יהודה. דאמר דבר שאין מתכוין אסור: בפסיק רישיה. והכא נמי הרוח מכבהו: כנגד המדורה. ואע"פ שרוח מנשבת ומבעיר האור: מאי טעמא דמאן דאסר. אין דרך להבעיר ברוח מצויה ולא פסיק רישיה ולא ימות הוא: אף כלי כפר שיחין. חרס העשוי מאותו עפר חזק הוא ואין משתבר אלמא לר' יוסי בגרם כבוי טפי מיקל מדרבנן: וכי תימא איפוך מתני'. ותני ברישא דברי ר' יוסי וחכמים אוסרין בכלי חרס חדשים כו': ור' יוסי דברייתא. דמשמע דבהנהו דפקעי מודה דהא כפר שיחין וכפר חנניה הוא דקשרי: לדבריהם קאמר להו. לדידי כל הכלים שרו דגרם כבוי מותר אלא לדידכו נהי דאסריתו גרם כבוי אודו לי מיהת דבהני אפילו גרם ליכא: כורך עליו גמי. קס"ד השתא כדי שלא ימחק את השם במים אלמא לרבנן גרם מחק אסור ולר' יוסי שרי: ובלבד שלא ישפשף. דהוי מוחק בידים: ותסברא. דהכא נמי דאצרכוה רבנן משום שלא ימחק הוא: האי גמי היכי דמי. להגין עליו: אי דמיהדק. שלא יכנסו בו מים וימחק הוי חצילה: ואי דלא מיהדק. לבשרו: עיילי ביה מיא. ואינו מגין מלמחוק: תיפוק ליה דמשום דיו. בלא גמי נמי חייץ דיו ומשני בלחה: מכל מקום קשיא. גמי לרבנן למה להו: מכלל דלר' יוסי כו'. בתמיה והא כתיב לא יראה בך ערות דבר (דברים כג): אלא אי איכא גמי הכי נמי. דמודה ר' יוסי דצריך לכרוך עליו גמי ולא סגי ליה לאנוחי ידיו עליו דילמא מישתלי ושקיל ליה לידיה:

תוספות

גרם כיבוי מי אמר. וא"ת הא קתני מתני' בין מלאים בין ריקנים ומאי רבותא איכא טפי במלאים מבריקנים אי לאו דמיירי בדרכן להשתבר וי"ל דס"ד דמיירי בכלים שאין דרכן להשתבר וקמ"ל דלא גזרינן אטו כלים שדרכן להשתבר:

מנער את הטבלא והיא נופלת ואם כבתה כבתה. אומר ר"י דמיירי דליכא שמן בנר דאי איכא שמן בנר חייב שהרי שופך ממנו והוי כמסתפק ממנו דחייב משום מכבה כדאמר בפ"ב דביצה (דף כב:) ובירושלמי מוקי לה בנר שכבה ולא קתני בהך ברייתא ואם כבתה כבתה ואתא לאשמעינן היתר טלטול ע"י ניעור לר' יהודה דאסר טלטול בנר שכבה אי נמי אפילו לר"ש ובנר גדול כגון קערה ועששית דמודה ר"ש כדאמר בפרק [כירה] (דף מד.) או כשיש אפר וגחלת אלא שכבה השלהבת:

פותח ונועל כדרכו. אע"פ שע"י כן מתנדנד הנר ומתרחק השמן מן השלהבת או מתקרב והוי מכבה או מבעיר אבל אין לפרש משום כיבוי דרוח דאחורי הדלת ליכא רוח ועוד דא"כ הוה ליה למימר פותח אדם דלת כנגד הנר כדקאמר בסמוך כנגד המדורה ועוד דמינה פותח נועל מאי איסורא איכא אלא כדפרישית ואי לאו משום כיבוי והבערה משום טלטול אין לאסור דבנעילת דלת לא חשיב טלטול וגם לא הוי בסיס לדבר האסור דבית חשוב הוא ובטל אגב בית אי נמי בשכח דלא הוי בסיס:

מר סבר גזרינן. הלכך צריך ליזהר שלא לפתוח הדלת לפני המדורה אפילו ברוח מצויה דהא לייט עלה אביי דהוי בתראה והנ"מ כשהמדורה קלת קרובה אצל הדלת:

והא איפכא שמעינן להו. לאו דווקא איפכא דר' יוסי דברייתא הוי כמו מתני' דאסר דרכו להשתבר אלא היינו איפכא דבמתניתין מחמיר ר' יוסי טפי מדרבנן ובברייתא מיקל טפי:

וכי תימא איפוך מתני' כו'. וא"ת מ"מ תקשה דבמתני' לא אסרי רבנן אלא חרס חדש ובברייתא אסרי אפי' ישן מדנקט כלי מתכות וי"ל דנקט בברייתא כלי מתכות משום דאין חילוק בהם בין חדשים לישנים וה"ה כלי חרס ישן:

והאמר רבה כו'. ואם תאמר ואמאי לא מפיך ברייתא דטפי אית לן לאפוכה ממתני' והוי אתי נמי שפיר הא דרבה בר תחליפא ונימא דרבנן לדברי ר' יוסי קאמרי ואינהו שרי אף בכלי חרס חדש וי"ל דהתלמוד לא קאמר אלא דאפילו מפיך מתני' לא אתי שפיר אלא על כרחך ברייתא אית לן לתרולי וכיון דאתינא להכי לא צריך להפוכה אלא למימר חסורי מיחסרא:

אי הכי קשה דרבנן אדרבנן. בלאו הכי הוה קשיא דרבנן אדרבנן אלא משום דהשתא פריך מכ"ש קאמר אי הכי [ט]:

הגהות הב"ח

(א) גמ' כנגד המדורה:

גליון הש"ס

גמ' הרי זה לא ירחוץ. עי' נדה דף סו ע"א תוס' ד"ה אם שמוך: שם דמנח ידיה עלויה. עי' בתרומת הדשן סימן [illegible]:

תורה אור השלם

א) וְנִתַּצְתֶּם אֶת מִזְבְּחֹתָם וְשִׁבַּרְתֶּם אֶת מַצֵּבֹתָם וַאֲשֵׁרֵיהֶם תִּשְׂרְפוּן בָּאֵשׁ וּפְסִילֵי אֱלֹהֵיהֶם תְּגַדֵּעוּן וְאִבַּדְתֶּם אֶת שְׁמָם מִן הַמָּקוֹם הַהוּא: לֹא תַעֲשׂוּן כֵּן לַייָ אֱלֹהֵיכֶם: [דברים יב, ג-ד]

ב) וְיוֹם הַשְּׁבִיעִי שַׁבָּת לַייָ אֱלֹהֶיךָ לֹא תַעֲשֶׂה כָל מְלָאכָה אַתָּה וּבִנְךָ וּבִתֶּךָ עַבְדְּךָ וַאֲמָתְךָ וּבְהֶמְתֶּךָ וְגֵרְךָ אֲשֶׁר בִּשְׁעָרֶיךָ: [שמות כ, י]

רב נסים גאון

מאי טעמא לייט עלה רב אי נימא דרב סבר לה כר' יהודה [illegible] במה מדליקין (לעיל דף כב) רב אמר אין הלכה כר' שמעון בגרירה מכלל דכר' יהודה סבירא ליה דפליג על ר' שמעון ואמר דבר שאינו מתכוין אסור ובסוף פ' שמונה שרצים (לעיל דף קיא) [illegible] הלכה כר' יהודה [illegible] ההיא

חשק שלמה על רבינו חננאל

א) עיין ערוך ערך ספרק.

ליקוטי רש"י

דתנא קמא שרי. [illegible] בסים. [illegible] לייט עלה. [illegible] כר' שמעון. דאמר [illegible] דבר שאין מתכוין מותר [illegible] מודה ר' שמעון בפסיק רישיה ולא ימות. [illegible] לא ירחוץ. [illegible] טבילה של מצוה. [illegible] כורך עליה גמי. [illegible] מתוך שאדם בהול על ממונו. [illegible]

רבינו חננאל

[illegible]

על בית יד של אונקלי שלו הרי זה דרך החיצונים: פונדא. גם היא מגעת עד למטה מטבורו של אדם וקורין לו בלשון פרסי פשק. ונקשר כחשב אפודה והיא אפוד האמורה בתורה ויש בה כיס כנגד הלב ותחת הידים: קנבוס של פשתן חלוק התחתון שלובשין אותו ונקרא [illegible]. חלוק הוא המלבוש העליון [illegible]: שני. ספרקים [illegible] [illegible]

The Gemara cites a related Amoraic ruling:

אָמַר רַב יְהוּדָה – **Rav Yehudah said:** פּוֹתֵחַ אָדָם דֶּלֶת כְּנֶגֶד מְדוּרָה בְּשַׁבָּת – **A person may open the door opposite a hearth fire on the Sabbath** even though wind blowing in through the door fans the fire.[11]

The Gemara records a negative reaction to this ruling as well:

לָיֵיט עֲלַהּ אַבַּיֵי – **Abaye condemned this** teaching of Rav Yehudah.

The Gemara inquires:

בְּמַאי עַסְקִינַן – **With what** case **are we dealing here?** אִילֵימָא בְּרוּחַ מְצוּיָה – **If you will say with** a case where **an ordinary wind** is blowing outdoors, מַאי טַעְמֵיהּ דְּמַאן דְּאָסַר – **what is the reasoning of the one** (Abaye) **who prohibits** opening the door? An ordinary wind blowing through a door does not commonly accelerate a fire and it is certainly not inevitable that it will do so![12] אִי בְּרוּחַ שֶׁאֵינָהּ מְצוּיָה – **And if** we are dealing **with an extraordinary wind,** מַאי טַעְמָא דְּמַאן דְּשָׁרֵי – **what is the reasoning of the one who permits** this? An unusually strong wind will certainly fan the fire! – ? –

The Gemara answers:

לְעוֹלָם בְּרוּחַ מְצוּיָה – **Actually,** we are dealing **with** the case of **an ordinary wind.** מַר סָבַר גָּזְרִינַן – **One master** (Abaye), however, holds that **we decree** a prohibition even in this case so that someone should not think it is permissible to open the door even when a strong wind blows; וּמַר סָבַר לֹא גָּזְרִינַן – **and the** other **master** (Rav Yehudah) **holds** that **we do not decree** such a prohibition.[13]

The Gemara cites the end of the Mishnah and analyzes it:

עוֹשִׂין מְחִיצָה כו׳ – AND WE MAY MAKE A PARTITION, etc. [in the path of the fire with all kinds of vessels, whether full or empty . . . R' Yose prohibits doing so with new earthenware vessels filled with water because they cannot withstand the fire and they burst and extinguish the fire].

The Gemara sets forth the basis of the dispute and presents a challenge to it from a Baraisa:

לְמֵימְרָא דְּרַבָּנָן סָבְרֵי גְּרַם כִּבּוּי מוּתָּר – Is this **to say that the Rabbis** (R' Shimon ben Nannas)[14] **hold** that **causing extinguishment is permitted,** וְרַבִּי יוֹסֵי סָבַר גְּרַם כִּבּוּי אָסוּר – **whereas R' Yose holds** that **causing extinguishment is prohibited?** וְהָא אִיפְּכָא שְׁמָעִינַן לְהוּ – **But we have heard the reverse from them!** דְּתַנְיָא – **For it was taught in a Baraisa:** עוֹשִׂין מְחִיצָה בְּכֵלִים רֵיקָנִין – ONE MAY MAKE A PARTITION in the path of the fire WITH EMPTY VESSELS, וּבִמְלֵאִין שֶׁאֵין דַּרְכָּן לְהִשְׁתַּבֵּר – AND WITH FULL ONES THAT ARE NOT PRONE TO BREAK when exposed to fire. וְאֵלּוּ מְלֵאִין שֶׁאֵין דַּרְכָּן לְהִשְׁתַּבֵּר – AND THESE ARE THE FULL ONES THAT ARE NOT PRONE TO BREAK: כְּלֵי מַתָּכוֹת – METAL VESSELS. רַבִּי יוֹסֵי אוֹמֵר – R' YOSE SAYS: אַף כְּלֵי כְּפַר שִׁיחִין וּכְלֵי כְּפַר חֲנַנְיָה אֵין דַּרְכָּן לְהִשְׁתַּבֵּר – EVEN THE earthenware VESSELS OF KFAR SHICHIN AND OF KFAR CHANANYAH ARE NOT PRONE TO BREAK.[15] In this Baraisa, both the Rabbis (the Tanna Kamma) and R' Yose agree that it is prohibited to cause extinguishment. However, in a reversal of their positions in the Mishnah, R' Yose is more *lenient* than the Rabbis in this regard, allowing the use of even certain earthenware vessels![16] – ? –

The Gemara notes a possible solution and rejects it:

וְכִי תֵּימָא אֵיפּוּךְ מַתְנִיתִין – **And if you will say** that we should **reverse** their positions in **our Mishnah,** i.e. revise the Mishnah so that R' Yose is the one who permits the use of all vessels while the Rabbis are the ones who forbid using new earthenware, וְרַבִּי יוֹסֵי דְּבָרַיְיתָא לְדִבְרֵיהֶם קָאָמַר – and then explain that when **R' Yose in the Baraisa** argues that the earthenware vessels of Kfar Shichin and Kfar Chananyah should also be permitted, **he says this** only **according to the position of [the Rabbis],** for he himself permits the use of *all* vessels[17] – this cannot be, as the Gemara will now explain. וּמִי מָצֵית אַפְּכַתְּ לַהּ – For **can you** indeed **reverse** the opinions recorded in **[the Mishnah]?** וְהָאָמַר רַבָּה בַּר תַּחְלִיפָא מִשְּׁמֵיהּ דְּרַב – **But Rabbah bar Tachlifa has said in the name of Rav:** מַאן תָּנָא גְּרַם כִּבּוּי אָסוּר – **Who is the Tanna** who holds **that causing extinguishment is prohibited?** רַבִּי יוֹסֵי – **R' Yose.** Thus, it is clear that the opinions in our Mishnah are correct as stated.

NOTES

purpose (see Mishnah and Gemara above, 29b-30a). The Tanna of this Baraisa is of the opinion that though R' Shimon concedes that one is forbidden to perform a permitted act that inevitably results in a forbidden act, he does so only if the inevitable consequence is *Biblically* prohibited, but not where it is only Rabbinically prohibited, as in this case. Rav, however, rules that R' Shimon prohibits even where the inevitable consequence is only Rabbinically prohibited.

[Since the halachah follows Rav in this matter, we learn that it is forbidden to engage in a permitted act that has an inevitable forbidden consequence even if that consequence is only Rabbinically forbidden (*Rashba*). This ruling is the subject of a great controversy: *Meiri* (here and 29b) and *Terumas HaDeshen* §64 dispute it, but *Magen Avraham* 314:5, *Hagahos HaGra* and *Hagahos R' Akiva Eiger* (there) rule like *Rashba;* cf. *Beis Meir, Orach Chaim* 321:14. See further, *Dagul MeiRevavah* to *Magen Avraham* 340:6.]

11. Thereby making it burn more intensely (*Rashi*). [A מְדוּרָה is a large fire such as is found in a fireplace.]

12. *Rashi; Mishnah Berurah* 277:10.

13. However, if there is no wind at all, it is certainly permitted to open the door (*Mishnah Berurah* 277:10 from *Magen Avraham*).

[In the case of a lamp, the concern was only for extinguishing the fire because a lamp's flame does not burn more intensely as a result of being fanned, as does a wood fire. On the other hand, a large wood fire is not extinguished by a wind blowing on it; thus, the concern in that case is only for accelerating the fire.]

14. R' Shimon ben Nannas is referred to as "the Rabbis" throughout this discussion because the halachah accords with his view (*Ritva MHK* ed. above ד״ה אין מדקתני סיפא; cf. *Rabbeinu Chananel*).

15. The clays of these areas produced exceptionally strong earthenware. Even new vessels formed from their clay would not break upon exposure to a fire (*Rashi*).

16. R' Yose broadens the category of vessels that may be used without fear of causing extinguishment, permitting even certain earthenware vessels. Thus, he is more lenient on this issue than the Rabbis, who allow only metal vessels (*Rashi*). Although this does not represent a complete reversal of their opinions in the Mishnah – for according to the Baraisa both agree that causing extinguishment is forbidden – it is nonetheless a reversal in the sense of who is more lenient and who is more stringent (*Tosafos*).

17. [The suggested revision is as follows: Since we see in the Baraisa that R' Yose is more lenient in regard to what type of vessels may be used in the firewall, we must conclude that his is the more lenient position in the Mishnah as well. Thus, we must correct the text of our Mishnah so that it attributes the *permission* to cause extinguishment through the use of new earthenware vessels to *R' Yose,* and the dissenting view that prohibits to the Rabbis (see *Rashi*). This, alone, however, would not suffice to answer the contradiction because] R' Yose in the Baraisa permits using the earthenware vessels of these two towns only because they do not commonly break when exposed to fire. This implies that he also forbids using earthenware vessels that break, because he too forbids גְּרַם כִּיבּוּי, *causing extinguishment.* Thus, to salvage this approach we must also say that when R' Yose argues in the Baraisa that using the earthenware vessels of Kfar Shichin and Kfar Chananyah should also be permitted, he is not expressing his own view; he is merely saying to the Rabbis that even according to their view – that causing extinguishment is forbidden – they should still permit using the earthenware vessels of these two towns because these do not commonly break. R' Yose himself, however, would permit using all earthenware vessels because he permits causing extinguishment (*Rashi*).

הוא דאמר כר' שמעון בן ננס אימר דאמר רבי שמעון בן ננס מפני שהוא מחרך גרם כיבוי מי אמר אין מדקתני סיפא רבי יוסי אוסר בכלי חרס חדשים מלאים מים שאינן יכולים לקבל את האור והן מתבקעין ומכבין את הדליקה מכלל דתנא קמא שרי ת"ר א נר שעל גבי טבלא מנער את הטבלא והיא נופלת ואם כבתה כבתה אמרי דבי רבי ינאי ב לא שנו אלא בשוכח אבל במניח נעשה בסיס לדבר האסור תנא נר שאחורי הדלת פותח ונועל כדרכו ואם כבתה כבתה ג לייט עלה רב אמר ליה רבינא לרב אחא בריה דרבא ואמרי לה רב אחא בריה דרבא לרב אשי מאי טעמא לייט עלה רב ד אילימא משום דרב סבר לה כרבי יהודה ותנא קתני לה כר' שמעון משום דרב סבר לה כר' יהודה כל דתני כר' שמעון מילט לייט ליה אמר ליה בהא אפילו ר' שמעון מודה ה דהא אביי ורבא דאמרי תרווייהו מודה רבי שמעון בפסיק רישיה ולא ימות אמר רב יהודה פותח אדם דלת כנגד (א) מדורה בשבת ו לייט עלה אביי במאי עסקינן אילימא ברוח מצויה מאי טעמיה דמאן דאסר אי ברוח שאינה מצויה מאי טעמא דמאן דשרי לעולם ברוח מצויה מר סבר גזרינן ומר סבר לא גזרינן: עושין מחיצה כו': למימרא דרבנן סברי גרם כבוי מותר ור' יוסי סבר גרם כבוי אסור והא איפכא שמעינן להו דתניא עושין מחיצה בכלים ריקנין ובמלאין שאין דרכן להשתבר ואלו מלאין שאין דרכן להשתבר כלי מתכות רבי יוסי אומר אף כלי כפר שיחין וכלי כפר חנניה אין דרכן להשתבר וכי תימא איפוך מתני' ורבי יוסי דברייתא לדבריהם קאמר ומי מצית אפכת לה והאמר רבה בר תחליפא משמיה דרבא מאן תנא גרם כבוי אסור ר' יוסי אלא לעולם לא תיפוך וברייתא כולה ר' יוסי היא וחסורי מחסרא והכי קתני עושין מחיצה בכלים ריקנין ובמלאים שאין דרכן להשתבר ואלו הן כלים שאין דרכן להשתבר כלי מתכות וכלי כפר חנניה נמי אין דרכן להשתבר שר' יוסי אומר אף כלי כפר שיחין וכלי כפר חנניה אין דרכן להשתבר ורמי דרבנן אדרבנן ורמי דרבי יוסי אדרבי יוסי ז דתניא ח הרי שהיה שם כתוב לו על בשרו • הרי זה לא ירחוץ ולא יסוך ולא יעמוד במקום הטינופת ט נזדמנה לו טבילה של מצוה כורך עליה גמי ויורד וטובל רבי יוסי אומר לעולם יורד וטובל כדרכו ובלבד שלא ישפשף שאני התם דאמר קרא א) ואבדתם את שמם מן המקום ההוא לא תעשון כן לה' אלהיכם עשייה הוא דאסור גרמא שרי אי הכי הכא נמי כתיב ב) לא תעשה [כל] מלאכה עשייה הוא דאסור גרמא שרי י מתוך שאדם בהול על ממונו אי שרית ליה אתי לכבויי אי הכי קשיא דרבנן אדרבנן ומה התם דאדם בהול על ממונו שרי הכא לא כל שכן ותסברא האי גמי היכי דמי אי דמיהדק קא הוי חציצה אי לא מיהדק עיילי ביה מיא תיפוק ליה משום דיו בלחה ז דתניא הדם והדיו והדבש והחלב יבשין חוצצין לחים אין חוצצין מכל מקום קשיא אלא אמר רבא בר רב שילא ח היינו טעמיהו דרבנן דקסברי אסור לעמוד בפני השם ערום מכלל דר' יוסי סבר מותר לעמוד בפני השם ערום דמנח ידיה עילויה לרבנן נמי • דמנח ידיה עילויה זימנין דמשתלי ושקיל ליה לר' יוסי נמי זימנין דמשתלי ושקיל ליה אלא אי דאיכא גמי ה"נ הב"ע לאהדורי אגמי רבנן סברי טבילה

רש"י

גמ' הוא דאמר כר"ש. דשרי לעכובי דליקה בעור גדי: גרם כיבוי. כי האי גוונא כשמגיע למים הוא כבה: מי אמר. דילמא הא דקתני במתני' ועושין מחיצה בכל הכלים לאו בחדשים המתבקעים קאמר: נר. דולק קרושיי"ל: אלא בשכח. דשכחו מבעוד יום על הטבלא שלא מדעת: אבל מניח נעשית. טבלא בסיס לדבר האסור ואסור לטלטלה כדי לנערה: לייט עליה. על כל המורין כן: כר' יהודה. דאמר דבר שאין מתכוין אסור: בפסיק רישיה. והכא נמי הרוח מכבהו: כנגד המדורה. ואע"פ שרוח מגשבת ומבעיר האור: מאי טעמא דמאן דאסר. אין דרך להבעיר ברוח מצויה ולא פסיק רישיה ולא ימות הוא: אף כלי כפר שיחין. חרס העשוי מאותו עפר חזק הוא ואין משתבר אלמא לר' יוסי בגרם כבוי טפי מיקל מדרבנן: וכי תימא איפוך מתני'. ותני ברישא דברי ר' יוסי וחכמים אוסרין בכלי חרס חדשים כו': ור' יוסי דברייתא. דמשמע דבהנהו דפקעי מודה דהא כפר שיחין וכפר חנניה הוא דקשרי: לדבריהם קאמר להו. לדידי כל הכלים שרו דגרם כבוי מותר אלא לדידכו נהי דאסריתו גרם כבוי אודו לי מיהת דבהני אפילו גרם ליכא: כורך עליו גמי. קס"ד השתא כדי שלא ימחק את השם במים אלמא לרבנן גרם מחק אסור ולר' יוסי שרי: ובלבד שלא ישפשף. דהוי מוחק בידים: ותסברא. דהכא נמי דאצרכוה רבנן משום שלא ימחק הוא: האי גמי היכי דמי. להגין עליו: אי דמיהדק. שלא יכנסו בו מים וימחק הוי חציצה: ואי דלא מיהדק. לבשרו: עיילי ביה מיא. ואינו מגין מלמחוק: תיפוק ליה דמשום דיו. בלא גמי נמי חייץ דיו ומשני בלחה: מכל מקום קשיא. גמי לרבנן למה להו: מכלל דלר' יוסי כו'. בתמיה והא כתיב לא יראה בך ערות דבר (דברים כג): אלא אי איכא גמי הכי נמי. דמודה ר' יוסי דצריך לכרוך עליו גמי ולא סגי ליה לאנוחי ידיו עליו דילמא מישתלי ושקיל ליה לידיה: טבילה

תוספות

גרם כיבוי מי אמר. וא"ת הא קתני מתני' בין מלאים בין ריקנים ומאי רבותא איכא טפי במלאים מבריקנים אי לאו דמיירי בדרכן להשתבר וי"ל דס"ד דמיירי בכלים שאין דרכן להשתבר וקמ"ל דלא גזרינן אטו כלים שדרכן להשתבר:

מנער את הטבלא והיא נופלת ואם כבתה כבתה. אומר ר"י דמיירי דליכא שמן בנר דאי איכא שמן בנר חייב שהרי שופך ממנו והוי כמסתפק ממנו דחייב משום מכבה כדאמר בפ"ב דביצה (דף כב:) ובירושלמי מוקי לה בנר שכבה ולא קתני בהך ברייתא ואם כבתה כבתה ואתא לאשמעינן היתר טלטול ע"י ניעור לר' יהודה דאסר טלטול בנר שכבה אי נמי אפילו לר"ש ובנר גדול כגון קערה ועששית דמודה ר"ש כדאמר בפרק [כירה] (דף מד.) או כשיש אפר וגחלת אלא שכבה השלהבת: פותח ונועל כדרכו. אע"פ שע"י כן מתנדנד הנר ומתרחק השמן מן השלהבת או מתקרב והוי מכבה או מבעיר אבל אין לפרש משום כיבוי דרוח דאחורי הדלת ליכא רוח ועוד דא"כ הוה ליה למימר פותח אדם דלת כנגד הנר כדקאמר בסמוך כנגד המדורה ועוד דתינח פותח נועל מאי איסורא איכא אלא כדפרישית ואי לאו משום כיבוי והבערה משום טלטול אין לאסור דבנעילת דלת לא חשיב טלטול וגם לא הוי בסיס לדבר האסור דבית חשוב הוא ובטל אגב בית אי נמי בשכח דלא הוי בסיס: מר סבר גזרינן. הלכך צריך ליזהר שלא לפתוח הדלת לפני המדורה אפילו ברוח מצויה דהא לייט עלה אביי דהוי בתרא והנ"מ כשהמדורה קצת קרובה אצל הדלת: והא איפכא שמעינן להו. לאו דווקא איפכא דר' יוסי דברייתא הוי כמו מתני' דאסר דרכו להשתבר אלא היינו איפכא דבמתניתין מחמיר ר' יוסי טפי מדרבנן ובברייתא מיקל טפי: וכי תימא איפוך מתני' כו'. וא"ת מ"מ תקשה דבמתני' לא אסרי רבנן אלא חרס חדש ובברייתא אסרי אפי' ישן מדנקט כלי מתכות וי"ל דנקט בברייתא כלי מתכות משום דאין חילוק בהם בין חדשים לישנים וה"ה כלי חרס ישן: והאמר רבה כו'. ואם תאמר ואמאי לא מפיך ברייתא דטפי אית לן לאפוכה ממתני' והוי אתי נמי שפיר הא דרבה בר תחליפא ונימא דרבנן לדברי ר' יוסי קאמרי ואינהו שרי אף בכלי חרס חדש וי"ל דהתלמוד לא קאמר אלא דאפילו מפיך מתני' לא אתי שפיר אלא על כרחיך ברייתא אית לן לתרוצי וכיון דאתינא להכי לא צריך להפוכה אלא למימר חסורי מיחסרא: אי הכי קשה דרבנן אדרבנן. בלאו הכי הוה קשיא דרבנן אדרבנן אלא משום דהשתא פריך מכ"ש קאמר אי הכי[ס]:

עין משפט נר מצוה

סג א ב מיי' פי"ב מהל' שבת הלכה ו סמג לאוין סה טוש"ע או"ח סימן רעז סעיף ג:
סד ג מיי' שם פ"ה הל' ח טוש"ע שם ס"א:
סה ד מיי' שם טוש"ע שם סעיף ג:
סו ה ו מיי' פ"ו מהל' יסודי התורה הל' ו סמג עשין ג:
סז ז מיי' פ"ב מהלכות מקואות הלכה ג סמג לאוין קיא טוש"ע יו"ד סימן קצח סעיף טו:
סח ח מיי' פ"ו מהל' יסודי התורה הל"ו:

ליקוטי רש"י

דתנא קמא שרי. דהתם כי מטי דליקה לכלים דליקה הוא דפקע להו וגרמא בעלמא הוא [לעיל מז:]. בסים. מושב אם כנו מתרגמינן בסיסיה [שם.]. לייט עלה. כל מאן דלייט ליה [קידושין לג:]. כל שיסמוך על זה [שם עא:]. כר' שמעון. דאמר במסכת שבת (מא:) דבר שאין מתכוין מותר [בכורות כה.]. מודה ר' שמעון בפסיק רישיה ולא ימות. כלומר אחתוך ראש בהמה זו בשבת ואיני רוצה שתמות דכיון דאי אפשר שלא תמות כמתכוין חשיב ליה, וכי אמרינן דבר שאין מתכוין מותר כגון היכא דאפשר ליה בלא איסור כגון גורר אדם מטה כסא וספסל ובלבד שלא יתכוין לעשות חריץ ואף על גב דאיכא למיחש דלמא עביד חריץ כיון דלא מתכוין להכי ואפשר לגרירה בלא חריץ כי עביד נמי חריץ דהוי מלאכה גמורה לא מיחייב אבל היכא דודאי עביד מודי [סוכה לג:]. לא ירחוץ. שלא ימחקנו ואזהרה למוחק את השם ואבדתם את שמם (דברים יב) וסמיך ליה לא תעשון כן וגו'. טבילה של מצוה. טבילת טהרה שהטבילה הכתוב עליו. כורך עליה גמי. להגין עליו [מפני] מחק שטף המים [יומא ח.]. לא תעשון כן. אזהרה למוחק את השם [דברים יב, ד]. מתוך שאדם בהול על ממונו. אי שרית ליה לאצולי בהצלה כולי האי מתוך שהוא בהול מינשי ליה שבת ואתי נמי לכבויי [לעיל קיז:]. אי שרי לאיעסוקי בהצלה כולי האי אתי לכבויי [לעיל ע"א].

רבינו חננאל

אמרינן בגמרא דפורפת על האבן ועל האגוז כו' תיבעי למאן דאמר מערימין תיבעי למ"ד אין מערימין. ואמר לאחרים בואו והצילו עמי שכן דרך בני אדם להשאיל כליו בשבת. פי' י"ח כלים דקא"ר יוסי [מקטורין] כמו מעיל. ובלשון ישמעאל כרכום שיש לו בית ראש ועוטה לו הלובשו ויש לו לולאות וקרסים (שהוא הווה) [שמחברן והוא] כמו מלבוש: אונקלי. בגד דקיקי שנקרא מערקה שלובש אדם על בשרו והולם כל גופו וכן שנינו (מגילה כ"ד) בענין תפלין של יד ציפהו זהב ונתנו על בית יד של אונקלי שלו הרי זה דרך החיצונים: פונדא. גם היא מגעת עד למטה מטבורו של אדם וקורין לו בלשון פרסי קשה. ונקשר כחשב אפודה והיא אפוד האמורה בתורה ויש בה כסים כסים כנגד הלב ותחת הידים: קבוס של פשתן. חלוק התחתון שלובשין אותו ונקרא גלאלה. חלוק הוא המלובש העליון וקורין לו ורבנין: שני. סרבלים ויש שגורס סרבליקין הם בלשון יון המכנסים ושמענו שאמר הגאון נט' דה' דם תפנקי שמלבישין בהן הידים עד האציל ויש בהן בתי אצבעות. שני מנעלים כמשמען: שני פרגוד. בלשון ישמעאל גודאשי: אנפליאות. גם הם מנעלים לשוקים...

מסורת הש"ס

א) לקמן קכה: ודף קמב:, ב) [חולין טו:], ג) לעיל עה. קג. קיא: קיז. קלג. [קמג.] ביצה לו. סוכה לג. כתובות ו. בכורות כה., ד) [קידושין לג. וש"נ], ה) יומא ח. כח. [מס' סופרים פ"ה הל"ב], ו) לעיל קיז:, ז) פסחים סה: מנחות כא. זבחים לה., ח) [ועי' תוס' עירובין כג: וביצה י: וכתובות ג: וב"מ לג. שבועות מה: ד"ה אי הכי].

הגהות הב"ח

(א) גמ' כנגד המדורה:

גליון הש"ס

גמ' הרי זה לא ירחוץ. עי' נדה דף סו ע"ב תוס' ד"ה אם תמצא: שם דמנח ידיה עלויה. עי' בתרומת הדשן סימן י:

תורה אור השלם

א) וְנִתַּצְתֶּם אֶת מִזְבְּחֹתָם וְשִׁבַּרְתֶּם אֶת מַצֵּבֹתָם וַאֲשֵׁרֵיהֶם תִּשְׂרְפוּן בָּאֵשׁ וּפְסִילֵי אֱלֹהֵיהֶם תְּגַדֵּעוּן וְאִבַּדְתֶּם אֶת שְׁמָם מִן הַמָּקוֹם הַהוּא: לֹא תַעֲשׂוּן כֵּן לַייָ אֱלֹהֵיכֶם: [דברים יב, ג-ד]

ב) וְיוֹם הַשְּׁבִיעִי שַׁבָּת לַייָ אֱלֹהֶיךָ לֹא תַעֲשֶׂה כָל מְלָאכָה אַתָּה וּבִנְךָ וּבִתֶּךָ עַבְדְּךָ וַאֲמָתְךָ וּבְהֶמְתֶּךָ וְגֵרְךָ אֲשֶׁר בִּשְׁעָרֶיךָ: [שמות כ, י]

רב נסים גאון

מאי טעמא לייט עלה רב אי נימא דרב סבר לה כר' יהודה תמצא ביאורו בפרק במה מדליקין (לעיל דף כב) רב אמר אין הלכה כר' שמעון בגרירה וכר' יהודה סבירא ליה דפליג על ר' שמעון ואסר דבר שאינו מתכוין ובסוף פ' שמונה שרצים (לעיל דף קיא) ובפרק בתולה נשאת (כתובות דף ו) הלכה כר' יהודה ושמואל אמר הלכה כר' שמעון ובפרק כל פסולי המוקדשין (דף לד) הרי מוכח למדנו שרב סבר דבר שאין מתכוין אסור כר' יהודה ההיא

חשק שלמה על רבינו חננאל

א) עיין ערוך ערך פסק:

The Gemara reconciles the Mishnah and the Baraisa:

אֶלָּא לְעוֹלָם לֹא תֵּיפוּךְ – **Rather, you should indeed not reverse** the positions in the Mishnah, but maintain the reading as we have it – that R' Yose forbids causing extinguishment. וּבָרַיְיתָא כּוּלָּהּ רַבִּי יוֹסֵי הִיא – **Instead,** explain **the entire Baraisa** to reflect **R' Yose's** opinion, וְחַסּוּרֵי מִחַסְּרָא וְהָכִי קָתָנֵי – **and [the text of the Baraisa] is deficient and this is how it should read:** עוֹשִׂין מְחִיצָּה בְּכֵלִים רֵיקָנִין וּבִמְלֵאִים שֶׁאֵין דַּרְכָּן לְהִשְׁתַּבֵּר – ONE MAY MAKE A PARTITION WITH EMPTY VESSELS, AND WITH FULL ONES THAT ARE NOT PRONE TO BREAK. וְאֵלּוּ הֵן כֵּלִים שֶׁאֵין דַּרְכָּן לְהִשְׁתַּבֵּר – AND THESE ARE THE VESSELS THAT ARE NOT PRONE TO BREAK: כְּלֵי מַתָּכוֹת – METAL VESSELS. וּכְלֵי כְּפַר שִׁיחִין וּכְלֵי כְּפַר חֲנַנְיָה נַמִּי אֵין דַּרְכָּן לְהִשְׁתַּבֵּר – AND THE earthenware VESSELS OF KFAR SHICHIN AND OF KFAR CHANANYAH ARE ALSO considered NOT PRONE TO BREAK, שֶׁרַבִּי יוֹסֵי אוֹמֵר – FOR R' YOSE SAYS: אַף כְּלֵי כְּפַר שִׁיחִין וּכְלֵי כְּפַר חֲנַנְיָה אֵין דַּרְכָּן לְהִשְׁתַּבֵּר – EVEN THE earthenware VESSELS OF KFAR SHICHIN AND OF KFAR CHANANYAH ARE NOT PRONE TO BREAK.

The Gemara notes contradictions to both sides of the dispute from a different Baraisa:

וְרָמֵי דְּרַבָּנָן אַדְּרַבָּנָן – **But contrast** this opinion **of the Rabbis** here **with the Rabbis'** opinion in the following Baraisa, וְרָמֵי דְּרַבִּי יוֹסֵי אַדְּרַבִּי יוֹסֵי – **and contrast** this opinion **of R' Yose** here **with R' Yose's** opinion there, and note the contradiction in both cases. דְּתַנְיָא – **For it was taught in a Baraisa:** הֲרֵי שֶׁהָיָה שֵׁם כָּתוּב לוֹ עַל בְּשָׂרוֹ – IF A PERSON HAD A NAME of God WRITTEN ON HIS SKIN, הֲרֵי זֶה לֹא יִרְחוֹץ וְלֹא יָסוּךְ – HE SHOULD NOT WASH OR ANOINT that area, since he will thereby erase the Name of God, which is prohibited,[18] וְלֹא יַעֲמוֹד בִּמְקוֹם הַטִּינּוֹפֶת – AND HE SHOULD NOT STAND IN A FILTHY PLACE.[19] נִזְדַּמְּנָה לוֹ טְבִילָה שֶׁל מִצְוָה – IF A MITZVAH-RELATED IMMERSION CAME HIS WAY,[20] כּוֹרֵךְ עָלֶיהָ גֶּמִי וְיוֹרֵד וְטוֹבֵל – HE SHOULD WRAP A blade of REED-GRASS OVER [THE NAME] AND THEN DESCEND into the *mikveh* AND IMMERSE himself.[21] רַבִּי יוֹסֵי אוֹמֵר – R' YOSE SAYS: לְעוֹלָם יוֹרֵד וְטוֹבֵל כְּדַרְכּוֹ – ACTUALLY, HE MAY DESCEND AND IMMERSE himself IN THE ORDINARY WAY, i.e. without tying a blade of reed-grass around it, וּבִלְבַד שֶׁלֹּא יְשַׁפְשֵׁף – AS LONG AS HE DOES NOT RUB the Name itself. R' Yose permits this because he is not erasing the Name directly but merely causing it to be erased, and only direct erasure of a Name (e.g. by rubbing it in the water) is forbidden.[22] Thus, we see in this Baraisa that R' Yose *permits* causing something forbidden to happen as long as one does not do it directly, whereas it is the Rabbis who forbid it – a reversal of their positions in regard to extinguishment! – ? –

The Gemara suggests a distinction that would reconcile R' Yose's opinions:

שַׁאנִי הָתָם – **It is different there** in the case of erasing the Name of God, דְּאָמַר קְרָא – **for Scripture states:** ,,וְאִבַּדְתֶּם אֶת־שְׁמָם מִן־הַמָּקוֹם הַהוּא לֹא־תַעֲשׂוּן כֵּן לַה׳ אֱלֹהֵיכֶם" – ***And you shall obliterate their names from that place. You shall not do so to Hashem, your God.***[23] Since the verse specifies that we should not *do* this, עֲשִׂיָּיה הוּא דְּאָסוּר – we may derive that **it is** only **doing** – i.e. direct erasure – **that is prohibited,** גְּרָמָא שְׁרֵי – but **causing** erasure **is permitted.**

The Gemara asks:

אִי הָכִי הָכָא נַמִּי כְּתִיב – **If so,** that the word "*do*" is interpreted to exclude causative action, then **here too,** regarding the Sabbath, **it is written:** ,,לֹא־תַעֲשֶׂה כָל־מְלָאכָה" – ***You shall not do any melachah,***[24] and we should therefore derive from this עֲשִׂיָּיה הוּא דְּאָסוּר גְּרָמָא שְׁרֵי – that **it is** only the actual **doing** of a *melachah* **that is prohibited,** but **causing** a *melachah* to occur **is permitted. – ? –**

The Gemara concedes that causation of *melachah* must be permitted on the Biblical level, and explains that R' Yose prohibits causing extinguishment for other reasons:

מִתּוֹךְ שֶׁאָדָם בָּהוּל עַל מָמוֹנוֹ – **Because a person is in a turmoil over** the threatened loss of **his property,** אִי שָׁרִית לֵיהּ אָתֵי לְכַבּוּיֵי – **if you permit him** to cause extinguishment, **he will come to extinguish** it directly. R' Yose therefore prohibits causing a fire's extinguishment.[25]

NOTES

18. The Gemara below will cite the source for this prohibition.

19. [I.e. in a place where there is excrement or urine (see *Rambam, Krias Shema* 3:4 and *Orach Chaim* 85:2).]

20. [I.e. the immersion necessary to render a person *tahor* from any of the conditions of *tumah* decreed by the Torah; see below, 121a.]

21. At this point, the Gemara assumes that the purpose of wrapping the reed-grass around the Name is to prevent its erasure by the *mikveh's* waters (*Rashi*).

22. Rubbing the Name is considered a direct act of erasure (*Rashi*). Merely submerging oneself in the water with the Name on his skin, however, is considered causative [גְּרָם] because the Name is not immediately erased, as a rule; rather the ink begins to loosen as a result of its contact with the water but does not dissolve or come off until some time later [as a result of the prolonged action of the water on the ink] (*Chazon Ish, Orach Chaim* 38:5). Moreover, since it is not certain that the water will erase the Name while he is submerged, his placing the Name in the water is considered no more than causing erasure, not direct erasure (*Rashba;* see further, *Chazon Ish, Yoreh Deah* 164:2; cf. *Igros Moshe, Orach Chaim* vol. I §6 for a different approach). Even so, it is only permissible because he is performing a mitzvah by immersing (as the Baraisa says, "If a mitzvah-related immersion came his way . . ."), but not for other purposes (*Chazon Ish* ibid., who explains on this basis why R' Yishmael above [115b] condemned the person who placed a bundle of blessings in a bucket of water; see also *Teshuvos Radbaz* §1420; *Noda BiYehudah Tinyana, Orach Chaim* end of §17; cf. *Teshuvos Chasam Sofer, Orach Chaim* §32 and *Yoreh Deah* §267; see further *Tashbetz* vol. I §2).

23. *Deuteronomy* 12:3-4. The previous verses speak of the requirement to destroy every vestige of idolatry in Eretz Yisrael. The Torah then goes on, in the verse cited here, to state a positive commandment to obliterate even the names of idols, and then a negative commandment against erasing the Name of God.

24. *Exodus* 20:10.

25. [This is the very reason given above by the Gemara (117b) to explain why the Rabbis prohibited saving more than three meals' worth of food. The Gemara extends this rationale to explain why R' Yose prohibits blocking the spread of a fire with methods that cause its extinguishment, even though he too agrees that this is not Biblically prohibited.]

[The Gemara has now concluded that all Tannaim agree that it is not prohibited to cause the erasure of a Divine Name as long as one does not do so directly. This raises the following question: If even *causing* erasure is permitted, why is one obligated to save Scriptures from a burning building? *R' Mordechai Gifter* (cited in *Igros Moshe, Orach Chaim* vol. I §6) answers that there are two issues here: erasure and degradation. The prohibition to erase God's Name is only through direct action, not causation. But there is a separate obligation not to allow the Name of God or His Scriptures to be degraded. It is this latter obligation that requires us to save Holy Scriptures from destruction. Although this obligation also requires us not to let a Divine Name be erased, it is waived where one needs to immerse in a *mikveh* because there is no degradation in allowing the Name to be erased for the performance of a mitzvah (see note 22). But if one can rescue Scriptures from a fire and does not do so, that is an impermissible degradation. This distinction is made by *Chazon Ish* as well (*Yoreh Deah* 164:2), in a slightly different context. [See *Meor Yisrael* (by *R' Ovadyah Yosef*) here who provides a separate Scriptural source for this latter obligation.]

[In his responsum, *R' Moshe Feinstein* disputes this distinction. He resolves the question by saying that Scriptures were treated by the Rabbis more stringently than a single Name of God, and it is only by Rabbinic decree that there is an obligation to save them from a fire. This decree was not extended to saving a Name written on a person's skin.]

עין משפט נר מצוה

סג א ב מיי׳ פ״ג מהל׳ שבת הלכה ו סמג לאוין סה טוש״ע או״ח סימן רעז סעיף ג:

סד ג מיי׳ שם הל׳ ח טוש״ע שם ס״ח:

סה ד מיי׳ שם טוש״ע שם סעיף ג:

סו ה ו מיי׳ פ״ו מהל׳ יסודי התורה הל׳ ו סמג עשין ג:

סז ז מיי׳ פ״ב מהלכות מקוואות הלכה ג סמג לאוין קלא טוש״ע יו״ד סימן קצח סעיף טו:

סח ח מיי׳ פ״ו מהל׳ יסודי התורה הל״ה:

גמרא

הוא דאמר כר׳ שמעון בן ננס איתמר דאמר רבי שמעון בן ננס מפני שהוא מחרך גרם כיבוי מי אמר אין מדקתני סיפא רבי יוסי אוסר בכלי חרס חדשים מלאים מים שאינן יכולים לקבל את האור והן מתבקעין ומכבין את הדליקה מכלל דתנא קמא שרי ת״ר א נר שעל גבי טבלא מנער את הטבלא והיא נופלת ואם כבתה כבתה אמרי דבי רבי ינאי ב לא א) שנו אלא בשוכח אבל במניח נעשה בסיס לדבר האסור תנא נר שאחורי הדלת פותח ונועל כדרכו ואם כבתה כבתה ג לייט עלה רב אמר ליה רבינא לרב אחא בריה דרבא ואמרי לה רב אחא בריה דרבא לרב אשי מאי טעמא לייט עלה רב ד אילימא משום דרב סבר לה כרבי יהודה ותנא קתני לה כר׳ שמעון משום דרב סבר לה כר׳ יהודה כל דתני כר׳ שמעון מילט לייט ליה והא אמר ליה בהא אפילו ר׳ שמעון מודה ה דהא אביי ורבא דאמרי תרוייהו מודה רבי שמעון בפסיק רישיה ולא ימות אמר רב יהודה פותח אדם דלת כנגד (א) מדורה בשבת ו לייט עלה אביי במאי עסקינן אילימא ברוח מצויה מאי טעמיה דמאן דאסר אי ברוח שאינה מצויה מאי טעמא דמאן דשרי לעולם ברוח מצויה מר סבר גזרינן ומר סבר לא גזרינן: עושין מחיצה כו׳: למימרא דרבנן סברי גרם כבוי מותר ור׳ יוסי סבר גרם כבוי אסור והא איפכא שמעינן להו דתניא עושין מחיצה בכלים ריקנין ובמלאין שאין דרכן להשתבר ואלו מלאין שאין דרכן להשתבר כלי מתכות רבי יוסי אומר אף כלי כפר שיחין וכלי כפר חנניה אין דרכן להשתבר וכי תימא איפוך מתני׳ ורבי יוסי דברייתא לדבריהם קאמר ומי מצית אפכת לה והאמר רבה בר תחליפא משמיה דרב מאן תנא גרם כבוי אסור ר׳ יוסי אלא לעולם לא תיפוך וברייתא כולה ר׳ יוסי היא וחסורי מחסרא והכי קתני עושין מחיצה בכלים ריקנין ובמלאים שאין דרכן להשתבר ואלו הן כלים שאין דרכן להשתבר כלי מתכות וכלי כפר חנניה נמי אין דרכן להשתבר שר׳ יוסי אומר אף כלי כפר שיחין וכלי כפר חנניה אין דרכן להשתבר ורמי דרבנן אדרבנן ורמי דרבי יוסי אדרבי יוסי ז) דתניא ח הרי שהיה שם כתוב לו על בשרו ° הרי זה לא ירחוץ ולא יסוך ולא יעמוד במקום הטינופת ט נזדמנה לו טבילה של מצוה כורך עליה גמי ויורד וטובל רבי יוסי אומר לעולם יורד וטובל כדרכו ובלבד שלא ישפשף שאני התם דאמר קרא א) ואבדתם את שמם מן המקום ההוא לא תעשון כן לה׳ אלהיכם עשייה הוא דאסור גרמא שרי אי הכי הכא נמי כתיב ב) לא תעשה [כל] מלאכה עשייה הוא דאסור גרמא שרי י) מתוך שאדם בהול על ממונו אי שרית ליה אתי לכבויי אי הכי קשיא דרבנן אדרבנן ומה התם דאדם בהול על ממונו שרי הכא לא כל שכן ותסברא האי גמי היכי דמי אי דמיהדק קא הוי חציצה אי לא מיהדק עיילי ביה מיא חציצה תיפוק ליה משום דיו בלחה ט) דתניא י הדם והדיו והדבש והחלב יבשין חוצצין לחים אין חוצצין מכל מקום קשיא אלא אמר רבא בר רב שילא ח היינו טעמייהו דרבנן דקסברי אסור לעמוד בפני השם ערום מכלל דר״י סבר מותר לעמוד בפני השם ערום דמנח ידיה עילויה לרבנן נמי ° דמנח ידיה עילויה זימנין דמשתלי ושקיל ליה לר׳ יוסי נמי זימנין דמשתלי ושקיל ליה אלא אי דאיכא גמי ה״נ הב״ע לאהדורי אגמי רבנן סברי טבילה

רש״י

גמ׳ הוא דאמר כר״ש. דשרי לעכובי דליקה בעור גדי: גרם כיבוי. כי האי גוונא כשמגיע למים הוא כבה: מי אמר. דילמא הא דקתני במתני׳ ועושין מחיצה בכל הכלים לאו במלאים המתבקעים קאמר: נר. דולק קרוש״ל: אלא בשכח. דשכחו מבעוד יום על הטבלא שלא מדעת: אבל מניח נעשית. טבלא בסיס לדבר האסור ואסור לטלטלה כדי לנערה: לייט עליה. על כל המורין כן: כר׳ יהודה. דאמר דבר שאין מתכוין אסור: בפסיק רישיה. והכא נמי הרוח מכבהו: כנגד המדורה. ואע״פ שרוח מנשבת ומבעיר האור: מאי טעמא דמאן דאסר. אין דרך להבעיר ברוח מצויה ולא פסיק רישיה ולא ימות הוא: אף כלי כפר שיחין. חרס העשוי מאותו עפר חזק הוא ואין משתבר אלמא לר׳ יוסי בגרם כבוי טפי מיקל מדרבנן: וכי תימא איפוך מתני׳. ותני ברישא דברי ר׳ יוסי וחכמים אוסרין בכלי חרס חדשים כו׳: ור׳ יוסי דברייתא. דמשמע דהכהו דפקעי מודה דהא כפר שיחין וכפר חנניה הוא דקשרי: לדבריהם קאמר להו. לדידי כל הכלים שרו דגרם כבוי מותר אלא לדידכו נמי דאסריתו גרם כבוי אודו לי מיהת דהני אפילו גרם ליכא: כורך עליו גמי. קס״ד השתא כדי שלא יימחק את השם במים אלמא לרבנן גרם מחק אסור ולר׳ יוסי שרי: ובלבד שלא ישפשף. דהוי מוחק בידים: ותסברא. דהכא גמי דאצרכוה רבנן משום שלא יימחק הוא: האי גמי היכי דמי. להגין עליו: אי דמיהדק. שלא יכנסו בו מים וימחק הוי חציצה: ואי דלא מיהדק. לבשרו עיילי ביה מיא. ולאו מגין מלמחוק: תיפוק ליה דמשום דיו. בלא גמי נמי חייץ דיו ומשני בלחה: מכל מקום קשיא. גמי לרבנן למה להו: מכלל דר׳ יוסי כו׳. בתמיה והא כתיב לא יראה בך ערות דבר (דברים כג): אלא אי איכא גמי הכי נמי. דמודה ר׳ יוסי דצריך לכרוך עליו גמי ולא סגי ליה לאנוחי ידיו עליו דילמא מישתלי ושקיל ליה לידיה:

תוספות

גרם כיבוי מי אמר. וא״ת הא קתני מתני׳ בין מלאים בין ריקנים ומאי רבותא איכא טפי במלאים מבריקנים אי לאו דמיירי בדרכן להשתבר וי״ל דס״ד דמיירי בכלים שאין דרכן להשתבר וקמ״ל דלא גזרינן אטו כלים שדרכן להשתבר:

מנער את הטבלא והיא נופלת ואם כבתה כבתה. אומר ר״י דמיירי דליכא שמן בנר דאי איכא שמן בנר חייב שהרי שופך ממנו והוי כמסתפק ממנו דחייב משום מכבה כדאמר בפ״ב דביצה (דף כב:) ובירושלמי מוקי לה בנר שכבה ולא קתני בהך ברייתא ואם כבתה כבתה ואתא לאשמעינן היתר טלטול ע״י ניעור לר׳ יהודה דאסר טלטול בנר שכבה אי נמי אפילו לר״ש ובנר גדול כגון קערה ועששית דמודה ר״ש כדאמר בפרק [כירה] (דף מד.) או כשיש אפר וגחלת אלא שכבה השלהבת: פותח ונועל כדרכו. אע״פ שע״י כן מתנדנד הנר ומתרחק השמן מן השלהבת או מתקרב והוי מכבה או מבעיר אבל אין לפרש משום כיבוי דרוח דאחורי הדלת ליכא רוח ועוד דא״כ הוה ליה למימר פותח אדם דלת כנגד הנר כדקאמר בסמוך כנגד המדורה ועוד דתינח פותח נועל מאי איסורא איכא אלא כדפרישית ואי לאו משום כיבוי והבערה משום טלטול אין לאסור דבנעילת דלת לא חשיב טלטול וגם לא הוי בסיס לדבר האסור דבית חשוב הוא ובטל אגב בית אי נמי בשכח דלא הוי בסיס: מר סבר גזרינן. הלכך צריך ליזהר שלא לפתוח הדלת לפני המדורה אפילו ברוח מצויה דהא לייט עלה אביי דהוי בתראה והנ״מ כשהמדורה קצת קרובה אצל הדלת: והא איפכא שמעינן להו. לאו דווקא איפכא דר׳ יוסי דברייתא הוי כמו מתני׳ דאסר דרכו להשתבר אלא היינו איפכא דבמתניתין מחמיר ר׳ יוסי טפי מדרבנן ובברייתא מיקל טפי: וכי תימא איפוך מתני׳ כו׳. וא״ת מ״מ תקשה דבמתני׳ לא אסרי רבנן אלא חרס חדש ובברייתא אסרי אפי׳ ישן מדנקט כלי מתכות וי״ל דנקט בברייתא כלי מתכות משום דאין חילוק בהם בין חדשים לישנים וה״ה כלי חרס ישן: והאמר רבה כו׳. ואם תאמר ואמאי לא מפיך ברייתא דטפי אית לן לאפוכה ממתני׳ והוי אתי נמי שפיר הא דרבה בר תחליפא ונימא דרבנן לדברי ר׳ יוסי קאמרי ואינהו שרי אף בכלי חרס חדש וי״ל דהתלמוד לא קאמר אלא דאפילו מפיך מתני׳ לא אתי שפיר אלא על כרחיך ברייתא אית לן לתרוצי וכיון דאתינא להכי לא צריך להפוכה אלא למימר חסורי מיחסרא: אי הכי קשה דרבנן אדרבנן. בלאו הכי הוה קשיא לרבנן אדרבנן אלא משום דהשתא פריך מכ״ש קאמר אי הכי (ד):

ליקוטי רש״י

דתנא קמא שרי. דהכא כי מטי דליקה לכלים כלים דליקה הוא דפקע להו וגרמא בעלמא הוא [לעיל מז:]. בסיס. מושב את הנר מתרגמינן בסיסיה [שם]. לייט עלה. כל מאן דלייט ליה [קידושין לג:]. כל שימצנו על זו [שם עא:]. כר׳ שמעון. דאמר במסכת שבת (מא:) דבר שאין מתכוין מותר [בכורות כה.]. מודה ר׳ שמעון בפסיק רישיה ולא ימות. כלומר אתמוך ראש בהמה זו בשבת ואינה רוצה שתמות כדין לדאי ניחא ליה, וכי אמרינן דבר שאין מתכוין מותר כגון גורר אדם מטה כסא וספסל ובלבד שלא יתכוין לעשות חריץ ואף על גב דאזיל למיעבד חריץ כיון דלא מתכוין לגרירה בלא חריץ כי עביד נמי חריץ דהוי מלאכה גמורה לא מתכוין אבל היכא דודאי עביד מודי [סוכה לג:]. לא ירחוץ. שלא ימחק את השם ולהכי למחוק את השם ולהכחיד את שמם (דברים יב) לא תעשון כן [יומא ח.]. טבילה של מצוה. טבילת טהרה שטבילה בזמנה מצוה. כורך עליו גמי. להגין עליו [מסכן] מחוק ערוב השם [יומא ח.]. לא תעשון כן. אזהרה למוחק את השם [דברים יב, ד]. מתוך שאדם בהול על ממונו. אי שרית ליה לאסתולי בהצלה כולי האי מתוך שהוא בהול מינשי ליה שבת ואתי נמי לכבויי [לעיל קיז:]. אי שרי לאעסוקי בהצלה כולי האי אתי לכבויי [לעיל ע״א].

רבינו חננאל

אמרינן בגמרא דפורפת על האבן ועל האגוז כו׳ תיובתי למאן דאמר מערימין תיובתי למ״ד אין מערימין. ואמר לאחרים בואו והצילו עמי שכן דרך בני אדם להשאיל כליו בשבת. פי׳ י״ח כלים דקא״ר יוסי [מקטורין] כמו מעיל. ובלשון ישמעאל כרכום שיש לו בית ראש ועושה לו להלבוש ויש לו לולאות וקרסים (שהוא הוהה) [שמחברן והוא] כמו מלבוש: אונקלי. בגד דקיקי שנקרא מערקה שלובש אדם על בשרו והולם כל גופו וכן שנינו (מגילה כ״ד) בענין תפלין של יד ציפהו זהב ונתנו על בית יד של אונקלי שלו הרי זה דרך החיצונים: פונדא. גם היא מגעת עד למטה מטבורו של אדם וקורין לו בלשון פרסי פשת. ונקשר כחשב אפודה והיא אפוד האמורה בתורה ויש בה כסים כסים כנגד הלב ותחת הידים: קנבוס של פשתן. חלוק התחתון שלובשין אותו ונקרא גלאלה. חלוק הוא המלובש העליון וקורין לו ורבנין: שני. ספרקים א) ויש שגורס סובריקין והם בלשון יון המכנסים ושמענו שאמר הגאון נט׳ דח׳ דם תפנקי שמלבישין בהן הידים עד האציל ויש בהן בתי אצבעות. שני מנעלים כמשמען: שני פרגוד. בלשון ישמעאל גודאבי: אנפליאות. גם הם מנעלים לשוקים עליון האנין שעל השוקים מן העור. ומעפורת וחגור שבמתנים וכובע הרי י״ח כלים: ר׳ שמעון בן ננס אומר פורשין עור של גדי כו׳. אמר רב יהודה טלית שאחז בה האור מצד אחד נותן עליה מים מצד אחר ואם כבתה כבתה. והא ודאי גרם כיבוי הוא. ואקשינן עליה ממתנית׳ דקתני פושטה ומתכסה בה אבל מים שהן גרם כיבוי לא קתני ואתנינן לאוקומיה לרב יהודה כ״ר שמעון בן ננס ולא קם. דר׳ שמעון בן ננס לא קאמר אלא מפני שהוא מחרך הא גרמא בידים לא קאמר אלא קם רב יהודה כרבנן. דתנן עושין מחיצה בכל הכלים בין מלאים בין ריקנין דשרו גרם כיבוי ור׳ יוסי אוסר גרם כיבוי והלכה כרבנן וכרב יהודה: נר שעל גבי טבלא איתא דאוקמה דבי ר׳ ינאי בשכח נר שעל גבי טבלא. אבל המניח נר על טבלא נעשה טבלא בסיס לנר שהיא מוקצה מחמת איסור ואסור לטלטוליה. ודתנא תנא קמיה דרב ולייט עלה רב. היכא דידע שבודאי כשפותח ונועל יכבה הנר מפני שהדלת נוגעת בו ומכבתו שאסור דבהא אפי׳ ר״ש מודה דהוי פסיק רישיה ולא ימות. אבל אי גרם בעלמא שרי: אמר רב יהודה אמר שמואל פותח אדם דלת כנגד המדורה בשבת ואינו חושש. ואע״פ שהרוח מלבה את האש. לייט עלה אביי דחשיב ליה כמבעיר את האש ואי רוח שאינה מצויה היא והוא שמניף ומושבה לא פליגי דאסיר. כי פליגי ברוח מצויה. (רב) [אביי] סבר גזרינן ברוח מצויה אטו רוח שאינה מצויה. ומר סבר לא גזרינן והלכתא כאביי וקאמרינן בגמרא דהכונס צאן לדיר בנזיקין המלבה ואין בליבויו כדי ללבותה פטור. ואקשינן אמאי פטור. ליהוי כי זורה ורוח מסייעתו. ואמרינן בה כמה טעמי. סימן ברו״ש. אמר אביי כגון שליבה מצד זה וליבתה הרוח מצד אחר ורבא אמר כגון שליבה ברוח מצויה וליבתו הרוח שאינה מצויה. רב זירא אמר דצמדא צמידי. רב אשי אמר היכא אמרינן זורה ורוח מסייעתו לענין שבת דמלאכת מחשבת אסרה תורה. אבל הכא גרמא בעלמא היא וגרמא בנזקין פטור. ש״מ דכיון דמשוי אורחא אפי׳ לרוח מצויה ללבות ומחשב לכן אסור בשבת דהיינו מלאכת מחשבת: סוגיא דשמעתא דר׳ יוסי מתיר בכלים מליאין מים כגון כלי מתכות וכלי כפר חנניה וכלי כפר שיחין שחרש שלהן חזק ואינן מתבקעין באור. ואע״פ שאין גרם כיבוי אסור כגון הני שקי. ור׳ יוסי דשרי

מסורת הש״ס

א) לקמן קכה: ודף קמב: ב) [חולין טו.] ג) לעיל עה. קג. קיז. קלג. [קמא.] ביצה לו. סוכה לג: כתובות ו. בכורות כה. ד) [קידושין לג. וש״נ] ה) יומא ח. כה. [מס׳ סופרים פ״ה הל״ב] ו) לעיל קיז: ז) פסחים סה: מנחות כא. זבחים לה. ח) [ועי׳ תוס׳ עירובין כג. ובכלים ה: וכתובות ג. וכ״ש לג. שבועות מה: ד״ה אי הכי]

הגהות הב״ח

(א) גמ׳ כנגד המדורה:

גליון הש״ס

גמ׳ הרי זה לא ירחוץ. עי׳ נדה דף סו ע״ב תוס׳ ד״ה לא סמוך: שם דמנח ידיה עליה. עי׳ בתרומת הדשן סימן י:

תורה אור השלם

א) וְנִתַּצְתֶּם אֶת מִזְבְּחֹתָם וְשִׁבַּרְתֶּם אֶת מַצֵּבֹתָם וַאֲשֵׁרֵיהֶם תִּשְׂרְפוּן בָּאֵשׁ וּפְסִילֵי אֱלֹהֵיהֶם תְּגַדֵּעוּן וְאִבַּדְתֶּם אֶת שְׁמָם מִן הַמָּקוֹם הַהוּא: לֹא תַעֲשׂוּן כֵּן לַייָ אֱלֹהֵיכֶם: [דברים יב, ג-ד]

ב) וְיוֹם הַשְּׁבִיעִי שַׁבָּת לַייָ אֱלֹהֶיךָ לֹא תַעֲשֶׂה כָל מְלָאכָה אַתָּה וּבִנְךָ וּבִתֶּךָ עַבְדְּךָ וַאֲמָתְךָ וּבְהֶמְתֶּךָ וְגֵרְךָ אֲשֶׁר בִּשְׁעָרֶיךָ: [שמות כ, י]

רב נסים גאון

מאי טעמא לייט עלה רב אי נימא דרב סבר לה כר׳ יהודה התמצא בירורו בפ׳ במה מדליקין (לעיל דף כב) רב אמר אין הלכה כר׳ שמעון בגרירה מכלל דכר׳ יהודה סבירא ליה דפליג על ר׳ שמעון ואסר דבר שאינו מתכוין ובסוף פ׳ שמונה שרצים (לעיל דף קיא) ובפרק בתולה נשאת (כתובות דף ו) הלכה אמר רב הלכה כר׳ יהודה ורב חייא בר אבין מתני לה בלא גברי רב אמר הלכה כר׳ יהודה ושמואל אמר הלכה כר׳ שמעון ותניא בבכורות בפרק כל פסולי המוקדשין (דף לד) הרי מיכן למדנו שרב סבר דבר שאינו מתכוין אסור כר׳ יהודה ההיא

חשק שלמה על רבינו חננאל

א) עיין ערוך ערך ספרק:

The Gemara now turns to the contradiction in the rulings of the Rabbis:

אִי הָכִי קַשְׁיָא דְּרַבָּנַן אַדְּרַבָּנַן – **If so,** then **a difficulty** presents itself **between** the opinion **of the Rabbis** in the Mishnah **and** the opinion **of the Rabbis** in the Baraisa: וּמָה הָתָם דְּאָדָם בָּהוּל עַל מָמוֹנוֹ שָׁרֵי – **For if** even **there,** in the case of a fire, **where a person is in turmoil over** the threatened loss of **his property,** and there is therefore reason to impose stringencies upon him, the Rabbis nevertheless **permitted** him to cause the fire's extinguishment, הָכָא לֹא כָּל שֶׁכֵּן – then **here,** where the person is not in turmoil concerning the Name on his skin, should the Rabbis **not surely** permit him to cause its erasure?[26]

The previous question assumes that the reason the Rabbis require the use of a reed-grass covering over the Name is to prevent its erasure. The Gemara answers the question by rejecting this premise:

וְתִסְבְּרָא – **And do you** really **think** that the Rabbis required the covering so as to prevent the Name's erasure? That cannot be, as we will now prove. הַאי גֶּמִי הֵיכִי דָּמֵי – For let us see: **This** blade of **reed-grass – how is it** fastened so as to protect the Name against erasure? אִי דְּמִיהַדַּק קָא הָוֵי חֲצִיצָה – **If it is tied tightly** over the Name, **it constitutes an interposition** that would invalidate the immersion;[27] אִי לֹא מִיהַדַּק עָיְילֵי בֵּיהּ מַיָּא – and **if it is not tied tightly, water will enter beneath it** and the grass will not protect the Name from being erased! – ? –

The Gemara challenges this proof:

חֲצִיצָה תֵּיפוּק לֵיהּ מִשּׁוּם דְּיוֹ – If you are concerned about **an interposition,** then **consider it** an interposition simply **because of the ink** forming the Name![28]

The Gemara answers this objection:

בְּלַחָה – We are dealing **with moist** ink, which is not deemed an interposition. דְּתַנְיָא – **For it was taught in a Baraisa:** הַדָּם וְהַדְּיוֹ הַדְּבַשׁ וְהֶחָלָב – BLOOD, INK, HONEY AND MILK, יְבֵשִׁין חוֹצְצִין – when they are DRY THEY CONSTITUTE AN INTERPOSITION; לַחִים אֵין חוֹצְצִין – when they are MOIST, THEY DO NOT CONSTITUTE AN INTERPOSITION. Thus, if not for the grass tied around the Name there would be no interposition.

The Gemara responds:

מִכָּל מָקוֹם קַשְׁיָא – **In any case,** the problem raised **is** still **difficult:** Why do the Rabbis require the reed-grass covering? What purpose does it serve?[29]

Because of this question, the Gemara is forced to explain the need for the covering – and the dispute between the Rabbis and R' Yose – in a completely different way:[30]

אֶלָּא אָמַר רָבָא בַּר רַב שִׁילָא – **Rather, Rava bar Rav Shila said:** הַיְינוּ טַעְמַיְיהוּ דְּרַבָּנַן – **This is the reasoning of the Rabbis:** דְּקָסָבְרֵי אָסוּר לַעֲמוֹד בִּפְנֵי הַשֵּׁם עָרוֹם – **For they hold it is forbidden to stand before the Name** while **naked.**[31] Since a person must immerse in a *mikveh* naked, the Rabbis required him to cover the Name with a loose-fitting covering.[32]

The Gemara turns to R' Yose's opinion:

מִכְּלָל דְּרַבִּי יוֹסֵי סָבַר מוּתָּר לַעֲמוֹד בִּפְנֵי הַשֵּׁם עָרוֹם – **This implies that R' Yose** – who does not require a covering – **holds** that **it is permitted to stand before a Name** while **naked.** How can this be?[33]

The Gemara replies:

דְּמַנַּח יְדֵיהּ עִילָּוֵיהּ – Indeed, R' Yose too forbids this. He permits the man to immerse without a covering **because he can** instead **place his hand over [the Name]** to cover it.

The Gemara counters:

לְרַבָּנַן נַמִּי דְּמַנַּח יְדֵיהּ עִילָּוֵיהּ – If so, **according to the Rabbis as well, he can place his hand over [the Name].** Why then do they require him to cover the Name with a blade of reed-grass?

The Gemara replies:

זִימְנִין דְּמִשְׁתְּלֵי וְשָׁקִיל לֵיהּ – They do so because **sometimes one forgets and removes [his hand],** leaving the Name exposed to his nakedness.

The Gemara asks:

לְרַבִּי יוֹסֵי נַמִּי זִימְנִין דְּמִשְׁתְּלֵי וְשָׁקִיל לֵיהּ – **According to R' Yose too** we should be concerned that **one sometimes forgets and removes [his hand].**

The Gemara therefore revises its previous explanation somewhat:

אֶלָּא אִי דְּאִיכָּא גֶּמִי הָכִי נַמִּי – **Rather, if there is a** blade of **reed-grass** readily available to cover the Name then R' Yose concedes that **this is indeed so:** One must cover the Name before immersing and cannot rely on remembering to keep his hand over it. הָכָא בְּמַאי עַסְקִינַן – But **with what case are we dealing here?** לְאַהֲדוּרֵי אַגְּמִי – Where it is necessary **to go after a reed-grass.** רַבָּנַן סָבְרֵי – In these circumstances, **the Rabbis hold**

NOTES

26. Actually, the contradiction concerning the Rabbis' position is a problem regardless of how we explain R' Yose's view, as the Gemara noted above. The Gemara prefaces its discussion of this contradiction with the words אִי הָכִי, *if so,* because the problem is more acute according to the previous explanation. It is not simply that the Rabbis' ruling in the Baraisa contradicts their ruling in the Mishnah; rather their ruling is actually contrary to the logic of the situation (*Tosafos*).

27. [When one immerses in a *mikveh,* there may be no *chatzitzah* (interposition) between his skin and the water. If a *chatzitzah* exists, the immersion is invalid.]

28. The Gemara's objection is this: It can be argued that neither the reed-grass covering nor the ink is legally considered a *chatzitzah,* since each covers only a minority of his body, and it may be that one is not ordinarily מַקְפִּיד, *particular,* about removing these. A *chatzitzah* of this kind [מִיעוּטוֹ וְאֵינוֹ מַקְפִּיד, *a minority that one is not particular about*] does not invalidate an immersion (*Eruvin* 4b). Thus, we could say that the Rabbis require the covering to be tied tightly. However, your question assumes that person is particular [מַקְפִּיד] regarding the covering, which is why you say that it cannot be tightly bound. By the same token, then, he is particular regarding the ink as well. Thus, the ink itself should constitute a *chatzitzah* and his immersion should be invalid even apart from the covering! (*Ritva MHK* ed.).

29. They cannot be discussing a case where it is bound tightly [since it would then constitute a *chatzitzah,* as we explained above]. Thus, they must be discussing a case where it is loosely wrapped. But if so, it does not protect the Name against erasure. Why then do the Rabbis require it? (*Rashi,* as explained by *Ritva MHK* ed.).

30. [I.e. their dispute in the case of the Name on his skin has nothing to do with the permissibility of causing its erasure and both agree that it is indeed permitted to do so. Thus, the Rabbis do not contradict their ruling in regard to extinguishing, for both here and there they hold that *causative action* [גְּרָמָא] is permitted. The reason they require the Name to be covered with a loose blade of reed-grass is an entirely different one, which the Gemara will now explain.]

31. This is based on the verse (*Deuteronomy* 23:15): *For Hashem your God walks within your camp . . . and your camp shall be holy; He shall not see in you any thing of nakedness . . .* [This verse is transgressed when one stands unclothed before a Name of God or a Sefer Torah] (*Rashi*).

32. [This suffices to cover the Name without constituting a *chatzitzah.*]

33. For this prohibition is derived from the verse cited above! (*Rashi*).

טְבִילָה בִּזְמַנָּהּ לַאו מִצְוָה – immersion at its appointed time is not a mitzvah,[1] **וּמְהַדְּרִינַן – and one should** therefore **go after** a reed-grass to cover the Name even if it means postponing the immersion. **וְרַבִּי יוֹסֵי סָבַר – R' Yose, however, holds: טְבִילָה בִּזְמַנָּהּ מִצְוָה וְלֹא מְהַדְּרִינַן – Immersion at its appointed time is a mitzvah,**[2] **and one should** therefore **not go after** a reed-grass if doing so will force him to postpone his immersion to the next day.

The Gemara questions whether this could be R' Yose's opinion: **וְסָבַר רַבִּי יוֹסֵי טְבִילָה בִּזְמַנָּהּ מִצְוָה – And does R' Yose** really **hold that immersion at its appointed time is a mitzvah? וְהָתַנְיָא – But it has been taught in a Baraisa:**[3] **הַזָּב וְהַזָּבָה הַמְצוֹרָע וְהַמְצוֹרַעַת בּוֹעֵל נִדָּה וּטְמֵא מֵת** – A *ZAV*, A *ZAVAH*, A *METZORA*, A *METZORAAS*, A MAN WHO COHABITS WITH A *NIDDAH* AND A PERSON *TAMEI* FROM A CORPSE[4] – if the seventh day of their purification period falls on Yom Kippur, **טְבִילָתָן בַּיּוֹם** – THEIR IMMERSION IS BY DAY,[5] despite the Yom Kippur restriction against washing. **נִדָּה וְיוֹלֶדֶת טְבִילָתָן בַּלַּיְלָה** – Similarly, if the immersion time for A *NIDDAH* AND A WOMAN WHO HAS GIVEN BIRTH falls on Yom Kippur night, THEIR IMMERSION IS AT NIGHT.[6] **בַּעַל קֶרִי טוֹבֵל וְהוֹלֵךְ כָּל הַיּוֹם כּוּלּוֹ** – A MAN WHO EXPERIENCES A SEMINAL EMISSION on Yom Kippur IMMERSES himself AT ANY POINT DURING THE ENTIRE DAY.[7] **רַבִּי יוֹסֵי אוֹמֵר** – R' YOSE SAYS: **מִן הַמִּנְחָה וּלְמַעְלָה אֵינוֹ צָרִיךְ לִטְבּוֹל** – If he experiences the emission FROM MINCHAH time FORWARD HE NEED NOT IMMERSE himself, since he is able to delay his immersion until the night.[8] It is evident from this that R' Yose does not hold that it is a mitzvah for someone to immerse himself at the appointed time. – ? –

The Gemara answers:

הַהִיא רַבִּי יוֹסֵי בְּרַבִּי יְהוּדָה הִיא – That R' Yose (of the Baraisa regarding Yom Kippur) **is** actually **R' Yose the son of R' Yehudah, דְּאָמַר דַּיָּהּ טְבִילָה בָּאַחֲרוֹנָה – who said,** in the case of a woman who had many different possible appointed times: IT IS SUFFICIENT FOR HER that she undergo ONE IMMERSION AT THE CONCLUSION of all the possible times, for immersion at the

---

NOTES

1. [I.e. there is no mitzvah for one to immerse himself immediately after the waiting period for his *tumah* concludes. Rather, one may choose to remain in a state of *tumah* as long as he wishes (or until it becomes necessary for him to purify himself, e.g. when he needs to go to the Temple). See next note.]

2. [The "appointed time" is the earliest day or night that one is allowed to immerse. This varies from *tumah* to *tumah.*]

The root of the dispute is how to understand the verse said in regard to a *baal keri* [a man who experienced a seminal emission]. The Torah states (*Deuteronomy* 23:12): וְהָיָה לִפְנוֹת־עֶרֶב יִרְחַץ בַּמָּיִם, *And it shall be, towards evening, that he shall immerse in waters,* i.e. in a *mikveh.* (A *baal keri* can immerse himself immediately after his emission and become *tahor* that night.) R' Yose views this as a commandment to immerse oneself that very day [though if he failed to do so he can still immerse himself and become *tahor* any day afterwards]. The Rabbis, however, assert that the Torah does not mean to set an obligation to immerse oneself that day but merely to advise the person to do so for his own benefit. For if he fails to immerse before the day turns to night, he will not became *tahor* until the following night, since a *tamei* who has immersed does not become *tahor* until the evening after his immersion (*Rashi*).

3. This Baraisa is found [with some alterations] in Tosefta *Yoma* 4:7 (*Rashi;* we have therefore explained the Baraisa here in accord with the reading found there). The Baraisa discusses what should be done by persons who are *tamei* if the first opportunity to immerse themselves falls on Yom Kippur. It is forbidden to wash on Yom Kippur [for the sake of pleasure or comfort]. For the sake of a mitzvah, however, it is permitted (see *Rashi* and below).

4. [See Glossary for a definition of these terms. A *metzoraas* is a female *metzora.* A man who cohabits with a *niddah* (in violation of the prohibition to do so) becomes *tamei* for seven days (*Leviticus* 15:24). All of those mentioned in this list are *tamei* for at least seven days.]

5. Although they require a seven-day waiting period before they can become *tahor,* these people may immerse themselves on the morning of that seventh day, from dawn on [though they should preferably wait until after sunrise; see *Megillah* 20a], because a part of this seventh day is counted for them as a full day. The Scriptural source for this is given in *Megillah* 20a (*Rashi*). [*Rashi's* explanation here of the source telescopes together two statements of the Gemara there, the first of which teaches that they may immerse themselves on the seventh day and the second of which teaches that they cannot immerse on the night of the seventh but must wait for daybreak.]

The Baraisa does not just mean that they may immerse themselves but rather that they *should* immerse themselves – so that they should be able to eat *terumah* that night [if they are Kohanim] (see *Rashi;* see note 8 below).

6. A *niddah* and a new mother must wait a *full* seven days; the earliest time they may immerse is the night following the seventh day. This is derived from the verse (*Leviticus* 15:19): שִׁבְעַת יָמִים תִּהְיֶה בְנִדָּתָהּ, *seven days she shall be in her state of separation.* The Gemara (*Pesachim* 90b) derives from the word תִּהְיֶה, *she shall be,* that she remains in her *niddah* state for the full seven days. [This requirement is extended to a new mother, as are many of the laws of *niddah* – see *Leviticus* 12:2.] The Baraisa teaches that if the seventh day of their purification period falls on Erev Yom Kippur, they immerse themselves that night, even though it is Yom Kippur (*Rashi*).

7. The Sages instituted that a man who has had a seminal emission should not study Torah [or pray] until he purifies himself by immersing in a *mikveh* (*Berachos* 22a). [Following his immersion, he may engage in Torah study and prayer immediately and need not wait for nightfall.] Thus, even if he does not have *terumah* to eat that night (see note 5), he should still immerse himself so that he may properly say the day's prayers. The Tanna goes further, however, and says that he should immerse himself at *any* point during the day – even if he experienced the emission after completing Minchah, when he could wait until after nightfall to immerse himself and then recite Maariv. (The Ne'ilah prayer is not an issue here because the Baraisa reflects the opinion of Rav that Ne'ilah may be recited after nightfall; *Rashi,* see *Yoma* 87a; cf. *Tosafos* and see *Ritva MHK* ed.). The reason is that immersion at its appointed time is itself a mitzvah. Therefore, even though he does not need to eat *terumah* that night or pray any more this day, he should still immerse himself on Yom Kippur afternoon (*Rashi;* see next note).

[The Rabbinic decree requiring a man to immerse after a seminal emission before studying Torah or praying is no longer in effect. Today immersion in such circumstances is regarded as a meritorious act but is not obligatory (see *Shulchan Aruch, Orach Chaim* 88 with *Mishnah Berurah*).]

8. Since he no longer needs to pray today nor to eat *terumah* tonight (see previous note), he need not immerse himself during Yom Kippur day – for R' Yose is of the opinion that there is no mitzvah to immerse oneself on the appointed day (*Rashi*).

[R' Yose states that he *need* not immerse himself on Yom Kippur day, which implies that he may do so if he wishes. Although R' Yose is of the opinion that there is no mitzvah to immerse oneself on the appointed day, immersion to purify oneself from *tumah* is nonetheless permitted on Yom Kippur (*Tosafos,* who infer that *Rashi* is of this opinion as well; cf. *Rashi* to *Yoma* 88a). Since R' Yose takes issue with the Tanna Kamma only in regard to a *baal keri* but not in regard to all the others listed in the Baraisa, it is clear that R' Yose agrees that the *zav, zavah,* etc. *should* immerse themselves on Yom Kippur. For this reason *Rashi* explained (in ד״ה הזב והזבה) that they should immerse themselves so as to be able to eat *terumah* that night. According to the Tanna Kamma, however, they should immerse themselves on Yom Kippur even if they have no *terumah* to eat – since immersion at the appointed time is itself a mitzvah.]

[In practice, *Shulchan Aruch* rules that nowadays neither a *niddah* nor a *baal keri* may immerse themselves on Yom Kippur or Tishah B'Av (*Orach Chaim* 554:8 and 613:11,12). See *Tur* and *Beis Yosef* there for an explanation of why this is so.] See also *Tosafos* to *Beitzah* 18b ד״ה כל.

טבילה בזמנה לאו מצוה ומהדרינן ור' יוסי סבר טבילה בזמנה מצוה ולא מהדרינן וסבר ר' יוסי טבילה בזמנה מצוה [א] והתניא [א] הזב והזבה המצורע והמצורעת בועל נדה וטמא מת טבילתן ביום נדה ויולדת טבילתן בלילה בעל קרי טובל והולך כל היום כולו ר' יוסי אומר מן המנחה ולמעלה אינו [ב] צריך לטבול התם ההיא ר' יוסי בר' יהודה היא [ג] דאמר דייה טבילה באחרונה: **מתני'** [ד] [ב] נכרי שבא לכבות אין אומרים לו כבה ואל תכבה מפני שאין שביתתו עליהן אבל קטן שבא לכבות אין שומעין לו מפני ששביתתו עליהן: **גמ'** [ה] א"ר אמי [ג] בדליקה התירו לומר כל המכבה אינו מפסיד נימא מסייע ליה נכרי שבא לכבות אין אומרים לו כבה ואל תכבה מפני שאין שביתתו עליהן כבה הוא דלא אמרינן ליה הא כל המכבה אינו מפסיד אמרינן ליה אימא סיפא אל תכבה לא אמרינן ליה וכל המכבה אינו מפסיד נמי לא אמרינן ליה אלא [ו] מהא ליכא למשמע מינה ת"ר [ז] מעשה ונפלה דליקה בחצירו של יוסף בן סימאי בשיחין ובאו אנשי גיסטרא של ציפורי לכבות מפני שאפטרופוס של מלך היה ולא הניחן מפני כבוד השבת ונעשה לו נס וירדו גשמים וכיבו לערב שיגר לכל אחד מהן שתי סלעין ולאפרכוס שבהן חמשים וכששמעו חכמים בדבר אמרו לא היה צריך לכך שהרי שנינו נכרי שבא לכבות אין אומרים לו כבה ואל תכבה: אבל [ד] קטן שבא לכבות אין שומעין לו מפני ששביתתו עליהן: שמעת מינה [ח] קטן אוכל נבלות ב"ד מצווין עליו להפרישו אמר רבי יוחנן [ה] בקטן העושה לדעת אביו דכוותה גבי נכרי דקא עביד לדעתיה דישראל מי שרי נכרי לדעתיה דנפשיה עביד: **מתני'** [ט] [ו] כופין קערה על גבי הנר בשביל שלא תאחוז בקורה ועל צואה של קטן ועל עקרב שלא תישך [י] א"ר יהודה מעשה בא לפני רבן יוחנן בן זכאי בערב ואמר חוששני לו מחטאת: **גמ'** רב יהודה ורב ירמיה בר אבא ורב חנן בר רבא איקלעו לבי אבין דמן נשיקיא לרב יהודה ורב ירמיה בר אבא אייתו

רש"י

טבילה בזמנה מצוה. דכתיב והיה לפנות ערב ירחץ במים (דברים כג): **לאו מצוה.** ואי לא משכח גמי האידנא לישתהי עד למחר ולמ"ד לאו מצוה קרא עלה טובה קמ"ל כדי שיעריב שמשו ביום לאחר טבילה שאם ימתין לטבול עד הלילה לא יהא לו הערב שמש עד ליל המחרת: **הזב והזבה כו'.** ברייתא זו אגב יוה"כ שנויה בתוספתא דיומא (פ"ד): הזב והזבה והמצורע ובועל נדה וטמא מת טובלין ביום. משהאיר המזרח ביום השביעי שלהם וטעמא (א) בפ"ב דמגילה (דף כ.) מקרא דביום השביעי מקצת שביעי ספירה ואם חל שביעי שלהם ביוה"כ טובלין כדרכן לאכול תרומה לערב: **נדה ויולדת.** טובלות כדרכן בלילי יוה"כ אם חל שביעי שלהם בערב יוה"כ שאינה יכולה לטבול ביום ז' דכתיב בה תהיה בנדתה בהוייתה תהא כל ז' (פסחים דף צ:): **בעל קרי.** שצריך טבילה לדברי תורה מדברי סופרים ואפי' אין (ב) אוכל טהרות לבו ביום: **טובל כל היום כולו.** ואע"פ שראה קרי מן המנחה ולמעלה לאחר שהתפלל תפלת המנחה שהרי הוא יכול להמתין עד שתחשך ויטבול לתפלת ערבית אפ"ה טובל ביו"כ מבעוד יום אע"פ שאסור ברחיצת הרשות דטבילה בזמנה מצוה: **ר' יוסי אומר מן המנחה ולמעלה.** אם ראה קרי לאחר שהתפלל תפלת מנחה שהרי הוא יכול להמתין עד שתחשך ויטבול ויתפלל תפלת ערבית ותפלת נעילה נמי ס"ל שיכול להתפלל בלילה כרב דאמר (יומא דף פז.) תפלת נעילה פוטרת של ערבית: **אין צריך לטבול.** ביום משום זמן טבילה דלאו מצוה לטבילה בזמנה: **דייה לטבילה שתהא באחרונה.** במסכת נדה בפרק המפלת גבי אשה שיצאה מלאה ובאה ריקנית ואינה יודעת מתי ילדה דמצרכינן לה ל"ה טבילות לספק ד' טבילות שעליה טבילת זכר לז' או טבילת נקבה לשבועיים ובלילה או שמא יולדת זכר בזוב וצריכה אף טבילת זבה ביום שבעה לספורים שלה או יולדת נקבה בזוב היתה ומשום דלא ידעינן מתי ילדה ואימתי מטי זמן טבילה דידה מצרכינן לה טבילה כל לילה וכל יום שיש לספוקי בזמן טבילתה ופליג ר' יוסי ברבי יהודה עלה ואמר דייה לטבילה שתהא באחרונה לסוף ספורים של נקבה דהיינו לסוף שלש שבועים שאם ילדה נקבה בזוב טמאה שבועיים ללידתה וז' נקיים בשביל הזיבה ולא אמרינן טבילה בזמנה מצוה: **מתני' אין אומרים לו כבה.** רבנן גזור על ° אמירה לנכרי משום שבות: **ולא תכבה.** אין צריך למחות בידו אלא יניחנו ויכבה: **שאין שביתתו.** של נכרי עליהן דישראל אינו מוזהר על שביתתו של נכרי שאינו עבדו: **גמ' כבה הוא דלא אמרינן ליה.** שעושהו שלוחו ממש: **הא כל המכבה אינו מפסיד כו'.** ונכרי מדעתיה דידיה עביד שריא: **אל תכבה הוא דלא אמרינן ליה.** שאינו צריך למחות בידו ומיהו גילוי דעתא דלא יפסיד בדבר נמי לא משתרי דאי גילוי דעתא שרי למה ליה למיתני סיפא אין צריך למחות: **אלא מהכא ליכא למישמע מיניה.** דודאי מתניתין לאו כולה דוקא אלא חדא מינייהו דוקא או רישא או סיפא ותנא אידך אטו ההיא ולא ידעינן הי מינייהו דוקא דנגמר מינייה: **גיסטרא.** שלטון: **אפטרופוס.** ממונה על ממונו: **שמעת מינה קטן אוכל נבילות בית דין מצווין להפרישו.** ותקשי לר' יוחנן[כ] דאמר ביבמות (דף קיד.) לרבה בר בר חנה דאירכסו ליה מפתחות של בית המדרש ברשות הרבים בשבת דבר טלי' וטליתא ליטיילי התם דאי משכחי להו מייתי להו: **על דעת אביו.** בקטן שידע להבחין שהכבוי זה נוח לאביו ועושה בשבילו: **נכרי אדעתיה דנפשיה עביד.** ואפילו יודע שנוח לו לישראל הוא להנאת עצמו מתכוין שיודע שלא יפסיד: **מתני' כופין קערה.** על גבי הנר. ובלבד שלא יכבה ואע"פ שנוטל כלי להצלת קורה שאינה ניטלת בשבת הא אותבינן מינה (דף מג.) לרבי יצחק דאמר אין כלי ניטל אלא לדבר הניטל ושנייה בצריך למקומו: **מעשה בא.** כפיית כלי על עקרב: **בערב.** מקום: **חוששני לו מחטאת.** כיון דלא היה עקרב רץ אחריו איני יודע אם חייב משום צידה אם לאו ומספקא לומר חייב חטאת הוא:

תוספות

הכי גרסי' ר' יוסי אומר מן המנחה ולמעלה אינו צריך לטבול. וכן גירסת רש"י ור"ת אבל לא גרסי' אינו יכול לטבול דאפי' מאן דסבר טבילה בזמנה לאו מצוה ° שרי לטבול כדמשמע בסוף מסכת יומא (דף פז:) דפריך לרב דאמר תפלת נעילה פוטרת של ערבית משום דקסבר דתפלת נעילה בלילה והתניא אור יוה"כ כו' נעילה מתפלל שבע ומתודה בערבית כו' ומשני תנאי היא דתניא כל חייבי טבילות טבילתן ביום נדה ויולדת טובלין בלילה בעל קרי טובל והולך עד המנחה דסבר תפלת נעילה בלילה וטבילה בזמנה לאו מצוה ר' יוסי אומר כל היום כולו טובל דתפלת נעילה ביום אלמא אע"ג דת"ק סבר דטבילה בזמנה לאו מצוה אפ"ה קתני כל חייבי טבילות טבילתן ביום אפילו טמא מת וטמא שרץ שאין צריכין טבילה לתפלה יכולין לטבול והא דפירש בקונטרס דר' יוסי כרב דאמר תפלת נעילה בלילה לא דק דבשלהי יומא (דף פח.) פריך מהך ברייתא דר' יוסי אדר"י דהכא קאמר מן המנחה ולמעלה א"צ לטבול ובההיא קאמר כל היום ומשני דהכא איירי בדצלי כבר תפלת נעילה והתם בדלא צלי ובכולהו רבי יוסי דלא כרב:

רבי יוסי בר' יהודה היא. וא"ת א"כ בשילהי יומא (דף פח.) מנא ליה לרב דההוא ת"ק דברייתא קמייתא דקאמר דבעל קרי טובל עד המנחה אתי' כוותיה דתפלת נעילה בלילה דילמא איירי בדצלי וטבילה בזמנה לאו מצוה ור' יוסי סבר מצוה ותנא קמא דהכא הוא ר' יוסי דהתם ויש לומר דסבר דר' יוסי דהכא ודהתם מסתמא חד תנא הוא ותרווייהו רבי יוסי ברבי יהודה דאיירי בטבילת בעל קרי ביו"כ וא"כ קשיא ר' יוסי בר' יהודה אדר' יוסי בר' יהודה וע"כ אית לן לשנויי הא דצלי והא דלא צלי:

אין אומרים לו כבה. אפי' באיסורא דרבנן אמירה לנכרי שבות כדאמרינן לקמן בפרק שואל (דף קנ.) לא יאמר אדם לחבירו שכור לי פועלים כו' דמוקי לה בחברו נכרי וכן מוכח בפרק הדר (דף סז:) גבי נייתי חמימי מגו ביתא:

אלא מהא ליכא למשמע מינה. מ"מ קי"ל כר' אמי ובירושלמי אמר שעשה ר' אמי מעשה כזה:

שמע מינה קטן אוכל נבלות בית דין מצווין עליו להפרישו. צ"ל דמוקי מתניתין כרבי יהודה דאמר מלאכה שאינה צריכה לגופה חייב עליה או כר"ש וכשצריך לאותו כיבוי כגון לעשות פחמין דבאיסורא דרבנן מוכח בפרק חרש (יבמות קיד.) דאין ב"ד מצווין להפרישו ונראה דמיירי בקטן שלא הגיע לחינוך דבהגיע לחינוך כיון שחייב לחנכו כ"ש דצריך להפרישו שלא יעשה עבירה וכל הנהו דפריך ביבמות הוה מצי לשנויי כשהגיע לחינוך אלא דניחא ליה לאוקמי בכל ענין והא דבעי לאיתויי התם דאין ב"ד מצווין להפרישו מדקתני תינוק יונק והולך וקתני ובגדול אסור משמע דוקא גדול אבל קטן אפי' בהגיע לחינוך שרי התם ע"כ גדול לאו דוקא בר עונשין דהא במסקנא מפרש טעמא משום דסתם תינוק מסוכן הוא אצל חלב והאי טעמא לא שייך אלא בבן שתים או שלש שנים:

כל

מסורת הש"ס

א) פסחים ל: יומא ו. פח. ע"ש [תוספתא יומא פ"ד ע"ש], ב) [נ"ל יבוא וכ"א ביומא פח.], ג) נדה כט: [ודף ל. יומא פח.], ד) יבמות קיד., ה) כתובות ט, ו) [ברכות כה. וש"נ], ז) [תוספתא פרק י"ד], ח) יבמות קיד. נדה מו: [גיטין נה.], ט) לעיל מג. קז., י) [לקמן קמו.], כ) וכן פירש הר"ן ותקשי לר' יוחנן וכו' וכבר הגיה הב"ח כבוד או"ח סי' שמג דבמקומות דידן איתא ר' פדת ור' יוחנן מספקי מספקא ליה וע' ב"מ סוף הלכות מאכלות אסורות הלכה כח.

הגהות הב"ח

(א) רש"י ד"ה הזב והזבה והמצורע וכו' וטעמא מפרש בפ"ב דמגילה: (ב) ד"ה בעל קרי וכו' אוכל טהרות הס"ד ותיבות לבו ביום נמחק:

גליון הש"ס

רש"י ד"ה אין אומרים לו וכו' אמירה לנכרי משום שבות. עי' רש"י דף טו ע"א ד"ה נהי דלגזירה: תוס' ד"ה הכי גרסי' וכו' שרי לטבול כדמשמע. ע"ל דף קיא ע"א תוס' ד"ה לא ס"ד:

רב נסים גאון

ההיא ר' יוסי בר' יהודה היא דתניא ר' יוסי בר' יהודה אומר דייה לטבילה באחרונה משכחת לה במס' נדה (דף כט) בפרק המפלת: שמעת מינה קטן אוכל נבלות בית דין מצווין עליו

ליקוטי רש"י

טבילה בזמנה מצוה. דכתיב (במדבר יט) וטהרו ביום השביעי וכבס בגדיו ורחץ לא כתיב לא זה אלא ללמד על הטבילה שתהא ביום השביעי. טבילה בזמנה לאו מצוה. והאי וטהרו דכתיב ביה למסכת קדושין בפרק שלישי [יומא ח.]. לאו מצוה ומהדרינן. והא היו לא גמי ימתין עד למחר ויטבול [שם פח.]. ורבי יוסי סבר. מצוה הלכך לא משכח גמי לא מהדר [שם ח.]. הזובה. זבה טבילתה ביום שביעי דכתיב (ויקרא טו) ואחר תטהר ואחר שבעת ימים תטהר מאחר כיון דמימה לה ספירה טהור ותמלת היום עבדה לה ספירה [פסחים צ:]. טבילתן ביום. כדיליף במסכת מגילה (כ.) מביום השביעי וכו' (במדבר יט) [יומא ו.]. נדה ויולדת. נדה דאורייתא שאינה סופרת נקיים אלא שבעה שם ימי הראייה אינה טובלת עד לאחר שקיעת החמה של שביעי הוי עד למחר. יולדת מיקש לנדה דכתיב (ויקרא יב) כימי נדת דותה תטמא [פסחים שם]. טבילתן בלילה נדה דכתיב (ויקרא טו) שבעת ימים [illegible]

עין משפט נר מצוה

סט א מיי' פ"א מהלכות מקוואות הלכה ה ופ"ג מהלכות שביתת עשור הלכה ג ג ופ"ד מהלכות איסורי ביאה הלכה ה סמג עשין רמג טוש"ע או"ח סימן תקנד סעיף ח ופי' מור"ם סעיף יא יב וטוש"ע יו"ד סימן קצז סעיף ג וסימן שפא סעיף ה [ברי"ף פ"ב דשבועות דף רלב וברא"ש בהלכות מקוואות סי' לט]:

ע ב מיי' פ"ו מהלכות שבת הלכה ד ופ"ב הלכה ז סמג לאוין סה טוש"ע או"ח סימן שלד סעיף כה:

עא ג מיי' פי"ב שם וסמג שם טוש"ע שם סעיף כו:

עב ד ה מיי' פי"ג שם ופכ"ד מהל' מאכלות אסורות הל' כח וסמג שם ולאוין קמח טוש"ע או"ח סימן שמג וטוש"ע יו"ד סימן שעג סעיף א בהגה"ה:

עג ו מיי' פ"י מהלכות שבת הלכה ד סמג לאוין סה טוש"ע או"ח סימן רעז סעיף ה וסימן שלד סעיף כב בהגה"ה:

רבינו חננאל

גרם מחיקת שם משום דאמר לך התם עשייה אסור גרמא שרי רבנן בשבת גרמא כמו מלאכת מחשבת היא ואסור. ואע"ג דכתיב לא תעשה כל מלאכה. (כל מלאכה) מדאורייתא עשייה אסורה מיהו גזרו רבנן אפי' גרמא משום דקי"ל אדם בהול על ממונו אי שרית ליה אתי לכבויי. תוב אקשינן דרבנן אדרבנן. התם בגרם מחיקת השם מצרכי ליה גמי לח. והכא שרו בגרם כיבוי. ואקשינן עלה האי גמי לח היכי דמי אי דקטר ומיהדק הוא גופיה חייץ בטבילה. ואי לא מיהדק עייל ביה מיא ומסיק לשם ולא מהני גמי לח לשם שכתוב בו בשר מידי ולא איפרקא הא קושיא. תוב אקשינן עליה ותיפוק ליה דהיו גופיה שהשם כתוב בו שחוצץ. ופרקינן הב"ע בדיו לחה שאינה חוצצת. דתניא הדם והדיו והדבש והחלב יבישין חוצצין לחין אין חוצצין. ופרקי' על קושיא הראשונה רבנן דאסרי לטבול עד שדרך על השם גמי לח לאו משום דסבירא להו גרם מחיקת השם אסור דכל גרמא שרי. והכא משום דאסור לעמוד בפני השם ערום מצריכי גמי לח. וכיון דלא צריך אלא לכסויי השם וממילא ידעינן שאין מהדק הגמי לח ולא איכפת ליה אי עיילי מיא דלא חייש לגרם מחיקה. ואקשינן וכי ר' יוסי מתיר לעמוד בפני השם. ושנינן לר' יוסי מכסהו לשם בידו ויטבול. א"ר אי הכי לרבנן נמי ניכסיה בידיה ונדחה זה הפירוק. ופרקינן לדברי הכל אסור לעמוד בפני השם ערום. ואי איכא גמי וכיוצא בו לכרוך על השם ולטבול טבילה בזמנה דכ"ע דכרוך. כי פליגי היכא דליכא מידי מצוי וצריך להדורי ולאתויי. ר' יוסי אומר טבילה בזמנה מצוה ואתיא מצוה זו ודחה לעמידת ערום בפני השם וטבול בדלא מיכסי א). ורבנן סברי טבילה בזמנה לאו מצוה הלכך לא הדרי.

חשק שלמה על רבינו חננאל

א) נראה דל"ל [illegible] ב) [illegible]

[illegible]

appointed time is not a mitzvah.[9] The R' Yose of our Baraisa (regarding a person with a Divine Name written on his skin) is a different Tanna,[10] who is of the opinion that immersion at the appointed time is a mitzvah.

Mishnah The Mishnah deals with one's reactions to others who set about extinguishing a fire for him: נָכְרִי שֶׁבָּא לְכַבּוֹת – **A gentile who comes to extinguish** a fire that has broken out in a Jew's home on the Sabbath, אֵין אוֹמְרִים לוֹ כַּבֵּה – **they may not say to him, "Extinguish** it,"[11] וְאַל תְּכַבֶּה – **nor** do they have to tell him, **"Do not extinguish** it,"[12] מִפְּנֵי שֶׁאֵין שְׁבִיתָתוֹ עֲלֵיהֶן – **because his resting is not their responsibility.**[13] אֲבָל קָטָן שֶׁבָּא לְכַבּוֹת – **However,** a Jewish **minor who comes to extinguish** the fire, אֵין שׁוֹמְעִין לוֹ – **they may not listen to him,** i.e. they may not allow him to do so, מִפְּנֵי שֶׁשְּׁבִיתָתוֹ עֲלֵיהֶן – **because his resting is their responsibility.**[14]

Gemara A ruling: אָמַר רַבִּי אַמִּי – **R' Ami said:** בִּדְלֵיקָה הִתִּירוּ לוֹמַר – **In a fire** situation, **[the Sages] permitted one to say** within earshot of nearby gentiles: כׇּל הַמְכַבֶּה אֵינוֹ מַפְסִיד – **"Anyone who extinguishes** the fire **will not lose"**; i.e. will not go unrewarded.[15]

The Gemara suggests a proof:

נֵימָא מְסַיַּיע לֵיהּ – **Let us say that [our Mishnah] supports [R' Ami]:** נָכְרִי שֶׁבָּא לְכַבּוֹת אֵין אוֹמְרִים לוֹ כַּבֵּה וְאַל תְּכַבֶּה – A GENTILE WHO COMES TO EXTINGUISH a fire, THEY MAY NOT SAY TO HIM, "EXTINGUISH it," NOR do they have to tell him, "DO NOT EXTINGUISH it," מִפְּנֵי שֶׁאֵין שְׁבִיתָתוֹ עֲלֵיהֶן – BECAUSE HIS RESTING IS NOT THEIR RESPONSIBILITY. כַּבֵּה הוּא דְּלֹא אַמְרִינַן לֵיהּ – **It is** only the direct command, **"Extinguish** it," **that we may not tell him,** because by doing so we are appointing him our agent; הָא כׇּל הַמְכַבֶּה אֵינוֹ מַפְסִיד אַמְרִינַן לֵיהּ – **but,** the implication is, **we could tell him, "Anyone who extinguishes** it **will not lose,"** because he would then be acting on his own.

The Gemara draws a contradictory inference from the second half of the Mishnah:

אֵימָא סֵיפָא – **But consider the end** of that citation: אַל תְּכַבֶּה לֹא אַמְרִינַן לֵיהּ – **We do not** have to **tell him, "Do not extinguish** it"; וְכׇל הַמְכַבֶּה אֵינוֹ מַפְסִיד נַמִּי לֹא אַמְרִינַן לֵיהּ – **but,** it is implied, **"Anyone who extinguishes** it **will not lose," we may not tell him either.**[16]

The Gemara concludes:

אֶלָּא מֵהָא לֵיכָּא לְמִשְׁמַע מִינָּהּ – **Rather, one cannot infer** a proof or disproof of R' Ami's ruling **from this** Mishnah.[17]

The Gemara cites a related incident:

תָּנוּ רַבָּנָן – **The Rabbis taught in a Baraisa:** מַעֲשֶׂה וְנָפְלָה דְלֵיקָה בַּחֲצֵירוֹ שֶׁל יוֹסֵף בֶּן סִימַאי בְּשִׁיחִין – THERE WAS AN INCIDENT IN WHICH THE COURTYARD OF YOSEF BEN SIMAI IN SHICHIN CAUGHT FIRE on the Sabbath, וּבָאוּ אַנְשֵׁי גִּיסְטְרָא שֶׁל צִיפּוֹרִי לְכַבּוֹת – AND

NOTES

9. The Gemara in *Niddah* (29b-30a) discusses the case of a woman who recently lost her pregnancy but is unable to recall exactly when this event occurred, whether the fetus was male or female, or whether it was accompanied by any unusual discharges of blood (see there for other details of this case). Thus, while it is clear that she is *tamei* due to childbirth, it is not clear whether this is a seven-day *tumah* (for the birth of a male) or a fourteen-day *tumah* (for the birth of a female), and whether she was a *zavah* at the time she gave birth, which would require her to purify herself from childbirth *tumah* before observing the seven clean days required of a *zavah.* Accordingly, there are four possible immersions required of her: an immersion on the eighth night (the night following the seventh day) in case her child was a male, an immersion on the fourteenth *day* (the seventh after the conclusion of her childbirth *tumah*) in case she was also a *zavah* (a *zavah* immerses by day, as the previous Baraisa stated), a third immersion that night in case her fetus was a female (for whom childbirth *tumah* lasts fourteen days), and a fourth immersion on the twenty-first day in case she gave birth to a female and was also a *zavah.* But since she does not know when she lost the pregnancy there are actually numerous possible times for each of these immersions to take place. Due to the uncertainty [as well as certain other factors mentioned there], the previous Tanna of the Baraisa stated that she must immerse herself thirty-five times to account for all the possibilities, because he is of the opinion that there is a mitzvah to immerse oneself at the appointed time. R' Yose the son of R' Yehudah rules that she need not immerse herself at all the possible times but only once – at the last of these times – because he is of the opinion that there is no mitzvah to immerse oneself at the appointed time (*Rashi*).

Thus, we may say that the R' Yose who maintains that a *baal keri* need not immerse himself on Yom Kippur after Minchah is actually R' Yose the son of R' Yehudah.

10. [When R' Yose is mentioned without a patronym the reference is generally to R' Yose bar Chalafta.]

11. I.e. they may not urge him on, even though he came for this purpose (*Mishnah Berurah* 334:63 with *Shaar HaTziyun;* cf. *Chidushei HaRan*), for the Rabbis decreed that a Jew may not instruct a non-Jew to perform a *melachah* on the Sabbath (*Rashi;* cf. *Rashi* to *Exodus* 12:16 with *Ramban* there; *Smag, Lo Saaseh* 75, cited by *Beis Yosef, Orach Chaim* end of *siman* 244).

[*Rashi* to *Avodah Zarah* 15a ד״ה כיון דזבנה קנייה places this decree in the category of speech prohibited under the rubric of מִמְּצוֹא חֶפְצְךָ וְדַבֵּר דָּבָר, *Pursuing your business and discussing the forbidden* (*Isaiah* 58:13). Elsewhere (below, 153a ד״ה מאי טעמא, and *Avodah Zarah* 22a ד״ה לא), *Rashi* explains that the gentile is considered the Jew's agent. Although in general only a Jew can become an agent of another Jew, in this case the Sages were stringent and considered even the gentile an agent (see *Hagahos Maimoniyos* 6:2; *Graz, Orach Chaim* 243:1; cf. *She'eilos U'Teshuvos Chasam Sofer, Orach Chaim* 84 and *Choshen Mishpat* 185).] See also below, 153a note 4.

12. They need not protest his actions either; rather, they may allow him to proceed and extinguish the fire (*Rashi*).

13. [The Torah requires a Jew to safeguard his own Sabbath observance, the Sabbath observance of his children and even that of his Canaanite slaves (see *Exodus* 20:10 and *Rashi* ad loc.). A Jew must even guarantee the Sabbath observance of his fellow Jews (see *Sotah* 37b with *Rashi*).] However, he is not obligated to ensure that non-Jews rest on the Sabbath (*Rashi*).

14. [The Gemara will discuss whose responsibility is meant here.]

15. Although such a statement effectively communicates the person's wish that a *melachah* be performed, the Rabbis did not proscribe this particular formula, since he has thereby not *commanded* anyone to do anything.

[R' Ami's ruling applies to any threat to property that appears suddenly on the Sabbath (*Orach Chaim* 334:26; see *Beis Yosef* who broadens the ruling's application still further; cf. *Mishnah Berurah* ad loc. §70).]

16. We are not required to object and restrain him, but neither are we allowed to place an incentive before him by indirectly revealing our wishes. For if such an indirect approach were permitted, why would the Mishnah not take note of it? The Mishnah should have taught: One may not say, "Extinguish it," but one may say, "Anyone who extinguishes will not lose" (*Rashi*).

17. Clearly, both parts of this Mishnah cannot be taken precisely, since they contradict one another. Rather, one of the statements and its implication is intended and the other statement is phrased as it is for stylistic symmetry. Since we do not know which is the precise statement, we are unable to draw any conclusions (*Rashi*).

טבילה בזמנה מצוה. דכתיב והיה לפנות ערב ירחץ במים (דברים כג): לאו מצוה. ואי לא משכח גמי האידנא לישתהי עד למחר ולמ"ד לאו מצוה קרא עצה טובה קמ"ל כדי שיעריב שמשו ביום לאחר טבילה שאם ימתין לטבול עד הלילה לא יהא לו הערב שמש עד ליל המחרת: הזב והזבה כו'. ברייתא זו אצל יוה"כ שנויה בתוספתא דיומא (פ"ד): הזב והזבה והמצורע ובועל נדה וטמא מת טובלין ביום. משהאיר המזרח ביום השביעי שלהם וטעמא (א) בפ"ב דמגילה (דף כ.) מקרא דביום השביעי מקצת שביעי ספירה ואם חל שביעי שלהם ביוה"כ טובלין כדרכן לאכול תרומה לערב: נדה ויולדת. טובלות כדרכן בלילי יוה"כ אם חל שביעי שלהם בערב יוה"כ שאינה יכולה לטבול ביום דכתיב בה תהיה בנדתה בהוייתה תהא כל ז' (פסחים דף צ:): בעל קרי. שצריך טבילה לדברי תורה מדברי סופרים ואפי' אין (ב) אוכל טהרות לבו ביום: טובל כל היום כולו. ואע"פ שראה קרי מן המנחה ולמעלה לאחר שהתפלל תפלת המנחה שהרי הוא יכול להמתין עד שתחשך ויטבול לתפלת ערבית אפ"ה טובל ביוה"כ מבעוד יום אע"פ שאסור ברחיצה הרשות לטבילה בזמנה מצוה: ר' יוסי אומר מן המנחה ולמעלה. אם ראה קרי לאחר שהתפלל תפלת מנחה שהרי הוא יכול להמתין עד שתחשך ויטבול ויתפלל תפלת ערבית ותפלת נעילה נמי ס"ל שיכול להתפלל בלילה כרב דאמר (יומא דף פז:) תפלת נעילה פוטרת של ערבית: אין צריך לטבול. ביום משום זמן טבילה לאו מצוה: דייה לטבילה שתהא באחרונה. במסכת נדה בפרק המפלת גבי אשה שילדה ואינה יודעת מה ילדה ובאה ריקנית ואינה יודעת מתי ילדה דמצרכינן לה ל"ה טבילות לספק ד' טבילות שעליה טבילת זכר לז' או טבילת נקבה לשבועים ובלילה או יולדת זכר בזוב וצריכה אף טבילה זה ביום שבעה לספורים שלה או יולדת נקבה בזוב היתה ומשום דלא ידעינן מתי ילדה ואימתי מטי זמן טבילה דידה מצרכינן לה טבילה כל לילה וכל יום שיש לספוקי בזמן טבילתה ופליג ר' יוסי ברבי יהודה עלה ואמר דייה לטבילה שתהא באחרונה לסוף ספורים של נקבה דהיינו לסוף שלש שבועים שאם ילדה נקבה בזוב טמאה שבועיים ללידתה וז' נקיים בשביל הזיבה ולא אמרינן טבילה בזמנה מצוה: מתני' אין אומרים לו כבה. רבנן גזור על אמירה לנכרי משום שבות: ולא תכבה. אין צריך למחות בידו אלא יניחנו ויכבה: שאין שביתתו. של נכרי עליהן דישראל אינו מוזהר על שביתתו של נכרי שאינו עבדו: גמ' כבה הוא דלא אמרינן ליה. שעושהו שלוחו ממש: הא כל המכבה אינו מפסיד כו'. ונכרי מדעתיה דידיה עביד שריא: אל תכבה הוא דלא אמרינן ליה. שאינו צריך למחות בידו ומיהו גילוי דעתא דלא יפסיד בדבר נמי לא משתרי דאי גילוי דעתא שרי למה ליה למיתני סיפא אין צריך למחות: אלא מהכא ליכא למישמע מיניה. דודאי מתניתין לאו כולה דוקא אלא חדא מינייהו דוקא או רישא או סיפא ותנא אידך אטו ההיא ולא ידעינן הי מינייהו דוקא דנגמר מיניה: גיסטרא. שלטון: אפטרופוס. ממונה על ממונו: שמעת מינה קטן אוכל נבילות בית דין מצווין להפרישו. ותקשי לר' יוחנן דאמר ביבמות (דף קיד.) לרבה בר בר חנה דאירכסו ליה מפתחות של בית המדרש ברשות הרבים בשבת דבר טלי' וטליתא ליטיילי התם דאי משכחי להו מייתי להו: על דעת אביו. בקטן שידע להבחין שהכבוי זה נוח לאביו ועושה בשבילו: נכרי אדעתיה דנפשיה עביד. ואפילו יודע שנוח לו לישראל הוא להנאת עצמו מתכוין שיודע שלא יפסיד: מתני' כופין קערה. של חרס: על גבי הנר. ובלבד שלא יכבה ואע"פ שנוטל כלי להצלת קורה שאינה ניטלת בשבת הא אותבינן מינה (דף מג.) לרבי יצחק דאמר אין כלי ניטל אלא לדבר הניטל ושנייה בצריך למקומו: מעשה בא. כפיית כלי על עקרב: בערב. מקום: חוששני לו מחטאת. כיון דלא היה עקרב רץ אחריו איני יודע אם חייב משום צידה אם לאו וחוששני לומר חייב חטאת הוא:

טבילה בזמנה לאו מצוה ומהדרינן ור' יוסי סבר טבילה בזמנה מצוה ולא מהדרינן וסבר ר' יוסי טבילה בזמנה מצוה והתניא הזב והזבה המצורע והמצורעת בועל נדה וטמא מת טבילתן ביום נדה ויולדת טבילתן בלילה בעל קרי טובל והולך כל היום כולו ר' יוסי אומר מן המנחה ולמעלה אינו צריך לטבול ההיא ר' יוסי בר' יהודה היא דאמר דייה טבילה באחרונה:

מתני' נכרי שבא לכבות אין אומרים לו כבה ואל תכבה מפני שאין שביתתו עליהן אבל קטן שבא לכבות אין שומעין לו מפני ששביתתו עליהן:

גמ' א"ר אמי בדליקה התירו לומר כל המכבה אינו מפסיד נימא מסייע ליה נכרי שבא לכבות אין אומרים לו כבה ואל תכבה מפני שאין שביתתו עליהן כבה הוא דלא אמרינן ליה הא כל המכבה אינו מפסיד אמרינן ליה אימא סיפא אל תכבה נמי לא אמרינן ליה וכל המכבה אינו מפסיד נמי לא אמרינן ליה אלא מהא ליכא למשמע מינה ת"ר מעשה ונפלה דליקה בחצירו של יוסף בן סימאי בשיחין ובאו אנשי גיסטרא של ציפורי לכבות מפני שאפטרופוס של מלך היה ולא הניחן מפני כבוד השבת ונעשה לו נס וירדו גשמים וכיבו לערב שיגר לכל אחד מהן שתי סלעין ולאפרכוס שבהן חמשים וכששמעו חכמים בדבר אמרו לא היה צריך לכך שהרי שנינו נכרי שבא לכבות אין אומרים לו כבה ואל תכבה: אבל קטן שבא לכבות אין שומעין לו מפני ששביתתו עליהן: שמעת מינה קטן אוכל נבלות ב"ד מצווין עליו להפרישו אמר רבי יוחנן בקטן העושה לדעת אביו דכוותה גבי נכרי דקא עביד לדעתיה דישראל מי שרי נכרי לדעתיה דנפשיה עביד:

מתני' כופין קערה על גבי הנר בשביל שלא תאחוז בקורה ועל צואה של קטן ועל עקרב שלא תישך א"ר יהודה מעשה בא לפני רבן יוחנן בן זכאי בערב ואמר חוששני לו מחטאת:

גמ' רב יהודה ורב ירמיה בר אבא ורב חנן בר רבא איקלעו לבי אבין דמן נשיקיא לרב יהודה ורב ירמיה בר אבא אייתו

הכי גרסי' ר' יוסי אומר מן המנחה ולמעלה אינו צריך לטבול. וכן גירסת רש"י ור"ת אבל לא גרסי' אינו יכול לטבול דאפי' מאן דסבר טבילה בזמנה לאו מצוה * שרי לטבול כדמשמע בסוף מסכת יומא (דף פח.) דפריך לרב דאמר תפלת נעילה פוטרת של ערבית משום דקסבר דתפלת נעילה בלילה והתניא אור יוה"כ כו' נעילה מתפלל שבע ומתודה בערבית כו' ומשני תנאי היא דתניא כל חייבי טבילות טבילתן ביום נדה ויולדת טובלין בלילה בעל קרי טובל והולך עד המנחה דסבר תפלת נעילה בלילה וטבילה בזמנה לאו מצוה ר' יוסי אומר כל היום כולו טובל דתפלת נעילה ביום אלמא אע"ג דת"ק סבר דטבילה בזמנה לאו מצוה אפ"ה קתני כל חייבי טבילות טבילתן ביום אפילו טמא מת וטמא שרץ שאין צריכין טבילה לתפלה יכולין לטבול והא דפירש בקונטרס דר' יוסי כרב דאמר תפלת נעילה בלילה לא דק דבשלהי יומא (דף פח.) פריך מהך ברייתא דר' יוסי אדר"י דהכא קאמר מן המנחה ולמעלה א"צ לטבול ובההיא קאמר כל היום ומשני דהכא איירי בדצלי כבר תפלת נעילה והתם בדלא צלי ובכולהו רבי יוסי דלא כרב: **רבי** יוסי בר' יהודה היא. וא"ת א"כ בשלהי יומא (דף פח.) מנא ליה לרב דההוא ת"ק דברייתא קמייתא דקאמר דבעל קרי טובל עד המנחה אתי' כוותיה דתפלת נעילה בלילה דילמא איירי בדצלי וטבילה בזמנה לאו מצוה ור' יוסי סבר מצוה ותנא קמא דהכא הוא ר' יוסי דהתם וי"ל דסבר דר' יוסי דהכא ודהתם מסתמא חד תנא הוא ותרוייהו רבי יוסי ברבי יהודה דאיירי בטבילת בעל קרי ביוה"כ וא"כ קשיא ר' יוסי בר' יהודה אדר' יוסי בר' יהודה וע"כ אית לן לשנויי הא דצלי והא דלא צלי: **אין** אומרים לו כבה. אפי' באיסורא דרבנן אמירה לנכרי שבות כדאמרינן לקמן בפרק שואל (דף קנ.) לא יאמר אדם לחבירו שכור לי פועלים כו' דמוקי לה בחברו נכרי וכן מוכח בפרק הדר (דף סז:) גבי נייתי חמימי מגו ביתא: **אלא** מהא ליכא למישמע מינה. מ"מ קי"ל כר' אמי וירושלמי אמר שעשה ר' אמי מעשה כזה: **שמע** מינה קטן אוכל נבלות בית דין מצווין עליו להפרישו. נ"ל דמוקי מתניתין כרבי יהודה דאמר מלאכה שאינה צריכה לגופה חייב עליה או כר"ש וכשצריך לאותו כיבוי כגון לעשות פחמין דבאיסורא דרבנן מוכח בפרק חרש (יבמות קיד.) דאין ב"ד מצווין להפרישו ונראה דמיירי בקטן שלא הגיע לחינוך דבהגיע לחינוך כיון שחייב לחנכו כ"ש דצריך להפרישו שלא יעשה עבירה וכל הנהו דפריך ביבמות הוה מצי לשנויי כשהגיע לחינוך אלא דניחא ליה לאוקמי בכל ענין והא דבעי לאיתויי התם דאין ב"ד מצווין להפרישו מדקתני תינוק יונק והולך וקתני ובגדול אסור משמע דוקא גדול אבל קטן אפי' בהגיע לחינוך שרי התם ע"כ גדול לאו דוקא בר עונשין דהא במסקנא מפרש טעמא משום דסתם תינוק מסוכן הוא אצל חלב והאי טעמא לא שייך אלא בבן שתים או שלש שנים:

הגהות הב"ח

(א) רש"י ד"ה הזב והזבה והמצורע וכו' וטעמא מפרש בפ"ב דמגילה: (ב) ד"ה בעל קרי וכו' אוכל טהרות הס"ד ותיבות לבו ביום נמחק:

גליון הש"ס

רש"י ד"ה אין אומרים לו וכו' אמירה לנכרי משום שבות. עי' ע"ז דף טו ע"א ברש"י ד"ה נכי לגרעינהו: תוס' ד"ה הכי וכו' שרי לטבול כדמשמע. ע"ל דף קיא ע"א תוס' ד"ה לא ס"ד:

רב נסים גאון

ההיא ר' יוסי בר' יהודה היא דתניא ר' יוסי בר' יהודה אומר דייה לטבילה באחרונה משכחת לה במס' נדה בפרק המפלת (דף כט):

ליקוטי רש"י

טבילה בזמנה מצוה. דכתיב (במדבר יט) וטהר ביום השביעי וכבס בגדיו ורחץ במים...

רבינו חננאל

גרם מחיקת שם משום דאמר לך התם עשייה אסור גרמא שרי רבנן בשבת גרמא כמו מלאכת מחשבת היא ואסור. ואע"ג דכתיב לא תעשה כל מלאכה. (כל מלאכה) מדאורייתא עשייה אסורה מיהו גזרו רבנן אפי' גרמא משום דקי"ל אדם בהול על ממונו אי שרית ליה אתי לכבויי. תוב אקשינן דרבנן אדרבנן. התם גרם מחיקת השם מצרכי ליה גמי לח. והכא שרו בגרם כיבוי. ואקשינן עלה האי גמי לח היכי דמי אי דקטר ומיהדק הוא גופיה חייץ בטבילה. ואי לא מיהדק עיילי ביה מיא ומסקי לשם ולא מהני גמי לח לשם שכתוב על בשרו מידי ולא איפרקא הא קושיא. תוב אקשינן עליה ותיפוק ליה דהוי גופיה שהשם כתוב בו שחוצץ. ופרקינן הב"א בדיו לחה שאינו חוצצת. דתניא הדם והדיו והדבש והחלב יבישין חוצצין לחין אין חוצצין. ופרקינן על קושיא הראשונה רבנן דאסרי לטבול עד דכריך על השם גמי לח לאו משום דסבירא להו גרם מחיקת השם אסור דכל גרמא שרי. והכא משום דאסור לעמוד לפני השם ערום מצרכי גמי לח. והיכן דלא צריך אלא לכסויי השם וממילא ידעינן שאין מהדק הגמי לח ולא איכפת ליה אי עיילי מיא דלא חייש לגרם מחיקה. ואקשינן והא ר' יוסי מתיר לעמוד בפני השם. ושנינן לר' יוסי מכסהו לשם בידו וטובל. אי הכי לרבנן נמי ניכסיה בידיה ונהדרה זה הפירוק. ופרקינן לדברי הכל אסור לעמוד בפני השם ערום. ואי איכא גמי ניכרוכו בו לכרוך על השם ולטבול בזמנה דכ"ע דכריך. כי פליגי היכא דליכא מידי מצוי וצריך להדור ואתרי. ר' יוסי אומר טבילה בזמנה מצוה ואתיא מצוה זו ודחה לעמידת ערום בפני השם וטובל בדלא מיכסי. ורבנן סברי טבילה בזמנה לאו מצוה הלכך לא הדרי

THE MEN OF THE Roman GOVERNOR OF TZIPPORI CAME TO EXTINGUISH it, מִפְּנֵי שֶׁאַפּוֹטְרוֹפּוֹס שֶׁל מֶלֶךְ הָיָה – BECAUSE [YOSEF BEN SIMAI] WAS THE KING'S TREASURER. וְלֹא הִנִּיחָן מִפְּנֵי כְּבוֹד הַשַּׁבָּת – HOWEVER, HE DID NOT ALLOW THEM to do so ON ACCOUNT OF THE HONOR OF THE SABBATH, וְנַעֲשָׂה לוֹ נֵס וְיָרְדוּ גְּשָׁמִים וְכִיבוּ – AND A MIRACLE OCCURRED ON HIS BEHALF AND RAIN FELL AND PUT OUT the fire. לָעֶרֶב שִׁיגֵּר לְכָל אֶחָד מֵהֶן שְׁתֵּי סְלָעִין – THAT NIGHT, after the Sabbath, HE SENT EVERY MEMBER OF [THE GARRISON] TWO *SELAIM*, וְלָאִפַּרְכוֹס שֶׁבָּהֶן חֲמִשִּׁים – AND TO THE LIEUTENANT AMONG THEM he sent FIFTY. וּכְשֶׁשָּׁמְעוּ חֲכָמִים בַּדָּבָר אָמְרוּ – AND WHEN THE SAGES HEARD OF THE MATTER, i.e. that he prevented the garrison from putting out the fire, THEY SAID: לֹא הָיָה צָרִיךְ לְכָךְ – HE DID NOT NEED TO DO THAT, שֶׁהֲרֵי שָׁנִינוּ נָכְרִי שֶׁבָּא לְכַבּוֹת אֵין אוֹמְרִים לוֹ כַּבֵּה וְאַל תְּכַבֶּה – FOR WE HAVE LEARNED IN THE MISHNAH: A GENTILE WHO COMES TO EXTINGUISH the fire, THEY MAY NOT SAY TO HIM, "EXTINGUISH it," NOR do they have to tell him, "DO NOT EXTINGUISH it."[18]

The Gemara cites the end of the Mishnah: אֲבָל קָטָן שֶׁבָּא לְכַבּוֹת אֵין שׁוֹמְעִין לוֹ מִפְּנֵי שֶׁשְּׁבִיתָתוֹ עֲלֵיהֶן – HOWEVER, A MINOR WHO COMES TO EXTINGUISH the fire, THEY MAY NOT LISTEN TO HIM, BECAUSE HIS RESTING IS THEIR RESPONSIBILITY.

The Gemara asks:

שְׁמַעַתְּ מִינַּהּ – **Shall we conclude from this** ruling קָטָן אוֹכֵל נְבֵלוֹת – that **if a minor is** discovered **eating *neveilah*** meat,[19] בֵּית דִּין מְצוּוִּין עָלָיו לְהַפְרִישׁוֹ – **the court is enjoined to separate him** from continuing?[20]

The Gemara responds with a new explanation of the Mishnah: אָמַר רַבִּי יוֹחָנָן – **R' Yochanan said:** There is no proof, because the Mishnah is dealing בְּקָטָן הָעוֹשֶׂה לְדַעַת אָבִיו – **with a minor who acts on behalf of his father's interest.**[21] We need not deter the minor, however, if he is pursuing his own interests.[22]

The Gemara questions this explanation:

דִּכְוָותָהּ גַּבֵּי נָכְרִי – **Now, the parallel** case to that one **regarding the gentile** דְּקָא עָבֵיד לְדַעְתֵּיהּ דְּיִשְׂרָאֵל – **is where he is acting on behalf of the Jew's interest.** מִי שָׁרֵי – But **is it permitted** to allow the gentile to extinguish the fire in such a situation?[23]

The Gemara replies:

נָכְרִי לְדַעְתֵּיהּ דְּנַפְשֵׁיהּ עָבֵיד – **A gentile** always **acts in his own self-interest.**[24]

Mishnah

כּוֹפִין קְעָרָה עַל גַּבֵּי הַנֵּר – **We may invert a bowl over a lamp** בִּשְׁבִיל שֶׁלֹּא תֶּאֱחוֹז בְּקוֹרָה – **in order that it** [i.e. the flame] **not catch onto the beam** that is on top of the lamp,[25] provided that one does not thereby extinguish the flame.[26] וְעַל צוֹאָה שֶׁל קָטָן – **And** one may invert a bowl **over the feces of a child;** וְעַל עַקְרָב שֶׁלֹּא תִּישֹׁךְ – **or over a scorpion so that it not sting.**[27] אָמַר רַבִּי יְהוּדָה – **R' Yehudah said:**

NOTES

18. Since the garrison acted of its own accord, he did not have to restrain them.

For suggestions as to the rationale for Yosef ben Simai's action, see *Rashba* to 122a ד"ה רבא אמר and *Maharsha* here.

19. *Neveilah* is the name given to an animal that died without having been ritually slaughtered. Its meat may not be eaten.

20. A minor himself is exempt from the observance of the commandments of the Torah. Nevertheless, it would seem from the fact that the Mishnah bids us to prevent a minor from extinguishing the fire that *we* ("the court") are charged with preventing him from transgressing. This conflicts with a ruling recorded in *Yevamos* 113b-114a, where the following incident is related: Rav Yitzchak bar Bisna lost the keys to the *beis hamidrash* in the *reshus harabim*. Since it was the Sabbath, he was not allowed to retrieve them. He presented the problem before another Amora, who advised him to take some little children to that area, without telling them about the lost keys, and have them play there. If they find the keys, they will bring them back on their own.

Clearly, this Amora maintains that one is not obligated to deter a child from desecrating the Sabbath. How would that Amora understand our Mishnah, which seems to teach the reverse? (*Rashi*).

[*Rashi* identifies this Amora as R' Yochanan; however in our version of the passage in *Yevamos* he is R' Pedas (see *Mesoras HaShas*).]

21. I.e. the child looks at his father who is standing over him, discerns that it is his father's wish that he extinguish the fire, and does so on his behalf. In this circumstance, it is as if the father has instructed him to extinguish (*Rashi* here and to *Yevamos* 114a ד"ה בעושה על דעת אביו).

[The exact prohibition violated by the father in this case is the subject of considerable discussion. Some assert that the tacit approval of the father is a form of "feeding" the child a forbidden thing, which is Biblically prohibited as derived by the Gemara in *Yevamos* 114a (לֹא תַאֲכִילוּם). If so, the same prohibition would apply even where the child extinguishes the fire for someone other than his father, and the Gemara would be understood as mentioning the father only because this is the usual case (*She'eilos U'Teshuvos Achiezer* vol. 3 81:25; see also *Shaar HaTziyun* 334:54 and *Beur Halachah* 266 ד"ה הגה). Other commentators indicate that the Gemara means specifically the father, and refers to the prohibition stated in *Exodus* 20:10: לֹא־תַעֲשֶׂה כָל־מְלָאכָה אַתָּה וּבִנְךָ, *you shall not do any work, you, your son* . . . (see *Rashi* ad loc.; *Rashba* below, 153b ד"ה כשהיא מהלכת; see also *Achiezer* ibid. 81:23 at length).]

22. Such as in the incident in *Yevamos*, where Rav Yitzchak did not tell the children that he had lost the keys, and they therefore did not realize that he would be pleased if they brought them back (*Rashi* to *Yevamos* ibid.).

23. The Mishnah draws a distinction between a gentile and a minor, everything else being equal. Both the minor and the gentile, then, can discern that the act of extinguishment fulfills the wishes of the person standing over them. Why must we stop a child from performing a prohibited act that benefits us, but not a gentile, since a gentile too may not be allowed to perform *melachah* for a Jew?

24. Even if he is aware that his deed benefits the Jew, he acts with his own interest in mind, because he knows that the Jew will reward him. Thus, the Jew need not stop him from extinguishing (*Rashi*).

25. *Rashi* explains that the bowl is an *earthenware* bowl. [A metal bowl, however, may not be used for this purpose, since placing it over a flame would constitute a *melachah* of הַבְעָרָה, *kindling* [should the metal become heated until it glows] (see *Mishnah Berurah* 277:22, from *Rambam, Hil. Shabbos* 12:1; see *Raavad, Maggid Mishneh* and *Lechem Mishneh* ad loc.).]

This Mishnah, which permits moving the bowl to protect the beam, seems to contradict the Amora R' Yitzchak, who holds (above, 43a) that a utensil may not be moved on the Sabbath for the sake of something that may *not* be moved on the Sabbath (such as the beam of a house). The Gemara there answers, though, that R' Yitzchak will explain our Mishnah as referring to where one wished to move the utensil for some permitted purpose; and since he is moving the utensil in any event, he may tailor its movement for the sake of the beam, which may not be moved (*Rashi*). [See *Sfas Emes* to 121b ד"ה בגמ' והלא היא עצמה, who seeks to explain the novelty taught by this ruling of the Tanna. However, that explanation, though it parallels *Rashi's* own explanation of a similar ruling on 128b (ד"ה כופין סל), is not without difficulty (as pointed out in the bracketed addition of *Sfas Emes'* son-in-law), and is also not suggested by *Rashi's* comments here.]

26. *Rashi*. [That is, one must cover the lamp in such a way that the air supply is not completely cut off, so that the flame is not smothered (*Matteh Yehudah*, cited in *Shaar HaTziyun* 277:26).]

27. This Tanna permits inverting the bowl over the scorpion even though he is thereby *trapping* it, which should constitute an *av melachah*.

There is a Tannaic dispute whether a *melachah* that is done for something other than its defined purpose [מְלָאכָה שֶׁאֵינָהּ צְרִיכָה לְגוּפָהּ] is Biblically forbidden (see 121b et al.). [See above, 93b note 34, where we have presented the dispute between *Rashi* and *Tosafos* regarding what constitutes a *melachah's* "defined purpose."] In the present case, where one is trapping the scorpion in order to keep it away from him, not in order to make use of it, he has done the *melachah* of trapping for a purpose other than its defined one. Apparently, this Tanna holds that

טבילה בזמנה לאו מצוה ומהדרינן ור' יוסי סבר טבילה בזמנה מצוה ולא מהדרינן וסבר ר' יוסי טבילה בזמנה מצוה והתניא [א]הזב והזבה המצורע והמצורעת בועל נדה וטמא מת טבילתן ביום נדה ויולדת טבילתן בלילה בעל קרי טובל והולך כל היום כולו ר' יוסי אומר מן המנחה ולמעלה אינו צריך לטבול ההיא ר' יוסי בר' יהודה היא דאמר דייה טבילה באחרונה: **מתני'** [ב]נכרי שבא לכבות אין אומרים לו כבה ואל תכבה מפני שאין שביתתו עליהן אבל קטן שבא לכבות אין שומעין לו מפני ששביתתו עליהן: **גמ'** א"ר אמי [ג]בדליקה התירו לומר כל המכבה אינו מפסיד נימא מסייע ליה נכרי שבא לכבות אין אומרים לו כבה ואל תכבה מפני שאין שביתתו עליהן כבה הוא דלא אמרינן ליה הא כל המכבה אינו מפסיד אמרינן ליה אימא סיפא אל תכבה לא אמרינן ליה וכל המכבה אינו מפסיד נמי לא אמרינן ליה אלא מהא ליכא למשמע מינה ת"ר מעשה ונפלה דליקה בחצירו של יוסף בן סימאי בשיחין ובאו אנשי גיסטרא של ציפורי לכבות מפני שאפטרופוס של מלך היה ולא הניחן מפני כבוד השבת ונעשה לו נס וירדו גשמים וכיבו לערב שיגר לכל אחד מהן שתי סלעין ולאפרכוס שבהן חמשים וכששמעו חכמים בדבר אמרו לא היה צריך לכך שהרי שנינו נכרי שבא לכבות אין אומרים לו כבה ואל תכבה: אבל [ד]קטן שבא לכבות אין שומעין לו מפני ששביתתו עליהן: שמעת מינה קטן אוכל נבלות ב"ד מצווין עליו להפרישו אמר רבי יוחנן [ה]בקטן העושה לדעת אביו דכוותה גבי נכרי דקא עביד לדעתיה דישראל מי שרי נכרי לדעתיה דנפשיה עביד: **מתני'** [ו]כופין קערה על גבי הנר בשביל שלא תאחוז בקורה ועל צואה של קטן ועל עקרב שלא תישך א"ר יהודה מעשה בא לפני רבן יוחנן בן זכאי בערב ואמר חוששני לו מחטאת: **גמ'** רב יהודה ורב ירמיה בר אבא ורב חנן בר רבא איקלעו לבי אבין דמן נשיקיא לרב יהודה ורב ירמיה בר אבא אייתו

רש"י

טבילה בזמנה מצוה. דכתיב והיה לפנות ערב ירחץ במים (דברים כג): **לאו מצוה.** ואי לא משכח גמי האידנא לישתהי עד למחר ולמ"ד לאו מצוה קרא עצה טובה קמ"ל כדי שיעריב שמשו ביום לאחר טבילה שאם ימתין לטבול עד הלילה לא יהא לו הערב שמש עד ליל המחרת: **הזב והזבה כו'.** ברייתא זו אלל יוה"כ שנויה בתוספתא דיומא (פ"ד): הזב והזבה והמצורע ובועל נדה וטמא מת טובלין ביום. משהאיר המזרח ביום השביעי שלהם וטעמא (א) בפ"ב דמגילה (דף כ.) מקרא דיום השביעי מקצת שביעי ספירה ואם חל שביעי שלהם ביוה"כ טובלין כדרכן לאכול תרומה לערב: **נדה ויולדת.** טובלות כדרכן בלילי יוה"כ אם חל שביעי שלהם בערב יוה"כ שאינה יכולה לטבול ביום ז' דכתיב בנדתה תהיה בהוייתה תהא כל ז' (פסחים דף נ:): **בעל קרי.** שצריך טבילה לדברי תורה מדברי סופרים ואפי' אין (ב) אוכל טהרות לבו ביום: **טובל כל היום כולו.** ואע"פ שראה קרי מן המנחה ולמעלה לאחר שהתפלל תפלת המנחה שהרי הוא יכול להמתין עד שתחשך ויטבול לתפלת ערבית אפ"ה טובל ביו"כ מבעוד יום אע"פ שאסור ברחילת משום דטבילה בזמנה מצוה: **ר' יוסי אומר מן המנחה ולמעלה.** אם ראה קרי לאחר שהתפלל תפלת מנחה שהרי הוא יכול להמתין עד שתחשך ויטבול ויתפלל תפלת ערבית ותפלת נעילה נמי ס"ל שיכול להתפלל בלילה כרב דאמר (יומא דף פז:) תפלת נעילה פוטרת של ערבית: **אין צריך לטבול.** ביום משום זמן טבילה דלאו מצוה טבילה בזמנה: **דייה לטבילה שתהא באחרונה.** במסכת נדה בפרק המפלת גבי אשה שילאה מלאה ובאה ריקנית ואינה יודעת מתי ילדה דמצרכינן לה ל"ה טבילות לספק ד' טבילות שעליה טבילת זכר לז' או טבילת נקבה לשבועיים ובלילה או שמא יולדת זכר בזוב וצריכה אף טבילת זבה ביום שבעה לספורים שלה או יולדת נקבה בזוב היתה ומשום דלא ידעינן מתי ילדה ואימתי מטי זמן טבילה דידה מצרכינן לה טבילה כל לילה וכל יום שיש לספוקי זמן טבילתה ופליג ר' יוסי ברבי יהודה עלה ואמר דייה לטבילה שתהא באחרונה לסוף ספורים של נקבה דהיינו לסוף שלש שבועים שאם ילדה נקבה בזוב טמאה שבועיים ללידתה וז' נקיים בשביל הזיבה ולא אמרינן טבילה בזמנה מצוה: **מתני' אין אומרים לו כבה.** רבנן גזור על אמירה לנכרי משום שבות: **ולא תכבה.** אין צריך למחות בידו אלא יניחנו ויכבה: **שאין שביתתו.** של נכרי עליהן דישראל אינו מוזהר על שביתתו של נכרי שאינו עבדו: **גמ' כבה הוא דלא אמרינן ליה.** ועושהו שלוחו ממש: **הא כל המכבה אינו מפסיד כו'.** ונכרי מדעתיה דידיה עביד שריא: **אל תכבה הוא דלא אמרינן ליה.** שאינו צריך למחות בידו ומיהו גילוי דעתא דלא יפסיד בדבר נמי לא משתרי דאי גילוי דעתא שרי למה ליה למיתני סיפא אין צריך למחות: **אלא מהכא ליכא למשמע מיניה.** דודאי מתניתין לאו כולה דוקא אלא חדא מינייהו דוקא או רישא או סיפא ותנא אידך אטו היא ולא ידעינן הי מינייהו דוקא דנגמר מיניה: **גיסטרא.** שלטון: **אפטרופוס.** ממונה על ממונו: **שמעת מינה קטן אוכל נבילות בית דין מצווין עליו להפרישו.** ותקשי לר' יוחנן דאמר ביבמות (דף קיד.) לרבה בר בר חנה דאירכסו ליה מפתחות של בית המדרש ברשות הרבים בשבת דבר טלי' וטליתא ליטיילי התם דאי משכחי להו מייתי להו: **על דעת אביו.** בקטן שידע להבחין שהכבוי זה נוח לאביו ועושה בשבילו: **נכרי אדעתיה דנפשיה עביד.** ואפילו יודע שנוח לו לישראל הוא להנאת עצמו מתכוין שיודע שלא יפסיד: **מתני' כופין קערה.** על גבי הנר. ובלבד שלא יכבה ואע"פ שנוטל כלי להצלת קורה שאינה ניטלת בשבת הא אותבינן מינה (דף מג.) לרבי יצחק דאמר אין כלי ניטל אלא לדבר הניטל ושנייה בצריך למקומו: **מעשה בא.** כפיית כלי על עקרב: **בערב.** מקום: **חוששני לו מחטאת.** כיון דלא היה עקרב רץ אחריו איני יודע אם חייב משום צידה אם לאו ומשני לומר חייב חטאת הוא: גמ'

תוספות

הכי גרסי' ר' יוסי אומר מן המנחה ולמעלה אינו צריך לטבול. וכן גירסת רש"י ור"ת אבל לא גרסי' אינו יכול לטבול דאפי' מאן דסבר טבילה בזמנה לאו מצוה ° שרי לטבול כדמשמע בסוף מסכת יומא (דף פז:) דפריך לרב דאמר תפלת נעילה פוטרת של ערבית משום דקסבר דתפלת נעילה בלילה והתניא אור יוה"כ כו' נעילה מתפלל שבע ומתודה בערבית כו' ומשני תנאי היא דתניא כל חייבי טבילות טבילתן ביום נדה ויולדת טובלין בלילה בעל קרי טובל והולך עד המנחה דסבר תפלת נעילה בלילה וטבילה בזמנה לאו מצוה ר' יוסי אומר כל היום כולו טובל דתפלת נעילה ביום אלמא אע"ג דת"ק סבר דטבילה בזמנה לאו מצוה אפ"ה קתני כל חייבי טבילות טבילתן ביום אפילו טמא מת וטמא שרץ שאין צריכין טבילה לתפלה יכולין לטבול והא דפירש בקונטרס דר' יוסי כרב דאמר תפלת נעילה בלילה לא דק דבשלהי יומא (דף פח.) פריך מהך ברייתא דר' יוסי אדר"י דהכא קאמר מן המנחה ולמעלה א"צ לטבול ובההיא קאמר כל היום ומשני דהכא איירי בדצלי כבר תפלת נעילה והתם בדלא צלי ובכולהו רבי יוסי דלא כרב:

רבי יוסי בר' יהודה היא. וא"ת א"כ בשילהי יומא (דף פח.) מנא ליה לרב דהוה ת"ק דברייתא קמייתא דקאמר דבעל קרי טובל עד המנחה אתי' כוותיה דתפלת נעילה בלילה דילמא איירי בדצלי וטבילה בזמנה לאו מצוה ור' יוסי סבר מצוה ותנא קמא דהכא הוא ר' יוסי דהתם ויש לומר דסבר דר' יוסי דהכא ודהתם מסתמא חד תנא הוא ותרוייהו רבי יוסי ברבי יהודה דאיירי בטבילת בעל קרי ביו"כ וא"כ קשיא ר' יוסי בר' יהודה אדר' יוסי בר' יהודה וע"כ אית לן לשנויי הא דצלי והא דלא צלי:

אין אומרים לו כבה. אפי' באיסורא דרבנן אמירה לנכרי שבות כדאמרינן לקמן בפרק שואל (דף קנ.) לא יאמר אדם לחבירו שכור לי פועלים כו' דמוקי לה בחברו נכרי וכן מוכח בפרק הדר (דף סו:) גבי נייתי חמימי מגו ביתא:

אלא מהא ליכא למישמע מינה. מ"מ קי"ל כר' אמי ובירושלמי אמר שעשה ר' אמי מעשה כזה:

שמע מינה קטן אוכל נבלות בית דין מצווין עליו להפרישו. נ"ל דמוקי מתניתין כרבי יהודה דאמר מלאכה שאינה צריכה לגופה חייב עליה או כר"ש וכשצריך לאותו כיבוי כגון לעשות פחמין דבאיסורא דרבנן מוכח בפרק חרש (יבמות קיד.) דאין ב"ד מצוין להפרישו ונראה דמיירי בקטן שלא הגיע לחינוך דבהגיע לחינוך כיון שחייב לחנכו כ"ש דצריך להפרישו שלא יעשה עבירה וכל הנהו דפריך ביבמות הוה מצי לשנויי כשהגיע לחינוך אלא דניחא ליה לאוקמי בכל ענין והא דבעי לאיתויי התם דאין ב"ד מצווין להפרישו מדקתני תינוק יונק והולך וקתני ובגדול אסור משמע דוקא גדול אבל קטן אפי' בהגיע לחינוך שרי התם ע"כ גדול לאו דוקא בר עונשין דהא במסקנא מפרש טעמא משום דסתם תינוק מסוכן הוא אצל חלב והאי טעמא לא שייך אלא בבן שתים או שלש שנים:

כל

עין משפט נר מצוה

סט א מיי' פ"א מהלכות מקוואות הלכה ו וסמ"ג מהלכות שביתת עשור הלכה ג ג וטוש"ע או"ח סימן תקנד סעיף ח:

ע ב מיי' פ"ו מהלכות שבת הלכה ז סמג לאוין סה טוש"ע או"ח סימן שלד סעיף כה:

עא ג מיי' פ"ב שם וסמג שם טוש"ע שם סעיף כו:

עב ד ה מיי' פי"ב שם וסמג שם וטוש"ע או"ח סימן שמג סעיף א בהגה"ה:

עג ו מיי' פכ"ה מהלכות שבת הלכה כו סמג לאוין סה טוש"ע או"ח סימן רעז סעיף ג וסימן שלד סעיף כה בהגה"ה:

רבינו חננאל

גרם מחיקת שם משום דאמר לך התם עשייה אסור גרמא שרי רבנן בשבת גרמא כמו מלאכת מחשבת היא ואסור. ואע"ג דכתיב לא תעשה כל מלאכה (דכתב) מדאורייתא עשייה אסורה מיהו גזרו רבנן אפי' גרמא משום דקי"ל אדם בהול על ממונו אי שרית ליה אתי לכבויי. תוב אקשינן דרבנן אדרבנן. התם בגרם מחיקת השם מצרכי ליה גמי לח. והכא שרו בגרם כיבוי. ואקשינן עלה האי גמי לח היכי דמי אי דקטור ומיהדק הוא גופיה חייץ בטבילה. ואי לא מיהדק עייל ביה מיא ומסקי לשם ולא מהני גמי לח לשם שכתוב על בשרו מידי ולא איפרקא הא קושיא. תוב אקשינן עליה ותיפוק ליה דהוה ליה גופיה שהשם כתוב בו שחוצץ. ופריקנן הב"ע בדיו לחה שאינו חוצצת. דתניא הדם והדיו והדבש והחלב יבישין חוצצין לחין אין חוצצין. ופרקי' על קושיא הראשונה רבנן דאסרי לטבול עד דכריך על השם גמי לח לאו משום דסבירא להו גרם מחיקת השם אסור דכל גרמא שרי. והכא משום דאסור לעמוד בפני השם ערום מצרכי גמי לח. וכיון דלא צריך אלא לכסויי השם ומפילו ידעינן שאין מהדק הגמי לח ולא איכפת ליה אי עייל מיא דלא חייש לגרם מחיקה. ואקשינן וכי ר' יוסי מתיר לעמוד בפני השם. ושנינן לר' יוסי מכסהו לשם בידו וטובל. אי הכי לרבנן נמי ניכסיה בידיה ונהדרה זה הפירוק. ופרקינן לדברי הכל אסור לעמוד בפני השם ערום. ואי איכא גמי וכיוצא בו לכרוך על השם ולטבול בזמניה דכ"ע דכריך. כי פליגי היכא דליכא מידי מצוי דצריך להדורי ולאתויי. ר' יוסי אומר טבילה בזמנה מצוה ואתיא מצוה זו ודחה לעמידת ערום בפני השם וטביל בדלא מיכסי (א). ורבנן סברי טבילה בזמנה לאו מצוה הלכך לא הדר.

מסורת הש"ס

א) פסחים נ: יומא ו. פח. ע"ש [תוספתא יומא פ"ד], ב) [ג"ל יבנה וכ"א ביומא פח.], ג) נדה כט: [ודף ל. יומא פח.], ד) יבמות קיד., ה) יבמות קיד., ו) כתובות ע., ז) [ברכות כה: וש"נ], ח) [תוספתא פרק י"ד], ט) [גיטין נה.], י) [לעיל מג. קו.], כ) [לקמן קמו.].

הגהות הב"ח

(א) רש"י ד"ה הזב והזבה והמצורע וכו' וטעמא מפרש בפ"ב דמגילה: (ב) ד"ה בעל קרי וכו' אוכל טהרות הס"ד ואח"כ מה"ד וכו' ואפי' אין אוכל טהרות לבו ביום נמחק:

גליון הש"ס

רש"י ד"ה אין אומרים לו וכו' אמירה לנכרי משום שבות. עי' ע"ז דף טו ע"א ברש"י ד"ה הא לצריכיה: תוס' ד"ה הכי גרסי' שרי לטבול כדמשמע. ע"ל דף קיא ע"א תוס' ד"ה לא קי:

רב נסים גאון

ההיא ר' יוסי בר' יהודה היא דתניא ר' יוסי בר' יהודה אומר דייה לטבילה באחרונה משכחת לה במס' נדה (דף כט) בפרק המפלת: שמעת מינה קטן אוכל נבילות בית דין מצווין עליו

ליקוטי רש"י

טבילה בזמנה מצוה. דכתיב (במדבר יט) ומטהרו ביום השביעי וכבס בגדיו ורחץ במים וטהר בערב...

חשק שלמה על רבינו חננאל: א) נראה דל"ל כאן לא בעי להדורי. ב) לפנינו בגמ' ליתא להך אוקימתא ע"ש.

מַעֲשֶׂה בָּא לִפְנֵי רַבָּן יוֹחָנָן בֶּן זַכַּאי בְּעָרָב – **The incident** of a person who inverted a bowl over a scorpion on the Sabbath **came before Rabban Yochanan ben Zakkai in** the Galilean city of **Arab,**[28] וְאָמַר חוֹשְׁשַׁנִי לוֹ מֵחַטָּאת – **and he said "I fear for him** that he is liable **for a *chatas*,"** for transgressing the *melachah* of *trapping.*[29]

Gemara The Gemara records an incident in which our Mishnah is discussed and explained:

רַב יְהוּדָה וְרַב יִרְמְיָה בַּר אַבָּא וְרַב חָנָן בַּר רָבָא אִיקְּלַעוּ לְבֵי אָבִין דְּמִן נַשִׁיקְיָא – **Rav Yehudah, Rav Yirmiyah bar Abba and Rav Chanan bar Rava visited the home of Avin from Nashikiya.** לְרַב יְהוּדָה וְרַב יִרְמְיָה בַּר אַבָּא – **For Rav Yehudah and Rav Yirmiyah bar Abba**

NOTES

such *melachah* is not Biblically forbidden (see *Tosafos* to 121b ד״ה כל המזיקין). [And though all agree that such *melachah* is forbidden, at any rate, by Rabbinic decree, the Rabbis suspended their decree to allow one to keep dangerous creatures at bay.]

[Alternatively, this Tanna holds that trapping a creature to keep it at bay is a *qualitatively* different act from trapping it for its use, and does not constitute the *melachah* of trapping altogether (see *Mishnah Berurah* 316:27).]

Alternatively, this Tanna holds that a scorpion is not a type of creature usually trapped for its use, and that one is not liable for trapping such creatures (see above, 107b). And though such trapping is nonetheless ordinarily forbidden Rabbinically, the Rabbis did not forbid it in this case [as above] (see *Beur Halachah* to 316:7, end of ד״ה נחשים וכו׳).

28. [Arab was a city in the Galilee where Rabban Yochanan ben Zakkai lived for eighteen years. During this period, he was asked only two questions in halachah, this one and the one mentioned below on 146a. He became incensed at their unconcern regarding the laws of the Torah and declared, "Galilee, O Galilee, how you hate the Torah! You will eventually become olive pickers," i.e. you will remain farmers and no Torah scholars will come forth from you (*Yerushalmi* 16:8 according to *Pnei Moshe*). Others render: You will eventually be overrun by bandits (*Korban HaEidah*).]

29. The scorpion had not been chasing anyone. [Thus, there was no immediate threat to life that would allow the performance of a Biblical *melachah.*] Rabban Yochanan ben Zakkai was therefore uncertain whether or not the fellow had become liable to a *chatas* (see *Rashi*).

[Seemingly, Rabban Yochanan ben Zakkai considers a *melachah* done for something other than its defined purpose (מְלָאכָה שֶׁאֵינָהּ צְרִיכָה לְגוּפָהּ) to be Biblically forbidden (this matter is disputed by the later Tannaim R' Yehudah and R' Shimon – see 121b note 13). Otherwise, he would not have entertained the possibility that the person who trapped the scorpion is liable to a *chatas,* as he did not do so for the defined purpose of making use of the trapped creature. R' Yehudah, who quotes this ruling of Rabban Yochanan ben Zakkai, does so in keeping with his own view that one *is* liable for a *melachah* done not for its defined purpose (see *Meiri*).]

[Possibly, a scorpion is considered an animal that is not usually trapped for its use (see above, note 27), and Rabban Yochanan ben Zakkai was uncertain whether one is liable for trapping such an animal [the issue is a Tannaic dispute above, 107b] (*Beur Halachah* to 316:7, end of ד״ה נחשים וכו׳).]

[R' Yehudah disputes the Tanna Kamma's permit to invert a bowl over a scorpion (that is not chasing anyone), by pointing to Rabban Yochanan ben Zakkai's uncertainty in the matter. If Rabban Yochanan ben Zakkai is concerned for the possibility of a *chatas* in this case, how can you – the Tanna Kamma – permit it outright!? (see *Beur Halachah* loc. cit.). See, however, the commentaries of *Ramaz* and *Hon Ashir,* who explain that R' Yehudah and the Tanna Kamma are not in dispute, but are rather discussing different situations.]

טבילה בזמנה לאו מצוה ומהדרינן ור' יוסי סבר טבילה בזמנה מצוה ולא מהדרינן וסבר ר' יוסי טבילה בזמנה מצוה והתניא הזב והזבה המצורע והמצורעת בועל נדה וטמא מת טבילתן ביום נדה ויולדת טבילתן בלילה בעל קרי טובל והולך כל היום כולו ר' יוסי אומר מן המנחה ולמעלה אינו צריך לטבול ההיא ר' יוסי בר' יהודה היא דאמר דייה טבילה באחרונה: **מתני'** נכרי שבא לכבות אין אומרים לו כבה ואל תכבה מפני שאין שביתתו עליהן אבל קטן שבא לכבות אין שומעין לו מפני ששביתתו עליהן: **גמ'** א"ר אמי בדליקה התירו לומר כל המכבה אינו מפסיד נימא מסייע ליה נכרי שבא לכבות אין אומרים לו כבה ואל תכבה מפני שאין שביתתו עליהן כבה הוא דלא אמרינן ליה הא כל המכבה אינו מפסיד אמרינן ליה אימא סיפא אל תכבה לא אמרינן ליה וכל המכבה אינו מפסיד נמי לא אמרינן ליה אלא מהא ליכא למשמע מינה ת"ר מעשה ונפלה דליקה בחצירו של יוסף בן סימאי בשיחין ובאו אנשי גיסטרא של ציפורי לכבות מפני שאפטרופוס של מלך היה ולא הניחן מפני כבוד השבת ונעשה לו נס וירדו גשמים וכיבו לערב שיגר לכל אחד מהן שתי סלעין ולאפרכוס שבהן חמשים וכששמעו חכמים בדבר אמרו לא היה צריך לכך שהרי שנינו נכרי שבא לכבות אין אומרים לו כבה ואל תכבה: אבל קטן שבא לכבות אין שומעין לו מפני ששביתתו עליהן: שמעת מינה קטן אוכל נבלות ב"ד מצווין עליו להפרישו אמר רבי יוחנן בקטן העושה לדעת אביו דכוותה גבי נכרי דקא עביד לדעתיה דישראל מי שרי נכרי לדעתיה דנפשיה עביד: **מתני'** כופין קערה על גבי הנר בשביל שלא תאחוז בקורה ועל צואה של קטן ועל עקרב שלא תישך א"ר יהודה מעשה בא לפני רבן יוחנן בן זכאי בערב ואמר חוששני לו מחטאת: **גמ'** רב יהודה ורב ירמיה בר אבא ורב חנן בר רבא איקלעו לבי אבין דמן נשיקיא לרב יהודה ורב ירמיה בר אבא אייתו

רש"י

טבילה בזמנה מצוה. דכתיב והיה לפנות ערב ירחץ במים (דברים כג): **לאו מצוה.** ואי לא משכח גמי האידנא לישהי עד למחר ולמ"ד לאו מצוה קרא עלה טובה קמ"ל כדי שיעריב שמשו ביום לאחר טבילה שאם ימתין לטבול עד הלילה לא יהא לו הערב שמש עד ליל המחרת: **הזב והזבה כו'.** ברייתא זו אלל יוה"כ שנויה בתוספתא דיומא (פ"ד): הזב והזבה והמצורע ובועל נדה וטמא מת טובלין ביום. משהאיר המזרח ביום השביעי שלהם וטעמא (א) בפ"ב דמגילה (דף כ.) מקרא דביום השביעי מקלת שביעי ספירה ואם חל שביעי שלהם ביוה"כ טובלין כדרכן לאכול תרומה לערב: **נדה ויולדת.** טובלות כדרכן בלילי יוה"כ אם חל שביעי שלהם בערב יוה"כ שאינה יכולה לטבול ביום ז' דכתיב בה תהיה בנדתה בהוייתה תהא כל ז' (פסחים דף ל:): **בעל קרי.** שצריך טבילה לדברי תורה מדברי סופרים ואפי' אין (ב) אוכל טהרות לבו ביום: **טובל כל היום כולו.** ואע"פ שראה קרי מן המנחה ולמעלה לאחר שהתפלל תפלת המנחה שהרי הוא יכול להמתין עד שתחשך ויטבול לתפלת ערבית אפ"ה טובל ביו"כ מבעוד יום אע"פ שאסור ברחילת הרשות דטבילה בזמנה מצוה: **ר' יוסי אומר מן המנחה ולמעלה.** אם ראה קרי לאחר שהתפלל תפלת מנחה שהרי הוא יכול להמתין עד שתחשך ויטבול ויתפלל תפלת ערבית ותפלת נעילה נמי ס"ל שיכול להתפלל בלילה כרב דאמר (יומא דף פז:) תפלת נעילה פוטרת של ערבית: **אין צריך לטבול.** ביום משום זמן טבילה דלאו מצוה לטבילה בזמנה: **דייה לטבילה שתהא באחרונה.** במסכת נדה בפרק המפלת גבי אשה שיצאה מלאה ובאה ריקנית ואינה יודעת מתי ילדה דמצרכינן לה צ"ה טבילות לספק ד' טבילות שעליה טבילת זכר לז' או טבילת נקבה לשבועיים ובלילה או שמא יולדת זכר בזוב וצריכה אף טבילת זבה ביום שבעה לספורים שלה או יולדת נקבה בזוב היתה ומשום דלא ידעינן מתי ילדה ואימתי מטי זמן טבילה דידה מצרכינן לה טבילה כל לילה וכל יום שיש לספוקי בזמן טבילתה ופליג ר' יוסי ברבי יהודה עלה ואמר דייה לטבילה שתהא באחרונה לסוף ספורים של נקבה דהיינו לסוף שלש שבועים שאם ילדה נקבה בזוב טמאה שבועיים ללידתה וז' נקיים בשביל הזיבה ולא אמרינן טבילה בזמנה מצוה: **מתני' אין אומרים לו כבה.** רבנן גזור על ° אמירה לנכרי משום שבות: **ולא תכבה.** אין צריך למחות בידו אלא יניחנו ויכבה: **שאין שביתתו.** של נכרי עליהן דישראל אינו מוזהר על שביתתו של נכרי שאינו עבדו: **גמ' כבה הוא דלא אמרינן ליה.** שעושהו שלוחו ממש: **הא כל המכבה אינו מפסיד כו'.** ונכרי מדעתיה דידיה עביד שריא: **אל תכבה הוא דלא אמרינן ליה.** שאינו צריך למחות בידו ומיהו גילוי דעתא דלא יפסיד בדבר נמי לא משתרי דאי גילוי דעתא שרי למה ליה למיתני סיפא אין צריך למחות: **אלא מהכא ליכא למישמע מיניה.** דודאי מתניתין לאו כולה דוקא אלא חדא מינייהו דוקא או רישא או סיפא ותנא אידך אטו ההיא ולא ידעינן הי מינייהו דוקא דנגמר מיניה: **גיסטרא.** שלטון: **אפטרופוס.** ממונה על ממונו: **שמעת מינה קטן אוכל נבילות בית דין מצווין להפרישו.** ותקשי לר' יוחנן דאמר ביבמות (דף קיד.) לרבה בר בר חנה דאירכסו ליה מפתחות של בית המדרש ברשות הרבים בשבת דבר טלי' וטליא ליטיילי התם דאי משכחי להו מייתי להו: **על דעת אביו.** בקטן שידע להבחין שהכבוי זה נוח לאביו ועושה בשבילו. ואפילו יודע שנוח לו לישראל הוא להנאת עצמו מתכוין שידע שלא יפסיד: **מתני' כופין קערה.** של חרס: **על גבי הנר.** ובלבד שלא יכבה ואע"פ שנוטל כלי להצלת קורה שאינה ניטלת בשבת הא אותבינן מינה (דף מג.) לרבי יצחק דאמר אין כלי ניטל אלא לדבר הניטל ושנייה בצריך למקומו: **מעשה בא.** כפיית כלי על עקרב: **בערב.** מקום: **חוששני לו מחטאת.** כיון דלא היה עקרב רץ אחריו איני יודע אם חייב משום צידה אם לאו וחוששני לומר חייב חטאת הוא:

גמ'

תוספות

הכי גרסי' ר' יוסי אומר מן המנחה ולמעלה אינו צריך לטבול. וכן גירסת רש"י ור"ת אבל לא גרסי' אינו יכול לטבול דאפי' מאן דסבר טבילה בזמנה לאו מצוה ° שרי לטבול כדמשמע בסוף מסכת יומא (דף פז:) דפריך לרב דאמר תפלת נעילה פוטרת של ערבית משום דקסבר דתפלת נעילה בלילה והתניא אור יוה"כ כו' נעילה מתפלל שבע ומתודה בערבית כו' ומשני תנאי היא דתניא כל חייבי טבילות טבילתן ביום נדה ויולדת טובלין בלילה בעל קרי טובל והולך עד המנחה דסבר תפלת נעילה בלילה וטבילה בזמנה לאו מצוה ר' יוסי אומר כל היום כולו טובל דתפלת נעילה ביום אלמא אע"ג דת"ק סבר דטבילה בזמנה לאו מצוה אפ"ה קתני כל חייבי טבילות טבילתן ביום אפילו טמא מת וטמא שרץ שאין צריכין טבילה לתפלה יכולין לטבול והא דפירש בקונטרס דר' יוסי כרב דאמר תפלת נעילה בלילה לא דק דבשלהי יומא (דף פח.) פריך מהך ברייתא דר' יוסי אדר"י דהכא קאמר מן המנחה ולמעלה א"צ לטבול ובההיא קאמר כל היום ומשני דהכא איירי בדצלי כבר תפלת נעילה והתם בדלא צלי ובכולהו רבי יוסי דלא כרב: **רבי** יוסי בר' יהודה היא. וא"ת א"כ בשילהי יומא (דף פח.) מנא ליה לרב דההוא ת"ק דברייתא קמייתא דקאמר דבעל קרי טובל עד המנחה אתי' כוותיה דתפלת נעילה בלילה דילמא איירי בדצלי וטבילה בזמנה לאו מצוה ור' יוסי סבר מצוה ותנא קמא דהכא הוא ר' יוסי דהתם וי"ל דסבר דר' יוסי דהכא ודהתם מסתמא חד תנא הוא ותרוייהו רבי יוסי ברבי יהודה דאיירי בטבילת בעל קרי ביו"כ וא"כ קשיא ר' יוסי בר' יהודה אדר' יוסי בר' יהודה וע"כ אית לן לשנויי הא דצלי והא דלא צלי: **אין** אומרים לו כבה. אפי' באיסורא דרבנן אמירה לנכרי שבות כדאמרינן לקמן בפרק שואל (דף קנ.) לא יאמר אדם לחבירו שכור לי פועלים כו' דמוקי לה בחברו נכרי וכן מוכח בפרק הדר (דף סז:) גבי נייתי חמימי מגו ביתא: **אלא** מהא ליכא למישמע מינה. מ"מ קי"ל כר' אמי וירושלמי אמר שעשה ר' אמי מעשה כזה: **שמע** מינה קטן אוכל נבלות בית דין מצווין עליו להפרישו. נ"ל דמוקי מתניתין כרבי יהודה דאמר מלאכה שאינה צריכה לגופה חייב עליה או כר"ש וכשצריך לאותו כיבוי כגון לעשות פחמין דבאיסורא דרבנן מוכח בפרק חרש (יבמות קיד.) דאין ב"ד מצווין להפרישו ונראה דמיירי בקטן שלא הגיע לחינוך דהגיע לחינוך כיון שחייב לחנכו כ"ש דצריך להפרישו שלא יעשה עבירה וכל הנהו דפריך ביבמות הוה מצי לשנויי כשהגיע לחינוך אלא דניחא ליה לאוקמי בכל ענין והא דבעי לאיתויי התם דאין ב"ד מצווין להפרישו מדקתני תינוק יונק והולך וקתני ובגדול אסור משמע דוקא גדול אבל קטן אפי' בהגיע לחינוך שרי התם ע"כ גדול לאו דוקא בר עונשין דהא במסקנא מפרש טעמא משום דסתם תינוק מסוכן הוא אצל חלב והאי טעמא לא שייך אלא בבן שתים או שלש שנים:

כל

הגהות הב"ח

(א) רש"י ד"ה הזב והזבה והמצורע וכו' וטעמא כדמפרש בפ"ב דמגילה: (ב) ד"ה בעל קרי וכו' אוכל טהרות הס"ד ואח"כ מה"ד לבו ביום נמחק:

גליון הש"ס

רש"י ד"ה אין אומרים לו וכו' אמירה לנכרי משום שבות. עי' ע"ז דף טו ע"א ברש"י ד"ה נהי לגרמיה: תוס' ד"ה הא כו' שרי לטבול כדמשמע. ע"ל דף קיא ע"א תוס' ד"ה מ"ד:

רב נסים גאון

ההיא ר' יוסי בר' יהודה היא דתניא ר' יוסי בר' יהודה אומר דייה לטבילה באחרונה משכחת לה במס' נדה (דף כט) בפרק המפלה. שמעת מינה קטן אוכל נבלות בית דין מצווין עליו

ליקוטי רש"י

רבינו חננאל

חשק שלמה על רבינו חננאל

עד א מיי' פ"ה מהלכות י"ט הלכה יד טוש"ע או"ח סימן שח סעיף טו:
עה ב ג מיי' פכ"ו מהל' שבת הלכה יג סמג לאוין סה טוש"ע או"ח סימן שח סעיף לד:
עו ד ה מיי' פי"א שם הלכה ד סמג שם טור שו"ע או"ח סימן שטז סעיף י:
עז ו מיי' פכ"ב שם הלכה ג ופכ"ו הלכה יג סמג שם טור שו"ע או"ח שם סעיף יא:
עח ז ח מיי' פי"א מהלכות שבת הל"ד סמג שם טור שו"ע שם סעיף י:
עט ט מיי' פכ"ו מהל' שבת הלכה יא סמג שם טור שו"ע או"ח סימן רעט סעיף ז:

כל המזיקין נהרגין בשבת. אף על גב דתנן במתניתין ועל עקרב שלא ישוך איצטריך לאשמעינן דהריגה נמי שרינן דסלקא דעתך דאסירא משום דמיפרסמא מילתא טפי מצלידה ומהאי טעמא נמי פליג רב הונא בסמוך ואסר הריגה:

ברצין אחריו וד"ה. פי' בקונט' דרבי יהושע בן לוי ברצין אחריו והוי פקוח נפש וברייתא באין רצין וכר"ש וקשה דא"כ תקשה מהך ברייתא לרבא בר רב הונא דשרי להרוג נחשים ועקרבים בשבת דע"כ באין רצין אחריו איירי דאי ברצין אחריו אמאי אין רוח חסידים נוחה הימנו לפירוש הקונטרס דברצין אחריו איכא פקוח נפש ועוד בניותי שהרג נחש ומיבעיא לן אי שפיר עבד תיפשוט מהכא דלא שרינן לר"ש באין רצין אלא ה' בלבד ועוד קשה לר"י דלישנא דהנא מתרצנא לה משמע לברייתא עצמה ונראה לר"י לפרש דברייתא ברצין אחריו וד"ה פירוש אפילו ר' יהודה מודה דחמשה שרי להרוג ברצין אחריו אבל שאר אסור להורגן אפילו רצין אחריו לר' יהודה ור' יהושע בן לוי כר"ש דשרי שאר (א) אפילו באין רצין אחריו ורב הונא דאסר בסמוך לא סבר כרבי יהושע בן לוי ונראה לר"י וכן פירש ר"ח שאין להקל כרבי יהושע בן לוי אלא כהנהו אמוראי דלקמן דלא שרו אלא בדריסה לפי תומו:

גמ' אייתו להו פורייתא. מטות לישב עליהן: לא אייתו ליה. והושיבוהו לארץ: מפני קטן. שלא יטפח בו ויתלכלך: א"ל. רב חנן שהיה כעוס ומתכוין להקניטו לר' אבין: והלא מוכנת לכלבים. ולמה לי לכפות כלי יפנוה משם שהרי ראויה לטלטל: דלא חזיא מאתמול. שהיום נולדה: נהרות המושכים כרגלי כל אדם. משום דמידי דנייד הוא ולא קני שביתה ואע"פ שבא מחוץ לתחום כל אדם מוליכן למקום שירצה ליכך מיהו שמעינן מינה דמותרין בטלטול ואע"ג דמאתמול לא הוי הני קמן כיון דלאורחייהו בהכי דעתיה עלייהו ה"נ כיון דלאורחיה דקטן בהכי דעתיה עליה לכלי מיתי יאכילנה לכלבים: א"ל ר' אבין. ואלא היכי אתנייה: צואה של תרנגולים. דלא חזיא לכלבים ושל קטן דקתני מתניתין שמטפח בה קטן קאמר ובשביל הקטן אמר כופין: תיפוק ליה דגרף של רעי הוא. דמאיס ולפנייה דהא קי"ל במסכת ביצה גרף של רעי מותר להוציאו לאשפה: וכי תימא גרף של רעי דמותר אגב מנא אין. הא דקי"ל מותר להוציאו משום דדמי במנא דגרף היינו כלי חרס העשוי לכך ואגב מנא הוא דשרי לטלטולי אבל בפני עצמו לא והכא לאו במנא רמי: באספרמקי. בשמים: בצוציתיה. זונבו שלמה בלאו מנא נמי מטלטלי ליה: ומשני באשפה. דלא רמי קמייהו ולא גרף של רעי הוא: קטן באשפה מאי בעי. התם הוא ומאי בעי קטן התם דקא מיכסי ליה בשביל קטן: ומשני בחצר. דשכיח קטן התם קס"ד בחצר דלאו אשפה וקפריך סוף סוף גרף של רעי הוא ומשני באשפה שבחצר: כל המזיקין. ההורגין: נהרגין בשבת. וקס"ד אפי' אין רצין אחריו ומשום דס"ל כר"ש דמלאכה שאינה צריכה לגופה מדרבנן הוא דאסירא והכא לא גזור: (נהרגין בשבת. אפי' אין רצין אחריו) משום דס"ל דסתמן הורגין הן: האמר חייב עליה. והיכי שרי במלאכה גמורה כשאין רצין אחריו דליכא פקוח נפש: ומאן לימא לן כו'. דרב יוסף הוא מתני ליה כדלקמן ולא בדבי ר' חייא ור' אושעיא מיתנייא וכל מתניתא דלא מתנייא בתוספתא דר' חייא ור' אושעיא איכא לספוקי במשבשתא ולא מותבינן מינה: אנא תנינא לה. במתניתא דידי ואנא אותבינא בבי מדרשא אדר' יהושע בן לוי: ואנא מתרצנא לה. דלא תיקשי

אייתו להו פורייתא לרב חנן בר רבא לא אייתו ליה אשכחיה מתני ליה לבריה ועל צואה של קטן מפני קטן א"ל אבין שטיא מתני שטותא לבניה ° והלא היא עצמה מוכנת לכלבים וכ"ת דלא חזיא ליה מאתמול א) והתניא א נהרות המושכין ומעיינות הנובעין הרי הן כרגלי כל אדם ואלא היכי אתנייה אימא ב על צואה של תרנגולים מפני קטן ותיפוק ליה דהוי גרף של רעי וכ"ת גרף של רעי אגב מנא אין איהו גופיה לא ג והא ב) ההוא עכבר דאישתכח באיספרמקי דרב אשי ואמר להו נקוטו בצוציתיה ואפקוה באשפה וקטן באשפה מאי בעי ליה בחצר חצר נמי גרף של רעי הוא [א] באשפה שבחצר: ועל עקרב שלא תישך: א"ר יהושע בן לוי כל המזיקין נהרגין בשבת מתיב רב יוסף ד חמשה נהרגין בשבת ואלו הן זבוב שבארץ מצרים וצירעה שבנינוה ועקרב שבחדייב ונחש שבא"י וכלב שוטה בכל מקום מני אילימא ג) ר' יהודה הא אמר מלאכה שאינה צריכה לגופה חייב עליה אלא לאו ר"ש והני הוא דשרי אחריני לא אמר ר' ירמיה ד) ומאן נימא לן דהא מתרצתא היא דילמא משבשתא היא אמר רב יוסף אנא מתנינא לה ואותיבנא לה ואנא מתריצנא לה ה ברצו אחריו ודברי הכל תני תנא קמיה דרבא בר רב הונא ההורג נחשים ועקרבים בשבת אין רוח חסידים נוחה הימנו א"ל ואותן חסידים אין רוח חכמים נוחה מהם ופליגא דרב הונא דרב הונא חזייה לההוא גברא דקא קטיל זיבורא א"ל שלימתינהו לכולהו ת"ר נזדמנו לו נחשים ועקרבים ו הרגן בידוע שנזדמנו לו להורגן לא הרגן בידוע שנזדמנו להורגו ונעשה לו נס מן השמים אמר עולא ואיתימא רבה בר בר חנה א"ר יוחנן בנישופין בו א"ר אבא בר כהנא פעם אחת נפל אחד בבהמ"ד ועמד ניותי אחד והרגו אמר רבי פגע בו כיוצא בו איבעיא להו פגע בו כיוצא בו דשפיר עביד או לא ת"ש דר' אבא בריה דר' חייא בר אבא ור' זירא הוו יתבי אקילעא דבי ר' ינאי נפק מילתא מבינייהו בעו מיניה מר' ינאי מהו להרוג נחשים ועקרבים בשבת אמר להו צירעה אני הורג נחש ועקרב לא כ"ש דילמא לפי תומו דאמר רב יהודה י רוק דורסו לפי תומו ואמר רב ששת ז נחש דורסו לפי תומו ואמר רב קטינא ח עקרב דורסו לפי תומו ו) אבא בר מרתא דהוא אבא בר מניומי הוה מסקי ביה דבי ריש גלותא זוזי אייתיוהו קא מצערא ליה הוה שדי רוקא אמר להו ריש גלותא אייתו מאנא סחיפו עליה אמר להו לא צריכתו הכי א"ר יהודה רוק דורסו לפי תומו אמר להו צורבא מרבנן הוא שבקוהו ז) אמר ר' אבא בר כהנא א"ר חנינא ט פמוטות של בית רבי מותר לטלטל בשבת א"ל ר' זירא בניטלין בידו אחת או בשתי ידים

כי אמר ר' יהושע בן לוי כל המזיקין נהרגין ברצין אחריו קאמר דפקוח נפש הוא: ודברי הכל. ואפי' לר' יהודה והא דחמשה נהרגין כשאין רצין אחריו ור' שמעון: אין רוח חסידים נוחה הימנו. דעתן של חסידים אינה מעורבת עמו שאין הגון בעיניהם על מה שעשה: נוחה. עריבה אין מתרצין במעשיו: אמר ליה. רבא לתנא: ואותן חסידים. השונאין אותו על כך אין רוח חכמים עריבה עמהם להיות נוחה ומיושבת במה שרואין במדת חסידים הללו דשפיר עביד דאי לא מזיקין השתא סופן להזיק בשעת כעסן: שלימתינהו לכולהו. הרגת את כולן כלומר מה אהני בהא אהכי טובא איכא אלמא לאו שפיר עבד והא דרבא פליג אדאבוה: שנזדמנו לו להורגן. לכך באו לידו שזימן לו המקום לאבדן לפי שהיו עתידות להזיק וגלגלו זכות על ידי זכאי: לא הרגן בידוע שנזדמנו לו להרוג אותו. והראה לו הקב"ה שחטא אלא שנעשה לו נס: בנישופין בו. בכה"ג קתני בידוע שנזדמנו להורגו נישופין כן דרך הנחש עושה כעין שריקה כשהוא רואה שונאו וכועס: ניותי. על שם מקומו וישראל היה: דשפיר עביד. וכיוצא בו דקאמר לאו לגנאי הוא אלא הנחש רודף ונעשה זה כיוצא בו: או לא. וכיוצא בו דקאמר לגנאי הוא: צרעה אני הורג. בשבת לכלות מזיקין ואף על פי שאינה מועדת כאלו: לא כל שכן. אלמא שפיר עביד: דילמא לפי תומו. לא שיעמוד עליו ויהרגנו להדיא אלא כשהוא הולך לתומו ונחש או עקרב בפניו אין צריך ליסטט ממנו אלא דורכו והולך ואם מת בדריכתו ימות הואיל ולא נתכוין ° דדבר שאין מתכוין לר' יהודה מדרבנן הוא ולענין מזיקין לא גזור: רוק דורסו לפי תומו. שאין מתכוין למרח ולאשוויי גומות דאף על גב דממילא ממרח הוא כי לא מיכוין שרי משום מאיסותא: הוה שדי רוקא. היה רוק מוטל לפניהם ושבת היתה: פמוטות. מנורות ולא של חוליות היו:

של

אמר [לעיל עג:]. שבכלונו לא תעשה ואינו צריך לעיקר (מחלתה) [תכליתה] כי הכא. ופלוגתייהו בהמצניע (לעיל לג:) גבי מוציא המת במטה חייב ואף על גב דהוצאת המת לא ניחא ליה ביה ור' שמעון פוטר [שם יב.]. חייב עליה. דמשום דאינה צריכה לגופה לא מיפטר הואיל וצריכה לדבר אחר מלאכת מחשבת הוא [שם לא:]. אלא ר"ש. דהוי מלאכה שאינה צריכה לגופה וכל מלאכה שאינה צריכה (לגופה) אלא לסלקה מעליו הוי מלאכה שאינה צריכה לגופה דברצונו לא באה לו ולא היה צריך לה הלכך לאו מלאכת מחשבת היא לר' שמעון [שם צג:]. ומאן נימא לן דהא מתרצתא וכו'. רבי חייא ורבי אושעיא סדרו את הברייתות ודקדקו בדברי כל חכם לומר כמו שאמר אבל יש תנאים הרבה שמוסיפים על משנתם בדדמי [חולין קמא.] ואמרינן (חולין קמא.) כל מתניתא דלא מיתנייא בי רבי חייא ורבי אושעיא לא תותבו מינה בבי מדרשא [ב"מ פה:]. אין רוח חכמים נוחה מהם. אין דעת חכמים נוחה עליהם במעשיו כלומר אין מחזיקין לו טובה [קידושין יז:]. אין רוח חכמה וחסידים ע"ש בגה"ש]. אין נחת רוח לחכמי ישראל במעשיו של זה אין דעתם נוחה עליהם הימנו על ידו [ב"מ מח.]. בנישופין בו. כשהנחש בא לנשוך הוא נושף כמין שריקה [בראשית ג, טו]. אקילעא. כניסת הבית חדר שלפני הטרקלין שקורין פורטיו"ז בלע"ז [ברכות כב:]. לפני הבית כעין בית שער וקורין פורטי"ק [שם מה:]. פמוטות. מנורה של מתכת [לעיל מד.]. בניטלין בידו אחת. בשתי ידים אסור לטלטלה דלאו לטלטולי עבידא דאדם קובע לה מקום [שם מה:].

מסורת הש"ס

א) ביצה לט. עירובין מו. מח. [תוספתא ביצה פ"ד], ב) ביצה לו:, ג) [לעיל עג: ושי"נ], ד) [פסחים לט:], ה) [גי' הרי"ף והרא"ש בשבת], ו) [יומא פד. יבמות קכ.], ז) [נ"ל ואמר].

הגהות הב"ח

(א) תוס' ד"ה ברצין וכו' כר"ש דשרי שאר מזיקין אפילו:

הגהות הגר"א

[א] גמרא באשפה שבחצר כו'. נ"ב גירסת הרי"ף בחצר אחרת.

רב נסים גאון

להפרישו מאי דשקלינן וטרינן בהא מילתא איתא במס' יבמות (דף קיד) בפרק חרש שנשא פיקחת: סוף סוף גרף של רעי הוא ונפקיה כבר פירשנו בפרק כירה כי עיקר השמועה שיש בה התרת זה הדבר בפרק משילין פירות (ביצה דף לו): ר' יהודה אומר כל מלאכה שאינה צריכה לגופה חייב עליה כבר פירשנו בפרק יציאות השבת ואמרנו כי עיקרה הן דברי ר' יהודה שאמרם כאן בזו המשנה מעשה בא לפני

ליקוטי רש"י

נהרות המושכין. היינו מים הנובעים שיש להם משך ולא נחתכו ממקום מקור נביעתן. ומעיינות הנובעין. ואין יוצאין מגבולות גבולין לימשך הלאה. הרי הן כרגלי כל אדם. אין להם שום שביתה כלל ולהכי שקן כרגלי הבעלים ואין מוליכן אלא כל אדם שמוליכן ברגליו הלכך מידי דנייד לית ליה שביתה והכי מפרשינן בעירובין בפרק מי שהוציאוהו [ביצה לט.]. כיון דנייד לא קני שביתה ואפילו הן של יחיד אינן כרגליו [עירובין מו.]. גרף של רעי. דתנא במסכת ביצה (לו:) מותר להוציאו לאשפה שבחצר [לעיל מג.]. שמותר לטלטלו ולפנותו לאשפה משום דמאיס [ביצה לו.]. גרף. כלי חרס המוכן לכך [לעיל שם]. אגב מנא. אין איהו גופיה לא. עמהם דוקא גרף נקט דלאו מנא שרי לטלטל את הרעי אגב מנא אבל בפני עצמו לא [ביצה לו.]. אילימא ר' יהודה. דתנן בפרק המצניע (לעיל צג:) גבי מוציא את המת במטה. מלאכה שאינה צריכה לגופה. כמו מוציא את המת לקברו שאינו צריך לגופו של מת אלא לפנות ביתו ואינו צריך לחפץ זה

גליון הש"ס

גמ' והלא היא עצמה מוכנת לכלבים. ע"ל דף קנ ע"ב תוס' ד"ה טמן: רש"י ד"ה דלמא לפי תומו וכו' דדבר שאין מתכוין דר"י מדרבנן. ע"ל דף מא ע"ב תוס' ד"ה מיחם:

רבינו חננאל

ביומא ליתעכבב עד לאורתא ולטבול. ומסקינן משום דסברי רבנן אע"ג דצלי ליה טבילה בזמנה מצוה ור' יוסי סבר טבילה בזמנה לאו מצוה היא ואי האי ר' יוסי בר' יהודה דגרסינן בנדה פרק המפלת בענין טועה. ר' יוסי בר"י אומר דייה לטבול באחרונה דקסבר טבילה בזמנה לאו מצוה היא. וזה רבי יוסי דהיה (אומר) שם כתוב על בשרו. אסיקנא בגמרא דשבת ימים (ביומא דף ח) דבטבילה בזמנה מצוה פליגי ונתבררה בסוף יום הכפורים דהא לר' יוסי בר' יהודה היא ואיכא אחריתי התם לר' יוסי דאמר כל היום כולו כשר לטבילה. דאלמא סבר טבילה בזמנה [מצוה] היא: א"ר אמי בדליקה התירו לומר כל המכבה אינו מפסיד. וכן הלכה: נכרי שבא לכבות אין אומרים לו כבה ואל תכבה אלא מניחין אותו. ואין אומרים לו כבה וגם אין מונעין אותו מלכבות. אבל קטן העושה לדעת אין מניחין אותו לכבות: אריב"ל כל המזיקין נהרגין. אסיקנא כשהן רצין אחריו. אבל אין רצין אחריו אין נהרגין אלא אלו בלבד. זבוב שבארץ מצרים. צירעה שבנינוה ועקרב שבחדייב ונחש שבא"י וכלב שוטה בכ"מ. פי' נישופין כדכתיב הוא ישופך ראש ואתה תשופנו עקב: רוק וכן נחש וכן עקרב אם דורסן לפי תומן שפיר דמי ושרי: א"ר חנינא פמוטות של בית רבי מותר לטלטלן בשבת. א"ל ר' זירא בניטלין בידו אחת

אַיְיתוּ לְהוּ פּוּרְיָיתָא – **they** [R' Avin's servants, on the instructions of their master] **brought couches** on which to recline, **לְרַב חָנָן בַּר רָבָא לֹא אַיְיתוּ לֵיהּ** – **but for Rav Chanan bar Rava they did not bring** a couch, but sat him instead on the ground.[1] **אַשְׁכְּחֵיהּ מַתְנֵי לֵיהּ לִבְרֵיהּ** – In the course of this visit, **[Rav Chanan bar Rava] found [R' Avin] teaching** our **Mishnah to his son** as follows: **וְעַל צוֹאָה שֶׁל קָטָן מִפְּנֵי קָטָן** – **"And** one may invert a bowl **over the feces of a child because of the child,"** i.e. so that the child should not handle it and become soiled. **אָמַר לֵיהּ** – **[Rav Chanan bar Rava] said to [R' Avin]: אָבִין שַׁטְיָא מַתְנֵי שְׁטוּתָא לִבְנֵיהּ** – **Avin the fool teaches foolishness to his son!**[2] **וַהֲלֹא הִיא עַצְמָהּ מוּכֶנֶת לִכְלָבִים** – **Why,** the reference cannot be to feces excreted by a child, as you explain, for **[that very excrement] itself is** considered **"prepared" for** the consumption of **dogs** (who nibble at a child's feces). Thus, it is not *muktzeh* at all and may be moved away, and the Mishnah would not say that one covers it with a bowl! **וְכִי תֵימָא דְּלֹא חַזְיָא לֵיהּ מֵאֶתְמוֹל** – **And perhaps you will say** in defense of your explanation **that** the child's excrement is *muktzeh* because **it was not fit for [the dog] from yesterday** (before the onset of the Sabbath), since it had not been excreted when the Sabbath began.[3] **וְהָתַנְיָא** – **Why,** this is not the law, **for it has been taught in a Baraisa: נַהֲרוֹת הַמּוֹשְׁכִין וּמַעְיָינוֹת הַנּוֹבְעִין הֲרֵי הֵן כְּרַגְלֵי כָל אָדָם** – Waters from FLOWING STREAMS AND GUSHING SPRINGS ARE permitted to be transported LIKE THE FEET OF ANY PERSON who happens to carry them at the moment.[4] In any event, we see from this Baraisa that the water one draws from the streams or springs is not *muktzeh* even though this particular water was distant and inaccessible to him at the onset of the Yom Tov. And the reason it is not *muktzeh* is that its becoming accessible on Yom Tov is predictable and expected. Thus, at the onset of Yom Tov, one *had* contemplated using this water when it would arrive on Yom Tov. Similarly, one expects the child to excrete feces on the Sabbath, and their accessibility to the dogs has been contemplated; thus, they are not *muktzeh* even if excreted on the Sabbath itself.[5] **וְאֶלָּא הֵיכִי אַתְנְיֵיהּ** – R' Avin asked Rav Chanan: **But how, then,** ***should*** **I teach the Mishnah to him?** If the Mishnah cannot refer to the feces excreted by a child, as you have just proven, then what *does* "the feces of a child" mean? **אֵימָא עַל צוֹאָה שֶׁל תַּרְנְגוֹלִים מִפְּנֵי קָטָן** – Rav Chanan bar Rava replied: **Say** that the Mishnah means that one may invert a bowl **"over the feces** ***of chickens*** **because of the child,"** i.e. so that the child should not handle it and become soiled.[6] Chicken feces are indeed *muktzeh* because they are not fit for dogs, and thus may only be covered but not moved.

The Gemara asks:[7]

וְתִיפּוֹק לֵיהּ דְּהָוֵי גְּרָף שֶׁל רְעִי – **But** even if the Tanna is referring to chicken excrement, which is *muktzeh,* **let it emerge to him** that one is permitted to move it away **because it is** tantamount to **"a vessel of excrement,"** whose clearing away the Rabbis permitted (though the excrement is *muktzeh*) because it is repulsive.[8] **וְכִי תֵימָא גְּרָף שֶׁל רְעִי אַגַּב מָנָא אִין** – **And perhaps you will say that** in the case of **"a vessel of excrement,"** where the *muktzeh* excrement is being moved indirectly **through** the movement **of the vessel** that contains it – **yes,** they permitted it; **אִיהוּ גּוּפֵיהּ לֹא** – but **[the excrement] itself – no,** they did not permit clearing it away.[9] Thus, in the present case, the chicken feces, which are lying on the ground rather than in a vessel, may not be moved. **וְהָא הַהוּא עַכְבָּר דְּאִישְׁתַּכַּח בְּאִיסְפַּרְמַקֵי דְּרַב אַשִׁי** – **Why,** I can show you that this is not so, for **there was** the incident of **the** dead **mouse that was found among the spices of Rav Ashi, וְאָמַר לְהוּ נְקוֹטוּ בְּצוּצִיתֵיהּ וְאַפְּקוּהּ** – **and [Rav Ashi] told them: Take hold** of it **by its tail and remove it.** We see, then, that something repulsive may be removed directly by hand from an area where it is offensive to people. Why, then, does the Tanna allow one only to cover the chicken feces but not to remove it?

The Gemara answers:

בְּאַשְׁפָּה – The Mishnah refers to chicken feces that are **in a trash pile.** Since they are not lying in a populated area that people should be repulsed by them, they may not be moved.[10]

The Gemara asks:

וְקָטָן בְּאַשְׁפָּה מַאי בָּעֵי לֵיהּ – **But what is a child doing in** the environs of **a trash heap,** that the Mishnah should have to state that one may cover the feces so that the child not become soiled?[11]

NOTES

1. *Rashi.* [Apparently, R' Avin did not consider Rav Chanan bar Rava to be of the same stature as his two colleagues, and so did not accord him the honor of ordering a couch for him.]

2. It is foolish to explain the Mishnah's phrase "the feces of a child" to mean the feces excreted by a child, as Rav Chanan will now explain.

Rav Chanan was angered [by the slight to his honor] and sought to annoy R' Avin [as a means of rebuke] (*Rashi*).

3. Thus, they would be *muktzeh* as *nolad* – something that has come into existence on the Sabbath, and was thus not "prepared" for use at the onset of the Sabbath (see *Rashi, Rashba* and *Ritva MHK* ed.).

4. Ordinarily, it is forbidden under the *techum* laws to move even an ownerless item on the Sabbath or Yom Tov more than two thousand *amos* from its "resting place" at the onset of the day (see *Eruvin* 45b for details). In this case, however, since the waters were in motion at the onset of the day, they do not "acquire" any legal "resting place" and they remain without any *techum* restrictions for the entire Yom Tov [or Sabbath] (see *Rashi* to *Beitzah* 39a ד״ה הרי הן כרגלי כל אדם; cf. *Tosafos* to *Eruvin* 45b ד״ה ביום טוב). Thus, any person can transport these waters on Yom Tov "like his feet" – i.e. as far as he himself is permitted to travel (*Rashi*).

5. The Rishonim raise the following difficulty: By the same logic offered here, an egg laid on the Sabbath should be permitted for consumption, since its accessibility was predictable and anticipated. Yet, such an egg represents the classic case of *nolad,* and is forbidden as *muktzeh*! The Rishonim answer that the case of the egg is different in that the egg before it is laid is considered to be part and parcel of the hen, which is *muktzeh* on the Sabbath (as slaughtering is forbidden). Thus, the egg acquires the *muktzeh* designation as well, which remains with it for the duration of the Sabbath (see *Ramban* et al.).

6. I.e. the Mishnah's words שֶׁל קָטָן, *"of" a child,* mean (chicken) feces that a child *might handle;* and because the child might handle it, we cover it (see *Rashi;* see also *Rambam, Peirush HaMishnah*). [Actually, as evident from what he had taught to his son, R' Avin had also understood that the Mishnah refers to covering the feces so that the child should not handle them. R' Avin, however, did not realize that this was the very meaning of the expression שֶׁל קָטָן, *of a child,* and therefore interpreted that expression to mean literally *a child's feces* – an interpretation that Rav Chanan bar Rava disproved.]

7. See *Hagahos Yavetz.*

8. Shmuel rules in *Beitzah* 36b that one may remove a vessel of excrement to the trash heap on the Sabbath (see *Rashi*).

9. We find that moving *muktzeh* indirectly (e.g. by moving a vessel that contains it) [טִלְטוּל מִן הַצַּד] is deemed a lesser movement of *muktzeh* than direct movement (see, for example, Gemara below, 123a).

[Generally, a vessel containing *muktzeh* becomes *muktzeh* itself, since it is a *base to,* and thus subordinate to, the *muktzeh* that it contains. Nevertheless, in the case of a vessel of excrement (which is repulsive and whose presence is demeaning to human dignity), it might be that the Sages were lenient and deemed the excrement to be subordinate to the vessel, so that one would be permitted to remove it (*Ritva MHK* ed.).]

10. [The permit to move "a vessel of excrement" is not a blanket one, but applies only where the repulsive matter is in a place that people are likely to come upon it and be repulsed by it.]

11. Typically, trash heaps were located in the public domain [where children would not wander unattended] (*Rashi*).

גמ' אייתו להו פורייתא. מטות לישב עליהן: לא אייתו ליה. והושיבוהו לארץ: מפני קטן. שלא יטפח בו ויתלכלך: א"ל. רב חנן שהיה כעוס ומתכוון להקניטו לר' אבין: והלא מוכנת לכלבים. ולמה לי לכפות כלי יפנוה משם שהרי ראויה לטלטל: דלא חזיא מאתמול.

אייתו להו פורייתא לרב חנן בר רבא לא אייתו ליה אשכחיה מתני ליה לבריה ועל צואה של קטן מפני קטן א"ל אבין שטיא מתני שטותא לבניה והלא היא עצמה מוכנת לכלבים וכ"ת דלא חזיא ליה מאתמול [ח] והתניא [א] נהרות המושכין ומעיינות הנובעין הרי הן כרגלי כל אדם ואלא היכי אתנייה אימא [ב] על צואה של תרנגולים מפני קטן ותיפוק ליה דהוי גרף של רעי וכ"ת גרף של רעי אגב מנא אין איהו גופיה לא [ג] והא [ד] ההוא עכבר דאישתכח באיספרמקי דרב אשי ואמר להו נקוטו בצוציתיה ואפקוה ואפקוה באשפה וקטן באשפה מאי בעי ליה בחצר חצר נמי גרף של רעי הוא [א] באשפה שבחצר: ועל עקרב שלא תישך: א"ר יהושע בן לוי כל המזיקין נהרגין בשבת מתיב רב יוסף חמשה נהרגין בשבת ואלו הן זבוב שבארץ מצרים וצירעה שבנינוה ועקרב שבחדייב ונחש שבא"י וכלב שוטה בכל מקום מני אילימא ר' יהודה האמר מלאכה שאינה צריכה לגופה חייב עליה אלא לאו ר"ש והני הוא דשרי אחריני לא אמר ר' ירמיה ומאן נימא לן דהא מתרצתא היא דילמא משבשתא היא אמר רב יוסף אנא מתנינא לה ואותיבנא לה ואנא מתריצנא לה ברצו אחריו ודברי הכל תני תנא קמיה דרבא בר רב הונא ההורג נחשים ועקרבים בשבת אין רוח חסידים נוחה הימנו א"ל ואותן חסידים אין רוח חכמים נוחה מהם ופליגא דרב הונא דרב הונא חזייה לההוא גברא דקא קטיל זיבורא א"ל שלימתינהו לכולהו ת"ר נזדמנו לו נחשים ועקרבים הרגן בידוע שנזדמנו לו להורגן לא הרגן בידוע שנזדמנו להורגו ונעשה לו נס מן השמים אמר עולא ואיתימא רבה בר בר חנה א"ר יוחנן בנישופין בו א"ר אבא בר כהנא פעם אחת נפל אחד בבהמ"ד ועמד ניותי אחד והרגו אמר רבי פגע בו כיוצא בו איבעיא להו פגע בו כיוצא בו דשפיר עביד או לא ת"ש דר' אבא בריה דר' חייא בר אבא ור' זירא הוו יתבי אקילעא דבי ר' ינאי נפק מילתא מבינייהו בעו מיניה מר' ינאי מהו להרוג נחשים ועקרבים בשבת אמר להו צירעה אני הורג נחש ועקרב לא כ"ש דילמא לפי תומו דאמר רב יהודה רוק דורסו לפי תומו ואמר רב ששת נחש דורסו לפי תומו ואמר רב קטינא עקרב דורסו לפי תומו אבא בר מרתא דהוא אבא בר מניומי הוה מסקי ביה דבי ריש גלותא זוזי אייתיוהו קא מצערא ליה הוה שדי רוקא אמר להו ריש גלותא אייתו מאנא סחיפו עלויה אמר להו לא צריכתו הכי א"ר יהודה רוק דורסו לפי תומו אמר להו צורבא מרבנן הוא שבקוהו אמר ר' אבא בר כהנא א"ר חנינא פמוטות של בית רבי מותר לטלטלן בשבת א"ל ר' זירא בניטלין בידו אחת או בשתי ידים

שהיום נולדה: נהרות המושכים כרגלי כל אדם. משום דמידי דנייד הוא ולא קני שביתה ואע"ג שבא מחוץ לתחום כל אדם מוליכין למקום שצריך לו ליכך מיהו שמעינן מינה דמותרין בטלטול ואע"ג דמאתמול לא הוי הכי קמן כיון דאורחייהו בהכי דעתיה עלייהו ה"נ כיון דאורחיה דקטן בהכי דעתיה עליה לכל מידי דחזי ליה לכלבים: א"ל ר' אבין. ואלא היכי אתנייה: צואה של תרנגולים. דלא חזיא לכלבים ושל קטן דקתני מתניתין שמטפח בה קטן קאמר ובשביל הקטן אמר כופין: תיפוק ליה דהגרף של רעי הוא. דמאיס ולפנייה דהא קי"ל במסכת ביצה גרף של רעי מותר להוציאו לאשפה: וכי תימא גרף של רעי דמותר אגב מנא אין. הא דקי"ל מותר להוציאו משום דרמי במנא דגרף היינו כלי חרס העשוי לכך ואגב מנא הוא דשרי לטלטולי אבל בפני עצמו לא והכא לאו במנא רמי: באיספרמקי. בשמים: בצוציתיה. בזנבו אלמא בלאו מנא נמי מטלטלי ליה: ומשני באשפה. דלא רמי קמייהו ולא גרף של רעי הוא: קטן באשפה מאי בעי. התם אשפה ברה"ר הוא ומאי בעי קטן התם דקא מיכסי ליה בשביל קטן: ומשני בחצר. דשכיח קטן התם קס"ד בחצר דלאו אשפה וקפריך סוף סוף גרף של רעי הוא ומשני באשפה שבחצר: כל המזיקין. ההורגין: נהרגין בשבת. וקס"ד אפי' אין רצין אחריו ומשום דס"ל כר"ש דמלאכה שאינה צריכה לגופה מדרבנן היא דאסירא והכא לא גזור: (נהרגין בשבת. אפי' אין רצין אחריו) משום דס"ל דסתמן הורגין הן: האמר חייב עליה. והיכי שרי במלאכה גמורה כשאין רצין אחריו דליכא פקוח נפש: ומאן לימא לן כו'. דרב יוסף הוא מתני ליה כדלקמן ולא בדבי ר' חייא ור' אושעיא מיתנייא וכל מתניתא דלא מתנייא בתוספתא דר' חייא ור' אושעיא איכא לספוקי במשבשתא ולא מותבינן מינה: אנא תנינא לה. במתניתא דידי ואנא אותבינא בבי מדרשא אדר' יהושע בן לוי: ואנא מתרצנא לה. דלא תיקשי כי אמר ר' יהושע בן לוי כל המזיקין נהרגין ברצין אחריו קאמר דפקוח נפש הוא: ודברי הכל. ואפי' לר' יהודה והא דחמשה נהרגין כשאין רצין אחריו ור' שמעון: אין רוח חסידים נוחה הימנו. דעתן של חסידים אינה מעורבת עמו שאין הגון בעיניהם על מה שעשה: נוחה. ערבה אין מתרצין במעשיו: אמר ליה. רבא לתנא: ואותן חסידים. השונאין אותו על כך אין רוח חכמים ערבה עמהם להיות נוחה ומיושבת במה שרואין במדת חסידים הללו דשפיר עביד דאי לא מזיקין השתא סופן להזיק בשעת כעסן: שלימתינהו לכולהו. הרגת את כולן כלומר מה אהני בהא אהכי טובא איכא אלמא לאו שפיר עבד והא דרבא פליג אדאבוה: שנזדמנו לו להורגן. לכך באו לידו שזימן לו המקום לאבדן לפי שהיו עתידות להזיק וגלגלו זכות על ידי זכאי: לא הרגן בידוע שנזדמנו לו להרוג אותו. והראה לו הקב"ה שחטא אלא שנעשה לו נס: בנישופין בו. בכה"ג קתני בידוע שנזדמנו להורגו נישופין כן דרך הנחש עושה כעין שריקה כשהוא רואה שונאו וכועס: ניותי. על שם מקומו וישראל היה: דשפיר עביד. וכיוצא בו דקאמר לאו לגנאי הוא אלא הנחש רודף ונעשה זה כיוצא בו: או לא. וכיוצא בו דקאמר לגנאי הוא: צרעה אני הורג. בשבת לכלות מזיקין ואף על פי שאינה מועדת כאלו: לא כל שכן. אלמא שפיר עביד: דילמא לפי תומו. לא שיעמוד עליו ויהרגנו להדיא אלא כשהוא הולך לתומו ונחש או עקרב בפניו אין צריך לישמט ממנו אלא דורכו והולך ואם מת בדריכתו ימות הואיל ולא נתכוון דדבר שאין מתכוין לר' יהודה מדרבנן הוא ולענין מזיקין לא גזור: רוק דורסו לפי תומו. שאין מתכוין למרח ולאשווי' גומות דאף על גב דממילא ממרח הוא כי לא מיכוין שרי משום מאיסותא: הוה שדי רוקא. היה רוק מוטל לפניהם ושבת היתה: פמוטות. מנורות ולא של חוליות היו:

של

כל המזיקין נהרגין בשבת. אף על גב דתנן במתניתין ועל עקרב שלא ישוך איצטריך לאשמעינן דהריגה נמי שרינן דסלקא דעתך דאסירא משום דמיפרסמא מילתא טפי מצידה ומהאי טעמא נמי פליג רב הונא בסמוך ואסר הריגה:

ברצין אחריו וד"ה. פי' בקונט' דרבי יהושע בן לוי ברצין אחריו והוי פקוח נפש וברייתא באין רצין וכר"ש וקשה דא"כ תקשה מהך ברייתא לרבא בר רב הונא דשרי להרוג נחשים ועקרבים בשבת דע"כ באין רצין אחריו איירי דאי ברצין אחריו אמאי אין רוח חסידים נוחה הימנו לפירוש הקונטרס דברצין אחריו איכא פקוח נפש ועוד בניותי שהרג נחש ומיבעיא לן אי שפיר עבד תיפשוט מהכא דלא שרינן לר"ש באין רצין אלא ה' בלבד ועוד קשה לר"י דלישנא דהנא מתרצנא לה משמע לברייתא עצמה ונראה לר"י לפרש דברייתא ברצין אחריו וד"ה פירוש אפילו ר' יהודה מודה דחמשה שרי להרוג ברצין אחריו אבל שאר אסור להורגן אפילו רצין אחריו לר' יהודה ור' יהושע בן לוי כר"ש דשרי שאר (א) אפילו באין רצין אחריו ורב הונא דאסר בסמוך לא סבר כרבי יהושע בן לוי ונראה לר"י וכן פירש ר"ח שאין להקל כרבי יהושע בן לוי אלא כהנהו אמוראי דלקמן דלא שרו אלא בדריסה לפי תומו:

עין משפט נר מצוה

עד א מיי' פ"ה מהלכות י"ט הלכה יז טוש"ע או"ח סימן שלב סעיף טו:

עה ב ג מיי' פכ"ו מהל' שבת הלכה יג סמג לאוין סה טוש"ע או"ח סימן שח סעיף לד:

עו ד ה מיי' פי"א שם הלכה ד סמג שם טור שו"ע או"ח סימן שטז סעיף י:

עז ו מיי' פכ"ו שם הלכה ג ופכ"ו הלכה יג סמג שם טור שו"ע או"ח שם סעיף יא:

עח ז ח מיי' פי"א מהלכות שבת הל"ד סמג שם טור שו"ע שם סעיף י:

עט ט מיי' פכ"ו מהל' שבת הלכה יב טור שו"ע או"ח סימן רעט סעיף ו:

גליון הש"ס

גמ' והלא היא עצמה מוכנת לכלבים. ע"ל דף יט ע"ב תוס' ד"ה שמן: רש"י ד"ה דלמא לפי תומו וכו' דדבר שאין מתכוין לר"י מדרבנן. ע"ל דף מא ע"ב תוס' ד"ה מיחם:

רבינו חננאל

ביומא ליתעכב עד לאורתא ולטבול. ומסקינן משום דסברי רבנן אע"ג דצלי ליה טבילה בזמנה מצוה ור' יוסי סבר טבילה בזמנה לאו מצוה היא האי ר' יוסי בר' יהודה דגרסינן בנדה פרק המפלת בבנין טועה. ר' יוסי בר"י אומר דייה לטבול באחרונה דקסבר טבילה בזמנה לאו מצוה היא. וזה רבי יוסי דהיה (אומר) שם כתוב על בשרו. אסיקנא בגמרא דשבעת ימים (ביומא דף ו') דבטבילה בזמנה מצוה פליגי ונתברר בסוף יום הכפורים דהא לר' יוסי בר' יהודה היא ואיכא אחריתי התם לר' יוסי דאמר כל היום כולו כשר לטבילה. דאלמא סבר טבילה בזמנה [מצוה] היא: א"ר אמי בדליקה התירו לומר כל המכבה אינו מפסיד. וכן הלכה: נכרי שבא לכבות אין אומרים לו כבה ואל תכבה אלא אין מניחין אותו. ואין אומרים לו כבה וגם אין מונעין אותו מלכבות. אבל קטן העושה לדעת אין מניחין אותו לכבות: אריב"ל כל המזיקין נהרגין. אסיקנא כשהן רצין אחריו. אבל אין רצין אחריו אין נהרגין אלא אלו בלבד. זבוב שבארץ מצרים. וצירעה שבנינוה ועקרב שבחדייב ונחש שבא"י וכלב שוטה בכ"מ. פי' נישופין כדכתיב הוא ישופך ראש ואתה תשופנו עקב: רוק נחש וכן עקרב אם דורסן לפי תומן שפיר דמי ושרי: א"ר חנינא פמוטות של בית רבי מותר לטלטלן בשבת. א"ל ר' זירא בניטלין בידו אחת

מסורת הש"ס

א) ביצה לט. עירובין מו. מח. [תוספתא ביצה פ"ד], ב) ביצה לו:, ג) [לעיל עג:], ד) [פסחים נט:], ה) [גי' הרי"ף והרא"ש בשבת], ו) [יומא פד. יבמות קכ.], ז) [ג"ל ואמר].

הגהות הב"ח

(א) תוס' ד"ה ברלין וכו' כר' שמעון דשרי שאר מזיקין אפילו:

הגהות הגר"א

[א] גמרא באשפה שבחצר כו'. נ"ב גירסת הרי"ף בחלר אחרת:

רב נסים גאון

להפרישו מאי דשקלינן וטרינן בהא מילתא איתא במס' יבמות (דף קיד) בפרק חרש שנשא פיקחת: סוף סוף גרף של רעי הוא ונפקה כבר פירשנו בפרק כירה כי עיקר השמועה שיש בה התרת זה הדבר בפרק משילין פירות (ביצה דף לו): ר' יהודה אומר כל מלאכה שאינה צריכה לגופה חייב עליה כבר פירשנו בפרק יציאות השבת ואמרנו כי עיקרה הן דברי ר' יהודה שאמרם כאן בזו המשנה מעשה באו לפני

ליקוטי רש"י

נהרות המושכין. היינו נהרות שיש להם משך להלאה ממקום מקור נביעתן. ומעיינות הנובעין. ואין עולין מגומות נביעתן לימשך הלאה. הרי הן כרגלי כל אדם. שאין להם קנין שביתה לא במקומן ולא כרגלי הבעלים ולא כרגלי המוליך דכל מידי דנייד לית ליה שביתה והכי מפרשינן בעירובין בפרק מי שהוליאוהו [ביצה לט.]. כיון דניידי לא קנו שביתה ואפילו הן של יחיד הן כרגליו [עירובין מו.]. גרף של רעי. דמאיס במסכת ביצה (לו:) מותר להוליאו לאשפה שבחלר [לעיל מז:]. מותר לטלטלו ולפנותו לאשפה [ביצה לו:] [ביצה כא:]. גרף. כלי חרס המוכן לכך [שם]. אגב מנא אין איהו גופיה לא. דדוקא גרף נקט דלאגב מנא שרי אבל בפני עצמו אינו ליטול את הרעי או דבר מאוס ממש בידו ולזורקו לא שרו ליה [ביצה לו:]. אילימא ר' יהודה. בפרק המלניע (לעיל לג:) גבי מוליא המת במטה. מלאכה שאינה צריכה לגופה. כמו מוליא את המת לקוברו אינו לריך לגופה דהוליאה ולא למת אלא לפנות ביתו ואילו לא היו

אחר [לעיל עג:]. שברלונו לא תעשה ואינו לריך לעיקר (תחלתה) [תכליתה] כי הכא. ופלוגתייהו בהמלניע (לעיל לג:) גבי מוליא המת במטה חייב ואף על גב דהולאת המת לא ניחא ליה ביה ור' שמעון פוטר [שם יב.]. חייב עליה. ... הואיל ולריכה לדבר אחר מלאכת מחשבת הוא [שם לא:]. אלא ר"ש. דהוי מלאכה שאינה לריכה לגופה וכל מלאכה שאינה לריכה (לגופה) אלא לסלקה מעליו הוי מלאכה שאינה לריכה לגופה דברלונו לא באה לו ... לאו מלאכת מחשבת היא לר' שמעון [שם צג:]. ומאן נימא לן דהא מתרצתא וכו'. רבי חייא ורבי אושעיא סדרו את הברייתות ודקדקו בדברי כל חכם לומר כמו שאמר אבל יש תנאים הרבה שמוסיפים על משנתם בדדמי [חולין קמא.] ... כל מתניתא דלא מיתנייא בי רבי חייא ורבי אושעיא לא מותבו מינה בבי מדרשא [ב"מ פה:]. אין רוח חכמים נוחה מהם. אין דעת חכמים נוחה עליהם במעשיו כלומר אין מחזיקין לו טובה [קידושין יז:]. אין רוח חכמה וחסידות בקרבו ... אין נחת רוח לחכמי ישראל במעשיו של זה אין דעתם נוחה עליהם הימנו על ידו [ב"מ מח.]. בנישופין בו. כשהנחש בא לנשוך הוא נושף כמין שריקה [בראשית ג, טו]. אקילעא. כניסת הבית חדר שלפני הטרקלין שקורין פורטיג"ו בלע"ז [ברכות כב:]. לפני הבית כעין בית שער וקורין פוריי"א [פסחים עב:]. פמוטות. מנורה של מתכת [לעיל מד.]. בניטלין בידו אחת. בשתי ידים אסור לטלטלה דלאו לטלטולי עבידא דאדם קובע לה מקום [שם מד.]

The Gemara answers:

בְּחָצֵר – The Mishnah means that the feces are lying **in a courtyard,** where children are present.

The Gemara asks:

חָצֵר נַמִּי גְּרָף שֶׁל רְעִי הוּא – But excrement in **a courtyard is also** a case of **"a vessel of excrement,"** since it is lying where people are present and will be repulsed by it. Thus, it may be moved directly! – ? –

The Gemara explains:

בְּאַשְׁפָּה שֶׁבְּחָצֵר – What we mean is that the feces lie **in a trash heap that is in a courtyard.** The feces may not be moved, because they are in a trash pile. Yet, one covers them with a bowl, since children are found in the vicinity.[12]

The Gemara moves on to the next part of the Mishnah, which states:

וְעַל עַקְרָב שֶׁלֹּא תִּישֹׁךְ – OR OVER A SCORPION SO THAT IT NOT STING.

The Gemara presents a ruling:

אָמַר רַבִּי יְהוֹשֻׁעַ בֶּן לֵוִי – **R' Yehoshua ben Levi said:** **כָּל הַמַּזִּיקִין נֶהֱרָגִין בְּשַׁבָּת** – **All lethal creatures may be killed on the Sabbath.**[13]

The Gemara challenges this ruling:

מֵתִיב רַב יוֹסֵף – **Rav Yosef challenged** this ruling **from a Baraisa:** **חֲמִשָּׁה נֶהֱרָגִין בְּשַׁבָּת וְאֵלּוּ הֵן** – FIVE lethal creatures MAY BE KILLED ON THE SABBATH, AND THEY ARE: **זְבוּב שֶׁבְּאֶרֶץ מִצְרַיִם** – THE FLY THAT IS IN THE LAND OF EGYPT; **וְצִירְעָה שֶׁבְּנִינְוֵה** – AND THE WASP THAT IS IN NINEVEH;[14] **וְעַקְרָב שֶׁבְּחַדְיָיב** – AND THE SCORPION THAT IS IN CHADYAV;[15] **וְנָחָשׁ שֶׁבְּאֶרֶץ יִשְׂרָאֵל** – AND THE SNAKE THAT IS IN THE LAND OF ISRAEL; **וְכֶלֶב שׁוֹטֶה בְּכָל מָקוֹם** – AND A MAD DOG IN ANY PLACE.[16]

Rav Yosef develops his challenge:

מַנִּי – Now, **who is** the Tanna of **this** Baraisa? **אִילֵימָא רַבִּי יְהוּדָה** – **If** you are **to say** that it is **R' Yehudah,** **הָא אָמַר מְלָאכָה שֶׁאֵינָהּ צְרִיכָה לְגוּפָהּ חַיָּיב עָלֶיהָ** – **why,** this cannot be, for **he says** that **one is liable for** performing **a labor that is not needed for its defined purpose.**[17] **אֶלָּא לָאו רַבִּי שִׁמְעוֹן** – **Must it not** be, **rather,** that the Tanna of the Baraisa is **R' Shimon,** who holds that one is *not* liable for performing a labor not needed for its defined purpose. **וְהָנֵי הוּא דְּשָׁרֵי אֲחֲרִינֵי לֹא** – **And,** as stated in this Baraisa, it is only **these** five dangerous creatures that **he permits** one to kill on the Sabbath as a matter of course, but **others not!** Thus, the Baraisa contradicts R' Yehoshua ben Levi.[18] – ? –

The Gemara seeks to defend R' Yehoshua ben Levi:

אָמַר רַבִּי יִרְמְיָה – **R' Yirmiyah said:** **וּמַאן נֵימָא לָן דְּהָא מַתְרֶצְתָּא הִיא** – **And who is to say to us that** the text of **this Baraisa is correct?** **דִּילְמָא מְשַׁבֶּשְׁתָּא הִיא** – **Perhaps it is a corrupt** version, from which no proof can be brought![19]

Rav Yosef responds:

אָמַר רַב יוֹסֵף – **Rav Yosef said:** **אֲנָא מַתְנֵינָא לַהּ וְאוֹתִיבְנָא לַהּ וַאֲנָא מְתָרֵיצְנָא לַהּ** – **I have this as a Baraisa** in my corpus of Baraisos,[20]

NOTES

12. From our Gemara, it would emerge that a child's feces are not *muktzeh* altogether, because they are fit for dogs (and the same is true of an adult's feces – *Rabbeinu Yerucham,* cited by *Beis Yosef* 308 ד״ה צואה של תרנגולים [except where they are collected in a "vessel of excrement," where they become repulsive even for dogs]). Chicken feces are *muktzeh,* but may be moved from a residential area, where people would be repulsed by them. *Ran,* however, apparently based on a different reading in the Gemara, does not distinguish at all between human feces and chicken feces; both are unfit for any Sabbath use and are *muktzeh,* and may be moved away only if they are in a residential area where people would be repulsed by them. This is also how *Beis Yosef* (loc. cit.) understands the ruling of *Tur* in this matter, and how he codifies the halachah in *Orach Chaim* 308:34 (but see *Beur HaGra* there).

13. Killing a living creature on the Sabbath constitutes the *melachah* of שׁוֹחֵט, *slaughtering.* Where one kills the creature in order to have use of its carcass, he has done the *melachah* for *its defined purpose* [לְגוּפָהּ] and is liable according to all opinions. However, when one kills the creature simply so that it not cause harm, he has performed a מְלָאכָה שֶׁאֵינָהּ צְרִיכָה לְגוּפָהּ, *melachah not needed for its defined purpose,* and whether or not such *melachah* is Biblically forbidden is the subject of a dispute between the Tannaim R' Yehudah and R' Shimon (see also 121a note 27).

At this point, the Gemara assumes that R' Yehoshua ben Levi [since he neglects to qualify his statement in any way] permits one to kill any lethal creature on the Sabbath even if the creature is not chasing anyone at the moment. Accordingly, his ruling is *not* based on the permit to perform any and all *melachah* to save a life, since no actual threat to life presently exists. Rather, he follows the view of R' Shimon, who holds that a *melachah* done for something other than its defined purpose is prohibited only Rabbinically. And in the case of lethal creatures, the Rabbis suspended their prohibition and allowed one to kill the creature in order to remove the potential danger, even though the creature is not presently threatening anyone (see *Rashi*). [Accordingly, R' Yehoshua ben Levi's permit is actually implicit in the Mishnah, where the Tanna Kamma allows inverting a bowl over a scorpion (for, in either case, what is being permitted is a *melachah* – hunting or killing – not needed for its defined purpose). Nonetheless, R' Yehoshua ben Levi would be teaching us that not only is inverting the bowl permitted, but even killing the scorpion is permitted, though the latter method is a more public display of Sabbath desecration (*Tosafos* ד״ה כל המזיקין). See, however, 121a note 27.]

14. [Nineveh is the capital of Assyria. This Baraisa, then, sheds light on the meaning of the verse in *Isaiah* 7:18, which describes the armies of Egypt and Assyria that will converge on Eretz Yisrael as *the fly that is in the uttermost part of the rivers of Egypt,* and *the bee that is in the land of Assyria.* Scripture chooses as its metaphor the murderous creatures indigenous to each region – the fly in Egypt, and the bee (a wasp is a type of bee) in Assyria (see *Rashash*).]

15. [חַדְיָיב, *Chadyav,* is probably the ancient kingdom of Adiabene, in what is today northern Iraq (see Schottenstein edition of *Kiddushin* 72a note 16).]

16. The Baraisa means that these five creatures may be killed on the Sabbath even if they are not presently chasing anyone [since the Baraisa does not qualify its statement in any way]. For the Baraisa considers these five creatures to be especially prone to attack people; thus, they are presently considered as posing not only a *potential* danger, but an *actual* danger (see *Rashi*).

[The Baraisa's list of five creatures is not meant to be exclusionary. The same will apply to any other creature known to be similarly dangerous and belligerent (*Beis Yosef* 316, in explanation of *Rambam's* formulation of this halachah; *Beur HaGra* to 316:10, cited in *Shaar HaTziyun* 316:71).]

17. Thus, even killing a creature simply in order to be rid of it is a Biblical *melachah,* which cannot be permitted unless one's life is in danger. And since these five creatures are not actually attacking anyone at the moment, there is no actual threat to life that would permit the performance of a Biblical *melachah* (see *Rashi*). [And though these five creatures are likely to become aroused eventually and attack, there is no need to kill them in order to forestall that eventuality, since one has the option of leaving the area. The permit to perform a Biblically forbidden *melachah* in order to save a life applies only where there is no other way to save the life (see *Ramban,* end of ד״ה ברצין אחריו ודברי הכל; see, however, *Meromei Sadeh* ד״ה שם מני אילימא).]

18. Who rules that according to R' Shimon, *all* potentially dangerous creatures – not only the five enumerated in the Baraisa – may be killed on the Sabbath even if they are not chasing anyone at the moment (see above, end of note 13).

19. As is clear from the Gemara below, this particular Baraisa was not part of the official collections of Baraisos redacted by R' Chiya and R' Oshaya. And the rule is that the accuracy of Baraisos not incorporated in those collections cannot be relied upon (see *Chullin* 141a-b). For these two sages were very careful to preserve the original texts of the Baraisos, whereas other sages would embellish the texts according to their own understanding (see *Rashi* ad loc.).

20. [And thus can attest to its correctness, even though it is not among the Baraisos taught by R' Chiya and R' Oshaya.]

עין משפט נר מצוה

עד א מיי' פ"ה מהלכות י"ט הלכה יד טוש"ע או"ח סימן שח סעיף טו:

עה ב ג מיי' פכ"ו מהל' שבת הלכה יג סמג לאוין סה טוש"ע או"ח סימן שח סעיף לד:

עו ד ה מיי' פי"א שם הלכה ד סמג שם טור שו"ע או"ח סימן שטז סעיף י:

עז ו מיי' שם הלכה ה ופכ"ו הלכה יג סמג שם טור שו"ע או"ח שם סעיף יא:

עח ז ח מיי' פי"א מהלכות שבת הל"ד סמג שם טור שו"ע שם סעיף י:

עט ט מיי' פכ"ו מהל' שבת הלכה יא טור שו"ע או"ח סימן רעט סעיף ז:

גליון הש"ס

גמ' והלא היא עצמה מוכנת לכלבים. ע"ל דף יט ע"ב תוס' ד"ה שמן: רש"י ד"ה דלמא לפי תומו וכו' דדבר שאין מתכוין לר"י מדרבנן. ע"ל דף מא ע"ב תוס' ד"ה מיחם:

רבינו חננאל

ביומא ליתעכב עד לאורתא ולטבול. ומסקינן משום דסברי רבנן אע"ג דצלי ליה טבילה בזמנה מצוה ור' יוסי סבר טבילה בזמנה לאו מצוה היא ואף ר' יוסי בר' יהודה דגרסינן בנדה פרק המפלת בענין טועה. ר' יוסי בר' אומר דייה לטבול באחרונה דקסבר טבילה בזמנה לאו מצוה היא. וזה רבי יוסי דהיה (אומר) שם כתוב על בשרו. אסיקנא בגמרא דשבעת ימים (ביומא דף ד) דבטבילה בזמנה מצוה פליגי ונתברה בסוף יום הכפורים דהא לר' יוסי בר' יהודה היא ואיכא אחריתי התם לר' יוסי דאמר כל היום כולו כשר לטבילה. דאלמא סבר טבילה בזמנה [מצוה] היא: א"ר אמי בדליקה התירו לומר כל המכבה אינו מפסיד. וכן הלכה: נכרי שבא לכבות אין אומרים לו כבה ואל תכבה אלא אין מניחין אותו. ואין אומרים לו כבה וגם אין מונעין אותו מלכבות. אבל קטן העושה לדעת אין מניחין אותו לכבות: אריב"ל כל המזיקין נהרגין. אסיקנא כשהן רצין אחריו. אבל אין רצין אחריו אין נהרגין אלא אלו בלבד. זבוב שבארץ מצרים. וצירעה שבנינוה ועקרב שבחדייב ונחש שבא"י וכלב שוטה בכ"מ. פי' נישופין כדכתיב הוא ישופך ראש ואתה תשופנו עקב: רוק ונחש וכן עקרב אם דורסן לפי תומו שפיר דמי ושרי: א"ר חנינא פמוטות של בית רבי מותר לטלטלן בשבת. א"ל ר' זירא בניטלין בידו אחת

תוספות

כל המזיקין נהרגין בשבת. אף על גב דתנן במתניתין ועל עקרב שלא ישוך איצטריך לאשמעינן דהריגה נמי שרינן דסלקא דעתך דאסירא משום דמיפרסמא מילתא טפי מצידה ומהאי טעמא נמי פליג רב הונא בסמוך ואסר הריגה:

ברצין אחריו וד"ה. פי' בקונט' דרבי יהושע בן לוי ברצין אחריו והוי פקוח נפש וברייתא באין רצין וכר"ש וקשה דא"כ תקשה מהך ברייתא לרבה בר רב הונא דשרי להרוג נחשים ועקרבים בשבת דע"כ באין רצין אחריו מיירי דאי ברצין אחריו אמאי אין רוח חסידים נוחה הימנו לפירוש הקונטרס דברצין אחריו איכא פקוח נפש ועוד בניותי שהרג נחש ומיבעיא לן אי שפיר עבד תיפשוט מהכא דלא שרינן לר"ש באין רצין אלא ה' בלבד ועוד קשה לר"י דלישנא דאנא מתרצנא לה משמע לברייתא עצמה ונראה לר"י לפרש דברייתא ברצין אחריו וד"ה פירוש אפילו ר' יהודה מודה דחמשה שרי להרוג ברצין אחריו אבל שאר אסור להורגן אפילו רצין אחריו לר' יהודה ור' יהושע בן לוי כר"ש דשרי שאר (א) אפילו באין רצין אחריו ורב הונא דאסר בסמוך לא סבר כרבי יהושע בן לוי ונראה לר"י וכן פירש ר"ח שאין להקל כרבי יהושע בן לוי אלא כהנהו אמוראי דלקמן דלא שרו אלא בדריסה לפי תומו:

א"ל

גמרא

אייתו להו פורייתא לרב חנן בר רבא לא אייתו ליה אשכחיה מתני ליה לבריה ועל צואה של קטן מפני קטן א"ל אבין שטיא מתני שטותא לבניה ° והלא היא עצמה מוכנת לכלבים וכ"ת דלא חזיא ליה מאתמול (א) והתניא [א] נהרות המושכין ומעיינות הנובעין הרי הן כרגלי כל אדם ואלא היכי אתנייה אימא [ב] על צואה של תרנגולים מפני קטן ותיפוק ליה דהוי גרף של רעי וכ"ת גרף של רעי אגב מנא אין איהו גופיה לא [ג] והא (ב) ההוא עכבר דאישתכח באיספרמקי דרב אשי ואמר להו נקוטו בצוציתיה ואפקוה באשפה וקטן באשפה מאי בעי ליה בחצר חצר נמי גרף של רעי הוא [א] באשפה שבחצר: ועל עקרב שלא תישך: א"ר יהושע בן לוי כל המזיקין נהרגין בשבת מתיב רב יוסף [ד] חמשה נהרגין בשבת ואלו הן זבוב שבארץ מצרים וצירעה שבנינוה ועקרב שבחדייב ונחש שבא"י וכלב שוטה בכל מקום מני אילימא (ג) ר' יהודה הא אמר מלאכה שאינה צריכה לגופה חייב עליה אלא לאו ר"ש והני הוא דשרי אחריני לא אמר ר' ירמיה (ד) ומאן נימא לן דהא מתרצתא היא דילמא משבשתא היא אמר רב יוסף אנא מתנינא לה ואותיבנא לה ואנא מתריצנא לה [ה] ברצו אחריו ודברי הכל תני תנא קמיה דרבא בר רב הונא ההורג נחשים ועקרבים בשבת אין רוח חסידים נוחה הימנו א"ל ואותן חסידים אין רוח חכמים נוחה מהם ופליגא דרב הונא דרב הונא חזייה לההוא גברא דקא קטיל זיבורא א"ל שלימתינהו לכולהו ת"ר נזדמנו לו נחשים ועקרבים (ה) הרגן בידוע שנזדמנו לו להורגן לא הרגן בידוע שנזדמנו להורגו ונעשה לו נס מן השמים אמר עולא ואיתימא רבה בר בר חנה א"ר יוחנן בנישופין בו א"ר אבא בר כהנא פעם אחת נפל אחד בבהמ"ד ועמד ניותי אחד והרגו אמר רבי פגע בו כיוצא בו איבעיא להו פגע בו כיוצא בו דשפיר עביד או לא ת"ש דר' אבא בריה דר' חייא בר אבא ור' זירא הוו יתבי אקילעא דבי ר' ינאי נפק מילתא מבינייהו בעו מיניה מר' ינאי מהו להרוג נחשים ועקרבים בשבת אמר להו צירעה אני הורג נחש ועקרב לא כ"ש דילמא לפי תומו דאמר רב יהודה [ו] רוק דורסו לפי תומו ואמר רב ששת [ז] נחש דורסו לפי תומו ואמר רב קטינא [ח] עקרב דורסו לפי תומו (ו) אבא בר מרתא דהוא אבא בר מניומי הוה מסקי ביה דבי ריש גלותא זוזי אייתיוהו קא מצערא ליה הוה שדי רוקא אמר להו ריש גלותא אייתו מאנא סחיפו עלויה אמר להו לא צריכתו הכי א"ר יהודה רוק דורסו לפי תומו אמר להו צורבא מרבנן הוא שבקוהו (ז) אמר ר' אבא בר כהנא א"ר חנינא [ט] פמוטות של בית רבי מותר לטלטלן בשבת א"ל ר' זירא בניטלין בידו אחת או בשתי ידים

רש"י

גמ' אייתו להו פורייתא. מטות לישב עליהן: **לא אייתו ליה.** והושיבוהו לארץ: **מפני קטן.** שלא יטפח בו ויתלכלך: **א"ל.** רב חנן שהיה כעוס ומתכוין להקניטו לר' אבין: **והלא מוכנת לכלבים.** ולמה לי לכפות כלי יפנוה משם שהרי ראויה לטלטל: **דלא חזיא מאתמול.** שהיום נולדה: **נהרות המושכים כרגלי כל אדם.** משום דמידי דנייד הוא ולא קני שביתה ואע"פ שבא מחוץ לתחום כל אדם מוליכן למקום שעירב לו לילך מיהו שמעינן מינה דמותרין בטלטול ואע"ג דמאתמול לא הוי הכי קמן כיון דאורחייהו בהכי דעתיה עלייהו ה"נ כיון דאורחיה דקטן בהכי דעתיה עליה דלכי תיתי יאכלנה לכלבים: **א"ל ר' אבין.** ואלא היכי אתנייה: **צואה של תרנגולים.** דלא חזיא לכלבים ושל קטן דקתני מתניתין שמטפח בה קטן קאמר ובשביל הקטן אמר כופין: **תיפוק ליה דגרף של רעי הוא.** דמאיס ולפנייה דהא קי"ל במסכת ביצה גרף של רעי מותר להוציאו לאשפה: **וכי תימא גרף של רעי דמותר אגב מנא אין.** הא דקי"ל מותר להוציאו משום דרמי במנא דגרף היינו כלי חרס העשוי לכך ואגב מנא הוא דשרי לטלטולי אבל בפני עצמו לא והכא לאו במנא רמי: **באספרמקי.** בשמים: **בצוציתיה.** בזנבו אלמא בלאו מנא נמי מטלטלי ליה: **ומשני באשפה.** דלא רמי קמייהו ולא גרף של רעי הוא: **קטן באשפה מאי בעי.** סתם אשפה ברה"ר הוא ומאי בעי קטן התם דקא מיכסי ליה בשביל קטן: **ומשני בחצר.** דשכיח קטן התם קס"ד בחצר דלאו אשפה וקפריך סוף סוף גרף של רעי הוא ומשני באשפה שבחצר: **כל המזיקין.** ההורגן: **נהרגין בשבת.** וקס"ד אפי' אין רצין אחריו ומשום דס"ל כר"ש דמלאכה שאינה צריכה לגופה מדרבנן היא דאסירא והכא לא גזור: (נהרגין בשבת. אפי' אין רצין אחריו) משום דס"ל דסתמן הורגין הן: **האמר חייב עליה.** והיכי שרי במלאכה גמורה כשאין רצין אחריו דליכא פקוח נפש: **ומאן לימא לן כו'.** דרב יוסף הוא מתני ליה כדלקמן ולא בדבי ר' חייא ור' אושעיא מיתנייא וכל מתניתא דלא מתנייא בתוספתא דר' חייא ור' אושעיא איכא לספוקי במשבשתא ולא מותבינן מינה: **אנא תנינא לה.** במתניתא דידי ואנא אותבינא בבי מדרשא אדר' יהושע בן לוי: **ואנא מתרצנא לה.** דלא תיקשי כי אמר ר' יהושע בן לוי כל המזיקין נהרגין ברצין אחריו קאמר דפקוח נפש הוא: **ודברי הכל.** ואפי' לר' יהודה והא דחמשה נהרגין כשאין רצין אחריו ור' שמעון: **אין רוח חסידים נוחה הימנו.** דעתן של חסידים אינה מעורבת עמו שאין הגון בעיניהם על מה שעשה: **נוחה.** עריבה אין מתרצין במעשיו: **אמר ליה.** רבא לתנא: **ואותן חסידים.** השונאין אותו על כך אין רוח חכמים עריבה עמהם להיות נוחה ומיושבת במה שרואין במדת חסידים הללו דשפיר עביד דאי לא מזיקין השתא סופן להזיק בשעת כעסן: **שלימתינהו לכולהו.** הרגת את כולן כלומר מה אהני בהא אכתי איכא טובא אלמא לאו שפיר עבד והא דרבא פליג אדאבוה: **שנזדמנו לו להורגן.** לכך באו לידו שזימן לו המקום לאבדן לפי שהיו עתידות להזיק וגלגלו זכות על ידי זכאי: **לא הרגן בידוע שנזדמנו לו להרוג אותו.** והראה לו הקב"ה שחטא אלא שנעשה לו נס: **בנישופין בו.** בכה"ג קתני בידוע שנזדמנו להורגו נישופין כן דרך הנחש עושה כעין שריקה כשהוא רואה שונאו וכועס: **ניותי.** על שם מקומו וישראל היה: **דשפיר עביד.** וכיוצא בו דקאמר לאו לגנאי הוא אלא הנחש רודף ונעשה זה כיוצא בו: **או לא.** וכיוצא בו דקאמר לגנאי הוא: **צרעה אני הורג.** בשבת לכלות מזיקין ואף על פי שאינה מועדת כאלו: **לא כל שכן.** אלמא שפיר עביד: **דילמא לפי תומו.** לא שיעמוד עליו ויהרגנו להדיא אלא כשהוא הולך לתומו ונחש או עקרב בפניו אין צריך ליזהר ממנו אלא דורכו והולך ואם מת בדריכתו ימות הואיל ולא נתכוין ° דדבר שאין מתכוין לר' יהודה מדרבנן הוא ולענין מזיקין לא גזור: **רוק דורסו לפי תומו.** שאין מתכוין למרח ולאשוו' גומות דאף על גב דממילא ממרח הוא כי לא מיכוין שרי משום מאיסותא: **הוה שדי רוקא.** היה רוק מוטל לפניהם ושבת היתה: **פמוטות.** מנורות ולא של חוליות היו:

של

מסורת הש"ס

א) ביצה לג. עירובין מו. מח. [תוספתא ביצה פ"ד], ב) ביצה לו:, ג) [לעיל עג: וש"נ], ד) [פסחים לג:], ה) [ג' הרי"ף והרא"ש בשבת], ו) [יומא פד. יבמות קכ.], ז) [נ"ל ואמר].

הגהות הב"ח

(א) תוס' ד"ה ברצין וכו' כר' שמעון דשרי שאר מזיקין אפילו:

הגהות הגר"א

[א] גמרא באשפה שבחצר כו'. נ"ב גירסת הרי"ף בחצר אחרת:

רב נסים גאון

להפרישו מאי דשקלינן וטרינן בהא מילתא איתא במס' יבמות (דף קיד) בפרק חרש שנשא פיקחת: סוף סוף גרף של רעי הוא ונפקיה כבר פירשנו בפרק כירה כי עיקר השמועה שיש בה התרת זה הדבר בפרק משילין פירות (ביצה דף לו): ר' יהודה אומר כל מלאכה שאינה צריכה לגופה חייב עליה כבר פירשנו בפרק יציאות השבת ואמרנו כי עיקרה מן דברי ר' יהודה שאמרם כאן בזו המשנה מעשה בא לפני

ליקוטי רש"י

נהרות המושכין. היינו שהם נהרות שיש להם משך ללכת ממקום מקור נביעתן: ומעיינות הנובעין. ואין יוצאין ממקום נביעתן לימשך הלאה. הרי הן כרגלי כל אדם. לא קנה שם שביתה לא במקומן ולא כרגלי הבעלים ולא כרגלי הממלא אלא כל אדם מוליכן כרגליו דכל מידי דנייד לית ליה שביתה והכי מפרשינן בעירובין בפרק מי שהוציאוהו [ביצה לט.]. כיון דניידי לא קני שביתה ואפילו הן של יחיד אינן כרגליו [עירובין מו.]. גרף של רעי. במסכת ביצה (לו:) מותר להוציאו לאשפה [לעיל מג:]. גרף. כלי חרס המוכן לכך [שם]. אגב מנא אין איהו גופיה לא. דדוקא גרף נקט דאגב מנא שרי לטלטולי אבל בפני עצמו לא [ביצה לו.]. אילימא ר' יהודה. בפרק המצניע (לעיל צג:) גבי מוציא את המת במטה. מלאכה שאינה צריכה לגופה. כמו מוציא את המת לקוברו [illegible]

מאי [לעיל עג.] שבדלתו לא תעשה ואינו צריך לעיקר (תחלתה) [תכליתה] כי הכא. ופלוגתייהו בהמצניע (לעיל צג:) גבי מוציא המת במטה חייב ואף על גב דהוצאת המת לא ניחא ליה ביה ור' שמעון פוטר [שם יב.]. חייב עליה. [illegible]

and I have raised the challenge from it **to [R' Yehoshua ben Levi's ruling], and I will reconcile [that ruling]** with the Baraisa by explaining that R' Yehoshua ben Levi refers[21] **בִּרְצוּ אַחֲרָיו – to where [the lethal creatures] were** actually **chasing after him, וְדִבְרֵי הַכֹּל – and** his ruling accords with **the opinion of all** Tannaim. For even R' Yehudah agrees that one may kill on the Sabbath any lethal creature that is actually chasing after him (or anyone else), since the actual threat to life overrides the Biblical prohibition against *melachah.* The Baraisa, however, refers to where one comes across a lethal creature that is *not* chasing after him (or anyone else), and it rules – in accordance with the view of R' Shimon – that one may kill the creature if it is one of the five enumerated by the Baraisa.[22]

The Gemara records another discussion regarding a Baraisa on this topic:

תָּנֵי תַּנָּא קַמֵּיהּ דְּרָבָא בַּר רַב הוּנָא – A teacher of Baraisos taught the following **in the presence of Rava bar Rav Huna: הַהוֹרֵג נְחָשִׁים וְעַקְרַבִּים בְּשַׁבָּת אֵין רוּחַ חֲסִידִים נוֹחָה הֵימֶנּוּ – IF ONE KILLS** poisonous **SNAKES OR SCORPIONS ON THE SABBATH,**[23] **THE SPIRIT OF PIOUS ONES IS NOT PLEASED WITH HIM,** for he has killed a creature on the Sabbath unnecessarily. **אָמַר לוֹ – [Rava bar Rav Huna] said to [the teacher of Baraisos]: וְאוֹתָן חֲסִידִים אֵין רוּחַ חֲכָמִים נוֹחָה מֵהֶם – And those pious ones,** who are displeased with the one who kills the snakes or scorpions on the Sabbath, **the spirit of the Sages is not pleased with *them*!**[24]

The Gemara notes:

וּפְלִיגָא דְּרַב הוּנָא – And the opinion **of Rav Huna** (as evident from the following incident) **disagrees** with the sentiment just expressed here by his son, Rava bar Rav Huna. **דְּרַב הוּנָא חַזְיֵיהּ לְהַהוּא גַּבְרָא דְּקָא קָטִיל זִיבּוּרָא – For Rav Huna** once **saw a certain person who was killing a bee** on the Sabbath. **אָמַר לֵיהּ – [Rav Huna] said to him** critically: **שְׁלֵימְתִּינְהוּ לְכוּלְּהוּ – Have you finished them all off!?**[25]

The Gemara cites a Baraisa on the topic of one who confronts a dangerous creature:

תָּנוּ רַבָּנָן – The Rabbis taught in a Baraisa: נִזְדַּמְּנוּ לוֹ נְחָשִׁים וְעַקְרַבִּים – IF poisonous **SNAKES AND SCORPIONS CROSSED ONE'S PATH, הֲרָגָן בְּיָדוּעַ שֶׁנִּזְדַּמְּנוּ לוֹ לְהוֹרְגָן – then IF HE KILLED THEM, ONE SHOULD KNOW THAT THEY CROSSED HIS PATH** for him **TO KILL THEM.**[26] **לֹא הֲרָגָן בְּיָדוּעַ שֶׁנִּזְדַּמְּנוּ לְהוֹרְגוֹ וְנַעֲשָׂה לוֹ נֵס מִן הַשָּׁמַיִם – IF HE DID NOT KILL THEM** and they did not harm him, **ONE SHOULD KNOW THAT THEY CROSSED HIS PATH TO KILL HIM, BUT A HEAVENLY MIRACLE WAS PERFORMED FOR HIM** and he was spared.[27]

The Gemara qualifies the Baraisa:

אָמַר עוּלָּא – Ulla said, וְאִיתֵימָא רַבָּה בַּר בַּר חָנָה אָמַר רַבִּי יוֹחָנָן – and some say it was **Rabbah bar bar Chanah** who **said** it **in the name of R' Yochanan: בְּנִישּׁוּפִין בּוֹ – The** last part of the Baraisa refers to **where they** [the snakes] **were hissing at him.** Only then does the Baraisa say that one should know that they were sent to kill him.[28]

An incident involving the killing of a dangerous creature:

אָמַר רַבִּי אַבָּא בַּר כַּהֲנָא – R' Abba bar Kahana said: פַּעַם אַחַת נָפַל אֶחָד בְּבֵית הַמִּדְרָשׁ – One time, [a poisonous snake] fell into the study hall on the Sabbath, **וְעָמַד נִיוָתִי אֶחָד וַהֲרָגוֹ – and a certain Nabatean**[29] **rose up and killed it, אָמַר רַבִּי –** whereupon **Rebbi said: פָּגַע בּוֹ כַּיּוֹצֵא בּוֹ – "One similar to it has struck it down!"**

The Gemara seeks to ascertain the intent of Rebbi's remark:

אִיבַּעְיָא לְהוּ – They inquired: פָּגַע בּוֹ כַּיּוֹצֵא בּוֹ דְּשַׁפִּיר עָבִיד – When he said, **"One similar to it has struck it down,"** did Rebbi mean **that he was doing the proper thing** by killing it,[30] **אוֹ לֹא – or** did he mean that he was **not** doing the proper thing?[31]

The Gemara replies:

תָּא שְׁמַע – Come, learn a proof from the following: **דְּרַבִּי אַבָּא בְּרֵיהּ דְּרַבִּי חִיָּיא בַּר אַבָּא וְרַבִּי זֵירָא הֲווּ יָתְבֵי אַקִּילְעָא דְּבֵי רַבִּי יַנַּאי – For** it once happened that **R' Abba the son of R' Chiya bar Abba and R' Zeira were sitting on the porch of R' Yannai's house, נְפַק מִילְּתָא מִבֵּינַיְיהוּ –** and **the** following **matter came up between them: בָּעוּ מִינֵּיהּ מֵרַבִּי יַנַּאי – They inquired of R' Yannai: מַהוּ לַהֲרוֹג נְחָשִׁים וְעַקְרַבִּים בְּשַׁבָּת – What is [the law]** regarding whether one is allowed **to kill** poisonous **snakes and scorpions on**

NOTES

21. *Rashi;* cf. *Tosafos;* see also *Ritva MHK* ed.

22. Thus, the following emerges from the Gemara here (according to *Rashi's* explanation): Lethal creatures can be divided into two groups – the five enumerated in the Baraisa (which are especially belligerent) and all others (which are not quick to attack a person, but are lethal to him if they do). The five belligerent ones may be killed on sight according to the opinion of R' Shimon, but not according to the opinion of R' Yehudah. If *any* lethal creature is actually chasing someone, then all agree that it may be killed, for the threat to life supersedes the Sabbath prohibitions.

23. That is, where they are not actually attacking anyone (*Rashi* below ד״ה ואותן חסידים, and *Tosafos* ד״ה ברצין אחריו).

24. Because the person who has killed the snakes or scorpions has done the right thing. For though these creatures pose no direct danger at present, they will ultimately pose a danger when aroused to attack (*Rashi*).

[*Tosafos* wonder why Rava bar Rav Huna's ruling in this matter is not contradicted by the Baraisa above, which has been interpreted as reflecting the lenient view of R' Shimon, yet permits killing only one of the five species enumerated there, where no one is presently being attacked. (This is one of the considerations that prompt *Tosafos* to explain the Gemara differently from *Rashi*; see *Leshon HaZahav* for a defense of *Rashi.*)]

25. I.e. what have you accomplished by killing this bee? There are still so many left! Thus, we see that Rav Huna does not allow killing bees indiscriminately on the Sabbath [even though they are in the category of potentially dangerous creatures] (*Rashi*). [*Tosafos* (end of ד״ה כל המזיקין) maintain that Rav Huna would in theory permit killing the bees, except that he forbids doing so because it is too public a display of Sabbath desecration.]

26. That is, God sent them his way in order to grant him the privilege of killing them. For these creatures were destined to cause harm, and God causes merit [in this case, the removal of danger] to come about through a meritorious person (*Rashi*). [Thus, one may take this as an indication that he is a meritorious person.]

27. And God wished to indicate to him that he had sinned in some way, and was deserving of punishment, but he was spared through a miracle (*Rashi*). [And the person should take this incident and its implications to heart, and be stirred to repentance.]

28. A snake hisses when it is aroused to attack its enemy (*Rashi*).

[Scorpions, though, do not hiss. Perhaps Ulla's qualification is said only with regard to snakes. In the case of scorpions, however, which are more prone to attack a person than snakes are, the person should regard himself as the beneficiary of a miracle even if there was no actual indication that the scorpion meant to attack him (see *Megadim Chadashim*). *R' Perachyah,* though, interprets נישופין בו as *attaching themselves to him* (or *attacking him* – see Appendix II op cit.) which can apply equally to a scorpion.]

29. I.e. a Jew from Nabatea [an ancient Arabic kingdom near Eretz Yisrael] (*Rashi*).

30. And Rebbi meant: The snake was dangerous and the one who killed it proved equally dangerous to the snake (see *Rashi*).

31. And Rebbi's comment was meant critically (*Rashi*). I.e. he is as evil as a snake [for he has desecrated the Sabbath by killing it] (*Chidushei HaRan*).

[The snake, though poisonous, was not of the species of "the snake that is in the Land of Israel," whose killing the Baraisa permits on the Sabbath (see *Hagahos Ben Aryeh*). Thus, the Gemara is uncertain whether Rebbi approved or disapproved of the Nabatean's actions.]

אייתו להו פורייתא לרב חנן בר רבא לא אייתו ליה אשכחיה מתני ליה לבריה ועל צואה של קטן מפני קטן א"ל אבין שטיא מתני שטותא לבניה ° והלא היא עצמה מוכנת לכלבים וכ"ת דלא חזיא ליה מאתמול ו) והתניא א נהרות המושכין ומעיינות הנובעין הרי הן כרגלי כל אדם ואלא היכי אתנייה אימא ב על צואה של תרנגולים מפני קטן ותיפוק ליה דהוי גרף של רעי וכ"ת גרף של רעי אגב מנא אין איהו גופיה לא ג) והא ההוא עכבר דאישתכח באיספרמקי דרב אשי ואמר להו נקוטו בצוציתיה ואפקוה באשפה וקטן באשפה מאי בעי ליה בחצר חצר נמי גרף של רעי הוא [א] באשפה שבחצר: ועל עקרב שלא תישך: א"ר יהושע בן לוי כל המזיקין נהרגין בשבת מתיב רב יוסף ד חמשה נהרגין בשבת ואלו הן זבוב שבארץ מצרים וצירעה שבנינוה ועקרב שבחדייב ונחש שבא"י וכלב שוטה בכל מקום מני אילימא ה) ר' יהודה הא אמר מלאכה שאינה צריכה לגופה חייב עליה אלא לאו ר"ש והני הוא דשרי אחריני לא אמר ר' ירמיה ז) ומאן נימא לן דהא מתרצתא היא דילמא משבשתא היא אמר רב יוסף אנא א"ל מתנינא לה ואותיבנא לה ואנא מתרצנא לה ה ברצו אחריו ודברי הכל תני תנא קמיה דרבא בר רב הונא ההורג נחשים ועקרבים בשבת אין רוח חסידים נוחה הימנו א"ל ואותן חסידים אין רוח חכמים נוחה מהם ופליגא דרב הונא דרב הונא חזייה לההוא גברא דקא קטיל זיבורא א"ל שלימתינהו לכולהו ת"ר נזדמנו לו נחשים ועקרבים ט הרגן בידוע שנזדמנו לו להורגן לא הרגן בידוע שנזדמנו להורגו ונעשה לו נס מן השמים אמר עולא ואיתימא רבה בר בר חנה א"ר יוחנן בנישופין בו א"ר אבא בר כהנא פעם אחת נפל אחד בבהמ"ד ועמד ניותי אחד והרגו אמר רבי פגע בו כיוצא בו איבעיא להו פגע בו כיוצא בו דשפיר עביד או לא ת"ש דר' אבא בריה דר' חייא בר אבא ור' זירא הוו יתבי אקילעא דבי ר' ינאי נפק מילתא מבינייהו בעו מיניה מר' ינאי מהו להרוג נחשים ועקרבים בשבת אמר להו צירעה אני הורג נחש ועקרב לא כ"ש דילמא לפי תומו דאמר רב יהודה י רוק דורסו לפי תומו ואמר רב ששת י נחש דורסו לפי תומו ואמר רב קטינא ה עקרב דורסו לפי תומו י) אבא בר מרתא דהוא אבא בר מניומי הוה מסקי ביה דבי ריש גלותא זוזי אייתיוהו קא מצערא ליה הוה שדי רוקא אמר להו ריש גלותא אייתו מאנא סחיפו עליה אמר להו לא צריכתו הכי א"ר יהודה רוק דורסו לפי תומו אמר להו צורבא מרבנן הוא שבקוהו ו) אמר ר' אבא בר כהנא א"ר חנינא ט פמוטות של בית רבי מותר לטלטלן בשבת א"ל ר' זירא בניטלין בידו אחת או בשתי ידים

רש"י

גמ' אייתו להו פורייתא. מטות לישב עליהן: לא אייתו ליה. והושיבוהו לארץ: מפני קטן. שלא יטפח בו ויתלכלך: א"ל. רב חנן שהיה כעוס ומתכוון להקניטו לר' אבין: והלא מוכנת לכלבים. ולמה לי לכפות כלי יפנה משם שהרי ראויה לטלטל: דלא חזיא מאתמול. שהיום נולדה: נהרות המושכים כרגלי כל אדם. משום דמידי דנייד הוא ולא קני שביתה ואע"פ שבא ממוך לתחום כל אדם מוליכן למקום שעירב לו לילך מיהו שמעינן מינה דמותרין בטלטול ואע"ג דמאתמול לא הוי הני קמן כיון דלמורקיהו בהכי דעתיה עלייהו ה"נ כיון דלמורקיה דקטן בהכי דעתיה עליה דלכי מיתי יאכילנה לכלבים: א"ל ר' אבין. ואלא היכי אתנייה: צואה של תרנגולים. דלא חזיא לכלבים ושל קטן דקתני מתניתין שמטפח בה קטן קאמר ובשביל הקטן אמר כופין: תיפוק ליה דגרף של רעי הוא. דמאיס ולפנייה דהא קי"ל במסכת ביצה גרף של רעי מותר להוציאו לאשפה: וכי תימא גרף של רעי דמותר אגב מנא אין. הא דקי"ל מותר להוציאו משום דרמי במנא דגרף היינו כלי חרס העשוי לכך ואגב מנא הוא דשרי לטלטולי אבל בפני עצמו לא והכא לאו במנא רמי: באספרמקי. בשמים: בצוציתיה. בזנבו אלמא בלאו מנא נמי מטלטלי ליה: ומשני באשפה. דלא רמי קמייהו ולא גרף של רעי הוא: קטן באשפה מאי בעי. סתם אשפה ברה"ר הוא ומאי בעי התם קטן דקא מיכסי ליה בשביל קטן: ומשני בחצר. דשכיח קטן התם קס"ד בחצר דלאו אשפה וקפריך סוף סוף גרף של רעי הוא ומשני באשפה שבחצר: כל המזיקין. ההורגן: נהרגין בשבת. וקס"ד אפי' אין רצין אחריו ומשום דס"ל כר"ש דמלאכה שאינה צריכה לגופה מדרבנן הוא דאסירא והכא לא גזור: (נהרגין בשבת. אפי' אין רצין אחריו) משום דס"ל דשמתן הורגן הן: האמר חייב עליה. והיכי שרי במלאכה גמורה כשאין רצין אחריו ליכא פקוח נפש: ומאן לימא לן כו'. דרב יוסף הוא מתני ליה כדלקמן ולא בדבי ר' חייא ור' אושעיא מיתנייה וכל מתניתא דלא מתנייא בתוספתא דר' חייא ור' אושעיא איכא לספוקי במשבשתא ולא מותבינן מינה: אנא תנינא לה. במתניתא דידי ואנא אותבינא בבי מדרשא אדר' יהושע בן לוי: ואנא מתרצנא לה. דלא תיקשי כי אמר ר' יהושע בן לוי כל המזיקין נהרגין ברצין אחריו קאמר דפקוח נפש הוא: ודברי הכל. ואפי' לר' יהודה והא דחמשה נהרגין כשאין רצין אחריו ור' שמעון: אין רוח חסידים נוחה הימנו. דעתן של חסידים אינה מעורבת עמו שאין הגון בעיניהם על מה שעשה: נוחה. עריבה אין מתרצין במעשיו: אמר ליה. רבא לתנא: ואותן חסידים. השונאין אותו על כך אין רוח חכמים עריבה עמהם להיות נוחה ומיושבת במה שרואין במדת חסידים הללו דשפיר עביד דאי לא מזיקין השתא סופן להזיק בשעת כעסן: שלימתינהו לכולהו. הרגת את כולן כלומר מה אהני בהא אהני טובא איכא אלמא לאו שפיר עבד והא דרבא פליג אדאבוה: שנזדמנו לו להורגן. לכך באו לידו שזימן לו המקום לאבדן לפי שהיו עתידות להזיק וגלגלו זכות על ידי זכאי: לא הרגן בידוע שנזדמנו לו להרוג אותו. והראה לו הקב"ה שחטא אלא שנעשה לו נס: בנישופין בו. בכה"ג קתני בידוע שנזדמנו להורגו נישופין כן דרך הנחש עושה כעין שריקה כשהוא רואה שונאו וכועס: ניותי. על שם מקומו וישראל היה: דשפיר עביד. וכיוצא בו דקאמר לאו לגנאי הוא אלא הנחש רודף ונעשה זה כיוצא בו: או לא. וכיוצא בו דקאמר לגנאי הוא: צרעה אני הורג. בשבת לכלות מזיקין ואף על פי שאינה מועדת כאלו: לא כל שכן. אלמא שפיר עביד: דילמא לפי תומו. לא שיעמוד עליו ויהרגנו להדיא אלא כשהוא הולך לתומו ונחש או עקרב בפניו אין צריך ליִשמט ממנו אלא דורכו והולך ואם מת בדריכתו ימות הואיל ולא נתכוין ° דדבר שאין מתכוין לר' יהודה מדרבנן הוא ולענין מזיקין לא גזור: רוק דורסו לפי תומו. שאין מתכוין למרח ולאשוויי גומות דאף על גב דממילא ממרח הוא כי לא מיכוין שרי משום מאיסותא: הוה שדי רוקא. היה רוק מוטל לפניהם ושבת היתה: פמוטות. מנורות ולא של חוליות היו:

של

תוספות

כל המזיקין נהרגין בשבת. אף על גב דתנן במתניתין ועל עקרב שלא ישוך אילטריך לאשמעינן דהריגה נמי שרינן דסלקא דעתך דלאסירא משום דמיפרסמא מילתא טפי מכלכלה ומהאי טעמא נמי פליג רב הונא בסמוך ואסר הריגה:

ברצין אחריו וד"ה. פי' בקונט' דרבי יהושע בן לוי ברצין אחריו והוי פקוח נפש וברייתא באין רצין וכר"ש וקשה דא"כ תקשה מהך ברייתא לרבא בר רב הונא דשרי להרוג נחשים ועקרבים בשבת דע"כ באין רצין אחריו מיירי דאי ברצין אחריו אמאי אין רוח חסידים נוחה הימנו לפירוש הקונטרס דברצין אחריו איכא פקוח נפש ועוד בעיא דההוא שהרג נחש ומיבעיא לן אי שפיר עבד תיפשוט מהכא דלא שרינן לר"ש באין רצין אלא ה' בלבד ועוד קשה לר"י דלישנא דהאי מתרצנא לה משמע דברייתא עצמה ונראה לר"י לפרש דברייתא ברצין אחריו וד"ה פירוש אפילו ר' יהודה מודה דמשמה שרי להרוג ברצין אחריו אבל שאר אסור להורגן אפילו רצין אחריו לר' יהודה ור' יהושע בן לוי כר"ש דשרי שאר (א) אפילו באין רצין אחריו ורב הונא דאסר בסמוך לא סבר כרבי יהושע בן לוי ונראה לר"י וכן פירש ר"ח שאין להקל כרבי יהושע בן לוי אלא כהנהו אמוראי דלקמן דלא שרו אלא בדריסה לפי תומו:

עין משפט נר מצוה

עד א מיי' פ"ה מהלכות י"ט הלכה יד טוש"ע או"ח סימן שצז סעיף טו:

עה ב ג מיי' פכ"ו מהל' שבת הלכה יג סמג לאוין סה טוש"ע או"ח סימן שח סעיף לד:

עו ד ה מיי' פי"א שם הלכה ד סמג שם טור שו"ע או"ח סימן שטז סעיף י:

עז ו מיי' פכ"א שם הלכה ג ופכ"ו הלכה יג סמג שם טור שו"ע או"ח שם סעיף יא:

עח ז ח מיי' פי"א מהלכות שבת הל"ד סמג שם טור שו"ע שם סעיף י:

עט ט מיי' פכ"ו מהל' שבת הלכה יא טור שו"ע או"ח סימן רעט סעיף ז:

גליון הש"ס

גמ' והלא היא עצמה מוכנת לכלבים. ע"ל דף יט ע"ב תוס' ד"ה שמן: רש"י ד"ה דלמא לפי תומו וכו' דדבר שאין מתכוין לר"י מדרבנן. ע"ל דף מא ע"ב תוס' ד"ה מיחס:

רבינו חננאל

ביומא ליתעכב עד לאורתא ולטבול. ומסקינן משום דסברי רבנן אע"ג דצלי ליה טבילה בזמנה מצוה ור' יוסי סבר טבילה בזמנה לאו מצוה היא האי ר' יוסי בר' יהודה דגרסינן בנדה פרק המפלת בענין טועה. ר' יוסי בר"י אומר דייה לטבול באחרונה דקסבר טבילה בזמנה לאו מצוה היא. וזה רבי יוסי דהיה (אומר) שם כתוב על בשרו. אסיקנא בגמרא דשבעת ימים (ביומא דף ז') דבטבילה בזמנה מצוה פליגי ונתבררה בסוף יום הכפורים דהא לר' יוסי בר' יהודה היא ואיכא אחריתי התם לר' יוסי דאמר כל היום כולו כשר לטבילה. דאלמא סבר טבילה בזמנה [מצוה] היא: א"ר אמי בדליקה התירו לומר כל המכבה אינו מפסיד. וכן הלכה: נכרי שבא לכבות אין אומרים לו כבה ואל תכבה אלא מניחין אותו. ואין אומרים לו כבה וגם אין מונעין אותו מלכבות. אבל קטן העושה לדעת אין מניחין אותו לכבות: אריב"ל כל המזיקין נהרגין. אסיקנא כשהן רצין אחריו. אבל אין רצין אחריו אין נהרגין אלא אלו בלבד. זבוב שבארץ מצרים. וצירעה שבנינוה ועקרב שבחדייב ונחש שבא"י וכלב שוטה בכ"מ. פי' נישופין כדכתיב הוא ישופך ראש ואתה תשופנו עקב: רוק וכן נחש וכן עקרב אם דורסן לפי תומן שפיר דמי ושרי: א"ר חנינא פמוטות של בית רבי מותר לטלטלן בשבת. א"ל ר' זירא בניטלין בידו אחת

מסורת הש"ס

א) ביצה לט. עירובין מו. מח. [תוספתא ביצה פ"ד], ב) ביצה לו:, ג) [לעיל עג: וש"נ], ד) [פסחים לט:], ה) [גי' הרי"ף והרא"ש בשבת], ו) [יומא פד. יבמות קכ.], ז) [צ"ל ואמר].

הגהות הב"ח

(א) תוס' ד"ה ברצין וכו' כר' שמעון דשרי שאר מזיקין אפילו:

הגהות הגר"א

[א] גמרא באשפה שבחצר כו'. נ"ב גירסת הרי"ף בחצר אחרת:

רב נסים גאון

להפרישו מאי דשקלינן וטרינן בהא מילתא איתא במס' יבמות (דף קיד) בפרק חרש שנשא פיקחת: סוף סוף גרף של רעי הוא ונפקיה כבר פירשנו בפרק כירה כי עיקר השמועה שיש בה התרת זה הדבר בפרק משילין פירות (ביצה דף לו): ר' יהודה אומר כל מלאכה שאינה צריכה לגופה חייב עליה כבר פירשנוה בפרק יציאות השבת ואמרנו כי עיקרה הן דברי ר' יהודה שאמרם כאן בזו המשנה מעשה בא לפני

ליקוטי רש"י

נהרות המושכין. היינו סתם נהרות שיש להם משך להלאה ממקום מקור נביעתן. ומעיינות הנובעין. ואין יוצאין מגומות נביעתן לימשך הלאה. הרי הן כרגלי כל אדם. אין להם שום שביתה לא במקומן ולא כרגלי הבעלים ולא כרגלי הממלא אלא כל אדם מוליכן ברגליו דכל מידי דנייד לית ליה שביתה והכי מפרשינן בעירובין בפרק מי שהוציאוהו [ביצה לט.]. כיון דניידי לא קנו שביתה ואפילו הן של יחיד אינן כרגליו [עירובין מו.]. גרף של רעי. דתניא במסכת ביצה (לו:) מותר להוציאו לאשפה שבחצר [לעיל מז.]. שמותר לטלטלו ולפנותו לאשפה מחמת מאוס כדאמרינן בפרק בתרא (ביצה לו:) [ביצה כא:]. גרף. כלי חרס המוכן לכך [לעיל שם]. אגב מנא אין איהו גופיה לא. דדוקא גרף נקט דאגב מנא שרי לטלטל את הרעי אבל בפני עצמו ליטול את הרעי או דבר מאוס ממש בידו ויוליכנו לא שרו ליה [ביצה לו:]. אילימא ר' יהודה. בפרק המצניע (לעיל צג:) גבי מוציא את המת במטה. מלאכה שאינה צריכה לגופה. כמו מוציא את המת לקוברו אינו צריך לגופה דהוצאה ולא למת אלא לפנות ביתו והוצאה הצריכה לגופה כגון שהוא צריך לחפץ זה במקום אחר [לעיל עג:]. שברצונו לא תעשה ואינו צריך לעיקר (תחלתה) [תכליתה] כי הכא. ופלוגתייהו בהמצניע (לעיל צג:) גבי מוציא המת במטה חייב ואף על גב דהוצאת המת לא ניחא ליה ביה ור' שמעון פוטר [שם יב.]. חייב עליה. דמשום אין צריכה לגופה לא מיפטר הואיל וצריכה לדבר אחר מלאכת מחשבת הוא [שם לא:]. אלא ר"ש. דהוי מלאכה שאינה צריכה לגופה וכל מלאכה שאינה צריכה (לגופה) אלא לסלקה מעליו הוי מלאכה שאינה צריכה לגופה דברצונו לא באה לו ולא היה צריך לה הלכך לאו מלאכת מחשבת היא לר' שמעון [שם צג:]. ומאן נימא לן דהא מתרצתא וכו'. רבי חייא ורבי אושעיא סדרו את הברייתות ודקדקו בדברי כל חכם לומר כמו שאמר אבל יש תנאים הרבה שמוסיפים על משנתם בדדמי [חולין קמא:]. ואמרינן (חולין קמא.) כל מתניתא דלא מיתנייא בי רבי חייא ורבי אושעיא לא תותבו מינה בבי מדרשא [ב"מ פה:]. אין רוח חכמים נוחה מהם. אין דעת חכמים נוחה עליהם במעשיו כלומר אין מחזיקין לו טובה [קידושין יז:]. אין רוח חכמה וחסידות בקרבו [ב"ק צד: ע"ש בגה"ש]. אין נחת רוח לחכמי ישראל במעשיו של זה אין דעתם נוחה עליהם הימנו על ידו [ב"מ מח.]. בנישופין בו. כשהנחש בא לנשוך הוא נושף כמין שריקה [בראשית ג, טו]. אקילעא. כניסת הבית חדר שלפני הטרקלין שקורין פורטיג"ו בלע"ז [ברכות כב:]. לפני הבית כעין בית שער וקורין פורייט"א [פסחים עב:]. פמוטות. מנורה של מתכת [לעיל מד.]. בניטלין בידו אחת. בשתי ידים אסור לטלטלה דלאו לטלטולי עבידא דאדם קובע לה מקום [שם מה:].

the Sabbath?[32] אָמַר לְהוּ – **He told them:** צִירְעָה אֲנִי הוֹרֵג – **I am accustomed to kill** even **a wasp** on the Sabbath![33] נָחָשׁ וְעַקְרָב לֹא כָּל שֶׁכֵּן – Is killing **a** poisonous **snake or scorpion not** permitted **all the more so!?** Thus, we must conclude that Rebbi was praising the Nabatean for killing the snake on the Sabbath.[34]

The Gemara rejects the proof:

דִּילְמָא לְפִי תוּמּוֹ – **Perhaps** R' Yannai meant only that one may kill the creatures on the Sabbath by treading on them **innocently,**[35] but R' Yannai would agree that one may not kill them deliberately.[36] דְּאָמַר רַב יְהוּדָה – **For Rav Yehudah said:** רוֹק דּוֹרְסוֹ לְפִי תוּמּוֹ – If **spittle** lies before him on the ground, **he may tread on it innocently.**[37] וְאָמַר רַב שֵׁשֶׁת – **And Rav Sheishess said:** נָחָשׁ דּוֹרְסוֹ לְפִי תוּמּוֹ – If a poisonous **snake** lies before him, **he may tread on it innocently.** וְאָמַר רַב קְטִינָא – **And Rav Ketina said:** עַקְרָב דּוֹרְסוֹ לְפִי תוּמּוֹ – If **a scorpion** lies before him, **he may tread on it innocently.**[38]

The Gemara records an incident in which one of the rulings just mentioned plays a role:

אַבָּא בַּר מַרְתָּא דְּהוּא אַבָּא בַּר מְנְיוּמֵי הֲוָה מַסְּקֵי בֵּיהּ דְּבֵי רֵישׁ גָּלוּתָא זוּזֵי – **Abba bar Marta, who is** also known as **Abba bar Manyumi,**[39] **owed money to members of the Exilarch's household.** אַיְיתְיוּהוּ קָא מְצַעֲרֵי לֵיהּ – So **they brought him** to the palace and **were tormenting him** to force him to pay the money. הֲוָה שְׁדֵי רוּקָא – **There was some spittle lying** on the ground before them (on the Sabbath). אָמַר לְהוּ רֵישׁ גָּלוּתָא אַיְיתוּ מָאנָא סְחִיפוּ עִלָּוֵיהּ – **The Exilarch said to them, "Bring a vessel and invert it over [the spittle]."**[40] אָמַר לְהוּ לֹא צְרִיכְתּוּ – **[Abba bar Marta] said to them, "You do not need** to do that. הָכִי אָמַר רַב יְהוּדָה רוֹק דּוֹרְסוֹ לְפִי תוּמּוֹ – **Thus did Rav Yehudah say:** If a person comes upon **spittle** lying on the ground, **he may tread on it innocently."**[41] אָמַר לְהוּ צוּרְבָא מֵרַבָּנָן הוּא שִׁבְקוּהוּ – Upon hearing this, **[the Exilarch] said to them, "**I see that **he is a young rabbinical scholar; leave him alone** and do not torment him."[42]

NOTES

32. [I.e. as a matter of course, even though they are not chasing anyone at the moment.]

33. In order to eliminate potential hazards, even though wasps are not as dangerous as snakes and scorpions (see *Rashi*).

34. [Perhaps, R' Yannai's position is considered indicative of Rebbi's because R' Yannai was his disciple and a member of his court (see *Rambam,* Introduction to *Yad HaChazakah* with *Raavad* and *Kesef Mishneh*).]

35. I.e. if one is walking along and [a wasp or] a snake or scorpion lies in his path, he need not [alter his stride to] avoid stepping on it. Rather, he may tread on it as he walks, and if it dies, it dies. This is permitted even according to R' Yehudah (who holds one liable for performing a *melachah* not needed for its defined purpose). For this is an instance of unintentional killing [since the person's primary intent is to walk, not to crush the creature, and the creature's death is *not* inevitable]. And even R' Yehudah holds that it is Biblically permitted to perform an act from which a *melachah* might result as an unintended side effect [דָּבָר שֶׁאֵין מִתְכַּוֵּן], since such a *melachah* does not qualify as a calculated act [מְלֶאכֶת מַחֲשֶׁבֶת]. Though performance of such an act is generally forbidden by Rabbinic decree, according to R' Yehudah, the Rabbis did not extend their decree to the case of lethal creatures [so that the number of these menaces might be reduced] (*Rashi;* see *Tosafos* to 41b ד״ה מיחם and to 95a ד״ה המכבד; see *Yoma* 34b and *Tosafos* there ד״ה הני מילי).

Ramban, however, objects and asserts that R' Yehudah forbids Biblically an act from which a *melachah* might result as an unintended side effect. Moreover, he maintains that R' Yannai's statement, "I am accustomed to kill even a wasp," indicates that he would kill it intentionally. Therefore, *Ramban* explains that R' Yannai is following the view of R' Shimon, who holds that it is Biblically permissible to do a *melachah* not needed for its defined purpose (see above, note 13). And though such *melachah* is generally forbidden Rabbinically, according to R' Shimon, the Rabbis suspended their decree with regard to eliminating dangerous creatures and permitted one to kill them intentionally. However, they required that one do so inconspicuously by *pretending* that he is stepping on the creature unintentionally, and this is what is meant by "treading on them innocently" (see *Ramban* et al.; see, also, *Orach Chaim* 316:10).

36. Thus, Rebbi's remark might have been meant critically, since the Nabatean killed the snake deliberately.

37. Rubbing spittle into an earthen floor often results in the leveling out of holes or other irregularities in the ground, which constitutes the *melachah* of *building.* The Amora Rav Yehudah rules that one may press the spittle into the ground by treading on it innocently – that is, by stepping on the spittle without any intention to level out the ground. And he need not be concerned about the leveling of the ground that might result from his actions. For the act of stepping on the spittle is an act that *might* produce an *unintended* forbidden consequence (a leveling of the ground) and [though such an act is generally forbidden Rabbinically according to the Tanna R' Yehudah] the Rabbis permitted it in this case in order to remove the repulsive spittle (see *Rashi*).

The Rishonim (*Ramban* et al.) understand that *Rashi* here explains "treading on it innocently" the same way he understands it above – namely, that one walks by normally and if he happens to tread on it in the normal course of his walking, so be it. *Sfas Emes* (end of ד״ה בגמ׳ א״ר יהודה), however, suggests that *Rashi* agrees here with the other Rishonim that one steps on the spittle *deliberately* (i.e. not necessarily in the course of his normal walking) but without intent to *level the ground.* [The main point of "innocently" according to *Rashi* is that the *melachah* which might ensue is being done *unintentionally.* Thus, in the case of stepping on the dangerous creature, it is the stepping itself that must be done unintentionally (i.e. in the course of normal walking). For to step on it deliberately would be a Biblical *melachah* (should the creature in fact die), since the sole *intent* of the act of *deliberately* stepping on the creature is to kill it. (The fact that the creature might *not* die as a result is a mitigating factor only where the act is *unintended,* not where it is intended.) In the case of spittle, however, the stepping itself may be deliberate, since the person's intent is to push the spittle into the ground, *not* to level the ground. Hence, even should the ground be leveled as a result, it would be viewed as an *unintended* act of leveling.] *Sfas Emes'* understanding of *Rashi* is apparently supported by the comments of *Beis Yosef* 316 ד״ה וכן ברוק שלפניו, and by his quoting of *Rashi's* phraseology in *Shulchan Aruch* 316:11 (regarding spittle) after following *Ramban* with regard to dangerous creatures in (316:10). See also *Magen Avraham* 316:24 and *Eliyahu Rabbah* there §11.

38. Thus, the Gemara does not resolve whether Rebbi's comment was an expression of approval or disapproval. [See, however, *Yefei Einayim,* who cites *Yerushalmi* as explaining that Rebbi's comment was an expression of disapproval.]

39. [Possibly, Marta was his mother and Manyumi his father (*Seder HaDoros,* entry on מרתא).]

40. Apparently, the sight of the spittle on the ground was repulsive to them, and there were no servants present to remove it, or it was lying in a place in which carrying is forbidden (e.g. a *karmelis*). See also *R' Perachyah.* [See, however, an alternative explanation in *Sfas Emes.*]

41. Thus, there is no need for you to cover it. You may simply tread on it as you walk by, and press it into the ground (see above, note 37; see, however, an alternative explanation in *Sfas Emes*).

42. [It seems strange that members of the Exilarch's household should seek to enforce payment of a debt on the Sabbath. Perhaps, the meaning here is not that they brought him to the palace and tormented him *on the Sabbath.* Rather, they would do so during the week. One Sabbath, however, he happened to be at the Exilarch's palace and related Rav Yehudah's teaching to them, whereupon the Exilarch commanded that they should no longer bother him. Alternatively, this represents another instance among several others in the Talmud where we find that members of the Exilarch's household behaved in a high-handed and improper manner (see *HaBoneh* in *Ein Yaakov*). *R' Perachyah,* however, explains that Abba bar Marta was being *detained* in the palace (which might mean that he had been imprisoned there during the week) and upon discovering that he was a Torah scholar, the Exilarch ordered his release.]

כל המזיקין נהרגין בשבת. אף על גב דתנן במתניתין ועל עקרב שלא ישוך איצטריך לאשמעינן דהריגה נמי שרינן דסלקא דעתך דאסירא משום דמיפרסמא מילתא טפי מצידה ומהאי טעמא נמי פליג רב הונא בסמוך ואסר הריגה:

ברצין אחריו וד"ה. פי' בקונט' דרבי יהושע בן לוי ברצין אחריו והוי פקוח נפש וברייתא באין רצין וכר"ש וקשה דא"כ תקשה מהך ברייתא לרבא בר רב הונא דשרי להרוג נחשים ועקרבים בשבת דע"כ באין רצין אחריו מיירי דאי ברצין אחריו אמאי אין רוח חסידים נוחה הימנו לפירוש הקונטרס דברצין אחריו איכא פקוח נפש ועוד בנויותי שהרג נחש ומיבעיא לן אי שפיר עבד תיפשוט מהכא דלא שרינן לר"ש באין רצין אלא ה' בלבד ועוד קשה לר"י דלישנא דאלא ממרגלא לה משמע לברייתא עצמה ונראה לר"י לפרש דברייתא ברצין אחריו וד"ה פירוש אפילו ר' יהודה מודה דחמשה שרי להרוג ברצין אחריו אבל שאר אסור להורגן אפילו רצין אחריו לר' יהודה ור' יהושע בן לוי כר"ש דשרי שאר (א) אפילו באין רצין אחריו ורב הונא דאסר בסמוך לא סבר כרבי יהושע בן לוי ונראה לר"י וכן פירש ר"ח שאין להקל כרבי יהושע בן לוי אלא כסתמא דמוריי לדלקמן דלא שרו אלא בדריסה לפי תומו:

אייתו להו פורייתא לרב חנן בר רבא לא אייתו ליה אשכחיה מתני ליה לבריה ועל צואה של קטן מפני קטן א"ל אבין שטיא מתני שטותא לבניה * והלא היא עצמה מוכנת לכלבים וכ"ת דלא חזיא ליה מאתמול (א) והתניא א נהרות המושכין ומעיינות הנובעין הרי הן כרגלי כל אדם ואלא היכי אתנייה אימא ב על צואה של תרנגולים מפני קטן ותיפוק ליה דהוי גרף של רעי וכ"ת גרף של רעי אגב מנא אין איהו גופיה לא ג והא ד ההוא עכבר דאישתכח באיספרמקי דרב אשי ואמר להו נקוטו בצוציתיה ואפקוה ואשפה וקטן באשפה מאי בעי ליה בחצר חצר נמי גרף של רעי הוא [א] באשפה שבחצר: ועל עקרב שלא תישך: א"ר יהושע בן לוי כל המזיקין נהרגין בשבת מתיב רב יוסף ה חמשה נהרגין בשבת ואלו הן זבוב שבארץ מצרים וצירעה שבנינוה ועקרב שבחדייב ונחש שבא"י וכלב שוטה בכל מקום מני אילימא ו ר' יהודה הא אמר מלאכה שאינה צריכה לגופה חייב עליה אלא לאו ר"ש והני הוא דשרי אחריני לא אמר ר' ירמיה ז ומאן נימא לן דהא מתרצתא היא דילמא משבשתא היא אמר רב יוסף אנא מתנינא לה ואותיבנא לה ואנא מתריצנא לה ח ברצו אחריו ודברי הכל תני תנא קמיה דרבא בר רב הונא ההורג נחשים ועקרבים בשבת אין רוח חסידים נוחה הימנו א"ל ואותן חסידים אין רוח חכמים נוחה מהם ופליגא דרב הונא דרב הונא חזייה לההוא גברא דקא קטיל זיבורא א"ל שלימתינהו לכולהו ת"ר נזדמנו לו נחשים ועקרבים ט הרגן בידוע שנזדמנו לו להורגן לא הרגן בידוע שנזדמנו להורגו ונעשה לו נס מן השמים אמר עולא ואיתימא רבה בר בר חנה א"ר יוחנן בנישופין בו א"ר אבא בר כהנא פעם אחת נפל אחד בבהמ"ד ועמד נויותי אחד והרגו אמר רבי פגע בו כיוצא בו איבעיא להו פגע בו כיוצא בו דשפיר עביד או לא ת"ש דר' אבא בריה דר' חייא בר אבא ור' זירא הוו יתבי אקילעא דבי ר' ינאי נפק מילתא מבינייהו בעו מיניה מר' ינאי מהו להרוג נחשים ועקרבים בשבת אמר להו צירעה אני הורג נחש ועקרב לא כ"ש דילמא לפי תומו דאמר רב יהודה י רוק דורסו לפי תומו ואמר רב ששת כ נחש דורסו לפי תומו ואמר רב קטינא ל עקרב דורסו לפי תומו מ אבא בר מרתא דהוא אבא בר מניומי הוה מסקי ביה דבי ריש גלותא זוזי אייתיוהו קא מצערא ליה הוה שדי רוקא אמר להו ריש גלותא אייתו מאנא סחיפו עלויה אמר להו לא צריכתו הכי א"ר יהודה רוק דורסו לפי תומו אמר להו צורבא מרבנן הוא שבקוהו נ אמר ר' אבא בר כהנא א"ר חנינא ס פמוטות של בית רבי מותר לטלטלן בשבת א"ל ר' זירא בניטלין בידו אחת או בשתי ידים

גמ' אייתו להו פורייתא. מטות לישב עליהן: **לא אייתו ליה.** והושיבוהו לארץ: מפני קטן. שלא יטפח בו ויתלכלך: **א"ל.** רב חנן שהיה כעוס ומתכוין להקניטו לר' אבין: והלא מוכנת לכלבים. ולמה לי לכפות כלי יפנה משם שהרי ראויה לטלטל: **דלא חזיא מאתמול.** שהיום נולדה: **נהרות המושכים כרגלי כל אדם.** משום דמידי דנייד הוא ולא קני שביתה ואע"פ שבא מחוץ לתחום כל אדם מוליכין למקום שעירב לו לילך מיהו שמעינן מינה דמותרין בטלטול ואע"ג דמאתמול לא הוו הני קמן כיון דאורחייהו בהכי דעתיה עלייהו ה"נ כיון דאורחיה דקטן בהכי דעתיה עליה דלכי מיתי יאכלוה לכלבים: **א"ל ר' אבין.** ואלא היכי אתנייה: **צואה של תרנגולים.** דלא חזיא לכלבים ושל קטן דקתני מתניתין מטפחת בה קטן קאמר ובשביל הקטן אמר כופין: **תיפוק ליה דגרף של רעי הוא.** דאמרים ולפניה דהא קי"ל במסכת ביצה גרף של רעי מותר להוציאו לאשפה: וכי תימא גרף של רעי דמותר אגב מנא אין. הא דקי"ל מותר להוציאו משום דלמי במנא דגרף היינו כלי חרס העשוי לכך ואגב מנא הוא דשרי לטלטולי אבל בפני עצמו לא והכא לאו במנא רמי: **באספרמקי.** בשמים: **בצוציתיה.** בזנבו דאלמא בלאו מנא נמי מטלטלי ליה: **ומשני באשפה.** דלא רמי קמייהו ולא גרף של רעי הוא: **קטן באשפה מאי בעי.** פתח אשפה ברה"ר הוא ומאי בעי קטן התם דקא מיכסי ליה בשביל קטן: **ומשני בחצר.** דשכיח קטן התם קס"ד בחצר דלאו אשפה וקפריך סוף סוף גרף של רעי הוא ומשני באשפה שבחצר: **כל המזיקין.** ההורגין: **נהרגין בשבת.** וקס"ד אפי' אין רצין אחריו ומשום דס"ל כר"ש דמלאכה שאינה צריכה לגופה מדרבנן היא דאסירא והכא לא גזור: (נהרגין בשבת. אפי' אין רצין אחריו) משום דס"ל דסתמן הורגין הן: **האמר חייב עליה.** והיכי שרי במלאכה גמורה כשאין רצין אחריו דליכא פקוח נפש: **ומאן לימא לן כו'.** דרב יוסף הוא מתני ליה כדלקמן ולא בדבי ר' חייא ור' אושעיא מיתנייא וכל מתניתא דלא מתנייא בתוספתא דר' חייא ור' אושעיא איכא לספוקי במשבשתא ולא מותבינן מינה: **אנא תנינא לה.** במתניתא דידי ואנא אותבינא בבי מדרשא אדר' יהושע בן לוי: **ואנא מתרצנא לה.** דלא תיקשי

כי אמר ר' יהושע בן לוי כל המזיקין נהרגין ברצין אחריו קאמר דפקוח נפש הוא: **ודברי הכל.** ואפי' לר' יהודה והא דחמשה נהרגין כשאין רצין אחריו ור' שמעון: **אין רוח חסידים נוחה הימנו.** דעתן של חסידים אינה מעורבת עמו שאין הגון בעיניהם על מה שעשה: נוחה. עריבה אין מתרצין במעשיו: **אמר ליה.** רבא לתנא: **ואותן חסידים.** השונאין אותו על כך אין רוח חכמים עריבה עמהם להיות נוחה ומיושבת במה שרואין במדת חסידים הללו דשפיר עביד דאי לא מזיקין השתא סופן להזיק בשעת כעסן: **שלימתינהו לכולהו.** הרגת את כולן כלומר מה אהני בהא אכתי טובא איכא אלמא לאו שפיר עבד והא דרבא פליג אדאבוה: **שנזדמנו לו להורגן.** לכך באו לידו שזימן לו המקום לאבדן לפי שהיו עתידות להזיק וגלגלו זכות על ידי זכאי: **לא הרגן בידוע שנזדמנו לו להרוג אותו.** והראה לו הקב"ה שחטא אלא שנעשה לו נס: **בנישופין בו.** בכה"ג קתני בידוע שנזדמנו להורגו נישופין כן דרך הנחש עושה כעין שריקה כשהוא רואה שונאו וכועס: **נויותי.** על שם מקומו וישראל היה: **דשפיר עביד.** וכיוצא בו דקאמר לאו לגנאי הוא אלא הנחש רודף ונעשה זה כיוצא בו: **או לא.** וכיוצא בו דקאמר לגנאי הוא: **צרעה אני הורג.** בשבת לכלות מזיקין ואף על פי שאינה מועדת כאלו: **לא כל שכן.** אלמא שפיר עביד: **דילמא לפי תומו.** לא שיעמוד עליו ויהרגנו להדיא אלא כשהוא הולך לתומו ונחש או עקרב בפניו אין צריך לישמט ממנו אלא דורכו והולך ואם מת בדריכתו ימות הואיל ולא נתכוין ° דדבר שאין מתכוין לר' יהודה מדרבנן הוא ולענין מזיקין לא גזור: **רוק דורסו לפי תומו.** שאין מתכוין למרח ולאשווי' גומות דאף על גב דממילא ממרח הוא כי לא מיכוין שרי משום מאיסותא: **הוה שדי רוקא.** היה רוק מוטל לפניהם ושבת היתה: **פמוטות.** מנורות ולא של חוליות היו:

של

עין משפט נר מצוה

עד א מיי' פ"ה מהלכות י"ט הלכה יד טוש"ע או"ח סימן שלג סעיף טו:
עה ב ג מיי' פכ"ו מהל' שבת הלכה יג סמג לאוין סה טוש"ע או"ח סימן שח סעיף לד:
עו ד ה מיי' פי"א שם הלכה ד סמג שם טור שו"ע או"ח סימן שטז סעיף י:
עז ו מיי' פכ"א שם הלכה ב ופכ"ו הלכה יג סמג שם טור שו"ע או"ח שם סעיף יא:
עח ז ח מיי' פי"א מהלכות שבת הל"ד סמג שם טור שו"ע שם סעיף י:
עט ט מיי' פכ"ו מהל' שבת הלכה יא טור שו"ע או"ח סימן רעט סעיף ז:

גליון הש"ס

גמ' והלא היא עצמה מוכנת לכלבים. ע"ל דף יט ע"ב תוס' ד"ה שמן: רש"י ד"ה דלמא לפי תומו וכו' דדבר שאין מתכוין לר"י מדרבנן. ע"ל דף מא ע"ב תוס' ד"ה מיחם:

רבינו חננאל

ביומא ליתעכב עד לאורתא ולטבול. ומסקינן משום דסברי רבנן אע"ג דצלי ליה טבילה בזמנה מצוה ור' יוסי סבר טבילה בזמנה לאו מצוה היא האי ר' יוסי בר' יהודה דגרסינן בנדה פרק המפלת בענין טועה. ר' יוסי בר"י אומר דייה לטבול באחרונה דקסבר טבילה בזמנה לאו מצוה היא. וזה רבי יוסי דהיה (אומר) שם כתוב על בשרו. אסיקנא בגמרא דשבעת ימים (ביומא דף ד') דבטבילה בזמנה מצוה פליגי ונתברבה בסוף יום הכפורים דהא לר' יוסי בר' יהודה היא ואיכא אחריתי התם לר' יוסי דאמר כל היום כולו כשר לטבילה. דאלמא סבר טבילה בזמנה [מצוה] היא: **א"ר** אמי בדליקה התירו לומר כל המכבה אינו מפסיד. וכן הלכה: **נכרי** שבא לכבות אין אומרים לו כבה ואל תכבה אלא מניחין אותו. ואין אומרים לו כבה וגם אין מונעין אותו מלכבות. אבל קטן העושה לדעת אין מניחין אותו לכבות: **אריב"ל** כל המזיקין נהרגין. אסיקנא כשהן רצין אחריו. אבל אין רצין אחריו אין נהרגין אלא אלו בלבד. זבוב שבארץ מצרים. וצירעה שבנינוה ועקרב שבחדייב ונחש שבא"י וכלב שוטה בכ"מ. פי' נישופין כדכתיב הוא ישופך ראש ואתה תשופנו עקב: רוק וכן נחש וכן עקרב אם דורסן לפי תומן שפיר דמי ושרי: **א"ר** חנינא פמוטות של בית רבי מותר לטלטלן בשבת. א"ל ר' זירא בניטלין בידו אחת

מסורת הש"ס

א) ביצה לט. עירובין מו. מח. [תוספתא ביצה פ"ד], ב) ביצה לו:, ג) [לעיל עג: וש"נ], ד) [פסחים לט:], ה) [גי' הרי"ף והרא"ש בשבת], ו) [יומא פד. יבמות קכ.], ז) [צ"ל ואמר].

הגהות הב"ח

(א) תוס' ד"ה ברצין וכו' כר' שמעון דשרי שאר מזיקין אפילו:

הגהות הגר"א

[א] גמרא באשפה שבחצר כו'. נ"ב גירסת הרי"ף בחצר אחרת:

רב נסים גאון

להפרישו מאי דשקלינן וטרינן בהא מילתא איתא במס' יבמות (דף קיד) בפרק חרש שנשא פיקחת: **סוף** סוף גרף של רעי הוא ונפקיה כבר פירשנו בפרק כירה כי עיקר השמועה שיש בה התרת זה הדבר בפרק משילין פירות (ביצה דף לו): **ר' יהודה** אומר כל מלאכה שאינה צריכה לגופה חייב עליה כבר פירשנוה בפרק יציאות השבת ואמרנו כי עיקרה הן דברי ר' יהודה שאמרם כאן בזו המשנה מעשה בא לפני

ליקוטי רש"י

נהרות המושכין. היינו סתם נהרות שיש להם משך להלאה ממקום מקור נביעתן. **ומעיינות הנובעין.** ואין יוצאין מגומות נביעתן לימשך הלאה. **הרי הן כרגלי כל אדם.** אין להם שום שביתה לא במקומן ולא כרגלי הבעלים ולא כרגלי הממלא אלא כל אדם מוליכן ברגליו דכל מידי דנייד לית ליה שביתה והכי מפרשינן בעירובין בפרק מי שהוציאוהו [ביצה לט.]. כיון דניידי לא קנו שביתה ואפילו הן של יחיד אינן כרגליו [עירובין מו.]. **גרף של רעי.** דתניא במסכת ביצה (לו:) מותר להוציאו לאשפה שבחצר [לעיל מז.]. שמותר לטלטלו ולפנותו לאשפה מחמת מאום כדאמרינן בפרק בתרא (ביצה לו:) [ביצה כא:]. **גרף.** כלי חרס המוכן לכך [לעיל שם]. **אגב מנא אין איהו גופיה לא.** דדוקא גרף נקט דאגב מנא שרי לטלטל את הרעי אבל בפני עצמו ליטול את הרעי או דבר מאוס ממש בידו ויוציאנו לא שרו ליה [ביצה לו:]. **אילימא ר' יהודה.** בפרק המצניע (לעיל לג:) גבי מוציא את המת במטה. **מלאכה שאינה צריכה לגופה.** כמו מוציא את המת לקוברו אינו צריך לגופה דהוצאה ולא למת אלא לפנות ביתו והוצאה הצריכה לגופה כגון שהוא צריך לחפץ זה במקום אחר [לעיל עג:]. שכרצונו לא תעשה ואינו צריך לעיקר (מתלתה) [מלאכה] כי הכא. ופלוגתייהו בהמצניע (לעיל לג:) גבי מוציא המת במטה חייב ואף על גב דהוצאת המת לא ניחא ליה ור' שמעון פוטר [שם יב.]. **חייב עליה.** דמשום אין צריכה לגופה לא מיפטר הואיל וצריכה לדבר אחר מלאכה מחשבת הוא [שם צג:]. **אלא ר"ש.** דהוי מלאכה שאינה צריכה לגופה וכל מלאכה שאינה צריכה (לגופה) לא מיחייב עלה לאו מלאכה מחשבת היא לר' שמעון [שם צג.]. **ומאן נימא לן דהא מתרצתא וכו'.** רבי חייא ורבי אושעיא סדרו את הברייתות ודקדקו בדברים על כל סתם ... ואמרינן (חולין קמא.) כל מתניתא דלא מיתנייא בי רבי חייא ורבי אושעיא משבשתא היא ולא מותבינן מינה בבי מדרשא [חולין קמא:]. **אין רוח חכמים נוחה מהם.** אין נחת רוח לחכמים ... [ב"מ מח.]. **בנישופין בו.** ... [בראשית ג, טו]. **אקילעא.** ... **פמוטות.** מנורה של מתכת [לעיל מד.]. **בניטלין בידו אחת.** בשתי ידים אסור ... [ברכות כב.]. לפני הבית כעין בית שער ... [פסחים עב.].

Having cited the report of R' Abba bar Kahana (regarding the snake that fell into the study hall), the Gemara cites three other statements of his:[43]

אָמַר רַבִּי אַבָּא בַּר כַּהֲנָא אָמַר רַבִּי חֲנִינָא – R' Abba bar Kahana said in the name of R' Chanina: **פָּמוּטוֹת שֶׁל בֵּית רַבִּי מוּתָּר לְטַלְטְלָן בְּשַׁבָּת – The candelabras of Rebbi's household may be moved on the Sabbath.**[44]

The Gemara inquires:

אָמַר לוֹ רַבִּי זֵירָא – R' Zeira said to him: **בְּנִיטָּלִין בְּיָדוֹ אַחַת אוֹ בִשְׁתֵּי יָדַיִם** – Are you referring to the smaller candelabras **that can be taken in one hand or** even those larger ones **that** require **two hands?**[45]

NOTES

43. *Rashi* to 122a ד״ה אי משום אימתא.

44. These candelabras were made in one piece, and not of several sections that fit together (*Rashi*). [A sectional candelabra, however, may *not* be moved on the Sabbath, as stated above on 46a. For we are concerned that it might fall and come apart and the person will reassemble it tightly, and thereby be guilty of making a utensil on the Sabbath (see *Ritva MHK* ed. here and *Rashi* ad loc.).] Also, they had not been burning on that Sabbath and they were not soiled; thus, they were not *muktzeh* (*R' Perachyah*).

45. A large candelabra is typically not meant to be moved, but is set down in a specific location with the intent that it remain there. This intent would possibly render it *muktzeh* (see *Rashi* to 122a ד״ה של בית אביך and above to 45b ד״ה בשתי ידים אסור לטלטלה).

R' Abba bar Kahana answers:

אָמַר לוֹ – He said to [R' Zeira]: כְּאוֹתָן שֶׁל בֵּית אָבִיךְ – Like those candelabras **of your father's house,** which are small.[1]

The second statement:

וְאָמַר רַבִּי אַבָּא בַּר כַּהֲנָא אָמַר רַבִּי חֲנִינָא – And R' Abba bar Kahana said in the name of R' Chanina: קְרוֹנוֹת שֶׁל בֵּית רַבִּי מוּתָּר לְטַלְטְלָן בְּשַׁבָּת – The wagons of Rebbi's household may be moved on the Sabbath.[2]

The Gemara inquires:

אָמַר לוֹ רַבִּי זֵירָא – R' Zeira said to him: בְּנִיטָּלִין בְּאָדָם אֶחָד אוֹ בִּשְׁנֵי בְנֵי אָדָם – Are you referring to wagons **that can be moved by one person or** even to those that cannot be moved **by** less than **two people?**

R' Abba bar Kahana answers:

אָמַר לוֹ – He said to him: כְּאוֹתָן שֶׁל בֵּית אָבִיךְ – Like those wagons **of your father's house.**[3]

The third statement:

וְאָמַר רַבִּי אַבָּא בַּר כַּהֲנָא – And R' Abba bar Kahana said: הִתִּיר לָהֶם רַבִּי חֲנִינָא לְבֵית רַבִּי לִשְׁתּוֹת יַיִן בִּקְרוֹנוֹת שֶׁל נָכְרִי בְּחוֹתָם אֶחָד – R' Chanina permitted the household of Rebbi to drink wine transported **in the wagons of a non-Jew on the basis of** only **one seal.**[4] **וְלֹא יָדַעְנָא – But I do not know אִי מִשּׁוּם דִּסְבַר לָהּ כְּרַבִּי אֱלִיעֶזֶר** – **if** R' Chanina permitted it **because he holds in accord with R' Eliezer** that one seal is always sufficient for wine,[5] **אִי מִשּׁוּם אֵימְתָא דְבֵי נְשִׂיאָה – or if** he permitted it only in this case, **because of the** non-Jew's **fear of the *Nasi's* house,** which would discourage him from tampering with the wine he is delivering there.[6]

Mishnah The first Mishnah on 121a taught that one may not instruct a non-Jew to perform an act prohibited to a Jew on the Sabbath. The following Mishnah discusses whether a Jew may benefit from a *melachah* already performed by a non-Jew:[7]

נָכְרִי שֶׁהִדְלִיק אֶת הַנֵּר – **If a gentile lit a lamp** for himself, **מִשְׁתַּמֵּשׁ לְאוֹרוֹ יִשְׂרָאֵל – a Jew may use its light; וְאִם בִּשְׁבִיל יִשְׂרָאֵל אָסוּר – but if** the gentile lit the lamp **for a Jew,** one **may not** use it.[8] **מִילֵּא מַיִם לְהַשְׁקוֹת בְּהֶמְתּוֹ** – **If [a gentile] drew water** with which **to water his** own **animal,**[9] **מַשְׁקֶה אַחֲרָיו יִשְׂרָאֵל – a Jew may water** his animal **after him; וְאִם בִּשְׁבִיל יִשְׂרָאֵל אָסוּר – but if** the gentile drew the water **for a Jew,** one **may not** use it.[10] **עָשָׂה נָכְרִי כֶּבֶשׁ לֵירֵד בּוֹ – If a gentile made a gangplank upon which to disembark** from a ship,[11] **יוֹרֵד אַחֲרָיו יִשְׂרָאֵל – a Jew may disembark after him; וְאִם בִּשְׁבִיל יִשְׂרָאֵל אָסוּר – but if** the gentile made the gangplank **for a Jew,** one **may not** use it.[12] **מַעֲשֶׂה בְּרַבָּן גַּמְלִיאֵל וּזְקֵנִים שֶׁהָיוּ בָּאִין בִּסְפִינָה – It once happened that Rabban Gamliel and the Elders were arriving on a ship,**[13] **וְעָשָׂה נָכְרִי כֶּבֶשׁ לֵירֵד בּוֹ – and a gentile made a gangplank on**

NOTES

1. But a large one may not be moved on the Sabbath because one set it in its place with the intent that it remain there (*Rashi;* see also *Rabbeinu Chananel*).

[Although this reasoning is advanced by Rabbah and Rav Yosef above (end of 45b), the Gemara there concludes that such "setting in place" is *not* a reason to prohibit moving a utensil on the Sabbath. Because of this consideration (and others), some Rishonim reject *Rashi's* explanation, and explain that R' Abba bar Kahana meant "like those of your father's house," which are *large;* even these may be moved on the Sabbath (see *Tosafos* here and to 35a ד״ה ואפילו בת תרי כורי; see also *Ramban* et al. here).]

2. This refers to passenger wagons (*Rashi*). The wagon is a "utensil" and thus is not *muktzeh.*

3. Here, too, the reference is to the smaller variety (see *Rabbeinu Chananel*). Other Rishonim maintain that here the reference is clearly to the larger variety (see *Ritva MHK* ed.).

4. A non-Jew's wine — or even a Jew's wine that was touched by a non-Jew — is forbidden Rabbinically (see above, 17b). Thus, kosher wine delivered to a Jew's home by a non-Jew is forbidden, unless the wine is in a sealed container that has not been tampered with. In *Avodah Zarah* 31a, the Tanna R' Eliezer holds that a single seal suffices for wine, while the Sages require a greater degree of security.

5. See preceding note.

6. Rebbi was the *Nasi* of the Jews by order of the Roman authorities. Thus, the non-Jew would be afraid to tamper with wine he was delivering to the *Nasi's* household [and that fear coupled with the single seal provides adequate assurance that he did not touch the wine] (*Rashi*).

7. Two distinct Rabbinic decrees are involved here: Firstly, one may not instruct a non-Jew to perform a *melachah* for him; secondly, one may not benefit from a *melachah* that a non-Jew performed for a Jew without being told. The Sages prohibited any Jew from benefiting from a non-Jew's *melachah* so that Jews will not come to instructing gentiles to perform *melachos* for them (*Rambam, Hil. Shabbos* 6:8; *Tosafos* here and to *Beitzah* 24b ד״ה ולערב; *Ramban, Rashba* et al.; *Beur Halachah* to *Orach Chaim* 515:1 ד״ה ויש מחמירין indicates that this is essentially *Rashi's* opinion as well, although *Rashi* and *Tosafos* dispute a related point on *Beitzah* 24b). Thus, in circumstances where one is clearly permitted to instruct a gentile to desecrate the Sabbath (see, for example, *Orach Chaim* 328:17), one is permitted to benefit from the gentile's actions (*Mishnah Berurah* 276:7).

The blanket prohibition against deriving benefit applies to Biblical *melachos* performed by a gentile. If, however, the gentile's action was only Rabbinically proscribed, then only the person for whom the benefit was intended is forbidden to enjoy it; all other Jews are permitted to enjoy it (see *Orach Chaim* 325:8,10 and *Mishnah Berurah* ad loc.).

[An apparent difficulty: There is a general principle that states: אֵין גּוֹזְרִין גְּזֵרָה לִגְזֵרָה, *we do not decree a safeguard for a safeguard.* Here, however, we seem to be doing just that: We prohibit the deriving of benefit from a gentile's *melachah* lest one instruct him to do the *melachah;* and instructing a gentile to perform a *melachah* is itself only Rabbinically prohibited!

Rambam (in his commentary to the Mishnah 4:1) explains that the principle of not decreeing a safeguard for a safeguard applies to a previously existing safeguard — i.e. the Rabbis may not issue a new decree to safeguard an established one. The Rabbis may, however, issue two decrees simultaneously — one to address the object of their concern, and another to support the main decree when they anticipate that the latter will not stand alone.]

8. I.e. no Jew may use it (*Rosh;* cf. *Meiri;* see previous note), by Rabbinical decree (*Rashi*).

9. This is an act of הוֹצָאָה, *transporting* something from a *reshus hayachid* (a private domain) to a *reshus harabim* (a public domain). The well from which the gentile draws his water is [at least ten handbreadths deep and is thus] a private domain. Where the gentile and his animal stand is a public domain (*Rashi*).

10. Clearly, a Jew may not water his animal with it, but may he himself drink it (may he use it to wash his hands, etc.)? *Tosafos* record a dispute on this question: *Rabbeinu Tam* contends that the Jew may use the water himself, since he could have climbed down into the well and drunk the water there. Hence, the gentile's action did not benefit him substantially. *Ri* and other Rishonim do not accept this reasoning, however. Both opinions are cited in *Orach Chaim* 325:10.

11. A gangplank is needed to disembark from a large ship (*Rashi*).

12. In all three cases no benefit may be derived for the duration of the Sabbath. Furthermore, the prohibition extends *after* the Sabbath for as long as it takes to duplicate the particular benefit. For example, in the case of the water drawn by a gentile on a Jew's behalf, no use may be made of this water until enough time has passed after the Sabbath to draw the same amount of water. The Sages applied this measure (בִּכְדֵי שֶׁיַּעֲשׂוּ) to many items produced in violation of the Sabbath (see *Rashi* ד״ה בכדי שיחמו חמין).

13. [The ship landed on the Sabbath.]

א"ל כאותן של בית אביך ואמר ר' אבא בר כהנא אמר ר' חנינא קרונות של בית רבי מותר לטלטלן בשבת א"ל ר' זירא בניטלין באדם אחד או בשני בני אדם א"ל כאותן של בית אביך ואמר ר' אבא בר כהנא התיר להם ר' חנינא לבית רבי לשתות יין בקרונות של נכרי [א] בחותם אחד ולא ידענא אי משום דסבר לה (א) כר' אליעזר אי משום אימתא דבי נשיאה: **מתני'** [ב] נכרי שהדליק את הנר משתמש לאורו ישראל ואם בשביל ישראל אסור מילא מים להשקות בהמתו משקה אחריו ישראל ואם בשביל ישראל אסור עשה נכרי כבש לירד בו יורד אחריו ישראל ואם בשביל ישראל אסור מעשה ברבן גמליאל וזקנים שהיו באין בספינה ועשה נכרי כבש לירד בו וירדו בו ר"ג וזקנים: **גמ'** וצריכא דאי אשמעינן נר משום דנר לאחד נר למאה אבל מים ליגזר דילמא אתי לאפושי בשביל ישראל וכבש ל"ל מעשה דרבן גמליאל וזקנים קמ"ל ת"ר [ג] נכרי שליקט עשבים מאכיל אחריו ישראל ואם בשביל ישראל אסור מילא מים להשקות בהמתו משקה אחריו ישראל ואם בשביל ישראל אסור [ד] בד"א שאין מכירו אבל מכירו אסור איני (ה) והאמר רב הונא אמר רבי חנינא [ה] מעמיד אדם בהמתו על גבי עשבים בשבת אבל לא על גבי מוקצה בשבת [ו] דקאים לה באפה ואזלא היא ואכלה אמר מר בד"א שאין מכירו אבל מכירו אסור הא רבן גמליאל מכירו הוה אמר אביי שלא בפניו הוה רבא אמר [ז] אפי' תימא בפניו נר לאחד נר למאה מיתיבי (ג) אמר להן רבן גמליאל הואיל ושלא בפנינו עשאו נרד בו אימא הואיל ועשאו נרד בו תא שמע [ח] עיר שישראל ונכרים דרין בתוכה והיתה בה מרחץ המרחצת בשבת אם רוב נכרים מותר לרחוץ בה מיד אם רוב ישראל ימתין בכדי שיחמו חמין התם כי מחממי אדעתא דרובא מחממי תא שמע [ט] נר הדלוק במסיבה אם רוב נכרים מותר להשתמש לאורה אם רוב ישראל אסור מחצה על מחצה אסור התם נמי כי מדלקי אדעתא

רש"י

של בית אביך. דקטנות היו אבל גדולות אדם קובע להם מקום: **קרונות.** עשויות לבני אדם: **אי משום דסבר** כרבי אליעזר. דאמר במסכת ע"ז (דף לא.) יין מותר בחותם אחד: **אי משום אימתא דבי נשיאה.** שהיה הנכרי המביאו ירא מן הנשיא שהיה שליט על פי המלכות ומשום דאיירי ר' אבא בר כהנא לעיל גבי נחש נקט כל הני בשמיה: **מתני' אם בשביל ישראל אסור.** מדרבנן: **מילא מים.** מבור ברה"ר: **כבש.** עושין בספינה גדולה לירד בו מספינה ליבשה: **גמ' נר לאחד נר למאה.** כיון דנכרי לצרכו הדליקו ליכא למימר דבשביל ישראל אפיש: **כבש למה לי.** הא דומיא דנר הוא כבש לאחד כבש למאה: **מאכיל אחריו ישראל.** את בהמתו ואחריו דוקא נקט בכולהו דנכרי לצורך עצמו עביד: **אבל מכירו אסור.** קס"ד דעביד נמי אדעתא דידיה: **מעמיד אדם בהמתו על גבי עשבים.** מחוברים: **בשבת.** לרעות וליכא למיגזר שמא יתלוש ויאכיל: **ואינו מעמידה** ע"ג מוקצה. שמא יטול בידו ויאכיל והא נמי מוקצין נינהו לגבי טלטול דאתמול הוו מחוברין: **דקאים ליה באפה.** שלא תפנה למקום אחר: **ואזלא ואכלה.** אבל הוא אינו עומד על העשבים קרוב להם דניחוש לשמא יטול ויאכיל: **מכירו הוה.** שהרי בספינה היה בא עמו: **שלא בפניו** הוה. כשעשאו לא היה רבן גמליאל שם דניכוין ליה: **נר לאחד נר למאה.** כבש לאחד כבש למאה אבל גבי עשבים כשהוא מכירו מרבה בשבילו: **הואיל ושלא בפנינו כו'.** קשיא לרבא דשמעינן מינה דבפניו אסור ואע"פ שאין כאן מרבה בשבילו: **אימא הואיל ועשאו נרד בו.** וטעמא לאו משום שלא בפניו הוא אלא הכי הוה מעשה: **מותר לרחוץ בה מיד.** למוצאי שבת: **בכדי שיחמו חמין.** שלא יהנה במה שהקדימו להם בשבת וכן בכל מעשה שבת נתנו חכמים שיעור להמתין לערב בכדי שיעשו והא הכא דחימום לאחד חימום למאה דקדרה אחת מחממין וקתני אם רוב ישראל דהוי דומיא דמכירו דמסיק אדעתיה לעשות אף בשבילו אסור ואע"ג דשלא בפניו וקשיא בין לאביי בין לרבא: **אדעתא דרובא מחממי.** ועיקר חילול השבת בשבילם אבל נכרי וישראל דנכרי אדעתא דנפשיה הוא דעביד שרי לאביי שלא בפניו ולרבא אפי' בפניו: **נר הדלוק במסיבה.** של בני אדם: **אם רוב ישראל אסור.** והא הכא דהוי דומיא דמכירו הואיל ורובא נינהו אסיק דעתיה להדליק אף בשבילם וקתני אסור: אדעתא

תוספות

אמר ליה כאותן של בית אביך. פי' שהם גדולים או קטנים דלית להו חזקי כמו שפירשתי לעיל (דף לה.): **משתמש** ישראל לאורה. ולא גזרינן שמא ידליק כדגזרינן בפ"ק דביצה (דף ג.) פירות הנושרין שמא יעלה ויתלוש ומשקין שזבו שמא יסחוט משום דסחיטה ותלישה הם קלים לעשות ואדם להוט אחריהם לפי שהן דבר אכילה אבל בכל הני דהכא אינן קלין לעשות כל כך ואין אדם להוט אחריהן: **ואם בשביל ישראל** אסור. נראה דאסור לכל ישראל דדוקא בתוך התחום דרבנן אמר בפרק בכל מערבין (עירובין דף מ.) ובאין לדין (ביצה דף כה.) הבא בשביל ישראל זה מותר לישראל אחר אבל באיסורא דאורייתא כי הכא לא ואע"ג דישראל המבשל בשבת בשוגג יאכל התם לא חיישינן אי שרית ליה לאכול דילמא אתי לבשולי במזיד דהא איכא איסור סקילה וחמיר עליה אבל בנכרי העושה לצורך ישראל אי שרית ליה אתי למימר לנכרי לעשות בשבילו ולא דמי להא דאמר לעיל (י) נכרי שבא לכבות אין אומרים לו כבה ואל תכבה והכא אסור כשעושה בשביל ישראל דכי אמרינן דנכרי אדעתא דנפשיה קא עביד הני מילי בכיבוי וכיוצא בו שאין ישראל נהנה במעשה הנכרי אבל הכא שגוף ישראל נהנה במעשה של נכרי לא אמרינן אדעתא דנפשיה קעביד הואיל והנכרי מתכוין להנאתו כך פירש רבינו שמשון הזקן: **משקה** אחריו ישראל ואם בשביל ישראל אסור. אומר ר"ת מדנקט בהמתו ולא נקט מילא מים לעצמו דוקא להשקות בהמתו אסור משום שלא היה יכול להביאה לתוך הבור אבל הוא עצמו שרי מטפס ועולה מטפס ויורד וכיון שיכול ליכנס לתוך הבור ולשתות לא אסרו לו בשביל שמילא אותם נכרי והא דאסרינן בגמרא נכרי שליקט עשבים לצורך ישראל אע"ג דישראל יכול להעמיד בהמתו על גבי העשבים במחובר אומר ר"ת דהתם נמי איירי בנכרי עברי דנהרא שלא היה יכול (ז) להביא הבהמה לשם ואע"ג דהך בבא דמילא מים משום חידוש הזכירה קתני לה כדמוכח בגמרא מיהא בהמתו משום איסורא נקט לה וה"ר אליהו הביא ראיה להתיר מפירות שיצאו חוץ לתחום וחזרו שלא הפסידו היתירן הראשון כדאמר בפרק מי שהוציאוהו (עירובין דף מא:) ה"ה המים שמתחילה היה יכול (א) לבא שם והביאו דרך רה"ר דשרו ולא דמי דהתם לא אתעבידא בהו איסורא דאורייתא מיהו לענין אותו ישראל עצמו לא מצינו חילוק ור"י אומר דה"ה לישראל עצמו אסור והאי דנקט בהמתו לאשמעינן רבותא דלא גזרינן דילמא אתי לאפושי בשביל ישראל שבהמה רגילה לשתות הרבה אבל ישראל עצמו פשיטא דשותה אחריו דליכא למיחש כולי האי דילמא אתי לאפושי דבדלייה אחת מושך הרבה לצורכו ולצורך ישראל ולפי זה אם נמשכו המים לצורך ישראל זה אסור לכל ישראל אי איכא איסורא דאורייתא כגון שמביאם דרך רה"ר או מרה"י לרה"ר אבל בכרמלית שרי לישראל אחר ויש שרצו לומר דדוקא שתיה אסורה אבל לרחוץ ידיו ורגליו ושאר תשמישין שרי כדאמר בפרק חרש (יבמות דף קיד.) רבי יצחק אירכסו ליה מפתחות דבי מדרשא כו' אמר ליה דבר טליא וטליתא ליטיילו התם דאי משכח להו מייתי להו אלמא יכולין ליהנות ממפתחות להשתמש בהם בשבת ואין נראה לר"י כלל דהתם אין עושין לדעת ישראל ועוד דהרי כבש ונר וכמה דברים לאסור להשתמש בהם בשבת כשנעשין לצורך ישראל ה"נ לא שנא שתיה לא שנא שאר תשמישין אסירי:

איני והאמר רב הונא אמר רב חנינא מעמיד אדם כו' אבל לא על גבי מוקצה. והני עשבים נמי מוקצין נינהו שנלקטו היום מן המחובר וא"ת ולימא דהך ברייתא רבי שמעון היא דלית ליה מוקצה וי"ל דמשני לה אפילו כר' יהודה א"נ מודה ר"ש במוקצה דמחובר כדפי' בקונטרס בפרק אין צדין (ביצה דף כד:) מדלא ליקטן מאתמול אקלינהו והוי כגרוגרות וצימוקים ובריש ביצה (דף ג.) לאסור פירות הנושרים משום גזירה שמא יעלה ויתלוש ולא אסר להו משום מוקצה משום דמוכנים לעורבים כי ההיא דבמקום שנהגו (פסחים דף נו:) והכא איירי כשאין הבהמה יכולה לבא ולאכול מן המחובר ולהכי הוי מוקצה א"נ עשבים מוקצין הם אפילו לר"ש לפי שאינו יושב ומצפה שילקטם אבל בנר יושב ומצפה מתי יכבה כדאמרינן לעיל (דף מו:) וכן פירות הנושרין יושב ומצפה מתי יפלו ולהכי אי לאו טעמא דשמא יעלה ויתלוש הוו שרו: **מעמיד** אדם בהמתו ע"ג עשבים בשבת. כדדרשי' במכילתין למען ינוח שורך וחמורך וגו' יכול לא יניחנו עוקר ת"ל למען ינוח ואין זה נוח אלא צער. ר"ת: **אמר** אביי שלא בפניו הוה. נראה לר"י דמודה אביי דנר לאחד נר למאה אלא דסבר דהכא אם היה בפניו עיקר היה נעשה לצורך ר"ג שהיה נשיא ושר וראש בספינה:

אהדרינהו

מסורת הש"ס

א) [ע"ז לא.], ב) [עירובין עט.], ג) [תוספתא פי"ד], ד) לקמן קנא. מכשירין פ"ב מ"ה, ה) [דף קכג.], ו) [ב"ק נו.], ז) להביא הבהמה לשם ואין זה דוחק לדומיא דמתני' איירי דאי בנכרי עברי דנהרא שאין הבהמה יכולה לילך לבור ואע"ג דהך בבא וכו' כצ"ל רש"ל.

הגהות הב"ח

(א) תוס' ד"ה משקה וכו' שמתחלה היה יכול לילך לשם והביאו נכרי דרך רה"ר:

ליקוטי רש"י

אם בשביל ישראל אסור. משום שמעשה בו איסור בשבילו. לישראל אחר נמי אסור דנכרי שהדליק את הנר מגן אם בשביל ישראל אסור ולא חלקו בינו לנכרו [ביצה כה. עיין בתוס' כאן ושם]. **מעמיד אדם בהמתו על גבי עשבים.** מחוברים לאכול ולא חיישינן דלמא עקר בידים ומאכיל לה דהא חמיר עליה איסור שבת אבל איסור מוקצה קיל ליה וחיישינן דלמא שקיל בידים וספי לה [עירובין עט.]. מעמיד משמע שאוחזה בידו ומוליכה [ב"ק נו:]. **דקאים לה באפה.** מתני' לאו דמוקים לה עלה בידים אלא קאי באפה שלא תלך במקום אחר ואיהי אזלה ואכלה וכולי האי לא גזור רבנן [עירובין שם]. שלא משכוה אלא עמדו בפניה לכל צד שלא תלך אנה ואנה אלא לאכול [ב"ק שם].

עין משפט נר מצוה

פ א מיי' פי"ג מהלכות מאכלות אסורות הל"י סמג לאוין קלח טור שו"ע יו"ד סימן קיח סעיף א וסימן קל סעיף ב:
פא ב מיי' פ"ו מהלכות שבת הלכה ב ג סמג לאוין סה טוש"ע או"ח סימן רעו סעיף א וסימן שכה סעיף יא ויב:
פב ג ד מיי' וסמג שם טוש"ע או"ח סימן שכה סעיף י יא:
פג ה ו מיי' פכ"א מהל' שבת הלכה לו סמג שם טוש"ע או"ח סימן שכד סעיף יג וסימן שכה סעיף יא:
פד ז מיי' פ"ו שם הל"ד וסמג שם טור שו"ע שם:
פה ח מיי' שם הלכה ז סמג שם טוש"ע או"ח סימן שכו סעיף יג:
פו ט מיי' שם הלכה ד סמג שם טוש"ע שם סימן רעו סעיף ב:

רבינו חננאל

או בב' ידים. אמר ליה כאותן של בית אביך ש"מ דניטלת בידו אחת שרי. ניטלת בב' ידים לא איתברירא לן בהדיא. וכן קרונות של בית רבי הניטלין בב' בני אדם לא איפשיטא. והתיר ר' חנינא לשתות יין הבא בקרונות של נכרים בחותם אחת ולא ידענא אי משום דסבר לה כר' אליעזר אי משום אימתא דבי נשיאה: **נכרי** שהדליק את הנר. ת"ר נכרי שליקט עשבים מאכיל אחריו ישראל ואם בשביל ישראל אסור. וכן מילא מים להשקות בהמתו וכו'. בד"א

רב נסים גאון

לפני רבן יוחנן בן זכאי בערב ואמר חושש אני לו מחטאת: **אי משום דסבר** לה כר' אליעזר דלא חייש לזיופא ומימרא דר' אליעזר במס' ע"ז אין מעמידין בהמה (דף לא) דתניא אחד הלוקח וא' השוכר בית כר' ר' אליעזר מתיר בשתייה ואמרו מר סבר כי פליגי רבנן עליה דר' אליעזר בחותם אחד כו' ובפ' השוכר את הפועלין (שם דף סט) אמרו וכי מאחר דקיימא לן כוותיה דרשב"ג וכוותיה דר' אליעזר דלא חייש לזיופא:

סליק פרק כל כתבי הקודש

which to disembark,[14] וְיָרְדוּ בוֹ רַבָּן גַּמְלִיאֵל וּזְקֵנִים – **and Rabban Gamliel and the Elders disembarked on it.**[15]

Gemara The Gemara explains why the Mishnah presented three illustrations of the same principle:

וּצְרִיכָא – **And it was necessary** to teach each of these cases, דְּאִי אַשְׁמְעִינַן נֵר – **for if [the Mishnah] had taught us** only the case of **a lamp,** מִשּׁוּם – I would have said that a Jew is allowed to benefit from the lamp **because** דְּנֵר לְאֶחָד נֵר לְמֵאָה – **a lamp** illuminates for **one** and **a lamp** illuminates for **one hundred.** Thus, since the gentile lit the lamp for himself, one cannot say that he did anything extra for the Jew. אֲבָל מַיִם לִיגְזַר דִּילְמָא אָתֵי לְאַפּוּשֵׁי בִּשְׁבִיל יִשְׂרָאֵל – **But** with regard to drawing **water,** it is proper **to decree** that a Jew may not use the remainder, for **perhaps [the gentile] will come to increase** the amount he draws **for the sake of the Jew.**

The Gemara asks:

וְכֶבֶשׁ לָמָּה לִי – **And why,** then, **do I** need the case of **the gangplank?**[16]

The Gemara answers:

מַעֲשֶׂה דְּרַבָּן גַּמְלִיאֵל וּזְקֵנִים קָמַשְׁמַע לָן – **[The Mishnah]** uses that case as an introduction to **inform us of the incident involving Rabban Gamliel and the Elders.**

The Gemara cites a Baraisa that qualifies the Mishnah's law:

תָּנוּ רַבָּנָן – **The Rabbis taught:** נָכְרִי שֶׁלִּיקֵּט עֲשָׂבִים – IF A GENTILE GATHERED GRASSES for his animal, מַאֲכִיל אַחֲרָיו יִשְׂרָאֵל – A JEW MAY FEED his own animal AFTER HIM;[17] וְאִם בִּשְׁבִיל יִשְׂרָאֵל אָסוּר – BUT IF a gentile gathered grasses FOR A JEW, a Jew MAY NOT use them.[18] מִילֵּא מַיִם לְהַשְׁקוֹת בְּהֶמְתּוֹ – If [A GENTILE] DREW WATER with which TO WATER HIS ANIMAL, מַשְׁקֶה אַחֲרָיו יִשְׂרָאֵל – A JEW MAY WATER his own animal AFTER HIM; וְאִם בִּשְׁבִיל יִשְׂרָאֵל אָסוּר – BUT IF a gentile drew water FOR A JEW, a Jew MAY NOT use it. בַּמֶּה דְּבָרִים אֲמוּרִים – REGARDING WHAT CIRCUMSTANCES ARE [THESE LENIENCIES] STATED? שֶׁאֵין מַכִּירוֹ – WHEN [THE GENTILE] DOES NOT KNOW [THE JEW]; only then may the Jew derive benefit from the remaining grasses and water. אֲבָל מַכִּירוֹ אָסוּר – HOWEVER, if [THE GENTILE] KNOWS [THE JEW], the Jew MAY NOT benefit from the gentile's labor.

The Gemara first questions how one is permitted to use grasses picked on the Sabbath:

אִינִי – **Is it** really **so?** וְהָאָמַר רַב הוּנָא אָמַר רַבִּי חֲנִינָא – **But Rav Huna has said in the name of R' Chanina:** מַעֲמִיד אָדָם בְּהֶמְתּוֹ עַל גַּבֵּי עֲשָׂבִים בְּשַׁבָּת – **A person may stand his animal over** still-attached **grasses on the Sabbath,** אֲבָל לֹא עַל גַּבֵּי מוּקְצֶה בְּשַׁבָּת – **but not over** ***muktzeh*** grasses **on the Sabbath.**[19] Since the grasses picked by the gentile were still attached to the ground at the onset of Shabbos, they remain *muktzeh* now. How, then, can a Jew bring his animal to feed on these grasses?

The Gemara answers:

דְּקָאִים לָהּ בְּאַפָּהּ – The Baraisa speaks of **where [the Jew] stands in front of [the animal],**[20] וְאַזְלָא הִיא וְאָכְלָה – **and [the animal] goes** of its own accord to the grass **and eats** it. This method is permitted.[21]

The Gemara now poses a question on the Mishnah from the Baraisa's qualifying statement:

אָמַר מַר – **Master said:** בַּמֶּה דְּבָרִים אֲמוּרִים – The Baraisa stated in its conclusion: REGARDING WHAT CIRCUMSTANCES ARE [THESE LENIENCIES] STATED? שֶׁאֵין מַכִּירוֹ – WHEN [THE GENTILE] DOES NOT KNOW [THE JEW]; אֲבָל מַכִּירוֹ אָסוּר – HOWEVER, if [THE GENTILE] KNOWS [THE JEW], the Jew MAY NOT benefit from the gentile's labor.[22] הָא רַבָּן גַּמְלִיאֵל מַכִּירוֹ הֲוָה – But **this** incident involving **Rabban Gamliel was** where **[the gentile] knew [the Jew],** since Rabban Gamliel and the gangplank builder had been traveling on the ship together! How, then, could Rabban Gamliel (and the Elders) disembark on the gangplank, which was built by the gentile on the Sabbath?

NOTES

14. I.e. he made it for himself.

15. Although disembarking on the Sabbath is prohibited if the ship traveled beyond its *techum* (see Mishnah, *Eruvin* 41b), one may leave the ship if it reaches within two thousand *amos* of the shore before the onset of the Sabbath. Rabban Gamliel determined that this was the case by looking through a telescope calibrated to resolve images up to a distance of two thousand *amos* (*Tosefta* 14:13; see also *Eruvin* 43b with *Rashi*). [This telescope was a hollow tube that operated on the principle that enables one to resolve a distant image by looking through a small hole.]

16. This case is analogous to that of the lamp, for here one can say: "a gangplank for one, a gangplank for one hundred" (*Rashi*). What, then, does it teach?

17. The use of the phrase "after him" in this example and the one to follow is meant precisely, and it connotes the case of a Jew who sees a gentile gathering grasses or drawing water without knowing the latter's intention. Only after he sees the gentile feed or water his animal may the Jew assume that the gentile acted on his own behalf, and the Jew may then use the grasses or water. However, if the Jew knows for certain at the time of the gathering or drawing that the gentile is acting in self-interest, the Jew may benefit from the feed or water immediately (*Rashi,* according to *Beur Halachah* 325:10 ד״ה להשקות מהם בהמתו).

18. Above (note 10), we noted that in *Rabbeinu Tam's* view where a gentile drew water for a Jew's animal, the Jew may himself use the water since he could have climbed down into the well and partaken of the water there. However, *Rabbeinu Tam* (ד״ה משקה) challenges his own opinion from the Baraisa here, which prohibits the grasses to the Jew's animal even though the Jew could have stood his animal over the attached grasses. *Rabbeinu Tam* thus explains that the Baraisa speaks of where it was impossible for the Jew to bring his animal to the grasses. See there and see *Baal HaMaor;* cf. *Chidushei HaRan,* who writes that their explanations are not compelling. See *Mishnah Berurah* 325 §64.

19. That is, one may pasture his livestock on the Sabbath, allowing them to eat grass still attached to the ground, but one may not lead them to already harvested grass or feed that is *muktzeh* (because it was not designated for use on the Sabbath prior to the onset of the Sabbath). In both cases, it is possible that the animal's owner may take the grass and feed it to the animal. The distinction between the cases lies in the severity of the potential Sabbath desecration. In the first case, uprooting the grass constitutes a Biblical *melachah;* since it is unlikely that one would carelessly perform it, the Sages saw no need to decree a safeguard. However, if one stands over his animal as it eats harvested *muktzeh* grass, it is possible that he will pick up some of the grass and feed it to his animal [for since *muktzeh* is a Rabbinic law, one may not be as careful in its observance]. As a safeguard for the laws of *muktzeh,* the Sages decreed that one may not stand his animal over *muktzeh* feed (*Ritva MHK* ed.; see also *Rashi*).

[One is generally obligated to prevent his animals from performing *melachos* on the Sabbath (שְׁבִיתַת בְּהֶמְתּוֹ). Nevertheless, one may allow his livestock to graze and uproot vegetation. This dispensation is based on a Scriptural exegesis found in *Mechilta, Mishpatim* 20 (see *Tosafos* ד״ה מעמיד, *Ritva* ibid.).]

20. [Literally: in its face.] I.e. he blocks its path so that the animal will not turn aside and wander off (*Rashi*).

21. Since the Jew is not standing near the pile of grass, there is no fear that he will grab a handful and feed it to his animal (*Rashi*).

[Although a Jew may not move or consume a *muktzeh* item, he may benefit from it in other ways. He may also let his animal eat it as long as he himself does not move it (see *Ramban*).]

22. At this point the Gemara assumes that if the gentile knows the Jew, he performs the *melachah* for both himself and the Jew, and for that reason [and not because he expended extra effort for the Jew] the grasses and the water are prohibited (*Rashi* above ד״ה אבל מכירו אסור).

גמרא

א"ל כאותן של בית אביך ואמר ר' אבא בר כהנא אמר ר' חנינא קרונות של בית רבי מותר לטלטלן בשבת א"ל ר' זירא בניטלין באדם אחד או בשני בני אדם א"ל כאותן של בית אביך ואמר ר' אבא בר כהנא התיר להם ר' חנינא לבית רבי לשתות יין בקרונות של נכרי א בחותם אחד ולא ידענא אי משום דסבר לה ה כר' אליעזר אי משום אימתא דבי נשיאה: **מתני'** ב נכרי שהדליק את הנר משתמש לאורו ישראל ואם בשביל ישראל אסור מילא מים להשקות בהמתו משקה אחריו ישראל ואם בשביל ישראל אסור עשה נכרי כבש לירד בו יורד אחריו ישראל ואם בשביל ישראל אסור מעשה ברבן גמליאל וזקנים שהיו באין בספינה ועשה נכרי כבש לירד בו וירדו בו ר"ג וזקנים: **גמ'** וצריכא דאי אשמעינן נר משום דנר לאחד נר למאה אבל מים ליגזור דילמא אתי לאפושי בשביל ישראל וכבש נמי ל"ל מעשה דרבן גמליאל וזקנים קמ"ל ת"ר ג נכרי שליקט עשבים מאכיל אחריו ישראל ואם בשביל ישראל אסור מילא מים להשקות בהמתו משקה אחריו ישראל ואם בשביל ישראל אסור ד בד"א שאין מכירו אבל מכירו אסור איני ו והאמר רב הונא אמר רבי חנינא ה מעמיד אדם בהמתו על גבי עשבים בשבת אבל לא על גבי מוקצה בשבת י דקאים לה באפה ואזלא היא ואכלה אמר מר בד"א שאין מכירו אבל מכירו אסור הא רבן גמליאל מכירו הוה אמר אביי שלא בפניו הוה רבא אמר ז אפי' תימא בפניו נר לאחד נר למאה מיתיבי ג אמר להן רבן גמליאל הואיל ושלא בפנינו עשאו נרד בו אימא הואיל ועשאו נרד בו תא שמע ז ח עיר שישראל ונכרים דרין בתוכה והיתה בה מרחץ המרחצת בשבת אם רוב נכרים מותר לרחוץ בה מיד אם רוב ישראל ימתין בכדי שיחמו חמין התם כי מחממי אדעתא דרובא מחממי תא שמע ט נר הדלוק במסיבה אם רוב נכרים מותר להשתמש לאורה אם רוב ישראל אסור מחצה על מחצה אסור התם נמי כי מדלקי אדעתא

רש"י

של בית אביך. דקטנות היו אבל גדולות אדם קובע להם מקום: קרונות. עשויות לבני אדם: **אי משום דסבר כרבי אליעזר.** דאמר במסכת ע"ז (דף לא.) יין מותר בחותם אחד: **אי משום אימתא דבי נשיאה.** שהיה הנכרי המביאו ירא מן הנשיא שהיה שליט על פי המלכות ומשום דאיירי ר' אבא בר כהנא לעיל גבי נתא נקט כל הני בשמיה: **מתני' אם בשביל ישראל אסור.** מדרבנן: **מילא מים.** מבור ברה"ר: **כבש.** עושין בספינה גדולה לירד בו מספינה ליבשה: **גמ' נר לאחד נר למאה.** כיון דנכרי לצרכו הדליקו ליכא למימר דבשביל ישראל אפיש: **כבש למה לי.** הא דומיא דנר הוא כבש לאחד כבש למאה: **מאכיל אחריו ישראל.** את בהמתו ואחריו דוקא נקט כלומר דנכרי לצורך עצמו עביד: **אבל מכירו אסור.** קס"ד דעביד נמי אדעתא דידיה: **מעמיד אדם בהמתו על גבי עשבים.** מחוברים: **בשבת.** לרעות וליכא למיגזר שמא יתלוש ויאכיל: **ואינו מעמידה ע"ג מוקצה.** שמא יטול בידו ויאכיל והא נמי מוקצין נינהו לגבי טלטול דאתמול הוו מחוברין: **דקאים ליה באפה.** שלא תפנה למקום אחר: **ואזלא ואכלה.** אבל הוא אינו עומד על העשבים קרוב להם דניחוש לשמא יטול ויאכיל: **מכירו הוה.** שהרי בספינה היה עמו: **שלא בפניו הוה.** כשעשאו לא היה רבן גמליאל שם דניכוין ליה: **נר לאחד נר למאה.** כבש לאחד כבש למאה אבל גבי עשבים כשהוא מכירו מרבה בשבילו: **הואיל ושלא בפנינו כו'.** קשיא לרבא דשמעינן מינה דבפניו אסור ואע"פ שאין כאן מרבה בשבילו: **אימא הואיל ועשאו נרד בו.** וטעמא לאו משום שלא בפניו הוא אלא הכי הוה מעשה: **מותר לרחוץ בה מיד.** למוצאי שבת: **בכדי שיחמו חמין.** שלא יהנה במה שהקדימו להחם בשבת וכן בכל מעשה שבת נתנו חכמים שיעור להמתין לערב בכדי שיעשו והא הכא דחימום לאחד חימום למאה דבבת אחת מחממין וקתני אם רוב ישראל דהוי דומיא דמכירו דמסיק דעתיה לעשות אף בשבילו אסור ואע"ג דשלא בפניו וקשיא בין לאביי בין לרבא: **אדעתא דרובא מחממי.** ועיקר חילול השבת בשבילם אבל נכרי וישראל דנכרי אדעתא דנפשיה הוא דעביד שרי לאביי שלא בפניו ולרבא אפי' בפניו: **נר הדלוק במסיבה.** של בני אדם: **אם רוב ישראל אסור.** והא הכא דהוי דומיא דמכירו הואיל ורובא נינהו אסיק דעתיה להדליק אף בשבילם וקתני אסור: **אדעתא**

תוספות

אמר ליה כאותן של בית אביך. פי' שהם גדולים או קטנים דלית להו מידקי כמו שפירשתי לעיל (דף קכא:): **משתמש** ישראל לאורה. ולא גזרינן שמא ידליק כדגזרינן בפ"ק דביצה (דף ג.) פירות הנושרין שמא יעלה ויתלוש ומשקין שזבו שמא יסחוט משום דסחיטה ותלישה הם קלים לעשות ואדם להוט אחריהם לפי שהן דבר אכילה אבל בכל הני דהכא אינן קלין לעשות כל כך ואין אדם להוט אחריהן: **ואם** בשביל ישראל אסור. נראה לאסור לכל ישראל דדוקא בתוך לתחום דרבנן אמר בפרק בכל מערבין (עירובין דף מ.) ובאין לדין (ביצה דף כה.) הבא בשביל ישראל זה מותר לישראל אחר אבל באיסורא דאורייתא כי הכא לא ואע"ג דישראל המבשל בשבת בשוגג יאכל התם לא חיישינן אי שרית ליה לאכול דילמא אתי לבשולי במזיד דהא איכא איסור סקילה וחמיר עליה אבל בנכרי העושה לצורך ישראל אי שרית ליה אתי למימר לנכרי לעשות בשבילו ולא דמי להא דאמר לעיל (ו) נכרי שבא לכבות אין אומרים לו כבה ואל תכבה והכא אסור כשעושה בשביל ישראל דכי אמרינן דנכרי אדעתא דנפשיה קא עביד הנ"מ בכיבוי וכיוצא בו שאין ישראל נהנה במעשה הנכרי אבל הכא שגוף ישראל נהנה במעשה של נכרי לא אמרינן אדעתא דנפשיה קעביד הואיל והנכרי מתכוין להנאתו כך פירש רבינו שמשון הזקן: **משקה** אחריו ישראל ואם בשביל ישראל אסור. אומר ר"ת מדנקט בהמתו ולא נקט מילא מים לעצמו דוקא להשקות בהמתו אסור משום שלא היה יכול להביאה לתוך הבור אבל הוא עצמו שרי דמטפס ועולה מטפס ויורד וכיון שיכול ליכנס לתוך הבור ולשתות לא אסרו לו בשביל שמילא אותם נכרי והא דאמרינן בגמרא נכרי שליקט עשבים לצורך ישראל אע"ג דישראל יכול להעמיד בהמתו על גבי העשבים במחובר אומר ר"ת דהתם נמי איירי בתרי עברי דנהרא שלא היה יכול (א) להביא הבהמה לשם ואע"ג דהך בבא דמילא מים משום חידוש דהיתרא קתני לה כדמוכח בגמרא מיהא בהמתו משום איסורא נקט לה וה"ר אליהו הביא ראיה להתיר מפירות שיצאו חוץ לתחום וחזרו שלא הפסידו היתירן הראשון כדאמר בפרק מי שהוציאוהו (עירובין דף מא:) ה"ה המים שמתחילה היה יכול (א) לבא שם והביאו דרך רה"ר דשרו ולא דמי דהתם לא אתעבידא בהו איסורא דאורייתא מיהו לענין אותו ישראל עצמו לא מצינו חילוק ור"י אומר דה"ה לישראל עצמו אסור והאי דנקט בהמתו לאשמעינן רבותא דלא גזרינן דילמא אתי לאפושי בשביל ישראל שבהמה רגילה לשתות הרבה אבל ישראל עצמו פשיטא דשותה אחריו דליכא למיחש כולי האי דילמא אתי לאפושי דבדלייה אחת מושך הרבה לצורכו ולצורך ישראל ולפי זה אם נמשכו המים לצורך ישראל זה אסור לכל ישראל אי איכא איסורא דאורייתא כגון שמביאם דרך רה"ר או מרה"י לרה"ר אבל בכרמלית שרי לישראל אחר ויש שרצו לומר דדוקא שתיה אסורה אבל לרחוץ ידיו ורגליו ושאר תשמישין שרי כדאמר בפרק חרש (יבמות דף קיד.) רבי ינאי אירכסו ליה מפתחות דבי מדרשא כו' אמר ליה דבר טליא וטליתא ליטיילו התם דאי משכח להו מייתי להו אלמא יכולין ליהנות ממפתחות להשתמש בהם בשבת ואין נראה לר"י כלל דהתם אין עושין לדעת ישראל ועוד דהרי כבש ונר וכמה דברים דאסור להשתמש בהם בשבת כשנעשין לצורך ישראל ה"נ לא שנא שתיה לא שנא שאר תשמישין אסירי:

איני והאמר רב הונא אמר רב חנינא מעמיד אדם כו' אבל לא על גבי מוקצה. והני עשבים נמי מוקצין נינהו שנלקטו היום מן המחובר וא"ת ולימא דהך ברייתא רבי שמעון היא דלית ליה מוקצה וי"ל דמשני לה אפילו כר' יהודה א"נ מודה ר"ש במוקצה דמחובר כדפי' בקונטרס בפרק אין לדין (ביצה דף כד:) מדלא ליקטן מאתמול אקצינהו והוי כגרוגרות וצימוקים ובריש ביצה (דף ג.) דאסר פירות הנושרים משום גזירה שמא יעלה ויתלוש ולא אסר להו משום מוקצה משום דמוכנים לעורבים כי ההיא דבמקום שנהגו (פסחים דף נו:) והכא איירי כשאין הבהמה יכולה לבא ולאכול מן המחובר ולהכי הוי מוקצה א"נ עשבים מוקצין הם אפילו לר"ש לפי שאינו יושב ומצפה שילקטום אבל בנר יושב ומצפה מתי יכבה כדאמרינן לעיל (דף מו:) וכן פירות הנושרין יושב ומצפה מתי יפלו ולהכי אי לאו טעמא דשמא יעלה ויתלוש הוו שרו: **מעמיד** אדם בהמתו ע"ג עשבים בשבת. כדדרשי' במכילתין למען ינוח שורך וחמורך וגו' יכול לא יניחנו תולש לא יניחנו עוקר ת"ל למען ינוח ואין זה נוח אלא צער. ר"ת: **אמר** אביי שלא בפניו הוה. נראה לר"י דמודה אביי דנר לאחד נר למאה אלא דסבר דהכא אם היה בפניו עיקר היה נעשה לצורך ר"ג שהיה נשיא ושר וראש בספינה:

אהדרינהו

מסורת הש"ס

א) [ע"ז לא.], ב) [עירובין עט.], ג) [תוספת' פי"ד], ד) לקמן קנא. מכשירין פ"ב מ"ה, ה) [ד"ה ואפילו], ו) [דף קכא.], ז) להביא הבהמה לשם ואין זה דוחק דדומיא דמתני' איירי הא בתרי עברי דנהרא שאין הבהמה יכולה לירד לבור ואע"ג דהך בבא וכו' כצ"ל רש"ל.

הגהות הב"ח

(א) תוס' ד"ה משקה וכו' שמתחלה היה יכול לילך ולשתות שם והביאו נכרי דרך רה"ר:

ליקוטי רש"י

אם בשביל ישראל אסור. משום שנעשה בו איסור בשבילו. לישראל אחר נמי אסור דנכרי שהדליק את הנר בשבת תנן אם בשביל ישראל אסור ולא חלקו בינו לחברו [ביצה כה. עיין בתוס' כאן ושם]. **מעמיד אדם בהמתו על גבי עשבים.** מחוברים לאכול ולא חיישינן דלמא עקר בידים ומאכיל לה דהא חמיר עליה איסור שבת אבל איסור מוקצה קיל ליה וחיישינן דלמא שקיל בידים וספי לה [עירובין עט.]. **מעמיד** משמע שאוחזה בידו ומוליכה [ב"ק נו:]. **דקאים לה באפה.** מתני' לאו דמוקים לה עלה בידים אלא קאי באפה שלא תלך במקום אחר ואיהי אזלה ואכלה וכולי האי לא גזור רבנן [עירובין שם]. שלא משכוה אלא עמדו בפניה לכל צד שלא תלך אנה ואנה אלא לאכול [ב"ק שם].

עין משפט נר מצוה

פ א מיי' פי"ג מהלכות מאכלות אסורות הל"י סמג לאוין קלח טור שו"ע יו"ד סימן קיח סעיף א וסימן קל סעיף ב:

פא ב מיי' פ"ו מהלכות שבת הלכה ב ג סמג לאוין סה טוש"ע או"ח סימן רעו סעיף א וסימן שכה סעיף יא ויב:

פב ג ד מיי' וסמג שם טוש"ע או"ח סימן שכה סעיף י יא:

פג ה ו מיי' פכ"א מהל' שבת הלכה לו סמג שם טוש"ע או"ח סימן שכד סעיף יג וסימן שכה סעיף יא:

פד ז מיי' פ"ו שם הל"ד וסמג שם טור שו"ע שם:

פה ח מיי' שם הלכה ז סמג שם טוש"ע או"ח סימן שכו סעיף יג:

פו ט מיי' שם הלכה ד סמג שם טוש"ע שם סימן רעו סעיף ב:

רבינו חננאל

או בב' ידים. אמר ליה כאותן של בית אביך ש"מ דניטלת בידו אחת שרי. ניטלת בב' ידים לא איתברירא לן בהדיא. וכן קרונות של בית רבי הניטלין בב' בני אדם לא איפשיטא. והתיר ר' חנינא לשתות יין הבא בקרונות של נכרים בחותם אחת ולא ידענא אי משום דסבר לה כר' אליעזר אי משום אימתא דבי נשיאה: **נכרי** שהדליק את הנר. ת"ר נכרי שליקט עשבים מאכיל אחריו ישראל ואם בשביל ישראל אסור. וכן מילא מים להשקות בהמתו וכו'. בד"א

רב נסים גאון

לפני רבן יוחנן בן זכאי בערב ואמר חושש אני לו מחטאת: **אי** משום דסבר לה כר' אליעזר דלא חייש לזיופא ומימרא דר' אליעזר במס' ע"ז אין מעמידין בהמה (דף לא) דתנא אחד הלוקח וא' השוכר בית כר' ר' אליעזר מתיר בשתייה ואמרו מר סבר כי פליגי רבנן עליה דר' אליעזר בחותם אחד כר' ובפ' השוכר את הפועלין (שם דף סט) אמרו וכי מאחר דקיימא לן כוותיה דרשב"ג וכוותיה דר' אליעזר דלא חייש לזיופא:

סליק פרק כל כתבי הקודש

The Gemara presents two answers:

אָמַר אַבָּיֵי – **Abaye said:** שֶׁלֹּא בְּפָנָיו הֲוָה – **[Rabban Gamliel] was not in [the gentile's] presence** when the latter made the gangplank; hence, the gentile had no intent to benefit him. רָבָא אָמַר – **Rava said:** אֲפִילּוּ תֵּימָא בְּפָנָיו – **Even if you say** that Rabban Gamliel *was* **in [the gentile's] presence** when the gangplank was constructed, its use would still be permitted – on the grounds that נֵר לְאֶחָד נֵר לְמֵאָה – **a lamp** illuminates for **one** and **a lamp** illuminates for **one hundred.** Similarly, the same gangplank that serves one passenger can serve one hundred, and so no extra effort was expended by the gentile on Rabban Gamliel's behalf.[23]

The Gemara challenges Rava's answer:

מֵיתִיבֵי – **They retorted** from the evidence of a Baraisa: אָמַר לָהֶן רַבָּן גַּמְלִיאֵל – RABBAN GAMLIEL SAID TO [THE ELDERS]: הוֹאִיל וְשֶׁלֹּא בְּפָנֵינוּ עֲשָׂאוֹ נֵרֵד בּוֹ – SINCE HE MADE [THE GANGPLANK] OUTSIDE OF OUR PRESENCE, LET US DISEMBARK ON IT.[24]

The Gemara reinterprets the Baraisa:

אֵימָא – **Say** that Rabban Gamliel meant thus: הוֹאִיל וַעֲשָׂאוֹ נֵרֵד בּוֹ – SINCE HE MADE IT and, in fact, expended no extra effort on our behalf, LET US DISEMBARK ON IT.[25]

The answers of both Abaye and Rava are challenged:

תָּא שְׁמַע – **Come, hear** a refutation from a Mishnah:[26] עִיר שֶׁיִּשְׂרָאֵל וְנָכְרִים דָּרִין בְּתוֹכָהּ – Regarding A CITY IN WHOSE MIDST both JEWS AND GENTILES DWELL, וְהָיְתָה בָּהּ מֶרְחָץ הַמַּרְחֶצֶת בְּשַׁבָּת – AND WHOSE public BATHHOUSE OPERATES ON THE SABBATH,[27] the law is as follows: אִם רוֹב נָכְרִים – IF A MAJORITY of the people who use the bathhouse on Saturday night[28] ARE GENTILES, מוּתָּר לִרְחוֹץ בָּהּ מִיָּד – a Jew IS PERMITTED TO BATHE IN IT IMMEDIATELY after the conclusion of the Sabbath.[29] אִם רוֹב יִשְׂרָאֵל – IF A MAJORITY of the users ARE JEWS, יַמְתִּין בִּכְדֵי שֶׁיֵּחַמּוּ חַמִּין – ONE MUST WAIT a length of time SUFFICIENT FOR WATER TO HEAT UP after the Sabbath. Now, the bathhouse waters are all heated at the same time, and a heating for one person is a heating for a hundred. Also, the heating is done outside the presence of Jews. Yet, where Jews are the majority, they are not allowed to benefit from the heating done on the Sabbath.[30] – ? –

The Gemara answers:

הָתָם כִּי מְחַמְּמֵי – **There, when [the bathhouse attendants] heat up** the water, אַדַּעְתָּא דְּרוּבָּא מְחַמְּמֵי – **they heat** them **with the majority in mind.** Thus, the act of Sabbath desecration is performed primarily for the Jews, and so the hot waters are prohibited. However, in the case of a single gentile and a single Jew, the gentile performs the *melachah* primarily for himself, and so the Jew may benefit from his labors.[31]

Another challenge, this time to Rava:

תָּא שְׁמַע – **Come, hear** a refutation from a Baraisa: נֵר הַדָּלוּק בִּמְסִיבָּה – Regarding A LAMP LIT AT A well-attended GATHERING, אִם רוֹב נָכְרִים מוּתָּר לְהִשְׁתַּמֵּשׁ לְאוֹרָהּ – IF A MAJORITY of the people there ARE GENTILES, [A JEW] IS PERMITTED TO USE ITS LIGHT; אִם רוֹב יִשְׂרָאֵל אָסוּר – IF A MAJORITY of the people ARE JEWS, ONE IS FORBIDDEN to use it. מֶחֱצָה עַל מֶחֱצָה אָסוּר – If the attendees are HALF Jewish AND HALF gentile, ONE IS FORBIDDEN to use the light.[32] – ? –

The Gemara answers:

הָתָם נַמִּי כִּי מַדְלְקֵי – **There, too, when they light** the lamp,

NOTES

23. *Rashi* implies that in Rava's view the gangplank would be prohibited not because the gentile constructed it for the Jews as well, as the Gemara originally thought, but only if he expended extra effort on the Jews' behalf [and here, because no extra effort was expended ("a gangplank for one, a gangplank for one hundred"), the gangplank is permitted to all]. According to Abaye, however, the prohibition applies whenever the Jew was in the gentile's presence, even when the latter expended no extra effort on the Jew's behalf (cf. *Tosafos*).

According to *Ritva's* understanding of the dispute, Abaye is mainly saying that benefiting from the gentile is permitted whenever the Jew was not in his presence; the rationale of "a lamp for one etc." is not needed to establish this. However, Abaye does accept the validity of that rationale to permit benefiting whenever the Jew was in the gentile's presence. [Conversely, Rava will concede that benefiting is always permitted when the Jew was not in the gentile's presence.]

According to *Ritva,* the following legal conclusions may be derived from the Gemara:

(a) In order for the prohibition against benefiting from a gentile's labor to apply, two conditions must be met: (1) The gentile performed the labor in the Jew's presence; and (2) the possibility exists that the gentile expended extra effort on the Jew's behalf (which would exclude the case of a lamp).

(b) When the labor was performed expressly on a Jew's behalf, benefiting from it is prohibited in every case. See, however, *Beur Halachah* 325:11 (ד"ה אם מכירו), who cites others that dispute these conclusions.

24. Rabban Gamliel's statement implies that had the gangplank been constructed in his presence, its use would be prohibited – even though the gentile had expended no extra effort on Rabban Gamliel's behalf (*Rashi*).

25. I.e. Rabban Gamliel did indeed say, "Since he made it outside of our presence . . ." However, he did not mean that this was the reason for permitting the gangplank's use; rather, that was simply how the incident transpired (*Rashi*).

26. *Machshirin* 2:5.

27. *Maharam* emends the Gemara to read: and whose bathhouse is heated up on the Sabbath. *Mishnah Berurah* 326 §37 notes that even though on Shabbos itself only non-Jews use the bathhouse, when the waters are reheated toward the end of the day, they are reheated for the benefit of the (Jewish) majority that uses the bathhouse on Saturday night.

28. See *Mishnah Berurah* ibid. §38.

29. There is no need to wait the length of time needed to heat up the bathhouse again (see note 12 above). [However, a Jew may not use the bathhouse on the Sabbath itself, since one is not allowed to bathe in hot water on the Sabbath (above, 39b; *Orach Chaim* 326:1; see *Mishnah Berurah* 326:5).]

30. This is a case where a gentile performs a single *melachah* for the sake of both himself and a Jew, inasmuch as Jews constitute a majority of the city and so it is as if the gentile who heated the bathhouse waters knew each Jew. Nevertheless, the Jews are not allowed to benefit, even though the heating was done outside their presence (a refutation of Abaye) and no extra effort was expended on their behalf (a refutation of Rava).

31. According to Abaye, the Jew may benefit from any *melachah* done outside his presence; according to Rava, he may benefit even if the *melachah* is done in his presence, so long as the gentile does not expend extra effort on the Jew's behalf (*Rashi*).

32. Here, too, since the majority of partygoers are Jewish, it is as if the gentile who lit the lamp knew each one, and thus lit for the Jews' benefit as well. And even though he expended no extra effort in doing so ("a lamp for one, a lamp for one hundred"), the Baraisa forbids the Jews to enjoy the light. [This, then, is a refutation of Rava, who permits the enjoyment of a lamp even when the Jew is in the gentile's presence at the time of kindling, which is apparently the case here] (*Rashi*).

Ritva MHK ed. notes that this challenge does not seem to add anything to the previous challenge. He explains that a bathhouse is different from a lamp. It is worthwhile to heat up a bathhouse only for a large number of people. Thus, in a small city with a Jewish majority, it is not practical to heat the entire bathhouse for a handful of gentiles. When the bathhouse is heated up, it is clearly done so solely for the Jews. However, if even one gentile needs illumination, it is worthwhile to light a lamp for him. Thus, even at a party with a majority of Jews, one can reasonably say that the gentile kindled the lamp solely for himself or for his fellow gentiles.

מסורת הש"ס

א) [ע"ז לא.], ב) [עירובין עט.], ג) [תוספתא פי"ד], ד) לקמן קנא. מכשירין פ"ב מ"ה, ה) [ד"ה ואפילו], ו) [דף קכא.], ז) להביא הבהמה לשם ואין זה דומה לדומיא דמתני' איירי האי בתרי עברי דנהרא שאין הבהמה יכולה לירד לבור ואע"ג דהך בבא וכו' כצ"ל רש"ל.

הגהות הב"ח

(א) תוס' ד"ה משקה וכו' שמתחלה היה יכול לילך ולשתות שם והביאו נכרי דרך רה"ר:

ליקוטי רש"י

אם בשביל ישראל אסור. משום שנעשה בו איסור בשבילו. לישראל אחר נמי אסור דנכרי שהדליק את הנר בשבת תנן אם בשביל ישראל אסור ולא חלקו בינו לחברו [ביצה כה. עיין בתוס' כאן ושם]. **מעמיד אדם בהמתו על גבי עשבים.** מחוברים לאכול ולא חיישינן דלמא עקר בידים ומאכיל לה דהא חמיר עליה איסור שבת אבל איסור מוקצה קיל ליה וחיישינן דלמא שקיל בידים וספי לה [עירובין עט.]. מעמיד משמע שאוחזה בידו ומוליכה [ב"ק נו:]. **דקאים לה באפה.** מתני' לאו דמוקים לה עלה בידים אלא קאי באפה שלא תלך במקום אחר ואיהי אזלה ואכלה וכולי האי לא גזור רבנן [עירובין שם]. שלא משכוה אלא עמדו בפניה לכל צד שלא תלך אנה ואנה אלא לאכול [ב"ק שם].

של בית אביך. דקטנות היו אבל גדולות אדם קובע להם מקום: **קרונות.** עגלות לבני אדם: **אי משום דסבר כרבי אליעזר.** דאמר במסכת ע"ז (דף לא.) יין מותר בחותם אחד: **אי משום אימתא דבי נשיאה.** שהיה הנכרי המביאו ירא מן הנשיא שהיה שליט על פי המלכות ומשום דאיירי ר' אבא בר כהנא לעיל גבי נחש נקט כל הני בשמיה: **מתני' אם בשביל ישראל אסור.** מדרבנן: **מילא מים.** מבור ברה"ר: **כבש.** עושין בספינה גדולה לירד בו מספינה ליבשה: **גמ' נר לאחד נר למאה.** כיון דנכרי לצרכו הדליקו ליכא למימר דבשביל ישראל אפיש: **כבש למה לי.** הא דומיא דנר הוא כבש לאחד כבש למאה: **מאכיל אחריו ישראל.** את בהמתו ואחריו דוקא נקט דכולהו דנכרי לצורך עצמו עביד: **אבל מכירו אסור.** קס"ד דעביד נמי אדעתא דידיה: **מעמיד אדם בהמתו על גבי עשבים.** מחוברים: **בשבת.** לרעות וליכא למיגזר שמא יתלוש ויאכיל: **ואינו מעמידה ע"ג מוקצה.** שמא יטול בידו ויאכיל והא נמי מוקצין נינהו לגבי טלטול דלאתמול הוו מחוברין: **דקאים ליה באפה.** שלא תפנה למקום אחר: **ואזלא ואכלה.** אבל הוא אינו עומד על העשבים קרוב להם דנימוס לשמא יטול ויאכיל: **מכירו הוה.** שהרי בספינה היה עמו: **שלא בפניו הוה.** כשעשאו לא היה רבן גמליאל שם דניכרון ליה: **נר לאחד נר למאה.** כבש לאחד כבש למאה אבל גבי עשבים כשהוא מכירו מרבה בשבילו: **הואיל ושלא בפנינו כו'.** קשיא לרבא דשמעינן מינה דבפניו אסור ואע"פ שאין כאן מרבה בשבילו: **אימא הואיל ועשאו נרד בו.** וטעמא לאו משום שלא בפניו הוא אלא הכי הוה מעשה: **מותר לרחוץ בה מיד.** למוצאי שבת: **בכדי שיחמו חמין.** שלא יהנה במה שהקדימו להחם בשבת וכן בכל מעשה שבת נתנו חכמים שיעור להמתין לערב בכדי שיעשו והא הכא דחימום לאחד חימום למאה דבבת אחת מחממין וקתני אם רוב ישראל דהוי דומיא דמכירו דמכירו למסיק אדעתיה לעשות אף בשבילו אסור ואע"ג דשלא בפניו וקשיא בין לאביי בין לרבא: **אדעתא דרובא מחממי.** ועיקר חילול השבת בשבילם אבל נכרי וישראל דנכרי אדעתא דנפשיה הוא דעביד שרי לאביי שלא בפניו ולרבא אפי' בפניו: **נר הדלוק במסיבה.** של בני אדם: **אם רוב ישראל אסור.** והא הכא דהוי דומיא דמכירו הואיל ורובא נינהו אסיק דעתיה להדליק אף בשבילם וקתני אסור: אדעתא

א"ל כאותן של בית אביך ואמר ר' אבא בר כהנא אמר ר' חנינא קרונות של בית רבי מותר לטלטל בשבת א"ל ר' זירא בניטלין באדם אחד או בשני בני אדם א"ל כאותן של בית אביך ואמר ר' אבא בר כהנא התיר להם ר' חנינא לבית רבי לשתות יין בקרונות של נכרי א בחותם אחד ולא ידענא אי משום דסבר לה א) כר' אליעזר אי משום אימתא דבי נשיאה: **מתני'** ב נכרי שהדליק את הנר משתמש לאורו ישראל ואם בשביל ישראל אסור מילא מים להשקות בהמתו משקה אחריו ישראל ואם בשביל ישראל אסור עשה נכרי כבש לירד בו יורד אחריו ישראל ואם בשביל ישראל אסור מעשה ברבן גמליאל וזקנים שהיו באין בספינה ועשה נכרי כבש לירד בו וירדו בו ר"ג וזקנים: **גמ'** וצריכא דאי אשמעינן נר משום דנר לאחד נר למאה אבל מים ליגזור דילמא אתי לאפושי בשביל ישראל וכבש ל"ל מעשה דרבן גמליאל וזקנים קמ"ל ת"ר ג נכרי שליקט עשבים מאכיל אחריו ישראל ואם בשביל ישראל אסור מילא מים להשקות בהמתו משקה אחריו ישראל ואם בשביל ישראל אסור ד בד"א שאין מכירו אבל מכירו אסור איני ו) והאמר רב הונא אמר רבי חנינא ה מעמיד אדם בהמתו על גבי עשבים בשבת אבל לא על גבי מוקצה בשבת ו דקאים לה באפה ואזלא היא ואכלה אמר מר בד"א שאין מכירו אבל מכירו אסור הא רבן גמליאל מכירו הוה אמר אביי שלא בפניו הוה רבא אמר ז אפי' תימא בפניו נר לאחד נר למאה מיתיבי ג) אמר להן רבן גמליאל הואיל ושלא בפנינו עשאו נרד בו אימא הואיל ועשאו נרד בו תא שמע ד) ח עיר שישראל ונכרים דרין בתוכה והיתה בה מרחץ המרחצת בשבת אם רוב נכרים מותר לרחוץ בה מיד אם רוב ישראל ימתין בכדי שיחמו חמין התם כי מחממי אדעתא דרובא מחממי תא שמע ט נר הדלוק במסיבה אם רוב נכרים מותר להשתמש לאורה אם רוב ישראל אסור מחצה על מחצה אסור התם נמי כי מדלקי אדעתא

אמר ליה כאותן של בית אביך. פי' שהם גדולים או קטנים דלאים להו מידקי כמו שפירשתי לעיל (דף לה.):

משתמש ישראל לאורה. ולא גזרינן שמא ידליק לגדורין כפ"ק דביצה (דף ג.) פירות הנושרין שמא יעלה ויתלוש ומשקין שזבו שמא יסחוט משום דסחיטה ותלישה הם קלים לעשות ואדם להוט אחריהם לפי שהן דבר אכילה אבל בכל הני דהכא אין קלין לעשות כל כך ואין אדם להוט אחריהן: **ואם** בשביל ישראל אסור. נראה דאסור לכל ישראל דדוקא בתוך התחום דרבנן אמר בפרק כל מערבין (עירובין דף מ.) ובאין צדין (ביצה דף כה.) הבא בשביל ישראל זה מותר לישראל אחר אבל באיסורא דאורייתא כי הכא לא ואע"ג דישראל המבשל בשבת בשוגג יאכל התם לא חיישינן אי שרית ליה לאכול דילמא אתי לבשולי במזיד דהא איכא איסור סקילה וחמיר עליה אבל בנכרי העושה לצורך ישראל אי שרית ליה אתי למימר לנכרי לעשות בשבילו ולא דמי להא דאמר לעיל ז) נכרי שבא לכבות אין אומרים לו כבה ואל תכבה והכא אסור כשעושה בשביל ישראל דכי אמרינן דנכרי אדעתא דנפשיה קא עביד הנ"מ בכיבוי וכיוצא בו שאין ישראל נהנה במעשה הנכרי אבל הכא שגוף ישראל נהנה במעשה של נכרי לא אמרינן אדעתא דנפשיה קעביד הואיל והנכרי מתכוין להנאתו כך פירש רבינו שמשון הזקן:

משקה אחריו ישראל ואם בשביל ישראל אסור. אומר ר"ת מדנקט בהמתו ולא נקט מילא מים לעצמו לא דווקא להשקות בהמתו אסור משום שלא היה יכול להביאה לתוך הבור אבל הוא עצמו שרי מטעם ועולה מטפס ויורד וכיון שיכול ליכנס לתוך הבור ולשתות לא אסרו לו בשביל שמילא אותם נכרי והא דאסרינן בגמרא נכרי שליקט עשבים לצורך ישראל אע"ג דישראל יכול להעמיד בהמתו על גבי העשבים המחובר אומר ר"ת דהתם נמי איירי בנכרי עברי דנהרא שלא היה יכול ז) להביא הבהמה לשם ואע"ג דהך בבא דמילא מים משום חידוש דהיתרא קתני לה כדמוכח בגמרא מיהא בהמתו משום איסורא נקט לה וה"ר אליהו הביא ראיה להתיר מפירות שיצאו חוץ לתחום וחזרו שלא הפסידו היתירן הראשון כדאמר בפרק מי שהוציאוהו (עירובין דף מא:) ה"ה המים שמתחילה היה יכול (א) לבא שם והביאו דרך רה"ר דשרו ולא דמי דהתם לא אתעבידא בהו איסורא דאורייתא מיהו לענין אותו ישראל עצמו לא מצינו חילוק ור"י אומר דה"ה לישראל עצמו אסור והאי דנקט בהמתו לאשמעינן רבותא דלא גזרינן דילמא אתי לאפושי בשביל ישראל שבהמה רגילה לשתות הרבה אבל ישראל עצמו פשיטא דשותה אחריו דליכא למיחש כולי האי דילמא אתי לאפושי דבדלייה אחת מושך הרבה לצרכו ולצורך ישראל ולפי זה אם נמשכו המים לצורך ישראל זה אסור לכל ישראל אי איכא איסורא דאורייתא כגון שמביאם דרך רה"ר או מרה"י לרה"ר אבל בכרמלית שרי לישראל אחר ויש שרצו לומר דדוקא שתיה אסורה אבל לרחוץ ידיו ורגליו ושאר תשמישין שרי כדאמר בפרק חרש (יבמות דף קיד.) רבי יצחק אירכסו ליה מפתחות דבי מדרשא כו' אמר ליה דבר טליא וטליתא ליטיילו התם דאי משכח להו מייתי להו אלמא יכולין ליהנות ממפתחות להשתמש בהם בשבת ואין נראה לר"י כלל דהתם אין עושין לדעת ישראל ועוד דהרי כבש ונר וכמה דברים דאסור להשתמש בהם בשבת כשנעשין לצורך ישראל ה"נ לא שנא שתיה לא שנא שאר תשמישין אסירי:

איני והאמר רב הונא אמר רב חנינא מעמיד אדם כו' אבל לא על גבי מוקצה. והני עשבים נמי מוקצין נינהו שנלקטו היום מן המחובר וא"ת ולימא דהך ברייתא רבי שמעון היא דלית ליה מוקצה וי"ל דמשני לה אפילו כר' יהודה א"נ מודה ר"ש במוקצה דמחובר כדפי' בקונטרס בפרק אין צדין (ביצה דף כד:) מדלא ליקטן מאתמול אקצינהו והוי כגרוגרות וצימוקים ובריש ביצה (דף ג.) דאסר פירות הנושרים משום גזירה שמא יעלה ויתלוש ולא אסר להו משום מוקצה משום דמוכנים לעורבים כי ההיא דמקום שנהגו (פסחים דף נו:) והכא איירי כשאין הבהמה יכולה לבא ולאכול מן המחובר ולהכי הוי מוקצה א"נ עשבים מוקצין הם אפילו לר"ש לפי שאינו יושב ומצפה שילקטום אבל בנר יושב ומצפה מתי יכבה כדאמרינן לעיל (דף מו:) וכן פירות הנושרין יושב ומצפה מתי יפלו ולהכי אי לאו טעמא דשמא יעלה ויתלוש הוו שרו: **מעמיד** אדם בהמתו ע"ג עשבים בשבת. כדדרשי' במכילתין למען ינוח שורך וחמורך וגו' יכול לא יניחנו תולש לא יניחנו עוקר ת"ל למען ינוח ואין זה נוח אלא צער. ר"ת: **אמר** אביי שלא בפניו הוה. נראה לר"י דמודה אביי דנר לאחד נר למאה אלא דסבר דהכא אם היה בפניו עיקר היה נעשה לצורך ר"ג שהיה נשיא ושר וראש בספינה:

אהדרינהו

עין משפט נר מצוה

פ א מיי' פי"ג מהלכות מאכלות אסורות הל"י סמג לאוין קלח טור שו"ע יו"ד סימן קיח סעיף א וסימן קל סעיף ג:
פא ב מיי' פ"ו מהלכות שבת הלכה ג ג סמג לאוין סה טוש"ע או"ח סימן רעו סעיף א וסימן שכה סעיף יא ויב:
פב ג ד מיי' וסמג שם טוש"ע או"ח סימן שכה סעיף י יא:
פג ה ו מיי' פכ"א מהל' שבת הלכה לו סמג שם טוש"ע או"ח סימן שכד סעיף יג וסימן שכה סעיף יא:
פד ז מיי' פ"ו שם הל"ד וסמג שם טור שו"ע שם:
פה ח מיי' שם הלכה ז סמג שם טוש"ע או"ח סימן שכו סעיף יג:
פו ט מיי' שם הלכה ד סמג שם טוש"ע שם סימן רעו סעיף ג:

רבינו חננאל

או בב' ידים. אמר ליה כאותן של בית אביך ש"מ דניטלת בידו אחת שרי. ניטלת בב' ידים לא איתברירא לן בהדיא. וכן קרונות של בית רבי הניטלין בב' בני אדם לא איפשיטא. והתיר ר' חנינא לשתות יין הבא בקרונות של נכרים בחותם אחת ולא ידענא אי משום דסבר לה כר' אליעזר אי משום אימתא דבי נשיאה: **נכרי** שהדליק את הנר. ת"ר נכרי שליקט עשבים מאכיל אחריו ישראל ואם בשביל ישראל אסור. וכן מילא מים להשקות בהמתו וכו'. בד"א

רב נסים גאון

לפני רבן יוחנן בן זכאי בערב ואמר חושש אני לו מחטאת: **אי** משום דסבר לה כר' אליעזר דלא חייש לזיופא ומימרא דר' אליעזר במס' ע"ז אין מעמידין בהמה (דף לא) דתניא אחד הלוקח וא' השוכר בית כו' ר' אליעזר מתיר בשתייה ואמרו מר סבר כי פליגי רבנן עליה דר' אליעזר בחותם אחד כו' ובפ' השוכר את הפועלין (שם דף סט) אמרו וכי מאחר דקיימא לן כוותיה דרשב"ג וכוותיה דר' אליעזר דלא חייש לזיופא:

סליק פרק כל כתבי הקודש

אדעתא דרובא מדלקי שמואל איקלע לבי אבין תורן אתא ההוא נכרי אדליק שרגא אהדרינהו שמואל לאפיה כיון דחזא דאייתי שטר וקא קרי אמר אדעתא דנפשיה הוא דאדליק אהדרינהו איהו לאפיה גבי שרגא:

הדרן עלך כל כתבי

כל הכלים ניטלין בשבת ודלתותיהן עמהן אע"פ שנתפרקו (בשבת) שאינן דומין לדלתות הבית לפי שאינן מן המוכן נוטל אדם קורנס לפצע בו את האגוזין קרדום לחתוך בו את הדבילה מגירה לגור בה את הגבינה מגריפה לגרוף בה את הגרוגרות את הרחת ואת המלגז לתת עליו לקטן את הכוש ואת הכרכר לתחוב בו מחט של יד ליטול בו את הקוץ ושל סקאים לפתוח בו את הדלת: **גמ'** כל הכלים ניטלין ואע"פ שנתפרקו בשבת ולא מיבעיא בחול אדרבה בשבת מוכנין על גבי אביהן בחול אין מוכנין על גבי אביהן אמר אביי הכי קאמר כל הכלים ניטלין בשבת ודלתותיהן עמהן אע"פ שנתפרקו בחול ניטלין בשבת ת"ר דלת של שידה ושל תיבה ושל מגדל נוטלין אבל לא מחזירין ושל לול של תרנגולים לא נוטלין ולא מחזירין בשלמא של לול של תרנגולים קסבר כיון דמחברי בארעא יש בנין בקרקע יש סתירה בקרקע אלא של שידה ושל תיבה ושל מגדל מאי קסבר אי קסבר יש בנין בכלים יש סתירה בכלים ואי אין סתירה בכלים אין בנין בכלים אמר אביי לעולם קסבר יש בנין בכלים ויש סתירה בכלים ושניטלו קאמר א"ל רבא [שתי תשובות בדבר] חדא דניטלין קתני ועוד מאי אבל לא מחזירין אלא אמר רבא קסבר אין בנין בכלים ואין סתירה בכלים וגזירה שמא יתקע: נוטל אדם קורנס כו': אמר רב יהודה קורנס של אגוזין לפצע בו את האגוזין אבל של נפחין לא קסבר דבר שמלאכתו לאיסור אפילו לצורך גופו אסור א"ל רבה אלא מעתה סיפא דקתני ואת הרחת ואת המלגז לתת עליו לקטן רחת ומלגז מי מייחדי ליה לקטן אלא אמר רבה קורנס של נפחין לפצע בו האגוזין קסבר
דבר

אהדרינהו שמואל לאפיה. מיירי שהיה לכל הפחות מחצה על מחצה דמשום ספק לא אהני נר לאחד נר למאה לא משתריא אלא היכא שהוא ניכר שהוא עושה לצרכו דתו לא גזרין אפילו במכירו שמא ירבה בשבילו: הדרן עלך כל כתבי

כל הכלים ניטלין בשבת ודלתותיהן עמהם גרסינן ול"ג כל הכלים ניטלין דטובא איכא דאין ניטלין כגון מסר הגדול ויתד של מחרישה דאפילו ר"ש מודה כדאיתא בשילהי מכילתין (דף קמז.) וכגון חלתא בת תרי כורי דאסר רבה בשילהי במה מדליקין (דף לה.) וכן תלוגרות לרבי יהודה ונר ישן מ"ר:

אדרבה בשבת מוכנין אגב אביהן. אע"ג דלקמן בפירקין (דף קכד:) אמר איפכא גבי שברי כלי חרס דשרי לטלטל יותר כשנשברו בע"ש משנשברו בשבת לא דמיא דהכא אכתי כלי הוא שעדיין עומד למלאכה ראשונה וראוי להתחבר הכיסוי עם הכלי אבל לקמן לא חשיב כלי אלא מחמת שעומד למלאכה אחרת הלכך כשנשבר בשבת אסור טפי דהוי נולד:

לעולם קסבר יש בנין בכלים כו'. וכשניטלו מטלטלין קאמר וה"פ הברייתא דלת של שידה תיבה ומגדל ניטלין פירוש מטלטלין כשניטלין ולא כפירוש הקונטרס דמפרש שניטלין דקתני היינו שניטלו קאמר כלומר כשניטל אין מחזירין אותן דלא יתכן לפרש כן ניטלין דסיפא אלא לשון טלטול הוא כדפרשתי ופריך והא (א) נמי ניטלין קתני ועוד מאי אבל לא מחזירין דלא שייך למיתני אמילתיה דלא (דמיא) [שייך] כלל למאי דאיירי בה דמעיקרא קאמר ניטלין שמותר לטלטל ואין בו איסור מוקצה והדר קאמר אבל לא מחזירין שהוא משום איסור בנין מאי ענין זה אצל זה לא שייך כה"ג למיתני אבל כלל:

רחת ומלגז מי מייחדי ליה לקטן. ורב יהודה ידע ליה לסיפא אלא דילמא הוה מוקי לה בשיחדה לכך ככל הנך דמתניתין ואם תאמר והאמר רב יהודה אמר שמואל בפרק אלו קשרים (לעיל דף קיג.) כלי קיואי מותר לטלטל בשבת דהיינו לצורך גופו אע"פ שמלאכתו לאיסור ואין לומר דמשמע דשמואל קאמר ליה וליה לא סבירא ליה מדבעי מיניה מרב יהודה כובד עליון וכובד התחתון מהו אין ולאו ורפיא בידיה משמע דס"ל הכי ועוד דרב יהודה גופיה בסוף כירה (לעיל ד' מו.) קאמר שרגא דמישחא שרי לטלטולי ואין לומר דמיירי כשייחדו להיתר כדמוקי רב יהודה הנך דמתני' דהא כלי קיואי לא משמע שייחדו דאם כן אפילו כובד העליון וכובד תחתון נמי ויש לומר דלא אסר רב יהודה אלא דומיא דפילוע אגוזים שהיא מלאכה גרועה לגבי קורנס שמיוחד למלאכה חשובה וכן כל הנך דמתניתין הוה אסור בלא ייחוד דמלאכת היתר שלהן מלאכה גרועה היא לגבי הנך כלים שמיוחדין למלאכה חשובה אבל כלי קיואי ושרגא דמישחא מותר לטלטל לצורך גופן דמלאכה שלהן חשובה יותר מפילוע אגוזים:
בסיכי

אדעתא דרובא. הלכך ישראל עיקר ומחצה על מחצה נמי ליכא למיקם עלה דמלתא דליכא למימר עיקר דעתיה דמדליק בשביל ישראל וליכא למימר עיקר דעתיה דמדליק בשביל נכרי אבל נכרי וישראל והמדליק עצמו משתמש לאורה ודאי עיקר אדעתא דידיה עביד וכיון דנר לאחד נר למאה שרי: תורן. מקום: דאייתי שטר. הסוה דאדלקה:

הדרן עלך כל כתבי

כל הכלים ניטלין בשבת ודלתותיהן עמהם. כל הכלים שיש להם דלתות כגון שידה תיבה ומגדל ניטלין בשבת ודלתות שיש להם בלדן עמהן ניטלין עמהן: ואע"פ שנתפרקו. הדלתות מן הכלים ניטלין ואין דומין לדלתות הבית שאין ניטלין לפי שדלתות הבית אינן מן המוכן לטלטל שאינן כלי אבל אלו הן כלי אגב אביהן: קורנס. מרטי"ל: דבילה. מאכל שעשאה עיגול עבה היא מאד וקשה כגבינה וצריך קורדום לחותכה: ומגירה. כעין סכין ויש בו פגימות הרבה: לגור בה את הגבינה. לחתכו ולחלקו לפי שמתהרכת לחתוך דבר עב: מגריפה. וודי"ל: לגרוף בה את הגרוגרות. מן המסיבות: רחת. פאל"א: מלגז. כמין עתר שקורין פורק"א של ברזל ולו ג' שיניים ומהפכין בו קש בגורן: לתת עליו לקטן. מזונות: כוש. פלך פושי"ל: כרכר. רא"ל: לתחוב בו. לאכול בו תותים וכל פרי רך: מחט של יד. מחט קטן שתופר בו בגדים: ושל סקאים. מחט גדולה שתופרים בה שקים: לפתוח בו את הדלת. מי שאבד מפתחו: **גמ' ולא מיבעיא** בחול. קא סלקא דעתך ואע"פ שנתפרקו אשבת דקתני רישא קאי ומשמע אע"פ שנתפרקו היום מותרים ולא מיבעיא אם נתפרקו מאתמול: אדרבה. מאי אע"פ שייך למתני הא ודאי נתפרקו בשבת איכא למישרי משום דכי קדיש יומא הוו מוכנין לטלטל אגב אביהן: הכי קאמר כו'. ואע"פ לא ארבותא דנתפרקו בשבת קאי אלא ארבותא דנתפרקו או בחול או בשבת קאי ולא מיבעיא כשהן מחוברין: נוטלין. משמע מסלקין אותן בשבת [(ה) מהיתר] ציר שלהן: לול. בנין העשוי לתרנגולין: לא נוטלין ולא מחזירין. כדמפרש ואזיל חזרתו בנין ממש הוא וסילוקו סתירה גמורה היא: מאי קסבר. שמתיר סילוקו ואוסר חזרתו: אי קסבר יש בנין בכלים. וחזרתו בנין על כרחיך אם יש בנין יש סתירה ואמאי נוטלין: ושניטלו קאמר. וה"ק דלת של תיבה שידה ומגדל שניטלו אין מחזירין: מאי אבל. כיון דלא תנא נוטלין לא שייך למיתני אבל: לעולם קסבר אין סתירה ואין בנין. הלכך נוטלין ומיהו אין מחזירין מדרבנן: גזירה שמא יתקע. בחוזקה בסכין ויתדות והוה ליה גמר מלאכה וחייב משום מכה בפטיש: קורנס של אגוזים. המיוחד לפליעת אגוזים הוא דקתני מתניתין דנוטלין אותו למלאכתו משום דעיקרו למלאכת היתר: אבל של נפחים. דעיקרו למלאכת איסור לא: לצורך גופו. שגופו צריך עוד למלאכה אחרת של היתר אין מטלטלין אותו לאותה מלאכה וכ"ש אם אין צריך לגופו אלא לפנות מקומו דאין מטלטלין: מי מייחדי לקטן. בשלמא כולהו הני דמתני' איכא לאוקמא בעשויין ומיוחדין לכך בר מהני דליכא דעביד להו להכי:
דבר

עין משפט נר מצוה

פז א טור שו"ע שם: א ב מיי' פכ"ב מהלכות שבת הלכה כה ופכ"ה הלכה יב סמג לאוין סה טוש"ע או"ח סימן שח סעיף ח: ב ג מיי' שם הלכה ז טוש"ע שם סעיף ג: ג ד מיי' שם הלכה ח טוש"ע שם סעיף יא: ד ה מיי' פכ"ה שם הלכה כה טור שו"ע שם סעיף ט: ה ו מיי' שם הלכה כו סמג שם טוש"ע או"ח סימן שיד סעיף א:

הגהות הב"ח

(א) תוס' ד"ה לעולם וכו' ופריך והא ניטלין קתני ולא תני נמי נתפרקו כו' ועוד מאי אבל:

רבינו חננאל

בנכרי שאינו מכירו אבל אם מכירו אסור. ת"ש עיר של ישראל ונכרים דרין כו':

הדרן עלך כל כתבי הקודש

פי"ז כל הכלים ניטלין בשבת כו'. באנו לפרש מתי נפרקו בשבת או אפי' בחול. ואוקמה אביי להא מתני' אע"פ שנתפרקו בחול ניטלין בשבת לפי שאינן דומין לדלתות הבית. כי דלתות הבית קבועין בקרקע ולא הוכנו להיטלטל. אבל הכלים הוכנו לטלטול וכ"ש דלתותיהן. ופשטה היא. ומפרקינן (א) גזירה שמא יתקע. פי' שמא יתקע בה מסמר או יתד וכדומה להן: נוטל אדם קורנס לפצוע בו אגוזים וכו'. בא רב יהודה להעמיד משנתנו זו בקורנס המוכן לפצוע אגוזים. ולא כל קורנס מותר. אלא זה בלבד. אבל קורנס של נפחים וכדומה להן אפילו לצורך גופו אסור. ואקשי' עלה רבה אלא מעתה סיפא דקתני ואת הרחת ואת המלגז לתת עליו לקטן. פי' לתת עליו מאכל לקטן כגון תבשיל. רחת ומלגז [מי] מכינין בנ"א לתבשיל

חשק שלמה על רבינו חננאל

א) נראה דחסר בדברי רבינו וצ"ל דלת של שידה ושל תיבה ושל מגדל נוטלין אבל לא מחזירין:

מסורת הש"ס

א) פירוש מזלג [ובמשנה שבמשניות איתא המזלג], ב) לעיל קז. סנהדרין פד:, ג) [תוספתא פרק טו], ד) [עירובין לה. ביצה י. יא: כב.], ה) רש"ל וכ"ה איתא מהיתר וכן איתא ברא"ש בד"ה לעולם, ו) [עי' לעיל לה. תוס' ד"ה ואפילו], ז) [לעיל לו.], ח) [לעיל מד.].

ליקוטי רש"י

קרדום. שמש קרדום עשוי כמין כלי אומנות שעושין בו אוכפות ומכרות שקורין אישי"ש ויש שעושין כעין כלי האומן שקורין ביזגוע"ה שראשו האחד דומה לקרדומות שלנו ולפעו השני דומה לכלי אומני אוכפות ומכרות הסוסים [ביצה לא.]. מגירה. שיר"ה בלע"ז וכמין סכין שיש בו פגימות הרבה וקוללת מהר [ב"ק קיט:]. סכין מלא פגימות ואין משופשות כשל מגל קליר אלא מכוונות שיש לפשטיה מורשא מכאן ומכאן כמספר פגימות אוגרת ומגירה בלעו ובלעז שיר"ה [חולין טו:]. שיג"א סכין מלא פגימות ומוכך מהר כעין שיש לעושי מסרקים [ערכין כג:]. שיג"א כעין סכין מלאה פגימות וממסר לקין בו עלים וכלי אומן הוא [ביצה שם]. מגריפה. כלי ברזל הוא ומלהיבים בו גרוגרות הנדבקות זו בזו [זבחים צט:]. כלי ברזל הוא שקורין וודי"ל שגורפין בו אפר הכירה וגם מבדלין בו תלוגים המודבקות זו לזו [חגיגה כ.]. וודי"ל הוא כעין כף [ערכין י:]. הרחת. פל"א שזורין המוגן ברוח מתוך המגולה [ב"מ קה.]. פל"ה בלע"ז כשכברי גדול צריך להגביה התבואה ברחת וזורק כלפי מעלה והרוח מוליך המוץ ודוחפת המוץ למרחוק [סוכה לו:]. מלגז. פורק"א בת שלש שיניים ומהפכין בה תבואה בגורן [לעיל צב.]. כוש. פלך פוז"ל בלע"ז שטווין בו [סוכה לז.]. כרכר. עץ יש לאורגין וראשו חד [לעיל פא.]. מחט של יד. היא מחט קטנה שתופרין בה בגדים ומשום דקתני לה להלן גבי ושל סקאין לפתוח בו את הדלת קרי ליה להא קטנה מחט של יד [סנהדרין פד:]. דלת של שידה. ודלתות שידה תיבה ומגדל דתנא מתניתין נוטלין יש תורת כלי עליהן דראויין לישב עליהן ולתת עליהן מזונות לקטן [לקמן קכו: עיי"ש]. שידה. כמין ארגז תלוי בעגלה למרכב נשים חשובות [עירובין יד:]. מרכבת נשים עגלה עשויה כקופסא [שם ל:]. מגדל. מנסטי"ר [שם יד:]. יש בנין בכלים. יש תורת בנין בכלים ובונה חייב בכל שהוא [ביצה כב.]. ואי אין סתירה בכלים. ואי בעי סתר ליה [עירובין לה.]. אין בנין בכלים. אין תורת בנין בכלים ואינו חייב אלא אם כן עשה בו מלאכה כגון ממחק או מחתך או אורג או תופר שהן אבות מלאכות לעצמם אבל וכו' משום בנין אין בונה אלא בבתים ואהלים [ביצה שם]. אין איסור בנין וסתירה בכלים אלא בבתים דנחייב בבנין כל דהו והעושה כלי או גומרו ביום טוב או בשבת משום מכה בפטיש הוא דמחייב שהוא חיוב לכל גמר מלאכה או אם הוא דבר שהוא מחליקו חייב משום ממחק ואם צריך קלוע חייב משום מחתך וכן אורג או מסך או תופר אבל בנין וסתירה לא שייך בהו לאתויי בסלוק וחזרה דהא דתנן (שבת קב:) הבונה כל שהוא בבתים תנן [שם יא:]. [מכאן שייך לדף קכג.] הא מני ר' נחמיה היא. דאמר בעירובין (לה.) אפי' תרווד ואפילו טלית אין ניטלין אלא לצורך תשמיש שהן מיוחדין לו [ביצה לב.]. את העלי. דף עב וכבד וכותשין בו חטים לטרגים וטיסני והוי מלאכתו לאיסור וקא סברי בית שמאי אסור לטלטלו ואפילו לצורך גופו שצריך לגוף הכלי למלאכה המותרת היום [שם י.]. מלאכתו לאיסור לכתוש במכתשת משום הכי אסרי ליה בית שמאי. שאסור לטלטלו. דלתעביד ליה לצורך יום טוב [שם יא.]. דקפיד עלייהו. שלא יתעקם ומייחד ליה מקום ומקלה ליה בידים ואפילו לר' שמעון אסור לטלטלו דמוקלה מחמת חסרון כיס אפילו ר' שמעון מודה [לקמן קכה:]. פגה. תאנה בוסר שטומנין אותה בתבן להתבשל ותבן מוקלה הוא ואסור לטלטלו כגון שהקצהו ללבון לבנים. וחררה שטמנה. אתמול בגחלים ועכשיו כבו ומכל מקום מוקצין הן אבל לא כבו לא דמתוך שנהפכים מכבה את התחתונות ומבעיר את העליונות כדאמרינן בכירה [עירובין עז.]. טלטול מן הצד. כלאחר יד [לעיל מג:]. האי פוגלא. [illegible] [לקמן קמא.]. [illegible] לטלטלה בשבת. [illegible] בגדולי. [illegible] ולא אמרו נקובה. [illegible] מעשהו ומיהו לענין שבת [illegible] [לעיל נב:]. תרגמא אביי אליבא דרבא. במקום (אביי) ובשבילו שתהא (משנה) זו מתורגמת לפי דבריו [סוטה יט. בסנהדרין רבא].

אַדַּעְתָּא דְּרוּבָּא מַדְלְקֵי – **they light** it **with the majority in mind.**[1]

A related incident:

שְׁמוּאֵל אִיקְּלַע לְבֵי אָבִין תּוֹרָן – **Shmuel** once **visited the house of Avin of Toran.**[2] אֲתָא הַהוּא נָכְרִי אַדְלִיק שְׁרָגָא – **A certain gentile came** and **lit a lamp.** אַהַדְרִינְהוּ שְׁמוּאֵל לְאַפֵּיה – **Shmuel turned his face** away so as not to benefit from the light.[3] כֵּיוָן דַּחֲזָא דְּאַיְיתִי שְׁטָר וְקָא קָרֵי – However, **once he saw that** [the gentile] who lit the lamp **brought a document and was reading it,** אָמַר – [Shmuel] **said** to himself, אַדַּעְתָּא דְנַפְשֵׁיהּ הוּא דְּאַדְלִיק – **"He lit with himself in mind."** אַהַדְרִינְהוּ אִיהוּ לְאַפֵּיה גַּבֵּי שְׁרָגָא – **Thereupon, [Shmuel] turned his face** back **toward the lamp.**[4]

הדרן עלך כל כתבי

WE SHALL RETURN TO YOU, KOL KISVEI

NOTES

1. Thus, the act of Sabbath desecration was performed primarily for the Jews, and so the light is forbidden. And even if the attendees are evenly divided between gentile and Jew, it is possible that the lamplighter intended to light primarily for the Jewish half (cf. *Rashi* below, 151a ד״ה רוחץ בה). However, in the case of a single gentile and a single Jew, and the gentile lamplighter himself uses the light, it is certain that he performed the *melachah* primarily for himself. Hence, the Jew may benefit from his labor, inasmuch as the gentile did not expend additional effort on the Jew's behalf ["a lamp for one . . ."] (*Rashi*).

2. Toran is a place (*Rashi*).

3. Most or half of the people present were Jews, so there was reason to believe that the gentile lit the lamp on their behalf (*Rosh;* see *Bais Yosef, Orach Chaim* 276 ד״ה ואיתא for alternative explanations of this incident from the *Yerushalmi;* see also *Beur Halachah* to 276:2 ד״ה ואם יש הוכחה).

4. *Rosh* writes that we assume that the gentile lit the lamp for the majority of Jews only when his intent is unclear. Where there is a definite indication that he lit for himself or another gentile, however, a Jew is permitted to use the light ("a lamp for one, a lamp for one hundred").

Chapter Seventeen

Introduction

The following chapter returns to the subject of *muktzeh*, which was previously discussed at length in Chapter Three (42b-47b). However, our chapter focuses on an aspect of these laws that was not covered previously. The earlier discussion centered on the dispute between R' Yehudah and R' Shimon concerning which classes of items are deemed to have been set aside from Sabbath use and thus rendered *muktzeh* (see Introduction to Chapter Three). Here, however, the focus will be on what is classified as a utensil in regard to the law of *muktzeh*, and on the special restrictions that pertain to moving certain categories of utensils on the Sabbath.

In general, something that is neither a utensil nor an edible food item (e.g. a stick or a stone) is deemed to be *inherently muktzeh* (see Introduction to Chapter Three). The Mishnah and Gemara in this chapter will discuss what preparation is necessary in order for such an object to become classified as a utensil, and thus, non-*muktzeh*. Similarly, they will discuss the circumstances in which the fragments of a utensil that broke retain their previous designation as non-*muktzeh*.

An object that is *muktzeh* is generally forbidden for consumption or other use, and may not be moved at all. We will learn in this chapter that there are also restrictions on moving certain utensils that are not *muktzeh* in the strict sense of the word (i.e. they were not completely "set aside" from Sabbath use).[1] However, these restrictions do not apply to all utensils, and are not as severe as those that apply to truly *muktzeh* objects. Thus, the utensils affected by the decree may not be moved about at will, but may be moved for certain purposes.

Specifically, the Gemara will deal with two categories of utensils. These are:

(a) **כְּלִי שֶׁמְּלַאכְתּוֹ לְהֶתֵּר** – *a utensil used [primarily] for work that is permitted [on the Sabbath].*

(b) **כְּלִי שֶׁמְּלַאכְתּוֹ לְאִסּוּר** – *a utensil used [primarily] for work that is forbidden [on the Sabbath].*

[For the sake of brevity, we shall often refer to utensils in these categories as "a permitted-use utensil" and "a forbidden-use utensil."]

The Gemara will also refer to several purposes for which it *might* be permitted to move utensils in these categories. These are:

(a) **לְצוֹרֶךְ גּוּפוֹ** – *for the sake of its use,* i.e. to use the utensil for some task that is permissible on the Sabbath.

(b) **לְצוֹרֶךְ מְקוֹמוֹ** – *for the sake of its place,* i.e. to make the place occupied by the utensil available for some other use.

(c) **מֵחַמָּה לְצֵל** – *from the sun to the shade,* i.e. to prevent the utensil from being damaged.

These issues will be clarified in the course of this chapter.

NOTES

1. The Gemara (123b,124b) provides reasons for these restrictions. Additional reasons are listed by *Rambam, Hil. Shabbos* 24:12-13, and were cited in the Introduction to Chapter Three, note 7.

אדעתא דרובא מדלקי שמואל איקלע לבי אבין תורן אתא ההוא נכרי אדליק שרגא אהדרינהו שמואל לאפיה כיון דחזא דאייתי שטר וקא קרי אמר [א] אדעתא דנפשיה הוא דאדליק אהדרינהו איהו לאפיה גבי שרגא:

הדרן עלך כל כתבי

כל [ג] הכלים ניטלין בשבת ודלתותיהן עמהן אע"פ שנתפרקו (בשבת) שאינן דומין לדלתות הבית לפי שאינן מן המוכן [ג] נוטל אדם קורנס לפצע בו את האגוזין קרדום לחתוך בו את הדבילה מגירה לגור בה את הגבינה מגריפה לגרוף בה את הגרוגרות את הרחת ואת [ה] המלגז לתת עליו לקטן את הכוש ואת הכרכר לתחוב בו [ו] מחט של יד ליטול בו את הקוץ ושל סקאים לפתוח בו את הדלת: **גמ'** כל הכלים ניטלין ואע"פ שנתפרקו בשבת ולא מיבעיא בחול אדרבה בשבת מוכנין על גבי אביהן בחול אין מוכנין על גבי אביהן אמר אביי הכי קאמר כל הכלים ניטלין בשבת ודלתותיהן עמהן אע"פ שנתפרקו בחול ניטלין בשבת ת"ר [ה] דלת של שידה ושל תיבה ושל מגדל נוטלין אבל לא מחזירין ושל לול של תרנגולים לא נוטלין ולא מחזירין בשלמא של לול של תרנגולים קסבר כיון דמחברי בארעא יש בנין בקרקע יש סתירה בקרקע אלא של שידה ושל תיבה ושל מגדל מאי קסבר אי קסבר יש בנין בכלים יש סתירה בכלים ואי אין סתירה בכלים אין בנין בכלים אמר אביי לעולם קסבר יש בנין בכלים ויש סתירה בכלים ושניטלו קאמר א"ל רבא [שתי תשובות בדבר] חדא דניטלין קתני ועוד מאי אבל לא מחזירין אלא אמר רבא קסבר [ו] אין בנין בכלים ואין סתירה בכלים וגזירה שמא יתקע: נוטל אדם קורנס כו': אמר רב יהודה קורנס של אגוזין לפצע בו את האגוזין אבל של נפחין לא קסבר דבר שמלאכתו לאיסור אפילו לצורך גופו אסור א"ל רבה אלא מעתה סיפא דקתני ואת הרחת ואת המלגז לתת עליו לקטן רחת ומלגז מי מייחדי ליה לקטן אלא אמר רבה קורנס של נפחין לפצע בו האגוזין קסבר
דבר

רש"י

אדעתא דרובא. הלכך ישראל עיקר ומחצה על מחצה נמי ליכא למיקם עלה דמלתא דאיכא למימר עיקר דעתיה דמדליק בשביל ישראל ואיכא למימר עיקר דעתיה דמדליק בשביל נכרי אבל נכרי וישראל והמדליק עצמו משתמש לאורה ודאי עיקר אדעתא דידיה עביד וכיון דנר לאחד נר למאה שרי: **תורן.** מקוס: **דאייתי שטר.** ההוא לאדלקה:

הדרן עלך כל כתבי

כל הכלים ניטלין בשבת ודלתותיהן עמהם. כל הכלים שיש להם דלתות כגון שידה תיבה ומגדל ניטלין בשבת ודלתות שיש להם בלדן עמהן ניטלין עמהן: **ואע"פ שנתפרקו.** הדלתות מן הכלים ניטלין ואין דומין לדלתות הבית שאין ניטלין לפי שדלתות הבית אינן מן המוכן לטלטל שאינן כלי אבל אלו הן כלי אגב אביהן: **קורנס.** מרטי"ל: **דבילה.** מאחר שעשאה עיגול עבה היא מאד וקשה כגבינה וצריך קורדום לחותכה: **ומגירה.** כעין סכין ויש בו פגימות הרבה: **לגור בה את הגבינה.** לחתכו ולחלקו לפי שממהרת לחתוך דבר עב: **מגריפה.** ווד"י: **לגרוף בה את הגרוגרות.** מן המכבות: **רחת.** פאל"א: **מלגז.** כמין עתר שקורין פורק"א של ברזל ולו ג' שיניים ומהפכין בו קש בגורן: **לתת עליו לקטן.** מזונות: **כוש.** פלך פוש"ל: **כרכר.** רא"ל: **לתחוב בו.** לאכול בו תותים וכל פרי רך: **מחט של יד.** מחט קטן שתופר בו בגדים: **ושל סקאים.** מחט גדולה שתופרים בה שקים: **לפתוח בו את הדלת.** מי שאבד מפתחו: **גמ' ולא מיבעיא בחול.** קא סלקא דעתך ואע"פ שנתפרקו אבשבת דקתני רישא קאי ומשמע אע"פ שנתפרקו היום מותרים ולא מיבעיא אם נתפרקו מאתמול: **אדרבה.** מאי אע"פ שייך למתני הא ודאי נתפרקו בשבת איכא למישרי משום דכי קדים יומא הוו מוכנין לטלטל אגב אביהן: **הכי קאמר כו'.** ואע"פ לא ארבותא דנתפרקו בשבת קאי אלא ארבותא דנתפרקו או בחול או בשבת קאי ולא מיבעיא כשהן מחוברין: **נוטלין.** משמע מסלקין אותן בשבת [מהיתר] ליר שלהן: **לול.** בנין העשוי לתרנגולין: **לא נוטלין ולא מחזירין.** כדמפרש ואזיל חזרתו בנין ממש הוא וסילוקו סתירה גמורה היא: **מאי קסבר.** שמתיר סילוקו ואוסר חזרתו: **אי קסבר יש בנין בכלים.** וחזרתו בנין על כרחיך אם יש בנין יש סתירה ואמאי נוטלין: **ושניטלו** קאמר. וה"ק דלת של תיבה שידה ומגדל שניטלו אין מחזירין: **מאי אבל.** כיון דלא תנא נוטלין לא שייך למיתני אבל: **לעולם קסבר אין** סתירה **ואין בנין.** הלכך נוטלין ומיהו אין מחזירין מדרבנן: **גזירה שמא יתקע.** בחוזקה בסכין ויתדות והוה ליה גמר מלאכה וחייב משום מכה בפטיש: **קורנס של אגוזים.** המיוחד לפליעת אגוזים הוא דקתני מתניתין דנוטלין אותו למלאכתו משום דעיקרו למלאכת היתר: **אבל של נפחים.** דעיקרו למלאכת איסור לא: **לצורך גופו.** שגופו צריך עוד למלאכה אחרת של היתר אין מטלטלין אותו לאותה מלאכה וכ"ש אם אין צריך לגופו אלא לפנות מקומו דאין מטלטלין: **מי מייחדי לקטן.** בשלמא כולהו הני דמתני' איכא לאוקמא בעשויין ומיוחדין לכך בר מהני דליכא דעביד להו להכי:
דבר

תוספות

אהדרינהו שמואל לאפיה. מיירי שהיה לכל הפחות מחצה על מחצה דמשום נר לאחד נר למאה לא משתריא אלא היכא שהוא ניכר שהוא עושה לצרכו דתו לא גזרינן אפילו במכירו שמא ירבה בשבילו: הדרן עלך כל כתבי

כל הכלים הניטלין בשבת דלתותיהן עמהם גרסינן ול"ג כל הכלים ניטלין דטובא איכא דאין ניטלין כגון מסר הגדול ויתד של מחרישה דאפילו ר"ש מודה כדאיתא בשילהי מכילתין (דף קמ.) וכגון חלתא[ו] בת תרי כורי דאסר רבה בשילהי במה מדליקין (דף לה.) וכן חצוצרות לרבי יהודה [ז] ונר ישן [ח] מ"ר: **אדרבה** בשבת מוכנין אגב אביהן. אע"ג דלקמן בפירקין (דף קכד:) אמר איפכא גבי שברי כלי חרס דשרי לטלטל יותר כשנשברו בע"ש משנשברו בשבת לא דמיא דהכא אכתי כלי הוא שעדיין עומד למלאכה ראשונה וראוי להתחבר הכיסוי עם הכלי אבל לקמן לא חשיב כלי אלא מחמת שעומד למלאכה אחרת הלכך כשנשבר בשבת אסור טפי דהוי נולד: **לעולם** קסבר יש בנין בכלים כו'. וכשניטלו מטלטלין קאמר וה"פ הברייתא דלת של שידה תיבה ומגדל ניטלין פירוש מטלטלין כשניטלין ולא כפירוש הקונטרס דמפרש שניטלין דקתני היינו שניטלו קאמר כלומר כשניטל אין מחזירין אותן דלא יתכן לפרש כן ניטלין דסיפא אלא לשון טלטול הוא כדפרשתי ופריך והא (א) נמי ניטלין קתני ועוד מאי אבל לא מחזירין דלא שייך למיתני אמילתיה דלא (דמיא) [שייך] כלל למאי דאיירי בה דמעיקרא קאמר ניטלין שמותר לטלטל ואין בו איסור מוקצה והדר קאמר אבל לא מחזירין שהוא משום איסור בנין מאי ענין זה אצל זה לא שייך כה"ג למיתני אבל כלל: **רחת** ומלגז מי מייחדי ליה לקטן. ורב יהודה ידע ליה לסיפא אלא דילמא הוה מוקי לה בשיחדה לכך ככל הנך דמתניתין ואם תאמר והאמר רב יהודה אמר שמואל בפרק אלו קשרים (לעיל דף קיג.) כלי קיואי מותר לטלטל בשבת דהיינו לצורך גופו אע"פ שמלאכתו לאיסור ואין לומר דמשמע דשמואל קאמר ליה וליה לא סבירא ליה מדבעי מיניה מרב יהודה כובד עליון וכובד התחתון מהו אין ולאו ורפיא בידיה משמע דס"ל הכי ועוד דרב יהודה גופיה בסוף כירה (לעיל ד' מו.) קאמר שרגא דמישחא שרי לטלטולי ואין לומר דמיירי כשייחדו להיתר כדמוקי רב יהודה הנך דמתני' דהא כלי קיואי לא משמע שייחדו דאם כן אפילו כובד העליון וכובד תחתון נמי ויש לומר דלא אסר רב יהודה אלא דומיא דפילוע אגוזים שהיא מלאכה גרועה לגבי קורנס שמיוחד למלאכה חשובה וכן כל הנך דמתניתין הוה אסור בלא ייחוד דמלאכת היתר שלהן מלאכה גרועה היא לגבי הנך כלים שמיוחדין למלאכה חשובה אבל כלי קיואי ושרגא דמישחא מותר לטלטל לצורך גופן דמלאכה שלהן חשובה יותר מפילוע אגוזים:
בסיכי

עין משפט נר מצוה

פז א טור שו"ע שם:
א ב מיי' פכ"ב מהלכות שבת הלכה כה וסכ"ה הלכה יג סמג לאוין סה טוש"ע או"ח סימן שח סעיף ח:
ב ג מיי' שם הלכה ז טוש"ע שם סעיף ג:
ג ד מיי' שם הלכה ח טוש"ע שם סעיף יא:
ד ה מיי' פכ"ב שם הלכה כה טור שו"ע שם סעיף ט:
ה ו מיי' שם הלכה כו סמג שם טוש"ע או"ח סימן שיד סעיף א:

הגהות הב"ח

(א) תוס' ד"ה לעולם וכו' ופריך והא ניטלין קתני ולא תני נמי נתפרקו כו' ועוד מאי אבל:

רבינו חננאל

בנכרי שאינו מכירו אבל אם מכירו אסור. ת"ש ציר של ישראל ונכרים דרין כו':

הדרן עלך כל כתבי הקודש

פי"ז כל הכלים ניטלין בשבת כו'. באנו לפרש מתני' נפרקו בשבת או אפי' בחול. ואוקמה אביי להא מתני' אע"פ שנתפרקו בחול ניטלין בשבת לפי שאינן דומין דלתות הכלים לדלתות הבית. כי דלתות הבית קבועין בקרקע ולא הוכנו להיטלטל. אבל הכלים הוכנו לטלטול וכ"ש דלתותיהן. ופשוטה היא. ומפרקינן (א) גזירה שמא יתקע. פי' שמא יתקע בה מסמר או יתד וכדומה להן: נוטל אדם קורנס לפצע בו אגוזים וכו'. בא רב יהודה להעמיד משנתנו זו בקורנס המוכן לפצוע אגוזים. ולא כל קורנס מותר. אלא זה בלבד. אבל קורנס של נפחים וכדומה להן אפילו לצורך גופו אסור. ואקשי' עלה רבה אלא מעתה סיפא דקתני ואת הרחת ואת המלגז לתת עליו לקטן. פי' לתת עליו מאכל לקטן כגון תבשיל. רחת ומלגז [מי] מכינין בי"א לתבשיל

חשק שלמה על רבינו חננאל

א) נראה דחסר בדברי רבינו ול"ל דלת של שידה ושל תיבה ושל מגדל נוטלין אבל לא מחזירין:

מסורת הש"ס

א) פירוש מזוג [ומגמגה שבשמשות אימת המזולג], ב) לעיל קו. סנהדרין פד:, ג) [תוספתא פרק יג], ד) [עירובין לה. ביצה י. יא: כב.], ה) רש"ל ובש"י איתא מסיכר וכן איתא ברא"ש בד"ה לעולם, ו) [עי' לעיל לה. תוס' ד"ה ואפילו], ז) [לעיל לו.], ח) [לעיל מד.].

ליקוטי רש"י

קרדום. פסס קרדוס עשוי כמין כלי אומנות שעושין בו חוכפות וקרגות שקורין איישי"ש ויש שעשוי כעין כלי האומן שקורין בירגו"ל...

אין תורת בנין בכלים ואינו חייב אלא אם כן עשה בו מלאכה כגון ממחק או מתחך או אורג או תופר שהן אבות מלאכות לעצמם אבל וכו' משום בנין אין בונה אלא בבתים ואהלים [ביצה שם]. אין איסור בנין וסתירה בכלים...
... כלי או גומרו ביום טוב או בשבת משום מכה בפטיש הוא דמחייב שהוא חיוב לכל גמר מלאכה או אם הוא דבר שהוא מחליקו חייב משום ממחק ואם צריך קלוע חייב משום מתחך וכן אורג או...
... לאחויי בקלוק ומורה דהא דתנן (שבת קב:) הבונה כל שהוא בבתים תנן [שם יא:]. [מכאן שייך לדף קכג.] הא מני ר' נחמיה היא. דאמר בערובין (לה.) אפי' תרווד ואפילו טלית אין ניטלין...
... את העלי. דף עב וכבד וכותשין בו חטים לטרגים וטיסני והוי מלאכתו לאיסור וקא סברי בית שמאי אסור לטלטלו ואפילו לצורך גופו שצריך לגוף הכלי למלאכה המותרת היום [שם י.]. מלאכתו...
... בית שמאי. שאסור לטלטלו. דלאעביד ליה לורך יום טוב [שם יא.]. דקפיד עלייהו. שלא יתעקם ומייחד ליה מקום ומקצה ליה בידים ואפילו לר' שמעון אסור לטלטלו דמוקצה מחמת חסרון כיס...
... מנה בוסר שטומנין אותה בתבן להתבשל ותבן מוקצה הוא ואסור לטלטלו כגון שהקצהו ללבון לבנים. וחררה שטמנה. אממול בגחלים ועכשיו כבו ומכל מקום מוקצין הן אבל לא כבו לא דמתוך שנהפכי...

Chapter Seventeen

Mishnah The Mishnah begins with a rule concerning the *muktzeh* status of utensils that have doors — for example, movable cabinets:

כָּל הַכֵּלִים נִיטָּלִין בְּשַׁבָּת – All utensils may be taken on the Sabbath וְדַלְתוֹתֵיהֶן עִמָּהֶן – and their doors with them, אַף עַל פִּי שֶׁנִּתְפָּרְקוּ (בשבת) **– even though they were detached;**[1] **שֶׁאֵינָן דּוֹמִין לְדַלְתוֹת הַבַּיִת – for they are not like house doors,** which if detached may not be moved, **לְפִי שֶׁאֵינָן מִן הַמּוּכָן – since [house doors] are not prepared** for Sabbath use.[2]

The Mishnah now lists specific uses for which certain utensils may be moved:

נוֹטֵל אָדָם קוּרְנָס – A person may take a hammer לְפַצֵּעַ בּוֹ אֶת הָאֱגוֹזִין – to crack open nuts with it,[3] **קַרְדּוֹם לַחְתּוֹךְ בּוֹ אֶת הַדְּבֵילָה – a hatchet to cut a cake of pressed figs with it,**[4] **מְגֵירָה לָגוֹר בָּהּ אֶת הַגְּבִינָה – a saw to slice cheese with it,**[5] **מַגְרֵיפָה לִגְרוֹף בָּהּ אֶת הַגְּרוֹגְרוֹת – a shovel to scoop up dried figs** from the bottom of a barrel **with it, אֶת הָרַחַת וְאֶת הַמַּלְגֵּז לָתֵת עָלָיו לַקָּטָן – a winnowing shovel or a pitchfork to put** food **on it for a child,**[6] **אֶת הַכּוּשׁ וְאֶת הַכַּרְכַּר לִתְחוֹב בּוֹ – a spindle or weaver's reed to spear** fruit **with it,**[7] **מַחַט שֶׁל יָד לִיטּוֹל בּוֹ אֶת הַקּוֹץ – a hand-needle to remove a splinter with it**[8] **וְשֶׁל סַקָּאִים לִפְתּוֹחַ בּוֹ אֶת הַדֶּלֶת – or a sackmaker's** needle **to open a door with it.**[9]

Gemara The Gemara analyzes the Mishnah's opening statement:

כָּל הַכֵּלִים נִיטָּלִין – The Mishnah implies that **all utensils may be taken,** and their doors may also be taken, **וְאַף עַל פִּי שֶׁנִּתְפָּרְקוּ בְּשַׁבָּת – even though they were detached on the Sabbath; וְלֹא מִיבַּעְיָא בְּחוֹל – and** this means that **certainly** if they were detached **on a weekday** they may be taken.[10] **אַדְּרַבָּה** – But **the contrary** would seem more logical! **בְּשַׁבָּת** – If they were detached **on the Sabbath, מוּכָנִין עַל גַּבֵּי אֲבִיהֶן** – then when the Sabbath arrived **they were prepared** for use **together with the main parts** of the utensils.[11] Thus, they should certainly remain non-*muktzeh* when they become detached. **בְּחוֹל** – But if they were detached **on a weekday, אֵין מוּכָנִין עַל גַּבֵּי אֲבִיהֶן** – then when the Sabbath arrived **they were not prepared** for use **together with the main parts** of the utensils. It is more novel to say that they are nevertheless non-*muktzeh*.[12] – ? –

The Gemara clarifies the Mishnah's statement:

אָמַר אַבַּיֵי – Abaye said: הָכִי קָאָמַר – This is what [the Mishnah] means to **say: כָּל הַכֵּלִים נִיטָּלִין בְּשַׁבָּת – All utensils may be taken on the Sabbath וְדַלְתוֹתֵיהֶן עִמָּהֶן – and their doors with them; אַף עַל פִּי שֶׁנִּתְפָּרְקוּ בְּחוֹל נִיטָּלִין בְּשַׁבָּת** – and **even though they were detached on a weekday they may be taken on the Sabbath.**[13]

NOTES

1. I.e. all utensils that have attached doors or lids, such as carriages, trunks or movable closets, may be moved on the Sabbath, and their doors may also be moved with them; there is no need to detach the door before moving the utensil. [Although the door might not be considered a non-*muktzeh* "utensil" by its own virtue,] it is non-*muktzeh* by virtue of having been attached to a real utensil (see also *Tiferes Yisrael*). Furthermore, even if the door became detached from the utensil, it remains non-*muktzeh* and one may move the door itself (*Rashi, Ritva MHK* ed.; see following note).

There are some utensils that are deemed *muktzeh* and may not be moved on the Sabbath (see below, 123a). However, when the Mishnah states, "All utensils may be moved," it refers to utensils that have doors or lids. These are generally used for storage and are thus in the category of כֵּלִים שֶׁמְּלַאכְתָּן לְהֶיתֵּר, *utensils used [primarily] for permitted work,* which are not *muktzeh* (*Ran,* following *Rashi;* see *Chasam Sofer;* cf. *Tosafos,* who emend the text). [*Rashi's* version of the text deletes the word בְּשַׁבָּת; see note 10.]

2. A house door is not considered "prepared" for Sabbath use when detached because it is not a utensil [and is therefore inherently *muktzeh*] (cf. *Rambam, Hil. Shabbos* 25:6 with *Maggid Mishneh, Rosh;* see *Beur Halachah* 308:10 ד״ה אין ניטלים). Thus, if a door came off its hinges it may not be moved at all. However, the door or lid of a utensil is deemed a "utensil" by virtue of its association with the main part of the utensil. Even if it became detached and is no longer part of the utensil, it retains the original designation and may still be moved (*Rashi;* cf. 126b note 1). The door or lid retains its non-*muktzeh* designation because it is still fit to be reattached to the utensil (*Tosafos* ד״ה אדרבה, *Ran, Mishnah Berurah* 308:35).

3. The Gemara will discuss whether the Mishnah refers to an ordinary, blacksmith's hammer, and permits using it for this purpose even though the hammer is a כְּלִי שֶׁמְּלַאכְתּוֹ לְאִיסּוּר, *a forbidden-use utensil* (see Chapter Introduction), or it refers only to a hammer that had been designated for cracking nuts, which is a כְּלִי שֶׁמְּלַאכְתּוֹ לְהֶיתֵּר, *a permitted-use utensil.* The same question applies to all the other utensils listed here.

4. After the figs were dried they were pressed into a circular cake. This cake was thick and hard, and a hatchet is required to cut it (*Rashi*).

5. Since a saw has a serrated edge, it cuts through a thick cheese quickly (*Rashi;* see *Beur Halachah* 308:3 ד״ה קורדום).

6. I.e. to pass food to a child who is on the opposite side of a stream and is unable to cross over (*Tiferes Yisrael;* cf. *Chidushei HaRan*).

7. I.e. to lift berries or pieces of soft fruit from a platter to one's mouth (*Rashi*). [The weaver's reed was a long spoke that was used in the weaving process to arrange the threads one beside the other (*Rav*). Ancient looms used the comb-like reed described above (in the appendices to Volumes II and III) to straighten the threads. A single reed was used to beat in the weft thread after it was passed through the warp.]

8. I.e. a sewing needle may be used to remove a splinter that is embedded in the skin (*Rashi;* see Gemara above, 107a, with note 12).

9. A large needle that is normally used for sewing sacks may be used to pick a lock by one who has misplaced his key (*Rashi*).

10. The Gemara understands the phrase "even if they were detached" as referring back to the Mishnah's opening phrase, which mentioned the Sabbath. Thus, the Mishnah means to state that the doors may be moved even if they became detached on the Sabbath itself. The implication is that if the doors were detached before the Sabbath they may certainly be moved on the Sabbath (*Rashi*). [Note that there is a version of the Mishnah text which reads explicitly "even if they were detached on the Sabbath." However, *Rashi* does not have that reading (*Ran*).]

11. Literally: with their fathers. [Since the *muktzeh* status of all objects is fixed during the twilight period (*bein hashemashos*) at the onset of the Sabbath,] it stands to reason that a door which was attached to a non-*muktzeh* utensil when the Sabbath began — and was thus "prepared" for use — remains permitted for use if it became detached on the Sabbath (*Rashi*) and is still fit for future use (*Tosafos* ד״ה אדרבה).

12. I.e. when they were not attached during *bein hashemashos,* it is novel to say that their suitability for reattachment to the utensils renders them non-*muktzeh* (see *Tosafos* ד״ה אדרבה). Yet the Mishnah's wording seems to imply that this rule is obvious! How are we to understand the Mishnah?

13. The phrase "even though," which emphasizes the novelty of the ruling, refers not to the point that the doors were detached *on the Sabbath,* but to the basic point that they were detached — either on a weekday or on the Sabbath. Thus, the Mishnah means to teach that the

אדעתא דרובא מדלקי שמואל איקלע לבי אבין תורן אתא ההוא נכרי אדליק שרגא אהדרינהו שמואל לאפיה כיון דחזא דאייתי שטר וקא קרי אמר ^אאדעתא דנפשיה הוא דאדליק אהדרינהו איהו לאפיה גבי שרגא:

הדרן עלך כל כתבי

כל ^בהכלים ניטלין בשבת ודלתותיהן עמהן אע"פ שנתפרקו (בשבת) שאינן דומין לדלתות הבית לפי שאינן מן המוכן ^גנוטל אדם קורנס לפצע בו את האגוזין קרדום לחתוך בו את הדבילה מגירה לגור בה את הגבינה מגריפה לגרוף בה את הגרוגרות את הרחת ואת [א] המלגז לתת עליו לקטן את הכוש ואת הכרכר לתחוב בו ^דמחט של יד ליטול בו את הקוץ ושל סקאים לפתוח בו את הדלת: **גמ'** כל הכלים ניטלין ואע"פ שנתפרקו בשבת ולא מיבעיא בחול אדרבה בשבת מוכנין על גבי אביהן בחול אין מוכנין על גבי אביהן אמר אביי הכי קאמר כל הכלים ניטלין בשבת ודלתותיהן עמהן אע"פ שנתפרקו בחול ניטלין בשבת ת"ר ^הדלת של שידה ושל תיבה ושל מגדל נוטלין אבל לא מחזירין ושל לול של תרנגולים לא נוטלין ולא מחזירין בשלמא של לול של תרנגולים קסבר כיון דמחברי בארעא יש בנין בקרקע יש סתירה בקרקע אלא של שידה ושל תיבה ושל מגדל מאי קסבר אי קסבר יש בנין בכלים יש סתירה בכלים ואי אין סתירה בכלים אין בנין בכלים אמר אביי לעולם קסבר יש בנין בכלים ויש סתירה בכלים ושניטלו קאמר א"ל רבא [שתי תשובות בדבר] חדא דניטלין קתני ועוד מאי אבל לא מחזירין אלא אמר רבא קסבר ^ואין בנין בכלים ואין סתירה בכלים וגזירה שמא יתקע: נוטל אדם קורנס כו': אמר רב יהודה קורנס של אגוזין לפצע בו את האגוזין אבל של נפחין לא קסבר דבר שמלאכתו לאיסור אפילו לצורך גופו אסור א"ל רבה אלא מעתה סיפא דקתני ואת הרחת ואת המלגז לתת עליו לקטן רחת ומלגז מי מייחדי ליה לקטן אלא אמר רבה קורנס של נפחין לפצע בו האגוזין קסבר דבר

רש"י

אדעתא דרובא. הלכך ישראל עיקר ומחצה על מחצה נמי ליכא למיקם עלה דמלתא דליכא למימר עיקר דעתיה דמדליק בשביל ישראל וליכא למימר עיקר דעתיה דמדליק בשביל נכרי אבל נכרי וישראל והמדליק עצמו משתמש לאורה ודאי עיקר אדעתא דידיה עביד וכיון דנר לאחד נר למאה שרי: תורן. מקום: דאייתי שטר. ההוא דאדלקה:

הדרן עלך כל כתבי

כל הכלים ניטלין בשבת ודלתותיהן עמהם. כל הכלים שיש להם דלתות כגון שידה תיבה ומגדל ניטלין בשבת ודלתות שיש להם בלדן עמהן ניטלין עמהן: **ואע"פ שנתפרקו.** הדלתות מן הכלים ניטלין ואין דומין לדלתות הבית שאין ניטלין לפי שדלתות הבית אינן מן המוכן לטלטל שאינן כלי אבל אלו הן כלי אגב אביהן: **קורנס.** מרטי"ל: **דבילה.** מאחר שעשאה עיגול עבה היא מאד וקשה כגבינה וצריך קורדום לחותכה: **ומגירה.** כעין סכין ויש בו פגימות הרבה: **לגור בה את הגבינה.** לחתכו ולחלקו לפי שממהרת לחתוך דבר עב: **מגריפה.** ודו"ל: **לגרוף בה את הגרוגרות.** מן המכביות: **רחת.** פאל"א: **מלגז.** כמין עתר שקורין פורק"א של ברזל ולו ג' שיניים ומהפכין בו קש בגורן: **לתת עליו לקטן.** מזונות: **כוש.** פלך פוש"ל: **כרכר.** רא"ל: **לתחוב בו.** לאכול בו תותים וכל פרי רך: **מחט של יד.** מחט קטן שתופר בו בגדים: **ושל סקאים.** מחט גדולה שתופרים בה שקים: **לפתוח בו את הדלת.** מי שאבד מפתחו: **גמ'** **ולא מיבעיא בחול.** קא סלקא דעתך ואע"פ שנתפרקו בשבת דקתני רישא קאי ומשמע אע"פ שנתפרקו היום מותרים ולא מיבעיא אם נתפרקו מאתמול: **אדרבה.** מאי אע"פ שייך למתני הא ודאי אם נתפרקו בשבת איכא למישרי משום דכי קדים יומא הוו מוכנין לטלטל אגב אביהן: **הכי קאמר כו'.** ואע"פ לא ארבותא דנתפרקו בשבת קאי אלא ארבותא דנתפרקו מו בחול או בשבת קאי ולא מיבעיא כשהן מחוברין: **נוטלין.** משמע מסלקין אותן בשבת [ג] מהיסתר] ליר שלהן: **לול.** בנין העשוי לתרנגולין: **לא נוטלין ולא מחזירין.** כדמפרש ואזיל חזרתו בנין ממש הוא וסילוקו סתירה גמורה היא: **מאי קסבר.** שמתיר סילוקו ואוסר חזרתו: **אי קסבר יש בנין בכלים.** וחזרתו בנין על כרחיך אם יש בנין יש סתירה ואמאי נוטלין: **ושניטלו** קאמר. וה"ק דלת של תיבה שידה ומגדל שניטלו אין מחזירין: **מאי אבל.** כיון דלא תנא נוטלין לא שייך למיתני אבל: **לעולם קסבר אין סתירה ואין בנין.** הלכך נוטלין ומיהו אין מחזירין מדרבנן: **גזירה שמא יתקע.** בחוזקה בסכין ויתדות והוה ליה גמר מלאכה וחייב משום מכה בפטיש: **קורנס של אגוזים.** המיוחד לפציעת אגוזים הוא דקתני מתניתין דנוטלין אותו למלאכתו משום דעיקרו למלאכת היתר: **אבל של נפחים.** דעיקרו למלאכת איסור לא: **לצורך גופו.** שגופו צריך עוד למלאכה אחרת של היתר אין מטלטלין אותו לאותה מלאכה וכ"ש אם אין צריך לגופו אלא לפנות מקומו דאין מטלטלין: **מי מייחדי לקטן.** בשלמא כולהו הני דמתני' איכא לאוקמא בעשויין ומיוחדין לכך בר מהני דליכא דעביד להו להכי:

תוספות

אהדרינהו שמואל לאפיה. מיירי שהיה לכל הספחות מחצה על מחצה דמשום נר לאחד נר למאה לא משתריא אלא היכא שהוא ניכר שהוא עושה לצרכו דהו לא גזרינן אפילו במכירו שמא ירבה בשבילו: הדרן עלך כל כתבי

כל הכלים ניטלין בשבת ודלתותיהן עמהם גרסינן ול"ג כל הכלים ניטלין דטובא איכא דאין ניטלין כגון מסר הגדול ויתד של מחרישה דאפילו ר"ש מודה כדאיתא בשילהי מכילתין (דף קנז.) וכגון מלתא [א] בת תרי כורי דאסר רבה בשילהי במה מדליקין (דף לה.) וכן תלולרות לרבי יהודה [ז] ונר ישן [ח] מ"ר: **אדרבה** בשבת מוכנין אגב אביהן. אע"ג דלקמן בפירקין (דף קכד:) אמר איפכא גבי שברי כלי חרס דשרי לטלטל יותר כשנשברו בע"ש משנשברו בשבת לא דמיא דהכא אכתי כלי הוא שעדיין עומד למלאכה ראשונה ורארי להתחבר הכיסוי עם הכלי אבל לקמן לא חשיב כלי אלא מחמת שעומד למלאכה אחרת הלכך כשנשבר בשבת אסור טפי דהוי נולד: **לעולם** קסבר יש בנין בכלים כו' וכשניטלו מטלטלין קאמר וה"פ הברייתא דלת של שידה תיבה ומגדל ניטלין פירוש מטלטלין כשניטלין ולא כפירוש הקונטרס דמפרש שניטלין דקתני היינו שניטלו קאמר כלומר כשניטל אין מחזירין אותן דלא יתכן לפרש כן ניטלין דסיפא אלא לשון טלטול הוא כדפרשתי ופריך והא [א] נמי ניטלין קתני ועוד מאי אבל לא מחזירין דלא שייך למיתני אמילתיה דלא (דמיא) [שייך] כלל למאי דאיירי בה דמעיקרא קאמר ניטלין שמותר לטלטל ואין בו איסור מוקצה והדר קאמר אבל לא מחזירין שהוא משום איסור בנין מאי ענין זה אצל זה לא שייך כה"ג למיתני אבל כלל: **רחת** ומלגז מי מייחדי ליה לקטן. ורב יהודה ידע ליה לסיפא אלא דילמא הוה מוקי לה בשיחדה לכך דכל הנך דמתניתין ואם תאמר והאמר רב יהודה אמר שמואל בפרק אלו קשרים (לעיל דף קיג.) כלי קיואי מותר לטלטל בשבת דהיינו לצורך גופו אע"פ שמלאכתו לאיסור ואין לומר דמשמע דשמואל קאמר ליה וליה לא סבירא ליה מדבעי מיניה מרב יהודה כובד עליון וכובד התחתון מהו אין ולאו ורפיא בידיה משמע דס"ל הכי ועוד דרב יהודה גופיה בסוף כירה (לעיל ד' מו.) קאמר שרגא דמישחא שרי לטלטולי ואין לומר דמיירי כשייחדו להיתר כדמוקי רב יהודה הנך דמתני' דהא כלי קיואי לא משמע שייחדו דאם כן אפילו כובד העליון וכובד תחתון נמי ויש לומר דלא אסר רב יהודה אלא דומיא דפילוע אגוזים שהיא מלאכה גרועה לגבי קורנס שמיוחד למלאכה חשובה וכן כל הנך דמתניתין הוה אסור בלא ייחוד דמלאכת היתר שלהן מלאכה גרועה היא לגבי הנך כלים שמיוחדין למלאכה חשובה אבל כלי קיואי ושרגא דמישחא מותר לטלטל לצורך גופן דמלאכה שלהן חשובה יותר מפילוע אגוזים:

עין משפט נר מצוה

פז א טור שו"ע שם:
א ב מיי' פכ"ב מהלכות שבת הלכה כה ופכ"ה הלכה יב סמג לאוין סה טוש"ע או"ח סימן שח סעיף ח:
ב ג מיי' שם הלכה ז טוש"ע שם סעיף ג:
ג ד מיי' שם הלכה ח טוש"ע שם סעיף יא:
ד ה מיי' פכ"ב שם הלכה כה טור שו"ע שם סעיף ט:
ה ו מיי' שם הלכה כו סמג שם טוש"ע או"ח סימן שיד סעיף א:

הגהות הב"ח

(א) תוס' ד"ה לעולם וכו' ופריך והא ניטלין קתני ולא תני נמי נתפרקו כו' ועוד מאי אבל:

רבינו חננאל

בנכרי שאינו מכירו אבל אם מכירו אסור. ת"ש עיר של ישראל ונכרים דרין כו':

הדרן עלך כל כתבי הקודש

פי"ז כל הכלים ניטלין בשבת כו'. באנו לפרש מתי נפרקו בשבת או אפי' בחול. ואוקמה אביי להא מתני' אע"פ שנתפרקו בחול ניטלין בשבת לפי שאינן דומין דלתות הכלים לדלתות הבית. כי דלתות הבית קבועין בקרקע ולא הוכנו להיטלטל. אבל הכלים הוכנו לטלטול וכ"ש דלתותיהן. ופשוטה היא. ומפרקינן (א) גזירה שמא יתקע. פי' שמא יתקע בה מסמר או יתד וכדומה להן: נוטל אדם קורנס לפצוע בו אגוזים וכו'. בא רב יהודה להעמיד משנתנו זו בקורנס המוכן לפצוע אגוזים. ולא כל קורנס מותר. אלא זה בלבד. אבל קורנס של נפחים וכדומה להן אפילו לצורך גופו אסור. ואקשי' עלה רבה אלא מעתה סיפא דקתני ואת הרחת ואת המלגז לתת עליו לקטן. פי' לתת עליו מאכל לקטן כגון תבשיל. רחת ומלגז [מי] מכינין בנ"א לתבשיל

חשק שלמה על רבינו חננאל

(א) נראה דחסר בדברי רבינו וצ"ל דלת של שידה ושל תיבה ושל מגדל נוטלין אבל לא מחזירין:

מסורת הש"ס

א) פירוש מזלג [ובמשנה שבמשניות איתא המזלג], ב) לעיל קז. סנהדרין פד:, ג) [תוספתא פרק טו], ד) [עירובין לה. ביצה י. יא: כב.], ה) רש"ל ובש"י איתא מהיכר וכן איתא ברא"ש בד"ה לעולם, ו) [עי' לעיל לה. תוס' ד"ה ואפילו], ז) [לעיל לו.], ח) [לעיל מד.].

ליקוטי רש"י

קרדום. קתם קרדום עשוי כמין כלי אומנות שעושין בו אוכפות וקרגות שקורין איסי"ש ויש שעשוי כעין כלי האומן שקורין בירגו"ה שראשו הקצר דומה לקרדומות שלנו וראשו השני דומה לכלי אומני אוכפות וקרגות הסוסים [ביצה לא.]. מגירה. סיי"ה בלע"ז וסכין הוא שיש בו פגימות הרבה וקוצצת מהר [ב"ק קיט:]. סכין מלא פגימות ואין משופעות כשל מגל קציר אלא מכוונות שיש לפגימה מורשא מכאן ומכאן כקסם פגימות אוגרת ומגירה בלעז סייג"א [חולין טו:]. סייג"א סכין מלא פגימות וחותך מהר כעין שיש לעושי מסריקות [ערכין כג:]. סיג"ה כעין סכין מלאה פגימות וממהר לקוץ בו עצים וכלי אומן הוא [ביצה שם]. מגריפה. כלי ברזל הוא וראשו רחב ומבדילים בו גרוגרות הנדבקות זו בזו [זבחים צג:]. כלי ברזל הוא שקורין וודי"ל שגופרין בו אפר הכירה וגם מבדילין בו תאנים המודבקות זו בזו [חגיגה כ.]. וודי"ל והוא כעין כף [ערכין י:]. הרחת. פל"א שזורין המוץ ברוח מתוך התבואה [ב"מ קה.]. פל"ה בלע"ז כשהכרי גדול צריך להגביה התבואה ברחת חורק כלפי מעלה והרוח מנשבת ודוחפת המוץ למרחוק [ב"ב כד:]. מלגז. פורק"א בת שלש שיניים ומהפכין בה תבואה בגורן [לעיל צב:]. כוש. פלך פוזי"ל בלע"ז שהנשים טוות בו [סוכה לז.]. כרכר. עץ יש לאורגין וראשו חד [לעיל פא.]. מחט של יד. היא מחט קטנה שתופרין בה בגדים ניטלת בשבת ליטול בה את הקוץ ומשום דקתני לה להנך גבי ושל שקאין לפתוח בו את הדלת קרי ליה להא קטנה מחט של יד [סנהדרין פד:]. דלת של שידה. ולדלתות שידה תיבה ומגדל דתנא מתניתין נוטלין יש תורת כלי עליהן דראויין ליישב עליהן ולתת עליהן מזונות לקטן [לקמן קכו: עיי"ש]. שידה. כמין ארגז מלוי בעגלה למרכב נשים חשובות [עירובין יד:]. מרכבת נשים עגלה עשויה כקופסא [שם ל:]. מגדל. מנשטי"ר [שם יד:]. יש בנין בכלים. יש תורת בנין בכלים ובונה חייב בכל שהוא [ביצה כב.]. ואי אין סתירה בכלים. ולאו בעי סתר ליה [עירובין לה.]. אין בנין בכלים. אין תורת בנין בכלים ואינו חייב אלא אם כן עשה בו מלאכה כגון ממחק או מורג או תופר שהן אבות מלאכות לעצמם אבל וכו' משום בנין אין בונה אלא בבתים ואהלים [ביצה שם]. אין איסור בנין וסתירה בכלים אלא בבתים דנחייב בבנין כל דהו והעושה כלי או גומרו ביום טוב או בשבת משום מכה בפטיש הוא דמחייב שהוא חיוב לכל גמר מלאכה או אם הוא דבר שהוא מחליקו חייב משום ממחק ואם צריך קלוע חייב משום מחתך וכן אורג או מסך או תופר אבל בנין וסתירה לא שייך בהו לאתויי בסלוק וחזרה דהא דתנן (שבת קכ:) הבונה כל שהוא בבתים תנן [שם יא:]. [מכאן שייך לדף קכג.] הא מני ר' נחמיה היא. דאמר בעירובין (לה.) אפי' טרווד ואפילו טלית אין ניטלין אלא לצורך תשמיש שהן מיוחדין לו [ביצה לב.]. את העלי. דף עב וכבד וכותשין בו חטים לטרגים וטיסני והוי מלאכתו לאיסור וקא סברי בית שמאי אסור לטלטלו ואפילו לצורך גופו שצריך לגוף הכלי למלאכה המותרת היום [שם י.]. מלאכתו לאיסור לכתוש במכתשת משום הכי אסרי ליה בית שמאי. שאסור לטלטלו. דלאעביד ליה לצורך יום טוב [שם יא.]. דקפיד עליהו. שלא יתעקם ומייחד ליה מקום ומקצה ליה בדיעה ואפילו לר' שמעון אסור לטלטלו דמוקצה מחמת חסרון כיס אפילו ר' שמעון מודה [לקמן קכה:]. פגה. תאנה בוסר שטומנין אותה בתבן להתבשל ותבן מוקצה הוא ואסור לטלטלו כגון שהקצהו ללבון לבנים. וחררה שטמנה. אסמול בגחלים ועכשיו כבו ומכל מקום מוקצין הן אבל לא כבו לא דמחוך שנהפכים מכבה את התחתונות ומבעיר את העליונות כדאמרינן בכריתות (כ.) [עירובין עו.]. מלמול מן הצד. כלאחר יד [לעיל מג:]. האי פוגלא. כגון שטומנין בקרקע להתקיים כשהא לתלוש מלמעלה למטה שרי אם היה ראשה מלמעלה ועוקצה מלמטה ומולגה מראשה העבה תחילה ועוקצה נמשך אחריה מותר לפי שהגומא רחבה מלמעלה ואין מזיזין הקרקע כשהוא שומטה אבל אם מולגה מלמטה שתחתונה נתון למעלה וראש עליונה שהוא עב נתון למטה והוא שומטה מסופה לראשה אסור לפי שהגומא קצרה מלמעלה וכשהוא מולגה מזיז העפר ומטלטלו ואף על גב דטלטול מן הצד הוא שמיה טלטול ואסור [לקמן קמא.]. מותר לטלטלה בשבת. בכלל דהא חזיא ליטול את הקוץ ותורת כלי עליה. ולא אמרו נקובה. טלוקה להכלוטיה אלא לענין טומאה בלבד דנקובה מקבלת טומאה ושאינה נקובה לא. בגולמי. שהוא גולם שנקלטה מן הסוט ועומדת לינקב הסם הוא דכל זמן שלא נקבה אינה מקבלת טומאה דהא לא נגמרת מלאכתה ולענין טומאה כלי מעשה כתיב (במדבר לא) שגמר כל מעשהו ומיהו לענין שבת שריא דזימנין דממליך עלה ומנח לה הכי ומשוי לה מנא לנטילת קוץ [לעיל נב:]. תרגמא אביי אליבא דרבא. במקום (אביי) ובשבילו שמהא (משנה) זו מתורגמת לפי דבריו [סוכה יט. בסוגיין רבא].

Having discussed the *muktzeh* status of detachable utensil doors, the Gemara turns to a discussion of whether such doors may be detached and reattached on the Sabbath without violating any *melachah*:[14]

תָּנוּ רַבָּנַן – The Rabbis taught in a Baraisa: דֶּלֶת שֶׁל שִׁידָּה וְשֶׁל תֵּיבָה וְשֶׁל מִגְדָּל – THE DOOR OF A CARRIAGE, OF A TRUNK OR OF A CLOSET נוֹטְלִין אֲבָל לֹא מַחֲזִירִין – MAY BE REMOVED from its socket BUT NOT REINSERTED on the Sabbath; וְשֶׁל לוּל שֶׁל תַּרְנְגוֹלִים – AND the door OF A CHICKEN COOP לֹא נוֹטְלִין וְלֹא מַחֲזִירִין – MAY BE NEITHER REMOVED NOR REINSERTED.[15]

The Gemara analyzes these rulings:

בִּשְׁלָמָא שֶׁל לוּל שֶׁל תַּרְנְגוֹלִים – **It is understandable** that the Tanna rules that the door **of a chicken coop** may be neither removed nor reinserted, כֵּיוָן קָסָבַר – because **he holds** that דִּמְחַבְּרֵי בְּאַרְעָא – **since [chicken coops] are attached to the ground** we apply to them the rule that יֵשׁ בִּנְיָן בְּקַרְקַע יֵשׁ סְתִירָה בְּקַרְקַע – the prohibition against **building applies to** items attached to **the ground** and the prohibition against **demolishing applies to** items attached to **the ground.** אֶלָּא שֶׁל שִׁידָּה וְשֶׁל תֵּיבָה וְשֶׁל מִגְדָּל – **But** concerning the door **of a carriage, of a trunk or of a closet,** which are not attached to the ground, but are utensils, מַאי קָסָבַר – **what does [the Tanna] hold?** אִי קָסָבַר יֵשׁ בִּנְיָן בְּכֵלִים – **If he holds** that the prohibition against **building applies to utensils,** יֵשׁ סְתִירָה בְּכֵלִים – he must agree that the prohibition against **demolishing** also **applies to utensils.**[16] וְאִי אֵין סְתִירָה בְּכֵלִים – **And if** the prohibition against **demolishing does not apply to utensils,** אֵין בִּנְיָן בְּכֵלִים – the prohibition against **building** also **should not apply to utensils!** How can he rule that removing the doors from their sockets is permitted but reinserting them is prohibited?

The Gemara answers:

אָמַר אַבָּיֵי – **Abaye said:** לְעוֹלָם קָסָבַר יֵשׁ בִּנְיָן בְּכֵלִים וְיֵשׁ סְתִירָה בְּכֵלִים – **Actually, [the Tanna] holds** that the prohibition against **building does apply to utensils and** the prohibition against **demolishing** also **applies to utensils,** וְשֶׁנִּיטְּלוּ קָאָמַר – **and he** means to **say** that ***if* [the doors] were removed** from their sockets they may not be reinserted; he does not permit removing them.[17]

Abaye's explanation is rejected:

אָמַר לֵיהּ רָבָא – **Rava said to him:** [שְׁתֵּי תְּשׁוּבוֹת בַּדָּבָר – **There are two rebuttals to this matter.**] חֲדָא דְּנוֹטְלִין קָתָנֵי – **Firstly, that [the Baraisa] states "may be removed,"** not "if they were removed." וְעוֹד – **And furthermore,** if the first clause does not mean that the doors may be removed, מַאי אֲבָל לֹא מַחֲזִירִין – **what is** the meaning of the following clause, which states ***"but* may not be reinserted"?**[18]

Rava therefore presents an alternative explanation:

אֶלָּא אָמַר רָבָא – **Rather, Rava said:** קָסָבַר אֵין בִּנְיָן בְּכֵלִים וְאֵין סְתִירָה בְּכֵלִים – **[The Tanna] holds** that the prohibition against **building does not apply to utensils and** the prohibition against **demolishing** also **does not apply to utensils,** וּגְזֵירָה שֶׁמָּא יִתְקַע – **but** he prohibits reinserting doors in their sockets on the Sabbath on account of **a decree** that was enacted out of concern that **perhaps one will wedge** them in.[19]

The Mishnah stated:

נוֹטֵל אָדָם קוּרְנָס וכו׳ – A PERSON MAY TAKE A HAMMER etc.

The Gemara discusses what type of hammer this refers to:

אָמַר רַב יְהוּדָה – **Rav Yehudah said:** קוּרְנָס שֶׁל אֱגוֹזִין לְפַצֵּעַ בּוֹ אֶת הָאֱגוֹזִין – The Mishnah means that one may take **a hammer** that had been designated **for** cracking open **nuts to crack open nuts with it,** אֲבָל שֶׁל נַפָּחִין לֹא – **but a blacksmith's** hammer may **not** be taken to crack open nuts.[20] קָסָבַר – **[Rav Yehudah] holds** that דָּבָר שֶׁמְּלַאכְתּוֹ לְאִיסּוּר – **something that is** ordinarily **used for work that is forbidden** on the Sabbath אֲפִילּוּ לְצוֹרֶךְ גּוּפוֹ אָסוּר – **may not** be taken **even for the sake of its use** in a permissible capacity.[21]

Rav Yehudah's interpretation is rejected:

אָמַר לֵיהּ רַבָּה – **Rabbah said to him:** אֶלָּא מֵעַתָּה – **But according to this,** סֵיפָא דְּקָתָנֵי – how will you interpret **the latter clause** of the Mishnah, **which states:** וְאֶת הָרַחַת וְאֶת הַמַּלְגֵּז לָתֵת עָלָיו לְקָטָן – One may take . . . A WINNOWING SHOVEL OR A PITCHFORK TO PUT food ON IT FOR A CHILD? רַחַת וּמַלְגֵּז מִי מְיַיחֲדֵי לֵיהּ לְקָטָן – **Are a winnowing shovel or a pitchfork ever**

NOTES

doors may be moved even after being detached from the utensils, and certainly while still attached (*Rashi*).

[It would seem that *Rashi's* version of the text read simply אַף עַל פִּי שֶׁנִּתְפָּרְקוּ, *even though they were detached,* rather than אַף עַל פִּי שֶׁנִּתְפָּרְקוּ בְּחוֹל, *even though they were detached* **on a weekday** (*Maharsha*).]

14. See *Sfas Emes* for an enlightening insight which directly relates this discussion to our subject of *muktzeh.*

15. As the Gemara will explain, inserting the pivots of a chicken-coop door in their sockets constitutes a genuine act of building, and removing them from their sockets constitutes a genuine act of demolishing. Thus, both acts are prohibited Biblically (*Rashi;* cf. *Rambam, Hil. Shabbos* 22:25 with *Maggid Mishneh;* see also *Chidushei HaRan* and *Orach Chaim* 313:5).

16. If the *melachah* of building is not limited to construction that is attached to the ground, but applies to movable utensils as well, the same must hold true regarding the *melachah* of demolishing, which is the opposite of building. Since the Tanna considers the reinsertion of the utensil doors into their sockets a violation of "building," he should consider their removal a violation of "demolishing" (see *Rashi*).

17. Abaye understands the first clause of the Baraisa as stating only one rule, namely: If the door of a carriage, trunk or closet was removed from its sockets it may not be reinserted (*Rashi;* cf. *Tosafos* ד״ה לעולם).

18. If the term נוֹטְלִין does not mean that the doors *may* be removed, it makes no sense to introduce the next clause with the word *but* (*Rashi;* cf. *Tosafos*).

19. Fastening the door securely would be the finishing touch of the utensil's assembly, and would be a violation of the *melachah* of מַכֶּה בְּפַטִּישׁ, *striking the final blow* (*Rashi,* as explained by editorial notes to the *Machon Devorah* edition of the *Tur* §308; see also *Mishnah Berurah* 308:37; cf. *Rif, Rambam* cited in note 15, *Ramban* to 102b; see also *Ran, Chazon Ish* 50:10 and 102b note 26). [This is a misprint in the printed versions of *Rashi* here. The word סכין should read סִיכִין, a type of peg (see above, 74b); see *Rashi* on the *Rif.*]

20. A hammer designated for cracking open nuts is a כְּלִי שֶׁמְּלַאכְתּוֹ לְהֶיתֵּר, *a permitted-use utensil.* A blacksmith's hammer, however, is כְּלִי שֶׁמְּלַאכְתּוֹ לְאִיסּוּר, *a forbidden-use utensil.* According to Rav Yehudah, the Mishnah permits using only the former type of hammer for cracking open nuts (*Rashi*).

Chazon Ish (43:1) states that R' Yehudah refers to a blacksmith's hammer that a person designated for use in cracking nuts. The Mishnah teaches that the designation is effective in altering the status of the hammer to that of a permitted-use utensil (see also *Sfas Emes*).

21. Certainly, Rav Yehudah will hold that it is forbidden to move this type of utensil for the sake of its place, i.e. to make the space that it occupies available for something else (*Rashi*). [The two reasons one might permit moving a forbidden-use utensil are the need to use it for a permitted function and the need for its place (see Chapter Introduction). Of these, the need to use the utensil itself is considered a more significant factor than the need for its place. Since Rav Yehudah prohibits taking a blacksmith's hammer for the sake of its use, he certainly prohibits moving it for the sake of its place (see below, 124a). However, he permits moving a nut-cracking hammer for the sake of its place. According to his view, the reason the Mishnah specifies that the hammer may be taken to crack open nuts (i.e. for the sake of its use) is to imply that a blacksmith's hammer may not be taken even for this purpose (*Ramban, Rashba, Ritva MHK* ed.; cf. *Sfas Emes*).]

אדעתא דרובא מדלקי שמואל איקלע לבי אבין תורן אתא ההוא נכרי אדליק שרגא אהדרינהו שמואל לאפיה כיון דחזא דאייתי שטר וקא קרי אמר אדעתא דנפשיה הוא דאדליק אהדרינהו איהו לאפיה גבי שרגא:

הדרן עלך כל כתבי

כל הכלים ניטלין בשבת ודלתותיהן עמהן אע"פ שנתפרקו (בשבת) שאינן דומין לדלתות הבית לפי שאינן מן המוכן נוטל אדם קורנס לפצע בו את האגוזין קרדום לחתוך בו את הדבילה מגירה לגור בה את הגבינה מגריפה לגרוף בה את הגרוגרות את הרחת ואת המלגז לתת עליו לקטן את הכוש ואת הכרכר לתחוב בו מחט של יד ליטול בו את הקוץ ושל סקאים לפתוח בו את הדלת: גמ' כל הכלים ניטלין ואע"פ שנתפרקו בשבת ולא מיבעיא בחול אדרבה בשבת מוכנין על גבי אביהן בחול אין מוכנין על גבי אביהן אמר אביי הכי קאמר כל הכלים ניטלין בשבת ודלתותיהן עמהן אע"פ שנתפרקו בחול ניטלין בשבת ת"ר דלת של שידה ושל תיבה ושל מגדל נוטלין אבל לא מחזירין ושל לול של תרנגולים לא נוטלין ולא מחזירין בשלמא של לול של תרנגולים קסבר כיון דמחברי בארעא יש בנין בקרקע יש סתירה בקרקע אלא של שידה ושל תיבה ושל מגדל מאי קסבר אי קסבר יש בנין בכלים יש סתירה בכלים ואי אין סתירה בכלים אין בנין בכלים אמר אביי לעולם קסבר יש בנין בכלים ויש סתירה בכלים ושניטלו קאמר א"ל רבא [שתי תשובות בדבר] חדא דניטלין קתני ועוד מאי אבל לא מחזירין אלא אמר רבא קסבר אין בנין ואין סתירה בכלים וגזירה שמא יתקע: נוטל אדם קורנס כו': אמר רב יהודה קורנס של אגוזין לפצע בו את האגוזין אבל של נפחין לא קסבר דבר שמלאכתו לאיסור אפילו לצורך גופו אסור א"ל רבה אלא מעתה סיפא דקתני ואת הרחת ואת המלגז לתת עליו לקטן רחת ומלגז מי מייחדי ליה לקטן אלא אמר רבה קורנס של נפחין לפצע בו האגוזין קסבר דבר

רש"י

אדעתא דרובא. הלכך ישראל עיקר ומחלה על מחלה נמי ליכא למיקם עלה דמלתא דליכא למימר עיקר דעתיה דמדליק בשביל ישראל וליכא למימר עיקר דעתיה דמדליק בשביל נכרי אבל נכרי וישראל והמדליק עצמו משתמש לאורה ודאי עיקר אדעתא דידיה עביד וכיון דנר לאחד נר למאה שרי: תורן. מקום: דאייתי שטר. הטוה לאדלקה:

הדרן עלך כל כתבי

כל הכלים ניטלין בשבת ודלתותיהן עמהם. כל הכלים שיש להם דלתות כגון שידה תיבה ומגדל ניטלין בשבת ודלתות שיש להם ניטלין עמהן: ואע"פ שנתפרקו. הדלתות מן הכלים ניטלין ואין דומין לדלתות הבית שאין ניטלין לפי שדלתות הבית אינן מן המוכן לטלטל שאינן כלי אבל אלו הן כלי אגב אביהן: קורנס. מרטי"ל: דבילה. מאחר שעשאה עיגול עבה היא מאד וקשה כגבינה וצריך קורדום לחותכה: ומגירה. כעין סכין ויש בו פגימות הרבה: לגור בה את הגבינה. לחתכו ולחלקו לפי שממהרת לחתוך דבר עב: מגריפה. ודיי"ל: לגרוף בה את הגרוגרות. מן התאנים: רחת. פאל"א: מלגז. כמין עתר שקורין פורק"א של ברזל ולו ג' שיניים ומהפכין בו קש בגורן: לתת עליו לקטן. מזונות: כוש. פלך פוסי"ל: כרכר. ראי"ל: לתחוב בו. לאכול בו תותים וכל פרי רך: מחט של יד. מחט קטן שתופר בו בגדים: ושל סקאים. מחט גדולה שתופרים בה שקים: לפתוח בו את הדלת. מי שאבד מפתחו: גמ' ולא מיבעיא בחול. קא סלקא דעתך ואע"פ שנתפרקו אבשבת דקתני רישא קאי ומשמע אע"פ שנתפרקו היום מותרים ולא מיבעיא אם נתפרקו מאתמש: אדרבה. מאי אע"פ שייך למתני הא ודאי נתפרקו בשבת איכא למישרי משום דכי קדיש יומא הוו מוכנין לטלטל אגב אביהן: הכי קאמר כו'. ואע"פ לא ארבותא דנתפרקו בשבת קאי אלא ארבותא דנתפרקו או בחול או בשבת קאי ולא מיבעיא כשהן מחוברין: נוטלין. משמע מסלקין אותן בשבת [מהיתר] ליר שלהן: לול. בנין העשוי לתרנגולין: לא נוטלין ולא מחזירין. כדמפרש ואזיל חזרתו בנין ממש הוא וסילוקו סתירה גמורה היא: מאי קסבר. שמתיר סילוקו ואוסר חזרתו: אי קסבר יש בנין בכלים. וחזרתו בנין על כרחיך אם יש בנין יש סתירה ואמאי נוטלין: ושניטלו קאמר. וה"ק דלת של תיבה שידה ומגדל שניטלו אין מחזירין: מאי אבל. כיון דלא תנא נוטלין לא שייך למיתני אבל: לעולם קסבר אין סתירה ואין בנין. הלכך נוטלין ומיהו אין מחזירין מדרבנן: גזירה שמא יתקע. בחוזקה בסכין ויתדות והוה ליה גמר מלאכה וחייב משום מכה בפטיש: קורנס של אגוזים. המיוחד לפליעת אגוזים הוא דקתני מתניתין דנוטלין אותו למלאכתו משום דעיקרו למלאכת היתר: אבל של נפחים. דעיקרו למלאכת איסור לא: לצורך גופו. שגופו צריך עוד למלאכה אחרת של היתר אין מטלטלין אותו לאותה מלאכה וכ"ש אם אין צריך לגופו אלא לפנות מקומו דאין מטלטלין: מי מייחדי לקטן. בשלמא כולהו הני דמתני' איכא לאוקמא בעשויין ומיוחדין לכך בר מהני דליכא דעביד להו להכי:

דבר

תוספות

אהדרינהו שמואל לאפיה. מיירי שהיה לכל הפחות מחלה על מחלה דמשום נר לאחד נר למאה לא משתריא אלא היכא שהוא ניכר שהוא עושה לצרכו דתו לא גזרינן אפילו במכירו שמא ירבה בשבילו:

הדרן עלך כל כתבי

כל הכלים הניטלין בשבת ודלתותיהן עמהם גרסינן ול"ג כל הכלים ניטלין דטובא איכא דאין ניטלין כגון מסר הגדול ויתד של מחרישה דאפילו ר"ש מודה כדאיתא בשילהי מכילתין (דף קנז.) וכגון מלתא [ז] בת תרי כורי דאמר רבה בשילהי במה מדליקין (דף לה.) וכן תלוסרות לרבי יהודה [ז] וכר ושן [ח] מ"ר: אדרבה בשבת מוכנין אגב אביהן. אע"ג דלקמן בפירקין (דף קכה.) אמר איפכא גבי שברי כלי חרס דשרי לטלטל יותר כשנשברו בע"פ משנשברו בשבת לא דמיא דהכא אפכי כלי הוא שעדיין עומד למלאכה ראשונה ולאו להתחבר הכיסוי עם הכלי אבל לקמן לא חשיב כלי אלא מחמת שעומד למלאכה אחרת הלכך כשנשבר בשבת אסור טפי דהוי נולד: לעולם קסבר יש בנין בכלים כו'. וכשניטלו מטלטלין קאמר וה"פ הבריית' דלת של שידה תיבה ומגדל ניטלין פירוש מטלטלין כשניטלין ולא כפירוש הקונטרס דמפרש שניטלין דקתני היינו שניטלו קאמר כלומר כשניטל אין מחזירין אותן דלא יתכן לפרש כן ניטלין דסיפא אלא לשון טלטול הוא כדפרשתי ופריך והא (א) נמי ניטלין קתני ועוד מאי אבל לא מחזירין דלא שייך למיתני אמילתיה דלא (דמיא) [שייך] כלל למאי דאיירי בה דמעיקרא קאמר ניטלין שמותר לטלטל ואין בו איסור מוקצה והדר קאמר אבל לא מחזירין שהוא משום איסור בנין מאי ענין זה אצל זה לא שייך כה"ג למיתני אבל כלל: רחת ומלגז מי מייחדי ליה לקטן. וכי יהודה ידע ליה לסיפא אלא דלמא לא מוקי לה בשיודה לכך כל הנך דמתניתין ואם תאמר והאמר רב יהודה אמר שמואל בפרק אלו קשרים (לעיל דף קיא:) כלי קיואי מותר לטלטל בשבת דהיינו לצורך גופו אע"פ שמלאכתו לאיסור ואין לומר דמשמע דשמואל קאמר ליה וליה לא סבירא ליה מדבעי מיניה מרב יהודה כובד עליון וכובד התחתון מהו אין ולאו ורפיא בידיה משמע דס"ל הכי ועוד דרב יהודה גופיה בסוף כירה (לעיל דף מו.) קאמר שרגא דמישחא שרי לטלטולי ואין לומר דמיירי כשייחדו להיתר כדמוקי רב יהודה הנך דמתני' דהא כלי קיואי לא משמע שייחדו דאם כן אפילו כובד העליון וכובד התחתון נמי ויש לומר דלא אסר רב יהודה אלא דומיא דפיצוע אגוזים שהיא מלאכה גרועה לגבי קורנס שמיוחד למלאכה חשובה וכן כל הנך דמתניתין הוי אסור בלא ייחוד דמלאכת היתר שלהן מלאכה גרועה היא לגבי הנך כלים שמיוחדין למלאכה חשובה אבל כלי קיואי ושרגא דמישחא מותר לטלטל לצורך גופן דמלאכה שלהן חשובה יותר מפילוע אגוזים:

בסיכי

עין משפט נר מצוה

פז א טור שו"ע שם: א ב מיי' פכ"ב מהלכות שבת הלכה כה ופכ"ה הלכה יב סמג לאוין סה טוש"ע או"ח סימן שח סעיף ח:

ב ג מיי' שם הלכה ז טוש"ע שם סעיף ג:

ג ד מיי' שם הלכה ו טוש"ע שם סעיף יא:

ד ה מיי' פכ"ב שם הלכה כה טור שו"ע שם סעיף ט:

ה ו מיי' שם הלכה כו סמג שם טוש"ע או"ח סימן שיד סעיף א:

הגהות הב"ח

(א) תוס' ד"ה לעולם וכו' ופריך והא ניטלין קתני ולא תני נמי נתפרקו כו' ועוד מאי אבל:

רבינו חננאל

בנכרי שאינו מכירו אבל אם מכירו אסור. ת"ש עיר של ישראל ונכרים הדרן כו'.

הדרן עלך כל כתבי הקודש

פי"ז כל הכלים ניטלין בשבת כו'. באנו לפרש מהו נפרקו בשבת או אפי' בחול. ואוקמה אביי להא מתני' אע"פ שנתפרקו בחול כל הכלים ניטלין בשבת לפי שאינן דומין דלתות הכלים לדלתות הבית. כי דלתות הבית קבועין בקרקע ולא הוכנו להיטלטל. אבל הכלים הוכנו לטלטל הן וכ"ש דלתותיהן. ופשוטה היא. ומפרקינן [לה] גזירה שמא יתקע. פי' שמא יתקע בה מסמר או יתד וכדומה להן: נוטל אדם קורנס לפצוע בו אגוזים וכו'. בא רב יהודה להעמיד משנתנו זו בקורנס המוכן לפצוע אגוזים. ולא כל קורנס מותר. אלא זה בלבד. אבל קורנס של נפחים וכדומה להן אפילו לצורך גופו אסור. ואקשי' עלה רבה אלא מעתה סיפא דקתני ואת הרחת ואת המלגז לתת עליו לקטן. פי' לתת עליו מאכל לקטן כגון תבשיל. רחת ומלגז [מי] מכינין בנ"א לתבשיל

חשק שלמה על רבינו חננאל

(א) נראה דמספר בדברי רבינו וצ"ל דלת של שידה ושל תיבה ושל מגדל נוטלין אבל לא מחזירין:

מסורת הש"ס

א) פירוש מלגז [ומגמגה] שבמשמעות איתא המזלג], ב) לעיל קו. סנהדרין סד:, ג) [תוספתא פרק יג], ד) [עירובין לה. ביצה י: יא: כב.], ה) רש"ל וכן איתא בחדושי הרשב"א, ו) [ע"ל לעיל לה. תוס' ד"ה ופסילין], ז) [לעיל לו.], ח) [לעיל מד.]

ליקוטי רש"י

קרדום. פאס קרדום עשוי כמין כלי אומנות שעושין בו אוכפות ומרגעות שקורין אייש"ש ויש שעשוי כעין כלי האומן שקורין בירגוו"ל שראשו האחד דומה לקרדומות שלנו וראשו השני דומה לכלי אומני אוכפות ומרגעות הסוסים [ביצה לא.]. מגירה. שיר"ה בלע"ז וסכין הוא שיש בו פגימות הרבה וקוללת מהר [ב"ק קיט:].

בנין בכלים. יש תורת בנין בכלים ובונה חייב בכל שהוא [ביצה כב.]. ואי אין סתירה בכלים. ואי בעי סתר ליה [עירובין לה.]. אין בנין בכלים. אין תורת בנין בכלים ואינו חייב אלא אם כן עשה בו מלאכה כגון ממחק או ממתך או אורג או תופר שהן אבות מלאכות לעצמם אבל וכו' משום בנין אין בונה אלא בבתים ואהלים [ביצה שם]. אין איסור בנין וסתירה בכלים אלא בבתים דנחייב בבנין כל דהו והעושה כלי או גומרו ביום טוב או בשבת משום מכה בפטיש הוא דמחייב שהוא חיוב לכל גמר מלאכה או אם הוא דבר שהוא מחליקו חייב משום ממחק ואם צריך קלוע חייב משום ממתך וכן אורג או תופר אבל בנין וסתירה לא שייך בהו לאמיובי בסלוק וחזרה דהא דתנן (שבת קב:) הבונה כל שהוא בבתים תנן [שם יא:]. [מכאן שייך לדף קכג.] הא מני ר' נחמיה היא. דאמר בערובין (לה.) אפי' מרווד ואפילו טלית אין ניטלין אלא לצורך תשמיש שהן מיוחדין לו [ביצה לב.]. את העלי. דף עב וככד וכותשין בו חטים לטרגים וטיסני והוי מלאכתו לאיסור וקא סברי בית שמאי אסור לטלטלו ואפילו לצורך גופו שצריך לגוף הכלי למלאכה המותרת היום [שם י.]. מלאכתו לאיסור לכתוש במכתשת משום הכי אסרי ליה בית שמאי. שאסור לטלטלו. דלאעביד ליה לצורך יום טוב [שם יא.]. דקפיד עלייהו. שלא יתעקם ומייחד ליה מקום ומקצה ליה בידים ואפילו לר' שמעון אסור לטלטלו דמוקצה מחמת חסרון כיס אפילו ר' שמעון מודה [לקמן קכה:]. פגה. תאנה בוסר שטומנין אותה בתבן להתבשל ותבן מוקצה הוא ואסור לטלטלו כגון שהקצהו ללבון לבנים. וחררה שטמנה. אממול בגחלים ועכשיו כבו ומכל מקום מוקצין הן אבל לא כבו לא דמתוך שנהפכים מכבה את התחתונות ומבעיר את העליונות כדאמרינן בכריתות (כ.) [עירובין עז.]. טלטול מן הצד. כלאחר יד [לעיל מג:]. האי פוגלא. לנון שטומנין בקרקע להתקיים כשבא לאלו מלמעלה למטה שרי אם היה ראשה מלמעלה ועוקצה מלמטה ותולה מראשה העבה תחילה ועוקצה נמשך אחריה מותר לפי שהגומא רחבה מלמעלה ואין מזיזין הקרקע כשהוא שומטה אבל אם תולה מלמטה למעלה שהתחתונה נתון למעלה וראש עליונה שהוא עב נתון למטה והוא שומטה מסופה לראשה אסור לפי שהגומא קצרה מלמעלה וכשהוא תולה מזיז העפר ומטלטלו ואף על גב דטלטול מן הצד הוא שמיה טלטול ואסור [לקמן קמא.]. מותר לטלטלה בשבת. במגר דהא חזיא ליטול את הקוץ ותורת כלי עליה. ולא אמרו נקובה. חלוקה להלכותיה אלא לענין טומאה בלבד דנקובה מקבלת טומאה ושאינה נקובה לא. בגולמי. שהוא גולם שנקללה מן המוט ועומדת לינקב הפס הוא דכל זמן שלא נקבה אינה מקבלת טומאה דהא לא נגמרת מלאכתה ולענין טומאה כלי מעשה כתיב (במדבר לא) שגמר כל מעשהו ומיהו לענין שבת שריא דזימנין דממליך עלה ומנח לה הכי ומשוי לה מנא לנטילת קוץ [לעיל נב:]. תרגמא אביי אליבא דרבא. במקום (אביי) ובשבילו שתהא (משנה) זו מתורגמת לפי דבריו [סוכה יט. בסוגיין רבא].

designated for the purpose of feeding **a child?**[22]

Rabbah therefore advances his own interpretation: אֶלָּא אָמַר רַבָּה – **Rather, Rabbah said:** קוּרְנָס שֶׁל נַפָּחִין לְפַצֵּעַ בּוֹ הָאֱגוֹזִין – The Mishnah means that one may take **a blacksmith's hammer to crack open nuts with it.** קָסָבַר – **[Rabbah] holds** that

NOTES

22. You may contend concerning all the other items mentioned in the Mishnah that we are dealing with utensils that were designated for the use that the Mishnah suggests. However, nobody ever designates a winnowing shovel or pitchfork for the purpose of passing food to a child (*Rashi;* see *Tosafos*). Obviously, the Mishnah refers to a winnowing shovel or pitchfork that are used primarily for winnowing – which is work that is prohibited on the Sabbath – and nevertheless, it allows using them for a permissible function. Thus, the Mishnah permits moving even a forbidden-use utensil for the sake of its use in a permissible capacity.

דָּבָר שֶׁמְּלַאכְתּוֹ לְאִיסּוּר – **something that is** ordinarily **used** primarily **for work that is forbidden** on the Sabbath לְצוֹרֶךְ גּוּפוֹ מוּתָּר – **may be** taken **for the sake of its use** in a permissible capacity.[1]

Rabbah's opinion is challenged:

אֵיתִיבֵיהּ אַבָּיֵי לְרַבָּה – **Abaye challenged Rabbah** on the basis of the following Baraisa: מְדוֹכָה – A MORTAR in which garlic is usually crushed – אִם יֵשׁ בָּהּ שׁוּם מְטַלְטְלִין אוֹתָהּ – IF IT CONTAINS GARLIC IT MAY BE MOVED on the Sabbath, וְאִם לָאו אֵין מְטַלְטְלִין אוֹתָהּ – BUT IF NOT IT MAY NOT BE MOVED, even for the sake of a permissible function. Thus, we see that a utensil which is used primarily for prohibited work may not be moved for the sake of its use.[2] – ? –

Rabbah responds:

אָמַר לֵיהּ – **He said to [Abaye]:** הָא מַנִּי – **Whose** opinion **is** reflected in **this** Baraisa? רַבִּי נְחֶמְיָה הִיא – **It is** the opinion of **R' Nechemyah,** דְּאָמַר אֵין כְּלִי נִיטָּל אֶלָּא לְצוֹרֶךְ תַּשְׁמִישׁוֹ – **who said** that **a utensil may be taken** on the Sabbath **only for the sake of its** designated **function.**[3]

Abaye issues another challenge:

אֵיתִיבֵיהּ – **He challenged [Rabbah]** on the basis of the following Baraisa: (בֵּית שַׁמַּאי אוֹמְרִים – BEIS SHAMMAI SAY: אֵין נוֹטְלִין אֶת הָעֱלִי לְקַצֵּב עָלָיו בָּשָׂר – ONE MAY NOT TAKE A PESTLE on Yom Tov TO CHOP MEAT UPON IT; וּבֵית הִלֵּל מַתִּירִין – BUT BEIS HILLEL PERMIT this.) וְשָׁוִין – HOWEVER, THEY AGREE שֶׁאִם קִצֵּב עָלָיו בָּשָׂר – THAT IF ONE HAS already CHOPPED MEAT ON [THE PESTLE] שֶׁאָסוּר לְטַלְטְלוֹ – HE MAY NOT MOVE IT afterwards for another purpose.[4] Thus, we see that something which is ordinarily used for prohibited work may not be moved for the sake of its use in a permissible capacity. – ? –

Rabbah's response is cited:

סָבַר לְשַׁנּוּיֵי לֵיהּ כְּרַבִּי נְחֶמְיָה – [Rabbah] initially **intended to answer [Abaye]** that this Baraisa also accords **with** the opinion **of R' Nechemyah.** כֵּיוָן דִּשְׁמַעָהּ לְהָא דְּאָמַר רַב חִינָּנָא בַּר שֶׁלֶמְיָא מִשְּׁמֵיהּ דְּרַב – However, **once he heard that which Rav Chinana bar Shelemya said in the name of Rav:** הַכֹּל מוֹדִים בְּסִיכֵּי זִירֵי וּמְזוֹרֵי – **All agree concerning spindles, clothespresses and mallets** that they may not be moved at all on the Sabbath,[5] דְּכֵיוָן דְּקָפֵיד עֲלַיְיהוּ – **because since [their owner] is particular about them** out of concern that they might be ruined, מְיַיחֵד לְהוּ מָקוֹם – **he designates a place for** storing **them** and sets them aside from Sabbath use[6] – הָנֵי נַמִּי – Rabbah said that with regard to **these** utensils **too** (i.e. a mortar and pestle) we may say that מְיַיחֵד לְהוּ מָקוֹם – **[the owner] designates a place for** storing **them** and sets them aside from Sabbath use. Therefore, all agree that they may not be moved on the Sabbath.[7]

The Gemara cites further opinions concerning which type of hammer our Mishnah permits using to crack open nuts:

אִיתְּמַר – **It was stated:** רַבִּי חִיָּיא בַּר אַבָּא אָמַר רַבִּי יוֹחָנָן – **R' Chiya bar Abba said in the name of R' Yochanan:** קוּרְנָס שֶׁל זֶהָבִים שָׁנִינוּ – **We learned** our Mishnah's ruling in regard to **a goldsmith's hammer.**[8] רַב שֶׁמֶן בַּר אַבָּא אָמַר – **Rav Shemen**

NOTES

1. However, Rabbah holds that this type of utensil may not be moved for the sake of its place (see below, 124a with *Rashi* ד״ה ודבר שמלאכתו לאיסור; *Rashba* to 122b).

2. The mortar is a utensil whose primary work (crushing garlic) is prohibited, for crushing spices is a *toladah* of the *melachah* of grinding. Since the Baraisa forbids moving an empty mortar — even for the sake of a permitted use, such as sitting on it — we learn that a forbidden-use utensil may not be moved for the sake of its use in a permissible capacity (*Rashi*).

It is, however, permitted to move the mortar when it contains garlic. The reason is that it is permitted to move a *muktzeh* utensil when it contains a non-*muktzeh* object (*Teshuvos HaRosh* 22:8, cited by *Beis Yosef, Orach Chaim* 308:5; see also *Rashi* and *Teshuvos R' Akiva Eiger* §22). [Others reject this explanation, contending that it is ordinarily forbidden to move a *muktzeh* utensil merely because it contains a non-*muktzeh* object. Only a corpse (which is *muktzeh*) is movable when a non-*muktzeh* object is placed upon it. This is a special dispensation allowed in order to preserve the dignity of the corpse, and does not pertain to other *muktzeh* objects (see below, 142b note 23). Rather, they explain that although the mortar is designated primarily for the prohibited work of crushing garlic, a legitimate aspect of its function is the storage of the garlic that is crushed. In this capacity, it performs permitted work. When actually serving in its legitimate permitted capacity, the mortar is treated as a permitted-use utensil [כְּלִי שֶׁמְּלַאכְתּוֹ לְהֶיתֵּר], which may be moved on the Sabbath. The same rule pertains to a pot. Since it is used primarily for cooking, it is categorized as a forbidden-use utensil. However, since the storage of cooked food is one of its legitimate functions, when it contains food it is treated as a permitted-use utensil (*Rashba, Ritva MHK* ed.; see also *Mishnah Berurah* 308:20,26 with *Beur Halachah* 308:2 ד״ה קורדום and *Chazon Ish* 47:11).]

3. R' Nechemyah's opinion is set forth below, 146a; see also the Mishnah on 124a. He holds that even a utensil that is designated for a permitted use may be moved only for its designated purpose (*Rashi;* see also *Rashi* to 124a ד״ה א״ל רבא). It follows that a utensil whose designated purpose is a prohibited one, such as a mortar, may not be moved at all (*Ritva MHK* ed.).

4. A pestle, since it is normally used for grinding, is seemingly classified as a forbidden-use utensil. Nevertheless, Beis Hillel permit taking it on Yom Tov to chop meat on it. However, Beis Hillel allow this only as a special dispensation to enhance the enjoyment of the Yom Tov meal. They concede to Beis Shammai that after one has chopped the meat that he needs for his meal, he may not take the pestle for a different purpose (*Rashi*).

5. Spindles [סִיכֵּי] are long spokes that are used to comb out silk fiber. Clothespresses [זִירֵי] are wooden beams that are used to press clothes with their weight. Mallets [מְזוֹרֵי] are wooden sticks that are used to beat clothes during the cleaning process (*Aruch,* cited by *Tosafos*). [*Rashi* states that the utensils listed here are used by dyers, but he does not specify their function. *Rashi* also cites an alternative explanation (which he rejects) that these utensils are parts of a loom.]

Rav said that all — i.e. even the Rabbis who dispute R' Nechemyah's ruling — agree that the listed utensils may not be moved on the Sabbath, even for the sake of their use in a permissible capacity (see *Rashi*).

6. The concern that these utensils might become misshapen, and subsequently damage clothes that are being cleaned or repaired, prompts the owner to disallow their use for other purposes (*Tosafos* ד״ה בסיכי). [And since their primary function is prohibited on the Sabbath they do not stand to be used at all (see *Shulchan Aruch HaGraz* 308:4).] Accordingly, it is prohibited to move them not because they are designated for a prohibited use, but because by setting them aside from Sabbath use the owner has made them *muktzeh* (*Rashi*). This is the category known as מוּקְצֶה מֵחֲמַת חֶסְרוֹן כִּיס, *muktzeh due to [fear of] monetary loss* (*Rashi* to 125b ד״ה קפיד עליה; *Ritva MHK* ed.; *Mishnah Berurah* 308:2; see Chapter Introduction).

7. Having heard Rav Chinana bar Shelemya's statement in the name of Rav, Rabbah retracted even his earlier rebuttal of Abaye's first challenge in favor of a more effective one. Rather than attributing the Baraisos concerning a mortar and pestle to R' Nechemyah, Rabbah responds that both a mortar and a pestle are unique in that one does not normally use them for anything other than their intended purpose, and stores them in a designated place when they are not in use. Therefore, all agree that they are *muktzeh* (see *Rashi;* cf. *Maharsha* to 123b and *Rashi* to 81a ד״ה מדוכה קטנה).

[The Gemara will revisit the subject of a mortar below, on 123b and 124a, and will offer another explanation of the Baraisos.]

8. Although a goldsmith is somewhat particular about the use of his hammer, as its surface must remain smooth to be suitable for flattening sheets of gold without puncturing them, he is not so particular that he sets it aside from all other uses, for the surface can always be smoothed out by striking it against an anvil. Therefore, the goldsmith's hammer

דבר שמלאכתו לאיסור לצורך גופו מותר איתיביה אביי לרבה (א) מדוכה אם יש בה שום מטלטלין אותה ואם לאו אין מטלטלין אותה א"ל הא מני ר' נחמיה היא דאמר (ג) אין כלי ניטל אלא לצורך תשמישו איתיביה (ד) ב"ש אומרים אין נוטלין את העלי לקצב עליו בשר (א ובה"מ מתירין) (ה) ושוין שאם קצב עליו בשר שאסור לטלטלו סבר לשנויי ליה כר' נחמיה כיון דשמעה להא דאמר רב חיננא בר שלמיא משמיה דרב הכל מודים בסיכי זיירי ומזורי דכיון דקפיד עלייהו מייחד להו מקום ה"נ מייחד להו מקום איתמר ר' חייא בר אבא אמר ר' יוחנן (ב) קורנס של זהבים שנינו רב שמן בר אבא אמר קורנס של בשמים שנינו מאן דאמר דבשמים כ"ש דזהבים מאן דאמר של זהבים אבל דבשמים קפיד עלייהו: ואת הכוש ואת הכרכר כו': (ו) ת"ר פגה שטמנה בתבן וחררה שטמנה (א) בגחלים אם מגולה מקצתה מותר לטלטלה ואם לאו אסור לטלטלה ר"א בן תדאי אומר (ג) תוחבין בכוש או בכרכר והן מנערות מאיליהם אמר רב נחמן הלכה כר"א בן תדאי למימרא דסבר רב נחמן (ז) טלטול מן הצד לא שמיה טלטול (ח) והאמר רב נחמן האי פוגלא מלמעל' למטה שרי ממטה למעלה אסיר הדר ביה רב נחמן מההיא: מחט של יד ליטול בה כו': שלח ליה רבא בריה דרבה לרב יוסף ילמדנו רבינו מחט שניטל חררה או עוקצה מהו א"ל תניתוה מחט של יד ליטול בה את הקוץ וכי מה איכפת ליה לקוץ בין נקובה לבין שאינה נקובה איתיביה (ט) מחט שניטל חררה או עוקצה טהורה אמר אביי טומאה אשבת קרמית (י) טומאה כלי מעשה בעינן לענין שבת מידי דחזי בעינן והא נמי חזיא למשקלא בה קוץ אמר רבא מאן דקמותיב שפיר קמותיב (כ) מדלענין טומאה לאו מנא הוא לענין שבת נמי לאו מנא הוא מיתיבי (ל) (ד) מחט בין נקובה בין שאינה נקובה מותר לטלטלה בשבת ולא אמרו נקובה אלא לענין טומאה בלבד (מ) תרגמא אביי אליבא דרבא בגולמי עסקינן זימנין דמימלך עלייהו ומשוי להו מנא (ה) אבל היכא דניטל חררה או עוקצה אדם זורקה לבין גרוטאות (נ) אסובי ינוקא רב נחמן (ס) אסיר ורב ששת (ו) שרי אמר רב נחמן מנא אמינא לה דתנן (ע) אין עושין אפיקטויזין

רש"י

דבר שמלאכתו לאיסור. אם לריך בשבת לגופו (ג) של מלאכה אחרת של היתר מותר: **מדוכה.** שדוכין בה שום: **אם יש בה שום מטלטלין אותה.** אגב השום: **ואם לאו אין מטלטלין.** כגון לישב עליה כיון דעיקר מלאכתו לשחיקה דהיא מלאכת איסור משום טוחן: **תשמישו.** תשמיש המיוחד לו: **ושוין.** ב"ש וב"ה שנחלקו בנוטלין את העלי לקצב עליו בשר ביו"ט: **שאם קצב עליו בשר.** שעשה לצורך שמחת יו"ט: **שאסור לטלטלו.** דהאי דקשרו ב"ה משום שמחת יו"ט קשרו אלמא משום דעלי מלאכתו לאיסור לכתישת טרגיס וטיסני וקליפת עלים לעבד בהן עורות אסור: **הכל מודים.** רבנן דאיפלגו אדר' נחמיה: **בסיכי זיירי ומזורי.** כלי אורגין לגרדים הן ובפירוש הלוי פירש כלי אורגין סיכי הן עמודין זיארי הן קנים שבשתי ומזורי כובד עליון ותחתון ולשון נראה לי דזיארי לשון עולרים הן כמו מעלרתא זיירא (ע"ז דף ס.): **דקפיד עלייהו.** האומן שלא יתקלקלו ושלא יתעקמו: **מייחד להם מקום.** מקלה להן בידים: **הני נמי.** (א) עלי ומדוכה: **קורנס של זהבים.** אע"פ דקפיד עליה קלת שלריך שיהא חלק לרדד טסין אפ"ה כיון שמתקן על ידי הכאה שמכה על הסדן לא מקפי ליה וכ"ש של שאר נפחים כרבה: **בשמים.** לשחוק בו: **קפיד עליה.** שלא ימאס: **פגה.** תאנה שלא בשלה כל לרכה וטומנין בתבן להתבשל ותבן מוקצה הוי לטיט: **אם מגולה מקצתה.** שיכול לאוחזו במקום המגולה דאפי' טלטול מן הצד ליכא שאין לריך להגביה התבן אלא מגביה מקום המגולה והתבן נשמט ונופל: **פוגלא.** לנון תלוש שהטמינו בארץ ונתגלה ראשו: **מלמעלה למטה שרי.** אם היה העליון שלה למעלה והקלר למטה וכשהוא שולפה שולפה מעליון שלה לתחתון שלה ורוחב הלנון למעלה מותר דליכא טלטול לעפר שכל שהרי נתגלה ראשו: **ממטה למעלה אסור.** שמזיז עפר לפי שהגומא קלרה מלמעלה ורוחב הלנון מלמטה ואע"ג דטלטול עפר מן הלד הוא שאינו אוחזו ממש בידו: **חררה.** חור שלה: **עוקצה.** פויינט"א: **מהו.** לטלטלה מי בטל תורת כלי מינה או לא: **כלי מעשה.** שמעשה שלו קיים: **ולא אמרו נקובה.** להיות תורת כלי עליה יותר משאין נקובה אלא לענין טומאה וקס"ד דבנטל חור שלה קאמר לענין טומאה בטל שם כלי מינה ולטלטול שרי: **בגולמי.** גולמי מחטין העומדות לינקב דנקובה נגמרה מלאכתה ושאינה נקובה אינה נגמרה מלאכתה הלכך לענין טומאה הוא דלא הוי כלי אבל בטלטול שריא דחזי לקוץ: **דמימליך.** ולא נקיב לה: **ומשוי לה מנא.** כמות שהיא ולנטילת קוץ: **גרוטאות.** שברי מתכות אדם זורק' לבין גרוטאו' ובטל שם כלי מינה: **אסובי ינוקא.** להחליק סדר אבריו כשהוא נולד אבריו מתפרקין ולריך ליישבן: **אסיר.** דדמי למתקן:

תוספות

בסיכי זיירי ומזורי. פי' בערוך (פ) סיכי הם יתדות המוכנין לנפץ בהן משי וכיולא בה תרגום יתדות סיכי זיירי כלי עץ כמו קרסים שכובשין בהן בגדים דתנן (לקמן דף קמא.) מכבש של בעלי בתים מזורי כלי עץ שהכובס מכה בו הבגדים על האבן שמלבנו ואלו כלים מקפיד עליהם שלא יתעקמו ולא יתפגמו שלא יתקלקלו הבגדים והמשי ומסיח דעתו מלטלטלן וכן מפרש בירושלמי זיירי דין עצר ביה מזורא דין חביט ביה ולפי' הקונט' דמפרש מזורי כובד עליון וכובד תחתון נ"ל דסבירא ליה כמאן דאסר בפרק אלו קשרים (לעיל דף קיג.): **הא** נמי מייחד לה מקום. מ"מ משום שמחת יו"ט מותר לטלטלו לקצב עליו בשר: (ל) **הדר** ביה רב נחמן מההיא. מסתברא דמההיא הדר ביה מדאמר בפרק תולין (לקמן דף קמא.) אמרי בי רב תנינא דלא כרב נחמן: **פגה** שהטמינה כו'. (ס) מיירי שהניחה שם ע"מ ליטלה אבל אם הניחה שם לכל השבת הוי בסיס לדבר האסור כדאמר לקמן בפרק נוטל (ד' קמב:) גבי אבן שעל פי החבית לא שנו אלא בשוכח אבל במניח נעשה בסיס לדבר האסור: **האי** פוגלא. וא"ת האי פוגלא היכי דמי אי במניח מ"ט דמאן דשרי מלמטה למעלה הא אפילו ניעור לא שרי כ"ש טלטול מן הצד ואי בשכח מ"ט דמאן דאסר אפי' טלטול גמור שרי לצורך לטלטל אגב היתר לקמן בפרק נוטל (קמא. וד' קמב:) במעות שעל גבי הכר בצריך למקומו דמטלטלו בעודן עליו ואבן שעל פי החבית כשהוא בין החביות מגביה ומטה כ"ש טלטול מן הצד וי"ל דמניח על מנת ליטלה איירי אע"ג דכשכח דמי כמו טמן וכיסה בדבר שאינו ניטל בסוף במה טומנין (לעיל דף נא.) דשרי לנער משום דאין מניח לכל השבת ובעצמות וקליפין דריש ביצה (ד' ב.) דשרי ב"ה לסלק את הטבלא ולנער מ"מ לא היה לו להניח באותו ענין שיצטרך טלטול מן הצד ועצמות וקליפין לא מסתייה דלא לינח בהן על גבי השלחן וטמן וכיסה דפרק במה טומנין (לעיל ד' נא.) אין לחוש כיון דאפשר בניעור דאפילו טלטול מן הצד אינו (ק): **מדלענין** טומאה לאו מנא לענין שבת נמי לאו מנא. תימה הא תנן לקמן (ר) כל הכלים הניטלין שבריהן ניטלין אע"ג דלענין טומאה לא הוי מנא כשנשבר אלא על ידי ייחוד לפי' הקונטרס דסוף המצניע (לעיל דף צה:) וי"ל דה"פ מדלענין טומאה (ש) לאו מנא אפי' על ידי ייחוד דכיון דניטל חררה או עוקצה לא מהני ביה ייחוד לענין שבת נמי לאו מנא היא אבל היכא דהוה מנא לענין טומאה ע"י ייחוד איכא למימר דהוי מנא לענין שבת אפי' בלא ייחוד כיון דיכול להיות כלי לענין טומאה וכן משמע בסמוך דתרגמא אביי אליבא דרבא בגולמי דזימנין דמימלך עלייהו ומשוי להו מנא משמע דלהכי מותר לטלטל אע"ג דטהורה היא דאכתי לא מימלך עלה כיון שראוי ליחדה להיות כלי (ת): **אסובי** ינוקא. לאו היינו לפופי ינוקא דשרי בפרק במה אשה (לעיל דף סו:) ולקמן בסוף חבית (דף קמז:) דהיינו שכורכין אותו בבגדים וקושרים בחגורה רחבה וכן פירש בקונטרס בסוף מפנין (ת) כי היכי דלא תקשי דרב נחמן אדרב נחמן דשרי התם לפופי והכא אסר אסובי והא דתנן בפ' חבית (שם) אין מעצבין את הקטן פריך לה התם אההיא דלפופי ומוקי לה בחומרי שדרה דמיחזי כבונה וקשה דמייתי לה מאין עושין אפיקטויזין שהוא תיקוני גברא כדפירש בקונטרס הוה ליה לאתויי מסיפא דאין מעצבין את הקטן דהוי נמי תקוני ינוקא ודמי טפי שהכל בקטן מענין אסובי ופירש רבינו תם דהכי נמי מייתי ונקט רישא (א) אין עושין אפיקטויזין כו' עד אין מעצבין:

וסכינה

עין משפט נר מצוה

ו א טוש"ע או"ח סימן תלט סעיף ה:
ז ב מיי' פכ"ה מהלכות שבת הלכה ז סמג לאוין סה טוש"ע או"ח סימן שח סעיף ג [ועי' בב"י]:
ח ג מיי' שם הלכה טו סמג שם טוש"ע או"ח סימן שיא סעיף ט:
ט ד ה מיי' שם הלכה ח סמג שם טוש"ע או"ח סימן שח סעיף יא:
י ו מיי' פ"כ מהלכות שבת הלכה"ד ופכ"א הלכה לא טור שו"ע או"ח סימן של סעיף ט:

רבינו חננאל

לתבשיל וכדומה לו. ולא מצא רב יהודה פירוקי והעמיד רבה משנתנו בקורנס של נפחים וה"ה לכל קורנס. ושמעינן מינה דכל דבר שמלאכתו אפי' לאיסור כגון מלאכת הקורנס של נפחים שהן עושי מלאכת כלי נחשת וברזל. ומלאכתם [זו] שהוכנו לכך אסורה בשבת. אם הוצרכו (לומר) [לדבר] שהוא מותר בשבת. כגון פיצוע האגוזים שהן הכנת מאכל ואינה מלאכה מותר. ואקשינן עליה והא מדוכה אם יש בה שום מטלטלין [אותה] ואם לאו אין מטלטלין אותה. דכיון שמלאכתה לאיסור היא אפי' לצורך גופה אין מטלטלין אותה. ופריק ליה מני מתניתא ר' נחמיה היא דאמר אין כלי ניטל אלא לצורך תשמישו. פי' מצאנו ר' נחמיה שאמר בפי' אפי' טלית ואפי' [תרווד] אין ניטלין אלא לצורך והיא טלית ללבישה. ותרווד לאכל בו ומתני' דקתני נוטל אדם קורנס לפצוע בו [וקרדום] (ומדוכה) דלא כר' נחמיה. ותוב אקשי' עליה ושוין שאם קצב עליו בשר ופשוטה היא. ומוקמינן להני מתניתא לדברי הכל ואפילו לרבנן ומודו רבנן במדוכה ובעלי דכיון דקפיד עליה מכין עליה מקום וגמר בדעתו שלא לטלטלן מאותו מקום. לפיכך אסור לטלטלן מן המקום המוכן להם. ודין אלו כדין סיכי זיירי ומזורי. פי' סיכי הן יתדות המוכנין לנער בהן משי וכדומה לו. והן תרגום של יתדות סיכי. זיירי. כלי עץ כגון קרשים שכובשין בהן הבגדים. כדתנן מכבש של בעלי בתים. מזורי כלי עץ שהכובס מכה בו הבגדים על אבן בעת שמלבנן. ואלו כולן קפיד עליהן שלא יתעוותו או יפגמו. שאם יפגמו יקרעו הבגדים והמשי. לפיכך מסיח דעתו מטלטלן ונעשו מוקצים ועל כן אסור לטלטלן. וכך זה מפורש בתלמוד א"י. בזייר די [במכונה] עצר ביה. במזורה. די חבוט ביה (בכיבאנא) די כתיש ביה. ונתבררו דברי משנתנו כי כל הקורנס מותר לפצוע בו אגוזין ואפי' קורנס של זהבים. ובקורנס של בשמים חלקו בו ר' חייא בר אבין ורב שמן בר אבא משמיה דרבי יוחנן. ר' חייא אוסר. ורב שמן מתיר. ומסתברא כר' חייא חדא דכיון דקפיד עליה דלא ליפגום

מסורת הש"ס

א) [לקמן קכד. תוספתא פי"ד], ב) [לעיל לו. וש"נ], ג) רש"ל מ"ז, ד) ביצה יא., ה) [לקמן קכד. ביצה יא.], ו) עירובין עז., ז) [לעיל מג: לקמן קמא.], ח) שם, ט) לעיל נב: כלים פי"ג מ"ה, י) [לעיל דף ס.], כ) [לעיל קיב.], ל) לעיל נב: [תוספ' דכלים ב"מ פ"ב], מ) [לעיל נב: וש"נ], נ) [בערוך פירש כשנפלה ערלת הגרון של תינוק משימה החיה אלבעה בפיו ומסלקת אותה הערלה ופעמי' שמקיא התינוק ע"כ הקשה לו והא אין עושין אפיקטויזין עכ"ל ועיין בהרא"ש מ"ש שם על הגליון], ס) ל"ל אוסר, ע) לקמן קמז., פ) [ערך זיירין], צ) שייך לקמן קודם ד"ה מדלענין, ק) [וער' תוס' לעיל דף נא. ד"ה או שטמן], ר) דף קכד:, ש) [וע"ע תוס' חולין דף נה. ד"ה שיעורן], ת) [דף קכט:].

הגהות הב"ח

(א) גמ' וחררה שטמנה. נ"ב לשון רש"י בעירובין דף עז וחררה שהטמינה אתמול בגחלים ועכשיו כבו ומכ"מ מוקלין הן אבל לא כבו לא דמתוך שנספי' מכבה את התחתונות ומבעיר את העליונות כדאמרינן בכריתות: (ב) רש"י ד"ה דבר שמלאכתו וכו' לגופו למלאכה כצ"ל ותיבת של נמחק:

גליון הש"ס

רש"י ד"ה הני נמי עלי ומדוכה. ע"ל פא ע"א ברש"י ד"ה מדוכה קטנה: תוס' ד"ה פגה שהטמינה וכו' מיירי שהניחה. עיין לעיל דף נא ע"א תוס' ד"ה או שטמן: תוס' ד"ה מדלענין וכו' לאו מנא אפילו ע"י יחוד. ע' לעיל דף מט ע"ב תוס' ד"ה לא אמרו: תוס' ד"ה אסובי ינוקא כו' אין עושין אפיקטויזין. וכה כתבו תוס' בשם ר"ת שבועות דף ט ע"ב ד"ה כדאמר. ושם מא ע"א ד"ה ומאן דתני. וגיטין דף פ ע"ב ד"ה זו דברי ר"מ. ובזיר דף נד ע"ב ד"ה למדני. ובכרכות דף מה ע"א תוס' ד"ה ג' שאכלו אינן רשאין לחלק. ובמעילה דף יב ע"ב תוס' ד"ה אלא המוקדשים: בעין משפט אות ו' מיי' פכ"א מהלכות שבת. לא נמצא שם מזה. וע"ש בהלכה ל"א ובהה"מ:

רב נסים גאון

הכל מודין בסיכי זיארי ומזורי. בגמרא דבני מערבא גרסי זיירה דו עצר בה מזורי דו חבט בה וסיכי הן יתידות וגלוי הוא הדבר וידוע לכל:

ליקוטי רש"י

[נדפס בדף קכב:]

כזיירי דמי. ותוב דהוא אשכחן דהוה תדיר קמי ר' יוחנן דהוה גריס ודייק. והוה מהדר תלמודיה עליה כל תלתין יומין: **ת"ר** פגה שטמנה בתבן וחררה שטמנה בגחלים אם מגולה מקצתה מותר לטלטלה ואם לאו אסור. אלעזר בן תדאי [אומר] תוחבן בכוש או בכרכר והן נגערות מאליהן. פי' פגה כדכתיב התאנה חנטה פגיה והן פירות שלא נתבשלו באילן וטמנן בתבן להתבשל בחמות התבן להוכשר לאכילה. וחררה ע"ג גחלים טמנה בהן ליאפות מבעו"י ובא בשבת לנוטלן ת"ק סבר אסור להסיר הגחלים או התבן מעליהן ולישלן. אלא אם מקצתן מגולין אוחז בידו המקום המגולה ושומטן ואם אין בהם מקום מגולה בחררה בלא גחלים. ובפגה בלא תבן אסור לטלטלן. ואלעזר בן תדאי סבר אע"פ שאין בהן מקום מגולה תוחבו בכוש או בכרכר. פי' נועץ בהן כוש והוא דתנן כוש שבלע את הצינורא או כרכר שהוא וכו'. ומגביהן ונופלין התבן או הגחלים מאליהן ואח"כ נוטלן בידו שלא נמצא טלטול הגחלים והתבן כדרכן אלא מן הצד. ואמר רב נחמן הלכה כאלעזר בן תדאי. ומקשינן וכי רב נחמן סבר דטלטול מן הצד לאו שמיה טלטול. והא רב נחמן בפרק ר' אליעזר אומר תולין. בסופו בגמרא הקש שע"ג המטה לא ינענענו בידו כו'. אמר רב נחמן האי פוגלא מלמעלן למטן שרי.

ממטן

bar Abba said: קוּרְנָס שֶׁל בַּשָּׂמִים שָׁנִינוּ – **We learned** it in regard to **a spice maker's hammer.**[9]

The Gemara clarifies this dispute:

מַאן דְּאָמַר דְּבַשָּׂמִים – **The one who said** that the ruling pertains to **a spice maker's [hammer]** holds that כָּל שֶׁכֵּן דְּזֶהָבִים – it **certainly** pertains to **a goldsmith's [hammer]** as well,[10] מַאן דְּאָמַר שֶׁל זֶהָבִים – whereas **the one who said** that it pertains to **a goldsmith's [hammer]** meant specifically this type of hammer, אֲבָל דְּבַשָּׂמִים קָפֵיד עֲלַיְיהוּ – **but** as for **a spice maker's [hammer],** he holds that **[the owner] is particular about it** and sets it aside from Sabbath use.[11]

The Mishnah stated:

וְאֶת הַכּוּשׁ וְאֶת הַכַּרְכָּר כו׳ – A SPINDLE OR WEAVER'S REED **etc.** [to spear fruit with it].

The Gemara cites a Baraisa which discusses an example of the Mishnah's ruling:

תָּנוּ רַבָּנָן – **The Rabbis taught in a Baraisa:** פַּגָּה שֶׁטְּמָנָהּ בְּתֶבֶן – AN UNRIPE FIG THAT WAS BURIED IN STRAW before the Sabbath in order for it to ripen,[12] וַחֲרָרָה שֶׁטְּמָנָהּ בְּגֶחָלִים – AND A CAKE THAT HAD BEEN BURIED IN COALS before the Sabbath[13] – אִם מְגוּלָּה מִקְצָתָהּ מוּתָּר לְטַלְטְלָהּ – IF PART OF [THE FIG OR CAKE] IS EXPOSED IT MAY BE MOVED on the Sabbath, וְאִם לָאו אָסוּר לְטַלְטְלָהּ – BUT IF NOT IT MAY NOT BE MOVED.[14] רַבִּי אֶלְעָזָר בֶּן תַּדָּאי אוֹמֵר – R' ELAZAR BEN TADDAI SAYS: תּוֹחֲבִין בְּכוּשׁ אוֹ בְּכַרְכָּר – Even if it is not exposed, ONE MAY SPEAR it WITH A SPINDLE OR A WEAVER'S REED and lift it וְהֵן מִנַּעֲרוֹת מֵאֵילֵיהֶם – AND [THE STRAW OR COALS] WILL FALL OFF BY THEMSELVES.[15]

A related comment is cited:

אָמַר רַב נַחְמָן – **Rav Nachman said:** הֲלָכָה כְּרַבִּי אֶלְעָזָר בֶּן תַּדָּאי – **The halachah follows R' Elazar ben Taddai.**

The Gemara asks:

לְמֵימְרָא דְּסָבַר רַב נַחְמָן – Is this **to say that Rav Nachman holds** that טִלְטוּל מִן הַצַּד לֹא שְׁמֵיהּ טִלְטוּל – **moving indirectly is not deemed moving** with respect to *muktzeh* and is therefore permitted? וְהָאָמַר רַב נַחְמָן – **But Rav Nachman has said:** הַאי פּוּגְלָא – **Concerning a radish** that had been plucked and was then buried in the ground to ripen, but is partially exposed, מִלְמַעְלָה לְמַטָּה שְׁרֵי – if it is lying **right side up it is permitted** to grasp the exposed part and lift it out of the ground, מִמַּטָּה לְמַעְלָה אָסִיר – but if it is lying **upside down it is forbidden** to lift it.[16] Thus, we see that Rav Nachman forbids the indirect movement of *muktzeh.* – ? –

The Gemara answers:

הֲדַר בֵּיהּ רַב נַחְמָן מֵהַהִיא – **Rav Nachman retracted that [ruling]** concerning a buried radish.[17]

The Mishnah stated:

מַחַט שֶׁל יָד לִיטּוֹל בָּהּ כו׳ – A HAND-NEEDLE TO REMOVE [a splinter] WITH IT **etc.**

The Gemara discusses the status of a *broken* needle:

שְׁלַח לֵיהּ רָבָא בְּרֵיהּ דְּרַבָּה לְרַב יוֹסֵף – **Rava the son of Rabbah sent** the following inquiry **to Rav Yosef:** יְלַמְּדֵנוּ רַבֵּינוּ – **Let our master teach us** מַחַט שֶׁנִּיטַּל חֲרָרָהּ אוֹ עוּקְצָהּ מַהוּ – **what** the law **is** concerning **a** sewing **needle whose eye or point was removed.** Does it lose its status as a utensil and become *muktzeh*?

אָמַר לֵיהּ – **[Rav Yosef] replied:** תְּנֵיתוּהָ – **We learned it in** our **Mishnah,** which states: מַחַט שֶׁל יָד לִיטּוֹל בָּהּ אֶת הַקּוֹץ – One may take . . . A HAND-NEEDLE (i.e. a sewing needle) TO REMOVE A SPLINTER WITH IT. וְכִי מָה אִיכְפַּת לֵיהּ לַקּוֹץ – **Now, what difference is there to the splinter** בֵּין נְקוּבָה לְבֵין שֶׁאֵינָהּ נְקוּבָה – **between [a needle] that has an eye and one that has no eye?** None! Since the Mishnah considers the removal of a splinter a valid use for a sewing needle, and the needle is fit for this task even after its eye is removed, it retains its status as a utensil and is not *muktzeh.*[18]

NOTES

is not considered *muktzeh.* Certainly, the Mishnah's rule applies to an ordinary blacksmith's hammer as well. This accords with Rabbah's explanation that a forbidden-use utensil may be taken for the sake of a permissible use (*Rashi*).

9. I.e. a hammer used for crushing spices (*Rashi*). This interpretation also accords with Rabbah's opinion, since the spice maker's hammer is designated for prohibited work. However, it does not accord with the opinion just stated by R' Chiya bar Abba, as the Gemara goes on to explain (*Ritva MHK* ed.). [The spice maker is somewhat particular that his hammer not be put to other uses, for it might become repugnant and unfit for crushing spices. Nevertheless, Rav Shemen bar Abba does not consider the hammer totally *muktzeh.*]

10. Since he does not consider the spice maker's hammer totally *muktzeh,* even in the face of the possibility that other uses will ruin it, he certainly will not consider the goldsmith's hammer *muktzeh.* The goldsmith's hammer is less prone to ruination since its surface can always be flattened against an anvil (*Ritva MHK* ed., following *Rashi's* [and our] version of the text; cf. *Ritva's* own reading and explanation).

11. Lest it become repugnant [in which case it will be unsalvageable] (*Rashi*).

12. Straw is commonly designated for use in the manufacture of cement and is therefore *muktzeh* (*Rashi*).

13. Dough had been placed in the coals before the Sabbath to bake, and now, on the Sabbath, the coals have been extinguished. Nevertheless, they are *muktzeh.*

While the coals are glowing, they may not be moved at all because the motion will kindle the upper coals and extinguish the lower ones, in violation of the *melachos* of *kindling* and *extinguishing.* After they have been extinguished, the only concern is for *muktzeh* (*Rashi* to *Eruvin* 77a, cited by *Bach*).

14. The fig or cake is, of course, not *muktzeh* (see *Tosafos* ד״ה פגה). If enough of the fig or cake is exposed for the person to grasp it, he may do so and lift it out of its *muktzeh* encasement. In this case, he is not deemed to be moving the *muktzeh* even indirectly, [which might be prohibited (see above, 43b)] since the *muktzeh* is not lifted at all but merely falls away from the buried object as the object rises (*Rashi;* cf. *Ritva MHK* ed. here and *Tosafos* to 43b-44a ד״ה דכ״ע). However, if the fig or cake is not sufficiently exposed, one may not remove it from beneath the *muktzeh* encasement.

15. R' Elazar ben Taddai holds that as long as one does not move the *muktzeh* directly, i.e. with his hand or implement, he may lift the buried object out of its encasement. Although the *muktzeh* covering will be lifted somewhat by the rising object before it falls off, and will thus be moved *indirectly,* R' Elazar ben Taddai permits the lifting (*Ran; Ritva MHK* ed., in explanation of *Rashi*).

16. Since the radish had previously been plucked, the *melachah* of harvesting is not applicable, and the only issue is that of moving the *muktzeh* earth indirectly. Now, the top of a radish is wider than its bottom. Therefore, if the radish was buried right side up and its top is exposed, one can grasp the wide top and lift the narrower bottom from the hole without any movement of the earth. However, if it was buried upside down with only the narrow bottom exposed, one who lifts it will automatically lift some earth that is resting on the wider top. Although this would merely constitute indirect movement of the earth, for the person would not be touching the earth, Rav Nachman forbids it (*Rashi;* see *Tosafos* ד״ה האי פוגלא).

17. The Gemara asserts that he retracted the ruling regarding the radish, rather than the other one, because the halachah actually permits the indirect movement of *muktzeh* for the sake of a non-*muktzeh* object (*Ritva MHK* ed.; see *Orach Chaim* 311:8). See also Gemara below, 141a.

18. Rav Yosef does not address the issue of a needle whose point broke off. However, his response implies somewhat that in such a case the needle is *muktzeh* [since there *is* a difference in regard to the removal of a splinter between a needle that has a point and one that has no point]. Nevertheless, this matter requires further analysis (see *Beur Halachah* 308:11 ד״ה וחדשה שלא ניקבה).

דבר שמלאכתו לאיסור לצורך גופו מותר איתיביה אביי לרבה [א] מדוכה אם יש בה שום מטלטלין אותה ואם לאו אין מטלטלין אותה א"ל הא מני ר' נחמיה היא דאמר [ג] אין כלי ניטל אלא לצורך תשמישו איתיביה [ג] (ד) ב"ש אומרים אין נוטלין את העלי לקצב עליו בשר [א] וב"ה מתירין) [ה] ושוין שאם קצב עליו בשר שאסור לטלטלו סבר לשנויי ליה כר' נחמיה כיון דשמעה להא דאמר רב חיננא בר שלמיא משמיה דרב הכל מודים בסיכי זיירי ומזורי דכיון דקפיד עלייהו מייחד להו מקום ה"נ מייחד להו מקום איתמר ר' חייא בר אבא אמר ר' יוחנן [ב] קורנס של זהבים שנינו רב שמן בר אבא אמר קורנס של בשמים שנינו מאן דאמר דבשמים כ"ש דזהבים מאן דאמר של זהבים אבל דבשמים קפיד עלייהו: ואת הכוש ואת הכרכר כו': [י] ת"ר פגה שטמנה בתבן וחררה שטמנה [א] בגחלים אם מגולה מקצתה מותר לטלטלה ואם לאו אסור לטלטלה ר"א בן תדאי אומר [ג] תוחבין בכוש או בכרכר והן מנערות מאליהם אמר רב נחמן הלכה כר"א בן תדאי למימרא דסבר רב נחמן [ו] טלטול מן הצד לא שמיה טלטול [ח] והאמר רב נחמן האי פוגלא מלמעל' למטה שרי ממטה למעלה אסיר הדר ביה רב נחמן מההיא: מחט של יד ליטול בה כו': שלח ליה רבא בריה דרבה לרב יוסף ילמדנו רבינו מחט שניטל חררה או עוקצה מהו א"ל תניתוה מחט של יד ליטול בה את הקוץ וכי מה איכפת ליה לקוץ בין נקובה לבין שאינה נקובה איתיביה [י] מחט שניטל חררה או עוקצה טהורה אמר אביי טומאה אשבת קרמית [י] טומאה כלי מעשה בעינן לענין שבת מידי דחזי בעינן והא נמי חזיא למשקלא בה קוץ אמר רבא מאן דקמותיב שפיר קמותיב [ס] מדלענין טומאה לאו מנא הוא לענין שבת נמי לאו מנא הוא מיתיבי [ל] [ד] מחט בין נקובה בין שאינה נקובה מותר לטלטלה בשבת ולא אמרו נקובה אלא לענין טומאה בלבד [מ] תרגמא אביי אליבא דרבא בגולמי עסקינן זימנין דמימלך עלייהו ומשוי להו מנא [ה] אבל היכא דניטל חררה או עוקצה אדם זורקה לבין גרוטאות [י] אסובי ינוקא רב נחמן [פ] אסיר ורב ששת [י] שרי אמר רב נחמן מנא אמינא לה דתנן [ע] אין עושין אפיקטויזין

רש"י

דבר שמלאכתו לאיסור. אם צריך בשבת לגופו (ג) של מלאכה אחרת של היתר מותר: מדוכה. שדוכין בה שום: אם יש בה שום מטלטלין אותה. אגב השום: ואם לאו אין מטלטלין. כגון לישב עליה כיון דעיקר מלאכתו לשחיקה דהיא מלאכת איסור משום טוחן: תשמישו. תשמיש המיוחד לו: ושוין. ב"ש וב"ה שנחלקו בנוטלין את העלי לקצב עליו בשר ביו"ט: שאם קצב עליו בשר. שעשה לצורך שמחת יו"ט: שאסור לטלטלו. דהאי דקשרו ב"ה משום שמחת יו"ט קשרו אלמא משום דעלי מלאכתו לאיסור לכתישת טרגים וטיסני וקליפת עלים לעבד בהן עורות אסור: הכל מודים. רבנן דאיפלגו אדר' נחמיה: בסיכי זיירי ומזורי. כלי צבעין הן ורבינו הלוי פירש כלי אורגין סיכי הן עמודין זיארי הן קנים שבשתי ומזורי כובד עליון ותחתון ולאשון נראה לי דזייארי לשון עוצרים הן כמו מעצרתא זיירא (ע"ז דף ס.): דקפיד עלייהו. האומן שלא יתלכלכו ושלא יתעקמו: מייחד להם מקום. מקלה להן בידים: הני נמי. [ס] עלי ומדוכה: קורנס של זהבים. אע"פ דקפיד עליה קצת שצריך שיהא חלק לרדד טסין אפ"ה כיון שמתקן על ידי הכאה שמכה על הסדן לא מקפי ליה וכ"ש של שאר נפחים כרבה: בשמים. לשחוק בו: קפיד עליה. שלא ימאס: פגה. תאנה שלא בשלה כל צרכה וטומנין בתבן להתבשל ותבן מוקצה הוי לטיט: אם מגולה מקצתה. שיכול לאוחזה במקום המגולה דאפי' טלטול מן הצד ליכא שאין צריך להגביה התבן אלא מגביה מקום המגולה והתבן נשמט ונופל: פוגלא. צנון תלוש שהטמינו בארץ ונתגלה ראשו: מלמעלה למטה שרי. אם היה העליון שלה למעלה והקצר למטה וכשהוא שולפה תולשה מעליון שלה לתחתון שלה ורוחב הצנון למעלה מותר דליכא טלטול לעפר כלל שהרי נתגלה ראשו: ממטה למעלה אסור. שמזיז עפר לפי שהגומא קצרה מלמעלה ורוחב הצנון מלמטה ואע"ג דטלטול עפר מן הצד הוא שאינו אוחזו ממש בידו: חררה. חור שלה: עוקצה. פויינט"א: מהו. לטלטלה מי בטל תורת כלי מינה או לא: כלי מעשה. שמעשה שלו קיים: ולא אמרו נקובה. להיות תורת כלי עליה יותר משאין נקובה אלא לענין טומאה וקס"ד דבנטל חור שלה קאמר דלענין טומאה בטל שם כלי מינה ולטלטול שרי: בגולמי. גולמי מחטין העשויות לינקב דנקובה נגמרה מלאכתה ושאינה נקובה אינה נגמרה הלכך לענין טומאה הוא דלא הוי כלי אבל בטלטול שריא דחזי לקוץ: דמימליך. ולא נקיב לה: ומשוי לה מנא. כמות שהיא ולנטילת קוץ: גרוטאות. שברי מתכות אדם זורק: לבין גרוטאות ובטל שם כלי מינה: אסובי ינוקא. להחליק סדר אבריו כשהוא נולד אבריו מתפרקין וצריך ליישבן: אסיר. דדמי למתקן:

תוספות

בסיכי זיירי ומזורי. פי' בערוך [פ] פי' סיכי הם יתדות המוכנין לנפץ בהן משי וכיוצא בה תרגום יתדות סיכי זיירי כלי עץ כמו קרשים שכובשין בהן בגדים דתנן (לקמן דף קמא.) מכבש של בעלי בתים מזורי כלי עץ שהכובס מכה בו הבגדים על האבן שמלבנו ואלו כלים מקפיד עליהם שלא יתעקמו ולא יתפגמו שלא יתקלקלו הבגדים והמשי ומסיח דעתו מלטלטלן וכן מפרש בירושלמי זיירי דין עכר ביה מזורא דין חביט ביה ולפי' הקונט' דמפרש מזורי כובד עליון וכובד תחתון נ"ל דסבירא ליה כמאן דאסר בפרק אלו קשרים (לעיל דף קיג.): הא נמי מייחד לה מקום. מ"מ משום שמחת יו"ט מותר לטלטלו לקצב עליו בשר: [ל] הדר ביה רב נחמן מההיא. מסתברא דמההיא הדר ביה מדאמר בפרק תולין (לקמן דף קמא.) אמרי בי רב תניא דלא כרב נחמן: פגה שהטמינה כו'. [ס] מיירי שהניחה שם ע"מ ליטלה אבל אם הניחה שם לכל השבת הוי בסיס לדבר האסור כדאמר לקמן בפרק נוטל (ד' קמב:) גבי אבן שעל פי החבית לא שנו אלא בשוכח אבל במניח נעשה בסיס לדבר האסור: האי פוגלא. וא"ת האי פוגלא היכי דמי אי במניח מ"ט דמאן דשרי מלמטה למעלה הא אפילו ניעור לא שרי כ"ש טלטול מן הצד ואי בשכח מ"ט דמאן דאסר אפי' טלטול גמור שרי לצורך לטלטל אגב היתר לקמן בפרק נוטל (קמא. וד' קמב:) במעות שעל גבי הכר בצריך למקומו דמטלטלו בעודן עליו ואבן שעל פי החבית כשהוא בין החביות מגביה ומטה כ"ש טלטול מן הצד וי"ל דמניח על מנת ליטלה איירי אע"ג דכשכח דמי כמו טמן וכיסה בדבר שאינו ניטל בסוף במה טומנין (לעיל דף נא.) דשרי לנער משום דלאו מניח לכל השבת ובעלמות וקליפין דריש ביצה (ד' ב.) דשרי ב"ה לסלק את הטבלא ולנער מ"מ לא היה לו להניח באותו ענין שיצטרך טלטול מן הצד ועצמות וקליפין לא מסתייה דלא לינח בהן על גבי השלחן וטמן וכיסה דפרק במה טומנין (לעיל ד' נא.) אין לחוש כיון דאפשר בניעור דאפילו טלטול מן הצד ליכא [ל]: מדלענין טומאה לאו מנא לענין שבת נמי לאו מנא. תימה הא תנן לקמן [ת] כל הכלים הניטלין שבריהן ניטלין אע"ג דלענין טומאה לא הוי מנא כשנשבר אלא על ידי ייחוד לפי' הקונטרס דסוף המצניע (לעיל דף צה:) י"ל דה"פ מלדענין טומאה [ס] לאו מנא אפי' על ידי ייחוד דכיון דניטל חררה או עוקצה לא מהני ביה ייחוד לענין שבת נמי לאו מנא היא אבל היכא דהוה מנא לענין טומאה ע"י ייחוד איכא למימר דהוי מנא לענין שבת אפי' בלא ייחוד כיון דיכול להיות כלי לענין טומאה וכן משמע בסמוך דמתרגמא אביי אליבא דרבא בגולמי דזימנין דמימלך עלייהו ומשוי להו מנא משמע דלהכי מותר לטלטל אע"ג דטהורה היא דלאכתי לא מימלך עלה כיון דיכול להיות כלי [פ]: אסובי ינוקא. לאו היינו לפופי ינוקא דשרי בפרק במה אשה (לעיל דף סו:) ולקמן בסוף חבית (דף קמז:) דהיינו שכורכין אותו בבגדים וקושרים בחגורה רחבה וכן פירש בקונטרס בסוף מפנין [פ] כי היכי דלא תקשי דרב נחמן אדרב נחמן דשרי התם לפופי והכא אסר אסובי והא דתנן בפ' חבית (שם) אין מעצבין את הקטן פריך לה התם אהשתא לפופי ומוקי לה בחומרי שדרה דמיחזי כבונה וקשה דמייתי לה מאן עושין אפיקטויזין שהוא תיקוני גברא לכדפירש בקונטרס הוה ליה לאתויי מסיפא דאין מעצבין את הקטן דהוי נמי תקוני ינוקא ודמי טפי שהכל בקטן מענין אסובי ופירש רבינו תם דהכי נמי מייתי ונקט רישא [ס] אין עושין אפיקטויזין כו' עד אין מעצבין: וסכינא

עין משפט נר מצוה

ו א טוש"ע או"ח סימן תלג סעיף ה:

ז ב מיי' פכ"ה מהלכות שבת הלכה ז סמג לאוין סה טוש"ע או"ח סימן שח סעיף ג [ועי' בב"י]:

ח ג מיי' שם הלכה טו סמג שם טוש"ע או"ח סימן שיא סעיף ט:

ט ד ה מיי' שם הלכה יב סמג שם טוש"ע או"ח סימן שח סעיף יא:

י ו מיי' פ"ג מהלכות שבת הלכה [ועי' פכ"א מהלכות] טור שו"ע או"ח סימן שלג סעיף ט:

רבינו חננאל

לתבשיל וכדומה לו. ולא מצא רב יהודה פירוקי והעמיד רבה משנתנו בקורנס של נפחים וה"ה לכל קורנס. ושמעינן מינה דכל דבר שמלאכתו אפי' לאיסור כגון מלאכת הקורנס של נפחים שהן עושי מלאכה כלי נחשת וברזל. ומלאכתם [זו] שהוכנו לכך אסורה בשבת. אם הוצרכו (לומר) [לדבר] שהוא מותר בשבת. כגון פיצוע האגוזים שהן הכנת מאכל ואינה מלאכה מותר. ואקשינן עליה והא מדוכה אם יש בה שום מטלטלין [אותה] ואם לאו אין מטלטלין אותה. דכיון שמלאכתה לאיסור היא אפי' לצורך גופה אין מטלטלין אותה. ופריק ליה מני מתניתא ר' נחמיה היא דאמר אין כלי ניטל אלא לצורך תשמישו. פי' מצאנו ר' נחמיה שאמר בפי' אפי' טלית [תרווד] אין ניטלין אלא לצורך והיא טלית ללבישה. ותרווד לאכל בו ומתני' דקתני נוטל אדם קורנס לפצע בו [וקרדום] (ומדוכה) דלא כר' נחמיה. ותוב אקשי' עליה ושוין שאם קצב עליו בשר ופשוטה היא. ומוקמינן להני מתניתא דרבי הכל ואפילו לרבנן ומודו רבנן במדוכה ובעלי דכיון דקפיד עליה מכין עליה מקום וגמר בדעתו שלא לטלטלן מאותו מקום. לפיכך אסור לטלטלן מן המקום המוכן להם. ודין אלו כדין סיכי זיירי ומזורי. פי' סיכי הן יתדות המוכנין לנער בהן משי וכדומה לו. והן תרגום של יתדות סיכי. זיירי. כלי עץ כגון קרשים שכובשין בהן הבגדים. כדתנן מכבש של בעלי בתים. מזורי כלי עץ שהכובס מכה בו הבגדים על אבן בעת שמלבנן. ואלו כולן קפיד עליהן שלא יתעוותו או יפגמו. שאם יפגמו לא יקרעו הבגדים והמשי. לפיכך מסיח דעתו מטלטלן ונעשו מוקצים ועל כן אסור לטלטלן. וכך זה מפורשין בתלמוד א"י. בזייר די [במכונא] עצר ביה. במזורה. די חבוט ביה (בכיבאגא) די כתיש ביה. ונתחברו דברי משנתנו כי כל הקורנס מותר לפצוע בו אגוזין ואפי' קורנס של זהבים. ובקורנס של בשמים חלקו בו ר' חייא בר אבין ורב שמן בר אבא משמיה דרבי יוחנן. ר' חייא אוסר. ורב שמן מתיר. ומסתברא כר' חייא דאי דכיון דקפיד עליה דלא ליפגם

מסורת הש"ס

א) [לקמן קכד. תוספתא פי"ד], ב) [לעיל לו. ב"ב], ג) רש"י מ"ו, ד) ביצה יא., ה) [לקמן קכד. ביצה יא.], ו) עירובין עז, ז) [לעיל מג. [לקמן קמא.], ח) שם, ט) לעיל נב: כלים פי"ג מ"ה, י) [לעיל דף ס.], כ) [לעיל קיג. ל) לקמן נב: [תוספ' דכלים ב"מ פ"ב], מ) [לעיל נב: וש"נ], נ) [בערוך פירש כשנפלה שלא הגרון של תינוק משימה המיה אלבעה בפיו ומסלקת אותה הערלה ועפמי' משקה המיתוק ע"כ הקשה לו והא אין עושין אפיקטויזין ע"כ ועיין בהרא"ש מ"ש שם על הגליון], ס) ל"ל אוסר, ע) לקמן קמז., פ) [ערך זיירי], צ) שייך לקמן קודם ד"ה מדלענין, ק) [ועי' תוס' לעיל דף נה. ד"ה או שטמן], ר) דף קכד:, ש) [וע"ע תוס' חולין דף נה. ד"ה סיעוך], ת) [דף קכד:].

הגהות הב"ח

(א) גמ' וחררה שטמנה. נ"ב לשון רש"י בעירובין דף עז ופגה וחררה שהטמינה לאפות בגחלים ועכשיו כבו ומכ"מ מוקצין הן אבל לא כבו לא דמתוק שנכספי' מכבה את המתמוטות ומבעיר את העליונות דלאמרינן בכירמות: (ב) רש"י ד"ה דבר שמלאכתו וכו' לגופו של מלאכה וכו' ומיבת של נמחק:

גליון הש"ס

רש"י ד"ה הני נמי עלי ומדוכה. ע"ל פא ע"א ברש"י ד"ה מדוכה קטנה: תוס' ד"ה פגה שהטמינה וכו' מיירי שהניחה. עיין לעיל דף נא ע"א תוס' ד"ה או שטמן: תוס' ד"ה מדלענין וכו' לאו מנא אפי' ע"י יחוד. עי' לעיל דף מט ע"ב תוס' ד"ה לא אמרו: תוס' ד"ה אסובי ינוקא כו' אין עושין אפיקטויזין. וכה כתבו תוס' בשם ר"ת שבועות דף יט ע"ב ד"ה לאמר. ושם פ"א ע"ב ד"ה ומאן דמני. ובגיטין דף פ ע"ב ד"ה ז דברי ר"מ. ובנזיר דף נד ע"ב ד"ה למדני. ובכרכות דף מה ע"א תוס' ד"ה ג' שאכלו אינן רשאין לחלק. ובמעילה דף יג ע"ב תוס' ד"ה אלה המוקדשים: בעין משפט אות ו' מיי' פכ"א מהלכות שבת. לא נמצא שם מזה. וע"ש בהלכה ל"א ובהה"מ:

רב נסים גאון

הכל מודין בסיכי זיארי ומזורי. בגמרא דבני מערבא גרסי זיירא דו עצר בה מזורי דו חבט בה כו סיכי הן יתידות וגלוי הוא הדבר וידוע לכל:

ליקוטי רש"י

[נדפס בדף קכב:]

כזירי דמי. ותוב להוא אשכחן דהוה תדיר קמי ר' יוחנן דהוה גריס ודייק. והוה מהדר תלמודיה עליה כל תלתין יומין: ת"ר פגה שטמנה בתבן וחררה שטמנה בגחלים אם מגולה מקצתה מותר לטלטלה ואם לאו אסור. אלעזר בן תדאי [אומר] תוחבן בכוש או בכרכר והן ננערות מאליהן. פי' מכתבינן התאנה חנטה פגה והן פירות שלא נתבשלו באילן וטמנן בתבן להתבשל בחמות התבן להוכשר לאכילה. וחררה ע"ג גחלים והן ליאפות מבעו"י ובא בשבת לנוטלן ת"ק סבר אסור להסיר הגחלים או התבן מעליהן ולטלן. אלא אם מקצתן מגולין אוחז בידו המקום המגולה ושומטן ואין בהם מקום מגולה בחררה בלא גחלים. ובפגה בלא תבן אסור לטלטל. ואלעזר בן תדאי סבר אע"פ שאין בהן מקום מגולה תוחבו בכוש או בכרכר. פי' נועץ בהן כוש והוא דתנן כוש שבלע את הציגורא או כרכר שהוא וכו'. ומגביהן ונופלין התבן או הגחלים מאליהן ואח"כ נוטלן בידו שלא נמצא טלטול הגחלים והתבן דרכו אלא מן הצד. ואמר רב נחמן הלכה כאלעזר בן תדאי. ומקשינן וכי רב נחמן סבר דטלטול מן הצד לאו שמיה טלטול. והא רב נחמן בפרק ש"ע הקש שע"ג המטה לא ינענעו בידו כו'. אמר רב נחמן האי פוגלא מלמעלן למטה שרי. ממטה

Rav Yosef's opinion is challenged:
אֵיתִיבֵיהּ – [Rava the son of Rabbah] challenged [Rav Yosef] on the basis of the following Mishnah:[19] מַחַט שֶׁנִּיטַל חֲרָרָהּ אוֹ עוּקְצָהּ טְהוֹרָה – A NEEDLE WHOSE EYE OR POINT HAS BEEN REMOVED IS *TAHOR,* i.e. is not susceptible to *tumah,* because it is not classified as a utensil.[20] Thus, we see that the removal of a needle's eye nullifies its status as a utensil. – ? –

The challenge is rebuffed:
אָמַר אַבַּיֵי – Abaye said: טוּמְאָה אַשַּׁבָּת קָרְמִית – **Do you** attempt to **contrast** the laws of ***tumah*** **with** the laws of **the Sabbath?** This is not a valid comparison for these laws are subject to different criteria. טוּמְאָה כְּלִי מַעֲשֶׂה בְּעִינַן – For an item to be susceptible to ***tumah,*** **we require** that it be ***a fashioned vessel,*** and once the eye or point of a needle is removed it does not fit into this category.[21] לְעִנְיַן שַׁבָּת מִידֵי דַּחֲזֵי בְּעִינַן – **Concerning the matter of the Sabbath,** however, for classification as non-*muktzeh* **we require** only **something that is fit** for use;[22] וְהָא נַמִּי חַזְיָא לְמִשְׁקְלָא בָּהּ קוֹץ – **and this** needle whose eye was removed **is also fit for** use in **the removal of a splinter.**

The Gemara cites a dissent to Abaye's rebuttal:
אָמַר רָבָא – Rava said: מַאן דְּקָמוֹתִיב שַׁפִּיר קָמוֹתִיב – **The one who challenged** Rav Yosef on the basis of the law of *tumah* **challenged** him **properly.** מִדִּלְעִנְיַן טוּמְאָה לָאו מָנָא הוּא – **Since concerning the matter of *tumah* [the needle whose eye was removed] is not** considered **a utensil,** לְעִנְיַן שַׁבָּת נַמִּי לָאו מָנָא הוּא – **so too, concerning the matter of the Sabbath it is not** considered **a utensil.**

Rava's opinion is challenged:
מֵיתִיבֵי – They challenged Rava on the basis of the following Baraisa: מַחַט בֵּין נְקוּבָה בֵּין שֶׁאֵינָהּ נְקוּבָה – WHETHER A NEEDLE IS PIERCED (i.e. it has an eye) OR IT IS NOT PIERCED, מוּתָּר לְטַלְטְלָהּ בְּשַׁבָּת – IT MAY BE MOVED ON THE SABBATH; וְלֹא אָמְרוּ נְקוּבָה אֶלָּא לְעִנְיַן טוּמְאָה בִּלְבַד – AND THEY SAID that being PIERCED makes a difference in the needle's classification ONLY CONCERNING THE MATTER OF *TUMAH.* Thus, we see that when a needle's eye is removed it retains its classification as a utensil in regard to *muktzeh* even though it is no longer considered a utensil in regard to *tumah.* – ? –

The challenge is rebuffed:
תַּרְגְּמָא אַבַּיֵי אַלִּיבָּא דְּרָבָא – **Abaye explained [the Baraisa] according to** the opinion **of Rava,** as follows: בְּגוֹלְמֵי עַסְקִינַן – In the Baraisa, **we are dealing with unfinished [needles].** Although these are not yet considered utensils in regard to *tumah* they are deemed non-*muktzeh,* זִימְנִין דְּמִימְלַךְ עֲלַיְיהוּ וּמְשַׁוֵּי לְהוּ מָנָא – because **sometimes one reconsiders** his plans **for them and** instead of piercing them he **designates them** in their current form **as a tool** for removing splinters.[23] אֲבָל הֵיכָא דְּנִיטַל חֲרָרָהּ אוֹ עוּקְצָהּ – **However, where** there was a finished needle and **its eye or point was removed,** אָדָם זוֹרְקָהּ לְבֵין גְּרוּטָאוֹת – **a person discards it among** his **metal scraps.** Therefore, it loses its designation as a utensil and becomes *muktzeh.*[24]

The Gemara digresses to an unrelated discussion in which one of the disputants cites our Mishnah in support of his opinion:
אַסּוּבֵי יְנוּקָא – **Straightening out** the limbs of **an infant** on the Sabbath – רַב נַחְמָן אָסִיר – **Rav Nachman forbids** it וְרַב שֵׁשֶׁת שָׁרֵי – **but Rav Sheishess permits** it.[25]

Rav Nachman cites a source for his opinion:
אָמַר רַב נַחְמָן – Rav Nachman said: מְנָא אֲמִינָא לָהּ – **From where do I** learn to **say this?** דִּתְנַן – **For we learned in a Mishnah:**[26] אֵין עוֹשִׂין

NOTES

19. *Keilim* 13:5.

20. Since it is no longer fit for its previous use, it is not considered a utensil and is thus not susceptible to *tumah.* Even if it was actually *tamei* before the breakage, it is now *tahor* (see *Keilim* 11:1).

21. In describing the golden vessels that were plundered in the Midianite war – and which were contaminated with corpse *tumah* – the Torah states (*Numbers* 31:51): כֹּל כְּלִי מַעֲשֶׂה, *every fashioned vessel* (see *Rashi* to 52b ד״ה בגולמי; see also above, 63b-64a). We learn from this that only a vessel that was fashioned for a specific use and still functions in that capacity is susceptible to *tumah* (see *Rashi*).

22. There is no requirement that a utensil be "fashioned" in order that it be deemed non-*muktzeh.* Even an ordinary stone that was designated for a common use before the Sabbath is not *muktzeh* (see *Orach Chaim* 308:22). [It follows that a utensil which no longer functions as it did before remains classified as non-*muktzeh,* if it can still be used in some other permitted capacity.]

23. With respect to *tumah,* the law is that only an item whose fashioning has been completed is considered a utensil. Since a needle that has not yet been pierced is in an unfinished state, it is not susceptible to *tumah.* With respect to the Sabbath, however, as long as something stands to be used in its current state it is deemed a utensil in the regard that it is not *muktzeh.* An unpierced needle may well be designated in its current state for the removal of splinters, and therefore, it may be moved on the Sabbath even if this designation has not been made (*Rashi, Tosafos* ד״ה מדלענין).

24. In this respect, there is no basis for differentiating between the laws of *tumah* and those of the Sabbath. Although the broken needle is still fit for use in the removal of a splinter, people generally do not save it for that purpose, but discard it immediately (*Ritva MHK* ed.). It is concerning this situation that Rava stated that since it is no longer considered a utensil in regard to *tumah* (i.e. it has lost its practical usefulness) it is also not considered a utensil in regard to the Sabbath. See *Tosafos* ד״ה מדלענין with *Maharsha* for further elaboration of Rava's opinion. See also 125a note 26.

25. The discussion pertains to an infant whose limbs were dislocated during birth and need straightening (i.e. repositioning). Rav Nachman forbids doing this on the Sabbath because "repairing" a human being is similar to repairing a utensil, which is prohibited Biblically. [It is a *toladah* of the *melachah* of striking the final blow.] Rav Sheishess, however, holds that there is no prohibition against "repairing" a human being when no medicinal remedy is employed. [Medical remedies are forbidden in non-critical situations by Rabbinical decree, lest one grind herbs to make medicine] (*Rashi* here and to 123b; cf. *Rabbeinu Chananel* et al.; see also *Rambam, Hil. Shabbos* 21:31 with *Maggid Mishneh*). [Obviously, the discussion pertains to a case where there is no critical need to straighten out the limbs immediately. Otherwise, all would agree that it is permitted.]

26. Below, 147a.

דבר שמלאכתו לאיסור לצורך גופו מותר איתיביה אביי לרבה מדוכה אם יש בה שום מטלטלין אותה ואם לאו אין מטלטלין אותה א"ל הא מני ר' נחמיה היא דאמר אין כלי ניטל אלא לצורך תשמישו איתיביה ב"ש אומרים אין נוטלין את העלי לקצב עליו בשר וב"ה מתירין ושוין שאם קצב עליו בשר שאסור לטלטלו סבר לשנויי ליה כר' נחמיה כיון דשמעה להא דאמר רב חיננא בר שלמיא משמיה דרב הכל מודים בסיכי זיירי ומזורי דכיון דקפיד עלייהו מייחד להו מקום ה"נ מייחד להו מקום איתמר ר' חייא בר אבא אמר ר' יוחנן קורנס של זהבים שנינו רב שמן בר אבא אמר קורנס של בשמים שנינו מאן דאמר דבשמים כ"ש דזהבים מאן דאמר של זהבים אבל דבשמים קפיד עלייהו: ואת הכוש ואת הכרכר כו': ת"ר פגה שטמנה בתבן וחררה שטמנה בגחלים אם מגולה מקצתה מותר לטלטלה ואם לאו אסור לטלטלה ר"א בן תדאי אומר תוחבין בכוש או בכרכר והן מנערות מאליהם אמר רב נחמן הלכה כר"א בן תדאי למימרא דסבר רב נחמן טלטול מן הצד לא שמיה טלטול והאמר רב נחמן האי פוגלא מלמעל' למטה שרי ממטה למעלה אסיר הדר ביה רב נחמן מההיא: מחט של יד ליטול בה כו': שלח ליה רבא בריה דרבה לרב יוסף ילמדנו רבינו מחט שניטל חררה או עוקצה מהו א"ל תניתוה מחט של יד ליטול בה את הקוץ וכי מה איכפת ליה לקוץ בין נקובה לבין שאינה נקובה איתיביה מחט שניטל חררה או עוקצה טהורה אמר אביי טומאה אשבת קרמית טומאה כלי מעשה בעינן לענין שבת מידי דחזי בעינן והא נמי חזיא למשקלא בה קוץ אמר רבא מאן דקמותיב שפיר קמותיב מדלענין טומאה לאו מנא הוא לענין שבת נמי לאו מנא הוא מיתיבי מחט בין נקובה בין שאינה נקובה מותר לטלטלה בשבת ולא אמרו נקובה אלא לענין טומאה בלבד תרגמא אביי אליבא דרבא בגולמי עסקינן זימנין דמימלך עלייהו ומשוי להו מנא אבל היכא דניטל חררה או עוקצה אדם זורקה לבין גרוטאות אסובי ינוקא רב נחמן אסיר ורב ששת שרי אמר רב נחמן מנא אמינא לה דתנן אין עושין אפיקטוויזין

רש"י

דבר שמלאכתו לאיסור. אם צריך בשבת לגופו (ג) של מלאכה אחרת של היתר מותר: מדוכה. שדוכין בה שום: אם יש בה שום מטלטלין אותה. אגב השום: ואם לאו אין מטלטלין. כגון לישב עליה כיון דעיקר מלאכתו לשחיקה דהיא מלאכת איסור משום טוחן: תשמישו. תשמיש המיוחד לו: ושוין. ב"ש וב"ה שנחלקו בנוטלין את העלי לקצב עליו בשר ביו"ט: שאם קצב עליו בשר. שעשה לצורך שמחת יו"ט: שאסור לטלטלו. דהאי דקשרו ב"ה משום שמחת יו"ט קשרו אלמא משום דעלי מלאכתו לאיסור לכתישת טרגיס וטיסני וקליפת עלים לעבד בהן עורות אסור: הכל מודים. רבנן דאיפלגו אדר' נחמיה: בסיכי זיירי ומזורי. כלי לבעין הן ורבינו הלוי פירש כלי אורגין סיכי הן עמודין זיזארי הן קנים שבשתי ומזורי כובד עליון ותחתון ולשון נראה לי דזיארי לשון עוצרים הן כמו מעצרתא זיירא (ע"ז דף ס.): דקפיד עלייהו. האומן שלא יתקלקלו ושלא יתעקמו: מייחד להם מקום. מקצה להן בידים: הני נמי. עלי ומדוכה: קורנס של זהבים. אע"פ דקפיד עליה קצת שצריך שיהא חלק לרדד טסין אפ"ה כיון שמתקן על ידי הכאה שמכה על הסדן לא מקפי ליה וכ"ש של שאר נפחים כרכה: בשמים. לשחוק בו: קפיד עליה. שלא יזהם: פגה. תאנה שלא בשלה כל צרכה וטומנין בתבן להתבשל ותבן מוקצה הוי לטיט: אם מגולה מקצתה. שיכול לאוחזה במקום המגולה דאפי' טלטול מן הצד ליכא שאין צריך להגביה התבן אלא מגביה מקום המגולה והתבן נשמט ונופל: פוגלא. צנון תלוש שהטמינו בארץ ונתגלה ראשו: מלמעלה למטה שרי. אם היה העליון שלה למעלה והקצר למטה וכשהוא שולפה אוצלה מעליון שלה לתחתון שלה ורוחב הצנון למעלה מותר דליכא טלטול לעפר כלל שהרי נתגלה ראשו: ממטה למעלה אסור. שמזיז עפר לפי שהגומא קצרה מלמעלה ורוחב הצנון מלמטה ואע"ג דטלטול עפר מן הצד הוא שאינו אוחזו ממש בידו: חררה. חור שלה: עוקצה. פויינט"א: מהו. לטלטלה מי בטל תורת כלי מינה או לא: כלי מעשה. שמעשה שלו קיים: ולא אמרו נקובה. להיות תורת כלי עליה יותר משאין נקובה אלא לענין טומאה וקס"ד דבנטל חור שלה קאמר לענין טומאה בטל שם כלי מינה ולטלטול שרי: בגולמי. גולמי מחטין העומדות לינקב דנקובה נגמרה מלאכתה ושאינה נקובה אינה נגמרה מלאכתה הלכך לענין טומאה הוא דלא הוי כלי אבל בטלטול שריא דחזי לקוץ: דמימליך. ולא נקיב לה: ומשוי לה מנא. כמות שהיא ולנטילת קוץ: גרוטאות. שברי מתכות אדם זורקה לבין גרוטאות ובטל שם כלי מינה: אסובי ינוקא. להחליק סדר אבריו כשהוא נולד אבריו מתפרקין וצריך ליישבן: אסיר. דדמי למתקן: אפיקטוויזין

תוספות

בסיכי זיירי ומזורי. פי' בערוך פי' סיכי הם יתדות המוכנין לנפץ בהן משי וכיוצא בה תרגום יתדות סיכי זיירי כלי עץ כמו קרקס שכובשין בהן בגדים דתנן (לקמן דף קמא.) מכבש של בעלי בתים מזורי כלי עץ שהכובס מכה בו הבגדים על האבן שמלבנו ואלו כלים מקפיד עליהם שלא יתעקמו ולא יתפגמו שלא יתקלקלו הבגדים והמשי ומסיח דעתו מלטלטלן וכן מפרש בירושלמי זיירי דין עצר ביה מזורה דין מבטש ביה ולפי' הקונט' דמפרש מזורי כובד עליון וכובד תחתון נ"ל דסבירא ליה כמאן דאסר בפרק אלו קשרים (לעיל דף קיג.): הא נמי מייחד לה מקום. מ"מ משום שמחת יו"ט מותר לטלטלו לקצב עליו בשר: הדר ביה רב נחמן מההיא. מסתברא דמההיא הדר ביה מדאמר בפרק תולין (לקמן דף קמא.) אמרי בי רב תניא דלא כרב נחמן: פגה שהטמינה כו'. מיירי שהניחה שם מע"ש ליטלה אבל אם הניחה שם לכל השבת הוי בסיס לדבר האסור כדאמר לקמן בפרק נוטל (ד' קמב:) גבי אבן שעל פי החבית לא שנו אלא בשוכח אבל במניח נעשה בסיס לדבר האסור: האי פוגלא. וא"ת האי פוגלא היכי דמי אי במניח מ"ט דמאן דשרי מלמטה למעלה הא אפילו ניעור לא שרי כ"ש טלטול מן הצד ואי בשכח מ"ט דמאן דאסר אפי' טלטול גמור שרי לצורך לטלטל אגב היתר לקמן בפרק נוטל (קמא. וד' קמב:) במעות שעל גבי הכר שצריך למקומו דמטלטלו בעודן עליו ואבן שעל פי החבית כשהוא בין החביות מגביה ומטה כ"ש טלטול מן הצד וי"ל דמניח על מנת ליטלה איירי אע"ג דכשכח דמי כמו טמן וכיסה בדבר שאינו ניטל בסוף במה טומנין (לעיל דף נא.) דשרי לנער משום דאין מניח לכל השבת ובעצמות וקליפין דריש ביצה (ד' ב.) דשרי ב"ה לסלק את הטבלא ולנער מ"מ לא היה לו להניח באותו ענין שיצטרך טלטול מן הצד ועצמות וקליפין לא מסתייה דלא לינח בהן על גבי השלחן וטמן וכיסה דפרק במה טומנין (לעיל ד' נא.) אין לחוש כיון דאפשר בניעור דאפילו טלטול מן הצד אינו: מדלענין טומאה לאו מנא לענין שבת נמי לאו מנא. תימה הא תנן לקמן כל הכלים הניטלין שבריהן ניטלין אע"ג דלענין טומאה לא הוי מנא כשנשבר אלא על ידי ייחוד לפי' הקונטרס דסוף המצניע (לעיל דף צה:) וי"ל דה"פ מדלענין טומאה לאו מנא אפי' על ידי ייחוד כיון דניטל חררה או עוקצה לא מהני ביה ייחוד לענין שבת נמי לאו מנא היא אבל היכא דהוי מנא לענין טומאה ע"י ייחוד איכא למימר דהוי מנא לענין שבת אפי' בלא ייחוד כיון דיכול להיות כלי לענין טומאה וכן משמע בסמוך דקתרגמא אביי אליבא דרבא בגולמי דזימנין דמימלך עלייהו ומשוי להו מנא משמע דלהכי מותר לטלטל אע"ג דטהורה היא דלהכי לא מימלך עלה כיון שראוי לייחדה להיות כלי: אסובי ינוקא. לאו היינו לפופי ינוקא דשרי בפרק במה אשה (לעיל דף סו:) ולקמן בסוף חבית (דף קמז:) דהיינו שכורכין אותו בבגדים וקושרים במגוה רפאה וכן פירש בקונטרס בסוף מפנין כי היכי דלא הוי מילתא לפופי והכא אסר אסובי והא דקתני בפ' חבית (שם) אין מעצבין את הקטן פריך לה התם אההיא דלפופי ומוקי לה בחומרי שדרה למיזחי כוונה וקשה דמייתי לה מאין עושין אפיקטוויזין שהוא תיקוני גברא דלפירש בקונטרס הוה ליה לאתויי מסיפא דאין מעצבין את הקטן דהוי נמי תקוני ינוקא ודמי טפי שהכל בקטן מעניין אסובי ופירש רבינו תם דהכי נמי מייתי ונקט רישא * אין עושין אפיקטוויזין כו' אין מעצבין: וסכינה

עין משפט נר מצוה

ו א טוש"ע או"ח סימן תלט סעיף ה:

ז ב מיי' פכ"ה מהלכות שבת הלכה ז סמג לאוין סה טוש"ע או"ח סימן שח סעיף ג [וער' בב"י]:

ח ג מיי' שם הלכה יג סמג שם טוש"ע או"ח סימן שיא סעיף ט:

ט ד ה מיי' שם הלכה ח סמג שם טוש"ע או"ח סימן שח סעיף יא:

י ו מיי' פ"ב מהלכות שבת הלכה יד ופכ"א הלכה לב טור שו"ע או"ח סימן של סעיף ט:

רבינו חננאל

לתבשיל וכדומה לו. ולא מצא רב יהודה פירוקי והעמיד רבה משנתנו בקורנס של נפחים וה"ה לכל קורנס. ושמעינן מינה דכל דבר שמלאכתו אפי' לאיסור כגון מלאכת הקורנס של נפחים שהן עושי מלאכת כלי נחשת וברזל. ומלאכתם [זו] שהוכנו לכך אסורה בשבת. אם הוצרכו (לומר) [לדבר] שהוא מותר בשבת. כגון פיצוע האגוזים שהן הכנת מאכל ואינה מלאכה מותר. ...

מסורת הש"ס

א) [לקמן קכז. תוספתא פי"ד], ב) [לעיל לו. וש"נ], ג) רש"ל מ"ז, ד) ביצה יא., ה) [לקמן קכז. ביצה יא.], ו) עירובין עז., ז) [לעיל מג: לקמן קמא.], ח) שם, ט) לעיל נב: כלים פי"ג מ"ה, י) [לעיל דף מ.], כ) [לעיל קיב.], ל) לעיל נב: [תוספ' דכלים ב"מ פ"ב], מ) [בערוך פירש כשנפלה ערלת הגרון של תינוק ...], נ) ל"ל אוסר, ס) לקמן קמז., ע) [ערך זיירי], פ) עיין לקמן קודם ד"ה מלטלטין, צ) [וער' תוס' לעיל דף נא. ד"ה אין טומנין], ק) דף קכד:, ר) [וע"ע תוס' חולין דף נה. ד"ה שיעורן], ש) [דף קכה:].

הגהות הב"ח

(א) גמ' וחררה שטמנה. נ"ב לשון רש"י בעירובין דף עז וחררה שהטמינה לאפות בגחלים ...

גליון הש"ס

רש"י ד"ה הני נמי עלי ומדוכה. ...

רב נסים גאון

הכל מודין בסיכי זיארי ומזורי. בגמרא דבני מערבא גרסי זיירה דו עצר בה מזורי דו חבט בה ...

ליקוטי רש"י

[נדפס בדף קכב:]

עין משפט נר מצוה

יא א מיי' פכ"ו מהל' שבת הלכה ז:
יב ב מיי' פ"א מהלכות כלים הלכה י:
יג ג מיי' שם פ"ב הל"ע:
יד ד ה מיי' פכ"ה מהל' שבת הלכה ט סמג לאוין סה טור ושו"ע או"ח סימן שח סעיף א:
טו ו מיי' שם הלכה ג טוש"ע שם סעיף ג ד:
טז ז מיי' פ"ה מהלכות תמידין ומוספין הלכה יא:
יז ח מיי' פ"א מהלכות ק"פ הלכה יד:

גליון הש"ס

תוס' ד"ה לא וכו' אשכחן במקדש. ע"ל דף קכו ע"א תוס' ד"ה והמונח:

רבינו חננאל

ממטן למעלן אסיר. פי' אם יש לאדם פוגלא טמונה בתבן או אפילו בעפר תיחוח עומדת כעין נטועה ראשה טמונה ועליה מגולין עכשיו כשבא לנוטלה אם אוחז בעלים ומושך הראש ומסלקה זהו ממעלה למטה. אע"פ כשמגביה התבן והעפר משתרבב במקומן ויורד שרי אבל לאחוז קצה הראש הטמונה ולהגביהה ממטה למעלה לא. אלמא שטלטול מן הצד שמיה טלטול. ומפרקינן הדר ביה מההיא. מחט שניטל חררה או עוקצה. פי' חרירה הנקב שלה. עוקצה ראשה הוא. חידודה תרגמה אביי אליבא דרבא בגלמי כלי הן פשוטין כדתנן גלמי כלי מתכות טהורין פשוטיהן טמאין ואלו הן וכו'. והן חוטי ברזל משוכין ותחתך אותן חתיכות חתיכות ולוקח מהן האומן כשיעור אורך מחט ומשוה ראשה האחת ונוקב הקצה השני ונעשה מחט. וקודם שיחדדנה וינקבנה נקראת אותה החתיכה גולם. כגון זו וכיוצא בה שהן עומדות להעשות כלי ניטלין בשבת. אבל מחט שניטל חררה או עוקצה אסור. גרוטאות הוא לשון יון. ופתרונו כלי מוכן להטיל בו התגר כלי נחושת או כלי ברזל שבורין שיזדמנו לו לקנותם קונה ומשליכם לאותו כלי כדי להתיכם. ונקראין גרוטאות ומיכן נהגו לקרות להתגר גרוטאות: אצובי יונקא. פי' כשנוטל ערלת הגרון של תינוק משימה החיה את אצבעותיה בפיו ומסלקת אותה הערלה. ופעמים שמקיא התינוק ועל זה אקשינן עלה והא אין עושין אפיקטויזין בשבת כו'. ורבותינו הגאונים אמרו פי' אחר. ואנו כתבנו מה שקבלנו מרבותינו: מתני' קנה של זיתים כו'. ואמרינן אמאי פשוטי כלי עץ הוא ואין מקבלין טומאה. ומפרקינן תנא משמיה דר' נחמיה בשעה שמהפך בו את הזיתים הופכו ורואה בו. ולא פי' מה הוא רואה בו. אבל פירשו בתלמוד א"י. קנה שהתקינו להיות בודק בו הזיתים. כיצד הוא יודע אם מלוכלך במשקה בידוע שנגמרה מלאכת המעטן. ואם לאו בידוע שלא נגמרה מלאכת המעטן. א"ל ר' מנא לא תני שמואל אלא להיות שולה בו הזיתים. ומשום כך יש בו בית קבול: אמר רב נחמן האי אוכלא דקצרי כיתד של מחרישה דמי. ואסור לטלטלו. אוכלא. אבן גדולה שנותן הכובס עליה היריעה שרוצה ללבנה והיא שרויה במים ומכה עליה במזורי. מכה ומהפך ומכה. ועוד שורה ומכה. ואחרי שילשים שוטחה ומניחה עליה. ועוד חוזר ושורה אותה פעם אחרת. ויש מי שפירש אוכלא דקצרי בדמות כלי שמנקבין אותו ומכבסין בו. אמר אביי חרבא דאושכפא וסכינא דאשכבתא וחצינא דנגרי כיתד של מחרישה דמו ואסור לטלטלם. חרבא דאושכפי. איזמל של שכף כדמתרגמינן עשה לך חרבות צורים. איזמלין חריפין. סכינא דאשכבתא. סכין המיוחדת לשחיטה בלבד. חצינא דנגרי הוא גרזן. וכל כלי המצאה של חרש כגון דקפדי אפגמיהו קבע ליה מקום ומסיח דעתו מלעשות בהן מלאכה אחרת הללו וכיוצא בהן שהן מוקצה מחמת חסרון כיס אסור לטלטלן בשבת. והרי מפורש בסוף פרק מי שהחשיך דכולהו הני היינו טעמא דאסירי משום דמוקצה מחמת חסרון כיס ניהו. ואפילו ר' שמעון מודה ביה דכל הני אסור לטלטלן בשבת: מקצוע של דבילה כלי ברזל שחותכין בו דבילה. וזומליסטרון תרווד שמהפך בו הקדירה. בראשונה היו אומרים שלשה כלים ניטלין בשבת מקצוע של דבילה וזומליסטרון של קדירה וסכין קטנה. כיון שנגדרו וחזרו לדקדק בשמירת שבת היו מתירין להן והולכין עד שהתירו הכל חוץ ממסר הגדול ויתד של מחרישה. א"ר אלעזר קנים ומקלות וגלוסטרא ומדוכה כולם קודם התרת כלים נשנו. קנים הם קנים של לחם הפנים. והן שנויין במס' מנחות.

וסכינא דאשכבתא. פירש בקונטרס סכין שהקצבים מקצבין בה בשר וי"מ סכין ששוחטין בה שמקפיד שלא תיפגם ויש ליזהר שלא לטלטלו אפי' לצורך גופו דהוי כיתד של מחרישה דאפי' ר"ש מודה כדאמרינן בסוף מכילתין (דף קנז.):

מקצוע של דבילה. לא חשיב אלא כלים דלאו בני קיבול דהא פשיטא דכוסות וקערות ולגוניות היו מטלטלין:

איתיביה אביי מדוכה. בשלמא לדידי מוקמינן לצורך מקומו וס"ל לשנויי כר' נחמיה כדשני לעיל ואביי נמי הוה ידע דהא משני ליה רבה הכי לעיל אלא פריך לרבא אולי יאמר מירוץ אחר ורבא לא בעי לשנויי כר' נחמיה דלית הלכתא כוותיה ורבה דמשני ליה כר' נחמיה משום דמשמע ליה אין מטלטלין אותה בשום ענין: הכא נמי מחמה לצל. והא דנקט שקצב עליו בשר אע"ג דלצורך גופו ומקומו נמי שרי לאשמעינן דאפילו בהא פליגי ב"ש דלא שרו מחמת שמחת יו"ט:

לא סידור קנים. אע"ג דלאו שבות (א) במקדש כמה שבותים * אשכחן במקדש ח) שגזרו פעמים לצורך כי הכא בקנים ומקלות לפי שהיו מחללים את השבת: ט) הרי היא ככל הכלים. אע"ג דקודם התרת כלים נשנית איכא למימר ככל הכלים כגון כוסות וקערות: הא

אפיקטויזין בשבת ורב ששת התם לאו אורחיה הכא אורחיה אמר רב ששת מנא אמינא לה דתנן מחט של יד ליטול בה את הקוץ ורב נחמן התם פקיד הכא לא פקיד: **מתני'** קנה של זיתים אם יש קשר בראשו מקבל טומאה ואם לאו אין מקבל טומאה א בין כך ובין כך ניטל בשבת: **גמ'** אמאי פשוטי כלי עץ הוא א) ב ופשוטי כלי עץ אינן מקבלין טומאה מ"ט ב) דומיא דשק בעינן תנא משמיה דר' נחמיה ג בשעה שמהפך בזיתים הופכו ורואה בו: **מתני'** ג) ר' יוסי אומר ד) כל הכלים ניטלין ד חוץ מן המסר הגדול ויתד של מחרישה: **גמ'** אמר ר"נ האי ה) אוכלא דקצרי כיתד של מחרישה דמיא אמר אביי ה חרבא דאושכפי וסכינא דאשכבתא וחצינא דנגרי כיתד של מחרישה דמי ת"ר ו) בראשונה היו אומרים שלשה כלים ניטלין בשבת מקצוע של דבילה וזוהמא ליסטרן של קדרה וסכין קטנה שעל גבי שלחן התירו וחזרו והתירו וחזרו והתירו עד שאמרו כל הכלים ניטלין בשבת חוץ מן מסר הגדול ויתד של מחרישה מאי התירו וחזרו והתירו וחזרו והתירו אמר אביי התירו דבר שמלאכתו להיתר לצורך גופו וחזרו והתירו דבר שמלאכתו להיתר לצורך מקומו וחזרו והתירו דבר שמלאכתו לאיסור לצורך גופו אין לצורך מקומו לא ועדיין בידו אחת אין בשתי ידיו לא עד שאמרו כל הכלים ניטלין בשבת ואפי' בשתי ידים א"ל רבא מכדי התירו קתני מה לי לצורך גופו מה לי לצורך מקומו אלא אמר רבא ו התירו דבר שמלאכתו להיתר בין לצורך גופו ובין לצורך מקומו וחזרו והתירו מחמה לצל וחזרו והתירו דבר שמלאכתו לאיסור לצורך גופו ולצורך מקומו אין מחמה לצל לא ועדיין באדם אחד אין בשני בני אדם לא עד שאמרו כל הכלים ניטלין בשבת אפילו בשני בני אדם ז) איתיביה אביי לרבא מדוכה אם יש בה שום מטלטלין אותה ואם לאו אין מטלטלין אותה הכא במאי עסקינן מחמה לצל איתיביה ח) ושוין שאם קצב עליו בשר שאסור לטלטלו הכא נמי מחמה לצל אמר ר' חנינא ט) בימי נחמיה בן חכליה נשנית משנה זו דכתיב א) בימים ההמה ראיתי ביהודה דורכים גתות בשבת ומביאים הערימות אמר ר' אלעזר קנין ומקלות גלוסטרא ומדוכה כולן קודם התרת כלים נשנו קנין דתנן י) ז לא סידור הקנין ולא נטילתן דוחה את השבת מקלות דתנן כ) ח מקלות דקין חלקין היו שם ומניחו על כתפו ועל כתף חבירו ותולה ומפשיט (ל) אמר) רבי אלעזר ארבעה עשר שחל להיות בשבת מניח ידו

אפיקטויזין. להקיא שותה משקים ומקיא ולא לרפואה אלא להריק את מעיו שיוכל לאכול ולשתות [היום] הרבה כדאמרי' בפרק חבית ואע"ג דלא גזור בה משום שחיקת סממנין דהא לאו לרפואה היא אסור משום דמתקן גברא: **הכא אורחיה.** והרי הוא כמי שמאכילו ומשקהו: **ליטול בה את הקוץ.** אלמא תקוני גברא במידי דלאו לרפואה דליכא משום שחיקת סממנין שרי: **פקיד.** הקוץ הזה אינו מחובר בו אלא מופקד ונתון שם והוצאה זו אינו תיקון: **הכא לא פקיד.** ודמי למלאכה שמסלקן ומכניסן למקום חבור: **מתני'** קנה של זיתים. לאחר מסיקתן לוקח במעטן וטמנן מתחמם בתוכו ונוח ללאת ויש לו קנה להפכן בו ולבדוק אם כמרו כל צרכן ומגיען לבית הבד: **אם יש קשר בראשו.** כעין פקק של קנה קולמוס: **מקבל טומאה.** דכלי הוא לפי שעב בראשו קלת: **ואם לאו.** לא דמי לכלי ובגמ' מפרש לה: **גמ' ואמאי.** כי יש בו קשר בראשו נהי נמי דקשר משוי ליה מנא מיהו פשוטי כלי עץ הוא שאפילו חלול הוא אין חללו עשוי לקבל כלום: **הופכו ורואה.** בחלל ראשו שמשחיר שם ע"י שהוא פקוק בקשר מן השמן הזב מן הזיתים ובודק בו אם הגיעו לעצור וזו היא לו קבלה בחלל שלו ואם לאו שאין קשר בראשו אין השמן נראית שם מפני שאינו פקוק וכולו חלל הילכך לאו לקבל הוא עשוי והוי פשוטי כלי עץ ובין כך ובין כך ניטל בשבת דהא כלי הוא להפוך בו זיתים: **מתני'** מסר הגדול. מגירה גדולה שעשויה לקצוץ קורות: **ויתד של מחרישה.** הוא כלי גדול העשוי כסכין שבו עושין חריץ של תלם המענה קולטר"א בלע"ז דהנך קפיד עלייהו ומייחד להם מקום דלא חזו למלאכה אחרת: **גמ' אוכלא דקצרי.** כלי נחושת העשוי כנפה נקבים נקבים והוא של כובסים ונותנו על הבגדים ומזלף בו המים עליהן וי"מ שמגמרין מוגמר מתחתיו והבגדים מונחין עליו ומתגמרין דרך הנקבים: **חרבא דאושכפי.** סכין של רצענין: **וסכינא דאשכבתא.** סכין של בית המקולין שהקצבין מקצבין בו בשר: **חצינא.** דולויר"א כל הני קפדי עלייהו משום דמפגמי ומקצי להו בידים: **ג' כלים.** ותו לא ולקמן אמרינן דבימי נחמיה בן חכליה בבית שני גזרו על טלטול כל הכלים כדי לגדור גדר להחמיר באיסורי שבת מפני שהיו מקילין בה: **מקצוע.** איזמל שמחתכין בו דבלה יעשהו במקלועות מתרגמינן באיזמליהון (ישעיה מד): **זוהמא לסטרון.** כף גדולה שמסלקין בו זוהמא של קדרה: **וסכין קטן.** שחותכין בו לחם ובשר ואוכלין דהני תדירין בתשמיש: **התירו.** עוד כשראו שחזרו להזהר קלת באיסור שבת וחזרו והתירו כשנזהרו יותר וחזרו והתירו ולקמיה מפרש מאי כולהו הנך התירו: **עד שאמרו.** עוד חזרו והתירו את הכל עד שאמרו הכל ניטלין חוץ מן המסר הגדול כו': **התירו.** לטלטל דבר שעיקר מלאכתו בחול להיתר לדבר המותר בשבת התירו לטלטל לצורך גופו אם הולרך להשתמש בגוף הכלי אבל לא משום שהולרך למקומו: **וחזרו והתירו.** את אלו לצורך מקומו: **וחזרו והתירו אף מי שמלאכתו לאיסור.** והולרך לו בשבת לגופו למלאכת היתר ומיהו לא הותרו אלו לצורך מקומו: **כל הכלים.** הללו שאמרנו חוץ מן המסר הגדול דלא שרי לא לצורך גופו ולא לצורך מקומו ואביי דמתרך הכי הדר ביה לגבי רבה דאמר לעיל קורנס של נפחים שניטו לדבר שמלאכתו לאיסור שרי לצורך גופו: **א"ל רבא מכדי.** לצורך התירו בפעם ראשונה: מה לי גופו מה לי מקומו. תרווייהו צורך ניהו: **מחמה לצל.** שאינו צריך לו עכשיו לא לגופו ולא למקומו אלא חס עליו שמא יתבקע בחמה: **עד שאמרו.** היינו עוד היתר אחרינא כל הכלים אפי' גדולים ומיהו לכדאוקימנא של היתר אפי' מחמה לצל ושל איסור לצורך גופו או מקומו: **אין מטלטלין אותה.** בשלמא לדידי אין מטלטלין אותה לצורך מקומה קאמר אלא לדידך אמאי: **משנה זו.** דלעיל בראשונה היו אומרין ג' כלים ותו לא משום דהוו מזלזלים בשבתות דכתיב בימים ההמה וגו': **קנים ומקלות כו'.** משניות הן כדמפרש ואזיל: **קודם התרת כלים.** מנין האחרון שהותרו כולן לצורך גופן לאביי ולרבא אף לצורך מקומו: **לא סידור הקנים.** שהיו נותנין במערכת לחם הפנים בין חלה לחלה להפרידן ליכנס הרוח ביניהן שלא יתעפשו: **ולא נטילתן.** מן המערכה ישנה: **דוחה את השבת.** אלא נכנס בע"ש ונוטל הקנים ולמחר מסלק המערכה הישנה ומסדר החדשה בלא קנים ולמוצאי שבת נכנס ונותן הקנים ביניהן זו נשנית קודם היתר מנין הראשון דהא מלאכתן להיתר וקאסר להו לצורך גופן: **מקלין דקין וחלקין היו.** בעזרה בפסח שחל להיות י"ד בחול:

מסורת הש"ס

א) [חולין כה.], ב) לעיל פב: חגיגה כו: מנחות לו: [בכורות לח.], ג) [משנה שבמשניות ליתא ר' יוסי אומר וכן מוכח מסוגיא דלקמן קנז. ע"ש אבל בעירובין לה. איתא סבר לה כר' יוסי דאמר כל הכלים ניטלין וכו' וע"ע וכן בר"ף ורא"ש איתא ר' יוסי אומר כל הכלים וכו'], ד) לקמן שם עירובין לה., ה) [גי' הערוך בערך אכל אובלא וע"ש פירושו בשני אופנים], ו) [תוספ' פט"ו], ז) [לקמן קכד.], ח) [תוספ' ביצה פ"א], ט) [עי' תוס' ב"ק לב. ד"ה בימין], י) מנחות נו., כ) פסחים סה., ל) [צ"ל ר' אלעזר אומר], מ) [וע"ע תוס' מנחות נה. ד"ה לא סידור ותוספות עירובין דף קג: ד"ה והעלוהו], נ) שייך לדף קכד ע"א.

הגהות הב"ח

(א) תוס' ד"ה לא סידור וכו' דלאו שבות. נ"ב ע"ל פרק המצניע דף צג ע"א תוס' ד"ה שרא דלמא:

תורה אור השלם

א) בַּיָּמִים הָהֵמָּה רָאִיתִי בִיהוּדָה דֹּרְכִים גִּתּוֹת בַּשַּׁבָּת וּמְבִיאִים הָעֲרֵמוֹת וְעֹמְסִים עַל הַחֲמֹרִים וְאַף יַיִן עֲנָבִים וּתְאֵנִים וְכָל מַשָּׂא וּמְבִיאִים יְרוּשָׁלִַם בְּיוֹם הַשַּׁבָּת וָאָעִיד בְּיוֹם מִכְרָם צָיִד: [נחמיה יג, טו]

רב נסים גאון

בשעה שמהפך בו זיתים הופכו ורואה בו. בגמ' דבני מערבא גרסי דבי ר' ינאי אמרי קנה שהתקינו להפך בו זיתים כיצד הוא יודע אם היה מלוכלך במשקה בידוע שנגמר מלאכת המעטן ואם לאו בידוע שלא נגמרה מלאכת המעטן אמר לון ר' לא תני שמואל אלא להיות שולה בו את הזיתים ומשום הכי אמרי דמקבל טומאה והואיל וכבלי קיבול דמי. אמר רב נחמן האי אוכלא דקצרי כיתד של מחרישה דמי אוכלא דקצרי הוא כלי שדומה לדלעת ומנוקב הוא כולו נקבין ובו מזלפין מים הכובסין על הבגדים ומשכחת לה בפ' כל ישראל יש להם חלק (סנהדרין דף צב) אמרו מנקבין אותו ככברה ואמר אביי כאוכלא דקצרי:

ליקוטי רש"י

אפיקטויזין. להקיא והוא בנוטריקון אפיק טפי זין מזון להוציא יותר מדאי [ב"ק ...]. **פקיד.** מופקד ועומד שם כנתון בכלי [לקמן קלג:]. **פשוטי כלי עץ.** אפילו נגמרה מלאכתן טהורין לאיתקש עץ לשק דכתיב (ויקרא יא) מכל כלי עץ או בגד או עור או שק מה שק מטלטל מלא וריקן אף כל מטלטל מלא וריקן [חגיגה כו:]. **דומיא דשק בעינן.** ... **כל הכלים ניטלין.** ... **חוץ מן המסר הגדול.** ... **ויתד של מחרישה.** ... **אוכלא דקצרי.** ... [לקמן קנז.]. **קצרי.** ... [נדרים כג.]. ... [המשך בדף קכד.]

אַפִּיקְטְוִיזִין בְּשַׁבָּת – ONE MAY NOT TAKE[1] AN EMETIC ON THE SABBATH.[2] I deduce from this that just as it is forbidden to "repair" one's body by taking an emetic, so too it is forbidden to "repair" an infant by straightening its limbs!

The proof is rebuffed:

וְרַב שֵׁשֶׁת – But Rav Sheishess retorts: הָתָם לָאו אוֹרְחֵיהּ – There, the emetic is not part of [the person's] normal conditioning, הָכָא אוֹרְחֵיהּ – whereas here, straightening the limbs is part of [the infant's] normal conditioning.[3]

Rav Sheishess now cites a source for his opinion:

אָמַר רַב שֵׁשֶׁת – Rav Sheishess said: מְנָא אֲמִינָא לָהּ – From where do I learn to say this? דִּתְנַן – For we learned in our Mishnah: מַחַט שֶׁל יָד לִיטּוֹל בָּהּ אֶת הַקּוֹץ – One may take ... A HAND-NEEDLE TO REMOVE A SPLINTER WITH IT. Thus, we see that there is no prohibition against "repairing" a human being where no medicinal remedy is employed!

The proof is rebuffed:

וְרַב נַחְמָן – But Rav Nachman retorts: הָתָם פְּקִיד – There, the splinter is an extraneous object that is merely embedded in the skin. Therefore, its removal is not considered a "repair." הָכָא לָא פְּקִיד – Here, however, the limbs are not merely embedded, but are actually attached to the body. Relocating them properly in their sockets is similar to repairing a utensil and is therefore prohibited.

Mishnah קָנֶה שֶׁל זֵיתִים – A cane for turning olives[4] – אִם יֵשׁ קֶשֶׁר בְּרֹאשׁוֹ מְקַבֵּל טוּמְאָה – if there is a knot at its end it is susceptible to *tumah,* וְאִם לָאו אֵין מְקַבֵּל טוּמְאָה – but if not, it is not susceptible to *tumah.*[5] בֵּין כָּךְ וּבֵין כָּךְ נִיטָּל בְּשַׁבָּת – In either case, it may be taken on the Sabbath.[6]

Gemara The Gemara analyzes the ruling that a cane with a knot at its end is susceptible to *tumah:*

אַמַּאי – Why is this so? פְּשׁוּטֵי כְּלֵי עֵץ הוּא – But [the cane] is a flat wooden utensil, i.e. one that has no receptacle, וּפְשׁוּטֵי כְּלֵי עֵץ אֵינָן מְקַבְּלִין טוּמְאָה – and flat wooden utensils are not susceptible to *tumah.* מַאי טַעְמָא – What is the reason that they are not susceptible to *tumah?* דּוּמְיָא דְשַׂק בְּעִינַן – Because it is required that a wooden utensil be analogous to a sack in order to be susceptible to *tumah.*[7] Why, then, is the cane susceptible to *tumah?*

The Gemara cites an answer:

תָּנָא מִשְּׁמֵיהּ דְּרַבִּי נְחֶמְיָה – A Tanna taught in the name of R' Nechemyah: בְּשָׁעָה שֶׁמְּהַפֵּךְ בַּזֵּיתִים – WHEN ONE TURNS OVER OLIVES with the cane, הוֹפְכוֹ וְרוֹאֶה בּוֹ – HE INVERTS IT AND LOOKS AT [THE END] to examine the oil that remains in the cavity formed by the knot. Thus, the cavity is used as a receptacle for oil.[8]

Mishnah רַבִּי יוֹסֵי אוֹמֵר – R' Yose says: כָּל הַכֵּלִים נִיטָּלִין – All utensils may be taken on the Sabbath, חוּץ מִן הַמַּסָּר הַגָּדוֹל וְיָתֵד שֶׁל מַחֲרֵישָׁה – except for a large saw and a colter.[9]

Gemara The Gemara lists other utensils that are subject to the Mishnah's rule:

אָמַר רַב נַחְמָן – Rav Nachman said: הַאי אוּכְלָא דְקַצָּרֵי כְּיָתֵד שֶׁל מַחֲרֵישָׁה דָּמְיָא – The launderer's riddle is similar to a colter and is therefore totally *muktzeh.*[10] אָמַר אַבַּיֵּי – Abaye said: חַרְבָּא דְּאוּשְׁכָּפֵי – A tanner's knife, וְסַכִּינָא דְּאַשְׁכַּבְתָּא – a butcher's

NOTES

1. Literally: make.

2. It is prohibited to induce vomiting by ingesting an emetic. This pertains to the inducement of vomiting not for purposes of health, but for the sake of emptying the digestive tract to enable oneself to continue eating and drinking. Since this is not done for one's health, the basis for the prohibition cannot be the rule against medicinal remedies. Rather, it is prohibited because it is considered a "repair" to the body (*Rashi;* cf. *Rashi* to 147b ד״ה אלא בסם).

3. Straightening an infant's limbs is akin to feeding it! [Since this task is normal and necessary, it is not considered a "repair" and is not analogous to the taking of an emetic for the sake of gorging oneself] (*Rashi*).

4. After olives were harvested, they were stored in a vat to soften until ready for pressing. A cane was used to turn over the olives in the vat to examine them for readiness (*Rashi*).

5. If the hollow cane is closed at its end by either a natural knot or an inserted plug, the cane is considered a utensil with respect to *tumah* susceptibility. However, if the cane is open at its end, it is not considered a utensil in this regard. The Gemara will clarify this ruling (see *Rashi* and *Rambam, Commentary;* see also *Sfas Emes*).

6. Since the cane is strong enough to be used for turning olives and has been designated for this purpose, it is considered a utensil with respect to the Sabbath laws and is not *muktzeh* (*Chidushei HaRan;* see also *Rashi* below ד״ה הופכו ורואה and *Shabbos Shel Mi*; see *Rambam, Hil. Shabbos* 26:7 with *Maggid Mishneh*).

7. The verse which teaches that various utensils are susceptible to *tumah* states (*Leviticus* 11:32): מִכָּל־כְּלִי־עֵץ אוֹ בֶגֶד אוֹ־עוֹר אוֹ שָׂק, *whether it is a wooden utensil, a garment, a leather or a sack.* By listing a wooden utensil together with a sack, the Torah teaches that it refers only to wooden utensils which, like a sack, are designed to contain things. Thus, a wooden utensil is susceptible to *tumah* only if it has a hollow in which things are meant to be contained (*Rashi* to *Chullin* 25a ד״ה טהורין). In our case, even if the cane does have a hollow, it is not meant to contain anything (*Rashi*).

8. The knot is slightly indented at the end of the cane, forming a small cavity. When the cane is inserted in the vat to turn over olives, some oil that oozes from the olives adheres to it and gathers in the cavity at its end. The oil-presser then examines it to better determine whether the olives are ready for pressing. Thus, the cane has a hollow that is used for containing oil and, on account of this hollow, it is deemed susceptible to *tumah*. By contrast, a cane that has no knot is not used to receive anything because no oil remains in its hollow interior. Therefore, it is not susceptible to *tumah*. [When this type of cane is used, the olives are tested for readiness by visual examination (*Tos. Yom Tov*).]

Whether it has a receptacle or not, the cane may be taken on the Sabbath because it is a bona-fide utensil that functions to turn over the olives (*Rashi*). [However, it is considered a forbidden-use utensil, and thus may be taken only for the sake of its use in a permissible capacity, or for the sake of its place (*Machatzis HaShekel* 313:4; see also *Beur Halachah* to 313:1 ד״ה שיהא ראוי and *Shabbos Shel Mi*).]

9. A large saw is one that is used to cut through beams. A colter is the large knifelike part of a plow that cuts into the ground to make furrows. These utensils are not fit to be used for other purposes [because they might be ruined]. Since the owner is particular about them, he designates a place for storing them, thus setting them aside and rendering them *muktzeh* (*Rashi;* see 123a note 6).

R' Yose teaches that every utensil may be moved — at least in some instances — except one that is set aside by its owner because of potential monetary loss (מוּקְצֶה מֵחֲמַת חֶסְרוֹן כִּיס). [The two items he listed are merely examples of such utensils.] However, R' Yose does not dispute the fact that there are restrictions on the movement of other utensils. For example, a forbidden-use utensil may not be moved other than for the sake of a permissible use or for the sake of its place (see *Ramban, Rashba* and *Ritva MHK* ed. above, 122b).

10. The launderer's riddle was a perforated copper vessel from which the launderer would pour water on clothing to rinse it. Others explain that clothes would be placed upon the riddle while incense was burned beneath it, and the scent would reach the clothing through the perforations (*Rashi;* cf. *Rabbeinu Chananel*). [Launderers were particular that their riddle not be used for any other purpose.]

אפיקטויזין בשבת ורב ששת התם לאו אורחיה הכא אורחיה אמר רב ששת מנא אמינא לה דתנן מחט של יד ליטול בה את הקוץ ורב נחמן התם פקיד הכא לא פקיד: **מתני'** קנה של זיתים אם יש קשר בראשו מקבל טומאה ואם לאו אין מקבל טומאה [א]בין כך ובין כך ניטל בשבת: **גמ'** אמאי פשוטי כלי עץ הוא [ב]ופשוטי כלי עץ אינן מקבלין טומאה מ"ט [ג]דומיא דשק בעינן תנא משמיה דר' נחמיה [ג]בשעה שמהפך בזיתים הופכו ורואה בו: **מתני'** [ג]ר' יוסי אומר [ד]כל הכלים ניטלין [ד]חוץ מן המסר הגדול ויתד של מחרישה: **גמ'** אמר ר"נ [ה]האי אוכלא דקצרי כיתד של מחרישה דמיא אמר אביי [ה]חרבא דאושכפי וסכינא דאשכבתא וחצינא דנגרי כיתד של מחרישה דמי ת"ר [ו]בראשונה היו אומרים שלשה כלים ניטלין בשבת מקצוע של דבילה וזוהמא ליסטרן של קדרה וסכין קטנה שעל גבי שלחן התירו והתירו וחזרו והתירו והתירו עד שאמרו כל הכלים ניטלין בשבת חוץ מן מסר הגדול ויתד של מחרישה מאי התירו וחזרו והתירו וחזרו והתירו אמר אביי התירו דבר שמלאכתו להיתר לצורך גופו וחזרו והתירו דבר שמלאכתו להיתר לצורך מקומו וחזרו והתירו דבר שמלאכתו לאיסור לצורך גופו אין לצורך מקומו לא ועדיין בידו אחת אין בשתי ידיו לא עד שאמרו כל הכלים ניטלין בשבת ואפי' בשתי ידים א"ל רבא מכדי התירו קתני מה לי לצורך גופו מה לי לצורך מקומו אלא אמר רבא [ו]התירו דבר שמלאכתו להיתר בין לצורך גופו ובין לצורך מקומו וחזרו והתירו מחמה לצל וחזרו והתירו דבר שמלאכתו לאיסור לצורך גופו ולצורך מקומו אין מחמה לצל לא ועדיין באדם אחד אין בשני בני אדם לא עד שאמרו כל הכלים ניטלין בשבת אפילו בשני בני אדם [ז]איתיביה אביי מדוכה אם יש בה שום מטלטלין אותה ואם לאו אין מטלטלין אותה הכא במאי עסקינן מחמה לצל איתיביה [ח]ושוין שאם קצב עליו בשר שאסור לטלטלו הכא נמי מחמה לצל אמר ר' חנינא [ט]בימי נחמיה בן חכליה נשנית משנה זו דכתיב [א]בימים ההמה ראיתי ביהודה דורכים גתות בשבת ומביאים הערימות אמר ר' אלעזר קנין ומקלות גלוסטרא ומדוכה כולן קודם התרת כלים נשנו קנין דתנן [י]לא סידור הקנין ולא נטילתן דוחה את השבת מקלות דתנן [כ]מקלות דקין חלקין היו שם ומניחו על כתפו ועל כתף חבירו ותולה ומפשיט ([ל]אמר) רבי אלעזר ארבעה עשר שחל להיות בשבת מניח ידו

תוספות

וסכינא דאשכבתא. פירש בקונטרס סכין שהקצבים מקלפין בה בשר וי"מ סכין ששוחטין בה שמקפיד שלא תיפגם ויש ליזהר שלא לטלטלו אפי' לצורך גופו דהוי כיתד של מחרישה דלפי' ר"ש מודה כדאמרינן בסוף מכילתין (דף קנז.):

מקצוע של דבילה. לא חשיב אלא כלים דלאו בני קיבול דהא פשיטא דכוסות וקערות ולגלוחיות היו מטלטלין:

איתיביה אביי מדוכה. בשלמא לדידי מוקמינן לצורך מקומו וה"מ לשנויי כר' נחמיה כדשני לעיל ואביי נמי הוה ידע דהא משני ליה רבה הכי לעיל אלא פריך לרבה אולי יאמר תירוץ אחר ורבה לא בעי לשנויי כר' נחמיה דלית הלכתא כוותיה ורבה דמשני ליה כר' נחמיה משום דמשמע ליה אין מטלטלין אותה כשום ענין: **הכא** נמי מחמה לצל. והא דנקט לקצב עליו בשר אע"ג דלצורך גופו ומקומו נמי שרי לאשמעינן דאפילו בהא פליגי ב"ש דלא שרו מחמת ממחת יו"ט:

לא סידור קנים. אע"ג דאין שבות במקדש (א) כמה שבותים אשכחן במקדש [מ]שגזרו פעמים לצורך כי הכא בקנים ומקלות לפי שהיו מחללים את השבת: [נ]**הרי** היא ככל הכלים. אע"ג דקודם התרת כלים נשנית איכא למימר ככל הכלים כעין כוסות וקערות: הא

רש"י

אפיקטויזין. להקיא שותה משקים ומקיא ולא לרפואה אלא להריק את מעיו שיוכל לאכול ולשתות [היום] הרבה כדאמרי' בפרק חבית ואע"ג דלא גזור בה משום שחיקת סממנין דהא לאו לרפואה היא אסור משום דמתקן גברא: **הכא אורחיה.** והרי הוא כמי שמאכילו ומשקהו: **ליטול בה את הקוץ.** אלמא תקוני גברא במידי דלאו לרפואה דליכא משום שחיקת סממנין שרי: **פקיד.** הקוץ הזה אינו מחובר בו אלא מופקד ונתון שם והולאה זו אינו תיקון: **הכא לא פקיד.** ודמי למלאכה שמסלקן ומכניסן למקום חבור: **מתני' קנה של זיתים.** לאחר מסיקתן צובר במעטן ושמן מתמצץ בתוכן ונוח ללאת ויש לו קנה להפכן בו ולבדוק אם כמרו כל צרכן ומגיעו לבית הבד: **אם יש קשר בראשו.** כעין פקק של קנה קולמוס: **מקבל טומאה.** דכלי הוא לפי שעב בראשו קלת: **ואם לאו.** לא דמי לכלי ובגמ' מפרש לה: **גמ' ואמאי.** כי יש בו קשר בראשו נמי דקשר משוי ליה מנא מיהו פשוטי כלי עץ הוא שאפילו חלול הוא אין חללו עשוי לקבל כלום: **הופכו ורואה.** בחלל ראשו שמשתייר שם ע"י שהוא פקוק בקשר מן השמן הזב מן הזיתים ובודק בו אם הגיעו לעצור וזו היא לו קבלה בחלל שלו ואם לאו שאין קשר בראשו אין השמן נראה שם מפני שאינו פקוק וכולו חלל הולך לאו לקבל עשוי והוי פשוטי כלי עץ ובין כך ובין כך ניטל בשבת דהא כלי הוא להפוך בו זיתים: **מתני' מסר הגדול.** מגירה גדולה שעשויה לקלוץ קורות: **ויתד של מחרישה.** הוא כלי גדול העשוי כסכין שבו עושין חריץ של תלם המענה קולטר"א בלע"ז הנך קפיד עליהו ומייחד להם מקום דלא מזו למלאכה אחרת: **גמ' אוכלא דקצרי.** כלי נחושת העשוי כפה נקבים נקבים והוא של כובסים ונותנו על הבגדים ומזלף בו המים עליהן וי"מ שמגהצין בו מגהץ מתחתיו והבגדים מונחין עליו ומתגהצין דרך הנקבים: **חרבא דאושכפי.** סכין של רצענין: **וסכינא דאשכבתא.** סכין של בית המקולין שהקצבין מקלפין בו בשר: **חצינא.** דולויר"א כל הני קפדי עליהו משום דמפגמי ומקצי להו בידים: **ג' כלים.** ותו לא ולקמן אמרינן דבימי נחמיה בן חכליה בבית שני גזרו על טלטול כל הכלים כדי לגדור גדר להחמיר לאיסורי שבת מפני שהיו מקילין בה: **מקצוע.** איזמל שמחתכין בו דבלה עיגולי מקצועות מתרגמינן באיזמליהון (ישעיה מד): **זוהמא ליסטרן.** כף גדולה שמסלקין בו זוהמא של קדרה: **וסכין קטן.** שמחתכין בו לחם ובשר ואוכלין והני תדירין בתשמישי: **התירו.** עוד כשראו שחזרו להזהר קלת לאיסור שבת וחזרו והתירו כשנזהרו יותר וחזרו והתירו ולקמיה מפרש מאי כולהו הנך התירו: **עד שאמרו.** עוד חזרו והתירו את הכל עד שאמרו הכל ניטלין חוץ מן המסר הגדול כו': **התירו.** לטלטל דבר שעיקר מלאכתו בחול להיתר לדבר המותר בשבת התירו לטלטל לצורך גופו אם הולך להשתמש בגוף הכלי אבל לא משום שהוצרך למקומו: **וחזרו והתירו.** אם אלו לצורך מקומו: **וחזרו והתירו אף מי שמלאכתו לאיסור.** והוצרך לו בשבת לגופו למלאכת היתר ומיהו לא הותרו אלו לצורך מקומו: **כל הכלים.** הללו שאמרנו חוץ מן המסר הגדול דלא שרי לא לצורך גופו ולא לצורך מקומו ואביי דמתרץ הכי הדר ביה לגבי רבה דאמר לעיל קורנס של נפחים שאינו לדבר שמלאכתו לאיסור שרי לצורך גופו: **א"ל רבא מכדי.** לצורך התירו בפעם ראשונה: **מה לי גופו מה לי מקום.** תרוייהו צורך נינהו: **מחמה לצל.** שאינו צריך לו עכשיו לא לגופו ולא למקומו אלא חס עליו שמא יתבקע בחמה: **עד שאמרו.** היינו עוד היתר אחרינא כל הכלים אפי' גדולים ומיהו לכדלוקימנא של היתר אפי' מחמה לצל ושל איסור לצורך גופו או מקומו: **אין מטלטלין אותה.** בשלמא לדידי אין מטלטלין אותה לצורך מקומה קאמר אלא לדידך אמאי: **משנה זו.** דלעיל בראשונה היו אומרים ג' כלים ותו לא משום דהוו מזלזלים בשבתות דכתיב בימים ההמה וגו': **קנים ומקלות כו'.** משניות הן דלמפרש ואזיל: **קודם התרת כלים.** מנין האחרון שהותרו כולן לצורך גופן ולרבא אף לצורך מקומן: **לא סידור הקנים.** שהיו נותנין במערכת לחם הפנים בין חלה לחלה להפרידן ליכנס הרוח ביניהן שלא יתעפשו: **ולא נטילתן.** מן המערכה ישנה: **דוחה את השבת.** אלא נכנס בע"ש ונוטל הקנים ולמחר מסלק המערכה הישנה ומסדר החדשה בלא קנים ולמוצאי שבת נכנס ונותן הקנים ביניהן זו נשנית קודם היתר מנין הראשון דהא מלאכתן להיתר ואסר להו לצורך גופן: **מקלין דקין וחלקין היו.** בעזרה בפסח שחל להיות י"ד בחול:

ידו

עין משפט נר מצוה

יא א מיי' פכ"ו מהל' שבת הלכה ז:
יב ב מיי' פ"ח מהלכות כלים הלכה י:
יג ג מיי' שם פ"ב הל"ב:
יד ד ה מיי' שם פכ"ה הל"ב שבת הלכה ט סמג לאוין סה טור וש"ע א"ח סימן שח סעיף ח:
טו ו מיי' שם הלכה ג טוש"ע שם סעיף ג ד:
טז ז מיי' פ"ה מהלכות תמידין ומוספין הלכה יא:
יז ח מיי' פ"ו מהלכות ק"פ הלכה יד:

גליון הש"ס

תוס' ד"ה לא וכו' אשכחן במקדש. ע"ל דף קכו ע"א תוס' ד"ה והמונח:

רבינו חננאל

ממטן למעלן אסיר. פי' אם יש לאדם פוגלא טמונה בתבן או אפילו בעפר תיחוח עומדת כעין נטועה ראשה טמונה ועליה מגולין עכשיו כשבא לנוטלה אם אוחזו בעלים ומושך הראש ומסלקה זהו ממעלה למטה. אע"פ כשמגביה התבן והעפר משתרבב במקומן ויורד שרי אבל לאחוז קצה הראש הטמונה ולהגביהה ממטה למעלה לא. אלמא שטלטול מן הצד שמיה טלטול. ומפרקינן הדר ביה מההיא. מחט שניטל חררה או עוקצה. פי' חרירה הנקב שלה. עוקצה ראשה הוא. חידודה תרגמה אביי אליבא דרבא בגלמי והן פשוטין כדתנן גלמי כלי מתכות טהורין פשוטיהן טמאין ואלו הן וכו'. והן חוטי ברזל משוכין וחותך אותן חתיכות חתיכות ולוקח מהן האומן כשיעור אורך מחט ומחדד ראשה האחת ונוקב הקצה השני ונעשה מחט. וקודם שיחדדנה וינקבנה נקראת אותה החתיכה גולם. כגון זו וכיוצא בה שהן עומדות להעשות כלי ניטלין בשבת. אבל מחט שניטל חררה או עוקצה אסור. גרוטאות הוא לשון יון. ופתרונו כלי מוכן להטיל בו התגר כלי נחושת או כלי ברזל שבורין שיזדמנו לו לקנותם קונה ומשליכם לאותו כלי כדי להתיכם. ונקראין גרוטאות ומיכן נהגו לקרות לתגר גרוטאות: **אסובי ינוקא.** פי' כשנופל ערלת הגרון של תינוק משימה החיה את אצבעותיה בפיו ומסלקת אותה הערלה. ופעמים שמקיא התינוק ועל זה אקשינן עלה והא אין עושין אפיקטויזין בשבת כו'. ורבותינו הגאונים אמרו פי' אחר. ואנן כתבנו מה שקבלנו מרבותינו: **מתני'** קנה של זיתים כו'. ואמרינן אמאי פשוטי כלי עץ הוא ואין מקבלין טומאה. ומפרקינן תנא משמיה דר' נחמיה בשעה שמהפך בו את הזיתים הופכן ורואה בו. ולא פי' מה הוא רואה בו. אבל פירשו בתלמוד א"י. קנה שהתקינו להיות בודק בו הזיתים. כיצד הוא יודע אם מלוכלך במשקה בידוע שנגמרה מלאכת המעטן. ואם לאו בידוע שלא נגמרה מלאכת המעטן. א"ל ר' מנא לא תני שמואל אלא להיות שולה בו הזיתים. כלומר יש בו בית קבול: אמר רב נחמן האי אוכלא דקצרי כיתד של מחרישה דמי. ואסור לטלטלו. אובלא. אבן גדולה שנותן הכובס עליה היריעה שרוצה ללבנה והיא שריה במים ומכה עליו במזורי. מכה והופך ומכה. ועוד שורה ומכה. ואחרי שילשים שוטחה ומייבשה. ועוד חוזר ושורה אותה פעם אחר שנתלבן היטב. וי"א כלי חרס מנוקב שכופין אותו על גחלים ומקטרין בגפרית הכלים ללבנן. אמר אביי חרבא דאשכפא. וסכינא דאשכבתא וחצינא דנגרי כיתד של מחרישה דמו ואסור לטלטלו. חרבא דאושכפי. איזמל של שכף כדמתרגמינן עשה לך חרבות צורים. איזמלין חריפין. סכינא דאשכבתא. סכין המיוחדת לשחיטה בלבד. חצינא דנגרי הוא גרזן. הני כיון דקפידי אפגמייהו קבע ליה מקום ומסיח דעתו מלעשות בהן מלאכה אחרת הלכך הללו וכיוצא בהן שהן מוקצה מחמת חסרון כיס אסור לטלטלן בשבת. והרי מפורש בסוף פרק מי שהחשיך דכולהו הני היינו טעמא דאסירי משום דמוקצה מחמת חסרון כיס נינהו. ואפילו ר' שמעון מודה דתנן סתמא לדברי הכל כל הכלים ניטלין בשבת חוץ מן המסר הגדול ויתד של מחרישה. מקצוע של דבילה כלי ברזל שחותכין בו דבילה. זומליסטרון תרווד שמהפך בו הקדירה. כדתנן זומליסטרא שנוטל כפה טמאה מפני המזלג וכו'. א"ר חנינא בימי נחמיה בן חכליה נשנית משנה זו דכתיב בימים ההמה ראיתי ביהודה דורכים גיתות בשבת. כיון שראום כך שהקילו בשבת אסרו להן כל הכלים ושרי להן הא דתנן רבנן. בראשונה היו אומרים שלשה כלים ניטלין בשבת מקצוע של דבילה וזומליסטרון של קדירה. וסכין קטנה. כיון שנגדרו וחזרו לדקדק בשמירת שבת היו מתירין להן והולכין עד שהתירו הכל חוץ ממסר הגדול ויתד של מחרישה. וכך הוא מפורש בתלמוד א"י: א"ר אלעזר קנים ומקלות וקלוסטרא ומדוכה כולם קודם התרת כלים נשנו. ולפיכך נשנו באיסור. קנים הם קנים של לחם הפנים. והן שנוין במס' מנחות

מסורת הש"ס

א) [חולין כה.], ב) לעיל סג: חגיגה כו: מנחות לו: [בכורות לח.], ג) [במשנה שבמשניות ליתא ר' יוסי אומר וכן מוכח מסוגיא דלקמן קנז. ע"ש אבל בעירובין לה. איתא סבר לה כר' יוסי דאמר כל הכלים ניטלין וכו' ול"ע וכן ברי"ף ורא"ש איתא ר' יוסי אומר כל הכלים וכו'], ד) לקמן קנז. עירובין לה., ה) [גי' הערוך בערך אבל אובלא וע"ש פירושו בשני אופנים], ו) [תוספ' פט"ו], ז) [לקמן קכד.], ח) ביצה יא. [תוספ' ביצה פ"א], ט) [עי' תוס' ב"ק לד. ד"ה בימי], י) מנחות לו., כ) פסחים סד., ל) [נ"ל ר' אלעזר אומר], מ) [וע"ע תוס' מנחות לז. ד"ה לא סדור ותוספות עירובין דף קב: ד"ה והעליון], נ) שייך לדף קכד ע"א.

הגהות הב"ח

(א) תוס' ד"ה לא סידור וכו' דאין שבות. נ"ב ע"ל פרק המצניע דף לה בתוס' ד"ה שרא ולמא:

תורה אור השלם

א) בַּיָּמִים הָהֵמָּה רָאִיתִי בִיהוּדָה דֹרְכִים גִּתּוֹת בַּשַּׁבָּת וּמְבִיאִים הָעֲרֵמוֹת וְעֹמְסִים עַל הַחֲמֹרִים וְאַף יַיִן עֲנָבִים וּתְאֵנִים וְכָל מַשָּׂא וּמְבִיאִים יְרוּשָׁלִַם בְּיוֹם הַשַּׁבָּת וָאָעִיד בְּיוֹם מִכְרָם צָיִד: [נחמיה יג, טו]

רב נסים גאון

בשעה שמהפך בו זיתים הופכו ורואה בו. בגמ' דבני מערבא גרסי דבי ר' ינאי אמרי קנה שהתקינו להפך בו זיתים כיצד הוא יודע אם היה מלוכלך במשקה בידוע שנגמר מלאכת המעטן ואם לאו בידוע שלא נגמרה מלאכת המעטן אמר לון ר' לא תני שמואל אלא להיות שולה בו את הזיתים ומשום הכי אמרי דמקבל טומאה והואיל וככלי קיבול דמי. אמר רב נחמן האי אוכלא דקצרי כיתד של מחרישה דמי אוכלא דקצרי הוא כלי שדומה לדלעת ומנוקב הוא כולו נקבין ובו מזלפין מים הכובסין על הבגדים ומשכחת לה בפ' כל ישראל יש להם חלק (סנהדרין דף צב) אמרו מנקבין אותו ככברה אמר אביי כאוכלא דקצרי:

ליקוטי רש"י

אפיקטויזין. להקיא והוא בנוטריקון אפיק טפי זין מזון האוכל יותר מדאי מוציא ומקיא [סוכה מ:]. **פקיד.** מופקד ועומד שם כנתון בכלי [לקמן קלג:]. **פשוטי כלי עץ.** אפילו נגמרה מלאכתן טהורין לאיתקש עץ לשק דכתיב (ויקרא יא) מכל כלי עץ או בגד או עור או שק מה שק מטלטל מלא וריקן אף כל מטלטל מלא וריקן [חולין כה.]. **דומיא דשק בעינן.** מקבל שהוא עשוי לקבל על ידו מה שנותנין לתוכו [לעיל סו:]. לענין טומאה הוקשו כלי עץ לשק דכתיב מכל כלי עץ אשר יפול עליו מהם במותם יטמא כלי עץ או בגד או עור או שק (ויקרא יא) [חגיגה כו:]. **כל הכלים ניטלין.** ואפילו מלאכתן לאיסור ור' שמעון היא. **חוץ מן המסר הגדול.** מגירה גדולה ויתד של מחרישה שמקפיד עליהן [לקמן קנז.]. **אוכלא דקצרי.** כלי שמשימין בו הכובסין בגדים [סנהדרין צב.]. **קצרי.** כך שמם בלשון ישמעאל ומלשון כובסין מתרגמינן [נדרים כג.] [המשך בדף קכד.]

knife כְּיָתֵד שֶׁל **וַחֲצִינָא דְּנַגָּרֵי – and a carpenter's adze** **מַחֲרֵישָׁה דָּמֵי – are similar to a colter** and are *muktzeh*.[11]

The Gemara discusses the origin of the Mishnah's rule:

תָּנוּ רַבָּנַן – The Rabbis taught in a Baraisa: בָּרִאשׁוֹנָה הָיוּ **אוֹמְרִים שְׁלֹשָׁה כֵלִים נִיטָּלִין בְּשַׁבָּת – ORIGINALLY, THEY SAID** that only **THREE UTENSILS MAY BE TAKEN ON THE SABBATH –** מַקְצוּעַ **שֶׁל דְּבֵילָה – THE KNIFE** used **FOR** cutting **A CAKE OF PRESSED FIGS, וְזוּהֲמָא לִיסְטְרָן שֶׁל קְדֵרָה – THE LADLE** used **FOR** skimming **FOAM OFF A POT, וְסַכִּין קְטַנָּה שֶׁעַל גַּבֵּי שֻׁלְחָן – AND A SMALL TABLE-KNIFE.**[12] **הִתִּירוּ וְחָזְרוּ וְהִתִּירוּ וְחָזְרוּ וְהִתִּירוּ –** Later, **THEY PERMITTED** movement of additional utensils, **THEY FURTHER PERMITTED AND THEY FURTHER PERMITTED, עַד שֶׁאָמְרוּ – UNTIL THEY** finally **SAID:** כָּל הַכֵּלִים נִיטָּלִין בְּשַׁבָּת חוּץ מִן מַסָּר הַגָּדוֹל וְיָתֵד **שֶׁל מַחֲרֵישָׁה – ALL UTENSILS MAY BE TAKEN ON THE SABBATH EXCEPT FOR A LARGE SAW AND A COLTER.**[13]

The Gemara analyzes the Baraisa:

מַאי הִתִּירוּ וְחָזְרוּ וְהִתִּירוּ וְחָזְרוּ וְהִתִּירוּ – What is the meaning of the statement, **"They permitted, they further permitted and they further permitted** etc."? **אָמַר אַבָּיֵי – Abaye said:** הִתִּירוּ דָּבָר **שֶׁמְּלַאכְתּוֹ לְהֶיתֵּר לְצוֹרֶךְ גּוּפוֹ –** First, **they permitted** taking **something that is used** primarily **for permitted work for the sake of its use;**[14] **וְחָזְרוּ וְהִתִּירוּ דָּבָר שֶׁמְּלַאכְתּוֹ לְהֶיתֵּר לְצוֹרֶךְ מְקוֹמוֹ –** then, **they further permitted** taking **something that is used** primarily **for permitted work for the sake of its place;** **וְחָזְרוּ וְהִתִּירוּ דָּבָר שֶׁמְּלַאכְתּוֹ לְאִיסּוּר –** then, **they further permitted** taking **something that is used** primarily **for prohibited work** **לְצוֹרֶךְ גּוּפוֹ אֵין לְצוֹרֶךְ מְקוֹמוֹ לֹא – only for the sake of its use,** but **not for the sake of its place.**[15] **וַעֲדַיִין בְּיָדוֹ אַחַת אֵין בִּשְׁתֵּי יָדָיו לֹא – Still,** it was permitted to take a utensil **only** if it could be moved **with one hand** but **not** if it needed to be moved **with two hands,**[16] **עַד שֶׁאָמְרוּ – until they** finally **said:** **כָּל הַכֵּלִים נִיטָּלִין בְּשַׁבָּת וַאֲפִילּוּ בִּשְׁתֵּי יָדַיִם – All utensils may be taken on the Sabbath even** if they must be taken **with two hands,** except for a large saw and a colter.[17]

Abaye's explanation is rejected and an alternate one is presented:

אָמַר לֵיהּ רָבָא – Rava said to him: **מִכְּדִי הִתִּירוּ קָתָנֵי – The fact is that [the Baraisa] teaches** that after the initial prohibition **they permitted** taking utensils for the sake of filling specific needs. **מַה לִּי לְצוֹרֶךְ גּוּפוֹ מַה לִּי לְצוֹרֶךְ מְקוֹמוֹ – What is the difference between** moving something **for the sake of its use and** moving it **for the sake of its place?** Either need is a legitimate one and there is no reason to differentiate between them![18] **אֶלָּא אָמַר רָבָא – Rather, Rava said:** הִתִּירוּ דָּבָר **שֶׁמְּלַאכְתּוֹ לְהֶיתֵּר בֵּין לְצוֹרֶךְ גּוּפוֹ וּבֵין לְצוֹרֶךְ מְקוֹמוֹ –** First, **they permitted** moving **something that is used** primarily **for permitted work both for the sake of its use and for the sake of its place;** **וְחָזְרוּ וְהִתִּירוּ מֵחַמָּה לַצֵּל –** then, **they further permitted** moving it **from the sun to the shade** for its protection, even when there is no need for its use or place;[19] **וְחָזְרוּ וְהִתִּירוּ דָּבָר שֶׁמְּלַאכְתּוֹ לְאִיסּוּר –** then, **they further permitted** moving **something that is used** primarily **for prohibited work** **לְצוֹרֶךְ גּוּפוֹ וּלְצוֹרֶךְ מְקוֹמוֹ אֵין מֵחַמָּה לַצֵּל לֹא – only for the sake of its use or the sake of its**

NOTES

11. People are particular not to use any of these cutting utensils for ordinary purposes, lest their blades be nicked. Thus, the owners actively set them aside from Sabbath use, rendering them *muktzeh* (*Rashi*).

The translation of סַכִּינָא דְּאַשְׁכַּבְתָּא as a butcher's knife follows *Rashi*. *Tosafos*, however, interpret it as a *slaughtering* knife, which is disqualified from use if it is nicked. According to this interpretation, ordinary butchers' knives are not *muktzeh*. See also *Orach Chaim* 308:1.

12. As the Gemara will explain below, in the days of Nechemyah ben Chachalyah (i.e. the beginning of the Second Commonwealth era) the Rabbis observed a laxity in Sabbath observance. To enhance the sanctity of the day, they decreed that most utensils not be moved on the Sabbath. [By prohibiting even the movement of utensils, the Rabbis ensured that people would not unwittingly use the utensils to perform prohibited *melachah* (see below, 124a, and *Rambam* and *Raavad, Hil. Shabbos* 24:12-13).] The initial decree was so wide-ranging that it forbade the movement of all utensils except those listed here. These were excluded from the prohibition due to the frequency with which they are needed (*Rashi*).

The prohibition never applied to eating implements such as cups, bowls, plates, etc., for these are in constant use and are rarely used for prohibited *melachah*. Among other implements, only the three frequently used ones listed here were excluded from the initial decree (*Ritva MHK* ed.; see also *Tosafos* ד״ה מקצוע, *Chasam Sofer, Sfas Emes* and *Mishnah Berurah* 308:23; cf. *Shulchan Aruch HaGraz* 308:16-17).

13. As the level of Sabbath observance improved, the Rabbis gradually eased their restriction and allowed more utensils to be moved. On three occasions they relaxed the prohibition somewhat, and finally, on a fourth occasion, they lifted it almost entirely and said that all utensils may be moved in some circumstances, except for a large saw and a colter [and similar utensils], which are *muktzeh* due to the concern for monetary loss. The Gemara goes on to elaborate on the gradual easing of the restriction (*Rashi;* see *Ritva MHK* ed.).

14. The first increment by which the Rabbis eased their decree was in extending permission to move, for the sake of its use, a utensil that is used primarily for work that is permitted on the Sabbath [כְּלִי שֶׁמְּלַאכְתּוֹ לְהֶיתֵּר]. [They also permitted using the utensil even for something other than its primary use, e.g. taking a key to pry a tightly fitting lid off a container.] However, they did not permit moving the utensil merely for the sake of making its place available for another object (*Rashi*).

15. The utensil that is used on a weekday primarily for work that is prohibited on the Sabbath [כְּלִי שֶׁמְּלַאכְתּוֹ לְאִיסּוּר] may be taken for the sake of using it for a task that is permitted on the Sabbath (e.g. taking a blacksmith's hammer to crack open nuts), but not for the sake of making its place available (*Rashi*).

16. The easing of the restrictions affected only small utensils that could be taken with one hand. Large, heavy utensils that could be lifted only with two hands remained forbidden (*Ritva MHK* ed.; see also *Rashi* below ד״ה עד שאמרו).

17. All utensils — including large ones that require two hands for lifting — may be taken on the Sabbath *in some circumstances,* except for the large saw and the colter, and similar items that are *muktzeh* due to concern for monetary loss, which may not be moved at all.

Thus, according to Abaye's interpretation, the final law is that a permitted-use utensil may be moved either for the sake of its use or for the sake of its place; and a forbidden-use utensil may be moved for the sake of its use but not for the sake of its place. Abaye has now retracted the position he took above (top of 123a) and acknowledges Rabbah's opinion (ibid.) that a blacksmith's hammer may be taken to crack open nuts (*Rashi*).

18. The need to utilize the space occupied by a utensil is no less justification for moving it than the need to utilize the utensil itself (*Rashi, Ritva MHK* ed.). Thus, when the Rabbis first eased the decree, they would not have differentiated between these needs.

19. That is, they permitted moving a permitted-use utensil out of the sun to prevent it from being damaged by the heat (*Rashi*). The prevention of damage to the utensil is also considered a need, although it is not as significant as the need to make use of the utensil or its place.

Moving a utensil from the sun to the shade is merely an example of movement for the sake of protecting it. One may similarly move a permitted-use utensil from a location where there is a danger of theft to a protected area (see below, 124b). However, it is prohibited to move even this type of utensil for no purpose at all (*Ran; Orach Chaim* 308:4). [As mentioned above, this restriction pertains only to implements used for ordinary permitted tasks. There is no restriction at all on the movement of eating implements (*Mishnah Berurah* 308:23; cf. *Shulchan Aruch HaGraz* 308:16-17).]

אפיקטויזין בשבת ורב ששת התם לאו אורחיה הכא אורחיה אמר רב ששת מנא אמינא לה דתנן מחט של יד ליטול בה את הקוץ ורב נחמן התם פקיד הכא לא פקיד: **מתני'** קנה של זיתים אם יש קשר בראשו מקבל טומאה ואם לאו אין מקבל טומאה א) בין כך ובין כך ניטל בשבת: **גמ'** אמאי פשוטי כלי עץ הוא ב) ופשוטי כלי עץ אינן מקבלין טומאה מ"ט ג) דומיא דשק בעינן תנא משמיה דר' נחמיה ד) בשעה שמהפך בזיתים הופכו ורואה בו: **מתני'** ה) ר' יוסי אומר ו) כל הכלים ניטלין ז) חוץ מן המסר הגדול ויתד של מחרישה: **גמ'** אמר ר"נ האי ח) אוכלא דקצרי כיתד של מחרישה דמיא אמר אביי ט) חרבא דאושכפי וסכינא דאשכבתא וחצינא דנגרי כיתד של מחרישה דמי ת"ר י) בראשונה היו אומרים שלשה כלים ניטלין בשבת מקצוע של דבילה וזוהמא ליסטרן של קדרה וסכין קטנה שעל גבי שלחן התירו וחזרו והתירו וחזרו והתירו עד שאמרו כל הכלים ניטלין בשבת חוץ מן מסר הגדול ויתד של מחרישה מאי התירו וחזרו והתירו וחזרו והתירו אמר אביי התירו דבר שמלאכתו להיתר לצורך גופו וחזרו והתירו דבר שמלאכתו להיתר לצורך מקומו וחזרו והתירו דבר שמלאכתו לאיסור לצורך גופו אין לצורך מקומו לא ועדיין בידו אחת אין בשתי ידיו לא עד שאמרו כל הכלים ניטלין בשבת ואפי' בשתי ידים א"ל רבא מכדי התירו קתני מה לי לצורך גופו מה לי לצורך מקומו אלא אמר רבא התירו דבר שמלאכתו להיתר בין לצורך גופו ובין לצורך מקומו וחזרו והתירו מחמה לצל וחזרו והתירו דבר שמלאכתו לאיסור לצורך גופו ולצורך מקומו אין מחמה לצל לא ועדיין באדם אחד אין בשני בני אדם לא עד שאמרו כל הכלים ניטלין בשבת אפילו בשני בני אדם כ) איתיביה אביי מדוכה אם יש בה שום מטלטלין אותה ואם לאו אין מטלטלין אותה הכא במאי עסקינן מחמה לצל איתיביה ל) ושוין שאם קצב עליו בשר שאסור לטלטלו הכא נמי מחמה לצל אמר ר' חנינא מ) בימי נחמיה בן חכליה נשנית משנה זו דכתיב א) בימים ההמה ראיתי ביהודה דורכים גתות בשבת ומביאים הערימות אמר ר' אלעזר קנין ומקלות גלוסטרא ומדוכה כולן קודם התרת כלים נשנו קנין דתנן נ) לא סידור הקנין ולא נטילתן דוחה את השבת מקלות דתנן ס) מקלות דקין חלקין היו שם ומניחו על כתפו ועל כתף חבירו ותולה ומפשיט (ע) אמר) רבי אלעזר ארבעה עשר שחל להיות בשבת מניח ידו

רש"י

אפיקטויזין. להקיא שותה משקים ומקיא ולא לרפואה אלא להריק את מעיו שיוכל לאכול ולשתות [היום] הרבה כדאמרי' בפרק חבית ואע"ג דלא גזור בה משום שחיקת סממנין דהא לאו לרפואה היא אסור משום דמתקן גברא: **הכא אורחיה.** והרי הוא כמי שמאכילו ומשקהו: **ליטול בה את הקוץ.** אלמא תקוני גברא במידי דלאו לרפואה לאו משום שחיקת סממנין שרי: **פקיד.** הקוץ הזה אינו מחובר בו אלא מופקד ומתון שם והוצאה זו אינו תיקון: **הכא לא פקיד.** ודמי למלאכה שמסדקין ומכניסין למקום חבור: **מתני' קנה של זיתים.** לאחר מסיקתן אוצר במעטן וטמנן ומתחמם בתוכן ונוח לצאת ויש לו קנה להפכן בו ולבדוק אם כמרו כל צרכן ומגיען לבית הבד: **אם יש קשר בראשו.** כעין פקק של קנה קולמוס: **מקבל טומאה.** דלכלי הוא לפי שעב בראשו קלת: **ואם לאו.** לא דמי לכלי ובגמ' מפרש לה: **גמ' ואמאי.** כי יש בו קשר בראשו נהי נמי דקשר משוי ליה מנא מיהו פשוטי כלי עץ הוא שאפילו חלול הוא אין חללו עשוי לקבל כלום: **הופכו ורואה.** בחלל ראשו שמשמיר שם ע"י שהוא פקוק בקשר מן השמן הזב מן הזיתים ובודק בו אם הגיעו לעצור וזו היא לו קבלה בחלל שלו ואם לאו שאין קשר בראשו אין השמן נראה שם מפני שאינו פקוק וכולו חלל הלכך לאו לקבל הוא עשוי והוי פשוטי כלי עץ ובין כך ובין כך ניטל בשבת דהא כלי הוא להפוך בו זיתים: **מתני' מסר הגדול.** מגירה גדולה שעשויה לקצוץ קורות: **ויתד של מחרישה.** הוא כלי גדול העשוי כסכין שבו עושין חריץ של תלם המענה קולטר"א בלע"ז הנך קפיד עלייהו ומייחד להם מקום דלא חזו למלאכה אחרת: **גמ' אוכלא דקצרי.** כלי נחושת העשוי כפיה נקבים נקבים והוא של כובסים ונותנו על הבגדים ומזלף בו המים על גביהן וי"א שמגמרין מתחתיו והבגדים מונחין עליו ומתגמרין דרך הנקבים: **חרבא דאושכפי.** סכין של רצענין: **וסכינא דאשכבתא.** סכין של בית המקולין שהקצבין מקלפין בו בשר: **חצינא.** דולויר"א כל הני קפדי עלייהו משום דמפגמי ומקצי להו בידים: **ג' כלים.** ותו לא ולקמן אמרינן דבימי נחמיה בן חכליה בבית שני גזרו על טלטול כל הכלים כדי לגדור גדר להחמיר באיסורי שבת מפני שהיו מקילין בה: **מקצוע.** איזמל שמחתכין בו דבלה יעשהו במקלועות מתרגמינן באיזמליהון (ישעיה מד): **זוהמא ליסטרן.** כף גדולה שמסלקין בו זוהמא של קדרה: **וסכין קטן.** שחותכין בו לחם ובשר ואוכלין דהני תדירין בתשמיש: **התירו.** עוד כשראו שחזרו להזהר קצת באיסור שבת וחזרו והתירו כשנזהרו יותר וחזרו והתירו ולקמיה מפרש מאי כולהו הנך התירו: **עד שאמרו.** עוד חזרו והתירו את הכל עד שאמרו הכל ניטלין חוץ מן המסר הגדול כו': **התירו.** לטלטל דבר שעיקר מלאכתו בחול להיתר לדבר המותר בשבת התירו לטלטל לצורך גופו אם הוצרך להשתמש בגוף הכלי אבל לא משום שהוצרך למקומו: **וחזרו והתירו.** את אלו לצורך מקומו: **וחזרו והתירו אף מי שמלאכתו לאיסור.** והוצרך לו בשבת לגופו למלאכת היתר ומיהו לא הותרו אלו לצורך מקומו: **כל הכלים.** הללו שאמרנו חוץ מן המסר הגדול דלא שרי לא לצורך גופו ולא לצורך מקומו ואביי דמתרץ הכי הדר ביה לגבי רבה דאמר לעיל קורנס של נפחים שנינו דדבר שמלאכתו לאיסור שרי לצורך גופו: **א"ל רבא מכדי.** לצורך התירו בפעם ראשונה: **מה לי גופו מה לי מקומו.** תרווייהו צורך נינהו: **מחמה לצל.** שאינו צריך לו עכשיו לא לגופו ולא למקומו אלא חס עליו שמא יתבקע בחמה: **עד שאמרו.** היינו עוד היתר אחרינא כל הכלים אפי' גדולים ומיהו לכדאוקימנא של היתר אפי' מחמה לצל ושל איסור לצורך גופו או מקומו: **אין מטלטלין אותה.** בשלמא לדידי אין מטלטלין אותה לצורך מקומה קאמר אלא לדידך אמאי: **משנה זו.** דלעיל בראשונה היו אומרין ג' כלים ותו לא משום דהוו מזלזלים בשבתות דכתיב בימים ההמה וגו': **קנים ומקלות כו'.** משניות הן כדמפרש ואזיל: **קודם התרת כלים.** מנין האחרון שהותרו כולן לצורך גופן לאביי ולרבא אף לצורך מקומו: **לא סידור הקנים.** שהיו נותנין במערכת לחם הפנים בין חלה לחלה להפרידן ליכנס הרוח ביניהן שלא יתעפשו: **ולא נטילתן.** מן המערכה ישנה: **דוחה את השבת.** אלא נכנס בע"ש ונוטל הקנים ולמחר מסלק המערכה הישנה ומסדר החדשה בלא קנים ולמוצאי שבת נכנס ונותן הקנים ביניהן וזו נשנית קודם היתר מנין הראשון דהא מלאכתן להיתר וקאסר להו לצורך גופן: **מקלין דקין וחלקין היו.** בעזרה בפסח שחל להיות י"ד בחול:

תוספות

וסכינא דאשכבתא. פירש בקונטרס סכין שהקצבים מקלפין בה בשר וי"מ סכין שמשחטין בה שמקפיד שלא תיפגם ויש ליזהר שלא לטלטלו אפי' לצורך גופו דהוי כיתד של מחרישה דלפי' ר"ש מודה כדאמרינן בסוף מכילתין (דף קנז.):

מקצוע של דבילה. לא חשיב אלא כלים דלאו בני קיבול דהא פשיטא דכוסות וקערות וצלוחיות היו מטלטלין:

איתיביה אביי מדוכה. בשלמא לדידי מוקמינן לצורך מקומו וה"מ לשנויי כר' נחמיה כדשני לעיל ואביי נמי הוה ידע דהא משני ליה רבה הכי לעיל אלא פריך לרבה אולי יאמר תירוץ אחר ורבא לא בעי לשנויי כר' נחמיה דלית הלכתא כוותיה ורבה דמשני ליה כר' נחמיה משום דמשמע ליה דאין מטלטלין אותם בשום ענין: **הכא** נמי מחמה לצל. והא דנקט קצב עליו בשר אע"ג דלצורך גופו ומקומו נמי שרי לאשמעינן דאפילו בהא פליגי ב"ש דלא שרו מחמת שמחת יו"ט:

לא סידור קנים. אע"ג דאין שבות (א) במקדש כמה שבותים * אשכחן במקדש ס) שגזרו פעמים לצורך כי הכא בקנים ומקלות לפי שהיו מחללים את השבת: **הרי** היא ככל הכלים. אע"ג דקודם התרת כלים נשנית איכא למימר ככל הכלים כעין כוסות וקערות:

עין משפט נר מצוה

יא א מיי' פכ"ו מהל' שבת הלכה ז:
יב ב מיי' פ"ב מהלכות כלים הלכה י:
יג ג מיי' שם פ"ב הל"ב:
יד ד ה מיי' פכ"ה מהל' שבת הלכה ט סמג לאוין סה טור ושו"ע או"ח סימן שח סעיף א:
טו ו מיי' שם הלכה ג טוש"ע שם סעיף ג ד:
טז ז מיי' פ"ה מהלכות תמידין ומוספין הלכה יא:
יז ח מיי' פ"א מהלכות ק"פ הלכה יד:

גליון הש"ס

תוס' ד"ה לא וכו' אשכחן במקדש. ע"ל דף קכו ע"א תוס' ד"ה והמונח:

רבינו חננאל

ממטן למעלן אסיר. פי' אם יש לאדם פוגלא טמונה בתבן או אפילו בעפר תיחוח עומדת כעין נטועה ראשה טמונה ועליה מגולין עכשיו כשבא לנוטלה אם אוחזו בעלים ומושך הראש ומסלקה זהו ממעלה למטה. אע"פ כשמגביה התבן והעפר משתרבב במקומן ויורד שרי אבל לאחוז קצה הראש הטמונה ולהגביהה ממטה למעלה לא. אלמא שטלטול מן הצד שמיה טלטול. ומפרקינן הדר ביה מההיא. מחט שניטל חררה או עוקצה. פי' חרירה הנקב שלה. עוקצה ראשה הוא. חידודה תרגמה אביי אליבא דרבא בגלמי והן פשוטין כדתנן גלמי כלי מתכות טהורין פשוטיהן טמאין ואלו הן וכו'. והן חוטי ברזל משוכין וחתך אותן חתיכות חתיכות ולוקח מהן האומן כשיעור אורך מחט ומחדד ראשה האחת ונוקב הקצה השני ונעשה מחט. וקודם שיחדדנה וינקבנה נקראת אותה החתיכה גולם. כגון זו וכיוצא בה שהן עומדות להעשות כלי ניטלין בשבת. אבל מחט שניטל חררה או עוקצה אסור. גרוטאות הוא לשון יון. ופתרונו כלי מוכן להטיל בו התגר כלי נחושת או כלי ברזל שבורין שיזדמנו לו לקנותם קונה ומשליכם לאותו כלי כדי להתיכם. ונקראין גרוטאות ומנהג נהגו לקרות להגר גרוטאות: אסובי יונקא. פי' כשנשפל ערלת הגרון של תינוק חיה משימה החיה את אצבעותיה בפיו ומסלקת אותה הערלה. ופעמים שמקיא התינוק ועל זה אקשינן עלה והא אין עושין אפיקטויזין בשבת כו'. ורבותינו הגאונים אמרו פי' אחר. ואנן כתבנו מה שקבלנו מרבותינו: מתני' קנה של זיתים כו' ואמרינן אמאי פשוטי כלי עץ הוא ואין מקבלין טומאה. ומפרקינן תנא משמיה דר' נחמיה בשעה שמהפך בו את הזיתים הופכו ורואה בו. ולא פי' מה הוא רואה בו. אבל פירשו בתלמוד א"י. קנה שהתקינו להיות בודק בו הזיתים. כיצד הוא יודע אם מלוכלך במשקה בידוע שנגמרה מלאכת המעטן. ואם לאו בידוע שלא נגמרה מלאכת המעטן. א"ל ר' מנא לא תני שמואל אלא להיות שולה בו הזיתים. כלומר יש בו בית קבול: **אמר** רב נחמן האי אוכלא דקצרי כיתד של מחרישה דמי. ואסור לטלטלה. אוכלא. אבן גדולה שנותן הכובס עליה היריעה כשהיא שרויה במים ומכה עליו במזורי. מכה ומהפך ומכה. ועוד שורה ומכה. ואחרי שישלים שוטחה ומייבשה. וחוזר ושורה אותה פעם אחר פעם עד שתתלבן היטב. וי"א כלי חרס מנוקב שכופין אותו ע"ג גחלים ומקטרין בגפרית הכלים ללבנן. אמר אביי חרבא דאשכפתא. וסכינא דאשכבתא וחצינא דנגרי כיתד של מחרישה דמו ואסור לטלטלם. חרבא דאושכפי. איזמל של שכף כדמתרגמינן עשה לך חרבות צורים. איזמלין חריפין. סכינא דאשכבתא. סכין המיוחדת לשחיטה בלבד. חצינא דנגרי הוא גרזן. והוא המעצד של חרש כיון דקפיד אפגמיהו קבע ליה מקום ומסיח דעתו מלעשות בהן מלאכה אחרת הללו וכיוצא בהן שהן מוקצה מחמת חסרון כיס אסור לטלטלן בשבת. והרי מפורש בסוף פרק מי שהחשיך דכולהו הני היינו טעמא דאסירי משום חסרון כיס נינהו. ואפילו ר' שמעון מודה דתנן סתמא לדברי הכל כל הכלים ניטלין בשבת חוץ מן המסר הגדול ויתד של מחרישה. מקצוע של דבילה כלי ברזל שחותכין בו דבילה. זומליסטרון תרווד שמהפך בו הקדירה. כדתנן זומליסטרא שנוטל כפה טמאה מפני המזלג וכו'. א"ר חנינא בימי נחמיה בן חכליה נשנית משנה זו דכתיב בימים ההמה ראיתי ביהודה דורכים גיתות בשבת. כיון שראום כך אסרו להן כל הכלים ושרי להן הא דתנן רבנן. בראשונה היו אומרים שלשה כלים ניטלין בשבת מקצוע של דבילה והומליסטרון של קדירה. וסכין קטנה. כיון שנגדרו וחזרו לדקדק בשמירת שבת היו מתירין להן הכל חוץ ממסר הגדול ויתד של מחרישה. וכך הוא מפורש בתלמוד א"י: **א"ר** אלעזר קנים ומקלות וקלוסטרא ומדוכה כולם קודם התרת כלים נשנו. ולפיכך נשנו באיסור. קנים הם קנים של לחם הפנים. והן שנוין במס' מנחות

מסורת הש"ס

א) [חולין כה.], ב) לעיל סו. חגיגה כו: מנחות צו: [בכורות לח.], ג) [במשנה שבמשניות ליתא ר' יוסי אומר וכן מוכח מסוגיא דלקמן קנז. ע"ש אלא בעירובין לה. איתא סבר לה כר' יוסי דאמר כל הכלים ניטלין וכו' וע"ע רש"י ע"ש ועיין ברי"ף ורא"ש איתא ר' יוסי אומר כל הכלים וכו'], ד) לקמן קנז. עירובין לה., ה) [גי' הערוך בערך אכל אובלא וע"ש פירושו בשני אופנים], ו) [תוספ' פט"ו], ז) [לקמן קכד.], ח) ביצה יא., ט) [תוספ' ביצה פ"א], י) [עי' תוס' ב"ק לד. ד"ה כיון], כ) מנחות נז., ל) פסחים סה., מ) [צ"ל ר' אלעזר אומר], נ) [וע"ע תוס' מנחות נז. ד"ה לא סדור ותוספות עירובין קב: ד"ה והעליון], ס) שייך לדף קכד. ע"א.

הגהות הב"ח

(א) תוס' ד"ה לא סידור וכו' דאין שבות. נ"ב ע"ל פרק המצניע דף צה בתוס' ד"ה שרא ואזלא:

תורה אור השלם

א) בַּיָּמִים הָהֵמָּה רָאִיתִי בִיהוּדָה דֹּרְכִים גִּתּוֹת בַּשַּׁבָּת וּמְבִיאִים הָעֲרֵמוֹת וְעֹמְסִים עַל הַחֲמֹרִים וְאַף יַיִן עֲנָבִים וּתְאֵנִים וְכָל מַשָּׂא וּמְבִיאִים יְרוּשָׁלִַם בְּיוֹם הַשַּׁבָּת וָאָעִיד בְּיוֹם מִכְרָם צָיִד: [נחמיה יג, טו]

רב נסים גאון

בשעה שמהפך בו זיתים הופכו ורואה בו. בגמ' דבני מערבא גרסי דבי ר' ינאי אמרי שולה בו זיתים כיצד הוא יודע אם היה מלוכלך במשקה בידוע שגמרה מלאכת המעטן ואם לאו בידוע שלא נגמרה מלאכת המעטן אמר לון ר' לא תני שמואל אלא להיות שולה בו את הזיתים ומשום הכי אמרי דמקבל טומאה והואיל וככלי קיבול דמי. אמר רב נחמן האי אוכלא דקצרי כיתד של מחרישה דמי אוכלא דקצרי הוא כלי שדומה לדלעת ומנוקב הוא כולו נקבין נקבין ובו מולפין מים הכובסים על הבגדים ומשכחת לה בפ' כל ישראל יש להם חלק (סנהדרין דף צב) אמר רב נחמן אותו ככברה מנוקבין אמר אביי כאוכלא דקצרי:

ליקוטי רש"י

אפיקטויזין. להקיא והוא בנטורקין אפיק טפי מן מזון האכול יותר מדאי מולא ומקיא [סוטה מ:]. **מופקד.** ועומד שם כמתון בו [לקמן קלג:]. **פשוטי כלי עץ.** אפילו נגמרה מלאכתן טהורין דאיתקש עץ לשק דכתיב (ויקרא יא) מכל כלי עץ או בגד או עור או שק מה שק כל מטלטל מלא וריקן [חולין כה.]. **דומיא דשק בעינן.** שקבול שלו עשוי לטלטל על ידו מה שנותנין לתוכו [לעיל סו:]. לענין טומאה הוקשו כלי עץ לשק דכתיב כל אשר יפול עליו מהם במותם יטמא מכל כלי עץ או בגד (ויקרא יא) [חגיגה כו:]. **כל הכלים ניטלין.** ואפילו מלאכתן לאיסור ור' שמעון היא. חוץ מן המסר הגדול. מגירה שהיא לאומנין לקוץ בה עצים ומוקצה מחמת חסרון כיס הוא שלא יפגמו חריצים שהוא עשוי כמסרק. ויתד של מחרישה. החופר את הקרקע קולטר"א בלע"ז [לקמן קנז.]. **אוכלא דקצרי.** כלי של כובסין שמנקב ומזלפין בו מים על הבגדים [סנהדרין צב.]. כלי שמשימין בו הכובסין בגדיהן [נדרים כג.]. **קצרי.** כך שמן של כובסין שמעתי אומרים על שם שמקצרין בגדי צמר כשדורסין אותן ברגליהן במים שקורין פולו"ר והיינו דמתרגמינן עין רוגל (ש"ב יז) עינא דקצרא [תענית כט:]. הכובס נקרא קצרי בלשון ארמי [ב"ק קיט:]. [המשך בדף קכד.]

place, but **not from the sun to the shade** for its protection. וַעֲדַיִין בְּאָדָם אֶחָד אֵין בִּשְׁנֵי בְנֵי אָדָם לֹא – **Still,** it was permitted **only** to move utensils that could be taken **by one person,** but **not** those that needed to be taken **by two people,** עַד שֶׁאָמְרוּ – **until they** finally **said:** כָּל הַכֵּלִים נִיטָּלִין בְּשַׁבָּת אֲפִילוּ בִּשְׁנֵי בְנֵי אָדָם – **All utensils may be taken on the Sabbath even** if they must be taken **by two people,** except for a large saw and a colter.[20]

Rava's explanation is challenged:

אֵיתִיבֵיהּ אַבַּיֵי – **Abaye challenged him** on the basis of the following Baraisa: מְדוֹכָה – A MORTAR in which garlic is usually crushed – אִם יֵשׁ בָּהּ שׁוּם מְטַלְטְלִין אוֹתָהּ – IF IT CONTAINS GARLIC IT MAY BE MOVED on the Sabbath, וְאִם לָאו אֵין מְטַלְטְלִין אוֹתָהּ – BUT IF NOT, IT MAY NOT BE MOVED.[21] I can interpret this as meaning that the mortar may not be moved for the sake of its place, but how will you accommodate the Baraisa's ruling?

Rava responds:

הָכָא בְּמַאי עַסְקִינַן – **What are we dealing with here?** מֵחַמָּה לְצֵל – It is with moving the mortar **from the sun to the shade** for its protection.[22]

Abaye presents another challenge:

אֵיתִיבֵיהּ – **He challenged [Rava]** on the basis of the following Baraisa: וְשָׁוִין – BUT THEY [Beis Shammai and Beis Hillel] AGREE concerning a pestle, שֶׁאִם קִצֵּב עָלָיו בָּשָׂר שֶׁאָסוּר לְטַלְטְלוֹ – THAT IF ONE HAS already CHOPPED MEAT ON IT HE MAY NOT MOVE IT on Yom Tov.[23] I can interpret this as meaning that the pestle may not be moved for the sake of its place, but how will you accommodate the Baraisa's ruling?

Rava responds:

הָכָא נַמִּי מֵחַמָּה לְצֵל – **Here, too,** we are dealing with moving the item **from the sun to the shade** for its protection.[24]

The Gemara explains when the original prohibition against moving utensils was enacted:

אָמַר רַבִּי חֲנִינָא – **R' Chanina said:** בִּימֵי נְחֶמְיָה בֶּן חֲכַלְיָה נִשְׁנֵית מִשְׁנָה זוֹ – **This teaching was taught in the days of Nechemiah ben Chachaliah.** דִּכְתִיב – **For it is stated:**[25] ,,בַּיָּמִים הָהֵמָּה רָאִיתִי בִיהוּדָה דֹרְכִים־גִּתּוֹת בַּשַּׁבָּת וּמְבִיאִים הָעֲרֵמוֹת" – ***During those days, I saw [people] in Judah pressing wine-vats on the Sabbath and bringing in the heaps [from the fields].***[26]

A related discussion is cited:

אָמַר רַבִּי אֶלְעָזָר – **R' Elazar said:** קָנִין וּמַקְלוֹת גְּלוּסְטְרָא וּמְדוֹכָה – The Tannaic teachings concerning **tubes, staffs, a knob and a mortar** כּוּלָּן קוֹדֶם הַתָּרַת כֵּלִים נִשְׁנוּ – **were all taught before** the movement of **utensils was permitted.**[27]

The Gemara elaborates:

קָנִין – The teaching concerning **tubes,** דִּתְנַן – **for we learned in a Mishnah:**[28] לֹא סִידּוּר הַקָּנִין וְלֹא נְטִילָתָן דּוֹחָה אֶת הַשַּׁבָּת – NEITHER THE ARRANGEMENT OF THE TUBES on the Temple *Shulchan* NOR THEIR REMOVAL OVERRIDES THE SABBATH laws.[29]

NOTES

20. All utensils – including those so large that they must be taken by two people – may be moved on the Sabbath *in some circumstances,* except for those that are *muktzeh* due to concern for monetary loss. According to Rava, the halachah is that a permitted-use utensil may be moved for the sake of its use or place, as well as for its own protection; and a forbidden-use utensil may be moved for the sake of its use or place, but not merely for its own protection (*Rashi*).

Rava further differs with Abaye in regard to the status of very large or heavy utensils that can be taken only by two people. Abaye forbids the movement of these utensils and permits taking only those that can be taken by one person, albeit with two hands. He considers larger utensils *muktzeh* because people set them down in a designated place due to the difficulty of moving them. Rava, however, holds that a utensil is never deemed *muktzeh* on account of its size. Although he mentions *two* people, he means that a utensil may be moved even if many people are needed to lift it (*Rashba, Ritva MHK* ed.; see above, 122a; see also *Orach Chaim* 308:2 with *Beur HaGra* and *Mishnah Berurah* §8; cf. *Re'ah,* cited by *Chidushei HaRan,* and see *Chasam Sofer*). The final halachah follows Rava in regard to all of these issues (see *Orach Chaim* 308:2-4).

21. The mortar is a forbidden-use utensil. See 123a note 2.

22. Abaye was certainly aware of this answer, but he challenged Rava in the hope of eliciting a more novel response. Abaye was also aware that Rava could respond that the Baraisa follows the view of R' Nechemyah, as Rabbah responded when Abaye challenged him with this Baraisa above, on 123a (*Tosafos* ד"ה איתיביה; see also *Ramban, Rashba, Ritva MHK* ed.; see ibid. for an alternative explanation).

23. See 123a note 4.

24. Thus, the Baraisa means that after one has used the pestle to chop meat on it he may not return it to its usual storage area, which is the equivalent of moving it from the sun to the shade for its protection (*Ritva MHK* ed.).

In the first segment of the Baraisa (cited on 123a), Beis Hillel state that one may take the pestle to chop meat on it. However, according to Rava, they actually hold that one may move the pestle for any legitimate need – whether for its use or its place. The reason the Baraisa focuses on the case of chopping meat is to bring out the point that Beis Shammai forbid the use of the pestle even for this purpose, which would enhance the enjoyment of Yom Tov (*Tosafos* ד"ה הכא נמי). Beis Shammai hold that one may not move a forbidden-use utensil even for the sake of its use (*Rashi* to *Beitzah* 10a and 11a).

[Note that the current interpretation of this Baraisa differs from the one offered by Rabbah above, on 123a.]

25. *Nehemiah* 13:15.

26. Nechemiah goes on to state (ibid. vs. 17-22) that he devoted himself to halting the Sabbath desecration and restoring the sanctity of the holy day. R' Chanina teaches that one of the measures Nechemiah employed was the enactment (together with the other Sages of his generation) of the prohibition against moving utensils. When the degree of Sabbath observance improved, the Sages gradually eased the restriction. The easing took place shortly after the decree was enacted, for as the Gemara implies, the initial teaching was in force only *during the days* of Nechemiah ben Chachaliah (*Tosafos* to *Bava Kamma* 94b end of ד"ה בימי רבי). [For a discussion of what law was in effect *before* Nechemiah's decree, see *Aruch HaShulchan* 308:4-5; cf. *Chasam Sofer's* introduction to *Beitzah – Mahadura Tinyana;* see also *Teshuvos Maimoni* to *Sefer Mishpatim* §20.]

27. The four Mishnahs and Baraisos that will be cited shortly all reflect the law that was in effect before the third level of permission was granted, i.e. before the movement of a forbidden-use utensil was permitted – according to Abaye for the sake of its use, and according to Rava even for the sake of its place (*Rashi*). [In fact, some of these teachings predate even the first level of permission, when the movement of permitted-use utensils was allowed.]

28. *Menachos* 96a.

29. In the Temple, twelve loaves of *panim* bread (*lechem hapanim*) were placed on the *Shulchan* (Table) every Sabbath and remained there until the following Sabbath, when new loaves were brought and the old ones were distributed among the Kohanim for consumption. The loaves were arranged on the *Shulchan* in two six-loaf columns. The loaves in each column did not rest on each other, for they might become moldy if there was no ventilation between them. Rather, two pillars stood on either side of the *Shulchan* and the pillars supported golden tubes that formed a series of shelves in the airspace above the *Shulchan.* [See diagram.] The bottom loaf in each column

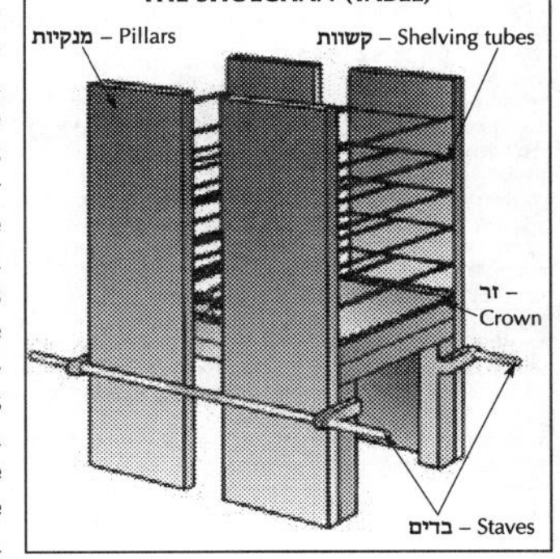

עין משפט
נר מצוה

יא א מיי' פכ"ו מהל' שבת הלכה ז:
יב ב מיי' פ"א מהלכות כלים הלכה יב:
יג ג מיי' שם פ"כ הל"ב:
יד ד ה מיי' פכ"ה מהל' שבת הלכה ט סמג לאוין סה טוש"ע או"ח סימן שח סעיף ח:
טו ו מיי' שם הלכה ג טוש"ע שם סעיף ג ד:
טז ז מיי' פ"ה מהלכות תמידין ומוספין הלכה יא:
יז ח מיי' פ"א מהלכות ק"פ הלכה יד:

גליון הש"ס

תוס' ד"ה לא וכו' אשכחן במקדש. ע"ל דף קכו ע"א תוס' ד"ה וסמוכות:

רבינו חננאל

ממטן למעלן אסיר. פי' אם יש לאדם פוגלא טמונה בתבן או אפילו בעפר תיחוח עומדת כעין נטועה ראשה טמונה ועליה מגולין עכשיו כשבא לנטלה אם אוחז בעלים ומושך הראש למטה. אע"פ כשמגביה התבן והעפר משתרבב במקומו ויורד שרי אבל לאחוז קצה הראש הטמונה ולהגביהה ממטה למעלה לא. שטלטול מן הצד שמיה טלטול. ומפרקינן הדר ביה מההיא. כגון מחט שניטל חררה או עוקצה. פי' חרירה הנקב שלה. עוקצה ראשה הוא. חרידה תרגמה אביי אליבא דרבא בגלמי והן פשוטין כדתנן גלמי כלי מתכות טהורין פשוטיהן טמאין ואלו הן וכו'. והן חוטי ברזל משוכין ותחתך אותן חתיכות חתיכות ולוקח מהן האומן כשיעור אורך מחט ונוקב הקצה השני ונעשה מחט. וקודם שיחדדנה וינקבנה נקראת אותה החתיכה גולם. כגון זו וכיוצא בה שהן עומדות להעשות כלי ניטלין בשבת. אבל מחט שניטל חררה או עוקצה אסור. גרוטאות הוא לשון יון. ופתרונו הוא כלי מוכן להטיל בו התגר כלי נחושת או כלי ברזל שבורין שיזדמנו לו לקנותם קונה ומשליכם לאותו כלי כדי להתיכם. ונקראין גרוטאות ומיכן נהגו לקרות לתגר גרוטאות: אסובי ינוקא. פי' כשנפל ערלת הגרון של תינוק משימה החיה את אצבעותיה בפיו ומסלקת אותה הערלה. ופעמים שמקיא התינוק ועל זה אקשינן עלה והא אין עושין אפיקטויזין בשבת כו'. ורבותינו הגאונים אמרו פי' אחר. ואנו כתבנו מה שקבלנו מרבותינו: מתני' קנה של זיתים כו'. ואמרינן אמאי פשוטי כלי עץ הוא ואין מקבלין טומאה. ומפרקינן תנא משמיה דר' נחמיה בשעה שהופכן בו את הזיתים הופכו ורואה בו. ולא פי' מה הוא רואה בו. אבל פירשו בתלמוד א"י. קנה שהתקינו להיות בודק בו הזיתים. כיצד הוא יודע אם מלוכלך במשקה בידוע שנגמרה מלאכת המעטן. ואם לאו בידוע שלא נגמרה מלאכת המעטן. א"ל ר' מנא לא תני שמואל אלא להיות שולה בו הזיתים. כלומר יש בו בית קבול: אמר רב נחמן האי אוכלא דקצרי כיתד של מחרישה דמי. ואסור לטלטלה. אוכלא. אבן גדולה שנותן הכובס עליה היריעה שרוצה ללבנה והיא שרויה במים ומכה עליו במזורי. מכה ומהפך ומכה. ועוד שורה ומכה. ואחרי שישלים שוטחה ומייבשה. ועוד חוזר ושורה אותה פעם אחר פעם עד שתתלבן היטב. וי"א כלי נחושת דומה לכף שיש לו נקבים הרבה שנותנין בו גחלים ומקטרין בגפרית הכלים ללבנן. אמר אביי חרבא דאושכפא וסכינא דאשכבתא וחצינא דנגרי כיתד של מחרישה דמו ואסור לטלטלן. חרבא דאושכפי. איזמל של שכף כדמתרגמינן עשה לך חרבות צורים. איזמלין חריפין. סכינא דאשכבתא. סכין המיוחדת לשחיטה בלבד. חצינא דנגרי הוא גרזן. הוא המעצד של חרש כיון דקפדי אפגמייהו קבע ליה מקום ומסיח דעתו מלעשות בהן מלאכה אחרת הללו וכיוצא בהן שהן מוקצה מחמת חסרון כיס אסור לטלטלן בשבת.

תוספות

וסכינא דאשכבתא. פירש בקונטרס סכין שהקצבים מקצבין בה בשר וי"מ סכין ששוחטין בה שמקפיד שלא תיפגם ויש ליזהר שלא לטלטלו אפי' לצורך גופו דהוי כיתד של מחרישה דאפי' ר"ש מודה כדאמרינן בסוף מכילתין (דף קנז.):

מקצוע של דבילה. לא חשיב אלא כלים דלאו בני קיבול דהא פשיטא דכוסות וקערות ולגלוסות היו מטלטלין:

איתיביה אביי מדוכה. בשלמא לדידי מוקמינן לצורך מקומו וה"נ לשנויי כר' נחמיה כדשני לעיל ואביי נמי הוה ידע דהא משני ליה רבה הכי לעיל אלא פריך לרבה אולי יאמר מירוץ אחר ורבה לא בעי לשנויי כר' נחמיה דלית הלכתא כוותיה ורבה דמשני ליה כר' נחמיה משום דמשמע ליה אין מטלטלין אותה בשום ענין:

הכא נמי מחמה לצל. והא דנקט דקצב עליו בשר אע"ג דלצורך גופו ומקומו נמי שרי לאשמעינן דאפילו בהא פליגי ב"ש דלא שרו מחמה לחמה יו"ט:

לא סידור קנים. אע"ג דלאין שבות (א) במקדש כמה שבותים * אשכחן במקדש שגזרו פעמים לצורך כי הכא בקנים ומקלות לפי שהיו מחללים את השבת:

הרי היא ככל הכלים. אע"ג דקודם התרת כלים נשנית היכא למימ' ככל הכלים כגון כוסות וקערות: הא

גמרא

אפיקטויזין בשבת ורב ששת התם לאו אורחיה הכא אורחיה אמר רב ששת מנא אמינא לה דתנן מחט של יד ליטול בה את הקוץ ורב נחמן התם פקיד הכא לא פקיד: **מתני'** קנה של זיתים אם יש קשר בראשו מקבל טומאה ואם לאו אין מקבל טומאה בין כך ובין כך ניטל בשבת: **גמ'** אמאי פשוטי כלי עץ הוא ופשוטי כלי עץ אינן מקבלין טומאה מ"ט דומיא דשק בעינן תנא משמיה דר' נחמיה בשעה שמהפך בזיתים הופכו ורואה בו: **מתני'** ר' יוסי אומר כל הכלים ניטלין חוץ מן המסר הגדול ויתד של מחרישה: **גמ'** אמר ר"נ האי אוכלא דקצרי כיתד של מחרישה דמיא אמר אביי חרבא דאושכפי וסכינא דאשכבתא וחצינא דנגרי כיתד של מחרישה דמי ת"ר בראשונה היו אומרים שלשה כלים ניטלין בשבת מקצוע של דבילה וזוהמא ליסטרון של קדרה וסכין קטנה שעל גבי שלחן התירו וחזרו והתירו וחזרו והתירו עד שאמרו כל הכלים ניטלין בשבת חוץ מן מסר הגדול ויתד של מחרישה מאי התירו וחזרו והתירו וחזרו והתירו אמר אביי התירו דבר שמלאכתו להיתר לצורך גופו וחזרו והתירו דבר שמלאכתו להיתר לצורך מקומו וחזרו והתירו דבר שמלאכתו לאיסור לצורך גופו אין לצורך מקומו לא ועדיין בידו אחת אין בשתי ידיו לא עד שאמרו כל הכלים ניטלין בשבת ואפי' בשתי ידים א"ל רבא מכדי התירו קתני מה לי לצורך גופו מה לי לצורך מקומו אלא אמר רבא התירו דבר שמלאכתו להיתר בין לצורך גופו ובין לצורך מקומו וחזרו והתירו מחמה לצל וחזרו והתירו דבר שמלאכתו לאיסור לצורך גופו ולצורך מקומו אין מחמה לצל לא ועדיין באדם אחד אין בשני בני אדם לא עד שאמרו כל הכלים ניטלין בשבת אפילו בשני בני אדם איתיביה אביי מדוכה אם יש בה שום מטלטלין אותה ואם לאו אין מטלטלין אותה הכא במאי עסקינן מחמה לצל איתיביה ושוין שאם קצב עליו בשר שאסור לטלטלו הכא נמי מחמה לצל אמר ר' חנינא בימי נחמיה בן חכליה נשנית משנה זו דכתיב א) בימים ההמה ראיתי ביהודה דורכים גתות בשבת ומביאים הערימות אמר ר' אלעזר קנין ומקלות גלוסטרא ומדוכה כולן קודם התרת כלים נשנו קנין דתנן לא סידור הקנין ולא נטילתן דוחה את השבת מקלות דתנן מקלות דקין חלקין היו שם ומניחו על כתפו ועל כתף חבירו ותולה ומפשיט (אמר) רבי אלעזר ארבעה עשר שחל להיות בשבת מניח ידו

רש"י

אפיקטויזין. להקיא שותה משקים ומקיא ולא לרפואה אלא להריק את מעיו שיוכל לאכול ולשתות [היום] הרבה כדאמרי' בפרק חבית ואע"ג דלא גזור בה משום שחיקת סממנין דהא לאו לרפואה היא אסור משום דמתקן גברא: הכא אורחיה. והרי הוא כמי שמאכילו ומשקהו: ליטול בה את הקוץ. אלמא תקוני גברא במידי דלאו לרפואה דליכא משום שחיקת סממנין שרי: פקיד. הקוץ הזה אינו מחובר בו אלא מופקד ונתון שם והוצאה זו אינו תיקון: הכא לא פקיד. ודמי למלאכה שמסלקן ומכניסן למקום חבור: מתני' קנה של זיתים. לאחר מסיקתן בוצר במעטן ושמנן מתאסף בתוכן ונוח לצאת ויש לו קנה להפכן בו ולבדוק אם כמרו כל צרכן ומגיען לבית הבד: אם יש קשר בראשו. כעין פקק של קנה קולמוס: מקבל טומאה. דכלי הוא לפי שעב בראשו קצת: ואם לאו. לא דמי לכלי וגמ' מפרש לה: גמ' ואמאי. כי יש בו קשר בראשו נמי כי קשר משוי ליה מנא מיהו פשוטי כלי עץ הוא שאפילו חלול הוא אין חללו עשוי לקבל כלום: הופכו ורואה. בחלל ראשו שמשחיר שם ע"י שהוא פקוק בקשר מן השמן הזב מן הזיתים ובודק בו אם הגיעו לעצור וזו היא לו קבלה בחלל שלו ואם לאו שאין קשר בראשו אין השמן נראה שם מפני שאינו פקוק וכולו חלל הלכך לאו לקבל הוא עשוי והוי פשוטי כלי עץ ובין כך ובין כך ניטל בשבת דהא כלי הוא להפוך בו זיתים: מתני' מסר הגדול. מגירה גדולה שעשויה לנסור קורות: ויתד של מחרישה. הוא כלי גדול העשוי כסכין שבו עושין חריץ של תלם המענה קולטר"א בלע"ז דהנך קפיד עלייהו ומייחד להם מקום דלא חזו למלאכה אחרת: גמ' אוכלא דקצרי. כלי נחושת העשוי כפה נקובה נקבים והוא של כובסים ונותן על הבגדים ומזלף בו המים עליהן וי"א שמגמרין מוגמר מתחתיו והבגדים מונחין עליו ומתגמרין דרך הנקבים: חרבא דאושכפי. סכין של רצענין: וסכינא דאשכבתא. סכין של בית המקולין שהקצבין מקצבין בו בשר: חצינא. דולויר"א כל הני קפדי עלייהו משום דמפגמי ומקצי להו בידים: ג' כלים. ותו לא ולקמן אמרינן דבימי נחמיה בן חכליה בבית שני גזרו על טלטול כל הכלים כדי לגדור גדר להחמיר באיסורי שבת מפני שהיו מקילין בה: מקצוע. איזמל שמחתכין בו דבלה יעשהו במקצועות מתרגמינן באיזמליהון (ישעיה מד): זוהמא ליסטרון. כף גדולה שמסלקין בו זוהמא של קדרה: וסכין קטן. שחותכין בו לחם ובשר ואוכלין דהני תדירין בתשמיש: התירו. עוד כשראו שחזרו להזהר קצת באיסור שבת וחזרו והתירו כשנזהרו יותר וחזרו והתירו ולקמיה מפרש מאי כולהו הנך התירו: עד שאמרו. עוד חזרו והתירו את הכל עד שאמרו הכל ניטלין חוץ מן המסר הגדול כו': התירו. לטלטל דבר שעיקר מלאכתו בחול להיתר לדבר המותר בשבת התירו לטלטל לצורך גופו אם הוצרך להשתמש בגוף הכלי אבל לא משום שהוצרך למקומו: וחזרו והתירו. את אלו לצורך מקומו: וחזרו והתירו אף מי שמלאכתו לאיסור. והוצרך לו בשבת לגופו למלאכת היתר ומיהו לא הותרו אלו לצורך מקומו: כל הכלים. הללו שאמרנו חוץ מן המסר הגדול דלא שרי לא לצורך גופו ולא לצורך מקומו ואביי דמתרץ הכי הדר ביה לגבי רבה דאמר לעיל קורנס של נפחים שניטו לדבר שמלאכתו לאיסור שרי לצורך גופו: א"ל רבא מכדי. לצורך התירו בפעם ראשונה: מה לי גופו מה לי מקומו. תרווייהו צורך נינהו: מחמה לצל. שאינו צריך לו עכשיו לא לגופו ולא למקומו אלא חס עליו שמא יתבקע בחמה: עד שאמרו. היינו עוד היתר אחרינא כל הכלים אפי' גדולים ומיהו לכדאוקימנא של היתר אפי' מחמה לצל ושל איסור לצורך גופו או מקומו: אין מטלטלין אותה. בשלמא לדידי אין מטלטלין אותה לצורך מקומה קאמר אלא לדידך אמאי: משנה זו. דלעיל בראשונה היו אומרין ג' כלים ותו לא משום דהוו מזלזלים בשבתות דכתיב בימים ההמה וגו': קנים ומקלות כו'. משניות הן כדמפרש ואזיל: קודם התרת כלים. מנין האחרון שהותרו כולן לצורך גופן לאביי ולרבא אף לצורך מקומו: לא סידור הקנים. שהיו נותנין במערכת לחם הפנים בין חלה לחלה להפרידן ליכנס הרוח ביניהן שלא יתעפשו: ולא נטילתן. מן המערכה ישנה: דוחה את השבת. אלא נכנס בע"ש ונוטל הקנים ולמחר מסלק המערכה הישנה ומסדר החדשה בלא קנים ולמוצאי שבת נכנס ונותן הקנים ביניהן זו נשנית קודם היתר מנין הראשון דהא מלאכתן להיתר וקאסר להו לצורך גופן: מקלין דקין וחלקין היו. בעזרה בפסח שחל להיות י"ד בחול:

מסורת הש"ס

א) [חולין כה.], ב) לעיל סג: חגיגה כו: מנחות נז: [בכורות לח.], ג) [במשנה שבמשניות ליתא ר' יוסי אומר וכן מוגה מתוס' דלקמן קנז. ע"ש אבל בעירובין לה. איתא סבר לה כר' יוסי דאמר כל הכלים ניטלין וכו' וע"ע וכן ברי"ף ורא"ש ליתא ר' יוסי אומר כל הכלים וכו'], ד) לקמן קנז. עירובין לה., ה) [גי' הערוך בערך אבל אובלא וע"ש פירושו בשני אופנים], ו) [תוספ' פט"ו], ז) [לקמן קכד.], ח) כילה פ"א, ט) [תוספ' כילה פ"ב], י) [עי' תוס' ב"ק לב. ד"ה בימין], כ) מנחות צו., ל) פסחים סד., מ) [נ"ל ר' אלעזר אומר], נ) [וע"ע תוס' מנחות נז. ד"ה לא סידור ותוספות עירובין דף קב: ד"ה והעלין], ס) שייך לדף קכד ע"א.

הגהות הב"ח

(א) תוס' ד"ה לא סידור וכו' דלאין שבות. נ"ב ע"ל פרק המצניע דף צד סוף ע"ב ד"ה שרא דלמא:

תורה אור השלם

א) בַּיָּמִים הָהֵמָּה רָאִיתִי בִיהוּדָה דֹּרְכִים גִּתּוֹת בַּשַּׁבָּת וּמְבִיאִים הָעֲרֵמוֹת וְעֹמְסִים עַל הַחֲמֹרִים וְאַף יַיִן עֲנָבִים וּתְאֵנִים וְכָל מַשָּׂא וּמְבִיאִים יְרוּשָׁלִַם בְּיוֹם הַשַּׁבָּת וָאָעִיד בְּיוֹם מִכְרָם צָיִד: [נחמיה יג, טו]

רב נסים גאון

בשעה שמהפך בו זיתים הופכו ורואה בו. בגמ' דבני מערבא גרסינן דבי ר' ינאי אמרי קנה שהתקינו להפך בו זיתים כיצד הוא יודע אם היה מלוכלך במשקה בידוע שנגמרה מלאכת המעטן ואם לאו בידוע שלא נגמרה מלאכת המעטן אמר לון ר' לא תני שמואל אלא להיות שולה בו את הזיתים ומשום הכי אמרי דמקבל טומאה הוא דהואיל וככלי קיבול דמי. אמר רב נחמן האי אוכלא דקצרי כיתד של מחרישה דמי אוכלא דקצרי הוא כלי שדומה לדלעת ומנוקב הוא כולו נקבים ובו מזלפין מים הכובסין על הבגדים ומשכחת לה בפ' כל ישראל יש להם חלק (סנהדרין דף צב) הללו אמרו מנקבין אותו ככברה אמר אביי כאוכלא דקצרי:

ליקוטי רש"י

אפיקטויזין. להקיא והוא כנוטריקון אפיק טפי זין מזון שאוכל יותר מדאי מוציא ומקיא [סוכה מ:]. פקיד. מופקד ועומד שם כנתון בכלי [לקמן קלג:]. פשוטי כלי עץ. אפילו נגמרה מלאכתן טהורין דאיתקש עץ לשק דכתיב (ויקרא יא) מכל כלי עץ או בגד או עור או שק מה שק מטלטל מלא וריקן [חולין כה.]. דומיא דשק בעינן. שקבול שלו עשוי לטלטל על ידו מה שמונח לתוכו [שם לב.]. לענין טומאה הוקשו כלי עץ לשק דכתיב כל אשר יפול עליו מהם במותם יטמא מכל כלי עץ או בגד או עור או שק (ויקרא יא) [חגיגה כו:]. כל הכלים ניטלין. ואפילו מלאכתן לאיסור. חוץ מן המסר הגדול. מגירה שהיא לחתוך בה קורות. ויתד של מחרישה. כלי העשוי לחפור בו קרקע שקורין קולטר"א [לקמן קנז.]. אוכלא דקצרי. כלי נחושת שמגמרין בו את הבגדים [סנהדרין צב:]. קצרי. כובסים [נדרים מג.]. רוגל (ע"ש יו) עיגל דקצרא [תענית כט:]. הכובס נקרא קצרא בלשון ארמי [ב"ק קיט:]. [המשך בדף קכד.]

רבינו חננאל (המשך)

והרי מפורש בסוף פרק מי שהחשיך דכולהו הני היינו טעמא דאסירי משום דמוקצה מחמת חסרון כיס נינהו. ואפילו ר' שמעון מודה להו בדבר סתמא להו כלים ניטלין בשבת חוץ מן המסר הגדול ויתד של מחרישה. מקצוע של דבילה כלי ברזל שחותכין בו דבילה. זומליסטרון תרווד שמהפך בו הקדירה. כדתנן זומליסטרון שניטל כפה טמא מפני המזלג. א"ר חנינא בימי נחמיה בן חכליה נשנית משנה זו דכתיב בימים ההמה ראיתי ביהודה דורכים גיתות בשבת. כיון שראו כך שקלו בשבת אסרו להן כל הכלים ושרי להן הא דתנן רבנן. כיון שנגדרו וחזרו לדקדק בשמירת שבת היו מתירין להן והולכין עד שהתירו הכל חוץ ממסר הגדול ויתד של מחרישה. וכך הוא מפורש בתלמוד א"י: א"ר אלעזר קנים ומקלות וגלוסטרא ומדוכה כולם קודם התרת כלים נשנו. ולפיכך נשנו באיסור. קנים הם קנים של לחם הפנים. והן שנויין במס' מנחות

מַקְלוֹת – The teaching concerning **staffs,** דִּתְנַן – **for we learned in a Mishnah:**[30] מַקְלוֹת דַּקִּין חֲלָקִין הָיוּ שָׁם – THERE WERE THIN, SMOOTH STAFFS THERE (in the Temple), וּמַנִּיחוֹ עַל כְּתֵפוֹ וְעַל כֶּתֶף חֲבֵירוֹ – AND ONE WOULD PLACE [A STAFF] ON HIS SHOULDER AND HIS FELLOW'S SHOULDER, וְתוֹלֶה וּמַפְשִׁיט – SUSPEND his slaughtered *pesach* offering from the staff AND FLAY it.[31] (אמר) רַבִּי אֱלִעָזָר [אוֹמֵר] – R' ELAZAR SAYS: אַרְבָּעָה עָשָׂר שֶׁחָל לִהְיוֹת בְּשַׁבָּת – WHEN THE FOURTEENTH of Nissan FELL ON THE SABBATH, מַנִּיחַ

NOTES

rested on the *Shulchan* proper, and the five upper loaves rested on the golden tubes (see *Menachos* 96a, 97a).

The loaves could not be removed, nor could new ones be placed on the *Shulchan,* while the tubes were in place [presumably because they were packed so tightly together]. Thus, it was necessary to remove the tubes from the pillars each week to allow for the replacement of the loaves. The Mishnah teaches that it was forbidden to arrange or remove the tubes on the Sabbath. Accordingly, a Kohen would enter the Temple and remove the tubes before the Sabbath, and leave the loaves stacked upon each other overnight. On the Sabbath day, he would remove the old loaves and stack the new ones upon each other in two columns, and after the Sabbath, he would return to lift the stacked loaves and insert the tubes between them. Now, the tubes were permitted-use utensils (since they had been designated to support the loaves), and nevertheless, the Mishnah forbids moving them on the Sabbath for the sake of their use. Perforce, this Mishnah was taught before permission to move a permitted-use utensil was granted (*Rashi;* cf. *Rashi* to *Menachos* 97a ד״ה אמאי לא דחי שבת; see *Tosafos* there ד״ה לא and *Ritva MHK* ed. here).

[Although Rabbinical decrees generally were not applied in the Temple, there are some exceptions. The necessity to bolster Sabbath observance prompted the Rabbis to apply the decree against moving utensils even in the Temple (*Tosafos* ד״ה לא סידור).]

30. *Pesachim* 64a.

31. The *pesach,* like other offerings, had to be flayed before its sacrificial parts could be placed upon the Altar (see above, 116b). To facilitate the flaying process, the animal was suspended. There were numerous hooks fixed into the walls and pillars of the Temple Courtyard for this purpose. However, since a multitude of *pesach* offerings would be brought simultaneously, the hooks were insufficient to accommodate all the offerings. Those who did not have access to a hook would suspend their offerings in the manner described here (Mishnah ibid.). This procedure was followed when the fourteenth of Nissan (i.e. the eve of Pesach, when the offering was brought) occurred on a weekday (*Rashi*).

יָדוֹ עַל כְּתֵף חֲבֵירוֹ – ONE WOULD PLACE HIS HAND ON HIS FELLOW'S SHOULDER וְיַד חֲבֵירוֹ עַל כְּתֵיפוֹ – AND HIS FELLOW'S HAND ON HIS SHOULDER, וְתוֹלֶה וּמַפְשִׁיט – SUSPEND the slaughtered *pesach* offering from their arms AND FLAY it.[1]

גְּלוֹסְטְרָא – The teaching concerning **a knob,** דִּתְנַן – **for we learned in a Mishnah:**[2] נֶגֶר שֶׁיֵּשׁ בְּרֹאשׁוֹ גְּלוֹסְטְרָא – A BOLT THAT HAS A KNOB ON ITS END[3] – רַבִּי יְהוֹשֻׁעַ אוֹמֵר – R' YEHOSHUA SAYS: שׁוֹמְטָהּ מִן פֶּתַח זֶה וְתוֹלָה בַּחֲבֵירוֹ בְּשַׁבָּת – ONE MAY DRAG IT away FROM THIS DOOR AND HANG IT ON ANOTHER ONE ON THE SABBATH.[4] רַבִּי טַרְפוֹן אוֹמֵר – R' TARFON SAYS: הֲרֵי הוּא כְּכָל הַכֵּלִים וּמִיטַּלְטֵל בֶּחָצֵר – IT IS LIKE ALL UTENSILS AND MAY BE MOVED in the usual manner WITHIN A COURTYARD.[5]

מְדוֹכָה – The teaching concerning **a mortar** הָא דַּאֲמָרַן – **is that which we mentioned** above.[6] Since all these Tannaic teachings forbid the movement of a utensil for the sake of its use, we must conclude that they were taught before this type of movement was permitted.[7]

R' Elazar's assertion is rejected:

אָמַר רַבָּה – **Rabbah said:** מִמַּאי – **On what basis** do you state that these teachings predate the permit to move all utensils? דִּילְמָא לְעוֹלָם אֵימָא לָךְ לְאַחַר הַתָּרַת כֵּלִים נִשְׁנוּ – **Perhaps I can actually tell you** that **they were taught after the permit to** move all **utensils was issued,** and their explanation is as follows: קָנִים טַעְמָא מַאי – Concerning the **tubes, what is the reason** for placing them in the *Shulchan*? מִשּׁוּם אִיפּוּשֵׁי – It is **because of** the concern for **decaying** of the *panim*-bread.[8] בְּהַאי פּוּרְתָּא לֹא מִיעַפַּשׁ – **In this small period,** i.e. from Friday afternoon until Sabbath morning, **it will not decay.** Thus, there is no real need to arrange or remove the tubes on the Sabbath.[9]

מַקְלוֹת – As for the **staffs** from which the *pesach* offerings are normally suspended, אֶפְשָׁר כְּרַבִּי אֱלְעָזָר – on the Sabbath **it is possible** to do **as R' Elazar** recommends and suspend the offerings from people's arms. Thus, there is no real need to take the staffs.

גְּלוֹסְטְרָא – The Mishnah concerning a bolt that has **a knob** at its end כִּדְרַבִּי יַנַּאי – can be explained **in accordance with** the clarification **of R' Yannai.** דְּאָמַר רַבִּי יַנַּאי – **For R' Yannai said:** בְּחָצֵר שֶׁאֵינָהּ מְעוֹרֶבֶת עָסְקִינַן – In this Mishnah **we are dealing with** the issue of moving the bolt to a different door within **a courtyard** whose houses have **not** been **joined with an** ***eruv,*** and in which it is therefore prohibited to take anything from one of the houses to the courtyard.[10] רַבִּי יְהוֹשֻׁעַ סָבַר תּוֹךְ הַפֶּתַח כִּלְפָנִים דָּמֵי – **R' Yehoshua holds** that **the hollow of the doorway is like the interior** of the house, וְקָמְטַלְטֵל מָנָא דְּבָתִּים בְּחָצֵר – **and** thus, when one removes the bolt from a doorway and transfers it to another one, **he is carrying a utensil from** inside one of **the houses across the courtyard.**[11] וְרַבִּי טַרְפוֹן סָבַר תּוֹךְ הַפֶּתַח כִּלְחוּץ דָּמֵי – **But R' Tarfon holds** that **the hollow of the**

NOTES

1. R' Eliezer teaches that on the Sabbath it was forbidden to take the staffs, and therefore, the people resorted to this measure to enable the flaying of the offerings to take place (*Rashi;* cf. *Rashi* to *Pesachim* 64b ד״ה שחל להיות בשבת). Now, the staffs were needed for the sake of their use, and thus, after the relaxation of the decree it would be permitted to take them. Perforce, R' Eliezer's teaching reflects the law that existed before the decree was modified.

2. *Keilim* 11:4, with a slight textual variation; see *Mesoras HaShas.*

3. The reference is to the bolt of a door that is wedged into a hole in a threshold to hold the door in place (*Rashi* to *Eruvin* 101b ד״ה נגר). The bolt has a knob at its end and is fit to be used as a pestle to chop garlic. Thus, it is categorized as a utensil (*Rashi* here and to *Eruvin* ibid.).

4. The bolt was commonly attached to the door with a cord (see *Eruvin* ibid.). R' Yehoshua teaches that if one needs to move the bolt to a different door on the Sabbath he may not carry it in the usual manner, but must drag it to the desired location. [Dragging the bolt is a form of indirect movement, which is subject to a more lenient rule (*Rav* to *Keilim* loc. cit.; see above, 44a note 2).] Now, the bolt is a permitted-use utensil (as it is designated for locking a door; see *Maharsha*), and nevertheless, R' Yehoshua forbids moving it in the usual manner even for the sake of its use. Perforce, his ruling reflects the law that applied prior to the modification of Nechemiah ben Chachaliah's decree (*Rashi;* see note 7).

5. I.e. it is like eating utensils, which even before the relaxation of the decree were allowed to be moved about at will within a courtyard that has an *eruv* (*Tosafos* to 123b ד״ה הרי היא). [Presumably, R' Tarfon's reasoning is that the bolt is used as frequently as eating utensils and is therefore in the same category.]

6. I.e. the Baraisa which states that a mortar may not be moved if it does not contain garlic. Although Rava interpreted that Baraisa as dealing only with moving the mortar from the sun to the shade, and Abaye interpreted it as dealing with moving the mortar merely for the sake of its place, [and thus, the Baraisa is relevant even nowadays,] those interpretations are forced. It is more reasonable to interpret the Baraisa literally as prohibiting all movement of the mortar and as having been taught prior to the modification of Nechemiah ben Chachaliah's decree (*Rashi*).

7. It seems unusual that the Tannaim R' Elazar, R' Yehoshua and R' Tarfon cited the law that was in effect before the restriction was eased. They lived several centuries after Nechemiah ben Chachaliah, and as mentioned above (123b note 26), the restriction was eased during his lifetime. This matter, therefore, requires further study (*Chasam Sofer* to 123b).

8. For we do not rely on the occurrence of a miracle to prevent the loaves from becoming moldy (*Rashi*). [Actually, this type of miracle did occur regularly, for when the loaves were removed from the *Shulchan* at the end of each week they were still warm as though they had just been removed from the oven (*Menachos* 96b).]

9. The old loaves would be stacked without the tubes only from Friday afternoon until Sabbath morning and the new loaves only from Sabbath morning until evening. There was no concern that they would spoil [due to lack of ventilation] in this short period (*Rashi*). Thus, the insertion or removal of the tubes on the Sabbath could not be rationalized as movement "for the sake of their use."

One might ask: Even if there was no outright need to move the tubes on the Sabbath to retard spoilage, it would certainly have been somewhat beneficial to insert and remove them on the Sabbath itself. Why does this slight necessity not qualify as the equivalent of moving a utensil from sunlight to shade – a secondary need that Rava deems sufficient in the case of a permitted-use utensil? The answer is that Rava would indeed permit moving the tubes nowadays for this purpose. However, the current interpretation is offered by Rabbah, who concurs with Abaye in prohibiting movement of any utensil from the sun to the shade (*Rashba, Ritva MHK* ed.; cf. *Meiri*; see Gemara below, after the Mishnah; see also *Chasam Sofer* and *R' Akiva Eiger;* cf. *Ran MHK* ed. to 123b; see *Chidushei R' Elazar Moshe Horowitz*).

10. When numerous homes open into a common courtyard, it is forbidden by Rabbinic decree to carry anything from one of the homes to the courtyard and vice versa – even if the courtyard is fully enclosed – unless the residents of the homes prepared an *eruv chatzeiros* (i.e. courtyard-*eruv,* consisting of a portion of bread collected from each of the homes). The reason is that in absence of an *eruv* (which has the effect of merging the various residences into one unit) each home is the private domain of its residents, whereas the courtyard is common to all the homes. Thus, transferring objects between the houses and courtyard resembles the Biblically prohibited *melachah* of transferring between private and public domains. However, even if no *eruv* was prepared, it is permitted to carry about within the enclosed courtyard any object that was there when the Sabbath began, since the courtyard is legally a private domain (*Rashi*). R' Yannai states that the Mishnah concerning a doorbolt deals with moving the bolt from the front door of one house to the front door of another house within a courtyard that has no *eruv.*

11. Therefore, R' Yehoshua permits only dragging the bolt, which is an indirect method of transferring it (*Rashi;* see *Rash* to *Keilim* 11:4). [It is ordinarily forbidden even to drag an item from a house to a courtyard whose houses have not been joined by an *eruv.* R' Yehoshua permits dragging only in our case, where the bolt is merely taken from the doorway, which appears like part of the courtyard (*Chidushei HaRan*).]

רש"י

ידו על כתף חברו. דלא מטלטלי מקלות: גלוסטרא. דתנן רבי יהושע אמר נגר שיש בראשו גלוסטרא שראשה עב וראוי לדוך בו שום ונועלין בו דלת: שומטה מפתח זה ותולה בחברו. ואע"ג דצריך לגופו לתלותו בחברו ולנעולה בו שומטו ע"י גרירה אבל טלטול גמור לא ואע"פ שמלאכתו להיתר לא שרי ליה לצורך גופו: מדוכה הא דאמרן. לעיל אע"ג דשנייה רבא לעיל מחמה לצל ואביי שנייה לצורך מקומו שינויי דחיקי נינהו אלא קודם התרת כלים נשנו: קנים טעמא מאי. מסדרין אותם במערכה: משום איעפושי. דלא סמכינן אניסא ומשום ההוא פורתא שהישנה מתעכבת בלא קנים מלילי שבת לשבת והחדשה משבת למוצ"ש לא מיעפשי: כדר"א. מניח ידו על כתף חבירו: שאינה מעורבת. שהרבה בתים פתוחים לה ולא עירבו דכלים ששבתו בבתים אסור להוציאן לחצר וששבתו בחצר מותר לטלטלן בחצר שהחצר כולו רשות לעצמו הוא והבתים מיוחדים לכל איש ביתו: תוך הפתח. שנטל הנגר משם: וקא מטלטל מנא דבית בחצר. הלכך שומטה אין דטלטול מן הצד היא אבל טלטול גמור לא: מדוכה רבי נחמיה היא. דאמר[ג] בעירובין (דף לה.) אפילו טלית ואפי' תרווד אין ניטלין אלא לצורך תשמיש המיוחד: מתני' ה"ג במתניתין כל הכלים ניטלין לצורך כו': גמ' מאי לצורך ומאי שלא לצורך אמר רבה כו'. לצורך דשרי תנא קמא היינו דבר שמלאכתו להיתר ומטלטלו לצורך גופו: שלא לצורך דבר שמלאכתו להיתר. ומטלטלו שלא לצורך גופו אבל צריך למקומו: ודבר שמלאכתו לאיסור לצורך גופו. הוא דאישתראי אם צריך לו למלאכת היתר אבל שלא לצורך גופו ואע"ג דצריך למקומו לא ורבה לטעמיה דאמר לעיל (דף קכג:) גבי קורנס של נפחים נמי מותר לצורך גופו: א"ל רבא כו' אלא אמר כו'. ולרבא דמוקי אליבא דרבי נחמיה דלצורך גופו ולצורך מקומו מותר ע"כ האי לצורך גופו כגון שזה התשמיש מיוחד לו דתניא לקמן בפרק חבית (דף קמו.) רבי נחמיה אומר אפילו תרווד ואפילו טלית אין ניטלין אלא לצורך תשמישן וצורך מקומו נמי לרבא כצורך גופו ותשמישו דמי ולרבה צורך גופו הוא דשרי רבי נחמיה ודוקא לתשמיש המיוחד לו ובין לרבה ובין לרבא דוקא דבר שמלאכתו להיתר אבל דבר שמלאכתו לאיסור אפילו לצורך גופו לא שרי רבי נחמיה דהאי צורך גופו לאו תשמיש המיוחד לו הוא דהא מיוחד למלאכת איסור: לרבה אליבא דרבי נחמיה. דאמר דבר שמלאכתו להיתר לצורך מקומו לא: הני קערות. לאחר אכילה היכי מטלטל להו לסלקן מלפניהו: ואם לאו אין מטלטלין אותה. בשלמא לרבה כגון דאין צריך לגופה [אלא למקומה] אלא לדידך אמאי: וכן בדלת. אוקימנא במסכת ביצה וכן הדלת אין סומכין בבקעת וביו"ט קיימי: והא בקעת ביו"ט מלאכתה להיתר היא. דלהסקה חזי וקיימא וקאסר לטלטלה לצורך גופו למלאכה אחרת וכל שכן לצורך מקומה: ומשני התם (ב) טעמא כיון דבשבת בקעת דהא אסור דהא בקעת בשבת מלאכתה לאיסור היא ביום טוב נמי אסור גזירה יו"ט אטו שבת: משילין פירות דרך ארובה ביום טוב. בהדיא תנן אבל לא בשבת פירות השטוחים על הגג לייבשן ורואה גשמים ממשמשים ובאין משילין לארץ דרך ארובת הגג דלא טריחא מילתא דנופלין מאליהן אלמא דלא גזרינן ופרכינן ומי לא גזרינן והתנן אין בין כו': לא קשיא הא. דתנן משילין דשרי טירחא ביו"ט משום איבוד ממון רבי יהושע היא שהתיר להעלות בהמה בהערמה מן הבור: והא. דאפשר בהערמה. דמיחזי כמאן דעביד לצורך יו"ט אבל גבי משילין דליכא הערמה לדמויי להתירא לא:

גמרא

ידו על כתף חבירו ויד חבירו על כתיפו ותולה ומפשיט גלוסטרא דתנן [א] א נגר שיש בראשו גלוסטרא ר' יהושע אומר שומטה מן פתח זה ותולה בחבירו בשבת ר' טרפון אומר הרי הוא ככל הכלים ומיטלטל בחצר מדוכה הא דאמרן אמר רבה ממאי דילמא לעולם אימא לך לאחר התרת כלים נשנו קנים טעמא מאי משום איעפושי בהאי פורתא לא מיעפש מקלות אפשר כר' אלעזר גלוסטרא כדרבי ינאי דאמר רבי ינאי בחצר שאינה מעורבת עסקינן רבי יהושע סבר תוך הפתח כלפנים דמי וקמטלטל מנא דבתים בחצר ור' טרפון סבר תוך הפתח כלחוץ דמי ומנא דחצר בחצר קא מטלטל מדוכה ר' נחמיה היא: **מתני'** ב כל הכלים ניטלין לצורך ושלא לצורך ג ר' נחמיה אומר אין ניטלין אלא לצורך: **גמ'** מאי לצורך ומאי שלא לצורך אמר ג רבה לצורך דבר שמלאכתו להיתר לצורך גופו שלא לצורך דבר שמלאכתו להיתר לצורך מקומו ודבר שמלאכתו לאיסור לצורך גופו אין לצורך מקומו לא ואתא רבי נחמיה למימר ואפילו דבר שמלאכתו להיתר לצורך גופו אין לצורך מקומו לא אמר ליה רבא לצורך מקומו שלא לצורך קרית ליה אלא אמר רבא ג לצורך דבר שמלאכתו להיתר בין לצורך גופו בין לצורך מקומו שלא לצורך ואפי' מחמה לצל ד ודבר שמלאכתו לאיסור לצורך גופו ולצורך מקומו אין מחמה לצל לא ואתא רבי נחמיה למימר ואפילו דבר שמלאכתו להיתר לצורך גופו ולצורך מקומו אין מחמה לצל לא יתיב רב ספרא ורב אחא בר הונא ורב הונא בר חנינא ויתבי וקאמרי לרבה אליבא דרבי נחמיה הני קערות היכי מטלטלינן אמר להו רב ספרא מידי דהוה אגרף של רעי אמר ליה אביי לרבה למר אליבא דרבי נחמיה הני קערות היכי מטלטלינן להו אמר להו רב ספרא חברין תרגמה מידי דהוה אגרף של רעי איתיביה אביי לרבא ה מדוכה אם יש בה שום מטלטלין אותה ואם לאו אין מטלטלין אותה הכא במאי עסקינן מחמה לצל איתיביה ו ושוין שאם קיצב עליו בשר שאסור לטלטלו הכא נמי מחמה לצל והא דתנן ז ה אין סומכין את הקדירה בבקעת וכן בדלת והא בקעת דביום טוב דבר שמלאכתו להיתר הוא אלמא דבר שמלאכתו להיתר בין לצורך גופו בין לצורך מקומו אסור התם (א) מאי טעמא כיון דבשבת דבר שמלאכתו לאיסור הוא גזירה יו"ט אטו שבת וכי תימא שבת גופיה תישתרי דהא דבר שמלאכתו להיתר לצורך גופו ולצורך מקומו שרי י הני מילי היכא דאיכא תורת כלי עליו היכא דליכא תורת כלי עליו לא ומי גזרינן והתנן ז משילין פירות דרך ארובה ביום טוב ח אבל לא בשבת ומי לא גזרינן והתנן ט אין בין יו"ט לשבת אלא אוכל נפש בלבד אמר רב יוסף לא קשיא הא ר' אליעזר הא רבי יהושע י דתניא אותו ואת בנו שנפלו לבור ר' אליעזר אומר מעלה את הראשון על מנת לשוחטו ושוחטו והשני עושה לו פרנסה במקומו בשביל שלא ימות ר' יהושע אומר מעלה את הראשון על מנת לשוחטו ואינו שוחטו ומערים ומעלה את השני רצה זה שוחט רצה זה שוחט כ ממאי דילמא עד כאן לא קאמר ר' אליעזר התם אלא דאפשר לפרנסה אבל היכא דלא אפשר לפרנסה לא אי נמי עד כאן לא קאמר רבי יהושע התם דאפשר בהערמה אבל היכא דלא אפשר בהערמה לא אלא אמר רב פפא לא קשיא הא בית שמאי הא בית הלל דתנן בית שמאי אומרים

אין

תוספות

הא ר"א. ההיא דאין בין אע"ג דבפ"ק דמגילה (דף ז:) דייקינן עלה הא לענין מכשירי אוכל נפש זה וזה שוין וקאמר מתני' דלא כרבי יהודה ור"א סבירא ליה כר"י ועדיפא מדרבי יהודה כדאמר בריש תולין (לקמן דף קלז:) איכא למימר דההוא תנא סבר לה כוותיה בחדא דגזרינן י"ט אטו שבת ופליג עליה במכשירין ועוד יש לומר דאין בין דפ"ק דמגילה מיירי במילי דאורייתא ואין בין דהכא היינו דתנן במשילין (ביצה ד' לז:) דמיירי במילי דשבות ואינו מענין אחד תדע דהכי פריך עלה בפ' משילין כדפריך הכא בשמעתא ולא פריך בפ"ק דמגילה והא דדייק התם הא לענין מכשירין זה וזה שוין לא דייק בפרק משילין:

הא

עין משפט נר מצוה

יח א מיי' פכ"ו מהלכות שבת הלכה ט סמג לאוין סה טוש"ע או"ח סימן שיג סעיף א:

יט ב ג מיי' פכ"ה שם הלכה ג סמג שם טוש"ע או"ח סימן שח סעיף ד:

כ ד מיי' שם טוש"ע שם סעיף ג:

כא ה מיי' פ"ד מהלכות יו"ט הלכה יא טור שו"ע או"ח סימן תקב סעיף ג:

כב ו מיי' פכ"ה מהל' שבת הלכה ו טוש"ע או"ח סימן שח סעיף ז:

כג ז מיי' פ"ה מהלכות יו"ט הלכה ה טור שו"ע או"ח סימן תקלא סעיף א:

כד ח טוש"ע או"ח סימן שלא סעיף ז:

כה ט מיי' פ"א מהלכות יו"ט הלכה א סמג לאוין עה טוש"ע או"ח סימן תצה סעיף א:

רבינו חננאל

שאסור בשבת סידורן ונטילתן מתוך לחם הפנים. מקלות מפורש במס' פסחים. בזמן שחל י"ד להיות בשבת אסר ר' אלעזר לטלטל מקל ולהניחו על כתיפו ועל כתף חבירו לתלות הפסח בו ולהפשיטו. וכן גלוסטרא. היא משנה בכלים פ' י"א שאסר ר' יהושע לטלטלה בשבת. תוספתא דכלים בתחלת בב"מ קלוסטרא ר' טרפון מטמא וחכמים מטהרין. ברוריה אומר שומטה מפתח זה ותולה בחבירו בשבת. כשנאמרו דברים לפני ר' יהושע אמר יפה אמר ברוריה. והוא ענין הזה בעירובין בסופו. מדוכה זו שאמרנו למעלה אלו כולן כלים הן וקודם התרת כלים נשנו שאסור לטלטלן בשבת. א) אבל אחר התרת כלים מותרין הן וחלק רבא על רבי אלעזר ואמר דלמא אחר התרת כלים נשנו ואסורין הן לעולם. ודבריו פשוטין הן: מתני' כל הכלים הניטלין לצורך ניטלין ושלא לצורך כו'. פירש רבא משנה זו לצורך דבר שמלאכתו להיתר כגון קערות וכוסות וכדומה להן. שמותר לכתחלה לטלטלן לאכול ולשתות בהן הללו מותרין לטלטלן בין לצורך גופו לאכול בהן בין לצורך מקומו לפנותן כדי לישב במקומן. דבר שמלאכתו לאיסור כגון קורנס של נפחים וכדומה לו לצורך גופו לאכול בהן (מותר) [כגון] לפצוע בו אגוזים מותר. אבל לצורך מקומן אסור. ורבי נחמיה אמר אפילו דבר שמלאכתו להיתר כגון קערות וכדומה להן לצורך גופו לאכול בהן מותר. אבל אחר שיאכל בהן אסור לטלטלן [לצורך] מקומן. ועל זה הקשה ליה אביי לרבה למר אליבא דר' נחמי' הני קערות כלומר שאינו מטלטל אלא לצורך אכילה בהן אחר שיאכל אדם האיך מטלטלן ומסלקן מן השולחן.

מסורת הש"ס

א) כלים פי"א מ"ד [ושם ליתא להך מימרא נגר שיש בראשו], ב) [לעיל לו. וש"נ], ג) [גי' הרי"ף והרא"ש אביי], ד) [לעיל קכג.], ה) [לקמן קמב:], ו) ביצה לב:, ז) ביצה לג., ח) לקמן קמו: ביצה כח. לו: מגילה ז: [תוספתא דמגילה פ"א], ט) ביצה לז. [תוספתא ביצה פ"ג], י) [ביצה לז. ע"ש], כ) [לקמן קמו.]

הגהות הב"ח

(א) גמ' התם היינו טעמא כיון דבשבת: (ב) רש"י ד"ה ומשני התם היינו טעמא:

גליון הש"ס

גמ' ומי גזרינן והתנן משילין. ע"ל דף כג ע"ב תוספות ד"ה גזירה:

ליקוטי רש"י

סכינא דאשכחתא. של בית המטבחים שמקבצים בו בשר [ב"מ קטו.]. זוהמא ליסטרון. כף גדולה שמסלקין בו זוהם הקדירה והקלחת לגלגין [שם לג.]. מדוכה. שדוכין בה שום. אם יש בה שום מטלטלין אותה. אגב השום. ואם לאו אין מטלטלין אותה. כיון דעיקר מלאכתו לשחיקה דהיא מלאכה איסור משום טוחן. ושוין. [illegible] שאם קצב עליו בשר. [illegible] שאסור לטלטל. [illegible]

[illegible]

חשק שלמה על רבינו חננאל

א) דברי רבינו כמות שהם אינם מובנים. [illegible]

doorway is like the exterior of the house and is part of the courtyard, וּמְנָא דְחָצֵר בֶּחָצֵר קָא מְטַלְטֵל – **and** thus, when one transfers the bolt, **he is carrying a utensil from the courtyard across the courtyard,** which is permitted.[12] מְדוֹכָה – As for the Baraisa concerning **a mortar,** רַבִּי נְחֶמְיָה הִיא – **it is** reflective of the opinion of **R' Nechemyah.**[13] Thus, all four teachings can have been taught after Nechemiah ben Chachaliah's restriction was relaxed.

Mishnah כָּל הַכֵּלִים נִיטָּלִין לְצוֹרֶךְ וְשֶׁלֹּא לְצוֹרֶךְ – **All utensils may be taken** either **out of necessity or not out of necessity.**[14] רַבִּי נְחֶמְיָה אוֹמֵר – **R' Nechemyah says:** אֵין נִיטָּלִין אֶלָּא לְצוֹרֶךְ – **They may not be taken except out of necessity.**

Gemara The Gemara seeks to clarify the opinions of the Tannaim:

מַאי לְצוֹרֶךְ וּמַאי שֶׁלֹּא לְצוֹרֶךְ – **What is** the meaning of **"out of necessity" and what is** the meaning of **"not out of necessity"?** אָמַר רַבָּה – **Rabbah said:** לְצוֹרֶךְ – The Tanna Kamma's statement that utensils may be taken **out of necessity** means that דָּבָר שֶׁמְּלַאכְתּוֹ לְהֶיתֵּר לְצוֹרֶךְ גּוּפוֹ – **something that is used** primarily **for permitted work** may be taken **for the sake of its use.** שֶׁלֹּא לְצוֹרֶךְ – The statement that they may be taken **not out of necessity** means that דָּבָר שֶׁמְּלַאכְתּוֹ לְהֶיתֵּר לְצוֹרֶךְ מְקוֹמוֹ – **something that is used** primarily **for permitted work** may be moved even **for the sake of its place.** וְדָבָר שֶׁמְּלַאכְתּוֹ לְאִיסּוּר – **However,** concerning **something that is used** primarily **for prohibited work,** the Tanna Kamma holds that לְצוֹרֶךְ גּוּפוֹ אֵין לְצוֹרֶךְ מְקוֹמוֹ לֹא – it may be moved **only for the sake of its use** but **not for the sake of its place.**[15] וְאָתָא רַבִּי נְחֶמְיָה לְמֵימַר – **And R' Nechemyah comes to say** that וַאֲפִילּוּ דָּבָר שֶׁמְּלַאכְתּוֹ לְהֶיתֵּר – **even something that is used** primarily **for permitted work** לְצוֹרֶךְ גּוּפוֹ אֵין לְצוֹרֶךְ מְקוֹמוֹ לֹא – may be moved **only for the sake of its use** but **not for the sake of its place.**[16]

Rabbah's interpretation is rejected and an alternative one is presented:

אָמַר לֵיהּ רָבָא – **Rava said to him:** לְצוֹרֶךְ מְקוֹמוֹ שֶׁלֹּא לְצוֹרֶךְ קָרֵית לֵיהּ – **Do you** mean to **call** the movement of a utensil **for the sake of its place** movement **not out of necessity?** Why, the need for its place is as legitimate a necessity as the need for its use! אֶלָּא אָמַר רָבָא – **Rather, Rava said:** לְצוֹרֶךְ – The Tanna Kamma's statement that utensils may be moved **out of necessity** means that דָּבָר שֶׁמְּלַאכְתּוֹ לְהֶיתֵּר בֵּין לְצוֹרֶךְ גּוּפוֹ בֵּין לְצוֹרֶךְ מְקוֹמוֹ – **something that is used** primarily **for permitted work** may be moved **either for the sake of its use or for the sake of its place.** שֶׁלֹּא לְצוֹרֶךְ – The statement that they may be moved **not out of necessity** means that something used primarily for permitted work may be moved וַאֲפִילּוּ מֵחַמָּה לְצֵל – **even from the sun to the shade** for its protection.[17] וְדָבָר שֶׁמְּלַאכְתּוֹ לְאִיסּוּר – **However,** concerning **something that is used** primarily **for prohibited work,** the Tanna Kamma holds that לְצוֹרֶךְ גּוּפוֹ וּלְצוֹרֶךְ מְקוֹמוֹ אֵין מֵחַמָּה לְצֵל לֹא – it may be moved **only for the sake of its use or for the sake of its place,** but **not from the sun to the shade** for its protection. וְאָתָא רַבִּי נְחֶמְיָה לְמֵימַר – **And R' Nechemyah comes to say** that וַאֲפִילּוּ דָּבָר שֶׁמְּלַאכְתּוֹ לְהֶיתֵּר – **even something that is used** primarily **for permitted work** לְצוֹרֶךְ גּוּפוֹ וּלְצוֹרֶךְ מְקוֹמוֹ אֵין מֵחַמָּה לְצֵל לֹא – may be moved **only for the sake of its use or for the sake of its place,** but **not from the sun to the shade** for its protection.[18]

A related discussion is cited:

יָתִיב רַב סַפְרָא וְרַב אַחָא בַּר הוּנָא וְרַב הוּנָא בַּר חֲנִינָא – **Rav Safra,**

NOTES

12. [Therefore, R' Tarfon allows carrying it from one doorway to another in the usual fashion. His statement that it is "like all other utensils" means that it is like the other utensils that were in the courtyard at the beginning of the Sabbath.]

13. Who permits moving a utensil only for the sake of its designated purpose (*Rashi*), and since the designated purpose of the mortar is a prohibited one, R' Nechemyah forbids moving it at all on the Sabbath (see 123a note 3). [This is the interpretation of the Baraisa that Rabbah himself proposed above, on 123a.]

14. The phrase "*All* utensils" actually refers only to permitted-use utensils, as will emerge from the Gemara (*Tosafos* above, 36a ד״ה הא ר׳ נחמיה; see also *Rambam, Commentary;* cf. *Rashash*). The Gemara will explain the meaning of "out of necessity or not out of necessity."

15. The Mishnah does not discuss the law with regard to forbidden-use utensils (see note 14). However, since we have interpreted it as teaching that a *permitted*-use utensil may be taken for the sake of either its use or its place, we may deduce that the more restricted forbidden-use utensil may be taken only for the sake of its use (cf. *Rashash*).

Rabbah does not consider the need for an object's place to be as significant as the need for its use. Thus, he limits the movement of a forbidden-use utensil to that which is for the sake of its use in a permissible capacity. Rabbah followed this reasoning above (bottom of 122b), when he stated that a blacksmith's hammer may be taken for the sake of using it to crack open nuts [i.e. a permissible use] (*Rashi*). [Abaye also took this position above, on 123b (see note 17 there).]

16. R' Nechemyah actually permits taking a utensil only for the sake of its *designated* use, but not for another permissible use (see note 18).

17. This is a lesser degree of necessity, and it can reasonably be called "not out of necessity." See 123b note 19.

18. The term "for the sake of its use" has a different meaning when applied to the opinion of R' Nechemyah than when applied to the opinion of the Tanna Kamma. The Tanna Kamma allows moving utensils for the sake of *any* permissible use. R' Nechemyah, however, allows moving a utensil only for the sake of its *designated* use, as he states explicitly in a Baraisa below, 146a (see also 123a note 3). Nevertheless, according to Rava, R' Nechemyah allows moving a permitted-use utensil for the sake of its place. Rava considers this a designated need, since after being used, utensils are commonly removed from their place and returned to storage. Rabbah, however, does not attach the same degree of significance to the need for a utensil's place, and therefore states that R' Nechemyah allows moving a permitted-use utensil only for the sake of its use – i.e. its designated use. Both Rabbah and Rava agree that R' Nechemyah permits moving only a permitted-use utensil. He cannot allow the movement of a forbidden-use utensil, even for the sake of its use, since its designated use is a prohibited one and he never allows putting a utensil to a secondary use (*Rashi,* as elaborated by *Tosafos* to 36a ד״ה הא ר׳ נחמיה; see *Rashba* here for a slightly different interpretation of *Rashi's* view; cf. *Rabbeinu Tam* cited by the above; see also *Ritva MHK* ed. and *Chidushei HaRan*). Thus, R' Nechemyah argues not only with the Tanna Kamma of our Mishnah, but also with the previous Mishnahs of our chapter, which allow taking a forbidden-use utensil at least for the sake of a permissible use.

At this point, let us review the respective opinions of Rabbah and Rava.

Rabbah's opinion: The Tanna Kamma allows moving a permitted-use utensil for the sake of any permissible use or the sake of its place; and a forbidden-use utensil for the sake of any permissible use, but not for the sake of its place. R' Nechemyah allows only moving a permitted-use utensil for the sake of its designated use.

Rava's opinion: The Tanna Kamma allows moving a permitted-use utensil for the sake of any permissible use or its place, as well as from the sun to the shade; and a forbidden-use utensil for the sake of any permissible use or its place, but not from the sun to the shade. R' Nechemyah allows only moving a permitted-use utensil for the sake of its designated use or the sake of its place.

ידו על כתף חבירו ויד חבירו על כתיפו ותולה ומפשיט גלוסטרא דתנן א נגר שיש בראשו גלוסטרא ר' יהושע אומר שומטה מן פתח זה ותולה בחבירו בשבת ר' טרפון אומר הרי הוא ככל הכלים ומיטלטל בחצר מדוכה הא דאמרן אמר רבה ממאי דילמא לעולם אימא לך לאחר התרת כלים נשנו קנים טעמא מאי משום איעפושי בהאי פורתא לא מיעפש מקלות אפשר כר' אלעזר גלוסטרא כדרבי ינאי דאמר רבי ינאי בחצר שאינה מעורבת עסקינן רבי יהושע סבר תוך הפתח כלפנים דמי וקמטלטל מנא דבתים בחצר ור' טרפון סבר תוך הפתח כלחוץ דמי ומנא דחצר בחצר קא מטלטל מדוכה ר' נחמיה היא: **מתני'** כל הכלים ניטלין לצורך ושלא לצורך ר' נחמיה אומר אין ניטלין אלא לצורך: **גמ'** מאי לצורך ומאי שלא לצורך אמר רבה לצורך דבר שמלאכתו להיתר לצורך גופו שלא לצורך דבר שמלאכתו להיתר לצורך מקומו ודבר שמלאכתו לאיסור לצורך גופו אין לצורך מקומו לא ואתא רבי נחמיה למימר ואפילו דבר שמלאכתו להיתר לצורך גופו אין לצורך מקומו לא אמר ליה רבא לצורך מקומו שלא לצורך קרית ליה אלא אמר רבא לצורך דבר שמלאכתו להיתר בין לצורך גופו בין לצורך מקומו שלא לצורך ואפי' מחמה לצל ודבר שמלאכתו לאיסור לצורך גופו ולצורך מקומו אין מחמה לצל לא ואתא רבי נחמיה למימר ואפילו דבר שמלאכתו להיתר לצורך גופו ולצורך מקומו אין מחמה לצל לא יתיב רב ספרא ורב אחא בר הונא ורב הונא בר חנינא ויתבי וקאמרי לרבה אליבא דרבי נחמיה הני קערות היכי מטלטלינן אמר להו רב ספרא מידי דהוה אגרף של רעי אמר ליה אביי לרבה למר אליבא דרבי נחמיה הני קערות היכי מטלטלינן להו אמר ליה רב ספרא חברין תרגמה מידי דהוה אגרף של רעי איתיביה אביי לרבא מדוכה אם יש בה שום מטלטלין אותה ואם לאו אין מטלטלין אותה הכא במאי עסקינן מחמה לצל איתיביה ושוין שאם קיצב עליו בשר שאסור לטלטלו הכא נמי מחמה לצל והא דתנן אין סומכין את הקדירה בבקעת וכן בדלת והא בקעת דביום טוב דבר שמלאכתו להיתר הוא אלמא דבר שמלאכתו להיתר בין לצורך גופו בין לצורך מקומו אסור התם (א) מאי טעמא כיון דבשבת דבר שמלאכתו לאיסור הוא גזירה יו"ט אטו שבת וכי תימא שבת גופיה תישתרי דהא דבר שמלאכתו לאיסור לצורך גופו ולצורך מקומו שרי הני מילי היכא דאיכא תורת כלי עליו היכא דליכא תורת כלי עליו לא ומי גזרינן והתנן משילין פירות דרך ארובה ביום טוב אבל לא בשבת ומי לא גזרינן והתנן אין בין יו"ט לשבת אלא אוכל נפש בלבד אמר רב יוסף לא קשיא הא ר' אליעזר הא רבי יהושע דתניא אותו ואת בנו שנפלו לבור ר' אליעזר אומר מעלה את הראשון על מנת לשוחטו ושוחטו והשני עושה לו פרנסה במקומו בשביל שלא ימות ר' יהושע אומר מעלה את הראשון על מנת לשוחטו ואינו שוחטו ומערים ומעלה את השני רצה זה שוחט רצה זה שוחט ממאי דילמא עד כאן לא קאמר ר' אליעזר התם אלא דאפשר לפרנסה אבל היכא דלא אפשר לפרנסה לא אי נמי עד כאן לא קאמר רבי יהושע התם דאפשר בהערמה אבל היכא דלא אפשר בהערמה לא אלא אמר רב פפא לא קשיא הא בית שמאי הא בית הלל דתנן בית שמאי אומרים אין

הא ר"א. ההיא דאין בין אע"ג דבפ"ק דמגילה (דף ז:) דייקינן עלה הא לענין מכשירי אוכל נפש זה וזה שוין וקאמר מתני' דלא כרבי יהודה ור"א סבירא ליה כר"י ועדיפא מדרבי יהודה כדאמר בריש חולין (לקמן דף קלז:) איכא למימר דההוא תנא סבר לה כוותיה בחדא דגזרינן י"ט אטו שבת ופליג עליה במכשירין ועוד יש לומר דאין בין דפ"ק דמגילה מיירי במילי דאורייתא ואין בין דהכא היינו דתנן במשילין (ביצה ד' לז:) דמיירי במילי דשבות ואינו מענין אחד תדע דהכי פריך עלה בפ' משילין כדפריך הכא בשמעתא ולא פריך בפ"ק דמגילה והא דדייק התם הא לענין מכשירין זה וזה שוין לא דייק בפרק משילין: הא

ידו על כתף חברו. דלא מטלטלי מקלות: גלוסטרא. דתנן רבי יהושע אמר נגר שיש בראשו גלוסטרא שראשו עב וראוי לדוך בו שום ונועלין בו דלת: שומטה מפתח זה ותולה בחברו. ואע"ג דצריך לגופו לתלותו בחברו ולנועלה בו שומטו ע"י גרירה אבל טלטול גמור לא ואע"פ שמלאכתו להיתר לא שרי ליה לצורך גופו: מדוכה הא דאמרן. לעיל אע"ג דשנייה רבא לעיל מחמה לצל ואביי שנייה לצורך מקומו שינויי דחיקי נינהו אלא קודם התרת כלים נשנו: קנים טעמא מאי. מסדרין אותם במערכה: משום איעפושי. דלא סמכינן אניסא ומשום ההוא פורתא שהישנה מתעכבת בלא קנים מלילי שבת לשבת והחדשה משבת למוצ"ש לא מיעפשי: כדר"א. מניח ידו על כתף חבירו: שאינה מעורבת. שהרבה בתים פתוחים לה ולא עירבו דכלים ששבתו בבתים אסור להוציאן לחצר וששבתו בחצר מותר לטלטלן בחצר שהחצר כולו רשות לעצמו הוא והבתים מיוחדים לכל איש ביתו: תוך הפתח. שנטל הנגר משם: וקא מטלטל מנא דבית בחצר. הלכך שומטה אין דטלטול מן הצד היא אבל טלטול גמור לא: מדוכה רבי נחמיה היא. דאמר בעירובין (דף לה.) אפילו טלית ואפי' תרווד אין ניטלין אלא לצורך תשמיש המיוחד: מתני' ה"ג במתניתין כל הכלים ניטלין לצורך כו': גמ' מאי לצורך ומאי שלא לצורך אמר רבה כו'. לצורך דשרי תנא קמא היינו דבר שמלאכתו להיתר ומטלטלו לצורך גופו: שלא לצורך דבר שמלאכתו להיתר. ומטלטלו שלא לצורך גופו אבל צריך למקומו: ודבר שמלאכתו לאיסור לצורך גופו. הוא דאישתראי אם צריך לו למלאכת היתר אבל שלא לצורך גופו ואע"ג דצריך למקומו לא ורבה לטעמיה דאמר לעיל (דף קכג:) גבי קורנס של נפחים נמי מותר לצורך גופו: א"ל רבא כו' אלא אמר כו'. ולרבא דמוקי אליבא דרבי נחמיה דלצורך גופו ולצורך מקומו מותר ע"כ האי לצורך גופו כגון שזה התשמיש מיוחד לו דתניא לקמן בפרק חבית (דף קמו.) רבי נחמיה אומר אפילו תרווד ואפילו טלית אין ניטלין אלא לצורך תשמישן ולצורך מקומו נמי לרבא כלצורך גופו ותשמישו דמי ולרבה לצורך גופו הוא דשרי רבי נחמיה ודוקא לתשמיש המיוחד לו ובין לרבה ובין לרבא דוקא דבר שמלאכתו להיתר אבל דבר שמלאכתו לאיסור אפילו לצורך גופו לא שרי רבי נחמיה דהאי לצורך גופו לאו תשמיש המיוחד לו הוא דהא מיוחד למלאכת איסור: לרבה אליבא דרבי נחמיה. דאמר דבר שמלאכתו להיתר לצורך מקומו לא: הני קערות. לאחר אכילה היכי מטלטל להו לסלקן מלפניו: ואם לאו אין מטלטלין אותה. בשלמא לרבה כגון דאין צריך לגופה [אלא למקומה] אלא לדידך אמאי: וכן בדלת. אוקימנא במסכת ביצה וכן הדלת אין סומכין בבקעת וביו"ט קיימי: והא בקעת ביו"ט מלאכתה להיתר היא. דלהסקה חזי וקיימא וקאסר לטלטלה לצורך גופו למלאכה אחרת וכל שכן לצורך מקומה: ומשני התם (ג) טעמא כיון דבשבת בקעת בשבת מלאכתה לאיסור היא ביום טוב נמי אסור גזירה י"ט אטו שבת: משילין פירות דרך ארובה ביום טוב. בהדיא תנן אבל לא בשבת פירות השטוחים על הגג לייבשן וראה גשמים ממשמשים ובאין משילן לארץ דרך ארובת הגג דלא טריחא מילתא דנופלין מאליהן אלמא דלא גזרינן ופרכינן ומי לא גזרינן והתנן אין בין כו': לא קשיא הא. דתנן משילין דשרי טירחא ביו"ט משום איבוד ממון רבי יהושע היא שהתיר להעלות בהמה בהערמה מן הבור: והא. דתנן אין בין כו' ר"א היא: דאפשר בהערמה. דמיחזי כמאן דעביד לצורך יו"ט אבל גבי משילין דליכא הערמה לדמויי להתירא לא: אין

Rav Acha bar Huna and Rav Huna bar Chanina were sitting together וְיָתְבֵי וְקָאָמְרֵי – **and as they sat they said:** לְרַבָּה אַלִּיבָּא דְּרַבִּי נְחֶמְיָה – According **to Rabbah's interpretation of** the opinion of **R' Nechemyah,** that even a permitted-use utensil may not be moved for the sake of its place, הָנֵי קְעָרוֹת הֵיכִי מְטַלְטְלִינַן – **how can we move bowls** off the table after a meal?[19] אָמַר לְהוּ רַב סַפְרָא – **Rav Safra said to [the others]:** מִידֵי דַּהֲוָה אַגְּרָף שֶׁל רְעִי – It is permitted to remove dirty dishes **because they are analogous to a vessel** used **for excrement,** which may be removed from one's presence due to the discomfort it engenders.[20]

A similar discussion:

אָמַר לֵיהּ אַבָּיֵי לְרַבָּה – **Abaye said to Rabbah:** לְמַר אַלִּיבָּא דְּרַבִּי נְחֶמְיָה – According **to master's interpretation of** the opinion of **R' Nechemyah,** הָנֵי קְעָרוֹת הֵיכִי מְטַלְטְלִינַן לְהוּ – **how may we move bowls** from the table after a meal? אָמַר לֵיהּ – **[Rabbah] replied:** רַב סַפְרָא חַבְרִין תַּרְגְּמָהּ – **Our colleague Rav Safra has** already **explained it** as follows: מִידֵי דַּהֲוָה אַגְּרָף שֶׁל רְעִי – **Because [dirty dishes] are analogous to a vessel** used **for excrement.**

The Gemara now cites a challenge to Rava's view:

אֵיתִיבֵיהּ אַבָּיֵי לְרָבָא – **Abaye challenged Rava** on the basis of the following Baraisa: מְדוֹכָה – A MORTAR in which garlic is usually crushed – אִם יֵשׁ בָּהּ שׁוּם מְטַלְטְלִין אוֹתָהּ – IF IT CONTAINS GARLIC IT MAY BE MOVED on the Sabbath, וְאִם לָאו אֵין מְטַלְטְלִין אוֹתָהּ – BUT IF NOT, IT MAY NOT BE MOVED. Rabbah can interpret this Baraisa as referring to a case where one does not need the use of the mortar but needs only its place. However, how will you interpret it?

Rava responds:

הָכָא בְּמַאי עַסְקִינַן – **What are we dealing with here?** מֵחַמָּה לְצֵל – It is with moving the mortar **from the sun to the shade** for its protection.[21]

Abaye poses another challenge:

אֵיתִיבֵיהּ – **He challenged [Rava]** on the basis of the following Baraisa: וְשָׁוִין – AND THEY [Beis Shammai and Beis Hillel] AGREE concerning a pestle שֶׁאִם קִיצֵּב עָלָיו בָּשָׂר שֶׁאָסוּר לְטַלְטְלוֹ – THAT IF ONE HAS already CHOPPED MEAT ON IT HE MAY NOT MOVE IT on Yom Tov. Rabbah can interpret this Baraisa as referring to a case where one does not need the use of the pestle but needs only its place. However, how will you interpret it?

Rava responds:

הָכָא נַמִּי מֵחַמָּה לְצֵל – **Here too,** we are dealing with moving it **from the sun to the shade.**[22]

The Gemara now cites a Mishnah that apparently contradicts both views:

וְהָא דִּתְנַן – **Now,** consider **that which we learned in a Mishnah:**[23] אֵין סוֹמְכִין אֶת הַקְּדֵירָה בְּבִקַּעַת – WE MAY NOT SUPPORT A POT WITH A PIECE OF WOOD on Yom Tov, וְכֵן בְּדֶלֶת – AND SO TOO A DOOR.[24] וְהָא בִּקַּעַת דְּבְיוֹם טוֹב דָּבָר שֶׁמְּלַאכְתּוֹ לְהֵיתֵּר הוּא – **Now, a piece of wood is, on Yom Tov,** classified as **something that is used** primarily **for permissible work,** since it stands to be burned as fuel for a cooking fire. Nevertheless, the Mishnah forbids taking it even for the sake of another use. אַלְמָא דָּבָר שֶׁמְּלַאכְתּוֹ לְהֵיתֵּר בֵּין לְצוֹרֶךְ גּוּפוֹ בֵּין לְצוֹרֶךְ מְקוֹמוֹ אָסוּר – **Thus,** we see that **something that is used** primarily **for permissible work may not** be taken **either for the sake of its use or for the sake of its place.**[25] – ? –

The Gemara responds:

הָתָם מַאי טַעְמָא – **What is the reason** for the prohibition **there,** in that case? כֵּיוָן דִּבְשַׁבָּת דָּבָר שֶׁמְּלַאכְתּוֹ לְאִיסּוּר הוּא – **Since on the Sabbath [a piece of wood] is** classified as **something that is used** primarily **for prohibited work,** since firewood may not be burned on the Sabbath, גְּזֵירָה יוֹם טוֹב אַטּוּ שַׁבָּת – **a decree** was enacted prohibiting its movement on **Yom Tov on account of** the concern that one might also move it on **the Sabbath.** וְכִי תֵּימָא – **And if you will say:** שַׁבָּת גּוּפֵיהּ תִּישְׁתְּרֵי – On **the Sabbath itself** it **should be permitted** to move the wood, דְּהָא דָּבָר שֶׁמְּלַאכְתּוֹ לְאִיסּוּר לְצוֹרֶךְ גּוּפוֹ וּלְצוֹרֶךְ מְקוֹמוֹ שְׁרֵי – **since something that is used** primarily **for prohibited work may be** moved either **for the sake of its use or for the sake of its place,** I will reply: הָנֵי מִילֵּי הֵיכָא דְּאִיכָּא תּוֹרַת כְּלִי עָלָיו – **That applies** only **where it is classified as a utensil,** הֵיכָא דְּלֵיכָּא תּוֹרַת כְּלִי עָלָיו לָא – but **where it is not classified as a utensil** one may **not** move it at all.[26]

The Gemara asks:

וּמִי גָּזְרִינַן – **Do we enact decrees** prohibiting doing things that are permissible on Yom Tov out of concern that people might do them on the Sabbath? וְהָתְנַן – **But we learned in a Mishnah:**[27] מַשִּׁילִין פֵּירוֹת דֶּרֶךְ אֲרוּבָּה בְּיוֹם טוֹב – WE MAY LOWER PRODUCE THROUGH A SKYLIGHT ON YOM TOV, אֲבָל לֹא בְּשַׁבָּת – BUT NOT ON THE SABBATH.[28] – ? –

NOTES

19. [The principle that eating implements were excluded from the decree against moving utensils on the Sabbath (see 123b note 12) does not hold true according to R' Nechemyah, who states explicitly in a Baraisa below (146a) that even a spoon may be taken only for the sake of its designated need (cf. *Chidushei R' Elazar Moshe Horowitz* to 123b; see *Maharsha* and *Rashash*).]

20. A special dispensation from the *muktzeh* law was granted for removing items such as a commode from one's presence, to alleviate discomfort (see *Beitzah* 36b).

Note that the assembled Rabbis initially found difficulty only with Rabbah's interpretation of R' Nechemyah's opinion. Seemingly, they could have asked even according to Rava's interpretation, that although we may remove a bowl from the table to create place for the next course, once the place is vacated how may we carry the bowl all the way back to its cupboard? Since they did not ask this question, we may deduce that according to Rava once permission is granted to lift an item from its location for the sake of making its place available one may carry it to any convenient location, even though the initial need is alleviated by moving it only a short distance (*Rashba, Ritva MHK* ed.; see also *Orach Chaim* 308:3 with *Mishnah Berurah* §13 and *Shaarei Teshuvah*).

21. See 123b notes 21 and 22.

22. See 123b notes 23 and 24.

23. *Beitzah* 32b.

24. The Gemara in *Beitzah* (33a) explains this as meaning that we may also not support a door with a piece of wood on Yom Tov (*Rashi*).

25. The Mishnah forbids taking the wood for the sake of a use other than its designated one. Certainly, then, it would prohibit taking the wood for the sake of its place (*Rashi*). Thus, the Mishnah contradicts the views of both Rabbah and Rava, who agree that a permitted-use utensil may be taken for the sake of either its use or its place (see *Rashba* to *Beitzah* 33a).

[It would seem that the Gemara could simply have answered that this Mishnah follows the view of R' Nechemyah. Apparently, the reason the Gemara did not advance this answer is that it did not wish to interpret an anonymous Mishnah as following R' Nechemyah's opinion.]

26. Something that is not classified as a utensil and is not edible for humans or animals is *muktzeh,* in the category of מוּקְצֶה מֵחֲמַת גּוּפוֹ, i.e. *inherently muktzeh* (*Beis Yosef,* introduction to *Orach Chaim* 308). [Thus, on the Sabbath, wood may not be moved at all. On Yom Tov, however, it is not *muktzeh* since it is fit for use as fuel for a fire, and it may be used in that capacity. Nevertheless, it may not be taken for other uses, due to the decree enacted out of concern that one might use the wood on the Sabbath. See 124b, end of note 3].

27. *Beitzah* 35b.

28. If one had spread produce (e.g. grain) on his roof to dry and he fears that oncoming rains will ruin them, he may throw them through a skylight into the house on Yom Tov. Large-scale moving of produce is usually considered excessive exertion which is prohibited Rabbinically

ידו על כתף חבירו. דלא מטלטלי מקלות: גלוסטרא. דתנן רבי יהושע אמר נגר שיש בראשו גלוסטרא שראשו עב וראוי לדוך בו שום ונועלין בו דלת: שומטה מפתח זה ותולה בחבירו. ואע"ג דלריך לגופו לתלותו בחבירו ולנעלה בו שומטו ע"י גרירה אבל טלטול גמור לא ואע"ג שמלאכתו להיתר לא שרי ליה לצורך גופו: מדוכה הא דאמרן. לעיל אע"ג דשנייה רבה לעיל מחמה לצל ואביי שנייה לצורך מקומו שינויי דחיקי נינהו אלא קודם התרת כלים נשנו: קנים טעמא מאי. מסדרין אותם במערכה: משום איעפושי. דלא סמכינן אניסא ומשום ההוא פורתא שהישנה מתעכבת בלא קנים מליל שבת לשבת והחדשה משבת למוצ"ש לא מיעפשי: כדר"א. מניח ידו על כתף חבירו: שאינה מעורבת. שהרבה בתים פתוחים לה ולא עירבו דכלים ששבתו בבתים אסור להוציאן לחצר וששבתו בחצר מותר לטלטלן בחצר שהחצר כולו רשות לעצמו הוא והבתים מיוחדים לכל אחד ביתו: תוך הפתח. שנטל הנגר משם: וקא מטלטל מנא דבית בחצר. הלכך שומטה אין דטלטול מן הלד היא אבל טלטול גמור לא: מדוכה רבי נחמיה היא. דאמר ובעירובין (דף לה.) אפילו טלית ואפי' תרווד אין ניטלין אלא לצורך תשמיש המיוחד: מתני' ה"ג במתניתין כל הכלים ניטלין לצורך כו': גמ' מאי לצורך ומאי שלא לצורך אמר רבה כו'. לצורך דשרי תנא קמא היינו דבר שמלאכתו להיתר ומטלטלו לצורך גופו: שלא לצורך דבר שמלאכתו להיתר. ומטלטלו שלא לצורך גופו אלא צריך למקומו: ודבר שמלאכתו לאיסור לצורך גופו. הוא דאשתרי אם צריך לו למלאכת היתר אבל שלא לצורך גופו ואע"ג דצריך למקומו לא ורבה לטעמיה דאמר לעיל (דף קכב:) גבי קורנס של נפחים נמי מותר לצורך גופו: א"ל רבא כו' אלא אמר כו'. ולרבה דמוקי אליבא דרבי נחמיה לצורך גופו ולצורך מקומו מותר ע"כ האי לצורך גופו כגון שזה התשמיש מיוחד לו דתניא לקמן בפרק מפנין (דף קכג.) רבי נחמיה אומר אפילו תרווד ואפילו טלית אין ניטלין אלא לצורך תשמישן ולצורך מקומו נמי לרבה כלומר גופו ותשמישו דמי ולרבה לצורך גופו הוא דשרי רבי נחמיה ודוקא לתשמיש המיוחד לו וכיון לרבה דוקא דבר שמלאכתו להיתר אבל דבר שמלאכתו לאיסור אפילו לצורך גופו לא שרי רבי נחמיה דהאי לורך גופו לאו תשמיש המיוחד לו הוא דהא מיוחד למלאכת איסור: לרבה אליבא דרבי נחמיה. דאמר דבר שמלאכתו להיתר לצורך מקומו לא: הני קערות. לאחר אכילה היכי מטלטל להו לסלקן מלפניהו: ואם לאו אין מטלטלין אותה. בשלמא לרבה כגון דאין צריך לגופה [אלא למקומה] אלא לדידך אמאי: וכן בדלת. אוקימנא במסכת ביצה וכן הדלת אין סומכין בבקעת וביו"ט קיימי: והא בקעת ביו"ט מלאכתה להיתר היא. להסקה חזי וקיימא וקאסר לטלטלה לצורך גופו למלאכה אחרת וכל שכן לצורך מקומה: ומשני התם (ב) טעמא כיון דבשבת אסור דהא בקעת בשבת מלאכתה לאיסור היא ביום טוב נמי אסור גזירה י"ט אטו שבת: משילין פירות דרך ארובה ביום טוב. בהדיא תנן אבל לא בשבת פירות השטוחים על הגג לייבשן ורואה גשמים ממשמשים ובאין משילן לארץ דרך ארובת הגג דלא טריחא מילתא דנופלין מאליהן אלמא דלא גזרינן ופרכינן ומי לא גזרינן והתנן אין בין כו': לא קשיא הא. דתנן משילין דשרי טירחא ביו"ט משום איבוד ממון רבי יהושע היא שהתיר להעלות בהמה בהערמה מן הבור: והא. דתנן אין בין כו' ר"א היא: דאפשר בהערמה. דמיחזי כמאן דעביד לצורך יו"ט אבל גבי משילין דליכא הערמה לדמויי להתירא לא:

ידו על כתף חבירו ויד חבירו על כתיפו ותולה ומפשיט גלוסטרא דתנן [א] נגר שיש בראשו גלוסטרא ר' יהושע אומר שומטה מן פתח זה ותולה בחבירו בשבת ר' טרפון אומר הרי הוא ככל הכלים ומיטלטל בחצר מדוכה הא דאמרן אמר רבה ממאי דילמא לעולם אימא לך לאחר התרת כלים נשנו קנים טעמא מאי משום איעפושי בהאי פורתא לא מיעפש מקלות אפשר כר' אלעזר גלוסטרא כדרבי ינאי דאמר רבי ינאי בחצר שאינה מעורבת עסקינן רבי יהושע סבר תוך הפתח כלפנים דמי וקמטלטל מנא דבתים בחצר ור' טרפון סבר תוך הפתח כלחוץ דמי ומנא דחצר בחצר קא מטלטל מדוכה ר' נחמיה היא: **מתני'** [ב] כל הכלים ניטלין לצורך ושלא לצורך ר' נחמיה אומר אין ניטלין אלא לצורך: **גמ'** מאי לצורך ומאי שלא לצורך אמר [ג] רבה לצורך דבר שמלאכתו להיתר לצורך גופו שלא לצורך דבר שמלאכתו להיתר לצורך מקומו ודבר שמלאכתו לאיסור לצורך גופו אין לצורך מקומו לא ואתא רבי נחמיה למימר ואפילו דבר שמלאכתו להיתר לצורך גופו אין לצורך מקומו לא אמר ליה רבא לצורך מקומו שלא לצורך קרית ליה אלא אמר רבא [ד] לצורך דבר שמלאכתו להיתר בין לצורך גופו בין לצורך מקומו שלא לצורך ואפי' מחמה לצל [ה] ודבר שמלאכתו לאיסור לצורך גופו ולצורך מקומו אין מחמה לצל לא ואתא רבי נחמיה למימר ואפילו דבר שמלאכתו להיתר לצורך גופו ולצורך מקומו אין מחמה לצל לא יתיב רב ספרא ורב אחא בר הונא ורב הונא בר חנינא ויתבי וקאמרי לרבה אליבא דרבי נחמיה הני קערות היכי מטלטלינן אמר להו רב ספרא מידי דהוה אגרף של רעי אמר ליה אביי לרבה לימא ליה רב ספרא חברין אליבא דרבי נחמיה הני קערות היכי מטלטלינן להו אמר ליה רב ספרא חברין תרגמה מידי דהוה אגרף של רעי איתיביה אביי לרבא [ו] מדוכה אם יש בה שום מטלטלין אותה ואם לאו אין מטלטלין אותה הכא במאי עסקינן מחמה לצל איתיביה [ז] ושוין שאם קיצב עליו בשר שאסור לטלטלו הכא נמי מחמה לצל והא דתנן [ח] אין סומכין את הקדירה בבקעת וכן בדלת והא בקעת דביום טוב דבר שמלאכתו להיתר הוא אלמא דבר שמלאכתו להיתר בין לצורך גופו בין לצורך מקומו אסור התם (א) מאי טעמא כיון דבשבת דבר שמלאכתו לאיסור הוא גזירה יו"ט אטו שבת וכי תימא שבת גופיה תישתרי דהא דבר שמלאכתו לאיסור לצורך גופו ולצורך מקומו שרי [ט] הני מילי היכא דאיכא תורת כלי עליו היכא דליכא תורת כלי עליו לא • ומי גזרינן והתנן [י] משילין פירות דרך ארובה ביום טוב [כ] אבל לא בשבת ומי לא גזרינן והתנן [ל] אין בין יו"ט לשבת אלא אוכל נפש בלבד אמר רב יוסף לא קשיא הא ר' אליעזר הא רבי יהושע [מ] דתניא אותו ואת בנו שנפלו לבור ר' אליעזר אומר מעלה את הראשון על מנת לשוחטו ושוחטו והשני עושה לו פרנסה במקומו בשביל שלא ימות ר' יהושע אומר מעלה את הראשון על מנת לשוחטו ואינו שוחטו ומערים ומעלה את השני רצה זה שוחט רצה זה שוחט [נ] ממאי דילמא עד כאן לא קאמר ר' אליעזר התם אלא דאפשר לפרנסה אבל היכא דלא אפשר לפרנסה לא אי נמי עד כאן לא קאמר רבי יהושע התם דאפשר בהערמה אבל היכא דלא אפשר בהערמה לא אלא אמר רב פפא לא קשיא הא בית שמאי הא בית הלל דתנן בית שמאי אומרים אין

הא ר"א. ההיא דאין בין אע"ג דבפ"ק דמגילה (דף ז:) דייקינן עלה הא לענין מכשירי אוכל נפש זה וזה שוין וקאמר מתני' דלא כרבי יהודה ור"א סבירא ליה כר"י ועדיפא מדרבי יהודה כדאמר בריש תולין (לקמן דף קלז:) איכא למימר דההוא תנא סבר לה כוותיה בחדא דגזרינן י"ט אטו שבת ופליג עליה במכשירין ועוד יש לומר דאין בין דפ"ק דמגילה איירי במילי דאורייתא ואין בין דהכא היינו דתנן במשילין (ביצה ד' לו:) דמיירי במילי דשבות ואינו מענין אחד תדע דהכי פריך עלה בפ' משילין כדפריך הכא בשמעתא ולא פריך בפ"ק דמגילה והא דדייק התם הא לענין מכשירין זה וזה שוין לא דייק בפרק משילין: הא

מסורת הש"ס

א) כלים פי"א מ"ד [וסם ליתא להך מימרא דנגר שיש בראשו], ב) [גי' הרי"ף והרא"ש אביי], ד) [לעיל קכג.], ה) [שם: וביצה יא.], ו) ביצה לב:, ז) ביצה לג., ח) לקמן קנ: ביצה כח. לו: מגילה ז: [תוספתא דמגילה פ"א], ט) [ביצה לז. ע"ש], י) [ביצה לז. תוספתא ביצה פ"ג], כ) [לקמן קמו.].

הגהות הב"ח

(א) גמ' התם היינו טעמא כיון דבשבת: (ב) רש"י ד"ה ומשני התם היינו טעמא:

גליון הש"ס

גמ' ומי גזרינן והתנן משילין. ע"ל דף כג ע"ב תוספות ד"ה גזירה:

ליקוטי רש"י

סכינא דאשכבתא. על בית שמקבצים בו בשר [ב"מ קטו.]. זוהמא ליסטרון. כף גדולה שמגלפין בו זוהם הקדירה [שם לב:]. מדוכה. שדוכין בה שום. אם יש בה שום מטלטלין אותה. אגב השום. ואם לאו אין מטלטלין אותה. כיון דעיקר מלאכתו למשיכה היא מלאכה איסור משום טוחן. ושוין. בית שמאי ובית הלל. שאם קיצב עליו בשר. שעשה לצורך שמחת יום טוב. שאסור לטלטלו. לא סידור הקנים. ידו על כתף חבירו. ותולה. גלוסטרא. שראשו עב ונועלין בו. שיש בראשו גלוסטרא. מחמה לצל. מידי דהוה אגרף של רעי. [ביצה לו.].

עין משפט נר מצוה

יח א מיי' פכ"ו מהלכות שבת הלכה ט סמג לאוין סה טוש"ע או"ח סימן שיג סעיף ה:
יט ב ג מיי' פכ"ה שם הלכה ג סמג שם טוש"ע או"ח סימן שח סעיף ד:
כ ד מיי' פ"ד שם טוש"ע שם סעיף ג:
כא ה מיי' פ"ד מהלכות יו"ט הלכה יא טור שו"ע או"ח סימן תקב סעיף ג:
כב ו מיי' פכ"ה מהל' שבת הלכה ו טוש"ע או"ח סימן שח סעיף ז:
כג ז מיי' פ"א מהלכות יו"ט הלכה ה טור שו"ע או"ח סימן תקכא סעיף א:
כד ח טוש"ע או"ח סימן שלה סעיף ז:
כה ט מיי' פ"ב מהלכות יו"ט הלכה ד סמג לאוין עט טוש"ע או"ח סימן תצח סעיף ט:

רבינו חננאל

שאסור בשבת סידורן ונטילתן מתוך לחם הפנים. מקלות מפורש במס' פסחים. בזמן שאמר ר' יד להיות בשבת אסר ר' אלעזר לטלטל מקל ולהניחו על כתיפו ועל כתף חבירו לתלות הפסח בו ולהפשיטו. וכן גלוסטרא. היא משנה בכלים פ' י"א שאסר ר' יהושע לטלטלה בשבת. תוספתא דכלים בתחלת בב"מ קלוסטרא ר' טרפון מטמא וחכמים מטהרין. ברורייה אומר שומטה מפתח זה ותולה בחבירו בשבת. כשנאמרו דברים לפני ר' יהושע אמר יפה אמר ברוריה. והא בענין הזה בעירובין בסופו. מדוכה זו שאמרנו למעלה אלו כולן כלים וקודם התרת כלים נשנו שאסור לטלטלן בשבת. א) אבל אחר התרת כלים מותרין הן וחלק רבא על רבי אלעזר ואמר דלמא אחר התרת כלים נשנו ואסורין הן לעולם. ודבריו פשוטין הן: מתני' כל הכלים הניטלין לצורך ניטלין לצורך ושלא לצורך כו'. פירש רבא משנה זו לצורך דבר שמלאכתו להיתר כגון קערות וכוסות וכדומה להן. שמותר לכתחלה לטלטלן לאכול ולשתות בהן הללו מותרין לטלטלן בין לצורך גופו לאכול בהן בין לצורך מקומו לפנותן כדי לישב במקומן. דבר שמלאכתו לאיסור כגון קורנס של נפחים וכדומה לו לצורך גופו (מותר) [כגון] לפצוע בו אגוזין מותר. אבל לצורך מקומן אסור. ורבי נחמיה אמר אפילו דבר שמלאכתו להיתר כגון קערות וכדומה להן לצורך גופו לאכול בהן מותר. אבל אחר שיאכל בהן אסור לטלטלן [לצורך] מקומן. ועל זה הקשה ליה אביי לרבה למר אליבא דר' נחמיה הני קערות כלומר שאינו מטלטלן אלא לצורך אכילה בהן אחר שיאכל אדם היאך מטלטל ומסלקן מן השולחן. והשיבו לו כבר נתקשה זה לרב ספרא חברין. ופירק מידי דהוה אגרף של רעי שמותר לטלטל לדברי הכל. דתניא בתוספתא גרף של רעי ושל מימי רגלים נוטלן ושופכן וכו' ובזמן שאמר רבה דברים הללו השיבו רבא לצורך מקומו שלא לצורך קרית ליה. אלא אמר [רבא] לצורך דבר שמלאכתו להיתר בין לצורך גופו בין לצורך מקומו. שלא לצורך אפילו מחמה לצל. ודבר שמלאכתו לאיסור לצורך גופו ולצורך מקומו אין. מחמה לצל לא. ואתא ר' נחמיה למימר ואפילו דבר שמלאכתו להיתר לצורך גופו ולצורך מקומו אין. מחמה לצל לא. מותיב אביי [לרבה] לדידך דאמרת דבר שמלאכתו לאיסור אפילו לצורך מקומו מטלטל הרי מדוכה שאינה מטלטלת אלא לצורך גופה אם יש בה שום. אבל אין בה שום לצורך מקומה אסור לטלטלו ופריק ליה הכא במאי עסקינן בשצריך לטלטלה להסירה מן החמה ולהניחה בצל. וכן שאר השמועה כולה פשוטה היא:

חשק שלמה על רבינו חננאל א) דברי רבינו כמות שהם אין להם הבנה. ונראה דל"ל אבל רבה כו' אבל לאחר התרת כלים וכו':

להניחה בצל מותר לטלטל. מדוכה. שדוכין בה שום. אם יש בה שום מטלטלין אותה. ואם לאו אין מטלטלין אותה. שאם קיצב עליו בשר. משילין פירות דרך ארובה ביום טוב. אין בין יום טוב לשבת אלא אוכל נפש. אותו ואת בנו. ואינו שוחטו. אבל היכא דלא אפשר בהערמה [ביצה שם].

The Gemara counters:

וּמִי לֹא גָּזְרִינַן – **Do we not enact** such **decrees?** וְהָתְנַן – **But we learned in a Mishnah:**[29] אֵין בֵּין יוֹם טוֹב לְשַׁבָּת אֶלָּא אוֹכֶל נֶפֶשׁ בִּלְבַד – THERE IS NO DIFFERENCE BETWEEN YOM TOV AND THE SABBATH EXCEPT in matters pertaining to FOOD PREPARATION.[30] – ? –

Faced with this contradiction, the Gemara states:

אָמַר רַב יוֹסֵף – **Rav Yosef said:** לֹא קַשְׁיָא – **There is no difficulty.** הָא רַבִּי אֱלִיעֶזֶר – **This [Mishnah]** follows **R' Eliezer,** הָא רַבִּי יְהוֹשֻׁעַ – whereas **this [Mishnah]** follows **R' Yehoshua.** דְּתַנְיָא – **For it was taught in a Baraisa:** אוֹתוֹ וְאֶת בְּנוֹ שֶׁנָּפְלוּ לְבוֹר – [AN ANIMAL] AND ITS OFFSPRING THAT FELL INTO A PIT on Yom Tov[31] – רַבִּי אֱלִיעֶזֶר אוֹמֵר – R' ELIEZER SAYS: מַעֲלֶה אֶת הָרִאשׁוֹן עַל מְנָת לְשׁוֹחֲטוֹ וְשׁוֹחֲטוֹ – ONE MAY RAISE THE FIRST animal IN ORDER TO SLAUGHTER IT AND he must then SLAUGHTER IT, וְהַשֵּׁנִי עוֹשֶׂה לוֹ פַּרְנָסָה בִּמְקוֹמוֹ בִּשְׁבִיל שֶׁלֹּא יָמוּת – AND FOR THE SECOND animal HE PROVIDES SUSTENANCE IN ITS PLACE in the pit SO THAT IT NOT DIE. רַבִּי יְהוֹשֻׁעַ אוֹמֵר – R' YEHOSHUA SAYS: מַעֲלֶה אֶת הָרִאשׁוֹן עַל מְנָת לְשׁוֹחֲטוֹ וְאֵינוֹ שׁוֹחֲטוֹ – ONE MAY RAISE THE FIRST animal ostensibly IN ORDER TO SLAUGHTER IT BUT HE NEED NOT SLAUGHTER IT then. וּמַעֲרִים וּמַעֲלֶה אֶת הַשֵּׁנִי – HE MAY THEN EMPLOY SUBTERFUGE TO RAISE THE SECOND animal.[32] רָצָה זֶה שׁוֹחֵט רָצָה זֶה שׁוֹחֵט – If HE WANTS HE MAY SLAUGHTER THIS first ONE, and if HE WANTS HE MAY SLAUGHTER THIS other ONE. Thus, R' Yehoshua rules leniently in regard to exertion on Yom Tov to preclude a financial loss while R' Eliezer rules stringently. Similarly, R' Yehoshua will permit lowering produce through a skylight out of concern for financial loss, while R' Eliezer will forbid it.[33]

The Gemara rejects this answer:

מִמַּאי – **On what basis** do you compare these cases: דִּילְמָא עַד כָּאן לֹא קָאָמַר רַבִּי אֱלִיעֶזֶר הָתָם – **Perhaps so far R' Eliezer stated** his stringent opinion **there,** in the case of animals that fell into a pit, אֶלָּא דְּאֶפְשָׁר לְפַרְנָסָה – **only because it is possible to provide sustenance for [the second animal]** in the pit, and thereby avoid the financial loss, אֲבָל הֵיכָא דְּלֹא אֶפְשָׁר לְפַרְנָסָה לֹא – **but** in a case **where it is not possible to provide [the endangered object] with sustenance** he would **not** forbid other measures. Thus, he might permit lowering produce through a skylight on Yom Tov to save it from the rain.[34] אִי נַמִּי – **Similarly,** a distinction can be drawn between the cases according to R' Yehoshua: עַד כָּאן לָא קָאָמַר ר׳ יְהוֹשֻׁעַ הָתָם – **So far R' Yehoshua stated** his lenient opinion only **there,** דְּאֶפְשָׁר בְּהַעֲרָמָה – **because it is possible to employ subterfuge,** אֲבָל הֵיכָא דְּלֹא אֶפְשָׁר בְּהַעֲרָמָה לֹא – **but** in a case **where it is not possible to employ subterfuge,** he would **not** rule leniently.[35] The dispute between R' Eliezer and R' Yehoshua is therefore not analogous to the matter of lowering produce through a skylight, and the contradiction between the two Mishnahs is still not resolved. – ? –

The Gemara advances another resolution to the contradiction:

אֶלָּא אָמַר רַב פָּפָּא – **Rather, Rav Pappa said:** לֹא קַשְׁיָא – There is **no difficulty.** הָא בֵּית שַׁמַּאי – **This** latter **[Mishnah],** which applies all the Sabbath Rabbinic prohibitions to Yom Tov, follows **Beis Shammai,** הָא בֵּית הִלֵּל – whereas **this** previous **[Mishnah],** which permits lowering produce through a skylight on Yom Tov, even though it is forbidden on the Sabbath, follows **Beis Hillel.** דִּתְנַן – **For we learned in a Mishnah:**[36] בֵּית שַׁמַּאי אוֹמְרִים – BEIS SHAMMAI SAY:

NOTES

on the Sabbath and Yom Tov. Nonetheless, the Sages granted a dispensation permitting one to drop the produce through a skylight on Yom Tov in order to preclude a financial loss, because the amount of labor involved is minimal. [However, one may not lift produce and drop it through a window, since this involves excessive exertion.] On the Sabbath, the Sages were more stringent, and prohibited even the minimal exertion involved in dropping produce through a skylight. Thus, we see that the Sages did not forbid activity on Yom Tov out of concern that one might do it on the Sabbath (*Rashi* here and to *Beitzah* 35b).

[There are certainly some activities that were prohibited on Yom Tov out of concern that one might do them on the Sabbath. The Gemara's point is to demonstrate that the Sages did not prohibit *moving* something on Yom Tov even when the same movement is forbidden on the Sabbath (see *Tosafos* above, 23b-24a, end of ד״ה גזירה).]

29. *Beitzah* 36b.

30. All Rabbinic decrees that apply on the Sabbath likewise apply on Yom Tov, with the exception of those related to food preparation, which is entirely permitted on Yom Tov (see *Tosafos* ד״ה הא ר״א).

31. Since hauling an animal out of a pit involves exertion, it is permitted on Yom Tov only if the animal is fit to be slaughtered and used on that day. According to Biblical law (see *Leviticus* 22:28), however, an animal and its offspring may not be slaughtered on the same day. Thus, it should be forbidden to remove both animals from the pit on Yom Tov since only one can be slaughtered (see *Mishnah Berurah* 498:57).

32. I.e. he may claim that the first animal did not meet his expectations, e.g. it was too thin, and that the animal which is still in the pit might be more desirable for the Yom Tov meal (*Rashi* to *Beitzah* 37a ד״ה דאפשר לאיערומי).

33. [However, all agree that in cases not involving financial loss there is no difference between the Sabbath and Yom Tov (except in matters pertaining to food preparation). Thus, Rava's answer – that moving wood was prohibited on Yom Tov because a similar prohibition applies on the Sabbath – is correct according to both Tannaim.]

34. No "provisions" can be placed on the roof to save the produce from the approaching rainstorm.

35. In R' Yehoshua's case, an observer would assume that the first animal had actually been raised to be slaughtered, but it was then found to be too thin. The second animal was therefore raised because it was more desirable for slaughter. In the other case, however, the produce is obviously being lowered for the sake of avoiding a financial loss. Perhaps R' Yehoshua grants the dispensation only in a case where the person's intention is not obvious (*Rashi*).

36. *Beitzah* 12a.

ידו על כתף חבירו. דלא מטלטלי מקלות: גלוסטרא. דתנן רבי יהושע אמר נגר שיש בראשו גלוסטרא שראשה עב וראוי לדוך בו שום ונועלין בו דלת: שומטה מפתח זה ותולה בחברו. ואע"ג דלריך לגופו לתלותו בחברו ולנועלה בו שומטו ע"י גרירה אבל טלטול גמור לא ואע"פ שמלאכתו להיתר לא שרי ליה לצורך גופו: מדוכה הא דאמרן. לעיל אע"ג דשנייה רבא לעיל מחמה לצל ואביי שנייה לצורך מקומו שינויי דחיקי נינהו אלא קודם התרת כלים נשנו: קנים טעמא מאי. מסדרין אותם במערכה: משום איעפושי. דלא סמכינן אניסא ומשום ההוא פורתא שהישנה מתעכבת בלא קנים מלילי שבת לשבת והחדשה משבת למו"ש לא מיעפשי: כדר"א. מניח ידו על כתף חבירו: שאינה מעורבת. שהרבה בתים פתוחים לה ולא עירבו דכלים ששבתו בבתים אסור להוציאן לחצר ושבתו בחצר מותר לטלטלן בחצר שהחצר כולו רשות לעצמו הוא והבתים מיוחדים לכל איש ביתו: תוך הפתח. שנטל הסגר משם: וקא מטלטל מנא דבית בחצר. הלכך שומטה אין דטלטול מן הצד היא אבל טלטול גמור לא: מדוכה רבי נחמיה היא. דאמר (לקמן) ובעירובין (דף לה.) אפילו טלית ואפי' תרווד אין ניטלין אלא לצורך תשמיש המיוחד: מתני' ה"ג במתניתין כל הכלים ניטלין לצורך כו': גמ' מאי לצורך ומאי שלא לצורך אמר רבה כו'. לצורך דשרי תנא קמא היינו דבר שמלאכתו להיתר ומטלטלו לצורך גופו: שלא לצורך דבר שמלאכתו להיתר. ומטלטלו שלא לצורך גופו אבל לריך למקומו: ודבר שמלאכתו לאיסור לצורך גופו. הוא דאשמעינן אם לריך לו למלאכת היתר אבל שלא לצורך גופו ואע"ג דלריך למקומו לא ורבה לטעמיה דאמר לעיל (דף קכג:) גבי קורנס של נפחים נמי מותר לצורך גופו: א"ל רבא כו' אלא אמר כו'. ולרבא דמוקי אליבא דרבי נחמיה דלצורך גופו ולצורך מקומו מותר ע"כ האי לצורך גופו כגון שזה התשמיש מיוחד לו דתניא לקמן בפרק חבית (דף קמו.) רבי נחמיה אומר אפילו תרווד ואפילו טלית אין ניטלין אלא לצורך תשמישן ולורך מקומו נמי לרבא כלורך גופו ותשמישו דמי ולרבה לורך גופו הוא דשרי רבי נחמיה ודוקא לתשמיש המיוחד לו ובין לרבה ובין לרבא דוקא דבר שמלאכתו להיתר אבל דבר שמלאכתו לאיסור אפילו לצורך גופו לא שרי רבי נחמיה דהאי לורך גופו לאו תשמיש המיוחד לו הוא דהא מיוחד למלאכת איסור: לרבה אליבא דרבי נחמיה. דאמר דבר שמלאכתו להיתר לצורך מקומו לא: הני קערות. לאחר אכילה היכי מטלטל להו לסלקן מלפניו: ואם לאו אין מטלטלין אותה. בשלמא לרבה כגון דאין לריך לגופה [אלא למקומה] אלא לדידך אמאי: וכן בדלת. אוקימנא במסכת ביצה וכן הדלת אין סומכין בבקעת וביו"ט קיימי: והא בקעת ביו"ט מלאכתה להיתר היא. דלהסקה חזי וקיימא וקאסר לטלטלה לצורך גופו למלאכה אחרת וכל שכן לצורך מקומה: ומשני התם (ב) טעמא כיון דבשבת אסור דהא בקעת בשבת מלאכתה לאיסור היא ביום טוב נמי אסור גזירה י"ט אטו שבת: משילין פירות דרך ארובה ביום טוב. בהדיא תנן אבל לא בשבת פירות השטוחים על הגג לייבשן ורואה גשמים ממשמשים ובאין משילן לארץ דרך ארובת הגג דלא טריחא מילתא דנופלין מאליהן אלמא דלא גזרינן ופרכינן ומי לא גזרינן והתנן אין בין כו': לא קשיא הא. דתנן משילין דשרי טירחא ביו"ט משום איבוד ממון רבי יהושע היא שהתיר להעלות בהמה בהערמה מן הבור: והא. דתנן אין בין כו' ר"א היא: דאפשר בהערמה. דמיחזי כמאן דעביד לצורך יו"ט אבל גבי משילין דליכא הערמה לדמויי להתירא לא:
אין

ידו על כתף חבירו ויד חבירו על כתיפו ותולה ומפשיט גלוסטרא דתנן[א] [א]נגר שיש בראשו גלוסטרא ר' יהושע אומר שומטה מן פתח זה ותולה בחבירו בשבת ר' טרפון אומר הרי הוא ככל הכלים ומיטלטל בחצר מדוכה הא דאמרן אמר רבה ממאי דילמא לעולם אימא לך לאחר התרת כלים נשנו קנים טעמא מאי משום איעפושי בהאי פורתא לא מיעפש מקלות אפשר כר' אלעזר גלוסטרא כדרבי ינאי דאמר רבי ינאי בחצר שאינה מעורבת עסקינן רבי יהושע סבר תוך הפתח כלפנים דמי וקמטלטל מנא דבתים בחצר ור' טרפון סבר תוך הפתח כלחוץ דמי ומנא דחצר בחצר קא מטלטל מדוכה ר' נחמיה היא: מתני' [ב] כל הכלים ניטלין לצורך ושלא לצורך [ג] ר' נחמיה אומר אין ניטלין אלא לצורך: גמ' מאי לצורך ומאי שלא לצורך אמר [ג] רבה לצורך דבר שמלאכתו להיתר לצורך גופו שלא לצורך דבר שמלאכתו להיתר לצורך מקומו ודבר שמלאכתו לאיסור לצורך גופו אין לצורך מקומו לא ואתא רבי נחמיה למימר ואפילו דבר שמלאכתו להיתר לצורך גופו אין לצורך מקומו לא אמר ליה רבא לצורך מקומו שלא לצורך קרית ליה אלא אמר רבא [ג] לצורך דבר שמלאכתו להיתר בין לצורך גופו בין לצורך מקומו שלא לצורך ואפי' מחמה לצל [ד] ודבר שמלאכתו לאיסור לצורך גופו ולצורך מקומו אין מחמה לצל לא ואתא רבי נחמיה למימר ואפילו דבר שמלאכתו להיתר לצורך גופו ולצורך מקומו אין מחמה לצל לא יתיב רב ספרא ורב אחא בר הונא ורב הונא בר חנינא ויתבי וקאמרי לרבה אליבא דרבי נחמיה הני קערות היכי מטלטלינן אמר להו רב ספרא מידי דהוה אגרף של רעי אמר ליה אביי לרבה למר אליבא דרבי נחמיה הני קערות היכי מטלטלינן להו אמר ליה רב ספרא חברין תרגמה מידי דהוה אגרף של רעי איתיביה אביי לרבא [ד] מדוכה אם יש בה שום מטלטלין אותה ואם לאו אין מטלטלין אותה הכא במאי עסקינן מחמה לצל איתיביה [ה] ושוין שאם קיצב עליו בשר שאסור לטלטלו הכא נמי מחמה לצל והא דתנן [ו] [ה] אין סומכין את הקדירה בבקעת וכן בדלת והא בקעת דביום טוב דבר שמלאכתו להיתר הוא אלמא דבר שמלאכתו להיתר בין לצורך גופו בין לצורך מקומו אסור התם (א) מאי טעמא כיון דבשבת דבר שמלאכתו לאיסור הוא גזירה יו"ט אטו שבת וכי תימא שבת גופיה תישתרי דהא דבר שמלאכתו לאיסור לצורך גופו ולצורך מקומו שרי [ו] הני מילי היכא דאיכא תורת כלי עליו היכא דליכא תורת כלי עליו לא ומי גזרינן והתנן [ז] משילין פירות דרך ארובה ביום טוב [ח] אבל לא בשבת ומי לא גזרינן והתנן [ט] [ט] אין בין יו"ט לשבת אלא אוכל נפש בלבד אמר רב יוסף לא קשיא הא ר' אליעזר הא רבי יהושע [י] דתניא אותו ואת בנו שנפלו לבור ר' אליעזר אומר מעלה את הראשון על מנת לשוחטו ושוחטו והשני עושה לו פרנסה במקומו בשביל שלא ימות ר' יהושע אומר מעלה את הראשון על מנת לשוחטו ואינו שוחטו ומערים ומעלה את השני רצה זה שוחט רצה זה שוחט [כ] ממאי דילמא עד כאן לא קאמר ר' אליעזר התם אלא דאפשר לפרנסה אבל היכא דלא אפשר לפרנסה לא אי נמי עד כאן לא קאמר רבי יהושע התם דאפשר בהערמה אבל היכא דלא אפשר בהערמה לא אלא אמר רב פפא לא קשיא הא בית שמאי הא בית הלל דתנן בית שמאי אומרים
אין

הא ר"א. ההיא דאין בין אע"ג דבפ"ק דמגילה (דף ז:) דייקינן עלה הא לענין מכשירי אוכל נפש זה וזה שוין וקאמר מתני' דלא כרבי יהודה ור"א סבירא ליה כר"י ועדיפא מדרבי יהודה כדאמר בריש חולין (לקמן דף קלז:) איכא למימר דההוא תנא סבר לה כוותיה בחדא דגזרינן י"ט אטו שבת ופליג עליה במכשירין ועוד יש לומר דאין בין דפ"ק דמגילה איירי במילי דאורייתא ואין בין דהכא היינו דתנן במשילין (ביצה ד' לז:) דמיירי במילי דשבות ואינו מענין אחד תדע דהכי פריך עלה בפ' משילין כדפריך הכא בשמעתא ולא פריך בפ"ק דמגילה והא דדייק התם הא לענין מכשירין זה וזה שוין לא דייק בפרק משילין:
הא

עין משפט נר מצוה

יח א מיי' פכ"ה מהלכות שבת הלכה ב סמג לאוין סה טוש"ע או"ח סימן שיג סעיף ה:

יט ב ג מיי' פכ"ה שם הלכה ג סמג שם טוש"ע או"ח סימן שח סעיף ד:

כ ד מיי' שם טוש"ע שם סעיף ג:

כא ה מיי' פ"ד מהלכות יו"ט הלכה יא טור שו"ע או"ח סימן תקב סעיף ג:

כב ו מיי' פכ"ה מהל' שבת הלכה ו טוש"ע או"ח סימן שח סעיף ז:

כג ז מיי' פ"ב מהלכות יו"ט הלכה ה טור שו"ע או"ח סימן תקמא סעיף א:

כד ח טוש"ע או"ח סימן שלב סעיף ב:

כה ט מיי' פ"ב מהלכות יו"ט הלכה ג סמג לאוין עה טוש"ע או"ח סימן תצח סעיף ט:

רבינו חננאל

שאסור בשבת סידורן ונטילתן מתוך לחם הפנים. מקלות מפורש במס' פסחים. בזמן שחל י"ד להיות בשבת אמר ר' אלעזר לטלטל מקל ולהניחו על כתיפו ועל כתף חבירו לתלות הפסח בו ולהפשיטו. וכן גלוסטרא. היא משנה בכלים פ' י"א שאמר ר' יהושע שטלטלה בשבת. תוספתא דכלים בתחלת בב"מ קלוסטרא ר' טרפון מטמא וחכמים מטהרין. ברוריה אומר שומטה מפתח זה ותולה בחבירו בשבת. כשנאמרו דברים לפני ר' יהושע אמר יפה אמר ברוריה. והוא בענין הזה בעירובין בסופו. מדוכה זו שאמרנו למעלה אלו כולן כלים הן אלו התרת כלים נשנו שאסור לטלטלן בשבת. (א) אבל אחר התרת כלים מותרין הן וחלק רבא על רבי אלעזר ואמר דלמא אחר התרת כלים נשנו ואסורין הן לעולם. ודבריו פשוטין הן: מתני' כל הכלים הניטלין לצורך ניטלין לצורך ושלא לצורך כו'. פירש רבא משנה זו לצורך דבר שמלאכתו להיתר כגון קערות וכוסות וכדומה להן. שמותר לכתחלה לטלטלן לאכול ולשתות בהן הללו מותרין לטלטלן בין לצורך גופו בין לצורך מקומו כגון לאכול בהן כדי לישב במקומן. דבר שמלאכתו לאיסור כגון קורנס של נפחים וכדומה לו לצורך גופו לאכול בהן (מותר) [כגון] לפצוע בו אגוזין מותר. אבל לצורך מקומו אסור. ורבי נחמיה אמר אפילו דבר שמלאכתו להיתר כגון קערות וכדומה להן לצורך גופו לאכול בהן מותר. אבל אחר שאכל בהן אסור לטלטלן [לצורך] מקומן. ועל זה הקשה ליה אביי לרבה למר אליבא דר' נחמיה הני קערות כלומר שאינו מטלטל אלא לצורך אכילה בהן אחר שאכל אדם האיך מטלטלן ומסלקן מן השולחן.

והשיבו לו כבר נתקשה זה לרב ספרא חברין. ופירק מידי דהוה אגרף של רעי שמותר לטלטל לדברי הכל. דתניא בתוספתא גרף של רעי ושל מימי רגלים נוטלן ושופכן וכו'. ובזמן שאמר רבה דברים הללו השיבו רבא לצורך דבר שמלאכתו להיתר בין לצורך גופו בין לצורך מקומו. שלא לצורך אפילו מחמה לצל. דבר שמלאכתו לאיסור לצורך גופו ולצורך מקומו אין. מחמה לצל לא. ואתא ר' נחמיה למימר אפילו דבר שמלאכתו להיתר לצורך גופו ולצורך מקומו אין. מחמה לצל לא. מותיב אביי (לרבה) [לרבא] לדידך דאמרת דבר שמלאכתו לאיסור אפילו לצורך מקומו מטלטל והרי מדוכה שאינה מטלטלת אלא לצורך גופה אם יש בה שום. אבל אין בה שום אסור לטלטלה ואפילו לצורך מקומה. ופירק ליה הכא במאי עסקינן בשצריך לטלטלה מחמה לצל וכן הא דתניא ושוין שאם קצב עליו בשר שאסור לטלטלו מחמה לצל. אבל לצורך מקומו מותר. וכן שאר השמועה כולה פשוטה.

חשק שלמה על רבינו חננאל
א) דברי רבינו כמות שהם אין להם הבנה. ונראה דל"ל אבל אחר התרת כלים נשנו ושרי. והיינו כמו שאמר רבה לעיל ודלמא לעולם אימא לך לאחר התרת כלים וכו':

מסורת הש"ס

א) כלים פי"א מ"ד [ושם ליתא להך מילתא נגר שיש בראשו], ב) [לעיל וש"נ], ג) [עי' הרי"ף והרא"ש אביי], ד) [לעיל קכב.], ה) [שם], ו) ביצה יא:, ז) ביצה לב: לו., ח) לקמן קלז: ביצה כח: לו: מגילה ז: [תוספתא דמגילה פ"א], ט) ביצה לו. [תוספתא ביצה פ"ג], י) [ביצה לז. ע"ש], כ) [לקמן קמו.].

הגהות הב"ח

(א) גמ' התם היינו טעמא כיון דבשבת: (ב) רש"י ד"ה ומשני התם היינו טעמא:

גליון הש"ס

גמ' ומי גזרינן והתנן משילין. ע"ל דף כג ע"ב תוספות ד"ה גזירה:

ליקוטי רש"י

סכינא דאשכבתא. על בית המטבחים שמקבצים בו בשר [ב"מ קטז.]. זוהמא ליספרון. כף גדולה שמקבצין בה זוהם הקדירה והקלפת לגלדין [שם לב.]. אותו כף שמוציאין את הקדרה ... [הוריות יג:]. מדוכה. שדוכין בה שום. אם יש בה שום מטלטלין אותה. אגב השום. ואם לאו אין מטלטלין אותה. כיון דעיקר מלאכתו לשחיקה היא מלאכה איסור משום טוחן. ושוין. בית שמאי ובית הלל שמטלטלין את העלי לקצב עליו בשר ביום טוב. שאם קצב עליו בשר. עשאה לצורך שמחת יום טוב. שאסור לטלטלו. דהאי דקשרו בית הלל משום שמחת יו"ט הוא דקשרו אלמא משום דעלי מלאכתו לאיסור לכתישת ערגים וטיסני וקליפת עלים לעבד בהן עורות אסור [לעיל ע"א]. דלמתעביד ליה לורך יום טוב [ביצה יא.]. לא סידור הקנין. במערכה ... [מנחות צז.]. חלקין. מחולקין ... [פסחים סה:]. ידו על כתף חבירו. ... שיש בראשו גלוסטרא. ... מחמה לצל. ... מידי דהוה אגרף של רעי. ... מותר

שבת (שם מז.). שמותר לטלטלו ולפנותו לאשפה מחמת מאוס כדאמרינן בפרק בתרא (ביצה לו:) [ביצה כא.]. גרף. כלי חרס המוכן לכך [לעיל שם]. מדוכה. שדוכין בה שום. אם יש בה שום מטלטלין אותה. אגב השום. ואם לאו אין מטלטלין אותה. כיון דעיקר מלאכתו לשחיקה היא מלאכה איסור משום טוחן. ושוין. בית שמאי ובית הלל ... שאם קצב עליו בשר. שאסור לטלטלו. ... [לעיל קכג.]. דלמתעביד ליה לורך יום טוב [ביצה יא.]. משילין פירות דרך ארובה. מי שהיו לו פירות בראש הגג ורואה גשמים ממשמשין ובאין משילן לארץ דרך ארובה ... [illegible]

[illegible] אין בין יום טוב לשבת. ... [illegible]

עין משפט
נר מצוה

כו א מיי' פ"א מהלכות יו"ט הלכה ד סמג לאוין עה טוש"ע או"ח סימן תקיח סעיף א:
כז ב מיי' פכ"ה מהלכו' שבת הלכה ג סמג לאוין שם טוש"ע או"ח סימן שח סעיף ג:
כח ג מיי' פכ"ו שם הלכה ב סמג שם טוש"ע שם סעיף מט:
כט ד מיי' פכ"ה מהל' שבת הלכה יג סמג שם טוש"ע או"ח סימן שח סעיף ו:
ל ה מיי' פכ"ו שם הלכה ב טוש"ע או"ח סימן שח סעיף יח:
לא ו ז ח מיי' שם הל' ג טוש"ע שם סעיף ז:

אין מוציאין. הוצאה שלא לצורך דלא אישתרי לכתחילה ביו"ט טפי מבשבת אלא אוכל נפש והנך דמשלין ב"ה: טלטול מי שמעת להו. דמשוי יו"ט לשבת: טלטול לאו צורך הוצאה. בתמיה הלכך אי מזלזלת בטלטול מזלזלת בהוצאה: להא דרבא. דאמר לצורך מקומו כלצורך גופו: מר. פוסו"ר: שלא יגנב. דומיא דמחמה לצל ואסור בדבר שמלאכתו לאיסור: שותא. (ב) מלודה: לאו למימרא כו'. למה לי לפרושי בהדיא דליתיב עלה לאו משום למימרא דהאי דשרי לטלטולי משום דלצורך גופו הוא: שקילו שותא מקמיה כהנא. דניתוב על מקומה קאמר ולצורך מקומה הוא דהוה: מחמה לצל הוה. במקום הרע לה היתה ואי לאו דפריש בהדיא ליתיב עלה מאן דחזי סבר דמחמה לצל שרי ולמקומה לא היה צריך דלימא שישב במקומה: בי סדיותא. כרים של לבד שקורין פילטר"א: בי שמשי. בחמה: אמר ליה שרי. רבא לטעמיה דאמר דבר שמלאכתו להיתר אף מחמה לצל מותר: אית לי אחריני. איני צריך לגופו: דכרבה סבירא לך. דאמר מחמה לצל אסור והלכה כרבא דאמר דבר שמלאכתו להיתר שרי לגמרי ודבר שמלאכתו לאיסור לצורך גופו ומקומו מותר מחמה לצל ושלא יגנב אסור: מכבדות. איסקוב"א שמכבדים בהן את השולחן: של מילתא. (ג) בגדים לכבד שולחן שמלאכתו להיתר: של תמרה. כעין שלנו לכבד את הבית דאסור משום אשויי גומות דמודה רבי שמעון בפסיק רישיה ולא ימות: לצורך גופו. למלאכת היתר: אלא מחמה לצל בהא לימא רבי אלעזר אף של תמרה. דבר שמלאכתו לאיסור ליכא מאן דשרי מחמה לצל: וכן אמר רבי אלעזר. של מילתא מותר של תמרה אסור מחמה לצל: מתני' מעין מלאכה. שום מלאכה ואפי' אינה מעין הראשונה: לצוק לתוכה מקפה. עבה דומיא דעיסה מעורבת במים: גמ' הואיל ומוכנין על גבי אביהן. כשקדש היום: מסיקין בכלים. ביו"ט שהרי ראוין לטלטל ויטלטל ויתנם לתוך האור: ואין מסיקין בשברי כלים. דהוו להו מוקצין ולא חזו לטלטול: עצים בעלמא נינהו. דהא מאתמול להסקה קיימי: וקתני אין מסיקין. ולא אמרינן מוכנין היו אגב אביהן אלא אמרינן נולד נינהו ואסירי: מר סבר מוכן הוא. כיון דראוי לשום מלאכה ומר סבר נולד הוה דמאתמול לאו להאי מלאכה הוה קאי הלכך מעין מלאכתו בעינן: הא רבי יהודה. מסיקין בכלים ואין מסיקין בשברי כלים דאית ליה מוקצה ונולד כלים לאו מוקצה נינהו שברים נולד נינהו: והא. דתני מסיקין בשניהם: רבי שמעון. דלית ליה מוקצה ולית ליה נולד: והא. דתניא אף בכלים אין מסיקין: רבי נחמיה היא. דאמר אין כלי ניטל אלא לצורך תשמישו המיוחד לו והאי לאו מיוחד הוא לו דלאו להסקה קאי: דאייתור. שהשלים בניינו וניתותר ומהשתא לא קיימי לבנין אלא לישב עליהם ותורת כלי עליהם: שרגינהו. אי סדרן זו על זו ודאי אקלינהו לצורך בנין אחר: בחצר. דשכיחי בה כלים שהחרס הזה ראוי להם לכיסוי ותורת כלי עליו: אבל לא בכרמלית. אפי' בתוך ד' אמות דלא שכיחי ביה מאני ולא חזי לכסויי: אפילו בכרמלית. הואיל ולאו רה"ר הוא שכיחי דאזלי ויתבי התם וחזי לכסות בו רוק: ורבא אמר אף ברה"ר. כיון דבחצר כלי הוא בעלמא נמי לא פקע שם כלי מיניה: בריתקא. שם רה"ר: איתווסאי מסאניה טינא. נתלכלך מנעלו בטיט: כפר ליה. מקנחו: אמר רבא לא מסתייה דלא גמירי. מה אסור מה מותר: אלא מיגמר נמי מגמרי. מלמדין שיבוש שבידם לאחרים: לדידי. לקינוח ואע"ג דלא שכיח הרי שם כלי עליו בחצר: שנתכתתה. החבית: (ד) מגופה. של חבית שנתכתתה החבית: היא. המגופה: ושבריה. של חבית ניטלין בשבת דחזו לכיסוי מנא: לא יספות. (ה) יתקן להתיר בליטותיו ועוקציו בשבת דעביד כלי והוי מכה בפטיש: ואם זרק. מגופה זו לאשפה בטלה מתורת כלי: זרקיה לגלימיה. בשבת לאשפה ה"נ דאסור לטלטולי:
מבעוד

[א] אין מוציאין את הקטן ואת הלולב ואת ספר תורה לרה"ר ובית הלל [א] מתירין אימר דשמעת להו לבית שמאי הוצאה טלטול מי שמעת להו [ב] וטלטול [ג] גופיה לאו משום הוצאה היא ואף רב סבר לה להא דרבא דאמר רב [ב] מר שלא יגנב זהו טלטול שלא לצורך ואסור טעמא שלא יגנב אבל לצורך גופו ולצורך מקומו מותר איני והא רב כהנא איקלע לבי רב ואמר אייתו ליה שותא לכהנא ליתיב עליה לאו למימרא דדבר שמלאכתו לאיסור לצורך גופו אין לצורך מקומו לא הכי אמר להו שקולו שותא מקמי כהנא ואי בעית אימא התם מחמה לצל הוה רב מרי בר רחל הוה ליה ההיא בי סדיותא בשמשא אתא לקמיה דרבא אמר ליה מהו לטלטולינהו אמר ליה שרי אית לי אחרינא חזו לאורחין אית לי נמי לאורחים אמר ליה גלית אדעתיך [ד] דכרבה סבירא לך [ה] לכולי עלמא שרי לדידך אסיר אמר רבי אבא אמר רבי חייא בר אשי [ג] אמר רב מכבדות של מילתא מותר לטלטלן בשבת אבל של תמרה לא רבי אלעזר אומר אף של תמרה במאי עסקינן אילימא לצורך גופו ולצורך מקומו בהא לימא רב של תמרה לא והא רב כרבא סבירא ליה אלא מחמה לצל בהא לימא ר' אלעזר אף של תמרה [א] לעולם מחמה לצל אימא וכן אמר רבי אלעזר: **מתני'** [ו] [ד] כל הכלים הניטלין בשבת שבריהן ניטלין עמהן ובלבד שיהו עושין מעין מלאכה שברי עריבה לכסות בהן את פי החבית שברי זכוכית לכסות בהן את פי הפך רבי יהודה אומר בלבד שיהו עושין מעין מלאכתן שברי עריבה לצוק לתוכן מקפה ושל זכוכית לצוק לתוכן שמן: **גמ'** אמר רב יהודה אמר שמואל מחלוקת שנשברו מערב שבת דמר סבר מעין מלאכתן אין מעין מלאכה אחרת לא ומר סבר אפילו מעין מלאכה אחרת אבל נשברו בשבת דברי הכל מותרין הואיל ומוכנין על גבי אביהן מותר מותיב רב זוטראי [ז] מסיקין בכלים ואין מסיקין בשברי כלים דנשברו אימת אילימא דנשברו מערב יום טוב עצים בעלמא נינהו אלא לאו ביום טוב וקתני מסיקין בכלים ואין מסיקים בשברי כלים אלא אי איתמר הכי איתמר אמר רב יהודה אמר שמואל מחלוקת שנשברו בשבת דמר סבר מוכן הוא ומר סבר נולד הוא אבל מערב שבת דברי הכל מותרין הואיל והוכנו למלאכה מבעוד יום תני חדא מסיקין בכלים ואין מסיקין בשברי כלים ותניא אידך [ח] כשם שמסיקין בכלים כך מסיקין בשברי כלים ותניא אידך אין מסיקין לא בכלים ולא בשברי כלים הא רבי יהודה הא רבי שמעון הא רבי נחמיה [ט] אמר רב נחמן [ה] הני ליבני דאישתיור מבניינא שרי לטלטולינהו דחזו למיזגא עלייהו שרגינהו ודאי אקצינהו אמר רב נחמן אמר שמואל [י] חרס קטנה מותר לטלטל בחצר אבל בכרמלית לא ורב נחמן דידיה אמר אפילו בכרמלית אבל ברה"ר לא ורבא אמר [ו] אפילו ברה"ר ואזדא רבא לטעמיה דרבא הוה קאזיל בריתקא דמחוזא אתווסאי מסאניה טינא אתא שמעיה שקל חספא וקא מכפר ליה רמו ביה רבנן קלא אמר לא מיסתייא דלא גמירי מיגמר נמי מגמרי אילו בחצר הואי מי לא הוה חזיא לכסויי ביה מנא הכא נמי חזיא לדידי אמר רב יהודה אמר שמואל מגופת חבית שנכתתה (א) מותר לטלטל בשבת תניא נמי הכי [י] מגופה שנכתתה היא ושבריה מותר לטלטלה בשבת ולא [כ] יספות ממנה שבר לכסות בה את הכלי ולסמוך בה כרעי המטה ואם זרקה באשפה אסור מתקיף לה רב פפא אלא מעתה זריק ליה לגלימיה ה"נ דאסור [ח] אלא אמר רב פפא
אם

הא רבי נחמיה. דסבירא ליה דאין כלי ניטל אלא לצורך תשמישו הרגיל בחול כדמפרש בפרק במה מדליקין (לעיל דף לו.) והאי נמי אין רגיל בחול לשרוף אותו: **ורבא** אמר אפילו ברה"ר. והני דנשברו בע"ש קאמר דאי בנשברו בשבת האמר בפרק נוטל (לקמן דף קמב:) דרבא אית ליה מוקצה וכל שכן נולד:
אס

רבינו חננאל

היא והלכתא כרבנן וכדמוקים לה רבה. דהכין סוגיא דשמעתא כולה. וזה שאמר רב שקולו שיתא מקמי כהנא. פי' שיתא שריתא והיא קורה כדמתרגמינן בצל קורתי בטלל שֵׁירוֹתִי. וי"א חבילה. וי"א רשת כדכתיב ויפרשו עליו גוים בשחתם נתפש. ושיתא היא שחתא. פי' מכבדת מטאטא שמכבדין הבית בהן. הנהו בי סדוותא. פי' כסתות והוא כגון כרים וכסתות: **מתני'** כל הכלים הניטלין בשבת שבריהן ניטלין [עמהן] ובלבד שיהו עושין מעין מלאכה וכו'. ר' יהודה אומר ובלבד שיהו עושין מעין מלאכתן כו'. פי' מקפה. מרק. בא רב יהודה משמיה דשמואל להעמיד מחלוקת ר' יהודה ות"ק כשנשברו מע"ש. ולא עמד אלא כשנשברו בשבת. דת"ק סבר מוכן הוא. ור' יהודה סבר מעין מלאכה אחרת כנולד הוא כדמפרש בגמרא דהכל שוחטין. אבל מע"ש דברי הכל מותרין. ואפילו לר' יהודה הואיל והוכנו למלאכה אחרת מבעו"י ואינו כנולד בשבת וקיי"ל כרבנן. וכלישנא בתרא דשמואל בין נשברו בשבת בין נשברו מע"ש. מעין מלאכה סגיא. תני חדא מסיקין בכלים ואין מסיקין בשברי כלים. פירוש בקעת שברי עצים שמסיקין בהן כדכתיב ויבקע עצי עולה. ותניא אידך כשם שמסיקין בכלים כך מסיקין בשברי כלים. ותניא אידך אין מסיקין לא בכלים ולא בשברי כלים לא קשיא הא ר' יהודה הא ר"ש הא ר' נחמיה. הא דתני אין מסיקין בשברי כלים ר' יהודה דמתניתין היא דחשיב בשברי כלים בנולד. והא דתני מסיקין בזה ובזה ר"ש היא דלית ליה מוקצה. ומיפרשא בגמ' דבמה מדליקין. והא דתני אין מסיקין לא בזה ולא בזה ר' נחמיה היא דאמר אין כלי ניטל אלא לצורך תשמישו. ומפורש במס' יו"ט פרק המביא כדי יין. והא דאמר רב נחמן אמר שמואל לענין ליבני דאישתייר מבניינא שרגינהו אקצינהו אפילו לר' שמעון דהני כגרוגרות וכצמוקים דמו. דאית ליה מוקצה. וזה שאמר חרס קטנה מותר לטלטלה בחצר. הואיל וראוי לכסות בו כלי שבחצר. אבל בכרמלית שאין בו כלי לא ורב נחמן סבר כיון שהמוציא מרשות הרבים לכרמלית או המכניס אינו חייב זימנין דעייל ליה לחצר וחזי ליה. ורבא סבר אפילו ברה"ר חזי לכפורי ביה טינא ושרי לטלטולי בטעמיה. וזה שאמר רב יהודה אמר שמואל מגופת חבית שנכתתה מותר לטלטלה. פי' מגופת כסוי שסותם פי החבית מלשון יגיפו הדלתות [ולא יספות]. פי' לא יחתוך הוא. כדתנן סופת באבטיח. ותניא נמי הכי כולן פשוטות הן.

מסורת הש"ס

א) ביצה יב. לז., ב) [ביצה לז. ע"ש ובפרש"י שם], ג) ס"א אמו טלטול לאו צורך הוצאה היא, ד) [גי' הרי"ף והרא"ש דכאביי], ה) [ע"ז כח:], ו) חולין יד:, ז) לעיל כח: כט. לקמן קמג. ביצה לב., ח) ביצה שם, ט) ביצה דף לא:, י) [תוספתא פרק ט"ו], כ) [ערוך בערך ספת פי' לא יחתוך. פי' אחר לא יחבר].

הגהות הב"ח

(א) גמ' אמר שמואל מגופת חבית שנכתתה היא ושבריה מותר וכו' מגופת חבית שנכתתה: (ב) רש"י ד"ה שותא מלודה. נ"ב וכן פי' בעל המאור על ההוא שותא דהוו מנחו עלה בי מרי דפ' הגוזל ומאכיל דף קיז אבל הכא פי' כמו שריתא דהיינו קורה כמו ההוא שריתא דבי ר' פדת דפ' המוצא תפילין דף קב ע"א: (ג) ד"ה של מילתא של בגדים הס"ד ואח"כ מ"ה מותר לכבד בהן השלחן: (ד) ד"ה שנתכתתה החבית (מגופה וכו' החבית) תא"מ ונ"ב ס"א אין זה: (ה) ד"ה לא יספות לא יתקן להסיר:

הגהות הגר"א

[א] גמ' לעולם מחמה לצל. נ"ב גי' הגאונים ורא"ש כר"ש סבירא ליה לדבר שאין מתכוין מותר:

רב נסים גאון

הא ר' יהודה והא ר' שמעון והא ר' נחמיה. דברי ר' יהודה ור"ש בפרק במה מדליקין (דף כט) אמר רב יהודה אמר רב מסיקין בכלים ואין מסיקין בשברי כלים דברי ר' יהודה ור' שמעון מתיר ודברי ר' נחמיה הן שנאמרו כן במשנה ר' נחמיה אומר אין ניטלין אלא לצורך וכמו שתירץ רבא ואמר ואתא ר' נחמיה למימר אפילו דבר שמלאכתו להיתר לצורך גופו ולצורך מקומו אין אבל מחמה לצל לא ובתוספתא (פט"ו) ר' נחמיה אומר אפילו טליתו ואפילו תרווד אין ניטלין אלא לצורך בברייתא שנאמר בה אין מסיקין לא בכלים ולא בשברי כלים הן דברי ר' נחמיה ובמס' יו"ט בפרק המביא כדי יין (דף לב) הזכירו עוד זה הדבר ואמרו תרי תנאי ואליבא דר' נחמיה כלומר קצת התנאים סוברין כי ר' (יהודה) [נחמיה] שאני ליה בין שבות שבת לשבות יום טוב:
דתנן

ליקוטי רש"י

אין מוציאין את הקטן וכו'. כל מילי דלאו לצורך אכילה [ביצה יב.]. דלא הותרה הוצאה שלא לצורך וגבי טלטול שלא לצורך נמי גזרינן ואפילו גבי הפסד ממון ולבית הלל דאמרי הוצאה שלא לצורך מותרת מן התורה בטלטול נמי לא גזור רבנן [שם לז.]. **ובית הלל מתירין.** לכולי עלמא יש הוצאה ליום טוב אלא שמן התורה הותרה לצורך ובית הלל אית להו כיון דהותרה לצורך הותרה מן התורה לגמרי אלא רבנן גזור במידי דהוי טרחא דלא צריך כגון אבנים אבל בקטן וספר תורה דצריכין להו ביום טוב לא גזור ובית שמאי לית להו מיגו ומידי דלצורך אכילה שהתורה התירתו הותר ושאינו לצורך אכילה באסורו עומד מן התורה [שם יב. עיי"ש ובתוס' שם]. **וטלטול גופיה לאו משום הוצאה היא.** תחילת הוצאה על ידי טלטול היא וכל מה שגזרו אינו אלא משום הוצאה והאי דלא גזרו על טלטול כלים ואוכלים מפני שלא יוכלו לעמוד בהן לבטל עונג שבת ושמחת יום טוב [שם לז.]. אי אין אסור הוצאה אין אסור טלטול שלא נאסר טלטול אלא משום הוצאה ומה שלא גזרו על כל טלטולים אפילו על אוכלים וכלים משום דאין גוזרין גזרה על הצבור אלא אם כן רוב צבור יכולין לעמוד בה [שם יב.]. **שותא.** מכמורת לדגים או לחיות [ב"ק קיז.]. **סדיותא.** סדיא. לבדין שקורין פלטר"ש ועשוין לקפלן תחתיו במקום הכר או הכסת [לקמן קמו:]. **שבריהן ניטלין.** אפילו נשתברו היום בשבת. **שיהו עושין מעין מלאכה.** שתהא תורת כלי עליהם. **מעין מלאכה.** כלומר אע"פ שאין ראויה למלאכה ממש אלא לכסוי בעלמא. **מעין מלאכתן.** הראשונה. **מקפה.** תבשיל עב דהיינו מעין עיסה [חולין יד:]. **מסיקין בכלים.** דבני טלטול נמי נינהו ומטלטלן נמי להסיקן. **ואין מסיקין בשברי כלים.** שנשברו ביום טוב דהשתא לא חזי לטלטול ואי משום דחזו להסקה אתמול לאו להכי קיימי [ביצה לב.]. שנשברו בו ביום דהוו להו נולד אבל בכלים מסיקין דהא חזו לטלטלן [לעיל כח:]. **כשם שמסיקין בכלים וכו'.** דלית להו מוקצה. **אין מסיקין לא בכלים.** דאין ניטלין אלא לצורך תשמישן וכל שכן בשברי כלים דנולד הוא והא רבי נחמיה היא ומציעתא רבי שמעון וקמייתא רבי יהודה [ביצה שם]. **דאישתיור מבניינא.** שנשתיירו לו לאחר שגמר בנינו. **שרי לטלטולינהו.** דמעתה לאו לבנין קיימי אלא למזגא עלייהו ותורת כלי עליהן [שם לא:]. **למיזגא.** להשען שכל הסבתן כך היתה יושב קצת ונשען קצת על שמאלו [לעיל מג.]. **שרגינהו.** סדרן זו על זו גלי דעתיה שמקצן לבנין ואסור לטלטלינהו [ביצה שם].

אֵין מוֹצִיאִין אֶת הַקָּטָן וְאֶת הַלּוּלָב וְאֶת סֵפֶר תּוֹרָה – **WE MAY NOT TAKE OUT A CHILD, A *LULAV* OR A TORAH SCROLL** לִרְשׁוּת הָרַבִּים – from a private domain **TO THE PUBLIC DOMAIN** on Yom Tov; וּבֵית הִלֵּל מַתִּירִין – **BUT BEIS HILLEL PERMIT** this. Similarly, Beis Hillel would permit one to lower produce through a skylight on Yom Tov whereas Beis Shammai would not.[1]

The Gemara attempts to reject this comparison as well: אֵימַר דִּשְׁמַעַתְּ לְהוּ לְבֵית שַׁמַּאי – **When can you say** that **you heard Beis Shammai** compare Yom Tov to the Sabbath? הוֹצָאָה – It is only in regard to **transferring** objects from a private to a public domain! טִלְטוּל מִי שְׁמַעַתְּ לְהוּ – In regard to merely **moving** something within a private domain, **did you hear them** make this comparison?[2]

The Gemara refutes this distinction: וְטִלְטוּל גּוּפֵיהּ לָאו מִשּׁוּם הוֹצָאָה הִיא – **Was moving itself not** prohibited **on account of** the concern that it might lead to **transferring?** Certainly it was! Therefore, since Beis Shammai compare Yom Tov to the Sabbath in regard to transferring, they must also compare it in regard to moving.[3]

Having rejected all the challenges, the Gemara cites a view concurring with that of Rava: וְאַף רַב סָבַר לָהּ לְהָא דְּרָבָא – **And Rav also concurs with that** opinion **of Rava,** who equates moving an object for the sake of its place with moving it for the sake of its use, דְּאָמַר רַב – **for Rav said:** מַר שֶׁלֹּא יִגָּנֵב – Moving **a hoe so that it not be stolen** – וְזֶהוּ טִלְטוּל שֶׁלֹּא לְצוֹרֶךְ וְאָסוּר – **this is** an example of **moving** something **"not out of necessity," and is forbidden.**[4] טַעְמָא שֶׁלֹּא יִגָּנֵב – This implies that **the reason** it is deemed "not out of necessity" **is** that one is moving it only **so that it not be stolen,** i.e. for its own protection, אֲבָל לְצוֹרֶךְ גּוּפוֹ וּלְצוֹרֶךְ מְקוֹמוֹ מוּתָּר – **but** moving it either **for the sake of its use or for the sake of its place** is permitted. Thus, Rav concurs with Rava.

The Gemara asks: אֵינִי – Is this **indeed** so? וְהָא רַב כַּהֲנָא אִיקְלַע לְבֵי רַב – **But Rav Kahana visited the house of Rav** on a Sabbath וְאָמַר – **and [Rav] said** to members of his household: אַיְיתוּ לֵיהּ שׁוּתָא לְכַהֲנָא לֵיתִיב עֲלֵיהּ – **"Bring the trap for Kahana to sit on."**[5] Why did Rav need to specify that the trap would be used as a seat? לָאו לְמֵימְרָא – Was it **not to say** by implication דְּדָבָר שֶׁמְּלַאכְתּוֹ לְאִיסּוּר לְצוֹרֶךְ גּוּפוֹ אֵין לְצוֹרֶךְ מְקוֹמוֹ לֹא – **that something** like a trap, **which is used** primarily **for prohibited work,** may be moved **only for the sake of its use,** such as sitting on it, but **not for the sake of its place?**

The Gemara answers: הָכִי אָמַר לְהוּ – In fact, the incident was not as you described it, but rather, **this is what [Rav] told them:** שְׁקוּלוּ שׁוּתָא מִקַּמֵּי כַּהֲנָא – **"Take away the trap from before Kahana."** Rav actually had them move the trap for the sake of making its place available for Rav Kahana to sit down. Thus, he holds that a forbidden-use utensil may be moved even for the sake of its place. וְאִי בָּעֵית אֵימָא – **Or, if you prefer, say** that the incident was as originally described, הָתָם מֵחַמָּה לְצֵל הֲוָה – but **there,** the trap **was** being moved **from the sun to the shade.**[6] Rav specified that he needed to use the trap as a seat to preclude the notion that he was sanctioning moving it for its own protection.

A related incident is cited: רַב מָרִי בַּר רָחֵל הֲוָה לֵיהּ הָהִיא בֵּי סַדְיָיתָא בְּשִׁמְשָׁא – **Rav Mari bar Rachel had some felt pillows** that were lying **in** the harmful rays **of the sun.** אֲתָא לְקַמֵּיהּ דְּרָבָא – **He came before Rava** אָמַר לֵיהּ מַהוּ לְטַלְטוּלִינְהוּ – and **said to him: What is** the law **with regard to moving them** indoors? אָמַר לֵיהּ שְׁרֵי – **[Rava] replied: It is permissible.**[7] אִית לִי אַחֲרִינָא – Rav Mari said: **I have others** available and do not need to use these. חֲזוּ לְאוֹרְחִין – Rava replied: **These are suitable for guests.**[8] אִית לִי נַמִּי לְאוֹרְחִים – Rav Mari retorted: **I also have** other pillows **for guests.** אָמַר לֵיהּ – **[Rava] said to him:** גַּלֵּית אַדַּעְתָּךְ דִּכְרַבָּה סְבִירָא לָךְ – **You have indicated that you concur with Rabbah,** who forbids moving a permitted-use utensil from the sun to the

NOTES

1. Beis Shammai hold that transferring from a private domain to a public domain is prohibited on Yom Tov for purposes not related to food preparation. [This prohibition applies even when one does so in order to fulfill a *mitzvah,* such as carrying out a *lulav* on Succos (*Tosafos* to *Beitzah* 12a ד״ה הג״ רש״י).] Beis Hillel, however, permit transferring on Yom Tov even for purposes unrelated to food preparation. The Gemara in Tractate *Beitzah* (12a) explains the basis for this dispute.

Beis Shammai would similarly forbid the moving of produce that is not being used for Yom Tov consumption, even if a financial loss was involved. It is they who authored the Mishnah which equates Yom Tov with the Sabbath in all respects other than food preparation. Beis Hillel, however, authored the Mishnah allowing one to lower produce through a skylight to avoid a financial loss (*Rashi*). The Gemara will clarify the analogy between the two cases.

2. [As explained in Tractate *Beitzah* (ibid.), the dispute between Beis Shammai and Beis Hillel is rooted in Biblical law. How can you draw an analogy from their dispute to our case, which involves a Rabbinical decree against moving things?]

3. [When Nechemiah ben Chachaliah decried the flagrant Sabbath desecration of his times, he mentioned specifically the widespread practice of transferring objects between domains (see *Nehemiah* 13:15). It follows that] Nechemiah's decree against handling utensils was enacted to prevent people from transferring those objects to the public domain (*Ritva MHK* ed.; *Raavad, Hil. Shabbos* 24:13; see *Mishbetzos Zahav,* beginning of §308). Therefore, it stands to reason that prohibitions which apply to acts of moving be governed by the stringencies that apply to transferring.

Rashi's version of the text [see also *Mesoras HaShas*] differs slightly from ours and reads: טִלְטוּל לַאו צוֹרֶךְ הוֹצָאָה, *Is moving* [an object within a private domain] *not necessary for transferring* [it to the public domain]? I.e. since every act of transferring to a public domain *begins* with an act of moving the object within the private domain, the stringencies that apply to transferring must be extended to moving as well (*Rashi*; see also *Rashi* to *Beitzah* 37a ד״ה אטו).

According to the Gemara's conclusion, the initial Mishnah cited above – which teaches that we may not support a pot with wood on Yom Tov, and which Rava explained as being based on equating the laws of Yom Tov to those of the Sabbath – follows Beis Shammai. Thus, it is halachically invalid. It is noteworthy, however, that the Gemara in Tractate *Beitzah* (33a) has an entirely different explanation for the Mishnah, according to which it is halachically valid. See *Ritva MHK* ed. here and *Rashba* to *Beitzah* 33a; cf. *Tos. HaRosh.* For further discussion of this topic, see *Baal HaMaor* and *Milchamos Hashem* to *Beitzah* 33a, and *Orach Chaim* 502:3.

4. Moving something to a secure location where it will be protected from theft is tantamount to moving it from the sun to the shade. This is prohibited in the case of a hoe, which is a forbidden-use utensil (*Rashi*).

5. [There was no chair available and Rav therefore requested that they bring a trap – which was a forbidden-use utensil, for trapping animals on the Sabbath is prohibited – to use as an improvised seat.]

6. I.e. it had been in an unprotected area and, upon Rav's request, would now be moved to a preferable location. Now, Rav did not intend for Rav Kahana to sit in the place where the trap had been. Thus, to an observer it might appear that Rav was allowing its movement for the sake of protecting it from possible damage. Therefore, he specified that it should be brought to another location for Rav Kahana to sit upon it there (*Rashi*).

7. Rava ruled in accordance with his own opinion that a permitted-use utensil may be moved from the sun to the shade (*Rashi*).

8. According to Rava, it was permitted to move them even if they were not needed at all. However, he told Rav Mari that even Rabbah would allow moving them in order that they be prepared for the use of guests (*Rashba, Ritva MHK* ed.; see *Taz* 308:2, cited by *Mishnah Berurah* 308:21; see also *Chidushei R' Elazar Moshe Horowitz*).

עין משפט נר מצוה

כו א מיי' פ"א מהלכות יו"ט הלכה ד סמג לאוין עה טוש"ע או"ח סימן תקיח סעיף א:
כז ב מיי' פכ"ה מהלכ' שבת הלכה ג סמג לאוין סה טוש"ע או"ח סימן שח סעיף ג:
כח ג מיי' פכ"ה שם הלכה ה סמג שם טוש"ע שם סעיף מט:
כט ד מיי' פכ"ה מהל' שבת הלכה יב סמג שם טוש"ע או"ח סימן שח סעיף ו:
ל ה מיי' פכ"ו שם הלכה ג טוש"ע או"ח סימן שח סעיף יז:
לא ו ז ח מיי' שם הל' ג טוש"ע שם סעיף ז:

גמרא

אין מוציאין את הקטן ואת הלולב ואת ספר תורה לרה"ר ובית הלל מתירין אימר דשמעת להו לבית שמאי הוצאה טלטול מי שמעת להו וטלטול גופיה לאו משום הוצאה היא ואף רב סבר לה להא דרבא דאמר רב מר שלא יגנב זהו טלטול שלא לצורך ואסור טעמא שלא יגנב אבל לצורך גופו ולצורך מקומו מותר איני והא רב כהנא איקלע לבי רב ואמר אייתו ליה שותא לכהנא ליתיב עליה לאו למימרא דדבר שמלאכתו לאיסור לצורך גופו אין לצורך מקומו לא הכי אמר להו שקולו שותא מקמי כהנא ואי בעית אימא התם מחמה לצל הוה רב מרי בר רחל הוה ליה ההיא בי סדיותא בשמשא אתא לקמיה דרבא אמר ליה מהו לטלטולינהו אמר ליה שרי אית לי אחרינא חזו לאורחין אית לי נמי לאורחים אמר ליה גלית אדעתיך דכרבה סבירא לך לכולי עלמא שרי לדידך אסיר אמר רבי אבא אמר רבי חייא בר אשי אמר רב מכבדות של מילתא מותר לטלטלן בשבת אבל של תמרה לא רבי אלעזר אומר אף של תמרה במאי עסקינן אילימא לצורך גופו ולצורך מקומו בהא לימא רב של תמרה לא והא רב כרבא סבירא ליה אלא מחמה לצל בהא לימא ר' אלעזר אף של תמרה [א] לעולם מחמה לצל אימא וכן אמר רבי אלעזר: **מתני'** כל הכלים הניטלין בשבת שבריהן ניטלין עמהן ובלבד שיהו עושין מעין מלאכה שברי עריבה לכסות בהן את פי החבית שברי זכוכית לכסות בהן את פי הפך רבי יהודה אומר ובלבד שיהו עושין מעין מלאכתן שברי עריבה לצוק לתוכן מקפה ושל זכוכית לצוק לתוכן שמן: **גמ'** אמר רב יהודה אמר שמואל מחלוקת שנשברו מערב שבת דמר סבר מעין מלאכה ומר סבר מעין מלאכתן מעין מלאכה אחרת לא ומר סבר אפילו מעין מלאכה אחרת אבל נשברו בשבת דברי הכל מותרין הואיל ומוכנין על גבי אביהן מותר מותיב רב זוטרא מסיקין בכלים ואין מסיקין בשברי כלים דנשברו אימת אילימא דנשברו מערב יום טוב עצים בעלמא נינהו אלא לאו ביום טוב וקתני מסיקין בכלים ואין מסיקין בשברי כלים אלא אי איתמר הכי איתמר אמר רב יהודה אמר שמואל מחלוקת שנשברו בשבת דמר סבר מוכן הוא ומר סבר נולד הוא אבל מערב שבת דברי הכל מותרין הואיל והוכנו למלאכה מבעוד יום תני חדא מסיקין בכלים ואין מסיקין בשברי כלים ותניא אידך כשם שמסיקין בכלים כך מסיקין בשברי כלים ותניא אידך אין מסיקין לא בכלים ולא בשברי כלים הא רבי יהודה הא רבי שמעון הא רבי נחמיה אמר רב נחמן הני ליבני דאישתיור מבניינא שרי לטלטולינהו דחזו למיזגא עלייהו שרגינהו ודאי אקצינהו אמר רב נחמן אמר שמואל חרס קטנה מותר לטלטל בחצר אבל בכרמלית לא ורב נחמן דידיה אמר אפילו בכרמלית אבל ברה"ר לא ורבא אמר אפילו ברה"ר ואזדא רבא לטעמיה דרבא הוה קאזיל בריתקא דמחוזא אתווסאי מסאניה טינא אתא שמעיה שקל חספא וקא מכפר ליה רמו ביה רבנן קלא אמר לא מיסתייא דלא גמירי מיגמר נמי מגמרי אילו בחצר הואי מי לא הוה חזיא לכסויי ביה מנא הכא נמי חזיא לדידי אמר רב יהודה אמר שמואל (א) מגופת חבית שנכתתה מותר לטלטלה בשבת תניא נמי הכי מגופה שנכתתה היא ושבריה מותר לטלטלה בשבת ולא יספות ממנה שבר לכסות בה את הכלי ולסמוך בה כרעי המטה ואם זרקה באשפה אסור מתקיף לה רב פפא אלא מעתה זריק ליה לגלימיה ה"נ דאסור אלא אמר רב פפא אם

רש"י

אין מוציאין. הוצאה שלא לצורך דלא אישתרי לכתחילה ביו"ט טפי מבשבת אלא אוכל נפש והנך דמשלין ב"ה: טלטול מי שמעת להו. דמשוי יו"ט לשבת: טלטול לאו צורך הוצאה. בתמיה הלכך אי מזלזלת בטלטול מזלזלת בהוצאה: להא דרבא. דאמר לורך מקומו כלורך גופו: מר. פושו"ר: שלא יגנב. דומיא דמחמה לצל ואסור בדבר שמלאכתו לאיסור: שותא. (ג) מלודה: לאו למימרא כו'. למה לי לפרושי בהדיא ליתיב עלה לאו משום למימרא דהאי דשרי לטלטולי משום דלצורך גופו הוא: שקילו שותא מקמיה כהנא. דניתוב על מקומה קאמר ולורך מקומה הוא דהוה: מחמה לצל הוה. במקום הרע לה היתה ואי לאו דפריש בהדיא ליתיב עלה מאן דחזי סבר דמחמה לצל שרי ולמקומה לא היה צריך דלימא שישב במקומה: בי סדיותא. כרים של בגד שקורין פילטר"א: בי שמשי. בחמה: אמר ליה שרי. רבא לטעמיה דאמר דבר שמלאכתו להיתר אף מחמה לצל מותר: אית לי אחריני. איני צריך לגופו: דכרבה סבירא לך. דאמר מחמה לצל אסור והלכה כרבא דאמר דבר שמלאכתו להיתר שרי לגמרי ודבר שמלאכתו לאיסור לצורך גופו ומקומו מותר מחמה לצל ושלא יגנב אסור: מכבדות. איסקוב"א שמכבדים בהן את השולחן: של מילתא. (ג) בגדים לכבד שולחן שמלאכתו להיתר: של תמרה. כעין שלנו לכבד את הבית דאסור משום אשויי גומות דמודה רבי שמעון בפסיק רישיה ולא ימות: לצורך גופו. למלאכת היתר: אלא מחמה לצל בהא לימא רבי אלעזר אף של תמרה. דבר שמלאכתו לאיסור ליכא מאן דשרי מחמה לצל: וכן אמר רבי אלעזר. של מילתא מותר של תמרה אסור מחמה לצל: מתני' מעין מלאכה. שום מלאכה ואפי' אינה מעין הראשונה: לצוק לתוכה מקפה. עבה דומיא דעיסה מעורבת במים: גמ' הואיל ומוכנין על גבי אביהן. כשקדש היום: מסיקין בכלים. ביו"ט שהרי ראוין לטלטל ויטלטל ויתנם לתוך האור: ואין מסיקין בשברי כלים. דהוו להו מוקצין ולא חזו לטלטול: עצים בעלמא נינהו. דהא מאתמול להסקה קיימי: וקתני אין מסיקין. ולא אמרינן מוכנין היו אגב אביהן אלא אמרינן נולד נינהו ואסירי: מר סבר מוכן הוא. כיון דראוי לשום מלאכה ומר סבר נולד הוה דמאתמול לאו להאי מלאכה הוה קאי הלכך מעין מלאכתו בעינן: הא רבי יהודה. מסיקין בכלים ואין מסיקין בשברי כלים דאית ליה מוקצה ונולד כלים לאו מוקצה נינהו שברים נולד נינהו: והא. דתני מסיקין בשניהם: רבי שמעון. דלית ליה מוקצה ולית ליה נולד: והא. דתניא אף בכלים אין מסיקין: רבי נחמיה היא. דאמר אין כלי ניטל אלא לצורך תשמישו המיוחד לו והאי לאו מיוחד הוא לו דלאו להסקה קאי: דאייתור. שהשלים בניינו ונשתייר ומהשתא לא קיימי לבנין אלא לישב עליהם ותורת כלי עליהם: שרגינהו. אי סדרן זו על זו ודאי אקצינהו לצורך בנין אחר: בחצר. דשכיחי בה כלים שהחרס הזה ראוי להם לכיסוי ותורת כלי עליו: אבל לא בכרמלית. אפי' בתוך ד' אמות דלא שכיחי ביה מאני ולא חזי לכסויי: אפילו בכרמלית. הואיל ולאו רה"ר הוא שכיחי דאזלי ויתבי התם וחזי לכסות בו רוק: ורבא אמר אף ברה"ר. כיון דבחצר כלי הוא בעלמא נמי לא פקע שם כלי מיניה: בריתקא. שם רה"ר: איתווסאי מסאניה טינא. נתלכלך מנעלו בטיט: כפר ליה. מקנחו: אמר רבא לא מסתייה דלא גמירי. מה אסור מה מותר: אלא מיגמר נמי מגמרי. מלמדין שיבוש שבידם לאחרים: לדידי. לקינוח ולע"ג דלא שכיח הרי שם כלי עליו בחצר: שנתכתתה. החבית: (ד) מגופה. של חבית שנתכתתה החבית: היא. המגופה: ושבריה. של חבית ניטלין בשבת דחזו לכיסוי מנא: לא יספות. (ה) יתקן להתיר בליטותיו ועוקציו בשבת דעביד כלי והוי מכה בפטיש: ואם זרק. מגופה זו לאשפה בטלה מתורת כלי: זרקיה לגלימיה. בשבת לאשפה ה"נ דאסור לטלטולי:

מבעוד

תוספות

הא רבי נחמיה. דסבירא ליה דאין כלי ניטל אלא לצורך תשמישו הרגיל בתוך כדמפרש בפרק במה מדליקין (לעיל דף לו.) והאי נמי אין רגיל בתוך לשרוף אותו: **ורבא** אמר אפילו ברה"ר. והני דנשברו בע"ש קאמר דאי בנשברו בשבת האמר בפרק נוטל (לקמן דף קמב:) דרבא אית ליה מוקצה וכל שכן נולד: אם

רבינו חננאל

היא והלכתא כרבנן וכדמוקים לה רבה. דהכין סוגיא דשמעתא כולה. וזה שאמר רב שקולו שיתא מקמי כהנא. פי' שיתא שריתא והיא קורה כדמתרגמינן בצל קורתי בטלל שירותי. וי"א חבילה. וי"א רשת כדכתיב ופרשו עליו גוים בשחתם נתפש. ושיתא היא שחתא. פי' מכבדת מטאטא שמכבדין הבית בהן. הנהו בי סדיותא. פי' כסתות שהוא כגון כרים וכסתות: מתני' כל הכלים הניטלין בשבת שבריהן ניטלין [עמהן] ובלבד שיהו עושין מעין מלאכה וכו'. ר' יהודה אומר ובלבד שיהו עושין מעין מלאכתן כו'. פי' מקפה. מרק. בא רב יהודה משמיה דשמואל להעמיד מחלוקת ר' יהודה ות"ק כשנשברו מע"ש. ולא עמד אלא כשנשברו בשבת. דת"ק סבר מוכן הוא. ור' יהודה סבר מעין מלאכה אחרת כנולד הוא כדמפרש בגמרא דהכל שוחטין. אבל מע"ש דברי הכל מותרין. ואפילו לר' יהודה הואיל והוכנו למלאכה אחרת מבעו"י ואינו כנולד בשבת וקיי"ל כרבנן. וכלישנא בתרא דשמואל בין נשברו בשבת בין נשברו מע"ש. מעין מלאכה סגיא. תני חדא מסיקין בכלים ואין מסיקין בשברי כלים. פירוש בקעת שברי עצים שמסיקין בהן כדכתיב ויבקע עצי עולה. ותניא אידך כשם שמסיקין בכלים כך מסיקין בשברי כלים. ותניא אידך אין מסיקין לא בכלים ולא בשברי כלים לא קשיא הא ר' יהודה הא ר"ש הא ר' נחמיה. הא דתני אין מסיקין בשברי כלים ר' יהודה דמתניתין היא דחשיב בשברי כלים בנולד. והא דתני מסיקין בזה ובזה ר"ש היא דלית ליה מוקצה. ומיפרשא בגמ' דבמה מדליקין. והא דתני אין מסיקין לא בזה ולא בזה ר' נחמיה היא דאמר אין כלי ניטל אלא לצורך תשמישו. ומפורש במס' יו"ט פרק המביא כדי יין. והא דאמר רב נחמן אמר שמואל לענין ליבני דאישתייר מבניינא שרגינהו אקצינהו אפילו לר' שמעון דהני כגרוגרות וכצמוקים דמו. דאית ליה מוקצה. וזה שאמר חרס קטנה מותר לטלטלה בחצר. הואיל וראוי לכסות בו כלי שבחצר. אבל בכרמלית שאין בו כלי לא ורב נחמן סבר כיון שהמוציא מרשות הרבים לכרמלית או המכניס אינו חייב זימנין דעייל ליה לחצר וחזי ליה. ורבא סבר אפילו ברה"ר חזי לכפורי ביה טינא ושרי לטלטולי בטעמיה. וזה שאמר רב יהודה אמר שמואל מגופת חבית שנכתתה מותר לטלטלה. פי' מגופת כסוי שסותם פי החבית מלשון יגיפו הדלתות [ולא יספות]. פי' לא יתחוך הוא. כדתנן סופת באבטיח. ותניא נמי הכי כולן פשוטות הן.

מסורת הש"ס

א) ביצה יב. לז. ב) [ביצה לז. ע"ש ובפרש"י שם], ג) ס"א אמו טלטול לאו צורך הוצאה היא, ד) [ע' הרי"ף והרא"ש דכאביי], ה) [ע"ז מג:] ו) חולין יד:, ז) לעיל כט: לקמן קמו., ח) ביצה לב., ט) ביצה שם, י) ביצה דף לא:, כ) [תוספתא פרק ט"ו], ל) [ערוך בערך ספת פי' לא יתחוך. פי' אחר לא יחבר].

הגהות הב"ח

(א) גמ' אמר שמואל מגופת חבית שנכתתה היא ושבריה מותר וכו' מגופת חבית שנכתתה: (ב) רש"י ד"ה שותא מלודה. נ"ב ע' לעיל דף קכג ... (ג) ד"ה של מילתא בגדים לכבד השולחן: (ד) ד"ה שנתכתתה החבית (מגופה וכו' החבית) תא"מ ונ"ב ס"א אין זה: (ה) ד"ה לא יספות לא יתקן הסיר:

הגהות הגר"א

[א] גמ' לעולם מחמה לצל. נ"ב ג' הגאונים ורא"ש סבירא ליה לדבר שאין מתכוין מותר:

רב נסים גאון

הא ר' יהודה והא ר' שמעון והא ר' נחמיה. דברי ר' יהודה ור"ש בפרק במה מדליקין (דף כט) אמר רב יהודה אמר רב מסיקין בכלים ואין מסיקין בשברי כלים דברי ר' יהודה ור' שמעון מתיר ודברי ר' נחמיה כן במשנה שנאמר אין ניטלין אלא לצורך וכמו שתירץ רבא ואמר ואתא ר' נחמיה למימר אפילו דבר שמלאכתו להיתר לצורך גופו ולצורך מקומו אין אבל מחמה לצל לא ובתוספתא (פט"ו) ר' נחמיה אומר אפילו טלית ואפילו תרווד אין ניטלין אלא לצורך ובברייתא שנאמר בה אין מסיקין לא בכלים ולא בשברי כלים הן דברי ר' נחמיה ובמס' יו"ט בפרק המביא כדי יין (דף לו) הזכירו עוד זה הדבר ואמרו תרי תנאי ואליבא דר' נחמיה כלומר קצת התנאים סוברין כי ר' (יהודה) [נחמיה] שאני ליה בין שבות שבת לשבות יום טוב: דתנן

ליקוטי רש"י

אין מוציאין את הקטן וכו'. כל מילי דלאו לצורך אכילה [ביצה יב.]. דלא הותרה הוצאה שלא לצורך וגבי טלטול שלא לצורך נמי גזרינן ואפילו גבי הפסד ממון ולבית הלל דאמרי הוצאה שלא לצורך הותרה ... התורה בטלטול נמי לא גזור רבנן [שם לז.]. ובית הלל מתירין. לכולי עלמא יש הוצאה ליום טוב הותרה לצורך ובית הלל אית להו כיון דהותרה לצורך הותרה מן התורה לגמרי אלא רבנן גזור ב... לריך כגון אבנים אבל בקטן וספר תורה דלריכינן להו ביום טוב לא גזור ובית שמאי לית להו מיגו ו... שהתורה התירתו הותר ושאינו לורך אכילה באסורו עומד מן התורה [שם יב. עיי"ש ובתוס' שם]. וטלטול גופיה לאו משום הוצאה היא. תחילת הוצאה על ידי טלטול היא וכל מה שגזרו אינו אלא משום הוצאה והאי דלא גזרו על טלטול כלים ואוכלים מפני שלא יוכלו לעמוד בהן לבטל עונג שבת ושמחת יום טוב [שם לז.]. אי אין אסור הוצאה ... שלא נאסר טלטול אלא משום הוצאה ומה שלא גזרו על כל טלטולים אפילו על אוכלים וכלים משום דאין גוזרין גזרה על הצבור אלא אם כן רוב צבור יכולין לעמוד בה [שם יב.]. שותא. מכמורת לדגים או לחיות [ב"ק קיז.]. סדיותא. ... שקורין פלטר"ש ועשויין לקפלן תחתיו במקום הכר או הכסת [לקמן קמו:]. שבריהן ניטלין. אפילו נשתברו היום בשבת. שיהו עושין מעין מלאכה. שתהא תורת כלי עליהם. מעין מלאכה. כלומר אע"פ שאין ראויה ... לכסוי בעלמא. מעין מלאכתן. הראשונה. מקפה. תבשיל עב דהיינו מעין עיסה [חולין יד:]. מסיקין בכלים. דכי טלטול נמי ניהו ומטלטלן נמי להסיקן. ואין מסיקין בשברי כלים. שנשברו ביום טוב דהשתא לא חזו ... להסקה אתמול לאו להכי קיימי [ביצה לב.]. שנשברו בו ביום דהוו להו נולד אבל בכלים מסיקין דהא חזו לטלטלן [לעיל כח:]. כשם שמסיקין בכלים וכו'. דלית להו מוקצה. אין מסיקין לא בכלים. דאין ניטלין אלא ... בן בשברי כלים דנולד הוא והא רבי נחמיה היא ומליעתא רבי שמעון וקמייתא רבי יהודה [ביצה שם]. דאישתיור מבניינא. שנשתיירו לו לאחר שגמר בנינו. שרי לטלטולינהו. דמעתה לאו לבנין קיימי אלא למזגא עלייהו [שם לא:]. למיזגא. להסב שכל הסבתן כך היתה יושב קצת ונשען קצת על שמאלו [לעיל מג.]. שרגינהו. סדרן זו על זו גלי דעתיה שמקצן לבנין ואסור לטלטלינהו [ביצה שם].

shade. Therefore, לְכוּלֵּי עָלְמָא שָׁרֵי לְדִידָךְ אָסִיר – **it is permitted for everybody else** to bring their pillows in from the sun, but **it is forbidden for you.**[9]

The Gemara cites a related discussion:

אָמַר רַבִּי אַבָּא אָמַר רַבִּי חִיָּיא בַּר אַשִׁי אָמַר רַב – **R' Abba said in the name of R' Chiya bar Ashi, who said in the name of Rav:** מְכַבְּדוֹת שֶׁל מֵילְתָא מוּתָּר לְטַלְטְלָן בְּשַׁבָּת – **Brooms of cloth may be moved on the Sabbath,** אֲבָל שֶׁל תְּמָרָה לֹא – **but** brooms **of palm** leaves may **not** be moved.[10] רַבִּי אֶלְעָזָר אוֹמֵר – **R' Elazar says:** אַף שֶׁל תְּמָרָה – **Even** brooms **of palm** leaves may be moved.

The Gemara analyzes this dispute:

בְּמַאי עָסְקִינַן – **With what** type of moving **are we dealing?** אִילֵימָא לְצוֹרֶךְ גּוּפוֹ וּלְצוֹרֶךְ מְקוֹמוֹ – **If you will say** it is with moving the broom **for the sake of its use** in a permitted capacity **or for the sake of its place,** בְּהָא לֵימָא רַב שֶׁל תְּמָרָה לֹא – **would Rav say in regard to this case** that when it is made **of palm** leaves it may **not** be moved? וְהָא רַב כְּרַבָּא סְבִירָא לֵיהּ – **But Rav concurs with Rava** and permits moving a forbidden-use utensil for the sake of its use or place! אֶלָּא מֵחַמָּה לְצֵל – **Rather,** you might say that we are dealing with moving the broom **from the sun to the shade** for its protection. בְּהָא לֵימָא רַבִּי אֶלְעָזָר אַף שֶׁל תְּמָרָה – **Would R' Elazar say in regard to this case** that **even** a broom **of palm** leaves may be moved? Why, nobody permits moving a forbidden-use utensil from the sun to the shade. – ? –

The Gemara answers by emending R' Elazar's opinion:

לְעוֹלָם מֵחַמָּה לְצֵל – **Actually,** we are dealing with moving the broom **from the sun to the shade,** אֵימָא וְכֵן אָמַר רַבִּי אֶלְעָזָר – **and say: R' Elazar said likewise** that brooms of cloth may be moved from the sun to the shade, but brooms of palm leaves may not.[11]

Mishnah The Mishnah turns to the issue of which broken utensils are non-*muktzeh*:

כָּל הַכֵּלִים הַנִּיטָּלִין בְּשַׁבָּת – **All utensils that may be taken on the Sabbath** – שִׁבְרֵיהֶן נִיטָּלִין עִמָּהֶן – **fragments of them may** also **be taken with them,**[12] וּבִלְבַד שֶׁיְּהוּ עוֹשִׂין מֵעֵין מְלָאכָה – **provided they can** still be used to **perform some sort of task.**[13] שִׁבְרֵי עֲרֵיבָה לְכַסּוֹת בָּהֶן אֶת פִּי הֶחָבִית – For example, **fragments of a mixing bowl** may be taken if they are fit **to be used to cover the mouth of a cask,** שִׁבְרֵי זְכוּכִית לְכַסּוֹת בָּהֶן אֶת פִּי הַפַּךְ – and **fragments of a glass,** if they are fit **to be used to cover the mouth of a flask.**[14] רַבִּי יְהוּדָה אוֹמֵר – **R' Yehudah says:** בִּלְבַד שֶׁיְּהוּ עוֹשִׂין מֵעֵין מְלַאכְתָּן – Fragments may be taken **provided** that **they can** still be used to **perform a semblance of their** former **task.** שִׁבְרֵי עֲרֵיבָה לָצוּק לְתוֹכָן מִקְפָּה – For example, **fragments of a mixing bowl** may be taken if they are fit **to pour porridge into them,** וְשֶׁל זְכוּכִית לָצוּק לְתוֹכָן שֶׁמֶן – **and** fragments **of a glass,** if they are fit **to pour oil into them.**[15]

Gemara The Gemara discusses the dispute cited in the Mishnah:

אָמַר רַב יְהוּדָה אָמַר שְׁמוּאֵל – **Rav Yehudah said in the name of Shmuel:** מַחְלוֹקֶת שֶׁנִּשְׁבְּרוּ מֵעֶרֶב שַׁבָּת – **The dispute** pertains to a case **where [the utensils] broke before the Sabbath,** and its basis is דְּמַר סָבַר – **that** one **master** (R' Yehudah) **holds** that the fragments retain their previous classification as a utensil מֵעֵין מְלַאכְתָּן אֵין מֵעֵין מְלָאכָה אַחֶרֶת לֹא – **only** if they can still be used to perform **a semblance of their** former **task,** but **not** if they can merely be used to perform **a different sort of task,**[16] וּמַר סָבַר – **whereas** the other **master** (the Tanna Kamma) **holds** that they retain their classification as a utensil אֲפִילּוּ מֵעֵין מְלָאכָה אַחֶרֶת – **even** if they can merely be used to perform **a different sort of task.** אֲבָל נִשְׁבְּרוּ בְּשַׁבָּת – **But if they broke on the**

NOTES

9. Rava was not penalizing Rav Mari, but merely informing him that since he concurred with Rabbah he was required to abide by that opinion (*Ritva MHK* ed.; see *Chasam Sofer* for illumination of Rava's discussion with Rav Mari).

The actual halachah follows Rava. Thus, a permitted-use utensil may be moved for any purpose [but not for no purpose at all; see 123b note 19], and a forbidden-use utensil may be moved for the sake of either its use or its place but not to protect it from loss (*Rashi*; see *Orach Chaim* 308:3-4).

10. "Brooms of cloth" are brushes with cloth bristles that are used to clear crumbs off a table (cf. *Rif*). These are permitted-use utensils. "Brooms of palm leaves" are ordinary brooms that are used to sweep floors. In Talmudic times, when most homes had dirt floors, these were classified as forbidden-use utensils. The reason is that it is forbidden to sweep a dirt floor on the Sabbath because one thereby smoothes out the indentations in the floor by filling them with dirt, thus violating the *melachah* of building (see above, 73b, with *Rashi* ד״ה בבית). Although one generally does not have this intent while sweeping, the unintended result is inevitable, and the rule is that one may not do an unintended act when the violation is inevitable [פְּסִיק רֵישֵׁיהּ] (*Rashi;* see General Introduction and above, 120b).

[Nowadays, since most houses have covered floors, it is permissible to sweep a floor on the Sabbath and a broom is therefore considered a permitted-use utensil (see *Orach Chaim* 308:49 with *Mishnah Berurah* §163 and *Beur Halachah* to 337:2 ד״ה ויש מחמירין).]

11. I.e. R' Elazar does not argue with Rav, but concurs with him (see *Rashi*). [See *Ritva MHK* ed., who cites another interpretation of this passage. See also *Rif, Baal HaMaor* and *Milchamos Hashem*.]

12. I.e. if any of these utensils broke, their fragments may be used on the Sabbath. The Gemara will discuss whether the utensils in question broke before the Sabbath or on the Sabbath. [In some versions, the word עִמָּהֶן, *with them,* is omitted. *Meleches Shlomo* approves of the omission. Cf. *Sfas Emes.*]

13. I.e. any sort of task, even one that is unrelated to the original function of the utensil (*Rashi*). Since these fragments are still functional, they do not lose their previous designation as utensils. Consequently, they are not *muktzeh* (*Ritva MHK* ed.). [Fragments of utensils that are no longer useful fit into the category of מוּקְצֶה מֵחֲמַת גּוּפוֹ, *inherently muktzeh,* like sticks and stones, and may not be moved for any purpose (*Mishnah Berurah* 308:28).]

14. [In Mishnaic times, it was common to use pieces of broken utensils as covers for casks and jugs. A shard fit for such use was therefore considered functional.] Fragments of a wooden mixing bowl must be large enough to cover a cask in order to retain their non-*muktzeh* classification, because smaller pieces are generally used as firewood (*Chidushei HaRan*).

Note that a stone does not qualify as a utensil on the basis of being suitable for use as the cover of a vessel, unless it is actually designated for that function. Only a shard, which was previously a utensil, qualifies on this basis (see *Ramban,* et al.).

15. A thick porridge is similar to dough (*Rashi*) which is normally kneaded in the mixing bowl. Thus, a fragment of a bowl that can be used to hold porridge is still fit for a semblance of its former task. Similarly, a fragment of a glass that can be used to hold oil is fit for a semblance of its former task (*Minchas Bikkurim* to *Tosefta* 15:9). The Gemara will explain this dispute.

16. R' Yehudah holds that, since the shard is unqualified for the task that gave the original implement its status as a utensil, it loses that classification. Its fitness for a new task is inconsequential unless [before the Sabbath] someone began using it or designated it for that task (*Ritva MHK* ed.).

עין משפט נר מצוה

כו א מיי' פ"א מהלכות יו"ט הלכה ד סמג לאוין עה טוש"ע או"ח סימן תקיח סעיף א:

כז ב מיי' פכ"ה מהלכות שבת הלכה ג סמג לאוין שם טוש"ע או"ח סימן שח סעיף ג:

כח ג מיי' פכ"ו שם הלכה ב סמג שם טוש"ע שם סעיף מט:

כט ד מיי' פכ"ה מהל' שבת הלכה יב סמג שם טוש"ע או"ח סימן שח סעיף ו:

ל ה מיי' פכ"ו שם הלכה ב טוש"ע או"ח סימן שח סעיף יז:

לא ו ז ח מיי' שם הל' ג טוש"ע שם סעיף ז:

רבינו חננאל

היא והלכתא כרבנן וכדמוקים לה רבה. דהכין סוגיא דשמעתא כולה. וזה שאמר רב שקולו שיתא מקמי כהנא. פי' שיתא שריתא והיא קורה כדמתרגמינן בצל קורתי בטל שירותי. וי"א חבילה. וי"א רשת כדכתיב ויפרשו עליו גוים בשחתם נתפש. ושיתא היא שחתא. פי' מכבדת מטאטא שמכבדין הבית בהן. הנהו בי סדוותא. כסתות והוא כגון כרים וכסתות: **מתני'** כל הכלים הניטלין בשבת שבריהן ניטלין [עמהן] ובלבד שיהו עושין מעין מלאכה וכו'. ר' יהודה אומר ובלבד שיהו עושין מעין מלאכתן כו'. פי' מקפה. מרק. בא רב יהודה משמיה דשמואל להעמיד מחלוקת ר' יהודה ות"ק כשנשברו מע"ש. ולא אמרו אלא כשנשברו בשבת. דת"ק סבר מוכן הוא. ור' יהודה סבר מעין מלאכה אחרת כנולד הוא כדמפרש בגמרא דהכל שוחטין. אבל מע"ש דברי הכל מותרין. ואפילו לר' יהודה הואיל והוכנו למלאכה אחרת מבעוד יום. אינו כנולד בשבת וקיי"ל כרבנן. וכלישנא בתרא דשמואל בין נשברו בשבת בין נשברו מע"ש. מעין מלאכה סגיא. תני חדא מסיקין בכלים ואין מסיקין בשברי כלים. פירוש בקעת שברי עצים שמסיקין בהן כדכתיב ויבקע עצי עולה. ותניא אידך כשם שמסיקין בכלים כך מסיקין בשברי כלים. ותניא אידך אין מסיקין לא בכלים ולא בשברי כלים לא קשיא הא ר' יהודה הא ר"ש הא ר' נחמיה. הא דתני אין מסיקין בשברי כלים ר' רחשיב דמתניתין בשברי כלים בנולד. והא דתני מסיקין ולא בזה ר"ש הא דלית ליה מוקצה. ומיפרשא בגמ' דבמה מדליקין. והא דתני אין מסיקין לא בזה ולא בזה ר' נחמיה היא דאמר אין כלי ניטל אלא לצורך תשמישו. ומפורש במס' יו"ט פרק המביא כדי יין. והא דאמר רב נחמן אמר שמואל לענין ליבני דאישתיור מבניינא שרגינהו ואקצינהו אפילו לר' שמעון דהני כגרוגרות וכצמוקים דמו. ודאית ליה מוקצה. וזה שאמר חרס קטנה מותר לטלטלה בחצר...

רב נסים גאון

הא ר' יהודה והא ר' שמעון והא ר' נחמיה. דברי ר' יהודה ור"ש בפרק במה מדליקין (דף כט) אמר רב יהודה אמר רב מסיקין בכלים ואין מסיקין בשברי כלים דברי ר' יהודה ור' שמעון מתיר ודברי ר' נחמיה הן במשנה שנאמרו אין ניטלין אלא לצורך וכמו שהתירו ר' נחמיה לומר אפילו דבר שמלאכתו להיתר לצורך גופו ולצורך מקומו אין אבל מחמה לצל לא ובתוספתא (פט"ו) ר' נחמיה אומר אפילו טליתו ואפילו תרוד או אין ניטלין אלא לצורך בברייתא שנאמר בה אין מסיקין לא בכלים ולא בשברי כלים הן דברי ר' נחמיה ובמס' יו"ט בפרק המביא כדי יין (דף לה) הזכיר עוד זה הדבר ואמרו תרי תנאי ואליבא דר' נחמיה כלומר קרא התנאים סוברין כי ר' [יהודה] [נחמיה] שאני ליה בין שבות שבת לשבות יום טוב: דתנן

ליקוטי רש"י

אין מוציאין את הקטן וכו'. כל מילי דלאו לורך אכילה [ביצה יב.]. דלא הותרה אלא

מסורת הש"ס

א) ביצה יב., לז., ב) [ביצה לז. ע"ש ובפרש"י שם], ג) ב"מ צח: ד) [עי' הרי"ף והרא"ש דכאביי], ה) [ע"ז כח:], ו) חולין יד:, ז) לעיל כח: כט. לקמן קמג, ח) ביצה לב., ט) ביצה שם, ע) ביצה לב: לא:, י) [תוספתא פרק ט"ו], כ) [ערוך בערך ספת פי' לא יחתוך. פי' אחר לא יחבר].

הגהות הב"ח

(א) גמ' אמר שמואל מגופת חבית שנכתתה היא ושבריה מותר וכו' מגופת חבית שנכתתה: (ג) רש"י ד"ה שותא מלודה. נ"ב וכן פי' בעל הערוך על השותא כמו שותא כדפירש בהגרול ואשכל דף קיז עיין שם. ולקמן פרק שני ביצה ובמקום: (ד) ד"ה של בגדים של מילתא וכו': (ד) ד"ה מגופה של חבית שנכתתה החבית (מגופה וכו' החבית) ... יספות לא יתקן להסיר:

הגהות הגר"א

[א] גמ' לעולם מחמה לצל. נ"ב גי' הגאונים וכו' ורב לדבר שאין מתכוין מותר:

אין מוציאין. הולאה שלא לצורך דלא איסתרי לכתחילה ביו"ט טפי מבשבת אלא אוכל נפש והך דמשילין ב"ה: טלטול מי שמעת להו. דמשוי יו"ט לשבת: טלטול לאו צורך הוצאה. בתמיה הלכך אי מזלזלת בטלטול מזלזלת בהולאה: להא דרבא. דאמר לורך מקומו כלורך גופו: מר. פוסו"ר: שלא יגנב. דומיא דמחמה לצל ואסור בדבר שמלאכתו לאיסור: שותא. (ג) מלודה: לאו למימרא כו'. למה לי לפרושי בהדיא דליתיב עלה לאו משום למימרא דהאי דשרי לטלטולי משום לצורך גופו הוא: שקילו שותא מקמיה כהנא. דניתוב על מקומה קאמר ולורך מקומה הוא דהוה: מחמה לצל הוה. במקום הרע לה היתה ואי לאו דפריש בהדיא ליתיב עלה מאן דחזי סבר דמחמה לצל שרי ולמקומה לא היה צריך דלימא שישב במקומה: בי סדיותא. כרים של צמר שקורין פילטר"א: בי שמשי. בחמה: אמר ליה שרי. רבא לטעמיה דאמר דבר שמלאכתו להיתר אף מחמה לצל מותר: אית לי אחריני. איני צריך לגופו: דכרבה סבירא לך. דאמר מחמה לצל אסור והלכה כרבא דאמר דבר שמלאכתו להיתר שרי לגמרי ודבר שמלאכתו לאיסור לצורך גופו ומקומו מותר מחמה לצל ושלא יגנב אסור: מכבדות. איסקוב"א שמכבדים בהן את השולחן: של מילתא. (ג) בגדים לכבד שולחן שמלאכתו להיתר: של תמרה. כעין שלנו לכבד את הבית לאסור משום אשויי גומות דמודה רבי שמעון בפסיק רישיה ולא ימות: לצורך גופו. למלאכת היתר: אלא מחמה לצל בהא לימא רבי אלעזר אף של תמרה. דבר שמלאכתו לאיסור ליכא מאן דשרי מחמה לצל: וכן אמר רבי אלעזר. של מילתא מותר של תמרה אסור מחמה לצל: **מתני'** מעין מלאכה. שום מלאכה ואפי' אינה מעין הראשונה: לצוק לתוכה מקפה. עבה דומיא לעיסה מעורבת במים: **גמ'** הואיל ומוכנין על גבי אביהן. כשקדש היום: מסיקין בכלים. ביו"ט שהרי ראוין לטלטל ויטלטל ויתנם לתוך האור: ואין מסיקין בשברי כלים. דהוו להו מוקצין ולא חזו לטלטול: עצים בעלמא נינהו. דהא מאתמול להסקה קיימי: וקתני אין מסיקין. ולא אמרינן מוכנין היו אגב אביהן אלא אמרינן נולד נינהו ואסירי: מר סבר מוכן הוא. כיון דלראוי לשום מלאכה ומר סבר נולד הוא דמאתמול לאו להאי מלאכה הוה קאי הלכך מעין מלאכתו בעינן: הא רבי יהודה. מסיקין בכלים ואין מסיקין בשברי כלים דאית ליה מוקצה ונולד כלים לאו מוקצה נינהו שברים נולד נינהו: והא. דתני מסיקין בשניהם: רבי שמעון. דלית ליה מוקצה ולית ליה נולד: והא. דתניא אף בכלים אין מסיקין: רבי נחמיה היא. דאמר אין כלי ניטל אלא לצורך תשמישו המיוחד לו והאי לאו מיוחד הוא לו דלאו להסקה קאי: דאישתיור. שהשלים בניינו וניתותר ומהשתא לא קיימי לבנין אלא לישב עליהם ותורת כלי עליהם: שרגינהו. אי סדרן זו על זו ודאי אקצינהו לצורך בנין אחר: בחצר. דשכיחי בה כלים שהחרס הזה ראוי להם לכיסוי ותורת כלי עליו: אבל לא בכרמלית. אפי' בתוך ד' אמות דלא שכיחי ביה מאני ולא חזי לכסויי: אפילו בכרמלית. הואיל ולאו רה"ר הוא שכיחי דאזלי ויתבי התם וחזי לכסות בו רוק: ורבא אמר אף ברה"ר. כיון דבחצר כלי הוא בעלמא נמי לא פקע שם כלי מיניה: בריתקא. שם רה"ר: איתווסאי מסאניה טינא. נתלכלך מנעלו בטיט: כפר ליה. מקנחו: אמר רבא לא מסתייה דלא גמירי. מה אסור מה מותר: אלא מיגמר נמי מגמרי. מלמדין שיבוש שבידם לאחרים: לדידי. לקינוח ואע"ג דלא שכיח הרי שם כלי עליו בחצר: שנכתתה. החבית: (ד) מגופה. של חבית שנכתתה החבית: היא. המגופה: ושבריה. של חבית ניטלין בשבת דחזו לכיסוי מנא: לא יספות. (ה) יתקן להתיר בליטותיו ועוקליו בשבת דעביד כלי והוי מכה בפטיש: ואם זרק. מגופה זו לאשפה בטלה מתורת כלי: זרקיה לגלימיה. בשבת לאשפה ה"נ דאסור לטלטולי:

מבעוד

הא רבי נחמיה. דסבירא ליה דאין כלי ניטל אלא לצורך תשמישו הרגיל בחול כדמפרש בפרק במה מדליקין (לעיל דף לו.) והאי נמי אין רגיל בחול לשרוף אותו: **ורבא** אמר אפילו ברה"ר. ובהני דנשברו בע"ש קאמר דאי בנשברו בשבת האמר בפרק נוטל (לקמן דף קמג:) דרבא אית ליה מוקצה וכל שכן נולד:

אם

אין מוציאין את הקטן ואת הלולב ואת ספר תורה לרה"ר ובית הלל מתירין אימר דשמעת להו לבית שמאי הוצאה טלטול מי שמעת להו וטלטול גופיה לאו משום הוצאה היא ואף רב סבר לה להא דרבא דאמר רב מר שלא יגנב זהו טלטול שלא לצורך ואסור טעמא שלא יגנב אבל לצורך גופו ולצורך מקומו מותר איני והא רב כהנא איקלע לבי רב ואמר אייתו ליה שותא לכהנא ליתיב עליה לאו למימרא דדבר שמלאכתו לאיסור לצורך גופו אין צורך מקומו לא הכי אמר להו שקולו שותא מקמי כהנא ואי בעית אימא התם מחמה לצל הוה רב מרי בר רחל הוה ליה ההיא בי סדיותא בשמשא אתא לקמיה דרבא אמר ליה מהו לטלטולינהו אמר ליה שרי איית לי אחרינא חזו לאורחין אית לי נמי לאורחים אמר ליה גלית אדעתיך דכרבה סבירא לך לכולי עלמא שרי לדידך אסיר אמר רבי אבא אמר רבי חייא בר אשי אמר רב מכבדות של מילתא מותר לטלטלן בשבת אבל של תמרה לא ורבי אלעזר אומר אף של תמרה במאי עסקינן אילימא לצורך גופו ולצורך מקומו בהא לימא רב של תמרה לא והא רב כרבא סבירא ליה אלא מחמה לצל בהא לימא ר' אלעזר אף של תמרה לעולם מחמה לצל אימא וכן אמר רבי אלעזר: **מתני'** [א] כל הכלים הניטלין בשבת שבריהן ניטלין עמהן ובלבד שיהו עושין מעין מלאכה שברי עריבה לכסות בהן את פי החבית שברי זכוכית לכסות בהן את פי הפך רבי יהודה אומר ובלבד שיהו עושין מעין מלאכתן שברי עריבה לצוק לתוכן מקפה ושל זכוכית לצוק לתוכן שמן: **גמ'** אמר רב יהודה אמר שמואל מחלוקת שנשברו מערב שבת דמר סבר מעין מלאכתן אין מעין מלאכה אחרת לא ומר סבר אפילו מעין מלאכה אחרת אבל נשברו בשבת דברי הכל מותרין הואיל ומוכנין על גבי אביהן מותיב רב זוטרא מסיקין בכלים ואין מסיקין בשברי כלים דנשברו אימת אילימא דנשברו מערב יום טוב עצים בעלמא נינהו אלא לאו ביום טוב וקתני מסיקין בכלים ואין מסיקים בשברי כלים אלא אי איתמר הכי איתמר אמר רב יהודה אמר שמואל מחלוקת שנשברו בשבת דמר סבר מוכן הוא ומר סבר נולד הוא אבל מערב שבת דברי הכל מותרין הואיל והוכנו למלאכה מבעוד יום תני חדא מסיקין בכלים ואין מסיקין בשברי כלים ותניא אידך כשם שמסיקין בכלים כך מסיקין בשברי כלים ותניא אידך אין מסיקין לא בכלים ולא בשברי כלים הא רבי יהודה הא רבי שמעון הא רבי נחמיה אמר רב נחמן הני ליבני דאישתיור מבניינא שרי לטלטולינהו דחזו למיזגא עליהו שרגינהו ודאי אקצינהו אמר רב נחמן אמר שמואל חרס קטנה מותר לטלטל בחצר אבל בכרמלית לא ורב נחמן דידיה אמר אפילו בכרמלית אבל ברה"ר לא ורבא אמר אפילו ברה"ר ואזדא רבא לטעמיה דרבא הוה קאזיל בריתקא דמחוזא אתווסאי מסאניה טינא אתא שמעיה שקל חספא וקא מכפר ליה רמו ביה רבנן קלא אמר לא מיסתייא דלא גמירי מיגמר נמי מגמרי אילו בחצר הואי מי לא הוה חזיא לכסויי ביה מנא הכא נמי חזיא לדידי אמר רב יהודה אמר שמואל מגופה שנכתתה (א) מותר לטלטלה בשבת תניא נמי הכי מגופה שנכתתה היא ושבריה מותר לטלטלה בשבת ולא יספות ממנה שבר לכסות בה את הכלי ולסמוך בה כרעי המטה ואם זרקה באשפה אסור מתקיף לה רב פפא אלא מעתה זריק ליה לגלימיה ה"נ דאסור אלא אמר רב פפא אם

מוקצה. וזה שאמר חרס קטנה מותר לטלטלה בחצר. הואיל וראוי לכסות בו כלי שבחצר. אבל בכרמלית שאין בו כלי לא ורב נחמן סבר כיון שהוציא מרשות הרבים לכרמלית או המכניס אינו חייב זימנין דעייל ליה לחצר וחזי ליה. ורבא סבר אפילו ברה"ר חזי לכסות ביה טינא ושרי לטלטולי בטעמיה. וזה שאמר רב יהודה אמר שמואל מגופת חבית שנכתתה מותר לטלטלה. פי' מגופת כסוי כסוי שסותם פי החבית מלשון יגיפו הדלתות [ולא יספות]. פי' לא יחתוך הוא. כדתנן סופת באבטיח. ותניא נמי הכי כולן פשוטות הן.

שלא לצורך וגבי טלטול שלא לצורך נמי גזרינן ואפילו גבי הפסד ממון ולבית הלל דאמרי הולאה התורה בטלטול נמי לא גזור רבנן [שם לז.]. ובית הלל מתירין. לכולי עלמא יש הולאה ליום הותרה לצורך ובית הלל אית להו כיון דהותרה לצורך הותרה מן התורה לגמרי אלא רבנן גזור צריך כגון אבנים אבל בקטן וספר תורה דצריכין להו ביום טוב לא גזור ובית שמאי לית להו [...] שהתורה התירתו הותר ושאינו צורך אכילה באסורו עומד מן התורה [שם יב. עיי"ש ובתוס' שם].

משום הוצאה היא. תחילת הולאה על ידי טלטול היא וכל מה שגזרו אינו אלא משום הולאה והאי דלא גזרו על טלטול כלים ו[...] טלטול כלים ואוכלים מפני שלא יוכלו לעמוד בהן לבטל עונג שבת ושמחת יום טוב [שם לז.]. אי אין אסור [...] משום הולאה ומה שלא גזרו על כל טלטולים אפילו על אוכלים וכלים משום דאין גוזרין גזרה על הצבור אלא אם כן רוב צבור יכולין לעמוד בה [שם יב.]. שותא. מכמורת לדגים או לחיות [ב"ק קיז.]. [...] לקפלן תחתיו במקום הכר או הכסת [לקמן קמו:]. שבריהן ניטלין. אפילו נשתברו היום בשבת. שיהו עושין מעין מלאכה. שתהא תורת כלי עליהם. מעין מלאכה. כלומר אע"פ שאין רא[...] [...]אכתן. הראשונה. מקפה. תבשיל עב דהיינו מעין עיסה [חולין יד:]. מסיקין בכלים. דהני טלטול נמי נינהו ומטלטלן נמי להסיקן. ואין מסיקין בשברי כלים. שנשברו ביום טוב דהשתא לא [...] להכי קיימי [ביצה לב.]. שנשברו בו ביום דהוו להו נולד אבל בכלים מסיקין דהא חזו לטלטלן [לעיל כח:]. כשם שמסיקין בכלים וכו'. דלית להו מוקצה. אין מסיקין לא בכלים. דאין ניטלין [...] [...] דאישתיור מבניינא. [...] שרי לטלטולינהו. [...] למיזגא. [...] שרגינהו. [...] [שם לא:]. [לעיל מג.] [ביצה שם].

Sabbath itself, דִּבְרֵי הַכֹּל מוּתָּרִין – **all agree** that **they are permitted** for use, הוֹאִיל וּמוּכָנִין עַל גַּבֵּי אֲבִיהֶן מוּתָּר – for **since** at the onset of the Sabbath **they were "prepared" by virtue of** being part of **the whole utensil,**[17] they remain **permitted** even after breaking.[18]

This explanation is rejected:

מוֹתִיב רַב זוּטְרָאי – **Rav Zutrai challenged** this on the basis of the following Baraisa: מַסִּיקִין בְּכֵלִים וְאֵין מַסִּיקִין בְּשִׁבְרֵי כֵלִים – WE MAY FUEL a fire WITH undamaged wooden UTENSILS on Yom Tov, BUT WE MAY NOT FUEL it WITH FRAGMENTS OF broken UTENSILS.[19] דְּנִשְׁבְּרוּ אֵימַת – In the Baraisa's case, **when did [the utensils] break?** אִילֵימָא דְּנִשְׁבְּרוּ מֵעֶרֶב יוֹם טוֹב – **If you will say that they broke before Yom Tov,** עֵצִים בְּעָלְמָא נִינְהוּ – then **[the fragments] are ordinary pieces of wood** and were certainly prepared before Yom Tov to be used as firewood.[20] אֶלָּא לָאו בְּיוֹם טוֹב – **Rather,** is it **not** clear that we are dealing with a case where they broke **on Yom Tov** itself? וְקָתָנֵי מַסִּיקִין בְּכֵלִים וְאֵין מַסִּיקִים בְּשִׁבְרֵי כֵלִים – **Yet [the Baraisa] teaches** that **we may fuel** a fire only **with** undamaged **utensils but may not fuel** it **with fragments of utensils.** Thus, there is a Tanna who holds that fragments of utensils which broke on Yom Tov are not considered prepared for use by virtue of having been part of the whole utensil at the onset of Yom Tov.[21] According to your explanation, we cannot attribute this Baraisa to any Tanna. – ? –

The Gemara therefore reinterprets our Mishnah's dispute:

אֶלָּא אִי אִיתְּמַר הָכִי אִיתְּמַר – **Rather, if** anything **was stated** in the name of Shmuel, **this is how it was stated:** אָמַר רַב יְהוּדָה אָמַר שְׁמוּאֵל – **Rav Yehudah said in the name of Shmuel:** מַחֲלוֹקֶת שֶׁנִּשְׁבְּרוּ בְּשַׁבָּת – **The dispute** pertains to a case **where [the utensils] broke on the Sabbath,** and its basis is דְּמָר סָבַר מוּכָן הוּא – **that** one **master** (the Tanna Kamma) **holds** that as long as a fragment can be used to perform some sort of task **it is** still considered **prepared** for use on the basis of its pre-Sabbath preparation, וּמָר סָבַר נוֹלָד הוּא – **whereas** the other **master** (R' Yehudah) **holds** that unless it can be used to perform a semblance of its former task **it is** considered ***nolad.***[22] אֲבָל מֵעֶרֶב שַׁבָּת דִּבְרֵי הַכֹּל מוּתָּרִין – **But** if the utensils broke **before the Sabbath,** – **all agree** that **[the fragments] are permitted** for use on the Sabbath, as long as they are fit for any sort of task, הוֹאִיל וְהוּכְנוּ לִמְלָאכָה מִבְּעוֹד יוֹם – **since they were prepared for** the new **task while it was yet day** before the Sabbath began.[23]

The Gemara contrasts the Baraisa cited above with two other Baraisas and explains them:

תָּנֵי חֲדָא – **It was taught in one Baraisa:** מַסִּיקִין בְּכֵלִים וְאֵין מַסִּיקִין בְּשִׁבְרֵי כֵלִים – WE MAY FUEL a fire WITH undamaged UTENSILS on Yom Tov, BUT WE MAY NOT FUEL a fire WITH FRAGMENTS OF broken UTENSILS. וְתַנְיָא אִידָךְ – **It was taught in another Baraisa:** כְּשֵׁם שֶׁמַּסִּיקִין בְּכֵלִים כָּךְ מַסִּיקִין בְּשִׁבְרֵי כֵלִים – JUST AS WE MAY FUEL a fire WITH undamaged UTENSILS, SO TOO MAY WE FUEL it WITH FRAGMENTS OF UTENSILS. וְתַנְיָא אִידָךְ – **And it was taught in** yet **another Baraisa:** אֵין מַסִּיקִין לֹא בְּכֵלִים וְלֹא בְשִׁבְרֵי כֵלִים – WE MAY NOT FUEL a fire, NEITHER WITH undamaged UTENSILS NOR WITH FRAGMENTS OF UTENSILS. The basis for this difference of opinion is the following: הָא רַבִּי יְהוּדָה – **This [Baraisa]** (the first) follows the view of **R' Yehudah,** הָא רַבִּי שִׁמְעוֹן – **this one** (the second) follow the view of **R' Shimon,** הָא רַבִּי נְחֶמְיָה – and **this one** (the third) follows the view of **R' Nechemyah.**[24]

Pursuant to its discussion of items that are no longer fit for their previous use, the Gemara cites a law:

אָמַר רַב נַחְמָן – **Rav Nachman said:** הָנֵי לִיבְנֵי דְּאִישְׁתַּיּוּר מִבִּנְיָינָא שָׁרֵי לְטַלְטוּלִינְהוּ – **The bricks that were left over from construction may be moved** on the Sabbath, דַּחֲזוּ לְמִיזְגָּא עֲלַיְיהוּ –

NOTES

17. Literally: their fathers.

18. As long as they are still fit to be used for some sort of task, their pre-Sabbath preparation for use remains in effect and they are not *muktzeh* (*Ritva MHK* ed.; see *Sfas Emes*).

19. Since whole utensils may be moved on Yom Tov, one is allowed to move them and toss them into a fire. Fragments of broken utensils, however, are *muktzeh* and may not be moved at all (*Rashi*). Now, since the Baraisa does not specify that it is dealing with fragments that are totally useless, its ruling presumably refers even to those that can be used for some sort of task, albeit not the former one. However, it obviously does not refer to fragments that are still fit for their former task, for those are certainly classified as utensils and the first clause *permitted* fueling a fire with utensils (*Ritva MHK* ed.).

20. *Rashi.* Unlike utensils that broke before the Sabbath, which arguably may require pre-Sabbath designation for a new task in order to be deemed non-*muktzeh* on the Sabbath, wooden utensils that broke before Yom Tov need no special designation in order to be non-*muktzeh* on Yom Tov. They obviously stand to be used as firewood (*Maharsha*).

21. And this pertains even if the fragments are still suitable for performing some sort of task (see note 19). Nevertheless, the Tanna holds that since they are no longer suitable for their former task or a semblance of it, their previous "preparation" is no longer in effect (see *Rashi* and following note).

22. *Nolad,* literally: newborn (i.e. newly formed), is a category of *muktzeh* which includes anything that came into existence on the Sabbath. This type of item cannot be deemed to have been prepared for use at the onset of the Sabbath. The classic example of *nolad* is a newly laid egg. In our case, the Tanna Kamma and R' Yehudah disagree whether a shard that is fit for some new use is prohibited under the category of *nolad*. The Tanna Kamma holds that anything that was functional previously and is still functional on the Sabbath is considered prepared, even if it is no longer fit for the original use. R' Yehudah, however, holds that if it is not fit for the same function as before, it is *nolad*. Since it serves in a new capacity, it is in effect not the utensil that was here when the Sabbath began. The Baraisa cited above, which forbids fueling a fire with fragments of a wooden utensil that broke on Yom Tov, follows R' Yehudah (*Rashi*; see note 24 for further clarification of the dispute).

23. [They are classified as utensils on the basis of their fitness even without specific designation for the new use.]

24. R' Yehudah and R' Shimon engage in a wide-ranging dispute regarding the extent of the *muktzeh* prohibitions. R' Yehudah applies these laws stringently, whereas R' Shimon applies them more leniently and permits certain categories that R' Yehudah considers *muktzeh*. Their dispute was discussed at length in the third chapter of this tractate (44a-46b; see also 126b note 28).

One facet of the dispute involves *nolad.* R' Yehudah forbids the use of *nolad* whereas R' Shimon permits it (see above, 45b, and *Beitzah* 2a). Thus, the Baraisa which prohibits fueling a fire with fragments of utensils that broke on Yom Tov and are fit for a different use than before, follows R' Yehudah. The Baraisa which permits fueling a fire with such fragments follows R' Shimon (see *Magen Avraham* 501:13 and *Chasam Sofer*; see also *Beur Halachah* 308:6 ד״ה לשום מלאכה, *Shaar HaTziyun* 501:29 and *Chazon Ish* 43:14-15).

The third Baraisa, which prohibits fueling a fire even with undamaged utensils, follows R' Nechemyah, who holds that a utensil may be taken only for its designated purpose. Since undamaged utensils are not designated for use as firewood, R' Nechemyah forbids taking them for this purpose (*Rashi;* see *Tosafos* ד״ה הא רבי נחמיה). R' Nechemyah also forbids fueling a fire with fragments of utensils that broke on Yom Tov, because he concurs with R' Yehudah concerning *nolad* (*Rashi* to *Beitzah* 32a).

We thus learn that the Tanna Kamma of our Mishnah, who permits the use of shards that broke on the Sabbath even if they are not fit for the same use as before, follows the opinion of R' Shimon (see *Ritva MHK* ed.). However, the identity of the Tanna Kamma is actually R' Meir, as we shall see below (125a note 10). [As a rule, anonymous Mishnaic opinions are attributable to R' Meir (see *Sanhedrin* 86a).]

אין מוציאין את הקטן ואת הלולב ואת ספר תורה לרה"ר ובית הלל מתירין אימר דשמעת להו לבית שמאי הוצאה טלטול מי שמעת להו וטלטול גופיה לאו משום הוצאה היא ואף רב סבר לה להא דרבא דאמר רב מר שלא יגנב זהו טלטול שלא לצורך ואסור טעמא שלא יגנב אבל לצורך גופו ולצורך מקומו מותר איני והא רב כהנא איקלע לבי רב ואמר אייתו ליה שותא לכהנא ליתיב עליה אם לאו למימרא דדבר שמלאכתו לאיסור לצורך גופו אין לצורך מקומו לא הכי אמר להו שקולו שותא מקמי כהנא ואי בעית אימא התם מחמה לצל הוה רב מרי בר רחל הוה ליה ההיא בי סדיותא בשמשא אתא לקמיה דרבא אמר ליה מהו לטלטולינהו אמר ליה שרי איתי לי אחרינא חזו לאורחין איתי לי נמי לאורחים אמר ליה גלית אדעתיך דכרבה סבירא לך לכולי עלמא שרי לדידך אסיר אמר רבי אבא אמר רבי חייא בר אשי אמר רב מכבדות של מילתא מותר לטלטלן בשבת אבל של תמרה לא רבי אלעזר אומר אף של תמרה במאי עסקינן אילימא לצורך גופו ולצורך מקומו בהא לימא רב של תמרה לא והא רב כרבא סבירא ליה אלא מחמה לצל בהא לימא ר' אלעזר אף של תמרה [א] לעולם מחמה לצל ואימא וכן אמר רבי אלעזר: **מתני'** כל הכלים הניטלין בשבת שבריהן ניטלין עמהן ובלבד שיהו עושין מעין מלאכה שברי עריבה לכסות בהן את פי החבית שברי זכוכית לכסות בהן את פי הפך רבי יהודה אומר ובלבד שיהו עושין מעין מלאכתן שברי עריבה לצוק לתוכן מקפה ושל זכוכית לצוק לתוכן שמן: **גמ'** אמר רב יהודה אמר שמואל מחלוקת שנשברו מערב שבת דמר סבר מעין מלאכתן אין מעין מלאכה אחרת לא ומר סבר אפילו מעין מלאכה אחרת אבל נשברו בשבת דברי הכל מותרין הואיל ומוכנין על גבי אביהן מותר מותיב רב זוטראי מסיקין בכלים ואין מסיקין בשברי כלים דנשברו אימת אילימא דנשברו מערב יום טוב עצים בעלמא נינהו אלא לאו ביום טוב וקתני מסיקין בכלים ואין מסיקים בשברי כלים אלא אי איתמר הכי איתמר אמר רב יהודה אמר שמואל מחלוקת שנשברו בשבת דמר סבר מוכן הוא ומר סבר נולד הוא אבל מערב שבת דברי הכל מותרין הואיל והוכנו למלאכה מבעוד יום תני חדא מסיקין בכלים ואין מסיקין בשברי כלים ותניא אידך כשם שמסיקין בכלים כך מסיקין בשברי כלים ותניא אידך אין מסיקין לא בכלים ולא בשברי כלים הא רבי יהודה הא רבי שמעון הא רבי נחמיה אמר רב נחמן הני ליבני דאישתיור מבנינא שרי לטלטולינהו דחזו למיזגא עלייהו שרגינהו ודאי אקצינהו אמר רב נחמן אמר שמואל חרס קטנה מותר לטלטל בחצר אבל בכרמלית לא ורב נחמן דידיה אמר אפילו בכרמלית אבל ברה"ר לא ורבא אמר אפילו ברה"ר ואזדא רבא לטעמיה דרבא הוה קאזיל בריתקא דמחוזא אתווסאי מסאניה טינא אתא שמעיה שקל חספא וקא מכפר ליה רמו ביה רבנן קלא אמר לא מיסתייא דלא גמירי מיגמר נמי מגמרי אילו בחצר הואי מי לא הוה חזיא לכסויי ביה מנא הכא נמי חזיא לדידי אמר רב יהודה אמר שמואל מגופת חבית שנשתברה מותר לטלטלה בשבת תניא נמי הכי מגופה שנשתברה היא ושבריה מותר לטלטלה בשבת ולא יספות ממנה שבר לכסות בה את הכלי ולסמוך בה כרעי המטה ואם זרקה באשפה אסור מתקיף לה רב פפא אלא מעתה זריק ליה לגלימיה ה"נ דאסור אלא אמר רב פפא אם

רש"י

אין מוציאין. הואיל שלא לצורך דלא אישתרי לכתחילה ביו"ט טפי מבשבת אלא אוכל נפש והך דמשילין ב"ה: טלטול מי שמעת להו. דמשוי יו"ט לשבת: טלטול לאו צורך הוצאה. בתמיה הלכך אי מזלזלת בטלטול מזלזלת בהוצאה: להא דרבא. דאמר לצורך מקומו כלצורך גופו: מר. פושו"ר: שלא יגנב. דומיא דמחמה לצל ואסור בדבר שמלאכתו לאיסור: שותא. (ב) מלודה: לאו למימרא כו'. למה לי לפרושי בהדיא דליתיב עלה לאו משום למימרא דהאי דשרי לטלטולי משום דלצורך גופו הוא: שקילו שותא מקמיה כהנא. דניתוב על מקומה קאמר ולצורך מקומה הוא דהוה: מחמה לצל הוה. במקום הרע לה היתה ואי לאו דפריש בהדיא ליתיב עלה מאן דחזי סבר דמחמה לצל שרי ולמקומה לא היה צריך דלימא שישב במקומה: בי סדיותא. כרים של לבד שקורין פילטר"א: בי שמשי. בחמה: אמר ליה שרי. רבא לטעמיה דאמר דבר שמלאכתו להיתר אף מחמה לצל מותר: אית לי אחריני. איני צריך לגופו: דכרבה סבירא לך. דאמר מחמה לצל אסור והלכה כרבא דאמר דבר שמלאכתו להיתר שרי לגמרי ודבר שמלאכתו לאיסור לצורך גופו ומקומו מותר מחמה לצל ושלא יגנב אסור: מכבדות. איסקוב"א שמכבדים בהן את השולחן: של מילתא. (ג) בגדים לכבד שולחן שמלאכתו להיתר: של תמרה. כעין שלנו לכבד את הבית לאסור משום דאשוי גומות ומודה רבי שמעון בפסיק רישיה ולא ימות: לצורך גופו. למלאכת היתר: אלא מחמה לצל בהא לימא רבי אלעזר אף של תמרה. דבר שמלאכתו לאיסור ליכא מאן דשרי מחמה לצל: וכן אמר רבי אלעזר. של מילתא של תמרה אסור מחמה לצל: מתני' מעין מלאכה. שום מלאכה ואפי' אינה מעין הראשונה: לצוק לתוכה מקפה. עבה דומיא דעיסה מעורבת במים: גמ' הואיל ומוכנין על גבי אביהן. כשקדש היום: מסיקין בכלים. ביו"ט שהרי ראוין לטלטל ויטלטל ויתנם לתוך האור: ואין מסיקין בשברי כלים. דהוו להו מוקצין ולא חזו לטלטול: עצים בעלמא נינהו. דהא מאתמול להסקה קיימי: וקתני אין מסיקין. ולא אמרינן מוכנין היו אגב אביהן אלא אמרינן נולד נינהו ואסירי: מר סבר מוכן הוא. כיון דראוי לשום מלאכה ומר סבר נולד הוא דמאתמול לאו להאי מלאכה הוה קאי הלכך מעין מלאכתו בעינן: הא רבי יהודה. מסיקין בכלים ואין מסיקין בשברי כלים דאית ליה מוקצה ונולד כלים לאו מוקצה נינהו שברים נולד נינהו: והא. דתני מסיקין בשניהם: רבי שמעון. דלית ליה מוקצה ולית ליה נולד: והא. דתניא אף בכלים אין מסיקין: רבי נחמיה היא. דאמר אין כלי ניטל אלא לצורך תשמישו המיוחד לו והאי לאו מיוחד הוא לו דלאו להסקה קאי: דאייתור. שהשלים בנייתו וניתותר ומהשתא לא קיימי לבנין אלא לישב עליהם ותורת כלי עליהם: שרגינהו. אי סדרן זו על זו ודאי אקצינהו לצורך בנין אחר: בחצר. דשכיחי בה כלים שהחרס הזה ראוי להם לכיסוי ותורת כלי עליו: אבל לא בכרמלית. אפי' בתוך ד' אמות דלא שכיחי ביה מאני ולא חזי לכסויי: אפילו בכרמלית. הואיל ולאו רה"ר הוא שכיחי דאזלי ויתבי התם וחזי לכסות בו רוק: ורבא אמר אף ברה"ר. כיון דאמר כלי הוא בעלמא נמי לא פקע שם כלי מיניה: בריתקא. שם רה"ר: איתווסאי מסאניה טינא. נתלכלך מנעלו בטיט: כפר ליה. מקנחו: אמר רבא לא מסתייה דלא גמירי. מה אסור מה מותר: אלא מיגמר נמי מגמרי. מלמדין שיבוש שבידם לאחרים: לדידי. לקינוח ואע"ג דלא שכיח הרי שם כלי עליו בחצר: שנתכתתה. החבית: (ד) מגופה. של חבית שנתכתתה החבית: היא. המגופה: ושבריה. של חבית ניטלין בשבת דחזו לכיסוי מנא: לא יספות. (ה) יתקן להסיר בליטותיו ועוקציו בשבת דעביד כלי והוי מכה בפטיש: ואם זרק. מגופה זו לאשפה בטלה מתורת כלי: זרקיה לגלימיה. בשבת לאשפה ה"נ דאסור לטלטולי: מבעוד

תוספות

הא רבי נחמיה. דסבירא ליה דאין כלי ניטל אלא לצורך תשמישו הרגיל בחול כדמפרש בפרק במה מדליקין (לעיל דף לו.) והאי נמי אין רגיל בחול לשרוף אותו: **ורבא** אמר אפילו ברה"ר. ובהני דנשברו בע"ש קאמר דאי בנשברו בשבת האמר בפרק נוטל (לקמן דף קמב:) דרבא אית ליה מוקצה וכל שכן נולד:

אס

עין משפט נר מצוה

כו א מיי' פ"א מהלכות יו"ט הלכה ה סמג לאוין עה טוש"ע או"ח סימן תקיח סעיף א:

כז ב מיי' פכ"ה מהלכ' שבת הלכה ג סמג לאוין סה טוש"ע או"ח סימן שח סעיף ג:

כח ג מיי' פכ"ו שם הלכה ז סמג שם טוש"ע שם סעיף מט:

כט ד מיי' פכ"ה מהל' שבת הלכה יב סמג שם טוש"ע או"ח סימן שח סעיף ו:

ל ה מיי' פכ"ו שם הלכה ב טוש"ע או"ח סימן שח סעיף ...:

לא ו ז ח מיי' שם הל' ג טוש"ע שם סעיף ז:

מסורת הש"ס

א) ביצה יב. לו. ב) [ביצה לג.] ע"ש ובפרש"י שם, ג) ס"א אסור טלטול לאו צורך הוצאה היא, ד) [ג' הרי"ף והרא"ש דאביי], ה) [ע"ז כח:] חולין יד:, ו) [לעיל קכג. לקמן קמג. ביצה לב.], ז) ביצה שם, ח) ביצה דף לג., ט) [תוספתא פרק ט"ו], י) [ערוך בערך ספת פי' לא יחתוך. פי' אחר לא יתכבר].

הגהות הגר"א

[א] גמ' לעולם מחמה לצל. נ"ב ג' הגאונים ולרא"ש כ"ג סבירא ליה דבדבר שאין מתכוין מותר:

רבינו חננאל

היא והלכתא כרבנן וכדמוקים לה רבה. דהכין סוגיא דשמעתא כולה. וזה שאמר רב שקולו שותא מקמי כהנא. פי' שותא שריתא והיא קורה כדמתרגמינן בצל קורתי בטלל שירותי. וי"א חבילה. וי"א רשת כדכתיב ויפרשו עליו גוים בשחתם נתפש. ושיתא היא שחתא. פי' מכבדות מטאטא שמכבדין הבית בהן. הנהו בי סדיותא. פי' כסתות והוא כגון כרים וכסתות. מתני' כל הכלים הניטלין בשבת שבריהן ניטלין [עמהן] ובלבד שיהו עושין מעין מלאכה וכו'. ר' יהודה אומר ובלבד שיהו עושין מעין מלאכתן כו'. פי' מקפה. מרק. בא רב יהודה משמיה דשמואל להעמיד מחלוקת ר' יהודה ות"ק כשנשברו מע"ש. ולא כשנשברו בשבת. דת"ק סבר מוכן הוא. ור' יהודה סבר מעין מלאכה אחרת כנולד הוא כדמפרש בגמרא דהכל שחשין. אבל מע"ש דברי הכל מותרין. ואפילו לר' יהודה הואיל והוכנו למלאכה אחרת מבעו"י ואינו כנולד בשבת וקי"ל כרבנן. וכלישנא בתרא דשמואל בין נשברו בשבת בין נשברו מע"ש. מעין מלאכה סגיא. תני חדא מסיקין בכלים ואין מסיקין בשברי כלים. פירוש בקעת שברי עצים שמסיקין בהן כדכתיב ויבקע עצי עולה. ותניא אידך כשם שמסיקין בכלים כך מסיקין בשברי כלים. ותניא אידך אין מסיקין לא בכלים ולא בשברי כלים לא קשיא הא ר' יהודה הא ר"ש הא ר' נחמיה. הא דתני אין מסיקין בשברי כלים ר' יהודה דמתניתין היא דחשיב בשברי כלים כנולד. והא דתני מסיקין בזה ובזה ר"ש היא דלית ליה מוקצה. ומפרשא בגמ' דבמה מדליקין. והא דתני אין מסיקין לא בזה ולא בזה ר' נחמיה היא דאמר אין כלי ניטל אלא לצורך תשמישו. ומפורש במס' יו"ט פרק המביא כדי יין. והא דאמר רב נחמן אמר שמואל לענין ליבני דאישתיור מבנינא שרגינהו אקצינהו אפילו לר' שמעון הני כגרוגרות וכצמוקים דמי. דאית ליה מוקצה. וזה שאמר חרס קטנה

רב נסים גאון

הא ר' יהודה והא ר' שמעון והא ר' נחמיה. דברי ר' יהודה ור"ש בפרק במה מדליקין [illegible]

[illegible]

because they are suitable to recline upon.[25] שַׁרְגִּינְהוּ וַדַּאי אַקְצִינְהוּ – However, **if one stacked them, he certainly set them aside** for use in future construction, and consequently, they are *muktzeh.*[26]

The Gemara cites a discussion concerning shards:

אָמַר רַב נַחְמָן אָמַר שְׁמוּאֵל – **Rav Nachman said in the name of Shmuel:** חֶרֶס קְטַנָּה מוּתָּר לְטַלְטֵל בְּחָצֵר – **A small earthenware shard may be moved about inside a courtyard,** אֲבָל בְּכַרְמְלִית לֹא – **but not in a** ***karmelis.***[27] וְרַב נַחְמָן דִּידֵיהּ אָמַר – **And Rav Nachman stated his own** opinion: אֲפִילּוּ בְּכַרְמְלִית – One may move it **even in a** ***karmelis,*** אֲבָל בִּרְשׁוּת הָרַבִּים לֹא – **but not in a public domain.**[28] וְרָבָא אָמַר – **But Rava said:** אֲפִילּוּ בִּרְשׁוּת הָרַבִּים – One may move it **even in a public domain.**[29] וְאַזְדָּא רָבָא לְטַעְמֵיהּ – **And Rava follows his own reasoning.** דְּרָבָא הֲוָה קָאָזִיל בְּרִי[ס]תְקָא[30] דִּמְחוֹזָא – **For Rava was** once **walking in the main thoroughfare of Mechoza,** אִתַּוּוּסַאי מְסָאנֵיהּ טִינָא – **and his shoes became soiled with mud.** אָתָא שַׁמָּעֵיהּ – **His servant came** along, שָׁקַל חַסְפָּא וְקָא מְכַפֵּר לֵיהּ – **took a shard** that had been lying in the public domain **and began to wipe** the mud **off for [Rava].** רָמוּ בֵּיהּ רַבָּנָן קָלָא – **The Rabbis** who had been accompanying Rava **shouted at him** to stop. אָמַר – **[Rava] thereupon said:** לָא מִיסְתַּיְיא דְּלָא גְּמִירֵי – **Not only did [these Rabbis] not learn** what is permitted and what is forbidden, מִיגְמַר נַמִּי מַגְמְרֵי – **they even teach others** their erroneous views! אִילּוּ בְּחָצֵר הֲוַאי – **If [the shard] were in a courtyard,** מִי לֹא הֲוָה חָזְיָא לְכַסּוּיֵי בֵּיהּ מָנָא – **would it not be fit to be used to cover a utensil?** הָכָא נַמִּי חָזְיָא לְדִידִי – **Here too,** in the public domain, **it is fit for me** to use to scrape mud off my shoes.[31]

A related ruling is cited:

אָמַר רַב יְהוּדָה אָמַר שְׁמוּאֵל – **Rav Yehudah said in the name of Shmuel:** מְגוּפַת חָבִית שֶׁנִּשְׁבְּרָה – **The lid of a cask that was shattered**[32] מוּתָּר לְטַלְטֵל בְּשַׁבָּת – **may be moved on the Sabbath.**[33]

The Gemara cites support for this ruling:

תַּנְיָא נַמִּי הָכִי – **It was taught similarly in a Baraisa:** מְגוּפָה שֶׁנִּשְׁבְּרָה – THE LID of a cask THAT WAS SHATTERED – הִיא וּשְׁבָרֶיהָ מוּתָּר לְטַלְטְלָהּ בְּשַׁבָּת – IT (i.e. the lid) AND THE SHARDS OF [THE CASK] MAY BE MOVED ON THE SABBATH; וְלֹא יִסְפּוֹת מִמֶּנָּה שֶׁבֶר – BUT ONE SHOULD NOT REPAIR ONE OF ITS SHARDS לְכַסּוֹת בָּהּ אֶת הַכֵּלִי – in order to be able TO COVER A VESSEL WITH IT וְלִסְמוֹךְ בָּהּ כַּרְעֵי הַמִּטָּה – OR TO SUPPORT THE LEGS OF A BED WITH IT.[34] וְאִם זְרָקָהּ בָּאַשְׁפָּה אָסוּר – AND IF ONE THREW [THE LID] IN A TRASH HEAP, IT IS FORBIDDEN for use on the Sabbath.[35]

The Baraisa's final ruling is questioned:

מַתְקִיף לָהּ רַב פָּפָּא – **Rav Pappa objected to this:** אֶלָּא מֵעַתָּה – **But now,** according to this will you also say that זָרִיק לֵיהּ לִגְלִימֵיהּ הָכִי נַמִּי דְּאָסוּר – if **one threw his garment** in a trash heap on the Sabbath **it is similarly forbidden** for use? A utensil should not lose its classification as such merely because it was discarded![36] – ? –

Rav Pappa therefore clarifies the Baraisa's rule:

אֶלָּא אָמַר רַב פָּפָּא – **Rather, Rav Pappa said:** This is what the Baraisa means:

NOTES

25. Building supplies are inherently *muktzeh*, for they are not utensils (*Beis Yosef, Orach Chaim* 308). However, when bricks were no longer needed for construction, they would normally be used as seats and therefore attained the status of utensils (*Rashi;* see *Ritva MHK* ed.; see also *Mishnah Berurah* 308:73).

26. For they revert back to the category of *inherently muktzeh* (*Mishnah Berurah* 308:74; cf. *Ritva MHK* ed.).

27. A *karmelis* is an area that resembles a public domain in certain respects and a private domain in others (see Introduction to Chapter One). It is Rabbinically prohibited to transfer items between either a private or public domain and a *karmelis,* or to carry something four *amos* in a *karmelis*.

Shmuel teaches that a shard may be moved about inside a courtyard, where there commonly are many vessels that are fit to be covered by the shard. Since it has this practical function, the shard retains its previous classification as a utensil and is not *muktzeh*. [This follows the opinion of the Tanna Kamma of our Mishnah.] However, one may not move a shard in a *karmelis,* even within four *amos*. A *karmelis* does not usually contain vessels for which the shard could serve as a cover, and thus, while in a *karmelis* the shard is *muktzeh* (*Rashi*).

28. Rav Nachman holds that a shard retains its classification as a utensil even in a *karmelis* because people often sit down in a *karmelis,* which is a relatively quiet area, and the shard has the practical function of being used to cover their spittle. Rav Nachman concedes, however, that a shard is *muktzeh* in a public domain, where it has no practical function (*Rashi*).

29. Rava holds that since the shard is considered a utensil when inside a courtyard it retains this classification even when found in a location where it is not useful (*Rashi;* see *Tosafos* ד״ה ורבא אמר and *Rashash*).

30. [Emendation follows *Dikdukei Soferim.*]

31. Although it is rarely needed for this purpose in the public domain [and would not qualify as a utensil on its basis], it may be used since it is deemed a utensil inside a courtyard (*Rashi;* see *Ritva MHK* ed. and *Chazon Ish* 43:16; cf. *Rabbeinu Chananel* and *Mishbetzos Zahav* 308:12). [See above, 46a note 16, where another episode involving Rava is explained on the basis of his opinion here.]

32. I.e. the cask was shattered but the lid is intact (*Rashi;* cf. *Chidushei HaRan*).

33. Because it is still fit to be used as a cover for other utensils (*Rashi*; see note 14). *Bach* emends the text to read: הִיא וּשְׁבָרֶיהָ מוּתָּר לְטַלְטֵל בְּשַׁבָּת, *it* (i.e. the lid) *and the fragments of [the cask] may be moved on the Sabbath.* The reference is to fragments that are fit to be used to cover vessels (see *Rashi*).

34. One should not smooth out the sharp edges of a shard to make it suitable for this use, since he would thereby be completing the formation of a utensil and would violate the *melachah* of מַכֶּה בְּפַטִּישׁ, *striking the final blow* (*Rashi*).

35. Since the Baraisa does not differentiate, this would seem to pertain whether one threw it in the trash heap before the Sabbath or on the Sabbath (see Gemara below).

36. Although a garment is fully functional and is thus more valuable than the lid of a broken cask, Rav Pappa argues that this is irrelevant. Since the lid was classified as a utensil at the onset of the Sabbath and is still somewhat useful, the fact that it was discarded should be inconsequential (*Ritva MHK* ed.; see also *Chidushei HaRan*).

אִם זְרָקָהּ מִבְּעוֹד יוֹם לָאַשְׁפָּה אֲסוּרָה – If one threw [the cover] in a trash heap while it was yet day before the Sabbath, **it is prohibited** for use on the Sabbath.[1]

The Gemara cites another related ruling:
אָמַר בַּר הַמְדּוּרִי אָמַר שְׁמוּאֵל – Bar Hamduri said in the name of Shmuel: קְרוּמִיּוֹת שֶׁל מַחְצֶלֶת מוּתָּר לְטַלְטְלָם בַּשַּׁבָּת – Shreds of reeds that became detached from **a mat may be moved on the Sabbath.**

The Gemara clarifies this ruling:
מַאי טַעְמָא – What is the reason that they are not *muktzeh*? **אָמַר רָבָא – Rava said: בַּר הַמְדּוּרִי אַסְבְּרָא לִי – Bar Hamduri explained it to me** as follows: **מַחְצֶלֶת גּוּפָא לְמַאי חַזְיָא – For what use is the mat itself suitable? לְכַסּוּיֵי בֵּיהּ עַפְרָא – To cover dust with it.**[2] **הָנֵי נַמִּי חַזְיָין לְכַסּוּיֵי בְּהוּ טִינוֹפֶת – These** detached shreds, **too, are suitable** to be used **to cover dirt with them.**[3]

Another related ruling:
שְׁיָרֵי – אָמַר רַבִּי זֵירָא אָמַר רַב – R' Zeira said in the name of Rav: פְּרוּזְמִיּוֹת אָסוּר לְטַלְטְלָן בְּשַׁבָּת – Remnants of a *tallis* may not be moved on the Sabbath. אָמַר אַבַּיֵי – Abaye said: בִּמְטַלְנִיּוֹת שֶׁאֵין בָּהֶן שָׁלֹשׁ עַל שָׁלֹשׁ – R' Zeira is dealing **with patches that are less than three** fingerbreadths **by three** fingerbreadths in size; **דְּלָא חַזְיָין לֹא לַעֲנִיִּים וְלֹא לַעֲשִׁירִים –** these are *muktzeh* **because they are unsuitable for** the use of **either paupers or people of means.**[4]

The Gemara now cites a related Baraisa:
תָּנוּ רַבָּנָן – The Rabbis taught in a Baraisa: שִׁבְרֵי תַנּוּר יָשָׁן – SHARDS OF AN OLD OVEN[5] **הֲרֵי הֵן כְּכָל הַכֵּלִים הַנִּיטָּלִין בֶּחָצֵר – ARE LIKE ALL** other **UTENSILS THAT MAY BE TAKEN IN A COURTYARD.**[6] **דִּבְרֵי רַבִּי מֵאִיר –** These are **THE WORDS OF R' MEIR. רַבִּי יְהוּדָה אוֹמֵר – R' YEHUDAH SAYS: אֵין נִיטָּלִין – THEY MAY NOT BE TAKEN.**[7] **הֵעִיד רַבִּי יוֹסֵי מִשּׁוּם רַבִּי אֱלִיעֶזֶר בֶּן יַעֲקֹב – R' YOSE TESTIFIED IN THE NAME OF R' ELIEZER BEN YAAKOV עַל שִׁבְרֵי תַנּוּר יָשָׁן – CONCERNING THE SHARDS OF AN OLD OVEN, שֶׁנִּיטָּלִין בְּשַׁבָּת – THAT THEY MAY BE TAKEN ON THE SABBATH; וְעַל כִּסּוּיוֹ – AND CONCERNING THE COVER OF [AN OVEN], שֶׁאֵינוֹ צָרִיךְ בֵּית יָד – THAT IT DOES NOT NEED A HANDLE** in order for one to be allowed to take it on the Sabbath.[8]

The Tannaic dispute is analyzed:
בְּמַאי קָמִיפַּלְגֵי – In what issue **do they disagree? אָמַר אַבַּיֵי – Abaye said: בְּעוֹשִׂין מֵעֵין מְלָאכָה וְאֵין עוֹשִׂין מֵעֵין מְלַאכְתָּן קָמִיפַּלְגֵי – They disagree concerning** a case **where [the shards] can** be used to **perform some sort of task** but **not** to **perform a semblance of their** former **task;**[9] **וְאַזְדָא רַבִּי יְהוּדָה לְטַעְמֵיהּ – and R' Yehudah follows his own reasoning** as set forth in our Mishnah, that such shards are *nolad* and may not be moved; **וְרַבִּי מֵאִיר לְטַעְמֵיהּ – and R' Meir** follows **his own reasoning** that such shards are considered prepared for use and may be moved.[10]

Abaye's explanation is rejected:
מַתְקִיף לָהּ רָבָא – Rava objected to this: אִי הָכִי – If so, אַדְּמִיפַּלְגֵי בְּשִׁבְרֵי תַנּוּר – instead of arguing specifically **about shards of an** old **oven, לִיפַּלְגוּ בְּשִׁבְרֵי כֵלִים בְּעָלְמָא – they should have argued about shards of any** broken **utensils. – ? –**

Rava therefore proposes an alternative explanation:
אֶלָּא אָמַר רָבָא – Rather, Rava said: בְּשִׁבְרֵי דְּהַאי תַּנּוּר קָמִיפַּלְגֵי – It is **regarding the shards of the following oven** that **they disagree. דִּתְנַן – For we learned in a Mishnah:**[11] **נְתָנוֹ עַל פִּי הַבּוֹר אוֹ עַל פִּי הַדּוּת –** If **ONE PLACED [AN OVEN] OVER THE MOUTH OF A PIT OR OVER THE MOUTH OF A CISTERN וְנָתַן שָׁם אֶבֶן – AND**

NOTES

1. In this case, the person has indicated before the Sabbath that the cover will no longer be used as a utensil (*Rashi*). Since it was not prepared for use when the Sabbath began, it is *muktzeh*. Now, if someone would discard an undamaged garment before the Sabbath it would not become *muktzeh*, for since it is a fine utensil we do not take into account its lack of desirability to its owner. However, the cover of a broken utensil does not necessarily stand to be used any longer, and thus, when one relegates it to the trash heap before the Sabbath, we recognize his act as stripping it of its classification as a utensil. It is only where the cover was prepared at the onset of the Sabbath that we say the owner cannot strip it of its classification on the Sabbath by discarding it (*Tosafos* ד״ה אם זרקה, *Ritva MHK* ed.).

2. I.e. to cover a pile of dust that one has prepared for spreading over excrement, and thus to prevent the dust from scattering. Alternatively, the meaning is that the mat is placed on the ground to prevent dust from rising (*Rashi*; see *Rashi* to *Rif*). [Mats were commonly used to sit upon. Bar Hamduri meant merely to point out one of the uses of a mat, for his explanation is based on the existence of this use.]

3. Thus, they can still be used to perform a semblance of their former task. Although the halachah follows the opinion that a fragment which is suitable for *any* task may be moved [and Shmuel himself followed this opinion above (see 124b note 27)], in our case it is necessary that the shreds be suitable for their former task. Shreds of reeds are so insignificant that when they become detached on a weekday, people discard them or use them as fuel for a fire. Therefore, if they were not suitable for their former task they would be deemed *muktzeh*, whether they became detached on a weekday or on the Sabbath. However, since they are suited for their former task, if they became detached *on the Sabbath* they are not *muktzeh*, for although they stand to be discarded they are still suited for the task for which they were prepared when the Sabbath began (*Rashba, Ritva MHK* ed.; cf. *Tosafos* ד״ה מחצלת and *Rif* as explained by *Chidushei HaRan*).

4. The smallest piece of fabric that is considered usable as a patch is one that is at least three fingerbreadths square. [Paupers use patches of this size to mend their garments. Even paupers, however, discard scraps that are smaller than three fingerbreadths square (see above, 26b).] If a piece of fabric tears off a *tallis*, people will not use it to cover dirt, for it is improper to assign a degrading function to something that had been designated for a mitzvah. Therefore, unless the scrap is large enough to be used as a patch, it is considered useless and is *muktzeh*. However, scraps of ordinary cloth may be moved even if they are smaller than this size, since they are suitable for use in covering dirt (*Rashi*, as explained by *Beur HaGra* to *Orach Chaim* 308:13; *Raavad* cited by *Ran, Rashba* and *Ritva MHK* ed.).

Others explain that Rav's ruling pertains to all scraps of cloth. If they are less than three fingerbreadths square, they are so insignificant that people automatically discard them. Thus, although they can conceivably be utilized to cover dirt, they are *muktzeh*. Even if they tear on the Sabbath they are *muktzeh*, since they are no longer suitable for the task for which they had been prepared (*Rambam, Hil. Shabbos* 26:6; *Rashba, Ritva MHK* ed.; see *Orach Chaim* 308:13; see also *Tosafos* to 127b ד״ה כיון, *Taz* 308:25 and *Chazon Ish* 43:19-20).

5. An "old" oven is one that was heated up at least once. Since its walls were hardened by the heat, its shards are somewhat useful (*Rashi*).

6. According to Rav Nachman and Rava (see 124b notes 28 and 29), this does not mean to exclude the shards from being moved [within four *amos*] in other areas, such as a *karmelis* or public domain (*Tosafos* ד״ה הרי הן).

7. The Gemara will proceed to explain the reasoning of each Tanna.

8. A dispute concerning this issue is cited in a Mishnah below, 126b, and is elaborated by the Gemara there (*Rashi*).

9. For example, the shards are suitable for use in covering casks, but not in baking (*Rashi*).

10. I.e. the Tanna Kamma of our Mishnah (on 124b) is R' Meir, and his dispute with R' Yehudah in this Baraisa follows the lines of their similar dispute in the Mishnah (*Rashi*). The reasoning behind each view was explained above, 124b note 24.

11. *Keilim* 5:6.

אם זרקה מבעוד יום לאשפה אסורה אמר בר המדורי אמר שמואל א קרומיות של מחצלת מותר לטלטלם בשבת מ"ט אמר רבא בר המדורי אסברא לי מחצלת גופא למאי חזיא לכסויי ביה עפרא הני נמי חזיין לכסויי בהו טינופת א"ר זירא אמר רב ב שירי פרומזיות אסור לטלטלן בשבת ג אמר אביי ג במטלניות שאין בהן ג' על ג' דלא חזיין לא לעניים ולא לעשירים: ת"ר ג שברי תנור ישן הרי הן ככל הכלים הניטלין בחצר דברי ר"מ ר' יהודה אומר אין ניטלין העיד ר' יוסי משום ר"א בן יעקב על שברי תנור ישן שניטלין בשבת ועל ד כיסויו שאינו צריך בית יד במאי קמיפלגי אמר אביי בעושין מעין מלאכה ואין עושין מעין מלאכתן קמיפלגי ואזדא ר' יהודה לטעמיה ור"מ לטעמיה מתקיף לה רבא אי הכי אדמיפלגי בשברי תנור ליפלגו בשברי כלים בעלמא אלא אמר רבא בשברי דהאי תנור קמיפלגי דתנן ה נתנו על פי הבור או על פי הדות ונתן שם אבן רבי יהודה אומר אם מסיק מלמטה והוא נסוק מלמעלה טמא ואם לאו טהור וחכמים אומרים הואיל והוסק מ"מ טמא ובמאי קמיפלגי בהאי קרא א תנור וכירים יותץ טמאים הם וטמאים יהיו לכם רבי יהודה סבר מחוסר נתיצה טמא שאין מחוסר נתיצה טהור ורבנן סברי טמאים יהיו לכם מ"מ ורבנן נמי הכתיב יותץ ההוא לאידך גיסא דסלקא דעתך אמינא כיון דחבריה בארעא כגופא דארעא דמי קמ"ל ואידך נמי הכתיב טמאים יהיו לכם ההיא כדרב יהודה אמר שמואל דאמר רב יהודה אמר שמואל מחלוקת בהיסק ראשון אבל בהיסק שני אפילו תלוי בצואר גמל אמר עולא והיסק ראשון לרבנן אפילו תלוי בצואר גמל מתקיף לה רב אשי אי הכי אדמיפלגי בשברי תנור ליפלגו בתנור גופה השתא תנור גופה לרבי יהודה לא הוי מנא שבריו מיבעיא אלא אמר רב אשי לעולם כדאמרן מעיקרא ובעושה מעשה טפקא ורבי מאיר לדבריו דרבי יהודה קאמר לדידי אפילו בעושין מעין מלאכה אלא לדידך אודי לי מיהא דכהאי גוונא מלאכתו הוא ורבי יהודה לא דמי התם הסקו מבפנים הכא הסקו מבחוץ התם מעומד הכא לאו מעומד: העיד ר' יוסי משום רבי אליעזר בן יעקב על שברי תנור ישן שניטלין בשבת ועל כיסויו שאינו צריך בית יד: אמר רבינא כמאן מטלטלינן האידנא כיסוי דתנורי דמתא מחסיא דאין להם בית אחיזה כמאן כר"א בן יעקב: **מתני'** ו האבן שבקירויה אם ממלאין בה ואינה נופלת ממלאין בה ואם לאו אין ממלאין בה

זמורה

רש"י

מבעוד יום. גלי דעתיה מאתמול דלאו מנא הוא: קרומיות של מחצלת. שנפרדו מן מחצלת ישנה: בר המדורי אסברא לי. בר המדורי פירש לי טעמו של דבר: לכסות בה עפרא. עומד לכסות בו צואה א"נ שלא יעלה האבק: שירי פרומזיות. טלימות כדאמר בסוכה (דף יא.) רמא תכלתא בפירמא לאינשי ביתיה: תנור ישן. שכבר הוסק ותכסיו קשים ומזו למלאכה: הרי הן ככל הכלים. לקמיה מפרש פלוגתייהו וטעמייהו: ועל כיסויו. של תנור שאינו צריך בית יד דבלאו בית אחיזה מטלטלין ליה ופלוגתא היא במתניתין דאיכא למ"ד בעינן בית אחיזה: מעין מלאכה. כגון לכסות בהן פי חבית: ואין עושין מעין מלאכתן. לאפות: ואזדא ר"מ לטעמיה. דאמר במתני' לא בעינן מעין מלאכתן: דהאי תנור. העשוי כעין זה שנשנו במשנה זו שאני מביא לך שלא נתקן כל צרכו מתחילתו ונשבר קמיפלגי: נתנו על פי הבור. תנורים שלהם עשוין כקדירות גדולות ואין להן שולים ומושיבו לארץ ומדביק טיט סביבותיו לעשותו עב שיחזיק חומו והיא קרויה טפילה והיא מגעת לארץ ומתוך כך הבל שלו קיים ואם נתנו על פי הבור או על פי הדות שהיא כעין בור אלא שהבור בחפירה והדות בבנין ונתן שם אבן בינו לבין דופן הבור לדוחקו שלא יפול ויהא עומד בחוזק: רבי יהודה אומר. אם דופנותיו למעלה קרובים לדופני הבור שלא הוצרך לתת ביניהם אלא אבן דקה ואין אויר ניכר בין דופני התנור לדופני הבור שיעכב את היסק התנור אלא יועילו לו דופני הבור להחזיק את חומו ושוליו קרובים לשולי הבור שאם מסיקין אותו מלמטה שעושין האור בבור והתנור ניסוק (א) מלמעלה בתוכו מאור דרך שוליו או שהתנור בתוך חלל הבור באויר והיסק עולה סביב דופנותיו וניסוק כגון שקצר מלמטה ורחב מלמעלה או הבור רחב מלמטה ופיו קצר טמא: ואם לאו. אלא נסוק כשאר תנורים מתוכו טהור כדמפרש טעמא דבעינן מחוסר נתילה שיהא קרוב להיות מחובר וכי אינו קרוב לארץ אין לך תנור נתוך מזה ואין לך לקיים בו תנור וכירים יותץ דנתילה לא שייכא אלא בבנין מחובר וכשאין מחובר שבירה שייכא ביה: טמאים הם וטמאים יהיו לכם. דכפל ביה קרא רבויא הוא שאע"פ שאינו מתוקן כל צרכו: ההוא לאידך גיסא. האי יותץ לאו לאגמורי קולא אתא ולמימר דאי ליכא לקיומי ביה נתילה כגון זה שאינו בנוי ומחובר וממילא הוא נתוך לליהוי טהור דהדר תנא ביה קרא וטמאים יהיו לכם לרבויי אלא לאגמורי חומרא אתא דלא תימא כל התנורים העשוים כהלכתן ומחוברים לארץ הרי הן כשאר בתים וכקרקע דמי הואיל וחברן ולא לקבל טומאה קמ"ל יותץ דאע"ג דשייכא ביה לשון נתילה כלומר דמחובר הוא טמא וכ"ש (ה) דמחוסר נתילה: בהיסק ראשון. שלא הוסק מעולם והיסק ראשון שנחלקו בו דההוא משוי ליה כלי כדתנן במס' כלים (פ"ה) איזהו גמר מלאכתו משיסיקנו לאפות בו סופגנין בההיא פליג ר' יהודה ואמר דאינו ראוי ליעשות כלי: אבל בהיסק שני. שמתחלה נעשה כשאר תנורים מחובר לארץ או לאבן עב והוסק שם ונעשה כלי וסוף נטלו משם ונתנו על פי הבור וכאן נטמא מודה ר' יהודה דאיתרבאי מוטמאים יהיו לכם: ואפילו תלוי בצואר גמל. אא"כ חלקו כדין טהרת תנור שצריך לשבור אף את חרסו ואינו נטהר בנטילתו שלם ממקומו: אמר עולא היסק ראשון לרבנן. דאמרי מריבוי דקרא ואע"ג דאין הבל שלו מתקיים יפה מקבל טומאה לא תימא נתנו ע"פ הבור דוקא אלא אפילו תלאו בצואר גמל והוסק שם היסק ראשון טמא: מתקיף לה רב אשי. אדרבא דאוקי פלוגתא דטלטול שברי תנור ישן דלעיל בשברים דכי האי תנור (ב) דהוא גופיה לר' יהודה לאו מנא הוא: כדאמרן מעיקרא. בעושין מעין מלאכה ולא מעין מלאכתן ושברי תנור מעליא קאמר ודקשיא לך אמאי נקט תנור ליפלוג בשברי כלי בהאי איצטריכא ליה ובעושין קצת מעין מלאכת אפייה כגון מעשה טפקא רעפים שקורין טובל"ש שמסיקין אותם ואופין בהן כך שברים אלו רחבים ומיהו אין להן תוך להסיקם מבפנים אלא מבחוץ כרעפים ולאו משום דבעי רבי מאיר מעין מלאכתן אלא משום דרבי יהודה נקט לה: ור"מ לדבריו דר' יהודה. נקט תנור וקאמר לדידי אפילו עושין מעין מלאכה כדאמר במתניתין: מעומד. בתנור אופין מעומד שהפת דבוקה לדופני התנור ועומדת ואינה מוטלת בשכיבה וע"ג שוליו כרעפים שהן שוכבות על לחכן: כיסוי דתנורי דמתא מחסיא. כיסוי תנור של אותו מקום לא היה להן בית אחיזה. תנור מפני שפיו למעלה יש לו כסוי שלא יצא הבל שלו לאחר שהדביק בו הפת מכסהו: מתני' האבן שבקירויה. דלעת יבישה חלולה וממלאין בה מים ומתוך שהיא קלה אינה שוקעת אלא צפה ונותנין בה אבן להכבידה: אם ממלאין בה ואינה נופלת. שקשורה יפה לפי שהקירויה שויא כלי: ואם לאו. הרי היא כשאר אבנים ואין מטלטל את הקירויה דשויא בסיס לאבן שנשאתה: זמורה

תוספות

אם זרקה מבעוד יום. השתא לא פריך אלא מעתה זרק לגלימא מבעוד יום דכיון דלא היה מוכן מבעו"י ליכא למימר לגלימי: **מחצלת** גופה למאי חזיא. לרווחא דמילתא מפרש הכי אע"ג דלא בעי מעין מלאכה לאשונה כדאמר רב נחמן לעיל חרס קטנה מותר לטלטלה בחצר משום דחזיא לכסויי בה מנא:

הרי הן ככל הכלים הניטלין בחצר. לאו דוקא בחצר לרב נחמן ולרבא דשרו בכרמלית וה"ה לר"ה:

בשעושין מעין מלאכה ואין עושין מעין מלאכתן. והא דנקט תנור ישן דשברי תנור חדש אין ראוין לכלום:

בשברי דהאי תנור קמיפלגי. לפי פירוש זה תימה הא דנקט תנור ישן דהיסק ראשון פליגי:

כמאן כר' אליעזר בן יעקב. וה"ה דה"מ למימר כרבי יוסי דסבר לקמן (ו) לטלטל כיסוי כלים שאין להם בית אחיזה ככלי דמכרעינהו בהכרעה אלא משום דמשנת ר' אליעזר בן יעקב קב ונקי: ואזדו

עין משפט נר מצוה

לב א מיי' פכ"ו מהל' שבת הלכה ח טור שו"ע או"ח סימן שח סעיף יב:
לג ב מיי' שם טוש"ע שם סעיף יג:
לד ג מיי' שם הל' יד:
לה ד מיי' פכ"ה מהל' שבת הלכה יג טור שו"ע או"ח סימן שח סעיף י:
לו ה מיי' פט"ו מהלכות כלים הלכה ח:
לז ו מיי' פכ"ה מהלכות שבת הלכה יח טוש"ע או"ח סימן שט סעיף ג:

רבינו חננאל

אתותסאי מסאני טינא. נטנפו מנעלין בטיט. פי' קרומיות. שירי מחצלאות שבלו. וזה שאמר ר' זירא אמר רב שירי פרומזיות אסור לטלטלן בשבת. פרומזיות. פירושו טליתות. כדאמרינן התם. רב יהודה רמי תכלתא בפרזמא דאינשי ביתיה. פי' תלא ציצית בטלית של אשתו. ופשוטה היא: ת"ר שברי תנור ישן. ס"א שירי תנור ישן הרי הן ככל הכלים וניטלין בחצר דברי ר' מאיר ר' יהודה אומר אין ניטלין. העיד ר' יוסי וכו'. ואמרינן במאי קא מיפלגי בעושין מלאכה ואין עושין מעין מלאכתן. ור"מ לטעמיה דהוא ת"ק דמתני'. וקיי"ל סתם משנה ר"מ דשרי. אע"פ שאין עושין מעין מלאכתן. ור' יהודה לטעמיה דאסר ולא קא שרי אלא בעושין מעין מלאכתן. ואתקף עליה רבא ולא מצא פירוק. ואוקים רבא פלוגתיהן בשברין דהאי תנור. דכיון דתנינן בפ' המביא כדי יין ת"ר תנור וכירים חדשים הרי הן ככל הכלים הניטלין בחצר. אבל אין סכין אותן שמן וכו' הוצרכו להודיע כי תנור חדש הראוי לאפות בו ניטל בחצר ושבריו כיוצא בו. ומצאנו חלוקה בתנור חדש לענין טומאה והאומר מקבל טומאה סבר הואיל ויתכן לאפות בו כלי גמור הוא. ושבריו כיוצא בו. והואיל וככלים חשובין ניטלין. ופירוש חלוקתן לענין טומאה וה"ה לטלטול. דתנן נתנו ע"פ הבור או ע"פ הדות ונתן שם אבן. ר' יהודה אומר אם מסיק מלמטה והוא ניסוק מלמעלה טמא ואם לאו טהור. וחכ"א הואיל והוסק מ"מ טמא. וכך פירושו תנור שנתנו ע"פ הבור או ע"פ הדות ונתן שם אבן בפי הבור או בפי הדות. סבר ר' יהודה אם מסיק מלמטה בבור או בדות וניסק מלמעלה התנור הרי הוא כבנוי בקרקע ונגמרה מלאכתו ונעשה כלי לאפות בו ומקבל טומאה ואם לאו לא נגמרה מלאכתו וחשוב הוא כקדירה שלא א) בפת' לה פת או לתת לתוכה תבשיל. שאין דרך התנור לאפות בו והוא תלוי. וחכ"א כיון שנגמר היסק הבור אבן ויכול להסיקו על האבן הרי הוא יכול לאפות בו. והיא כלי לקבל טומאה. וחלוקתן בזה הפסוק תנור וכירים יותץ. ר' יהודה סבר מדאמר קרא יותץ מכלל

שצריך להיות בנוי ואם [לאו] אינו כלי. ורבנן סברי טמאים מ"מ ואפילו אינו בנוי: תוספתא ומודה ר' יהודה בתנור שנתנו ע"פ הבור או ע"פ הדות ונתן שם אבן ומירחו בטיט מן הצדדים שהוא טמא. וחכ"א בין כך ובין כך טמא. ועל זו הדרך סוגיא ואתקיף לה רב אשי לרבא על זה שאמר ולא מצא פירוקו והעמיד רב אשי דברי אביי חזיק דבריו ולא בטעמו. אלא העמיד חלוקתם בשברי תנור שאופין עליהם מעשה טפקא. ופירושו שנותנין זה השבר ע"ג אבנים ומסיקין אש מלמטה ומרתיחין אותן השברין ומדבקין הפת מלמעלה וקיי"ל כר' אליעזר בן יעקב דהא רבינא פירש דמטלטלינן כיסוי דתנורי כר' אליעזר: מתני' האבן שבקירויה וכו'. פי' מביאין קרא יבשה ומוציאין בני מעיה ועושה אותה חללה. ועושין אותה כגון דרנוקא לדלות בה מים מן הבור והיא קלה ואינה שוקעת במים אלא היא צפה ע"פ המים ואין יכולין למלאות בה מים וכשרוצין להכבידה נותנין בתוכה אבן מהודקת שלא תהיה מתנדנדת וממלאין בה מים מן הבורות. וזה פי' האבן שבקירויה: את

מסורת הש"ס

א) [עי' תוספות לקמן קמ: ד"ה כיון וכו'], ב) [סוכה כז.], ג) [תוספ' פט"ו], ד) כלים פ"ה מ"ו, ה) בתוס' יו"ט פכ"ה דכלים משנה ו העתיק לשון רש"י וכ"ש שאינו מחוסר נתילה וכו"ל, ו) [דף קמו:].

הגהות הב"ח

(א) רש"י ד"ה ר' יהודה וכו' והתנור ניסוק בתוכו מלמעלה לאור: (ב) ד"ה מתקיף וכו' הלי תנור הס"ד ואח"כ מ"ה כתנור גופיה:

רב נסים גאון

דתנן נתנו על פי הבור או על פי הדות וכו'. זו המשנה במס' כלים בפרק ה' (משנה ו) תנור שנתנו בו עפר עד חציו מן העפר ולמטה מטמא במגע ולמעלה מטמא באויר נתנו על פי הבור או על פי הדות וכו' ועיקר זה הוא מה שנאמר בתורת כהנים (פ' שמיני פ"ט) [אין] מה כלי חרס בשמו אף תנור בשמו [תנור] שמו ת"ל אך מאימתי מקבל טומאה משיסקנו כדי לאפות בו סופגנין יותץ טמאים הם

תורה אור השלם

א) וְכֹל אֲשֶׁר יִפֹּל מִנִּבְלָתָם עָלָיו יִטְמָא תַּנּוּר וְכִירַיִם יֻתָּץ טְמֵאִים הֵם וּטְמֵאִים יִהְיוּ לָכֶם: [ויקרא יא, לה]

ליקוטי רש"י

תנור וכירים. (כלים יא) כלים המטלטלין הם והם של חרס ויש להן תוך ושופת את הקדרה על נקב החלל ושניהם פיהם למעלה. יותץ. שאין לכלי חרס טהרה בטבילה [ויקרא יא, לה].

חשק שלמה על רבינו חננאל

א) נ"ל שלא נגמרה מלאכתו ראויה לאפות.

HE PLACED A STONE THERE to wedge the oven in,[12] רַבִּי יְהוּדָה אוֹמֵר – R' YEHUDAH SAYS: אִם מַסִּיק מִלְּמַטָּה וְהוּא נִסּוֹק מִלְּמַעְלָה – IF ONE CAN HEAT the oven by lighting a fire UNDERNEATH it, on the floor of the pit or cistern, AND IT WILL BE HEATED effectively ABOVE,[13] טָמֵא – IT IS *TAMEI;*[14] וְאִם לָאו טָהוֹר – BUT IF NOT, IT IS *TAHOR.*[15] וַחֲכָמִים אוֹמְרִים – BUT THE SAGES SAY: הוֹאִיל וְהוּסַּק מִכָּל מָקוֹם טָמֵא – SINCE [THE OVEN] WAS HEATED BY ANY MEANS, IT IS *TAMEI.*[16]

The Gemara pauses to analyze this Mishnah:

וּבְמַאי קָמִיפַּלְגִי – **In what** issue **do they** (R' Yehudah and the Sages) **disagree?** בְּהַאי קְרָא – It is **in** regard to the interpretation of **the following verse:** "תַּנּוּר וְכִירַיִם יֻתָּץ – *An oven or a stove* (that became *tamei*) *shall be demolished,* טְמֵאִים הֵם וּטְמֵאִים יִהְיוּ לָכֶם" – *they are tamei and shall remain tamei to you.*[17] רַבִּי יְהוּדָה סָבַר – **R' Yehudah holds** that since the verse employs the expression "shall be *demolished,*" it implies that מְחוּסַּר נְתִיצָה טָמֵא – an oven **that** is somewhat attached to the ground so that it **lacks "demolishing" can be *tamei,*** שֶׁאֵין מְחוּסַּר נְתִיצָה טָהוֹר – whereas **one that** is not attached to the ground at all so that it **does not lack "demolishing" is** always ***tahor.***[18] וְרַבָּנַן סָבְרֵי – **But the Rabbis hold** that the superfluous phrase at the end of the verse, "טְמֵאִים יִהְיוּ לָכֶם" – ***[they] shall remain tamei to you,*** teaches that מִכָּל מָקוֹם – they are susceptible to *tumah* **in all cases,** whether they are attached to the ground or not.[19]

The Gemara seeks to clarify the Rabbis' view:

וְרַבָּנַן נַמִּי – **But** according to **the Rabbis too,** הָכְתִיב "יֻתָּץ" – **why,** the expression ***shall be demolished* is written,** and this implies that only an attached oven can become *tamei.* – ? –

The Gemara answers:

הַהוּא לְאִידָךְ גִּיסָא – The Rabbis hold that **that** expression should be interpreted **the opposite way** – not as restricting the class of ovens that are susceptible to *tumah* to those that are attached to the ground, but as expanding it to include *even* those that are attached to the ground![20] דְּסַלְקָא דַּעְתָּךְ אֲמִינָא – **For you might have thought** it appropriate **to say** that כֵּיוָן דְּחַבְּרֵיהּ בְּאַרְעָא כְּגוּפָא דְּאַרְעָא דָּמֵי – **since [the oven] was attached to the ground it is like the ground itself** and is not susceptible to *tumah.*[21] קָא מַשְׁמַע לָן – **[The Torah]** therefore **informs us,** through the expression *shall be demolished,* that even though an oven is attached to the ground it is susceptible to *tumah.*[22]

The Gemara now seeks to clarify R' Yehudah's view:

וְאִידָךְ נַמִּי – **Now,** according to **the other** Tanna (R' Yehudah), **too,** הָכְתִיב "טְמֵאִים יִהְיוּ לָכֶם" – **why, it is written:** ***shall remain tamei to you,*** which would seem to include even ovens that were not attached to the ground as being susceptible to *tumah.* – ? –

NOTES

12. The ancient oven consisted of a large earthenware cylinder, shaped like a bottomless pot, that was ordinarily placed on the ground. To facilitate the retention of heat, clay would be applied to the entire outer surface of the oven, from top to bottom, to thicken its walls and to form an airtight seal where the oven met the ground. A fire would be lit on the ground inside the oven, and a pot would be suspended above it or dough would be plastered to the interior oven wall.

The Mishnah cited here deals with a case where a person did not place the oven on the ground, but suspended it in the opening of a pit or cistern, using a stone to wedge it in place. Thus, the pit or cistern would in effect serve as an extension of his oven, which has no bottom of its own, and the fire would be lit at the bottom of the pit or cistern. [The cistern we are dealing with is shaped like a pit, but is an above-ground structure] (*Rashi;* cf. *Rambam, Commentary* and *Mishnah Acharonah* to *Keilim* 5:6). See diagram.

13. This would be the case if the oven fits snugly into the mouth of the pit so that only a thin stone was needed to wedge it in, leaving no noticeable gap through which heat can escape; and furthermore (cf. *Chidushei HaRan*), the pit is relatively shallow so that the heat rising from a fire on its floor through the open bottom of the oven will be sufficient for baking. Alternatively, if the oven is narrower on bottom than on top, or the pit is wider on bottom than on top, the oven may be suspended *inside* the pit so that the heat will envelop the oven and penetrate it through its walls, thereby making baking in the oven possible (*Rashi;* see *Chazon Ish, Keilim* 7:21-22). See diagram.

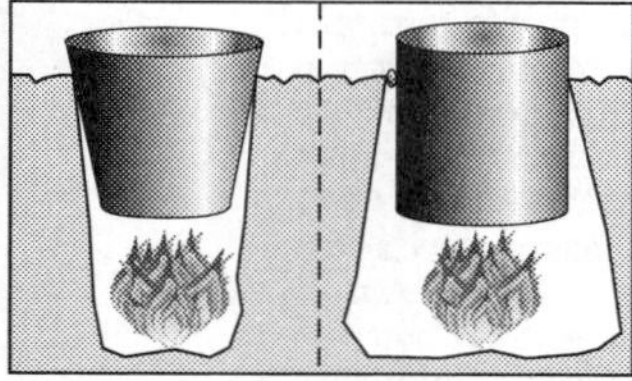

14. [I.e. it is susceptible to *tumah.*] Since the wedged oven can be heated effectively in its current position, it is considered sufficiently attached to the ground to be susceptible to *tumah* [even though it was not cemented down] (*Rashi;* see following notes for further clarification).

15. If a fire lit on the floor of the pit will not generate enough heat inside the oven for baking, but the fire must be lit in the oven itself on a makeshift floor [for example, on a stone that is placed in the pit,] the oven is not susceptible to *tumah.* As the Gemara will explain shortly, R' Yehudah derives from Scripture that an oven becomes susceptible to *tumah* only if it is attached to the ground in some measure. In the case where it is merely wedged into the mouth of a pit or cistern, it is considered "attached" if it can be heated by means of a fire on the floor of the pit, but not if it requires heating from its own makeshift floor (*Rashi;* see *Tiferes Yisrael* to *Keilim* 5:6 and *Chazon Ish* ibid.).

16. The Sages do not consider it necessary for an oven to be attached to the ground in order for it to become susceptible to *tumah* (see below). All agree, however, that an oven attains *tumah* susceptibility only upon being heated up for the first time, since the first heating completes the hardening of the oven walls (see *Keilim* 5:1, cited by *Rashi* below ד״ה בהיסק ראשון).

The relevance of this dispute to our discussion of *muktzeh* will be explained below, after the Gemara's clarification of the dispute.

17. *Leviticus* 11:35. The verse teaches that ovens (and other earthenware vessels) cannot be purified of their *tumah* through immersion in a *mikveh*. The *tumah* departs only when they are smashed (*Rashi* ad loc.).

18. The expression "demolishing" is appropriate only to structures that are attached to the ground. "Breaking" is the appropriate term for describing the destruction of ordinary vessels. By employing the former expression, the verse implies that an oven becomes susceptible to *tumah* only if it is first attached to the ground in some measure. One that is not attached to the ground at all is already demolished (albeit not "broken") and thus cannot become susceptible to *tumah* (*Rashi*).

[This limitation pertains only to ovens, which do not function properly unless they are attached to the ground (see *Rashi* ד״ה טמאים הם and ד״ה אמר עולא). Other vessels are susceptible to *tumah* only when *not* attached to the ground (see Gemara below and *Mishnah Acharonah* ibid.).]

19. The superfluous expression comes to include even an imperfect oven in the law of *tumah* susceptibility (*Rashi*).

20. I.e. the verse does not mean to teach that *only* attached ovens are susceptible to *tumah,* for the statement *they shall remain tamei to you* has included detached ovens in the law of *tumah.* Rather, the verse means to teach that *even* attached ovens are susceptible to *tumah* (*Rashi*; see *Maharsha* and *Chazon Ish* ibid. §24).

21. One might think that it should be regarded like a house, which is not susceptible to *tumah* because it is built upon the ground (*Rashi*).

22. The expression "shall be demolished" teaches that even an oven that requires demolition, i.e. one that is attached to the ground, is susceptible to *tumah*. Certainly, an oven that is unattached, and is like other utensils in that it does not require demolition, is susceptible to *tumah* (*Rashi*, as quoted by *Tos. Yom Tov* to *Keilim* 5:6).

[The reason an oven is subject to the unique rule of being susceptible to *tumah* even when attached to the ground is that it is actually a utensil, but is commonly attached to the ground to enhance its effectiveness (see *Mishnah Acharonah* ibid.).]

אם זרקה מבעוד יום לאשפה אסורה אמר בר המדורי אמר שמואל קרומיות של מחצלת מותר לטלטלם בשבת מ"ט אמר רבא בר המדורי אסברא לי מחצלת גופא למאי חזיא לכסויי ביה עפרא הני נמי חזיין לכסויי בהו טינופת א"ר זירא אמר רב שירי פרוזמיות אסור לטלטלן בשבת אמר אביי במטלניות שאין בהן ג' על ג' דלא חזיין לא לעניים ולא לעשירים: ת"ר שברי תנור ישן הרי הן ככל הכלים הניטלין בחצר דברי ר"מ ר' יהודה אומר אין ניטלין העיד ר' יוסי משום ר"א בן יעקב על שברי תנור ישן שניטלין בשבת ועל כיסויו שאינו צריך בית יד במאי קמיפלגי אמר אביי בעושין מעין מלאכה ואין עושין מעין מלאכתן קמיפלגי ואזדא ר' יהודה לטעמיה ור"מ לטעמיה מתקיף לה רבא אי הכי אדמיפלגי בשברי תנור ליפלגו בשברי כלים בעלמא אלא אמר רבא בשברי דהאי תנור קמיפלגי דתנן נתנו על פי הבור או על פי הדות ונתן שם אבן רבי יהודה אומר אם מסיק מלמטה והוא נסוק מלמעלה טמא ואם לאו טהור וחכמים אומרים הואיל והוסק מ"מ טמא ובמאי קמיפלגי בהאי קרא תנור וכירים יותץ טמאים הם וטמאים יהיו לכם רבי יהודה סבר מחוסר נתיצה טמא שאין מחוסר נתיצה טהור ורבנן סברי טמאים יהיו לכם מ"מ ורבנן נמי הכתיב יותץ ההוא לאידך גיסא דסלקא דעתך אמינא כיון דחבריה בארעא כגופא דארעא דמי קמ"ל ואידך נמי הכתיב טמאים יהיו לכם ההיא כדרב יהודה אמר שמואל דאמר רב יהודה אמר שמואל מחלוקת בהיסק ראשון אבל בהיסק שני אפילו תלוי בצואר גמל אמר עולא והיסק ראשון לרבנן אפילו תלוי בצואר גמל מתקיף לה רב אשי אי הכי אדמיפלגי בשברי תנור ליפלגו בתנור גופה השתא תנור גופה לרבי יהודה לא הוי מנא שבריו מיבעיא אלא אמר רב אשי לעולם כדאמרן מעיקרא ובעושה מעשה טפקא ורבי מאיר לדבריו דרבי יהודה קאמר לדידי אפילו בעושין מעין מלאכה אלא לדידך אודי לי מיהא דכהאי גוונא מלאכתו הוא ורבי יהודה לא דמי התם הסקו מבפנים הכא הסקו מבחוץ התם מעומד הכא לאו מעומד: העיד ר' יוסי משום רבי אליעזר בן יעקב על שברי תנור ישן שניטלין בשבת ועל כיסויו שאינו צריך בית יד: אמר רבינא כמאן מטלטלינן האידנא כיסוי דתנורי דמתא מחסיא דאין להם בית אחיזה כמאן כר"א בן יעקב: **מתני'** האבן שבקירויה אם ממלאין בה ואינה נופלת ממלאין בה ואם לאו אין ממלאין בה זמורה

רש"י

מבעוד יום. גלי דעתיה מאתמול דלאו מנא הוא: קרומיות של מחצלת. שנפרדו מן מחצלת ישנה: בר המדורי אסברא לי. בר המדורי פירש לי טעמו של דבר: לכסות בה עפרא. עומד לכסות בו צואה א"נ שלא יעלה האבק: שירי פרוזמיות. טליתות כדאמר בסוכה (דף יא.) רמא תכלתא בפירזמא דאינשי ביתיה: תנור ישן. שכבר הוסק ותרסיו קשים וחזו למלאכה: הרי הן ככל הכלים. לקמיה מפרש פלוגתייהו וטעמייהו: ועל כיסויו. של תנור שאינו צריך בית יד דלאו בית אחיזה מטלטלין ליה ופלוגתא היא במתניתין דאיכא למ"ד בעינן בית אחיזה: מעין מלאכה. כגון לכסות בהן פי חבית: ואין עושין מעין מלאכתן. לאפות: ואזדא ר"מ לטעמיה. דאמר במתני' לא בעינן מעין מלאכתן: דהאי תנור. העשוי כעין זה ששנוי במשנה זו שאני מביא לך שלא נתקן כל צרכו מתחילתו ובשבר קמיפלגי: נתנו על פי הבור. תנורים שלהם עשוין כקדירות גדולות ואין להן שולים ומושיבו לארץ ומדביק טיט סביבותיו לעשותו עב שיחזיק חומו והיא קרויה טפילה והיא מגעת לארץ ומתוך כך הבל שלו קיים ואם נתנו על פי הבור או על פי הדות שהיא כעין בור אלא שהבור בחפירה והדות בבנין ונתן שם אבן בינו לבין דופן הבור לדוחקו שלא יפול ויהא עומד באויר: רבי יהודה אומר. אם דופנותיו למעלה קרובים לדופני הבור שלא הוצרך לתת ביניהם אלא אבן דקה ואין אויר ניכר בין דופני התנור לדופני הבור שיעכב את היסק התנור אלא יועילו לו דופני הבור להחזיק את חומו ושוליו קרובים לשולי הבור שאם מסיקין אותו מלמטה שעושין האור בבור והתנור ניסוק (א) מלמעלה בתוכו מאור דרך שוליו או שהתנור בתוך חלל הבור באויר וההיסק עולה סביב דופנותיו וניסוק כגון שקצר מלמטה ורחב מלמעלה או הבור רחב מלמטה ופיו קצר טמא: ואם לאו. אלא נסוק כשאר תנורים מתוכו טהור כדמפרש טעמא דבעינן מחוסר נתיצה שיהא קרוב להיות מחובר וכי אינו קרוב לארץ אין לך תנור נתוץ מזה ואין לך לקיים בו תנור וכירים יותץ דנתיצה לא שייכא אלא בבנין מחובר וכשאין מחובר שבירה שייכא ביה: טמאים הם וטמאים יהיו לכם. דכפל ביה קרא רבויא הוא שאע"פ שאינו מתוקן כל צרכו: ההוא לאידך גיסא. האי יותץ לאו לאגמורי קולא אתא ולמימר דאי ליכא לקיומי ביה נתיצה כגון זה שאינו בנוי ומחובר וממילא הוא נתוץ דליהוי טהור דהדר תנא ביה קרא וטמאים יהיו לכם לרבויי אלא לאגמורי חומרא אתא דלא תימא כל התנורים העשוים כהלכתן ומחוברים לארץ הרי הן כשאר בתים וכקרקע דמי הואיל וחברן ולא לקבל טומאה קמ"ל יותץ דאע"ג דשייכא ביה לשון נתיצה כלומר דמחובר הוא טמא וכ"ש (ה) דמחוסר נתיצה: בהיסק ראשון. שלא הוסק מעולם והיסק ראשון שנחלקו בו דההוא משוי ליה כלי כדתנן במס' כלים (פ"ה) איזהו גמר מלאכתו משיסיקנו לאפות בו סופגנין בההיא פליג ר' יהודה ואמר דאינו ראוי ליעשות כלי: אבל בהיסק שני. שמתחלה נעשה כשאר תנורים מחובר לארץ או לאבן עב והוסק שם ונעשה כלי וסוף נטלו משם ונתנו על פי הבור וכאן נטמא מודה ר' יהודה דאיתרבאי מוטמאים יהיו לכם: ואפילו תלוי בצואר גמל. אא"כ חלקו כדין טהרת תנור שצריך לשבור אף את חרסו ואינו נטהר בנטילתו שלם ממקומו: אמר עולא היסק ראשון לרבנן. דאמרי מריבוי דקרא ואע"ג דאין הבל שלו מתקיים יפה מקבל טומאה לא תימא נתנו ע"פ הבור דוקא אלא אפילו תלאו בצואר גמל והוסק שם היסק ראשון טמא: מתקיף לה רב אשי. אדרבא דאוקי פלוגתא דטלטול שברי תנור ישן לעיל בשברים דכי האי תנור (ג) דהוא גופיה לר' יהודה לאו מנא הוא: כדאמרן מעיקרא. בעושין מעין מלאכה ולא מעין מלאכתן ושברי תנור מעליא קאמר ודקשיא לך אמאי נקט תנור ליפלוג בשברי כלי בהאי איצטריכא ליה ובעושין קצת מעין מלאכת אפייה כגון מעשה טפקא רעפים שקורין טובל"ש שמסיקין אותם ואופין בהן כך שברים אלו רקיקים ומיהו אין להן תוך להסיקם מבפנים אלא מבחוץ כרעפים ולאו משום דבעי רבי מאיר מעין מלאכתן אלא משום דרבי יהודה נקט לה: ור"מ לדבריו דר' יהודה. נקט תנור וקאמר לדידי אפילו עושין מעין מלאכה כדאמר במתניתין: מעומד. בתנור אופין מעומד שהפת דבוקה בדופני התנור ועומדת ואינה מוטלת בשכיבה ע"ג שוליו כרעפים שהן שוכבות על רחבן: כיסוי דתנורי דמתא מחסיא. כיסוי תנור של אותו מקום לא היה להן בית אחיזה. תנור מפני שפיו למעלה יש לו כסוי שלא יצא הבל שלו לאחר שהדביק בו הפת מכסהו: **מתני'** האבן שבקירויה. דלעת יבישה חלולה וממלאין בה מים ומתוך שהיא קלה אינה שואבת אלא צפה ונותנין בה אבן להכבידה: אם ממלאין בה ואינה נופלת. שקשורה יפה לפי הקירויה שויא כלי: ואם לאו. הרי היא כשאר אבנים ואין מטלטל את הקירויה דשויא בסיס לאבן שנושאתה: זמורה

תוספות

אם זרקה מבעוד יום. השתא לא פריך אלא מעתה זרק לגלימא מבעוד יום דכיון דלא היה מוכן מבעו"י ליכא לדמויי לגלימי: מחצלת גופה למאי חזיא. לרווחא דמילתא מפרש הכי אע"ג דלא בעי מעין מלאכה ראשונה כדאמר רב נחמן לעיל חרס קטנה מותר לטלטלה בחצר משום דחזיא לכסויי בה מנא: הרי הן ככל הכלים הניטלין בחצר. לאו דוקא בחצר לרב נחמן ולרבא דשרו בכרמלית ורה"ר: בשעושין מעין מלאכה ואין עושין מעין מלאכתן. והא דנקט תנור ישן דשברי תנור חדש אין ראוין לכלום: בשברי דהאי תנור קמיפלגי. לפי תירוץ זה תימה הא דנקט תנור ישן דבהיסק ראשון פליגי: כמאן כר' אליעזר בן יעקב. ה"ה דה"מ למימר כרבי יוסי דשרי לקמן לטלטל כיסוי כלים שאין להם בית אחיזה בכלי דמחבריהו בארעא אלא משום דמשנת ר' אליעזר בן יעקב קב ונקי: ואזדו

רבינו חננאל

אתווסאי מסאני טינא. נטנפו מנעלין בטיט. פי' קרומיות. שירי מחצלאות שבלו. וזה שאמר ר' זירא אמר רב שירי פרוזמיות אסור לטלטלן בשבת. פרוזמיות. פירושו טליתות. כדאמרינן התם. רב יהודה רמי תכלתא בפריזמא דאינשי ביתיה. פי' תלא ציצית בטלית של אשתו. ופשוטה היא: ת"ר שברי תנור ישן. ס"א שירי תנור ישן הרי הן ככל הכלים וניטלין בחצר דברי ר' מאיר ר' יהודה אומר אין ניטלין. העיד ר' יוסי וכו'. ואמרינן במאי קא מיפלגי בעושין מלאכה ואין עושין מעין מלאכתן. ור"מ לטעמיה דהוא ת"ק דמתני'. וקיי"ל סתם משנה ר"מ דשרי. אע"פ שאין עושין מעין מלאכתן. ור' יהודה לטעמיה דאסר ולא קא שרי אלא בעושין מעין מלאכתן. ואתקף עליה רבא ולא מצא פירוק. ואוקים רבא פלוגתיהן בשברין דהאי תנור. דכיון דתנינן בפ' המביא כדי יין ת"ר תנור וכירים חדשים הרי הן ככל הכלים הניטלין בחצר. אבל אין סכין אותן שמן וכו' הוצרכו להודיע כי תנור חדש הראוי לאפות בו ניטל בחצר ושבריו כיוצא בו. ומצאנו חלוקה בתנור חדש לענין טומאה והאומר מקבל טומאה סבר הואיל ויתכן לאפות בו כלי גמור הוא. ושבריו כיוצא בו. והואיל וככלים חשובין ניטלין. ופירשו חלוקתן לענין טומאה וה"ה לטלטול. דתנן נתנו ע"פ הבור או ע"פ הדות ונתן שם אבן. ר' יהודה אומר אם מסיק מלמטה והוא ניסוק מלמעלה טמא ואם לאו טהור. וחכ"א הואיל והוסק מ"מ טמא. וכך פירושו תנור שנתנו ע"פ הבור או ע"פ הדות ונתן שם אבן בפי הבור או בפי הדות. סבר ר' יהודה אם מסיק מלמטה בבור או בדות וניסק מלמעלה התנור הרי הוא כבנוי בקרקע ונגמרה מלאכתו ונעשה כלי לאפות בו ומקבל טומאה ואם לאו לא נגמרה מלאכתו וחשוב הוא כקדירה שלא א) בפת' לה פת או לתת לתוכה תבשיל. שאין דרך התנור לאפות בו והוא תלוי. וחכ"א כיון שנתן בפי הבור אבן ויכול להסיקו על האבן הרי הוא יכול לאפות בו. והיא כלי לקבל טומאה. וחלוקתן בזה הפסוק תנור וכירים יותץ. ר' יהודה סבר מדאמר קרא יותץ מכלל שצריך להיות בנוי ואם [לאו] אינו כלי. ורבנן סברי טמאים מ"מ ואפילו אינו בנוי: **תוספתא** ומודה ר' יהודה בתנור שנתנו ע"פ הבור או ע"פ הדות ונתן שם אבן ומירחו בטיט מן הצדדים שהוא טמא. וחכ"א בין כך ובין כך טמא. ועל זו הדרך סוגיא דהא שמעתא. ואתקיף לה רב אשי לרבא על זה שאמר ולא מצא פירוקי והעמיד רב אשי דברי אביי וחיזק דבריו ולא בטעמו. אלא העמיד חלוקתם בשברי תנור שאופין עליהם מעשה טפקא. ופירושו שנותנין זה השבר ע"ג אבנים ומסיקין אש מלמטה ומרתיחין אותן השברין ומדבקין הפת מלמעלה וקיי"ל כר' אליעזר ור"מ דהא רבינא פירש דמטלטלינן כיסוי דתנורי כר' אליעזר: **מתני'** האבן שבקירויה וכו'. פי' מביאין קרא יבשה ומוציאין בני מעיה ועושה אותה חלול דהנוקא לדלות בה מים מן הבור והיא קלה ואינה שוקעת במים אלא היא צפה ע"פ המים ואין יכולין למלאות בה מים וכשרוצין להכבידה נותנין בתוכה אבן מהודקת שלא תהיה מתנדנדת וממלאין בה מים מן הבורות. וזה פי' האבן שבקירויה: את

עין משפט נר מצוה

לב א מיי' פכ"ו מהל' שבת הלכה ח טור שו"ע או"ח סימן שח סעיף יג:
לג ב מיי' שם טוש"ע שם סעיף יג:
לד ג מיי' שם הל' יד:
לה ד מיי' פכ"ה מהל' שבת הלכה יג טור שו"ע או"ח סימן שח סעיף ז:
לו ה מיי' פט"ו מהלכות כלים הלכה ח:
לז ו מיי' פכ"ה מהלכות שבת הלכה יח טוש"ע או"ח סימן שט סעיף ג:

מסורת הש"ס

א) [עי' תוספות לקמן קמ: ד"ה כיון וכו'], ב) [סוכה מו.], ג) [תוספ' פט"ו], ד) כלים פ"ה מ"ו, ה) כתוס' יו"ט פכ"ה דכלים משנה ו העתיק לשון רש"י וכ"ש שאינו מחוסר נתיצה וכצ"ל, ו) [דף קכו:].

הגהות הב"ח

(א) רש"י ד"ה רבי יהודה וכו' והתנור ניסוק בתוכו מלמעלה לאור: (ג) ד"ה מתקיף וכו' דהאי תנור הס"ד ואח"כ מ"ה בתנור גופיה:

רב נסים גאון

דתנן נתנו על פי הבור או על פי הדות וכו'. זו המשנה במס' כלים בפרק ה' (משנה ו) תנור שנתן בו עפר עד חציו מעפר ולמטה מטמא במגע מעפר ולמעלה מטמא באויר נתנו על פי הבור או על פי הדות וכו' ועיקר זה הוא מה שנאמר בתורת כהנים (פ' שמיני פ"ט) [אין] מה כלי חרש בשמו אף תנור בשמו תנור שלא הוסק [תנור] שמו ת"ל אך מאימתי מקבל טומאה משיסיקנו כדי לאפות בו סופגנין יותץ טמאים הם

תורה אור השלם

א) וְכֹל אֲשֶׁר יִפֹּל מִנִּבְלָתָם עָלָיו יִטְמָא תַּנּוּר וְכִירַיִם יֻתָּץ טְמֵאִים הֵם וּטְמֵאִים יִהְיוּ לָכֶם: [ויקרא יא, לה]

ליקוטי רש"י

תנור וכירים. (כלים יא) כלים המטלטלין הם והם של חרס ויש להן תוך ושופת את הקדרה על נקב החלל ושניהם פיהם למעלה. יותץ. שאין לכלי חרס טהרה בנתיצה [ויקרא יא, לה].

חשק שלמה על רבינו חננאל

א) נ"ל שלא נגמרה שאינה ראויה לאפות.

The Gemara answers:

הַהִיא כִּדְרַב יְהוּדָה אָמַר שְׁמוּאֵל – **That** superfluous phrase can be interpreted **in accordance with** a teaching of **Rav Yehudah in the name of Shmuel.** דְּאָמַר רַב יְהוּדָה אָמַר שְׁמוּאֵל – **For Rav Yehudah said in the name of Shmuel:** מַחֲלוֹקֶת בְּהֶיסֵּק רִאשׁוֹן – **The dispute** between the Rabbis and R' Yehudah **pertains to the** very **first heating** of the oven.[23] אֲבָל בְּהֶיסֵּק שֵׁנִי – **But as for the second** or subsequent **heating,** all agree that אֲפִילּוּ תָּלוּי בְּצַוַּאר גָּמָל – **even if [the oven] is** detached from the ground and **suspended from the neck of a camel** while a fire is lit underneath, it remains susceptible to *tumah.* The verse *shall remain tamei for you* comes to teach us this law.[24]

The Gemara cites a final clarification of the Rabbis' view:

אָמַר עוּלָּא – **Ulla said:** וְהֶיסֵּק רִאשׁוֹן לְרַבָּנַן – **And the first heating** renders an oven susceptible to *tumah,* **according to the Rabbis** who do not require that it be attached to the ground, אֲפִילּוּ תָּלוּי בְּצַוַּאר גָּמָל – **even if it is suspended from the neck of a camel** for the heating.[25]

At any rate, R' Yehudah holds that a new oven does not become classified as a utensil with regard to *tumah* susceptibility unless it is attached to the ground for the first heating, whereas the Rabbis hold that it becomes classified as a utensil regardless of the circumstances of the first heating. Rava says that this very dispute finds expression with regard to the law of *muktzeh* in the Baraisa cited above. The Baraisa deals with the shards of an oven that was heated up for the first time while detached from the ground and then broke. R' Yehudah, who does not consider the oven a utensil while it is intact, holds that the shards too are not considered utensils and are therefore *muktzeh.* R' Meir, however, concurs with the Rabbis who consider the oven a utensil, and therefore he holds that when it breaks, its shards are non-*muktzeh.*[26]

Rava's explanation of the Baraisa is also rejected:

מַתְקִיף לָהּ רַב אַשִׁי – **Rav Ashi objected to this:** אִי הָכִי – **If so,** אַדְּמִיפַּלְגֵי בְּשִׁבְרֵי תַנּוּר – **instead of arguing about the shards of the oven** after it broke, לִיפַּלְגוּ בְּתַנּוּר גּוּפֵהּ – **they should have argued about** the status of **the oven itself** while it is undamaged! הַשְׁתָּא תַּנּוּר גּוּפֵהּ לְרַבִּי יְהוּדָה לֹא הָוֵי מָנָא – For **if even the oven itself is, according to R' Yehudah, not** considered **a utensil,** שִׁבְרָיו מִיבַּעְיָא – **is it necessary** to state that **its shards** are not considered utensils and are *muktzeh*?[27]

Rav Ashi therefore advances his own explanation of the Baraisa:

אֶלָּא אָמַר רַב אַשִׁי – **Rather, Rav Ashi said:** לְעוֹלָם כְּדַאֲמָרָן מֵעִיקָּרָא – **Actually, it is as we stated above,** that the dispute pertains to shards that are suitable to be used for some sort of task but not for a semblance of their former task.[28] וּבְעוֹשֶׂה מַעֲשֵׂה טַפְקָא – **And** specifically, it pertains to a case **where [the shards] can be used** for baking **in the manner of tiles,** by being heated from underneath to bake a dough that is resting on top of them.[29] וְרַבִּי מֵאִיר לְדִבְרָיו דְּרַבִּי יְהוּדָה קָאָמַר – **And R' Meir** focused on this case because he **spoke according to the opinion of R' Yehudah,** as follows: לְדִידִי אֲפִילּוּ בְּעוֹשִׂין מֵעֵין מְלָאכָה – **According to my [opinion],** shards may be moved **even if they can** be used to **perform any sort of task.** אֶלָּא לְדִידָךְ – **But** even **according to your [opinion],** that the shards must be suitable for a semblance of their former task, אוֹדִי לִי מִיהָא דְּכְהַאי גַּוְונָא מְלַאכְתּוֹ הוּא – **at least concede to me that in this case,** where the shards of an oven can be used for baking in the manner of tiles, **[the current use]** is similar to **their** former **task** and they may therefore be moved. וְרַבִּי יְהוּדָה – **But R' Yehudah** holds that לֹא דָּמֵי – **[the current use] is not similar** to the former one. הָתָם הֶסֵּקוֹ מִבִּפְנִים – **There,** while the oven was intact, **it would be heated from the inside,** הָכָא הֶסֵּקוֹ מִבַּחוּץ – whereas **here,** once it has

NOTES

23. An oven becomes classified as a utensil — and thereby susceptible to *tumah* — when it is heated up for the first time and its walls are hardened (see *Keilim* 5:1). R' Yehudah's argument that an oven's susceptibility to *tumah* depends on its being attached to the ground pertains only to the first heating of the oven. He holds that it is not fit to become classified as a functional utensil unless it is attached to the ground for the heating (*Rashi*).

24. R' Yehudah concedes that, once an oven attained classification as a utensil by being heated up while attached to the ground or to a thick stone, it retains this classification even if it is subsequently detached from the ground. It thus remains susceptible to *tumah* if one placed it loosely in the mouth of a pit, and even if one suspended it in the air. This is what the phrase *shall remain tamei to you* comes to teach — that as long as the oven is intact it remains susceptible to *tumah*. The only way for an oven that had been classified as a utensil to lose this classification is through shattering (*Rashi*).

25. I.e. one should not think that the Rabbis require that an oven be at least placed into the mouth of a pit for the first heating in order for *tumah* susceptibility to devolve upon it. It is not so, for since the Rabbis expound the phrase *they shall remain tamei to you* as including in the law of *tumah* those ovens that do not retain heat effectively, they learn to include even one that was completely suspended in the air for its first heating (*Rashi*).

Let us briefly summarize the two opinions: R' Yehudah holds that the phrase *shall be demolished* teaches that since a detached oven does not function properly, an oven does not become classified as a utensil and susceptible to *tumah* unless it is attached to the ground for the first heating. He concedes, however, that once an oven has attained classification as a utensil it retains this status even if subsequently detached from the ground, as indicated by the phrase *shall remain tamei to you.*

The Rabbis hold that the phrase *shall remain tamei to you* teaches that an oven which was never attached to the ground is considered a utensil and susceptible to *tumah,* notwithstanding its poor quality. The phrase *shall be demolished* teaches that *even* an oven that is attached to the ground is susceptible to *tumah,* unlike other attached items.

26. *Rashi.* The Baraisa's reference to an "old" oven does not preclude this interpretation, because in the context of *muktzeh* "old" means merely that the oven's walls were hardened through at least one heating so that the shards are suitable for use (see *Rashi* above ד״ה תנור ישן; cf. *Tosafos* ד״ה בשברי; see *Maginei Shlomo, Sfas Emes* and *Chazon Ish* ibid.).

[See *Ramban, Rashba, Ritva* (*MHK* ed.) and *Chidushei HaRan* for a discussion of the analogy between the laws of *tumah* and those of *muktzeh*, and a comparison of our Gemara with the one above, 123a, which differentiates between these laws.]

27. [Thus, in the previous Baraisa, R' Yehudah should have stated the novel law that the oven is *muktzeh* even while intact, and we would have known that if it breaks, its shards are certainly *muktzeh.*]

28. And the shards come from an oven that was heated up while properly attached to the ground [so that all agree that the oven itself was non-*muktzeh* while intact] (*Rashi*).

29. Rav Ashi says this in response to the objection raised to this interpretation above — namely, why does the dispute focus on the shards of an *oven* when the same dispute could apply to the shards of any broken utensil? Rav Ashi explains that it was necessary to state the dispute in regard to shards that can be used for baking in this makeshift manner. That is, the shards are large enough for bread to be baked upon them, but unlike an oven, which is a round structure that is heated from within, the shards have no interior. They are merely curved fragments, similar to tiles or shingles, that can be placed above a fire and thus utilized for baking dough that rests on top of them. This function bears some resemblance to their former one.

Now, since R' Meir is the Tanna Kamma of our Mishnah, he clearly holds that even suitability for a function that is completely dissimilar to the former one would allow the shards to be moved. However, as the Gemara goes on to explain, he focused on the case of shards that can, like tiles, be used for baking, for the sake of disputing R' Yehudah's opinion (*Rashi*).

אם זרקה מבעוד יום לאשפה אסורה אמר בר המדורי אמר שמואל (א)קרומיות של מחצלת מותר לטלטלם בשבת מ״ט אמר רבא בר המדורי אסברא לי מחצלת גופא למאי חזיא לכסויי ביה עפרא הני נמי חזיין לכסויי בהו טינופת א״ר זירא אמר רב (ב)שירי פרוזמיות אסור לטלטלן בשבת (ג)אמר אביי (ב)במטלניות שאין בהן ג׳ על ג׳ דלא חזיין לא לעניים ולא לעשירים: ת״ר (ג)שברי תנור ישן הרי הן ככל הכלים הניטלין בחצר דברי ר״מ ר׳ יהודה אומר אין ניטלין העיד ר׳ יוסי משום ר״א בן יעקב על שברי תנור ישן שניטלין בשבת ועל (ד)כיסויו שאינו צריך בית יד במאי קמיפלגי אמר אביי בעושין מעין מלאכה ואין עושין מעין מלאכתן קמיפלגי ואזדא ר׳ יהודה לטעמיה ור״מ לטעמיה מתקיף לה רבא אי הכי אדמיפלגי בשברי תנור ליפלגו בשברי כלים בעלמא אלא אמר רבא בשברי דהאי תנור קמיפלגי דתנן (ה)נתנו על פי הבור או על פי הדות ונתן שם אבן רבי יהודה אומר אם מסיק מלמטה והוא נסוק מלמעלה טמא ואם לאו טהור וחכמים אומרים הואיל והוסק מ״מ טמא ובמאי קמיפלגי בהאי קרא (א)תנור וכירים יותץ טמאים הם וטמאים יהיו לכם רבי יהודה סבר מחוסר נתיצה טמא שאין מחוסר נתיצה טהור ורבנן סברי טמאים יהיו לכם מ״מ ורבנן נמי הכתיב יותץ ההוא לאידך גיסא דסלקא דעתך אמינא כיון דחבריה בארעא כגופא דארעא דמי קמ״ל ואידך נמי הכתיב טמאים יהיו לכם ההיא כדרב יהודה אמר שמואל דאמר רב יהודה אמר שמואל מחלוקת בהיסק ראשון אבל בהיסק שני אפילו תלוי בצואר גמל אמר עולא והיסק ראשון לרבנן אפילו תלוי בצואר גמל מתקיף לה רב אשי אי הכי אדמיפלגי בשברי תנור ליפלגו בתנור גופה השתא תנור גופה לרבי יהודה לא הוי מנא שבריו מיבעיא אלא אמר רב אשי לעולם כדאמרן מעיקרא ובעושה מעשה טפקא ורבי מאיר לדבריו דרבי יהודה קאמר לדידי אפילו בעושין מעין מלאכה אלא לדידך אודי לי מיהא דכהאי גוונא מלאכתו הוא ורבי יהודה לא דמי התם הסקו מבפנים הכא הסקו מבחוץ התם מעומד הכא לאו מעומד: העיד ר׳ יוסי משום רבי אליעזר בן יעקב על שברי תנור ישן שניטלין בשבת ועל כיסויו שאינו צריך בית יד: אמר רבינא כמאן מטלטלינן האידנא כיסוי דתנורי דמתא מחסיא דאין להם בית אחיזה כמאן כר״א בן יעקב: **מתני׳** (ו)האבן שבקירויה אם ממלאין בה ואינה נופלת ממלאין בה ואם לאו אין ממלאין בה

זמורה

רש״י

מבעוד יום. גלי דעתיה מאתמול דלאו מנא הוא: **קרומיות של מחצלת.** שנפרדו מן מחצלת ישנה: **בר המדורי אסברא לי.** בר המדורי פירש לי טעמו של דבר: **לכסות בה עפרא.** עומד לכסות בו צואה א״נ שלא יעלה האבק: **שירי פרוזמיות.** טליתות כדאמר בסוכה (דף יח.) רמא תכילתא בפירמא לדאינשי ביתיה: **תנור ישן.** שכבר הוסק וחרסיו קשים וחזו למלאכה: **הרי הן ככל הכלים.** לקמיה מפרש פלוגתייהו וטעמייהו: **ועל כיסויו.** של תנור שאינו צריך בית יד דבלאו בית אחיזה מטלטלין ליה ופלוגתא היא במתניתין דאיכא למ״ד בעינן בית אחיזה: **מעין מלאכה.** כגון לכסות בהן פי חבית: **ואין עושין מעין מלאכתן.** לאפות: **ואזדא ר״מ לטעמיה.** דאמר במתני׳ לא בעינן מעין מלאכתן: **דהאי תנור.** העשוי כעין זה ששנו במשנה זו שאני מביא לך שלא נתקן כל צרכו מתחילתו ושבר קמיפלגי: **נתנו על פי הבור.** תנורים שלהם עשוין כקדירות גדולות ואין להן שולים ומושיבו לארץ ומדביק טיט סביבותיו לעשותו עב שיחזיק חומו והיא קרויה טפילה והיא מגעת לארץ ומתוך כך הבל שלו קיים ואם נתנו על פי הבור או על פי הדות שהיא כעין בור אלא שהבור בחפירה והדות בבנין ונתן שם אבן בינו לבין דופן הבור לדוחקו שלא יפול ויהא עומד באויר: **רבי יהודה אומר.** אם דופנותיו למעלה קרובים לדופני הבור שלא הוצרך לתת בינתים אלא אבן דקה ואין אויר ניכר בין דופני התנור לדופני הבור שיעכב את היסק התנור אלא יועילו לו דופני הבור להחזיק את חומו ושוליו קרובים לשולי הבור שאם מסיקין אותו מלמטה שעושין האור בבור והתנור ניסוק (א) מלמעלה בתוכו מאור דרך שוליו או שהתנור בתוך חלל הבור באויר והיסק עולה סביב דופנותיו וניסוק כגון שקצר מלמטה ורחב מלמעלה או הבור רחב מלמטה ופיו קצר טמא: **ואם לאו.** אלא נסוק כשאר תנורים מתוקן טהור כדמפרש טעמא דבעינן מחוסר נתיצה שיהא קרוב להיות מחובר וכי אינו קרוב לארץ אין לך תנור נתוץ מזה ואין לך לקיים בו תנור וכירים יותץ דנתילה לא שייכא אלא בבנין מחובר וכשאין מחובר שבירה שייכא ביה: **טמאים הם וטמאים יהיו לכם.** דכפל ביה קרא רבויא הוא שאע״פ שאינו מתוקן כל צרכו: **ההוא לאידך גיסא.** האי יותץ לאו לאגמורי קולא אתא ולמימר דאי ליכא לקיומי ביה נתילה כגון זה שאינו בנוי ומחובר וממילא הוא נתוץ דליהוי טהור דהדר תנא ביה קרא וטמאים יהיו לכם לרבויי אלא לאגמורי חומרא אתא דלא תימא כל התנורים העשוים כהלכתן ומחוברים לארץ הרי הן כשאר בתים וכקרקע דמי הואיל וחברן ולא לקבל טומאה קמ״ל יותץ דאע״ג דשייכא ביה לשון נתילה כלומר דמחובר הוא טמא וכ״ש (א) דמחוסר נתילה: **בהיסק ראשון.** שלא הוסק מעולם והיסק ראשון שנחלקו בו דההוא משוי ליה כלי כדתנן במס׳ כלים (פ״ה) איזהו גמר מלאכתו משיסיקנו לאפות בו סופגנין בההיא פליג ר׳ יהודה ואמר דאינו ראוי ליעשות כלי: **אבל בהיסק שני.** שמתחלה נעשה כשאר תנורים מחובר לארץ או לאבן עב והוסק שם ונעשה כלי וסוף נטלו משם ונתנו על פי הבור וכאן נטמא מודה ר׳ יהודה דאיתרבאי מוטמאים יהיו לכם: **ואפילו תלוי בצואר גמל.** אא״כ חלקו כדין טהרת תנור שצריך לשבור אף את חרסו ואינו נטהר בנטילתו שלם ממקומו: **אמר עולא היסק ראשון לרבנן.** דאמרי מריבוי דקרא ואע״ג דאין הבל שלו מתקיים יפה מקבל טומאה לא תימא נתנו ע״פ הבור דוקא אלא אפילו תלאו בצואר גמל והוסק שם היסק ראשון טמא: **מתקיף לה רב אשי.** אדרבא דאוקי פלוגתא דטלטול שברי תנור ישן דלעיל בשברים דכי האי תנור (ב) דהוא גופיה לר׳ יהודה לאו מנא הוא: **כדאמרן מעיקרא.** בעושין מעין מלאכה ולא מעין מלאכתן ושברי תנור מעליא קאמר ודקשיא לך אמאי נקט תנור ליפלוג בשברי כלי בהאי איצטריכא ליה דבעושין קצת מעין מלאכת אפייה כגון מעשה טפקא רעפים שקורין טוילל״ש שמסיקין אותם ואופין בהן כך שברים אלו רחבים ומיהו אין להן תוך להסיקם מבפנים אלא מבחוץ כרעפים ולאו משום דבעי רבי מאיר מעין מלאכתן אלא משום דרבי יהודה נקט לה: **ור״מ לדבריו דר׳ יהודה.** נקט תנור וקאמר לדידי אפילו עושין מעין מלאכה כדאמר במתניתין: **מעומד.** בתנור אופין מעומד שהפת דבוקה בדופני התנור ועומדת ואינה מוטלת בשכיבה ע״ג שוליו כרעפים שהן שוכבות על רחבן: **כיסוי דתנורי דמתא מחסיא.** כיסוי תנור של אותו מקום לא היה להן בית אחיזה. תנור מפני שפיו למעלה יש לו כסוי שלא יצא הבל שלו לאחר שהדביק בו הפת מכסהו: **מתני׳ האבן שבקירויה.** דלעת יבישה חלולה וממלאין בה מים ומתוך שהיא קלה אינה שואבת אלא צפה ונותנין בה אבן להכבידה: **אם ממלאין בה ואינה נופלת.** שקשורה יפה לפי הקירויה שויא כלי: **ואם לאו.** הרי היא כשאר אבנים ואין מטלטל את הקירויה דשויא בסיס לאבן שנושאתה:

זמורה

תוספות

אם זרקה מבעוד יום. השתא לא פריך אלא מעתה זרק לגלימא מבעוד יום דכיון דלא היה מוכן מבעו״י ליכא לדמויי לגלימי:

מחצלת גופה למאי חזיא. לרווחא דמילתא מפרש הכי אע״ג דלא בעי מעין מלאכה ראשונה כדאמר רב נחמן לעיל חרס קטנה מותר לטלטלה בחצר משום דחזיא לכסויי בה מנא:

הרי הן ככל הכלים הניטלין בחצר. לאו דוקא בחצר לרב נחמן ולרבא דשרו בכרמלית וה״ה ר״ה:

בשעושין מעין מלאכה ואין עושין מעין מלאכתן. והא דנקט תנור ישן דשברי תנור חדש אין ראוין לכלום:

בשברי דהאי תנור קמיפלגי. לפי תירוץ זה תימה הא דנקט תנור ישן דבהיסק ראשון פליגי:

כמאן כר׳ אליעזר בן יעקב. ה״ה דה״מ למימר כרבי יוסי דשרי לקמן (ו) לטלטל כיסוי כלים שאין להם בית אחיזה בכלי דחברינהו בארעא אלא משום דמשנת ר׳ אליעזר בן יעקב קב ונקי:

ואזדו

מסורת הש״ס

א) [עי׳ תוספות לקמן קמו: ד״ה כיון וכו׳], ב) [סוכה טז.], ג) [תוספ׳ פט״ו], ד) כלים פ״ח מ״ז, ה) [בתוס׳ יו״ט פכ״ה דכלים משנה ג העתיק לשון רש״י וכ״ש שאינו מחוסר נתיצה וכו׳], ו) [דף קכו:].

הגהות הב״ח

(א) רש״י ד״ה ר׳ יהודה וכו׳ והתנור ניסוק בתוכו מלמעלה לאור: (ב) ד״ה מתקיף וכו׳ האי תנור הס״ד ואח״כ מ״ה כתנור גופיה:

רב נסים גאון

דתנן נתנו על פי הבור או על פי הדות וכו׳. זו המשנה במס׳ כלים בפרק ה׳ (משנה ו) תנור שנתן בו עפר עד חציו מעפר ולמטה מטמא במגע מעפר ולמעלה טמא באויר נתנו על פי הבור או על פי הדות וכו׳ ועיקר זה הוא מה שנאמר בתורת כהנים (פ׳ שמיני פ״ט) [אין מה כלי חרש שמו אף תנור שמו תנור שלא הוסק [תנור] שמו ת״ל אך מאימתי מקבל טומאה משיסיקנו כדי לאפות בו סופגנין יותץ טמאים הם

תורה אור השלם

א) וְכֹל אֲשֶׁר יִפֹּל מִנִּבְלָתָם עָלָיו יִטְמָא תַּנּוּר וְכִירַיִם יֻתָּץ טְמֵאִים הֵם וּטְמֵאִים יִהְיוּ לָכֶם: [ויקרא יא, לה]

ליקוטי רש״י

תנור וכירים. (כלים יא) כלים המטלטלין הם והם של חרס ויש להן תוך ושופת את הקדרה על נקב החלל ושניהם פיהם למעלה. יותץ. שאין לכלי חרס טהרה בטבילה [ויקרא יא, לה].

חשק שלמה על רבינו חננאל

א) נ״ל שלא נגמרה מלאכתו לאפות.

עין משפט נר מצוה

לב א מיי׳ פכ״ו מהל׳ שבת הלכה ח טוש״ע או״ח סימן שח סעיף יב:
לג ב מיי׳ שם טוש״ע שם סעיף יג:
לד ג מיי׳ שם הל׳ יד:
לה ד מיי׳ פכ״ה מהל׳ שבת הלכה יג טוש״ע או״ח סימן שח סעיף ו:
לו ה מיי׳ פט״ו מהלכות כלים הלכה ח:
לז ו מיי׳ פכ״ה מהלכות שבת הלכה יב טוש״ע או״ח סימן שח סעיף ג:

רבינו חננאל

אתוסאי מסאני טינא. נטנפו מנעלין בטיט. פי׳ קרומיות. שירי מחצלאות שבלו. וזה שאמר ר׳ זירא אמר רב שירי פרוזמיות אסור לטלטלן בשבת. פירושו פרוזמיות. טליתות. כדאמרינן התם. רב יהודה רמי תכלתא בפריזמא דאינשי ביתיה. פי׳ תלא ציצית בטלית של אשתו. ופשוטה היא: ת״ר שברי תנור ישן. ס״א שירי תנור ישן הרי הן ככל הכלים וניטלין בחצר דברי ר׳ מאיר ר׳ יהודה אומר אין ניטלין. העיד ר׳ יוסי וכו׳. ואמרינן במאי קא מיפלגי בעושין מלאכה ואין עושין מעין מלאכתן. ור״מ לטעמיה דהוא ת״ק דמתני׳. וקיי״ל סתם משנה ר״מ דשרי. אע״פ שאין עושין מעין מלאכתן. ור׳ יהודה לטעמיה דאסר ולא קא שרי אלא בעושין מעין מלאכתן. ואתקף עליה רבא ולא מצא פירוק. ואוקים רבא פלוגתיהן בשברין דהאי תנור. דכיון דתנינן בפ׳ המביא כדי יין ת״ר תנור וכירים חדשים הרי הן ככל הכלים הניטלין בחצר. אבל אין סכין אותן שמן וכו׳ הוצרכו להודיע כי תנור חדש הראוי לאפות בו ניטל בחצר ושבריו כיוצא בו. ומצאנו חלוקה בתנור חדש לענין טומאה והאומר מקבל טומאה סבר הואיל ויתכן לאפות בו כלי גמור הוא. ושבריו כיוצא בו. והואיל וככלים חשובין ניטלין. ופירשו חלוקתן לענין טומאה וה״ה לטלטול. דתנן נתנו ע״פ הבור או ע״פ הדות ונתן שם אבן. ר׳ יהודה אומר אם מסיק מלמטה והוא ניסוק מלמעלה טמא ואם לאו טהור. וחכ״א הואיל והוסק מ״מ טמא. וכך פירושו תנור שנתנו ע״פ הבור או ע״פ הדות ונתן שם אבן בפי הבור או בפי הדות. סבר ר׳ יהודה אם מסיק מלמטה בבור או בדות וניסק מלמעלה התנור הרי הוא כבנוי בקרקע ונגמרה מלאכתו ונעשה כלי לאפות בו ומקבל טומאה ואם לאו לא נגמרה מלאכתו וחשוב הוא כקדירה שלא א) בפת׳ לה פת או לתת לתוכה תבשיל. שאין דרך התנור לאפות בו והוא תלוי. וחכ״א כיון שנתן בפי הבור אבן ויכול להסיקו על האבן הרי הוא יכול לאפות בו. והיא כלי לקבל טומאה. וחלוקתן בזה הפסוק תנור וכירים יותץ. ר׳ יהודה סבר מדאמר קרא יותץ מכלל שצריך להיות בנוי ואם [לאו] אינו כלי. ורבנן סברי טמאים מ״מ ואפילו אינו בנוי: **תוספתא** ומודה ר׳ יהודה בתנור שנתנו ע״פ הבור או ע״פ הדות ונתן שם אבן ומירחו בטיט מן הצדדים שהוא טמא. וחכ״א בין כך ובין כך טמא. ועל זו הדרך סוגיא דהא שמעתא. ואתקיף לה רב אשי לרבא על זה שאמר ולא מצא פירוקו והעמיד רב אשי דברי אביי חזיק דבריו ולא בטעמו. אלא העמיד חלוקתם בשברי תנור שאופין עליהם מעשה טפקא. ופירושו שנותנין זה השבר ע״ג אבנים ומסיקין אש מלמטה ומרתיחין אותן השברין ומדבקין הפת מלמעלה וכי׳ כר׳ אליעזר ור״מ דהא ורבינא פירש דמטלטלינן כיסוי דתנורי כר׳ אליעזר. פי׳ מביאין קרא יבשה ומוציאין כל מעיה ועושה אותה כגון דרנוקא לדלות בה מים מן הבור והיא אינה שוקעת במים אלא היא צפה ע״פ המים ואין יכולין למלאות בה מים וכשרוצין להכבידה נותנין בתוכה אבן מהודקת שלא תהיה מתנדנדת וממלאין בה מים מן הבורות. וזה פי׳ האבן שבקירוי׳:

את

been shattered, **[the shards] must be heated from the outside,** by a fire that is underneath them. הָתָם מְעוּמָּד – Furthermore, **there,** while the oven was intact, dough would be baked **in a standing position,** i.e. while attached vertically to the oven walls, הָכָא לָאו מְעוּמָּד – whereas **here,** once the oven has shattered, the dough is **not** baked **in a standing position,** but must be lying on top of the shards. Thus, the function of the shards is not similar to their former task.

The Baraisa stated:

הֵעִיד רַבִּי יוֹסֵי מִשּׁוּם רַבִּי אֱלִיעֶזֶר בֶּן יַעֲקֹב – R' YOSE TESTIFIED IN THE NAME OF R' ELIEZER BEN YAAKOV עַל שִׁבְרֵי תַנּוּר יָשָׁן שֶׁנִּיטָּלִין בְּשַׁבָּת – CONCERNING THE SHARDS OF AN OLD OVEN, THAT THEY MAY BE TAKEN ON THE SABBATH; וְעַל כִּיסּוּיוֹ שֶׁאֵינוֹ צָרִיךְ בֵּית יָד – AND CONCERNING ITS COVER, THAT IT DOES NOT NEED A HANDLE in order for one to be allowed to move it on the Sabbath.

The Gemara comments:

אָמַר רָבִינָא – **Ravina said:** כְּמַאן מְטַלְטְלִינַן הָאִידָּנָא כִּיסּוּי דְתַנּוּרֵי דְּמָתָא מְחַסְיָא – **In accordance with whom do we nowadays move the oven-covers of the town of Mechasya,** דְּאֵין לָהֶם בֵּית אֲחִיזָה – **which do not have handles?** כְּמַאן – **In accordance with whom?** כְּרַבִּי אֱלִיעֶזֶר בֶּן יַעֲקֹב – It is **in accordance with R' Eliezer ben Yaakov.**[30]

Mishnah This Mishnah discusses the law of a *muktzeh* object that is attached to a non-*muktzeh* object and functions as part of it:

הָאֶבֶן שֶׁבַּקֵּירוּיָה – **A stone that is in a gourd-shell**[31] – אִם מְמַלְּאִין בָּהּ וְאֵינָהּ נוֹפֶלֶת – **if** water **can be drawn with [the gourd-shell] without [the stone's] falling out,** for it is securely attached, מְמַלְּאִין בָּהּ – **we may draw** water **with it** on the Sabbath; וְאִם לָאו אֵין מְמַלְּאִין בָּהּ – **but if not, we may not draw** water **with it.**[32]

NOTES

30. As a rule, the halachah follows opinions stated by R' Eliezer ben Yaakov (see *Tosafos* ד״ה כמאן and *Yevamos* 37a; see 126b note 17, where this view will be explained further).

31. Dry gourd-shells, or dry pumpkin-shells, were used as buckets to draw water. Since the shell is light, it will not sink into the water unless a stone is placed in it to weigh it down (*Rashi*).

32. If the stone is securely fastened to the shell, it is regarded as part of the latter and is therefore deemed a utensil, and is not *muktzeh*. However, if it is not securely attached, it remains *muktzeh* like any other stone. Since the stone was placed in the shell before the Sabbath, the shell has been rendered a *base to muktzeh* and may not be used to draw water [or for any other purpose] (*Rashi*; see *Rashash*; see also *Shaar HaTziyun* 309:11).

אם זרקה מבעוד יום לאשפה אסורה אמר בר המדורי אמר שמואל [א]קרומיות של מחצלת מותר לטלטלם בשבת מ"ט אמר רבא בר המדורי אסברא לי מחצלת גופא למאי חזיא לכסויי ביה עפרא הני נמי חזיין לכסויי בהו טינופת א"ר זירא אמר רב (א) שירי פרוזמיות אסור לטלטלן בשבת (ב) אמר אביי [ב]במטלניות שאין בהן ג' על ג' דלא חזיין לא לעניים ולא לעשירים: ת"ר (ג) [ג]שברי תנור ישן הרי הן ככל הכלים הניטלין בחצר דברי ר"מ ר' יהודה אומר אין ניטלין העיד ר' יוסי משום ר"א בן יעקב על שברי תנור ישן שניטלין בשבת ועל [ד]כיסויו שאינו צריך בית יד במאי קמיפלגי אמר אביי בעושין מעין מלאכה ואין עושין מעין מלאכתן קמיפלגי ואזדא ר' יהודה לטעמיה ור"מ לטעמיה מתקיף לה רבא אי הכי אדמיפלגי בשברי תנור ליפלגו בשברי כלים בעלמא אלא אמר רבא בשברי דהאי תנור קמיפלגי דתנן (ד) [ה]נתנו על פי הבור או על פי הדות ונתן שם אבן רבי יהודה אומר אם מסיק מלמטה והוא נסוק מלמעלה טמא ואם לאו טהור וחכמים אומרים הואיל והוסק מ"מ טמא ובמאי קמיפלגי בהאי קרא (א) תנור וכירים יותץ טמאים הם וטמאים יהיו לכם רבי יהודה סבר מחוסר נתיצה טמא שאין מחוסר נתיצה טהור ורבנן סברי טמאים יהיו לכם מ"מ ורבנן נמי הכתיב יותץ ההוא לאידך גיסא דסלקא דעתך אמינא כיון דחבריה בארעא כגופא דארעא דמי קמ"ל ואידך נמי הכתיב טמאים יהיו לכם ההיא כדרב יהודה אמר שמואל דאמר רב יהודה אמר שמואל מחלוקת בהיסק ראשון אבל בהיסק שני אפילו תלוי בצואר גמל אמר עולא והיסק ראשון לרבנן אפילו תלוי בצואר גמל מתקיף לה רב אשי אי הכי אדמיפלגי בשברי תנור ליפלגו בתנור גופה השתא תנור גופה לרבי יהודה לא הוי מנא שבריו מיבעיא אלא אמר רב אשי לעולם כדאמרן מעיקרא ובעושה מעשה תפקא ורבי מאיר לדבריו דרבי יהודה קאמר לדידי אפילו בעושין מעין מלאכה אלא לדידך אודי לי מיהא דכהאי גוונא מלאכתו הוא ורבי יהודה לא דמי התם הסקו מבפנים הכא הסקו מבחוץ התם מעומד הכא לאו מעומד: העיד ר' יוסי משום רבי אליעזר בן יעקב על שברי תנור ישן שניטלין בשבת ועל כיסויו שאינו צריך בית יד: אמר רבינא כמאן מטלטלינן האידנא כיסוי דתנורי דמתא מחסיא דאין להם בית אחיזה כמאן כר"א בן יעקב: **מתני'** [ו]האבן שבקירויה אם ממלאין בה ואינה נופלת ממלאין בה ואם לאו אין ממלאין בה

זמורה

רש"י

מבעוד יום. גלי דעתיה מאתמול דלאו מנא הוא: קרומיות של מחצלת. שנפרדו מן מחצלת ישנה: בר המדורי אסברא לי. בר המדורי פירש לי טעמו של דבר: לכסות בה עפרא. עומד לכסות בו צואה אע"ג שלא יעלה האבק: שירי פרוזמיות. טליתות כדאמר בסוכה (דף יא.) רמא תכילתא בפירזמא דאינשי ביתיה: תנור ישן. שכבר הוסק וחרסיו קשים וחזו למלאכה: הרי הן ככל הכלים. לקמיה מפרש פלוגתייהו וטעמייהו: ועל כיסויו. של תנור שאינו צריך בית יד דבלאו בית אחיזה מטלטלין ליה ופלוגתא היא במתניתין דאיכא למ"ד בעינן בית אחיזה: מעין מלאכה. כגון לכסות בהן פי חבית: ואין עושין מעין מלאכתן. לאפות: ואזדא ר"מ לטעמיה. דאמר במתני' לא בעינן מעין מלאכתן: דהאי תנור. העשוי כעין זה ששנוי במשנה זו שאני מגלה לך שלא נתקן כל צרכו מתחלתו ובשבר קמיפלגי: נתנו על פי הבור. תנורים שלהם עשוין כקדירות גדולות ואין להן שולים ומושיבו לארץ ומדביק טיט סביבותיו לעשותו עב שיחזיק חומו והיא קרויה טפילה והיא מגעת לארץ ומתוך כך הבל שלו קיים ואם נתנו על פי הבור או על פי הדות שהיא כעין בור אלא שהבור בחפירה והדות בבנין ונתן שם אבן בינו לבין דופן הבור לדוחקו שלא יפול ויהא עומד באויר: רבי יהודה אומר. אם דופנותיו למעלה קרובים לדופני הבור שלא הוצרך לתת בינתים אלא אבן דקה ואין אויר ניכר בין דופני התנור לדופני הבור שיעכב את היסק התנור אלא יועילו לו דופני הבור להחזיק את חומו ושוליו קרובים לשולי הבור שאם מסיקין אותו מלמטה שעושין האור בבור והתנור ניסוק (א) מלמעלה בתוכו מאור דרך שוליו או שהתנור בתוך חלל הבור באויר וההיסק עולה סביב דופנותיו וניסוק כגון שקצר מלמטה ורחב מלמעלה או הבור רחב מלמטה ופיו קצר טמא: ואם לאו. אלא נסוק כשאר תנורים מתוכו טהור כדמפרש טעמא דבעינן מחוסר נתיצה שיהא קרוב להיות מחובר וכי אינו קרוב לארץ אין לך תנור נתוץ מזה ואין לך לקיים בו תנור וכירים יותץ דנתיצה לא שייכא אלא בבנין מחובר וכשאין מחובר שבירה שייכא ביה: טמאים הם וטמאים יהיו לכם. דכפל ביה קרא רבויא הוא שאע"פ שאינו מתוקן כל צרכו: ההוא לאידך גיסא. האי יותץ לאו לאגמורי קולא אתא ולמימר דאי ליכא לקיומי ביה נתיצה כגון זה שאינו בנוי ומחובר וממילא הוא נתוץ ליהוי טהור דהדר תנא ביה קרא וטמאים יהיו לכם לרבויי אלא לאגמורי חומרא אתא דלא תימא כל התנורים העשוים כהלכתן ומחוברים לארץ הרי הן כשאר בתים וכקרקע דמי הואיל וחברן ולא לקבל טומאה קמ"ל יותץ דאע"ג דשייכא ביה לשון נתיצה כלומר דמחובר הוא טמא וכ"ש (ה) דמחוסר נתיצה: בהיסק ראשון. שלא הוסק מעולם והיסק ראשון שנחלקו בו דההוא משוי ליה כלי כדתנן במס' כלים (פ"ה) איזהו גמר מלאכתו משיסיקנו לאפות בו סופגנין בההיא פליג ר' יהודה ואמר דאינו ראוי ליעשות כלי: אבל בהיסק שני. שמתחלה נעשה כשאר תנורים מחובר לארץ או לאבן עב והוסק שם ונעשה כלי וסוף נטלו משם ונתנו על פי הבור וכאן נטמא מודה ר' יהודה דאיתרבאי מוטמאים יהיו לכם: ואפילו תלוי בצואר גמל. אא"כ חלקו כדין טהרת תנור שצריך לשבור אף את חרסו ואינו נטהר בנטילתו שלם ממקומו: אמר עולא היסק ראשון לרבנן. דאמרי מריבוי דקרא ואע"ג דאין הבל שלו מתקיים יפה מקבל טומאה לא תימא נתנו ע"פ הבור דוקא אלא אפילו תלאו בצואר גמל והוסק שם היסק ראשון טמא: מתקיף לה רב אשי. אדרבא דאוקי פלוגתא דטלטול שברי תנור ישן דלעיל בשברים דכי האי תנור (ב) דהוא גופיה לר' יהודה לאו מנא הוא: כדאמרן מעיקרא. בעושין מעין מלאכה ולא מעין מלאכתן ושברי תנור מעליא קאמר ודקשיא לך אמאי נקט תנור ליפלוג בשברי כלי בהאי איצטריכא ליה ובעושין קצת מעין מלאכת אפייה כגון מעשה טפקא רעפים שקורין טולי"ש שמסיקין אותם ואופין בהן כך שברים אלו רחבים ומיהו אין להן תוך להסיקם מבפנים אלא מבחוץ כרעפים ולאו משום דבעי רבי מאיר מעין מלאכתן אלא משום דרבי יהודה נקט לה: ור"מ לדבריו דר' יהודה. נקט תנור וקאמר לדידי אפילו עושין מעין מלאכה כדאמר במתניתין: מעומד. בתנור אופין מעומד שהפת דבוקה בדופני התנור ועומדת ואינה מוטלת בשכיבה ע"ג שוליו כרעפים שהן שוכבות על רחבן: כיסוי דתנורי דמתא מחסיא. כיסוי תנור של אותו מקום לא היה להן בית אחיזה. תנור מפני שפיו למעלה יש לו כסוי שלא יצא הבל שלו לאחר שהדביק בו הפת מכסהו: **מתני'** האבן שבקירויה. דלעת יבישה חלולה וממלאין בה מים ומתוך שהיא קלה אינה שואבת אלא צפה ונותנין בה אבן להכבידה: אם ממלאין בה ואינה נופלת. שקשורה יפה לפי הקירויה שויא כלי: ואם לאו. הרי היא כשאר אבנים ואין מטלטל את הקירויה דשויא בסים לאבן שנעשתה:

זמורה

תוספות

אם זרקה מבעוד יום. השתא לא פריך אלא מעתה זרק לגלימא מבעוד יום דכיון דלא היה מוכן מבעו"י ליכא לדמויי לגלימי:

מחצלת גופה למאי חזיא. לרווחא דמילתא מפרש הכי אע"ג דלא בעי מעין מלאכה ראשונה כדאמר רב נחמן לעיל חרס קטנה מותר לטלטלה בחצר משום דחזיא לכסויי בה מנא:

הרי הן ככל הכלים הניטלין בחצר. לאו דוקא בחצר לרב נחמן ולרבא דשרו בכרמלית ורה"ר:

בשעושין מעין מלאכה ואין עושין מעין מלאכתן. והא דנקט תנור ישן דשברי תנור חדש אין ראוין לכלום:

בשברי דהאי תנור קמיפלגי. לפי תירוץ זה תימה הא דנקט תנור ישן דבהיסק ראשון פליגי:

כמאן כר' אליעזר בן יעקב. ה"ה דה"מ למימר כרבי יוסי דשרי לקמן (ו) לטלטל כיסוי כלים שאין להם בית אחיזה בכלי דמכרינהו בארעא אלא משום דמשנת ר' אליעזר בן יעקב קב ונקי:

ואזדו

מסורת הש"ס

א) [עי' תוספות לקמן קמו: ד"ה כיון וכו'], ב) [סוכה טז.], ג) [תוספ' פע"ז], ד) כלים פ"ה מ"ג, ה) בתוס' יו"ט פכ"ה דכלים משנה ו העתיק לשון רש"י וכ"ש שאינו ממוסר נתילה וכצ"ל, ו) [דף קמו:].

הגהות הב"ח

(א) רש"י ד"ה ר' יהודה וכו' והתנור ניסוק בתוכו מלמעלה לאור: (ב) ד"ה מתקיף וכו' האי תנור הס"ד ואח"כ מ"ה בתנור גופיה:

רב נסים גאון

דתנן נתנו על פי הבור או על פי הדות וכו'. זו המשנה במס' כלים בפרק ה' (משנה ו) תנור שנתן בו עפר עד חציו מעפר ולמטה מטמא במגע מעפר ולמעלה מטמא באויר נתנו על פי הבור או על פי הדות וכו' ועיקר זה הוא מה שנאמר בתורת כהנים (פ' שמיני פ"ט) [אין] מה כלי חרס בשמו אף תנור בשמו תנור שלא הוסק [תנור] שמו ת"ל אך מאימתי מקבל טומאה משיסיקנו כדי לאפות בו סופגנין יותץ טמאים הם

תורה אור השלם

א) וְכֹל אֲשֶׁר יִפֹּל מִנִּבְלָתָם עָלָיו יִטְמָא תַּנּוּר וְכִירַיִם יֻתָּץ טְמֵאִים הֵם וּטְמֵאִים יִהְיוּ לָכֶם: [ויקרא יא, לה]

ליקוטי רש"י

תנור וכירים. [כלים יא] כלים המטלטלין הם והם של חרס ויש להן תוך ושופת את הקדירה על נקב החלל ושניהם פיהם למעלה. יותץ. שאין לכלי חרס טהרה בנתיצה [ויקרא יא, לה].

חשק שלמה על רבינו חננאל

א) נ"ל שלא נגמרה מלאכה ראויה לאפות.

עין משפט נר מצוה

לב א מיי' פכ"ו מהל' שבת הלכה ח טור שו"ע או"ח סימן שח סעיף יג:
לג ב מיי' שם טוש"ע שם סעיף יג:
לד ג מיי' שם הל' יד:
לה ד מיי' פכ"ה מהל' שבת הלכה יג טור שו"ע או"ח סימן שח סעיף י:
לו ה מיי' פט"ו מהלכות כלים הלכה ט:
לז ו מיי' פכ"ה מהלכות שבת הלכה יח טוש"ע או"ח סימן שט סעיף ג:

רבינו חננאל

אתוותאי מסאני סיינא. נטנפו מגעלין בטיט. פי' קרומיות. שירי מחצלאות שבלו. וזה שאמר ר' זירא אמר רב שירי פרוזמיות אסור לטלטלן בשבת. פרוזמיות. פירושו טליתות. כדאמרינן התם. רב יהודה רמי תכלתא בפרוזמא דאינשי ביתיה. פי' תלא ציצית בטלית של אשתו. ופשוטה היא: ת"ר שברי תנור ישן. ס"א שירי תנור ישן הרי הן ככל הכלים וניטלין בחצר דברי ר' מאיר ר' יהודה אומר אין ניטלין. העיד ר' יוסי וכו'. ואמרינן במאי קא מיפלגי בעושין מלאכה ואין עושין מעין מלאכתן. ור"מ לטעמיה דהוא ת"ק דמתני'. וקיי"ל סתם משנה ר"מ דשרי. אע"פ שאין עושין מעין מלאכתן. ור' יהודה לטעמיה דאסר ולא קא שרי אלא בעושין מעין מלאכתן. ואתקף עליה רבא ולא מצא פירוק. ואוקים רבא פלוגתיהן בשברין דהאי תנור. דכיון דתנינן בפ' המביא כדי יין ת"ר תנור וכירים חדשים הרי הן ככל הכלים הניטלין בחצר. אבל אין סכין אותן שמן וכו' הוצרכו להודיע כי תנור חדש הראוי לאפות בו ניטל בחצר ושבריו כיוצא בו. ומצאנו חלוקה בתנור חדש לענין טומאה והאומר מקבל טומאה סבר הואיל ויתכן לאפות בו כלי גמור הוא. ושבריו כיוצא בו. הואיל וככלים חשובין ניטלין. ופירוש חלוקתן לענין טומאה וה"ה לטלטול. דתנן נתנו ע"פ הבור או ע"פ הדות ונתן שם אבן. ר' יהודה אומר אם מסיק מלמטה והוא ניסוק מלמעלה טמא ואם לאו טהור. וחכ"א הואיל והוסק מ"מ טמא. וכך פירושו תנור שנתנו ע"פ הבור או ע"פ הדות ונתן שם אבן בפני הבור או בפני הדות. סבר ר' יהודה אם מסיק מלמטה בבור או בדות וניסק מלמעלה התנור הרי הוא כבנוי בקרקע ונגמרה מלאכתו ונעשה כלי לאפות בו ומקבל טומאה ואם לאו לא נגמרה מלאכתו וחשוב הוא כקדירה שלא א) בפת' לה פת או לתת לתוכה תבשיל. שאין דרך התנור לאפות בו והוא תלוי. וחכ"א כיון שנתנו בפי הבור או בפי הדות ונתן על האבן ויכול להסיקו לאפות בו. הרי הוא יכול לקבל טומאה. וחלוקתן בזה הפסוק תנור וכירים יותץ. ר' יהודה סבר מדאמר קרא יותץ מכלל שצריך להיות בנוי ואם [לאו] אינו כלי. ורבנן סברי טמאים מ"מ ואפילו אינו בנוי: **תוספתא** ומודה ר' יהודה בתנור שנתנו ע"פ הבור או ע"פ הדות ונתן שם אבן ומירחו בטיט מן הצדדים שהוא טמא. וחכ"א בין כך ובין כך טמא. ועל זו הדרך סוגיא דהא שמעתא. ואתקיף לה רב אשי לרבא על זה שאמר ולא מצא פירוקי והעמיד רב אשי דברי אביי וחיזק דבריו ולא בטעמו. אלא העמיד חלוקתם בשברי תנור שאופין עליהם מעשה טפקא. ופירושו שנותנין זה השבר ע"ג השברין ומדבקין הפת מלמעלה וקיי"ל כר' אליעזר ור"מ דהא רבינא פירש דמטלטלינן כיסוי דתנורי כר' אליעזר: **מתני'** האבן שבקירויה וכו'. פי' מביאין קרא יבשה ומוציאין בני מעיה ועושה אותה חללה ודוקא לדלות בה מים מן הבור והיא קלה ואינה שוקעת במים אלא היא צפה ע"פ המים ואין יכולין למלאות בה מים וכשרוצין להכבידה נותנין בתוכה אבן מהודקת שלא תהיה מתנדנדת וממלאין בה מים מן הבורות. וזה פי' האבן שבקירויה:

את

זמורה שהיא קשורה בטפיח ממלאין בה בשבת [א] פקק החלון ר"א אומר בזמן שהוא קשור ותלוי פוקקין בו ואם לאו אין פוקקין בו וחכ"א בין כך ובין כך פוקקין בו:

גמ' [ב] תנן התם אבן שעל פי החבית מטה על צידה והיא נופלת אמר רבה א"ר אמי א"ר יוחנן [ג] [א] לא שנו אלא בשוכח אבל במניח נעשה בסים לדבר האסור ורב יוסף א"ר אסי א"ר יוחנן לא שנו אלא בשוכח אבל במניח נעשה כיסוי להחבית אמר רבה [ד] מותבינן אשמעתין האבן שבקירויה אם ממלאין בה ואינה נופלת ממלאין בה ולא היא התם כיון דהדקה שויא דופן אמר רב יוסף ומותבינן אשמעתין אם לאו אין ממלאין בה ולא היא התם כיון דלא הדקה בטולי בטלה במאי קמיפלגי מר סבר בעינן מעשה ומר סבר לא בעינן מעשה ואזדו לטעמייהו דכי אתא רב דימי א"ר חנינא ואמרי לה א"ר זירא א"ר חנינא פעם אחת הלך רבי למקום אחד ומצא נדבך של אבנים ואמר לתלמידיו צאו וחשבו כדי שנשב עליהן למחר ולא הצריכן רבי למעשה ור' יוחנן אמר הצריכן רבי למעשה מאי אמר להו [ב] רבי אמי אמר צאו ולמדום אמר להו רבי אסי אמר צאו ושפשפום אמר להו איתמר ר' יוסי בן שאול אמר סואר של קורות הוה ור' יוחנן בן שאול אמר גשוש של ספינה הוה מ"ד גשוש כ"ש סואר ומ"ד סואר אבל גשוש קפיד עליה: זמורה שהיא קשורה כו': [ג] קשורה אין לא קשורה לא לימא מתניתין דלא כרשב"ג דתניא [ה] חריות של דקל שגדרן לעצים ונמלך עליהן לישיבה צריך לקשור רבן שמעון בן גמליאל אומר אין צריך לקשור אמר רב ששת אפי' תימא רשב"ג הכא במאי עסקינן במחוברת באביה אי הכי קא משתמש במחובר לקרקע למטה מג' רב אשי אמר [ד] אפי' תימא בתלושה גזירה שמא יקטום: פקק החלון כו': [ו] אמר רבה בר בר חנה א"ר יוחנן [ה] הכל מודים שאין עושין אהל עראי בתחלה ביו"ט וא"צ לומר בשבת לא נחלקו אלא להוסיף שר"א אומר אין מוסיפין ביו"ט וא"צ לומר בשבת [ו] וחכ"א מוסיפין בשבת וא"צ לומר ביו"ט: מאי בין כך ובין כך אמר ר' אבא אמר רב כהנא בין

רש"י

זמורה. של גפן: שהיא קשורה בטפיח. פך ששואבין בו מן הבור או מן המעין: ממלאין בה. דשויא כלי להך זמורה: ותלוי. שאינו נגרר בארץ שהחבל שהוא קשור בו אינו מגיע לארץ: אין פוקקין בו. דמיחזי כמוסיף על הבנין: בין כך ובין כך. בגמרא מפרש לה: גמ' תנן התם. לקמן בהאי מסכתא: האבן שעל פי החבית. והוצרך ליטול מן היין שבתוכה: מטה. החבית על צדה והיא נופלת: לא שנו. דמותר לטלטל החבית והאבן עליה דקתני ואם היתה בין חביות שירא להטותה שם שלא תפול האבן על החבית שבצדה מגביה ומטה על צדה והיא נופלת: בשוכח. האבן עליה שלא במתכוין: אבל במניח נעשית. החבית בסיס לאבן שהיא דבר האיסור ואין מטלטל את החבית: ורב יוסף א"ר אסי. לקולא אמר ר' יוחנן לא שנו דהוצרך להטות את החבית ולא ניתן לטלטל האבן להדיא: אלא בשוכח. דלא נתכוין לעשותה כלי: אבל במניח נעשה. האבן כיסוי לחבית ומגלה אותה כדרכה: אשמעתין. על שמועה שלי שאמרתי במניח אין האבן נעשה כלי: ממלאין בה. אלמא אבן נעשה כלי: דהדקה. שקשרה יפה: ואם לאו אין ממלאין. ולא אמרינן נעשה כלי בהנחה בעלמא וקשיא לדידי דאמרי לעיל במניח נעשה כיסוי לחבית: ולא היא. לא קשיא לי דהתם הואיל ובלא קשירה לא חזיא למלאות דהא נפלה והאי לאו הדקה בטולי בטלה מתורת כלי גלי דעתיה דלא חשיב ליה אבל כיסוי חבית הנחה משויא ליה כלי: ואזדו לטעמייהו. ר' אמי ור' אסי: נדבך של אבנים. אבנים סדורות ומוקצות לבנין: מאי אמר להו. מאי מעשה הצריכן לרבי יוחנן: צאו ולמדום. סדרו אותם והשיבום כדי שלא נצטרך ליגע בהם למחר לפי שאין הזמנה במעשה [ח] כל דהו] מועלת לאבן לעשותה כלי ור' אמי לטעמיה דאמר לעיל אין אבן נעשית כלי בהנחה: למדום. כדאמרי' במו"ק (דף יב.) עושה להם למודים לסדר נסרים על פי הבור: ושפשפום. מן הטיט שיהו נאות לישב ולמחר תלמדום דבמעשה כל דהו נעשה כלי: סואר של קורות. הוה ולא אבנים: סואר. סדר של קורות חדשות שמסדרין אותן לבנין כדי שלא יתעקמו: גשוש. עץ ארוך שמגששים בו המים לפני הספינה לידע שהוא בעומקן שתוכל ספינה להלך בהן: קפיד עליה. שלא יתעקם ומייחד ליה מקום ומקצה ליה בידים ואפי' לר"ש אסור לטלטלו דמוקצה מחמת חסרון כיס אפי' ר"ש מודה: שאינה קשורה לא. ואפי' יש עקמומית כראשה כעין מזלג שראוי לתלות בה טפיח ולמלאות וחשב עליה: שגדרן לעצים. שחתכן להסיק: צריך לקשור. מע"ש: באביה. בגפן: והא קא משתמש במחובר. ואפילו קשורה מבעוד יום ליאסר: למטה מג'. סמוך לקרקע וכגון לשאוב מן המעין שאינו עמוק ומותר להשתמש באילן למטה מג' כדאמרי' בפרק בתרא דעירובין (דף צט:) היו שרשים גבוהין מן הארץ ג' לא ישב עליהם: גזירה שמא יקטום. שמא למחר תהיה לו ארוכה ויקטמנה מתוך שהיא רכה ונוחה לקטום ונמצא עושה כלי וחייב משום מכה בפטיש אבל בחריות לישיבה ליכא למיגזר הכי: הכל מודים שאין עושין אהל עראי. לפרוס מחצלת על ד' מחיצות או על ד' קונדסים להיות לו לאהל אבל מחצלה גג ולאו אהל הוא ושרי לפורסה לצניעות כדאמרי' בעירובין (דף ד.) בעובדא דשמואל ופקק החלון מתני' [ט] משום דבנין קבוע הוא ומיחזי כמוסיף על הבנין: להוסיף. כגון שהיה מחצלת פרוסה עליהן וכרוכה ונשאר בה אויר ולמחר פושטה דומיא דפקק דמוסיף בעלמא הוא: בין

תוספות

ואזדו לטעמייהו. תימה היכי הוה רבי אסי לטעמיה אדרבה פליגי דהכא קאמר ר' אסי נעשה כיסוי לחבית בהנחה גרידא בלא שום מעשה וגבי נדבך אמר ר' אסי לאו ושפשפום אמר להו דהיינו מעשה שהצריכן רבי ועוד קשה גבי נדבך קאמר דסגי בשפשוף ולקמן גבי כיסוי כלים א"ר אסי א"ר יוחנן והוא שיש בהם תורת כלי ויש לומר דכיסוי חבית סגי לה בהנחה שדרכו לעשותו כל דהו דלא בעי תיקון ומעשה גמור כשאר כיסוי כלים ונדבך של אבן מסותת ומרובע לבנין סגי להו בשפשוף שאין צריך עוד תיקון ומ"מ הוי ר' אסי לטעמיה דכי היכי דמיקל רבי אסי גבי נדבך ה"נ הכא והא דקאמר ר' אסי בפרק במה טומנין (לעיל דף נ.) חריות של דקל ישב אע"פ שלא קשר התם רב אסי גרסינן אי נמי ראויין הם לישיבה טפי מאבנים:

הכל מודים שאין עושין אהל עראי בתחלה. פי' בקונ' דלא אסיר אהל אלא למעלה בגג אבל בדפנות לא כדמוכח בעובדא דשמואל בכל גגות (עירובין דף לד.) דאיתמר חצר כותל שנפרצה רב אמר אין מטלטלין אלא בד' אמות ושמואל אמר זה מטלטל עד עיקר המחילה וזה מטלטל עד עיקר המחילה והא דרב לאו בפירוש איתמר אלא מכללא דשמואל הוה יתיב בההוא חצר נפל גודא דביני ביני אמר להו שמואל שקולו גלימא נגודי ליה אהדרינהו רב לאפיה כו' ושמואל למה ליה למיעבד הכי האמר זה מטלטל עד עיקר המחילה כו' שמואל לצניעותא בעלמא הוא דעבד אלמא משמע דאהל דדפנות שרי למיעבד הכי ורב שהיה מקפיד לאו משום עשיית אהל דשרי כדפרישית אלא הוה קפיד אמאי דהוו מטלטלין גלימא ד' אמות בחצר וקשה דע"כ שייך איסור אהל אפילו בדפנות כדאיתא בעירובין בפרק מי שהוציאוהו (דף מד. ושם) גבי עשיית דופן סוכה דפריך התם והאמר רבה בר בר חנה אמר רבי יוחנן הכל מודים שאין עושין אהל עראי בתחילה ומשני הא בדופן שלישית והא בדופן רביעית אלא נראה לר"ת דשפיר שייך בדפנות אהל היכא דמחילה מועלת להיתר והכי בדופן שלישית דהויא מחילה ומכשר ליה לסוכה חשיב עשיית אהל בתחלה אבל דופן רביעית אינה אלא תוספת בעלמא הואיל וכבר הסוכה היתה כשרה ועיקר פלוגתין דר"א ורבנן איתא באהל כעשיית דופן דפקק החלון משמע בחלון שבכותל דאי בגג מיירי הוה ליה למימר ארובה כמו שמצינו משלין פירות דרך ארובה (ביצה דף לה:) ומיהו באהל שבגגג נמי פליגי כדמוכח לקמן בפרק תולין (דף קלח:) דמייתי הך גבי טלית משמרת שהיא כעין גג וכן משמע בפרק בתרא דעירובין (דף קב.) דקאמר הנהו דיכרי דהוו בי רב הונא דיממא בעו טולא ובלילייא בעו אוירא אתא לקמיה דרב אמר ליה כרוך בודיא ושייר בה טפח דלמחר הוא מוסיף על אהל עראי ומותר ומשמע דהיינו נמי תוספת אהל עראי דפליגי רבי אליעזר ורבנן ועובדא דשמואל דכל

הלכך במחצלה סגי: שאין עושין אהל עראי. לפרוס מחצלת על ד' מחיצות או על ד' קונדסים להיות לו לאהל אבל מחצלה גג וזוקא גג אבל מחילה לאו אהל הוא ושרי לפורסה לצניעות כדאמרי' בעירובין (דף ד.) בעובדא דשמואל ופקק החלון מתני' [ט] משום דבנין קבוע הוא ומיחזי כמוסיף על הבנין: להוסיף. כגון שהיה מחצלת פרוסה עליהן וכרוכה ונשאר בה אויר ולמחר פושטה דומיא דפקק דמוסיף בעלמא הוא:

(לג.) לתלות בו שיהו לא יקטמנו או קטמו חייב חטאת: הכל מודים. ר"א ומחלוקתו נחלקו במוספת אהל עראי גבי פקק חלון דאיכא למאן דאמר פוקקין בו ואף על גב דמוסיף על אהל עראי הוא ומודים שאין עושין אהל עראי בתחלה (לקמן קמו.) דלפילו רבנן לא שרו אלא להוסיף ולא פסקו תוספת אהל מותר: אלא להוסיף. כגון פקק החלון ואיירי בשבת בפרק כל הכלים (שבת קכה.) ורבנן שרי למעבד לה להוסיף. (עירובין פט.)

עין משפט נר מצוה

לח א מיי' פכ"ה מהל' שבת הלכה יז סמג לאוין סה טוש"ע או"ח סימן שח סעיף כב וסימן שט סעיף ד:

לט ב מיי' שם הל' כא סמג שם טור שו"ע או"ח סימן שח סעיף כג:

מ ג מיי' פכ"ב מהלכות שבת הלכה ז:

מא ד ה מיי' פכ"ב מהל' שבת הלכה כז סמג לאוין סה טוש"ע או"ח סימן שטו סעיף א:

מב ו מיי' שם טוש"ע שם סעיף ג:

רבינו חננאל

וזה שאמר רבי צאו ולמדום עשו להם לימודים. יש מי שאומר עיינו בהן. כלומר לימוד בעינן בלא מעשה ור"א לימודים כגון הא ששנינו במסכת משקין. ר' יהודה אומר עושה לו לימודים בשביל שלא יחמיץ. והן כיסויים עצים ועליהם טיט (שרוצים מעשים) [שהצריכן למעשה] וראיתן הא דגרסינן בבמה טומנין תני רבה בר רב הונא קמי דרב חריות של דקל שגדרן לעצים ונמלך עליהם לישיבה צריך לקשר רשב"ג אומר אין צריך לקשר. ואמרינן מאן תנא דפליג עליה דרשב"ג. ר' חנינא בן עקביא היא שהלך למקום א' ומצא חריות של דקל שגרום לעצים כו': פיסקא זמורה שהיא קשורה בטפיח כו'. זמורה היא כגון אמיר והיא זמורה של כרם ארוכה כמו חבל וטפיח הוא כלי בדלי. ואמרה המשנ' אם זמורה זו היתה קשורה בטפיח ממלאין בה בשבת שעשאה מאתמול במקום חבל ועשה בה מעשה. ואם לאו אסור לחשב עליו בשבת להיותו בחבל. ואקשינן לימא מתניתין דלא כרשב"ג. דהא רשב"א בחריות שגדרן לעצים ונמלך עליהן לישיבה אין צריך לקשר. ופירק רב ששת זמורה זו מחוברת באביה. כלומר מחוברת בקרקע. ואם לא קשרה מאתמול לא ביטלה. ואינה דומה לחריות של דקל שהן גרודין. ואקשינן אי הכי היכי משתמש במחובר ופרקינן למטה משלשה. כדתנן היו שרשים גבוהין מן הארץ שלשה טפחים לא ישב עליהן. אם גבוהין ג' טפחים הוא דאסירא. הא בפחות מותר לישב עליהן. מיהא שמעינן דפחות מג' במחובר לקרקע כקרקע דמי ומותר להשתמש בו. ויש שאומרים כי המים הם קרובים בפחות משלש' ולא אתי למחתך. רב אשי אמר אפילו תימא בתלושה גזירה שמא יקטום: מתני' פקק החלון. כגון מסך העשוי לסתום החלון בין אם הוא מגבר בין מזולתו בזמן ששקשור ותלוי פוקקין בו. ואם לאו אין פוקקין בו. אמר (רבא) [רבה] בר בר חנה א"ר יוחנן הכל מודין שאין עושין אהל עראי בתחלה ביו"ט. ואין צ"ל בשבת. לא נחלקו אלא להוסיף. פי' שאם היה בו פקק פוקק במקצת החלון. ר' אליעזר אוסר למושכו כנגד כל החלון.

מסורת הש"ס

א) לקמן קלו: עירובין מד. סוכה כט. ב) [לקמן קמב:] ע"ש, ג) [לעיל קכ: לקמן קמב: ע"ש, ד) [קידושין כ:] וש"נ, ה) לעיל נ. ולקמן קנו:, ו) לקמן קלז: עירו' מד. פו ו, ז) [תוספתא סוכה פ"א], ח) גי' רש"א, ט) גי' רש"ל הוי למעלה בגג ולא מן הצד אבל הכ"ן מקיים פי' רש"י דהכא.

רב נסים גאון

את שיש לו נחיצה ואת שאין לו נחיצה אין לו טומאה: אי הכי קא משתמש במחובר לקרקע למטה מג' מכלל כי מה שיהיה מדבר המחובר לקרקע קרוב מהארץ פחות מג' טפחים מותר להשתמש בו ואין איסור משום שבות [רק] מה שהוא גבוה מן הארץ ג' טפחים ותמצא עיקר זה במשנה במס' עירובין בפרק המוצא תפילין (דף צט) אילן שהוא מיסך על הארץ אם אין נופו גבוה מן הארץ ג' טפחים לא ישב עליו ודבר זה אין בו חלוקה אבל חלקו רבא ורב ששת בשרשי אילן הבאים מלמעלה מג' לתוך ג' ובפ' בכל מערבין (שם דף לג:) תניא נתנו באילן בתוך ג' מותר לטלטל. סליק פרק כל הכלים

ליקוטי רש"י

פקק החלון. כגון ארובה הגג [לקמן קלז:]. שהוא קשור ותלוי. שם כל שעה. פוקקין בו. כיון דמוכן ועומד לכך אין זה לא בונה ולא מוסיף. ואם לאו אין פוקקין בו. דדמי כמוסיף הוא על סתימת אהל [סוכה כז:]. דדמי לבונה שמוסיף על סתימת הבית והוא על פי שעראי הוא אסור יחזור ויפתחנו [עירובין מד.]. מטה על צידה. מטה חבית על צדה כדי שהאבן צריך ליטול מן היין והאבן נופלת ולא עשאה בידים היתה בין החביות וירא שלא תפול האבן על החביות ותשברנה מגביה לחבית כולה ומטלקה מבין החביות ושם מטה על לדה. אלא בשוכח. שכח האבן עליה בין השמשות ולא מדעת [לקמן קמב:]. מותבינן אשמעתין. יש לי להשיב על דברי [קידושין ג:]. משמעות שמעתא [גיטין לח:]. אלדידיה גופיה קא מותיב [מנחות מט.]. סואר של קורות. כן קורות הערוכות על גבי קרקע זו על גב זו ועומדות לבנין [סוכה כ:]. המוסכמות לארץ על בנין [ביצה לא:]. גשוש של ספינה. כני אדם ממששים בכלונסות את עומק המים ואין מניחין לילך הספינה אלא במקום עמוק שמא תעמד לילך ותשקע לארץ במקום מושבה [לעיל ק:]. חריות. ענפים קשים כעין משוקים שדלאות של גלפין ונפלו עלין להן קרי לחן חריות. שגדרן. [קלעתו] כל [לקטום] ממרים קרי גדירה. צריך לקשור. לקשרם יחד מבעוד יום להוכיח שלישיבה עומדים ואם לא קשרם יחד אסור לטלטלן למחר דלא קא ממחשבה [שם נ:]. קא משתמש במחובר. דשימוש אילן שבות הוא כדתנן (ביצה לו:) אלו הן משום שבות לא עולין באילן [עירובין לב.]. למטה מג'. כל למטה מג' אמרינן כגון שאם אילן מותר (עירובין צט:) היו שרשים גבוהין מן הארץ שלשה לא ישב עליהן [שם לג.]. שמא יקטום. שמא יקצוץ ויתקננה לכך. אבל לחריות לא גזרו דתנן קומתן כלי דליכא למיגזר שמא יקטום.

(לג.) לתלות בו שיהו לא יקטמנו או קטמו חייב חטאת

זְמוֹרָה שֶׁהִיא קְשׁוּרָה בְּטָפִיחַ – **A vine that is tied to a pitcher**[1] – מְמַלְאִין בָּהּ בְּשַׁבָּת – **we may draw** water **with it on the Sabbath.**[2]

The Mishnah discusses a variant case:

פְּקַק הַחַלּוֹן – **A window shutter**[3] – רַבִּי אֱלִיעֶזֶר אוֹמֵר – **R' Eliezer says:** בִּזְמַן שֶׁהוּא קָשׁוּר וְתָלוּי – **When it is attached** to the building by a rope **and** the rope is so short that the shutter is **suspended** when not in use, פּוֹקְקִין בּוֹ – **we may shutter** the window **with it** on the Sabbath; וְאִם לָאו – **but if** the shutter is **not** suspended in this manner, אֵין פּוֹקְקִין בּוֹ – **we may not shutter** the window **with it.**[4] וַחֲכָמִים אוֹמְרִים – **But the Sages say:** בֵּין כָּךְ וּבֵין כָּךְ פּוֹקְקִין בּוֹ – **In either case we may shutter** the window **with it.**[5]

Gemara The Gemara cites a discussion related to the Mishnah's opening rule:

תְּנַן הָתָם – **We learned in a Mishnah elsewhere:**[6] אֶבֶן שֶׁעַל פִּי הֶחָבִית – A STONE THAT IS ON THE OPENING OF A CASK – מַטָּה עַל צִידָּהּ וְהִיא נוֹפֶלֶת – ONE MAY TILT [THE CASK] ON ITS SIDE SO THAT [THE STONE] FALLS OFF. If it was among other casks which might break if the stone would fall against them, one may lift the cask as is, remove it to a safe location and there tilt it on its side so that the stone falls off.[7] אָמַר רַבָּה אָמַר רַבִּי אַמִּי אָמַר רַבִּי יוֹחָנָן – **Rabbah said in the name of R' Ami, who said in the name of R' Yochanan:** לֹא שָׁנוּ אֶלָּא בְּשׁוֹכֵחַ – **They taught** this **only** concerning a case **where one forgot** the stone on top of the cask, אֲבָל בְּמַנִּיחַ – **but** in a case **where one left** it there intentionally before the Sabbath, נַעֲשָׂה בָּסִיס לְדָבָר הָאָסוּר – **[the cask] has become a base to a forbidden object** and may not be moved.[8] וְרַב יוֹסֵף אָמַר רַבִּי אַסִּי אָמַר רַבִּי יוֹחָנָן – **But Rav Yosef said in the name of R' Assi, who said in the name of R' Yochanan:** לֹא שָׁנוּ אֶלָּא בְּשׁוֹכֵחַ – **They taught** this **only** concerning a case **where one forgot** the stone on top of the cask, אֲבָל בְּמַנִּיחַ – **but** in a case **where one left** it there intentionally נַעֲשָׂה כִּיסּוּי לְהֶחָבִית – **it has become** classified as **a cover to the cask** and may be lifted outright.[9]

Rabbah cites a possible challenge to his version of R' Yochanan's opinion and then deflects it:

אָמַר רַבָּה – **Rabbah said:** מוֹתְבִינַן אַשְׁמַעְתִּין – **We can challenge our principle** from the Mishnah, which states: הָאֶבֶן שֶׁבַּקֵּירוּיָה – A STONE THAT IS IN A GOURD-SHELL – אִם מְמַלְאִין בָּהּ וְאֵינָהּ נוֹפֶלֶת מְמַלְאִין בָּהּ – IF WE CAN DRAW water WITH [THE GOURD-SHELL] WITHOUT [THE STONE'S] FALLING OUT, WE MAY DRAW WATER WITH IT. Thus, we see that when a stone is placed in a utensil it itself becomes part of the utensil, and thus, non-*muktzeh*![10] וְלֹא הִיא – **But** actually, **this is not** a contradiction to our view, הָתָם כֵּיוָן דְּהִדְקָהּ שַׁוְיָא דּוֹפֶן – for **there,** in the Mishnah's case, **since [the person] fastened [the stone] securely** to the shell **he has made it** part of **the** shell's

NOTES

1. A branch from a grapevine was tied to a pitcher to facilitate drawing water from a well or cistern (*Rashi*). [The particulars of the case are discussed in the Gemara.]

2. By tying the branch to the pitcher, one has made it part of the utensil (*Rashi*). [This explanation reflects only one of the Gemara's interpretations of this ruling; see notes 27 and 30.]

3. A board or anything else used to close a window (*Orach Chaim* 313:1). [This applies even to the shutter of a skylight, where the placing of the shutter is more akin to making an *ohel* (see *Mishnah Berurah* 313:1, *Chasam Sofer* here and *Rashi* below, 137b ד״ה פקק).]

4. Since it rests on the ground, when one picks it up to shut the window he appears to be adding to the structure, in violation of the *melachah* of בּוֹנֶה, *building* (*Rashi, Rav*). [Due to the appearance of building, this act is prohibited Rabbinically.] However, when the shutter is suspended, it has already been defined as part of the structure and putting it in the window is merely a matter of returning it to its former position (*Ritva MHK* ed.).

[Under the law of *muktzeh,* there would be no requirement that the shutter be suspended. Even if a plain board is used as the shutter, the *maximum* preparatory act that could be required to give it the status of a non-*muktzeh* utensil (i.e. a shutter) would be to attach it to the building (and perhaps, even this preparatory act is not required; see following note). It is to preclude the appearance of building that the shutter must be attached *and* suspended (*Rashba, Ritva MHK* ed.).]

5. The Gemara (126a) will explain this as meaning that one may use the shutter even if it is not tied to the building at all. The Sages hold that placing the shutter in the window temporarily is not prohibited under the *melachah* of building. [The Gemara will elaborate this point.] Furthermore, they hold that even if the shutter is a plain board it need not be attached to the structure in order to be classified as a non-*muktzeh* utensil. The mere designation of the board for this use suffices (see *Tosafos* to 126a ד״ה בין קשור, *Rashba* and *Ritva MHK* ed. there; see also *Rosh* §8, *Orach Chaim* 313:1 and 126a note 1; see Gemara, 126a, for an alternative explanation of the Sages' opinion).

According to *Rashi's* explanation of the Gemara (126a), even R' Eliezer agrees that merely designating the board as a shutter suffices to render it non-*muktzeh.* He requires both attaching and suspending it on account of the concern for building (see *Chasam Sofer, Beur HaGra* to *Orach Chaim* 313:1 and *Avnei Nezer* 224:14).

6. Below, 142b.

7. If one needs to take wine from the cask, he may not handle the stone to remove it, since it is *muktzeh*. Rather, he must tilt the cask so that the stone falls off. However, if this might cause damage, one may lift the cask and carry it to a safe location before tilting it (*Rashi* here and to 142b).

8. The rule that if the cask is among other casks one may carry it to another location before tilting it pertains only to a case where one left the stone on the cask unintentionally. If he left it there intentionally (i.e. in order to cover the cask and to leave it covered on the Sabbath), he may not lift the cask because it is a base to *muktzeh*. [Although he has designated the stone as a cover to the cask, its status is not elevated to that of a utensil, but it remains *muktzeh* (see below).] Nevertheless, he may tilt the cask in its place so that the stone falls off (*Rashi*, as explained by *R' Akiva Eiger*; cf. *Maharsha*).

[Ordinarily, something that is a base to a *muktzeh* item may not even be tilted to make the *muktzeh* item fall off, because the base itself attains the *muktzeh* status of the item that is resting on it. In our case, however, the cask does not serve the stone as a bona fide base. To the contrary, *the stone serves it* as a lid! Therefore, one is restricted only from lifting the cask while the stone is on it and thereby lifting the stone itself, but not from tilting the cask. If, however, one would place the stone on the cask so that it should rest there for the Sabbath, the cask would be serving it as a base and he would be forbidden even to tilt the cask (*R' Akiva Eiger,* thus resolving an apparent contradiction between *Rashi's* comments here and his comments to a similar Gemara on 142b [cited there in note 7]; see also *Baal HaMaor, Ritva MHK* ed.; cf. *Milchamos Hashem* and *Chasam Sofer*).]

9. According to Rav Yosef in the name of R' Assi, R' Yochanan qualified the Mishnah's rule in a lenient fashion. The Mishnah indeed refers exclusively to a case in which the stone was left on top of the cask inadvertently. However, the qualification is that if one left it there intentionally to serve as a lid, he is not required to tilt the cask so that the stone should fall off. Rather, he may lift the stone itself and replace it at will, for by using it as a lid he has elevated its status to that of a utensil (*Rashi;* see 126b note 14).

10. In our Mishnah's case, the stone becomes classified as a utensil by being placed in the shell [to serve as a weight]. This would seem to contradict the version of R' Yochanan's opinion cited by Rabbbah in the name of R' Ami — that a stone which is placed on a cask [to serve as its cover] does not become classified as a utensil (*Rashi*, as explained by *R' Akiva Eiger;* see also *Baal HaMaor* and *Ritva MHK* ed.).

זמורה שהיא קשורה בטפיח ממלאין בה בשבת ה) פקק החלון ר"א אומר בזמן שהוא קשור ותלוי פוקקין בו ואם לאו אין פוקקין בו וחכ"א בין כך ובין כך פוקקין בו: גמ' ג) תנן התם אבן שעל פי החבית מטה על צידה והיא נופלת אמר רבה א"ר אמי א"ר יוחנן א לא שנו אלא בשוכח אבל במניח נעשה בסים לדבר האסור ורב יוסף א"ר אסי א"ר יוחנן לא שנו אלא בשוכח אבל במניח נעשה כיסוי להחבית אמר רבה ד) מותבינן אשמעתין האבן שבקירויה אם ממלאין בה ואינה נופלת ממלאין בה ולא היא התם כיון דהדקה שויא דופן אמר רב יוסף ומותבינן אשמעתין אם לאו אין ממלאין בה ולא היא התם כיון דלא הדקה בטולי בטלה במאי קמיפלגי מר סבר בעינן מעשה ומר סבר לא בעינן מעשה ואזדו לטעמייהו דכי אתא רב דימי א"ר חנינא ואמרי לה א"ר זירא א"ר חנינא פעם אחת הלך רבי למקום אחד ומצא נדבך של אבנים ואמר לתלמידיו צאו וחשבו כדי שנשב עליהן למחר ולא הצריכן רבי למעשה ור' יוחנן אמר הצריכן רבי למעשה מאי אמר להו ג) רבי אמי אמר צאו ולמדום אמר להו רבי אסי אמר צאו ושפשפום אמר להו איתמר ר' יוסי בן שאול אמר סואר של קורות הוה ור' יוחנן בן שאול אמר גשוש של ספינה הוה מ"ד גשוש כ"ש סואר ומ"ד סואר אבל גשוש קפיד עליה: זמורה שהיא קשורה כו': ג) קשורה אין לא קשורה לא לימא מתניתין דלא כרשב"ג דתניא ה) חריות של דקל שגדרן לעצים ונמלך עליהן לישיבה צריך לקשור רבן שמעון בן גמליאל אומר אין צריך לקשור אמר רב ששת אפי' תימא רשב"ג הכא במאי עסקינן במחוברת באביה אי הכי קא משתמש במחובר לקרקע למטה מג' רב אשי אמר ד) אפי' תימא בתלושה גזירה שמא יקטום: פקק החלון כו': ז) אמר רבה בר בר חנה א"ר יוחנן ה) הכל מודים שאין עושין אהל עראי בתחלה ביו"ט וא"צ לומר בשבת לא נחלקו אלא להוסיף שר"א אומר אין מוסיפין ביו"ט וא"צ לומר בשבת י) וחכ"א מוסיפין בשבת וא"צ לומר ביו"ט: וחכ"א בין כך ובין כך פוקקין בו: מאי בין כך ובין כך אמר ר' אבא אמר רב כהנא

בין

רש"י

זמורה. של גפן: שהיא קשורה בטפיח. פך ששואבין בו מן הבור או מן המעין: ממלאין בה. דשויא כלי להך זמורה: ותלוי. שאינו נגרר בארץ שהחבל שהוא קשור בו אינו מגיע לארץ: אין פוקקין בו. דמיחזי כמוסיף על הבנין: בין כך ובין כך. בגמרא מפרש לה: גמ' תנן התם. לקמן בהאי מסכתא: האבן שעל פי החבית. והולך ליטול מן היין שבתוכה: מטה. החבית על לדה והיא נופלת: לא שנו. דמותר לטלטל החבית והאבן עליה דקתני ואם היתה בין חביות שירא להטותה שם שלא תפול האבן על החבית שבלדה מגביה ומטה על לדה והיא נופלת: בשוכח. האבן עליה שלא במתכוין: אבל במניח נעשית. החבית בסיס לאבן שהיא דבר האיסור ואין מטלטל את החבית: ורב יוסף א"ר אסי. לקולא אמר ר' יוחנן לא שנו דהולך להטות את החבית ולא נימן לטלטל האבן להדיא אלא בשוכח. דלא נתכוון לעשותה כלי: אבל במניח נעשה. האבן כיסוי לחבית ומגלה אותה כדרכה: אשמעתין. על שמועה שלי שאמרתי במניח אין האבן נעשה כלי: ממלאין בה. אלמא אבן נעשה כלי: דהדקה. שקשרה יפה: ואם לאו אין ממלאין. ולא אמרינן נעשה כלי בהנחה בעלמא וקשיא לדידי דאמרי לעיל במניח נעשה כיסוי לחבית: ולא היא. לא קשיא לי דהתם הואיל ובלא קשירה לא חזיא למלאות דהא נפלה והאי לאו הדקה בטולי בטלה מתורת כלי גלי דעתיה דלא חשיב ליה אבל כיסוי חבית הנחה משויא ליה כלי: ואזדו לטעמייהו. ר' אמי ור' אסי: נדבך של אבנים. אבנים סדורות ומוקצות לבנין: מאי אמר להו. מאי מעשה הצריכן לרבי יוחנן: צאו ולמדום. סדרו אותם והשיבום כדי שלא נצטרך ליגע בהם למחר לפי שאין הזמנה במעשה [ח) כל דהו] מועלת לאבן לעשותה כלי ור' אמי לטעמיה דאמר לעיל אין אבן נעשית כלי בהנחה: למדום. כדאמרי' במו"ק (דף יב.) עושה להם למודים לסדר נסרים על פי הבור: ושפשפום. מן הטיט שיהו נאות לישב ולמחר תלמדום דבמעשה כל דהו נעשה כלי: סואר של קורות. הוה ולא אבנים: סואר. סדר של קורות חדשות שמסדרין אותן לבנין כדי שלא יתעקמו: גשוש. עץ ארוך שמגששים בו המים לפני הספינה לידע שהוא בעומקו שתוכל ספינה להלך בהן: קפיד עליה. שלא יתעקם ומייחד ליה מקום ומקצה ליה בידים ואפי' לר"ש אסור לטלטלו דמוקצה מחמת חסרון כיס אפי' ר"ש מודה: שאינה קשורה לא. ואפי' יש עקמומית בראשה כעין מזלג שראוי לתלות בה טפיח ולמלאות וישב עליה: שגדרן לעצים. שחתכן להיסק: צריך לקשור. מע"ש: באביה. בגפן: והא קא משתמש במחובר. ואפילו קשורה מבעוד יום ליתסר: למטה מג'. סמוך לקרקע וכגון לשאוב מן המעין שאינו עמוק ומותר להשתמש באילן למטה מג' כדאמרי' בפרק בתרא דעירובין (דף לט:) היו שרשיו גבוהין מן הארץ ג' לא ישב עליהם: גזירה שמא יקטום. שמא למחר תהיה לו ארוכה ויקטמנה מתוך שהיא רכה ונוחה לקטום ונמצא עושה כלי וחייב משום מכה בפטיש אבל בחריות לישיבה ליכא למיגזר הכי הלכך במחשבה סגי: שאין עושין אהל עראי. לפרוס מחצלת על ד' מחילות או על ד' קונדסים להיות צל לאהל מן החמה ודוקא גג אבל מחילה לאו אהל הוא ושרי לפורסה לצניעות כדאמרי' בעירובין (ד' לד.) בעובדא דשמואל ופקק החלון דמתני' ט) משום דבנין קבוע הוא ומיחזי כמוסיף על הבנין: להוסיף. כגון שהיה מחצלת פרוסה עליהן וכרוכה ונשאר בה אויר ולמחר פושטה דומיא דפקק דמוסיף בעלמא הוא:

בין

תוספות

ואזדו לטעמייהו. תימה היכי הוה רבי אסי לטעמיה דלרבה פליגי דהכא קאמר ר' אסי נעשה כיסוי לחבית בהנחה גרידא בלא שום מעשה וגבי נדבך אמר ר' אסי לאו ושפשפום אמר להו דהיינו מעשה שהצריכן רבי ועוד קשה גבי נדבך קאמר דסגי בשפשוף ולקמן גבי כיסוי כלים א"ר אסי א"ר יוחנן והוא שיש בהם תורת כלי ויש לומר דכיסוי חבית סגי לה בהנחה שדרכו לעשותו כל דהו דלא בעי תיקון ומעשה גמור כשאר כיסוי כלים ונדבך של אבן מסותת ומרובע לבנין סגי להו בשפשוף שאין צריך עוד תיקון ומ"מ הוי ר' אסי לטעמיה דכי היכי דמיקל רבי אסי גבי נדבך ה"נ הכא והא דקאמר ר' אסי בפרק במה טומנין (לעיל דף נ.) חריות של דקל ישב לע"פ שלא קשר התם רב אסי גרסינן אי נמי דאיירי הם לישיבה טפי מאבנים:

הכל מודים שאין עושין אהל עראי בתחלה. פי' בקונ' דלא אסיר אלא אהל למעלה בגג אבל דפנות לא כדמוכח בעובדא דשמואל בכל גגות (עירובין דף צד.) דאיתמר מחצלת שנפרצה רב אמר אין מטלטלין אלא בד' אמות ושמואל אמר זה מטלטל עד עיקר המחילה וזה מטלטל עד עיקר המחילה והא דרב לאו בפירוש איתמר אלא מכללא דשמואל הוה יתיב בההוא חצר נפל גודא דביני ביני אמר להו שמואל שקולו גלימא נגודי ליה אהדרינהו רב לאפיה כו' ושמואל למה ליה למיעבד הכי האמר זה מטלטל עד עיקר המחילה כו' שמואל לצניעותא בעלמא הוא דעבד אלמא משמע דאהל דדפנות שרי למיעבד הכי ורב שהיה מקפיד לאו משום עשיית אהל דשרי כדפרישית אלא הוה קפיד אמאי דהוו מטלטלין גלימא ד' אמות בחצר וקשה דע"כ שייך איסור אהל אפילו בדפנות כדאיתא בעירובין בפרק מי שהוציאוהו (דף מד. ושם) גבי עשיית דופן סוכה דפריך התם והאמר רבה בר בר חנה אמר רבי יוחנן הכל מודים שאין עושין אהל עראי בתחילה ומשני הא בדופן שלישית והא בדופן רביעית אלא נראה לר"ת דשפיר שייך בדפנות אהל היכא דמחילה מועלת להיתר ולהכי בדופן שלישית דהויא מחילה ומכשר ליה לסוכה חשיב עשיית אהל בתחלה אבל דופן רביעית אינה אלא תוספת בעלמא הואיל וכבר הסוכה היתה כשרה ועיקר פלוגתין דר"א ורבנן איתא באהל כבעשיית דופן דפקק החלון משמע בחלון שבכותל דאי בגג מיירי הוה ליה למימר ארובה כמו ששנינו משילין פירות דרך ארובה (ביצה דף לה:) ומיהו באהל שבגג נמי פליגי כדמוכח לקמן בפרק תולין (דף קלח:) דמייתי הך גבי תליית משמרת שהיא כעין גג וכן משמע בפרק בתרא דעירובין (דף קב.) דאמר הנהו דיכרי דהוו בי רב הונא בימאמא בעו טולא ובליליא בעו אוירא אתא לקמיה דרב אמר ליה כרוך בודיא ושייר בה טפח דלמחר הוא מוסיף על אהל עראי ומותר ומשמע דהיינו נמי תוספת אהל עראי דפליגי רבי אליעזר ורבנן ועובדא דשמואל

דכל

עין משפט נר מצוה

לח א מיי' פכ"ה מהל' שבת הלכה יח סמג לאוין סה טוש"ע או"ח סימן שח סעיף כב וסימן שט סעיף ד:

לט ב מיי' שם הל' כא סמג שם טור שו"ע או"ח סימן שח סעיף כא:

מ ג מיי' פכ"ג מהלכות שבת הלכה ז:

מא ד ה מיי' פכ"ב מהל' שבת הלכה כז סמג לאוין סה טוש"ע או"ח סימן שטו סעיף א:

מב ו מיי' שם טוש"ע שם סעיף ג:

רבינו חננאל

וזה שאמר רבי צאו ולמדום עשו להם לימודים. יש מי שאומר עיינו בהן. כלומר לימוד בעינן בלא מעשה וי"א לימודים כגון זה ששנינו במסכת משקין. ר' יהודה אומר עושה לו לימודים בשביל שלא יתמיקו. והן כיסויי עצים ועליהם טיט (שרוצים מעשים) [שהצריכן למעשה] וראייתן הא דגרסינן בבמה טומנין תני רבה בר רב הונא קמי דרב חריות של דקל שגדרום לעצים ונמלך עליהם לישיבה צריך לקשר רשב"ג אומר אין צריך לקשר. ואמרינן מאן תנא דפליג עליה דרשב"ג. ר' חנינה בר עקביא היא שהלך למקום א' ומצא חריות של דקל שגדורים לעצים כו': פיסקא זמורה שהיא קשורה בטפיח כו'. זמורה היא כגון אמיר והיא זמורה של כרם ארוכה כמו חבל וטפיח הוא כלי בדלי. ואמרה המשנה אם זמורה זו היתה קשורה בזה הכלי ממלאין בה בשבת שעשאה מאתמול במקום חבל ועשה בה מעשה ואם לאו אסור לחשב עליו בשבת להיותו בחבל. ואמרינן לימא מתניתין דלא כרשב"ג. דהא רשב"ג בחריות שגדרן לעצים ונמלך עליהן לישיבה אין צריך לקשר. ופירק רב ששת זמורה זו מחוברת באביה. כלומר מחוברת בקרקע. ואם לא קשרה מאתמול לא בטלה. ואינה דומה לחריות של דקל שהן גרודין. ואקשינן אי הכי היכי משתמש במחובר ופרקינן למטה משלשה. כדתנן היו שרשין גבוהין מן הארץ שלשה טפחים לא ישב עליהן. אם גבוהין ג' טפחים הוא אסורה. הא בפחות מותר לישב עליהן. מיהא שמעינן דפחות מג' במחובר לקרקע כקרקע דמי ומותר להשתמש בו. ויש שאומרים כי המים הם קרובים בפחות משלש' ולא אתי למחתך. רב אשי אמר אפילו תימא בתלושה גזירה שמא יקטום: מתני' פקק החלון. כגון מסך העשוי לסתום החלון בין אם הוא מבגד בין מזולתו בזמן שקשור ותלוי פוקקין בו. ואם לאו אין פוקקין בו. אמר (רבא) [רבה] בר בר חנה א"ר יוחנן הכל מודים שאין עושין אהל עראי בתחלה ביו"ט. ואין צ"ל בשבת. לא נחלקו אלא להוסיף. פי' שאם היה בו פקק פוקק במקצת החלון. ר' אליעזר אוסר למשכן כנגד כל החלון. וחכמים מתירים (וזהו) להוסיף כיוצא בו בסוף המוצא תפילין הנהו דכרי דהוו לרב הונא דבימאמא בעו טולא ובליליא בעו אוירא. ואמר ליה רב כרוך בודיא עלייהו ושייר בה טפח ולמחר פרסיה

מסורת הש"ס

א) לקמן קלו: עירובין מד. סוכה מ:, ב) [לקמן קמב: ע"ש], ג) [לעיל קב: לקמן קמב: ע"ש], ד) [קידושין נ: וש"נ], ה) לעיל נ. ולקמן קסו:, ו) לקמן קלו: עירו' מד. סו:, ז) [תוספתא סוכה פ"א], ח) גי' רש"ל, ט) גי' רש"ל הוי למעלה בגג ולא מן הצד אבל הכ"ן מקיים פי' רש"י דהכא.

רב נסים גאון

את שיש לו נתיצה ואת שאין לו נתיצה אין לו טומאה: אי הכי קא משתמש במחובר לקרקע למטה מג' מכלל כי מה שיהיה מדבר המחובר לקרקע קרוב מהארץ פחות מג' טפחים מותר להשתמש בו ואין איסור משום שבות [רק] מה שהוא גבוה מן הארץ ג' טפחים ותמצא עיקר זה במשנה במס' עירובין בפרק המוצא תפילין (דף צט) אילן שהוא מיסך על הארץ אם אין נופו גבוה מן הארץ ג' טפחים לא ישב עליהן ודבר זה אין בו חלוקה אבל חלוקה רבא ורב ששת בשרשי אילן הבאים מלמעלה מג' לתוך ג' ובפ' בכל מערבין (שם דף לג) תניא נתנו באילן בתוך ג' מותר לטלטל: סליק פרק כל הכלים

ליקוטי רש"י

פקק החלון. כגון ארובת הגג [לקמן קלז:]. שהוא קשור ותלוי. שם כל שעה. פוקקין בו. כיון דמתוקן ועומד לכך אין זה לא בונה ולא מוסיף. ואם לאו אין פוקקין בו. דמוסיף הוא על סתימת אהל [סוכה כז:]. דדמי לבונה שמוסיף על סתימת הבית ואף על פי שעראי הוא שהרי יחזור ויפתחנו [עירובין מד.]. מטה על צידה. מטה חבית על לדה אם צריך ליטול מן היין והאבן נופלת ולא יטלנה בידים היתה בין החביות וירא שלא תפול האבן על החביות וישברם מגביה לחבית כולה ומסלקה מבין החביות ושם מטה על לדה. אלא בשוכח. ששכח האבן עליה בין השמשות ולא מדעת [לקמן קמב:]. מותבינן אשמעתין. יש לי להשיב על דברי [קידושין נ:]. אשמועת עצמינו [גיטין לח:]. אדידיה גופיה קא מותיב [מנחות מט.]. סואר של קורות. הן קורות הערוכות על גבי קרקע זו על גב זו ועומדות לבנין [סוכה כ:]. המושכבות לארך של בנין [ביצה לא:]. גשוש של ספינה. בני אדם ממשמשים בכלונסות את עומק המים ואין מניחין לילך הספינה אלא במקום עמוק שמא תשבר לילך ולשכון לארץ במקום מושבה [לעיל ק:]. חריות. ענפים קשים כעין משוקמין שדלמות של לולבין ונטלו עלין שלהן קרי להו חריות [לעיל נ.]. שגדרן. [קלצתן] [וקיטנו] ממחיים קרי גדירה. צריך לקשור. לקשרם יחד מבעוד יום להוכיח שלישיבה עומדים ואם לא קשרם יחד אסור לטלטלן למחר דלא הוי יחוד במחשבה [שם ג.]. קא משתמש במחובר. דשימוש אילן שבות הוא כדתנן (ביצה לו:) אלו הן משום שבות לא עולין באילן [עירובין לב.]. למטה מג'. דכל למטה משלשה אפילו באילן לא גזרו עליו דהוי כארעא סמיכתא והכי נמי תנן בפרק בתרא (עירובין לט:) היו שרשיו גבוהין מן הארץ שלשה לא ישב עליהן [שם לג.]. שמא יקטום. מן הענף וזיין דקטמיה הוה ליה כמתקן כלי כדתנן במסכת ביצה (לג:) לתלות בו שיניו לא יקטמנו ואם קטמו חייב חטאת [עירובין שם]. הכל מודים. ר"א ומחלוקתו שנחלקו בתוספת אהל עראי הוא מודה שאין עושין את האהל לכתחלה בשבת בפרק כל הכלים (שבת קכה:) [שם]. אלא להוסיף. כגון פקק זה שאינו אלא תוספת עראי על האהל דאפילו רבנן לא שרו אלא להוסיף כגון פקק חלון דמתני' דמוסיף בעלמא הוא וברייתא שרי למיעבד דופן לכתחלה [עירובין מד.].

wall.[11] In our case, however, where he merely placed the stone on the cask but did not fasten it, it is not considered part of the utensil.

Rav Yosef similarly cites a possible challenge to his version of R' Yochanan's opinion, and deflects it:

אָמַר רַב יוֹסֵף – Rav Yosef said: וּמוֹתְבִינַן אַשְׁמַעְתִּין – And we challenge our principle from the latter clause of our Mishnah, which states: **אִם לָאו אֵין מְמַלְאִין בָּהּ** – But **IF NOT** (i.e. if we cannot draw water with the shell without the stone's falling out) **WE MAY NOT DRAW** water **WITH IT.** Thus, we see that a stone which is merely placed in a vessel but not fastened to it does not become classified as a utensil![12] **וְלָא הִיא – But** actually, **this is not** a contradiction to our view, **הָתָם כֵּיוָן דְּלָא הַדְּקָהּ בַּטּוּלֵי בַּטְּלָהּ** – for **there,** in the Mishnah's case, **since he did not fasten it securely** to the shell **he nullified its** possible **classification** as a utensil, as it is unsuitable for being used in drawing water.[13] In our case, however, merely placing the stone on top of the cask suffices to designate it as a lid.

The Gemara analyzes the dispute:

בְּמַאי קָמִיפַּלְגִי – In what issue **do they disagree? מַר סָבַר בְּעִינַן מַעֲשֶׂה** – One **master** (Rabbah in the name of R' Ami in the name of R' Yochanan) **holds** that **a** significant **act** of preparation **is required** to turn the stone into a utensil,[14] **וּמַר סָבַר לֹא בְּעִינַן מַעֲשֶׂה – whereas** the other **master** (Rav Yosef in the name of R' Assi in the name of R' Yochanan) **holds** that **no** significant **act** of preparation **is required,** but merely placing the stone on the cask suffices.[15]

The Gemara cites another instance of this dispute:

וְאָזְדוּ לְטַעְמַיְיהוּ – And they (R' Ami and R' Assi) **follow their own reasoning. דְּכִי אֲתָא רַב דִּימִי אָמַר רַבִּי חֲנִינָא – For when Rav Dimi came** to Babylonia **he said in the name of R' Chanina, וְאָמְרִי לָהּ אָמַר רַבִּי זֵירָא אָמַר רַבִּי חֲנִינָא** – **and others say** that **Rav Zeira said in the name of R' Chanina: פַּעַם אַחַת הָלַךְ רַבִּי לְמָקוֹם אֶחָד – Rebbi once went to a certain place** before the Sabbath **וּמָצָא נִדְבָּךְ שֶׁל אֲבָנִים – and found a row of stones** that had been prepared for building,[16] **וְאָמַר לְתַלְמִידָיו – and he said to his students, צְאוּ וְחַשְּׁבוּ כְּדֵי שֶׁנֵּשֵׁב עֲלֵיהֶן לְמָחָר – "Go out and have intent** that those stones be designated as seats, **so that we may sit on them tomorrow," וְלֹא הִצְרִיכָן רַבִּי לְמַעֲשֶׂה – and Rebbi did not require them** to perform any **act** of preparation.[17] **וְרַבִּי יוֹחָנָן אָמַר – But R' Yochanan said: הִצְרִיכָן רַבִּי לְמַעֲשֶׂה – Rebbi did require them** to perform **an act. מַאי אָמַר לְהוּ** – According to R' Yochanan, **what did [Rebbi] tell them** to do? **רַבִּי אַמִּי אָמַר – R' Ami said: צְאוּ וְלַמְּדוּם אָמַר לְהוּ – He told them, "Go out and position [the stones],** so that we will not *need* to move them on the Sabbath."[18] **רַבִּי אַסִּי אָמַר** – But **R' Assi said: צְאוּ וְשַׁפְשְׁפוּם אָמַר לְהוּ – He told them, "Go out and wipe [the stones] clean,** so that we will be *allowed* to move them on the Sabbath."[19] Thus, R' Assi holds that a minor act such as wiping a stone clean is sufficient to give it the classification of a utensil, whereas R' Ami holds that such a minor act is insufficient. This is the same reasoning they follow in the case of a stone that was placed on top of a cask as a cover.

The Gemara cites other versions of the incident involving Rebbi:

אִיתְּמַר – It was stated: רַבִּי יוֹסֵי בֶּן שָׁאוּל אָמַר – R' Yose ben Shaul said: סְנָאר שֶׁל קוֹרוֹת הֲוָה – It was a stack of beams that Rebbi sent his students to prepare for Sabbath use.[20] **וְרַבִּי יוֹחָנָן בֶּן שָׁאוּל אָמַר – And R' Yochanan ben Shaul said: גָּשׁוֹשׁ שֶׁל סְפִינָה הֲוָה – It was the sounding pole of a ship.**[21]

The Gemara explains the difference between these views:

מַאן דְּאָמַר גָּשׁוֹשׁ – The one who said that it was **a sounding pole** holds that **כָּל שֶׁכֵּן סְנָאר – certainly,** Rebbi would have allowed sitting on **a stack** of beams on the basis of his students' minimal preparation.[22] **וּמַאן דְּאָמַר סְנָאר – But the one who said** it was **a stack** of beams holds that Rebbi's lenient ruling was limited to this case, **אֲבָל גָּשׁוֹשׁ קָפֵיד עֲלֵיהּ – but** as for **a sounding pole, [the owner] is particular about it** since it can easily be ruined by

NOTES

11. The Mishnah is perforce dealing with a case where the stone is fastened to the shell, for otherwise it would fall out when the shell is lowered into a well.

12. This would seem to contradict R' Yochanan's opinion as cited by Rav Yosef in the name of R' Assi — that a stone can become classified as a utensil by merely being placed on top of a cask as a lid (*Rashi*).

13. An unfastened stone does not help make the shell fit for drawing water, for it will fall out and the shell will float. Thus, one who places the stone in the shell without fastening it indicates that he does not want to make it part of the utensil, but merely wishes to store it there. Its status therefore does not change on account of this act and it remains *muktzeh* as before (*Rashi, Ritva MHK* ed.; see *Chidushei HaRan*).

14. I.e. one must do some physical preparation to the stone itself [such as shaping or smoothing it] (*Baal HaMaor;* see also *Rashi* below ד״ה צאו ולמדים).

15. However, one *must* do the minimal act of placing the stone on the cask before the Sabbath (*Baal HaMaor, Ritva MHK* ed.; see also *Rashi* below ד״ה ושפשפום and *Tosafos* ד״ה ואזדו לטעמייהו).

16. The stones were thus *muktzeh* (see 124b note 25).

17. According to R' Chanina's version of the event, the mere advance intent to use the stones on the Sabbath — without the performance of even a minimal act — sufficed to elevate them to the class of utensils. Once so classified, it would be permitted to move them about on the Sabbath for the purpose of sitting. The reason Rebbi required his students to go out to the stones was that the intent could be effective only if they first determined that the stones were suitable for use as seats (*Ritva MHK* ed.; cf. *Milchamos Hashem*).

Note that it would have been permitted to sit on the stones on the Sabbath *without* moving them about, even if they had not been designated for this use in advance. It is prohibited only to move *muktzeh*, not to touch it, and thus, sitting on a *muktzeh* object is permitted. Even if sitting on it will make the *muktzeh* object shift, it is permitted when another seat is not available, since one who sits on it merely moves it indirectly. Rebbi wanted the stones to be designated as utensils so that his students would be allowed to rearrange them on the Sabbath (see *Ritva MHK* ed., *Magen Avraham* 308:41 and *Mishnah Berurah* 308:82).

18. R' Ami holds that a minimal act of preparation is insufficient to turn a stone into a utensil. Since it was unfeasible for the students to do a significant preparatory act to the stones, Rebbi told them to position the stones properly to enable sitting on them the next day without any need to touch [i.e. move] them (*Rashi*, as printed, which reflects the reading of *Maharshal* and *Maharam*; see *Maharsha* and *Beis Yosef, Orach Chaim* 308, for a variant reading; cf. *Rambam, Hil. Shabbos* 25:21 with *Maggid Mishneh* and *Mishnah Berurah* 308:89; see also *Chazon Ish* 42:12).

19. According to R' Assi, the minimal act of wiping the stones clean sufficed to turn them into utensils and allow positioning them on the Sabbath itself (*Rashi*; see *Tosafos* ד״ה ואזדו לטעמייהו; cf. *Milchamos Hashem*).

20. He sent them out not to prepare stones as seats, but to prepare new beams that stood to be used for construction and had been stacked to prevent warping (*Rashi*).

21. This is the pole that is used to sound the water and determine whether it is deep enough for the ship to remain afloat (*Rashi*).

[As shall emerge from the Gemara's clarification, both of these Amoraim hold that Rebbi sent his students out to designate the item in question as a utensil, either through mere intent (as R' Chanina stated), or through a minimal act (as R' Assi stated). He did not send them out to position the item and preclude the need to move it (as R' Ami stated).

22. It is more novel to say that a sounding pole can be rendered non-*muktzeh* through minimal preparation for Sabbath use, than to say this regarding a stack of beams (see following note).

זמורה שהיא קשורה בטפיח ממלאין בה בשבת [א] פקק החלון ר"א אומר בזמן שהוא קשור ותלוי פוקקין בו ואם לאו אין פוקקין בו וחכ"א בין כך ובין כך פוקקין בו: **גמ'** [ג] תנן התם אבן שעל פי החבית מטה על צידה והיא נופלת אמר רבה א"ר אמי א"ר יוחנן [א] לא שנו אלא בשוכח אבל במניח נעשה בסים לדבר האסור ורב יוסף א"ר אסי א"ר יוחנן לא שנו אלא בשוכח אבל במניח נעשה כיסוי להחבית אמר רבה [ד] מותבינן אשמעתין האבן שבקירויה אם ממלאין בה ואינה נופלת ממלאין בה ולא היא התם כיון דהדקה שויא דופן אמר רב יוסף ומותבינן אשמעתין אם לאו אין ממלאין בה ולא היא התם כיון דלא הדקה בטולי בטלה במאי קמיפלגי מר סבר בעינן מעשה ומר סבר לא בעינן מעשה ואזדו לטעמייהו דכי אתא רב דימי א"ר חנינא ואמרי לה א"ר זירא א"ר חנינא פעם אחת הלך רבי למקום אחד ומצא נדבך של אבנים ואמר לתלמידיו צאו וחשבו כדי שנשב עליהן למחר ולא הצריכן רבי למעשה ור' יוחנן אמר הצריכן רבי למעשה מאי אמר להו [ב] רבי אמי אמר צאו ולמדום אמר להו רבי אסי אמר צאו ושפשפום אמר להו איתמר ר' יוסי בן שאול אמר סואר של קורות הוה ור' יוחנן בן שאול אמר גשוש של ספינה הוה מ"ד גשוש כ"ש סואר ומ"ד סואר אבל גשוש קפיד עליה: זמורה שהיא קשורה כו': [ג] קשורה אין לא קשורה לא לימא מתניתין דלא כרשב"ג דתניא [ז] חריות של דקל שגדרן לעצים ונמלך עליהן לישיבה צריך לקשור רבן שמעון בן גמליאל אומר אין צריך לקשור אמר רב ששת אפי' תימא רשב"ג הכא במאי עסקינן במחוברת באביה אי הכי קא משתמש במחובר לקרקע למטה מג' רב אשי אמר [ד] אפי' תימא בתלושה גזירה שמא יקטום: פקק החלון כו': [י] אמר רבה בר בר חנה א"ר יוחנן [ז] [ה] הכל מודים שאין עושין אהל עראי בתחלה ביו"ט וא"צ לומר בשבת לא נחלקו אלא להוסיף שר"א אומר אין מוסיפין ביו"ט וא"צ לומר בשבת [י] וחכ"א מוסיפין בשבת וא"צ לומר ביו"ט: וחכ"א בין כך ובין כך פוקקין בו: מאי בין כך ובין כך אמר ר' אבא אמר רב כהנא
בין

זמורה. של גפן: **שהיא קשורה בטפיח.** פך ששואבין בו מן הבור או מן המעין: **ממלאין בה.** דשויא כלי להך זמורה: **ותלוי.** שאינו נגרר בארץ שהחבל שהוא קשור בו אינו מגיע לארץ: **אין פוקקין בו.** דמיחזי כמוסיף על הבנין: **בין כך ובין כך.** בגמרא מפרש לה: **גמ' תנן התם.** לקמן בהאי מסכתא: **האבן שעל פי החבית.** והולכך ליטול מן היין שבתוכה: **מטה.** החבית על לדה והיא נופלת: **לא שנו.** דמותר לטלטל החבית והאבן עליה דקתני ואם היתה בין חביות שירא להטותה שם שלא תפול האבן על החביות שבלדה מגביה ומטה על לדה והיא נופלת: **בשוכח.** האבן עליה שלא במתכוין: **אבל במניח נעשית.** החבית בסיס לאבן שהיא דבר האיסור ואין מטלטל את החבית: **ורב יוסף א"ר אסי.** לקולא אמר ר' יוחנן לא שנו דהולכך להטות את החבית ולא ניתן לטלטל האבן להדיא: **אלא בשוכח.** דלא נתכוון לעשותה כלי: **אבל במניח נעשה.** האבן כיסוי לחבית ומגלה אותה כדרכה: **אשמעתין.** על שמועה שלי שאמרתי במניח אין האבן נעשה כלי: **ממלאין בה.** אלמא אבן נעשה כלי: **דהדקה.** שקשרה יפה: **ואם לאו אין ממלאין.** ולא אמרינן נעשה כלי בהנחה בעלמא וקשיא לידי דאמרי לעיל במניח נעשה כיסוי לחבית: **ולא היא.** לא קשיא לי דהתם הואיל ובלא קשירה לא חזיא למלאות דהא נפלה והיא לאו הדקה בטולי בטלה מתורת כלי גלי דעתיה דלא חשיב ליה אבל כיסוי חבית הנחה משויא ליה כלי: **ואזדו לטעמייהו.** ר' אמי ור' אסי: **נדבך של אבנים.** אבנים סדורות ומוקצות לבנין: **מאי אמר להו.** מאי מעשה הצריכן לרבי יוחנן: **צאו ולמדום.** סדרו אותם והשיבום כדי שלא נצטרך ליגע בהם למחר לפי שאין הזמנה במעשה [ס כל דהו] מועלת לאבן לעשותה כלי ור' אמי לטעמיה דאמר לעיל אין אבן נעשית כלי בהנחה: **למדום.** כדאמרי' במו"ק (דף יב.) עושה להם למודים לסדר נסרים על פי הבור: **ושפשפום.** מן הטיט שיהו נאות לישב ולמחר תלמודם דבמעשה כל דהו נעשה כלי: **סואר של קורות.** הוה ולא אבנים: **סואר.** סדר של קורות חדשות שמסדרין אותן לבנין כדי שלא יתעקמו: **גשוש.** עץ ארוך שמגששים בו המים לפני הספינה לידע שהוא בעומקו שתוכל ספינה להלך בהן: **קפיד עליה.** שלא יתעקם ומייחד ליה מקום ומקלה ליה בידים ואפי' לר"ש אסור לטלטלו דמוקלה מחמת חסרון כים אפי' ר"ש מודה: **שאינה קשורה לא.** ואפי' יש עקמומית בראשה כעין מזלג שראוי לתלות בה טפיח ולמלאות וחישב עליה: **שגדרן לעצים.** שחתכן להיסק: **צריך לקשור.** מע"ש: **באביה.** בגפן: **והא קא משתמש במחובר.** ואפילו קשורה מבעוד יום ליתסר: **למטה מג'.** סמוך לקרקע וכגון לשאוב מן המעין שאינו עמוק ומותר להשתמש באילן למטה מג' כדאמרי' בפרק בתרא דעירובין (דף לט:) היו שרשיו גבוהין מן הארץ ג' לא ישב עליהם: **גזירה שמא יקטום.** שמא למחר תהיה לו ארוכה ויקטמנה מתוך שהיא רכה ונוחה לקטום ונמצא עושה כלי וחייב משום מכה בפטיש אבל בחריות ליכא למיגזר הכי הלכך במחשבה סגי: **שאין עושין אהל עראי.** לפרוס מחצלת על ד' מחילות או על ד' קונדסים להיות צל לאהל מן החמה ודוקא גג אבל מחילה לאו אהל הוא ושרי לפורסה לצניעות כדאמרי' בעירובין (ד' לד.) בעובדא דשמואל ופקק החלון דמתני' [ט] משום דבנין קבוע הוא ומיחזי כמוסיף על הבנין: **להוסיף.** כגון שהיה מחצלת פרוסה עליהן וכרוכה ונשאר בה אויר ולמחר פושטה דומיא דפקק דמוסיף בעלמא הוא:
בין

ואזדו לטעמייהו. תימה היכי הוה רבי אסי לטעמיה אדרבה פליגי דהכא קאמר ר' אסי נעשה כיסוי לחבית בהנחה גרידא בלא שום מעשה וגבי נדבך אמר ר' אסי צאו ושפשפום אמר להן דהיינו מעשה שהצריכן רבי ועוד קשה גבי נדבך קאמר דסגי בשפשוף ולקמן גבי כיסוי כלים א"ר אסי א"ר יוחנן והוא שיש בהם תורת כלי ויש לומר דכיסוי חבית סגי לה בהנחה שדרכו לעשותו כל דהו דלא בעי תיקון ומעשה גמור כשאר כיסוי כלים ונדבך של אבן מסותת ומרובע לבנין סגי להו בשפשוף שאין צריך עוד תיקון ומ"מ הוי ר' אסי לטעמיה דכי היכי דמיקל רבי אסי גבי נדבך ה"נ הכא והא דקאמר ר' אסי בפרק במה טומנין (לעיל דף נ.) חריות של דקל ישב אע"פ שלא קשר התם רב אשי גרסינן אי נמי ראויין הם לישיבה טפי מאבנים:

הכל מודים שאין עושין אהל עראי בתחלה. פי' בקונ' דלא אסיר אהל אלא למעלה בגג אבל בדפנות לא כדמוכח בעובדא דשמואל בכל גגות (עירובין דף לד.) דאיתמר חצר כותל שנפרצה רב אמר אין מטלטלין אלא בד' אמות ושמואל אמר זה מטלטל עד עיקר המחיצה וזה מטלטל עד עיקר המחיצה והא דרב לאו בפירוש איתמר אלא מכללא דשמואל הוה יתיב בההוא חצר נפל גודא דביני ביני אמר להו שמואל שקולו גלימא נגודי ליה אהדרינהו רב לאפיה כו' ושמואל למה ליה למיעבד הכי האמר זה מטלטל עד עיקר המחיצה כו' שמואל לצניעותא בעלמא הוא דעבד אלמא משמע דאהל דדפנות שרי למיעבד הכי ורב שהיה מקפיד לאו משום עשיית אהל דשרי כדפרישית אלא הוה קפיד אמאי דהוו מטלטלין גלימא ד' אמות בחצר וקשה דע"כ שייך איסור אהל אפילו בדפנות כדאיתא בעירובין בפרק מי שהוציאוהו (דף מד. ושם) גבי עשיית דופן סוכה דפריך התם והאמר רבה בר בר חנה אמר רבי יוחנן הכל מודים שאין עושין אהל עראי בתחילה ומשני הא בדופן שלישית והא בדופן רביעית אלא נראה לר"ת דשפיר שייך בדפנות אהל היכא דמחיצה מועלת להיתר ולהכי בדופן שלישית דהויא מחיצה ומכשר ליה לסוכה חשיב עשיית אהל בתחלה אבל דופן רביעית אינה אלא תוספת בעלמא הואיל וכבר הסוכה היתה כשרה ועיקר פלוגתין דר"א ורבנן איתא באהל כבעשיית דופן דפקק החלון משמע בחלון שבכותל דאי בגג מיירי הוה ליה למימר ארובה כמו ששנינו משילין פירות דרך ארובה (ביצה דף לה:) ומיהו באהל שבגג נמי פליגי כדמוכח לקמן בפרק תולין (דף קלח:) דמייתי הך גבי תליית משמרת שהיא כעין גג וכן משמע בפרק בתרא דעירובין (דף קב.) דאמר הנהו דיכרי דהוו בי רב הונא ביממא בעו טולא ובליליא בעו אוירא אתא לקמיה דרב אמר ליה כרוך בודיא ושייר בה טפח דלמחר הוה מוסיף על אהל עראי ומותר ומשמע דהיינו נמי תוספת אהל עראי דפליגי רבי אליעזר ורבנן ועובדא דשמואל
דכל

ר' אליעזר אוסר למושכן כנגד כל החלון. וחכמים מתירים (וזהו) להוסיף כיוצא בו בסוף המוצא תפילין הנהו דכרי דהוו לרב הונא דביממא בעו טולא ובליליא בעו אוירא. ואמר ליה רב כרוך בודיא עלייהו ושייר בה טפח ולמחר פרסיה

משתמש במחובר. דשימוש אילן שבות הוא כדתנן (ביצה לו:) אלו הן משום שבות לא עולין באילן [עירובין לב.]. דכל למטה משלשה אפילו באילן לא גזרו עליו דהוי כארעא סמיכתא והכי נמי תנן בפרק בתרא (עירובין לט:) היו שרשיו גבוהין מן הארץ שלשה לא ישב עליהן [שם לג.]. **שמא יקטום.** מן הענף וכיון דקטמיה הוה ליה כמתקן כלי

(לג.) לתלות בו שיהו לא יקטמנו ואם קטמו חייב חטאת [לקמן קמו:]. **הכל מודים.** ר"א ומחלוקתו שנחלקו בתוספת אהל עראי גבי פקק חלון דאיכא למאן דאמר פוקקין בו ואף על גב דמוסיף על אהל עראי הוא מודים שאין עושין אהל עראי לכתחילה בשבת בפרק כל הכלים (שבת קכה:) [עירובין פו:]. **אלא להוסיף.** כגון פקק זה שאינו אלא תוספת עראי על האהל [לקמן קלז:]. דאפילו רבנן לא שרו אלא להוסיף כגון פקק חלון דתוספת בעלמא הוא ובריית' שרי למיעבד דופן רביעית לכתחילה [עירובין מד.].

עין משפט נר מצוה

לח א מיי' פכ"ה מהל' שבת הלכה יז סמג לאוין סה טוש"ע או"ח סימן שח סעיף כב וסימן שט סעיף ד:

לט ב מיי' שם הל' כא סמג שם טור שו"ע או"ח סימן שח סעיף כב:

מ ג מיי' פכ"ב מהלכות שבת הלכה ג:

מא ד מיי' פכ"ב מהל' שבת הלכה כז סמג לאוין סה טוש"ע או"ח סימן שטו סעיף א:

מב ה מיי' שם טוש"ע שם סעיף ג:

רבינו חננאל

וזה שאמר רבי צאו ולמדום עשו להם לימודים. יש מי שאומר עיינו בהן. כלומר לימוד בעינן בלא מעשה ור"א לימודים כגון זה ששנינו במסכת משקין. ר' יהודה אומר עושה לו לימודים בשביל שלא יחמיץ. והן כיסויי עצים ועליהם טיט (שרופים) [שהצריכן למעשה] וראיתן הא דגרסינן בפרק במה טומנין אמר רב הונא קמי דרב חריות של דקל שגדרום לעצים ונמלך עליהם לישיבה צריך לקשר רשב"ג אומר אין צריך לקשר. ואמרינן מאן תנא דפליגא עליה דרשב"ג. ר' חנינה בן עקביא היא שהלך למקום א' ומצא חריות של דקל שגרודים לעצים כו': **פיסקא** זמורה שהיא קשורה בטפיח כו'. זמורה היא כגון אמיר והיא זמורה של כרם ארוכה כמו חבל וטפיח הוא כלי בדיל. ואמרה המשנ' אם זמורה זו היתה קשורה בזה הכלי ממלאין בה בשבת שעשאה מאתמול במקום חבל ועשה בה מעשה ואם לאו אסור לטלטלה בשבת להיותו בחבל. ואמרינן לימא מתניתין דלא כרשב"ג. דהא רשבג"א בחריות שגדרן לעצים ונמלך עליהן לישיבה אין צריך לקשר. ופריק רב ששת זמורה זו מחוברת באביה. כלומר מחוברת בקרקע. והא לא קשרה מאתמול לא ביטלה. ואינה דומה לחריות של דקל שהן גרודין. ואקשינן אי הכי היכי משתמש במחובר ופרקינן למטה משלשה. כדתנן היו שרשין גבוהין מן הארץ שלשה טפחים לא ישב עליהן. אם גבוהין ג' טפחים הוא דאסירו. הא בפחות מותר לישב עליהן. מיהא שמעינן דפחות מג' במחובר לקרקע דמי ומותר להשתמש בו. ויש שאומרים כי המים הם קרובים במשלש' ולא אתי למתחך. רב אשי אמר אפילו תימא בתלושה גזירה שמא יקטום: **מתני'** פקק החלון. כגון מסך העשוי לסתום החלון בין אם הוא מבד בין מוזלתו בזמן שקשור ותלוי פוקקין בו. ואם לאו אין פוקקין בו. אמר (רבא) [רבה] בר חנה א"ר יוחנן הכל מודין שאין עושין אהל עראי בתחלה ביו"ט. ואין צ"ל בשבת. לא נחלקו אלא להוסיף. פי' שאם היה בו פקק פוקק במקצת החלון.

מסורת הש"ס

א) לקמן קלז: עירובין מד. סוכה מו. ב) [לקמן קמב:] ג) [לעיל קב: לקמן קמב: ע"ש], ד) [קידושין נ: וש"נ], ה) לעיל נ. ו) [לקמן קלז: עירו' מד. פו:], ז) [תוספתא סוכה פ"א], ח) גי' רש"ל, ט) גי' רש"ל הוי למעלה בגג ולא מן הצד אבל כל הכי מקיים פי' רש"י דהכא.

רב נסים גאון

את שיש לו נתיצה ואת שאין לו נתיצה אין לו טומאה: **אי הכי קא משתמש במחובר למטה מג'** מכלל כל מה שיהיה מדבר המחובר לקרקע קרוב מהארץ פחות מג' טפחים מותר להשתמש בו ואין איסור משום שבות [רק] מה שהוא גבוה מן הארץ ג' טפחים ומצא עיקר זה במשנה במס' עירובין בפרק המוצא תפלין (דף צט) אילן שהוא מיסך על הארץ אם אין נופו גבוה מן הארץ ג' טפחים לא ישב עליהן ודבר זה אין בו חלוקה אבל רבא ורב ששת בשרשי אילן הבאים מלמעלה מג' לתוך ג' ובפ' עירובין (שם דף לג) בכל מערבין תניא נתנו באילן בתוך ג' מותר לטלטל: סליק פרק כל הכלים

ליקוטי רש"י

פקק החלון. כגון ארובת הגג [לקמן קלז:]. **שהוא קשור ותלוי.** שם כל שעה. **פוקקין בו.** כיון דמתוקן ועומד לכך אין זה כבונה ולא מוסיף. **ואם לאו אין פוקקין בו.** דמוסיף הוא על סתימת אהל [סוכה כו:]. דדמי לבונה שמוסיף על סתימת הבית ולא שהוא על שערי פי שערים הוא שהוי יחזור ויפתחנו [עירובין קב.]. **מטה על צידה.** מטה חבית על לדה אם צריך ליטול מן היין והאבן נופלת ולא ניחוש דנוגע בשהיה בין החביות וירא שלא תפול האבן על החביות ותשברם ונכרסם מגביה לחבית כולה ומלקה מכין לצד אחר חבית וכם מטה על לדה. **אלא בשוכח.** שמם האבן עליה בין השמשות ולא מדעת [לקמן קמב:]. **מותבינן אשמעתין.** על דברי בשמועת עצמינו [גיטין לה:]. אדידיה גופיה קא מותיב [מנחות מט.]. **סואר של קורות.** הן קורות הסדורות על גבי קרקע זו על גב זו ועומדות לבנין [סוכה כג:]. המוקצות לאותך על גב מן הסתכלו לבנין [ביצה לא:]. **גשוש של ספינה.** כני אדם שמשתמשים בכלונסות את עומק המים ואין מניחין לילך הספינה במקום עמוק שמא תטבע ומשכן לארץ במקום משוכה [לעיל ק:]. **חריות.** ענפים קשים כגון מקלות של לולבין ונפלו עלין שלהן קרי להו חריות. **שגדרן.** כל [לקטם] לשון גדירה. **צריך לקשור.** לקשרם יחד מבעוד יום להוכיח שלישיבה עומדים ואם לא קשרם יחד אסור לטלטל דהכי מלא ולמחר לטלטל דהוי יחד בתמשכה [שם נ.].

bending, and he sets it aside from use. Therefore, a minimal degree of preparation cannot render it non-*muktzeh*.[23]

The Mishnah stated:

וּזְמוֹרָה שֶׁהִיא קְשׁוּרָה כו׳ – A VINE THAT IS TIED etc. [to a pitcher – we may draw water with it on the Sabbath].

The Gemara analyzes this ruling:

קְשׁוּרָה אֵין – The Mishnah implies that if the vine is **tied** to the pitcher we may **indeed** draw water with it, **לֹא קְשׁוּרָה לֹא** – but if it is **not tied** to the pitcher we may **not** suspend the pitcher from it and draw water.[24] **לֵימָא מַתְנִיתִין דְּלָא כְּרַבָּן שִׁמְעוֹן בֶּן גַּמְלִיאֵל** – **Shall we say** that **our Mishnah does not accord with Rabban Shimon ben Gamliel? דְּתַנְיָא** – **For it was taught in a Baraisa:** **חֲרָיוֹת שֶׁל דֶּקֶל שֶׁגְּדָרָן לְעֵצִים** – If one had HARDENED BRANCHES OF A DATE PALM THAT ONE HARVESTED FOR FIREWOOD, which are *muktzeh,* **וְנִמְלַךְ עֲלֵיהֶן לִישִׁיבָה** – AND HE then CHANGED HIS MIND REGARDING THEM and decided to use them FOR SITTING, **צָרִיךְ לִקְשׁוֹר** – HE MUST TIE them into bundles before the Sabbath in order to render them non-*muktzeh*.[25] **רַבָּן שִׁמְעוֹן בֶּן גַּמְלִיאֵל אוֹמֵר** – RABBAN SHIMON BEN GAMLIEL SAYS: **אֵין צָרִיךְ לִקְשׁוֹר** – HE NEED NOT TIE them. It is sufficient if he merely intends before the Sabbath to sit on them. Shall we say that our Mishnah does not accord with this view?[26]

The Gemara answers:

אָמַר רַב שֵׁשֶׁת – **Rav Sheishess said:** **אֲפִילּוּ תֵּימָא רַבָּן שִׁמְעוֹן בֶּן גַּמְלִיאֵל** – **You can even say** that the Mishnah accords with **Rabban Shimon ben Gamliel,** **הָכָא בְּמַאי עָסְקִינַן** – for **what are we dealing with here,** in our Mishnah? **בִּמְחוּבֶּרֶת בְּאָבִיהָ** – It is with a case **where [the vine] is** still **attached to its parent** (i.e. the body of the grapevine). Even Rabban Shimon ben Gamliel agrees that in this instance it must be tied to the pitcher before it can be permitted for use.[27]

The Gemara wonders how the Mishnah can possibly be dealing with an attached vine:

אִי הָכִי קָא מִשְׁתַּמֵּשׁ בִּמְחוּבָּר לַקַּרְקַע – But **if so, one** who draws water **will be making use of something that is attached to the ground,** which is prohibited.[28] – ? –

The Gemara answers:

לְמַטָּה מִשְּׁלֹשָׁה – We are dealing with a short vine that is **within three** *tefachim* of the ground. It is permitted to make use of an attached item that is within three *tefachim* of the ground.[29]

The Gemara cites an alternative answer to the original question: **רַב אַשִׁי אָמַר** – **Rav Ashi said:** **אֲפִילּוּ תֵּימָא בִּתְלוּשָׁה** – **You can even say** that the Mishnah is dealing **with a detached [vine].** Nevertheless, Rabban Shimon ben Gamliel concedes that it must be tied to the pitcher before the Sabbath **גְּזֵירָה שֶׁמָּא יָקְטוֹם** – on account of **a decree** that was enacted out of concern that **perhaps one will** find the vine too long for his purpose and will **cut** it down to size.[30]

The Mishnah stated:

פְּקַק הַחַלּוֹן כו׳ – A WINDOW SHUTTER – etc. [R' Eliezer says: When it is attached to the building by a rope and the rope is so short that the shutter is suspended, we may shutter the window with it on the Sabbath; but if the shutter is not suspended in this manner, we may not shutter the window with it. But the Sages say: In either case we may shutter the window with it.]

The dispute is clarified:

אָמַר רַבָּה בַּר בַּר חָנָה אָמַר רַבִּי יוֹחָנָן – **Rabbah bar bar Chanah said in the name of R' Yochanan:** **הַכֹּל מוֹדִים שֶׁאֵין עוֹשִׂין אֹהֶל עֲרַאי בַּתְּחִלָּה בְּיוֹם טוֹב** – **All** [both R' Eliezer and the Sages] **agree that we may not erect** even **a temporary structure initially on Yom Tov,** **וְאֵין צָרִיךְ לוֹמַר בְּשַׁבָּת** – **and it need not be said** that this is forbidden **on the Sabbath.**[31]

NOTES

23. A sounding pole is מוּקְצֶה מֵחֲמַת חֶסְרוֹן כִּיס, *muktzeh due to [fear of] monetary loss.* The owner consciously sets such an object aside from use and puts it in a designated place for the duration of the Sabbath. Even the Tanna R' Shimon, who is lenient concerning other categories of *muktzeh*, recognizes this category. Thus, a significant act of preparation is required to make it permitted for Sabbath use (*Rashi;* see *Ritva MHK* ed., *Chidushei HaRan* and *Tosafos* to *Beitzah* 2b ד״ה אין מבקעין). [A minimal act suffices to "prepare" for use something that would have been *muktzeh* due to a mere lack of preparation (e.g. stones or beams that lack designation as utensils). However, when something was actively set aside from use, a significant act is required to undo its designation.]

24. Even if the vine has a crook by which the pitcher can be lowered into the well, and one had intent before the Sabbath to use the vine for this purpose, he may not do so (*Rashi*).

25. Merely intending before the Sabbath to use them for sitting is insufficient to give them the classification of utensils. One must tie them together to demonstrate their new designation (*Rashi* above, 50a).

26. [Why, above (50a) we said that the halachah follows Rabban Shimon ben Gamliel!]

27. Since an attached vine does not stand to be used for any purpose, its status cannot be elevated to that of a utensil through mere intent to use it, but only through a genuine act of preparation [such as tying it to the pitcher] (*Ritva MHK* ed.; cf. *Chidushei HaRan*).

28. The Rabbis forbade the use of trees on the Sabbath (e.g. leaning on a tree), due to the concern that one might deliberately tear off branches, leaves or fruit and violate the *melachah* of קוֹצֵר, *reaping* (see *Beitzah* 36b and *Orach Chaim* 336:1). Thus, if a vine is attached to its parent, one may not utilize it as a handle for a pitcher even if one tied it to the pitcher before the Sabbath (*Rashi*).

29. The Mishnah thus means that one may use a short vine that is tied to a pitcher to draw water from a shallow well (*Rashi*). [Any vine or branch that is within three tefachim of the ground is considered like the ground itself, rather than a separate growth (*Rabbeinu Chananel*; see *Eruvin* 99b-100a).]

30. By cutting the vine down to the right size, one will be fashioning it into a utensil, thus violating the *melachah* of מַכֶּה בְּפַטִּישׁ, *striking the final blow*. The Rabbis therefore required the person to tie the vine to his pitcher before the Sabbath, ensuring that he will take heed of its size at that time. They enacted this decree only in regard to a vine, which is relatively soft and easy to cut, out of concern that one might find it too long and cut it shorter. In the case of hardened palm branches, however, this concern does not exist. Therefore, according to Rabban Shimon ben Gamliel, it is sufficient for one who wishes to use them as seats to designate them for this purpose before the Sabbath (*Rashi*). [In either case, intent suffices to render the item non-*muktzeh*. A vine requires advance tying to the pitcher to remove the concern that one might cut it down to size on the Sabbath.]

An obvious question arises: Why is it that in this case intent suffices to render the item non-*muktzeh*, whereas above, in the case of a stone used as a cover for a cask, R' Ami and R' Assi agreed that intent is insufficient and they even debated whether the minimal act of placing it on the cask suffices? The answer is that intent suffices for an item that is commonly designated for the intended task. However, for an item that is rarely designated for the intended task, a preparatory act is required (*Magen Avraham* 308:43, *Mishnah Berurah* 308:92,95; see *Baal HaMaor* and *Milchamos Hashem* for a lengthy discussion of this and related topics).

Note that the question of whether intent alone is sufficient pertains to intent before the Sabbath to use an item for a certain purpose on that Sabbath. If one permanently designates an item for a certain task, it becomes classified as a utensil on that basis, even if this type of item is rarely designated for this task (*Orach Chaim* 308:22 with *Mishnah Berurah* §93).

31. I.e. we may not spread a mat over a frame or over a walled enclosure for shade. By spreading the mat where there was previously no roof, one is making a structure (viz. a roof) from the start. Although this roof is a temporary one, all agree that its construction is prohibited.

However, the prohibition against erecting a temporary structure from the start pertains only to making a roof. It is permitted to create

לח א מיי' פכ"ה מהל' שבת הלכה יז סמג לאוין סה טוש"ע או"ח סימן שח סעיף כב וסימן שח סעיף ד:
לט ב מיי' שם הל' כא סמג שם טור שו"ע או"ח סימן שח סעיף כב:
מ ג מיי' פכ"ג מהלכות שבת הלכה ז:
מא ד ה מיי' פכ"ב מהל' שבת הלכה כח סמג לאוין סה טוש"ע או"ח סימן שטו סעיף א:
מב ו מיי' שם טוש"ע שם סעיף ג:

רבינו חננאל

הא שאמר רבי צאו ולמדום עשו להם לימודים. יש מי שאומר עיינו בהן. כלומר לימוד עיינן בלא מעשה וי"א לימודים כגון זה ששנינו במסכת משקין. ר' יהודה אומר עושה לו לימודים בשביל שלא יחמיץ. והן כיסויי עצים ועליהם טיט (שרוצים מעשים) [שהצריכן למעשה] וראיתן הא דגרסינן בהמה טומנין תני רבה בר רב הונא קמי דרב חריות של דקל שגדרום לעצים ונמלך עליהם לישיבה צריך לקשר רשב"ג אומר אין צריך לקשר. ואמרינן מאן תנא דפליג עליה דרשב"ג. ר' חנינא בן עקביא היא שהלך למקום א' ומצא חריות של דקל שגדרום לעצים כו': **פיסקא** זמורה שהיא קשורה בטפיח כו'. זמורה היא כגון אמיר והיא זמורה של כרם ארוכה כמו חבל וטפיח הוא כלי בדלי. ואמרה המשנ' אם זמורה זו היתה קשורה בזה הכלי ממלאין בה בשבת שעשאה מאתמול במקום חבל ועשה בה מעשה ואם לאו אסור לחשוב עליו בשבת להיותו כחבל. ואמרינן לימא מתניתין דלא כרשב"ג. דהא רשב"ג בחריות שגדרן לעצים ונמלך עליהן לישיבה אין צריך לקשר. ופריק רב ששת זמורה זו מחוברת באביה. כלומר מחוברת בקרקע. ואינה כו לא קשרה מאתמול לא ביטלה. ואינה דומה לחריות של דקל שהן גרודין. ואקשינן אי הכי משתמש במחובר ופוקקין למטה משלשה. כדתנן היו שרשין גבוהין מן הארץ שלשה טפחים לא ישב עליהן. אם גבוהין ג' טפחים הוא דאסירו. הא בפחות מותר לישב עליהן. מיהא שמעינן דפחות מג' במחובר לקרקע כקרקע דמי ומותר להשתמש בו. ויש שאומרים כי המים הם קרובים בפחות משלש'. ולא אתי למחתך. רב אשי אמר אפילו תימא בתלושה גזירה שמא יקטום. **מתני'** פקק החלון. כגון מסך העשוי לסתום החלון בין אם הוא מבגד בין מזולתו בזמן שקשור ותלוי פוקקין בו. ואם לאו אין פוקקין בו. אמר (רבא) [רבה] בר בר חנה א"ר יוחנן הכל מודים שאין עושין אהל עראי בתחלה ביו"ט ואין צ"ל בשבת. לא נחלקו אלא להוסיף. פי' שאם היה בו פקק פוקק במקצת החלון.

ואזדו לטעמייהו. תימה היכי הוה רבי אסי לטעמיה אדרבה פליגי דהכא קאמר ר' אסי נעשה כיסוי לחבית בהנחה גרידא בלא שום מעשה וגבי נדבך אמר ר' אסי לאו ושפשפום אמר להן דהיינו מעשה שהצריכן רבי ועוד קשה גבי נדבך קאמר דסגי בשפשוף ולקמן גבי כיסוי כלים א"ר אסי א"ר יוחנן והוא שיש בהם תורת כלי ויש לומר דכיסוי חבית סגי לה בהנחה שדרכו לעשותו כל דהו דלא בעי תיקון ומעשה גמור כשאר כיסוי כלים ונדבך של אבן מסותת ומרובע לבנין סגי להו בשפשוף שאין צריך עוד תיקון ומ"מ הוי ר' אסי לטעמיה דכי היכי דמיקל רבי אסי גבי נדבך ה"נ הכא והא דקאמר ר' אסי בפרק במה טומנין (לעיל דף נ.) חריות של דקל ישב אע"פ שלא קשר התם רב אסי גרסינן אי נמי ראויין הם לישיבה טפי מאבנים:

הכל מודים שאין עושין אהל עראי בתחלה. פי' בקונ' דלא אסיר אהל אלא למעלה בגג אבל בדפנות לא כדמוכח בעובדא דשמואל בכל גגות (עירובין דף לד.) דאיתמר חצר כותל שנפרצה רב אמר אין מטלטלין אלא בד' אמות ושמואל אמר זה מטלטל עד עיקר המחיצה וזה מטלטל עד עיקר המחיצה והא דרב לאו בפירוש איתמר אלא מכללא דשמואל הוה יתיב בההוא חצר נפל גודא דביני אמר להו שמואל שקולו גלימא נגודי ליה אהדרינהו רב לאפיה כו' ושמואל למה ליה למיעבד הכי האמר זה מטלטל עד עיקר המחיצה כו' שמואל לצניעותא בעלמא הוא דעבד אלמא משמע דאהל דדפנות שרי למיעבד הכי ורב שהיה מקפיד לאו משום עשיית אהל דשרי כדפרישית אלא הוה קפיד אמאי דהוו מטלטלין גלימא ד' אמות בחצר וקשה דע"כ שייך איסור אהל אפילו בדפנות כדאיתא בעירובין בפרק מי שהוליאוהו (דף מד. ושם) גבי עשיית דופן סוכה דפריך התם והאמר רבה בר בר חנה אמר רבי יוחנן הכל מודים שאין עושין אהל עראי בתחילה ומשני הא בדופן שלישית והא בדופן רביעית אלא נראה לר"ת דשפיר שייך בדפנות אהל היכא דמחיצה מועלת להיתר ולהכי בדופן שלישית דהויא מחיצה ומכשר ליה לסוכה חשיב עשיית אהל בתחלה אבל דופן רביעית אינה אלא תוספת בעלמא הואיל וכבר הסוכה היתה כשרה ועיקר פלוגתין דר"א ורבנן איתא באהל כבעשיית דופן דפקק החלון משמע בחלון שבכותל דאי בגג מיירי הוה ליה למימר ארובה כמו ששנינו משילין פירות דרך ארובה (בילה דף לה:) ומיהו באהל שבגג נמי פליגי כדמוכח לקמן בפרק תולין (דף קלח:) דמייתי הך גבי טליית משמרת שהיא כעין גג וכן משמע בפרק בתרא דעירובין (דף קב.) דאמר הנהו דיכרי דהוו בי רב הונא בימאמא בעו טולא ובליליא בעו אוירא אתא לקמיה דרב אמר ליה כרוך בודיא ושייר בה טפח דלמחר הוא מוסיף על אהל עראי ומותר ומשמע דהיינו נמי תוספת אהל עראי דפליגי רבי אליעזר ורבנן ועובדא דשמואל דכל

זמורה שהיא קשורה בטפיח ממלאין בה בשבת ^א פקק החלון ר"א אומר בזמן שהוא קשור ותלוי פוקקין בו ואם לאו אין פוקקין בו וחכ"א בין כך ובין כך פוקקין בו: **גמ'** ^ב תנן התם אבן שעל פי החבית מטה על צידה והיא נופלת אמר רבה א"ר אמי א"ר יוחנן ^ג לא שנו אלא בשוכח אבל במניח נעשה בסים לדבר האסור ורב יוסף א"ר אסי א"ר יוחנן לא שנו אלא בשוכח אבל במניח נעשה כיסוי להחבית אמר רבה ^ד מותבינן אשמעתין האבן שבקירויה אם ממלאין בה ואינה נופלת ממלאין בה ולא היא התם כיון דהדקה שויא דופן אמר רב יוסף ומותבינן אשמעתין אם לאו אין ממלאין בה ולא היא התם כיון דלא הדקה בטולי בטלה במאי קמיפלגי מר סבר בעינן מעשה ומר סבר לא בעינן מעשה ואזדו לטעמייהו דכי אתא רב דימי א"ר חנינא ואמרי לה א"ר זירא א"ר חנינא פעם אחת הלך רבי למקום אחד ומצא נדבך של אבנים ואמר לתלמידיו צאו וחשבו כדי שנשב עליהן למחר ולא הצריכן רבי למעשה ור' יוחנן אמר הצריכן רבי למעשה מאי אמר להו ^ב רבי אמי אמר צאו ולמדום אמר להו רבי אסי אמר צאו ושפשפום איתמר ר' יוסי בן שאול אמר סואר של קורות הוה ור' יוחנן בן שאול אמר גשוש של ספינה הוה מ"ד גשוש כ"ש סואר ומ"ד סואר אבל גשוש קפיד עליה: זמורה שהיא קשורה כו': ^ג קשורה אין לא קשורה לא לימא מתניתין דלא כרשב"ג דתניא ^ה חריות של דקל שגדרן לעצים ונמלך עליהן לישיבה צריך לקשור רבן שמעון בן גמליאל אומר אין צריך לקשור אמר רב ששת אפי' תימא רשב"ג הכא במאי עסקינן במחוברת באביה אי הכי קא משתמש במחובר לקרקע למטה מג' רב אשי אמר ^ו אפי' תימא בתלושה גזירה שמא יקטום: פקק החלון כו': ^ז אמר רבה בר בר חנה א"ר יוחנן ^ח הכל מודים שאין עושין אהל עראי בתחלה ביו"ט וא"צ לומר בשבת לא נחלקו אלא להוסיף שר"א אומר אין מוסיפין ביו"ט וא"צ לומר בשבת ^י וחכ"א מוסיפין בשבת וא"צ לומר ביו"ט: וחכ"א בין כך ובין כך פוקקין בו: מאי בין כך ובין כך אמר ר' אבא אמר רב כהנא בין

זמורה. של גפן: שהיא קשורה בטפיח. פך ששואבין בו מן הבור או מן המעין: ממלאין בה. דשויא כלי להך זמורה: ותלוי. שאינו נגרר בארץ שהחבל שהוא קשור בו אינו מגיע לארץ: אין פוקקין בו. דמיחזי כמוסיף על הבנין: בין כך ובין כך. בגמ' מפרש לה: **גמ'** תנן התם. לקמן בהאי מסכתא: האבן שעל פי החבית. והולכך ליטול מן היין שבתוכה: מטה. החבית על צדה והיא נופלת: לא שנו. דמותר לטלטל החבית והאבן עליה דקתני ואם היתה בין חביות שירא להטותה שם שלא תפול האבן על החביות שבצדה מגביה ומטה על צדה והיא נופלת: בשוכח. שהאבן עליה שלא במתכוין: אבל במניח. נעשית. החבית בסיס לאבן ואין מטלטל את החבית: ורב יוסף א"ר אסי. לקולא אמר ר' יוחנן לא שנו דהולכך להטות את החבית ולא נימן לטלטל האבן להדיא: אלא בשוכח. דלא נתכוון לעשותה כלי: אבל במניח נעשה. האבן כיסוי לחבית ומגלה אותה כדרכה: אשמעתין. על שמועה שלי שאמרתי במניח אין האבן נעשה כלי: ממלאין בה. אלמא אבן נעשה כלי: דהדקה. שקשרה יפה: ואם לאו אין ממלאין. ולא אמרינן נעשה כלי בהנחה בעלמא וקשיא לדידי דאמרי לעיל במניח נעשה כיסוי לחבית: ולא היא. לא קשיא לי דהתם הואיל ובלא קשירה לא חזיא למלאות דהא נפלה והאי לאו הדקה בטולי בטלה מתורת כלי גלי דעתיה דלא חשיב ליה אבל כיסוי חבית הנחה משויא ליה כלי: ואזדו לטעמייהו. ר' אמי ור' אסי: נדבך של אבנים. אבנים סדורות לבנין: מאי אמר להו. מאי מעשה הצריכן לרבי יוחנן: צאו ולמדום. סדרו אותם והשיבום כדי שלא נצטרך ליגע בהם למחר לפי שאין הזמנה כמעשה [^ד כל דהו] מועלת לאבן לעשותה כלי ור' אמי לטעמיה דאמר לעיל אין אבן נעשית כלי בהנחה: למדום. כדאמרי' במו"ק (דף יב.) עושה להם למודים לסדר נסרים על פי הבור: ושפשפום. מן הטיט שיהו נאות לישב ולמחר תלמודים דבמעשה כל דהו נעשה כלי: אלא בשוכח. שאבן עליה יכול לטלטלו הכא. אלא אבנים. סואר של קורות. הוא ולא אבנים: סואר. סדר של קורות חדשות שמסדרין אותן לבנין כדי שלא יתעקמו: גשוש. עץ ארוך שמגששים בו המים לפני הספינה לידע שהוא בעומקו שתוכל ספינה להלך בהן: קפיד עליה. שלא יתעקם ומייחד ליה מקום ומקלה ליה בידים ואפי' לר"ש אסור לטלטלו דמוקצה מחמת חסרון כיס אפי' ר"ש מודה: שאינה קשורה לא. ואפי' יש עקמומית בראשה כעין מזלג שראוי לתלות בה טפיח ולמלאות וחישב עליה: שגדרן לעצים. שחתכן להיסק: צריך לקשור. מע"ש: באביה. בגפן: והא קא משתמש במחובר. ואפילו קשורה מבעוד יום ליתסר: למטה מג'. סמוך לקרקע וכגון לשאוב מן המעין שאינו עמוק ומותר להשתמש באילן למטה מג' כדאמרי' בפרק בתרא דעירובין (דף צט:) היו שרשיו גבוהין מן הארץ ג' לא ישב עליהם: גזירה שמא יקטום. שמא למחר תהיה לו ארוכה ויקטמנה מתוך שהיא רכה ונוחה לקטום ונמצא עושה כלי וחייב משום מכה בפטיש אבל בחריות ליכא למיגזר הכי הלכך במחשבה סגי: שאין עושין אהל עראי. לפרוס מחצלת על ד' מחיצות או על ד' קונדסים להיות צל לאהל מן החמה ודוקא גג אבל מחיצה לאו אהל הוא ושרי לפורסה לצניעות כדאמרי' בעירובין (דף לד.) בעובדא דשמואל ופקק החלון דמתני' ^ט משום דבנין קבוע הוא ומיחזי כמוסיף על הבנין: להוסיף. כגון שהיה מחצלת פרוסה עליהן וכרוכה ונשאר בה אויר ולמחר פושטה דומיא דפקק דמוסיף בעלמא הוא:

א) לקמן קלז: עירובין מד. סוכה מו. ב) לקמן קמב: ג) [לקמן קמב: ע"ש], ד) [לעיל קכ: לקמן קמב: ע"ש], ה) [קידושין נ. וש"נ], ו) [לעיל נ. ולקמן קכו.], ז) [לקמן קלז: עירו' מד. סוכה מו.] ח) [תוספת' פ"א], ט) [גי' רש"ל, ו) גי' רש"ל הוי למעלה בגג ולא למטה לכל דבר מקיים פי' רש"י דהכא.

רב נסים גאון

את שיש לו נחיצה ואת שאין לו נחיצה אין לו טומאה: אי הכי קא משתמש במחובר למטה מג' מכלל כי מה שיהיה מדבר המחובר לקרקע קרוב מהארץ פחות מג' טפחים מותר להשתמש בו ואין איסור משום שבות [רק] מה שהוא גבוה מן הארץ ג' טפחים ותמצא עיקר זה במשנה במס' עירובין בפרק המוצא תפילין (דף צט) אילן שהוא מיסך על הארץ אם אין נופו גבוה מן הארץ ג' טפחים לא ישב עליהן ודבר זה אין בו חלוקה אבל חלקו רבא ורב ששת בשרשי אילן הבאים מלמעלה מג' לתוך ג' (בפ' כל מערבין [שם דף לג:]) תניא נתנו באילן בתוך ג' מותר לטלטל: סליק פרק כל הכלים

ליקוטי רש"י

פקק החלון. כגון ארובה הגג [לקמן קלז:]. שהוא קשור ותלוי. שם כל שעה. פוקקין בו. כיון דמתוקן ועומד לכך אין זו כבונה ולא מוסיף. ואם לאו אין פוקקין בו. דמוסיף הוא על סתימת הבית [סוכה כו:]. דדמי לבונה שמוסיף על סתימת הבית וזה שמוסיף על שעראי הוא שהרי יחזור ויפתחנו [עירובין מד.]. מטה על צידה. מטה חבית על לדה והיא נופלת צריך ליטול מן היין והאבן נוטלה ולא יטלנה בידים דהיה בין החביות וירא שלא תפול האבן על החביות ותשברנה מגביה לחבית כולה והאבן עליה ומוליכה חוץ לחביות וטה על לדה. אלא בשוכח. אבל בשוכח שאבן עליה יכול לטלטלו הכא. סואר של קורות. הוא ולא אבנים [לקמן קמב:]. מותבינן אשמעתין. יש לי להשיב על דברי [קידושין נ:]. אשמעתין. לדידיה גופיה קא מותיב [מנחות מט.]. סואר של קורות. הן קורות העריכות על גבי קרקע זו על גב זו ועומדות לבנין [סוכה כ:]. שהו אוצר בנין. מתוקנות לבנות את ביתו [ביצה לא:]. גשוש של ספינה. כני אדם מתמשמשים בכלונסות את עומק המים ולפי מה ספינה שלא מקום עמוק שמא יכנס למקום מושכה [לעיל קו:]. חריות. ענפים קשים כען משמקשקן מלרפות שמכם שנגר שבגרנו ובעטו ולא שגר עילו כן קרויין גבין. שגדרן. ממזרים קרי גדירה. צריך לקשור. לקטוס יחד מבעוד יום שלישיה עומדים ושם לא קשרם יחד אסור לטלטל דלא הוי יחוד. קא

(לב:) לתלות בו שיהיו לא יקטמנו ושם קטמו חייב סטלא (לקמן קמב:). הכל מודים. ר"א ומחלוקתו שנחלקו בתוספת אהל עראי גבי פקק החלון לחלכה ללמדך פוקקין בו ואף על גב דאהל עראי הוא מודה שאין עושין אהל עראי בתחלה שבשבת בפרק כל הכלים (שבת קכה:) [עירובין מד.]. אלא להוסיף. כגון פקק זה שאינו אלא תוספת אהל עראי על האהל (לקמן קלז:). דלפילו רבנן לא שרו אלא להוסיף כגון פקק חלון דתוספת בעלמא הוא ובריחא שרי למיעבד דופן לכתחלה (עירובין מד.).

משתמש במחובר. דשימוש הוא לכמתן דלאו הן משום שבות הוא עולין באילן (בילה לו:) ולא משום שבות הוא עולין באילן (עירובין לג:) היו שרשיו גבוהין וכל למטה משלשה אפילו באילן לא גזרו עלו דהוי כלארעא סמיכה והכי נמי מתן בפרק בתרא (עירובין לג:) היו שרשיו גבוהין מן הארץ שלשה לא ישב עליהן (שם לג.). שמא יקטום. מן הענף ונתיה נמי לקמן במחט מריב שמנה דבנין מירב שריה כלמיות כן מלאכה (שם לג.).

ר' אליעזר אוסר למושכן כנגד כל החלון. וחכמים מתירים (וזהו) להוסיף כיוצא בו בסוף המוצא תפילין הנהו דיכרי דהוו לרב הונא דביממא בעו טולא ובליליא בעו אוירא. ואמר ליה רב כרוך בודיא ושייר בה טפח ולמחר פרשיה

לֹא נֶחְלְקוּ אֶלָּא לְהוֹסִיף – **They disagree only** whether one is permitted **to make a** temporary **addition** to an existing structure.[32] שֶׁרַבִּי אֱלִיעֶזֶר אוֹמֵר – **For** in such a case **R' Eliezer says:** אֵין מוֹסִיפִין בְּיוֹם טוֹב – **We may not make** even **a** temporary **addition** to a building **on Yom Tov,** וְאֵין צָרִיךְ לוֹמַר בְּשַׁבָּת – **and, it need not be said** that it is forbidden **on the Sabbath;** וַחֲכָמִים אוֹמְרִים – **while the Sages say:** מוֹסִיפִין בְּשַׁבָּת – **We may make a** temporary **addition** to a building even **on the Sabbath,** וְאֵין צָרִיךְ לוֹמַר בְּיוֹם טוֹב – **and it need not be said** that we may do so **on Yom Tov.**[33]

The Mishnah stated:

וַחֲכָמִים אוֹמְרִים בֵּין כָּךְ וּבֵין כָּךְ פּוֹקְקִין בּוֹ – **BUT THE SAGES SAY: IN EITHER CASE WE MAY SHUTTER** the window **WITH IT.**

The Gemara clarifies the Sages' opinion:

מַאי בֵּין כָּךְ וּבֵין כָּךְ – **What is** the meaning of **"in either case"?** Does it mean that we may shutter the window whether the shutter is suspended in the air or not, but it must be attached to the building? Or, perhaps, it means that we may shutter with it whether it is attached to the building or not. אָמַר רַבִּי אַבָּא אָמַר רַב כַּהֲנָא – **R' Abba said in the name of Rav Kahana:**

NOTES

a temporary wall from the start, for example, by spreading a privacy curtain. The construction of a wall is prohibited only if it is of a permanent nature (*Rashi*, as explained by *Ran*; see also *Chasam Sofer*, and see following notes; cf. *Tosafos*).

32. For example, if a folded mat was partially covering an enclosure, is one permitted to unfold the mat on the Sabbath or Yom Tov and cover the remaining open space (*Rashi*; see following note).

33. Thus, R' Eliezer forbids unfolding a mat that had been covering part of an area, whereas the Sages permit it. In essence, R' Eliezer holds that it is forbidden Rabbinically to make a temporary *addition* wherever it is prohibited Biblically to make the entire structure from the start. The Sages, however, do not forbid the temporary addition. This very dispute finds expression in our Mishnah, which deals with shuttering a window that is in a permanent wall. Since it would be prohibited to build the wall from the start, R' Eliezer forbids adding a shutter to it temporarily. He therefore states that one may close a window only with a shutter that is suspended from the wall by a short rope, so that it was previously defined as part of the structure. The Sages, on the other hand, permit shuttering the window even with an unsuspended shutter, since this merely constitutes a temporary addition to the structure [see further, 126a] (*Rashi*, as explained by *Ran, Rashba* and *Ritva MHK* ed.; cf. explanation of *Maharshal,* whose emendation of the *Rashi* text is cited in a marginal gloss and by *Maharsha*; see Gemara below).

בֵּין קָשׁוּר בֵּין שֶׁאֵינוֹ קָשׁוּר – The Sages mean that we may use the shutter **whether it is attached** to the building **or it is not attached,** וְהוּא שֶׁמְּתוּקָּן – **provided that it was prepared** for use as a shutter before the Sabbath.[1]

R' Abba's explanation is questioned:

אָמַר לֵיהּ רַבִּי יִרְמְיָה – **R' Yirmiyah said to [R' Abba]:** וְלֵימָא מַר – **Let master** rather **say** that the Sages mean we may use the shutter בֵּין תָּלוּי וּבֵין שֶׁאֵינוֹ תָּלוּי וְהוּא שֶׁקָּשׁוּר – **whether it is suspended** in the air **or it is not suspended, provided that it is attached** to the building![2] דְּאָמַר רַבָּה בַּר בַּר חָנָה אָמַר רַבִּי יוֹחָנָן – **For Rabbah bar bar Chanah said in the name of R' Yochanan:** כְּמַחְלוֹקֶת כָּאן – **Just as** the Tannaim of our Mishnah are in **dispute here,** concerning the case of a window shutter, כָּךְ מַחְלוֹקֶת בְּנֶגֶר הַנִּגְרָר – **so too,** they are in **dispute concerning** the case of **a door bolt that drags** on the ground, i.e. it is tied to the door but the cord is so long that the bolt reaches the ground.[3] דִּתְנַן – **For we learned in a Mishnah:**[4] נֶגֶר הַנִּגְרָר – A DOOR BOLT THAT DRAGS on the ground – נוֹעֲלִין בּוֹ בַּמִּקְדָּשׁ – ONE MAY LOCK a door WITH IT IN THE TEMPLE, אֲבָל לֹא בַּמְּדִינָה – BUT NOT IN THE PROVINCES, i.e. outside the Temple. וְהַמּוּנָּח – AND [A BOLT] THAT is completely unattached and RESTS on the ground כָּאן וְכָאן אָסוּר – IS PROHIBITED BOTH HERE AND THERE, i.e. in the Temple and the provinces.[5] רַבִּי יְהוּדָה אוֹמֵר – R' YEHUDAH SAYS: הַמּוּנָּח בַּמִּקְדָּשׁ – THE [BOLT] THAT is unattached and RESTS on the ground is permitted IN THE TEMPLE, וְהַנִּגְרָר בַּמְּדִינָה – AND THE ONE THAT is attached but DRAGS on the ground is completely permitted, even IN THE PROVINCES.[6] וְתַנְיָא – **And** the following elaboration **was taught in a Baraisa:** אֵיזֶהוּ נֶגֶר הַנִּגְרָר – WHAT IS the definition of THE BOLT THAT DRAGS on the ground, שֶׁנּוֹעֲלִין בּוֹ בַּמִּקְדָּשׁ אֲבָל לֹא בַּמְּדִינָה – WHICH MAY BE USED TO LOCK a door IN THE TEMPLE BUT NOT IN THE PROVINCES?[7] כֹּל שֶׁקָּשׁוּר וְתָלוּי וְרֹאשׁוֹ מַגִּיעַ לָאָרֶץ – ANY bolt THAT IS ATTACHED to the door AND SUSPENDED from it, BUT ITS END REACHES THE GROUND.[8] רַבִּי יְהוּדָה אוֹמֵר – R' YEHUDAH SAYS: זֶה אַף בַּמְּדִינָה מוּתָּר – THIS type of bolt IS PERMITTED EVEN IN THE PROVINCES.[9] אֶלָּא אֵיזֶהוּ שֶׁבַּמְּדִינָה אָסוּר – RATHER, WHAT IS the definition of [A BOLT] THAT IS PROHIBITED IN THE PROVINCES? כֹּל שֶׁאֵינוֹ לֹא קָשׁוּר וְלֹא תָלוּי – ANY bolt THAT IS NEITHER ATTACHED to the door NOR SUSPENDED from it, וְשׁוֹמְטוֹ וּמַנִּיחוֹ בְּקֶרֶן זָוִית – AND instead, ONE REMOVES IT AND LEAVES IT IN A CORNER after use. וְאָמַר רַבִּי יְהוֹשֻׁעַ בַּר אַבָּא מִשְּׁמֵיהּ דְּעוּלָּא – **And R' Yehoshua bar Abba said in the name of Ulla:** מַאן תַּנָּא נֶגֶר הַנִּגְרָר – **Who is the Tanna** Kamma **who taught** that **a bolt which** is attached to the door but **drags** on the ground may not be used in the provinces? רַבִּי אֱלִיעֶזֶר הִיא – **It is R' Eliezer,** who said in our Mishnah concerning a window shutter that it may not be used unless it is attached to the building *and* suspended in the air. This implies that R' Yehudah follows the opinion of the Sages of our Mishnah, who dispute R' Eliezer's ruling concerning a window shutter. Since R' Yehudah concedes that a bolt must at least be attached to the door in order for its use to be permitted in the provinces, it follows that the Sages require that a shutter be attached to the building for its use to be permitted. Thus, you should interpret the Sages' statement, "in either case, we may shutter the window with it," as meaning that we may use the shutter whether it is suspended in the air or drags on the ground, but it must certainly be attached to the building.[10] – ? –

R' Abba defends his interpretation of the Sages' opinion:

אָמַר לֵיהּ – **He said to [R' Yirmiyah]:** אֲנָא דְּאָמְרִי כִּי הַאי תַּנָּא – **I stated** my interpretation **in accordance with** the view of **this** other **Tanna,** who permits even the use of a bolt that is unattached. דְּתַנְיָא – **For it was taught in a Baraisa:** קָנֶה שֶׁהִתְקִינוֹ בַּעַל הַבַּיִת לִהְיוֹת פּוֹתֵחַ וְנוֹעֵל בּוֹ – A ROD THAT A HOMEOWNER PREPARED FOR USE IN UNLOCKING AND LOCKING

NOTES

1. I.e. one mentally designated it for use as a shutter before the Sabbath. No preparatory act is required, in accordance with the opinion of Rabban Shimon ben Gamliel [cited on 125b; see notes 26 and 30 there] (*Rashi,* as explained by *Ritva MHK* ed.; *Tosafos* ד״ה בין קשור).

2. I.e. say that the Sages dispute R' Eliezer only in regard to his requirement that the shutter be suspended in the air. Thus, whereas R' Eliezer holds that even where the shutter is attached to the building, if it drags on the ground, lifting and inserting it in the window falls under the prohibition of [making a temporary addition to a] building, the Sages will hold that even if it drags on the ground there is no prohibition, provided the shutter is attached to the building. Why do you interpret the Sages' opinion leniently, as disputing even the requirement that the shutter be attached? (*Rashi,* as explained by *Chasam Sofer*; see note 10).

3. And since, as we shall see, in the case of a door bolt the Sages permit its use only when it is attached to the door, it follows that in our case, too, the Sages permit the use of a shutter only when it is attached to the building.

The door bolt referred to here is a peg that is wedged into a hole in the threshold to lock the door (*Rashi*).

4. *Eruvin* 102a.

5. The use of a bolt that is not tied to the door at all is a Biblical violation, for the act of inserting it into the threshold is a genuine act of building, like driving a nail into a wall. Therefore, it is prohibited in all locations – both in the Temple and in the provinces. However, if the bolt is tied to the door, it has been designated for this purpose and has already been rendered a part of the structure from before the Sabbath. Therefore, its use does not constitute building on the Biblical level. Nevertheless, if the cord is so long that the bolt reaches the ground, it does not appear to be attached to the door and its use *resembles* an act of building. The Rabbis therefore prohibited the use of a bolt unless it is suspended above the ground. However, like most Rabbinic decrees, this prohibition does not apply in the Temple, but only in the provinces (*Rashi* here and to *Eruvin* 102a).

[*Tosafos* (ד״ה והמונח) argue that even if the bolt is not attached at all there is no Biblical prohibition, since one does not append it to the building indefinitely. They therefore explain our Gemara differently (see 126b note 6 for further elaboration).]

6. R' Yehudah is of the opinion that once a bolt was designated for this purpose before the Sabbath, its use does not constitute an act of building on the Biblical level, even if it is not attached to the door (*Rashi*). The designation for use as a lock defines the bolt as a utensil, and it is no longer regarded as construction material. Since one does not append a utensil to the building, its insertion in the threshold is not considered an act of construction (see *Rashi* to *Eruvin* 102a ד״ה כשאין ניטל באיגדו; see also *Milchamos Hashem, Rosh* with *Korban Nesanel* §9, *Beur HaGra* to *Orach Chaim* 313:2 and *Beur Halachah* to 313:1 ד״ה יהא קשור). Thus, the use of this bolt is permitted in the Temple. However [since the unattached bolt looks like an ordinary peg], its use *appears* like building and is therefore prohibited Rabbinically in the provinces (*Rashi* to *Eruvin* 102a ד״ה והמונח; cf. *Tosafos* here ד״ה והמונח). When the bolt is attached to the door, there is not even a Rabbinical prohibition against its use, according to R' Yehudah, since there is not even the appearance of building (see *Avnei Nezer* 224:14).

7. [According to the Tanna Kamma.]

8. I.e. its upper end is suspended but its lower end reaches the ground (*Rashi*). Actually, even if both ends reach the ground, the bolt may be used in the Temple. The Baraisa focuses on the case where one of its ends reaches the ground to teach that *even* a bolt that rests only partially on the ground is still forbidden in the provinces (*Tosafos* ד״ה שקשור; see also *Rashi* ד״ה והמונח).

9. R' Yehudah also does not differentiate between a bolt that rests partially on the ground and one that rests entirely on the ground, but permits the use of both types in the provinces (ibid.).

10. *Rashi.* You should say that the Sages concede that the shutter must be attached to the building to preclude the *appearance* of building [for if it is not attached with a rope, it appears to be a permanent addition rather than a temporary one] (*Rashi,* as understood by *Beur HaGra, Orach Chaim* 313:1 and *Avnei Nezer* 224:14).

בין קשור בין שאינו קשור והוא שמתוקן א"ל ר' ירמיה ולימא מר בין תלוי ובין שאינו תלוי והוא שקשור דאמר רבה בר בר חנה א"ר יוחנן כמחלוקת כאן כך מחלוקת בנגר הנגרר דתנן נגר הנגרר נועלין בו במקדש אבל לא במדינה והמונח כאן וכאן אסור ר' יהודה אומר המונח במקדש והנגרר במדינה ותניא איזהו נגר הנגרר שנועלין בו במקדש אבל לא במדינה כל שקשור ותלוי וראשו מגיע לארץ ר' יהודה אומר זה אף במדינה מותר אלא איזהו שבמדינה אסור כל שאינו לא קשור ולא תלוי ושומטו ומניחו בקרן זוית ואמר רבי יהושע בר אבא משמיה דעולא מאן תנא נגר הנגרר ר"א היא א"ל אנא דאמרי כי האי תנא דתניא קנה שהתקינו בעה"ב להיות פותח ונועל בו בזמן שקשור ותלוי בפתח פותח ונועל בו אין קשור ותלוי אין פותח ונועל בו רשב"ג אומר מתוקן אע"פ שאינו קשור אמר רב יהודה בר שילת אמר רב אסי א"ר יוחנן הלכה כרשב"ג ומי אמר רבי יוחנן הכי והתנן כל כסויי הכלים

שיש

רש"י

בין קשור כו'. כלומר אפילו קשירה לא צריך: והוא שמתוקן. מוכן מאתמול לכך: א"ל רבי ירמיה. אמאי פשיט ליה מר לקולא: לימא מר. דלא פליגי רבנן אלא אתלויה דרבי אליעזר בעי קשור ותלוי ואפילו קשור אם ראשו נגרר לארץ חשיב ליה רבי אליעזר כשומטו מן הקרקע ובונה בו לכתחלה ורבנן אמרי ליה בין תלוי בין נגרר פוקקין בו ובלבד שיהא קשור: דאמר רבה בר בר חנה. בתלייה הוא דפליגי ולא בקשירה דמדמי לה לפלוגתא דנגר הנגרר והתם לדברי הכל קשור בעינן: נגר. יתד שתוקעין בחור שבמפתן ונועלין בו את הדלת: הנגרר. כלמפרש שקשור בדלת אלא שראשו נגרר לארץ: נועלין בו במקדש. דכיון דקשור בו מיוחד ועומד הוא לכך וכבר נבנה בנין זה מבעוד יום ואין בו אלא גזירת שבות מדרבנן ואין שבות במקדש: והמונח. שאינו קשור כלל אלא כשהוא שומטו מן החור מניחו ע"ג קרקע הלכך כשתוקעו בשבת בונה הוא ואיסורא דאורייתא הוא אף במקדש: המונח מותר במקדש. דכיון דמתוקן מאתמול להכי לאו בונה הוא: שקשור ותלוי. ראשו העליון אבל ראשו התחתון מגיע לארץ: מאן תנא נגר הנגרר. אסור דבעי תרתי: ר"א היא. דאמר גבי פקק החלון תרתי בעינן מכלל דר' יהודה כרבנן אלמא רבנן קשירה בעו: כי האי תנא. דלפי' קשירה לא בעי כרבן שמעון בן גמליאל דאמר מתוקן בהזמנה בעלמא ואע"פ שאינו קשור: שהתקינו. שהזמינו: אמר רב יהודה גרסינן ולא גרסינן ואמר:

תוספות

דכל גגות (עירובין צ.) דפריך ושמואל למה ליה למיעבד הכי וקאמר זה מטלטל כו' לאו משום דאי הוה אמר אין מטלטלין בו אלא בד' אמות דאז הוה ניחא ליה אלא אז נמי היה קשה היכי עביד הכי כיון דמתחלה מתרת לטלטל בחצר הוה כעשיית אהל עראי בתחלה ואסור כדפרישית לעיל ומהאי טעמא היה מקפיד רב דס"ל שאין מטלטלין אלא בד' אלא משום דהש"ס לא ידע דסבר שמואל דזה מטלטל עד עיקר המחיצה ניחא למיפרך למה הוצרך לעשות מחיצה:

בין קשור בין שאינו קשור והוא שמתוקן. נראה לר"ת דלאו בתיקון של מעשה אלא במחשבה בעלמא כדמוכח לקמן דאמר כרשב"ג ס"ל דאמר מתוקן אע"פ שאינו קשור דהיינו במחשבה ומשמע דלגמרי ס"ל כוותיה דגבי ר' יוחנן דוקא הוא דאמר בסמוך סבר לה כוותיה בחדא ופליג עליה בחדא ופריך ולימא מר בין תלוי בין שאינו תלוי והוא שקשור כרבי יהודה דבעי קשירה וטעמא משום טלטול ולא משום בנין דאי משום בנין מאי ראיה מנגר שצריך קשירה לפקק והא בפקק לא שייך בנין אלא תוספת אהל עראי ותוספת אהל עראי שרו רבנן בלא שום קשירה כדמוכח במי שהוליכוהו (שם מד.): **והמונח** כאן וכאן אסור. פי' רש"י שכשתוקעו בשבת בונה הוא ואיסורא דאורייתא איכא ואינו משמע שיהא בו איסורא דאורייתא כיון שאינו מבטלו שם אלא נראה לר"ת דכולה מילתא בנגר הנגרר ליכא איסורא אלא משום טלטול וכי ההיא דקנה שהתקינו בעה"ב להיות פותח ונועל בו דמיירי משום טלטול ואפ"ה בעי ר"א קשור ותלוי יותר משאר כלי תשמיש שדי להם בתיקונם לפי שהם תשמיש בית מידי דהוי אכיסוי קרקעות שהחמירו בהם להצריכם בית אחיזה אע"ג דהכי משום שבות נאסר טלטולם במקדש כקנים וכמקלות דלעיל אבל בשום בנין ליכא איסורא כלל אפילו מדרבנן וקשה לר"ת מנלן דאפליגו רבי אליעזר ורבנן בתוספת אהל עראי כיון דאפליגו בטלטול דילמא בחד הוא דאיפליגו ותירץ ר"ת בספר הישר דא"כ הוה ליה למנקט פלוגתייהו במילתא דלא שייכא ביה תוספת אהל כי ההיא דנגר הנגרר ומדנקט פלוגתא בפקק החלון דשייך ביה תוספת אהל ש"מ דפליגי באהל וליכא למימר דדווקא באהל פליגי ולא בטלטול דהא בההיא דנגר לא שייך אלא איסור טלטול אפ"ה איפלוג בה ר"א ורבנן דע"כ איבעי לן למימר דת"ק דנגר היינו ר"א דרבנן שרו אפילו בפקק החלון כ"ש בנגר דלא שייך איסור אהל אלא איסור טלטול אלא ודאי בתרתי פליגי דר"א אסר בפקק החלון ומשום טלטול בשאין תורת כלי גמור עליו ואפי' יש עליו תורת כלי גמור כגון שיש לו בית יד אסור מ"מ משום תוספת אהל עראי כיון דבטלי' בפקק ורבנן דשרו אפי' אין עליו תורת כלי דלית להו לא משום טלטול ולא משום אהל: **רבי** יהודה אומר כו'. ובעירובין מסקינן אמר רב יהודה אמר שמואל הלכה כרבי יהודה וקשה לר"י דהא שמואל גופיה סבר לעיל בפרק במה טומנין (דף נ.) גבי חריות של דקל שגדרן לעצים דבמחשבה בעלמא סגי דאיתמר רב (יהודה) אומר קושר ושמואל אמר חושב וקאמר התם דשמואל ס"ל כרשב"ג דאמר חריות של דקל שגדרן לעצים ונמלך עליהן לישיבה א"צ לקשר וא"כ היכי קאמר הלכה כרבי יהודה דבעי קשירה משום איסור טלטול דהא לא שייך איסור בנין בההיא דנגר הנגרר אלא איסור טלטול ומשום איסור טלטול בעי רבי יהודה קשירה כדפירשתי וליכא לפרושי דבנגר הנגרר דהכא לאפוקי מאיסור בנין הוא דבעי קישור אבל משום איסור טלטול לא הוה בעי קישור אלא במחשבה בעלמא כרשב"ג א"כ מאי קא מהדר ליה ר' אבא בר כהנא לר' ירמיה אנא דאמרי כי האי תנא כו' דילמא מאי דלא בעי התם רשב"ג אלא מתוקן אע"פ שאינו קשור היינו משום דהתם ליכא אלא איסור טלטול דהתם ודאי לא איירי מידי בבנין דקאמר קנה שהתקינו בעה"ב להיות פותח ונועל (א) ומדקתני פותח ונועל משמע שאינו נועל באותו קנה עצמו דהוה ליה למיתני שהתקינו לנעול בו אלא משמע שהוא כעין מפתחות שלנו שיש מהם שמושכין המנעול שבדלת לכאן ולכאן כך הקנה מושך המנעול אבל הקנה עצמו אינו במקום המנעול א"כ פשיטא דכה"ג לא שייך בנין בהאי קנה אלא משום איסור טלטול הוא ומיהו אין ראיה מזה דבהאי קנה מיירי כדפרישית מדקתני פותח ונועל דהא כה"ג קתני בתוספתא חבילי עצים וסוכה של קוצים שעשאן דלת לפירצה ולחצר אם היו קשורות ותלויות פותחין ונועלין בהן אם לאו כו' מיהו אומר ר"י דאפילו הוה מפרש ההיא דקנה שהתקינו כו' דשייך ביה בנין ובמקום מנעול הוה ולהכי פשיט מיניה רבי אבא בר כהנא דס"ל כרשב"ג דאמר דכי הוי מתוקן אע"פ שאינו קשור נפיק מתורת איסור בנין לא הוי אתי שפיר (דה"א) מדקאמר הש"ס בסמוך וכ"ת הכא נמי דאיכא תורת כלי עליהן והתניא חריות של דקל כו' והיכי מוכח מההיא דחריות של דקל דהא דאמר מתוקן אע"פ שאינו קשור היינו בלא תורת כלי אלא במחשבה בעלמא דלמא באיסור טלטול הוא דלא מצריך רשב"ג אלא מחשבה אבל לאיסור בנין הוה בעי שיתקנוהו ויכינוהו ויעשו בו מעשה שיהא תורת כלי עליו על כן נראה לר"י דבהכי פליגי רבי אבא בר כהנא ורבי יוחנן ורב יהודה דעירובין (דף קב.) דלאיהו סבירא להו דבההיא דנגר לא שייך אלא איסור טלטול ואיהו ס"ל דשייך בנין בנגר הנגרר ולהכי בעי קישור לאפוקי מאיסור בנין והשתא אתיא שמעתין שפיר דלא מיירי מידי באיסור בנין לא בההוא דנגר ולא בההיא דקנה והשתא נמי ההיא דקנה משום טלטול. מ"ר:

שקשור ותלוי וראשו מגיע לארץ. פירוש ראשו העליון תלוי וראשו התחתון מגיע לארץ כדפירש בקונטרס ונראה לרשב"א דאפילו שני הראשים מונחים לארץ אלא שקשור דשרי במקדש והאי דנקט כהאי גוונא לאשמעינן דאפ"ה אסור במדינה והשתא אתי שפיר הא דתנן במשנה והמונח כאן וכאן אסור היינו שאינו קשור ולא תלוי כלל דאי אמרת דוקא נקט ראשו מגיע לארץ אבל שני הראשים מונחין בארץ אסור במקדש אע"פ שקשור אם כן השתא לא הוי מונח דרבי יהודה כמונח דתנא קמא דמונח דרבי יהודה על כרחיך היינו שאינו לא קשור ולא תלוי ושומטו ומניחו בקרן זוית דאי אמרת כמו מונח דת"ק שני ראשים מונחים לארץ אלא שקשורין היכי קאמר המונח במקדש ההוא אפילו במדינה שרי דלא אסר רבי יהודה אלא דוקא שאינו קשור כלל:

וכ"ת

מסורת הש"ס

א) עירובין קב., ב) [נ"ל מותר במקדש], ג) [תוספ' פט"ו].

הגהות הב"ח

(א) תום' ד"ה ר' יהודה וכו' פותח ונועל בו מדקתני פותח ונועל בו משמע:

גליון הש"ס

גמ' שנועלין בו במקדש אבל לא במדינה. עיין פי"א מ"ד דכלים:

ליקוטי רש"י

נגר. קבילי"א שתוחבין אותו בחור שבאיסקופה לנעול הדלת [עירובין קא:]. נגר הנגרר. שקשור בדלת אבל אינו תלוי שהחבל ארוך ומתוך שנגרר אינו נראה כקשור וכשאין בראשו גלוסטרא קאמר. נועלין בו במקדש. דשבות בעלמא הוא דאינו בונה ממש הואיל וקשור לכך אלא הואיל ונגרר מיחזי כבונה ואין שבות דרבנן במקדש דלא גזרו שם. והמונח. שאינו קשור כלל הוי בנין ממש. והמונח כאן וכאן אסור. דכיון שאינו קשור שם בנין גמור הוא כשאר נגרים שנועלים בכותלים והבונה כל שהוא חייב ומלאכה דאורייתא לא הותרה במקדש חוץ מהקרבת תמידין ומוספין וקרבנות צבור שדוחין את השבת מגזירת הכתוב. המונח במקדש. ר' יהודה סבר לאו בנין ממש הוא אלא דומה לבנין ובמקדש לא גזרו שבות [שם קב.].

עין משפט נר מצוה

מג א ב מיי' פכ"ב מהלכות שבת הלכה ל ופכ"ו הלכה י סמג לאוין סה טוש"ע או"ח סימן שיג סעיף א:

מד ג מיי' פכ"ו שם הלכה י:

רבינו חננאל

עליהן מוסיף על אהלי עראי הוא ושפיר דמי. וחכ"א בין כך ובין כך פוקקין בו. ומיבעיא לן מאי בין כך ובין כך אמר רבה בר כהנא בין קשור בין שאינו קשור אותו פקק פוקקין בו. והוא שמתוקן. כלומר שהתקינו לפקק בו. היכי דמי תיקון זה כדאמרינן בסוף המוצא תפילין: ת"ר סיכי קמצים וחבילי עצים שהתקינן לפירצה שבחצר. בזמן שקשורין ותלוין נועלין בשבת ואין צ"ל ביו"ט. א"ל ר' ירמיה ולימא מר בין תלוי בין שאינו תלוי והוא שקשור כלומר כבר נעשה בו מעשה לשום כלי. דאמר רבה ב"ב חנה א"ר יוחנן כמחלוקת כאן בפקק החלון כך חלוקתן בנגר הנגרר בקשור ותלוי בלבד. אבל לא לענין מקדש ומדינה. ותניא בסוף עירובין. איזהו נגר הנגרר שנועלין בו במקדש אבל לא במדינה: שומטו ומניחו בקרן זוית. דייקינן מינה מדקתני ושומטו ומניחו מכלל שאם הוא קשור שאם אינו יכול לשומטו ולהניחו בקרן זוית שפיר דמי. ואמרינן מאן תנא נגר הנגרר צריך להיות קשור ותלוי ר' אליעזר והא ר' יוחנן סבר כי חכמים חלוקין על ר' אליעזר סבירא להו כר' יהודה דאסר בשאינו קשור ולא תלוי ולא בתלוי אבל אם הוא קשור אע"פ שאינו תלוי שרי. וא"ל ר' אבא לר' ירמיה אנא דאמרי והוא שמתוקן אע"פ שאינו לא קשור ולא תלוי כי הא מתניתא דתני בקנה שהתקינו בעה"ב להיות פותח ונועל בו. ואמר רשב"ג מתוקן אע"פ שאינו קשור ואמר משמיה דר' יוחנן הלכה כרשב"ג דקאי רשב"ג כחכמים. ואקשינן היכי אמר ר' יוחנן הלכה

a door[11] – בִּזְמַן שֶׁקָּשׁוּר וְתָלוּי בַּפֶּתַח – WHEN IT IS ATTACHED to the wall AND SUSPENDED IN THE DOORWAY, פּוֹתֵחַ וְנוֹעֵל בּוֹ – HE MAY USE IT TO UNLOCK AND LOCK the door; אֵין קָשׁוּר וְתָלוּי – but if IT IS NOT ATTACHED AND SUSPENDED, אֵין פּוֹתֵחַ וְנוֹעֵל בּוֹ – HE MAY NOT USE IT TO UNLOCK AND LOCK the door. רַבָּן שִׁמְעוֹן בֶּן גַּמְלִיאֵל אוֹמֵר – RABBAN SHIMON BEN GAMLIEL SAYS: מְתוּקָּן – Once the rod was PREPARED for this purpose, one may use it אַף עַל פִּי שֶׁאֵינוֹ קָשׁוּר – EVEN IF IT IS NOT ATTACHED to the wall. In my opinion, the Sages of our Mishnah follow Rabban Shimon ben Gamliel.[12]

A related ruling is cited:

אָמַר רַב יְהוּדָה בַּר שִׁילַת אָמַר רַב אַסִּי אָמַר רַבִּי יוֹחָנָן – Rav Yehudah bar Shilas said in the name of Rav Assi, who said in the name of R' Yochanan: הֲלָכָה כְּרַבָּן שִׁמְעוֹן בֶּן גַּמְלִיאֵל – The halachah follows Rabban Shimon ben Gamliel.

The Gemara questions the veracity of this ruling:

וּמִי אָמַר רַבִּי יוֹחָנָן הָכִי – Did R' Yochanan actually **say this? וְהָתְנַן – But we learned in a Mishnah:**[13] כָּל כִּסּוּיֵי הַכֵּלִים – ALL VESSEL-COVERS

NOTES

11. The rod would be inserted in a hole in the wall near the door to keep the door closed. Thus, it served in the same capacity as a bolt (*Magen Avraham* 313:2, *Mishnah Berurah* 313:4; see also *Milchamos Hashem*; cf. *Tosafos* ד״ה רבי יהודה אומר).

12. According to Rabban Shimon ben Gamliel, the only preparation required is mental designation for this purpose (*Rashi*). The designation alone defines the rod as a utensil, thus eliminating the appearance of building (*Avnei Nezer* 224:14). Accordingly, I interpret the Sages' statement in our Mishnah as meaning that one may use a shutter whether it is attached to the building or it is unattached. The only requirement is that it be designated for this purpose in advance of the Sabbath (see *Orach Chaim* 313:1).

See *Chasam Sofer* for an explanation of why R' Abba assumed that the Sages of our Mishnah follow Rabban Shimon ben Gamliel rather than R' Yehudah.

13. Below, 126b.

א בין קשור בין שאינו קשור והוא שמתוקן א"ל ר' ירמיה ולימא מר בין תלוי ובין שאינו תלוי והוא שקשור דאמר רבה בר בר חנה א"ר יוחנן כמחלוקת כאן כך מחלוקת בנגר הנגרר (א) דתנן נגר הנגרר נועלין בו במקדש אבל לא במדינה והמונח כאן וכאן אסור ר' יהודה אומר המונח (ב) במקדש והנגרר במדינה ותניא איזהו נגר הנגרר ° שנועלין בו במקדש אבל לא במדינה כל שקשור ותלוי וראשו מגיע לארץ ר' יהודה אומר ב זה אף במדינה מותר אלא איזהו שבמדינה אסור כל שאינו לא קשור ולא תלוי ושומטו ומניחו בקרן זוית ואמר רבי יהושע בר אבא משמיה דעולא מאן תנא נגר הנגרר ר"א היא א"ל אנא דאמרי כי האי תנא דתניא (ג) קנה שהתקינו בעה"ב להיות פותח ונועל בו בזמן שקשור ותלוי בפתח פותח ונועל בו אין קשור ותלוי אין פותח ונועל בו רשב"ג אומר מתוקן אע"פ שאינו קשור אמר רב יהודה בר שילת אמר רב אסי א"ר יוחנן ג הלכה כרשב"ג ומי אמר רבי יוחנן הכי והתנן כל כסויי הכלים

שיש

רש"י

בין קשור כו'. כלומר אפילו קשירה לא צריך: והוא שמתוקן. מוכן מאתמול לכך: א"ל רבי ירמיה. אמאי פשיט ליה מר לקולא: לימא מר. דלא פליגי רבנן אלא אתלויה דרבי אליעזר בעי קשור ותלוי ואפילו קשור אם ראשו נגרר לארץ חשיב ליה רבי אליעזר כשומטו מן הקרקע ובונה בו לכתחלה ורבנן אמרי ליה בין תלוי בין נגרר פוקקין בו ובלבד שיהא קשור: דאמר רבה בר בר חנה. בתלייה הוא דפליגי ולא בקשירה דמדמי לה לפלוגתא דנגר הנגרר והתם לדברי הכל קשור בעינן: נגר. יתד שתוקעין בחור שבמפתן ונועלין בו את הדלת: הנגרר. כדמפרש שקשור בדלת אלא שראשו נגרר לארץ: נועלין בו במקדש. דכיון דקשור בו מיוחד ועומד הוא לכך וכבר נבנה בנין זה מבעוד יום ואין בו אלא גזירת שבות מדבריהם ואין שבות במקדש: והמונח. שאינו קשור כלל אלא כשהוא שומטו מן החור מניחו ע"ג קרקע הלכך כשתוקעו בשבת בונה הוא ואיסורא דאורייתא הוא אף במקדש: המונח מותר במקדש. דכיון דמתוקן מאתמול להכי לאו בונה הוא: שקשור ותלוי. ראשו העליון אבל ראשו התחתון מגיע לארץ: מאן תנא נגר הנגרר. אסור דבעי תרתי: ר"א היא. דאמר גבי פקק החלון תרתי בעינן מכלל דר' יהודה כרבנן אלמא רבנן קשירה בעו: כי האי תנא. דאפי' קשירה לא בעי כרבן שמעון בן גמליאל דאמר מתוקן בהזמנה בעלמא ואע"פ שאינו קשור: שהתקינו. שהזמינו: אמר רב יהודה גרסינן ולא גרסינן ואמר:

שיש

תוספות

דכל גגות (עירובין לז.) דפריך ושמואל למה ליה למיעבד הכי וקאמר זה מטלטל כו' לאו משום דאי הוה אמר אין מטלטלין בו אלא בד' אמות דאז הוה ניחא ליה אלא אז נמי היה קשה היכי עביד הכי כיון דמחילה מתרת לטלטל בחצר הוה כעשיית אהל עראי בתחלה ואסור כדפרישית לעיל ומהאי טעמא היה מקפיד רב דס"ל שאין מטלטלין אלא בד' אלא משום דהש"ס ידע דסבר שמואל דזה מטלטל עד עיקר המחילה ניחא למיפרך למה הוצרך לעשות מחילה:

בין קשור בין שאינו קשור והוא שמתוקן. נראה לר"ת דלאו בתיקון של מעשה אלא במחשבה בעלמא כדמוכח לקמן דאמר כרשב"ג ס"ל דאמר מתוקן אע"פ שאינו קשור דהיינו במחשבה ומשמע דלגמרי ס"ל כוותיה דגבי ר' יוחנן דוקא הוא דאמר בסמוך סבר לה כוותיה בחדא ופליג עליה בחדא ופריך ולימא מר בין תלוי בין שאינו תלוי והוא שקשור כרבי יהודה דבעי קשירה וטעמא משום טלטול ולא משום בנין דאי משום בנין מאי ראיה מנגר שצריך קשירה לפקק והא בפקק לא שייך בנין אלא תוספת אהל עראי ותוספת אהל עראי שרו רבנן בלא שום קשירה כדמוכח במי שהוציאוהו (שם מד.):

והמונח כאן וכאן אסור. פי' רש"י שכשתוקעו בשבת בונה הוא ואיסורא דאורייתא איכא ואינו משמע שיהא בו איסורא דאורייתא כיון שאינו מבטלו שם אלא נראה לר"ת דכולה מילתא בנגר הנגרר ליכא איסורא אלא משום טלטול וכי ההיא דקנה שהתקינו בעה"ב להיות פותח ונועל בו דמיירי משום טלטול ואפ"ה בעי ר"א קשור ותלוי יותר משאר כלי תשמיש שדי להם במקומם לפי שהם תשמיש בית מידי דהוי אכיסוי קרקעות שהתמירו בהם להצריכם בית אחיזה אע"ג דהוי משום שבות נאסר טלטולם במקדש כקנים ומקלות דלעיל אבל בשום בנין ליכא איסורא כלל אפילו מדרבנן וקשה לר"ת מנלן דפליגי רבי אליעזר ורבנן בתוספת אהל עראי כיון דאפליגו בטלטול דילמא בחד הוא דאפליגו ומיהך ר"ת בספר הישר דא"כ הוה ליה לאקשויי פלוגתייהו במילתא דלא שייכא ביה תוספת אהל כי ההיא דנגר הנגרר ומדנקט פלוגתא דפקק החלון דשייך ביה תוספת אהל ש"מ דפליגי באהל וליכא למימר דדווקא באהל פליגי ולא בטלטול דהא בההיא דנגר לא שייך אלא איסור טלטול אפ"ה איפלוג בה ר"א ורבנן דע"כ איבעי לן למימר דת"ק דנגר היינו ר"א דרבנן שרו אפילו בפקק החלון כ"ש בנגר דלא שייך איסור אהל אלא איסור טלטול ולא בתרתי פליגי דר"א אסר בפקק החלון ומשום טלטול דבאין תורת כלי גמור עליו ואפי' יש עליו תורת כלי גמור כגון שיש לו בית יד אסור מ"מ משום תוספת אהל עראי כיון דבטלי' בפקק ורבנן דשרו אפי' אין עליו תורת כלי דלית להו לא משום טלטול ולא משום אהל:

רבי יהודה אומר כו'. ובעירובין מסקינן אמר רב יהודה אמר שמואל הלכה כרבי יהודה וקשה לר"י דהא שמואל גופיה סבר לעיל בפרק במה טומנין (דף נ.) גבי חריות של דקל שגדרן לעצים דבמחשבה בעלמא סגי דאיתמר רב (יהודה) אומר קושר ושמואל אמר חושב וקאמר התם דשמואל ס"ל כרשב"ג דאמר חריות של דקל שגדרן לעצים ונמלך עליהן לישיבה א"צ לקשר וא"כ היכי קאמר הלכה כרבי יהודה דבעי קשירה משום איסור טלטול דהא לא שייך איסור בנין בההיא דנגר הנגרר אלא איסור טלטול ומשום איסור טלטול בעי רבי יהודה קשירה כדפירשתי וליכא לפרושי דבנגר הנגרר דהכא לאפוקי מאיסור בנין הוא דבעי קשירה אבל משום איסור טלטול לא הוה בעי קישור אלא במחשבה בעלמא כרשב"ג א"כ מאי קא מהדר ליה ר' אבא בר כהנא לר' ירמיה אנא דאמרי כי האי תנא כו' דילמא מאי דלא בעי התם רשב"ג אלא מתוקן אע"פ שאינו קשור היינו משום דהתם ליכא אלא איסור טלטול דהתם ודאי לא מיירי מידי בבנין דקאמר קנה שהתקינו בעה"ב להיות פותח ונועל (א) ומדקתני פותח ונועל משמע שאינו נועל באותו קנה עצמו דהוה ליה למיתני שהתקינו לנעול בו אלא משמע שהוא כעין מפתחות שלנו שיש מהם שמושכין המנעול שבדלת לכאן ולכאן כך הקנה מושך המנעול אבל הקנה עצמו אינו במקום המנעול א"כ פשיטא דהכ"ג לא שייך בנין בהאי קנה אלא משום איסור טלטול הוא ומיהו אין ראיה מזה דבהאי קנה מיירי כדפירשית מדקתני פותח ונועל דהא כה"ג קתני בתוספתא חבילי עצים וסוכה של קוצים שעשאן דלת לפירצה ולחצר אם היו קשורות ותלויות פותחין ונועלין בהן אם לאו כו' מיהו אומר ר"י דאפילו הוה מפרש ההיא דקנה שהתקינו כו' דשייך ביה בנין ובמקום מנעול הוה והכי פשיט מיניה רבי אבא בר כהנא דס"ל כרשב"ג דאמר דכי הוי מתוקן אע"פ שאינו קשור נפיק מתורת איסור בנין לא הוי אתי שפיר (דה"א) מדקאמר הש"ס בסמוך וכ"ת הכא נמי דליכא תורת כלי עליהן והתניא חריות של דקל כו' והיכי מוכח מההיא דחריות של דקל דהא דאמר מתוקן אע"פ שאינו קשור היינו בלא תורת כלי אלא במחשבה בעלמא דלמא באיסור טלטול הוא דלא מצריך רשב"ג אלא מחשבה אבל באיסור בנין הוה בעי שיתקנוהו ויכינוהו ויעשו בו מעשה שיהא תורת כלי עליו על כן נראה לר"י דבהכי פליגי רבי אבא בר כהנא ורבי יוחנן ורב יהודה דעירובין (דף קב.) דלאינהו סבירא להו דבההיא דנגר לא שייך אלא איסור טלטול ואיהו ס"ל דשייך בנין בנגר הנגרר והכי בעי קשור לאפוקי מאיסור בנין והשתא אתיא שמעתין שפיר דלא מיירי מידי באיסור בנין לא בההוא דנגר ולא בההיא דקנה והשתא נמי ההיא דקנה משום טלטול. מ"ר:

שקשור ותלוי וראשו מגיע לארץ. פירוש ראשו העליון תלוי וראשו התחתון מגיע לארץ כדפירש בקונטרס ונראה לרשב"א דאפילו שני הראשים מונחים לארץ אלא שקשור דשרי במקדש והאי דנקט כהאי גוונא לאשמעינן דאפ"ה אסור במדינה והשתא אתי שפיר הא דתנן במשנה והמונח כאן וכאן אסור היינו שאינו קשור ולא תלוי כלל דאי אמרת דוקא נקט ראשו מגיע לארץ אבל שני הראשים מונחין בארץ אסור במקדש אע"פ שקשור אם כן השתא לא הוי מונח דרבי יהודה כמונח דתנא קמא דמונח דרבי יהודה על כרחיך היינו שאינו לא קשור ולא תלוי ושומטו ומניחו בקרן זוית דאי אמרת כמו מונח דת"ק שני ראשים מונחים בארץ אלא שקשורין היכי קאמר המונח במקדש הוא אפילו במדינה שרי דלא אסר רבי יהודה אלא דוקא שאינו קשור כלל:

וכ"ת

עין משפט נר מצוה

מג א ב מיי' פכ"ב מהלכות שבת הלכה ל ופכ"ו הלכה י סמג לאוין סה טוש"ע או"ח סימן שיג סעיף א:

מד ג מיי' פכ"ו שם הלכה י:

רבינו חננאל

עליהן מוסיף על אהלי עראי הוא ושפיר דמי. וחכ"א בין כך ובין כך פוקקין בו. ומיבעיא לן מאי בין כך ובין כך אמר רבה בר כהנא בין קשור בין שאינו קשור אותו פקק פוקקין בו. והוא שמתוקן. כלומר שהתקינו לפקק בו. היכי דמי תיקון זה כדאמרינן בסוף המוצא תפילין: ת"ר סיכי קמצים וחבילי עצים שהתקינן לפירצה שבחצר. בזמן שקשורין ותלוין נועלין בשבת ואין צ"ל ביו"ט. א"ל ר' ירמיה ולימא מר בין תלוי בין שאינו תלוי והוא שקשור כלומר כבר נעשה בו מעשה לשום כלי. דאמר רבה ב"ב חנה א"ר יוחנן כמחלוקת כאן בפקק החלון כך חלוקתן בנגר הנגרר בקשור ותלוי בלבד. אבל לא לענין מקדש ומדינה. ותניא בסוף עירובין. איזהו נגר הנגרר שנועלין בו במקדש אבל לא במדינה: שומטו ומניחו בקרן זוית. דייקינן מינה מדקתני ושומטו ומניחו מכלל שאם הוא קשור שאם אינו יכול לשומטו ולהניחו בקרן זוית שפיר דמי. ואמרינן מאן תנא נגר הנגרר צריך להיות קשור ותלוי ר' אליעזר והא ר' יוחנן סבר כי חכמים חלוקין על ר' אליעזר סבירא להו כר' יהודה דאסר בשאינו קשור ולא תלוי ולא בתלוי אבל אם הוא קשור אע"פ שאינו תלוי שרי. וא"ל ר' אבא לר' ירמיה אנא דאמרי והוא שמתוקן אע"פ שאינו לא קשור ולא תלוי כי הא מתניתא דתני בקנה שהתקינו בעה"ב להיות פותח ונועל בו. ואמר רשב"ג מתוקן אע"פ שאינו קשור ואמר משמיה דר' יוחנן הלכה כרשב"ג דקאי רשב"ג כחכמים. ואקשינן היכי אמר ר' יוחנן הלכה

מסורת הש"ס

א) עירובין קב., ב) [נ"ל מותר במקדש], ג) [תוספ' פט"ו].

הגהות הב"ח

(א) תוס' ד"ה ר' יהודה וכו' פותח ונועל בו מדקתני פותח ונועל בו משמע:

גליון הש"ס

גמ' שנועלין בו במקדש אבל לא במדינה. עיין פי"א מ"ד דכלים:

ליקוטי רש"י

נגר. קביל"א שתוחבין אותו בחור שבאיסקופה לנעול הדלת [עירובין קא:]. נגר הנגרר. שקשור בדלת אבל אינו תלוי שהחבל ארוך ומתוך שנגרר אינו נראה כקשור וכשאין בראשו גלוסטרא קאמר. נועלין בו במקדש. דשבות בעלמא הוא דאינו בונה ממש הואיל וקשור לכך אלא הואיל ונגרר מיחזי כבונה ואין שבות דרבנן במקדש דלא גזרו שם. והמונח. שאינו קשור כלל הוי בנין ממש. והמונח כאן וכאן אסור. דכיון שאינו קשור שם בנין גמור הוא כשאר נגרים שנועלים בכותלים והבונה כל שהוא חייב ומלאכה דאורייתא לא הותרה במקדש חוץ מהקרבת תמידין ומוספין וקרבנות צבור שדוחין את השבת מגזירת הכתוב. המונח במקדש. ר' יהודה סבר לאו בנין ממש הוא אלא דומה לבנין ובמקדש לא גזרו שבות [שם קב.].

עין משפט נר מצוה

מה א ב ג מיי' פכ"ה מהלכות שבת הלי"ג טוש"ע או"ח סימן שח סעיף י:

א ד ה מיי' פכ"א מהל' שבת הלכה ג ופכ"ו הלכה טו סמג לאוין סה טוש"ע או"ח סימן שלג סעיף א:

שיש להם בית אחיזה ניטלין בשבת ואמר רב יהודה בר שילא אמר רב אסי אמר רבי יוחנן והוא שיש תורת כלי עליהן וכי תימא הכא נמי דאיכא תורת כלי עליו ומי בעי רשב"ג תורת כלי עליו והתניא (א) חריות של דקל שגדרן לשם עצים ונמלך עליהן לישיבה צריך לקשר רשב"ג אומר אין צריך לקשר רבי יוחנן סבירא ליה כוותיה בחדא ופליג עליה בחדא דרש רבי יצחק נפחא אפתחא דריש גלותא הלכה כרבי אליעזר מתיב רב עמרם (ב) ומדבריהם למדנו שפוקקין ומודדין וקושרין בשבת א"ל [אביי] מאי דעתיך משום דקתני סתמא נגר הנגרר נמי סתמא היא ואפי' הכי (ג) מעשה רב: **מתני'** (ד) כל כיסוי הכלים שיש להם בית אחיזה ניטלין בשבת א"ר יוסי בד"א (א) בכיסוי קרקעות אבל בכיסוי הכלים בין כך ובין כך ניטלין בשבת: **גמ'** אמר רב יהודה בר שילא א"ר אסי א"ר יוחנן (ב) והוא שיש תורת כלי עליהן דכ"ע בכסוי קרקעות אם יש להן בית אחיזה אין אי לא לא כסוי הכלים אע"ג דאין להן בית אחיזה כי פליגי בכלים דחברינהו בארעא מ"ס גזרינן (ג) ומ"ס לא גזרינן לישנא אחרינא כי פליגי בכיסוי תנור מר מדמי ליה לכיסוי קרקע ומר מדמי ליה לכיסוי כלים:

הדרן עלך כל הכלים

מפנין (ה) (ד) אפילו ארבע וחמש קופות של תבן ושל תבואה מפני האורחים ומפני בטול בהמ"ד (ו) אבל לא את האוצר מפנין תרומה טהורה ודמאי ומעשר ראשון שניטלה תרומתו ומעשר שני והקדש שנפדו והתורמוס היבש מפני שהוא מאכל (ז) לעזים (ח) אבל לא את הטבל ולא את מעשר [ראשון] שלא נטלה תרומתו ולא את מעשר שני והקדש שלא נפדו ולא (ט) את הלוף ולא את החרדל ר' שמעון בן גמליאל (י) מתיר בלוף מפני שהוא מאכל עורבין חבילי קש וחבילי עצים וחבילי זרדים אם התקינן למאכל בהמה מטלטלין אותן ואם לאו אין מטלטלין אותן: **גמ'** השתא חמש מפנין ארבע מיבעיא (כ) אמר רב חסדא ארבע מחמש (ל) איכא דאמרי (ה) ארבע מאוצר קטן) וחמש מאוצר גדול ומאי אבל לא את האוצר שלא יתחיל באוצר תחלה ומני רבי יהודה היא דאית ליה מוקצה ושמואל אמר ארבע וחמש כדאמרי

תוספות

וכי תימא הכא נמי דאיכא תורת כלי עליו. פי' בקונטרס שיהא ראוי לעשות שום תשמיש אחר ואין נראה לר"ת כי למה יש לנו להצריך שלדבר אחר יהא ראוי כיון שראוי לדבר זה אלא נראה לר"ת דה"פ דאיכא תורת כלי עליו שתיקנו ועשה בו מעשה והכינו לכך שמאחר שלכך תיקנו והכינו לכך יש תורת כלי עליו אפילו אינו ראוי לדבר אחר כמו חריות של דקל שאין ראוין לשום תשמיש אלא לישיבה אף על פי כן (ד) יכול להכינם ולטלטלם בשבת ואבנים נמי אמרינן לעיל לאו ושיפשפו ועוד אי תורת כלי עליהם ממש לריכה למימר דכלי ניטל לצורך גופו והא דאמרי' בעירובין (ד' קב.) נגר הנגרר עשה לו בית יד מהו א"ל בוכנא קאמרת פירוש ושרי לאו משום דאי לא הוה כבוכנא ע"י הבית יד הוה הוה אסור דאפילו לא חזי למילתא אחריתי כיון שתקנוהו בידים לכך היה מותר אפי' בלא בית יד אלא נראה לר"י דהסיא מיירי בנקמז דאסור לעיל מיני' בסמוך משום דמיחזי כבונה פי' שנועץ הנגר בתוך הנקב שבמפתן עד (ה) בתוך הארץ כדפירש בקונטרס התם ועלה קאי הא עשה לו בית יד באותו נגר שנקמז אי נמי שמואל לטעמיה דסבר לטעמא דרבי יהודה משום בנין אפילו בלא נעילה נגר בארץ וכן נראה יותר כי נקמז אין פתרונו נעילה בארץ אלא דומה שהוא מעין נשמט רק שאינו נשמט ממש כדמוכח בברייתא שהבאתי למעלה דקתני נגר אם נשמט כולו אסור נקמז מותר רבי יהודה אומר נקמז אע"פ שאינו נשמט ולא נודע פירוש נקמז היטב ובירושלמי גרסינן נגר דר' אליעזר הוה קטיר בגמי נשמט אסור נקמז רבי יעקב בר אחא מורה כראשי אצבעותיו (ו):

ומדבריהן למדנו שפוקקין ומודדין. ואע"ג דטפיח לא מבטל ליה כמו פקק כדאמרי' בפרק הישן (סוכה דף כא.) גבי סדין איכא למימר דמבטל ליה טפי מסדין ולא מצי למימר נמי פקק דמלוה שאני כדאמרי' בשילהי מכילתין (ד' קמ:) גבי מדידה דהתם לא הוי איסור כל כך אלא משום דהוי כעובדא דחול אבל פקק דמשום תוספת אהל דדמי לבנין ליכא למישרי משום מלוה:

הדרן עלך כל הכלים

מפנין ארבע וחמש קופות. בירושלמי מפרש כמה שיעור קופות כההוא דתנינן (ם) שלשה קופות של שלשה סאין:

של

רש"י

שיש להן בית אחיזה. בית יד: ה"ג ואמר רב יהודה **והוא שיש תורת כלי עליהן.** שהכיסוי ראוי לתשמיש (א) עצמו הוא דניטלין בשבת ואם אין תורת כלי עליו לא אמרינן כיסוי כלי הוה כלי ודלתות שידה תיבה ומגדל דתנא מתני' נוטלין יש תורת כלי עליהן דראוין לישב עליהן ולתת עליהן מזונות לקטן ולקמן מפרש אמאי בעינן בית אחיזה הואיל ותורת כלי עליהן אלמא לרבי יוחנן מידי דליכא תורת כלי עליו לא מטלטלין והאי קנה מאי תורת כלי עליו איכא אי משום דפותח ונועל בו אין זו תורת כלי עליו אלא תורת בנין: **וכ"ת הכא נמי דאיכא תורת כלי עליו.** שראוי להפך בו זיתים או לפצע בו אגוזים (ב): (מ) (תורת כלי עליו. אפי' אינו ראוי לדבר אחר): **סבירא ליה כוותיה בחדא.** דמתוקן ואע"פ שאינו קשור: **ופליג עליה בחדא.** דבעי תורת כלי: **הלכה כרבי אליעזר.** דבעינן קשור ותלוי: **מדבריהם למדנו.** בפ' בתרא בימי אביו של ר' לדוק ובימי אבא שאול בן בטנית שפקקו את המאור בטפיח וקשרו את המקידה בגמי לידע אם יש בגיגית פותח טפח והתם מפרש לה וקתני מדבריהם למדנו: **שפוקקין.** את המאור בדבר שאינו קשור ותלוי: **וקושרין.** קשר שאינו של קיימא לכתחלה: **ומודדין.** מקוה ומטלניות: **מאי דעתיך.** דמותבת לרבי יצחק נפחא מהא מצי לשנויי לך הא מני רבנן היא ואי משום דקתני לה סתמא מותבת ליה דמדסתם לן כרבנן הלכתא כוותייהו: **נגר הנגרר נמי סתמא.** קתני לה וסתם לן בהא כרבי אליעזר דאסור: **מעשה רב.** למילף מיניה דכיון דסמיך למיעבד עובדא לקולא ש"מ הלכתא היא: **מתני' בכיסוי קרקע.** כגון כיסוי בור ודות דהוי כבונה אי לאו דמוכחא בית אחיזה דילה דלמשקיל ואהדורי עביד: **גמ' א"ר יוחנן והוא שיש תורת כלי עליהם.** דכיסויין הללו חזו לתשמיש דעלמא אבל כיסוי כלי לא אמרינן כלי הוא: **ודכ"ע.** משום דאוקמא ר' יוחנן בשיש תורת כלי עליהן איצטריכא ליה למימר דכי פליגי רבנן בכלים דחברינהו בארעא פליגי דאילו כלים דעלמא אע"ג דלית להו לכיסויהן בית אחיזה מיטלטלי דכיון דאיכא תורת כלי עליהן קיימי מה לי איכא בית אחיזה מה לי ליכא בית אחיזה אלא בכיסוי כלים המחוברי' לקרקע כגון תנור וכירים הוא דפליגי משום דדמו במקצת לכיסוי בור ודות וגזרינן הני אטו הני:

הדרן עלך כל הכלים

מפנין. אם צריך למקומן להושיב שם אורחים להסב בסעוד' או תלמידים לדרשה ולא חיישינן לטרחא דשבת: **אבל לא את האוצר.** מפרש בגמרא: **מפנין תרומה טהורה.** כלומר ומהו מפנין דבר הראוי כגון אלו תרומה טהורה דחזי לבהמת כהן אבל תרומה טמאה לא דאפילו לבהמת כהן לא חזיא בשבת דאע"ג דבחול חזיא כדתניא בכל שעה בפסחים (דף לב.) שאם רצה כהן מרילה לפני הכלב בשבת וביום טוב לא חזיא דזו היא ביעורה מן העולם או להיסק או לבהמה ואין מבערין תרומה טמאה וקדשים טמאין ביום טוב ואין מדליקין בשמן שריפה ביום טוב כדתנן (לעיל דף כג:) ואוקימנא (י) טעמא משום דאין שורפין קדשים ביום טוב: (ג) **לוף.** מין קטניות שאינו ראוי חי אפילו לבהמה: **לעורבין.** כגון עשירים שמגדלין עורבין לגדולה: **זרדים.** מין קנים הם שמורידים כשהן רכים ואוכלים אותם: **גמ' ארבע מחמש.** אם לא היה שם אלא כשיעור ה' קופות לא יפנה אלא ד' מהם שאסור לגמור את האוצר דילמא חזי גומות בקרקעיתו ומשוי להו: **מאוצר גדול.** ואם יש הרבה אין מפנין אלא חמש דחיישינן לטירחא: **מאי אבל לא את האוצר.** שלא יגמור את האוצר לא מלית אמרת דהא מרישא שמעינן ארבע וחמש: **תחלה.** אם לא התחיל בו להסתפק ממנו כבר למאכלו או למאכל בהמתו דאם כן הוה ליה מוקצה ומתניתין רבי יהודה היא:

רבינו חננאל

כרשב"ג ורשב"ג שרי אע"פ דליכא תורת כלי עליו. ור' יוחנן שמעי' ליה דבעי תורת כלי. ואוקימנא בקנה שהתקינו להיות נועל ופותח בו בדאיכא תורת כלי עליו והא א"ר יוחנן הלכתא כרשב"ג. אבל בחריות של דקל שגדרן לעצים דשרי רשב"ג בלא קישור לא סבר לזה ר' יוחנן כוותיה. ועליהן [אמר דר'] יוחנן סבר לה כוותיה בחדא ופליג עליה בחדא: **דרש** ר' יצחק נפחא אפתחא דבי ריש גלותא הלכתא כר' אלעזר שאין פוקקין (עליו) [בו] אם [לא שהוא] קשור ותלוי. ואותבה ר' (עולא) [רב עמרם] מהא דתנן בסוף שבת מדבריהן למדנו שפוקקין ומודדין וקושרין בשבת. א"ל אביי לרב (עזרא) [עמרם] למה אותביתיה מהא מפני שהיא שנויה סתם. וקיי"ל הלכה כסתם משנה. נגר הנגרר נמי סתמא היא. והיא שנויה סתם אליבא דר' אלעזר. ושני ליה אע"פ דהא סתמא והא סתמא. הא סתמא דפוקקין ומודדין וקושרין בשבת עבדו בה עובדא ומעשה רב חו הלכה למעשה והלכתא כחכמים ונדחה דרישא דר' יצחק נפחא. ואמרינן בתלמוד א"י. א"ר יוחנן אתיא יחידאה דהכא סתמא דתמן. ויחידאה דתמן כסתמא דהכא. פי' יחידאה דהכא דהוא ר' אלעזר דפקק החלון בסתמא דנגר נגרר [ויחידאי דנגר הנגרר] (דהוא ר' יהודה כסתמא) [דפקק החלון דחכ"א] בין כך ובין כך פוקקין בו: **כל** כסויי הכלים שיש להן בית אחיזה ניטלין בשבת. א"ר יוסי בד"א בכסויי קרקעות וכו'. א"ר יהודה בר שילא א"ר אסי א"ר יוחנן והוא שיש תורת כלי עליהן. ואמרינן כולי עלמא בכסוי קרקעות אם יש להן בית אחיזה שרי ואי לא אסיר לטלטלן. כגון כסויי הבארות וכסויי הדות וכיוצא בהן. כסויי כלים כגון כדות ופיטסים וכיוצא בהן אע"פ (שהן) [שאין] להן בית אחיזה מותר לטלטלן לגלותם ולכסותם. כי פליגי בכסויי כלים וחיברו בקרקע. ר' יוסי לא גזר ות"ק סבר גזרינן והלכתא כוותיה:

הדרן עלך פרק כל הכלים

פי"ח מפנין אפילו ד' וה' קופות של תבן. פי' מפנין מעתיקין התבואה ממקום למקום מלשון ורצה הכהן ופנו את הבית. אקשינן על משנתנו. השתא ה' מפנין ד' מיבעיא ופריק רב חסדא ארבע מחמש וה' מאוצר גדול. ומאי אבל לא את האוצר שלא יתחיל באוצר תחלה ומני ר"י היא דאית ליה מוקצה ובא שמואל ופריק פירוק אחר ודברים פשוטין הן. אבל סוגיא דשמעתא כרב חסדא דמתניתא סתמא תנן כוותיה. שאין מתחילין

מסורת הש"ס

א) לעיל ג. [ודף קכה:], ב) לקמן קנז., ג) [לעיל קמ. וש"נ], ד) רש"ל מ"ז וכן בס"י ליתא, ה) ביצה לה:, ו) [שם לו.], ז) ס"א לעניים, ח) [עי' תוס' לקמן קכח. ד"ה אבל], ט) [ב"מ קיג:], י) [עי' תוס' לקמן קכח. ד"ה רשב"ג], כ) [עי' תוס' לעיל ס: ד"ה השתא ע"ש דהעתיקו אמר רב חסדא ד' מאולר קטן ה' מאולר גדול], ל) ל"ג ברי"ף ורש"ל, מ) ס"א ל"ג ומ"כ שלפני רש"י היה הגירסא בגמרא אמר בריית' דחריות אלמא לא בעי רשב"ג תורת כלי עליו ומליין רש"י בזה, נ) [שם כג:], ס) [בכלים פי"ג מ"ב].

הגהות הב"ח

(א) רש"י ד"ה ה"ג וכו' לתשמיש לעצמו הוא: (ב) ד"ה וכ"ת הכא וכו' אגוזים הס"ד. ואח"כ מ"ה אין צריך לקשר אלמא דאיכא תורת כלי עליו: (ג) רש"י ד"ה לוף מז"מ. ונ"ב ס"א תורמוס: (ד) תוס' ד"ה וכי תימא וכו' אלא לישיבה אעפ"כ. נ"ב ועי' באשר"י: (ה) בא"ד עד לתוך הארץ: (ו) בא"ד מורה בראשי אצבעותיו סס V:

רב נסים גאון

פי"ח ר' יהודה היא דאמר מוקצה ור' שמעון לית ליה מוקצה אצל כל פחמא (פי' עיקר הדברים) בפרק במה מדליקין וכבר פירשנו זה בפרק יציאות השבת:

ליקוטי רש"י

חריות. ענפים קשים כעין משהוקשו שדלאות של לולבין ונפלו עלין שלהן קרי להן חריות [לעיל נ.]. **שגדרן לעצים.** שחתכן להיסק [שם קכה:]. **שגדרן.** כל [קלילן] [קלילת] תמרים קרי גדירה. **צריך לקשר.** לקשרם יחד מבעוד יום להוכיח שלישיבה עומדים ואם לא קשרם יחד אסור לטלטלן דאמר דלא הוי יחוד ממחשבה [שם נ.]. **שפוקקין.** כרבנן דאמרי פוקקין פקק החלון. **ומודדין.** להתלמד על דבר הוראה [לקמן קנז.]. **מפני האורחים.** שזימן לאכול ואין מקום להסב. **בטול בית המדרש.** שאין לתלמידים מקום לישב [ביצה לה:]. **דמאי.** תבואה הנלקחת מעם הארץ והיא נקראת דמאי ספק עישרה ספק לא עישרה וחייבו חכמים להפריש מעשרותיה מספק [פסחים לה.]. ספק מעושר ספק אינו מעושר דרוב עמי הארץ מעשרין הן ומותרא לרבנן היא [עירובין יז:]. לקחם מעם הארץ ומפרש פירותיהן ספק אין מעושרין [סוכה לה:]. **ומעשר ראשון.** של לויים. **שניטלה תרומתו.** תרומת מעשר לכהן ומכאן ואילך המעשר מותר לזרים [פסחים שם]. קס"ד תרומת מעשר שלו שעל הלוי להפריש [ברכות מה. ע"ש בב"ח]. קס"ד תרומת מעשר שהלוי נותן לכהן וכ"ש תרומה גדולה שיש על ישראל להפריש והפרישו קודם שנתנו המעשר ללוי [לקמן קכז:]. **ומעשר שני.** מעשר שני שנפדה להתירו באכילה חוץ לירושלים ואת פדיונו יעלה לירושלים ויאכל [ברכות שם].

תורמוס. מין קטנית עגול כמין עדשה ורחב כמעה קטנה [ביצה כה:]. **ולא את מעשר שני.** חוץ לירושלים [פסחים שם]. **שלא נפדו.** ואע"ג דמצי פריק להו השתא מיהא לא מפרק [עירובין לא.]. **ולא את הלוף ולא את החרדל.** מטלטלין בשבת שאינם ראוין היום [illegible] **זרדים.** מין קנים הם [illegible] **התקינן.** הזמינן [לקמן קכח.].

נִיטָּלִין בְּשַׁבָּת – MAY שֶׁיֵּשׁ לָהֶם בֵּית אֲחִיזָה – THAT HAVE HANDLES BE TAKEN ON THE SABBATH. וְאָמַר רַב יְהוּדָה בַּר שִׁילָא אָמַר רַב אַסִּי אָמַר רַבִּי יוֹחָנָן – And Rav Yehudah bar Shila said in the name of Rav Assi, who said in the name of R' Yochanan: וְהוּא שֶׁיֵּשׁ תּוֹרַת כְּלִי עֲלֵיהֶן – This rule is applicable only if [the covers] can function as utensils by being used for some task; otherwise they are *muktzeh*.[1] Thus, R' Yochanan considers something that does not function as a utensil to be *muktzeh*! How can he have ruled that the halachah follows Rabban Shimon ben Gamliel, who permits using a rod to lock a door on the basis of its mere designation for this purpose? Why, the rod does not function as a utensil![2] וְכִי תֵּימָא – And if you should say that הָכָא נַמִּי דְּאִיכָּא תּוֹרַת כְּלִי עָלָיו – here too, in Rabban Shimon ben Gamliel's case, we are dealing with [a rod] that can function as a utensil,[3] I will retort: וּמִי בָּעֵי רַבָּן שִׁמְעוֹן בֶּן גַּמְלִיאֵל תּוֹרַת כְּלִי עָלָיו – But does Rabban Shimon ben Gamliel require that something be a functional utensil in order for it to be non-*muktzeh*? וְהָתַנְיָא – Why, it was taught in a Baraisa: חֲרָיוֹת שֶׁל דֶּקֶל שֶׁגְּדָרָן לְשֵׁם עֵצִים – If one had HARDENED BRANCHES OF A DATE PALM THAT HE HAD HARVESTED FOR FIREWOOD, which are *muktzeh*, וְנִמְלַךְ עֲלֵיהֶן לִישִׁיבָה – AND HE then CHANGED HIS MIND REGARDING THEM and decided to use them FOR SITTING, צָרִיךְ לִקְשֹׁר – HE MUST TIE them into bundles before the Sabbath in order to render them non-*muktzeh*.[4] רַבָּן שִׁמְעוֹן בֶּן גַּמְלִיאֵל אוֹמֵר – RABBAN SHIMON BEN GAMLIEL SAYS: אֵין צָרִיךְ לִקְשֹׁר – HE NEED NOT TIE them. It is sufficient if he merely designates them as seats before the Sabbath. Clearly, when Rabban Shimon ben Gamliel permitted the use of a rod for locking a door, he was dealing with a rod that was merely designated for that purpose before the Sabbath, but does not necessarily function as a utensil.[5] – ? –

The Gemara answers:

רַבִּי יוֹחָנָן סְבִירָא לֵיהּ כְּוָותֵיהּ בַּחֲדָא – R' Yochanan concurs with [Rabban Shimon ben Gamliel] in one respect, for he permits the use of a rod as a lock even though it is not attached to the door, וּפְלִיג עֲלֵיהּ בַּחֲדָא – but he disagrees with him in one respect, for he requires that the rod be able to function as a utensil, whereas Rabban Shimon ben Gamliel permits its use on the basis of mere designation for this purpose.[6]

A related discussion is cited:

דָּרַשׁ רַבִּי יִצְחָק נַפְחָא אַפִּתְחָא דְרֵישׁ גָּלוּתָא – R' Yitzchak Nafcha discoursed at the entrance to the house of the Exilarch: הֲלָכָה כְּרַבִּי אֱלִיעֶזֶר – The halachah follows R' Eliezer, who stated in our Mishnah that a shutter may be used to close a window only if it is attached to the building and suspended in the air.

This ruling is challenged:

מָתִיב רַב עַמְרָם – Rav Amram challenged this on the basis of the following Mishnah:[7] וּמִדִּבְרֵיהֶם לָמַדְנוּ שֶׁפּוֹקְקִין וּמוֹדְדִין וְקוֹשְׁרִין בְּשַׁבָּת – AND FROM THEIR WORDS WE LEARNED THAT WE MAY SHUTTER, MEASURE AND TIE ON THE SABBATH.[8] The Mishnah teaches that we may shutter a window even with something that is not attached to the building. – ? –

An attempt is made to rebuff the challenge:

אָמַר לֵיהּ [אַבַּיֵי] – [Abaye] said to [Rav Amram]: מַאי דַּעְתִּיךְ – What is your intention in posing this challenge? Why, one can readily respond that the Mishnah you cited follows the opinion of the Sages of our Mishnah, but nevertheless, the halachah follows R' Eliezer! מִשּׁוּם דְּקָתָנֵי סְתָמָא – Presumably, your intention is that the Mishnah you cited is authoritative, because it teaches its ruling anonymously, and the halachah generally follows anonymous Mishnahs. נֶגֶר הַנִּגְרָר נַמִּי סְתָמָא הִיא – But the Mishnah which teaches that a bolt which is attached to the door but drags

NOTES

1. R' Yochanan holds that a vessel-cover is not classified as a utensil — and is thus *muktzeh* — unless it is useful in some capacity other than merely covering the vessel. Its usefulness as a cover alone does not define it as a utensil. He understands the Mishnah and Baraisa above (122b), which rule that even the door of a carriage, trunk or closet may be taken on the Sabbath, as basing their ruling on the fact that the doors are suitable for some other use, such as sitting upon them or putting food for a child on them (cf. 122b note 2). The Gemara below (after the Mishnah) will explain why, if the vessel-covers are useful utensils in their own right, it is additionally necessary for them to have handles in order for their movement to be permitted (*Rashi*).

[Others explain that R' Yochanan does not require the covers to be useful in another capacity, for their function as covers alone can suffice to define them as utensils. Rather, he is dealing with plain boards that are being implemented as vessel-covers. In contrast with the opinion of Rabban Shimon ben Gamliel, who requires only that an article be mentally designated for a task in order for it to be considered a utensil, R' Yochanan requires that it undergo a preparatory act, such as shaping (*Tosafos* ד״ה וכי תימא, *Rashba, Ritva MHK* ed.; see *Rosh, Maharsha, Chasam Sofer* and *Sfas Emes* for further discussion of *Rashi's* view; see also note 14).]

2. Its function as a bolt does not serve to define it as a utensil, for that is, rather, a function of construction (*Rashi*).

3. For example, it is suitable for turning over olives in a vat to test their ripeness (see 123b note 6), or for cracking open nuts (*Rashi*).

4. See 125b note 25.

5. For we have seen that Rabban Shimon ben Gamliel considers an article non-*muktzeh* on the basis of merely being designated for some use before the Sabbath (*Rashi,* as emended by *Bach;* see following note).

6. R' Yochanan concurs with Rabban Shimon ben Gamliel that even the use of an unattached bolt is not prohibited on account of building. However, he disagrees insofar as he considers a bolt *muktzeh* unless it can also function as a utensil (*Chidushei R' Elazar Moshe Horowitz,* whose explanation follows *Rashi*).

We have explained the previous passage (126a-b) in accordance with *Rashi*. However, *Tosafos* point out a basic difficulty with this approach. How can the Gemara cite Rabban Shimon ben Gamliel's ruling concerning hardened palm branches as proof that he considers designation sufficient even in regard to a rod that will be used to bolt a door? Why, in the case of palm branches, the only consideration is that of *muktzeh*, whereas in the case of a rod there is the additional consideration of the appearance of building (according to *Rashi's* explanation)! Perhaps Rabban Shimon ben Gamliel requires that the rod undergo physical preparation as a utensil so that its use should not have the appearance of building (see *Tosafos* to 126a ד״ה והמונח and ד״ה ר׳ יהודה אומר with *Maharsha*). *Tosafos* therefore explain that the insertion of a door bolt in a wall or threshold is not an act of building at all, and the only consideration throughout the previous *sugya* was that of *muktzeh*.

However, *Rashi* apparently holds that since in the case of palm branches, where the Tanna Kamma requires tying them, Rabban Shimon ben Gamliel says that the only preparation required is mental designation for the task, and in the case of a rod Rabban Shimon ben Gamliel similarly states that it need not be tied to the door but must merely be "prepared," it is obvious that here, too, the only preparation he requires is that of mental designation. The designation defines the rod as a utensil, thus rendering it non-*muktzeh* and *also* eliminating the appearance of building (see *Maharshal*, *Chasam Sofer* to 126a and *Avnei Nezer* 224:14). See also *Baal HaMaor, Milchamos Hashem, Rosh* with *Korban Nesanel* §9, and *Chazon Ish* §42 for lengthy discussions of this subject.

7. Below, 157a.

8. The beginning of this Mishnah cites an incident that occurred in the times of R' Tzadok's father and Abba Shaul ben Batnis, in which they stopped up a window with an earthenware jug to preclude the spread of corpse-*tumah* from one house to another via the window. They also tied a reed to a *tefach*-wide cup with a temporary knot, so as to be able to thrust the cup into an overhead aperture and measure whether it was wide enough to preclude the spread of *tumah*. See Gemara, 157a-b, for further details.

The Mishnah concludes that we learn from this incident that one may shutter a window (even with something that was not attached to the structure), measure (when the performance of a mitzvah necessitates this), and tie (a temporary knot) on the Sabbath (*Rashi*).

וכי תימא הכא נמי דאיכא תורת כלי עליו. פי' בקונטרס שיהא ראוי לעשות שום תשמיש אחר ואין נראה לר"ת כי למה יש לנו להצריך שלדבר אחר יהא ראוי כיון שראוי לדבר זה אלא נראה לר"ת דה"פ דליכא תורת כלי עליו שתיקנו ועשה בו מעשה והכינו לכך שמאחר שלכך תיקנו והכינו לכך יש תורת כלי עליו אפילו אינו ראוי לדבר אחר כמו חריות של דקל שאינן ראוין לשום תשמיש אלא לישיבה אף על פי כן (ד) יכול להכניס ולטלטל בשבת ואבנים נמי אמרינן לעיל לאו ושיפשפו ועוד אי תורת כלי עליהם ממש לריכא למימר דכלי ניטל לצורך גופו והא דאמרי' בעירובין (ד' קא.) נגר הנגרר עשה לו בית יד מהו א"ל בוכנא קאמרת פירוש ושרי לאו משום דלאי לא הוה כבוכנא ע"י הבית יד הוה אסור דאפילו לא חזי למילתא אחריתי כיון שתקנוהו בידים לכך היה מותר אפי' בלא בית יד אלא נראה לר"י דההיא מיירי בנקמז דאסור לעיל מיני' בסמוך משום דמיחזי כבונה פי' שנועץ הנגר בתוך הנקב שבמפתן עד (ה) בתוך הארץ כדפירש בקונטרס התם ועלה קאי הא עשה לו בית יד באותו נגר שנקמז אי נמי שמואל לטעמיה דסבר דטעמא דרבי יהודה משום בנין אפילו בלא נעילת נגר בארץ וכן נראה יותר כי נקמז אין פתרונו נעילה בארץ אלא דומה שהוא מעין נשמט רק שאינו נשמט ממש כדמוכח בברייתא שהביא למעלה דקתני נגר אם נשמט כולו אסור נקמז מותר רבי יהודה אומר נקמז אע"פ שאינו נשמט ולא נודע פירוש נקמז היטב ובירושלמי גרסינן נגר דר' אליעזר הוה קטיר בגמי נשמט אסור נקמז רבי יעקב בר אחא מורה כראשי אצבעותיו (ו):

ומדבריהן למדנו שפוקקין ומודדין. ואע"ג דטפיח לא מבטל ליה כמו פקק כדאמרי' בפרק הישן (סוכה דף כח.) גבי סדין איכא למימר דמבטל ליה טפי מסדין ולא מצי למימר נמי פקק דמלוה שאני כדאמרי' בשילהי מכילתין (ד' קמ:) גבי מדידה דהתם לא הוי איסור כל כך אלא משום דהוי כעובדא דחול אבל פקק דמשום תוספת אהל דדמי לבנין ליכא למישרי משום מלוה:

הדרן עלך כל הכלים

מפנין ארבע וחמש קופות. בירושלמי מפרש כמה שיעור קופות כההוא דתנינן שלשה קופות של שלשה סאין: של

שיש להם בית אחיזה ניטלין בשבת ואמר רב יהודה בר שילא אמר רב אסי אמר רבי יוחנן והוא שיש תורת כלי עליהן וכי תימא הכא נמי דאיכא תורת כלי עליו ומי בעי רשב"ג תורת כלי עליו והתניא חריות של דקל שגדרן לשם עצים ונמלך עליהן לישיבה צריך לקשר רשב"ג אומר אין צריך לקשר רבי יוחנן סבירא ליה כוותיה בחדא ופליג עליה בחדא דרש רבי יצחק נפחא אפתחא דריש גלותא הלכה כרבי אליעזר מתיב רב עמרם ומדבריהם למדנו שפוקקין ומודדין וקושרין בשבת א"ל [אביי] מאי דעתיך משום דקתני סתמא נגר הנגרר נמי סתמא היא ואפ' הכי מעשה רב: **מתני'** (ד) כל כיסוי הכלים שיש להם בית אחיזה ניטלין בשבת א"ר יוסי בר"א בכיסוי קרקעות אבל בכיסוי הכלים בין כך ובין כך ניטלין בשבת: **גמ'** אמר רב יהודה בר שילא א"ר אסי א"ר יוחנן והוא שיש תורת כלי עליהן דכ"ע כסוי קרקעות אם יש להן בית אחיזה אין אי לא לא כסוי הכלים אע"ג דאין להם בית אחיזה כי פליגי בכלים דחברינהו בארעא מ"ס גזרינן ומ"ס לא גזרינן לישנא אחרינא כי פליגי בכיסוי תנור מר מדמי ליה לכיסוי קרקע ומר מדמי ליה לכיסוי כלים:

הדרן עלך כל הכלים

מפנין אפילו ארבע וחמש קופות של תבן ושל תבואה מפני האורחים ומפני בטול בהמ"ד אבל לא את האוצר מפנין תרומה טהורה ודמאי ומעשר ראשון שניטלה תרומתו ומעשר שני והקדש שנפדו והתורמוס היבש מפני שהוא מאכל לעזים אבל לא את הטבל ולא את מעשר [ראשון] שלא נטלה תרומתו ולא את מעשר שני והקדש שלא נפדו ולא את הלוף ולא את החרדל ר' שמעון בן גמליאל מתיר בלוף מפני שהוא מאכל עורבין חבילי קש וחבילי עצים וחבילי זרדים אם התקינן למאכל בהמה מטלטלין אותן ואם לאו אין מטלטלין אותן: **גמ'** השתא חמש מפנין ארבע מיבעיא אמר רב חסדא ארבע מחמש (איכא דאמרי ארבע מאוצר קטן) וחמש מאוצר גדול ומאי אבל לא את האוצר שלא יתחיל באוצר תחלה ומני רבי יהודה היא דאית ליה מוקצה ושמואל אמר ארבע וחמש כדאמרי

שיש להן בית אחיזה. בית יד: ה"ג ואמר רב יהודה והוא שיש תורת כלי עליהן. שהכיסוי ראוי לתשמיש (א) עלמו הוא דניטלין בשבת ואם אין תורת כלי עליו לא אמרינן כיסוי כלי הוה כלי ודלתות שידה תיבה ומגדל דתנא מתני' נוטלין יש תורת כלי עליהן דראוין לישב עליהן ולתת עליהן מזונות לקטן ולקמן מפרש אמאי בעינן בית אחיזה הואיל ותורת כלי עליהן אלמא לרבי יוחנן מידי דליכא תורת כלי עליו לא מטלטלין והאי קנה מאי תורת כלי עליו איכא אי משום דפותח ונועל בו אין זו תורת כלי עליו אלא תורת בנין: **וכ"ת הכא נמי דאיכא תורת כלי עליו.** שראוי להפך בו זיתים או לפצע בו אגוזים (ב): (תורת כלי עליו. אפי' אינו ראוי לדבר אחר): **סבירא ליה כוותיה בחדא.** דמתוקן ואע"פ שאינו קשור: **ופליג עליה בחדא.** דבעי תורת כלי: **הלכה כרבי אליעזר.** דבעינן קשור ותלוי: **מדבריהם למדנו.** בפ' בתרא בימי אביו של ר' צדוק ובימי אבא שאול בן בטנית שפקקו את המאור בטפיח וקשרו את המקידה בגמי לידע אם יש בגיגית פותח טפח והתם מפרש לה וקתני מדבריהם למדנו: **שפוקקין.** את המאור בדבר שאינו קשור ותלוי: **וקושרין.** קשר שאינו של קיימא לכתחלה: **ומודדין.** מקוה ומטלניות: **מאי דעתיך.** דמותבת לרבי יצחק נפחא מהא מצי לשנויי לך הא מני רבנן היא ואי משום דקתני לה סתמא מותבת ליה דמדסתם לן כרבנן הלכתא כוותייהו: **נגר הנגרר נמי סתמא.** קתני לה וסתם לן בהא כרבי אליעזר דאסור: **מעשה רב.** למילף מיניה דכיון דסמיך למיעבד עובדא לקולא ש"מ הלכתא היא: **מתני' בכיסוי קרקע.** כגון כיסוי בור ודות דהוי כבונה אי לאו דמוכחא בית אחיזה דילה דלמשקיל ולאהדורי עביד: **גמ' א"ר יוחנן והוא שיש תורת כלי עליהם.** דכיסויין הללו חזו לתשמיש דעלמא אבל כיסוי כלי לא אמרינן כלי הוא: **ודכ"ע.** משום דאוקמא ר' יוחנן בשיש תורת כלי עליהן איצטריכא ליה למימר דכי פליגי רבנן בכלים דחברינהו בארעא פליגי דאילו כלים דעלמא אע"ג דלית להו לכיסוייהן בית אחיזה מיטלטלי דכיון דאיכא תורת כלי עליהן קיימי מה לי איכא בית אחיזה מה לי ליכא בית אחיזה אלא בכיסוי כלים המחוברי' לקרקע כגון תנור וכירים הוא דפליגי משום דדמו במקצת לכיסוי בור ודות וגזרינן הני אטו הני:

הדרן עלך כל הכלים

מפנין. אם צריך למקומן להושיב שם אורחים להסב בסעוד' או תלמידים לדרשה ולא חיישינן לטירחא דשבת: **אבל לא את האוצר.** מפרש בגמרא: **מפנין תרומה טהורה.** כלומר ומהו מפנין דבר הראוי כגון אלו תרומה טהורה דחזי לבהמת כהן אבל תרומה טמאה לא דאפילו לבהמת כהן לא חזיא בשבת דאע"ג דבחול חזיא כדתניא בכל שעה בפסחים (דף לב.) שאם רצה כהן מטילה לפני הכלב בשבת וביום טוב לא חזיא דזו היא ביעורה מן העולם או להיסק או לבהמה ואין מבערין תרומה טמאה וקדשים טמאין ביום טוב כדתנן (לעיל דף כג:) ואין מדליקין בשמן שריפה ביום טוב ואוקימנא טעמא משום דאין שורפין קדשים ביום טוב: (ג) **לוף.** מין קטניות שאינו ראוי חי אפילו לבהמה: **לעורבין.** כגון עשירים שמגדלין עורבין לגדולה: **זרדים.** מין קנים הם שמורידים כשהן רכים ואוכלים אותם: **גמ' ארבע מחמש.** אם לא היה שם אלא כשיעור ה' קופות לא יפנה אלא ד' מהם שאסור לגמור את האוצר דילמא חזי גומות בקרקעיתו ומשוי להו: **מאוצר גדול.** ואם יש הרבה אין מפנין אלא חמש דחיישינן לטירחא: **מאי אבל לא את האוצר.** שלא יגמור את האוצר לא מצית אמרת דהא מרישא שמעינן ארבע וחמש: **תחלה.** אם לא התחיל בו להסתפק ממנו כבר למאכלו או למאכל בהמתו דאם כן הוה ליה מוקצה ומתניתין רבי יהודה היא:

עין משפט נר מצוה

מה א ב ג מיי' פכ"ה מהלכות שבת הל"ג טוש"ע או"ח סימן שח סעיף י:

א ד ה מיי' פכ"ו מהל' שבת הלכה ג ועי' בפ"ד מהל' הלכה טו סמג לאוין סה טוש"ע או"ח סימן שלג סעיף א:

רבינו חננאל

כרשב"ג ורשב"ג שרי אע"פ דליכא תורת כלי עליו. ור' יוחנן שמעי' ליה דבעי תורת כלי. ואוקימנא בקנה שתקנו להיות נועל ופותח בו בדאיכא תורת כלי עליו והא א"ר יוחנן הלכתא כרשב"ג. אבל בחריות של דקל שגדרן לעצים דשרי רשב"ג בלא קשור לא סבר לה ר' יוחנן כוותיה. ועליהן [אמר דר'] יוחנן סבר לה כוותיה בחדא ופליג עליה בחדא: דרש ר' יצחק נפחא אפתחא דבי ריש גלותא הלכתא כר' אלעזר שאין פוקקין (עליו) [בין אם] [לא] קשור ותלוי. ואותבה ר' (עולא) [רב עמרם] מהא דתנן בסוף שבת מדבריהן למדנו שפוקקין ומודדין וקושרין בשבת. א"ל אביי לרב (עזרא) [עמרם] למה אותביתה מהא מפני שהיא שנויה סתם. וקיי"ל הלכה כסתם משנה. נגר הנגרר נמי סתמא היא. והיא שנויה סתם אליבא דר' אלעזר. ושני ליה אע"פ דהא סתמא והא סתמא. הא סתמא דפוקקין ומודדין וקושרין בשבת עבדו בה עובדא ומעשה רב הוא הלכה למעשה והלכתא כחכמים ונדחה דרשה דר' יצחק נפחא. ואמרינן בתלמוד א"י. א"ר יוחנן אתיא יחידאה דהכא כסתמא דתמן. ויחידאה דתמן כסתמא דהכא. פי' יחידאה דפקק החלון בסתמא דנגר נגרר [ויחידאי דנגר הנגרר] (דהוא ר' יהודה כסתמא) [דפקק החלון דהא"א] בין כך ובין כך פוקקין בו: כל כסויי הכלים שיש להן בית אחיזה ניטלין בשבת. א"ר יוסי בר"א בכסוי קרקעות וכו'. א"ר יהודה בר שילא א"ר אסי א"ר יוחנן והוא שיש תורת כלי עליה. ואמרינן כולי עלמא בכסוי קרקעות אם יש להן בית אחיזה שרי ואי לא אסיר לטלטלן. כגון כסויי הבארות וכסויי הדות וכיוצא בהן. כסויי כלים כגון כדות ופיטסים וכיוצא בהן אע"פ (שהן) [שאין] להן בית אחיזה מותר לטלטלן לגלותם ולכסותם. כי פליגי בכסויי כלים וחיברו בקרקע. ר' יוסי לא גזר ות"ק סבר גזרינן והלכתא כוותיה:

הדרן עלך פרק כל הכלים

פי"ח מפנין אפילו ד' וה' קופות של תבן. פי' מפנין מעתיקין התבואה ממקום למקום מלשון ותצוה הכהן ופנו את הבית. אקשינן על משנתנו. השתא ה' מפנין ד' מיבעיא ופריק רב חסדא ארבע מחמש וכו' גדול. ומאי אבל לא את האוצר שלא יתחיל באוצר תחלה ומני ר"י היא דאית ליה מוקצה ובא שמואל ופריק פירוק אחר והדברים פשוטין הן. אבל סוגיא דשמעתא כרב חסדא דמתניתא סתמא תנן כוותיה. שאין מתחלין

מסורת הש"ס

א) לעיל ג. [ודף קכה:], ב) לקמן קנז., ג) [לעיל כח. וש"נ], ד) רש"ל מ"ז וכן בס"י ליתא, ה) ביצה לה:, ו) [שם לו.], ז) ס"ח לעניים, ח) [עי' תוס' לקמן קמג. ד"ה אבל], ט) [כ"מ קיג.], י) [עי' תוס' לקמן קמג. ד"ה רשב"ג], כ) [עי' תוס' לעיל מ: ד"ה השמא ע"ש דהעתיקו אמר רב חסדא ד' מאוצר קטן ה' מאוצר גדול], ל) ל"ג רב"י ורש"ל, מ) מ"ז ל"ג ומ"ח שלפני רש"י היה הגירסא בגמרא אחר בריית' דחריות אלמא לא בעי רשב"ג תורת כלי עליו ומלין רש"י ע"ש, נ) [שם כג:], ס) [בשקלים פ"ג מ"ב].

הגהות הב"ח

(א) רש"י ד"ה ש"ג וכו' לתשמיש לעלמו הוא: (ב) ד"ה וכ"ת הכא וכו' אגוזים הס"ד. ואח"כ מ"ה אין לריך לקשר אלמא דליכא תורת כלי עליו: (ג) רש"י ד"ה לוף מין. נ"ב ... (ד) תוס' ד"ה וכי תימא וכו' אלא לישיבה אפ"ה. נ"ב ועי' באשר"י: (ה) באד עד לתוך הארץ: (ו) באד מורה כראשי אלבעותיו

רב נסים גאון

פי"ח ר' יהודה היא דאמר מוקצה ור' שמעון לית ליה מוקצה אצל כל פתחא (פי' עיקר הדברים) בפרק במה מדליקין והכבר פירשנוהו זה בפרק יציאות השבת:

ליקוטי רש"י

חריות. ענפים קשים כעין משמוקשו שדלתות של לולבין ונפלו עלין שלהן קרי להן חריות [לעיל נ.]. שגדרן לעצים. שחתכן להיסק [שם קכה:]. שגדרן. כל (לקיטת) [קלילת] תמרים קרי גדירה. צריך לקשר. לקשרם יחד מבעוד יום להוכיחם שלישיבה עומדים ואם לא קשרם יחד אסור לטלטלן למחר דלא הוי יחוד שמחשבה [שם נ.]. שפוקקין. כרבנן דאמרי פוקקין פקק החלון. ומודדין. למדוד על דבר סולה לקמן קנז. מפני האורחים. זימון להושיב בו מדרש [ביצה לה:]. מפני ביטול בית המדרש. שאין מקום לתלמידים מקום לישב [ביצה לה:]. דמאי. תבואה הנלקחת מעם הארץ והיא נקראת דמאי ספק עישר ספק לא עישר והחמירו חכמים להפריש מעשרותיו מספק [פסחים לה.]. ספק מעשר ספק אינו מעשר דרוב עמי הארץ מעשרין הן ומומרא דרבנן הוא [עירובין יז.]. האוצר ותפס פירושים ספק לאכון מעשרין [סוכה לה:]. ומעשר ראשון. של ליים. שניטלה תרומתו. תרומת מעשר

on the ground may not be used as a lock in the provinces **is also an anonymous one,** and it follows the opinion of R' Eliezer.[9] Why do you attach greater significance to the Mishnah that you cited?

The challenge is upheld:

וַאֲפִילוּ הָכִי מַעֲשֶׂה רַב – **Nevertheless, practice is greater** proof than an ordinary ruling. Since the Mishnah cited by Rav Amram based its ruling on the actual practice of Tannaim, it is more authoritative.[10]

Mishnah (כָּל) כִּיסּוּי הַכֵּלִים שֶׁיֵּשׁ לָהֶם בֵּית אֲחִיזָה – **(All) vessel-covers that have handles** נִיטָּלִין בְּשַׁבָּת – **may be taken on the Sabbath.**[11] אָמַר רַבִּי יוֹסֵי – **R' Yose said:** בַּמֶּה דְּבָרִים אֲמוּרִים – **Regarding what** type of covers **was this stated?** בְּכִיסּוּי קַרְקָעוֹת – **Regarding covers of** holes in **the ground.**[12] אֲבָל בְּכִיסּוּי הַכֵּלִים – **But regarding covers of vessels,** בֵּין כָּךְ וּבֵין כָּךְ נִיטָּלִין בְּשַׁבָּת – **in either case,** i.e. whether they have handles or not, **they may be taken on the Sabbath.**[13]

Gemara The Mishnah's ruling is qualified:

אָמַר רַב יְהוּדָה בַּר שִׁילָא אָמַר רַבִּי אַסִּי אָמַר רַבִּי יוֹחָנָן – **Rav Yehudah bar Shila said in the name of R' Assi, who said in the name of R' Yochanan:** וְהוּא שֶׁיֵּשׁ תּוֹרַת כְּלִי עֲלֵיהֶן – **This** rule **is** applicable **only if [the covers] can function as utensils** by being used for some task; otherwise, they are *muktzeh*.[14]

In light of R' Yochanan's qualification, the Gemara proceeds to clarify the dispute cited in the Mishnah.[15]

דְּכוּלֵּי עָלְמָא – **All** (i.e. the Tanna Kamma and R' Yose) **agree** that כִּסּוּי קַרְקָעוֹת – regarding **covers of** holes in **the ground** the rule is that אִם יֵשׁ לָהֶן בֵּית אֲחִיזָה אִין – **if they have handles** they may **indeed** be taken, אִי לֹא לֹא – but **if not** they may **not** be taken, because their removal and return appear like acts of demolishing and building. כִּסּוּי הַכֵּלִים – Regarding **covers of** movable **utensils,** the rule is that אַף עַל גַּב דְּאֵין לָהֶם בֵּית אֲחִיזָה – **even if they do not have handles** they may be taken, provided, as R' Yochanan said, that they are functional utensils in their own right.[16] כִּי פְּלִיגֵי – **When do they disagree?** בְּכֵלִים דְּחַבְּרִינְהוּ בְּאַרְעָא – It is **regarding** covers of **utensils that were attached to the ground** and are thus similar to holes in the ground. מַר סָבַר גָּזְרִינַן – One **master** (the Tanna Kamma) **holds** that **[the Rabbis] decreed** that when they have no handles the covers of these utensils not be taken, due to their similarity to covers of holes. וּמַר סָבַר לָא גָּזְרִינַן – **And** the other **master** (R' Yose) **holds** that **[the Rabbis] did not** enact this **decree.** Thus, the covers may be taken even if they have no handles.

לִישָּׁנָא אַחֲרִינָא – **An alternative version** of this explanation is as follows: כִּי פְּלִיגֵי – **When do they disagree?** בְּכִיסּוּי תַּנּוּר – It is **regarding the cover of an oven,** which is a utensil that is attached to the ground. מַר מְדַמֵּי לֵיהּ לְכִיסּוּי קַרְקַע – One **master** (the Tanna Kamma) **compares it to the cover of** a hole in **the ground,** וּמַר מְדַמֵּי לֵיהּ לְכִיסּוּי כֵּלִים – **and** the other **master** (R' Yose) **compares it to the cover of** ordinary **utensils.**[17]

הדרן עלך כל הכלים

WE SHALL RETURN TO YOU, KOL HAKEILIM

NOTES

9. As explained above, on 126a. [Although R' Yehudah's dissenting opinion is also recorded in that Mishnah, the opinion of R' Eliezer is cited anonymously (i.e. as that of the Tanna Kamma) and is thus treated as a majority opinion (see *Tosafos* to *Yevamos* 42b ד״ה סתם ואח״כ מחלוקת and *Teshuvos HaRashba* §114).]

10. Even when a sage says that the halachah follows a certain view, he might be stating only what appears to be correct in the course of his study at that time. Hence, such a decision may not be relied upon in actual practice. But when a sage rules in an actual incident, he gives the matter his full consideration and reaches a definite conclusion (*Rashbam* to *Bava Basra* 130b ד״ה ומר סבר מעשה רב).

11. Some editions delete the word כָּל, *All,* for as the Gemara explains, certain vessel-covers may be taken even if they have no handle (*Maharshal,* cited in marginal gloss).

12. For example, covers of pits or cisterns (or manholes). One who places a plain cover over a hole in the ground appears to be building, i.e. permanently blocking up the hole. Conversely, one who removes the cover from such a hole appears to be demolishing, i.e. opening a sealed hole. The cover must have a handle so that it will be obvious that it is designed to be removed and replaced (*Rashi*; see *Shaar HaTziyun* 308:46; see also *Beur Halachah* to 308:10 ד״ה אין ניטלין).

13. The Gemara will clarify the dispute.

14. See note 1. This ruling of Rav Yehudah bar Shila in the name of R' Assi in the name of R' Yochanan, seems to contradict a ruling stated previously (on 125b; see note 9 there) by Rav Yosef in the name of R' Assi in the name of R' Yochanan. According to that previous report, R' Assi said in the name of R' Yochanan that a stone which was placed on a keg becomes designated as a non-*muktzeh* cover on the mere basis of having been placed there for that purpose — even though the stone is not a functional utensil. Some suggest that Rav Yehudah bar Shila and Rav Yosef disagree as to the true opinion of R' Assi in the name of R' Yochanan (one explanation of *Rabbeinu Tam,* cited by *Rashba* and *Ritva MHK* ed., and by *Maharshal* to 125b). However, for possible resolutions of the contradiction, see *Tosafos* to 125b ד״ה ואזדו לטעמייהו, *Rashba* and *Ritva MHK* ed.

15. Since R' Yochanan has qualified the Mishnah as pertaining to covers that are functional utensils in their own right, it behooves us to explain why the Tanna Kamma additionally requires a handle even for vessel-covers. Since they are functional utensils, they are certainly not *muktzeh*! (*Rashi*).

16. [Actually, the halachah does not follow R' Yochanan (as quoted by Rav Yehudah bar Shila) in this regard. Rather, it follows Rabban Shimon ben Gamliel, who stated that the mere pre-Sabbath designation of an article for use as a cover suffices to make it non-*muktzeh.* Thus, vessel-covers need neither to have handles nor to be functional utensils. They need merely be mentally designated as such in advance, or used to cover the utensil before the Sabbath (see *Orach Chaim* 308:10 with *Mishnah Berurah* §45).]

17. *Tosafos,* cited by *Maharshal,* state that the two versions of the explanation differ only in language, but are substantively the same. However, it is clear from other Rishonim that in their view there is a substantive difference between the two versions. This emerges from the following observation made by the Rishonim:

A Baraisa above (125a) cited R' Yose's testimony in the name of R' Eliezer ben Yaakov that the cover of an oven does not require a handle, and the Gemara there commented that this opinion was followed in actual practice. Accordingly, *Rif* there cited this practice as halachah. Yet *Rif* here rules that the halachah follows the Tanna Kamma, who states that a handle is required for the cover of a utensil that is attached to the ground! The Rishonim resolve this apparent contradiction by explaining that *Rif* differentiates between utensils that are completely buried in the ground with only their lips protruding and those that stand above ground but are merely cemented to it (like ovens). Only buried utensils might be confused with holes in the ground, and therefore, it is only with regard to the covers of such utensils that the Tanna Kamma requires handles. Covers of attached utensils in the class of ovens, which stand above the ground, do not require handles, since these utensils would not be confused with holes. Thus, R' Eliezer ben Yaakov's opinion above conforms with the Tanna Kamma's opinion here (*Ran; Ramban, Rashba* and *Ritva MHK* ed. to 125a; see also *Rambam, Hil. Shabbos* 25:13 and *Orach Chaim* 308:10).

Now, this explanation can fit only with our Gemara's first version, and indeed, *Rif* cites this version exclusively. The second version states explicitly that according to the Tanna Kamma even oven-covers require handles. Thus, we learn from the Rishonim that the two versions differ in whether the decree, which according to the Tanna Kamma was enacted, extends even to the covers of utensils in the class of ovens. See also *Baal HaMaor, Milchamos Hashem* and *Rosh* here.

שיש להם בית אחיזה ניטלין בשבת ואמר רב יהודה בר שילא אמר רב אסי אמר רבי יוחנן והוא שיש תורת כלי עליהן וכי תימא הכא נמי דאיכא תורת כלי עליו ומי בעי רשב"ג תורת כלי עליו והתניא [א] חריות של דקל שגדרן לשם עצים ונמלך עליהן לישיבה צריך לקשר רשב"ג אומר אין צריך לקשר רבי יוחנן סבירא ליה כוותיה בחדא ופליג עליה בחדא דרש רבי יצחק נפחא אפתחא דריש גלותא הלכה כרבי אליעזר מתיב רב עמרם [ב] ומדבריהם למדנו שפוקקין ומודדין וקושרין בשבת א"ל [אביי] מאי דעתיך משום דקתני סתמא נגר הנגרר נמי סתמא היא ואפ' הכי [ג] מעשה רב: **מתני'** ([ד] כל) כיסוי הכלים שיש להם בית אחיזה ניטלין בשבת א"ר יוסי בד"א [א] בכיסוי קרקעות אבל בכיסוי הכלים בין כך ובין כך ניטלין בשבת: **גמ'** אמר רב יהודה בר שילא א"ר אסי א"ר יוחנן [ב] והוא שיש תורת כלי עליהן דכ"ע כסוי קרקעות אם יש להן בית אחיזה אין אי לא לא כסוי הכלים אע"ג דאין להם בית אחיזה כי פליגי בכלים דחברינהו בארעא מ"ס גזרינן [ג] ומ"ס לא גזרינן לישנא אחרינא כי פליגי בכיסוי תנור מר מדמי ליה לכיסוי קרקע ומר מדמי ליה לכיסוי כלים:

הדרן עלך כל הכלים

מפנין [ד] [ה] אפילו ארבע וחמש קופות של תבן ושל תבואה מפני האורחים ומפני בטול בהמ"ד [ו] אבל לא את האוצר מפנין תרומה טהורה ודמאי ומעשר ראשון שניטלה תרומתו ומעשר שני והקדש שנפדו והתורמוס היבש מפני שהוא מאכל [ז] לעזים [ח] אבל לא את הטבל ולא את מעשר [ראשון] שלא נטלה תרומתו ולא את מעשר שני והקדש שלא נפדו ולא [ט] את הלוף ולא את החרדל ר' שמעון בן גמליאל [י] מתיר בלוף מפני שהוא מאכל עורבין חבילי קש וחבילי עצים וחבילי זרדים אם התקינן למאכל בהמה מטלטלין אותן ואם לאו אין מטלטלין אותן: **גמ'** השתא חמש מפנין ארבע מיבעיא [כ] אמר רב חסדא ארבע מחמש ([ל] איכא דאמרי [מ] ארבע מאוצר קטן) וחמש מאוצר גדול ומאי אבל לא את האוצר שלא יתחיל באוצר תחלה ומני רבי יהודה היא דאית ליה מוקצה ושמואל אמר ארבע וחמש כדאמרי

רש"י

שיש להן בית אחיזה. בית יד: ה"ג ואמר רב יהודה והוא שיש תורת כלי עליהן. שהכיסוי ראוי לתשמיש (א) עלמו הוא דניטלין בשבת ואם אין תורת כלי עליו לא אמרינן כיסוי כלי הוה כלי ודלתות שידה תיבה ומגדל דתנא מתני' נוטלין יש תורת כלי עליהן דראוין ליֵשב עליהן ולתת עליהן מזונות לקטן ולקמן מפרש אמאי בעינן בית אחיזה הואיל ותורת כלי עליהן אלמא לרבי יוחנן מידי דליכא תורת כלי עליו לא מטלטלין והאי קנה מאי תורת כלי עליו איכא אי משום דפותח ונועל בו אין זו תורת כלי עליו אלא תורת בנין: וכ"ת הכא נמי דאיכא תורת כלי עליו. שראוי להפך בו זיתים או לפצע בו אגוזים (ב): [מ] (תורת כלי עליו. אפי' אינו ראוי לדבר אחר): סבירא ליה כוותיה בחדא. דמתוקן ואע"פ שאינו קשור: ופליג עליה בחדא. דבעי תורת כלי: הלכה כרבי אליעזר. דבעינן קשור ותלוי: מדבריהם למדנו. בפ' בתרא בימי אביו של ר' לדוק ובימי אבא שאול בן בטנית שפקקו את המאור בטפיח וקשרו את המקידה בגמי לידע אם יש בגיגית פותח טפח והתם מפרש לה וקתני מדבריהם למדנו: שפוקקין. את המאור בדבר שאינו קשור ותלוי: וקושרין. קשר שאינו של קיימא לכתחלה: ומודדין. מקוה ומטלניות: מאי דעתיך. דמותבת לרבי יצחק נפחא מהא מלי לשנויי לך הא מני רבנן היא ואי משום דקתני לה סתמא מותבת ליה דמדסתם לן כרבנן הלכתא כוותייהו: נגר הנגרר נמי סתמא. קתני לה וסתם לן בהא כרבי אליעזר דאסור: מעשה רב. למילף מיניה דכיון דסמיך למיעבד עובדא לקולא ש"מ הלכתא היא: **מתני'** בכיסוי קרקע. כגון כיסוי בור ודות דהוי כבונה אי לאו דמוכחא בית אחיזה דילה דלמשקיל ולאהדורי עביד: **גמ'** א"ר יוחנן והוא שיש תורת כלי עליהם. דכיסויין הללו חזו לתשמיש דעלמא אבל כיסוי כלי לא אמרינן כלי הוא: ודכ"ע. משום דאוקמא ר' יוחנן בשיש תורת כלי עליהן איצטריכא ליה למימר דכי פליגי רבנן בכלים דחברינהו בארעא פליגי דאילו כלים דעלמא אע"ג דלית להו לכיסוייהן בית אחיזה מיטלטלי דכיון דבאיכא תורת כלי עליהן קיימי מה לי איכא בית אחיזה מה לי ליכא בית אחיזה אלא בכיסוי כלים המחוברי' לקרקע כגון תנור וכירים הוא דפליגי משום דדמו במקצת לכיסוי בור ודות וגזרינן הני אטו הני:

הדרן עלך כל הכלים

מפנין. אם צריך למקומן להושיב שם אורחים להסב בסעוד' או תלמידים לדרשה ולא חיישינן לטרחא דשבת: אבל לא את האוצר. מפרש בגמרא: מפנין תרומה טהורה. כלומר ומהו מפנין דבר הראוי כגון אלו תרומה טהורה דחזי לבהמת כהן לא דאפילו לבהמת כהן לא חזיא בשבת דאע"ג דבטול הואי כדתניא בכל שעה בפסחים (דף לג.) שאם רלה כהן מרילה לפני הכלב בשבת וביום טוב לא חזיא היא דזו היא ביעורה מן העולם או לאדם או לבהמה ואין מבערין תרומה טמאה וקדשים טמאין ביום טוב כדתנן (לעיל דף כג:) ואין מדליקין בשמן שריפה ביום טוב ואוקימנא [י] טעמא משום דאין שורפין קדשים ביום טוב: (ג) לוף. מין קטניות שאינו ראוי חי אפילו לבהמה: לעורבין. כגון עשירים שמגדלין עורבין לגדולה: זרדים. מין קנים הם שמורדים כשהן רכים ואוכלים אותם: **גמ'** ארבע מחמש. אם לא היה שם אלא כשיעור ה' קופות לא יפנה אלא ד' מהם שאסור לגמור את האולר דילמא חזי גומות בקרקעיתו ומשוי להו: מאוצר גדול. ואם יש הרבה אין מפנין אלא חמש דחיישינן לטירחא: מאי אבל לא את האוצר. שלא יגמור את האולר לא מלית אמרת דהא מרישא שמעינן ארבע וחמש תחלה. אם לא התחיל בו להסתפק ממנו כבר למאכלו או למאכל בהמתו דאם כן הוה ליה מוקלה ומתניתין רבי יהודה היא: כדאמרי

תוספות

וכי תימא הכא נמי דאיכא תורת כלי עליו. פי' בקונטרס שיהא ראוי לעשות שום תשמיש אחר ואין נראה לר"ת כי למה יש לנו להצריך שלדבר אחר יהא ראוי כיון שראוי לדבר זה אלא נראה לר"ת דה"פ דאיכא תורת כלי עליו שתיקנו ועשה בו מעשה והכינו לכך שמאחר שלכך תיקנו והכינו לכך יש תורת כלי עליו אפילו אינו ראוי לדבר אחר כמו חריות של דקל שאינן ראוין לשום תשמיש אלא לישיבה אף על פי כן (ד) יכול להכניס ולטלטלם בשבת ולהכניס נמי אמרינן לעיל לאו ושיפשפו ועוד אי תורת כלי עליהם ממש לריכא למימר דכלי ניטל לצורך גופו והא דאמרי' בעירובין (ד' קב.) נגר הנגרר עשה לו בית יד מהו א"ל בוכנא קאמרת פירוק ושרי לאו משום דלאי לא הוה כבוכנא ע"י הבית יד הוה הוה אסור דאפילו לא חזי למילתא אחריתי כיון שתקנוהו בידים לכך היה מותר אפי' בלא בית יד אלא נראה לר"י דהסיא מיירי בנקמז דאסור לעיל מיני' בסמוך משום דמיחזי כבונה פי' שנועץ הנגר בתוך הנקב שבמפתן עד (ה) בתוך הארץ כדפירש בקונטרס התם ועלה קאי הא עשה לו בית יד באותו נגר שנקמז אי נמי שמואל לטעמיה דסבר דטעמא דרבי יהודה משום בנין אפילו בלא נעילה נגר בארץ וכן נראה יותר כי נקמז אין פתרונו נעילה בארץ אלא דומה שהוא מעין נשמט רק שאינו נשמט ממש כדמוכח בברייתא שהביא למעלה דקתני נגר אם נשמט כולו אסור נקמז מותר רבי יהודה אומר נקמז אע"פ שאינו נשמט ולא נודע פירוש נקמז היטב ובירושלמי גרסינן נגר דר' אליעזר הוה קטיר בגמי נשמט אסור נקמז רבי יעקב בר אחא מורה כרבנן לאבעותיה (ו):

ומדבריהם למדנו שפוקקין ומודדין. ואע"ג דטפיח לא מבטל ליה כמו פקק דאמרי' בפרק הישן (סוכה דף כח.) גבי סדין איכא למימר דמבטל ליה טפי מסדין ולא מלי למימר נמי דפקק דמצוה שאני כדאמרי' בשילהי מכילתין (ד' קנז:) גבי מדידה דהתם לא הוי איסור על כך אלא משום דהוי כעובדא דחול אבל פקק דמשום תוספת אהל דמי לבנין ליכא למישרי משום מצוה:

הדרן עלך כל הכלים

מפנין ארבע וחמש קופות. בירושלמי מפרש כמה שיעור קופות כההוא דתנינן (ז) שלשה קופות של שלשה סאין: של

עין משפט נר מצוה

מה א ב ג מיי' פכ"ה מהלכות שבת הלכ"ג טוש"ע או"ח סימן שח סעיף י:

א ד ה מיי' פכ"ו מהל' שבת הלכה ג ופכ"ה הלכה טו סמג לאוין סה טוש"ע או"ח סימן שלג סעיף א:

רבינו חננאל

כרשב"ג ורשב"ג שרי אע"פ דליכא תורת כלי עליו. ור' יוחנן שמעי' ליה דבעי תורת כלי. ואוקימנא בקנה שהתקינו להיות נועל ופותח בו בדאיכא תורת כלי עליו ובהא א"ר יוחנן הלכתא כרשב"ג. אבל בחריות של דקל שגדרן לעצים דשרי רשב"ג בלא קישור לא סבר לזה ר' יוחנן כוותיה. ועליהן [אמר דר'] יוחנן סבר לה כוותיה בחדא ופליג עליה בחדא: **דרש** ר' יצחק נפחא אפתחא דבי ריש גלותא הלכתא כר' אלעזר שאין פוקקין (עליו) [בו] אם [לא שהוא] קשור ותלוי. ואותבה ר' (עולא) [רב עמרם] מהא דתנן בסוף שבת מדבריהן למדנו שפוקקין ומודדין וקושרין בשבת. א"ל אביי לרב (עזרא) [עמרם] למה אותיבתיה מהא מפני שהיא שנויה סתם. וקיי"ל הלכה כסתם משנה. נגר הנגרר נמי סתמא היא. והיא שנויה סתם אליבא דר' אלעזר. ושני ליה אע"פ דהא סתמא והא סתמא. הא סתמא דפוקקין ומודדין וקושרין בשבת עבדו בה עובדא ומעשה רב וזו הלכה למעשה והלכתא כחכמים ונדחה דרישא דר' יצחק נפחא. ואמרינן בתלמוד א"י. א"ר יוחנן אתיא יחידאה דהכא סתמא דתמן. ויחידאה דתמן כסתמא דהכא. פי' יחידאה דהכא דהוא ר' אלעזר דפקק החלון בסתמא דנגר נגרר [ויחידאי דנגר הנגרר] (דהוא ר' יהודה כסתמא) [דפקק החלון דחכ"א] בין כך ובין כך פוקקין בו: **כל** כסויי הכלים שיש להן בית אחיזה ניטלין בשבת. א"ר יוסי בד"א בכסויי קרקעות וכו'. א"ר יהודה בר שילא א"ר אסי א"ר יוחנן והוא שיש תורת כלי עליהן. ואמרינן כולי עלמא כסויי קרקעות אם יש להן בית אחיזה שרי ואי לא אסור לטלטל. כגון כסויי הבארות וכסויי הדות וכיוצא בהן. כסויי כלים כגון כדות ופיטסים וכיוצא בהן אע"פ (שהן) [שאין] להן בית אחיזה מותר לטלטלן ולכסותם. כי פליגי בכסויי כלים וחיברן בקרקע. ר' יוסי לא גזר ורבנן סבר גזרינן והלכתא כוותיה:

הדרן עלך פרק כל הכלים

פי"ח מפנין אפילו ד' וה' קופות של תבן. פי' מפנין מעתיקין ממקום למקום מלשון ורצה הכהן ופנו את הבית. אקשינן על משנתנו. השתא ה' מפנין ד' מיבעיא ופריק רב חסדא ארבע מחמש וה' מאוצר גדול. ומאי אבל לא את האוצר שלא יתחיל באוצר תחלה ומני ר"י היא דאית ליה מוקצה ובא שמואל ופריק פירוק אחר ודברים פשוטין הן. אבל סוגיא דשמעתא כרב חסדא דמתניתא סתמא תנן כוותיה. שאין מתחילין

מסורת הש"ס

א) לעיל נ. [ודף קכה:], ב) לקמן קנז., ג) [לעיל כא. וש"נ], ד) רש"ל מ"ז וכן בס"י ליתא, ה) ביצה לה:, ו) [שם לו.], ז) פ"ח לעניים, ח) [עי' תוס' לקמן קמג. ד"ה אבל], ט) [ב"מ קיג.], י) [עי' תוס' לקמן קמג. ד"ה רשב"ג], כ) [עי' תוס' לעיל ס: ד"ה הסמא ע"ש דהשמיטו אמר רב חסדא ד' מאוצר קטן ה' מאוצר גדול], ל) ל"ג ברי"ף ורא"ש, מ) מ"א ל"ג ומ"כ שלפני רש"י היה הגירסא בגמרא אחר כך בחריות דמתירים אלמא לא בעי רשב"ג תורת כלי עליו ומליין רש"י בזה, נ) [שם כג:], ס) [בתקילים פ"ג מ"ב].

הגהות הב"ח

(א) רש"י ד"ה ה"ג וכו' לתשמיש לעצמו הוא: (ב) ד"ה וכ"ת הכא וכו' אגוזים הס"ד. ואח"כ מ"ה אין צריך לקשר אלמא דאיכא תורת כלי עליו: (ג) רש"י ד"ה לוף וכו' מו"מ. ונ"ב פ"א סורמוס: (ד) תוס' ד"ה וכי תימא וכו' לישיבה אפ"כ. נ"ב ועיי' בפ"ק: (ה) באד עד לתוך הארץ: (ו) באד מורה כרבנן לאבעותיה מה V:

רב נסים גאון

פי"ח ר' יהודה היא דאמר מוקצה ור' שמעון לית ליה מוקצה אצל כל פחמא (פי' עיקר הדברים) בפרק במה מדליקין והכבר פירשנו זה בפרק יציאות השבת:

ליקוטי רש"י

חריות. ענפים קשים כעין שמתקינין שדלופין של לולבין ונשלו עלין שלהן קרי להן חריות [לעיל נ.]. שגדרן לעצים. שחתכן להסיק [שם קנה:]. שגדרן. כל [קליטת] תמרים קרי גדירה. צריך לקשר. לקשרם יחד מבעוד יום להוכיח שלישיבה עומדים ואם לא קשרם יחד אסור לטלטלן למחר דלא הוי יחוד למחשבה [שם נ.]. שפוקקין. כרבנן דאמרי פוקקין פקק החלון. ומודדין. להתלמד על דבר הורלה [שם כג.]. מפני האורחים. זימון לאכול ואין מקום להסב. בטול בית המדרש. שאין לתלמידים מקום להושיב לישב [ביצה לו:]. דמאי. תבואה הנלקחת מעם הארץ והיא נקראת דמאי ספק עישרו ספק לא עישרו וחכמים הפרישו מעשרותיו מספק [פסחים לה.]. ספק מעושר ספק אינו מעושר דרוב עמי הארץ מעשרין הן ומומלא דרבנן היא [עירובין יז:]. לקמן מעם הארץ ומכס פירותיו ספק לאין מעושרין [סוכה לה:]. ומעשר ראשון. שניטלה תרומתו. לוים. תרומת מעשר

לכהן ומכאן ואילך המעשר מותר לזרים [פסחים שם]. קס"ד תרומת מעשר שלו שעל הלוי להפריש [ברכות מז. עיי"ש בב"ח]. קס"ד תרומת מעשר שהלוי נותן לכהן וכ"ש תרומה גדולה שיש על ישראל להפריש והפרישו קודם שנתן המעשר ללוי [לקמן קכז:]. ומעשר שני. מעשר שני שנפדה להוציאו באכילה חוץ לירושלים ולא פדיוו עולה לירושלים ויאכל [ברכות שם].

תורמוס. מין קטנית עגול כמין עדשה ורחב כמעה קטנה [ביצה כה:]. ולא את מעשר שני. חוץ לירושלים [פסחים שם]. שלא נפדו. ואע"ג דמלי פריק להו השתא מיהא לא מפרק [עירובין לא.]. ולא את הלוף ולא את החרדל. מין קטנית ואינו ראוי למאכל בהמה חי ואפילו לעופות. מפני שהוא מאכל עורבים. ישראל בני מלכים הם ועורבים לגוי ולוף גדל ונאכל [ב"מ קיג:]. זרדים. מין קנים הם ועומדים לשריפה [לעיל קנ.]. התקינן. הזמינן [לקמן קכח.]. רכין זורדין אותם למאכל אדם נתקשו מעט ראוין למאכל בהמה ובמחשבה יעבו וקשות אוגדין אותם ועושין לאין בהמה אוכלתם ולכי יבשי עומדים להיסק [סוכה יב.].

Chapter Eighteen

Mishnah The Rabbis prohibited certain activities on the Sabbath because they involve excessive exertion.[1] The Rabbis, however, relaxed this prohibition (subject to certain conditions) where the exertion is needed for the performance of a *mitzvah,* the care of animals or the care of the ill.[2] These exemptions are discussed in the Mishnahs of this chapter.

מְפַנִּין אֲפִילוּ אַרְבַּע וְחָמֵשׁ קוּפּוֹת שֶׁל תֶּבֶן וְשֶׁל תְּבוּאָה – **We may clear away** on the Sabbath **even four or five boxes**[3] **of straw or of grain** מִפְּנֵי הָאוֹרְחִים וּמִפְּנֵי בִטּוּל בֵּית הַמִּדְרָשׁ – **because of guests or because of curtailment of** attendance at **the study hall,**[4] אֲבָל לֹא אֶת הָאוֹצָר – **but not a store** of straw or grain.[5]

The Mishnah proceeds to delineate the types of items that may be cleared away:

מְפַנִּין תְּרוּמָה טְהוֹרָה – **We may clear away** ***terumah*** **that is** ***tahor;***[6] וּדְמַאי – **and** ***demai;***[7] וּמַעֲשֵׂר רִאשׁוֹן שֶׁנִּיטְּלָה תְּרוּמָתוֹ – **and** ***maaser rishon*** **whose** ***terumah*** **has been taken;**[8] וּמַעֲשֵׂר שֵׁנִי וְהֶקְדֵּשׁ שֶׁנִּפְדּוּ – **and** ***maaser sheni***[9] **or consecrated produce that was redeemed;**[10] וְהַתּוּרְמוּס הַיָּבֵשׁ – **and dried** ***turmos,***[11] מִפְּנֵי שֶׁהוּא מַאֲכָל לְעִזִּים – **because it is food for goats.**[12] אֲבָל לֹא אֶת הַטֶּבֶל – **However,** we may **not** clear away ***tevel;***[13] וְלֹא אֶת מַעֲשֵׂר [רִאשׁוֹן] שֶׁלֹּא נִטְּלָה תְּרוּמָתוֹ – **nor** ***maaser [rishon]*** **whose** ***terumah*** **has not been taken;**[14]

NOTES

1. See note 4.

2. See *Meiri.*

3. The reference is to a box of a specific size (*Rashba* to 127a ד״ה ה״ג רש״י; *Ritva MHK* ed. there ד״ה למעוטי and ד״ה ותניא אידך), each box having a three-*se'ah* capacity (*Tosafos,* from *Yerushalmi*; see also *Rabbeinu Chananel,* who gives the combined total of the boxes as a *lesech,* or fifteen *se'ah*; cf. *Ramban* to 127a ד״ה ה״ג תבואה צבורה, who asserts that according to the *Bavli,* the boxes can be even larger).

4. I.e. one may remove several large boxes of straw or grain [which are not *muktzeh* – see note 6] to make room to seat guests for the meal, or to seat students for a Torah lecture. Though moving such large amounts of straw or grain would generally be forbidden on the Sabbath because of the excessive exertion entailed [and the appearance of weekday activity (see *Chidushei HaRan*)], the Rabbis permitted the exertion where it is needed in order to facilitate the performance of a *mitzvah* (*Rashi*; see also *Rif* and *Rosh*). [The guests referred to here are people who, for whatever reason, cannot eat in their homes (e.g. they are traveling). Hence, providing their needs fulfills the mitzvah of *hachnasas orchim.* Simply inviting friends for the Sabbath meal, however, is considered optional rather than a mitzvah (see *Rama* 333:1).]

[Where one desires the extra room for a non-mitzvah purpose, some Rishonim permit the clearing away of one or two boxes (*Rambam* and *Ramban,* as interpreted by *Beis Yosef* 333; see also *Mishnah Berurah* 333:1-2). *Rosh* and *Ran,* however, rule that in such cases, no amount of straw or produce may be cleared away. (See also *Rambam, Hil. Shabbos* 26:15, *Darchei Moshe HaAroch* 333 and *Taz* 333:1.)]

5. The Gemara will explain the meaning of this phrase (*Rashi*). [We use the word "store" here in the sense of a quantity of stored straw or produce.]

6. After harvesting his crop, a farmer separates its *terumah* (also called *terumah gedolah*; generally, 1/50 of the crop is separated as *terumah*) and gives it to the Kohen. *Terumah* may not be eaten by a non-Kohen, but only by a Kohen, the members of his household and – if animal food – his animals.

The Mishnah now makes the point that the permit to move the straw and grain is a dispensation only with regard to the ordinary restrictions against excessive exertion on the Sabbath. But the *muktzeh* restrictions were not relaxed; thus, only such items which are not *muktzeh* may be moved.

Terumah that is *tahor* is fit to be eaten by a Kohen's animal (*Rashi,* as found in our texts; see also *Ran*; cf. *Rashi* printed alongside *Rif*). [Stored grain is generally not fit for human consumption. Still, it is not *muktzeh* because it can be fed to animals. See, however, the difficulties raised by *Rashash.*]

Terumah that is *tamei,* however, must be destroyed and thus is *muktzeh,* as it is not fit for any use on the Sabbath. Though feeding *terumah* that is *tamei* to a Kohen's animal is generally an acceptable means of destroying the *terumah* [see *Pesachim* 32a], that may not be done on the Sabbath, since the eradication of disqualified sanctified foods may not be done on the Sabbath or festivals even if the eradication does not involve any forbidden *melachah* [see above, end of 23b; see also note 48 there] (*Rashi*; see also *Rashi* to *Beitzah* 27b ד״ה חלה, and note 10 in the Schottenstein edition there). [*Rashi's* assertion that feeding an animal *terumah* that is *tamei* is generally an acceptable means of destroying the *terumah* is disputed by *Baal HaMaor, Ramban* et al. here and by *Tosafos* to *Beitzah* 27b.]

7. *Demai* is produce obtained from an *am ha'aretz* (an unlearned person, who – although basically an observant Jew – is one whose observance of certain laws, especially those with numerous and complex details, cannot be relied upon due to his ignorance). The Sages decreed that such produce may not be eaten until it has been tithed, because they observed that a sizable minority of unlearned people had become lax in separating tithes other than *terumah* (see *Sotah* 48a). On the Biblical level, however, one would be permitted to assume that *demai* was already tithed, since the majority of *amei ha'aretz* do tithe their produce. [According to many commentators, *demai* is a composite of דָּא מַאי, *what is this?* (*Rambam, Commentary to the Mishnah* and *Rav* to *Berachos* 7:1; see also *Aruch* ע׳ דמאי).]

Though it is forbidden to tithe produce – even *demai* – on the Sabbath, *demai* is not considered *muktzeh,* for reasons that will be explained in the Gemara.

8. After separating *terumah,* the farmer separates *maaser rishon* (the first tithe) – one-tenth of the remaining crop – and gives it to the Levi. The Levi, in turn, must separate one-tenth of the *maaser rishon* he has received as *terumah* (*terumas maaser*) for the Kohen; and until he does so, the *maaser rishon* is *tevel* and may not be eaten. Thus, "*maaser rishon* whose *terumah* has been taken" means that the *terumas maaser* has been separated, rendering the rest of the *maaser rishon* permissible. [The Gemara will explain why the Mishnah had to state the seemingly obvious ruling that *maaser rishon* whose *terumah* has been taken is not *muktzeh.*]

9. In the first, second, fourth and fifth years of the seven-year *shemittah* cycle, the farmer separates *maaser sheni* (the second tithe) from the remainder of his crop (after the *terumah* and *maaser rishon* have been removed). The farmer either brings this second tithe to Jerusalem and eats it there, or he may redeem the *maaser sheni* with money, which he brings to Jerusalem to buy food to be eaten there (see *Deuteronomy* 14:22-26).

10. The redemption of the original *maaser sheni* or of the consecrated produce removes its sanctity, allowing it to be consumed as ordinary food anywhere; thus, the redeemed produce is not *muktzeh.* [Here, too, the Gemara will explain why the Mishnah had to state the seemingly obvious ruling that the redeemed produce is not *muktzeh.*]

11. [Lupine, a type of bean.]

12. Since dried *turmos* is used as goat feed, it is not *muktzeh.* [To be fit for human consumption, however, lupine must be cooked extensively (see above, 74a-b; *Beitzah* 25b with *Rashi*).] Some texts read here: לַעֲנִיִּים, *for poor people,* rather than לְעִזִּים, *for goats.*

13. Grain that has been processed to the point that it is obligated in *terumah* and tithes is called *tevel* until the *terumah* and tithes have been separated. *Tevel* may not be eaten [nor may it be fed to animals once it has been brought into storage (see *Rashi* to *Avodah Zarah* 41b ד״ה כדי שתהא and *Tosafos* there ד״ה ומכניסה)].

14. At first glance, this would seem to mean that the *terumas maaser* was not separated from the *maaser rishon,* in which case the *maaser rishon* remains *tevel* and is forbidden for consumption. But the ruling that such

שיש להם בית אחיזה ניטלין בשבת ואמר רב יהודה בר שילא אמר רב אסי אמר רבי יוחנן והוא שיש תורת כלי עליהן וכי תימא הכא נמי דאיכא תורת כלי עליו ומי בעי רשב"ג תורת כלי עליו והתניא [א] חריות של דקל שגדרן לשם עצים ונמלך עליהן לישיבה צריך לקשר רשב"ג אומר אין צריך לקשר רבי יוחנן סבירא ליה כוותיה בחדא ופליג עליה בחדא דרש רבי יצחק נפחא אפתחא דריש גלותא הלכה כרבי אליעזר מתיב רב עמרם [ג] ומדבריהם למדנו שפוקקין ומודדין וקושרין בשבת א"ל [אביי] מאי דעתיך משום דקתני סתמא נגר הנגרר נמי סתמא היא ואפ' הכי מעשה רב: **מתני'** [ד] (כל) כיסוי הכלים שיש להם בית אחיזה ניטלין בשבת א"ר יוסי בד"א [א] בכיסוי קרקעות אבל בכיסוי הכלים בין כך ובין כך ניטלין בשבת: **גמ'** אמר רב יהודה בר שילא א"ר אסי א"ר יוחנן [ה] והוא שיש תורת כלי עליהן דכ"ע כסוי קרקעות אם יש להן בית אחיזה אין אי לא לא כסוי הכלים דאין להם בית אחיזה כי פליגי בכלים דחברינהו בארעא מ"ס גזרינן [ו] ומ"ס לא גזרינן לישנא אחרינא כי פליגי בכיסוי תנור מר מדמי ליה לכיסוי קרקע ומר מדמי ליה לכיסוי כלים:

הדרן עלך כל הכלים

מפנין [ז] אפילו ארבע וחמש קופות של תבן ושל תבואה מפני האורחים ומפני בטול בהמ"ד [ח] אבל לא את האוצר מפנין תרומה טהורה ודמאי ומעשר ראשון שניטלה תרומתו ומעשר שני והקדש שנפדו והתורמוס היבש מפני שהוא מאכל [ט] לעזים [י] אבל לא את הטבל ולא את מעשר [ראשון] שלא נטלה תרומתו ולא את מעשר שני והקדש שלא נפדו ולא [כ] את הלוף ולא את החרדל ר' שמעון בן גמליאל [ל] מתיר בלוף מפני שהוא מאכל עורבין חבילי קש וחבילי עצים וחבילי זרדים אם התקינן למאכל בהמה מטלטלין אותן ואם לאו אין מטלטלין אותן: **גמ'** השתא חמש מפנין ארבע מיבעיא [מ] אמר רב חסדא ארבע מחמש ([נ] איכא דאמרי [ה] ארבע מאוצר קטן) וחמש מאוצר גדול ומאי אבל לא את האוצר שלא יתחיל באוצר תחלה ומני רבי יהודה היא דאית ליה מוקצה ושמואל אמר ארבע וחמש כדאמרי

רש"י

שיש להן בית אחיזה. בית יד: ה"ג ואמר רב יהודה והוא שיש תורת כלי עליהן. שהכיסוי ראוי לתשמיש (א) עצמו הוא דניטלין בשבת ואם אין תורת כלי עליו לא אמרינן כיסוי כלי הוה כלי ודלתות שידה תיבה ומגדל דתנא מתני' נוטלין יש תורת כלי עליהן דראויין לישב עליהן ולתת עליהן מזונות לקטן ולקמן מפרש אמאי בעינן בית אחיזה הואיל ותורת כלי עליהן אלמא לרבי יוחנן מידי דליכא תורת כלי עליו לא מטלטלין והאי קנה מאי תורת כלי עליו איכא אי משום דפותח ונועל בו אין זו תורת כלי עליו אלא תורת בנין: **וכ"ת הכא נמי דאיכא תורת כלי עליו.** שראוי להפך בו זיתים או לפצע בו אגוזים (ב): (תורת כלי עליו. אפי' אינו ראוי לדבר אחר): **סבירא ליה כוותיה בחדא.** דמתוקן ואע"פ שאינו קשור: **ופליג עליה בחדא.** דבעי תורת כלי: **הלכה כרבי אליעזר.** דבעינן קשור ותלוי: **מדבריהם למדנו.** בפ' בתרא בימי אביו של ר' צדוק ובימי אבא שאול בן בטנית שפקקו את המאור בטפיח וקשרו את המקידה בגמי לידע אם יש בגיגית פותח טפח והתם מפרש לה וקתני מדבריהם למדנו: **שפוקקין.** את המאור בדבר שאינו קשור ותלוי: **וקושרין.** קשר שאינו של קיימא לכתחלה: **ומודדין.** מקוה ומטלניות: **מאי דעתיך.** דמותבת לרבי יצחק נפחא מהא מצי לשנויי לך הא מני רבנן היא ואי משום דקתני לה סתמא מותבת ליה דמדסתם לן כרבנן הלכתא כוותייהו: **נגר הנגרר נמי סתמא.** קתני לה וסתם לן בהא כרבי אליעזר דאסור: **מעשה רב.** למילף מיניה דכיון דסמיך למיעבד עובדא לקולא ש"מ הלכתא היא: **מתני' בכיסוי קרקע.** כגון כיסוי בור ודות דהוי כבונה אי לאו דמוכחא בית אחיזה דילה דלמשקיל ואהדורי עביד: **גמ' א"ר יוחנן והוא שיש תורת כלי עליהם.** דכיסויין הללו חזו לתשמיש דעלמא אבל כיסוי כלי לא אמרינן כלי הוא: **ודכ"ע.** משום דאוקמא ר' יוחנן בשיש תורת כלי עליהן איצטריכא ליה למימר דכי פליגי רבנן בכלים דחברינהו בארעא פליגי דאילו כלים דעלמא אע"ג דלית להו לכיסויהן בית אחיזה מיטלטלי דכיון דאיכא תורת כלי עליהן קיימי מה לי איכא בית אחיזה מה לי ליכא בית אחיזה אלא בכיסוי כלים המחוברי' לקרקע כגון תנור וכירים הוא דפליגי משום דדמו במקצת לכיסוי בור ודות וגזרינן הני אטו הני:

הדרן עלך כל הכלים

מפנין. אם צריך למקומן להושיב שם אורחים להסב בסעוד' או תלמידים לדרשה ולא חיישינן לטרחא דשבת: **אבל לא את האוצר.** מפרש בגמרא: **מפנין תרומה טהורה.** כלומר ומהו מפנין דבר הראוי כגון אלו תרומה טהורה דחזי לבהמת כהן אבל תרומה טמאה לא דאפילו לבהמת כהן לא חזיא בשבת ... שאם רצה כהן מטילה לפני הכלב בשבת וביום טוב לא חזיא ... או לבהמה ואין מבערין תרומה טמאה וקדשים טמאין ביום טוב כדתנן (לעיל דף כג:) ואין מדליקין בשמן שריפה ביום טוב ואוקימנא טעמא משום דאין שורפין קדשים ביום טוב: (ג) **לוף.** מין קטניות שאינו ראוי אפי' לבהמה: **לעורבין.** כגון עשירים שמגדלין עורבין לגדולה: **זרדים.** מין קנים הם שמוציאים בשכן רכים ואוכלים אותם: **גמ' ארבע מחמש.** אם לא היה שם אלא כשיעור ה' קופות לא יפנה אלא ד' מהם שאסור לגמור כל האוצר דילמא אתי לאשוויי גומות בקרקעיתו ומשוי להו: **מאוצר גדול.** ואם יש הרבה אין מפנין אלא כמה דמיישינן לטירחא: **מאי אבל לא את האוצר.** שלא יגמור את האוצר לא מלי אמרת דהא מרישא שמעינן ארבע וחמש: **תחלה.** אם לא התחיל בו להסתפק ממנו כבר למאכלו או למאכל בהמתו דהוה ליה מוקצה ומתניתין רבי יהודה היא: **כדאמרי**

תוספות

וכי תימא הכא נמי דאיכא תורת כלי עליו. פי' בקונטרס שיהא ראוי לעשות שום תשמיש אחר ואין נראה לר"ת כי למה יש לנו להצריך שלדבר אחר יהא ראוי אחר כיון שראוי לדבר זה אלא נראה לר"ת דה"ק דאיכא תורת כלי עליו שתיקנו ועשה בו מעשה והכינו לכך שמאחר שלכך תיקנו והכינו לכך יש תורת כלי עליו אפילו אינו ראוי לדבר אחר כמו חריות של דקל שאינן ראוין לשום תשמיש אלא לישיבה אף על פי כן (ד) יכול להכינם ולטלטלם בשבת ואגנים נמי אמרינן לעיל לאו ושיפשפו ועוד אי תורת כלי עליהם ממש צריכה למימר דכלי ניטל לצורך גופו והא דאמרי' בעירובין (ד' קב.) נגר הנגרר עשה לו בית יד מהו א"ל בוכנא קאמרת פירוש ושרי לאו משום דלאו הכי לא הוה כבוכנא ע"י הבית יד הוה הוה אסור דאפילו לא חזי למילתא אחריתי כיון שתקנוהו בידים לכך היה מותר אפי' בלא בית יד אלא נראה לר"ת דהסיא מיירי בנקמז דאסור לעיל מיני' בסמוך משום דמיחזי כבונה פי' שנועץ הנגר בתוך הנקב שבמפתן עד (ה) בתוך הארץ כדפירש בקונטרס התם ועלה קאי הא עשה לו בית יד בלאותו נגר שנקמז אי נמי שמואל לטעמיה דסבר דטעמא דרבי יהודה משום בנין אפילו בלא נעילת נגר בארץ וכן נראה יותר כי נקמז אין פתרונו נעילה בארץ אלא דומה שהוא מעין נשמט רק שאינו נשמט ממש כדמוכח בברייתא שהביא למעלה דקתני נגר אם נשמט כולו אסור נקמז מותר רבי יהודה אומר נקמז אע"פ שאינו נשמט ולא נודע פירוש נקמז היטב ובירושלמי גרסינן נגר דר' אליעזר הוה קטיר בגמי נשמט אסור נקמז רבי יעקב בר אחא מורה בראשי אצבעותיו (ו):

ומדבריהן למדנו שפוקקין ומודדין. ואע"ג דטפיח לא מבטל ליה כמו פקק כדאמרי' בפרק הישן (סוכה דף כח.) גבי סדין איכא למימר דמבטל ליה טפי מסדין ולא מצי למימר נמי פקק דמצוה שאני כדאמרי' בשילהי מכילתין (ד' קנז:) גבי מדידה דהתם לא הוי איסור כל כך אלא משום דהוי כעובדא דחול אבל פקק דמשום תוספת אהל דדמי לבנין ליכא למישרי משום מצוה:

הדרן עלך כל הכלים

מפנין ארבע וחמש קופות. בירושלמי מפרש כמה שיעור קופות כההוא דתנין [ס] שלשה קופות של שלשה סאין:

של

עין משפט נר מצוה

מה א ב ג מיי' פכ"ה מהלכות שבת הל"ג טוש"ע או"ח סימן שח סעיף י:
א ד ה מיי' פכ"א מהל' שבת הלכה ג ופכ"ו הלכה טו סמג לאוין סה טוש"ע או"ח סימן שלג סעיף א:

רבינו חננאל

כרשב"ג ורשב"ג שרי אע"פ דליכא תורת כלי עליו. ור' יוחנן שמעי' ליה דבעי תורת כלי. ואוקימנא בקנה שהתקינו להיות בו נועל ופותח בו דאיכא תורת כלי עליו ובהא א"ר יוחנן הלכתא כרשב"ג. אבל בחריות של דקל שגדרן לעצים דשרי רשב"ג בלא קישור לא סבר לה ר' יוחנן כוותיה. ועליהן [אמר ד"ר] יוחנן סבר לה כוותיה בחדא ופליג עליה בחדא: דרש ר' יצחק נפחא אפתחא דבי ריש גלותא הלכתא כר' אליעזר שאין פוקקין (עליו) [בו] אם [לא] שהוא קשור ותלוי. ואותבה ר' (עולא) [רב עמרם] מהא דתנן בסוף שבת מדבריהן למדנו שפוקקין ומודדין וקושרין בשבת. א"ל אביי לרב (עזרא) [עמרם] למה אותיבתיה מהא מפני שהיא שנויה סתם. וקי"ל הלכה כסתם משנה. נגר הנגרר נמי סתמא היא. והיא שנויה סתם אליבא דר' אלעזר. ושני ליה אע"פ דהא סתמא והא סתמא. דפוקקין ומודדין וקושרין בשבת שעשו בה עובדא למעשה והלכתא כחכמים ונדחה דרישא דר' יצחק נפחא. ואמרינן בתלמוד א"י. א"ר יוחנן אתיא יחידאה דהכא סתמא דתמן. ויחידאה דתמן כסתמא דהכא. פי' יחידאה דהכא דהוא ר' אלעזר דפקק החלון בסתמא דנגר נגרר [ויחידאי דנגר הנגרר] (דהוא ר' יהודה כסתמא) [דפקק החלון דהכ"א] בין כך ובין כך פוקקין בו: כל כסויי הכלים שיש להן בית אחיזה ניטלין בשבת. א"ר יוסי בד"א בכסויי קרקעות וכו'. א"ר יהודה בר שילא א"ר אסי א"ר יוחנן והוא שיש תורת כלי עליהן. ואמרינן כולי עלמא בכסוי קרקעות אם יש להן בית אחיזה שרי ואי לא אסיר לטלטל. כגון כסויי הבארות וכסויי הדות וכיוצא בהן. כסויי כלים כגון כדות ופיטסים וכיוצא בהן אע"פ (שהן) [שאין] להן בית אחיזה מותר לטלטלן לגלותם ולכסותם. כי פליגי בכסויי כלים וחיבורו בקרקע. ר' יוסי לא גזר ות"ק סבר גזרינן והלכתא כוותיה:

הדרן עלך פרק כל הכלים

פי"ח מפנין אפילו ד' וה' קופות של תבן. פי' מפנין מעתיקין התבואה ממקום למקום מלשון וצוה הכהן ופנו את הבית. אקשינן על משנתנו. השתא ה' מפנין ד' מיבעיא ופריק רב חסדא ארבע מחמש וה' מאוצר גדול. ומאי אבל לא את האוצר שלא יתחיל באוצר תחלה ומני ר"י היא דאית ליה מוקצה ובא שמואל ופריק פירוק אחר ודברים פשוטין הן. אבל סוגיא דשמעתא כרב חסדא דמתניתא סתמא תנן כוותיה. שאין מתחילין

רב נסים גאון

פי"ח ר' יהודה היא דאמר מוקצה ור' שמעון לית ליה מוקצה אצל כל פחמא (פי' עיקר הדברים בפרק במה מדליקין וכבר פירשנו זה בפרק יציאות השבת:

וְלֹא אֶת מַעֲשֵׂר שֵׁנִי וְהֶקְדֵּשׁ שֶׁלֹּא נִפְדּוּ – nor *maaser sheni* or consecrated produce that was not redeemed;[15] וְלֹא אֶת הַלּוּף – nor *luf;*[16] וְלֹא אֶת הַחַרְדָּל – nor mustard.[17] רַבָּן שִׁמְעוֹן בֶּן גַּמְלִיאֵל מַתִּיר בְּלוּף – Rabban Shimon ben Gamliel permits clearing away *luf,* מִפְּנֵי שֶׁהוּא מַאֲכַל עוֹרְבִין – because it is food for ravens.[18] חֲבִילֵי קַשׁ – As regards bundles of stubble וַחֲבִילֵי עֵצִים – and bundles of twigs[19] וַחֲבִילֵי זְרָדִים – and bundles of tender reeds,[20] אִם הִתְקִינָן לְמַאֲכַל בְּהֵמָה מְטַלְטְלִין אוֹתָן – if one has set them aside for use as animal feed, we may move them; וְאִם לָאו אֵין מְטַלְטְלִין אוֹתָן – and if one has not set them aside for use as animal feed, we may not move them.[21]

Gemara The Mishnah ruled that we may clear away "even four or five boxes" of straw or grain. The Gemara examines the expression "four or five boxes," and asks:

הַשְׁתָּא חָמֵשׁ מְפַנִּין – Now that we may clear away even five boxes, as stated in the Mishnah, אַרְבַּע מִיבַּעְיָא – was it necessary for the Mishnah to state that we may also clear four boxes?[22]

The Gemara answers:

אָמַר רַב חִסְדָּא – Rav Chisda said: The Mishnah means as follows: אַרְבַּע מֵחָמֵשׁ – One may clear away a maximum of four boxes from a store of produce containing only five boxfuls[23] (אִיכָּא דְּאָמְרֵי אַרְבַּע מֵאוֹצָר קָטָן – others report a variant reading of the preceding: One may clear away four boxes from a small store[24]), וְחָמֵשׁ מֵאוֹצָר גָּדוֹל – and a maximum of five boxes from a large store of produce.[25] וּמַאי אֲבָל לֹא אֶת הָאוֹצָר – And accordingly what does "but not the store" mean?[26] שֶׁלֹּא יַתְחִיל בָּאוֹצָר תְּחִלָּה – It means that one may not begin taking produce from a previously unused store.[27] וּמַנִּי – And accordingly, whose view is reflected by this Mishnah? רַבִּי יְהוּדָה הִיא דְּאִית לֵיהּ מוּקְצֶה – It is the view of R' Yehudah, who holds a broad application of *muktzeh.*[28]

The Gemara presents a different explanation of the formulation "four or five boxes":

וּשְׁמוּאֵל אָמַר – And Shmuel says: אַרְבַּע וְחָמֵשׁ – The Mishnah uses the expression "four or five boxes"

NOTES

maaser rishon is *muktzeh* would then be obvious and unnecessary. The Mishnah must therefore intend something else, as the Gemara (128a) will explain.

15. Since it is not redeemed, the *maaser sheni* may not be eaten outside Jerusalem, nor may the consecrated produce be eaten at all. [Here, too, the Gemara will explain the Mishnah's need to state what seems to be obvious.]

16. *Luf* is a type of legume that is inedible when raw even to livestock and domestic fowl (see *Rashi* [as it appears in our versions and as cited here by *Rav*] and *Rashi* to *Bava Metzia* 113b ד״ה לא את הלוף). Since one may not cook on the Sabbath, the raw *luf* is *muktzeh* (*Rashi* to *Bava Metzia* loc. cit.).

[*Rambam* (*Peirush HaMishnah*) writes that *luf* is undoubtedly a type of onion. See also *Peirush HaMishnah* to *Sheviis* 5:2, where *Rambam* cites a *Yerushalmi* to this effect.]

17. Mustard is edible only after it is ground. Since grinding is forbidden on the Sabbath, the unground mustard is *muktzeh* (see *Rashi* to *Bava Metzia* loc. cit.; cf. *Tiferes Yisrael* here).

18. Wealthy people would breed ravens as a status symbol (*Rashi*) or for ornamental and entertainment purposes (*Rashi* to *Bava Metzia* 112b ד״ה לעורבין). Even the Tanna Kamma agrees that *luf* is not *muktzeh* for those who actually raise ravens. Rabban Shimon ben Gamliel asserts that it is not *muktzeh* even for common folk. The Gemara will explain his rationale.

[Based on a Baraisa cited below (128a), *Tosafos* (ad loc. ד״ה רשב״ג) explain that Rabban Shimon ben Gamliel permits *even luf,* and *certainly* mustard.]

19. I.e. bundles of tender twigs that can be used as fodder (*Beis Yosef* 308).

20. *Rashi*; cf. *Rav*. These, too, can be used as fodder.

21. Since they are generally used as kindling. Thus, they are *muktzeh* unless expressly set aside as animal feed (*Beis Yosef* loc. cit.).

22. Why did the Mishnah not state simply: "We may clear away even five boxes ..."? [The expression "four or five" and similarly worded expressions abound in the Talmud. See *Tosafos* to 60b ד״ה השתא, who discuss why the Gemara sometimes questions this usage and sometimes does not. See also *Tos. Yom Tov.*]

23. Because the Rabbis forbade one to clear away an entire store of produce, since one would thereby expose the floor under the produce. The Rabbis were concerned that one might notice holes or depressions in the exposed ground [caused by burrowing rodents that are common in store areas (*Meiri*)] and come to level out the ground intentionally [which would constitute the *melachah* of בּוֹנֶה, *building*] (*Rashi*; see *Ran* to 127a; cf. *Baal HaMaor* and *Chasam Sofer*).

[It would seem that the restriction against clearing away the entire store requires one to clear away the produce from the top down, leaving a thin layer of produce across the entire floor (see *R' Perachyah*). It may be, however, that one *is* permitted to clear a section of the store down to the ground. And the concern that one will come to level out the ground applies only when one clears out a store entirely, in order to transform it into a guest area. (There would seem to be some indication of this latter approach in *Chidushei HaRan*; see also *Ran to Rif,* p. 50a ד״ה ושמואל אמר.)]

24. [I.e. a store containing only five boxfuls of produce. Though the wording of the variant differs from the preceding, the substance is the same.]

25. [I.e. one containing more than five boxfuls.] Even though removing more than five boxfuls would not expose the floor of the large store, the Rabbis were concerned about the excessive exertion involved, and therefore limited a person to five boxfuls (*Rashi*).

26. According to Rav Chisda's interpretation, we cannot explain "but not the store" to mean that one may not remove *all* the boxes from the store [which would be the simplest interpretation of these words], since the Mishnah has already taught that law by stating the otherwise redundant word "four," as Rav Chisda has just explained (*Rashi*; cf. *Baal HaMaor* and *Korban Nesanel* §30).

27. I.e. one may not clear away straw or grain from a store whose contents one has not begun to use for human or animal consumption before the Sabbath. For since the store was not designated for consumption at the onset of the Sabbath, the Tanna considers its contents *muktzeh* (*Rashi*).

28. We have learned earlier in this tractate (44a-46b) that R' Yehudah and R' Shimon differ markedly with regard to the laws of *muktzeh*. Although all accept the basic prohibition of *muktzeh,* they disagree about the extent of these restrictions. R' Shimon is more lenient, and so is described as holding אֵין מוּקְצֶה, *there is no [broad application of] muktzeh.* R' Yehudah is more stringent; his opinion is reported to be יֵשׁ מוּקְצֶה, *there is [a broad application of] muktzeh.*

As has been explained there, their dispute stems from a disagreement over how to interpret the basic rule that whatever was set aside from being used on the Sabbath is *muktzeh*. According to R' Yehudah, this includes any object that in the normal course of events does not stand to be used on the Sabbath. Since the owner did not intend or expect to use the object, it lacks "preparation" for Sabbath use and is *muktzeh*. R' Shimon, on the other hand, holds that the mere fact that an object does not stand to be used is not a consideration. Rather, as long as something is fit for use, it is not rendered *muktzeh* unless the owner consciously sets it aside (*Chasam Sofer's* introduction to *Beitzah – Mahadura Tinyana; Afikei Yam* vol. II §19; *Kehillos Yaakov, Beitzah* §4; see *Rashi* to *Beitzah* 2a ד״ה ואי דלא אחזו and 26b ד״ה קא סלקא דעתין).

Thus, with respect to the store of produce that has not yet been touched, R' Yehudah would prohibit the produce as *muktzeh,* since the person had not planned on using it on the Sabbath. [And even should he decide to use it now, it would remain *muktzeh,* due to the principle of מִיגּוֹ דְּאִתְקְצַאי לְבֵין הַשְּׁמָשׁוֹת אִתְקְצַאי לְכוּלֵּי יוֹמָא, *since it is muktzeh during the twilight period (at the beginning of the Sabbath), it remains muktzeh for the entire day.*]

כִּדְאָמְרֵי אִינְשֵׁי – **as people speak.** In popular speech, one will state a smaller amount and then a larger amount, as a way of saying: If the smaller amount suffices, fine; if not, take even more.[1] וְאִי בָּעֵי אֲפִילוּ טוּבָא נַמִּי מְפַנִּין – **But if one wants,** then **even more** than five **may be cleared away.**[2] וּמַאי אֲבָל לֹא אֶת הָאוֹצָר – **And** accordingly, **what is** the meaning of the Mishnah's next statement **"but not the store"?** שֶׁלֹּא יִגְמוֹר כּוּלּוֹ – It means **that one should not finish** clearing out the store of produce in **its entirety,** thereby exposing the floor, דִּילְמָא אָתֵי [לְ]אַשְׁוּוּיֵי גּוּמוֹת – **lest he come to level holes** that he might find in the just-exposed floor.[3] אֲבָל אַתְחוּלֵי מַתְחִיל – **But one may** in fact **begin** taking produce from a previously unused store. וּמַנִּי – **And** accordingly **whose** view is reflected by **this** Mishnah? רַבִּי שִׁמְעוֹן הִיא דְּלֵית לֵיהּ מוּקְצֶה – **It is the view of R' Shimon, who does not hold** a broad interpretation **of *muktzeh.***[4]

The Gemara cites a Baraisa:

תָּנוּ רַבָּנָן – **The Rabbis taught in a Baraisa:** אֵין מַתְחִילִין בָּאוֹצָר תְּחִילָּה – WE MAY NOT BEGIN taking produce from A previously unused STORE.[5] אֲבָל עוֹשֶׂה בּוֹ שְׁבִיל כְּדֵי שֶׁיִּכָּנֵס וְיֵצֵא – BUT ONE MAY MAKE A PATH THROUGH IT [the unused store of produce] SO THAT HE CAN ENTER AND LEAVE.

The Gemara points out an apparent contradiction in the Baraisa:

עוֹשֶׂה בּוֹ שְׁבִיל – You say that ONE MAY MAKE A PATH THROUGH IT? וְהָא אָמַרְתְּ אֵין מַתְחִילִין – **But you have** just **said** in the first part of the Baraisa that WE MAY NOT BEGIN taking produce from the unused store (because the stored produce is *muktzeh*)! If it is *muktzeh,* how can it be moved for the purpose of clearing a path?

The Gemara answers:

הָכִי קָאָמַר – **This is what [the Baraisa] means:** עוֹשֶׂה בּוֹ שְׁבִיל בְּרַגְלָיו בִּכְנִיסָתוֹ וּבִיצִיאָתוֹ – **One may make a path through it with his legs when he enters and when he leaves** the storage area.[6]

The Gemara cites and explains a relevant Baraisa:

תָּנוּ רַבָּנָן – **The Rabbis taught in a Baraisa:** תְּבוּאָה צְבוּרָה – In the case of PILED GRAIN,[7] בִּזְמַן שֶׁהִתְחִיל בָּהּ מֵעֶרֶב שַׁבָּת – WHEN ONE HAS STARTED partaking OF IT BEFORE THE SABBATH, מוּתָּר לְהִסְתַּפֵּק מִמֶּנָּה בְּשַׁבָּת – IT IS PERMITTED TO TAKE PROVISIONS FROM IT ON THE SABBATH.[8] וְאִם לָאו אָסוּר לְהִסְתַּפֵּק מִמֶּנָּה בְּשַׁבָּת – AND IF he did NOT start partaking of it before the Sabbath, IT IS FORBIDDEN TO TAKE PROVISIONS FROM IT ON THE SABBATH, for it is *muktzeh.* דִּבְרֵי רַבִּי שִׁמְעוֹן – These are THE WORDS OF R' SHIMON. רַבִּי אַחָא מַתִּיר – R' ACHA, however, PERMITS partaking of the grain in either event.

The Gemara asks:

כְּלַפֵּי לַיָּיא – **Towards where** does this face? I.e. the matter seems inverted. R' Shimon is always permitting what others consider to be *muktzeh* situations, and here he is ruling stringently![9] – ? –

The Gemara concedes this point and replies:

אֶלָּא אֵימָא – **Rather,** emend the Baraisa and **say** it as follows: דִּבְרֵי רַבִּי אַחָא – At the point following the first and stringent position, the Baraisa should read: These are THE WORDS OF R' ACHA.[10] וְרַבִּי שִׁמְעוֹן מַתִּיר – BUT R' SHIMON PERMITS partaking of the grain in either event (in keeping with his usual, lenient definition of *muktzeh*).[11]

The Baraisa just cited spoke of "piled grain." The Gemara now defines that term:

תָּנָא – **An** explanatory **Baraisa taught:** כַּמָּה שִׁיעוּר תְּבוּאָה צְבוּרָה – WHAT IS THE AMOUNT that constitutes "PILED GRAIN"?[12] לֶתֶךְ – A *LESECH.*[13]

NOTES

1. *Rashi.* [Thus, "four" and "five" are not meant as specific limits in different situations, as Rav Chisda interpreted, but rather as a popular way of expressing that one may clear away as much as necessary (see *Meiri* here and *Tosafos* to 60b ד״ה השתא).]

2. *Rashi.* [See, however, *Rashba* who cites the reading of the *She'iltos* that omits this last phrase, and according to which Shmuel, too, agrees that one may not clear away more than five boxes. See also *Tos. HaRosh.*]

3. [Rav Chisda's interpretation also accepted the law that one may not clear away the store in its entirety, but explained it to be implicit in the Mishnah's first statement, and therefore had to explain the words "but not the store" differently (see above, 126b note 26; see also next note).]

4. Rav Chisda, who interpreted the word "four" to indicate that one may not clear away an entire store (see above), had to interpret "but not the store" to mean that one may not begin a previously unused store – a position held by R' Yehudah. Shmuel, however, who explains "four or five" to be a popular expression, can explain "but not the store" to mean simply that one may not clear away the entire store. Accordingly, the Mishnah has not addressed the issue of beginning an unused store, and Shmuel can say that the Mishnah in fact follows R' Shimon's position on the question of *muktzeh,* which permits clearing or taking produce from a previously unused store.

5. This Baraisa reflects the view of R' Yehudah, who considers the produce in a previously unused store to be *muktzeh* [see Gemara above] (*Rabbeinu Chananel*; *Rif* [see *Ran*]; cf. *Ritva MHK* ed., and see also *Rambam, Hil. Shabbos* 26:15 with *Maggid Mishneh* and *Aruch HaShulchan* 333:3).

6. This is permitted, since one may move *muktzeh* with parts of his body other than his hands [טִלְטוּל בְּגוּפוֹ], such as by pushing it with his feet or elbow (see Mishnah below, 141a; *Orach Chaim* 311:8).

[*Chazon Ish* (*Orach Chaim* 47:12-13) infers from the Gemara's language here ("when he enters and when he leaves") that the permit to move *muktzeh* with one's body applies only where the *muktzeh* is moved as the incidental result of a different activity (e.g. walking in and out of the storage area). *Mishnah Berurah* (308:13), however, understands the permit to apply even where one means simply to move the *muktzeh.* See the extensive treatment of this matter by *R' Shlomo Zalman Auerbach,* printed at the end of *Shemiras Shabbos Ke-Hilchasah* vol. I p. 558. See also 141a note 5..]

7. The fact that it is piled up indicates that it was designated for storage rather than for immediate use (*Rashi*).

8. To feed his animal (*Rashi*). It is not *muktzeh,* because he had begun using the grain before Shabbos.

9. *Rashi.* [Moreover, given R' Shimon's definition of *muktzeh* (see above, 126b note 28), he should certainly permit the initial use of a new store of grain, since such grain was not consciously set aside.]

10. [R' Acha follows R' Yehudah's broader application of *muktzeh,* and prohibits moving the piled grain.]

11. [For although the piled grain constitutes an untouched store, it is not deemed *muktzeh,* in the view of R' Shimon, as it was not consciously set aside.]

12. And is thus considered a "store" of grain, which is *muktzeh* unless one began to partake of it before Shabbos. This Baraisa is elaborating R' Acha's (stringent) position, since according to R' Shimon the question is irrelevant, as stored grain is not *muktzeh* in his view no matter how large the store (see *Rashba,* in explanation of *Rashi's* reading; see, however, *Ramban* et al. for a different reading and interpretation).

13. A *lesech* is half a *kor,* or fifteen *se'ah* (*Rashi*). A pile containing less than a *lesech,* however, is not considered a "store" and is thus not *muktzeh* even if one did not begin partaking of it before Shabbos (*Ohr Zarua, Hil. Shabbos* §87).

The volume of a *lesech* mentioned here is equal to the combined volume of the five boxes mentioned in the Mishnah [each containing three *se'ah* – see 126b note 3] (*Rabbeinu Chananel*). [Rav Chisda explained that when the Mishnah states that four boxes may be cleared away, it means that four can be cleared away *from a small store.* In light of *Rabbeinu Chananel's* present observation, we understand that the Mishnah refers to the smallest of stores, which – as stated here – contains a *lesech,* or five boxes worth. See also how *Ramban* et al. utilize *Rabbeinu Chananel's* observation.]

כדאמרי אינשי ואי בעי אפילו טובא נמי: מפנין א ומאי א) אבל לא את האוצר שלא יגמור כולו (א) דילמא אתי לאשויי גומות אבל אתחולי מתחיל ומני ר"ש היא דלית ליה מוקצה ת"ר ב אין מתחילין באוצר תחילה אבל עושה בו שביל כדי שיכנס ויצא עושה בו שביל והא אמרת אין מתחילין הכי קאמר עושה בו שביל ברגליו בכניסתו וביציאתו תנו רבנן תבואה ג) צבורה בזמן שהתחיל בה מע"ש מותר להסתפק ממנה בשבת ואם לאו אסור להסתפק ממנה בשבת דברי ר"ש ר' אחא מתיר כלפי לייא אלא אימא דברי ר' אחא ג ורבי שמעון מתיר תנא כמה שיעור תבואה ג) צבורה לתך בעא מיניה רב נחומי בר זכריה מאביי שיעור תבואה ד) צבורה בכמה אמר ליה הרי אמרו שיעור תבואה צבורה לתך איבעיא להו הני ארבע וחמש קופות דקאמר בארבע וחמש קופות אין טפי לא אלמא למעוטי בהילוכא עדיף או דילמא למעוטי משוי עדיף ת"ש דתני חדא מפנין אפילו ארבע וחמש קופות של כדי שמן ושל כדי יין ותניא אידך בעשר ובחמש עשרה מאי לאו בהא קמיפלגי דמר סבר מעוטי בהילוכא עדיף ומר סבר מעוטי במשוי עדיף לא ד דכ"ע מעוטי בהילוכא עדיף ומי סברת בעשר ובחמש עשרה אקופות קאי אכדין קאי ולא קשיא הא דמשתקלי חד חד בקופה והא דמישתקלי תרי תרי והא דמשתקלי תלתא תלתא ובדקורי דהרפניא איבעיא להו הני ארבע וחמש דקאמר אע"ג דאית ליה אורחין טובא או דילמא הכל לפי האורחין ואת"ל הכל לפי האורחין חד גברא מפני לכולהו או דילמא גברא (ב) גברא מפני לנפשיה ת"ש דאמר רבה אמר רבי חייא פעם אחת הלך רבי למקום אחד וראה מקום דחוק לתלמידים ויצא לשדה ומצא שדה מלאה עומרים ועימר רבי כל השדה כולה ה) (שמע מינה הכל לפי האורחין) ורב יוסף א"ר הושעיא פעם אחת הלך ר' חייא למקום אחד וראה מקום דחוק לתלמידים ויצא לשדה ומצא שדה מלאה עומרים ועימר ר' חייא כל השדה כולה ה שמע מינה הכל לפי האורחין ועדיין תבעי לך חד גברא מפני ליה לכולא או דילמא כל גברא וגברא מפני לנפשיה ת"ש ועימר רבי ולטעמיך רבי בדנפשיה עימר ו אלא צוה ועימר ולעולם כל חד וחד מפני לנפשיה: מפני האורחין וכו': א"ר יוחנן ז גדולה הכנסת אורחין כהשכמת בית המדרש דקתני מפני האורחין ומפני בטול בית המדרש ורב דימי מנהרדעא אמר יותר מהשכמת בית המדרש דקתני מפני האורחין והדר ומפני בטול בית המדרש ו) אמר רב יהודה אמר רב ז גדולה הכנסת אורחין מהקבלת פני שכינה דכתיב א ויאמר ז) (ה') אם נא מצאתי חן בעיניך אל נא תעבור וגו' א"ר אלעזר בא וראה שלא כמדת הקב"ה מדת בשר ודם מדת ב"ו אין קטן יכול לומר לגדול המתן עד שאבא אצלך ואילו בהקדוש ברוך הוא כתיב ויאמר ח) (ה') אם נא מצאתי וגו' אמר רב יהודה בר שילא א"ר אסי א"ר יוחנן ח ששה דברים אדם אוכל פירותיהן בעולם הזה והקרן קיימת לו לעולם הבא ואלו הן הכנסת אורחין וביקור חולים ט) ועיון תפלה והשכמת בית המדרש והמגדל בניו לתלמוד תורה ט והדן את חברו לכף זכות איני והא אנן י) תנן אלו דברים שאדם עושה אותם ואוכל פירותיהן בעולם הזה והקרן קיימת לו לעולם הבא ואלו הן כיבוד אב ואם וגמילות חסדים והבאת שלום שבין אדם לחברו י ות"ת כנגד כולם [הני אין מידי אחרינא לא] הני

רש"י

כדאמרי אינשי. משכון קטן תחילה ואם יאמרוך ליותר יפנה יותר משום הכי נקט ד' ברישא והדר חמשה וה"ה אפילו טובא: שלא יגמור. משום אשווי גומות: ברגליו. מפנה ברגליו לכאן ולכאן דרך הליכתו דלא הוי טלטול: תבואה צבורה. מוכחא מילתא דהוקצה לאוצר: להסתפק. להאכיל לבהמתו: כלפי לייא. כנגד היכן פונה הדבר הזה האמור להיפך ר"ש מתיר מוקצה בכל מקום וכאן הוא מחמיר: לייא. היכן כגון תלבי לנהרא כגני לייא דברכות (דף נח.): לתך. אבל בציר מהכי לאו אוצר הוא: לתך. חצי כור הוא ט"ו סאין: בד' וה' קופות אין טפי לא. בקופות עצמן הוא יפנה וימלאם אם ירצה או שק בכתפו שיעור קופה בפעם אחת אבל טפי להלך יותר מה' פעמים כגון לפנות בכלים קטנים וירבה בהילוך לא: למעוטי בהילוכא עדיף. ואע"ג דאפושי משוי הוא: או דילמא מעוטי משוי עדיף. ואם בא לפנות בכלים קטנים כשיעור ה' קופות מותר ולרב חסדא קבעי לה דאמר ה' דוקא: בי' ובט"ו. קס"ד אקופות קאי לומר שמפנה בקופות קטנות וירבה בהילוך: אכדין קאי. ולא פליגי והכי קאמר בי' בט"ו יפנה באותן ה' קופות: הא דמשתקלי חדא חדא בקופה. הך דתניא ד' וה' ולא נחת למניינא דכדין איירי בכדין גדולים דמשתקלי חדא בקופה והך דתנא בי' וט"ו איירי בכדים בינונים ובכדין קטנים עשר כדמשתקלי תרי תרי בקופה ט"ו כדמשתקלי תלתא תלתא בקופה דקטנים: כי דקורי דהרפניא. ל) בכדין של הרפניא: איבעיא להו. אליבא דרב חסדא: דחוק לתלמידים. שאין מקום לתלמידים להושיב: ועימר. פנה את העומרים וכרמלית הואי ובפחות פחות מד' אמות: ת"ש ועימר רבי. אלמא חד גברא פנינהו: רבי בנפשיה עימר. בתמיה וכי אורחיה דנשיא בהכי: כהשכמת ביהמ"ד. מדשוי להו במתני' כי הדדי: מהשכמת בית המדרש. דתנא דידן אקדמה ברישא: אל נא תעבור. והניחו והלך לקבל האורחים: ועיון תפלה. לכוין בתפלתו: הכי

תוספות

של כדי שמן ושל כדי יין. והא דתנן בפ' המביא (ביצה דף כט:) כדי יין לא יביאם בסל ובקופה היינו ממקום רחוק למיחזי כעובדין דחול אבל הכא בביתו: דכולי עלמא למעוטי בהלוכא עדיף. לא מצי למימר למעוטי במשוי עדיף דהשתא דקתני ד' וה' קופות לא מצי סבר הכי דא"כ הוה ליה למיתני בעשר וט"ו כשיעור ה' קופות וא"ת והא תנן בפרק אין צדין (שם דף כה.) שחטה בשדה לא יביאנה במוט ובמוטה אלא מביאה לאיבריה אף על גב דמפיש בהילוכא התם שאני דאיכא טירחא יותר מדאי להביאה שלימה א"נ משום דמיחזי כמוליכה למכור בשוק והא דאמרינן בריש שואל (לקמן דף קמח.) היכי ליעבד דמליא בחצבא רבא מימלי בחצבא זוטא קא מפשה בהילוכא דמליא בחצבא זוטא ממלא בחצבא רבא קא מפשה במשוי התם כיון שנהגו למלאות המים בחצבא רבא או בחצבא זוטא קשה להם לשנות ממדות שנהגו: אע"ג דאית ליה אורחין טובא או דילמא הכל לפי האורחין. מכאן יש להוכיח דהא דתנן במתניתין ד' וה' קופות הוי אפי' בשביל אדם אחד דאי הוי נמי לפי האורחין אמאי נקט ד' וה' ועוד מדלא מספקא ליה אי חד מפני כולהו או כל חד לנפשיה אלא בא"ל הכל לפי האורחין משמע הא אם אמר אף על גב דאית ליה אורחין טובא ליכא לאיסתפוקי ואי אמרינן דד' וה' קופות הוי לפי האורחין אכתי איכא לספוקי אי חד גברא מפני לכולהו או כל חד מפני לנפשיה אלא משמע דפשיטא דד' וה' אינן לפי האורחין אלא אפילו לצורך אדם אחד: ולטעמיך רבי בנפשיה עימר. פי' כל השדה כולה: דכתיב ויאמר ה' אם נא מצאתי חן וגו'. קסבר כמאן דאמר בשבועות (דף לה:) דהאי השם קדש דאיכא מאן דאמר התם שהוא חול שלמלאכים היה מדבר שהיה מזמינם: אוכל מפירותיהן בעולם הזה. בפ"ק דקדושין (דף לט:) מפ' דהיינו אם היתה מ) שקולה מכרעת דשכר מצות בהאי עלמא ליכא: כיון

מסורת הש"ס

א) [ביצה לו.], ב) [מלת צבורה ליתא בשאלתות פרשת ויחי סי' יא], ג) [ג"ז ליתא שם], ד) [ג"ז ליתא שם], ה) [ס"א מ"ש], ו) [שבועות לה:], ז) [נ"ל אדני], ח) [נ"ל אדני], ט) [עי' תוספות לעיל קיח: ד"ה עיון ותוספות ברכות לב: ד"ה כל ותוס' ב"ב קסד: ד"ה עיון], י) פאה פ"ק מ"א קדושין לט: ע"ש, כ) ס"א, ל) [ועי' בפרש"י ב"מ פד. ותוס' חולין ל: ד"ה דקורא], מ) והך משנה דהכא פליגא אר' יעקב דס"ל בסוף פרק קמא דקדושין שכר מצוה כו' רש"ל. ואפשר לפרש כוונת התוספות בלא הגה"ה שהולים לייתב גם למאי דלא מירלו התם הקושיא בלומן אמר דהכי מלות הקרן כולה קיימת לעוה"ב לאפוקי שכר מלות וממכלי תוס' ד"ה לפרש כן דשכר מלוה בהאי עלמא ליכא אליבא דכ"ע ולא פליגי התם אר"י בפירות ודוק כ"מ ומהרש"א גרס דשכר מצוה בהאי עלמא ליכא.

עין משפט נר מצוה

ב א מיי' פכ"ו מהל' שבת הלכה טו טוש"ע שם: ג ב ג מיי' שם הלכה יד וטו: ד ד טוש"ע שם סעיף ג: ה ה ו מיי' וסמג שם טוש"ע שם ס"ג: ו ז מיי' פי"ד מהלכות אבל הלכה ב: ז ח סמג עשין יג: ח ט מיי' פ"ו מהלכות דעות הלכה ז ופכ"ג מהלכות סנהדרין הלכה י טוש"ע ח"מ סימן יז סעיף י: ט י מיי' פ"ג מהלכות ת"ת הלכה ג סמג שם טוש"ע י"ד סימן רמו סעיף יח:

רבינו חננאל

מתחילין באוצר תחלה ולא בתבואה צבורה. ומדבעא רב נחומי כמה שיעורי תבואה צבורה. ותנא כמה שיעור תבואה צבורה לתך ש"מ דהלכתא כהני מתניתא מדקט[ר]חינן לפרושי טעמייהו ויש מי שאומר הלכתא כשמואל דמוקים למתניתין כרבי שמעון דלית ליה מוקצה והלכתא כוותיה. ולתך זה האמור כאן הוא שיעור הקופות ששנינו במשנתנו. ואע"ג דלא איתאמרא בהדיא בגמרא דילן הא איתפרש בתלמוד א"י. ר' זעירא שאל לר' יאשיה כמה שעור הקופות. א"ל נלמד סתום מן המפורש דתנינן תמן בג' קופות של ג' ג' סאין תורמין את הלשכה. ושיעור לתך חצי כור והוא ט"ו סאין. נמצא שעור המשנה והברייתא שיעור אחד. וכדאוקמה רב חסדא למתני' ד' מה'. והכין שמעתא דא סלקא ועלה קמבעיא לן מעוטי בהלוכא עדיף או מעוטי במשוי עדיף. ואמרי' ת"ש דתני חדא מפנין אפילו ד' וה' קופות של כדי יין וכדי שמן. ותניא אידך בעשר ובחמש עשרה. ואוקימנא להו דכ"ע מעוטי בהילוכא עדיף. ושיעורם אחד הם. ואכדין קאי ולא אקופות והא מתניתא דקתני חמש הכין פירושא. חמש כדות גדולות שאין מכילה הקופה יותר מכדה אחת. והא מתניתא דקתני בעשר ובחמש עשרה בעשר כדות בחמש קופות והן בינוניות שנמצאו ב' כדות בכל קופה והא דתני ט"ו ג' כדות בכל קופה והא דמשתקלי תלת כדי בכל קופה כגון דקורי הרפניא פי' כדות שעושין בהרפניא והן קטנות ונוטלות ג' ג' בקופה שנמצא שיעור משקל כל כדה קטנה סאה והבינונית סאה וחצי. והגדולה ג' סאין. ותוב איבעיא לן הני דקא מפנינן ד' או ה' קופות מפני האורחין אע"פ דאית ליה אורחין הרבה אין לו רשות לפנות יותר מזה השיעור או דילמא הכל לפי האורחין ועוד בעיא אחרת כשמפנין אחד מפנה לכולן או כל אחד מפנה לעצמו ואיפשיטא שמעתא הכל לפי האורחין אם יש לו אורחין הרבה מפנין להן כל צרכן. ובאנו לדקדק מדקתני ועימר רבי את כל השדה שאחד מפנה לכולן (ולא עמר) [ודחינן וליטעמיך] וכי ר' בעצמו עימר אלא צוה ועימרו. ולעולם כל חד וחד לנפשיה וכיון דלא איפשיט בהדיא חד מפנהו לכולהו מחמרינן לפנויי כל דחד וחד לנפשיה דאיסורא הוא. וסתמא לחומרא. זה נכון לפנות כל אחד לעצמו ומסתייעא הא מילתא מהא (לעיל דף קכ"ה ע"ב) דא"ר חנניה פעם אחד הלך רבי למקום אחד ומצא נדבך של אבנים ואמר לתלמידיו צאו וחשבו כדי שנשב עליהן למחר ולא סמך במחשבתו שלו אלא הצריך כל אחד לעצמו וכדר' אסי ור' אמי אליבא דר' יוחנן כל אחד כטעמיה. פי' נדבך של אבנים אבנים סדורות זו ע"ג זו. ושפשפום לשפשפם ברגליהם. סואר של קורות קורות נתונות זו ע"ג זו. גשוש בלשון ישמעאל עירים ספינות. נגדר בלשון ישמעאל מתרו ופינוי לבית המדרש ולאורחים והכנת מקום לישיבתם שניהם שוין בדבר מצוה ושאר השמועה פשוטה היא. והא דתנן מפנין ד' ה' קופות. ה"מ לדבר מצוה מדקתני מפני האורחין ומפני

הגהות הב"ח

(א) גמ' שלא יגמור כולו (דילמא וכו' גומות) תא"מ ונ"ב ס"א נמחק: (ב) שם או דילמא גברא וגברא:

גליון הש"ס

גמרא גדולה הכנסת אורחים. עי' ב"מ דף פו ע"ב ובתוספות שם ד"ה מזייה:

תורה אור השלם

א) וַיֹּאמַר אֲדֹנָי אִם נָא מָצָאתִי חֵן בְּעֵינֶיךָ אַל נָא תַעֲבֹר מֵעַל עַבְדֶּךָ: [בראשית יח, ג]

רב נסים גאון

כמה שיעור תבואה לתך. הלתך הוא חצי כור והוא ט"ו כי הכור הוא ל' סאה והכור והחומר מדה אחת כי תרגום חומר כורא כמו שאתה מוצא ביחזקאל (מה) האיפה והבת תוכן אחד להם ואמר התרגום מכילת וביתא טוקס חד יהי לכון סכום תלת סאין למיסב מעשר כורא הרי נתברר לו מכן כי החומר הוא כור וכי הבת היא ג' סאין ואמר אחר כך כי עשרת הבתים חומר נמצא שיעור הכור ל' סאין ושם אמר (הושע ג) וחומר שעורים ולתך שעורים ואמרו חכמינו בפרק גיד הנשה (חולין דף צב) אלו ארבעים וחמשה צדיקים החומר ל' ולתך ט"ו הרי מ"ה נתקיים לך כי הכור הוא שני לתכים: שמא

ליקוטי רש"י

שלא יגמור כולו. לא לא היו שם אלא ארבע או חמש קופות שהתירו לו במקום שיש יותר כאן לא התירו לפנותן כולן ולגלות את הרצפה דלמא הוי בה גומא ומשוה לה [ביצה לו.]. אשוויי גומות. דמלאכה הוא בשבת דהוי כבנין [עירובין קד.]. כלפי לייא. שתי מלות כלפי היכן נוטה דבר זה. לייא. היכן ותבירו בברכות בפרק הרואה (נח.) תלבי לנהרא כגני לייא חרסים שבורים להיכן הולכין [פסחים ה:]. כלפי היכא נהפך דבר זה [לעיל צג:]. כנגד איפוא הדבר הזה סובב [כתובות טו.]. כנגד איפוא הפכת הדבר צריך לייא איפוא כדאמר בברכות (נח.) כגני לייא כדים שבורים להיכן הולכים [סוטה מד.]. כנגד מה שונה כאן ולאן הדבר נוטה כדאמרינן בברכות (נח.) תלבי לנהרא כגני לייא הקדירות שלמות הולכין לנהר לשאוב בהן מים אבל השבורין להיכן הולכין [שב"מ ב"ב קד:]. דקורי דהרפנאי. כלים שעושין בהרפניא [ב"מ פד.]. ויאמר [אדני] אם נא וגו'. דבר אחר, קודש הוא והיה אומר להקב"ה להמתין לו עד שירוץ ויכנים את האורחים [בראשית יח, ג ועי' כאן בתוס']. כתיב לעיל מינה וירא עליו ה' והדר כתיב והנה שלשה אנשים ואמר להקב"ה אל נא תעבור מעל עבדך המתן לי כאן עד שאכניס האורחין [שבועות לה:]. והדן את חברו לכף זכות. ברואה חבירו עושה דבר שאתה יכול להכריעו לצד עבירה ולצד זכות הכריעו לזכות ואל תחשדהו בעבירה [שם ל.]. על כל שתשמע עליו אמור שנתכוון לטובה עד שתדע בבירור שאינו כן שאם אתה תדין כן ידונו אותך מן השמים לזכות כמו שמפורש בפרק מפנין [אבות פ"א מ"ו]. והבאת שלום. תשלום שכר גדול להבאת שלום שאוכל פירותיהן בעולם הזה והקרן קיימת לו לעולם הבא כגמילות חסדים דכתיב בהו ימצא חיים צדקה בעולם הבא וכבוד בעולם הזה [יבמות קט:].

The Gemara relates an Amoraic discussion about this same point:

בְּעָא מִינֵּיהּ רַב נְחוּמִי בַּר זְכַרְיָה מֵאַבַּיֵּי – **Rav Nechumi bar Zecharyah inquired of Abaye:** שִׁיעוּר תְּבוּאָה צְבוּרָה בְּכַמָּה – **What is the amount** that constitutes **"piled grain"?** אָמַר לֵיהּ – **[Abaye] said to him:** הֲרֵי אָמְרוּ שִׁיעוּר תְּבוּאָה צְבוּרָה לֶתֶךְ – **Indeed, [the Sages] have said** that **the amount** which constitutes **"piled grain" is a** ***lesech.***

The Gemara presents an inquiry concerning our Mishnah:

אִיבַּעְיָא לְהוּ – **They inquired:** הָנֵי אַרְבַּע וְחָמֵשׁ קוּפּוֹת דְּקָאָמַר – Regarding **these "four or five boxes" that [the Tanna] mentions** in the Mishnah, בְּאַרְבַּע וְחָמֵשׁ קוּפּוֹת אֵין טְפֵי לֹא – does he mean that this volume of stored material may be moved **only** ***in*** **four or five** large **boxes,** but **not** in **a greater number** of containers, requiring a greater number of trips? אַלְמָא לְמַעוּטֵי בְּהִילּוּכָא עֲדִיף – **Thus,** he would be teaching that **it is better to reduce the** amount of **walking,** even though this increases the weight of each load.[14] אוֹ דִילְמָא לְמַעוּטֵי מַשּׂוֹי עֲדִיף – **Or perhaps** the Tanna agrees that **it is better to reduce the** weight of each **load,** even though this increases the number of trips.[15] – **?** –

The Gemara seeks to resolve this inquiry:

תָּא שְׁמַע – **Come, learn** a resolution through the analysis of two Baraisos. דְּתָנֵי חֲדָא – **For one Baraisa teaches:** מְפַנִּין אֲפִילוּ אַרְבַּע וְחָמֵשׁ קוּפּוֹת שֶׁל כַּדֵּי שֶׁמֶן וְשֶׁל כַּדֵּי יַיִן – WE MAY CLEAR AWAY EVEN FOUR OR FIVE BOXES OF JUGS OF OIL OR OF JUGS OF WINE. וְתַנְיָא אִידָךְ – **But another Baraisa teaches:** בְּעֶשֶׂר וּבַחֲמֵשׁ עֶשְׂרֵה – One may clear away the contents of even four or five boxes of jugs of oil or of jugs of wine IN TEN OR FIFTEEN. Apparently, this means that he may do so in ten or fifteen *boxes.* Thus, whereas the first Baraisa restricts the person to the movement of five boxes of jugs, the second Baraisa allows him to move the jugs even in fifteen boxes. מַאי לָאו בְּהָא קָמִיפְלְגֵי – **Is it not that [these Baraisos] argue with regard to the following** issue? דְּמַר סָבַר מַעוּטֵי בְּהִילּוּכָא עֲדִיף – **That one master** [the Tanna of the first Baraisa, who restricts the person to five boxes] **holds that reducing the** amount of **walking is better,** וּמַר סָבַר מַעוּטֵי בְּמַשּׂוֹי עֲדִיף – **whereas the other master** [the Tanna of the second Baraisa, who allows even ten or fifteen boxes] **holds that reducing the load is better.** Therefore, he states that the five large boxfuls of jugs may be transported even in ten or fifteen smaller boxes, since the increased number of trips is offset by the lighter weight of each load.

Thus, the Gemara argues, it emerges that the point of law inquired about is in fact a matter of dispute between the Tannaim of these Baraisos.

The Gemara rejects this resolution:

לֹא דְּכוּלֵּי עָלְמָא מַעוּטֵי בְּהִילּוּכָא עֲדִיף – **No.** You have no proof that the Baraisos argue about this matter. Rather, it might be that **everyone** [i.e. both Baraisos] **agrees that reducing the walking is preferable,**[16] and that the person is therefore limited to carrying five large boxes in five trips. וּמִי סָבְרַתְּ בְּעֶשֶׂר וּבַחֲמֵשׁ עֶשְׂרֵה אַקּוּפּוֹת קָאֵי – **And** as regards the phraseology of the second Baraisa, **do you you think that "in ten or fifteen" refers to** the number of **boxes** carried out of the storage area? אַכַּדִּין קָאֵי – No! **It refers to** the number of **jugs** placed within the five boxes that are carried out, וְלָא קַשְׁיָא – **and there is no contradiction** at all between the different amounts listed in the Baraisos, as we will now show: הָא דְּמִשְׁתַּקְלֵי חַד חַד בְּקוּפָּה – **This** statement of the first Baraisa, that one may move five boxes of oil or wine jugs, refers to **where** the jugs are so large that **they can be transported only one at a time in** a large **box.** וְהָא דְּמִישְׁתַּקְלֵי תְּרֵי תְּרֵי – **And this** statement of the second Baraisa, that "ten [jugs]" may be taken, refers to **where** the jugs are of intermediate size, so that **they can be transported two at a time** in a large box. וְהָא דְּמִשְׁתַּקְלֵי תְּלָתָא תְּלָתָא – **And this** statement of the second Baraisa, that "fifteen [jugs]" may be taken, refers to **where** the jugs are small enough so that **they can be transported three at a time** in a box, וּבְדִקוּרֵי דְהַרְפַּנְיָא – **such as in** the case of **the small jugs of Harpania.**[17]

The Gemara inquires further into the ruling of the Mishnah:

אִיבַּעְיָא לְהוּ – **They inquired:** הָנֵי אַרְבַּע וְחָמֵשׁ דְּקָאָמַר – Regarding **these four or five** boxes **that [the Tanna] mentions** in the

NOTES

14. Perhaps "four or five boxes" means that one should transport the five boxfuls *in* five boxes, and the Mishnah means to limit not only the *volume* of material being cleared (five boxfuls), but also the number of *trips* made in clearing it. That is, one may not make more than five trips in clearing away the produce, though he may carry a full large box or equivalently loaded sack on each trip, despite its heavy weight (see *Rashi*). The greater the number of trips, the greater the commotion and disturbance of the Sabbath atmosphere. Hence, it is better to minimize the number of trips (*Tur*).

[The Gemara here mentions *in "four or" five boxes* because that is the expression used by the Mishnah. The primary reference here, however, is to *five* – the maximum allowed by the Mishnah (according to Rav Chisda's interpretation, which is the interpretation presumed by this inquiry – see end of next note). The Gemara does not apparently doubt, though, that one may make five trips using partially empty boxes even if he could have reduced the number of trips by filling each box (e.g. where he needs to clear away only three or four boxfuls).]

15. [Reducing the weight of each load reduces the exertion required to transport each one, though it necessitates making a greater number of trips.]

According to this possibility, by stating "four or five boxes," the Mishnah means only to limit the volume of material to be cleared to four or five *boxfuls* (see *Maharsha* ד״ה תוס׳ בד״ה דכ״ע). The Tanna does *not,* however, mean to restrict the person to five trips using large boxes. Rather, if the person wishes, he may carry lighter loads spread over a greater number of trips (*Rashi*). [The Gemara cannot mean that the person *must* use smaller containers spread over a greater number of trips (as a simple reading of our Gemara would suggest), for the Mishnah's statement that one may clear away "four or five boxes" surely implies that moving the produce in the boxes themselves is permitted. Therefore, we must say that the Gemara merely considers the possibility that making a greater number of trips using smaller containers is *permitted,* not *mandatory.* And the expression עֲדִיף is used here in the sense of "equally acceptable" (or "important") rather than "superior" (*Korban Nesanel* §90, in explanation of *Rashi*; see also *Tosafos* to *Berachos* 50a ד״ה אלא ש״מ, where other instances of this usage of עֲדִיף are given). Alternatively, the Gemara means it is indeed *better* to decrease the weight of each load and increase the number of trips *where one desires to do so* (*Chidushei HaRan*).]

This inquiry presumes the view of Rav Chisda, that the Mishnah allows a maximum of five boxfuls (*Rashi*). [According to Shmuel, however, it is certainly permitted to reduce the size of the containers and increase the number of trips, since in his view the only restriction intended by the Mishnah is that one not clear out the entire store.]

16. See *Tosafos* ד״ה דכולי עלמא (with *Maharsha* and *Rashash*), who explain why the Gemara could not have said the reverse – namely, that both Baraisos hold that reducing the *load* is preferable. [*Ohr Zarua, Hil. Shabbos* §87, however, maintains that the Gemara could have said the reverse; its *choice* of attributing to both Baraisos the view that reducing the walking is preferable, though, indicates that this is the halachah.]

17. The second Baraisa agrees that these ten or fifteen jugs should be transported in no more than five trips, by carrying one large box of jugs on each trip (*Rashi* ד״ה אכדין).

כדאמרי אינשי ואי בעי אפילו טובא נמי מפנין א ומאי א אבל לא את האוצר שלא יגמור כולו (א) דילמא אתי לאשווי גומות אבל אתחולי מתחיל ומני ר"ש היא דלית ליה מוקצה ת"ר ב אין מתחילין באוצר תחילה אבל עושה בו שביל כדי שיכנס ויצא עושה בו שביל והא אמרת אין מתחילין הכי קאמר עושה בו שביל ברגליו בכניסתו וביציאתו תנו רבנן תבואה ג צבורה בזמן שהתחיל בה מע"ש מותר להסתפק ממנה בשבת ואם לאו אסור להסתפק ממנה בשבת דברי ר"ש ר' אחא מתיר כלפי לייא אלא אימא דברי ר' אחא ג ורבי שמעון מתיר תנא כמה שיעור תבואה ג צבורה לתך בעא מיניה רב נחומי בר זכריה מאביי שיעור תבואה ד צבורה בכמה אמר ליה הרי אמרו שיעור תבואה צבורה לתך איבעיא להו הני ארבע וחמש קופות דקאמר בארבע וחמש קופות אין טפי לא אלמא למעוטי בהילוכא עדיף או דילמא למעוטי משווי עדיף ת"ש דתני חדא מפנין אפילו ארבע וחמש קופות של כדי שמן ושל כדי יין ותניא אידך בעשר ובחמש עשרה מאי לאו בהא קמיפלגי דמר סבר מעוטי בהילוכא עדיף ומר סבר מעוטי במשוי עדיף לא ד דכ"ע מעוטי בהילוכא עדיף ומי סברת בעשר ובחמש עשרה אקופות קאי אכדין קאי ולא קשיא הא דמשתקלי חד חד בקופה והא דמישתקלי תרי תרי והא דמשתקלי תלתא תלתא ובדקורי דהרפניא איבעיא להו הני ארבע וחמש דקאמר אע"ג דאית ליה אורחין טובא או דילמא הכל לפי האורחין ואת"ל הכל לפי האורחין חד גברא מפני לכולהו או דילמא גברא (ב) גברא מפני לנפשיה ת"ש דאמר רבה אמר רבי חייא פעם אחת הלך רבי למקום אחד וראה מקום דחוק לתלמידים ויצא לשדה ומצא שדה מלאה עומרים ועימר רבי כל השדה כולה ו (שמע מינה הכל לפי האורחין) ורב יוסף א"ר הושעיא פעם אחת הלך ר' חייא למקום אחד וראה מקום דחוק לתלמידים ויצא לשדה ומצא שדה מלאה עומרים ועימר ר' חייא כל השדה כולה ה שמע מינה הכל לפי האורחין ועדיין תבעי לך חד גברא מפני ליה לכולא או דילמא כל גברא וגברא מפני לנפשיה ת"ש ועימר רבי ולטעמיך רבי בדנפשיה עימר ו אלא צוה ועימר ולעולם כל חד וחד מפני לנפשיה: מפני האורחין וכו': א"ר יוחנן ● גדולה הכנסת אורחין כהשכמת בית המדרש דקתני מפני האורחין ומפני בטול בית המדרש ורב דימי מנהרדעא אמר יותר מהשכמת בית המדרש דקתני מפני האורחין והדר ומפני בטול בית המדרש ז אמר רב יהודה אמר רב ז גדולה הכנסת אורחין מהקבלת פני שכינה דכתיב א ויאמר ז (ה') אם נא מצאתי חן בעיניך אל נא תעבור וגו' א"ר אלעזר בא וראה שלא כמדת הקב"ה מדת בשר ודם מדת ב"ו אין קטן יכול לומר לגדול המתן עד שאבא אצלך ואילו בהקדוש ברוך הוא כתיב ויאמר ח (ה') אם נא מצאתי וגו' אמר רב יהודה בר שילא א"ר אסי א"ר יוחנן ח ששה דברים אדם אוכל פירותיהן בעולם הזה והקרן קיימת לו לעולם הבא ואלו הן הכנסת אורחין וביקור חולים ט ועיון תפלה והשכמת בית המדרש והמגדל בניו לתלמוד תורה ט והדן את חבירו לכף זכות איני והא אנן י תנן אלו דברים שאדם עושה אותם ואוכל פירותיהן בעולם הזה והקרן קיימת לו לעולם הבא ואלו הן כיבוד אב ואם וגמילות חסדים והבאת שלום שבין אדם לחבירו ות"ת כנגד כולם י [הני אין מידי אחרינא לא] הני

רש"י

כדאמרי אינשי. חשבון קטן תחילה ואם יצטרך ליותר יפנה יותר משום הכי נקט ד' ברישא והדר חמשה וה"ה אפילו טובא: **שלא יגמור.** משום אשווי גומות: **ברגלו.** מפנה ברגליו לכאן ולכאן דרך הליכתו דלא הוי טלטול: **תבואה צבורה.** מוכחא מילתא דהוקצה לאוצר: **להסתפק.** להאכיל לבהמתו: **אסור דברי ר"ש ורבי אחא כו':** **כלפי לייא.** כנגד היכן פונה הדבר הזה שאמור להיפך ר"ש מתיר מוקצה בכל מקום וכאן הוא מחמיר: **לייא.** היכן כגון תלבי לנהרא כגני לייא דברכות (דף נח.): **לתך.** אבל בציר מהכי לאו אוצר הוא: **לתך.** חצי כור הוא ט"ו סאין: **בד' וה' קופות אין טפי לא.** בקופות עצמן הוא יפנה וימלאם אם ירצה או שק בכתפו שיעור קופה בפעם אחת אבל טפי להלך יותר מה' פעמים כגון לפנות בכלים קטנים וירבה בהילוך לא: **למעוטי בהילוכא עדיף.** ואע"ג דאפושי משוי הוא: **או דילמא מעוטי משוי עדיף.** ואם בא לפנות בכלים קטנים כשיעור ה' קופות מותר ולרב חסדא קבעי לה דאמר ה' דוקא: **בי' ובט"ו.** קס"ד אקופות קאי לומר שמפנה בקופות קטנות וירבה בהילוך: **אכדין קאי.** ולא פליגי והכי קאמר בי' בט"ו יפנה באותן ה' קופות: **הא דמשתקלי חדא חדא בקופה.** הך דתניא ד' וה' ולא נחת למניינא דכדין איירי בכדין גדולים דמשתקלי חדא בקופה והך דתני בי' וט"ו איירי בכדים בינונים ובכדין קטנים עשר כדמשתקלי תרי תרי בקופה ט"ו כדמשתקלי תלתא תלתא בקופה דקטנים: **כי דקורי דהרפניא.** כי כדין של הרפניא: **איבעיא להו.** אליבא דרב חסדא: **דחוק לתלמידים.** שאין מקום לתלמידים להושיב: **ועימר.** פנה את העומרים ובכרמלית הואי ובפחות פחות מד' אמות: **ת"ש ועימר רבי.** אלמא חד גברא פנינהו: **רבי בנפשיה עימר.** בתמיה וכי אורחיה דנשיא בהכי: **כהשכמת ביהמ"ד.** מדשוי להו במתני' כי הדדי: **מהשכמת בית המדרש.** דתנא לידן אקדמה ברישא: **אל נא תעבור.** והניחו והלך לקבל האורחים: **ועיון תפלה.** לכוין בתפלתו: הכי

תוספות

של כדי שמן ושל כדי יין. והא דתנן בפ' המביא (ביצה דף כט:) כדי יין לא יביאם בסל ובקופה היינו ממקום רחוק דמיחזי כעובדין דחול אבל הכא קרוב הוא: **דכולי** עלמא למעוטי בהלוכא עדיף. לא מצי למימר למעוטי במשוי עדיף דהשתא דקתני ד' וה' קופות לא מצי סבר הכי דא"כ הוה ליה למיתני בעשר וט"ו כשיעור ה' קופות וא"ת והא תנן בפרק אין צדין (שם דף כה.) שחטה בשדה לא יביאנה במוט ובמוטה אלא מביאה לאיברים אף על גב דמפיש בהילוכא התם שאני דאיכא טירחא יותר מדאי להביאה שלימה א"נ משום דמיחזי כמוליכה למכור בשוק והא דאמרינן בריש שואל (לקמן דף קמח.) היכי ליעבד דמליא בחצבא רבא לימלי בחצבא זוטא הא מפשא בהילוכא דמליא בחצבא זוטא תמלא בחצבא רבא הא מפשא במשוי התם כיון שנהגו למלאות המים בחצבא רבא או בחצבא זוטא קשה להם לשנות מכמות שנהגו: **אע"ג** דאית ליה אורחין טובא או דילמא הכל לפי האורחין. מכאן יש להוכיח דהא דתנן במתניתין ד' וה' קופות הוי אפי' בשביל אדם אחד דאי הוי נמי לפי האורחין אמאי נקט ד' וה' ועוד מדלא מספקא ליה אי חד מפני כולהו או כל חד לנפשיה אלא בהא"ל הכל לפי האורחין משמע דהא אם אמר אף על גב דאיתרמו ליה אורחין טובא ליכא לאיספוקי ואי אמרינן דד' וה' קופות הוי לפי האורחין הכי איכא לספוקי אי חד גברא מפני לכולהו או כל חד מפני לנפשיה אלא משמע דפשיטא דד' וה' אין לפי האורחין אלא אפילו לצורך אדם אחד: **ולטעמיך** רבי בנפשיה עימר. פי' כל השדה כולה: **דכתיב** ויאמר ה' אם נא מצאתי חן וגו'. קסבר כמאן דאמר בשבועות (דף לה:) דהאי השם קדש דאיכא מאן דאמר התם שהוא חול שאמר למלאכים היה מדבר שהיו מזומנים: **אוכל** מפירותיהן בעולם הזה. בפ"ק דקדושין (דף לט:) מפ' דהיינו אם היתה ח שקולה מכרעת דשכר מלות בהאי עלמא ליכא:

מסורת הש"ס

א) [ביצה לו.], ב) [מלת צבורה ליתא בשאלתות פרשת וירא סי' יא], ג) [ג"ז ליתא שם], ד) [ג"ז ליתא שם], ה) רש"ל מ"ז, ו) [שבועות לה:], ז) [ג"ז אדני], ח) [ג"ז אדני], ט) [עי' תוספות לעיל קיח: ד"ה עיון ותוספות ברכות לב: ד"ה כל ותוס' ב"ב קסד: ד"ה עיון], י) פאה פ"ק מ"א קדושין לט: ע"ש, כ) פ"א, ל) [ועי' תוספות ב"מ פד. ותוס' חולין ד. ד"ה דקולא], מ) והך משנה הכהל פליגא אר' יעקב דס"ל בסוף פרק קמא דקדושין דשכר מלוה בהאי עלמא ליכא

עין משפט נר מצוה

ב א מיי' פכ"ו מהל' שבת הלכה טו טוש"ע שם:
ג ב ג מיי' שם הלכה יד וטו:
ד ד טוש"ע שם סעיף ב:
ה ה ו מיי' וסמג שם טוש"ע שם ס"ק:
ו ז מיי' פ"ד מהלכות אבל הלכה ב:
ז ח סמג עשין יב:
ח ט מיי' פ"ה מהלכות דעות הלכה ז ופכ"ג מהלכות סנהדרין הלכה י טוש"ע ח"מ סימן יז סעיף י:
ט י מיי' פ"ג מהלכות ת"ת הלכה ג סמג שם טוש"ע י"ד סימן רמו סעיף יח:

רבינו חננאל

מתחילין באוצר תחלה ולא בתבואה צבורה. ומדבעא רב נחומי כמה שיעורי תבואה צבורה. ותנא כמה שיעור תבואה צבורה לתך ש"מ דהלכתא כהני מתניתא מדקט[ר]חינן לפרושי טעמייהו ויש מי שאומר הלכתא כשמואל דמוקים למתניתין כרבי שמעון דלית ליה מוקצה והלכתא כוותיה. ולתך זה האמור כאן הוא שיעור הקופות ששנינו במשנתנו. ואע"ג דלא איתאמרא בהדיא בגמרא דילן הא איתפרש בתלמוד א"י. ר' זעירא שאל לר' יאשיה כמה שעור הקופות. א"ל נלמד סתום מן המפורש דתנינן תמן בג' קופות של ג' ג' סאין תורמין את הלשכה. ושיעור לתך חצי כור והוא ט"ו סאין. נמצא שעור המשנה והברייתא שיעור אחד. וכדאוקמה רב חסדא למתני' ד' מה'. והכין שמעתא דא סלקא ועלה קמבעיא לן מעוטי בהלוכא עדיף או מעוטי במשוי עדיף. ואמרי' ת"ש דתני חדא מפנין אפילו ד' וה' קופות של כדי יין וכדי שמן. ותניא אידך בעשר ובחמש עשרה. ואוקימנא להו דכ"ע מעוטי בהילוכא עדיף. ושיעורם אחד הם. ואכדין קאי ולא אקופות והא מתניתא דקתני חמש הכין פירושא. חמש כדות גדולות שאין מכילה הקופה יותר מכדה אחת. והא מתניתא דקתני בעשר ובחמש עשרה בעשר כדות בחמש קופות והן בינוניות שנמצאו ב' כדות בכל קופה והא דתני ט"ו ג' כדות בכל קופה והא דמשתקלי תלת כדי בכל קופה כגון דקורי הרפניא פי' כדות שעושין בהרפניא והן קטנות ונוטלות ג' ג' בקופה שנמצא שיעור משקל כל כדה קטנה סאה והבינונית סאה וחצי. והגדולה ג' סאין. ותוב איבעיא לן הני דקא מפנינן ד' או ה' קופות מפני האורחין אע"פ דאית ליה אורחין הרבה אין לו רשות לפנות יותר מזה השיעור או דילמא הכל לפי האורחין ועוד בעיא אחרת כשמפנין אחד מפנה לכולן או כל אחד מפנה לעצמו ואיפשיטא שמעתא הכל לפי האורחין אם יש לו אורחין הרבה מפנין להן כל צרכן. ובאנו לדקדק מדקתני ועימר רבי את כל השדה שאחד מפנה לכולן (ולא עמר) [ודחינן וליטעמיך] וכי ר' בעצמו עימר אלא צוה ועימרו. ולעולם כל חד וחד לנפשיה וכיון דלא איפשיט בהדיא חד מפנהו לכולהו מחמרינן לפנויי כל דחד וחד לנפשיה דאיסורא הוא. וסתמא לחומרא. זה נכון לפנות כל אחד לעצמו ומסתייעא הא מילתא מהא (לעיל דף קכ"ה ע"ב) דא"ר חנניה פעם אחד הלך רבי למקום אחד ומצא נדבך של אבנים ואמר לתלמידיו צאו וחשבו כדי שנשב עליהן למחר ולא סמך במחשבתו שלו אלא הצריך כל אחד לעצמו וכדר' אסי ור' אמי אליבא דר' יוחנן כל אחד כטעמיה. פי' נדבך של אבנים אבנים סדורות זו ע"ג זו. ושפשפום לשפשפם ברגליהם. סואר של קורות קורות נתונות זו ע"ג זו. גשוש בלשון ישמעאל עירים ספינות. נגדר בלשון ישמעאל מתרו ופינוי לבית המדרש ולאורחים והכנת מקום לישיבתם שניהם שוין בדבר מצוה ושאר השמועה פשוטה היא. והא דתנן מפנין ד' ה' קופות. ה"מ לדבר מצוה מדקתני מפני האורחין ומפני

הגהות הב"ח

(א) גמ' שלא יגמור כולו (דילמא וכו' גומות) תא"מ וניב"ב נמחק: (ב) שם או דילמא גברא וגברא:

גליון הש"ס

גמרא גדולה הכנסת אורחים. עי' ב"מ דף פו ע"א ובתוספות שם ד"ה מזייה:

תורה אור השלם

א) וַיֹּאמַר אֲדֹנָי אִם נָא מָצָאתִי חֵן בְּעֵינֶיךָ אַל נָא תַעֲבֹר מֵעַל עַבְדֶּךָ: [בראשית יח, ג]

רב נסים גאון

כמה שיעור תבואה לתך. הלתך הוא חצי כור והוא ט"ו כי הכור הוא ל' סאה והכור והחומר מדה אחת כי תרגום חומר כורא כמו שאתה מוצא ביחזקאל (מה) האיפה והבת תוכן אחד להם ואמר התרגום מכילה וביתא טוקס חד יהי לכון סכום תלת סאין למיסב משער כורא הרי נתברר לו מיכן כי החומר הוא כור וכי הבת היא ג' סאין ואמר אחר כך כי עשרת הבתים חומר נמצא שיעור הכור ל' סאין ושם אמר (הושע ג) וחומר שעורים ולתך שעורים ואמרו חכמנו בפרק גיד הנשה (חולין דף צב) אלו ארבעים וחמשה צדיקים החומר ל' ולתך ט"ו הכל מ"ה נתקיים לך כי הכור הוא שני לתכים: שמא

ליקוטי רש"י

שלא יגמור כולו. אם לא היו שם אלא ארבע או חמש קופות שהתירו לו במקום שיש יותר כאן לא התירו לפנותן כולן ולגלות את הקרקע דלמא הוי בה גומא ומשוה לה [ביצה לו.]. **אשוויי גומות.** דמלאכה הוא בשבת דהוי כבנין [עירובין קד.]. **כלפי לייא.** שתי מלות כלפי היכן נוטה דבר זה. לייא. היכן וחבירו בברכות בפרק הרואה (נח.) תלבי לנהרא כגני לייא תרסים שבורים להיכן הולכין [פסחים ה:]. כלפי היכא נהפך דבר זה [לעיל צג:]. כנגד איפוא הדבר הזה סובב [כתובות טו.]. כנגד איפוא הפכת דבריך לייא איפוא כדאמר בברכות (נח.) כגני לייא כדים שבורים להיכן הולכים [סוטה מד.]. כנגד מה שונה כאן ולאן הדבר נוטה כדאמרינן בברכות (נח.) תלבי לנהרא כגני לייא הקדירות שלמות הולכין לנהר לשאוב בהן מים אבל השבורין להיכן הולכין [רשב"ם ב"ב קד:]. **דקורי דהרפנאי.** סלים שעושין בהרפניא [ב"מ פד.]. **ויאמר [אדני] אם נא וגו'.** דבר אחר, קודש הוא והיה אומר להקב"ה להמתין לו עד שירוץ ויכנים את האורחים [בראשית יח, ג ועי' כאן בתוס']. כתיב לעיל מינה וירא עליו ה' והדר כתיב והנה שלשה אנשים ואמר להקב"ה אל נא תעבור מעל עבדך המתן לי כאן עד שאכנים האורחין [שבועות לה:]. **והדן את חברו לכף זכות.** ברואה חבירו עושה דבר שאתה יכול להכריעו לצד עבירה ולצד זכות הכריעו לזכות ואל תחשדהו בעבירה [שם ל.]. על כל שתשמע עליו אמור שנתכוון לטובה עד שתדע בבירור שאינו כן שאם אתה תדין כן ידונו אותך מן השמים לזכות כמו שמפורש בפרק מפנין [אבות פ"א מ"ו]. **והבאת שלום.** תשלום שכר גדול להבאת שלום שאוכל פירותיהן בעולם הזה והקרן קיימת לו לעולם הבא כגמילות חסדים דכתיב בהו ימצא חיים צדקה בעולם הבא וכבוד בעולם הזה [יבמות קט:].

Mishnah, אַף עַל גַּב דְּאִית לֵיהּ אוֹרְחִין טוּבָא – does this refer **even to where he has many guests?**[18] אוֹ דִילְמָא הַכֹּל לְפִי הָאוֹרְחִין – **Or perhaps it all depends on the** number of **guests** (or attendees), and the Mishnah means to limit one to clearing away no more than five boxes *per guest.*[19] – ? –

The Gemara takes the inquiry a step further:

וְאִם תִּמְצֵי לוֹמַר הַכֹּל לְפִי הָאוֹרְחִין – **And if you will conclude and say** that indeed **it all depends on the** number **of guests,** and that the Mishnah means to limit the clearing away to five boxes per guest, we can still inquire in the case of many guests: חַד גַּבְרָא מְפַנֵּי לְכוּלְּהוּ – **May one person clear away** the grain or straw **for all of them?** אוֹ דִילְמָא גַּבְרָא גַּבְרָא מְפַנֵּי לְנַפְשֵׁיהּ – **Or perhaps** no one person may clear away more than five boxes, rather **each person clears away for himself** the five boxes of space that he needs.[20] – ? –

The Gemara seeks to resolve these inquiries:

תָּא שְׁמַע – **Come, learn** a resolution from the following: דְּאָמַר רַבָּה אָמַר רַבִּי חִיָּיא – **For Rabbah said in the name of R' Chiya:** פַּעַם אַחַת הָלַךְ רַבִּי לְמָקוֹם אֶחָד – **One time, Rebbi went to a certain place** to lecture on the Sabbath, וְרָאָה מָקוֹם דָּחוּק לַתַּלְמִידִים – **and he saw that the place** selected as the lecture site **was too cramped for the disciples,** וְיָצָא לַשָּׂדֶה וּמָצָא שָׂדֶה מְלֵאָה עוֹמָרִים – **so he went out to the fields and found a field filled with bundles** of produce, וְעִימֵּר רַבִּי כָּל הַשָּׂדֶה כּוּלָּהּ – **and Rebbi cleared away**[21] all the bundles from **the entire field** to make room for the disciples.[22] (שְׁמַע מִינָּהּ הַכֹּל לְפִי הָאוֹרְחִין – **Learn from this that it all depends on the** number of **guests.**)[23]

A similar report:

וְרַב יוֹסֵף אָמַר רַבִּי הוֹשַׁעְיָא – **And Rav Yosef said in the name of R' Hoshaya:** פַּעַם אַחַת הָלַךְ רַבִּי חִיָּיא לְמָקוֹם אֶחָד – **One time, R' Chiya went to a certain place** to lecture on the Sabbath, וְרָאָה מָקוֹם דָּחוּק לַתַּלְמִידִים – **and he saw that the place** selected as the lecture site **was too cramped for the disciples,** וְיָצָא לַשָּׂדֶה וּמָצָא שָׂדֶה מְלֵאָה עוֹמָרִים – **so he went out to the fields and found a field filled with bundles** of produce, וְעִימֵּר רַבִּי חִיָּיא כָּל הַשָּׂדֶה כּוּלָּהּ – **and R' Chiya cleared away** all the bundles from **the entire field** to make room for the disciples.

The Gemara therefore reasons:

שְׁמַע מִינָּהּ הַכֹּל לְפִי הָאוֹרְחִין – **Learn from this** (i.e. these two reports) that when the Mishnah states a maximum of five boxes, **it all depends on the number of guests** (or disciples).

The Gemara has indeed resolved the first inquiry, concluding that the Mishnah means that a maximum of five boxes *per guest* may be cleared away. The Gemara adds:

וַעֲדַיִין תִּבָּעֵי לָךְ חַד גַּבְרָא מְפַנֵּי לֵיהּ לְכוּלָּא – **But you can still inquire whether one person may clear away all** the space needed for all the guests, אוֹ דִילְמָא כָּל גַּבְרָא וְגַבְרָא מְפַנֵּי לְנַפְשֵׁיהּ – **or** whether **perhaps each person clears away for himself** the five boxes of space that he needs. – ? –

The Gemara seeks to resolve this inquiry as well:

תָּא שְׁמַע – **Come, learn** a resolution from the report cited above, which states: וְעִימֵּר רַבִּי – **"So Rebbi cleared away** all the bundles . . ." This implies that he did so himself, proving that one person *may* clear away the space needed for all the disciples or guests, even though he is personally clearing away far more than five boxes.

The Gemara challenges this proof:

וּלְטַעְמֵיךְ רַבִּי בְּדִנַפְשֵׁיהּ עִימֵּר – **And according to your reasoning,** that you interpret the report to mean literally that Rebbi cleared out the field himself, can it really be that **Rebbi himself cleared away** the bundles? Why, Rebbi was the *Nasi,* and it was certainly not befitting for him to do so![24] אֶלָּא צִוָּה וְעִימְּרוּ – **Rather,** the report means only that **he instructed** the others **to clear away** the bundles, וּלְעוֹלָם כָּל חַד וְחַד מְפַנֵּי לְנַפְשֵׁיהּ – **and in fact each one clears away for himself** the five boxes of space that he needs. Thus the second inquiry remains unresolved.

The Gemara now moves on to discuss the next phrase in the Mishnah, which states:

מִפְּנֵי הָאוֹרְחִין וכו׳ – One may clear away . . . BECAUSE OF GUESTS **etc.** [or because of curtailment of attendance at the study hall].

The Gemara derives a lesson from the examples stated in our Mishnah:

אָמַר רַבִּי יוֹחָנָן – **R' Yochanan said:** גְּדוֹלָה הַכְנָסַת אוֹרְחִין כְּהַשְׁכָּמַת בֵּית הַמִּדְרָשׁ – **Receiving guests**[25] **is as great as rising early to** attend **the study hall.**[26] דְּקָתָנֵי מִפְּנֵי הָאוֹרְחִין וּמִפְּנֵי בִּטּוּל בֵּית הַמִּדְרָשׁ – **For the Mishnah** equates the two when it **states** that produce may be cleared away BECAUSE OF GUESTS OR BECAUSE OF CURTAILMENT OF attendance at THE STUDY HALL. וְרַב דִּימִי מִנְּהַרְדְּעָא אָמַר יוֹתֵר מֵהַשְׁכָּמַת בֵּית הַמִּדְרָשׁ – **And Rav Dimi from Nehardea says:** Receiving guests is even **greater than rising early to** attend **the study hall.** דְּקָתָנֵי מִפְּנֵי הָאוֹרְחִין – **For the Mishnah states** BECAUSE OF GUESTS first, וַהֲדַר וּמִפְּנֵי בִּטּוּל בֵּית הַמִּדְרָשׁ – **and** only **then** does it state OR BECAUSE OF CURTAILMENT OF attendance at THE STUDY HALL.

The Gemara expounds further on the virtue of receiving guests:

אָמַר רַב יְהוּדָה אָמַר רַב – **Rav Yehudah said in the name of Rav:** גְּדוֹלָה הַכְנָסַת אוֹרְחִין מֵהַקְבָּלַת פְּנֵי שְׁכִינָה – **Receiving guests is greater than greeting the Divine Presence.** דִּכְתִיב ,,וַיֹּאמַר ה׳ אִם־נָא מָצָאתִי חֵן בְּעֵינֶיךָ אַל־נָא תַעֲבֹר וגו׳ ״ – **For it is written:** *And*

NOTES

18. And "five boxes" is the maximum number that can be cleared away, whether there is one guest (or attendee at a lecture) or many (see *Tosafos*).

19. [See *Orach Chaim* 333:3.] This inquiry presumes Rav Chisda's interpretation of the Mishnah (*Rashi*). [According to Shmuel's interpretation, however, the Mishnah means that one may clear away as much as he needs, as long as he does not clear away the entire store.]

20. [The Gemara does not mean specifically that each person must clear away *for himself.* It is perfectly acceptable if someone else clears away the space for him, as long as no one person is clearing away more than five boxes (see *Orach Chaim* 333:3).]

21. [The word עִימֵּר, which means literally *he gathered together,* is used here in the sense of *he cleared away* (see *Meiri* and *Ritva MHK* ed.; cf. *Rashash*), since the case involved the moving away of bundled (*gathered together*) produce.]

22. [Though] the field was a *karmelis* [in which it is Rabbinically forbidden to transport something four *amos* or more], Rebbi moved each bundle less than four *amos* at a time (*Rashi*). [Ordinarily, moving an object less than four *amos* at a time in a public domain or *karmelis* is also forbidden Rabbinically, where the total distance moved is four *amos* or more (*Orach Chaim* 349:5; cf. *Hagahos R' Akiva Eiger* ad loc.). Nevertheless, it was permitted for Rebbi to do so in this case, because it was an instance of performing a Rabbinic *melachah* (carrying in a *karmelis*) in a manner that would be forbidden only Rabbinically even if the *melachah* were Biblical (less than four *amos* at a time) in order to fulfill a mitzvah (allow the disciples to attend a lecture) (שְׁבוּת דִּשְׁבוּת בִּמְקוֹם מִצְוָה) (*Rashash*; see also *Beur Halachah* ad loc.).]

[Though the Mishnah forbids one to clear away an entire store, lest one come to level holes in the ground, this concern does not apply in a field, as stated in the Gemara above, 113a. (*Ohr Same'ach* to *Rambam, Hil. Shabbos* 26:15, however, advances a different reason for why it was permitted to clear out the entire field.)]

23. [Some editions delete the words in parentheses (considering them unnecessary, as the Gemara will state them at the end of the identical proof cited next).]

24. See *Rashi*; cf. *Tosafos.*

25. [I.e. receiving wayfarers into one's home; see above, 126b note 4.]

26. Cf. *Hagahos Yavetz.*

כדאמרי אינשי ואי בעי אפילו טובא נמי מפנין ומאי אבל לא את האוצר שלא יגמור כולו (א) דילמא אתי לאשווי גומות אבל אתחולי מתחיל ומני ר"ש היא דלית ליה מוקצה ת"ר אין מתחילין באוצר תחילה אבל עושה בו שביל כדי שיכנס ויצא עושה בו שביל והא אמרת אין מתחילין הכי קאמר עושה בו שביל ברגליו בכניסתו וביציאתו תנו רבנן תבואה צבורה בזמן שהתחיל בה מע"ש מותר להסתפק ממנה בשבת ואם לאו אסור להסתפק ממנה בשבת דברי ר"ש ר' אחא מתיר כלפי לייא אלא אימא דברי ר' אחא ורבי שמעון מתיר תנא כמה שיעור תבואה צבורה לתך בעא מיניה רב נחומי בר זכריה מאביי שיעור תבואה צבורה בכמה אמר ליה הרי אמרו שיעור תבואה צבורה לתך איבעיא להו הני ארבע וחמש קופות דקאמר בארבע וחמש קופות אין טפי לא אלמא למעוטי בהילוכא עדיף או דילמא למעוטי משווי עדיף ת"ש דתני חדא מפנין אפילו ארבע וחמש קופות של כדי שמן ושל כדי יין ותניא אידך בעשר ובחמש עשרה מאי לאו בהא קמיפלגי דמר סבר מעוטי בהילוכא עדיף ומר סבר מעוטי במשוי עדיף לא דכ"ע מעוטי בהילוכא עדיף ומי סברת בעשר ובחמש עשרה אקופות קאי אכדין קאי ולא קשיא הא דמשתקלי חד חד בקופה והא דמישתקלי תרי תרי והא דמשתקלי תלתא תלתא ובדקורי דהרפניא איבעיא להו הני ארבע וחמש דקאמר אע"ג דאית ליה אורחין טובא או דילמא הכל לפי האורחין ואת"ל הכל לפי האורחין חד גברא מפני לכולהו או דילמא גברא (ב) גברא מפני לנפשיה ת"ש דאמר רבה אמר רבי חייא פעם אחת הלך רבי למקום אחד וראה מקום דחוק לתלמידים ויצא לשדה ומצא שדה מלאה עומרים ועימר רבי כל השדה כולה (שמע מינה הכל לפי האורחין) ורב יוסף א"ר הושעיא פעם אחת הלך ר' חייא למקום אחד וראה מקום דחוק לתלמידים ויצא לשדה ומצא שדה מלאה עומרים ועימר ר' חייא כל השדה כולה שמע מינה הכל לפי האורחין ועדיין תבעי לך חד גברא מפני ליה לכולא או דילמא כל גברא וגברא מפני לנפשיה ת"ש ועימר רבי ולטעמיך רבי בדנפשיה עימר אלא צוה ועימר ולעולם כל חד וחד מפני לנפשיה: מפני האורחין וכו': א"ר יוחנן גדולה הכנסת אורחין כהשכמת בית המדרש דקתני מפני האורחין ומפני בטול בית המדרש ורב דימי מנהרדעא אמר יותר מהשכמת בית המדרש דקתני מפני האורחין והדר ומפני בטול בית המדרש אמר רב יהודה אמר רב גדולה הכנסת אורחין מהקבלת פני שכינה דכתיב ויאמר (ה') אם נא מצאתי חן בעיניך אל נא תעבור וגו' א"ר אלעזר בא וראה שלא כמדת הקב"ה מדת בשר ודם מדת ב"ו אין קטן יכול לומר לגדול המתן עד שאבא אצלך ואילו בהקדוש ברוך הוא כתיב ויאמר (ה') אם נא מצאתי וגו' אמר רב יהודה בר שילא א"ר אסי א"ר יוחנן ששה דברים אדם אוכל פירותיהן בעולם הזה והקרן קיימת לו לעולם הבא ואלו הן הכנסת אורחין וביקור חולים ועיון תפלה והשכמת בית המדרש והמגדל בניו לתלמוד תורה והדן את חברו לכף זכות איני והא אנן תנן אלו דברים שאדם עושה אותם ואוכל פירותיהן בעולם הזה והקרן קיימת לו לעולם הבא ואלו הן כיבוד אב ואם וגמילות חסדים והבאת שלום שבין אדם לחבירו ות"ת כנגד כולם [הני אין מידי אחרינא לא] הני

רש"י

כדאמרי אינשי. חשבון קטן תחילה ואם יצטרך ליותר יפנה יותר משום הכי נקט ד' ברישא והדר חמשה וה"ה אפילו טובא: שלא יגמור. משום אשויי גומות: ברגלו. מפנה ברגלו לכאן ולכאן דרך הליכתו דלא הוי טלטול: תבואה צבורה. מוכחא מילתא דהוקצה לאוצר: להסתפק. להאכיל לבהמתו: אסור דברי ר"ש ורבי אחא כו': כלפי לייא. כנגד היכן פונה הדבר הזה האמור להיפך ר"ש מתיר מוקצה בכל מקום וכאן הוא מחמיר: לייא. היכן כגון אבלי לנהרא כגני לייא דברכות (דף נח.): לתך. אבל בציר מהכי לאו אוצר הוא: לתך. חצי כור הוא ט"ו סאין: בד' וה' קופות אין טפי לא. בקופות עצמן הוא יפנה וימלאם אם ירצה או שק בכתפו שיעור קופה בפעם אחת אבל טפי להלך יותר מה' פעמים כגון לפנות בכלים קטנים וירבה בהילוך לא: למעוטי בהילוכא עדיף. ואע"ג דאפושי משוי הוא: או דילמא מעוטי משוי עדיף. ואם בא לפנות בכלים קטנים כשיעור ה' קופות מותר ולרב חסדא קבעי לה דאמר ה' דוקא: בי' ובט"ו. קס"ד אקופות קאי לומר שמפנה בקופות קטנות וירבה בהילוך: אכדין קאי. ולא פליגי והכי קאמר בי' בט"ו יפנה באותן ה' קופות: הא דמשתקלי חדא חדא בקופה. הך דתניא ד' וה' ולא נחת למניינא דכדין איירי בכדין גדולים דמשתקלי חדא בקופה והך דתנא בי' וט"ו איירי בכדים בינונים ובכדין קטנים עשר כדמשתקלי תרי תרי בקופה ט"ו כדמשתקלי תלתא תלתא בקופה דקטנים: בי דקורי דהרפניא. בכדין של הרפניא: איבעיא להו. אליבא דרב חסדא: דחוק לתלמידים. שאין מקום לתלמידים להושיב: ועימר. פנה את העומרים וכרמלית הואי ובפחות פחות מד' אמות: ת"ש ועימר רבי. אלמא חד גברא פניהו: רבי בנפשיה עימר. בתמיה וכי אורחיה דנשיא בהכי: כהשכמת ביהמ"ד. מדשוי להו במתני' כי הדדי: מהשכמת בית המדרש. דתנא דידן אקדמה ברישא: אל נא תעבור. והניחו והלך לקבל האורחים: ועיון תפלה. לכוין בתפלתו:

תוספות

של כדי שמן ושל כדי יין. והא דתנן בפ' המביא (ביצה דף כט:) כדי יין לא יביאם בסל ובקופה היינו ממקום רחוק דמיחזי כעובדין דחול אבל הכא בביתו:

דכולי עלמא למעוטי בהלוכא עדיף. לא מצי למימר למעוטי במשוי עדיף דההיא דקתני ד' וה' קופות לא מצי סבר הכי דא"כ הוה ליה למיתני בעשר וט"ו כשיעור ה' קופות וא"ת והא תנן בפרק אין לדין (שם דף כה.) שחטה בשדה לא יביאנה במוט ובמוטה אלא מביאה לאיברים אף על גב דמפיש בהילוכא התם שאני דאיכא טירחא יותר מדאי להביאה שלימה א"נ משום דמיחזי כמוליכה למכור בשוק והא דאמרינן בריש שואל (לקמן דף קמח.) היכי ליעבד דמליא בחצבא רבא תימלי בחצבא זוטא קא מפשא בהילוכא דמליא בחצבא זוטא תמלא בחצבא רבא קא מפשא במשוי התם כיון שנהגו למלאות המים בחצבא רבא או בחצבא זוטא קשה להם לשנות מכמות שנהגו:

אע"ג דאית ליה אורחין טובא או דילמא הכל לפי האורחין. מכאן יש להוכיח דהא דתנן במתניתין ד' וה' קופות הוי אפי' בשביל אדם אחד דאי הוי נמי לפי האורחין אמאי נקט ד' וה' ועוד מדלא מספקא ליה אי חד מפני כולהו או כל חד לנפשיה אלא בא"ל הכל לפי האורחין משמע הא אם אמר אף על גב דאיתרמו ליה אורחין טובא ליכא לאיסתפוקי ואי אמרינן דד' וה' קופות הוי לפי האורחין אכתי איכא לספוקי אי חד גברא מפני לכולהו או כל חד מפני לנפשיה אלא משמע דפשיטא דד' וה' אינן לפי האורחין אלא אפילו לצורך אדם אחד:

ולטעמיך רבי בנפשיה עימר. פי' כל השדה כולה:

דכתיב ויאמר ה' אם נא מצאתי חן וגו'. קסבר כמאן דאמר בשבועות (דף לה:) דהאי השם קדש דאיכא מאן דאמר התם שהוא חול שלמלאכים היה מדבר שהיה מזומנים:

אוכל מפירותיהן בעולם הזה. בפ"ק דקדושין (דף לט:) מפ' דהיינו אם היתה שקולה מכרעת דשכר מצות בהאי עלמא ליכא: כיון

עין משפט נר מצוה

ב א מיי' פכ"ו מהל' שבת הלכה טו טוש"ע שם:
ג ב ג מיי' שם הלכה יד ועוו:
ד ד טוש"ע שם סעיף ג:
ה ה ו מיי' ומגג שם טוש"ע שם ס"ג:
ו ז מיי' פי"ד מהלכות אבל הלכה ג:
ז ח סמג עשין יג:
ח ט מיי' פ"ה מהלכות דעות הלכה ז ופכ"ג מהלכות סנהדרין הלכה י טוש"ע ח"מ סימן יז סעיף י:
ט י מיי' פ"ג מהלכות ת"ת הלכה ג סמג שם טוש"ע י"ד סימן רמו סעיף יח:

רבינו חננאל

מתחילין באוצר תחלה ולא בתבואה צבורה. ומדבעא רב נחומי כמה שיעורי תבואה צבורה. ותנא כמה שיעור תבואה צבורה לתך ש"מ דהלכתא כהני מתניתא מדקטנ[ר]חינן לפרושי טעמייהו ויש מי שאומר הלכתא כשמואל דמוקים למתניתין כרבי שמעון דלית ליה מוקצה והלכתא כוותיה. ולתך זה האמור כאן הוא שיעור הקופות ששנינו במשנתנו. ואע"ג דלא איתאמרא בהדיא בגמרא דילן הא איתפרש בתלמוד א"י. ר' זעירא שאל לר' יאשיה כמה שעור הקופות. א"ל נלמד סתום מן המפורש דתנינן תמן בג' קופות של ג' ג' סאין תורמין את הלשכה. ושיעור לתך חצי כור והוא ט"ו סאין. נמצא שעור המשנה והברייתא שיעור אחד. וכדאוקמה רב חסדא למתני' ד' מה'. והכין שמעתא דא סלקא ועלה קמבעיא לן מעוטי בהלוכא עדיף או מעוטי במשוי עדיף. ואמרי' ת"ש דתני חדא מפנין אפילו ד' וה' קופות של כדי יין וכדי שמן. ותניא אידך בעשר ובחמש עשרה. ואוקימנא להו דכ"ע מעוטי בהילוכא עדיף. ושיעורם אחד הם. ואכדין קאי ולא אקופות והא מתניתא דקתני חמש הכין פירושא. חמש כדות גדולות שאין מכילה הקופה יותר מכדה אחת. והא מתניתא דקתני בעשר ובחמש עשרה בעשר כדות בחמש קופות והן בינוניות שנמצאו ב' כדות בכל קופה והא דתני ט"ו ג' כדות בכל קופה והא דמשתקלי תלת כדי בכל קופה כגון דקורי הרפניא פי' כדות שעושין בהרפניא והן קטנות ונוטלות ג' ג' בקופה שנמצא שיעור משקל כל כדה קטנה סאה והבינונית סאה וחצי. והגדולה ג' סאין. ותוב איבעיא לן הני דקא מפנינן ד' או ה' קופות מפני האורחין אע"פ דאית ליה אורחין הרבה אין לו רשות לפנות יותר מזה השיעור או דילמא הכל לפי האורחין ועוד בעיא אחרת כשמפנין אחד מפנה לכולן או כל אחד מפנה לעצמו ואיפשיטא שמעתא הכל לפי האורחין אם יש לו אורחין הרבה מפנין להן כל צרכן. ובאנו לדקדק מדקתני ועימר רבי את כל השדה שאחד מפנה לכולן (ולא עמר) [ודחינן וליטעמיך] וכי ר' בעצמו עימר אלא צוה ועימרו. ולעולם כל חד וחד לנפשיה וכיון דלא איפשיט בהדיא חד מפנהו לכולהו מחמרינן לפנויי כל דחד וחד לנפשיה דאיסורא הוא. וסתמא לחומרא. זה נכון לפנות כל אחד לעצמו ומסתייעא הא מילתא מהא (לעיל דף קכ"ה ע"ב) דא"ר חנניה פעם אחד הלך רבי למקום אחד ומצא נדבך של אבנים ואמר לתלמידיו צאו וחשבו כדי שנשב עליהן למחר ולא סמך במחשבתו שלו אלא הצריך כל אחד לעצמו וכדר' אסי ור' אמי אליבא דר' יוחנן כל אחד כטעמיה. פי' נדבך של אבנים אבנים סדורות זו ע"ג זו. ושפשפום לשפשפם ברגליהם. סואר של קורות קורות נתונות זו ע"ג זו. גשוש בלשון ישמעאל עירים ספינות. נגדר בלשון ישמעאל מתרו ופינוי לבית המדרש ולאורחים והכנת מקום לישיבתם שניהם שוין בדבר מצוה ושאר השמועה פשוטה היא. והא דתנן מפנין ד' ה' קופות. ה"מ לדבר מצוה מדקתני מפני האורחין ומפני

מסורת הש"ס

א) [ביצה לו.], ב) [מלת צבורה ליתא בשאלתות פרשת וילא פרי יח], ג) [ג"ז ליתא שם], ד) [ג"ז ליתא שם], ה) בש"מ מ"ז, ו) [שבועות לה:], ז) [צ"ל אדני], ח) [צ"ל אדני], ט) [עי' תוספות לעיל קיח: ד"ה עיון ותוספות ברכות לב: ד"ה כל ותוס' ב"ב קסד: ד"ה עיון], י) פאה פ"א מ"א קדושין לט: ע"ש, כ) פ"א, ל) [ועי' בפרש"י ב"מ פד. ותוס' חולין ד. ד"ה דקורי], מ) והך משנה דהכא פליגא אר' יעקב דס"ל בפרק קמא דקדושין דשכר מצוה בהאי עלמא ליכא

הגהות הב"ח

(א) גמ' שלא יגמור כולו (דילמא וכו' גומות) תא"מ ונ"ב ס"א נמחק: (ב) שם או דילמא גברא וגברא:

גליון הש"ס

גמרא גדולה הכנסת אורחים. עי' ב"מ דף פו ע"ב ובתוספות שם ד"ה מזיה:

תורה אור השלם

א) וַיֹּאמַר אֲדֹנָי אִם נָא מָצָאתִי חֵן בְּעֵינֶיךָ אַל נָא תַעֲבֹר מֵעַל עַבְדֶּךָ: [בראשית יח, ג]

רב נסים גאון

כמה שיעור תבואה לתך. הלתך הוא חצי כור והוא ט"ו סאין כי הכור הוא ל' סאה והכור והחומר מדה אחת כי תרגום חומר כורא כמו שאתה מוצא ביחזקאל (מה) האיפה והבת תוכן אחד להם והם התרגום מכילתא וביאנא טופס קד יהי לכון סכום תלת סאין למיסב מעשר כורא ... נתברר לו מיכן כי החומר הוא כור וכי הבת היא ג' סאין ואמר אחר כך כי עשרה הבתים חומר נמצא שיעור הכור ל' סאין ושם אמר (הושע ג) וחומר שעורים ולתך שעורים ואמרו חכמינו בפרק גיד הנשה (חולין דף צב) אלו ארבעים וחמשה צדיקים החומר ל' ולתך ט"ו הכל מ"ה נתקיים לך כי הכור הוא לתך שני לתכים: שמא

ליקוטי רש"י

שלא יגמור כולו. אם לא היו שם אלא ארבע או חמש קופות שהתירו לו במקום שיש יותר כאן לא התירו לפנותן כולן ולגלות את הקרקע שמא ימצא בה גומא ומשוה לה [ביצה לו.]. אשוויי גומות. דמלאכה הוא בשבת דהוי כבונין [עירובין קד.]. כלפי לייא. שתי מלות כלפי היכן נוטה דבר זה. לייא. היכן ותבירו בברכות בפרק הרואה (נח.) אבלי לנהרא כגני לייא חרסים שבורים להיכן [פסחים ח:]. כלפי היכא נהפך דבר זה [לעיל צג:]. כנגד איפוא הדבר הזה סובב [כתובות טו.]. כנגד איפוא הפכת דברך ... בברכות (נח.) כגני לייא כדים שבורים להיכן הולכים [סוטה מד.]. כנגד מה שונה כאן ולאן הדבר נוטה כדמתבירן בברכות (נח.) אבלי לנהרא כגני לייא הקדירות שלמות הולכין לנהר לשאוב בהן מים אבל השבורין להיכן הולכין [רשב"ם ב"ב קד:]. דקורי דהרפנאי. כלים שעושין בהרפניא [ב"מ פד.]. ויאמר [אדני] אם נא וגו'. דבר אחר, קודש הוא והיה אומר להקב"ה להמתין לו עד שירוץ ויכניס את האורחים [בראשית יח, ג ועי' כאן בתוס']. כתיב לעיל מינה וירא עליו ה' והדר כתיב והנה שלשה אנשים ואמר להקב"ה אל נא תעבור מעל עבדך המתן לי כאן עד שאכניס האורחין [שבועות לה:]. והדן את חבירו לכף זכות. כשרואה חבירו עושה דבר שאתה יכול להכריעו לצד עבירה ולצד זכות הכריעו לזכות ואל תחשדהו בעבירה [שם ל.]. על כל שתשמע עליו אמור שנתכוון לטובה עד שתדע בבירור שאינו כן שאם אתה תדין כן ידונו אותך מן השמים לזכות כמו שמפורש בפרק מפנין [אבות פ"א מ"ו]. והבאת שלום. תשלום שכר גדול להבאת שלום שאוכל פירותיהן בעולם הזה והקרן קיימת לו לעולם הבא כגמילות חסדים דכתיב בהו ימצא חיים צדקה וכבוד בעולם הזה [יבמות קט.].

***[Abraham] said, "My Lord, if I have now found favor in Your eyes, please do not pass away** from Your servant."*[27]

Another observation on that verse:

אָמַר רַבִּי אֶלְעָזָר בֹּא וּרְאֵה שֶׁלֹּא כְּמִדַּת הַקָּדוֹשׁ בָּרוּךְ הוּא מִדַּת בָּשָׂר וָדָם – R' Elazar said: Come and observe how unlike the way of the Holy One, Blessed is He, is the way of flesh and blood. מִדַּת בָּשָׂר וָדָם – According to **the way of flesh and blood,** אֵין קָטָן יָכוֹל לוֹמַר לְגָדוֹל הַמְתֵּן עַד שֶׁאָבֹא אֶצְלְךָ – **one of lower station cannot tell one of higher station, "Wait** here for me **until I come** back **to you."** וְאִילּוּ בְּהַקָּדוֹשׁ בָּרוּךְ הוּא כְּתִיב ,,וַיֹּאמַר ה׳ אִם־נָא מָצָאתִי וְגוֹ׳ " – **Whereas with regard to the Holy One, Blessed is He, it is written:** ***And [Abraham] said, "My Lord, if I have now found** favor in Your eyes, please do not pass away from Your servant."*

The Gemara elaborates further on the virtue of welcoming guests:

אָמַר רַב יְהוּדָה בַּר שִׁילָא אָמַר רַבִּי אַסִּי אָמַר רַבִּי יוֹחָנָן – Rav Yehudah bar Shila said in the name of R' Assi, who said in the name of R' Yochanan: שִׁשָּׁה דְּבָרִים אָדָם אוֹכֵל פֵּירוֹתֵיהֶן בָּעוֹלָם הַזֶּה – In the case of **six precepts, a person** who fulfills them **enjoys their fruits in this world,** וְהַקֶּרֶן קַיֶּימֶת לוֹ לָעוֹלָם הַבָּא – **but the principal remains intact for him** to enjoy **in the World to Come.** וְאֵלּוּ הֵן – **And these are [the six]:** הַכְנָסַת אוֹרְחִין – **receiving guests,** וּבִיקּוּר חוֹלִים – **and visiting the sick,** וְעִיּוּן תְּפִלָּה – **and concentration during prayer,**[28] וְהַשְׁכָּמַת בֵּית הַמִּדְרָשׁ – **and rising early to** attend **the study hall,** וְהַמְגַדֵּל בָּנָיו לְתַלְמוּד תּוֹרָה – **and one who raises his children to the study of Torah,** וְהַדָּן אֶת חֲבֵירוֹ לְכַף זְכוּת – **and one who judges his fellow favorably.**[29]

The Gemara asks:

אֵינִי – **Is it** indeed **so** as R' Yochanan says? וְהָא אֲנַן תְּנַן – **Why, we have learned in a Mishnah:**[30] אֵלּוּ דְּבָרִים שֶׁאָדָם עוֹשֶׂה אוֹתָם – THESE ARE THE PRECEPTS THAT A PERSON PERFORMS THEM וְאוֹכֵל פֵּירוֹתֵיהֶן בָּעוֹלָם הַזֶּה – AND ENJOYS THEIR FRUITS IN THIS WORLD וְהַקֶּרֶן קַיֶּימֶת לוֹ לָעוֹלָם הַבָּא – WHILE THE PRINCIPAL REMAINS INTACT FOR HIM IN THE WORLD TO COME: וְאֵלּוּ הֵן – THESE ARE: כִּיבּוּד אָב וָאֵם – HONORING one's FATHER AND MOTHER, וּגְמִילוּת חֲסָדִים – AND BESTOWING KINDNESS, וַהֲבָאַת שָׁלוֹם שֶׁבֵּין אָדָם לַחֲבֵירוֹ – AND BRINGING about PEACE BETWEEN ONE PERSON AND ANOTHER; וְתַלְמוּד תּוֹרָה כְּנֶגֶד כּוּלָּם – AND STUDYING TORAH IS EQUAL TO ALL OF THEM combined. הָנֵי אִין מִידֵי אַחֲרִינָא לֹא – The Mishnah implies that for **these** four precepts – **yes,** one reaps the incidental benefits in this world while the principal remains intact for him in the World to Come; but **other things – no,** they do not have this quality.[31] – ? –

NOTES

27. *Genesis* 18:3. The preceding two verses relate how God appeared to Abraham while he was sitting at the entrance to his tent; Abraham then saw three wayfarers standing nearby and ran to welcome them into his home. In the present verse, the Torah relates how Abraham – prior to running out to welcome the wayfarers – asked God to please wait for him while he interrupted to receive the wayfarers. Abraham's behavior, then, indicates that receiving guests is greater than greeting the Divine presence. [See *Haamek Davar* to *Genesis* 18:2; see also *Maharal* here, and *Michtav M'Eliyahu* II pp. 180-181.]

[The Gemara in *Shevuos* (35b) observes that Rav's exposition reflects the view that in this verse Abraham is addressing God, and the word אֲדֹנָי is the Holy name of God. (Our Gemara texts here read: ה׳, but this should be emended to read אֲדֹנָי, as in the verse, since ה׳ is used exclusively as a shorthand form of the Ineffable Name – see *Mesoras HaShas*; see also *Emes LeYaakov*.) Another view in the Gemara there, however, takes the word אֲדֹנָי in the verse to be mundane, meaning *my masters*; accordingly, the verse means that after Abraham reached the wayfarers, he begged them not to pass by, but to remain and avail themselves of his hospitality (see *Tosafos*).]

28. *Rashi*; see also *Tosafos* above, 118b ד״ה עיון תפלה.

29. [I.e. where his fellow's actions admit positive or negative interpretations, he gives his fellow the benefit of the doubt. (See 127b note 21.)]

30. *Pe'ah* 1:1.

31. [R' Yochanan's list is entirely different than that of the Mishnah!]

כדאמרי אינשי ואי בעי אפילו טובא נמי מפנין *ומאי א) אבל לא את האוצר שלא יגמור כולו (א) דילמא אתי לאשוויי גומות אבל אתחולי מתחיל ומני ר"ש היא דלית ליה מוקצה ת"ר ב אין מתחילין באוצר תחילה אבל עושה בו שביל כדי שיכנס ויצא עושה בו שביל והא אמרת אין מתחילין הכי קאמר עושה בו שביל ברגליו בכניסתו וביציאתו תנו רבנן תבואה ג צבורה שהתחיל בה מע"ש מותר להסתפק ממנה בשבת ואם לאו אסור להסתפק ממנה בשבת דברי ר"ש ר' אחא מתיר כלפי לייא אלא אימא דברי ר' אחא ג ורבי שמעון מתיר תנא כמה שיעור תבואה ד צבורה לתך בעא מיניה רב נחומי בר זכריה מאביי שיעור תבואה ה צבורה בכמה אמר ליה הרי אמרו שיעור תבואה צבורה לתך איבעיא להו הני ארבע וחמש קופות דקאמר בארבע וחמש קופות אין טפי לא אלמא למעוטי בהילוכא עדיף או דילמא למעוטי משוי עדיף ת"ש דתני חדא מפנין אפילו ארבע וחמש קופות של כדי שמן ושל כדי יין ותניא אידך בעשר ובחמש עשרה מאי לאו בהא קמיפלגי דמר סבר מעוטי בהילוכא עדיף ומר סבר מעוטי במשוי עדיף לא ד דכ"ע מעוטי בהילוכא עדיף ומי סברת בעשר ובחמש עשרה אקופות קאי אכדין קאי ולא קשיא הא דמשתקלי חד חד בקופה והא דמישתקלי תרי תרי והא דמשתקלי תלתא תלתא ובדקורי דהרפניא איבעיא להו הני ארבע וחמש דקאמר אע"ג דאית ליה אורחין טובא או דילמא הכל לפי האורחין ואת"ל הכל לפי האורחין חד גברא מפני לכולהו או דילמא גברא (ב) גברא מפני לנפשיה ת"ש דאמר רבה אמר רבי חייא פעם אחת הלך רבי למקום אחד וראה מקום דחוק לתלמידים ויצא לשדה ומצא שדה מלאה עומרים ועימר רבי כל השדה כולה ו (שמע מינה הכל לפי האורחין) ורב יוסף א"ר הושעיא פעם אחת הלך ר' חייא למקום אחד וראה מקום דחוק לתלמידים ויצא לשדה ומצא שדה מלאה עומרים ועימר ר' חייא כל השדה כולה ה שמע מינה הכל לפי האורחין ועדיין תבעי לך חד גברא מפני ליה לכולא או דילמא כל גברא וגברא מפני לנפשיה ת"ש ועימר רבי ולטעמיך רבי בדנפשיה עימר ו אלא צוה ועימר ולעולם כל חד וחד מפני לנפשיה: מפני האורחין וכו': א"ר יוחנן ה גדולה הכנסת אורחין כהשכמת בית המדרש דקתני מפני האורחין ומפני בטול בית המדרש ורב דימי מנהרדעא אמר יותר מהשכמת בית המדרש דקתני מפני האורחין והדר ומפני בטול בית המדרש ו אמר רב יהודה אמר רב ז גדולה הכנסת אורחין מהקבלת פני שכינה דכתיב א ויאמר ז (ה') אם נא מצאתי חן בעיניך אל נא תעבור וגו' א"ר אלעזר בא וראה שלא כמדת הקב"ה מדת בשר ודם מדת ב"ו אין קטן יכול לומר לגדול המתן עד שאבא אצלך ואילו בהקדוש ברוך הוא כתיב ויאמר ח (ה') אם נא מצאתי וגו' אמר רב יהודה בר שילא א"ר אסי א"ר יוחנן ח ששה דברים אדם אוכל פירותיהן בעולם הזה והקרן קיימת לו לעולם הבא ואלו הן הכנסת אורחין וביקור חולים ט ועיון תפלה והשכמת בית המדרש והמגדל בניו לתלמוד תורה ט והדן את חברו לכף זכות איני והא אנן תנן י אלו דברים שאדם עושה אותם ואוכל פירותיהן בעולם הזה והקרן קיימת לו לעולם הבא ואלו הן כיבוד אב ואם וגמילות חסדים והבאת שלום שבין אדם לחברו י ות"ת כנגד כולם כ [הני אין מידי אחרינא לא]

הני

רש"י

כדאמרי אינשי. תשבון קטן תחילה ואם יצטרך ליותר יפנה יותר משום הכי נקט ד' ברישא והדר חמשה וה"ה אפילו טובא: שלא יגמור. משום אשויי גומות: ברגלו. מפנה ברגלו לכאן ולכאן דרך הליכתו דלא הוי טלטול: תבואה צבורה. מוכחא מילתא דהוקצה לאוצר: להסתפק. להאכיל לבהמתו: אסור דברי ר"ש ורבי אחא כו': כלפי לייא. כנגד היכן פונה הדבר הזה האמור להיפך ר"ש מתיר מוקצה בכל מקום וכאן הוא מחמיר: לייא. היכן כגון אנבי לנהרא כגני לייא דברכות (דף נח.): לתך. אבל בציר מהכי לאו אוצר הוא: לתך. חצי כור הוא ט"ו סאין: בד' וה' קופות אין טפי לא. בקופות עצמן הוא יפנה וימלאם אם ירצה או שק בכתפו שיעור קופה בפעם אחת אבל טפי להלך יותר מה' פעמים כגון לפנות בכלים קטנים וירבה בהילוך לא: למעוטי בהילוכא עדיף. ואע"ג דאפושי משוי הוא: או דילמא מעוטי משוי עדיף. ואם בא לפנות בכלים קטנים כשיעור ה' קופות מותר ולרב חסדא קבעי לה דאמר ה' דוקא: בי' ובט"ו. קס"ד אקופות קאי לומר שמפנה בקופות קטנות וירבה בהילוך: אכדין קאי. ולא פליגי והכי קאמר בי' בט"ו יפנה באותן ה' קופות: הא דמשתקלי חדא חדא בקופה. הך דתניא ד' וה' ולא נחת למניינא דכדין איירי בכדין גדולים דמשתקלי חדא בקופה והך דתנא בי' וט"ו איירי בכדים בינונים ובכדין קטנים עשר כדמשתקלי תרי תרי בקופה ט"ו כדמשתקלי תלתא תלתא בקופה דקטנים: כי דקורי דהרפניא. ל) בכדין של הרפניא: איבעיא להו. אליבא דרב חסדא: דחוק לתלמידים. שאין מקום לתלמידים להושיב: ועימר. פנה את העומרים וכרמלית הואי ובפחות פחות מד' אמות: ת"ש ועימר רבי. אלמא חד גברא פנינהו: רבי בנפשיה עימר. בתמיה וכי אורחיה דנשיא בהכי: כהשכמת ביהמ"ד. מדשוי להו במתני' כי הדדי: מהשכמת בית המדרש. דתנא דידן אקדמה ברישא: אל נא תעבור. והניחו והלך לקבל האורחים: ועיון תפלה. לכוין בתפלתו:

הכי

תוספות

של כדי שמן ושל כדי יין. והא דתנן בפ' המביא (ביצה דף כט:) כדי יין לא יביאם בסל ובקופה היינו ממקום רחוק דמיחזי כעובדין דחול אבל הכא הכל בביתו: דכולי עלמא למעוטי בהלוכא עדיף. לא מצי למימר למעוטי במשוי עדיף דההיא דקתני ד' וה' קופות לא מצי סבר הכי דא"כ הוה ליה למיתני בעשר וט"ו כשיעור ה' קופות וא"ת והא תנן בפרק אין צדין (שם דף כה.) שחטה בשדה לא יביאנה במוט ובמוטה אלא מביאה לאיברים אף על גב דמפיש בהילוכא התם שאני דאיכא טירחא יותר מדאי להביאה שלימה א"נ משום דמיחזי כמוליכה למכור בשוק והא דאמרינן בריש שואל (לקמן דף קמח.) היכי ליעבד דמליא בחצבא רבא תימלי בחצבא זוטא קא מפשא בהילוכא דמליא בחצבא זוטא תמלא בחצבא רבא קא מפשא במשוי התם כיון שנהגו למלאות המים בחצבא רבא או בחצבא זוטא קשה להם לשנות מכמות שנהגו: אע"ג דאית ליה אורחין טובא או דילמא הכל לפי האורחין. מכאן יש להוכיח דהא דתנן במתניתין ד' וה' קופות הוי אפי' בשביל אדם אחד דאי הוי נמי לפי האורחין אמאי נקט ד' וה' ועוד מדלא מספקא ליה אי חד מפני כולהו או כל חד לנפשיה אלא בא"ת הכל לפי האורחין משמע הא אם אמר אף על גב דאיתרמו ליה אורחין טובא ליכא לאיסתפוקי ואי אמרינן דד' וה' קופות הוי לפי האורחין אכתי איכא לספוקי אי חד גברא מפני לכולהו או כל חד מפני לנפשיה אלא משמע דפשיטא דד' וה' אינן לפי האורחין אלא אפילו לצורך אדם אחד: ולטעמיך רבי בנפשיה עימר. פי' כל השדה כולה: דכתיב ויאמר ה' אם נא מצאתי חן וגו'. קסבר כמאן דאמר בשבועות (דף לה:) דהאי השם קדש דאיכא מאן דאמר התם שהוא חול שלמלאכים היה מדבר שהיה מזמינם: אוכל מפירותיהן בעולם הזה. בפ"ק דקדושין (דף לט:) מפ' דהיינו אם היתה מ) שקולה מכרעת דשכר מצות בהאי עלמא ליכא:

כיון

עין משפט נר מצוה

ב א מיי' פכ"ו מהל' שבת הלכה טו טוש"ע שם:
ג ב ג מיי' שם הלכה יד וטוש"ע שם:
ד ד טוש"ע שם סעיף ג:
ה ה ו מיי' וסמג שם טוש"ע שם ס"ג:
ו ז מיי' פי"ד מהלכות אבל הלכה ב:
ז ח סמג עשין יג:
ח ט מיי' פ"ה מהלכות דעות הלכה ז וסה"ג מהלכות סנהדרין הלכה י טוש"ע ח"מ סימן יז סעיף י:
ט י מיי' פ"ג מהלכות ת"ת הלכה ג סמג שם טוש"ע י"ד סימן רמו סעיף יח:

רבינו חננאל

מתחילין באוצר תחלה ולא בתבואה צבורה. ומדבעא רב נחומי כמה שיעורי תבואה צבורה. ותנא כמה שיעור תבואה צבורה לתך ש"מ דהלכתא כהני מתניתא מדקדק[ו]חינן לפרושי טעמייהו ויש מי שאומר הלכתא כשמואל דמוקים למתניתין כרבי שמעון דלית ליה מוקצה והלכתא כוותיה. ולתך זה האמור כאן הוא שיעור הקופות ששנינו במשנתנו. ואע"ג דלא איתאמרא בהדיא בגמרא דילן הא איתפרש בתלמוד א"י. ר' זעירא שאל לר' יאשיה כמה שיעור הקופות. א"ל נלמד סתום מן המפורש דתנינן תמן בג' קופות של ג' ג' סאין תורמין את הלשכה. ושיעור לתך חצי כור והוא ט"ו סאין. נמצא שיעור המשנה והברייתא שיעור אחד. ובדאוקמה רב חסדא למתני' [illegible] והכין שמעתא דא סלקא ועלה קמבעיא לן מעוטי בהלוכא עדיף או מעוטי במשוי עדיף. ואמרי' ת"ש דתני חדא מפנין אפילו ד' וה' קופות של כדי יין וכדי שמן. ותניא אידך בעשר ובחמש עשרה. ואוקימנא להו דכ"ע מעוטי בהילוכא עדיף. ושיעורם אחד הם. ואכדין קאי ולא אקופות והא מתניתא דקתני חמש הכין פירושא. חמש כדות גדולות שאין מכילה הקופה יותר מכדה אחת. והא מתניתא דקתני בעשר ובחמש עשרה בעשר כדות בחמש קופות והן בינוניות שנמצאו ב' כדות בכל קופה הא דתני ט"ו ג' כדות בכל קופה והן דמשתקלי תלת בכל קופה כגון דקורי הרפניא פי' כדות שעושין בהרפניא והן קטנות ונוטלות ג' ג' בקופה שנמצא שיעור משקל כל כדה קטנה סאה והבינונית סאה וחצי. והגדולה ג' סאין. ותוב איבעיא לן הני דקא מפנינן ד' או ה' קופות מפני האורחין אע"פ דאית ליה אורחין הרבה אין לו רשות לפנות יותר מזה השיעור או דילמא הכל לפי האורחין ואם תמצא לומר [illegible] כשמפנין אחד מפנה לכולן או כל אחד מפנה לעצמו ואיפשיטא שמעתא הכל לפי האורחין אם יש לו אורחין הרבה מפנין להן כל צרכן. ובאנו לדקדק מדקתני ועימר רבי את כל השדה שאחד מפנה לכולן (ולא עמר) [והדרן וליטעמיך] וכי ר' בעצמו עימר אלא צוה ועימרו. ולעולם כל חד וחד לנפשיה וכיון דלא איפשיט בהדיא חד מפנה לכולהו מחמרינן לפנויי כל דחד וחד לנפשיה דאיסורא הוא. וסתמא לחומרא. זה נכון [illegible] מהא (לעיל דף קכ"ה ע"ב) דא"ר חנניה פעם אחד הלך רבי למקום אחד ומצא נדבך של אבנים ואמר לתלמידיו צאו וחשבו כדי שנשב עליהן למחר ולא סמך במחשבתו שלו אלא הצריך כל אחד לעצמו [illegible] כטעמיה. פי' נדבך של אבנים אבנים סדורות זו ע"ג זו. ושפשפום לשפשפם [illegible] זו. גשוש בלשון ישמעאל עירים ספינות. נגדר בלשון ישמעאל מתרו ופינוי [illegible] שניהם שוין בדבר מצוה ושאר השמועה פשוטה היא. והא דתנן מפנין ד' וה' [illegible]

רב נסים גאון

כמה שיעור תבואה לתך. הלתך הוא חצי כור והוא ט"ו כי הכור הוא ל' סאה והכור והחומר מדה אחת כי תרגום חומר כורא כמו שאתה מוצא ביחזקאל (מה) האיפה והבת תוכן אחד להם ואמר התרגום מכילת וביתא טוקס חד יהי לכון סכום תלת סאין למיסב מעשר כורא הרי נתברר לו מיכן כי החומר הוא כור וכי הבת היא ג' סאין ואמר אחר כך כי עשרת הבתים חומר נמצא שיעור הכור ל' ושם אמר (הושע ג) וחומר שעורים ולתך שעורים ואמרו חכמינו בפרק גיד הנשה (חולין דף צב.) אלו ארבעים וחמשה צדיקים החומר ל' ולתך ט"ו הכל מ"ה נתקיים לך כי הכור הוא שני לתכים:

שמא

מסורת הש"ס

א) [ביצה לו.], ב) [מלת צבורה ליתא בשאלתות פרשת ויקהל סי' יא], ג) [ג"י ליתא שם], ד) [ג"י ליתא שם], ה) רש"ל מ"ז, ו) [שבועות לה:], ז) [צ"ל אדנין], ח) [צ"ל אדנין], ט) [עי' תוספות לעיל קיח: ד"ה עיון ותוספות ברכות לג: ד"ה כל ותוס' ב"ב קסד: ד"ה שלשה], י) פאה פ"א מ"א קדושין לט: ע"ש, כ) [illegible], ל) [illegible], מ) [illegible]

הגהות הב"ח

(א) גמ' שלא יגמור כולו (דילמא וכו' גומות) תא"מ וג"ב ס"ל נמחק: (ב) שם או דילמא גברא וגברא:

גליון הש"ס

גמרא גדולה הכנסת אורחים. עי' ב"מ דף פו ע"ב ותוספות שם ד"ה מיד:

תורה אור השלם

א) וַיֹּאמַר אֲדֹנָי אִם נָא מָצָאתִי חֵן בְּעֵינֶיךָ אַל נָא תַעֲבֹר מֵעַל עַבְדֶּךָ: [בראשית יח, ג]

ליקוטי רש"י

שלא יגמור כולו. אם לא היו שם אלא ארבע או חמש קופות שהתירו לו במקום שיש יותר כאן לא התירו לפנות כולן ולגלות את הקרקע דאמר הוי בה גומא ומשוה לה [ביצה לו.]. אשויי גומות. דמלאכה הוא בשבת דהוי כבנין [עירובין קד.]. כלפי לייא. [illegible] היכן נוטה דבר זה. לייא. היכן ומצירו בברכות בפרק הרואה (נח.) אנבי לנהרא כגני לייא תרסים שבורים [פסחים ה:]. כלפי היכא נהפך דבר זה [לעיל צג:]. כנגד איפוא הדבר הזה קוכב [כתובות טו.]. כנגד איפוא הפכת דבריך [illegible] בברכות (נח.) כגני לייא כדים שבורים להיכן הולכים [סוטה מד.]. כנגד מה שונה כאן ולאן הדבר נוטה [illegible] (נח.) אנבי לנהרא כגני לייא הקדירות שלמות הולכין לנהר לשאוב בהן מים אבל השבורין להיכן הולכין [ב"ב קד:]. דקורי דהרפנאי. סלים שעושין בהרפניא [ב"מ פד.]. ויאמר [אדני] אם נא וגו'. דבר אחר, קודש הוא [illegible] להמתין לו עד שירוץ ויכניס את האורחים [בראשית יח, ג ועי' כאן בתוס']. כתיב לעיל מינה וירא עליו ה' [illegible] אנשים ואמר להקב"ה אל נא תעבור מעל עבדך המתן לי כאן עד שאכניס האורחין [שבועות לה:]. והדן את חברו לכף זכות. כרואה חבירו עושה דבר שאתה יכול להכריעו לצד עבירה ולצד זכות הכריעו לזכות ואל תחשדהו בעבירה [שם ל.]. על כל שתשמע עליו אמור שנתכוון לטובה עד שתדע בבירור שאינו [illegible] בפרק מפנין [אבות פ"א מ"ו]. והבאת שלום. תשלום שכר גדול להבאת שלום שאוכל פירותיהן בעולם הזה והקרן קיימת לו לעולם הבא כגמילות חסדים דכתיב בהו ימצא חיים צדקה [illegible]

עין משפט נר מצוה

י א מיי' פכ"ה מהלכות שבת הלכה כ:
יא ב שם הלכה יב:
יב ג מיי' פ"ט מהלכות מעשר הלכה ג:
יג ד מיי' פ"ג מהלכות תרומות הלכה יג טור י"ד סימן שלא:
יד ה מיי' פכ"ה מהל' שבת הלכה יט:

גמרא

הני נמי (בגמילות חסדים שייכי ל"א הני) בהני שייכי ת"ר הדן חבירו לכף זכות דנין אותו לזכות ומעשה באדם אחד שירד מגליל העליון ונשכר אצל בעה"ב אחד בדרום שלש שנים ערב יוה"כ אמר לו תן לי שכרי ואלך ואזון את אשתי ובני אמר לו אין לי מעות אמר לו תן לי פירות אמר לו אין לי תן לי קרקע אין לי תן לי בהמה אין לי תן לי כרים וכסתות אין לי הפשיל כליו לאחוריו והלך לביתו בפחי נפש לאחר הרגל נטל בעה"ב שכרו בידו ועמו משוי ג' חמורים אחד של מאכל ואחד של משתה ואחד של מיני מגדים והלך לו לביתו אחר שאכלו ושתו נתן לו שכרו אמר לו בשעה שאמרת לי תן לי שכרי ואמרתי אין לי מעות במה חשדתני אמרתי שמא פרקמטיא בזול נזדמנה לך ולקחת בהן ובשעה שאמרת לי תן לי בהמה ואמרתי אין לי בהמה במה חשדתני אמרתי שמא מושכרת ביד אחרים בשעה שאמרת לי תן לי קרקע ואמרתי לך אין לי קרקע במה חשדתני אמרתי שמא מוחכרת ביד אחרים (א) היא ובשעה שאמרתי לך אין לי פירות במה חשדתני אמרתי שמא אינן מעושרות ובשעה שאמרתי לך אין לי כרים וכסתות במה חשדתני אמרתי שמא הקדיש כל נכסיו לשמים א"ל העבודה כך היה הדרתי כל נכסי בשביל הורקנוס בני שלא עסק בתורה וכשבאתי אצל חבירי בדרום התירו לי כל נדרי ואתה כשם שדנתני לזכות המקום ידין אותך לזכות ת"ר מעשה בחסיד אחד שפדה ריבה אחת בת ישראל ולמלון השכיבה תחת מרגלותיו למחר ירד וטבל ושנה לתלמידיו ואמר להן בשעה שהשכבתיה תחת מרגלותי במה חשדתוני אמרנו שמא יש בנו תלמיד שאינו בדוק לרבי בשעה שירדתי וטבלתי במה חשדתוני אמרנו שמא מפני טורח הדרך אירע קרי לרבי אמר להם העבודה כך היה ואתם כשם שדנתוני לכף זכות המקום ידין אתכם לכף זכות תנו רבנן פעם אחת הוצרך דבר אחד לתלמידי חכמים אצל מטרוניתא אחת שכל גדולי רומי מצויין אצלה אמרו מי ילך אמר להם ר' יהושע אני אלך הלך רבי יהושע ותלמידיו כיון שהגיע לפתח ביתה חלץ תפיליו ברחוק ארבע אמות ונכנס ונעל הדלת בפניהן אחר שיצא ירד וטבל ושנה לתלמידיו ואמר להן בשעה שחלצתי תפילין במה חשדתוני אמרנו כסבור רבי לא יכנסו דברי קדושה במקום טומאה בשעה שנעלתי במה חשדתוני אמרנו שמא דבר מלכות יש בינו לבינה בשעה שירדתי וטבלתי במה חשדתוני אמרנו שמא ניתזה צינורא מפיה על בגדיו של רבי אמר להם העבודה כך היה ואתם כשם שדנתוני לזכות המקום ידין אתכם לזכות: **מפנין תרומה טהורה וכו':** פשיטא לא צריכא דמנחה ביד ישראל מהו דתימא כיון דלא חזיא ליה אסור קמ"ל כיון דחזיא לכהן שפיר דמי: **ודמאי (וכו'):** דמאי הא לא חזי ליה כיון דאי בעי מפקר ליה לנכסיה והוה עני וחזיא ליה השתא נמי חזי ליה דתנן מאכילין את העניים דמאי ואת האכסניא דמאי ואמר רב הונא תנא ב"ש אומרים אין מאכילין את העניים דמאי ואת האכסניא דמאי ובה"א מאכילין את העניים דמאי ואת האכסניא דמאי: **ומעשר ראשון שניטלה תרומתו וכו':** פשיטא לא צריכא שהקדימו בשבולים ונטלה הימנו תרומת מעשר ולא נטלה הימנו תרומה גדולה וכי הא דא"ר אבהו אר"ל מעשר ראשון שהקדימו בשבולין פטור מתרומה גדולה שנא' והרמותם ממנו תרומת ה' מעשר מן המעשר מעשר מן המעשר אמרתי לך ולא תרומה גדולה ותרומת מעשר מן המעשר א"ל רב פפא לאביי א"ה אפי' הקדימו בכרי נמי ליפטר א"ל עליך אמר קרא מכל מתנותיכם תרימו וגו' ומה ראית האי אידגן והאי לא אידגן: **ומעשר שני וכו':** פשיטא לא צריכא שנתן את הקרן ולא נתן את החומש הא קמ"ל דאין חומש מעכב: **והתורמס היבש כו':** דווקא יבש אבל לח לא מ"ט כיון דמריר לא אכלה: אבל

רש"י

ה"ג הני נמי בהני שייכי. הכנסת אורחים וביקור חולים היינו גמילות חסדים ועיון תפלה היינו בכלל גמילות חסדים דכתיב (משלי יא) גומל נפשו איש חסד (א) השכמת בית המדרש וגידול בנים לתלמוד תורה היינו תלמוד תורה דן את חבירו לכף זכות היינו בכלל הבאת שלום דמתוך שהוא מכריעו לזכות ואמר לא חטא לי בזאת אנוס היה או לטובה נתכוון הוא שלום ביניהן ורבי יוחנן ופרק לך אתא דבכלל ג' דמתניתין איתנהו להנך ו' ואיכא נמי לכבוד אב ואם ורבי יוחנן לא פליג עליה: **בפחי נפש.** בדאבון נפש: **מוחכרת.** שנותנה לחברו בכך וכך כורין לשנה: (ב) כל היכא דאמרינן מעשה בחסיד אחד או ברבי יהודה בן בבא או רבי יהודה ברבי אלעאי: **ריבה.** נערה: **שאינו בדוק לרבי.** שאינו מכיר במדותיו לסמוך עליו והניחה אצלנו: **מטרוניתא.** נכרית: **דבר מלכות.** ולריך להעלימו: **צינורא.** רוק וגזרו על הנכרים שיהיו כזבים לכל דבריהם: **מאכילין לעניים דמאי.** לא אסרוהו עליהם מפני שהרבים לחזור על פתח ע"ה וסמכו על שרוב עמי הארץ מעשרין: **אכסניא.** (ג) חיל של מלך ישראל ומטיל על בני העיר לפרנסן: **שניטלה תרומתו.** קס"ד תרומת מעשר שהלוי נותן לכהן וכ"ש תרומה גדולה שיש על ישראל להפרים והפרישו קודם שנתן המעשר ללוי: **שהקדימו בשבולין.** לתרומה ישראל היה לו להפרים תרומה גדולה תחילה דכתיב (שמות כב) מלאתך ודמעך לא תאחר מלאתך אלו בכורים מכאן שהמקדים תרומה לבכורים לוקה ודמעך זו תרומה שאם הקדים מעשר לתרומה לוקה והנ"מ משנתמרח בכרי לוקה אם הקדים מעשר לתרומה אבל הקדים למעשר קודם לתרומה בשבלים אינו לוקה: **והרמותם ממנו.** בלוים כתיב גבי תרומת מעשר: **מכל מתנותיכם וגו'.** נמי בלוים כתיב גבי תרומת מעשר וקאמר את כל תרומת ה' כל משמע כל לד תרומה שבו: **האי.** דנתמרח: **אידגן.** וחלה עליו חובת תרומה כדכתיב (דברים יח) ראשית דגנך הלכך כי שקלה לוי בעי אהדורי לכהן תרי ממאה שבו ברישא והדר אחד מעשרה: **דמריר.** שהוא מר: שלא

תוספות

כיון דחזיא לכהן שפיר דמי. אע"ג דאמר בשילהי כירה (לעיל דף מז.) דבגדי עניים לעשירים לא הכא לכ"ע חזיא אלא איסורא הוא דרביע עליה אבל התם לא חזו מחמת גריעותא ומההוא טעמא נמי לא אמרינן התם טעמא דבסמוך דאי בעי מפקר לנכסיה והא דאמר בפרק כל הכלים (לעיל ד' קכה.) שירי פרוזמיות שאין בהן ג' על ג' אין מטלטלין אותן משמע הא יש בהן שלש על שלש מטלטלים היינו לעניים א"נ אפילו לעשירים בבית עניים: **דאי** בעי מפקר לנכסיה. הוה מצי למימר כדלעיל כיון דחזי אלא כיון דמשכח טעמא דאפי' לדידיה מצי חזי אמר ובפרק כל שעה (פסחים דף לה:) ובפרק שלשה שאכלו (ברכות ד' מז.) אילטריך להאי טעמא: **האי** אידגן. מדנקט אידגן משמע אפי' לא ראה פני הבית תימה אכתי אפילו הקדימו בכרי נמי לא לחייב אלא באידגן וראה פני הבית וי"ל דאי לא כתב והרמותם ה"א דכולם חייבין אפילו לא אידגן השתא דכתי' קרא מוקמי ליה במסתבר דהיינו לא אידגן שאפילו ראה פני הבית לא היה חייב א"נ י"ל הא דנקט אידגן היינו ככל דינו שראה פני הבית אלא דמילתא דפסיקא נקט דאיכא למאן דאמר בבבא מציעא (ד' פח:) דלא בעינן ראיית פני הבית אלא בזיתים וענבים דלאו בני גורן נינהו: **הא** קמ"ל דאין חומש מעכב. ואף על גב דמבעיא לן בפרק הזהב (שם דף נד.) אי מעכב אי לא ולא פשיט מהכא משום דהוה מצי למידחי דאגב אחרינא תנייה: אבל

רבינו חננאל

ומפני ביטול בהמ"ד שהן מצות כדרב יהודה אמר שמואל דאמר גדול הכנסת אורחין. וכדר' יוחנן דאמר אחד משׁשה דברים שאדם אוכל מפירותיהן בעוה"ז והקרן קיימת לו לעולם הבא: **מפנין** תרומה טהורה אע"פ שהיא בביתו של ישראל הואיל וראויה לכהן היום מטלטלין אותה ושפיר דמי וכן דמאי והדמאי כיון דאילו הפקיר כל נכסיו ויהיה עני מותר לאוכלו אע"פ שעכשיו לא הפקיר נכסיו מותר לטלטלו. והוא הלוקח תבואה מעם הארץ שאינו יודע אם הוציא מעשר ממנה אם לאו כי התרומה לא נחשדו עמי הארץ עליה (ודאי) והיו מפרישין אחד מחמשים והוא בבינונית ונתנו לכהן אבל המעשר היו הרבה ע"ה שלא היו מפרישין אותו ונותנין ללוי. וחייבו חכמים הקונה מעם הארץ שאינו יודע אם הוציא מעשר ממנה אם לאו להפריש מזו התבואה חלק אחד ממאה שהיא תרומת מעשר שהוא א' וכל תרומה כאוכל תרומה והוא עון מיתה. וזה פירושו ישראל שיש לו מאה סאין תבואה חייב לתת לכהן ב' סאין מהן והיא נקראת תרומה גדולה וחייב לתת עשרה מהן פחות מעט והוא נקרא מעשר ראשון וחייב הלוי לתת מן העשרה סאין שנתן לו ישראל סאה אחת לכהן והוא שאמר הכתוב והרמותם ממנו תרומת ה' מעשר מן המעשר. נמצא הסאה שביד כהן שהיא תרומת מעשר שנתן לו הלוי אחד ממאה מן התבואה שביד ישראל וכיון שראו שע"ה לא היו מפרישין מעשר לכהן שחייב בו מיתה [לכן חייבהו להפריש] אבל המעשר שהוא בלאו לא חייבהו מספק. וזה מפורש בגמרא יומא א) פ"ק דיוחנן העביר הודיית המעשר בסוף מס' סוטה ודמאי זה כיון שהוא ספק מעושר ספק אינו מעושר התירוהו מפני חיי נפש לאכסניא ולעניים (בפירושו). וזה שאמר ר"ל מעשר ראשון שהקדימו בשבלין פטור מתרומה גדולה פי' חייבה התורה להפריש תרומה ומעשר מן הדגן שכבר נעשה גורן כדכתיב ראשית דגנך תירושך ויצהרך כו' ואינו נקרא דגן אלא אחרי דישתו בגורן והעמדתו כרי והתורה אמרה להפריש מן הדגן ראשון תרומה גדולה ואחריו מעשר ראשון. ואחריו שנה ראשונה ושניה מעשר שני [illegible] להפריש כל אלו אלא אחרי [illegible] עשרה עומרין שבלין וקודם [illegible] תרומת מעשר לכהן שהשבלין [illegible] עליו רב פפא למה הוצרכת [illegible] ליפטר ולא יהא חייב הלוי [illegible] מתנותיכם תרימו שכולל הכל.

מסורת הש"ס

א) מ"א ל"ג, ב) [כרי"ף וכרא"ש ליתא ערב הרגל], ג) [illegible], ד) [נ"ל להם], ה) [נ"ל להם], ו) ברכות דף מז. [illegible], ז) ברכות מז. דמאי פ"ג מ"א עירובין לא:, ח) פסחים לה:, ט) ברכות שם עירובין לא: פסחים לה: ביצה יג:, י) תמורה ה., כ) [illegible], ל) לפרנסן והוזין עניים [illegible], מ) [וע"ע תוספות עירובין לא. ד"ה דאמר ותוס' סוכה לה: ד"ה דאי בעי].

הגהות הב"ח

(א) גמ' אמרתי שמא מוחכרת ביד אחרים ובשעה כצ"ל ותיבת היא נמחק: (ג) רש"י ד"ה אכסניא חיל של מלך ישראל. נ"ב כך פירש"י בפרק בכל מערבין דף לא וכן בפרק כל שעה דף לה אבל התוספות בפ' ג' שאכלו פי' עוד פי' אחר חיל של נכרים כו' וע"ש דף מז:

גליון הש"ס

רש"י ד"ה כל היכא דאמרינן מעשה וכו'. עיין [illegible] תמורה דף טו ע"ב:

תורה אור השלם

א) וְאֶל הַלְוִיִּם תְּדַבֵּר וְאָמַרְתָּ אֲלֵהֶם כִּי תִקְחוּ מֵאֵת בְּנֵי יִשְׂרָאֵל אֶת הַמַּעֲשֵׂר אֲשֶׁר נָתַתִּי לָכֶם מֵאִתָּם בְּנַחֲלַתְכֶם וַהֲרֵמֹתֶם מִמֶּנּוּ תְּרוּמַת יְיָ מַעֲשֵׂר מִן הַמַּעֲשֵׂר: [במדבר יח, כו]

ב) מִכֹּל מַתְּנֹתֵיכֶם תָּרִימוּ אֵת כָּל תְּרוּמַת יְיָ מִכָּל חֶלְבּוֹ אֶת מִקְדְּשׁוֹ מִמֶּנּוּ: [במדבר יח, כט]

רב נסים גאון

שמא ניתזה צינורא מפיה על רבי. פי' צינורא שנתזה מפי האדם כשהוא מדבר למטרונית והיא נכרית ונגע בו מרוקה הוצרך לטבול כי רוקן של נכרים גזרו עליו חכמים טומאה ועיקר זה הוא מה שאמר הכתוב בענין הזב (ויקרא טו) וכי ירוק הזב בטהור יכול אפילו רקק ולא נגע יהא טמא ת"ל בטהור ובתוספתא זבין בפרק חמישי אמרו ורירו וכיחו ומימי האף שלו הרי הן כרוקו דמעת עינו ודם מגפתו וחלב האשה מטמאין טומאת משקה [illegible] אבל לא בנכרים והחכמים הם [illegible] (דף לד) כשאמר בית שמי דם [illegible] אין מי שחולק בו כי הוא טמא [illegible] רוקה ומימי רגליה דשכיחי [illegible] מסכת שקלים (פ"ח מ"א) שנינו כל [illegible] ר' אבון בשם ר' יהושע קצרין של [illegible] כותית כל הרוקין שבעיר טמאין [illegible] כבר נתבאר לך עכשיו ונתקיים מכל [illegible] אמרו ספיקות באושא גזור עליהן [illegible] (דף מז) אמרו עליו על רבי ישמעאל [illegible] אחיו ושימש תחתיו ובחומר בקודש [illegible] טהורה ודמאי. כבר פירשנו דמאי בפ'

ליקוטי רש"י

[illegible] הלוי וקידמו כדי שלא יחסרנו הכהן [illegible] לו ליטול תרומה גדולה תחלה אחד [illegible] שהופרשה תרומה גדולה מן העמרים [illegible] שלא הורמה תרומה גדולה ממעשרו [illegible] פטור הלוי מתרומה גדולה שבמעשר [illegible]. **עליך אמר קרא.** כדי שלא [illegible] א' מחמשים לתרומה גדולה ויחזור [illegible] את כל תרומת ה', ובלוים כתיב ולהכי [illegible] [עירובין שם]. [המשך בדף קכח.]

The Gemara answers:

הָנֵי נַמֵּי (בגמילות חסדים שייכי ל״א הני) בְּהָנֵי שַׁיְיכֵי – **These** precepts enumerated by R' Yochanan **are also related to** and thus included in **those** enumerated by the Mishnah.[1]

One of the precepts enumerated by R' Yochanan is "judging one's fellow man favorably." The Gemara now cites three incidents that exemplify this virtue:

תָּנוּ רַבָּנַן – **The Rabbis taught in a Baraisa:** הַדָּן חֲבֵירוֹ לְכַף זְכוּת דָּנִין אוֹתוֹ לִזְכוּת – ONE WHO JUDGES HIS FELLOW MAN FAVORABLY IS HIMSELF JUDGED FAVORABLY.[2] וּמַעֲשֶׂה בְּאָדָם אֶחָד – AND THERE WAS THE INCIDENT INVOLVING A CERTAIN MAN שֶׁיָּרַד מִגָּלִיל הָעֶלְיוֹן – WHO WENT DOWN FROM UPPER GALILEE וְנִשְׂכַּר אֵצֶל בַּעַל הַבַּיִת אֶחָד בַּדָּרוֹם שָׁלֹשׁ שָׁנִים – AND ENTERED THE EMPLOY OF A CERTAIN HOMEOWNER IN THE SOUTH FOR THREE YEARS.[3] עֶרֶב יוֹם הַכִּפּוּרִים – ON THE EVE OF YOM KIPPUR following his three years of work,[4] אָמַר לוֹ – [THE WORKER] SAID TO [THE HOMEOWNER]: תֵּן לִי שְׂכָרִי וְאֵלֵךְ וְאָזוּן אֶת אִשְׁתִּי וּבָנַי – "GIVE ME MY WAGES, AND I WILL GO AND PROVIDE FOR MY WIFE AND CHILDREN." אָמַר לוֹ אֵין לִי מָעוֹת – [THE HOMEOWNER] REPLIED TO HIM: "I HAVE NO MONEY." אָמַר לוֹ תֵּן לִי פֵּירוֹת – SAID [THE WORKER] TO HIM: "Then GIVE ME my wages in the form of PRODUCE." אָמַר לוֹ אֵין לִי – HE SAID TO [THE WORKER]: "I HAVE NONE." תֵּן לִי קַרְקַע – Said the worker: "Then GIVE ME LAND." אֵין לִי – Replied his employer: "I HAVE NONE." תֵּן לִי בְּהֵמָה – Said the worker: "Then GIVE ME LIVESTOCK." אֵין לִי – Replied the employer: "I HAVE NONE." תֵּן לִי כָּרִים וּכְסָתוֹת – Said the worker: "Then GIVE ME PILLOWS AND CUSHIONS." אֵין לִי – Replied his employer: "I HAVE NONE." הִפְשִׁיל כֵּלָיו לַאֲחוֹרָיו – Unable to obtain any of the wages due him, [THE WORKER] SLUNG HIS BELONGINGS OVER HIS BACK וְהָלַךְ לְבֵיתוֹ בְּפַחֵי נֶפֶשׁ – AND RETURNED HOME DEJECTEDLY. לְאַחַר הָרֶגֶל – AFTER THE FESTIVAL,[5] נָטַל בַּעַל הַבַּיִת שְׂכָרוֹ בְּיָדוֹ – THE HOMEOWNER TOOK [THE WORKER'S] WAGES IN HIS HAND וְעִמּוֹ מַשּׂוֹי שְׁלֹשָׁה חֲמוֹרִים – ALONG WITH THREE DONKEY-LOADS OF goods – אֶחָד שֶׁל מַאֲכָל – ONE donkey-load OF FOOD, וְאֶחָד שֶׁל מִשְׁתֶּה – AND ONE OF DRINK וְאֶחָד שֶׁל מִינֵי מְגָדִים – AND ONE OF VARIOUS SWEET DELICACIES – וְהָלַךְ לוֹ לְבֵיתוֹ – AND TRAVELED TO HIS former worker's HOUSE in the Upper Galilee. אַחַר שֶׁאָכְלוּ וְשָׁתוּ נָתַן לוֹ שְׂכָרוֹ – AFTER THEY HAD EATEN AND DRUNK, HE PAID [THE WORKER] HIS WAGES.[6] אָמַר לוֹ – HE then SAID TO [THE WORKER]: בְּשָׁעָה שֶׁאָמַרְתָּ לִי תֵּן לִי שְׂכָרִי – "WHEN YOU SAID TO ME, 'GIVE ME MY WAGES,' וְאָמַרְתִּי אֵין לִי מָעוֹת – AND I SAID, 'I HAVE NO MONEY,' בַּמֶּה חֲשַׁדְתַּנִי – OF WHAT DID YOU SUSPECT ME?" אָמַרְתִּי שֶׁמָּא פְּרַקְמַטְיָא בְּזוֹל נִזְדַּמְּנָה לְךָ וְלָקַחְתָּ בָּהֶן – The worker replied: "I SAID to myself that PERHAPS UNDERPRICED MERCHANDISE CAME YOUR WAY AND YOU BOUGHT it WITH [THE MONIES] that you would have otherwise used to pay my wages.[7] וּבְשָׁעָה שֶׁאָמַרְתָּ לִי תֵּן לִי בְּהֵמָה – The employer pressed on: "AND WHEN YOU SAID TO ME, 'GIVE ME LIVESTOCK,' וְאָמַרְתִּי אֵין לִי בְּהֵמָה – AND I SAID TO YOU, 'I HAVE NO LIVESTOCK,' בַּמֶּה חֲשַׁדְתַּנִי – OF WHAT DID YOU SUSPECT ME?" אָמַרְתִּי שֶׁמָּא מוּשְׂכֶּרֶת בְּיַד אֲחֵרִים – The worker replied: "I SAID to myself that PERHAPS THEY WERE LEASED TO OTHERS." בְּשָׁעָה שֶׁאָמַרְתָּ לִי תֵּן לִי קַרְקַע – Continued the employer: "And WHEN YOU SAID TO ME, 'GIVE ME LAND,' וְאָמַרְתִּי לְךָ אֵין לִי קַרְקַע – AND I SAID TO YOU, 'I HAVE NO LAND,' בַּמֶּה חֲשַׁדְתַּנִי – OF WHAT DID YOU SUSPECT ME?" אָמַרְתִּי שֶׁמָּא מוּחְכֶּרֶת בְּיַד אֲחֵרִים הִיא – The worker replied: "I SAID to myself that PERHAPS IT WAS LEASED TO OTHERS."[8] וּבְשָׁעָה שֶׁאָמַרְתִּי לְךָ אֵין לִי פֵּירוֹת – The employer asked further: "AND WHEN I SAID TO YOU, 'I HAVE NO PRODUCE,' בַּמֶּה חֲשַׁדְתַּנִי – OF WHAT DID YOU SUSPECT ME?" אָמַרְתִּי שֶׁמָּא אֵינָן מְעוּשָּׂרוֹת – The worker answered: "I SAID to myself that PERHAPS you could not give it to me because IT WAS NOT TITHED."[9] וּבְשָׁעָה שֶׁאָמַרְתִּי לְךָ אֵין לִי כָּרִים וּכְסָתוֹת בַּמֶּה חֲשַׁדְתַּנִי – The employer continued: "AND WHEN I SAID

NOTES

1. The six precepts listed by R' Yochanan are: (a) receiving guests; (b) visiting the sick; (c) concentration during prayer; (d) rising early to attend the study hall; (e) raising one's children to the study of Torah; and (f) judging one's fellow favorably. The first two precepts ("receiving guests" and "visiting the sick") are clearly included in "bestowing kindness" (number two in the Mishnah's list). Similarly, "concentration during prayer" is a form of "bestowing kindness," for it is written in *Mishlei* (11:17): גֹּמֵל נַפְשׁוֹ אִישׁ חָסֶד, *One who bestows goodness to himself is a man of kindness.* [Certainly, one who prays sincerely is bestowing goodness upon himself. Moreover,] the word נַפְשׁוֹ used in this verse can be understood as a direct allusion to prayer, as we find in *I Samuel* 1:15: וָאֶשְׁפֹּךְ אֶת־נַפְשִׁי לִפְנֵי ה׳, *and I poured out my "nefesh"* [i.e. prayer] *before Hashem.* "Rising early to attend the study hall" and "raising one's children to the study of Torah" are included in "studying Torah" mentioned by the Mishnah. And "judging one's fellow favorably" is included in the precept of "bringing peace between people." For when one judges his fellow's negative actions against him favorably, by assuming that his fellow was coerced or that he really intended to benefit him, they are at peace with one another.

Thus, R' Yochanan simply means to elaborate on the Mishnah, by showing how these six precepts are in fact contained in three of the four listed by the Mishnah. These, together with the fourth precept mentioned by the Mishnah – honoring one's father and mother – (whose inclusion R' Yochanan does not dispute), comprise the precepts whose incidental benefits one enjoys in this world, while the principal remains intact for him in the World to Come (*Rashi,* as emended by *Mesoras HaShas,* based on the way *Rashi's* comments are cited by *Rash* to *Peah* 1:1; see also *Ritva MHK* ed.).

2. By God (*She'iltos* §40). Alternatively, it means that he is judged favorably by his fellow man (see *Sfas Emes*).

3. The homeowner was the Tanna R' Eliezer ben Horkenos, and the employee was R' Akiva (see *She'iltos* §40) before he became a scholar. Thus, even before R' Akiva became a scholar, he was possessed of sterling character [as will emerge from the incident cited here] (*Chasam Sofer* from *Teshuvos Rama MiFano* §63; see also *Haamek She'eilah* to *She'iltos* loc. cit., from *Kesubos* end of 62b, and *Maharsha* to *Kesubos* ad loc.).

4. See *She'iltos* loc. cit.

5. [I.e. Succos, which occurs five days after Yom Kippur.]

6. [See *Chasam Sofer,* who discusses the *ribbis* implications of the employer giving the three extra donkey-loads of goods to his worker in addition to the delayed wages. See also *Hagahos Yavetz.*]

7. [And the worker could not be paid with that merchandise itself, since the employer had subsequently consecrated it – see Gemara below (*Chasam Sofer*; cf. *Maharsha*).]

Apparently, it would be permitted for the employer to buy underpriced merchandise with money he would eventually need to pay his worker, as long as the worker's wages are not yet due. If the merchandise is not underpriced, though, the employer should rather keep the money on hand than place himself in a position where he will not be able to fulfill his obligation to pay the worker when the wages come due. Once the wages are due, however, then the employer is Biblically prohibited from spending the money that he owes the worker, regardless of the commercial opportunities. In the present case, R' Akiva surmised that the money had been spent on underpriced merchandise before his wages had come due (see *Sfas Emes*; see also *Ahavas Chesed* I:9:10 with note 26 there). [In *She'iltos'* version of the incident, however, R' Akiva saw that R' Eliezer still had money in his possession, and surmised that R' Eliezer wanted to *withhold* the money for himself in order to buy underpriced fields and vineyards. Apparently, then, we must say that R' Akiva did not wish to demand his wages immediately where this would cause financial hardship to his employer, and R' Eliezer knew this (see *Haamek She'eilah* loc. cit.).]

8. חֲכִירוּת is the leasing of land to a tenant-farmer, who pays for his lease with a fixed amount of produce from the crops that he grows (*Rashi*).

9. And one is not permitted to give untithed produce to an unlearned person, which is what the worker was [see above, note 3] (*Sfas Emes*). [As to why the employer could not have tithed his produce then and there, see *Maharsha,* and *Haamek She'eilah* loc. cit.)

עין משפט נר מצוה

י א מיי׳ פכ״ה מהלכות שבת הלכה כ:
יא ב שם הלכה יט:
יב ג מיי׳ פ״י מהלכות מעשר הלכה יא:
יג ד מיי׳ פ״ג מהלכות תרומות הלכה יג טור י״ד סימן שלא:
יד ה מיי׳ פכ״ה מהל׳ שבת הלכה יט:

כיון דחזיא לכהן שפיר דמי. אע״ג דאמר בשילהי כירה (לעיל דף מז.) דבגדי עניים לעשירים לא הכא לכ״ע חזיא אלא איסורא הוא דרביע עליה אבל התם לא חזו מחמת גריעותא ומהאי טעמא נמי לא אמרינן התם טעמא דבסמוך דאי בעי מפקר לנכסיה והא דאמר בפרק כל הכלים (לעיל דף קכה.) שירי פרוזמיות שאין בהן ג׳ על ג׳ אין מטלטלין אותן משמע הא יש בהן שלש על שלש מטלטלים היינו לעניים א״נ אפילו לעשירים בבית עניים: **דאי** בעי מפקר לנכסיה. הוה מצי למימר כדלעיל כיון דחזי אלא כיון דמשכח טעמא דאפי׳ לדידיה מצי חזי אמר ובפרק כל שעה (פסחים דף לה:) ובפרק שלשה שאכלו (ברכות ד׳ מז.) איצטריך להאי טעמא: **האי** אידגן. מדנקט אידגן משמע אפי׳ לא ראה פני הבית תימה אכתי אפילו הקדימו בכרי נמי לא לחייב אלא באידגן וראה פני הבית וי״ל דאי לא כתב והרמותם ה״א דכולם חייבין אפילו לא אידגן השתא דכתי׳ קרא מוקמי ליה במסתבר דהיינו לא אידגן שאפילו ראה פני הבית לא היה חייב א״נ י״ל הא דנקט אידגן היינו ככל דינו שראה פני הבית אלא דמילתא דפסיקא נקט דאיכא למאן דאמר בבבא מציעא (ד׳ פח:) דלא בעינן ראיית פני הבית אלא בזיתים וענבים דלאו בני גורן נינהו: **הא** קמ״ל דאין חומש מעכב. ואף על גב דמבעיא לן בפרק הזהב (שם דף נד.) אי מעכב אי לא ולא פשיט מהכא משום דהוה מצי למידחי דלאגב אחרינא תנייה: אבל

הני נמי (א) (בגמילות חסדים שייכי ל״א הני) בהני שייכי ת״ר הדן חבירו לכף זכות דנין אותו לזכות ומעשה באדם אחד שירד מגליל העליון ונשכר אצל בעה״ב אחד בדרום שלש שנים ערב ב יוה״כ אמר לו תן לי שכרי ואלך ואזון את אשתי ובני אמר לו אין לי מעות אמר לו תן לי פירות אמר לו אין לי תן לי קרקע אין לי תן לי בהמה אין לי תן לי כרים וכסתות אין לי הפשיל כליו לאחוריו והלך לביתו בפחי נפש לאחר הרגל נטל בעה״ב שכרו בידו ועמו משוי ג׳ חמורים אחד של מאכל ואחד של משתה ואחד של מיני מגדים והלך לו לביתו אחר שאכלו ושתו נתן לו שכרו אמר לו בשעה שאמרת לי תן לי שכרי ואמרתי אין לי מעות במה חשדתני אמרתי שמא פרקמטיא בזול נזדמנה לך ולקחת בהן ובשעה שאמרת לי תן לי בהמה ואמרתי אין לי בהמה במה חשדתני אמרתי שמא מושכרת ביד אחרים בשעה שאמרת לי תן לי קרקע ואמרתי לך אין לי קרקע במה חשדתני אמרתי שמא מוחכרת ביד אחרים (א) היא ובשעה שאמרתי לך אין לי פירות במה חשדתני אמרתי שמא אינן מעושרות ובשעה שאמרתי לך אין לי כרים וכסתות במה חשדתני אמרתי שמא הקדיש כל נכסיו לשמים א״ל העבודה כך היה הדרתי כל נכסי בשביל הורקנוס בני שלא עסק בתורה וכשבאתי אצל חבירי בדרום התירו לי כל נדרי ואתה כשם שדנתני לזכות המקום ידין אותך לזכות ת״ר ג מעשה בחסיד אחד שפדה ריבה אחת בת ישראל ולמלון השכיבה תחת מרגלותיו למחר ירד וטבל ושנה לתלמידיו ואמר (ד) להן) בשעה שהשכבתיה תחת מרגלותי במה חשדתוני אמרנו שמא יש בנו תלמיד שאינו בדוק לרבי בשעה שירדתי וטבלתי במה חשדתוני אמרנו שמא מפני טורח הדרך אירע קרי לרבי אמר להם העבודה כך היה ואתם כשם שדנתוני לכף זכות המקום ידין אתכם לכף זכות תנו רבנן פעם אחת הוצרך דבר אחד לתלמידי חכמים אצל מטרוניתא אחת שכל גדולי רומי מצויין אצלה אמרו מי ילך אמר להם ר׳ יהושע אני אלך הלך רבי יהושע ותלמידיו כיון שהגיע לפתח ביתה חלץ תפיליו ברחוק ארבע אמות ונכנס ונעל הדלת בפניהן אחר שיצא ירד וטבל ושנה לתלמידיו ואמר (ה) להן) בשעה שחלצתי תפילין במה חשדתוני אמרנו כסבור רבי לא יכנסו דברי קדושה במקום טומאה בשעה שנעלתי במה חשדתוני אמרנו שמא דבר מלכות יש בינו לבינה בשעה שירדתי וטבלתי במה חשדתוני אמרנו שמא ניתזה צינורא מפיה על בגדיו של רבי אמר להם העבודה כך היה ואתם כשם שדנתוני לזכות המקום ידין אתכם לזכות: מפנין תרומה טהורה וכו׳: פשיטא לא צריכא א דמנחה ביד ישראל מהו דתימא כיון דלא חזיא ליה אסור קמ״ל כיון דחזיא לכהן שפיר דמי: ב ודמאי (וכו׳): דמאי הא לא חזי ליה ו כיון דאי בעי מפקר ליה לנכסיה והוה עני וחזיא ליה השתא נמי חזי ליה ז דתנן ג מאכילין את העניים דמאי ואת האכסניא דמאי ואמר רב הונא תנא ב״ש אומרים אין מאכילין את העניים דמאי ואת האכסניא דמאי וב״ה אומרים מאכילין את העניים דמאי ואת האכסניא דמאי: ומעשר ראשון שניטלה תרומתו וכו׳: פשיטא לא צריכא שהקדימו בשבולים ונטלה הימנו תרומת מעשר ולא נטלה הימנו תרומה גדולה וכי הא ח דא״ר אבהו אר״ל ד מעשר ראשון שהקדימו בשבולין פטור מתרומה גדולה שנא׳ א והרמותם ממנו תרומת ה׳ מעשר מן המעשר מעשר מן המעשר אמרתי לך ולא תרומה גדולה ותרומת מעשר מן המעשר ט א״ל רב פפא לאביי א״ה אפי׳ הקדימו בכרי נמי ליפטר א״ל עליך אמר קרא ב מכל מתנותיכם תרימו וגו׳ ומה ראית האי אידגן והאי לא אידגן: ומעשר שני וכו׳: פשיטא ה לא צריכא שנתן את הקרן ולא נתן את החומש הא קמ״ל דאין חומש מעכב: והתורמס היבש כו׳: דווקא יבש אבל לח לא מ״ט כיון דמריר לא אכלה: אבל

רש״י

ה״ג הני נמי בהני שייכי. הכנסת אורחים וביקור חולים היינו גמילות חסדים ועיון תפלה היינו בכלל גמילות חסדים דכתיב (משלי יא) גומל נפשו איש חסד השכמת בית המדרש וגידול בנים לתלמוד תורה היינו תלמוד תורה דן את חבירו לכף זכות בכלל הבאת שלום דמתוך שהוא מכריעו לזכות ואמר לא חטא לי בזאת אנוס היה או לטובה נתכוון יש שלום ביניהן ורבי יוחנן לפרש לך אתא דבכלל ג׳ דמתניתין איתנהו להנך ו׳ ואיכא נמי לכבוד אב ואם ורבי יוחנן לא פליג עליה: **בפחי נפש.** בדאבון נפש: **מוחכרת.** שנותנה לחברו בכך וכך כורין לשנה: כל היכא דאמרינן ז מעשה בחסיד אחד או רבי יהודה בן בבא או רבי יהודה ברבי אלעאי: **ריבה.** נערה: **שאינו בדוק לרבי.** שאינו מכיר במדותיו לסמוך עליו והניחה אצלנו: **מטרוניתא.** נכרית: **דבר מלכות.** וצריך להעלימו: **צינורא.** רוק וגזרו על הנכרים שיהיו כזבים לכל דבריהם: **מאכילין לעניים דמאי.** לא אסרוהו עליהם מפני שצריכים לחזור על פתח ע״ה וסמכו על שרוב עמי הארץ מעשרין: **אכסניא.** (ב) חיל של מלך ישראל ומטילו על בני העיר לפרנסן ח: **שניטלה תרומתו.** קס״ד תרומת מעשר שהלוי נותן לכהן וכ״ש תרומה גדולה שיש על ישראל להפריש והפרישו קודם שנתן המעשר ללוי: **שהקדימו בשבולין.** לתרומה ישראל היה לו להפריש תרומה גדולה תחילה דכתיב (שמות כב) מלאתך ודמעך לא תאחר מלאתך אלו בכורים מכאן שהמקדים תרומה לבכורים לוקה ודמעך זו תרומה שאם הקדים מעשר לתרומה לוקה והנ״מ משנתמרח בכרי לוקה אם הקדים מעשר לתרומה אבל הקדים למעשר קודם לתרומה בשבלים אינו לוקה: **והרמותם ממנו.** בלוים כתיב גבי תרומת מעשר: **מכל מתנותיכם וגו׳.** נמי בלוים כתיב גבי תרומת מעשר וקאמר את כל תרומת ה׳ כל משמע כל לד תרומה שבו: **האי.** דנתמרח: **אידגן.** ונלה עליו חובת תרומה לדכתיב (דברים יח) ראשית דגנך הלכך כי שקלה לוי בעי להדורי לכהן תרי ממאה שבו בריבא והדר אחד מעשרה: **דמריר.** שהוא מר: שלא

[Hebrew]

רבינו חננאל

ומפני ביטול בהמ״ד שהן מצות כדרב יהודה אמר שמואל דאמר גדול הכנסת אורחין. וכדר׳ יוחנן דאמר אחד משמשה דברים שאדם אוכל מפירותיהן בעוה״ז והקרן קיימת לו לעולם הבא: **מפנין** תרומה טהורה אע״פ שהיא בביתו של ישראל הואיל וראויה לכהן היום מטלטלין אותה ושפיר דמי וכן דמאי והדמאי כיון דאילו הפקיר כל נכסיו ויהיה עני מותר לאוכלו אע״פ שעכשיו לא הפקיר נכסיו מותר לטלטלו. והוא הלוקח תבואה מעם הארץ שאינו יודע אם הוציא מעשר ממנה אם לאו כי התרומה לא נחשדו עמי הארץ עליה (ודאי) והיו מפרישין אחד מחמשים והוא בבינונית ונתנו לכהן אבל המעשר היו הרבה ע״ה שלא היו מפרישין אותו ונותנין ללוי. וחייבו חכמים הקונה מעם הארץ שאינו יודע אם הוציא מעשר ממנה אם לאו להפריש מזו התבואה חלק אחד ממאה שהיא תרומת מעשר שהוא א׳ וכל תרומה כאוכל תרומה והוא עון מיתה. וזה פירושו ישראל שיש לו מאה סאין תבואה חייב לתת לכהן ב׳ סאין מהן והיא נקראת תרומה גדולה

TO YOU, 'I HAVE NO PILLOWS OR CUSHIONS,' OF WHAT DID YOU SUSPECT ME?" אָמַרְתִּי שֶׁמָּא הִקְדִּישׁ כָּל נְכָסָיו לַשָּׁמַיִם – The worker replied: "I SAID to myself that PERHAPS [MY EMPLOYER] HAS CONSECRATED ALL HIS POSSESSIONS TO HEAVEN." אָמַר לֵיהּ הָעֲבוֹדָה כָּךְ הָיָה – Whereupon [THE EMPLOYER] EXCLAIMED TO HIM: "BY THE Divine SERVICE![10] SO IT WAS! הִדַּרְתִּי כָּל נְכָסַי – I HAD VOWED ALL MY POSSESSIONS to Heaven בִּשְׁבִיל הוּרְקָנוֹס בְּנִי שֶׁלֹּא עָסַק בַּתּוֹרָה – BECAUSE OF MY SON HURKANOS WHO DID NOT OCCUPY HIMSELF IN TORAH study, so I did not wish him to benefit from them. וּכְשֶׁבָּאתִי אֵצֶל חֲבֵירַי בַּדָּרוֹם – AND WHEN I CAME TO MY COLLEAGUES IN THE SOUTH, הִתִּירוּ לִי כָּל נְדָרַי – THEY ANNULLED FOR ME ALL MY VOWS.[11] וְאַתָּה כְּשֵׁם שֶׁדַּנְתַּנִי לִזְכוּת – AND AS FOR YOU – JUST AS YOU HAVE JUDGED ME FAVORABLY, הַמָּקוֹם יָדִין אוֹתְךָ לִזְכוּת – so MAY THE OMNIPRESENT JUDGE YOU FAVORABLY."

A second incident:

תָּנוּ רַבָּנָן – The Rabbis taught in a Baraisa: מַעֲשֶׂה בְּחָסִיד אֶחָד – THERE WAS AN INCIDENT INVOLVING A CERTAIN PIOUS MAN[12] שֶׁפָּדָה רִיבָה אַחַת בַּת יִשְׂרָאֵל – WHO RANSOMED A YOUNG JEWISH GIRL from captivity, וְלַמָּלוֹן הִשְׁכִּיבָהּ תַּחַת מַרְגְּלוֹתָיו – AND when they arrived AT THE INN where he and his disciples were to spend the night, HE LAY HER DOWN AT HIS FEET. לְמָחָר יָרַד וְטָבַל וְשָׁנָה לְתַלְמִידָיו – THE FOLLOWING MORNING, HE DESCENDED AND IMMERSED HIMSELF in a *mikveh* AND then TAUGHT Torah to HIS DISCIPLES. וְאָמַר (לָהֶן) בְּשָׁעָה שֶׁהִשְׁכַּבְתִּיהָ תַּחַת מַרְגְּלוֹתַי – AND HE SAID TO THEM: "WHEN I LAID HER AT MY FEET, בַּמֶּה חֲשַׁדְתּוּנִי – OF WHAT DID YOU SUSPECT ME?" אָמַרְנוּ שֶׁמָּא יֵשׁ בָּנוּ תַּלְמִיד שֶׁאֵינוֹ בָּדוּק לְרַבִּי – His disciples answered: "WE SAID to ourselves that PERHAPS THERE IS AMONG US A DISCIPLE WHO HAS NOT BEEN sufficiently SCRUTINIZED BY MASTER, thus master could not entrust the girl to our care." בְּשָׁעָה שֶׁיָּרַדְתִּי וְטָבַלְתִּי בַּמֶּה חֲשַׁדְתּוּנִי – The pious man asked further, "And WHEN I DESCENDED AND IMMERSED MYSELF in the *mikveh* before teaching Torah to you, OF WHAT DID YOU SUSPECT ME?"[13] אָמַרְנוּ שֶׁמָּא מִפְּנֵי טוֹרַח הַדֶּרֶךְ אֵירַע קֶרִי לְרַבִּי – The disciples replied: "WE SAID to ourselves that PERHAPS BECAUSE OF THE EXERTION OF TRAVEL, THE MASTER EXPERIENCED A SEMINAL EMISSION."[14] אָמַר לָהֶם הָעֲבוֹדָה כָּךְ הָיָה – Whereupon [THE PIOUS MAN] SAID TO THEM, "BY THE Divine SERVICE! SO IT WAS! וְאַתֶּם כְּשֵׁם שֶׁדַּנְתּוּנִי לְכַף זְכוּת הַמָּקוֹם יָדִין אֶתְכֶם לְכַף זְכוּת – AND AS FOR YOU – JUST AS YOU HAVE JUDGED ME FAVORABLY, so MAY THE OMNIPRESENT JUDGE YOU FAVORABLY."

A third incident:

תָּנוּ רַבָּנָן – The Rabbis taught in a Baraisa: פַּעַם אַחַת הוּצְרַךְ דָּבָר אֶחָד לְתַלְמִידֵי חֲכָמִים אֵצֶל מַטְרוֹנִיתָא אַחַת – ONE TIME, A CERTAIN communal MATTER MADE IT NECESSARY FOR THE SAGES to APPROACH A CERTAIN non-Jewish NOBLEWOMAN שֶׁכָּל גְּדוֹלֵי רוֹמִי מְצוּיִין אֶצְלָהּ – WHO WAS FREQUENTED BY ALL THE PATRICIANS OF ROME.[15] אָמְרוּ מִי יֵלֵךְ – [THE SAGES] SAID to one another: "WHO WILL GO represent us before this noblewoman?" אָמַר לָהֶם רַבִּי יְהוֹשֻׁעַ אֲנִי אֵלֵךְ – R' YEHOSHUA SAID TO THEM, "I WILL GO." הָלַךְ רַבִּי יְהוֹשֻׁעַ וְתַלְמִידָיו – So R' YEHOSHUA AND HIS DISCIPLES WENT to her home. כֵּיוָן שֶׁהִגִּיעַ לְפֶתַח בֵּיתָהּ – AS R' YEHOSHUA APPROACHED THE DOOR OF HER HOUSE, חָלַץ תְּפִילָּיו בְּרִחוּק אַרְבַּע אַמּוֹת – HE REMOVED HIS TEFILLIN AT A DISTANCE OF FOUR *AMOS*, handed them to his disciples,[16] וְנִכְנַס וְנָעַל הַדֶּלֶת בִּפְנֵיהֶן – AND ENTERED AND CLOSED THE DOOR BEFORE THEM, so that they could not enter after him. אַחַר שֶׁיָּצָא יָרַד וְטָבַל וְשָׁנָה לְתַלְמִידָיו – AFTER HE LEFT her house, HE DESCENDED AND IMMERSED HIMSELF in a *mikveh* AND then TAUGHT Torah to HIS DISCIPLES. וְאָמַר (לָהֶן) בְּשָׁעָה שֶׁחָלַצְתִּי תְּפִילִּין בַּמֶּה חֲשַׁדְתּוּנִי – AND HE SAID TO THEM: "WHEN I REMOVED THE TEFILLIN, OF WHAT DID YOU SUSPECT ME?"[17] אָמַרְנוּ כִּסְבוּר רַבִּי לֹא יִכָּנְסוּ דִּבְרֵי קְדוּשָּׁה בִּמְקוֹם טוּמְאָה – They answered: "WE SAID to ourselves that MASTER REASONS: HOLY ARTICLES SHALL NOT ENTER A DEFILED PLACE." בְּשָׁעָה שֶׁנָּעַלְתִּי בַּמֶּה חֲשַׁדְתּוּנִי – He then asked them: "And WHEN I CLOSED THE DOOR, thereby secluding myself with the woman,[18] OF WHAT DID YOU SUSPECT ME"? אָמַרְנוּ שֶׁמָּא דְּבַר מַלְכוּת יֵשׁ בֵּינוֹ לְבֵינָהּ – They replied: "WE SAID to ourselves that PERHAPS THERE IS a confidential GOVERNMENTAL MATTER that must be discussed between HIM AND HER." בְּשָׁעָה שֶׁיָּרַדְתִּי וְטָבַלְתִּי בַּמֶּה חֲשַׁדְתּוּנִי – R' Yehoshua continued: "And WHEN I DESCENDED AND IMMERSED MYSELF in the *mikveh* before teaching you Torah, OF WHAT DID YOU SUSPECT ME?"[19] אָמַרְנוּ שֶׁמָּא נִיתְּזָה צִינּוֹרָא מִפִּיהָ עַל בְּגָדָיו שֶׁל רַבִּי – The disciples replied: "WE SAID to ourselves that PERHAPS some SPITTLE SPURTED FROM HER MOUTH ONTO MASTER'S CLOTHING."[20] אָמַר לָהֶם הָעֲבוֹדָה כָּךְ הָיָה – Whereupon HE SAID TO THEM: "BY THE Divine SERVICE! SO IT WAS! וְאַתֶּם כְּשֵׁם שֶׁדַּנְתּוּנִי לִזְכוּת הַמָּקוֹם יָדִין אֶתְכֶם לִזְכוּת – AND AS FOR YOU – JUST AS YOU HAVE JUDGED ME FAVORABLY, so MAY THE OMNIPRESENT JUDGE YOU FAVORABLY."[21]

NOTES

10. This is a form of oath. One swears by linking his words to an object of sanctity (see *Tos. Yom Tov* to *Kesubos* 2:9; see *Maharsha* here, and *Megadim Chadashim*).

11. Three judges or one expert sage can release a person from his vows (see *Rambam, Hil. Shevuos* 6:1-2 and *Hil. Nedarim* 4:5, with sources cited in *Kesef Mishneh* ad loc.).

12. Whenever the Talmud speaks of an anonymous "pious man," it refers either to R' Yehudah ben Bava or R' Yehudah the son of R' Ila'i (*Rashi*; see also *Ritva MHK* ed., *Chasam Sofer* and *Rashash*).

13. Ezra enacted that one who emits semen must immerse himself in a *mikveh* before uttering words of Torah. Thus, the pious man's curious actions lent credence to the suspicion that he had sinned with the girl. [Though Ezra's enactment was rescinded in later generations, it is possible that pious people would adhere to it voluntarily, so that this would have been expected of this pious man as well (*Ritva MHK* ed.; see also *Rashash*).]

14. Which also necessitates an immersion.

15. For debauchery.

16. *Meiri*; see also *Hagahos Yavetz.*

17. [Since one may not wear tefillin during cohabitation, the fact that he removed them before entering would give rise to the suspicion that he intended to cohabit with her.]

18. Since one of the Eighteen Enactments forbids a man to seclude himself with a non-Jewess (see above, 17b note 17), we must say that this incident took place before those enactments were promulgated (*Hagahos R' Elazar Moshe Horowitz*). See, however, *Hagahos Yavetz.*

19. See note 13.

20. The spittle of a *zav* [or *zavah*] is an *av hatumah* that renders the one who touches or carries it *tamei* (see *Leviticus* 15:8; *Keilim* 1:3). Although on a Biblical level a gentile (while alive) cannot become *tamei* or transmit *tumah*, the Rabbis decreed that all gentiles shall have the *tumah* status of the *zav* (see above, 17b). Thus, the falling of the gentile noblewoman's spittle on R' Yehoshua's clothing would render him *tamei* [as one who, in effect, "carried" the spittle of a *zavah*] (see *Rashi*).

[The basic Rabbinic decree that a gentile shall have the status of a *zav* preceded the Eighteen Enactments (see 17b note 28). Thus, even though there was no enactment against seclusion with a non-Jewess at the time (see above, note 18), it had already been decreed that gentile women shall have the status of a *zavah* (*Hagahos R' Elazar Moshe Horowitz*).]

[Though there is no requirement whatever for one who has become *tamei* through a *zav* to immerse himself in a *mikveh* before uttering words of Torah, R' Yehoshua was apparently personally stringent and desired to teach Torah only in a state of *taharah* (where possible). See *Rashash.*]

21. From these cases, we learn that one is obligated to strain the limits of credibility in order to justify the actions of a pious person even though the evidence points strongly to sinful behavior. However, in the case of an ordinary person, not known to be especially pious, one is obligated to judge him favorably only where the evidence does not point more

י א מיי' פכ"ה מהלכות שבת הלכה כ:
יא ב שם הלכה יט:
יב ג מיי' פ"י מהלכות מעשר הלכה יא:
יג ד מיי' פ"ג מהלכות תרומות הלכה יג טור י"ד סימן שלא:
יד ה מיי' פכ"ה מהל' שבת הלכה יט:

רבינו חננאל

ומפני ביטול בהמ"ד שהן מצות כדרב יהודה אמר שמואל דאמר גדול הכנסת אורחין. וכדר' יוחנן דאמר אחד משׁשה דברים שאדם אוכל מפירותיהן בעוה"ז והקרן קיימת לו לעולם הבא: **מפנין** תרומה טהורה אע"פ שהיא בביתו של ישראל הואיל וראויה לכהן היום מטלטלין אותה ושפיר דמי וכן דמאי והדמאי כיון דאילו הפקיר כל נכסיו ויהיה עני מותר לאוכלו אע"פ שעכשיו לא הפקיר נכסיו מותר לטלטלו. והוא הלוקח תבואה מעם הארץ שאינו יודע אם הוציא מעשר ממנה אם לאו כי התרומה לא נחשדו עמי הארץ עליה (ודאי) והיו מפרישין אחד מחמשים והוא בבינונית ונתנו לכהן אבל המעשר היו הרבה ע"ה שלא היו מפרישין אותו ונותנין ללוי. וחייבו חכמים הקונה מעם הארץ שאינו יודע אם הוציא מעשר ממנה אם לאו להפריש מזו התבואה חלק אחד ממאה שהיא תרומת מעשר שהוא א' וכל תרומה כאוכל תרומה והוא עון מיתה. וזה פירושו ישראל שיש לו מאה סאין תבואה חייב לתת לכהן ב' סאין מהן והיא נקראת תרומה גדולה וחייב לתת עשרה מהן פחות מעט והוא נקרא מעשר ראשון וחייב הלוי לתת מן העשרה סאין שנתן לו ישראל סאה אחת לכהן והוא שאמר הכתוב והרמותם ממנו תרומת ה' מעשר מן המעשר. נמצא הסאה שביד כהן שהיא תרומת מעשר שנתן לו הלוי אחד ממאה מן התבואה שביד ישראל וכיון שראו שע"ה לא היו מפרישין מעשר לכהן שחייב בו מיתה [לכן חייבוהו להפריש] אבל המעשר שהוא בלאו לא חייבוהו מספק. וזה מפורש בגמרא יומא א) פ"ק דיוחנן העביר הודיית המעשר בסוף מס' סוטה ודמאי זה כיון שהוא ספק מעושר ספק אינו מעושר התירוהו מפני חיי נפש לאכסניא ולעניים (בפירושו). וזה שאמר ר"ל מעשר ראשון שהקדימו בשבלין פטור מתרומה גדולה פי' חייבה התורה להפריש תרומה ומעשר מן הדגן שכבר נעשה גורן כדכתיב ראשית דגנך תירושך ויצהרך כו' ואינו נקרא …

כיון דחזיא לכהן שפיר דמי. אע"ג דאמר בשילהי כירה (לעיל דף מז.) דבגדי עניים לעשירים לא איסורא הוא דרביע עליה אבל התם לא חזו טעמא נמי לא אמרינן התם טעמא דבסמוך דאי בעי מפקר לנכסיה והא דאמר בפרק כל הכלים (לעיל ד' קכה.) שירי פרוזמיות שאין בהן ג' על ג' אין מטלטלין אותן משמע הא יש בהן שלש על שלש מטלטלים היינו לעניים א"נ אפילו לעשירים בבית עניים: **דאי** בעי מפקר לנכסיה. הוה מצי למימר כדלעיל כיון דחזי אלא כיון דמשכח טעמא דאפי' לדידיה מצי חזי אמר ובפרק כל שעה (פסחים דף לה:) ובפרק שלשה שאכלו (ברכות ד' מז.) איצטריך להאי טעמא[ח]: **האי** אידגן. מדנקט אידגן משמע אפי' לא ראה פני הבית תימה אכתי אפילו הקדימו בכרי נמי לא לחייב אלא באידגן וראה פני הבית וי"ל דאי לא כתב והרמותם ה"א דכולם חייבין אפילו לא אידגן השתא דכתי' קרא מוקמי ליה במסתבר דהיינו לא אידגן שאפילו ראה פני הבית לא היה חייב א"נ י"ל הא דנקט אידגן היינו ככל דינו שראה פני הבית אלא דמילתא דפסיקא נקט דאיכא למאן דאמר בבבא מציעא (ד' פח:) דלא בעינן ראיית פני הבית אלא בזיתים וענבים דלאו בני גורן נינהו: **הא** קמ"ל דאין חומש מעכב. ואף על גב דמבעיא לן בפרק הזהב (שם דף נד.) אי מעכב אי לא ולא פשיט מהכא משום דהוה מצי למידחי דלגבי אתרינה תניא: אבל

ה"ג הני נמי בהני שייכי. הכנסת אורחים וביקור חולים היינו גמילות חסדים ועיון תפלה היינו בכלל גמילות חסדים דכתיב (משלי יא) גומל נפשו איש חסד [ו] השכמת בית המדרש וגידול בנים לתלמוד תורה היינו תלמוד תורה דן את חבירו לכף זכות בכלל הבאת שלום דמתוך שהוא מכריעו לזכות ואמר לא חטא לי בזאת אנוס היה או לטובה נתכוון יש שלום ביניהן ורבי יוחנן לפרש לך אתא דבכלל ג' דמתניתין איתנהו להנך ו' ואיכא נמי לכבוד אב ואם ורבי יוחנן לא פליג עליה: **בפחי נפש.** בדאבון נפש: **מוחכרת.** שנותנה לחבירו בכך וכך כורין לשנה: [ט] כל היכא דאמרינן מעשה בחסיד אחד או רבי יהודה בן בבא או רבי יהודה ברבי אלעאי: **ריבה.** נערה: **שאינו בדוק לרבי.** שאינו מכיר במדותיו לסמוך עליו ולהניחה אצלנו: **מטרוניתא.** נכרית: **דבר מלכות.** וצריך להעלימו: **צינורא.** רוק וגזרו על הנכרים שיהיו כזבים לכל דבריהם: **מאכילין לעניים דמאי.** לא אסרוהו עליהם מפני שצריכים לחזור על פתח ע"ה וסמכו על שרוב עמי הארץ מעשרין: **אכסניא.** (ב) חיל של מלך ישראל ומטילו על בני העיר לפרנסן[י]: **שניטלה תרומתו.** קס"ד תרומת מעשר שהלוי נותן לכהן וכ"ש תרומה גדולה שיש על ישראל להפריש והפרישו קודם שנתן המעשר ללוי: **שהקדימו בשבולין.** לתרומה ישראל היה לו להפריש תרומה גדולה תחילה דכתיב (שמות כב) מלאתך ודמעך לא תאחר מלאתך אלו בכורים ודמעך זו תרומה מכאן שמקדים תרומה לבכורים לוקח ודמעך זו תרומה שאם הקדים מעשר לתרומה לוקה והנ"מ משנתמרח בכרי לוקה אם הקדים מעשר לתרומה אבל הקדימו למעשר קודם לתרומה בשבלים אינו לוקה: **והרמותם ממנו.** מכל מתנותיכם וגו'. נמי בלוים כתיב גבי תרומת מעשר וקאמר את כל תרומת ה' כל משמע כל צד תרומה שבו: **האי.** דנתמרח: **אידגן.** וחלה עליו חובת תרומה כדכתיב (דברים יח) ראשית דגנך הלכך כי שקלה לוי בעי אהדורי לכהן תרי ממאה שבו ברישא והדר אחד מעשרה: **דמריר.** שהוא מר: אבל

הני נמי [א] (בגמילות חסדים שייכי ל"א הני) בהני שייכי ת"ר הדן חבירו לכף זכות דנין אותו לזכות ומעשה באדם אחד שירד מגליל העליון ונשכר אצל בעה"ב אחד בדרום שלש שנים ערב [ב] יוה"כ אמר לו תן לי שכרי ואלך ואזון את אשתי ובני אמר לו אין לי מעות אמר לו תן לי פירות אמר לו אין לי תן לי קרקע אין לי תן לי בהמה אין לי תן לי כרים וכסתות אין לי הפשיל כליו לאחוריו והלך לביתו בפחי נפש לאחר הרגל נטל בעה"ב שכרו בידו ועמו משוי ג' חמורים אחד של מאכל ואחד של משתה ואחד של מיני מגדים והלך לו לביתו אחר שאכלו ושתו נתן לו שכרו אמר לו בשעה שאמרת לי תן לי שכרי ואמרתי אין לי מעות במה חשדתני אמרתי שמא פרקמטיא בזול נזדמנה לך ולקחת בהן ובשעה שאמרת לי תן לי בהמה ואמרתי אין לי בהמה במה חשדתני אמרתי שמא מושכרת ביד אחרים בשעה שאמרת לי תן לי קרקע ואמרתי לך אין לי קרקע במה חשדתני אמרתי שמא מוחכרת ביד אחרים (א) היא ובשעה שאמרתי לך אין לי פירות במה חשדתני אמרתי שמא אינן מעושרות ובשעה שאמרתי לך אין לי כרים וכסתות במה חשדתני אמרתי שמא הקדיש כל נכסיו לשמים א"ל העבודה כך היה הדרתי כל נכסי בשביל הורקנוס בני שלא עסק בתורה וכשבאתי אצל חבירי בדרום התירו לי כל נדרי ואתה כשם שדנתני לזכות המקום ידין אותך לזכות ת"ר [ג] מעשה בחסיד אחד שפדה ריבה אחת בת ישראל ולמלון השכיבה תחת מרגלותיו למחר ירד וטבל ושנה לתלמידיו ואמר [ד] להן בשעה שהשכבתיה תחת מרגלותי במה חשדתוני אמרנו שמא יש בנו תלמיד שאינו בדוק לרבי בשעה שירדתי וטבלתי במה חשדתוני אמרנו שמא מפני טורח הדרך אירע קרי לרבי אמר להם העבודה כך היה ואתם כשם שדנתוני לכף זכות המקום ידין אתכם לכף זכות תנו רבנן פעם אחת הוצרך דבר אחד לתלמידי חכמים אצל מטרוניתא אחת שכל גדולי רומי מצויין אצלה אמרו מי ילך אמר להם ר' יהושע אני אלך הלך רבי יהושע ותלמידיו כיון שהגיע לפתח ביתה חלץ תפיליו ברחוק ארבע אמות ונכנס ונעל הדלת בפניהן אחר שיצא ירד וטבל ושנה לתלמידיו ואמר [ה] להן בשעה שחלצתי תפילין במה חשדתוני אמרנו כסבור רבי לא יכנסו דברי קדושה במקום טומאה בשעה שנעלתי במה חשדתוני אמרנו שמא דבר מלכות יש בינו לבינה בשעה שירדתי וטבלתי במה חשדתוני אמרנו שמא ניתזה צינורא מפיה על בגדיו של רבי אמר להם העבודה כך היה ואתם כשם שדנתוני לזכות המקום ידין אתכם לזכות: מפנין תרומה טהורה וכו': פשיטא לא צריכא [א] דמנחה ביד ישראל מהו דתימא כיון דלא חזיא ליה אסור קמ"ל כיון דחזיא לכהן שפיר דמי: [ב] ודמאי (וכו'): דמאי הא לא חזי ליה [ו] כיון דאי בעי מפקר ליה לנכסיה והוה עני וחזיא ליה השתא נמי חזי ליה [ז] דתנן [ג] מאכילין את העניים דמאי ואת האכסניא דמאי ואמר רב הונא תנא ב"ש אומרים אין מאכילין את העניים דמאי ואת האכסניא דמאי וב"ה אומרים מאכילין את העניים דמאי ואת האכסניא דמאי: ומעשר ראשון שניטלה תרומתו וכו': פשיטא לא צריכא שהקדימו בשבולים ונטלה הימנו תרומת מעשר ולא נטלה הימנו תרומה גדולה וכי הא [ח] דא"ר אבהו אר"ל [ד] מעשר ראשון שהקדימו בשבולין פטור מתרומה גדולה שנא' [א] והרמותם ממנו תרומת ה' מעשר מן המעשר מעשר מן המעשר אמרתי לך ולא תרומה גדולה ותרומת מעשר מן המעשר [ט] א"ל רב פפא לאביי א"ה אפי' הקדימו בכרי נמי ליפטר א"ל עליך אמר קרא [ב] מכל מתנותיכם תרימו וגו' ומה ראית האי אידגן והאי לא אידגן: ומעשר שני וכו': פשיטא [ה] לא צריכא שנתן את הקרן ולא נתן את החומש הא קמ"ל דאין חומש מעכב: והתורמס היבש וכו': דווקא יבש אבל לח לא מ"ט כיון דמריר לא אכלה: אבל

א) פ"א ל"ג, ב) [גרי"ף ובא"ש ליתא ערב הרגל], ג) אבות דר"נ פ"ח ועי"ש, ד) [ל"ל להם], ה) [ל"ל להם], ו) ברכות דף מז. וש"נ, ז) ברכות מז. דמאי פ"ג מ"א, ח) פסחים לה: ביצה יג:, ח) ברכות שם עירובין לא: פסחים לה: ביצה יג., ט) תמורה ה:, י) [ע"ש תוספות עירובין לא. ד"ה דמאי ותוס' סוכה לה: ד"ה לאי בעי].

הגהות הב"ח

(א) גמ' אמרתי שמא מוחכרת ביד אחרים ובשעה כו"ל ותיבת היא נמחק: (ב) רש"י ד"ה אכסניא חיל של מלך ישראל. נ"ב כך פירש בפרק כלל מערבין דף לא ובן בפרק כל שעה דף לה אבל התוספות כת' ג' שאלו פי' עוד פי' אחר חיל של נכרים כו' וע"ש דף מו:

גליון הש"ס

רש"י ד"ה כל היכא דאמרינן מעשה וכו'. עיין דבר נחמד בזה בברכות הוצא תמורה דף טו ע"ב:

תורה אור השלם

א) וְאֶל הַלְוִיִּם תְּדַבֵּר וְאָמַרְתָּ אֲלֵהֶם כִּי תִקְחוּ מֵאֵת בְּנֵי יִשְׂרָאֵל אֶת הַמַּעֲשֵׂר אֲשֶׁר נָתַתִּי לָכֶם מֵאִתָּם בְּנַחֲלַתְכֶם וַהֲרֵמֹתֶם מִמֶּנּוּ תְּרוּמַת יְיָ מַעֲשֵׂר מִן הַמַּעֲשֵׂר: [במדבר יח, כו]

ב) מִכֹּל מַתְּנֹתֵיכֶם תָּרִימוּ אֵת כָּל תְּרוּמַת יְיָ מִכָּל חֶלְבּוֹ אֶת מִקְדְּשׁוֹ מִמֶּנּוּ: [במדבר יח, כט]

רב נסים גאון

שמא צינורא ניתזה מפיה על רבי. פי' צינורא שניתזה מפי האדם כשהוא מדבר למטרונית והיא נכרית ונגע בו מרוקה הוצרך לטבול כי הרוק של נכרים גזרו עליו חכמים טומאה ועיקר זה הוא מה שאמר הקב"ה בענין הזב (ויקרא טו) וכי ירוק הזב בטהור יכול אפילו רקק ולא נגע יהא טמא ת"ל בטהור ובתוספתא …

חשק שלמה על רבינו חננאל

ליקוטי רש"י

מטרוניתא. שרה (עירובין דף סח.). **דחזיא ליה.** לכהן הוא דחזיא (ביצה יג:). **אכסניא.** חיל של מלך ישראל (פסחים לה:). **שהקדימו בשבולים.** … **והרמותם ממנו.** … **מכל מתנותיכם תרימו וגו'.** … **ומה ראית.** …

The Gemara now resumes its elaboration of our Mishnah, which stated:

מְפַנִּין תְּרוּמָה טְהוֹרָה וכו' – WE MAY CLEAR AWAY *TERUMAH* THAT IS *TAHOR* etc. for it is not *muktzeh.*

The Gemara asks:

פְּשִׁיטָא – **It is obvious** that *terumah* which is *tahor* is not *muktzeh,* for the Kohen may eat it on the Sabbath! Why did the Mishnah have to state this?

The Gemara answers:

לֹא צְרִיכָא דְּמַנְחָה בְּיַד יִשְׂרָאֵל – **No. It is** a **necessary** ruling (i.e. the Mishnah refers to) **where [the *terumah*] rests in the possession of a Yisrael** [i.e. a non-Kohen], who may not eat it. מַהוּ דְּתֵימָא כֵּיוָן דְּלָא חַזְיָא לֵיהּ אָסוּר – For in this case **I might have said** that **since it is not fit for him,** as he is not a Kohen, **it is prohibited** to him as *muktzeh* and he may not move it. קָא מַשְׁמַע לָן – To dispel this notion, **[the Mishnah] informs us** כֵּיוָן דְּחַזְיָא לְכֹהֵן שַׁפִּיר דָּמֵי – that **since it is fit for a Kohen, it is fine** for the non-Kohen to move it as well.

The Mishnah then stated:

וּדְמַאי (וכו') – **AND** one may clear away ***DEMAI,*** for it is not *muktzeh.*

The Gemara asks:

דְּמַאי – Is ***demai*** in fact not *muktzeh*? הָא לֹא חֲזֵי לֵיהּ – **Why, it is not fit for him** to eat on the Sabbath![22] – ? –

The Gemara answers:

כֵּיוָן דְּאִי בָּעֵי מַפְקַר לֵיהּ לְנִכְסֵיהּ – **Since, if [the owner] so desired, he could renounce ownership of his possessions**[23] וַהֲוָה עָנִי וְחַזְיָא לֵיהּ – **and** thereby **become a pauper and** thus **[the *demai*] would be fit for him,**[24] הַשְׁתָּא נַמִּי חֲזֵי לֵיהּ – **now too,** although he has *not* made himself into a pauper, **it is deemed fit for him,** and thus non-*muktzeh.*[25] The Gemara cites the source for its assertion that a pauper may eat *demai*: דִּתְנַן – **For we have learned in a Mishnah:**[26] מַאֲכִילִין אֶת הָעֲנִיִּים דְּמַאי וְאֶת הָאַכְסַנְיָא דְּמַאי – WE MAY FEED PAUPERS *DEMAI*[27] and we may feed TRAVELING SOLDIERS *DEMAI.*[28] וְאָמַר רַב הוּנָא – **And Rav Huna said:** תָּנָא בֵּית שַׁמַּאי אוֹמְרִים אֵין מַאֲכִילִין אֶת הָעֲנִיִּים דְּמַאי – **A Baraisa teaches:** BEIS SHAMMAI SAY: WE MAY NOT FEED PAUPERS *DEMAI* וְאֶת הָאַכְסַנְיָא דְּמַאי – NOR may we feed TRAVELING SOLDIERS *DEMAI.* וּבֵית הִלֵּל אוֹמְרִים מַאֲכִילִין אֶת הָעֲנִיִּים דְּמַאי – BUT BEIS HILLEL SAY: WE MAY FEED PAUPERS *DEMAI* וְאֶת הָאַכְסַנְיָא דְּמַאי – AND we may feed TRAVELING SOLDIERS *DEMAI.*[29]

Next, our Mishnah stated:

וּמַעֲשֵׂר רִאשׁוֹן שֶׁנִּיטְּלָה תְּרוּמָתוֹ וכו' – And one may clear away *MAASER RISHON* WHOSE *TERUMAH* HAS BEEN REMOVED.[30]

The Gemara asks:

פְּשִׁיטָא – **It is obvious** that *maaser rishon* whose *terumah* has been removed is not *muktzeh,* for it is food that is perfectly permissible to all! Why did the Mishnah have to state this?

The Gemara answers:

לֹא צְרִיכָא שֶׁהִקְדִּימוֹ בְּשִׁבֳּלִים – **No! It is** a **necessary** ruling (i.e. the Mishnah refers to) **where one advanced** the separation of **[the *maaser rishon*]** ahead of the *terumah gedolah* while the grain was still **in ears,**[31] וְנִטְּלָה הֵימֶנּוּ תְּרוּמַת מַעֲשֵׂר – **and** only ***terumas maaser* was taken from [this *maaser rishon*]**

NOTES

strongly to guilt than to innocence. Where the evidence points to guilt, however, one is not obligated to judge the ordinary person favorably, though it is nonetheless a pious practice to do so (see *Meiri,* and *Rambam, Commentary to the Mishnah,* to *Avos* 1:6).

22. Since one may not eat *demai* without first tithing it, and it is forbidden to tithe produce on the Sabbath! (see 126b note 7).

23. See end of note 25.

24. For a pauper is permitted to eat *demai* as is, as the Gemara will presently show.

25. [The fact that the *demai* is *potentially* fit for him on this Sabbath is sufficient to deem it non-*muktzeh.*]

Earlier, the Gemara stated that *terumah* is not *muktzeh* for a non-Kohen because it is fit for a Kohen. Similarly, the Gemara could have said here simply that *demai* is not *muktzeh* for an ordinary person because it is fit for a pauper. Nevertheless, since the Gemara finds a way of considering the *demai* fit even for the person himself, it prefers presenting that reason. Moreover, there are other instances in which the Mishnah lists *demai* together with these other items, and the Gemara there *must* resort to the reason that *demai* is potentially fit for the person himself. [Therefore, the Gemara presents that reason here as well] (see *Tosafos*).

Alternatively, the reason used by the Gemara for *terumah* would *not* apply to *demai.* In the case of *terumah,* which is indeed destined to be eaten by a Kohen, the fact that it is fit for the Kohen suffices to render it non-*muktzeh* even while in the possession of a non-Kohen. *Demai,* however, though fit for a pauper, is not *destined* to be eaten by him, since in all probability the owner himself will tithe it and then consume it himself. Thus, its present suitability for the pauper is not sufficient to deem it non-*muktzeh,* and the Gemara must resort to the reason that the *demai* is potentially suitable for the person himself (*Ramban* et al.).

[From the Gemara here, which states that one could make *demai* fit for himself on the Sabbath by renouncing his possessions, it would seem that one is permitted to renounce ownership (הֶפְקֵר) on the Sabbath, and that such renunciation is not included in the Rabbinic ban against conducting transactions (מִקָּח וּמִמְכָּר) on the Sabbath (*Meiri*). There is considerable discussion of this issue in the Rishonim and Acharonim – see *Gilyon Maharsha* and *Chasam Sofer* here; see also *Shaar HaMelech, Hil. Lulav* 8:2, *Hagahos R' Akiva Eiger* to *Orach Chaim,* end of §13, and in responsum I:174; *Rashash* to *Eruvin* 71a; *Sdei Chemed* Vol. II p. 191; see also *Kehillos Yaakov* to *Beitzah* §12.]

26. *Demai* 3:1.

27. The Rabbis did not wish to curtail the food sources available to poor people, who must go door to door for food. Therefore, the Rabbis exempted paupers from the law of *demai,* so that they would be able to obtain food from the homes of *amei ha'aretz* (whose food is *demai*) as well. In this, the Rabbis relied on the fact that most *amei ha'aretz* do tithe their produce properly (*Rashi*; cf. *Rambam, Commentary to the Mishnah* ad loc.).

28. The reference is to situations in which a Jewish king requires the local citizenry to feed the [Jewish] soldiers passing through their districts (*Rashi*; cf. *Hagahos HaBach*). It is permitted to feed the soldiers *demai,* since they are presently removed from home and property and dependent on public support, and thus in the category of "paupers" (*Rashi* to *Eruvin* 31b).

29. [Thus, what the Mishnah states as an unchallenged ruling is actually the view of Beis Hillel and is disputed by Beis Shammai. The end result, however, is the same, since the halachah follows Beis Hillel.]

30. See 126b note 9. At this point, the Gemara assumes the Mishnah to mean that the *terumas maaser* was separated and *certainly* the *terumah gedolah* as well (*Rashi*).

31. The proper sequence in separating the required portions from produce is: *bikkurim, terumah gedolah* and *maaser rishon.* For the Torah states (*Exodus* 22:28): מְלֵאָתְךָ וְדִמְעֲךָ לֹא תְאַחֵר, *You shall not delay your bikkurim and terumah* [see *Temurah* 4a]. From this we derive that one who inverts the proper sequence and separates *terumah gedolah* before *bikkurim,* or *maaser rishon* before *terumah gedolah,* has transgressed a prohibition and is subject to lashes (*Rashi*; see *Terumos* 3:6,7). One incurs lashes, however, only if he inverts the order after the raw processing of the grain ends with the threshed and winnowed grain being smoothed in a pile [מֵירוּחַ בִּכְרִי], which triggers the absolute tithing obligation. But if he inverts the order before the grain is smoothed in a pile [which the Gemara here refers to as "while the grain is still in ears"], then he does not incur lashes for the inversion (*Rashi*; see *Minchas Chinuch* 72:2,6; see also *Afikei Yam* I:44, who addresses at length the apparent contradiction between *Rashi's* comments here and his comments to the end of *Beitzah* 13a ד"ה קנסא).

The Gemara explains that the Mishnah here refers to where the Levi preempted the Kohen by asking the farmer to separate and give him the *maaser rishon* before separating the *terumah gedolah* for the Kohen. In

עין משפט
נר מצוה

י א מיי' פכ"ה מהלכות שבת הלכה כ:
יא ב שם הלכה יט:
יב ג מיי' פ"י מהלכות מעשר הלכה יא:
יג ד מיי' פ"ג מהלכות תרומות הלכה יג טור י"ד סימן שלא:
יד ה מיי' פכ"ה מהל' שבת הלכה יט:

רבינו חננאל

ומפני ביטול בהמ"ד שהן מצות כדרב יהודה אמר שמואל דאמר גדול הכנסת אורחין. וכדר' יוחנן דאמר אחד משׁשה דברים שאדם אוכל מפירותיהן בעוה"ז והקרן קיימת לו לעולם הבא: **מפנין** תרומה טהורה אע"פ שהיא בביתו של ישראל הואיל וראויה לכהן היום מטלטלין אותה ושפיר דמי וכן דמאי והדמאי כיון דאילו הפקיר כל נכסיו ויהיה עני מותר לאוכלו אע"פ שעכשיו לא הפקיר נכסיו מותר לטלטלו. והוא הלוקח תבואה מעם הארץ שאינו יודע אם הוציא מעשר ממנה אם לאו כי התרומה לא נחשדו עמי הארץ עליה (ודאי) והיו מפרישין אחד מחמשים והוא בבינונית ונתנו לכהן אבל המעשר היו הרבה ע"ה שלא היו מפרישין אותו ונותנין ללוי. וחייבו חכמים הקונה מעם הארץ שאינו יודע אם הוציא מעשר ממנה אם לאו להפריש מזו התבואה חלק אחד ממאה שהיא תרומת מעשר שהוא א' וכל תרומה כאוכל תרומה והוא עון מיתה. וזה פירוש ישראל שיש לו מאה סאין תבואה חייב לתת לכהן ב' סאין מהן והיא נקראת תרומה גדולה וחייב לתת עשרה מהן פחות מעט והוא נקרא מעשר ראשון וחייב הלוי לתת מן העשרה סאין שנתן לו ישראל סאה אחת לכהן והוא שאמר הכתוב והרמותם ממנו תרומת ה' מעשר מן המעשר. נמצא הסאה שביד כהן שהיא תרומת מעשר שנתן לו הלוי אחד ממאה מן התבואה שביד ישראל וכיון שראו שעם הארץ לא היו מפרישין מעשר לכהן שחייב בו מיתה [לכן חייבוהו להפריש] אבל המעשר שהוא בלאו לא חייבוהו מספק. וזה מבואר במסכת יומא א) פ"ק דיוחנן העביר הודיית המעשר בסוף מס' סוטה ודמאי זה כיון שהוא ספק מעשר ספק אינו מעשר התירוהו מפני חיי נפש לאכסניא ולעניים (כפירוש). וזה שאמר ר"ל מעשר ראשון שהקדימו בשבלין פטור מתרומה גדולה פי' חייבה התורה להפריש תרומה ומעשר מן הדגן שכבר נעשה גורן כדכתיב ראשית דגנך תירושך ויצהרך ואינו נקרא דגן אלא אחרי דישתו בגורן והעמדתו כרי והתורה אמרה להפריש מן הדגן תרומה גדולה ואחריו מעשר ראשון. ואחריו שנה ראשונה ושניה מעשר [illegible]

כיון דחזיא לכהן שפיר דמי. אע"ג דאמר בשילהי כירה (לעיל דף מז.) דבגדי עניים לעשירים לא הכא לכ"ע חזיא אלא איסורא הוא דרביע עליה אבל התם לא חזו מחמת גריעותא ומהאי טעמא נמי לא אמרינן התם טעמא דבסמוך דאי בעי מפקר לנכסיה והא דאמר בפרק כל הכלים (לעיל ד' קכד.) שירי פרוזמיות שאין בהן ג' על ג' אין מטלטלין אותן משמע הא יש בהן שלש על שלש מטלטלים היינו לעניים א"נ אפילו לעשירים בבית עניים: **דאי** בעי מפקר לנכסיה. הוה מצי למימר כדלעיל כיון דחזי אלא כיון דמשכח טעמא דאפי' לדידיה מצי חזי אמר ובפרק כל שעה (פסחים דף לה:) ובפרק שלשה שאכלו (ברכות ד' מז.) איצטריך להאי טעמא מ): **האי** אידגן. מדנקט אידגן משמע אפי' לא ראה פני הבית תימה אכתי אפילו הקדימו בכרי נמי לא לחייב אלא באידגן ורואה פני הבית וי"ל דאי לא כתב והרמותם ה"א דכולם חייבין אפילו לא אידגן השתא דכתי' קרא מוקמי ליה כמסתבר דהיינו לא אידגן שאפילו ראה פני הבית לא היה חייב א"נ י"ל הא דנקט אידגן היינו ככל דינו שראה פני הבית אלא דמילתא דפסיקא נקט דאיכא למאן דאמר בבבא מציעא (ד' פח:) דלא בעינן ראיית פני הבית אלא בזיתים וענבים דלאו בני גורן נינהו: **הא** קמ"ל דאין חומש מעכב. ואף על גב דמבעיא לן בפרק הזהב (שם דף נג:) אי מעכב אי לא ולא פשיט מהכא משום דהוה מצי למידחי דלאגב אחרינא תנייה: אבל

הני נמי א) (בגמילות חסדים שייכי ל"א הני) בהני שייכי ת"ר הדן חבירו לכף זכות דנין אותו לזכות ומעשה באדם אחד שירד מגליל העליון ונשכר אצל בעה"ב אחד בדרום שלש שנים ערב ב) יוה"כ אמר לו תן לי שכרי ואלך ואזון את אשתי ובני אמר לו אין לי מעות אמר לו תן לי פירות אמר לו אין לי תן לי קרקע אין לי תן לי בהמה אין לי תן לי כרים וכסתות אין לי הפשיל כליו לאחוריו והלך לביתו בפחי נפש לאחר הרגל נטל בעה"ב שכרו בידו ועמו משוי ג' חמורים אחד של מאכל ואחד של משתה ואחד של מיני מגדים והלך לו לביתו אחר שאכלו ושתו נתן לו שכרו אמר לו בשעה שאמרת לי תן לי שכרי ואמרתי אין לי מעות במה חשדתני אמרתי שמא פרקמטיא בזול נזדמנה לך ולקחת בהן ובשעה שאמרת לי תן לי בהמה ואמרתי אין לי בהמה במה חשדתני אמרתי שמא מושכרת ביד אחרים בשעה שאמרת לי תן לי קרקע ואמרתי לך אין לי קרקע במה חשדתני אמרתי שמא מוחכרת ביד אחרים (א) היא ובשעה שאמרתי לך אין לי פירות במה חשדתני אמרתי שמא אינן מעושרות ובשעה שאמרתי לך אין לי כרים וכסתות במה חשדתני אמרתי שמא הקדיש כל נכסיו לשמים א"ל העבודה כך היה הדרתי כל נכסי בשביל הורקנוס בני שלא עסק בתורה וכשבאתי אצל חבירי בדרום התירו לי כל נדרי ואתה כשם שדנתני לזכות המקום ידין אותך לזכות ת"ר ג) מעשה בחסיד אחד שפדה ריבה אחת בת ישראל ולמלון השכיבה תחת מרגלותיו למחר ירד וטבל ושנה לתלמידיו ואמר ד) (להן) בשעה שהשכבתיה תחת מרגלותי במה חשדתוני אמרנו שמא יש בנו תלמיד שאינו בדוק לרבי בשעה שירדתי וטבלתי במה חשדתוני אמרנו שמא מפני טורח הדרך אירע קרי לרבי אמר להם העבודה כך היה ואתם כשם שדנתוני לכף זכות המקום ידין אתכם לכף זכות תנו רבנן פעם אחת הוצרך דבר אחד לתלמידי חכמים אצל מטרוניתא אחת שכל גדולי רומי מצויין אצלה אמרו מי ילך אמר להם ר' יהושע אני אלך הלך רבי יהושע ותלמידיו כיון שהגיע לפתח ביתה חלץ תפיליו ברחוק ארבע אמות ונכנס ונעל הדלת בפניהן אחר שיצא ירד וטבל ושנה לתלמידיו ואמר ה) (להן) בשעה שחלצתי תפילין במה חשדתוני אמרנו כסבור רבי לא יכנסו דברי קדושה במקום טומאה בשעה שנעלתי במה חשדתוני אמרנו שמא דבר מלכות יש בינו לבינה בשעה שירדתי וטבלתי במה חשדתוני אמרנו שמא ניתזה צינורא מפיה על בגדיו של רבי אמר להם העבודה כך היה ואתם כשם שדנתוני לזכות המקום ידין אתכם לזכות: **מפנין** תרומה טהורה וכו': פשיטא לא צריכא א) דמנחה ביד ישראל מהו דתימא כיון דלא חזיא ליה אסור קמ"ל כיון דחזיא לכהן שפיר דמי: ב) ודמאי (וכו'): דמאי הא לא חזי ליה ו) כיון דאי בעי מפקר ליה לנכסיה והוה עני וחזיא ליה השתא נמי חזי ליה ז) דתנן ג) מאכילין את העניים דמאי ואת האכסניא דמאי ואמר רב הונא תנא ב"ש אומרים אין מאכילין את העניים דמאי ואת האכסניא דמאי וב"ה אומרים מאכילין את העניים דמאי ואת האכסניא דמאי: **ומעשר** ראשון שניטלה תרומתו וכו': פשיטא לא צריכא שהקדימו בשבולים ונטלה הימנו תרומת מעשר ולא נטלה הימנו תרומה גדולה וכי הא ח) דא"ר אבהו אר"ל ד) מעשר ראשון שהקדימו בשבולין פטור מתרומה גדולה שנא' א) והרמותם ממנו תרומת ה' מעשר מן המעשר מעשר מן המעשר אמרתי לך ולא תרומה גדולה ותרומת מעשר מן המעשר ט) א"ל רב פפא לאביי א"ה אפי' הקדימו בכרי נמי ליפטר א"ל עליך אמר קרא ב) מכל מתנותיכם תרימו וגו' ומה ראית האי אידגן והאי לא אידגן: **ומעשר** שני וכו': פשיטא ה) לא צריכא שנתן את הקרן ולא נתן את החומש הא קמ"ל דאין חומש מעכב: **והתורמס** היבש כו': דוקא יבש אבל לח לא מ"ט כיון דמריר לא אכלה: אבל

ה"ג הני נמי בהני שייכי. הכנסת אורחים וביקור חולים היינו גמילות חסדים ועיון תפלה היינו בכלל גמילות חסדים דכתיב (משלי יא) גומל נפשו איש חסד ה) השכמת בית המדרש וגידול בנים לתלמוד תורה היינו תלמוד תורה דן את חבירו לכף זכות בכלל הבאת שלום דמתוך שהוא מכריעו לזכות ואמר לא חטא לי בזאת אנוס היה או לטובה נתכוון יש שלום ביניהן ורבי יוחנן לפרש לך אתא דבכלל ג' דמתניתין איתנהו להנך ו' ואיכא נמי לכבוד אב ואם ורבי יוחנן לא פליג עליה: **בפחי** נפש. בדאבון נפש: **מוחכרת.** שנותנה לחברו בכך וכך כורין לשנה: ° כל היכא דאמרינן ו) מעשה בחסיד אחד או רבי יהודה בן בבא או רבי יהודה ברבי אלעאי: **ריבה.** נערה: **שאינו** בדוק לרבי. שאינו מכיר במדותיו לסמוך עליו ולהניחה אצלנו: **מטרוניתא.** נכרית: דבר מלכות. וצריך להעלימו: **צינורא.** רוק וגזרו על הנכרים שיהיו כזבים לכל דבריהם: **מאכילין** לעניים דמאי. לא אסרוהו עליהם מפני שצריכים לחזור על פתח ע"ה וסמכו על שרוב עמי הארץ מעשרין: **אכסניא.** (ג) חיל של מלך ישראל ומטילו על בני העיר לפרנסן ל): **שניטלה** תרומתו. קס"ד תרומת מעשר שהלוי נותן לכהן וכ"ש תרומה גדולה שיש על ישראל להפריש והפרישו קודם שנתן המעשר ללוי: **שהקדימו** בשבולין. לתרומה ישראל היה לו להפריש תרומה גדולה תחילה דכתיב (שמות כב) מלאתך ודמעך לא תאחר מלאתך אלו בכורים מכאן שהמקדים תרומה לבכורים לוקה ודמעך זו תרומה שאם הקדים מעשר לתרומה לוקה והנ"מ משנתמרח בכרי לוקה אם הקדים מעשר לתרומה אבל הקדים למעשר קודם לתרומה בשבלים אינו לוקה: **והרמותם** ממנו. בלוים כתיב גבי תרומת מעשר: **מכל** מתנותיכם וגו'. נמי בלוים כתיב גבי תרומת מעשר וקאמר את כל תרומת ה' כל משמע כל לד תרומה שבו: **האי.** דנתמרח. **אידגן.** וחלה עליו חובת תרומה כדכתיב (דברים יח) ראשית דגנך הלכך כי שקלה לוי בעי אהדורי לכהן תרי ממאה שבו בראשה והדר אחד מעשרה: **דמריר.** שהוא מר: שלא

מסורת הש"ס

א) ס"א ל"ג, ב) [ברי"ף וברא"ש איתא ערב הרגל], ג) אבות דר"נ פ"ח וע"ש, ד) [נ"ל להם], ה) [נ"ל להם], ו) ברכות דף מז. וש"נ, ז) ברכות מז. דמאי פ"ג מ"א עירובין יז: לא. פסחים לה: סוכה לה:, ח) ברכות שם עירובין לא: פסחים לה: ביצה יג:, ט) תמורה ה:, י) כאן חסר ונפש היינו תפלה דכתי' גבי חנה ואשפוך את נפשי לפני ה' ש"א א ע' רש"י ברכות ה: ד"ה טורף נפשו וכן הובא בר"ש פאה פ"א מ"א, כ) [ב"ק קג:], ל) לפרנסן והוין כעניים כיון שאינם בבתיהם כצ"ל, מ) [וע"ע תוספות עירובין לא. ד"ה דמאי ותוס' סוכה לה: ד"ה דאי בעי].

הגהות הב"ח

(א) גמ' אמרתי שמא מוחכרות ביד אחרים ובשעה כצ"ל ותיבת היא נמחק: (ב) רש"י ד"ה אכסניא חיל של מלך ישראל. נ"ב כך פירש"י בפרק בכל מערבין דף לא וכן בפרק כל שעה דף לה אבל התוספות בפ' ג' שאכלו פי' עוד פי' אחר חיל של נכרים כו' וע"ש דף מו:

גליון הש"ס

רש"י ד"ה כל היכא דאמרינן מעשה וכו'. עיין דבר נחמד בזה בכרכות הזהב תמורה דף טו ע"ב:

תורה אור השלם

א) וְאֶל הַלְוִיִּם תְּדַבֵּר וְאָמַרְתָּ אֲלֵהֶם כִּי תִקְחוּ מֵאֵת בְּנֵי יִשְׂרָאֵל אֶת הַמַּעֲשֵׂר אֲשֶׁר נָתַתִּי לָכֶם מֵאִתָּם בְּנַחֲלַתְכֶם וַהֲרֵמֹתֶם מִמֶּנּוּ תְּרוּמַת יְיָ מַעֲשֵׂר מִן הַמַּעֲשֵׂר: [במדבר יח, כו]

ב) מִכֹּל מַתְּנֹתֵיכֶם תָּרִימוּ אֵת כָּל תְּרוּמַת יְיָ מִכָּל חֶלְבּוֹ אֶת מִקְדְּשׁוֹ מִמֶּנּוּ: [במדבר יח, כט]

רב נסים גאון

שמא ניתזה צינורא מפיה על רבי. פי' צינורא שינתז מפי האדם כשהוא מדבר למטרונית והיא נכרית ונגע בו מרוקה הוצרך לטבול כי רוקן של נכרים גזרו עליו חכמים טומאה ועיקר זה הוא מה שאמר הקב"ה בענין הזב (ויקרא טו) וכי ירוק הזב בטהור יכול אפילו רקק ולא נגע בו יהא טמא ת"ל בטהור והתוספתא זבין בפרק חמישי אמרו ורירו וכיחו ומימי האף שלו הרי הן כרוקו דמעת עינו ודם מגפתו וחלב האשה מטמאין טומאת משקה [illegible]

זובו ורוקו ומימי רגליו מטמאים טומאה חמורה וזאת התורה מיוחדת בישראל בלבד אבל לא בנכרים והחכמים הם שגזרו עליהם שיהו כזבין לכל דבריהם ותמצא ביאור כזה במס' נדה בפרק בנות כותים (דף לד) כשאמר בית שמאי דם הנכרית טהור [illegible] ...וגורסין בתלמוד בני מערבא ר' אבון בשם ר' יהושע בן לוי [illegible] ...ומכאן אמרו ספיקות באושא גזרו עליהן [illegible] (חגיגה דף כג) תמצא גזירת צינורא דעם הארץ וזה בענין הקודש: **מפנין** תרומה טהורה ודמאי. כבר פירשנו דמאי בפ' [illegible]

וזהו שנת שלישית אינו מפריש מעשר [שני] אלא מעשר עני. ושנה ראשונה ושניה מעשר שני. ואינו חייב לאכול אלא אחר שיקצור ויגדיש ויעמיד כרי ויעשה גורן לפיכך אמר ר"ל אם בא ישראל מן השבולים... [illegible] ...מעכב

חשק שלמה על רבינו חננאל א) כ"ה דף ט ע"א ונכפל קושט דמשנה דיוחנן כ"ג העביר הודיית המעשר ובגמ' שם כצ"ל:

ליקוטי רש"י

מטרוניתא. שרת נכרית [ב"מ פג:]. **וחזיא ליה.** דרוב עמי הארץ מעשרין הן ומותרת לעניים כדתנן מאכילין את העניים ואת האכסניא... **אכסניא.** חיל של מלך... [illegible] **שהקדימו בשבולים.** [illegible] **וכי הא דא"ר אבהו.** [illegible] **מכל מתנותיכם תרימו.** [illegible] **ומה ראית.** [illegible]

וְלֹא נִטְּלָה הֵימֶנּוּ תְּרוּמָה גְּדוֹלָה – but *terumah gedolah* **was not taken from it.** וְכִי הָא דְּאָמַר רַבִּי אַבָּהוּ אָמַר רֵישׁ לָקִישׁ – **And** our Mishnah is **in accordance** with (and thus corroborates) **that which R' Abahu said in the name of Reish Lakish:** מַעֲשֵׂר רִאשׁוֹן שֶׁהִקְדִּימוֹ בְּשִׁבּוֹלִין – ***Maaser rishon*** **that one advanced** ahead of the *terumah gedolah* while the grain was still **in ears** פָּטוּר מִתְּרוּמָה גְּדוֹלָה – **is exempt from** ***terumah gedolah.*** שֶׁנֶּאֱמַר ,,וַהֲרֵמֹתֶם מִמֶּנּוּ תְּרוּמַת ה' מַעֲשֵׂר מִן־הַמַּעֲשֵׂר'' – **For it states** in reference to *maaser rishon:* ***And you shall separate from it Hashem's terumah, a tithe of the tithe,***[32] which we interpret as indicating: ,,מַעֲשֵׂר מִן־הַמַּעֲשֵׂר'' אָמַרְתִּי לְךָ – ***A tithe of the tithe*** **is what I** [G-d] **have told you,** the Levi, to separate as *terumah* from the tithe, וְלֹא תְּרוּמָה גְּדוֹלָה וּתְרוּמַת מַעֲשֵׂר מִן הַמַּעֲשֵׂר – **but not** both ***terumah gedolah*** **and** ***terumas maaser*** from **the tithe.**[33]

The Gemara questions Reish Lakish's teaching:

אָמַר לֵיהּ רַב פָּפָּא לְאַבַּיֵי – **Rav Pappa said to Abaye:** אִי הָכִי – **If** it is **so** that this verse specifically exempts *maaser rishon* from *terumah gedolah,* as Reish Lakish maintains, אֲפִילוּ הִקְדִּימוֹ בִּכְרִי נַמִּי לִיפְּטַר – then **even if one advanced [the** ***maaser rishon*****]** ahead of the *terumah gedolah* after the grain was heaped **in a** finished **pile, [the** ***maaser rishon*****] should also be exempt** from *terumah gedolah*! Yet, the law is clearly that the Levi *must* separate *terumah gedolah* in this case.[34] – ? –

Abaye responds:

אָמַר לֵיהּ עָלֶיךָ אָמַר קְרָא ,,מִכֹּל מַתְּנֹתֵיכֶם תָּרִימוּ וגו' '' – **He said to [Rav Pappa]:** In response **to** the question **you** raise, **Scripture states:** ***From all your gifts you shall separate*** *all of Hashem's terumah.*[35]

The Gemara asks:

וּמָה רָאִיתָ – **And what have you seen** that leads you to apply the first verse (which exempts the Levi from *terumah gedolah*) to the situation in which he preempted the Kohen while the grain was in ears, and the second verse (which obligates the Levi in *terumah gedolah*) to the situation in which he preempted the Kohen after the grain was smoothed in a pile? Perhaps the verses should be applied in the reverse way![36] – ? –

The Gemara answers:

הַאי אִידְגַּן – **This** produce that has been smoothed in a pile **has been rendered "grain,"** וְהַאי לֹא אִידְגַּן – **whereas this** produce that is still in ears **has not been rendered "grain."**[37]

The Mishnah then states:

וּמַעֲשֵׂר שֵׁנִי וכו' – **AND** one may clear away ***MAASER SHENI*** **etc.** [or consecrated produce that was redeemed].

The Gemara asks:

פְּשִׁיטָא – **It is obvious** that redeemed *maaser sheni* or redeemed consecrated produce is not *muktzeh,* for it is perfectly permissible food permitted to all! Why did the Mishnah have to state this?

The Gemara answers:

לֹא צְרִיכָא שֶׁנָּתַן אֶת הַקֶּרֶן וְלֹא נָתַן אֶת הַחוֹמֶשׁ – **No! It is a necessary** ruling (i.e. the Mishnah refers to) **where [the owner] gave the principal** (the actual value of the item he is redeeming) **but he did not give the** required additional **fifth.**[38] הָא קָא מַשְׁמַע לָן דְּאֵין חוֹמֶשׁ מְעַכֵּב – **Thus [the Mishnah] informs us** (by stating that *maaser sheni* or consecrated produce redeemed in this way is not *muktzeh*) **that** the failure to add **the** additional **fifth does not hold back** the redemption from taking effect.[39]

The Mishnah stated:

וְהַתּוּרְמוֹס הַיָּבֵשׁ כו' – **AND** one may clear away **DRIED** ***TURMOS*** **etc.** [because it is food for goats].

The Gemara comments:

דַּוְקָא יָבֵשׁ אֲבָל לַח לֹא – The Mishnah means **specifically dried** *turmos,* but **moist** (i.e. fresh) *turmos* is *muktzeh* and may **not** be cleared away. מַאי טַעְמָא – **What is the reason** that a moist *turmos* is *muktzeh*? כֵּיוָן דְּמָרִיר לֹא אָכְלָה – For **since it is bitter** when moist, even **[a goat] would not eat** it.

NOTES

this way, the Levi increases his take by two percent – the percentage (on average) that the farmer's crop would have been reduced by the removal of *terumah gedolah* before the *maaser rishon* tithe (see *Rashi* to *Eruvin* 31b et al.).

32. *Numbers* 18:26.

33. The verse does not state merely: *And you shall separate from it maaser from the maaser,* but rather: *And you shall separate from it "Hashem's terumah," maaser from the maaser.* With this extra expression, the Torah indicates that the only aspect of "Hashem's *terumah*" separated by the Levi from his *maaser* is the *terumah* identified in the subsequent phrase – a tithe of the tithe – and not any additional *terumah.* Therefore, even when the Levi obtained his *maaser rishon* before the *terumah* was separated, thus causing the Kohen to lose some of his *terumah* (two percent of the *maaser rishon*), he is exempted by Scriptural decree from having to repay that *terumah* from the *maaser* (see *Rashi* to *Beitzah* 13b).

Thus, our Mishnah states the case of "*maaser rishon* whose *terumah* was taken" in order to teach us that when the Levi preempts the Kohen while the grain is still in ears, there is indeed no *terumah gedolah* obligation on that *maaser rishon,* and that is why it is not *muktzeh.*

34. [This is clearly so, as even Reish Lakish stated that the *terumah gedolah* is preempted only if the normal sequence of separation was altered while the grain was still *in ears.*]

35. Ibid. verse 29. This is stated in reference to the Levi's obligation to separate *terumas maaser.* The expression *"All" of Hashem's terumah"* implies that in certain instances there is another aspect of *terumah* – besides the *terumas maaser* – that the Levi must separate from the *maaser rishon* (*Rashi*). This other aspect is the *terumah gedolah,* and the instance in which it must be separated is where the Levi preempted the *terumah gedolah* after the grain had already been smoothed in a pile.

36. *Rashi* to *Beitzah* (13b). [*Tosafos* there (see also *Ritva MHK* ed. here) question what sense it would make to apply the verses in the reverse way. How could one entertain the notion that if the *terumah gedolah* is preempted after piling, the Levi need not separate it, but if it is preempted in ears, he must? *Tos. HaRosh* here (citing *Maharam MeRotenburg*) answers that perhaps the Torah obligated the Levi to separate the *terumah gedolah* only if he preempted it before piling, when he should have realized that *terumah gedolah* had not yet been separated, but not if he preempted the *terumah gedolah* after piling, when he might have thought that it had already been separated.]

37. Produce attains the status of "grain" only after its raw processing has been completed [i.e. it has been smoothed in a pile] (see *Rashi* to *Berachos* 47b, and *Eruvin* 31b). Therefore, that is the point at which the *obligation* to separate *terumah* [and tithes] takes effect, as the verse (*Deuteronomy* 18:4) states: רֵאשִׁית דְּגָנְךָ. . . תִּתֶּן־לוֹ, *The first of your "grain" . . . shall you give to [the Kohen].* It stands to reason, then, that the verse *requiring* the Levi to restitute the preempted *terumah gedolah* to the Kohen refers to the case in which the Levi preempted it after the Kohen had already become entitled to it – i.e. after the grain has been smoothed in a pile. (Therefore, the Levi first separates two percent of his *maaser rishon* as *terumah gedolah,* and then ten percent of the remainder as *terumas maaser.*) And it stands to reason that the verse *exempting* the Levi from making restitution of the preempted *terumah gedolah* to the Kohen refers to the case in which the Levi preempted it before the Kohen had become entitled to it – i.e. while the grain was still in ears (see *Rashi*).

38. When one redeems his own *maaser sheni* or consecrated object, he must add a fifth. The fifth is not added when redeeming someone else's item (see *Leviticus* 27:13 and 31, with *Rashi*).

39. See *Rashash* to the Mishnah above.

The Gemara now examines the Mishnah's list of objects that are *muktzeh* and may not be cleared away. The Mishnah stated: **אֲבָל לֹא אֶת הַטֶּבֶל וכו׳** – **HOWEVER,** one may **NOT** clear away ***TEVEL*** **etc.**

The Gemara asks:

פְּשִׁיטָא – **It is obvious** that *tevel* is *muktzeh,* for it may not be eaten until it is tithed, and one may not tithe produce on the Sabbath. Why did the Mishnah have to state that it may not be cleared away?

The Gemara answers:

לֹא צְרִיכָא בְּטֶבֶל טָבוּל מִדְּרַבָּנָן – **No! It is** a **necessary** ruling **in** the case of ***tevel*** **that requires tithing** only **Rabbinically,** **שֶׁזְּרָעוֹ בְּעָצִיץ שֶׁאֵינוֹ נָקוּב** – such as **where one planted [the produce] in an unperforated flowerpot.**[1] And the Mishnah teaches that although the produce is fit for eating on the Biblical level, it is deemed *muktzeh* because it is unfit for eating on the Rabbinic level.

The Mishnah's list of *muktzeh* items continues with:

וְלֹא מַעֲשֵׂר רִאשׁוֹן וכו׳ – **NOR *MAASER RISHON* etc.** [whose *terumah* has not been taken].

Apparently, this means that the *terumas maaser* has not been taken from it.[2] Accordingly, the Gemara asks:

פְּשִׁיטָא – **It is obvious** that *maaser rishon* whose *terumas maaser* has not been taken is *muktzeh,* as it is bona fide *tevel* that has not been tithed. Why did the Mishnah have to state that it may not be cleared away?

The Gemara answers:

לֹא צְרִיכָא שֶׁהִקְדִּימוֹ בְּכְרִי – **No! It is** a **necessary** ruling (i.e. the Mishnah refers to) **where one advanced** the separation of **[the *maaser rishon*]** ahead of the *terumah gedolah* after the grain had been heaped **in a** finished **pile,** **שֶׁנִּטַּל מִמֶּנּוּ מַעֲשֵׂר** – and **where *terumas maaser* has been taken from [the *maaser rishon*]** **וְלֹא נִטְּלָה מִמֶּנּוּ תְּרוּמָה גְּדוֹלָה** – **but *terumah gedolah* has not been taken from it.**[3] And there is thus a novelty in the Mishnah's ruling that such produce may not be eaten. **מַהוּ דְּתֵימָא כִּדְאָמַר לֵיהּ רַב פָּפָּא לְאַבַּיֵי** – For **you might have said as Rav Pappa said to Abaye;**[4] viz. that the verse which exempts the *maaser rishon* from *terumah gedolah* if the Levi preempts the Kohen while the grain is in ears should also exempt it from *terumah gedolah* even if he preempts the Kohen after the grain is piled.[5] **קָא מַשְׁמַע לָן כִּדְשַׁנֵּי לֵיהּ אַבַּיֵי** – Therefore, **[the Tanna] informs us** otherwise – **as Abaye had answered [Rav Pappa];**[4] viz. that a second verse serves to obligate the *maaser rishon* in *terumah gedolah* where the Levi preempts the Kohen after the grain has already been piled.[6]

The Mishnah's list of *muktzeh* items continues with:

וְלֹא אֶת מַעֲשֵׂר שֵׁנִי וכו׳ – **NOR *MAASER SHENI* etc.** [or consecrated produce that was not redeemed].

The Gemara asks:

פְּשִׁיטָא – **It is obvious** that these items are *muktzeh* if not redeemed![7] Why did the Mishnah have to state this?

The Gemara answers:

לֹא צְרִיכָא – **No! It is** a **necessary** ruling (i.e. the Mishnah refers to) **דְּנִפְדּוּ וְלֹא נִפְדּוּ כְּהִלְכָתָן** – **where they were,** in fact, **redeemed, but they were not redeemed properly.** **מַעֲשֵׂר שֶׁפְּדָאוֹ עַל גַּבֵּי אֲסִימוֹן** – In the case of ***maaser** sheni,* this would refer to **where one redeemed it** by attempting to transfer its sanctity **onto an unminted slug,** rather than onto a minted coin. And a redemption done in such a manner is not effective, **דְּרַחֲמָנָא אָמַר ,,וְצַרְתָּ הַכֶּסֶף בְּיָדְךָ״** – **for the Merciful One says** in His Torah: ***And you shall bind ("vetzarta") the money in your hand.***[8] This verse indicates that the *maaser sheni* may be deconsecrated only onto **דָּבָר שֶׁיֵּשׁ בּוֹ צוּרָה** – **something that has an image,** i.e. a minted coin, and not an unminted slug.[9] **הֶקְדֵּשׁ שֶׁחִילְּלוֹ עַל גַּבֵּי קַרְקַע** – In the case of **consecrated produce** "redeemed but not redeemed properly" would refer to **where one deconsecrated it onto real property.** And a deconsecration of consecrated items done by substituting land for them is ineffective, **דְּרַחֲמָנָא אָמַר ,,וְנָתַן הַכֶּסֶף . . . וְקָם לוֹ״** – **for the Merciful One says** in His Torah: ***And he shall pay the [redemption] money . . . and it*** [the consecrated object] ***will be secured to him.***[10] We derive from this verse that deconsecration onto real property is ineffective.[11]

The Mishnah's list of *muktzeh* items continues with:

וְלֹא אֶת הַלּוּף – **NOR *LUF.*** [R' Shimon ben Gamliel, however, permits clearing away *luf,* because it is food for ravens.]

The Gemara cites a Baraisa that discusses the dispute between the Tanna Kamma and R' Shimon ben Gamliel:

תָּנוּ רַבָּנָן – **The Rabbis taught in a Baraisa:** **מְטַלְטְלִין אֶת הֶחָצָב** – **WE MAY MOVE** cut ***CHATZAV***[12] on the Sabbath, **מִפְּנֵי שֶׁהוּא מַאֲכָל לִצְבָיִים** – **BECAUSE IT IS FOOD FOR DEER,** **וְאֶת הַחַרְדָּל מִפְּנֵי שֶׁהוּא**

NOTES

1. Since the produce does not draw its nourishment from the ground, it is not Biblically subject to tithing. Rabbinically, however, such produce does require tithing.

2. *Rashi.*

3. [In contrast to the first part of the Mishnah (*maaser rishon whose terumah has been taken*), where "*terumah*" referred to *terumas maaser,* here (in the case of *maaser rishon whose terumah has* **not** *been taken*) "*terumah*" refers to *terumah gedolah.*]

4. At the end of 127b.

5. Accordingly, even in the present case the *maaser rishon* would be fully tithed and fit for consumption.

6. Accordingly, the *maaser rishon* is still *tevel* and thus *muktzeh* until its *terumah gedolah* is separated.

7. For these items (*maaser sheni* outside of Jerusalem, or consecrated produce anywhere) cannot be eaten without being redeemed, and it is forbidden to redeem them on the Sabbath.

8. *Deuteronomy* 14:25. The verse is discussing taking the redemption money of *maaser sheni* to Jerusalem. [Now, the Torah could have written simply וְלָקַחְתָּ הַכֶּסֶף בְּיָדְךָ, *And you shall take the money in your hand.* The unusual choice of the verb וְצַרְתָּ, *and you shall bind,* indicates that we are to expound it in the sense of וְצַרְתָּ, *and you shall engrave with an image,* i.e. the silver should be a minted coin.

9. [Thus, whereas the redemption of other sacred articles can generally be accomplished by substituting for them most any item of value, the redemption of *maaser sheni* requires specifically its replacement with minted coins (see *Rambam, Hil. Maaser Sheni* 4:2,9 with commentaries).]

Our Mishnah teaches us that if one redeemed the *maaser sheni* with an unminted slug, the *maaser-sheni* produce remains unredeemed and it is therefore *muktzeh* outside of Jerusalem (see *Tosafos*).

10. *Tosafos* point out that there is no such verse in the Torah. The Gemara is rather citing an abbreviated paraphrase of *Leviticus* 27:19 (which deals with one who has consecrated his ancestral field and now wishes to redeem it), which states: וְיָסַף חֲמִשִׁית כֶּסֶף־עֶרְכְּךָ עָלָיו וְקָם לוֹ, *And he shall add a fifth of the money of assessment to it and [the field] shall be assured to him.*

11. *Tosafos* explain the hermeneutic mechanism by which the Gemara derives from the word "money" used in the verse that real property, which is dissimilar to money in that it is immovable, cannot be used to redeem the field.

12. *Chatzav* is a grass whose roots grow straight down and do not spread to the sides. It is the grass that Joshua used to demarcate the various portions in Eretz Yisrael [see *Bava Basra* 56a with *Rashbam*] (*Rashi*).

אבל לא את הטבל וכו': פשיטא לא צריכא בטבל טבול מדרבנן (א) שזרעו בעציץ שאינו נקוב: ולא מעשר ראשון וכו': פשיטא לא צריכא שהקדימו בכרי שנטל ממנו מעשר ולא נטלה ממנו תרומה גדולה מהו דתימא כדאמר ליה רב פפא לאביי קמ"ל כדשני ליה אביי: ולא את מעשר שני וכו': פשיטא לא צריכא דנפדו ולא נפדו כהלכתן מעשר שפדאו על גבי אסימון דרחמנא אמר וצרת הכסף בידך דבר שיש בו צורה הקדש שחיללו על גבי קרקע דרחמנא אמר ונתן הכסף וקם לו: ולא את הלוף: ת"ר מטלטלין את החצב מפני שהוא מאכל לצביים ואת החרדל מפני שהוא מאכל ליונים רשב"ג אומר אף מטלטלין שברי זכוכית מפני שהוא מאכל לנעמיות אמר ליה רבי נתן אלא מעתה חבילי זמורות יטלטלו מפני שהוא מאכל לפילין ורשב"ג נעמיות שכיחי פילין לא שכיחי אמר אמימר והוא דאית ליה נעמיות אמר רב אשי לאמימר אלא דקאמר ליה ר' נתן לרשב"ג חבילי זמורות יטלטל מפני שהוא מאכל לפילין אי אית ליה פילין אמאי לא אלא ראוי ה"נ ראוי אמר אביי רשב"ג ורבי שמעון ורבי ישמעאל ורבי עקיבא כולהו סבירא להו כל ישראל בני מלכים הם רשב"ג הא דאמרן ר' שמעון דתנן בני מלכים סכין על גבי מכותיהן שמן וורד שכן דרכן של בני מלכים לסוך בחול ר"ש אומר כל ישראל בני מלכים הם ר' ישמעאל ור' עקיבא דתניא הרי שהיו נושין בו אלף מנה ולבוש איצטלא בת ק' מנה מפשיטין אותו ומלבישין אותו איצטלא הראויה לו תנא משום רבי ישמעאל ותנא משום רבי עקיבא כל ישראל ראוין לאותה איצטלא: חבילי קש וחבילי כו': תנו רבנן חבילי קש וחבילי עצים (ג) וחבילי זרדים אם התקינן למאכל בהמה מטלטלין אותן ואם לאו אין מטלטלין אותן רשב"ג אומר חבילין הניטלין ביד אחד מותר לטלטלן בשתי ידים אסור לטלטלן חבילי סיאה אזוב וקורנית הכניסן לעצים אין [א] מסתפק מהן בשבת למאכל בהמה מסתפק מהן בשבת וקוטם ביד ואוכל ובלבד שלא יקטום בכלי ומולל ואוכל ובלבד שלא ימלול בכלי הרבה דברי רבי יהודה וחכמים אומרים מולל בראשי אצבעותיו ואוכל ובלבד שלא ימלול בידו הרבה כדרך שהוא עושה בחול וכן באמיתא וכן בפיגם וכן בשאר מיני תבלין מאי אמיתא ניניא סיאה אמר רב יהודה (סיאה) צתרי אזוב אברתא קורנית קורניתא שמה והא ההוא דאמר להו מאן בעי קורניתא ואישתכח חשי אלא סיאה צתרי אזוב אברתא קורניתא חשי: איתמר בשר מליח מותר לטלטלו בשבת [ב] תפל רב הונא אמר מותר לטלטלו רב חסדא אמר אסור לטלטלו רב הונא אמר מותר לטלטלו והא רב הונא תלמיד דרב הוה ורב כר' יהודה סבירא ליה דאית ליה מוקצה במוקצה לאכילה סבר לה כרבי יהודה במוקצה לטלטל סבר לה כרבי שמעון רב חסדא אמר אסור לטלטלו והא רב יצחק בר אמי איקלע לבי רב חסדא וחזא ההוא בר אווזא דהוו קא מטלטלו ליה משמשא לטולא ואמר רב חסדא חסרון כיס קא חזינן הכא שאני בר אווזא דחזי לאומצא ת"ר דג מליח מותר לטלטלו דג תפל אסור לטלטלו בשר בין תפל ובין מליח מותר לטלטלו (וסתמא כרבי שמעון) תנו רבנן מטלטלין את העצמות מפני שהוא מאכל לכלבים בשר

רש"י

שלא ניטלה תרומתו. קא סלקא דעתך שלא ניטלה תרומה גדולה שלו: אסימון. שאין עליו צורה: חצב. עשב שמשתרש בעומק כנגדו ואין שרשיו מתפשטין וכו' תיחם יהושע את הארץ לישראל: נעמיות. בנות היענה: יטלטלו. ראוי הוא להיות לו פילין ולהאכילן: על מכותיהן. בשבת ולא גזר משום שחיקת סממנין: שכן דרכן לסוך. בלא מכה הלכך לאו מוכחא מילתא דלרפואה: התקינן. הזמינן: אסור לטלטלן. ואפילו הזמינם למאכל בהמה דטירחא היא: סיאה אזוב וקורנית. לקמיה מפרש לה: הכניסן לעצים. לייבשן: שלא יקטום בכלי. כדרך חול כדאמרן (לעיל דף עד:) האי מאן דפריס סילקא דמי לטוחן. במילתיה דרבי יהודה גרסינן מולל ואוכל ובלבד שלא ימלול בכלי הרבה וחכמי' אומרים מולל בראשי אצבעותיו ובלבד שלא ימלול בידו הרבה כדרך חול כך מצאתי בתוספתא דרבנן מחמרי דבכולי ידא אסור אלא בראשי אצבעותיו ומהו מולל כגון אם בא לאכול הזרע מולל השרביטין שהזרע בתוכם: וכן באמיתא. לקמיה מפרש מאי אמיתא: ניניא. מינטא"י: פיגם. רוד"א: צתרי. שדריא"ה לוי"ה ל"א פוליאול: אברתא. איסופ"א: חשי. שדריא"ה וללשון הראשון לא פורש: בשר תפל. שאינו מלוח ומאן דגריס תפוח היא היא: מותר לטלטלו. דלית ליה מוקצה בטלטול: במוקצה לאכילה סבר לה כר' יהודה. כלומר באיסור מוקצה לענין אכילה סבר לה כרבי יהודה לאסר לאוכלו (ג) ובאיסור מוקצה לטלטול סבר לה כרבי שמעון: בר אווזא. שחוט: משמשא לטולא. שלא יסריח: ואמר להו רב חסדא חסרון כיס קא חזינא הכא. שאתם מניחים אותה בשמש ומתחמם וסלקוהו על פיו מחמה לצל: באומצא. כשהוא חי אוכלין אותו בלא מלח: דג תפל אסור לטלטלו. דאינו ראוי לכלום ולכלבים לאו דעתיה למישדייה אבל מליח נאכל חי על ידי מלחו:

תוספות

אבל לא את הטבל. והא דאמר (ד) רבה בפרק כירה (לעיל דף מג.) טבל מוכן הוא אצל שבת שאם עבר ותיקנו מתוקן ה"מ לענין ביטול כלי מהיכנו שלא החמירו כמו לענין טלטול בידים:

שפדאו אגב אסימון. הא דנקט אסימון היינו דלא כרבי דוסא דפרק הזהב (ב"מ דף מז:) והוה מצי למימר מעות הניתנות סימן לבית המרחץ לד"ה אלא משום דאם כן מאי קמ"ל אבל השתא קמ"ל כרבנן:

ונתן הכסף וקם לו. אין הפסוק כן אלא ויסף חמישית כסף ערכך עליו וקם לו (ויקרא כז) ודרך הש"ס לקצר ולומר בלשון אחר קצר כי ההיא דפרק הדר (עירובין דף סה.) רבי חנינא ביומא דרתח לא מצלי שנאמר בצר אל יורה ובפרק הרואה (ברכות דף נה:) שנאמר כל החלומות הולכים אחר הפה וקשה לר"י נימא כסף דוקא וכ"ת דשוה כסף ככסף הדא דגבי נזקין מצרכינן קרא ישיב לרבות שוה כסף ועוד דאם כן אפילו קרקע נמי ומנלן למעוטי קרקע ואומר ר"י דמכלל ופרט נפקא כדתנן בבכורות בפרק יש בכור לנחלה (דף נא.) אין פודין לא בעבדים ולא בקרקעות ולא בהקדשות ומפרש בגמרא דבעי למימר ולא הקדשות בכל אלו לענין פדיון בכור דרשינן התם כלל ופרט ופדויו מבן חדש כלל כסף פרט תפדה חזר וכלל מה הפרט מפורש דבר המיטלטל כו' ה"נ איכא למימר בפדיון הקדשות ונתן כלל כסף פרט וקם לו חזר וכלל כו' מיהו בת"כ דריש ליה מקרא אחרינא וכל ערכך יהיה בשקל הקדש מה ת"ל לפי שנאמר (ה) תפדה יכול בעבדים ושטרות וקרקעו' ת"ל בשקל הקדש אין לי אלא סלעים מניין לרבות כל דבר המיטלטל ת"ל ופדה בערכך א"כ למה נאמר בשקל פרט לעבדים ושטרות וקרקעות אלא כן דרך הש"ס שאינו מביא עיקר הדרשה כמו שרגיל להביא (כתובות דף מו:) בנעוריה בית אביה כל שבח נעורים לאביה אע"ג דההוא בהפרת נדרים הוא דכתיב וכן הרבה:

רשב"ג אומר אף מטלטלין שברי זכוכית. משמע דמודה לת"ק דמתיר חרדל והא דתנן רשב"ג מתיר בלוף וכל שכן דמתיר בחרדל:

הכניסן לעצים אין מסתפק. איכא למימר דה"ק הא סתמא נעשה כמי שהכניסן למאכל בהמה כי היכי דלא תקשה רישא לסיפא:

דחזי לאומצא. מכאן ראיה דדס האברים שלא פירש מותר דקאמר דחזי לאומצא אע"ג דלא מליח:

דג תפל אסור לטלטלו. תימה מדשרי בשר תפל אלמא כר"ש אתיא א"כ דג תפל נמי לישרי כמו בשר תפל וי"ל דדג תפל אינו ראוי לכלבים אי נמי כר' יהודה אתיא ודג תפל אע"פ שראוי לכלבים אסור לטלטלו דכל מידי דחזי לאינש לא מקצה לכלבים בשר תפל מותר לטלטלו לרבי יהודה מפני שהוא מאכל לחיה:

מטלטלין את העצמות. לר' יהודה דאית לי' מוקצה איירי כגון שלא הי' עליה' בשר מאתמול:

גליון הש"ס

הגהות הב"ח

הגהות הגר"א

תורה אור השלם

רב נסים גאון

רבינו חננאל

ליקוטי רש"י

מַאֲכָל לְיוֹנִים – AND also MUSTARD, BECAUSE IT IS FOOD FOR DOVES.[13] רַבָּן שִׁמְעוֹן בֶּן גַּמְלִיאֵל אוֹמֵר – RABBAN SHIMON BEN GAMLIEL SAYS: אַף מְטַלְטְלִין שִׁבְרֵי זְכוּכִית – WE MAY EVEN MOVE GLASS SHARDS, מִפְּנֵי שֶׁהוּא מַאֲכָל לְנַעֲמִיּוֹת – BECAUSE IT IS FOOD FOR OSTRICHES.[14] אָמַר לֵיהּ רַבִּי נָתָן – R' NASSAN SAID TO HIM: אֶלָּא מֵעַתָּה – BUT according to your reasoning, IT SHOULD FOLLOW חֲבִילֵי זְמוֹרוֹת יְטַלְטְלוּ – that BUNDLES OF VINES MAY BE MOVED as well, מִפְּנֵי שֶׁהוּא מַאֲכָל לְפִילִין – BECAUSE IT IS FOOD FOR ELEPHANTS! And since no one maintains that bundles of vines may be moved, surely your reasoning is disproved!

The Gemara explains Rabban Shimon ben Gamliel's view:

וְרַבָּן שִׁמְעוֹן בֶּן גַּמְלִיאֵל – **But Rabban Shimon ben Gamliel** would answer to R' Nassan that vines cannot be compared to glass shards. נַעֲמִיּוֹת שְׁכִיחִי – For **ostriches are common;**[15] therefore, glass shards, which are fed to them, are considered "prepared" and are thus not *muktzeh.* פִּילִין לֹא שְׁכִיחִי – **Elephants,** however, **are not common;** therefore, bundles of vines, though they are fit for elephants, are not considered "prepared" for such use, and are thus deemed *muktzeh.*

The Gemara presents an Amoraic dispute concerning Rabban Shimon ben Gamliel's position:

אָמַר אֲמֵימַר – **Ameimar said:** וְהוּא דְּאִית לֵיהּ נַעֲמִיּוֹת – Rabban Shimon ben Gamliel permits the moving of glass shards **provided that [the person]** in fact **has ostriches** in his possession. Thus, his glass shards are considered "prepared" to be fed to the ostriches. But if he does not own any ostriches, then even Rabban Shimon ben Gamliel agrees that the glass shards are *muktzeh.*

Rav Ashi challenges Ameimar's assertion:

אָמַר רַב אַשִׁי לַאֲמֵימַר – **Rav Ashi said to Ameimar:** אֶלָּא דְּקָאָמַר לֵיהּ רַבִּי נָתָן לְרַבָּן שִׁמְעוֹן בֶּן גַּמְלִיאֵל – **But** how will you explain **that which R' Nassan says to Rabban Shimon ben Gamliel** in the Baraisa: חֲבִילֵי זְמוֹרוֹת יְטַלְטֵל מִפְּנֵי שֶׁהוּא מַאֲכָל לְפִילִין – "But according to your reasoning, it should follow that ONE MAY MOVE BUNDLES OF VINES as well, BECAUSE IT IS FOOD FOR ELEPHANTS"? אִי אִית לֵיהּ פִּילִין אַמַּאי לֹא – Now, **if [the person]** actually **has elephants** in his possession, as emerges from your interpretation of Rabban Shimon ben Gamliel's position,[16] then **why** in fact would one **not** be permitted to move the vines? Certainly, they are "prepared" for the elephants' use by the owner and obviously would not be *muktzeh*! אֶלָּא רָאוּי – **Rather,** R' Nassan's objection must involve the case in which the person does not actually have elephants, so that the vines are merely **fit** for elephants, not actually "prepared" for them. הָכִי נַמִּי רָאוּי – **So, too,** must Rabban Shimon ben Gamliel's ruling involve the case in which the person does not actually have ostriches, so that the glass shards are merely **fit** for ostriches, not actually "prepared" for them.

Abaye presents a list of Tannaim who follow the rationale that underlies Rabban Shimon ben Gamliel's ruling in this matter:

אָמַר אַבַּיֵי – **Abaye said:** רַבָּן שִׁמְעוֹן בֶּן גַּמְלִיאֵל וְרַבִּי שִׁמְעוֹן וְרַבִּי יִשְׁמָעֵאל וְרַבִּי עֲקִיבָא – **Rabban Shimon ben Gamliel, R' Shimon, R' Yishmael and R' Akiva** כּוּלְּהוּ סְבִירָא לְהוּ כָּל יִשְׂרָאֵל בְּנֵי מְלָכִים הֵם – **all hold that all** the people of **Israel are** considered **princes.**

Abaye proceeds to demonstrate his assertion: רַבָּן שִׁמְעוֹן בֶּן גַּמְלִיאֵל הָא דַּאֲמָרָן – That this is the view of **Rabban Shimon ben Gamliel** is evident from **that which we have just stated.**[17] רַבִּי שִׁמְעוֹן – That **R' Shimon** also subscribes to this view is evident from the following: דִּתְנַן – **For we learned in a Mishnah:**[18] בְּנֵי מְלָכִים סָכִין עַל גַּבֵּי מַכּוֹתֵיהֶן שֶׁמֶן וֶורֶד – PRINCES MAY SMEAR ROSE OIL ON THEIR WOUNDS on the Sabbath, שֶׁכֵּן דַּרְכָּן שֶׁל בְּנֵי מְלָכִים לָסוּךְ בְּחוֹל – FOR SUCH IS THEIR CUSTOM TO SMEAR rose oil on their bodies even ON WEEKDAYS.[19] רַבִּי שִׁמְעוֹן אוֹמֵר – R' SHIMON SAYS: כָּל יִשְׂרָאֵל בְּנֵי מְלָכִים הֵם – ALL of ISRAEL ARE PRINCES. Therefore, any Jew may apply rose oil to his wounds on the Sabbath.[20]

רַבִּי יִשְׁמָעֵאל וְרַבִּי עֲקִיבָא – That **R' Yishmael and R' Akiva** also subscribe to this view is evident from the following: דְּתַנְיָא – **For it was taught in a Baraisa:** הֲרֵי שֶׁהָיוּ נוֹשִׁין בּוֹ אֶלֶף מָנֶה – IF [CREDITORS] HAD A CLAIM AGAINST HIM FOR ONE THOUSAND *MANEH* וְלָבוּשׁ אִיצְטְלָא בַּת מֵאָה מָנֶה – AND HE WAS CLOTHED IN A very expensive CLOAK WORTH ONE HUNDRED *MANEH,* מַפְשִׁיטִין אוֹתוֹ – WE STRIP HIM of it וּמַלְבִּישִׁין אוֹתוֹ אִיצְטְלָא הָרְאוּיָה לוֹ – AND WE CLOTHE HIM instead in A CLOAK THAT IS SUITABLE TO HIM.[21] תָּנָא מִשּׁוּם רַבִּי יִשְׁמָעֵאל – However, **it was taught in a**

NOTES

13. Seemingly, the Tanna Kamma of this Baraisa (who rules that [unground] mustard is not *muktzeh*) disputes the Tanna Kamma of our Mishnah (who rules that [unground] mustard is *muktzeh*). See *Rashba* and *Ran MHK* ed., who explain what the rationale for the dispute would be. Alternatively, there is, in fact, no halachic dispute between the Baraisa and Mishnah; the different rulings merely reflect different local conditions. In the place of the Baraisa's Tanna, doves were common [hence, he rules that unground mustard is not *muktzeh*]. In the place of the Mishnah's Tanna, doves were not common [hence, he rules that unground mustard is *muktzeh*] (*Ran MHK* ed., in explanation of *Rif* and *Rambam*). From this it emerges that an item fit for animals that are commonly found is not *muktzeh* and — as the Gemara will soon state — even for one who does not own such animals, whereas one fit for animals that are not commonly found is *muktzeh* (see *Orach Chaim* 308:29).

14. This is the בַּת הַיַּעֲנָה, *bas hayaanah,* mentioned in *Leviticus* 11:16, among the non-kosher birds (*Rashi*; see *Targum Onkelos* ad loc.). This is identified as the ostrich (*Rav Saadiah Gaon*; *Chizkuni*). [The ostrich swallows glass shards or other grit to aid digestion, in the same way that other birds use gravel.]

15. Ostriches [which are indigenous to the Arabian peninsula, east of Eretz Yisrael] were kept as pets by the royalty (see *Ran*).

16. If Rabban Shimon ben Gamliel permits the movement of glass shards only where the person owns ostriches, then R' Nassan's objection from the parallel case of elephants must also refer to where the person owns elephants.

17. Rabban Shimon ben Gamliel has stated (in the Mishnah) that *luf* is not *muktzeh* because it is food for ravens; similarly (as he states in the Baraisa), glass shards are not *muktzeh* because they are food for ostriches. Even though only the wealthy and aristocratic raise ravens and ostriches as pets, Rabban Shimon ben Gamliel rules that *luf* and glass shards are not *muktzeh* for any Jew. His rationale (as Abaye teaches us) is that all Jews are considered royalty. Hence, anything fit for use by royalty is considered fit for all Jews. [This rationale is necessary according to Rav Ashi (above), who demonstrates that Rabban Shimon ben Gamliel rules glass shards to be non-*muktzeh* even if the person does not own ostriches.]

18. Above, 111a. The Mishnah there discusses the use of medicines on the Sabbath. Generally, a healthy person who suffers from a localized pain or ailment [which is not severe enough to confine him to bed] is not permitted to use medication on the Sabbath. The Rabbis prohibited this so that people would not inadvertently grind herbs on the Sabbath (medicines generally being prepared from ground herbs), which would constitute the *melachah* of *grinding.*

19. Rose oil is expensive, and most people would reserve it only for medicinal purposes. Princes, however, owing to their wealth, use rose oil to anoint themselves (a non-medicinal practice) even during the week. Therefore, when they apply it to a wound on the Sabbath, it is not *evident* that they are doing so for medicinal purposes, and the Rabbis therefore did not forbid them to do so (see *Rashi*).

20. For anything used by royalty is permitted for all Jews (see, though, *Rashi* to 111b ד״ה דאילו ר״ש סבר מסי, and 111a note 25).

21. When collecting a debt, a lender cannot strip a borrower of all his assets, but must allow him to keep certain essentials (see *Bava Metzia* 113b, *Rashi* ד״ה ומפץ). Clothing is considered essential. However, if the borrower is wearing clothing that is considered excessively expensive for his social station, we force him to sell it, so that after using some of the proceeds to buy more appropriate clothing he can pay the lender the difference.

אבל לא את הטבל וכו': פשיטא לא צריכא בטבל טבול מדרבנן (א) שזרעו בעציץ שאינו נקוב: **ולא מעשר ראשון וכו':** פשיטא לא צריכא שהקדימו בכרי שנטל ממנו מעשר ולא נטלה ממנו תרומה גדולה מהו דתימא כדאמר ליה רב פפא לאביי קמ"ל כדשני ליה אביי: **ולא את מעשר שני וכו':** פשיטא לא צריכא דנפדו ולא נפדו כהלכתן מעשר שפדאו על גבי אסימון דרחמנא אמר א) וצרת הכסף בידך דבר שיש בו צורה הקדש שחיללו על גבי קרקע דרחמנא אמר ב) ונתן הכסף וקם לו: **ולא את הלוף:** ת"ר מטלטלין את החצב מפני שהוא מאכל לצביים ואת החרדל מפני שהוא מאכל ליונים רשב"ג אומר אף מטלטלין שברי זכוכית מפני שהוא מאכל לנעמיות אמר ליה רבי נתן אלא מעתה חבילי זמורות יטלטלו מפני שהוא מאכל לפילין ורשב"ג נעמיות שכיחי פילין לא שכיחי אמימר אמר והוא דאית ליה נעמיות אמר רב אשי לאמימר אלא דקאמר ליה ר' נתן לרשב"ג חבילי זמורות יטלטל מפני שהוא מאכל לפילין אי אית ליה פילין אמאי לא אלא ראוי ה"נ ראוי אמר אביי רשב"ג ורבי שמעון ורבי ישמעאל ורבי עקיבא כולהו סבירא להו כל ישראל בני מלכים הם רשב"ג הא דאמרן ר' שמעון דתנן בני מלכים סכין על גבי מכותיהן שמן וורד שכן דרכן של בני מלכים לסוך בחול ר"ש אומר כל ישראל בני מלכים הם ר' ישמעאל ור' עקיבא דתניא הרי שהיו נושין בו אלף מנה ולבוש איצטלא בת ק' מנה מפשיטין אותו ומלבישין אותו איצטלא הראויה לו תנא משום רבי ישמעאל ותנא משום רבי עקיבא כל ישראל ראוין לאותה איצטלא:

חבילי קש וחבילי כו': תנו רבנן חבילי קש וחבילי עצים (ב) וחבילי זרדים אם התקינן למאכל בהמה מטלטלין אותן ואם לאו אין מטלטלין אותן רשב"ג אומר חבילין הניטלין ביד אחד מותר לטלטלן בשתי ידים אסור לטלטלן חבילי סיאה אזוב וקורנית הכניסן לעצים אין [א] מסתפק מהן בשבת למאכל בהמה מסתפק מהן בשבת וקוטם ביד ואוכל ובלבד שלא יקטום בכלי ומולל ואוכל ובלבד שלא ימלול בכלי הרבה דברי רבי יהודה וחכמים אומרים מולל בראשי אצבעותיו ואוכל ובלבד שלא ימלול בידו הרבה כדרך שהוא עושה בחול וכן באמיתא וכן בפיגם וכן בשאר מיני תבלין מאי אמיתא ניניא סיאה אמר רב יהודה (סיאה) צתרי אזוב אברתא קורנית קורניתא שמה והא ההוא דאמר להו מאן בעי קורניתא ואישתכח חשי אלא סיאה צתרי אזוב אברתא קורניתא חשי: איתמר בשר מליח מותר לטלטלו בשבת בשר [ב] תפל רב הונא אמר מותר לטלטלו רב חסדא אמר אסור לטלטלו רב הונא אמר מותר לטלטלו והא רב הונא תלמיד דרב הוה ורב כר' יהודה סבירא ליה דאית ליה מוקצה במוקצה לאכילה סבר לה כרבי יהודה במוקצה לטלטל סבר לה כרבי שמעון רב חסדא אמר אסור לטלטלו והא רב יצחק בר אמי איקלע לבי רב חסדא וחזא ההוא בר אווזא דהוו קא מטלטלו ליה משמשא לטולא ואמר רב חסדא חסרון כיס קא חזינן הכא שאני בר אווזא דחזי לאומצא ת"ר דג מליח מותר לטלטלו דג תפל אסור לטלטלו בשר בין תפל ובין מליח מותר לטלטלו (וסתמא כרבי שמעון) תנו רבנן מטלטלין את העצמות מפני שהוא מאכל לכלבים בשר

רש"י

שלא ניטלה תרומתו. קא סלקא דעתך שלא ניטלה תרומת מעשר שלו: **אסימון.** שאין עליו צורה: **חצב.** עשב שמשתרש בעומק כנגדו ואין שרשיו מתפשטין ובו [ח] תיחם יהושע את הארץ לישראל: **נעמיות.** בנות היענה: **יטלטלו.** ראוי הוא להיות לו פילין ולהאכילן: **על מכותיהן.** בשבת ולא גזר משום שחיקת סממנין: **שכן דרכן לסוך.** בלא מכה הלכך לאו מוכחא מילתא דלרפואה: **התקינן.** הזמינן: **אסור לטלטלן.** ואפילו הזמינם למאכל בהמה דטירחא היא: **סיאה אזוב וקורנית.** לקמיה מפרש לה: **הכניסן לעצים.** לייבשן: **שלא יקטום בכלי.** כדרך חול כדאמרן (לעיל דף עד:) האי מאן דפריס סילקא דמי לטוחן. במילתיה דרבי יהודה גרסינן מולל ואוכל ובלבד שלא ימלול בכלי הרבה וחכמי' אומרים מולל בראשי אצבעותיו ובלבד שלא ימלול בידו הרבה כדרך חול כך מצאתי בתוספתא דרבנן מחמרי דבכולי ידא אסור אלא בראשי אצבעותיו ומהו מולל כגון אם בא לאכול הזרע מולל השרביטין שהזרע בתוכם: **וכן באמיתא.** לקמיה מפרש מאי אמיתא: **ניניא.** מינטא"י: **פיגם.** רוד"א: **צתרי.** שדריא"ה לו"ה ל"א פוליאול: **אברתא.** איסני"א: **חשי.** שדריא"ה וללשון הראשון לא פורש: **בשר תפל.** שאינו מלוח ומאן דגריס תפוח היא היא: **מותר לטלטלו.** דלית ליה מוקצה בטלטול: **במוקצה לאכילה סבר לה כר' יהודה.** כלומר באיסור מוקצה לענין אכילה סבר לה כרבי יהודה לאסר לאוכלו (ג) ובאיסור מוקצה לטלטול סבר לה כרבי שמעון: **בר אווזא.** שחוט: **משמשא לטולא.** שלא יסריח: **ואמר להו רב חסדא חסרון כיס חזינא הכא.** שאתם מניחים אותה בשמש ומתחמם וסלקוהו על פיו מחמה לצל: **באומצא.** כשהוא חי אוכלין אותו בלא מלח: **דג תפל אסור לטלטלו.** דאינו ראוי לכלוס ולכלבים לאו דעתיה למישדייה אבל מליח נאכל חי על ידי מלחו:

תוספות

אבל לא את הטבל. והא דאמר (ד) רבה בפרק כירה (לעיל דף מג.) טבל מוכן הוא אצל שבת שאם עבר ותיקנו מתוקן ה"מ לענין ביטול כלי מהיכנו שלא החמירו כמו לענין טלטול בידים: **שפדאו אגב אסימון.** הא דנקט אסימון היינו דלא כרבי דוסא דפרק הזהב (ב"מ דף מז:) והוה מצי למימר מעות הניתנות סימן לבית המרחץ לד"ה אלא משום דאם כן מאי קמ"ל אבל השתא קמ"ל כרבנן: **ונתן הכסף וקם לו.** אין הפסוק כן אלא ויסף חמישית כסף ערכך עליו וקם לו (ויקרא כז) ודרך הש"ס לקצר ולומר בלשון אחר קצר כי ההיא דפרק הדר (עירובין דף סה.) רבי חנינא ביומא דרתח לא מצלי שנאמר בצר אל יורה ובפרק הרואה (ברכות דף נה:) שנאמר כל החלומות הולכים אחר הפה וקשה לר"י נימא כסף דוקא וכ"ת דשוה כסף ככסף הוא דגבי נזקין מצרכינן קרא ישיב לרבות שוה כסף ועוד דאם כן אפילו קרקע נמי ומנלן למעוטי קרקע ואומר ר"י דמכלל ופרט נפקא כדתנן בבכורות בפרק יש בכור לנחלה (דף נא.) אין פודין לא בעבדים ולא בקרקעות ולא בהקדשות ומפרש בגמרא דבעי למימר ולא הקדשות בכל אלו לענין פדיון בכור דרשינן התם כלל ופרט ופדויו מבן חדש כלל כסף פרט תפדה חזר וכלל מה הפרט מפורש דבר המיטלטל כו' ה"נ איכא למימר בפדיון הקדשות ונתן כלל כסף פרט וקם לו חזר וכלל כו' מיהו בת"כ דריש ליה מקרא אחרינא וכל ערכך יהיה בשקל הקדש מה ת"ל לפי שנאמר (ה) תפדה יכול בעבדים ושטרות וקרקעו' ת"ל בשקל הקדש אין לי אלא סלעים מניין לרבות כל דבר המיטלטל ת"ל ופדה בערכך א"כ למה נאמר בשקל פרט לעבדים ושטרות וקרקעות אלא כן דרך הש"ס שאינו מביא עיקר הדרשה כמו שרגיל להביא [ס] (כתובות דף מו:) בנעוריה בית אביה כל שבח נעורים לאביה אע"ג דההוא בהפרת נדרים הוא דכתיב וכן הרבה: **רשב"ג אומר אף מטלטלין שברי זכוכית.** משמע דמודה לת"ק דמתיר חרדל והא דתנן רשב"ג מתיר בלוף וכל שכן דמתיר בחרדל: **הכניסן לעצים אין מסתפק.** איכא למימר דה"ק הא סתמא נעשה כמי שהכניסן למאכל בהמה כי היכי דלא תקשה רישא לסיפא: **דחזי לאומצא.** מכאן ראיה דדם האברים שלא פירש מותר דקאמר דחזי לאומצא אע"ג דלא מליח [ע]: **דג תפל אסור לטלטלו.** תימה מדשרי בשר תפל אלמא כר"ש אתיא אם כן דג תפל נמי לישרי כמו בשר תפל וי"ל דדג תפל אינו ראוי לכלבים אי נמי כר' יהודה אתיא ודג תפל אע"פ שראוי לכלבים אסור לטלטלו דכל מידי דחזי לאינש לא מקצה לכלבים בשר תפל מותר לטלטלו לרבי יהודה מפני שהוא מאכל לחיה: **מטלטלין את העצמות.** לר' יהודה דאית לי' מוקצה מיירי כגון שלא הי' עליה' בשר מאתמול:

עין משפט נר מצוה

טו א ב ג מיי' פכ"ה מהל' שבת הל' יט:
טז ד ה מיי' פכ"ו מהל' שבת הל' [טו] יח סמג לאוין סה טוש"ע א"ח סימן שח סעיף כט:
יז ו מיי' פ"ח מהלכות מלוה ולוה הלכה ז ופ"ג מהלכות ערכין הל' טו סמג עשין לג טוש"ע ח"מ סימן צז סעיף כג:
יח ז מיי' פכ"ו מהלכות שבת הלכה יט סמג לאוין סה ועשין קלה טוש"ע א"ח סימן שח סעיף לא:
יט ח ט מיי' שם הלכה יא סמג שם טוש"ע א"ח סימן שכא סעיף א וסימן שיט סעיף ו:
כ י מיי' פכ"ו שם הלכה טו סמג שם טוש"ע א"ח סי' שח סעיף לב:
כא כ מיי' שם טוש"ע א"ח סי' שח סעיף לג:
כב ל מיי' שם טוש"ע שם סעיף כט בהגה"ה:

גליון הש"ס

גמ' והא ר"ה תלמיד דרב. ביצה דף מ ע"א. ב"ק קטו ע"א. ועיין ב"ב דף קנ ע"א תוספות ד"ה שלמו לכ"ע: שם במוקצה לטלטל ס"ל כר' שמעון. עיין לעיל דף יט ע"ב תוספות ד"ה רבי כרבי דוסי ולקמן דף קלט ע"ב ושייך לדף קנב ע"א תוספות ד"ה אלא דכשרא. ועיין במהרש"א ביצה דף ב ע"ב בתוספות ד"ה אין מוכנין:

הגהות הגר"א

[א] גמ' אין מסתפק מהן בשבת למאכל בהמה. נ"ב למאכל מסתפק מהן בשבת: [ב] שם מותר לטלטל בשבת בשר תפל. נ"ב גי' הגאונים והרי"ף תפוח. ועי' רש"י.

תורה אור השלם

א) וְנָתַתָּה בַּכָּסֶף וְצַרְתָּ הַכֶּסֶף בְּיָדְךָ וְהָלַכְתָּ אֶל הַמָּקוֹם אֲשֶׁר יִבְחַר יְיָ אֱלֹהֶיךָ בּוֹ: [דברים יד, כה]
ב) וְאִם גָּאֹל יִגְאַל אֶת הַשָּׂדֶה הַמַּקְדִּישׁ אֹתוֹ וְיָסַף חֲמִשִׁית כֶּסֶף עֶרְכְּךָ עָלָיו וְקָם לוֹ: [ויקרא כז, יט]

רבינו חננאל

מעכב: אסימון מטבע שאין עליו צורה. ולא את הלוף ולא את החרדל. רשב"ג מתיר בלוף וכו' והא דרשב"ג פשוטה חבילי קש וחבילי עצים וכו'. חצבי עשב הוא והוא העשב (שכן) [שבו] תיחם יהושע לישראל את הארץ. הא מתני' סתמא היא וכוותה עבדינן דהא מתנית' נמי דברי הכל הוא. ורשב"ג דאמר אין מותר לטלטל אלא חבילה הניטלת בידו אחת מוקמינן ליה בחבילות שהכניסן למאכל בהמה דכל סתם של תורה לחומרא עבדינן. ותוב מתניתין סתמא תני וכוותה עבדינן וליכא לאוקמא רשב"ג מפרש דהא לא קתני אימתי ולא במה: חבילי סיאה. ציתרי. אזוב אברתא. וקורנית (האשי) [חשי] כולן מיני אזוב הן. הכניסן לעצים להדליק מהן אין מסתפק מהן בשבת למאכל בהמה מסתפק מהן בשבת א) דקיי"ל אבל דחזי ליה וקוטם ואוכל ובלבד שלא יקטום בכלי ובמלילה חלקו ר' יהודה וחכמים והלכה כחכמים וכן בפיגם וכן בשאר מיני תבלין וקיי"ל כחכמים. אמיתא. נענע. בשר תפוח חלק בו רב הונא ורב חסדא. רב הונא אמר מותר לטלטלו ורב חסדא אמר אסור לטלטלו. והלכתא כרב הונא דרב חסדא לגבי רב הונא תלמיד הוא. ותוב הא רב הונא קאי כר' שמעון ואפילו רב חסדא קאי כר' יהודה במוקצה לאכילה במוקצה לטלטול כר' שמעון סבירא ליה ואי חזי לאומצא פי' ואם ראוי להאכל נא אפי' רב חסדא מודה שמותר לטלטלו

חשק שלמה על רבינו חננאל א) אולי צ"ל וה"ק אם הכניסן למאכל בהמה דקיי"ל לדעתי אבל דחזי ליה. ועי' תוס' כאן ד"ה הכניסן.

מסורת הש"ס

א) [בכלל מליעא מו:], ב) [תוספתא פרק טו], ג) ב"מ קיג:, ד) לעיל קיא., ה) [על מז. וש"נ], ו) פי' מעיל ומגורה, ז) [תוספתא פרק טו], ח) [שם], ט) נ"ל פיאה, י) [לקמן קמ. ע"ש], כ) [ביצה מ.], ל) רש"ל מ"ז, מ) [ב"ב ט.], נ) [שייך לעיל קמו: על המשנה], ס) [תמורה מקום זה לא דק דלדרבה שם בכתובות מו: וכן שם מ: ובקדושין ג: פריך הש"ס לקמן ליה ומפיק ג"כ דהספיק בהפרת נדרים הוא דכתיב אבל כותבם לגמרא דכ"ק. וע"ש תוספות ד"ה כיון וע"ע בתוס' עירובין טו: ד"ה בכתיבה וכו' מבואר היטב וע"ע תוספות מו"ק ח. ד"ה נ"ל ומגילה כ. ד"ה ראיו ודף כ. ד"ה דכתיב וביבמות סח. ד"ה לי בה וסנהדרין לד: ד"ה דכתיב והכאים קח. ד"ה והמורה ובכורות טו. ד"ה עדות וסוכה ג. ד"ה כי יקריב בכורות ה. ד"ה טוב], ע) [וע"ע תוס' חולין יד: ד"ה ובקנין].

הגהות הב"ח

(א) גמ' בטבל טבול מדרבנן וכגון שזרע בעציץ: (ב) שם וחבילי עצים וחבילי זרדין) תא"מ ונ"ב ע"י כמה שכתב הטור א"ח סי' ש"מ משמע להדיא דלא גרסי בברייתא וחבילי זרדין אלא במתניתין גרסינן וחבילי זרדין ע"ש: (ג) רש"י ד"ה במוקצה וכו' לאסור לאוכלו ובאיסור מוקצה לטלטול סבר: (ד) תוס' ד"ה אבל וכו' והא דאמר רב יוסף בפרק כירה: (ה) בא"ד וה"נ תמן וכו' לפי שנא' ופדה בערכך יכול בעבדים:

רב נסים גאון

בפרק שלשה שאכלו כאחת כי הוא הדבר הנדמה דמי מתוקן ומי אינו מתוקן ובארנו שם עיקר גדירתו: אסימון הוא מטבע בפ' הזהב (ב"מ דף מז) מאי אסימון פולסא ומה שהוא בענין זה אסימון לפדות בו את המעשר שני כי הכתוב פי' שצריך מטבע שיש עליו צורה דכתיב (דברים יד) וצרת הכסף בידך דבר שיש עליו צורה: ת"ר מטלטלין את החצב זה חצב הוא צמח משלח שרשיו למטה בקרקע בצדק בלא הטייה והוא מה שאמרו בפרק חזקת הבתים (ב"ב דף נה) אמר ר' אסי אמר ר' יוחנן המצר והחצב מפסיקין ברשות הגר וכו' ואמרו מאי חצוצא אמר רב יהודה אמר רב שבו תיחם יהושע את הארץ לישראל

ליקוטי רש"י

האי אידנן. הלי נתמרמם ככרי לידנן וכגון דנקלה לתו לרב ממנה לכתוב ומתוכו לנטלה תרומה גדולה לכתוב להפריש לשגך [פסחים שם].

Baraisa in the name of R' Yishmael, וְתָנָא מִשּׁוּם רַבִּי עֲקִיבָא – **and it was taught in a** different **Baraisa in the name of R' Akiva:** כָּל יִשְׂרָאֵל רְאוּיִין לְאוֹתָהּ אִיצְטְלָא – ALL of ISRAEL ARE FIT FOR THAT expensive CLOAK.[22] The borrower is therefore not required to sell it for a less expensive one.

The Gemara cites the final case of *muktzeh* listed in the Mishnah:

חֲבִילֵי קַשׁ וַחֲבִילֵי כו׳ – As regards BUNDLES OF STUBBLE AND BUNDLES OF etc. [twigs and bundles of tender reeds, if one has set them aside for use as animal feed, we may move them; and if not, we may not move them].

The Gemara cites a Baraisa that discusses this ruling:

תָּנוּ רַבָּנָן – **The Rabbis taught in a Baraisa:** חֲבִילֵי קַשׁ וַחֲבִילֵי עֵצִים – As regards BUNDLES OF STUBBLE AND BUNDLES OF TWIGS וַחֲבִילֵי זְרָדִים – AND BUNDLES OF TENDER REEDS, אִם הִתְקִינָן לְמַאֲכַל בְּהֵמָה מְטַלְטְלִין אוֹתָן – IF ONE HAS SET THEM ASIDE FOR use as ANIMAL FEED, WE MAY MOVE THEM on the Sabbath; וְאִם לָאו אֵין מְטַלְטְלִין אוֹתָן – AND IF one has NOT set them aside for use as animal feed, WE MAY NOT MOVE THEM.[23] רַבָּן שִׁמְעוֹן בֶּן גַּמְלִיאֵל אוֹמֵר – RABBAN SHIMON BEN GAMLIEL SAYS: חֲבִילִין הַנִּיטָּלִין בְּיָד אֶחָד מוּתָּר לְטַלְטְלָן – Even if they have been set aside as animal feed, only BUNDLES THAT CAN BE MOVED WITH ONE HAND IT IS PERMITTED TO MOVE, בִּשְׁתֵּי יָדַיִם אָסוּר לְטַלְטְלָן – but those which can be moved only WITH TWO HANDS IT IS FORBIDDEN TO MOVE.[24] חֲבִילֵי סִיאָה אֵזוֹב וְקוֹרָנִית – As regards BUNDLES OF *SI'AH, EIZOV* AND *KORANIS,*[25] הִכְנִיסָן לְעֵצִים – IF ONE BROUGHT THEM IN to be dried and used FOR fireWOOD, אֵין מִסְתַּפֵּק מֵהֶן בְּשַׁבָּת – ONE MAY NOT PARTAKE OF THEM ON THE SABBATH. לְמַאֲכַל בְּהֵמָה – If, however, one brought them in for use AS ANIMAL FEED, מִסְתַּפֵּק מֵהֶן בְּשַׁבָּת – ONE MAY PARTAKE OF THEM ON THE SABBATH.[26] וְקוֹטֵם בְּיָד וְאוֹכֵל – AND one may BREAK them into small pieces BY HAND AND EAT THEM,[27] וּבִלְבַד שֶׁלֹּא יִקְטוֹם בִּכְלִי – PROVIDED THAT HE DOES NOT BREAK them into small pieces WITH A UTENSIL.[28] ומולל ואוכל – AND ONE MAY RUB the pods to remove AND EAT the seeds,[29] וּבִלְבַד שֶׁלֹּא יָמְלוֹל בִּכְלִי הַרְבֵּה דִּבְרֵי רַבִּי יְהוּדָה – PROVIDED THAT HE DOES NOT RUB A LOT of them WITH A UTENSIL; these are THE WORDS OF R' YEHUDAH.[30] וַחֲכָמִים אוֹמְרִים – BUT THE SAGES SAY: מוֹלֵל בְּרָאשֵׁי אֶצְבְּעוֹתָיו וְאוֹכֵל – HE MAY RUB the pods WITH THE TIPS OF HIS FINGERS to remove AND EAT the seeds, וּבִלְבַד שֶׁלֹּא יָמְלוֹל בְּיָדוֹ הַרְבֵּה – PROVIDED THAT HE DOES NOT ROLL A LOT of them WITH HIS entire HAND כְּדֶרֶךְ שֶׁהוּא עוֹשֶׂה בְּחוֹל – IN THE MANNER THAT HE DOES ON WEEKDAYS.[31] וְכֵן בְּאָמִיתָא – AND THE SAME law applies TO

NOTES

22. For all of Israel are considered royalty; thus, the expensive cloak indeed befits a person of his station.

23. In the absence of designation to the contrary, these items are assumed to be set aside for use as firewood. Therefore, where they have not been designated as animal feed, they are *muktzeh* (*Rashba*; cf. *Rabbeinu Chananel*). [This is in contrast to glass shards (in the Baraisa above), which are not *muktzeh* (in the view of Rabban Shimon ben Gamliel there) because they are *fit* for ostriches, even though the glass shards have not been *designated* for that purpose. For even in the absence of being designated as ostrich feed, glass shards are *not* set aside for any *muktzeh* purpose. Hence, their fitness as ostrich feed renders them non-*muktzeh* (*Rashba*).]

[*Rashba* (to 155a ד״ה קסבר שווי אוכלין) explains the Mishnah here to mean only that the undesignated bundles are *muktzeh* as long as one has not decided to feed them to his animal, e.g. he wishes to move them to use the space they occupy or to sit on them. But if he decides now, on the Sabbath, to feed them to his animal, he may do so and they cease to be *muktzeh* (according to R' Shimon). See also *Tos. R' Akiva* to 24:4 and *Beur Halachah* to 324:5.]

24. Though the heavy bundles are not *muktzeh,* they may not be moved because of the excessive exertion involved (*Rashi*).

25. The Gemara below will identify these items (*Rashi*). [These are legumes that are generally fed to animals, but will sometimes be eaten by people (*Meiri*; see also next note).]

26. [The Baraisa seems to give conflicting indications as to what the law would be if one did not designate them for any specific purpose. The first part of the Baraisa ("if one brought them in *for use as wood,* one may not partake of them on the Sabbath") implies that they are *muktzeh* only if specifically designated for use as firewood; but in the absence of designation, they are not *muktzeh.* The second part of the Baraisa ("[If one brought them in for use] *as animal feed,* one may partake of them on the Sabbath"), however, implies that they are not *muktzeh* only if specifically designated for use as animal feed; but in the absence of designation, they are *muktzeh. Tosafos* therefore explain the Baraisa to mean that if one brought them in for use as firewood, they are *muktzeh.* But if one did not designate them specifically as firewood, then the assumption is that they will be used as animal feed; accordingly, *it is as if* they have been designated as animal feed, and they are not *muktzeh.* It is not necessary, though, to *designate* them as animal feed in order to remove the *muktzeh* status. (There are many other instances where Mishnahs and Baraisos are interpreted in similar fashion – see, for example, Gemara above, 91b; below, 145a; *Succah* 19b-20a; *Kiddushin* 17a.)]

27. Though he has designated them for use as animal feed, they are somewhat fit for human consumption as well (*Mishnah Berurah* 321:4; see also note 25 above).

28. The normal, weekday manner of preparing these items as food would be to dice them finely with a utensil. To do so on the Sabbath, however, would be [Biblically] forbidden, as we learned earlier (74b) that dicing beets finely is akin to *grinding* [i.e. a *toladah* of *grinding* – *Eglei Tal, Meleches Tochein* 3:7] (*Rashi*; cf. *Tos. Rid* here). Therefore, on the Sabbath, one may not cut them into pieces with a utensil, but only by hand. [See also the comments of *Tos. Rid* here.]

[*Beis Yosef* (*Orach Chaim* 321 ד״ה אסור לחתוך) infers from *Rashi's* comments here that one is liable for breaking vegetables into fine pieces only if he does so with a utensil. (He adds, however, that it might be Rabbinically forbidden to do so with one's hand.)]

29. See *Rashi.* [See, though, *Ran* to *Beitzah* p. 6a ד״ה ואיכא למידק.]

30. Dislodging the seeds from the pod in the usual fashion – that is, either by beating the pod with a utensil, or by opening the pod and plucking the seeds – would constitute *threshing.* Obviously, then, dislodging the seeds on the Sabbath can be permitted only if one alters in some way the usual manner of doing so (see *Shulchan Aruch HaRav, Orach Chaim* 319:9).

Apparently, R' Yehudah means that one may rub the pods even with a utensil (cf. *Chidushei R' Moshe Kazis*), so that the seeds fall out, provided that he does not do many pods at a time, but only the amount he wishes to eat immediately [i.e. at that meal (*Chidushei R' Moshe Kazis*)].

[The commentators do not explain why R' Yehudah's method of rubbing the pods on the Sabbath constitutes an alteration of the usual manner of threshing. Perhaps the usual manner is *beating* the pods with a utensil, whereas R' Yehudah allows only *rubbing* with a utensil. Or perhaps dislodging the seeds to eat immediately rather than to put aside is not considered the manner of threshing, according to R' Yehudah. It should be noted, however, that early editions of the Gemara do not contain the word הַרְבֵּה, *a lot,* in R' Yehudah's ruling, and this was added to the Gemara text by *Maharshal,* based on the reading cited by *Rashi* from Tosefta (*Dikdukei Soferim* §8). According to the reading found in these early editions, R' Yehudah would be ruling that one may not rub the pods with a utensil altogether (and that this is the alteration of the normal manner of threshing!). *Dikdukei Soferim* (ibid.) suggests that the word הַרְבֵּה, *a lot,* be deleted from *Rashi's* citation of the text as well (see, however, *Rashi* to *Rif*). Indeed, the Tosefta, which *Rashi* cites as the source for his reading, is quoted by *Ritva MHK* ed. without the critical word הַרְבֵּה, *a lot.* See also *Minchas Bikkurim* to Tosefta 15:12.]

31. The Sages require that one deviate from the normal way of rubbing pods; that is, instead of the usual rubbing of the pods between the palms of one's hands, one may rub them only between the tips of his fingers. Moreover, they require that one not rub more than a few pods at a time [i.e. only what he needs for immediate consumption]. These two conditions ensure that one will rub the pods in a manner sufficiently different from the weekday manner [so that one not come to thresh the pods in a

אבל לא את הטבל וכו': פשיטא לא צריכא בטבל טבול מדרבנן (א) שזרעו בעציץ שאינו נקוב: ולא מעשר ראשון וכו': פשיטא לא צריכא שהקדימו בכרי שנטל ממנו מעשר ולא נטלה ממנו תרומה גדולה מהו דתימא כדאמר ליה רב פפא לאביי קמ"ל כדשני ליה אביי: ולא את מעשר שני וכו': פשיטא לא צריכא דנפדו ולא נפדו כהלכתן מעשר שפדאו על גבי אסימון דרחמנא אמר א) וצרת הכסף בידך דבר שיש בו צורה הקדש שחיללו על גבי קרקע דרחמנא אמר ב) ונתן הכסף וקם לו: ולא את הלוף: ת"ר מטלטלין את החצב מפני שהוא מאכל לצביים ואת החרדל מפני שהוא מאכל ליונים רשב"ג אומר אף מטלטלין שברי זכוכית מפני שהוא מאכל לנעמיות אמר ליה רבי נתן אלא מעתה חבילי זמורות יטלטלו מפני שהוא מאכל לפילין ורשב"ג נעמיות שכיחי פילין לא שכיחי אמר אמימר והוא דאית ליה נעמיות אמר רב אשי לאמימר אלא דקאמר ליה ר' נתן לרשב"ג חבילי זמורות יטלטל מפני שהוא מאכל לפילין אי אית ליה פילין אמאי לא אלא ראוי ה"נ ראוי: אמר אביי רשב"ג ורבי שמעון ורבי ישמעאל ורבי עקיבא כולהו סבירא להו כל ישראל בני מלכים הם רשב"ג הא דאמרן ר' שמעון דתנן בני מלכים סכין על גבי מכותיהן שמן וורד שכן דרכן של בני מלכים לסוך בחול ר"ש אומר כל ישראל בני מלכים הם ר' ישמעאל ור' עקיבא דתניא הרי שהיו נושין בו אלף מנה ולבוש איצטלא בת ק' מנה מפשיטין אותו ומלבישין אותו איצטלא הראויה לו תנא משום רבי ישמעאל ותנא משום רבי עקיבא כל ישראל ראוין לאותה איצטלא:

חבילי קש וחבילי כו': תנו רבנן חבילי קש וחבילי עצים (ג) וחבילי זרדים אם התקינן למאכל בהמה מטלטלין אותן ואם לאו אין מטלטלין אותן רשב"ג אומר חבילין הניטלין ביד אחד מותר לטלטלן בשתי ידים אסור לטלטלן חבילי סיאה אזוב וקורנית הכניסן לעצים אין [א] מסתפק מהן בשבת למאכל בהמה מסתפק מהן בשבת וקוטם ביד ואוכל ובלבד שלא יקטום בכלי ומולל ואוכל ובלבד שלא ימלול בכלי הרבה דברי רבי יהודה וחכמים אומרים מולל בראשי אצבעותיו ואוכל ובלבד שלא ימלול בידו הרבה כדרך שהוא עושה בחול וכן באמיתא וכן בפיגם וכן בשאר מיני תבלין מאי אמיתא נינייא סיאה אמר רב יהודה (סיאה) צתרי אזוב אברתא קורנית קורניתא שמה והא ההוא דאמר להו מאן בעי קורניתא ואישתכח חשי אלא סיאה צתרי אזוב אברתא קורניתא חשי: איתמר בשר מליח מותר לטלטלו בשבת בשר [ב] תפל רב הונא אמר מותר לטלטלו רב חסדא אמר אסור לטלטלו רב הונא אמר מותר לטלטלו והא רב הונא תלמיד דרב הוה ורב כר' יהודה סבירא ליה דאית ליה מוקצה לאכילה סבר לה כרבי יהודה במוקצה לטלטל סבר לה כרבי שמעון רב חסדא אמר אסור לטלטלו והא רב יצחק בר אמי איקלע לבי רב חסדא וחזא ההוא בר אווזא דהוו קא מטלטלו ליה משמשא לטולא ואמר רב חסדא חסרון כיס קא חזינן הכא שאני בר אווזא דחזי לאומצא ת"ר דג מליח מותר לטלטלו דג תפל אסור לטלטלו בשר בין תפל ובין מליח מותר לטלטלו (ד) (וסתמא כרבי שמעון) תנו רבנן מטלטלין את העצמות מפני שהוא מאכל לכלבים בשר

רש"י

שלא ניטלה תרומתו. קא סלקא דעתך שלא ניטלה תרומת מעשר שלו: אסימון. שאין עליו צורה: חצב. עשב שמשריש בעומק כנגדו ואין שרשיו מתפשטין ובו תיחם יהושע את הארץ לישראל: נעמיות. בנות היענה: יטלטלו. ראוי הוא להיות לו פילין ולהאכילן: על מכותיהן. בשבת ולא גזר משום שחיקת סממנין: שכן דרכן לסוך. בלא מכה הלכך לאו מוכחא מילתא דלרפואה: התקינן. הזמינן: אסור לטלטלן. ואפילו הזמינם למאכל בהמה דטירחא היא: סיאה אזוב וקורנית. לקמיה מפרש לה: הכניסן לעצים. לייבשן: שלא יקטום בכלי. כדרך חול כדאמרן (לעיל דף עד:) האי מאן דפריס סילקא דמי לטוחן. במילתיה דרבי יהודה גרסינן מולל ואוכל ובלבד שלא ימלול בכלי הרבה וחכמי' אומרים מולל בראשי אצבעותיו ובלבד שלא ימלול בידו הרבה כדרך חול כך מצאתי בתוספתא דרבנן מחמרי דבכולי ידא אסור אלא בראשי אצבעותיו ומהו מולל כגון אם בא לאכול הזרע מולל השרביטין שהזרע בתוכם: וכן באמיתא. לקמיה מפרש מאי אמיתא: נינייא. מינטא"י: פיגם. רוד"א: צתרי. שדריא"ה לוי"ה לי"א פוליאול: אברתא. איסני"א: חשי. שדריא"ה וללשון הראשון לא פורש: בשר תפל. שאינו מלוח ומאן דגרים תפוח היא היא: מותר לטלטלו. דלית ליה מוקצה בטלטול: במוקצה לאכילה סבר לה כר' יהודה. כלומר באיסור מוקצה לענין אכילה סבר לה כרבי יהודה דאסר לאוכלו (ג) ובאיסור מוקצה לטלטול סבר לה כרבי שמעון: בר אווזא. שחוט: משמשא לטולא. שלא יסריח: ואמר להו רב חסדא חסרון כיס חזינא הכא. שאתם מניחים אותה בשמש ומתחמם וסלקוהו על פיו מחמה לצל: באומצא. כשהוא חי אוכלין אותו בלא מלח: דג תפל אסור לטלטלו. דאינו ראוי לכלום ולכלבים לא עבדיה למישדייה אבל מליח נאכל חי על ידי מלחו: בשר

תוספות

אבל לא את הטבל. והא דאמר (ד) רבה בפרק כירה (לעיל דף מג.) טבל מוכן הוא אצל שבת שאם עבר ותיקנו מתוקן ה"מ לענין ביטול כלי מהיכנו שלא החמירו כמו לענין טלטול בידים: שפדאו אגב אסימון. הא דנקט אסימון היינו דלא כרבי דוסא דפרק הזהב (ב"מ דף מז:) והוה מצי למימר מעות הניתנות סימן לבית המרחץ לד"ה אלא משום דאם כן מאי קמ"ל אבל השתא קמ"ל כרבנן:

ונתן הכסף וקם לו. אין הפסוק כן אלא ויסף חמישית כסף ערכך עליו וקם לו (ויקרא כז) ודרך הש"ס לקצר ולומר בלשון אחר קצר כי ההיא דפרק הדר (עירובין דף סה.) רבי חנינא ביומא דרתח לא מצלי שנאמר בצר אל יורה ובפרק הרואה (ברכות דף נה:) שנאמר כל החלומות הולכים אחר הפה וקשה לר"י נימא כסף דווקא וכ"ת דשוה כסף ככסף הדא דגבי נזקין מרבינן קרא ישיב לרבות שוה כסף ועוד דאם כן אפילו קרקע נמי ומנלן למעוטי קרקע ואומר ר"י דמכלל ופרט נפקא כדתנן בבכורות בפרק יש בכור לנחלה (דף נא.) אין פודין לא בעבדים ולא בקרקעות ולא בהקדשות ומפרש בגמרא דבעי למימר ולא הקדשות בכל אלו לענין פדיון בכור דרשינן התם כלל ופרט ופדויו מבן חדש כלל כסף פרט תפדה חזר וכלל מה הפרט מפורש דבר המיטלטל כו' ה"נ איכא למימר בפדיון הקדשות ונתן כלל כסף פרט וקם לו חזר וכלל כו' מיהו בת"כ דריש ליה מקרא אחרינא וכל ערכך יהיה בשקל הקדש מה ת"ל לפי שנאמר (ה) תפדה יכול בעבדים ושטרות וקרקעו' ת"ל בשקל הקדש אין לי אלא סלעים מניין לרבות כל דבר המיטלטל ת"ל ופדה בערכך א"כ למה נאמר בשקל פרט לעבדים ושטרות וקרקעות אלא כן דרך הש"ס שאינו מביא עיקר הדרשה כמו שרגיל להביא (כתובות דף מו:) בנעוריה בית אביה כל שבח נעורים לאביה אע"ג דההוא בהפרת נדרים הוא דכתיב וכן הרבה:

רשב"ג אומר אף מטלטלין שברי זכוכית. משמע דמודה לת"ק דמתיר חרדל והא דתנן רשב"ג מתיר בלוף וכל שכן דמתיר בחרדל:

הכניסן לעצים אין מסתפק. איכא למימר דה"ק הא סתמא נעשה כמי שהכניסן למאכל בהמה כי היכי דלא תקשה רישא לסיפא:

דחזי לאומצא. מכאן ראיה דדם האברים שלא פירש מותר דקאמר דחזי לאומצא אע"ג דלא מליח:

דג תפל אסור לטלטלו. תימה מדשרי בשר תפל אלמא כר"ש אתיא אם כן דג תפל נמי לישרי כמו בשר תפל וי"ל דדג תפל אינו ראוי לכלבים אי נמי כר' יהודה אתיא ודג תפל אע"פ שראוי לכלבים אסור לטלטלו דכל מידי דחזי לאינש לא מקצה לכלבים בשר תפל מותר לטלטלו לרבי יהודה מפני שהוא מאכל לחיה:

מטלטלין את העצמות. לר' יהודה דאית לי' מוקצה מיירי כגון שלא הי' עליה' בשר מאתמול:

עין משפט נר מצוה

טו א ב מיי' פכ"ה מהל' שבת הל' יט:

טז ג ד מיי' פכ"ה מהל' שבת הל' [...] ועיין [...] סמג לאוין [...] טוש"ע א"ח סימן שח סעיף כט:

יז ו מיי' פ"א מהלכות מלוה ולוה הלכה ז ופ"ג מהלכות ערכין [...] סמג עשין [...]:

יח ז מיי' פכ"א מהלכות שבת הלכה יט סמג לאוין סה [...] טוש"ע א"ח סימן שכא סעיף [...]:

יט ח ט מיי' שם ופכ"ה [...] טוש"ע א"ח סימן שכא [...]:

כ י מיי' שם הלכה [...] טוש"ע א"ח [...]:

כא כ מיי' שם טוש"ע א"ח [...]:

כב ל מיי' שם טוש"ע א"ח [...]:

גליון הש"ס

גמ' והא ר"ה תלמיד דרב. [...]

הגהות הגר"א

[א] גמ' אין מסתפק מהן בשבת למאכל בהמה. נ"ב למאכל מסתפק מהן [...]: [ב] שם מותר לטלטל בשבת בשר תפל. נ"ב [...]

תורה אור השלם

א) וְנָתַתָּה בַּכָּסֶף וְצַרְתָּ הַכֶּסֶף בְּיָדְךָ וְהָלַכְתָּ אֶל הַמָּקוֹם אֲשֶׁר יִבְחַר יְיָ אֱלֹהֶיךָ בּוֹ: (דברים יד, כה)

ב) וְאִם גָּאֹל יִגְאַל אֶת הַשָּׂדֶה הַמַּקְדִּישׁ אֹתוֹ וְיָסַף חֲמִשִׁית כֶּסֶף עֶרְכְּךָ עָלָיו וְקָם לוֹ: (ויקרא כז, יט)

רבינו חננאל

מעבב: אסימון מטבע שאין עליו צורה. ולא את הלוף ולא את החרדל. [...] רשב"ג מתיר בלוף [...] והא דרשב"ג פשוטה חבילי קש וחבילי עצים וכו'. חצב: עשב הוא [...] יהושע לישראל את הארץ. [...]

מסורת הש"ס

א) [בכמה מקומות [...]], ב) [תוספתא פרק טו], ג) ב"מ [...], ד) [לעיל [...]], ה) [...], ו) פי' [...], ז) [תוספתא פרק טו], ח) [...], ט) [...], י) [...], כ) [...], ל) [...] [...]

הגהות הב"ח

(א) גמ' בטבל טבול מדרבנן וכגון שזרעו בעציץ: (ב) שם [...] (ג) רש"י ד"ה במוקצה [...] ובאיסור מוקצה [...] (ד) תוס' ד"ה אבל וכו' [...]

רב נסים גאון

בפרק שלשה שאכלו כאחת כי הוא הדבר [...] אסימון [...]

ליקוטי רש"י

האי אידנן. [...]

AMISA,[32] וְכֵן בְּפֵיגָם – AND THE SAME applies TO RUE, וְכֵן בִּשְׁאָר מִינֵי תַבְלִין – AND THE SAME applies TO OTHER TYPES OF SPICES.

The Gemara identifies the plants listed in the Baraisa:

מַאי אֲמִיתָא – What is *amisa?* נִינְיָא – **Mint.** סִיאָה – What is *si'ah?* אָמַר רַב יְהוּדָה – **Rav Yehudah said:** (סיאה) צַתְרֵי – It is *tzasrei.*[33] אֵזוֹב – What is *eizov?* אַבַּרְתָּא – **Hyssop.** קוֹרָנִית – What is *koranis?* קוֹרָנִיתָא שְׁמָהּ – **Its name is** *koranisa.*[34]

The Gemara asks:

וְהָא הַהוּא דְּאָמַר לְהוּ – **But** there was **this** merchant **who said to** [others], מַאן בָּעֵי קוֹרָנִיתָא – **"Who wants** to buy *koranisa?"* וְאִישְׁתַּכַּח חַשֵׁי – **and it was found** that he was offering *chashei* for sale.[35] – ? –

The Gemara answers:

אֶלָּא סִיאָה צַתְרֵי – **Rather,** the list of identifications given above should read as follows: ***Si'ah*** is ***tzasrei*** (as above), אֵזוֹב אַבַּרְתָּא – *eizov* is **hyssop** (as above) קוֹרָנִיתָא חַשֵׁי – and *koranisa* (or: *koranis,* as it is called in the Baraisa) is ***chashei.***

The Gemara discusses the *muktzeh* status of certain types of meat:

אִיתְּמַר – **It was said:** בָּשָׂר מָלִיחַ מוּתָּר לְטַלְטְלוֹ בְּשַׁבָּת – If one has raw but **salted meat, it is permitted to move it on the Sabbath.**[36] בָּשָׂר תָּפֵל – In the case of raw **meat that is unsalted,**[37] רַב הוּנָא אָמַר מוּתָּר לְטַלְטְלוֹ – **Rav Huna says: It is permitted to move it,**[38] רַב חִסְדָּא אָמַר אָסוּר לְטַלְטְלוֹ – whereas **Rav Chisda says: It is forbidden to move it.**[39]

The Gemara questions the assertion that Rav Huna considers raw, unsalted meat to be non-*muktzeh*:

רַב הוּנָא אָמַר מוּתָּר לְטַלְטְלוֹ – Can it be that **Rav Huna says** with regard to raw, unsalted meat that **it is permitted to move it?** וְהָא רַב הוּנָא תַּלְמִיד דְּרַב הֲוָה – **But Rav Huna was a disciple of Rav,** וְרַב כְּרַבִּי יְהוּדָה סְבִירָא לֵיהּ – **and Rav holds**[40] **in accordance with** the view of **R' Yehudah,** דְּאִית לֵיהּ מוּקְצֶה – **who holds** a broad interpretation of ***muktzeh*** and certainly considers raw, unsalted meat *muktzeh.*[41] How, then, can Rav Huna maintain that one is permitted to move it?

The Gemara answers:

בְּמוּקְצֶה לַאֲכִילָה סָבַר לָהּ כְּרַבִּי יְהוּדָה – **Concerning** ***muktzeh*** **with regard to eating** it, **[Rav] holds in accordance with** the view **of R' Yehudah,** that it is forbidden to eat *muktzeh.* בְּמוּקְצֶה לְטַלְטֵל סָבַר לָהּ כְּרַבִּי שִׁמְעוֹן – But **concerning** ***muktzeh*** **with regard to moving** it, **[Rav] holds in accordance with** the view of **R' Shimon,** that it is permitted to move *muktzeh.*[42]

The Gemara now questions the assertion that Rav Chisda forbids one to move raw, unsalted meat on the Sabbath:

רַב חִסְדָּא אָמַר אָסוּר לְטַלְטְלוֹ – Can it be that **Rav Chisda says** with regard to raw, unsalted meat that **it is forbidden to move it?** וְהָא רַב יִצְחָק בַּר אַמֵּי אִיקְּלַע לְבֵי רַב חִסְדָּא – **Why, Rav Yitzchak bar Ami visited the home of Rav Chisda** on the Sabbath, וַחֲזָא הַהוּא בַּר אַוָּוזָא – **and saw a certain** slaughtered **duck** (which was unsalted and uncooked) דַּהֲוּו קָא מְטַלְטְלוּ לֵיהּ מִשִּׁמְשָׁא לְטוּלָּא – **that [the servants] were carrying from the sun to the shade,** וְאָמַר רַב חִסְדָּא – **because Rav Chisda had said** to them,[43] upon observing the raw meat lying in the sun, חֶסְרוֹן כִּיס קָא חָזֵינַן הָכָא – **"We see here a financial loss** (should the meat remain in the sun)." Thus we see that Rav Chisda permits the movement of

NOTES

Biblically forbidden way; see beginning of note 30] (see *Rashi*; *Shevisas HaShabbos, Meleches Dash* §5; and *Shulchan Aruch HaRav* loc. cit.). [*Shulchan Aruch HaRav* explains that employing even the *normal* method of rubbing to extract the seeds (viz. rolling the pods between the palms of the hand) would not constitute a Biblical violation, which requires either dislodging the seeds with a tool designed for this task, or actually extracting the seeds by hand. Nevertheless, the Sages require the two departures from the Rabbinically forbidden normal manner of rubbing, so that one not come to commit a Biblical violation.]

[From the Gemara in *Beitzah* (12b), it would appear that there is no permissible way whatsoever to rub ears of grain on the Sabbath to release the kernels. The Rishonim propose various resolutions – see *Baal HaMaor, Milchamos, Ran* and *Rashba* here, and *Ran* to *Beitzah* p. 6a ד״ה ואיכא למידק.]

32. The Gemara will define this immediately below.

33. *Rashi,* quoting his teacher R' Yitzchak HaLevi, identifies this as "sadrei" in Old French [savory (an aromatic herb)]. Alternatively, *Rashi* identifies it as "poliol" in Old French [pennyroyal (a type of mint)].

34. [I.e. there is no other name for it; it is known only as *koranis* or *koranisa.*]

35. *Rashi* identifies *chashei* as "sadrei" in Old French [savory], and notes that this identification is acceptable according to the alternative definition given above for *tzasrei* (see note 33). But it does not fit with R' Yitzchak HaLevi's definition of *tzasrei* as "sadrei" (ibid.) [for *tzasrei* and *chashei* cannot be the same thing]. Rather, according to R' Yitzchak HaLevi, the identity of *chashei* remains unknown.

[At any rate, this incident involving the merchant shows that *koranisa* is *chashei,* and is not known *only* by the name *koranis* or *koranisa* by which the Baraisa refers to it. (See, however, *Rashash.*)

36. [Since salted meat, though uncooked, is edible as is.]

37. *Rashi* cites an alternative version: בָּשָׂר תָּפוּחַ, but explains that it is substantively the same as our version, and also means *unsalted meat* (see *Rashi* to *Rif* ד״ה בשר תפוח, and *Derishah, Orach Chaim* 308:13 ד״ה בשר חי at the end; cf. *Derishah's* first explanation there and *Chasam Sofer* here). [Other Rishonim, however, explain the alternative version to mean *spoiled meat*; see *Rashba.*]

38. Because he holds that it is permitted to move *muktzeh* on the Sabbath (*Rashi*).

As mentioned above, the Tannaim R' Yehudah and R' Shimon dispute the scope of *muktzeh* (see 126b note 28). Thus, there is a large range of items that R' Yehudah considers *muktzeh* and R' Shimon does not. Raw, unsalted meat (which cannot be salted on the Sabbath – see *Orach Chaim* 321:5 and *Mishnah Berurah* there §21) falls within this range. [In the view of *Rashi* and *Tosafos* (see *Tos. R' Akiva* to 24:4), R' Shimon does not consider it *muktzeh,* though it has been set aside and is presently unfit for human consumption, since it is in the final analysis presently fit for animal consumption (see also *Bach* 308 ד״ה בשר חי, and *Taz* 308:20). Cf. *Rashba* here ד״ה ה״ג רש״י, and above ד״ה מתני׳ חבילי קש; *Magen Avraham* 308:56.] It is such "*muktzeh*" (i.e. that which is *muktzeh* according to R' Yehudah) that Rav Huna permits one to move (in keeping with R' Shimon's position). Certainly, however, Rav Huna agrees that one may not move those items which even R' Shimon deems *muktzeh.*

39. Rav Chisda follows the opinion of R' Yehudah, who considers such meat *muktzeh.* For even though the raw meat is fit to be fed to dogs, one sets it aside from such use, planning instead to prepare it after the Sabbath for human consumption (see *Tosafos* below ד״ה דג תפל, and *Bach* and *Taz* loc. cit.).

40. Above, 19b (see *Ritva MHK* ed.; see also Gemara below, end of 156b).

41. Because it is set aside for human consumption, and it is unfit for that purpose in its present state (see note 39).

42. *Rashi.* I.e. in principle, Rav sides with R' Shimon's more lenient interpretation of *muktzeh* and thus allows one to move the items that are debated by R' Yehudah and R' Shimon. However, Rav adopts the stringency that one may not *eat muktzeh* (see *Chasam Sofer*; see *Afikei Yam* II:17 ד״ה ויובן מאוד). [*Maharsha* to *Beitzah* 33a adds that Rav prohibits *any* usage of the *muktzeh;* he permits only moving it. See also *Rashba* above, 29a ד״ה כי ארליק.]

[The Rishonim point out various passages where Rav seems to adopt R' Yehudah's approach even with regard to moving *muktzeh,* and they therefore attach certain conditions to the Gemara's sweeping statement here, as interpreted by *Rashi* (*Ramban* et al.; see also *Tosafos* to 19b ד״ה הני כרכי). Moreover, the Rishonim also cite the approach of *Rabbeinu Tam,* who explains the Gemara's statement here differently than *Rashi* does (*Rashba* et al.).]

43. See *Rashi.*

אבל לא את הטבל וכו': פשיטא לא צריכא בטבל טבול מדרבנן (א) שזרעו בעציץ שאינו נקוב: ולא מעשר ראשון וכו': פשיטא לא צריכא שהקדימו בכרי שנטל ממנו מעשר ולא נטלה ממנו תרומה גדולה מהו דתימא כדאמר ליה רב פפא לאביי קמ"ל כדשני ליה אביי: ולא את מעשר שני וכו': פשיטא לא צריכא דנפדו ולא נפדו כהלכתן מעשר שפדאו על גבי אסימון דרחמנא אמר א) וצרת הכסף בידך דבר שיש בו צורה הקדש שחיללו על גבי קרקע דרחמנא אמר ב) ונתן הכסף וקם לו: ולא את הלוף: ת"ר מטלטלין את החצב מפני שהוא מאכל לצביים ואת החרדל מפני שהוא מאכל ליונים רשב"ג אומר אף מטלטלין שברי זכוכית מפני שהוא מאכל לנעמיות אמר ליה רבי נתן אלא מעתה חבילי זמורות יטלטלו מפני שהוא מאכל לפילין ורשב"ג נעמיות שכיחי פילין לא שכיחי אמימר והוא דאית ליה נעמיות אמר רב אשי לאמימר אלא דקאמר ליה ר' נתן לרשב"ג חבילי זמורות יטלטל מפני שהוא מאכל לפילין אי אית ליה פילין אמאי לא אלא ראוי ה"נ ראוי אמר אביי רשב"ג ורבי שמעון ורבי ישמעאל ורבי עקיבא כולהו סבירא להו כל ישראל בני מלכים הם רשב"ג הא דאמרן ר' שמעון דתנן בני מלכים סכין על גבי מכותיהן שמן וורד שכן דרכן של בני מלכים לסוך בחול ר"ש אומר כל ישראל בני מלכים הם ר' ישמעאל ור' עקיבא דתניא הרי שהיו נושין בו אלף מנה ולבוש איצטלא בת ק' מנה מפשיטין אותו ומלבישין אותו איצטלא הראויה לו תנא משום רבי ישמעאל ותנא משום רבי עקיבא כל ישראל ראוין לאותה איצטלא: חבילי קש וחבילי כו': תנו רבנן חבילי קש וחבילי עצים (ב) וחבילי זרדים אם התקינן למאכל בהמה מטלטלין אותן ואם לאו אין מטלטלין אותן רשב"ג אומר חבילין הניטלין ביד אחד מותר לטלטלן בשתי ידים אסור לטלטלן חבילי סיאה אזוב וקורנית הכניסן לעצים אין [א] מסתפק מהן בשבת למאכל בהמה מסתפק מהן בשבת וקוטם ביד ואוכל ובלבד שלא יקטום בכלי ומולל ואוכל ובלבד שלא ימלול בכלי הרבה דברי רבי יהודה וחכמים אומרים מולל בראשי אצבעותיו ואוכל ובלבד שלא ימלול בידו הרבה כדרך שהוא עושה בחול וכן באמיתא וכן בפיגם וכן בשאר מיני תבלין מאי אמיתא ניניא סיאה אמר רב יהודה (סיאה) צתרי אזוב אברתא קורנית קורניתא שמה והא ההוא דאמר להו מאן בעי קורניתא ואישתכח חשי אלא סיאה צתרי אזוב אברתא קורניתא חשי: איתמר בשר מליח מותר לטלטלו בשבת בשר [ב] תפל רב הונא אמר מותר לטלטלו רב חסדא אמר אסור לטלטלו רב הונא אמר מותר לטלטלו והא רב הונא תלמיד דרב הוה ורב כר' יהודה סבירא ליה דאית ליה מוקצה לאכילה סבר לה כרבי יהודה במוקצה לטלטל סבר לה כרבי שמעון רב חסדא אמר אסור לטלטלו והא רב יצחק בר אמי איקלע לבי רב חסדא וחזא ההוא בר אווזא דהוו קא מטלטלו ליה משמשא לטולא ואמר רב חסדא חסרון כיס קא חזינן הכא שאני בר אווזא דחזי לאומצא ת"ר דג מליח מותר לטלטלו דג תפל אסור לטלטלו בשר בין תפל ובין מליח מותר לטלטלו (ו) (וסתמא כרבי שמעון) תנו רבנן מטלטלין את העצמות מפני שהוא מאכל לכלבים בשר

רש"י

שלא ניטלה תרומתו. קא סלקא דעתך שלא ניטלה תרומת מעשר שלו: אסימון. שאין עליו צורה: חצב. עשב שמשתרש בעומק כנגדו ואין שרשיו מתפשטין ובו תיחם יהושע את הארץ לישראל: נעמיות. בנות היענה: יטלטלו. ראוי הוא להיות לו פילין ולהאכילן: על מכותיהן. בשבת ולא גזר משום שחיקת סממנין: שכן דרכן לסוך. בלא מכה הלכך לאו מוכחא מילתא דלרפואה: התקינן. הזמינן: אסור לטלטלן. ואפילו הזמינם למאכל בהמה דטירחא היא: סיאה אזוב וקורנית. לקמיה מפרש לה: הכניסן לעצים. לייבשן: שלא יקטום בכלי. כדרך חול כדאמרן (לעיל דף עד:) האי מאן דפריס סילקא דמי לטוחן. במילתיה דרבי יהודה גרסינן מולל ואוכל ובלבד שלא ימלול בכלי הרבה וחכמי' אומרים מולל בראשי אצבעותיו ובלבד שלא ימלול בידו הרבה כדרך חול כך מצאתי בתוספתא דרבנן מחמרי דבכולי ידא אסור אלא בראשי אצבעותיו ומהו מולל כגון אם בא לאכול הזרע מולל השרביטין שהזרע בתוכם: וכן באמיתא. לקמיה מפרש מאי אמיתא: ניניא. מינטא"י: פיגם. רוד"א: צתרי. סדריא"ה לוי"ה ל"א פוליאול: אברתא. איסופ"א: חשי. סדריא"ה וללשון הראשון לא פורש: בשר תפל. שאינו מלוח ומאן דגרים תפוח היא היא: מותר לטלטלו. דלית ליה מוקצה בטלטול: במוקצה לאכילה סבר לה כר' יהודה. כלומר באיסור מוקצה לענין אכילה סבר לה כרבי יהודה דאסר לאוכלו (ג) ובאיסור מוקצה לטלטול סבר לה כרבי שמעון: בר אווזא. שחוט: משמשא לטולא. שלא יסריח: ואמר להו רב חסדא חסרון כיס חזינא הכא. שאתם מניחים אותה בשמש ומתחמם וסלקוהו על פיו מחמה לצל: באומצא. כשהוא חי אוכלין אותו בלא מלח: דג תפל אסור לטלטלו. דאינו ראוי לכלוס ולכלבים לאו דעתיה למישדייה אבל מליח נאכל חי על ידי מלחו:

תוספות

אבל לא את הטבל. והא דאמר (ד) רבה בפרק כירה (לעיל דף מג.) טבל מוכן הוא אצל שבת שאם עבר ותיקנו מתוקן ה"מ לענין ביטול כלי מהיכנו שלא התמירו כמו לענין טלטול בידים:

שפדאו אגב אסימון. הא דנקט אסימון היינו דלא כרבי דוסא דפרק הזהב (ב"מ דף מז:) והוא הדין למימר מעות הניתנות סימן לבית המרחץ לר"ה אלא משום דאם כן הוי קמ"ל אלא השתא קמ"ל כרבנן:

ונתן הכסף וקם לו. אין הפסוק כן אלא ויסף חמישית כסף ערכך עליו וקם לו (ויקרא כז) ולכך הש"ס קצר ולומר בלשון אחר קצר כי ההיא דפרק הדר (עירובין דף סה.) רבי חנינא ביומא דרתח לא מצלי שנאמר בצר אל יורה ובפרק הרואה (ברכות דף נה:) שנאמר כל החלומות הולכים אחר הפה וקשה לר"י נימא כסף דוקא וכו"ת דשוה כסף ככסף הלא דגבי זוזין מרבינן קרא יתיר לרבות שוה כסף ועוד דאם כן אפילו קרקע נמי ומנלן למעוטי קרקע ואומר ר"י דמכלל ופרט נפקא כדתנן בבכורות בפרק יש בכור לנחלה (דף נא.) אין פודין לא בעבדים ולא בקרקעות ולא בהקדשות ומפרש בגמרא דבעי למימר ולא הקדשות בכל אלו לענין פדיון בכור דרשינן התם כלל ופרט ופדויו מבן חדש כלל בערכך פרט כסף חמשת שקלים חזר וכלל מה הפרט מפורש דבר המיטלטל כו' ה"נ איכא למימר בפדיון הקדשות ונתן כלל כסף פרט וקם לו חזר וכלל כו' מיהו בת"כ דריש ליה מקרא אחרינא וכל ערכך יהיה בשקל הקדש מה ת"ל שנאמר (ה) תפדה יכול בעבדים ושטרות וקרקעות ת"ל בשקל הקדש אין לי אלא סלעים מנין לרבות כל דבר המיטלטל ת"ל ופדה בערכך א"כ למה נאמר בשקל פרט לעבדים ושטרות וקרקעות אלא כן דרך הש"ס שאינו מביא עיקר הדרשה כמו שרגיל להביא (ו) (כתובות דף מו:) בנעוריה בית אביה כל שבח נעורים לאביה אע"ג דההוא בהפרת נדרים הוא דכתיב וכן הרבה:

רשב"ג אומר אף מטלטלין שברי זכוכית. משמע דמודה לת"ק דמתיר חרדל והא דתנן רשב"ג מתיר בלוף ולא שכן דמתיר בחרדל:

הכניסן לעצים אין מסתפק. איכא למימר דה"ק הא סתמא נעשה כמי שהכניסן למאכל בהמה כי היכי דלא תקשה רישא לסיפא:

דחזי לאומצא. מכאן ראיה דדם האברים שלא פירש מותר דקאמר דחזי לאומצא אע"ג דלא מליח:

דג תפל אסור לטלטלו. תימה מאי שנא בשר תפל אלמא כר"ש אתיא אם כן דג תפל נמי לישרי כמו בשר תפל וי"ל דדג תפל אינו ראוי לכלבים כי נמי כר' יהודה אתיא ודג תפל אע"פ שראוי לכלבים אסור לטלטלו דכל מידי דחזי לאיניש לא מקצה לכלבים בשר תפל מותר לטלטלו לרבי יהודה מפני שהוא מאכל לחיה:

מטלטלין את העצמות. לר' יהודה דאית לי' מוקצה מיירי כגון שלא הי' עליה' בשר מאתמול:

עין משפט נר מצוה

טו א ב ג מיי' פכ"ה מהל' שבת הל' יט:
טז ד ה מיי' פכ"ה מהל' שבת הל' [טו] סמג לאוין סה טוש"ע א"ח סימן שח סעיף כט:
יז ו ז מיי' פכ"ו מהלכות מלוה ולוה הלכה ז וס"ג מהלכות ערכין הלכה יב סמג עשין קא טוש"ע ח"מ סימן צז סעיף כג:
יח ז מיי' פכ"א מהלכות שבת הלכה יט סמג לאוין סה ועשין קלה טוש"ע א"ח סימן שכא סעיף ט:
יט ח ט מיי' שם פכ"ה הלכה יב סמג שם טוש"ע א"ח סימן שח סעיף לב ובסימן שכד סעיף ז:
כ י מיי' שם הלכה טו סמג שם טוש"ע א"ח סי' שם סעיף לג:
כא כ מיי' שם טוש"ע שם סעיף לג:
כב ל מיי' שם טוש"ע שם סעיף כט בהג"ה:

גליון הש"ס

גמ' והא רב הונא תלמיד דרב. ביצה דף ב ע"א. ב"ק קטו ע"א. ועיין ב"ב דף קנב ע"ב תוספות ד"ה שלחו ליה: שם במוקצה לטלטל ס"ל כר' שמעון. עיין לעיל דף יט ע"ב תוספות ד"ה הני כרכי. ולקמן דף קלט ע"ב ודף קמ ע"א תוספות ד"ה אלא. ועיין ביצה דף כו ע"א בתוספות ד"ה אין קוטמין:

הגהות הגר"א

[א] גמ' אין מסתפק מהן בשבת למאכל בהמה. נ"ב למאכל מסתפק מהן בשבת: [ב] שם מותר לטלטל בשבת בשר תפל. נ"ב גי' הגאונים ורי"ף תפוח. ועי' רשב"א:

תורה אור השלם

א) וְנָתַתָּה בַּכָּסֶף וְצַרְתָּ הַכֶּסֶף בְּיָדְךָ וְהָלַכְתָּ אֶל הַמָּקוֹם אֲשֶׁר יִבְחַר יְיָ אֱלֹהֶיךָ בּוֹ: [דברים יד, כה]

ב) וְאִם גָּאֹל יִגְאַל אֶת הַשָּׂדֶה הַמַּקְדִּישׁ אֹתוֹ וְיָסַף חֲמִשִׁית כֶּסֶף עֶרְכְּךָ עָלָיו וְקָם לוֹ: [ויקרא כז, יט]

רבינו חננאל

מעבב: אסימון מטבע שאין עליו צורה. ולא את הלוף ולא את החרדל. רשב"ג מתיר בלוף וכו' והא דרשב"ג פשוטה חבילי קש וחבילי עצים וכו'. חצב: עשב הוא והוא העשב (שכן) [שבו] תיחם יהושע לישראל את הארץ. הא מתני' סתמא היא וכוותה קי"ל דהא מתניתי' נמי דברי הכל הוא. ורשב"ג דאמר אין מותר לטלטל אלא חבילה הניטלת בידו אחת מוקמינן ליה בחבילות שהכניסן למאכל בהמה דכל סתם של תורה לחומרא עבדינן. ותרוב מתניתין כוותה תנא וכוותה עבדינן וליכא

רב נסים גאון

בפרק שלשה שאכלו כאחת כי הוא הדבר הנדמה דמי מתוקן ומי אינו מתוקן ובארנו שם עיקר גזירתו: אסימון בפרק הזהב (ב"מ דף מז) מאי אסימון פולסא ומה שהוא כצנין זה אסור לפדות בו את המעשר שני כי הכתוב פי' שצריך מטבע שיש עליו צורה דכתיב (דברים יד) וצרת הכסף בידך דבר שיש עליו צורה: ת"ר מטלטלין את החצב זה חצב צמח שלשה שרשיו למטה בקרקע בצדק בלא הטייה והוא מה שאמרו בפרק חזקת הבתים (ב"ב דף נה) אמר ר' אסי אמר ר' יוחנן המצר והחצב מפסיקין בנכסי הגר וכו' ואמרו מאי חצובא אמר רב יהודה אמר רב שבו תיחם יהושע את הארץ לישראל

הגהות הב"ח

(א) גמ' בטבל טבול מדרבנן וכגון שזרעו: (ב) שם וחבילי עצים (וחבילי זרדים) תא"מ ונ"ב עי' כמה שכתב הטור א"ח סי' ש"ח משמע דגרסי' בגמ' וחבילי זרדים: (ג) רש"י ד"ה במוקצה וכו' דאסר לאוכלו ובמוקצה לענין טלטול סבר: (ד) תוס' ד"ה אבל וכו' דאמר רב יוסף בפרק כירה: (ה) ד"ה ונתן וכו' ופדה בערכך יכול בעבדים:

ליקוטי רש"י

האי אידנן. הלי דנחמכם כבר לאידנן וכין דאקרא דכן נעשה כבר על תרומה כלכמים לאשית לבנך [פסחים שם]. ...

בעציץ שאינו נקוב. דטבל שלו מדרבנן [יומא פה:]. ולא מעשר ראשון שלא נטלה תרומתו. קא סלקא דעתך שלא נטלה תרומת מעשר שלו ...

raw, unsalted meat on the Sabbath. How is that to be reconciled with the view attributed to him above?

The Gemara answers:

שָׁאנֵי בַּר אַוָּוזָא דַּחֲזֵי לְאוּמְצָא – The raw meat of **a duck is different** from other raw meats (whose movement Rav Chisda *does* prohibit), **for it is fit to be eaten raw.**[44]

The Gemara cites a relevant Baraisa:

תָּנוּ רַבָּנָן – The Rabbis taught in a Baraisa: דָּג מָלִיחַ – As regards raw, SALTED FISH, מוּתָּר לְטַלְטְלוֹ – IT IS PERMITTED TO MOVE IT on the Sabbath.[45] דָּג תָּפֵל – But as regards raw, UNSALTED FISH, אָסוּר לְטַלְטְלוֹ – IT IS FORBIDDEN TO MOVE IT on the Sabbath.[46] בָּשָׂר – As regards raw MEAT, however, בֵּין תָּפֵל וּבֵין מָלִיחַ מוּתָּר לְטַלְטְלוֹ – WHETHER IT IS UNSALTED OR SALTED, IT IS PERMITTED TO MOVE IT.[47] (וּסְתָמָא כְּרַבִּי שִׁמְעוֹן) – **And the unattributed Baraisa** that we have just presented **follows** the opinion of **R' Shimon.)**[48]

The Gemara cites another Baraisa that discusses the *muktzeh* status of certain types of meat:

תָּנוּ רַבָּנָן – The Rabbis learned in a Baraisa: מְטַלְטְלִין אֶת הָעֲצָמוֹת – WE MAY MOVE BONES, מִפְּנֵי שֶׁהוּא מַאֲכָל לִכְלָבִים – BECAUSE THEY ARE FOOD FOR DOGS,

NOTES

44. Since it is tender (see *Bach* and *Taz* loc. cit.; cf. *Rashba* here).

[It emerges from this Gemara that one may eat raw, unsalted meat (as long as it is rinsed off to remove the blood on the surface), even though he is ingesting the blood that remains absorbed in the meat, which has not been purged through salting or roasting (see *Tosafos*; see *Yoreh Deah* 67:2).]

45. [For it is fit to eat as is.]

46. For it is unfit as is for human consumption. And though it is presently fit for dogs, one has set it aside from such use, since he wishes to use it after the Sabbath for human consumption (see *Rashi*). Thus, this Baraisa accords with R' Yehudah's position that something is *muktzeh* and may not be moved if fit for animal use, but set aside and presently unfit for human use [see above, note 39] (see *Tosafos*, second explanation, which *Bach* loc. cit. maintains is *Rashi's* position as well).

47. Although this Baraisa follows R' Yehudah's view (see previous note), it nonetheless rules that raw, unsalted meat may be moved. For it follows the view that "all Israel are considered princes" (see Gemara above), and it is the practice of royalty to keep beasts as pets and feed them raw meat [but not raw fish]. And since raw meat is not *muktzeh* for royalty [who certainly keep raw meat to feed their beasts], it is not deemed *muktzeh* for any Jew (see *Tosafos* here and to 128b ד״ה בשר תפוח; *Bach* loc. cit.).

48. *Maharshal* deletes these words from the text, and it is evident that they did not appear in the texts of *Rashi* or *Tosafos* (see preceding two notes).

אבל לא את הטבל וכו': פשיטא לא צריכא בטבל טבול מדרבנן (א) שזרעו בעציץ שאינו נקוב: ולא מעשר ראשון וכו': פשיטא לא צריכא שהקדימו בכרי שנטל ממנו מעשר ולא נטלה ממנו תרומה גדולה מהו דתימא כדאמר ליה רב פפא לאביי קמ"ל כדשני ליה אביי: ולא את מעשר שני וכו': פשיטא לא צריכא דנפדו ולא נפדו כהלכתן מעשר שפדאו על גבי אסימון דרחמנא אמר וצרת הכסף בידך דבר שיש בו צורה הקדש שחיללו על גבי קרקע דרחמנא אמר ונתן הכסף וקם לו: ולא את הלוף: ת"ר מטלטלין את החצב מפני שהוא מאכל לצביים ואת החרדל מפני שהוא מאכל ליונים רשב"ג אומר אף מטלטלין שברי זכוכית מפני שהוא מאכל לנעמיות אמר ליה רבי נתן אלא מעתה חבילי זמורות יטלטלו מפני שהוא מאכל לפילין ורשב"ג נעמיות שכיחי פילין לא שכיחי אמר אמימר והוא דאית ליה נעמיות אמר רב אשי לאמימר אלא דקאמר ליה ר' נתן לרשב"ג חבילי זמורות יטלטל מפני שהוא מאכל לפילין אי אית ליה פילין אמאי לא אלא ראוי ה"נ ראוי אמר אביי רשב"ג ורבי שמעון ורבי ישמעאל ורבי עקיבא כולהו סבירא להו כל ישראל בני מלכים הם רשב"ג הא דאמרן ר' שמעון דתנן בני מלכים סכין על גבי מכותיהן שמן וורד שכן דרכן של בני מלכים לסוך בחול ר"ש אומר כל ישראל בני מלכים הם ר' ישמעאל ור' עקיבא דתניא הרי שהיו נושין בו אלף מנה ולבוש איצטלא בת ק' מנה מפשיטין אותו ומלבישין אותו איצטלא הראויה לו תנא משום רבי ישמעאל ותנא משום רבי עקיבא כל ישראל ראוין לאותה איצטלא:

חבילי קש וחבילי כו': תנו רבנן חבילי קש וחבילי עצים (ג) וחבילי זרדים אם התקינן למאכל בהמה מטלטלין אותן ואם לאו אין מטלטלין אותן רשב"ג אומר חבילין הניטלין ביד אחד מותר לטלטלן בשתי ידים אסור לטלטלן חבילי סיאה אזוב וקורנית הכניסן לעצים אין [א] מסתפק מהן בשבת למאכל בהמה מסתפק מהן בשבת וקוטם ביד ואוכל ובלבד שלא יקטום בכלי ומולל ואוכל ובלבד שלא ימלול בכלי הרבה דברי רבי יהודה וחכמים אומרים מולל בראשי אצבעותיו ואוכל ובלבד שלא ימלול בידו הרבה כדרך שהוא עושה בחול וכן באמיתא וכן בפיגם וכן בשאר מיני תבלין מאי אמיתא ניניא סיאה אמר רב יהודה (סיאה) צתרי אזוב אברתא קורנית קורניתא שמה והא ההוא דאמר להו מאן בעי קורניתא ואישתכח חשי אלא סיאה צתרי אזוב אברתא קורניתא חשי: איתמר בשר מליח מותר לטלטלו בשבת בשר [ב] תפל רב הונא אמר מותר לטלטלו רב חסדא אמר אסור לטלטלו רב הונא אמר מותר לטלטלו והא רב הונא תלמיד דרב הוה ורב כר' יהודה סבירא ליה דאית ליה מוקצה במוקצה לאכילה סבר לה כרבי יהודה במוקצה לטלטל סבר לה כרבי שמעון רב חסדא אמר אסור לטלטלו והא רב יצחק בר אמי איקלע לבי רב חסדא וחזא ההוא בר אווזא דהוו קא מטלטלו ליה משמשא לטולא ואמר רב חסדא חסרון כיס קא חזינן הכא שאני בר אווזא דחזי לאומצא ת"ר דג מליח מותר לטלטלו דג תפל אסור לטלטלו בשר בין תפל ובין מליח מותר לטלטלו (ד) וסתמא כרבי שמעון) תנו רבנן מטלטלין את העצמות מפני שהוא מאכל לכלבים

בשר

רש"י

שלא ניטלה תרומתו. קא סלקא דעתך שלא ניטלה תרומת מעשר שלו: **אסימון.** שאין עליו צורה: **חצב.** עשב שמשרש בעומק כנגדו ואין שרשיו מתפשטין ובו (ח) תיחם יהושע את הארץ לישראל: **נעמיות.** בנות היענה: **יטלטלו.** ראוי הוא להיות לו פילין ולהאכילן: **על מכותיהן.** בשבת ולא גזר משום שחיקת סממנין: **שכן דרכן לסוך.** בלא מכה הלכך לאו מוכחא מילתא דלרפואה: **התקינן.** הזמינן: **אסור לטלטלן.** ואפילו הזמינם למאכל בהמה דטירחא היא: **סיאה אזוב וקורנית.** לקמיה מפרש לה: **הכניסן לעצים.** לייבשן: **שלא יקטום בכלי.** כדרך חול כדאמרן (לעיל דף עד:) האי מאן דפריס סילקא דמי לטוחן. במילתיה דרבי יהודה גרסינן מולל ואוכל ובלבד שלא ימלול בכלי הרבה וחכמי' אומרים מולל בראשי אצבעותיו ובלבד שלא ימלול בידו הרבה כדרך חול כך מצאתי בתוספתא דרבנן מחמרי דבכולי ידא אסור אלא בראשי אצבעותיו ומהו מולל כגון אם בא לאכול הזרע מולל השבלין שהזרע בתוכם: **וכן באמיתא.** לקמיה מפרש מאי אמיתא: **ניניא.** מינטא"י: **פיגם.** רוד"א: **צתרי.** סדריא"ה לוי"ה ל"א פוליאול: **אברתא.** איסני"א: **חשי.** סדריא"ה וללשון הראשון לא פורש: **בשר תפל.** שאינו מלוח ומאן דגריס תפוח היא היא: **מותר לטלטלו.** דלית ליה מוקצה בטלטול: **במוקצה לאכילה סבר לה כר' יהודה.** כלומר באיסור מוקצה לענין אכילה סבר לה כרבי יהודה דאסר לאוכלו (ג) ובאיסור מוקצה לטלטול סבר לה כרבי שמעון: **בר אווזא.** שחוט: **משמשא לטולא.** שלא יסריח: **ואמר להו רב חסדא חסרון כיס חזינא הכא.** שאתם מניחים אותה בשמש ומתחמם וסלקוהו על פיו מחמה לצל: **באומצא.** כשהוא חי אוכלין אותו בלא מלח: **דג תפל אסור לטלטלו.** דאינו ראוי לכלום ולכלבים לאו דעתיה למישדייה אבל מליח נאכל חי על ידי מלחו:

בשר

תוספות

אבל לא את הטבל. והא דאמר (ד) רבה בפרק כירה (לעיל דף מג.) טבל מוכן הוא אצל שבת שאם עבר ותיקנו מתוקן ה"מ לענין ביטול כלי מהיכנו שלא החמירו כמו לענין טלטול בידים: **שפדאו** אגב אסימון. הא דנקט אסימון היינו דלא כרבי דוסא דפרק הזהב (ב"מ דף מז:) והוה מצי למימר מעות הניתנות סימן לבית המרחץ לד"ה אלא משום דאם כן מאי קמ"ל אבל השתא קמ"ל כרבנן: **ונתן** הכסף וקם לו. אין הפסוק כן אלא ויסף חמישית כסף ערכך עליו וקם לו (ויקרא כז) ודרך הש"ס לקצר ולומר בלשון אחר קצר כי ההיא דפרק הדר (עירובין דף סה.) רבי חנינא ביומא דרתח לא מצלי שנאמר בצר אל יורה ובפרק הרואה (ברכות דף נה:) שנאמר כל החלומות הולכים אחר הפה וקשה לר"י נימא כסף דוקא וכ"ת דשוה כסף ככסף הלא דגבי נזקין מרבינן קרא ישיב לרבות שוה כסף ועוד דאם כן אפילו קרקע נמי ומנלן למעוטי קרקע ואומר ר"י דמכלל ופרט נפקא כדתנן בבכורות בפרק יש בכור לנחלה (דף נא.) אין פודין לא בעבדים ולא בקרקעות ולא בהקדשות ומפרש בגמרא דבעי למימר ולא הקדשות בכל אלו לענין פדיון בכור דרשינן התם כלל ופרט ופדויו מבן חדש כלל כסף פרט תפדה חזר וכלל מה הפרט מפורש דבר המיטלטל כו' ה"נ איכא למימר בפדיון הקדשות ונתן כלל כסף פרט וקם לו חזר וכלל כו' מיהו בת"כ דריש ליה מקרא אחרינא וכל ערכך יהיה בשקל הקדש מה ת"ל לפי שנאמר (ה) תפדה יכול בעבדים ושטרות וקרקעו' ת"ל בשקל הקדש אין לי אלא סלעים מניין לרבות כל דבר המיטלטל ת"ל ופדה בערכך א"כ למה נאמר בשקל פרט לעבדים ושטרות וקרקעות אלא כן דרך הש"ס שאינו מביא עיקר הדרשה כמו שרגיל להביא (ט) (כתובות דף מו:) בנעוריה בית אביה כל שבח נעורים לאביה אע"ג דההוא בהפרת נדרים הוא דכתיב וכן הרבה: **רשב"ג** אומר אף מטלטלין שברי זכוכית. משמע דמודה לת"ק דמתיר חרדל והא דתנן רשב"ג מתיר בלוף וכל שכן דמתיר בחרדל: **הכניסן** לעצים אין מסתפק. איכא למימר דה"ק הא סתמא נעשה כמי שהכניסן למאכל בהמה כי היכי דלא תקשה רישא לסיפא: **דחזי** לאומצא. מכאן ראיה דדם האברים שלא פירש מותר דקאמר דחזי לאומצא אע"ג דלא מליח (פ): **דג** תפל אסור לטלטלו. תימה מדשרי בשר תפל אלמא כר"ש אתיא אם כן דג תפל נמי לישרי כמו בשר תפל וי"ל דדג תפל אינו ראוי לכלבים אי נמי כר' יהודה אתיא ודג תפל אע"פ שראוי לכלבים אסור לטלטלו דכל מידי דחזי לאינש לא מקצה לכלבים בשר תפל מותר לטלטלו לרבי יהודה מפני שהוא מאכל לחיה: **מטלטלין** את העצמות. לר' יהודה דאית לי' מוקצה מיירי כגון שלא הי' עליה' בשר מאתמול:

בשר

כג א מיי' פכ"ה מהל' שבת הלכה כה סמג לאוין סה טוש"ע א"ח סימן שח סעיף לט:
כד ב מיי' פכ"ה שם הלכה כו סמג שם טוש"ע שם סעיף מא:
כה ג מיי' שם הלכה כו וסמג שם טוש"ע א"ח סימן שה סעיף יט:
כו ד מיי' פי"ג מהלכות רולח וש"מ הלכה יג סמג עשין סה ש"פ ולאוין קסט טוש"ע ח"מ סימן רעב סעיף ט בהג"ה:
כז ה ו מיי' פכ"ה מהל' שבת הלכה כו סמג לאוין סה טוש"ע א"ח סי' שח סעיף מ:
כח ז שם סעיף מא:
כט ח מיי' פ"ג מהל' שחיטה הל' יד סמג עשין סג טוש"ע יו"ד סי' כד סעיף כ [וכרב אלפס חולין פ"ב דף רפא]:
ל ט י מיי' פ"ד מהל' יו"ט הלכה טו סמג לאוין עה טוש"ע א"ח סימן תקכב סעיף א וסימן שלב סעיף א:
לא כ מיי' שם טוש"ע שם ס"ד:
לב ל מ נ מיי' פ"ב מהלכות שבת הלכה יא סמג לאוין סה טוש"ע א"ח סי' של סעיף א:

בשר תפוח מפני שהוא מאכל לחיה מים מגולין מפני שהן ראויין לחתול רשב"ג אומר כל עצמן אסור לשהותן מפני הסכנה: **מתני׳** [א]כופין את הסל לפני האפרוחים כדי שיעלו וירדו תרנגולת שברחה דוחין אותה עד שתכנס מדדין עגלין וסייחין [ב] (א) אשה מדדה את בנה אמר רבי יהודה [ג]אימתי בזמן שהוא נוטל אחת ומניח אחת אבל אם היה גורר אסור: **גמ׳** אמר רב יהודה אמר רב בהמה שנפלה לאמת המים מביא כרים וכסתות ומניח תחתיה ואם עלתה עלתה מיתיבי [ג]בהמה שנפלה לאמת המים עושה לה פרנסה במקומה בשביל שלא תמות פרנסה אין כרים וכסתות לא לא קשיא [ג]הא דאפשר בפרנסה הא דאי אפשר בפרנסה אפשר בפרנסה אין ואי לא מביא כרים וכסתות ומניח תחתיה והא [ד]קא מבטל כלי מהיכנו סבר מבטל כלי מהיכנו דרבנן [ה]צער בעלי חיים דאורייתא ואתי דאורייתא ודחי דרבנן: [ח]תרנגולת שברחה וכו': דוחין אין מדדין לא תנינא להא דת"ר [ו]מדדין בהמה חיה ועוף בחצר אבל לא את התרנגולת תרנגולת מאי טעמא לא אמר אביי משום דמקפיא נפשה תני חדא מדדין בהמה וחיה ועוף בחצר אבל לא ברה"ר והאשה מדדה את בנה [ז]ברה"ר ואצ"ל בחצר ותניא אידך אין עוקרין בהמה וחיה ועוף אפילו בחצר אבל דוחין בהן שיכנסו הא גופא קשיא אמרת אין עוקרין אבל דדויי מדדינן (ב) הדר אמרת דוחין אין מדדין לא אמר אביי סיפא אתאן לתרנגולת אמר אביי [ח]האי מאן דשחיט תרנגולת לכבשינהו לכרעיה בארעא אי נמי נידל להו מידל דדילמא מנח להו לטופריה בארעא ועקר להו לסימנים: **מתני׳** [ט]אין מילדין את הבהמה ביום טוב אבל מסעדין ומילדין את האשה בשבת וקורין לה חכמה ממקום למקום ומחללין עליה את השבת וקושרין את הטיבור רבי יוסי אומר [י]אף חותכין [י]וכל צרכי מילה עושין בשבת: **גמ׳** כיצד מסעדין רב יהודה אמר אוחז את הולד שלא יפול לארץ רב נחמן אמר דוחק בבשר כדי שיצא הולד תניא כוותיה דרב יהודה [ט]כיצד מסעדין [י]אוחזין את הולד שלא יפול לארץ ונופח לו בחוטמו ונותן לו דד לתוך פיו כדי שינק אמר רשב"ג [כ]מרחמין היינו על בהמה טהורה ביו"ט היכי עביד אמר אביי מביא בול של מלח ומניח לה בתוך הרחם כדי שתזכור צערה ותרחם עליו ומזלפין מי שליא על גבי ולד כדי שתריח ריחו ותרחם עליו ודוקא טהורה אבל טמאה לא מ"ט טמאה לא מרחקא ולדא ואי מרחקא ולדא לא מקרבא: [ל]מילדין את האשה וכו': מכדי תנא ליה מילדין את האשה וקורין לה חכמה ממקום למקום ומחללין עליה את השבת לאתויי מאי לאתויי הא דתנו רבנן [מ]אם היתה צריכה לנר חבירתה מדלקת לה את הנר ואם היתה צריכה לשמן חבירתה מביאה לה שמן ביד ואם אינו ספק ביד מביאה בשערה ואם אינו ספק בשערה מביאה לה בכלי אמר מר אם היתה צריכה לנר חבירתה מדלקת לה את הנר פשיטא [נ]לא צריכא בסומא מהו דתימא כיון דלא חזיא אסור קא משמע לן איתובי מיתבא דעתה סברא אי איכא מידי חזיא חבירתא ועבדה לי: אם היתה צריכה לשמן וכו': [ס]תיפוק ליה משום סחיטה רבה ורב יוסף דאמרי תרווייהו אין סחיטה בשיער רב אשי אמר אפי' תימא יש סחיטה בשיער מביאה לה בכלי דרך שערה [ע]דכמה דאפשר לשנויי משנינן אמר רב יהודה אמר שמואל חיה כל זמן שהקבר פתוח בין אמרה צריכה אני [פ]בין לא אמרה צריכה אני מחללין עליה את השבת נסתם הקבר בין אמרה צריכה

בשר תפוח. מסריח: **לחתול.** לא מזיק ליה ארס דנחש שאף הנחשים היא אוכלת: **מפני הסכנה.** שמא ישתה אדם מהם: **מתני׳ כופין סל בפני האפרוחים.** אשמעינן דכלי ניטל לדבר שאינו ניטל בשבת ורבי יצחק משני לה בפ"ג בצריך למקומו: **שברחה.** מן הבית: **דוחין.** בידים: **מדדין עגלים.** אוחז בצוארו ובצדדין וגוררו ומסייעו (ג) ומנענע לו ברגליו: **אשה מדדה את בנה.** אוחזתו בזרועותיו מאחוריו ומסייעתו והוא מניע רגליו והולך: **שנוטל אחת ומניח אחת.** שהתינוק מניע את רגליו כשמניח אחת מגביה אחת: **אבל גורר אסור.** מפני שנושאתו: **גמ׳ ואי לא.** כגון שהמים עמוקין: **והא קמבטל כלי מהיכנו.** דמשהניחם תחתיה אין יכול לטלטלן דדומה לסותר בנין (ד) מדרבנן: **צער בעלי חיים דאורייתא.** שנאמר עזוב תעזוב עמו ואיכא מאן דדריש טעמא דקרא משום צער בעלי חיים באלו מציאות (ב"מ דף לב:): **מדדין לא.** שלא יהא אוחזה בגפיה ורגליה נוגעין לארץ ומוליכה: **דמקפיא נפשה.** מגבהת עצמה מן הארץ ונמצא זה מטלטל אבל אווזים כשאוחזין בגפיהן הן מהלכין ברגליהן ומיהו ברה"ר לא משום שמא יגביהם מן הארץ ונמצא נושאן דסתמא כרבנן דפליגי עליה דרבי נתן בהמצניע (לעיל דף צד.) גבי המוציא חיה ועוף בין חיין בין שחוטין חייב והאשה מדדה את בנה אפילו ברה"ר דאי נמי מגביה ליה חי נושא את עצמו דהכי מוקמינן התם דבאדם מודו רבנן לרבי נתן: **מקפיא.** כגון אקפו ידייכו דחגיגה (דף טו:): **אין עוקרין.** רגליה לגמרי מן הארץ דמוקצה היא לטלטלה: **דדויי מדדינן.** אוחזה בשני צדדיה בידו ומדדה והוה טלטול טפי מדחייה שדוחפה מאחריה: **סיפא.** דקתני דוחין אבל לא מדדין: **אתאן לתרנגולת.** ורישא בשאר עופות: **לכבשינהו לכרעיה בארעא.** כדי שיתכפלו ולא יוכל להתחזק עליהן: **אי נמי לידלינהו.** יגביהנו שלא יהו רגליו נוגעות לארץ: **מתני׳ מסעדין.** מפרש בגמרא: **חכמה.** מילדת: **אין מילדין את הבהמה ביום טוב.** דאיכא טרחא יתירה: **אבל מסעדין.** אותה בי"ט: **ומיילדין אשה בשבת.** ואין צריך לומר שמסעדין וכל שכן ביום טוב: **וקושרין הטיבור.** של ולד שהוא ארוך שאם לא יתקשר ויכרך בשום דבר יצאו מעיו אם יגביהו התינוק: **גמ׳ דוחק.** בבשר של בהמה לפנים שיהא הולד בולט לחוץ: **ונופח לו בחוטמו.** שנחיריו סתומין לו בדירין: **ונותן דד.** של אמו בתוך פיו: **מרחמין.** מאהבין את ולדה עליה: **בול של מלח.** מלא אגרוף דכייב לה וזוכרת צער לידה ומרחמה את הולד אם רחקתו: **מי שליא.** שורין את השליא במים: **לא מרחקה.** אין דרכה לרחק: **מביאה לה שמן.** דרך רה"ר: **ביד.** בכפה ולא בכלי דכמה דאפשר משנינן: **בשערה.** סכה שערה שמן וכשבאה אצלה מקנחתו ואין כאן חילול שבת כיון שאין דרך הוצאה בכך: **פשיטא.** דהא פקוח נפש דוחה שבת: **תיפוק ליה משום סחיטה.** למה לא הביאה לה בכלי שלא תחלל שבת בהוצאה הכא נמי הא קמחללה בסחיטה: **אין סחיטה בשיער.** שהוא קשה ואין בולע: **דרך שערה.** כורכת הכלי בראשה בשערה: **חיה.** יולדת: **קבר.** בית הרחם: צריכה

בשר תפוח מפני שהוא מאכל לחיה. תימה לימא מפני שהוא מאכל לכלבים וי"ל דכרבי יהודה אתיא ואינו מסריח כפירוש הקונטרס אלא חזי ליה וכל מידי דחזי ליה לאינש לא מקצה לכלבים אבל מפני שהוא מאכל לחיה מותר לטלטלו דכל ישראל בני מלכים הם ורב חסדא דלא שרי בשר תפל מהאי טעמא לית ליה כל ישראל בני מלכים:

אין עוקרין בהמה חיה ועוף. לספרים דגרסי רה"ר הך ברייתא פליגא אקמייתא בתרתי דדייקין הא לדדויי מדדין אפילו ברה"ר ולעיל קתני דווקא בחצר ותו סיפא דמוקמת לתרנגולת דאין מדדין ברה"ר ולעיל קתני דאפי' בחצר לא ולספרים דגרסי אין עוקרין בהמה חיה ועוף בחצר אתי שפיר:

קמ"ל איתובי מיתבא דעתה. אע"ג דבפרק בתרא דיומא (דף פג.) אמר חולה אין מאכילין אותו ביוה"כ אלא ע"פ מומחה והכא (ה) שריא משום יתובי דעתא היינו שיותר יכולה היולדת להסתכן על ידי פחד שתפחד שמא אין עושין יפה מה שהיא צריכה ממה שיסתכן החולה ברעב: רבה

א) [לעיל מג.], ב) ס"א ברה"ר, ג) [תוספתא פט"ו], ד) [לעיל מג. וש"נ וע"ש תוספות ד"ה דמבטל], ה) [ב"מ לב:], ו) [בס"א מ"מ סימן של סעיף ד פסק הלכתא כרבי יוסי וכן דעת הרמב"ם], ז) לקמן קלג., ח) [תוספ' פט"ו], ט) [לעיל קח: לקמן קמח. ע"ש], י) ס"א בין אמרה איני צריכה, כ) [ע"ל לעיל בפ"ג מג:].

הגהות הב"ח

(א) במשנה ואשה מדדה: (ב) גמ' והדר אמרת: (ג) רש"י ד"ה מדדין וכו' ומסייעו לילך ומנענע: (ד) ד"ה והא קא מבטל וכו' לסותר בנין מבטל כלי מהיכנו מדרבנן צער בעלי חיים: (ה) תוס' ד"ה קמ"ל וכו' והכא שריא משום וכו' היינו לפי שיותר:

גליון הש"ס

גמרא תיפוק ליה משום סחיטה. עיין לקמן דף קמה ע"א תוספות ד"ה כבסים:

רב נסים גאון

כדי שיתפרשו תחומין אחד מחבירו ויאמינו בכך לענין עירובין של תחומים ושיתופים כי השרשים שהן משלח בקרקע מוכיחים על הגבולים ועל פי זה אמרו שם במסכת יום טוב (פרק אין צדין דף כה) חצובא מקטע רגליהון דרשיעיא שהוא דבר שאין בו רוח חיים ובצמיחתו משלח שרשיו בארץ במשפט והרשעים מעקמין דרכיהם ואין הולכין בדרכיו של הקב"ה כמו שראוי להם לכך דרכם באפילה: צער בעלי חיים דאורייתא מה שאמר הקב"ה (שמות כג) כי תראה חמור שונאך רובץ תחת משאו ואמרו בבא מציעא בפרק אלו מציאות (דף לב) מצוה מן התורה לפרוק דקסבר תנא דידן צער בעלי חיים דאורייתא ורבי יוסי הגלילי סבר צער בעלי חיים דרבנן וסבר (אביי) [רב יהודה] בכאן כתנא קמא דצער בעלי חיים דאורייתא וביטול כלי מהיכנו דרבנן משכחת לה בפרק כירה (לעיל דף מב) דתנן אין נותנין כלי תחת הנר לקבל בו את השמן ואמר רב חסדא אין נותנין כלי תחת התרנגולת לקבל ביצתה כו' ופירש רב יוסף טעמא בכך ואמר היינו טעמא דרב חסדא דקא מבטל כלי מהיכנו והא מדרבנן הוא:

סליק פרק מפנין

ליקוטי רש"י

מים מגולין. מים שנשארו מגולין בלילה ספק שתה מהן נחש ספק לא שתה וקיימא לן דאסירי [חולין ט:]. עושה לה פרנסה. כל לשון פרנסה לשון עסק לצורכיה הוא קונדר"ס בלע"ז כמו (כתובות סב.) וכמו מוליכין למזונות (שם סט.) [גיטין סה:]. כל צורך סיפוק קרי פרנסה קונדר"ס בלע"ז [ב"מ מו.]. והא קא מבטל כלי מהיכנו. שהיה מוכן מתחלה לטלטלו ועכשיו עושהו מוקצה [לעיל מג. ע"ש בתוס' ובפנ"י]. אסור לבטל כלי במקום שלא יוכל עוד ליטלו [משם] דהוי כקובע לו מקום ומחברו בטיט ודמי למלאכה וכלי זה יהא אסור לטלטלו [שם מב:]. כרים וכסתות כשמניחן תחת דבר שאין ניטל מבטלן מהיכנן דשוב לסותר [לקמן קנד:]. מקפיא. לשון דבר הצף ואין מכביד כדמתרגמינן ויצף הברזל וקפא ברזלא (מ"ב ו) [חגיגה טו:]. טופריה. צפרניו [לעיל סג:]. בול של מלח. מלא אגרוף של מלח שמעתי [זבחים סג:].

רבינו חננאל

לטלטלו: דג תפל אסור לטלטלו בשר חי ובין מליח מותר לטלטלו. ת"ר מטלטלין את העצמות מפני שהן מאכל לכלבים בשר תפוח מפני שהוא מאכל לחיה וזו היא דתניא כוותיה דרב הונא מים מגולין מפני שהן ראוין לחתול. ומתניתא אלין הלכתא אינון דליכא דפליג. ואליבא דב"ה נשנו דתנן ב"ה אומרים מגביהין מעל השלחן עצמות וקליפין: כופין את הסל לפני האפרוחים שיעלו וישרדו. בהמה שנפלה לאמת המים אם אפשר לה בפרנסה עושין לה פרנסה. ואם אי אפשר לה בפרנסה מביא כרים וכסתות ומניח תחתיה ואם עלתה עלתה ואף על גב דמבטל כלי מהיכנו. מדרבנן היא. וצער ב"ח דאורייתא ואתא דאורייתא ודחה דרבנן. תרנגולת שברחה דוחין אותה עד שתכנס אבל אין מדדין אותה אפי' בחצר משום דמקפיא נפשה וא"ש ששאר בהמה חיה ועוף מדדין בחצר אבל לא ברה"ר וכ"ש תרנגולת אפילו בחצר לא אלא אסור לדדותם אפילו בחצר. האשה מדדה את בנה ברה"ר וכ"ש בחצר והוא דאמר ר' יהודה אימתי בזמן שנוטל אחת ומניח אחת אבל אם היה גורר אסור [היינו] ברה"ר בלבד שאם נוטל התינוק רגלו האחת ונשען על רגלו האחרת נמצא כמהלך אבל אם אינו נשען על רגליו אלא כשמדדתו גורר רגליו נמצאת נושאתו ברה"ר ואסור אבל בחצר מותר לטלטלו. אמר אביי מאן דשחיט תרנגולת ליכבשינה לכרעתא בארעא. אי נמי תידלינהו דילמא מנח להן ... ועקרה להו לסימנים הלכתא היא: **מתני׳** אין מילדין את הבהמה ביו"ט אבל מסעדין כיצד מסעדין. ... אוחז בולד שלא יפול לארץ והלכתא כמותו. דתניא כוותיה. כיצד מסעדין אוחז בולד שלא יפול לארץ ... בחוטמו ונותן דד לתוך פיו כדי שיינק כו'. וקיי"ל דמסעדין ומרחמין דתנינן ביו"ט אבל לא בשבת ... בשבת וקורין לה חכמה ממקום למקום ומחללין עליה את השבת. ואסיקנא שמדלקת לה חברתה ... היא סומא מותר להדליק לה נר בשבת דקיי"ל ייתובי מייתבא דעתה סברא אי איכא מידי חזייא ... ואם היתה צריכה לשמן מביאה לה שמן כרב אשי דאמר מביאה לה בכלי דרך שערה נועצת כלי של שמן בשערה כדי שלא [יהא] הוצאה ביד כדרך המוציאין ומסקנא כמה דאית לשנויי ... מר זוטרא מתני אמר רב יהודה אמר שמואל חיה כל זמן שהקבר פתוח. בין אמרה צריכה אני ובין אמרה איני צריכה מחללין עליה את השבת. נסתם (הכלי) [הקבר] אמרה צריכה

בָּשָׂר תָּפוּחַ – and we may move SPOILED[1] MEAT, מִפְּנֵי שֶׁהוּא מַאֲכָל לְחַיָּה – BECAUSE IT IS FOOD FOR BEASTS.[2] מַיִם מְגוּלִּין – WATERS THAT WERE EXPOSED and thus unfit for human and even animal consumption[3] are nevertheless not *muktzeh,* מִפְּנֵי שֶׁהֵן רְאוּיִין לְחָתוּל – BECAUSE THEY ARE FIT FOR CATS.[4] רַבָּן שִׁמְעוֹן בֶּן גַּמְלִיאֵל אוֹמֵר – RABBAN SHIMON BEN GAMLIEL SAYS: כָּל עַצְמָן אָסוּר לְשַׁהוֹתָן – THE VERY [WATERS] THEMSELVES ONE IS FORBIDDEN TO KEEP in existence מִפְּנֵי הַסַּכָּנָה – BECAUSE OF the DANGER that they pose to one who might drink them! Certainly, then, they are *muktzeh.*[5]

Mishnah כּוֹפִין אֶת הַסַּל לִפְנֵי הָאֶפְרוֹחִים – WE MAY INVERT A BASKET IN FRONT OF CHICKS כְּדֵי שֶׁיַּעֲלוּ וְיֵרְדוּ – SO THAT THEY MAY CLIMB UP to AND DOWN from their nests.[6] תַּרְנְגוֹלֶת שֶׁבָּרְחָה – IF A HEN ESCAPED,[7] דּוֹחִין אוֹתָהּ עַד שֶׁתִּכָּנֵס – WE MAY PUSH HER[8] UNTIL SHE ENTERS.[9] מְדַדִּין עֲגָלִין וּסְיָיחִין – WE MAY HELP CALVES AND YOUNG DONKEYS WALK.[10] אִשָּׁה מְדַדָּה אֶת בְּנָהּ – A WOMAN MAY HELP HER young CHILD WALK.[11] אָמַר רַבִּי יְהוּדָה – R' YEHUDAH SAID: אֵימָתַי – WHEN may she help the child walk?[12] בִּזְמַן שֶׁהוּא נוֹטֵל אַחַת וּמַנִּיחַ אַחַת – WHEN HE LIFTS ONE foot AND PUTS DOWN THE OTHER foot. אֲבָל אִם הָיָה גּוֹרֵר אָסוּר – BUT IF HE WAS DRAGGING his feet as his mother pulled him, IT IS FORBIDDEN for her to propel him through the public domain.[13]

Gemara The Mishnah has taught that the *muktzeh* prohibitions were relaxed in the face of an animal's distress. The Gemara presents a related ruling:

אָמַר רַב יְהוּדָה אָמַר רַב – **Rav Yehudah said in the name of Rav:** בְּהֵמָה שֶׁנָּפְלָה לְאַמַּת הַמַּיִם – **If an animal fell into a stream of water** on the Sabbath, and is unable to extricate herself, מֵבִיא כָּרִים וּכְסָתוֹת וּמַנִּיחַ תַּחְתֶּיהָ – **one may bring pillows and cushions and place** them **beneath her**[14] so that she can step up on them and climb out, וְאִם עָלְתָה עָלְתָה – **and if she emerges** from the stream as a result, **she emerges.**[15]

The Gemara asks:

מֵיתִיבֵי – **They challenged** Rav's ruling on the basis of the following Baraisa: בְּהֵמָה שֶׁנָּפְלָה לְאַמַּת הַמַּיִם – IF AN ANIMAL FELL INTO A STREAM OF WATER, עוֹשֶׂה לָהּ פַּרְנָסָה בִּמְקוֹמָהּ – ONE SUPPLIES HER WITH PROVISIONS IN HER present LOCATION (assuming that this entails no *melachah*) בִּשְׁבִיל שֶׁלֹּא תָּמוּת – SO THAT SHE SHOULD NOT DIE of hunger.

The Gemara develops its challenge:

פַּרְנָסָה אִין – The Baraisa implies that supplying her with **provisions – yes,** this is permitted; כָּרִים וּכְסָתוֹת לֹא – but placing **pillows and cushions** into the stream so that she can step up on them and climb out – **no,** this is not allowed.[16] Thus, this Baraisa contradicts the ruling of Rav, who permits placing objects into the stream. – ? –

The Gemara answers:

לֹא קַשְׁיָא – **It is not difficult.** הָא דְּאֶפְשָׁר בְּפַרְנָסָה – **This** ruling

NOTES

1. *Rashi;* cf. *Tosafos.* [Although in his comments to the Gemara above *Rashi* indicated that תָּפוּחַ means *unsalted,* he maintains that in the present context it refers to *spoiled* meat (see *Derishah* cited above, 128a note 37).]

2. Spoiled meat is edible only to beasts and not to dogs. Thus, the Baraisa did not state – as it did with regard to bones – that it is fit for dogs (*Ran MHK* ed. to 128a, end of ד״ה איתמר בשר חי; cf. *Rashba* there and *Tosafos* here; see also *Aruch HaShulchan* 308:57).

3. One may not drink or give his animals to drink from water or wine that was left uncovered, because a snake might have drunk from it and injected venom into it (see *Terumos* 8:4-5 and *Avodah Zarah* 30a-b; *Tur, Yoreh Deah* 116). [Nowadays, however, that snakes are uncommon, these laws no longer apply (*Shulchan Aruch* ibid. §1; see, however, *Pischei Teshuvah* ibid. §1).]

4. It is not dangerous for cats to drink snake venom, as evident from the fact that they eat venomous snakes. Thus, exposed water is fit for cats and therefore not *muktzeh* (*Rashi;* see also *Rashi* to *Avodah Zarah* 30b ד״ה בשונרא).

5. *Chasdei Dovid* to Tosefta 15:10.

6. With this ruling, the Mishnah teaches us that one is permitted on the Sabbath to move a utensil [the basket] for the sake of a *muktzeh* item [the chicks – see *Tosafos* to 45b ד״ה הכא במאי עסקינן] (*Rashi*).

Actually, there is the Amora R' Yitzchak (above, 43a) who holds that it is *forbidden* to move a utensil for the sake of a *muktzeh* item, and the Gemara there challenges him from this Mishnah. R' Yitzchak is therefore forced to explain (ibid.) that the Mishnah here refers to where one wished to move the utensil for some permitted purpose; and the Mishnah is ruling that since the person is moving the utensil in any event, he may tailor its movement for the sake of the *muktzeh* item (*Rashi*).

7. I.e. from the house (*Rashi*). [*Rashi* means to explain that the Mishnah here does not use the expression שֶׁבָּרְחָה, *that escaped,* in the sense of a hen that abandoned the eggs on which she was sitting (as the expression is used in *Pesachim* 55b), but rather in the sense of a chicken that ran away, and is thus in danger of being hurt (see *Bach* 308 ד״ה תרנגולת).]

8. I.e. [even] with one's hands (*Rashi* to *Rif; Ran*).

9. Ordinarily, it would be forbidden even to push the chicken, which is *muktzeh,* since one may not move even part of a *muktzeh* item (*Tiferes Yisrael;* see *Ran* ד״ה ונמצא פסקן של דברים; see also *Bach* loc. cit.). However, since she is exposed to injury or distress when outside her usual, protected area, the Rabbis permitted pushing her in order to alleviate or forestall the suffering of a living creature (ibid.; see also *Mishnah Berurah* 308:152). [Similarly, though it is generally forbidden Rabbinically to "trap" a domesticated animal that has escaped (*Orach Chaim* 316:12), the Rabbis permitted it where necessary to alleviate or forestall the animal's suffering (*Tiferes Yisrael*).]

10. That is, one may take hold of the animal's neck and sides and nudge it so that it moves its legs on its own (see *Rashi* and *Rashi* to *Rif;* see also *Rashash*). [This is not permitted, however, in the previous case of the chicken, for reasons that the Gemara will explain.]

By walking the animal in this way, one is moving a portion of a *muktzeh* item, which is generally forbidden (see preceding note). The Mishnah refers, however, to where the animal is exposed to injury or distress in its present location. Therefore, the Rabbis permitted this minimal movement of *muktzeh* in order to alleviate or forestall the suffering of a living creature (see references cited in preceding note).

If pushing or helping the animal walk is insufficient to alleviate the animal's suffering, some permit even *carrying* the animal to safety [which is a greater degree of moving *muktzeh* than "pushing" or "helping to walk"], but others forbid this (see *Mishnah Berurah* 305:70).

11. That is, she may support the child by holding his arms from behind, and the child moves his legs and walks (*Rashi*). [Certainly, a child is not *muktzeh.* Here, the Mishnah is teaching us that she may help the child walk even in a public domain, and this does not constitute carrying, nor is there the concern that she will actually carry him – see Baraisa cited in the Gemara below.]

12. R' Yehudah is explaining, rather than disputing, the previous ruling (*Rif;* see *Eruvin* 81b).

13. Dragging is tantamount to carrying outright (see *Rashi*) and is thus forbidden in a public domain – or even in a *karmelis* (see *Beur Halachah* to 308:41 ד״ה שלא תתגררהו at length, but see there for a discussion of *Ran's* view).

14. I.e. he may place them in the stream so that the animal will be able to climb on top of them, whereupon they will be under her.

15. That is to say: But one may not physically lift the animal out, because the animal is *muktzeh.* [See, however, note 18 below.]

16. [The reason for prohibiting this would be that one effectively renders the pillows and cushions immovable on the Sabbath – see Gemara below.]

בשר תפוח מפני שהוא מאכל לחיה. תימה לימא מפני שהוא מאכל לכלבים וי"ל דכרבי יהודה אתיא ואינו מסריח כפירוש הקונטרס אלא חזי ליה וכל מידי דחזי ליה לאינש לא מקצה לכלבים אבל מפני שהוא מאכל לחיה מותר לטלטלו דכל ישראל בני מלכים הם ורב חסדא דלא שרי בשר תפל מהאי טעמא לית ליה כל ישראל בני מלכים:

אין עוקרין בהמה חיה ועוף. לספרים דגרסי רה"ר הך ברייתא פליגא אקמייתא בתרתי דדייקינן הא דדויי מדדין אפילו ברה"ר ולעיל קתני דווקא בחצר ועוד סיפא דמוקמת לתרנגולת דאין מדדין ברה"ר ולעיל קתני דאפי' בחצר לא ולספרים דגרסי אין עוקרין בהמה חיה ועוף בחצר אתי שפיר:

קמ"ל איתובי מיתבא דעתה. אע"ג דבפרק בתרא דיומא (דף פג.) אמר חולה אין מאכילין אותו ביוה"כ אלא ע"פ מומחה והכא (ה) שריא משום יתובי דעתא היינו שיותר יכולה היולדת להסתכן על ידי פחד שתתפחד שמא אין עושין יפה מה שהיא צריכה ממה שיסתכן החולה ברעב:

רבא

בשר תפוח מפני שהוא מאכל לחיה מים מגולין מפני שהן ראויין לחתול רשב"ג אומר כל עצמן אסור לשהותן מפני הסכנה:

מתני' [א] כופין את הסל לפני האפרוחים כדי שיעלו וירדו תרנגולת שברחה דוחין אותה עד שתכנס מדדין עגלין וסייחין (א) אשה מדדה את בנה אמר רבי יהודה אימתי בזמן שהוא נוטל אחת ומניח אחת אבל אם היה גורר אסור: **גמ'** אמר רב יהודה אמר רב בהמה שנפלה לאמת המים מביא כרים וכסתות ומניח תחתיה ואם עלתה עלתה מיתיבי בהמה שנפלה לאמת המים עושה לה פרנסה במקומה בשביל שלא תמות פרנסה אין כרים וכסתות לא לא קשיא הא דאפשר בפרנסה הא דאי אפשר בפרנסה אפשר בפרנסה אין ואי לא מביא כרים וכסתות ומניח תחתיה והא קא מבטל כלי מהיכנו סבר מבטל כלי מהיכנו דרבנן צער בעלי חיים דאורייתא ואתי דאורייתא ודחי דרבנן:

תרנגולת שברחה וכו': דוחין אין מדדין לא תנינא להא דת"ר מדדין בהמה חיה ועוף בחצר אבל לא את התרנגולת תרנגולת מאי טעמא לא אמר אביי משום דמקפיא נפשה תני חדא מדדין בהמה וחיה ועוף בחצר אבל לא ברה"ר והאשה מדדה את בנה ברה"ר ואצ"ל בחצר ותניא אידך אין עוקרין בהמה וחיה ועוף בחצר אבל מדדין אותן בחצר קשיא הא גופא קשיא אמרת אין עוקרין אבל דדויי מדדינן (ג) הדר אמרת דוחין אין מדדין לא אמר אביי סיפא אתאן לתרנגולת אמר אביי האי מאן דשחיט תרנגולת לכבשינהו לכרעיה בארעא אי נמי נידל להו מידל דדילמא מנח להו לטופריה בארעא ועקר להו לסימנים:

מתני' אין מילדין את הבהמה ביום טוב אבל מסעדין ומילדין את האשה בשבת וקורין לה חכמה ממקום למקום ומחללין עליה את השבת וקושרין את הטיבור רבי יוסי אומר אף חותכין וכל צרכי מילה עושין בשבת: **גמ'** כיצד מסעדין רב יהודה אמר אוחז את הולד שלא יפול לארץ רב נחמן אמר דוחק בבשר כדי שיצא הולד תניא כוותיה דרב יהודה כיצד מסעדין אוחזין את הולד שלא יפול לארץ ונופח לו בחוטמו ונותן לו דד לתוך פיו כדי שינק אמר רשב"ג מרחמין היינו על בהמה טהורה ביו"ט היכי עביד אמר אביי מביא גוש של מלח ומניח לה בתוך הרחם כדי שתזכור צערה ותרחם עליו ומזלפין מי שליא על גבי ולד כדי שתריח ריחו ותרחם עליו ודוקא טהורה אבל טמאה לא מ"ט טמאה לא מרחקא ולדא ואי מרחקא ולדא לא מקרבא: מילדין את האשה וכו': מכדי תנא ליה מילדין את האשה וקורין לה חכמה ממקום למקום ומחללין עליה את השבת לאתויי מאי לאתויי הא דתנו רבנן אם היתה צריכה לנר חבירתה מדלקת לה את הנר ואם היתה צריכה לשמן חבירתה מביאה לה שמן ביד ואם אינו ספק ביד מביאה בשערה ואם אינו ספק בשערה מביאה לה בכלי אמר מר אם היתה צריכה לנר חבירתה מדלקת לה את הנר פשיטא לא צריכא בסומא מהו דתימא כיון דלא חזיא אסור קא משמע לן איתובי מיתבא דעתה סברא אי איכא מידי חזיא חברתא ועבדה לי: אם היתה צריכה לשמן וכו': תיפוק ליה משום סחיטה רבה ורב יוסף דאמרי תרווייהו אין סחיטה בשיער רב אשי אמר אפי' תימא יש סחיטה בשיער מביאה לה בכלי דרך שערה דכמה דאפשר לשנויי משנינן אמר רב יהודה אמר שמואל חיה כל זמן שהקבר פתוח בין אמרה צריכה אני בין לא אמרה צריכה אני מחללין עליה את השבת נסתם הקבר בין אמרה

צריכה

בשר תפוח. מסריח: לחתול. לא מזיק ליה ארס דנחש שאף הנחשים היא אוכלת: מפני הסכנה. שמא ישתה אדם מהם: **מתני'** כופין סל בפני האפרוחים. אשמעינן דכלי ניטל לדבר שאינו ניטל בשבת ורבי יצחק משני לה בפ"ג בצריך למקומו: שברחה. מן הבית: דוחין. בידים: מדדין עגלים. אוחז בצוארו ובצדדין וגוררו ומסייעו (ג) ומנענע לו ברגליו: אשה מדדה את בנה. אוחזתו בזרועותיו מאחוריו ומסייעתו והוא מניע רגליו והולך: שנוטל אחת ומניח אחת. שהתינוק מניע את רגליו כשמניח אחת מגביה אחת: אבל גורר אסור. מפני שנושאתו: **גמ'** ואי לא. כגון שהמים עמוקין: והא קמבטל כלי מהיכנו. דמשהכניסם תחתיה אין יכול לטלטלן דדומה לסותר בנין (ד) מדרבנן: צער בעלי חיים דאורייתא. שנאמר עזוב תעזוב עמו ואיכא מאן דדריש טעמא דקרא משום צער בעלי חיים באלו מציאות (ב"מ דף לב:): מדדין לא. שלא יהא אוחזה בגפיה ורגליה נוגעין לארץ ומוליכה: דמקפיא נפשה. מגבהת עצמה מן הארץ ונמצא זה מטלטל אבל אווזים כשאוחזין בגפיהן הן מהלכין ברגליהן ומיהו ברה"ר לא משום שמא יגביהם מן הארץ ונמצא נושאן דסתמא כרבנן דפליגי עליה דרבי נתן בהמצניע (לעיל דף צד.) גבי המוציא חיה ועוף בין חיין בין שחוטין חייב והאשה מדדה את בנה אפילו ברה"ר דאי נמי מגביה ליה חי נושא את עצמו דהכי מוקמינן התם דבאדם מודו רבנן לרבי נתן: מקפיא. כגון אקפו ידייכו דחגיגה (דף טז:): אין עוקרין. רגליה לגמרי מן הארץ דמוקצה היא לטלטלה: דדויי מדדינן. אוחזה בשני צדדיה בידו ומדדה והוה טלטול טפי מדחייה שדחפה מאחריה: סיפא. דקתני דוחין אבל לא מדדין: אתאן לתרנגולת. ורישא בשאר עופות: לכבשינהו לכרעיה בארעא. כדי שיתכפלו ולא יוכל להתחזק עליהן: אי נמי לידלינהו. יגביהנו שלא יהו רגליו נוגעות לארץ: **מתני'** מסעדין. מפרש בגמרא: חכמה. מילדת: אין מילדין את הבהמה ביום טוב. דאיכא טרחא יתירה: אבל מסעדין. אותה בי"ט: ומיילדין אשה בשבת. ואין צריך לומר שמסעדין וכל שכן ביום טוב: וקושרין הטיבור. של ולד שהוא ארוך שאם לא יתקשר ויכרך בשום דבר יצאו מעיו אם יגביהו התינוק: **גמ'** דוחק. בבשר של בהמה לפנים שיהא הולד בולט לחוץ: ונופח לו בחוטמו. שנחיריו סתומין לו ברירין: ונותן דד. של אמו בתוך פיו: מרחמין. מאהבין את ולדה עליה: גוש של מלח. מלא אגרוף דכייב לה וזוכרת צער לידה ומרחמה את הולד אם רחקתו: מי שליא. שורין את השליא במים: לא מרחקה. אין דרכה לרחק: מביאה לה שמן. דרך רה"ר: ביד. בכפה ולא בכלי דכמה דאפשר משנינן: בשערה. ככה שערה שמן וכשבאה אצלה מקנחתו ואין כאן חילול שבת כיון שאין דרך הוצאה בכך: פשיטא. דהא פקוח נפש דוחה שבת: תיפוק ליה משום סחיטה. למה לא הביאה לה בכלי שלא תחלל שבת בהוצאה הכא נמי הא קמחללה בסחיטה: אין סחיטה בשיער. שהוא קשה ואין בולע: דרך שערה. כורכת הכלי בראשה בשערה: חיה. יולדת: קבר. בית הרחם:

לריכה

of the Baraisa (which, by implication, does not allow placing pillows and cushions in the stream) refers to **where it is possible** to alleviate the animal's suffering by supplying her **with provisions,** הָא דְּאִי אֶפְשָׁר בְּפַרְנָסָה – whereas **this** ruling of Rav (which permits placing pillows and cushions in the stream) refers to **where it is not possible** to alleviate the animal's suffering merely by supplying her **with provisions.**[17] Accordingly, the Baraisa means that אֶפְשָׁר בְּפַרְנָסָה אִין – where it is **possible** to merely supply her **with provisions – yes,** that is all that should be done, but one should not place pillows and cushions underneath her. וְאִי לֹא – **But if** it is **not** possible to alleviate her suffering with provisions, מֵבִיא כָּרִים וּכְסָתוֹת וּמַנִּיחַ תַּחְתֶּיהָ – then **he brings pillows and cushions and places them beneath her** so that she may climb out.[18]

The Gemara asks further concerning the ruling of Rav Yehudah in the name of Rav:

וְהָא קָא מְבַטֵּל כְּלִי מֵהֵיכָנוֹ – **But he is nullifying the preparedness of a utensil** by placing the pillow or cushion under the animal![19] How is one permitted to do so?

The Gemara answers:

סָבַר מְבַטֵּל כְּלִי מֵהֵיכָנוֹ דְּרַבָּנָן – **He** [Rav] **holds** that whereas the prohibition against **nullifying the preparedness of a utensil is Rabbinic,** צַעַר בַּעֲלֵי חַיִּים דְּאוֹרַיְיתָא – the concern for **the distress of live creatures is a Biblical** precept.[20] וְאָתֵי דְּאוֹרַיְיתָא וְדָחֵי דְּרַבָּנָן – **Therefore, the Biblical** concern for the distress of the animal **comes and overrides the Rabbinical** prohibition against nullifying the utensil's preparedness.

The Gemara cites the next ruling of the Mishnah:

תַּרְנְגוֹלֶת שֶׁבָּרְחָה וכו׳ – IF A HEN ESCAPED **etc.** [we may push her until she enters].

The Gemara comments:

דּוֹחִין אִין – The Mishnah implies that **pushing** the hen – **yes,** this is permitted; מְדַדִּין לֹא – **but helping** her **walk,**[21] which the Mishnah permits with regard to calves and foals – **no,** this is forbidden.[22] תָּנֵינָא לְהָא דְּתָנוּ רַבָּנָן – **We have** thus **learned** by inference **from the Mishnah that which the Rabbis taught** explicitly **in the** following **Baraisa:** מְדַדִּין בְּהֵמָה חַיָּה וְעוֹף בֶּחָצֵר – WE MAY HELP AN ANIMAL, BEAST OR BIRD WALK IN A COURTYARD,[23] אֲבָל לֹא אֶת הַתַּרְנְגוֹלֶת – BUT NOT A HEN.

The Gemara explains:

תַּרְנְגוֹלֶת מַאי טַעְמָא לֹא – **What is the reason** that one may **not** help **a hen** walk? אָמַר אַבָּיֵי – **Abaye said:** מִשּׁוּם דְּמַקְפְּיָא נַפְשָׁהּ – **Because** when one grasps her wings **she will** tend to **lift herself** off the ground, whereupon it emerges that the person is not merely helping her walk, but actually carrying her, and carrying *muktzeh* is prohibited.[24]

The Gemara cites two Baraisos concerning the laws of "helping to walk" on the Sabbath:

תָּנֵי חֲדָא – **One Baraisa states:** מְדַדִּין בְּהֵמָה וְחַיָּה וְעוֹף בֶּחָצֵר – WE MAY HELP AN ANIMAL, BEAST OR BIRD WALK IN A COURTYARD, אֲבָל לֹא בִּרְשׁוּת הָרַבִּים – BUT NOT IN A PUBLIC DOMAIN.[25] וְהָאִשָּׁה מְדַדָּה אֶת בְּנָהּ בִּרְשׁוּת הָרַבִּים – HOWEVER, A WOMAN MAY HELP HER CHILD WALK even IN A PUBLIC DOMAIN,[26] וְאֵין צָרִיךְ לוֹמַר בֶּחָצֵר – AND NEEDLESS TO SAY she may do so IN A COURTYARD.

A second Baraisa:

וְתַנְיָא אִידָךְ – **And another Baraisa states:** אֵין עוֹקְרִין בְּהֵמָה וְחַיָּה וְעוֹף בֶּחָצֵר – WE MAY NOT LIFT AN ANIMAL, BEAST OR BIRD completely off the ground even IN A COURTYARD (where there is no prohibition against "carrying"),[27] אֲבָל דּוֹחִין בָּהֶן שֶׁיִּכָּנְסוּ – BUT WE MAY PUSH THEM SO THEY WILL ENTER their enclosures.

The Gemara asks:

הָא גּוּפָא קַשְׁיָא – **This** second Baraisa **is self-contradictory.** אָמְרַתְּ אֵין עוֹקְרִין – On one hand **you say** in the Baraisa that WE MAY NOT LIFT the animal off the ground, which implies:

NOTES

17. For example, the water is too deep (*Rashi* ד״ה ואי לא), so that no matter how much food is given to her on location, she will not be able to survive, due to the distress she suffers from the deep water (*Chidushei HaRan*).

18. [If this, too, does not succeed in helping the animal extricate itself, some permit actually lifting the animal out, while others forbid it (see above, end of note 10).]

19. When the animal climbs upon the pillow or cushion, it becomes a base for the *muktzeh* animal, rendering the base itself *muktzeh* and legally immovable (see *Rashi* to 43a ד״ה מפני; cf. *Chidushei HaRan* and *Rambam* cited at the end of this note). And the Rabbis prohibited rendering the utensil immovable in this way, because it is akin to סוֹתֵר, *dismantling,* the utensil (see *Rashi* here, with *Aruch HaShulchan* 265:7). [Alternatively, it is akin to בּוֹנֶה, *building,* since one is in effect affixing the utensil to its place (*Rashi* to 42b ד״ה כלי תחת הנר).]

[The Gemara above (43a) explains that inverting a basket so that the chicks can use it to climb up or step down, which our Mishnah permits, does not constitute nullifying the basket from its preparedness, since it is permitted to move the basket when the chicks are no longer on it. In the case of the pillows and cushions, however, the animal might remain atop them, should it be unable to climb out of the stream (see *Rashba; Chidushei HaRan;* see also above, 43a, end of note 17, and references cited there). Alternatively, because they become soaked with water, the pillows and cushions are effectively rendered unusable for the duration of the Sabbath, and are thus nullified from their preparedness (*Chidushei HaRan; Rambam, Hil. Shabbos* 25:26 with *Maggid Mishneh*).]

20. This reflects the view of the one (see *Bava Metzia* 32b) who understands that concern for the suffering of animals is the rationale for the Biblical command (*Exodus* 23:5) to help unload an animal that has buckled under its load (*Rashi;* see, however, *Chasam Sofer* [*Mechon Chasam Sofer* ed.] here; see further, *Bava Metzia* 32b note 1).

21. By grasping her wings and guiding her along as her feet walk across the ground (*Rashi*).

22. For the Mishnah does not mention the permit to "help walk" [which entails a greater degree of moving *muktzeh* than mere pushing] until the next case, regarding calves and foals.

23. I.e. but not in the public domain. [This will be explained below, in note 25.]

24. [See above, note 10.] Other birds, such as geese, however, do not tend to lift themselves off the ground when grasped by their wings; hence, helping them walk [in a courtyard or other enclosure] in this manner is permitted (see *Rashi;* cf. *Rambam, Hil. Shabbos* 25:26 and *Chasam Sofer* here).

25. This Tanna forbids helping the animal walk in a public domain [even in order to alleviate the animal's distress] out of concern that one might come to lift the animal outright and carry it four *amos,* thereby transgressing the Biblical *melachah* of carrying in a public domain. And though Tannaim above (94a) debate whether one is liable for carrying a live animal on the Sabbath, this Baraisa reflects the view of the Sages there, who do not apply the principle of "a live creature carries itself" to carrying an animal (*Rashi*).

It is permitted, however, to help the animal walk in a courtyard (save in the case of a hen, which has the *tendency* to lift itself off the ground), since even if the person will lift the animal and carry it he will have transgressed only the Rabbinic precept of *muktzeh.* [Whether it is permitted to help an animal walk in a *karmelis* (in which carrying is Rabbinically forbidden) is debated by the authorities (see *Mishnah Berurah* 308:150).]

["Pushing" the animal, however, is permitted even in the public domain, because there is no concern that this will lead the person to actually carry the animal (see *Bach,* end of 308 ד״ה ומ״ש דוקא בחצר and *Shaar HaTziyun* 308:121).]

26. For even if she were to forget and actually carry him, she would not transgress a Biblical *melachah,* since (as agreed by all Tannaim – see 94a) one is not liable for carrying a live [and mobile] human being (*Rashi;* see also *Beur Halachah,* cited above in note 13).

27. For it is forbidden to lift the animal, which is *muktzeh,* off the ground (*Rashi*).

בשר תפוח מפני שהוא מאכל לחיה מים מגולין מפני שהן ראויין לחתול רשב"ג אומר כל עצמן אסור לשהותן מפני הסכנה: **מתני'** (א) [א] כופין את הסל לפני האפרוחים כדי שיעלו וירדו תרנגולת שברחה דוחין אותה עד שתכנס מדדין עגלין וסייחין [ב] (א) אשה מדדה את בנה אמר רבי יהודה [ב] אימתי בזמן שהוא נוטל אחת ומניח אחת אבל אם היה גורר אסור: **גמ'** אמר רב יהודה אמר רב בהמה שנפלה לאמת המים מביא כרים וכסתות ומניח תחתיה ואם עלתה עלתה מיתיבי [ג] בהמה שנפלה לאמת המים עושה לה פרנסה במקומה בשביל שלא תמות פרנסה אין כרים וכסתות לא לא קשיא [ג] הא דאפשר בפרנסה הא דאי אפשר בפרנסה אפשר בפרנסה אין ואי לא מביא כרים וכסתות ומניח תחתיה והא [ד] קא מבטל כלי מהיכנו סבר מבטל כלי מהיכנו דרבנן [ה] צער בעלי חיים דאורייתא ואתי דאורייתא ודחי דרבנן: [ה] תרנגולת שברחה וכו': דוחין אין מדדין לא תנינא להא דת"ר [ו] מדדין בהמה חיה ועוף בחצר אבל לא את התרנגולת תרנגולת מאי טעמא לא אמר אביי משום דמקפיא נפשה תני חדא מדדין בהמה וחיה ועוף בחצר אבל לא ברה"ר והאשה מדדה את בנה [ז] ברה"ר ואצ"ל בחצר ותניא אידך אין עוקרין בהמה וחיה ועוף בחצר אבל דוחין בהן שיכנסו הא גופא קשיא אמרת אין עוקרין אבל דדויי מדדינן (ג) הדר אמרת דוחין אין מדדין לא אמר אביי סיפא אתאן לתרנגולת אמר אביי [ח] האי מאן דשחיט תרנגולת לכבשינהו לכרעיה בארעא אי נמי ניזל להו מידל דדילמא מנח להו לטופריה בארעא ועקר להו לסימנים: **מתני'** [ט] אין מילדין את הבהמה ביום טוב אבל מסעדין ומילדין את האשה בשבת וקורין לה חכמה ממקום למקום ומחללין עליה את השבת וקושרין את הטיבור רבי יוסי אומר [י] אף חותכין [י] וכל צרכי מילה עושין בשבת: **גמ'** כיצד מסעדין רב יהודה אמר אוחז את הולד שלא יפול לארץ רב נחמן אמר דוחק בבשר כדי שיצא הולד תניא כוותיה דרב יהודה [ח] כיצד מסעדין [ל] אוחזין את הולד שלא יפול לארץ ונופח לו בחוטמו ונותן לו דד לתוך פיו כדי שינק אמר רשב"ג [ט] מרחמין היינו על בהמה טהורה ביו"ט היכי עביד אמר אביי מביא בול של מלח ומניח לה בתוך הרחם כדי שתזכור צערה ותרחם עליו ומזלפין מי שליא על גבי ולד כדי שתריח ריחו ותרחם עליו ודוקא טהורה אבל טמאה לא מ"ט טמאה לא מרחקא ולדא ואי מרחקא ולדא לא מקרבא: [ל] מילדין את האשה וכו': מכדי תנא ליה מילדין את האשה וקורין לה חכמה ממקום למקום ומחללין עליה את השבת לאתויי מאי לאתויי הא דתנו רבנן [מ] אם היתה צריכה לנר חבירתה מדלקת לה את הנר ואם היתה צריכה לשמן חבירתה מביאה לה שמן בידה ואם אינו ספק ביד מביאה בשערה ואם אינו ספק בשערה מביאה לה בכלי אמר מר אם היתה צריכה לנר חבירתה מדלקת לה את הנר פשיטא [נ] לא צריכא בסומא מהו דתימא כיון דלא חזיא אסור קא משמע לן איתובי מיתבא דעתה סברא אי איכא מידי חזיא חברתא ועבדה לי: אם היתה צריכה לשמן וכו': [ס] תיפוק ליה משום סחיטה רבה ורב יוסף דאמרי תרוייהו אין סחיטה בשיער רב אשי אמר אפי' תימא יש סחיטה בשיער מביאה לה בכלי דרך שערה [ע] דכמה דאפשר לשנויי משנינן אמר רב יהודה אמר שמואל חיה כל זמן שהקבר פתוח בין אמרה צריכה אני [פ] בין לא אמרה צריכה אני מחללין עליה את השבת נסתם הקבר בין אמרה צריכה

תוספות

בשר תפוח מפני שהוא מאכל לחיה. תימה לימא מפני שהוא מאכל לכלבים וי"ל דכרבי יהודה אתיא ואינו מסריח כפירוש הקונטרס אלא חזי ליה וכל מידי דחזי ליה לאינש לא מקרה לכלבים אבל מפני שהוא מאכל לחיה מותר לטלטלו דכל ישראל בני מלכים הם ורב חסדא דלא שרי בשר תפל מהאי טעמא לית ליה כל ישראל בני מלכים:

אין עוקרין בהמה חיה ועוף. לספרים דגרסי רה"ר הך ברייתא פליגא אקמייתא בתרתי דדייקינן הא דדויי מדדין אפילו ברה"ר ולעיל קתני דווקא בחצר ותו סיפא דמוקמת לתרנגולת דאין מדדין ברה"ר ולעיל קתני דאפי' בחצר לא ולספרים דגרסי אין עוקרין בהמה חיה ועוף בחצר אתי שפיר:

קמ"ל איתובי מיתבא דעתה. אע"ג דבפרק בתרא דיומא (דף פג.) אמר חולה אין מאכילין אותו ביוה"כ אלא ע"פ מומחה והכא (ה) שריא משום יתובי דעתה היינו שיותר יכולה היולדת להסתכן על ידי פחד שתפחד שמא אין עושין יפה מה שהיה צריכה ממה שיסתכן החולה ברעב: רבא

רש"י

בשר תפוח. מסריח: לחתול. לא מזיק ליה ארס דנחש שאף הנחשים היא אוכלת: מפני הסכנה. שמא ישתה אדם מהם: **מתני'** כופין סל בפני האפרוחים. אשמעינן דכלי ניטל לדבר שאינו ניטל בשבת ורבי יצחק פליג (בפ"ג) בצריך למקומו: שברחה. מן הבית: דוחין. בידים: מדדין עגלים. אוחז בצוארו ובצדדין וגוררו ומסייעו (ג) ומנענע לו ברגליו: אשה מדדה את בנה. אוחזתו בזרועותיו מאחוריו ומסייעתו והוא מניע רגליו והולך: שנוטל אחת ומניח אחת. שהתינוק מניע את רגליו כשמניח אחת מגביה אחת: אבל גורר אסור. מפני שנושאתו: **גמ'** ואי לא. כגון שהמים עמוקין: והא קמבטל כלי מהיכנו. דמשהניחם תחתיה אין יכול לטלטלן דדומה לסותר בנין (ד) מדרבנן: צער בעלי חיים דאורייתא. שנאמר עזוב תעזוב עמו ואיכא מאן דדריש טעמא דקרא משום צער בעלי חיים באלו מציאות (ב"מ דף לב:): מדדין לא. שלא יהא אוחזה בגפיה ורגליה נוגעין לארץ ומוליכה: דמקפיא נפשה. מגבהת עצמה מן הארץ ונמצא זה מטלטל אבל אווזים כשאוחזין בגפיהן הן מהלכין ברגליהן ומיהו ברה"ר לא משום שמא יגביהם מן הארץ ונמצא נושאן דסתמא כרבנן דפליגי עליה דרבי נתן בהמצניע (לעיל דף צד.) גבי המוציא חיה ועוף בין חיין בין שחוטין חייב והאשה מדדה את בנה אפילו ברה"ר דאי נמי מגביה ליה חי נושא את עצמו דהכי מוקמינן התם דבאדם מודו רבנן לרבי נתן: מקפיא. כגון אקפו ידייכו דחגיגה (דף טו:): אין עוקרין. רגליה לגמרי מן הארץ דמוקצה היא לטלטלה: דדויי מדדינן. אוחזה בשני לדדיה בידו ומדדה והוה טלטול טפי מדחייה שדחפה מאחריה: סיפא. דקתני דוחין אבל לא מדדין: אתאן לתרנגולת. ורישא בשאר עופות: לכבשינהו לכרעיה בארעא. כדי שיתכפלו ולא יוכל להתחזק עליהן: אי נמי לידלינהו. יגביהנו שלא יהו רגליו נוגעות לארץ: **מתני'** מסעדין. מפרש בגמרא: חכמה. מילדת: אין מילדין את הבהמה ביום טוב. דאיכא טרחא יתירה: אבל מסעדין. אותה בי"ט: ומיילדין אשה בשבת. ואין צריך לומר שמסעדין וכל שכן ביום טוב: וקושרין הטיבור. של ולד שהוא ארוך שאם לא יתקשר ויכרך בשום דבר יצאו מעיו אם יגביהו התינוק: **גמ'** דוחק. בבשר של בהמה לפנים שיהא הולד בולט לחוץ: ונופח לו בחוטמו. שנחיריו סתומין לו ברירין: ונותן דד. של אמו בתוך פיו: מרחמין. מאהבין את ולדה עליה: בול של מלח. מלא אגרוף דכייב לה וחוכרת צער לידה ומרחמה את הולד אם רחקתו: מי שליא. שורין את השליא במים: לא מרחקה. אין דרכה לרחק: מביאה לה שמן. דרך רה"ר: ביד. בכפה ולא בכלי דכמה דאפשר משנינן: בשערה. סכה שערה שמן וכשבאה אצלה מקנחתו ואין כאן חילול שבת כיון שאין דרך הוצאה בכך: פשיטא. דהא פקוח נפש דוחה שבת: תיפוק ליה משום סחיטה. למה לא הביאה לה בכלי שלא תחלל שבת בהוצאה הכא נמי הא קמחללה בסחיטה: אין סחיטה בשיער. שהוא קשה ואין בולע: דרך שערה. כורכת הכלי בראשה בשערה: חיה. יולדת: קבר. בית הרחם: צריכה

אֲבָל דִּדּוּיֵי מְדַדִּינָן – But with respect to helping them walk, we may help them walk. הָדַר אָמְרַתְּ – Then you say in the Baraisa that דּוֹחִין אֵין מְדַדִּין לֹא – WE MAY PUSH the animal, which implies: pushing – yes, this is permitted; but helping them walk – no, this is forbidden.[28] Thus, the Baraisa provides conflicting indications regarding the permissibility of helping an animal walk. – ? –

The Gemara answers:

אָמַר אַבַּיֵי – Abaye said: סֵיפָא אֲתָאן לְתַרְנְגוֹלֶת – In the latter part of the Baraisa (which indicates that only "pushing" is permitted, but not "helping to walk"), we come to the case of a hen (i.e. that part of the Baraisa refers specifically to a hen) which one may not "help walk," as explained above. The first part of the Baraisa (which indicates that "helping to walk" *is* permitted) refers to other fowl and animals.[29]

Abaye digresses to teach another ruling specifically related to a chicken's physical tendencies:

אָמַר אַבַּיֵי – Abaye said: הַאי מַאן דְּשָׁחִיט תַּרְנְגוֹלֶת – One who slaughters a rooster[30] לִכְבְשִׁינְהוּ לְכַרְעֵיהּ בְּאַרְעָא – should press its legs to the ground,[31] אִי נַמִּי נִידַל לְהוּ מִידַל – or else lift them entirely off the ground, דְּדִילְמָא מַנַּח לְהוּ לְטוּפְרֵיהּ בְּאַרְעָא – lest it plant its claw in the ground and attempt to pull away from the slaughterer, וְעָקַר לְהוּ לְסִימָנִים – thereby dislodging the pipes from their connection to the jaw, invalidating the slaughter.[32]

Mishnah אֵין מְיַלְּדִין אֶת הַבְּהֵמָה בְּיוֹם טוֹב – We may not deliver an animal of its young on Yom Tov,[33] אֲבָל מְסַעֲדִין – but we may assist it in its delivery.[34] וּמְיַלְּדִין אֶת הָאִשָּׁה בְּשַׁבָּת – But we deliver a woman of her child even on the Sabbath.[35] וְקוֹרִין לָהּ חֲכָמָה מִמָּקוֹם לְמָקוֹם – And we summon a midwife for her even from one place to another, distant place.[36] וּמְחַלְּלִין עָלֶיהָ אֶת הַשַּׁבָּת – And we desecrate the Sabbath on her account.[37] וְקוֹשְׁרִין אֶת הַטִּיבּוּר – And we tie the umbilical cord of the newborn child on the Sabbath.[38] רַבִּי יוֹסֵי אוֹמֵר אַף חוֹתְכִין – R' Yose says: We also sever it.[39] וְכָל צָרְכֵי מִילָה עוֹשִׂין בְּשַׁבָּת – And we perform all the requirements of circumcision on the Sabbath.[40]

Gemara The Mishnah stated that although we may not directly deliver an animal of its young on Yom Tov, we may "assist" in its delivery. The Gemara explains the nature of this assistance:

כֵּיצַד מְסַעֲדִין – In what way may we assist the animal in its delivery? רַב יְהוּדָה אוֹמֵר – Rav Yehudah says: אוֹחֵז אֶת הַוָּלָד שֶׁלֹּא יִפּוֹל לָאָרֶץ – One grasps the newborn animal after it emerges from the womb so that it not fall to the ground. רַב נַחְמָן אָמַר – Rav Nachman says: דּוֹחֵק בַּבָּשָׂר כְּדֵי שֶׁיֵּצֵא הַוָּלָד – One may press the mother's flesh inward so that the fetus should emerge.[41]

The Gemara cites a Baraisa in support of Rav Yehudah's explanation:

תַּנְיָא כְּוָותֵיהּ דְּרַב יְהוּדָה – The Rabbis taught a Baraisa consistent

NOTES

28. Helping an animal walk (by holding its sides) entails a greater degree of moving *muktzeh* than mere pushing (*Rashi*). Thus, if the Baraisa states only that "pushing" is permitted, we can infer that "helping to walk" is forbidden.

29. To summarize: One may help a toddler walk (but not carry him) even in the public domain. Animals who are in distress may be nudged to safety even in the public domain, and (with the exception of chickens) be helped to walk in a courtyard (and possibly, even in a *karmelis*). One may not, however, help a chicken walk even in the house, since it tends to lift itself off the ground, which would cause the person to carry *muktzeh*.

30. [We have followed *Ritva MHK* ed., who emends the text to read תַּרְנְגוֹלָא, *a male chicken,* rather than תַּרְנְגוֹלֶת, *a female chicken,* since the female does not exhibit the problematic tendency that the Gemara will describe. (See, however, *Aruch HaShulchan, Yoreh Deah* 24:49.)]

31. So that the legs buckle and cannot be used in that position by the rooster to put up resistance to the slaughterer (see *Rashi*).

32. The two "pipes" – the foodpipe and windpipe – are attached to the jaw. The *shechitah* of a bird requires that most of one pipe be severed (and preferably most of both), but the *shechitah* is invalid if a pipe is dislodged from its place of attachment to the jaw (see *Chullin* 9a, with *Tosafos* ד״ה כולהו תנינהו and *Tosafos* there to 44a ד״ה והאיכא עיקור סימנים; see also Gemara there, 10a, with *Rashi* ד״ה שחט את הושט).

33. That is, we may not take hold of the fetus in the womb and pull it out (*Rambam, Commentary to the Mishnah*) even on Yom Tov [and certainly not on the Sabbath, whose laws are more stringent], because actively delivering the fetus in this manner involves excessive exertion (*Rashi*). Alternatively, actively delivering the fetus is a Biblical *melachah* (*Rashba*), namely, the *melachah* of מַכֶּה בְּפַטִּישׁ, *striking the final blow* (*Ritva MHK* ed.; cf. *Be'er Avraham,* cited in note 74 to *Rashba MHK* ed.; see also *Tosafos* to *Avodah Zarah* 26a ד״ה סבר and *Meromei Sadeh* here).

34. On Yom Tov [but not on the Sabbath] (see *Rashi;* cf. *Rosh;* see *Chasam Sofer* [*Mechon Chasam Sofer* ed.] and *Shaar HaTziyun* 332:2). The Gemara will explain what is meant here by "assisting" the animal in delivery.

35. [During childbirth (within the time frame delineated in the Gemara below) the life of a woman is considered endangered. Therefore, all Sabbath restrictions – Rabbinic as well as Biblical – are waived to ensure her well-being.] Since the Mishnah permits actively delivering her of the child on the Sabbath, it goes without saying that merely assisting her in delivery is permitted, and that these permits certainly apply on Yom Tov as well (*Rashi*).

36. Even if this entails traveling beyond the *techum* – the boundary within which a person is permitted to travel on the Sabbath. [The Rabbis forbade a person to travel more than two thousand *amos* away from what was legally defined as his "place of residence" at the onset of the Sabbath. According to some Rishonim, traveling more than twelve *mil* (twenty-four thousand *amos*) away from one's place of residence is Biblically forbidden (see *Rif* to *Eruvin,* end of chapter 1; *Rambam, Hil. Shabbos* 27:1). Other Rishonim, however, maintain that there is no Biblical limit whatsoever on the distance one may travel on the Sabbath (see *Baal HaMaor* and *Milchamos* to *Rif* loc. cit.).]

37. The Gemara will explain what the Mishnah means to add with this clause.

38. For if we do not tie it and it gets caught on something, the newborn's intestines will extrude when he is lifted (*Rashi*).

39. So that the mother not inadvertently tug at the umbilical cord and pull it out of the infant's navel, endangering the infant (see *Meiri* and *Chidushei HaRan;* see also 129b note 25).

Tosafos (to 129b ד״ה כל האמור) maintain that cutting the umbilical cord does not involve any Biblical *melachah.* Other commentators, however, disagree (see *Mishnah Berurah* 330:27). In either event, it is permitted to cut the cord on Sabbath (in R' Yose's view), because not doing so poses a threat to the infant's life. The Tanna Kamma, however, holds that once the cord is tied, leaving it uncut does not pose a significant threat to the infant (see *Chidushei HaRan*). [*Tosafos* (loc. cit.), however, explain that even R' Yose does not consider leaving the cord uncut a threat to life; nevertheless, he permits cutting it to alleviate the infant's pain, since there is no Biblical *melachah* involved.]

40. The Mishnah will enumerate these requirements in the next chapter, on 133a. [See *Tosafos* there ד״ה עושין.]

41. Applying pressure to the mother at strategic points on the outside causes the fetus to bulge out, thereby helping it emerge from the womb (see *Rashi*).

בשר תפוח מפני שהוא מאכל לחיה מים מגולין מפני שהן ראוין לחתול רשב"ג אומר כל עצמן אסור לשהותן מפני הסכנה:

מתני' כופין את הסל לפני האפרוחים כדי שיעלו וירדו תרנגולת שברחה דוחין אותה עד שתכנס מדדין עגלין וסייחין (א) אשה מדדה את בנה אימתי בזמן שהוא נוטל אחת ומניח אחת אבל אם היה גורר אסור:

גמ' אמר רב יהודה אמר רב בהמה שנפלה לאמת המים מביא כרים וכסתות ומניח תחתיה ואם עלתה עלתה מיתיבי בהמה שנפלה לאמת המים עושה לה פרנסה במקומה בשביל שלא תמות פרנסה אין כרים וכסתות לא לא קשיא הא דאפשר בפרנסה הא דאי אפשר בפרנסה אפשר בפרנסה אין ואי לא מביא כרים וכסתות ומניח תחתיה והא קא מבטל כלי מהיכנו דרבנן צער בעלי חיים דאורייתא ואתי דאורייתא ודחי דרבנן: תרנגולת שברחה וכו': דוחין אין מדדין לא תנינא להא דת"ר מדדין בהמה חיה ועוף בחצר אבל לא את התרנגולת תרנגולת מאי טעמא לא אמר אביי משום דמקפיא נפשה תני חדא מדדין בהמה וחיה ועוף בחצר אבל לא ברה"ר והאשה מדדה את בנה ברה"ר ואצ"ל בחצר ותניא אידך אין עוקרין בהמה וחיה ועוף בחצר אבל דוחין בהן שיכנסו הא גופא קשיא אמרת אין עוקרין אבל דדויי מדדינן (ג) הדר אמרת דוחין אין מדדין לא אמר אביי סיפא אתאן לתרנגולת אמר אביי האי מאן דשחיט תרנגולת לכבשינהו לכרעיה בארעא אי נמי נידל להו מידל דדילמא מנח להו לטופריה בארעא ועקר להו לסימנים:

מתני' אין מילדין את הבהמה ביום טוב אבל מסעדין ומילדין את האשה בשבת וקורין לה חכמה ממקום למקום ומחללין עליה את השבת וקושרין את הטיבור רבי יוסי אומר אף חותכין וכל צרכי מילה עושין בשבת:

גמ' כיצד מסעדין רב יהודה אמר אוחז את הולד שלא יפול לארץ רב נחמן אמר דוחק בבשר כדי שיצא הולד תניא כוותיה דרב יהודה כיצד מסעדין אוחזין את הולד שלא יפול לארץ ונופח לו בחוטמו ונותן לו דד לתוך פיו כדי שינק אמר רשב"ג מרחמין היינו על בהמה טהורה ביו"ט היכי עביד אמר אביי מביא בול של מלח ומניח לה בתוך הרחם כדי שתזכור צערה ותרחם עליו ומזלפין מי שליא על גבי ולד כדי שתריח ריחו ותרחם עליו ודוקא טהורה אבל טמאה לא מ"ט טמאה לא מרחקא ולדא ואי מרחקא ולדא לא מקרבא: מילדין את האשה וכו': מכדי תנא ליה מילדין את האשה וקורין לה חכמה ממקום למקום ומחללין עליה את השבת לאתויי מאי לאתויי הא דתנו רבנן אם היתה צריכה לנר חבירתה מדלקת לה את הנר ואם היתה צריכה לשמן חבירתה מביאה לה שמן ביד ואם אינו ספק ביד מביאה בשערה ואם אינו ספק בשערה מביאה לה בכלי אמר מר אם היתה צריכה לנר חבירתה מדלקת לה את הנר פשיטא לא צריכא בסומא מהו דתימא כיון דלא חזיא אסור קא משמע לן איתובי מיתבא דעתה סברא אי איכא מידי חזיא חברתא ועבדה לי: אם היתה צריכה לשמן וכו': תיפוק ליה משום סחיטה רבה ורב יוסף דאמרי תרוייהו אין סחיטה בשיער רב אשי אמר אפי' תימא יש סחיטה בשיער דכמה דאפשר לשנויי משנינן אמר רב יהודה אמר שמואל חיה כל זמן שהקבר פתוח בין אמרה צריכה אני בין לא אמרה צריכה אני מחללין עליה את השבת נסתם הקבר בין אמרה
צריכה

רש"י

בשר תפוח. מסריח: לחתול. לא מזיק ליה ארס דנחש שאף הנחשים היא אוכלת: מפני הסכנה. שמא ישתה אדם מהם: **מתני'** כופין סל בפני האפרוחים. אשמעינן דכלי ניטל לדבר שאינו ניטל בשבת ורבי יצחק משני לה בפ"ג בצריך למקומו: שברחה. מן הבית: דוחין. בידים: מדדין עגלים. אוחז בצוארו ובצלדין וגוררו ומסייעו (ג) ומנענע לו ברגליו: אשה מדדה את בנה. אוחזתו בזרועותיו מאחוריו ומסייעתו והוא מניע רגליו והולך: שנוטל אחת ומניח אחת. שהתינוק מניע את רגליו כשמניח אחת מגביה אחת: אבל גורר אסור. מפני שנושאתו: **גמ'** ואי לא. כגון שהמים עמוקין: והא קמבטל כלי מהיכנו. דמשהניחם תחתיה אין יכול לטלטלן דדומה לסותר בנין (ד) מדרבנן: צער בעלי חיים דאורייתא. שנאמר עזוב תעזוב עמו ואיכא מאן דדריש טעמא דקרא משום צער בעלי חיים באלו מציאות (ב"מ דף לב:): מדדין לא. שלא יהא אוחז בגפיה ורגליה נוגעין לארץ ומוליכה: דמקפיא נפשה. מגבהת עצמה מן הארץ ונמצא זה מטלטל אבל אוחזים כשאוחזין בגפיהן הן מהלכין ברגליהן ומיהו ברה"ר לא משום שמא יגביהם מן הארץ ונמצא נושאן דסתמא כרבנן דפליגי עליה דרבי נתן בהמצניע (לעיל דף צד.) גבי המוציא חיה ועוף בין חיין בין שחוטין חייב והאשה מדדה את בנה אפילו ברה"ר דאי נמי מגביה ליה חי נושא את עצמו דהכי מוקמינן התם דבאדם מודו רבנן לרבי נתן: מקפיא. כגון אקפו ידייכו דחגיגה (דף טו:): אין עוקרין. רגליה לגמרי מן הארץ דמוקצה היא לטלטלה: דדויי מדדינן. אוחזה בשני צדדיה בידו ומדדה והוה טלטול טפי מדחייה שדחפה מאחריה: סיפא. דקתני דוחין אבל לא מדדין: אתאן לתרנגולת. ורישא בשאר עופות: לכבשינהו לכרעיה בארעא. כדי שיתכפלו ולא יוכל להתחזק עליהן: אי נמי לידלינהו. יגביהנו שלא יהו רגליו נוגעות לארץ: **מתני'** מסעדין. מפרש בגמרא: חכמה. מילדת: אין מילדין את הבהמה ביום טוב. דאיכא טרחא יתירה: אבל מסעדין. אותה בי"ט: ומיילדין אשה בשבת. ואין צריך לומר שמסעדין וכל שכן ביום טוב: וקושרין הטיבור. של ולד שהוא ארוך שאם לא יתקשר ויכרך בשום דבר יצאו מעיו אם יגביהו התינוק: **גמ'** דוחק. בבשר של בהמה לפנים שיהא הולד בולט לחוץ: ונופח לו בחוטמו. שנחיריו סתומין לו בריריו: ונותן דד. של אמו בתוך פיו: מרחמין. מאהבין את ולדה עליה: בול של מלח. מלא אגרוף דכיון לה חוכרת צער לידה ומרחמה את הולד אם רחקתו: מי שליא. שורין את השליא במים: לא מרחקא. אין דרכה לרחק: מביאה לה שמן. דרך רה"ר: ביד. בכפה ולא בכלי דכמה דאפשר משנינן: בשערה. ספה שערה שמן וכשבאה אצלה מקנחתו ואין כאן חילול שבת כיון שאין דרך הוצאה בכך: פשיטא. דהא פקוח נפש דוחה שבת: תיפוק ליה משום סחיטה. למה לא הביאה לה בכלי שלא תחלל שבת בהוצאה הכא נמי הא קמחללה בסחיטה: אין סחיטה בשיער. שהוא קשה ואין בולע: דרך שערה. כורכת הכלי בראשה בשערה: חיה. יולדת: קבר. בית הרחם:
צריכה

תוספות

בשר תפוח מפני שהוא מאכל לחיה. תימה לימא מפני שהוא מאכל לכלבים וי"ל דכרבי יהודה אתיא ולאו מטריח כפירוש הקונטרס אלא חזי ליה וכל מידי דחזי ליה לאינו לא מקלה לכלבים אבל מפני שהוא מאכל לחיה מותר לטלטלו דכל ישראל בני מלכים הם ורב חסדא דלא שרי בשר תפל מהאי טעמא לית ליה כל ישראל בני מלכים:

אין עוקרין בהמה חיה ועוף. לספרים דגרסי רה"ר הך ברייתא פליגא אקמייתא בתרתי דדייקינן הא דדויי מדדינן אפילו ברה"ר ולעיל קתני דווקא בחצר ותו סיפא דמוקמת לתרנגולת דאין מדדין ברה"ר ולעיל קתני דאפי' בחצר לא ולספרים דגרסי אין עוקרין בהמה חיה ועוף בחצר אתי שפיר:

קמ"ל איתובי מיתבא דעתה. אע"ג דבפרק בתרא דיומא (דף פג.) אמר חולה אין מאכילין אותו ביוה"כ אלא ע"פ מומחה והכא (ה) שריא משום יתובי דעתא היינו שיותר יכולה היולדת להסתכן על ידי פחד שתפחד שמא אין עושין יפה מה שהיא צריכה ממה שיסתכן החולה ברעב:
רבא

עין משפט נר מצוה

כג א מיי' פכ"ה מהל' שבת הלכה כה סמג לאוין סה טוש"ע א"ח סימן שח סעיף לט:
כד ב מיי' פי"ח שם הלכה טז סמג שם טוש"ע שם סעיף מא:
כה ג מיי' פכ"ה שם הלכה כו וסמג שם טוש"ע א"ח סימן שה סעיף יט:
כו ד מיי' פי"ג מהלכות רוצח וש"ג הלכה יג סמג עשין פ פא ולאוין קסט טוש"ע ח"מ סימן ערב סעיף ט בהג"ה:
כז ה ו מיי' פכ"ה מהל' שבת הלכה כו סמג לאוין סה טוש"ע א"ח סי' שח סעיף מ:
כח ז שם סעיף מא:
כט ח [מיי' פ"ג מהל' שחיטה הל' יד] סמג עשין סג טוש"ע י"ד סי' כד סעיף כ [וברב אלפס חולין פ"ב דף רסא]:
ל ט י מיי' פ"ד מהל' יו"ט הלכה טז סמג לאוין עה טוש"ע א"ח סימן שלב סעיף א וסימן תקכג סעיף ג:
לא כ מיי' שם טוש"ע שם ס"ד:
לב ל מ נ מיי' פ"ב מהלכות שבת הלכה יא סמג לאוין סה טוש"ע א"ח סי' של סעיף א:

גליון הש"ס

גמרא תיפוק ליה משום סחיטה. עיין לקמן דף קמה ע"א תוספות ד"ה כבשים:

רבינו חננאל

לטלטלו: דג תפל אסור לטלטלו בשר בין חי ובין מליח מותר לטלטלו. ת"ר מטלטלין את העצמות מפני שהן מאכל לכלבים בשר תפוח מפני שהוא מאכל לחיה וזו היא דתניא כוותיה דרב הונא מים מגולין מפני שהן ראוין לחתול. ומתניתא אלין הלכתא אינון דליכא דפליג. ואליבא דב"ה נשנו דתנן ב"ה אומרים מגביהין מעל השלחן עצמות וקליפין: כופין את הסל לפני האפרוחים שיעלו ושירדו. בהמה שנפלה לאמת המים אם אפשר לה בפרנסה עושין לה פרנסה במקומה. ואם אי אפשר לה בפרנסה מביא כרים וכסתות ומניח תחתיה ואם עלתה עלתה ואף על גב דמבטל כלי מהיכנו. מדרבנן היא. וצער ב"ח דאורייתא ואתא דאורייתא ודחה דרבנן. תרנגולת שברחה דוחין אותה עד שתכנס אבל אין מדדין אותה אפי' בחצר משום דמקפיא נפשה ואע"פ ששאר בהמה חיה ועוף מדדין בחצר אבל לא ברה"ר תרנגולת אפילו בחצר לא אלא אסור לדדותם אפילו בחצר. האשה מדדה את בנה ברה"ר וכ"ש בחצר והא דאמר ר' יהודה אימתי בזמן שנוטל אחת ומניח אחת אבל אם היה גורר אסור [היינו] ברה"ר בלבד שאם נוטל התינוק רגלו אחת ונשען על רגלו האחרת נמצא כמהלך אבל אם אינו נשען על רגליו אלא כשמדדתו גורר רגליו נמצאת נושאתו ברה"ר ואסור אבל בחצר מותר לטלטלו ולשאת אותו והא דאמר אביי האי מאן דשחיט תרנגולת ליכבשינה לכרעתא בארעא. אי נמי תידלינהו דילמא מנח להן לטופראה בארעא ועקרה להו לסימנים הלכתא היא: מתני' אין מילדין את הבהמה ביו"ט אבל מסעדין כיצד מסעדין. רב יהודה אומר אוחז בולד שלא יפול לארץ והלכתא כמותו. דתניא כוותיה. כיצד מסעדין אוחז בולד שלא יפול לארץ ונופחין לו בחוטמו ונותן לו דד לתוך פיו כדי שיינק כו'. וקיי"ל דמסעדין ומרחמין דתנינן ביו"ט אבל לא בשבת ומילדין את האשה בשבת וקורין לה חכמה ממקום למקום ומחללין עליה את השבת. ואסיקנא שמדלקת לה חברתה את הנר ואפילו אם היא סומא מותר להדליק לה נר בשבת דקיי"ל ייתובי מייתבא דעתה סברא אי איכא מידי חזייא חברתאי ועבדא לי. ואם היתה צריכה לשמן מביאה לה שמן כרב אשי דאמר מביאה לה בכלי דרך שערה נועצת כלי של שמן בשערה כדי שלא [יהא] הוצאה ביד כדרך המוציאין ומסקנא כמה דאית לשנויי משנינן ואם צריכה למאכל מביאין לה. מר זוטרא מתני אמר רב יהודה אמר שמואל חיה כל זמן שהקבר פתוח. פירוש הקבר בית הרחם. בין אמרה צריכה אני ובין אמרה איני צריכה מחללין עליה את השבת. נסתם (הכלי) [הקבר] אמרה
צריכה

מסורת הש"ס

א) [לעיל מג.], ב) ס"א ברה"ר, ג) [תוספתא פט"ו], ד) [לעיל מג. וש"נ וע"ש תוספות ד"ה דמבטל], ה) [ב"מ לב:], ו) [בש"ע א"ח סימן ש"ל סעיף ז פסק הלכתא כרבי יוסי וכן דעת הרמב"ם], ז) לקמן קלג., ח) [תוספ' פט"ו], ט) [לעיל קח: לקמן קמח. ביצה ג.], י) ס"א בין אמרה איני צריכה, כ) [נ"ל לעיל כפ"ג מג:].

הגהות הב"ח

(א) במשנה ואשה מדדה: (ב) גמ' והדר אמרת: (ג) רש"י ד"ה מדדין וכו' ומסייעו לילך ומנענע: (ד) ד"ה והא קא מבטל וכו' לסותר בנין מבטל כלי מהיכנו מדרבנן לער בעלי חיים: (ה) תוס' ד"ה קמ"ל וכו' והכא שרינא משום וכו' היינו לפי שיותר:

רב נסים גאון

כדי שיתפרשו תחומין אחד מחבירו ויאמינו בכך לענין עירובן של תחומים ושיתופם כי השרשים שהוא משלח בקרקע מוכיחים על הגבולים ועל פי זה אמרו שם במסכת יום טוב (פרק אין צדין דף כה) חצובא מקטע רגליהון דרשיעיא שהוא דבר שאין בו רוח חיים ובצמיחתו משלח שרשיו בארץ במשפט והרשעים מעקמין דרכיהם ואין הולכין בדרכיו של הקב"ה כמו שראוי להם לכן דרכם באפילה: צער בעלי חיים דאורייתא מה שאמר הקב"ה (שמות כג) כי תראה חמור שונאך רובץ תחת משאו ואמרו בבא מציעא בפרק אלו מציאות (דף לב) מצוה מן התורה לפרוק דקסבר תנא דידן צער בעלי חיים דאורייתא ורבי יוסי הגלילי סבר צער בעלי חיים דרבנן וסבר (אביי) [רב יהודה] בכאן כתנא קמא דצער בעלי חיים דאורייתא וביטול כלי מהיכנו דרבנן משכחת לה בפרק כירה (לעיל דף מב) דתנן אין נותנין כלי תחת הנר לקבל בו את השמן ואמר רב חסדא אין נותנין כלי תחת התרנגולת לקבל ביצתה כו' ופירש רב יוסף טעמא בכך ואמר היינו טעמא דרב חסדא דקא מבטל כלי מהיכנו והא מרבנן הוא:

סליק פרק מפנין

ליקוטי רש"י

מים מגולין. מים שנשארו מגולין בלילה ספק שתה מהן נחש ספק לא שתה וקיימא לן דאסירי [חולין ט:]. עושה לה פרנסה. כל לשון פרנסה לשון עשיית צרכיה הוא קונדי"ר בלע"ז כמו לפרנסה שמין באב (כתובות סח.) וכמו מוליאין לפרנסה ואין מוליאין למזונות (שם סט.) [גיטין סה:]. כל צורך סיפוק קרי פרנסה קונדרי"ר בלע"ז [ב"מ מו.]. והא קא מבטל כלי מהיכנו. שהיה מוכן מתחלה לטלטלו ועכשיו עושהו מוקצה [לעיל מג. ע"ש בתוס' ובפנ"י]. אסור לבטל כלי מהיכנו להושיב כלי במקום שלא יוכל עוד ליטלו [משם] דהוי כקובע לו מקום ומחברו בטיט ודמי למלאכה וכלי זה משיפול בו המוקצה יהא אסור לטלטלו [שם מב:]. כרים וכסתות כשמניחן תחת דבר שאין ניטל מבטלן מהיכנן דשוב לא יטלם משם ודמי לסותר [לקמן קנד:]. מקפיא. לשון דבר הצף ואין מכביד כדמתרגמינן ויצף הברזל וקפא ברזלא (מ"ב ו) [חגיגה טו:]. טופריה. צפרניו [לעיל סג:]. בול של מלח. מלא אגרוף של מלח שמעתי [זבחים סב.].

with the explanation of Rav Yehudah: כֵּיצַד מְסַעֲדִין – IN WHAT WAY MAY WE ASSIST an animal in childbirth (on Yom Tov)? אוֹחֲזִין אֶת הַוָּלָד שֶׁלֹּא יִפּוֹל לָאָרֶץ – WE GRASP THE NEWBORN after it emerges from the womb so THAT IT NOT FALL TO THE GROUND, וְנוֹפֵחַ לוֹ בְּחוֹטְמוֹ – AND ONE BLOWS INTO ITS NOSTRIL to clear its nasal passages of mucus, וְנוֹתֵן לוֹ דַּד לְתוֹךְ פִּיו כְּדֵי שֶׁיִּנַק – AND WE PLACE THE mother's TEAT INTO ITS MOUTH SO THAT IT SHOULD SUCKLE. אָמַר רַבָּן שִׁמְעוֹן בֶּן גַּמְלִיאֵל – RABBAN SHIMON BEN GAMLIEL SAID: מְרַחֲמִין הָיִינוּ עַל בְּהֵמָה טְהוֹרָה בְּיוֹם טוֹב – WE USED TO ENDEAR TO A KOSHER SPECIES OF ANIMAL its newborn ON YOM TOV.[42]

The Gemara explains:

הֵיכִי עָבִיד – What does one do? אָמַר אַבָּיֵי – Abaye said: מֵבִיא בּוּל שֶׁל מֶלַח וּמַנִּיחַ לָהּ בְּתוֹךְ הָרֶחֶם – One brings a fist-size lump of salt and places it into [the mother's] womb כְּדֵי שֶׁתִּזְכּוֹר צַעֲרָהּ וּתְרַחֵם עָלָיו – so that she should remember (because of the pain caused by the salt) her labor pain and have pity on [the newborn]. וּמְזַלְפִין מֵי שִׁלְיָא עַל גַּבֵּי וָלָד – And we dash water of the afterbirth[43] on the newborn כְּדֵי שֶׁתָּרִיחַ רֵיחוֹ וּתְרַחֵם עָלָיו – so that she should smell its scent and have pity on [the newborn].

The Gemara adds:

וְדַוְקָא טְהוֹרָה – And we employ these devices on Yom Tov only for a kosher species of animal, אֲבָל טְמֵאָה לֹא – but not for a non-kosher species of animal. מַאי טַעְמָא – What is the reason that we do not employ these devices for non-kosher species? טְמֵאָה לֹא מְרַחֲקָא וַלְדָּא – Because a non-kosher species of animal does not generally reject the offspring she has borne,[44] וְאִי מְרַחֲקָא וַלְדָּא – and even if she does on rare occasion reject the offspring she has borne, לֹא מְקָרְבָא – she will not reaccept it even if these devices are employed.[45]

The Gemara moves on to the next part of the Mishnah, which stated:

מְיַלְּדִין אֶת הָאִשָּׁה וכו׳ – WE DELIVER A WOMAN of her child etc. [even on the Sabbath, and we summon for her a midwife . . . and we desecrate the Sabbath on her account].

The Gemara seeks to understand what the Mishnah means to teach by the last phrase "and we desecrate the Sabbath on her account":

מִכְּדִי – Now, let us see. תְּנָא לֵיהּ מְיַלְּדִין אֶת הָאִשָּׁה – The Mishnah has already stated that WE DELIVER A WOMAN of her child on the Sabbath, וְקוֹרִין לָהּ חֲכָמָה מִמָּקוֹם לְמָקוֹם – and that WE SUMMON FOR HER A MIDWIFE FROM PLACE TO PLACE. וּמְחַלְּלִין עָלֶיהָ אֶת הַשַּׁבָּת לְאֲתוּיֵי מַאי – What permit, then, does the Mishnah's next statement AND WE DESECRATE THE SABBATH ON HER ACCOUNT come to include that we do not already know on the basis of the Mishnah's previous statements?[46]

The Gemara answers:

לְאֲתוּיֵי הָא דְּתָנוּ רַבָּנַן – It comes to include that law which the Rabbis taught explicitly in the following Baraisa: אִם הָיְתָה צְרִיכָה לְנֵר – IF SHE [the woman giving birth] NEEDED A LAMP lit, חֲבֵירְתָּהּ מַדְלֶקֶת לָהּ אֶת הַנֵּר – HER FRIEND LIGHTS THE LAMP FOR HER.[47] וְאִם הָיְתָה צְרִיכָה לְשֶׁמֶן – AND IF SHE NEEDED OIL,[48] חֲבֵירְתָּהּ מְבִיאָה לָהּ שֶׁמֶן בַּיָּד – HER FRIEND BRINGS HER OIL even through the public domain, if necessary, IN the palm of HER HAND.[49] וְאִם אֵינוֹ סָפֵק בַּיָּד – AND IF the amount of oil that she can bring IN the palm of HER HAND IS INSUFFICIENT, מְבִיאָה בִּשְׂעָרָהּ – then SHE BRINGS oil to her IN HER HAIR.[50] וְאִם אֵינוֹ סָפֵק בִּשְׂעָרָהּ – AND IF the amount of oil that she can bring IN HER HAIR IS also INSUFFICIENT, מְבִיאָה לָהּ בִּכְלִי – then SHE BRINGS oil TO HER IN A CONTAINER in the usual manner.

NOTES

42. But not on the Sabbath (*Rabbeinu Chananel; Meiri;* cf. *Bach* 332 end of ד״ה אין מילדין). [Animals sometimes reject their offspring, which then die of neglect. Various ploys are used to endear the rejected newborn to its mother, as the Gemara will now explain.]

43. That is, water in which the afterbirth is steeped (*Rashi*). Alternatively, this refers to the amniotic fluid itself (see *Rambam, Hil. Yom Tov* 4:16).

44. [Thus, in all probability, what appears to us as her rejection of her young is not really that at all.]

45. Therefore, one may not employ these devices for a non-kosher species of animal on Yom Tov, since these devices serve no useful function [that we should permit the exertion and/or *muktzeh* violations that they entail].

46. The Mishnah has already stated that "delivering her" and "summoning a midwife for her [from beyond the *techum*]" are permitted, though they involve Sabbath desecration. Why would I not know on the basis of those statements that *any* desecration of the Sabbath that she requires is similarly permitted?

There is a difficulty here. According to *Rashi's* explanation above that "delivering a fetus" on the Sabbath or festival involves only the Rabbinic prohibition against "excessive exertion" (see note 33), the two permits mentioned explicitly in the Mishnah ("delivering" and "summoning the midwife from beyond the *techum*") involve strictly Rabbinic prohibitions. Why, then, does the Gemara here not answer quite simply that the Mishnah's third statement ("and we desecrate the Sabbath on her account") comes to add the very important ruling that we perform even *Biblically* forbidden *melachos* on her behalf!? Because of this difficulty, *Rashba* (cited in note 33) and others reject *Rashi's* explanation that "delivering the fetus" entails no more than "excessive exertion," and explain instead that it involves a *Biblically* forbidden *melachah* (which explains why the Gemara here considers the Mishnah's third statement superfluous). *Tos. Yom Tov* (to the Mishnah) suggests that the Gemara here understands the larger *techum* measure (twelve *mil*) to be Biblical, and that accounts for why it considers the Mishnah's third statement superfluous. That explanation, however, is also difficult, since even those who understand the twelve-*mil* limit to be Biblical agree that there is no death penalty incurred for violating it; the Mishnah's third statement, then, would still be necessary to teach that one may perform for the woman even *melachos* that are capital offenses (see *Tiferes Yisrael* [*Boaz*] to the Mishnah).

47. A woman giving birth has more peace of mind when the area is illuminated (see Gemara below), and the Sages determined that this peace of mind can be critical to her survival. Therefore, the Baraisa rules that we light a lamp for her if necessary (see *Tos. Yeshanim* to *Yoma* 83a; *Mishnah Berurah* 330:3; see also *Tosafos* here ד״ה קמ״ל).

We light the lamp as a matter of course, even if she or the one attending her does not request it. What the Baraisa means by "*if* she needed a lamp" is: if it was nighttime or the room was dark, and the natural sources of light are insufficient (*Mishnah Berurah* ibid.). Alternatively, the Baraisa might mean that we light the lamp only if she or the one attending her claims that it is necessary (see *Beur Halachah* ad loc.).

48. [Presumably, the oil provides her with a comfort that the Sages deemed critical for her survival.]

49. Carrying oil in the palm of one's hand constitutes a deviation from the normal way of carrying, and is thus not Biblically forbidden even though one is transporting the oil four *amos* in the public domain [or from domain to domain]. And though the saving of a life overrides the Sabbath, permitting if necessary even the performance of a Biblical *melachah,* we avoid where possible performing a Biblical *melachah* by doing the act in an altered fashion (see *Rashi;* see also Gemara below, and note 56).

50. I.e. she soaks her hair in oil, and she wrings it out when she returns to the woman giving birth. In this way, she avoids transporting the oil in a Biblically prohibited fashion, since carrying in one's hair is a deviation from the norm [Mishnah above, 92a] (*Rashi*).

בשר תפוח מפני שהוא מאכל לחיה מים מגולין מפני שהן ראוין לחתול רשב"ג אומר כל עצמן אסור לשהותן מפני הסכנה: מתני' א) כופין את הסל לפני האפרוחים כדי שיעלו וירדו תרנגולת שברחה דוחין אותה עד שתכנס מדדין עגלין וסייחין (א) אשה מדדה את בנה אמר רבי יהודה אימתי בזמן שהוא נוטל אחת ומניח אחת אבל אם היה גורר אסור: גמ' אמר רב יהודה אמר רב בהמה שנפלה לאמת המים מביא כרים וכסתות ומניח תחתיה ואם עלתה עלתה מיתיבי בהמה שנפלה לאמת המים עושה לה פרנסה במקומה בשביל שלא תמות פרנסה אין כרים וכסתות לא לא קשיא הא דאפשר בפרנסה הא דאי אפשר בפרנסה אפשר בפרנסה אין ואי לא מביא כרים וכסתות ומניח תחתיה והא קא מבטל כלי מהיכנו סבר מבטל כלי מהיכנו דרבנן צער בעלי חיים דאורייתא ואתי דאורייתא ודחי דרבנן: תרנגולת שברחה וכו': דוחין אין מדדין לא תנינא להא דת"ר מדדין בהמה חיה ועוף בחצר אבל לא את התרנגולת תרנגולת מאי טעמא לא אמר אביי משום דמקפיא נפשה תני חדא מדדין בהמה וחיה ועוף בחצר אבל לא ברה"ר והאשה מדדה את בנה ברה"ר ואצ"ל בחצר ותניא אידך אין עוקרין בהמה וחיה ועוף בחצר אבל דוחין בהן שיכנסו הא גופא קשיא אמרת אין עוקרין אבל דדויי מדדינן הדר אמרת (ב) דוחין אין מדדין לא אמר אביי סיפא אתאן לתרנגולת אמר אביי האי מאן דשחיט תרנגולת לכבשינהו לכרעיה בארעא אי נמי נידל להו מידל דדילמא מנח להו לטופריה בארעא ועקר להו לסימנים: מתני' אין מילדין את הבהמה ביום טוב אבל מסעדין ומילדין את האשה בשבת וקורין לה חכמה ממקום למקום ומחללין עליה את השבת וקושרין את הטיבור רבי יוסי אומר אף חותכין וכל צרכי מילה עושין בשבת: גמ' כיצד מסעדין רב יהודה אמר אוחז את הולד שלא יפול לארץ רב נחמן אמר דוחק בבשר כדי שיצא הולד תניא כוותיה דרב יהודה כיצד מסעדין אוחזין את הולד שלא יפול לארץ ונופח לו בחוטמו ונותן לו דד לתוך פיו כדי שינק אמר רשב"ג מרחמין היינו על בהמה טהורה ביו"ט היכי עביד אמר אביי מביא בול של מלח ומניח לה בתוך הרחם כדי שתזכור צערה ותרחם עליו ומזלפין מי שליא על גבי ולד כדי שתריח ריחו ותרחם עליו ודוקא טהורה אבל טמאה לא מ"ט טמאה לא מרחקא ולדא ואי מרחקא ולדא לא מקרבא: מילדין את האשה וכו': מכדי תנא ליה מילדין את האשה וקורין לה חכמה ממקום למקום ומחללין עליה את השבת לאתויי מאי לאתויי הא דתנו רבנן אם היתה צריכה לנר חבירתה מדלקת לה את הנר ואם היתה צריכה לשמן חבירתה מביאה לה שמן ביד ואם אינו ספק ביד מביאה בשערה ואם אינו ספק בשערה מביאה לה בכלי אמר מר אם היתה צריכה לנר חבירתה מדלקת לה את הנר פשיטא לא צריכא בסומא מהו דתימא כיון דלא חזיא אסור קא משמע לן איתובי מיתבא דעתה סברא אי איכא מידי חזיא חבירתא ועבדה לי: אם היתה צריכה לשמן וכו': תיפוק ליה משום סחיטה רבה ורב יוסף דאמרי תרווייהו אין סחיטה בשיער רב אשי אמר אפי' תימא יש סחיטה בשיער מביאה לה בכלי דרך שערה דכמה דאפשר לשנויי משנינן אמר רב יהודה אמר שמואל חיה כל זמן שהקבר פתוח בין אמרה צריכה אני בין לא אמרה צריכה אני מחללין עליה את השבת נסתם הקבר בין אמרה צריכה

רש"י

בשר תפוח. מסריח: לחתול. לא מזיק ליה ארס דנחש שאף הנחשים היא אוכלת: מפני הסכנה. שמא ישתה אדם מהם: מתני' כופין סל בפני האפרוחים. אשמעינן דכלי ניטל לדבר שאינו ניטל בשבת ורבי יצחק משני לה בפ"ג בצריך למקומו: שברחה. מן הבית: דוחין. בידים: מדדין עגלים. אוחז בצוארו ובצדדין וגוררו ומסייעו (ג) ומנענע לו ברגליו: אשה מדדה את בנה. אוחזתו בזרועותיו מאחוריו ומסייעתו והוא מניע רגליו והולך: שנוטל אחת ומניח אחת. שהתינוק מניע את רגליו כשמניח אחת מגביה אחת: אבל גורר אסור. מפני שנושאתו: גמ' ואי לא. כגון שהמים עמוקין: והא קמבטל כלי מהיכנו. דמשהכניסם תחתיה אין יכול לטלטלן דדומה לסותר בנין (ד) מדרבנן: צער בעלי חיים דאורייתא. שנאמר עזוב תעזוב עמו ואיכא מאן דדריש טעמא דקרא משום צער בעלי חיים באלו מציאות (ב"מ דף לב:): מדדין לא. שלא יהא אוחזה בגפיה ורגליה נוגעין לארץ ומוליכה: דמקפיא נפשה. מגבהת עצמה מן הארץ ונמצא זה מטלטל אבל אווזים כשאוחזין בגפיהן הן מהלכין ברגליהן ומיהו ברה"ר לא משום שמא יגביהם מן הארץ ונמצא נושאן דסתמא כרבנן דפליגי עליה דרבי נתן בהמצניע (לעיל דף צד.) גבי המוציא חיה ועוף בין חיין בין שחוטין חייב והאשה מדדה את בנה אפילו ברה"ר דאי נמי מגביה ליה חי נושא את עצמו דהכי מוקמינן התם דבאדם מודו רבנן לרבי נתן: מקפיא. כגון אקפו ידייכו דחגיגה (דף טו:): אין עוקרין. רגליה לגמרי מן הארץ דמוקצה היא לטלטלה: דדויי מדדינן. אוחזה בשני צדדיה בידו ומדדה והוה טלטול טפי מדחייה שדוחפה מאחריה: סיפא. דקתני דוחין אבל לא מדדין: אתאן לתרנגולת. ורישא בשאר עופות: לכבשינהו לכרעיה בארעא. כדי שיתכפלו ולא יוכל להתחזק עליהן: אי נמי לידלינהו. יגביהנו שלא יהו רגליו נוגעות לארץ: מתני' מסעדין. מפרש בגמרא: חכמה. מילדת: אין מילדין את הבהמה ביום טוב. דאיכא טרחא יתירה: אבל מסעדין. אותה בי"ט: ומיילדין אשה בשבת. ואין צריך לומר שמסעדין וכל שכן ביום טוב: וקושרין הטיבור. של ולד שהוא ארוך שאם לא יתקשר ויכרך בשום דבר יצאו מעיו אם יגביהו התינוק: גמ' דוחק. בבשר של בהמה לפנים שיהא הולד בולט לחוץ: ונופח לו בחוטמו. שנחיריו סתומין לו בריריו: ונותן דד. של אמו בתוך פיו: מרחמין. מאהבין את ולדה עליה: בול של מלח. מלא אגרוף דכייב לה חוכרת צער לידה ומרחמה את הולד אם רחקתו: מי שליא. שורין את השליא במים: לא מרחקה. אין דרכה לרחק: מביאה לה שמן. דרך רה"ר: ביד. בכפה ולא בכלי דכמה דאפשר משנינן: בשערה. סכה שערה שמן וכשבאה אצלה מקנחתו ואין כאן חילול שבת כיון שאין דרך הוצאה בכך: פשיטא. דהא פקוח נפש דוחה שבת: תיפוק ליה משום סחיטה. למה לא הביאה לה בכלי שלא תחלל שבת בהוצאה הכא נמי הא קמחללה בסחיטה: אין סחיטה בשיער. שהוא קשה ואין בולע: דרך שערה. כורכת הכלי בראשה בשערה: חיה. יולדת: קבר. בית הרחם: צריכה

תוספות

בשר תפוח מפני שהוא מאכל לחיה. תימה לימא מפני שהוא מאכל לכלבים וי"ל דכרבי יהודה אתיא ואינו מקצה לכלבים כפירוש הקונטרס אלא חזי ליה וכל מידי דחזי ליה לאינש לא מקצה לכלבים אבל מפני שהוא מאכל לחיה מותר לטלטלו דכל ישראל בני מלכים הם ורב חסדא דלא שרי בשר תפל מהאי טעמא לית ליה כל ישראל בני מלכים:

אין עוקרין בהמה חיה ועוף. לספרים דגרסי רה"ר הך ברייתא פליגא אקמייתא בתרתי דדייקינן הא דדויי מדדין אפילו ברה"ר ולעיל קתני דווקא בחצר ותו סיפא דמוקמת לתרנגולת דאין מדדין ברה"ר ולעיל קתני דאפי' בחצר לא ולספרים דגרסי אין עוקרין בהמה חיה ועוף בחצר אתי שפיר: קמ"ל איתותבי מיתבא דעתה. אע"ג דבפרק בתרא דיומא (דף פג.) אמר חולה אין מאכלין אותו ביוה"כ אלא ע"פ מומחה והכא (ה) שריא משום יתובי דעתא היינו שיותר יכולה היולדת להסתכן על ידי פחד שתפחד שמא אין עושין יפה מה שהיא צריכה ממה שיסתכן החולה ברעב: רבה

עין משפט נר מצוה

כג א מיי' פכ"ה מהל' שבת הלכה כה סמג לאוין סה טוש"ע א"ח סימן שח סעיף לט:
כד ב מיי' פי"ח שם הלכה טו סמג שם טוש"ע שם סעיף מא:
כה ג מיי' פכ"ה שם הלכה כו וסמג שם טוש"ע א"ח סימן שה סעיף יט:
כו ד מיי' פי"ג מהלכות רוצח וש"נ הלכה יג סמג עשין פ פא ולאוין קסט טוש"ע ח"מ סימן ערב סעיף ט בהג"ה:
כז ה ו מיי' פכ"ה מהל' שבת הלכה כו סמג לאוין סה טוש"ע א"ח סי' שח סעיף מ:
כח ז שם סעיף מא:
כט ח [מיי' פ"ג מהל' שחיטה הל' יד] סמג עשין סג טוש"ע י"ד סי' כד סעיף כ [וברב אלפס חולין פ"ב דף רסא]:
ל ט י מיי' פ"ד מהל' יו"ט הלכה טו סמג לאוין עה טוש"ע א"ח סימן שלב סעיף א וסימן תקכג סעיף ג:
לא כ מיי' שם טוש"ע שם ס"ד:
לב ל מ נ מיי' פ"ב מהלכות שבת הלכה יא סמג לאוין סה טוש"ע א"ח סי' של סעיף א:

גליון הש"ס

גמרא תיפוק ליה משום סחיטה. עיין לקמן דף קמה ע"א תוספות ד"ה כבשים:

רבינו חננאל

לטלטלו: דג תפל אסור לטלטלו בשר בין חי ובין מליח מותר לטלטלו. ת"ר מטלטלין את העצמות מפני שהן מאכל לכלבים בשר תפוח מפני שהוא מאכל לחיה וזו היא דתניא כוותיה דרב הונא מים מגולין מפני שהן ראוין לחתול. ומתניתא אלין הלכתא אינון דליכא דפליג. ואליבא דב"ה נשנו דתנן ב"ה אומרים מגביהין מעל השלחן עצמות וקליפין: כופין את הסל לפני האפרוחים שיעלו וירדו. בהמה שנפלה לאמת המים אם אפשר לה בפרנסה עושין לה פרנסה במקומה. ואם אי אפשר לה בפרנסה מביא כרים וכסתות ומניח תחתיה ואם עלתה עלתה ואף על גב דמבטל כלי מהיכנו. מדרבנן היא. וצער ב"ח דאורייתא ואתא דאורייתא ודחה דרבנן. תרנגולת שברחה דוחין אותה עד שתכנס אבל אין מדדין אותה אפי' בחצר משום דמקפיא נפשה ואע"פ ששאר בהמה חיה ועוף מדדין בחצר אבל לא ברה"ר תרנגולת אפילו בחצר לא אלא אסור לדדותם אפילו בחצר. האשה מדדה את בנה ברה"ר וכ"ש בחצר והא דאמר ר' יהודה אימתי בזמן שנוטל אחת ומניח אחת אבל אם היה גורר אסור [היינו] ברה"ר בלבד שאם נוטל התינוק רגלו אחת ונשען על רגלו האחרת נמצא כמהלך אבל אם אינו נשען על רגליו אלא כשמדדתו גורר רגליו נמצאת נושאתו ברה"ר ואסור אבל בחצר מותר לטלטלו ולשאת אותו והא דאמר אביי מאן דשחיט תרנגולת ליכבשינה לכרעתא בארעא. אי נמי תידלינהו דילמא מנח להן לטופראה בארעא ועקרה להו לסימנים הלכתא היא: מתני' אין מילדין את הבהמה ביו"ט אבל מסעדין כיצד מסעדין. רב יהודה אומר אוחז בולד שלא יפול לארץ והלכתא כמותו. דתניא כוותיה. כיצד מסעדין אוחז בולד שלא יפול לארץ ונופחו לו בחוטמו ונותן דד לתוך פיו כדי שיינק כו'. וקיי"ל דמסעדין ומרחמין דתנינן ביו"ט אבל לא בשבת ומילדין את האשה בשבת וקורין לה חכמה ממקום למקום ומחללין עליה את השבת. ואסיקנא שמדלקת לה חברתה את הנר ואפילו אם היא סומא מותר להדליק לה נר בשבת דקיי"ל יתובי מייתבא דעתה סברא אי איכא מידי חזייא חברתאי ועבדא לי. ואם היתה צריכה לשמן מביאה לה שמן כרב אשי דאמר מביאה לה בכלי דרך שערה נועצת כלי של שמן בשערה כדי שלא [יהא] הוצאה ביד כדרך המוציאין ומסקנא כמה דאית לשנויי משנינן ואם צריכה למאכל מביאין לה. מר זוטרא מתני אמר רב יהודה אמר שמואל חיה כל זמן שהקבר פתוח. פירוש הקבר בית הרחם. בין אמרה צריכה אני ובין אמרה איני צריכה מחללין עליה את השבת. נסתם (הכלי) [הקבר] אמרה צריכה

מסורת הש"ס

א) [לעיל מג.], ב) ס"א ברה"ר, ג) [תוספתא פט"ו], ד) [לעיל מג. וע"ש תוספות ד"ה דמבטל], ה) [ב"מ לב:], ו) [בע"א ס"ן סימן ש"ל סעיף ד ספק הלכתא כרבי יוסי וכן דעת הרמב"ם], ז) לקמן קנג., ח) [תוספ' פט"ו], ט) [לעיל קח: לקמן קמח. עיי"ש], י) ס"א בין אמרה איני צריכה, כ) [ל"ל לעיל בפ"ג מג.].

הגהות הב"ח

(א) במשנה ואשה מדדה: (ב) גמ' והדר אמרת: (ג) רש"י ד"ה מדדין וכו' ומסייעו לילך ומנענע: (ד) ד"ה והא קא מבטל וכו' לסותר בנין מבטל כלי מהיכנו מדרבנן צער בעלי חיים: (ה) תוס' ד"ה קמ"ל וכו' והכלא שריא משום וכו' היינו לפי שיותר:

רב נסים גאון

כדי שיתפרשו תחומין אחד מחבירו ראמינו בכך לענין עירובין של תחומים ושיתופם כי השרשים שהוא משלח בקרקע מוכיחים על הגבולים ועל פי זה אמרו שם במסכת יום טוב (פרק אין צדין דף כה) חצובא מקטע רגליהון דרשיעיא שהוא דבר שאין בו רוח חיים ובצמיחתו משלח שרשיו בארץ במשפט והרשעים מעקמין דרכיהם ואין הולכין בדרכיו של הקב"ה כמו שראוי להם לכן דרכם באפילה: צער בעלי חיים דאורייתא מה שאמר הקב"ה (שמות כג) כי תראה חמור שונאך רובץ תחת משאו ואמרו בבא מציעא בפרק אלו מציאות (דף לב) מצוה מן התורה לפרוק דקסבר תנא דידן צער בעלי חיים דאורייתא ורבי יוסי הגלילי סבר צער בעלי חיים דרבנן וסבר (אביי) [רב יהודה] בבבא קמא דצער בעלי חיים דאורייתא וביטול כלי מהיכנו משכחת לה בפרק כירה (לעיל דף מב) דתנן אין נותנין כלי תחת הנר לקבל בו את השמן ואמר רב חסדא אין נותנין כלי תחת התרנגולת לקבל ביצתה כו' ופירש רב יוסף טעמא בכך ואמר היינו טעמא דרב חסדא דקא מבטל כלי מהיכנו והא מדרבנן הוא:

סליק פרק מפנין

ליקוטי רש"י

מים מגולין. מים שנשארו מגולין בלילה ספק שתה מהן נחש ספק לא שתה וקיימא לן דאסירי [חולין ט.]. פרנסה. לשון פרנסה צריכה בלע"ז (כתובות סה.) וכמו מוליכין לפרנסה ואין מוליכין למזונות (שם סט.) [גיטין סה:]. כל צורך סיפוק קרי פרנסה קונדר"ר בלע"ז [ב"מ מו.]. והא קא מבטל כלי מהיכנו. שהיה מוכן מתחלה לטלטלו ועכשיו עושהו מוקצה [לעיל מג. ע"ש בתוס' ובפנ"י]. אסור לבטל כלי במקום שלא יוכל עוד ליטלו [משם] דהוי כקובע לו מקום ומחברו בטיט ודמי למלאכה וכלי זה יהא אסור לטלטלו [שם מב:]. כרים וכסתות כשמניחן תחת דבר שאין ניטל מבטלן מהיכן לסותר [לקמן קנד:]. מקפיא. לשון דבר הצף ואין מכביד כדמתרגמינן ויצף הברזל וקפא ברזלא. טופריה. צפרניו [לעיל סג:]. בול של מלח. מלא אגרוף של מלח שמעתי [זבחים].

The Gemara again quotes a portion of this Baraisa (in order to question it):

אָמַר מַר – **The master said** in the Baraisa: אִם הָיְתָה צְרִיכָה לְנֵר – IF SHE NEEDED A LAMP, חֲבֵירְתָּהּ מַדְלֶקֶת לָהּ אֶת הַנֵּר – HER FRIEND MAY LIGHT THE LAMP FOR HER.

The Gemara asks:

פְּשִׁיטָא – **It is obvious** that we may light the lamp for her, since her life is in danger and her needs therefore override the Sabbath prohibitions.[51] – ? –

The Gemara answers:

לֹא צְרִיכָא בְּסוּמָא – **No, it is** a **necessary** ruling **in the case of a blind woman** who is giving birth. מַהוּ דְתֵימָא כֵּיוָן דְּלָא חָזְיָא אָסוּר – For in that case, **you might have said** that **since she cannot see** and thus derives no direct benefit from the lamp, **it is prohibited** to light the lamp for her. קָא מַשְׁמַע לָן – To dispel this notion, **the Baraisa informs us** that it is permitted nonetheless to light the lamp for her, אַיְתוּבֵי מְיַתְּבָא דַּעְתָּהּ – because **her mind is put at ease,** סָבְרָא אִי אִיכָּא מִידֵי – for **she reasons, "if there is something** pertaining to my well-being that must be done, חָזְיָא חֲבֵירְתָּא וְעָבְדָה לִי – my **friend will** more readily **see** it in the light **and do** it **for me."**[52]

The Baraisa stated:

אִם הָיְתָה צְרִיכָה לְשֶׁמֶן וכו׳ – IF SHE NEEDED OIL etc. [her friend brings it in the palm of her hand; and if this is insufficient, she brings it in her hair; and if this, too, is insufficient, she brings it in a container in the usual manner].

The Gemara asks:

תֵּיפּוּק לֵיהּ מִשּׁוּם סְחִיטָה – Granted that by carrying the oil in her hair she does not commit any Biblically forbidden act of "carrying," but **it should emerge** that she commits a Biblically forbidden act **because of the prohibition** against **"squeezing out"** on the Sabbath.[53] What, then, have we accomplished by advising her to soak her hair with the oil to avoid the Biblical *melachah* of carrying the oil in a container in the usual manner, if as a result she will have to commit the Biblical *melachah* of squeezing the oil out of her hair!?

The Gemara answers:

רַבָּה וְרַב יוֹסֵף דְּאָמְרֵי תַּרְוַויְיהוּ – **Rabbah and Rav Yosef both say:** אֵין סְחִיטָה בְּשֵׂיעָר – **There is no** Biblical violation of **"squeezing out"** involved **in** the squeezing out of **hair.**[54]

A second answer:

רַב אַשִׁי אָמַר – **Rav Ashi said:** אֲפִילוּ תֵּימָא יֵשׁ סְחִיטָה בְּשֵׂיעָר – **Even if you say that there is** a Biblical violation of **"squeezing out"** involved **in** the squeezing out of **hair,** there is no difficulty.[55] For what the Baraisa means by "she brings it in her hair" is that מְבִיאָה לָהּ בִּכְלִי דֶּרֶךְ שַׂעֲרָהּ – **she brings** it **to her** ***in a container*** **by means of her hair,** i.e. she carries the container in her hair. דִּכְמָה דְּאֶפְשָׁר לְשַׁנּוּיֵי מְשַׁנִּינַן – **For as much as it is possible to deviate** from the normal method of doing a necessary *melachah,* **we must deviate,** to avoid as much as possible doing the necessary *melachah* in the Biblically forbidden manner.[56]

NOTES

51. See *Rashi.* [That is, certainly a woman giving birth feels more secure in an illuminated environment, and that sense of security is crucial for her survival.]

52. And the Sages determined that even this peace of mind is critical to her well-being (see above, note 47; see also *Igros Moshe, Orach Chaim* I:132).

Thus, the Baraisa teaches us (and the Mishnah as well, by stating the additional clause "and we desecrate the Sabbath on her account") that we may perform even a Biblical *melachah* on the Sabbath to provide for the needs of a woman who is giving birth (or the needs of some other dangerously ill person), even if providing those needs does not directly address a threat to life (see next paragraph).

[Some Rishonim maintain that we desecrate the Sabbath to do *anything* for a critically ill person that would usually be done for him on a weekday (since all aspects of his care can be said to contribute to sustaining his life). Other Rishonim, however, allow desecration of the Sabbath only for needs that have more direct impact on his survival. See *Beur Halachah* to 328:4 ד״ה כל שרגילים, who discusses this issue at great length.]

53. Squeezing oil out of the material into which it is absorbed is akin to squeezing it out of the olive, which is Biblically forbidden as מְפָרֵק, *disengaging [an absorbed food or liquid],* a *toladah* of דָּשׁ, *threshing* (see *Tosafos* to *Kesubos* 6a ד״ה האי מסוכרייתא; *Meiri* below to 145a, end of ד״ה מה שאמרו במסוביתא; see also *Beur Halachah* to 302:9, end of ד״ה אסור and *Igros Moshe, Orach Chaim* I:133.).

54. Since the liquid is not absorbed into the hair fibers themselves, which are non-absorbent (see *Rashi*), but simply into the spaces between them.

Rashba asks: If squeezing out the hair does not constitute a *melachah,* then why does the Baraisa state that it is preferable to bring the oil in the palm of her hand than in her hair? On the contrary, carrying the oil in the hair – which is more of a deviation from the norm than carrying it in the palm of the hand – should be the preferred option! [See Gemara below, where the Gemara implies that not only must we deviate where possible from the norm, but we must deviate *to the greatest degree possible* from the norm.] *Beis Yosef* (beginning of 330; also *Kesef Mishneh, Hil. Shabbos* 2:11) answers that although there is no Biblical *melachah* violated by squeezing the oil out of the hair, it is nonetheless forbidden Rabbinically [as stated in *Maggid Mishneh, Hil. Shabbos* 9:11]. Therefore, it is preferable to bring the oil in violation of one Rabbinic precept (carrying the oil in the palm of the hand) than in violation of two Rabbinic precepts (carrying the oil in the hair and then squeezing it out on arrival). See also *Ran MHK* ed. here.

55. Rav Ashi might not mean to dispute the assertion of Rabbah and Rav Yosef that there is no Biblical *melachah* committed by squeezing out hair, but only to say that we can answer the Gemara's question even without resorting to that principle (*Beis Yosef* and *Kesef Mishneh* loc. cit.).

56. Though it would seem that carrying a container in one's hair is more of a deviation than carrying oil in the palm of the hand, the former option is preferable, because it entails carrying less oil [as she can wipe her palm on the body of the woman who needs it]. Were the oil to be placed in a container, however, more oil would have to be carried in order to obtain the same amount, since some oil adheres to the walls of the container (*Ritva MHK* ed.). [Thus, a lesser deviation in transporting a smaller amount is preferable to a greater deviation in transporting a greater amount.]

[Actually, the principle that we must deviate from the norm as much as possible when performing the necessary *melachah* on the Sabbath is not Rav Ashi's innovation, but is implicit in the Baraisa's order of preferences for transporting the oil needed by the woman (see *Rashi* above ד״ה ביד). Perhaps, then, this clause "for as much as it is possible to deviate, we must deviate" is not a continuation of Rav Ashi's statement, but is rather the Gemara's elaboration on the Baraisa itself, which the Gemara does not state until after the difficulty with the Baraisa's ruling is resolved.]

The Rishonim emphasize that a deviation in performing the necessary *melachah* should be employed only if it does not cause any delay in providing the necessary service for the dangerously ill person (*Ritva MHK* ed.; *Chidushei HaRan; Rama, Orach Chaim* 328:12; see *Mishnah Berurah* there §35, and 330:5). Moreover, some authorities maintain that the Gemara's requirement to opt for a deviation from the norm where possible applies only to the case of a woman who gives birth (since her dangerous situation is a natural condition rather than a result of illness, and only rarely do women die in childbirth). In the case of a person who is dangerously *ill,* however, no deviation whatsoever need be employed (*Maggid Mishneh, Hil. Shabbos* 2:11, according to the opinion of *Rambam* there; *Mishnah Berurah* 330:5). Other authorities, however, do not distinguish between the two cases, and require deviation from the norm, where possible, in either event (*Ramban,* cited by *Maggid Mishneh* there; *Rama, Orach Chaim* 328:12).

עין משפט
נר מצוה

כג א מיי' פכ"ה מהל' שבת הלכה כה סמג לאוין סה טוש"ע א"ח סימן שח סעיף לט:
כד ב מיי' פי"ח שם הלכה טו סמג שם טוש"ע שם סעיף מא:
כה ג מיי' פכ"ה שם הלכה כו וסמג שם טוש"ע א"ח סימן שה סעיף יט:
כו ד מיי' פי"ג מהלכות רוצח וש"מ הלכה יג סמג עשין פ פא ולאוין קסט טוש"ע ח"מ סימן ערב סעיף ט בהג"ה:
כז ה ו מיי' פכ"ה מהל' שבת הלכה כו סמג לאוין סה טוש"ע א"ח סי' שח סעיף מ:
כח ז שם סעיף מא:
כט ח [מיי' פ"ג מהל' שחיטה הל' יד] סמג עשין סג טוש"ע י"ד סי' כד סעיף כ [וברב אלפס חולין פ"ג דף רסא]:
ל ט י מיי' פ"ד מהל' יו"ט הלכה טו סמג לאוין עה טוש"ע א"ח סימן שלב סעיף א וסימן תקכג סעיף ג:
לא כ מיי' שם טוש"ע שם ס"ד:
לב ל מ נ מיי' פ"ב מהלכות שבת הלכה יא סמג לאוין סה טוש"ע א"ח סי' של סעיף א:

גליון הש"ס

גמרא תיפוק ליה משום סחיטה. עיין לקמן דף קמה ע"א תוספות ד"ה כבסים:

רבינו חננאל

לטלטלו: דג תפל אסור לטלטלו בשר בין חי ובין מליח מותר לטלטלו. ת"ר מטלטלין את העצמות מפני שהן מאכל לכלבים בשר תפוח מפני שהוא מאכל לחיה וזו היא דתניא כוותיה דרב הונא מים מגולין מפני שהן ראוין לחתול. ומתניתא אלין הלכתא אינון דליכא דפליג. ואליבא דב"ה נשנו דתנן ב"ה אומרים מגביהין מעל השלחן עצמות וקליפין: כופין את הסל לפני האפרוחים שיעלו וישדו. בהמה שנפלה לאמת המים אם אפשר לה בפרנסה עושין לה פרנסה במקומה. ואם אי אפשר לה בפרנסה מביא כרים וכסתות ומניח תחתיה ואם עלתה עלתה ואף על גב דמבטל כלי מהיכנו. מדרבנן היא. וצער ב"ח דאורייתא ואתא דאורייתא ודחה דרבנן. תרנגולת שברחה דוחין אותה עד שתכנס אבל אין מדדין אותה אפי' בחצר משום דמקפיא נפשה ואע"פ ששאר בהמה חיה ועוף מדדין בחצר אבל לא ברה"ר תרנגולת אפילו בחצר לא אלא אסור לדדותם אפילו בחצר. האשה מדדה את בנה ברה"ר וכ"ש בחצר והא דאמר ר' יהודה אימתי בזמן שנוטל אחת ומניח אחת אבל אם היה גורר אסור [היינו] ברה"ר בלבד שאם נוטל התינוק רגלו אחת ונשען על רגלו האחרת נמצא כמהלך אבל אם אינו נשען על רגליו אלא כשמדדתו גורר רגליו נמצאת נושאתו ברה"ר ואסור אבל בחצר מותר לטלטלו ולשאת אותו והא דאמר אביי מאן דשחיט תרנגולת ליכבשינהו לכרעיה בארעא. אי נמי תידלינהו דילמא מנח להו לטופראה בארעא ועקרה להו לסימנים כבר פירשנוה: מתני' אין מילדין את הבהמה ביו"ט אבל מסעדין. כיצד מסעדין. רב יהודה אומר אוחז בולד שלא יפול לארץ ונופחו לו בחוטמו ונותן לו דד לתוך פיו כדי שיינק כו'. וקי"ל דמסעדין ומרחמין ביו"ט אבל לא בשבת. ומילדין את האשה בשבת וקורין לה חכמה ממקום למקום ומחללין עליה את השבת. ואסיקנא שמדלקת לה חברתה את הנר ואפילו אם היא סומא מותר להדליק לה נר בשבת דקי"ל יתובי מיתבא דעתה סברא אי איכא מידי חזייא חברתאי ועבדא לי. ואם היתה צריכה לשמן מביאה לה בכלי דרך שערה כרב אשי דאמר כמה דאפשר לשנויי משנינן. ואם צריכה למאכל מביאין לה. מר זוטרא מתני אמר רב יהודה אמר שמואל חיה כל זמן שהקבר פתוח בין אמרה צריכה אני ובין אמרה איני צריכה מחללין עליה את השבת. נסתם הקבר (הכלי) [הקבר] אמרה צריכה

בשר תפוח מפני שהוא מאכל לחיה. תימה לימא מפני שהוא מאכל לכלבים וי"ל דכרבי יהודה אתיא ואינו מסריח כפירוש הקונטרס אלא חזי ליה וכל מידי דחזי ליה לאינש לא מקצה לכלבים אבל מפני שהוא מאכל לחיה מותר לטלטלו דכל ישראל בני מלכים הם ורב חסדא דלא שרי בשר תפל מההיא טעמא לית ליה כל ישראל בני מלכים: אין עוקרין בהמה חיה ועוף. לספרים דגרסי רה"ר הך ברייתא פליגא אקמייתא בתרתי דדייקינן הא דדווי מדדין אפילו ברה"ר ולעיל קתני דווקא בחצר ותו סיפא דמוקמא לתרנגולת דאין מדדין ברה"ר ולעיל קתני דאפי' בחצר לא ולספרים דגרסי אין עוקרין בהמה חיה ועוף בחצר אתי שפיר: קמ"ל איתובי מיתבא דעתה. אע"ג דבפרק בתרא דיומא (דף פג.) אמר חולה אין מאכילין אותו ביוה"כ אלא ע"פ מומחה והכא (ה) שריא משום יתובי דעתא היינו שיותר יכולה היולדת להסתכן על ידי פחד שתפחד שמא אין עושין יפה מה שהיא צריכה ממה שיסתכן החולה ברעב:

רבא

בשר תפוח מפני שהוא מאכל לחיה מים מגולין מפני שהן ראויין לחתול רשב"ג אומר כל עצמן אסור לשהותן מפני הסכנה: מתני' [א] כופין את הסל לפני האפרוחים כדי שיעלו וירדו תרנגולת שברחה דוחין אותה עד שתכנס מדדין עגלין וסייחין (א) אשה מדדה את בנה [ב] אמר רבי יהודה אימתי בזמן שהוא נוטל אחת ומניח אחת אבל אם היה גורר אסור: גמ' אמר רב יהודה אמר רב בהמה שנפלה לאמת המים מביא כרים וכסתות ומניח תחתיה ואם עלתה עלתה מיתיבי [ג] בהמה שנפלה לאמת המים עושה לה פרנסה במקומה בשביל שלא תמות פרנסה אין כרים וכסתות לא לא קשיא [ג] הא דאפשר בפרנסה הא דאי אפשר בפרנסה אפשר בפרנסה אין ואי לא מביא כרים וכסתות ומניח תחתיה והא [ד] קא מבטל כלי מהיכנו סבר מבטל כלי מהיכנו דרבנן [ה] [ד] צער בעלי חיים דאורייתא ואתי דאורייתא ודחי דרבנן: [ה] תרנגולת שברחה וכו': דוחין אין מדדין לא תנינא להא דת"ר [ו] מדדין בהמה חיה ועוף בחצר אבל לא את התרנגולת תרנגולת מאי טעמא לא אמר אביי משום דמקפיא נפשה תני חדא מדדין בהמה וחיה ועוף בחצר אבל לא ברה"ר והאשה מדדה את בנה [ז] ברה"ר ואצ"ל בחצר ותניא אידך אין עוקרין בהמה וחיה ועוף בחצר אבל דוחין בהן שיכנסו הא גופא קשיא אמרת אין עוקרין אבל דדויי מדדינן (ב) הדר אמרת דוחין אין מדדין לא אמר אביי סיפא אתאן לתרנגולת אמר אביי [ח] האי מאן דשחיט תרנגולת לכבשינהו לכרעיה בארעא אי נמי נידל להו מידל דדילמא מנח להו לטופריה בארעא ועקר להו לסימנים: מתני' [ט] אין מילדין את הבהמה ביום טוב אבל מסעדין ומילדין את האשה בשבת וקורין לה חכמה ממקום למקום ומחללין עליה את השבת וקושרין את הטיבור רבי יוסי אומר [י] אף חותכין [י] וכל צרכי מילה עושין בשבת: גמ' כיצד מסעדין רב יהודה אמר אוחז את הולד שלא יפול לארץ רב נחמן אמר דוחק בבשר כדי שיצא הולד תניא כוותיה דרב יהודה [ס] כיצד מסעדין [י] אוחזין את הולד שלא יפול לארץ ונופח לו בחוטמו ונותן לו דד לתוך פיו כדי שינק אמר רשב"ג [כ] מרחמין היינו על בהמה טהורה ביו"ט היכי עביד אמר אביי מביא בול של מלח ומניח לה בתוך הרחם כדי שתזכור צערה ותרחם עליו ומזלפין מי שליא על גבי ולד כדי שתריח ריחו ותרחם עליו ודוקא טהורה אבל טמאה לא מ"ט טמאה לא מרחקא ולדא ואי מרחקא ולדא לא מקרבא: [ל] מילדין את האשה וכו': מכדי תנא ליה מילדין את האשה וקורין לה חכמה ממקום למקום ומחללין עליה את השבת לאתויי מאי לאתויי הא דתנו רבנן [מ] אם היתה צריכה לנר חבירתה מדלקת לה את הנר ואם היתה צריכה לשמן חבירתה מביאה לה שמן ביד ואם אינו ספק ביד מביאה בשערה ואם אינו ספק בשערה מביאה לה בכלי אמר מר אם היתה צריכה לנר חבירתה מדלקת לה את הנר פשיטא [נ] לא צריכא בסומא מהו דתימא כיון דלא חזיא אסור קא משמע לן איתובי מיתבא דעתה סברא אי איכא מידי חזיא חבירתא ועבדה לי: אם היתה צריכה לשמן וכו': [ס] תיפוק ליה משום סחיטה רבה ורב יוסף דאמרי תרוייהו אין סחיטה בשיער רב אשי אמר אפי' תימא יש סחיטה בשיער מביאה לה בכלי דרך שערה [ע] דכמה דאפשר לשנויי משנינן אמר רב יהודה אמר שמואל חיה כל זמן שהקבר פתוח בין אמרה צריכה אני [פ] בין לא אמרה צריכה אני מחללין עליה את השבת נסתם הקבר בין אמרה צריכה

צריכה

בשר תפוח. מסריח: לחתול. לא מזיק ליה ארס דנחש שאף הנחשים היא אוכלת: מפני הסכנה. שמא ישתה אדם מהם: מתני' כופין סל בפני האפרוחים. שמעינן דכלי ניטל לדבר שאינו ניטל בשבת ורבי יצחק משני לה בפ"ג כצריך למקומו: שברחה. מן הבית: דוחין. בידים: מדדין עגלים. אוחז בצוארו ובלדדין וגוררו ומסייעו (ג) ומנענע לו ברגליו: אשה מדדה את בנה. אוחזתו בזרועותיו מאחוריו ומסייעתו והוא מניע רגליו והולך שנוטל אחת ומניח אחת. שהתינוק מניע את רגליו כשמניח אחת מגביה אחת: אבל גורר אסור. מפני שנושאתו: גמ' ואי לא. כגון שהמים עמוקין: והא קמבטל כלי מהיכנו. דמשהכניסם תחתיה אין יכול לטלטלן דדומה לסותר בנין (ד) מדרבנן: צער בעלי חיים דאורייתא. שנאמר עזוב תעזוב עמו ואיכא מאן דדריש טעמא דקרא משום צער בעלי חיים בבבא מציעא (ב"מ דף לב:): מדדין לא. שלא יהא אוחזה בגפיה ורגליה נוגעין לארץ ומוליכה: דמקפיא נפשה. מגבהת עצמה מן הארץ ונמצא זה מטלטל אבל אווזים כשאוחזין בגפיהן הן מהלכין ברגליהן ומיהו ברה"ר משום שמא יגביהם מן הארץ ונמצא נושאן דסתמא כרבנן דפליגי עליה דרבי נתן בהמצניע (לעיל דף צד.) גבי המוציא חיה ועוף בין חיין בין שחוטין חייב והאשה מדדה את בנה אפילו ברה"ר דלאו נמי מגביה ליה חי נושא את עצמו ואע"ג דהכי מוקמינן התם דבאדם מודו רבנן לרבי נתן: מקפיא. כגון אקפו יידיכו דחגיגה (דף טו:): אין עוקרין. רגליה לגמרי מן הארץ דמוקצה היא לטלטלה: דדויי מדדינן. אוחזה בשני לדדיה בידו ומדדה והוה טלטול טפי מדמייה שדוחקה מאחריה: סיפא. דקתני דוחין אבל לא מדדין אתאן לתרנגולת. ורישא בשאר עופות: לכבשינהו לכרעיה בארעא. כדי שיכפפו ולא יוכל להתחזק עליהן: אי נמי לידלינהו. יגביהם שלא יהו רגליו נוגעות לארץ: מתני' מסעדין. מפרש בגמרא: חכמה. מילדת: אין מילדין את הבהמה ביום טוב. דאיכא טרחא יתירה: אבל מסעדין. אותה ביו"ט: ומילדין אשה בשבת. ואין צריך לומר שמסעדין וכל שכן ביום טוב: וקושרין הטיבור. של ולד שהוא ארוך שאם לא יתקשר ויכרך בשום דבר יצאו מעיו אם יגביהו התינוק: גמ' דוחק. בבשר של בהמה לפניו שיהא הולד בולט לחוץ: ונופח לו בחוטמו. שנקביו סתומין לו בריר: ונותן דד. של אמו בתוך פיו: מרחמין. מקרבין את הולד אליה: בול של מלח. מלא אגרוף דכייל לה זוכרת לצער לידה ומרחמת את הולד אם רחקתו: מי שליא. שורין את השליא במים: לא מרחקא. אין דרכה לרחק: מביאה לה שמן. דרך רה"ר: ביד. בכפה ולא בכלי דלכמה דאפשר משנינן: בשערה. סכה שערה שמן ומביאה אלא מקנחתו ואין כאן חילול שבת כיון שאין דרך הוצאה בכך: פשיטא. דהא פקוח נפש דוחה שבת: תיפוק ליה משום סחיטה. למה לא הביאה לה בכלי שלא תחלל שבת בהוצאה הכא נמי הא קמחללה בסחיטה: אין סחיטה בשיער. שהוא קשה ואין בולע: דרך שערה. כורכת הכלי בראשה בשערה: חיה. יולדת: קבר. בית הרחם:

מסורת הש"ס

א) [לעיל מג.], ב) ס"א ברה"ר, ג) [תוספתא פט"ו], ד) [לעיל מג. וש"נ וע"ש תוספות ד"ה למטלטל], ה) [ב"מ לב:], ו) [בס"א מ"ח סימן ש"ל סעיף ד ספק הלכתא כרבי יוסי וכן דעת הרמב"ם], ז) לקמן קלג., ח) [תוספ' פט"ו], ט) [לעיל קח: לקמן קמח. ביצה ג.], י) ס"א בין אמרה איני צריכה, כ) [לעיל בפ"ג מג.]

הגהות הב"ח

(א) במשנה ואשה מדדה: (ב) גמ' והדר אמרת: (ג) רש"י ד"ה מדדין וכו' ומסייעו לילך ומנענע: (ד) ד"ה והא קא מבטל וכו' לסותר בנין מבטל כלי מהיכנו מדרבנן צער בעלי חיים: (ה) תוס' ד"ה קמ"ל וכו' והכא שריא משום וכו' היינו לפי שיותר:

רב נסים גאון

כדי שיתפרשו תחומין אחד מחבירו ויאמינו בכך לענין עירובין של תחומים ושיתופם כי השרשים שהוא משלח בקרקע מוכיחים על הגבולים ועל פי זה אמרו שם במסכת יום טוב (פרק אין צדין דף כה:) חצובא מקטע רגליהון דרשיעיא שהוא דבר שאין בו רוח חיים ובצמיחתו משלח שרשיו בארץ במשפט והרשעים מעקמין דרכיהם ואין הולכין בדרכיו של הקב"ה כמו שראוי להם לכן דרכם באפילה: צער בעלי חיים דאורייתא מה שאמר הקב"ה (שמות כג) כי תראה חמור שונאך רובץ תחת משאו ואמרו בבא מציעא בפרק אלו מציאות (דף לב) מצוה מן התורה לפרוק דקסבר תנא דידן צער בעלי חיים דאורייתא ורבי יוסי הגלילי סבר צער בעלי חיים דרבנן וסבר (אביי) [רב יהודה] בבאן כתנא קמא דצער בעלי חיים דאורייתא וביטול כלי מהיכנו מדרבנן מהלכה ליה בפרק כירה (לעיל דף מב) דתנן אין נותנין כלי תחת הנר לקבל בו את השמן ואמר רב חסדא אין נותנין כלי תחת התרנגולת לקבל ביצתה ופירש רב יוסף טעמא בכך ואמר היינו טעמא דרב חסדא דקא מבטל כלי מהיכנו והא מרבנן הוא:

סליק פרק מפנין

ליקוטי רש"י

מים מגולין. מים שנשארו מגולין בלילה ספק שתה מהן נחש ספק לא שתה וקיימא לן דאסירי [חולין ט:]. עושה לה פרנסה. כל צרכה הוא קונדרי"ר בלע"ז כמו לפרנסה ממון בלבד [מועדות כה.]. מולידין לממות [שם סט.] [גיטין סה:]. כל לורך קרי פרנסה קונדרי"ר בלע"ז [ב"מ מו.]. והא קא מבטל כלי מהיכנו. מבטל כלי מהיכנו שעושהו מוקצה [לעיל מג.]. כרים וכסתות כשמניחן תחת הבהמה אין נוטלין אותן משם כל השבת [שם מג:]. מקפיא. לשון דבר הצף ואין מכביד עצמו [חגיגה טו:]. בול של מלח. מלא אגרוף [זבחים סג.]. טופריה. צפרניו [לעיל קכ:].

The Gemara now explains the circumstances under which we desecrate the Sabbath for a woman in labor or one who has just given birth:

אָמַר רַב יְהוּדָה אָמַר שְׁמוּאֵל – **Rav Yehudah said in the name of Shmuel:**[57] חַיָּה – In the case of **a woman who has just given birth,**[58] כָּל זְמַן שֶׁהַקֶּבֶר פָּתוּחַ – **as long as the womb is open,**[59] בֵּין אָמְרָה צְרִיכָה אֲנִי בֵּין לֹא אָמְרָה צְרִיכָה אֲנִי – then **whether she says, "I need** it,"[60] **or whether she does not say, "I need** it," but her friends say that she does need it,[61] מְחַלְּלִין עָלֶיהָ אֶת הַשַּׁבָּת – **we desecrate the Sabbath on her account** in order to provide that need.[62] נִסְתַּם הַקֶּבֶר – Once **the womb has closed,** בֵּין אָמְרָה – then **whether she says,**

NOTES

57. [The Gemara itself will present two versions of this ruling of Shmuel, and the Rishonim have variant texts for each of the Gemara's two versions – each with its own halachic ramifications. See *Rif, Rosh* (with *Korban Nesanel*), *Ran, Tur* and *Maharshal.* We will explain the Gemara according to the readings found in our text and in *Rashi.*]

58. Although the word חַיָּה appears in Scripture as a reference [according to some interpretations] to *a midwife* [see *Exodus* 1:19 with *Rashi*], in the Talmud it is used to refer to the woman who has given birth (*Tos. HaRosh*).

59. The Gemara will explain what time period is meant by "the womb is open."

60. That is, she says she needs a thing generally considered essential for a woman who has just given birth (*Ramban* et al.; see also end of note 52 above).

61. *Rashi,* printed on 129a (whose comments seem to refer to the Gemara here; see, however, *Rosh* §5). I.e. it is a need normally considered essential for a woman who has just given birth [see preceding note] (see *Mishnah Berurah* 330:12, with *Shaar HaTziyun* §8).

62. According to the reading found in our texts, it emerges only that we desecrate the Sabbath for a perceived need whether or not she says that she needs it. But if she says explicitly, "I do *not* need it," then we would not desecrate the Sabbath to provide that need (see *Ran,* and *Korban Nesanel* 5:3). *Rashi's* reading (in his comments printed at the beginning of 129a – see preceding note) seems to be: *whether she says, "I need," or whether she says, "I do not need"* . . . Accordingly, even if she protests that she does not need it, we desecrate the Sabbath to provide that need (see also *Orach Chaim* 330:4).

צְרִיכָה אֲנִי – **"I need it,"**[1] בֵּין לֹא אָמְרָה צְרִיכָה אֲנִי – **or whether she does not say, "I need it,"** אֵין מְחַלְּלִין עָלֶיהָ אֶת הַשַּׁבָּת – **we do not desecrate the Sabbath on her account** to provide that need.[2]

The Gemara comments regarding the above citation of Shmuel's ruling:

רַב אַשִׁי מַתְנֵי הָכִי – **Rav Ashi teaches** Shmuel's ruling in **this** way that was just stated. מַר זוּטְרָא מַתְנֵי הָכִי – **Mar Zutra,** however, **teaches** Shmuel's ruling according to **this** following version: אָמַר רַב יְהוּדָה אָמַר שְׁמוּאֵל – **Rav Yehudah said in the name of Shmuel:** חַיָּה – In the case of **a woman who has just given birth,** כָּל זְמַן שֶׁהַקֶּבֶר פָּתוּחַ – **as long as the womb is** still **open,** בֵּין אָמְרָה צְרִיכָה אֲנִי וּבֵין אָמְרָה אֵין צְרִיכָה אֲנִי – then **whether she says, "I need it," or whether she says, "I do not need it,"** מְחַלְּלִין עָלֶיהָ אֶת הַשַּׁבָּת – **we desecrate the Sabbath on her account.**[3] נִסְתַּם הַקֶּבֶר – Once **the womb has closed,** אָמְרָה צְרִיכָה אֲנִי מְחַלְּלִין עָלֶיהָ אֶת הַשַּׁבָּת – then **if she says, "I need it," we desecrate the Sabbath on her account.**[4] לֹא אָמְרָה צְרִיכָה אֲנִי אֵין מְחַלְּלִין עָלֶיהָ אֶת הַשַּׁבָּת – **If she does not say, "I need it,"** then **we do not desecrate the Sabbath on her account.**

The Gemara seeks to ascertain which version of Shmuel's ruling we follow in practice:

אָמַר לֵיהּ רָבִינָא לְמָרֵימָר – **Ravina said to Mereimar:** מַר זוּטְרָא מַתְנֵי לְקוּלָּא – **Mar Zutra teaches a lenient [version]** of Shmuel's ruling, וְרַב אַשִׁי מַתְנֵי לְחוּמְרָא – **whereas Rav Ashi teaches a stringent [version]** of that ruling.[5] הִלְכְתָא כְּמַאן – **In accordance with whom is the halachah?**

Mereimar answers:

אָמַר לֵיהּ – **He said to [Ravina]:** הֲלָכָה כְּמַר זוּטְרָא – **The halachah is in accordance with** the version taught by **Mar Zutra,** סְפֵק נְפָשׁוֹת לְהָקֵל – because in matters of **uncertainty involving life** and death, we are bidden **to rule leniently.**[6] We therefore must follow Mar Zutra's more lenient position.

Shmuel's ruling speaks of desecrating the Sabbath on account of a woman whose "womb is open." The Gemara now defines that term:

מֵאֵימָתַי פְּתִיחַת הַקֶּבֶר – **From when is the womb** of a woman giving birth regarded as **open?** אָמַר אַבַּיֵי – **Abaye said:** מִשָּׁעָה שֶׁתֵּשֵׁב עַל הַמַּשְׁבֵּר – **From the moment she sits on the birthing stool.**[7] רַב הוּנָא בְּרֵיהּ דְּרַב יְהוֹשֻׁעַ אָמַר – **Rav Huna the son of Rav Yehoshua says:** מִשָּׁעָה שֶׁהַדָּם שׁוֹתֵת וְיוֹרֵד – **From the moment that the blood is dripping down** (as a result of labor), וְאָמְרֵי לָהּ – **or,** as **others report it:** מִשָּׁעָה שֶׁחַבְרוֹתֶיהָ נוֹשְׂאוֹת אוֹתָהּ בְּאַגַּפֶּיהָ – **from the moment** that the labor is so intense **that her friends** must **support her by her arms** because she cannot walk on her own.[8]

The Gemara continues:

עַד מָתַי פְּתִיחַת הַקֶּבֶר – And **until when is the womb** considered **open?** אָמַר אַבַּיֵי – **Abaye said:** שְׁלֹשָׁה יָמִים – It is considered open for **three days.** רָבָא אָמַר מִשְּׁמֵיהּ דְּרַב יְהוּדָה – But **Rava says in the name of Rav Yehudah:** שִׁבְעָה – It is considered open for **seven days,** וְאָמְרֵי לָהּ – **or,** as **others report it:** שְׁלֹשִׁים – **thirty days.**[9]

The Gemara cites a ruling from the Sages of Nehardea regarding desecrating the Sabbath on account of a woman who has given birth:

אָמְרֵי נְהַרְדְּעֵי – **The Nehardeans say:** חַיָּה – There are three stages in the recovery of **a woman who has** just **given birth,** with corresponding differences in the circumstances under which we may desecrate the Sabbath on her account: ג׳ ז׳ ול׳ – **three** days, **seven** days **and thirty** days.[10] ג׳ בֵּין אָמְרָה צְרִיכָה אֲנִי וּבֵין אָמְרָה לֹא צְרִיכָה אֲנִי – Until the end of **three** days, **whether she says, "I need it," or whether she says, "I do not need it,"**

NOTES

1. That is, she claims that a particular thing generally done for a woman after the womb has closed (but which entails *melachah*) is essential for her [and could put her at risk if it is not done now] (see *Ramban*).

2. Since the deprivation of that need is not assumed to be a threat to her life at that stage; moreover, it is only a question of waiting until after the Sabbath to provide her with that need (see *Ramban*).

3. I.e. even though she explicitly says that I do not need this treatment or preparation, since her friends say that she does in fact require it, we do not listen to her (see *Rashi*). [This is in contrast to Rav Ashi's version, as found in our texts above, from which it emerges that if she says explicitly she does not need it, we listen to her and do not desecrate the Shabbos – see 128b note 62.]

[If, however, the attending midwife or doctor concurs with her that she does not need it, we accept what they say, and do not desecrate the Sabbath (*Rashba,* citing *Ramban* [in *Toras HaAdam*]; see *Mishnah Berurah* 330:13; cf. *Aruch HaShulchan* 330:5).]

4. Here, Mar Zutra's version is fundamentally more lenient than Rav Ashi's. For whereas Rav Ashi's version has it that once the womb has closed we do not desecrate the Sabbath for her regardless of what she says, Mar Zutra's version has it that if she claims that she needs a particular thing, we desecrate the Sabbath for her even after the womb has closed.

5. For according to Mar Zutra's version, we desecrate the Sabbath for a woman even after her womb has closed, if she insists that she needs a particular thing (see preceding note). [And, according to the reading found above in our texts, there is a second leniency in that only Mar Zutra's version bids us to desecrate the Sabbath for a woman whose womb has *not* closed but insists that she does not need a thing usually deemed necessary (see note 3).]

6. [That is, to adopt the lenient position that suspends a prohibition in a particular situation because it considers that situation to be life threatening.]

The directive to adopt the lenient position in matters of life and death is contained in the verse (*Numbers* 35:25): וְהִצִּילוּ הָעֵדָה, *And the congregation shall rescue* [which bids us to do our utmost to vindicate someone accused of a capital crime – see, for example, *Pesachim* 12a and *Rosh Hashanah* 26a] (*Rashi* to *Kesubos* 15a et al.; cf. *Tosafos* to *Bava Basra* 50b).

7. I.e. the chair or bed from which she intends to deliver her child. This indicates that her delivery is imminent. [See *Sidrei Taharah* (194:25), who asserts that as long as her labor has begun in earnest and she requests the midwife's presence, she is considered at the stage of "sitting on the birthing stool," even if she has not actually mounted it.]

From this moment on, we may desecrate the Sabbath on her account. [Obviously, our desecration of the Sabbath to summon a midwife (or doctor) must be done earlier, to ensure her presence at the delivery. This summoning may be done, if necessary, as soon as the woman thinks that her contractions might be starting (see *Mishnah Berurah* 330:9).]

8. Some maintain that the "dripping of blood" is an earlier stage of labor than "sitting on the birthing stool" (see *Rabbeinu Chananel* and *Rif*), whereas others maintain that the dripping of blood is a later stage of labor (see *Rambam, Commentary to the Mishnah,* and *Beur Halachah* to 330:3 ד״ה כיון). *Ramban* (*Toras HaAdam* [Chavel ed. p. 31], cited by *Tur* 330), however, asserts that the sequence of events varies from woman to woman, and that we may desecrate the Sabbath for the woman giving birth as soon as she exhibits any of the three signs mentioned here.

9. There is a question whether these days are counted from the moment the womb opens or from the actual time of birth (see *Beur Halachah* 330:4 ד״ה כל שלשים and *Aruch HaShulchan* 330:7). [There is also a question whether in regard to these laws the day refers to a full twenty-four hours or whether it ends with nightfall (see *Mishnah Berurah* 330:10; see *Tosafos* to *Gittin* 8b ד״ה אע״ג).]

Tosafos here assert that Abaye and the two versions of Rava are not in fact disagreeing, but are rather referring to the various sets of law that correspond to the three stages of the woman's recovery, as set forth by the Sages of Nehardea in the coming Gemara.

10. That is, from the beginning [see preceding note] until the end of three days, from the end of three days until the end of seven, and from the end of seven until the end of thirty (*Rashi*).

עין משפט נר מצוה

לג א ב ג מיי' פ"ב מהל' שבת הלכה יג סמג לאוין סה טוש"ע א"ח סימן של סעיף ג:

לד ד מיי' שם טוש"ע שם ס"ד:

לה ה מיי' שם הלכה י סמג שם טוש"ע א"ח סי' שכח סעיף יז:

לו ו מיי' שם הלכה יד סמג שם טוש"ע א"ח סימן של סעיף ו:

לז ז מיי' וסמג שם טוש"ע א"ח סימן שכח סעיף יח:

רש"י

צריכה אני. לחילול: בין שאמרה אין צריכה אני. וחברותיה אומרות שהיא צריכה מחללין: באגפיה. בזרועותיה שאינה יכולה להלך: חיה ג' ימים וז' ימים ול' יום. הוזכרו בה לחילוק הלכות חילול שבת ל' מז' עד השלמת ל' וכן ז' מג' עד השלמת ז': כל צרכי חולה. והא חיה עד ל' יום סתמא חולה היא: דבר שאין בו סכנה. חולה שאם לא יעשו לו רפואה זו אין מסוכן למות ומ"מ צריך הוא לה: אומר לארמאי ועושה. אבל דבר שיש בו סכנה ישראל עצמו עושה לו: לטבילה. עד ל' יום לא תטבול מפני הצינה: שאין בעלה עמה. והיא טובלת לטהרות: בעלה מחממה.

גמרא

[א] צריכה אני בין לא אמרה צריכה אני אין מחללין עליה את השבת רב אשי מתני הכי מר זוטרא מתני הכי אמר רב יהודה אמר שמואל חיה כל זמן שהקבר פתוח בין אמרה צריכה אני ובין אמרה אין צריכה אני מחללין עליה את השבת נסתם הקבר אמרה [ב] צריכה אני מחללין עליה את השבת לא אמרה צריכה אני אין מחללין עליה את השבת א"ל רבינא למרימר מר זוטרא מתני לקולא ורב אשי מתני לחומרא הלכתא כמאן א"ל הלכה כמר זוטרא [ג] ספק נפשות להקל מאימתי פתיחת הקבר אמר אביי [א] משעה שתשב על המשבר רב הונא בריה דרב יהושע אמר [ב] משעה שהדם שותת ויורד ואמרי לה [ג] משעה שחברותיה נושאות אותה באגפיה עד מתי פתיחת הקבר אמר אביי שלשה ימים רבא אמר משמיה דרב יהודה שבעה ואמרי לה שלשים אמרי נהרדעי [ד] חיה ג' ז' ול' ג' בין אמרה צריכה אני ובין [ד] אמרה לא צריכה אני מחללין עליה את השבת ז' אמרה צריכה אני מחללין עליה את השבת אמרה לא צריכה אני אין מחללין עליה את השבת ל' אפי' אמרה צריכה אני אין מחללין עליה את השבת אבל עושין ע"י ארמאי [ה] כדרב עולא בריה דרב עילאי דאמר כל צרכי חולה נעשין ע"י ארמאי בשבת [ו] וכדרב המנונא דאמר רב המנונא [ה] [ז] דבר שאין בו סכנה [ח] אומר לנכרי ועושה אמר רב יהודה אמר שמואל לחיה ל' יום למאי הלכתא אמרי נהרדעי לטבילה אמר רבא לא אמרן אלא שאין בעלה עמה אבל בעלה עמה בעלה מחממה כי הא דברתיה דרב חסדא טבלה בגו תלתין יומין שלא בפני בעלה ואצטניאת ואמטוי לערסה בתריה דרבא לפומבדיתא [ט] אמר רב יהודה אמר שמואל [ו] עושין מדורה לחיה בשבת (בימות הגשמים) סבור מינה לחיה אין לחולה לא בימות הגשמים אין בימות החמה לא ([י] ולא היא לא שנא חיה ולא שנא חולה לא שנא בימות הגשמים ולא שנא בימות החמה מדאתמר) אמר רב חייא בר אבין אמר שמואל [ז] הקיז דם ונצטנן עושין לו מדורה אפי' בתקופת תמוז צלחו ליה תכתקא לשמואל צלחו ליה תכתקא דשאגא רב יהודה צלחו ליה פתורא דיונה לרבה צלחו ליה שרשיפא וא"ל אביי לרבה והא קעבר מר משום [א] בל תשחית [כ] א"ל בל תשחית דגופאי עדיף לי אמר רב יהודה אמר רב לעולם ימכור אדם קורות ביתו ויקח [ל] מנעלים לרגליו הקיז דם ואין לו מה יאכל ימכור מנעלים שברגליו ויספיק מהן צרכי סעודה מאי צרכי סעודה רב אמר בשר ושמואל אמר יין רב אמר בשר נפשא חלף נפשא ושמואל אמר יין סומקא חלף סומקא: (סימן שנמסר) [מ] שמואל ביומא דעביד מילתא עבדי ליה תבשילא דטחלי ר' יוחנן שתי עד דנפיק תיהיא מאוניה ורב נחמן שתי עד דקפי טחליה רב יוסף שתי עד דנפיק מריבדא דכוסילתא רבא מהדר אחמרא בר תלתא טרפי אמר להו רב נחמן בר יצחק לרבנן במטותא מיניכו ביומא דהקזה אמרו לביתייכו נחמן איקלע לגבן וכולהו ערומי אערומי אסירי בר מהאי ערמה דשרי מאן דעביד מילתא ולא אפשר ליה לישקול זוזא מכא וליזיל לשב חנותא עד דטעים שיעור רביעתא ואי לא ליכול שב תמרי אוכמתא ולישוף משחא בצידעיה וניגני בשמשא אבלט אשכחיה לשמואל דגני בשמשא א"ל חכימא דיהודאי בישא מי הוי טבא א"ל יומא דהקזה הוא ולא היא אלא איכא יומא דמעלי בה שמשא בכוליה שתא יומא דנפלה ביה תקופת [נ] תמוז וסבר לא איגלי ליה: (היקיל ברוח טעמא שהה סימן) רב ושמואל דאמרי תרוייהו כל המקיל בסעודת הקזת דם מקילין לו מזונותיו מן השמים ואומרים הוא על חייו לא חס אני אחוס עליו רב ושמואל דאמרי תרוייהו האי מאן דעביד מילתא לא ליתיב היכא דכריך זיקא דילמא שפי ליה אומנא ומוקים ליה ארביעתא ואתי זיקא ושאיף מיניה ואתי לידי סכנה שמואל הוה רגיל ועבד מילתא בביתא דשב לביניא ואריחא יומא חדא עבד וארגיש בנפשיה בדק וחסר חד אריחא רב ושמואל דאמרי תרוייהו האי מאן דעביד מילתא ליטעום מידי והדר ליפוק דאי לא טעים מידי אי פגע בשכבא יריקא אפיה אי פגע במאן דקטל נפשא מית אי פגע

בדבר

תוספות

רבא משמיה דרב יהודה אמר שבעה. לכאורה משמע דרבא לטעמיה דבפרק הדר (עירובין דף סח.) גבי ההוא ינוקא דאישתפוך חמימיה אמר להו רבא נשיילה לאימיה אם צריכה ניחיימו אגב אימיה דמסתמא ביום שמיני היה קודם מילה שהיה צריך חמין למולו דלאחר מילה מסוכן הוא ובלא אימיה ביום שמיני מחללין עליו שבת והיינו לאחר שבעה דנכנסה הקבר בעינן צריכה מיהו ללישנא דאמרי לה לרבא שלשים תיקשי למה צריכה ועוד דבקונטרס פי' התם ניחיימו אגב אימיה ע"י נכרי וכן פירש ר"ח לכך יש לפרש דאביי ורבא ואמרי לה מר אמר חדא ומר אמר חדא ולא פליגי וכולהו קיימו כנהרדעי [פ]:

מי

רש"י

לאחר טבילה בתשמיש והגוף מתחמם מן הגוף: מדורה. היסק גדול: הקיז דם. וכ"ש חולה: צלחו ליה תכתקא דשאגא. לא מצאו עצים מוכנים להיסק ביום הקזה וגוה ובקעו כסא של תדהר שהוא מעולה בדמים: פתורא דיונה. מין ארז הוא ורבינו הלוי אמר (א) בו"ש: [ס] רבא צלחו ליה שרשיפא. ספסל: ויקח מנעלים. שאין לך בזוי מן המהלך יחף בשוק: (מאי) צרכי סעודה. (צרכי) סעודת הקזה: ביומא דמלתא. דהקזה: דטחלי. טחול סומקא חלף סומקא: עד דנפיק תיהי. הריח: מאוניה. מאזניו מריחין היין: מריבדא דכוסילתא. נקבי כלי האומן שבבשרו פלימ"א: עד דקפי טחליה. טחול שלו לף ביין: בר תלתא טרפי. בן ג' שנים שטענה אמו משנקלט ג' עלין חדשין: לרבנן. לתלמידיו: אמרו נחמן איקלע לגבן. הרבו בסעודה כאילו אני סועד אצלכם: בר מהדיא ערמה. דמפרש ואזיל: ולא אפשר ליה. לקנות יין: לשקול זוזא מכא. זוז רע ופחות שאינו יוצא בהוצאה: ולייזיל לשב חנותא. ודרך הלוקחים לטועמו תחלה שיהא טוב ויטעום וכשיתן לו הזוז והחנווני ימצאנו רע ולא יקבלנו והוא ילך לחנות אחרת ויעשה כן: ואי לא. דאין לו זוז רע: ולישוף משחא בצידעיה. ברקתו והתמריס והשומן מחממין אותו: בישא מי הוה טבא. חום השמש שהוא קשה לאדם כלום מטיב לו: היכא דכריך זיקא. [ע] אינדרו"ן שיש בו חלונות והרוח נכנסת בהם נכרכת ומתגלגלת באינדרו"ן: דילמא שפי ליה אומנא. מריקו מדמו כמו השופה יין לחבירו (ב"מ דף ס.): ומוקי ליה ארביעתא. לא הניח בו דם אלא כדי חייו דהיינו רביעית והדר אתי ליה זיקא ושייף ליה מדם הנותר בגופו ומחסרו משיעורו ומסתכן: שב לביני ואריחא. עובי החומה ז' לבינים מוטלין לרחבן זה אצל זה דכל לבינה ג"ט ואריחא אריח חצי לבינה טפח ומחצה: ארגיש בנפשיה. הרגיש בעצמו שהוא נחלש: חסר חד אריחא. החומה היתה חסירה מעוביה אריח:

בדבר

רבינו חננאל

צריכה אני מחללין עליה את השבת אמרה איני צריכה אין מחללין עליה את השבת ומסקינן לה לשמעתא דא"ל מרימר לרבינא הלכתא כי הא דמר זוטרא ספק נפשות להקל והוצרכנו לדקדק מאימתי פתיחת הקבר כדי לחלל באותו העת את השבת לעשות צרכי החיה. ואמר אביי משתשב על המשבר. ואמר רב הונא בריה דרב יהושע משעה שהדם שותת ויורד כו' ודייקי מדלא אמר רב הונא עד שיתחיל הדם להיות שותת ש"מ קודם שתשב על המשבר קאמר וכאביי עבדינן (א) ולא מחללי שבתא אלא עד שיהא שותת. קדם שותת ויורד ותשב על המשבר אבל בהא דאמר אביי משום רב יהודה עד מתי פתיחת הקבר ג' ימים בלבד אין הלכה כמותו. ולא כרבא דאמר משמיה דרב יהודה שבעה. אלא קיי"ל כנהרדעא דאמרי חיה ג' ז' ושלשים. ג' בין אמרה צריכה אני בין אמרה איני צריכה מחללין עליה את השבת. ז' אמרה צריכה אני מחללין עליה את השבת אמרה איני צריכה אין מחללין עליה את השבת. סתמא עבדינן כמר זוטרא לקולא. שלשים אפילו אמרה צריכה אני אין מחללין עליה את השבת. אלא עושין לה ע"י ארמאי כדרב עולא בריה דרב עילאי דאמר כל צרכי הולד נעשין ע"י ארמאי בשבת וכדרב המנונא דאמר דבר שאין בו סכנה אומר לנכרי ועושה. חיה לא תטבול בתוך שלשים יום שמא תצטנן אמר רבא לא אמרן אלא שאין בעלה עמה. אבל בעלה [עמה בעלה] מחממה. אמר רב יהודה אמר שמואל עושין מדורות לחיה בשבת סבור מינה לחיה אין לחולה לא [בימות הגשמים אין] בימות החמה לא וכו' ומסקינן משמא דשמואל הקיז דם ונצטנן עושין לו מדורה ואפילו בתקופת תמוז. שמעינן מינה אפילו לחולה ואפילו בימות החמה. שמואל צלחו ליה תכתקא דשאגא. פי' שמואל הקיז דם ולא היה לו עצים מוכנים להדליק ולהתחמם בהן ובקעו לו שידה שהיו עציה עצי שאגא והן יקרים להודיע שאם יתמהמה עד שיביאו לו עצים יסתכן וכדתרגם ויבקע עצי העולה וצלח אעי דעלתא. רב יהודה צלחו ליה פתורא פי' שולחן העשוי מעצי יָנָס והן יקרים פי' יאבנוס. ורבה צלחו ליה שרשיפא והוא הדום לכסא וכולן טעם אחד. שאם לא ימהרו להתחמם יסתכנו

מסורת הש"ס

א) ג' רא"ש אמרה צריכה אני מחללין לא אמרה צריכה אין כו', ב) ג' רא"ש אמרה איני צריכה אין מחללין לא אמרה איני צריכה מחללין, ג) [יומא פג. פד: כתובות טו. ב"ק מד: ל. ב"ב נ: סנהדרין עט.], ד) בס"י הגירסא לא אמרה צריכה וכן לקמן, ה) [בילה כב.], ו) [בילה שם וכן בשאלתות פרש' שמות סי' לח איתא ואמר רב המנונא דבר שאין בו וכו'], ז) [שם ע"ש], ח) [עיין רש"י גיטין ח: ד"ה כדאמר רבא], ט) עירובין עט:, י) ס"א ז"א וה"ג לא איתמר אמר ר"ח כו', כ) [לקמן קמ:], ל) [עיין פסחים קיב.], מ) [חולין קיא.], נ) ס"א טבת, ס) כן גי' הערוך בערך שרפרף אולם הגאון מהרי"ף הגיה כאן שא"ל רבה, ע) אין זה בלעז כ"א לשון תלמוד' אכסדרא דבי רב כאינדרונא מעלית' מנחות לג:, פ) [ועי' תוס' בגיטין ח: ד"ה אע"ג].

הגהות הב"ח

(א) רש"י ד"ה פתורא דיונה וכו' בוי"ש. נ"ב עלי ברותים:

גליון הש"ס

גמ' משעה שתשב על המשבר. עיין פ"ו מ"ד דאהלות בר"ש:

תורה אור השלם

א) כִּי תָצוּר אֶל עִיר יָמִים רַבִּים לְהִלָּחֵם עָלֶיהָ לְתָפְשָׂהּ לֹא תַשְׁחִית אֶת עֵצָהּ לִנְדֹּחַ עָלָיו גַּרְזֶן כִּי מִמֶּנּוּ תֹאכֵל וְאֹתוֹ לֹא תִכְרֹת כִּי הָאָדָם עֵץ הַשָּׂדֶה לָבֹא מִפָּנֶיךָ בַּמָּצוֹר: [דברים כ, יט]

ליקוטי רש"י

שאגא. ס"פ בלע"ז [ר"ה כג. ועי' ב"ב פ:]. ריבדא דכוסילתא. פולטויר"ה דפלמוס"ה בלע"ז רידא ניקור כוסילתא, כלי אומן מקיז [כתובות לט:]. רידא פוינור"א בלע"ז כוסילתא שם כלי המקיז פלגמ"ל [סנהדרין צג:]. כלי אומן המקיז בכתפים רידא מכת הכלי ובלע"ז פיינד"א [ע"ז כז.]. אבלט. שם חכם נכרי היה [לקמן קנו:].

חשק שלמה על רבינו חננאל

א) נ"ל ולא מחללי שבתא עד שתהא הדם שותת ויורד ותשב על המשבר וכו'. וכ"כ הרי"ף כאן משמיה דרבוותא. ופשוט דכוונתו על דברי רבינו כאן:

מְחַלְּלִין עָלֶיהָ אֶת הַשַּׁבָּת – **we desecrate the Sabbath on her account.** ז׳ אָמְרָה צְרִיכָה אֲנִי – From the end of three until the end of seven, **if she says, "I need it,"** מְחַלְּלִין עָלֶיהָ אֶת הַשַּׁבָּת – **we desecrate the Sabbath on her account.** אָמְרָה לֹא צְרִיכָה אֲנִי – If **she says, "I do not need it,"** אֵין מְחַלְּלִין עָלֶיהָ אֶת הַשַּׁבָּת לִי – **we do not desecrate the Sabbath on her account.**[11] אֲפִילוּ אָמְרָה צְרִיכָה אֲנִי – From the end of seven until the end of **thirty, even if she says, "I need it,"** אֵין מְחַלְּלִין עָלֶיהָ אֶת הַשַּׁבָּת – **we do not desecrate the Sabbath on her account,** אֲבָל עוֹשִׂין עַל יְדֵי אַרְמַאי – **but we do it** for her on the Sabbath **through a gentile.**[12] כִּדְרַב עוּלָּא בְּרֵיהּ דְּרַב עִילַּאי – And this last ruling is **in accordance with** the ruling **of Rav Ulla the son of Rav Illai,** דְּאָמַר כָּל צָרְכֵי חוֹלֶה נַעֲשִׂין עַל יְדֵי אַרְמַאי בְּשַׁבָּת – **who says** that **all** things necessary to provide for **the needs of a sick person**[13] **may be done through a gentile on the Sabbath,** וּכְדְרַב הַמְנוּנָא – **and** it is also **in accordance with** the similar ruling **of Rav Hamnuna,** דְּאָמַר רַב הַמְנוּנָא – **for Rav Hamnuna said:** דָּבָר שֶׁאֵין בּוֹ סַכָּנָה אוֹמֵר לְנָכְרִי וְעוֹשֶׂה – In the case of **something** needed by a sick person, but **which does not entail a threat to life** if withheld from him, **one may say to a gentile that he should do** it for him on the Sabbath.[14]

Another ruling regarding a woman who has given birth:

אָמַר רַב יְהוּדָה אָמַר שְׁמוּאֵל – **Rav Yehudah said in the name of Shmuel:** לְחַיָּה שְׁלֹשִׁים יוֹם – **For a woman who has given birth,** there is a time limit of **thirty days.**

The Gemara inquires:

לְמַאי הִלְכְתָא – In regard **to what law** was this ruling said?[15]

The Gemara answers:

אָמְרֵי נְהַרְדְּעֵי לִטְבִילָה – **The Nehardeans say:** In regard **to immersion.** That is, a woman should not immerse herself in a *mikveh* for thirty days after childbirth, because she is then particularly sensitive to the cold.[16]

Rava qualifies this law:

אָמַר רָבָא – **Rava said:** לֹא אֲמָרָן אֶלָּא שֶׁאֵין בַּעְלָהּ עִמָּהּ – **We said** this law **only** in cases **where her husband is not with her** at home.[17] אֲבָל בַּעְלָהּ עִמָּהּ בַּעְלָהּ מְחַמְּמָהּ – **But if her husband is with her** at home, in which case she will have relations with him after immersion, then she may immerse without concern for the ill effects of the cold, because **her husband warms her.**[18]

The Gemara cites a supporting incident:

כִּי הָא דִּבְרַתֵּיהּ דְּרַב חִסְדָּא – As in **this** incident **involving the daughter of Rav Chisda,** טְבַלָה בְּגוֹ תְּלָתִין יוֹמִין שֶׁלֹּא בִּפְנֵי בַעְלָהּ – who **immersed herself within thirty days** of childbirth **when her husband was not present,** וְאִצְטְנִיאַת – **and she became chilled;** וְאַמְטוּי לְעַרְסָהּ בָּתְרֵיהּ דְּרָבָא לְפוּמְבְּדִיתָא – **whereupon they transported** her in **her sickbed in pursuit of** her husband **Rava** all the way **to Pumbedisa** so that she could be warmed by him.[19]

Another ruling by Rav Yehudah in the name of Shmuel regarding a woman after childbirth:

אָמַר רַב יְהוּדָה אָמַר שְׁמוּאֵל – **Rav Yehudah said in the name of Shmuel:** עוֹשִׂין מְדוּרָה לְחַיָּה בְּשַׁבָּת (בימות הגשמים) – **We may make** a large **fire on the Sabbath to** warm **a woman who has given birth.**[20]

The Gemara comments:

סְבוּר מִינָּהּ – **They understood from [this ruling]** לְחַיָּה אֵין לְחוֹלֶה לֹא – that **for a woman who has given birth – yes,** we may kindle a fire on the Sabbath as a matter of course; but **for a sick person – no,** we may not kindle it as a matter of course.[21] בִּימוֹת הַגְּשָׁמִים אֵין בִּימוֹת הַחַמָּה לֹא – They also understood from this ruling that **during the winter**[22] **– yes,** we may kindle a fire

NOTES

11. But if she says nothing, then we do desecrate the Sabbath on her account [as if she said that she does need it] (*Rosh*).

12. Although the Rabbis forbade one to instruct a gentile to do *melachah* for a Jew on the Sabbath (see Mishnah above, 121a; Gemara below, 150a), the Rabbis allowed doing so for the needs of a person who is bedridden or systemically ill even if his life is not in danger (see *Orach Chaim* 328:17).

13. Who is not in danger, but bedridden or systemically ill (see preceding note).

14. If it does entail a threat to life, however, then the Jew himself does the necessary *melachah* (*Rashi*).

Some maintain that Rav Hamnuna refers to a critically ill person, and he distinguishes between the person's critical needs (for which *melachah* is done through a Jew) and his non-critical needs (for which *melachah* is done by a gentile). Others, however, maintain that Rav Hamnuna refers to a person who is not critically ill. In the case of a critically ill person, however, *melachah* is done by a Jew to provide even his non-critical needs (see *Rambam, Hil. Shabbos* 2:14, with *Raavad, Maggid Mishneh* and *Kesef Mishneh; Beur Halachah* to 328:4 ד״ה כל שרגילים; see above, 128b end of note 52). [An issue that hinges on this dispute is the meaning of Rav Hamnuna's expression "something which does not entail a threat to life." Does he mean that the *illness* is not critical, or that the illness is critical but the *need* is not?]

15. This statement cannot have meant, as the previous one did, that until thirty days *melachah* may be done for her through a gentile, for if so, he would have addressed the laws regarding the first two stages as well – until three days and until seven (*Rashba;* see *Chasam Sofer* [*Mechon Chasam Sofer* ed.]).

16. [The *mikvaos* in those days were usually situated in caves or other cold places, and were seldom heated.]

17. So that she will not have relations with him after immersion. Rather, she wishes to immerse herself in order to prepare or eat *tohoros* (*Rashi*).

18. During relations, one body is warmed by the other (*Rashi*).

19. [The daughter of Rav Chisda was Rava's wife; see *Yevamos* 34b.] See *Tosafos Niddah* 15b ד״ה אפילו who record that Rava's wife was indeed healed from her chill by the warmth of her husband.

20. Since her life is endangered by the cold, we must desecrate the Sabbath and kindle a fire to warm her.

Some Rishonim explain that Shmuel refers here to a woman who has given birth within the past thirty days. Although a woman who has given birth is generally not considered to be in danger after seven days (as taught by the Nehardeans above), Shmuel teaches us here that with regard to the cold a woman who has given birth is considered to be endangered for thirty days. Thus, whereas all her other *melachah* needs are done on the Sabbath through a gentile once seven days have elapsed, her warming needs are done on the Sabbath through a Jew until thirty days have elapsed (see *Maggid Mishneh* to *Hil. Shabbos* 2:14). *Beur Halachah* (to 330:6 ד״ה כל שלשים), however, demonstrates that many other Rishonim understand Shmuel here as referring specifically to a woman within three or seven days of having given birth. [And Shmuel is teaching that adequate heat is considered critical for her during this time (see, however, *Aruch HaShulchan* 330:9).]

21. According to those who interpret Shmuel's ruling as referring to a woman within *thirty* days of childbirth (the stage at which she is not considered to be in danger – except with respect to cold, according to their interpretation), the parallel case of a "sick person" refers to one who is *not* critically ill. Thus, whereas the non-critical woman who has given birth is considered to be in danger with regard to cold, the non-critical sick person is not considered to be in danger at all – even with regard to cold.

According to those who interpret Shmuel's ruling as referring to a woman within three or seven days of childbirth (a stage at which she is considered to be in danger), however, the parallel case of a "sick person" refers to one who *is* critically ill. And the present assumption is that a critically ill person (with the exception of a woman who has given birth) is not considered endangered with regard to cold [or with regard to the need for fire, at any rate, since his need for warmth can be provided for with warm clothing] (see *Maggid Mishneh* and *Beur Halachah* loc. cit.).

22. [Literally: during the days of rain. In countries with a Mediterranean climate, the winter is the rainy season.]

צריכה אני. לחילול: **בין שאמרה אין צריכה אני.** וחברותיה אומרות שהיא צריכה מחללין: **באגפיה.** בזרועותיה שאינה יכולה להלך: **חיה ג' ימים וז' ימים ול' יום.** הוזכרו כה לחילוק הלכות חילול שבת ל' מז' עד השלמת ל' וכן ז' מג' עד השלמת ז': **כל צרכי חולה.** והא חיה עד ל' יום סתמא חולה היא: **דבר שאין בו סכנה.** חולה שאם לא יעשו לו רפואה זו אין מסוכן למות ומ"מ צריך הוא לה: **אומר לארמאי ועושה.** אבל דבר שיש בו סכנה ישראל עצמו עושה לו: **לטבילה.** עד ל' יום לא תטבול מפני הצינה: **שאין בעלה עמה.** והיא טובלת לטהרות: **בעלה מחממה.** לאחר טבילה בתשמיש והגוף מתחמם מן הגוף: **מדורה.** היסק גדול: **הקיז דם.** וכ"ש חולה: **צלחו ליה תכתקא דשאגא.** לא מצאו עצים מוכנים להיסק ביום הקזה ולוה ובקעו כסא של תדהר שהוא מעולה בדמים: **פתורא דיונה.** מין ארז הוא ורבינו הלוי אמר (א) בוי"ש: ס) **רבא צלחו ליה שרשיפא.** ספסל: **ויקח מנעלים.** שאין לך בזוי מן המהלך יחף בשוק: (**מאי**) **צרכי סעודה.** (צרכי) סעודת הקזה: **ביומא דמלתא.** דהקזה: **דטחלי.** טחול סומקא חלף סומקא: **עד דנפיק תיהי.** הריח: **מאוניה.** מאזניו מריחין היין: **מריבדא דכוסילתא.** נקבי כלי האומן שבבשרו פלימ"א: **עד דקפי טחליה.** טחול שלו צף ביין: **בר תלתא טרפי.** בן ג' שנים שטענה אמו משנקלט ג' עלין חדשין: **לרבנן.** לתלמידיו: **אמרו נחמן איקלע לגבן.** הרבו בסעודה כאילו אני סועד אצלכם: **בר מהאי ערמה.** דמפרש ואזיל: **ולא אפשר ליה.** לקנות יין: **לשקול זוזא מכא.** זוז רע ופחות שאינו יוצא בהוצאה: **וליזיל לשב חנותא.** ודרך הלוקחים לטועמו תחלה שיהא טוב ויטעום וכשיתן לו הזוז והחנווני ימצאנו רע ולא יקבלנו והוא ילך לחנות אחרת ויעשה כן: **ואי לא.** דאין לו זוז רע: **ולישוף משחא בצידעיה.** ברקתו והתמרים והשומן מחממין אותו: **בישא מי הוה טבא.** חום השמש שהוא קשה לאדם כלום מטיב לו: **היכא דכריך זיקא.** ע) אינדרו"ן שיש בו חלונות והרוח נכנסת בהם נכרכת ומתגלגלת באינדרו"ן: **דילמא שפי ליה אומנא.** מריקו מדמו כמו השופה יין לחבירו (ב"מ דף ס.): **ומוקי ליה ארביעתא.** לא הניח בו דם אלא כדי חייו דהיינו רביעית והדר אתי ליה זיקא ושייף ליה מדם הנותר בגופו ומחסרו משיעורו ומסתכן: **שב לביני ואריחא.** עובי החומה ז' לבינים מוטלין לרחבן זה אצל זה דכל לבינה ג"ט ואריחא אריח חצי לבינה טפח ומחצה: **ארגיש בנפשיה.** הרגיש בעצמו שהוא נחלש: **חסר חד אריחא.** החומה היתה חסירה מעוביה אריח: בדבר

רבא משמיה דרב יהודה אמר שבעה. לכאורה משמע דרבא לטעמיה דבפרק הדר (עירובין דף סח.) גבי ההוא ינוקא דאישתפוך חמימיה אמר להו רבא נישיילה לאימיה אם צריכה ניחיימו אגב אימיה דמסתמא ביום שמיני היה קודם מילה שהיה צריך חמין למולו דלאחר מילה מסוכן הוא ובלא אימיה ביום שמיני מחללין עליו שבת והיינו לאחר שבעה דבנסתם הקבר בעינן צריכה מיהו ללישנא דאמרי לה לרבא שלשים תיקשי למה צריכה ועוד דבקונטרס פי' התם ניחיימו אגב אימיה ע"י נכרי וכן פירש ר"ח לכך יש לפרש דאביי ורבא ואמרי לה מר אמר חדא ומר אמר חדא ולא פליגי וכולהו קיימו כנהרדעי ס): מי

צריכה אני בין לא אמרה צריכה אני אין מחללין עליה את השבת רב אשי מתני הכי מר זוטרא מתני הכי אמר רב יהודה אמר שמואל חיה כל זמן שהקבר פתוח בין אמרה צריכה אני ובין אמרה אין צריכה אני מחללין עליה את השבת נסתם הקבר אמרה צריכה אני מחללין עליה את השבת לא אמרה צריכה אני אין מחללין עליה את השבת א"ל רבינא למרימר מר זוטרא מתני לקולא ורב אשי מתני לחומרא הלכתא כמאן א"ל הלכה כמר זוטרא ספק נפשות להקל מאימתי פתיחת הקבר אמר אביי משעה שתשב על המשבר רב הונא בריה דרב יהושע אמר משעה שהדם שותת ויורד ואמרי לה משעה שחברותיה נושאות אותה באגפיה עד מתי פתיחת הקבר אמר אביי שלשה ימים רבא אמר משמיה דרב יהודה שבעה ואמרי לה שלשים אמרי נהרדעי חיה ג' ז' ול' ג' בין אמרה צריכה אני ובין אמרה לא צריכה אני מחללין עליה את השבת ז' אמרה צריכה אני מחללין עליה את השבת אמרה לא צריכה אני אין מחללין עליה את השבת ל' אפי' אמרה צריכה אני אין מחללין עליה את השבת אבל עושין ע"י ארמאי כדרב עולא בריה דרב עילאי דאמר כל צרכי חולה נעשין ע"י ארמאי בשבת וכדרב המנונא דאמר רב המנונא דבר שאין בו סכנה אומר לנכרי ועושה אמר רב יהודה אמר שמואל לחיה ל' יום למאי הלכתא אמרי נהרדעי לטבילה אמר רבא לא אמרן אלא שאין בעלה עמה אבל בעלה עמה בעלה מחממה כי הא דברתיה דרב חסדא טבלה בגו תלתין יומין שלא בפני בעלה ואצטניאת ואמטוי לערסה בתריה דרבא לפומבדיתא אמר רב יהודה אמר שמואל עושין מדורה לחיה בשבת (בימות הגשמים) סבור מינה לחיה אין לחולה לא בימות הגשמים אין בימות החמה לא (ולא היא ל"ש חיה ול"ש חולה ל"ש בימות הגשמים ול"ש בימות החמה מדאתמר) אמר רב חייא בר אבין אמר שמואל הקיז דם ונצטנן עושין לו מדורה אפי' בתקופת תמוז שמואל צלחו ליה תכתקא דשאגא רב יהודה צלחו ליה פתורא דיונה רבה צלחו ליה שרשיפא וא"ל אביי לרבה והא קעבר מר משום א בל תשחית א"ל בל תשחית דגופאי עדיף לי אמר רב יהודה אמר רב לעולם ימכור אדם קורות ביתו ויקח מנעלים לרגליו הקיז דם ואין לו מה יאכל ימכור מנעלים שברגליו ויספיק מהן צרכי סעודה מאי צרכי סעודה רב אמר בשר ושמואל אמר יין רב אמר בשר נפשא חלף נפשא ושמואל אמר יין סומקא חלף סומקא: (סימן שנמסר) שמואל ביומא דעבד מילתא עבדי ליה תבשילא דטחלי ר' יוחנן שתי עד דנפיק תיהיא מאוניה ורב נחמן שתי עד דקפי טחליה רב יוסף שתי עד דנפיק מריבדא דכוסילתא רבא מהדר אחמרא בר תלתא טרפי אמר להו רב נחמן בר יצחק לרבנן במטותא מינייכו ביומא דהקזה אמרו לביתייכו נחמן אקלע לגבן וכולהו ארעומי אסירי בר מהאי ערמה דשרי מאן דעביד מילתא ולא אפשר ליה לישקול זוזא מכא וליזיל לשב חנותא עד דטעים שיעור רביעתא ואי לא ליכול שב תמרי אוכמתא ולישוף מישחא בצידעיה וניגני בשמשא אבלט אשכחיה לשמואל דגני בשמשא א"ל חכימא דיהודאי בישא מי הוי טבא א"ל יומא דהקזה הוא ולא היא אלא איכא יומא דמעלי בה שמשא בכולה שתא יומא דנפלה ביה תקופת י) תמוז וסבר לא איגלי ליה: (היקיל ברוח טעמא שהה סימן) רב ושמואל דאמרי תרוייהו כל המקיל בסעודת הקזת דם מקילין לו מזונותיו מן השמים ואומרים הוא על חייו לא חס אני אחוס עליו רב ושמואל דאמרי תרוייהו האי מאן דעביד מילתא לא ליתיב היכא דכריך זיקא דילמא שפי ליה אומנא ומוקים ליה ארביעתא ואתי זיקא ושאיף מיניה ואתי לידי סכנה שמואל הוה רגיל ועבד מילתא בביתא דשב לביניא ואריחא יומא חדא עבד וארגיש בנפשיה בדק וחסר חד אריחא רב ושמואל דאמרי תרוייהו האי מאן דעביד מילתא ליטעום מידי והדר ליפוק דאי לא טעים מידי אי פגע בשבבא ירקא אפיה אי פגע במאן דקטל נפשא מית אי פגע בדבר

עין משפט נר מצוה

לג א ב ג מיי' פ"ב מהל' שבת הלכה יג סמג לאוין סה טוש"ע א"ח סימן של סעיף ג:
לד ד מיי' שם טוש"ע שם ס"ד:
לה ה מיי' שם הלכה י סמג שם טוש"ע א"ח סי' שכ סעיף ח:
לו ו מיי' שם הלכה יד סמג שם טוש"ע א"ח סימן של סעיף ו:
לז ז מיי' וסמג שם טוש"ע א"ח סימן שכח סעיף יח:

רבינו חננאל

צריכה אני מחללין עליה את השבת אמרה איני צריכה אין מחללין עליה את השבת ומסקינן לה לשמעתא דא"ל מרימר לרבינא הלכתא כי הא דמר זוטרא ספק נפשות להקל והוצרכנו לדקדק מאימתי פתיחת הקבר כדי לחלל באותו העת את השבת לעשות צרכי החיה. ואמר אביי משתשב על המשבר. ואמר רב הונא בריה דרב יהושע משעה שהדם שותת ויורד כו' ודייקי מדלא אמר רב הונא עד שיתחיל הדם להיות שותת ש"מ קודם שתשב על המשבר קאמר וכאביי עבדינן א) ולא מחללי שבתא אלא עד שיהא שותת. קדם שותת ויורד ותשב על המשבר אבל בהא דאמר אביי משום רב יהודה עד מתי פתיחת הקבר ג' ימים בלבד אין הלכה כמותו. ולא כרבא דאמר משמיה דרב יהודה שבעה. אלא קיי"ל כנהרדעא דאמרי חיה ג' ז' ושלשים. ג' בין אמרה צריכה אני בין אמרה איני צריכה מחללין עליה את השבת. ז' אמרה צריכה אני מחללין עליה את השבת אמרה איני צריכה אין מחללין עליה את השבת. סתמא עבדינן כמר זוטרא לקולא. שלשים אפילו אמרה צריכה אני אין מחללין עליה את השבת. אלא עושין לה ע"י ארמאי כדרב עולא בריה דרב עילאי דאמר כל צרכי הולד נעשין ע"י ארמאי בשבת וכדרב המנונא דאמר דבר שאין בו סכנה אומר לנכרי ועושה. חיה לא תטבול בתוך שלשים יום שמא תצטנן אמר רבא לא אמרן אלא שאין בעלה עמה. אבל בעלה [עמה בעלה] מחממה. אמר רב יהודה אמר שמואל עושין מדורות לחיה בשבת סבור מינה לחיה אין לחולה לא [בימות הגשמים אין] בימות החמה לא וכו' ומסקינן משמא דשמואל הקיז דם ונצטנן עושין לו מדורה ואפילו בתקופת תמוז. שמעינן מינה אפילו לחולה ואפילו בימות החמה. שמואל צלחו ליה תכתקא דשאגא. פי' שמואל הקיז דם ולא היה לו עצים מוכנים להדליק ולהתחמם בהן ובקעו לו שידה שהיו עציה עצי שאגא והן יקרים להודיע שאם יתחמם עד שיביאו לו עצים יסתכן וכדתרגם ויבקע עצי העולה וצלח אעי דעלתא. רב יהודה צלחו ליה פתורא פי' שולחן העשוי מעצי יַנֵס והן יקרים פי' יאבנוס. ורבה צלחו ליה שרשיפא והוא הדום לכסא וכולן טעם אחד. שאם לא ימהרו להתחמם יסתכנו

מסורת הש"ס

א) ג' רא"ש אמרה צריכה אני מחללין לא אמרה צריכה אין כו', ב) ג' רא"ש אמרה איני צריכה אין מחללין לא אמרה איני צריכה מחללין, ג) [יומא פג. פד: כתובות טו. ב"ק מד: ל. ב"ב נ: סנהדרין עט.], ד) בס"י הגירסא לא אמרה צריכה וכן לקמן, ה) [נילה כג.], ו) [בנילה שם וכן בשאלתות פרש' שמות סי' לט איתא ואמר רב המנונא דבר שאין בו וכו'], ז) [שם ע"ש], ח) [עיין רש"י גיטין ח: ד"ה כדאמר רבא], ט) עירובין עט., י) פ"א ז"א וה"ג לא איתמר אמר ר"ח כו', כ) [לקמן קמ:], ל) [עיין פסחים קיב.], מ) [חולין קיא.], נ) פ"א טבת, ס) כן ג' הערוך בערך שרפרף אולם הגאון מהרי"ף הגיה כאן שצ"ל רבה, ע) אין זה בלעז כ"א לשון תלמוד' אכסדרא דבי רב כאינדרונא מעלית' מנחות לג:, פ) [וע"ע תוס' בגיטין ח: ד"ה אע"ג].

הגהות הב"ח

(א) רש"י ד"ה פתורא דיונה וכו' בוי"ש. נ"ב עצי ברושים:

גליון הש"ס

גמ' משעה שתשב על המשבר. עיין פ"ז מ"ד דאהלות בר"ש:

תורה אור השלם

א) כִּי תָצוּר אֶל עִיר יָמִים רַבִּים לְהִלָּחֵם עָלֶיהָ לְתָפְשָׂהּ לֹא תַשְׁחִית אֶת עֵצָהּ לִנְדֹּחַ עָלָיו גַּרְזֶן כִּי מִמֶּנּוּ תֹאכֵל וְאֹתוֹ לֹא תִכְרֹת כִּי הָאָדָם עֵץ הַשָּׂדֶה לָבֹא מִפָּנֶיךָ בַּמָּצוֹר: [דברים כ, יט]

ליקוטי רש"י

שאגא. ש"פ בלע"ז [ר"ה כג. ועי' ב"ב פ:]. **ריבדא דכוסילתא.** פוטוויי"א דפלמות"ה בלע"ז רידא ניקור כוסילתא, כלי אומן מקיז [כתובות לט:]. רידא פוניי"א בלע"ז כוסילתא שם כלי המקיז פלנמא"ל [סנהדרין צג:]. כלי אומן המקיז בכתפים רידא מכת הכלי ובלע"ז פיינדר"א [ע"ז כז.]. **אבלט.** שם חכם נכרי היה [לקמן קנו:].

חשק שלמה על רבינו חננאל

א) נ"ל ולא מחללי שבתא עד שתהא הדם שותת ויורד ותשב על המשבר וכו'. וכ"כ הרי"ף כאן משמיה דרבוותא. ופשוט דכוונתו על דברי רבינו כאן:

for her; but **during the summer**[23] – **no,** we may not kindle it, since it is not a critical need for her during the summer. (**וְלָא הִיא – But it is not so,** i.e. both these assumptions are incorrect. **לָא שְׁנָא חַיָּה וְלָא שְׁנָא חוֹלֶה – There is no difference** in this matter whether the patient is **a woman who has given birth or a** different **sick person. לָא שְׁנָא בִּימוֹת הַגְּשָׁמִים וְלָא שְׁנָא בִּימוֹת הַחַמָּה – And there is no difference** whether it is **during the winter or during the summer.** At all times and for other sick people as well [not only women who have given birth], the kindling is permitted. **מִדְּאִתְּמַר – For this can be seen from that which was stated:**)[24] **אָמַר רַב חִיָּיא בַּר אָבִין אָמַר שְׁמוּאֵל – Rav Chiya bar Avin said in the name of Shmuel: הִקִּיז דָּם וְנִצְטַנֵּן – If one let blood and became chilled, עוֹשִׂין לוֹ מְדוּרָה – we make for him a** large **fire** even on the Sabbath,[25] **אֲפִילּוּ בִּתְקוּפַת תַּמּוּז – even at the time of the Tammuz** (summer) **solstice,** when the weather is hot.[26]

Having introduced the matter of kindling a fire to warm someone who has let blood, the Gemara elaborates on this matter: **שְׁמוּאֵל צַלְחוּ לֵיהּ תַּכְתְּקָא דְּשָׁאגָא** – On one occasion, **Shmuel** let blood and, on his instructions, **they chopped up for him a chair** made **of** expensive ***shaga*-wood,**[27] to fuel a fire to warm him, since no other firewood could be found.

A similar incident:

רַב יְהוּדָה צַלְחוּ לֵיהּ פְּתוֹרָא דְּיַוְנָה – Similarly, on one occasion **Rav Yehudah** let blood and **they chopped up for him a table** made **of *yavnah*-wood**[28] to fuel a fire to warm him.

A third such incident:

לְרַבָּה צַלְחוּ לֵיהּ שַׁרְשִׁיפָא – For Rabbah, after he had let blood, **they chopped up a footstool,** to fuel a fire, **וְאָמַר לֵיהּ אַבַּיֵי לְרַבָּה – whereupon Abaye said to Rabbah: וְהָא קָעָבַר מָר מִשּׁוּם בַּל תַּשְׁחִית – But master** (by instructing them to chop up this stool) **is transgressing the prohibition "do not destroy"** useful items![29] **אָמַר לֵיהּ – [Rabbah] answered him: בַּל תַּשְׁחִית דְּגוּפַאי עָדִיף לִי** – The prohibition **"do not destroy" with respect to my body is more important for me,** i.e. I am required to ruin the piece of furniture in order to forestall a ruination of my health.[30]

A similar ruling concerning the importance of proper care following bloodletting:

אָמַר רַב יְהוּדָה אָמַר רַב – Rav Yehudah said in the name of Rav: לְעוֹלָם יִמְכּוֹר אָדָם קוֹרוֹת בֵּיתוֹ וְיִקַּח מִנְעָלִים לְרַגְלָיו – One should always sell even **the beams of his house,** if necessary, **to buy shoes for his feet.**[31] **הִקִּיז דָּם וְאֵין לוֹ מַה יֹּאכַל** – Nevertheless, **if one let blood and has nothing to eat** afterwards, **יִמְכּוֹר מִנְעָלִים שֶׁבְּרַגְלָיו וְיַסְפִּיק מֵהֶן צָרְכֵי סְעוּדָה – he should sell** even **the shoes that are on his feet and provide himself from** the money he receives for **them with the requirements of a meal,** for it is essential that one obtain the proper nourishment after bloodletting.

The Gemara explains:

מַאי צָרְכֵי סְעוּדָה – What are "the requirements of a meal" that are essential after bloodletting? **רַב אָמַר בָּשָׂר – Rav says, "Meat," וּשְׁמוּאֵל אָמַר יַיִן** – whereas **Shmuel says, "Wine."**

The Gemara explains their respective reasonings:

רַב אָמַר בָּשָׂר נַפְשָׁא חֲלַף נַפְשָׁא – Rav say that **meat** is essential because he reasons that one must ingest **"life"** (i.e. meat) **in place of "life"** (i.e. the blood that was drained from him).[32] **וּשְׁמוּאֵל אָמַר יַיִן סוּמָּקָא חֲלַף סוּמָּקָא – But Shmuel says** that [red] **wine** is essential, because one must ingest **"red"** (wine) **in place of "red"** (blood).

The Gemara's presentation of various other incidents highlighting the importance of proper nutrition following bloodletting is prefaced by a mnemonic for the names of the Amoraim involved:

(**סִימָן שֶׁנִּמְסַר – A mnemonic: SHeNiMSaR.**[33]) **שְׁמוּאֵל בְּיוֹמָא דְּעָבֵד מִילְתָא – On the day that Shmuel underwent the procedure** of bloodletting, **עָבְדֵי לֵיהּ תַּבְשִׁילָא דְּטַחְלֵי – they made for him a cooked dish** made **of spleen.**[34] **רַבִּי יוֹחָנָן שָׁתֵי עַד דְּנָפֵיק תֵּיהְיָא מֵאוּנֵּיהּ** – After bloodletting, **R' Yochanan would drink** wine **until the scent came out of his ears. וְרַב נַחְמָן שָׁתֵי עַד דְּקָפֵי טַחְלֵיהּ – And Rav Nachman would drink** wine after blood-letting **until his spleen floated in wine. רַב יוֹסֵף שָׁתֵי עַד דְּנָפֵיק מֵרִיבְדָּא דְּכוּסִילְתָא – Rav Yosef would drink** wine after blood-letting **until [the scent] came out from the puncture** in the vein **made by the** bloodletter's **lancet. רָבָא מְהַדֵּר אַחַמְרָא בַּר תְּלָתָא טַרְפֵי – Rava**

NOTES

23. [Literally: during the days of the sun.]

24. Some texts omit the passage in parenthesis (and substitute simply the word אִיתְּמַר, *it was said*). The variant reading is also the one found in our versions of the parallel text in *Eruvin* 79b. See below, note 26.

25. See however *Maharsha, Chidushei Aggados.*

26. If a fire may be kindled [on the Sabbath] — even during the summer — for a person who has let blood and is chilled, then certainly it may be done for a person who is truly ill [and is chilled] (*Rashi;* see *Bach* 330 ד"ה ועושין). Thus, we see that when Shmuel ruled above that we may kindle a fire on the Sabbath for a woman who has given birth, he was referring not only to a woman who has given birth, but to other sick people as well [see note 21, regarding which sick people are meant], and not only to the winter but even to the summer — unlike what "they understood" from his ruling.

[This conclusion (that both inferences originally made from Shmuel's ruling are rejected) is explicit according to the reading found in our texts (see note 24). *Rambam* (*Hil. Shabbos* 2:14), however, apparently did not have this reading, and he explains that the distinction between a woman who has given birth and other sick people is never rejected. Thus, he rules that one may kindle a fire for a woman who has given birth — even during the summer — but *not* for a sick person (see *Maggid Mishneh* ad loc.).]

27. *Shaga* is the Aramaic of *tidhar* [mentioned in *Isaiah* 41:19] (*Rashi*). It is a type of *erez* tree (see *Bava Basra* 80b).

28. Another type of *erez* tree (see *Rashi*).

29. In the passage concerning the laws of warfare, the Torah states (*Deuteronomy* 20:19): כִּי־תָצוּר אֶל־עִיר יָמִים רַבִּים לְהִלָּחֵם עָלֶיהָ לְתָפְשָׂהּ לֹא־תַשְׁחִית אֶת־עֵצָהּ, *When you besiege a city for many days to wage battle against it to take it, you shall not destroy its trees.* As evident from this Gemara, this prohibition "do not destroy" applies even in non-warfare situations, and not only to trees but to all useful items (see *Rambam, Hil. Melachim* 6:8,10 with *Kesef Mishneh*).

30. [Apparently, Abaye was not aware initially that being chilled after bloodletting is dangerous. See, however, *Maharsha, Chidushei Aggados,* and *Hagahos R' Elazar Moshe Horowitz;* see also *Yad David (Basra).*]

31. For there is nothing more degrading than one who walks barefoot in public (*Rashi;* cf. *Maharsha*). Thus, one should rather be without a roof over his head than without shoes.

32. "Blood" is referred to here as "life," following the Scriptural precedent found in *Leviticus* 17:11,14 and *Deuteronomy* 12:23 (see *Maharsha, Chidushei Aggados*). The blood lost during bloodletting must be replenished with meat (i.e. red meat — see *Nedarim* 54b) [which has a high blood content (from a chemical, though not necessarily legal, standpoint)].

[The Gemara's expression "life in place of life" (instead of "blood in place of blood") is borrowed from *Exodus* 21:23 (also *Leviticus* 24:18); see also *Targum Onkelos* ad loc.]

33. [SHeNiMSaR: **SH=Sh**muel; **N**=R' YochaNan; **M**=Rav NachMan; **S**=Rav YoSef; **R=R**ava.]

34. [In keeping with Shmuel's insistence above on] "red in place of red" [the spleen is particularly red] (see *Rashi*).

צריכה אני. לחילול: בין שאמרה אין צריכה אני. וחברותיה אומרות שהיא צריכה מחללין: באגפיה. בזרועותיה שאינה יכולה להלך: חיה ג' ימים וז' ימים ול' יום. הוזכרו כאן לחילוק הלכות חילול שבת ל' מז' עד השלמת ל' וכן ז' מג' עד השלמת ז': כל צרכי חולה. והא חיה עד ל' יום סתמא חולה היא: דבר שאין בו סכנה. חולה שאם לא יעשו לו רפואה זו אין מסוכן למות ומ"מ צריך הוא לה: אומר לארמאי ועושה. אבל דבר שיש בו סכנה ישראל עצמו עושה לו: לטבילה. עד ל' יום לא תטבול מפני הצינה: שאין בעלה עמה. והיא טובלת לטהרות: בעלה מחממה. לאחר טבילה בתשמיש והגוף מתחמם מן הגוף: מדורה. היסק גדול: הקיז דם. וכ"ש חולה: צלחו ליה תכתקא דשאגא. לא מצאו עצים מוכנים להיסק ביום הקזה וצוה ובקעו כסא של תדהר שהוא מעולה בדמים: פתורא דיונה. מין ארז הוא ורבינו הלוי אמר (א) בור"ש: [פ] רבא צלחו ליה שרשיפא. ספסל: ויקח מנעלים. שאין לך בזוי מן המהלך יחף בשוק: (מאי) צרכי סעודה. (צרכי) סעודת הקזה: ביומא דמלתא. דהקזה: דטחלי. טחול סומקא חלף סומקא: עד דנפיק תיהי. הריח: מאוניה. מאזניו מריקין היין: מריבדא דכוסילתא. נקבי כלי האומן שבבשרו פלימ"א: עד דקפי טחליה. טחול שלו צף ביין: בר תלתא טרפי. בן ג' שנים שטענה אמו משנקלט ג' עלין חדשין: לרבנן. לתלמידיו: אמרו נחמן איקלע לגבן. הרבו בסעודה כאילו אני סועד אצלכם: בר מהאי ערמה. דמפרש ואזיל: ולא אפשר ליה. לקנות יין: לישקול זוזא מכא. זוז רע ופחות שאינו יוצא בהוצאה: וליזיל לשב חנותא. ודרך הלוקחים לטועמו תחלה שיהא טוב ויטעום וכשיתן לו הזוז והחנווני ימצאנו רע ולא יקבלנו והוא ילך לחנות אחרת ויעשה כן: ואי לא. דאין לו זוז רע: ולישוף משחא בצידעיה. ברקתו והתמרים והשומן מחממין אותו: בישא מי הוה טבא. חום השמש שהוא קשה לאדם כלום מטיב לו: היכא דכריך זיקא. [ע] אינדרו"ן שיש בו חלונות והרוח נכנסת בהם נכרכת ומתגלגלת באינדרו"ן: דילמא שפי ליה אומנא. מריקו מדמו כמו השופה יין לחבירו (ב"מ דף ס.): ומוקי ליה ארביעתא. לא הניח בו דם אלא כדי חייו דהיינו רביעית והדר אתי ליה זיקא ושייף ליה מדם הנותר בגופו ומחסרו משיעורו ומסתכן: שב לביני ואריחא. עובי החומה ז' לבינים מוטלין לרחבן זה אצל זה דכל לבינה ג"ט ואריחא אריח חצי לבינה טפח ומחצה: ארגיש בנפשיה. הרגיש בעצמו שהוא נחלש: חסר חד אריחא. החומה היתה חסירה מעוביה אריח: בדבר

[א] צריכה אני בין לא אמרה צריכה אני אין מחללין עליה את השבת רב אשי מתני הכי מר זוטרא מתני הכי אמר רב יהודה אמר שמואל חיה כל זמן שהקבר פתוח בין אמרה צריכה אני ובין אמרה אין צריכה אני מחללין עליה את השבת נסתם הקבר אמרה [ב] צריכה אני מחללין עליה את השבת לא אמרה צריכה אני אין מחללין עליה את השבת א"ל רבינא למרימר מר זוטרא מתני לקולא ורב אשי מתני לחומרא הלכתא כמאן א"ל הלכה כמר זוטרא [ג] ספק נפשות להקל מאימתי פתיחת הקבר אמר אביי [*] משעה שתשב על המשבר רב הונא בריה דרב יהושע אמר [ג] משעה שהדם שותת ויורד ואמרי לה [ג] משעה שחברותיה נושאות אותה באגפיה עד מתי פתיחת הקבר אמר אביי שלשה ימים רבא אמר משמיה דרב יהודה שבעה ואמרי לה שלשים אמרי נהרדעי [ד] חיה ג' ז' ול' ג' בין אמרה צריכה אני ובין [ה] אמרה לא צריכה אני מחללין עליה את השבת ז' אמרה צריכה אני מחללין עליה את השבת אמרה לא צריכה אני אין מחללין עליה את השבת ל' אפי' אמרה צריכה אני אין מחללין עליה את השבת אבל עושין ע"י ארמאי [ו] כדרב עולא בריה דרב עילאי דאמר כל צרכי חולה נעשין ע"י ארמאי בשבת [ז] וכדרב המנונא דאמר רב המנונא [ח] דבר שאין בו סכנה אומר לנכרי ועושה אמר רב יהודה אמר שמואל לחיה ל' יום למאי הלכתא אמרי נהרדעי לטבילה אמר רבא לא אמרן אלא שאין בעלה עמה אבל בעלה עמה בעלה מחממה כי הא דברתיה דרב חסדא טבלה בגו תלתין יומין שלא בפני בעלה ואצטניאת ואמטוי לערסה בתריה דרבא לפומבדיתא [ט] אמר רב יהודה אמר שמואל [י] עושין מדורה לחיה בשבת (בימות הגשמים) סבור מינה לחיה אין לחולה לא בימות הגשמים אין בימות החמה לא [כ] ולא היא ל"ש חיה ול"ש חולה ל"ש בימות הגשמים ול"ש בימות החמה מדאתמר) אמר רב חייא בר אבין אמר שמואל [ז] הקיז דם ונצטנן עושין לו מדורה אפי' בתקופת תמוז שמואל צלחו ליה תכתקא דשאגא רב יהודה צלחו ליה פתורא דיונה לרבה צלחו ליה שרשיפא וא"ל אביי לרבה והא קעבר מר משום [א] בל תשחית [ל] א"ל בל תשחית דגופאי עדיף לי אמר רב יהודה אמר רב לעולם ימכור אדם קורות ביתו ויקח [מ] מנעלים לרגליו הקיז דם ואין לו מה יאכל ימכור מנעלים שברגליו ויספיק מהן צרכי סעודה מאי צרכי סעודה רב אמר בשר ושמואל אמר יין רב אמר בשר נפשא חלף נפשא ושמואל אמר יין סומקא חלף סומקא: (סימן שנמסר) [נ] שמואל ביומא דעבד מילתא עבדי ליה תבשילא דטחלי ר' יוחנן שתי עד דנפיק תיהיא מאוניה ורב נחמן שתי עד דקפי טחליה רב יוסף שתי עד דנפיק מריבדא דכוסילתא רבא מהדר אחמרא בר תלתא טרפי אמר להו רב נחמן בר יצחק לרבנן במטותא מינייכו ביומא דהקזה אמרו לביתייכו נחמן אקלע לגבן וכולהו ארעומי אסירי בר מהאי ערמה דשרי מאן דעביד מילתא ולא אפשר ליה לישקול זוזא מכא וליזיל לשב חנותא עד דטעים שיעור רביעתא ואי לא ליכול שב תמרי אוכמתא ולישוף מישחא בצידעיה וניגני בשמשא אבלט אשכחיה לשמואל דגני בשמשא א"ל חכימא דיהודאי בישא מי הוי טבא א"ל יומא דהקזה הוא ולא היא אלא איכא יומא דמעלי בה שמשא בכוליה שתא יומא דנפלה ביה תקופת [ס] תמוז וסבר לא איגלי ליה: (היקיל ברוח טעמא שהה סימן) רב ושמואל דאמרי תרוייהו כל המקיל בסעודת הקזת דם מקילין לו מזונותיו מן השמים ואומרים הוא על חייו לא חס אני אחוס עליו רב ושמואל דאמרי תרוייהו האי מאן דעביד מילתא לא ליתיב היכא דכריך זיקא דילמא שפי ליה אומנא ומוקים ליה ארביעתא ואתי זיקא ושאיף מיניה ואתי לידי סכנה שמואל הוה רגיל ועבד מילתא בביתא דשב לביניא ואריחא יומא חדא עבד וארגיש בנפשיה בדק וחסר חד אריחא רב ושמואל דאמרי תרוייהו האי מאן דעביד מילתא ליטעום מידי והדר ליפוק דאי לא טעים מידי אי פגע בשכבא ירקא אפיה אי פגע במאן דקטל נפשא מית אי פגע בדבר

תוספות

רבא משמיה דרב יהודה אמר שבעה. לכאורה משמע דרבא לטעמיה דבפרק הדר (עירובין דף סח.) גבי ההוא ינוקא דאישתפוך חמימיה אמר להו רבא נישיילה לאימיה אם צריכה ניחיימו אגב אימיה דמסתמא ביום שמיני היה קודם מילה שהיה צריך חמין למולו דלאחר מילה מסוכן הוא ובלא אימיה ביום שמיני מחללין עליו שבת והיינו לאחר שבעה דנסתם הקבר בעינן צריכה מיהו ללישנא דאמרי לה לרבא שלשים תיקשי למה צריכה ועוד דבקונטרס פי' התם ניחיימו אגב אימיה ע"י נכרי וכן פירש ר"ח לכך יש לפרש דאביי ורבא ואמרי לה מר אמר חדא ומר אמר חדא ולא פליגי וכולהו קיימו כנהרדעי [פ]: מי

עין משפט נר מצוה

לג א ב ג מיי' פ"ב מהל' שבת הלכה יג סמג לאוין סה טוש"ע א"ח סימן של סעיף ג:

לד ד מיי' שם טוש"ע שם ס"ד:

לה ה מיי' שם הלכה י סמג שם טוש"ע א"ח סי' שכח סעיף יז:

לו ו מיי' שם הלכה יד סמג שם טוש"ע א"ח סימן של סעיף ו:

לז ז מיי' וסמג שם טוש"ע א"ח סימן שכח סעיף יח:

רבינו חננאל

צריכה אני מחללין עליה את השבת אמרה איני צריכה אין מחללין עליה את השבת ומסקינן לה לשמעתא דא"ל מרימר לרבינא הלכתא כי הא דמר זוטרא ספק נפשות להקל והוצרכנו לדקדק מאימתי פתיחת הקבר כדי לחלל באותו העת את השבת לעשות צרכי החיה. ואמר אביי משתשב על המשבר. ואמר רב הונא בריה דרב יהושע משעה שהדם שותת ויורד כו' ודייקי מדלא אמר רב הונא עד שיתחיל הדם להיות שותת ש"מ קודם שתשב על המשבר קאמר וכאביי עבדינן א) ולא מחללי שבתא אלא עד שיהא שותת. קדם שותת ויורד ותשב על המשבר אבל בהא דאמר אביי משום רב יהודה עד מתי פתיחת הקבר ג' ימים בלבד אין הלכה כמותו. ולא כרבא דאמר משמיה דרב יהודה שבעה. אלא קיי"ל כנהרדעא דאמרי חיה ג' ז' ושלשים. ג' בין אמרה צריכה אני בין אמרה איני צריכה מחללין עליה את השבת. ז' אמרה צריכה אני מחללין עליה את השבת אמרה איני צריכה אין מחללין עליה את השבת. סתמא עבדינן כמר זוטרא לקולא. שלשים אפילו אמרה צריכה אני אין מחללין עליה את השבת. אלא עושין לה ע"י ארמאי כדרב עולא בריה דרב עילאי דאמר כל צרכי הולד נעשין ע"י ארמאי בשבת וכדרב המנונא דאמר דבר שאין בו סכנה אומר לנכרי ועושה. חיה לא תטבול בתוך שלשים יום שמא תצטנן אמר רבא לא אמרן אלא שאין בעלה עמה. אבל בעלה [עמה בעלה] מחממה. אמר רב יהודה אמר שמואל עושין מדורות לחיה בשבת סבור מינה לחיה אין לחולה לא ו[בימות הגשמים אין] בימות החמה לא וכו' ומסקינן משמא דשמואל הקיז דם ונצטנן עושין לו מדורה ואפילו בתקופת תמוז. שמעינן מינה אפילו לחולה ואפילו בימות החמה. שמואל צלחו ליה תכתקא דשאגא. פי' שמואל הקיז דם ולא היה לו עצים מוכנים להדליק ולהתחמם בהן ובקעו מדי שידה שהיו עציה עצי שאגא והן יקרים להודיע שאם יתחממה לא עצים יסתכן וכדתרגם שאם לא יזהרו להתחמם יסתכנו

ריבקא עצי הערלה וצלח אעי דעלתא. רב יהודה צלחו ליה פתורא פי' שולחן העשוי מעצי יָנָס והן יקרים פי' אבנוס. ורבה צלחו ליה שרשיפא והוא הדום לכסא וכולן טעם אחד.

מסורת הש"ס

א) גי' רא"ש אמרה צריכה אני מחללין לא אמרה צריכה אין כו', ב) גי' רא"ש אמרה איני צריכה אין מחללין לא אמרה איני צריכה מחללין, ג) [יומא פג. פד: כתובות טו. ב"ק מד: ל. ב"ב נ: סנהדרין עט.], ד) בס"י הגירסא לא אמרה צריכה וכן לקמן, ה) [ביצה כב.], ו) [ביצה שם וכן בשאלתות פרש' שמות סי' לא איתא ואמר רב המנונא דבר שאין בו וכו'], ז) [שם ע"ש], ח) [עיין רש"י גיטין ח: ד"ה כדאמר רבא], ט) עירובין עט:, י) ס"א ז"א וה"ג לא איתמר אמר ר"ח כו', כ) [לקמן קמ:], ל) [עיין פסחים קיב.], מ) [חולין קיא.], נ) ס"א טבת, ס) כן גי' הערוך בערך שרפרף אולם הגאון מהרי"ף הגיה כאן של"ל רבה, ע) אין זה בלעז כ"א לשון תלמו' אכסדרא דבי רב כאינדרונא מעלים' מנחות לג:, פ) [וע"ע תוס' בגיטין ח: ד"ה אע"ג].

הגהות הב"ח

(א) רש"י ד"ה פתורא דיונה וכו' בוי"ש. נ"ב עלי ברותים:

גליון הש"ס

גמ' משעה שתשב על המשבר. עיין פ"ז מ"ד דאהלות בר"ש:

תורה אור השלם

א) כִּי תָצוּר אֶל עִיר יָמִים רַבִּים לְהִלָּחֵם עָלֶיהָ לְתָפְשָׂהּ לֹא תַשְׁחִית אֶת עֵצָהּ לִנְדֹּחַ עָלָיו גַּרְזֶן כִּי מִמֶּנּוּ תֹאכֵל וְאֹתוֹ לֹא תִכְרֹת כִּי הָאָדָם עֵץ הַשָּׂדֶה לָבֹא מִפָּנֶיךָ בַּמָּצוֹר: [דברים כ, יט]

ליקוטי רש"י

שאגא. ס"פ בלע"ז [ר"ה כג. ועי' ב"ב פ:]. ריבדא דכוסילתא. פונטור"א בלע"ז דלאמו"ה [חולין קיא.], ריבדא כוסילתא, כלי אומן מקיז [כתובות נט:]. ריבדא פונטור"א בלע"ז כוסילתא שם כלי אומן [סנהדרין צג:]. כלי אומן המקיז בכתפים ריבדא מכת הכלי ובלע"ז פיינדר"א [ע"ז כח:]. אבלט. שם חכם נכרי היה [לקמן קנו:].

חשק שלמה על רבינו חננאל

א) נ"ל ולא מחללי שבתא עד שתהא שותת וכו' ... על המשבר וכו'. וכל' הרי"ף כאן משמיה דרבותא. ופשוט דסמוכות על דברי רבינו כאן:

would seek wine of a "three-leaf" [vine].[35] אָמַר לְהוּ רַב נַחְמָן בַּר יִצְחָק לְרַבָּנָן – Rav Nachman bar Yitzchak said to his disciples, the Rabbis of the academy: בְּמָטוּתָא מִינַּיְיכוּ – I beg of you, בְּיוֹמָא דְהַקָּזָה – on the day of your undergoing bloodletting, אִמְרוּ לְבֵיתְהַיְיכוּ נַחְמָן אִקְּלַע לְגַבָּן – tell your wives, "Rav Nachman will be visiting us."[36]

The Gemara cites another ruling regarding bloodletting:

וְכוּלְּהוּ אַעֲרוֹמֵי אֲסִירֵי – And all deception is forbidden, בַּר מֵהַאי עַרְמָה דִשְׁרֵי – except for this following deception, which is permitted (in order to preserve one's health). מַאן דְּעָבֵיד מִילְּתָא וְלָא אֶפְשַׁר לֵיהּ – One who undergoes the procedure of bloodletting and it is not possible for him to buy wine, for lack of funds, לִישְׁקוֹל זוּזָא מְכָא – should take a worn-out *zuz*, which is no longer accepted as currency,[37] וְלֵיזִיל לְשַׁב חָנְוָתָא – and he should go to seven wine shops and sample the wine, עַד דְּטָעִים שִׁיעוּר רְבִיעֲתָא – until he has sipped the volume of a *reviis* of wine.[38] וְאִי לָא – And if he does not have a worn coin with which to employ this deception, לֵיכוּל שַׁב תַּמְרֵי אוּכָּמָתָא – he should eat seven black dates וְלִישׁוּף מִישְׁחָא בְּצִידְעֵיהּ – and rub oil into his temples,[39] וְנֵיגְנֵי בְּשִׁמְשָׁא – and sleep in the sun.

A related incident:

אַבְלֵט אַשְׁכְּחֵיהּ לִשְׁמוּאֵל דְּגָנֵי בְּשִׁמְשָׁא – Avlet[40] found Shmuel sleeping in the sun. אָמַר לֵיהּ חַכִּימָא דִיהוּדָאֵי בִּישָׁא מִי הָוֵה טָבָא – He said to [Shmuel], "Wise man of the Jews! Can bad become good?" I.e. can exposure to the sun, which is unhealthy, have beneficial effects? אָמַר לֵיהּ – [Shmuel] said to him: יוֹמָא דְהַקָּזָה הוּא – It is the day of bloodletting. Therefore, sleeping in the sun is beneficial.[41]

The Gemara however adds:

וְלָא הִיא – But it was not so. Shmuel had not undergone bloodletting that day.[42] אֶלָּא אִיכָּא יוֹמָא דְּמַעֲלֵי בֵּהּ שִׁמְשָׁא בְּכוּלֵּיהּ שַׁתָּא – Rather, there is one day in the entire year that exposure to the sun is beneficial, יוֹמָא דְנָפְלָה בֵּיהּ תְּקוּפַת תַּמּוּז – that is, the day on which the Tammuz (summer) solstice falls. וְסָבַר לָא אֲגַלֵּי לֵיהּ – And Shmuel reasoned, "I shall not reveal this to him."

The Gemara's citation of four teachings by Rav and Shmuel regarding proper care following bloodletting is prefaced with a mnemonic for those teachings:

(הֵיקִיל בְּרוּחַ טַעְמָא שָׁהָה סִימָן) – He is lenient with the wind, the taste waited. A mnemonic.)

The first teaching:

רַב וּשְׁמוּאֵל דְּאָמְרֵי תַּרְוַיְיהוּ – Rav and Shmuel both say: כֹּל הַמֵּקֵל בִּסְעוּדַּת הַקָּזַת דָּם – If someone is lax about the meal following bloodletting, מְקִילִין לוֹ מְזוֹנוֹתָיו מִן הַשָּׁמַיִם – then from the Heavenly [court] they are lax about supplying his provisions, וְאוֹמְרִים הוּא עַל חַיָּיו לֹא חָס אֲנִי אָחוּס עָלָיו – for they say, "If he does not show concern for his own life, shall I show concern for him?"

A second teaching:

רַב וּשְׁמוּאֵל דְּאָמְרֵי תַּרְוַיְיהוּ – Rav and Shmuel both say: הַאי מַאן דְּעָבֵיד מִילְּתָא – One who undergoes the procedure of bloodletting לָא לֵיתִיב הֵיכָא דְּכָרֵיךְ זִיקָא – should not sit where the wind swirls.[43] דִּילְמָא שָׁפֵי לֵיהּ אוּמָּנָא – For we are concerned that the bloodletter might have overly drained him of blood וּמוֹקֵים לֵיהּ אַרְבִיעֲתָא – and reduced it to the bare minimum of one *reviis* necessary to sustain life. וְאָתֵי זִיקָא וְשָׁאֵיף מִינֵּיהּ – And the wind might come and draw from him just a bit more blood,[44] וְאָתֵי לִידֵי סַכָּנָה – and he will come to a life-threatening situation.

The Gemara records a related incident, which highlights the extreme sensitivity to the wind of a person who has let blood:

שְׁמוּאֵל הֲוָה רָגִיל וְעָבַד מִילְּתָא בְּבֵיתָא דְשַׁב לְבֵינָא וַאֲרִיחָא – Shmuel was accustomed to undergo the procedure of bloodletting in a house made of walls that were seven-and-a-half bricks thick,[45] so that he would be well insulated from the chilling effects of the wind. יוֹמָא חֲדָא עֲבַד וְאַרְגִּישׁ בְּנַפְשֵׁיהּ – One day he underwent bloodletting in that house, as usual, and felt a certain weakness in himself. בְּדַק וְחָסַר חַד אֲרִיחָא – So he examined the walls of the house and found one half brick of the wall's usual thickness missing.

The third teaching:

רַב וּשְׁמוּאֵל דְּאָמְרֵי תַּרְוַיְיהוּ – Rav and Shmuel both say: הַאי מַאן דְּעָבֵיד מִילְּתָא – One who undergoes the procedure of bloodletting לִיטְעוֹם מִידֵי וַהֲדַר לִיפּוּק – should eat something first and then leave the house. דְּאִי לָא טָעִים מִידֵי – For if he does not eat anything before leaving, he exposes himself to a host of dangers: אִי פָּגַע בְּשִׁכְבָא יַרְקָא אַפֵּיהּ – If he meets up with a corpse, his face will turn green. אִי פָּגַע בְּמַאן דְּקָטַל נַפְשָׁא – If he meets up with a murderer, מָיֵית – he will die. אִי פָּגַע – If he meets up with

NOTES

35. That is, a vine that had produced three sets of leaves since taking root; in other words, a vine that was three years old (*Rashi*, as found in our texts). [*Sfas Emes* objects that the fruit of a vine less than three years old would have been forbidden in any event as *orlah*. It should be noted, though, that *Rashash* emends *Rashi's* comments here to read מִשֶּׁנִּלְקַט, *from when it was picked*, rather than מִשֶּׁנִּקְלַט, *from when it took root*. Accordingly, *Rashi* would mean that the wine had been aged for three years. And, as stated in *Rashi* to *Pesachim* 42b ד״ה עתיק עתיקי (cited here by *Mitzpeh Eisan*), wine that is three years old benefits the entire body.]

36. Apparently, Rav Nachman was instructing his disciples to deceive their wives into believing that he would be visiting, so that the husbands would be able to eat the large meal that the wives would prepare in anticipation of their honored guest. [And deception is permitted in this case, as in the Gemara's next ruling.] See, however, *Rashi*, whose reading seems to have been simply: אִמְרוּ נַחְמָן אִקְּלַע לְגַבָּן, *Say that Nachman is visiting* (without the critical word לְבֵיתְהַיְיכוּ, *to your wives;* see also *Dikdukei Soferim*) – i.e. "Make believe that I was your guest." Accordingly, no deception is involved. Rav Nachman simply meant that they should eat as liberally as they would had they been hosting him.

37. *Rashi;* see also *Rashi* to *Bava Kamma* 37a ד״ה זוזא מכא. [Such a disused coin would likely be available even to a very poor man.]

38. It was the common practice for a customer to first sample the wine before purchasing it. Here, the poor man would sip the wine and agree to buy it, but the seller would refuse to accept the worn coin as payment. The poor man would then go to another wine merchant and employ the same subterfuge, and then to another, until he had sipped a total of a *reviis* of wine.

[This subterfuge, though deceptive, does not constitute theft, since the worn coin has value and is sometimes accepted as payment. The poor man is perfectly willing to buy the wine if the seller accepts the coin, and no one is forcing the seller to refuse it (see *Hagahos Yavetz* here and to *Bava Kamma* 37a).]

39. The eating of the dates and the rubbing of the oil warm him (*Rashi*).

40. A non-Jewish sage and astrologer (*Rashi* to 156b ד״ה אבלט).

41. [As the Gemara has just said with regard to the poor man who cannot afford to drink wine after letting blood.]

42. *Ritva MHK* ed.

43. I.e. in a portico, which has many openings, so that the wind enters from many points and swirls around (*Rashi*).

44. [I.e. the chilling effect of the wind will draw blood away from the vital organs, leaving them without the requisite minimum of a *reviis*.]

45. A brick is three *tefachim* by three *tefachim*. An אֲרִיחַ is a half brick [three *tefachim* by $1\frac{1}{2}$ *tefachim*] (*Rashi*). Thus, the walls were $22\frac{1}{2}$ *tefachim* (nearly four *amos*) thick!

עין משפט נר מצוה

לג א ב ג מיי' פ"ב מהל' שבת הלכה יג סמג לאוין סה טוש"ע א"ח סימן של סעיף ג:
לד ד מיי' שם טוש"ע שם ס"ד:
לה ה מיי' שם הלכה י סמג שם טוש"ע א"ח סי' שכח סעיף יז:
לו ו מיי' שם הלכה יד סמג שם טוש"ע א"ח סימן של סעיף ו:
לז ז מיי' וסמג שם טוש"ע א"ח סימן שכח סעיף יח:

גמרא

(א) צריכה אני בין לא אמרה צריכה אני אין מחללין עליה את השבת רב אשי מתני הכי מר זוטרא מתני הכי אמר רב יהודה אמר שמואל חיה כל זמן שהקבר פתוח בין אמרה צריכה אני ובין אמרה אין צריכה אני מחללין עליה את השבת נסתם הקבר (ב) אמרה צריכה אני מחללין עליה את השבת לא אמרה צריכה אני אין מחללין עליה את השבת א"ל רבינא למרימר מר זוטרא מתני לקולא ורב אשי מתני לחומרא הלכתא כמאן א"ל הלכה כמר זוטרא (ג) ספק נפשות להקל מאימתי פתיחת הקבר אמר אביי (א) משעה שתשב על המשבר רב הונא בריה דרב יהושע אמר (ב) משעה שהדם שותת ויורד ואמרי לה (ג) משעה שחברותיה נושאות אותה באגפיה עד מתי פתיחת הקבר אמר אביי שלשה ימים רבא אמר משמיה דרב יהודה שבעה ואמרי לה שלשים אמרי נהרדעי (ד) חיה ג' ז' ול' ג' בין אמרה צריכה אני ובין (ה) אמרה לא צריכה אני מחללין עליה את השבת ז' אמרה צריכה אני מחללין עליה את השבת אמרה לא צריכה אני אין מחללין עליה את השבת ל' אפי' אמרה צריכה אני אין מחללין עליה את השבת אבל עושין ע"י ארמאי (ו) כדרב עולא בריה דרב עילאי דאמר כל צרכי חולה נעשין ע"י ארמאי בשבת (ז) וכדרב המנונא דאמר רב המנונא (ח) דבר שאין בו סכנה (ט) אומר לנכרי ועושה אמר רב יהודה אמר שמואל לחיה ל' יום למאי הלכתא אמרי נהרדעי לטבילה אמר רבא לא אמרן אלא שאין בעלה עמה אבל בעלה עמה בעלה מחממה כי הא דברתיה דרב חסדא טבלה בגו תלתין יומין שלא בפני בעלה ואצטניאת ואמטוי לערסה בתריה דרבא לפומבדיתא (י) אמר רב יהודה אמר שמואל (כ) עושין מדורה לחיה בשבת (בימות הגשמים) סבור מינה לחיה אין לחולה לא בימות הגשמים אין בימות החמה לא (ל) ולא היא לא שנא חיה ולא שנא חולה לא שנא בימות הגשמים ולא שנא בימות החמה מדאתמר) אמר רב חייא בר אבין אמר שמואל (ל) הקיז דם ונצטנן עושין לו מדורה אפי' בתקופת תמוז שמואל צלחו ליה תכתקא דשאגא רב יהודה צלחו ליה פתורא דיונה רבה צלחו ליה שרשיפא וא"ל אביי לרבה והא קעבר מר משום (א) בל תשחית (ס) א"ל בל תשחית דגופאי עדיף לי אמר רב יהודה אמר רב לעולם ימכור אדם קורות ביתו ויקח (נ) מנעלים לרגליו הקיז דם ואין לו מה יאכל ימכור מנעלים שברגליו ויספיק מהן צרכי סעודה מאי צרכי סעודה רב אמר בשר ושמואל אמר יין רב אמר בשר נפשא חלף נפשא ושמואל אמר יין סומקא חלף סומקא: (סימן שנמסר) (מ) שמואל ביומא דעבד מילתא עבדי ליה תבשילא דטחלי ר' יוחנן שתי עד דנפיק תיהיא מאוניה ורב נחמן שתי עד דקפי טחליה רב יוסף שתי עד דנפיק מריבדא דכוסילתא רבא מהדר אחמרא בר תלתא טרפי רב נחמן בר יצחק אמר להו לרבנן במטותא מיניכו ביומא דהקזה אמרו לביתיכו נחמן איקלע לגבן וכולהו ארעומי אסירי בר מהאי ערמה דשרי מאן דעביד מילתא ולא אפשר ליה לישקול זוזא מכא וליזיל לשב חנותא עד דטעים שיעור רביעתא ואי לא ליכול שב תמרי אוכמתא ולישוף מישחא בצידעיה וניגני בשמשא אבלט אשכחיה לשמואל דנגני בשמשא א"ל חכימא דיהודאי בישא מי הוי טבא א"ל יומא דהקזה הוא ולא היא אלא איכא יומא דמעלי בה שמשא בכוליה שתא יומא דנפלה ביה תקופת (ע) תמוז וסבר לא איגלי ליה: (היקיל ברוח טעמא שהה סימן) רב ושמואל דאמרי תרוייהו כל המקיל בסעודת הקזת דם מקילין לו מזונותיו מן השמים ואומרים הוא על חייו לא חס אני אחוס עליו רב ושמואל דאמרי תרוייהו האי מאן דעביד מילתא לא ליתיב היכא דכריך זיקא דילמא שפי ליה אומנא ומוקים ליה ארביעתא ואתי זיקא ושאיף מיניה ואתי לידי סכנה שמואל הוה רגיל ועבד מילתא בביתא דשב לביניא ואריחא יומא חדא עבד וארגיש בנפשיה בדק וחסר חד אריחא רב ושמואל דאמרי תרוייהו האי מאן דעביד מילתא ליטעום מידי והדר ליפוק דאי לא טעים מידי אי פגע בשכבא ירקא אפיה אי פגע במאן דקטל נפשא מית אי פגע

בדבר

רש"י

צריכה אני. לחילול: בין שאמרה אין צריכה אני. וחברותיה אומרות שהיא צריכה מחללין: באגפיה. בזרועותיה שאינה יכולה להלך: חיה ג' ימים וז' ימים ול' יום. הוזכרו כאן לחילוק הלכות חילול שבת ל' מז' עד השלמת ל' וכן ז' מג' עד השלמת ז': כל צרכי חולה. והא חיה עד ל' יום שתמאת חולה היא: דבר שאין בו סכנה. חולה שאם לא יעשו לו רפואה זו אין מסוכן למות ומ"מ צריך הוא לה: אומר לארמאי ועושה. אבל דבר שיש בו סכנה ישראל עצמו עושה לו: לטבילה. עד ל' יום לא תטבול מפני הצינה: שאין בעלה עמה. והיא טובלת לטהרות: בעלה מחממה. לאחר טבילה בתשמיש והגוף מתחמם מן הגוף: מדורה. היסק גדול: הקיז דם. וכ"ש חולה: צלחו ליה תכתקא דשאגא. לא מצאו עצים מוכנים להיסק ביום הקזה ולזה ובקעו כסא של מדהר שהוא מעולה בדמים: פתורא דיונה. מין ארז הוא ורבינו הלוי אמר (א) כו"ש: רבא צלחו ליה שרשיפא. ספסל: ויקח מנעלים. שאין לך בזוי מן המהלך יחף בשוק: (מאי) צרכי סעודה. (לרכי) סעודת הקזה: ביומא דמלתא. דהקזה: דטחלי. טחול סומקא חלף סומקא: עד דנפיק תיהי. הריח: מאוניה. מאזניו מריחין היין: מריבדא דכוסילתא. נקבי כלי האומן שהקיזו פלימ"א: עד דקפי טחליה. טחול שלו צף ביין: בר תלתא טרפי. בן ג' שנים שטענה אמו משנקלט ג' עלין חדשין: לרבנן. לתלמידיו: אמרו נחמן איקלע לגבן. הכריזו בסעודה כאילו אני קובע אצלכם: בר מהאיא ערמה. דמפרש ואזיל: ולא אפשר ליה. לקנות יין: לשקול זוזא מכא. זוז רע ופחות שאינו יוצא בהוצאה: וליזיל לשב חנותא. ודרך הלוקחים לטועמו תחלה שיהא טוב ויטעום וכשיתן לו הזוז והחנווני ימצאהו רע ולא יקבלנו והוא ילך לחנות אחרת ויעשה כן: ואי לא. דאין לו זוז רע: ולישוף משחא בצידעיה. ברקתו והתמרים והשומן מחממין אותו: בישא מי הוה טבא. חום השמש שהוא קשה לאדם כלום מטיב לו: היכא דכריך זיקא. (ע) אינדרו"ן שיש בו חלונות והרוח נכנסת בהם נכרכת ומתגלגלת באינדרו"ן: דילמא שפי ליה אומנא. מריקו מדמו כמו השופה יין לחבירו (ב"מ דף ס.): ומוקי ליה ארביעתא. לא הניח בו דם אלא כדי חייו דהיינו רביעית והדר אתי ליה זיקא ושייף ליה מדם הנותר בגופו ומחסרו משיעורו ומסתכן: שב לביני ואריחא. עובי החומה ז' לבינים מוטלין לרחבן זה אצל זה דכל לבינה ג"ט ואריחא אריח חצי לבינה טפח ומחצה: ארגיש בנפשיה. הרגיש בעצמו שהוא נחלש: חסר חד אריחא. החומה היתה חסירה מעוביה אריח:

בדבר

תוספות

רבא משמיה דרב יהודה אמר שבעה. לכאורה משמע דרבא לטעמיה דבפרק הדר (עירובין דף סח.) גבי ההוא ינוקא דאשתפוך חמימיה אמר להו רבא נישיליה לאימיה אם צריכה ניחימו אגב אימיה דמסתמא ביום שמיני היה קודם מילה שהיה צריך חמין למולו דלאחר מילה מסוכן הוא ובלא אימיה ביום שמיני מחללין עליו שבת והיינו לאחר שבעה דבנסתם הקבר בעינן צריכה מיהו לגירסא דאמרי לה לרבא שלשים תיקשי למה צריכה ועוד דבקונטרס פי' התם ניחימו אגב אימיה ע"י נכרי וכן פירש ר"ח לכך יש לפרש לאביי ורבא ואמרי לה מר אמר חדא ומר אמר חדא ולא פליגי וכולהו קיימו כנהרדעי (פ):

מי

רבינו חננאל

צריכה אני מחללין עליה את השבת אמרה איני צריכה אין מחללין עליה את השבת ומסקינן לה לשמעתא דא"ל מרימר לרבינא הלכתא כי הא דמר זוטרא ספק נפשות להקל והוצרכנו לדקדק מאימתי פתיחת הקבר כדי לחלל באותו העת את השבת לעשות צרכי החיה. ואמר אביי משתשב על המשבר. ואמר רב הונא בריה דרב יהושע משעה שהדם שותת ויורד כו' ודייקי מדלא אמר רב הונא עד שיתחיל הדם להיות שותת ש"מ קודם שתשב על המשבר קאמר וכאביי עבדינן א) ולא מחללי שבתא אלא עד שיהא שותת. קדם שותת ויורד ותשב על המשבר אבל בהא דאמר אביי משום רב יהודה עד מתי פתיחת הקבר ג' ימים בלבד אין הלכה כמותו. ולא כרבא דאמר משמיה דרב יהודה שבעה. אלא קיי"ל כנהרדעא דאמרי חיה ג' ז' ושלשים. ג' בין אמרה צריכה אני בין אמרה איני צריכה מחללין עליה את השבת. ז' אמרה צריכה אני מחללין עליה את השבת אמרה איני צריכה אין מחללין עליה את השבת. סתמא עבדינן כמר זוטרא לקולא. שלשים אפילו אמרה צריכה אני אין מחללין עליה את השבת. אלא עושין לה ע"י ארמאי כדרב עולא בריה דרב עילאי דאמר כל צרכי הולד נעשין ע"י ארמאי בשבת וכדרב המנונא דאמר דבר שאין בו סכנה אומר לנכרי ועושה. חיה לא תטבול בתוך שלשים יום שמא תצטנן אמר רבא לא אמרן אלא שאין בעלה עמה. אבל בעלה [עמה בעלה] מחממה. אמר רב יהודה אמר שמואל עושין מדורות לחיה בשבת סבור מינה לחיה אין לחולה לא [בימות הגשמים אין] בימות החמה לא וכו' ומסקינן משמא דשמואל הקיז דם ונצטנן עושין לו מדורה ואפילו בתקופת תמוז. שמעינן מינה אפילו לחולה ואפילו בימות החמה. שמואל צלחו ליה תכתקא דשאגא. פי' שמואל הקיז דם ולא היה לו עצים מוכנים להדליק ולהתחמם בהן ובקעו לו שידה שהיו עציה עצי שאגא והן יקרים להודיע שאם יתמהמה עד שיביאו לו עצים יסתכן וכדתרגם ויבקע עצי העולה וצלח אעי דעלתא. רב יהודה צלחו ליה פתורא פי' שולחן העשוי מעצי יַנָס והן יקרים פי' יאבנוס. ורבה צלחו ליה שרשיפא והוא הדום לכסא וכולן טעם אחד. שאם לא ימהרו להתחמם יסתכנו

מסורת הש"ס

א) גי' רא"ש אמרה צריכה אני מחללין לא אמרה צריכה אין כו', ב) גי' רא"ש אמרה איני צריכה אין מחללין לא אמרה איני צריכה מחללין, ג) [יומא פג. פד: כתובות טו. ב"ק מד: ל. ב"ב נ: סנהדרין עט.], ד) בס"י הגירסא לא אמרה צריכה וכן לקמן, ה) [ביצה כב.], ו) [ביצה שם וכן בשאלתות פרש' שמות סי' לח איתא ואמר רב המנונא דבר שאין בו וכו'], ז) [שם ע"ש], ח) [עיין רש"י גיטין ח: ד"ה כדאמר רבא], ט) עירובין עט:, י) ס"א ז"א וה"ג לא איתמר אמר ר"ח כו', כ) [לקמן קמ:], ל) [עיין פסחים קיב.], מ) [חולין קיא.], נ) ס"א טבת, ס) כן גי' הערוך בערך שרפרף אולם הגאון מהרי"ף הגיה כאן שצ"ל רבה, ע) אין זה בלעז כ"א לשון תלמו' אכסדרא דבי רב כאינדרונא מעלית' מנחות לג:, פ) [וע"ע תוס' בגיטין ח: ד"ה אע"ג].

הגהות הב"ח

(א) רש"י ד"ה פתורא דיונה וכו' בוי"ש. נ"ב עלי ברותים:

גליון הש"ס

גמ' משעה שתשב על המשבר. עיין פ"ז מ"ד דאהלות בר"ש:

תורה אור השלם

א) כִּי תָצוּר אֶל עִיר יָמִים רַבִּים לְהִלָּחֵם עָלֶיהָ לְתָפְשָׂהּ לֹא תַשְׁחִית אֶת עֵצָהּ לִנְדֹּחַ עָלָיו גַּרְזֶן כִּי מִמֶּנּוּ תֹאכֵל וְאֹתוֹ לֹא תִכְרֹת כִּי הָאָדָם עֵץ הַשָּׂדֶה לָבֹא מִפָּנֶיךָ בַּמָּצוֹר: [דברים כ, יט]

ליקוטי רש"י

שאגא. ש"פ בלע"ז [ר"ה כג. ועי' ב"ב פ:]. ריבדא דכוסילתא. פולטויר"א דפלמוא"ה בלע"ז רידלא ניקור כוסילתא, כלי אומן מקיז [כתובות לט:]. רידלא פוניור"א בלע"ז כוסילתא שם כלי המקיז פלנמא"ל [סנהדרין צג:]. כלי אומן המקיז בכתפים רידלא מכת הכלי ובלע"ז פיינדר"א [ע"ז כז.]. אבלט. שם חכם נכרי היה [לקמן קנו:].

חשק שלמה על רבינו חננאל

א) נ"ל ולא מחללי שבתא עד שתהא הדם שותת ויורד ותשב על המשבר וכו'. וכ"כ הרי"ף כאן משמיה דרבוותא. ופשוט דכוונתו על דברי רבינו כאן:

בדבר אחר קשה לדבר אחר רב ושמואל דאמרי תרוייהו א האי מאן דעביד מילתא לישהי פורתא והדר ליקום דאמר מר ב ה' דברים קרובין למיתה יותר מן החיים ואלו הן ב אכל ועמד שתה ועמד ישן ועמד הקיז דם ועמד ג שימש מטתו ועמד אמר שמואל פורסא דדמא כל תלתין יומין ד ובין הפרקים ימעט ובין הפרקים יחזור וימעט ואמר שמואל פורסא דדמא חד בשבתא ארבעה ומעלי שבתא אבל שני וחמישי לא דאמר מר מי שיש לו זכות אבות יקיז דם בשני ובחמישי שב"ד של מעלה ושל מטה שוין כאחד בתלתא בשבתא מאי טעמא לא משום דקיימא ליה מאדים ה בזווי מעלי שבתא נמי קיימא בזווי ° כיון דדשו ביה רבים א שומר פתאים ה' אמר שמואל ד' דהוא ד' ד' דהוא ארביסר ד' דהוא עשרים וארבעה ד' דליכא ארבע בתריה סכנתא ר"ח ושני לו חולשא שלישי לו סכנה מעלי יומא טבא חולשא מעלי יומא דעצרתא סכנתא ה וגזרו רבנן אכולהו מעלי יומא טבא משום יומא טבא דעצרת דנפיק ביה זיקא ושמיה טבוח דאי לא קבלו ישראל תורה הוה טבח להו לבשרייהו ולדמייהו אמר שמואל אכל חטה והקיז דם לא הקיז אלא לאותה חטה והנ"מ לרפואה אבל לאוקולי מיקיל המקיז דם שתייה לאלתר אכילה עד חצי מיל איבעיא להו שתייה לאלתר מעלי אבל בתר הכי קשי או דילמא לא קשי ולא מעלי תיקו איבעיא להו אכילה עד חצי מיל הוא דקמעלי הא בתר הכי ומקמי הכי קשי או דילמא לא קשי ולא מעלי תיקו ג מכריז רב מאה קרי בזוזא מאה רישי בזוזא מאה שפמי ולא כלום אמר רב יוסף כי הוינן בי רב הונא יומא דמפגרי ביה רבנן אמרי האידנא יומא דשפמי הוא ולא ידענא מאי קאמרי: וקושרין הטבור: ת"ר ד קושרין הטבור ר' יוסי אומר אף חותכין וטומנין השליא כדי שיחם הולד אמר רשב"ג בנות מלכים טומנות בספלים של שמן בנות עשירים בספוגים של צמר בנות עניים במוכין ה אמר רב נחמן אמר רבה בר אבוה אמר רב הלכה כר' יוסי ואמר רב נחמן אמר רבה בר אבוה אמר רב מודים חכמים לר' יוסי בטבור של שני תינוקות שחותכין מ"ט דמנתחי אהדדי ואמר רב נחמן אמר רבה בר אבוה אמר רב ו כל האמור בפרשת תוכחה עושין לחיה בשבת שנאמר ב ומולדותיך ביום הולדת אותך לא כרת שרך ובמים לא רחצת למשעי והמלח לא המלחת והחתל לא חתלת ומולדותיך ביום הולדת מכאן שמיילדים את הולד בשבת לא כרת שרך מכאן שחותכין הטבור בשבת ובמים לא רחצת למשעי מכאן שרוחצין הולד בשבת והמלח לא המלחת מכאן שמולחין הולד בשבת והחתל לא חתלת מכאן שמלפפין הולד בשבת:

הדרן עלך מפנין

רש"י

בדבר אחר. מזיק: קשה לדבר אחר. לרעת שהמזיקים מנוגעים הם כדאמרינן בקדושין (דף מט:) י' קבים נגעים ירדו לעולם תשעה נטלו מזיקים: אכל ועמד. מהר לעמוד מתמול אחר שאכל שובעו: פורסא דדמא. זמן הקזה כמו כפרוס הפסח (שקלים פ"ג מ"א): בין הפרקים. פירקי שנותיו כגון לאחר מ' שנה: ימעט. בהקזה לא יקיז בכל חדש אלא לג' חדשים: ובין הפרקים יחזור וימעט. לאחר ששים יקיז לג' חדשים לפי שאין כחו עליו ואין דמו רב וגופו מלטנן כשמחסר דמו: שב"ד של מעלה ושל מטה שוין. אלא נדון בכל יום וב"ד יושבין בעיירות בב' ובה' מתקנת עזרא ואילך (ב"ק דף פב.) וכיון דיום הדין ופקידה הוא עונותיו מזכירים: דקיימא ליה מאדים בזווי. שמזל מאדים משמש בו בשעות זוגות ומזל מאדים ממונה על החרב ועל הדבר ועל הפורעניות והזוגות קשין שהן רשות לשדים כדאמר בפסחים (דף קי:) והפורעניות מוכנין של"ם חנכ"ל סדר השעות כשנתלו המאורות והמזלות שעה ראשונה של ד' בשבת שימש שבתאי ובשניה צדק ואחריו מאדים ואחריו חמה ואחריו נוגה ואחריו כוכב ואחריו לבנה נמצאו ז' המזלות לז' השעות וחוזרים חלילה לעולם נמצא כסדר זה לעולם סימני מזלות המשמשין בתחלת לילי השבוע כלנ"ש חל"ם מוצאי שבת שעה ראשונה של כוכב תחלת ליל ראשון לדק וכן בסדר הזה וסדר תחלת סימני הימים חל"ם כלנ"ש שעה ראשונה של אחד בשבת חמה ושל שני בשבת לבנה ושל שלישי בשבת מאדים נמצא מאדים חוזר בו חלילה בשעה שמינית ביום והיא זוגות אבל שאר ימים אין מאדים בזוגות שלהם אם לא בלילה ובלילה אין דרך להקיז: מעלי שבתא נמי קיימא מאדים בזווי. שהרי שעה ראשונה של יום נוגה לפי הסדר של חל"ם כלנ"ש בתחלת הימים וכיון שתחלתו נוגה וסדר הליכתן של"ם חנכ"ל נמצאו מתחילין לחזור חלילה בשעה רביעית נמצא מאדים בשעה ששית: כיון דדשו ביה רבים. הורגלו בו מפני דזמינן שיהיו קרובים לסעודת שבת ואמרינן בפירקין דלעיל (ד' קיח:) כבוד שבת בדגים גדולים ובמסכת ע"ז (ד' כט:) אמרינן שני לדם לדג: ארבע דהוא ד'. ד' בשבת שהוא ד' לחדש או ארביסר לחדש או כ"ד לחדש כולהון קשה להקזה: ד' דליכא ד' בתריה. שאין ד' ימים עד סוף החדש ואיכא דאמרי דליכא ד' בשבת בתריה בלאותו חדש ולאו כן: ה"ג ר"ח ושני לו חולשא שלישי לו סכנתא: אכל חטה והקיז דם לא הקיז אלא לחטה. שהאוכל מכביד את האדם והקזה שאחר אכילה אינו מועיל אלא לאותו כובד: והנ"מ. במקיז לרפואה: אבל אקולי. מי שיש לו דם המכביד עליו אפי' לאחר אכילה מקיז ומיקל: מאה רישי בזוזא. כלומר אם יהיו בזול מאד קנה ראשי בהמה ואם לאו אל תקח שאינן בריאין לאכול: מאה קרי. דלועין: מאה שפמי. כמו על שפם (ויקרא יג) גרנו"ן בלעז שפמים של בהמה: יומא דמפגרי ביה רבנן. שהיו התלמידים מתעגלין מלבא בבית המדרש קרי ליה יומא דשפמי כלומר היום הזה אבד לנו ואין בו תועלת: וטומנין את השליא. כדמפרש רשב"ג שהיא רפואה להתחמם הולד: ספוגין של צמר. למר מנופץ: של שני תינוקות. תאומים וקשורין עבורן זה בזה: משום דמנתחי מהדדי. זה אילך וזה אילך ונמצאו מסוכנין: בפרשת תוכחה. שהוכיח יחזקאל לישראל את חסדי הקב"ה שעמהן: תוכחה. לשון לכו ונוכחה (ישעיה א) להתווכח ולהודיע מי הוא שסרח על שכנגדו: למשעי. לטוח ולהחליק בשרו: שמולחין. ובשרו מתקשה: מלפפין. אנוולופ"ר בלע"ז ולאו היינו אסוקי יוקא דאמרן לעיל בפרק כל הכלים (דף קכג.) דהא שמעינן ליה לרב נחמן דאסר אלא י) לפופי בעלמא כמו שעושין ° בחגורות ופסיקיאות: הדרן עלך מפנין

תוספות

מי שיש לו זכות אבות. וקודם תקנת עזרא אע"פ שהיו דנין בכל יום שהיו צריכים לא היו קובעים לישב בכל יום:

דקאי מאדים בזווי. ברביעי נמי קאי מאדים בזווי בסוף היום אלא לא חשו חכמים לכך דאין דרך להקיז כל כך בסמוך ללילה:

דליכא ארבע בתריה. שאין ד' ימים עד סוף החדש כדפירש בקונטרס דליכא למימר רביעי בשבת דהא ד' דהוא עשרין וארבע היינו דליכא רביעי בתריה:

מאה רישי בזוזא מאה קרי בזוזא. לפירוש הקונטרס תימה מה שייך הכא ור"ח גריס מאה קרני בזוזא ומפרש מאה רישי מאה ראשי בני אדם (ונראה) שהיה מנהג קצוב לספר לגלח בזוזא וכן מנהג ק' קרני להקיז בזוזא כמו קרנא דאומנא (לקמן דף קמד:) אבל מאה שפמי לתקן השפה בולא כלום דבשכר גילוח והקזה היה מתקן השפה וביום שהיה מתקן שפמו לא היה נוטל כלום ועל כן היה למשל כל מי שהיה יגע ולא עלה בידו שכרו היו קורין אותו יומא דשפמי: מפגרי רבנן. תשש כחם והיו מתחלשין ולא יכלו למיגרס כדכתיב (ש"א ל) וירדוף דוד הוא וארבע מאות איש (עמו) ויעמדו מאתים איש אשר פגרו מעבור את נחל הבשור:

כל האמור בפרשת תוכחה. לאו מקרא מפיק אלא אסמכתא כיון שבא בפרשת תוכחה אם כן צער הוא אם אין עושין והקילו חכמים לעשות וכולהו אין בהן איסורא דאורייתא:

הדרן עלך מפנין

עין משפט נר מצוה

לח א מיי' פ"ד מהלכות דעות הלכה יח:
לט ב מיי' שם הל' ג:
מ ג מיי' שם הלכה יט טוש"ע א"ח סי' רמ סעיף טו:
מא ד מיי' פ"ד מהלכות דעות הלכה יח:
מב ה ש"ע א"ח סימן תסח סעי' י בהג"ה:
מג ו מיי' פ"ב מהלכות שבת הלכה יא יג סמג לאוין סה טוש"ע א"ח סימן של סעיף ז:

רבינו חננאל

יסתכנו. פי' זוזא מכא. זוז מעוך שנמעך מטבע הצורה ונראה כאסימון. דעביד מלתא. באותו היום שמקיז דם. פורסא דדמא כל תלתין יומין. פי' גבול הדם לבחורים כל שלשים יום. בין הפרקים הגיע לחמשים שנה ימעט. יוציא משנים חדשים [או] ג' חדשים. פעם אחת עוד בין הפרקים בא בימים יחזור ימעט משנה חדשים לששה חדשים או משנה לשנה וזה הפי' קיבלנוהו מרבותינו קבלה: בתלתא קאי מאדים בזוזי. פי' בשתי שעות שהן זוגות יום שלישי שעה שמינית מאדים ושעה שתים ועשרים מאדים ושכך סידור הכוכבים חל"ם כצנ"ש בימים נמצא יום אחד שעה ראשונה כוכב חמה יום שני שעה ראשונה כוכב לבנה. יום ג' שעה ראשונה כוכב מאדים יום ד' שעה ראשונה כוכב [כוכב]. יום ה' שעה ראשונה כוכב צדק יום ו' שעה ראשונה כוכב נוגה. יום ז' שעה ראשונה כוכב שבתי וסידורן חל"ם כצנ"ש בימים כצנ"ש חל"ם בלילות וסידוריהן חנכ"ל שצ"ם. וכיון שביום ג' עומד מאדים בשעה שמינית והן זוגות ובשעה כ"ב והן זוגות חיישינן לסכנה. וכיוצא בזה בשני ובחמישי משום הכי חיישינן לסכנה. כי מאדים הוא ממונה על הדם ואקשינן עלה והא יום ו' הוא דמעלי שבתא דקאי מאדים בשעה ששית ובשעה עשרים והן זוגות. ואמרת פורסא דדמא חד בשבא וארבעה ומעלי שבתא. ולא מצאו לו פירוק. והשיב אע"פ שהוא כן כיון דדשו בה רבים להקיז ביום ששי שומר פתאים ה'. מאה רישי בזוזי מאה קרני בזוזא שפמי ולא כלום פי' היה מנהג קצוב כי הספר מגלח מאה ראשי כלומר מאה ראשי בני אדם נוטל שכרו זוז אחד וכן (א' מדוגמא) [חמשים] מאה קרן כלומר מאה קרן של זכוכית והוא ריבדא דכוסילתא נוטל בשכרו בק' קרן זוז אחד. אבל לתקן הזקן וליטול השפה ולתקנו לא היה מנהג ליקח האומן כלום אלא אותן בני אדם שמגלח ראשם או עושה להן ריבדא דכוסילתא נוטל שכרו כאשר אמרנו מתקן זקנם ונוטל שפמם בחנם. וכן היה הדין ויום שהיה האומן עושה השפמות לא היה נוטל שכר והיה הולך לביתו ריקם. ועל כן היה למשל כל מי שהיה יגע ולא [היה] עולה בידו (סבר) [שכר] היה קורא אותו יומא דשפמי. מיפגרי תשש כחם והוו מתחלשי יגעים ויעפים ולא יכלי למיגרס כדכתיב וירדף דוד הוא וארבע מאות איש ויעמדו מאתים איש אשר פגרו מעבור וגו' הוו אמרי יומא דשפמי א): וקושרין את הטיבור. ר' יוסי אומר אף חותכין את הטיבור כל צרכי מילה עושין בשבת אמר רב נחמן אמר רבה בר אבוה הלכה כרבי יוסי שחותכין בשבת טיבור תינוק אחד. וכן תינוקות שבזה אפילו חכמים מודים שמחתך מ"ט משום (דמתחזי) [דמנתחו] אהדדי. ואמר רב נחמן אמר רבה בר אבוה אמר רב כל האמור בפרשת תוכחה עושין לחיה בשבת שנא' ומולדותיך ביום הולדת אותך מיכן שמיילדין לחיה בשבת לא כרת שרך מיכן שחותכין את הטיבור בשבת ובמים לא רוחצת למשעי מיכן שמרחיצין את הולד והחתל לא חתלת מיכן שמלפפין הולד בשבת ואמרינן בתלמוד א"י ומחללין עליה את השבת שמואל אמר עושין לה מדורה אפילו בתקופת תמוז וקושרין את הטיבור כהדא אמתיה דבר קפרא נפקא מיילדה בשבת אתת ושאלת לר' וא' לה אזלון ושאלון לחייתא. אמרה לה זילי עבידי כמנהגך אמרה ליה ליכא חייא. אמר לה ליכא מנהג אמר לה איזיל חתיך כר' יוסי כבמתניתא וכל צרכי חיה עושין בשבת תני השליא הזאת בשבת עשירין טומנין אותה בשמן והעניים בתבן ובחול אלו ואלו טומנין אותה בארץ כדי ליתן ערבון בארץ [לארץ]: הדרן עלך מפנין

חשק שלמה על רבינו חננאל א) עיין בערוך ערך פגר:

מסורת הש"ס

א) גיטין ע., ב) [עיין תוספות עירובין נו. ד"ה ואין], ג) [מכאן עד יומא דשפמי ממלא פירוש יפה בערוך ערך פגר בשינוי הנוסח], ד) [תוספתא פט"ו], ה) [לפני הרא"ש והטור לא היה כתוב הא דאמר רב נחמן הלכה כר' יוסי ועיין ב"י א"ח סימן של], ו) [וכן איתא לעיל סו: לפופי יוקא בשבת שפיר דמי וע"ש בפרש"י וכן עוד לקמן קמז: ובפרש"י שם], ז) [וע"ע תוספות כתובות ג. ד"ה שכמי דינין].

גליון הש"ס

גמרא כיון דדשו ביה רבים שומר פתאים. עיין תה"ד סי' רי"א: רש"י ד"ה מלפפים וכו' בחגורות ופסיקיאות. עיין לקמן דף קמז ע"ב רש"י ד"ה במוזרי שדרה וצ"ע. ועי' בתשובת אדמת הקדש חלק א"ח סי' מ:

תורה אור השלם

א) שֹׁמֵר פְּתָאיִם יְיָ דַּלּוֹתִי וְלִי יְהוֹשִׁיעַ: [תהלים קטז, ו]

ב) וּמוֹלְדוֹתַיִךְ בְּיוֹם הוּלֶּדֶת אֹתָךְ לֹא כָרַּת שָׁרֵּךְ וּבְמַיִם לֹא רֻחַצְתְּ לְמִשְׁעִי וְהָמְלֵחַ לֹא הֻמְלַחַתְּ וְהָחְתֵּל לֹא חֻתָּלְתְּ: [יחזקאל טז, ד]

ליקוטי רש"י

אכל ועמד. מיד קודם ששהה מעט [גיטין ע.]. מוכין. כל דבר רך קרוי מוכין כגון למר גפן ותלישי למר רך של בהמה וגרירת בגדים בלויים [לעיל מז:]. ביום הולדת אותך. פושניא"ה בלע"ז כשנכרתי כך במצרים היית בלי שום תיקון ולפי שדימה הדבר ללידה הזכיר כאן תיקוני הולד. שרך. כמו טבורך. למשעי. לנקות לחים הסלע תרגומו שעיעות כיפה אפלנמנ"ט בלע"ז ומנחם חבר למשעי לשון שעשועים. לא המלחת. מכאן שמולחין את הולד כדי שיתקשה בשרו. והחתל. לשון כריכה בבגדים וכן (איוב לח) וערפל חתולתו הוא שמלפפין את הוולד [יחזקאל טז, ד]. שמלפפין הולד בשבת. לכורכו בבגדים וקושרו בחגורה רחבה ומתישבין פרקי אבריו שהן רכין ונעקמין במכלי הלידה וקורין אנגלוטור"ש בלע"ז [לעיל סו:] כמו שעושין לקטן שיתתקנו אבריו ולא יתעקמו [לקמן קמז:]. מעטפתו מלפפתו. לשון מלבוש המיטוק בחגורה [ע"ז ה.].

בְּדָבָר אַחֵר – **"that other thing,"** i.e. a swine, **קָשֶׁה לְדָבָר אַחֵר** – **it is harmful with regard to "that other thing,"** i.e. *tzaraas.*[1]

The fourth teaching of Rav and Shmuel:

רַב וּשְׁמוּאֵל דְּאָמְרֵי תַּרְוַיְיהוּ – **Rav and Shmuel both say:** **הַאי מַאן דְּעָבִיד מִילְּתָא** – **One who undergoes the procedure** of bloodletting **לִישְׁהֵי פּוּרְתָּא וַהֲדַר לֵיקוּם** – **should wait a little and** only **then get up** to go. **דְּאָמַר מַר** – **For the master has said:**[2] **חֲמִשָּׁה דְּבָרִים קְרוֹבִין לְמִיתָה יוֹתֵר מִן הַחַיִּים** – **Five things** bring a person **closer to death than to life,** **וְאֵלּוּ הֵן** – **and these are:** **אָכַל וְעָמַד** – **if one eats and stands up** immediately; **שָׁתָה וְעָמַד** – **if one drinks and stands up** immediately; **יָשֵׁן וְעָמַד** – **if one sleeps and stands up** immediately; **הִקִּיז דָּם וְעָמַד** – **if one undergoes bloodletting and stands up** immediately; **שִׁימֵּשׁ מִטָּתוֹ וְעָמַד** – **and if one engages in conjugal relations and stands up** immediately.

Shmuel presents additional guidelines for bloodletting:

אָמַר שְׁמוּאֵל – **Shmuel said:** **פּוּרְסָא דְּדְמָא כָּל תְּלָתִין יוֹמִין** – **The time for** letting **blood is every thirty days.**[3] **וּבֵין הַפְּרָקִים יִמַעֵט** – **And** when one reaches the point **between the** first two **stages of life,**[4] **he should decrease** the frequency of bloodletting.[5] **וּבֵין הַפְּרָקִים יַחֲזוֹר וִימַעֵט** – **And** upon reaching the point **between the** next two **stages** of life,[6] **he should again decrease** the frequency of bloodletting.[7]

Additional guidelines:

וְאָמַר שְׁמוּאֵל – **And Shmuel** also **said:** **פּוּרְסָא דִּדְמָא חַד בְּשַׁבְּתָא אַרְבְּעָה וּמַעֲלֵי שַׁבְּתָא** – **The** appropriate **time for** one to let **blood is** either on a **Sunday, Wednesday or Friday.** **אֲבָל שֵׁנִי וַחֲמִישִׁי לֹא** – **But** on a **Monday or Thursday,** one should **not** let blood. **דְּאָמַר מַר** – **For the master said:** **מִי שֶׁיֵּשׁ לוֹ זְכוּת אָבוֹת יַקִּיז דָּם בְּשֵׁנִי וּבַחֲמִישִׁי** – Only **one who has ancestral merit** to protect him **can** take the risk and **let** his **blood on a Monday or Thursday.** And why is it dangerous to let blood on Monday or Thursday? **שֶׁבֵּית דִּין שֶׁל מַעְלָה וְשֶׁל מַטָּה שָׁוִין כְּאֶחָד** – **Because the Heavenly court and the lower** (earthly) **one are** in session **at the same time.**[8] **בִּתְלָתָא בְּשַׁבְּתָא מַאי טַעְמָא לֹא** – And **what is the reason** that one should **not** let blood **on the third day of the week** (on Tuesday)? **מִשּׁוּם דְּקַיְימָא לֵיהּ מַאְדִּים בְּזוּגֵי** – **Because** on Tuesday the influence of **Mars prevails during the pairs** (i.e. the even hours) of the day.[9]

NOTES

1. [In Talmudic parlance "that other thing" is a euphemism for both a swine and for *tzaraas*. Here, the Gemara apparently does not refer to the Biblical *tzaraas,* but rather to a *tzaraas*-like skin disease.] Swine are infected with skin diseases, as evident from the Gemara in *Kiddushin* (49b), which states that swine took nine of the ten measures of *tzaraas* that descended to this world (*Rashi*). Thus, one who meets up with a swine immediately after bloodletting, without eating something first, exposes himself to the danger of contracting skin diseases from it.

2. See *Gittin* 70a.

3. That is, one should undergo bloodletting every thirty days (see *Hagahos Yavetz*).

4. I.e. after reaching the age of forty (*Rashi;* cf. *Rabbeinu Chananel*).

5. That is, he should let blood every two months rather than monthly (*Rashi;* cf. *Rabbeinu Chananel*).

6. I.e. after reaching the age of sixty (*Rashi*).

7. To once every three months (*Rashi;* cf. *Rabbeinu Chananel*). For at this age, one no longer has the same strength and his blood is not as warm, so that his body becomes chilled when he loses blood (*Rashi*).

8. [As stated in *Rosh Hashanah* 16a,] a person is subject to Heavenly judgment every day. And by Ezra's enactment (following his return from the Babylonian exile), the earthly courts convene in the cities every Monday and Thursday [*Bava Kamma* 82a]. And since the Heavenly court convenes when the earthly ones do, Mondays and Thursdays are times of Heavenly judgment, when special notice is taken of a person's sins [and he is then most susceptible to punishment] (*Rashi*). It is therefore advisable for one to avoid dangerous activities [such as bloodletting] at such times, since Divine judgment is executed more readily when one is in a dangerous situation (see above, 32a and *Rosh Hashanah* 16b; see also above, 31b note 31; see *Sfas Emes*).

9. There are seven celestial bodies that exert their respective astrological influences on earthly affairs in hourly rotation (unrelated to their positions in the sky at that moment – see *Rashi* to *Eruvin* 56a ד"ה ואין תקופה מושכת; cf. the responsum of *Rambam,* cited in *Ritva MHK* ed. ד"ה כיון דרשו). These seven bodies are the sun, the moon and the five planets visible on Earth to the naked eye (Mercury, Venus, Mars, Saturn and Jupiter). The sequence of influences is שצ"ם חנכ"ל, which is an acronym for: שַׁבְּתַאי, *Saturn;* צֶדֶק, *Jupiter;* מַאְדִּים, *Mars;* חַמָּה, *the sun;* נוֹגַהּ, *Venus;* כּוֹכָב, *Mercury;* and לְבָנָה, *the moon.* This cycle of influences began at the beginning of the fourth day of Creation, when the celestial bodies were placed in the firmament. Thus, at the first hour of the first Tuesday night of creation, שַׁבְּתַאי, *Saturn,* exerted its influence, followed by צֶדֶק, *Jupiter,* in the second hour, מַאְדִּים, *Mars,* in the third hour, and so on (see *Rashi;* see also *Rashi* to *Eruvin* 56a ד"ה ואין תקופה מושכת). The effect this constantly repeating cycle has on each hour of the week is shown in the following chart. [Note that the influence which prevails at any given hour of a particular day is the same each and every week. For there are seven hourly influences, and every point in one week is separated from the same point in the previous week by exactly 168 hours – a multiple of seven (7×24).]

Mars' influence predisposes the world to war, epidemic and other misfortune. And, as taught in *Pesachim* 110b, anything associated with "pairs" is particularly susceptible to demonic influences. Thus, one must especially avoid dangerous activities, such as bloodletting, when Mars is dominant during an even-numbered hour, for two negative influences then coincide. Now, as can be seen on the accompanying chart, Mars is ascendant on Tuesday during the eighth hour of the daytime. Therefore, one should not let blood on Tuesday [lest he come to do so during the dangerous eighth hour of the day – see end of note] (*Rashi*).

S	F	T	W	T	M	S	HR.	
מ	ל	ח	ש	נ	צ	כ	1	NIGHT
ח	ש	נ	צ	כ	מ	ל	2	
נ	צ	כ	מ	ל	ח	ש	3	
כ	מ	ל	ח	ש	נ	צ	4	
ל	ח	ש	נ	צ	כ	מ	5	
ש	נ	צ	כ	מ	ל	ח	6	
צ	כ	מ	ל	ח	ש	נ	7	
מ	ל	ח	ש	נ	צ	כ	8	
ח	ש	נ	צ	כ	מ	ל	9	
נ	צ	כ	מ	ל	ח	ש	10	
כ	מ	ל	ח	ש	נ	צ	11	
ל	ח	ש	נ	צ	כ	מ	12	
ש	נ	צ	כ	מ	ל	ח	1	DAY
צ	כ	מ	ל	ח	ש	נ	2	
מ	ל	ח	ש	נ	צ	כ	3	
ח	ש	נ	צ	כ	מ	ל	4	
נ	צ	כ	מ	ל	ח	ש	5	
כ	מ	ל	ח	ש	נ	צ	6	
ל	ח	ש	נ	צ	כ	מ	7	
ש	נ	צ	כ	מ	ל	ח	8	
צ	כ	מ	ל	ח	ש	נ	9	
מ	ל	ח	ש	נ	צ	כ	10	
ח	ש	נ	צ	כ	מ	ל	11	
נ	צ	כ	מ	ל	ח	ש	12	

Shaded boxes indicate when Mars is dominant during an even-numbered hour.

Though Mars is also ascendant during even hours on other days [e.g. Sunday and Wednesday], this occurs during the nighttime hours, when it is unusual to let blood in any event [and there is thus no concern that one will come to do so] (*Rashi*). [The twelfth daytime hour of Wednesday is also deemed "nighttime" in this regard, for it is unusual for one to let blood so late in the day (*Tosafos*).]

The influence of Mars also prevails during even daytime hours on Monday, Thursday and Friday, but the Gemara has already explained a better reason for not letting blood on Monday and Thursday (see *Chidushei HaRan*), and will raise the question of Friday shortly. Alternatively, now that the Gemara has introduced the consideration of the coincidence of negative influences, it emerges that this is also the reason for not letting blood on Monday or Thursday (ibid.).

Earlier in the note, we assumed that letting blood any time Tuesday is discouraged lest one come to do so during the inauspicious eighth daytime hour of that day. Indeed, this assumption seems implicit in *Tosafos* ד"ה דקאי. *Chidushei HaRan,* however, suggests that when Mars prevails during an even hour [of a particular daytime or nighttime period], the entire period becomes inauspicious. An exception to this is the coincidence of Mars' domain with the last hour of the daytime period (as occurs on Wednesday), since that hour is reckoned as part of the following night in regard to these matters.

עין משפט נר מצוה

לח א מיי׳ פ״ד מהלכות דעות הלכה יח:
לט ב מיי׳ שם הל׳ ג:
מ ג מיי׳ שם הלכה יט טוש״ע א״ח סי׳ רמ סעיף טו:
מא ד מיי׳ פ״ד מהלכות דעות הלכה יח:
מב ה ש״ע א״ח סימן תסח סעי׳ י בהג״ה:
מג ו מיי׳ פ״ב מהלכות שבת הלכה יא יג סמג לאוין סה טוש״ע א״ח סימן של סעיף ז:

מסורת הש״ס

א) גיטין ע., ב) [עיין תוספות עירובין ע. ד״ה ואין], ג) [עי׳ ערוך ערך יומא דשפמי ממלא פירוש יפה בערוך ערך פגר בשינוי הטעם], ד) [תוספתא פט״ו], ה) [לקמן קמ״ט ושם הוא הטעור לא היה כתוב הא דאמר רב נחמן הלכה כר׳ יוסי ועיין רש״י לקמן שם], ו) [וכן איתא לעיל סו: דלפופי ינוקא בשבתא שפיר דמי וע״ש בפרש״י וכן עוד לקמן קמו: ובפרש״י שם], ז) [וע״ע תוספות כתובות ו. ד״ה שבתי דיען].

גמרא

בדבר אחר קשה לדבר אחר רב ושמואל דאמרי תרווייהו ^א^ האי מאן דעביד מילתא לישהי פורתא והדר ליקום דאמר מר ^ה^ ה׳ דברים קרובין למיתה יותר מן החיים ואלו הן ^ב^ אכל ועמד שתה ועמד ישן ועמד הקיז דם ועמד ^ג^ שימש מטתו ועמד אמר שמואל פורסא דדמא כל תלתין יומין ^ד^ ובין הפרקים ימעט ובין הפרקים יחזור וימעט ואמר שמואל פורסא דדמא חד בשבתא ארבעה ומעלי שבתא אבל שני וחמישי לא דאמר מר מי שיש לו זכות אבות יקיז דם בשני ובחמישי שב״ד של מעלה ושל מטה שוין כאחד בתלתא בשבתא מאי טעמא לא משום דקיימא ליה מאדים ^ז^ בזווי מעלי שבתא נמי קיימא בזווי ^ו^ כיון דדשו ביה רבים ^א^ שומר פתאים ה׳ אמר שמואל ד׳ דהוא ד׳ ד׳ דהוא ארביסר ד׳ דהוא עשרים וארבעה ד׳ דליכא ארבע בתריה סכנתא ר״ח ושני לו חולשא שלישי לו סכנה מעלי יומא טבא חולשא מעלי יומא דעצרתא סכנתא ^ה^ וגזרו רבנן אכולהו מעלי יומא טבא משום יומא טבא דעצרת דנפיק ביה זיקא ושמיה טבוח דאי לא קבלו ישראל תורה הוה טבח להו לבשרייהו ולדמייהו אמר שמואל אכל חטה והקיז דם לא הקיז אלא לאותה חטה והנ״מ לרפואה אבל לאוקולי מיקל המקיז דם שתייה לאלתר אכילה עד חצי מיל איבעיא להו שתייה לאלתר מעלי אבל בתר הכי קשי או דילמא לא קשי ולא מעלי תיקו איבעיא להו אכילה עד חצי מיל הוא דקמעלי הא בתר הכי ומקמי הכי קשי או דילמא לא קשי ולא מעלי תיקו ^ג^ מכריז רב מאה קרי בזוזא מאה רישי בזוזא מאה שפמי ולא כלום אמר רב יוסף כי הוינן בי רב הונא יומא דמפגרי ביה רבנן אמרי האידנא יומא דשפמי הוא ולא ידענא מאי קאמרי: וקושרין הטבור: ת״ר ^ז^ קושרין הטבור ר׳ יוסי אומר אף חותכין וטומנין השליא כדי שיחם הולד אמר רשב״ג בנות מלכים טומנות בספלים של שמן בנות עשירים בספוגים של צמר בנות עניים במוכין ^ח^ אמר רב נחמן אמר רבה בר אבוה אמר רב הלכה כר׳ יוסי ואמר רב נחמן אמר רבה בר אבוה אמר רב מודים חכמים לר׳ יוסי בטבור של שני תינוקות שחותכין מ״ט דמנתחי אהדדי ואמר רב נחמן אמר רבה בר אבוה אמר רב ^י^ כל האמור בפרשת תוכחה עושין לחיה בשבת שנאמר ^ב^ ומולדותיך ביום הולדת אותך לא כרת שרך ובמים לא רחצת למשעי והמלח לא המלחת והחתל לא חתלת ומולדותיך ביום הולדת מכאן שמיילדים את הולד בשבת לא כרת שרך מכאן שחותכין הטבור בשבת ובמים לא רחצת למשעי מכאן שרוחצין הולד בשבת והמלח לא המלחת מכאן שמולחין הולד בשבת והחתל לא חתלת מכאן שמלפפין הולד בשבת:

הדרן עלך מפנין

תוספות

מי שיש לו זכות אבות. וקודם תקנת עזרא אע״פ שהיו דנין בכל יום שהיו נריכים לא היו קובעים לישב בכל יום ^ו^:

דקאי מאדים בזווי. ברביעי נמי קאי מאדים בזווי בסוף היום אלא לא חשו חכמים לכך דאין דרך להקיז כל כך בסמוך ללילה: **דליכא** ארבע בתריה. שאין ד׳ ימים עד סוף החדש כדפירש בקונטרס דליכא למימר רביעי בשבת דהא ד׳ דהוא עשרין וארבע היינו דליכא רביעי בתריה:

מאה רישי בזוזא מאה קרי בזוזא. לפירוש הקונטרס תימה מה שייך הכא ור״ח גרים מאה קרני בזוזא ומפרש מאה רישי מאה ראשי בני אדם (ונראה) שהיה מנהג קצוב לספר לגלח בזוזא וכן מנהג ק׳ קרני להקיז בזוזא כמו קרנא דאומנא (לקמן דף קנד:) אבל מאה שפמי לתקן השפה בזולא כלום דבשכר גילוח והקזה היה מתקן השפה וכיום שהיה מתקן שפמו לא היה נוטל כלום ועל כן היה למשל כל מי שהיה יגע ולא עלה בידו שכרו היו קורין אותו יומא דשפמי: **מפגרי** רבנן. תשש כחם והיו מתחלשין ולא יכלו למיגרס כדכתיב (ש״א ל) וירדוף דוד הוא וארבע מאות איש ויעמדו מאתים איש אשר פגרו מעבור את נחל הבשור: **כל** האמור בפרשת תוכחה. לאו מקרא מפיק אלא אסמכתא כיון שבא בפרשת תוכחה אם כן לער הוא אם אין עושין והקילו חכמים לעשות וכלום אין כהן איסורא דאורייתא:

הדרן עלך מפנין

רש״י

בדבר אחר. מזיר: קשה לדבר אחר. לרעת שהחזירים מנוגעים הם כדאמרינן בקדושין (דף מט:) י׳ קבים נגעים ירדו לעולם תשעה נטלו חזירים: אבל ועמד. מהר לעמוד פתאום אחר שאכל שובעו: פורסא דדמא. זמן הקזה כמו כפרוס הפסח (שקלים פ״ג מ״א): בין הפרקים. פירקי שנותיו כגון לאחר מ׳ שנה: ימעט. בהקזה לא יקיז בכל חדש אלא לג׳ חדשים: ובין הפרקים יחזור וימעט. לאחר ששים יקיז לג׳ חדשים לפי שאין כמו עליו ואין דמו הם וגופו מלטנן כשמתקר דמו: שב״ד של מעלה ושל מטה שוין. אדם נדון בכל יום וב״ד יושבין בעיירות בב׳ ובה׳ מתקנת עזרא ואילך (ב״ק דף פב.) וכיון דיום הדין ופקידה היא עוונותיו מזכרים: דקיימא ליה מאדים בזווי. שמזל מאדים משמש בו בשעות זוגות ומזל מאדים ממונה על החרב ועל הדבר ועל הפורעניות והזוגות קשין שהן רשות לשדים כדאמר בפסחים (דף קי:) והפורעניות מוכנין של״מ חנכ״ל סדר השעות כשנתלו המאורות והמזלות שעה ראשונה של ד׳ בשבת שימש שבתאי ובשניה לדק ואחריו מאדים ואחריו חמה ואחריו נוגה ואחריו כוכב ואחריו לבנה נמלאו ז׳ המזלות לז׳ השעות וחוזרים חלילה לעולם נמלא בסדר זה לעולם סימני מזלות המשמשין בתחלת לילי השבוע כלנ״ש חל״מ מולאי שבת שעה ראשונה שלו כוכב תחלה ליל שני לבנה וכן בסדר הזה וסדר תחלת סימני הימים חל״ם כלנ״ש שעה ראשונה של אחד בשבת חמה ושל שני בשבת לבנה ושל שלישי בשבת מאדים נמלא מאדים חוזר בו חלילה בשעה שמינית ביום והיא זוגות ואבל שאר ימים אין מאדים בזוגות שלהם אם לא בלילה ובלילה אין דרך להקיז: מעלי שבתא נמי קיימא מאדים בזווי. שהרי שעה ראשונה של יום נוגה לפי הסדר של חל״ם כלנ״ש תחלת הימים וכיון שתחלתו נוגה וסדר דליכתן של״ם חנכ״ל נמלאו מתחלין לחזור חלילה בשעה רביעית נמלא מאדים בשעה ששית: כיון דדשו ביה רבים. הורגלו בו מפני דזמנן שיהיו קרובים לסעודת שבת ואמרינן בפירקין דלעיל (ד׳ קיח:) כבוד שבת בדגים גדולים ובמסכת ע״ז (ד׳ כט:) אמרינן שני לדם דג: ארבע דהוא ד׳. ד׳ בשבת שהוא ד׳ לחדש או ארביסר לחדש או כ״ד לחדש כולהון קשה להקזה: ד׳ דליכא ד׳ בתריה. שאין ד׳ ימים עד סוף החדש וליכא דאמרי דליכא ד׳ בשבת בתריה באותו חדש ואינו כן: ה״ג ר״ח ושני לו חולשא שלישי לו סכנתא: אכל חטה והקיז דם לא הקיז אלא לחטה. שהאוכל מכביד את האדם והקזה שאחר אכילה אינו מועיל אלא לאותו כובד: וה״מ. במקיז לרפואה: אבל אקולי. מי שיש לו דם המכביד עליו אפי׳ לאחר אכילה מקיז ומיקל: מאה רישי בזוזא. כלומר אם יהיו בזול מאד קנה ראשי בהמה ואם לאו אל תקח שאינן בריאין לאכול: מאה קרי. דלועין: מאה שפמי. כמו על שפם (ויקרא יג) גרוינו״ן בלעז שפתים של בהמה: יומא דמפגרי ביה רבנן. שהיו התלמידים מתעצלין מלבא בבית המדרש קרי ליה יומא דשפמי כלומר היום הזה אבד לו ואין בו תועלת: וטומנין את השליא. כדמפרש רשב״ג שהיא רפואה להתחמם הולד: ספוגין של צמר. למר מנופץ: של שני תינוקות. תאומים וקשורין טבורן זה בזה: משום דמנתחי מהדדי. זה אילך וזה אילך ונמצאו מסוכנין: בפרשת תוכחה. שהוכיח יחזקאל לישראל את חסדי הקב״ה שעמהן: תוכחה. לשון לכו ונוכחה (ישעיה א) להתווכח ולהודיע מי הוא שסרח על שכנגדו: למשעי. לטוח ולהחליק בשרו: שמולחין. ובשרו מתקשה: מלפפין. אנמליי״ן בלע״ז ולאו היינו אסוקי ינוקא דאמרן לעיל בפרק כל הכלים (דף קכג.) דהא שמעינן ליה לרב נחמן דאסר אלא ^ו^ לפופי בעלמא כמו שעושין ^*^ בחגורות ופסיקיאות: **הדרן עלך מפנין**

רבינו חננאל

יסתכנו. פי׳ זוזא מכא. זה מעוך שנמעך מטבע הצורה ונראה כאסימון. דעביד מלתא. באותו היום שמקיז דם. פורסא דדמא כל תלתין יומין. פי׳ גבול הדם לבחורים כל שלשים יום. בין הפרקים הגיע לחמשים שנה ימעט. יוציא משנים חדשים [או] ג׳ חדשים. פעם אחת עוד בין הפרקים בא בימים יחזור ימעט משה חדשים לששה חדשים או משנה לשנה וזה הפי׳ קיבלנוהו מרבותינו קבלה: **בתלתא** קאי מאדים בזוי. פי׳ בשתי שעות שהן זוגות יום שלישי שעה שמינית מאדים ושעה שתים ועשרים מאדים ושכן סידור הכוכבים חל״ם כצנ״ש בימים נמצא יום אחד שעה ראשונה כוכב חמה יום שני שעה ראשונה כוכב לבנה. יום ג׳ שעה ראשונה כוכב מאדים יום ד׳ שעה ראשונה כוכב [כוכב]. יום ה׳ שעה ראשונה כוכב צדק יום ו׳ שעה ראשונה כוכב נוגה. יום ז׳ שעה ראשונה כוכב שבתי וסידורן חל״ם כצנ״ש בימים כצנ״ש חל״ם בלילות וסידוריהן חנכ״ל שצ״ם. וכיון שביום ג׳ עומד מאדים בשעה שמינית והן זוגות ובשעה כ״ב והן זוגות חיישינן לסכנה. וכיוצא בזה בשני ובחמישי משום הכי חיישינן לסכנה. כי מאדים הוא ממונה על הדם ואקשינן עלה והא יום ו׳ הוא דמעלי שבתא דקאי מאדים בשעה ששית ובשעה עשרים והן זוגות. ואמרת פורסא דדמא חד בשבא וארבעה ומעלי שבתא. ולא מצאו לו פירוק. והשיב אע״פ שהוא כן כיון דדשו בה רבים להקיז ביום ששי שומר פתאים ה׳. מאה רישי בזוזי מאה קרני בזוזא שפמי ולא כלום פי׳ היה מנהג קצוב כי הספר מגלח מאה ראשי כלומר מאה ראשי בני אדם נוטל שכרו זוז אחד וכן (א׳ מדוגמא) [חמשים] מאה קרן כלומר מאה קרן של זכוכית והוא ריבדא דכוסילתא נוטל בשכרו בק׳ קרן זוז אחד. אבל לתקן הזקן וליטול השפה ולתקנו לא היה מנהג ליקח האומן כלום אלא אותן בני אדם שמגלח ראשם או עושה להן ריבדא דכוסילתא נוטל שכרו כאשר אמרנו מתקן זקנם ונוטל שפמם בחנם. וכן היה הדין ויום שהיה האומן עושה השפמות לא היה נוטל שכר והיה הולך לביתו ריקם. ועל כן היה למשל כל מי שהיה יגע ולא [היה] עולה בידו (סבר) [שכר] היה קורא אותו יומא דשפמי. מיפגרי תשש כחם והוו מתחלשי יגעים ויעפים ולא יכלי למיגרס כדכתיב וירדף דוד הוא וארבע מאות איש ויעמדו מאתים איש אשר פגרו מעבור וגו׳ הוו אמרי יומא דשפמי ^א^: **וקושרין** את הטיבור. ר׳ יוסי אומר אף חותכין את הטיבור כל צרכי מילה עושין בשבת אמר רב נחמן אמר רבה בר אבוה הלכה כרבי יוסי שחותכין בשבת טיבור תינוק אחד וכ״ש טיבור ב׳ תינוקות שבזה אפילו חכמים מודים שמחתך מ״ט משום (דמתחזי) [דמנתחו] אהדדי. ואמר רב נחמן אמר רבה בר אבוה אמר רב כל האמור בפרשת תוכחה עושין לחיה בשבת שנא׳ ומולדותיך ביום הולדת אותך מיכן שמיילדין לחיה בשבת לא כרת שרך מיכן שחותכין את הטיבור בשבת ובמים לא רוחצת למשעי מיכן שמרחיצין את הוולד בשבת והחתל לא חתלת מיכן שמלפפין הולד בשבת ואמרינן בתלמוד א״י ומחללין עליה את השבת שמואל אמר עושין לה מדורה אפילו בתקופת תמוז וקושרין את הטיבור כהדא אמתיה דבר קפרא נפקא מיילדה בשבת אתת ושאלת לר׳ וא׳ לה אזלון ושאלון לחייתא. אמרה לה ליכא חייא. אמר לה זילי עבידי כמנהגך אמרה ליה ליכא מנהג אמר לה איזיל חתיך כר׳ יוסי כבמתניתא וכל צרכי חיה עושין בשבת תני השליא הזאת בשבת עשירין טומנין אותה בשמן והעניים בתבן ובחול אלו ואלו טומנין אותה בארץ כדי ליתן ערבון בארץ [לארץ]: **הדרן עלך מפנין**

חשק שלמה על רבינו חננאל א) עיין בערוך ערך פגר:

גליון הש״ס

גמרא כיון דדשו ביה רבים שומר פתאים. עיין תוס׳ פ״ד סי׳ ר״ח: רש״י ד״ה מלפפים וכו׳ בחגורות ופסיקיאות. עיין לקמן דף קמז ע״ב תוס׳ ד״ה ובלבד שלא יבא לידי השוואה. ועי׳ בתשובה לאדמה הקודם חלק א״ח סי׳ מ:

תורה אור השלם

א) שֹׁמֵר פְּתָאיִם יְיָ דַּלּוֹתִי וְלִי יְהוֹשִׁיעַ: [תהלים קטז, ו]

ב) וּמוֹלְדוֹתַיִךְ בְּיוֹם הוּלֶּדֶת אֹתָךְ לֹא כָרַּת שָׁרֵּךְ וּבְמַיִם לֹא רֻחַצְתְּ לְמִשְׁעִי וְהָמְלֵחַ לֹא הֻמְלַחַתְּ וְהָחְתֵּל לֹא חֻתָּלְתְּ: [יחזקאל טז, ד]

ליקוטי רש״י

אכל ועמד. מיד קודם ששהה מעט [גיטין ע.]. מוכין. כל דבר רך קרוי מוכין כגון למר גפן ותלישי למר של בהמה וגרירת בגדים בלויים [לעיל מז:]. ביום הולדת אותך. פוטמיא״ה בלע״ז כשנחתך הטבור קשור בו הכל בלי שום תיקון ולפי שדימה הדבר לכריה הזכיר כאן תיקוני הולד. שרך. כמו שרירך. למשעי. לנקות לחוח הסלע תרגומו שעיעות כיפה אפלאנמנ״ט בלע״ז ומנהג הכל למשעי לשון שעשועים. לא המלחת. מכאן שמולחין את הולד כדי שיתקשו׳ בשרו. והחתל. לשון כורכין בבגדים וכן (איוב לח) וערפל חתולתו שמלפפין את הולד בשבת. לכורכו בבגדים וקושרו בחגורה רחבה ומתיישבין פרקי אבריו שהן רכין ונשמטין במכבלי הלידה וקורין אנמלוטוי״ר בלע״ז [לעיל סו:]. אונמלוטי״א כמו שעושין לקטן שיתיישבו אבריו ולא יתעקם [לקמן קמז:]. מלפפתו. מעטפתו לשון מלבוש כמו מלפפין את התינוק בשבת [ע״ז ה.].

The Gemara asks:

מַעֲלֵי שַׁבְּתָא נַמִי קַיְימָא בְּזָווֵי – But **on Friday** the influence of **[Mars] also prevails during the even [hours]** of the day,[10] and still Shmuel lists it as one of the allowable times for bloodletting! – ? –

The Gemara answers:

כֵּיוָן דְּדָשׁוּ בֵּיהּ רַבִּים – **Since many have trampled** a beaten path **upon it** (i.e. since it has become common practice to let blood on Friday),[11] we say that "שֹׁמֵר פְּתָאִים ה׳" – *Hashem protects the heedless.*[12]

Additional guidelines:

אָמַר שְׁמוּאֵל – **Shmuel said:** **ד׳ דְּהוּא אַרְבָּעָה** – Letting blood on **the fourth** day of the week (Wednesday) **that is** also **the fourth** day of the month, **ד׳ דְּהוּא אַרְבֵּיסַר** – or letting blood on **the fourth day** of the week **that is** also **the fourteenth** day of the month, **ד׳ דְּהוּא עֶשְׂרִים וְאַרְבָּעָה** – or letting blood on **the fourth** day of the week **that is** also **the twenty-fourth** day of the month, **ד׳ דְּלֵיכָּא אַרְבַּע בַּתְרֵיהּ** – or letting blood on **the fourth** day of the week **where there are not four** days **after it** in the month.[13] **סַכַּנְתָּא** – **is dangerous.** **רֹאשׁ חוֹדֶשׁ וְשֵׁנִי לוֹ חוּלְשָׁא** – Letting blood on **the first of the month or the next day** causes **weakness.** **שְׁלִישִׁי לוֹ סַכָּנָה** – Letting blood on **the third** day of the month **is** actually **dangerous.** **מַעֲלֵי יוֹמָא טָבָא חוּלְשָׁא** – Letting blood on **the eve of** (i.e the day before) **Yom Tov** causes **weakness,** **מַעֲלֵי יוֹמָא דַעֲצַרְתָּא סַכַּנְתָּא** – but on **the eve of Shavuos**[14] it is actually **dangerous.** **וְגָזְרוּ רַבָּנָן אַכּוּלְּהוּ מַעֲלֵי יוֹמָא טָבָא** – **Therefore, the Rabbis decreed** that one should not let blood **on the eve of *any* Yom Tov,** **מִשּׁוּם יוֹמָא טָבָא דַעֲצֶרֶת** – **because of** the concern that one might come to do so on the eve of **the Yom Tov of Shavuos** when there is actual danger, **דְּנָפִיק בֵּיהּ זִיקָא וּשְׁמֵיהּ טְבוֹחַ** – **for on it** [this day before Shavuos] **a wind blows whose name is *Tevoach*** ("Slaughtering"), **דְּאִי לֹא קִבְּלוּ יִשְׂרָאֵל תּוֹרָה** – **for had Israel not accepted the Torah,**[15] **הֲוָה טָבַח לְהוּ לְבִשְׂרַייהוּ וּלְדָמַייהוּ** – **[this wind] would have slaughtered them – their flesh and their blood.**[16]

Another teaching:

אָמַר שְׁמוּאֵל – **Shmuel said:** **אָכַל חִטָּה וְהִקִּיז דָּם** – **If one ate wheat and** then **let** his **blood,** **לֹא הִקִּיז אֶלָּא לְאוֹתָהּ חִטָּה** – **he has let** blood **only for the sake of that wheat.**[17] **וְהָנֵי מִילֵּי לִרְפוּאָה** – **But this** statement regarding the uselessness of letting blood after eating **applies only** where one wishes to let blood **for** general **therapeutic purposes.** **אֲבָל לְאוֹקוּלֵי מֵיקַל** – **But** if one is letting blood **to lighten** the burden of excess blood in his body, **he may lighten** it even after eating and accomplish his purpose.

Another teaching:

הַמַּקִּיז דָּם שְׁתִיָּה לְאַלְתַּר – **If one lets** his **blood, drinking** should follow **immediately;** **אֲכִילָה עַד חֲצִי מִיל** – **eating** should wait **until** the time it takes to walk **half a *mil*** elapses.

The Gemara analyzes this statement:

אִיבַּעְיָא לְהוּ – **They inquired:** **שְׁתִיָּה לְאַלְתַּר מְעַלֵּי** – Does it mean that **drinking immediately** after letting blood **is beneficial,** **אֲבָל בָּתַר הָכִי קָשֵׁי** – **but** drinking **after this** (after "immediately") **is detrimental?** **אוֹ דִילְמָא לֹא קָשֵׁי וְלֹא מְעַלֵּי** – **Or perhaps** it means only that drinking sometime later is **neither detrimental nor beneficial.**

The Gemara concludes:

תֵּיקוּ – **Let [this matter] stand** unresolved.

אִיבַּעְיָא לְהוּ – **They inquired:** **אֲכִילָה עַד חֲצִי מִיל הוּא דְקָמְעַלֵּי** – Does it mean that **eating at an interval of** exactly the time it takes to walk **half a *mil* is beneficial,** **הָא בָּתַר הָכִי וּמִקַּמֵּי הָכִי קָשֵׁי** – **but** eating **after this** time **or before this** time **is detrimental?** **אוֹ דִילְמָא לֹא קָשֵׁי וְלֹא מְעַלֵּי** – **Or perhaps** it means only that eating before or after this time is **neither detrimental nor beneficial.**

The Gemara concludes:

תֵּיקוּ – **Let [this matter] stand** unresolved.

Rav offers advice on other health-related matters:[18]

מַכְרִיז רַב – **Rav announced:** **מְאָה קָרֵי בְּזוּזָא** – If **one hundred gourds** go **for a *zuz*,** one should buy them; **מְאָה רֵישֵׁי בְּזוּזָא** – if **one hundred** animal **heads** go **for a *zuz*,** one should buy them.[19] **מְאָה שִׂפְּמֵי וְלֹא כְלוּם** – But even if **one hundred** animal **lips cost nothing,** one should not bother taking them, for they serve no benefit.

The Gemara notes:

אָמַר רַב יוֹסֵף – Upon hearing this advice of Rav, **Rav Yosef remarked:** **כִּי הֲוֵינַן בֵּי רַב הוּנָא יוֹמָא דִּמְפַגְּרֵי בֵּיהּ רַבָּנָן** – **When we were in Rav Huna's academy** on **the day that the Rabbis** (i.e. the disciples) **were lazy** about coming to the study hall,[20] **אָמְרֵי הָאִידְנָא יוֹמָא דְשִׂפְּמֵי הוּא** – **[people] would say, "Today is a lip day,"** **וְלָא יָדַעְנָא מַאי קָאָמְרֵי** – **and I did not understand what they were saying.** Now, however, that I have heard this teaching of Rav about the worthlessness of animal lips, I realize that they meant to say, "Today is a worthless day, which accomplished nothing."

NOTES

10. That is, during the sixth hour of the daytime (see chart in preceding note).

11. It is healthful for one to eat fish on the day following bloodletting (as stated in *Avodah Zarah* 29a). Financial conditions forced many people to consider fish an expensive luxury, and they would not eat fish except on Shabbos, when it is a mitzvah to do so in honor of the holy day (see above, 118b). Therefore, it became the practice for these people to delay bloodletting until Friday so that they could eat fish on the following day (*Rashi*).

12. *Psalms* 116:6. That is, though a particular behavior should be considered dangerous, the fact that it has become common practice causes God to protect His heedless children from the harmful effects of their imprudent actions.

[We apply this principle only in cases where we see that the overwhelming majority of people are, in fact, not harmed by such behavior. But where we find that a significant number of people *do* suffer harm from it (since it is evident that God is *not* protecting the heedless in this case) it is forbidden (see *Igros Moshe, Choshen Mishpat* II:76).]

13. For example, a Wednesday that falls on the twenty-seventh of the month, so that there are less than four days remaining to the month (see *Rashi*).

14. For the reason the Gemara will state shortly.

15. [Shavuos falls on the day the Israelites received the Torah at Sinai.]

16. Apparently, the Gemara here means that had the Jews not accepted the Torah the following day, this wind would have slaughtered them. *Chasam Sofer* (*Derashos* II p. 294a), however, understands this Gemara as referring to Israel's declaration of נַעֲשֶׂה וְנִשְׁמַע, *We will do and we will listen* (*Exodus* 24:7), which the Jews proclaimed on the fifth of Sivan (Erev Shavuos) [see *Rashi* to *Exodus* 24:4]. Had they not made this declaration, the wind would have slaughtered them on that very day.

[*Maharsha* (*Chidushei Aggados* to *Sanhedrin* 43b) vocalizes the wind's name as טָבוּחַ, *Tavuach* (the slaughtered one). He explains that it is none other than the Satan, who is the Evil Inclination, who is the spirit of the Angel of Death, who stands ready to slaughter Israel if they do not accept the Torah. But if Israel does accept the Torah, then Israel instead "slaughters" (i.e. overcomes and subjugates) the Evil Inclination, which is why it is called here טָבוּחַ, *the slaughtered one,* rather than טוֹבֵחַ, *the slaughterer.*]

17. Eating brings a certain heaviness upon a person. The efficacy of the bloodletting afterwards is spent entirely on alleviating that heaviness, and has no further therapeutic effect (see *Rashi*). [Thus, one loses the benefits of bloodletting by doing so right after eating.]

18. This follows *Rashi's* explanation of the next passage. [According to the reading and explanation of *Rabbeinu Chananel* (cited by *Tosafos*), however, the next passage also relates to bloodletting.]

19. I.e. one should buy gourds or animal heads only if they are extremely cheap, for they are not good sources of nutrition (see *Rashi*).

20. *Rashi.* [*Tosafos,* however, explain that the reference is to a day on which the Rabbis were weak and could not study properly.]

עין משפט
נר מצוה

לח א מיי' פ"ד מהלכות דעות הלכה יח:
לט ב מיי' שם הל' ג:
מ ג מיי' שם הלכה יט טוש"ע א"ח סי' רמ סעיף טו:
מא ד מיי' פ"ד מהלכות דעות הלכה יח:
מב ה ש"ע א"ח סימן תסח סעי' י בהג"ה:
מג ו מיי' פ"ב מהלכות שבת הלכה יא יג סמג לאוין סה טוש"ע א"ח סימן של סעיף ז:

מי שיש לו זכות אבות. וקודם תקנת עזרא אע"פ שהיו דנין בכל יום שהיו רגילים לא היו קובעים לישב בכל יום:

דקאי מאדים בזווי. ברביעי נמי קאי מאדים בזווי בסוף היום אלא לא חשו חכמים לכך דאין דרך להקיז כל כך בסמוך ללילה:

דליכא ארבע בתריה. שאין ד' ימים עד סוף החדש לפירש בקונטרס דליכא למימר רביעי בשבת דהא ד' דהוא עשרין וארבע היינו דליכא רביעי בתריה:

מאה רישי בזוזא מאה קרי בזוזא. לפירוש הקונטרס תימה מה שייך הכא ור"ח גריס מאה קרני בזוזא ומפרש מאה רישי מאה ראשי בני אדם (ונראה) שהיה מנהג קבוע לספר לגלח בזוזא וכן מנהג ק' קרני להקיז בזוזא כמו קרנא דאומנא (לקמן דף קנד:) אבל מאה שפמי לתקן השפה בולא כלום דבשכר גילוח והקזה היה מתקן השפה וכיוס שהיה מתקן שפמו לא היה נוטל כלום ועל כן היה למשל כל מי שהיה יגע ולא עלה בידו שכרו היו קורין אותו יומא דשפמי: **מפגרי** רבנן. תשש כחם והיו מתחלשין ולא יכלו למיגרס כדכתיב (ש"א ל) וירדוף דוד הוא וארבע מאות איש ויעמדו מאתים איש אשר פגרו מעבור את נחל הבשור: **כל** האמור בפרשת תוכחה. לאו מקרא מפיק אלא מסמכא כיון שבא בפרשת תוכחה אם כן לער הוא אם אין עושין והקילו חכמים לעשות וכולהו אין בהן איסורא לאורייתא:

הדרן עלך מפנין

בדבר אחר קשה לדבר אחר רב ושמואל דאמרי תרוייהו אהאי מאן דעביד מילתא לישהי פורתא והדר ליקום דאמר מר ה' דברים קרובין למיתה יותר מן החיים ואלו הן באכל ועמד שתה ועמד ישן ועמד הקיז דם ועמד גשימש מטתו ועמד אמר שמואל פורסא דדמא כל תלתין יומין דובין הפרקים ימעט ובין הפרקים יחזור וימעט ואמר שמואל פורסא דדמא חד בשבתא ארבעה ומעלי שבתא אבל שני וחמישי לא דאמר מר מי שיש לו זכות אבות יקיז דם בשני ובחמישי שב"ד של מעלה ושל מטה שוין כאחד בתלתא בשבתא מאי טעמא לא משום דקיימא ליה מאדים בזווי מעלי שבתא נמי קיימא בזווי כיון דדשו ביה רבים אשומר פתאים ה' אמר שמואל ד' דהוא ד' ד' דהוא ארביסר ד' דהוא עשרים וארבעה ד' דליכא ארבע בתריה סכנתא ר"ח ושני לו חולשא שלישי לו סכנה מעלי יומא טבא חולשא מעלי יומא דעצרתא סכנתא הוגזרו רבנן אכולהו מעלי יומא טבא משום יומא טבא דעצרת דנפיק ביה זיקא ושמיה טבוח דאי לא קבלו ישראל תורה הוה טבח להו לבשרייהו ולדמייהו אמר שמואל אכל חטה והקיז דם לא הקיז אלא לאותה חטה והנ"מ לרפואה אבל לאוקולי מיקיל המקיז דם שתייה לאלתר אכילה עד חצי מיל איבעיא להו שתייה לאלתר מעלי אבל בתר הכי קשי או דילמא לא קשי ולא מעלי תיקו איבעיא להו אכילה עד חצי מיל הוא דקמעלי הא בתר הכי ומקמי הכי קשי או דילמא לא קשי ולא מעלי תיקו ימכריז רב מאה קרי בזוזא מאה רישי בזוזא מאה שפמי ולא כלום אמר רב יוסף כי הוינן בי רב הונא יומא דמפגרי ביה רבנן אמרי האידנא יומא דשפמי הוא ולא ידענא מאי קאמרי: וקושרין הטבור: ת"ר זקושרין הטבור ר' יוסי אומר אף חותכין וטומנין השליא כדי שיחום הולד אמר רשב"ג בנות מלכים טומנות בספלים של שמן בנות עשירים בספוגים של צמר בנות עניים במוכין חאמר רב נחמן אמר רבה בר אבוה אמר רב הלכה כר' יוסי ואמר רב נחמן אמר רבה בר אבוה אמר רב מודים חכמים לר' יוסי בטבור של שני תינוקות שחותכין מ"ט דמנתחי אהדדי ואמר רב נחמן אמר רבה בר אבוה אמר רב טכל האמור בפרשת תוכחה עושין לחיה בשבת שנאמר בומולדותיך ביום הולדת אותך לא כרת שרך ובמים לא רחצת למשעי והמלח לא המלחת והחתל לא חתלת ומולדותיך ביום הולדת מכאן שמיילדים את הולד בשבת לא כרת שרך מכאן שחותכין הטבור בשבת ובמים לא רחצת למשעי מכאן שרוחצין הולד בשבת והמלח לא המלחת מכאן שמולחין הולד בשבת והחתל לא חתלת מכאן שמלפפין הולד בשבת:

הדרן עלך מפנין

בדבר אחר. קשה לדבר אחר. לרעת שהחזירים מנוגעים הם כדאמרינן בקדושין (דף מט:) י' קבים נגעים ירדו לעולם תשעה נטלו חזירים: **אכל ועמד**. מהר לעמוד מאחר שאכל: **פורסא דדמא**. זמן הקזה כמו כפרוס הפסח (שקלים פ"ג מ"א): **בין הפרקים**. פירקי שנותיו כגון לאחר מ' שנה: **ימעט**. בהקזה לא יקיז בכל חדש אלא לג' חדשים: **ובין הפרקים יחזור וימעט**. לאחר ששים יקיז לג' חדשים לפי שאין כחו עליו ואין דמו חם וגופו מצטנן כשמחסר דמו: **שב"ד של מעלה ושל מטה שוין**. אלה נדון בכל יום וב"ד יושבין בעיירות בב' ובה' מתקנת עזרא ואילך (ב"ק דף פב.) וכיון דיום הדין ופקידה היא עונותיו נזכרים: **דקיימא ליה מאדים בזווי**. שמזל מאדים משמש בו בשעות זוגות ומזל מאדים ממונה על החרב ועל הדבר ועל הפורעניות והזוגות קשין שכן רשות לשדים כדאמר בפסחים (דף קי:) והפורעניות מוכנין של"ם חנכ"ל סדר השעות כשנתלו המאורות והמזלות שעה ראשונה של ד' בשבת שימש שבתאי ובשניה צדק ואחריו מאדים ואחריו חמה ואחריו נוגה ואחריו כוכב ואחריו לבנה נמצאו ז' המזלות לז' השעות ומחזרים חלילה לעולם נמצא בסדר זה לעולם סימני מזלות המשמשין בתחלת לילי השבוע כלנ"ש חל"ם מוצאי שבת שעה ראשונה שלו כוכב תחלת ליל שני לבנה וכן בסדר הזה וסדר תחלת סימני הימים חל"ם כלנ"ש שעה ראשונה של אחד בשבת חמה ושל שני בשבת לבנה ושל שלישי בשבת מאדים נמצא מאדים חוזר בו חלילה בשעה שמינית ביום והיא זוגות אבל שאר ימים אין מאדים בזוגות שלהם אם לא בלילה ובלילה אין דרך להקיז: **מעלי שבתא נמי קיימא מאדים בזווי**. שהרי שעה ראשונה של יום נוגה לפי הסדר של חל"ס כלנ"ש תחלת הימים וכיון שתחלתו נוגה וסדר הליכתן של"ס חנכ"ל נמצאו מתחילין לחזור חלילה בשעה רביעית נמצא מאדים בשעה ששית: **כיון דדשו ביה רבים**. הורגלו בו מפני דוחקן שיהיו קרובים לסעודת שבת ואמרינן בפירקין דלעיל (ד' קיח:) כבוד שבת בדגים גדולים ובמסכת ע"ז (ד' כט:) אמרינן שני לדם דג: **ארבע דהוא ד'**. ד' בשבת שהוא ד' לחדש או ארביסר לחדש או כ"ד לחדש כולהון קשה להקזה: **ד' דליכא ד' בתריה**. שאין ד' ימים עד סוף החדש ואיכא דאמרי דליכא ד' בשבת בתריה באותו חדש ואינו כן: ה"ג ר"ח ושני לו חולשא שלישי לו סכנתא: **אכל חטה והקיז דם לא הקיז אלא לחטה**. שהאוכל מכביד את האדם והקזה שאחר אכילה אינו מועיל אלא לאותו כובד: **וה"מ**. במקיז לרפואה: **אבל אקולי**. מי שיש לו דם המכביד עליו אפי' לאחר אכילה מקיז ומיקל: **מאה רישי בזוזא**. כלומר אם יהיו בזול מאד קנה ראשי בהמה ואם לאו אל תקח שאינן בריאין לאכול: **מאה קרי**. דלועין: **מאה שפמי**. כמו על שפם (ויקרא יג) גרוינו"ן בלעז שפתים של בהמה: **יומא דמפגרי ביה רבנן**. שהיו התלמידים מתעצלין מלבא בבית המדרש קרי ליה יומא דשפמי כלומר היום הזה אבד לו ואין בו תועלת: **וטומנין את השליא**. כדמפרש רשב"ג שהיא רפואה להתחמם הולד: **ספוגין של צמר**. צמר מנופץ: **של שני תינוקות**. תאומים וקשורין טבורן זה בזה: **משום דמנתחי מהדדי**. זה אילך וזה אילך ונמצאו מסוכנין: **בפרשת תוכחה**. שהוכיח יחזקאל לישראל את חסדי הקב"ה שעמהן: **תוכחה**. לשון לכו ונוכחה (ישעיה א) להתווכח ולהודיע מי הוא שסרח על שכנגדו: **למשעי**. לטוח ולהחליק בשרו: **שמולחין**. ובשרו מתקשה: **מלפפין**. אנמליו"ן בלע"ז ולאו היינו אסוקי יונקא דאמרן לעיל בפרק כל הכלים (דף קכג.) דהא שמעינן ליה לרב נחמן דאסר אלא י) לפופי בעלמא כמו שעושין ° בחגורות ופסיקיאות: **הדרן עלך מפנין**

רבינו חננאל

יסתכנו. פי' זווא מכא. זהו מעוך שנמעך מטבע הצורה ונראה כאסימון. דעביד מלתא. באותו היום שמקיז דם. פורסא דדמא כל תלתין יומין. פי' בגבול הדם לבחורים כל שלשים יום. בין הפרקים הגיע לחמשים שנה ימעט. יוציא משנים חדשים [או] ג' חדשים. פעם אחת עוד בין הפרקים בא בימים יחזור ימעט משלשה חדשים לששה חדשים או משנה לשנה וזה הפי' קיבלנוהו מרבותינו קבלה: בתלתא קאי מאדים בזווי. פי' בשתי שעות שהן זוגות יום שלישי שעה שמינית מאדים ושעה שתים ועשרים מאדים ושכך סידור הכוכבים חל"ם כנצ"ש בימים נמצא יום אחד שעה ראשונה כוכב חמה יום שני שעה ראשונה כוכב לבנה. יום ג' שעה ראשונה כוכב מאדים יום ד' שעה ראשונה כוכב [כוכב]. יום ה' שעה ראשונה כוכב צדק יום ו' שעה ראשונה כוכב נוגה. יום ז' שעה ראשונה כוכב שבתי וסידורן חל"ם כנצ"ש בימים כנצ"ש חל"ם בלילות וסידורן חנכ"ל שצ"ם. וכיון שביום ג' עומד מאדים בשעה שמינית והן זוגות ובשעה כ"ב והן זוגות חיישינן לסכנה. וכיוצא בזה בשני חיישינן משום הכי חיישינן לסכנה. כי מאדים הוא ממונה על הדם ואקשינן עלה והא יום ו' הוא דמעלי שבתא דקאי מאדים בשעה ששית ובשעה עשרים והן זוגות. ואמרת פורסא דדמא חד בשבא וארבעה ומעלי שבתא. ולא מצאו לו פירוק. והשיב אע"פ שהוא כן כיון דדשו בה רבים להקיז ביום ששי שומר פתאים ה'. מאה רישי בזוזי מאה קרני בזוזא שפמי ולא כלום פי' היה מנהג קבוע כי הספר מגלח מאה ראשי כלומר מאה ראשי בני אדם נוטל שכרו זוז אחד וכן (א' מדוגמא) [חמשים] מאה קרן כלומר מאה קרן של זכוכית והוא ריבדא דכוסילתא נוטל בשכרו בק' קרן זוז אחד. אבל לתקן הזקן וליטול השפה ולתקנו לא היה מנהג ליקח האומן כלום אלא אותן בני אדם שמגלח ראשם או עושה להן ריבדא דכוסילתא נוטל שכרו כאשר אמרנו מתקן זקנם ונוטל שפמם בחנם. וכן היה הדין ויום שהיה האומן עושה השפמות לא היה נוטל שכר והיה הולך לביתו ריקם. ועל כן היה למשל כל מי שהיה יגע ולא [היה] עולה בידו (סבר) [שכר] היה קורא אותו יומא דשפמי. מיפגרי תשש כחם והוו מתחלשי יגעים ויעפים ולא יכלי למיגרס כדכתיב וירדף דוד הוא וארבע מאות איש ויעמדו מאתים איש אשר פגרו מעבור וגו' הוו אמרי יומא דשפמי א): וקושרין את הטיבור. ר' יוסי אומר אף חותכין את הטיבור כל צרכי מילה עושין בשבת אמר רב נחמן אמר רבה בר אבוה הלכה כרבי יוסי שחותכין בשבת טיבור תינוק אחד וכ"ש טיבור ב' תינוקות שבזה אפילו חכמים מודים שמתחך מ"ט משום (דמתחזי) [דמנתחו] אהדדי. ואמר רב נחמן אמר רבה בר אבוה אמר רב כל האמור בפרשת תוכחה עושין לחיה בשבת שנא' ומולדותיך ביום הולדת אותך מיכן שמיילדין לחיה בשבת לא כרת שרך מיכן שחותכין את הטיבור בשבת ובמים לא רוחצת למשעי מיכן שמרחיצין את הולד בשבת והחתל לא חתלת מיכן שמלפפין הולד בשבת ואמרינן בתלמוד א"י ומחללין עליה את השבת שמואל אמר עושין לה מדורה אפילו בתקופת תמוז וקושרין את הטיבור כהדא אמתיה דבר קפרא נפקא מיילדה בשבתא אתת ושאלת לר' וא' לה אזלון ושאלון לחייתא. אמרה לה ליכא חייא. אמר לה זילי עבידי כמנהגך אמרה ליה ליכא מנהג אמר לה איזיל חתיך כר' יוסי כבמתניתא וכל צרכי חיה עושין בשבת תני השליא הזאת בשבת עשירין טומנין אותה בשמן והעניים בתבן ובחול אלו ואלו טומנין אותה בארץ כדי ליתן ערבון בארץ [לארץ]: הדרן עלך מפנין

חשק שלמה על רבינו חננאל א) עיין בערוך ערך פגר:

מסורת הש"ס

א) גיטין ע., ב) [עיין תוספות עירובין נו. ד"ה ואין], ג) [מכאן עד יומא דשפמי ממלא פירוש יפה בערוך ערך פגר בשינוי הנוסח], ד) [תוספתא פט"ו], ה) [לפי הרא"ש והטור לא היה כתוב הא דאמר רב נחמן הלכה כר' יוסי ועיין ב"י א"ח סימן של], ו) [וכן איתא לעיל סו: לפופי יונקא בשבת שפיר דמי וע"ש בפרש"י ועוד לקמן קמז: ובפרש"י שם], ז) [וע"ע תוספות כתובות ג. ד"ה שבקי דיינין].

גליון הש"ס

גמרא כיון דדשו ביה רבים שומר פתאים. עיין תוס' פ"ק ר"ה ... רש"י ד"ה מלפפין וכו' בחגורות ופסיקיאות. עיין לקמן דף קמז ע"ב ... בתשובת אדמת הקדש חלק א"ח סי' מ:

תורה אור השלם

א) שֹׁמֵר פְּתָאיִם יְיָ דַּלּוֹתִי וְלִי יְהוֹשִׁיעַ: (תהלים קטז, ו)

ב) וּמוֹלְדוֹתַיִךְ בְּיוֹם הוּלֶּדֶת אֹתָךְ לֹא כָרַּת שָׁרֵּךְ וּבְמַיִם לֹא רֻחַצְתְּ לְמִשְׁעִי וְהֻמְלֵחַ לֹא הֻמְלַחַתְּ וְהָחְתֵּל לֹא חֻתָּלְתְּ: (יחזקאל טז, ד)

ליקוטי רש"י

אכל ועמד. מיד קודם שסהה מעט [גיטין ע.]. מוכין. כל דבר רך קרוי מוכין כגון צמר גפן ותלישי צמר רך של בהמה וגרירת בגדים בלויים [לעיל מז:]. ביום הולדת אותך. פוטנ"א בלע"ז כשנתפרש בן במצרים הייתה בלי שום תיקון ולפי שדימה הדבר ללידה הזכיר כאן תיקוני הולד. שרך. כמו שרכך. למשעי. להחליק. מכאן שמולחין את הולד כדי שיתקשה בשרו. והחתל. לשון כריכה בבגדים וכן (איוב לח) וערפל חתולתו והוא שמלפפין את הולד [יחזקאל טז, ד]. שמלפפין הולד בשבת. לכורכו בבגדים וקושרין בחגורה ומיישבין פרקי אבריו שהן רכין ונשמטין בחבלי הלידה וקורין אונמלוטי"ר בלע"ז [לעיל סו:]. אונמלוטי"א כמו שעושין לקטן שיתיישבו אבריו ולא יתעקם [לקמן קמז:]. מלפפתו. מעטפתו לשון מלבוש כמו מלפפין את התינוק בשבת [ע"ז ה.].

The Mishnah stated:

וְקוֹשְׁרִין הַטַּבּוּר – AND WE TIE THE UMBILICAL CORD of a newborn on the Sabbath. R' Yose says: We also sever it.

The Gemara cites a Baraisa that also mentions this dispute:

תָּנוּ רַבָּנָן – **The Rabbis taught in a Baraisa:** קוֹשְׁרִין הַטַּבּוּר – WE TIE THE UMBILICAL CORD of a newborn on the Sabbath. רַבִּי יוֹסֵי אוֹמֵר אַף חוֹתְכִין – R' YOSE SAYS: WE ALSO SEVER IT.

The Baraisa continues:

וְטוֹמְנִין הַשִּׁלְיָא כְּדֵי שֶׁיֵּחַם הַוָּלָד – AND WE MAY ENVELOP THE PLACENTA SO THAT THE NEWBORN WILL BE WARM.[21] אָמַר רַבָּן שִׁמְעוֹן בֶּן גַּמְלִיאֵל – RABBAN SHIMON BEN GAMLIEL SAID: בְּנוֹת מְלָכִים טוֹמְנוֹת בִּסְפָלִים שֶׁל שֶׁמֶן – THE DAUGHTERS OF ROYALTY ENVELOP the placenta IN BOWLS OF OIL. בְּנוֹת עֲשִׁירִים בִּסְפוֹגִים שֶׁל צֶמֶר – THE DAUGHTERS OF THE WEALTHY envelop it IN WADS OF combed WOOL. בְּנוֹת עֲנִיִּים בְּמוֹכִין – THE DAUGHTERS OF THE POOR envelop it IN SOFT RAGS.

The Gemara rules on the dispute between the Tanna Kamma and R' Yose:

אָמַר רַב נַחְמָן אָמַר רַבָּה בַּר אֲבוּהָ אָמַר רַב – **Rav Nachman said in the name of Rabbah bar Avuha, who said in the name of Rav:** הֲלָכָה כְּרַבִּי יוֹסֵי – **The halachah follows R' Yose,** who states that we do cut the umbilical cord on the Sabbath.

Rav Nachman comments further on this dispute:

וְאָמַר רַב נַחְמָן אָמַר רַבָּה בַּר אֲבוּהָ אָמַר רַב – **And Rav Nachman said in the name of Rabbah bar Avuha, who said in the name of Rav:** מוֹדִים חֲכָמִים לְרַבִּי יוֹסֵי בְּטַבּוּר שֶׁל שְׁנֵי תִינוֹקוֹת שֶׁחוֹתְכִין – **The Sages** [Tanna Kamma] **concede to R' Yose in** the case of **the umbilical cord of** newborn **twins that we cut** it on the Sabbath. מַאי טַעְמָא – **What is the reason** that the Sages concede in this case? דְּמִנַּתְחֵי אַהֲדָדֵי – **Because [the twin newborns]** would tend to **pull away from one another,** which would dislodge the cord[22] and place them in danger.[23]

A third comment of Rav Nachman in this matter:

וְאָמַר רַב נַחְמָן אָמַר רַבָּה בַּר אֲבוּהָ אָמַר רַב – **And Rav Nachman said in the name of Rabbah bar Avuha, who said in the name of Rav:** כָּל הָאָמוּר בְּפָרָשַׁת תּוֹכֵחָה עוֹשִׂין לְחַיָּה בְּשַׁבָּת – **Whatever is mentioned in the "Passage of Remonstration" we may do for a woman who has given birth** (i.e. for her newborn child) **on the Sabbath.** שֶׁנֶּאֱמַר ,,וּמוֹלְדוֹתַיִךְ – **For it states** in the "Passage of Remonstration":[24] ***And in regard to your birth:*** בְּיוֹם הוּלֶּדֶת אוֹתָךְ לֹא־כָרַּת שָׁרֵּךְ – ***On the day of your birth, your umbilical cord was not cut,*** וּבְמַיִם לֹא־רֻחַצְתְּ לְמִשְׁעִי – ***nor were you washed with water to smooth [the skin];*** וְהָמְלֵחַ לֹא הֻמְלַחַתְּ – ***nor were you salted at all,*** וְהָחְתֵּל לֹא חֻתָּלְתְּ'' – ***nor were you swaddled at all . . .*** The Gemara expounds the various elements mentioned in the verse:[25] ,,וּמוֹלְדוֹתַיִךְ בְּיוֹם הוּלֶּדֶת'' – מִכָּאן שֶׁמְּיַילְּדִים אֶת הַוָּלָד בְּשַׁבָּת – ***And in regard to your birth: On the day of your birth*** – **from here** we see **that we deliver a child on the Sabbath.** ,,לֹא־כָרַּת שָׁרֵּךְ'' מִכָּאן שֶׁחוֹתְכִין הַטַּבּוּר בְּשַׁבָּת – ***Your umbilical cord was not cut*** – **from here** we see **that we cut the umbilical cord on the Sabbath.**[26] ,,וּבְמַיִם לֹא־רֻחַצְתְּ לְמִשְׁעִי'' מִכָּאן שֶׁרוֹחֲצִין הַוָּלָד בְּשַׁבָּת – ***Nor were you washed with water to smooth [the skin]*** – **from here** we see **that we wash a newborn on the Sabbath.**[27] ,,וְהָמְלֵחַ לֹא הֻמְלַחַתְּ'' מִכָּאן שֶׁמּוֹלְחִין הַוָּלָד בְּשַׁבָּת – ***Nor were you salted at all*** – **from here** we see **that we "salt" a newborn on the Sabbath.**[28] ,,וְהָחְתֵּל לֹא חֻתָּלְתְּ'' מִכָּאן שֶׁמְּלַפְּפִין הַוָּלָד בְּשַׁבָּת – ***Nor were you swaddled at all*** – **from here** we see **that we swaddle the newborn on the Sabbath.**[29]

הדרן עלך מפנין

WE WILL RETURN TO YOU, MEFANIN

NOTES

21. Enveloping the placenta warms the newborn through means unknown to science [דֶּרֶךְ סְגוּלָּה] (see *Mishnah Berurah* 330:26). On weekdays, the placenta would be enveloped by burying it in the earth (see *Rabbeinu Chananel* and *Meiri,* citing *Yerushalmi*). But since this is forbidden on the Sabbath, some other means of envelopment must be used, as the Baraisa goes on to describe.

22. [E.g. where the two cords are connected to the same placenta.]

23. [Translation follows *Rashi,* who apparently reads מֵהֲדָדֵי rather than אַהֲדָדֵי.]

24. *Ezekiel* 16:4. In this passage, God remonstrates against Israel's ingratitude to Him. He compares her to an abandoned newborn girl, left lying filthy and neglected in the field [the infant nation of Israel enslaved in Egypt]. A benefactor [God] passes by and raises her to womanhood [the time of the Exodus], whereupon he vows to take her as his wife [to be His nation]. Yet, after he has beautified her and adorned her, she is disloyal to him and strays after other men.

The verse cited here depicts the newborn of the parable lying in its neglected state.

25. The verse mentions various things that had not been done for the neglected newborn, from which we infer that depriving the newborn of these things causes discomfort to it. And since none of these things involves a Biblical *melachah,* the Rabbis permitted doing them on the Sabbath to alleviate the newborn's discomfort (*Tosafos*). [As noted above (128b note 39), however, other authorities consider some of the things mentioned in this verse to involve a Biblical *melachah,* and it is permitted to do them on the Sabbath because neglecting to do so would endanger the newborn's life. See also *Radak* ad loc., *Rambam, Hil. Shabbos* 2:14 and *Beur Halachah* to 330:7 ד״ה הולד שנולד.]

26. [This exposition reflects the view of R' Yose, who rules that the umbilical cord be cut on the Sabbath.]

27. With warm water. Generally, it is Rabbinically forbidden to wash the entire body with warm water on the Sabbath, even if the water was heated before the Sabbath (see *Orach Chaim* 326). In the case of a newborn, however, the Rabbis permitted one to wash the entire body with water heated before the Sabbath in order to alleviate his discomfort.

Alternatively, failing to bathe the newborn in warm water (after cutting the umbilical cord) is considered a danger to his life, and accordingly it is permitted even to heat the necessary water on the Sabbath (see *Rambam, Hil. Shabbos* 2:14 and *Beur Halachah* to 330:7 ד״ה הולד שנולד).

28. I.e. we apply salt to his skin in order to harden it (*Rashi*). Alternately, "salting" refers not to the application of actual salt, but rather to a powder made of ground myrtle and the like (see *Rambam, Commentary to the Mishnah* and *Mishnah Berurah* 330:23).

29. In order to force the bones and joints that were bent or dislodged during delivery back into place (*Ritva MHK* ed.; *Rashi* to 66b ד״ה לפופי). This is not the same procedure as אַסּוּבֵי יְנוּקָא, *straightening the infant,* which Rav Nachman himself forbids above [123a, because it is akin to מְתַקֵּן, *repairing*] (*Rashi*). There, the reference is to straightening the bones by hand, whereas here the infant is simply swaddled (*Ritva MHK* ed.; see also *Tosafos* to 123a ד״ה אסובי). See, however, *Rosh* 17:3 and *Korban Nesanel* there §8. See also *Rashi* to the end of 147b ד״ה בחומרי שדרה (cited here by *Gilyon HaShas*).

Chapter Nineteen

Introduction

This chapter elaborates upon various laws of circumcision (*bris milah*), especially as they relate to the Sabbath. Hence, the chapter is called "R' Eliezer of *Milah.*" [Chapters 13 and 20 also begin with the words, "R' Eliezer says," and they are called הָאוֹרֵג ("One who weaves") and תּוֹלִין ("We may suspend"), respectively.] The actual circumcision consists of cutting off the foreskin of the male member and afterward exposing the corona. This is followed by drawing some blood from, and then bandaging, the wound. Various antiseptics are usually applied to the wound prior to bandaging. During the Mishnaic era the common practice was to apply cumin and a mixture of wine with oil.

In order to perform a *bris milah,* one must be equipped with a knife or scalpel. Making the knife and transporting it to the location of the circumcision are obviously not part of the circumcision itself, but *are* considered מַכְשִׁירֵי מִילָה, *preliminaries to* [literally: those [things] that prepare or enable] *the circumcision.*

As a general rule, an act that causes bleeding is prohibited on the Sabbath, for it is a *toladah* of *slaughtering* (see above, 107a note 3). However, as the Torah specifies the day of *milah* – וּבַיּוֹם הַשְּׁמִינִי יִמּוֹל בְּשַׂר עָרְלָתוֹ, *And on the eighth day the flesh of his foreskin shall be circumcised* (*Leviticus* 12:3) – the Gemara (see below, 132a; *Sanhedrin* 59b) derives that the act of *bris milah* in its proper time (i.e. on the eighth day) overrides the *melachah* restrictions of the Sabbath and festivals. [A *bris* that has been delayed for any reason (underweight, ill health, etc.), however, may *not* be rescheduled for a Sabbath or festival (see below, 132b).] There is, however, a Tannaic dispute as to whether activities regarded as preliminaries to the circumcision also override the Sabbath *melachah* restrictions; this dispute is the subject of the first Mishnah in our chapter.

Chapter Nineteen

Mishnah The final Mishnah in the preceding chapter concluded with the statement, "And we may perform all requirements of circumcision on the Sabbath" (128b). Our Mishnah elaborates on this dictum, discussing whether the preliminaries to *milah* also override the Sabbath *melachah* restrictions:[1]

רַבִּי אֱלִיעֶזֶר אוֹמֵר – **R' Eliezer says:** אִם לֹא הֵבִיא כְּלִי מֵעֶרֶב שַׁבָּת – **If one did not bring an instrument** for circumcising **on the Sabbath eve,**[2] מְבִיאוֹ בְּשַׁבָּת מְגוּלֶּה – **he should bring it exposed**[3] **on the Sabbath** itself;[4] וּבַסַּכָּנָה מְכַסֵּהוּ עַל פִּי עֵדִים – **and in** times of **danger,**[5] **he should cover it in the presence of witnesses.**[6] וְעוֹד אָמַר רַבִּי אֱלִיעֶזֶר – **And R' Eliezer said further:** כּוֹרְתִים עֵצִים לַעֲשׂוֹת פֶּחָמִין לַעֲשׂוֹת (כלי) בַּרְזֶל – **We may fell trees to make charcoal in order to make** an instrument of **iron.**[7]

כְּלָל אָמַר רַבִּי עֲקִיבָא – But **R' Akiva stated a general rule:** כָּל מְלָאכָה שֶׁאֶפְשָׁר לַעֲשׂוֹתָהּ מֵעֶרֶב שַׁבָּת – **Any labor that can be performed on the Sabbath eve** אֵינָהּ דּוֹחָה אֶת הַשַּׁבָּת – **does not push aside the Sabbath** *melachah* restrictions,[8] (ומילה) שֶׁאִי אֶפְשָׁר לַעֲשׂוֹתָהּ מֵעֶרֶב שַׁבָּת – and any labor **that cannot be performed on the Sabbath eve**[9] דּוֹחָה אֶת הַשַּׁבָּת – **does push aside the Sabbath** restrictions.

Gemara The Gemara discusses the first part of R' Eliezer's first ruling:

אִיבַּעְיָא לְהוּ – **[The sages] inquired:** טַעְמָא דְּרַבִּי אֱלִיעֶזֶר – **Is R' Eliezer's reason** for requiring that the knife be carried exposed under normal circumstances מִשּׁוּם חִבּוּבֵי מִצְוָה – **because of** the opportunity it presents for expressing **love of the commandment** of circumcision,[10] אוֹ דִּילְמָא מִשּׁוּם חֲשָׁדָא – **or is it, perhaps, because of** the need to avert **suspicion** that he is carrying other, personal effects?[11]

The Gemara elucidates the question:

לְמַאי נַפְקָא מִינָּהּ – **What practical difference does this make?** לְאַתּוּיֵי מְכוּסֶּה עַל פִּי עֵדִים – **To include** the option of the knife being **covered in the presence of witnesses,** as follows: אִי אָמְרַתְּ מִשּׁוּם חִבּוּבֵי מִצְוָה – **If you say** that R' Eliezer rules that the knife be carried exposed **because of** the **love of the commandment** of *milah* that will thereby be proclaimed, מְגוּלֶּה אִין מְכוּסֶּה לֹא – then the knife should **indeed** be carried **exposed,** but **not covered** (i.e. even with the knowledge of witnesses). אֶלָּא אִי אָמְרַתְּ מִשּׁוּם חֲשָׁדָא – **However, if you say** that the knife must be carried exposed **because of suspicion,** אֲפִילּוּ מְכוּסֶּה שַׁפִּיר דָּמֵי – **it is well even** if it is **covered** in the presence of witnesses. מַאי – **What,** then, is the reason for R' Eliezer's ruling?

The Gemara answers:

אִיתְּמַר – **It was stated:** אָמַר רַבִּי לֵוִי – **R' Levi stated:** לֹא אָמְרָהּ רַבִּי אֱלִיעֶזֶר אֶלָּא לְחִבּוּבֵי מִצְוָה – **R' Eliezer stated [his ruling] only for the purpose** of proclaiming one's **love for the**

NOTES

1. *Rashi;* see *Maharam,* who writes that *Rashi* is explaining why R' Eliezer does not mention that he is discussing *milah*. See also *Rashba.*

2. That is, he did not bring the circumcision knife on Friday to the house where the infant's Sabbath circumcision is scheduled to take place (*Rashi*).

3. The Gemara will discuss why R' Eliezer requires that the knife be exposed while being carried to the circumcision house (*Rashi*).

4. [This leniency derives from R' Eliezer's holding that the preliminaries to *milah* override the Sabbath restrictions.]

Tosafos ask: Why advise that the knife be carried to the infant, an act that is normally Biblically prohibited on the Sabbath (i.e. as the *melachah* of transferring)? Carry instead the infant to the location of the knife, which involves no Biblical *melachah* prohibition (see *Maharsha, Maharam* and *Maharam Schiff*), inasmuch as חַי נוֹשֵׂא אֶת עַצְמוֹ, *a living creature supports its own weight* [see above, 94a, and notes there]! *Tosafos* answer that since the infant requires his mother's care after the circumcision and she is presumably insufficiently recovered from childbirth to go to him, it will be necessary to carry the child back to his mother. Now, since the infant has been weakened by the circumcision, he is unable to aid in his own carriage during the return trip. Hence, returning him to his mother will involve the same prohibition as carrying the knife to the circumcision house, and for that reason the latter act is permitted. [Cf. *Ramban,* who argues that even *before* circumcision the child of only eight days is too young to aid in his own carriage. See *Tosafos* above, 94a ד״ה אבל, who suggest this argument themselves. See *R' Akiva Eiger* to 128b at length.] See further in *Tosafos* here for a second answer.

5. At times when the gentiles prohibited the performance of circumcision upon pain of death [and the *milah* knife therefore cannot be carried openly]. This occurred specifically during the Roman occupation of Israel (*Rashi;* see *Me'ilah* 17a, *Mechilta* 20:6), during the reign of Hadrian. It was one of the prime causes of the Bar Kochba uprising (*Doros HaRishonim* vol. 4 [of the reprinted edition, published in Jerusalem 1967] ch. 27).

6. [Literally: upon the word of witnesses.] The witnesses can later attest that he carried the knife for purposes of performing a mitzvah, thereby deflecting from him any suspicion of wrongdoing (*Rashi;* see *Shoshanim LeDavid*).

7. If there is no knife available, we may even fell trees to make the charcoal necessary to forge iron in order to make a knife. R' Eliezer teaches us here that even preliminaries that are further removed from the circumcision, and which could have easily been performed before the Sabbath, also override the *melachah* restrictions.

It is apparent from several commentators that the word כְּלִי, *an instrument,* did not appear in their editions of the Mishnah. According to those editions, the text states: to *make iron.* That is, the circumcision knife is called simply a piece of iron (not an *iron instrument*) to teach that even according to R' Eliezer's lenient opinion, the iron may not be fashioned into a finished instrument on the Sabbath. Rather, one may forge it only into a sharp piece, since that is sufficient for performing a circumcision (*Tiferes Yisrael*). See also *Gra* to *Yoreh Deah* 264:17.

8. R' Akiva argues with R' Eliezer, who permits the performance of preliminaries to a mitzvah (that involve a *melachah* – see below, 131b) on the Sabbath. R' Akiva maintains, on the other hand, that when a preliminary can be performed before the Sabbath, one may not perform it on the Sabbath (*Rashi*). [R' Eliezer and R' Akiva argue similarly in *Pesachim* 66a and *Menachos* 96a.]

9. Such as the circumcision itself, which may not be performed before the eighth day (*Rashi*). [See *Chazon Yechezkel* on Tractate *Shabbos* for a discussion of preliminaries that cannot be performed before the Sabbath].

10. That is, carrying the knife for all to see proclaims that the mitzvah of *milah* is dear to a person, for he even desecrates the Sabbath for its sake (*Rashi*).

11. In the second part of the ruling (the case of times of danger), R' Eliezer's purpose in requiring that the knife be covered in the presence of witnesses is certainly to avert suspicion (see note 6 above). Thus, we see that suspicion is certainly a concern. However, the Gemara will now explain that where there is no danger, it is possible that R' Eliezer ruled the knife be carried exposed for a different reason as well – to express one's love for the mitzvah of *milah* – in which case one may not carry it concealed, even with the knowledge of witnesses. On the other hand, perhaps even here R' Eliezer remains concerned only about suspicion, and so would permit concealing the knife in the presence of witnesses in times of non-danger as well (*Rashi*).

מסורת הש"ס

א) [נזכר לקמן קלו. ובעירובין קב: קג.], ב) ס"א ל"ג, ג) פסחים סו. סט: יבמות יד. מנחות עב. נו., ד) ס"א ל"ג, ה) יבמות יד. חולין קטו. ע"ש, ו) [צ"ל דטווסא עיין בערוך פירושו], ז) חולין קיג., ח) יומא עה., ט) לעיל מט., י) [ברכות נג: לעיל מט. וש"נ], כ) [דף קכח:], ל) ס"א, מ) [צ"ל שנזכר], נ) [צ"ל עליה].

הגהות הב"ח

(א) רש"י ד"ה ומשני וכו' ומאי קרי להו: (ב) תוס' ד"ה ר' אליעזר וכו' ואז הוי כפות. נ"ב עיין בפרק המצניע דף לד ע"א: (ג) באו"ד כדי למהר המצוה. נ"ב עיין בסוף עירובין דף קג ע"ב בתוספות ד"ה מה לי: (ד) ד"ה שש וכו' וכן אמרי' במדרש ויעש אברהם:

תורה אור השלם

א) לֹא תֹאכְלוּ כָל נְבֵלָה לַגֵּר אֲשֶׁר בִּשְׁעָרֶיךָ תִּתְּנֶנָּה וַאֲכָלָהּ אוֹ מָכֹר לְנָכְרִי כִּי עַם קָדוֹשׁ אַתָּה לַייָ אֱלֹהֶיךָ לֹא תְבַשֵּׁל גְּדִי בַּחֲלֵב אִמּוֹ: [דברים יד, כא]

ב) שָׂשׂ אָנֹכִי עַל אִמְרָתֶךָ כְּמוֹצֵא שָׁלָל רָב: [תהלים קיט, קסב]

ג) וַיִּשְׁמַע מֹשֶׁה אֶת הָעָם בֹּכֶה לְמִשְׁפְּחֹתָיו אִישׁ לְפֶתַח אָהֳלוֹ וַיִּחַר אַף יְיָ מְאֹד וּבְעֵינֵי מֹשֶׁה רָע: [במדבר יא, י]

ד) אִם תִּשְׁכְּבוּן בֵּין שְׁפַתָּיִם כַּנְפֵי יוֹנָה נֶחְפָּה בַכֶּסֶף וְאֶבְרוֹתֶיהָ בִּירַקְרַק חָרוּץ: [תהלים סח, יד]

ליקוטי רש"י

כורתים עצים בשבת לעשות פחמין. לנו ביום כדי לעשות ברזל לאיזמל של מילה דקסבר ר"א מכשירי מצוה דומין כמצוה עצמה [יבמות יד.]. רבי אליעזר אית ליה מכשירי מצוה דוחין את השבת ואם אין לו איזמל למול בו בשבת כורתין עצים ועושין פחמין ועושין איזמל [חולין קטז.]. לעשות כלי ברזל. לעשות איזמל למול בו [עירובין קב:]. היו אוכלין בשר עוף בחלב. דלרבי יוסי הגלילי אפילו איסורא דרבנן לית ליה בעוף. רישבא. לייד עופות רישבא לשון אין פורקין [חולין קטז. ועי' רש"י בהגרי"ב]. פורס גבן לגבי חיה ועוף [יז:]. דטווסא. פוולין [חולין שם]. ת"ל בחלב אמו. מי שיש לו חלב אמו יצא בשר עוף שאין לו חלב אם [מכות שם]. שש אנכי על אמרתך. וכשהיינו לדרשוהו על המילה שהיה דוד בבית המרחץ וראה עצמו בלא ציצית ובלא תפילין ובלא תורה אמר אוי לי שאני ערום מכל מצות כיון שנסתכל במילה שמח ואמר בנאתו (מבית המרחץ) שש אנכי על אמרתך המילה שמתחלה נתנה במאמר ולא בדבור שנאמר (בראשית יז) ויאמר אלהים אל אברהם ואתה את בריתי תשמור [תהלים קיט, קסב]. זו מילה שניתנה במאמר ולא בדיבור ויאמר ה' אל אברהם ואתה את בריתי תשמור (בראשית יז) ומצינו שדוד שמח עליה שנאמר למנצח על השמינית (תהלים ו) כשהיה בבית המרחץ וראה עצמו בלא תורה ובלא מצות כיון (שנסתכל) [שנזכר] במילה שמח [מגילה טז:]. על עסקי משפחותיו. על עריות הנאסרות להם [במדבר יא, י]. שלא יפיח. שיכול להעמיד עצמו בשעת הרוח. שלא יישן בהם. שוטר שלא יישן בהן כל הגופים נקיים בהפחה שיכולין להעמיד עצמן. יקרו את מוחו. יקרו את מוחו שהוא תחת התפילין, ינקרו לשון ניקור עינים. קסדור. מגיסטרא"ל שהיה ממונה על כך [לעיל מט.]. שם פקידות ומלוכה. כנפי יונה. כדמפרש לקמיה מפני שהם מצות והם מגינין לישראל והוא להם ככנפים ליונה שהיא נמשלת ליונה והמצות ככנפים [לעיל שם]. כנפי יונה. פלומ"א בלע"ז. נחפה בכסף. בכספה ומחמדה של תורה ומצות. ואברותיה. כנפיה. בירקרק חרוץ. פמר דומה כן לגבע המרוץ הוא זהב ולכך נמנו המשורר אלא הכסף וירקרק המרוץ הוא הזהב אשר יוצא מארץ החוילה ולכך קראו ירקרק כמו (ויקרא יג) לבן אדמדם שאינו לא לבן ולא אדום לכך נכפל ירקרק אדמדם [תהלים סח, יד]. כנפיה מגינות עליה. מן הנץ ומכל עוף ואדם הבא עליה היא נלחמת ומכה בראש גפיה מה שאין כן בשאר עופות [לעיל שם]. או בורחת או נלחמת בראשי אגפיה [ברכות נג:].

רבי אליעזר אומר אם לא הביא כלי מע"ש מביאו בשבת מגולה ובסכנה מכסהו ע"פ עדים ועוד אמר ° ר"א כורתים עצים לעשות פחמין לעשות (כלי) ברזל כלל אמר ר"ע כל מלאכה שאפשר לעשותה מע"ש אינה דוחה את השבת (ומילה) שאי אפשר לעשותה מע"ש דוחה את השבת: גמ' איבעיא להו טעמא דר"א משום חבובי מצוה או דילמא משום חשדא למאי נפקא מינה לאתויי מכוסה ע"פ עדים אי אמרת משום חבובי מצוה מגולה אין מכוסה לא אלא אי אמרת משום חשדא אפי' מכוסה שפיר דמי מאי איתמר א"ר לוי לא אמרה ר"א אלא לחבובי מצוה תניא נמי הכי מביאו מגולה ואין מביאו מכוסה דברי ר"א אמר רב אשי מתני' נמי דיקא דקתני ובשעת הסכנה מכסהו ע"פ עדים בסכנה אין שלא בסכנה לא שמע מינה משום חבובי מצוה שמע מינה תניא אידך מביאו מגולה ואין מביאו מכוסה דברי ר"א ר' יהודה אומר משום ר"א נוהגין היו בשעת הסכנה שהיו מביאין מכוסה ע"פ עדים איבעיא להו עדים דקאמר איהו וחד או דילמא הוא ותרי ת"ש ובסכנה מכסהו ע"פ עדים אי אמרת • בשלמא הוא ותרי שפיר אלא אי אמרת הוא וחד מאי עדים שראוים להעיד במקום אחר: ועוד אמר ר"א: ת"ר במקומו של ר"א היו כורתין עצים לעשות פחמין לעשות ברזל בשבת במקומו של ר' יוסי הגלילי היו אוכלין בשר עוף בחלב לוי איקלע לבי יוסף רישבא קריבו ליה רישא דטוותא בחלבא לא אכל כי אתא לקמיה דרבי א"ל אמאי לא תשמתינהו א"ל אתריה דר' יהודה בן בתירה הוה ואמינא דילמא דרש להו כר' יוסי הגלילי דתנן ר' יוסי הגלילי אומר נאמר לא תאכלו כל נבלה ונאמר לא תבשל גדי בחלב אמו את שאסור משום נבלה אסור לבשל בחלב עוף שאסור משום נבלה יכול יהא אסור לבשל בחלב ת"ל בחלב אמו יצא עוף שאין לו חלב אם א"ר יצחק עיר אחת היתה בא"י שהיו עושין כר"א והיו מתים בזמנן ולא עוד אלא שפעם אחת גזרה מלכות הרשעה גזרה על ישראל על המילה ועל אותה העיר לא גזרה: תניא רשב"ג אומר כל מצוה שקיבלו עליהם בשמחה כגון מילה דכתיב שש אנכי על אמרתך כמוצא שלל רב עדיין עושין אותה בשמחה וכל מצוה שקבלו עליהם בקטטה כגון עריות דכתיב וישמע משה את העם בוכה למשפחותיו על עסקי משפחותיו עדיין עושין אותה בקטטה דליכא כתובה דלא רמו בה תיגרא תניא ר"ש בן אלעזר אומר כל מצוה שמסרו ישראל עצמן עליהם למיתה בשעת גזרת המלכות כגון עבודת כוכבים ומילה עדיין היא מוחזקת בידם וכל מצוה שלא מסרו ישראל עצמן עליה למיתה בשעת גזרת המלכות כגון תפילין עדיין היא מרופה בידם דא"ר ינאי תפילין צריכין גוף נקי כאלישע בעל כנפים מאי היא אמר אביי שלא יפיח בהם רבא אמר שלא יישן בהם ואמאי קרו ליה בעל כנפים שפעם אחת גזרה מלכות הרשעה גזרה על ישראל שכל המניח תפילין על ראשו יקרו את מוחו והיה אלישע מניח תפילין ויצא לשוק וראהו קסדור אחד רץ מלפניו ורץ אחריו כיון שהגיע אצלו נטלן מראשו ואחזן בידו א"ל מה בידך אמר לו כנפי יונה פשט את ידו ונמצאו בה כנפי יונה לפיכך היו קורין אותו בעל כנפים • מאי שנא כנפי יונה דא"ל ולא א"ל שאר עופות משום דדמיא כנסת ישראל ליונה שנאמר כנפי יונה נחפה בכסף ואברותיה בירקרק חרוץ מה יונה זו כנפיה מגינות עליה אף ישראל מצות מגינות עליהן: א"ר אבא בר רב אדא א"ר יצחק פעם אחת שכחו ולא הביאו איזמל מערב שבת והביאוהו בשבת [דרך גגות ודרך חצירות] שלא

רש"י

רבי אליעזר אומר אם לא הביא כלי. איזמל למול את התינוק וקאי אמתניתין דפרקין לעיל דסליק מיניה וכל צרכי מילה עושין בשבת: מגולה. בפני הכל ובגמרא מפרש אמאי מצריך ליה לגלוייה: ובסכנה. שגזרו ארמאים על המילה: מכסהו ע"פ עדים. שיעידו שאיזמל של מצוה הוא מביא ולא יחשדוהו: כלל אמר ר"ע. נחלק על ר"א במכשירי מצוה שאין דומין הואיל ואפשר לעשותן מע"ש: ושאי אפשר לעשות מע"ש. כגון מילה עצמה שא"א לה ליעשות דזמנה ביום השמיני דוחה שבת: גמ' טעמא דר"א. דאמר מגולה אין מכוסה לא: משום חיבוב מצוה. להודיע שחביבה מצוה עליו שמחלל שבת עליה: משום חשדא. שלא יחשדוהו שהוא נושא שאר חפציו וסיפא דמתני' דקתני ובסכנה מכסהו ע"פ עדים ודאי משום חשדא הוא אלא רישא מיבעיא לן דוקא מגולה קאמר אבל מכוסה לא ומשום חיבוב שלא בשעת הסכנה לא ומשום חיבוב מצוה או לאו דוקא מגולה דטעמיה משום חשדא וה"ה למכוסה על פי עדים: אי אמרת בשלמא הוא ותרי שפיר. היינו דמיקרו עדים אלא הוא וחד מי מיקרי עדים איהו לגביה נפשיה מי מיקרי עד: ומשני שראוים להעיד במקום אחר. לעולם הכא עדות לא שייכא דלאפוקי מחשדא בעלמא הוא ואין כאן לא דיני ממונות ולא דיני נפשות שיהו שנים (א) ומאי קרו להו עדים דאיכא גילוי מילתא ע"י השני ושנים קרו עדים בעדות אחריתי שאינו נוגע בה: לעשות ברזל. לאיזמל של מילה: היו אוכלין בשר עוף בחלב. כדלקמן: רישבא. לייד עופות: נאמר לא תאכלו כל נבלה ונאמר. באותו פסוק עצמו לא תבשל גדי משמע כל האסור משום נבלה נוהג בו איסור בשר בחלב: שש אנכי על אמרתך. אמירה יחידה שקדמה לשאר אמירות והיא מילה שישראל עושין וששים עליה דכל שאר מצות אינן מוכיחות כל שעה כגון תפילין ומזוזה וציצית דאינן כשהוא בשדה וערום בבית המרחץ אבל זו מעיד עליהם לעולם כדאמרינן במנחות (דף מג:) בדוד שראה עצמו בבית המרחץ ונצטער אמר אוי לי שאני ערום מכל מצות כיון שנסתכל במילה נתיישבה דעתו: בשמחה. שעושין משתה: על עסקי משפחותיו. שנאסר להם קרובות: מרופה. רפויה: דא"ר ינאי תפילין צריכות גוף נקי. שלא יפיח אלמא לא זהירי בהו ושמעינן מינה דלא מסרו עליה אלא אלישע לבדו: יקרו. פוריי"ר בלעז לשון יקרוה עורבי נחל (משלי ל) ולשון תנקר לא נעלה (במדבר טז): את מוחו. שכנגד תפילין: קסדור. ממונה: מגינות עליהן. אינה נלחמת בחרטומיה אלא בכנפיה:

דרך

תוספות

רבי אליעזר אומר אם לא הביא כלי כו' מביאו בשבת מגולה. ° וא"ת ויביאו התינוק אצל כלי דהשתא ליכא איסור שבת כלל דהאי נושא את עצמו וי"ל דקטן צריך לאמו הוא ואחר המילה היה צריך להחזירו לאמו ואז הוי כפות (ב) לפי שהוא חולה כדאמרינן ביומא (דף סו:) אפי' תימא ר' נתן חולה שאני וגם אמו שהיא מסוכנת לא תוכל לבא אצל התינוק ועוד י"ל כיון דיותר בקל יביא הכלי משיביא התינוק שרי ר"א כדי למהר המצוה כדמוכח בגמרא דקאמר פעם אחת שכחו ולא הביאו איזמל מע"ש והביאו בשבת שלא ברצונו שהביאו דרך חצרות וגגות וקרפיפות והיו יכולין להביא דרך רה"ר אלמא דשרי ר"א דרך רה"ר דהוי דאורייתא (ג) ° כדי למהר המצוה אע"פ שיכול לעשות [בענין] דליכא אלא איסורא דרבנן:

שש אנכי. במדרש (שוחר טוב) למנצח על השמינית כתיב הנדרש על המילה שהיא בשמיני וכן אמרי' (ד) (פר"א פ' כ"ט) ויעש אברהם משתה גדול ביום הגמל את יצחק ביום ה"ג מל את יצחק דהיינו ביום השמיני דמילה כמנין ה"ג. ר"ת:

אמר ליה כנפי יונה. הרי שלא מסר עצמו לומר תפילין הן. רבינו שמואל:

שלא

עין משפט נר מצוה

א א מיי' פ"ב מהלכות מילה הלכה ו סמג עשין כח טוש"ע א"ח סי' שלא סעיף ו וטוש"ע י"ד סימן רסו סעיף ג:

ב ב טוש"ע י"ד סימן רסה סעיף יג:

ג ג מיי' פכ"ב מהלכות איסורי ביאה הל' יח סמג לאוין קכד:

גליון הש"ס

גמרא בשלמא הוא ותרי. עיין תשובת הרלנ"ח ס"א סי' פ"ט: תוס' ד"ה רבי אליעזר וכו' וא"ת ויביאו התינוק. עיין לעיל דף לד ע"א תוספות ד"ה אבל אדם: באו"ד כדי למהר המצוה. עיין עירובין דף קג ע"ב תוספות ד"ה מה לי:

רבינו חננאל

פרק יט

רבי אליעזר אומר אם לא הביא כלי מערב שבת מביאו בשבת מגולה וכו' ואיבעיא לן האי דקתני ר' אליעזר אומר מביאו מגולה משום חבובי מצוה הוא או משום שלא יחשדוהו שהוציא חפציו טמונים לפיכך מגליהו שיראו שסכין של מצוה הוא. ופשטנא דמשום חבובי מצוה הוא היכא דליכא סכנה ותוב איבעיא לן האי דתנא במתניתא רבי יהודה משום רבי אליעזר [אומר] נוהגים היינו בסכנה מביאין אותו (בסכנה) מכוסה ע"פ עדים הני עדים שנים אחרים זולתו המביאו או דלמא הוא ואחרים ולא איפשטא בהדיא: לוי איקלע לבי יוסף רישבא קריבו ליה רישא דטווסא בחלבא לא אכל כי אתא לקמיה דר' א"ל מ"ט לא שמתינהו א"ל אתרא דר' יהודה בן בתירא ואמרי דלמא דריש להו כרבי יוסי הגלילי דסבר יצא עוף שאין לו חלב אם: א"ר יצחק עיר אחת היתה בא"י שהיו עושין כר' אליעזר והיו מתיה מתין בזמנן ולא עוד אלא שפעם אחת גזרה מלכות הרשעה גזרה על ישראל על המילה ועל אותה העיר לא גזרה: (א) כל השבת ואין הלכה כר"א ולא כר' יוסי הגלילי שמתיר בשר עוף בחלב ולא כרבי ינאי שאמר תפילין צריכין גוף נקי כאלישע ומפרשי רבנן כי לא אמר רבי ינאי אלא בשעת הגזרה וסמיך דהוא עריק ועבדי ליה נס אמר ראובן בר רב אדא א"ר יצחק פעם אחת שכחו ולא הביאו איזמל מע"ש והביאוהו

חשק שלמה על רבינו חננאל

א) נראה דל"ל לאחר כל השבת הזה מ"מ אין הלכה כר"א וכו':

commandment of *milah*. Hence, the knife may not be carried concealed, even with the knowledge of witnesses.

The Gemara adduces support for R' Levi's explanation from R' Eliezer's own words:

תַּנְיָא נַמִּי הָכִי – It was also taught thus in a Baraisa: מְבִיאוֹ מְגוּלֶּה וְאֵין מְבִיאוֹ מְכוּסֶּה – **HE SHOULD BRING [THE KNIFE] EXPOSED, AND HE SHOULD NOT BRING IT COVERED.** דִּבְרֵי רַבִּי אֱלִיעֶזֶר – These are **THE WORDS OF R' ELIEZER.** R' Eliezer insists that the knife be carried exposed – i.e. so as to publicize one's love for the mitzvah of *milah*.[12]

Another proof of the above:

אָמַר רַב אַשִׁי – Rav Ashi said: מַתְנִיתִין נַמִּי דַּיְקָא דְּקָתָנֵי – This can also be inferred from a precise reading of **our Mishnah, for [the Mishnah]** afterward **states:** וּבִשְׁעַת הַסַּכָּנָה מְכַסֵּהוּ עַל פִּי עֵדִים – **AND IN TIMES OF**[13] **DANGER, HE SHOULD COVER IT IN THE PRESENCE OF WITNESSES.** בְּסַכָּנָה אִין – R' Eliezer states specifically that **in** times of **danger, yes** – one may indeed cover the knife and transport it, שֶׁלֹּא בְּסַכָּנָה לֹא – which implies **that not in** times of **danger** one may **not** cover and carry it.[14] שְׁמַע מִינָּהּ מִשּׁוּם חִבּוּבֵי מִצְוָה – **Derive from this specific mention of danger,** then, that R' Eliezer rules the knife be carried exposed **because of** the **love of the commandment** of *milah* that will thereby be expressed. שְׁמַע מִינָּהּ – Indeed, **derive** it **from [that].**

The Gemara discusses the question of whether technically valid witnesses are required for concealing and carrying the *milah* knife in times of danger:

תַּנְיָא אִידָךְ – It was taught in another Baraisa: מְבִיאוֹ מְגוּלֶּה וְאֵין מְבִיאוֹ מְכוּסֶּה – **HE SHOULD BRING [THE KNIFE] EXPOSED, AND HE SHOULD NOT BRING IT COVERED.** דִּבְרֵי רַבִּי אֱלִיעֶזֶר – These are **THE WORDS OF R' ELIEZER.** רַבִּי יְהוּדָה אוֹמֵר מִשּׁוּם רַבִּי אֱלִיעֶזֶר – **R' YEHUDAH SAYS IN THE NAME OF R' ELIEZER:** נוֹהֲגִין הָיוּ בִּשְׁעַת הַסַּכָּנָה – **IN TIMES OF DANGER THEY WOULD FOLLOW THE PRACTICE** שֶׁהָיוּ מְבִיאִין מְכוּסֶּה עַל פִּי עֵדִים – **OF BRINGING** the knife **CONCEALED WITH THE KNOWLEDGE OF WITNESSES.** אִיבַּעְיָא לְהוּ – And apropos of R' Yehudah's statement **[the sages] inquired:** עֵדִים דְּקָאָמַר אִיהוּ וְחַד – Regarding the **witnesses** of **which [R' Yehudah] spoke,** are they simply **he,** the bearer of the knife, **and one** other person,[15] אוֹ דִילְמָא הוּא וּתְרֵי – **or perhaps he and two** others are meant?[16]

The Gemara answers:

תָּא שְׁמַע – Come and **hear** a proof that two technically valid witnesses are required, for R' Eliezer states in our Mishnah: וּבְסַכָּנָה מְכַסֵּהוּ עַל פִּי עֵדִים – **AND IN** times of **DANGER, HE SHOULD COVER IT IN THE PRESENCE OF WITNESSES.** אִי אָמְרַתְּ בִּשְׁלָמָא הוּא וּתְרֵי שַׁפִּיר – Now, **it is well if you say** that **he,** the bearer, **and two** others are meant, for that is what the Mishnah refers to as "witnesses."[17] אֶלָּא אִי אָמְרַתְּ הוּא וְחַד – **But if you say** that **he and** only **one** other are meant, מַאי עֵדִים – **what** do you mean when you talk about **"witnesses"?**[18]

The Gemara refutes this proof:

שֶׁרְאוּיִים לְהָעִיד בְּמָקוֹם אַחֵר – In truth, the Mishnah means the bearer and only one other person,[19] and nevertheless we refer to "the two witnesses" **because they must be qualified to testify in another case.**[20]

The Mishnah stated:

וְעוֹד אָמַר רַבִּי אֱלִיעֶזֶר – AND R' ELIEZER SAID FURTHER: We may fell trees to make charcoal in order to make [an instrument of] iron (i.e. a circumcision knife).

The Gemara cites a Baraisa that refers to this ruling:

תָּנוּ רַבָּנָן – The Rabbis taught: בִּמְקוֹמוֹ שֶׁל רַבִּי אֱלִיעֶזֶר – **IN R' ELIEZER'S PLACE** of residence הָיוּ כּוֹרְתִין עֵצִים לַעֲשׂוֹת פֶּחָמִין לַעֲשׂוֹת בַּרְזֶל – **THEY WOULD FELL TREES TO MAKE CHARCOAL IN ORDER TO MAKE IRON** for a circumcision knife – בְּשַׁבָּת – all **ON THE SABBATH,** as per R' Eliezer's lenient ruling. בִּמְקוֹמוֹ שֶׁל רַבִּי יוֹסֵי הַגְּלִילִי – **IN R' YOSE HAGLILI'S PLACE** of residence הָיוּ אוֹכְלִין בְּשַׂר עוֹף בְּחָלָב – **THEY WOULD EAT FOWL MEAT WITH MILK** products.[21]

The Gemara records an incident that relates to the second part of the Baraisa:

לֵוִי אִיקְלַע לְבֵי יוֹסֵף רִישְׁבָּא – Levi once **visited the house of Yosef, the trapper of fowl.** קָרִיבוּ לֵיהּ רֵישָׁא דְטַוְותָא בְּחַלְבָא – They

NOTES

12. *Chidushei HaRan* (*MHK* ed.) explains that the proof comes from the double expression. That is, since the Baraisa states "exposed," then certainly we know that he should not bring it "covered." The implication then is that the knife should not be covered *even in the presence of witnesses.*

13. The word בִּשְׁעַת, *in times of,* does not actually appear in the Mishnah.

14. If under normal circumstances the knife may be carried covered, then R' Eliezer should have just stated: ". . . he should bring it exposed, or covered in the presence of witnesses." From this we could infer that in times of danger, when it is impossible to bring the knife exposed, he should bring it covered in the presence of witnesses. For that reason R' Eliezer specifically mentioned "times of danger" – to teach that only then may the knife be covered (*Maharam;* see also *Ritva MHK* ed.).

15. And, since a person is disqualified from testifying about himself, R' Yehudah uses the term "witnesses" loosely (see also below, note 20). [See *Leshon HaZahav,* who explains why the Gemara is asking this question on the Baraisa and not on our Mishnah; see also note 17 below.]

16. Perhaps R' Yehudah requires technically qualified witnesses [and the minimum number for any testimony is two].

17. Since the Mishnah states, "he covers it in the presence of witnesses," the implication is that the full complement of two *other,* impartial observers is required. [This is in contrast to the Baraisa, where the phrase, "bringing (the knife) concealed with the knowledge of witnesses," lends itself more easily to the interpretation that the carrier is one of the two witnesses.] Hence, two people besides the bearer must know that the latter carried the knife in order to perform the mitzvah of *milah* (*Rashi,* as explained by *Maharam Schiff* and *Leshon HaZahav*).

18. If only the bearer and one other person were meant, the phrase, "and he covers it in the presence of witnesses," would be inappropriate, since a person is disqualified from testifying about himself (*Rashi*). See also previous note.

19. The function here of "witnesses" is only to reveal the bearer's intent in carrying the knife; hence, this is not a formal testimony, such as is found in capital or monetary cases, that requires two [technically valid] witnesses (*Rashi*).

20. In truth, the revelation of the bearer's intent comes only from the second person. However, there is a requirement that these two people qualify as witnesses in a case where they are both not involved (i.e. they cannot be relatives). The Mishnah teaches us this by referring to the two of them as "witnesses" (see *Rashi, Tos. Yom Tov* to Mishnah, and *Ritva MHK* ed.; see also *Rashash* and *Hagahos R' Elazar Moshe Horowitz*).

21. The Torah commands three times: לֹא־תְבַשֵּׁל גְּדִי בַּחֲלֵב אִמּוֹ, *You shall not cook a kid in its mother's milk* (*Exodus* 23:19, 34:26; *Deuteronomy* 14:21). This prohibition applies not only to the meat of a kid in its mother's milk, but to the meat of any kosher domestic animal in the milk of any kosher domestic animal (see Mishnah in *Chullin* 113a). The verse is stated three times so as to intimate three distinct prohibitions: 1) against cooking meat and milk together; 2) against eating the milk and meat that were cooked together; and 3) against deriving any benefit from them (ibid. 115b). See also *Chullin* 114b for another derivation of these prohibitions.

Three authorities are quoted in the Mishnah in *Chullin* (113a) – the Tanna Kamma, R' Akiva and R' Yose HaGlili. Regarding whether eating the meat of fowl with milk is also Biblically prohibited, both R' Akiva and R' Yose hold that it is not; R' Akiva, however, maintains that it is Rabbinically forbidden, while R' Yose (who will be cited in the Gemara below) maintains that it is entirely permitted (see ibid. 116a). The Tanna Kamma's view in this matter is disputed by Rishonim. *Rambam* contends (*Hil. Mamrim* 2:9) that it coincides with R' Akiva's opinion, while according to *Tosafos* (ibid. ד״ה בשר), the Tanna Kamma holds that eating fowl with milk is *Biblically* prohibited (see *Yoreh Deah* 87:3 with *Shach*).

עין משפט נר מצוה

א א מיי' פ"ב מהלכות מילה הלכה ו סמג עשין כח טוש"ע א"ח סי' שלא סעיף ו וטוש"ע י"ד סימן רסו סעיף ג:

ב ב טוש"ע י"ד סימן רסה סעיף יב:

ג ג מיי' פכ"ב מהלכות איסורי ביאה הל' יט סמג לאוין קכו:

מסורת הש"ס

א) [מכאן לקמן קלו. ועירובין קב.], ב) פ"ל ע"ג, ג) פסחים סו. סט: יבמות יד. מנחות עב. צו., ד) ס"ל ע"ג, ה) יבמות יד. חולין קטו. ע"ש, ו) [ע"ל דטווסא עיין בערוך טירוס], ז) חולין קיג., ח) יומא עה., ט) לעיל מט., י) [ברכות נג: לעיל מט. וש"נ], כ) [דף קמז.], ל) ס"א, מ) [ע"ל סנטר], נ) [ע"ל עליהן].

מתני' וגמ'

רבי אליעזר אומר אם לא הביא כלי מע"ש מביאו בשבת מגולה ובסכנה מכסהו ע"פ עדים ועוד אמר ר"א כורתים עצים לעשות פחמין לעשות (כלי) ברזל כלל אמר ר"ע כל מלאכה שאפשר לעשותה מע"ש אינה דוחה את השבת (ומילה) שאי אפשר לעשותה מע"ש דוחה את השבת: **גמ'** איבעיא להו טעמא דר"א משום חבובי מצוה או דילמא משום חשדא למאי נפקא מינה לאתויי מכוסה ע"פ עדים אי אמרת משום חבובי מצוה מגולה אין מכוסה לא אלא אי אמרת משום חשדא אפי' מכוסה שפיר דמי מאי איתמר א"ר לוי לא אמרה ר"א אלא לחבובי מצוה תניא נמי הכי מביאו מגולה ואין מביאו מכוסה דברי ר"א אמר רב אשי מתני' נמי דיקא דקתני ובשעת הסכנה מכסהו ע"פ עדים בסכנה אין שלא בסכנה לא שמע מינה משום חבובי מצוה שמע מינה תניא אידך מביאו מגולה ואין מביאו מכוסה דברי ר"א ר' יהודה אומר משום ר"א נוהגין היו בשעת הסכנה שהיו מביאין מכוסה ע"פ עדים איבעיא להו עדים דקאמר איהו וחד או דילמא הוא ותרי ת"ש ובסכנה מכסהו ע"פ עדים אי אמרת בשלמא הוא ותרי שפיר אלא אי אמרת הוא וחד מאי עדים שראוים להעיד במקום אחר: ועוד אמר ר"א: ת"ר במקומו של ר"א היו כורתין עצים לעשות פחמין לעשות ברזל בשבת במקומו של ר' יוסי הגלילי היו אוכלין בשר עוף בחלב לוי איקלע לבי יוסף רישבא קריבו ליה רישא דטווסא בחלבא לא אכל כי אתא לקמיה דרבי א"ל אמאי לא תשמתינהו א"ל אתריה דר' יהודה בן בתירה הוה ואמינא דילמא דרש להו כר' יוסי הגלילי דתנן ר' יוסי הגלילי אומר נאמר לא תאכלו כל נבלה ונאמר לא תבשל גדי בחלב אמו את שאסור משום נבלה אסור לבשל בחלב עוף שאסור משום נבלה יכול יהא אסור לבשל בחלב ת"ל בחלב אמו יצא עוף שאין לו חלב אם א"ר יצחק עיר אחת היתה בא"י שהיו עושין כר"א והיו מתים בזמנן ולא עוד אלא שפעם אחת גזרה מלכות הרשעה גזרה על ישראל על המילה ועל אותה העיר לא גזרה: תניא רשב"ג אומר כל מצוה שקיבלו עליהם בשמחה כגון מילה דכתיב שש אנכי על אמרתך כמוצא שלל רב עדיין עושין אותה בשמחה וכל מצוה שקבלו עליהם בקטטה כגון עריות דכתיב וישמע משה את העם בוכה למשפחותיו על עסקי משפחותיו עדיין עושין אותה בקטטה דליכא כתובה דלא רמו בה תיגרא תניא ר"ש בן אלעזר אומר כל מצוה שמסרו ישראל עצמן עליהם למיתה בשעת גזרת המלכות כגון עבודת כוכבים ומילה עדיין היא מוחזקת בידם וכל מצוה שלא מסרו ישראל עצמן עליה למיתה בשעת גזרת המלכות כגון תפילין עדיין היא מרופה בידם דא"ר ינאי תפילין צריכין גוף נקי כאלישע בעל כנפים מאי היא אמר אביי שלא יפיח בהם רבא אמר שלא יישן בהם ואמאי קרו ליה אלישע בעל כנפים שפעם אחת גזרה מלכות הרשעה גזרה על ישראל שכל המניח תפילין על ראשו יקרו את מוחו והיה אלישע מניח תפילין ויצא לשוק וראהו קסדור אחד רץ מלפניו ורץ אחריו כיון שהגיע אצלו נטלן מראשו ואחזן בידו א"ל מה בידך אמר לו כנפי יונה פשט את ידו ונמצאו בה כנפי יונה לפיכך היו קורין אותו בעל כנפים מאי שנא כנפי יונה דא"ל ולא א"ל שאר עופות משום דדמיא כנסת ישראל ליונה שנאמר כנפי יונה נחפה בכסף ואברותיה בירקרק חרוץ מה יונה זו כנפיה מגינות עליה אף ישראל מצות מגינות עליהן: א"ר אבא בר רב אדא א"ר יצחק פעם אחת שכחו ולא הביאו איזמל מערב שבת והביאוהו בשבת [דרך גגות ודרך חצירות] שלא

רש"י

רבי אליעזר אומר אם לא הביא כלי. איזמל למול את התינוק וקאי אמתניתין דפרקין דלעיל דסליק מיניה וכל צרכי מילה עושין בשבת: מגולה. בפני הכל ובגמרא מפרש מאי מצריך ליה לגלויה: ובסכנה. שגזרו ארמאים על המילה: מכסהו ע"פ עדים. שיעידו שאיזמל של מצוה הוא מביא ולא יחשדוהו: כלל אמר ר"ע. נחלק על ר"א במכשירי מצוה שאין דוחין הואיל ואפשר לעשותן מע"ש: [ושאי אפשר לעשות מע"ש. כגון] מילה עצמה שא"א לה ליעשות דזמנה ביום השמיני דוחה שבת: גמ' טעמא דר"א. דאמר מגולה אין מכוסה לא: משום חיבוב מצוה. להודיע שחביבה מצוה עליו שמחלל שבת עליה: משום חשדא. שלא יחשדוהו שהוא נושא שאר חפציו וסיפא דמתני' דקתני ובסכנה מכסהו ע"פ עדים ודאי משום חשדא הוא אלא רישא מיבעיא לן דוקא מגולה קאמר אבל מכוסה ע"פ עדים שלא בשעת הסכנה לא ומשום חיבוב מצוה או לאו דוקא מגולה דטעמיה משום חשדא והוא"ה למכוסה על פי עדים: אי אמרת בשלמא הוא ותרי שפיר. היינו דמיקרו עדים אלא הוא וחד מי מיקרי עדים איהו לגביה נפשיה מי מיקרי עד: ומשני שראוים להעיד במקום אחר. לעולם הכא עדות לא שייכא דלאפוקי מחשדא בעלמא הוא ואין כאן לא דיני ממונות ולא דיני נפשות שיהו שנים (א) ומאי קרו להו עדים דאיכא גילוי מילתא ע"י השני ושנים קרו עדים בעדות אחריני שאינו נוגע בה: לעשות ברזל. לאיזמל של מילה: היו אוכלין בשר עוף בחלב. כדלקמן: רישבא. לייד עופות: נאמר לא תאכלו כל נבלה ונאמר. באותו פסוק עצמו לא תבשל גדי משמע כל האסור משום נבלה נוהג בו איסור בשר בחלב: שש אנכי על אמרתך. אמירה יחידה שקדמה לשאר אמירות והיא מילה שישראל עושין וששים עליה לכל שאר מצות אינן מוכיחות כל שעה כגון תפילין ומזוזה וציצית דאינן כשהוא בשדה וערום בבית המרחץ אבל זו מעיד עליהם לעולם כדאמרינן במנחות (דף מג:) בדוד שראה עצמו בבית המרחץ ונצטער אמר אוי לי שאני ערום מכל מצות כיון שנסתכל במילה נתיישבה דעתו: בשמחה. שעושין משתה: על עסקי משפחותיו. שנאסר להם קרובות: מרופה. רפויה: דא"ר ינאי תפילין צריכות גוף נקי. שלא יפיח אלמא לא זהירי בהו ושמעינן מינה דלא מסרו עליה אלא אלישע לבדו: יקרו. פוריי"ר בלעז לשון יקרוה עורבי נחל (משלי ל) ולשון תנקר לא נעלה (במדבר טז) את מוחו. שכנגד תפילין: קסדור. ממונה: מגינות עליהן. אינה נלחמת בחרטומיה אלא בכנפיה: דרך

תוספות

רבי אליעזר אומר אם לא הביא כלי כו' מביאו בשבת מגולה. ° וא"ת ויביאו התינוק אצל כלי דהשתא ליכא איסור שבת כלל דהחי נושא את עצמו וי"ל דקטן צריך לאמו הוא ואחר המילה היה צריך להחזירו לאמו ואז הוי כפות (ב) לפי שהוא חולה כדאמרינן ביומא (דף סו:) אפי' תימא ר' נתן חולה שאני וגם אמו שהיא מסוכנת לא תוכל לבא אצל התינוק ועוד י"ל כיון דיותר בקל יביא הכלי משיביא התינוק שרי ר"א כדי למהר המצוה כדמוכח בגמרא דאמר פעם אחת שכחו ולא הביאו אזמל מע"ש והביאו בשבת שלא ברצונו שהביאו דרך חצרות וגגות וקרפיפות והיו יכולין להביא דרך רה"ר אלמא דשרי ר"א דרך רה"ר דהוי דאורייתא (ג) ° כדי למהר המצוה אע"פ שיכול לעשות [בענין] דליכא אלא איסורא דרבנן:

שש אנכי. במדרש (שוחר טוב) למנצח על השמינית כתיב הנדרש על המילה שהיא בשמיני וכן אמרי' (ד) (פר"א פ' כ"ט) ויעש אברהם משתה גדול ביום הגמל את יצחק ביום ה"ג מל את יצחק דהיינו ביום השמיני דמילה כמנין ה"ג. ר"ת: **אמר** ליה כנפי יונה. הרי שלא מסר עצמו לומר תפילין הן. רבינו שמואל: שלא

גליון הש"ס

גמרא בשלמא הוא ותרי. עיין תשובת הרלנ"ח סי' פ"ט: תוס' ד"ה רבי אליעזר וכו' ואת"ו ויביאו התינוק. עיין לעיל דף לד ע"א תוספות ד"ה אבל אדם: בא"ד כדי למהר המצוה. עיין עירובין דף קג ע"ב תוספות ד"ה מה לי:

הגהות הב"ח

(א) רש"י ד"ה ומאי וכו' ומאי קרי להו: (ב) תוס' ד"ה ר' אליעזר וכו' ואז הוי כפות. נ"ב עיין בפרק המלביש דף קי ע"א: (ג) בא"ד כדי למהר המצוה. נ"ב עיין בסוף עירובין דף קג ע"ב בתוספות ד"ה מה לי: (ד) ד"ה שש וכו' וכן אמרי' במדרש ויעש אברהם:

תורה אור השלם

א) לא תאכלו כל נבלה לגר אשר בשעריך תתננה ואכלה או מכר לנכרי כי עם קדוש אתה ליי' אלהיך לא תבשל גדי בחלב אמו: [דברים יד, כא]

ב) שש אנכי על אמרתך כמוצא שלל רב: [תהלים קיט, קסב]

ג) וישמע משה את העם בכה למשפחתיו איש לפתח אהלו ויחר אף יי' מאד ובעיני משה רע: [במדבר יא, י]

ד) אם תשכבון בין שפתים כנפי יונה נחפה בכסף ואברותיה בירקרק חרוץ: [תהלים סח, יד]

ליקוטי רש"י

כורתים עצים בשבת לעשות פחמין. לנו ביום כדי לעשות ברזל איזמל של מילה דקסבר ר"א מכשירי מצוה דוחין שבת כמצוה עצמה [יבמות יד.]. כי ר' אליעזר אית ליה מכשירי מצוה דוחין את השבת כמצוה עצמה. לעשות כלי ברזל. לעשות איזמל למול בו [עירובין קב:]. היו אוכלין בשר עוף בחלב. לדברי יוסי הגלילי אפילו איסורא דרבנן ליכא [חולין קטז.]. רישבא. שם. דטווסא. [חולין שם]. ת"ל בחלב אמו. מי שיש לו חלב אם יצא עוף שאין לו חלב אם [יבמות שם]. שש אנכי

רבינו חננאל

פרק יט

רבי אליעזר אומר אם לא הביא כלי מערב שבת מביאו בשבת מגולה וכו' ואיבעיא לן האי דקתני ר' אליעזר אומר מביאו מגולה משום חבובי מצוה הוא או משום שלא יחשדוהו שהוציא חפציו טמונים לפיכך מגליהו שיראו שסכין של מצוה הוא. ופשטנא דמשום חבובי מצוה הוא היכא דליכא סכנה ותוב איבעיא לן האי דתנא במתניתא רבי יהודה משום רבי אליעזר [אומר] נוהגים היינו בסכנה מביאין אותו (בסכנה) מכוסה ע"פ עדים הני עדים שנים אחרים זולתו המביאו או דלמא הוא ואחרים ולא איפשטא בהדיא: **לוי** איקלע לבי יוסף רישבא קריבו ליה רישא דטווסא בחלבא לא אכל כי אתא לקמיה דר' א"ל מ"ט לא שמתינהו א"ל אתרא דר' יהודה בן בתירא ואמרי דלמא דריש להו כרבי יוסי הגלילי דסבר יצא עוף שאין לו חלב אם: **א"ר** יצחק עיר אחת היתה בא"י שהיו עושין כר' אליעזר והיו מתיה מתין בזמנן ולא עוד אלא שפעם אחת גזרה מלכות הרשעה גזרה על ישראל על המילה ועל אותה העיר לא גזרה א) כל השבח ואין הלכה כר"א ולא כר' יוסי הגלילי שמתיר בשר עוף בחלב ולא כרבי ינאי שאמר תפילין צריכין גוף נקי כאלישע בעל כנפים ומפרשי רבנן כי לא אמר רבי ינאי אלא בשעת הגזרה וסמיך דהוא עריק ועבדי ליה נס אמר ראבין בר רב אדא א"ר יצחק פעם אחת שכחו ולא הביאו איזמל מע"ש והביאוהו

חשק שלמה על רבינו חננאל

א) נראה דצ"ל לאמר כל השבח הזה מ"מ אין הלכה כר"א וכו':

על אמרתך. ורבותינו דרשוהו על המילה שהיה דוד בבית המרחץ וראה עצמו בלא ציצית ובלא תפילין ובלא תורה אמר אוי לי שאני ערום מכל מצות כיון שנסתכל במילה שמח ואמר על אמרתך המילה שמתחלה נתנה במאמר ולא בדבור שנאמר (בראשית יז) ואתה את בריתי תשמור ויאמר אלהים אל אברהם ולא נאמר וידבר [תהלים קיט, קסב]. למנצח על השמינית (תהלים ו) על מילה שניתנה בשמיני [מנחות מג:]. על עסקי משפחותיו. על עריות הנאסרות להם [במדבר יא, י]. שלא יפיח. שיכול להעמיד עצמו בשעת הכרח. שלא יישן בהם. שמא יפיח או ירגא. קסדור. ממונה. מגינות עליה. שהיא נלחמת בכנפיה [לעיל מט.]. כנפי יונה. כשמסתכלין כנפיה של יונה כנסת ישראל נמשלה ליונה [לעיל שם]. נחפה בכסף. בכספם ובממונם של תורה ומצות. ואברותיה. כנפיה. בירקרק חרוץ. בזהב מובחר [תהלים סח, יד]. כנפיה מגינות עליה. שאינה נלחמת בחרטומה אלא בכנפיה [ברכות נג:].

served [Levi] a peacock's[22] **head in milk,** לֹא אֲכַל – **but he did not eat** it. כִּי אֲתָא לְקַמֵּיהּ דְּרַבִּי אֲמַר לֵיהּ – **When [Levi] later came before Rebbi, he said to [Rebbi]:** אַמַּאי לֹא תְשַׁמְּתִינְהוּ – **Why do you not excommunicate [the members of Yosef's household]** for violating the prohibition against eating meat with milk? אֲמַר לֵיהּ – **[Rebbi] said to [Levi]** in reply: אַתְרֵיהּ דְּרַבִּי יְהוּדָה בֶּן בְּתֵירָה הֲוָה – **[That] was R' Yehudah ben Beseirah's town,**[23] וַאֲמֵינָא דִּילְמָא דָּרֵשׁ לְהוּ כְּרַבִּי יוֹסֵי הַגְּלִילִי – **and I thought** that **perhaps [R' Yehudah] expounds [the Scriptures] as** does **R' Yose HaGlili,** דִּתְנַן – **for we learned in a Mishnah:**[24] רַבִּי יוֹסֵי הַגְּלִילִי אוֹמֵר – R' YOSE HAGLILI SAYS: נֶאֱמַר ,,לֹא תֹאכְלוּ כָל־נְבֵלָה" – IT IS STATED, *YOU SHALL NOT EAT ANY CARCASS,*[25] וְנֶאֱמַר ,,לֹא־תְבַשֵּׁל גְּדִי בַּחֲלֵב אִמּוֹ" – AND IT IS STATED in that selfsame verse, *YOU SHALL NOT COOK A KID IN ITS MOTHER'S MILK.* אֶת שֶׁאָסוּר מִשּׁוּם נְבֵלָה – The inclusion of both prohibitions in one verse implies that THAT WHICH IS PROHIBITED UNDER THE CATEGORY OF "CARCASS" אָסוּר לְבַשֵּׁל בְּחָלָב – IS FORBIDDEN TO BE COOKED WITH MILK. עוֹף – Accordingly, FOWL, שֶׁאָסוּר מִשּׁוּם נְבֵלָה – WHICH IS PROHIBITED UNDER THE CATEGORY OF "CARCASS," יָכוֹל יְהֵא אָסוּר לְבַשֵּׁל בְּחָלָב – ONE MIGHT think IS also FORBIDDEN TO BE COOKED WITH MILK. תַּלְמוּד לוֹמַר ,,בַּחֲלֵב אִמּוֹ" – SCRIPTURE therefore STATES, *IN ITS MOTHER'S MILK,* יָצָא עוֹף שֶׁאֵין לוֹ חֲלֵב אֵם – whereby FOWL IS EXCLUDED from the prohibition, SINCE IT HAS NO MOTHER'S MILK.

The Gemara mentions the reward of a city that followed R' Eliezer's ruling:[26]

אָמַר רַבִּי יִצְחָק – **R' Yitzchak said:** עִיר אַחַת הָיְתָה בְּאֶרֶץ יִשְׂרָאֵל שֶׁהָיוּ עוֹשִׂין כְּרַבִּי אֱלִיעֶזֶר – **There was one city in the Land of Israel whose** inhabitants **acted in accordance with R' Eliezer's** rulings, וְהָיוּ מֵתִים בִּזְמַנָּן – **and they would die** only **in their** proper **time.**[27] וְלֹא עוֹד אֶלָּא שֶׁפַּעַם אַחַת – **And not only that, but once** גָּזְרָה מַלְכוּת הָרְשָׁעָה גְּזֵרָה עַל יִשְׂרָאֵל עַל הַמִּילָה – **the evil regime** (i.e. the Romans) **issued a decree on** all of **Israel against circumcision,** וְעַל אוֹתָהּ הָעִיר לֹא גָּזְרָה – **and on that city** that adhered to R' Eliezer's rulings **they did not** so **decree.**[28]

The Gemara presents aggadic teachings on the subject of the performance of circumcision:

תַּנְיָא – **It was taught in a Baraisa:** רַבָּן שִׁמְעוֹן בֶּן גַּמְלִיאֵל אוֹמֵר – RABBAN SHIMON BEN GAMLIEL SAYS: כָּל מִצְוָה שֶׁקִּיבְּלוּ עֲלֵיהֶם בְּשִׂמְחָה – ANY COMMANDMENT THAT [THE JEWISH PEOPLE] ACCEPTED UPON THEMSELVES WITH JOY – כְּגוֹן מִילָה דִּכְתִיב – SUCH AS CIRCUMCISION, AS IT IS WRITTEN,[29] ,,שָׂשׂ אָנֹכִי עַל־אִמְרָתֶךָ כְּמוֹצֵא שָׁלָל רָב" – *I REJOICE OVER YOUR WORD, LIKE ONE WHO FINDS ABUNDANT SPOILS*[30] – עֲדַיִין עוֹשִׂין אוֹתָהּ בְּשִׂמְחָה – THEY STILL PERFORM WITH JOY.[31] וְכָל מִצְוָה שֶׁקִּבְּלוּ עֲלֵיהֶם בִּקְטָטָה – AND ANY COMMANDMENT THAT [THE JEWISH PEOPLE] ACCEPTED UPON THEMSELVES CONTENTIOUSLY – כְּגוֹן עֲרָיוֹת דִּכְתִיב – SUCH AS the prohibition against INCESTUOUS RELATIONS, AS IT IS WRITTEN,[32] ,,וַיִּשְׁמַע מֹשֶׁה אֶת־הָעָם בֹּכֶה לְמִשְׁפְּחֹתָיו" – *AND MOSES HEARD THE PEOPLE WEEPING BY THEIR FAMILIES,* עַל עִסְקֵי מִשְׁפְּחוֹתָיו – which we expound to mean that they wept OVER THEIR FAMILY AFFAIRS[33] – עֲדַיִין עוֹשִׂין אוֹתָהּ בִּקְטָטָה – THEY STILL OBSERVE CONTENTIOUSLY,[34] דְּלֵיכָּא כְּתוּבָּה דְּלֹא רָמוּ בַּהּ תִּיגְרָא – FOR THERE IS NO MARRIAGE CONTRACT CONCERNING WHICH [THE PARTIES] DO NOT QUARREL.[35]

Another aggadic teaching about *milah:*

תַּנְיָא – **It was taught in a Baraisa:** רַבִּי שִׁמְעוֹן בֶּן אֶלְעָזָר אוֹמֵר – R' SHIMON BEN ELAZAR SAYS: כָּל מִצְוָה שֶׁמָּסְרוּ יִשְׂרָאֵל עַצְמָן עֲלֵיהֶם לְמִיתָה – ANY COMMANDMENT FOR WHICH THE JEWISH PEOPLE GAVE THEMSELVES OVER TO DEATH בִּשְׁעַת גְּזֵרַת הַמַּלְכוּת – AT

NOTES

22. *Aruch;* cf. *Shabbos Shel Mi.*

23. I.e. Yosef and the members of his household resided in a place where R' Yehudah ben Beseirah was the central rabbinic authority.

24. *Chullin* 113a. See above, note 21.

25. *Deuteronomy* 14:21. The verse refers to the carcass (*neveilah*) of an animal that was not slaughtered according to the procedure prescribed by the Torah.

26. [R' Eliezer ruled in the Mishnah that even the preliminaries to *milah* override the Sabbath *melachah* restrictions.]

Citing *Raavad, Ritva* (*MHK* ed.) explains that since the halachah was not yet established in favor of R' Akiva and against R' Eliezer, it was permitted to follow the latter's ruling. Hence, the people of this city were rewarded for fulfilling the verse, *You shall not deviate from the word that they will tell you* (*Deuteronomy* 17:11). [See also *Maharshal* here.]

27. That is, no one in that city died prematurely.

Ben Yehoyada explains the appropriateness of the reward: The Midrash teaches that Sabbath observance and *milah* are both very great mitzvos, each equivalent to all the other mitzvos of the Torah. The only indication of which of these two is greater is the fact that *milah* overrides the Sabbath *melachah* restrictions. Hence, one who publicizes *milah's* superiority by carrying the circumcision knife on the Sabbath in an exposed way, in accordance with R' Eliezer's dictum, merits to live out the full measure of his years, for in reference to the blood of *milah* the prophet states: *By your blood you shall live* (*Ezekiel* 16:6). See also *Maharsha.*

28. In adhering to R' Eliezer's rulings they displayed their love for the mitzvah of *milah,* and for that reason they were rewarded (see *Tosafos* to *Yevamos* 14a ד״ה במקומו).

29. *Psalms* 119:162.

30. *Your word,* in the singular, implies a single "word" (commandment) – one that was incumbent upon the Jews before any other. This "word" is *milah,* which was commanded to our patriarch Abraham in *Genesis* ch. 17 (see *Rashi* to *Megillah* 16b and *Emes LeYaakov* here). King David is stating that there is a unique joy (שָׂשׂוֹן) associated with *milah.* This is because of all the mitzvos, only *milah* is in constant evidence. That is, one leaves behind his *mezuzah* when he goes to work in the field, and one must remove his tefillin and *tzitzis* when he repairs to the bathhouse. Circumcision, on the other hand, is a constant testimony that the Jewish people have been sanctified by God's commandments, and so it calls for a special joyfulness (*Rashi,* as explained by *Yad David* [*Basra*] and *Leshon HaZahav;* see also *Rif* in *Ein Yaakov*).

King David uttered this verse after visiting a bathhouse, where he became distressed upon realizing that he was bereft of all mitzvos. However, his mind was eased when he recalled his circumcision (ibid.; see *Menachos* 43b; cf. *Tosafos*).

Maharal (*Chidushei Aggados*) offers a different interpretation of *milah's* uniqueness: The foreskin is considered an extraneous aspect of the (male) body (see *Nedarim* 31b), and so its removal through *milah* completes the infant's physical formation. For that reason the Jews joyfully accepted the mitzvah of *milah* upon themselves, for one naturally rejoices when attaining completeness and perfection.

31. I.e. with a festive meal (*Rashi*). See also *Tosafos* ד״ה שש.

32. *Numbers* 11:10.

33. They wept over the fact that certain relatives (see *Leviticus* ch. 18) were now prohibited to one another in marriage (*Rashi*).

Maharal (ibid.) explains the reason for their weeping: Whereas *milah* is a completion and thus a cause for joy, the forbidden-relation prohibitions are a sundering of what is naturally attached – and thus a cause for weeping. Indeed, the forbidden relations are referred to as שְׁאֵר בְּשָׂרוֹ (*Leviticus* 18:6), which *Targum Onkelos* renders קָרִיב בִּסְרֵיהּ, *a relation of his flesh.* Now, inasmuch as the goal of marriage is for the man and woman to become בָּשָׂר אֶחָד, *one flesh* (*Genesis* 2:24), it is most natural for a person to want to attain that goal with someone who is already "a relation of his flesh." When the Torah proscribed such unions, however, the people wept, for they were now being separated from those to whom they were naturally attached.

34. I.e. in the context of legitimate marital unions.

35. The reference is to dispute over financial matters – such as the dowry, the marriage contract (*kesubah*), and other stipulations.

רבי אליעזר אומר אם לא הביא כלי מע"ש מביאו בשבת מגולה ובסכנה מכסהו ע"פ עדים ועוד אמר א) ר"א כורתים עצים לעשות פחמין לעשות ב) (כלי) ברזל ג) כלל אמר ר"ע א כל מלאכה שאפשר לעשותה מע"ש אינה דוחה את השבת ד) (ומילה) שאי אפשר לעשותה מע"ש דוחה את השבת:

גמ' איבעיא להו טעמא דר"א משום חבובי מצוה או דילמא משום חשדא למאי נפקא מינה לאתויי מכוסה ע"פ עדים אי אמרת משום חבובי מצוה מגולה אין מכוסה לא אלא אי אמרת משום חשדא אפי' מכוסה שפיר דמי מאי איתמר א"ר לוי לא אמרה ר"א אלא לחבובי מצוה תניא נמי הכי מביאו מגולה ואין מביאו מכוסה דברי ר"א אמר רב אשי מתני' נמי דיקא דקתני ובשעת הסכנה מכסהו ע"פ עדים בסכנה אין שלא בסכנה לא שמע מינה משום חבובי מצוה שמע מינה תניא אידך מביאו מגולה ואין מביאו מכוסה דברי ר"א ר' יהודה אומר משום ר"א נוהגין היו בשעת הסכנה שהיו מביאין מכוסה ע"פ עדים איבעיא להו עדים דקאמר איהו וחד או דילמא הוא ותרי ת"ש ובסכנה מכסהו ע"פ עדים אי אמרת ° בשלמא הוא ותרי שפיר אלא אי אמרת הוא וחד מאי עדים שראוים להעיד במקום אחר: ועוד אמר ר"א: ה) ת"ר במקומו של ר"א היו כורתין עצים לעשות פחמין לעשות ברזל בשבת במקומו של ר' יוסי הגלילי היו אוכלין בשר עוף בחלב לוי איקלע לבי יוסף רישבא קריבו ליה רישא ו) דטוותא בחלבא לא אכל כי אתא לקמיה דרבי א"ל אמאי לא תשמתינהו א"ל אתריה דר' יהודה בן בתירה הוה ואמינא דילמא דרש להו כר' יוסי הגלילי ז) דתנן ר' יוסי הגלילי אומר נאמר א) לא תאכלו כל נבלה ונאמר א) לא תבשל גדי בחלב אמו את שאסור משום נבלה אסור לבשל בחלב עוף שאסור משום נבלה יכול יהא אסור לבשל בחלב ת"ל בחלב אמו יצא עוף שאין לו חלב אם א"ר יצחק עיר אחת היתה בא"י שהיו עושין כר"א והיו מתים בזמנן ולא עוד אלא שפעם אחת גזרה מלכות הרשעה גזרה על ישראל על המילה ועל אותה העיר לא גזרה: תניא רשב"ג אומר כל מצוה שקיבלו עליהם בשמחה כגון מילה דכתיב ב) שש אנכי על אמרתך כמוצא שלל רב ב עדיין עושין אותה בשמחה וכל מצוה שקבלו עליהם בקטטה ג כגון עריות דכתיב ג) וישמע משה את העם בוכה למשפחותיו ח) על עסקי משפחותיו עדיין עושין אותה בקטטה דליכא כתובה דלא רמו בה תיגרא תניא ר"ש בן אלעזר אומר כל מצוה שמסרו ישראל עצמן עליהם למיתה בשעת גזרת המלכות כגון עבודת כוכבים ומילה עדיין היא מוחזקת בידם וכל מצוה שלא מסרו ישראל עצמן עליה למיתה בשעת גזרת המלכות כגון תפילין עדיין היא מרופה בידם ט) דא"ר ינאי תפילין צריכין גוף נקי כאלישע בעל כנפים מאי היא אמר אביי שלא יפיח בהם רבא אמר שלא יישן בהם ואמאי קרו ליה אלישע בעל כנפים שפעם אחת גזרה מלכות הרשעה גזרה על ישראל שכל המניח תפילין על ראשו יקרו את מוחו והיה אלישע מניח תפילין ויצא לשוק וראהו קסדור אחד רץ מלפניו ורץ אחריו כיון שהגיע אצלו נטלן מראשו ואחזן בידו א"ל מה בידך אמר לו כנפי יונה פשט את ידו ונמצאו בה כנפי יונה לפיכך היו קורין אותו בעל כנפים י) ומאי שנא כנפי יונה דא"ל ולא א"ל שאר עופות משום דדמיא כנסת ישראל ליונה שנאמר ד) כנפי יונה נחפה בכסף ואברותיה בירקרק חרוץ מה יונה זו כנפיה מגינות עליה אף ישראל מצות מגינות עליהן: א"ר אבא בר רב אדא א"ר יצחק פעם אחת שכחו ולא הביאו איזמל מערב שבת והביאוהו בשבת [דרך גגות ודרך חצירות] שלא

רש"י

רבי אליעזר אומר אם לא הביא כלי. איזמל למול את התינוק וקאי אמתניתין דפרקין דלעיל ק) דסליק מיניה וכל צרכי מילה עושין בשבת: מגולה. בפני הכל ובגמרא מפרש אמאי מצריך ליה לגלוייה: ובסכנה. שגזרו ארמאים על המילה: מכסהו ע"פ עדים. שיעידו שאיזמל של מצוה הוא מביא ולא יחשדוהו: כלל אמר ר"ע. נחלק על ר"א במכשירי מצוה שאין דוחין הואיל ואפשר לעשותן מע"ש: ל) [ושאי אפשר לעשות מע"ש. כגון] מילה עצמה שא"א לה ליעשות דזמנה ביום השמיני דוחה שבת: גמ' טעמא דר"א. דאמר מגולה אין מכוסה לא: משום חיבוב מצוה. להודיע שחביבה מצוה עליו שמחלל שבת עליה: משום חשדא. שלא יחשדוהו שהוא נושא שאר חפציו וסיפא דמתני' דקתני ובסכנה מכסהו ע"פ עדים ודאי משום חשדא הוא אלא רישא מיבעיא לן דוקא מגולה קאמר אבל מכוסה ע"פ עדים שלא בשעת הסכנה לא ומשום חיבוב מצוה או לאו דוקא מגולה דטעמיה משום חשדא וה"ה למכוסה על פי עדים: אי אמרת בשלמא הוא ותרי שפיר. היינו דמיקרו עדים אלא הוא וחד מי מיקרי עדים איהו לגביה נפשיה מי מיקרי עד: ומשני שראוים להעיד במקום אחר. לעולם הכא עדות לא שייכא דלאפוקי מחשדא בעלמא הוא ואין כאן לא דיני ממונות ולא דיני נפשות שיהו שנים (א) ומאי קרו להו עדים דאיכא גילוי מילתא ע"י השני ושנים קרו עדים בעדות אחריתי שאינו נוגע בה: לעשות ברזל. לאיזמל של מילה: היו אוכלין בשר עוף בחלב. כדלקמן: רישבא. לייד עופות: נאמר לא תאכלו כל נבלה ונאמר. באותו פסוק עצמו לא תבשל גדי משמע כל האסור משום נבלה נוהג בו איסור בשר בחלב: שש אנכי על אמרתך. אמירה יחידה שקדמה לשאר אמירות והיא מילה שישראל עושין ושש עליה דכל שאר מצות אינן מוכיחות כל שעה כגון תפילין ומזוזה וציצית דאינן כשהוא בשדה וערום בבית המרחץ אבל זו מעיד עליהם לעולם כדאמרינן במנחות (דף מג:) בדוד שראה עצמו בבית המרחץ ונצטער אמר אוי לי שאני ערום מכל מצות כיון מ) שנסתכל במילה נתיישבה דעתו: בשמחה. שעושין משתה: על עסקי משפחותיו. שנאסר להם קרובות: מרופה. רפויה: דא"ר ינאי תפילין צריכות גוף נקי. שלא יפיח אלמא לא זהירי בהו ושמעינן מינה דלא מסרו עליה אלא אלישע לבדו: יקרו. פוריי"ר בלעז לשון יקרוה עורבי נחל (משלי ל) ולשון תנקר לא נעלה (במדבר טז): את מוחו. שכנגד תפילין: קסדור. ממונה: מגינות נ) עליהן. אינה נלחמת בחרטומיה אלא בכנפיה:

תוספות

רבי אליעזר אומר אם לא הביא כלי כו' מביאו בשבת מגולה. ° וא"ת ויביאו התינוק אצל כלי דהשתא ליכא איסור שבת כלל דהחי נושא את עצמו וי"ל דקטן צריך לאמו הוא ואחר המילה היה צריך להחזירו לאמו ואז הוי כפות (ב) לפי שהוא חולה כדאמרינן ביומא (דף סו:) אפי' תימא ר' נתן חולה שאני וגם אמו שהיא מסוכנת לא תוכל לבא אצל התינוק ועוד י"ל כיון דיותר בקל יביא הכלי משיביא התינוק שרי ר"א כדי למהר המצוה כדמוכח בגמרא דאמר פעם אחת שכחו ולא הביאו איזמל מע"ש והביאו בשבת שלא ברצונו שהביאו דרך חצרות וגגות וקרפיפות והיו יכולין להביא דרך רה"ר אלמא דשרי ר"א דרך רה"ר דהוי דאורייתא (ג) ° כדי למהר המצוה אע"פ שיכול לעשות [בענין] דליכא אלא איסורא דרבנן:

שש אנכי. במדרש (שוחר טוב) למנצח על השמינית כתיב הנדרש על המילה שהיא בשמיני וכן אמרי' (ד) (פר"א פ' כ"ט) ויעש אברהם משתה גדול ביום הגמל את יצחק ביום ה"ג מל את יצחק דהיינו ביום השמיני דמילה כמנין ה"ג. ר"ת: **אמר** ליה כנפי יונה. הרי שלא מסר עצמו לומר תפילין הן. רבינו שמואל: שלא

עין משפט נר מצוה

א א מיי' פ"ב מהלכות מילה הלכה ו סמג עשין כח טוש"ע א"ח סי' שלא סעיף ו וטוש"ע י"ד סימן רסו סעיף ב:

ב ב טוש"ע י"ד סימן רסו סעיף יב:

ג ג מיי' פכ"ב מהלכות איסורי ביאה הל' יט סמג לאוין קכו:

גליון הש"ס

גמרא בשלמא הוא ותרי. עיין תשובת הרא"ש כלל ס"ח סי' פ"ט: תוס' ד"ה רבי אליעזר וכו' וא"ת ויביאו התינוק. עיין לעיל דף לד ע"א תוספות ד"ה אבל אדם: באד"ה כדי למהר המצוה. עיין עירובין דף קג ע"ב תוספות ד"ה מה לי:

רבינו חננאל

פרק יט

רבי אליעזר אומר אם לא הביא כלי מערב שבת מביאו בשבת מגולה וכו' ואיבעיא לן האי דקתני ר' אליעזר אומר מביאו מגולה משום חבובי מצוה הוא או משום שלא יחשדוהו שהוציא חפציו טמונים לפיכך מגלהו שיראו שסכין של מצוה הוא. ופשטנא דמשום חבובי מצוה הוא היכא דליכא סכנה ותוב איבעיא לן האי דתנא במתניתא רבי יהודה משום רבי אליעזר [אומר] נוהגים היינו בסכנה מביאין אותו (בסכנה) מכוסה ע"פ עדים הני עדים שנים אחרים זולתו המביאו או דלמא הוא ואחרים ולא איפשטא בהדיא: לוי איקלע לבי יוסף רישבא קריבו ליה רישא דטווסא בחלבא לא אכל כי אתא לקמיה דרבי א"ל מ"ט לא שמתינהו א"ל אתרא דר' יהודה בן בתירא ואמרי דלמא דריש להו כר' יוסי הגלילי דסבר יצא עוף שאין לו חלב אם: א"ר יצחק עיר אחת היתה בא"י שהיו עושין כר' אליעזר והיו מתין בזמנן ולא עוד אלא שפעם אחת גזרה מלכות הרשעה גזרה על ישראל על המילה ועל אותה העיר לא גזרה (א) כל השבת ואין הלכה כר"א ולא כר' יוסי הגלילי שמתיר בשר עוף בחלב ולא כרבי ינאי שאמר תפילין צריכין גוף נקי כאלישע בעל כנפים ומפרשי רבנן כי לא אמר רבי ינאי אלא בשעת הגזרה וסמיך דהוה צריך ועבדי ליה נס אמר ראובן בר רב אדא א"ר יצחק פעם אחת שכחו ולא הביאו איזמל מע"ש והביאוהו

חשק שלמה על רבינו חננאל

א) נראה דצ"ל לאמר כל השבת הוא מ"מ אין הלכה כר"א וכו':

מסורת הש"ס

א) [מכות כה. ועירובין קג.], ב) פי' לי"ג, ג) פסחים סו. יבמות יד. מנחות עב. ד) [ל"ג], ה) יבמות יד. חולין קטז. ע"ש, ו) [צ"ל דטווסא עיין בערוך פירושו], ז) חולין קיג., ח) יומא עה., ט) לעיל מט. ע"ש, י) [ברכות נג:], כ) [דף קכח:], ל) [צ"ל שמכרו], מ) [צ"ל עליה].

הגהות הב"ח

(א) רש"י ד"ה ומשני וכו' ומאי קרי להו: (ב) תוס' ד"ה ר' אליעזר וכו' ואז הוי כפות. נ"ב עיין בפרק המצניע דף לד ע"א: (ג) באד"ה כדי למהר המצוה. נ"ב עיין בסוף עירובין דף קג ע"ב בתוספות ד"ה מה לי: (ד) ד"ה שש וכו' וכן אמרי' במדרש ויעש אברהם:

תורה אור השלם

א) לֹא תֹאכְלוּ כָל נְבֵלָה לַגֵּר אֲשֶׁר בִּשְׁעָרֶיךָ תִּתְּנֶנָּה וַאֲכָלָהּ אוֹ מָכֹר לְנָכְרִי כִּי עַם קָדוֹשׁ אַתָּה לַייָ אֱלֹהֶיךָ לֹא תְבַשֵּׁל גְּדִי בַּחֲלֵב אִמּוֹ: [דברים יד, כא]

ב) שָׂשׂ אָנֹכִי עַל אִמְרָתֶךָ כְּמוֹצֵא שָׁלָל רָב: [תהלים קיט, קסב]

ג) וַיִּשְׁמַע מֹשֶׁה אֶת הָעָם בֹּכֶה לְמִשְׁפְּחֹתָיו אִישׁ לְפֶתַח אָהֳלוֹ וַיִּחַר אַף יְיָ מְאֹד וּבְעֵינֵי מֹשֶׁה רָע: [במדבר יא, י]

ד) אִם תִּשְׁכְּבוּן בֵּין שְׁפַתָּיִם כַּנְפֵי יוֹנָה נֶחְפָּה בַכֶּסֶף וְאֶבְרוֹתֶיהָ בִּירַקְרַק חָרוּץ: [תהלים סח, יד]

ליקוטי רש"י

כורתים עצים בשבת לעשות פחמין. לבו ביום כדי לעשות ברזל איזמל של מילה דקסבר ר"א מכשירי מצוה דוחין שבת כמצוה עצמה [יבמות יד.]. רבי אליעזר אית ליה מכשירי מצוה דוחין את השבת כמצוה שדוחה את השבת ואם אין לו איזמל למולו בשבת כורתין עצים לעשות פחמין ועושין איזמל [חולין קטז.]. לעשות כלי ברזל. לעשות איזמל למול בו [עירובין קג.]. היו אוכלין בשר עוף בחלב. כדברי יוסי הגלילי דאפילו איסורא דרבנן לית ליה בעוף. רישבא. לייד עופות ריקבה לשון צייד [חולין שם]. דטוותא. פורגין ריקבין ליונים [חולין שם ע"ש בהגר"ב]. ... דטוותא. פוגין [חולין שם]. ת"ל בחלב אמו. מי שיש לו חלב אם ... שש אנכי

[illegible]

A TIME OF A GOVERNMENT EDICT directed at that commandment – כְּגוֹן עֲבוֹדַת כּוֹכָבִים וּמִילָה – SUCH AS an edict to perform IDOLATRY[36] OR to refrain from performing CIRCUMCISION[37] – עֲדַיִין הִיא מוּחְזֶקֶת בְּיָדָם – IS STILL HELD FIRMLY IN THEIR HANDS. וְכָל מִצְוָה שֶׁלֹּא מָסְרוּ יִשְׂרָאֵל עַצְמָן עָלֶיהָ לְמִיתָה – AND ANY COMMANDMENT FOR WHICH THE JEWISH PEOPLE DID NOT GIVE THEMSELVES OVER TO DEATH בִּשְׁעַת גְּזֵרַת הַמַּלְכוּת – AT THE TIME OF A GOVERNMENT EDICT directed at the commandment – כְּגוֹן תְּפִלִּין – SUCH AS the wearing of TEFILLIN[38] – עֲדַיִין הִיא מְרוּפָּה בְּיָדָם – IS STILL HELD WEAKLY IN THEIR HANDS.

The Gemara establishes that the Jewish people as a whole were not totally dedicated to the mitzvah of tefillin:

דְּאָמַר רַבִּי יַנַּאי – **For R' Yannai said:** תְּפִלִּין צְרִיכִין גּוּף נָקִי כֶּאֱלִישָׁע בַּעַל כְּנָפַיִם – **Tefillin require** their wearer to maintain **a clean body, as Elisha the Winged One**[39] maintained.

The Gemara explains R' Yannai's teaching:

מַאי הִיא – **What is it** that constitutes "a clean body"? אָמַר אַבַּיֵי שֶׁלֹּא יָפִיחַ בָּהֶם – **Abaye said: That one should not pass wind** while dressed **with them.**[40] רָבָא אָמַר שֶׁלֹּא יִישַׁן בָּהֶם – **Rava said: That one should not sleep in them.**[41] From the fact that R' Yannai singled out Elisha as one who maintains a clean body, we can infer that the people did not do so, and thus they were not totally dedicated to the mitzvah of tefillin.[42]

The Gemara now explains how Elisha earned his title:

וְאַמַּאי קָרוּ לֵיהּ ,,אֱלִישָׁע בַּעַל כְּנָפַיִם" – **And why did they call him "Elisha the Winged One"?** שֶׁפַּעַם אַחַת גָּזְרָה מַלְכוּת הָרְשָׁעָה גְּזֵרָה עַל יִשְׂרָאֵל – **Because once the evil** Roman **government issued a decree against Israel,** שֶׁכָּל הַמַּנִּיחַ תְּפִלִּין עַל רֹאשׁוֹ – ruling **that** in the case of **anyone who dons tefillin on his head,** יִקְּרוּ אֶת מוֹחוֹ – **they would gouge out his brain** (which lies beneath the head tefillin).[43] וְהָיָה אֱלִישָׁע מַנִּיחַ תְּפִלִּין וְיָצָא לַשּׁוּק – **But Elisha would don tefillin and go out into the marketplace** in defiance of the decree. וְרָאָהוּ קַסְדּוֹר אֶחָד – One day **a certain official spied him.** רָץ מִלְּפָנָיו וְרָץ אַחֲרָיו – **[Elisha] ran from [the official] and [the official] ran after him.** כֵּיוָן שֶׁהִגִּיעַ אֶצְלוֹ – **As [the official] caught up to him,** נְטָלָן מֵרֹאשׁוֹ וַאֲחָזָן בְּיָדוֹ – **[Elisha] took [the tefillin] from his head and grasped them inside his hand.** אָמַר לֵיהּ מַה בְּיָדְךָ – **[The official] said to him: What is in your hand?** אָמַר לוֹ כַּנְפֵי יוֹנָה – **[Elisha] answered him: Dove's wings.** פָּשַׁט אֶת יָדוֹ וְנִמְצְאוּ בָּהּ כַּנְפֵי יוֹנָה – Whereupon **[Elisha] opened his hand and in it dove's wings were found.** לְפִיכָךְ הָיוּ קוֹרְאִין אוֹתוֹ בַּעַל כְּנָפַיִם – **Therefore,** on account of this miracle, **they would call him** "Elisha **the Winged One.**"[44]

The Gemara inquires about a particular detail of the incident:

מַאי שְׁנָא כַּנְפֵי יוֹנָה דְּאָמַר לֵיהּ – **What is unique about dove's wings that** caused **[Elisha]** to **answer [the official]** as he did, וְלֹא אָמַר לֵיהּ שְׁאָר עוֹפוֹת – **and not answer him** that he was holding wings from any of the **other birds?**[45]

The Gemara answers:

מִשּׁוּם דְּדָמְיָא כְּנֶסֶת יִשְׂרָאֵל לְיוֹנָה – Elisha mentioned dove's wings specifically **because the Congregation of Israel resembles a dove,** שֶׁנֶּאֱמַר ,,כַּנְפֵי יוֹנָה נֶחְפָּה בַכֶּסֶף וְאֶבְרוֹתֶיהָ בִּירַקְרַק חָרוּץ" – **for it is said** of Israel:[46] [You will be like] ***the wings of a dove covered with silver and her pinions with brilliant gold.*** מַה יוֹנָה זוּ כְּנָפֶיהָ מְגִינּוֹת עָלֶיהָ – This analogy teaches that **just as** in the case of **this dove its wings protect it,**[47] אַף יִשְׂרָאֵל מִצְוֹת מְגִינּוֹת עֲלֵיהֶן – **so** in the case of **Israel** – the **commandments** that they observe **protect them.** Since the commandments, of which donning tefillin is one, are compared to the wings of a dove, and since Elisha was in need of the commandments' protection, it is fitting that he refer to his tefillin specifically as *dove's* wings.

The Gemara records an incident that relates to the first part of R' Eliezer's ruling:

אָמַר רַבִּי אַבָּא בַּר רַב אַדָּא אָמַר רַבִּי יִצְחָק – **R' Abba bar Rav Adda said in the name of R' Yitzchak:** פַּעַם אַחַת שָׁכְחוּ וְלֹא הֵבִיאוּ אִיזְמֵל מֵעֶרֶב שַׁבָּת – **Once they forgot and did not bring a knife** to the place of circumcision **on the Sabbath eve,** וֶהֱבִיאוּהוּ בְּשַׁבָּת [דֶּרֶךְ גַּגּוֹת וְדֶרֶךְ חֲצֵירוֹת][48] – **and** then **they brought it on the Sabbath by way of** adjoining **roofs and courtyards** –[49]

NOTES

36. [E.g. the wicked emperors Antiochus and Caligula demanded idol worship of their Jewish subjects.]

37. See Mishnah and Gemara above.

38. The Gemara below will discuss an edict banning tefillin.

39. The Gemara will presently explain how Elisha earned this sobriquet.

40. When one feels the urge to pass wind, he must be able to contain himself (*Rashi* above, 49a ד״ה שלא יפיח) until he first removes his tefillin (*Tosafos* there ד״ה אביי).

41. He must be able to restrain himself from falling asleep while wearing tefillin, lest while asleep he pass wind or experience a seminal emission (*Rashi* ibid. ד״ה שלא יישן בהם; cf. *Tosafos* there ד״ה שלא, and see note 8 there).

42. See *Chidushei HaRan, Rashba* and *Maharam,* who infer from the story that follows that only Elisha was totally dedicated to the mitzvah (*Rashi,* as explained by *Maharam*). However, *Tosafos* understand that the Gemara's proof comes from Elisha himself, below, for even he (in the incident that the Gemara will relate) failed to give up his life for the sake of the mitzvah of tefillin (see *Maharam* and *Maharam Schiff*). See end of note 44 below.

43. The Romans prohibited the wearing of head tefillin specifically because these tefillin sit exposed for all to see (while the arm tefillin are covered), and of them Scripture states (*Deuteronomy* 28:10): *And all the peoples of the earth will see that the Name of God is proclaimed over you, and they will fear you* [see *Menachos* 35b] (*Maharsha, Ben Yehoyada*).

44. Although Elisha did not sprout wings, he was termed "the Winged One" because he maintained a clean body like that of an angel (*Maharsha*).

Nothing in the story the Gemara has related indicates that Elisha maintained a clean body while wearing tefillin. However, since a miracle was performed for him on account of his tefillin, it is to be assumed that he was scrupulous in keeping all the laws of that mitzvah, one of which is the requirement to maintain a clean body (*Tosafos* above, 49a ד״ה כאלישע).

See *Ritva* (*MHK* ed.), who discusses why all the Jews did not give up their lives for the mitzvah of tefillin, and if they were obligated to do so. See also above, 49a note 13.

45. Certainly, Elisha needed to say something to save himself; however, it would have sufficed had he answered simply "wings," without specifying dove's wings (*Maharsha*).

46. *Psalms* 68:14.

47. Unlike other birds, the dove uses its wings (rather than its beak) to fend off attackers (*Rashi* here and above, 49a; see note 12 there).

48. Some versions of the Gemara do not contain the words in brackets (see *Rashash*).

49. In this incident an *eruv chatzeiros* was not prepared before the onset of the Sabbath, and so carrying an object even through adjoining courtyards or roofs is Rabbinically forbidden (*Rashi,* top of next *amud*).

The following points will serve as an introduction to this passage:

(a) Transferring from one private domain (*reshus hayachid*) to another is *Biblically* permitted.

(b) However, the Rabbis prohibited this if the two domains are owned by different people. Nevertheless, to allow transferring in such a case, the Rabbis instituted *eruvei chatzeiros* (see *Eruvin* chs. 1-3,6).

(c) In ancient times the houses surrounded and opened into a common courtyard, and the Rabbis also prohibited carrying from the separately-owned houses to the courtyard without an *eruv chatzeiros.*

(d) These prohibitions apply when transferring vessels out of a house. Whether the Rabbis prohibited transferring between other types of private domains (e.g. from courtyard to roof, roof to roof, courtyard to courtyard), is a three-way dispute in *Eruvin* 89a, and it appears in the Gemara below.

רבי אליעזר אומר אם לא הביא כלי מע"ש מביאו בשבת מגולה ובסכנה מכסהו ע"פ עדים ועוד אמר ר"א כורתים עצים לעשות פחמין לעשות (כלי) ברזל כלל אמר ר"ע כל מלאכה שאפשר לעשותה מע"ש אינה דוחה את השבת (ומילה) שאי אפשר לעשותה מע"ש דוחה את השבת:

גמ' איבעיא להו טעמא דר"א משום חבובי מצוה או דילמא משום חשדא למאי נפקא מינה לאתויי מכוסה ע"פ עדים אי אמרת משום חבובי מצוה מגולה אין מכוסה לא אלא אי אמרת משום חשדא אפי' מכוסה שפיר דמי מאי איתמר א"ר לוי לא אמרה ר"א אלא לחבובי מצוה תניא נמי הכי מביאו מגולה ואין מביאו מכוסה דברי ר"א אמר רב אשי מתני' נמי דיקא דקתני ובשעת הסכנה מכסהו ע"פ עדים בסכנה אין שלא בסכנה לא שמע מינה משום חבובי מצוה שמע מינה תניא אידך מביאו מגולה ואין מביאו מכוסה דברי ר"א ר' יהודה אומר משום ר"א נוהגין היו בשעת הסכנה שהיו מביאין מכוסה ע"פ עדים איבעיא להו עדים דקאמר איהו וחד או דילמא הוא ותרי ת"ש ובסכנה מכסהו ע"פ עדים אי אמרת ° בשלמא הוא ותרי שפיר אלא אי אמרת הוא וחד מאי עדים שראוים להעיד במקום אחר: ועוד אמר ר"א: ת"ר במקומו של ר"א היו כורתין עצים לעשות פחמין לעשות ברזל בשבת במקומו של ר' יוסי הגלילי היו אוכלין בשר עוף בחלב לוי איקלע לבי יוסף רישבא קריבו ליה רישא דטוותא בחלבא לא אכל כי אתא לקמיה דרבי א"ל אמאי לא תשמתינהו א"ל אתריה דר' יהודה בן בתירה הוה ואמינא דילמא דרש להו כר' יוסי הגלילי דתנן ר' יוסי הגלילי אומר נאמר לא תאכלו כל נבלה ונאמר לא תבשל גדי בחלב אמו את שאסור משום נבלה אסור לבשל בחלב עוף שאסור משום נבלה יכול יהא אסור לבשל בחלב ת"ל בחלב אמו יצא עוף שאין לו חלב אם א"ר יצחק עיר אחת היתה בא"י שהיו עושין כר"א והיו מתים בזמנן ולא עוד אלא שפעם אחת גזרה מלכות הרשעה גזרה על ישראל על המילה ועל אותה העיר לא גזרה: תניא רשב"ג אומר כל מצוה שקיבלו עליהם בשמחה כגון מילה דכתיב שש אנכי על אמרתך כמוצא שלל רב עדיין עושין אותה בשמחה וכל מצוה שקבלו עליהם בקטטה כגון עריות דכתיב וישמע משה את העם בוכה למשפחותיו על עסקי משפחותיו עדיין עושין אותה בקטטה דליכא כתובה דלא רמו בה תיגרא תניא ר"ש בן אלעזר אומר כל מצוה שמסרו ישראל עצמן עליהם למיתה בשעת גזרת המלכות כגון עבודת כוכבים ומילה עדיין היא מוחזקת בידם וכל מצוה שלא מסרו ישראל עצמן עליה למיתה בשעת גזרת המלכות כגון תפילין עדיין היא מרופה בידם דא"ר ינאי תפילין צריכין גוף נקי כאלישע בעל כנפים מאי היא אמר אביי שלא יפיח בהם רבא אמר שלא יישן בהם ואמאי קרו ליה אלישע בעל כנפים שפעם אחת גזרה מלכות הרשעה גזרה על ישראל שכל המניח תפילין על ראשו יקרו את מוחו והיה אלישע מניח תפילין ויצא לשוק וראהו קסדור אחד רץ מלפניו ורץ אחריו כיון שהגיע אצלו נטלן מראשו ואחזן בידו א"ל מה בידך אמר לו כנפי יונה פשט את ידו ונמצאו בה כנפי יונה לפיכך היו קוראין אותו בעל כנפים מאי שנא כנפי יונה דא"ל ולא א"ל שאר עופות משום דדמיא כנסת ישראל ליונה שנאמר כנפי יונה נחפה בכסף ואברותיה בירקרק חרוץ מה יונה זו כנפיה מגינות עליה אף ישראל מצות מגינות עליהן: א"ר אבא בר רב אדא א"ר יצחק פעם אחת שכחו ולא הביאו איזמל מערב שבת והביאוהו בשבת [דרך גגות ודרך חצירות] שלא

רש"י

רבי אליעזר אומר אם לא הביא כלי. איזמל למול את התינוק וקאי אמתניתין דפרקין דלעיל דסליק מיניה וכל צרכי מילה עושין בשבת: מגולה. בפני הכל ובגמרא מפרש אמאי מצריך ליה לגלוייה: ובסכנה. שגזרו ארמאים על המילה: מכסהו ע"פ עדים. שיעידו שאיזמל של מצוה הוא מביא ולא יחשדוהו: כלל אמר ר"ע. נחלק על ר"א במכשירי מצוה שאין דוחין הואיל ואפשר לעשותן מע"ש: [ושאי אפשר לעשות מע"ש. כגון] מילה עצמה שא"א לה ליעשות דזמנה ביום השמיני דוחה שבת: גמ' טעמא דר"א. דאמר מגולה אין מכוסה לא: משום חיבוב מצוה. להודיע שמחבבה מצוה עליו שמחלל שבת עליה: משום חשדא. שלא יחשדוהו שהוא נושא שאר חפציו וסיפא דמתני' דקתני ובסכנה מכסהו ע"פ עדים ודאי משום חשדא הוא אלא רישא מיבעיא לן דוקא מגולה קאמר אבל מכוסה ע"פ עדים שלא בשעת הסכנה לא ומשום חיבוב מצוה או לאו דוקא מגולה דטעמיה משום חשדא וה"ה למכוסה על פי עדים: אי אמרת בשלמא הוא ותרי שפיר. היינו דמיקרו עדים אלא הוא וחד מי מיקרי עדים איהו לגביה נפשיה מי מיקרי עד: ומשני שראוים להעיד במקום אחר. לעולם הכא עדות לא שייכא דלאפוקי מחשדא בעלמא הוא ואין כאן לא דיני ממונות ולא דיני נפשות שיהו שנים (א) ומאי קרו להו עדים דאיכא גילוי מילתא ע"י השני ושנים קרו עדים בעדות אחריתי שאינו נוגע בה: לעשות ברזל. לאיזמל של מילה: היו אוכלין בשר עוף בחלב. כדלקמן: רישבא. לייד עופות: נאמר לא תאכלו כל נבלה ונאמר. באותו פסוק עצמו לא תבשל גדי משמע כל האסור משום נבלה נוהג בו איסור בשר בחלב: שש אנכי על אמרתך. אמירה יחידה שקדמה לשאר אמירות והיא מילה שישראל עושין וששים עליה דכל שאר מצות אינן מוכיחות כל שעה כגון תפילין ומזוזה וציצית דאינן כשהוא בשדה וערום בבית המרחץ אבל זו מעיד עליהם לעולם כדאמרינן במנחות (דף מג:) בדוד שראה עצמו בבית המרחץ ונצטער אמר אוי לי שאני ערום מכל מצות כיון שנסתכל במילה נתיישבה דעתו: בשמחה. שעושין משתה: על עסקי משפחותיו. שנאסר להם קרובות: מרופה. רפויה: דא"ר ינאי תפילין צריכות גוף נקי. שלא יפיח אלמא לא זהירי בהו ושמעינן מינה דלא מסרו עליה אלא אלישע לבדו: יקרו. פוריי"ר בלעז לשון יקרוה עורבי נחל (משלי ל) ולשון תנקר לא נעלה (במדבר טז): את מוחו. שכנגד תפילין: קסדור. ממונה: מגינות עליהן. אינה נלחמת בחרטומיה אלא בכנפיה:
דרך

תוספות

רבי אליעזר אומר אם לא הביא כלי כו' מביאו בשבת מגולה. ° וא"ת ויביאו התינוק אצל כלי דהשתא ליכא איסור שבת כלל דהחי נושא את עצמו וי"ל דקטן צריך לאמו הוא ואחר המילה היה צריך להחזירו לאמו ואז הוי כפות (ב) לפי שהוא חולה כדאמרינן ביומא (דף סו:) אפי' תימא ר' נתן חולה שאני וגם אמו שהיא מסוכנת לא תוכל לבא אצל התינוק ועוד י"ל כיון דיותר בקל יביא הכלי משיביא התינוק שרי ר"א כדי למהר המצוה כדמוכח בגמרא דאמר פעם אחת שכחו ולא הביאו איזמל מע"ש והביאו בשבת שלא ברצונו שהביאו דרך חצרות וגגות וקרפיפות והיו יכולין להביא דרך רה"ר אלמא דשרי ר"א דרך רה"ר דהוי דאורייתא (ג) ° כדי למהר המצוה אע"פ שיכול לעשות [בענין] דליכא אלא איסורא דרבנן:

שש אנכי. במדרש (שוחר טוב) למנצח על השמינית כתיב הנדרש על המילה שהיא בשמיני וכן אמרי' (ד) (פר"א פ' כ"ט) ויעש אברהם משתה גדול ביום הגמל את יצחק ביום ה"ג מל את יצחק דהיינו ביום השמיני דמילה כמנין ה"ג. ר"ת: אמר ליה כנפי יונה. הרי שלא מסר עצמו לומר תפילין הן. רבינו שמואל:
שלא

עין משפט נר מצוה

א א מיי' פ"ב מהלכות מילה הלכה ו סמג עשין כח טוש"ע א"ח סי' שלא סעיף ו וטוש"ע י"ד סימן רסו סעיף ב:
ב ב טוש"ע י"ד סימן רסה סעיף יב:
ג ג מיי' פכ"ב מהלכות איסורי ביאה הל' יח סמג לאוין קכד:

גליון הש"ס

גמרא בשלמא הוא ותרי. עיין תשובת הרא"ש כלל סי' פ"ט: תוס' ד"ה רבי אליעזר וכו' וא"ת ויביאו התינוק. עיין לעיל דף לד ע"א תוספות ד"ה אבל אדם: בא"ד כדי למהר המצוה. עיין ערובין דף קג ע"ב תוספות ד"ה מה לי:

רבינו חננאל

פרק יט

רבי אליעזר אומר אם לא הביא כלי מערב שבת מביאו בשבת מגולה וכו' ואיבעיא לן האי דקתני ר' אליעזר אומר מביאו מגולה משום חבובי מצוה הוא או משום שלא יחשדוהו שהוציא חפציו טמונים לפיכך מגליהו שיראו שסכין של מצוה הוא. ופשטנא דמשום חבובי מצוה הוא היכא דליכא סכנה ותוב איבעיא לן האי דתנא במתניתא רבי יהודה משום רבי אליעזר [אומר] נוהגים היינו בסכנה מביאין אותו (בסכנה) מכוסה ע"פ עדים הני עדים שנים אחרים זולתו המביאו או דלמא הוא ואחרים ולא איפשטא בהדיא: לוי איקלע לבי יוסף רישבא קריבו ליה רישא דטווסא בחלבא לא אכל כי אתא לקמיה דר' א"ל מ"ט לא שמתינהו א"ל אתרא דר' יהודה בן בתירא ואמרי דלמא דריש להו כרבי יוסי הגלילי דסבר יצא עוף שאין לו חלב אם: א"ר יצחק עיר אחת היתה בא"י שהיו עושין כר' אליעזר והיו מתיה מתין בזמנן ולא עוד אלא שפעם אחת גזרה מלכות הרשעה גזרה על ישראל על המילה ועל אותה העיר לא גזרה א) כל השבח ואין הלכה כר"א ולא כר' יוסי הגלילי שמתיר בשר עוף בחלב ולא כרבי ינאי שאמר תפילין צריכין גוף נקי כאלישע בעל כנפים ומפרשי רבנן כי לא אמר רבי ינאי אלא בשעת הגזרה וסמיך דהוא עריק ועבדי ליה נס אמר ראבין בר רב אדא א"ר יצחק פעם אחת שכחו ולא הביאו איזמל מע"ש והביאוהו

חשק שלמה על רבינו חננאל

א) נראה דצ"ל לאחר כל השבח הזה מ"מ אין הלכה כר"א וכו':

מסורת הש"ס

א) [מכאן לקמן קלו. ועירובין קג: קג.], ב) פ"א ל"ג, ג) פסחים סו. סט: יבמות יד. מנחות עב. נג., ד) פ"א ל"ג, ה) יבמות יד. חולין קטז. ע"ש, ו) [נ"ל דטווסא עיין בערוך פירושו], ז) חולין קיג., ח) יומא עה., ט) לעיל מט., י) [ברכות נג: לעיל מט. וש"נ], כ) [דף קמז:], ל) פ"א, מ) [נ"ל שנזכר], נ) [נ"ל עליה].

הגהות הב"ח

(א) רש"י ד"ה ומשני וכו' ומאי קרי להו: (ב) תוס' ד"ה ר' אליעזר וכו' ואז הוי כפות. נ"ב עיין בפרק המלניע דף לג ע"א: (ג) בא"ד כדי למהר המצוה. נ"ב עיין בסוף עירובין דף קג ע"ב בתוספות ד"ה מה לי: (ד) ד"ה שש וכו' וכן אמרי' במדרש ויעש אברהם:

תורה אור השלם

א) לֹא תֹאכְלוּ כָל נְבֵלָה לַגֵּר אֲשֶׁר בִּשְׁעָרֶיךָ תִּתְּנֶנָּה וַאֲכָלָהּ אוֹ מָכֹר לְנָכְרִי כִּי עַם קָדוֹשׁ אַתָּה לַיָי אֱלֹהֶיךָ לֹא תְבַשֵּׁל גְּדִי בַּחֲלֵב אִמּוֹ: [דברים יד, כא]

ב) שָׂשׂ אָנֹכִי עַל אִמְרָתֶךָ כְּמוֹצֵא שָׁלָל רָב: [תהלים קיט, קסב]

ג) וַיִּשְׁמַע מֹשֶׁה אֶת הָעָם בֹּכֶה לְמִשְׁפְּחֹתָיו אִישׁ לְפֶתַח אָהֳלוֹ וַיִּחַר אַף יְיָ מְאֹד וּבְעֵינֵי מֹשֶׁה רָע: [במדבר יא, י]

ד) אִם תִּשְׁכְּבוּן בֵּין שְׁפַתָּיִם כַּנְפֵי יוֹנָה נֶחְפָּה בַכֶּסֶף וְאֶבְרוֹתֶיהָ בִּירַקְרַק חָרוּץ: [תהלים סח, יד]

ליקוטי רש"י

כורתים עצים בשבת לעשות פחמין. לבו ביום כדי לעשות ברזל איזמל של מילה דקסבר ר"א מכשירי מצוה דוחין שבת כמצוה עצמה [יבמות יד.]. רבי אליעזר אית ליה מכשירי מצוה דוחין את השבת כמצוה שדוחה את השבת ואם אין לו איזמל למולו בשבת כורתין עצים לעשות פחמין ועושין איזמל [חולין קטז.]. לעשות כלי ברזל. לעשות איזמל למול בו [עירובין קג:]. היו אוכלין בשר עוף בחלב. דכרבי יוסי הגלילי אפילו איסורא דרבנן ליכא ליה בעוף. רישבא. לייד עופות רישבא לשון אין פורסין רישבן ליונים [חולין שם וע"ש בהגרי"ב]. פורס נשבין לצוד מיני ועוף [לעיל יז:]. דטוותא. פוא"ן [חולין שם]. ת"ל בחלב אמו. מי שיש לו חלב אמו יצא בשר עוף שאין לו חלב אם [יבמות שם]. שש אנכי על אמרתך. ורבותינו דרשוהו על המילה שהיה דוד בבית המרחץ וראה עצמו בלא ציצית ובלא תפילין ובלא תורה אמר אוי לי שאני ערום מכל מצות כיון שנסתכל במילה שמח ואמר בלבו (מבית המרחץ) שש אנכי על אמרתך המילה שמתחלה נתנה במאמר ולא בדבור שנאמ' (בראשית יז) ויאמר אלהים אל אברהם ואתה את בריתי תשמור [תהלים קיט, קסב]. זו מילה שנתנה במאמר ולא בדיבור ויאמר ה' אל אברהם ואתה את בריתי תשמור (בראשית יז) ומצינו שדוד שמח עליה שנאמר למנצח על השמינית (תהלים ו) כשהיה בבית המרחץ וראה עצמו בלא תורה ובלא מצות כיון (שנסתכל) [שנזכר] במילה שמח [מגילה טז:]. על עסקי משפחותיו. על עריות הנאסרות להם [במדבר יא, י]. שלא יפיח. שיכול להעמיד עצמו בשעת הרוח. שלא יישן בהם. שמא יפיח או יראה קרי אבל אם יכול להזהר שלא יישן כהן כל הגופים נקיים בהפסה שיכולין להעמיד עצמן. יקרו את מוחו. ינקרו את מוחו שהוא תחת התפילין, ינקרו לשון ניקור עיים. קסדור. מנישטרא"ל שהיה ממונה על כך [לעיל מט.]. שם פקידות הוא כגון קרדיוט והוא שוטר [יומא יא.]. כנפי יונה. כדמפרש לקמיה מפני שהם מצות והם מגינין לישראל והוא להם ככנפים ליונה שהיא נמשלת ליונה והמצות ככנפים [לעיל שם]. כנפי יונה. פלומ"א בלע"ז. נחפה בכסף. בכספה ומחמדה של תורה ומצות. ואברותיה. כנפיה שעופפת בהן. בירקרק חרוץ. פתר דונש בן לברט החרוץ הוא זהב ולכך נתנו המשורר אצל הכסף וירקרק הוא הזהב אשר יוצא מארץ החוילה ומארץ כוש זהב טוב מאד מאד לא הוא ירוק ולא הוא אדום ולכך קראו ירקרק כמו (ויקרא יג) לבן אדמדם שאינו לא לבן ולא אדום לכך נכפל ירקרק אדמדם [תהלים סח, יד]. כנפיה מגינות עליה. מן הגנה ומכל עוף ואדם הבא עליה היא נלחמת ומכה בראש גפיה מה שאין כן בשאר עופות [לעיל שם]. או נורמת או נלחמת בראשי אגפיה [ברכות נג:].

שלא ברצון ר"א דשרי אפי' ברה"ר. קשה לר"י הא אמרינן לקמן בפירקין (דף קלג.) כל מקום שאתה מוצא עשה ולא תעשה אם אתה יכול לקיים את שניהם מוטב כו' והכא כיון דאפשר לקיים את שניהם להביאו דרך גגות וחצירות וקרפיפות אמאי יביאו אותו דרך רה"ר וליכא למימר דלגבי מילה דגלי רחמנא בה דדחי שבת כדדרשינן לקמן לא אמרינן הכי דהא לקמן (ד) גבי בשר אפי' במקום בהרת יקוץ כו' אמרינן כדר"ל דאמר ר"ל כל מקום שאתה מוצא כו': ומי שרי והתניא. וא"ת ולוקמי שהביאו דרך חצר מעורבת דהוי כרצון חכמים ושלא כרצון ר"א דשרי אפי' דרך רה"ר וי"ל דהכא"ג לא הוה (ה) שרי ר"א מן רה"ר כיון שיכול להביאו דרך חצר מעורבת בהיתר גמור א"נ לישנא דשכחו לא משמע כן דאי היתה מעורבת לא ה"ל למימר שכחו אלא לא חשו להביאו מע"ש כיון דבשבת אפשר להביאו בהיתר גמור אבל כי מסיק ברצון ר"ש אתי שפיר דקאמר שכחו שאם היו זוכרין מע"ש היו מביאין משום דפליגי רבנן עליה:

ברצון ר"ש. ה"ה דהוה מצי למימר ברצון ר"מ שהביאו דרך גגות מגג לגג או דרך חצרות מחצר לחצר דמוכח בפרק כל גגות (עירובין דף פט.) דלית ליה כל גגות העיר רשות אחת הן וכן חצרות וקרפיפות אלא נקט ר' שמעון דקי"ל כוותיה: לכלים ששבתו לתוכו. וכן היה אותו אזמל:

דרבי אליעזר שמותי הוא. מב"ש וכן מוכח בירושלמי במסכת תרומות בפרק סאה תרומה דתנן התם סאה תרומה טמאה שנפלה למאה סאין טהורין בית שמאי אוסרים וב"ה מתירין כו' עד לאחר שהודו ר"א אומר תירום ותישרף ואמר בגמרא (ו) בן פזי ורבי אייבו בר נגרי הוו יתבין ואמרי תנינן אחר שהודו ר"א אומר תירום ותישרף מי הודה למי א"ר אסי מתניתין אמרה כן לאחר שהודו ר"א אומר תירום ותישרף ר"א לאו שמותי הוא הרי משמע דשמותי הוא מתלמידי ב"ש דמינה קא פשיט דב"ש הודו לב"ה. ר"ת:

ניתקו חצרות ונעשו בתים. פירוש וחשיב כאילו אין כאן חצר כלל שהחצר נעשה בית וכשלא עירבו חשיבי בתים כליתנהו ומיהו חצר לא חשיב כליתא אע"פ שאסור לטלטל מתוכו למבוי כיון שאין (ז) דרך מפסיק בינו למבוי לא חשוב [כסתום] אבל בתים כסתומות חשיבי כיון שהחצר מפסיק בינם למבוי ודוקא היכא דלא נשתתפו בעינן בתים וחצרות פתוחין לתוכו אבל נשתתפו לא בעינן ומשני אפשר דמבטלי רשות גבי חד דהשתא איכא בית דלא חשיב כסתום ולא אמר נמי ניתקו חצרות כולם כיון דשאר הבתים אסורין בחצר ופריך בית איכא בתים ליכא ולא מצי למימר דבטלי רשות גבי תרי שהם היו אוסרין זה על זה ולא מצי למימר שהשנים עירבו דהא מדקאמר רב לא עירבו משמע לא עירבו כלל:

שלא ברצון ר"א מתקיף לה רב יוסף שלא ברצון ר"א אדרבה ר"א הוא דשרי וכי תימא שלא ברצון ר"א דשרי אפילו ברה"ר אלא ברצון רבנן דאסרו דרך רה"ר ושרו דרך גגות דרך חצירות וקרפיפות ומי שרי והתניא [ט] כשם שאין מביאין אותו דרך רה"ר כך אין מביאין אותו לא דרך גגות ולא דרך קרפיפות ולא דרך חצירות אלא אמר רב אשי שלא ברצון ר"א ומחלוקתו אלא ברצון ר"ש [י] דתנן ר"ש אומר אחד [כ] גגות (א) ואחד קרפיפות ואחד חצירות כולן רשות אחד הן לכלים ששבתו בתוכן ולא לכלים ששבתו בתוך הבית בעא מיניה רבי זירא מר' אסי מבוי שלא נשתתפו בו מהו לטלטל בכולו מי אמרינן כחצר דמי מה חצר אע"ג דלא ערבו מותר לטלטל בכולו האי נמי אע"ג דלא נשתתפו בו מותר לטלטל בכולו או דילמא לא דמי לחצר דחצר אית ליה ד' מחיצות האי לית ליה ד' מחיצות א"נ חצר אית ליה דיורין האי לית ביה דיורין שתיק ולא א"ל ולא מידי זימנין אשכחיה דיתיב וקא אמר אמר ר"ש בן לקיש משום ר' יהודה הנשיא פעם אחת שכחו ולא הביאו איזמל מע"ש והביאוהו בשבת והיה הדבר קשה לחכמים היאך מניחין דברי חכמים ועושין כר"א חדא דר"א שמותי [ל] הוא ועוד יחיד ורבים [מ] הלכה כרבים וא"ר אושעיא שאילית את רבי יהודה הגוזר ואמר לי מבוי שלא נשתתפו בו הוה ואייתוהו מהאי רישא להאי רישא א"ל ס"ל למר מבוי שלא נשתתפו (ב) מותר לטלטל בכולו וא"ל אין א"ל והא זימנין בעאי מינך ולא אמרת לי (ג) הכי [נ] דילמא אגב שיטפך רהיט לך גמרך א"ל אין אגב שיטפא רהיטנא לי גמרי [ס] איתמר אמר רבי זירא אמר רב מבוי שלא נשתתפו בו אין מטלטלין בו אלא בד' אמות אמר אביי הא מילתא אמרה רבי זירא ולא פירשה עד דאתא רבה בר אבוה ופירשה דאמר רב נחמן אמר רבה בר אבוה אמר רב [ג] מבוי שלא נשתתפו בו עירבו חצירות עם בתים אין מטלטלין בו אלא בד' אמות לא עירבו חצירות עם בתים מותר לטלטל בכולו אמר ליה רב חנינא חוזאה לרבה מאי שנא כי עירבו חצירות עם בתים דניתקו חצירות ונעשו בתים ורב לטעמיה [י] דאמר רב [ד] אין המבוי ניתר בלחי וקורה עד שיהו בתים

דרך גגות ודרך חצירות. שלא עירבו זו עם זו ואיכא איסורא דרבנן: שלא ברצון ר"א ומחלוקתו. קאמר דר"א אפילו ברה"ר שרי ואינהו דאיימו לדרך אחרות גלי דעתייהו דאין מכשירי מילה דוחין שבת ושלא ברצון החולקין עליו דאסרי דרך אחרות דהעמידו חכמים דבריהם לאיסור [ט] שבת אף במקום כרת: אלא ברצון ר"ש. שמתיר אף לדבר הרשות: דתנן ר"ש אומר אחד גגות כו' כולן. ואפילו הן של בעלים הרבה מטלטלין מזה לזה דלא אסרו מרשות לרשות אלא בתים: קרפיפות. אם של בית סאתים הוא מטלטל בכולו ואם יותר ולא הוקף לדירה קרי ליה רשות אחת לגבי חבירו או לגבי חצר לטלטל ד' אמות מזה וד' אמות מזה להוציא ולהכניס מזה לזה: ששבתו בתוכן. שבשקדש היום היו בתוכו ולא בתוך הבית דאילו שבתו כלים בבית לא מיבעיא היכא דלא עירבו בני החצר דאפילו מבית לחצר לא יוציאו כלי הבית אלא אפילו עירבו ומטלטל מבית לחצר לא יוציאו כלי הבית מחצר זו לחברתה שלא עירבו עמה: שלא נשתתפו בו. עירוב לחצירות למבוי קרי שיתוף: מהו לטלטל. בתוכו בכולו כלים ששבתו בתוכו ולהוציא מן החצר לתוכו פשיטא לן דאסור וכן ממנו לחצר: מה חצר אע"ג דלא עירבו. הרבה בתים שבחצר ביחד ואסור להכניס ולהוציא מבתים לחצר ומחצר לבתים: מותר לטלטל בכולו. מה שנמצא בתוכו או בגדיו שהוציאן מן הבית לתוכו דרך מלבוש [פ] פושטן ומטלטלן בכולו לדברי הכל דג' מחלוקות הן בעירובין בפרק כל גגות לדברי ר' מאיר גגין רשות לעצמן ומטלטלין מזה לזה ואפילו של בעלים הרבה וחצרות רשות לעצמן לטלטל מזו לזו בלא עירוב כלים ששבתו בתוכם אבל לא מגגין לחצרות וקרפיפות רשות לעצמן ולדברי חכמים גגין וחצרות רשות אחת וקרפיפות רשות אחת ולדברי ר"ש כולן רשות אחת חוץ מן הבתים: א"נ חצר אית ביה דיורין. כלומר עשויה להשתמש בה תדיר: האי אין בו דיורין. שהדיורין בבתים הן והבתים פתוחין לחצירות וחצירות למבוי: זימנין. פעם אחרת: אשכחיה. רבי זירא לר' אסי: שמותי הוא. ברכוהו כדאמרינן בהזהב (ב"מ דף נט:) ובתלמוד ירושלמי [צ] מפ' שמותי הוא מתלמידי שמאי היה: וא"ר אושעיא. לאותן שהיה קשה עליהן מה ששמעו: שאילית את רבי יהודה הגוזר. המל את התינוקות: ואייתוהו מהאי רישא. שהיה התינוק בבית שבראש המבוי ואיזמל בבית שבראש האחר שכנגדו עד כאן דברי ר' אסי: א"ל. רבי זירא אלמא ס"ל למר מדאמר ליה להא ולא קשיא לך ביה מידי סבירא לך מותר לטלטל בכולו: הכי גרסינן והא זמנין בעאי מינך ולא אמרת דילמא אגב שיטפא אתיא לך. כשהיית שטוף בגרסתך לחזור על שמועה זו דר"ל עם מרוצת גרסתך אתיא לך הך דר' אושעיא בהדא דאיתמר עלה: ולא פירשה. אימתי מותר ואימתי אסור: עירבו חצרות. שבמבוי עם בתיהם שבני הבתים מוציאין לחצרותיהן שעירבו בתים הפתוחים לחצר יחד וכן בני חצר האחרת אבל בני החצרות לא נשתתפו במבוי: אין מטלטלין. במבוי אפי' כלים ששבתו בתוכו אלא בד': לא עירבו חצרות עם בתיהן. שאסורים בני הבתים להוציא מבתיהן לחצריהם: מותר לטלטל בכולו. כלים ששבתו בתוכו ולקמיה מפרש טעמא: ונעשו בתים. בטלו לגבי הבתים ואין שם חצרות עליהם: בתים

עין משפט נר מצוה

ד א מיי' פ"ב מהלכות מילה הלכה ו סמג עשין כח טוש"ע א"ח סימן שלא סעיף ו וטוש"ע י"ד סימן רסו סעיף ג:

ה ב מיי' פ"ג מהלכות עירובין הלכה יח סמג עשין דרבנן א טוש"ע א"ח סימן שעב סעיף א:

ו ג מיי' פ"ה מהלכות עירובין הלכה טו סמג שם טוש"ע א"ח סימן שפח:

ז ד מיי' פי"ז מהלכות שבת הלכה יז סמג שם טוש"ע א"ח סימן שסג סעיף כו:

גליון הש"ס

רש"י ד"ה מותר לטלטל בכולו וכו' פושטן ומטלטלן. תמוי לי הא מ"מ כיון דשבתו בבית אסור לטלטלן וכדאיתא להדיא עירובין דף צא בכמתא וקודלא ועש"נ: תוספות ד"ה דר"א שמותי וכו' וכן מוכח בירושלמי. עיין בילה דף לב ע"ב תוספות ד"ה ואומר:

רבינו חננאל

בשבת שלא כרצון רבי אליעזר ושקלינן וטרינן בה ואוקמא רב אשי שלא כרצון ר' אליעזר דשרי אפילו דרך רה"ר ושלא ברצון מחלוקתו והן החכמים שחולקים על ר' אליעזר ואומרים אפילו דרך גגות ודרך חצירות וכו' דרבי עקיבא סבירא ליה כוותיהון אלא כרצון ר' שמעון דשרי דרך גגות דתנן ר' שמעון אומר אחד גגות ואחד חצירות ואחת קרפיפות כו'. בעא ר' זירא מר' אמי מבוי שלא נשתתפו בו מהו לטלטל בכולו כו' ושתק ולא השיב לו זמנין אשכחיה דאמר אמר ר"ל משום רבי יהודה נשיאה פעם אחת שכחו ולא הביאו אזמל מע"ש והביאוהו בשבת והיה הדבר קשה לחכמים היאך מניחין דברי חכמים ועושין כר' אליעזר שהן דברי יחיד ועוד דר' אליעזר שמותי הוא כלומר מתלמידי שמאי הוא. א"ר אושעיא שאלית את ר' יהודה הגוזר פי' המל ואמר לי מבוי שלא נשתתפו בו הוה ואתיוה מהאי רישא להאי רישא אמינא ליה סבירא ליה למר מבוי שלא נשתתפו בו מותר לטלטל בכולו א"ל אין כו'. אתמר ר' זירא אמר רב מבוי שלא נשתתפו בו אין מטלטלין בו אלא בארבע. ר' זירא לא פירש שמועה זו היטב עד דאתא רב נחמן אמר רבה בר אבוה ופרשה משמיה דרב הכי מבוי שלא נשתתפו בו אם עירבו חצרות עם בתיהם אין מטלטלין בו אלא בארבע לא עירבו חצרות עם בתיהם מותר לטלטל בכולו א"ל רב חנינא חוזאה לרבא מפני מה כי עירבו עם בתיהם אין מטלטלין באותו מבוי אלא בארבע דניתקו חצרות ונעשו בתים כלומר כיון שעירבו נעשו בתי החצר והחצר רשות אחת ורב לטעמיה דאמר אין מבוי ניתר בלחי וקורה עד שיהו

מסורת הש"ס

א) פסחים לב., ב) עירובין כב: לה. עד. פט. לא., ג) [נדה ז:], ד) [לעיל ס:] ברכות ט. וש"נ, ה) [נדה נג:], ו) עירובין לא:, ז) עירובין ה. [ע"ש ל"ש] ושם עג:, ח) ג"ל שבות, ט) סוף פרק ט דשביעית, י) [וע"ע תוספות נדה ז: ד"ה שמותי הוא], כ) בס"א ר"ל לדבריו דס"ל דבתים אין לה ולא"כ אינו ניתר בלחי וקורה ולא גם לס"ל ר"ש דרשות א' הן ולא"כ גם חצר אין לה ולא"כ היאך אמר חצר ותירות איכא ועי' בטוש"ע סימן שעב וברמב"ם פ"ג מה"ע ומשמע ליה לר"ש מהר דניתר בלחי וקורה כמ"ש התוספות לקמן דבטלי רשות לגבי חד ואמן חד עירבו ולא דוחה התוספות להקשות בין על עירבו ובין על לא עירבו וכדי שלא אמר דזהו מקשה המקשה באומרו בתים איכא חצרות ליכא בעירבו ע"כ פירשו התוספות דמ"ש ניתקו חצירות פירום וחשיב כאילו כו'.

הגהות הב"ח

(א) גמ' אחד גגות ואחד חצרות ואחד קרפיפות רשות אחת: (ב) שם שלא נשתתפו בו מותר: (ג) שם ולא אמרת לי דילמא כו' ותיבת הכי נמחק: (ד) תום' ד"ה שלא וכו' דהא לקמן דף קלג ע"א: (ה) ד"ה ומי שרי וכו' לא הוה שרי ר"א דרך רה"ר כיון: (ו) ד"ה דרבי אליעזר וכו' ואמר בגמרא רבי יהודה בן פזי: (ז) ד"ה ניתקו וכו' כיון שאין דבר מפסיק:

ליקוטי רש"י

שאין מביאין אותו. איזמל למילה. כך אין מביאין אותו וכו'. אף על גב דרשויות דרבנן נינהו [פסחים צב.]. אחד גגות כו'. כולן רשות אחת לטלטל כלים ששבתו בגג זה לגג זה חבירו ולא אמרינן כשם שדיורין חלוקין למטה כך חלוקין למעלה וכלים ששבתו בחצר זו מוציאין לחברתה וכן לקרפף וכן מחצר ולקרפף מן הגגין הוציא וכולן רשות אחת לענין שבת וכלם שבתו בבית וטלטל בבית אפילו במקום ביתו ואין לריך לעבור מחצר לחצר אלא באלו בשביל כלים שבתו בבית להוציאם לחצר אחרת [עירובין עד.]. וגגות וקרפיפות שאינן יותר מבית סאתים הוציא וכולם לענין שמשתמשין מיוחד ותדיר רשות אחת הן ומטלטלין מזה לזה ואפילו מחצר של רבים לחצר רבים בלא עירוב ולית ליה לר"ש שמעון עירובי חצרות אלא משום הימר כלי הבית. לכלים ששבתו בתוכן. כלים ששבתו באחד מהן מוציאין אותן מזה לזה. ולא לכלים ששבתו בתוך הבית. והביאום לחצירן על ידי שעירבו בני החצר אסור להוציאן מחצירו לחצר אחרת אם לא עירבו שתי החצירות יחד [שם פט.]. והוציאן לחצר אסור להוציאן מחצר לקרפף או לגג דבית וקרפף שתי

שֶׁלֹּא בִּרְצוֹן רַבִּי אֱלִיעֶזֶר – but **not with the approval of R' Eliezer.**

The Gemara asks:

מַתְקִיף לָהּ רַב יוֹסֵף – **Rav Yosef objects to [this last point]:** שֶׁלֹּא בִּרְצוֹן רַבִּי אֱלִיעֶזֶר – You say **"not with the approval of R' Eliezer"?!** אַדְּרַבָּה רַבִּי אֱלִיעֶזֶר הוּא דְּשָׁרֵי – **On the contrary, it is R' Eliezer who permits** carrying a knife on the Sabbath to the place of circumcision! וְכִי תֵּימָא – **And if you will say** that R' Abba means: שֶׁלֹּא בִּרְצוֹן רַבִּי אֱלִיעֶזֶר דְּשָׁרֵי אֲפִילּוּ בִּרְשׁוּת הָרַבִּים – **Not with the approval of R' Eliezer, who permits** carrying the knife **even in the public domain**[1] (where the prohibition is Biblical),[2] אֶלָּא בִּרְצוֹן רַבָּנָן דְּאָסְרוּ דֶּרֶךְ רְשׁוּת הָרַבִּים – **but with the approval of the Rabbis, who prohibited** carrying the knife **through the public domain**[3] וְשָׁרוּ דֶּרֶךְ גַּגּוֹת דֶּרֶךְ חֲצֵירוֹת וְקַרְפֵּיפוֹת – **but permitted** carrying it **by way of roofs, courtyards and *karpafs***[4] – וּמִי שָׁרֵי – such an interpretation is untenable, **for would [the Rabbis]** really **permit** carrying a circumcision knife by way of roofs, courtyards, etc.? וְהָתַנְיָא – **But it was taught in a Baraisa** that presents the Rabbis' position: כְּשֵׁם שֶׁאֵין מְבִיאִין אוֹתוֹ דֶּרֶךְ רְשׁוּת הָרַבִּים – JUST AS WE MAY NOT BRING [A CIRCUMCISION KNIFE] THROUGH THE PUBLIC DOMAIN, כָּךְ אֵין מְבִיאִין אוֹתוֹ לֹא דֶּרֶךְ גַּגּוֹת – SO WE MAY NOT BRING IT BY WAY OF adjoining ROOFS, וְלֹא דֶּרֶךְ קַרְפֵּיפוֹת וְלֹא דֶּרֶךְ חֲצֵירוֹת – NOR BY WAY OF adjoining *KARPAFS,* NOR BY WAY OF adjoining COURTYARDS.[5] Hence, the Rabbis would not have approved of the transporting action employed in R' Abba's case.[6] – ? –

The Gemara advances a different understanding of R' Abba's last statement:

אֶלָּא אָמַר רַב אַשִׁי – **Rather, Rav Ashi said:** שֶׁלֹּא בִּרְצוֹן רַבִּי אֱלִיעֶזֶר וּמַחֲלוֹקְתּוֹ – R' Abba means that they transported the knife in this manner **not with the approval of R' Eliezer and his opposition,**[7] אֶלָּא בִּרְצוֹן רַבִּי שִׁמְעוֹן – **but with the approval of R' Shimon,** who permits such transporting outright, דִּתְנַן – **for we learned in a Mishnah:**[8] רַבִּי שִׁמְעוֹן אוֹמֵר – R' SHIMON SAYS: אֶחָד גַּגּוֹת וְאֶחָד קַרְפֵּיפוֹת וְאֶחָד חֲצֵירוֹת – Adjoining ROOFS, *KARPAFS* AND COURTYARDS[9] כּוּלָּן רְשׁוּת אֶחָד הֵן – ARE ALL ONE DOMAIN[10] לְכֵלִים שֶׁשָּׁבְתוּ בְּתוֹכָן – FOR UTENSILS THAT WERE RESTING IN THEM at the onset of the Sabbath,[11] וְלֹא לְכֵלִים שֶׁשָּׁבְתוּ בְּתוֹךְ הַבַּיִת – BUT NOT FOR UTENSILS THAT WERE RESTING INSIDE THE HOUSE at that time.[12] Inasmuch as R' Abba's case involves a knife that was resting in an outdoor enclosure at the onset of the Sabbath,[13] R' Shimon would approve its transport through these enclosures to the place of circumcision.[14]

The Gemara continues its discussion of areas without the proper *eruvin*:

בָּעָא מִינֵּיהּ רַבִּי זֵירָא מֵרַבִּי אַסִּי – **R' Zeira inquired of R' Assi:** מָבוֹי שֶׁלֹּא נִשְׁתַּתְּפוּ בּוֹ – In the case of **an alley in which [the courtyards] were not merged,**[15] מַהוּ לְטַלְטֵל בְּכוּלּוֹ – **what is**

NOTES

1. And so, according to R' Eliezer, it would not be necessary to carry the knife by way of adjoining courtyards and roofs.

2. [The Gemara below (133a) rules that even where the Torah allows a positive commandment (עֲשֵׂה) to override a prohibition (לֹא תַעֲשֶׂה), one may not violate the prohibition if it is possible to comply with both mitzvos. Hence, ask *Tosafos,* how can R' Eliezer permit carrying in the public domain, a Biblical violation, when the circumcision can just as effectively be performed if the knife is transported by way of adjoining courtyards or roofs (which entails only a Rabbinic violation)? *Tos. HaRosh* answers that since the performance of the positive commandment (*milah*) is hastened by violating the prohibition (inasmuch as the public domain is an easier and more direct route), this is regarded as a case in which it is impossible to comply with both mitzvos (cf. *Maharam*). See also *Chidushei HaRan* at the beginning of this chapter.]

3. The reference is to the view of R' Akiva, who stated in the Mishnah that when a preliminary to a mitzvah can be performed before the Sabbath, one may not perform it on the Sabbath.

4. [A *karpaf* is an enclosed area not used for residential purposes.] The Gemara is speaking of carrying from a roof, courtyard or *karpaf* into a roof, courtyard or *karpaf,* suggesting that it is permitted without an *eruv.*

5. [In other words, just as preliminaries to *milah* that can be performed on the Sabbath eve do not override the Biblical prohibition against transporting, so they do not override the Rabbinic prohibition against same; and transporting between the areas mentioned in the Baraisa is at least Rabbinically forbidden.]

The Rabbis enacted their prohibition against carrying through such areas even when it means not fulfilling the mitzvah of *milah,* which carries the penalty of *kares* [excision] (*Rashi* ד״ה שלא ברצון רבי אליעזר ומחלוקתו; see *Pesachim* 92a).

[The Rishonim discuss at length if this prohibition applies when a non-Jew is asked to transport the knife (אֲמִירָה לְעַכּוּ״ם), and if there are circumstances when such transporting would be allowed.]

6. The Gemara seeks to find a condoning Tanna because R' Abba's statement, "not with the approval of R' Eliezer," implies the existence of an opposing opinion (*Maharam*).

7. R' Eliezer holds that even a preliminary to a mitzvah overrides the Sabbath prohibitions, whereas the bearers of the knife in R' Abba's case, by eschewing the direct route of the public domain, demonstrated that they reject R' Eliezer's opinion. Nor, obviously, did they accept the Rabbis' prohibition against carrying by way of roofs, courtyards and *karpafs,* for they indeed transported the knife using such a route (*Rashi*).

8. [*Eruvin* 89a.] R' Meir, also cited there, would likewise have approved; nevertheless, the Gemara mentions R' Shimon because the halachah follows his opinion (*Tosafos*).

9. [In the text of the Mishnah "courtyards" is listed before "*karpafs.*" *Bach* emends here accordingly.]

The Mishnah speaks of a *karpaf* not larger than two *beis se'ah* (5,000 sq. *amos*). If it exceeds that size and is not enclosed for residential use, one may not carry in it a distance of four *amos,* although one may transfer an object from it to another *karpaf* or courtyard (or the reverse) as long as the distance carried is less than four *amos* in the *karpaf* (*Rashi*). [See above, 7a, and *Eruvin* 67b; see *Rashash,* who asks on *Rashi,* and see *Chasam Sofer* above, 80a.]

10. Even if they are owned by different people, we may carry from one such outdoor area to another without the benefit of an *eruv,* for the Rabbis prohibited only the transfer from *houses* to these areas, or the reverse (*Rashi*). See *Eruvin* 89a ff.

11. Any object that was in such an outdoor enclosure when the Sabbath began may be freely moved throughout these contiguous areas without the benefit of an *eruvei chatzeiros* (see *Rashi* to *Eruvin* 89a ד״ה ר׳ שמעון).

12. Certainly, one may not carry such an object to a courtyard, roof, etc. without having made an *eruv.* Moreover, even if one did prepare an *eruv* and lawfully transferred the object from house to courtyard, for example, he may not carry it to another courtyard without having merged with that courtyard [inasmuch as the object retains the status of its original resting place] (*Rashi*; see below, note 15).

13. *Tosafos* ד״ה לכלים. [According to *Maharsha* (on *Rashi* ד״ה ואייתוהו), *Rashi* holds that in R' Shimon's view it is permitted *in the case of milah* to transport an object from a house [where it was located at the onset of Shabbos] even into an area where it would otherwise be permitted to do so. See there, and see note 26 below.]

14. Presumably, the place of circumcision was not a house (cf. *Maharsha* cited in the previous note; see *Tosafos* ד״ה מי).

15. In the common layout of streets and houses in Talmudic times, several houses would open into a courtyard and several courtyards would lead into an alley (*mavoi*), through which the residents of the courtyards would pass to reach the street (the *reshus harabim,* or public domain).

Typically, a *mavoi* was a dead-end alley, closed on three sides and open only on the fourth side, where it met the *reshus harabim.* This is known as a מָבוֹי סָתוּם, *closed mavoi.* The closed *mavoi* is, under Biblical law, a *reshus hayachid* (a private domain), and on the Biblical level one is permitted to carry in it. The Sages, however, were apprehensive that people might confuse a *mavoi* with a *reshus harabim,* and extend the

שלא ברצון ר"א מתקיף לה רב יוסף שלא ברצון ר"א אדרבה ר"א הוא דשרי וכי תימא שלא ברצון ר"א דשרי אפילו ברה"ר אלא ברצון רבנן דאסרו דרך רה"ר ושרו דרך גגות דרך חצירות וקרפיפות ומי שרי והתניא *כשם שאין מביאין אותו דרך רה"ר כך אין מביאין אותו לא דרך גגות ולא דרך קרפיפות ולא דרך חצירות אלא אמר רב אשי שלא ברצון ר"א ומחלוקתו אלא ברצון ר"ש דתנן ר"ש אומר אחד גגות (א) ואחד קרפיפות ואחד חצירות כולן רשות אחד הן לכלים ששבתו בתוכן ולא לכלים ששבתו בתוך הבית בעא מיניה רבי זירא מר' אסי מבוי שלא נשתתפו בו מהו לטלטל בכולו מי אמרינן כחצר דמי מה חצר אע"ג דלא ערבו מותר לטלטל בכולו האי נמי אע"ג דלא נשתתפו בו מותר לטלטל בכולו או דילמא לא דמי לחצר דחצר אית ליה ד' מחיצות האי לית ליה ד' מחיצות א"נ חצר אית ליה דיורין האי לית ביה דיורין שתיק ולא א"ל ולא מידי זימנין אשכחיה דיתיב וקא אמר אמר ר"ש בן לקיש משום ר' יהודה הנשיא פעם אחת שכחו ולא הביאו איזמל מע"ש והביאוהו בשבת והיה הדבר קשה לחכמים היאך מניחין דברי חכמים ועושין כר"א חדא דר"א שמותי הוא ועוד יחיד ורבים הלכה כרבים וא"ר אושעיא שאילית את רבי יהודה הגוזר ואמר לי מבוי שלא נשתתפו בו הוה ואייתוהו מהאי רישא להאי רישא א"ל ס"ל למר מבוי שלא נשתתפו (ב) מותר לטלטל בכולו וא"ל אין א"ל והא זימנין בעאי מינך ולא אמרת לי (ג) הכי דילמא אגב שיטפך רהיט לך גמרך א"ל אין אגב שיטפא רהיטא לי גמרי איתמר אמר רבי זירא אמר רב מבוי שלא נשתתפו בו אין מטלטלין בו אלא בד' אמות אמר אביי הא מילתא אמרה רבי זירא ולא פירשה עד דאתא רבה בר אבוה ופירשה דאמר רב נחמן אמר רבה בר אבוה אמר רב מבוי שלא נשתתפו בו עירבו חצירות עם בתים אין מטלטלין בו אלא בד' אמות לא עירבו חצירות עם בתים מותר לטלטל בכולו אמר ליה רב חנינא חוזאה לרבה מאי שנא כי עירבו חצירות עם בתים דניתקו חצירות ונעשו בתים ורב לטעמיה דאמר רב אין המבוי ניתר בלחי וקורה עד שיהו בתים

רש"י

דרך גגות ודרך חצירות. שלא עירבו זו עם זו ואיכא איסורא דרבנן: שלא ברצון ר"א ומחלוקתו. קאמר דר"א אפילו ברה"ר שרי ואינהו לאייתו לדרך חצרות גלי אדעתייהו דאין מכשירי מילה דוחין שבת ושלא ברצון החלוקין עליו דאסרי דרך חצרות דהעמידו חכמים דבריהם לאיסור שבת אף במקום כרת: אלא ברצון ר"ש. שמתיר אף לדבר הרשות: דתנן ר"ש אומר אחד גגות כו' כולן. ואפילו הן של בעלים הרבה מטלטלין מזו לזו דלא אסרו מרשות לרשות אלא בתים: קרפיפות. אם של בית סאתים הוא מטלטל בכולו ואם יותר ולא הוקף לדירה קרי ליה רשות אחת לגבי חבירו או לגבי חצר לטלטל ד' אמות בזה וד' אמות בזה להוציא ולהכניס מזה לזה: ששבתו בתוכן. שכשקדש היום היו בתוכו ולא בתוך הבית דאילו שבתו כלים בבית לא מיבעיא היכא דלא עירבו בני בתי החצר דאפילו מבית לחצר לא יוציאו כלי הבית אלא אפילו עירבו ומטלטל מבית לחצר לא יוציאו כלי הבית מחצר זו לחברתה שלא עירבו עמה: שלא נשתתפו בו. עירוב לחצירות למבוי קרי שיתוף: מהו לטלטל. בתוכו בכולו כלים ששבתו בתוכו ולהוציא מן החצר לתוכו פשיטא לן דאסור וכן ממנו לחצר: מה חצר אע"ג דלא עירבו. הרבה בתים שבחצר ביחד ואסור להכניס ולהוציא מבתים לחצר ומחצר לבתים: מותר לטלטל בכולו. מה שנמצא בתוכו או בגדיו שהוציאן מן הבית לתוכו דרך מלבוש פושטן ומטלטלן בכולו לדברי הכל דג' מחלוקות הן בעירובין בפרק כל גגות לדברי ר' מאיר גגין רשות לעצמן ומטלטלין מזה לזה ואפילו של בעלים הרבה וחצרות רשות לעצמן לטלטל מזו לזו בלא עירוב כלים ששבתו בתוכם אבל לא מגגין לחצרות וקרפיפות רשות לעצמן ולדברי חכמים גגין וחצרות רשות אחת וקרפיפות רשות אחת ולדברי ר"ש כולן רשות אחת חוץ מן הבתים: א"נ חצר אית ביה דיורין. כלומר עשויה להשתמש בה תדיר: האי אין בו דיורין. שהדיורין בבתים הן והבתים פתוחין לחצירות וחצירות למבוי: זמנין. פעם אחרת: אשכחיה. רבי זירא לר' אסי: שמותי הוא. כדמוכח בהזהב (ב"מ דף נט:) ובתלמוד ירושלמי מפ' שמותי הוא מתלמידי שמאי היה: וא"ר אושעיא. לאותן שהיה קשה עליהן מה ששמעו: שאילית את רבי יהודה הגוזר. המל את התינוקות: ואייתוהו מהאי רישא. שהיה התינוק בבית שבראש המבוי ואיזמל בבית שבראש האחר שכנגדו עד כאן דברי ר' אסי: א"ל. רבי זירא אלמא ס"ל למר מדאמר ליה להא ולא קשיא לך ביה מידי סבירא לך מותר לטלטל בכולו: הכי גרסינן והא זמנין בעאי מינך ולא אמרת דילמא אגב שיטפא אתיא לך. כשהיית שטוף בגרסתך לחזור על שמועה זו דר"ל עם מרוצת גרסתך אתיא לך הך דר' אושעיא בהדא דאיתמר עלה: ולא פירשה. אימתי מותר ואימתי אסור: עירבו חצרות. שבמבוי עם בתיהם שבני הבתים מוציאין לחצרותיהן שעירבו בתים הפתוחים לחצר יחד וכן בני חצר האחרת אבל בני החצרות לא נשתתפו במבוי: אין מטלטלין. במבוי אפי' כלים ששבתו בתוכו אלא בד': לא עירבו חצרות עם בתיהן. שאסורים בני הבתים להוציא מבתיהן לחצריהם: מותר לטלטל בכולו. כלים ששבתו בתוכו ולקמיה מפרש טעמא: ונעשו בתים. בטלו לגבי הבתים ואין שם חצרות עליהם: בתים

תוספות

שלא ברצון ר"א דשרי אפי' ברה"ר. קשה לרשב"א הא אמרינן לקמן בפירקין (דף קלג.) כל מקום שאתה מוצא עשה ולא תעשה אם אתה יכול לקיים את שניהם מוטב כו' והכא כיון דאפשר לקיים את שניהם להביאו דרך גגות וחצירות וקרפיפות אמאי יביאו אותו דרך רה"ר וליכא למימר דלגבי מילה דגלי רחמנא בה דדחי שבת כדדרשינן לקמן לא אמרינן הכי דהא לקמן (ד) גבי בשר אפי' במקום בהרת יקוץ כו' אמרינן כדר"ל דאמר ר"ל כל מקום שאתה מוצא כו': ומי שרי והתניא. וא"ת ולוקמי שהביאו לדרך חצר מעורבת דהוי כרצון חכמים ושלא כרצון ר"א דשרי אפי' לדרך רה"ר וי"ל דבכה"ג לא הוה (ה) שרי ר"א מן רה"ר כיון שיכול להביאו לדרך חצר מעורבת בהיתר גמור א"נ לישנא דשכחו לא משמע כן דאי היתה מעורבת לא ה"ל למימר שכחו אלא לא חשו להביאו מע"ש כיון דבשבת אפשר להביאו בהיתר גמור אבל כי מסיק כרצון ר"ש אתי שפיר דקאמר שכחו שאם היו מכירין מע"ש היו מביאין משום דפליגי רבנן עליה: ברצון ר"ש. ה"ה דהוה מצי למימר כרבנן כר"מ שהביאו דרך גגות מגג לגג או דרך חצרות מחצר לחצר דלמוכח בפרק כל גגות (עירובין דף פט.) דלית ליה כל גגות העיר רשות אחת הן וכן חצרות וקרפיפות אלא נקט ר' שמעון דקיי"ל כוותיה: לכלים ששבתו לתוכו. וכן היה אותו איזמל: דרבי אליעזר שמותי הוא. מב"ש וכן מוכח בירושלמי במסכת תרומות בפרק סאה תרומה דתנן התם סאה תרומה טמאה שנפלה למאה סאין טהורין בית שמאי אוסרים וב"ה מתירין כו' עד לאחר שהודו ר"א אומר תירום ותישרף ואמר בגמרא (ו) בן פזי ורבי אייבו בר נגרי הוו יתבין ואמרי תנינן אחר שהודו ר"א אומר תירום ותישרף מי הודה למי א"ר אסי מתניתין אמרה כן לאחר שהודו ר"א אומר תירום ותישרף ר"א לאו שמותי הוא הרי משמע דשמותי הוא מתלמידי ב"ש דמינה קא פשיט דב"ש הודו לב"ה. ר"ת: ניתקו חצרות ונעשו בתים. פירוש וחשיב כאילו אין כאן חצר כלל שהחצר נעשה בית וכשלא עירבו חשיבי בתים כליתנהו ומיהו חצר לא חשיב כליתא אע"פ שאסור לטלטל מתוכו למבוי כיון שאין (ז) דרך מפסיק בינו למבוי לא חשוב [כסתום] אבל בתים כסתומות חשיבי כיון שהחצר מפסיק בינם למבוי ודוקא היכא דלא נשתתפו בעינן בתים וחצרות פתוחין לתוכו אבל נשתתפו לא בעינן ומשני אפשר דמבטלי רשות גבי חד דהשתא איכא בית דלא חשיב כסתום ולא אמר נמי ניתקו חצרות כולם כיון דשאר הבתים אסורין בחצר ופריך בית איכא בתים ליכא ולא מצי למימר דבטלי רשות גבי תרי שהם היו אוסרין זה על זה ולא מצי למימר שהשנים עירבו דהא מדקאמר רב לא עירבו משמע לא עירבו כלל: אפשר

עין משפט נר מצוה

ד א מיי' פ"ב מהלכות מילה הלכה ו סמג עשין כח טוש"ע א"ח סימן שלא סעיף ו וטוש"ע י"ד סימן רסו סעיף ב:

ה ב מיי' פ"ג מהלכות עירובין הלכה יח סמג עשין דרבנן א טוש"ע א"ח סימן שעב סעיף א:

ו ג מיי' פ"ה מהלכות עירובין הלכה טו סמג שם טוש"ע א"ח סימן שפח:

ז ד מיי' פי"ז מהלכות שבת הלכה ח סמג שם טוש"ע א"ח סימן שסג סעיף כו:

גליון הש"ס

רש"י ד"ה מותר לטלטל בכולו וכו' פושטן ומטלטלן. תמוה לי הא מ"מ כיון דשבתו בבית אסור לטלטלן ובלבישה להדיא עירובין דף לא בכותמא וקולרא וצ"ע: תוספות ד"ה דר"א שמותי וכו' וכן מוכח בירושלמי. עיין ביצה דף לד ע"ב תוספות ד"ה אומר:

רבינו חננאל

בשבת שלא כרצון רבי אליעזר ושקלינן וטרינן בה ואוקמא רב אשי שלא כרצון ר' אליעזר דשרי אפילו דרך רה"ר ושלא ברצון מחלוקתו והן החכמים שחולקים על ר' אליעזר ואומרים אפילו דרך גגות ודרך חצירות וכו' דרבי עקיבא סבירא ליה כוותיהון אלא כרצון ר' שמעון דשרי דרך גגות דתנן ר' שמעון אומר אחד גגות ואחד קרפיפות ואחת חצירות ואחת קרפיפות כו'. בעא ר' זירא מר' אמי מבוי שלא נשתתפו בו מהו לטלטל בכולו כו' ושתק מיניה ולא השיב לו זמנין אשכחיה דאמר אמר ר"ל משום רבי יהודה נשיאה פעם אחת שכחו ולא הביאו אזמל מע"ש והביאוהו בשבת והיה הדבר קשה לחכמים היאך מניחין דברי חכמים ועושין כר' אליעזר חדא דברי יחיד ועוד רבי אליעזר שמותי הוא כלומר מתלמידי שמאי הוא. א"ר אושעיא שאילית את ר' יהודה הגוזר פי' המל ואמר לי מבוי שלא נשתתפו בו הוה ואתיוה מהאי רישא להאי רישא אמינא ליה סבירא ליה למר מבוי שלא נשתתפו בו מותר לטלטל בכולו א"ל אין כו'. אתמר ר' זירא אמר רב מבוי שלא נשתתפו בו אין מטלטלין בו אלא בד' אמות. א"ר זירא לא פירשה שמועה זו היטב עד דאתא רב נחמן אמר רבה בר אבוה ופרשה משמיה דרב הכי מבוי שלא נשתתפו בו אם עירבו חצרות עם בתיהם אין מטלטלין בו מותר לטלטל בכולו א"ל רב חנינא חוזאה לרבא מפני מה כי עירבו עם בתיהם אין מטלטלין באותו מבוי אלא בארבע דניתקו חצרות ונעשו בתים כלומר כיון שעירבו נעשו בתי החצר והחצר רשות אחת ורב לטעמיה דאמר אין מבוי ניתר בלחי וקורה עד שיהו

מסורת הש"ס

א) פסחים לב., ב) עירובין כב: לה. עד. פט. צא., ג) [נדה ז:], ד) [לעיל קל. ברכות ט. וש"נ], ה) [נדה נג:], ו) עירובין ג:, ז) עירובין ה. [ע"ש] ושם עג:, ח) ל"ל שבות, ט) סוף פרק ט דשביעית, י) [וע"ע תוספות נדה ז: ד"ה שמותי הוא], [illegible]

הגהות הב"ח

(א) גמ' אחד גגות ואחד חצירות ואחד קרפיפות רשות אחת: (ב) שם שלא נשתתפו בו מותר: (ג) שם ולא אמרת לי דילמא כצ"ל ותיבת הכי נמחק: (ד) תוס' ד"ה שלא וכו' דהא לקמן. נ"ב דף קלג ע"א: (ה) ד"ה ומי שרי וכו' דרך רה"ר כיון: (ו) ד"ה דרבי אליעזר וכו' ואמר בגמרא רבי יהודה בן פזי: (ז) ד"ה ניתקו וכו' כיון שאין דרך מפסיק:

ליקוטי רש"י

שאין מביאין אותו. איזמל למילה. כך אין מביאין אותו וכו'. אף על גב דרשויות דרבנן נינהו [פסחים צב.]. אחד גגות. כולן רשות אחת לטלטל כלים ששבתו בגג זה לגג חבירו [illegible]

רשויות הן ואפילו דחד גברא [שם כג.]. חצר אע"ג דלא עירבו. ואוסרים בני הבתים זה על זה שאין יכולין להוציא מן הבתים לחצר בלא עירוב מפני שהבית רשות מיוחדת לו והחצר רשות חבירו מושל בה ונמצא מוציא מר[שות] ... שלא להוציא מרשות היחיד לרשות היחיד גזירה דילמא אתי לאפוקי מרשות היחיד לרשות הרבים אבל בחצר מותר לטלטל בה [שם יב:]. שמותי. לשון שמחה שהרי ברכוהו כדאמרינן בהזהב (ב"מ נט:) הלכך לא עבדינן כוותיה ... הלכה כרבים. דאחרי רבים להטות כתיב (שמות כג) [ב"ק קטז.]. שיטפך. ריהטך [נדה נג:]. [מכאן שייך לדף קלא.] בתים וחצרות. בתים פתוחין לחצירות וחצירות למבוי שכן היה דרכן שאין בתים פתוחין אלא לחצרין ו... בהש"ס ובמשנה אינו אלא לפני הבית אבל שאחורי הבית מוקלה או רחבה קרי ליה [עירובין ה.]. שתי חצירות פתוחות לתוכו ובית פתוח לכל חצר שכן היו דירותיהן לפני כל בית היה חצר [שם יב: ע"ש בתוס']. מה הבאה האמורה בעומר מכשירין דוחין את השבת. כדכתיב ביה וביום השביעי תשבות בחריש ובקציר תשבות בא ללמדך מה חריש אין לך חריש של מצוה ואפילו לזרוע לצורך עומר ושתי הלחם שהרי אם מצא חרוש אינו חורש ואני אוסרו לך בשבת ... אוסר לך בשל רשות אני אוסר לך יצא קציר העומר שהוא מצוה שאפילו מצא קצור מצוה לקצור ויש לך ללמוד מכאן שדוחה את השבת [ר"ה ט.]. מופני. צריך שתהא גזירה שוה זו משתי תיבות מופנין למדרש זה שלא יהו צריכי[ן] ... שמופנין ללמוד גזירה שוה הוי ליה כמאן דכתיב דרשא בקרא בהדיא ואין משיבין עליה. דאי לאו מופני. אמרינן לגופן באו ולא ילפינן להא מילתא מינייהו [לעיל סד.].

[the law] regarding whether one is permitted **to carry in its entirety?**[16] מִי אַמְרִינַן כְּחָצֵר דָּמֵי – That is, **do we say that [an alley] is like a courtyard,** מַה חָצֵר אַף עַל גַּב דְּלֹא עֵרְבוּ – in that **just as** in the case of **a courtyard, even though [its residents] did not merge** before the Sabbath,[17] מוּתָּר לְטַלְטֵל בְּכוּלּוֹ – one is nonetheless **permitted to carry in its entirety,**[18] הַאי נַמִּי – so in the case of **this** *mavoi* **as well,** אַף עַל גַּב דְּלֹא נִשְׁתַּתְּפוּ בּוֹ – **even though [its courtyards] were not merged in it,** מוּתָּר לְטַלְטֵל בְּכוּלּוֹ – one is **permitted to carry in its entirety?** אוֹ דִילְמָא לֹא דָּמֵי לְחָצֵר – **Or, perhaps, [an alley] is not like a courtyard,** דְּחָצֵר אִית לֵיהּ אַרְבַּע מְחִיצוֹת – **for a courtyard has four** proper **partitions,**[19] הַאי לֵית לֵיהּ אַרְבַּע מְחִיצוֹת – while **this** *mavoi* **does not have four partitions.**[20] אִי נַמִּי חָצֵר אִית לֵיהּ דִּיוּרִין – **Alternatively, a courtyard has residents,**[21] הַאי לֵית בֵּיהּ דִּיוּרִין – while **this** *mavoi* **does not have residents.**[22] – ? –

The Gemara reports what transpired after R' Zeira posed this question:

שָׁתִיק וְלֹא אָמַר לֵיהּ וְלֹא מִידִי – **[R' Assi] was silent, and said nothing to [R' Zeira]** in reply. זִימְנִין אַשְׁכְּחֵיהּ דְּיָתֵיב וְקָאָמַר – However, on **another occasion [R' Zeira] found [R' Assi] sitting,** and at that time **[R' Assi] said:** אָמַר רַבִּי שִׁמְעוֹן בֶּן לָקִישׁ מִשּׁוּם רַבִּי יְהוּדָה הַנָּשִׂיא – **R' Shimon ben Lakish said in the name of R' Yehudah HaNasi:** פַּעַם אַחַת שָׁכְחוּ וְלֹא הֵבִיאוּ אִיזְמֵל מֵעֶרֶב שַׁבָּת – **Once they forgot and did not bring a knife on the Sabbath eve** to the place of a Sabbath circumcision, וֶהֱבִיאוּהוּ בְּשַׁבָּת – **and** then **they brought it on the Sabbath** itself; וְהָיָה הַדָּבָר קָשֶׁה לַחֲכָמִים – **and the matter was difficult for the** local **sages** to understand, הֵיאַךְ מַנִּיחִין דִּבְרֵי חֲכָמִים וְעוֹשִׂין כְּרַבִּי אֱלִיעֶזֶר – **how [these people] could disregard the opinion of the Sages** of the Mishnah[23] **and act in accordance with** the ruling of **R' Eliezer,**[24] for two reasons: חֲדָא דְּרַבִּי אֱלִיעֶזֶר שַׁמּוּתִי הוּא – **One, because R' Eliezer was excommunicated** by his colleagues,[25] וְעוֹד יָחִיד וְרַבִּים הֲלָכָה כְּרַבִּים – **and, moreover,** because the rule is that in a dispute between **an individual and a majority, the halachah accords with** the view of **the majority.**

Having concluded his quotation of Reish Lakish, R' Assi continues to relate:

וְאָמַר רַבִּי אוֹשַׁעְיָא – **And** subsequently **R' Oshaya said** to those sages who were displeased with the Sabbath knife-carrying: שְׁאֵילִית אֶת רַבִּי יְהוּדָה הַגּוֹזֵר וְאָמַר לִי – **I** once **asked R' Yehudah the Circumciser** about the particulars of this case **and he told me** that מָבוֹי שֶׁלֹּא נִשְׁתַּתְּפוּ בּוֹ הָוָה – **it was** in **an alley in which [the courtyards] were not merged** via a *shituf* that this episode occurred, וְאַיְיתוּהוּ מֵהַאי רֵישָׁא לְהַאי רֵישָׁא – **and they brought [the knife] from this end** of the alley, where it was resting at the onset of the Sabbath, **to this** other **end,** where the circumcision was to be performed.[26] This concludes R' Assi's statement, which R' Zeira heard at their second encounter.

The Gemara now records R' Zeira's reaction to the statement:

אָמַר לֵיהּ – **[R' Zeira]** thereupon **said to [R' Assi]:** סְבִירָא לֵיהּ לְמָר – Inasmuch as master related R' Oshaya's explanation of the incident and himself voiced no objection to the people's actions, **master** presumably **holds** that in the case of מָבוֹי שֶׁלֹּא נִשְׁתַּתְּפוּ – **an alley in which [the courtyards] were not merged** via a *shituf,* מוּתָּר לְטַלְטֵל בְּכוּלּוֹ – one is **permitted to carry in its entirety,** for in that incident they carried the circumcision knife

NOTES

practice of carrying within a *mavoi* to the *reshus harabim* as well (*Rashi* to *Eruvin* 2a). Alternatively, since the *mavoi* is completely open to the *reshus harabim,* people might erroneously conclude that the alley was part of the *reshus harabim* and carry from the *reshus harabim* into it [and thus transgress the prohibition of carrying from a *reshus harabim* to a *reshus hayachid*] (*Rabbeinu Yehonasan; Meiri; R' Yeshayah HaAcharon* to *Eruvin* 2a).

Whatever the consideration, the Rabbis prohibited carrying in a *mavoi* unless a certain adjustment is made to the open end of the *mavoi* to demonstrate that it and the *reshus harabim* are two separate entities (see note 38 below). In addition, the Rabbis prohibited carrying from a courtyard into a *mavoi* without a *shitufei mevo'os,* which merges all the courtyards (much as an *eruvei chatzeiros* merges all the houses of a courtyard [see *Orach Chaim* 386:1 and 387]. The Gemara now questions whether permission to carry within the *mavoi* applies even if the residents of the courtyards opening into the *mavoi* did not, in addition, prepare a *shitufei mevo'os.*

16. It is obvious that in this case one may not carry from the *mavoi* into a courtyard (or the reverse), since a *shitufei mevo'os* was not prepared. The Gemara asks only if an object that was resting in the *mavoi* at the onset of *Shabbos* may be carried more than four *amos* in the *mavoi* on *Shabbos* (see *Rashi*). [For perhaps, just as one may not carry from the *mavoi* to a courtyard, so carrying four *amos* within the *mavoi* is prohibited, since a *mavoi* without a *shituf* could be considered a Rabbinic public domain.]

Maharsha understands that the Gemara poses its question even according to R' Shimon (even though he *permits* carrying from courtyard to *mavoi*). Cf. *Netziv* and *Leshon HaZahav.*

17. I.e. even if they did not prepare an *eruvei chatzeiros* [a device that allows us to view all the houses opening into the courtyard as owned by a single consortium (composed of all the residents of the courtyard)], which permits the residents to carry from their houses into the courtyard, and the reverse (*Rashi*).

18. According to all three opinions cited in the Mishnah in *Eruvin* (89a), one may carry throughout the entirety of a courtyard an object that was resting in the courtyard at the onset of Shabbos, or a garment that one was wearing as he went on Shabbos from his house into the courtyard, where he subsequently removed the garment (*Rashi*). [*R' Akiva Eiger* questions *Rashi's* case of the garment, since it rested in the house at the onset of Shabbos. See *Rashash* and *Netziv* at length, and see *Beur Halachah* to 372:1 ד״ה שמא.]

19. [Thereby rendering it a totally enclosed private domain, in whose entirety carrying is permitted despite the absence of an *eruv,* which prohibits carrying between house and courtyard.]

20. Rather, it has only an adjustment on the fourth side (see note 38 below). Thus, since the courtyards did not prepare a *shituf,* it is possible that this adjustment loses its classification as a partition (*Ritva MHK* ed.).

21. I.e. it is used by the residents of the surrounding houses as an extension of their residence (*Rashi*) [giving it the appearance of a private domain] (see also *Menachem Meishiv Nefesh*).

22. Rather, the residents occupy the houses and use the courtyard, but only pass through the *mavoi* to reach the street (see *Rashi*) [giving it the appearance of a public domain] (see also *Menachem Meishiv Nefesh*).

23. The Sages ascribe to the view of R' Akiva, who said that if a preliminary to a mitzvah (e.g. carrying a knife to the location of a circumcision) can be performed before the Sabbath, it may not be performed on the Sabbath.

24. Who said that a circumcision knife may be brought on the Sabbath, even by way of the public domain.

25. For refusing to yield to the majority opinion in the incident of the "*Achnai* oven," as detailed in *Bava Metzia* 59b (*Rashi*). Alternatively, שַׁמּוּתִי derives from שַׁמַּאי, meaning that R' Eliezer was a disciple of Shammai (ibid., from *Yerushalmi Sheviis* ch. 9; see also *Tosafos*). [According to the second interpretation, the Sages were displeased with the people following R' Eliezer's ruling because the halachah generally does not accord with Beis Shammai.]

26. And so, in fact, the people did not abandon the majority opinion in favor of R' Eliezer, whose leniency involved carrying in the public domain.

Rashi states that the knife was brought from *a house* at one end of the *mavoi* to another *house* at the other end. From this *Maharsha* concludes that *Rashi* argues with *Tosafos* (see note 13 above). However, *Maharam Schif* emends the text of *Rashi.* See also *Menachem Meishiv Nefesh* and *Hagahos Ben Aryeh.*

שלא ברצון ר"א מתקיף לה רב יוסף שלא ברצון ר"א אדרבה ר"א הוא דשרי וכי תימא שלא ברצון ר"א דשרי אפילו ברה"ר אלא ברצון רבנן דאסרו דרך רה"ר ושרו דרך גגות דרך חצירות וקרפיפות ומי שרי [ה] והתניא [א] כשם שאין מביאין אותו דרך רה"ר כך אין מביאין אותו לא דרך גגות ולא דרך קרפיפות ולא דרך חצירות אלא אמר רב אשי שלא ברצון ר"א ומחלוקתו אלא ברצון ר"ש [ו] דתנן ר"ש אומר אחד [ב] גגות (א) ואחד קרפיפות ואחד חצירות כולן רשות אחד הן לכלים ששבתו בתוכן ולא לכלים ששבתו בתוך הבית בעא מיניה רבי זירא מר' אסי מבוי שלא נשתתפו בו מהו לטלטל בכולו מי אמרינן כחצר דמי מה חצר אע"ג דלא ערבו מותר לטלטל בכולו האי נמי אע"ג דלא נשתתפו בו מותר לטלטל בכולו או דילמא לא דמי לחצר דחצר אית ליה ד' מחיצות האי לית ליה ד' מחיצות א"נ חצר אית ליה דיורין האי לית ביה דיורין שתיק ולא א"ל ולא מידי זימנין אשכחיה דיתיב וקא אמר אמר ר"ש בן לקיש משום ר' יהודה הנשיא פעם אחת שכחו ולא הביאו איזמל מע"ש והביאוהו בשבת והיה הדבר קשה לחכמים היאך מניחין דברי חכמים ועושין כר"א חדא דר"א שמותי [ז] הוא ועוד יחיד ורבים [ח] הלכה כרבים וא"ר אושעיא שאילית את רבי יהודה הגוזר ואמר לי מבוי שלא נשתתפו בו הוה ואייתוהו מהאי רישא להאי רישא א"ל ס"ל למר מבוי שלא נשתתפו (ב) מותר לטלטל בכולו וא"ל אין א"ל והא זימנין בעאי מינך ולא אמרת לי (ג) הכי [ט] דילמא אגב שיטפך רהיט לך גמרך א"ל אין אגב שיטפא רהיטא לי גמרי [י] איתמר אמר רבי זירא אמר רב מבוי שלא נשתתפו בו אין מטלטלין בו אלא בד' אמות אמר אביי הא מילתא אמרה רבי זירא ולא פירשה עד דאתא רבה בר אבוה ופירשה דאמר רב נחמן אמר רבה בר אבוה אמר רב [ג] מבוי שלא נשתתפו בו עירבו חצירות עם בתים אין מטלטלין בו אלא בד' אמות לא עירבו חצירות עם בתים מותר לטלטל בכולו אמר ליה רב חנינא חוזאה לרבה מאי שנא כי עירבו חצירות עם בתים דניתקו חצירות ונעשו בתים ורב לטעמיה [י] דאמר רב [ד] אין המבוי ניתר בלחי וקורה עד שיהו

בתים

דרך גגות ודרך חצירות. שלא עירבו זו עם זו ואיכא איסורא דרבנן: שלא ברצון ר"א ומחלוקתו. קאמר דר"א אפילו ברה"ר שרי ואינהו דאייתו דרך חצרות גלי אדעתייהו דאין מכשירי מילה דוחין שבת ושלא ברצון החלוקין עליו דאסרי דרך חצרות דהעמידו חכמים דבריהם לאיסור [ס] שבת אף במקום כרת: אלא ברצון ר"ש. שמתיר אף לדבר הרשות: דתנן ר"ש אומר אחד גגות כו' כולן. ואפילו הן של בעלים הרבה מטלטלין מזה לזה דלא אסרו מרשות לרשות אלא בתים: קרפיפות. אם של בית סאתים הוא מטלטל בכולו ואם יותר ולא הוקף לדירה קרי ליה רשות אחת לגבי חבירו או לגבי חצר לטלטל ב' אמות בזה וב' אמות בזה להוציא ולהכניס מזה לזה: ששבתו בתוכן. שכשקדש היום היו בתוכו ולא בתוך הבית דאילו שבתו כלים בבית לא מיבעיא היכא דלא עירבו בני בתי החצר דאפילו מבית לחצר לא יוציאו כלי הבית אלא אפילו עירבו ומטלטל מבית לחצר לא יוציאו כלי הבית מחצר זו לחברתה שלא עירבו עמה: שלא נשתתפו בו. עירוב דחצירות במבוי קרי שיתוף: מהו לטלטל. בתוכו בכולו כלים ששבתו בתוכו ולהוציא מן החצר לתוכו פשיטא לן דאסור וכן ממנו לחצר: מה חצר אע"ג דלא עירבו. הרבה בתים שבחצר ביחד ואסור להכניס ולהוציא מבתים לחצר ומחצר לבתים: מותר לטלטל בכולו. מה שנמצא בתוכו או בגדיו שהוציאן מן הבית לתוכו דרך מלבוש ° פושטן ומטלטלן בכולו לדברי הכל דג' מחלוקות הן בעירובין בפרק כל גגות לדברי ר' מאיר גגין רשות לעצמן ומטלטלין מזה לזה ואפילו של בעלים הרבה וחצרות רשות לעצמן לטלטל מזו לזו בלא עירוב כלים ששבתו בתוכם אבל לא מגגין לחצרות וקרפיפות רשות לעצמן ולדברי חכמים גגין וחצרות רשות אחת וקרפיפות רשות אחת ולדברי ר"ש כולן רשות אחת חוץ מן הבתים: א"נ חצר אית ביה דיורין. כלומר עשויה להשתמש בה תדיר: האי אין בו דיורין. שהדיורין בבתים הן והבתים פתוחין לחצירות וחצירות למבוי: זמנין. פעם אחרת: אשכחיה. רבי זירא לר' אסי: שמותי הוא. ברכוהו כדאמרינן בהזהב (ב"מ דף נט:) ובתלמוד ירושלמי [ט] מפ' שמותי הוא מתלמידי שמאי היה: וא"ר אושעיא. לאותן שהיה קשה עליהן מה ששמעו: שאילית את רבי יהודה הגוזר. המל את התינוקות: ואייתוהו מהאי רישא. שהיה התינוק בבית שבראש המבוי ואיזמל בבית שבראש האחר שכנגדו עד כאן דברי ר' אסי: א"ל. רבי זירא אלמא ס"ל למר מדאמר ליה להא ולא קשיא לך ביה מידי סבירא לך מותר לטלטל בכולו: הכי גרסינן והא זמנין בעאי מינך ולא אמרת דילמא אגב שיטפא אתיא לך. כשהיית שטוף בגרסתך לחזור על שמועה זו דר"ל עם מרוצת גרסתך אתיא לך הך דר' אושעיא בהדא דאיתמר עלה: ולא פירשה. אימתי מותר ואימתי אסור: עירבו חצרות. שבמבוי עם בתיהם שבני הבתים מוציאין לחצרותיהן שעירבו בתים הפתוחים לחצר יחד וכן בני חצר האחרת אבל בני החצרות לא נשתתפו במבוי: אין מטלטלין. במבוי אפי' כלים ששבתו בתוכו אלא בד': לא עירבו חצרות עם בתיהן. שאסורים בני הבתים להוציא מבתיהן לחצריהם: מותר לטלטל בכולו. כלים ששבתו בתוכו ולקמיה מפרש טעמא: ונעשו בתים. בטלו לגבי הבתים ואין שם חצרות עליהם:

בתים

שלא ברצון ר"א דשרי אפי' ברה"ר. קשה לרשב"א הא אמרינן לקמן בפירקין (דף קלג.) כל מקום שאתה מוצא עשה ולא תעשה אם אתה יכול לקיים את שניהם מוטב כו' והכא כיון דאפשר לקיים את שניהם להביאו דרך גגות וחצירות וקרפיפות אמאי יביאו אותו דרך רה"ר וליכא למימר דלגבי מילה דגלי רחמנא בה דדחי שבת כדדרשינן לקמן לא אמרינן הכי דהא לקמן (ד) גבי בשר אפי' במקום בהרת יקוץ כו' אמרינן כדר"ל דאמר ר"ל כל מקום שאתה מוצא כו': ומי שרי והתניא. וא"ת ולוקמי שהביאו דרך חצר מעורבת דהוי כרצון חכמים ושלא כרצון ר"א דשרי אפי' דרך רה"ר וי"ל דבכה"ג לא הוה (ה) שרי ר"א מן רה"ר כיון שיכול להביאו דרך חצר מעורבת בהיתר גמור א"נ לישנא דשכחו לא משמע כן דאי היתה מעורבת לא ה"ל למימר שכחו אלא לא חשו להביאו מע"ש כיון דבשבת אפשר להביאו בהיתר גמור אבל כי מסיק ברצון ר"ש אתי שפיר דקאמר שכחו שאם היו נזכרין מע"ש היו מביאין משום דפליגי רבנן עליה:

ברצון ר"ש. ה"ה דהוה מצי למימר כרצון ר"מ שהביאו דרך גגות מגג לגג או דרך חצרות מחצר לחצר כדמוכח בפרק כל גגות (עירובין דף פט.) דלית ליה כל גגות העיר רשות אחד הן וחצרות וקרפיפות אלא נקט ר' שמעון דקי"ל כוותיה: לכלים ששבתו לתוכו. וכן היה אותו איזמל:

דרבי אליעזר שמותי הוא. מב"ש ° וכן מוכח בירושלמי במסכת תרומות בפרק סאה תרומה דתנן התם סאה תרומה טמאה שנפלה למאה סאין טהורין בית שמאי אוסרים וב"ה מתירין כו' עד לאחר שהודו ר"א אומר תירום ותישרף ואמר בגמרא (ו) בן פזי ורבי לייבו בר נגרי הוו יתבין ואמרי תנינן אחר שהודו ר"א אומר תירום ותישרף מי הודה למי א"ר אסי מתניתין אמרה כן לאחר שהודו ר"א אומר תירום ותישרף ר"א לאו שמותי הוא הרי משמע דשמותי הוא מתלמידי ב"ש דמינה קא פשיט דב"ש הודו לב"ה. ר"ת:

ניתקו חצרות ונעשו בתים. פירוש וחשיב כאילו אין כאן חצר כלל שהחצר נעשה בית וכשלא עירבו חשיבי בתים כליתנהו ומיהו חצר לא חשיב כליתא אע"פ שאסור לטלטל [ס] מתוכו למבוי כיון שאין (ז) דרך מפסיק בינו למבוי לא חשוב [כסתום] אבל בתים כסתומות חשיבי כיון שהחצר מפסיק בינם למבוי ודוקא היכא דלא נשתתפו בעינן בתים וחצרות פתוחין לתוכו אבל נשתתפו לא בעינן ומשני אפשר למבטלי רשות גבי חד דהשתא איכא בית דלא חשיב כסתום ולא אמר נמי ניתקו חצרות כולם כיון דשאר הבתים אסורין בחצר ופריך בית איכא בתים ליכא ולא מצי למימר דבטלי רשות גבי תרי שהם היו אוסרין זה על זה ולא מצי למימר שהשנים עירבו דהא מדקאמר רב לא עירבו משמע לא עירבו כלל:

אפשר

עין משפט
נר מצוה

ד א מיי' פ"ב מהלכות מילה הלכה ו סמג עשין כח טוש"ע א"ח סימן שלא סעיף ו וטוש"ע י"ד סימן רסו סעיף ג:
ה ב מיי' פ"ג מהלכות עירובין הלכה יח סמג עשין דרבנן א טוש"ע א"ח סימן שעב סעיף א:
ו ג מיי' פ"ה מהלכות עירובין הלכה טו סמג שם טוש"ע א"ח סימן שסה:
ז ד מיי' פי"ז מהלכות שבת הלכה יז סמג שם טוש"ע א"ח סימן שסג סעיף כו:

גליון הש"ס

רש"י ד"ה מותר לטלטל בכולה וכו' פושטן ומטלטלן. תמי' לי הא מ"מ כיון דשבתו בבית אסור לטלטלן וכדאיתא להדיא עירובין דף לא בכמתא וקודלא ולע"ג: תוספות ד"ה דר"א שמותי וכו' וכן מוכח בירושלמי. עיין בילה דף לד ע"ב תוספות ד"ה ואומר:

רבינו חננאל

בשבת שלא כרצון רבי אליעזר ושקלינן וטרינן בה ואוקמא רב אשי שלא כרצון ר' אליעזר דשרי אפילו דרך רה"ר ושלא ברצון מחלוקתו והם החכמים שחולקים על ר' אליעזר ואומרים אפילו דרך גגות ודרך חצירות וכו' דרבי עקיבא סבירא ליה כוותיהון אלא כרצון ר' שמעון דשרי דרך גגות דתנן ר' שמעון אומר אחד גגות ואחד חצירות ואחת קרפיפות כו'. בעא ר' זירא מר' אמי מבוי שלא נשתתפו בו מהו לטלטל בכולו כו' ושתק ר' אמי ולא השיב לו זמנין אשכחיה דאמר ר"ל משום רבי יהודה נשיאה פעם אחת שכחו ולא הביאו אזמל מע"ש והביאוהו בשבת והיה הדבר קשה לחכמים היאך מניחין דברי חכמים ועושין כר' אליעזר שהן דברי יחיד ועוד רבי אליעזר שמותי הוא כלומר מתלמידי שמאי הוא. א"ר אושעיא שאילית את ר' יהודה הגוזר פי' המל ואמר לי מבוי שלא נשתתפו בו הוה ואתיוה מהאי רישא להאי רישא אמינא ליה סבירא ליה למר מבוי שלא נשתתפו בו מותר לטלטלו בכולן א"ל אין כו'. אתמר ר' זירא אמר רב מבוי שלא נשתתפו בו אין מטלטלין בו אלא בארבע. ר' זירא לא פירש שמועה זו היטב עד דאתא רב נחמן אמר רבה בר אבוה ופרשה משמיה דרב הכי מבוי שלא נשתתפו בו אם עירבו חצרות עם בתיהם אין מטלטלין בו אלא בארבע לא עירבו חצרות עם בתיהם מותר לטלטל בכולו א"ל רב חנינא חוזאה לרבא מפני מה כי עירבו עם בתיהם אין מטלטלין באותו מבוי אלא בארבע דניתקו חצרות ונעשו בתים כלומר כיון שעירבו נעשו בתי החצר והחצר רשות אחת ורב לטעמיה דאמר אין מבוי ניתר בלחי וקורה עד שיהו

מסורת הש"ס

א) פסחים לג., ב) עירובין כג: לה. עד. פט. צא., ג) [נדה ז:], ד) [לעיל ס:] ברכות ט. וש"נ, ה) [נדה נג:], ו) עירובין לא:, ז) עירובין ה. [ע"ש ל"ש] ושם עג:, ח) נ"ל שבוע, ט) סוף פרק ט דשביעית, י) [וע"ע תוספות נדה ז: ד"ה שמותי הוא], כ) פי' ר"ל לדבריו דס"ל דבתים [illegible]

הגהות הב"ח

(א) גמ' אחד גגות ואחד חצרות ואחד קרפיפות רשות אחת: (ב) שם שלא נשתתפו בו מותר: (ג) שם ולא אמרת לי דילמא כו' ומיבת הכי נמחק: (ד) תוס' ד"ה שלא וכו' דהא לקמן. נ"ב דף קלג ע"א: (ה) ד"ה ומי שרי וכו' שרי ר"א דרך רה"ר כיון: (ו) ד"ה דרבי אליעזר וכו' ואמר בגמרא רבי יהודה בן פזי: (ז) ד"ה ניתקו וכו' כיון שאין דבר מפסיק:

ליקוטי רש"י

שאין מביאין אותו. איזמל למילה. כך אין מביאין אותו וכו'. אף על גב דרשויות דרבנן ניינהו [פסחים צב.]. אחד גגות כו'. כולן רשות אחת לטלטל כלים ששבתו בגג זה לגג חבירו [illegible] ששבתו בתוך הבית. [illegible]

רשויות הן ואפילו דמד גברא [שם כג:]. חצר אע"ג דלא עירבו. ואוסרים בני הבתים זה על זה שאין יכולין להוציא מן הבתים לחצר בלא עירוב מפני שהבית רשות מיוחדת לו וחצר רשות חבירו מושל בה ונמצא מוציא מרשות לרשות ורבנן גזור שלא להוציא מרשות היחיד לרשות היחיד גזירה דילמא אתי לאפוקי מרשות היחיד לרשות הרבים אבל בחצר מותר לטלטל בה [שם יב:]. שמותי. לשון שמתא שהרי ברכוהו כדאמרינן בהזהב (ב"מ נט:) הלכך לא עבדינן כוותיה [נדה ז:]. הלכה כרבים. דאמרי רבים להטות כתיב (שמות כג) [ב"ק קטז.]. שיטפך. ריצתך [נדה נג:]. [מכאן שייך לדף קלא.] בתים וחצרות. בתים פתוחין לחצירות וחצירות למבוי שכן היה דרכן שאין בתים פתוחין אלא לחצריהן וכל חצר האמור בהש"ס ובמשנה אינו אלא לפני הבית אבל שאחורי הבית מוקצה או רחבה קרי ליה [עירובין ה.]. שתי חצירות פתוחות לתוכו ובית פתוח לכל חצר שכן היו דירותיהן לפני כל בית היה חצר [שם יב: ע"ש בתוס']. מה הבאה האמורה בעומר מכשירין דוחין את השבת. כדכתיב ביה וביום השביעי תשבות בחריש ובקציר תשבות בא ללמדך מה חריש אין לך חריש של מצוה ואפילו לזרוע לצורך עומר ושתי הלחם שהרי אם מצא חרוש אינו חורש ואני אוסרו לך בשבת אף קציר שאני אוסר לך בשל רשות אני אוסר לך יצא קציר העומר שהוא מצוה שאפילו מצא קצור מצוה לקצור ויש לך ללמוד מכאן שדוחה את השבת [ר"ה ט.]. מופני. צריך שתהא גזירה שוה זו משתי תיבות מופנין למדרש זה שלא יהו צריכין לגופן ומאחר שמופנין ללמוד גזירה שוה הוי ליה כמאן דכתיב דרשא בקרא בהדיא ואין משיבין עליה. דאי לאו מופני. אמרינן לגופן באו ולא ילפינן להא מילתא מינייהו [לעיל סד.].

from one end of the *mavoi* to the other![27] וְאָמַר לֵיהּ אִין – **And [R' Assi] said to [R' Zeira]** in reply: **Indeed,** so I hold. אָמַר לֵיהּ – Whereupon **[R' Zeira] said to [R' Assi]:** וְהָא זִימְנִין בְּעַאי מִינָּךְ – **But** there was **an occasion when I inquired of you** about this very matter, וְלֹא אָמַרְתְּ לִי הָכִי[28] – **and you did not answer me.** דִּילְמָא אַגַּב שִׁיטְפָךְ רְהִיט לָךְ גְּמָרָךְ – **Perhaps through the flow of your [learning] your tradition came running back to you?**[29] אָמַר לֵיהּ אִין – **[R' Assi] said to [R' Zeira]** in reply: **Indeed,** it is so. אַגַּב שִׁיטְפָא רְהִיטָא לִי גְּמָרִי – **Through the flow** of my learning **my tradition came running back to me.**

R' Zeira himself cites another opinion on this issue: אִיתְּמַר – **It was stated:** אָמַר רַבִּי זֵירָא אָמַר רַב – **R' Zeira said in the name of Rav:** מָבוֹי שֶׁלֹּא נִשְׁתַּתְּפוּ בּוֹ – In the case of **an alley in which [the courtyards] were not merged** via a *shituf,* אֵין מְטַלְטְלִין בּוֹ אֶלָּא בְּאַרְבַּע אַמּוֹת – **we may carry in it only within** a distance of **four** ***amos.***

The Gemara comments:

אָמַר אַבַּיֵי – **Abaye said:** הָא מִילְּתָא אֲמָרָהּ רַבִּי זֵירָא וְלֹא פֵּירְשָׁהּ – **R' Zeira stated this opinion, but he did not explain it** well.[30] עַד דְּאָתָא רַבָּה בַּר אֲבוּהָ וּפֵירְשָׁהּ – Indeed, we were unsure of its precise application **until Rabbah bar Avuha came and explained it,** דְּאָמַר רַב נַחְמָן אָמַר רַבָּה בַּר אֲבוּהָ אָמַר רַב – **for Rav Nachman said in the name of Rabbah bar Avuha,** who said it **in the name of Rav:** מָבוֹי שֶׁלֹּא נִשְׁתַּתְּפוּ בּוֹ – In the case of **an alley in which [the courtyards] were not merged** via a *shituf* – עֵירְבוּ חֲצֵירוֹת עִם בָּתִּים – if the **courtyards** of the alley **merged with** the **houses** of the courtyards,[31] אֵין מְטַלְטְלִין בּוֹ אֶלָּא בְּאַרְבַּע אַמּוֹת – **we may carry in [the alley] only within** a distance of **four** ***amos;***[32] לֹא עֵירְבוּ חֲצֵירוֹת עִם בָּתִּים – however, if the **courtyards did not merge with** the **houses** via *eruvei chatzeiros,*[33] מוּתָּר לְטַלְטֵל בְּכוּלּוֹ – one is **permitted to carry in [the alley's] entirety** any object that was located in the alley at the onset of *Shabbos.*[34]

The Gemara asks:

אָמַר לֵיהּ רַב חֲנִינָא חוֹזָאָה לְרַבָּה – **Rav Chanina Choza'ah said to Rabbah:** מַאי שְׁנָא כִּי עֵירְבוּ חֲצֵירוֹת עִם בָּתִּים – **Why is it different when** the **courtyards merged with** the **houses?**[35] דְּנִיתְּקוּ חֲצֵירוֹת וְנַעֲשׂוּ בָּתִּים – Presumably, **because** as a result of the *eruvei chatzeiros* the **courtyards have been removed** from their normative legal status **and transformed into houses.**[36] וְרַב לְטַעְמֵיהּ דְּאָמַר רַב – **And Rav,** who authored the ruling that it is forbidden to carry in a *mavoi,* **follows his own reasoning** in the matter, **for Rav said** elsewhere:[37] אֵין הַמָּבוֹי נִיתָּר בְּלֶחִי וְקוֹרָה – Carrying in **an alley is not rendered permissible by virtue of a sidepost or crossbeam**[38] עַד שֶׁיְּהוּ – **unless there are**

NOTES

27. [According to the opinion that the Gemara's question accorded only with the Rabbis who argued with R' Shimon (see note 16 above), one may ask: Perhaps R' Oshaya held like R' Shimon?! See *Leshon HaZahav* for an answer.]

28. In *Rashi's* text the word הָכִי does not appear, and so we have deleted it in the translation.

29. Perhaps in the flow of your reviewing Reish Lakish's statement you suddenly recalled R' Oshaya's explanation of how the knife was brought (*Rashi*). [Our elucidation follows *Rashi,* whose text reads אַגַּב שִׁיטְפָךְ אַתְיָא לָךְ; see *Rashash* for another explanation based on the textual version printed in our texts of the Gemara.]

30. He did not explain if carrying four *amos* or more in the *mavoi* is prohibited in all cases (see *Rashi*).

31. I.e. if the residents of the courtyards prepared *eruvei chatzeiros* to enable themselves to carry from their houses into their own courtyards, and from courtyard to adjoining courtyard, even though they failed to prepare a *shitufei mevo'os* to permit carrying between the various courtyards and the *mavoi* (*Rashi*).

32. This stringency applies even to objects that were located in the *mavoi* at the onset of *Shabbos* (*Rashi*).

33. So that the residents are forbidden to carry from their houses even into their own courtyards (*Rashi*).

34. The Gemara below will explain the reason for these different rulings.

35. Rav Chanina Choza'ah asks rhetorically why in that case one may not carry four *amos* or more.

36. I.e. the courtyards have, in the legal sense, been subsumed by the houses, and are no longer considered courtyards (*Rashi*).

37. *Eruvin* 73b; see also ibid. 5a.

38. Above (note 15), we noted that the Rabbis prohibited carrying in a *mavoi* unless an adjustment is made at its open end. Rav here mentions the two prescribed adjustments (either of which is effective): (a) a *lechi* (sidepost), which is placed at the side of the entrance to the *mavoi.* The *lechi* must be at least ten *tefachim* high, but may be of any width or thickness; (b) a *korah* (crossbeam), which is placed atop the entrance to the *mavoi.* The *korah* must be at least a *tefach* wide, and must reach from one side of the *mavoi* to the other.

בָּתִּים וַחֲצֵרוֹת פְּתוּחִין לְתוֹכוֹ – **houses and courtyards opening into [the alley].**[1] וְהָכָא בָּתִּים אִיכָּא חֲצֵרוֹת לֵיכָּא – **And here,** where the courtyards have been nullified vis-a-vis the houses by the *eruvei chatzeiros,* **there are houses** opening into the alley but **there are no courtyards.** Hence, a mere sidepost or crossbeam placed at the *mavoi's* open end does not constitute a proper partition, and so it is prohibited to carry more than four *amos* in the *mavoi.*

Rav Chanina Choza'ah now articulates his challenge:

כִּי לֹא עֵירְבוּ נַמִּי – According to this explanation, in the case **where [the courtyards] did not merge** with the houses **as well,** לֶיחֱזִינְהוּ לְהָנֵי בָּתִּים כְּמַאן דִּסְתִימֵי דָּמוּ – **let us perceive these houses as if they were sealed** vis-a-vis the *mavoi,*[2] וַחֲצֵרוֹת אִיכָּא וּבָתִּים לֵיכָּא – **and** so **there are courtyards** opening into the *mavoi* **but there are no houses.** Why, then, did Rav rule that here one *may* carry in the *mavoi's* entirety?

The Gemara responds:

אֶפְשָׁר דִּמְבַטְּלֵי לֵיהּ רְשׁוּתָא דְּכוּלְּהוּ לְגַבֵּי חַד – **It is possible for [the owners]** of the houses in each courtyard **to renounce their rights** in the courtyard **in favor of one** of the houses in that courtyard.[3]

The Gemara rejects this answer:

סוֹף סוֹף בַּיִת אִיכָּא בָּתִּים לֵיכָּא – **In the final analysis,** with such an arrangement **there is** indeed one **house** per courtyard opening into the *mavoi,* but **there is not** the required multiple **houses.** Rav requires that each of the (minimum two) courtyards opening into the *mavoi* contains at least two houses. – ? –

The Gemara again attempts to deflect Rav Chanina Choza'ah's challenge:

אֶפְשָׁר דְּמִצַּפְרָא וְעַד פַּלְגָא דְיוֹמָא לְגַבֵּי חַד – **It is possible that from** Shabbos **morning until midday** the owners of each house in each courtyard can renounce their rights in their courtyard **in favor of one** house, מִפַּלְגֵיהּ דְּיוֹמָא וּלְפַנְיָא לְגַבֵּי חַד – and **from midday to evening** renounce them **in favor of one** other house.[4] In that way each courtyard will contain two houses, and both of them will "open into the *mavoi.*"

The Gemara rejects this solution as well:

סוֹף סוֹף בְּעִידְּנָא דְּאִיתֵיהּ לְהַאי לֵיתֵיהּ לְהַאי – **In the final analysis, at the time this** residence **is** the legal "house" of the courtyard, **this** other residence **is not.** Hence, at any given moment the courtyard lacks the requisite two houses.

The Gemara explains the reasoning of Rav's ruling differently:

אֶלָּא אָמַר רַב אַשִׁי – **Rather, Rav Ashi said:**[5] מִי גָּרַם לַחֲצֵרוֹת שֶׁיֵּאָסְרוּ – **What caused the courtyards to be prohibited** with regard to carrying into the *mavoi?*[6] בָּתִּים – The **houses!**[7] וְלֵיכָּא – **And** here, where *eruvei chatzeiros* were not prepared, **[the houses] are not** a factor, and so Rav permits carrying in the *mavoi's* entirety.[8]

The Gemara returns to the subject of the Mishnah, and expands upon R' Eliezer's opinion:

אָמַר רַבִּי חִיָּיא בַּר אַבָּא אָמַר רַבִּי יוֹחָנָן – **R' Chiya bar Abba said in the name of R' Yochanan:** לֹא לְכֹל אָמַר רַבִּי אֱלִיעֶזֶר מַכְשִׁירֵי מִצְוָה דּוֹחִין אֶת הַשַּׁבָּת – **Not for all** commandments **did R' Eliezer**

NOTES

1. In order to qualify as a *mavoi,* the alley must serve as a passageway to and from the *reshus harabim* for residents of at least two inner courtyards containing at least two houses each (*Rashi*). Otherwise, the alley would have the status of a courtyard, which cannot be adjusted with a *lechi* or *korah,* but needs a more substantial adjustment at its fourth, open end (see *Eruvin* 12b and *Orach Chaim* 363:2,3).

2. Since *eruvei chatzeiros* were not prepared, carrying from the houses into the courtyards is prohibited. Hence, the courtyards effectively intervene between the houses and the *mavoi,* in which case it cannot be said that houses as well "open into the *mavoi*" (*Rashi;* see *Tosafos* above, 130b ד״ה ניתקו).

3. [Where no *eruvei chatzeiros* were made, the Sages sanctioned what is known as בִּטּוּל רְשׁוּת – the *renunciation of* one's *rights* in his domain. That is, since the Rabbinic prohibition against carrying from house to courtyard derives from the fact that each house is a private domain and the courtyard resembles a public domain (being jointly owned by the home owners), the Sages further declared that if these owners "renounce" their "ownership" in the courtyard (which they are permitted to do even on the Sabbath), the courtyard now "belongs" to only one person. He is then allowed to carry from his house to the courtyard (see *Eruvin* ch. 6 for all the details and ramifications of this law).

Hence, even without an *eruv chatzeiros,* the "renouncing of rights" is a completely proper and legal way to permit carrying from house to courtyard on the Sabbath.] Accordingly, in such a case, the entire courtyard would "belong" to that house, and so carrying from the house into the courtyard would be permitted even without an *eruv.* Hence, it could be said that both house and courtyard "open into the *mavoi*" (*Rashi;* see *Tosafos* ibid. for why this remedy does not resurrect the problem of the houses subsuming the courtyard).

4. For Rav is the sage who holds (in *Eruvin* 68b) that one resident of a courtyard (where no *eruv* was prepared) may relinquish his rights in the courtyard to a fellow resident, who in turn may relinquish those rights back to the first – all on the same Shabbos (*Tosafos*).

5. The Gemara will now abandon its previous explanation – that Rav's ruling derives from his requiring that both houses and courtyards open into the *mavoi* before a sidepost or crossbeam constitutes a legal closure for the *mavoi's* fourth side. Rather, as long as there physically exist two courtyards and two houses, the requirement is met – and the legalisms of the permissibility of carrying have no impact. Rather, the Gemara will now explain that Rav is being consistent with his ruling in *Eruvin* 74a (see, however, *Shabbos Shel Mi*), where the Gemara cites R' Shimon's ruling that "roofs, *karpafs* and courtyards are all (considered) one domain for articles resting in them at the onset of Shabbos, but not for articles resting in the house (at that time)." Apropos of this, Rav stated that the halachah follows R' Shimon, but only if the residents of each courtyard did *not* prepare an *eruvei chatzeiros.* For since the residents would then be forbidden to carry from their houses to their courtyard, it is unlikely that articles that rested in the houses at the onset of Shabbos would ultimately be transferred to another courtyard, since generally they would not be present in the first courtyard. However, where *eruvei chatzeiros* were made, so that household articles would be found in the courtyard, the Rabbis forbade carrying from courtyard to *mavoi,* lest one carry a household article there. In such a case, a *shituf mevo'os* (which merges all the courtyards) is needed to permit carrying from courtyard to *mavoi.* It is on this basis that we can understand Rav's ruling.

6. I.e. what creates the need for a *shitufei mevo'os* to allow carrying from the courtyards into the *mavoi* (according to Rav)? (*Rashi*).

7. Without the houses, the courtyards and *mavoi* would be considered a single domain (as per R' Shimon), and carrying from one area to the other would be permitted (*Rashi*).

8. [Rav permits carrying within a *mavoi* that lacks a *shituf* if there are no *eruvei chatzeiros* between the house and courtyards, and forbids carrying there if *eruvei chatzeiros* were made.] Now, failure to prepare *eruvei chatzeiros* is legally tantamount to preparing a *shitufei mevo'os when we determine the mavoi's legal status,* for since it is now permitted to carry from *mavoi* to courtyard (see note 5 above), the *mavoi* and courtyard are seen as one combined domain. Carrying from the courtyards to the *mavoi,* then, is permitted as if a *shituf* were actually prepared, for the *mavoi* and courtyard are now seen as one domain. Thus, one may carry throughout the entirety of the *mavoi* [since the *mavoi* and courtyard are as one and one may carry in the courtyard], also as if a *shituf* were prepared (see *Rashi;* see also *Maharam Schiff*). However, where *eruvei chatzeiros* were made, so that according to Rav it is forbidden to carry from courtyard to *mavoi,* the houses and courtyard form one domain, while the *shituf*-lacking *mavoi* constitutes a different domain – one where the Sages forbade carrying four *amos* (see *Ritva MHK* ed. and *Sfas Emes* for further elaboration. See *Chidushei HaRan* for a different explanation of the Gemara).

[*Tosafos* state that the final ruling would be that even where *eruvei chatzeiros* were prepared, carrying is permitted in the *mavoi's* entirety,

ֿ בתים וחצרות פתוחין לתוכו והכא בתים איכא חצרות ליכא כי לא עירבו נמי ליחזינהו להני בתים כמאן דסתימי דמו וחצרות איכא ובתים ליכא אפשר דמבטלי ליה רשותא דכולהו לגבי חד סוף סוף בית איכא בתים ליכא אפשר דמצפרא ועד פלגא דיומא לגבי חד מפלגיה דיומא ולפניא לגבי חד סוף סוף בעידנא דאיתיה להאי ליתיה להאי אלא אמר רב אשי מי גרם לחצרות שיאסרו בתים וליכא אמר ר' חייא בר אבא א"ר יוחנן • לא לכל אמר ר' אליעזר מכשירי מצוה דוחין את השבת שהרי שתי הלחם חובת היום הן ולא למדן ר"א אלא מגזירה שוה דתניא ר' אליעזר אומר מניין למכשירי שתי הלחם שדוחין את השבת נאמרה הבאה בעומר ונאמרה הבאה בשתי הלחם מה הבאה האמורה בעומר מכשירין דוחין את השבת אף הבאה האמורה בשתי הלחם מכשירין דוחין את השבת מופני דאי לא מופני איכא למיפרך מה לעומר שכן אם מצא קצור קוצר תאמר בשתי הלחם שאם מצא קצור אינו קוצר לאי אפנויי מופני מכדי כתיב א) והבאתם את עומר ראשית קצירכם אל הכהן ב) ביום הביאכם למה לי ש"מ לאפנויי ואכתי מופנה מצד אחד הוא ושמעינן ליה לר' אליעזר ג) דאמר מופנה מצד אחד למידין ומשיבין ג) תביאו רבויא הוא למעוטי מאי אילימא למעוטי לולב ד) והתניא לולב וכל מכשיריו דוחין את השבת דברי ר"א ואלא למעוטי סוכה והתניא סוכה וכל מכשיריה דוחין את השבת דברי ר"א ואלא למעוטי מצה והתניא מצה וכל מכשיריה דוחין את השבת דברי רבי אליעזר ואלא למעוטי שופר והתניא שופר וכל מכשיריו דוחין את השבת דברי ר"א אמר רב אדא בר אהבה למעוטי ציצית לטליתו ומזוזה לפתחו תניא נמי הכי ושוין שאם צייץ טליתו ועשה מזוזה לפתחו שהוא חייב מאי טעמא אמר רב יוסף לפי שאין קבוע להם זמן אמר ליה אביי אדרבה מדאין קבוע להם זמן כל

בתים וחצרות. שני בתים פתוחים לשתי חצרות שתים לכל חצר ושתי חצרות פתוחות למבוי: **כמאן דסתימי דמי.** דהא לגבי מבוי כמאן דסתימי הוו דהא חצרות מפסיקות בינתים שאין הבתים מוליכין להם: **אפשר דמבטלי.** בני הבתים שבחצר רשות שיש להם בחצר לגבי חד מינייהו והוי כל החצר שלו ומותר להוציא מביתו לחצר: **סוף סוף בית איכא.** בכל חצר בתים ליכא ורב בעי שני בתים לכל חצר: **אלא אמר רב אשי.** טעמא לאו משום בתים וחצרות פתוחות לתוכו הוא דרב בין עירבו בין לא עירבו מכיון דפתוחי שתי חצרות למבוי ושני בתים לכל חצר תורת מבוי עליו וניתר בלחי וקורה והיינו טעמא דכי עירבו בחצרות ולא נשתתפו במבוי אסור לטלטל בו וכי לא עירבו שרי: **מי גרם לחצירות שיאסרו.** על המבוי להצריכו שיתוף להוציא מן החצירות לתוכו: **בתים.** הוא דגרמי לו דאי לאו משום בתים הוו להו חצרות ומבוי רשות אחת דרב דאמרה להא מלתא כר"ש סבירא ליה דאמר בעירובין (דף עד.) גג וחצר וקרפף ומבוי כולן רשות אחת הן ומטלטלין מזה לזה ואמר רב עלה הלכה כר' שמעון והוא שלא עירבו בתים עם החצרות דלא שכיחי מאני דבתים בחצר הלכך לענין טלטול בתוכו נמי כי לא עירבו חצרות עם הבתים שרי דהוו להו כמו שנשתתפו בו דמי גרם לו למבוי ליאסר ולהצטרך לשיתוף בתים גרמו לו ולאים שהרי נסתלקו ממנו ומותר להוציא מן החצרות למבוי כאילו נשתתפו וכשנשתתפו לא מספקא לן דמותר לטלטל בכולן: **לא לכל אמר רבי אליעזר.** לא בכל מכשירי מצוה אמר כן ולקמן מפרש הי מכשירי מצוה אתא למעוטי: **שתי הלחם.** דעצרת חובת יום הן ואין לאחרן עד למחר: **ולא למדן רבי אליעזר.** דלפיכך תדחה שבת אלא בגזירה שוה ואי בכל מכשירי מצוה שעיקר המצוה נוהגת בשבת אמר מכשיריה כמותה למה לי גזירה שוה: **מה הבאה האמורה בעומר מכשיריה.** דהיינו קצירה טחינה והרקדה שלא דוחין את השבת כדאמרינן במנחות (דף עב.) בחריש ובקציר תשבות מה חריש רשות אף קציר רשות יצא קצירת העומר שהיא מצוה: **שכן (א) מצא קצור.** שלא לשם עומר מצוה לקצור לשמה דכתיב וקצרתם והבאתם הלכך קצירה גופה מצוה היא תאמר בשתי הלחם שלא נאמר בהן קצירה: **לאו.** באמת: **מצד אחד.** הבאה דעומר מופנה הבאה דשתי הלחם אינה מופנה דלצריכה לגופה: **ושמעינן ליה לרבי אליעזר דאמר.** גזירה שוה שאינה מופנה משני לדדיה אלא מצד אחד למדין ממנה אם אין להשיב אבל אם יש להשיב משיבין ובמסכת יבמות בפרק מצות חליצה ה) שמעינן ליה דאמר הכי דקתני חליצה בשמאל פסולה ורבי אליעזר מכשיר דלא יליף רגל רגל ממצורע והא תניא ר"א אומר מניין לרציעה שהיא באזן ימנית נאמר כאן אוזן ונאמר להלן אוזן וכו' ומשנינן אזן אזן מופנה רגל רגל לא מופנה והאי לאו מופנה דקאמרינן משני לדדין קאמר דרגל דכתיב בחליצה איצטריכא לגופה אבל מצד אחד מופנה הוא דפרשת מצורע • מופנה הוא ההיא לעני דכולהו כתיבן במצורע עשיר: **תביאו ריבויא הוא.** דהא והקרבתם מנחה חדשה סמיך ומאי למיכתב ממושבותיכם לחם תנופה ותביאו יתירה הוא: **למעוטי מאי.** הא דאמר רבי יוחנן לעיל לא לכל אמר רבי אליעזר למעוטי הי מכשירים אתי דלא דחי שבת: **וכל מכשיריו.** כגון לקוצצו מן המחובר ולאוגדו: **למעוטי ציצית.** שלא יתלנה בטליתו בשבת כדמפרש טעמא ולקמיה: כל

אפשר דמבטלי רשות כו'. וא"ת כי עירבו חצרות נמי עם בתים מלינן למימר שיש חצר למבוי כגון שביטלו אותו של חצר זה לרשות דכולהו שיש להם במבוי לבני חצר אחרת ויכולין לטלטל מן החצר למבוי הא לא בעי לאקשויי • דליכא למ"ד בעירובין (דף סו:) אין ביטול רשות מחצר לחצר ועוד דבלאו הכי פריך שפיר: **מפלגא** דיומא לפניא. רב לטעמיה דאמר במסכת עירובין (דף סח:) מבטלין וחוזרין ומבטלין: **מי** גרם לחצירות. אנן קי"ל דאפילו עירבו חצרות עם בתים מותר לטלטל (ג) דהא רב דאמר בעירובין לטעמיה דפסיק כרבי שמעון דוקא בלא עירבו אבל רבי יוחנן פסיק כר"ש בין עירבו בין לא עירבו וכר' יוחנן קי"ל: **לא** לכל אמר רבי אליעזר מכשירי מצוה דוחין את השבת. לקמן מפרש דאתא למעוטי ציצית ומזוזה וה"פ לא (ג) כל מצות הנוהגות בשבת אמר ר' אליעזר שמכשירין ידחו שבת שהרי שתי הלחם כו' ומשמע דלכאורה דאי לא דאשכחן דמצריך ר' אליעזר ג"ש הוה גמרינן לציצית ומזוזה ממילה וניימא דמכשיריה ידחו שבת ותימה הוא היכי שייך למילף ציצית ומזוזה ממילה דמילה דין הוא דמכשיריה דוחין שבת דהיא עצמה דוחה שבת אבל ציצית ומזוזה אין במלותן דחיית שבת:

תאמר בשתי הלחם שאם מצא קצור אינו קוצר. תימה מאי קא פריך דהיא גופא נילף מינה מה העומר שאף על פי שמצא קצור קוצר אף שתי הלחם אם מצא קצור קוצר ונילף מינה תרתי מכשירין וקצירה ומיהו ר"ם דהא לא דמי דנילף מינה קצירה שהרי בעצרת יהיו כל החיטין והשעורין קצורים ולא משמע דצריך ג"ש אלא (ד) מכשירין דדמו שבת ומ"מ י"ל דהא לא מצי למימר נילף קצירה דמהיכא נפקא לן קצירת העומר דדחיא שבת מדכתיב בחריש ובקציר תשבות כדדרשינן במנחות בשילהי ר' ישמעאל (דף עב.) מה חריש רשות אף קציר רשות יצא קצירת העומר שהיא מצוה וגלי רחמנא דליכא למילף אלא לגבי העומר דכתיב ביה נמי קציר ולא לגבי שתי הלחם דלא כתיב בהו קציר ועל כרחך ודאי היינו טעמא דיליף גבי עומר קצירה משום דכתיב ביה קציר דלאו הכי מ"מ

דיליף טפי גבי עומר מגבי שתי הלחם דהכא נמי מימה ילא קצירת שתי הלחם שהיא מצוה: **ושוין** שאם צייץ טליתו כו' מ"מ כו'. תימה מה צריך טעם לזה אלא משום דלא אשכחן דלריבינו קרא לכל איכך מלרכינן קרא לקמן דלא גמרי מהדדי ומיהו יש לומר דאיכא למילף ציצית ומזוזה מסוכה דמאי פרכת שכן נוהגת בלילות כבימים מזוזה נמי נוהג בלילות כבימים וכן ציצית לרבנן דפליגי עליה דרבי שמעון בפרק התכלת (מנחות דף מג.) דלא דרשי וראיתם אותו פרט לכסות לילה אלא • פרט לכסות סומא ולהאי טעמא דפרישית דמסוכה יליף לריך לומר דליכא (ה) אם עבר זמנה בטלה דאי לאו הכי איכא למפרך מה לסוכה שכן אם עבר זמנה בטלה דמסתבר דמילה אם עבר זמנה לא בטלה שאותה מילה עצמה שהוה מחייב בשמיני הוא עושה בתשיעי שאם מל בשמיני לא היה מחוי ומל בתשיעי אבל (ו) סוכה ציצית ומזוזה בכל יומא מחייב בהן ואפילו קיימם היום חייב לקיימם למחר הלכך כשעבר היום ולא עשאם מצות היום לא יקיים עוד לעולם ולא תאמר ומסוכה היכי מצי למילף וכן כל הני דלקמן דפריך ניכתוב רחמנא בהאי ומיתי הנך וניגמרו מיניה אלדרבה נגמר מכיפוד אל ולא ומבנין בית המקדש דלא דמו שבת כלאיתא

ירוטין ה. יב: עג: [ל"ט], ג) [נ"ל מיום], ג) יבמות ע:, ה) סוכה מג., ו) [דף קב.].

הגהות הב"ח

(א) רש"י ד"ה שכן אם מצא: (ב) תוס' ד"ה מי גרם וכו' מותר לטלטל בכולי דהא רב: (ג) ד"ה לא לכל וכו' וה"פ לא לכל מצות: (ד) ד"ה תאמר וכו' אלא למכשירין: (ה) ד"ה ושוין וכו' דליכא ומזוזה אם עבר: (ו) באד"ה אבל ליכא ומזוזה כל"ל ותיבת סוכה נמחק:

גליון הש"ס

גמרא לא לכל אר"א מכשירי מצוה. עי' בס' בני חיי בסוף הספר בלקוטי: רש"י ד"ה ושמעי' ליה לר"א וכו' מופנה הוא ההיא דעני. עי' כתב"י יבמות דף ע ע"ב ד"ה ושמעי' לי' לר"א וע"ש: תוס' ד"ה אפשר וכו' דאיכא למ"ד בעירובין. עי' עירובין דף ע ע"ב תוס' ד"ה אלא פשיטא: תוס' ד"ה ושוין וכו' אלא פרט לכסות סומא. וכ"כ רש"י סוכה יא ע"א ד"ה לפרומה. ועיין בשער המלך פ"ג מהל' ציצית:

תורה אור השלם

א) דַּבֵּר אֶל בְּנֵי יִשְׂרָאֵל וְאָמַרְתָּ אֲלֵהֶם כִּי תָבֹאוּ אֶל הָאָרֶץ אֲשֶׁר אֲנִי נֹתֵן לָכֶם וּקְצַרְתֶּם אֶת קְצִירָהּ וַהֲבֵאתֶם אֶת עֹמֶר רֵאשִׁית קְצִירְכֶם אֶל הַכֹּהֵן: [ויקרא כג, י]

ב) וּסְפַרְתֶּם לָכֶם מִמָּחֳרַת הַשַּׁבָּת מִיּוֹם הֲבִיאֲכֶם אֶת עֹמֶר הַתְּנוּפָה שֶׁבַע שַׁבָּתוֹת תְּמִימֹת תִּהְיֶינָה: [ויקרא כג, טו]

ג) מִמּוֹשְׁבֹתֵיכֶם תָּבִיאוּ לֶחֶם תְּנוּפָה שְׁתַּיִם שְׁנֵי עֶשְׂרֹנִים סֹלֶת תִּהְיֶינָה חָמֵץ תֵּאָפֶינָה בִּכּוּרִים לַיהוָה: [ויקרא כג, יז]

ליקוטי רש"י

ושמעינן ליה לר' אליעזר דאמר מופנה מצד אחד למידין ומשיבין. בפרק מצות חליצה (יבמות קד.) שמעינן לרבי אליעזר דאמר מופנה מצד אחד למדין ומשיבין גבי חליצה בשמאל פסולה ור' אליעזר מכשיר ואמרינן מ"ט דר"א לא יליף רגל רגל ממצורע דכתיב ביה ימנית וקרא דהאי הלכתא דכתיב בה בהאי כתיב רגל כרגל ימנית ולא הוי גמי למיבעי ולמכתבינהו דכתיב וכמחין בפ"ק (י.) מופנה הוא לגמרינהו דהוה רגל רגל דליכא לאפנויי ר' אליעזר כסבירא ליה בשמאל לגמר מיניה ואם לאו כדיליף מנתבר ובכלל אוזן אוזן לפתחו נמי דלא נחיה ולא יליף רגל רגל מופנה דלא מופנה אלא מצד אחד משמע דר"א לא יליף רגל רגל ואפ"ה לא ממצורע ובדבור ליה ושמע מינה מופנה מצד אחד למידין ומשיבין.

בתים וחצרות פתוחין לתוכו והכא כיון שערבו כאלו אין שם חצר וכולן (בתים) [חצרות] נינהו ואפי' נשתתפו כיון שאין שם בתים אין שיתוף מועיל באותו מבוי. כך יש לומר כי לא עירבו נמי כיון שהן אסורין להוציא מן הבית לחצר חשוב אותן הבתים כאלו סתומין הן שאין להן רשות להשתמש מן הבתים לחצר וחצר איכא בית ליכא. לטעמיה דרב היאך מטלטלין במבוי שאין לו בית ומפרק יתכן שיבטלו כל בני החצר רשותם לגבי חד וכיון שמבטלין רשותם לגביה יש לו להוציא מן הבית לחצר כדתנן נתנו לו רשותן הוא מותר והם אסורים וקיי"ל הא דתנן נתנו לו רשותם רשות מעיקרא מקודם א) שיבטל הויא רשותא לגבייהו ואקשינן וכיון שבטלו כל בני חצר רשותם לגבי חד נעשו כל הבתים שלו וכולן כבית אחד הן חשובין ורב לא אמר אלא בתים ומיעוטי בתי' שנים והכא ליכא שני בתים והיאך מתיר רב. ופרקי' עוד כגון שבני חצר בטלו רשותן מן הבקר עד חצי היום לגבי ראובן בפירוש ומחצי היום ולהלן לגבי שמעון שנמצאו ראובן ושמעון שניהם מותרין בחצר זו הא דהוא שמעינן לרב דאמר מבטלין וחוזרין ומבטלין ואקשינן תוב סוף סוף בעת שמותר לזה להשתמש בחצר זה אסור לחבירו ואותה העת אין שם בחצר אלא בית ראובן בלבד ומחצי היום ולהלן בית שמעון לבדו ואין לראובן בה רשות להשתמש. ומ"מ לא תמצא ב' בתים מותרין בחצר זו בעת אחת. ופירק רב אשי פירוק אחר ואמר מי גרם לחצרות הללו הפתוחות למבוי להיאסר הן מלטלטל בהן בתים מפני אלו הבתים שהן פתוחין לתוכן ולא עירבו אבל אלו היו בהן בתים מותרין היו השותפים שם לטלטל בה בכולה. שהן כמו קרפף שמותר השותבת בו לטלטל בכולן וגם המבוי לא נאסר בהן טלטול אי לא מפני הבתים שהן פתוחים לתוכה ואינם. כלומר כיון שלא עירבו חשובים כאלו סתומים הם ואינם כלל. הלא אילו היו סתומין היה הטלטול מותר בהם עכשיו יהיה מותר ועמדו דברי רב אשי ועיקר דברי רב ופירושם בעירובין פרק הדר עם הנכרי בחצר ופירשנום שם. ושמעינן מינה דרבנן פליגי עלי' ר' שמעון דשרי דרך גגות חצירות דרך קרפיפות ואע"ג דאמר רב הלכתא כר' שמעון בפרק כל גגות העיר רשות אחת הן לגבי

חשק שלמה על רבינו חננאל

א) נראה דל"ל דקיי"ל כר"י בעירובין סט ע"ב דמטמן רשות משמשתן:

רב נסים גאון

ואכתי מופנה מצד א' הוא ושמעי' ליה לר' אליעזר דאמר מופנה מצד אחד למידין ומשיבין. דע שאע"פ

שלא מצאנו לר' אליעזר בפירוש שאמר דבר זה ידועים אנחנו אותו מדבריהם במס' נדה בפרק המפלת (דף כב) מופנה מצד אחד לר' ישמעאל למידין ואין משיבין לרבנן למידין ומשיבין והואיל ור' אליעזר א) עומר כר' ישמעאל כי אנו מוצאין ר' יהושע חבירו של ר' אליעזר אומר (ע"ז דף כט ע"ב) ישמעאל אחי ועם זה לא נחלק בחלוקה בזה הדבר אלא ר' ישמעאל והשאר שוו כלם בדבר אחד כי מופנה מצד אחד למדין ומשיבין ידענו כי ר' אליעזר בכלל החכמים ששוו עומד וסובר כמותן שאילו היה חולק עליהן בדבר זה היה נזכר עם ר' ישמעאל וכיון שלא הזכירה החלוקה אלא ברי' ישמעאל בלבד נתברר כי ר' אליעזר אינו שוה לו וכרבנן סבירא ליה ומיכן אמרנו ושמעינן ליה לר' אליעזר דאמר מופנה מצד אחד למדין ומשיבין לפי שכל החכמים שהיו באותו הדור שוו בדבר זה חוץ מר' ישמעאל שהוזכר בפירוש שהוא חולק: איצטריך

ממצורע והכא מנין לרציעה שהיא באוזן ימנית כו' ומשנינן אוזן אוזן מופנה רגל רגל לא מופנה לאו מופנה מצד אחד דלגבי מצורע מופנה הוא כדאמר ולא מופנה לגמרי אבל רגל דחליצה לא מופנה כלל אלא לגופו [עי' בגה"ש כאן ושם]. לולב וכל מכשיריו. כלומר מקוציה ואפילו לקוצצו מן המחובר ולאוגדו [סוכה מג.]

חשק שלמה על רב נסים גאון א) אין הלשון מדויק. ולמנם כוונתו שהרי ר"א היה מרבה ר' יהושע ואם היה לבו לדבר כמותו היה להזכירו עם ר"י. ועי' בחשק"ש כאן בד"ה ושמעינן. ובילקוט מ"ט ע"ב לא הוסיף ול"ע:

say that the **preliminaries of a commandment override the Sabbath** labor restrictions,[9] שֶׁהֲרֵי שְׁתֵּי הַלֶּחֶם חוֹבַת הַיּוֹם הֵן – **for the Two Loaves** of leavened bread offered on Shavuos[10] **are an obligation of** that holy **day** itself, and may not be postponed to the morrow, וְלֹא לְמָדָן רַבִּי אֱלִיעֶזֶר אֶלָּא מִגְּזֵירָה שָׁוָה – **and yet R' Eliezer derived [their law]**[11] **only from a *gezeirah shavah*** derivation,[12] דְּתַנְיָא – **as was taught in a Baraisa:** רַבִּי אֱלִיעֶזֶר אוֹמֵר – **R' ELIEZER SAYS:** מִנַּיִין לְמַכְשִׁירֵי שְׁתֵּי הַלֶּחֶם שֶׁדּוֹחִין אֶת הַשַּׁבָּת – **FROM WHERE** do we know that **THE PRELIMINARIES** to the mitzvah of offering the **TWO LOAVES OVERRIDE THE SABBATH** labor restrictions? From the following *gezeirah shavah* interpretation: נֶאֶמְרָה הֲבָאָה בָּעוֹמֶר – A form of the word **"BRINGING" IS STATED IN CONNECTION WITH THE *OMER*** offering,[13] וְנֶאֶמְרָה הֲבָאָה בִּשְׁתֵּי הַלֶּחֶם – **AND** a form of the word **"BRINGING" IS STATED IN CONNECTION WITH THE TWO LOAVES** offering.[14] מַה הֲבָאָה הָאֲמוּרָה בָּעוֹמֶר – **JUST AS** in the **"BRINGING" STATED IN CONNECTION WITH THE *OMER*** מַכְשִׁירִין דּוֹחִין אֶת הַשַּׁבָּת – the **PRELIMINARIES**[15] **OVERRIDE THE SABBATH** *melachah* restrictions,[16] אַף הֲבָאָה הָאֲמוּרָה בִּשְׁתֵּי הַלֶּחֶם – **SO TOO** in the **"BRINGING" STATED IN CONNECTION WITH THE TWO LOAVES** מַכְשִׁירִין דּוֹחִין אֶת הַשַּׁבָּת – the **PRELIMINARIES OVERRIDE THE SABBATH** restrictions.

The Gemara comments:

דְּאִי לֹא מוּפְנֵי אִיכָּא מוּפְנֵי – This *gezeirah shavah* must be **free,**[17] לְמִיפְרַךְ – **for if it were not free, there are** the following grounds **to refute** it: מַה לָעוֹמֶר שֶׁכֵּן אִם מָצָא קָצוּר קוֹצֵר – **Whereas the *Omer*** is special, **for indeed if he**[18] **found** barley already **cut,**[19] **he must cut** other stalks specifically for the sake of the mitzvah,[20] תֹּאמַר בִּשְׁתֵּי הַלֶּחֶם – **can you say** the same **of the Two Loaves** offering, שֶׁאִם מָצָא קָצוּר אֵינוֹ קוֹצֵר – **where if he found** the grain already **cut he need not cut** other stalks?![21]

The Gemara confirms this assessment:

לָאֵי אַפְנוּיֵי מוּפְנֵי – **Indeed! [The Biblical passage] is** redundant and thus **completely free** for this derivation, מִכְּדִי כְּתִיב – for **since it is written** previously in the passage that deals with the *Omer* itself,[22] ,,וַהֲבֵאתֶם אֶת־עֹמֶר רֵאשִׁית קְצִירְכֶם אֶל־הַכֹּהֵן'' – ***You shall bring an Omer from your first harvest to the Kohen,*** ,,מִיּוֹם הֲבִיאֲכֶם'' לָמָּה לִי – **why** do **I** need the phrase, ***from the day of your bringing** the Omer,* at the

NOTES

for we rule like R' Yochanan (in Tractate *Eruvin*), who holds that the halachah accords with R' Shimon in *all* cases. Thus, one is *always* permitted to carry from courtyard to *mavoi,* making them one legal domain – which allows carrying throughout the *mavoi* (even without a *shituf*) just as carrying within and through a courtyard is permitted. See also *Tos. HaRosh.*

One final point: According to *Rashi,* it seems that Rav disputes the previous Gemara's reasoning (that of R' Zeira and R' Oshaya), which permits carrying four *amos* in a *mavoi* under *all* circumstances. Rav would permit it only where it is permitted to carry between a *mavoi* and a courtyard [i.e. when they are considered one domain]. See *Netziv.*

9. *Tosafos* explain R' Chiya to mean that the law that preliminaries (involving *melachos*) of mitzvos performed on Shabbos override the Shabbos restrictions does not apply to all mitzvos. While the preliminaries of *most* mitzvos do (even though the mitzvah itself is not a *melachah* and thus need not override; see *Tos. HaRosh* and *Maharam* on *Tosafos*), R' Chiya comes to exclude *some* mitzvos – i.e. those lacking a Scriptural basis for overriding. R' Chiya will proceed to prove this statement, and below the Gemara will reveal which commandments are actually excluded from R' Eliezer's leniency.

10. See *Leviticus* 23:17.

11. The law that a preliminary action for the offering of the Two Loaves – e.g. baking them – may also be performed on the Sabbath (*Rashi*).

12. [A *gezeirah shavah* is one of the thirteen methods of Biblical exegesis propounded by R' Yishmael in the introduction to *Sifra.* The rule states that two similar words that appear in two different places in the Torah are so written in order to infer from one to the other (either to clarify an explicit law of the Torah, or to derive a new law). *Rashi* to *Succah* (11b ד"ה לא ילפינן) writes that a sage was not authorized to innovate a *gezeirah shavah;* rather, he could use one only if it was a tradition received from his teacher.] Now, if R' Eliezer held generally that *all* preliminaries override the *melachah* restrictions, why did he have to rely on a *gezeirah shavah* to establish that law in the case of the Two Loaves? Rather, we see from that case that R' Eliezer's leniency is not universally applied (*Rashi*).

13. מִיּוֹם הֲבִיאֲכֶם אֶת־עֹמֶר הַתְּנוּפָה – *From the day of your bringing the Omer of the waving* (*Leviticus* 23:15). The *Omer* offering consists of barley flour, and is brought on the 16th of Nissan.

14. תָּבִיאוּ לֶחֶם תְּנוּפָה שְׁתַּיִם – *You shall bring two loaves of waving* (ibid. v. 17).

15. Such as reaping, grinding and sifting barley for the offering (*Rashi*).

16. This law is derived [with respect to reaping] exegetically in *Menachos* 72a (*see Rashi*). See *Ishei Yisrael* and *Maharam Schiff,* who explain how we derive all preliminaries from reaping.

17. There are three types of *gezeirah shavah* interpretations: (a) *free on both sides* – both of the similar words that comprise the *gezeirah shavah* are superfluous in their respective contexts, for no other derivation is made from either of them. Thus, both are "open," serving no other purpose than to form the *gezeirah shavah;* (b) *free on one side* – only one of the similar words is extra, while the other is not; (c) *not free at all* – neither word is superfluous, since both are used for other derivations.

A *gezeirah shavah* of the first variety, which is free on both sides, is – according to all authorities – an absolute teaching, and even though many distinctions may be found between the side that teaches and its counterpart, nevertheless, such a *gezeirah shavah* cannot be refuted. Since it is free on both sides, we regard the teaching as one expressly written in the Torah, and for that reason it cannot be challenged.

A *gezeirah shavah* that is free on one side is, according to one opinion in the Gemara (*Niddah* 22b-23a), considered valid only if it cannot be refuted. However, if it can be shown that the side that teaches is either more superior (if we want to derive a stringency) or deficient (if we want to derive a leniency) than the other side, then the *gezeirah shavah* may be rebutted – in much the same manner as a *kal vachomer* is refuted. A second opinion in the Gemara, however, maintains that even a *gezeirah shavah* that is free on one side is considered an absolute, irrefutable teaching. Thus, according to that opinion, the only practical difference between a *gezeirah shavah* that is free on two sides and one that is free on one side is that when presented with the choice of learning from one or the other, we select the former as the source of the teaching. According to this approach, a *gezeirah shavah* that is free on neither side is not valid at all.

Another approach in the Gemara (ibid.) is that a *gezeirah shavah* free on neither side is valid if not successfully challenged. And according to this view, the practical difference between a *gezeirah shavah* that is free on one side and one that is free on neither side is that when presented with the opportunity to learn from one or the other, we select the former as the source of instruction.

18. The one sent into the fields to reap barley from the new crop for the *Omer* offering.

19. I.e. if someone had already harvested barley without intending to bring it as the *Omer* offering (*Rashi*).

20. For Scripture states (*Leviticus* 23:10): *When you enter the Land . . . you shall reap* (וּקְצַרְתֶּם) *its harvest and bring* (וַהֲבֵאתֶם) *an Omer* [implying that the reaping, too, must be done for the sake of the mitzvah; see *Rashi* and *Ritva MHK* ed.]. Thus, Scripture indicates that the reaping itself is an actual mitzvah; and since it has the status of an actual mitzvah, perhaps that is why it overrides the Sabbath restrictions.

21. In the Two Loaves passage, reaping is not mentioned (*Rashi, Ritva MHK* ed.). Hence, it ranks as a mere preliminary to the mitzvah, and so we may not infer from the *Omer* passage that its preliminaries override the Sabbath restrictions. [If this is a valid *gezeirah shavah,* however, we would derive that all actions involved in bringing the Two Loaves – i.e. even the preliminaries – override the Sabbath.]

See *Tosafos* (with *Maharsha* and *Maharam*), who discuss why indeed we cannot derive with the *gezeirah shavah* this very law – i.e. that reaping grain for the Two Loaves is itself a mitzvah, and if the one sent into the fields finds grain already harvested, he must reap anew.

22. *Leviticus* 23:10.

בתים וחצרות פתוחין לתוכו והכא בתים איכא חצרות ליכא כי לא עירבו נמי ליחזינהו להני בתים כמאן דסתימי דמו וחצרות איכא ובתים ליכא אפשר דמבטלי ליה רשותא דכולהו לגבי חד סוף סוף בית איכא בתים ליכא אפשר דמצפרא ועד פלגא דיומא לגבי חד מפלגיה דיומא ולפניא לגבי חד סוף סוף בעידנא דאיתיה להאי ליתיה להאי אלא אמר רב אשי מי גרם לחצרות שיאסרו בתים וליכא אמר ר' חייא בר אבא א"ר יוחנן ° לא לכל אמר ר' אליעזר מכשירי מצוה דוחין את השבת שהרי שתי הלחם חובת היום הן ולא למדן ר"א אלא מגזירה שוה דתניא ר' אליעזר אומר מניין למכשירי שתי הלחם שדוחין את השבת נאמרה הבאה בעומר ונאמרה הבאה בשתי הלחם מה הבאה האמורה בעומר מכשירין דוחין את השבת אף הבאה האמורה בשתי הלחם מכשירין דוחין את השבת מופני דאי לא מופני איכא למיפרך מה לעומר שכן אם מצא קצור קוצר תאמר בשתי הלחם שאם מצא קצור אינו קוצר לאי אפנויי מופני מכדי כתיב א) והבאתם את עומר ראשית קצירכם אל הכהן ב) ביום הביאכם למה לי ש"מ לאפנויי ואכתי מופנה מצד אחד הוא ושמעינן ליה לר' אליעזר ג) דאמר מופנה מצד אחד למידין ומשיבין ג) תביאו רבויא הוא למעוטי מאי אילימא למעוטי לולב ד) והתניא לולב וכל מכשיריו דוחין את השבת דברי ר"א ואלא למעוטי סוכה והתניא סוכה וכל מכשיריה דוחין את השבת דברי ר"א ואלא למעוטי מצה והתניא מצה וכל מכשיריה דוחין את השבת דברי רבי אליעזר ואלא למעוטי שופר והתניא שופר וכל מכשיריו דוחין את השבת דברי ר"א אמר רב אדא בר אהבה למעוטי ציצית לטליתו ומזוזה לפתחו תניא נמי הכי ושוין שאם צייץ טליתו ועשה מזוזה לפתחו שהוא חייב מאי טעמא אמר רב יוסף לפי שאין קבוע להם זמן אמר ליה אביי אדרבה מדאין קבוע להם זמן כל

רש"י

בתים וחצרות. שני בתים פתוחים לשתי חצרות שתים לכל חצר ושתי חצרות פתוחות למבוי: כמאן דסתימי דמי. דהא לגבי מבוי כמאן דסתימי הוו דהא חצרות מפסיקות בינתים שאין הבתים מוציאין להם: אפשר דמבטלי. בני הבתים שבחצר רשות שיש להם בחצר לגבי חד מינייהו והוי כל החצר שלו ומותר להוציא מביתו לחצר: סוף סוף בית איכא. בכל חצר בתים ליכא ורב בעי שני בתים לכל חצר: אלא אמר רב אשי. טעמא לאו משום בתים וחצרות פתוחות לתוכו הוא דרב בין עירבו בין לא עירבו מכיון דפתוחי שתי חצרות למבוי ושני בתים לכל חצר תורת מבוי עליו ויתיר בלחי וקורה והיינו טעמא דכי עירבו החצרות ולא נשתתפו במבוי אסור לטלטל בו וכי לא עירבו שרי: מי גרם לחצירות שיאסרו. על המבוי להצריכו שיתוף להוציא מן החצירות לתוכו: בתים. הוא דגרמי לו דאי לאו משום בתים הוו להו חצרות ומבוי רשות אחת דרב דאמרה להא מלתא כר"ש סבירא ליה דאמר בעירובין (דף עב.) גג וחצר וקרפף ומבוי כולן רשות אחת הן ומטלטלין מזה לזה ואמר רב עלה הלכה כר' שמעון והוא שלא עירבו בתים עם החצרות דלא שכיחי מאני דבתים בחצר הלכך לענין טלטול בתוכו נמי כי לא עירבו חצרות עם הבתים שרי דהוו להו כמו שנשתתפו בו דמי גרם לו למבוי ליאסר ולהצטרך לשיתוף בתים גרמו לו ואינם שהרי נסתלקו ממנו ומותר להוציא מן החצרות למבוי כאילו נשתתפו ובנשתתפו לא מספקא לן דמותר לטלטל בכולו: לא לכל אמר רבי אליעזר. לא בכל מכשירי מצוה אמר כן ולקמן מפרש למעוטי מאי: שתי הלחם. דעצרת חובת יום הן ואין לאחרן עד למחר: ולא למדן רבי אליעזר. דלפיים תדחה שבת אלא בגזירה שוה ואי בכל מכשירי מצוה שעיקר המצוה נוהגת בשבת אמר מכשיריה כמותה למה לי גזירה שוה: מה הבאה האמורה בעומר מכשיריה. דהיינו קצירה טחינה והרקדה שלו דוחין את השבת כדאמרינן במנחות (דף עב:) בחריש ובקציר תשבות מה חריש רשות אף קציר רשות יצא קצירת העומר שהיא מצוה: שכן (א) מצא קצור. שלא לשם עומר מצוה לקצור לשמה דכתיב וקצרתם והבאתם הלכך קצירה גופיה מצוה היא תאמר בשתי הלחם שלא נאמר בהן קצירה: לאי. באמת: מצד אחד. הבאה דעומר מופנה הבאה דשתי הלחם אינה מופנה דצריכה לגופה: ושמעינן ליה לרבי אליעזר דאמר. גזירה שוה שאינה מופנה משני צדדיה אלא מצד אחד למדין ממנה אם אין להשיב אבל אם יש להשיב משיבין ובמסכת יבמות בפרק מצות חליצה ה) שמעינן ליה דאמר הכי דקתני חליצה בשמאל פסולה ורבי אליעזר מכשיר דלא יליף רגל רגל ממצורע ופרכינן ורבי אליעזר לא יליף ממצורע והא תניא ר"א אומר מניין לרציעה שהיא באוזן ימנית נאמר כאן אוזן ונאמר להלן אוזן וכו' ומשנינן אוזן אוזן מופנה רגל רגל לא מופנה והאי לאו מופנה דקאמרינן משני צדדין קאמר דרגל דכתיב בחליצה איצטריכא לגופה אבל מצד אחד מופנה הוא דפרשת מצורע ° מופנה הוא ההיא דעני דכולהו כתיבין במצורע עשיר: תביאו ריבויא הוא. דהא מוהקרבתם מנחה חדשה סמיך ומאי למיכתב ממושבותיכם לחם תנופה ותביאו יתירה הוא: למעוטי מאי. הא דאמר רבי יוחנן לעיל לא לכל אמר רבי אליעזר למעוטי הי מכשירים אתי דלא דחי שבת: וכל מכשיריו. כגון לקוצצו מן המחובר: למעוטי ציצית. שלא יתלנה בטליתו בשבת כדמפרש טעמא ואזיל:

תוספות

אפשר דמבטלי רשות כו'. וא"ת כי עירבו חצרות נמי עם בתים מצינן למימר שיש חצר למבוי כגון שביטלו אותו של חצר זה לרשות דכולהו שיש להם במבוי לבני חצר אחרת ויכולין לטלטל מן החצר למבוי הא לא בעי לאקשויי ° דליכא למ"ד בעירובין (דף סו:) אין ביטול רשות מחצר לחצר ועוד דבלאו הכי פריך שפיר:

מפלגא דיומא לפניא. רב לטעמיה דאמר במסכת עירובין (דף סט.) מבטלין וחוזרין ומבטלין: מי גרם לחצרות. אלמא קי"ל דאפילו עירבו חצרות עם בתים מותר לטלטל (ב) דהא רב דאסר בעירבו לטעמיה דפסיק כרבי שמעון דוקא בלא עירבו אבל רבי יוחנן פסיק כר"ש בין עירבו בין לא עירבו וכר' יוחנן קי"ל: לא לכל אמר רבי אליעזר מכשירי מצוה דוחין את השבת. לקמן מפרש דאתא למעוטי ציצית ומזוזה וה"פ לא (ג) כל מצות הנוהגות בשבת אמר ר' אליעזר שמכשיריהן ידחו שבת שהרי שתי הלחם כו' ומשמע לכאורה דאי לא דאשכחן דמצריך ר' אליעזר ג"ש הוה גמרינן ציצית ומזוזה ממילה וניחא דמכשיריה דחו שבת ותימה הוא היכי שייך למילף ציצית ומזוזה ממילה דמילה דין הוא דמכשיריה דוחין שבת דהיא עצמה דוחה שבת אבל ציצית ומזוזה אין במצותן דחיית שבת:

תאמר בשתי הלחם שאם מצא קצור אינו קוצר. תימה מאי קא פריך דהיא גופה נילף מינה מה העומר שאף על פי שמצא קצור קוצר אף שתי הלחם אם מצא קצור קוצר ונילף מינה תרתי מכשירין וקצירה ותירץ ר"ת דהא לא דמי דנילף מינה קצירה שהרי בעצרת יהיו כל החיטין והשעורין קצורים ולא משמע דאתיא ג"ש אלא (ד) מכשירין דדחו שבת א"נ י"ל דהא לא מצי למימר נילף קצירה דמהיכא נפקא לן קצירת העומר דדחיא שבת מדכתיב בחריש ובקציר תשבות כדדרשינן במנחות בשילהי ר' ישמעאל (דף עב.) מה חריש רשות אף קציר רשות יצא קצירת העומר שהיא מצוה וגלי רחמנא דליכא למילף אלא לגבי העומר דכתיב ביה נמי קציר ולא לגבי שתי הלחם דלא כתיב בהו קציר ועל כרחיך ודאי היינו טעמא דיליף גבי עומר קצירה משום דכתיב ביה קציר דאי לאו הכי מ"ש דיליף טפי גבי עומר מגבי שתי הלחם דהכא נמי נימא יצא קצירת שתי הלחם שהיא מצוה: ושוין שאם צייץ טליתו כו' מ"ט כו'. תימה מה צריך טעם לזה אלא משום דלא אשכחן דרבינהו קרא דכל איך מצרכינן קרא לקמן דלא גמרי מהדדי ומיהו יש לומר דאיכא למילף ציצית ומזוזה מסוכה דמאי פרכת שכן נוהגת בלילות כבימים מזוזה נמי נוהג בלילות כבימים וכן ציצית לרבנן דפליגי עליה דרבי שמעון בפרק התכלת (מנחות דף מג.) דלא דרשי וראיתם אותו פרט לכסות לילה אלא ° פרט לכסות סומא ולהאי טעמא דפרישית דמסוכה יליף צריך לומר דציצית (ה) אם עבר זמנה בטלה דאי לאו הכי איכא למפרך מה לסוכה שכן אם עבר זמנה בטלה דמסתבר דמילה אם עבר זמנה לא בטלה שאותה מילה עצמה שהוא מחייב בשמיני הוא עושה בתשיעי שאם מל בשמיני לא היה חוזר ומל בתשיעי אבל (ו) סוכה ציצית ומזוזה בכל יומא מיחייב בהן אפילו קיימם היום חייב לקיימם למחר הלכך כשעבר היום ולא עשאם מצות היום לא יקיים עוד לעולם ואם תאמר ומסוכה היכי מצי למילף וכן כל הנך דלקמן דפריך ניכתוב רחמנא בהאי וניתי הנך וניגמרו מיניה אדרבה נגמר מכיבוד אב ואם ומבנין בית המקדש דלא דחו שבת כדאיתא

רבינו חננאל

בתים וחצרות פתוחין לתוכו והכא כיון שערבו כאלו אין שם חצר וכולן (בתים) [חצרות] נינהו ואפי' נשתתפו כיון שאין שם בתים אין שתוף מועיל באותו מבוי. כך יש לומר כי לא עירבו נמי כיון שהן אסורין להוציא מן הבית לחצר חשוב אותן הבתים כאלו סתומין הן שאין להם רשות להשתמש מן הבתים לחצר וחצר איכא בית ליכא. לטעמיה דרב היאך מטלטלין במבוי שאין לו בית ומפרק יתכן שאין כל בני החצר רשותם לגבי חד וכיון שמבטלין רשותם לגביה יש לו להוציא מן הבית לחצר כדתנן נתנו לו רשותם הוא מותר והן אסורין וקיי"ל הא דתנן נתנו לו רשותם רשותם מעיקרא קודם א) שיבטלו הרשות לגבייהו ואקשינן וכיון שבטלו כל בני חצר רשותם לגבי חד נעשו כל הבתים שלו וכולהו כבית אחד הן חשובין ורב לא אמר אלא בתים ומיעוטי בתי' שנים והכא ליכא שני בתים והיאך מתיר רב. ופרקינן עוד כגון שבני חצר בטלו רשותן מן הבקר עד חצי היום לגבי ראובן בפירוש ומחצי היום ולהלן לגבי שמעון שנמצא ראובן ושמעון שניהם מותרין בחצר זו הא שמעינן לרב דאמר מבטלין וחוזרין ומבטלין ואקשינן תוב סוף סוף בעת שמותר לזה להשתמש בחצר זה אסור לחבירו ואותה העת אין שם בחצר אלא בית ראובן בלבד ומחצי היום ולהלן בית שמעון לבדו ואין לראובן בה רשות להשתמש. ומ"ש תמצא ב' בתים מותרין בחצר זו בעת אחת. ופריק רב אשי פירוק אחר ואמר מי גרם לחצרות הללו הפתוחות למבוי להיאסר בהן טלטול המבוי מפני אלו הבתים שהן פתוחין לתוכן ולא עירבו שאלו לא היו בהן בתים מותרין היו השובתים שם לטלטל בה בכולה. שהן כמו קרפף שמותר השובת בו לטלטל בכולו וגם המבוי לא נאסר בהן טלטול אי לא מפני הבתים שהן פתוחים לתוכה ואינם. כלומר כיון שלא עירבו תחשבם כאלו סתומים הם ואינם כלל. הלא אילו היו סתומין היה הטלטול מותר בהם עכשיו יהיה מותר ועמדו דברי רב אשי ועיקר דברי רב ופירושם בעירובין פרק הדר עם הנכרי בחצר ופירשנום שם. ושמעינן מינה דרבנן פליגי על ר' שמעון דשרי דרך גגות ודרך חצירות ודרך קרפיפות ואע"ג דאמר רב הלכתא כר' שמעון בפרק כל גגות העיר רשות אחת הן לגבי

חשק שלמה על רבינו חננאל

א) נראה דר"ל דקי"ל כר"ש בעירובין סט ע"ב דנותנין רשות ומסתלקין:

רב נסים גאון

ואכתי מופנה מצד א' הוא ושמעי' ליה לר' אליעזר דאמר מופנה מצד אחד למדין ומשיבין. דע שאע"פ שלא מצאנו לר' אליעזר בפירוש שאמר דבר זה ידועים אנחנו אותו מדבריהם במס' נדה בפרק המפלת (דף כב) מופנה מצד

מסורת הש"ס

א) [עירובין ה. יב: עג: עד.], ב) [נ"ל מיום], ג) יבמות ע:, ד) סוכה מג., ה) [דף קד.].

הגהות הב"ח

(א) רש"י ד"ה שכן אם מצא: (ב) תוס' ד"ה מי גרם וכו' מותר לטלטל בכולו דהא רב: (ג) ד"ה לא לכל וכו' וה"פ לא לכל מצות: (ד) ד"ה תאמר וכו' אלא למכשירין: (ה) ד"ה ושוין וכו' דציצית ומזוזה אם עבר: (ו) בא"ד אבל ציצית ומזוזה כו"ל ותיבת סוכה נמחק:

גליון הש"ס

גמרא לא לכל אר"א מכשירי מצוה. עי' בס' כני חיא בסוף הספר בלקוטי: רש"י ד"ה ושמעי' ליה לר"א וכו' מופנה הוא ההיא דעני. עי' יבמות דף ע ע"ב ד"ה ושמעי' לי' וע"ע: תוס' ד"ה אפשר דאיכא למ"ד בעירובין. עי' עירובין דף עג ע"ב תוס' ד"ה אלא פשיטא: תוס' ד"ה ושוין וכו' אלא פרט לכסות סומא. וכ"כ רש"י סוכה יא ע"א לפרושה. ועיין בשער המלך פ"ג מהל' ציצית:

תורה אור השלם

א) דַּבֵּר אֶל בְּנֵי יִשְׂרָאֵל וְאָמַרְתָּ אֲלֵהֶם כִּי תָבֹאוּ אֶל הָאָרֶץ אֲשֶׁר אֲנִי נֹתֵן לָכֶם וּקְצַרְתֶּם אֶת קְצִירָהּ וַהֲבֵאתֶם אֶת עֹמֶר רֵאשִׁית קְצִירְכֶם אֶל הַכֹּהֵן: (ויקרא כג, י)

ב) וּסְפַרְתֶּם לָכֶם מִמָּחֳרַת הַשַּׁבָּת מִיּוֹם הֲבִיאֲכֶם אֶת עֹמֶר הַתְּנוּפָה שֶׁבַע שַׁבָּתוֹת תְּמִימֹת תִּהְיֶינָה: (ויקרא כג, טו)

ג) מִמּוֹשְׁבֹתֵיכֶם תָּבִיאוּ לֶחֶם תְּנוּפָה שְׁתַּיִם שְׁנֵי עֶשְׂרֹנִים סֹלֶת תִּהְיֶינָה חָמֵץ תֵּאָפֶינָה בִּכּוּרִים לַה': (ויקרא כג, יז)

ליקוטי רש"י

ושמעינן ליה לר' אליעזר דאמר מופנה מצד אחד למדין ומשיבין. בפרק מצות חליצה (יבמות קד.) שמעינן לרבי אליעזר דאמר מופנה מצד אחד למדין ומשיבין דקתני חליצה בשמאל פסולה ור' אליעזר מכשיר ... רגל ממצורע והתניא מנין לרציעה שהיא בימין כו' ומשנינן אוזן אוזן מופנה רגל רגל לא מופנה ... למדין ומשיבין.

חשק שלמה על רב נסים גאון

א) אין הלשון מדויק ...

beginning of the Two Loaves passage?[23] שְׁמַע מִינָּהּ לְאַפְנוּיֵי – Rather, **derive from [the superfluous mention of "bringing"]** that the second verse is **free** for interpretation.

The Gemara asks:

וְאַכַּתִּי מוּפְנֶה מִצַּד אֶחָד הוּא – **But still [the *gezeirah shavah*] is free on** only **one side,**[24] וְשָׁמְעִינַן לֵיהּ לְרַבִּי אֱלִיעֶזֶר דְּאָמַר – **and we have heard that R' Eliezer has said:** מוּפְנֶה מִצַּד אֶחָד לְמֵידִין וּמְשִׁיבִין – With regard to a *gezeirah shavah* that is **free on one side, we may derive** laws from it, **but we may** also **raise objections** to refute it.[25] Since in our case we may argue that reaping the *Omer* grain is an actual mitzvah while reaping the Two Loaves grain is not, we cannot derive via a *gezeirah shavah* that the latter labor is likewise performed on the Sabbath.

The Gemara deflects the challenge and revives R' Eliezer's *gezeirah shavah* teaching:

תָּבִיאוּ רִבּוּיָא הוּא – The phrase ***you shall bring*** (in the Two Loaves passage) **is** also **extraneous,**[26] and is thus free for interpretation; hence, the *gezeirah shavah* is actually free on both sides, and cannot be refuted.

R' Yochanan stated above that in R' Eliezer's view the preliminaries of not all mitzvos may be performed on the Sabbath. The Gemara therefore inquires:

לְמַעוּטֵי מַאי – **What** does R' Yochanan come **to exclude?** Which preliminaries do not override the Sabbath restrictions?

The Gemara considers and rejects various possibilities:

אִילֵימָא לְמַעוּטֵי לוּלָב – **If** you wish **to say** that R' Yochanan comes **to exclude** the preliminaries to the mitzvah of ***lulav,***[27] can that be? וְהָתַנְיָא – **But it has been taught in a Baraisa:** לוּלָב וְכָל מַכְשִׁירָיו דּוֹחִין אֶת הַשַּׁבָּת – The mitzvah of ***LULAV* AND ALL ITS PRELIMINARIES OVERRIDE THE SABBATH** restrictions. דִּבְרֵי רַבִּי אֱלִיעֶזֶר – These are **THE WORDS OF R' ELIEZER.**[28] וְאֶלָּא לְמַעוּטֵי סוּכָּה – **And** does he come, **rather, to exclude** the preliminaries to the mitzvah of ***succah?***[29] וְהָתַנְיָא – **But it was taught** otherwise **in a Baraisa:** סוּכָּה וְכָל מַכְשִׁירֶיהָ דּוֹחִין אֶת הַשַּׁבָּת – The mitzvah of ***SUCCAH* AND ALL ITS PRELIMINARIES OVERRIDE THE SABBATH** restrictions. דִּבְרֵי רַבִּי אֱלִיעֶזֶר – These are **THE WORDS OF R' ELIEZER.** וְאֶלָּא לְמַעוּטֵי מַצָּה – **And** does he come, **rather, to exclude** the preliminaries to the mitzvah of **matzah?**[30] וְהָתַנְיָא – **But it was taught** otherwise **in a Baraisa:** מַצָּה וְכָל מַכְשִׁירֶיהָ דּוֹחִין אֶת הַשַּׁבָּת – The mitzvah of **MATZAH AND ALL ITS PRELIMINARIES OVERRIDE THE SABBATH** restrictions. דִּבְרֵי רַבִּי אֱלִיעֶזֶר – These are **THE WORDS OF R' ELIEZER.** וְאֶלָּא לְמַעוּטֵי שׁוֹפָר – **And** does he come, **rather, to exclude** the preliminaries to the mitzvah of ***shofar?***[31] וְהָתַנְיָא – **But it was taught** otherwise **in a Baraisa:** שׁוֹפָר וְכָל מַכְשִׁירָיו דּוֹחִין אֶת הַשַּׁבָּת – The mitzvah of ***SHOFAR* AND ALL ITS PRELIMINARIES OVERRIDE THE SABBATH** restrictions. דִּבְרֵי רַבִּי אֱלִיעֶזֶר – These are **THE WORDS OF R' ELIEZER.**

The Gemara finally identifies the preliminaries that are not performed on the Sabbath:

אָמַר רַב אַדָּא בַּר אַהֲבָה – **Rav Adda bar Ahavah said:** לְמַעוּטֵי צִיצִית לְטַלִּיתוֹ וּמְזוּזָה לְפִתְחוֹ – In fact, R' Yochanan comes **to exclude** the preliminaries to the mitzvos of having ***tzitzis* on one's garment**[32] **and** affixing **a *mezuzah* to one's doorway.**[33]

The Gemara adduces Tannaic support for this answer:

תַּנְיָא נַמִּי הָכִי – **It was also taught thus in a Baraisa:** וְשָׁוִין – **AND [THE OPINIONS]** of R' Eliezer and R' Akiva **ARE SIMILAR** in this respect, שֶׁאִם צִיֵּיץ טַלִּיתוֹ וְעָשָׂה מְזוּזָה לְפִתְחוֹ – **IN THAT IF ONE TIED FRINGES TO HIS** four-cornered **GARMENT, OR MADE** (i.e. wrote) **A *MEZUZAH* FOR HIS DOORWAY,** שֶׁהוּא חַיָּיב – **HE IS OBLIGATED** to bring a *chatas* offering.[34] The Baraisa thus indicates that the preliminaries mentioned by Rav Adda bar Ahavah do not override the Sabbath restrictions.

The Gemara asks:

מַאי טַעְמָא – **What,** indeed, **is the reason** that these preliminaries are prohibited?[35]

The Gemara answers:

אָמַר רַב יוֹסֵף – **Rav Yosef said:** לְפִי שֶׁאֵין קָבוּעַ לָהֶם זְמַן – **Because [the mitzvos of *tzitzis* and *mezuzah*] have no fixed time** for their performance. Since they need not be performed on the Sabbath, there is no compelling reason to allow their preliminaries, which each constitute an *av melachah,* to override the Sabbath restrictions.

This explanation is challenged:

אָמַר לֵיהּ אַבַּיֵי – **Abaye said to [Rav Yosef]:** אַדְּרַבָּה – **On the contrary!** מִדְּאֵין קָבוּעַ לָהֶם זְמַן – **Since [the mitzvos of *tzitzis* and *mezuzah*] have no fixed time,**

NOTES

23. *Leviticus* 23:15. [Scripture could just as well have written, "from the day of the *Omer.*"]

24. Although there is an extraneous mention of "bringing" with respect to the *Omer,* the one mention of "bringing" in the Two Loaves passage (*you shall bring two loaves of waving;* ibid. v. 17) is needed for itself (*Rashi*).

25. See note 17 above; see *Rashi* for an explanation of where R' Eliezer's opinion is indicated.

26. תָּבִיאוּ (*you shall bring*) appears near the beginning of verse 17: *From your dwelling places you shall bring two loaves of waving.* Now, at the end of the preceding verse the Torah states (with reference to the Two Loaves): *You shall offer a new meal offering to Hashem.* The Torah could have stated simply, "You shall offer a new meal offering to Hashem from your dwelling places, two loaves of waving." *You shall bring* is thus superfluous, and open for the *gezeirah shavah* (*Rashi*). See *Rashash, Mitzpeh Eisan* and *Tz'lach* ד״ה תביאו.

27. The mitzvah is to take a branch of a date palm on Succos (see *Leviticus* 23:40). Its preliminary would be to cut the palm branch off the tree [which is the *melachah* of reaping] (*Rashi, Ritva MHK* ed.). See also *Rashi* to *Succah* 43a ד״ה למכשירי.

28. The Gemara below (131b) will present the derivation for this case, as well as for those that follow.

29. The mitzvah is to dwell in booths during the seven-day Succos festival (see *Leviticus* 23:42). Its preliminaries would be the various labors involved in building a booth.

30. The mitzvah is to eat unleavened bread on the Pesach festival (see *Leviticus* 23:6). Its preliminaries would be, for example, grinding the grain, sifting the flour, kneading and baking the dough.

31. The mitzvah is to blow a ram's horn on Rosh Hashanah (see *Leviticus* 23:24). The preliminaries would be the various labors involving in making a *shofar* horn [e.g. מַכֶּה בְּפַטִּישׁ, *striking the final blow,* which one performs when he forms a utensil].

32. [*Tzitzis* are fringes that must be worn on each corner of a four-cornered garment (see *Numbers* 15:37-41).] Tying the *tzitzis* onto the corners, an *av melachah* (primary labor), is the preliminary to this mitzvah (*Rashi;* see *Ritva MHK* ed., who mentions the making of the *tzitzis* threads; see *Chasam Sofer* ד״ה והי׳ אפשר לומר).

33. [A *mezuzah* is a small scroll containing the passages of *Deuteronomy* 6:4-9 and 11:13-21 that is affixed to the right doorpost.] Writing those passages, an *av melachah,* is the preliminary to this mitzvah (*Ritva MHK* ed.; see *Chasam Sofer* ibid., who suggests that the *melachah* of building may be involved as well).

34. If his violation was unintentional (see *Ritva MHK* ed.).

35. The Gemara below will teach that the Torah specifically sanctioned the Sabbath performance of each of the other preliminaries. Hence, it wonders here why the Torah did not extend this leniency to the preliminaries of *tzitzis* and *mezuzah* (*Ritva MHK* ed.). Alternatively, the Gemara asks why – despite the Torah's silence in the matter – R' Eliezer did not derive these two preliminaries from the ones that do override the Sabbath (see *Tosafos* et al.).

בתים וחצרות פתוחין לתוכו והכא בתים איכא חצרות ליכא כי לא עירבו נמי ליחזינהו להני בתים כמאן דסתימי דמו וחצרות איכא ובתים ליכא אפשר דמבטלי ליה רשותא דכולהו לגבי חד סוף סוף בית איכא בתים ליכא אפשר דמצפרא ועד פלגא דיומא לגבי חד מפלגיה דיומא ולפניא לגבי חד סוף סוף בעידנא דאיתיה להאי ליתיה להאי אלא אמר רב אשי מי גרם לחצרות שיאסרו בתים וליכא אמר ר' חייא בר אבא א"ר יוחנן לא לכל אמר ר' אליעזר מכשירי מצוה דוחין את השבת שהרי שתי הלחם חובת היום הן ולא למדן ר"א אלא מגזירה שוה דתניא ר' אליעזר אומר מניין למכשירי שתי הלחם שדוחין את השבת נאמרה הבאה בעומר ונאמרה הבאה בשתי הלחם מה הבאה האמורה בעומר מכשירין דוחין את השבת אף הבאה האמורה בשתי הלחם מכשירין דוחין את השבת מופני דאי לא מופני איכא למיפרך מה לעומר שכן אם מצא קצור קוצר תאמר בשתי הלחם שאם מצא קצור אינו קוצר לאי אפנויי מופני מכדי כתיב א) והבאתם את עומר ראשית קצירכם אל הכהן ב) ביום הביאכם למה לי ש"מ לאפנויי ואכתי מופנה מצד אחד הוא ושמעינן ליה לר' אליעזר ג) דאמר מופנה מצד אחד למידין ומשיבין ג) תביאו רבויא הוא למעוטי מאי אילימא למעוטי לולב והתניא ד) לולב וכל מכשיריו דוחין את השבת דברי ר"א ואלא למעוטי סוכה והתניא סוכה וכל מכשיריה דוחין את השבת דברי ר"א ואלא למעוטי מצה והתניא מצה וכל מכשיריה דוחין את השבת דברי רבי אליעזר ואלא למעוטי שופר והתניא שופר וכל מכשיריו דוחין את השבת דברי ר"א אמר רב אדא בר אהבה למעוטי ציצית לטליתו ומזוזה לפתחו תניא נמי הכי ושוין שאם צייץ טליתו ועשה מזוזה לפתחו שהוא חייב מאי טעמא אמר רב יוסף לפי שאין קבוע להם זמן אמר ליה אביי אדרבה מדאין קבוע להם זמן כל

רש"י

בתים וחצרות. שני בתים פתוחים לשתי חצרות שתים לכל חצר ושתי חצרות פתוחות למבוי: כמאן דסתימי דמי. דהא לגבי מבוי כמאן דסתימי הוו דהא חצרות מפסיקות בינתים שאין הבתים מוציאין להם: אפשר דמבטלי. בני הבתים שבחצר רשות שיש להם בחצר לגבי חד מינייהו והוי כל החצר שלו ומותר להוציא מביתו לחצר: סוף סוף בית איכא. בכל חצר בתים ליכא ורב בעי שני בתים לכל חצר: אלא אמר רב אשי. טעמא לאו משום בתים וחצרות פתוחות לתוכו הוא דרב בין עירבו בין לא עירבו מכיון דפתיחי שתי חצרות למבוי ושני בתים לכל חצר תורת מבוי עליו ונימר בלחי וקורה והיינו טעמא דכי עירבו בחצרות ולא נשתתפו במבוי אסור לטלטל בו וכי לא עירבו שרי: מי גרם לחצירות שיאסרו. על המבוי להצריכו שיתוף להוציא מן החצירות לתוכו: בתים. הוא דגרמי לו דאי לאו משום בתים הוו להו חצרות ומבוי רשות אחת דרב דאמר להא מלתא כר"ש סבירא ליה דאמר בעירובין (דף עד.) גג וחצר וקרפף ומבוי כולן רשות אחת הן ומטלטלין מזה לזה ואמר רב עלה הלכה כר' שמעון והוא שלא עירבו בתים עם החצרות דלא שכיחי מאני דבתים בחצר הלכך לענין טלטול בתוכו נמי כי לא עירבו חצרות עם הבתים שרי דהוה להו כמו שנשתתפו בו דמי גרם לו למבוי ליאסר ולהצטרך לשיתוף בתים גרמו לו ואינם שהרי נסתלקו ממנו ומותר להוציא מן החצרות למבוי כאילו נשתתפו ובנשתתפו לא מספקא לן דמותר לטלטל בכולן: לא לכל אמר רבי אליעזר. לא בכל מכשירי מצוה אמר כן ולקמן מפרש הי מכשירי מצוה אתא למעוטי: שתי הלחם. דעצרת חובת יום הן ואין לאחרן עד למחר: ולא למדן רבי אליעזר. דאפייתם תדחה שבת אלא בגזירה שוה ואי בכל מכשירי מצוה שעיקר המצוה נוהגת בשבת אמר מכשיריה כמותה למה לי גזירה שוה: מה הבאה האמורה בעומר מכשיריה. דהיינו קצירה טחינה והרקדה שלה דוחין את השבת כדאמרינן במנחות (דף עב.) בחריש ובקציר תשבות מה חריש רשות אף קציר רשות יצא קצירת העומר שהיא מצוה: שכן (א) מצא קצור. שלא לשם עומר מצוה לקצור לשמה דכתיב וקצרתם והבאתם הלכך קצירה גופיה מצוה היא תאמר בשתי הלחם שלא נאמר בהן קצירה: לאי. באמת: מצד אחד. הבאה דעומר מופנה הבאה דשתי הלחם אינה מופנה דצריכה לגופה: ושמעינן ליה לרבי אליעזר דאמר. גזירה שוה שאינה מופנה משני צדדיה אלא מצד אחד למדין ממנה אם אין להשיב אבל אם יש להשיב משיבין ובמסכת יבמות בפרק מצות חליצה (ה) שמעינן ליה דאמר הכי דקתני חליצה בשמאל פסולה ורבי אליעזר מכשיר דלא יליף רגל רגל ממצורע ופרכינן ורבי אליעזר לא יליף ממצורע והא תניא ר"א אומר מניין לרציעה שהיא באוזן ימנית נאמר כאן אוזן ונאמר להלן אוזן וכו' ומשנינן אזן מופנה רגל רגל לא מופנה והאי לאו מופנה דקאמרינן משני צדדין קאמר דרגל דכתיב בחליצה איצטריכא לגופה אבל מצד אחד מופנה הוא דפרשת מצורע * מופנה הוא שהיא דעני דכולהו כתיבן במצורע עשיר: תביאו ריבויא הוא. דהא אוהקרבתם מנחה חדשה סמיך ומאי למיכתב ממושבותיכם לחם תנופה ותביאו יתירה הוא: למעוטי מאי. הא דאמר רבי יוחנן לעיל לא לכל אמר רבי אליעזר למעוטי הי מכשירי אמרה דלא דחו שבת: וכל מכשיריו. כגון לקוצצו מן המחובר: למעוטי ציצית. שלא יתלנה בשבת דכמתקן מנא הוא. ואזיל:

תוספות

אפשר דמבטלי רשות כו'. וא"ת כי עירבו חצרות נמי עם בתים מצינן למימר שיש חצר למבוי כגון שביטלו אותו של חצר זה לרשות דכולהו שיש להם במבוי לבני חצר אחרת ויכולין לטלטל מן החצר למבוי הא לא בעי לאקשויי * דאיכא למ"ד בעירובין (דף סו:) אין ביטול רשות מחצר לחצר ועוד דבלאו הכי פריך שפיר: מפלגא דיומא לפניא. רב לטעמיה דאמר במסכת עירובין (דף סח:) מבטלין וחוזרין ומבטלין: מי גרם לחצרות. אנן קי"ל דאפילו עירבו חצרות עם בתים מותר לטלטל (ב) דהא רב דאסר בעירבו לטעמיה דפסיק כרבי שמעון דוקא בלא עירבו אבל רבי יוחנן פסיק כר"ש בין עירבו בין לא עירבו וכר' יוחנן קי"ל: לא לכל אמר רבי אליעזר מכשירי מצוה דוחין את השבת. לקמן מפרש דאתא למעוטי ציצית ומזוזה וה"פ לא (ג) כל מצות הנוהגות בשבת אמר ר' אליעזר שמכשירין ידחו שבת שהרי שתי הלחם כו' ומשמע לכאורה דאי לא דאשכחן דמצריך ר' אליעזר ג"ש הוה גמרינן לציצית ומזוזה ממילה ונימא דמכשיריה דחו שבת ותימה הוא היכי שייך למילף ציצית ומזוזה ממילה דמילה דין הוא דמכשיריה דוחין שבת דהיא עצמה דוחה שבת אבל ציצית ומזוזה אין במצותן דחיית שבת:

תאמר בשתי הלחם שאם מצא קצור אינו קוצר. תימה מאי קא פריך דהיא גופה נילף מינה מה העומר שאף על פי שמצא קצור קוצר אף שתי הלחם אם מצא קצור קוצר ונילף מינה תרתי מכשירין וקצירה ותירץ ר"ת דהא לא דמי דנילף מינה קצירה שהרי בעצרת יהיו כל החיטין והשעורין קצורים ולא משמע דאתיא ג"ש אלא (ד) מכשירין דדחו שבת א"נ י"ל דהא לא מצי למימר נילף קצירה דמהיכא נפקא לן קצירת העומר דדחיא שבת מדכתיב בחריש ובקציר תשבות כדדרשינן במנחות בשילהי ר' ישמעאל (דף עב.) מה חריש רשות אף קציר רשות יצא קצירת העומר שהיא מצוה וגלי רחמנא דליכא למילף אלא לגבי העומר דכתיב ביה נמי קציר ולא לגבי שתי הלחם דלא כתיב בהו קציר ועל כרחיך ודאי היינו טעמא דיליף גבי עומר קצירה משום דכתיב ביה קציר דאי לאו הכי מ"ש דיליף טפי גבי עומר מגבי שתי הלחם דהכא נמי נימא יצא קצירת שתי הלחם שהיא מצוה:

ושוין שאם צייץ טליתו כו' מ"ט כו'. תימה מה צריך טעם לזה אלא משום דלא אשכחן דרבינהו קרא דכל אינך מצרכינן קרא לקמן דלא גמרי מהדדי ומיהו יש לומר דאיכא למילף ציצית ומזוזה מסוכה דמאי פרכת שכן נוהגת בלילות כבימים מזוזה נמי נוהג בלילות כבימים וכן ציצית לרבנן דפליגי עליה דרבי שמעון בפרק התכלת (מנחות דף מג.) דלא דרשי ולאיתם אותו פרט לכסות לילה אלא * פרט לכסות סומא ולהאי טעמא דפרישית דמסוכה יליף צריך לומר דציצית (ה) אם עבר זמנה בטלה דאי לאו הכי איכא למפרך מה לסוכה שכן אם עבר זמנה בטלה דמסתבר דמילה אם עבר זמנה לא בטלה שאותה מילה עצמה שהוא מחייב בשמיני הוא עושה בתשיעי שאם מל בשמיני לא היה חוזר ומל בתשיעי אבל (ו) סוכה ציצית ומזוזה בכל יומא מיחייב בהן ואפילו קיימם היום חייב לקיימם למחר הלכך כשעבר היום ולא עשאם מצות היום לא יקיים עוד לעולם ולא תאמר ומסוכה היכי מצי למילף וכן כל הנך דלקמן דפריך ליכתוב רחמנא בהאי וניתי הנך ונגמרו מיניה אדרבה נגמר מכיבוד אב ואם ומבנין בית המקדש דלא דחו שבת כדלקמן:

רבינו חננאל

בתים וחצרות פתוחין לתוכו והכא כיון שערבו כאלו אין שם חצר וכולן (בתים) [חצרות] נינהו ואפי' נשתתפו כיון שאין שם בתים אין שתוף מועיל באותו מבוי. כך יש לומר כי לא עירבו נמי כיון שהן אסורין להוציא מן הבית לחצר חשוב אותן הבתים כאלו סתומין הן שאין להם רשות להשתמש מן הבתים לחצר וחצר איכא בית ליכא. לטעמיה דרב היאך מטלטלין במבוי שאין לו בית ומפרק יתכן שיבטלו כל בני החצר רשותם לגבי חד וכיון שמבטלין רשותם לגביה יש לו להוציא מן הבית לחצר כדתנן נתנו לו רשותם הוא מותר והם אסורים וקיי"ל הא דתנן נתנו לו רשותם רשותם מעיקרא מקודם א) שיבטל הויא רשותא לגבייהו ואקשינן וכיון שבטלו כל בני חצר רשותם לגבי חד נעשו כל הבתים שלו וכולן כבית אחד הן חשובין ורב לא אמר אלא בתים ומיעוטי בתי' שנים והכא ליכא שני בתים והיאך מתיר רב. ופרקי' עוד כגון שבני חצר בטלו רשותן מן הבקר עד חצי היום לגבי ראובן בפירוש ומחצי היום ולהלן לגבי שמעון שנמצאו ראובן ושמעון שניהם מותרין בחצר זו דהא שמעינן לרב דאמר מבטלין וחוזרין ומבטלין ואקשינן תוב סוף סוף בעת שמותר לזה להשתמש בחצר זה אסור לחבירו ואותה העת אין שם בחצר אלא בית ראובן בלבד ומחצי היום ולהלן בית שמעון לבדו ואין לראובן בה רשות להשתמש. ומ"מ לא תמצא ב' בתים מותרין בחצר זו בעת אחת. ופירק רב אשי פירוק אחר ואמר מי גרם לחצרות הללו הפתוחות למבוי להיאסר בהן טלטול בתים מפני אלו הבתים שהן פתוחין לתוכן ולא עירבו שאלו לא היו בהן בתים מותרין היו השובתים שם לטלטל בה בכולה. שהן כמו קרפף שמותר השובת בו לטלטל בכולן וגם המבוי לא נאסר בהן טלטול אי לא מפני הבתים שהן פתוחים לתוכה ואינם. כלומר כיון שלא עירבו תחשבם כאלו סתומים הם ואינם כלל. הלא אלו היו סותמין היה הטלטול מותר להם עכשיו יהיה מותר ועמדו דברי רב אשי ועיקר דברי רב ופירושו בעירובין פרק הדר עם הנכרי בחצר ופירשנוהו שם. ושמעינן מינה דרבנן פליגי על ר' שמעון דשרי דרך גגות דרך חצירות ודרך קרפיפות ואע"ג דאמר רב הלכתא כר' שמעון בפרק כל גגות העיר רשות אחת הן לגבי

חשק שלמה על רבינו חננאל

א) נראה דר"ל דקיי"ל כביטול לעירובין שט"ע דטעמו דבטלו רשות משמשין.

רב נסים גאון

ואכתי מופנה מצד א' הוא ושמעי' ליה לר' אליעזר דאמר מופנה מצד אחד למידין ומשיבין. דע שאע"פ

מסורת הש"ס

א) [עירובין ה. יג: עג: עד.], ב) [ל"ל מיום], ג) יבמות ע:, ד) סוכה מג., ה) [דף קד.]

הגהות הב"ח

(א) רש"י ד"ה שכן מצא. נ"ב ... (ב) תוס' ד"ה מי גרם וכו' מותר לטלטל בכולו וכו': (ג) ד"ה לא לכל וכו' וה"פ לא לכל מצות: (ד) ד"ה תאמר וכו' אלא לענין מכשירין: (ה) ד"ה ושוין וכו' דציצית ומזוזה אם עבר: (ו) בא"ד אבל ציצית ומזוזה וכו':

גליון הש"ס

גמרא לא לכל אר"א מכשירי מצוה. עי' בס' בני חיי"א בקונ' הספר בלקוטי: רש"י ד"ה ושמעי' ליה לר"א וכו' מופנה הוא ההיא דעני. עי' ברש"י יבמות דף ע ע"ב ד"ה ושמעי' לי' לר"א ול"ע: תוס' ד"ה אפשר דאיכא למ"ד בעירובין. עי' עירובין דף ע ע"ב תוס' ד"ה אלא פשיטא: תוס' ד"ה ושוין וכו' אלא פרט לכסות סומא. וכ"כ רש"י סוכה דף יא ע"ב ד"ה לפרזמא: ועיין בשער המלך פ"ג מהל' ציצית:

תורה אור השלם

א) דַּבֵּר אֶל בְּנֵי יִשְׂרָאֵל וְאָמַרְתָּ אֲלֵהֶם כִּי תָבֹאוּ אֶל הָאָרֶץ אֲשֶׁר אֲנִי נֹתֵן לָכֶם וּקְצַרְתֶּם אֶת קְצִירָהּ וַהֲבֵאתֶם אֶת עֹמֶר רֵאשִׁית קְצִירְכֶם אֶל הַכֹּהֵן: [ויקרא כג, י]

ב) וּסְפַרְתֶּם לָכֶם מִמָּחֳרַת הַשַּׁבָּת מִיּוֹם הֲבִיאֲכֶם אֶת עֹמֶר הַתְּנוּפָה שֶׁבַע שַׁבָּתוֹת תְּמִימֹת תִּהְיֶינָה: [ויקרא כג, טו]

ג) מִמּוֹשְׁבֹתֵיכֶם תָּבִיאוּ לֶחֶם תְּנוּפָה שְׁתַּיִם שְׁנֵי עֶשְׂרֹנִים סֹלֶת תִּהְיֶינָה חָמֵץ תֵּאָפֶינָה בִּכּוּרִים לַה': [ויקרא כג, יז]

ליקוטי רש"י

ושמעינן ליה לר' אליעזר דאמר מופנה מצד אחד למידין ומשיבין. בפרק מצות חליצה (יבמות קד.) שמעינן לרבי אליעזר דאמר מופנה מצד אחד למדין ומשיבין דקתני חליצה בשמאל פסולה ורבי אליעזר מכשיר ...

שלא מצאנו לר' אליעזר בפירוש שאמר דבר זה יודעים אנחנו אותו מדבריהם במס' נדה בפרק המפלת ... ממצורע והתניא מנין לרציעה שהיא בימין כו' ומשנינן אזן אזן מופנה רגל רגל לא מופנה ...

כל שעתא ושעתא זמניה הוא אלא אמר רב נחמן א"ר יצחק ואיתימא רב הונא בריה דרב יהושע א) הואיל ובידו להפקירן: אמר מר לולב וכל מכשיריו דוחין את השבת דברי ר"א מנא ליה לר"א הא אי מעומר ושתי הלחם שכן צורך גבוה אלא אמר קרא א) ביום ב) ביום אפילו בשבת ולמאי הלכתא אילימא לטלטול איצטריך קרא למישרי טלטול אלא למכשיריו ורבנן ההוא מיבעי ליה ביום ולא בלילה ור"א ביום ולא בלילה מנא ליה נפקא ליה א) מושמחתם לפני ה' אלהיכם שבעת ימים ימים ולא לילות ורבנן איצטריך ס"ד אמינא נילף שבעת ימים (א) מסוכה מה להלן ב) ימים ואפילו לילות אף כאן ימים ואפילו לילות קמ"ל וליכתוב רחמנא בלולב וניתו הנך ונילפו מיניה משום דאיכא למיפרך מה ללולב שכן טעון ארבעה מינים: סוכה וכל מכשיריה דוחין את השבת דברי רבי אליעזר מנא ליה לר"א הא אי מעומר ושתי הלחם שכן צורך גבוה הוא אי מלולב שכן טעון ארבעה מינים אלא גמר ב) שבעת ימים (ב) מלולב מה להלן מכשיריו דוחין את השבת אף כאן נמי מכשיריו דוחין את השבת וליכתוב רחמנא בסוכה וניתי הנך וניגמור מיניה משום דאיכא למיפרך מה לסוכה שכן נוהגת בלילות כבימים: מצה וכל מכשיריה דוחין את השבת דברי ר"א מנא ליה לר"א הא אי מעומר ושתי הלחם שכן צורך גבוה אי מלולב שכן טעון ארבעה מינים אי מסוכה שכן נוהגת בלילות כבימים אלא גמר ג) חמשה עשר ד) חמשה עשר מחג הסוכות מה להלן מכשיריה דוחין את השבת אף כאן מכשיריה דוחין את השבת וליכתוב רחמנא במצה וניתו הנך וליגמור מיניה משום דאיכא למיפרך מה למצה שכן נוהגת בנשים כבאנשים: שופר וכל מכשיריו דוחין את השבת דברי ר"א מנא ליה לר"א הא אי מעומר ושתי הלחם שכן צורך גבוה אי מלולב שכן טעון ארבעה מינים אי מסוכה שכן נוהגת בלילות כבימים אי ממצה שכן נוהגת בנשים כבאנשים אלא אמר קרא ה) יום תרועה יהיה לכם ביום אפילו בשבת ולמאי אילימא לתקיעה הא ג) תנא דבי שמואל ה) כל מלאכת עבודה לא תעשו יצתה תקיעת שופר ורדיית הפת שהיא חכמה ואינה מלאכה אלא למכשירין ורבנן ההוא מיבעי ליה ביום ולא בלילה ור"א ביום ולא בלילה מנא ליה נפקא ליה ו) מביום הכפורים תעבירו שופר בכל ארצכם וגמרי מהדדי וליכתוב רחמנא בשופר וליתו הנך וליגמרו מיניה מתקיעת שופר דראש השנה ליכא למיגמר שכן מכנסת זכרונות של ישראל לאביהן שבשמים מתקיעות [שופר] דיוה"כ ליכא למיגמרי ד) דאמר מר תקעו ב"ד שופר נפטרו עבדים לבתיהם ושדות חוזרות לבעליהן: (אמר מר) מילה וכל מכשיריה דוחין את השבת דברי רבי אליעזר מנא ליה לר"א הא אי מכולהו גמר כדאמרינן ועוד מה להנך שכן

רש"י

כל שעתא זמניה הוא. וכיון שיש לו טלית בכל יום שמשהה בלא ציצית עובר בעשה ° ואפילו מונחת בקופסא הלכך כל יומא רמיא מצותיה עליה: הואיל ובידו להפקירן. ונפקי מרשותיה ולאו עליה רמיא חובתיה: אי מעומר ושתי הלחם. וגמר במה מלינו: ביום ואפילו בשבת. מדלא כתיב בראשון לדרשא אתא בכל יום שהוא ראשון לחג: ולמאי איצטריך לרבויי. להאי ואפילו בשבת אי נימא לטלטל כדמשמע קרא לקיחה טלטול בעלמא הוא ועדיין במתן תורה לא נאסר טלטול דאיצטריך קרא למישרי להאי: אלא למכשיריו. דאיסורא דאורייתא הוא: מה להלן ימים ואפילו לילות. כדילפינן במסכת סוכה (דף מג.): ולכתוב רחמנא בלולב. דמכשירין דחו: וניתו. עומר ושתי הלחם מיניה ולמה ליה דכתביה בכולהו: אי מלולב. במה מלינו מלולב שהוא מצוה ומכשיריו דוחין אף סוכה שהיא מצוה מכשיריה דוחין: גמר ז' ימים כו'. ובג"ש אתי ליה ואע"ג דאינה מופנה משני לדדים דהא גבי לולב חד שבעת ימים הוא דכתיב ודרשינן לר' אליעזר למעוטי לילות כיון דגלי רחמנא בעומר ושתי הלחם ולולב גילוי מילתא בעלמא הוא ולא פרכינן עלה גימגום (ג): וניתו הנך. עומר ושתי הלחם מינה: אי מסוכה שכן נוהגת בלילות כבימים. ואילו מצה לילה הראשון חובה ותו לא כדאמרינן בפסחים (דף קכ.): ונכתוב רחמנא. בהדיא במצה ונגמרו הנך כולהו מיניה: בנשים כבאנשים. כדילפינן בפסחים (ד' מג:) לא תאכל עליו חמץ שבעת ימים וגו' כל שישנו בבל תאכל חמץ ישנו בקום אכול מצה ונשים איתנהו בבל תאכל חמץ דכל מצות לא תעשה בין שהזמן גרמא בין שאין הזמן גרמא חייבות לאפוקי סוכה ולולב דליתנהו בנשים דמצות עשה שהזמן גרמא היא: ולמאי. האי קרא הי מילתא דתרועה אתא למישרי בשבת אי לתקיעה לא איצטריך דאפילו תקיעת הרשות לית בה איסורא דאורייתא: מלאכת עבודה. של טורח: וגמרי מהדדי. במסכת ראש השנה (דף לג:) שאין תלמוד לומר בחדש השביעי דהא בכמה קראי כתב לן דיוה"כ בחודש השביעי מה ת"ל בחודש השביעי שיהו כל תרועות משל חדש זה שוות: נפטרו עבדים לבתיהם. קריאת דרור דיובל תלויה בה הלכך חשיבא: אי מכולהו. מאחת מכולן. איכא למיפרך בכל הנך חדא לד חמור האמור בה לעיל:

שאם

תוספות

כדאיתא בפ"ק דיבמות (דף ו.) וי"ל דהכא הכי גמרי מה מלינו בהנך שמלות נוהגות בשבת ומכשיריה דחו שבת אף כל שמלות נוהגות בשבת מכשיריה דחו שבת הלכך לא שייך למילף מכיבוד דהיינו המלוה עלמה ולא מכשיריה דשחוט לי בשל לי היינו כיבוד עלמו כשמתקן לו מאכלו והבנין נמי הוי מלוה אחת שלוה הקדוש ברוך הוא לבנות בית המקדש: סד"א נילף שבעת ימים משבעת ימים מסוכה. וא"ת היכי תיסק אדעתיה לדון ג"ש הא אין אדם דן ג"ש מעלמו אא"כ למדה מרבו וי"ל דשמא בעלמא ניתנה למדרש ה): קמ"ל. ° ולא ידענא השתא האי שבעת ימים למאי אתיא דאע"ג דדרשינן בפ"ק דפסחים (דף ה.) מה שביעי שביעי לחג אף ראשון ראשון לחג הא איכא למידרש משבעה בלא ימים: שכן טעון ארבעה מינים. אף על גב דעומר ושתי הלחם נמי מביאין עמהן כבשים ויין לניסוך ושמן למנחות שאני ד' מינין שבלולב דמעכבין זה את זה כדאמר בפרק הקומץ (מנחות דף כ.) ובפרק התכלת (שם דף מה:) [אמרינן] הכבשים אין מעכבין לא את העומר ולא את שתי הלחם ו) והיינו טעון ד' מינין שאין מלות לולב כלל בלא ד' מינין אבל באלו יכולה להיות מלוותן בלא ד' מינין. הר"ב פור"ת: אי מעומר כו'. הכא לא דייקא תלמודא למילף מבינייהו דהכי אורחיה דתלמודא זימנין דייק וזימנין לא דייק ואי הוה דייק הוה משכח פירכ' הרב פור"ת א"נ מילתא דאתיא במה הלד טרח וכתב לה קרא כמו מילתא דאתיא בקל וחומר והאי דקאמר תלמודא ניכתוב רחמנא בהאי ותיתי אידך מיניה פירוש ומאי לריך קרא היינו משום דאי בלא מה הלד הוה מלי למילף הך מלוה מאידך לא הוה כתב רחמנא קרא כיון דהוה פשוט כל כך דלא דמי למילתא דאתיא בק"ו דהוא פשוט יותר: שבעת ימים (ד) מלולב. מופנה הוה משני לדדים גבי לולב לא איצטריך דאע"ג דדרשינן ימים ולא לילות מיהו לא הוה לריך למיכתב שבעת כלל דהוה מלי למיכתב ושמחת לפני וגו' בימים והוי לשון שבעת מיותר לג"ש וא"ת ור' אליעזר היכי דריש ימים ולא לילות כיון דאית ליה ג"ש היא גופה נילף מסוכה מה להלן ימים אפילו לילות אף לולב ימים ואפי' לילות ויש לומר דלית לן למילף בג"ש מילתא דלשון ג"ש גופא מוכחא דאינו כן דימים משמע ולא לילות: ואי מסוכה שכן נוהגת בלילות כבימים. משמע דבעי למימר תאמר במלה שאינה נוהגת בלילות כבימים ואדרבה עיקר מלותה בלילה הראשון שנאמר בערב תאכלו מלות (שמות יב) והכי הוה מלי למימר שכן נוהגת בימים ובלילות: נפקא ליה מביום הכפורים. וגמרינן מהדדי כדדרשינן בראש השנה ז) שיהו כל התקיעות של חודש השביעי שוות כדפירש בקונטרס ורבנן סברי דלא שייך לאקשויי אלא לומר שסדר תקיעות יהיו שוין לענין סדר תקיעות מייתי לה התם אבל לזמן דיום ודאי לא איתקש דע"כ זמנם אינו שוה שזה בראש חודש וזה בעשור לחודש:

והתניא

רבינו חננאל

אזמל לא שרינן בכי האי גוונא דבהדיא קיי"ל הלכתא כרבנן א) וככלליה דרבי עקיבא דאמר כל מלאכה שאפשר לה לעשות מע"ש אינ' דוחה את השבת והבאת אזמל כיון שאפשר לו להביאו מע"ש ולא הביאו אין הבאתו דוחה את השבת אפילו לענין עשיית פסח דכרת הוא לא מייתינן אזמל למול בנו או עבדו כדי שיותר לו לעשות פסח ולא שנא להו לרבנן לא דרך רה"ר ולא דרך גגות וקרפיפות וחצרות הכל אחד הוא ובכל אסור ואשכחנן בתלמוד א"י עובדא ולא הביאוהו בשבת. ואמרינן בכל מקום (רב עביד) מעשה רב דגמרינן מינה. וזה הוא המעשה. ר' שמואל בר אבודומי הוה ליה עובדא למגזר לרב ששעא בריה אנשיון למיתי אזמל שאל לר' [מנא]. אמר להון ידחה למחר. שאל לר' יצחק בן אלעזר אמר להון משחוק [קונדיטון] לא אנשיתון ומיתי אזמל אנשיתון ידחה למחר: א"ר חייא בר אבא. א"ר יוחנן לא לכל א"ר אליעזר מכשירי מצוה דוחין את השבת שהרי שתי הלחם חובת היום הן ולא למדם ר' אליעזר אלא מג"ש נאמרה הבאה בעומר שנאמר והבאתם את עומר וגו' ונאמרה הבאה בשתי הלחם שנאמר ממושבותיכם תביאו לחם תנופה שתים וגו'. מנין שהעומר דוחה שבת. גרסינן באחרית פרק ר' ישמעאל אומר העומר היה בא בשבת מג' סאין וכו'. ת"ר תקריב את מנחת בכוריך מה ת"ל לפי שמצות העומר להביא מן הקמה מניין שאם לא מצא קמה יביא מן העומרין ת"ל תקריב כו' עד תקריב לפי שמצותו לקצור בלילה. מניין שאם קצר ביום כשר ודוחה שבת ת"ל תקריב כל שהוא תקריב מ"מ תקריב אפי' בשבת תקריב אפי' בטומאה. ותוב תניא (בתו"כ) בסוף פרשת אמור אל הכהנים (ובפסחים עו ובמנחות עב) רבי אומר וידבר משה את מועדי ה' מה ת"ל לפי שלא למדנו שדוחין את השבת אלא הפסח והתמיד שכתוב בהן במועדו מניין לרבות העומר והקרב עמו. שתי הלחם והקרב עמהן ת"ל וידבר משה את מועדי ה' קבעו מועד אחד לכולן ופשוטה היא בהלכה כולה. ואפי' ר' אליעזר שמתיר במכשירי מצוה מודה. שאם צייץ טליתו ועשה מזוזה בפתחו בשבת שהוא חייב ואמרינן מ"ש הני ואוקימנא הואיל ובידו להפקירן. פי' כי הציצית הוא חובת הבגד וכיון שהפקיר אינו בגדו וכן הבית כיוצא בו.

חשק שלמה על רבינו חננאל

א) עיין הגהות הגר"א כאן דגרס כל הרגלים שהביא רבינו ע"ש.

מסורת הש"ס

א) [עי' תוספות מנחות מד. ד"ה כל טלית], ב) סוכה מג., ג) לעיל קיז: ע"ש ר"ה כט:, ד) ר"ה ח:, ה) עיין מהרש"א, ו) [כדאיתא בפ' התכלת מה:], ז) [דף לג:].

הגהות הב"ח

(א) גמ' נילף שבעת ימים משבעת ימים מסוכה: (ב) שם אלא גמר שבעת ימים שבעת ימים מלולב: (ג) רש"י ד"ה גמר ז' ימים וכו' גימגום הס"ד ואחר כך מ"ה ונכתוב רחמנא בהדיא במצה ונגמרו הנך עומר ושתי הלחם ולולב מינה: (ד) תוס' ד"ה שבעת ימים משבעת ימים מלולב מופנה הוה משני לדדין דגבי לולב נמי לא איצטריך:

גליון הש"ס

רש"י ד"ה כל שעתא וכו' ואפילו מונחת בקופסא. עי' מנחות דף מד ע"א תוס' ד"ה כל טלית: תוס' ד"ה קמ"ל ולא ידענא. כעין זה לעיל דף קיח ע"ב תוס' ד"ה אלו היו וש"נ:

תורה אור השלם

א) וּלְקַחְתֶּם לָכֶם בַּיּוֹם הָרִאשׁוֹן פְּרִי עֵץ הָדָר כַּפֹּת תְּמָרִים וַעֲנַף עֵץ עָבֹת וְעַרְבֵי נָחַל וּשְׂמַחְתֶּם לִפְנֵי יְיָ אֱלֹהֵיכֶם שִׁבְעַת יָמִים: [ויקרא כג, מ]

ב) בַּסֻּכֹּת תֵּשְׁבוּ שִׁבְעַת יָמִים כָּל הָאֶזְרָח בְּיִשְׂרָאֵל יֵשְׁבוּ בַּסֻּכֹּת: [ויקרא כג, מב]

ג) וּבַחֲמִשָּׁה עָשָׂר יוֹם לַחֹדֶשׁ הַזֶּה חַג הַמַּצּוֹת לַייָ שִׁבְעַת יָמִים מַצּוֹת תֹּאכֵלוּ: [ויקרא כג, ו]

ד) דַּבֵּר אֶל בְּנֵי יִשְׂרָאֵל לֵאמֹר בַּחֲמִשָּׁה עָשָׂר יוֹם לַחֹדֶשׁ הַשְּׁבִיעִי הַזֶּה חַג הַסֻּכּוֹת שִׁבְעַת יָמִים לַייָ: [ויקרא כג, לד]

ה) וּבַחֹדֶשׁ הַשְּׁבִיעִי בְּאֶחָד לַחֹדֶשׁ מִקְרָא קֹדֶשׁ יִהְיֶה לָכֶם כָּל מְלֶאכֶת עֲבֹדָה לֹא תַעֲשׂוּ יוֹם תְּרוּעָה יִהְיֶה לָכֶם: [במדבר כט, א]

ו) וְהַעֲבַרְתָּ שׁוֹפַר תְּרוּעָה בַּחֹדֶשׁ הַשְּׁבִעִי בֶּעָשׂוֹר לַחֹדֶשׁ בְּיוֹם הַכִּפֻּרִים תַּעֲבִירוּ שׁוֹפָר בְּכָל אַרְצְכֶם: [ויקרא כה, ט]

ליקוטי רש"י

ביום אפילו בשבת. דמשמע כל יום ויום וקרא יתירא הוא דהא כבר כתיב בראשון. איצטריך קרא למישרי טלטול. דרבנן אסור ועדיין לא נאסר טלטול כל עיקר. אלא למכשיריו. ללמוד שמכשירי לולב דוחין את השבת ואפילו לקוצצו מן המחובר ולאוגדו [סוכה מג.]. בנשים כבאנשים. אכילת מצה ליל ראשון שהוא חובה כדכתיב (שמות יב) בערב תאכלו מצות וחמץ גרס לה בע"ו בניסן ונשים חייבות באכילת מצה כדאמר בפסחים (מג:) נשים חייבות באכילת מצה דבר תורה שנאמר שבעת ימים תאכל עליו מצות כל שישנו בבל תאכל חמץ ישנו בקום אכול מצה ונשים איתנהו בבל תאכל חמץ דמצות לא תעשה היא [קידושין לד.]. ורדיית הפת. לרדיית הפת שבות היא שהיא חכמה ואינה מלאכה [לעיל ג:].

כָּל שַׁעְתָּא וְשַׁעְתָּא זְמַנֵּיהּ הוּא – **each and every moment is its** fixed **time!**[1] Hence, since failure to make *tzitzis* or a *mezuzah* on the Sabbath results in the transgression of the commandment incumbent upon the individual, the preliminaries should also be permitted at that time. – ? –

The Gemara offers a different explanation for the exclusion of these preliminaries:

אֶלָּא אָמַר רַב נַחְמָן אָמַר רַבִּי יִצְחָק – **Rather, Rav Nachman said in the name of R' Yitzchak,** וְאִיתֵּימָא רַב הוּנָא בְּרֵיהּ דְּרַב יְהוֹשֻׁעַ – **and some say** that he said it in the name of **Rav Huna the son of Rav Yehoshua:** הוֹאִיל וּבְיָדוֹ לְהַפְקִירָן – Tying *tzitzis* and writing a *mezuzah* scroll are prohibited on the Sabbath **since one can renounce ownership** of his garment and his house, in which case the obligations attached to these items would no longer be incumbent upon him.[2] Since such a potential exists, the Torah did not permit any desecration of the Sabbath in the cases of *tzitzis* and *mezuzah.*

The Gemara above (131a) mentioned preliminaries to various other mitzvos that do, in fact, override the Sabbath *melachah* restrictions. The Gemara now begins to establish the Biblical sources for these leniencies:

אָמַר מַר – **Master said:** The Gemara above quoted the following Baraisa: לוּלָב וְכָל מַכְשִׁירָיו דּוֹחִין אֶת הַשַּׁבָּת – The mitzvah of LULAV AND ALL ITS PRELIMINARIES OVERRIDE THE SABBATH restrictions. דִּבְרֵי רַבִּי אֱלִיעֶזֶר – These are THE WORDS OF R' ELIEZER. מְנָא לֵיהּ לְרַבִּי אֱלִיעֶזֶר הָא – Now, **from where** does **R' Eliezer** derive **this** law? אִי מֵעוֹמֶר וּשְׁתֵּי הַלֶּחֶם – **If** you say he derives it **from the** ***Omer*** **and Two Loaves** offerings,[3] that cannot be – שֶׁכֵּן צוֹרֶךְ גָּבוֹהַּ – **for indeed** each is **a necessity for the Most High.**[4] אֶלָּא אָמַר קְרָא ,,בַּיּוֹם'' – **Rather, the verse states**[5] with reference to *lulav* and the three other species: *You shall take for yourselves* ***on the first day*** (i.e. of the seven-day Succos festival). ,,בַּיּוֹם'' – The fact that the verse stated ***on the first day,*** and not simply "on the first," implies: אֲפִילוּ בְּשַׁבָּת – *on any day* that is the first day of the festival – i.e. **even on the Sabbath.** וּלְמַאי הִלְכְתָא – **And for what** novel **ruling** is this interpretation meant? אִילֵימָא לְטַלְטוּל – **If we say** that it is meant **for handling,** i.e. to teach that handling the *lulav* is permitted even when the first day of Succos falls on Shabbos, and the *muktzeh* prohibition does not prevent the mitzvah's fulfillment,[6] that cannot be – אִיצְטְרִיךְ קְרָא לְמִישְׁרֵי טִלְטוּל – for **is a verse needed to permit handling?!**[7] אֶלָּא לְמַכְשִׁירָיו – **Rather,** the interpretation is meant **for** a ruling about **[*lulav's*] preliminaries,**[8] to teach that they may be performed even when the first day of Succos falls on Shabbos.

The Gemara asks:

וְרַבָּנָן – **And the Rabbis,** who disagree with R' Eliezer and maintain that preliminaries to a mitzvah may not be performed on the Sabbath – what do they do with the extraneous *on the . . . day*?

The Gemara answers:

הַהוּא מִיבְּעֵי לֵיהּ בַּיּוֹם וְלֹא בַּלַּיְלָה – **That** verse **is needed** to teach that the mitzvah of *lulav* applies **during the day and not at night.**

The Gemara then asks:

וְרַבִּי אֱלִיעֶזֶר בַּיּוֹם וְלֹא בַּלַּיְלָה מְנָא לֵיהּ – **And from where** does **R' Eliezer,** who derives the law of preliminaries from the superfluous *on the . . . day,* know that the mitzvah of *lulav* applies **during the day and not at night?**

The Gemara answers:

נָפְקָא לֵיהּ מִ,,וּשְׂמַחְתֶּם לִפְנֵי ה' אֱלֹהֵיכֶם שִׁבְעַת יָמִים'' – **He derives** that law **from** the conclusion of that verse, ***and you shall rejoice before Hashem, your God, for seven days,*** יָמִים וְלֹא לֵילוֹת – which implies that the mitzvah of *lulav* is to be performed during those **days and not** those **nights.**[9]

The Gemara then asks:

וְרַבָּנָן – **And the Rabbis?** Why do they not derive the "day and not night" law from there, thereby freeing *on the . . . day* (at the

NOTES

1. And for every day that one fails to attach *tzitzis* to his garment or affix a *mezuzah* to his doorpost, he violates a positive commandment of the Torah (*Rashi*). [Our Gemara states כָּל שַׁעְתָּא וְשַׁעְתָּא, *each and every moment; Rashi,* however, writes בְּכָל יוֹם, *every day.* See *Megadim Chadashim,* who discuss this.]

Rashi writes that the violation occurs even in the case of a four-cornered garment that one has purchased but is not wearing. The Rishonim dispute this point, since the established halachah is that the *tzitzis* obligation applies only when a garment is being worn (see *Rambam, Hil. Tzitzis* 3:10, and *Orach Chaim* 19:1). See *Rashba* for an explanation of why *Rashi* chose to explain our Gemara according to the other opinion; see also *Beis HaLevi* I:4 at length. [Whether, in fact, one violates the mitzvah of *tzitzis* if he wears a four-cornered garment without *tzitzis* on the Sabbath, see *Magen Avraham* 13:8, and *Chasam Sofer* here.]

2. In commanding the mitzvah of *tzitzis* the Torah states (*Deuteronomy* 22:12): *You shall make for yourselves twisted threads on the four corners of your garment.* The specification of ***your garment*** (כְּסוּתְךָ) implies that one who wears an ownerless or borrowed garment is entirely exempt from the mitzvah (i.e. under Biblical law; under Rabbinic law *tzitzis* must be attached after thirty days). Similarly, regarding *mezuzah* scrolls, the Torah states (ibid. 6:9 and 11:20): *And write them on the doorposts of your house.* The phrase ***your house*** (בֵּיתֶךָ) implies that one who lives in an ownerless or borrowed house is likewise exempt from the mitzvah (see *Ramban, Rashba* et al.). [According to *Ramban, Rashba, Rosh* (*Hil. Mezuzah* 15) and *Tosafos* to *Avodah Zarah* (21a ד״ה הא), he is absolutely exempt under Biblical law, but is Rabbinically obligated to affix a *mezuzah* after thirty days. However, *Tosafos* in *Menachos* (44a ד״ה טלית) write that while the post-thirty-day obligation to attach *tzitzis* is only Rabbinic, the post-thirty-day obligation to affix a *mezuzah* is Biblical.] *Meiri* writes that this renouncing of ownership (of one's garment or house) may take place on the Sabbath as well (see also *Magen Avraham* 13:8 and *Ishei Yisrael;* cf. *Netziv*).

3. [That the preliminaries (e.g. reaping, grinding, sifting) to the mitzvah of *Omer* override the Sabbath restrictions is derived exegetically in *Menachos* 72a. That the preliminaries to the mitzvah of Two Loaves override the Sabbath is derived from the case of *Omer* via a *gezeirah shavah* (above, 131a).] The Gemara now mentions the possibility of deriving *lulav* from *Omer* and Two Loaves through a מָה מָּצִינוּ, *mah matzinu* (literally: what do we find?) interpretation (*Rashi*). [The *mah matzinu* is an analogy that teaches that a law known to apply to one or more cases should apply to every other similar case.]

4. The *Omer* and Two Loaves are offerings to God, and so it is understandable that their preliminaries override the Sabbath restrictions. Taking a *lulav* on Succos is a personal mitzvah, not an offering, and thus cannot be analogized via a *mah matzinu* to the *Omer* and Two Loaves.

5. *Leviticus* 23:40.

6. [And the exposition of the verse would refer to the mitzvah itself and not its preliminaries], inasmuch as the verse mandates a "taking" of the *lulav,* which is an act of handling (*Rashi*). [As for why a *lulav* would be considered *muktzeh,* see *Tosafos* to *Succah* 42b ד״ה טלטול.]

7. At the time the Torah was given, *muktzeh* was permitted [it was only later proscribed by Rabbinic edict (see chs. 17 and 21 in this tractate)]. Hence, no special verse is needed to permit handling (i.e. taking) the *lulav* (*Rashi, Ritva MHK* ed.).

8. Namely, cutting the branch off the palm tree (*Ritva MHK* ed.), which is the Biblically prohibited *melachah* of reaping (see *Rashi*).

9. Although the conclusion of the verse refers to the Temple, where the *lulav* was to be taken for all seven days of the festival (as opposed to all other places, where under Torah law it is taken only on the first day), still, the word יָמִים, *days,* implies that the mitzvah in the Temple is to be performed only during the day; and from there we can infer that in all other places as well it is to be performed only during the day (*Ritva MHK* ed.).

כל שעתא ושעתא זמניה הוא אלא אמר רב נחמן א"ר יצחק ואיתימא רב הונא בריה דרב יהושע א) הואיל ובידו להפקירן: אמר מר לולב וכל מכשיריו דוחין את השבת דברי ר"א מנא ליה לר"א הא אי מעומר ושתי הלחם שכן צורך גבוה אלא אמר קרא א) ביום ב) ביום אפילו בשבת ולמאי הלכתא אילימא לטלטול איצטריך קרא למישרי טלטול אלא למכשיריו ורבנן ההוא מיבעי ליה ביום ולא בלילה ור"א ביום ולא בלילה מנא ליה נפקא ליה א) מושמחתם לפני ה' אלהיכם שבעת ימים ימים ולא לילות ורבנן איצטריך ס"ד אמינא נילף שבעת ימים (א) מסוכה מה להלן ב) ימים ואפילו לילות אף כאן ימים ואפילו לילות קמ"ל וליכתוב רחמנא בלולב וניתו הנך ונילפו מיניה משום דאיכא למיפרך מה ללולב שכן טעון ארבעה מינים: סוכה וכל מכשיריה דוחין את השבת דברי רבי אליעזר מנא ליה לר"א הא אי מעומר ושתי הלחם שכן צורך גבוה הוא אי מלולב שכן טעון ארבעה מינים אלא גמר (ב) ג) שבעת ימים מלולב מה להלן מכשיריו דוחין את השבת אף כאן נמי מכשירין דוחין את השבת וליכתוב רחמנא בסוכה וניתי הנך וניגמור מיניה משום דאיכא למיפרך מה לסוכה שכן נוהגת בלילות כבימים: מצה וכל מכשיריה דוחין את השבת דברי ר"א מנא ליה לר"א הא אי מעומר ושתי הלחם שכן צורך גבוה אי מלולב שכן טעון ארבעה מינים אי מסוכה שכן נוהגת בלילות כבימים אלא גמר ג) חמשה עשר ד) חמשה עשר מחג הסוכות מה להלן מכשיריה דוחין את השבת אף כאן מכשיריה דוחין את השבת וליכתוב רחמנא במצה וניתו הנך וליגמור מיניה משום דאיכא למיפרך מה למצה שכן נוהגת בנשים כבאנשים: שופר וכל מכשיריו דוחין את השבת דברי ר"א מנא ליה לר"א הא אי מעומר ושתי הלחם שכן צורך גבוה אי מלולב שכן טעון ארבעה מינים אי מסוכה שכן נוהגת בלילות כבימים אי ממצה שכן נוהגת בנשים כבאנשים אלא אמר קרא ה) יום תרועה יהיה לכם ביום אפילו בשבת ולמאי אילימא לתקיעה הא ג) תנא דבי שמואל ו) כל מלאכת עבודה לא תעשו יצתה תקיעת שופר ורדיית הפת שהיא חכמה ואינה מלאכה אלא למכשירין ורבנן ההוא מיבעי ליה ביום ולא בלילה ור"א ביום ולא בלילה מנא ליה נפקא ליה ו) מביום הכפורים תעבירו שופר בכל ארצכם וגמרי מהדדי וליכתוב רחמנא בשופר וליתו הנך וליגמרו מיניה מתקיעת שופר דראש השנה ליכא למיגמר שכן מכנסת זכרונות של ישראל לאביהן שבשמים מתקיעות [שופר] דיוה"כ ליכא למיגמרי ז) דאמר מר תקעו ב"ד שופר נפטרו עבדים לבתיהם ושדות חוזרות לבעליהן: (אמר מר) מילה וכל מכשיריה דוחין את השבת דברי רבי אליעזר מנא ליה לר"א הא אי מכולהו גמר כדאמרינן ועוד מה להנך

שכן

רש"י

כל שעתא זמניה הוא. וכיון שיש לו טלית בכל יום שמשהה בלא ציצית עובר בעשה ° ואפילו מונחת בקופסא הלכך כל יומא רמיא מלותיה עליה: הואיל ובידו להפקירן. ונפקי מרשותיה ולאו עליה רמיא חובתיה: אי מעומר ושתי הלחם. וגמר במה מלינו: ביום ואפילו בשבת. מדלא כתיב בראשון לדרשא אתא בכל יום שהוא ראשון לחג: ולמאי איצטריך לרבויי. להאי ואפילו בשבת אי נימא לטלטל כדמשמע קרא לקיחה טלטול בעלמא הוא ועדיין במתן תורה לא נאסר טלטול דאיצטריך קרא למישרי להאי: אלא למכשיריו. דאיסורא דאורייתא הוא: מה להלן ימים ואפילו לילות. כדילפינן במסכת סוכה (דף מג.): ולכתוב רחמנא בלולב. דמכשירין דחו: וניתו. עומר ושתי הלחם מיניה ולמה ליה דכתביה בכולהו: אי מלולב. במה מלינו מלולב שהוא מלוה ומכשיריו דוחין אף סוכה שהיא מלוה מכשיריה דוחין: גמר ז' ימים כו'. ובג"ש אתי ליה ואע"ג דאינה מופנה משני לדדים דהא גבי לולב חד שבעת ימים הוא דכתיב ודרשינן לר' אליעזר למעוטי לילות כיון דגלי רחמנא בעומר ושתי הלחם ולולב גילוי מילתא בעלמא הוא ולא פרכינן עלה גימגום (ג): וניתו הנך. עומר ושתי הלחם מינה: אי מסוכה שכן נוהגת בלילות כבימים. ואילו מלה לילה הראשון חובה ותו לא כדאמרינן בפסחים (דף קכ.): ונכתוב רחמנא. בהדיא במלה ונגמרו הנך כולהו מיניה: בנשים כבאנשים. כדילפינן בפסחים (ד' מג:) לא תאכל עליו חמץ שבעת ימים וגו' כל שישנו בבל תאכל חמץ ישנו בקום אכול מלה ונשים איתנהו בבל תאכל חמץ דכל מלות לא תעשה בין שהזמן גרמא בין שאין הזמן גרמא חייבות לאפוקי סוכה ולולב דליתנהו בנשים דמלות עשה שהזמן גרמא היא: ולמאי. האי קרא הי מילתא דתרועה אתא למישרי בשבת אי לתקיעה לא איצטריך דאפילו תקיעת הרשות לית בה איסורא דאורייתא: מלאכת עבודה. של טורח: וגמרי מהדדי. במסכת ראש השנה (דף לג:) שאין תלמוד לומר בחדש השביעי דהא בכמה קראי כתב לן דיוה"כ בחודש השביעי מה ת"ל בחודש השביעי שיהו כל תרועות משל חדש השביעי שוות: נפטרו עבדים לבתיהם. קריאת דרור דיובל תלויה בה הלכך חשיבא: אי מכולהו. מאחת מכולן: כדאמרינן. איכא למיפרך בכל הנך חדא לד חמור האמור בה לעיל:

שאם

תוספות

כדאיתא בפ"ק דיבמות (דף ו.) וי"ל דהכא הכי גמרי מה מלינו בהנך שמלות נוהגות בשבת ומכשיריה דחו שבת אף כל שמלות נוהגות בשבת מכשיריה דחו שבת הלכך לא שייך למילף מכיבוד דהיינו המלוה עלמה ולא מכשיריה דשפוט לי בשל לי היינו כיבוד עלמו כשמתקן לו מאכלו והבנין נמי הוי מלוה אחת שלוה הקדוש ברוך הוא לבנות בית המקדש: סד"א נילף שבעת ימים משבעת ימים מסוכה. וא"ת היכי מיסק אדעתיה לדון ג"ש הא אין אדם דן ג"ש מעלמו אא"כ למדה מרבו וי"ל דשמא בעלמא ניתנה למדרש ז): קמ"ל. ° ולא ידענא השתא האי שבעת ימים למאי אתיא דאע"ג דדרשינן בפ"ק דפסחים (דף ה.) מה שביעי שביעי לחג אף ראשון לחג ראשון לחג הא איכא למידרש משבעה בלא ימים: שכן טעון ארבעה מינים. אף על גב דעומר ושתי הלחם נמי מביאין עמהן כבשים ויין לניסוך ושמן למנחות שאני ד' מינין שבלולב דמעכבין זה את זה כדאמר בפרק הקומץ (מנחות דף כז.) ובפרק התכלת (שם דף מד:) [אמרינן] הכבשים אין מעכבין לא את העומר ולא את שתי הלחם ז) והיינו טעון ד' מינין שאין מלות לולב כלל בלא ד' מינין אבל בלאו יכולה להיות מלוותן בלא ד' מינין. הר"ב פור"ח: אי מעומר כו'. הכא לא דייקא תלמודא למילף מבינייהו דהכי אורחיה דתלמודא זימנין דייק וזימנין לא דייק ואי הוה דייק הוה משכח פירכ' הרב פור"ח א"נ מילתא דאתיא במה הלד טרח וכתב לה קרא כמו מילתא דאתיא בקל וחומר והאי דקאמר תלמודא ניכתוב רחמנא בהאי ותיתי אידך מיניה פירוש ומאי לריך קרא היינו משום דאי בלא מה הלד הוה מלי למילף הך מלוה מאידך לא הוה כתב רחמנא קרא כיון דהוה פשוט כל כך דלא דמי למילתא דאתיא בק"ו דהוה פשוט יותר: שבעת ימים (ד) מלולב. מופנה הוה משני לדדים גבי לולב לא איצטריך דאע"ג דדרשינן ימים ולא לילות מיהו לא הוה לריך למיכתב שבעת כלל דהוה מלי למיכתב ושמחתם לפני וגו' בימים והוי לשון שבעת מיותר לג"ש וא"ת ור' אליעזר היכי דריש ימים ולא לילות כיון דאית ליה ג"ש היא גופה נילף מסוכה מה להלן ימים אפילו לילות אף לולב ימים ואפי' לילות ויש לומר דלית לן למילף בג"ש מילתא דלשון ג"ש גופה מוכחא דלינו כן דימים משמע ולא לילות: ואי מסוכה שכן נוהגת בלילות כבימים. משמע דבעי למימר תאמר במלה שאינה נוהגת בלילות כבימים ואדרבה עיקר מלותה בלילה הראשון שנאמר בערב תאכלו מלות (שמות יב) והכי הוה מלי למימר שכן נוהגת בימים ובלילות: נפקא ליה מביום הכפורים. וגמרינן מהדדי כדדרשינן בראש השנה ז) שיהו כל התקיעות של חודש השביעי שוות כדפירש בקונטרס ורבנן סברי דלא שייך לאקשויי אלא לומר שסדר תקיעות יהיו שוין לענין סדר תקיעות מייתי לה התם אבל לזמן דיום ודאי לא איתקש דעי"כ זמנם אינו שוה שזה בראש חודש וזה בעשור לחודש:

והתניא

רבינו חננאל

אזמל לא שרינן בכי האי גוונא דבהדיא קיי"ל הלכתא כרבנן א) וככלליה דרבי עקיבא דאמר כל מלאכה שאפשר לה לעשות מע"ש אינ' דוחה את השבת והבאת אזמל כיון שאפשר לו להביאו מע"ש ולא הביאו אין הבאתו דוחה את השבת אפילו לענין עשיית פסח דכרת הוא לא מייתינן אזמל למול בנו או עבדו כדי שיותר לו לעשות פסח ולא שנא להו לרבנן לא דרך רה"ר ולא דרך גגות וקרפיפות וחצרות הכל אחד הוא ובכל אסור ואשכחנן בתלמוד א"י עובדא ולא הביאוהו בשבת. ואמרינן בכל מקום (רב עביד) מעשה רב דגמרינן מינה. וזה הוא המעשה. ר' שמואל בר אבודומי הוה ליה עובדא למגזר לרב ששעא בריה אנשיון למיתי אזמל שאל לר' [מנא]. אמר להון ידחה למחר. שאל לר' יצחק בן אלעזר אמר להון משחוק [קונדיטון] לא אנשיתון ומיתי אזמל אנשיתון ידחה למחר: א"ר חייא בר אבא. א"ר יוחנן לא לכל א"ר אליעזר מכשירי מצוה דוחין את השבת שהרי שתי הלחם חובת היום הן ולא למדם ר' אליעזר אלא מג"ש נאמרה הבאה בעומר שנאמר והבאתם את עומר וגו' ונאמרה הבאה בשתי הלחם שנאמר ממושבותיכם תביאו לחם תנופה שתים וגו'. מנין שהעומר דוחה שבת. גרסינן באחרית פרק ר' ישמעאל אומר העומר היה בא בשבת מג' סאין וכו'. ת"ר תקריב את מנחת בכוריך מה ת"ל לפי שמצות העומר להביא מן הקמה מניין שאם לא מצא קמה יביא מן העומרין ת"ל תקריב כו' עד תקריב לפי שמצותו לקצור בלילה. מניין שאם קצר ביום כשר ודוחה שבת ת"ל תקריב כל שהוא תקריב מ"מ תקריבו אפי' בשבת אפילו ביום בטומאה. ותוב תניא (בתו"כ) בסוף פרשת אמור אל הכהנים (ובפסחים עז ובמנחות עב) רבי אומר וידבר משה את מועדי ה' מה ת"ל לפי שלא למדנו שדוחין את השבת אלא הפסח והתמיד שכתוב בהן במועדו מניין לרבות העומר והקרב עמו. שתי הלחם והקרב עמהן שידחו שבת ת"ל וידבר משה את מועדי ה' קבעו מועד אחד לכולן ופשוטה היא זו הלכה כולה. ואפי' ר' אליעזר שמתיר במכשירי מצוה מודה. שאם ציצית טליתו ועשה מזוזה בפתחו בשבת שהוא חייב ואמרינן מ"ש הני אוקימנא הואיל ובידו להפקירן. פי' כי הציצית הוא חובת הבגד וכיון שהפקיר אינו בגדו וכן הבית כיוצא בו.

חשק שלמה על רבינו חננאל

א) עיין היטב ברי"ף כאן דדחה כל הראיות שהביא רבינו ע"ש:

מסורת הש"ס

א) [עי' תוספות מנחות מד. ד"ה טלית], ב) סוכה מג., ג) לעיל קח: ע"ש ר"ה כט:, ד) ר"ה ח:, ה) עיין מהרש"א, ו) [כדאיתא בפ' המכללת מה:], ז) [דף לג:].

הגהות הב"ח

(א) גמ' נילף שבעת ימים משבעת ימים מסוכה: (ב) שם אלא גמר שבעת ימים מלולב: (ג) רש"י ד"ה גמר ז' ימים וכו' גימגום הס"ד ואחר כך מ"ה ונכתוב רחמנא בהדיא בסוכה וניתי הנך עומר ושתי הלחם ולולב מינה: (ד) תוס' ד"ה שבעת ימים משבעת ימים מלולב מופנה הוה משני לדדין דגבי לולב נמי לא איצטריך:

גליון הש"ס

רש"י ד"ה כל שעתא וכו' ואפי' מונחת בקופסא. עי' מנחות דף מד ע"א תוס' ד"ה טלית: תוס' ד"ה קמ"ל ולא ידענא. כעין זה לעיל דף קיט ע"ב תוס' ד"ה אלו היו וכו':

תורה אור השלם

א) וּלְקַחְתֶּם לָכֶם בַּיּוֹם הָרִאשׁוֹן פְּרִי עֵץ הָדָר כַּפֹּת תְּמָרִים וַעֲנַף עֵץ עָבֹת וְעַרְבֵי נָחַל וּשְׂמַחְתֶּם לִפְנֵי יְיָ אֱלֹהֵיכֶם שִׁבְעַת יָמִים: [ויקרא כג, מ]

ב) בַּסֻּכֹּת תֵּשְׁבוּ שִׁבְעַת יָמִים כָּל הָאֶזְרָח בְּיִשְׂרָאֵל יֵשְׁבוּ בַּסֻּכֹּת: [ויקרא כג, מב]

ג) וּבַחֲמִשָּׁה עָשָׂר יוֹם לַחֹדֶשׁ הַזֶּה חַג הַמַּצּוֹת לַייָ שִׁבְעַת יָמִים מַצּוֹת תֹּאכֵלוּ: [ויקרא כג, ו]

ד) דַּבֵּר אֶל בְּנֵי יִשְׂרָאֵל לֵאמֹר בַּחֲמִשָּׁה עָשָׂר יוֹם לַחֹדֶשׁ הַשְּׁבִיעִי הַזֶּה חַג הַסֻּכּוֹת שִׁבְעַת יָמִים לַייָ: [ויקרא כג, לד]

ה) וּבַחֹדֶשׁ הַשְּׁבִיעִי בְּאֶחָד לַחֹדֶשׁ מִקְרָא קֹדֶשׁ יִהְיֶה לָכֶם כָּל מְלֶאכֶת עֲבֹדָה לֹא תַעֲשׂוּ יוֹם תְּרוּעָה יִהְיֶה לָכֶם: [במדבר כט, א]

ו) וְהַעֲבַרְתָּ שׁוֹפַר תְּרוּעָה בַּחֹדֶשׁ הַשְּׁבִעִי בֶּעָשׂוֹר לַחֹדֶשׁ בְּיוֹם הַכִּפֻּרִים תַּעֲבִירוּ שׁוֹפָר בְּכָל אַרְצְכֶם: [ויקרא כה, ט]

ליקוטי רש"י

ביום אפילו בשבת. דמשמע כל יום ויום וקרא יתירא הוא דמלי למכתב בראשון. איצטריך קרא למישרי טלטול. דרבנן עדיין לא גזור טלטול בעולם ולא הכתוב להתירו כאן. אלא למכשירי. לא הכתוב ללמדך שמכשירי לולב דוחין את השבת כלומר תיקוניה ואפילו לקוללו מן המחובר ולאגדו [סוכה מג.]. בנשים כבאנשים. אכילת מלה ליל ראשון שהוא חובה כדכתיב (שמות יב) בערב תאכלו מלות וזמן גרם לה בט"ו בניסן ונשים חייבות באכילת מלה דבר תורה שנאמר לא תאכל עליו חמץ שבעת ימים תאכל עליו מלות כל שישנו בבל תאכל חמץ ישנו בקום אכול מלה ונשים איתנהו בבל תאכל חמץ דמלות לא תעשה היא [קידושין לד.]. ורדיית הפת. דרדיית הפת שבות היא שהיא חכמה ו...

beginning of the verse) to teach that the preliminaries to the mitzvah of *lulav* override the Sabbath restrictions?

The Gemara answers:

אִיצְטְרִיךְ – [*On the . . . day*] is indeed **needed** to teach the "day and not night" law, סָלְקָא דַּעְתָּךְ אָמִינָא – for **it would have occurred to you** that **I might say** נֵילַף "שִׁבְעַת יָמִים" מִסּוּכָּה – that **we should learn** a *gezeirah shavah* of ***for seven days****/for seven days* **from** the passage of **succah,**[10] as follows: מַה לְהַלָּן יָמִים וַאֲפִילוּ לֵילוֹת – **Just as there** we learn that one must dwell in a succah during the festival's **days and even nights,**[11] אַף כָּאן יָמִים וַאֲפִילוּ לֵילוֹת – **so here** we could derive that one must take a *lulav* for the festival's **days and even nights.** קָא מַשְׁמַע לָן – [***On the . . . day***] thus **informs us** that the mitzvah of *lulav* applies only during the day.[12]

With regard to R' Eliezer's law of preliminaries, the Gemara has identified different sources for the cases of *lulav, Omer* and Two Loaves.[13] The Gemara therefore asks: וְלִיכְתּוֹב רַחֲמָנָא בְּלוּלָב – **But let the Merciful One write** a sanction for preliminaries to override the Sabbath restrictions **in** the passage of ***lulav,*** וְנֵיתוּ הָנָךְ וְנֵילְפוּ מִינֵּיהּ – **and let the other** two cases – the *Omer* and Two Loaves offerings – **come and be derived from it!**[14] Why are three separate teachings necessary?

The Gemara answers:

מִשּׁוּם דְּאִיכָּא לְמִיפְרַךְ – **Because there are** grounds **to refute** the *mah matzinu* teaching, as follows: מַה לְלוּלָב שֶׁכֵּן טָעוּן אַרְבָּעָה מִינִים – **Whereas** the mitzvah of ***lulav*** is unique, **for indeed it requires** the taking of **four species,**[15] the same cannot be said of the mitzvos of *Omer* and Two Loaves.[16] Hence, because *Omer* and Two Loaves lack this attribute of *lulav,* the law of preliminaries cannot be inferred to them.

The Gemara now establishes the source for the second set of preliminaries mentioned above:

סוּכָּה וְכָל מַכְשִׁירֶיהָ דּוֹחִין אֶת הַשַּׁבָּת – The Baraisa stated: The mitzvah of SUCCAH AND ALL ITS PRELIMINARIES OVERRIDE THE SABBATH restrictions. דִּבְרֵי רַבִּי אֱלִיעֶזֶר – These are THE WORDS OF R' ELIEZER. מְנָא לֵיהּ לְרַבִּי אֱלִיעֶזֶר הָא – Now, **from where does R' Eliezer** derive **this** law? אִי מֵעוֹמֶר וּשְׁתֵּי הַלֶּחֶם – **If** you say he derives it **from the *Omer* and Two Loaves** offerings,[17] that cannot be – שֶׁכֵּן צוֹרֶךְ גָּבוֹהַּ הוּא – **for indeed [each] is a necessity for the Most High.**[18] אִי מִלּוּלָב – **If** you say he derives it **from** the mitzvah of ***lulav,***[19] that also cannot be – שֶׁכֵּן טָעוּן אַרְבָּעָה מִינִים – **for indeed [that mitzvah] requires** the taking of **four species.**[20] Since *succah* lacks this attribute of *lulav,* the law of preliminaries cannot be inferred to it. אֶלָּא גָּמַר "שִׁבְעַת יָמִים" מִלּוּלָב – **Rather, [R' Eliezer] learned** a *gezeirah shavah* of ***for seven days****/for seven days* **from** the passage of ***lulav,***[21] as follows: מַה לְהַלָּן מַכְשִׁירָיו דּוֹחִין אֶת הַשַּׁבָּת – **Just as there** we learn[22] that [***lulav's***] **preliminaries override the Sabbath** restrictions, אַף כָּאן נַמִּי מַכְשִׁירָיו דּוֹחִין אֶת הַשַּׁבָּת – **so here** derive that **[succah's] preliminaries also override the Sabbath** restrictions.[23]

The Gemara asks:

וְלִיכְתּוֹב רַחֲמָנָא בְּסוּכָּה – **But let the Merciful One write** the law of preliminaries **in** the passage of ***succah,***[24] וְנֵיתֵי הָנָךְ וְנִיגְמוֹר מִינֵּיהּ – **and let these other** two cases – the *Omer* and Two Loaves

NOTES

10. *Leviticus* 23:42 states: בַּסֻּכֹּת תֵּשְׁבוּ שִׁבְעַת יָמִים, *You shall dwell in booths for seven days.* Hence, the phrase שִׁבְעַת יָמִים, *for seven days,* which is stated with reference to the mitzvah of *lulav* in the Temple (at the conclusion of ibid. v. 40, just quoted by the Gemara), can be used for a *gezeirah shavah* to the mitzvah of dwelling in a *succah.* [See *Tosafos* with *Maharsha, Maharam* and *Maharam Schif* regarding the possibility of innovating a *gezeirah shavah.*]

11. The Gemara (*Succah* 43a-b) derives this via a *gezeirah shavah* from the passage of מִלּוּאִים, *the consecration* of the Kohanim for service in the Tabernacle (*Leviticus* ch. 8).

12. I.e. and in the Temple as well (see *Ritva MHK* ed.).

The question arises: Since *on the . . . day* is needed to preclude the *gezeirah shavah* teaching from succah ("days and even nights"), how does R' Eliezer, who uses *on the . . . day* to derive that *lulav's* preliminaries override the Sabbath, know that the mitzvah of *lulav* does not apply at night? *Chidushei HaRan* explains that, in R' Eliezer's view, logic precludes learning the *gezeirah shavah* from succah to *lulav,* for since a *succah* is supposed to be one's dwelling on Succos, it is understandable that the mitzvah applies to a *full* day – i.e. including the nighttime. However, one does not take a *lulav for a full day* in any event; hence, the word יָמִים (*days*) at the end of v. 40 must teach that the *lulav* is taken only during the day (i.e. in the Temple, from which we derive the law for all other places). See *Rashba* for a different explanation.

13. The Gemara has just established that R' Eliezer derives that *lulav's* preliminaries override the Sabbath from *on the . . . day.* For the sources in the other two cases, see note 3 above.

14. Via the *mah matzinu* rule of exegesis, which states that when the Torah reveals a law in one passage, that law may be applied to all other cases that logically appear to be similar.

15. A *lulav* (palm branch), an *esrog* (citron), *hadassim* (myrtle branches) and *aravos* (willow branches); see *Leviticus* 23:40.

16. Although animal sacrifices, wine libations and oil are brought with the *Omer* and Two Loaves offerings, they are regarded as separate mitzvos. The taking of the four species, on the other hand, is considered one mitzvah. Alternatively, failure to bring any of the accompaniments to the *Omer* or Two Loaves does not disqualify either offering, whereas failure to take any of the four species invalidates the mitzvah's performance (*Tos. HaRosh;* see also *Tosafos*).

17. I.e. through a *mah matzinu* exegesis; see note 3 above.

18. Whereas dwelling in a *succah* is a personal mitzvah; see note 4 above.

19. Again, through a *mah matzinu* exegesis, as follows: Just as we find that *lulav* is a mitzvah and its preliminaries override the Sabbath restrictions, so in the case of *succah,* which is also a *mitzvah,* its preliminaries should override the Sabbath restrictions (*Rashi*).

20. See above, note 15.

21. The common phrase שִׁבְעַת יָמִים (*for seven days*) appears in *Leviticus* ch. 23 with reference to the mitzvah of *lulav* (*and you shall rejoice before Hashem, your God, for seven days* – v. 40) and with reference to the mitzvah of *succah* (*you shall dwell in booths for seven days* – v. 42).

22. From the extraneous בַּיּוֹם, *on the . . . day* (ibid. v. 40).

23. Although the Gemara was unable to learn from *lulav* to *succah* through a *mah matzinu* derivation, it is able to do so through a *gezeirah shavah* (*Rashi*).

However, the Rishonim point out that this *gezeirah shavah* is not free on both sides (see above, 131a note 17), since R' Eliezer requires the mention of *for seven days* in the *lulav* passage to teach that the mitzvah of *lulav* does not apply at night. Hence, the refutation used against the *mah matzinu* attempt (*lulav* is unique, in that it requires the taking of four species) can also be employed to undermine the *gezeirah shavah* (for R' Eliezer holds that a *gezeirah shavah* free on one side can be refuted; see above, 131a). *Rashi, Ramban, Rashba* and others thus explain that this is not an ordinary *gezeirah shavah.* Rather, inasmuch as the Torah has already established the law of preliminaries in the cases of *Omer,* Two Loaves and *lulav,* the "common word" analogy that exists between *lulav* and *succah* serves simply to indicate that the leniency applies to the mitzvah of succah as well. Since this is a mere revelation of a law (גִּלּוּי מִלְּתָא בְּעָלְמָא) as opposed to an actual *gezeirah shavah* teaching, it is impervious to the refutation posed against the *mah matzinu.* See *Tosafos* for a different explanation, and see *Maharsha* for an explanation of why the other Rishonim eschewed *Tosafos'* approach.

24. I.e. let the Torah state a *gezeirah shavah* between *lulav* and *succah* that is free on both sides, and is thus irrefutable (*Maharam,* in explanation of *Rashi;* cf. *Ritva MHK* ed. and *Maharam Schif*).

כל שעתא ושעתא זמניה הוא אלא אמר רב נחמן א"ר יצחק ואיתימא רב הונא בריה דרב יהושע הואיל ובידו להפקירן: אמר מר לולב וכל מכשיריו דוחין את השבת דברי ר"א מנא ליה לר"א הא אי מעומר ושתי הלחם שכן צורך גבוה אלא אמר קרא ביום ביום אפילו בשבת ולמאי אילימא לטלטול איצטריך קרא למישרי טלטול אלא למכשיריו ורבנן ההוא מיבעי ליה ביום ולא בלילה ור"א ביום ולא בלילה מנא ליה נפקא ליה א) מושמחתם לפני ה' אלהיכם שבעת ימים ימים ולא לילות ורבנן איצטריך ס"ד אמינא נילף שבעת ימים (א) מסוכה מה להלן ב) ימים ואפילו לילות אף כאן ימים ואפילו לילות קמ"ל וליכתוב רחמנא בלולב וניתו הנך ונילפו מיניה משום דאיכא למיפרך מה ללולב שכן טעון ארבעה מינים: סוכה וכל מכשיריה דוחין את השבת דברי רבי אליעזר מנא ליה לר"א הא אי מעומר ושתי הלחם שכן צורך גבוה הוא אי מלולב שכן טעון ארבעה מינים אלא גמר ב) שבעת ימים (ב) מלולב מה להלן מכשיריו דוחין את השבת אף כאן נמי מכשיריו דוחין את השבת וליכתוב רחמנא בסוכה וניתי הנך וניגמור מיניה משום דאיכא למיפרך מה לסוכה שכן נוהגת בלילות כבימים: מצה וכל מכשיריה דוחין את השבת דברי ר"א מנא ליה לר"א הא אי מעומר ושתי הלחם שכן צורך גבוה אי מלולב שכן טעון ארבעה מינים אי מסוכה שכן נוהגת בלילות כבימים אלא גמר ג) חמשה עשר ד) חמשה עשר מחג הסוכות מה להלן מכשיריה דוחין את השבת אף כאן מכשיריה דוחין את השבת וליכתוב רחמנא במצה וניתו הנך וליגמור מיניה משום דאיכא למיפרך מה למצה שכן נוהגת בנשים כבאנשים: שופר וכל מכשיריו דוחין את השבת דברי ר"א מנא ליה לר"א הא אי מעומר ושתי הלחם שכן צורך גבוה אי מלולב שכן טעון ארבעה מינים אי מסוכה שכן נוהגת בלילות כבימים אי ממצה שכן נוהגת בנשים כבאנשים אלא אמר קרא ה) יום תרועה יהיה לכם ביום אפילו בשבת ולמאי אילימא לתקיעה הא ג) תנא דבי שמואל ה) כל מלאכת עבודה לא תעשו יצתה תקיעת שופר ורדיית הפת שהיא חכמה ואינה מלאכה אלא למכשירין ורבנן ההוא מיבעי ליה ביום ולא בלילה ור"א ביום ולא בלילה מנא ליה נפקא ליה ו) מביום הכפורים תעבירו שופר בכל ארצכם וגמרי מהדדי וליכתוב רחמנא בשופר וליתו הנך וליגמרו מיניה מתקיעת שופר דראש השנה ליכא למיגמר שכן מכנסת זכרונות של ישראל לאביהן שבשמים מתקיעות [שופר] דיוה"כ ליכא למיגמרי ד) דאמר מר תקעו ב"ד שופר נפטרו עבדים לבתיהם ושדות חוזרות לבעליהן: (אמר מר) מילה וכל מכשיריה דוחין את השבת דברי רבי אליעזר מנא ליה לר"א הא אי מכולהו גמר כדאמרינן ועוד מה להנך שכן

רש"י

כל שעתא זמניה הוא. וכיון שיש לו טלית בכל יום שמשהה בלא ציצית עובר בעשה ואפילו מונחת בקופסא הלכך כל יומא רמיא מצותיה עליה: הואיל ובידו להפקירן. ונפקי מרשותיה ולאו עליה רמיא חובתיה: אי מעומר ושתי הלחם. וגמר במה מצינו: ביום ואפילו בשבת. מדלא כתיב בראשון לדרשה אתא בכל יום שהוא ראשון לחג: ולמאי איצטריך לרבויי. להאי ואפילו בשבת אי נימא לטלטל כדמשמע קרא לקיחה טלטול בעלמא הוא ועדיין במתן תורה לא נאסר טלטול דאיצטריך קרא למישרי להאי: אלא למכשיריו. דאיסורא דאורייתא הוא: מה להלן ימים ואפילו לילות. כדילפינן במסכת סוכה (דף מג.): וליכתוב רחמנא בלולב. דמכשירין דחו: וניתו. עומר ושתי הלחם מיניה ולמה ליה דכתביה בכולהו: אי מלולב. במה מצינו מלולב שהוא מצוה ומכשיריו דוחין אף סוכה שהיא מצוה מכשיריה דוחין: גמר ז' ימים כו'. ובג"ש אתי ליה ואע"ג דאינה מופנה משני צדדים דהא גבי לולב חד שבעת ימים הוא דכתיב ודרשינן לר' אליעזר למעוטי לילות כיון דגלי רחמנא בעומר ושתי הלחם ולולב גילוי מילתא בעלמא הוא ולא פרכינן עלה גימגום (ג): וניתו הנך. עומר ושתי הלחם מינה: אי מסוכה שכן נוהגת בלילות כבימים. ואילו מצה לילה הראשון חובה ותו לא כדאמרינן בפסחים (דף קכ.): ונכתוב רחמנא. בהדיא במצה ונגמרו הנך כולהו מיניה: בנשים כבאנשים. כדילפינן בפסחים (ד' מג:) לא תאכל עליו חמץ שבעת ימים וגו' כל שישנו בבל תאכל חמץ ישנו בקום אכול מצה ונשים איתנהו בבל תאכל חמץ דכל מצות לא תעשה בין שהזמן גרמא בין שאין הזמן גרמא חייבות לאפוקי סוכה ולולב דליתנהו בנשים דמצות עשה שהזמן גרמא היא: ולמאי. האי קרא הי מילתא דתרועה אתא למישרי בשבת אי לתקיעה לא איצטריך דאפילו תקיעת הרשות ליכא בה איסורא דאורייתא: מלאכת עבודה. של טורח: וגמרי מהדדי. במסכת ראש השנה (דף לג:) שאין תלמוד לומר בחדש השביעי דהא בכמה קראי כתב לן דיוה"כ בחודש השביעי מה ת"ל בחודש השביעי שיהו כל תרועות משל חדש השביעי שוות: נפטרו עבדים לבתיהם. קריאת דרור דיובל תלויה בה הלכך חשיבא: אי מכולהו. מאחת מכולן: כדאמרינן. איכא למיפרך בכל הנך חדא לד חמור האמור בה לעיל: שאם

תוספות

כדאיתא בפ"ק דיבמות (דף ו.) וי"ל דהכא הכי גמרי מה מצינו בהנך שמצות נוהגות בשבת ומכשיריה דחו שבת אף כל שמצות נוהגות בשבת מכשיריה דחו שבת הלכך לא שייך למילף מכיבוד דהיינו המצוה עצמה ולא מכשיריה דשחוט לי בשל לי היינו כיבוד עצמו כשמתקן לו מאכלו והבנין נמי הוי מצוה אחת שצוה הקדוש ברוך הוא לבנות בית המקדש: **סד"א** נילף שבעת ימים משבעת ימים מסוכה. וא"ת היכי תיסק אדעתיה לדון ג"ש הא אין אדם דן ג"ש מעצמו אא"כ למדה מרבו וי"ל דשמא בעלמא ניתנה למדרש: **קמ"ל.** ולא ידענא השתא האי שבעת ימים למאי אתיא דאע"ג דדרשינן בפ"ק דפסחים (דף ה.) מה שביעי שביעי לחג אף ראשון ראשון לחג הא איכא למידרש משבעה בלא ימים:

שכן טעון ארבעה מינים. אף על גב דעומר ושתי הלחם נמי מביאין עמהן כבשים ויין לניסוך ושמן למנחות שאני ד' מינין שבלולב דמעכבין זה את זה כדאמר בפרק הקומץ (מנחות דף כז.) ובפרק התכלת (שם דף מה:) [אמרינן] הכבשים אין מעכבין לא את העומר ולא את שתי הלחם והיינו טעון ד' מינין שאין מצות לולב כלל בלא ד' מינין אבל באלו יכולה להיות מצוותן בלא ד' מינין. הר"ב פור"ת: **אי** מעומר כו'. הכא לא דייקא תלמודא למילף מבינייהו דהכי אורחיה דתלמודא זימנין דייק וזימנין לא דייק ואי הוה דייק הוה משכח פירכ' הרב פור"ת א"נ מילתא דאתיא במה הצד טרח וכתב לה קרא כמו מילתא דאתיא בקל וחומר והאי דקאמר תלמודא ניכתוב רחמנא בהאי ותיתי אידך מיניה פירוש ומאי צריך קרא היינו משום דאי בלא מה הצד הוה מצי למילף הך מצוה מאידך לא הוה כתב רחמנא קרא כיון דהוה פשוט כל כך דלא דמי למילתא דאתיא בק"ו דהוא פשוט יותר: **שבעת** ימים (ד) מלולב. מופנה הוה משני צדדים גבי לולב לא איצטריך דאע"ג דדרשינן ימים ולא לילות מיהו לא הוה צריך למיכתב שבעת כלל דהוה מצי למיכתב ושמחת לפני וגו' בימים והוי לשון שבעת מיותר לג"ש וא"ת ור' אליעזר היכי דריש ימים ולא לילות כיון דאית ליה ג"ש היא גופה נילף מסוכה מה להלן ימים אפילו לילות אף לולב ימים ואפי' לילות וי"ל דלית לן למילף בג"ש מילתא דלשון ג"ש גופא מוכחא דאינו כן דימים משמע ולא לילות:

ואי מסוכה שכן נוהגת בלילות כבימים. משמע דבעי למימר תאמר במצה שאינה נוהגת בלילות כבימים ואדרבה עיקר מצותה בלילה הראשון שנאמר בערב תאכלו מצות (שמות יב) והכי הוה מצי למימר שכן נוהגת בימים ובלילות:

נפקא ליה מביום הכפורים. וגמרינן מהדדי כדדרשינן בראש השנה שיהו כל התקיעות של חודש השביעי שוות כדפירש בקונטרס ורבנן סברי דלא שייך לאקשויי אלא לומר שסדר תקיעות יהיו שוין לענין סדר תקיעות מייתי לה התם אבל לזמן דיום ודאי לא איתקש דע"כ זמנם אינו שוה שזה בראש חודש וזה בעשור לחודש: והתניא

רבינו חננאל

אזמל לא שרינן בכי האי גוונא דבהדיא קיי"ל הלכתא כרבנן א) וכלליה דרבי עקיבא דאמר כל מלאכה שאפשר לה לעשות מע"ש אינ' דוחה את השבת והבאת אזמל כיון שאפשר לו להביאו מע"ש ולא הביאו אין הבאתו דוחה את השבת אפילו לענין עשיית פסח דכרת הוא לא מייתינן אזמל למול בנו או עבדו כדי שיותר לו לעשות פסח ולא שנא להו לרבנן לא דרך רה"ר ולא דרך גגות וקרפיפות וחצרות הכל אחד הוא ובכל אסור ואשכחנן בתלמוד א"י עובדא ולא הביאוהו בשבת. ואמרינן בכל מקום (רב עביד) מעשה רב דגמרינן מינה. וזה הוא המעשה. ר' שמואל בר אבודומי הוה ליה עובדא למגזר לרב ששעא בריה אנשיון למיתי אזמל שאל לר' [מנא]. אמר להון ידחה למחר. שאל לר' יצחק בן אלעזר אמר להון משחוק [קונדיטון] לא אנשיתון ומיתי אזמל אנשיתון ידחה למחר: א"ר חייא בר אבא. א"ר יוחנן לא לכל א"ר אליעזר מכשירי מצוה דוחין את השבת שהרי שתי הלחם חובת היום הן ולא למדם ר' אליעזר אלא מג"ש נאמרה הבאה בעומר שנאמר והבאתם את עומר וגו' ונאמרה הבאה בשתי הלחם שנאמר ממושבותיכם תביאו לחם תנופה שתים וגו'. מנין שהעומר דוחה שבת. גרסינן באחרית פרק ר' ישמעאל אומר העומר היה בא בשבת מג' סאין וכו'. ת"ר תקריב את מנחת בכוריך מה ת"ל לפי שמצות העומר להביא מן הקמה מניין שאם לא מצא קמה יביא מן העומרין ת"ל תקריב כו' עד תקריב לפי שמצותו לקצור בלילה. מניין שאם קצר ביום כשר ודוחה שבת ת"ל תקריב כל שהוא תקריב מ"מ תקריבו אפי' בשבת אפילו ביום בטומאה. ותוב תניא (בתר"כ) בסוף פרשת אמור אל הכהנים (ובפסחים עז ובמנחות עב) רבי אומר וידבר משה את מועדי ה' מה ת"ל לפי שלא למדנו שדוחין את השבת אלא הפסח והתמיד שכתוב בהן במועדו מניין לרבות העומר והקרב עמו. שתי הלחם והקרב עמהן שידחו שבת ת"ל וידבר משה את מועדי ה' קבעו מועד אחד לכולן ופשוטה היא זו ההלכה כולה. ואפי' ר' אליעזר שמתיר במכשירי מצוה מודה. שאם צייץ טליתו ועשה מזוזה בפתחו בשבת שהוא חייב ואמרינן מ"ש הני ואוקימנא הואיל ובידו להפקירן. פי' כי הציצית הוא חובת הבגד וכיון שהפקיר אינו בגדו וכן הבית כיוצא בו.

חשק שלמה על רבינו חננאל

א) עיין היטב בר"ן פ"ק דר"ה כאן דדחה כל הראיות שהביא רבינו ע"ש:

מסורת הש"ס

א) [עי' תוספות מנחות מד. ד"ה טלית], ב) סוכה מג., ג) לעיל קוז: ע"ש ד"ה כמו, ד) ר"ה מ:, ה) עיין מהרש"ם, ו) [כדאיתא בפ' התכלת מה:], ז) [דף לג:].

הגהות הב"ח

(א) גמ' נילף שבעת ימים משבעת ימים מסוכה: (ב) שם אלא גמר שבעת ימים מלולב: (ג) רש"י ד"ה גמר ז' ימים וכו' גימגום הס"ד ואחר כך מ"ה וניתו הנך וכו' ונכתוב רחמנא בהדיא במצה וניתי הנך עומר ושתי הלחם ולולב מינה: (ד) תוס' ד"ה שבעת ימים משבעת ימים מלולב מופנה הוה משני צדדין דגבי לולב נמי לא איצטריך:

גליון הש"ס

רש"י ד"ה כל שעתא וכו' ואפי' מונחת בקופסא. עי' מנחות דף מד ע"א תוס' ד"ה טלית: תוס' ד"ה ולא ידענא. כעין זה לעיל דף קיט ע"ב תוס' ד"ה אלו היו וש"נ:

תורה אור השלם

א) וּלְקַחְתֶּם לָכֶם בַּיּוֹם הָרִאשׁוֹן פְּרִי עֵץ הָדָר כַּפֹּת תְּמָרִים וַעֲנַף עֵץ עָבֹת וְעַרְבֵי נָחַל וּשְׂמַחְתֶּם לִפְנֵי יְיָ אֱלֹהֵיכֶם שִׁבְעַת יָמִים: [ויקרא כג, מ]

ב) בַּסֻּכֹּת תֵּשְׁבוּ שִׁבְעַת יָמִים כָּל הָאֶזְרָח בְּיִשְׂרָאֵל יֵשְׁבוּ בַּסֻּכֹּת: [ויקרא כג, מב]

ג) וּבַחֲמִשָּׁה עָשָׂר יוֹם לַחֹדֶשׁ הַזֶּה חַג הַמַּצּוֹת לַייָ שִׁבְעַת יָמִים מַצּוֹת תֹּאכֵלוּ: [ויקרא כג, ו]

ד) דַּבֵּר אֶל בְּנֵי יִשְׂרָאֵל לֵאמֹר בַּחֲמִשָּׁה עָשָׂר יוֹם לַחֹדֶשׁ הַשְּׁבִיעִי הַזֶּה חַג הַסֻּכּוֹת שִׁבְעַת יָמִים לַייָ: [ויקרא כג, לד]

ה) וּבַחֹדֶשׁ הַשְּׁבִיעִי בְּאֶחָד לַחֹדֶשׁ מִקְרָא קֹדֶשׁ יִהְיֶה לָכֶם כָּל מְלֶאכֶת עֲבֹדָה לֹא תַעֲשׂוּ יוֹם תְּרוּעָה יִהְיֶה לָכֶם: [במדבר כט, א]

ו) וְהַעֲבַרְתָּ שׁוֹפַר תְּרוּעָה בַּחֹדֶשׁ הַשְּׁבִעִי בֶּעָשׂוֹר לַחֹדֶשׁ בְּיוֹם הַכִּפֻּרִים תַּעֲבִירוּ שׁוֹפָר בְּכָל אַרְצְכֶם: [ויקרא כה, ט]

ליקוטי רש"י

ביום אפילו בשבת. דמשמע כל היום ואפילו יום וקרא יתירא הוא דמצי למכתב בראשון. איצטריך קרא למישרי טלטול. דרבנן עדיין לא נאסר טלטול בעולם וגם לא נכתב לתחום. אלא למכשיריו. כל הכתוב ללמדך שמכשירי לולב דוחין את השבת כלומר תיקוניו ואפילו לקוצצו מן המחובר ולאגדו [סוכה מג.]. בנשים כבאנשים. אכילת מצה ליל ראשון שהוא חובה כדכתיב (שמות יב) בערב תאכלו מצות חמץ גרס לה בט"ו בניסן ונשים חייבות באכילת מצה כדאמר בפסחים (מג:) נשים חייבות באכילת מצה דבר תורה שנאמר לא תאכל עליו חמץ שבעת ימים תאכל עליו מצות כל שישנו בבל תאכל חמץ ישנו בקום אכול מצה ונשים איתנהו בבל תאכל חמץ דמצות לא תעשה היא [קידושין לד.]. ורדיית הפת. לרדיית הפת שבות היא שהיא חכמה ואינה מלאכה [לעיל ג:].

offerings – **come and be derived from it.**[25] Why are the *Omer* and Two Loaves teachings necessary?

The Gemara answers:

מִשּׁוּם דְּאִיכָּא לְמִיפְרַךְ – Because there are grounds **to refute** the *mah matzinu* teaching, as follows: **מַה לְסוּכָּה שֶׁכֵּן נוֹהֶגֶת בַּלֵּילוֹת כְּבַיָּמִים – Whereas** the mitzvah of ***succah*** is unique, **for indeed it operates by nights as by days,** the same cannot be said of the mitzvos of *Omer* and Two Loaves.[26] Hence, because *Omer* and Two Loaves lack this attribute of *succah,* the law of preliminaries cannot be inferred to them.

The Gemara now establishes the source for the third set of preliminaries mentioned above:

מַצָּה וְכָל מַכְשִׁירֶיהָ דּוֹחִין אֶת הַשַּׁבָּת – The Baraisa stated: The mitzvah of **MATZAH AND ALL ITS PRELIMINARIES OVERRIDE THE SABBATH** restrictions. **דִּבְרֵי רַבִּי אֱלִיעֶזֶר** – There are **THE WORDS OF R' ELIEZER. מְנָא לֵיהּ לְרַבִּי אֱלִיעֶזֶר הָא – Now, from where** does **R' Eliezer** derive **this** law? **אִי מֵעוֹמֶר וּשְׁתֵּי הַלֶּחֶם – If** you say he derives it **from the *Omer* and Two Loaves** offerings through a *mah matzinu* exegesis, that cannot be – **שֶׁכֵּן צוֹרֶךְ גָּבוֹהַּ – for indeed** each is **a necessity for the Most High.**[27] **אִי מִלּוּלָב – If** you say he derives it **from** the mitzvah of ***lulav*** through a *mah matzinu,* that also cannot be – **שֶׁכֵּן טָעוּן אַרְבָּעָה מִינִים – for indeed [that mitzvah] requires** the taking of **four species.**[28] Since matzah lacks this attribute of *lulav,* the law of preliminaries cannot be inferred to it. **אִי מִסּוּכָּה** – And **if** you say R' Eliezer derives it **from** the mitzvah of ***succah*** through a *mah matzinu,* that cannot be – **שֶׁכֵּן נוֹהֶגֶת בַּלֵּילוֹת כְּבַיָּמִים – for indeed [succah] operates by nights as by days.** Since matzah lacks this attribute of *succah,*[29] the law of preliminaries cannot be inferred to it. **אֶלָּא גָּמַר ,,חֲמִשָּׁה עָשָׂר" ,,חֲמִשָּׁה עָשָׂר" מֵחַג הַסּוּכּוֹת – Rather, [R' Eliezer] learned** a *gezeirah shavah* of ***fifteenth/fifteenth*** **from the festival of Succos,**[30] as follows: **מַה לְהַלָּן מַכְשִׁירֶיהָ דּוֹחִין אֶת הַשַּׁבָּת – Just as there** we learn[31] that **[succah's] preliminaries override the Sabbath** restrictions, **אַף כָּאן מַכְשִׁירֶיהָ דּוֹחִין אֶת הַשַּׁבָּת – so here** derive that **[matzah's] preliminaries override the Sabbath** restrictions.

The Gemara asks:

וְלִיכְתּוֹב רַחֲמָנָא בְּמַצָּה – But let the Merciful One write the law of preliminaries explicitly **in** the passage of **matzah, וְנֵיתוֹ הָנָךְ וְלִיגְמוֹר מִינֵּיהּ – and let** all **the other** cases **come and be derived from it!**[32] Why are separate teachings required for each mitzvah?

The Gemara answers:

מִשּׁוּם דְּאִיכָּא לְמִיפְרַךְ – Because there are grounds **to refute** the *mah matzinu* teaching, as follows: **מַה לְמַצָּה שֶׁכֵּן נוֹהֶגֶת בְּנָשִׁים כְּבַאֲנָשִׁים – Whereas** the mitzvah of matzah is unique, **for indeed it operates with respect to women as with respect to men,**[33] the same cannot be said of the mitzvos of *succah* and *lulav.*[34] Hence, because those two mitzvos lack this attribute of matzah, the law of preliminaries cannot be inferred to them.

The Gemara now establishes the source for the final set of preliminaries mentioned above:

שׁוֹפָר וְכָל מַכְשִׁירָיו דּוֹחִין אֶת הַשַּׁבָּת – The Baraisa stated: The mitzvah of ***SHOFAR* AND ALL ITS PRELIMINARIES OVERRIDE THE SABBATH** restrictions. **דִּבְרֵי רַבִּי אֱלִיעֶזֶר** – These are **THE WORDS OF R' ELIEZER. מְנָא לֵיהּ לְרַבִּי אֱלִיעֶזֶר הָא – Now, from where** does **R' Eliezer** derive **this** law? **אִי מֵעוֹמֶר וּשְׁתֵּי הַלֶּחֶם – If** you say he derives it **from the *Omer* and Two Loaves** offerings, that cannot be – **שֶׁכֵּן צוֹרֶךְ גָּבוֹהַּ – for indeed** each is **a necessity for the Most High,** while *shofar* is a personal mitzvah. **אִי מִלּוּלָב – If** you say he derives it **from** the mitzvah of ***lulav,*** that too cannot be – **שֶׁכֵּן טָעוּן אַרְבָּעָה מִינִים – for indeed [that mitzvah] requires** the taking of **four species,** a unique attribute whose existence precludes a *mah matzinu* teaching. **אִי מִסּוּכָּה** – Further, **if** you say that R' Eliezer derives it **from** the mitzvah of ***succah,*** that cannot be – **שֶׁכֵּן נוֹהֶגֶת בַּלֵּילוֹת כְּבַיָּמִים – for indeed [that mitzvah] operates by nights as by days,** which likewise precludes a *mah matzinu* teaching.[35] **אִי מִמַּצָּה** – Finally, **if** you say he derives it **from** the mitzvah of **matzah,** that also cannot be – **שֶׁכֵּן נוֹהֶגֶת בְּנָשִׁים כְּבַאֲנָשִׁים – for indeed [that mitzvah] operates with respect to women as with respect to men,**[36] while *shofar* does not.[37] Hence, because *shofar* lacks this attribute of matzah, a *mah matzinu* teaching from the latter to the former is impossible.

The Gemara finally identifies the source:

אֶלָּא אָמַר קְרָא ,,יוֹם תְּרוּעָה יִהְיֶה לָכֶם" – Rather, the verse states,[38] ***It shall be a day of shofar-sounding for you,*** which

NOTES

25. I.e. from *succah* through a *mah matzinu* exegesis. [The Gemara has already refuted a *mah matzinu* from *lulav,* and is not inclined to essay a "common feature" exegesis from multiple sources (see *Tosafos* ד"ה אי).]

26. These offerings are brought only during the day.

27. Whereas eating matzah on Passover is a personal mitzvah; see note 4 above.

28. See above, note 15.

29. Actually, since the principal obligation to eat matzah occurs at night (the night of the 15th of Nissan; see *Pesachim* 120a), one cannot say "matzah does not operate by night." Rather, the Gemara is only verbalizing the refutation as it did above, but actually means thus: ". . . for indeed [the mitzvah of *succah]* operates during the day and at night." That is, one pronounces a blessing over the mitzvah of dwelling in a *succah* at any time during the entire seven days of the festival. With regard to the mitzvah of eating matzah, however, one pronounces a blessing only on the first night of Pesach (*Tos. HaRosh;* see *Rashi; Tosafos,* and *Ritva MHK* ed.).

30. The common phrase חֲמִשָּׁה עָשָׂר (*fifteenth*) appears in *Leviticus* ch. 23 with reference to the mitzvah of matzah (*And on the fifteenth day of this month* [i.e. Nissan] . . . *you shall eat matzos* – v. 6) and with reference to the mitzvah of *succah* (*But on the fifteenth day of the seventh month* [i.e. Tishrei] . . . *you shall celebrate Hashem's festival* – v. 39).

31. Through a *gezeirah shavah* from *lulav.*

32. Let the Torah explicitly teach that the preliminaries to the mitzvah of matzah override the Sabbath restrictions, and then extend this leniency to the preliminaries of all the other mitzvos (*Omer,* Two Loaves et al.) [through a *mah matzinu* interpretation] (*Rashi*).

33. Although women are obligated to observe all negative commandments of the Torah, they are exempt from those positive commandments that must be performed at a particular time (מִצְוֹת עֲשֵׂה שֶׁהַזְּמַן גְּרָמָן) [see *Kiddushin* 29a]. However, eating matzah on the night of the fifteenth of Nissan, which is a time-bound mitzvah, is an exception to the rule. The Gemara (*Pesachim* 43b) derives this from a juxtaposition of the negative commandment against eating leavened bread and the positive commandment to eat matzah in one verse (*Deuteronomy* 16:3): לֹא־תֹאכַל עָלָיו חָמֵץ שִׁבְעַת יָמִים תֹּאכַל־עָלָיו מַצּוֹת, *You shall not eat leavened bread with it* [i.e. the *pesach* offering]; *for seven days you shall eat matzos because of it.* The juxtaposition implies that anyone who is obligated to refrain from eating leavened bread is also obligated to eat matzah. Since women must observe all the negative commandments, they are obligated to eat matzah (*Rashi*).

34. These time-bound positive commandments are not Scripturally excluded from the general rule, and so women are exempt from performing them (*Rashi*).

Regarding the obligation of women, vis-a-vis the *Omer* and Two Loaves offerings, see *Rashash.*

35. Since the mitzvah of hearing the *shofar*-blasts applies only during the day.

36. See above, note 33.

37. *Shofar* is a time-bound positive commandment that follows the general rule; hence, women are exempt from performing it.

38. *Numbers* 29:1.

כל שעתא ושעתא זמניה הוא אלא אמר רב נחמן א"ר יצחק ואיתימא רב הונא בריה דרב יהושע ה) הואיל ובידו להפקירן: אמר מר לולב וכל מכשיריו דוחין את השבת דברי ר"א מנא ליה לר"א הא אי מעומר ושתי הלחם שכן צורך גבוה אלא אמר קרא א) ביום ג) ביום אפילו בשבת ולמאי הלכתא אילימא לטלטול איצטריך קרא למישרי טלטול אלא למכשיריו ורבנן ההוא מיבעי ליה ביום ולא בלילה ור"א ביום ולא בלילה מנא ליה נפקא ליה א) ושמחתם לפני ה' אלהיכם שבעת ימים ולא לילות ורבנן איצטריך ס"ד אמינא נילף שבעת ימים (א) מסוכה מה להלן ב) ימים ואפילו לילות אף כאן ימים ואפילו לילות קמ"ל וליכתוב רחמנא בלולב וניתו הנך ונילפו מיניה משום דאיכא למיפרך מה ללולב שכן טעון ארבעה מינים: סוכה וכל מכשיריה דוחין את השבת דברי רבי אליעזר מנא ליה לר"א הא אי מעומר ושתי הלחם שכן צורך גבוה הוא אי מלולב שכן טעון ארבעה מינים אלא גמר ב) שבעת ימים (ג) מלולב מה להלן מכשיריו דוחין את השבת אף כאן נמי מכשיריו דוחין את השבת וליכתוב רחמנא בסוכה וניתי הנך ונגמור מיניה משום דאיכא למיפרך מה לסוכה שכן נוהגת בלילות כבימים: מצה וכל מכשיריה דוחין את השבת דברי ר"א מנא ליה לר"א הא אי מעומר ושתי הלחם שכן צורך גבוה אי מלולב שכן טעון ארבעה מינים אי מסוכה שכן נוהגת בלילות כבימים אלא גמר ג) חמשה עשר ד) חמשה עשר מחג הסוכות מה להלן מכשיריה דוחין את השבת אף כאן מכשיריה דוחין את השבת וליכתוב רחמנא במצה וניתו הנך וליגמור מיניה משום דאיכא למיפרך מה למצה שכן נוהגת בנשים כבאנשים: שופר וכל מכשיריו דוחין את השבת דברי ר"א מנא ליה לר"א הא אי מעומר ושתי הלחם שכן צורך גבוה אי מלולב שכן טעון ארבעה מינים אי מסוכה שכן נוהגת בלילות כבימים אי ממצה שכן נוהגת בנשים כבאנשים אלא אמר קרא ה) יום תרועה יהיה לכם ביום אפילו בשבת ולמאי אילימא לתקיעה הא ו) תנא דבי שמואל ה) כל מלאכת עבודה לא תעשו יצתה תקיעת שופר ורדיית הפת שהיא חכמה ואינה מלאכה אלא למכשירין ורבנן ההוא מיבעי ליה ביום ולא בלילה ור"א ביום ולא בלילה מנא ליה נפקא ליה ו) מביום הכפורים תעבירו שופר בכל ארצכם וגמרי מהדדי וליכתוב רחמנא בשופר וליתו הנך וליגמרו מיניה מתקיעת שופר דראש השנה ליכא למיגמר שכן מכנסת זכרונות של ישראל לאביהן שבשמים מתקיעות [שופר] דיוה"כ ליכא למיגמרי ז) דאמר מר תקעו ב"ד שופר נפטרו עבדים לבתיהם ושדות חוזרות לבעליהן: (אמר מר) מילה וכל מכשיריה דוחין את השבת דברי רבי אליעזר מנא ליה לר"א הא אי מכולהו גמר כדאמרינן ועוד מה להנך שכן

תוספות

כדאיתא בפ"ק דיבמות (דף ו.) וי"ל דהכא הכי גמרי מה מצינו בהנך שמצות נוהגות בשבת ומכשיריה דחו שבת אף כל שמצות נוהגות בשבת מכשיריה דחו שבת הלכך לא שייך למילף מכיבוד דהיינו המצוה עצמה ולא מכשיריה דפשוט לי בשל לי היינו כיבוד עצמו כשמתקן לו מאכלו והבנין נמי הוי מצוה אחת שצוה הקדוש ברוך הוא לבנות בית המקדש: **סד"א** נילף שבעת ימים משבעת ימים מסוכה. וא"ת היכי תיסק אדעתיה לדון ג"ש הא אין אדם דן ג"ש מעצמו אא"כ למדה מרבו וי"ל דשמא בעלמא ניתנה למדרש[ה]:

קמ"ל. ולא ידענא השתא האי שבעת ימים למאי אתיא דאע"ג דדרשינן בפ"ק דפסחים (דף ה.) מה שביעי שביעי לחג אף ראשון ראשון לחג הא איכא למידרש משבעה בלא ימים:

שכן טעון ארבעה מינים. אף על גב דעומר ושתי הלחם נמי מביאין עמהן כבשים ויין לניסוך ושמן למנחות שאני ד' מינין שבלולב דמעכבין זה את זה כדאמר בפרק הקומץ (מנחות דף מ.) ובפרק התכלת (שם דף מה:) [אמרינן] הכבשים אין מעכבין לא את העומר ולא את שתי הלחם[ו] והיינו טעון ד' מינין שאין מצות לולב כלל בלא ד' מינין אבל באלו יכולה להיות מצוותן בלא ד' מינין. הר"ב פור"ת: **אי** מעומר כו'. הכא לא דייקא תלמודא למילף מבינייהו דהכי אורחיה דתלמודא זימנין דייק וזימנין לא דייק ואי הוה דייק הוה משכח פירכ' הרב פור"ת א"נ מילתא דאתיא במה הצד טרח וכתב לה קרא כמו מילתא דאתיא בקל וחומר והאי דקאמר תלמודא ניכתוב רחמנא בהאי ותיתי אידך מיניה פירוש ומאי צריך קרא היינו משום דאי בלא מה הצד הוה מצי למילף הך מצוה מאידך לא הוה כתב רחמנא קרא כיון דהוה פשוט כל כך דלא דמי למילתא דאתיא בק"ו דהוא פשוט יותר: **שבעת** ימים (ד) מלולב. מופנה הוה משני לדדים גבי לולב לא איצטריך דאע"ג דדרשינן ימים ולא לילות מיהו לא הוה צריך למיכתב שבעת כלל דהוה מצי למיכתב ושמחת לפני וגו' בימים והוי לשון שבעת מיותר לג"ש וא"ת ור' אליעזר היכי דריש ימים ולא לילות כיון דאית ליה ג"ש היא גופה נילף מסוכה מה להלן ימים אפילו לילות אף לולב ימים ואפי' לילות ויש לומר דלית לן למילף בג"ש מילתא דלשון ג"ש גופא מוכחא דאינו כן דימים משמע ולא לילות: **ואי** מסוכה שכן נוהגת בלילות כבימים. משמע דבעי למימר תאמר במצה שאינה נוהגת בלילות כבימים ואדרבה עיקר מצותה בלילה הראשון שנאמר בערב תאכלו מצות (שמות יב) והכי הוה מצי למימר שכן נוהגת בימים ובלילות: **נפקא** ליה מביום הכפורים. וגמרינן מהדדי כדדרשינן בראש השנה[ז] שיהו כל התקיעות של חודש השביעי שוות כדפירש בקונטרס ורבנן סברי דלא שייך לאקשויי אלא לומר שסדר תקיעות יהיו שוין דלענין סדר תקיעות מייתי לה התם אבל לזמן דיום ודאי לא איתקש דע"כ זמנם אינו שוה שזה בראש חודש וזה בעשור לחודש: והתניא

רש"י

כל שעתא זמניה הוא. וכיון שיש לו טלית בכל יום שמשהה בלא ציצית עובר בעשה ° ואפילו מונחת בקופסא הלכך כל יומא רמיא מצותיה עליה: הואיל ובידו להפקירן. ונפקי מרשותיה ולאו עליה רמיא חובתיה: אי מעומר ושתי הלחם. וגמר במה מצינו: ביום ואפילו בשבת. מדלא כתיב בראשון לדרשא אתא בכל יום שהוא ראשון לחג: ולמאי איצטריך לרבויי. להאי ואפילו בשבת אי נימא לטלטל כדמשמע קרא לקיחה טלטול בעלמא הוא ועדיין במתן תורה לא נאסר טלטול דאיצטריך קרא למישרי להאי: אלא למכשיריו. דאיסורא דאורייתא הוא: מה להלן ימים ואפילו לילות. כדילפינן במסכת סוכה (דף מג.): וליכתוב רחמנא בלולב. דמכשירין דחו: וניתו. עומר ושתי הלחם מיניה ולמה ליה דכתביה בכולהו: אי מלולב. במה מצינו מלולב שהוא מצוה ומכשיריו דוחין אף סוכה שהיא מצוה מכשיריה דוחין: גמר ז' ימים כו'. ובג"ש אתי ליה ואע"ג דאינה מופנה משני לדדים דהא גבי לולב חד שבעת ימים הוא דכתיב ודרשינן לר' אליעזר למעוטי לילות כיון דגלי רחמנא בעומר ושתי הלחם ולולב גילוי מילתא בעלמא הוא ולא פרכינן עלה גימגום (ג): וניתו הנך. עומר ושתי הלחם מינה: אי מסוכה שכן נוהגת בלילות כבימים. ואילו מצה לילה הראשון חובה ותו לא כדאמרינן בפסחים (דף קכ.): ונכתוב רחמנא. בהדיא במצה ונגמרו הנך כולהו מיניה: בנשים כבאנשים. כדילפינן בפסחים (ד' מג:) לא תאכל עליו חמץ שבעת ימים וגו' כל שישנו בבל תאכל חמץ ישנו בקום אכול מצה ונשים איתנהו בבל תאכל חמץ דכל מצות לא תעשה בין שהזמן גרמא בין שאין הזמן גרמא חייבות לאפוקי סוכה ולולב דליתנהו בנשים דמצות עשה שהזמן גרמא היא: ולמאי. האי קרא הי מילתא דתרועה אתא למישרי בשבת אי לתקיעה לא איצטריך דאפילו תקיעת הרשות לית בה איסורא דאורייתא: מלאכת עבודה. של טורח: וגמרי מהדדי. במסכת ראש השנה (דף לג:) שאין תלמוד לומר בחדש השביעי דהא בכמה קראי כתב לן דיוה"כ בחודש השביעי מה ת"ל בחודש השביעי שיהו כל תרועות משל חדש השביעי שוות: נפטרו עבדים לבתיהם. קריאת דרור דיובל תלויה בה הלכך חשיבא: אי מכולהו. מאחת מכולן: כדאמרינן. איכא למיפרך בכל הנך חדא לד חמור האמור בה לעיל: שאם

רבינו חננאל

אזמל לא שרינן בכי האי גוונא דבהדיא קיי"ל הלכתא כרבנן א) וככלליה דרבי עקיבא דאמר כל מלאכה שאפשר לה לעשות מע"ש אינ' דוחה את השבת והבאת אזמל כיון שאפשר לו להביאו מע"ש ולא הביאו אין הבאתו דוחה את השבת אפילו לענין עשיית פסח דכרת הוא לא מייתינן אזמל למול בנו או עבדו כדי שיותר לו לעשות פסח ולא שנא להו לרבנן לא דרך רה"ר ולא דרך גגות וקרפיפות וחצרות הכל אחד הוא ובכל אסור ואשכחנן בתלמוד א"י עובדא ולא הביאוהו בשבת. ואמרינן בכל מקום (רב עביד) מעשה רב דגמרינן מינה. וזה הוא המעשה. ר' שמואל בר אבודומי הוה ליה עובדא למגזר לרב ששעא בריה אנשיון למיתי אזמל שאל לר' [מנא]. אמר להון ידחה למחר. שאל לר' יצחק בן אלעזר אמר להון משחוק [קונדיטון] לא אנשיתון ומיתי אזמל אנשיתון ידחה למחר: א"ר חייא בר אבא. א"ר יוחנן לא לכל א"ר אליעזר מכשירי מצוה דוחין את השבת שהרי שתי הלחם חובת היום הן ולא למדם ר' אליעזר אלא מג"ש נאמרה הבאה בעומר שנאמר והבאתם את עומר וגו' ונאמרה הבאה בשתי הלחם שנאמר ממושבותיכם תביאו לחם תנופה שתים וגו'. מנין שהעומר דוחה שבת. גרסינן באחרית פרק ר' ישמעאל אומר העומר היה בא בשבת מג' סאין וכו'. ת"ר תקריב את מנחת בכוריך מה ת"ל לפי שמצות העומר להביא מן הקמה מניין שאם לא מצא קמה יביא מן העומרין ת"ל תקריב כו' עד תקריב לפי שמצותו לקצור בלילה. מניין שאם קצר ביום כשר ודוחה שבת ת"ל תקריב כל שהוא תקריב מ"מ תקריבו אפי' בשבת אפילו ביום בטומאה. ותוב תניא (בתו"כ) בסוף פרשת אמור אל הכהנים (ובפסחים עז ובמנחות עב) רבי אומר וידבר משה את מועדי ה' מה ת"ל לפי שלא למדנו שדוחין את השבת אלא הפסח והתמיד שכתוב בהן במועדו מניין לרבות העומר והקרב עמו. שתי הלחם והקרב עמהן שידחו שבת ת"ל וידבר משה את מועדי ה' קבעו מועד אחד לכולן ופשוטה היא זו הלכה כולה. ואף ר' אליעזר שמתיר במכשירי מצוה מודה. שאם צייץ טליתו ועשה מזוזה בפתחו בשבת שהוא חייב ואמרינן מ"ש הני ואוקימנא הואיל ובידו להפקירן. פי' כי הציצית הוא חובת הבגד וכיון שהפקיר אינו בגדו וכן הבית כיוצא בו.

חשק שלמה על רבינו חננאל

א) עיין היטב בר"ף כאן דלמה לא הלכות שהביא רבינו ע"ש.

מסורת הש"ס

א) [עי' תוספות מנחות מד. ד"ה טלית], ב) סוכה מג., ג) לעיל קח: ע"ש ר"ה כט:, ד) ר"ה מ:, ה) עיין מהרש"ם, ו) [כדאיתא בפ' התכלת מה:], ז) [דף לג:].

הגהות הב"ח

(א) גמ' נילף שבעת ימים משבעת ימים מסוכה: (ג) שם אלא גמר שבעת ימים משבעת ימים מלולב: (ג) רש"י ד"ה גמר ז' ימים וכו' גימגום הס"ד ואחר כך מ"ה ונכתוב רחמנא בהדיא בסוכה וניתי הנך עומר ושתי הלחם ולולב מינה: (ד) תוס' ד"ה שבעת ימים משבעת ימים מלולב מופנה הוה משני לדדין דגבי לולב נמי לא איצטריך:

גליון הש"ס

רש"י ד"ה כל שעתא וכו' ואפי' מונחת בקופסא. עי' מנחות דף מד ע"א תוס' ד"ה טלית: תוס' ד"ה קמ"ל ולא ידענא. כעין זה לעיל דף קיט ע"ב תוס' ד"ה אלו היו וש"נ:

תורה אור השלם

א) וּלְקַחְתֶּם לָכֶם בַּיּוֹם הָרִאשׁוֹן פְּרִי עֵץ הָדָר כַּפֹּת תְּמָרִים וַעֲנַף עֵץ עָבֹת וְעַרְבֵי נָחַל וּשְׂמַחְתֶּם לִפְנֵי יְיָ אֱלֹהֵיכֶם שִׁבְעַת יָמִים: [ויקרא כג, מ]

ב) בַּסֻּכֹּת תֵּשְׁבוּ שִׁבְעַת יָמִים כָּל הָאֶזְרָח בְּיִשְׂרָאֵל יֵשְׁבוּ בַּסֻּכֹּת: [ויקרא כג, מב]

ג) וּבַחֲמִשָּׁה עָשָׂר יוֹם לַחֹדֶשׁ הַזֶּה חַג הַמַּצּוֹת לַייָ שִׁבְעַת יָמִים מַצּוֹת תֹּאכֵלוּ: [ויקרא כג, ו]

ד) דַּבֵּר אֶל בְּנֵי יִשְׂרָאֵל לֵאמֹר בַּחֲמִשָּׁה עָשָׂר יוֹם לַחֹדֶשׁ הַשְּׁבִיעִי הַזֶּה חַג הַסֻּכּוֹת שִׁבְעַת יָמִים לַייָ: [ויקרא כג, לד]

ה) וּבַחֹדֶשׁ הַשְּׁבִיעִי בְּאֶחָד לַחֹדֶשׁ מִקְרָא קֹדֶשׁ יִהְיֶה לָכֶם כָּל מְלֶאכֶת עֲבֹדָה לֹא תַעֲשׂוּ יוֹם תְּרוּעָה יִהְיֶה לָכֶם: [במדבר כט, א]

ו) וְהַעֲבַרְתָּ שׁוֹפַר תְּרוּעָה בַּחֹדֶשׁ הַשְּׁבִעִי בֶּעָשׂוֹר לַחֹדֶשׁ בְּיוֹם הַכִּפֻּרִים תַּעֲבִירוּ שׁוֹפָר בְּכָל אַרְצְכֶם: [ויקרא כה, ט]

ליקוטי רש"י

ביום אפילו בשבת. דמשמע כל דהו יום וקרא יתירא הוא דמצי למכתב בראשון. איצטריך קרא למישרי טלטול. דרבנן עדיין לא נאסר טלטול בעולם ולא הכתוב להתירו כאן. אלא למכשיריו. לא הכתוב ללמדך שמכשירי לולב דוחין את השבת כלומר מקוציו ואפילו לקוצצו מן המחובר ולאוגדו [סוכה מג.]. בנשים כבאנשים. אכילת מצה ליל ראשון שהוא חובה כדכתיב (שמות יב) בערב תאכלו מצות חמץ גרס לה בע"ו בניסן ונשים חייבות כדאמר בפסחים (מג:) נשים חייבות באכילת מצה דבר תורה שנאמר לא תאכל עליו חמץ שבעת ימים תאכל עליו מצות כל שישנו בבל תאכל חמץ ישנו בקום אכול מצה ונשים איתנהו בבל תאכל חמץ דמצות לא תעשה היא [קידושין לד.]. ורדיית הפת. לרדיים הפת שבום היא שהיא חכמה ואינה מלאכה [לעיל ג:].

implies: בְּיוֹם אֲפִילוּ בְּשַׁבָּת – You shall sound the shofar **on the day** of Rosh Hashanah, whenever that may be – i.e. **even on the Sabbath.**[39] וּלְמַאי – **Now, why** is this necessary? For which aspect of the *shofar*-sounding does the Torah create this leniency? אִילֵימָא לִתְקִיעָה – **If we say** it is **for the** actual **blowing,** to permit it when Rosh Hashanah falls on the Sabbath (in which case the leniency applies to the mitzvah itself and not to its preliminaries), that cannot be – הָא תָּנָא דְּבֵי שְׁמוּאֵל – **for [one of the sages] of Shmuel's academy taught:** ,,כָּל־מְלֶאכֶת עֲבֹדָה לֹא תַעֲשׂוּ" – Scripture states,[40] ***You shall do no laborious work*** [i.e. on Rosh Hashanah].[41] יָצְתָה תְּקִיעַת שׁוֹפָר וּרְדִיַּית הַפַּת – **Excluded** from this prohibition are the **blowing of a *shofar* and the removal of bread** (from an oven),[42] שֶׁהִיא חָכְמָה וְאֵינָהּ מְלָאכָה – **since [each] is** just **a skill and** is **not** considered creative **work.**[43] From here we see that even a discretionary *shofar*-blowing is Biblically permitted on Yom Tov and Shabbos; certainly, then, no special verse is needed to teach that the actual mitzvah of *shofar*-blowing may be performed on the Sabbath. אֶלָּא לְמַכְשִׁירִין – **Rather,** we must say that the extraneous word *day* comes **for the preliminaries** to the mitzvah of *shofar,*[44] to teach that they override the Sabbath restrictions.

The Gemara asks:

וְרַבָּנָן – **And the Rabbis,** who disagree with R' Eliezer and maintain that preliminaries to a mitzvah may not be performed on the Sabbath – what do they do with the extraneous word *day*?

The Gemara answers:

הַהוּא מִיבְּעֵי לֵיהּ בַּיּוֹם וְלֹא בַּלַּיְלָה – **That** word **is needed** to teach that the mitzvah of *shofar* applies **during the day and not at night.**

The Gemara then asks:

וְרַבִּי אֱלִיעֶזֶר בַּיּוֹם וְלֹא בַּלַּיְלָה מְנָא לֵיהּ – **And from where** does **R' Eliezer,** who derives the law of preliminaries from the superfluous *day,* know that the mitzvah of *shofar* applies **during the day and not at night?**

The Gemara answers:

נָפְקָא לֵיהּ מִ,,בְּיוֹם הַכִּפֻּרִים תַּעֲבִירוּ שׁוֹפָר בְּכָל־אַרְצְכֶם" – **He derives** that law **from** that which is written about a different *shofar* sounding:[45] *You shall sound a broken blast on the shofar, in the seventh month . . .* ***on the Day of Atonement you shall sound the shofar throughout your Land.*** וְגָמְרֵי מֵהֲדָדֵי – **Now,** it was unnecessary to state *in the seventh month* in this verse, since several other verses teach that Yom Kippur occurs in the seventh month. The extraneous phrase thus teaches that **[the laws]** of the various *shofar*-soundings performed in the seventh month **are derived from one another.**[46] Hence, just as the *shofar*-sounding of *Yovel* is performed during the day and not at night,[47] so on Rosh Hashanah we sound the *shofar* by day and not at night.[48]

The Gemara now asks vis-a-vis R' Eliezer's opinion:

וְלִיכְתּוֹב רַחֲמָנָא בְּשׁוֹפָר – **But let the Merciful One write** the law of preliminaries **in** the passage of ***shofar,***[49] וְלֵיתוּ הָנָךְ וְלִיגְמְרוּ מִינֵּיהּ – **and let all the other** cases **come and be derived from it** through a *mah matzinu* exegesis! Why are separate teachings required for each mitzvah?

The Gemara answers that a *mah matzinu* teaching is not feasible in this instance:

מִתְּקִיעַת שׁוֹפָר דְּרֹאשׁ הַשָּׁנָה לֵיכָּא לְמִיגְמַר – **It is impossible to derive** the law of preliminaries **from the *shofar*-blowing of Rosh Hashanah,** שֶׁכֵּן מַכְנֶסֶת זִכְרוֹנוֹת שֶׁל יִשְׂרָאֵל לַאֲבִיהֶן שֶׁבַּשָּׁמַיִם – **for indeed [that blowing] brings Israel's remembrances unto their Father in Heaven,** for a good judgment.[50] מִתְּקִיעוֹת [שׁוֹפָר] דְּיוֹם הַכִּפּוּרִים לֵיכָּא לְמִיגְמַרֵי – Further, **it is impossible to derive** this law **from the *shofar*-blowings of Yom Kippur,**[51] דְּאָמַר מַר – **for master has said:**[52] תָּקְעוּ בֵּית דִּין שׁוֹפָר – Once the members of each **court have sounded a shofar,** נִפְטְרוּ עֲבָדִים לְבָתֵּיהֶם – the Jewish **slaves are released** and may return **to their homes,** וְשָׂדוֹת חוֹזְרוֹת לְבַעֲלֵיהֶן – **and the** ancestral **fields revert to their** original **owners.**[53]

NOTES

39. The word יוֹם, *day,* in the verse is extraneous, since the Torah could have stated simply: "There shall be a shofar-sounding for you." The extra word is therefore available for exegesis (*Ritva MHK* ed.).

40. *Numbers* 29:1.

41. Our text is precisely repeated in *Rosh Hashanah* 29b; however, in the Gemara above (117b) the teaching is presented by a different authority (a sage from the academy of R' Yishmael), who cites a different verse לֹא־תַעֲשֶׂה כָל־מְלָאכָה, *you shall not do any work* [i.e. on the Sabbath] (*Exodus* 20:10). See *Ramban, Rashba* and *Ritva* (*MHK* ed.) to 117b at length.

42. [In Talmudic times, bread was baked by pressing the dough onto the interior wall of a hot oven.] Removing bread from the oven wall after it is baked is forbidden Rabbinically as עוּבְדָא דְחוֹל, *a weekday activity* (*Ran* to *Rif,* folio 1b).

43. *Ritva* (*MHK* ed.) notes that even if removing freshly-baked bread from an oven were a *melachah,* it would nonetheless be permitted on Rosh Hashanah, since all food-preparation labors are permitted on Yom Tov. *Ritva* thus explains that the Gemara is teaching that removing bread is allowed even if the bread is being baked not for the sake of Yom Tov. [See also *Ritva* (*MHK* ed.) to 117b, where he writes that, in truth, the verse is needed only for removing bread from an oven, since one might have thought that this act is included in the *melachah* of baking. However, no verse is needed for blowing a *shofar,* since that act was never performed during the construction of the Mishkan and it would not be a *melachah* in any event (see also *Ran* to *Rif* folio 1b).]

44. See above, 131a note 31.

45. *Leviticus* 25:9, which commands a *shofar*-sounding on Yom Kippur of the Jubilee (*Yovel*) year.

46. The superfluous phrase, *in the seventh month,* teaches that the various mitzvos of *shofar*-blowing performed in the month of Tishrei are legally comparable to one another (*Rashi,* from *Rosh Hashanah* 33b).

47. Since the verse states *on the **Day** of Atonement* (see *Sifra* to verse).

48. The Rabbis maintain, on the other hand, that the Scriptural equating of the two *shofar* soundings cannot involve matters of time, since in this aspect they are inherently dissimilar (one sounding occurs on the first day of the month, while the other takes place on the tenth) [see *Tosafos, Tos. HaRosh, Rashba, Ritva MHK* ed.]. The Rabbis understand, rather, that the soundings are equated with respect to the order of the blasts, or the blessings pronounced in conjunction with them (see ibid.). R' Eliezer holds, however, that once we are deriving laws from the Yom Kippur sounding, all laws may be derived (*Ritva MHK* ed.).

49. Via the extraneous word *day.*

50. Because the Rosh Hashanah mitzvah of *shofar*-blowing is uniquely invested with this significance, it cannot serve as the instructive source of a *mah matzinu,* to teach that the preliminaries to all other mitzvos also override the Sabbath restrictions.

51. See *Maharam Schif,* who explains how R' Eliezer knows that these *shofar*-blowings override the Yom Kippur restrictions.

52. R' Yishmael, the son of R' Yochanan ben Beroka, in *Rosh Hashanah* 8b.

53. [Although *Yovel* ushers in the emancipation of Jewish slaves and the reversion of ancestral plots of land to their original owners (see *Leviticus* 25:8-13), these "freedoms" are not triggered on Rosh Hashanah (i.e. the first day) of the Jubilee year. Rather, R' Yishmael teaches there in Tractate *Rosh Hashanah,* the slaves enter into a ten-day transitional period, in which they are no longer subjugated to their masters but are not free to return home. Only when the *shofar* is sounded on Yom Kippur are the promised freedoms of *Yovel* actualized.] Hence, since *Yovel's* "proclamation of freedom" (see *Leviticus* ibid. vs. 9,10) is contingent upon the *shofar* blast, that mitzvah is considered (uniquely) significant, and thus cannot serve as a source for teaching

כל שעתא ושעתא זמניה הוא אלא אמר רב נחמן א"ר יצחק ואיתימא רב הונא בריה דרב יהושע הואיל ובידו להפקירן: אמר מר לולב וכל מכשיריו דוחין את השבת דברי ר"א מנא ליה לר"א הא אי מעומר ושתי הלחם שכן צורך גבוה אלא אמר קרא א) ביום ב) ביום אפילו בשבת ולמאי הלכתא אילימא לטלטול איצטריך קרא למישרי טלטול אלא למכשיריו ורבנן ההוא מיבעי ליה ביום ולא בלילה ור"א ביום ולא בלילה מנא ליה נפקא ליה א) משמחתם לפני ה' אלהיכם שבעת ימים ימים ולא לילות ורבנן איצטריך ס"ד אמינא נילף שבעת ימים (א) מסוכה מה להלן ימים ואפילו לילות אף כאן ימים ואפילו לילות קמ"ל וליכתוב רחמנא בלולב וניתו הנך ונילפו מיניה משום דאיכא למיפרך מה ללולב שכן טעון ארבעה מינים: סוכה וכל מכשיריה דוחין את השבת דברי רבי אליעזר מנא ליה לר"א הא אי מעומר ושתי הלחם שכן צורך גבוה הוא אי מלולב שכן טעון ארבעה מינים אלא גמר (ב) שבעת ימים מלולב מה להלן מכשיריו דוחין את השבת אף כאן נמי מכשיריו דוחין את השבת וליכתוב רחמנא בסוכה וניתי הנך ונגמור מיניה משום דאיכא למיפרך מה לסוכה שכן נוהגת בלילות כבימים: מצה וכל מכשיריה דוחין את השבת דברי ר"א מנא ליה לר"א הא אי מעומר ושתי הלחם שכן צורך גבוה אי מלולב שכן טעון ארבעה מינים אי מסוכה שכן נוהגת בלילות כבימים אלא גמר חמשה עשר חמשה עשר מחג הסוכות מה להלן מכשיריה דוחין את השבת אף כאן מכשיריה דוחין את השבת וליכתוב רחמנא במצה וניתו הנך וליגמור מיניה משום דאיכא למיפרך מה למצה שכן נוהגת בנשים כבאנשים: שופר וכל מכשיריו דוחין את השבת דברי ר"א מנא ליה לר"א הא אי מעומר ושתי הלחם שכן צורך גבוה אי מלולב שכן טעון ארבעה מינים אי מסוכה שכן נוהגת בלילות כבימים אי ממצה שכן נוהגת בנשים כבאנשים אלא אמר קרא ה) יום תרועה יהיה לכם ביום אפילו בשבת ולמאי אילימא לתקיעה הא תנא דבי שמואל ה) כל מלאכת עבודה לא תעשו יצתה תקיעת שופר ורדיית הפת שהיא חכמה ואינה מלאכה אלא למכשירין ורבנן ההוא מיבעי ליה ביום ולא בלילה ור"א ביום ולא בלילה מנא ליה נפקא ליה ו) מביום הכפורים תעבירו שופר בכל ארצכם וגמרי מהדדי וליכתוב רחמנא בשופר וליתו הנך וליגמרו מיניה מתקיעת שופר דראש השנה ליכא למיגמר שכן מכנסת זכרונות של ישראל לאביהן שבשמים מתקיעות [שופר] דיוה"כ ליכא למיגמרי ז) דאמר מר תקעו ב"ד שופר נפטרו עבדים לבתיהם ושדות חוזרות לבעליהן: (אמר מר) מילה וכל מכשיריה דוחין את השבת דברי רבי אליעזר מנא ליה לר"א הא אי מכולהו גמר כדאמרינן ועוד מה להנך שכן

רש"י

כל שעתא זמניה הוא. וכיון שיש לו טלית בכל יום שמשהה בלא ציצית עובר בעשה * ואפילו מונחת בקופסא הלכך כל יומא רמיא מצותיה עליה: הואיל ובידו להפקירן. ונפקי מרשותיה ולאו עליה רמיא חובתיה: אי מעומר ושתי הלחם. וגמר במה מצינו: ביום ואפילו בשבת. מדלא כתיב בראשון לדרשא אתא בכל יום שהוא ראשון לחג: ולמאי איצטריך לרבויי. להאי ואפילו בשבת אי נימא לטלטל כדמשמע קרא לקיחה טלטול בעלמא הוא ועדיין במתן תורה לא נאסר טלטול דאיצטריך קרא למישרי להאי: אלא למכשיריו. דאיסורא דאורייתא הוא: מה להלן ימים ואפילו לילות. כדילפינן במסכת סוכה (דף מג.): וליכתוב רחמנא בלולב. דמכשירין דחו: וניתו. עומר ושתי הלחם מיניה ולמה ליה דכתביה בכולהו: אי מלולב. במה מצינו מלולב שהוא מצוה ומכשיריו דוחין אף סוכה שהיא מצוה מכשיריה דוחין: גמר ז' ימים כו'. ובג"ש אתי ליה ואע"ג דאינה מופנה משני לדדים דהא גבי לולב חד שבעת ימים הוא דכתיב ודרשינן לר' אליעזר למעוטי לילות כיון דגלי רחמנא בעומר ושתי הלחם ולולב גילוי מילתא בעלמא הוא ולא פרכינן עלה גימגום (ג): וניתו הנך. עומר ושתי הלחם מינה: אי מסוכה שכן נוהגת בלילות כבימים. ואילו מצה לילה הראשון חובה ותו לא כדאמרינן בפסחים (דף קכ.): ונכתוב רחמנא. בהדיא במצה ונגמרו הנך כולהו מיניה: בנשים כבאנשים. כדילפינן בפסחים (ד' מג:) לא תאכל עליו חמץ שבעת ימים וגו' כל שישנו בבל תאכל חמץ ישנו בקום אכול מצה ונשים איתנהו בבל תאכל חמץ דכל מצות לא תעשה בין שהזמן גרמא בין שאין הזמן גרמא חייבות לאפוקי סוכה ולולב דליתנהו בנשים דמצות עשה שהזמן גרמא היא: ולמאי. האי קרא הי מילתא אי לתרועה אתא למישרי בשבת אי לתקיעה לא איצטריך דאפילו תקיעת הרשות ליכא בה איסורא דאורייתא: מלאכת עבודה. של טורח: וגמרי מהדדי. במסכת ראש השנה (דף לג:) שאין תלמוד לומר בחדש השביעי דהא בכמה קראי כתב לן דיוה"כ בחודש השביעי מה ת"ל בחודש השביעי שיהו כל תרועות משל חדש השביעי שוות: נפטרו עבדים לבתיהם. קריאת דרור דיובל תלויה בה הלכך חשיבא: אי מכולהו. מאחת מכולהו. איכא למיפרך בכל הנך חדא לד חמור האמור בה לעיל: שאם

תוספות

כדאיתא בפ"ק דיבמות (דף ו.) וי"ל דהכא הכי גמרי מה מצינו בהנך שמצות נוהגות בשבת ומכשיריה דחו שבת אף כל שמצות נוהגות בשבת מכשיריה דחו שבת הלכך לא שייך למילף מכיבוד דהיינו המצוה עצמה ולא מכשיריה דשחוט לי בשל לי היינו כיבוד עצמו כשמתקן לו מאכלו והבנין נמי הוי מצוה אחת שצוה הקדוש ברוך הוא לבנות בית המקדש: **סד"א** נילף שבעת ימים משבעת ימים מסוכה. וא"ת היכי תיסק אדעתיה לדון ג"ש הא אין אדם דן ג"ש מעצמו אא"כ למדה מרבו וי"ל דשמא בעלמא ניתנה למדרש ט): **קמ"ל.** * ולא ידענא השתא האי שבעת ימים למאי אתיא דאע"ג דדרשינן בפ"ק דפסחים (דף ה.) מה שביעי שביעי לחג אף ראשון ראשון לחג הא איכא למידרש משבעה בלא ימים: **שכן** טעון ארבעה מינים. אף על גב דעומר ושתי הלחם נמי מביאין עמהן כבשים ויין לניסוך ושמן למנחות שאני ד' מינין שבלולב דמעכבין זה את זה כדאמר בפרק הקומץ (מנחות דף מ.) ובפרק התכלת (שם דף מה:) [אמרינן] הכבשים אין מעכבין לא את העומר ולא את שתי הלחם י) והיינו טעון ד' מינין שאין מצות לולב כלל בלא ד' מינין אבל באלו יכולה להיות מצוותן בלא ד' מינין. הר"ב פור"ת: **אי** מעומר כו'. הכא לא דייקא תלמודא למילף מבינייהו דהכי אורחיה דתלמודא זימנין דייק וזימנין לא דייק ואי הוה דייק הוה משכח פירכ' הרב פור"ת א"נ מילתא דאתיא במה הצד טרח וכתב לה קרא כמו מילתא דאתיא בקל וחומר והאי דקאמר תלמודא ניכתוב רחמנא בהאי ותיתי אידך מיניה פירוש ומאי צריך קרא היינו משום דאי בלא מה הצד הוה מצי למילף הך מצוה מאידך לא הוה כתב רחמנא קרא כיון דהוה פשוט כל כך דלא דמי למילתא דאתיא בק"ו דהוא פשוט יותר: **שבעת** ימים (ד) מלולב. מופנה הוא משני לצדדים גבי לולב לא איצטריך דאע"ג דדרשינן ימים ולא לילות מיהו לא הוה צריך למיכתב שבעת כלל דהוה מצי למיכתב ושמחת לפני וגו' בימים והוי לשון שבעת מיותר לג"ש וא"ת ור' אליעזר היכי דריש ימים ולא לילות כיון דאית ליה ג"ש היא גופה נילף מסוכה מה להלן ימים אפילו לילות אף לולב ימים ואפי' לילות ויש לומר דלית לן למילף בג"ש מילתא דלשון ג"ש גופא מוכחא דלאו כן דימים משמע ולא לילות: **ואי** מסוכה שכן נוהגת בלילות כבימים. משמע דבעי למימר תאמר במצה שאינה נוהגת בלילות כבימים ואדרבה עיקר מצותה בלילה הראשון שנאמר בערב תאכלו מצות (שמות יב) והכי הוה מצי למימר שכן נוהגת בימים ובלילות: **נפקא** ליה מביום הכפורים. וגמרינן מהדדי כדדרשינן בראש השנה י) שיהו כל התקיעות של חודש השביעי שוות כדפירש בקונטרס ורבנן סברי דלא שייך לאקשויי אלא לומר שסדר תקיעות יהיו שוין לענין סדר תקיעות מייתי לה התם אבל לזמן דיום ודאי לא איתקש דע"כ זמנם אינו שוה זה בראש חודש וזה בעשור לחודש: והתניא

רבינו חננאל

אזמל לא שרינן בכי האי גונא דבהדיא קיי"ל הלכתא כרבנן א) וככלליה דרבי עקיבא דאמר כל מלאכה שאפשר לה לעשות מע"ש אינ' דוחה את השבת והבאת אזמל כיון שאפשר לו להביאו מע"ש ולא הביאו אין הבאתו דוחה את השבת אפילו לענין עשיית פסח דכרת הוא לא מייתינן אזמל למול בנו או עבדו כדי שיותר לו לעשות פסח ולא שנא להו לרבנן לא דרך רה"ר ולא דרך גגות וקרפיפות וחצרות הכל אחד הוא ובכל אסור ואשכחנן בתלמוד א"י עובדא ולא הביאוהו בשבת. ואמרינן בכל מקום (רב עביד) מעשה רב דגמרינן מינה. וזה הוא המעשה. ר' שמואל בר אבודומי הוה ליה עובדא למגזר לרב ששא בריה אנשיון למיתי אזמל שאל לר' [מנא]. אמר להון ידחה למחר. שאל לר' יצחק בן אלעזר אמר להון משחוק [קונדיטון] לא אנשיתון ומיתי אזמל אנשיתון ידחה למחר: א"ר חייא בר אבא. א"ר יוחנן לא לכל א"ר אליעזר מכשירי מצוה דוחין את השבת שהרי שתי הלחם חובת היום הן ולא למדם ר' אליעזר אלא מג"ש נאמרה הבאה בעומר שנאמר והבאתם את עומר וגו' ונאמרה הבאה בשתי הלחם שנאמר ממושבותיכם תביאו לחם תנופה שתים וגו'. מנין שהעומר דוחה שבת. גרסינן באחרית פרק ר' ישמעאל אומר העומר היה בא בשבת מג' סאין וכו'. ת"ר תקריב את מנחת בכוריך מה ת"ל לפי שמצות העומר להקריב מן הקמה מנין שאם לא מצא קמה יביא מן העומרין ת"ל תקריב כו' עד תקריב לפי שמצותו לקצור בלילה. מניין שאם קצר ביום כשר ודוחה שבת ת"ל תקריב כל שהוא תקריב מ"מ תקריבו אפי' בשבת אפילו בטומאה. ותוב תניא (בתו"כ) בסוף פרשת אמור אל הכהנים (ובפסחים עז ובמנחות עב) וידבר משה את מועדי ה' מה ת"ל לפי שלא למדנו שדוחין את השבת אלא התמיד והפסח שכתוב בהן במועדו מניין לרבות העומר והקרב עמו. שתי הלחם והקרב עמהן שידחו שבת ת"ל וידבר משה וגו' קבען מועד אחד לכולן ופשוטה היא זו הלכה כולה. ואפי' ר' אליעזר שמתיר במכשירי מצוה מודה. שאם צריך טליתו ועשה מזוזה בפתחו לעשות בשבת שהוא חייב ואמרינן מ"ש הני ואוקימנא הואיל ובידו להפקירן. פי' כי הציצית הוא חובת הבגד וכיון שהפקיר אינו בגדו וכן הבית כיוצא בו.

חשק שלמה על רבינו חננאל

א) עיין היטב בר"ן כאן דלפסה לא הראיות שהביא רבינו ע"ש.

מסורת הש"ס

א) [עי' תוספות מנחות מד. ד"ה טלית], ב) סוכה מג., ג) לעיל קלו: ע"ש ר"ה כט:, ד) ר"ה ל:, ה) עיין מהרש"ם, ו) [כדאיתא בפ' התכלת מה:], ז) [דף לג:].

הגהות הב"ח

(א) גמ' נילף שבעת ימים משבעת ימים מסוכה: (ב) שם אלא גמר שבעת ימים מלולב: (ג) רש"י ד"ה גמר ז' ימים וכו' גימגום הס"ד ואח"כ מ"ה וניתו הנך עומר ושתי הלחם: ונכתוב רחמנא בהדיא במצה ונגמרו הנך כולהו מיניה: (ד) תוס' ד"ה שבעת ימים משבעת ימים מלולב מופנה הוא משני לצדדין דגבי לולב נמי לא איצטריך:

גליון הש"ס

רש"י ד"ה כל שעתא וכו' ואפי' מונחת בקופסא. עי' מנחות דף מד ע"א תוס' ד"ה טלית: תוס' ד"ה קמ"ל ולא ידענא. כעין זה לעיל דף קיח ע"ב תוס' ד"ה אלו הוו וש"נ:

תורה אור השלם

א) וּלְקַחְתֶּם לָכֶם בַּיּוֹם הָרִאשׁוֹן פְּרִי עֵץ הָדָר כַּפֹּת תְּמָרִים וַעֲנַף עֵץ עָבֹת וְעַרְבֵי נָחַל וּשְׂמַחְתֶּם לִפְנֵי יְיָ אֱלֹהֵיכֶם שִׁבְעַת יָמִים: [ויקרא כג, מ]

ב) בַּסֻּכֹּת תֵּשְׁבוּ שִׁבְעַת יָמִים כָּל הָאֶזְרָח בְּיִשְׂרָאֵל יֵשְׁבוּ בַּסֻּכֹּת: [ויקרא כג, מב]

ג) וּבַחֲמִשָּׁה עָשָׂר יוֹם לַחֹדֶשׁ הַזֶּה חַג הַמַּצּוֹת לַייָ שִׁבְעַת יָמִים מַצּוֹת תֹּאכֵלוּ: [ויקרא כג, ו]

ד) דַּבֵּר אֶל בְּנֵי יִשְׂרָאֵל לֵאמֹר בַּחֲמִשָּׁה עָשָׂר יוֹם לַחֹדֶשׁ הַשְּׁבִיעִי הַזֶּה חַג הַסֻּכּוֹת שִׁבְעַת יָמִים לַייָ: [ויקרא כג, לד]

ה) וּבַחֹדֶשׁ הַשְּׁבִיעִי בְּאֶחָד לַחֹדֶשׁ מִקְרָא קֹדֶשׁ יִהְיֶה לָכֶם כָּל מְלֶאכֶת עֲבֹדָה לֹא תַעֲשׂוּ יוֹם תְּרוּעָה יִהְיֶה לָכֶם: [במדבר כט, א]

ו) וְהַעֲבַרְתָּ שׁוֹפַר תְּרוּעָה בַּחֹדֶשׁ הַשְּׁבִעִי בֶּעָשׂוֹר לַחֹדֶשׁ בְּיוֹם הַכִּפֻּרִים תַּעֲבִירוּ שׁוֹפָר בְּכָל אַרְצְכֶם: [ויקרא כה, ט]

ליקוטי רש"י

ביום אפילו בשבת. דמשמע כל דהו יום וקרא יתירא הוא דהוי למכתב בראשון. איצטריך קרא למישרי טלטול. דרכנן עדיין לא נאסר טלטול בשבת ולא הכתוב להתיר כאן. אלא למכשיריו. לא הכתוב ללמדך שמכשירי לולב דוחין את השבת כלומר מיקוץ ואפילו לקוללו [סוכה מג.]. בנשים כבאנשים. אכילת מצה ליל ראשון שהוא חובה מכתיב (שמות יב) בערב תאכלו מצות ונשים חייבות כדאמר בפסחים (מג:) נשים חייבות באכילת מצה דבר תורה שנאמר לא תאכל עליו חמץ שבעת ימים תאכל עליו מצות כל שישנו בבל תאכל חמץ ישנו בקום אכול מצה [קידושין לד.]. ורדיית הפת. לרדות הפת מן התנור שהיא חכמה ואינה מלאכה [לעיל ג:].

The Gemara now inquires about R' Eliezer's source for the law of preliminaries in the case of *milah* itself:

(אָמַר מַר) מִילָה וְכָל מַכְשִׁירֶיהָ דּוֹחִין אֶת הַשַּׁבָּת – **(Master said:)** A Baraisa taught: The mitzvah of CIRCUMCISION AND ALL ITS PRELIMINARIES OVERRIDE THE SABBATH restrictions. דִּבְרֵי רַבִּי אֱלִיעֶזֶר – These are THE WORDS OF R' ELIEZER. מְנָא לֵיהּ לְרַבִּי אֱלִיעֶזֶר הָא – Now, **from where** did **R' Eliezer** derive **this** law? אִי מִכּוּלְּהוּ גָּמַר – If you say **he derived** it **from** any one of **all [the cases]** mentioned above (through a *mah matzinu* exegesis), that cannot be – כִּדְאַמְרִינָן – for it is possible to refute each *mah matzinu* by ascribing a unique stringency to each instructive case, **as we have said** above.[54] וְעוֹד – **And, furthermore,** we can offer this new retort: מַה לְהָנָךְ – **Whereas** each of **these** other mitzvos is unique,

NOTES

that the preliminaries to the other mitzvos also override the Sabbath restrictions (*Rashi, Ritva MHK* ed.). [See *Minchas Chinuch* §331.]

54. E.g. "whereas the mitzvah of *lulav* is unique, for indeed it requires the taking of four species . . ."

שֶׁכֵּן אִם עָבַר זְמַנָּהּ בָּטְלָה – **for indeed if its** prescribed **time lapsed, [the obligation] is voided,**[1] the same cannot be said of the mitzvah of circumcision.[2] Hence, because *milah* lacks this stringency, the law of preliminaries cannot be inferred to it.

The Gemara identifies R' Eliezer's Biblical source:

אֶלָּא הַיְינוּ טַעְמָא דְּרַבִּי אֱלִיעֶזֶר – **Rather, this is R' Eliezer's reason** for holding that *milah's* preliminaries override the Sabbath restrictions: דְּאָמַר קְרָא ,,וּבַיּוֹם הַשְּׁמִינִי יִמּוֹל בְּשַׂר עָרְלָתוֹ" – **Because the verse states,**[3] ***And on the eighth day the flesh of his foreskin shall be circumcised,*** which implies: וַאֲפִילּוּ בְּשַׁבָּת – You shall perform the preliminaries to *milah*[4] on the eighth day, whenever that may be – i.e. **and even on the Sabbath** day.[5]

The Gemara asks:

וְלִיכְתּוֹב רַחֲמָנָא בְּמִילָה – **But let the Merciful One write** the law of preliminaries **in** the passage of **circumcision,**[6] וְלֵיתוּ הָנָךְ וְלִיגְמוּר מִינַּהּ – **and let** all **the other** cases **come and be derived from it** through a *mah matzinu* exegesis! Why are separate teachings required for each mitzvah?

The Gemara answers:

מִשּׁוּם דְּאִיכָּא לְמִיפְרַךְ – **Because there are** grounds **to refute** the *mah matzinu* teaching, as follows: מָה לְמִילָה שֶׁכֵּן נִכְרְתוּ עָלֶיהָ שְׁלֹשׁ עֶשְׂרֵה בְּרִיתוֹת – **Whereas** the mitzvah of **circumcision** is unique, **for indeed thirteen covenants were made over it,**[7] the same cannot be said of any of the other mitzvos. Hence, because *milah* is invested with this special significance, it cannot serve as the instructive source of a *mah matzinu* to teach the law of preliminaries universally.

The Gemara now debates the Biblical source for circumcision itself overriding the Sabbath restrictions:

עַד כָּאן לֹא פְּלִיגֵי רַבָּנָן עֲלֵיהּ אֶלָּא בְּמַכְשִׁירֵי מִילָה – **Only until here do the Rabbis argue** with R' Eliezer **in this matter** – i.e. only **concerning the preliminaries to** the mitzvah of **circumcision.** אֲבָל מִילָה גּוּפָהּ – **However,** with regard to the **circumcision itself,** דִּבְרֵי הַכֹּל דּוֹחָה שַׁבָּת – **the opinion of all** is that **it overrides** the **Sabbath** restrictions. מְנָלַן – **From where** do **we** know this?

The Gemara offers one answer:

אָמַר עוּלָּא הֲלָכָה – **Ulla said:** It is **a law** taught orally to Moses on Mt. Sinai, and is not derived from the Written Torah. וְכֵן אָמַר רַבִּי יִצְחָק הֲלָכָה – **And so said R' Yitzchak:** It is **a law** taught orally to Moses on Mt. Sinai.

The Gemara rejects this answer:

מֵיתִיבֵי – **They objected** on the evidence of a Baraisa: מִנַּיִין לְפִיקּוּחַ נֶפֶשׁ שֶׁדּוֹחֶה אֶת הַשַּׁבָּת – **FROM WHERE** is it derived **THAT SAVING A LIFE OVERRIDES THE SABBATH** restrictions? רַבִּי אֶלְעָזָר בֶּן עֲזַרְיָה אוֹמֵר – **R' ELAZAR BEN AZARYAH SAYS:** It is derived from the following *kal vachomer* (a fortiori) argument: מָה מִילָה שֶׁהִיא אַחַת מֵאֵיבָרָיו שֶׁל אָדָם – **INASMUCH AS CIRCUMCISION, WHICH IS** a fulfillment of only a single mitzvah in **ONE OF A PERSON'S LIMBS,** דּוֹחָה אֶת הַשַּׁבָּת – **OVERRIDES THE SABBATH** restrictions, קַל וָחוֹמֶר לְפִיקּוּחַ נֶפֶשׁ – **ALL THE MORE SO SAVING A LIFE,** which enables the endangered person to continue fulfilling all the mitzvos of the Torah, שֶׁדּוֹחָה אֶת הַשַּׁבָּת – **SHOULD OVERRIDE THE SABBATH** restrictions.[8] וְאִי סָלְקָא דַּעְתָּךְ הֲלָכָה – **Now, if it enters your mind** that the source for *milah's* power to override the Sabbath is **a law** taught orally to Moses at Sinai, קַל וָחוֹמֶר מֵהֲלָכָה מִי אָתֵי – **can a *kal vachomer* come from** such **a law?** וְהָתַנְיָא – **But it was** explicitly **taught** otherwise **in a Baraisa:** אָמַר לוֹ רַבִּי אֶלְעָזָר (בֶּן עֲזַרְיָה) עֲקִיבָא – **R' ELAZAR**[9] **(BEN AZARYAH) SAID TO [R' AKIVA]: "AKIVA!** עֶצֶם כִּשְׂעוֹרָה מְטַמֵּא הֲלָכָה – That **A BARLEY-SIZED BONE CONTAMINATES** a *nazir* through touching or carrying it so that the *nazir* is obligated to shave his head and recommence his *nezirus* **IS AN** oral **LAW** taught to Moses at Sinai. וּרְבִיעִית דָּם קַל וָחוֹמֶר – **AND** from there you sought to derive that contamination by **A QUARTER-*log*** of a corpse's **BLOOD** likewise causes him to shave and recommence his *nezirus,* through **A *KAL VACHOMER*** argument.[10] וְאֵין דָּנִין קַל וָחוֹמֶר מֵהֲלָכָה – **BUT WE DO NOT REASON** via **A *KAL VACHOMER* FROM AN** oral **LAW,** inasmuch as the Thirteen Rules of Biblical Exegesis cannot be applied to the Oral Law." From here we may conclude that the law that *milah* overrides the Sabbath, which is the basis of the first Baraisa's *kal vachomer* (through which we derive that saving a life also overrides the Sabbath), cannot be an oral law from Sinai. – ? –

The Gemara suggests a different Biblical source for the law that *milah* overrides the Sabbath:

אֶלָּא אָמַר רַבִּי אֶלְעָזָר – **Rather, R' Elazar said:** אַתְיָא ,,אוֹת" ,,אוֹת" – **[The law of overriding]** for *milah* **is derived** through the *gezeirah shavah* of ***sign/sign.***[11]

NOTES

1. Therefore, the Torah allowed its preliminaries to override the Sabbath restrictions (*Rashi*).

2. The mitzvah of *milah* may be performed up until the moment of one's death (see *Rambam, Hil. Milah* 1:2, with *Raavad* and *Kesef Mishneh*). Each of the other mitzvos, on the other hand, has a circumscribed appointed time: *Omer* on the second day of Pesach, Two Loaves on Shavuos, *lulav* on the first day of Succos (the Biblical requirement). And even in the case of succah, which operates for all seven days of the festival, on each day there is a separate obligation to dwell in a succah. Hence, if the Shabbos restrictions are observed, that day's mitzvah will have been voided (*Tos. HaRosh, Tosafos* above, 131a ד"ה ושוין; see also *Rashba* here).

3. *Leviticus* 12:3.

4. Scripture perforce refers to the preliminaries, since the Gemara below learns from a different source that *milah* itself overrides the Sabbath (see *Rashi, Ritva MHK* ed.).

5. The Torah could have stated simply, "And on the eighth, the flesh..." [since the previous verse speaks of the childbirthing mother as being ritually contaminated *for a seven-**day** period*] (*Rashi* below ד"ה ביום ואפילו בשבת). Hence, the word יוֹם, *day,* in our verse is superfluous, and thus available for exegesis.

6. Via the extraneous word *day.*

7. In the passage wherein Abraham receives the commandment of circumcision (*Genesis* 17:1-22), the word *covenant* appears thirteen times [which indicates the mitzvah's great importance] (*Rashi;* see *Rashash*).

8. Our elucidation of the Baraisa's *kal vachomer* follows *Rashba* and *Ran* (*MHK* ed.). See *Tos. HaRosh* and *Ritva* (*MHK* ed.) for a different interpretation.

9. *Menachem Meishiv Nefesh* and *Rashash* emend this to read "R' Eliezer."

10. One of a *nazir's* obligations is to avoid becoming ritually contaminated by a human corpse (*Numbers* 6:6). If he does become *tamei* in this fashion, he must shave his head according to the procedure outlined there (ibid. vs. 9-12) and begin his *nezirus* count anew. However, not every case of corpse *tumah* triggers the shaving requirement. The Mishnah in *Nazir* (54a; see also 49b) teaches that a *nazir* does not shave and recommence his *nezirus* for *tumah* contracted from a quarter-*log* of corpse's blood. In the *kal vachomer* argument referenced by R' Eliezer (which originally appears in a Mishnah ibid. 56b), R' Akiva attempts to prove otherwise, as follows: If a barley-sized human bone, which does not contaminate a person via a roof (*tumas ohel*), causes a *nazir* to shave through touching or carrying it, then a quarter-*log* of blood, which does contaminate a person via a roof, should certainly cause a *nazir* to shave through contracting *tumah* from it (*Rashi*).

11. With reference to *Shabbos* the Torah states כִּי אוֹת הוּא, *it is a sign* (*Exodus* 31:13), and with reference to circumcision it states וְהָיָה לְאוֹת בְּרִית, *and it shall be a sign of the covenant* (*Genesis* 17:11). The common word *sign* intimates that just as there in the first passage the word refers to Shabbos, so here in the passage of *milah* it refers to Shabbos – i.e. to teach that Shabbos is a time for *milah* (*Rashi;* see *Ritva MHK* ed.; cf. *Tos. HaRosh*).

שכן אם עבר זמנה בטלה אלא היינו טעמא דרבי אליעזר דאמר קרא (א) וביום השמיני ימול בשר ערלתו ואפילו בשבת וליכתוב רחמנא במילה וליתו הנך וליגמור מיניה משום דאיכא למיפרך מה למילה שכן נכרתו עליה שלש עשרה בריתות: ע"כ לא פליגי רבנן עליה אלא במכשירי מילה אבל מילה גופה דברי הכל דוחה שבת מנלן אמר עולא הלכה וכן אמר רבי יצחק הלכה מיתיבי (ב) מניין לפיקוח נפש שדוחה את השבת רבי אלעזר בן עזריה אומר מה מילה שהיא אחת מאיבריו של אדם דוחה את השבת קל וחומר לפיקוח נפש שדוחה את השבת ואי סלקא דעתך הלכה קל וחומר מהלכה מי אתי והתניא (ג) אמר לו רבי אליעזר (ג בן עזריה) עקיבא עצם כשעורה מטמא הלכה ורביעית דם קל וחומר ואין דנין קל וחומר מהלכה אלא אמר רבי אלעזר אתיא (ב) אות (ג) אות אלא מעתה תפילין דכתיב בהן (ד) אות לידחי שבת אלא אתיא (ה) ברית (ו) ברית לידחי שבת אלא אתיא גדול דכתיב ביה (ו) ברית לידחי שבת אלא אתיא ציצית דכתיב ביה (ח) דורות לידחי שבת אלא אמר רב נחמן בר יצחק דנין אות ברית ודורות מאות ברית ודורות לאפוקי הנך דחד חד הוא דכתיב בהן ור' יוחנן אמר אמר קרא (א) ביום (ט) ביום אפילו בשבת אמר ליה ריש לקיש לרבי יוחנן אלא מעתה מחוסרי כפרה דכתיב בהו ביום הכי נמי דדחו שבת ההוא מיבעי ליה ביום ולא בלילה האי נמי מיבעי ליה ביום ולא בלילה ההוא (ז) מבן שמנת ימים נפקא האי נמי (ט) מביום צוותו נפקא אע"ג דנפקא מביום צוותו אצטריכא סד"א הואיל וחס רחמנא עליה לאתויי בדלות בלילה נמי ליתי קמ"ל מתקיף לה רבינא אלא מעתה יהא זר כשר בהן ויהא אונן כשר בהן הא אהדריה קרא רב אחא בר יעקב אמר קרא (א) שמיני שמיני אפילו בשבת האי שמיני מיבעי ליה למעוטי שביעי שביעי מבן שמנת ימים נפקא ואכתי מיבעי ליה חד למעוטי שביעי וחד למעוטי תשיעי דאי מחד הוה אמינא שביעי הוא דלא מטא זמניה אבל משמיני ואילך זמניה הוא אלא מחוורתא כדרבי יוחנן תניא כוותיה דרבי יוחנן ודלא כרב אחא בר יעקב שמיני ימול אפילו בשבת ומה אני מקיים (י) מחלליה מות יומת בשאר מלאכות חוץ ממילה או אינו אלא אפי' מילה ומה אני מקיים שמיני ימול חוץ משבת ת"ל ביום אפילו בשבת אמר רבא האי תנא מעיקרא מאי קא ניחא ליה ולבסוף מאי קא קשיא ליה הכי קאמר שמיני ימול אפילו בשבת ומה אני מקיים מחלליה מות יומת בשאר מלאכו' חוץ ממילה אבל מילה דחיא מ"ט ק"ו הוא ומה צרע' שדוחה את העבודה

ועבודה

רש"י

שאם עבר זמנן בטלין. הילכך דחו: **וביום השמיני ימול ואפילו בשבת.** ומילה גופה דדחיא שבת אמרינן לקמן הלכה למשה מסיני איצטריך ליה ביום למכשיריה: **י"ג בריתות.** נאמרו לאברהם בפרשת מילה (בראשית יז): **והא תניא.** במסכת נזיר: **עקיבא עצם כשעורה הלכה.** שהיה ר"ע דן ק"ו מניין לרביעית דם המת שהנזיר מגלח על אהלה ק"ו מה עצם כשעורה שאינו מטמא באהל נזיר מגלח על מגעו ומשאו רביעית דם שמטמאה באהל דכתיב ועל כל נפש מת לא יבא אינו דין שהנזיר מגלח עליה ואמר ליה רבי אלעזר עקיבא עצם כשעורה הלכה למשה מסיני שיהא נזיר מגלח עליה ורביעית דם אתה בא ללמוד ממנה בק"ו ואין דנין קל וחומר מהלכה דלא ניתנה תורה שבעל פה לידרש בי"ג מדות: **אתיא אות אות.** בשבת כתיב (שמות לא) כי אות היא ובמילה כתיב (בראשית יז) והיה לאות ברית מה להלן שבת אף כאן שבת: **אלא מעתה.** אי הך ג"ש לאות המאמורה בשבת נאמרה בסיני לידרש שתיבה זו לדרשה נאמרה ליגמר מינה נמי לתפילין: **אלא אתיא ברית ברית.** ההוא לאות לא נאמרה בסיני ואין אדם דן גזרה שוה מעצמו אלא הך דברית נאמרה בסיני ובשבת כתיב ברית (שמות לא) לדורותם ברית עולם: **גדול.** בן שלש עשרה דהוי מילה שלא בזמנה: **דכתיב ביה ברית.** וערל זכר אשר לא ימול וגו' את בריתי הפר (בראשית יז) והאי קרא בגדול כתיב מדמחייב ליה כרת שאם לא מלו אביו חייב הוא למול את עצמו ולידחי שבת ואנן אמרינן לקמן דאפילו יום טוב אינו דוחה אלא בזמנה: **דורות. דורות.** בשבת כתיב לדורותם ברית עולם ובמילת קטן כתיב (שם) ובן שמנת ימים ימול לכם כל זכר לדורותיכם: **ביום ואפילו בשבת.** מדלא כתיב בשמיני ימול ולר' אליעזר דאפקיה למכשירין מילה עצמה הלכה היא ופיקוח נפש לא אתיא ליה בק"ו ממילה אלא מקראי נפקא ליה כדאמרינן בפרק בתרא דיומא (ה): **מחוסרי כפרה.** כל טמאין שהוצרכו לקרבן זב וזבה יולדת ומצורע נאמר בהן וביום השמיני: **ביום צותו.** את בני ישראל להקריב את קרבניהם (ויקרא ז) ביום ולא בלילה: **אלא מעתה.** משום דהוכשר להביא בדלות מכשירין בה שאר פסולין: **יהא זר ואונן כשר בהן.** אונן אף שלא נקבר מתו פסול לעבודה דכתיב (שם כא) בכהן גדול לאביו ולאמו לא יטמא ומן המקדש לא יצא ולא יחלל והכי משמע אף ביום שמתו אביו ואמו אינו צריך לצאת מן המקדש אלא מקריב אונן ולא יחלל ועבודתו לא תהא מחוללת בכך הא אחר שלא יצא חילל: **הא אהדריה קרא.** לפסול בהן לילה דכתיב בהו וביום כדאמרינן וכיון דלענין לילה תורת כל הקרבנות עליהן לענין זר ואונן נמי תורת קרבן עליהן: **שמיני.** כל שהוא שמיני ואפילו בשבת וביום למעוטי לילה: **תניא כוותיה דר' יוחנן.** דיליף מוביום: **מעיקרא מאי ניחא ליה.** לאוקמי שמיני דווקא ואפילו בשבת ודחי מחלליה מות יומת אצל שאר מלאכות מאיזה טעם נראה לו כן: **ולבסוף.** כשהיפך דבריו ואמר או אינו אלא אפי' מילה בכלל מחלליה מות יומת דהוא דוקא ודחי שמיני ימול אצל שאר ימים: **מאי קשיא ליה.** בטעמא הראשון: **אבל מילה דחיא.** שבת בק"ו ותיגמר מיניה למידחי מחלליה מות יומת אצל שאר מלאכות ולמימר שמיני דווקא קאמר ואפי' ביום שבת: **ומה צרעת שדוחה את העבודה.** אזהרה שהזהירה תורה על הצרעת שלא לקוץ בהרתו כדתניא (מכות דף כב.) השמר בנגע הצרעת אזהרה בקוצץ בהרתו הכתוב מדבר והתמיהה תורה באזהרה זו לדחות העבודה כדקיימא לן בפסחים (דף סז.) דטומאת מת נדחית בקרבן צבור ולא זבין ומצורעי' ובטלים לעשות פסח ולא אמרינן יקוצו בהרתן ויאכלו פסחים או הכהן יקוץ בהרתו ויעבוד אם הכהנים טמאין והקהל טהורין:

תוספות

והתניא אמר ליה רבי אליעזר כו'. ול"ג והתנן דכל זה אינו במשנה: **ההיא** מבן שמונת ימים נפקא. תימה דתניא בת"כ ומייתי לה בפרק הערל (יבמות עב:) השמיני ימול לתניא יכול בין ביום ובין בלילה ת"ל ביום אין לי אלא שנימול לח' נימול לט' לי' ולי"א מניין שאינו נימול אלא ביום ת"ל וביום ובפ"ב דמגילה (דף כ:) נמי אמר אין מוהלין אלא ביום דכתיב וביום השמיני ויש לומר דסמיך אבן שמנת ימים ודרשא פשוטה נקט: **אלא** מעתה יהא זר ואונן כשר בהן. לאו דווקא נקט זר דהא בכולהו בזב וזבה ויולדת ומצורע כתב בהו כהן: **הא** אהדריה קרא. והוה ליה דבר שיצא מן הכלל לידון בדבר החדש לאתויי בדלות שאי אתה יכול להחזירו לכללו לפסול לילה ואונן עד שיחזירנו הכתוב לכללו בפירוש הרי החזירה בפירוש ופסל לילה וה"ה אונן וקשה ואמאי לא קאמר דאהדריה קרא מדכתיב כהן ולא זר ושמא לשום דרשה אחריתי אתא: **תניא** כוותיה דרבי יוחנן ודלא כרב אחא בר יעקב. ודלא כרב נחמן בר יצחק דאמר אתיא אות ברית דורות לא הוי דאיהו מודה דדרשינן ביום כדדרשינן בברייתא ואות ברית דורות אתא למכשירין וביום למילה גופה ולית ליה למילה הלכה אע"ג דר' יוחנן אית ליה (י) הלכה לר' אליעזר [כדפי' רש"י והאי ברייתא דדרשי ביום אתיא כרבנן דביום] איצטריך למילה גופה והכי לא קאמר אלא דלא כרב אחא דברייתא מוכחא בהדיא דלא בעיא למדרש שמיני ימול. מ"ר: **מה** צרעת שדוחה את העבודה. תימה ולימא קל וחומר איפכא ותדחה עבודה את הצרעת שיקוץ בהרתו כדי לעשות עבודה ומה שבת שדוחה את המילה ומילה דוחה את הצרעת עבודה דוחה אותה לצרעת שנדחה מפני מילה אינו דין שתהא עבודה דוחה אותה והא דאמרינן בפסחים בפרק אלו דברים (דף סז.) וישלחו מן המחנה כל צרוע וכל זב וכל טמא לנפש אם טמאי מתים משתלחין זבים ומצורעים לא כ"ש אלא יש לך שעה שזבין ומצורעים משתלחים ואין טמאי מתים משתלחים ואיזה זה פסח הבא בטומאה

רבינו חננאל

עד כאן לא פליגי ר' אליעזר ורבנן אלא במכשירי מילה אבל במילה עצמה דברי הכל דחיא שבת. מנלן עולא ור' אסי ור' יצחק נפחא כולהי אימרי הלכה ומותבינן עליהן. מניין לפקוח נפש שדוחה' שבת נענה ר' אלעזר בן עזריה ואמר ומה מילה שהיא אחד מאבריו של אדם דוחה שבת ק"ו לפקוח נפש שדוחה את השבת ואי ס"ד הלכה ק"ו מהלכה (מייתי) [מי אתין]. והתניא א"ל ר' עקיבא עצם כשעורה הלכה ורביעית דם ק"ו ואין דנין ק"ו מהלכה וכו' לבטלו וזה מפורש בנזיר פר' כ"ג ונזיר אין מטמאין לקרוביהן וכו'. ובטלו דברי מי שאמר הלכה היא ובא ר' אלעזר ללמדו בג"ש באות אות משבת. ונדחו דבריו ובא רב נחמן בר יצחק ולמדו באות ברית ודורו' בשבת כתיב לעשות את השבת לדורותם ברית עולם ביני ובין בני ישראל אות היא לעולם במילה כתיב ואתה את בריתי תשמור אתה וזרעך אחריך לדורותם וכתיב ונמלתם את בשר ערלתכם והיתה לאות ברית ביני וביניכם. ר' יוחנן אמר אמר קרא וביום השמיני ימול בשר ערלתו ביום אפילו בשבת אקשינן עליה ר"ל אי הכי אפילו מחוסרי כפרה כגון מצורע והזבה דכתי' בהן וביום השמיני יקח שני כבשים וגו' ובזבה כתיב וביום השמיני תקח לה שתי תורים הכי נמי כיון דכתיב בהו וביום יקריבו קרבנותיהם אפילו בשבת והא קיי"ל אין קרבן יחיד דוחה את השבת ופירק לו זה שכתוב במחוסר כפרה וביום למעוטי לילה. עוד הקשה לו ר"ל וכל קשיא שהקשה לו פירק ר' יוחנן וחזר רבינא להתקיף על פירוק ר' יוחנן ופריק סד"א הואיל וחס רחמנא עליה לאתויי בדלות בלילה נמי ליתי קמ"ל וביום. התקיף רבינא אי הכי אמ' דחס עליהן או אינו כשר בהן ולא יטריחם להמתין עד שימצאו כהן טהור כשר לטהרם ופריק הא אהדריה קרא כלומר אע"פ שחס עליו והקל בקרבנו החזיר לטהרת הכהן שנאמר והביא אותם ביום השמיני לטהרתו אל הכהן וגו' ואתא רב אחא בר יעקב עוד להוציא שהמילה מותרת בשבת מדכתיב וביום השמיני ימול כלומר איזה יפול שמיני אין לך לא להקדים ולא לאחר ונתקשה ולא עמדו דבריו ואמרינן אלא מחוורתא כר' יוחנן דאפקיה מן וביום. וסוגיא דשמעתיה כר' יוחנן ודתניא כוותי' ולא כר' אחא בר יעקב:

רב נסים גאון

איצטריך סלקא דעתך אמינא הואיל וחס רחמנא עליה לאיתויי בדלות בלילה נמי ליתי קמ"ל מתקיף לה רבינא [אלא] מעתה יהא זר ואונן כשר בהן חייבנו הקב"ה בתורת הקרבנות שנקריבם ביום ולא בלילה שנאמר (ויקרא ז) אשר צוה ה' את משה ביום צותו את בני ישראל ופירש ביום צותו ולמדנו

לכל הקרבנות כולם שאינן כשירין אלא ביום ובפרק הקורא את המגילה (דף כ) שנינו כל היום כשר לסמיכה לשחיטה כו' ובתלמוד אמרו לסמיכה ולשחיטה דכתיב (ויקרא ג) וסמך ושחט ואיתקש סמיכה לשחיטה ובשחיטה כתיב (שם יט) ביום זבחכם [illegible] כמו שאמרה המשנה (זבחים דף טו) כל הזבחים שקיבל דמן זר ואונן כולם פסולין ובגמ' גרסי זר מנלן דתני לוי (ויקרא כב) דבר אל אהרן ואל בניו וינזרו מקדשי בני ישראל ולא יחללו כלומר בני ישראל [illegible] מן הקדשים ולא יקריבו אותן שלא יחללום שאם יקרבו אליהם ויקריבו אותם [illegible] ומן המקדש לא יצא ולא יחלל הא אחר שלא יצא חילל וכשאמרנו כי המחוסר כפרה [illegible] ידוע הוא לפי שכתב כן במקום אחר ביום צותו וממנו ידענו חיוב הקרבת כל הקרבנות [illegible] שאנו צריכין לאותו דבר מפני שמצאנו שהקל כאן על המצורע ואמר בו [illegible] ביום היה עולה על דעתנו הואיל והיקל עליו הכתוב שדי לו בשתי תורים [illegible] ולא היינו לומדין משפטו משאר הקרבנות שנאמר בהן ביום צותו הילכך [illegible] תורים או שני בני יונה מה שאין כן בזולתו לא נלמוד משאר הקרבנות [illegible] זה ראוי להיות הזר והאונן וכל המנויין

מסורת הש"ס

א) [תוספתא פט"ו] יומא פה. ב) מכילתא פרשת כי תשא, ג) פסחים סו: נזיר נז., ד) [סנהדרין נט:], ה) [דף פה:], ו) [ס"א הלכך].

תורה אור השלם

א) וּבַיּוֹם הַשְּׁמִינִי יִמּוֹל בְּשַׂר עָרְלָתוֹ: [ויקרא יב, ג]

ב) וּנְמַלְתֶּם אֵת בְּשַׂר עָרְלַתְכֶם וְהָיָה לְאוֹת בְּרִית בֵּינִי וּבֵינֵיכֶם: [בראשית יז, יא]

ג) וְאַתָּה דַּבֵּר אֶל בְּנֵי יִשְׂרָאֵל לֵאמֹר אַךְ אֶת שַׁבְּתֹתַי תִּשְׁמֹרוּ כִּי אוֹת הִוא בֵּינִי וּבֵינֵיכֶם לְדֹרֹתֵיכֶם לָדַעַת כִּי אֲנִי יְיָ מְקַדִּשְׁכֶם: [שמות לא, יג]

ד) וְהָיָה לְךָ לְאוֹת עַל יָדְךָ וּלְזִכָּרוֹן בֵּין עֵינֶיךָ לְמַעַן תִּהְיֶה תּוֹרַת יְיָ בְּפִיךָ כִּי בְּיָד חֲזָקָה הוֹצִאֲךָ יְיָ מִמִּצְרָיִם: [שמות יג, ט]

ה) וְשָׁמְרוּ בְנֵי יִשְׂרָאֵל אֶת הַשַּׁבָּת לַעֲשׂוֹת אֶת הַשַּׁבָּת לְדֹרֹתָם בְּרִית עוֹלָם: [שמות לא, טז]

ו) וְעָרֵל זָכָר אֲשֶׁר לֹא יִמּוֹל אֶת בְּשַׂר עָרְלָתוֹ וְנִכְרְתָה הַנֶּפֶשׁ הַהִוא מֵעַמֶּיהָ אֶת בְּרִיתִי הֵפַר: [בראשית יז, יד]

ז) וּבֶן שְׁמֹנַת יָמִים יִמּוֹל לָכֶם כָּל זָכָר לְדֹרֹתֵיכֶם יְלִיד בָּיִת וּמִקְנַת כֶּסֶף מִכֹּל בֶּן נֵכָר אֲשֶׁר לֹא מִזַּרְעֲךָ הוּא: [בראשית יז, יב]

ח) דַּבֵּר אֶל בְּנֵי יִשְׂרָאֵל וְאָמַרְתָּ אֲלֵהֶם וְעָשׂוּ לָהֶם צִיצִת עַל כַּנְפֵי בִגְדֵיהֶם לְדֹרֹתָם וְנָתְנוּ עַל צִיצִת הַכָּנָף פְּתִיל תְּכֵלֶת: [במדבר טו, לח]

ט) אֲשֶׁר צִוָּה יְיָ אֶת מֹשֶׁה בְּהַר סִינָי בְּיוֹם צַוֹּתוֹ אֶת בְּנֵי יִשְׂרָאֵל לְהַקְרִיב אֶת קָרְבְּנֵיהֶם לַייָ בְּמִדְבַּר סִינָי: [ויקרא ז, לח]

י) וּשְׁמַרְתֶּם אֶת הַשַּׁבָּת כִּי קֹדֶשׁ הִוא לָכֶם מְחַלְלֶיהָ מוֹת יוּמָת כִּי כָּל הָעֹשֶׂה בָהּ מְלָאכָה וְנִכְרְתָה הַנֶּפֶשׁ הַהִוא מִקֶּרֶב עַמֶּיהָ: [שמות לא, יד]

ליקוטי רש"י

מה מילה. שהיא תיקון אחד מאיבריו של אדם דוחה את השבת לפי שחייבין עליה כרת לאחר זמן כך שנויה בתוספתא דשבת [יומא פה:]. **והתניא אמר לו וכו'.** דר"א ור"ע במסכת נזיר דאמרינן התם רביעית דם אין הנזיר מגלח על מגעה ועל משאה וקאמר ר' עקיבא קל וחומר ומה עצם כשעורה שאין מטמא (את כל) אדם באהל הנזיר מגלח על מגעה ועל משאה רביעית דם שמטמאה (את כל) אדם באהל אינו דין שהנזיר מגלח על מגעה ועל משאה אמר לו ר"א לר"ע עצם כשעורה שהנזיר מגלח על מגעה ומשאה הלכה למשה מסיני ואין כתוב בתורה ורביעית דם אתה בא ללמוד ממנה בקל וחומר ואין דנין קל וחומר מהלכה אלא מדבר הכתוב בתורה [פסחים פא:]. **מחלליה.** הנוהג בה חול [שמות לא, יד].

The Gemara objects to this answer as well:

אֶלָּא מֵעַתָּה – But according to that,[12] **תְּפִילִּין דִּכְתִיב בְּהֶן ,,אוֹת״** – the mitzvah of **tefillin, concerning which** the word ***sign*** **is** also **written,**[13] **לִידְחֵי שַׁבָּת – should** likewise **override the Sabbath** restrictions,[14] and we know that it does not. Hence, *sign/sign* is not an authentic *gezeirah shavah.*[15] – ? –

The Gemara essays a different source:

אֶלָּא אַתְיָא ,,בְּרִית״ ,,בְּרִית״ – Rather, [the law of overriding] for *milah* **is derived** through the *gezeirah shavah* of ***covenant/covenant.***[16]

The Gemara again objects:

גָּדוֹל דִּכְתִיב בֵּיהּ ,,בְּרִית״ – But the *milah* of an uncircumcised **adult, concerning whom** the word ***covenant*** **is** also **written,**[17] **לִידְחֵי שַׁבָּת – should** likewise **override the Sabbath** restrictions, and we know that it does not.[18] Hence, *covenant/covenant* is not an authentic *gezeirah shavah.* – ? –

The Gemara offers yet another source:

אֶלָּא אַתְיָא ,,דֹּרוֹת״ ,,דֹּרוֹת״ – Rather, [the law of overriding] for *milah* **is derived** through the *gezeirah shavah* of ***generations/generations.***[19]

The Gemara rejects this answer as well:

צִיצִית דִּכְתִיב בֵּיהּ ,,דֹּרוֹת״ – But the preliminaries[20] to the mitzvah of ***tzitzis*** (ritual fringes), **concerning which** a variation of the word ***generations*** **is** also **written,**[21] **לִידְחֵי שַׁבָּת – should** likewise **override the Sabbath** restrictions, and we know that they do not. Hence, *generations/generations* is not an authentic *gezeirah shavah.* – ? –

The Gemara finally identifies a legitimate *gezeirah shavah*:

אֶלָּא אָמַר רַב נַחְמָן בַּר יִצְחָק – Rather, Rav Nachman bar Yitzchak said: **דָּנִין ,,אוֹת״ ,,בְּרִית״ וְ,,דֹרוֹת״ – We learn** about that mitzvah (i.e. *milah*) concerning which is written the words ***sign, covenant*** **and** ***generations*** **מִ,,אוֹת״ ,,בְּרִית״ וְ,,דֹרוֹת״ – from** the Sabbath, which is also associated with the words ***sign, covenant*** **and** ***generations*** – **לְאַפּוּקֵי הָנָךְ – to exclude these** other mitzvos,[22] **דְּחַד חַד הוּא דִּכְתִיב בְּהֶן – for** only **one** of these **words is written by each of them.**[23] Hence, the Rabbis and R' Eliezer derive that *milah* itself overrides the Sabbath restrictions from the *gezeirah shavah* of "*sign, covenant* and *generations,*" which exists between Shabbos and *milah.*

The Gemara presents a different source for *milah* overriding the Sabbath:

וְרַבִּי יוֹחָנָן אָמַר – But R' Yochanan said: **אָמַר קְרָא ,,בַּיּוֹם״** – The Rabbis derive that *milah* itself overrides the Sabbath from that which **the verse stated,** ***on the*** *eighth* ***day,***[24] which implies: **בַּיּוֹם אֲפִילּוּ בְּשַׁבָּת** – You shall perform the mitzvah of *milah* **on the** eighth **day,** whenever that may be – i.e. **even on the Sabbath** day.[25]

R' Yochanan's interpretation is challenged:

אָמַר לֵיהּ רֵישׁ לָקִישׁ לְרַבִּי יוֹחָנָן – Reish Lakish said to R' Yochanan: **אֶלָּא מֵעַתָּה – But according to that,**[26] **מְחוּסְּרֵי כַּפָּרָה דִּכְתִיב בְּהוּ ,,בַּיּוֹם״** – then with regard to the purification offerings of **those who lack atonement,**[27] **concerning which** the phrase ***on the eighth day*** **is** also **written,**[28] **הָכִי נַמִּי דָּחוּ שַׁבָּת – it should also be true that they override the Sabbath** restrictions, and we know they do not.[29] Hence, *on*

NOTES

12. [Literally: but from now.] That is, if the word *sign* in the Shabbos passage was stated at Sinai for purposes of *gezeirah shavah* interpretation (*Rashi*).

13. *Deuteronomy* 6:8 and 11:18.

14. I.e. we should derive a parallel *gezeirah shavah* from Shabbos to tefillin (*Rashi*).

The Rishonim question why the mitzvah of tefillin needs to override the Sabbath restrictions. Donning tefillin is not a *melachah,* and wearing them into the public domain is Biblically permitted (i.e. even according to those who hold that tefillin are not worn on *Shabbos;* see above, 61a), since they are considered apparel. The Rishonim explain that the Gemara refers to the manufacturing of tefillin, which encompasses all the preliminaries to the mitzvah. For similar reasons, the Gemara below refers to the making, not wearing, of *tzitzis.* The questioner thus reasons as follows: Where the Rabbis can apply the *gezeirah shavah* of *sign/sign* to a mitzvah (viz. *milah*), they do. But where there is no need to do so (e.g. in the cases of tefillin and *tzitzis*), they should apply it to the preliminaries (see *Ramban, Rashba, Ran MHK* ed.).

15. That is, it was not stated at Sinai; nor was it innovated by the Sages, since the rules of exegesis preclude the Sages from creating their own *gezeiros shavos* (*Rashi* ד״ה אלא אתיא ברית וכו׳).

16. The word בְּרִית (*covenant*) is mentioned in reference to Shabbos (לְדֹרֹתָם בְּרִית עוֹלָם, *an eternal covenant for their generations – Exodus* 31:16), and it is mentioned with reference to *milah* (see note 11 above). This commonality teaches that just as there in the first passage *covenant* refers to Shabbos, so here in the passage of *milah* it refers to Shabbos – i.e. to teach that Shabbos is a time for *milah.*

17. The Torah states (*Genesis* 17:14): *An uncircumcised male . . . shall be cut off from [his] people; he has invalidated My covenant.* The verse perforce speaks of an adult, for it imposes the penalty of *kares* (excision), and a male whose father has failed to circumcise him becomes obligated to circumcise himself when he reaches adulthood (age thirteen) [and would incur excision if he died uncircumcised; see *Rambam, Hil. Milah* 1:2] (*Rashi*).

18. The Gemara below (132b) teaches that a *milah* not performed on the eighth day [and, of course, an adult's *milah* is not] does not override even the Yom Tov restrictions against *melachah* (*Rashi, Ritva MHK* ed.).

19. A variation of the word דורות (*generations*) is written in reference to Shabbos (see note 16 above), and a different variation is written with reference to the *milah* of an infant (וּבֶן־שְׁמֹנַת יָמִים יִמּוֹל לָכֶם כָּל־זָכָר לְדֹרֹתֵיכֶם, *At the age of eight days every male among you shall be circumcised, throughout your generations – Genesis* 17:12) [*Rashi*]. See *Maharshal*.

20. See note 14 above.

21. *Numbers* 15:38.

22. Viz. tefillin, the circumcision of an adult, and *tzitzis.*

23. *Milah* and Shabbos share all three common words, and are thus linked by an authentic *gezeirah shavah.* Tefillin, *tzitzis* and an adult's circumcision each share only one common word with Shabbos, and so their commonality with Shabbos is incomplete; hence, a *gezeirah shavah* to any of these three mitzvos is precluded.

24. This is the verse cited above, from which R' Eliezer derived that *milah's* preliminaries override the Sabbath. It reads in full: *And on the eighth day the flesh of his foreskin shall be circumcised* (*Leviticus* 12:3).

25. [See note 5 above.] According to R' Yochanan's interpretation, R' Eliezer, who uses this verse for *milah's* preliminaries, understands the law for *milah* itself to be a *Halachah LeMoshe MiSinai* (an oral Sinaitic law). Accordingly, he holds that the power of "saving a life" to override the Sabbath is derived not via a *kal vachomer* from *milah* (a proposition the Gemara above proved untenable when *milah's* law is characterized as a *Halachah LeMoshe MiSinai*), but via one of the Scriptural exegeses found in *Yoma* 85b (*Rashi*).

26. [Literally: but from now.] That is, if an extraneous mention of the word *day* implies that a passage's mitzvah is to be performed even on the Sabbath day.

27. This term refers to *tamei* individuals, such as a *metzora, zav, zavah* and a woman who has given birth, who must bring sacrifices to attain complete purification (*Rashi*). See *Kereisos* 8b.

28. With regard to a *metzora* Scripture states (*Leviticus* 14:10): *On the eighth day he shall take two unblemished sheep* etc. See also ibid. 15:14 for a *zav,* and ibid. v. 29 for a *zavah.* [With regard to a woman who has given birth the word *day* is not stated (see *Rashash*).] In each of these contexts the Torah could have stated simply, "And on the eight, he/she shall take . . ." Hence, the word *day* in each verse is superfluous, and thus is theoretically available for exegesis.

29. Only certain public sacrifices may be offered on the Sabbath (see *Rashi* to the beginning of the next *amud,* ד״ה ועבודה).

שכן אם עבר זמנה בטלה אלא היינו טעמא דרבי אליעזר דאמר קרא א) וביום השמיני ימול בשר ערלתו ואפילו בשבת וליכתוב רחמנא במילה וליתו הנך וליגמור מיניה משום דאיכא למיפרך מה למילה שכן נכרתו עליה שלש עשרה בריתות: ע"כ לא פליגי רבנן עליה אלא במכשירי מילה אבל מילה גופה דברי הכל דוחה שבת מנלן אמר עולא הלכה וכן אמר רבי יצחק הלכה מיתיבי מניין לפיקוח נפש שדוחה את השבת רבי אלעזר בן עזריה אומר מה מילה שהיא אחת מאבריו של אדם דוחה את השבת קל וחומר לפיקוח נפש שדוחה את השבת ואי סלקא דעתך הלכה קל וחומר מהלכה מי אתי והתניא אמר לו רבי אלעזר (בן עזריה) עקיבא עצם כשעורה מטמא הלכה ורביעית דם קל וחומר ואין דנין קל וחומר מהלכה אלא אמר רבי אלעזר אתיא ב) אות ג) אות אלא מעתה תפילין דכתיב בהן ד) אות לידחי שבת אלא אתיא ה) ברית ו) ברית אלא מעתה גדול דכתיב ביה ז) ברית לידחי שבת אלא אתיא ח) דורות ט) דורות אלא מעתה ציצית דכתיב ביה י) דורות לידחי שבת אלא אמר רב נחמן בר יצחק דנין אות ברית ודורות מאות ברית ודורות לאפוקי הנך דחד חד הוא דכתיב בהן ור' יוחנן אמר אמר קרא א) ביום ביום אפילו בשבת אמר ליה ריש לקיש לרבי יוחנן אלא מעתה מחוסרי כפרה דכתיב בהו ביום הכי נמי דדחו שבת ההוא מיבעי ליה ביום ולא בלילה האי נמי מיבעי ליה ביום ולא בלילה ההוא ז) מבן שמנת ימים נפקא האי נמי ט) מביום צוותו נפקא אע"ג דנפקא מביום צוותו אצטריכא סד"א הואיל וחס רחמנא עליה לאתויי בדלות בלילה נמי ליתי קמ"ל מתקיף לה רבינא אלא מעתה יהא זר כשר בהן ויהא אונן כשר בהן הא אהדריה קרא רב אחא בר יעקב אמר קרא א) שמיני שמיני אפילו בשבת האי שמיני מיבעי ליה למעוטי שביעי מבן שמנת ימים נפקא ואכתי מיבעי ליה חד למעוטי שביעי וחד למעוטי תשיעי דאי מחד הוה אמינא שביעי הוא דלא מטא זמניה אבל משמיני ואילך זמניה הוא אלא מחוורתא כדרבי יוחנן תניא כוותיה דרבי יוחנן ודלא כרב אחא בר יעקב שמיני ימול אפילו בשבת ומה אני מקיים י) מחלליה מות יומת בשאר מלאכות חוץ ממילה או אינו אלא אפי' מילה ומה אני מקיים שמיני ימול חוץ משבת ת"ל ביום אפילו בשבת אמר רבא האי תנא מעיקרא מאי קא ניחא ליה ולבסוף מאי קא קשיא ליה הכי קאמר שמיני ימול אפילו בשבת ומה אני מקיים מחלליה מות יומת בשאר מלאכו' חוץ ממילה אבל מילה דחיא מ"ט ק"ו הוא ומה צרע' שדוחה את העבודה ועבודה

רש"י

שאם עבר זמנן בטלין. הילכך דמו: וביום השמיני ימול ואפילו בשבת. ומילה גופה דדחיא שבת אמרינן לקמן הלכה למשה מסיני איתר ליה ביום למכשיריה: י"ג בריתות. נאמרו לאברהם בפרשת מילה (בראשית יז): והא תניא. במסכת נזיר: עקיבא עצם כשעורה הלכה. שהיה ר"ע דן ק"ו מניין לרביעית דם שהנזיר מגלח על אהלה ק"ו מה עצם כשעורה שאינו מטמא באהל נזיר מגלח על מגעו ומשאו רביעית דם שמטמאה באהל דכתיב ועל כל נפש מת לא יבא אינו דין שהנזיר מגלח עליה ואמר ליה רבי אלעזר עקיבא עצם כשעורה הלכה למשה מסיני שיהא נזיר מגלח עליה ורביעית דם אתה בא ללמוד ממנה בק"ו ואין דנין קל וחומר מהלכה שבעל פה ניתנה תורה לידרש בי"ג מדות: אתיא אות אות. בשבת כתיב (שמות לא) כי אות היא ובמילה כתיב (בראשית יז) והיה לאות ברית מה להלן שבת אף כאן שבת: אלא מעתה. אי הך ג"ש לאות האמורה בשבת נאמרה בסיני לידרש שהיא זו לדרשה נאמרה ליגמר מינה נמי לתפילין: אלא אתיא ברית ברית. ההוא לאות לא נאמרה בסיני ואין אדם דן גזרה שוה מעצמו אלא הך דברית נאמרה בסיני ובשבת כתיב ברית (שמות לא) לדורותם ברית עולם: גדול. בן שלש עשרה דהוי מילה שלא בזמנה: דכתיב ביה ברית. וערל זכר אשר לא ימול וגו' את בריתי הפר (בראשית יז) והאי קרא בגדול כתיב מדמחייב ליה כרת שאם לא מלו אביו חייב למול את עצמו ולידחי שבת ואנן אמרינן לקמן דאפילו יום טוב אינה דוחה אלא בזמנה: דורות דורות. בשבת כתיב לדורותם ברית עולם ובמילת קטן כתיב (שם) ובן שמנת ימים ימול לכם כל זכר לדורותיכם: ביום ואפילו בשבת. מדלא כתיב בשמיני ימול ולר' אליעזר דאפקיה למכשירין מילה עצמה הלכה היא ופיקוח נפש לא אתיא ליה בק"ו ממילה אלא מקראי נפקא ליה כדאמרינן בפרק בתרא דיומא: מחוסרי כפרה. כל טמאין שהוצרכו לקרבן זב וזבה יולדת ומצורע נאמר בהן וביום השמיני: ביום צותו. את בני ישראל להקריב את קרבניהם (ויקרא ז) ביום ולא בלילה: אלא מעתה. משום דהוכשר להביא בדלות מכשירין בה שאר פסולין: יהא זר ואונן כשר בהן. אונן עד שלא נקבר מתו פסול לעבודה דכתיב (שם כא) בכהן גדול לאביו ולאמו לא יטמא ומן המקדש לא יצא ולא יחלל והכי משמע אף ביום שמתו אביו ואמו אינו צריך לצאת מן המקדש אלא מקריב אונן ולא יחלל ועבודתו לא תהא מחוללת בכך הא אחר שלא יצא חילל: הא אהדריה קרא. לפסול בהן לילה דכתיב בהו וביום כדאמרינן וכיון דלענין לילה תורת כל הקרבנות עליהן לענין זר ואונן נמי תורת קרבן עליהן: שמיני. כל שהוא שמיני ואפילו בשבת וביום למעוטי לילה: תניא כוותיה דר' יוחנן. דיליף מוביום: מעיקרא מאי ניחא ליה. לאוקמי שמיני דווקא ואפילו בשבת ודחי מחלליה מות יומת אצל שאר מלאכות מאיזה טעם נראה לו כן: ולבסוף. כשהיפך דבריו ואמר או אינו אלא אפי' מילה בכלל מחלליה מות יומת ודחי שמיני ימול אצל שאר ימים: מאי קשיא ליה. בטעמא הראשון: אבל מילה דחיא. שבת בק"ו ותיגמר מיניה למידחי מחלליה מות יומת אצל שאר מלאכות ולמימר שמיני דווקא קאמר ואפי' ביום שבת: ומה צרעת שדוחה את העבודה. אזהרה שהזהירה תורה על הצרעת שלא לקוץ בהרתו כדתניא (מכות דף כב.) השמר בנגע הצרעת אזהרה בקוצץ בהרתו הכתוב מדבר והתמידה תורה באזהרה זו לדחות העבודה דקיימא לן בפסחים (דף סו.) דטומאת מת נדחית בקרבן צבור ולא זבין ומצורעין ובטלים לעשות פסח ולא אמרינן יקוצו בהרתן ויאכלו פסחים או הכהן יקוץ בהרתו ויעבוד אם הכהנים טמאין בצרעת והקהל טהורין:

תוספות

והתניא אמר ליה רבי אלעזר כו'. ול"ג והתנן דכל זה אינו במשנה: ההיא מבן שמונת ימים נפקא. תימה דתניא בת"כ ומייתי לה בפרק הערל (יבמות עב:) השמיני ימול דתניא יכול בין ביום ובין בלילה ת"ל ביום אין לי אלא שנימול לח' נימול לט' לי' ולי"א מניין שאינו נימול אלא ביום ת"ל וביום ובפ"ב דמגילה (דף כ:) נמי אמר אין מוהלין אלא ביום דכתיב וביום השמיני ויש לומר דסמיך אבן שמנת ימים ודרשא פשוטה נקט: אלא מעתה יהא זר ואונן כשר בהן. לאו דווקא נקט זר דהא בכולהו בזב וזבה ויולדת ומצורע כתב בהו כהן: הא אהדריה קרא. והוה ליה דבר שיצא מן הכלל לידון בדבר החדש לאתויי בדלות שאי אתה יכול להחזירו לכללו לפסול לילה ואונן עד שיחזירנו הכתוב לכללו בפירוש הרי החזירה בפירוש ופסל לילה וה"ה אונן וקשה ואמאי לא קאמר דאהדריה קרא מדכתיב כהן ולא זר ושמא לשום דרשא אחריתי אתא: תניא כוותיה דרבי יוחנן ודלא כרב אחא בר יעקב. ודלא כרב נחמן בר יצחק דלאמר אתיא אות ברית דורות לא הוי דאיהו מודה דדרשינן ביום כדדרשינן בברייתא ואות ברית דורות אתא למכשירין וביום למילה גופה ולית ליה למילה הלכה אע"ג דר' יוחנן אית ליה הלכה לר' אליעזר [כדפי' רש"י והאי ברייתא דדרשי ביום אתיא כרבנן דביום] איצטריך למילה גופה ולהכי לא קאמר אלא דלא כרב אחא דברייתא מוכחא בהדיא דלא בעיא למדרש שמיני ימול. מ"ר: מה צרעת שדוחה את העבודה. תימה ולימא קל וחומר איפכא ותדחה עבודה את הצרעת שיקוץ בהרתו כדי לעשות עבודה ומה שבת שדוחה את המילה ומילה דוחה את הצרעת עבודה דוחה אותה צרעת שנדחה מפני מילה אינו דין שתהא עבודה דוחה אותה והא דאמרינן בפסחים בפרק אלו דברים (דף סו.) וישלחו מן המחנה כל צרוע וכל זב וכל טמא לנפש אם טמאי מתים משתלחין זבים ומצורעים לא כ"ש אלא יש לך שעה שזבין ומצורעים משתלחים ואין טמאי מתים משתלחים ואיזה זה פסח הבא בטומאה

תורה אור השלם

א) וּבַיּוֹם הַשְּׁמִינִי יִמּוֹל בְּשַׂר עָרְלָתוֹ: [ויקרא יב, ג]

ב) וּנְמַלְתֶּם אֵת בְּשַׂר עָרְלַתְכֶם וְהָיָה לְאוֹת בְּרִית בֵּינִי וּבֵינֵיכֶם: [בראשית יז, יא]

ג) וְאַתָּה דַּבֵּר אֶל בְּנֵי יִשְׂרָאֵל לֵאמֹר אַךְ אֶת שַׁבְּתֹתַי תִּשְׁמֹרוּ כִּי אוֹת הִוא בֵּינִי וּבֵינֵיכֶם לְדֹרֹתֵיכֶם לָדַעַת כִּי אֲנִי יְיָ מְקַדִּשְׁכֶם: [שמות לא, יג]

ד) וְהָיָה לְךָ לְאוֹת עַל יָדְךָ וּלְזִכָּרוֹן בֵּין עֵינֶיךָ לְמַעַן תִּהְיֶה תּוֹרַת יְיָ בְּפִיךָ כִּי בְּיָד חֲזָקָה הוֹצִאֲךָ יְיָ מִמִּצְרָיִם: [שמות יג, ט]

ה) וְשָׁמְרוּ בְנֵי יִשְׂרָאֵל אֶת הַשַּׁבָּת לַעֲשׂוֹת אֶת הַשַּׁבָּת לְדֹרֹתָם בְּרִית עוֹלָם: [שמות לא, טז]

ו) וְעָרֵל זָכָר אֲשֶׁר לֹא יִמּוֹל אֶת בְּשַׂר עָרְלָתוֹ וְנִכְרְתָה הַנֶּפֶשׁ הַהִוא מֵעַמֶּיהָ אֶת בְּרִיתִי הֵפַר: [בראשית יז, יד]

ז) וּבֶן שְׁמֹנַת יָמִים יִמּוֹל לָכֶם כָּל זָכָר לְדֹרֹתֵיכֶם יְלִיד בָּיִת וּמִקְנַת כֶּסֶף מִכֹּל בֶּן נֵכָר אֲשֶׁר לֹא מִזַּרְעֲךָ הוּא: [בראשית יז, יב]

ח) דַּבֵּר אֶל בְּנֵי יִשְׂרָאֵל וְאָמַרְתָּ אֲלֵהֶם וְעָשׂוּ לָהֶם צִיצִת עַל כַּנְפֵי בִגְדֵיהֶם לְדֹרֹתָם וְנָתְנוּ עַל צִיצִת הַכָּנָף פְּתִיל תְּכֵלֶת: [במדבר טו, לח]

ט) אֲשֶׁר צִוָּה יְיָ אֶת מֹשֶׁה בְּהַר סִינָי בְּיוֹם צַוֹּתוֹ אֶת בְּנֵי יִשְׂרָאֵל לְהַקְרִיב אֶת קָרְבְּנֵיהֶם לַייָ בְּמִדְבַּר סִינָי: [ויקרא ז, לח]

י) וּשְׁמַרְתֶּם אֶת הַשַּׁבָּת כִּי קֹדֶשׁ הִוא לָכֶם מְחַלְלֶיהָ מוֹת יוּמָת כִּי כָּל הָעֹשֶׂה בָהּ מְלָאכָה וְנִכְרְתָה הַנֶּפֶשׁ הַהִוא מִקֶּרֶב עַמֶּיהָ: [שמות לא, יד]

ליקוטי רש"י

רב נסים גאון

the . . . day cannot imply "even on the Sabbath day." – ? –

R' Yochanan deflects the challenge:

הַהוּא מִיבָּעֵי לֵיהּ בַּיּוֹם וְלֹא בַּלַּיְלָה – That superfluous *on the . . . day,* written vis-a-vis those who lack atonement, **is needed** to teach that their offerings are brought **during the day and not at night.** Hence, it is not free to teach that their offerings are brought and slaughtered even on the Sabbath.

Reish Lakish counters:

הַאי נַמִּי מִיבָּעֵי לֵיהּ בַּיּוֹם וְלֹא בַּלַּיְלָה – If so, say that **this** *on the . . . day* in the *milah* passage **is also needed** to teach that circumcision is performed **during the day and not at night.** Accordingly, it cannot teach that *milah* overrides the Sabbath. – ? –

R' Yochanan answers:

הַהוּא מ,,בֶן־שְׁמֹנַת יָמִים" נַפְקָא – That law **is derived from** a different verse:[30] ***At the age of eight days*** *every male among you shall be circumcised.* The word *days* is extraneous, and thus teaches that *milah* must be performed during the day.[31]

Reish Lakish again counters:

הַאי נַמִּי מ,,בְּיוֹם צַוֹּתוֹ" נַפְקָא – By the same token, since **this** law (that these offerings must be brought during the day) **also is derived from** a different verse,[32] viz. ***on the day [God] commanded*** *the Children of Israel to bring their offerings,*[33] *on the . . . day* in each passage is free to teach that that particular *tamei's* offering overrides the Sabbath restrictions! – ? –

R' Yochanan replies:

אַף עַל גַּב דְּנַפְקָא מ,,בְּיוֹם צַוֹּתוֹ" – Even though [the law] that sacrifices are brought only by day **is derived** generally **from *on the day [God] commanded,*** **אִצְטְרִיכָא – it is necessary** to repeat it vis-a-vis those who lack atonement, **סַלְקָא דַּעְתָּךְ אָמִינָא** – for **it would enter your mind** that **I might say: הוֹאִיל וְחָס רַחֲמָנָא עֲלֵיהּ לְאַתּוּיֵי בְּדַלּוּת – Since the Merciful One had compassion on [this *tamei*],** allowing him **to bring** a lesser sacrifice **in his poverty,**[34] **בַּלַּיְלָה נַמִּי לֵיתֵי – let him bring** it **at night as well.**[35] **קָא מַשְׁמַע לָן** – *[On the . . . day]* in each passage thus **informs us** that the *tamei's* sacrifice must be brought during the day.

The Gemara objects:

מַתְקִיף לָהּ רָבִינָא – Ravina challenges [R' Yochanan's reply]: אֶלָּא מֵעַתָּה – But according to that,[36] **יְהֵא זָר כָּשֵׁר בָּהֶן – let a "stranger"** (i.e. a non-Kohen) **be qualified for [their bringing], וִיהֵא אוֹנֵן כָּשֵׁר בָּהֶן – and let an *onein***[37] **be qualified for [their bringing].**[38] – ? –

The Gemara answers:

הָא אֶהְדְּרֵיהּ קְרָא – The verse *on the . . . day* explicitly **returned [the purification offering]** of the one lacking atonement to the general category of Temple offerings.[39] R' Yochanan's interpretation is thus still valid.

A different verse is suggested as the source for *milah's* overriding the Sabbath:

רַב אַחָא בַּר יַעֲקֹב אָמַר – Rav Acha bar Yaakov said: אָמַר קְרָא ,,שְׁמִינִי" – The Rabbis derive that *milah* itself overrides the Sabbath from that which **the verse stated,** *on the **eighth** day,*[40] which implies: **שְׁמִינִי אֲפִילּוּ בְּשַׁבָּת** – You shall perform the mitzvah of *milah* on whatever happens to be the **eighth** day – i.e. **even on the Sabbath.**[41]

The Gemara challenges this interpretation:

הַאי ,,שְׁמִינִי" מִיבָּעֵי לֵיהּ לְמַעוּטֵי שְׁבִיעִי – This word ***eighth*** **is needed to exclude** the performing of *milah* on the **seventh** day, or earlier.[42] Hence, it is not free to teach that *milah* overrides the Sabbath. – ? –

The Gemara responds:

שְׁבִיעִי מ,,בֶן־שְׁמֹנַת יָמִים" נַפְקָא – That *milah* is not performed on the **seventh** day **is derived from** the other verse:[43] ***At the age of eight days*** *every male among you shall be circumcised.* Hence, the word *eighth* is free for exegesis.

NOTES

30. *Genesis* 17:12.

31. This follows *Tosafos.* Cf. *Tos. HaRosh,* who maintains that for linguistic reasons this law cannot be inferred from the expression שְׁמֹנַת יָמִים, *eight days* (see there for another interpretation, and see *Torah Temimah* to *Genesis* 17:12 §31, who explains *Tosafos'* interpretation).

32. *Leviticus* 7:38, which speaks generally of the Temple offerings.

33. *On the day* implies: but not at night (*Rashi*).

34. One lacking atonement who is impoverished may bring two turtledoves (תורים) or two doves (יונים) instead of the animal sacrifices (see *Leviticus* 12:8 and 14:21-22). [A *zav* and *zavah* always bring one of these bird offerings, and *Meiri* implies that this in itself is called a sacrifice brought בְּדַלּוּת (*in poverty*).]

35. The Gemara here invokes the eleventh of R' Yishmael's Thirteen Rules of Biblical Exegesis. This rule states: כָּל דָּבָר שֶׁהָיָה בִּכְלָל וְיָצָא לִדּוֹן בְּדָבָר הֶחָדָשׁ, אִי אַתָּה יָכוֹל לְהַחֲזִירוֹ לִכְלָלוֹ, עַד שֶׁיַּחֲזִירֶנּוּ הַכָּתוּב לִכְלָלוֹ בְּפֵרוּשׁ, *Anything that was included in a general statement, but was then singled out to be treated as a new case, cannot be returned to its general statement unless Scripture returns it explicitly to its general statement.* This means that if a certain item was included in a general category, and was then specifically mentioned in connection with a new law that contradicts the general law, then the terms of the general law can no longer apply to the item unless the Torah expressly declares that they do. Here, the *tamei's* purification offering was singled out from the general category of Temple sacrifices and was given a unique law (that it may be a bird offering if offered in poverty). The Gemara thus argues that other terms of the general law (viz. that an offering is not valid at night) no longer apply to it (*Ran, MHK* ed.). See also *Tosafos* ד״ה הא אהדרי׳; cf. *Chidushei HaRan.*

36. I.e. if these purification offerings were singled out from the general category and cannot be returned there unless Scripture does so explicitly.

37. [An *onein* is a person who is observing the first stage of mourning, which is called *aninus. Aninus* lasts until the end of the day on which the death occurs (see *Zevachim* 99b-101a). If burial is delayed, *aninus* is Rabbinically extended until the day of burial.] If an ordinary Kohen performs a Temple service while he is an *onein,* he invalidates that service (see *Rashi*).

38. Ravina argues: Although a "stranger" (a non-Kohen) and an *onein* are ordinarily disqualified from performing the sacrificial service, let the case of the one lacking atonement be special in this aspect as well, and permit these individuals to offer the sacrifices of those lacking atonement.

The Rishonim question how the Gemara could suggest that a non-Kohen be so qualified, when it is explicitly stated in each passage that a Kohen performs the service. *Ramban* explains that perhaps the Torah is merely stating its preference; when no Kohen is present, however, a non-Kohen may offer the sacrifice so as not to delay the full purification of the one lacking atonement. *Ritva* (*MHK* ed.) contends that the "stranger" in our Gemara refers to a Kohen who is not wearing his priestly garments while performing the service, a condition that ordinarily invalidates the service. See *Tosafos* ד״ה הא, *Rashba* and *Ritva* (*MHK* ed.) for other explanations.

39. As the Gemara stated above, *on the . . . day* teaches that the *tamei's* offering must conform to the general rule that Temple sacrifices are brought by day and not at night. The verse thereby returns the *tamei's* offering to the general category of Temple sacrifices. Hence, just as *on the . . . day's* law applies to the *tamei's* offering, so do the laws that disqualify an *onein* and non-Kohen from performing the service (*Rashi, Tosafos* et al.; cf. *Rabbeinu Chananel*).

40. See above, notes 24 and 25.

41. And *on the . . . day* comes to exclude performing the circumcision at night (*Rashi*).

42. That is, the word *eighth* is needed for itself – to teach that the proper time for *milah* is not before the eighth day.

43. *Genesis* 17:12.

א) [תוספתא פט"ז] יומא פה: מכילתא פרשת כי תשא, ב) [פסחים סח: נזיר נז.], ג) [פסחים סח: ונזיר ליתא], ד) [סנהדרין נט:], ה) [דף פה:], ו) [פ"ח הלכך].

תורה אור השלם

א) וּבַיּוֹם הַשְּׁמִינִי יִמּוֹל בְּשַׂר עָרְלָתוֹ: [ויקרא יב, ג]

ב) וּנְמַלְתֶּם אֵת בְּשַׂר עָרְלַתְכֶם וְהָיָה לְאוֹת בְּרִית בֵּינִי וּבֵינֵיכֶם: [בראשית יז, יא]

ג) וְאַתָּה דַּבֵּר אֶל בְּנֵי יִשְׂרָאֵל לֵאמֹר אַךְ אֶת שַׁבְּתֹתַי תִּשְׁמֹרוּ כִּי אוֹת הִוא בֵּינִי וּבֵינֵיכֶם לְדֹרֹתֵיכֶם לָדַעַת כִּי אֲנִי יְיָ מְקַדִּשְׁכֶם: [שמות לא, יג]

ד) וְהָיָה לְךָ לְאוֹת עַל יָדְךָ וּלְזִכָּרוֹן בֵּין עֵינֶיךָ לְמַעַן תִּהְיֶה תּוֹרַת יְיָ בְּפִיךָ כִּי בְּיָד חֲזָקָה הוֹצִאֲךָ יְיָ מִמִּצְרָיִם: [שמות יג, ט]

ה) וְשָׁמְרוּ בְנֵי יִשְׂרָאֵל אֶת הַשַּׁבָּת לַעֲשׂוֹת אֶת הַשַּׁבָּת לְדֹרֹתָם בְּרִית עוֹלָם: [שמות לא, טז]

ו) וְעָרֵל זָכָר אֲשֶׁר לֹא יִמּוֹל אֶת בְּשַׂר עָרְלָתוֹ וְנִכְרְתָה הַנֶּפֶשׁ הַהִוא מֵעַמֶּיהָ אֶת בְּרִיתִי הֵפַר: [בראשית יז, יד]

ז) וּבֶן שְׁמֹנַת יָמִים יִמּוֹל לָכֶם כָּל זָכָר לְדֹרֹתֵיכֶם יְלִיד בָּיִת וּמִקְנַת כֶּסֶף מִכֹּל בֶּן נֵכָר אֲשֶׁר לֹא מִזַּרְעֲךָ הוּא: [בראשית יז, יב]

ח) דַּבֵּר אֶל בְּנֵי יִשְׂרָאֵל וְאָמַרְתָּ אֲלֵהֶם וְעָשׂוּ לָהֶם צִיצִת עַל כַּנְפֵי בִגְדֵיהֶם לְדֹרֹתָם וְנָתְנוּ עַל צִיצִת הַכָּנָף פְּתִיל תְּכֵלֶת: [במדבר טו, לח]

ט) אֲשֶׁר צִוָּה יְיָ אֶת מֹשֶׁה בְּהַר סִינָי בְּיוֹם צַוֹּתוֹ אֶת בְּנֵי יִשְׂרָאֵל לְהַקְרִיב אֶת קָרְבְּנֵיהֶם לַייָ בְּמִדְבַּר סִינָי: [ויקרא ז, לח]

י) וּשְׁמַרְתֶּם אֶת הַשַּׁבָּת כִּי קֹדֶשׁ הִוא לָכֶם מְחַלְלֶיהָ מוֹת יוּמָת כִּי כָּל הָעֹשֶׂה בָהּ מְלָאכָה וְנִכְרְתָה הַנֶּפֶשׁ הַהִוא מִקֶּרֶב עַמֶּיהָ: [שמות לא, יד]

ליקוטי רש"י

מה מילה. שהיא תיקון אחד מאבריו של אדם דוחה את השבת...

שכן אם עבר זמנה בטלה אלא היינו טעמא דרבי אליעזר דאמר קרא א) וביום השמיני ימול בשר ערלתו ואפילו בשבת וליכתוב רחמנא במילה וליתו הנך וליגמור מיניה משום דאיכא למיפרך מה למילה שכן נכרתו עליה שלש עשרה בריתות: ע"כ לא פליגי רבנן עליה אלא במכשירי מילה אבל מילה גופה דברי הכל דוחה שבת מנלן אמר עולא הלכה וכן אמר רבי יצחק הלכה מיתיבי ב) מניין לפיקוח נפש שדוחה את השבת רבי אלעזר בן עזריה אומר מה מילה שהיא אחת מאיבריו של אדם דוחה את השבת קל וחומר לפיקוח נפש שדוחה את השבת ואי סלקא דעתך הלכה קל וחומר מהלכה מי אתי והתניא ג) אמר לו רבי אלעזר (ג) בן עזריה) עקיבא עצם כשעורה מטמא הלכה ורביעית דם קל וחומר ואין דנין קל וחומר מהלכה אלא אמר רבי אלעזר אתיא ב) אות ג) אות אלא מעתה תפילין דכתיב בהן ד) אות לידחי שבת אלא אתיא ב) ברית ה) ברית גדול דכתיב ביה ו) ברית לידחי שבת אלא אתיא ז) דורות ה) דורות ציצית דכתיב ביה ח) דורות לידחי שבת אלא אמר רב נחמן בר יצחק דנין אות ברית ודורות מאות ברית ודורות לאפוקי הנך דחד חד הוא דכתיב בהן ור' יוחנן אמר אמר קרא א) ביום ז) ביום אפילו בשבת אמר ליה ריש לקיש לרבי יוחנן אלא מעתה מחוסרי כפרה דכתיב בהו ביום הכי נמי דדחו שבת ההוא מיבעי ליה ביום ולא בלילה האי נמי מיבעי ליה ביום ולא בלילה ההוא ז) מבן שמנת ימים נפקא האי נמי ט) מביום צוותו נפקא אע"ג דנפקא מביום צוותו אצטריכא סד"א הואיל וחס רחמנא עליה לאתויי בדלות בלילה נמי ליתי קמ"ל מתקיף לה רבינא אלא מעתה יהא זר כשר בהן ויהא אונן כשר בהן הא אהדריה קרא רב אחא בר יעקב אמר אמר קרא א) שמיני שמיני אפילו בשבת האי שמיני מיבעי ליה למעוטי שביעי שביעי מבן שמנת ימים נפקא ואכתי מיבעי ליה חד למעוטי שביעי וחד למעוטי תשיעי דאי מחד הוה אמינא שביעי הוא דלא מטא זמניה אבל משמיני ואילך זמניה הוא אלא מחוורתא כדרבי יוחנן תניא כוותיה דרבי יוחנן ודלא כרב אחא בר יעקב שמיני ימול אפילו בשבת ומה אני מקיים י) מחלליה מות יומת בשאר מלאכות חוץ ממילה או אינו אלא אפי' מילה ומה אני מקיים שמיני ימול חוץ משבת ת"ל ביום אפילו בשבת אמר רבא האי תנא מעיקרא מאי קא ניחא ליה ולבסוף מאי קא קשיא ליה הכי קאמר שמיני ימול אפילו בשבת ומה אני מקיים מחלליה מות יומת בשאר מלאכו' חוץ ממילה אבל מילה דחיא מ"ט ק"ו הוא ומה צרע' שדוחה את העבודה ועבודה

שאם עבר זמנן בטלין. הילכך דחו: **וביום השמיני ימול ואפילו בשבת.** ומילה גופה דדחיא שבת אמרינן לקמן הלכה למשה מסיני איתך ליה ביום למכשיריה: י"ג בריתות. נאמרו לאברהם בפרשת מילה (בראשית יז): **והא תניא.** במסכת נזיר: **עקיבא עצם כשעורה הלכה.** שהיה ר"ע דן ק"ו מניין לרביעית דם המת שהנזיר מגלח על אהלה ק"ו מה עצם כשעורה שאינו מטמא באהל נזיר מגלח על מגעו ומשאו רביעית דם שמטמאה באהל דכתיב ועל כל נפש מת לא יבא אינו דין שהנזיר מגלח עליה ואמר ליה רבי אלעזר עקיבא עצם כשעורה הלכה למשה מסיני שיהא נזיר מגלח עליה ורביעית דם אתה בא ללמוד ממנה בק"ו ואין דנין קל וחומר מהלכה דלא ניתנה תורה שבעל פה לידרש בי"ג מדות: **אתיא אות אות.** בשבת כתיב (שמות לא) כי אות היא ובמילה כתיב (בראשית יז) והיה לאות ברית מה להלן שבת אף כאן שבת: **אלא מעתה.** אי הך ג"ש לאות האמורה בשבת נאמרה בסיני לידרש שתיבה זו לדרשה נאמרה ליגמר מינה נמי לתפילין: **אלא אתיא ברית ברית.** ההוא לאות לא נאמרה בסיני ואין אדם דן גזרה שוה מעצמו אלא הך דברית ברית נאמרה בסיני ובשבת כתיב ברית (שמות לא) לדורותם ברית עולם: **גדול.** בן שלש עשרה דהוי מילה שלא בזמנה: **דכתיב ביה ברית.** וערל זכר אשר לא ימול וגו' את בריתי הפר (בראשית יז) והאי קרא בגדול כתיב מדמחייב ליה כרת שאם לא מלו אביו חייב למול את עצמו ולידחי שבת ואנן אמרינן לקמן דאפילו יום טוב אינה דוחה אלא בזמנה: **דורות דורות.** בשבת כתיב לדורותם ברית עולם ובמילת קטן כתיב (שם) ובן שמנת ימים ימול לכם כל זכר לדורותיכם: **ביום ואפילו בשבת.** מדלא כתיב בשמיני ימול ולר' אליעזר דאפקיה למכשירין מילה עצמה הלכה היא ופיקוח נפש לא אתיא ליה בק"ו ממילה אלא מקראי נפקא ליה כדאמרינן בפרק בתרא דיומא ה): **מחוסרי כפרה.** כל טמאין שהוצרכו לקרבן זב וזבה יולדת ומצורע נאמר בהן וביום השמיני: **ביום צותו.** את בני ישראל להקריב את קרבניהם (ויקרא ז) ביום ולא בלילה: **אלא מעתה.** משום דהוכשר להביא בדלות מכשירין בה שאר פסולין: **יהא זר ואונן כשר בהן.** אונן עד שלא נקבר מתו פסול לעבודה דכתיב (שם כא) בכהן גדול לאביו ולאמו לא יטמא ומן המקדש לא יצא ולא יחלל והכי משמע אף ביום שמתו אביו ואמו אינו צריך לצאת מן המקדש אלא מקריב אונן ולא יחלל ועבודתו לא תהא מחוללת בכך הא אחר שלא יצא חילל: **הא אהדריה קרא.** לפסול בהן לילה דכתיב בהו וביום כדאמרינן וכיון דלענין לילה תורת כל הקרבנות עליהן לענין זר ואונן נמי תורת קרבן עליהן: **שמיני.** כל שהוא שמיני ואפילו בשבת וביום למעוטי לילה: **תניא כוותיה דר' יוחנן.** דיליף מביום: **מעיקרא מאי ניחא ליה.** לאוקמי שמיני דווקא ואפילו בשבת ודחי מחלליה מות יומת אצל שאר מלאכות מאיזה טעם נראה לו כן: **ולבסוף.** כשהפך דבריו ואמר או אינו אלא אפי' מילה בכלל מחלליה מות יומת והוא דוקא ודחי שמיני ימול אצל שאר ימים: **מאי קשיא ליה.** בטעמא הראשון: **אבל מילה דחיא.** שבת בק"ו ומיגמר מיניה למידחי מחלליה מות יומת אצל שאר מלאכות ולמימר שמיני דווקא קאמר ואפי' ביום שבת: **ומה צרעת שדוחה את העבודה.** שהכהן שהוא צרוע אינו עובד עבודה והכהן שהוא מצורע אסור לו לקוץ בהרתו דכתיב (מכות דף כב.) השמר בנגע הצרעת אזהרה בקוצץ בהרתו הכתוב מדבר והמקרא מוכיח כן דזה לדבר אחר השמר... הרי זה לוקה ובכל מקום שנאמר השמר פן ואל אינו אלא לא תעשה... והכי מפרש לה בפרק ...

והתניא אמר ליה רבי אלעזר כו'. ול"ג והתנן דכל זה אינו במשנה: **ההיא** מבן שמונת ימים נפקא. תימה דתניא בת"כ ומייתי לה בפרק הערל (יבמות עב:) השמיני ימול דתניא יכול בין ביום ובין בלילה ת"ל ביום אין לי אלא שמיני למ' נימול לט' לי' ולי"א מניין שאינו נימול אלא ביום ת"ל וביום ובפ"ב דמגילה (דף כ:) נמי אמר אין מוהלין אלא ביום דכתיב וביום השמיני ויש לומר דסמיך אבן שמנת ימים ודרשה פשוטה נקט: **אלא** מעתה יהא זר ואונן כשר בהן. לאו דווקא נקט זר דהא בכולהו בזב וזבה ויולדת ומצורע כתב בהו כהן:

הא אהדריה קרא. והוה ליה דבר שיצא מן הכלל לידון בדבר החדש לאתויי בדלות שאי אתה יכול להחזירו לכללו לפסול לילה ואונן עד שיחזירנו הכתוב לכללו בפירוש הרי החזירו בפירוש לפסול לילה וה"ה אונן וקשה ואמאי לא קאמר לאהדריה קרא מדכתיב כהן ולא זר ושמא לפום דרשה אחריתי אתא:

תניא כוותיה דרבי יוחנן ודלא כרב אחא בר יעקב. ודלא כרב נחמן בר יצחק דאמר אתיא אות ברית דורות לא הוי דאיהו מודה דדרשינן ביום כדדרשינן בברייתא ואות ברית דורות אתא למכשירין וביום למילה גופה ולית ליה למילה הלכה אע"ג דר' יוחנן אית ליה י) הלכה לר' אליעזר [כדפי' רש"י והאי ברייתא דדרשי ביום אתיא כרבנן דביום] איצטריך למילה גופה ולהכי לא קאמר אלא דלא כרב אחא דברייתא מוכחא בהדיא דלא בעיא למדרש שמיני ימול. מ"ר: **מה** צרעת שדוחה את העבודה. תימה ולימא קל וחומר איפכא ותדחה עבודה את הצרעת שיקוץ בהרתו כדי לעשות עבודה ומה שבת שדוחה את המילה ומילה דוחה את הצרעת עבודה דוחה אותה צרעת שנדחה מפני מילה אינו דין שתהא עבודה דוחה אותה והא דאמרינן בפסחים בפרק אלו דברים (דף סז.) וישלחו מן המחנה כל צרוע וכל זב וכל טמא לנפש אם טמאי מתים משתלחין זבים ומצורעים לא כ"ש אלא יש לך שעה שזבין ומצורעים משתלחים ואין טמאי מתים משתלחים ואיזה זה פסח הבא בטומאה

רבינו חננאל

עד כאן לא פליגי ר' אליעזר ורבנן אלא במכשירי מילה אבל במילה עצמה דברי הכל דוחה שבת. מנלן עולא ור' אסי ור' יצחק נפשא כולהו אימרי הלכה ומותבינן עליהון. מניין לפקוח נפש שדוחה שבת נענה ר' אלעזר בן עזריה ואמר ומה מילה שהיא אחד מאבריו של אדם דוחה שבת ק"ו לפקוח נפש שדוחה את השבת ואי ס"ד הלכה ק"ו מהלכה (מיתי) [מי אתי]. והתניא א"ל ר' עקיבא עצם כשעורה הלכה ורביעית דם ק"ו ואין דנין ק"ו מהלכה וכו' לבטולי הא מפורש בנזיר פר' כ"ג ונזיר אין מטמאין לקרוביהן וכו'. ובטלו דברי מי שאמר הלכה היא ובא ר' אלעזר ללמוד בג"ש באות אות משבת. ונדחו דבריו וגם ר' נחמן בר יצחק ולמדו באות ברית ודורו' בשבת כתיב לעשות את השבת לדורותם ברית עולם ביני ובין בני ישראל אות היא לעולם ובמילה כתיב ואתה את בריתי תשמור אתה וזרעך אחריך לדורותם וכתיב ונמלתם את בשר ערלתכם והיתה לאות ברית ביני וביניכם. ר' יוחנן אמר קרא וביום השמיני ימול בשר ערלתו ביום אפילו בשבת אקשינן עליה ר"ל אי הכי אפילו מחוסרי כפרה כגון מצורע והזבה דכתי' בהן וביום השמיני יקח שני כבשים וגו' ובזבה כתיב וביום השמיני תקח לה שתי תורים הכי נמי כיון דכתיב בהו וביום יקריבו קרבנותיהם ואפילו בשבת והא קיי"ל אין קרבן יחיד דוחה את השבת ופירק לו זה שכתוב במחוסרי כפרה וביום למעוטי לילה. עוד הקשה לו ר"ל כל קושיא שהקשה לו פירק ר' יוחנן וחזר רבינא להתקיף על פירוקו דר' יוחנן ופריק סד"א הואיל וחס רחמנא עליה לאתויי בדלות בלילה נמי ליתי קמ"ל וביום. התקיף רבינא אי הכי אמ' דחס עליהן או אינו כשר כהן זר ולא יטריחם להמתין עד שימצאו כהן טהור כשר לטהרם ופריק הא אהדריה קרא כלומר אע"פ שחס עליו והקל בקרבנו החזיר לטהרת הכהן שנאמר והביאו אותם ביום השמיני לטהרתו אל הכהן וגו' ואתא רב אחא בר יעקב עוד להוציא שהמילה מותרת בשבת מדכתיב וביום השמיני ימול כלומר איזה יום שמיני אין לך לא להקדים ולא לאחר ונתקשה ולא עמדו דבריו ואמרינן לא מחוורתא כר' יוחנן דאפקיה מן וביום. וסוגיא דשמעתיה כר' יוחנן ודחינא כוותי' ולא כר' אחא בר יעקב:

רב נסים גאון

איצטריך סלקא דעתך אמינא הואיל וחס רחמנא עליה לאיתויי בדלות בלילה נמי ליתי קמ"ל מתקיף לה רבינא [אלא] מעתה יהא זר ואונן כשר בהן הא אהדריה קרא כבר חייבנו הקב"ה בתורת הקרבנות שנקריבם ביום ולא בלילה שנאמר (ויקרא ז) אשר צוה ה' את משה ביום צותו את בני ישראל ופירש ביום צותו ביום למדנו

לכל הקרבנות כולם שאינן כשירין אלא ביום ובפרק הקורא את המגילה (דף כ:) ...

The Gemara counters:

וְאַכַּתִּי מִיבָּעֵי לֵיהּ חַד לְמַעוּטֵי שְׁבִיעִי – **Still, one** of those verses **is needed to exclude** the performing of *milah* on the **seventh** day, וְחַד לְמַעוּטֵי תְּשִׁיעִי – **and one** is needed **to exclude** the performing of *milah* on the **ninth** day.[44] דְּאִי מֵחַד – **For if** we were to expound **from** just **one** of those verses, הֲוָה אָמֵינָא שְׁבִיעִי הוּא – **I would think** that **it is** *milah* on the **seventh** day that the Torah precludes, דְּלֹא מְטָא זִמְנֵיהּ – **since [the mitzvah's] time has not arrived.** אֲבָל מִשְּׁמִינִי וְאֵילָךְ זִמְנֵיהּ הוּא – **But from the eighth** day **and onward is its** primary **time.** Accordingly, the word *eighth* is not free to teach that *milah* overrides the Sabbath, for it teaches me that *only* the eighth day is the proper time for the mitzvah of *milah*. – ? –

The Gemara concludes:

אֶלָּא מְחַוַּורְתָּא כִּדְרַבִּי יוֹחָנָן – **Rather,** the answer is **clear according to** the explanation of **R' Yochanan,** who said above that the Rabbis derive the law for *milah* itself from *on the . . . day.*

The Gemara adduces support for R' Yochanan's derivation:

תַּנְיָא כְּוָותֵיהּ דְּרַבִּי יוֹחָנָן – **It was taught in a Baraisa in accordance with R' Yochanan** וּדְלֹא כְּרַב אַחָא בַּר יַעֲקֹב – **and not in accordance with Rav Acha bar Yaakov,**[45] as follows: "שְׁמִינִי יִמּוֹל" – Scripture states,[46] *And on the* EIGHTH *day the flesh of his foreskin* SHALL BE CIRCUMCISED, which means: אֲפִילּוּ בְּשַׁבָּת – You shall perform the mitzvah of *milah* on whatever happens to be the eighth day – i.e. EVEN ON THE SABBATH. וּמָה אֲנִי מְקַיֵּים "מְחַלְלֶיהָ מוֹת יוּמָת" – AND HOW DO I ESTABLISH the verse,[47] *[SABBATH'S] DESECRATORS SHALL BE PUT TO DEATH?* בִּשְׁאָר מְלָאכוֹת חוּץ מִמִּילָה – WITH REGARD TO those who perform any of THE OTHER forbidden LABORS BESIDES CIRCUMCISION. אוֹ אֵינוֹ אֶלָּא אֲפִילּוּ מִילָה – OR, indeed, IT IS NOT so, BUT EVEN CIRCUMCISION is prohibited on pain of death. וּמָה אֲנִי מְקַיֵּים "שְׁמִינִי יִמּוֹל" – AND HOW then DO I ESTABLISH the verse, *And on the* EIGHTH *day the flesh of his foreskin* SHALL BE CIRCUMCISED? חוּץ מִשַּׁבָּת – It means that the time for *milah* is the eighth day, EXCEPT when that day is THE SABBATH. תַּלְמוּד לוֹמַר "בַּיּוֹם" – To preclude the latter interpretation THE TORAH STATES, *ON THE . . . DAY,* which implies: אֲפִילּוּ בְּשַׁבָּת – You shall perform the mitzvah of *milah* on the eighth day, whenever that may be – i.e. EVEN ON THE SABBATH day.

The Gemara now analyzes the Baraisa:

אָמַר רָבָא – **Rava said:** הַאי תַּנָּא מֵעִיקָּרָא מַאי קָא נִיחָא לֵיהּ – **Why to this Tanna was it originally appropriate** to interpret *on the eighth* literally[48] and *its desecrators* loosely,[49] וּלְבַסּוֹף מַאי קָא קַשְׁיָא לֵיהּ – **and in the end**[50] **what was difficult to him** about his initial reasoning?

The Gemara explains the Tanna's thinking:

הָכִי קָאָמַר – **[The Tanna] was saying thus:** "שְׁמִינִי יִמּוֹל" – *And on the* ***eighth*** *day the flesh of his foreskin* ***shall be circumcised*** teaches that *milah* is to be performed on the eighth day אֲפִילּוּ בְּשַׁבָּת – **even** when it falls **on the Sabbath.** וּמָה אֲנִי מְקַיֵּים "מְחַלְלֶיהָ מוֹת יוּמָת" – **And how do I establish** ***its desecrators shall be put to death?*** בִּשְׁאָר מְלָאכוֹת חוּץ מִמִּילָה – **With regard to** those who perform any of **the other** forbidden **labors besides circumcision.** אֲבָל מִילָה דָּחְיָא – **However, circumcision overrides** the Sabbath restrictions. מַאי טַעְמָא – **What is the reason?** קַל וָחוֹמֶר הוּא – **It is a** ***kal vachomer*** argument that establishes this,[51] as follows: וּמָה צָרַעַת – **Inasmuch as** the ***tzaraas*** prohibition[52] is stringent, שֶׁדּוֹחָה אֶת הָעֲבוֹדָה – **for it overrides the** sacrificial **service** obligation,[53]

NOTES

44. That is, the verses teach that neither day is the proper time for *milah*.

45. [Who derives that *milah* overrides the Sabbath from the word *eighth.*] The Rishonim debate whether the Gemara also means to reject the interpretation of Rav Nachman bar Yitzchak, who derived (above) the law for *milah* from the *gezeirah shavah* of "*sign, covenant* and *generations.*" See *Tosafos* with *Maharam, Ramban, Ritva* (*MHK* ed.) and *Ran* (*MHK* ed.).

46. *Leviticus* 12:3.

47. *Exodus* 31:14.

48. As sanctioning *milah* even when the eighth day is Shabbos (*Rashi, Ritva MHK* ed.).

49. As referring only to those who perform any of the other forbidden labors (*Rashi*).

50. When the Tanna reversed his thinking and interpreted *its desecrators* literally (as including even *milah* on the eighth day) and *on the eighth* loosely (as referring only to *milah* on a weekday) [*Rashi;* cf. *Ritva MHK* ed.].

[See *Rashash*, who asks: Perhaps the Tanna originally held like Rav Acha bar Yaakov, and reversed his thinking based on the challenge mentioned in the Gemara earlier!]

51. Thus compelling the Tanna to interpret *on the eighth* literally [see note 48] and *its desecrators* loosely [see note 49] (*Rashi*).

52. The Torah states (*Deuteronomy* 24:8), הִשָּׁמֶר בְּנֶגַע־הַצָּרַעַת, *Take heed concerning the affliction of tzaraas,* which the Gemara (*Makkos* 22a) interprets as a prohibition against cutting off any whitish spot on the skin that, in conjunction with certain other symptoms, signifies a condition of *tzaraas* [see *Leviticus* ch. 13] (*Rashi*).

53. That is, Kohanim are forbidden to cut off a *tzaraas* spot on their bodies even if it means that there will be no eligible Kohanim to perform the sacrificial service, and a non-Kohen is forbidden to cut off a *tzaraas* spot to qualify himself to bring a *pesach* offering (*Rashi*, from *Pesachim* 67a; see there and *Meiri* here; see also *Tosafos* and *Tos. HaRosh* here).

שכן אם עבר זמנה בטלה אלא היינו טעמא דרבי אליעזר דאמר קרא א) וביום השמיני ימול בשר ערלתו ואפילו בשבת וליכתוב רחמנא במילה וליתו הנך וליגמור מיניה משום דאיכא למיפרך מה למילה שכן נכרתו עליה שלש עשרה בריתות: ע"כ לא פליגי רבנן עליה אלא במכשירי מילה אבל מילה גופה דברי הכל דוחה שבת מנלן אמר עולא הלכה וכן אמר רבי יצחק הלכה מיתיבי א) מניין לפיקוח נפש שדוחה את השבת רבי אלעזר בן עזריה אומר מה מילה שהיא אחת מאיבריו של אדם דוחה את השבת קל וחומר לפיקוח נפש שדוחה את השבת ואי סלקא דעתך הלכה קל וחומר מהלכה מי אתי והתניא ב) אמר לו רבי אליעזר (ג) בן עזריה) עקיבא עצם כשעורה הלכה ורביעית דם קל וחומר ואין דנין קל וחומר מהלכה אלא אמר רבי אלעזר אתיא ב) אות ג) אות אלא מעתה תפילין דכתיב בהן ד) אות לידחי שבת אלא אתיא ב) ברית ה) ברית גדול דכתיב ביה ו) ברית לידחי שבת אלא אתיא ז) דורות ח) דורות ציצית דכתיב ביה ח) דורות לידחי שבת אלא אמר רב נחמן בר יצחק דנין אות ברית ודורות מאות ברית ודורות לאפוקי הנך דחד חד הוא דכתיב בהן ור' יוחנן אמר אמר קרא א) ביום ז) ביום אפילו בשבת אמר ליה ריש לקיש לרבי יוחנן אלא מעתה מחוסרי כפרה דכתיב בהו ביום הכי נמי דדחו שבת ההוא מיבעי ליה ביום ולא בלילה האי נמי מיבעי ליה ביום ולא בלילה ההוא ו) מבן שמנת ימים נפקא האי נמי ט) מביום צוותו נפקא אע"ג דנפקא מביום צוותו אצטריכא סד"א הואיל וחס רחמנא עליה לאתויי בדלות בלילה נמי ליתי קמ"ל מתקיף לה רבינא אלא מעתה יהא זר כשר בהן ויהא אונן כשר בהן הא אהדריה קרא רב אחא בר יעקב אמר קרא א) שמיני שמיני אפילו בשבת האי שמיני מיבעי ליה למעוטי שביעי שביעי מבן שמנת ימים נפקא ואכתי מיבעי ליה חד למעוטי שביעי וחד למעוטי תשיעי דאי מחד הוה אמינא שביעי הוא דלא מטא זמניה אבל משמיני ואילך זמניה הוא אלא מחוורתא כדרבי יוחנן תניא כוותיה דרבי יוחנן ודלא כרב אחא בר יעקב שמיני ימול אפילו בשבת ומה אני מקיים י) מחלליה מות יומת בשאר מלאכות חוץ ממילה או אינו אלא אפי' מילה ומה אני מקיים שמיני ימול חוץ משבת ת"ל ביום אפילו בשבת אמר רבא האי תנא מעיקרא מאי קא ניחא ליה ולבסוף מאי קא קשיא ליה הכי קאמר שמיני ימול אפילו בשבת ומה אני מקיים מחלליה מות יומת בשאר מלאכו' חוץ ממילה אבל מילה דחיא מ"ט ק"ו הוא ומה צרע' שדוחה את העבודה ועבודה

רש"י

שאם עבר זמנן בטלין. הילכך דחו: וביום השמיני ימול ואפילו בשבת. ומילה גופה דדחיא שבת אמרינן לקמן הלכה למשה מסיני איתר ליה ביום למכשיריה: י"ג בריתות. נאמרו לאברהם בפרשת מילה (בראשית יז): והא תניא. במסכת נזיר: עקיבא עצם כשעורה הלכה. שהיה ר"ע דן ק"ו מניין לרביעית דם המת שהנזיר מגלח על אהלה ק"ו מה עצם כשעורה שאינו מטמא באהל נזיר מגלח על מגעו ומשאו רביעית דם שמטמאה באהל דכתיב ועל כל נפש מת לא יבא אינו דין שהנזיר מגלח עליה ואמר ליה רבי אלעזר עקיבא עצם כשעורה הלכה למשה מסיני שיהא נזיר מגלח עליה ורביעית דם אתה בא ללמוד ממנה בק"ו ואין דנין קל וחומר מהלכה דלא ניתנה תורה שבעל פה לידרש בי"ג מדות: אתיא אות אות. בשבת כתיב (שמות לא) כי אות היא ובמילה כתיב (בראשית יז) והיה לאות ברית מה להלן שבת אף כאן שבת: אלא מעתה. אי הך ג"ש דאות האמורה בשבת נאמרה בסיני לידרש שתיבה זו לדרשה נאמרה ליגמר מינה נמי לתפילין: אלא אתיא ברית ברית. הכא דאות אות לא נאמרה בסיני ואין אדם דן גזרה שוה מעצמו אלא הך דברית ברית נאמרה בסיני ובשבת כתיב ברית (שמות לא) לדורותם ברית עולם: גדול. בן שלש עשרה דהוי מילה שלא בזמנה: דכתיב ביה ברית. וערל זכר אשר לא ימול וגו' את בריתי הפר (בראשית יז) והאי קרא בגדול כתיב מדמחייב ליה כרת שאם לא מלו אביו חייב למול את עצמו ולידחי שבת ואנן אמרינן לקמן דאפילו יום טוב אינה דוחה אלא בזמנה: דורות דורות. בשבת כתיב לדורותם ברית עולם ובמילת קטן כתיב (שם) ובן שמנת ימים ימול לכם כל זכר לדורותיכם: ביום ואפילו בשבת. מדלא כתיב בשמיני ימול ולר' אליעזר דאפקיה למכשירין מילה עצמה הלכה היא ופיקוח נפש לא אתיא ליה בק"ו ממילה אלא מקרא נפקא ליה כדאמרינן בפרק בתרא דיומא ט): מחוסרי כפרה. כל טמאין שהוצרכו לקרבן זב וזבה יולדת ומצורע נאמר בהן וביום השמיני: ביום צותו. את בני ישראל להקריב את קרבניהם (ויקרא ז) ביום ולא בלילה: אלא מעתה. משום דהוכשר להביא בדלות מכשירין בה שאר פסולין: יהא זר ואונן כשר בהן. אונן עד שלא נקבר מתו פסול לעבודה דכתיב (שם כא) בכהן גדול לאביו ולאמו לא יטמא ומן המקדש לא יצא ולא יחלל והכי משמע אף ביום שמתו אביו ואמו אינו צריך לצאת מן המקדש אלא מקריב אונן ולא יחלל ועבודתו לא תהא מחוללת הא כהן אחר שלא יצא חילל: הא אהדריה קרא. לפסול בהן לילה דכתיב בהו וביום כדאמרינן וכיון דלענין לילה תורת כל הקרבנות עליהן לענין זר ואונן נמי תורת קרבן עליהן: שמיני. כל שהוא שמיני ואפילו בשבת וביום למעוטי לילה: תניא כוותיה דר' יוחנן. דיליף מוביום: מעיקרא מאי ניחא ליה. לאוקמי שמיני דווקא ואפילו בשבת ודחי מחלליה מות יומת אכל שאר מלאכות מאיזה טעם נראה לו כן: ולבסוף. כשהיפך דבריו ואמר או אינו אלא אפי' מילה בכלל מחלליה מות יומת דהוא דוקא ודחי שמיני ימול אכל שאר ימים: מאי קשיא ליה. בטעמא הראשון: אבל מילה דחיא. שבת בק"ו ותיגמר מיניה למידחי מחלליה מות יומת אכל שאר מלאכות ולמימר שמיני דווקא קאמר ואפי' ביום שבת: ומה צרעת שדוחה את העבודה. אזהרה שהזהירה תורה על הצרעת שלא לקוץ בהרתו כדתניא (מכות דף כב.) השמר בנגע הצרעת אזהרה בקוצץ בהרתו הכתוב מדבר והמחוסר כפרה מחמת הצרעת דוחה את העבודה כדקיימא לן בפסחים (דף סז.) דטומאת מת נדחית בקרבן ציבור ולא זבין ומצורעי' ובטלים לעשות פסח ולא אמרינן יקוץ בהרתו ויאכלו פסחים ולא הכהן יקוץ בהרתו ויעבוד אם הכהנים טמאין בצרעת והקהל טהורין: ועבודה

תוספות

והתניא אמר ליה רבי אליעזר כו'. ול"ג והתנן דכל זה אינו במשנה: ההיא מבן שמונת ימים נפקא. תימה דמניה בת"כ ומייתי לה בפרק הערל (יבמות עב:) השמיני ימול דמניה יכול בין ביום ובין בלילה ת"ל ביום אין לי אלא שנימול לח' נימול לט' לי' ולי"א מניין נימול אלא ביום ת"ל וביום ובפ"ב דמגילה (דף כ.) נמי אמר אין מוהלין אלא ביום דכתיב וביום השמיני ויש לומר דסמיך אבן שמנת ימים ודרשה פשוטה נקט: אלא מעתה יהא זר ואונן כשר בהן. לאו דווקא נקט זר דהא בכולהו בזב וזבה ויולדת ומצורע כתב בהו כהן:

הא אהדריה קרא. והוה ליה דבר שילא מן הכלל לידון בדבר החדש לאתויי בדלות שאי אתה יכול להחזירו לכללו לפסול לילה ואונן עד שיחזירנו הכתוב לכללו בפירוש הרי החזירה בפירוש ופסל לילה וה"ה אונן וקשה ואמאי לא קאמר דאהדריה קרא מדכתיב כהן ולא זר ושמא לשום דרשא אחריתי אתא:

תניא כוותיה דרבי יוחנן ודלא כרב אחא בר יעקב. ודלא כרב נחמן בר יצחק דאמר אתיא אות ברית דורות לא הוי דאיהו מודה דדרשינן ביום כדדרשינן בברייתא ואות ברית דורות אתא למכשירין וביום למילה גופה ולית ליה למילה הלכה אע"ג דר' יוחנן אית ליה י) הלכה לר' אליעזר [כדפי' רש"י והאי ברייתא דדרשי ביום אתיא כרבנן דביום] איצטריך למילה גופה ולהכי לא קאמר אלא דלא כרב אחא דברייתא מוכחא בהדיא דלא בעיא למדרש שמיני ימול. מ"ר: מה צרעת שדוחה את העבודה. תימה ולימא קל וחומר איפכא ותדחה עבודה את הצרעת שיקוץ בהרתו כדי לעשות עבודה ומה שבת שדוחה את המילה ומילה דוחה את הצרעת עבודה דוחה אותה צרעת שנדחה מפני מילה אינו דין שתהא עבודה דוחה אותה והא דאמרינן בפסחים בפרק אלו דברים (דף סז.) וישלחו מן המחנה כל צרוע וכל זב וכל טמא לנפש אם טמאי מתים משתלחין זבים ומצורעים לא כ"ש אלא יש לך שעה שזבין ומצורעים משתלחים ואין טמאי מתים משתלחים ואיזה זה פסח הבא בטומאה

תורה אור השלם

א) וּבַיּוֹם הַשְּׁמִינִי יִמּוֹל בְּשַׂר עָרְלָתוֹ: [ויקרא יב, ג]

ב) וּנְמַלְתֶּם אֵת בְּשַׂר עָרְלַתְכֶם וְהָיָה לְאוֹת בְּרִית בֵּינִי וּבֵינֵיכֶם: [בראשית יז, יא]

ג) וְאַתָּה דַּבֵּר אֶל בְּנֵי יִשְׂרָאֵל לֵאמֹר אַךְ אֶת שַׁבְּתֹתַי תִּשְׁמֹרוּ כִּי אוֹת הִוא בֵּינִי וּבֵינֵיכֶם לְדֹרֹתֵיכֶם לָדַעַת כִּי אֲנִי יְיָ מְקַדִּשְׁכֶם: [שמות לא, יג]

ד) וְהָיָה לְךָ לְאוֹת עַל יָדְךָ וּלְזִכָּרוֹן בֵּין עֵינֶיךָ לְמַעַן תִּהְיֶה תּוֹרַת יְיָ בְּפִיךָ כִּי בְּיָד חֲזָקָה הוֹצִאֲךָ יְיָ מִמִּצְרָיִם: [שמות יג, ט]

ה) וְשָׁמְרוּ בְנֵי יִשְׂרָאֵל אֶת הַשַּׁבָּת לַעֲשׂוֹת אֶת הַשַּׁבָּת לְדֹרֹתָם בְּרִית עוֹלָם: [שמות לא, טז]

ו) וְעָרֵל זָכָר אֲשֶׁר לֹא יִמּוֹל אֶת בְּשַׂר עָרְלָתוֹ וְנִכְרְתָה הַנֶּפֶשׁ הַהִוא מֵעַמֶּיהָ אֶת בְּרִיתִי הֵפַר: [בראשית יז, יד]

ז) וּבֶן שְׁמֹנַת יָמִים יִמּוֹל לָכֶם כָּל זָכָר לְדֹרֹתֵיכֶם יְלִיד בָּיִת וּמִקְנַת כֶּסֶף מִכֹּל בֶּן נֵכָר אֲשֶׁר לֹא מִזַּרְעֲךָ הוּא: [בראשית יז, יב]

ח) דַּבֵּר אֶל בְּנֵי יִשְׂרָאֵל וְאָמַרְתָּ אֲלֵהֶם וְעָשׂוּ לָהֶם צִיצִת עַל כַּנְפֵי בִגְדֵיהֶם לְדֹרֹתָם וְנָתְנוּ עַל צִיצִת הַכָּנָף פְּתִיל תְּכֵלֶת: [במדבר טו, לח]

ט) אֲשֶׁר צִוָּה יְיָ אֶת מֹשֶׁה בְּהַר סִינָי בְּיוֹם צַוֹּתוֹ אֶת בְּנֵי יִשְׂרָאֵל לְהַקְרִיב אֶת קָרְבְּנֵיהֶם לַייָ בְּמִדְבַּר סִינָי: [ויקרא ז, לח]

י) וּשְׁמַרְתֶּם אֶת הַשַּׁבָּת כִּי קֹדֶשׁ הִוא לָכֶם מְחַלְלֶיהָ מוֹת יוּמָת כִּי כָּל הָעֹשֶׂה בָהּ מְלָאכָה וְנִכְרְתָה הַנֶּפֶשׁ הַהִוא מִקֶּרֶב עַמֶּיהָ: [שמות לא, יד]

מסורת הש"ס

א) [תוספתא פט"ז] יומא פה: מכילתא פרשת כי תשא, ב) פסחים פא: [נזיר מ.], ג) [בפסחים ובנזיר ליתא], ד) [סנהדרין נט:], ה) [דף פה:], ו) [ס"א הלכך].

ליקוטי רש"י

מה מילה. שהיא תיקון אחד מאבריו של אדם דוחה את השבת לפי שמיניין עליה כרת לאחר זמן כן שנינו בתוספתא דשבת [יומא פה:]. והתניא אמר לו וכו'. דר"א ור"ע במסכת נזיר דאמרינן התם רביעית דם אין הנזיר מגלח על מגעה ועל משאה וקאמר ר' עקיבא קל וחומר ומה עצם כשעורה שאין מטמא (את כל) אדם באהל הנזיר מגלח על מגעה ועל משאה רביעית דם שמטמאה (את כל) אדם באהל אינו דין שהנזיר מגלח על מגעה ועל משאה אמר לו ר"א עקיבא עצם כשעורה שהנזיר מגלח על מגעה ועל משאה הלכה למשה מסיני ואתה בא ללמוד ממנה בקל וחומר ואין דנין קל וחומר מהלכה אלא מדבר כתוב [פסחים פא.]. מחלליה. הנוהג בה חול [שמות לא, יד].

רבינו חננאל

עד כאן לא פליגי ר' אליעזר ורבנן אלא במכשירי מילה אבל במילה עצמה דברי הכל דחיא שבת. מנלן עולא ור' אסי ור' יצחק נפחא כולהו אמרי הלכה ומותבינן עליהון. מניין לפקוח נפש שדוחה שבת נענה ר' אלעזר בן עזריה ואמר ומה מילה שהיא אחד מאבריו של אדם דוחה את השבת ק"ו לפקוח נפש שדוחה את השבת ואי ס"ד הלכה ק"ו מהלכה (מי"ת) [מי אתי]. והתניא א"ל ר' עקיבא עצם כשעורה הלכה ורביעית דם ק"ו ואין דנין ק"ו מהלכה כו' לבטלו וזה מפורש בנזיר פר' כ"ג ונזיר אין מטמאין לקרוביהן וכו'. ובטלו דברי מי שאמר הלכה היא ובא ר' אליעזר ללמדו בג"ש באות אות משבת. ונדחו דבריו וגם רב נחמן בר יצחק ולמדו באות ברית דורו' בשבת כתיב לעשות את השבת לדורותם ברית עולם ביני ובין בני ישראל אות היא לעולם ובמילה כתיב וזאת בריתי אשר תשמרו אתה וזרעך אחריך לדורותם וכתיב ונמלתם את בשר ערלתכם והיתה לאות ברית ביני וביניכם. ר' יוחנן אמר אמר קרא וביום השמיני ימול בשר ערלתו ביום אפילו בשבת אקשינן עליה א"ה אי הכי אפילו מחוסרי כפרה כגון מצורע והזבה דכתי' בהן וביום השמיני יקח שני כבשים וגו' ובזבה כתיב וביום השמיני תקח לה שתי תורים הכי נמי כיון דכתיב בהו וביום יקריבו קרבנותיהם אפילו בשבת והא קיי"ל אין קרבן יחיד דוחה את השבת ופריק לו זה שכתוב במחוסרי כפרה וביום למעוטי לילה. עוד הקשה לו ר"ל וכל קשיא שהקשה לו פירק לו ר' יוחנן וחזר רבינא להתקיף על פירוק ר' יוחנן ופריק סד"א הואיל וחס רחמנא עליה לאתויי בדלות בלילה נמי ליתי קמ"ל וביום. התקיף רבינא אי הכי אמ' דחס עליהן אינו כשר כהן ולא יטריחם להמתין עד שימצאו כהן טהור כשר לטהרם ופריק הא אהדריה קרא כלומר אע"פ שחס עליו והקל בקרבנו החזיר לטהרת הכהן שנאמר והביא אותם ביום השמיני לטהרתו אל הכהן וגו'. ואתא רב אחא בר יעקב עוד להוציא שהמילה מותרת בשבת מדכתיב וביום השמיני ימול כלומר איזה יפול שמיני אין לך לא להקדים ולא לאחר ונתקשה לו ועמדו דבריו ואמרינן אלא מחוורתא כר' יוחנן דאפקיה מן ביום. וסוגיא דשמעתיה כר' יוחנן ודתניא כוותי' ולא כר' אחא בר יעקב:

רב נסים גאון

איצטריך סלקא דעתך אמינא הואיל וחס רחמנא עליה לאיתויי בדלות בלילה נמי ליתי קמ"ל [רבינא] מתקיף לה רבינא [אלא] מעתה יהא זר ואונן כשר בהן חייבנו הקב"ה בתורת הקרבנות שנקריבם ביום ולא בלילה שנאמר (ויקרא ז) אשר צוה ה' את משה ביום צותו את בני ישראל ופירש ביום צותו לעולם

לכל הקרבנות כולם שאינן כשרין אלא ביום ובפרק הקורא את המגילה (דף כ:) שנינו כל היום כשר לסמיכה לשחיטה כו' ובתלמוד אמרו לסמיכה ולשחיטה דכתיב (ויקרא ג) וסמך ושחט ואיתקש סמיכה לשחיטה ובשחיטה כתיב (שם יט) ביום זבחכם לקמיצה והגשה והזייה בכולהו כתיב ביום צוותו והזהיר האונן והזר כמו שאמרה המשנה (זבחים דף טו:) כל הזבחים שקיבל דמן זר ואונן כולם פסולין ובגמ' גרסי זר מנלן דתני לוי (ויקרא כב) דבר אל אהרן ואל בניו וינזרו מקדשי בני ישראל ולא יחללו [illegible]

ח א מיי' פ"א מהל' מילה הלכה ט ופ"י מהל' טומאת צרעת הלכה ה סמג עשין מח טוש"ע יו"ד סי' רסו סעיף ח:

ט ב מיי' פ"א מהלכות מילה שם סמג שם טוש"ע שם סעיף ב:

ועבודה דוחה את השבת מילה דוחה אותה שבת שנדחית מפני העבודה אינו דין שתהא מילה דוחה אותה ומאי או אינו דקאמר הדר אמר וממאי דצרעת חמורה דילמא שבת חמורה שכן יש בה עונשין ואזהרות הרבה (א) אי נמי) וממאי משום דחמירא צרעת היא דילמא משום גברא הוא דלא חזי ומה אני מקיים א) שמיני ימול חוץ משבת • תלמוד לומר א) ביום אפילו בשבת: תנו רבנן מילה דוחה את הצרעת בין בזמנה בין שלא בזמנה ב) יום טוב אינה דוחה אלא בזמנה בלבד מנהני מילי דתנו רבנן א) ימול בשר ערלתו • ואע"פ שיש שם בהרת יקוץ ומה אני מקיים ב) השמר בנגע הצרעת בשאר מקומות חוץ ממילה או אינו אלא אפילו מילה ומה אני מקיים ימול בשר ערלתו בזמן שאין בה בהרת ת"ל בשר ואע"פ שיש שם בהרת אמר רבא האי תנא מעיקרא מאי ניחא ליה ולבסוף מאי קשיא ליה הכי קאמר ימול בשר ערלתו ואע"פ שיש בהרת ומה אני מקיים השמר בנגע הצרעת בשאר מקומות חוץ ממילה אבל מילה דוחה את הצרעת מ"ט דאתיא מק"ו ומה שבת חמורה מילה דוחה אותה צרעת לא כ"ש ומאי או אינו דקאמר הדר קאמר ממאי דשבת חמירא דילמא צרעת חמירא שכן דוחה את העבודה ועבודה דוחה את השבת ת"ל בשר ואע"פ שיש שם בהרת לישנא אחרינא מילה דוחה את הצרעת מ"ט דאתי עשה ודחי לא תעשה ומאי או אינו דקאמר הדר קאמר אימר דאמרינן דאתי עשה ודחי את לא תעשה לא תעשה גרידא האי עשה ולא תעשה הוא ומה אני מקיים ימול בשר ערלתו בזמן שאין בה בהרת ת"ל בשר ואע"פ שיש שם בהרת תינח גדול דכתיב בהו ג) בשר קטן נמי כתיב ביה א) בשר בינוני מנלן אמר אביי אתיא מביניא מגדול לא אתיא שכן ענוש כרת מקטן לא אתיא שכן מילה בזמנה הצד השוה שבהן שכן נימולין ודוחין את הצרעת אף כל שנימולין דוחין את הצרעת רבא אמר מילה בזמנה דוחה לא צריכא קרא מק"ו אתיא ומה שבת דחמירא דוחה צרעת לא כל שכן אמר ליה רב ספרא לרבא ממאי דשבת חמירא דילמא צרעת חמירא שכן דוחה את העבודה ועבודה דוחה את השבת התם לאו משום דחמירא צרעת אלא משום דגברא הוא דלא חזי אמאי ויקוץ בהרתו ויעבוד מחוסר טבילה הוא תינח נגעים טמאים נגעים ג) טהורים מאי איכא למימר אלא א"ר אשי ג) היכא אמרינן דאתי עשה ודחי ל"ת כגון מילה בצרעת א"נ ציצית וכלאים דבעידנא דמתעקר לאו קא מוקי' עשה הכא בעידנא דמתעקר ללאו לא קא מוקים עשה והא דרבא ורב ספרא תנאי

תורה אור השלם

א) וּבַיּוֹם הַשְּׁמִינִי יִמּוֹל בְּשַׂר עָרְלָתוֹ: [ויקרא יב, ג]

ב) הִשָּׁמֶר בְּנֶגַע הַצָּרַעַת לִשְׁמֹר מְאֹד וְלַעֲשׂוֹת כְּכֹל אֲשֶׁר יוֹרוּ אֶתְכֶם הַכֹּהֲנִים הַלְוִיִּם כַּאֲשֶׁר צִוִּיתִם תִּשְׁמְרוּ לַעֲשׂוֹת: [דברים כד, ח]

ג) וְעָרֵל זָכָר אֲשֶׁר לֹא יִמּוֹל אֶת בְּשַׂר עָרְלָתוֹ וְנִכְרְתָה הַנֶּפֶשׁ הַהִוא מֵעַמֶּיהָ אֶת בְּרִיתִי הֵפַר: [בראשית יז, יד]

וַעֲבוֹדָה דּוֹחָה אֶת הַשַּׁבָּת – **and the** sacrificial **service** obligation is itself stringent, for it **overrides the Sabbath** restrictions,[1] מִילָה דּוֹחָה אוֹתָהּ – and yet the mitzvah of **circumcision overrides [the *tzaraas* prohibition],**[2] שַׁבָּת שֶׁנִּדְחֵית מִפְּנֵי הָעֲבוֹדָה – then with regard to the **Sabbath, which is overridden on account of the** sacrificial **service,** אֵינוֹ דִּין שֶׁתְּהֵא מִילָה דּוֹחָה אוֹתָהּ – **is it not logical that circumcision should override it?!**[3] It was the logic of this *kal vachomer* that initially caused the Tanna to interpret *on the eighth* literally and *its desecrators* loosely.

The Gemara now explains why the Tanna changed his mind:

וּמַאי אוֹ אֵינוֹ דְּקָאָמַר – **And what is** the explanation for **[the Tanna] stating, "OR,** indeed, **IT IS NOT** so," which implies that he was reversing himself and now maintains that *milah is* included in the verse, *its desecrators shall be put to death*? What difficulty forced the Tanna to retract?

The Gemara answers:

הֲדַר אָמַר – **[The Tanna] subsequently said** to himself: וּמִמַּאי דְּצָרַעַת חֲמוּרָה – **From what** proof do we know **that the *tzaraas*** prohibition **is** more **stringent** than the Sabbath restrictions, which was the very premise of our *kal vachomer* argument? דִּילְמָא שַׁבָּת חֲמוּרָה – **Perhaps the Sabbath is** more **stringent,** שֶׁכֵּן יֵשׁ בָּהּ עוֹנָשִׁין וְאַזְהָרוֹת הַרְבֵּה – **for indeed it carries many penalties and prohibitions.** (אִי נַמִי) וּמִמַּאי מִשּׁוּם דַּחֲמִירָא[4] צָרַעַת הִיא – **And** as for the fact that the *tzaraas* prohibition overrides the sacrificial service,[5] **from what** proof do we know that it does so **because *tzaraas* is** inherently more **stringent** than the service? דִּילְמָא מִשּׁוּם גַּבְרָא הוּא דְּלָא חֲזֵי – Perhaps the reason we do not advise the Kohen to remove the *tzaraas* spot and then bring the sacrifice is **because he is** still **not a** ritually **fit person.**[6] And if so, the entire *kal vachomer* is undermined.[7] Hence, *its desecrators shall be put to death* should encompass even *milah* on the eighth day. וּמָה אֲנִי מְקַיֵּים ,,שְׁמִינִי יִמּוֹל" – **And how,** then, **do I establish** the verse, *On the* **eighth** *day the flesh of his foreskin* **shall be circumcised**? חוּץ מִשַּׁבָּת – It perforce means that *milah* shall be performed on every "eighth" day **except for the Sabbath.**[8]

The Tanna now concludes:

תַּלְמוּד לוֹמַר ,,בַּיּוֹם" – And to preclude this very interpretation **the Torah states, *on the . . . day,*** which implies: אֲפִילּוּ בְּשַׁבָּת – You shall perform the mitzvah of *milah* on the eighth day, whenever that may be – i.e. **even on the Sabbath** day. The Tanna thus uses R' Yochanan's exegesis to prove that *milah,* indeed, overrides the Sabbath restrictions. R' Yochanan's exegesis is thereby corroborated.

The Gemara stated above that the mitzvah of *milah* overrides the *tzaraas* prohibition.[9] The Gemara now discusses the Biblical source of this law:

תָּנוּ רַבָּנָן – **The Rabbis taught** in a Baraisa: מִילָה דּוֹחָה אֶת הַצָּרַעַת – The mitzvah of CIRCUMCISION OVERRIDES THE *TZARAAS* prohibition בֵּין בִּזְמַנָּהּ בֵּין שֶׁלֹּא בִּזְמַנָּהּ – WHETHER it is performed AT ITS proper TIME[10] OR NOT AT ITS proper TIME.[11] יוֹם טוֹב אֵינָהּ דּוֹחָה אֶלָּא בִּזְמַנָּהּ בִּלְבַד – However, [CIRCUMCISION] OVERRIDES the FESTIVAL *melachah* restrictions ONLY when performed AT ITS proper TIME.[12]

The Gemara asks:

מְנָהָנֵי מִילֵּי – **From where** do we derive **this law** that *milah* overrides the *tzaraas* prohibition, when Scripture expressly states: *Take heed concerning the affliction of tzaraas*?[13]

The Gemara cites another Baraisa to answer:

דְּתָנוּ רַבָּנָן – It is **as the Rabbis taught:** ,,יִמּוֹל בְּשַׂר עָרְלָתוֹ" – Scripture states,[14] ***THE FLESH OF HIS FORESKIN SHALL BE CIRCUMCISED,*** which means: וְאַף עַל פִּי שֶׁיֵּשׁ שָׁם בַּהֶרֶת יָקוֹץ – AND EVEN THOUGH a ***BAHERES*** spot (a type of *tzaraas*) IS THERE on the foreskin, HE SHALL CUT it OFF. וּמָה אֲנִי מְקַיֵּים ,,הִשָּׁמֶר בְּנֶגַע־הַצָּרַעַת" – AND HOW, then, DO I ESTABLISH the verse,[15] ***TAKE HEED CONCERNING THE AFFLICTION OF TZARAAS,*** which prohibits the removal of *tzaraas*? בִּשְׁאָר מְקוֹמוֹת חוּץ מִמִּילָה – That verse applies IN all OTHER PLACES BESIDES CIRCUMCISION.[16] אוֹ אֵינוֹ אֶלָּא אֲפִילּוּ מִילָה – OR, indeed, IT IS NOT so, BUT EVEN CIRCUMCISION is included in the prohibition against cutting off *tzaraas*. וּמָה אֲנִי מְקַיֵּים ,,יִמּוֹל בְּשַׂר עָרְלָתוֹ" – AND HOW, then, DO I ESTABLISH the verse, ***THE FLESH OF HIS FORESKIN SHALL BE CIRCUMCISED?*** בִּזְמַן שֶׁאֵין בָּהּ בַּהֶרֶת – That verse applies only AT A TIME WHEN THERE IS NO ***BAHERES*** spot ON [THE FORESKIN]. תַּלְמוּד לוֹמַר ,,בָּשָׂר" – To preclude the latter interpretation THE TORAH STATES, ***THE FLESH,*** which teaches: וְאַף עַל פִּי שֶׁיֵּשׁ שָׁם בַּהֶרֶת – AND EVEN THOUGH a

NOTES

1. The daily (*tamid*) offerings, the *mussaf* offerings and all public offerings whose times are fixed are all brought on the Sabbath (*Rashi*).

2. I.e. one performs the mitzvah even if a *tzaraas* spot is found on the foreskin and will be cut off as a result of the circumcision. The Gemara below will derive this sanction from Scripture (*Rashi*).

3. That is, if *milah* overrides a mitzvah (*tzaraas*) that overrides a mitzvah (sacrificial service) that overrides the Sabbath, then certainly *milah* itself should override the Sabbath.

4. *Maharam* (and it would appear *Rashi* as well) deletes אִי נַמִי, *alternatively,* from the text, on the grounds that the Gemara is not presenting a second refutation but is developing the first (cf. *Mesoras HaShas*). Our translation follows *Maharam's* approach. [See also *Maharsha* on *Tosafos* ד"ה הדר אמר. See *Meromei Sadeh,* who explains why indeed according to *Maharam's* text two arguments are needed.]

5. A key element of the *kal vachomer's* premise that *tzaraas* is more stringent than the sacrificial service.

6. Even after the *tzaraas* is removed, a *metzora* must immerse himself in a *mikveh* and wait until evening until he becomes completely purified and fit for service. Hence, the Kohen is in any event prevented from performing the service on that day. Thus, the Kohen is presently unfit for service [and is not under the obligation of that mitzvah (see, for example, *Pesachim* 69a,b)]; his not performing the service is not due to the prohibition against cutting off *tzaraas*. We thus have no basis to say that the *tzaraas* prohibition is more stringent than the sacrificial service (see *Rashi* and *Ritva MHK* ed.). [See further in *Rashi* ד"ה מחוסר, where he adds that tomorrow's service does not obligate the Kohen today to override the *tzaraas* prohibition; see also note 46 below.]

7. If *tzaraas* does not actually override the sacrificial service, it is not necessarily a "stringent" mitzvah. Hence, there is no compelling logic to say that *milah* should override the Sabbath because it overrides *tzaraas*.

8. That is, the verse is interpreted loosely, as referring only to the weekdays (*Rashi*).

9. See note 2 above.

10. On the eighth day.

11. After the eighth day, such as when an infant's *milah* must be postponed because of illness (*Rashi*).

12. [And all the more so does this law apply to Shabbos, whose desecration carries the penalty of *kares.*]

The Gemara below (133a) will derive this law from Scripture (*Ritva MHK* ed.; see there for a discussion of whether *milah* is permissible on the second day of Yom Tov, which was instituted for the diaspora only by Rabbinic decree).

13. *Ritva MHK* ed.; see above, 132a note 52.

14. *Leviticus* 12:3.

15. *Deuteronomy* 24:8.

16. I.e. *Take heed* . . . is to be interpreted loosely, as not including the case of circumcision.

עין משפט נר מצוה

ח א מיי' פ"א מהל' מילה הלכה ט ופ"י מהל' טומאת צרעת הלכה ה סמג עשין סח טוש"ע י"ד סי' רסו סעיף א:

ט ב מיי' פ"א מהלכות מילה שם סמג שם טוש"ע שם סעיף ב:

גליון הש"ס

גמ' ת"ל ביום אפי' בשבת. עיין חולין דף פד ע"ב ברש"י ד"ה שתלה ול"ע: שם ואע"פ שיש שם בהרת. עיין בר"ש רפ"ג דמלה: תוס' ד"ה האי וכו' שכן נכרתו עליה י"ג בריתות. ע' יבמות ה' ע"א תוד"ה שכן:

תורה אור השלם

א) וּבַיּוֹם הַשְּׁמִינִי יִמּוֹל בְּשַׂר עָרְלָתוֹ: [ויקרא יב, ג]

ב) הִשָּׁמֶר בְּנֶגַע הַצָּרַעַת לִשְׁמֹר מְאֹד וְלַעֲשׂוֹת כְּכֹל אֲשֶׁר יוֹרוּ אֶתְכֶם הַכֹּהֲנִים הַלְוִיִּם כַּאֲשֶׁר צִוִּיתִם תִּשְׁמְרוּ לַעֲשׂוֹת: [דברים כד, ח]

ג) וְעָרֵל זָכָר אֲשֶׁר לֹא יִמּוֹל אֶת בְּשַׂר עָרְלָתוֹ וְנִכְרְתָה הַנֶּפֶשׁ הַהִוא מֵעַמֶּיהָ אֶת בְּרִיתִי הֵפַר: [בראשית יז, יד]

ועבודה דוחה את השבת מילה דוחה אותה שבת שנדחית מפני העבודה אינו דין שתהא מילה דוחה אותה ומאי או אינו דקאמר הדר אמר וממאי דצרעת חמורה דילמא שבת חמורה שכן יש בה עונשין ואזהרות הרבה (א) אי נמי) וממאי משום דחמירא צרעת היא דילמא משום גברא הוא דלא חזי ומה אני מקיים א) שמיני ימול חוץ משבת • תלמוד לומר א) ביום אפילו בשבת: תנו רבנן א מילה דוחה את הצרעת בין בזמנה בין שלא בזמנה ב יום טוב אינה דוחה אלא בזמנה בלבד מנהני מילי דתנו רבנן א) ימול בשר ערלתו • ואע"פ שיש שם בהרת יקוץ ומה אני מקיים ב) השמר בנגע הצרעת בשאר מקומות חוץ ממילה או אינו אלא אפילו מילה ומה אני מקיים ימול בשר ערלתו בזמן שאין בה בהרת ת"ל בשר ואע"פ שיש שם בהרת אמר רבא האי תנא מעיקרא מאי ניחא ליה ולבסוף מאי קשיא ליה הכי קאמר ימול בשר ערלתו ואע"פ שיש שם בהרת ומה אני מקיים השמר בנגע הצרעת בשאר מקומות חוץ ממילה אבל מילה דוחה את הצרעת מ"ט דאתיא מק"ו ומה שבת חמורה מילה דוחה אותה צרעת לא כ"ש ומאי או אינו דקאמר הדר קאמר ממאי דשבת חמירא דילמא צרעת חמירא שכן דוחה את העבודה ועבודה דוחה את השבת ת"ל בשר ואע"פ שיש שם בהרת לישנא אחרינא מילה דוחה את הצרעת מ"ט דאתי עשה ודחי לא תעשה ומאי או אינו דקאמר הדר קאמר אימר דאמרינן דאתי עשה ודחי את לא תעשה לא תעשה גרידא האי עשה ולא תעשה הוא ומה אני מקיים ימול בשר ערלתו בזמן שאין בה בהרת ת"ל בשר ואע"פ שיש שם בהרת תינח גדול דכתיב בהו ג) בשר קטן נמי כתיב ביה א) בשר בינוני מנלן אמר אביי אתיא מבינייא מגדול לא אתיא שכן ענוש כרת מקטן לא אתיא שכן מילה בזמנה הצד השוה שבהן שכן נימולין ודוחין את הצרעת אף כל שנימולין דוחין את הצרעת רבא אמר מילה בזמנה דוחה לא צריכא קרא מק"ו אתיא ומה שבת דחמירא דוחה צרעת לא כל שכן אמר ליה רב ספרא לרבא ממאי דשבת חמירא דילמא צרעת חמירא שכן דוחה את העבודה ועבודה דוחה את השבת התם לאו משום דחמירא צרעת אלא משום דגברא הוא דלא חזי אמאי ויקוץ בהרתו ויעבוד מחוסר טבילה הוא תינח נגעים טמאים נגעים ג) טהורים מאי איכא למימר אלא א"ר אשי ד) היכא אמרינן דאתי עשה ודחי ל"ת כגון מילה בצרעת א"נ ציצית וכלאים דבעידנא דמתעקר לאו קא מוקי' עשה הכא בעידנא דמתעקר ללאו לא קא מוקים עשה והא דרבא ורב ספרא תנאי

רש"י

ועבודה. חמורה היא שדוחה שבת בתמידין ומוספין וקרבנות צבור שזמנם קבוע: מילה דוחה אותה. את הצרעת כדתניא לקמן ימול בשר ערלתו אפילו במקום בהרת יקוץ: ומה או אינו דקאמר. דמשמע או אינו כן כמו שאמרנו אלא אפי' מילה נמי בכלל מחלליה מאי קשיא ליה דקא הדר ביה: הדר אמר תנא. לנפשיה ממאי דצרעת חמורה משבת דתימא ק"ו: דילמא שבת חמורה כו'. דהאי דצרעת דוחה עבודה ממאי דמשום חומרא דצרעת היא דילמא הא דלא אמרינן ליה יקוץ משום דגברא דלא חזי הוא כדלקמן דאי נמי קייץ מחוסר טבילה והערב שמש והיום לא יעבוד (א) וטבול יום דמצורע כמצורע הילכך מחלליה מות יומת אפילו במילה ועל כרחך שמיני ימול תדחה אלא שאר ימים: בין שלא בזמנה. כגון קטן חולה והמתינו לו עד שיבריא: בשר. ריבויא הוא ולדרשה: ה"ג ל"א מאי טעמא אתי עשה ודחי לא תעשה. מ"ט מילה דוחה צרעת דאתי עשה דימול ודחי לא תעשה דהשמר (ב) לך דהכי קי"ל בפ"ק דיבמות (דף ג:) דאתי עשה ודחי לא תעשה: האי עשה ולא תעשה הוא. השמר לא תעשה הוא ולעשות ככל אשר יורו (דברים כד) היינו עשה: תינח גדול. בר עונשין דכתיב ביה בשר וערל זכר אשר לא ימול את בשר ערלתו (בראשית יז) והאי בבר עונשין משתעי מדמחייב ליה כרת וקטן נמי בזמנה ביום השמיני כתיב ביה בשר וביום השמיני ימול בשר ערלתו: בינוני. כגון שלא בזמנה ולאו בר עונשין ואביו מצווה עליו נפקא לן מהמול לכם כל זכר (קדושין דף כט.): אתיא מבינייא. הצד השוה שבהן שנימולו ודוחין את הצרעת אף אני אביא בינוני שנימול וידחה הצרעת: לא צריכא קרא כו'. וכי אתיא קרא לשלא בזמנה של בינוני: דגברא לא חזי. קס"ד מפני שהוא טמא והיינו דפריך ויקוץ ויטהר ויעבוד: מחוסר טבילה. ולא חזי לעבודה בהאי יומא ומשום למחר ליתא לעבודה דהא קטן לא מדחי: נגעים טהורים. כגון קטן ופרחה בכולה וכולהו מיתרבו לאיסור קציצה בסיפרי אין לי אלא משנזקק לטומאה עד שלא נזקק לטומאה מנין ת"ל לכל אשר יורו: אלא אמר רב אשי. הא דאמרינן דשבת חמירא מצרעת אע"ג דדחייה לעבודה ולאו חומרא דידה הוא אלא היינו טעמא כי אמרינן אתי עשה ודחי לא תעשה כגון מילה בצרעת דבשעת קצילה דמיעקר לאו מקיים עשה וכן ציצית דכלאים בשעת לבישה מיעקר לאו ומקיים עשה אבל צרעת הנקצצת בשעת עבודה בעידנא דמיעקר לאו דקצילה אכתי לא מקיים עשה דעבודה הילכך מידחיא עבודה ממילה ולאו חומרא דצרעת הוא:

תנאי

תוספות

בטומאה אלמא דצרעת דוחה את העבודה נימא דהיינו כל זמן שהיא עליו ובק"ו נילף שיקוץ בהרתו כדי לעשות עבודה ועוד קשה לימא רציחה תוכיח שדוחה את העבודה ואינו דוחה שבת אף אני אביא מילה וכי תימא מילה עדיפא שדוחה צרעת הדוחה את העבודה אכתי נימא קבורת מת מצוה תוכיח דעדיפא ממילה שדוחה את המילה מולאחותו הדוחה את הצרעת הדוחה את העבודה הדוחה את השבת אפילו הכי לא דחיא שבת ויש לומר דהכי נמי הוה מצי למימר איפכא ורציחה תוכיח או קבורת מת מצוה תוכיח אלא דניחא ליה לומר שיהא דוחה דנפקא ליה מביום דמילה דחיא שבת ועושה מתחילה ק"ו להעמיד דבריו וסותרו אחר כך שאינו ק"ו כלל ד) ופריך ליה מיניה וביה: **הדר אמר ממאי דשבת חמירא דילמא צרעת חמירא.** תימה דבברייתא דלעיל מסיק איפכא דלאו משום דצרעת חמירא אלא משום (ג) גברא דלא חזי ורבא גופיה סבירא ליה הכי לקמן ועוד למאי דקאמר השתא מנלן דצרעת דוחה את העבודה אימא דעבודה דוחה הצרעת מק"ו ומה שבת חמורה [צרעת לא כ"ש ואומר ר"י דלהאי לישנא] צריך לומר דגרסינן רבה הכא ולית ליה דרבא דלקמן דטעמא משום דגברא לא חזי וסבירא ליה כרב ספרא דפליג עליה דרבא לקמן והא דפשיט להו לרבה ורב ספרא דצרעת דוחה עבודה מצי למימר דמקרא נפקא להו אבל רבא דס"ל גברא לא חזי לדידיה לא בעי קרא ועוד נראה לרשב"א ה) דאפי' ליכא קרא דצרעת דוחה עבודה אתי שפיר אפילו לרב ספרא דלא קאמר רב ספרא שיהא הטעם ודאי דצרעת דוחה עבודה משום חומרא דצרעת אלא איכא למימר הכי ואיכא למימר הכי הילכך בברייתא דלעיל סתר ק"ו דקאמר וממאי דצרעת חמירא דילמא משום גברא דלא חזי והכא ולקמן על מילתא דרבא דחינן בע"א ממאי דשבת חמירא דילמא צרעת חמירא שכן דוחה את העבודה חיל הכא קא מדמי ליה חיל הכא קא מדמי ליה ומהאי טעמא נמי ליכא למילף ביה ק"ו דעבודה תדחי צרעת דשבת דחמורה דוחה צרעת לא כ"ש דדילמא אין לתלות משום חומרא אלא משום (ג) גברא לא חזי: **האי עשה ולא תעשה הוא.** השמר היינו לאו ולעשות היינו עשה כדפי' בקונטרס ואע"ג דאמר בסוף פרק הקומץ (מנחות דף לו:) השמר דלאו לאו השמר דעשה עשה מכל מקום לאו מצות עשה הוא אלא לא תעשה ו) דאמר רחמנא הזהר פן תקוץ בהרת תימה היכי מצינן למימר דלעשות אתא לעשה הא אמר לקמן דאיצטריך לעשות אי אתה עושה אבל אתה עושה בסיב שעל גבי רגלו ויש לפרש דעשה שמעינן מדכתיב ז) לשמור ואם תאמר והא אמר בסמוך היכא אמרינן דאתי עשה ודחי את לא תעשה כגון מילה בצרעת אלמא דליכא בצרעת אלא לאו ואר"ת דלא נקטינן אלא לסימנא בעלמא ואם תאמר והא דקי"ל דאין עשה דוחה את לא תעשה ועשה נגמר ממילה בצרעת דדמי וי"ל מה למילה • שכן נכרתו עליה י"ג בריתות ח): **רבא** אמר מילה בזמנה לא צריכא קרא. והילכך האי בשר דכתיב בה אם אינו ענין לזמנה תנהו ענין לשלא בזמנה ואו אינו דקתני הוה מפרש רבא כלישנא אחרינא:

ואביי

רבינו חננאל

ת"ר מילה דוחה צרעת בין בזמנה בין שלא בזמנה. פי' כתיב בצרעת השמר בנגע הצרעת ואמרו חכמים כ"מ שנאמר השמר פן ואל אינו אלא בל"ת. כלומר השמר אזהרה הוא שלא לעשות וכיון דכתיב השמר הנה הזהיר שלא לחתוך הצרעת (מכל מקום) [בכל מקום] שהיא והתיר במילה אם יש צרעת בערלה מותר לו לחתוך הערלה והצרעת עמה בין ביום השמיני שהוא זמן המילה כדכתיב וביום השמיני ימול בשר ערלתו. בין אירע לו אונס כגון חולי לקטן וכדומה לו ולא מל בשמיני חייב לימול כל זמן שיסור האונס והיא הנקראת מילה שלא בזמנה כלומר שאינה ביום השמיני וגם במילה שאינה ביום השמיני יש למל לחתוך הערלה אע"פ שיש בה צרעת והתורה שהזהירה שלא לחתוך הצרעת לגבי מילה התירה. ובאנו לברר זה הפי' שפירשנו מזו הברייתא. דת"ר ימול בשר ערלתו ואע"פ שיש שם בהרת ומה אני מקיים השמר בנגע הצרעת בשאר מקומות חוץ ממילה או אינו אלא אפי' מילה ומה אני מקיים ימול בשר ערלתו בזמן שאין שם בהרת ת"ל בשר אע"פ שיש שם בהרת לא תעשה בצרעת שנאמר השמר פן עשה שנא' ולעשות ופשוטה היא תינח גדול כתיב ביה בשר שנאמר וערל זכר אשר לא ימול את בשר ערלתו ונכרתה הנפש ההיא מעמיה את בריתי הפר. מדכתיב ונכרתה שמעינן מינה שהוא גדול ואם לא מל אותו אביו ונשאר ערל וגדל חייב למול עצמו קטן נמי כתיב ביה בשר שנאמר וביום השמיני ימול בשר ערלתו. ודרשת בשר אע"פ שיש שם בהרת אלו השנים הגדול שהוא בר עונשין והקטן שהוא בן שמונה ימים שכתב בהם בשר מילה דוחה את ערלתם אבל בינוני שאינו לא גדול בן עונשין ולא קטן בן שמונת ימים אלא בינוני שהוא מבן שמונה ימים ולמעלה הן חסר והן יתר עד שיגיע להתחייב בעונשים מנ"ל שמילתו דוחה צרעת. ופירק אביי ואמר אתיא מבינייא כלומר משניהם מן הגדול ומן הקטן. ודברים פשוטין הן. ודברי רבא ורב ספרא פשוטין הן. אמר רב אשי היכא אמרינן דאתי עשה ודוחה לא תעשה כגון מילה בצרעת כלומר אם יש צרעת בערלה בחתיכת הערלה והצרעת עליה נתקיימה המילה שפיר וכן כלאים בציצית. אבל זה שאמר ויקוץ בהרתו ויעבור חתיכת הצרעת להכשיר הכהן לעבוד עבודה אינו דומה לאלו שיתכן שיחתוך הצרעת מעליו והוא לא יעשה עבודה והנה נעקרה אזהרתו שלא לחתוך הצרעת שהוא לאו כמו שפירשנו למעלה. ולא נתקיימה עבודתו שהוא עשה נגעים טהורין שפוסלין בכהנים מפורש בבכורות פ"ז (מה:) דתנן הכושי והגיחור והלווקר והננס והחרש והשוטה והשכור ובעלי נגעים טהורין פסולין באדם וכשרין בבהמה כו' פי' כל זמן שיש בכהן נגעים טהורים פסול לעבודה חתכו טהר מיד ואין צריך טבילה:

מסורת הש"ס

א) רש"ל מ"ז והג"י גרס א"נ ממאי ויש ליישב אותה הגירסא דמקשה שני קושיות וה"פ דהוכחה שלו היא כיון דלא אמרינן דיקוץ בהרתו ויעבוד כמו שפרש"י והא ודאי די"ל ק"ו איפכא דיקוץ בהרתו בשביל עבודה כמו שהקשו התוס' אך כאשר מוכן בשום פעם דאי אפשר לו לקוץ הבהרת ואעפ"כ לא יעבוד ודאי לאו חומרא דעבודה הוא אלא חומרא דצרעת ולפי זה מקשה הכא דילמא שבת חמירא שכן יש בה כו' וא"כ דשבת חמירא מצרעת אסור לו לקוץ בהרת בשבת וא"כ שוב לא יכול ללמוד הק"ו איפכא דיקוץ בהרתו משום עבודה הא כבר נתנה העבודה לידחות מפני הצרעת בשבת וממילא נתבטל גם הק"ו הזה, ב) [עיין תוס' שבועות ד. ד"ה בקוצץ], ג) נדה ס: כתובות מ., ד) גיר' הרש"ל ופריך ליה מיניה וביה ונוכל לומר דהאי תנא כאו אינו דקאמר כולה ופריך ואימא איפכא או מת מצוה תוכיח עכ"ל ואין הגירסא זו מוכרחת דא"א לפרש כן בדברי רבה שעליו הקשו תוס', ה) ואפילו לסברא זו גרסי' רבה, ו) ועיין תוס' בעירובין דף צו. ד"ה השמר, ז) גיר' רש"ל ועי"ל תרי לעשות כתיבי בקרא זה חדא לעשה וחדא לעושה בסיב וכו' וכן פירש"י השמר לא תעשה הוא ולעשות ככל אשר יורו היינו עשה וא"ת והא אמר כו', ח) [וע"ע תוס' כתובות מ. ד"ה ניתי].

הגהות הב"ח

(א) רש"י ד"ה דילמא שבת וכו' לטבול יום: (ב) ד"ה ה"ג ל"א וכו' דהשמר דהכי כצ"ל ותיבת לך נמחק: (ג) תוס' ד"ה הדר וכו' אלא משום דגברא:

ליקוטי רש"י

בין שלא בזמנה. כגון גר שנתגייר וקטן שנולד אביו ועבר זמנו [פסחים פד.]. השמר בנגע הצרעת. ולאמרין בקוצץ בהרתו הכתוב מדבר והשמר הוא לא תעשה [מכות כב.]. שלא תתלוש סימני טומאה ולא תקוץ את הבהרת [דברים כד, ח]. כגון מילה בצרעת. דכתיב (דברים כד) השמר בנגע הצרעת ותניא בקוצץ בהרתו הכתוב מדבר ותניא בגמרא דאם לא הביא כלי במסכת שבת (קלב:) ימול בשר ערלתו אפילו במקום בהרת יקוץ אי נמי ציצית בכלאים דכתיב (דברים כב) לא תלבש שעטנז וסמיך ליה גדילים תעשה לך דבשעת מילה או בשעת לבישת הטלית מעקר לאו ומקיים עשה [ביצה ח:].

רב נסים גאון

המגורין במשנה שפסולין להקריב כשרים להקריב קרבנותיו של מצורע לפי שיצא מכללם ונבדל מהם חוץ מהקרבת קרבן בלילה שאמר בו הכתוב וביום השמיני בלבד ועמד זה הקושיא רוו ההתקפה ואמרנו קשיא ומקצת הגורסין אין מעמידין הדבר אלא שגורסין כך כיון דאהדריה קרא אהדריה כלומר אילו לא כתב וביום היינו אומרים מדחס רחמנא עליה לאיתויי בדלות בלילה נמי ליתי ויהא זר ואונן כשר בקרבנותיו והיינו מפרישין אותו לענין דיניו מכלל הקרבנות אבל הואיל ונאמר בו וביום השמיני באר לנו בזה חזרתו לכלל הקרבנות בכל עניניו והשבתו אליהן בכל תנאותיהן חוץ מקרבן עולה ויורד המפורש בו בלבד וזה שהוצרכתי לפרש דבר זה לפי שראיתיו מסובך אצל כל התלמידים וביארתיו כדי שיתגלה ויתברר: **אימור** דאמרי' אתי עשה ודחי לא תעשה לא תעשה גרידא לא תעשה ועשה מי דחי לא תעשה גרידא הוא לא תעשה הכי יחיד א) שאין עמו כרת כמו (דברים כה) לא תחסום שור בדישו (שם כב) לא תחרוש בשור ובחמור (ויקרא יט) לא תקיפו פאת ראשכם ודומה להם ויתוסף עם זה מה שנאמר במבטא השמר פן ואל כגון (דברים כד) השמר בנגע הצרעת (שמות לד) פן תכרת ברית ליושב הארץ (שם טז) אל יצא איש ממקומו גם הן אזהרות לאו ומי שיעבר עליהם עובר על לא תעשה כמו שאמרו בתלמוד (עירובין דף צו וש"נ) השמר פן ואל אינו אלא לשון לא תעשה ומה שנמצא בתורה ממצות לא תעשה מה שאין בו כרת ולא מיתת בית דין ולא ניתוסף עליו עשה אותו דבר הוא הנקרא לאו גרידא ודינו שכשאירע עם מצות עשה במקום אחד נקיים מצות עשה ולא נחוש לאזהרות לאו ועיקר זה מצוי במסכת יבמות בפ' א' (דף ג) וכן אמרו שם אימור דאמרי'

חשק שלמה על רב נסים גאון א) נ"ל לא תעשה יחידי שאין עמו כרת:

BAHERES spot **IS THERE** on the foreskin, you may perform the circumcision.[17]

The Gemara now analyzes the Baraisa:

אָמַר רָבָא – Rava[18] **said: הָאי תַּנָּא מֵעִיקָּרָא מַאי נִיחָא לֵיהּ – Why to this Tanna was it originally appropriate** to interpret the *milah* verse literally[19] and the *tzaraas* verse loosely,[20] **וּלְבַסּוֹף מַאי קַשְׁיָא לֵיהּ – and in the end**[21] **what was difficult to him** about his initial reasoning?

Rava explains the Tanna's thinking:

הָכִי קָאָמַר – [The Tanna] was saying thus: ,,יִמּוֹל בְּשַׂר עָרְלָתוֹ" – *The flesh of his foreskin shall be circumcised* teaches that the foreskin is cut off in all cases – **וְאַף עַל פִּי שֶׁיֵּשׁ בַּהֶרֶת** – i.e. **and even though there is** a ***baheres*** spot on it. **וּמָה אֲנִי מְקַיֵּים ,,הִשָּׁמֶר בְּנֶגַע הַצָּרַעַת" – And how do I establish *Take heed concerning the affliction of tzaraas*? בִּשְׁאָר מְקוֹמוֹת חוּץ מִמִּילָה** – That verse applies **in all other places besides circumcision. אֲבָל מִילָה דּוֹחָה אֶת הַצָּרַעַת – However, circumcision overrides the *tzaraas*** prohibition. **מַאי טַעְמָא – What is the reason? דְּאַתְיָא מִקַּל וָחוֹמֶר – Because it is derived from a *kal vachomer*** argument, as follows: **וּמָה שַׁבָּת חֲמוּרָה – Since Sabbath** law **is** more **stringent** than *tzaraas* law[22] **מִילָה דּוֹחָה אוֹתָהּ** – and nevertheless the mitzvah of **circumcision overrides it,**[23] **צָרַעַת לֹא כָּל שֶׁכֵּן – should** circumcision, **not certainly** override the ***tzaraas*** prohibition?!

Rava now explains why the Tanna changed his mind:

וּמַאי אוֹ אֵינוֹ דְּקָאָמַר – And what is the explanation for **[the Tanna] stating, "OR,** indeed, **IT IS NOT** so," which implies that he was reversing himself and now maintains that *milah is* included in the prohibition against cutting off *tzaraas*? What difficulty forced the Tanna to retract?

Rava answers:

הָדַר קָאָמַר – [The Tanna] subsequently said to himself: **מִמַּאי דְּשַׁבָּת חֲמִירָא – From what** proof do we know **that Sabbath** law **is** more **stringent** than the *tzaraas* prohibition?[24] **דִּילְמָא צָרַעַת חֲמִירָא – Perhaps** the ***tzaraas*** prohibition **is more stringent, שֶׁכֵּן דּוֹחָה אֶת הָעֲבוֹדָה – for indeed it overrides the** sacrificial **service וַעֲבוֹדָה דּוֹחָה אֶת הַשַּׁבָּת – and the** sacrificial **service** in turn **overrides the Sabbath.**[25] If so, the *kal vachomer* argument is undermined. **תַּלְמוּד לוֹמַר ,,בָּשָׂר"** – To preclude such a conclusion **the Torah states, *the flesh*** – an extraneous word that teaches: **וְאַף עַל פִּי שֶׁיֵּשׁ שָׁם בַּהֶרֶת – And even though** a ***baheres*** spot **is there** on the foreskin and will inevitably be cut off, you may nonetheless perform the circumcision.

The Gemara presents a different interpretation of the Tanna's thinking:

לִישָּׁנָא אַחֲרִינָא – Another version[26] of the Gemara's elucidation of the Baraisa: **מִילָה דּוֹחָה אֶת הַצָּרַעַת** – The Tanna initially derived from the verse, *the flesh of his foreskin shall be circumcised,* that **circumcision overrides the *tzaraas*** prohibition. **מַאי טַעְמָא – What is the reason? דְּאָתֵי עֲשֵׂה וְדָחֵי לֹא תַעֲשֶׂה – Because the positive commandment** of *milah* **comes and overrides the negative commandment** against cutting off *tzaraas* (*Take heed concerning the affliction of tzaraas*).[27] **וּמַאי אוֹ אֵינוֹ דְּקָאָמַר – And what is** the explanation for **[the Tanna] stating, "OR,** indeed, **IT IS NOT** so," which implies a retraction? **אֵימַר הָדַר קָאָמַר – [The Tanna] subsequently said** to himself: **דְּאַמְרִינַן דְּאָתֵי עֲשֵׂה וְדָחֵי אֶת לֹא תַעֲשֶׂה – One could say that we say that a positive commandment comes and overrides a negative commandment לֹא תַעֲשֶׂה גְּרֵידָא** – when the former conflicts with **only a negative commandment. הַאי עֲשֵׂה וְלֹא תַעֲשֶׂה הוּא** – However, **this is** a case of a positive commandment in conflict with another **positive commandment and a negative commandment.**[28] Under these circumstances the two positive commandments offset one another; accordingly, *milah* cannot override the *tzaraas* prohibition.[29] **וּמָה אֲנִי מְקַיֵּים ,,יִמּוֹל בְּשַׂר עָרְלָתוֹ" – And how,** then, **do I establish *the flesh of his foreskin shall be circumcised*? בִּזְמַן שֶׁאֵין בָּהּ בַּהֶרֶת** – That verse applies only **at a time when there is no *baheres*** spot **on [the foreskin]. תַּלְמוּד לוֹמַר ,,בָּשָׂר"** – To preclude this conclusion

NOTES

17. The word בָּשָׂר, *flesh,* in *Leviticus* 12:3 is extraneous, since the Torah could have stated simply, "And on the eighth day his foreskin shall be circumcised." *Flesh* is therefore available to teach that *milah* overrides the *tzaraas* prohibition (*Ritva MHK* ed.; see also *Rashi*).

18. See *Tosafos* ד״ה הדר, who emend this to "Rabbah." See also note 40 below.

19. As sanctioning *milah* even when it involves cutting off a *tzaraas* spot.

20. As not including *milah* in the prohibition.

21. When the Tanna reversed his thinking and interpreted the *milah* verse loosely (as applying only when there is no *tzaraas*) and the *tzaraas* verse literally (as prohibiting also *milah*).

22. For it contains many penalties and prohibitions [as the Gemara mentioned above] (*Ritva MHK* ed.).

23. R' Yochanan derived this from *on the . . . day* (above, 132a, where the Gemara also expressed its preference for his exegesis).

24. The Tanna's *kal vachomer* was predicated on the premise that the law of Shabbos is more stringent than that of *tzaraas,* for its point was that since *milah* can override the Sabbath, it can certainly override the less stringent *tzaraas* prohibition.

25. Although the Gemara explained above that the Tanna of the previous Baraisa reversed himself on the grounds that the law of Shabbos is more stringent than that of *tzaraas* (for it contains many penalties and prohibitions), that statement was not a firm conclusion. Rather, from the two Baraisos together we see that there are arguments on either side as to whether Shabbos or *tzaraas* is more stringent. And, in fact, the Tanna of each Baraisa was ultimately compelled to cite a verse to resolve the issue of *milah's* power to override each prohibition (*Tos. HaRosh*).

26. In the texts of *Ramban* and *Ran MHK* ed. the words לִישָּׁנָא אַחֲרִינָא (*another version*) do not appear. Accordingly, they understand that the Gemara has until now been speaking of an eighth-day *milah,* and now begins to speak of a deferred *milah.* However, in the texts of *Ritva* and *Rashba* (and, it would appear, *Rashi*), the words do appear. See there for an explanation of how the law of overriding is derived for a deferred *milah* according to the first version, where the scriptural proof concerns only an eighth-day *milah.*

27. Reish Lakish teaches (below, 133a; *Nazir* 41a, 58a; see *Yevamos* 3b-6b) that when a positive commandment and a prohibition are in conflict, if some way can be found to fulfill the former without violating the latter, that way must be pursued. But if fulfilling the positive commandment necessarily involves violating the prohibition, then one must perform the positive commandment.

28. *Deuteronomy* 24:8 states in full: *Take heed concerning the tzaraas affliction* [this is the prohibition against cutting off *tzaraas*], *to be very careful and to act; according to everything that the Kohanim, the Levites, shall teach you – as I have commanded them – you shall be careful to perform* [this is a positive commandment to follow the Kohen's directions during the verification-of-*tzaraas* procedure; see *Leviticus* ch. 13] (*Rashi, Ritva MHK* ed.).

29. *Rashba* asks how the Tanna could have initially thought that it did. [Since both are positive commandments, why would one be stronger than the other?!] He explains that the Tanna had viewed *milah* as the stronger positive commandment because it carries the penalty of *kares* (excision) for its non-fulfillment, and because thirteen covenants were made over it (see above, 132a note 7). For this reason the Tanna originally thought that *milah* overrode the positive commandment of *tzaraas* [as well as its prohibition]. (See *Rashba* for other examples of one positive commandment potentially superseding another, and see *Ritva MHK* ed. for a different answer to the question.)

ועבודה דוחה את השבת מילה דוחה אותה שבת שנדחית מפני העבודה אינו דין שתהא מילה דוחה אותה ומאי או אינו דקאמר הדר אמר וממאי דצרעת חמורה דילמא שבת חמורה שכן יש בה עונשין ואזהרות הרבה (א אי נמי) וממאי משום דחמירא צרעת היא דילמא משום גברא הוא דלא חזי ומה אני מקיים א) שמיני ימול חוץ משבת • תלמוד לומר א) ביום אפילו בשבת: תנו רבנן א מילה דוחה את הצרעת בין בזמנה בין שלא בזמנה ב יום טוב אינה דוחה אלא בזמנה בלבד מנהני מילי דתנו רבנן א) ימול בשר ערלתו • ואע"פ שיש שם בהרת יקוץ ומה אני מקיים ב) השמר בנגע הצרעת בשאר מקומות חוץ ממילה או אינו אלא אפילו מילה ומה אני מקיים ימול בשר ערלתו בזמן שאין בה בהרת ת"ל בשר ואע"פ שיש שם בהרת אמר רבא האי תנא מעיקרא מאי ניחא ליה ולבסוף מאי קשיא ליה הכי קאמר ימול בשר ערלתו ואע"פ שיש בהרת ומה אני מקיים השמר בנגע הצרעת בשאר מקומות חוץ ממילה אבל מילה דוחה את הצרעת מ"ט דאתיא מק"ו ומה שבת חמורה מילה דוחה אותה צרעת לא כ"ש ומאי או אינו דקאמר הדר קאמר ממאי דשבת חמירא דילמא צרעת חמירא שכן דוחה את העבודה ועבודה דוחה את השבת ת"ל בשר ואע"פ שיש שם בהרת לישנא אחרינא מילה דוחה את הצרעת מ"ט דאתי עשה ודחי לא תעשה ומאי או אינו דקאמר הדר קאמר אימר דאמרינן דאתי עשה ודחי את לא תעשה לא תעשה גרידא האי עשה ולא תעשה הוא ומה אני מקיים ימול בשר ערלתו בזמן שאין בה בהרת ת"ל בשר ואע"פ שיש שם בהרת תינח גדול דכתיב בהו ג) בשר קטן נמי כתיב ביה א) בשר בינוני מנלן אמר אביי אתיא מבינייא מגדול לא אתיא שכן ענוש כרת מקטן לא אתיא שכן מילה בזמנה הצד השוה שבהן שכן נימולין ודוחין את הצרעת אף כל שנימולין דוחין את הצרעת רבא אמר מילה בזמנה דוחה לא צריכא קרא מק"ו אתיא ומה שבת דחמירא דוחה צרעת לא כל שכן אמר ליה רב ספרא לרבא ממאי דשבת חמירא דילמא צרעת חמירא שכן דוחה את העבודה ועבודה דוחה את השבת התם לאו משום דחמירא צרעת אלא משום דגברא הוא דלא חזי אמאי ויקוץ בהרתו ויעבוד מחוסר טבילה הוא תינח נגעים טמאים ג) טהורים מאי איכא למימר אלא א"ר אשי ג) היכא אמרינן דאתי עשה ודחי ל"ת כגון מילה בצרעת א"נ ציצית וכלאים דבעידנא דמתעקר לאו קא מוקי' עשה הכא בעידנא דמתעקר ללאו לא קא מוקים עשה והא דרבא ורב ספרא תנאי

רש"י

ועבודה. תמורה היא שדוחה שבת בתמידין ומוספין וקרבנות צבור שזמנם קבוע: מילה דוחה אותה. את הצרעת כדתניא לקמן ימול בשר ערלתו אפילו במקום בהרת יקוץ: ומה או אינו דקאמר. דמשמע או אינו כן כמו שאמרנו אלא אפי' מילה נמי בכלל השמר. מאי קשיא ליה דקא הדר ביה: הדר אמר תנא. לנפשיה ממאי דצרעת חמורה משבת דקיימא ק"ו: דילמא שבת חמורה כו'. דהאי דצרעת דוחה עבודה ממאי משום חומרא דצרעת היא דילמא הא דלא אמרינן ליה יקוץ משום דגברא דלא חזי הוא כדלקמן דאי נמי קייץ מחוסר טבילה והערב שמש והיום לא יעבוד (א) וטבול יום דמצורע כמצורע הילכך מחללה מות יומת אפילו במילה ועל כרחך שמיני ימול תדחה אלא שאר ימים: בין שלא בזמנה. כגון קטן חולה והמתינו לו עד שיבריא: בשר. ריבויא הוא ולדרשה: ה"ג לא מאי טעמא אתי עשה ודחי לא תעשה. מ"ט מילה דוחה צרעת דהאי עשה דימול ודחי לא תעשה דהשמר (ב) לך דהכי ק"ל בפ"ק דיבמות (דף ג:) דאתי עשה ודחי לא תעשה: האי עשה ולא תעשה הוא. השמר לא תעשה הוא ולעשות ככל אשר יורו (דברים כד) היינו עשה: תינח גדול. בר עונשין דכתיב ביה בשר וערל זכר אשר לא ימול את בשר ערלתו (בראשית יז) והאי בבר עונשין משתעי מדמחייב ליה כרת וקטן נמי בזמנה ביום השמיני כתיב ביה בשר וביום השמיני ימול בשר ערלתו: בינוני. כגון שלא בזמנה ולאו בר עונשין ואביו מצווה עליו דנפקא לן מהמול לכם כל זכר (קדושין דף כט.): אתיא מבינייא. הלך הפוכה שבהן שנימולין ודוחין את הצרעת אף אביא בינוני שנימול ודחה הצרעת: לא צריכא קרא כו'. וכי אתיא קרא לשלא בזמנה של בינוני: דגברא לא חזי. קס"ד מפני שהוא טמא והיינו דפריך ויקוץ ויטהר ויעבוד: מחוסר טבילה. ומשום למחר דליתא לעבודה דההיא יומא לא מדחי: נגעים טהורין. כגון בהק ופרחה בכוליה וכולהו איתרבו לאיסור קצילה בספרי אין לי אלא משנזקק לטומאה עד שלא נזקק לטומאה מניין ת"ל ככל אשר יורו: אלא אמר רב אשי. הא דאמרינן שבת חמירא מצרעת אע"ג דדחייה צרעת לעבודה לאו חומרא דידה הוא אלא היינו טעמא כי אמרינן אתי עשה ודחי לא תעשה כגון מילה בצרעת דבשעת קצילה דמיעקר לאו מקיים עשה וכן ציצית דכלאים בשעת לבישה מיעקר לאו ומקיים עשה אבל צרעת הנקצצת משום עבודה בעידנא דמיעקר לאו דקצילה אכתי לא מקיים עשה דעבודה הילכך מידחיא עבודה ממילה ולאו חומרא דצרעת הוא: תנאי.

תוספות

בטומאה אלמא דצרעת דוחה את העבודה נימא דהיינו כל זמן שהיא עליו ובק"ו נילף שיקוץ בהרתו כדי לעשות עבודה ועוד קשה לימא רציחה תוכיח שדוחה את העבודה ואינו דוחה שבת אף אני אביא מילה וכי תימא מילה עדיפא שדוחה צרעת הדוחה את העבודה אכתי נימא קבורת מת מצוה תוכיח דעדיפא ממילה שדוחה את המילה מולאחותו הדוחה את הצרעת הדוחה את העבודה הדוחה את השבת אפילו הכי לא דחיא שבת ויש לומר דהכי נמי הוה מצי למימר איפכא ורציחה תוכיח או קבורת מת מצוה תוכיח אלא דניחא ליה לומר שיהא דוחה דנפקא ליה מביום דמילה דחיא שבת ועושה מתחילה ק"ו להעמיד דבריו וסותרו אחר כך שאינו ק"ו כלל ד) ופריך ליה מיניה וביה: הדר אמר ממאי דשבת חמירא דילמא צרעת חמירא. תימה דבברייתא דלעיל מסיק איפכא דלאו משום דצרעת חמירא אלא משום (ג) גברא דלא חזי ורבא גופיה סבירא ליה הכי לקמן ועוד למאי דקאמר השתא מנלן דצרעת דוחה את העבודה אימא דעבודה דוחה הצרעת מק"ו ומה שבת חמורה [צרעת לא כ"ש ואומר ר"י דלהאי לישנא] צריך לומר דגרסינן רבה הכא ולית ליה דרבא דלקמן דטעמא משום דגברא לא חזי וסבירא ליה כרב ספרא דפליג עליה דרבא לקמן והא דפשיט להו לרבה ורב ספרא דצרעת דוחה עבודה מצי למימר דמקרא נפקא להו אבל רבא דס"ל גברא לא חזי לדידיה לא בעי קרא ועוד נראה לרשב"א ה) דאפי' ליכא קרא דצרעת דוחה עבודה אתי שפיר אפילו לרב ספרא דלא קאמר רב ספרא שיהא הטעם ודאי דצרעת דוחה עבודה משום חומרא דצרעת אלא איכא למימר הכי ואיכא למימר הכי הילכך בברייתא דלעיל סתר ק"ו דקאמר וממאי דצרעת חמירא דילמא משום גברא דלא חזי והכא ולקמן על מילתא דרבא דחינן בע"א ממאי דשבת חמירא דילמא צרעת חמירא שכן דוחה את העבודה וח"ל הכא קא מדחי ליה וח"ל הכא קא מדחי ליה ומהאי טעמא נמי ליכא למילף ביה ק"ו דעבודה תדחי צרעת דשבת דחמורה דוחה צרעת לא כ"ש דדילמא אין לתלות משום חומרא אלא משום (ג) גברא לא חזי: האי עשה ולא תעשה הוא. השמר היינו לאו ולעשות היינו עשה כדפי' בקונטרס ואע"ג דאמר בסוף פרק הקומץ (מנחות דף לו:) השמר דלאו לאו השמר דעשה עשה מכל מקום לאו מצות עשה הוא אלא לא תעשה ו) דאמר רחמנא הזהר פן תקוץ בהרת תימה היכי מצינן למימר דלעשות אתא לעשה הא אמר לקמן דאיצטריך לעשות אי אתה עושה אבל אתה עושה בסיב שעל גבי רגלו ויש לפרש דעשה שמעינן מדכתיב ז) לשמור ואם תאמר והא אמר בסמוך היכא אמרינן דאתי עשה ודחי את לא תעשה כגון מילה בצרעת אלמא דליכא בצרעת אלא לאו וא"ר"ת דלא נקטינן אלא לסימנא בעלמא ואם תאמר והא דקי"ל דאין עשה דוחה את לא תעשה ועשה נגמר ממילה בצרעת דדחי וי"ל מה למילה • שכן נכרתו עליה י"ג בריתות: רבא אמר מילה בזמנה לא צריכא קרא. והילכך האי דכתיב בה אם אינו ענין לזמנה תנהו ענין לשלא בזמנה ואו אינו דקתני הוה מפרש רבה כלישנא אחרינא: ולאביי

עין משפט נר מצוה

ח א מיי' פ"א מהל' מילה הלכה ט ופ"י מהל' טומאת צרעת הלכה ה סמג עשין כח וטוש"ע י"ד סי' רסו סעיף ב: ט ב מיי' פ"א מהלכות מילה שם סמג שם טוש"ע שם סעיף ג:

גליון הש"ס

גמ' ת"ל ביום אפי' בשבת. עיין חולין דף פד ע"ב בתוס' ד"ה שולפו וצ"ע: שם ואע"פ שיש שם בהרת. עיין ברש"י רפ"ק דמלה: תוס' ד"ה האי וכו' שכן נכרתו עליה י"ג בריתות. עי' יבמות ה' ע"א תוס' ד"ה שכן:

תורה אור השלם

א) וּבַיּוֹם הַשְּׁמִינִי יִמּוֹל בְּשַׂר עָרְלָתוֹ: [ויקרא יב, ג]

ב) הִשָּׁמֶר בְּנֶגַע הַצָּרַעַת לִשְׁמֹר מְאֹד וְלַעֲשׂוֹת כְּכֹל אֲשֶׁר יוֹרוּ אֶתְכֶם הַכֹּהֲנִים הַלְוִיִּם כַּאֲשֶׁר צִוִּיתִם תִּשְׁמְרוּ לַעֲשׂוֹת: [דברים כד, ח]

ג) וְעָרֵל זָכָר אֲשֶׁר לֹא יִמּוֹל אֶת בְּשַׂר עָרְלָתוֹ וְנִכְרְתָה הַנֶּפֶשׁ הַהִוא מֵעַמֶּיהָ אֶת בְּרִיתִי הֵפַר: [בראשית יז, יד]

רבינו חננאל

ת"ר מילה דוחה צרעת בין בזמנה בין שלא בזמנה. פי' כתיב בצרעת השמר בנגע הצרעת ואמרו חכמים כ"מ שנאמר השמר פן ואל אינו אלא בל"ת. כלומר השמר אזהרה הוא שלא לעשות וכיון שנאמר השמר הנה הזהיר שלא לחתוך הצרעת (מכל מקום) [בכל מקום] שהיא והתיר במילה אם יש צרעת בערלה מותר לו לחתוך הערלה והצרעת עמה בין ביום השמיני שהוא זמן המילה כדכתיב וביום השמיני ימול בשר ערלתו. בין אירע לו אונס כגון חולי לקטן וכדומה לו ולא מל בשמיני חייב לימול כל זמן שיסור האונס והיא הנקראת מילה שלא בזמנה כלומר שאינה ביום השמיני וגם במילה שאינה ביום השמיני יש למל לחתוך הערלה אע"פ שיש בה צרעת והתורה שהזהירה שלא לחתוך הצרעת לגבי מילה התירה. ובאנו לברר זה הפי' שפירשנו מזו הברייתא. דת"ר ימול בשר ערלתו ואע"פ שיש שם בהרת ומה אני מקיים השמר בנגע הצרעת בשאר מקומות חוץ ממילה או אינו אלא אפי' מילה ומה אני מקיים ימול בשר ערלתו בזמן שאין שם בהרת ת"ל בשר אע"פ שיש שם בהרת לא תעשה בצרעת שנאמר השמר פן עשה שנא' ולעשות ופשוטה היא תינח גדול כתיב ביה בשר שנאמר וערל זכר אשר לא ימול את בשר ערלתו ונכרתה הנפש ההיא מעמיה את בריתי הפר. מדכתיב ונכרתה שמעינן מינה שהוא גדול ואם לא מל אותו אביו ונשאר ערל וגדל חייב למול עצמו קטן נמי כתיב ביה בשר [illegible]

מסורת הש"ס

[illegible]

הגהות הב"ח

(א) רש"י ד"ה דילמא שבת וכו' וטבול יום: (ב) ד"ה ה"ג וכו' דהשמר דהכי כצ"ל ותיבת לך נמחק: (ג) תוס' ד"ה הדר וכו' אלא משום דגברא:

ליקוטי רש"י

[illegible]

רב נסים גאון

[illegible]

[illegible]

חשק שלמה על רב נסים גאון [illegible]

the Torah states, ***the flesh,*** which teaches: וְאַף עַל פִּי שֶׁיֵּשׁ שָׁם בַּהֶרֶת – **And even though a** ***baheres*** spot **is there** on the foreskin and will inevitably be cut off, you may perform the circumcision.

According to both interpretations of the Baraisa, the Tanna derives that *milah* overrides the *tzaraas* prohibition from the extraneous word *flesh.* The Gemara therefore asks:

תֵּינַח גָּדוֹל – That exegesis is indeed **appropriate** for the category of uncircumcised **adult,**[30] דִּכְתִיב בְּהוּ ,,בָּשָׂר" – **for** the word ***flesh*** **is written** superfluously **with regard to them.**[31] קָטָן נַמִּי כְּתִיב בֵּיהּ ,,בָּשָׂר" – **With regard to an** eight-day-old **infant as well,** the word ***flesh*** **is written.**[32] בֵּינוֹנִי מְנָלַן – However, **from where** do **we** derive that the *tzaraas* of a child in the **middle** category[33] may likewise be cut off during the course of circumcision?

The Gemara answers:

אָמַר אַבַּיֵי – **Abaye said:** אַתְיָא מִבֵּינַיָא – **It is derived from the two [other categories]** through a "common feature" exegesis, as follows: מִגָּדוֹל לֹא אַתְיָא – **[The middle category] cannot be derived** directly **from** the case of **a** legal **adult,**[34] שֶׁכֵּן עָנוּשׁ כָּרֵת – **for indeed** an adult who dies uncircumcised **is punished** with **excision.** Since the case of an uncircumcised minor lacks this stringency, the law of overriding (the *tzaraas* prohibition) cannot be inferred to it through a *mah matzinu.* מִקָּטָן לֹא אַתְיָא – Further, **[the middle category] cannot be derived** directly **from** the case of **an** eight-day-old **infant,**[34] שֶׁכֵּן מִילָה בִּזְמַנָּהּ – **for indeed** that case involves **circumcision at its** proper **time.** Since the middle category lacks this significance, we cannot infer that it, too, overrides the *tzaraas* prohibition. הַצַּד הַשָּׁוֶה שֶׁבָּהֶן – Rather, **the feature common to** both of **them** [the adult and the eight-day-old] שֶׁכֵּן נִימּוֹלִין וְדוֹחִין אֶת הַצָּרַעַת – **is that they are indeed** subject to be **circumcised and [their circumcisions] override the** ***tzaraas*** prohibition. אַף כֹּל שֶׁנִּימּוֹלִין דּוֹחִין אֶת הַצָּרַעַת – So **too,** in the case of **all** others **who are** subject to be **circumcised,**[35] **[their circumcisions] override the** ***tzaraas*** prohibition.

The Gemara offers a different interpretation of the Baraisa's exegesis of the extraneous word *flesh*:

רָבָא אָמַר – **Rava said:** מִילָה בִּזְמַנָּהּ דּוֹחָה לֹא צְרִיכָא קְרָא – To establish that **circumcision at its** proper **time overrides** the *tzaraas* prohibition **does not require a** superfluous **verse,**[36] מִקַּל וָחוֹמֶר אַתְיָא – for indeed **[that law] is derived via a** ***kal vachomer*** argument,[37] as follows: וּמַה שַּׁבָּת דַּחֲמִירָא דּוֹחָה – **Since Sabbath** law **is** more **stringent** than *tzaraas* law[38] – and nevertheless the mitzvah of **[circumcision at its proper time] overrides** it,[39] צָרַעַת לֹא כָּל שֶׁכֵּן – **shouldn't** that category of *milah* **certainly** override the weaker ***tzaraas*** prohibition?![40]

Rava's exegesis is challenged:

אָמַר לֵיהּ רַב סַפְרָא לְרָבָא – **Rav Safra said to Rava:** מִמַּאי דְּשַׁבָּת חֲמִירָא – **From what** proof do we know **that Sabbath** law **is** more **stringent** than the *tzaraas* prohibition, which is the very premise of your *kal vachomer*? דִּילְמָא צָרַעַת חֲמִירָא – **Perhaps** the ***tzaraas*** prohibition **is** more **stringent,** שֶׁכֵּן דּוֹחָה אֶת הָעֲבוֹדָה – **for indeed it overrides the** sacrificial **service**[41] וַעֲבוֹדָה דּוֹחָה אֶת הַשַּׁבָּת – **and the** sacrificial **service overrides the Sabbath.**[42] Hence, your *kal vachomer* argument is undermined.[43] – ? –

Rava responds:

הָתָם – Your point **there,** that *tzaraas* law overrides the sacrificial service, לַאו מִשּׁוּם דַּחֲמִירָא צָרַעַת – **is not because** ***tzaraas*** law **is** inherently more **stringent** than the service, אֶלָּא מִשּׁוּם דְּגַבְרָא הוּא דְּלָא חֲזֵי – **but because [the Kohen] is not a** ritually **fit person.** Hence, you have no proof that *tzaraas* law is inherently more stringent than Sabbath law.

Rav Safra understood Rava to mean that the Kohen is rendered

NOTES

30. I.e. males age thirteen or older, who are subject to the punishments of the Torah (*Rashi*).

31. *Genesis* 17:14 states: וְעָרֵל זָכָר אֲשֶׁר לֹא־יִמּוֹל אֶת־בְּשַׂר עָרְלָתוֹ וְנִכְרְתָה הַנֶּפֶשׁ הַהִוא מֵעַמֶּיהָ, *An uncircumcised male the flesh of whose foreskin will not be circumcised – that soul shall be cut off from its people.* Inasmuch as the verse prescribes the punishment of *kares,* it perforce speaks of a legal "adult." Inclusion of the extraneous *flesh* in the verse thus indicates that an adult's circumcision overrides the *tzaraas* prohibition (*Rashi*). [Even though the Gemara has until now been expounding *Leviticus* 12:3, the word *flesh* in *Genesis* 17:14 is also extraneous, and the same exegesis (see note 17 above) can be made there as well.]

32. *Leviticus* 12:3 states: וּבַיּוֹם הַשְּׁמִינִי יִמּוֹל בְּשַׂר עָרְלָתוֹ, *On the eighth day the flesh of his foreskin shall be circumcised.* Here the superfluous word *flesh* also teaches that a *milah* performed at its proper time (the eighth day) likewise overrides the *tzaraas* prohibition (*Rashi*).

33. I.e. a minor whose circumcision occurs after the eighth day. Since he is not liable to punishment, he is not included in *Genesis* 17:14 (see note 31 above); and the verses that do obligate first his father and then the community to circumcise him (*Genesis* 21:4 and 17:10, respectively – see *Kiddushin* 29a) do not contain an extraneous word (*flesh*) (*Rashi*).

34. I.e. through a *mah matzinu* derivation.

35. I.e. minors whose circumcision occurs after the eighth day – the middle category.

36. I.e. the word *flesh* in *On the eighth day the flesh of his foreskin shall be circumcised* (*Leviticus* 12:3).

37. Hence, *Leviticus* 12:3 is free to teach that the delayed *milah* of a minor (the middle category) also overrides the *tzaraas* prohibition, thereby obviating the need for a "common feature" exegesis (see *Rashi,* et al.).

Tosafos explain that Rava is employing here the "if it has no application" (אִם אֵינוֹ עִנְיָן) rule of interpretation, which states that if a verse cannot be explained as referring to its own subject matter (because of a difficulty or redundancy), it may be explained as referring to a related matter. Here, although *Leviticus* 12:3 specifies the *milah* of an eight-day-old, its teaching is not needed for that category (since the law of overriding *tzaraas* is derived there through a *kal vachomer*). Hence, we may explain that the verse extends the law of overriding *tzaraas* to the middle category of *milah.* See also note 40 below.

38. See note 22 above.

39. See note 23 above.

40. Rava perforce subscribes to the second version of the Gemara's elucidation of the Baraisa, inasmuch as in the first version the Tanna concludes that *tzaraas* is more stringent than *milah* (*Tosafos, Rashba,* second explanation in *Ramban;* see also note 18 above; cf. *Ran* [*MHK* ed.] and first explanation in *Ramban*).

41. See above, 132a note 53.

42. See note 1 above.

43. *Rashba* notes that if the law of *tzaraas* is more stringent than Sabbath law, one could derive through a *kal vachomer* that *milah* at its proper time overrides the Sabbath restrictions, as follows: Since *milah* overrides the *tzaraas* prohibition, it certainly overrides the weaker Sabbath restrictions. Hence, R' Yochanan's verse (*on the . . . day*) is free to teach that the *preliminaries* to *milah* also override the Sabbath. It would seem, then, that this is Rav Safra's position, for he contends that *tzaraas* law is more stringent than Sabbath law. But how, asks *Rashba,* can Rav Safra reject the view of the Rabbis (who hold that *milah's* preliminaries *do not* override the Sabbath) and embrace the view of R' Eliezer (who holds that they do)? *Rashba* thus explains that Rav Safra does not actually maintain that *tzaraas* law is more stringent than Sabbath law. Rather, he is suggesting that position for the sole purpose of attempting to rebut Rava's *kal vachomer* (see also *Tosafos* and *Ritva MHK* ed.).

עין משפט נר מצוה

ח א מיי' פ"א מהל' מילה הלכה ט ופ"י מהל' טומאת צרעת הלכה ה סמג עשין שם טוש"ע י"ד סי' רסו סעיף ח:

ט ב מיי' פ"א מהלכות מילה שם סמג שם טוש"ע שם סעיף ב:

ועבודה דוחה את השבת מילה דוחה אותה שבת שנדחית מפני העבודה אינו דין שתהא מילה דוחה אותה ומאי או אינו דקאמר הדר אמר וממאי דצרעת חמורה דילמא שבת חמורה שכן יש בה עונשין ואזהרות הרבה (א) אי נמי) וממאי משום דחמירא צרעת היא דילמא משום גברא הוא דלא חזי ומה אני מקיים א) שמיני ימול חוץ משבת ת"ל לומר א) ביום אפילו בשבת: תנו רבנן א מילה דוחה את הצרעת בין בזמנה בין שלא בזמנה ב יום טוב אינה דוחה אלא בזמנה בלבד מנהני מילי דתנו רבנן א) ימול בשר ערלתו ואע"פ שיש שם בהרת יקוץ ומה אני מקיים ב) השמר בנגע הצרעת בשאר מקומות חוץ ממילה או אינו אלא אפילו מילה ומה אני מקיים ימול בשר ערלתו בזמן שאין בה בהרת ת"ל בשר ואע"פ שיש שם בהרת אמר רבא האי תנא מעיקרא מאי ניחא ליה ולבסוף מאי קשיא ליה הכי קאמר ימול בשר ערלתו ואע"פ שיש בהרת ומה אני מקיים השמר בנגע הצרעת בשאר מקומות חוץ ממילה אבל מילה דוחה את הצרעת מ"ט דאתיא מק"ו ומה שבת חמורה מילה דוחה אותה צרעת לא כ"ש ומאי או אינו דקאמר הדר קאמר ממאי דשבת חמירא דילמא צרעת חמירא שכן דוחה את העבודה ועבודה דוחה את השבת ת"ל בשר ואע"פ שיש שם בהרת לישנא אחרינא מילה דוחה את הצרעת מ"ט דאתי עשה ודחי לא תעשה ומאי או אינו דקאמר הדר קאמר אימר דאמרינן דאתי עשה ודחי את לא תעשה לא תעשה גרידא האי עשה ולא תעשה הוא ומה אני מקיים ימול בשר ערלתו בזמן שאין בה בהרת ת"ל בשר ואע"פ שיש שם בהרת תינח גדול דכתיב בהו ג) בשר קטן נמי כתיב ביה א) בשר ביוני מנלן אמר אביי אתיא מבינייא מגדול לא אתיא שכן ענוש כרת מקטן לא אתיא שכן מילה בזמנה הצד השוה שבהן שכן נימולין ודוחין את הצרעת אף כל שנימולין דוחין את הצרעת רבא אמר מילה בזמנה דוחה לא צריכא קרא מק"ו אתיא ומה שבת דחמירא דוחה צרעת לא כל שכן אמר ליה רב ספרא לרבא ממאי דשבת חמירא דילמא צרעת חמירא שכן דוחה את העבודה ועבודה דוחה את השבת התם לאו משום דחמירא צרעת אלא משום דגברא הוא דלא חזי אמאי ויקוץ בהרתו ויעבוד מחוסר טבילה הוא תינח נגעים טמאים ג) טהורים מאי איכא למימר אלא א"ר אשי ג) היכא אמרינן דאתי עשה ודחי ל"ת כגון מילה בצרעת א"נ ציצית וכלאים דבעידנא דמתעקר לאו קא מוקי' עשה הכא בעידנא דמתעקר ללאו לא קא מוקים עשה והא דרבא ורב ספרא תנאי

רש"י

ועבודה. חמורה היא שדוחה שבת בתמידין ומוספין וקרבנות לבור שזמנם קבוע: מילה דוחה אותה. את הצרעת כדתניא לקמן ימול בשר ערלתו אפילו במקום בהרת יקוץ: ומה או אינו דקאמר. דמשמע או אינו כן כמו שאמרנו אלא אפי' מילה נמי בכלל מחלליה מאי קשיא ליה דקא הדר ביה: הדר אמר תנא. לנפשיה ממאי דלרעת חמורה משבת דתימא ק"ו: דילמא שבת חמורה כו'. דהאי דלרעת דוחה עבודה ממאי דמשום חומרא דלרעת היא דילמא הא דלא אמרינן ליה יקוץ משום דגברא דלא חזי הוא כדלקמן דאי נמי קייץ מחוסר טבילה והערב שמש והיום לא יעבוד (א) וטבול יום דמלורע כמלורע הילכך מחלליה מות יומת אפילו במילה ועל כרחך שמיני ימול תדחה אלל שאר ימים: בין שלא בזמנה. כגון קטן חולה והמתינו לו עד שיבריא: בשר. ריבויא הוא ולדרשה: ה"ג ל"א מאי טעמא אתי עשה ודחי לא תעשה. מ"ט מילה דוחה לרעת דאתי עשה דימול ודחי לא תעשה דהשמר (ב) לך דהכי קי"ל בפ"ק דיבמות (דף ג:) דאתי עשה ודחי לא תעשה: האי עשה ולא תעשה הוא. השמר לאו הוא ולעשות ככל אשר יורו (דברים כד) היינו עשה: תינח גדול. בר עונשין דכתיב ביה בשר וערל זכר אשר לא ימול את בשר ערלתו (בראשית יז) והאי בבר עונשין משתעי מדמחייב ליה כרת וקטן נמי בזמנה ביום השמיני כתיב ביה בשר וביום השמיני ימול בשר ערלתו: ביוני. כגון שלא בזמנה ולאו בר עונשין ואביו מצווה עליו נפקא לן מהמול לכם כל זכר (קדושין דף כט.): אתיא מבינייא. הצד השוה שבהן שנימולו ודוחין את הצרעת אף אני אביא בינוני שנימול וידחה הצרעת: לא צריכא קרא כו'. וכי אתיא קרא לשלא בזמנה של בינוני: דגברא לא חזי. קס"ד מפני שהוא טמא והיינו דפריך ויקוץ ויטהר ויעבוד: מחוסר טבילה. ולא חזי לעבודה בהאי יומא ומשום למחר דליתא לעבודה קמן לא מדחי: נגעים טהורין. כגון בהק ופרחה בכוליה ובכולהו איתרבו לאיסור קציצה בסיפרי אין לי אלא משנזקק לטומאה עד שלא נזקק לטומאה מניין ת"ל ככל אשר יורו: אלא אמר רב אשי. הא דאמרינן שבת חמירא מצרעת אע"ג דדחייה צרעת לעבודה לאו חומרא דידה הוא אלא היינו טעמא כי אמרינן אתי עשה ודחי לא תעשה כגון מילה בצרעת דבשעת קציצה דמיעקר לאו מקיים עשה וכן ציצית דכלאים בשעת לבישה מיעקר לאו ומקיים עשה אבל צרעת הנקצצת משום עבודה בעידנא דמיעקר לאו דקציצה אכתי לא מקיים עשה דעבודה הילכך מידחיא עבודה ממילא ולאו חומרא דצרעת הוא: תנאי

תוספות

בטומאה אלמא דצרעת דוחה את העבודה נימא דהיינו כל זמן שהיא עליו ובק"ו נילף שיקוץ בהרתו כדי לעשות עבודה ועוד קשה לימא רציחה תוכיח שדוחה את העבודה ואינו דוחה שבת אף אני אביא מילה וכי תימא מילה עדיפא שדוחה צרעת הדוחה את העבודה אכתי נימא קבורת מת מצוה תוכיח דעדיפא ממילה שדוחה את המילה מולאחותו הדוחה את הצרעת הדוחה את העבודה הדוחה את השבת אפילו הכי לא דחיא שבת ויש לומר דהכי נמי הוה מצי למימר איפכא ורציחה תוכיח או קבורת מת מצוה תוכיח אלא דניחא ליה לומר שיהא דוחה דנפקא ליה מביום דמילה דחיא שבת ועושה מתחילה ק"ו להעמיד דבריו וסותרו אחר כך שאינו ק"ו כלל ד) ופריך ליה מיניה וביה: הדר אמר ממאי דשבת חמירא דילמא צרעת חמירא. תימה דבברייתא דלעיל מסיק איפכא דלאו משום דצרעת חמירא אלא משום (ג) גברא דלא חזי ורבא גופיה סבירא ליה הכי לקמן ועוד למאי דקאמר השתא מנלן דצרעת דוחה את העבודה אימא דעבודה דוחה צרעת מק"ו ומה שבת חמורה [צרעת לא כ"ש ולומר ר"י דלהאי לישנא] צריך לומר דגרסינן רבה הכא ולית ליה דרבא לקמן לטעמא משום דגברא לא חזי וסבירא ליה כרב ספרא דפליג עליה דרבא לקמן והא דפשיטא להו לרבה ורב ספרא דצרעת דוחה עבודה מצי למימר דמקרא נפקא להו אבל רבא דס"ל גברא לא חזי לדידיה בעי קרא ועוד נראה לר"י (ד) דאפי' ליכא קרא דצרעת דוחה עבודה אתי שפיר אפילו לרב ספרא דלא קאמר רב ספרא שיהא הטעם ודאי דצרעת דוחה עבודה משום חומרא דצרעת אלא איכא למימר הכי ואיכא למימר הכי הילכך בברייתא דלעיל סתר ק"ו דקאמר וממאי דצרעת חמירא דילמא משום גברא דלא חזי והכא ולקמן על מילתא דרבא דחינן בע"א ממאי דשבת חמירא דילמא צרעת חמירא שכן דוחה את העבודה וחיל הכא קא מדחי ליה וחיל הכא קא מדחי ליה ומהאי טעמא נמי ליכא למילף ביה ק"ו דעבודה תדחי צרעת דשבת דחמורה דוחה צרעת לא כ"ש דדילמא אין לתלות משום חומרא אלא משום (ג) גברא לא חזי: האי עשה ולא תעשה הוא. השמר היינו לאו ולעשות היינו עשה כדפי' בקונטרס ואע"ג דאמר בסוף פרק הקומץ (מנחות דף לו:) השמר דלאו לאו השמר דעשה עשה מכל מקום לאו מצות עשה הוא אלא לא תעשה ו) דאמר רחמנא הזהר פן תקוץ בהרת תימה היכי מצינן למימר דלעשות אתא לעשה הא אמר לקמן דאיצטריך לעשות אי אתה עושה אבל אתה עושה בסיב שעל גבי רגלו ויש לפרש דעשה שמעינן מדכתיב ז) לשמור ואם תאמר והא אמר בסמוך היכא אמרינן דאתי עשה ודחי את לא תעשה כגון מילה בצרעת אלמא דליכא בצרעת אלא לאו ואר"ת דלא נקטינן אלא לסימנא בעלמא ואם תאמר והא דקי"ל דאין עשה דוחה את לא תעשה ועשה נגמר ממילה בצרעת דדחי וי"ל מה למילה * שכן נכרתו עליה י"ג בריתות ח): רבא אמר מילה בזמנה לא צריכא קרא. והילכך האי בשר דכתיב בה אם אינו ענין לזמנה תנהו ענין לשלא בזמנה ואו אינו דקתני הוה מפרש רבא כלישנא אחרינא: ואביי

גליון הש"ס

גמ' ת"ל ביום אפי' בשבת. עיין חולין דף פד ע"ב ברש"י ד"ה שולאה ול"ע: שם ואע"פ שיש שם בהרת. עיין ברש"ם רפ"ב דמלה: תוס' ד"ה האי וכו' שכן נכרתו עליה י"ג בריתות. עי' יבמות ה' ע"א תוס' ד"ה שכן:

תורה אור השלם

א) וּבַיּוֹם הַשְּׁמִינִי יִמּוֹל בְּשַׂר עָרְלָתוֹ: [ויקרא יב, ג]

ב) הִשָּׁמֶר בְּנֶגַע הַצָּרַעַת לִשְׁמֹר מְאֹד וְלַעֲשׂוֹת כְּכֹל אֲשֶׁר יוֹרוּ אֶתְכֶם הַכֹּהֲנִים הַלְוִיִּם כַּאֲשֶׁר צִוִּיתִם תִּשְׁמְרוּ לַעֲשׂוֹת: [דברים כד, ח]

ג) וְעָרֵל זָכָר אֲשֶׁר לֹא יִמּוֹל אֶת בְּשַׂר עָרְלָתוֹ וְנִכְרְתָה הַנֶּפֶשׁ הַהִוא מֵעַמֶּיהָ אֶת בְּרִיתִי הֵפַר: [בראשית יז, יד]

רבינו חננאל

ת"ר מילה דוחה צרעת בין בזמנה בין שלא בזמנה. פי' כגון בהרת בנגע הצרעת ואמרו חכמים כ"מ שנאמר השמר פן ואל אינו אלא בל"ת. כלומר השמר אזהרה הוא שלא לעשות וכיון דכתיב השמר הנה הזהיר שלא לחתוך הצרעת (מכל מקום) [בכל מקום] שהיא והתיר במילה אם יש בערלה בהרת מותר לו לחתוך הערלה והצרעת עמה בין ביום השמיני ובין שלא בזמן המילה כדכתיב וביום השמיני ימול בשר ערלתו. בין אירע לו אונס כגון חולי לקטן וכדומה לו ולא מל בשמיני חייב לימול כל זמן שיסור ממנו החולי וזו היא הנקראת מילה שלא בזמנה כלומר שאינה ביום השמיני וגם במילה שאינה ביום השמיני יש למל לחתוך הערלה אע"פ שיש בה צרעת והתורה שהזהירה שלא לחתוך הצרעת לגבי זה המילה התירה. ובאנו לברר זה הפי' שפירשנו מזו הברייתא. דת"ר ימול בשר ערלתו ואע"פ שיש שם בהרת ומה אני מקיים השמר בנגע הצרעת בשאר מקומות חוץ ממילה או אינו אלא אפי' מילה ומה אני מקיים ימול בשר ערלתו בזמן שאין שם בהרת ת"ל בשר ואע"פ שיש שם בהרת לא תעשה בצרעת שנאמר השמר פן עשה שנא' ולעשות ופשוטה היא תינח גדול כתיב ביה בשר שנאמר וערל זכר אשר לא ימול את בשר ערלתו ונכרתה הנפש ההיא מעמיה את בריתי הפר. מדכתיב ונכרתה שמעינן מינה שהוא גדול ואם לא מל אותו אביו ונשאר ערל חייב למול את עצמו קטן נמי כתיב ביה בשר שנאמר וביום השמיני ימול בשר

הגהות הב"ח

(א) רש"י ד"ה דילמא שבת וכו' לא יעבוד וטבול יום: (ב) ד"ה ה"ג ל"א וכו' דהשמר הכי קי"ל ומיבעי לך נמחק: (ג) תוס' ד"ה הדר וכו' אלא משום דגברא:

ליקוטי רש"י

בין שלא בזמנה. כגון גר שנתגייר וקטן שנולד לאביו ולא מהלו [שבת סד.]. השמר בנגע הצרעת. ולמדנו בקוצץ בהרת שהוא לא תעשה והשמר הוא בבל תעשה [מכות כב.]. שלא תתלוש סימני טומאה ולא תקוץ את הבהרת [דברים כד, ח]. כגון מילה בצרעת. דכתיב (דברים כד) השמר בנגע הצרעת ומילה דוחה ימול בשר ערלתו אפילו במקום בהרת יקוץ אי נמי ציצית בכלאים (דברים כב) לא תלבש שעטנז וסמיך ליה גדילים תעשה לך דכשאתה מטיל ציצית לטלית מתעקר לאו ומקיים עשה [ביצה ח.].

רב נסים גאון

tamei by the *tzaraas,* and for that reason is prevented from serving.[44] He therefore asks:

אַמַּאי – Why should the Kohen be disqualified on account of *tumah?* **וְיָקוֹץ בַּהַרְתּוֹ וְיַעֲבוֹד – Let him cut off his *baheres*** spot **and** then **perform the service!**[45] That he does not do so is, perforce, because he *is forbidden* to cut off the *baheres.* Hence, the *tzaraas* prohibition *is* inherently more stringent than the sacrificial service, and so my argument persists and your *kal vachomer* is undermined. – ? –

Rava responds:

מְחוּסַּר טְבִילָה הוּא – Cutting off the *baheres* will not help, because **[the Kohen] is lacking immersion** in a *mikveh* and is even then disqualified for the remainder of the day.[46] Hence, you have no proof that *tzaraas* law is more stringent than Sabbath law.

Rav Safra persists:

תֵּינַח נְגָעִים טְמֵאִים – Your answer is **appropriate** for **impure afflictions** such as a *baheres* spot, which require immersion in a *mikveh* and waiting until evening before purification is achieved. **נְגָעִים טְהוֹרִים – But** in the case of **pure afflictions,**[47] which do not require immersion and waiting,[48] **מַאי אִיכָּא לְמֵימַר – what is there to say?** Perforce the Kohen does not cut them off and then serve because he is forbidden to do so,[49] and *tzaraas* law overrides the service. But according to you, Rava, let the positive commandment of performing the sacrificial service come and override the prohibition against cutting off all *tzaraas* afflictions![50] The fact that it does not indicates that the *tzaraas* prohibition *is* inherently more stringent than the sacrificial service, and so my argument persists and your *kal vachomer* is undermined. – ? –

The Gemara defuses Rav Safra's challenge:

אֶלָּא אָמַר רַב אַשִׁי – Rather, Rav Ashi said:[51] **הֵיכָא אַמְרִינַן דְּאָתֵי עֲשֵׂה וְדָחֵי לֹא תַעֲשֶׂה – Where do we say that a positive commandment comes and overrides a negative commandment?** **כְּגוֹן מִילָה בְּצָרַעַת** – It is, **for example,** in the case of **circumcision with *tzaraas*** present on the foreskin[52] – **אִי נַמִּי צִיצִית וְכִלְאַיִם** – and **alternatively,** in the case of ***tzitzis* and** the presence of ***kilayim***[53] – **דִּבְעִידָּנָא דְּמִתְעַקַּר לָאו קָא מוּקִים עֲשֵׂה** – **where at the** very **moment the negative commandment is violated one fulfills the positive commandment.**[54] **הָכָא בְּעִידָּנָא דְּמִתְעַקַּר לָלָאו** – **Here,** however, **at the moment the negative commandment** against cutting off *tzaraas* **is violated** **לֹא קָא מוּקִים עֲשֵׂה – [the Kohen] is not fulfilling the positive commandment** of performing the sacrificial service, since he cuts off the *tzaraas* as a preliminary to serving. Thus, the service cannot override *tzaraas;* Rava's *kal vachomer* is perforce resurrected.[55]

The Gemara comments:

וְהָא דְּרָבָא וְרַב סַפְרָא – And this dispute **of Rava and Rav Safra**

NOTES

44. *Rashi.*

45. And since he can do so, he is fit now for the service, and therefore must do so.

46. See note 6 above.

Rashash points out that the Kohen requires many other purification procedures, such as sprinklings and shavings (see *Leviticus* ch. 14). He suggests that the Gemara is speaking of a "confined" *metzora* (see *Megillah* 8b), who does not require any of these measures.

47. Such as *tzaraas* that covers the entire flesh (*Leviticus* 13:12-13), or faint white spots called *bohak* (ibid. v. 39). In either case the affliction does not contaminate the person (*Rashi*; cf. *Tosafos* to *Shevuos* 4a ד״ה בקוצץ and *Tos. Rid* here).

48. Nevertheless, the Kohen is disqualified for service as long as the pure afflictions remain, since he is a בַּעַל מוּם (*blemished*) [*Chidushei HaRan, Tos. HaRosh; see also Rashash*].

49. The Rabbis derived from *Deuteronomy* 24:8 (*according to everything that the Kohanim . . . shall teach you* – see note 28 above) that cutting off even the non-contaminating afflictions is forbidden (*Rashi* and *Chidushei HaRan;* see *Mishneh LaMelech* to *Hil. Tumas Tzaraas* 10:1; cf. *Ramban, Ritva* [*MHK* ed.] and *Ran* [*MHK* ed.], who write that this prohibition is a received tradition).

50. Here, where there is no *tumah,* the Kohen is fit for service! See *Ritva MHK* ed.

51. Rava's *kal vachomer* was based on the proposition that Sabbath law is more stringent than *tzaraas* law. However, Rav Safra contended that *tzaraas* law is more stringent, and his proof was partially predicated on the fact that *tzaraas* law overrides the sacrificial service. Rav Ashi now debunks that premise, claiming that *tzaraas* law is not inherently more stringent than the service. Rather, he argues, it is only because the crucial condition of simultaneity has not been met that the positive commandment of performing the service does not override the prohibition against cutting off *tzaraas* (*Rashi*). [That is, *tzaraas* does not actually override the service. Rather, since for technical reasons *tzaraas* law cannot be overriden by the service, the *tzaraas* remains, and automatically the service cannot be performed.]

52. Actually, the Gemara established above that the passage of *tzaraas* involves both a positive and a negative commandment, which a single positive commandment (such as *milah*) cannot override. Hence, the Gemara is simply presenting the case of *milah* and *tzaraas* as an example of the fulfillment of a positive commandment (*milah*) occurring simultaneously with the violation of a negative commandment [cutting off *tzaraas*] (*Tosafos* ד״ה האי, *Ramban, Ran* (*MHK* ed.); cf. *Rashba* below, 133a ד״ה וכן הא; see also *Mishneh LaMelech* to *Hil. Tumas Tzaraas* 10:5).

53. [The Torah prohibits the wearing of a garment that has in it a mixture of wool and linen threads (כִּלְאַיִם, *kilayim*). Now, it is a positive Torah commandment to attach fringes (צִיצִית, *tzitzis*) to the corners of one's four-cornered garments. The *tzitzis* at each corner should include a thread of blue-dyed wool (תְּכֵלֶת, *techeiles*). One who wishes to wear a four-cornered garment of linen must attach *tzitzis* to it, despite the fact that the garment will then contain both linen and wool threads.] This, indeed, is the source in *Yevamos* for the law that a positive commandment overrides a negative one (see there 4a-5b). Some Rishonim here question, however, whether the case of *tzitzis* and *kilayim* itself contains all the requisites for an "override" situation. See *Ramban* (see, however, notes from *R' Issur Zalman*), *Chidushei HaRan* and *Ran* (*MHK* ed.).

54. I.e. the circumciser cuts off the foreskin and the *tzaraas* simultaneously; one wears the *tzitzis* and the mixture of wool and linen simultaneously (*Rashi*).

55. See note 51. *Ritva* (*MHK* ed.) states that the Gemara could also have established that the service cannot override *tzaraas* law (even if *tzaraas* is *not inherently* more stringent than the service) for the reason that a positive commandment cannot override a positive and a negative commandment. See there and *Rashba* below, 133a ד״ה וכן הא.

דְּתַנְיָא תַּנָּאֵי הִיא – is actually a controversy between Tannaim, – for it was taught in a Baraisa: "בָּשָׂר" – The Torah states,[1] *On the eighth day the* FLESH *of his foreskin shall be circumcised.* וְאַף עַל פִּי שֶׁיֵּשׁ שָׁם בַּהֶרֶת יָמוּל – The extraneous word *flesh* teaches: AND EVEN THOUGH a *BAHERES* spot IS THERE on the foreskin and will inevitably be cut off, HE SHALL PERFORM THE CIRCUMCISION. דִּבְרֵי רַבִּי יֹאשִׁיָּה – These are THE WORDS OF R' YOSHIYAH. רַבִּי יוֹנָתָן אוֹמֵר – However, R' YONASAN SAYS: אֵינוֹ צָרִיךְ – A verse IS NOT NEEDED to teach this law, for it may be derived by *kal vachomer* argument, as follows: שַׁבָּת חֲמוּרָה – Since SABBATH law IS STRINGENT דּוֹחָה – and nevertheless the mitzvah of [CIRCUMCISION AT ITS PROPER TIME] OVERRIDES it, צָרַעַת לֹא כָּל שֶׁכֵּן – SHOULD that category of *milah* NOT CERTAINLY override the weaker *TZARAAS* prohibition?![2]

The Gemara discusses the first opinion of the Baraisa:

אָמַר מָר – Master said: "בָּשָׂר" – The Baraisa stated: In the Torah it is written, *On the eighth day the* FLESH *of his foreskin shall be circumcised.* אַף עַל פִּי שֶׁיֵּשׁ שָׁם בַּהֶרֶת יָמוּל – The extraneous word *flesh* teaches that EVEN THOUGH a *BAHERES* spot IS THERE on the foreskin, HE SHALL PERFORM THE CIRCUMCISION. דִּבְרֵי רַבִּי יֹאשִׁיָּה – These are THE WORDS OF R' YOSHIYAH. הָא לָמָּה לִי קְרָא – Now, why do I [need] a verse to teach this law? דָּבָר שֶׁאֵין מִתְכַּוֵּין הוּא – [Cutting off the *baheres*] in the course of circumcising is an unintentional act,[3] וְדָבָר שֶׁאֵין מִתְכַּוֵּין מוּתָּר – and an unintentional act is permitted. – ? –

The Gemara answers:

אָמַר אַבַּיֵּי – Abaye said: לֹא נִצְרְכָא אֶלָּא לְרַבִּי יְהוּדָה – [The verse] is needed only according to R' Yehudah, דְּאָמַר דָּבָר שֶׁאֵין מִתְכַּוֵּין אָסוּר – who said that an unintentional act is forbidden.[4] Because he concurs with R' Yehudah's view, R' Yoshiyah requires a Scriptural teaching to permit the unintentional cutting off of *baheres.*[5]

A different explanation:

רָבָא אָמַר – Rava said: אֲפִילּוּ תֵּימָא רַבִּי שִׁמְעוֹן – You can even say that R' Yoshiyah's exegesis accords with R' Shimon,[6] מוֹדֶה רַבִּי שִׁמְעוֹן בִּפְסִיק רֵישֵׁיהּ וְלֹא יָמוּת – for R' Shimon concedes that one is liable in the case of an inevitable consequence.[7] Here, it is inevitable that the *baheres* will be cut off along with the foreskin. Hence, without the verse even R' Shimon would prohibit the circumcision.

The Gemara wonders:

וְאַבַּיֵּי לֵית לֵיהּ הַאי סְבָרָא – And Abaye[8] does not agree with this understanding of the matter?! וְהָא אַבַּיֵּי וְרָבָא דְּאָמְרֵי תַּרְוַיְיהוּ – But Abaye and Rava have both said: מוֹדֶה רַבִּי שִׁמְעוֹן בִּפְסִיק רֵישֵׁיהּ וְלֹא יָמוּת – R' Shimon concedes that one is liable in the case of an inevitable consequence. – ? –

The Gemara answers:

בָּתַר דִּשְׁמָעָהּ מֵרָבָא סְבָרָהּ – After [Abaye] heard [this] qualification of R' Shimon's opinion from Rava, he contemplated and accepted it. However, his explanation of the Baraisa was issued beforehand.

The Gemara presents a different version of the Abaye-Rava dialogue:

אִיכָּא דְּמַתְנֵי לְהָא דְּאַבַּיֵּי וְרָבָא אַהָא – There are those who teach this disagreement of Abaye and Rava as concerning this following verse:[9] "הִשָּׁמֶר בְּנֶגַע־הַצָּרַעַת לִשְׁמֹר מְאֹד וְלַעֲשׂוֹת" – *Take heed concerning the affliction of tzaraas, to be very careful and to do.* "לַעֲשׂוֹת" – *To do* implies: אִי אַתָּה עוֹשֶׂה – Intentionally cutting off *baheres* – you may not do it; אֲבָל עוֹשֶׂה אַתָּה בְּסִיב שֶׁעַל גַּבֵּי רַגְלוֹ – however, you may do unintentionally with the bast on one's foot וּבְמוֹט שֶׁעַל גַּבֵּי כְּתֵיפוֹ – and with the pole on one's shoulder, וְאִם עָבְרָה עָבְרָה – and if [the *baheres*] comes off, it comes off.[10]

The Gemara asks:

וְהָא לָמָּה לִי קְרָא – But why do I [need] a verse to teach this law?

NOTES

1. *Leviticus* 12:3.

2. Like Rava, R' Yonasan derives via a *kal vachomer* that *milah* on the eighth day overrides the *tzaraas* prohibition. This frees *Leviticus* 12:3 to teach the law of overriding in the case of a minor's delayed *milah* (the middle category). R' Yoshiyah, on the other hand, eschews the *kal vachomer.* Like Rav Safra, he applies the verse to the case of *milah* on the eighth day [and would derive the law of overriding in the case of a minor's delayed *milah* through Abaye's "common feature" exegesis (above, 132b)] (see *Rashi*).

3. As explained in the General Introduction, when a person performs a permissible act (e.g. circumcision) and as a consequence a second, forbidden but foreseeable act also occurs (e.g. *tzaraas* is cut off), this second act is classified as דָּבָר שֶׁאֵינוֹ מִתְכַּוֵּין, *an unintentional act.* In this category the person performing the permissible act is aware that the prohibited act may occur, but does not intend for it to occur. [Our Gemara is one of the sources that extend this rule to all other areas of the Torah; see also, for example, above, 29b.]

See *Rashba* and *Ritva* (*MHK* ed.), who discuss at length whether the classification of *a labor not needed for its defined purpose* [מְלָאכָה שֶׁאֵינָהּ צְרִיכָה לְגוּפָהּ] (see General Introduction for a description of that category) applies here, since the circumciser apparently intends for the very act he is performing (cutting), but wants a different objective (*milah*). See also *Sfas Emes.*

4. R' Yehudah maintains that since the person realizes that a prohibition may be violated as a result of his action, he is responsible for that unintended violation should it actually occur. [Consequently, he is not permitted to engage in the permissible act because of the possibility that he will violate the prohibition. See, for example, *Beitzah* 23a.]

5. From here we see that R' Yehudah regards the unintended act as *Biblically* forbidden, inasmuch as Scripture must expressly sanction it in our case of circumcision (*Rashba*). However, with regard to Sabbath law, R' Yehudah regards the unintentional commission of a *melachah* as only Rabbinically prohibited, since it is not מְלֶאכֶת מַחֲשֶׁבֶת, *a calculated labor* (*Tosafos* above, 41b ד״ה מיחם; *Rashi* above, 121b ד״ה דילמא).

6. R' Shimon disputes R' Yehudah in the matter of דָּבָר שֶׁאֵינוֹ מִתְכַּוֵּין, *an unintentional act,* maintaining that one is not responsible for a prohibition violated unintentionally (e.g. see above, 22a). Consequently, as long as a person does not intend for the prohibited act to occur, he is permitted to engage in the permissible act even when it leads to the occurrence of the prohibited act.

7. Although R' Shimon allows the performance of a permitted act that also has an unintended forbidden consequence, he does so only if the forbidden consequence is a *possible* result, not an *inevitable* one. If the performance of the permissible act will *inevitably* result in the occurrence of the prohibited act, R' Shimon agrees that it is forbidden. This qualification is known as פְּסִיק רֵישֵׁיהּ וְלֹא יָמוּת – literally: *Its head is cut off and it should not die?* (see above, 75a note 25). We shall refer to it simply as *the rule of the inevitable consequence.* According to all authorities, this rule operates Biblically with regard to Sabbath law as well (see *Rambam, Hil. Shabbos* 1:6 and *Tosafos* above, 41b ד״ה מיחם).

8. Who said that R' Yehudah's exegesis accords only with R' Yehudah.

9. *Deuteronomy* 24:8.

10. That is, you may go about and do your normal activities, even pulling tight the bast strings to tie your shoes or carrying a burden on your shoulder, and you need not be concerned that you will inadvertently scrape off a *baheres* spot on your foot or shoulder.

Rashi deletes the words אִי אַתָּה עוֹשֶׂה אֲבָל from the text, for the sentence then implies that the second part of the verse is a negative commandment, whereas the Gemara established above (132b) that it is a positive commandment. According to *Rashi,* then, the Gemara reads: . . . *to be very careful; but to do* – i.e. you may do your normal activities as long as you do not *intend* to cut off the *tzaraas* (which still implies that intending to cut off is forbidden, and this implied prohibition has the force of a positive commandment; see *Rashba* at length).

תנאי היא דתניא א) א) בשר ואף על פי שיש שם בהרת ימול דברי רבי יאשיה רבי יונתן אומר אינו צריך שבת חמורה דוחה צרעת לא כ"ש: אמר מר בשר אע"פ שיש שם בהרת ימול דברי רבי יאשיה ג) הא למה לי קרא דבר שאין מתכוין הוא ודבר שאין מתכוין מותר אמר אביי לא נצרכא אלא לרבי יהודה דאמר דבר שאין מתכוין אסור רבא אמר אפילו תימא ר"ש מודה ר"ש בפסיק רישיה ולא ימות ואביי לית ליה האי סברא והא ג) אביי ורבא דאמרי תרוייהו מודה רבי שמעון בפסיק רישיה ולא ימות בתר דשמעה מרבא סברה איכא דמתני להא דאביי ורבא אהא ב) השמר בנגע הצרעת לשמור מאד ולעשות ד) לעשות אי אתה עושה א אבל (א) עושה אתה בסיב שעל גבי רגלו ובמוט שעל גבי כתיפו ואם עברה עברה והא למה לי קרא דבר שאין מתכוין הוא ודבר שאין מתכוין מותר אמר אביי לא נצרכא אלא לרבי יהודה דאמר דבר שאין מתכוין אסור ורבא אמר אפילו תימא רבי שמעון ומודה רבי שמעון בפסיק רישיה ולא ימות ואביי לית ליה האי סברא והא אביי ורבא דאמרי תרוייהו מודה ר' שמעון בפסיק רישיה ולא ימות לבתר דשמעיה מרבא סברה ואביי אליבא דרבי שמעון האי בשר מאי עביד ליה אמר רב עמרם באומר לקוץ בהרתו הוא מתכוין תינח גדול קטן מאי איכא למימר אמר רב משרשיא באומר אבי הבן לקוץ בהרת דבנו הוא קא מתכוין ואי איכא אחר ליעביד אחר ה) דאמר ר"ש בן לקיש ב כל מקום שאתה מוצא עשה ולא תעשה אם אתה יכול לקיים שניהם מוטב ואם לאו יבא עשה וידחה לא תעשה דליכא אחר: אמר מר יום טוב אינה דוחה אלא בזמנה בלבד מנא הני מילי ו) אמר חזקיה וכן תנא דבי חזקיה אמר קרא ג) לא תותירו ממנו ז) עד בקר שאין ת"ל עד בקר מה ת"ל עד בקר בא הכתוב ליתן לו בקר שני לשריפתו אביי אמר קרא ח) עולת שבת בשבתו ולא עולת חול בשבת ולא עולת חול בי"ט רבא אמר אמר קרא ט) הוא לבדו יעשה לכם הוא ולא מכשירין לבדו ולא מילה שלא בזמנה דאתיא מק"ו רב אשי אמר י) שבתון עשה הוא והוה ליה י"ט עשה ול"ת ואין עשה דוחה את לא תעשה ועשה: כלל אמר ר"ע וכו': כ) אמר רב יהודה אמר רב הלכה כר"ע ותנן נמי גבי פסח כי האי גוונא ג כלל אמר ר"ע כל מלאכה שאפשר לה לעשותה מע"ש אינה דוחה את השבת שחיטה שאי אפשר לעשותה מע"ש דוחה את השבת ואמר רב יהודה אמר רב הלכה כר"ע וצריכא דאי אשמעינן גבי מילה התם הוא דמכשירין (ב) אפשר לעשות מאתמול לא דחו שבת דליכא כרת אבל פסח דאיכא כרת אימא לידחו שבת ואי אשמעינן גבי פסח משום דלא נכרתו עליה י"ג בריתות אבל מילה דנכרתו עליה י"ג בריתות אימא לידחו שבת צריכא:

מתני' ל) ד עושין כל צרכי מילה [בשבת] מוהלין ופורעין ומוצצין ונותנין עליה איספלנית וכמון ה אם לא שחק מע"ש מ) לועס בשיניו ונותן אם לא טרף יין ושמן מע"ש ינתן זה בעצמו וזה בעצמו ואין עושין לה חלוק לכתחילה אבל כורך עליה סמרטוט אם לא התקין מע"ש כורך על אצבעו ומביא ואפי' מחצר אחרת:

גמ'

רש"י

תנאי היא. דאיכא דנפקא ליה מילה בזמנה מק"ו כרבא וכי אתא קרא לשלא בזמנה ואיכא דלא נפקא ליה בק"ו ואיצטריך למילה בזמנה כרב ספרא ושלא בזמנה אתיא מביניא: **לרבי יהודה.** רבי יאשיה דמצריך קרא להכי כרבי יהודה סבירא ליה: **מודה ר' שמעון בפסיק כו'.** הילכך אי לא רבי קרא לא עבדי: **סברה.** נתן בה דעתיה וקבל ממנו: ה"ג **לעשות עושה אתה בסיב שעל רגלו ובמוט שעל גבי כתיפו.** ואינו צריך להזהר מלדחות סיב שקושר מנעלו ברגלו ומלישא משאוי על כתיפו: **ואם עברה.** הבהרת בכך עברה ואינו חושש לה להכי כתיב לעשות שמותר לעשות מלאכתו: **ואביי אליבא דר' שמעון.** מעיקרא מקמי דסברה האי בשר מאי עביד ליה: **באומר לקוץ.** גדול שהוא בר עונשין ואומר למוהל לקוץ בהרתו בכוונה ליטהר: **קטן.** דלא ידע לכווני מאי איכא למימר ועל כרחיך בתרוייהו כתיב בשר כדאמרי' לעיל ובשר דכתיב גבי קטן ביום השמיני ל"ל: **באומר אבי הבן לקוץ.** דמתכוין לטהרו והוא מוזהר דלא ליעבד בידים ובמתכוין: **ואי איכא אחר.** שאינו חושש לטהרו ליעבד אחר ולא ליקו אב להתם ואע"ג דכייה קרא שהרי אתה יכול לקיים שניהם שלא עקיבת לאו לר' שמעון דהא אחר לא מיכוין ולא עבר ואמר ר"ש לקיים כו' וכיוון לחאי אתא: **שאין תלמוד לומר עד בקר.** תניינא והנותר ממנו עד בקר דמאי למכתב והנותר באש תשרפו (ג) אלא אשריפה קאי והכי קאמר והנותר ממנו בזמן שאסרתי לך דהיינו בקר ראשון כשיבא בקר שני שהוא מולו של מועד תשרפו אבל בי"ט לא אלמא מידי דמול לא עדיפא בי"ט ופסח קרבן י"ד בניסן הוא שהוא חול ומילה שלא בזמנה נמי מידי דמול הוא דבשבת זו לא היה זמנה: **ולא עולת חול בי"ט.** אבל תמיד של עי"ט אין קרבין בי"ט ומילה שלא בזמנה נמי כעולת חול בי"ט דמי: **דאתיא בק"ו.** שמלאכה ומה לרעת שדוחה עבודה מילה שלא בזמנה דוחה אותה כדאמרינן לעיל (ד) שבת שנדחית מפני עבודה אינו דין שמילה שלא בזמנה דוחה אותה והכי איצטריך לבדו: **ואין עשה.** דמילה דוחה לא תעשה ועשה אבל בזמנה איתרבי מביום אפילו בשבת: **גבי פסח.** כל מלאכה שאפשר לה לעשות מע"ש כגון הבאתו מחוץ לתחום וחתיכת יבלתו: **וצריכא.** למימר בתרוייהו הלכה כר"ע דמכשירין לא דחו: **מילה בזמנה ליכא כרת.** דקטן לאו בר עונשין הוא ואבוה לא מיחייב עליה כרת: **מתני' מוהלין.** חותך את הערלה: **ופורעין.** את העור המכסה ראש הגיד: **ומוצצין.** את הדם ואף על גב דהיא עשיית חבורה שאין הדם ניתק ממקורו אלא על ידי (ה) המצילה: **איספלנית.** תחבושת: **לועס בשיניו.** כמה דאפשר לשנויי משנינן: **לא טרף יין ושמן.** כך היו רגילין והיא רפואה שמערבין וטורפין בקערה יין ושמן יחד כדרך שטורפין ביצים בקערה: **חלוק.** כעין כיס דחוק היו עושין ומלבישים את ראש הגיד עד העטרה וקושרים שם כדי שלא יחזור העור לכסות את הגיד: **לא התקין.** לא הזמין: **כורך על ידו.** דרך מלבוש לשנותו מדרך הוצאה בחול:

תוספות

ואביי אליבא דר' שמעון. ולרבי יונתן לא מיבעיא ליה דמוקי ליה בינוני ולאביי נמי דאמר לעיל דבינוני אתי מביניא מצי למימר דסבר ר' יונתן מילתא דאתי בק"ו טרח וכתב לה קרא:

באומר לקוץ בהרתו הוא מתכוין. וא"ת אם כן אמאי קאמר אביי לא נצרכא אלא לרבי יהודה הא לר"ש נמי איצטריך כדאמר הכא ויש לומר דלשון ברייתא משמע דמיירי בלא מתכוין מדלא קתני בשר אע"ג דמתכוין לקוץ בהרת ימול:

ותנן נמי גבי פסח כה"ג אמר רב יהודה אמר רב הלכה כר"ע. והכא לא פריך הילכתא למשיחא משום דנפקא מינה גבי מילה אע"ג דגבי מילה נמי פסיק הכי מ"מ לאלומי פיסקא דמילה פסיק נמי גבי פסח אגב דפסיק גבי מילה דתילף מינה שפסק ברור הוא לכל דבר מ):

וצריכא דאי אשמועינן. אדרב יהודה קאי דפסיק כר"ע הכא והתם דאי אדרבי עקיבא א"כ בפ' שתי הלחם (מנחות דף צו.) דקתני נמי כלל אמר ר"ע הוה ליה למימר וצריכא וכן פירש בקונטרס ט):

עושין כל צרכי מילה בשבת. אע"ג דלעיל נמי קתני (ו) בשילהי מפנין (ד' קכח.) התם תני לה אגב גררא דמילי דתינוק אבל הכא עיקר:

גדול

עין משפט נר מצוה

י א מיי' פ"ו מהלכות טומאת צרעת הלכה א סמג לאוין שמג:
יא ב מיי' פ"ג מהלכות מילה הלכה ו:
יב ג מיי' פ"א מהלכות קרבן פסח הלכה יח סמג עשין רכג:
יג ד מיי' פ"ב מהלכות מילה הל' ו סמג עשין כח טוש"ע א"ח סי' של סעיף א טוש"ע י"ד סי' רסו סעיף ב:
יד ה מיי' שם הל' ז סמג שם טוש"ע א"ח שם סעיף ו וטוש"ע י"ד שם סעיף ג:

גליון הש"ס

רש"י ד"ה שאין ת"ל וכו' י"ד בניסן הוא שהוא חול. עיין טורי אבן במגילה בחגיגה מלואים דף ט ע"ב ד"ה אף כאן:

רבינו חננאל

מודה ר' שמעון בפסיק רישי' ולא ימות פי' כי ר' שמעון מודה בדבר שהוא ברור כגון אדם שחותך ראש אדם ואומר שאין כוונתו להמיתו אלא להוציא את ממנו שאין שומעין לו אלא דנין אותו דין כל הורג נפש כך כל דבר שמתברר (מעשין) [שיעשה] לאותה מלאכה אין אומרין שלא היתה כוונתו לכך. והכא אפילו ר' שמעון מודה. ואביי אליבא דר' שמעון קודם שישמע מרבא. מודה ר' שמעון בפסיק רישיה ולא ימות דהוה מוקים ליה כר' יהודה ולא כר' שמעון הוה אמר דר"ש פליג נמי בהא דסבר ר' שמעון חתיכות הערלה והצרעת עליה דבר שאין מתכוין הוא ואין כוונתו לחתוך הצרעת אלא למול בנו וכי האי לר' שמעון שרי ולא צריך קרא למשרייה אם כן אביי אליבא דר' שמעון האי בשר ערלתו מאי עביד ליה אמר רב משרשיא באומר לקוץ בהרתו הוא מתכוין כלומר בדבר מוכיח שמתכוין לקוץ בהרתו בא הכתוב להתירו ואקשינן תינח גדול פי' שיש בו דעת יש לומר כן מתכוין לקוץ בהרתו קטן שאין בו דעת למה כתוב בו בשר להתיר חתיכת צרעת במילה ואמרי' קטן נמי מתכוין אביו בזה כשמול לבנו לחתוך בהרת בנו ואמרי' בעת שיש בהרת בערלת הקטן ימול אחר זולתו אבי הבן. שהאחר אין מתכוין לחתוך הבהרת ודבר שאין מתכוין לר' שמעון שרי ולא הוה צריך קרא למישריה דאמר רבי שמעון בן לקיש כל מקום שאתה מוצא עשה ולא תעשה פי' כגון זה עשה שנאמר וביום השמיני ימול בשר ערלתו. לא תעשה השמר בנגע הצרעת שהוא לאו כאשר פירשנו למעלה. ואם יש בהרת בערלה וימול אחר זולתו אבי הבן נתקיימה המילה שהיא עשה ונתקיימה חתיכת הצרעת

מסורת הש"ס

א) [יומא לד:], ב) [שם], ג) לעיל קג. קז: קלה: [בכורות כה:], ד) [פסחים כה:], ה) תוספתא נגעים פ"ג, ו) לעיל כד:, ז) [פסחים פג:], ח) [לעיל דף קכח:], ט) [ע' תוס' יומא יג: ד"ה הלכה ותוס' זבחים מה. ד"ה הלכתא], י) [ולמיגמר דר"ש לא קפי גריסתא], כ) לעיל קלא:, ל) תוספתא פי"ט, מ) [ע' תוס' ד"ה עושין וכו' קתני לה בשילהי].

הגהות הב"ח

(א) גמ' אבל אתה עושה אותו בסיב: (ב) שם לאפשר לעשות: (ג) רש"י ד"ה שאין ת"ל וכו' באש תשרפו אלא אשריפה קאי וכו' דמול דבי"ט לא: (ד) ד"ה דאתיא וכו' כדאמרינן לעיל י"ט שנדחים: (ה) ד"ה ומוצצין וכו' אלא ע"י (המצילה) מז"מ וכ"ב פ"א: (ו) תוס' ד"ה עושין וכו' קתני לה בשילהי.

תורה אור השלם

א) וּבַיּוֹם הַשְּׁמִינִי יִמּוֹל בְּשַׂר עָרְלָתוֹ: [ויקרא יב, ג]
ב) הִשָּׁמֶר בְּנֶגַע הַצָּרַעַת לִשְׁמֹר מְאֹד וְלַעֲשׂוֹת כְּכֹל אֲשֶׁר יוֹרוּ אֶתְכֶם הַכֹּהֲנִים הַלְוִיִּם כַּאֲשֶׁר צִוִּיתִם תִּשְׁמְרוּ לַעֲשׂוֹת: [דברים כד, ח]
ג) וְלֹא תוֹתִירוּ מִמֶּנּוּ עַד בֹּקֶר וְהַנֹּתָר מִמֶּנּוּ עַד בֹּקֶר בָּאֵשׁ תִּשְׂרֹפוּ: [שמות יב, י]
ד) עֹלַת שַׁבַּת בְּשַׁבַּתּוֹ עַל עֹלַת הַתָּמִיד וְנִסְכָּהּ: [במדבר כח, י]
ה) וּבַיּוֹם הָרִאשׁוֹן מִקְרָא קֹדֶשׁ וּבַיּוֹם הַשְּׁבִיעִי מִקְרָא קֹדֶשׁ יִהְיֶה לָכֶם כָּל מְלָאכָה לֹא יֵעָשֶׂה בָהֶם אַךְ אֲשֶׁר יֵאָכֵל לְכָל נֶפֶשׁ הוּא לְבַדּוֹ יֵעָשֶׂה לָכֶם: [שמות יב, טז]
ו) דַּבֵּר אֶל בְּנֵי יִשְׂרָאֵל לֵאמֹר בַּחֹדֶשׁ הַשְּׁבִיעִי בְּאֶחָד לַחֹדֶשׁ יִהְיֶה לָכֶם שַׁבָּתוֹן זִכְרוֹן תְּרוּעָה מִקְרָא קֹדֶשׁ: [ויקרא כג, כד]

רב נסים גאון

דאתי עשה ודחי לא תעשה לא תעשה שיש בה כרת מי דחי ותו לא תעשה גרידא מנלן דדחי דכתיב [illegible]

[illegible]

חשק שלמה על רבינו חננאל א) חסר קצת וכצ"ל ופי' חזקיה דילפינן לה מנותר מן הקדשים וכו':

ליקוטי רש"י למה לי קרא. [illegible]

דָּבָר שֶׁאֵין מִתְכַּוֵּין הוּא – [Removing the *baheres*] while engaged in a routine activity **is an unintentional act,** וְדָבָר שֶׁאֵין מִתְכַּוֵּין מוּתָּר – **and an unintentional act is permitted.** – ? –

The Gemara answers:

אָמַר אַבַּיֵי – **Abaye said:** לֹא נִצְרְכָא אֶלָּא לְרַבִּי יְהוּדָה – [The verse] **is needed only according to R' Yehudah,** דְּאָמַר דָּבָר שֶׁאֵין מִתְכַּוֵּין אָסוּר – **who said** that **an unintentional act is forbidden.** Hence, Scripture must expressly condone the inadvertent removal of *baheres.*

A different explanation:

וְרָבָא אָמַר – **But Rava said:** אֲפִילּוּ תֵּימָא רַבִּי שִׁמְעוֹן – **You can even say** that the verse accords with **R' Shimon,** וּמוֹדֶה רַבִּי שִׁמְעוֹן בִּפְסִיק רֵישֵׁיהּ וְלֹא יָמוּת – **and R' Shimon concedes** that one is liable **in** the case of **an inevitable consequence.** The verse thus teaches that even though the *baheres* will inevitably come off as a result of the routine activity, the activity is nonetheless permitted.[11]

The Gemara wonders:

וְאַבַּיֵי לֵית לֵיהּ הַאי סְבָרָא – **And Abaye**[12] **does not agree with this understanding** of the matter?! וְהָא אַבַּיֵי וְרָבָא דְּאָמְרֵי תַּרְוַיְיהוּ – **But Abaye and Rava have both said:** מוֹדֶה רַבִּי שִׁמְעוֹן בִּפְסִיק רֵישֵׁיהּ וְלֹא יָמוּת – **R' Shimon concedes** that one is liable **in** the case of **an inevitable consequence.** – ? –

The Gemara answers:

לְבָתַר דִּשְׁמָעֵיהּ מֵרָבָא סְבָרָהּ – **After** [Abaye] **heard** [this] qualification of R' Shimon's opinion **from Rava, he contemplated** and **accepted it.**

The Gemara revisits the first version of the Abaye-Rava dialogue, and asks:

וְאַבַּיֵי – **And Abaye,** when he initially held that R' Yoshiyah's exegesis accords only with R' Yehudah, אַלִּיבָּא דְּרַבִּי שִׁמְעוֹן הַאי ,,בָּשָׂר" מַאי עָבֵיד לֵיהּ – **what did he do with** the extraneous word *flesh* **according to the opinion of R' Shimon?**[13]

The Gemara answers:

אָמַר רַב עַמְרָם – **Rav Amram said:** בְּאוֹמֵר לָקוּץ בַּהַרְתּוֹ הוּא מִתְכַּוֵּין – He interprets it as **concerning** an adult **who tells** his circumciser **to cut off his *baheres*** spot, **intending** thereby to attain purification. The word *flesh* teaches that entertaining such intent in the case of *milah* is permitted.[14]

The Gemara objects:

תִּינַח גָּדוֹל – [This] interpretation **is appropriate** for the case of an uncircumcised **adult,** who has the mental capacity to entertain an intent for purification. קָטָן מַאי אִיכָּא לְמֵימַר – But in the case of an uncircumcised **minor,** who lacks such mental capacity, **what is there to say?**[15]

The Gemara answers:

אָמַר רַב מְשַׁרְשִׁיָּא – **Rav Mesharshiya said:** בְּאוֹמֵר אֲבִי הַבֵּן לָקוּץ בַּהֶרֶת דִּבְנוֹ הוּא קָא מִתְכַּוֵּין – Abaye interprets it as **concerning** where **the child's father**[16] **states**[17] that he means **to cut off his son's *baheres*** spot, **intending** thereby to effect his son's purification. Although normally one may not cut off another party's *tzaraas* for that purpose,[18] the word *flesh* teaches that in the case of a minor's *milah* it is permitted.

The Gemara objects to this interpretation as well:

וְאִי אִיכָּא אַחֵר – **But if there is another** person who can take responsibility for the minor's circumcision,[19] לִיעָבֵיד אַחֵר – **let the other** person **perform** that function,[20] דְּאָמַר רַבִּי שִׁמְעוֹן בֶּן לָקִישׁ – **for R' Shimon ben Lakish said:** כָּל מָקוֹם שֶׁאַתָּה מוֹצֵא עֲשֵׂה וְלֹא תַעֲשֶׂה – **Wherever you encounter a positive commandment and a prohibition** in conflict with one another, אִם אַתָּה יָכוֹל לְקַיֵּים שְׁנֵיהֶם מוּטָב – **if you can observe both of them, it is preferable.**[21] וְאִם לָאו – **But if not,** i.e. if fulfilling the positive commandment necessarily involves violating the prohibition, יָבֹא עֲשֵׂה וְיִדְחֶה לֹא תַעֲשֶׂה – then **let the positive com-**

NOTES

11. *Ran* (*MHK* ed.). According to the first version, then, there is a verse that permits *circumcising* a *tzaraas*-infected foreskin when the cutting off of the *tzaraas* is inevitable. According to the second version, however, a different verse *always* allows the unintentional cutting off of *tzaraas,* even when it is inevitable. If so, the Rishonim ask: Inasmuch as the inadvertent but inevitable removal of *tzaraas* is sanctioned (by the verse *to do*) when one's action is discretionary, then certainly it is permitted when the action is a mitzvah! Why, then, is *the flesh of his foreskin* needed to teach that *milah* may be performed on a *tzaraas*-infected foreskin? *Rashba* answers that the case of the second verse is where the person's action (e.g. carrying the pole) is but an indirect cause (גְּרָמָא) of the cutting off; it is for that reason that it is permitted. *Chasam Sofer* contends, however, that the inevitability of outcome would render the act a direct cause. Cf. *Chidushei HaRan,* who characterizes the inadvertent removal as a מִתְעַסֵּק (*unwitting act*), which is permitted. *Ramban* and *Ran* (*MHK* ed.) answer that the *milah* verse teaches that circumcision is permitted even when one intends to cut off the *tzaraas for purposes of purifying the contaminated individual.* Only in the case of *milah* is such intent condoned; in discretionary cases it is not. See also *Rashash,* and Gemara below (which further explains the first version).

12. Who said that the verse accords only with R' Yehudah.

13. Abaye originally understood that R' Yoshiyah's exegesis of the word *flesh* (viz. that the unintentional cutting off of *baheres* during circumcision is permitted) was needed only according to R' Yehudah, who holds that an unintentional violation is generally forbidden. The Gemara thus asks how Abaye would then have interpreted the extraneous *flesh* according to R' Shimon, who – Abaye held at the time – permits an unintentional violation even when it is inevitable.

Ritva (*MHK* ed.) notes that Abaye would eschew using *flesh* to teach the *baheres* law for the middle category of *milah* (a minor's delayed circumcision), since Abaye derives it in that case through a "common feature" exegesis (above, 132b). See, further, *Tosafos* ד״ה ואביי with *Maharam.*

14. *Rashi.* As for why *Rashi* mentions a circumciser, see *Yad David* [*Basra*]. In any event, though, the adult being circumcised, who is obligated in the mitzvah, establishes that which the circumciser effects, and so the circumciser is only his agent (conclusion of *Mishneh LaMelech, Hil. Tumas Tzaraas* 10:1). See also note 20 below.

Tosafos ask: Inasmuch as R' Shimon indeed derives this law from the word *flesh,* why did Abaye initially say that the verse is needed only according to R' Yehudah? They explain that Abaye is interpreting R' Yoshiyah's exegesis, and R' Yoshiyah stated, "And even though *baheres* is there, he may perform the circumcision," which implies that R' Yoshiyah is discussing an unintentional removal of *baheres.* Had he meant an intentional removal, he would have stated more explicitly: "And even though he intends to cut off the *baheres* . . ."

15. The extraneous word *flesh* (בָּשָׂר) is written twice – with regard to both an uncircumcised minor and an uncircumcised adult (see above, 132b notes 31 and 32). How, then, would Abaye interpret the former mention of the word according to R' Shimon? (*Rashi*).

16. Who has the primary obligation to circumcise his minor son (*Ritva MHK* ed., from *Kiddushin* 29a).

17. See *Ritva MHK* ed. here, who suggests that the father need not actually verbalize this; rather, *we presume* (אֲנַן סַהֲדֵי) that his intent is for purification.

18. See *Mishnah LaMelech* ibid. See also *Minchas Chinuch* 584:2 ד״ה ולשון הר״מ, and *Rashi* here.

19. And who, not being the child's father, will not intend for the circumcision to effect the child's purification (*Rashi*).

20. And let the father not attend the circumcision (*Rashi*). [*Rashi's* comment implies that if the father is present, the *mohel* is his agent and does his bidding, and if so, the *mohel* transgresses when he cuts off the *tzaraas* since the father intended for his son's purification (see *Mishneh LaMelech* ibid. and *Minchas Chinuch* 584:5 ד״ה וע׳ ברש״י שבת).]

21. If you can find some way to fulfill the positive commandment without violating the prohibition, you must opt for that way of performing the positive commandment.

תנאי היא דתניא א) בשר ואף על פי שיש שם בהרת ימול דברי רבי יאשיה רבי יונתן אומר אינו צריך שבת חמורה דוחה צרעת לא כ"ש: אמר מר בשר אע"פ שיש שם בהרת ימול דברי רבי יאשיה ה) הא למה לי קרא דבר שאין מתכוין הוא ודבר שאין מתכוין מותר אמר אביי לא נצרכא אלא לרבי יהודה דאמר דבר שאין מתכוין אסור רבא אמר אפילו תימא ר"ש מודה ר"ש בפסיק רישיה ולא ימות ואביי לית ליה האי סברא והא ג) אביי ורבא דאמרי תרווייהו מודה רבי שמעון בפסיק רישיה ולא ימות בתר דשמעה מרבא סברה איכא דמתני להא דאביי ורבא אהא ב) השמר בנגע הצרעת לשמור מאד ולעשות ד) לעשות אי אתה עושה *אבל (א) עושה אתה בסיב שעל גבי רגלו ובמוטט שעל גבי כתיפו ואם עברה עברה והא למה לי קרא דבר שאין מתכוין הוא ודבר שאין מתכוין מותר אמר אביי לא נצרכא אלא לרבי יהודה דאמר דבר שאין מתכוין אסור ורבא אמר אפילו תימא רבי שמעון ומודה רבי שמעון בפסיק רישיה ולא ימות ואביי לית ליה האי סברא והא אביי ורבא דאמרי תרווייהו מודה ר' שמעון בפסיק רישיה ולא ימות לבתר דשמעיה מרבא סברה ואביי אליבא דרבי שמעון האי בשר מאי עביד ליה אמר רב עמרם באומר לקוץ בהרתו הוא מתכוין תינח גדול קטן מאי איכא למימר אמר רב משרשיא באומר אבי הבן לקוץ בהרת דבנו הוא קא מתכוין ואי איכא אחר ליעביד אחר ו) דאמר ר"ש בן לקיש ב כל מקום שאתה מוצא עשה ולא תעשה אם אתה יכול לקיים שניהם מוטב ואם לאו יבא עשה וידחה לא תעשה דליכא אחר: אמר מר יום טוב אינה דוחה אלא בזמנה בלבד מנא הני מילי ז) אמר חזקיה וכן תנא דבי חזקיה אמר קרא ג לא תותירו ממנו ח) עד בקר שאין ת"ל עד בקר מה ת"ל עד בקר בא הכתוב ליתן לו בקר שני לשריפתו אביי אמר אמר קרא ד) עולת שבת בשבתו ולא עולת חול בשבת ולא עולת חול בי"ט רבא אמר אמר קרא ה) הוא לבדו יעשה לכם הוא ולא מכשירין לבדו ולא מילה שלא בזמנה דאתיא מק"ו רב אשי אמר ו) שבתון עשה הוא והוה ליה י"ט עשה ול"ת ואין עשה דוחה את לא תעשה ועשה: כלל אמר ר"ע וכו': אמר רב יהודה אמר רב הלכה כר"ע ותנן נמי גבי פסח כי האי גוונא ט) ג כלל אמר ר"ע כל מלאכה שאפשר לה לעשותה מע"ש אינה דוחה את השבת שחיטה שאי אפשר לעשותה מע"ש דוחה את השבת ואמר רב יהודה אמר רב הלכה כר"ע וצריכא דאי אשמעינן גבי מילה התם הוא דמכשירין (ג) אפשר לעשות מאתמול לא דחו שבת דליכא כרת אבל פסח דאיכא כרת אימא לידחו שבת ואי אשמעינן גבי פסח משום דלא נכרתו עליה י"ג בריתות אבל מילה דנכרתו עליה י"ג בריתות אימא לידחו שבת צריכא:

מתני' י) ד עושין כל צרכי מילה [בשבת] מוהלין ופורעין ומוצצין ונותנין עליה איספלנית וכמון ה אם לא שחק מע"ש ט) לועס בשיניו ונותן אם לא טרף יין ושמן מע"ש ינתן זה בעצמו וזה בעצמו ואין עושין לה חלוק לכתחילה אבל כורך עליה סמרטוט אם לא התקין מע"ש כורך על אצבעו ומביא ואפי' מחצר אחרת:

גמ'

רש"י

תנאי היא. דליכא דנפקא ליה מילה בזמנה מק"ו כרבה וכי אתא קרא לשלא בזמנה ואיכא דלא נפקא ליה בק"ו ואיצטריך למילה בזמנה כרב ספרא ושלא בזמנה אתיא מבינה: לרבי יאשיה דמצריך קרא להכי כרבי יהודה סבירא ליה: מודה ר' שמעון בפסיק כו'. הילכך אי לא רבי קרא לא עבדי: סברה. נתן בה דעתיה וקבל ממנו: ה"ג לעשות עושה אתה בסיב שעל רגלו ובמוטט שעל גבי כתיפו. ואינו צריך להזהר ט) מלדחות סיב שקושר מנעלו ברגלו ומלישא משאוי על כתיפו: ואם עברה. הבהרת בכך עברה ואינו חושש לה להכי כתיב לעשות שמותר לעשות מלאכתו: ואביי אליבא דר' שמעון. מעיקרא מקמי דסברה האי בשר מאי עביד ליה: באומר לקוץ. גדול שהוא בר עונשין ואומר למוהל לקוץ בהרתו בכוונה ליטהר: קטן. דלא ידע לכווני מאי איכא למימר ועל כרחיך בתרוייהו כתיב בשר דאמרי' לעיל ובשר דכתיב גבי קטן ביום השמיני ל"ל: באומר אבי הבן לקוץ. למתכוין לטהרו והוא מוהל דלא לעבד בידים ובמתכוין: ואי איכא אחר. שאינו חושש לטהרו ליעבד אחר ולא ליקו אב להפס ואע"ג דרבייה קרא שהרי אתה יכול לקיים עשה בלא עקירת לאו לר' שמעון דהא אחר לא מיכוין ולא עבר ואמר ריש לקיש כו' ורבויא למאי אתא: שאין תלמוד לומר עד בקר. מכניא והנותר ממנו עד בקר דמאי למכתב והנותר באש תשרפו (ג) אלא אשריפה קאי והכי קאמר והנותר ממנו בזמן שאמרתי לך דהיינו בקר ראשון כשיבא בקר שני שהוא חולו של מועד תשרפו אבל בי"ט לא אלמא מידי דחול לא עבדינן בי"ט ופסח קרבן י"ד בניסן הוא שהוא חול ומילה שלא בזמנה נמי מידי דחול הוא דבשבת זו לא היה זמנה: ולא עולת חול בי"ט. אבל תמיד של עי"ט אין קרבין בי"ט ומילה שלא בזמנה נמי כעולת חול בי"ט דמי: דאתיא בק"ו. שתחלה ומה צרעת שדוחה עבודה מילה שלא בזמנה דוחה אותה כדאמרינן לעיל (ד) שבת שנדחית מפני עבודה אינו דין שמילה שלא בזמנה דוחה אותה להכי איצטריך לבדו: ואין עשה. דמילה דוחה לא תעשה ועשה אבל בזמנה איתרבי מביום אפילו בשבת: גבי פסח. כל מלאכה שאפשר לה לעשות מע"ש כגון הבאתו מחוץ לתחום וחתיכת יבלתו: וצריכא. למימר בתרוייהו הלכה כר"ע דמכשירין לא דמו: מילה בזמנה ליכא כרת. דקטן לאו בר עונשין הוא ואבוה לא מיחייב עליה כרת: מתני' מוהלין. חותך את הערלה: ופורעין. את העור המכסה ראש הגיד: ומוצצין. את הדם ואף על גב דהיא עשיית חבורה שאין הדם ניתק ממיבורו אלא על ידי (ה) המלילה: איספלנית. תחבושת: לועס בשיניו. כמה דאפשר לשנויי משנינן: לא טרף יין ושמן. כך היו רגילין והיא רפואה שמערבין וטורפין בקערה יין ושמן יחד כדרך שטורפין ביצים בקערה: חלוק. כעין כיס דחוק היו עושין ומלבישים את ראש הגיד עד העטרה וקושרים שם כדי שלא יחזור העור לכסות את הגיד: לא התקין. לא הזמין: כורך על ידו. דרך מלבוש לשנותו מדרך הוצאה בחול:

תוספות

ואביי אליבא דר' שמעון. ולרבי יונתן לא מיבעיא ליה דמוקי ליה בינוני ולאביי נמי איכא למימר לעיל דבינוני אתי מבינה מאי למימר דסבר כר' יונתן מילתא דאתי בק"ו טרח וכתב לה קרא: באומר לקוץ בהרתו הוא מתכוין. וא"ת אם כן אמאי קאמר אביי לא נצרכא אלא לרבי יהודה הא לר"ש נמי איצטריך כדאמר הכא וי"ל דלשון ברייתא משמע דמיירי בלא מתכוין מדלא קתני בשר אע"ג דמתכוין לקוץ בהרת ימול:

ותנן נמי גבי פסח כה"ג אמר רב יהודה אמר רב הלכה כר"ע. והכא לא פריך הילכתא למשיחא משום דנפקא מינה גבי מילה אע"ג דגבי מילה נמי פסיק הכי מ"מ איצטריך איפסקא דמילה פסיק נמי גבי פסח אגב דפסיק גבי מילה דהלכה למילף מינה שפסק ברור הוא לכל דבר ט):

וצריכא דאי אשמעינן. אליבא דרב יהודה קאי דפסיק כר"ע הכא והתם דלאו לדרבי עקיבא א"כ בפ' שתי הלחם (מנחות דף צו:) דקתני נמי כלל אמר ר"ע הכא לא אמר ורבינא וכן פירש בקונטרס י):

עושין כל צרכי מילה בשבת. אע"ג דלעיל נמי קתני (ו) בשילהי מפנין (ד' קכז.) התם תני לה אגב גררא דמילי דמינוק אבל הכא עיקר:

גדול

עין משפט נר מצוה

י א מיי' פ"א מהלכות טומאת צרעת הלכה ח סמג לאוין שפ:
יא ב מיי' פ"ב מהלכות מילה הלכה ו:
יב ג מיי' פ"א מהלכות קרבן פסח הלכה יח סמג עשין רנג:
יג ד מיי' פ"ב מהלכות מילה הל' ו סמג עשין כח טוש"ע א"ח סי' שלא סעיף א טוש"ע י"ד סי' רסו סעיף ב:
יד ה מיי' שם הל' ז סמג שם וטוש"ע א"ח שם סעיף ז וטוש"ע י"ד שם סעיף ג:

גליון הש"ס

רש"י ד"ה שאין ת"ל וכו' י"ד בניסן הוא שהוא חול. עיין כתובות לקמן במגילה בלשני מלואים דף מז ע"ב ד"ה אף כאן:

רבינו חננאל

מודה ר' שמעון בפסיק רישי' ולא ימות פי' כי ר' שמעון מודה בדבר שהוא ברור כגון אדם שחותך ראש אדם ואומר שאין כוונתו להמיתו אלא להוציא את ממונו שאין שומעין לו אלא דנין אותו דין כל הורג נפש כך כל דבר שמתברר (מעשין) [שיעשה] לאותה מלאכה אין אומרין שלא היתה כוונתו לכך. וכה"ג אפילו ר' שמעון מודה. ואביי אליבא דר' שמעון קודם שישמע מרבא. מודה ר' שמעון בפסיק רישיה ולא ימות דהוה מוקים ליה כר' יהודה ולא כר' שמעון הוה אמר דר"ש פליג נמי בהא דסבר ר' שמעון חתיכות הערלה והצרעת עליה דבר שאין מתכוון הוא שאין כוונתו לחתוך הצרעת אלא למול בנו וכי האי לר' שמעון שרי ולא צריך קרא למשרייה אם כן אביי אליבא דר' שמעון האי בשר ערלתו מאי עביד ליה אמר רב משרשיה באומר לקוץ בהרתו הוא מתכוין כלומר בדבר מוכיח שמתכוין לקוץ בהרתו בא הכתוב להתירו ואקשינן תינח גדול פי' שיש בו דעת יש לומר כן מתכוין לקוץ בהרתו קטן שאין בו דעת למה כתוב בו בשר להתיר חתיכת צרעת במילה ואמרי' קטן נמי מתכוין אביו בזה במולו לבנו לחתוך בהרת בנו ואמרי' בעת שיש בהרת בערלת הקטן ימול אחר זולתו אבי הבן. שהאחר אין מתכוין לחתוך הבהרת ודבר שאין מתכוין לר' שמעון שרי ולא הוה צריך קרא למישריה דאמר רבי שמעון בן לקיש כל מקום שאתה מוצא עשה ולא תעשה פי' כגון זה עשה שנאמר וביום השמיני ימול בשר ערלתו. לא תעשה השמר בנגע הצרעת שהוא לאו כאשר פירשנו למעלה. ואם יש בהרת בערלה וימול אחר זולתו אבי הבן נתקיימה המילה שהיא עשה ונתקיימה חתיכת הצרעת שלא בכוונה שלא הזהירה התורה אלא במתכוין והאחר לא נתכוין ואין אומר יבא עשה וידחה לא תעשה אלא אם אין כח כלל לקיים שניהם ופרקינן דליכא אחר ואם נאמר להמתין עד שיבא אחר וימול ביטלנו וביום השמיני ימול שהוא עשה: ובאנו לפרש עוד תשלום הברייתא: אמר מר י"ט אינו דוחה אלא בזמנו. פי' אין מילה דוחה י"ט אלא הנימול ביום ח' שהוא זמנו בלבד ואמרינן מנא הני מילי ופירשו חזקיה א) מן הקדשים שטעונין שריפה והוא עשה כדכתיב

מסורת הש"ס

א) [יומא לד:], ב) [שם], ג) לעיל קג. קיא: קיז. קכ: ולקמן קמג. [בכורות כה. סוכה לג. כתובות ו. כריתות כ.], ד) תוספתא נגעים פ"ב, ה) יבמות ז: נזיר מא. נח. מנחות מ:, ו) לעיל כד: פסחים פג: תמורה ד: ע"ש, ז) [ע"ל עד בקר והנותר ממנו עד בקר באש תשרופו וכו' ליתא בדפוסים], ח) פסחים סו. סט: יבמות יד. מנחות עב., ט) [עי' תוס' עמוד ב' ד"ה לוקחן], י) [ועי' תוס' יומא יב. ד"ה ..., וזבחים מה. ד"ה הלכתא, וכו'] ט) [ועי' תוס' כתובות ה. ד"ה אלא לכאן]

הגהות הב"ח

(א) גמ' אבל אתה עושה אותו בסיב: (ב) שם דלעשות לעשות: (ג) רש"י ד"ה שאין ת"ל וכו' והנותר באש תשרפו אלא אשריפה קאי וכו': (ד) ד"ה דאתיא וכו' כדאמרינן לעיל: (ה) ד"ה ומוצצין וכו' ע"י המצילה: (ו) תוס' ד"ה עושין וכו' קתני לה בשילהי:

תורה אור השלם

א) וּבַיּוֹם הַשְּׁמִינִי יִמּוֹל בְּשַׂר עָרְלָתוֹ: [ויקרא יב, ג]
ב) הִשָּׁמֶר בְּנֶגַע הַצָּרַעַת לִשְׁמֹר מְאֹד וְלַעֲשׂוֹת כְּכֹל אֲשֶׁר יוֹרוּ אֶתְכֶם הַכֹּהֲנִים הַלְוִיִּם כַּאֲשֶׁר צִוִּיתִם תִּשְׁמְרוּ לַעֲשׂוֹת: [דברים כד, ח]
ג) וְלֹא תוֹתִירוּ מִמֶּנּוּ עַד בֹּקֶר וְהַנֹּתָר מִמֶּנּוּ עַד בֹּקֶר בָּאֵשׁ תִּשְׂרֹפוּ: [שמות יב, י]
ד) עֹלַת שַׁבַּת בְּשַׁבַּתּוֹ עַל עֹלַת הַתָּמִיד וְנִסְכָּהּ: [במדבר כח, י]
ה) וּבַיּוֹם הָרִאשׁוֹן מִקְרָא קֹדֶשׁ וּבַיּוֹם הַשְּׁבִיעִי מִקְרָא קֹדֶשׁ יִהְיֶה לָכֶם כָּל מְלָאכָה לֹא יֵעָשֶׂה בָהֶם אַךְ אֲשֶׁר יֵאָכֵל לְכָל נֶפֶשׁ הוּא לְבַדּוֹ יֵעָשֶׂה לָכֶם: [שמות יב, טז]
ו) דַּבֵּר אֶל בְּנֵי יִשְׂרָאֵל לֵאמֹר בַּחֹדֶשׁ הַשְּׁבִיעִי בְּאֶחָד לַחֹדֶשׁ יִהְיֶה לָכֶם שַׁבָּתוֹן זִכְרוֹן תְּרוּעָה מִקְרָא קֹדֶשׁ: [ויקרא כג, כד]

רב נסים גאון

דאתי עשה ודחי לא תעשה גרידא לא תעשה שיש בה כרת מי דחי ותו לא תעשה גרידא מנלן דדחי דכתיב (דברים כב) לא תלבש שעטנז וכתיב גדילים תעשה לך ידענו כי זה לא תעשה אינו שוה בכל דבר אלא מיוחד הוא וכי הציווי שנאמר אחריו הוא תנאי עליו וכי לא בא להזהיר אלא על לבישת כלאים חוץ ממצות ציצית אבל מה שהוא מעורב מחוטי פשתן עם הטלית של צמר שהיא מצוה אינו נכנס בזו האזהרה אלא מותר הוא ואמרו חכמים שדבר זה עיקר הוא שנסמך עליו וכי כל אזהרה שאין עמה כרת שבתורה כך היא דרכה שבעת שאירע חיוב מצות עשה נדחה האזהרה שהיא לא תעשה ונקיים הציוי שהוא עשה ותבוא מצות עשה ותדחה לא תעשה כי האזהרה של לאו על זה התנאי נאמרה ובזה הפירוש שפירשנו יסיר מלבך ספק גדול שמסתפקין בו בני אדם ושואלין עליו והוא שאומרין מאחר שאנו יודעין שאזהרת לאו קשה מציווי עשה היאך יבא עשה וידחה האזהרה של לאו שהיא חמורה

חשק שלמה על רבינו חננאל א) חסר קצת וכצ"ל ופי' חזקיה דילפינן זה מנותר מן הקדשים וכו':

ליקוטי רש"י

למה לי קרא. בשר לרבות המנוגע דמאי למכתב ימול ערלתו וכתב בשר לרבות בשר האמור בנגעים (ויקרא יג) אדם כי יהיה בעור בשרו למה לי קרא הא דבר שאינו מתכוין הוא [יומא לד:]. אפילו תימא ר"ש. דאמר במסכת שבת (מא:) דבר שאין מתכוין מותר [בכורות כה.]. מודה ר' שמעון בפסיק רישיה ולא ימות. כאומר אחתוך ראש בהמה זו בשבת ואיני רוצה שתמות דמיון דלאי אפשר שלא תמות כמתכוין חשיב ליה וכי אמרינן דבר שאין מתכוין מותר כגון היכא דאפשר ליה בלא איסור כגון גורר אדם מטה כסא וספסל ובלבד שלא יתכוין לעשות חריץ ואף על גב דאיכא למיחש דלמא עביד חריץ כיון דלא מתכוין להכי ואפשר לגרירה בלא חריץ כי עביד נמי חריץ דהוי מלאכה גמורה לא מיחייב אבל היכא דלאי עביד מודי [סוכה לג:]. השמר בנגע הצרעת. בקוצץ בהרתו הכתוב מדבר והשמר הוא לא תעשה [מכות כב.]. שלא תתלוש סימני טומאה ולא תקוץ את הבהרת [דברים כד, ח]. דאמר וכו' כל מקום שאתה מוצא עשה. [illegible]

mandment come and override the prohibition. Here, the positive commandment of *milah* ostensibly conflicts with the prohibition against cutting off *tzaraas* to effect purification. However, there exists a way to perform the former without violating the latter — i.e. to have an outside party, who will not intend for purification, oversee the minor's circumcision. Since according to Reish Lakish that is the required approach, the word *flesh* cannot refer to the case of the child's father, or agent, who will have intent for his son's purification. With regard to what case, then, does *flesh* come to teach?[22]

The Gemara answers:

דְּלֵיכָּא אַחֵר – Indeed, it teaches as to **where there is no** person **other** than the father who can oversee the minor child's circumcision. And so, according to Abaye's initial understanding of R' Shimon's opinion, the word *flesh* instructs that a father may intend for circumcision to effect his minor son's purification from *tzaraas*.[23]

The Gemara revisits a Baraisa cited above (132b), to discuss its second half:

אָמַר מַר – **Master said:** **יוֹם טוֹב אֵינָהּ דוֹחָה אֶלָּא בִּזְמַנָּהּ בִּלְבַד** – The Baraisa stated: The mitzvah of [THE CIRCUMCISION] OVERRIDES the FESTIVAL *melachah* restrictions ONLY when performed AT ITS proper TIME. **מְנָא הָנֵי מִילֵּי** – **From where** do we know **this law?**[24]

The Gemara answers:

אָמַר חִזְקִיָּה וְכֵן תָּנָא דְּבֵי חִזְקִיָּה – **Chizkiyah said, and so** one **of** the sages from **Chizkiyah's academy taught:** **אָמַר קְרָא** – **The verse states:**[25] **"לֹא־תוֹתִירוּ מִמֶּנּוּ עַד־בֹּקֶר"** – *You shall not leave any of it until morning; and that which is left of it until morning you shall burn in fire.* **שֶׁאֵין תַּלְמוּד לוֹמַר "עַד־בֹּקֶר"** – Now, **it is not [necessary for] the Torah to state** ***until morning*** a second time.[26] **מַה תַּלְמוּד לוֹמַר "עַד־בֹּקֶר"** – **What,** then, **does the Torah** come **to teach** with the second ***until morning?*** **בָּא הַכָּתוּב לִיתֵּן לוֹ בֹּקֶר שֵׁנִי לִשְׂרֵיפָתוֹ** – **Scripture comes to give [the** ***pesach*** **offering] a second morning** (i.e. the first morning of Chol HaMoed) **for its burning.**[27]

The Gemara offers a different source:

אַבַּיֵי אָמַר אָמַר קְרָא – **Abaye said: The verse states**[28] with respect to the Sabbath *mussaf* offering, **"עֹלַת שַׁבַּת בְּשַׁבַּתּוֹ"** – ***The olah offering of each Sabbath on its own Sabbath,*** which implies that a Sabbath *olah* is burned on the Sabbath **וְלֹא עוֹלַת חוֹל בְּשַׁבָּת** – **but a weekday** ***olah*** is **not** burned **on the Sabbath** **וְלֹא עוֹלַת חוֹל בְּיוֹם טוֹב** – **and a weekday** ***olah*** is **not** burned **on a festival day.**[29]

A third source for the Baraisa's law:

רָבָא אָמַר אָמַר קְרָא – **Rava said: The verse states**[30] with regard to the Festival Days: **"הוּא לְבַדּוֹ יֵעָשֶׂה לָכֶם"** – *No work may be done on them, except for what must be eaten for any person* —***only that***[31] ***may be done for you.*** **"הוּא" וְלֹא מַכְשִׁירִין** – Although the verse sanctions the performance on Yom Tov of any *melachah* needed for the preparation of meals, the superfluous word ***that*** implies: **But** one may **not** perform a *melachah* to accomplish any of the **preliminaries** to food preparation, such as manufacturing a spit, knife or oven for cooking.[32] **"לְבַדּוֹ" וְלֹא מִילָה שֶׁלֹּא בִּזְמַנָּהּ** – Further, the extraneous word ***only*** teaches: **But** one may **not** perform on Yom Tov or Shabbos **a circumcision not at its** proper **time,**[33] **דְּאָתְיָא מִקַּל וָחוֹמֶר** – the opposite of **which** could **have been derived through a** ***kal vachomer.***[34]

NOTES

22. See *Ritva* (*MHK* ed.) and *Chidushei HaRan,* who explain that the Gemara finds the verse difficult, for it is unreasonable that Scripture would contravene an accepted principle of exegesis.

Regarding why this is a case of "it is possible to observe both [conflicting commandments]," see *Beis HaLevi* I:10, *Maharatz Chayes* and *Melo HaRo'im.*

23. [According to the Gemara's conclusion, it matters not if the father so intends, since removal of the *tzaraas* is an inevitable consequence (פְּסִיק רֵישָׁא) of the circumcising. Hence, the verse comes to permit *milah* even in such a case.] Cf. *Ramban* to 111a citing *Aruch,* who understands that this passage accords with Rava as well (and, according to the conclusion, Abaye as well). See also *Maharam Schif* here.

24. I.e. why not say that the positive commandment of *milah* overrides the prohibition against performing *melachah* on Yom Tov? (*Chidushei HaRan, Maharam Schif*).

25. *Exodus* 12:10, which instructs as to the disposition of the leftovers of the *pesach* offering (*korban pesach*), which is consumed on the night of the fifteenth of Nissan, the night of Yom Tov.

26. Rather, it would have sufficed to say, "and that which is left of it you shall burn in fire" [inasmuch as "until morning" appears in the beginning of the verse] (*Rashi*).

27. The second *until morning* perforce refers to the leftovers' burning, so that the verse implicitly reads as follows: ". . . and that which is left of it at the time burning is prohibited (i.e. the morning of Yom Tov, 15 Nissan) shall be kept until the second morning (under Biblical law, the first morning of Chol HaMoed, 16 Nissan), and shall be burned at that time." Now, the *pesach* sacrifice is considered a "weekday" matter, since the time of its offering is Yom Tov eve (14 Nissan, a regular weekday). For that reason the burning of its leftovers may not be performed on the holy Yom Tov day. Similarly, *milah* after the eighth day is also considered a "weekday" matter vis-a-vis Yom Tov (since the eighth day, its proper time, fell on a weekday), and thus may not be performed on that holy day (*Rashi*). [When the eighth day falls on Yom Tov, however, the *milah* is considered one of the mitzvos of that holy day.]

28. *Numbers* 28:10.

29. That is, limbs from the afternoon *tamid* sacrifice of the day before Yom Tov may not be offered the following night (when they would ordinarily be brought on the Altar — see *Berachos* 2a). [See above, 24b note 28, as to how Yom Tov is implicated by a verse that speaks only of the Sabbath.] Now, since *milah* not at its proper time corresponds to burning the limbs of a weekday *olah* (see note 27 above), it too may not be performed on Yom Tov (*Rashi*).

30. *Exodus* 12:16.

31. The words *only that* are extraneous, since the verse could have stated, ". . . except for what must be eaten for any person may be done for you" (*Rashi* above, 24b ד״ה הוא לבדו). Rava now enumerates the two exclusions implied by these two extra words.

32. See *Beitzah* 28b, where this matter is debated by Tannaim.

33. I.e. a circumcision performed after the eighth day, the case of the Baraisa.

34. That is, if not for the exclusionary word לְבַדּוֹ (*only*), we could derive through a *kal vachomer* that even a deferred *milah* overrides the Sabbath and Yom Tov restrictions. The argument would run as follows: Since deferred *milah* overrides a mitzvah (*tzaraas* law) that overrides a mitzvah (the sacrificial service) that overrides Sabbath and Yom Tov law, then certainly deferred *milah* itself should override Sabbath and Yom Tov law. The word *only* teaches that it does not (*Rashi*), and is the third source for the Baraisa's law.

The Gemara stated this *kal vachomer* above, on 132b. The Rishonim question *Rashi's* rendering of the *kal vachomer,* since Rava himself rejected it there, for he held that Sabbath law is more stringent than *tzaraas* law (see *Tosafos* above, 24b ד״ה ולא, and *Ritva MHK* ed. here). *Tosafos* (ibid.) suggest deleting the words דְּאָתְיָא מִקַּל וָחוֹמֶר, since now we assume that Yom Tov law is only a prohibition, which can be overridden by the positive commandment of *milah;* hence, the verse is needed to teach that Yom Tov law is not overridden. Others point out, however, that Rava himself certainly holds that Yom Tov law encompasses both a positive and a negative commandment. Hence, a *kal vachomer* is needed to create the need for a verse. They therefore suggest other, viable *kal vachomer* arguments. See *Tosafos* ibid. and *Rabbeinu Chananel* here; and see *Ritva* (*MHK* ed.), who writes in defense of *Rashi.*

תנאי היא דתניא (א) בשר ואף על פי שיש שם בהרת ימול דברי רבי יאשיה רבי יונתן אומר אינו צריך שבת חמורה דוחה צרעת לא כ"ש: אמר מר בשר אע"פ שיש שם בהרת ימול דברי רבי יאשיה והא למה לי קרא דבר שאין מתכוון הוא ודבר שאין מתכוון מותר אמר אביי לא נצרכא אלא לרבי יהודה דאמר דבר שאין מתכוון אסור רבא אמר אפילו תימא ר"ש מודה ר"ש בפסיק רישיה ולא ימות ואביי לית ליה האי סברא והא אביי ורבא דאמרי תרווייהו מודה רבי שמעון בפסיק רישיה ולא ימות בתר דשמעה מרבא סברה איכא דמתני להא דאביי ורבא אהא השמר בנגע הצרעת לשמור מאד ולעשות לעשות אי אתה עושה אבל (א) עושה אתה בסיב שעל גבי רגלו ובמוט שעל גבי כתיפו ואם עברה עברה והא למה לי קרא דבר שאין מתכוון הוא ודבר שאין מתכוון מותר אמר אביי לא נצרכא אלא לרבי יהודה דאמר דבר שאין מתכוון אסור ורבא אמר אפילו תימא רבי שמעון ומודה רבי שמעון בפסיק רישיה ולא ימות ואביי לית ליה האי סברא והא אביי ורבא דאמרי תרוייהו מודה ר' שמעון בפסיק רישיה ולא ימות לבתר דשמעיה מרבא סברה ואביי אליבא דרבי שמעון האי בשר מאי עביד ליה אמר רב עמרם באומר לקוץ בהרתו הוא מתכוין תינח גדול קטן מאי איכא למימר אמר רב משרשיא באומר אבי הבן לקוץ בהרת דבנו הוא קא מתכוין ואי איכא אחר ליעביד אחר דאמר ר"ש בן לקיש כל מקום שאתה מוצא עשה ולא תעשה אם אתה יכול לקיים שניהם מוטב ואם לאו יבא עשה וידחה לא תעשה דליכא אחר: אמר מר יום טוב אינה דוחה אלא בזמנה בלבד מנא הני מילי אמר חזקיה וכן תנא דבי חזקיה אמר קרא לא תותירו ממנו עד בקר שאין ת"ל עד בקר מה ת"ל עד בקר בא הכתוב ליתן לו בקר שני לשריפתו אביי אמר אמר קרא עולת שבת בשבתו ולא עולת חול בשבת ולא עולת חול בי"ט רבא אמר אמר קרא הוא לבדו יעשה לכם הוא ולא מכשירין לבדו ולא מילה שלא בזמנה דאתיא מק"ו רב אשי אמר שבתון עשה הוא והוה ליה י"ט עשה ול"ת ואין עשה דוחה את לא תעשה ועשה: כלל אמר ר"ע וכו': אמר רב יהודה אמר רב הלכה כר"ע ותנן נמי גבי פסח כי האי גוונא כלל אמר ר"ע כל מלאכה שאפשר לה לעשותה מע"ש אינה דוחה את השבת שחיטה שאי אפשר לעשותה מע"ש דוחה את השבת ואמר רב יהודה אמר רב הלכה כר"ע וצריכא דאי אשמעינן גבי מילה התם הוא דמכשירין (ג) אפשר לעשות מאתמול לא דחו שבת דליכא כרת אבל פסח דאיכא כרת אימא לידחו שבת ואי אשמעינן גבי פסח משום דלא נכרתו עליה י"ג בריתות אבל מילה דנכרתו עליה י"ג בריתות אימא לידחו שבת צריכא:

מתני' עושין כל צרכי מילה [בשבת] מוהלין ופורעין ומוצצין ונותנין עליה איספלנית וכמון אם לא שחק מע"ש לועס בשיניו ונותן אם לא טרף יין ושמן מע"ש ינתן זה בעצמו וזה בעצמו ואין עושין לה חלוק לכתחילה אבל כורך עליה סמרטוט אם לא התקין מע"ש כורך על אצבעו ומביא ואפי' מחצר אחרת: **גמ'**

רש"י

תנאי היא. דאיכא דנפקא ליה מילה בזמנה מק"ו כרבא וכי אתא קרא לשלא בזמנה ואיכא דלא נפקא ליה בק"ו ואיצטריך למילה בזמנה כרב ספרא ושלא בזמנה אתיא מבינייא: **לרבי יהודה.** רבי יאשיה דמצריך קרא להכי כרבי יהודה סבירא ליה: **מודה ר' שמעון בפסיק רישיה.** הילכך אי לא רבי קרא לא עבדי: **סברה.** נתן בה לעמיה וקבל ממנו: ה"ג לעשות עושה אתה בסיב שעל רגלו ובמוט שעל גבי כתיפו. ואינו צריך להזהר מללבוש סיב שקושר מנעלו ברגלו ומלשאת משאוי על כתיפו: **ואם עברה.** הבהרת בכך עברה ואינו חושש לה להכי כתיב לעשות שמותר לעשות מלאכתו: **ואביי אליבא דר' שמעון.** מעיקרא מקמי דסברה האי בשר מאי עביד ליה: **באומר לקוץ.** גדול שהוא בר עונשין ואומר למוהל לקוץ בהרתו בכוונה ליטהר: **קטן.** דלא ידע לכווני מאי איכא למימר ועל כרחין בתרוייהו כתיב בשר כדאמרי' לעיל ובשר דכתיב גבי קטן כתיב ביום השמיני ל"ל: **באומר אבי הבן לקוץ.** דמתכוין לטהרו והוא מוזהר לא ליעבד בידים ובמתכוין: **ואי איכא אחר.** שאינו חושש לטהרו ליעבד אחר ולא ליקו לא להתם ואע"ג דרבייה קרא שהרי אתה יכול לקיים עשה בלא עקירת לאו לר' שמעון דהא אחר לא מיכוין ולא עבר ואמר ריש לקיש כו' ורבויא למאי אתא: **שאין תלמוד לומר עד בקר.** מניינא והנותר ממנו עד בקר למאי למכתב והנותר באש תשרפו (ג) אלא אשריפה קאי והכי קאמר והנותר ממנו זמנן שאסרתי לך דהיינו בקר ראשון כשיבא בקר שני שהוא חולו של מועד תשרפו אבל בי"ט לא אלמא מידי דחזי לחול לא עבדינן בי"ט ופסח קרבן הוא י"ד בניסן הוא שהוא חול ומילה שלא בזמנה נמי מידי דחזי לחול הוא דבשבת זו לא היה זמנה: **ולא עולת חול בי"ט.** אבל תמיד של ע"ש אין קרבין בי"ט ומילה שלא בזמנה נמי כעולת חול בי"ט דמי: **דאתיא בק"ו.** שמלה ומה לרעת שדוחה עבודה מילה שלא בזמנה דוחה אותה כדאמרינן לעיל (ד) שבת שנדחית מפני עבודה אינו דין שמילה שלא בזמנה דוחה אותה להכי איצטריך לבדו: **ואין עשה.** דמילה דוחה לא תעשה ועשה אבל בזמנה איתרבי מביום אפילו בשבת: **גבי פסח.** כל מלאכה שאפשר לה לעשות מע"ש כגון הבאתו מחוץ לתחום וחתיכת יבלתו: **וצריכא.** למימר בתרוייהו הלכה כר"ע דמכשירין לא דחו: **מילה בזמנה ליכא כרת.** דקטן לאו בר עונשין הוא ואבוה לאו מיחייב עליה כרת: **מתני' מוהלין.** חותך את הערלה: **ופורעין.** את העור המכסה ראש הגיד: **ומוצצין.** את הדם ואף על גב דהיא עשיית חבורה שאין הדם נימצה מחיבורו אלא על ידי (ה) המציצה: **איספלנית.** מתבושת. כמה דאפשר לשנויי משנינן: **לועס בשיניו. לא טרף יין ושמן.** כך היו רגילין והיא רפואה שמערבין וטורפין בקערה יין ושמן יחד כדרך שטורפין ביצים בקערה: **חלוק.** כעין כיס דחוק היו עושין ומלבישים את ראש הגיד עד העטרה וקושרים שם כדי שלא יחזור העור לכסות את הגיד: **לא התקין.** לא הזמין: **כורך על ידו.** דרך מלבוש לשנותו מדרך הוצאה בחול:

תוספות

ואביי אליבא דר' שמעון. ולרבי יוחנן לא מיבעיא ליה דמוקי ליה בינוי ולאביי נמי דאמר לעיל דבינוי אתי מבינייא מאי למימר דסבר כר' יוחנן מילתא דאתי בק"ו טרח וכתב לה קרא: **באומר לקוץ בהרתו הוא מתכוין.** וא"ת אם כן אמאי קאמר אביי לא נצרכא אלא לרבי יהודה הא לר"ש נמי איצטריך כדאמר הכא וי"ל דמשמע דלשון ברייתא משמע דמיירי בלא מתכוין מדלא קתני בשר אע"ג דמתכוין לקוץ בהרת ימול:

ותנן נמי גבי פסח כה"ג אמר רב יהודה אמר רב הלכה כר"ע. והכא לא פריך הילכתא למשיחא משום דנפקא מינה גבי מילה אע"ג דגבי מילה נמי פסיק הכי מ"מ לאלומי פיסקא דמילה פסיק נמי גבי פסח אגב דפסיק גבי מילה דמילף מינה שפסק ברור הוא לכל דבר (מ):

וצריכא דאי אשמעינן. אדרב יהודה קאי דפסיק כר"ע הכא והתם דלאו אדרבי עקיבא א"כ בפ' שתי הלחם (מנחות דף צו.) דקתני נמי כלל אמר ר"ע הוה ליה למימר וצריכא וכן פירש בקונטרס (ס):

עושין כל צרכי מילה בשבת. אע"ג דלעיל נמי קתני (ו) בשילהי מפנין (ד' קכח.) התם תני לה אגב גררא דמילי דמינוק אבל הכא עיקר:

גדול

עין משפט נר מצוה

י א מיי' פ"י מהלכות טומאת צרעת הלכה ח סמג לאוין שנג:
יא ב מיי' פ"א מהלכות יו"ט הלכה ו:
יב ג מיי' פ"א מהלכות קרבן פסח הלכה יח סמג עשין רכג:
יג ד מיי' פ"ב מהלכות מילה הל' ו סמג עשין כח טוש"ע א"ח סי' שלא סעיף ו וטוש"ע י"ד סי' רסו סעיף ב:
יד ה מיי' שם הל' ז סמג שם וטוש"ע א"ח שם וטוש"ע י"ד שם סעיף ג:

גליון הש"ס

רש"י ד"ה שאין ת"ל וכו' י"ד בניסן הוא שהוא חול. עיין כעין זה לקמן במגילה בלבני מלואים דף מז ע"ב ד"ה אף כאן:

רבינו חננאל

מודה ר' שמעון בפסיק רישי' ולא ימות פי' כי ר' שמעון מודה בדבר שהוא ברור כגון אדם שחותך ראש אדם ואומר שאין כוונתו להמיתו אלא להוציא את ממונו שאין שומעין לו אלא דנין אותו דין כל הורג נפש כך כל דבר שמתברר (מעשין) [שיעשה] לאותה מלאכה אין אומרין שלא היתה כוונתו לכך. וכה"ג אפילו ר' שמעון מודה. ואביי אליבא דר' שמעון קודם שישמע מרבא. מודה ר' שמעון בפסיק רישיה ולא ימות דהוה מוקים ליה כר' יהודה ולא כר' שמעון הוה אמר דר"ש פליג נמי בהא דסבר ר' שמעון חתיכות הערלה והצרעת עליה דבר שאין מתכוון הוא שאין כוונתו לחתוך הצרעת אלא למול בנו וכי האי לר' שמעון שרי ולא צריך קרא למשרייה אם כן אביי אליבא דר' שמעון האי בשר ערלתו מאי עביד ליה אמר רב משרשיה באומר לקוץ בהרתו הוא מתכוין כלומר בדבר מוכיח שמתכוין לקוץ בהרתו בא הכתוב להתירו ואקשינן תינח גדול פי' שיש בו דעת יש לומר כן מתכוין לקוץ בהרתו קטן שאין בו דעת למה כתוב בו בשר להתיר חתיכת צרעת במילה ואמרי' קטן נמי מתכוין אביו בזה במולו לבנו לחתוך בהרת בנו ואמרי' בעת שיש בהרת בערלת הקטן ימול אחר זולתו אבי הבן. שהאחר אין מתכוין לחתוך הבהרת ודבר שאין מתכוין לר' שמעון שרי ולא הוה צריך קרא למישריה דאמר רבי שמעון בן לקיש כל מקום שאתה מוצא עשה ולא תעשה פי' כגון זה עשה שנאמר וביום השמיני ימול בשר ערלתו. לא תעשה השמר בנגע הצרעת שהוא לאו כאשר פירשנו למעלה. ואם יש בהרת בערלה וימול אחר זולתו אבי הבן נתקיימה המילה שהיא עשה ונתקיימה חתיכת הצרעת שלא בכוונה שלא הזהירה התורה אלא במתכוין והאחר לא נתכוין ואין אומר יבא עשה וידחה לא תעשה אלא אם אין כח כלל לקיים שניהם ופרקינן דליכא אחר ואם נאמר להמתין עד שיבא אחר וימול ביטלנו וביום השמיני ימול שהוא עשה: ובאנו לפרש עוד תשלום הברייתא: **אמר** מר י"ט אינו דוחה אלא בזמנו. פי' אין מילה דוחה י"ט אלא הנימול ביום ח' שהוא זמנו בלבד ואמרינן מנא הני מילי ופירשו חזקיה א) מן הקדשים שטעונין שריפה והוא עשה כדכתיב

חשק שלמה על רבינו חננאל א) חסר קלת ונ"ל ופי' חזקיה דילפינן זה מנותר מן הקדשים וכו':

מסורת הש"ס

א) [יומא לד:], ב) [שם], ג) לעיל קלב. קיז. קלג: ולק' קמג. [ביצה לו.] סוכה לג: כתובות ו. בכורות כה., ד) [תוספתא נגעים פ"ב], ה) יבמות כ: נזיר מא. נח. מנחות מ., ו) לעיל כד: פסחים פג: תמורה ד:, ז) [תוספתא פי"ב], ח) יבמות ד: ע"ש, ט) [צ"ל] עד בקר והנותר ממנו עד בקר באש תשרפו וכ"ה בפסחים], מ) [פסחים סט.], ס) יבמות יד. מנחות מה. ובע"י, ע) [לעיל דף קכח], פ) [ער' תוס' מגילה עמוד ב' ד"ה לעשן], צ) נ"ל מלוזוק, ק) [וע"ע תוס' יומא יג. ד"ה הלכה כר"ע וכו' ...], ר) [ואלמתא דר"ש לא כעי לריכותא דלאמשמעי' כל דוכתא מאי דדמי שבת כ"ד תוס' בחמכות].

הגהות הב"ח

(א) גמ' אבל אתה עושה אותו בסיב: (ב) שם למספר לעשות: (ג) רש"י ד"ה שאין וכו' ולא חנא באש תשרפו אלא אשריפה קאי וכו' דלמשריפה קאי וכו' הוא דכ"ש זו לא: (ד) ד"ה דאתיא וכו' כדאמרינן לעיל ע"י שנדחים: (ה) ד"ה ומוצצין וכו' אלא ע"י (המלילה) מו"מ וכ"נ מ"א סכורה: (ו) תוס' ד"ה עושין וכו' קתני לה בשילהי:

תורה אור השלם

א) וּבַיּוֹם הַשְּׁמִינִי יִמּוֹל בְּשַׂר עָרְלָתוֹ: [ויקרא יב, ג]
ב) הִשָּׁמֶר בְּנֶגַע הַצָּרַעַת לִשְׁמֹר מְאֹד וְלַעֲשׂוֹת כְּכֹל אֲשֶׁר יוֹרוּ אֶתְכֶם הַכֹּהֲנִים הַלְוִיִּם כַּאֲשֶׁר צִוִּיתִם תִּשְׁמְרוּ לַעֲשׂוֹת: [דברים כד, ח]
ג) וְלֹא תוֹתִירוּ מִמֶּנּוּ עַד בֹּקֶר וְהַנֹּתָר מִמֶּנּוּ עַד בֹּקֶר בָּאֵשׁ תִּשְׂרֹפוּ: [שמות יב, י]
ד) עֹלַת שַׁבַּת בְּשַׁבַּתּוֹ עַל עֹלַת הַתָּמִיד וְנִסְכָּהּ: [במדבר כח, י]
ה) וּבַיּוֹם הָרִאשׁוֹן מִקְרָא קֹדֶשׁ וּבַיּוֹם הַשְּׁבִיעִי מִקְרָא קֹדֶשׁ יִהְיֶה לָכֶם כָּל מְלָאכָה לֹא יֵעָשֶׂה בָהֶם אַךְ אֲשֶׁר יֵאָכֵל לְכָל נֶפֶשׁ הוּא לְבַדּוֹ יֵעָשֶׂה לָכֶם: [שמות יב, טז]
ו) דַּבֵּר אֶל בְּנֵי יִשְׂרָאֵל לֵאמֹר בַּחֹדֶשׁ הַשְּׁבִיעִי בְּאֶחָד לַחֹדֶשׁ יִהְיֶה לָכֶם שַׁבָּתוֹן זִכְרוֹן תְּרוּעָה מִקְרָא קֹדֶשׁ: [ויקרא כג, כד]

רב נסים גאון

דאתי עשה ודחי לא תעשה לא תעשה גרידא לא תעשה שיש בה כרת מי דחי ותו לא תעשה גרידא מנלן דדחי דכתיב (דברים כב) לא תלבש שעטנז וכתיב גדילים תעשה לך ידענו כי זה לא תעשה אינו שוה בכל דבר אלא מיוחד הוא וכי הציווי שנאמר אחריו הוא תנאי עליו וכי לא בא להזהיר אלא על לבישת כלאים חוץ ממצות ציצית אבל מה שהוא מעורב מחוטי פשתן עם הטלית של צמר שהיא מצוה אינו נכנס בזו האזהרה אלא מותר הוא ואמרו חכמים שדבר זה עיקר הוא שנסמך עליו וכי כל אזהרה שאין עמה כרת שבתורה כך היא דרכה שבעת שאירע חיוב מצות עשה נדחה האזהרה שהיא לא תעשה ונקיים הציווי שהוא עשה ותבוא מצות עשה ותדחה לא תעשה כי האזהרה שנאמרה לא על זה התנאי נאמרה ובזה הפירוש שפירשנו יסיר מלבך ספק גדול שמסתפקין בו בני אדם ושואלין עליו ואומרים מאחר שאנו יודעין שאזהרת לאו קשה מציווי עשה היאך יבא עשה וידחה האזהרה של לאו שהיא חמורה

ליקוטי רש"י

למה לי קרא. בשר לרבות המנוגע דמאי למכתב ימול ערלתו וכתב בשר לרבות בשר האמור בנגעים (ויקרא יג) אדם כי יהיה בעור בשרו למה לי קרא הא דבר שאינו מתכוין הוא [יומא לד:]. **אפילו תימא ר"ש.** דאמר במסכת שבת (מא:) דבר שאין מתכוין מותר [בכורות כה.]. **מודה ר' שמעון בפסיק רישיה ולא ימות.** כלומר אחתוך ראש בהמה זו בשבת ואיני רוצה שתמות דכיון דלאי אפשר שלא תמות כמתכוין חשיב ליה וכי אמרינן דבר שאין מתכוין מותר כגון גורר אדם מטה כסא וספסל ובלבד שלא יתכוין לעשות חריץ ואף על גב דליכא למיחש דלמא עביד חריץ כיון דלא מתכוין להכי ואפשר לגרירה בלא חריץ כי עביד נמי חריץ דהוי מלאכה גמורה לא ודאי עביד מודי [סוכה לג:]. **השמר בנגע הצרעת.** בקוצץ בהרתו הכתוב מדבר והשמר הוא לא תעשה [מכות כב.]. שלא תתלוש סימני טומאה ולא תקוץ את הבהרת [דברים כד, ח]. **דאמר וכו' כל מקום שאתה מוצא עשה.** [illegible]

The Gemara presents one final source for the Baraisa's law:

רַב אַשִׁי אָמַר – **Rav Ashi said:** "שַׁבָּתוֹן" – The verse,[35] *On the first day **a solemn rest** and on the eighth day a solemn rest,* עֲשֵׂה הוּא – **constitutes a positive commandment,** for its implication is: rest on that day. וַהֲוָה לֵיהּ יוֹם טוֹב עֲשֵׂה וְלֹא תַעֲשֶׂה – **And so** work on **Yom Tov is** prohibited by both **a positive and a negative**[36] **commandment,** וְאֵין עֲשֵׂה דּוֹחֶה אֶת לֹא תַעֲשֶׂה וַעֲשֵׂה – **and a** single **positive commandment** (such as a deferred *milah*) **does not override** the opposing combination of **a negative and a positive commandment.**[37]

The Gemara now turns to the next part of the Mishnah, which stated:

כְּלָל אָמַר רַבִּי עֲקִיבָא וכו' – R' AKIVA STATED A GENERAL RULE etc. [Any labor that can be performed on the Sabbath eve does not override the Sabbath (*melachah* restrictions), (and any labor) that cannot be performed on the Sabbath eve does override the Sabbath (restrictions).]

R' Akiva argues with R' Eliezer, who permits the performance of preliminaries to a mitzvah on the Sabbath. R' Akiva maintains, however, that when a preliminary can be performed before the Sabbath, one may not perform it on the Sabbath. An Amora now rules in the matter:

אָמַר רַב יְהוּדָה אָמַר רַב – **Rav Yehudah said in the name of Rav:** הֲלָכָה כְּרַבִּי עֲקִיבָא – **The law accords with** the opinion of **R' Akiva.**

The Gemara notes that Rav issued a similar ruling in another case:

וּתְנַן נַמִּי גַּבֵּי פֶּסַח כִּי הַאי גַּוְונָא – **And we also learned like this in** another **Mishnah**[38] **with regard to** the **Passover** sacrifice:

כְּלָל אָמַר רַבִּי עֲקִיבָא – R' AKIVA STATED A GENERAL RULE: כָּל מְלָאכָה שֶׁאֶפְשָׁר לָהּ לַעֲשׂוֹתָהּ מֵעֶרֶב שַׁבָּת – ANY LABOR THAT CAN BE PERFORMED ON THE SABBATH EVE[39] אֵינָהּ דּוֹחָה אֶת הַשַּׁבָּת – DOES NOT OVERRIDE THE SABBATH restrictions. שְׁחִיטָה שֶׁאִי אֶפְשָׁר לַעֲשׂוֹתָהּ מֵעֶרֶב שַׁבָּת – However, SLAUGHTERING the Passover sacrifice, WHICH IS IMPOSSIBLE TO DO ON THE SABBATH EVE,[40] דּוֹחָה אֶת הַשַּׁבָּת – DOES OVERRIDE THE SABBATH restrictions. וְאָמַר רַב יְהוּדָה אָמַר רַב – **And** apropos of this ruling as well **Rav Yehudah said in the name of Rav:** הֲלָכָה כְּרַבִּי עֲקִיבָא – **The law accords with** the opinion of **R' Akiva.**[41]

The Gemara comments:

וּצְרִיכָא – **And it is necessary** for Rav Yehudah to instruct in both cases that the halachah accords with R' Akiva,[42] דְּאִי אַשְׁמְעִינַן גַּבֵּי מִילָה – **for if he had taught us** his preference only **with regard to** the dispute over **circumcision,** הָתָם הוּא – I would have thought **it is there** דְּמַכְשִׁירִין אֶפְשָׁר לַעֲשׂוֹת מֵאֶתְמוֹל לֹא דָּחוּ שַׁבָּת – **that preliminaries** that **can be performed yesterday**[43] **do not override the Sabbath** restrictions, דְּלֵיכָּא כָּרֵת – **since there is no** penalty of **excision** for the mitzvah's non-fulfillment.[44] אֲבָל פֶּסַח – **But** with regard to the **Passover** sacrifice, דְּאִיכָּא כָּרֵת – **where there is excision** for the mitzvah's non-fulfillment, אֵימָא לִידְחוּ שַׁבָּת – **I would say** that **[its preliminaries] should override** the **Sabbath** restrictions.[45] וְאִי אַשְׁמְעִינַן גַּבֵּי פֶּסַח – **And,** conversely, **if [Rav Yehudah] had taught us** that the halachah accords with R' Akiva only **with regard to** the dispute over the **Passover** sacrifice, I would have thought it is there that preliminaries that can be performed beforehand do not override the Sabbath, מִשּׁוּם דְּלֹא נִכְרְתוּ עָלֶיהָ שְׁלֹשׁ עֶשְׂרֵה בְּרִיתוֹת – **inasmuch as thirteen covenants were not made over** the mitzvah of **[the Passover offering].** אֲבָל מִילָה – **But** with regard to the mitzvah of **circumcision,** דְּנִכְרְתוּ עָלֶיהָ שְׁלֹשׁ עֶשְׂרֵה בְּרִיתוֹת – **over which thirteen covenants were made,**[46] אֵימָא לִידְחוּ שַׁבָּת – **I would say** that **[its preliminaries] should override** the **Sabbath** restrictions.[47]

The Gemara concludes:

צְרִיכָא – **It is** therefore **necessary** for Rav Yehudah to instruct in both cases that the halachah follows R' Akiva, who held that the preliminaries to a mitzvah may not be performed on the Sabbath when they can be performed beforehand.

Mishnah The Mishnah now discusses the circumcision operation itself, explaining which of its various elements may be performed on the Sabbath, and how:[48]

עוֹשִׂין כָּל צָרְכֵי מִילָה [בְּשַׁבָּת] – **We may perform all the necessities of circumcision on the Sabbath:**[49]

NOTES

35. E.g. *Leviticus* 23:39, which speaks of the two Biblical Yom Tov days in the Succos festival.

36. *You shall not do any laborious work* (ibid. v.35).

37. That an eighth-day *milah* is performed on Shabbos and Yom Tov, however, is derived from R' Yochanan's extraneous *on the ... day* (*Rashi*). See above, 132a,b. *Maharsha* (132b) asks: But we have learned that *milah does* override a positive and a negative commandment, i.e. *tzaraas*?! See there for his answer, and see *Kovetz He'aros, Yevamos* 7:1,2; *Maharam Schif* here; *Divrei Yechezkel* 12.

38. *Pesachim* 66a.

39. Such as bringing the *pesach* lamb to Jerusalem, which involves going beyond one's Sabbath boundary (*techum*), or cutting off a wart on its body (*Rashi*).

40. The *pesach* offering must be slaughtered on the fourteenth of Nissan. When that date falls on the Sabbath, there is no option but to slaughter it at that time (*Ritva MHK* ed.).

41. The Rishonim question why the Gemara does not object to Rav Yehudah's deciding the issue in this matter of sacrificial law, as it does in other places (*Sanhedrin* 51b, *Zevachim* 45a) where the law being decided is irrelevant until the Holy Temple is rebuilt. *Tosafos* answer that Rav Yehudah ruled here in favor of R' Akiva in order to give added weight to his parallel ruling in the *milah* case. See *Ramban, Ritva* (*MHK* ed.) and *Ran* (*MHK* ed.) for other explanations.

42. Who rules that the preliminaries to a mitzvah may not be performed on Shabbos when they can be performed beforehand (*Rashi;* see also *Tosafos, Ritva MHK* ed.).

43. I.e. on the Sabbath eve.

44. That is, if an infant is not circumcised at the proper time (the eighth day), he does not incur the *kares* penalty, for a minor is exempt from all punishments of the Torah. Nor does the father receive *kares,* since *kares* is not prescribed for violating the obligation to have one's son circumcised (*Rashi;* see *Ritva MHK* ed.).

45. I.e. I would say that in this case the halachah does not accord with R' Akiva (*Ritva MHK* ed.). Hence, Rav Yehudah must inform us that it does.

46. See above, 132a note 7.

47. I.e. I would say that in this case the halachah does not accord with R' Akiva (*Ritva MHK* ed.). Hence, Rav Yehudah must inform us that it does.

48. In order to understand this Mishnah properly, one must familiarize himself with the various steps of the circumcision procedure. Prior to circumcision, the corona has two coverings: The outer covering is a thick layer of skin called the foreskin; beneath it lies a thin membrane. The *mohel* first cuts off the foreskin. This act is called מִילָה, *circumcision.* He then tears the membrane and pulls it back, thereby exposing the corona. This is called פְּרִיעָה, *uncovering.* He next performs מְצִיצָה, *drawing the blood,* and then dresses the wound.

49. Although this general rule has already been stated at the end of the preceding chapter (128b), it is mentioned there incidentally, since the Mishnah there states other rules concerning infants. Here, however, is its proper place (*Tosafos*).

תנאי היא דתניא בשר ואף על פי שיש שם בהרת ימול דברי רבי יאשיה רבי יונתן אומר אינו צריך שבת חמורה דוחה צרעת לא כ"ש: אמר מר בשר אע"פ שיש שם בהרת ימול דברי רבי יאשיה הא למה לי קרא דבר שאין מתכוין הוא ודבר שאין מתכוין מותר אמר אביי לא נצרכא אלא לרבי יהודה דאמר דבר שאין מתכוין אסור רבא אמר אפילו תימא ר"ש מודה ר"ש בפסיק רישיה ולא ימות ואביי לית ליה האי סברא והא אביי ורבא דאמרי תרווייהו מודה רבי שמעון בפסיק רישיה ולא ימות בתר דשמעה מרבא סברה איכא דמתני להא דאביי ורבא אהא השמר בנגע הצרעת לשמור מאד ולעשות לעשות אי אתה עושה אבל (א) עושה אתה בסיב שעל גבי רגלו ובמוט שעל גבי כתיפו ואם עברה עברה והא למה לי קרא דבר שאין מתכוין הוא ודבר שאין מתכוין מותר אמר אביי לא נצרכא אלא לרבי יהודה דאמר דבר שאין מתכוין אסור ורבא אמר אפילו תימא רבי שמעון ומודה רבי שמעון בפסיק רישיה ולא ימות ואביי לית ליה האי סברא והא אביי ורבא דאמרי תרווייהו מודה ר' שמעון בפסיק רישיה ולא ימות לבתר דשמעיה מרבא סברה ואביי אליבא דרבי שמעון האי בשר מאי עביד ליה אמר רב עמרם באומר לקוץ בהרתו הוא מתכוין תינח גדול קטן מאי איכא למימר אמר רב משרשיא באומר אבי הבן לקוץ בהרת דבנו הוא קא מתכוין ואי איכא אחר ליעביד אחר דאמר ר"ש בן לקיש כל מקום שאתה מוצא עשה ולא תעשה אם אתה יכול לקיים שניהם מוטב ואם לאו יבא עשה וידחה לא תעשה דליכא אחר: אמר מר יום טוב אינה דוחה אלא בזמנה בלבד מנא הני מילי אמר חזקיה וכן תנא דבי חזקיה אמר קרא לא תותירו ממנו עד בקר והנותר ממנו עד בקר וגו' שאין ת"ל עד בקר מה ת"ל עד בקר בא הכתוב ליתן לו בקר שני לשריפתו אביי אמר אמר קרא עולת שבת בשבתו ולא עולת חול בשבת ולא עולת חול בי"ט רבא אמר אמר קרא הוא לבדו יעשה לכם הוא ולא מכשירין לבדו ולא מילה שלא בזמנה דאתיא מק"ו רב אשי אמר שבתון עשה הוא והוה ליה י"ט עשה ול"ת ואין עשה דוחה את לא תעשה ועשה: כלל אמר ר"ע וכו': אמר רב יהודה אמר רב הלכה כר"ע ותנן נמי גבי פסח כי האי גוונא כלל אמר ר"ע כל מלאכה שאפשר לה לעשותה מע"ש אינה דוחה את השבת שחיטה שאי אפשר לעשותה מע"ש דוחה את השבת ואמר רב יהודה אמר רב הלכה כר"ע וצריכא דאי אשמועינן גבי מילה התם הוא דמכשירין (ג) אפשר לעשות מאתמול לא דחו שבת דליכא כרת אבל פסח דאיכא כרת אימא לידחו שבת ואי אשמעינן גבי פסח משום דלא נכרתו עליה י"ג בריתות אבל מילה דנכרתו עליה י"ג בריתות אימא לידחו שבת צריכא:

מתני' עושין כל צרכי מילה [בשבת] מוהלין ופורעין ומוצצין ונותנין עליה איספלנית וכמון אם לא שחק מע"ש לועס בשיניו ונותן אם לא טרף יין ושמן מע"ש ינתן זה בעצמו וזה בעצמו ואין עושין לה חלוק לכתחילה אבל כורך עליה סמרטוט אם לא התקין מע"ש כורך על אצבעו ומביא ואפי' מחצר אחרת: **גמ'**

רש"י

תנאי היא. דליכא דנפקא ליה מילה בזמנה מק"ו כרבא וכי אתא קרא לשלא בזמנה ואיכא דלא נפקא ליה בק"ו ואיצטריך למילה בזמנה כרב ספרא ושלא בזמנה אתיא מבינייא: **לרבי יהודה.** רבי יאשיה דמצריך קרא להכי כרבי יהודה סבירא ליה: **מודה ר' שמעון בפסיק רישיה** ולא ימות. הילכך אי לא רבי קרא לא עבדי: **סברה.** נתן בה דעתיה וקבל ממנו: ה"ג **לעשות עושה אתה בסיב שעל רגלו ובמוט שעל גבי כתיפו.** ואינו צריך להזהר מלדחות סיב שקושר מנעלו ברגלו ומלישא משאוי על כתיפו: **ואם עברה.** הבהרת בכך עברה ואינו חושש לה להכי כתיב לעשות שמותר לעשות מלאכתו: **ואביי אליבא דר' שמעון.** מעיקרא מקמי דסברה האי בשר מאי עביד ליה: **באומר לקוץ.** גדול שהוא בר עונשין ואומר למוהל לקוץ בהרתו בכוונה ליטהר: **קטן.** דלא ידע לכוין מאי איכא למימר ועל כרחיך בתרוייהו כתיב בשר כדאמרי' לעיל ובשר דכתיב גבי קטן ביום השמיני ל"ל: **באומר אבי הבן לקוץ.** דמתכוין לטהרו והוא מוהר דלא ליעבד בידים ומתכוין: **ואי איכא אחר.** שאינו חושש לטהרו ליעבד אחר ולא ליקו אב להתם ואע"ג דרבייה קרא שהרי אתה יכול לקיים עשה בלא עקירת לאו לר' שמעון דהא אחר לא מיכוין ולא עבר ואמר [...]ר' ורבויא למאי אתא: **שאין תלמוד לומר עד בקר.** תניינא והנותר ממנו עד בקר דמאי למכתב והנותר באש תשרפו (ג) אלא אשריפה קאי והכי קאמר והנותר ממנו בזמן שאמרתי לך דהיינו בקר ראשון כשיבא בקר שני שהוא חולו של מועד תשרפו אבל בי"ט לא אלמא מידי דחול לא עבדינן בי"ט ופסח קרבן י"ד בניסן הוא שהוא חול ומילה שלא בזמנה נמי מידי דחול הוא דבשבת זו לא היה זמנה: **ולא עולת חול בי"ם.** אבל תמיד של עי"ט אין קרבין בי"ט ומילה שלא בזמנה נמי כעולת חול בי"ט דמי: **דאתיא בק"ו.** מצרעת ומה צרעת שדוחה עבודה מילה שלא בזמנה דוחה אותה כדאמרינן לעיל (ד) שבת שנדחית מפני עבודה אינו דין שמילה שלא בזמנה דוחה אותה להכי איצטריך לבדו: **ואין עשה.** דמילה דוחה לא תעשה ועשה אבל בזמנה איתרבי מביום השמיני בשבת: **גבי פסח.** כל מלאכה שאפשר לה לעשות מע"ש כגון הבאתו מחוץ לתחום ותחיכת יבלתו: **וצריכא.** למימר בתרוייהו הלכה כר"ע דמכשירין לא דחו: **מילה בזמנה ליכא כרת.** דקטן לאו בר עונשין הוא והאב לא מיחייב עליה כרת: **מתני' מוהלין.** חותך את הערלה: **ופורעין.** את העור המכסה ראש הגיד: **ומוצצין.** את הדם ואף על גב דהיא עשיית חבורה שאין הדם ניתק מחיבורו אלא על ידי (ה) המצילה: **איספלנית.** מתחבושת: **לועס בשיניו.** כמה דאפשר לשנויי משנינן: **לא טרף יין ושמן.** כך היו רגילין והיא רפואה שמערבין וטורפין בקערה יין ושמן יחד מלכך שטורפין ביצים בקערה: **חלוק.** כעין כיס דחוק היו עושין ומלבישים את ראש הגיד עד העטרה וקושרים שם כדי שלא יחזור העור לכסות את הגיד: **לא התקין.** לא הזמין: **כורך על ידו.** דרך מלבוש לשנותו מדרך הוצאה בחול:

תוספות

ואביי אליבא דר' שמעון. ולרבי יונתן לא מיבעיא ליה דמוקי ליה בינוני ולאביי נמי דאמר לעיל דבינוני אתי מבינייא מצי למימר דסבר ר' יונתן מילתא דאתי בק"ו טרח וכתב לה קרא: **באומר לקוץ בהרתו הוא מתכוין.** וא"ת אם כן מאי קאמר אביי לא נצרכא אלא לרבי יהודה הא לר"ש נמי איצטריך כדאמר הכא וי"ל דלשון ברייתא משמע דמיירי בלא מתכוין מדלא קתני בשר אע"ג דמתכוין לקוץ בהרת ימול: **ותנן נמי גבי פסח כה"ג אמר רב יהודה אמר רב הלכה כר"ע.** והכא לא פריך הילכתא למשיחא משום דנפקא מינה גבי מילה אע"ג דגבי מילה נמי פסיק הכי מ"מ לאלומי פיסקא דמילה פסיק נמי גבי פסח אגב דפסיק גבי מילה דתילף מינה שפסק ברור הוא לכל דבר: **וצריכא דאי אשמועינן.** אדרב יהודה קאי דפסיק כר"ע הכא והתם דלאי אדרבי עקיבא א"כ בפ' שתי הלחם (מנחות דף צו.) דקתני נמי כלל אמר ר"ע הוה ליה למימר וצריכא וכן פירש בקונטרס: **עושין כל צרכי מילה בשבת.** אע"ג דלעיל נמי קתני (ו) בשילהי מפנין (ד' קכח.) התם תני לה אגב גררא דמילי דתינוק אבל הכא עיקר:

עין משפט נר מצוה

י א מיי' פ"א מהלכות טומאת צרעת הלכה א סמג לאוין שמג:
יא ב מיי' פ"ב מהלכות מילה הלכה ו:
יב ג מיי' פ"ח מהלכות קרבן פסח הלכה יח סמג עשין רגג:
יג ד מיי' פ"ב מהלכות מילה הל' ו סמג עשין כח טוש"ע א"ח סי' שלא סעיף ח טוש"ע י"ד סי' רסו סעיף ב:
יד ה מיי' שם הל' ז סמג שם טוש"ע א"ח שם סעיף ז וטוש"ע י"ד שם סעיף ג:

גליון הש"ס

רש"י ד"ה שאין ת"ל וכו' י"ד בניסן הוא שהוא חול. עיין כתובות שהוא חול. עיין כתובות אבן במגילה באבני מלואים דף מז ע"ב ד"ה אף כאן:

רבינו חננאל

מודה ר' שמעון בפסיק רישי' ולא ימות פי' כי ר' שמעון מודה בדבר שהוא ברור כגון אדם שחותך ראש אדם ואומר שאין כוונתו להמיתו אלא להוציא את ממונו שאין שומעין לו אלא דנין אותו דין כל הורג נפש כך כל דבר שמתברר (מעשין) [שיעשה] לאותה מלאכה אין אומרין שלא היתה כוונתו לכך. וכה"ג אפילו ר' שמעון מודה. ואביי אליבא דר' שמעון קודם שישמע מרבא. מודה ר' שמעון בפסיק רישיה ולא ימות דהוה מוקים ליה כר' יהודה ולא כר' שמעון הוה אמר דר"ש פליג נמי בהא דסבר ר' שמעון חתיכות הערלה והצרעת עליה דבר שאין מתכוון הוא שאין כוונתו לחתוך הצרעת אלא למול בנו וכי האי לר' שמעון שרי ולא צריך קרא למשרייה אם כן אביי אליבא דר' שמעון האי בשר ערלתו מאי עביד ליה אמר רב משרשיה באומר לקוץ בהרתו הוא מתכוין כלומר בדבר מוכיח שמתכוין לקוץ בהרתו בא הכתוב להתירו ואקשינן תינח גדול פי' שיש בו דעת יש לומר כן מתכוין לקוץ בהרתו קטן שאין בו דעת למה כתוב בו בשר להתיר חתיכת צרעת במילה ואמרי' קטן נמי מתכוין אביו בזה במולו לבנו לחתוך בהרת בנו ואמרי' בעת שיש בהרת בערלת הקטן ימול אחר זולתו אבי הבן. שהאחר אין מתכוין לחתוך הבהרת ודבר שאין מתכוין לר' שמעון שרי ולא הוה צריך קרא למשריה דאמר רבי שמעון בן לקיש כל מקום שאתה מוצא עשה ולא תעשה פי' כגון זה עשה שנאמר וביום השמיני ימול בשר ערלתו. לא תעשה השמר בנגע הצרעת שהוא לאו כאשר פירשנו למעלה. ואם יש בהרת בערלה וימול אחר זולתו אבי הבן נתקיימה המילה שהיא עשה ונתקיימה חתיכת הצרעת

מסורת הש"ס

א) [יומא לד:], ב) [שם], ג) לעיל עה. קג. קיא: קיז. קכ: ולק' קמג. [ביצה לו.] סוכה לג: כתובות ו. בכורות כה., ד) תוספתא נגעים פ"ג, ה) יבמות כ: נזיר מא. נח. מנחות מ., ו) לעיל כד: פסחים סג: תמורה ד: ע"ש, ז) [צ"ל עד בקר והנותר ממנו עד בקר באש תשרופו וכ"א בפסחים], ח) [פסחים סט:], ט) פסחים סו. סט: יבמות יד. מנחות עב. ודף צו., י) [לעיל דף קכח:], כ) [עי' תוס' עמוד ב ד"ה לועס], ל) צ"ל מלדחוק, מ) [וע"ע תוס' יומא יג. ד"ה הלכה ותוס' זבחים מה. ד"ה הלכתא], נ) [ואמילתא דר"ע לא בעי צריכותא דאשמעי' בכל דוכתא מאי דדמי שבת כ"כ תוס' במנחות].

הגהות הב"ח

(א) גמ' אבל אתה עושה אותו בסיב: (ב) שם דאפשר לעשות: (ג) רש"י ד"ה שאין ת"ל וכו' באש תשרפו אלמא דאשריפה קאי וכו' דחול הוא דבי"ט זו לא: (ד) ד"ה דאתיא וכו' כדאמרינן לעיל י"ט שנדחים: (ה) ד"ה ומוצצין וכו' אלא ע"י (המצילה) תו"מ ונ"ב ס"א מבורה: (ו) תוס' ד"ה עושין וכו' קתני לה בשילהי:

תורה אור השלם

א) וּבַיּוֹם הַשְּׁמִינִי יִמּוֹל בְּשַׂר עָרְלָתוֹ: [ויקרא יב, ג]
ב) הִשָּׁמֶר בְּנֶגַע הַצָּרַעַת לִשְׁמֹר מְאֹד וְלַעֲשׂוֹת כְּכֹל אֲשֶׁר יוֹרוּ אֶתְכֶם הַכֹּהֲנִים הַלְוִיִּם כַּאֲשֶׁר צִוִּיתִם תִּשְׁמְרוּ לַעֲשׂוֹת: [דברים כד, ח]
ג) וְלֹא תוֹתִירוּ מִמֶּנּוּ עַד בֹּקֶר וְהַנֹּתָר מִמֶּנּוּ עַד בֹּקֶר בָּאֵשׁ תִּשְׂרֹפוּ: [שמות יב, י]
ד) עֹלַת שַׁבַּת בְּשַׁבַּתּוֹ עַל עֹלַת הַתָּמִיד וְנִסְכָּהּ: [במדבר כח, י]
ה) וּבַיּוֹם הָרִאשׁוֹן מִקְרָא קֹדֶשׁ וּבַיּוֹם הַשְּׁבִיעִי מִקְרָא קֹדֶשׁ יִהְיֶה לָכֶם כָּל מְלָאכָה לֹא יֵעָשֶׂה בָהֶם אַךְ אֲשֶׁר יֵאָכֵל לְכָל נֶפֶשׁ הוּא לְבַדּוֹ יֵעָשֶׂה לָכֶם: [שמות יב, טז]
ו) דַּבֵּר אֶל בְּנֵי יִשְׂרָאֵל לֵאמֹר בַּחֹדֶשׁ הַשְּׁבִיעִי בְּאֶחָד לַחֹדֶשׁ יִהְיֶה לָכֶם שַׁבָּתוֹן זִכְרוֹן תְּרוּעָה מִקְרָא קֹדֶשׁ: [ויקרא כג, כד]

רב נסים גאון

דאתי עשה ודחי לא תעשה ועשה. [...]

[illegible]

חשק שלמה על רבינו חננאל [illegible]

ליקוטי רש"י

[illegible]

מוֹהֲלִין וּפוֹרְעִין וּמוֹצְצִין – **We may circumcise,**[50] **uncover** the corona,[51] **draw** the blood,[52] **וְנוֹתְנִין עָלֶיהָ אִיסְפְּלָנִית וְכַמּוֹן** – **and place a bandage and cumin upon it.**[53] **אִם לֹא שָׁחַק מֵעֶרֶב שַׁבָּת** – **If one did not crush** the cumin **on the Sabbath eve,** **לוֹעֵס בְּשִׁינָּיו וְנוֹתֵן** – **he may chew** it **with his teeth and apply** it.[54] **אִם לֹא טָרַף יַיִן וָשֶׁמֶן מֵעֶרֶב שַׁבָּת** – **If one did not vigorously mix wine and oil on the Sabbath eve,**[55] **יִנָּתֵן זֶה בְּעַצְמוֹ וְזֶה בְּעַצְמוֹ** – **each of these** ingredients **should be placed** in the bowl **by itself.**[56] **וְאֵין עוֹשִׂין לָהּ חָלוּק לְכַתְּחִילָּה** – **And we may not in the first place fashion a shirtlike bandage for [the member],**[57] **אֲבָל כּוֹרֵךְ עָלֶיהָ סְמַרְטוּט** – **but one may wrap a piece of cloth around it.**[58] **אִם לֹא הִתְקִין מֵעֶרֶב שַׁבָּת** – **If he did not prepare** even an ordinary cloth[59] **on the Sabbath eve,** **כּוֹרֵךְ עַל אֶצְבָּעוֹ וּמֵבִיא** – **he may wrap** one **around his finger**[60] **and bring** it; **וַאֲפִילוּ מֵחָצֵר אַחֶרֶת** – **and** he may bring it **even from another courtyard.**[61]

NOTES

50. I.e. cut off the foreskin (*Rashi*).

51. By tearing and pulling back the thin membrane under the foreskin, one uncovers the corona (*Rashi*).

The uncovering of the corona is mandatory. Therefore, if the circumciser fails to expose the corona, the infant is considered uncircumcised (*Ritva MHK* ed., from Mishnah below, 137b).

52. The blood is drawn out of the wound to prevent it from coagulating under the skin and causing the member to swell (*Tiferes Yisrael*).

Normally, one who causes blood to flow on the Sabbath (where it can be considered a constructive act) performs a *toladah* of *slaughtering*. However, in this instance drawing blood is permissible, since it is done to prevent a potentially fatal condition from developing (*Ritva MHK* ed.; see *Rashi*).

Some authorities hold that aside from any medical considerations, drawing out the blood is an inherent part of the mitzvah of circumcision (see *Sefer HaBris,* pp. 185, 216-226).

53. These are applied for therapeutic purposes (*Ritva MHK* ed.). The cumin must be crushed to be effective, as is evident below.

54. Crushing cumin on the Sabbath in the normal manner is a *toladah* of *grinding,* and is ordinarily prohibited. Hence, although crushing for therapeutic purposes in a case of *milah* would be allowed, since the circumcised person is considered critically ill (חוֹלֶה שֶׁיֵּשׁ בּוֹ סַכָּנָה), we perform it in the most unusual manner possible (*Rashi*). See *Tosafos* (on next *amud,* ד״ה לועס), as to whether this is always the rule in cases of "saving a life" (פִּקּוּחַ נֶפֶשׁ); see *Sfas Emes.*

55. In Mishnaic times it was customary to mix wine and oil by beating them in a bowl (as we do with eggs), and then apply the mixture to the incision as a medication (*Rashi*).

Beating wine with oil on the Sabbath is prohibited by Rabbinic decree, as is beating eggs, for the reason that it appears as though one is preparing food for cooking. Although this is only a Rabbinic prohibition, it nonetheless operates even when the mixture is needed for post-circumcision medication (*Tiferes Yisrael*), for it can be performed in the manner presently described in the Mishnah.

56. [Literally: this one by itself and this one by itself.] Although one may not vigorously mix them, he may pour first the wine and then the oil (or vice versa) into the same bowl, and if they become mixed, so be it (*Meiri;* cf. *Tos. Rabbi Akiva Eiger* §159).

57. After medications are applied to the circumcision wound, the wound is bandaged. During the Mishnaic era, it was common to employ for this purpose a cloth shaped like a finger, with openings at either end. This bandage would be drawn over the corona, thereby preventing the skin from growing back over it (*Rashi, Rav*).

Fashioning such a bandage on the Sabbath is prohibited because it is tantamount to making a utensil (and the purpose here is not to address a life-threatening situation). Hence, such a bandage may be used for circumcision only if it has been prepared before the Sabbath (*Meiri*).

58. If one did not prepare a shirtlike bandage before the Sabbath, he may wrap an ordinary piece of cloth around the corona.

59. I.e. he did not bring it to the site of the circumcision (*Tiferes Yisrael* §25; see also *Rashi* and *Meiri*).

60. He should wrap the cloth around his finger [thus "wearing" it] and transport it in this irregular manner (*Rashi*).

The prohibition against carrying on the Sabbath does not apply to the clothing one is wearing. However, this is true only of normal clothing. One may not "wear" an article that is not considered apparel. Hence, wrapping a cloth around one's finger and walking with it into the public domain is permitted only in order to bandage the circumcision (see *Tiferes Yisrael*). See *Rashash* here.

61. By Rabbinic enactment it is prohibited to carry articles from one property to another unless the owners have merged their properties by means of an *eruv chatzeiros* [explained at length in the General Introduction]. The circumcision bandage, however, may be brought from another person's property [i.e. even from one courtyard to another] in the manner prescribed above even if no *eruv* [or *shituf*] has been prepared (*Rav*).

The Mishnah implies that carrying from the public domain is, however, forbidden – even if the cloth is wrapped around one's finger. See *Tos. R' Akiva Eiger* §158 and *Rashash,* who discuss this. See also *Chidushei HaRan* and *Meiri.*

The Rishonim below (134b) discuss the time it became apparent that the bandage or cumin was lacking [i.e. after the *milah,* or even before]; and what can be done when the Mishnah's advice cannot be followed. See also *Keren Orah* here at length.

מסורת הש"ס

א) [יומא לד:], ב) [שם], ג) לעיל עא. קג. קיא: קיז. קכ: ולק' קמג. [ביצה לו.] סוכה לג: כתובות ו. בכורות כה., ד) תוספתא נגעים פ"ג, ה) יבמות ג: נזיר מא. נח. מנחות מ., ו) לעיל כד: פסחים סג: תמורה ד: ע"ש, ז) [נ"ל עד בקר והנותר ממנו עד בקר באש תשרפו וכ"א בפסחים], ח) [פסחים סט:], ט) פסחים סו. סט: יבמות יד. מנחות עב. ודף לו., י) [לעיל דף קכח:], כ) [עי' תוס' עמוד ב ד"ה לועס], ל) נ"ל מלדמוק, מ) [וע"ע תוס' יומא יג. ד"ה הלכה ותוס' זבחים מה. ד"ה הלכתא], נ) [ומילתא דר"ע לא בעי לריכותא דלאשמעי' בכל דוכתא מאי דלמי שבת כ"כ תוס' במנחות].

הגהות הב"ח

(א) גמ' אבל אתה עושה אותו בסיב: (ב) שם דאפשר לעשות: (ג) רש"י ד"ה שאין ת"ל וכו' בלא תשרפו אלא לאשריפה קאי וכו' דמול הוא דבי"ט זו לא: (ד) ד"ה דאתיא וכו' כדאמרינן לעיל י"ט שנדחים: (ה) ד"ה ומוצצין וכו' אלא ע"י (המצילה) תא"מ ונ"ב ס"א מבורה: (ו) תוס' ד"ה עושין וכו' קתני לה בשילהי:

תורה אור השלם

א) וּבַיּוֹם הַשְּׁמִינִי יִמּוֹל בְּשַׂר עָרְלָתוֹ: [ויקרא יב, ג]

ב) הִשָּׁמֶר בְּנֶגַע הַצָּרַעַת לִשְׁמֹר מְאֹד וְלַעֲשׂוֹת כְּכֹל אֲשֶׁר יוֹרוּ אֶתְכֶם הַכֹּהֲנִים הַלְוִיִּם כַּאֲשֶׁר צִוִּיתִם תִּשְׁמְרוּ לַעֲשׂוֹת: [דברים כד, ח]

ג) וְלֹא תוֹתִירוּ מִמֶּנּוּ עַד בֹּקֶר וְהַנֹּתָר מִמֶּנּוּ עַד בֹּקֶר בָּאֵשׁ תִּשְׂרֹפוּ: [שמות יב, י]

ד) עֹלַת שַׁבַּת בְּשַׁבַּתּוֹ עַל עֹלַת הַתָּמִיד וְנִסְכָּהּ: [במדבר כח, י]

ה) וּבַיּוֹם הָרִאשׁוֹן מִקְרָא קֹדֶשׁ וּבַיּוֹם הַשְּׁבִיעִי מִקְרָא קֹדֶשׁ יִהְיֶה לָכֶם כָּל מְלָאכָה לֹא יֵעָשֶׂה בָהֶם אַךְ אֲשֶׁר יֵאָכֵל לְכָל נֶפֶשׁ הוּא לְבַדּוֹ יֵעָשֶׂה לָכֶם: [שמות יב, טז]

ו) דַּבֵּר אֶל בְּנֵי יִשְׂרָאֵל לֵאמֹר בַּחֹדֶשׁ הַשְּׁבִיעִי בְּאֶחָד לַחֹדֶשׁ יִהְיֶה לָכֶם שַׁבָּתוֹן זִכְרוֹן תְּרוּעָה מִקְרָא קֹדֶשׁ: [ויקרא כג, כד]

רב נסים גאון

דאתי עשה ודחי לא תעשה לא תעשה גרידא לא תעשה שיש בה כרת מי דחי ותו לא תעשה גרידא מנלן דדחי דכתיב (דברים כב) לא תלבש שעטנז וכתיב גדילים תעשה לך ידענו כי זה לא תעשה אינו שוה בכל דבר אלא מיוחד הוא וכי הציווי שנאמר אחריו הוא תנאי עליו וכי לא בא להזהיר אלא על לבישת כלאים חוץ ממצות ציצית אבל מה שהוא מעורב מחוטי פשתן עם הטלית של צמר שהיא מצוה אינו נכנס בזו האזהרה אלא מותר הוא ואמרו חכמים שדבר זה עיקר הוא שנסמך עליו וכי כל אזהרה שאין עמה כרת שבתורה כך היא דרכה שבעת שאירע חיוב מצות עשה נדחה האזהרה שהיא לא תעשה ונקיים הציווי שהוא עשה ותבוא מצות עשה ותדחה לא תעשה כי האזהרה של לאו על זה התנאי נאמרה ובזה הפירוש שפירשנו יסיר מלבך ספק גדול שמסתפקין בו בני אדם ושואלין עליו והוא שאומרין מאחר שאנו יודעין שאזהרת לאו קשה מציווי עשה היאך יבא עשה וידחה האזהרה של לאו שהיא חמורה

עין משפט נר מצוה

י א מיי' פ"י מהלכות טומאת צרעת הלכה א סמג לאוין שסג:

יא ב מיי' פ"ג מהלכות מילה הלכה ו:

יב ג מיי' פ"א מהלכות קרבן פסח הלכה יח סמג עשין רגג:

יג ד מיי' פ"ב מהלכות מילה הל' ו סמג עשין כח טוש"ע א"ח סי' שלא סעיף א טוש"ע י"ד סי' רסו סעיף ב:

יד ה מיי' שם הל' ז סמג שם וטוש"ע א"ח שם סעיף ז וטוש"ע י"ד שם סעיף ג:

גליון הש"ס

רש"י ד"ה שאין ת"ל וכו' י"ד בניסן הוא שהוא חול. עיין בטורי אבן במגילה באבני מלואים דף ה ע"ב ד"ה אף כאן:

רבינו חננאל

מודה ר' שמעון בפסיק רישי' ולא ימות פי' כי ר' שמעון מודה בדבר שהוא ברור כגון אדם שחותך ראש אדם ואומר שאין כוונתו להמיתו אלא להוציא את ממונו שאין שומעין לו אלא דנין אותו דין כל הורג נפש כך כל דבר שמתברר (מעשין) [שיעשה] לאותה מלאכה אין אומרין שלא היתה כוונתו לכך. וכה"ג אפילו ר' שמעון מודה. ואביי אליבא דר' שמעון קודם שישמע מרבא. מודה ר' שמעון בפסיק רישיה ולא ימות דהוה מוקים ליה כר' יהודה ולא כר' שמעון הוה אמר דר"ש פליג נמי בהא דסבר ר' שמעון חתיכות הערלה והצרעת עליה דבר שאין מתכוון הוא שאין כוונתו לחתוך הצרעת אלא למול בנו וכי האי לר' שמעון שרי ולא צריך קרא למשרייה אם כן אביי אליבא דר' שמעון האי בשר ערלתו מאי עביד ליה אמר רב משרשיה באומר לקוץ בהרתו הוא מתכוין כלומר בדבר מוכיח שמתכוין לקוץ בהרתו בא הכתוב להתירו ואקשינן תינח גדול פי' שיש בו דעת יש לומר כן מתכוין לקוץ בהרתו קטן שאין בו דעת למה כתוב בו בשר להתיר חתיכת צרעת במילה ואמרי' קטן נמי מתכוין אביו בזה במולו לבנו לחתוך בהרת בנו ואמרי' בעת שיש בהרת בערלת הקטן ימול אחר זולתו אבי הבן. שהאחר אין מתכוין לחתוך הבהרת ודבר שאין מתכוין לר' שמעון שרי ולא הוה צריך קרא למישריה דאמר רבי שמעון בן לקיש כל מקום שאתה מוצא עשה ולא תעשה פי' כגון זה עשה שנאמר וביום השמיני ימול בשר ערלתו. לא תעשה השמר בנגע הצרעת שהוא לאו כאשר פירשנו למעלה. ואם יש בהרת בערלה וימול אחר זולתו אבי הבן נתקיימה המילה שהיא עשה ונתקיימה חתיכת הצרעת שלא בכוונה שלא הזהירה התורה אלא במתכוין והאחר לא נתכוין ואין אומר יבא עשה וידחה לא תעשה אלא אם אין כח כלל לקיים שניהם ופרקינן דליכא אחר ואם נאמר להמתין עד שיבא אחר וימול ביטלנו וביום השמיני ימול שהוא עשה: ובאנו לפרש עוד תשלום הברייתא: **אמר** מר י"ט אינו דוחה אלא בזמנו. פי' אין מילה דוחה י"ט אלא הנימול ביום ח' שהוא זמנו בלבד ואמרינן מנא הני מילי ופירשו חזקיה א) מן הקדשים שטעונין שריפה והוא עשה כדכתיב

חשק שלמה על רבינו חננאל א) חסר קלת וכל"ל ופי' חזקיה דילפינן זה מנותר מן הקדשים וכו':

גמרא

תנאי היא דתניא א) בשר ואף על פי שיש שם בהרת ימול דברי רבי יאשיה רבי יונתן אומר אינו צריך שבת חמורה דוחה צרעת לא כ"ש: אמר מר בשר אע"פ שיש שם בהרת ימול דברי רבי יאשיה הא למה לי קרא דבר שאין מתכוין הוא ודבר שאין מתכוין מותר אמר אביי לא נצרכא אלא לרבי יהודה דאמר דבר שאין מתכוין אסור רבא אמר אפילו תימא ר"ש מודה ר"ש בפסיק רישיה ולא ימות ואביי לית ליה האי סברא והא אביי ורבא דאמרי תרוייהו מודה רבי שמעון בפסיק רישיה ולא ימות בתר דשמעה מרבא סברה איכא דמתני להא דאביי ורבא אהא השמר בנגע הצרעת לשמור מאד ולעשות לעשות אי אתה עושה אבל (א) עושה אתה בסיב שעל גבי רגלו ובמוט שעל גבי כתיפו ואם עברה עברה והא למה לי קרא דבר שאין מתכוין הוא ודבר שאין מתכוין מותר אמר אביי לא נצרכא אלא לרבי יהודה דאמר דבר שאין מתכוין אסור ורבא אמר אפילו תימא רבי שמעון ומודה רבי שמעון בפסיק רישיה ולא ימות ואביי לית ליה האי סברא והא אביי ורבא דאמרי תרוייהו מודה ר' שמעון בפסיק רישיה ולא ימות לבתר דשמעיה מרבא סברה ואביי אליבא דרבי שמעון האי בשר מאי עביד ליה אמר רב עמרם באומר לקוץ בהרתו הוא מתכוין תינח גדול קטן מאי איכא למימר אמר רב משרשיא באומר אבי הבן לקוץ בהרת דבנו הוא קא מתכוין ואי איכא אחר ליעביד אחר דאמר ר"ש בן לקיש כל מקום שאתה מוצא עשה ולא תעשה אם אתה יכול לקיים שניהם מוטב ואם לאו יבא עשה וידחה לא תעשה דליכא אחר: אמר מר יום טוב אינה דוחה אלא בזמנה בלבד מנא הני מילי אמר חזקיה וכן תנא דבי חזקיה אמר קרא לא תותירו ממנו עד בקר שאין ת"ל עד בקר מה ת"ל עד בקר בא הכתוב ליתן לו בקר שני לשריפתו אביי אמר אמר קרא עולת שבת בשבתו ולא עולת חול בשבת ולא עולת חול בי"ט רבא אמר אמר קרא הוא לבדו יעשה לכם הוא ולא מכשירין לבדו ולא מילה שלא בזמנה דאתיא מק"ו רב אשי אמר שבתון עשה הוא והוה ליה י"ט עשה ול"ת ואין עשה דוחה את לא תעשה ועשה: כלל אמר ר"ע וכו': אמר רב יהודה אמר רב הלכה כר"ע ותנן נמי גבי פסח כי האי גוונא כלל אמר ר"ע כל מלאכה שאפשר לה לעשותה מע"ש אינה דוחה את השבת שחיטה שאי אפשר לעשותה מע"ש דוחה את השבת ואמר רב יהודה אמר רב הלכה כר"ע וצריכא דאי אשמעינן גבי מילה התם הוא דמכשירין (ב) אפשר לעשות מאתמול לא דחו שבת דליכא כרת אבל פסח דאיכא כרת אימא לידחו שבת ואי אשמעינן גבי פסח משום דלא נכרתו עליה י"ג בריתות אבל מילה דנכרתו עליה י"ג בריתות אימא לידחו שבת צריכא:

מתני' עושין כל צרכי מילה [בשבת] מוהלין ופורעין ומוצצין ונותנין עליה איספלנית וכמון אם לא שחק מע"ש לועס בשיניו ונותן אם לא טרף יין ושמן מע"ש ינתן זה בעצמו וזה בעצמו ואין עושין לה חלוק לכתחילה אבל כורך עליה סמרטוט אם לא התקין מע"ש כורך על אצבעו ומביא ואפי' מחצר אחרת:

גמ'

רש"י

תנאי היא. דלהכי דנפקא ליה מילה בזמנה מק"ו כרבה וכי אתא קרא לשלא בזמנה ולהכי לא נפקא ליה בק"ו ואיצטריך למילה בזמנה כרב ספרא ושלא בזמנה אתיא מבינייא: **לרבי יהודה.** רבי יאשיה דמצריך קרא להכי כרבי יהודה סבירא ליה: **מודה ר' שמעון בפסיק רישיה.** הילכך אי לאו קרא לא עבדי: **סברה.** נתן בה דעתיה וקבל ממנו: ה"ג לעשות עושה אתה בסיב שעל רגלו ובמוט שעל גבי כתיפו. ואינו צריך להזהר מלכרוך סיב שקושר מנעלו ברגלו ומלשאת משאוי על כתיפו: **ואם עברה.** הבהרת בכך עברה ואינו חושש לה להכי כתיב לעשות שמותר לעשות מלאכתו: **ואביי אליבא דר' שמעון.** מעיקרא מקמי דסברה האי בשר מאי עביד ליה: **באומר לקוץ.** גדול שהוא בר עונשין ואומר למוהל לקוץ בהרתו בכוונה ליטהר: **קטן.** דלא ידע לכווני מאי איכא למימר ועל כרחך בתרווייהו כתיב בשר כדאמרי' לעיל ובשר דכתיב גבי קטן ביום השמיני ל"ל: **באומר אבי הבן לקוץ.** דמתכוין לטהרו והוא מוהל דלא ליעבד בידים ומתכוין: **ואי איכא אחר.** שאינו חושש לטהרו ליעבד אחר ולא ליקו אב להסם ואע"ג דרבייה קרא שהרי אתה יכול לקיים עשה בלא עקירת לאו לר' שמעון דהא אחר לא מיכוין ולא עבר ואמר ריש לקיש כו' ורבויא למאי אתא: **שאין תלמוד לומר עד בקר.** (ג) מנותר ממנו עד בקר והנותר ממנו עד בקר באש תשרפו אלא אשריפה קאי והכי קאמר והנותר ממנו זמנו שאמרתי לך דהיינו בקר ראשון כשיבא בקר שני שהוא חולו של מועד תשרפו אבל בי"ט לא אלמא מידי דחול לא עבדינן בי"ט ופסח קרבן י"ד בניסן הוא שהוא חול ומילה שלא בזמנה נמי מידי דחול הוא דבשבת זו לא היה זמנה: **ולא עולת חול בי"ט.** אלא תמיד של י"ט אין קרבין בי"ט מילה שלא בזמנה נמי כעולת חול בי"ט דמי: **דאתיא בק"ו.** שמתחלה ומה צרעת שדוחה עבודה מילה שלא בזמנה דוחה אותה כדאמרינן לעיל (ד) שבת שנדחית מפני עבודה אינו דין שמילה שלא בזמנה דוחה אותה להכי איצטריך לבדו: **ואין עשה.** דמילה דוחה לא תעשה ועשה אבל בזמנה איתרבי מביום אפילו בשבת: **גבי פסח.** כל מלאכה שאפשר לה לעשות מע"ש כגון הבאתו מחוץ לתחום וחתיכת יבלתו: **וצריכא.** למימר בתרוייהו הלכה כר"ע: **דמכשירין לא דחו.** מילה בזמנה: **ליכא כרת.** דקטן לאו בר עונשין הוא ואבוה לא מיחייב עליה כרת: **מתני' מוהלין.** חותכין את הערלה: **ופורעין.** את העור המכסה ראש הגיד: **ומוצצין.** את הדם ואף על גב דהיא עשיית חבורה שאין הדם ניתק ממקומו אלא על ידי (ה) המצילה: **איספלנית.** מתבושת: **לועס בשיניו.** כמה דאפשר לשנויי משנינן: **לא טרף יין ושמן.** כך היו רגילין והיא רפואה שמערבין וטורפין בקערה יין ושמן יחד כדרך שטורפין ביצים בקערה: **חלוק.** כעין כיס דחוק היו עושין ומלבישים את ראש הגיד עד העטרה וקושרים שם כדי שלא יחזור העור לכסות את הגיד: **לא התקין.** לא הזמין: **כורך על ידו.** דרך מלבוש לשנותו מדרך הוצאה בחול:

תוספות

ואביי אליבא דר' שמעון. ולרבי יונתן לא מיבעיא ליה דמוקי ליה בינוני ולאביי נמי דאמר לעיל דבינוני אתי מבינייא מצי למימר דסבר ר' יונתן מילתא דאתי בק"ו טרח וכתב לה קרא: **באומר לקוץ בהרתו הוא מתכוין.** וא"ת אם כן אמאי קאמר אביי לא נצרכא אלא לרבי יהודה הא לר"ש נמי איצטריך כדאמר הכא ויש לומר דלשון ברייתא משמע דמיירי בלא מתכוין מדלא קתני בשר אע"ג דמתכוין לקוץ בהרת ימול:

ותנן נמי גבי פסח כה"ג אמר רב יהודה אמר רב הלכה כר"ע. והכא לא פריך הילכתא למשיחא משום דנפקא מינה גבי מילה אע"ג דגבי מילה נמי פסיק הכי מ"מ לאלומי פיסקא דמילה פסיק נמי גבי פסח אגב דפסיק גבי מילה דמילף מינה שפסק ברור הוא לכל דבר (נ): **וצריכא.** דאי אשמעינן. תימה דרב יהודה קאי דפסיק כר"ע הכא והתם דלאו דברי עקיבא א"כ בפ' שתי הלחם (מנחות דף צו.) דקתני נמי כלל אמר ר"ע הוה ליה למימר וצריכא וכן פירש בקונטרס (ט): **עושין כל צרכי מילה בשבת.** אע"ג דלעיל נמי קתני (ו) בשילהי מפנין (דף קכח:) התם תני לה אגב גררא דמילי דמיתוק אבל הכא עיקר:

גדול

ליקוטי רש"י

למה לי קרא. בשר לרבות המנוגע דמאי למכתב ימול ערלתו וכתב בשר לרבות בשר האמור בנגעים (ויקרא יג) אדם כי יהיה בעור בשרו למה לי קרא הא דבר שאינו מתכוין הוא [יומא לד:]. **אפילו תימא ר"ש.** דאמר במסכת שבת (מא:) דבר שאין מתכוין מותר [בכורות כה.]. **מודה ר' שמעון בפסיק רישיה ולא ימות.** בתמיה דאי אפשר שלא תמות כמתכוין חשיב ליה וכי אמרינן דבר שאין מתכוין מותר כגון היכא דאפשר ליה בלא איסור כגון גורר אדם מטה כסא וספסל ובלבד שלא יתכוין לעשות חריץ ואף על גב דליכא למימש דלמא עביד חריץ כיון דלא מתכוין להכי ואפשר לגרירה בלא חריץ כי עביד נמי חריץ דהוי מלאכה גמורה לא מיחייב אבל היכא דודאי עביד מודי [סוכה לג:]. **השמר בנגע הצרעת.** בקוצץ בהרתו הכתוב מדבר והשמר הוא לא תעשה [מכות כב.]. שלא תתלוש סימני טומאה ולא תקוץ את הבהרת [דברים כד, ח]. **דאמר וכו' כל מקום שאתה מוצא עשה.** כגון גדילים תעשה לך ולא תעשה לא תלבש שעטנז [אם אתה יכול] לקיים את שניהם [מוטב] ואם לאו וכו' [נזיר נח. ע"ש בב"ח ובמנחות מ.]. **מנא הני מילי.** דאי לא ממעט לה קרא אית לן למימר ליתי עשה וידחה את לא תעשה כל מלאכה [ועי' כאן במהרש"א]. **שאין תלמוד לומר עד בקר.** זימנא אחריתי אלא והנותר ממנו באש תשרפו דהא כתיב עד בקר ברישא [לעיל כד:]. **מה ת"ל עד בוקר וכו' בקר שני.** ...

עין משפט
נר מצוה

טו א מיי' פ"ב מהלכות מילה הל' ו וטוש"ע א"ח סי' שלא סעיף ב וטוש"ע י"ד סי' רסו סעיף ב:

טז ב מיי' פ"ז מהל' לולב הלכה ו ופ"ג מהל' ס"ת הל' ו סמג עשין כח וג' ולאוין שסד טוש"ע א"ח סימן תרנו:

יז ג מיי' פ"א מהלכות דעות הלכה ו:

יח ד מיי' פ"ב מהלכות קידוש החדש הל' ד:

יט ה מיי' פ"ה מהל' תמידין ומוספין הל' ד סמג עשין קצ:

כ ו מיי' פ"ב מהלכות שגגות הלכה ט:

כא ז מיי' פ"ב מהל' מילה הל' ו סמג עשין כח טוש"ע י"ד סי' רסד סעיף ג:

כב ח טוש"ע א"ח סי' שלא סעיף ד:

תורה אור השלם

א) עָזִּי וְזִמְרָת יָהּ וַיְהִי לִי לִישׁוּעָה זֶה אֵלִי וְאַנְוֵהוּ אֱלֹהֵי אָבִי וַאֲרֹמְמֶנְהוּ: [שמות טו, ב]

ב) וְנָתַתָּ עַל הַשֻּׁלְחָן לֶחֶם פָּנִים לְפָנַי תָּמִיד: [שמות כה, ל]

ג) וְעָרֵל זָכָר אֲשֶׁר לֹא יִמּוֹל אֶת בְּשַׂר עָרְלָתוֹ וְנִכְרְתָה הַנֶּפֶשׁ הַהִוא מֵעַמֶּיהָ אֶת בְּרִיתִי הֵפַר: [בראשית יז, יד]

רבינו חננאל

והנותר ממנו עד בוקר באש תשרופו ואין שריפת קדשים דוחה יו"ט דתנן בגמרא בפ' כיצד צולין את הפסח. דתנן העצמות והגידים והנותר ישרפו בששה עשר חל ששה עשר להיות בשבת ישרפו בי"ז שאינו דוחה לא את השבת ולא את יו"ט וקיימא לן דמילה שלא בזמנה אפילו יו"ט אינו דוחה דתנן שני יו"ט של ר"ה נימול לי"ב ללמדך שאין עשה דוחה יו"ט כן המילה שלא בזמנה אינה דוחה י"ט ואין לומר אי הכי אפי' מילה בזמנה כי מילה בזמנה בפירוש אמרה תורה וביום ואפי' בשבת וכ"ש ביו"ט. אביי פירשו מעולת שבת בשבתו כו' רבא אמר הוא ולא מכשיריו פי' עשיית אוכל נפש דוחה יו"ט ולא מכשירי אוכל נפש. כגון חטיבת עצים מן היער לבשל ביו"ט וכדומה (לו) [הוא] לבדו ולא מילה שלא בזמנה הבאה בק"ו והוו ק"ו שאמר רבא ומה אוכל נפש שאינו בא באזהרת יו"ט (מנוח שדוחה) [דוחה] אינה דוחה שמחה לשחוט ולבשל ולאפות וכיוצא בהן מילה שלא בזמנה שאע"פ שהיא שלא בזמנה מצוה היא ומעכבתו מלאכול בתרומה. אינו דין שדוחה יו"ט לא לבו למעט המילה שלא בזמנה. רב אשי אמר שבת שבתון עשה הוא וי"ט עשה ול"ת עשה שבתון ולא תעשה כל מלאכה לא תעשה ונמצא כתוב ביו"ט עשה ול"ת והמילה עשה לבדו. ולא אתי עשה ודחי לא תעשה ועשה דיו"ט: מתני' כלל א"ר עקיבא כל מלאכה שאפשר [לעשות] מע"ש דוחה את השבת וכו'.

גמ' מכדי קתני. במתניתין: כולהו. כל דברים העשוים למילה מוהלין ופורעין ומוצצין כו' למה לי דתנן כללא ברישא עושין כל צרכי מילה: ציצין. שיורי ערלה ובמתני' (ג) מפרש אלו הן ציצין המעכבין ויש שאינן מעכבין כגון בשר שאינה חופה רוב העטרה אלא מיעוטה ומה היא עטרה שורה גבוה המקפת בגיד סביב שממנה הגיד משפע ויורד לצד הקרקע ומשפע ויורד לצד הגוף: המל. בשבת: כל זמן שהוא עוסק בה. שלא סילק ידו אם ראה שנשתיירו בה ציצין בין מעכבין את המילה שאינה כשרה עד שיחתכם בין שאין מעכבין חוזר וחותך דכולא חדא מילתא היא והרי ניתנה שבת לדחות אצלה: פירש. שסילק ידיו: על המעכבין חוזר. שהרי הן כמילה עצמה: ועל שאין מעכבין אינו חוזר. דהוי כהתחלה בפני עצמה ועל אלו לא ניתן לחלל את השבת והיינו דקתני כל צרכי מילה ואפילו ציצין שאין מעכבין חוזר עליהם כל זמן שלא פירש: מאן תנא פירש אינו חוזר. ומשום דפירש חשיב ליה חזרה מילתא לנפשה והואיל ולא עיכוב מצוה ניהו לא הדר: מפשיט הפסח עד החזה (ד). והיינו פירש דתנן במסכת תמיד (פ"ד מ"ג) גבי הפשיטו שהיה מתחיל מן הרגלים והיה מפשיט ויורד עד שמגיע לחזה הגיע לחזה חתך את הראש ונתנו למי שזכה בו ואח"כ הכרעיים ומירק והפשיט כו' שמעי' מיניה משהגיע לחזה סילק ידיו מן ההפשט והתחיל להתעסק בניתוח קצת וגבי עולה דכולה כליל מירק והפשיט ומנתח הידים תחילה אחר הראש וגבי פסח נמי משהפשיט עד החזה דיכול להוציא אימוריו (ה) בלא נימין קורעו ומוציאן מיד והוה ליה פירש מן ההפשט וקאמר רבי ישמעאל שוב אינו גומר ומפשיט משום דכיון דפירש הויא חזרה מילתא דאתחלתא לנפשה ושלא לצורך גבוה דומיא דציצין דלא מעכבין: דלא בעינן זה אלי ואנוהו. דאחר נטילת האימורין אין הידור מצוה ביפוי בשר אבל יפוי מילה מצוה היא: הוי דומה לו. ולשון אנוהו אני והוא אעשה עצמי כמותו לדבק בדרכיו: בין שנראה. החדש: בעליל. בגילוי לכל ויש לדעת שראוהו בית דין והקרובים להם ואין צריך לרואין חוץ לתחום לחלל שבת ולבא ולהעיד לפני ב"ד מחללין: ר' יוסי אומר כו'. אלמא אע"ג דאיכא מצוה כיון דלאו לצורך גבוה הוא לא מחללינן והכא נמי פירש דהוי אתחלתא דחילול כי הכא בלא צורך גבוה לא מחללינן: לא ניתנה שבת לדחות. אפילו בהתחלתה דהא נראה בעליל אבל הכא כיון שנתנה שבת לדחות להתחיל בה המילה הכי נמי דכי פירש והדר לאו אתחלתא לנפשה היא והוי כמו שלא פירש וגומר כל מצותו: רבנן דפליגי עליה דרבי יוסי. גבי לחם הפנים: ארבעה כהנים נכנסין. להיכל בשבת לסדר לחם הפנים: שני סדרים. שתים מערכות של לחם: שני בזיכין. שתי כפות מלאות לבונה דכתיב (ויקרא כד) ונתת על המערכת לבונה זכה: מקדימין לפניהם שנים ליטול. מן השלחן שני סדרים הישנים: ושנים ליטול שני בזיכין. והשלחן היה נתון ארכו ממזרח למערב ואלו עומדין מזה לרוחב השלחן בצפון ואלו עומדין כנגדו לדרום ודווקא מכניסין לצפון לפי שצפון ענין חשיבות היא כדאמרינן במסכת סוכה (דף נו.) גבי חילוק לחם הפנים למשמרה הנכנסת והיוצאת הנכנסין חולקין בצפון כדי שיראו (ו) נכנסין: רבי יוסי אומר אפילו אלו נוטלין. תחילה ומסלקין כולה מן השלחן ולאחר שעה מניחין אלו: אף זה תמיד. ומה אני מקיים תמיד שלא ילין שלחן בלא לחם ולרבנן אי שקלי ושבקי ליה והדר מסדרי לא מיקרי להו תמיד אלא התחלה אחריתי ונמצא שמתעכב שלחן בלא לחם וגבי פירש נמי כי הדר אתי מילתא אחריתי היא ולרבי יוסי דאמר כי שבקי והדר מתחלי נמי תמיד הוא דחדא מילתא הוא הכא נמי פירש חוזר אע"פ שאין מעכבין דכולה גמר מילתא היא: מהלקטין. בציצין המעכבין: מני. כרת זו של מי הוא: אמר רב כהנא אומן. ענוש כרת ובשבת קאי שחילל שבת ולא עשה מצוה: ונימא אנא עבדי פלגא. כלומר הואיל וכשהתחיל ברשות התחיל וחבורה שעשה ברשות עשה אמאי חייב נימא להו לכו אתם וסיימו המלאכה: אלא אמר רב פפא. בגדול שמל קמיירי ובחול וענוש כרת דקאמר משום מילה קאמר דעדיין ערל הוא: וכגון דאתא בין השמשות. דכל היום כשר למילה ז) ואמרו ליה לא מספקת לגמור ביום כהילכתה ותעשה חבורה בשבת בלא מצוה וענוש כרת ומיהו מיתה ליכא דלא אתרו ביה למיתה ולא קבל עליו התראה וכרת איכא דאתחלה ברשות לא התחיל ולא ניתנה שבת לדחות אצלו בשעה זו: מהו דתימא. מתניתין לא אשמעינן דמחלל שבתא עלה דדם מיפקד פקיד ועומד שם כנתון בכלי ובמציצה אין חבורה ואין כאן איסור תורה ומשום הכי שרי ולאו משום סכנה ואומנא דלא מייץ בחול לאו סכנתא היא ולא ניעבריה: קא משמע לן דדם חיבורי מיחבר. כשיוצא ע"י מציצה ואפילו הכי שרי משום סכנה מדקתני במתני' גבי איספלנית וכמון: שב מינאי תרבא. ז' מנות של חלב: וחדא דקירא. שעוה: קירא וקלבא רישינא. הוא זפת של עץ שמוציאים ממנו שלא ע"י האור והיא לבנה: קרעינהו למנייהו. שהפסיד להם לגלות רפואה זו: שבקי לכו חדא. שלא גיליתי:

גמ' מכדי קתני כולהו כל צורכי מילה לאתויי מאי לאתויי הא דת"ר א) המל כל זמן שהוא עוסק במילה חוזר בין על הציצין המעכבין את המילה בין על הציצין שאין מעכבין את המילה פירש על ציצין המעכבין את המילה חוזר על ציצין שאין מעכבין את המילה אינו חוזר מאן תנא פירש אינו חוזר אמר רבה בר בר חנה אמר רבי יוחנן רבי ישמעאל בנו של ר' יוחנן בן ברוקה היא דתניא ב) ארבעה עשר שחל להיות בשבת מפשיט (ג) אדם הפסח עד החזה דברי רבי ישמעאל בנו של ר' יוחנן בן ברוקה וחכ"א מפשיטין את כולו ממאי עד כאן לא קאמר ר' ישמעאל בנו של ר' יוחנן בן ברוקה התם (א) משום דלא בעינן א) זה אלי ואנוהו אבל הכא דבעינן זה אלי ואנוהו הכי נמי ג) דתניא זה אלי ואנוהו התנאה לפניו במצות עשה סוכה נאה ולולב נאה ושופר נאה ציצית נאה ספר תורה נאה וכתוב בו לשמו בדיו נאה בקולמוס נאה בלבלר אומן וכורכו בשיראין נאין אבא שאול אומר ואנוהו הוי דומה לו ד) מה הוא חנון ורחום אף אתה היה חנון ורחום אלא אמר רב אשי הא מני רבי יוסי היא דתנן ה) בין שנראה בעליל ובין שלא נראה בעליל מחללין עליו את השבת רבי יוסי אומר נראה בעליל אין מחללין עליו את השבת ממאי דילמא עד כאן לא קאמר ר' יוסי התם (ב) דלא ניתנה שבת לידחות אבל הכא דניתנה שבת לידחות הכי נמי אלא אמרי נהרדעי רבנן דפליגי עליה דרבי יוסי היא דתנן ו) ארבעה כהנים נכנסין שנים בידם שני סדרים ושנים בידם שני בזיכין וארבעה מקדימין לפניהם שנים ליטול שני סדרים ושנים ליטול שני בזיכין המכניסין עומדים בצפון ופניהם לדרום והמוציאין עומדים בדרום ופניהם לצפון אלו מושכים ואלו מניחין טפחו של זה בצד טפחו של זה משום שנאמר ב) לפני (ה') תמיד ר' יוסי אומר אפילו אלו נוטלין ואלו מניחין אף זה היה תמיד ת"ר מהלקטין את המילה ואם לא הילקט ענוש כרת מני א"ר כהנא אומן מתקיף לה רב פפא אומן לימא להו אנא עבדי פלגא דמצוה אתון עבידיתו פלגא דמצוה אלא אמר רב פפא גדול מתקיף לה רב אשי גדול בהדיא כתיב ביה ג) וערל זכר אשר לא ימול אלא אמר רב אשי לעולם אומן ז) וכגון דאתא בין השמשות דשבת ואמרו ליה לא מספקת ואמר להו מספקינא ועבד ולא איספק ואישתכח דחבורה הוא דעבד וענוש כרת: מוצצין וכו': אמר רב פפא ז) האי אומנא דלא מייץ סכנה הוא ועברינן ליה פשיטא מדקא מחללי עליה שבתא סכנה הוא מהו דתימא האי דם מיפקד פקיד קמ"ל חבורי מיחבר ודומיא דאיספלנית וכמון מה איספלנית וכמון כי לא עביד סכנה הוא אף ה"נ כי לא עביד סכנה הוא: ונותנין עליה איספלנית: אמר אביי ט) אמרה לי אם איספלניתא דכולהון כיבי שב מינאי תרבא וחדא קירא רבא אמר קירא וקלבא רישינא דרשה רבא במחוזא קרעינהו בני מנוומי אסיא למנייהו אמר להו שבקי לכו חדא דאמר שמואל ח) האי מאן דמשי אפיה ולא נגיב טובא נקטרו ליה חספניתא

גדול בהדיא כתיב ביה. אע"ג דבכמה דוכתין תניא מה שבהדיא בפסוק איבעי (ז) למתני גדול שלא מל ענוש כרת:

לועס בשיניו. אף על גב דלאחר מילה חולה שיש בו סכנה הוא מ"מ כמה דאפשר לשנויי משנינן: הגה

מסורת הש"ס

א) לעיל קנז. מנחות סג: [תוספתא פסחים פ"ד], ב) נזיר ב: ג) ע"ש סוכה יא: מכילתא פרשת בשלח [מס' שירה פ"ג], ד) ר"ה כא: ה) מנחות צט: ו) קידושין לט: ז) פסחים ז: יומא כח: [מגילה ג.], ח) [שייך למשנה הקודמת].

הגהות הב"ח

(א) גמ' התם אלא משום דלא: (ב) שם ר' יוסי התם אלא משום דלא ניתנה שבת: (ג) רש"י ד"ה ציצין וכו' ובמתני'. נ"ב לקמן דף קלז סוף ע"א: (ד) ד"ה מפשיט וכו' עד החזה הפסק עד וכו': (ה) בא"ד להוציא אימוריו. נ"ב בפרק כל כתבי דף קטז: (ו) ד"ה ושנים ליטול וכו' כדי שיראו שהן נכנסין: (ז) תוס' ד"ה גדול וכו' איבעי ליה למיתני:

רב נסים גאון

חמורה ממנו ומדרך הידוע שהחמור דוחה הקל ולא עוד אלא שפעמים שעולה על דעתן שיש בענין הזה ענין חזרה בדבר הראשון והתשובה הוא מה שהקדמנו שאזהרה של לאו כך נאמרה מיוחדת וכי הציווי של עשה תנאי הוא בה וכן אמרו רז"ל (ספרי פ' תצא) מחלליה מות יומת וביום השבת שני כבשים בני שנה שניהן בדיבור אחד נאמרו ערות אשת אחיך ויבמה יבוא עליה שניהם בדיבור אחד נאמרו מה שאי אפשר לבשר ודם לומר שנא' אחת דיבר אלהים שתים זו שמענו כי הוא ספק גדול והרי לפני דבר זה ושמור אותו גלינו אותו ומזה העיקר אמרו רז"ל בתלמוד כל מקום שאתה מוצא עשה ולא תעשה אם אתה יכול לקיים את שניהם מוטב ואם לאו יבא עשה וידחה לא תעשה וסבר (רבינא) [רבא] כי לא תעשה שבקודש מוצא מזה העיקר וכי לא תדחה מפני עשה ולא שוה עמו רב אשי בדבר זה כמו שנאמר בשחיטת קדשים בפרק דם חטאת (דף צז) אמאי וניתי עשה ונידחי לא תעשה אמר רבינא אין עשה דוחה לא תעשה שבמקדש דתניא כו' רב אשי אמר עקר דשבת וערות אשת אחיך וכו' ...

ליקוטי רש"י

ציצין. רצועות של בשר שנשארו מן הערלה [לקמן קלז.]. חתיכות בשר שלא נפרעת המילה כהלכתה [יבמות מז:]. שנשתיירו שלא חתך כל הערלה [שם עא:]. עד החזה. ממשיך מרגליו האחרונים עד החזה שיוכל להוציא אימורים שהקטר חלב ... מפשיט מידי עד אורתא לצורך הדיוט הוא [לעיל קטז:]. בעליל. שנראה הלבנה בעליל לכל העולם גילוי הוא בלשון המשנה בין שנראה בעליל בין שלא נראה בעליל כו' [תהלים יב, ז]. נראה בעליל אין מחללין. לפי שאין צורך [ר"ה כא:]. ללכת ולהעיד לב"ד שהרי א"כ כיון דבעליל נראה ב"ד נמי ראוהו [מנחות ...]. נכנסין. ... של לחם הפנים שתים שתי המערכות שש המערכת [שם ז.]. שני בזיכין. לשני קומצי לבונה שנותנין על שתי המערכות שנאמר (ויקרא כד) ונתת על המערכת לבונה זכה [שמות כה, כט]. ליטול שני בזיכין. ... השלחן והן מסירין את הלחם באפילה כדכתיב והיה ללחם לאזכרה [סוכה נו:]. המכניסין עומדים בצפון. דהכי שפיר [מלתא] דאותן [ה]מסדרין (העבודה) יהו בצפון דקדושת צפון חמירא. ופניהם ... ומערב מונחין ורחבן לצפון ולדרום. לעצמן ואלו מניחין אחר שסילקו אף זה היה תמיד כדמפרש טעמא בגמ' דאין ... [מנחות צט:]. אלו מושכים. ועד שלא יגביהו הן מן השלחן אלו מניחין. אפילו אלו נוטלין. ... אפילו סילק את הישנה שחרית וסידר את החדשה ערבית אף זו היתה תמיד ומהו תמיד שלא ילין שולחן בלא לחם אבל לרבנן טפחו של זה מסדר בצד טפחו של מסלק [מגילה כא.]. מיפקד פקיד. כנוס ועומד ואינו נבלע להיות יוצאו על ידי חבורה [כתובות ה:]. אמרה לי אם. אומנתו היתה [כתובות לט: ע"ש בב"ח]. וקלבא. רשינ"א שבחביות של יין [ב"ק פה. וע"ע ביצה לג: ד"ה במוסתקי].

... אמר רב הלכה כר' עקיבא: מתני' עושין כל צרכי מילה בשבת מוהלין ופורעין כו' אמרינן כי מכדי ... מוהלין ופורעין ומוצצין כו' עושין כל צרכי מילה למה לי לאתויי הא דתנו רבנן המל כל זמן שעוסק במילה חוזר בין על הציצין המעכבין את המילה בין על הציצין שאינן מעכבין את המילה פירש על ציצין המעכבין את המילה חוזר ושאין מעכבין אינו חוזר. ואמרינן מאן תנא פירש ואתא רבה בר בר חנה לאוקומה כר' (שמעון) [ישמעאל] בר' יוחנן בן ...

Gemara The Gemara ponders the Mishnah's first statement:

מִכְּדִי קָתָנֵי כּוּלְהוּ – **Inasmuch as [the Tanna]** specifically **states all** the stages of the *milah* procedure,[1] כָּל צוֹרְכֵי מִילָה לְאֵתוּיֵי מַאי – **what does "ALL THE NECESSITIES OF CIRCUMCISION"** come **to include?**[2]

The Gemara answers:

לְאֵתוּיֵי הָא דְּתָנוּ רַבָּנָן – It comes **to include this** action of **which the Rabbis taught** in a Baraisa: הַמָּל – With regard to ONE WHO CIRCUMCISES on the Sabbath and notices that the foreskin has not been completely removed – כָּל זְמַן שֶׁהוּא עוֹסֵק בַּמִּילָה – SO LONG AS HE IS still ENGAGED IN performing THE CIRCUMCISION[3] חוֹזֵר בֵּין עַל הַצִּיצִין הַמְעַכְּבִין אֶת הַמִּילָה – HE MAY RETURN BOTH TO THE SHREDS THAT IMPEDE the validity of THE CIRCUMCISION[4] בֵּין עַל הַצִּיצִין שֶׁאֵין מְעַכְּבִין אֶת הַמִּילָה – AND TO THE SHREDS THAT DO NOT IMPEDE the validity of THE CIRCUMCISION,[5] and cut them off.[6] פֵּירַשׁ – However, if HE WITHDREW from the act of circumcising (having decided that the circumcision was completed), עַל צִיצִין הַמְעַכְּבִין אֶת הַמִּילָה חוֹזֵר – HE MAY RETURN TO THE SHREDS THAT IMPEDE the validity of THE CIRCUMCISION and cut them off,[7] עַל צִיצִין שֶׁאֵין מְעַכְּבִין אֶת הַמִּילָה אֵינוֹ חוֹזֵר – but HE MAY NOT RETURN TO THE SHREDS THAT DO NOT IMPEDE THE CIRCUMCISION.[8] Thus, when the Tanna of our Mishnah stated "all the necessities of circumcision," he meant to include the case of non-impeding shreds, teaching that even these may be cut off so long as the *mohel* is still engaged in the act of circumcising.

The Gemara inquires:

מַאן תַּנָּא פֵּירַשׁ אֵינוֹ חוֹזֵר – **Who is the Tanna** that holds that once **[the *mohel*] withdraws** from the act of circumcising, **he may not return** to and cut off the non-impeding shreds?[9]

The Gemara answers:

אָמַר רַבָּה בַּר בַּר חָנָה אָמַר רַבִּי יוֹחָנָן – **Rabbah bar bar Chanah said in the name of R' Yochanan:** רַבִּי יִשְׁמָעֵאל בְּנוֹ שֶׁל רַבִּי יוֹחָנָן בֶּן בְּרוֹקָה הִיא – **It is R' Yishmael, the son of R' Yochanan ben Berokah,** דְּתַנְיָא – **for it was taught in a Baraisa:** אַרְבָּעָה עָשָׂר שֶׁחָל לִהְיוֹת בְּשַׁבָּת – When the FOURTEENTH day of Nissan[10] FALLS ON THE SABBATH,[11] מַפְשִׁיט (אָדָם)[12] הַפֶּסַח עַד הֶחָזֶה – ONE SKINS THE PASSOVER sacrifice AS FAR AS THE BREAST,[13] and does not resume skinning. דִּבְרֵי רַבִּי יִשְׁמָעֵאל בְּנוֹ שֶׁל רַבִּי יוֹחָנָן בֶּן בְּרוֹקָה – These are THE WORDS OF R' YISHMAEL, THE SON OF R' YOCHANAN BEN BEROKAH.[14] וַחֲכָמִים אוֹמְרִים מַפְשִׁיטִין אֶת כּוּלוֹ – BUT THE SAGES SAY: WE SKIN ITS ENTIRE carcass.[15] Hence, it is R' Yishmael the son of R' Yochanan ben Berokah who holds that cessation from an action renders a return to that action a separate and distinct act.

The Gemara challenges this answer:

מִמַּאי – **From what** proof do you say this?! עַד כָּאן לֹא קָאָמַר רַבִּי יִשְׁמָעֵאל בְּנוֹ שֶׁל רַבִּי יוֹחָנָן בֶּן בְּרוֹקָה הָתָם – Perhaps **R' Yishmael the son of R' Yochanan ben Berokah did not say** that the skinning may be resumed **there** only[16] מִשּׁוּם דְּלֹא בָּעִינָן ,,זֶה אֵלִי וְאַנְוֵהוּ" – **because we do not require** a fulfillment of the verse,[17] ***This is my God and I will beautify Him,*** in that case.[18]

NOTES

1. "We may circumcise, uncover [the corona], draw [the blood] etc." (*Rashi*).

2. That is, once the Tanna is expressly sanctioning each step of circumcision, his initial, general statement ("We may perform all the necessities of circumcision on the Sabbath") is superfluous. The Gemara thus seeks to know what additional action the Tanna means implicitly to permit (*Rashi*).

3. I.e. he has not withdrawn his hands from performing the circumcision (*Rashi*).

4. The Mishnah below (137a) teaches that if shreds of the foreskin cover a majority of the corona (the ridge surrounding the member, from which it tapers off in both directions; see also *Rashi* below, 137a ד״ה עטרה, and to *Yevamos* 47b ד״ה עטרה, and see below, 137b), the circumcision is not valid until they are removed (*Rashi*).

5. These are shreds that cover less than a majority of the corona. The circumcision is valid even if they are not removed.

6. [Since the *mohel* did not disengage from the act of circumcising] there is no legal distinction between the two types of shreds; rather, cutting them both is considered one act of circumcision, whose performance overrides the Sabbath *melachah* restrictions (*Rashi*).

Chidushei HaRan writes that one is considered still engaged in the mitzvah also while he is engaged in uncovering the corona (פְּרִיעָה), and thus may return to and cut off the non-impeding shreds. See *Mishnah Berurah* 331:4.

7. [Since the circumcision is still not valid] it is as if he is now performing a full and proper act of circumcision (*Rashi;* cf. *Ritva MHK* ed.).

8. Since a valid circumcision has already been performed, cutting these shreds would be tantamount to commencing a new act of circumcising. However, the Torah did not sanction a desecration of the Sabbath for this remaining foreskin (*Rashi*).

It should be noted that the Baraisa does not actually mention the Sabbath. Indeed, *Rambam* understands that the Baraisa's rulings apply during the week as well (see *Hil. Milah* 2:4). See also *Beis HaLevi* II:47, and *Chidushei HaGriz* on *Rambam* (*Hil. Chanukah* 4:1).

9. I.e. which Tanna holds that cessation from an action renders a return to that action a distinct and separate act, so that here the circumciser is forbidden to resume the *milah* by cutting off the non-impeding shreds? (*Rashi*).

10. Pesach eve, when the *pesach* sacrifice is slaughtered and its innards offered.

11. In which case the slaughtering of the *pesach* lamb and the burning of its innards override the Sabbath restrictions [as does the skinning of the animal (which is also a *melachah*), since it is performed for the burning of the innards (see note 14 below)].

12. Translation follows emendation of *Mesoras HaShas*.

13. At which point he ceases skinning, makes an incision there, and removes the animal's innards (*Rashi*).

14. The purpose of skinning before removing the innards was to ensure that no wool or hairs from the animal (a kid) would stick to the innards as they were removed, for these parts were to be burned on the Altar. [Hence, the skinning was performed even on the Sabbath, since it was a necessary stage of the offering.] For this purpose, however, it sufficed to skin the animal until its breast, whereupon the innards could be cleanly removed. Now, the method of skinning a sacrifice in the Temple was modeled after the skinning of the daily *tamid* offering. That is, first they skinned it to the breast, then stopped and cut from the animal, and then they completed the skinning. Here, too, with regard to the *pesach* offering, when the skinning reached the breast (a sufficient amount for removing the innards without attracting any wool or hairs), they stopped and removed the innards (see *Rashi, Ramban* and *Leshon HaZahav* here). A resumption of the skinning would now be considered a new act of skinning that is unnecessary for the offering. Indeed, R' Yishmael the son of R' Yochanan ben Berokah disallows this. Similarly, avers R' Yochanan, R' Yishmael would disallow the resumption of *milah* to cut off non-impeding shreds, since they are analogous to the continued skinning of the *pesach* sacrifice (*Rashi*).

15. I.e. after removing the innards, we complete the skinning (*Ritva MHK* ed.; cf. *Chidushei HaRan*; see also *Hagahos R' Elazar Moshe Horowitz*).

16. *Bach* inserts the word אֶלָּא, *only,* into the text.

17. *Exodus* 15:2.

18. As the Gemara states below, the verse teaches that one must beautify himself before God through the embellished performance of mitzvos. In the *pesach* case, however, the verse is inapplicable, since skinning effects no embellishment of the mitzvah once the innards are removed. For that reason R' Yishmael did not permit its resumption (*Rashi*).

גמ' מכדי קתני כולהו כל צורכי מילה לאתויי מאי לאתויי הא דת"ר המל כל זמן שהוא עוסק במילה חוזר בין על הציצין המעכבין את המילה בין על הציצין שאין מעכבין את המילה פירש על ציצין המעכבין את המילה חוזר על ציצין שאין מעכבין את המילה אינו חוזר מאן תנא פירש אינו חוזר אמר רבה בר בר חנה אמר רבי יוחנן רבי ישמעאל בנו של ר' יוחנן בן ברוקה היא דתניא ארבעה עשר שחל להיות בשבת מפשיט (אדם) הפסח עד החזה דברי רבי ישמעאל בנו של ר' יוחנן בן ברוקה וחכ"א מפשיטין את כולו ממאי עד כאן לא קאמר ר' ישמעאל בנו של ר' יוחנן בן ברוקה התם משום דלא בעינן זה אלי ואנוהו אבל הכא דבעינן זה אלי ואנוהו הכי נמי דתניא זה אלי ואנוהו התנאה לפניו במצות עשה לפניו סוכה נאה ולולב נאה ושופר נאה ציצית נאה ספר תורה נאה וכתוב בו לשמו בדיו נאה בקולמוס נאה בלבלר אומן וכורכו בשיראין נאין אבא שאול אומר ואנוהו הוי דומה לו מה הוא חנון ורחום אף אתה היה חנון ורחום אלא אמר רב אשי הא מני רבי יוסי היא דתנן בין שנראה בעליל ובין שלא נראה בעליל מחללין עליו את השבת רבי יוסי אומר נראה בעליל אין מחללין עליו את השבת ממאי דילמא עד כאן לא קאמר ר' יוסי התם דלא ניתנה שבת לידחות אבל הכא דניתנה שבת לידחות הכי נמי אלא אמרי נהרדעי רבנן דפליגי עליה דרבי יוסי היא דתנן ארבעה כהנים נכנסין שנים בידם שני סדרים ושנים בידם שני בזיכין וארבעה מקדימין לפניהם שנים ליטול שני סדרים ושנים ליטול שני בזיכין המכניסין עומדים בצפון ופניהם בדרום והמוציאין עומדים בדרום ופניהם לצפון אלו מושכים ואלו מניחין טפחו של זה בצד טפחו של זה משום שנאמר לפני (ה') תמיד ר' יוסי אומר אפילו אלו נוטלין ואלו מניחין אף זה היה תמיד ת"ר מהלקטין את המילה ואם לא הילקט ענוש כרת מני א"ר כהנא אומן מתקיף לה רב פפא אומן לימא להו אנא עבדי פלגא דמצוה אתון עבדיתו פלגא דמצוה אלא אמר רב פפא גדול מתקיף לה רב אשי גדול בהדיא כתיב ביה וערל זכר אשר לא ימול אלא אמר רב אשי לעולם אומן וכגון דאתא בין השמשות דשבת ואמרו ליה לא מספקת ואמר להו מספקינא ועבד ולא איסתפק ואישתכח דחבורה הוא דעבד וענוש כרת: מוצצין וכו': אמר רב פפא האי אומנא דלא מייץ סכנה הוא ועברינן ליה פשיטא מדקא מחללי עליה שבתא סכנה הוא מהו דתימא האי דם מיפקד פקיד קמ"ל חבורי מיחבר ודומיא דאיספלנית וכמון מה איספלנית וכמון כי לא עביד סכנה הוא אף ה"נ כי לא עביד סכנה הוא: ונותנין עליה איספלנית: אמר אביי אמרה לי אם איספלניתא דכולהון כיבי שב מינאי תרבא וחדא קירא רבא אמר קירא וקלבא רישינא דרשה רבא במחוזא קרעינהו בני מנומי אסיא למנייהו אמר להו שבקי לכו חדא דאמר שמואל האי מאן דמשי אפיה ולא נגיב טובא נקטרו ליה חספניתא

רש"י

גמ' מכדי קתני. במתניתין: **כולהו.** כל דברים העשוים למילה מוהלין ופורעין ומוצצין כו' למה לי דתנן כללא ברישא עושין כל צרכי מילה: **ציצין.** שיורי ערלה ובמתני' (ג) מפרש אלו הן ציצין המעכבין ויש שאין מעכבין כגון בשר שאינה חופה רוב העטרה אלא מיעוטו ומה היא עטרה שורה גבוה המקפת בגיד סביב שממנה הגיד משפע ויורד לצד הקרקע ומשפע ויורד לצד הגוף: **המל.** בשבת: **כל זמן שהוא עוסק בה.** שלא סילק ידו אם ראה שנשתיירו בה ציצין בין מעכבין את המילה שאינה כשרה עד שיחתכם בין שאין מעכבין חוזר וחותך דכולה חדא מילתא היא והרי ניתנה שבת לדחות אצלה: **פירש.** שסילק ידיו: **על המעכבין חוזר.** שהרי הן כמילה עצמה: **ועל שאין מעכבין אינו חוזר.** דהוי כהתחלה בפני עצמה ועל אלו לא ניתן לדחות את השבת והיינו דקתני כל צרכי מילה ואפילו ציצין שאין מעכבין חוזר עליהם כל זמן שלא פירש: **מאן תנא פירש אינו חוזר.** ומשום דפירש חשיב ליה מילתא לנפשה והואיל ולא עיכוב מצוה ניהו לא הדר: **מפשיט הפסח עד החזה** (ד). והיינו פירש דתנן במסכת תמיד (פ"ד מ"ג) גבי הפשטו שהיה מתחיל מן הרגלים והיה מפשיט ויורד עד שמגיע לחזה הגיע לחזה חתך את הראש ונתנו למי שזכה בו ואח"כ הכרעיים ומירק והפשיט כו' שמעי' מיניה משהגיע לחזה סילק ידיו מן ההפשט והתחיל להתעסק בניתוח קצת וגבי עולה דכולה כליל מירק והפשיט ומנתח הידים תחילה אחר הראש וגבי פסח נמי משהפשיטו עד החזה דיכול להוציא אימוריו (ה) בלא נימין קורעו ומוציאן מיד והוה ליה פירש מן ההפשט וקאמר רבי ישמעאל שוב אינו גומר ומפשיט משום דכיון דפירש הוא חזרה מילתא דאתחלתא לנפשה ושלא לצורך גבוה דומיא דציצין דלא מעכבין: **דלא בעינן זה אלי ואנוהו.** לאחר נטילת האימורין אין הידור מצוה ביפוי בשר אבל יפוי מילה מצוה היא: **הוי דומה לו.** ולשון אנוהו אני והוא לעשה עצמי כמותו לדבק בדרכיו: **בין שנראה.** החדש: **בעליל.** בגלוי לכל ויש לדעת שראוהו בית דין והקרובים להם ואין צריך לראויין חוץ לתחום לחלל שבת ולבא ולהעיד לפני ב"ד מחללין: **ר' יוסי אומר כו'.** אלמא אע"ג דאיכא מצוה כיון דלאו לצורך גבוה הוא לא מחללין והכא נמי פירש דהוי אתחלתא דמילתא לחילול כי הכא בלא צורך גבוה לא מחללין: **לא ניתנה שבת לדחות.** אפילו בהתחלתה דהא נראה בעליל אבל הכא כיון שנתנה שבת לדחות להתחיל בה המילה הכי נמי דכי פירש והדר לאו אתחלתא לנפשה היא והוי כמו שלא פירש וגומר כל מצותו: **רבנן דפליגי עליה דרבי יוסי.** גבי לחם הפנים: **ארבעה כהנים נכנסין.** להיכל בשבת לסדור לחם הפנים: **שני סדרים.** שתים מערכות של לחם: **שני בזיכין.** שתי כפות מלאות לבונה כדכתיב (ויקרא כד) ונתת על המערכת לבונה זכה: **מקדימין לפניהם שנים ליטול.** מן השלחן שני סדרים הישנים: **ושנים ליטול שני בזיכין.** והשלחן היה נתון ארכו ממזרח למערב ואלו עומדין מזה לרוחב השלחן בצפון ואלו עומדין לנגדו לדרום ודווקא מכניסין לצפון דכל צפון ענין חשיבות היא כדאמרינן במסכת סוכה (דף נו.) גבי חילוק לחם הפנים למשמרה הנכנסת והיוצאת הנכנסין חולקין בצפון כדי שיראו (ו) נכנסין: **רבי יוסי אומר אפילו אלו נוטלין.** תחילה ומסלקין כולה מן השלחן ולאחר שעה מניחין אלו: **אף זה תמיד.** ומה אני מקיים תמיד שלא ילין שלחן בלא לחם ולרבנן אי שקלי ושבקי ליה והדר מסדרי לא מיקרי להו תמיד אלא התחלה אחריתי ונמצא שמתעכב שלחן בלא לחם וגבי פירש נמי כי הדר אתי מילתא אחריתי היא ולרבי יוסי דאמר כי שבקי והדר מתחלי נמי תמיד הוא דחדא מילתא הוא הכא נמי פירש חוזר אע"פ שאין מעכבין דכולה גמר מילתא היא: **מהלקטין.** בצילין המעכבין: **מני.** כרת זו של מי הוא: **אמר רב כהנא אומן.** ענוש כרת ובשבת קאי שחילל שבת ולא עשה מצוה: **ונימא אנא עבדי פלגא.** כלומר הואיל וכשהתחיל ברשות התחיל וחבורה שעשה ברשות עשה אמאי חייב נימא להו לכו אתם וסיימו המלאכה: **אלא אמר רב פפא.** בגדול שמל קמיירי ובמול וענוש כרת דקאמר משום מילה קאמר דעדיין ערל הוא: **וכגון דאתא בין השמשות.** דכל היום כשר למילה [ז] ואמרו ליה לא מספקת לגמור ביום כהילכתה ותעשה חבורה בשבת בלא מצוה וענוש כרת ומיהו מיתה ליכא דלא אתרו ביה למיתה ולא קבל עליו התראה וכרת איכא דלאתחלה ברשות לא התחיל ולא ניתנה שבת לדחות אצלו בשעה זו: **מהו דתימא.** מתניתין לא אשמעינן דמחלל שבתא עלה דדם מיפקד פקיד ועומד שם כנתון בכלי ובמציצה אין חבורה ואין כאן איסור תורה ומשום הכי שרי ולאו משום סכנה דלא מייץ במול לאו סכנתא היא ולא ניעבריה: **קא משמע לן דדם חיבורי מיחבר.** כשיוצא ע"י מציצה ואפילו הכי שרי משום סכנה מדקתני במתני' גבי איספלנית וכמון: **שב מינאי תרבא.** ז' מנות של חלב: **וחדא דקירא.** שעוה: **קירא וקלבא רישינא.** הוא זפת של עץ שמוציאים ממנו שלא ע"י האור והיא לבנה: **קרעינהו למנייהו.** שהפסיד להם לגלות רפואה זו: **שבקי לכו חדא.** שלא גיליתי: **חספניתא**

תוספות

גדול בהדיא כתיב ביה. אע"ג דבכמה דוכתין תניא מה שבהדיא בפסוק איבעי (ז) למתני גדול שלא מל ענוש כרת:

לועם [ח] בשיניו. אף על גב דאחר מילה חולה שיש בו סכנה הוא מ"מ כמה דאפשר לשנויי משנינן: הכא

עין משפט נר מצוה

טו א מיי' פ"ב מהלכות מילה הל' ד ו טוש"ע א"ח סי' שלא סעיף ג וטוש"ע י"ד סי' רסו סעיף ג:

טז ב מיי' פ"ז מהל' ס"ת הלכה ד ופ"ז מהל' לולב הל' ו סמג עשין כה ולאוין שסד טוש"ע א"ח סימן תרנו:

יז ג מיי' פ"א מהלכות דעות הלכה ו:

יח ד מיי' פ"ג מהלכות קידוש החדש הל' ד:

יט ה מיי' פ"ה מהל' תמידין ומוספין הל' ד סמג עשין קצ:

כ ו מיי' פ"א מהלכות שגגות הלכה ט:

כא ז מיי' פ"ב מהל' מילה הל' ג סמג עשין כח טוש"ע י"ד סי' רסד סעיף ג:

כב ח טוש"ע א"ח סי' ד סעיף כ:

תורה אור השלם

א) עָזִּי וְזִמְרָת יָהּ וַיְהִי לִי לִישׁוּעָה זֶה אֵלִי וְאַנְוֵהוּ אֱלֹהֵי אָבִי וַאֲרֹמְמֶנְהוּ: [שמות טו, ב]

ב) וְנָתַתָּ עַל הַשֻּׁלְחָן לֶחֶם פָּנִים לְפָנַי תָּמִיד: [שמות כה, ל]

ג) וְעָרֵל זָכָר אֲשֶׁר לֹא יִמּוֹל אֶת בְּשַׂר עָרְלָתוֹ וְנִכְרְתָה הַנֶּפֶשׁ הַהִוא מֵעַמֶּיהָ אֶת בְּרִיתִי הֵפַר: [בראשית יז, יד]

רבינו חננאל

והנותר ממנו עד בוקר באש תשרופו ואין שריפת קדשים דוחה יו"ט דתנינן בגמרא בפ' כיצד צולין את הפסח. דתנן העצמות והגידים והנותר ישרפו בששה עשר חל ששה עשר להיות בשבת ישרפו בי"ז שאינו דוחה לא את השבת ולא את יו"ט וקיימא לן דמילה שלא בזמנה אפילו יו"ט אינו דוחה דתנן שני יו"ט של ר"ה נימול לי"ב ללמדך שאין עשה דוחה י"ט כן המילה שלא בזמנה אינה דוחה י"ט ואין לומר אי הכי אפי' מילה בזמנה כי מילה בזמנה בפירוש אמרה תורה וביום ואפי' בשבת וכ"ש י"ט אביי פירשו מעולת שבת בשבתו כו' רבא אמר הוא ולא מכשיריו פי' עשיית אוכל נפש דוחה י"ט ולא מכשירי אוכל נפש. כגון חטיבת עצים מן היער לבשל ביו"ט וכדומה (לו) [הוא] לבדו ולא מילה שלא בזמנה הבאה בק"ו וזהו ק"ו שאמר רבא ומה אוכל נפש שאע"פ שהיא באזהרת שמחה אינה (מנוח שדוחה) [דוחה] יו"ט לשחוט ולבשל ולאפות וכיוצא בהן מילה שלא בזמנה שאע"פ שהיא בלא זמנה מצוה היא ומעכבתו מלאכול בתרומה. אינו דין שדוחה י"ט בא לבדו למעט המילה שלא בזמנה. רב אשי אמר שבת שבתון עשה הוא וי"ט עשה ול"ת עשה שבתון ולא תעשה כל מלאכה לא תעשה נמצא כתיב ביו"ט עשה ול"ת והמילה עשה בלבד. ולא אתי עשה דמילה ודחי את לא תעשה ועשה דיו"ט: **מתני' כלל** א"ר עקיבא כל מלאכה שאפשר [לעשות] מע"ש דוחה את השבת וכו'.

אמר רב יהודה אמר רב הלכה כר' עקיבא: **מתני' עושין** כל צרכי מילה בשבת מוהלין ופורעין כו' אמרינן כי מכדי קתני מוהלין ופורעין ומוצצין כו' עושין כל צרכי מילה למה לי לאתויי הא דתנו רבנן המל כל זמן שעוסק במילה חוזר בין על ציצין המעכבין את המילה בין על הציצין שאינן מעכבין את המילה פירש על ציצין המעכבין את המילה חוזר על שאין מעכבין אינו חוזר. ואמרינן מאן תנא פירש ואתא רבה בר בר חנה לאוקומה כר' (שמעון) [ישמעאל] בר' יוחנן בן

מסורת הש"ס

א) לעיל קנו: מנחות סג: [תוספתא פסחים פ"ד], ב) נ"ל את, ג) [נזיר ג: ע"ש] סוכה יא: מכילתא פרשת בשלח [מס' סופרים פ"ג הל' יג], ד) ר"ה כב. מנחות סד., ה) מנחות ז: צט:, ו) [קידושין לא: ושם נסמן], ז) פסחים ד. יומא כט: [מגילה כ.], ח) [שייך לעמוד א במשנה].

הגהות הב"ח

(א) גמ' מפשיט אלא משום דלא: (ב) שם ר' יוסי התם אלא משום דלא ניתנה בשבת: (ג) רש"י ד"ה ציצין וכו' ובמתני'. נ"ב לקמן דף קלז סוף ע"א: (ד) ד"ה מפשיט עד וכו': (ה) באד אימוריו. נ"ב ע"ל בפרק כל כתבי דף קטז בסוף הדף: (ו) ד"ה ונכנסין ליטול וכו' כדי שיראו שלא נשנו: (ז) תוס' ד"ה גדול וכו' איבעי ליה למיתני:

רב נסים גאון

חמורה ממנו ודרך הידוע שהחמור דוחה הקל ולא עוד אלא שפעמים שעולה על דעתך שיש בענין הזה ענין חזרה בדבור הראשון והתשובה הוא מה שהקדמנו שהאזהרה של לאו כך נאמרה מיוחדת וכי הציווי של עשה תנאה הוא בה וכן אמרו רז"ל (ספרי פ' תצא) מחלליה מות יומת וביום השבת שני כבשים בני שנה שניהן בדבור אחד נאמרו ערות אשת אחיך ויבמה יבוא עליה שניהן בדיבור אחד נאמרו מה שאי אפשר לומר בשר ודם לומר שנא' אחת דיבר אלהים שתים זו שמענו הבן דבר זה שמור וזכור כי הוא ספק גדול והרי גלינו אותו ומזה העיקר אמרו רז"ל בתלמוד כל מקום שאתה מוצא עשה ולא תעשה אם אתה יכול לקיים את שניהם מוטב ואם לאו יבא עשה וידחה את לא תעשה וסבר (רבינא) [רבא] כי לא תעשה שבקודש מוצא מזה העיקר וכי לא ידחה מפני עשה ולא שום עמו רב אשי בדבר זה כמו שנאמר בשחיטת קדשים בפרק דם חטאת (דף צז) אמאי וניתי עשה ונידחי לא תעשה ועשה ורבא אין עשה דוחה את לא תעשה שבמקדש דתניא כו' רב אשי אמר עשה דוחה את לא תעשה ועשה ובמס' נזירות בפ' ג' מינין (נזיר נח) אמרו עוד ומאי דקא מדלי ליה (ומאן דמוקים) לקרא למידרש לא תעשה ועשה לאו גרידא מנא ליה יליף מגדילים דאמר קרא לא תלבש שעטנז גדילים תעשה לך מהן וכל מה שאתה מוצא בתלמוד דאתי עשה ודחי לא תעשה מזה העיקר שהקדימו לא תעשה נאמר בלאו גרידא לבד אבל לא תעשה ועשה וכל שכן לא תעשה שיש בו כרת אין עשה דוחה אותו ואנו מבארין לך זה ונאמר

ליקוטי רש"י

ציצין. רצועות של בשר שנשארו מן הערלה [לקמן קלז.]. חתיכות בשר שלא נפרעת המילה כהלכתה [יבמות מז:]. שנשתיירו שלא חתך כל הערלה [שם עא:]. **עד החזה.** מתחיל מרגליו האחרונים עד החזה שיוכל להוציא אימורים שהקטר חלביו דוחין שבת ותו לא מפשיט מידי עד אורתא דצורך הדיוט הוא [לעיל קטז:]. **בעליל.** שנראה הלבנה בעליל לכל העולם [מנחות סד.]. בעליל לי גילוי הוא בלשון המשנה בין שנראה בעליל בין שלא נראה בעליל כו' [תהלים יב, ז]. **נראה בעליל אין מחללין.** לפי שאין צורך [ר"ה כא:]. ללכת ולהעיד לב"ד שהרי א"ל כיון דבעליל נראה ב"ד נמי ראוהו [מנחות שם]. **נכנסין.** ביום השבת. **שני סדרים.** של לחם הפנים שתים המערכות של המערכת [שם ז.]. **שני בזיכין.** לשני קומצי לבונה שנותנין על שתי המערכות שנאמר (ויקרא כד) ונתת על המערכת לבונה זכה [שמות כה, כט]. **ליטול שני בזיכין.** ומקטירין שני בזיכי לבונה שסילקו מעל השלחן והן מתירין את הלחם באכילה כדכתיב והיה ללחם לאזכרה [סוכה נו:]. **המכניסין עומדים בצפון.** דהכי שפיר [מלתא] דאומן [ה]מסדרין (העבודה) יהו בצפון דקדושת צפון עדיף. **ופניהם לדרום.** וסתמא כמאן דאמר שולחנות מזרח ומערב מונחין ורחבן צפון ודרום. **אלו מושכים.** ועד שלא יגביהו הן מן השלחן אלו מניחין. **אפילו אלו נוטלין.** לגמרי ואלו מניחין אחר שסילקו אף זה היה תמיד כדמפרש טעמא בגמ' דאין תמיד אלא שלא ילין שולחן לילה אחד בלא לחם [מנחות צט:]. אפילו סילק את הישנה שחרית וסידר את החדשה ערבית אף זו היתה תמיד ומהו תמיד שלא ילין שולחן בלא לחם אבל לרבנן טפחו של זה מסדר בצד טפחו של מסלק [מגילה כא.]. **מיפקד פקיד.** כמו פקדון כנוס ועומד ואינו נבלע להיות יוצאו על ידי חבורה [כתובות ה:]. **אמרה לי אם.** אומנתו היתה [כתובות לט: ע"ש בב"ח]. **וקלבא.** רשינ"א שבחביות של יין [ב"ק פה. וע"ע ביצה לג: ד"ה במוסתקי].

אֲבָל הָכָא דִּבְעֵינַן ,,זֶה אֵלִי וְאַנְוֵהוּ'' – **But here** in the case of *milah,* **where we require** a fulfillment of ***This is my God and I will beautify Him,***[19] הָכִי נַמִּי – **it is indeed so** that R' Yishmael would condone a resumption of the *milah*![20] – ? –

The Gemara proceeds to elucidate the concept of "beautifying oneself through mitzvos":

דְּתַנְיָא – **For it was taught in a Baraisa:** ,,זֶה אֵלִי וְאַנְוֵהוּ'' – Scripture states, ***THIS IS MY GOD AND I WILL BEAUTIFY HIM,*** which implies:[21] הִתְנָאֵה לְפָנָיו בְּמִצְוֹת – BEAUTIFY ONESELF BEFORE HIM IN the fulfillment of THE COMMANDMENTS.[22] עֲשֵׂה לְפָנָיו סוּכָּה נָאָה – For example, MAKE BEFORE HIM A BEAUTIFUL *SUCCAH,* וְלוּלָב נָאֶה וְשׁוֹפָר נָאֶה – A BEAUTIFUL *LULAV* AND A BEAUTIFUL *SHOFAR,* צִיצִית נָאָה סֵפֶר תּוֹרָה נָאֶה – BEAUTIFUL *TZITZIS*[23] and A BEAUTIFUL TORAH SCROLL; וּכְתוֹב בּוֹ לִשְׁמוֹ בִּדְיוֹ נָאֶה – AND WRITE IN IT FOR HIS SAKE[24] WITH BEAUTIFUL INK, בְּקוּלְמוֹס נָאֶה בְּלַבְלָר אוּמָּן – A BEAUTIFUL PEN[25] and AN EXPERT SCRIBE, וְכוֹרְכוֹ בְּשִׁירָאִין נָאִין – AND WRAP [THE TORAH] IN BEAUTIFUL SILKS. אַבָּא שָׁאוּל אוֹמֵר – ABBA SHAUL SAYS: ,,וְאַנְוֵהוּ'' הֱוֵי דּוֹמֶה לוֹ – The word *V'ANVEIHU* implies: BE LIKE HIM.[26] מַה הוּא חַנּוּן וְרַחוּם – JUST AS [GOD] IS GRACIOUS AND COMPASSIONATE, אַף אַתָּה הֱיֵה חַנּוּן וְרַחוּם – YOU ALSO SHOULD BE GRACIOUS AND COMPASSIONATE.

The Gemara again attempts to identify the Tanna who holds that the *mohel* does not return to and cut off the non-impeding shreds of foreskin once he has completed his act:

אֶלָּא אָמַר רַב אַשִׁי – **Rather, Rav Ashi said:** הָא מַנִּי – **Who is this** Tanna? רַבִּי יוֹסֵי הִיא דִּתְנַן – **It is R' Yose, for we learned in a Mishnah:**[27] בֵּין שֶׁנִּרְאָה בַּעֲלִיל – WHETHER [THE NEW MOON] IS CLEARLY VISIBLE to everyone[28] וּבֵין שֶׁלֹּא נִרְאָה בַּעֲלִיל – OR WHETHER IT IS NOT CLEARLY VISIBLE to everyone, מְחַלְּלִין עָלָיו אֶת הַשַּׁבָּת – WE DESECRATE THE SABBATH BECAUSE OF IT.[29] רַבִּי יוֹסֵי אוֹמֵר – R' YOSE SAYS: נִרְאָה בַּעֲלִיל – If [THE NEW MOON] IS CLEARLY VISIBLE to everyone, אֵין מְחַלְּלִין עָלָיו אֶת הַשַּׁבָּת – WE DO NOT DESECRATE THE SABBATH BECAUSE OF IT.[30]

The Gemara challenges this answer as well:

מִמַּאי – **From what** proof do you say that the Tanna is R' Yose?! דִּילְמָא עַד כָּאן לָא קָאָמַר רַבִּי יוֹסֵי הָתָם – **Perhaps R' Yose did not say there** that witnesses may leave their *techum* to testify only because[31] in that case דְּלֹא נִיתְּנָה שַׁבָּת לִידָּחוֹת – **the Sabbath is not** – even in the first place – **given to be overridden.**[32] אֲבָל הָכָא דְּנִיתְּנָה שַׁבָּת לִידָּחוֹת – **But here** in the case of *milah,* **where the Sabbath is given to be overridden** in the first place,[33] הָכִי נַמִּי – **it is indeed so** that R' Yose would condone a resumption of the *milah*![34] Thus, he may not be the Tanna of the Baraisa.

The Gemara finally identifies the Tanna of the Baraisa:

אֶלָּא אָמְרֵי נְהַרְדְּעֵי – **Rather,** the sages **of Nehardea said:** רַבָּנַן דִּפְלִיגֵי עֲלֵיהּ דְּרַבִּי יוֹסֵי הִיא – **It is the rabbis who argue with R' Yose** in the matter of the *lechem hapanim* (*panim* bread),[35] דִּתְנַן – **for we learned in a Mishnah:**[36] אַרְבָּעָה כֹּהֲנִים נִכְנָסִין – Each Shabbos FOUR KOHANIM ENTER the Sanctuary to perform the service of the *lechem hapanim,* שְׁנַיִם בְּיָדָם שְׁנֵי סְדָרִים – TWO carrying IN THEIR HANDS the TWO ARRANGEMENTS of *lechem hapanim*[37] וּשְׁנַיִם בְּיָדָם שְׁנֵי בָזִיכִין – AND TWO carrying IN THEIR HANDS the TWO SPOONS of frankincense.[38] וְאַרְבָּעָה מַקְדִּימִין לִפְנֵיהֶם – AND FOUR other Kohanim PRECEDE THEM, שְׁנַיִם לִיטּוֹל שְׁנֵי סְדָרִים – TWO TO TAKE AWAY the TWO old ARRANGEMENTS of *lechem hapanim* וּשְׁנַיִם לִיטּוֹל שְׁנֵי בָזִיכִין – AND TWO TO TAKE AWAY the TWO SPOONS from the previous week. הַמַּכְנִיסִין עוֹמְדִים בַּצָּפוֹן וּפְנֵיהֶם לַדָּרוֹם – THOSE WHO ARE BRINGING IN STAND ON THE NORTH side of the Table FACING SOUTH, וְהַמּוֹצִיאִין עוֹמְדִים בַּדָּרוֹם

NOTES

19. Since the circumcision is embellished when the remaining, non-impeding shreds are removed (*Rashi*).

20. [Because such an embellishment would perhaps automatically constitute a continuation of the act of circumcision.] Hence, R' Yishmael may not be the Tanna who holds that cessation from an action would render a return to that action a separate and distinct act.

21. The Baraisa will present two interpretations of the verse. The Gemara's previous suggestion accords with the first one.

22. Since it is patently impossible to beautify God, the Tanna Kamma understands that Scripture must mean that one should beautify himself before God through the embellished performance of mitzvos (*Maharsha*).

23. *Rosh* to *Succah* (3:12) adds: "a beautiful garment." See also *Mishnah Berurah* 24:9.

24. See *Binyan Shlomo* §6, cited by *Megadim Chadashim,* who discusses why the Baraisa chose to mention the intent requirement here. See also *Sfas Emes* here.

25. *Rashi* to *Yoma* 70a implies that his text read: "a beautiful parchment." *Meiri* implies that by קולמוס the Baraisa means a beautiful script. See also *Ben Yehoyada;* cf. *Sfas Emes.*

26. Abba Shaul understands that אַנְוֵהוּ is a contraction of two words, אֲנִי וָהוּא (*I and He*), and thus implies: *I* shall make myself like *Him* (God) by emulating and cleaving to His ways (*Rashi;* cf. *Ritva MHK* ed. and *Maharsha*).

27. *Rosh Hashanah* 21b.

28. [Before the fixed calendar was instituted,] the sanctification of the new Jewish month (*Kiddush HaChodesh*) was performed by the *beis din* in Jerusalem, who rely upon the testimony of two witnesses who sighted the new moon. A previous Mishnah there teaches that they may come to Jerusalem even on the Sabbath. This Mishnah speaks of where potential witnesses located outside of the *beis din's* Sabbath boundary (*techum*) were certain that the new moon was visible to observers within that boundary [e.g. the moon was high above the horizon (*Rav*), or the night sky was free of clouds (*Tiferes Yisrael*)], and these observers would not have to desecrate the Sabbath in order to testify (*Rashi;* see following note).

29. The Tanna Kamma holds that even when the new moon is clearly visible throughout the Land and so their testimony is probably unnecessary, witnesses are permitted to violate the prohibition against traveling beyond one's Sabbath boundary in order to report their sightings to *beis din* (*Rashi*).

30. R' Yose holds that since in this case traveling to testify will apparently serve no sacred purpose (since other witnesses are available in the *beis din's techum*), one may not desecrate the Sabbath despite the fact that he *is* performing the mitzvah. Similarly, contends Rav Ashi, R' Yose would hold that since cutting off the non-impeding shreds serves no sacred purpose (since the circumcision is already valid), one may not desecrate the Sabbath in order to complete the *milah* (*Rashi;* see also *Ritva MHK* ed.; see also *Hagahos R' Elazar Moshe Horowitz*).

31. *Bach* inserts אֶלָּא מִשּׁוּם, *only because,* into the text.

32. Since it is obvious that the new moon is visible to those living in the *beis din's techum* [the mitzvah itself loses its power to override] (*Rashi*).

33. I.e. one lawfully commences an eighth-day *milah* on the Sabbath (*Rashi*).

34. I.e. perhaps he does not regard the resumption as a new beginning and a separate act, but merely as the completion of an act of circumcision, as if it were never interrupted (*Rashi*).

35. Twelve specially baked loaves of *lechem hapanim* rested at all times on the Table (*Shulchan*) in the Tabernacle and Holy Temple. They were arranged in two columns of six loaves each. The bread was baked each Friday, and on the Sabbath the old loaves were removed (and divided among the ministering Kohanim), and were replaced by new loaves (see *Leviticus* 24:5-9). The Mishnah cited below describes this replacement procedure.

36. *Menachos* 99b.

37. I.e. each of these two Kohanim carried one stack of six loaves.

38. *Leviticus* 24:7 states: *You shall put pure frankincense on each stack* (*Rashi*). Each of these two Kohanim carried one spoon filled with frankincense.

עין משפט
נר מצוה

טו א מיי' פ"ב מהלכות מילה הל' ד ו טוש"ע א"ח סי' שלא סעיף ב וטוש"ע י"ד סי' רסו סעיף ב:
טז ב מיי' פ"ז מהל' ק"ח הלכה ד ופ"ז מהל' לולב הל' ו סמג עשין כח ולאוין שסד טוש"ע א"ח סימן תרנו:
יז ג מיי' פ"א מהלכות דעות הלכה ו:
יח ד מיי' פ"ג מהלכות קידוש החדש הל' ד:
יט ה מיי' פ"ה מהל' תמידין ומוספין הל' ד סמג עשין קצ:
כ ו מיי' פ"ב מהלכות שגגות הלכה ט:
כא ז מיי' פ"ב מהל' מילה הל' ב סמג עשין כח טוש"ע י"ד סי' רסד סעיף ג:
כב ח טוש"ע א"ח סי' ד סעיף כ:

תורה אור השלם
א) עָזִּי וְזִמְרָת יָהּ וַיְהִי לִי לִישׁוּעָה זֶה אֵלִי וְאַנְוֵהוּ אֱלֹהֵי אָבִי וַאֲרֹמְמֶנְהוּ: [שמות טו, ב]
ב) וְנָתַתָּ עַל הַשֻּׁלְחָן לֶחֶם פָּנִים לְפָנַי תָּמִיד: [שמות כה, ל]
ג) וְעָרֵל זָכָר אֲשֶׁר לֹא יִמּוֹל אֶת בְּשַׂר עָרְלָתוֹ וְנִכְרְתָה הַנֶּפֶשׁ הַהִוא מֵעַמֶּיהָ אֶת בְּרִיתִי הֵפַר: [בראשית יז, יד]

רבינו חננאל
והנותר ממנו עד בוקר באש תשרופו ואין שריפת קדשים דוחה יו"ט דתנינן בגמרא בפ' כיצד צולין את הפסח. דתנן העצמות והגידים והנותר ישרפו בששה עשר חל ששה עשר להיות בשבת ישרפו בי"ז שאינו דוחה את השבת ולא את יו"ט וקיימא לן דמילה שלא בזמנה אפילו יו"ט אינו דוחה דתנן שני יו"ט של ר"ה נימול לי"ב ללמדך שאין עשה דוחה י"ט כן המילה שלא בזמנה אינה דוחה י"ט ואין לומר אי הכי אפי' מילה בזמנה כי מילה בזמנה בפירוש אמרה תורה וביום ואפי' בשבת וכ"ש י"ט אביי פירשו מעולת שבת בשבתו כו' רבא אמר הוא ולא מכשיריו פי' עשיית אוכל נפש דוחה י"ט ולא מכשירי אוכל נפש. כגון חטיבת עצים מן היער לבשל ביו"ט וכדומה (לו) [הוא] לבדו ולא מילה שלא בזמנה הבאה בק"ו וזהו ק"ו שאמר רבא ומה אוכל נפש שאע"פ שהיא באזהרת שמחה אינה (מנוח שדוחה) [דוחה] יו"ט לשחוט ולבשל ולאפות וכיוצא בהן מילה שלא בזמנה שאע"פ שהיא בלא זמנה מצוה היא ומעכבתו מלאכול בתרומה. אינו דין שדוחה י"ט בא לבדו למעט המילה שלא בזמנה. רב אשי אמר שבת שבתון עשה הוא וי"ט עשה ול"ת עשה שבתון ולא תעשה כל מלאכה לא תעשה נמצא כתיב ביו"ט עשה ול"ת והמילה עשה בלבד. ולא אתי עשה דמילה ודחי את לא תעשה ועשה דיו"ט: מתני' כלל א"ר עקיבא כל מלאכה שאפשר [לעשות] מע"ש דוחה את השבת וכו'.

אמר רב יהודה אמר רב הלכה כר' עקיבא: מתני' עושין כל צרכי מילה בשבת מוהלין ופורעין כו' אמרינן כי מכדי קתני מוהלין ופורעין ומוצצין כו' עושין כל צרכי מילה למה לי לאתויי הא דתנו רבנן המל כל זמן שעוסק במילה חוזר בין על הציצין שאינן מעכבין את המילה בין על ציצין המעכבין את המילה פירש על ציצין המעכבין את המילה חוזר על שאין מעכבין אינו חוזר. ואמרינן מאן תנא פירש ואתא רבה בר בר חנה לאוקומה כר' (שמעון) [ישמעאל] בר' יוחנן בן

גמ' מכדי קתני. במתניתין: כולהו. כל דברים העושים למילה מוהלין ופורעין ומוצצין כו' למה לי דתנן כללא ברישא עושין כל צרכי מילה: ציצין. שיורי ערלה ובמתני' (ג) מפרש אלו הן ציצין המעכבין ויש שאין מעכבין כגון בשר שאינו חופה רוב העטרה אלא מיעוטה ומה היא עטרה שורה גבוה המקפת בגיד סביב שממנה הגיד משפע ומשפע ויורד לצד הקרקע ומשפע ויורד לצד הגוף: המל. בשבת: כל זמן שהוא עוסק בה. שלא סילק ידו אם ראה שנשתיירו בה ציצין בין מעכבין את המילה שאינה כשרה עד שיחתכם בין שאין מעכבין חוזר ומותך דכולא חדא מילתא היא והרי ניתנה שבת לדחות אצלה: פירש. סילק ידיו: על המעכבין חוזר. שהרי הן כמילה עצמה: ועל שאין מעכבין אינו חוזר. דהוי כהתחלה בפני עצמה ועל אלו לא ניתן לחלל את השבת והיינו דקתני כל צרכי מילה ואפילו ציצין שאין מעכבין חוזר עליהם כל זמן שלא פירש: מאן תנא פירש אינו חוזר. ומשום דפירש חשיב ליה חזרה מילתא לנפשה והואיל ולא עיכוב מלוה ניהו לא הדר: מפשיט הפסח עד החזה (ד). והיינו פירש דתנן במסכת תמיד (פ"ד מ"ג) גבי הפשיטו שהיה מתחיל מן הרגלים והיה מפשיט ויורד עד שמגיע לחזה הגיע לחזה חתך את הראש ונתנו למי שזכה בו ואח"כ הכרעיים ומירק והפשיט כו' שמעי' מיניה משהגיע לחזה סילק ידיו מן ההפשט והתחיל להתעסק בניתוח קלת וגבי עולה דכולה כליל מירק והפשיט ומנתח הידים תחילה אחר הראש וגבי פסח נמי משהפשיט עד החזה דיכול להוציא אימוריו (ה) בלא נימין קורעו ומוציאן מיד והוה ליה פירש מן ההפשט וקאמר רבי ישמעאל שוב אינו גומר ומפשיט משום דכיון דפירש הויא חזרה מילתא דאתחלתא לנפשה ושלא לצורך גבוה דומיא דציצין דלא מעכבין: דלא בעינן זה אלי ואנוהו. דאחר נטילת האימורין אין הידור מלוה ביפוי בשר אבל יפוי מילה מלוה היא: הוי דומה לו. ולשון אנוהו אני והוא אעשה עלמי כמותו לדבק בדרכיו: בין שנראה. החדש: בעליל. בגילוי לכל ויש לדעת שראוהו בית דין והקרובים להם ואין לריך לרואין חוץ לתחום לחלל שבת ולבא ולהעיד לפני ב"ד מחללין: ר' יוסי אומר כו'. אלמא אע"ג דאיכא מלוה כיון דלאו לצורך גבוה הוא לא מחללינן והכא נמי פירש דהוי אתחלתא דחילול כי הכא בלא צורך גבוה לא מחללינן: לא ניתנה שבת לדחות. אפילו בהתחלתה דהא נראה בעליל אבל הכא כיון שנתנה שבת לדחות להתחיל בה המילה הכי נמי דכי פירש והדר לאו אתחלתא לנפשה היא והוי כמו שלא פירש וגומר כל מלותו: רבנן דפליגי עליה דרבי יוסי. גבי לחם הפנים: ארבעה כהנים נכנסין. להיכל בשבת לסדור לחם הפנים: שני סדרים. שתים מערכות של לחם: שני בזיכין. שתי כפות מלאות לבונה כדכתיב (ויקרא כד) ונתת על המערכת לבונה זכה: מקדימין לפניהם שנים ליטול. מן השלחן שני סדרים הישנים: ושנים ליטול שני בזיכין. והשלחן היה נתון ארכו ממזרח למערב ואלו עומדין מזה לרוחב השלחן בצפון ואלו עומדין לנגדו לדרום ודווקא מכניסין לצפון דכל צפון ענין חשיבות היא כדאמרינן במסכת סוכה (דף נו.) גבי חילוק לחם הפנים למשמרה הנכנסת והיוצאת הנכנסין חולקין בצפון כדי שיראו (ו) נכנסין: רבי יוסי אומר אפילו אלו נוטלין. תחילה ומסלקין כולה מן השלחן ולאחר שעה מניחין אלו: אף זה תמיד. ומה אני מקיים תמיד שלא ילין שלחן בלא לחם ולרבנן אי שקלי ושבקי ליה והדר מסדרי לא מיקרי להו תמיד אלא התחלה אחריתי ונמצא שמתעכב שלחן בלא לחם וגבי פירש נמי כי הדר אתי מילתא אחריתי היא ולרבי יוסי דאמר כי שבקי והדר מתחלי נמי תמיד הוא דחדא מילתא הוא הכא נמי פירש חוזר אע"פ שאין מעכבין דכולה גמר מילתא היא: מהלקטין. בציצין המעכבין: מני. כרת זו של מי הוא: אמר רב כהנא אומן. ענוש כרת ובשבת קאי שחילל שבת ולא עשה מלוה: ונימא אנא עבדי פלגא. כלומר הואיל וכשהתחיל ברשות התחיל וחבורה שעשה ברשות עשה אמאי חייב נימא להו לכו אתם וסיימו המלאכה: אלא אמר רב פפא. בגדול שמל קמיירי ובחול וענוש כרת דקאמר משום מילה קאמר דעדיין ערל הוא: וכגון דאתא בין השמשות. דכל היום כשר למילה י) ואמרו ליה לא מספקת לגמור ביום כהילכתה ותעשה חבורה בשבת בלא מלוה וענוש כרת ומיהו מיתה ליכא דלא אתרו ביה למיתה ולא קבל עליו התראה וכרת איכא דאתחלה ברשות לא התחיל ולא ניתנה שבת לדחות אצלו בשעה זו: מהו דתימא. מתניתין לא אשמעינן דמחלל שבתא עלה דדם מיפקד פקיד ועומד שם כנתון בכלי ובמציצה אין חבורה ואין כאן איסור תורה ומשום הכי שרי ולאו משום סכנה ואומנא דלא מייץ בחול לאו סכנתא היא ולא ניעבריה: קא משמע לן דדם חיבורי מיחבר. כשיולא ע"י מציצה ואפילו הכי שרי משום סכנה מדקתני במתני' גבי איספלנית וכמון: שב מינאי תרבא. ז' מנות של חלב: וחדא דקירא. שעוה: קירא וקלבא רישינא. הוא זפת של עץ שמוציאים ממנו שלא ע"י האור והיא לבנה: קרעינהו למנייהו. שהפסיד להם לגלות רפואה זו: שבקי לכו חדא. שלא גיליתי: חספניתא

גדול בהדיא כתיב ביה. אע"ג דבכמה דוכתין תנינן מה שבהדיא בפסוק איבעי (ז) למתני גדול שלא מל ענוש כרת:

לועס בשיניו. אף על גב דאחר מילה מוצה שיש בו סכנה הוא מ"מ כמה דאפשר לשנויי משנינן: הכא

גמ' מכדי קתני כולהו כל צורכי מילה לאתויי מאי לאתויי הא דת"ר א המל כל זמן שהוא עוסק במילה חוזר בין על הציצין המעכבין את המילה בין על הציצין שאין מעכבין את המילה פירש על ציצין המעכבין את המילה חוזר על ציצין שאין מעכבין את המילה אינו חוזר מאן תנא פירש אינו חוזר אמר רבה בר בר חנה אמר רבי יוחנן רבי ישמעאל בנו של ר' יוחנן בן ברוקה היא דתניא א) ארבעה עשר שחל להיות בשבת מפשיט (ב) אדם) הפסח עד החזה דברי רבי ישמעאל בנו של ר' יוחנן בן ברוקה וחכ"א מפשיטין את כולו ממאי עד כאן לא קאמר ר' ישמעאל בנו של ר' יוחנן בן ברוקה התם (א) משום דלא בעינן א) זה אלי ואנוהו אבל הכא דבעינן זה אלי ואנוהו הכי נמי ג) דתניא זה אלי ואנוהו ב התנאה לפניו במצות עשה לפניו סוכה נאה ולולב נאה ושופר נאה ציצית נאה ספר תורה נאה וכתוב בו לשמו בדיו נאה בקולמוס נאה בלבלר אומן וכורכו בשיראין נאין אבא שאול אומר ואנוהו הוי דומה לו ג מה הוא חנון ורחום אף אתה היה חנון ורחום אלא אמר רב אשי הא מני רבי יוסי היא דתנן ד) ד בין שנראה בעליל ובין שלא נראה בעליל מחללין עליו את השבת רבי יוסי אומר נראה בעליל אין מחללין עליו את השבת ממאי דילמא עד כאן לא קאמר ר' יוסי התם (ב) דלא ניתנה שבת לידחות אבל הכא דניתנה שבת לידחות הכי נמי אלא אמרי נהרדעי רבנן דפליגי עליה דרבי יוסי היא דתנן ה) ה ארבעה כהנים נכנסין שנים בידם שני סדרים ושנים בידם שני בזיכין וארבעה מקדימין לפניהם שנים ליטול שני סדרים ושנים ליטול שני בזיכין המכניסין עומדים בצפון ופניהם לדרום והמוציאין עומדים בדרום ופניהם לצפון אלו מושכים ואלו מניחין טפחו של זה כנגד טפחו של זה משום שנאמר ב) לפני (ה') תמיד ר' יוסי אומר אפילו אלו נוטלין ואלו מניחין אף זה היה תמיד ת"ר מהלקטין את המילה ואם לא הילקט ענוש כרת מני א"ר כהנא אומן מתקיף לה רב פפא לימא להו אנא עבדי פלגא דמצוה אתון עבידתו פלגא דמצוה אלא אמר רב פפא גדול מתקיף לה רב אשי גדול בהדיא כתיב ביה ג) וערל זכר אשר לא ימול אלא אמר רב אשי לעולם אומן י וכגון דאתא בין השמשות דשבת ואמרו ליה לא מספקת ואמר להו מספקינא ועבד ולא איסתפק ואישתכח דחבורה הוא דעבד וענוש כרת: מוצצין וכו': אמר רב פפא ז האי אומנא דלא מייץ סכנה הוא ועברינן ליה פשיטא מדקא מחללי עליה שבתא סכנה הוא מהו דתימא האי דם מיפקד פקיד קמ"ל חבורי מיחבר ודומיא דאיספלנית וכמון מה איספלנית וכמון כי לא עביד סכנה הוא אף ה"נ כי לא עביד סכנה הוא: ונותנין עליה איספלנית: אמר אביי י אמרה לי אם איספלניתא דכולהון כיבי שב מינאי תרבא וחדא קירא רבא אמר קירא וקלבא רישינא דרשה רבא במחוזא קרעינהו בני מגיומי אסיא למנייהו אמר להו שבקי לכו חדא דאמר שמואל ח האי מאן דמשי אפיה ולא נגיב טובא נקטרו ליה חספניתא

מסורת הש"ס

א) לעיל קטו: מנחות סג: [תוספתא פסחים פ"ד], ב) נ"ל את, ג) [נזיר ב: ע"ש] סוכה יא: מכילתא פרשת בשלח [מס' סופרים פ"ג הל' יג], ד) ר"ה כא: מנחות סד., ה) מנחות ז. לט:, ו) [קידושין לא: ושם נסמן], ז) פסחים ד. יומא כח: (מגילה כ.), ח) [שייך לעמוד א במשנה].

הגהות הב"ח

(א) גמ' התם אלא משום דלא: (ב) שם ר' יוסי התם אלא משום דלא ניתנה בשבת: (ג) רש"י ד"ה ציצין וכו' ובמתני'. נ"ב לקמן דף קלז סוף ע"א: (ד) ד"ה מפשיטין את הפסח עד וכו': (ה) בא"ד להוציא אימוריו. נ"ב ע"ל בפרק כל כתבי דף קטז בסוף הדף: (ו) ד"ה ושנים ליטול וכו' כדי שיראו שהן נכנסין: (ז) תוס' ד"ה גדול וכו' איבעי ליה למיתני:

רב נסים גאון

חמורה ממנו ומדרך הידוע שהחמור דוחה הקל ולא עוד אלא שפעמים שעולה על דעתן שיש בענין הזה ענין חזרה בדבר הראשון והתשובה הוא מה שהקדמנו שהאזהרה של לאו כך נאמרה מיוחדת וכי הציווי של עשה תנאי הוא בה וכן אמרו רז"ל (ספרי פ' תצא) מחלליה מות יומת וביום השבת שני כבשים בני שנה שניהן בדיבור אחד נאמרו ערות אשת אחיך ויבמה יבוא עליה שניהן בדיבור אחד נאמרו מה שאי אפשר לבשר ודם לומר שאי אחת דיבר אלהים שתים זו שמענו הבן דבר זה ושמור אותו כי הוא ספק גדול והרי גלינו אותו ומזה העיקר אמרו רז"ל בתלמוד כל מקום שאתה מוצא עשה ולא תעשה אם אתה יכול לקיים את שניהם מוטב ואם לאו יבא עשה וידחה לא תעשה והסבר (רבינא) [רבא] כי לא תעשה שבקודש מוצא מזה העיקר וכי לא ידחה מפני עשה ולא שוה עצו רב אשי בדבר זה כי שנאמר בשחיטות קדשים בפרק דם חטאת (דף צז) אמאי וניתי עשה ונידחי לא תעשה אמר רבא אין עשה דוחה את לא תעשה שבמקדש ואין עשה דוחה את לא תעשה ועשה ובמס' נזירות בפ' שלשה מינין (דף נח) אמרו עוד (ומאי דקאמר) מורי ליה [ומאן דמוקים] לקרא למידחא לאו תעשה ועשה לאו גרידא מנא ליה יליף מגדילים דאמר קרא לא תלבש שעטנז וכתיב גדילים תעשה לך מהן וכל מה שתמצא בתלמוד דאתי עשה ודחי לא תעשה העיקר שהקדמנו הוא וזה הדין בלאו גרידא לבד אבל לא תעשה שיש בו כרת אין עשה דוחה אותו ואנו מבארין לך זה ונאמר

ליקוטי רש"י

ציצין. רלועות של בשר שנשארו מן הערלה [לקמן קלז.]. חתיכות בשר שלא נפרעת המילה כהלכתה [יבמות מז:]. שנשתיירו שלא חתך כל [שם עא.]. עד החזה. מתחיל מרגליו המאחרונים עד החזה שיוכל להוציא אימורים שהקטר חלב מפשיט מידי עד אורתא לצורך הדיוט הוא [לעיל קטז:]. בעליל. שנראה הלבנה בעליל לכל העולם גילוי הוא בלשון המשנה בין שנראה בעליל בין שלא נראה בעליל כו' [תהלים יב, ז]. נראה בעליל שאין לורך [ר"ה כא:]. ללכת ולהעיד לב"ד שהרי א"ל כיון דבעליל נראה ב"ד נמי ראוהו [מנחות

וּפְנֵיהֶם לַצָּפוֹן – WHILE THOSE WHO ARE TAKING OUT STAND ON THE SOUTH side FACING NORTH.[39] אֵלּוּ מוֹשְׁכִים וְאֵלּוּ מַנִּיחִין – THESE WITHDRAW AND THESE PLACE DOWN,[40] טִפְחוֹ שֶׁל זֶה בְּצַד טִפְחוֹ שֶׁל זֶה – WITH THE HAND OF THIS ALONGSIDE THE HAND OF THIS,[41] מִשּׁוּם שֶׁנֶּאֱמַר ,,לְפָנַי (ה׳) תָּמִיד" – FOR IT IS STATED: *You shall place show bread BEFORE ME CONTINUOUSLY.*[42] רַבִּי יוֹסֵי אוֹמֵר – R' YOSE SAYS: אֲפִילּוּ אֵלּוּ נוֹטְלִין וְאֵלּוּ מַנִּיחִין – EVEN if THESE Kohanim TAKE AWAY all the bread from the Table AND, only later, THESE other Kohanim PLACE the new loaves DOWN, אַף זֶה הָיָה תָּמִיד – THIS ALSO IS considered "CONTINUOUSLY."[43]

The Gemara further discusses the matter of impeding foreskin shreds:

תָּנוּ רַבָּנָן – **The Rabbis taught** in a Baraisa: מְהַלְקְטִין אֶת הַמִּילָה – WE MUST TRIM[44] the shreds of foreskin that impede the validity of THE CIRCUMCISION, וְאִם לֹא הִילְקֵט עָנוּשׁ כָּרֵת – AND IF [THE SHREDS] ARE NOT TRIMMED,[45] HE IS PUNISHED with EXCISION.

The Gemara asks:

מַנִּי – **Whose is it?** I.e. who is punished with excision?

The Gemara ventures an answer:

אָמַר רַב כָּהֲנָא אוּמָּן – **Rav Kahana said:** It is the **expert** surgeon who performed the partial circumcision.[46]

An objection:

מַתְקִיף לָהּ רַב פַּפָּא – **Rav Pappa challenges [this answer]:** אוּמָּן – **An expert** surgeon!? לֵימָא לְהוּ – **Let him say to [the others present]:** אֲנָא עֲבַדִי פַּלְגָא דְּמִצְוָה – **I have performed half of the commandment;** אַתּוּן עַבְדִיתוּ פַּלְגָא דְּמִצְוָה – now **you perform** the other **half of the commandment.**[47]

The Gemara offers a different answer:

אֶלָּא אָמַר רַב פַּפָּא גָּדוֹל – **Rather, Rav Pappa said:** The Baraisa speaks of **an** uncircumcised **adult** who was later partially circumcised. Since the remaining shreds cover a majority of the corona, he remains uncircumcised; hence, it is he who is liable to the *kares* penalty.[48]

The Gemara again objects:

מַתְקִיף לָהּ רַב אַשִׁי – **Rav Ashi challenges [this answer]:** גָּדוֹל בְּהֶדְיָא כְּתִיב בֵּיהּ – **[The excision penalty] is expressly written with regard to an** uncircumcised **adult,** for Scripture states:[49] ,,וְעָרֵל זָכָר אֲשֶׁר לֹא־יִמּוֹל. . .'' – ***An uncircumcised male the flesh of whose foreskin will not be circumcised*** *– that soul shall be cut off from its people.* Why would the Baraisa repeat an explicit teaching of the Torah?[50]

The Gemara finally arrives at a correct interpretation of the Baraisa:

אֶלָּא אָמַר רַב אַשִׁי – **Rather, Rav Ashi said:** לְעוֹלָם אוּמָּן – **In truth,** the Baraisa speaks of **an expert** surgeon who performed a partial and invalid circumcision, וּכְגוֹן דְּאָתָא בֵּין הַשְּׁמָשׁוֹת דְּשַׁבָּת – **and in a case where he came at the twilight of the Sabbath**[51] וְאָמְרוּ לֵיהּ לֹא מְסַפְּקַת – and [the people] **said to him: You lack sufficient** time to complete a proper circumcision before the Sabbath day concludes. Hence, you will be making a wound on the Sabbath without performing a mitzvah, an act which is punishable by *kares.*[52] וְאָמַר לְהוּ מְסַפְּקִינָא – **And he said to them** in reply: **I do have sufficient** time to perform a valid circumcision. וְעָבַד וְלֹא אִיסְתַּפֵּק – **And he** began **performing**

NOTES

39. The Table was placed in the Sanctuary lengthwise along an east-west axis. The Kohanim arranging the new bread and frankincense took up positions on the north side of the Table, while the other group stood facing them along the south side. Inasmuch as the "arrangers" performed a more sanctified service than the "removers," it is appropriate that the former stood in the north, for the north side is considered more prominent. This is evidenced by the fact that the קָדְשֵׁי קָדָשִׁים, *most-holy offerings,* are slaughtered in the northern portion of the Temple Courtyard (*Rashi* here and, regarding the last point, to *Menachos* 99b [as explained by *Tos. Yom Tov* there]).

40. The Kohanim standing to the south of the *Shulchan* gradually pull the breads of the previous week off the *Shulchan,* while those standing to the north place down the new breads as the old ones are removed (*Rashi* to *Menachos* ibid.).

41. I.e. the hand of the arranger was alongside the hand of the remover.

42. *Exodus* 25:30, which teaches that the *Shulchan* shall never be bereft of show bread.

43. According to R' Yose, the word תָּמִיד (*continuously*) teaches only that the Table may not be empty overnight [i.e. until a new day]. R' Yose thus countenances a substantial interruption between the removal of the old loaves and the arranging of the new, for he views the same-day replacement as a continuation of the original placement and not as a new action. By the same token, we can surmise, he would allow a *mohel* to return to and cut off non-impeding shreds, since he views the resumption not as a new act of circumcising but as a completion of the original mitzvah.

According to the Rabbis, however, even the slightest interruption between the removal of the old loaves and the arranging of the new constitutes a violation of the "continuously" requirement, for the interruption renders the arranging a new placement of bread. From this we may conclude that they would regard a withdrawal from *milah* after a majority of the foreskin has been cut as rendering any resumption a new act of circumcising, which would be forbidden on the Sabbath because a valid *milah* has already been performed. It is the Rabbis of this Mishnah, then, who hold that a cessation from an action renders a return to that action a distinct and separate act (*Rashi*).

The question arises: Perhaps the Rabbis would allow a resumption of *milah* to remove non-impeding shreds in order to embellish the mitzvah? See *Shaagas Aryeh* 50, who discusses this point.

44. Literally: cause to be collected.

45. I.e. if the *milah* is not completed, and the impeded shreds remain.

46. According to Rav Kahana, the Baraisa speaks of a Sabbath circumcision, and the circumciser receives *kares* because he desecrates the Sabbath [by wounding the child] without performing a mitzvah [the *milah* is invalid] (*Rashi*).

47. That is, the circumciser can claim that when he began the circumcision and made the initial wound, he did so with the permission of the Torah. Why, then, should he be liable, when someone else can simply complete the procedure? (*Rashi*). [As to whether it is permitted in the first place to use two circumcisers on the Sabbath, see *Shaagas Aryeh* 59, *Hagahos Chochmas Manoach,* and *Chasam Sofer.*]

48. And the Baraisa speaks of a weekday.

49. *Genesis* 17:14.

50. While it is common for a Baraisa to teach an explicit law of the Torah, when it does so it does so in a straightforward manner. Hence, instead of saying, "We must trim etc.," the Baraisa should have stated, "An uncircumcised adult is punished with *kares*" (*Tosafos*).

51. *Milah* may be performed at any time during the day (*Rashi*). This *mohel* came just before the conclusion of the Sabbath day. [The Gemara apparently means that the *mohel* came just prior to בֵּין הַשְּׁמָשׁוֹת (*twilight*), before there was a doubt whether night had fallen. See *Rambam, Hil. Shegagos* 2:9, and *Teshuvos R' Akiva Eiger* 174; cf. second interpretation in *Chidushei HaRan*.]

52. The circumciser is not executed by *beis din,* although Sabbath desecration is punishable by stoning, since [the case is that] he was not warned that he would receive that particular punishment, nor did he accept upon himself any warning. He *is* punished with *kares,* however, because he did not commence the circumcision with permission. At such a late hour, when performing a valid *milah* is an impossibility, the mitzvah of *milah* does not override the Sabbath *melachah* restrictions (*Rashi*). The Baraisa thus means that if this *mohel* did not trim the impeding shreds on time, or quickly enough, he is punished with *kares* (excision).

Even though this *mohel* thought that he could complete the *milah* before the end of Shabbos, he is not considered an unintentional desecrator (שׁוגג), since he was forewarned. Cf. *Rambam, Hil. Shegagos* 2:9 (with *Kesef Mishneh*), who does rule the *mohel* an unintentional desecrator, but not an unavoidable one (אונס). See also *Tos. HaRosh* here.

טו א מיי' פ"ב מהלכות מילה הל' ד ו טוש"ע א"ח סי' שלא סעיף ג וטוש"ע י"ד סי' רסו סעיף כ:

טז ב מיי' פ"ז מהל' ס"ת הלכה ד ופ"ו מהל' לולב הל' ו סמג עשין כח ולאוין שסד טוש"ע א"ח סימן תרנו:

יז ג מיי' פ"א מהלכות דעות הלכה ו:

יח ד מיי' פ"ג מהלכות קידוש החדש הל' ד:

יט ה מיי' פ"ה מהל' תמידין ומוספין הל' ד סמג עשין קצ:

כ ו מיי' פ"ב מהלכות שגגות הלכה ב:

כא ז מיי' פ"ב מהל' מילה הל' ב סמג עשין כח טוש"ע י"ד סי' רסד סעיף ג:

כב ח טוש"ע א"ח סי' ד סעיף כ:

תורה אור השלם

א) עָזִּי וְזִמְרָת יָהּ וַיְהִי לִי לִישׁוּעָה זֶה אֵלִי וְאַנְוֵהוּ אֱלֹהֵי אָבִי וַאֲרֹמְמֶנְהוּ: [שמות טו, ב]

ב) וְנָתַתָּ עַל הַשֻּׁלְחָן לֶחֶם פָּנִים לְפָנַי תָּמִיד: [שמות כה, ל]

ג) וְעָרֵל זָכָר אֲשֶׁר לֹא יִמּוֹל אֶת בְּשַׂר עָרְלָתוֹ וְנִכְרְתָה הַנֶּפֶשׁ הַהִוא מֵעַמֶּיהָ אֶת בְּרִיתִי הֵפַר: [בראשית יז, יד]

רבינו חננאל

והנותר ממנו עד בוקר באש תשרופו ואין שריפת קדשים דוחה י"ט דתנינן בגמרא בפ' כיצד צולין את הפסח. דתנן העצמות והגידים והנותר ישרפו בששה עשר חל ששה עשר להיות בשבת ישרפו בי"ז שאינו דוחה את השבת ולא את יו"ט וקיימא לן דמילה שלא בזמנה אפילו יו"ט אינו דוחה דתנן שני יו"ט של ר"ה נימול לי"ב ללמדך שאין עשה דוחה י"ט כן המילה שלא בזמנה אינה הכי אפי' מילה בזמנה כי מילה בזמנה בפירוש אמרה תורה וביום ואפי' בשבת וכ"ש י"ט אביי פירשו מעולת שבת בשבתו כו' רבא אמר הוא ולא מכשיריו פי' עשיית אוכל נפש דוחה י"ט ולא מכשירי אוכל נפש. כגון חטיבת עצים מן היער לבשל ביו"ט וכדומה (לו) [הוא] לבדו ולא מילה שלא בזמנה הבאה בק"ו והוא ק"ו שאמר רבא ומה אוכל נפש שאע"פ שהיא באזהרת שמחה אינה [דוחה] (מנות שדוחה) י"ט לשחוט ולבשל ולאפות וכיוצא בהן מילה שלא בזמנה שאע"פ שהיא בלא כנה מצוה היא ומעכבתו מלאכול בתרומה. אינו דין שדוחה י"ט בא לבדו למעט המילה שלא בזמנה. רב אשי אמר שבת שבתון עשה הוא וי"ט עשה ול"ת עשה שבתון ולא תעשה כל מלאכה לא תעשה נמצא כתיב ביו"ט עשה ול"ת והמילה עשה בלבד. ולא אתי עשה דמילה ודחי את לא תעשה ועשה דיו"ט: מתני' כלל א"ר עקיבא כל מלאכה שאפשר [לעשות] מע"ש דוחה את השבת וכו'.

אמר רב הלכה כר' עקיבא: מתני' עושין כל צרכי מילה בשבת מוהלין ופורעין כו' אמרינן כי מכדי [קתני] מוהלין ופורעין ומוצצין כו' עושין כל צרכי מילה למה לי לאתויי הא דתנו רבנן המל כל זמן שעוסק במילה חוזר בין על הציצין המעכבין את המילה בין על הציצין שאינן מעכבין את המילה פירש על ציצין המעכבין את המילה חוזר [על שאינן מעכבין] אינו חוזר. ואמרינן מאן תנא פירש ואתא רבה בר בר חנה לאוקומה כר' (שמעון) [ישמעאל] בר' יוחנן בן

גמ' מכדי קתני. במתניתין: כולהו. כל דברים העשוים למילה מוהלין ופורעין ומוצצין כו' למה לי דתנן כללא ברישא עושין כל צרכי מילה: ציצין. שיורי ערלה ובמתני' (ג) מפרש אלו הן ציצין המעכבין ויש שאין מעכבין כגון בשר שאינה חופה רוב העטרה אלא מיעוטה ומה היא עטרה חורה גבוה המקפת בגיד סביב שממנה הגיד משפע ויורד לצד הקרקע ומשפע ויורד לצד הגוף: המל. בשבת: כל זמן שהוא עוסק בה. שלא סילק ידו אם ראה שנשתיירו בה ציצין בין מעכבין את המילה שאינה כשרה עד שיחתכם בין שאין מעכבין חוזר ומחתך דכולה חדא מילתא היא והרי ניתנה שבת לדחות אצלה: פירש. שסילק ידיו: על המעכבין חוזר. שהרי הן כמילה עצמה: ועל שאין מעכבין אינו חוזר. דהוי כהתחלה בפני עצמה ועל אלו לא ניתן לחלל את השבת והיינו דקתני כל צרכי מילה ואפילו ציצין שאין מעכבין חוזר עליהם כל זמן שלא פירש: מאן תנא פירש אינו חוזר. ומשום דפירש חשיב ליה חזרה מילתא לנפשה והואיל ולא עיכוב מצוה נינהו לא הדר: מפשיט הפסח עד החזה (ד). והיינו פירש דתנן במסכת תמיד (פ"ד מ"ג) גבי הפשיטו שהיה מתחיל מן הרגלים והיה מפשיט ויורד עד שמגיע לחזה הגיע לחזה חתך את הראש ונתנו למי שזכה בו ואח"כ הכרעיים ומירק והפשיט כו' שמעי' מיניה משהגיע לחזה סילק ידיו מן ההפשט והתחיל להתעסק בניתוח קצת וגבי עולה דכולה כליל מירק והפשיט ומנתח הידים תחילה אחר הראש וגבי פסח נמי משהפשיט עד החזה דיכול להוציא אימוריו (ה) בלא נימין קורעו ומוציאן מיד והוה ליה פירש מן ההפשט וקאמר רבי ישמעאל שוב אינו גומר ומפשיט משום דכיון דפירש הויא חזרה מילתא דאתחלתא לנפשה ושלא לצורך גבוה דומיא דצילין דלא מעכבין: דלא בעינן זה אלי ואנוהו. דלאחר נטילת האימורין אין הידור מצוה ביפוי בשר אבל יפוי מילה מצוה היא: הוי דומה לו. ולשון אנוהו אני והוא אעשה עצמי כמותו לדבק בדרכיו: בין שנראה. החדש: בעליל. בגילוי לכל ויש לדעת שראוהו בית דין והקרובים להם ואין צריך לרואין חוץ לתחום לחלל שבת ולבא ולהעיד לפני ב"ד מחללין: ר' יוסי אומר כו'. אלמא אע"ג דאיכא מצוה כיון דלאו לצורך גבוה הוא לא מחללינן והכא נמי פירש דהוי אתחלתא דחילול כי הכא בלא צורך גבוה לא מחללינן: לא ניתנה שבת לדחות. אפילו בהתחלתה דהא נראה בעליל אבל הכא כיון שנתנה שבת לדחות להתחיל בה המילה הכי נמי דכי פירש והדר לאו אתחלתא לנפשה היא והוי כמו שלא פירש וגומר כל מצותו: רבנן דפליגי עליה דרבי יוסי. גבי לחם הפנים: ארבעה כהנים נכנסין. להיכל בשבת לסדור לחם הפנים: שני סדרים. שתים מערכות של לחם: שני בזיכין. שתי כפות מלאות לבונה כדכתיב (ויקרא כד) ונתת על המערכת לבונה זכה: מקדימין לפניהם שנים ליטול. מן השלחן שני סדרים הישנים: ושנים ליטול שני בזיכין. והשלחן היה נתון ארכו ממזרח למערב ואלו עומדין מזה לרוחב השלחן בצפון ואלו עומדין לנגדו לדרום ודווקא מכניסין לצפון דכל צפון ענין חשיבות היא כדאמרינן במסכת סוכה (דף נו.) גבי חילוק לחם הפנים למשמרה הנכנסת והיוצאת הנכנסין חולקין בצפון כדי שיראו (ו) נכנסין: רבי יוסי אומר אפילו אלו נוטלין. תחילה ומסלקין כולה מן השלחן ולאחר שעה מניחין אלו: אף זה תמיד. ומה אני מקיים תמיד שלא ילין שלחן בלא לחם ולרבנן אי שקלי ושבקי ליה והדר מסדרי לא מיקרי להו תמיד אלא התחלה אחריתי ונמצא שמתעכב שלחן בלא לחם וגבי פירש נמי כי הדר אתי מילתא אחריתי היא ולרבי יוסי דאמר כי שבקי והדר מתחלי נמי תמיד הוא דחדא מילתא הוא הכא נמי פירש חוזר אע"פ שאין מעכבין דכולה גמר מילתא היא: מהלקטין. בציצין המעכבין: מני. כרת זו של מי הוא: אמר רב כהנא אומן. ענוש כרת ובשבת קאי שחילל שבת ולא עשה מצוה: ונימא אנא עבדי פלגא. כלומר הואיל וכשהתחיל ברשות התחיל וחבורה שעשה ברשות עשה אמאי חייב נימא להו לכו אתם וסיימו המלאכה: אלא אמר רב פפא. בגדול שמל קמיירי ובמזיד וענוש כרת דקאמר משום מילה קאמר דעדיין ערל הוא: וכגון דאתא בין השמשות. דכל היום כשר למילה [ז] ואמרו ליה לא מספקת לגמור ביום כהילכתה ותעשה חבורה בשבת בלא מצוה וענוש כרת ומיהו מיתה ליכא דלא אתרו ביה למיתה ולא קבל עליו התראה וכרת איכא דאתחלה ברשות לא התחיל ולא ניתנה שבת לדחות אלא בשעה זו: מהו דתימא. מתניתין לא אשמעינן דמחלל שבתא עלה דדם מיפקד פקיד מופקד ועומד שם כנתון בכלי ובמציצה אין חבורה ואין כאן איסור תורה ומשום הכי שרי ולאו משום סכנה ואומנא דלא מייץ בחול לאו סכנתא היא ולא ניעבריה: קא משמע לן דדם חיבורי מיחבר. כשיוצא ע"י מצילה ואפילו הכי שרי משום סכנה מדקתני במתני' גבי איספלנית וכמון: שב מינאי תרבא. ז' מנות של חלב: וחדא דקירא. שעוה: קירא וקלבא רישינא. הוא זפת של עץ שמוציאים ממנו שלא ע"י האור והיא לבנה: קרעינהו למנייהו. שהפסיד להם לגלות רפואה זו: שבקי לכו חדא. שלא גיליתי:

גדול בהדיא כתיב ביה. אע"ג דבכמה דוכתין תניא מה שבהדיא בפסוק איצטי (ז) למתני גדול שלא מל ענוש כרת:

לועס בשיניו. אף על גב דאמר מילה מולה שיש בו סכנה הוא מ"מ כמה דאפשר לשנויי משנינן הכא

גמ' מכדי קתני כולהו כל צורכי מילה לאתויי מאי לאתויי הא דת"ר [א]המל כל זמן שהוא עוסק במילה חוזר בין על הציצין המעכבין את המילה בין על הציצין שאין מעכבין את המילה פירש על ציצין המעכבין את המילה חוזר על ציצין שאין מעכבין את המילה אינו חוזר מאן תנא פירש אינו חוזר אמר רבה בר בר חנה אמר רבי יוחנן רבי ישמעאל בנו של ר' יוחנן בן ברוקה היא דתניא [ב]ארבעה עשר שחל להיות בשבת מפשיט (ג) אדם) הפסח עד החזה דברי רבי ישמעאל בנו של ר' יוחנן בן ברוקה וחכ"א מפשיטין את כולו ממאי עד כאן לא קאמר ר' ישמעאל בנו של ר' יוחנן בן ברוקה התם (א) משום דלא בעינן [א] זה אלי ואנוהו אבל הכא דבעינן זה אלי ואנוהו הכי נמי [ג]דתניא זה אלי ואנוהו [ד]התנאה לפניו במצות עשה סוכה נאה ולולב נאה ושופר נאה ציצית נאה ספר תורה נאה וכתוב בו לשמו בדיו נאה בקולמוס נאה בלבלר אומן וכורכו בשיראין נאין אבא שאול אומר ואנוהו הוי דומה לו מה הוא חנון ורחום אף אתה היה חנון ורחום אלא אמר רב אשי הא מני רבי יוסי היא דתנן [ד]בין שנראה בעליל ובין שלא נראה בעליל מחללין עליו את השבת רבי יוסי אומר נראה בעליל אין מחללין עליו את השבת ממאי דילמא עד כאן לא קאמר ר' יוסי התם (ב) דלא ניתנה שבת לידחות אבל הכא דניתנה שבת לידחות הכי נמי אלא אמרי נהרדעי רבנן דפליגי עליה דרבי יוסי היא דתנן [ה]ארבעה כהנים נכנסין שנים בידם שני סדרים ושנים בידם שני בזיכין וארבעה מקדימין לפניהם שנים ליטול שני סדרים ושנים ליטול שני בזיכין המכניסין עומדים בצפון ופניהם לדרום והמוציאין עומדים בדרום ופניהם לצפון אלו מושכים ואלו מניחין טפחו של זה בצד טפחו של זה משום שנאמר [ב]לפני (ה') תמיד ר' יוסי אומר אפילו אלו נוטלין ואלו מניחין אף זה היה תמיד ת"ר מהלקטין את המילה ואם לא הילקט ענוש כרת מני א"ר כהנא אומן מתקיף לה רב פפא אומן לימא להו אנא עבדי פלגא דמצוה אתון עבדיתו פלגא דמצוה אלא אמר רב פפא גדול מתקיף לה רב אשי גדול בהדיא כתיב ביה [ג]וערל זכר אשר לא ימול אלא אמר רב אשי לעולם אומן וכגון דאתא בין השמשות דשבת ואמרו ליה לא מספקת ואמר להו מספקינא ועבד ולא איסתפק ואישתכח דחבורה הוא דעבד וענוש כרת: מוצצין וכו': אמר רב פפא האי אומנא דלא מייץ סכנה הוא ועברינן ליה פשיטא מדקא מחללי עליה שבתא סכנה הוא מהו דתימא האי דם מיפקד פקיד קמ"ל חבורי מיחבר ודומיא דאיספלנית וכמון מה איספלנית וכמון כי לא עביד סכנה הוא אף ה"נ כי לא עביד סכנה הוא: ונותנין עליה איספלנית: אמר אביי אמרה לי אם איספלניתא דכולהון כיבי שב מינאי תרבא וחדא קירא רבא אמר קירא וקלבא רישינא דרשה רבא במחוזא קרעינהו בני מנומי אסיא למנייהו אמר להו שבקי לכו חדא דאמר שמואל [ה]האי מאן דמשי אפיה ולא נגיב נקטרו ליה חספניתא

א) לעיל קנו: מנחות סג: [תוספתא פסחים פ"ד], ב) צ"ל את, ג) [נזיר ב: ע"ש] סוכה יא: מכילתא פרשה בשלח [מס' שירתא פ"ג הל' יג], ד) ר"ה כ: מנחות צט:, ה) מנחות ז. לט:, ו) [קידושין לא: ושם נסמן], ז) פסחים ד. יומא כח: (מגילה כ.), ח) [שייך לעמוד א' במשנה].

הגהות הב"ח

(א) גמ' התם אלא משום דלא: (ב) שם ר' יוסי התם אלא משום דלא ניתנה: (ג) רש"י ד"ה ציצין וכו' ובמתני' נ"ב לקמן דף קלז סוף ע"א: (ד) ד"ה מפשיט את הפסח עד וכו': (ה) בא"ד להוציא אימוריו. נ"ב ע"ל בפרק כל כתבי דף קטו ע"ב בסוף הדף: (ו) ד"ה ושנים ליטול וכו' כדי שירוו שאין נכנסין: (ז) תוס' ד"ה גדול וכו' איצטי ליה למיתני:

רב נסים גאון

חמורה ממנו ומדרך הידוע שהחמור דוחה הקל ולא עוד אלא שפעמים שעולה על דעתך שיש בענין הזה ענין חזרה בדבר הראשון והתשובה הוא מה שהקדמנו שהאזהרה של לאו כך נאמרה מיוחדת וכי הציווי של עשה תנאי הוא בה וכן אמרו רז"ל (ספרי פ' תצא) מחלליה מות יומת וביום השבת שני כבשים בני שנה שניהן בדיבור אחד נאמרו ערות אשת אחיך ויבמה יבוא עליה שניהן בדיבור אחד נאמרו מה שאי אפשר לבשר ודם לומר שנא' אחת דיבר אלהים שתים זו שמענו הבן דבר זה ושמור אותו כי הוא ספק גדול והרי גלינו אותו ומזה העיקר אמרו רז"ל בתלמוד כל מקום שאתה מוצא עשה ולא תעשה אם אתה יכול לקיים את שניהם מוטב ואם לאו יבא עשה וידחה לא תעשה וסבר (רבינא) [רבא] כי לא תעשה שבקודש מוצא מזה העיקר וכי לא ידחה מפני עשה ולא שוה עמו רב אשי בדבר זה כמו שנאמר בשחיטת קדשים בפרק דם חטאת (דף צז) אמאי וניתי עשה ונידחי לא תעשה אמר רבינא אין עשה דוחה את לא תעשה שבמקדש דתניא כו' רב אשי אמר לא יקדש עשה הוא ואין עשה דוחה את לא תעשה ועשה ובמס' נזירות בפ"ב דנזירין (דף נח) אמרו עוד (ומאי דקא מודי ליה) [ומאן דמוקים] לקרא למידחא לא תעשה ועשה לאו גרידא מנא ליה יליף מגדילים דאמר קרא לא תלבש שעטנז הא גדילים תעשה לך מהן וכל מה שתמצא בתלמוד דאתי עשה ודחי לא תעשה מזה העיקר שהקדימו הוא וזה הדין בלאו גרידא בלבד אבל לא תעשה ועשה וכל שכן לא תעשה שיש בו כרת אין עשה דוחה אותם ואנו מבארין לך זה ונאמר

ליקוטי רש"י

ציצין. רצועות של בשר שנשארו מן הערלה [לקמן קלז.]. חתיכות בשר שלא נפרעת המילה כהלכתה [יבמות מז:]. שנשתיירו שלא חתך כל הערלה [שם עא:]. עד החזה. מתחיל מרגליו האחרונים עד החזה שיוכל להוציא אימורים שהקטר חלביו דוחין שבת ותו לא מפשיט מידי עד אורתא דלצורך הדיוט הוא [לעיל קטז:]. בעליל. שנראה הלבנה בעליל לכל העולם [מנחות סד.]. בעליל לי' גילוי הוא בלשון המשנה בין שנראה בעליל בין שלא נראה בעליל כו' [תהלים יב, ז]. נראה בעליל אין מחללין. לפי שאין צורך [ר"ה כא:]. ללכת ולהעיד לב"ד שהרי א"א כיון דבעליל נראה ב"ד נמי ראוהו [מנחות ...] ...יים. של לחם הפנים שתים המערכות של המערכת [שם ז.]. שני בזיכין. לשני קומצי לבונה שנותנין על שתי המערכות שנאמר (ויקרא כה) ונתת על המערכת לבונה זכה [שמות כה, כט]. ליטול שני בזיכ... של השלחן והן מתירין את הלחם באכילה כדכתיב והיה ללחם לאזכרה [סוכה נו:]. המכניסין עומדים בצפון. דהכי שפיר [מלתא] דאותן [ה]מסדרין (העבודה) יהו בצפון דקדושת צפון חמירא. ופניהם ... מזרח ומערב מונחין ורוחבן לצפון ודרום. ועד שלא יגביהו הן מן השלחן אלו מניחין. אלו מושכים. לעצמן ואלו מניחין אחר שסילקו אף זה היה תמיד כדמפרש טעמא בגמ' דאין תמ... לחם [מנחות צט:]. אפילו סילק את הישנה שחרית וסידר את החדשה ערבית אף זו היתה תמיד ומהו תמיד שלא ילין שולחן בלא לחם אבל לרבנן טפחו של זה מסדר בצד טפחו של מסלק [מגילה כא.]. מיפ... כנוס ועומד ואינו נבלע להיות יציאתו על ידי חבורה [כתובות ה:]. אמרה לי אם. אומנתו היתה [כתובות לט: ע"ש בב"ח]. וקלבא. רשינ"א שבחביות של יין [ב"ק פה. וע"ע ביצה לג: ד"ה במוסתקי].

the *milah* **and** – in fact – **he did not have sufficient** time. וְאִישְׁתַּכַּח דְּחַבּוּרָה הוּא דַּעֲבַד – **And so it resulted that it was an** unsanctioned **wound that he made** on the child, וְעָנוּשׁ כָּרֵת – **and he is punished** with **excision.**

In specifying the stages of *milah* that may be performed on Shabbos, the Mishnah stated:

מוֹצִצִין וכו׳ – WE MAY DRAW the blood **etc.**

The Gemara discusses the nature of this procedure, and the legal ramifications involved:

אָמַר רַב פָּפָּא – **Rav Pappa said:** הַאי אוּמָּנָא דְּלָא מָיֵיץ סַכָּנָה הוּא – **This expert** surgeon **who does not draw** blood from the wound **is** responsible for creating **a danger** to the person being circumcised, וְעַבְרִינַן לֵיהּ – **and so we dismiss him.**

The Gemara exclaims:

פְּשִׁיטָא – This is **obvious!** מִדְּקָא מְחַלְּלֵי עֲלֵיהּ שַׁבְּתָא – **Since we desecrate the Sabbath because of [the blood],** as the Mishnah teaches, סַכָּנָה הוּא – then certainly **it is a danger,** and we dismiss anyone who fails to draw it from the wound. What, then, is Rav Pappa teaching us?

The Gemara explains the need for Rav Pappa's dictum:

מַהוּ דְּתֵימָא – Without Rav Pappa's teaching, **what is it that you would have said?** הַאי דָּם מִיפְקַד פָּקִיד – That **this blood is** now **stored up** as if in a vessel.[53] קָא מַשְׁמַע לָן חַבּוּרֵי מִיחַבַּר – **[Rav Pappa]** therefore **informs us** that **[this blood]** cannot be drawn without **causing a wound,**[54] and yet the Mishnah sanctions that procedure because the blood *is* a danger to the circumcised individual's health. It is for that reason that we dismiss a circumciser who omits the drawing procedure. וְדוּמְיָא דְּאִיסְפְּלָנִית וְכַמּוֹן – **And** the reason for the Mishnah's law of **[drawing blood] is the same as that** for the application of **a bandage and cumin** to the wound: מָה אִיסְפְּלָנִית וְכַמּוֹן – **Just as** with regard to **a bandage and cumin** כִּי לֹא עָבִיד סַכָּנָה הוּא – **if he does not do** as prescribed **it is a danger,** and so these procedures are permitted, אַף הָכָא נַמִּי כִּי לֹא עָבִיד סַכָּנָה הוּא – **here as well** with regard to drawing blood, **if he does not do** as prescribed **it is a danger,** and therefore drawing is permitted.

The Mishnah next stated:

וְנוֹתְנִין עָלֶיהָ אִיסְפְּלָנִית – AND WE MAY PLACE A BANDAGE and cumin UPON [THE WOUND].

The Gemara debates the superiority of various types of bandages and salves:[55]

אָמַר אַבַּיֵי אָמְרָה לִי אֵם – **Abaye said: Mother**[56] **told me** that אִיסְפְּלָנִיתָא דְּכוּלְּהוֹן כִּיבֵי – **a salve** compress **for all pains** is made of שַׁב מִינָּאֵי תַּרְבָּא וַחֲדָא קִירָא – **seven parts**[57] **of fat and one of wax.** רָבָא אָמַר קִירָא וְקַלְבָּא רִישִׁינָא[58] – **Rava said:** The best compress is made of **wax and resin.**

The Gemara relates:

דְּרָשָׁהּ רָבָא בְּמְחוֹזָא – **Rava** once **taught [this medical secret]** publicly **in** the town of **Mechoza,** קָרְעִינְהוּ בְּנֵי מַנְיוּמֵי אַסְיָא לְמָנַיְיהוּ – and **the family of Manyumi the physician tore their garments** in despair and vexation.[59] אָמַר לְהוּ – However, **[Rava] said to them:** שַׁבְקִי לְכוּ חֲדָא – **I have left for you one** secret cure, which I have not revealed, דְּאָמַר שְׁמוּאֵל – **for Shmuel has said:** הַאי מַאן דְּמָשֵׁי אַפֵּיהּ וְלֹא נָגֵיב טוּבָא – Regarding **this one who washes his face and does not dry** it **well,** נִקְטְרוּ לֵיהּ

NOTES

53. I.e. the blood is not "connected" to the body in such a way that drawing it out would involve making a wound, which would be a violation of Sabbath law. Rather, it is "stored" there, and is released through the drawing act (מְצִיצָה) as if a door is being opened (see *Rashi* to *Kesubos* 5b ד״ה מיפקד פקיד). See also *Tos. Rid* here. We would therefore conclude that the Mishnah is not sanctioning a desecration of the Sabbath with regard to drawing blood; the blood, then, perhaps poses no danger – and a circumciser who fails to draw it need not be dismissed (*Rashi*).

54. I.e. the blood is absorbed in the body, so that drawing it out constitutes a Sabbath desecration. See *Tosafos* to *Kesubos* 5b ד״ה דם; see also *Rambam, Hil. Milah* 2:2.

55. It would appear that when the Mishnah mentions אִיסְפְּלָנִית, it refers to a bandage that contains a medicinal ointment (salve).

56. Abaye was an orphan. He often quoted the nurse who raised him, referring to her as "mother" (see *Kiddushin* 31b). For several examples see below, 134a.

57. *Rashi;* cf. *Hagahos Yavetz.*

58. It would appear from *Rashi* that רִישִׁינָא is a foreign word that should be deleted from the text of the Gemara. The translation of the word is "resin."

59. For Rava's revelation would cause them financial loss (*Rashi, Chidushei HaRan*).

חַסְפַּנִיתָא – **boils will break out on [his face].**[1] מַאי תַּקַּנְתֵּיהּ – And **what is his remedy?** לִימְשֵׁי טוּבָא בְּמַיָּא דְּסִילְקָא – **Let him wash well in water** in which **beets** have been cooked.

The Mishnah then stated:

לֹא שָׁחַק מֵעֶרֶב שַׁבָּת – If ONE DID NOT CRUSH the cumin ON THE SABBATH EVE, he may chew [it] with his teeth and apply [it]. If one did not vigorously mix wine and oil on the Sabbath eve, each of these [ingredients] should be placed [in the bowl] by itself.

The Gemara cites a companion Baraisa:

תָּנוּ רַבָּנָן – **The Rabbis taught:** דְּבָרִים שֶׁאֵין עוֹשִׂין לַמִּילָה בְּשַׁבָּת – THINGS THAT WE MAY NOT DO FOR A CIRCUMCISION ON THE SABBATH עוֹשִׂין לָהּ בְּיוֹם טוֹב – WE MAY DO FOR IT ON A FESTIVAL DAY. שׁוֹחֲקִין לָהּ כַּמּוֹן – Namely, WE MAY CRUSH CUMIN FOR IT, וְטוֹרְפִין לָהּ יַיִן וְשֶׁמֶן – AND WE MAY VIGOROUSLY MIX WINE AND OIL FOR IT.

The Gemara inquires:

אָמַר לֵיהּ אַבַּיֵּי לְרַב יוֹסֵף – **Abaye said to Rav Yosef:** מַאי שְׁנָא כַּמּוֹן בְּיוֹם טוֹב – For **what** reason **is** the law of **cumin different on a festival day?** דַּחֲזֵי לִקְדֵרָה – **Because [cumin] is fit for a pot.**[2] יַיִן וְשֶׁמֶן חֲזֵי נַמִּי בְּשַׁבָּת לְחוֹלֶה – By the same token, **wine and oil are fit also on the Sabbath for a sick person,**[3] דְּתַנְיָא – **for it was taught in a Baraisa:** אֵין טוֹרְפִין יַיִן וְשֶׁמֶן לְחוֹלֶה בְּשַׁבָּת – WE MAY NOT VIGOROUSLY MIX WINE AND OIL FOR A SICK PERSON ON THE SABBATH. אָמַר רַבִּי שִׁמְעוֹן בֶּן אֶלְעָזָר מִשּׁוּם רַבִּי מֵאִיר – However, R' SHIMON BEN ELAZAR SAID IN THE NAME OF R' MEIR: אַף טוֹרְפִין יַיִן וְשֶׁמֶן – WE MAY ALSO VIGOROUSLY MIX WINE AND OIL for a sick person.[4] אָמַר רַבִּי שִׁמְעוֹן בֶּן אֶלְעָזָר – R' SHIMON BEN ELAZAR SAID further: פַּעַם אַחַת חָשׁ רַבִּי מֵאִיר בְּמֵעָיו – ONCE R' MEIR WAS EXPERIENCING INTESTINAL PAIN וּבִקַּשְׁנוּ לִטְרוֹף לוֹ יַיִן וְשֶׁמֶן – AND WE WANTED TO MIX VIGOROUSLY OIL AND WINE as a medication FOR HIM, וְלֹא הִנִּחָנוּ – AND HE DID NOT ALLOW US. אָמַרְנוּ לוֹ דְּבָרֶיךָ יִבָּטְלוּ בְּחַיֶּיךָ – WE SAID TO HIM: "SHALL YOUR WORDS BE NULLIFIED IN YOUR LIFETIME?!"[5] אָמַר לָנוּ – And HE SAID TO US in reply: אַף עַל פִּי שֶׁאֲנִי אוֹמֵר כָּךְ וַחֲבֵירַי אוֹמְרִים כָּךְ – "EVEN THOUGH I SAY THUS[6] AND MY COLLEAGUES SAY THUS,[7] and you would expect that I would adhere to my own opinion, מִיָּמַי לֹא מְלָאַנִי לִבִּי לַעֲבוֹר עַל דִּבְרֵי חֲבֵירַי – THROUGHOUT all MY DAYS I HAVE NEVER PRESUMED TO TRANSGRESS THE WORDS OF MY COLLEAGUES."

Abaye draws the following conclusion from the Baraisa, and thereby completes his question to Rav Yosef:

הוּא נִיהוּ דְּמַחְמִיר אַנַּפְשֵׁיהּ – Now, **it is [R' Meir] who was strict on himself** in this matter of mixing oil and wine. אֲבָל לְכוּלֵּי עָלְמָא שָׁרֵי – **However, for everyone else he permits** it. Why does it seem otherwise from our Mishnah?[8]

Rav Yosef responds:

הָתָם לָא בָּעֵי לִיכָּא – **There** in the Baraisa, which speaks of preparing medication for sick people in general, **[the mixture]** of oil and wine **does not require a** vigorous **beating** and thorough blending.[9] הָכָא בָּעֵי לִיכָּא – But **here** in our Mishnah, which concerns specifically a circumcised individual, **[the mixture] does require a** vigorous **beating** and thorough blending for it to be optimally effective, and this R' Meir also forbids.

The Gemara asks:

הָכָא נַמִּי נִיעַבִיד וְלֹא לֵילַךְ – But **here also** in the case of *milah*, **let us prepare** a mixture of oil and wine **and not** vigorously **beat** it!?[10]

The Gemara answers:

הַיְינוּ דְּקָתָנֵי – **This** moderate level of blending **is** precisely **what** our Mishnah prescribed when **it stated** נוֹתֵן זֶה בִּפְנֵי עַצְמוֹ וְזֶה בִּפְנֵי עַצְמוֹ – that **one may place "each of these"** ingredients into the bowl **"by itself."**[11]

The Gemara digresses to present other laws of Yom Tov discussed by Abaye and Rav Yosef:[12]

תָּנוּ רַבָּנָן – **The Rabbis taught** in a Baraisa: אֵין מְסַנְּנִין אֶת הַחַרְדָּל בִּמְסַנֶּנֶת שֶׁלּוֹ – WE MAY NOT STRAIN MUSTARD SEED THROUGH ITS OWN STRAINER on Yom Tov,[13] וְאֵין מְמַתְּקִין אוֹתוֹ בְּגַחֶלֶת – NOR MAY WE SWEETEN IT WITH A BURNING COAL.[14]

NOTES

1. *Rashi.* Cf. *Mesoras HaShas,* who cites *Aruch's* interpretation of חַסְפַּנִיתָא as *scabs,* which more precisely fits the literal translation of נִקְטְרוּ (*shall be knotted* [or *tied*]).

2. I.e. it is an ingredient for cooking, which is permitted on Yom Tov. Hence, preparing cumin for use in cooking by crushing it in the normal manner is permitted on Yom Tov (see *Orach Chaim* 504). Similarly, one may vigorously mix wine and oil for cooking on Yom Tov.

3. I.e. one who is not dangerously ill (*Rashi*). [For a dangerously ill person (חוֹלֶה שֶׁיֵּשׁ בּוֹ סַכָּנָה), any *melachah* may be performed.] Abaye is asking that just as we find that even a Biblical *melachah* (viz. crushing cumin) is permitted on Yom Tov because it is "fit for a pot" (see *Rashash*), similarly, vigorously mixing wine and oil *in the normal manner* should be permitted, since it is permitted for a sick person (according to one Tanna) when mixing is impossible to perform on the Sabbath eve. Thus, the Gemara will proceed to show that the Tanna of our Mishnah (R' Meir; see *Rashi* ד״ה אבל) holds that vigorously mixing wine and oil for a sick person is permitted on the Sabbath. Hence, is it not logical that the Sages would permit it in the case of *milah* as well?

See *Gra* to *Yoreh Deah* 266:10, who writes that the unusual procedures recommended by our Mishnah must be performed *before* the circumcision (i.e. before the child becomes a sick person). According to this opinion, the Gemara's need to cite Yom Tov as a comparison is more understandable. See *Keren Orah* to 133a above. See also *Hagahos R' Elazar Moshe Horowitz;* cf. *Sfas Emes.*

4. R' Meir holds that the Rabbinic prohibition against mixing wine and oil (because it resembles a preparation for cooking) does not apply to a sick person. As for the general prohibition against healing on the Sabbath, Tosefta (13:8,9) implies that it would not apply in this case, since a healthy person would anoint himself with the mixture of oil and wine. However, *Maggid Mishneh* (*Hil. Shabbos* 2:10) implies that the Baraisa speaks of someone with a systemic illness (חוֹלֶה כָּל גּוּפוֹ), for whom healing is permitted.

5. As a sick person, R' Meir qualified for his own leniency. They thus asked why he did not avail himself of it.

6. That vigorous mixing is permitted.

7. The Tanna Kamma, articulating the position of the Rabbis, says that it is forbidden.

8. The general rule is that an anonymous Mishnah reflects the opinion of R' Meir (סְתָם מִשְׁנָה ר׳ מֵאִיר). Our Mishnah (133a) falls into this category. Why, then, does it teach that wine and oil may be placed in the bowl separately, but not vigorously mixed? (*Rashi;* see note 3 above).

9. Hence, R' Meir there condones a moderate blending (see *Rashi*). [Such beating does not necessarily appear as if it's being done for cooking.]

10. That is, let the Mishnah at least sanction the moderate level of blending that the Baraisa sanctioned for sick people in general (see *Rashi*).

11. According to *Meiri,* it would seem, the Gemara means that a therapeutic effect is had with the minimal mixing that results from adding both ingredients to the same bowl. Cf. *R' Akiva Eiger* (§159) to Mishnayos, who understands that the Gemara refers here too to a non-vigorous mixing. See above, 133a note 56. See also *Chidushei HaRan* here, who cites both explanations of our Gemara.

12. I.e. other laws concerning which Abaye asked of Rav Yosef, "Why is this law different from . . ." (*Ritva MHK* ed.).

13. As the Gemara will explain below, straining separates the seed from the outer husks (*Rashi*).

14. [In order to render mustard more palatable] a burning coal was customarily buried inside a mound of mustard seeds. The smothered coal became extinguished, and extinguishing is forbidden on Yom Tov (see *Rashi, Ritva MHK* ed.).

חספניתא. פניו מתבקעות ואני אומר שהוא מין שחין שקורין אינייר"א והוא (בגרב) ובחרס שכתוב בתורה (דברים כח) וחספניתא תרגום של חרס: **במיא דסילקא.** מרק תרדין: **חזי לחולה.** שאין בו סכנה: **יבטלו.** דהאי נמי חולה הוא: **אבל לכולי עלמא שרי.** ר"מ וסתם מתני' ר"מ ואמאי תנן נותן זה בעצמו וזה בעצמו: **התם.** גבי שאר חולים: **לא בעו ליכא.** לטרפו ולערבו יפה יפה: **ולא לילך.** לא יערבנו כל כך: ומתרך היינו דקתני נותן זה בעצמו וזה בעצמו. שמערב ואינו לוכך: **אין מסננין את החרדל.** בי"ט: **במסננת שלו.** טעמא מפרש לקמיה דמיחזי כבורר שמשליך הסובין שלו: **ואין ממתקין אותו בגחלת.** כדרך שרגילין לכבות לתוכו את הגחלת או אבן ניסוקת: **נותנין ביצה במסננת של חרדל.** ומסננה בתוכו לייפות מראיתו: **לא מיחזי כבורר.** שכולה יוצאה דרך המסננת ואין משתייר שם פסולת: **בגחלת של עץ.** אסור דשייך בה כיבוי לפי שעושה פחם גחלת של מתכת לא שייך בה כיבוי דאינו נעשה פחם: **ומ"ש מבישרא אגומרי.** שצולין בי"ט ואע"ג דמכבה: **לא אפשר.** לצלות מאתמול דביומא שביחא טפי אבל חרדל אפשר מאתמול: **לגבן.** גבינה: **מאי שנא מלישה.** שלשין פת ביום טוב והאי נמי ללישה דמיא: **לא אפשר.** דפת חמה מעליא טפי הכא אפשר מאתמול: **אימא אף גבינתא בת יומא מעליא.** וכ"ש דאתמול: **לפניה לסטריה לעילאי.** לאימרא שבשפת פיה יהפוך ויקפל למעלה שלא תהא סמוכה לבשרו מפני שראש מקום חתך הבגד שם הוא ויוצאין ממנו גרדין שקורין פיינד"ץ ודלמא מדביקא גרדא מיניה במכה וכשבא להפשיט החלוק מעל המילה ישמוט ויקרע את ראש הגיד ומשוי ליה כרות שפכה: **אימיה דאביי.** אומנתו: **עבדא.** לתינוקות הבאים לידה לתקן מילתן: **כיסתתא לפלגא.** דמילה כיס היתה עושה של בגד לפנים בתוך החלוק ותופרתו מתוכו בתוך החלוק ומגיע למטה עד חצי החלוק כדי לחוץ בין האימרא ובין המילה: **לייתי בליתא.** מעט שחק של בגד שיהא בו אימרא לפי שהאימרא מהדקה יפה בבשר שלא ישמט החלוק מן הגיד: **וליפכיה לשפתיה לתתאי.** לתחתית ראש הגיד יתן השפה וראש השני החלק יהא למעלה: **ולעפפיה לעילאי.** אותו ראש העליון החלוק יקפל ויקפול כלפי חוץ מפני הגרדין שלא ידבקו במכה: **דלא ידיע ביה מפקתיה.** שאין ניכר בו נקב בית הרעי ששם הוצאת זבלו: **לישייפיה מישחא.** שהשמן מגהיל הבשר: **ולוקמיה להדי יומא.** נגד השמש: **והיכא דזיג.** שצלול כזכוכית בידוע שהחלל כנגדו: **בשערתא.** בראש השעורה שהוא חדוד: **דזריף.** מנפחו אינפליי"ר בלע"ז: **דלא מייץ.** שלא יכול לינק: **מיקר הוא דקר פומיה.** נצטננו שפתיו ואין בו כח למוץ בהן: **לייתו כסא דגומרי.** תשטח גחלים על דף או על כלי: **ולוקמה להדי פומיה.** ויעמיד אצל פיו: **דחיים פומיה.** שיתחמם פיו: **ומייץ.** וינק: **דלא מינשתא.** שאין נשימה ניכרת בו שאין דופק כנגד לבו כדרך כל אדם: **לינפפיה בנפוותא.** ינפו עליו בנפה שקורין ונ"ן: **דלא מעוי.** אין רוחו נכנס ויוצא יפה אליינ"א בלע"ז: **סילתא דאימיה.** שליא שנולדה עמו: **ולישרקיה עליה.** יחליקנה על בשרו כמו אישתרוקי אישתריקו (ע"ג ד' מ:) אשאולדי"ר: **דקטין.** שהוא דק: **מקוטנא לאולמא.** השליא ראשה אחד קצר וראשה אחד רחב יחליקוה עליו מראש הקצר יתחילו וימשוכו לצד הרחב כלומר כן ירחיב זה ויתעבה: **ואי אלים.** לישרקיה עליה מאולמא לקוטנא: **דסומק.** כל בשרו אדום: **לא איבלע ביה דמיה.** בבשרו דעכשיו כל דמו מלוי בין עור לבשר וכשמוהלין אותו יוצא כל דמו: **ליתרחו ליה.** ימתינו מלמולו: **לא נפל ביה דמא.** לא בא בו דם ומתוך כך חלש הוא ואין בו כח וממהר לחלוש ולמות: **לכרכי הים.** ה"ג ראיתיו שהיה ירוק הצצתי בו ולא היה בו דם ברית תרתי לגריעותא חדא דאי מהיל ליה לא נפק מיניה דמא והטפת דם ברית מצוה דכתיב (זכריה ט) גם את בדם בריתך ועוד דמסוכן הוא ומשום חולשא שלא נולד בו עדיין דם:

א) **חספניתא** מאי תקנתיה לימשי טובא במיא דסילקא: **לא שחק מערב שבת:** תנו רבנן דברים שאין עושין למילה בשבת עושין לה ביו"ט א שוחקין לה כמון וטורפין לה יין ושמן א"ל אביי לרב יוסף מאי שנא כמון בי"ט דחזי לקדרה יין ושמן חזי נמי בשבת לחולה דתניא ג) אין טורפין יין ושמן לחולה בשבת אמר ר"ש בן אלעזר משום ר"מ אף טורפין יין ושמן א"ר שמעון בן אלעזר פעם אחת חש רבי מאיר במעיו ובקשנו לטרוף לו יין ושמן ולא הנחנו אמרנו לו דבריך יבטלו בחייך אמר לנו אע"פ שאני אומר כך וחבירי אומרים כך ד) מימי לא מלאני לבי לעבור על דברי חבירי הוא ניהו דמחמיר אנפשיה אבל לכולי עלמא שרי התם לא בעי ליכא הכא בעי ליכא הכא נמי ניעביד ולא לילך היינו דקתני נותן זה בפני עצמו וזה בפני עצמו: ת"ר ב אין מסננין את החרדל במסננת שלו ואין ממתקין אותו בגחלת א"ל אביי לרב יוסף מאי שנא מהא ה) דתנן נותנים ביצה במסננת של חרדל א"ל התם לא מיחזי כבורר הכא מיחזי כבורר ואין ממתקין אותו בגחלת והתניא ממתקין אותו בגחלת לא קשיא ג כאן בגחלת של מתכת כאן בגחלת של עץ א"ל אביי לרב יוסף מ"ש ו) מבישרא אגומרי א"ל התם לא אפשר הכא אפשר א"ל אביי לרב יוסף מהו לגבן א"ל ד אסור מ"ש מלישה א"ל התם לא אפשר הכא אפשר והא אמרי נהרדעי גבינה בת יומא מעליא הכי קאמרי דאפילו גבינה בת יומא מעליא: **אין עושין לה חלוק כו':** אמר אביי ז) אמרה לי אם ה האי חלוק דינוקא לפניה לסיטרא ו לעילאי דילמא מידביק (א) גרדא מיניה ואתי לידי כרות שפכה אימיה דאביי עבדא כיסתתא לפלגא אמר אביי האי ינוקא דלית ליה חלוק לייתי בליתא דאית ליה שיפתא וליכרכיה לשיפתא לתתאי ועייף ליה לעילאי ואמר אביי אמרה לי אם האי ינוקא דלא ידיע מפקתיה לשייפיה מישחא ולוקמיה להדי יומא והיכא דזיג ליקרעיה בשערתא שתי וערב אבל בכלי מתכות לא משום דזריף ואמר אביי אמרה לי אם האי ינוקא דלא מייץ מיקר (ב) דקר פומיה מאי תקנתיה ליתו כסא גומרי ולינקטיה ליה להדי פומיה דחיים פומיה ומייץ ואמר אביי אמרה לי אם האי ינוקא דלא ח) מנשתיה לינפפיה בנפוותא ומנשתיה ואמר אביי אמרה לי אם האי ינוקא דלא ט) מעוי ליתו סליתא דאימיה ולישרקיה עילויה ומעוי ואמר אביי אמרה לי אם האי ינוקא דקטין לייתו לסילתא דאימיה ולישרקיה עילויה מקוטנא לאולמא ואי אלים מאולמא לקוטנא ואמר אביי אמרה לי אם ז האי ינוקא דסומק דאכתי לא איבלע ביה דמא י) ליתרחו ליה עד דאיבלע ביה דמא ולימהלוה דירוק ואכתי לא נפל ביה דמיה ליתרחו עד דנפל ביה דמיה ולימהלוה כ) דתניא א"ר נתן פעם אחת הלכתי לכרכי הים ובאת אשה אחת לפני שמלה בנה ראשון ומת שני ומת שלישי הביאתו לפני ראיתיו שהוא אדום אמרתי לה המתיני לו עד שיבלע בו דמו המתינה לו עד שנבלע בו דמו ומלה אותו וחיה והיו קורין אותו נתן הבבלי על שמי שוב פעם אחת הלכתי למדינת קפוטקיא ובאת אשה אחת לפני שמלה בנה ראשון ומת שני ומת שלישי הביאתו לפני ראיתיו שהוא ירוק הצצתי בו ולא ראיתי בו דם ברית אמרתי לה המתיני לו עד שיפול בו דמו והמתינה לו ומלה אותו וחיה והיו קורין שמו נתן הבבלי על שמי:

מתני'

הכא מיחזי כבורר. מיהו בורר לא הוי שגם הפסולת ראוי לאכילה ולא דמי למשמרת דריש תולין (לקמן ד' קלז:) דאיכא למ"ד חייב משום בורר: מי

מסורת הש"ס

א) [פי' בערוך ערך קרס הצומח בעור הפנים ומתקלף. ערוך], ב) [תוספ' פי"ג], ג) לקמן קלט:, ד) [ביצה כג.], ה) [קידושין לא: וכו'], ו) [גי' הערוך בערך עבר אבראי], ז) [פי' שאין יכול להסתפק ערוך ע' עסס], ח) [פי' שאין מוציא הבל ממוטמו ערוך], ט) [גי' הערוך ליתרחו ועי' במוסף הערוך ערך תרח וכרש"י], י) [יבמות סד: ד"ה מלתי גבי, גיטין סז: חולין מז: תוספ' פט"ז ע"ש], כ) [בתרגום ירושלמי לישא ועיין כמ"ש פירש רש"י וחספניתא הסקין שבפני אדם].

הגהות הב"ח

(א) גמ' דילמא מידביק גרדא מיניה: (ב) שם מיקר הוא דקר:

גליון הש"ס

גמ' מימי לא מלאני לבי. לעיל דף קיא ע"ב:

ליקוטי רש"י

מיא דסילקא. מים שבשלו בהן תרדין [יומא עו.]. **נותנין ביצה במסננת.** שהחרדל נתון בה להסתנן וקולטת את הפסולת ואף הביצה החלמון שלה נוטף ומתמתק עמו והוה ליה לחרדל למראה והחלבון שהוא קשור נשאר למעלה ורבינו הלוי פירש מינונה ולא לתוך חרדל שבחוץ היא ולא לתוך חרדל לשרי משום שינוי וזולך לתוך הקערה שהוא כלי שני ומתלבן המבשל [לקמן קלט: ועי' כאן בהגהות ר' שמחה מדעסוי וע"ש במהרש"א שם]. **כרות שפכה.** מי שנכרת לו מן הגיד מן העטרה ולמעלה לצד הגוף והוא אינו מוליד [ע"ז כו:]. שנכרת הגיד ואינו יורה קילוח כחץ זרע אלא שותת ושותת ואינו מוליד (יבמות עה:). [דברים כג, ב]. **דזיג.** לשון זכוכית [פסחים עד:]. **המתיני לו.** לאין לך דבר העומד בפני פיקוח נפש חוץ מעבודת כוכבים וגילוי עריות ושפיכות דמים. **שיבלע בו דמו.** שיהא דמו נבלע בבשרו שהיה דמו הולך בין עור לבשר והוי כמי שאין לו דם והדם הוא הנפש ומתוך שאין בו דם הוא מת במכה קלה [חולין מז:].

עין משפט נר מצוה

כג א מיי' פ"ב מהלכות מילה הל' יד סמג עשין כח טוש"ע י"ד סי' רסו סעיף ו:
כד ב ג מיי' פכ"ג מהל' שבת הלכה יב סמג לאוין סה טוש"ע או"ח סי' תקי סעיף ג [וברב אלפס בילה פ"ב קעג: ע"ש ובא"ח סם סי' כג]:
כה ד שם סעיף ה:
כו ה טוש"ע י"ד סי' רסד סעיף ג בהג"ה:
כז ו ז מיי' פ"א מהל' מילה הלכה יח טוש"ע י"ד סי' רסג סעיף א:

רבינו חננאל

[illegible]

רב נסים גאון

[illegible]

Abaye inquires:

אָמַר לֵיהּ אַבַּיֵי לְרַב יוֹסֵף – **Abaye said to Rav Yosef:** מַאי שְׁנָא מֵהָא דִּתְנַן – For **what** reason is the Baraisa's first ruling **different from this** other law **that we learned in a Mishnah:**[15] נוֹתְנִים בֵּיצָה בִּמְסַנֶּנֶת שֶׁל חַרְדָּל – WE MAY PUT A raw EGG INTO A MUSTARD STRAINER and strain it in order to improve the mustard's appearance. Since this act is permitted even on Shabbos, why is straining mustard through its own strainer forbidden on Yom Tov, when preparing and cooking food is permitted?

Rav Yosef responds:

אָמַר לֵיהּ – **[Rav Yosef] said to [Abaye]:** הָתָם לָא מֶיחֱזֵי כְּבוֹרֵר – **There** in the case of the egg **it does not appear as though he is sorting;**[16] הָכָא מֶיחֱזֵי כְּבוֹרֵר – **here** in the case of mustard seed **it appears as though he is sorting.**[17]

The Gemara now quotes the second ruling of the Baraisa:

וְאֵין מְמַתְּקִין אוֹתוֹ בְּגַחֶלֶת – NOR MAY WE SWEETEN IT WITH A BURNING COAL.

The Gemara cites a conflicting ruling:

וְהָתַנְיָא – **But it was taught in** another **Baraisa:** מְמַתְּקִין אוֹתוֹ בְּגַחֶלֶת – WE MAY SWEETEN [MUSTARD SEED] WITH A BURNING COAL.

The contradiction is resolved:

לָא קַשְׁיָא – In truth, there is **no difficulty.** כָּאן בְּגַחֶלֶת שֶׁל מַתֶּכֶת – **Here** in the lenient ruling we speak **of a glowing metal coal,** כָּאן בְּגַחֶלֶת שֶׁל עֵץ – while **there** in the stringent ruling we speak **of a glowing wooden coal.**[18]

Abaye inquires:

אָמַר לֵיהּ אַבַּיֵי לְרַב יוֹסֵף – And apropos of this discussion **Abaye said to Rav Yosef:** מַאי שְׁנָא מִבִּישְׂרָא אַגּוּמְרֵי – For **what** reason is this stringent ruling **different from** the case of roasting **meat on burning coals,** which is permitted on Yom Tov even though the dripping juices of the meat will inevitably extinguish the wooden coals?[19]

Rav Yosef responds:

אָמַר לֵיהּ – **[Rav Yosef] said to [Abaye]:** הָתָם לֹא אֶפְשָׁר – **There it is impossible** to roast the meat on Yom Tov eve and have it be as tasty as when it is roasted on Yom Tov itself. Hence, roasting it on Yom Tov is permitted. הָכָא אֶפְשָׁר – **Here,** however, **it is possible** to sweeten the mustard on Yom Tov eve and not suffer any deterioration in taste on Yom Tov itself. Hence, sweetening, which involves extinguishing, is not permitted on Yom Tov.[20]

Abaye himself introduces a third line of halachic inquiry:

אָמַר לֵיהּ אַבַּיֵי לְרַב יוֹסֵף – **Abaye said to Rav Yosef:** מַהוּ לְגַבֵּן – **What is [the law]** regarding whether one is permitted **to make cheese** on Yom Tov?[21] אָמַר לֵיהּ אָסוּר – **[Rav Yosef] answered him: It is forbidden.** מַאי שְׁנָא מִלִּישָׁה – Whereupon Abaye inquired: For **what** reason is cheese making **different from kneading** dough (for baking bread), which is permitted on Yom Tov? Since cheese making resembles kneading, it too should be permitted.[22] – ? –

Rav Yosef's answer:

אָמַר לֵיהּ – **[Rav Yosef] said to [Abaye]** in reply: הָתָם לֹא אֶפְשָׁר – **There it is impossible** to knead dough for immediate baking on Yom Tov eve[23] and have warm bread on Yom Tov. Hence, because warm fresh bread is tastier than yesterday's goods, kneading is permitted on Yom Tov. הָכָא אֶפְשָׁר – **Here,** however, **it is possible** to make cheese on Yom Tov eve and not suffer any deterioration in its taste on Yom Tov itself.[24] Hence, cheese making is not permitted on Yom Tov.

The Gemara asks:

וְהָא אָמְרֵי נְהַרְדָּעֵי גְּבִינָה בַּת יוֹמָא מְעַלְּיָא – **But** the sages **of Nehardea have said** that **freshly made**[25] **cheese is excellent!** Since freshly made cheese is of exceptional quality, why is cheese making not permitted on Yom Tov?

The Gemara answers:

הָכִי קָאָמְרֵי – **[The sages of Nehardea]** actually **said thus:** דַּאֲפִילּוּ גְּבִינָה בַּת יוֹמָא מְעַלְּיָא – It is true **that** *even* **freshly made cheese is excellent**! But cheese made yesterday is better still! Hence, because cheese made on Yom Tov eve is actually superior, cheese making is prohibited on Yom Tov itself.[26]

The Mishnah next stated:

אֵין עוֹשִׂין לָהּ חָלוּק כו׳ – WE MAY NOT in the first place FASHION A SHIRTLIKE BANDAGE FOR [THE MEMBER] **etc.** [but one may wrap a piece of cloth around it].[27]

NOTES

15. Below, 139b; see there note 26.

16. [Sorting is one of the thirty-nine primary labors. It involves separating inedible matter from food by hand or with a sieve (or strainer).] Passing the egg through a strainer does not resemble straining (see 140a note 1 for the reason why; see also *Leshon HaZahav* to 139b).

17. However, this is not actually sorting, since the material left in the strainer is also edible (see 140a note 1). Hence, it is only Rabbinically forbidden (*Tosafos;* cf. *Ritva MHK* ed.; see *Shaar HaTziyun* 510:8).

18. As explained above (note 14), sweetening mustard seed necessarily results in the extinguishing of the burning coal. Now, the Biblical *melachah* of extinguishing involves dousing a burning object in order to make charcoal for kindling. Since wood can be made into charcoal, it may not be used for sweetening mustard. Since metal cannot become charcoal, it may be used for the sweetening procedure (*Rashi;* see *Ritva MHK* ed. and *Mishnah Berurah* 510:15).

19. On Yom Tov, extinguishing for purposes of preparing food is permitted (*Rashi*).

20. We have elucidated the Gemara according to *Rashi's* commentary, which implies that extinguishing for purposes of preparing food is permitted on Yom Tov. The halachah is indeed so decided in *Orach Chaim* 507:4. However, *Rif* (to *Beitzah* 23a; folio 12a) rules that such extinguishing is prohibited, and he has a different text and a different interpretation of our Gemara. See *Rif* there, *Meiri* here, and *Beur Halachah* to 507:4. See also *Chidushei HaRan* here for yet another interpretation of our Gemara.

21. The Gemara above (95a) establishes that cheese making is prohibited at least Rabbinically. See *Ran* to *Rif* (folio 12b) in *Beitzah, Hagahos Rav Betzalel Ronsburg* here, *Mitzpeh Eisan* and *Melo HaRo'im.*

22. Cheese making involves squeezing curds together to form one mass. This is the concept of kneading (see *Rabbeinu Chananel*). [See above, 95a, where the Gemara suggests that cheese making resembles the *melachah* of building (בּוֹנֶה). See *Tosafos* there ד״ה והרודה.]

23. In the time of the Gemara (and until the advent of refrigeration), baking took place shortly after the dough was formed.

24. For cheese is eaten cold [and the passage of a day does not affect its freshness].

25. Literally: of the [same] day.

26. *Ritva* (*MHK* ed.) notes that the prohibition against performing on Yom Tov *melachos* that can be performed beforehand applies – under Biblical law – only to preliminary food preparations (מַכְשִׁירֵי אוֹכֶל נֶפֶשׁ), such as kneading dough (see *Beitzah* 28b). Cheese making, however, is a *melachah* that produces the food itself. *Ritva* therefore concludes that the Gemara's prohibition against cheese making on Yom Tov is only Rabbinic in origin. See, however, *Rashi* to *Beitzah* 23b (ד״ה אין), where he writes that even actual food-preparation *melachos* are prohibited on Yom Tov when they can be performed beforehand (cf. *Tosafos* ibid. ד״ה אין, *Rosh* and *Ran* there). See *Rabbeinu Chananel* here and *Baal HaMaor* to *Beitzah* (12a,b on pages of *Rif*), who explain our Gemara differently.

27. See above, 133a note 57.

ᵃ) חספניתא מאי תקנתיה לימשי טובא במיא דסילקא: לא שחק מערב שבת: תנו רבנן דברים שאין עושין למילה בשבת עושין לה ביו"ט ᵃשוחקין לה כמון וטורפין לה יין ושמן א"ל אביי לרב יוסף מאי שנא כמון בי"ט דחזי לקדרה יין ושמן חזי נמי בשבת לחולה דתניא ᵃאין טורפין יין ושמן לחולה בשבת אמר ר"ש בן אלעזר משום ר"מ אף טורפין יין ושמן א"ר שמעון בן אלעזר פעם אחת חש רבי מאיר במעיו ובקשנו לטרוף לו יין ושמן ולא הנחנו אמרנו לו דבריך יבטלו בחייך אמר לנו אע"פ שאני אומר כך וחבירי אומרים כך ᵃמימי לא מלאני לבי לעבור על דברי חבירי הוא ניהו דמחמיר אנפשיה אבל לכולי עלמא שרי התם לא בעי ליכא הכא בעי ליכא הכא נמי ניעביד ולא לילך היינו דקתני נותן זה בפני עצמו וזה בפני עצמו: ת"ר ᵇאין מסננין את החרדל במסננת שלו ואין ממתקין אותו בגחלת א"ל אביי לרב יוסף מאי שנא מהא ᵃדתנן נותנים ביצה במסננת של חרדל א"ל התם לא מיחזי כבורר הכא מיחזי כבורר ואין ממתקין אותו בגחלת והתניא ממתקין אותו בגחלת לא קשיא ᵍכאן בגחלת של עץ כאן בגחלת של מתכת א"ל אביי לרב יוסף מ"ש ᵃמבישרא אגומרי א"ל התם לא אפשר הכא אפשר א"ל אביי לרב יוסף מהו לגבן א"ל ᵈאסור מ"ש מלישה א"ל התם לא אפשר הכא אפשר והא אמרי נהרדעי גבינה בת יומא מעליא הכי קאמרי דאפילו גבינה בת יומא מעליא: אין עושין לה חלוק כו': אמר אביי ᵉאמרה לי אם ʰהאי חלוק דינוקא לפניה לסיטרא ⁱלעילאי דילמא מדביק (א) גרדא מיניה ואתי לידי כרות שפכה אימיה דאביי עבדא כיסתתא לפלגא אמר אביי האי ינוקא דלית ליה חלוק לייתי בליתא דאית ליה שיפתא וליכרכיה לשיפתא לתתאי ועייף ליה לעילאי ואמר אביי אמרה לי אם האי ינוקא דלא ידיע מפקתיה לשייפיה משחא ולוקמיה להדי יומא והיכא דזיג ליקרעיה בשערתא שתי וערב אבל בכלי מתכות לא משום דזריף ואמר אביי אמרה לי אם האי ינוקא דלא מייץ מיקר (ב) דקר פומיה מאי תקנתיה ליתו כסא גומרי ולינקטיה ליה להדי פומיה דחיים פומיה ומייץ ואמר אביי אמרה לי אם האי ינוקא דלא ʲמנשתיה לינפפיה בנפוותא ומנשתיה ואמר אביי אמרה לי אם האי ינוקא דלא ᵏמעוי ליתו סליתא דאימיה ולישרקיה עילויה ומעוי ואמר אביי אמרה לי אם האי ינוקא דקטין לייתו לסילתא דאימיה ולישרקיה עילויה מקוטנא לאולמא ואי אלים מאולמא לקוטנא ואמר אביי אמרה לי אם ˡהאי ינוקא דסומק דאכתי לא איבלע ביה דמא ᵐליתרחו ליה עד דאיבלע ביה דמא ולימהלוה ⁿדירוק ואכתי לא נפל ביה דמיה ליתרחו ליה עד דנפל ביה דמיה ולימהלוה ᵒדתניא א"ר נתן פעם אחת הלכתי לכרכי הים ובאת אשה אחת לפני שמלה בנה ראשון ומת שני ומת שלישי הביאתו לפני ראיתיו שהוא אדום אמרתי לה המתיני לו עד שיבלע בו דמו המתינה לו עד שנבלע בו דמו ומלה אותו וחיה והיו קורין אותו נתן הבבלי על שמי שוב פעם אחת הלכתי למדינת קפוטקיא ובאת אשה אחת לפני שמלה בנה ראשון ומת שני ומת שלישי הביאתו לפני ראיתיו שהוא ירוק הצצתי בו ולא ראיתי בו דם ברית אמרתי לה המתיני לו עד שיפול בו דמו והמתינה לו ומלה אותו וחיה והיו קורין שמו נתן הבבלי על שמי:

מתני'

רש"י

חספניתא. פניו מתבקעות ואני אומר שהוא מין שחין שקורין אינייר"א והוא (בגרב) ובחרס שכתוב בתורה (דברים כח) ⁰ וחספניתא תרגום של חרס: במיא דסילקא. מרק תרדין: חזי לחולה. שאין בו סכנה: יבטלו. דהאי נמי חולה הוא: אבל לכולי עלמא שרי. ר"מ וסתם מתני' ר"מ ואמאי תנן נותן זה בעצמו וזה בעצמו: התם. גבי שאר חולים: לא בעו ליכא. לטרפו ולערבו יפה יפה: ולא לילך. לא יערבנו כל כך: ומתרץ היינו דקתני נותן זה בעצמו וזה בעצמו. שמערב ואינו לוכך: אין מסננין את החרדל. בי"ט: במסננת שלו. טעמא מפרש לקמיה דמיחזי כבורר שמשליך הסובין שלו: ואין ממתקין אותו בגחלת. כדרך שרגילין לכבות לתוכו את הגחלת או אבן ניסוקת: נותנין ביצה במסננת של חרדל. ומסננה בתוכו ליפות מראיתו: לא מיחזי כבורר. שכולה יוצאה דרך המסננת ואין משתייר שם פסולת: בגחלת של עץ. אסור דשייך בה כיבוי לפי שעושה פחם גחלת של מתכת לא שייך בה כיבוי דאינו נעשה פחם: ומ"ש מבישרא אגומרי. שצולין בי"ט ואע"ג דמכבה: לא אפשר. לצלות מאתמול דביומא שביחא טפי אבל חרדל אפשר מאתמול: לגבן. גבינה: מאי שנא מלישה. שלשין פת ביום טוב והאי נמי ללישה דמיא: לא אפשר. דפת חמה מעליא טפי הכא אפשר מאתמול: אימא אף גבינתא בת יומא מעליא. וכ"ש דאתמול: לפניה לסטריה לעילאי. לאימרה שבשפת פיה יהפוך ויקפל למעלה שלא תהא סמוכה לבשרו מפני שראש מקום חתך הבגד שם הוא ויוצאין ממנו גרדין שקורין פיינ"ץ ולמא מדביקה גרדמא מיניה במכה וכשבא להפשיט החלוק מעל המילה ישמוט ויקרע את ראש הגיד ומשוי ליה כרות שפכה: אימיה דאביי. אומנתו: עבדא. לתינוקות הבאים לידה לתקן מילתן: כיסתתא לפלגא. דמילה כיס היתה עושה של בגד לפניו בתוך החלוק ותופרתו מתוך בתוך החלוק ומגיע למטה עד חצי החלוק כדי לחוץ בין האימרא ובין המילה: לייתי בליתא. מעט סמרטוט שלא יהא בו אימרה לפי שהאימרה מהדקה יפה בבשר שלא ישמט החלוק מן הגיד: וליכרכיה לשפתיה לתתאי. למתחית ראש הגיד יתן השפה וראש השני החלוק יהא למעלה: ועיפפיה לעילאי. אותו ראש העליון החלוק יקפל ויקפול כלפי חוץ מפני הגרדין שלא ידבקו במכה: דלא ידיע ביה מפקתיה. שאין ניכר בו נקב בית הרעי שהוא הולאת זבלו: לישייפיה משחא. שהשמן מגהיל הבשר: ולוקמיה להדי יומא. נגד השמש: והיכא דזיג. שגלול מזכוכית בידוע שהחלל כנגדו: בשערתא. בראש השעורה שהוא חדוד: דזריף. מנפחו אינפליי"ר בלע"ז: דלא מייץ. שלא יכול לינק: מיקר הוא דקר פומיה. נצטננו שפתיו ואין בו כח למוץ בהן: לייתו כסא דגומרי. תשטת גחלים על דף או על כלי: ולוקמה להדי פומיה. ויעמיד אצל פיו: דחיים פומיה. שיתחמם פיו: ומייץ. וינק: דלא מינשתא. שאין נשימה ניכרת בו שאין דופק כנגד לבו כדרך כל אדם: לינפפיה בניפוותא. יניפו עליו בנפה שקורין וא"ן: דלא מעוי. אין רוחו נכנס ויוצא יפה אליינ"א בלע"ז: סילתא דאימיה. שיליא שנולדה עמו: ולישרקיה עליה. ימליקנה על בשרו כמו אישתרוקי אישתריקו (ע"ג ד' מ:) אשאולדי"ר: דקטין. שהוא דק: מקוטנא לאולמא. השליא ראשה א' קצר וראשה אחד רחב ימליקוה עליו מראש הקצר יתחילו וימשוכו לצד הרחב כלומר כן ירחיב זה ויתעבה: ואי אלים. ולא מחמת בריאות אלא נפוח לישרקיה עליה מאולמא לקוטנא: דסומק. כל בשרו אדום: לא איבלע ביה דמיה. בבשרו דעכשיו כל דמו מלוי בין עור לבשר וכשמוהלין אותו יוצא כל דמו: ליתרחו ליה. ימתינו מלמולו: לא נפל ביה דמא. לא בא בו דם ומתוך כך חלש הוא ואין בו כח וממהר לחלוש ולמות: לכרכי הים. ה"ג ראיתיו שהיה ירוק הצצתי בו ולא היה בו דם ברית תרתי לגריעותא חדא דלאי מהיל ליה לא נפק מיניה דמא והטפת דם ברית מצוה כדכתיב (זכריה ט) גם את בדם בריתך ועוד דמסוכן הוא ומשום חולשא שלא נולד בו עדיין דם:

תוספות

הכא מיחזי כבורר. מיהו בורר לא הוי שגם הפסולת ראוי לאכילה ולא דמי למשמרת דריש תולין (לקמן ד' קלט:) דלהכא למ"ד חייב משום בורר: מי

עין משפט נר מצוה

כג א מיי' פ"ב מהלכות מילה הל' יד סמג עשין כח טוש"ע י"ד סי' רסו סעיף ו:

כד ב ג מיי' פ"ג מהל' י"ט הלכה יא סמג לאוין עה טוש"ע א"ח סי' תקי סעיף ד [וברב אלפס ביצה פ"ב קנ: ע"ש וברא"ש שם סי' כג]:

כה ד שם סעיף ה:

כו ה טוש"ע י"ד סי' רסד סעיף ג בהג"ה:

כז ו ז מיי' פ"א מהל' מילה הלכה יז טוש"ע י"ד סי' רסג סעיף א:

מסורת הש"ס

א) [פי' כעין קרום הצומח בעור הפנים ומתקלף. ערוך], ב) [תוספ' פי"ג], ג) [לקמן קלט:], ד) [ביצה כג.], ה) [קידושין לג: וש"נ], ו) [גי' הערוך בערך ספר אבראי"ן], ז) [פי' שאין יכול להשמין ערוך ע' שמש], ח) [פי' שאין מולים הכל מתוכמו ערוך], ט) [גי' הערוך ליתרחוהו ועי' כתוספ' הערוך ערך סרח וכר"ש גיטין סח: ד"ה סיבוא גבי], י) חולין מז: [תוספ' פ"ע], כ) [במסכת סלמוני ליתא וכע"ז כע"ש פירש רש"י ותוספתא סקדין שכמוני אדם].

הגהות הב"ח

(א) גמ' דילמא מדביק גרדמא מיניה: (ב) שם מיקר הוא דקר:

גליון הש"ס

גמ' מימי לא מלאני לבי. לעיל דף קיט ע"ב:

ליקוטי רש"י

מיא דסילקא. מים שנתבשלו בהן תרדין [יומא עז.]. נותנים ביצה במסננת. שהחלמון נכנס בה להסתנן וקולטת את הפסולת ואף הביצה החלמון שלה מתקן עמו והוא ליה לחרדל למראה והחלבון וכובד החלמון לתוך של חרדל קולט שם [לקמן קלט: ועי' כאן בהגהות ר' שמחה מדסוי"א ועי' במהרש"א שם]. כרות שפכה. מי שנכרת לו מן הגיד מן העטרה ולמעלה לצד הגוף והוא אינו מוליד [ע"ג כו:]. שנכרת הגיד ונקב אינו יורה קילוח אלא שופך ונוטף ואינו מוליד [יבמות עה:]. דזיג. [דברים כב, ב]. המתיני לו. דאין לך דבר העומד בפני פיקוח נפש חוץ מעבודת כוכבים וגילוי עריות ושפיכות דמים. שיבלע בו דמו. שיהא דמו הולך בין עור לבשר והוי כמי שאין לו דם ומתוך שאין לו הנפש מת מהמכה קלה [חולין מז:].

רבינו חננאל

ברוקה. ולא קמה ופשוטה היא ובא רב אשי להעמידה כר' יוסי דנראה בעליל ואיפשיטא במנחות בתחלת פ' ר' ישמעאל הכי לאו א"ר יוסי התם כיון דאפשר לא טרחינן הכא נמי כיון דאפשר לא טרחינן ונדחת גם זו ואתו נהרדעי ואוקמוה כרבנן דפליגי עליה דר' יוסי במנחות פרק שתי הלחם גילושות דתנן ד' כהנים נכנסים ב' בידם ב' סדרים וב' בידם ב' בזיכין וד' מקדמין לפניהם ב' ליטול ב' סדרים וב' ליטול ב' הבזיכין המכניסין עומדין בצפון ופניהם לדרום והמוציאין עומדים בדרום ופניהם לצפון. אלו מושכין ואלו מניחין טפחיים של זה בצד טפחו של זה שנא' לפני תמיד. ר' יוסי אומר אפילו אלו נוטלין ואלו מניחין אף זו היתה תמיד. שמעינן מדבריהם שאמר' אלו מושכין ואלו מניחין. פי' מושכין את לחם הפנים לא שמערין אותו מעל השלחן כולו אלא מושכין אותו מעט מעט ומתגלה מקצת השלחן ובאותו מקצת המגולה מניחין הלחם המכניסין החדש. וכן עושין טפחו של זה בצד טפחו של זה וסבירא להו שאם נטלו הישן מעל השלחן אין מחזירין אותו אלא כיון שסילק הלחם הישן ונשאר השלחן שעה אחת בלא לחם עבור על הכתוב לפני תמיד ואע"פ שיש לו רשות להדר הא חדש [הוא] מהא שמעינן שהפורש מן המצוה אין לו עוד לחזור עליה להדרה. ומצאנו בתלמוד א"י המל יכול מיכן לשתי מילות אחת למילה ואחת לפריעה. אחת למילה ואחת לציצין כדברי ר' עקיבא ולר' ישמעאל דסבירא ליה דברה תורה כלשון בני אדם נפקא ליה מהא דא"ר יהודה בן פזי אז אמרה חתן דמים למולות מיכן ב' מילות למילה ולפריעה למילה ולציצין: ת"ר מהלקטין את המילה ואם לא הלקטו ענוש כרת. פי' מהלקטין יש מי שאומר מלקטין הציצין המעכבין את המילה כולן וכן סבירא לן ויש מי שאומר מהלקטין מלשון ילקוט שהערלה היא כמו ילקוט ובתוכו העטרה וצריך לחתוך הילקוט כולו לגלות העטרה ואם לא חתכו כולו כאלו לא מל והמל אם לא הילקט בשבת כל הציצין המעכבין את המילה כאלו לא מל וחילל השבת וענוש כרת. והאי דאמרו לא מספקת אינה התראה ואינו מתכוון לחלל את השבת אלא לעשות מצוה מכוון וכיון שלא עשה חייב (כדרבי) [כרת] מפני שלא הניח כיון שנכנסה השבת מוצצין. אע"ג דהאי דם מחבר הוא כיון דאי' סכנה דמיא לאספלנית וכמון ועבדינן לה בשבת פי' אספלנית רטייה: קירא שעוה והיא פסולת הדבש: חספניתא כעין קרום הצומח בעור הפנים ומתקלף ובלשון ישמעאל אל כופה סילקא בלשון ישמעאל סילק: טורפין. מערבין. פי' סילתא שיליא

רב נסים גאון

ונאמר כי כל מצות לא תעשה שבתורה שענש בה כרת לא דחיא לה מצות עשה כי התנאי שנא' בערות אשת אחיך שהוא היתר היבום בה שנאמר (דברים כה) יבמה יבא עליה לא בא אלא באשת אח גרידתא שאינה אסורה אלא משום אשת אח בלבד אבל באחות אשתו שהיא אשת אחיו ודומה לה מן ט"ו נשים המנויין במשנה לא נאמר בהן תנאי להתיר הייבום ואילו נשאו ראובן ושמעון שתי אחיות ומת ראובן ובן אין לו אין לאשתו על שמעון לא חליצה ולא ייבום ולא אתי עשה דאמר רחמנא יבמה יבא עליה ודחי (ויקרא יח) ואשה אל אחותה לא תקח שענש בה הכתוב כרת ובזה אמרה המשנה ט"ו נשים פוטרות צרותיהן וכו' ואמרו בתלמוד (יבמות דף ח) בסוף הדבר רבא אמר ערוה לא צריכא קרא דאין עשה דוחה את לא תעשה שיש בו כרת וכמו כן אם יהיה לא תעשה שאין בו כרת אבל נוסף עליו עשה שנמצא באותה מצוה עשה ולא תעשה אין לנו נמי לדחותה במצות עשה לפי שיצאת מן כלל לאו גרידא מפני הציווי שנתוסף עליה ואפילו שתי מצות עשה שהן זו כנגד זו ואין אחת מכרעת מחברתה אין לנו לדחות אחת מהן מפני האחרת כמו שנאמר בתלמוד בפרק תמיד נשחט (פסחים דף נט) בשלמא לתנא קמא יבא עשה דפסח שיש בה כרת וידחה עשה דהשלמה שאין בו כרת אלא לר' ישמעאל בנו של ר' יוחנן בן ברוקא מכדי האי עשה והאי עשה מאי אולמיה דהאי עשה מהאי עשה וכל שכן אם יהיה עשה ולא תעשה שמן הדין לקיים אותם יותר מלקיים העשה בלבד שכנגדם אלא אם יהיה דבר מיוחד שייחדו הכתוב או החכמים שנעשה כמו שהוא מפורש ואנו מזכירים עיקר שתקיש לו כל מה שתמצא מזה הענין ונאמר הקב"ה ביום אחד לחודש השביעי שהוא יום ראש השנה (ויקרא כג) יהיה לכם שבתון זה מקרא מלא בציווי השביתה ואמר עוד מלאכת עבודה לא תעשו הזהיר בו מלעשות מלאכות מיוחדות נמצא עלינו בקידוש היום עצמו עשה ולא תעשה ועוד ציונו בו לתקוע בשופר שנאמר (במדבר כט) יום תרועה יהיה לכם ובעת שלא תיקננו השופר מערב יום טוב והוצרכנו ביום טוב עצמו לתקוע בשופר לקיים המצוה ואי אפשר להיות דבר זה אלא עד שנחתוך השופר ונתקן אותו ונחלל קדושת היום ראוי לנו שנניח מצות שופר שהיא עשה ולא נחלל היום שיש בחיוב קידושו עשה ולא תעשה שאי אפשר שיבא עשה בלבד וידחה עשה ולא תעשה יחדו וכגון זה מילה שלא בזמנה והוא מי שנתאחר לאחר יום ח' מחמת חולי שאירע לתינוק או מפני הספק כמו ששנינו (לקמן דף קלו) בין השמשות ערב שבת נימול לי' יום טוב אחר שבת נמול לי"א וכשתהיה מילה שלא בזמנה אינה מותרת ביום טוב כי יום טוב יש בו עשה ולא תעשה ולא יבוא עשה של מילה ודחי עשה ולא תעשה של יום טוב אלא בזמנה שהוא יום ח' ודאי שבו נאמר (ויקרא יב) וביום השמיני ימול ואמרו בפירוש וביום ואפי' בשבת אבל שלא בזמנה אפי' יום טוב אינה דוחה שאין עשה דוחה את לא תעשה ועשה שבו וביאור זה כי הקב"ה צוה הנזיר שיגדל שער ראשו מאחר שהקדים האזהרה

The Gemara discusses the manufacture of this bandage:

אָמַר אַבַּיֵי אָמְרָה לִי אֵם – **Abaye said: Mother told me**[28] that **הַאי חָלוּק דִּינוּקָא לְפַנְיֵהּ לְסִיטְרָא לְעֵילָאִי** – **the hem of this infant's shirtlike bandage should be turned upward,**[29] **דִּילְמָא מִידַּבִּיק גַּרְדָּא מִינֵּיהּ וְאָתֵי לִידֵי** – **lest a thread from it stick** to the wound – **and,** when the bandage is removed, **[the infant] כְּרוּת שָׁפְכָה** – **becomes genitally mutilated.**[30] **אִימֵּיהּ דְּאַבַּיֵי עָבְדָא כִּיסְתָּתָא לְפַלְגָא** – But **Abaye's mother**[31] **would** herself **make** for those infants whose circumcisions she arranged **a lining**[32] **for half** of the bandage.[33]

Abaye himself dispenses advice:

אָמַר אַבַּיֵי – **Abaye said:** **הַאי יָנוּקָא דְּלֵית לֵיהּ חָלוּק** – For **this infant who does not have a shirtlike bandage,** **לַיְיתֵי בְּלִיתָא דְּאִית לֵיהּ שִׂיפְתָא** – **bring a rag that has a hem**[34] **וְלִיכְרְכֵיהּ לְשִׂיפְתָא לְתַתָּאִי** – **and tie the hem around at the bottom,**[35] **וְעָיֵיף לֵיהּ לְעֵילָאִי** – **and double over [the top end] upward.**[36]

More advice from Abaye's nurse:

וְאָמַר אַבַּיֵי אָמְרָה לִי אֵם – **And Abaye said** further: **Mother told me** that **הַאי יָנוּקָא דְּלָא יְדִיעַ מַפַּקְתֵּיהּ** – for **this infant whose anus is not discernible,** **לִשְׁוְיפֵיהּ מִישְׁחָא וְלוֹקְמֵיהּ לַהֲדֵי יוֹמָא** – **rub him with oil**[37] **and stand him against the sun,**[38] **וְהֵיכָא דְּזִיג** – **and where [the skin] appears transparent**[39] **לִיקַרְעֵיהּ בִּשְׂעַרְתָּא שְׁתִי וָעֵרֶב** – **tear it crosswise with** the head of **a barley grain,** which is sharp. **אֲבָל בִּכְלֵי מַתָּכוֹת לֹא** – **However,** do **not** tear it **with a metal instrument,** **מִשּׁוּם דְּזָרִיף** – **because [that] causes inflammation.**

More advice:

וְאָמַר אַבַּיֵי אָמְרָה לִי אֵם – **And Abaye** also **said: Mother told me** that **הַאי יָנוּקָא דְּלָא מָיֵיץ** – regarding **this infant who [cannot] suckle,** **מֵיקַר [הוּא] דְּקַר פּוּמֵּיהּ** – **it is** because **his mouth is cold.**[40] **מַאי תַּקַּנְתֵּיהּ** – **What is his remedy?** **לַיְתוּ כָּסָא גּוּמְרֵי** – **Bring a cup of burning coals,**[41] **וְלִינְקְטֵיהּ לֵיהּ לַהֲדֵי פּוּמֵּיהּ** – **and stand it near [the infant's] mouth** **דְּחָיִים פּוּמֵּיהּ** – **so that his mouth will become warm,** **וּמָיֵיץ** – **and** then **he will suckle.**

More advice:

וְאָמַר אַבַּיֵי אָמְרָה לִי אֵם – **And Abaye** also **said: Mother told me** that **הַאי יָנוּקָא דְּלָא מְנַשְׁתֵּיהּ** – for **this infant who does not breathe,**[42] **לִינְפְּפֵיהּ בְּנַפְוָותָא** – **fan him with a fan** **וּמְנַשְׁתֵּיהּ** – **and he will breathe.**

More advice:

וְאָמַר אַבַּיֵי אָמְרָה לִי אֵם – **And Abaye** also **said: Mother told me** that **הַאי יָנוּקָא דְּלָא מְעַוֵּי** – for **this infant who does not breathe easily,** **לַיְיתוּ סִלְיְתָא דְּאִימֵּיהּ** – **bring his mother's afterbirth** **וְלִישַׁרְקֵיהּ עִילָוֵיהּ** – **and slide it over [his flesh],** **וּמְעַוֵּי** – **and he will breathe easily.**

More advice:

וְאָמַר אַבַּיֵי אָמְרָה לִי אֵם – **And Abaye** also **said: Mother told me** that **הַאי יָנוּקָא דְּקָטִין** – for **this infant who is emaciated,** **לַיְיתוּ לְסִילְ[וֹ]תָא דְּאִימֵּיהּ** – **bring his mother's afterbirth** **וְלִישַׁרְקֵיהּ עִילָוֵיהּ מִקּוּטְנָא לְאוּלְמָא** – **and slide it over [his flesh] from** its **narrow end to** its **wide end.**[43] **וְאִי אָלִים** – **And if [the infant] is bloated,**[44] **מֵאוּלְמָא לְקוּטְנָא** – slide the afterbirth over him **from** its **wide end to** its **narrow end.**

One final piece of advice from Abaye's nurse:

וְאָמַר אַבַּיֵי אָמְרָה לִי אֵם – **And Abaye** also **said: Mother told me** that **הַאי יָנוּקָא דְּסוּמָק** – regarding **this infant who is red,**[45] **דְּאַכַּתִּי לֹא אִיבְּלַע בֵּיהּ דְּמָא** – it is **because** his **blood is still not absorbed into [his flesh];**[46] **לִיתַרְחוּ לֵיהּ עַד דְּאִיבְּלַע בֵּיהּ דְּמָא** – therefore, **wait for him until** his **blood is absorbed into [his flesh]** **וְלִימְהֲלוּהּ** – **and** then **circumcise him.** **דִּירוֹק וְאַכַּתִּי לֹא נָפַל בֵּיהּ דְּמֵיהּ** – In the case of an infant **who is yellow, and** the reason is that **he is still blood deficient,**[47] **לִיתַרְחוּ עַד דְּנָפַל בֵּיהּ דְּמֵיהּ** – **wait until he is full blooded** **וְלִימְהֲלוּהּ** – **and** then **circumcise him.**[48]

The Gemara adduces Tannaic support for this last piece of advice:

דְּתַנְיָא – **For it was taught in a Baraisa:** **אָמַר רַבִּי נָתָן** – **R' NASSAN SAID:** **פַּעַם אַחַת הָלַכְתִּי לִכְרַכֵּי הַיָּם** – **ONCE I WENT TO** visit **THE SEA TOWNS,**[49] **וּבָאת אִשָּׁה לְפָנַי** – **AND A WOMAN CAME BEFORE ME** **שֶׁמָּלָה בְּנָהּ רִאשׁוֹן וּמֵת** – **WHO HAD CIRCUMCISED HER FIRST SON AND HE DIED,** **שֵׁנִי וּמֵת** – her **SECOND** son **AND HE DIED,** **שְׁלִישִׁי הֱבִיאַתּוּ לְפָנַי** – and now **SHE BROUGHT** her **THIRD** son **BEFORE ME,** seeking guidance. **רְאִיתִיו שֶׁהוּא אָדוֹם** – **I SAW**

NOTES

28. See above, 133b note 56.

29. I.e. he should fold up the edge of the hem, so that the loose threads of the material should be on the outside of the bandage, away from the flesh (*Rashi*).

30. See *Deuteronomy* 23:2 and *Rashi* there ד״ה כרות שפכה.

31. I.e. nurse (*Rashi*). [Here, Abaye is not *quoting* his surrogate mother (i.e. his nurse). Hence, one might think that the Gemara actually refers to Abaye's real mother. *Rashi* therefore teaches us that this, too, is a reference to Abaye's surrogate mother.]

32. Literally: covering.

33. See *Maharshal,* who has our text of the Gemara. That which *Rashi* adds in his commentary, "[for half] of the circumcision," is apparently the text deleted by *Maharshal* (*Menachem Meishiv Nefesh*). Be that as it may, Abaye's nurse left the loose threads at the hem on the inside but lined the garment halfway down, so that the lining intervened between the hem and the wound (*Rashi*).

34. The hem will keep the rag pressed to the flesh, thereby preventing it from slipping off the member (*Rashi*).

35. That is, tie the hemmed end of the rag below the head of the member [well away from the wound] (*Rashi*).

36. I.e. toward the outside, so that any threads that may be sticking out from the rag cannot stick to the wound (*Rashi*).

37. For oil brightens the skin (*Rashi*).

38. Literally: against the day.

39. An indication that the anal aperture is just on the other side (*Rashi*).

40. That is, his lips have become chilled, and he lacks the strength to suck with them (*Rashi*). [Emendation follows *Rashi* and *Hagahos HaBach.*]

41. I.e. spread out burning coals on a board or implement (*Rashi*).

42. That is, his breathing is not discernible, for his chest does not heave as it normally should (*Rashi*).

Mesoras HaShas cites *Aruch,* who translates דְּלָא מְנַשְׁתֵּיהּ as "who cannot urinate" (לְהַשְׁתִּין).

43. The afterbirth is narrow at one end and wide at the other. Abaye's nurse advises that one should slide the afterbirth over the emaciated infant's flesh, beginning with the narrow end and gradually tilting to the wide end, in a gesture that suggests: This child should broaden and grow more corpulent (*Rashi*).

44. Due to a medical condition (*Rashi*).

45. His entire body has a reddish hue (*Rashi*).

46. Rather, his blood is now located between the skin and the flesh. Should he be circumcised at this time, he will bleed to death (*Rashi*).

47. [Literally: his blood has still not fallen in him.] In this condition he is extremely weak, and could not survive a circumcision (*Rashi, Ritva MHK* ed.).

In *Tur* and *Shulchan Aruch* it is written that the yellow coloring is a sign of blood deficiency. Apparently their text read, as before, דְּאַכַּתִּי לֹא נָפַל בֵּיהּ דְּמָא, "*because* he is still blood deficient."

48. See *Emes LeYaakov* here, who discusses whether it is necessary to wait another seven days, as is the case of one who is systemically ill (חולה כל גופו) and then recovers (see below, 137a).

49. The coastal cities, such as Tyre.

חספניתא. פניו מתבקעות ואני אומר שהוא מין שחין שקורין לויינ"א והוא (בגרב) ובחרס שכתוב בתורה (דברים כח) ט) וחספניתא תרגום של חרס: במיא דסילקא. מרק תרדין: חזי לחולה. שאין בו סכנה: יבטלו. דהלא נמי חולה הוא: אבל לכולי עלמא שרי. ר"מ וקסם מתני' ר"מ ואמאי תנן נותן זה בעצמו וזה בעצמו: התם. גבי שאר חולים: לא בעו ליכא. לטרפו ולערבו יפה יפה: ולא לילך. לא יערבנו כל כך: ומתרך היינו דקתני נותן זה בעצמו וזה בעצמו. שמערב ואינו טורף: אין מסננין את החרדל. בי"ט: במסננת שלו. טעמא מפרש לקמיה דמיחזי כבורר שמשליך הסובין שלו:

א) חספניתא מאי תקנתיה לימשי טובא במיא דסילקא: לא שחק מערב שבת: תנו רבנן דברים שאין עושין למילה בשבת עושין לה ביו"ט **א** שוחקין לה כמון וטורפין לה יין ושמן א"ל אביי לרב יוסף מאי שנא כמון ביו"ט דחזי לקדרה יין ושמן חזי נמי בשבת לחולה דתניא **ב)** אין טורפין יין ושמן לחולה בשבת אמר ר"ש בן אלעזר משום ר"מ אף טורפין יין ושמן א"ר שמעון בן אלעזר פעם אחת חש רבי מאיר במעיו ובקשנו לטרוף לו יין ושמן ולא הנחנו אמרנו לו דבריך יבטלו בחייך אמר לנו אע"פ שאני אומר כך וחבירי אומרים כך **ב** מימי לא מלאני לבי לעבור על דברי חבירי הוא ניהו דמחמיר אנפשיה אבל לכולי עלמא שרי התם לא בעי ליכא הכא בעי ליכא הכא נמי ניעביד ולא ליליך היינו דקתני נותן זה בפני עצמו וזה בפני עצמו: ת"ר **ג** אין מסננין את החרדל במסננת שלו ואין ממתקין אותו בגחלת א"ל אביי לרב יוסף מאי שנא מהא **ג)** דתנן נותנים ביצה במסננת של חרדל א"ל התם לא מיחזי כבורר הכא מיחזי כבורר ואין ממתקין אותו בגחלת והתניא ממתקין אותו בגחלת לא קשיא **ד** כאן בגחלת של מתכת כאן בגחלת של עץ א"ל אביי לרב יוסף מ"ש **ד)** מבישרא אגומרי א"ל התם לא אפשר הכא אפשר א"ל אביי לרב יוסף מהו לגבן א"ל **ה** אסור מ"ש מלישה א"ל התם לא אפשר הכא אפשר והא אמרי נהרדעי גבינה בת יומא מעליא הכי קאמרי דאפילו גבינה בת יומא מעליא: אין עושין לה חלוק כו': אמר אביי **ו** אמרה לי אם **ה)** האי חלוק דינוקא לפניה לסיטרא **ו)** לעילאי דילמא מדביק (א) גרדא מיניה ואתי לידי כרות שפכה אימיה דאביי עבדא כיסתתא לפלגא אמר אביי האי ינוקא דלית ליה חלוק לייתי בליתא דאית ליה שיפתא וליכרכיה לשיפתא לתתאי ועייף ליה לעילאי ואמר אביי אמרה לי אם האי ינוקא דלא ידיע מפקתיה לשייפיה מישחא ולוקמיה להדי יומא והיכא דזיג ליקרעיה בשערתא שתי וערב אבל בכלי מתכות לא משום דזריף ואמר אביי אמרה לי אם האי ינוקא דלא מייץ מיקר (ב) דקר פומיה מאי תקנתיה לייתו כסא גומרי ולינקטיה ליה להדי פומיה דחיים פומיה ומייץ ואמר אביי אמרה לי אם האי ינוקא דלא **ז)** מנשתיה לינפפיה בנפוותא ומנשתיה ואמר אביי אמרה לי אם האי ינוקא דלא **ח)** מעוי ליתו סליתא דאימיה ולישרקיה עילויה ומעוי ואמר אביי אמרה לי אם האי ינוקא דקטין לייתו לסילתא דאימיה ולישרקיה עילויה מקוטנא לאולמא ואי אלים מאולמא לקוטנא ואמר אביי אמרה לי אם **ז** האי ינוקא דסומק דאכתי לא איבלע ביה דמא **ט)** ליתרחו ליה עד דאיבלע ביה דמא ולימהלוה **י)** דירוק ואכתי לא נפל ביה דמיה ליתרחו ליה עד דנפל ביה דמיה ולימהלוה **ח** דתניא א"ר נתן פעם אחת הלכתי לכרכי הים ובאת אשה אחת לפני שמלה בנה ראשון ומת שני ומת שלישי הביאתו לפני ראיתיו שהוא אדום אמרתי לה המתיני לו עד שיבלע בו דמו המתינה לו עד שנבלע בו דמו ומלה אותו וחיה והיו קורין אותו נתן הבבלי על שמי שוב פעם אחת הלכתי למדינת קפוטקיא ובאת אשה אחת לפני שמלה בנה ראשון ומת שני ומת שלישי הביאתו לפני ראיתיו שהוא ירוק הצצתי בו ולא ראיתי בו דם ברית אמרתי לה המתיני לו עד שיפול בו דמו והמתינה לו ומלה אותו וחיה והיו קורין שמו נתן הבבלי על שמי:

מתני'

רש"י

ואין ממתקין אותו בגחלת. כדרך שרגילין לכבות לתוכו את הגחלת או אבן ניסוקת: נותנין ביצה במסננת של חרדל. ומסננה בתוכו לייפות מראיתו: לא מיחזי כבורר. שכולה יוצאה דרך המסננת ואין משתייר שם פסולת: בגחלת של עץ. אסור דשייך בה כיבוי לפי שעושה פחם גחלת של מתכת לא שייך בה כיבוי דאינו נעשה פחם: ומ"ש מבישרא אגומרי. שצולין בי"ט ואע"ג דמכבה: לא אפשר. לצלות מאתמול דביומא שביחא טפי אבל חרדל אפשר מאתמול: לגבן. גבינה: מאי שנא מלישה. שלשין פת ביום טוב והאי נמי ללישה דמיא: לא אפשר. דפת חמה מעליא טפי הכא אפשר מאתמול: אימא אף גבינתא בת יומא מעליא. וכ"ש דאתמול: לפניה לסטריה לעילאי. לאימרא שבשפת פיה יהפוך ויקפל למעלה שלא תהא סמוכה לבשרו מפני שראש מקום חתך הבגד שם הוא ויוצאין ממנו גרדין שקורין פיינד"ץ ודלמא מדביקא גרדתא מיניה במכה וכשבא להפשיט החלוק מעל המילה ישמוט ויקרע את ראש הגיד ומשוי ליה כרות שפכה: אימיה דאביי. אומנתו: עבדא. לתינוקות הבאים לידה לתקן מילתן: כיסתתא לפלגא. דמילה כיס היתה עושה של בגד לפנים בתוך החלוק ותופרתו מתוכו בתוך החלוק ומגיע למטה עד חצי החלוק כדי לחוץ בין האימרא ובין המילה: לייתי בליתא. מעט שחק של בגד שיהא בו אימרא לפי שהאימרא מהדקה יפה בבשר שלא ישמט החלוק מן הגיד: וליכרכיה לשפתיה לתתאי. לתחתית ראש הגיד יתן השפה וראש השני החלק יהא למעלה: ולעפפיה לעילאי. אותו ראש העליון החלוק יקפל ויקפול כלפי חוץ מפני הגרדין שלא ידבקו במכה: דלא ידיע ביה מפקתיה. שאין ניכר בו נקב בית הרעי ששם הוצאת זבלו: לישייפיה מישחא. שהשמן מאהיל הבשר: ולוקמיה להדי יומא. נגד השמש: והיכא דזיג. שנראה כזכוכית בידוע שהחלל כנגדו: בשערתא. בראש השעורה שהוא חדוד: דזריף. מנפחו אינפלי"ר בלע"ז: דלא מייץ. שלא יכול לינק: מיקר הוא דקר פומיה. נצטננו שפתיו ואין בו כח למוץ בהן: לייתו כסא דגומרי. תשטח גחלים על דף או על כלי: ולוקמה להדי פומיה. ויעמיד אצל פיו: דחיים פומיה. שיתחמם פיו: ומייץ. וינק: דלא מינשתא. שאין נשימה ניכרת בו שאין דופק כנגד לבו כדרך כל אדם: לינפפיה בניפוותא. יניפו עליו בנפה שקורין ואן: דלא מעוי. אין רוחו נכנס ויוצא יפה אליינ"א בלע"ז: סילתא דאימיה. שליא שנולדה עמו: ולישרקיה עליה. יחליקנה על בשרו כמו אישתרוקי אישתריקו (ע"ג ד' מ:) אשאולדי"ר: דקטין. שהוא דק: מקוטנא לאולמא. השליא ראשה א' קצר וראשה אחד רחב יחליקוה עליו מראש הקצר יתחילו וימשוכו לצד הרחב כלומר כן ירחיב זה ויתעבה: ואי אלים. ולא מחמת בריאות אלא נפוח לישרקיה עליה מאולמא לקוטנא: דסומק. כל בשרו אדום: לא איבלע ביה דמיה. בבשרו דעכשיו כל דמו מלוי בין עור לבשר וכשמוהלין אותו יוצא כל דמו: ליתרחו ליה. ימתינו מלמולו: לא נפל ביה דמא. לא בא בו דם ומתוך כך חלש הוא ואין בו כח וממהר לחלוש ולמות: לכרכי הים. ה"ג ראיתיו שהיה ירוק הצצתי בו ולא היה בו דם ברית תרתי לגריעותא חדא דאי מהיל ליה לא נפק מיניה דמא והטפת דם ברית מצוה כדכתיב (זכריה ט) גם את בדם בריתך ועוד דמסוכן הוא ומשום חולשא שלא נולד בו עדיין דם:

מתני'

תוספות

הכא מיחזי כבורר. מיהו בורר לא הוי שגם הפסולת ראוי לאכילה ולא דמי למשמרת דריש תולין (לקמן ד' קלז.) דליכא למ"ד חייב משום בורר:

מי

מסורת הש"ס

א) [פי' כעין קרום הצומח בעור הפנים ומתקלף. ערוך], ב) [תוספ' פי"ג], ג) לקמן קלט., ד) [ביצה כג.], ה) [קידושין לב. וש"נ], ו) [גי' הערוך בערך טער אבראין], ז) [פי' שאין יכול להשמין ערוך ע' שתם], ח) [פי' שאין מוציא הבל מתוך מעיו ערוך], ט) [גי' הערוך ליתרחו ועי' במוסף הערוך ערך תרח וכרש"י גיטין סח: ד"ה תרחי גבי], י) חולין מז: [תוספ' פט"ו ע"ש], כ) [בתרגום שלפנינו ליתא ובע"ן כן: פירש רש"י חספניתא סדקין שבכפי אדם].

הגהות הב"ח

(א) גמ' דילמא מידביק גרדתא מיניה: (ב) שם מיקר הוא דקר:

גליון הש"ס

גמ' מימי לא מלאני לבי. לעיל דף קיח ע"ב:

ליקוטי רש"י

מיא דסילקא. מים שבשלו בהן תרדין [יומא עז.]. נותנים ביצה במסננת. חרדל נתון בה להסתנן וקולטת את הפסולת ואף הביצה החלמון שבה צולל ומתמקן עמו ונותן ליה לחרדל למראה והחלבון שהוא קשור נשאר למעלה ורבינו הלוי פירש קיטונה של ביצה לתוך מסננת של חרדל היא ולא דמי לבורר דשרי משום שינוי ויורד לתוך הקערה המבשל בכלי שני ומסנן [לקמן קלט:] ועי' כאן בהגהות ר' שמחה מדסויא וע"ע בהגהות הרש"א. כרות שפכה. מי שנכרתה לו הגיד מן העטרה ולמעלה לצד הגוף ואינו יורה קילוח ואינו מוליד [עי' כה:]. שנכרת הגיד ואינו יורה קילוח זרע אלא שותת ושופך ואינו מוליד (יבמות עה:) [דברים כג, ב]. דזיג. לשון זכוכית [פסחים עד:]. המתיני לו. לאין לך דבר העומד בפני פיקוח נפש חוץ מעבודת כוכבים וגילוי עריות ושפיכות דמים. שיבלע בו דמו. שיהא דמו הולך בין עור לבשר והרי כמי שאין לו דם והדם הוא הנפש ומתוך כך אין בו כח ומתוך הוא מת מכה קלה [חולין מז:].

עין משפט נר מצוה

כג א מיי' פ"ב מהלכות מילה הל' יוד סמג עשין כח טוש"ע י"ד סי' רסו סעיף ו:

כד ב ג מיי' פ"ג מהל' י"ט הלכה יח סמג לאוין עה טוש"ע א"ח סי' תקי סעיף ג [וכרב אלפס ביצה פ"ב קלג: ע"ש וברא"ש שם סי' כג]:

כה ד שם סעיף ה:

כו ה טוש"ע י"ד סי' רסד סעיף ג בהג"ה:

כז ו ז מיי' פ"א מהל' מילה הלכה יח טוש"ע י"ד סי' רסג סעיף א:

רבינו חננאל

ברוקה. ולא קמה ופשוטה היא ובא רב אשי להעמידה כר' יוסי דנראה בעליל ואיפשיטא במנחות בתחלת פ' ר' ישמעאל הכי לאו א"ר יוסי התם כיון דאפשר לא טרחינן הכא נמי כיון דאפשר לא טרחינן ונדחת גם זו ואתו נהרדעי ואוקמוה כרבנן דפליגי עליה דר' יוסי במנחות פרק שתי הלחם גילושות דתנן ד' כהנים נכנסים ב' בידם ב' סדרים וב' בידם ב' בזיכין וד' מקדמין לפניהם ב' ליטול ב' סדרים וב' ליטול ב' בזיכין המכניסין עומדין בצפון ופניהם לדרום והמוציאין עומדים בדרום ופניהם לצפון. אלו מושכין ואלו מניחין טפחיים של זה בצד טפחו של זה שנא' לפני תמיד. ר' יוסי אומר אפילו אלו נוטלין ואלו מניחין אף זו היתה תמידי. שמעינן מדבריהם שאו' אלו מושכין ואלו מניחין. פי' מושכין את לחם הפנים לא שמערין אותו מעל השלחן כולו אלא מושכין אותו מעט מעט ומתגלה מקצת השלחן ובאותו מקצת המגולה מניחין הלחם המכניסין החדש. וכן עושין טפחו של זה בצד טפחו של זה וסבירא להו שאם נטלו הישן מעל השלחן אין מחזירין אותו אלא כיון שסילק הלחם הישן ונשאר השלחן שעה אחת בלא לחם עברו על הכתוב לפני תמיד ואע"פ שיש לו רשות להדר הא חדש [הוא] מהא שמעינן שהפורש מן המצוה אין לו עוד לחזור עליה להדרה. ומצאנו בתלמוד א"י המל ימול מיכן לשתי מילות אחת למילה ואחת לפריעה. אחת למילה ואחת לציצין כדברי ר' עקיבא ולר' ישמעאל דסבירא ליה דברה תורה כלשון בני אדם נפקא ליה מהא דא"ר יהודה בן פזי אז אמרה חתן דמים למולות מיכן ב' מילות למילה ולפריעה למילה ולציצין: ת"ר מהלקטין את המילה ואם לא הלקטו ענוש כרת. פי' מהלקטין יש מי שאומר מלקטן הציצין המעכבין את המילה כולן וכן סבירא לן ויש מי שאומר מהלקטין מלשון ילקוט שהערלה היא כמו ילקוט ובתוכו העטרה וצריך לחתוך הילקוט כולו לגלות העטרה ואם לא חתכו כולו כאלו לא מל והמל אם לא הילקט בשבת כל הציצין המעכבין את המילה כאלו לא מל וחילל השבת וענוש כרת. והאי דאמרו לא מספקת אינה התראה ואינו מתכוון לחלל את השבת אלא לעשות מצוה מכוון וכיון שלא עשה חייב (כדרבי) [כרת] מפני שלא הניח כיון שנכנסה השבת מרצין. אע"ג דהאי דם מחבר הוא כיון דאי' סכנה דמיא לאספלנית וכמון ועבדינן לה בשבת פי' אספלנית רטייה: קירא שעוה והיא פסולת הדבש: **חספניתא** כעין קרום הצומח בעור הפנים ומתקלף ובלשון ישמעאל אל כופה סילקא בלשון ישמעאל סילק: **טורפין**. מערבין. פי' סילתא שיליא

רב נסים גאון

ונאמר כי כל מצות לא תעשה שבתורה שענש בה כרת לא דחיא לה מצות עשה כי התנאי שנא' בערות אשת אחיך שהוא היתר היבום בה שנאמר (דברים כה) יבמה יבא עליה לא בא אלא באשת אח גרידתא שאינה אסורה אלא משום אשת אח בלבד אבל באחות אשתו שהיא אשת אחיו ודומה לה מן ט"ו נשים המנויין במשנה לא נאמר בהן תנאי להתיר הייבום ואילו נשאו ראובן ושמעון שתי אחיות ומת ראובן ובן אין לו אין לאשתו על שמעון לא חליצה ולא ייבום ולא אתי עשה דאמר רחמנא יבמה יבא עליה ודחי (ויקרא יח) ואשה אל אחותה לא תקח שענש בה הכתוב כרת ובזה אמרה המשנה ט"ו נשים פוטרות צרותיהן וכו' ואמרו בתלמוד (יבמות דף ח) בסוף הדבר רבא אמר ערוה לא צריכא קרא דאין עשה דוחה את לא תעשה שיש בו כרת וכמו כן אם יהיה לא תעשה שאין בו כרת אבל נוסף עליו עשה שנמצא באותה מצוה עשה ולא תעשה אין לנו נמי לדחותה במצות עשה לפי שיצאת מן כלל לאו גרידא מפני הציורי שנתוסף עליה ואפילו שתי מצות עשה שהן זו כנגד זו ואין אחת מכרעת מחברתה אין לנו לדחות אחת מהן מפני האחרת כמו שנאמר בתלמוד בפרק תמיד נשחט (פסחים דף נט) בשלמא לתנא קמא יבא עשה דפסח שיש בה כרת וידחה עשה דהשלמה שאין בו כרת אלא לר' ישמעאל בנו של ר' יוחנן בן ברוקא מכדי האי עשה והאי עשה מאי אולמיה דהאי עשה מהאי עשה וכל שכן אם יהיה עשה ולא תעשה שמן הדין לקיים אותם יותר מלקיים העשה בלבד שכנגדם אלא אם יהיה דבר מיוחד שייחדו הכתוב או החכמים שנעשה כמו שהוא מפורש ואנו מזכירים עיקר שתקיש לו כל מה שתמצא מזה הענין ונאמר אמר הקב"ה ביום אחד לחודש השביעי שהוא יום ראש השנה (ויקרא כג) יהיה לכם שבתון זה מקרא מלא בציוי השביתה ואמר עוד מלאכת עבודה לא תעשו הזהיר בו מלעשות מלאכות מיוחדות נמצא עלינו בקידוש היום עצמו עשה ולא תעשה עוד ציונו בו לתקוע בשופר שנאמר (במדבר כט) יום תרועה יהיה לכם ובעת שלא תיקננו השופר מערב יום טוב והוצרכנו ביום טוב עצמו לתקוע בשופר לקיים המצוה ואי אפשר להיות דבר זה אלא עד שנחתוך השופר ונתקן אותו ונחלל קדושת היום ראוי לנו שנניח מצות שופר שהיא עשה ולא נחלל היום שיש בחיוב קידושו עשה ולא תעשה שאי אפשר שיבא עשה בלבד וידחה עשה ולא תעשה יחדו וכגון זה מילה שלא בזמנה והוא מי שנתאחר לאחר יום ח' מחמת חולי שאירע לתינוק או מפני הספק כמו ששנינו (לקמן דף קלז) בין השמשות ערב שבת נימול לי' יום טוב אחר שבת נמול לי"א וכשתהיה מילה שלא בזמנה אינה מותרת ביום טוב כי יום טוב יש בו עשה ולא תעשה ולא יבוא עשה של מילה ודחי עשה ולא תעשה של יום טוב אלא בזמנה שהוא יום ח' ודאי שבו נאמר (ויקרא יב) וביום השמיני ימול ואמרו בפירוש וביום ואפי' בשבת אבל שלא בזמנה אפי' יום טוב אינה דוחה שאין עשה דוחה את לא תעשה ועשה אלא נזיר מצורע כי פירש בראיות ברורות שעשה ידחה את לא תעשה ועשה שבו וביאור זה כי הקב"ה צוה הנזיר שיגדל שער ראשו מאחר שהקדים

האזהרה

THAT [THE INFANT] WAS RED, אֲמַרְתִּי לָהּ הַמְתִּינִי עַד שֶׁיִּבָּלַע בּוֹ דָּמוֹ – and I TOLD [THE WOMAN]: "WAIT FOR HIM UNTIL HIS BLOOD IS ABSORBED INTO [HIS FLESH]."[50] הִמְתִּינָה לוֹ עַד שֶׁנִּבְלַע בּוֹ דָּמוֹ – SHE WAITED FOR HIM UNTIL HIS BLOOD WAS ABSORBED INTO [HIS FLESH], וּמָלָה אוֹתוֹ וְחָיָה – AND then SHE CIRCUMCISED HIM, AND HE LIVED. וְהָיוּ קוֹרִין אוֹתוֹ נָתָן הַבַּבְלִי עַל שְׁמִי – AND THEY CALLED [THE CHILD] NASSAN THE BABYLONIAN AFTER ME.[51]

R' Nassan continues his discourse:

שׁוּב פַּעַם אַחַת הָלַכְתִּי לִמְדִינַת קַפּוֹטְקִיָא – ON ANOTHER OCCASION I TRAVELED TO THE PROVINCE OF CAPPADOCIA,[52] וּבָאת אִשָּׁה אַחַת לְפָנַי – AND ONE WOMAN CAME BEFORE ME שֶׁמָּלָה בְּנָהּ רִאשׁוֹן וּמֵת – WHO HAD CIRCUMCISED HER FIRST SON AND HE DIED, שֵׁנִי וּמֵת – her SECOND son AND HE DIED, שְׁלִישִׁי הֱבִיאַתּוּ לְפָנַי – and now SHE BROUGHT her THIRD son BEFORE ME, seeking guidance. רְאִיתִיו שֶׁהוּא יָרוֹק – I SAW THAT [THE INFANT] WAS YELLOW. הֵצַצְתִּי בּוֹ – I LOOKED CLOSELY AT HIM, וְלֹא רָאִיתִי בּוֹ דַּם בְּרִית – AND I DID NOT SEE IN HIM any COVENANTAL BLOOD.[53] אֲמַרְתִּי לָהּ הַמְתִּינִי לוֹ עַד שֶׁיִּפּוֹל בּוֹ דָּמוֹ – I then SAID TO [THE MOTHER]: "WAIT FOR HIM UNTIL HE IS FULL BLOODED, and then circumcise your son." וְהִמְתִּינָה לוֹ – AND SHE WAITED FOR HIM until he became full blooded, וּמָלָה אוֹתוֹ וְחָיָה – AND then SHE CIRCUMCISED HIM, AND HE LIVED. וְהָיוּ קוֹרִין שְׁמוֹ נָתָן הַבַּבְלִי עַל שְׁמִי – AND THEY CALLED HIS NAME NASSAN THE BABYLONIAN AFTER ME.

NOTES

50. See *Yevamos* 64b, which discusses the case of a male infant whose two older brothers died on account of *milah.* See also *Noda BiYehudah* (*Tinyana* 164), and *Chasam Sofer* to *Yoreh Deah* 245, who speak about our Gemara.

51. Literally: after my name.

52. A district of Asia Minor.

53. [I.e. there was no blood in the member – no blood whose flow would be caused by circumcision.] *Rashi* emends the Gemara to read: ". . . and there was no covenantal blood in him."

Through his examination R' Nassan discovered two obstacles to this child's immediate circumcision: (a) The state of weakness engendered by the deficiency of blood rendered *milah* a threat to the child's life. (b) The very validity of the *milah* was precluded since no blood would flow from the incision, and the issuance of such "covenantal blood" is a requirement of circumcision (see *Zechariah* 9:11) [*Rashi*]. See *Sefer Cheifetz Hashem* by *R' Chaim ibn Atar,* who discusses why *Rashi* mentioned two obstacles here.

חספניתא. פניו מתבקעות ואני אומר שהוא מין שאין שקורין לינייר"א והוא (כגרב) ובחרס שכתוב בתורה (דברים כח) ותספניתא תרגום של חרס: במיא דסילקא. מרק תרדין: חזי לחולה. שאין בו סכנה: יבטלו. דהאי נמי מולה הוא: אבל לכולי עלמא שרי. ר"מ וסתם מתני' ר"מ ואמאי תנן נותן זה בעצמו וזה בעצמו: התם. גבי שאר חולים: לא בעי ליכא. לטרפו ולערבו יפה יפה: ולא לילך. לא יערבנו כל כך: ומתרץ היינו דקתני נותן זה בעצמו וזה בעצמו. שמערב ואינו לוכך: אין מסננין את החרדל. בי"ט: במסננת שלו. טעמא מפרש לקמיה למיחזי כבורר שמשליך הסובין שלו: ואין ממתקין אותו בגחלת. כדרך שרגילין לכבות לתוכו את הגחלת או אבן ניסוקת: נותנין ביצה במסננת של חרדל. ומסננה בתוכו לייפות מראיתו: לא מיחזי כבורר. שכולה יוצאה דרך המסננת ואין משייר שם פסולת: בגחלת של עץ. אסור דשייך בה כיבוי לפי שעושה פחם גחלת של מתכת לא שייך בה כיבוי דאינו נעשה פחם: ומ"ש מבישרא אגומרי. שצולין בי"ט ואע"ג דמכבה: לא אפשר. לצלות מאתמול דיומא שביחא טפי אבל חרדל אפשר מאתמול: לגבן. גבינה: מאי שנא מלישה. שלשין פת ביום טוב והאי נמי לישה דמיא: לא אפשר. דפת חמה מעליא טפי הכא אפשר מאתמול: אימא אף גבינתא בת יומא מעליא. וכ"ש דאתמול: לפניה לסטריה לעילאי. לאימרא שבשפת פיה יהפוך ויקפל למעלה שלא תהא סמוכה לבשרו מפני שראש מקום חתך הבגד שם הוא ויוצאין ממנו גרדין שקורין פיינד"ן ודלמא מדביקא גרדא מיניה במכה וכשבא להפשיט החלוק מעל המילה ישמוט ויקרע את ראש הגיד ומשוי ליה כרות שפכה: אימיה דאביי. אומנתו: עבדא. לתינוקות הבאים לידה לתקן מילתן: כיסתתא לפלגא. דמילה כיס היתה עושה של בגד לפניס בתוך החלוק ומופרתו מתוכו בתוך החלוק ומגיע למטה עד חצי החלוק כדי לחוץ בין האימרא ובין המילה: לייתי בליתא. מעט שחק של בגד שיהא בו אימרא לפי שהאימרא מהדקה יפה בבשר שלא ישמט החלוק מן הגיד: וליפכיה לשפתיה לתתאי. לתחתית ראש הגיד יתן השפה וראש השני החלק יהא למעלה: ולעפפיה לעילאי. אותו ראש העליון החלוק יקפל ויקפול כלפי חוץ מפני הגרדין שלא ידבקו במכה: דלא ידיע ביה מפקתיה. שאין ניכר בו נקב בית הרעי ששם הוצאת זבלו: לישייפיה מישחא. שהשמן מגהיל הבשר: ולוקמיה להדי יומא. נגד השמש: והיכא דזיג. שצלול כזכוכית בידוע שחלל כנגדו: בשערתא. כראש השעורה שהוא חדוד: דזריף. מנפחו אינפלי"ר בלע"ז: דלא מייץ. שלא יכול לינק: מיקר הוא דקר פומיה. נצטננו שפתיו ואין בו כח למוץ בהן: לייתו כסא דגומרי. תשטח גחלים על דף או על כלי: ולוקמה להדי פומיה. ויעמיד אצל פיו: דחיים פומיה. שיתחמם פיו: ומייץ. וינק: דלא מינשתא. שאין נשימה ניכרת בו שאין דופק כנגד לבו כדרך כל אדם: לינפפיה בניפוותא. יניפו עליו בנפה שקורין וא"ן: דלא מעוי. אין רוחו נכנס ויוצא יפה אליינ"א בלע"ז: סילתא דאימיה. שיליא שנולדה עמו: ולישרקיה עליה. יחליקנה על בשרו כמו אשתרוקי אשתריקו (ע"ג ד' מ:) אשאולדי"ר: דקטין. שהוא דק: מקוטנא לאולמא. השליא ראשה א' קצר וראשה אחד רחב יחליקוה עליו מראש הקצר יתחילו וימשכו לצד הרחב כלומר כן ירחיב זה ויתעבה: ואי אלים. ולא מחמת בריאות אלא נפוח לישרקיה עליה מאולמא לקוטנא: דסומק. כל בשרו אדום: לא איבלע ביה דמיה. בבשרו דעכשיו כל דמו מצוי בין עור לבשר וכשמוהלין אותו יוצא כל דמו: ליתרחו ליה. ימתינו מלמולו: לא נפל ביה דמא. לא בא בו דם ומתוך כך חלש הוא ואין בו כח וממהר לחלוש ולמות: לכרכי הים. ה"ג ראיתיו שהיה ירוק הצצתי בו ולא היה בו דם ברית תרתי לגריעותא חדא דאי מהיל ליה לא נפק מיניה דמא והטפת דם ברית מצוה כדכתיב (זכריה ט) גם את בדם בריתך ועוד דמסוכן הוא ומשום חולשא שלא נוצר בו עדיין דם:

א) חספניתא מאי תקנתיה לימשי טובא במיא דסילקא: לא שחק מערב שבת: תנו רבנן דברים שאין עושין למילה בשבת עושין לה ביו"ט א שוחקין לה כמון וטורפין לה יין ושמן א"ל אביי לרב יוסף מאי שנא כמון בי"ט דחזי לקדרה יין ושמן חזי נמי בשבת לחולה דתניא ב) אין טורפין יין ושמן לחולה בשבת אמר ר"ש בן אלעזר משום ר"מ אף טורפין יין ושמן אמר ר"ש בן אלעזר פעם אחת חש רבי מאיר במעיו ובקשנו לטרוף לו יין ושמן ולא הנחנו אמרנו לו דבריך יבטלו בחייך אמר לנו אע"פ שאני אומר כך וחבירי אומרים כך ג) מימי לא מלאני לבי לעבור על דברי חבירי הוא ניהו דמחמיר אנפשיה אבל לכולי עלמא שרי התם לא בעי ליכא הכא בעי ליכא הכא נמי ניעביד ולא לילך היינו דקתני נותן זה בפני עצמו וזה בפני עצמו: ת"ר ב אין מסננין את החרדל במסננת שלו ואין ממתקין אותו בגחלת א"ל אביי לרב יוסף מאי שנא מהא ד) דתנן נותנים ביצה במסננת של חרדל א"ל התם לא מיחזי כבורר הכא מיחזי כבורר ואין ממתקין אותו בגחלת והתניא ממתקין אותו בגחלת לא קשיא ג כאן בגחלת של מתכת כאן בגחלת של עץ א"ל אביי לרב יוסף מ"ש ה) מבישרא אגומרי א"ל התם לא אפשר הכא אפשר א"ל אביי לרב יוסף מהו לגבן א"ל ד אסור מ"ש מלישה א"ל התם לא אפשר הכא אפשר והא אמרי נהרדעי גבינה בת יומא מעליא הכי קאמרי דאפילו גבינה בת יומא מעליא: אין עושין לה חלוק כו': אמר אביי ו) אמרה לי אם ה האי חלוק דינוקא לפניה לסיטרא ז) לעילאי דילמא מידביק (א) גרדא מיניה ואתי לידי כרות שפכה אימיה דאביי עבדא כיסתתא לפלגא אמר אביי האי ינוקא דלית ליה חלוק לייתי בליתא דאית ליה שיפתא וליכרכיה לשיפתא לתתאי ועייף ליה לעילאי ואמר אביי אמרה לי אם האי ינוקא דלא ידיע מפקתיה לשייפיה מישחא ולוקמיה להדי יומא והיכא דזיג ליקרעיה בשערתא שתי וערב אבל בכלי מתכות לא משום דזריף ואמר אביי אמרה לי אם האי ינוקא דלא מייץ מיקר (ב) דקר פומיה מאי תקנתיה לייתו כסא גומרי ולינקטיה ליה להדי פומיה דחיים פומיה ומייץ ואמר אביי אמרה לי אם האי ינוקא דלא ח) מנשתיה לינפפיה בנפוותא ומנשתיה ואמר אביי אמרה לי אם האי ינוקא דלא ט) מעוי ליתו סליתא דאימיה ולישרקיה עילויה ומעוי ואמר אביי אמרה לי אם האי ינוקא דקטין ליתו לסילתא דאימיה ולישרקיה עילויה מקוטנא לאולמא ואי אלים מאולמא לקוטנא ואמר אביי אמרה לי אם ו האי ינוקא דסומק דאכתי לא איבלע ביה דמא ט) ליתרחו ליה עד דאיבלע ביה דמא ולימהלוה י) דירוק ואכתי לא נפל ביה דמיה ליתרחו עד דנפל ביה דמיה ולימהלוה ז דתניא א"ר נתן פעם אחת הלכתי לכרכי הים ובאת אשה אחת לפני שמלה בנה ראשון ומת שני ומת שלישי הביאתו לפני ראיתיו שהוא אדום אמרתי לה המתיני לו עד שיבלע בו דמו המתינה לו עד שנבלע בו דמו ומלה אותו וחיה והיו קורין אותו נתן הבבלי על שמי שוב פעם אחת הלכתי למדינת קפוטקיא ובאת אשה אחת לפני שמלה בנה ראשון ומת שני ומת שלישי הביאתו לפני ראיתיו שהוא ירוק הצצתי בו ולא ראיתי בו דם ברית אמרתי לה המתיני לו עד שיפול בו דמו והמתינה לו ומלה אותו וחיה והיו קורין שמו נתן הבבלי על שמי:

מתני'

הכא מיחזי כבורר. מיהו בורר לא הוי שגם הפסולת ראוי לאכילה ולא דמי למשמרת דריש תולין (לקמן ד' קלט:) דליכא למ"ד חייב משום בורר: מי

מסורת הש"ס

א) [פי' כעין קרוס הצומח בעור הפנים ומתקלף. ערוך], ב) [תוספ' פי"ג], ג) לקמן קלט:, ד) [ביצה כג.], ה) [קידושין לא: וסם נסמן], ו) [גי' הערוך בערך סטר אבראי], ז) [פי' שאין יכול להסמין ערוך ע' שמם], ח) [פי' שאין מוציא הבל מפומו ערוך], ט) [גי' הערוך ליתרהו ועי' במוסף הערוך ערך תרה וברש"י גיטין סח: ד"ה תרתי גבי], י) חולין מז: [תוספ' פט"ו ע"ש], כ) [במרגוס שלפנינו ליתא ובע"ז כט: פירש רש"י חוספניתא סדקין שבפני אדם].

הגהות הב"ח

(א) גמ' דילמא מידביק גרדא מיניה: (ב) שם מיקר הוא דקר:

גליון הש"ס

גמ' מימי לא מלאני לבי. לעיל דף קיח ע"ב:

ליקוטי רש"י

מיא דסילקא. מים שבשלו בהן תרדין [יומא עז.]. נותנים ביצה במסננת. שהחרדל נתון בה להסתנן וקולטת את הפסולת ואף הבילה החלמון שלה טורף ומסתנן עמו והוא ליה לחרדל למראה והחלבון שהוא קשור נשאר למעלה ורבינו הלוי פירש סינונה של בילה לתוך תבשיל היא ולא לתוך חרדל ובמסננת של חרדל הוא דשרי משום שינוי ויורד לתוך הקערה שהוא כלי שני ומתלבן התבשיל [לקמן קלט: ועי' כאן בהגהות ר' שמחה מדעסויא וע"ע במהרש"א שם]. כרות שפכה. מי שנכרת לו מן הגיד מן העטרה ולמעלה לצד הגוף ושוב אינו מוליד [ע"ז כו.]. שנכרת הגיד ושוב אינו יורה קילוח זרע אלא שופך ושותת ואינו מוליד (יבמות עה:) [דברים כג, ב]. דזיג. לשון זכוכית [פסחים עד:]. המתיני לו. דאין לך דבר העומד בפני פיקוח נפש חוץ מעבודת כוכבים וגילוי עריות ושפיכות דמים. שיבלע בו דמו. שיהא דמו נבלע בבשרו שהיה דמו הולך בין עור לבשר והוי כמי שאין לו דם והדם הוא הנפש ומתוך שאין בו מיום הוא מת במכה קלה [חולין מז:].

עין משפט נר מצוה

כג א מיי' פ"ב מהלכות מילה הל' יוד סמג עשין כח טוש"ע י"ד סי' רסו סעיף ו:

כד ב ג מיי' פ"ג מהל' י"ט הלכה יז סמג לאוין עה טוש"ע א"ח סי' תקי סעיף ג [וברב אלפס בילה פ"ב קנג: ע"ש וברא"ש שם סי' כג]:

כה ד שם סעיף ה:

כו ה טוש"ע י"ד סי' רסד סעיף ג בהג"ה:

כז ו ז מיי' פ"א מהל' מילה הלכה יח טוש"ע י"ד סי' רסג סעיף א:

רבינו חננאל

ברוקה. ולא קמה ופשוטה היא ובא רב אשי להעמידה כר' יוסי דנראה בעליל ואיפשיטא במנחות בתחלת פ' ר' ישמעאל הכי לאו א"ר יוסי התם כיון דאפשר לא טרחינן הכא נמי כיון דאפשר לא טרחינן ונדחת גם זו ואתו נהרדעי ואוקמוה כרבנן דפליגי עליה דר' יוסי במנחות פרק שתי הלחם נילושות דתנן ד' כהנים נכנסים ב' בידם ב' סדרים וב' בידם ב' בזיכין וד' מקדמין לפניהם ב' ליטול ב' סדרים וב' ליטול ב' בזיכין המכניסין עומדין בצפון ופניהם לדרום והמוציאין עומדים בדרום ופניהם לצפון. אלו מושכין ואלו מניחין טפחיים של זה בצד טפחו של זה שנא' לפני תמיד. ר' יוסי אומר אפילו אלו נוטלין ואלו מניחין אף זו היתה תמידי. שמעינן מדבריהם שאר' אלו מושכין ואלו מניחין. פי' מושכין את לחם הפנים לא שמערין אותו מעל השלחן כולו אלא מושכין אותו מעט מעט ומתגלה מקצת השלחן ובאותו מקצת המגולה מניחין הלחם המכניסין החדש. וכן עושין טפחו של זה בצד טפחו של זה וסבירא להו שאם נטלו הישן מעל השלחן אין מחזירין אותו אלא כיון שסילק הלחם הישן ונשאר השלחן שעה אחת בלא לחם עברו על הכתוב לפני תמיד ואע"פ שיש לו רשות להדר הא חדש [הוא] מהא שמעינן שהפורש מן המצוה אין לו עוד לחזור עליה להדרה. ומצאנו בתלמוד א"י המל ימול מיכן לשתי מילות אחת למילה ואחת לפריעה. אחת למילה ואחת לציצין כדברי ר' עקיבא ולר' ישמעאל דסבירא ליה דברה תורה כלשון בני אדם נפקא ליה מהא דא"ר יהודה בן פזי אז אמרה חתן דמים למולות מיכן ב' מילות למילה ולפריעה למילה ולציצין: ת"ר מהלקטין את המילה ואם לא הלקטו ענוש כרת. פי' מהלקטין יש מי שאומר מלקטן הציצין המעכבין את המילה כולן וכן סבירא לן ויש מי שאומר מהלקטין מלשון ילקוט שהערלה היא כמו ילקוט ובתוכו העטרה וצריך לחתוך הילקוט כולו לגלות העטרה ואם לא חתכו כולו כאלו לא מל והמל אם לא הילקט בשבת כל הציצין המעכבין את המילה כאלו לא מל וחילל השבת וענוש כרת. והאי דאמרו לא מספקת אינה התראה ואינו מתכוון לחלל את השבת אלא לעשות מצוה מכוון וכיון שלא עשה חייב (כדרבי) [כרת] מפני שלא הניח כיון שנכנסה השבת מוצצין. אע"ג דהאי דם מחבר הוא כיון דאי' סכנה דמיא לאספלנית וכמון ועבדינן לה בשבת פי' אספלנית רטיה: קירא שעוה והיא פסולת הדבש: חספניתא כעין קרום הצומח בעור הפנים ומתקלף ובלשון ישמעאל אל כופה סילקא בלשון ישמעאל סילק: טורפין. מערבין. פי' סילתא שיליא

רב נסים גאון

ונאמר כי כל מצות לא תעשה שבתורה שענש בה כרת לא דחיא לה מצות עשה כי התנאי שנא' בערות אשת אחיך שהוא היתר היבום בה שנאמר (דברים כה) יבמה יבא עליה לא בא אלא באשת אח גרידתא שאינה אסורה אלא משום אשת אח בלבד אבל באחות אשתו שהיא אשת אחיו ודומה לה מן ט"ו נשים המנויין במשנה לא נאמר בהן תנאי להתיר הייבום ואילו נשאו ראובן ושמעון שתי אחיות ומת ראובן ובן אין לו אין לאשתו על שמעון לא חליצה ולא ייבום ולא אתי עשה דאמר רחמנא יבמה יבא עליה ודחי (ויקרא יח) ואשה אל אחותה לא תקח שענש בה הכתוב כרת ובזה אמרה המשנה ט"ו נשים פוטרות צרותיהן וכו' ואמרו בתלמוד (יבמות דף ח) בסוף הדבר רבא אמר ערוה לא צריכא קרא דאין עשה דוחה את לא תעשה שיש בו כרת וכמו כן אם יהיה לא תעשה שאין בו כרת אבל נוסף עליו עשה שנמצא באותה מצוה עשה ולא תעשה אין לנו נמי לדחותה במצות עשה לפי שיצאת מן כלל לאו גרידא מפני הציווי שנתוסף עליה ואפילו שתי מצות עשה שהן זו כנגד זו ואין אחת מכרעת מחברתה אין לנו לדחות אחת מהן מפני האחרת כמו שנאמר בתלמוד בפרק תמיד נשחט (פסחים דף נט) בשלמא לתנא קמא יבא עשה דפסח שיש בה כרת וידחה עשה דהשלמה שאין בו כרת אלא לר' ישמעאל בנו של ר' יוחנן בן ברוקא מכדי האי עשה והאי עשה מאי אולמיה דהאי עשה מהאי עשה וכל שכן אם יהיה עשה ולא תעשה שמן הדין לקיים אותם יותר מלקיים העשה בלבד שכנגדם אלא אם יהיה דבר מיוחד שייחדו הכתוב או החכמים שנעשה כמו שהוא מפורש ואנו מזכירים עיקר שתקיש לו כל מה שתמצא מזה הענין ונאמר אמר הקב"ה ביום אחד לחודש השביעי שהוא יום ראש השנה (ויקרא כג) יהיה לכם שבתון זה מקרא מלא בציוי השביתה ואמר עוד מלאכת עבודה לא תעשו הזהיר בו מלעשות מלאכות מיוחדות נמצא עלינו בקידוש היום עצמו עשה ולא תעשה ואמר עוד ציונו בו לתקוע בשופר שנאמר (במדבר כט) יום תרועה יהיה לכם ובעת שלא תיקננו השופר מערב יום טוב והוצרכנו ביום טוב עצמו לתקוע בשופר לקיים המצוה ואי אפשר להיות דבר זה אלא עד שנתחוך השופר ונתקן אותו ונחלל קדושת היום ראוי לנו שנניח מצות שופר שהיא עשה ולא נחלל היום שיש בחיוב קידושו עשה ולא תעשה שאי אפשר שיבא עשה בלבד וידחה עשה ולא תעשה יחדו וכגון זה מילה שלא בזמנה והוא מי שנתאחר לאחר יום ח' מחמת חולי שאירע לתינוק או מפני הספק כמו ששנינו (לקמן דף קלז) בין השמשות ערב שבת נימול לי' יום טוב אחר שבת נמול לי"א וכשתהיה מילה שלא בזמנה אינה מותרת ביום טוב כי יום טוב יש בו עשה ולא תעשה ולא יבוא עשה של מילה ודחי עשה ולא תעשה של יום טוב אלא בזמנה שהוא יום ח' ודאי שבו נאמר (ויקרא יב) וביום השמיני ימול ואמרו בפירוש וביום ואפי' בשבת אבל שלא בזמנה אפי' יום טוב אינה דוחה שאין עשה דוחה את לא תעשה ועשה אלא נזיר מצורע כי פירש בראיות ברורות שעשה ידחה את לא תעשה ועשה שבו וביאור זה כי הקב"ה צוה הנזיר שיגדל שער ראשו מאחר שהקדים האזהרה

עין משפט נר מצוה

כח א מיי' פ"ב מהל' מילה הלכה ח ופ"ב מהל' שבת הלכה יד סמג עשין כח טוש"ע א"ח סי' שלא סעיף ט:
כט ב ג מיי' פכ"א מהל' שבת הלכה כו טוש"ע א"ח סי' שכח סעיף כב:
ל ד ה מיי' שם טוש"ע שם סעיף כג:

מסורת הש"ס

א) לעיל פו. ע"ש, ב) רש"ל מ"ז וא"ל למחוק וקאי למאי דהסכים רבא לפי דסבר דדיקא כוותייהו ולא הסיר מ"ק אפי' לזלף ביום ג'.

מתני' ומזלפין עליו. את החמין: ביד. אבל לא בכלי ובגמ' פריך הא אמרת רישא מרחיצין דמשמע כדרכו והדר תני אפילו לזלף עליו בכלי אסור: ספק. כגון ספק בן ח' חדשים [וספק בן ט'] דהוא כאבן בעלמא ואין מילתו דוחה שבת (וספק בן ט'): ר' יהודה מתיר באנדרוגינוס. דלאיתרבי מקראי כדמפרש בגמ' לקמן: גמ' והא אמרת רישא מרחיצין. ואפילו כדרכו: כיצד קתני. מרחיצין דרישא לאו כדרכו הוא דתנא סיפא לפרושי כיצד מרחיצין כגון לזלף ביד ואפילו ביום ראשון: תניא כוותיה דרבא כו' ה"ג ביום השלישי מזלפין עליו ביד ולא גרסינן אבל לא בכלי: אתאן לת"ק. הך סיפא תנא קמא אמרה דאילו ר"א אפילו הרחצה כדרכו שרי: משום דגדול לא סליק בישרא הייא. היינו טעמא דמעשה שכם לאו ראיה גמורה היא משום דגדול אין מכה שבבשרו מעלה ארוכה מהר אבל קטן נתרפא מידי סכנתו מהר: אורי ליה כשמעתיה. התיר לו הרחצה כדרכו ביום ראשון שחל להיות בשבת: איחלש. נעשה חולה והיה דואג שמא על כך נענש: אמר בהדי תרגימנא דסבי למה לי. מה היה לי לחלוק כנגד זקנים הללו רב יהודה ורבה בר אבוה שפירשו שאסור להרחיץ: אי אמרת בשלמא ת"ק מזלפין. ביום ראשון קאמר ולא איירי בהרחצה כלל אלא בזילוף היינו דאתא ר"א בן עזריה ופליג ואמר מרחיצין: אלא אי אמרת. תנא קמא נמי מרחיצין אמר בשני הימים ולא פליג ר"א אלא איום שלישי דקאמר ת"ק מזלפין אף מרחיצין ביום השלישי מיבעי ליה: הוו בה. דייקי בה: דאי ס"ד הרחצת מילה מי גרע מחמין על גבי מכה. דשרי והכא אסרי רבנן בשלישי ([ג] לגמרי): ולא שני כו'. והכא גבי מילה בהוחמו בשבת עסקינן הלכך בשלישי דליכא סכנתא לא: אמר אביי אנא בעאי דאישני ליה. אני הייתי רוצה לתרץ אתקפתא זו כדשני ליה רב יוסף מפני שסכנה היא לו: וקדם רב יוסף ושנייא ליה. דודאי מתניתין חמין שהוחמו בשבת נמי שרי בימים הראשונים ולר"א אף בשלישי מפני שמניעת חמין סכנה היא לו: אין נותנין כו'. קס"ד גזרה משום שחיקת סמנין כשמואל דטעמיה משום הכי הוא והיינו דקאמר אבל נותן חוץ למכה דלא מוכחא מילתא דלרפואה: מוך יבש וספוג יבש. דלאו לרפואה היא אלא שלא ישרטו בגדיו הקשים מכתו: אבל לא כתיתין יבישים (א) וגמי יבש. חתיכות בגדים דקות משום דמסו וגזרו משום שחיקת סמנין: קשיא כתיתין אכתיתין. רישא שרי מוך יבש דהיינו כתיתין וסיפא אסר כתיתין: חדתי. חדשים שלא היו על גבי מכה מעולם מסו עתיקי לא מסו: ה"ג שמע מינה הני כתיתין מסו: ערלתו ודאי דוחה השבת. דבהאי קרא וביום השמיני דילפינן מיניה אפילו בשבת כתיב בסיפיה ערלתו דמשמע מיעוטא ערלתו של זה ולא של אחר ולמעוטי ספק אתא: אנדרוגינוס

מתני' מרחיצין את הקטן בין לפני המילה ובין לאחר המילה ומזלפין עליו ביד אבל לא בכלי ר"א בן עזריה (א) אומר מרחיצין את הקטן ביום השלישי שחל להיות בשבת שנאמר (א) ויהי ביום השלישי בהיותם כואבים ספק ואנדרוגינוס אין מחללין עליו את השבת ורבי יהודה מתיר באנדרוגינוס: **גמ'** והא אמרת רישא מרחיצין רב יהודה ורבה בר אבוה דאמרי תרוייהו כיצד תני מרחיצין את הקטן בין לפני מילה בין לאחר מילה כיצד מזלפין עליו ביד אבל לא בכלי אמר רבא והא מרחיצין קתני אלא אמר רבא הכי קתני מרחיצין את הקטן בין מלפני מילה בין לאחר המילה ביום הראשון כדרכו וביום השלישי שחל להיות בשבת מזלפין עליו ביד אבל לא בכלי ר"א בן עזריה אומר מרחיצין את הקטן ביום השלישי שחל להיות בשבת שנאמר ויהי ביום השלישי בהיותם כואבים תניא כוותיה דרבא מרחיצין הקטן בין לפני מילה בין לאחר מילה ביום ראשון כדרכו וביום השלישי שחל להיות בשבת מזלפין עליו ביד ר"א בן עזריה אומר מרחיצין את הקטן ביום השלישי שחל להיות בשבת ואע"פ שאין ראיה לדבר זכר לדבר שנאמר ויהי ביום השלישי בהיותם כואבים וכשהן מזלפין אין מזלפין לא בכוס ולא בקערה ולא בכלי אלא ביד אתאן לתנא קמא מאי אע"פ שאין ראיה לדבר זכר לדבר משום דגדול לא סליק ביה בישרא הייא ההוא קטן דאתא לקמיה דרבא אורי ליה כשמעתיה איחלש רבא אמר אנא בהדי תרגימנא דסבי למה לי אמרו ליה רבנן לרבא והתניא כוותיה דמר אמר להו מתניתין כוותיהו דיקא ממאי מדקאמר רבי אלעזר בן עזריה אומר מרחיצין את הקטן ביום השלישי שחל להיות בשבת אי אמרת בשלמא תנא קמא מזלפין קאמר היינו דקאמר ליה ר"א בן עזריה מרחיצין אלא אי אמרת תנא קמא מרחיצין ביום הראשון קאמר ומזלפין ביום השלישי האי רבי אלעזר בן עזריה אומר מרחיצין אף מרחיצין מיבעי ליה כי אתא רב דימי אמר רבי אלעזר הלכה כר"א בן עזריה הוו בה במערבא הרחצת כל גופו או הרחצת מילה אמר להו ההוא מרבנן ורבי יעקב שמיה מסתברא הרחצת כל גופו דאי ס"ד הרחצת מילה מי גרע מחמין על גבי מכה דאמר רב אין מונעין חמין ושמן מעל גבי מכה בשבת מתקיף לה רב יוסף ולא שני לך בין חמין שהוחמו בשבת לחמין שהוחמו מע"ש מתקיף לה רב דימי וממאי דהכא בחמין שהוחמו בשבת פליגי דילמא בחמין שהוחמו בע"ש פליגי אמר אביי אנא בעאי דאישני ליה וקדם רב יוסף ושני ליה מפני שסכנה הוא לו איתמר נמי כי אתא רבין א"ר אבהו א"ר אלעזר ואמרי לה א"ר אבהו א"ר יוחנן א הלכה כר"א בן עזריה בין בחמין שהוחמו בשבת בין בחמין שהוחמו מע"ש בין הרחצת כל גופו בין הרחצת מילה מפני שסכנה היא לו: גופא אמר רב אין מונעין חמין ושמן מעל גבי מכה בשבת ושמואל אמר נותן חוץ למכה ושותת ויורד למכה מיתיבי ב אין נותנין שמן וחמין על גבי מוך ליתן על גבי מכה בשבת התם משום סחיטה תא שמע אין נותנין חמין ושמן על גבי מוך שעל גבי מכה בשבת התם נמי משום סחיטה תניא כוותיה דשמואל ג אין נותנין חמין ושמן על גבי מכה בשבת אבל נותנין חוץ למכה ושותת ויורד למכה תנו רבנן ד נותנין על גבי המכה מוך יבש וספוג יבש אבל לא גמי יבש ולא כתיתין יבשין קשיא כתיתין אכתיתין לא קשיא ה הא בחדתי הא בעתיקי אמר אביי שמע מינה הני כתיתין מסו: ספק ואנדרוגינוס כו': תנו רבנן (ב) ערלתו ערלתו ודאי דוחה את השבת ולא

מי גרע מחמין על גבי מכה. וסיפי אסרי רבנן בשלישי אע"ג דליכא למימר דרך אמרה למילתיה כר"א בן עזריה דפסקינן לעיל הלכתא כוותיה משמע ליה דלכ"ע קאמר ועוד דאפילו לר"א בן עזריה פריך דמשמע דשרי בשלישי משום סכנה מדמייתי קרא ויהי ביום השלישי ורב איירי במכה שאין בה סכנה: **ואין** מונעין חמין ושמן. פירש ה"ר יוסף פורת בשם רבינו שמואל דבמעורבת יחד איירי דאי כל חד באפי נפשיה מאי קמ"ל בשמן מתני' היא בפ' שמנה שרצים (לעיל דף קיא.) אבל סך הוא את השמן והיינו אפילו על גבי מכה מדקתני בני מלכים סכין ע"ג מכותיהן שמן וורד מכלל דבשאר שמן מותר לאחר אפילו ע"ג מכה ושמואל נמי היכי הוה פליג: ולא

הגהות הב"ח

(א) רש"י ד"ה אבל לא כתיתין יבישים חתיכות כצ"ל ותיבות וגמי יבש נמחק:

תורה אור השלם

א) וַיְהִי בַיּוֹם הַשְּׁלִישִׁי בִּהְיוֹתָם כֹּאֲבִים וַיִּקְחוּ שְׁנֵי בְנֵי יַעֲקֹב שִׁמְעוֹן וְלֵוִי אֲחֵי דִינָה אִישׁ חַרְבּוֹ וַיָּבֹאוּ עַל הָעִיר בֶּטַח וַיַּהַרְגוּ כָּל זָכָר: [בראשית לד, כה]

ב) וּבַיּוֹם הַשְּׁמִינִי יִמּוֹל בְּשַׂר עָרְלָתוֹ: [ויקרא יב, ג]

ליקוטי רש"י

מרחיצין את הקטן ביום השלישי. דאף ביום שלישי מסוכן הוא [לעיל פו.]. **ויהי ביום השלישי בהיותם כואבים.** ולאו למימרא דביום השלישי כאיב ליה טפי מיומא קמא אלא לכך המתינו שמעון ולוי עד יום השלישי כדי שיהו חלושין ביותר שנכאבו ג' ימים והכי מוכח בפ' ר"א דמילה [ר"ן נדרים לא: ועי' בר"ן כאן]. **אנדרוגינוס.** שיש לו זכרות ונקבות [רשב"ם ב"ב קכו.].

רבינו חננאל

מקוטמא לאולמא ממקום הדק לעבה: ת"ר דברים שאין עושין למילה בשבת עושין לה ביו"ט שוחקין כמון וטורפין לה יין ושמן יין בפ"ע ושמן בפ"ע אבל ע"י ליכא [אסור]. פי' ליכא עירוב יין ושמן להוליך השמן בתוך היין על [ידין] עירבוב. (אבל) א"ל אביי לרבה מהו לגבן. פי' לגבן ביו"ט לקפות גבינה לקבץ פיתותי החלב הקפוי ולעשותם חריץ של גבינה. א"ל אסור לגבן. א"ל והלא גיבון כמו לישת העיסה שנותן מים בקמח ומולל בידיו ועושה פתיתין ומוסיף מים ומקבץ הפתיתין ועושה אותם עיסה. כך מקפה החלב בטוכמסו ואחר שיקפה בכלי ויעמוד מכניס ידו ופיתתו. ואח"כ מכניס ידו ומגבן מתוך הכיס. הנה גיבון ולישה מלאכתן שוה מפני מה זה מותר וזה אסור ופירק לו קמח אי אפשר לאוכלו אלא ע"י לישה ביומו. והחלב אפשר לאכלו חלב או לעשותו גבינה בערב. אקשינן עלה והא אמרו נהרדעי גבינה בת יומא מעליא והנה היא כמו הלישה וכשם שהפת חמה מעליא כך הגבינה בת יומא מעליא ופריק ליה הכי קאמר אפילו בת יומא מעליא מכלל שבת שנים ושלשה ימים מעליא טפי ואפילו בת יומא מעליא: אין עושין למילה חלוק לכתחילה אבל כורך עליה סמרטוט: מתניתין מרחיצין את הקטן בין לפני המילה ובין לאחר המילה ומזלפין עליו אבל לא בכלי. ואקשי היאך קתני מזלפין מכלל שרחיצה אסורה והא רישא דמתניתין קתני מרחיצין ופרקי' רב יהודה ורבה בר אבוה אמר כך סידור המשנה מרחיצין את הקטן בין לפני המילה ובין לאחר המילה. והרחצה זו כיצד היא ע"י זילוף היא ביד אבל לא בכלי. ואקשי עליהו רבה והא מרחיצין קתני וזילוף אינה רחיצה ופריק רבא משנתנו הא דקתני מרחיצין ביום ראשון של מילה אם היא שבת רחיצה כדרכו בין לפני המילה בין לאחר המילה וביום השלישי שחל להיות בשבת מזלפין ביד אבל לא בכלי ותניא כוותיה דרבא ואע"ג דתניא כוותיה לפום דקדוקא דמתניתין לא מיתוקמה כתירוציה דהא רבה כנפשיה אורי כשמעתיה ואיחלש ועיין במתניתין שפיר וחזא דלכאורה כתירוציה רהטא. וכי עיין בה דקיימא לן דאין עשה דחי לא תעשה ועשה ליגמר מנזיר דאתי עשה ודחי לא תעשה ועשה אלא מנזיר לא גמרינן שכן ישנן בשאלה ובארו כי דבר זה הוא מיוחד בו לבדו ולא בזולתו וכי בכל התורה כולה לא אתי עשה ודחי לא תעשה

רב נסים גאון

האזהרה עליו שלא יגלחנו שנאמר (במדבר ו) גדל פרע שער ראשו אחר שאמר תער לא יעלה על ראשו הרי הוא בדבר זה מוזהר בלאו ומצווה בעשה וחייב המצורע בעת טהרתו לגלח כל שער שבגופו שנאמר (ויקרא יד) והיה ביום השביעי יגלח את כל שערו וכשיתנגע הנזיר בצרעת ויגיע יום ז' שהוא חייב לגלח בו אמרו חכמים שמצות גילוח של צרעת דוחה עשה ולא תעשה שיש עליו לענין נזירותו וכי מה שאמר הכתוב לענין מצורע את ראשו אחר שאמר יגלח את כל שערו לא בא אלא לענין נזיר שנאמר בו תער לא יעבור על ראשו לומר כי זו המצוה אינו חייב בה אלא בעת שלא תהיה בו צרעת אבל בעת שיהיה בגופו צרעת יגלח את ראשו אפי' שער ראשו שהזהרתיו שלא יגלחנו בימי נזירותו חייב לגלח אם היה צרוע נתקיים לנו מזה שבנזיר מצורע לבדו יבא עשה ודחי לא תעשה ועשה ובראש מס' יבמות (דף ה) אמרו אלא

ועשה והזהר לשמור אלו העיקרים שפירשנו שמהן מתבארים לך כל דבר כשתמצא בתלמוד מעין אלו הענינים: **תינח** גדול דכתיב ביה בשר קטן נמי כתיב ביה בשר בינוני מגלן פי' כבר ידענו כי הקטנים פטורים ממצות והשכר והעונש הם תלויין בחיוב המצות ומאחר שנדע כי לא חייב הכתוב במצות אלא לפי שיש בו עניני החיוב כגון שהביא ב' שערות ושהגיע למספר שני האנשים ושיצא מגבול הנערות אז הוא בן עונשין וכיון שראינו שענש הכתוב מי שלא נימול שנאמר (בראשית יז) וערל זכר אשר לא ימול את בשר ערלתו ונכרתה וגו' ידענו כי דבר זה מיוחד הוא באנשים גדולים ולא בנערים ומצאנו כתב בו בשר ערלתו להודיענו שהמילה דוחה את הצרעת על דרך העיקר שהקדמנו דאתי עשה ודחי לא תעשה וכי בעת שתהיה בערלה בהרת ימול ויחתוך אותה וידחה מה שכתוב (דברים כד) השמר בנגע הצרעת והוצרכנו שיבאר לנו דבר זה להסיר מדעתנו מה שהיה עולה עליו שמה היינו סוברים כי זה שכתב (שם) לשמור מאד ולעשות הוא דבר מוסף על הלאו והוה ליה לא תעשה ועשה ואין המילה דוחה אותן שאין עשה דוחה את לא תעשה ועשה והסיר ממנו סברא זו והודיענו שהוא לא תעשה בלבד והמילה דוחה אותה וזהו שאמרו תינח גדול דכתב ביה בשר והקטן נמי שהוא בן ח' ימים נאמר בו וביום השמיני ימול בשר ערלתו ידענו כי המילה ביום ח' תדחה (עוד) את הצרעת נשאר לנו לשאול על הבינוני והוא שעברו עליו ח' ימים ולא נימול מפני מאורע שאירע לו כגון שהיה חולה או שהיה בו ספק התחיה המילה ראויה בו בעת שיש בהרת בערלתו או לא ולפיכך אמרו בינוני מנלן ובאה התשובה משם אביי דאתיא מבינייא ומשם רבא מילה בזמנה [לא] צריכא קרא כו' ופירוש על דעת אביי שהמילה מותרת בבינוני במקום שיש בהרת נלמוד מגדול וקטן כמו ששנינו (ריש ספרא) בבנין אב משני כתובים הצד השוה שבהן כו' וכן הוא הילוך הדבר בכאן כי הבינוני לא יתכן שנלמוד מן הגדול לפי שהגדול ענוש כרת לכך התירו בו הכתוב חתיכת הבהרת אבל הבינוני שאין בו חיוב כרת אין דבר זה מותר בו וכמו כן לא נלמוד דבר זה מן הקטן כי הקטן מילתו בזמנה ביום ח' והיא דוחה את השבת ולפיכך התיר הכתוב חתיכת הבהרת אבל הבינוני שאין מילתו בזמנה לא ומאחר שלא יכולנו ללמוד דבר זה מאחד מהן חיברנו אותם ביחד וקיימנו דבר עיקר מהם שהבינוני מותר לחתוך בהרת מערלתו וכן הילוכו של דבר בענין זה בינוני מנלן אמר אביי אתיא מבניינא מה לגדול שכן ענוש כרת קטן יוכיח שאינו ענוש כרת מה לקטן שכן מילה בזמנה גדול יוכיח שאין מילה בזמנה וחזר הדין הצד השוה שבהן שמילתו דוחה את הצרעת אף אני אביא בינוני שתהא מילתו דוחה את הצרעת ורבא לא הוצרך לדבר זה כי הוא סובר כי בשר ערלתו שנאמר בבן שמנת ימים לא בא להתיר מילת בן שמונת ימים במקום שיש בהרת כי זה נלמדנו מקל וחומר השתא שבת חמורה דוחה צרעת קלה לא כל שכן והואיל ואינו צריך לבן ח' ימים הועיל להתיר המילה בבינוני במקום שיש בהרת: **לא** צריכא אפי' ר' יהודה דאמר דבר שאינו מתכוין אסור כבר פירשנו זה בפ' כירה. לבדו ולא מילה שלא בזמנה

Mishnah In Mishnaic times it was customary to bathe the infant in hot water twice, once prior to the circumcision to enable him to withstand the ordeal, and once again afterward as a therapeutic measure. Failure to perform either of these washings possibly endangered the infant's life (see Gemara below). Hence, the Rabbis permitted otherwise forbidden hot-water bathing on the Sabbath (see above, 39b, 40a) when the circumcision is performed on that day. In addition, some consider the infant critically ill on the third day following *milah* and thus allow him to be bathed in hot water then as well, even though it is Shabbos.[1] The following Mishnah and Gemara discuss these bathings:

מַרְחִיצִין אֶת הַקָּטָן – **We may bathe the infant** in hot water[2] בֵּין לִפְנֵי הַמִּילָה וּבֵין לְאַחַר הַמִּילָה – **both before the circumcision and after the circumcision,**[3] וּמְזַלְּפִין עָלָיו בַּיָּד אֲבָל לֹא בִכְלִי – **and we may sprinkle** hot water **upon him by hand, but not with a utensil.**[4] רַבִּי אֶלְעָזָר בֶּן עֲזַרְיָה אוֹמֵר – **R' Elazar ben Azaryah says:** מַרְחִיצִין אֶת הַקָּטָן בַּיּוֹם הַשְּׁלִישִׁי שֶׁחָל לִהְיוֹת בְּשַׁבָּת – **We may bathe the infant on the third day** following his circumcision **when it falls on the Sabbath,**[5] שֶׁנֶּאֱמַר ,,וַיְהִי בַיּוֹם הַשְּׁלִישִׁי בִּהְיוֹתָם כֹּאֲבִים״ – **for it is stated:**[6] ***And it came to pass on the third day, when they were in pain.***[7]

סָפֵק וְאַנְדְּרוֹגִינוּס[8] – In the case of **a questionable one**[9] **or an androgyne,**[10] אֵין מְחַלְּלִין עָלָיו אֶת הַשַּׁבָּת – **we may not desecrate the Sabbath on his behalf.**[11] וְרַבִּי יְהוּדָה מַתִּיר בְּאַנְדְּרוֹגִינוּס – **But R' Yehudah permits** it **in [the case of] an androgyne.**[12]

Gemara The Gemara notes a contradiction between the first two statements of the Mishnah:

וְהָא אָמְרַתְּ רֵישָׁא מַרְחִיצִין – **But you,** the Tanna, **have stated** in **the first part** of the Mishnah that **we may bathe** the infant in hot water even in the normal manner, and then you stated that we may only sprinkle the water upon him by hand! What, indeed, do you mean to say?

The Gemara offers an interpretation:

רַב יְהוּדָה וְרַבָּה בַּר אֲבוּהּ דְּאָמְרֵי תַּרְוַיְיהוּ – **Rav Yehudah and Rabbah bar Avuha both say** that כֵּיצַד תָּנֵי – **[the second statement] is teaching how** the "bathing" mentioned in the first statement is to be performed.[13] מַרְחִיצִין אֶת הַקָּטָן – That is, the Tanna first tells us that WE MAY BATHE THE INFANT בֵּין לִפְנֵי מִילָה בֵּין לְאַחַר מִילָה – BOTH BEFORE the CIRCUMCISION AND AFTER the CIRCUMCISION – but not in the normal fashion. כֵּיצַד – **How,** then, shall we bathe him? The Tanna explains:

NOTES

1. Today, these bathings are not considered necessary to safeguard the child's health (*Orach Chaim* 331:9), due to changes in the human constitution over the course of centuries (*Mishnah Berurah* ibid. §31).

2. Heating the water is a preliminary to the mitzvah of *milah*. According to R' Eliezer (above, 130a), it may be performed even on the Sabbath; according to R' Akiva (ibid.), it may not. The Rishonim (above, 130b) discuss at length the permissibility of heating water on Shabbos for a circumcision through the agency of a non-Jew, according to R' Akiva. The Rishonim here also discuss the permissibility of heating water (even according to R' Akiva) for the post-*milah* bathing, when a possible danger to the infant's life already exists. See, however, *Meiri* סוד״ה מרחיצין.

3. With regard to the pre-*milah* bathing, when no danger to the infant yet exists, *Ran* explains that although the Rabbis disallowed bathing in hot water on the Sabbath (even when the water was heated beforehand), bathing an infant for circumcision was not included in the prohibition [i.e. the Rabbis did not require postponing the *milah* for the sake of their prohibition – (אִסּוּר שְׁבוּת) see above, 130b]. This is because the Rabbis enacted the prohibition at a time when bathhouse attendants were suspected of heating water on the Sabbath while claiming that it was heated on Friday. Since this suspicion is not relevant in *milah* situations [inasmuch as only a small amount of water is needed for bathing the infant], bathing for *milah* was never included in the prohibition. See also *Rashba* and *Ran MHK* ed.; see *Kesef Mishneh* to *Hil. Milah* 2:8 (at end) for another explanation. [*Ran MHK* ed. limits this leniency, however, to water that was heated *before* Shabbos; cf. *Rashba.*]

4. [I.e. not in a *somewhat* unusual manner, but only in a completely unusual one – see below, note 16.] The first statement of the Mishnah ("We may bathe . . .") implies that the infant may be bathed in the ordinary manner, while the second statement – in seeming contradiction – prohibits even sprinkling water upon him with a utensil, insisting on a *completely* unusual manner. The Gemara will immediately address this difficulty (*Rashi*). [See *Rashash* for a discussion of the etymology of מְזַלְּפִין.]

5. The Gemara will identify the points of contention between the Tanna Kamma and R' Elazar ben Azaryah.

6. *Genesis* 34:25, with regard to the male population of Shechem, who had circumcised themselves.

7. On the third day after the males of Shechem were circumcised, Shimon and Levy seized the opportunity to attack the city. The verse thus implies that on the third day the people were especially vulnerable because the pain is very acute, from which we may derive that a danger to the infant's life exists on the third day following circumcision.

The Rishonim debate whether the verse teaches that the danger exists *also* on the third day (i.e. and certainly on the [first and] second days as well), or whether it exists only on [the first and] third days. *Ramban, Rashba, Ritva* (*MHK* ed.) and *Rashi* (see here ד״ה אלא אי אמרת, and above, 86a ד״ה מנין) all subscribe to the former view, while *Rif* and *Rambam* (*Hil. Milah* 2:8; see also *Hil. Shabbos* 2:14 with *Maggid Mishneh*) adopt the latter view. Hence, according to *Ramban* et al., R' Elazar's leniency applies to the second day as well; according to *Rambam* and *Rif,* it does not.

The Rishonim explain that although the danger to life was even greater on the first and second days (as per the first view above), Shimon and Levi nonetheless waited until the third day to attack because the condition of weakness, a cumulative result of the pain, was greatest on that day.

8. *Meiri* implies that a new Mishnah begins here; cf. *Sfas Emes.*

9. I.e. a baby possibly born during the eighth month of pregnancy (*Rashi*).

The ordinary incubation period for a fetus is nine months. Some fetuses mature earlier and are born during the seventh month. However, the Sages determined that a child born after being formed in eight months cannot live, and halachah thus considers him not to be alive (the Gemara's expression is: *he is like a stone*). Accordingly, his circumcision does not override the Sabbath restrictions. Consequently, if there is uncertainty as to whether a child was born during the eighth month of pregnancy, his circumcision is not performed on the Sabbath either (see *Rashi*). A "seventh-month" child, however, is considered viable, and his circumcision does override the Sabbath (Gemara below, 135a). Cf. *Meiri* and *Tos. R' Akiva Eiger* (160), who – citing the Gemara below (136a) – understand that the Mishnah refers to a case where a doubt exists as to which day is the child's eighth day after birth.

10. An individual possessing both male and female organs (*Tiferes Yisrael*).

This person's sexual status in matters of halachah is doubtful (*Rashi* below, 135a), and the obligation to circumcise him is therefore uncertain. See *Gra* to *Yoreh Deah* 262:7; cf. *Tosafos* below, 135a ד״ה ולא, with *Maharsha.*

11. Since in both cases the obligation to circumcise is uncertain, the *milah* is postponed until after the Sabbath.

12. As the Gemara explains below (137a), R' Yehudah derives an absolute *milah* obligation for such an infant from an inclusionary verse (*Rashi*).

13. That is, the Tanna never meant in the first statement that the bathing should be performed in the normal fashion (*Rashi*).

עין משפט נר מצוה

כח א מיי׳ פ"ב מהל׳ מילה הלכה ח ופ"כ מהל׳ שבת הלכה יד סמג עשין כח טוש"ע א"ח סי׳ שלא סעיף ט:
כט ב ג מיי׳ פכ"א מהל׳ שבת הלכה כו טוש"ע א"ח סי׳ שכח סעיף כב:
ל ד ה מיי׳ שם טוש"ע שם סעיף כג:

מתני׳ מרחיצין את הקטן בין לפני המילה ובין לאחר המילה ומזלפין עליו ביד אבל לא בכלי ר"א בן עזריה א) אומר מרחיצין את הקטן ביום השלישי שחל להיות בשבת שנאמר א) ויהי ביום השלישי בהיותם כואבים ספק ואנדרוגינוס אין מחללין עליו את השבת ורבי יהודה מתיר באנדרוגינוס: **גמ׳** והא אמרת רישא מרחיצין רב יהודה ורבה בר אבוה דאמרי תרוייהו כיצד תני מרחיצין את הקטן בין לפני מילה בין לאחר מילה כיצד מזלפין עליו ביד אבל לא בכלי אמר רבא והא מרחיצין קתני אלא אמר רבא הכי קתני מרחיצין את הקטן בין מלפני מילה בין לאחר המילה ביום הראשון כדרכו וביום השלישי שחל להיות בשבת מזלפין עליו ביד אבל לא בכלי ר"א בן עזריה אומר מרחיצין את הקטן ביום השלישי שחל להיות בשבת שנאמר ויהי ביום השלישי בהיותם כואבים תניא כוותיה דרבא מרחיצין הקטן בין לפני מילה בין לאחר מילה ביום ראשון כדרכו וביום השלישי שחל להיות בשבת מזלפין עליו ביד ר"א בן עזריה אומר מרחיצין את הקטן ביום השלישי שחל להיות בשבת ואע"פ שאין ראיה לדבר זכר לדבר שנאמר ויהי ביום השלישי בהיותם כואבים וכשהן מזלפין אין מזלפין לא בכוס ולא בקערה ולא בכלי אלא ביד אתאן לתנא קמא מאי אע"פ שאין ראיה לדבר זכר לדבר משום דגדול לא סליק ביה בישרא הייא קטן סליק ביה בישרא הייא ההוא דאתא לקמיה דרבא אורי ליה כשמעתיה איחלש רבא אמר אנא בהדי תרגימנא דסבי למה לי אמרו ליה רבנן לרבא והתניא כוותיה דמר אמר להו מתניתין כוותייהו דיקא ממאי מדקאמר רבי אלעזר בן עזריה אומר מרחיצין את הקטן ביום השלישי שחל להיות בשבת אי אמרת בשלמא תנא קמא מזלפין קאמר היינו דקאמר ליה ר"א בן עזריה מרחיצין אלא אי אמרת תנא קמא מרחיצין ביום הראשון קאמר ומזלפין ביום השלישי האי רבי אלעזר בן עזריה אומר מרחיצין אף מרחיצין מיבעי ליה כי אתא רב דימי אמר רבי אלעזר הלכה כר"א בן עזריה הוו בה במערבא הרחצת כל גופו או הרחצת מילה אמר להו ההוא מרבנן ורבי יעקב שמיה מסתברא הרחצת כל גופו דאי ס"ד הרחצת מילה מי גרע מחמין על גבי מכה דאמר רב אין מונעין חמין ושמן מעל גבי מכה בשבת מתקיף לה רב יוסף ולא שני לך בין חמין שהוחמו בשבת לחמין שהוחמו מע"ש מתקיף לה רב דימי וממאי דהכא בחמין שהוחמו בשבת פליגי דילמא בחמין שהוחמו בע"ש פליגי אמר אביי אנא בעאי דאישני ליה וקדם רב יוסף ושני ליה מפני שסכנה הוא לו איתמר נמי כי אתא רבין א"ר אבהו א"ר אלעזר ואמרי לה א"ר אבהו א"ר יוחנן א הלכה כר"א בן עזריה בין בחמין שהוחמו בשבת בין בחמין שהוחמו מע"ש בין הרחצת כל גופו בין הרחצת מילה מפני שסכנה היא לו: גופא אמר רב אין מונעין חמין ושמן מעל גבי מכה בשבת ושמואל אמר נותן חוץ למכה ושותת ויורד למכה מיתיבי ב אין נותנין שמן וחמין על גבי מוך ליתן על גבי מכה בשבת התם משום סחיטה תא שמע אין נותנין חמין ושמן על גבי מוך שעל גבי מכה בשבת התם נמי משום סחיטה תניא כוותיה דשמואל ג אין נותנין חמין ושמן על גבי מכה בשבת אבל נותנין חוץ למכה ושותת ויורד למכה תנו רבנן ד נותנין על גבי המכה מוך יבש וספוג יבש אבל לא גמי יבש ולא כתיתין יבשין קשיא כתיתין אכתיתין לא קשיא ה הא בחדתי הא בעתיקי אמר אביי שמע מינה הני כתיתין מסו: ספק ואנדרוגינוס כו': תנו רבנן ב) ערלתו ודאי דוחה את השבת ולא

רש"י

מתני׳ ומזלפין עליו. את החמין: ביד. אבל לא בכלי וגמ׳ פריך הא אמרת רישא מרחיצין דמשמע כדרכו והדר תני אפילו לזלף עליו בכלי אסור: ספק. כגון ספק בן ח׳ חדשים [וספק בן ט׳] דהוא כאבן בעלמא ולאו מילתו דוחה שבת (וספק בן ט׳): ר׳ יהודה מתיר באנדרוגינוס. דלאתרבי מקרא כדמפרש בגמ׳ לקמן: **גמ׳** והא אמרת רישא מרחיצין. ואפילו כדרכו: כיצד קתני. מרחיצין דרישא לאו כדרכו הוא דהנא סיפא לפרושי כיצד מרחיצין כגון לזלף ביד ואפילו ביום ראשון: תניא כוותיה דרבא כו׳ ה"ג ביום השלישי מזלפין עליו ביד ולא גרסינן אבל לא בכלי: אתאן לת"ק. הך סיפא תנא קמא אמרה דאילו ר"א אפילו הרחצה כדרכו שרי: משום דגדול לא סליק בישרא הייא. היינו טעמא דמעשה שכם לאו ראיה גמורה היא משום דגדול אין מכה שבבשרו מעלה ארוכה מהר אבל קטן נתרפא מידי סכנתו מהר: אורי ליה כשמעתיה. התיר לו הרחצה כדרכו ביום ראשון שחל להיות בשבת: איחלש. נעשה חולה והיה דואג שמא על כך נענש: אמר בהדי תרגמנא דסבי למה לי. מה היה לי לחלוק כנגד זקנים הללו רב יהודה ורבה בר אבוה שפירשו שאסור להרחיץ: אי אמרת בשלמא ת"ק מזלפין. ביום ראשון קאמר ולא איירי בהרחצה כלל אלא בזילוף היינו דאתא ר"א בן עזריה ופליג ואמר מרחיצין: אלא אי אמרת. תנא קמא נמי מרחיצין אמר בשני הימים ולא פליג ר"א אלא ביום שלישי דקאמר ת"ק מזלפין אף מרחיצין ביום השלישי מיבעי ליה: הוו בה. דייקי בה: דאי ס"ד הרחצת מילה מי גרע מחמין על גבי מכה. דשרי והכא אסרי רבנן בשלישי (ג גמרי׳) ולא שני כו׳. והכא גבי מילה בהוחמו בשבת עסקינן הלכך בשלישי דליכא סכנתא לא: אמר אביי אנא בעאי דאישני ליה. אני הייתי רוצה לתרץ אתקפתא זו דכשני ליה רב יוסף מפני שסכנה היא לו: וקדם רב יוסף ושנייא ליה. דוחי מתניתין חמין שהוחמו בשבת נמי שרי בימים הראשונים ולר"א אף בשלישי מפני שמניעת חמין סכנה היא לו: אין נותנין כו׳. קס"ד גזרה משום סחיטת סמנין כשמואל דלטעמיה משום הכי הוא והיינו דקאמר אבל נותן חוץ למכה דלא מוכחא מילתא דלרפואה: מוך יבש וספוג יבש. דלאו לרפואה היא אלא שלא ישרטו בגדיו הקשים מכתו: אבל לא כתיתין יבשים (א) וגמי יבש. חתיכות בגדים דקות משום דמסו וגזרו משום שחיקת סמנין: קשיא כתיתין אכתיתין. רישא שרי מוך יבש דהיינו כתיתין וסיפא אסר כתיתין: חדתי. חדשים שלא היו על גבי מכה מעולם מסו עתיקי לא מסו: ה"ג שמע מינה הני כתיתין מסו: ערלתו ודאי דוחה השבת. דבהאי קרא וביום השמיני דילפינן מיניה אפילו בשבת כתיב בסיפיה ערלתו דמשמע מיעוטא ערלתו של זה ולא של אחר ולמעוטי ספק אתא:
אנדרוגינוס

תוספות

מי גרע מחמין על גבי מכה. והיכי אסרי רבנן בשלישי אע"ג דליכא למימר דרב אמרה למילתיה כר"א בן עזריה דפסקינן לעיל הלכתא כוותיה משמע ליה דלכ"ע קאמר ועוד דאפילו לר"א בן עזריה פריך דמשמע דשרי בשלישי משום סכנה מדמייתי קרא ויהי ביום השלישי וכל איירי במכה שאין בה סכנה: **ואין** מונעין חמין ושמן. פירש ה"ר יוסף פורת בשם רבינו שמואל דבמעורבת יחד איירי דאי כל חד לחודיה מאי קמ"ל בשמן מתני׳ היא בפ׳ שמנה שרצים (לעיל דף קיא.) אבל סך הוא את השמן והיינו אפילו על גבי מכה מדקתני בני מלכים סכין ע"ג מכותיהן שמן וורד מכלל דבשאר שמן מותר לאחר אפילו ע"ג מכה ושמואל נמי היכי הוה פליג: ולא

רבינו חננאל

מקוטמא לאולמא ממקום הדק לעבה: **ת"ר** דברים שאין עושין למילה בשבת עושין לה ביו"ט שוחקין כמון וטורפין לה יין ושמן יין בפ"ע ושמן בפ"ע אבל ע"י ליכא [אסור]. פי׳ ליכא עירוב יין ושמן להוליך השמן בתוך היין על [ידי] עירבוב. (אבל) א"ל אביי לרבה מהו לגבן. פי׳ לגבן ביו"ט לקפות גבינה לקבץ פיתותי החלב הקפוי ולעשותם חריץ של גבינה. א"ל אסור לגבן. א"ל והלא גיבון כמו לישת העיסה שנותן מים בקמח ומולל בידיו ועושה פתיתין ומוסיף מים ומקבץ הפתיתין ועושה אותם עיסה. כך מקפה החלב בטוכמסו ואחר שיקפה בכלי ויעמוד מכניס ידו ופיתתו. ואח"כ מכניס ידו ומגבן מתוך הכיס. הנה גיבון ולישה מלאכתן שוה מפני מה זה מותר וזה אסור ופירק לו קמח אי אפשר לאוכלו אלא ע"י לישה ביומו. והחלב אפשר לאכלו חלב או לעשותו גבינה בערב. אקשינן עלה והא אמרו נהרדעי גבינה בת יומא מעליא והנה היא כמו הלישה וכשם שהפת חמה מעליא כך הגבינה בת יומא מעליא ופריק ליה הכי קאמר אפילו בת יומא מעליא מכלל שבת שנים ושלשה ימים מעליא טפי ואפילו בת יומא מעליא: **אין** עושין למילה חלוק לכתחילה אבל כורך עליה סמרטוט: **מתניתין** **מרחיצין** את הקטן בין לפני המילה ובין לאחר המילה ומזלפין עליו אבל לא בכלי. ואקשי היאך קתני מזלפין מכלל שרחיצה אסורה והא רישא דמתניתין קתני מרחיצין ופרקי׳ רב יהודה ורבה בר אבוה אמר כך סידור המשנה מרחיצין את הקטן בין לפני המילה ובין לאחר המילה. והרחצה זו כיצד היא ע"י זילוף היא ביד אבל לא בכלי. ואקשי עליהו רבה והא מרחיצין קתני וזילוף אינה רחיצה ופריק רבא משנתנו הא דקתני מרחיצין ביום ראשון של מילה אם היא שבת רחיצה כדרכו בין לפני המילה בין לאחר המילה וביום השלישי שחל להיות בשבת מזלפין ביד אבל לא בכלי ותניא כוותיה דרבא ואע"ג דתניא כוותיה לפום דקדוקא דמתניתין לא מיתוקמה כתירוציה דהא רבה כנפשיה אורי כשמעתיה ואיחלש ועיין במתניתין שפיר וחזא דלכאורה כתירוציה רהטא. וכי עיין בה

מסורת הש"ס

א) לעיל פו. ע"ש, ב) רש"ל מ"ז ואו"ל למחוק ולא גרסינן הספקים כצד לפי דמפר דליקו כותיהו ולא הסדר מ"ק אפי׳ לזלף ביום ג׳.

הגהות הב"ח

(א) רש"י ד"ה אבל לא כתיתין יבשים חתיכות כצ"ל ותיבות וגמי יבש נמחק:

תורה אור השלם

א) וַיְהִי בַיּוֹם הַשְּׁלִישִׁי בִּהְיוֹתָם כֹּאֲבִים וַיִּקְחוּ שְׁנֵי בְנֵי יַעֲקֹב שִׁמְעוֹן וְלֵוִי אֲחֵי דִינָה אִישׁ חַרְבּוֹ וַיָּבֹאוּ עַל הָעִיר בֶּטַח וַיַּהַרְגוּ כָּל זָכָר: (בראשית לד, כה)
ב) וּבַיּוֹם הַשְּׁמִינִי יִמּוֹל בְּשַׂר עָרְלָתוֹ: (ויקרא יב, ג)

ליקוטי רש"י

מרחיצין את הקטן ביום השלישי. לפי שביום שלישי מסוכן הוא [לעיל פו.]. ויהי ביום השלישי בהיותם כואבים. ולאו למימרא דביום השלישי כאיב ליה טפי מיומא קמא אלא לכך המתינו שמעון ולוי עד יום השלישי כדי שיהו חלושין ביותר שנכאבו ג׳ ימים וכל כמה שנוקף כאיב טפי [ר"ן נדרים לא: ועי׳ ר"ן כאן]. אנדרוגינוס. שיש לו זכרות ונקבות [רשב"ם ב"ב קכו.].

רב נסים גאון

האזהרה עליו שלא יגלחנו שנאמר (במדבר ו) גדל פרע שער ראשו אחר שאמר תער לא יעלה על ראשו הרי הוא בדבר זה מוזהר בלאו ומצווה בעשה וחייב המצורע בעת טהרתו לגלח כל שער שבגופו שנאמר (ויקרא יד) והיה ביום השביעי יגלח את כל שערו וכשיתנגע הנזיר בצרעת ויגיע יום ז׳ שהוא חייב לגלח בו אמרו חכמים שמצות גילוח של צרעת דוחה עשה ולא תעשה שיש עליו לענין נזירותו וכי מה שאמר הכתוב לענין מצורע את ראשו אחר שאמר יגלח את כל שערו לא בא אלא לענין נזיר שנאמר בו תער לא יעבור על ראשו לומר כי זה המצוה אינו חייב בה אלא בעת שלא תהיה בו צרעת אבל בעת שיהיה בגופו צרעת יגלח את ראשו אפי׳ שער ראשו שהזהירתו שלא יגלחנו בימי נזירותו חייב לגלח אם היה צרוע נתקיים לנו מזה שבנזיר מצורע לבדו יבא עשה ודחי לא תעשה ועשה ובראש מס׳ יבמות (דף ה) אמרו אלא דקיימא לן דאין עשה דחי לא תעשה ועשה ליגמר מנזיר דאתי עשה ודחי לא תעשה ועשה אלא מנזיר לא גמרינן שכן ישנו בשאלה ובארו כי דבר זה הוא מיוחד בו לבדו ולא בזולתו וכי בכל התורה כולה לא אתי עשה ודחי לא תעשה ועשה והזהר לשמור אלו העיקרים שפירשנו שמהן מתבארים לך כל דבר כשתמצא בתלמוד מעין אלו הענינים: **תינח** גדול דכתיב ביה בשר קטן נמי כתיב ביה בשר בינוני מנלן פי׳ כבר ידענו כי הקטנים פטורים ממצות והשכר והעונש הם תלויין בחיוב המצות ומאחר שנדע כי לא חייב הכתוב במצות אלא לפי שיש בו עניני החיוב כגון שהביא ב׳ שערות ושהגיע למספר שני האנשים ושיצא מגבול הנערות אז הוא בן עונשין וכיון שראינו שענש הכתוב מי שלא נימול שנאמר (בראשית יז) וערל זכר אשר לא ימול את בשר ערלתו ונכרתה וגו׳ ידענו כי דבר זה מיוחד הוא באנשים גדולים ולא בנערים ומצאנו כתב בו בשר ערלתו להודיענו שהמילה דוחה את הצרעת על דרך העיקר שהקדמנו דאתי עשה ודחי לא תעשה וכי בעת שתהיה בערלה בהרת ימול ויחתוך אותה וידחה מה שכתוב (דברים כד) השמר בנגע הצרעת והוצרכנו שיבאר לנו דבר זה להסיר מדעתנו מה שהיה עולה עליו שמה היינו סוברים כי זה שכתב (שם) לשמור מאד ולעשות הוא דבר מוסף על הלאו והוה ליה לא תעשה ועשה ואין המילה דוחה אותן שאין עשה דוחה את לא תעשה ועשה והסיר ממנו סברא זו והודיענו שהוא לא תעשה בלבד והמילה דוחה אותה וזהו שאמרו תינח גדול דכתב ביה בשר והקטן נמי שהוא בן ח׳ ימים נאמר בו וביום השמיני ימול בשר ערלתו ידענו כי המילה ביום ח׳ תדחה (עוד) את הצרעת נשאר לנו לשאול על הבינוני והוא שעברו עליו ח׳ ימים ולא נימול מפני מאורע שאירע לו כגון שהיה חולה או שהיה בו ספק התחיה המילה ראויה בו בעת שיש בהרת בערלתו או לא ולפיכך אמרו בינוני מנלן ובאה התשובה משם אביי דאתיא מבינייא ומשם רבא מילה בזמנה [לא] צריכא קרא כו׳ ופירוש על דעת אביי שהמילה מותרת בבינוני במקום שיש בהרת נלמוד מגדול וקטן כמו ששנינו (ריש ספרא) בבנין אב משני כתובים הצד השוה שבהן כו׳ וכן הוא הילוך הדבר בכאן כי הבינוני לא יתכן שנלמוד מן הגדול לפי שהגדול ענוש כרת לכך התירו בו הכתוב חתיכת הבהרת אבל הבינוני שאין בו חיוב כרת אין דבר זה מותר בו וכמו כן לא נלמוד דבר זה מן הקטן כי הקטן מילתו בזמנה ביום ח׳ והיא דוחה את השבת ולפיכך התיר הכתוב חתיכת הבהרת אבל הבינוני שאין מילתו בזמנה לא ומאחר שלא יכולנו ללמוד דבר זה מאחד מהן חיברנו אותם ביחד וקיימנו דבר עיקר מהם שהבינוני מותר לחתוך בהרת מערלתו וכן הילוכו של דבר בענין זה בינוני מנלן אמר אביי אתיא מבינייא מה לגדול שכן ענוש כרת קטן יוכיח שאינו ענוש כרת מה לקטן שכן מילה בזמנה גדול יוכיח שאין מילה בזמנה וחזר הדין הצד השוה שבהן שמילתו דוחה את הצרעת אף אני אביא בינוני שתהא מילתו דוחה את הצרעת ורבא לא הוצרך לדבר זה כי הוא סובר כי בשר ערלתו שנאמר בבן שמנת ימים לא בא להתיר מילת בן שמונת ימים במקום שיש בהרת כי זה נלמדנו מקל וחומר השתא שבת חמורה דוחה צרעת קלה לא כל שכן והואיל ואינו צריך לבן ח׳ ימים הועיל להתיר המילה בבינוני במקום שיש בהרת: **לא** צריכא אפי׳ ר׳ יהודה דאמר דבר שאינו מתכוין אסור כבר פירשנו זה בפ׳ כירה. לבדו ולא מילה שלא בזמנה

מְזַלְּפִין עָלָיו בַּיָּד אֲבָל לֹא בִּכְלִי – WE MAY SPRINKLE hot water UPON HIM BY HAND, BUT NOT WITH A UTENSIL.[14]

This interpretation is challenged:

אָמַר רָבָא – Rava said: וְהָא מַרְחִיצִין קָתָנֵי – But [the Tanna Kamma] states, WE MAY BATHE, which implies that we may bathe the infant normally! If he meant sprinkling, he should have said so. – ? –

Another interpretation is advanced:

אֶלָּא אָמַר רָבָא – Rather, Rava said: הָכִי קָתָנֵי – [The Tanna Kamma] actually stated thus: מַרְחִיצִין אֶת הַקָּטָן – We may bathe the infant in hot water, בֵּין מִלִּפְנֵי מִילָה בֵּין לְאַחַר הַמִּילָה – both before the circumcision and after the circumcision, בַּיּוֹם הָרִאשׁוֹן כְּדַרְכּוֹ – on the first day in the normal fashion; וּבַיּוֹם הַשְּׁלִישִׁי שֶׁחָל לִהְיוֹת בְּשַׁבָּת – and on the third day, when it falls on the Sabbath, מְזַלְּפִין עָלָיו בַּיָּד אֲבָל לֹא בִּכְלִי – we may sprinkle hot water upon him by hand, but not with a utensil. רַבִּי אֶלְעָזָר בֶּן עֲזַרְיָה אוֹמֵר – And in disagreement with the Tanna Kamma's second ruling R' Elazar ben Azaryah says: מַרְחִיצִין אֶת הַקָּטָן בַּיּוֹם הַשְּׁלִישִׁי שֶׁחָל לִהְיוֹת בְּשַׁבָּת – We may bathe the infant in the normal manner even on the third day when it falls on the Sabbath, שֶׁנֶּאֱמַר ,,וַיְהִי בַיּוֹם הַשְּׁלִישִׁי בִּהְיוֹתָם כֹּאֲבִים" – for it is stated: *And it came to pass on the third day, when they were in pain.*[15]

The Gemara adduces Tannaic support for Rava's interpretation:

תַּנְיָא כְּוָותֵיהּ דְּרָבָא – It was taught in a Baraisa in accordance with the interpretation of Rava: מַרְחִיצִין הַקָּטָן בֵּין לִפְנֵי מִילָה בֵּין לְאַחַר מִילָה – WE MAY BATHE THE INFANT, BOTH BEFORE the CIRCUMCISION AND AFTER the CIRCUMCISION, בַּיּוֹם רִאשׁוֹן כְּדַרְכּוֹ – ON THE FIRST DAY IN THE NORMAL FASHION; וּבַיּוֹם הַשְּׁלִישִׁי שֶׁחָל לִהְיוֹת בְּשַׁבָּת – AND ON THE THIRD DAY, WHEN IT FALLS ON THE SABBATH, מְזַלְּפִין עָלָיו בַּיָּד – WE MAY SPRINKLE hot water UPON HIM BY HAND. רַבִּי אֶלְעָזָר בֶּן עֲזַרְיָה אוֹמֵר – R' ELAZAR BEN AZARYAH SAYS: מַרְחִיצִין אֶת הַקָּטָן בַּיּוֹם הַשְּׁלִישִׁי שֶׁחָל לִהְיוֹת בְּשַׁבָּת – WE MAY BATHE THE INFANT in the normal manner even ON THE THIRD DAY WHEN IT FALLS ON THE SABBATH, וְאַף עַל פִּי שֶׁאֵין רְאָיָה לַדָּבָר – AND EVEN THOUGH THERE IS NO absolute Scriptural PROOF FOR THE MATTER, זֵכֶר לַדָּבָר שֶׁנֶּאֱמַר – there is A Scriptural ALLUSION TO THE MATTER, FOR IT IS STATED: ,,וַיְהִי בַיּוֹם הַשְּׁלִישִׁי בִּהְיוֹתָם כֹּאֲבִים" – *AND IT CAME TO PASS ON THE THIRD DAY, WHEN THEY WERE IN PAIN.* וּכְשֶׁהֵן מְזַלְּפִין – AND WHEN THEY SPRINKLE hot water upon the infant, אֵין מְזַלְּפִין לֹא בְּכוֹס וְלֹא בִּקְעָרָה וְלֹא בִּכְלִי – THEY MAY SPRINKLE WITH NEITHER A CUP, NOR A PLATE, NOR A VESSEL; אֶלָּא בַּיָּד – RATHER, they must do so BY HAND.[16]

The Gemara comments:

אֲתָאן לְתַנָּא קַמָּא – With the last ruling,[17] we have come back to the opinion of the Tanna Kamma.[18]

The Gemara inquires regarding one point of the Baraisa:

מַאי אַף עַל פִּי שֶׁאֵין רְאָיָה לַדָּבָר זֵכֶר לַדָּבָר – What is meant by the statement, "AND EVEN THOUGH THERE IS NO PROOF FOR THE MATTER, [there is] AN ALLUSION TO THE MATTER"? The verse expressly states that on the third day following circumcision the men of Shechem experienced great pain, and were presumably in physical danger. – ? –

The Gemara answers:

מִשּׁוּם דְּגָדוֹל לֹא סָלִיק בִּישְׂרָא הָיָיא – This is not an absolute proof because in the case of an adult, wounded flesh does not heal[19] quickly, קָטָן סָלִיק בֵּיהּ בִּישְׂרָא הָיָיא – whereas in the case of a child, wounded flesh does heal quickly.[20]

The Gemara records a related incident:

הַהוּא דַּאֲתָא לְקַמֵּיהּ דְּרָבָא – There was once a certain [person] who came before Rava to inquire whether he was permitted to bathe an infant normally on the day of circumcision, which was the Sabbath. אוֹרֵי לֵיהּ כִּשְׁמַעְתֵּיהּ – [Rava] instructed [the man] according to his own teaching,[21] answering in the affirmative. אִיחַלַּשׁ רָבָא – Subsequently, Rava became weak and ill, and began to worry that his illness was a punishment for ruling as he did. אָמַר – He said to himself: אֲנָא בַּהֲדֵי תַּרְגִּימְנָא דְּסָבֵי לָמָּה לִי – Why did I have to take issue with the interpretation of the elders, Rav Yehudah and Rabbah bar Avuha?[22] אָמְרוּ לֵיהּ רַבָּנָן לְרָבָא – Whereupon the Rabbis said to Rava: וְהָתַנְיָא כְּוָותֵיהּ דְּמָר – But it was taught in a Baraisa in accordance with master's (Rava's) interpretation of the Mishnah! Why does he now have doubts? אָמַר לְהוּ – [Rava] said to them in reply: מַתְנִיתִין כְּוָותַיְיהוּ דַּיְקָא – Although the Baraisa conforms with my interpretation of the Mishnah, the wording of the Mishnah itself is more precise according to their interpretation. מִמַּאי – From what evidence do I say this? מִדְּקָאָמַר רַבִּי אֶלְעָזָר בֶּן עֲזַרְיָה אוֹמֵר – From that which [the Mishnah] states, R' ELAZAR BEN AZARYAH SAYS: מַרְחִיצִין אֶת הַקָּטָן בַּיּוֹם הַשְּׁלִישִׁי שֶׁחָל לִהְיוֹת בְּשַׁבָּת – WE MAY BATHE THE INFANT ON THE THIRD DAY WHEN IT FALLS ON THE SABBATH. אִי אָמְרַתְּ בִּשְׁלָמָא תַּנָּא קַמָּא מְזַלְּפִין קָאָמַר – Now, it is well if you say the Tanna Kamma stated that we must sprinkle even on the first day, and he never mentioned normal bathing at all; הַיְינוּ דְּקָאָמַר לֵיהּ רַבִּי אֶלְעָזָר בֶּן עֲזַרְיָה מַרְחִיצִין – this is why R' Elazar ben Azaryah came and said to him in utter disagreement: "We may actually bathe the infant." אֶלָּא אִי אָמְרַתְּ תַּנָּא קַמָּא מַרְחִיצִין בַּיּוֹם הָרִאשׁוֹן קָאָמַר – But if you say the Tanna Kamma also stated that we may bathe the infant on the first day and the second, וּמְזַלְּפִין בַּיּוֹם הַשְּׁלִישִׁי – and he stated that we sprinkle only on the third day,[23]

NOTES

14. The Tanna Kamma holds that this unusual method must be employed on the day of circumcision [and that it is forbidden even to sprinkle on the third day; see *Maharsha* and *Leshon HaZahav,* and see note 26 below]. R' Elazar ben Azaryah maintains, however, that bathing normally is permitted on all three days (*Rashi;* see also *Rashi* below ד"ה אי, and note 7 above). See *Ran* to *Rif, Chidushei HaRan* and *Ritva MHK* ed.

15. According to Rava, both the Tanna Kamma and R' Elazar ben Azaryah hold that normal bathing is permitted on the first two days. They argue only with regard to the third day: The Tanna Kamma maintains that normal bathing is then forbidden, and R' Elazar allows it (see *Rashi* below ד"ה אלא אי אמרת; see also *Ritva MHK* ed.).

16. It would appear that sprinkling with a utensil is not a sufficient deviation from the norm.

17. "And when they sprinkle etc."

18. [The anonymous final statement is a resumption of the Tanna Kamma's utterance and not a continuation of R' Elazar ben Azaryah's words, inasmuch as R' Elazar permits even normal bathing on the third day (*Rashi*).] The Baraisa thus confirms Rava's interpretation of the Mishnah – that the Tanna Kamma and R' Elazar argue only with regard to the third day (see note 15 above).

19. Literally: grow.

20. The adult males of Shechem experienced great pain even on the third day after circumcision because the wound of an adult is slow to heal. An infant, on the other hand, heals quickly. Perhaps, then, the third day for an infant is not sufficiently dangerous to warrant the leniency of a normal bathing (see *Rashi*). See *Sfas Emes.*

21. According to Rava's interpretation of the Mishnah, both the Tanna Kamma and R' Elazar ben Azaryah maintain that normal bathing is permitted on the first two days following *milah.*

22. Who understood that in the Tanna Kamma's view, normal bathing is prohibited even on the day of circumcision. Rava was ruing his failure to rule in accordance with the other sages' stringent interpretation of the Tanna Kamma's opinion.

23. I.e. if the Tanna Kamma concurs with R' Elazar ben Azaryah with regard to the first and second days, and argues with him only regarding the third day – which is Rava's own interpretation (see *Rashi*).

כח א מיי' פ"ב מהל' מילה הלכה ט ופ"ב מהל' שבת הלכה יד סמג עשין כח טוש"ע א"ח סי' שלא סעיף ט:
כט ב ג מיי' פכ"א מהל' שבת הלכה כה טוש"ע א"ח סי' שכח סעיף כב:
ל ד ה מיי' שם טוש"ע שם סעיף כג:

רבינו חננאל

מקוטמא לאולמא ממקום הדק לעבה: ת"ר דברים שאין עושין לו בשבת עושין לה ביו"ט שוחקין כמון וטורפין לה יין ושמן יין בש"ע אבל ע"י ליכא [אסור]. פי' ליבא עירוב יין ושמן להוליך השמן בתוך היין על [ידי] עירובו. (אבל) א"ל אביי לרבה מהו לגבן. פי' לגבן ביו"ט לקפות גבינה לקבץ פיתותי החלב הקפוי ולעשותם חריץ של גבינה. א"ל אסור לגבן. א"ל והלא גיבון כמו לישת העיסה שנותן מים בקמח ומולל בידיו ועושה פתיתין ומוסיף מים ומקבץ הפתיתין ועושה אותם עיסה. כך מקפה החלב בשטכמוס ואחר שיקפה בכלי ויעמוד מכניס ידו ופותח. ואח"כ מכניס ידו ומגבן מתוך הכיס. הנה גיבון ולישה מלאכתן שוה מפני מה זה מותר וזה אסור ופריק לו קמח אי אפשר לאוכלו אלא ע"י לישה ביומו. והחלב אפשר לאכלו חלב או לעשותו גבינה בערב. אקשינן עלה והא אמרו נהרדעי גבינה בת יומא מעליא והנה היא כמו הלישה וכשם שהפת חמה מעליא כך הגבינה בת יומא מעליא ופריק ליה הכי קאמר אפילו בת יומא מעליא מכלל שבת שנים ושלשה ימים מעליא ספי מעליא בת יומא מעליא: אין עושין למילה חלוק לכתחילה אבל כורך עליה סמרטוט: מתניתין מרחיצין את הקטן בין לפני המילה ובין לאחר המילה ומזלפין עליו אבל לא בכלי. ואקשי היאך קתני מזלפין מכלל שרחיצה אסורה והא רישא דמתניתין קתני מרחיצין ופרקי' רב יהודה ורבה בר אבוה אמר כך סידור המשנה מרחיצין את הקטן בין לפני המילה ובין לאחר המילה. והרחצה זו רחיצה היא ע"י זילוף היא ביד אבל לא בכלי. ואקשי' עליהו רבה והא מרחיצין קתני וזילוף אינה רחיצה ופריק רבא משנתנו הא דקתני מרחיצין ביום ראשון של מילה אם היא שבת רחיצה כדרכו בין לפני המילה בין לאחר המילה וביום השלישי שחל להיות בשבת מזלפין ביד אבל לא בכלי ותניא כוותיה דרבא ואע"ג דתניא כוותיה לפום דקדוקא דמתניתין לא מיתוקמה כתירוציה דהא רבה כנפשיה אורי כשמעתיה ואיחלש ועיין במתניתין שפיר וחזא דלכאורה כתירוציה והטא. וכי עיין בה

מתני' מרחיצין את הקטן בין לפני המילה ובין לאחר המילה ומזלפין עליו ביד אבל לא בכלי ר"א בן עזריה (א) אומר מרחיצין את הקטן ביום השלישי שחל להיות בשבת שנאמר א) ויהי ביום השלישי בהיותם כואבים ספק ואנדרוגינוס אין מחללין עליו את השבת ורבי יהודה מתיר באנדרוגינוס: **גמ'** והא אמרת רישא מרחיצין רב יהודה ורבה בר אבוה דאמרי תרוייהו כיצד תני מרחיצין את הקטן בין לפני מילה בין לאחר מילה כיצד מזלפין עליו ביד אבל לא בכלי אמר רבא והא מרחיצין קתני אלא אמר רבא הכי קתני מרחיצין את הקטן בין מלפני מילה בין לאחר המילה ביום הראשון כדרכו וביום השלישי שחל להיות בשבת מזלפין עליו ביד אבל לא בכלי ר"א בן עזריה אומר מרחיצין את הקטן ביום השלישי שחל להיות בשבת שנאמר ויהי ביום השלישי בהיותם כואבים תניא כוותיה דרבא מרחיצין הקטן בין לפני מילה בין לאחר מילה ביום ראשון כדרכו וביום השלישי שחל להיות בשבת מזלפין עליו ביד ר"א בן עזריה אומר מרחיצין את הקטן ביום השלישי שחל להיות בשבת שנאמר ויהי ביום השלישי בהיותם כואבים וכשהן מזלפין אין מזלפין לא בכוס ולא בקערה ולא בכלי אלא ביד אתאן לתנא קמא מאי אע"פ שאין ראיה לדבר זכר לדבר משום דגדול לא סליק ביה בישרא הייא קטן סליק ביה בישרא הייא ההוא דאתא לקמיה דרבא אורי ליה כשמעתיה איחלש אמר אנא בהדי תרגימנא דסבי למה לי אמרו ליה רבנן לרבא והתניא כוותיה דמר אמר להו מתניתין כוותייהו דיקא ממאי מדקאמר רבי אלעזר בן עזריה אומר מרחיצין את הקטן ביום השלישי שחל להיות בשבת אי אמרת בשלמא תנא קמא מזלפין קאמר היינו דקאמר ליה ר"א בן עזריה מרחיצין אלא אי אמרת תנא קמא מרחיצין ביום הראשון קאמר ומזלפין ביום השלישי האי רבי אלעזר בן עזריה אומר מרחיצין אף מרחיצין מיבעי ליה כי אתא רב דימי אמר רבי אלעזר הלכה כר"א בן עזריה הוו בה במערבא הרחצת כל גופו או הרחצת מילה אמר להו ההוא מרבנן ורבי יעקב שמיה מסתברא הרחצת כל גופו דאי ס"ד הרחצת מילה מי גרע מחמין על גבי מכה דאמר רב אין מונעין חמין ושמן מעל גבי מכה בשבת מתקיף לה רב יוסף ולא שני לך בין חמין שהוחמו בשבת לחמין שהוחמו מע"ש מתקיף לה רב דימי וממאי דהכא בחמין שהוחמו בשבת פליגי דילמא בחמין שהוחמו בע"ש פליגי אמר אביי אנא בעאי דאישני ליה וקדם רב יוסף ושני ליה מפני שסכנה הוא לו איתמר נמי כי אתא רבין א"ר אבהו א"ר אלעזר ואמרי לה א"ר אבהו א"ר יוחנן א הלכה כר"א בן עזריה בין בחמין שהוחמו בשבת בין בחמין שהוחמו מע"ש בין הרחצת כל גופו בין הרחצת מילה מפני שסכנה היא לו: גופא אמר רב אין מונעין חמין ושמן מעל גבי מכה בשבת ושמואל אמר נותן חוץ למכה ושותת ויורד למכה מיתיבי ב אין נותנין שמן וחמין על גבי מוך ליתן על גבי מכה בשבת התם משום סחיטה תא שמע אין נותנין חמין ושמן על גבי מוך שעל גבי מכה בשבת התם נמי משום סחיטה תניא כוותיה דשמואל ג אין נותנין חמין ושמן על גבי מכה בשבת אבל נותנין חוץ למכה ושותת ויורד למכה תנו רבנן ד נותנין על גבי המכה מוך יבש וספוג יבש אבל לא גמי יבש ולא כתיתין יבשין קשיא כתיתין אכתיתין לא קשיא ה הא בחדתי הא בעתיקי אמר אביי שמע מינה הני כתיתין מסו: ספק ואנדרוגינוס כו': תנו רבנן ב) ערלתו ודאי דוחה את השבת ולא

רש"י

מתני' ומזלפין עליו. את החמין: ביד. אבל לא בכלי ובגמ' פריך הא אמרת רישא מרחיצין דמשמע כדרכו והדר תני אפילו לזלף עליו בכלי אסור: ספק. כגון ספק בן ח' חדשים [וספק בן ט'] דהוא כאבן בעלמא ואין מילתו דוחה שבת (וספק בן ט'): ר' יהודה מתיר באנדרוגינוס. דלימרבי מקראי כדמפרש בגמ' לקמן: **גמ'** והא אמרת רישא מרחיצין. ואפילו כדרכו: כיצד קתני. מרחיצין דרישא לאו כדרכו הוא דתנא סיפא לפרושי כיצד מרחיצין כגון לזלף ביד ואפילו ביום ראשון: תניא כוותיה דרבא כו' ה"ג ביום השלישי מזלפין עליו ביד ולא גרסינן אבל לא בכלי: אתאן לת"ק. הך סיפא תנא קמא אמרה דאילו ר"א אפילו הרחצה כדרכו שרי: משום דגדול לא סליק בישרא הייא. היינו טעמא דמעשה שכם לאו ראיה גמורה היא משום דגדול אין מכה שבבשרו מעלה ארוכה מהר אבל קטן נתרפא מידי סכנתו מהר: אורי ליה כשמעתיה. התיר לו הרחצה כדרכו ביום ראשון שחל להיות בשבת: איחלש. נעשה חולה והיה דואג שמא על כך נענש: אמר בהדי תרגימנא דסבי למה לי. מה היה לי לחלוק כנגד זקנים הללו רב יהודה ורבה בר אבוה שפירשו שאסור להרחיץ: אי אמרת בשלמא ת"ק מזלפין. ביום ראשון קאמר ולא איירי בהרחצה כלל אלא בזילוף היינו דאתא ר"א בן עזריה ופליג ואמר מרחיצין: אלא אי אמרת. תנא קמא נמי מרחיצין אמר בשני הימים ולא פליג ר"א אלא איום שלישי דקאמר ת"ק מזלפין אף מרחיצין ביום השלישי מיבעי ליה: הוו בה. דייקי בה: דאי ס"ד הרחצת מילה מי גרע מחמין על גבי מכה. דשרי והכא אסרי רבנן בשלישי (לגמרי): ולא שני כו'. והכא גבי מילה בהוחמו בשבת עסקינן הלכך בשלישי ליכא סכנתא לא: אמר אביי אנא בעאי דאישני ליה. אני הייתי רוצה לתרץ אתקפתא זו כדשני ליה רב יוסף מפני שסכנה היא לו: וקדם רב יוסף ושנייא ליה. דודאי מתניתין חמין שהוחמו בשבת נמי שרי בימים הראשונים ולר"א אף בשלישי מפני שמניעת חמין סכנה היא לו: אין נותנין כו'. קס"ד גזרה משום שחיקת סממנין כשמואל דטעמיה משום הכי הוא והיינו דקאמר אבל נותן מוך למכה דלא מוכחא מילתא דלרפואה: מוך יבש וספוג יבש. דלאו לרפואה היא אלא שלא יסרטו בגדיו הקשים מכתו: אבל לא כתיתין יבישים (א) וגמי יבש. חתיכות בגדים דקות משום דמסו וגזרו משום שחיקת סממנין: קשיא כתיתין אכתיתין. רישא שרי מוך יבש דהיינו כתיתין וסיפא אסר כתיתין: חדתי. חדשים שלא היו על גבי מכה מעולם מסו עתיקי לא מסו: ה"ג שמע מינה הני כתיתין מסו: ערלתו ודאי דוחה השבת. דהאי קרא וביום השמיני דילפינן מיניה אפילו בשבת כתיב בסיפיה ערלתו דמשמע מיעוטא ערלתו של זה ולא של אחר ולמעוטי ספק אתא: אנדרוגינוס

תוספות

מי גרע מחמין על גבי מכה. והיכי אסרי רבנן בשלישי אע"ג דליכא למימר דרב אמרה למילתיה כר"א בן עזריה דפסקינן לעיל הלכתא כוותיה משמע ליה לכל"ע קאמר ועוד דאפילו לר"א בן עזריה פריך דמשמע דשרי בשלישי משום סכנה מדמייתי קרא ויהי ביום השלישי ורב לא איירי במכה שאין בה סכנה: **ואין** מונעין חמין ושמן. פירש ה"ר יוסף פורת בשם רבינו שמואל דבמעורבת יחד איירי דאי כל חד באפי נפשיה מאי קמ"ל בשמן מתני' היא בפ' שמנה שרצים (לעיל דף קיא.) אבל כך הוא את השמן והיינו אפילו על גבי מכה מדקתני בני מלכים סכין ע"ג מכותיהן שמן וורד מכלל דבשאר שמן מותר ולאחר אפילו ע"ג מכה ושמואל נמי היכי הוה פליג: ולא

מסורת הש"ס

א) לעיל פו. ע"ש, ב) רש"ל מ"ז וא"ל למחוק וקאי למאי דהקשים רבא לפי דסבר דדיקא כוותייהו ולא התיר ת"ק אפי' לזלף ביום ג'.

הגהות הב"ח

(א) רש"י ד"ה אבל לא כתיתין יבישים חתיכות כצ"ל ותיבות וגמי יבש נמחק:

תורה אור השלם

א) וַיְהִי בַיּוֹם הַשְּׁלִישִׁי בִּהְיוֹתָם כֹּאֲבִים וַיִּקְחוּ שְׁנֵי בְנֵי יַעֲקֹב שִׁמְעוֹן וְלֵוִי אֲחֵי דִינָה אִישׁ חַרְבּוֹ וַיָּבֹאוּ עַל הָעִיר בֶּטַח וַיַּהַרְגוּ כָּל זָכָר: [בראשית לד, כה]

ב) וּבַיּוֹם הַשְּׁמִינִי יִמּוֹל בְּשַׂר עָרְלָתוֹ: [ויקרא יב, ג]

ליקוטי רש"י

מרחיצין **את** הקטן ביום השלישי. דאף ביום שלישי מסוכן הוא [לעיל פו.]. **ויהי ביום השלישי בהיותם כואבים.** ולאו למימרא דביום השלישי כתיב ליה טפי מיומא קמא אלא לכך המתינו שמעון ולוי עד יום השלישי כדי שיהו חלושין ביותר שנכאבו ג' ימים והכי מוכח בפ' ר"א דמילה [ר"ן נדרים לא: ועי' בר"ן כאן]. **אנדרוגינוס.** שיש לו זכרות ונקבות [רשב"ם ב"ב קכו.].

רב נסים גאון

האזהרה עליו שלא יגלחנו שנאמר (במדבר ו) גדל פרע שער ראשו אחר שאמר תער לא יעלה על ראשו הרי הוא בדבר זה מוזהר בלאו ומצווה בעשה וחייב המצורע בעת טהרתו לגלח כל שער שבגופו שנאמר (ויקרא יד) והיה ביום השביעי יגלח את כל שערו וכשיתנגע הנזיר בצרעת ויגיע יום ז' שהוא חייב לגלח בו אמרו חכמים שמצות גילוח של צרעת דוחה עשה ולא תעשה שיש עליו לענין נזירותו וכי מה שאמר הכתוב לענין מצורע את ראשו אחר שאמר יגלח את כל שערו לא בא אלא לענין נזיר שנאמר בו תער לא יעבור על ראשו לומר כי זו המצוה אינו חייב בה אלא בעת שלא תהיה בו צרעת אבל בעת שיהיה בגופו צרעת יגלח את ראשו אפי' שער ראשו שהזהרתיו שלא יגלחנו בימי נזירותו חייב לגלח אם היה צרוע נתקיים לנו מזה שבנזיר מצורע לבדו יבא עשה ודחי לא תעשה ועשה ובראש מס' יבמות (דף ה) אמרו אלא דקיימא לן דאין עשה דחי לא תעשה ועשה ליגמר מנזיר דאתי עשה ודחי לא תעשה ועשה אלא מנזיר לא גמרינן שכן ישנן בשאלה ובארו כי דבר זה הוא מיוחד בו לבדו ולא בזולתו וכי בכל התורה כולה לא אתי עשה ודחי לא תעשה ועשה והזהר לשמור אלו העיקרים שפירשנו שמהן מתבארים לך כל דבר כשתמצא בתלמוד מעין אלו הענינים: **תינח** גדול דכתיב ביה בשר קטן נמי כתיב ביה בשר בינוני מנלן פי' כבר ידענו כי הקטנים פטורים ממצות והשכר והעונש הם תלויין בחיוב המצות ומאחר שנדע כי לא חייב הכתוב במצות אלא לפי שיש בו עניני החיוב כגון שהביא ב' שערות ושהגיע למספר שני האנשים ושיצא מגבול הנערות אז הוא בן עונשין וכיון שראינו שענש הכתוב מי שלא נימול שנאמר (בראשית יז) וערל זכר אשר לא ימול את בשר ערלתו ונכרתה וגו' ידענו כי דבר זה מיוחד הוא באנשים גדולים ולא בנערים ומצאנו כתב בו בשר ערלתו להודיענו שהמילה דוחה את הצרעת על דרך העיקר שהקדמנו דאתי עשה ודחי לא תעשה וכי בעת שתהיה בערלה בהרת ימול ויחתוך אותה וידחה מה שכתוב (דברים כד) השמר בנגע הצרעת והוצרכנו שיבאר לנו דבר זה להסיר מדעתנו מה שהיה עולה עליו שמה היינו סוברים כי זה שכתב (שם) לשמור מאד ולעשות הוא דבר מוסף על הלאו והוה ליה לא תעשה ועשה ואין המילה דוחה אותן שאין עשה דוחה את לא תעשה ועשה והסיר ממנו סברא זו והודיענו שהוא לא תעשה בלבד והמילה דוחה אותה וזהו שאמרו תינח גדול דכתב ביה בשר והקטן נמי שהוא בן ח' ימים נאמר בו וביום השמיני ימול בשר ערלתו ידענו כי המילה ביום ח' תדחה (עוד) את הצרעת נשאר לנו לשאול על הבינוני והוא שעברו עליו ח' ימים ולא נימול מפני מאורע שאירע לו כגון שהיה חולה או שהיה בו ספק התהיה המילה ראויה בו בעת שיש בהרת בערלתו או לא ולפיכך אמרו בינוני מנלן ובאה התשובה משם אביי דאתיא מביניא ומשם רבא מילה בזמנה [לא] צריכא קרא כו' ופירוש על דעת אביי שהמילה מותרת בבינוני במקום שיש בהרת נלמוד מגדול וקטן כמו ששנינו (ריש ספרא) בבנין אב משני כתובים הצד השוה שבהן כו' וכן הוא הילוך הדבר בכאן כי הבינוני לא יתכן שנלמוד מן הגדול לפי שהגדול ענוש כרת לכך התירו בו הכתוב חתיכת הבהרת אבל הבינוני שאין בו חיוב כרת אין דבר זה מותר בו וכמו כן לא נלמוד דבר זה מן הקטן כי הקטן מילתו בזמנה ביום ח' והיא דוחה את השבת ולפיכך התיר הכתוב חתיכת הבהרת אבל הבינוני שאין מילתו בזמנה לא ומאחר שלא יכולנו ללמוד דבר זה מאחד מהן חיברנו אותם ביחד וקיימנו דבר עיקר מהם שהבינוני מותר לחתוך בהרת מערלתו וכן הילוכו של דבר בענין זה בינוני מנלן אמר אביי אתיא מבניינא מה לגדול שכן ענוש כרת קטן יוכיח שאינו ענוש כרת מה לקטן שכן מילה בזמנה גדול יוכיח שאין מילה בזמנה וחזר הדין הצד השוה שבהן שמילתו דוחה את הצרעת אף אני אביא בינוני שתהא מילתו דוחה את הצרעת ורבא לא הוצרך לדבר זה כי הוא סובר כי בשר ערלתו שנאמר בבן שמנת ימים לא בא להתיר מילת בן שמונת ימים במקום שיש בהרת כי זה נלמדנו מקל וחומר השתא שבת חמורה דוחה צרעת קלה לא כל שכן והואיל ואינו צריך לבן ח' ימים הועיל להתיר המילה בבינוני במקום שיש בהרת: **לא** צריכא אפי' ר' יהודה דאמר דבר שאינו מתכוין אסור כבר פירשנו זה בפ' כירה. לבדו ולא מילה שלא בזמנה

הָאי רַבִּי אֶלְעָזָר בֶּן עֲזַרְיָה אוֹמֵר מַרְחִיצִין – then **this** phrase of the Mishnah, **"R' ELAZAR BEN AZARYAH SAYS: 'WE MAY BATHE** the infant on the third day,' " is imprecisely worded. אַף מַרְחִיצִין מִיבָּעֵי לֵיהּ – **It should have** stated, **"We may** ***also*** **bathe** [him] on the third day," inasmuch as R' Elazar is merely extending the unanimous ruling of the first two days to the third day.[24]

The Gemara reports a decision on the dispute between the Tanna Kamma and R' Elazar ben Azaryah:

כִּי אֲתָא רַב דִּימִי – **When Rav Dimi came** from Eretz Yisrael to Babylonia, אָמַר רַבִּי אֶלְעָזָר – **he said** in the name of **R' Elazar:** הֲלָכָה כְּרַבִּי אֶלְעָזָר בֶּן עֲזַרְיָה – **The law accords with** the opinion of **R' Elazar ben Azaryah.**[25] הֲוּוּ בָּהּ בְּמַעֲרְבָא – **They pondered [this opinion] in the West** (Eretz Yisrael): הַרְחָצַת כָּל גּוּפוֹ אוֹ הַרְחָצַת מִילָה – When R' Elazar ben Azaryah sanctioned bathing as opposed to sprinkling, did he permit **bathing of [the infant's] entire body, or** only **bathing of the circumcision** wound?

An answer is ventured:

אָמַר לְהוּ הַהוּא מֵרַבָּנָן וְרַבִּי יַעֲקֹב שְׁמֵיהּ – **One of the Rabbis said to [his colleagues], and R' Yaakov was his name:** מִסְתַּבְּרָא הַרְחָצַת כָּל גּוּפוֹ – **It is logical** that **bathing of [the infant's] entire body** was permitted, דְּאִי סַלְקָא דַעְתָּךְ הַרְחָצַת מִילָה – **for if it enters your mind** that R' Elazar ben Azaryah sanctioned only **bathing of the circumcision** wound, מִי גָּרַע מֵחַמִּין עַל גַּבֵּי מַכָּה – **is [that case] worse than** applying **hot water upon an** ordinary **wound** on the Sabbath, which is permitted? דְּאָמַר רַב – **For Rav said:** אֵין מוֹנְעִין חַמִּין וְשֶׁמֶן מֵעַל גַּבֵּי מַכָּה בְּשַׁבָּת – **We do not prevent hot water and oil from** being applied **upon an** ordinary **wound on the Sabbath.**[26]

An objection is raised:

מַתְקִיף לָהּ רַב יוֹסֵף – **Rav Yosef challenges [R' Yaakov's answer]:** וְלֹא שָׁנֵי לָךְ בֵּין חַמִּין שֶׁהוּחַמּוּ בְּשַׁבָּת – **But,** R' Yaakov, **do you not differentiate between hot water that was heated on the Sabbath** לְחַמִּין שֶׁהוּחַמּוּ מֵעֶרֶב שַׁבָּת – **and hot water that was heated on the Sabbath eve?!**[27]

The Gemara objects to this objection:

מַתְקִיף לָהּ רַב דִּימִי – **Rav Dimi challenges [Rav Yosef's argument]:** וּמִמַּאי דְהָכָא בְּחַמִּין שֶׁהוּחַמּוּ בְּשַׁבָּת פְּלִיגֵי – **And from what** proof do you say **that here** in the Mishnah **[the Rabbis and R' Elazar ben Azaryah] argue in [the case of] hot water that was heated on the Sabbath?** דִּילְמָא בְּחַמִּין שֶׁהוּחַמּוּ בְּעֶרֶב שַׁבָּת פְּלִיגֵי – **Perhaps they argue in [the case of] hot water that was heated on the Sabbath eve,** and the point of contention between them *is* whether the entire body may be bathed![28] – ? –

Another Amora responds:

אָמַר אַבָּיֵי – **Abaye said:** אֲנָא בְּעָאִי דְּאִישַׁנֵּי לֵיהּ – **I wanted to answer [Rav Dimi's objection]** as Rav Yosef subsequently did, וְקָדַם וְשַׁנֵּי לֵיהּ רַב יוֹסֵף – **but Rav Yosef anticipated** me **and he answered it:** מִפְּנֵי שֶׁסַּכָּנָה הוּא לוֹ – The Mishnah certainly allows hot water that was heated on the Sabbath as well,[29] **because** to withhold hot water **is a danger for [the infant].**[30] אִיתְּמַר נַמִּי – **It was stated also** by other Amoraim that the Mishnah speaks of actual danger: כִּי אֲתָא רָבִין – **When Ravin came** from Eretz Yisrael to Babylonia, אָמַר רַבִּי אַבָּהוּ אָמַר רַבִּי אֶלְעָזָר – he reported that **R' Abahu said in the name of R' Elazar** – וְאָמְרֵי לָהּ אָמַר רַבִּי אַבָּהוּ אָמַר רַבִּי יוֹחָנָן – **and some quote it** that **R' Abahu said in the name of R' Yochanan:** הֲלָכָה כְּרַבִּי אֶלְעָזָר בֶּן עֲזַרְיָה – **The law accords with** the opinion of **R' Elazar ben Azaryah,**[31] בֵּין בְּחַמִּין שֶׁהוּחַמּוּ בְּשַׁבָּת – **whether in [the case of] hot water that was heated on the Sabbath** בֵּין בְּחַמִּין שֶׁהוּחַמּוּ מֵעֶרֶב שַׁבָּת – **or hot water that was heated on the Sabbath eve,** בֵּין הַרְחָצַת כָּל גּוּפוֹ – **whether** with regard to **bathing of [the infant's] entire body** בֵּין הַרְחָצַת מִילָה – **or bathing of the circumcision** wound – מִפְּנֵי שֶׁסַּכָּנָה הִיא לוֹ – **because** to withhold hot water from the entire body **is a danger for him.**[32]

The Gemara now fully quotes and discusses an Amoraic dictum that was mentioned briefly in the previous passage:

גּוּפָא – Let us return to the statement **itself:** אָמַר רַב – **Rav said:** אֵין מוֹנְעִין חַמִּין וְשֶׁמֶן מֵעַל גַּבֵּי מַכָּה בְּשַׁבָּת – **We do not prevent hot water and oil from** being applied **upon an** ordinary **wound on the Sabbath.** וּשְׁמוּאֵל אָמַר – **But Shmuel said:** נוֹתֵן חוּץ לַמַּכָּה – **One should place** the hot water and oil **outside**

NOTES

24. Rava argues thus even though the Baraisa that supports him does not state "also" (see *Rashba* and *Ran MHK* ed.; see also *Maharsha* and *Leshon HaZahav*).

25. Who, according to both interpretations of the Mishnah presented above, permits normal bathing on all three days.

26. [From the Gemara below it is apparent that Rav is addressing the question of whether this constitutes an act of healing, which is forbidden on the Sabbath. Nevertheless, we see from here that it is permitted to bathe a limb with a wound with hot water on Shabbos. And even Shmuel, who prohibits (below) the direct application of hot water and oil, would allow hot water alone (see *Korban Nesanel* 3:5 and *Mishnah Berurah* 328 §74).]

Since the Tanna Kamma (representing the Rabbis) prohibits even sprinkling hot water on the third day [according to the interpretation of Rav Yehudah and Rabbah bar Avuha, which Rava himself praises as being more consistent with the Mishnah's wording], he and R' Elazar must be debating the case of the entire body, for everyone agrees that the wound itself may even be bathed normally with hot water on the Sabbath. [Hence, R' Elazar, who espouses the lenient view, perforce sanctions bathing the entire body] (*Rashi,* as explained by *Maharsha* and *Mesoras HaShas,* who thereby retain the parenthesized לְגַמְרֵי, *entirely; cf. Maharshal,* who deletes it; cf. *Rashba* and *Ran MHK* ed., who challenge *Rashi's* interpretation and advance a different one). See *Tosafos,* who explain that the proof comes directly from R' Elazar's words as well.

27. Rav Yosef argues: Our Mishnah speaks of water heated on Shabbos itself. This case is more stringent (see above, 39b), and is usually forbidden even for one limb. Thus, when the third day after *milah* falls on Shabbos, the Rabbis prohibit even sprinkling just on the wound, since in their opinion the child is no longer in danger (*Rashi*). R' Elazar allows even a normal bathing of the wound, for he holds that a danger exists. Thus, we have no proof as to whether or not the entire body may be bathed according to R' Elazar ben Azaryah [for perhaps the danger does not warrant bathing the entire body] (see *Maharsha*).

28. For, as Rav has taught, bathing only the wound is certainly permitted in such a case. And so R' Elazar permits bathing the entire body even on the third day. But perhaps no one allows the use of water heated on the Sabbath itself.

29. According to R' Elazar ben Azaryah, on all three days; according to the Rabbis, on the first two days (*Rashi*).

30. And since there is an actual danger, certainly water heated on Shabbos is also permitted; hence, the dispute in the Mishnah is whether this danger exists on the third day as well. [Nevertheless, it is still possible that the danger does not warrant bathing the entire body; see *Maharsha,* cited in note 27 above. See also *Sfas Emes.*]

31. See note 25 above.

32. Ravin adds to Rav Yosef's opinion in that he holds that bathing the entire body is also necessary in order to avoid the danger (see *Maharsha*).

The Rishonim (cited above in note 3) discuss at length the reason for allowing bathing before the circumcision, when there is not yet any danger. They also discuss the circumstances under which it would be permissible actually to heat water for a circumcision. See there.

עין משפט
נר מצוה

כח א מיי' פ"ב מהל' מילה הלכה ח ופ"ב מהל' שבת הלכה יד סמג עשין כח טוש"ע א"ח סי' של"א סעיף ט:
כט ב ג מיי' פכ"א מהל' שבת הלכה כו טוש"ע א"ח סי' שכח סעיף כב:
ל ד ה מיי' שם טוש"ע שם סעיף כג:

מתני' ומזלפין עליו. את החמין: ביד. אבל לא בכלי ובגמ' פריך הא אמרת רישא מרחיצין דמשמע כדרכו והדר תני אפילו לזלף עליו בכלי אסור: ספק. כגון ספק בן ח' חדשים [וספק בן ט'] דהוא כאבן בעלמא ואין מילתו דוחה שבת (וספק בן ט'): ר' יהודה מתיר באנדרוגינוס. דאיתרבי מקרא כדמפרש בגמ' לקמן: גמ' והא אמרת רישא מרחיצין. ואפילו כדרכו: כיצד קתני. מרחיצין דרישא לאו כדרכו הוא דתנא סיפא לפרושי כילד מרחיצין כגון לזלף ביד ואפילו ביום ראשון: תניא כוותיה דרבא כו' ה"ג ביום השלישי מזלפין עליו ביד ולא גרסינן אבל לא בכלי: אתאן לת"ק. הך סיפא תנא קמא אמרה דאילו ר"א אפילו הרחצה כדרכו שרי: משום דגדול לא סליק בישרא הייא. היינו טעמא דמעשה שכם לאו ראיה גמורה היא משום דגדול אין מכה שבבשרו מעלה ארוכה מהר אבל קטן נתרפא מידי סכנתו מהר: אורי ליה כשמעתיה. התיר לו הרחצה כדרכו ביום ראשון שחל להיות בשבת: איחלש. נעשה חולה והיה דואג שמא על כך נענש: אמר בהדי תרגימנא דסבי למה לי. מה היה לי לחלוק כנגד זקנים הללו רב יהודה ורבה בר אבוה שפירשו שאסור להרחיץ: אי אמרת בשלמא ת"ק מזלפין. ביום ראשון קאמר ולא איירי בהרחצה כלל אלא בזילוף היינו דאתא ר"א בן עזריה ופליג ואמר מרחיצין: אלא אי אמרת. תנא קמא נמי מרחיצין אמר בשני הימים ולא פליג ר"א אלא איום שלישי דקאמר ת"ק מזלפין אף מרחיצין ביום השלישי מיבעי ליה: הוו בה. דייקי בה: דאי ס"ד הרחצת מילה מי גרע מחמין על גבי מכה. דשרי והכא אסרי רבנן בשלישי (ג) לגמרי): ולא שני כו'. והכא גבי מילה בהוחמו בשבת עסקינן הלכך בשלישי דליכא סכנתא לא: אמר אביי אנא בעאי דאישני ליה. אני הייתי רוצה לתרץ אתקפתא זו כדשני ליה רב יוסף מפני שסכנה היא לו: וקדם רב יוסף ושנייא ליה. דודאי מתניתין חמין שהוחמו בשבת נמי שרי בימים הראשונים ולר"א אף בשלישי מפני שמניעת חמין סכנה היא לו: אין נותנין כו'. קס"ד גזרה משום שחיקת סמנין כשמואל דטעמיה משום הכי הוא והיינו דקאמר אבל נותן חוץ למכה דלא מוכחא מילתא דלרפואה: מוך יבש וספוג יבש. דלאו לרפואה היא אלא שלא ישרטו בגדיו הקשים מכתו: אבל לא כתיתין יבישים (א) וגמי יבש. חתיכות בגדים דקות משום דמסו וגזרו משום שחיקת סמנין: קשיא כתיתין אכתיתין. רישא שרי מוך יבש דהיינו כתיתין וסיפא אסר כתיתין: חדתי. חדשים שלא היו על גבי מכה מעולם מסו עתיקי לא מסו: ה"ג שמע מינה הני כתיתין מסו: ערלתו ודאי דוחה השבת. דבהאי קרא וביום השמיני דילפינן מיניה אפילו בשבת כתיב בסיפיה ערלתו דמשמע מיעוטא ערלתו של זה ולא של אחר ולמעוטי ספק אתא: אנדרוגינוס

מתני' מרחיצין את הקטן בין לפני המילה ובין לאחר המילה ומזלפין עליו ביד אבל לא בכלי ר"א בן עזריה אומר מרחיצין את הקטן ביום השלישי שחל להיות בשבת שנאמר א) ויהי ביום השלישי בהיותם כואבים ספק ואנדרוגינוס אין מחללין עליו את השבת ורבי יהודה מתיר באנדרוגינוס: גמ' והא אמרת רישא מרחיצין רב יהודה ורבה בר אבוה דאמרי תרוייהו כיצד תני מרחיצין את הקטן בין לפני מילה בין לאחר מילה כיצד מזלפין עליו ביד אבל לא בכלי אמר רבא והא מרחיצין קתני אלא אמר רבא הכי קתני מרחיצין את הקטן בין מלפני מילה בין לאחר המילה ביום הראשון כדרכו וביום השלישי שחל להיות בשבת מזלפין עליו ביד אבל לא בכלי ר"א בן עזריה אומר מרחיצין את הקטן ביום השלישי שחל להיות בשבת שנאמר ויהי ביום השלישי בהיותם כואבים תניא כוותיה דרבא מרחיצין הקטן בין לפני מילה בין לאחר מילה ביום ראשון כדרכו וביום השלישי שחל להיות בשבת מזלפין עליו ביד ר"א בן עזריה אומר מרחיצין את הקטן ביום השלישי שחל להיות בשבת ואע"פ שאין ראיה לדבר זכר לדבר שנאמר ויהי ביום השלישי בהיותם כואבים וכשהן מזלפין אין מזלפין לא בכוס ולא בקערה ולא בכלי אלא ביד אתאן לתנא קמא מאי אע"פ שאין ראיה לדבר זכר לדבר משום דגדול לא סליק ביה בישרא הייא קטן סליק ביה בישרא הייא ההוא דאתא לקמיה דרבא אורי ליה כשמעתיה איחלש רבא אמר אנא בהדי תרגימנא דסבי למה לי אמרו ליה רבנן לרבא והתניא כוותיה דמר אמר להו מתניתין כוותייהו דיקא ממאי מדקאמר רבי אלעזר בן עזריה אומר מרחיצין את הקטן ביום השלישי שחל להיות בשבת אי אמרת בשלמא תנא קמא מזלפין קאמר היינו דקאמר ליה ר"א בן עזריה מרחיצין אלא אי אמרת תנא קמא מרחיצין ביום הראשון קאמר ומזלפין ביום השלישי האי רבי אלעזר בן עזריה אומר מרחיצין אף מרחיצין מיבעי ליה כי אתא רב דימי אמר רבי אלעזר הלכה כר"א בן עזריה הוו בה במערבא הרחצת כל גופו או הרחצת מילה אמר להו ההוא מרבנן ורבי יעקב שמיה מסתברא הרחצת כל גופו דאי ס"ד הרחצת מילה מי גרע מחמין על גבי מכה דאמר רב אין מונעין חמין ושמן מעל גבי מכה בשבת מתקיף לה רב יוסף ולא שני לך בין חמין שהוחמו בשבת לחמין שהוחמו מע"ש מתקיף לה רב דימי וממאי דהכא בחמין שהוחמו בשבת פליגי דילמא בחמין שהוחמו בע"ש פליגי אמר אביי אנא בעאי דאישני ליה וקדם ושני ליה רב יוסף מפני שסכנה הוא לו איתמר נמי כי אתא רבין א"ר אבהו א"ר אלעזר ואמרי לה א"ר אבהו א"ר יוחנן הלכה כר"א בן עזריה בין בחמין שהוחמו בשבת בין בחמין שהוחמו מע"ש בין הרחצת כל גופו בין הרחצת מילה מפני שסכנה היא לו: גופא אמר רב אין מונעין חמין ושמן מעל גבי מכה בשבת ושמואל אמר נותן חוץ למכה ושותת ויורד למכה מיתיבי ב) אין נותנין שמן וחמין על גבי מוך ליתן על גבי מכה בשבת התם משום סחיטה תא שמע אין נותנין חמין ושמן על גבי מוך שעל גבי מכה בשבת התם נמי משום סחיטה תניא כוותיה דשמואל ג) אין נותנין חמין ושמן על גבי מכה בשבת אבל נותנין חוץ למכה ושותת ויורד למכה תנו רבנן ד) נותנין על גבי המכה מוך יבש וספוג יבש אבל לא גמי יבש ולא כתיתין יבשין קשיא כתיתין אכתיתין לא קשיא ה) הא בחדתי הא בעתיקי אמר אביי שמע מינה הני כתיתין מסו: ספק ואנדרוגינוס כו': תנו רבנן ו) ערלתו ערלתו ודאי דוחה את השבת ולא

מי גרע מחמין על גבי מכה. והיכי אסרי רבנן בשלישי אע"ג דאיכא למימר דרב אמרה למילתיה כר"א בן עזריה דפסקינן לעיל הלכתא כוותיה משמע ליה דלכ"ע קאמר ועוד דאפילו לר"א בן עזריה פריך דמשמע דשרי בשלישי משום סכנה מדמייתי קרא ויהי ביום השלישי ורב איירי במכה שאין בה סכנה: ואין מונעין חמין ושמן. פירש ה"ר יוסף פורת בשם רבינו שמואל דבמעורבת יחד איירי דאי כל חד באפי נפשיה מאי קמ"ל בשמן מתני' היא בפ' שמונה שרצים (לעיל דף קיא.) אבל סך הוא את השמן והיינו אפילו על גבי מכה מדקתני בני מלכים סכין ע"ג מכותיהן שמן וורד מכלל דבשאר שמן מותר לאחר אפילו ע"ג מכה ושמואל נמי היכי הוה פליג: ולא

רבינו חננאל

מקוטמא לאולמא ממקום הדק לעבה: ת"ר דברים שאין עושין למילה בשבת עושין לה ביו"ט שוחקין כמון וטורפין לה יין ושמן יין בפ"ע ושמן בפ"ע אבל ע"י ליכא [אסור]. פי' ליכא עירוב יין ושמן להוליך השמן בתוך היין על [ידין] עירבוב. (אבל) א"ל אביי לרבה מהו לגבן. פי' לגבן ביו"ט לקפות גבינה לקבץ פיתותי החלב הקפוי ולעשותם חריץ של גבינה. א"ל אסור לגבן. א"ל והלא גיבון כמו לישת העיסה שנותן מים בקמח ומולל בידיו ועושה פתיתין ומוסיף מים ומקבץ הפתיתין ועושה אותם עיסה. כך מקפה החלב בטוכמסו ואחר שיקפה בכלי ויעמוד מכניס ידו ופיתתו. ואח"כ מכניס ידו ומגבן מתוך הכיס. הנה גיבון ולישה מלאכתן שוה מפני מה זה מותר וזה אסור ופירק לו קמח אי אפשר לאוכלו אלא ע"י לישה ביומו. והחלב אפשר לאכלו חלב או לעשותו גבינה בערב. אקשינן עלה והא אמרו נהרדעי גבינה בת יומא מעליא והנה היא כמו הלישה וכשם שהפת חמה מעליא כך הגבינה בת יומא מעליא ופריק ליה הכי קאמר אפילו בת יומא מעליא מכלל שבת שנים ושלשה ימים מעליא טפי ואפילו בת יומא מעליא: אין עושין למילה חלוק לכתחילה אבל כורך עליה סמרטוט: מתניתין: מרחיצין את הקטן בין לפני המילה ובין לאחר המילה ומזלפין עליו אבל לא בכלי. ואקשי היאך קתני מזלפין מכלל שרחיצה אסורה והא רישא דמתניתין קתני מרחיצין ופרקי' רב יהודה ורבה בר אבוה אמר כך סידור המשנה מרחיצין את הקטן בין לפני המילה ובין לאחר המילה. והרחצה זו כיצד היא ע"י זילוף היא ביד אבל לא בכלי. ואקשי עליהו רבה והא מרחיצין קתני וזילוף אינה רחיצה ופריק רבא משנתנו הא דקתני מרחיצין ביום ראשון של מילה אם היא שבת רחיצה כדרכו בין לפני המילה בין לאחר המילה וביום השלישי שחל להיות בשבת מזלפין ביד אבל לא בכלי ותניא כוותיה דרבא ואע"ג דתניא כוותיה לפום דקדוקא דמתניתין לא מיתוקמה כתירוציה דהא רבה כנפשיה אורי כשמעתיה ואיחלש ועיין במתניתין שפיר וחזו דלאורה כתירוציה דרבא. וכי עיין בה

מסורת הש"ס

א) לעיל פו. ע"ש, ב) רש"ל מ"ז וא"ל למחוק וקאי למאי דהסכים רבא לפי דסבר דדיקא כוותייהו ולא התיר ת"ק אפי' לזלף ביום ג'.

הגהות הב"ח

(א) רש"י ד"ה אבל לא כתיתין יבישים חתיכות כצ"ל ותיבות וגמי יבש נמחק:

תורה אור השלם

א) וַיְהִי בַיּוֹם הַשְּׁלִישִׁי בִּהְיוֹתָם כֹּאֲבִים וַיִּקְחוּ שְׁנֵי בְנֵי יַעֲקֹב שִׁמְעוֹן וְלֵוִי אֲחֵי דִינָה אִישׁ חַרְבּוֹ וַיָּבֹאוּ עַל הָעִיר בֶּטַח וַיַּהַרְגוּ כָּל זָכָר: [בראשית לד, כה]

ב) וּבַיּוֹם הַשְּׁמִינִי יִמּוֹל בְּשַׂר עָרְלָתוֹ: [ויקרא יב, ג]

ליקוטי רש"י

מרחיצין את הקטן ביום השלישי. דאף ביום שלישי מסוכן הוא [לעיל פו.]. ויהי ביום השלישי בהיותם כואבים. ולאו למימרא דביום השלישי כאיב ליה טפי מיומא קמא אלא לכך הסמיכו שמעון ולוי עד יום השלישי כדי שיהו חלושין ביותר שנכאבו ג' ימים והכי מוכח בפ' ר"א דמילה [ר"ן נדרים לא: ועי' בר"ן כאן]. אנדרוגינוס. שיש לו זכרות ונקבות [רשב"ם ב"ב קכו.].

רב נסים גאון

האזהרה עליו שלא יגלחנו שנאמר (במדבר ו) גדל פרע שער ראשו ואחר שאמר תער לא יעלה על ראשו הרי הוא בדבר זה מוזהר בלאו ומצווה בעשה וחייב המצורע בעת טהרתו לגלח כל שער שבגופו שנאמר (ויקרא יד) והיה ביום השביעי יגלח את כל שערו וכשיתנגע הנזיר בצרעת ויגיע יום ז' שהוא חייב לגלח בו אמרו חכמים שמצות גילוח של צרעת דוחה עשה ולא תעשה שיש עליו לענין נזירותו וכי מה שאמר תער לא יעבור על ראשו לא בא אלא לענין נזיר שאמר בו תער לא יעבור על ראשו אינו לומר כי זו המצוה אינו חייב בה אלא בעת שלא תהיה בו צרעת אבל בעת שיהיה בגופו צרעת יגלח את ראשו אפי' שער ראשו שהזהירו שלא יגלחנו בימי נזירותו חייב לגלח אם היה צרוע נתקיים לנו מזה שבנזיר מצורע לבדו יבא עשה ודחי לא תעשה ועשה ובראש מס' יבמות (דף ה) אמרו אלא דקיימא לן דאין עשה דוחי לא תעשה ועשה ליגמר מנזיר דאתי עשה ודחי לא תעשה ועשה אלא מנזיר לא גמרינן שכן ישנן בשאלה ובארו כי דבר זה הוא מיוחד בו לבדו ולא בזולתו ולא בכל התורה כולה לא אתי עשה ודחי לא תעשה ועשה

ועשה והזהר לשמור אלו העיקרים שפירשנו שמהן מתבארים לך כל דבר כשתמצא בתלמוד מעין אלו הענינים: תינח גדול דכתיב ביה בשר ערלתו [illegible]

בחיוב המצות ומאחר שנדע כי לא חייב הכתוב במצות אלא לפי שיש בו [illegible]

וערל זכר אשר לא ימול את בשר ערלתו ונכרתה [illegible]

[illegible]

the wound, וְשׁוֹתֵת וְיוֹרֵד לַמַּכָּה – **and they flow gently down to the wound.**[33]

Rav's opinion is challenged:

מֵיתִיבֵי – **They challenged** this **from a Baraisa:** אֵין נוֹתְנִין שֶׁמֶן וְחַמִּין – WE MAY NOT PUT OIL AND HOT WATER עַל גַּבֵּי מוֹךְ – ONTO A SOFT CLOTH לִיתֵּן עַל גַּבֵּי מַכָּה בְּשַׁבָּת – TO PLACE UPON A WOUND ON THE SABBATH.[34] – ? –

The Gemara defuses the challenge:

הָתָם מִשּׁוּם סְחִיטָה – The prohibition **there** in the Baraisa is **on account of squeezing,** not grinding.[35] Hence, the Baraisa does not validate Shmuel's opinion, which is a safeguard against grinding.

The Gemara mounts another challenge:

תָּא שְׁמַע – **Come, learn** a disproof of Rav, for a different Baraisa states: אֵין נוֹתְנִין חַמִּין וְשֶׁמֶן עַל גַּבֵּי מוֹךְ – WE MAY NOT PUT HOT WATER AND OIL ONTO A SOFT CLOTH שֶׁעַל גַּבֵּי מַכָּה בְּשַׁבָּת – THAT IS resting UPON A WOUND ON THE SABBATH.[36] – ? –

This challenge as well is defused:

הָתָם נַמִּי מִשּׁוּם סְחִיטָה – **There also** the prohibition is **on account of squeezing,** not grinding.[37] Hence, the Baraisa does not validate Shmuel's opinion, which is a safeguard against grinding.

Shmuel's position is finally corroborated:

תַּנְיָא כְּוָותֵיהּ דִּשְׁמוּאֵל – **It was** explicitly **taught in a Baraisa in accordance with** the opinion of **Shmuel:**[38] אֵין נוֹתְנִין חַמִּין וְשֶׁמֶן עַל גַּבֵּי מַכָּה בְּשַׁבָּת – WE MAY NOT PLACE HOT WATER AND OIL UPON A WOUND ON THE SABBATH, אֲבָל נוֹתְנִין חוּץ לַמַּכָּה – BUT WE MAY PLACE them OUTSIDE THE WOUND וְשׁוֹתֵת וְיוֹרֵד לַמַּכָּה – AND THEY FLOW GENTLY DOWN TO THE WOUND.

The Gemara cites a related Baraisa:

תָּנוּ רַבָּנָן – **The Rabbis taught:** נוֹתְנִין עַל גַּבֵּי הַמַּכָּה מוֹךְ יָבֵשׁ וּסְפוֹג יָבֵשׁ – WE MAY PLACE UPON THE WOUND A DRY CLOTH OR A DRY SPONGE,[39] אֲבָל לֹא גְּמִי יָבֵשׁ וְלֹא כְּתִיתִין יְבֵשִׁין – BUT NOT A DRY REED AND NOT DRY CLOTH RAGS.[40]

The Gemara asks:

קַשְׁיָא כְּתִיתִין אַכְּתִיתִין – The rule of **cloth rags** in the first part of the Baraisa **is contradictory to** the rule of **cloth rags** in the second part![41] – ? –

The Gemara reconciles the two rulings:

לֹא קַשְׁיָא – This is **not difficult!** הָא בְּחַדְתֵּי – **This** second ruling deals **with new** rags,[42] which have a healing effect; thus, as a safeguard, the Tanna prohibits their use. הָא בְּעַתִּיקֵי – **This** first ruling, on the other hand, deals **with old** rags, which do not have a healing effect; hence, there is no need to prohibit their use.[43]

The Gemara concludes:

אָמַר אַבָּיֵי – **Abaye said:** שְׁמַע מִינָּהּ הָנֵי כְּתִיתִין מַסּוּ – **Derive from [the Baraisa]** that **these** new **cloth rags cause healing.**

The Gemara returns to the Mishnah, which stated:

סָפֵק וְאַנְדְּרוֹגִינוּס כו׳ – In the case of A QUESTIONABLE ONE OR AN ANDROGYNE etc. [we may not desecrate the Sabbath on his behalf. But R' Yehudah permits (it) in the case of an androgyne.]

The Gemara cites a related Baraisa:

תָּנוּ רַבָּנָן – **The Rabbis taught:** ,,עָרְלָתוֹ״ – Scripture states: *On the eighth day the flesh of* HIS FORESKIN *shall be circumcised.*[44] ,,עָרְלָתוֹ״ וַדַּאי דּוֹחָה אֶת הַשַּׁבָּת – The exclusionary *his foreskin* teaches that circumcising THE FORESKIN OF ONE WHO IS CERTAIN[45] OVERRIDES THE SABBATH restrictions,

---

NOTES

33. Rav and Shmuel argue over whether the direct placement of oil and hot water on a wound is included in the general prohibition against healing on the Sabbath, which itself is a Rabbinic safeguard (גְּזֵירָה) lest one come to grind herbs (a Biblical *melachah*) for medicinal purposes. Rav holds that it is not, while Shmuel disagrees. Shmuel thus recommends having the oil and hot water flow down to the wound, which avoids the appearance of having placed them for medicinal purposes, and is therefore permitted.

34. The Gemara assumes that the Tanna's prohibition is due to the Rabbinic safeguard that protects one from grinding herbs on the Sabbath (a Biblical *melachah*) for medicinal purposes (see previous note). The Baraisa thus validates Shmuel's opinion, and refutes Rav's (*Rashi*).

35. I.e. the Tanna forbade placing oil and hot water on a soft cloth lest one come to squeeze the contents of the cloth onto the wound, which is a Biblical *melachah*. See *Orach Chaim* 320:15-18 with *Mishnah Berurah*.

36. Here, since the cloth is already on the wound, the Gemara assumes that a Rabbinic safeguard against squeezing is unnecessary. Rather, the Tanna is concerned about grinding for medicinal purposes, and so his prohibition parallels – and thus confirms – that of Shmuel.

37. Even though the cloth rests on the wound, the Tanna was concerned that its contents would be squeezed into the wound.

38. See *Sefer Cheifetz Hashem*.

39. These serve no healing purpose, but merely protect the wound from being scratched by one's stiff clothing (*Rashi*).

40. כְּתִיתִין are thin strips of cloth. These and dry reeds have a healing effect, and so their use was Rabbinically prohibited as a safeguard lest one come to grind herbs for medicinal purposes (*Rashi*).

41. In the first part the Tanna sanctions the use of a dry מוֹךְ which is a cloth rag, and in the second part he prohibits the use of dry cloth rags (*Rashi*).

42. I.e. rags that were never before placed on a wound (*Rashi*).

43. *Rashi;* cf. *Chidushei HaRan*; see *Rosh,* end of §3.

44. *Leviticus* 12:3. As the Gemara taught above (132a), this verse teaches that *milah* on the eighth day overrides the Sabbath *melachah* restrictions. The word עָרְלָתוֹ (*his foreskin*), written at the end of the verse, implies an exclusion: *His* foreskin shall be cut off on the Sabbath, but not another's foreskin (*Rashi*).

45. I.e. one whose obligation to undergo circumcision is certain.

וְלֹא סָפֵק דּוֹחֶה אֶת הַשַּׁבָּת – BUT circumcising ONE WHO IS QUESTIONABLE[1] DOES NOT OVERRIDE THE SABBATH.[2] עָרְלָתוֹ וַדַּאי דּוֹחָה אֶת הַשַּׁבָּת – Furthermore, *his foreskin* teaches that circumcising THE FORESKIN OF ONE WHO IS CERTAIN OVERRIDES THE SABBATH, וְלֹא אַנְדְּרוֹגִינוּס דּוֹחֶה אֶת הַשַּׁבָּת – BUT circumcising AN ANDROGYNE DOES NOT OVERRIDE THE SABBATH. רַבִּי יְהוּדָה אוֹמֵר – However, R' YEHUDAH SAYS: אַנְדְּרוֹגִינוּס דּוֹחֶה אֶת הַשַּׁבָּת – The circumcision of AN ANDROGYNE DOES OVERRIDE THE SABBATH, וְעָנוּשׁ כָּרֵת – AND, in fact, an uncircumcised androgyne is PUNISHED with *KARES*. עָרְלָתוֹ וַדַּאי דּוֹחָה אֶת הַשַּׁבָּת – The Baraisa continues: *His foreskin* teaches further that circumcising THE FORESKIN OF ONE WHO IS CERTAIN OVERRIDES THE SABBATH, וְלֹא נוֹלָד בֵּין הַשְּׁמָשׁוֹת דּוֹחֶה אֶת הַשַּׁבָּת – BUT circumcising ONE WHO WAS BORN DURING TWILIGHT DOES NOT OVERRIDE THE SABBATH.[3] עָרְלָתוֹ וַדַּאי דּוֹחָה אֶת הַשַּׁבָּת – Furthermore, the verse teaches that circumcising THE FORESKIN OF ONE WHO IS CERTAIN OVERRIDES THE SABBATH, וְלֹא נוֹלָד כְּשֶׁהוּא מָהוּל דּוֹחֶה אֶת הַשַּׁבָּת – BUT circumcising ONE WHO WAS BORN CIRCUMCISED DOES NOT OVERRIDE THE SABBATH, שֶׁבֵּית שַׁמַּאי אוֹמְרִים צָרִיךְ לְהַטִּיף מִמֶּנּוּ דַּם בְּרִית – FOR BEIS SHAMMAI SAY that ONE MUST CAUSE COVENANTAL BLOOD TO FLOW FROM [A NATURALLY CIRCUMCISED INFANT],[4] וּבֵית הִלֵּל אוֹמְרִים אֵינוֹ צָרִיךְ – WHILE BEIS HILLEL SAY that IT IS NOT NECESSARY.

The Baraisa now presents a conflicting Tannaic interpretation of the Beis Shammai-Beis Hillel dispute:

אָמַר רַבִּי שִׁמְעוֹן בֶּן אֶלְעָזָר – R' SHIMON BEN ELAZAR SAID: לֹא נֶחְלְקוּ בֵּית שַׁמַּאי וּבֵית הִלֵּל עַל נוֹלָד כְּשֶׁהוּא מָהוּל – BEIS SHAMMAI AND BEIS HILLEL DID NOT DISAGREE OVER the case of ONE WHO WAS BORN CIRCUMCISED; שֶׁצָּרִיךְ לְהַטִּיף מִמֶּנּוּ דַּם בְּרִית – indeed, all agree that ONE MUST CAUSE COVENANTAL BLOOD TO FLOW FROM [THE INFANT] מִפְּנֵי שֶׁעָרְלָה כְּבוּשָׁה הִיא – BECAUSE we suspect that IT IS A SUPPRESSED FORESKIN.[5] עַל מַה נֶחְלְקוּ – OVER WHAT case, then, DID THEY DISAGREE? עַל גֵּר שֶׁנִּתְגַּיֵּיר כְּשֶׁהוּא מָהוּל – OVER the case of A CONVERT[6] WHO CONVERTED to Judaism WHEN HE WAS already CIRCUMCISED,[7] שֶׁבֵּית שַׁמַּאי אוֹמְרִים צָרִיךְ לְהַטִּיף מִמֶּנּוּ דַּם בְּרִית – FOR BEIS SHAMMAI SAY that ONE MUST CAUSE COVENANTAL BLOOD TO FLOW FROM [SUCH A CONVERT],[8] וּבֵית הִלֵּל אוֹמְרִים אֵין צָרִיךְ לְהַטִּיף מִמֶּנּוּ דַּם בְּרִית – WHILE BEIS HILLEL SAY that ONE NEED NOT CAUSE COVENANTAL BLOOD TO FLOW FROM HIM.

The Baraisa above mentioned various cases of doubt excluded by the verse *his foreskin*. The Gemara now inquires about one of them:

אָמַר מַר – **Master said:** וְלֹא סָפֵק דּוֹחֶה אֶת הַשַּׁבָּת – The Rabbis stated at the beginning of the Baraisa: *His foreskin* teaches that circumcising ONE WHO IS QUESTIONABLE DOES NOT OVERRIDE THE SABBATH. לְאֵתוּיֵי מַאי – However, inasmuch as the Baraisa proceeds to specify other excluded cases of doubt,[9] **what** does the ambiguously phrased first case come **to include?**

The Gemara answers:

לְאֵתוּיֵי הָא דְּתָנוּ רַבָּנָן – It comes **to include this** case about **which the Rabbis taught** in a Baraisa: בֶּן שִׁבְעָה מְחַלְּלִין עָלָיו אֶת הַשַּׁבָּת – WE VIOLATE THE SABBATH FOR A CHILD born IN THE SEVENTH month of pregnancy,[10] וּבֶן שְׁמוֹנָה אֵין מְחַלְּלִין עָלָיו אֶת הַשַּׁבָּת – BUT WE DO NOT VIOLATE THE SABBATH FOR A CHILD born IN THE EIGHTH month of pregnancy.[11] סָפֵק בֶּן שִׁבְעָה סָפֵק בֶּן שְׁמוֹנָה – If there is A QUESTION WHETHER it is A CHILD OF THE SEVENTH month OR A CHILD OF THE EIGHTH month,[12] אֵין מְחַלְּלִין עָלָיו אֶת הַשַּׁבָּת – WE DO NOT VIOLATE THE SABBATH FOR HIM. The Tanna now explains the rationale for his second ruling: בֶּן שְׁמוֹנָה הֲרֵי הוּא כְּאֶבֶן – For A CHILD OF THE EIGHTH month[13] IS treated LIKE A STONE, וְאָסוּר לְטַלְטְלוֹ – AND so one is FORBIDDEN TO MOVE HIM;[14] אֲבָל אִמּוֹ שׁוֹחָה וּמְנִיקַתּוֹ – HOWEVER, HIS MOTHER MAY BEND OVER HIM AND (without handling the infant) NURSE HIM מִפְּנֵי הַסַּכָּנָה – BECAUSE OF THE DANGER posed to her by the excessive amount of milk she is carrying.[15]

NOTES

1. I.e. one whose obligation to undergo circumcision is doubtful.

2. The Baraisa proceeds to specify different cases of doubt. The Gemara will explain to which case this first, general exclusion refers (*Rashi*). [*Ritva* (*MHK* ed.) explains that the derivations to follow are, in reality, one derivation — that of the general "one who is questionable." For that reason the Baraisa can seemingly learn many cases from the same exclusionary phrase.]

Tosafos question why any case of doubt requires a verse to teach that the circumcision does not override the Sabbath. Certainly logic dictates that the Sabbath not be desecrated on account of an uncertain obligation. *Tosafos* answer that indeed this teaching is not needed for an ordinary case of doubt, but only for some of the unusual cases cited by the Baraisa below. It is mentioned in regard to a case of doubt only by way of *asmachta*, a Scriptural support for a Rabbincal teaching. See *Leshon HaZahav* and *Minchas Chinuch* (*Mitzvah* 2; §17 in *Machon* ed.) for other answers to this question.

3. Since there is a question whether twilight is part of the outgoing or the incoming day, one born during twilight on Friday may not be circumcised on the next Shabbos day, for perhaps he was born on Friday and the following Shabbos is, in fact, the *ninth* day after his birth, not the eighth. Similarly, one born during twilight on Shabbos may not be circumcised on the next Shabbos day, for perhaps he was born at night and the next Shabbos is only the *seventh* day.

4. For Beis Shammai hold that perhaps there is a suppressed foreskin (see *Rashi* ד״ה אנדרוגינוס, and next note). And even so, they concede that this letting-of-blood requirement does not override the Sabbath restrictions (*Rashi*).

For a discussion of what a "letting-of-blood" accomplishes for a suppressed foreskin, see *Chazon Ish* 62:27, *Kehillos Yaakov* §48 and *Megadim Chadashim*.

5. I.e. we are concerned that perhaps there is a foreskin, but it is suppressed into the flesh of the member and is not visible (see *Rashi* above ד״ה אנדרוגינוס). [The Gemara below will debate, however, whether the Tanna means a doubtful, or a certain, suppressed foreskin.]

6. Such as an Arab (*Rashi*) or ancient Gibeonite (*Ritva MHK* ed.). These people traditionally circumcised their males at infancy.

7. Here, we obviously do not suspect the existence of a suppressed foreskin (*Rashi*), for a complete circumcision has already been performed.

8. The conversion process entails accepting upon oneself the Torah's commandments, circumcision (for a male), and immersion in a *mikveh*. Beis Shammai require that the circumcision aspect be fulfilled here at least in a token manner.

9. The androgyne, the infant born during twilight, and the infant born ostensibly circumcised (*Rashi* above ד״ה אנדרוגינוס; *Ritva MHK* ed.).

10. If a child is born during the seventh month of pregnancy, he is considered viable, and we may circumcise him on the eighth day when it falls on the Sabbath. [From *Rashi* (ד״ה בן ח׳) it is clear that the Baraisa speaks of circumcising on the Sabbath. However, *Tur* cites it regarding the more general question of saving the infant's life through desecrating the Sabbath. See *Beur Halachah* to 330:7 ד״ה או ספק בן ד׳, for a discussion of these opinions.]

11. A child born during the eighth month of pregnancy is regarded as a corpse, and there is no mitzvah to circumcise him (cf. *Sfas Emes*); hence, we do not desecrate the Sabbath for the sake of his circumcision. And although the *melachah* of slaughtering (of which *milah* is a *toladah* — see Chapter Introduction) cannot be performed on a corpse (see below, 136a), the Sabbath desecration referred to here is the performance of those preliminaries to *milah* that involve *melachos;* and our Baraisa implicitly rules like R' Eliezer, who sanctions (above, 130a) the performance of such preliminaries on the Sabbath [and is teaching us that for a child born in the eighth month we do not desecrate the Sabbath] (*Rashi;* see also *Ritva MHK* ed.).

12. This is the ambiguous first case of the previous Baraisa — "one who is questionable."

13. I.e. an infant born during the eighth month.

14. The infant is classified as *muktzeh*.

15. Failure to relieve herself of the milk poses a danger to the mother's health (*Rashi*), and so we are not concerned that she might move the child while nursing (*Tosafos;* cf. *Rashi* to *Yevamos* 80b, cited here

ולא ספק דוחה את השבת ערלתו ודאי דוחה את השבת א) ולא אנדרוגינוס דוחה את השבת רבי יהודה אומר אנדרוגינוס דוחה את השבת וענוש כרת ערלתו ודאי דוחה את השבת ב) ולא נולד בין השמשות דוחה את השבת ערלתו ודאי דוחה את השבת ג) ולא נולד כשהוא מהול דוחה את השבת שב"ש אומרים צריך להטיף ממנו דם ברית וב"ה אומרים אינו צריך ד) א"ר שמעון בן אלעזר לא נחלקו ב"ש וב"ה ה) על נולד כשהוא מהול שצריך להטיף ממנו דם ברית מפני שערלה כבושה היא על מה נחלקו על גר שנתגייר כשהוא מהול שב"ש אומרים ו) צריך להטיף ממנו דם ברית וב"א א"צ להטיף ממנו דם ברית: אמר מר ולא ספק דוחה את השבת לאתויי מאי לאתויי הא דתנו רבנן ז) בן שבעה מחללין עליו את השבת ובן ח' אין מחללין עליו את השבת ספק בן ז' ספק בן ח' אין מחללין עליו את השבת ח) בן שמונה הרי הוא כאבן ואסור לטלטלו אבל אמו שוחה ומניקתו מפני הסכנה איתמר רב אמר הלכה כת"ק ושמואל אמר הלכה כר"ש בן אלעזר רב אדא בר אהבה אתיליד ליה ההוא ינוקא כשהוא מהול אהדריה אתליסר מהולאי עד דשוייה כרות שפכה אמר תיתי לי דעברי אדרב אמר ליה רב נחמן ואדשמואל לא עבר אימר דאמר שמואל בחול בשבת מי אמר (א) הוא סבר ודאי ערלה כבושה היא דאיתמר רבה אמר חיישינן שמא ערלה כבושה היא רב יוסף אמר ודאי ערלה כבושה היא אמר רב יוסף מנא אמינא לה דתניא רבי אליעזר הקפר אומר לא נחלקו ב"ש וב"ה על נולד כשהוא מהול שצריך להטיף ממנו דם ברית על מה נחלקו לחלל עליו את השבת ב"ש אומרים מחללין עליו את השבת וב"ה אומרים אין מחללין עליו את השבת לאו מכלל דת"ק סבר מחללין עליו את השבת ודילמא ת"ק דברי הכל אין מחללין קאמר אם כן רבי אליעזר הקפר טעמא דב"ש אתא לאשמעינן דילמא ה"ק ט) לא נחלקו ב"ש וב"ה בדבר זה: י) אמר ר' אסי כל שאמו טמאה לידה נימול לשמונה וכל שאין אמו טמאה לידה אין נימול לשמנה שנאמר א) אשה כי תזריע וילדה זכר וטמאה וגו' וביום השמיני ימול בשר ערלתו א"ל אביי דורות הראשונים יוכיחו שאין אמו טמאה לידה ונימול לשמנה א"ל י) נתנה תורה ונתחדשה

אנדרוגינוס. ספק הוא ונולד בין השמשות נמי ספק זמנו הוא ספק אינו זמנו וכן נולד מהול ספק שמא ערלה כבושה היא שהעור דבוק בבשר ולקמיה פריך ספק קמא לאתויי מאי הואיל ותני כל הני ספיקי: **רבי יהודה אומר כו'.** לקמיה יליף מילתיה: **שב"ש אומרים צריך להטיף כו'.** ואפילו הכי מודו דשבת לא דחי: **שצריך להטיף.** חיישינן שמא ערלה כבושה היא: **על גר.** דליכא שום ספק ערלה כגון ערבי מהול: **בן ח' אין מחללין עליו.** שהרי כמת הוא ואין מילתו מילה ולי קשיא א"כ לאו חילול הוא שהרי הוא כמחתך בבשר מת לקמן נמי מוקי האי חילול במכשירי מילה וליכא לר' אליעזר: **מפני הסכנה.** מפני שחלב הרבה (ב) בדדיה ומביאה לידי חולי: **כת"ק.** דליכא דב"ה דאמר א"צ להטיף ממנו דם ברית: **אהדריה אתליסר מהולאי.** שיטיפו ממנו דם ברית ולא רצו משום דשבת הואי ואפילו לב"ש ספק הוא ואין מחללין: **עד דשוייה כרות שפכה.** והוא עצמו מלו ועשאו כרות שפכה שחתך מן הגיד: **אדרב.** דאמר א"צ להטיף: **בשבת מי אמר.** הא ספיקא הוא: **והוא סבר.** רב אדא סבר דודאי ערלה כבושה היא ומחללין: **חיישינן.** הא דאמר ר"ש בן אלעזר לדברי הכל צריך להטיף אספיקא קאמר ובחול שמא ערלה כבושה היא ולענין שבת נמי ודאי לא מחללין: **ודאי ערלה כבושה היא.** ומחללין: **לאו מכלל דת"ק.** דר' אליעזר הקפר סבר לדברי הכל מחללין ואנא דאמרי כוותיה: **ה"ג וממאי דילמא מכלל דת"ק סבר דברי הכל אין מחללין א"כ רבי אליעזר טעמא דב"ש אתא לאשמעינן כו'.** א"כ דתנא לעיל מיניה אמר דברי הכל אין מחללין ר' אליעזר הקפר דאתא לאיפלוגי ולמימר דלאו דברי הכל הוא דהא לב"ש מחללין מאי רבותא אשמעינן דב"ש פליגי בה הא ב"ש במקום ב"ה אינה משנה ומשנינן דילמא הכי קאמר ר' אליעזר לת"ק דאמר בשבת לדברי הכל אין מחללין ופלוגתייהו בחול דלב"ה א"צ להטיף ממנו דם ברית הא ליתא דלא נחלקו בדבר זה אלא ודאי צריך ובשבת הוא דפליגי וטעמא דב"ה אתא לאשמעינן דבחול צריך ולאפוקי מת"ק דאמר לב"ה לא צריך: **כל שאין אמו טמאה לידה.** כגון יוצא דופן ונכרית שילדה ולאחר נתגיירה אין בנה ממתין עד שמנה אלא נימול מיד: **דורות הראשונים.** מאברהם עד מתן תורה שנתנה מילה ולא נהגו טומאה: ונתחדשה

ולא ספק דוחה את השבת. נראה לר"י דאצטריך בעלמא הוא ולא איצטריך קרא להכי דהיכי תיסוק אדעתיה לחלל את השבת ולא ידענא אם הוא בר חיוב מילה או לא כדמפרש לקמן דספק נולד לז' או לח' ומשום נולד בין השמשות לא איצטריך נמי קרא למעוטי דמיבטל מצות מילה בשמיני מספיקא בשב ואל תעשה ואל יחלל שבת בידים מספק אלא נראה לר"י דעיקר האי קרא אתא לאנדרוגינוס שאינו דוחה שבת ונולד כשהוא מהול ומיהו לא מחד ערלתו נפקי דאין סברא לומר שקולים ויבואו שניהם מקרא אחד תרי קראי כתיבי חד במילה בזמנה וביום השמיני ימול בשר ערלתו וחד במילה שלא בזמנה ט) וערל זכר אשר לא ימול בשר ערלתו (בראשית יז) א"כ קרא אתא לאנדרוגינוס ונולד כשהוא מהול מסברא ידעינן דאין צריך להטיף דם ברית ר"י. אי נמי עיקר קרא לנולד כשהוא מהול ולאנדרוגינוס לא צריך קרא דהא נפקא ליה לר' יהודה לקמן דאנדרוגינוס טעון מילה מדכתיב כל זכר ורבנן הוו דרשי לדרשה אחריתי:

לא נחלקו על נולד כשהוא מהול שצריך להטיף ממנו דם ברית כו' על מה נחלקו על גר שנתגייר. השתא משמע דיותר יש להצריך הטפה לנולד כשהוא מהול מלנתגייר כשהוא מהול דהא לנולד כ"ע מודו ובגר איכא פלוגתא וא"כ לקמן דפסיק רב הלכה כת"ק ומשמע דכוותיה קי"ל מדקאמר רב אדא בר אהבה תיתי לי דעברי אדרב וכיון דקי"ל כת"ק בנולד כשהוא מהול שאין צריך להטיף ממנו דם ברית כ"ש גר שנתגייר כשהוא מהול וה"ג לא פסקו כן אלא פסקו דקטן א"צ וגר צריך ובקטן ודאי כדין פסקו כשמועתנו ובגר נמי נראה לר"י שסמכו אההיא דיבמות דפרק החולץ (דף מו:) דתניא הרי שבא ואמר מלתי ולא טבלתי מטבילין אותו ומה בכך דברי רבי יהודה ור' יוסי אומר אין מטבילין ואת"ל דא"צ להטיף ממנו דם ברית בנתגייר כשהוא מהול לרבי יוסי אמאי אין מטבילין הרי הוא מהול לפנינו מאי נפקא מינה אם לא מלו אותו ב"ד לא יהא אלא ערבי מהול וגבעוני מהול אלא ודאי צריך להטיף ממנו דם ברית ולכך אין מטבילין דאינו גר עד שימול ויטבול ונראה לרשב"א לתת טעם בדבר שהרי הסברא הפוכה מסברא דשמעתין והיינו טעמא דבין קטן שנולד כשהוא מהול ובין גר שנתגייר כשהוא מהול דין הוא דשניהם היו טעונים הטפת דם ברית אי לאו דדרשינן הכא דקטן אין צריך להטיף ממנו משום דכתיב ערלתו ודוקא בקטן דגלי גלי בגר דלא גלי לא גלי ור"ח פסק איפכא מה"ג:

בן שמנה הרי הוא כאבן ואסור לטלטלו. נראה לר"י דעכשיו מותר לטלטל כל תינוקות שאין אנו בקיאין וכולם כמו ספק בן ח' ספק בן ט' ופעמים שהאשה מתעברת סמוך לטבילתה ופעמים שאינה מתעברת ומותר למולו בשבת ממ"נ כדאמרינן לקמן (דף קלו.) אפילו הוא בן שמנה ודאי כגון שלא בא על אשתו אלא פעם אחת ופירש וילדה לסוף ח' אפילו הכי נראה לר"י דמותר לטלטלו ולמולו בשבת אם אין ריעותא בשערו ובציפרניו כדאמר בפרק הערל (יבמות דף פ:) דאמרינן האי בר שבעה הוא ואישתהוי אישתהי: **מפני** הסכנה. סכנת חלב כשיש הרבה בדדין ולא חיישינן שמא תטלטל אותו ולא (ג) ידע רשב"א מאי איריא מפני הסכנה דאפילו לא יהא אלא צערא בעלמא מותר י) אפילו (ד) היא לחלוב עצמה ולהוציא חלב שבדדין אע"פ שהיא מלאכה שאינה צריכה לגופה דהמיר איסורא טפי מאיסור טלטול נראה דשרי מידי דהוה אמפיס מורסא דשרינן משום צערא: **מכלל** דת"ק סבר ד"ה מחללין. ר' אליעזר הקפר ור"ש בן אלעזר תרוייהו קיימי את"ק והא"ק ליה ר"א הקפר לר"ש בן אלעזר לא כך יש להשיב על דברי ת"ק אלא הכי אית לן למימר לא נחלקו כו' והשתא דייק שפיר מכלל דת"ק סבר וכו'. פירוש רשב"א:

עין משפט נר מצוה

לא א ב ג מיי' פ"א מהל' מילה הלכה יא סמג עשין כח טוש"ע י"ד סי' רסו סעי' י וטוש"ע י"ד סי' רסה סעי' יב:
לב ד מיי' שם הלכה ט סמג שם טוש"ע י"ד סי' רסג סעי' ד:
לג ה מיי' שם וסמג שם טוש"ע י"ד סי' רסח סעי' א:
לד ו מיי' פ"א מהל' מילה הלכה יד ופכ"א מהל' שבת הלכה יד וטוש"ע א"ח סי' של סעי' ז וטוש"ע י"ד סי' רסו סעי' יא בהג"ה:

רבינו חננאל

יאות איתעבד ליה כתירוצא דרב יהודה ורבה בר אבוה. דאי כתירוצי' דידיה דאוקמא למתניתין שאמרו חכמים מרחיצין ביום ראשון בשבת כדרכו ומזלפין ביום שלישי שחל להיות בשבת ר' אלעזר בן עזריה אומר אף מרחיצין ביום שלישי שחל להיות בשבת היה צריך לומר מפני שאמרו חכמים יום ג' שחל להיות בשבת מזלפין בא הוא ואמר מזלפין ואף מרחיצין אלא מכיון (כולא) [דלא] אמר כך שמעינן מינה שלא הזכירו חכמים ביום ג' שחל להיות בשבת לא רחיצה ולא זילוף. וממילא שמעינן דלית להו לרבנן ביום השלישי לא רחיצה ולא זילוף. ר' אלעזר בן עזריה אומר מרחיצין את המילה ביום השלישי שחל להיות בשבת שנאמר ויהי ביום השלישי בהיותם כואבים וכ"ש ביום ראשון וקיי"ל כר' אלעזר בן עזריה דאמר' א"ר אבהו א"ר יוחנן הלכה כר' אלעזר בן עזריה בין בחמין שהוחמו בשבת ובין בחמין שהוחמו בע"ש. בין הרחצה כל גופו בין הרחצה מילה. מפני שסכנה היא לו: גופא אמר רב אין נותנין חמין ושמן ע"ג מכה בשבת ושמואל אמר נותנין חוץ למכה ושותת ויורד למכה. ואע"ג דקיי"ל רב ושמואל הלכה כרב באיסורי הכא הלכה כשמואל דתניא כוותיה. אין נותנין חמין ושמן ע"ג מכה בשבת אבל נותן חוץ למכה ושותת ויורד למכה. תני רב נותנין ע"ג מכה מוך יבש וספוג יבש אבל לא גמי יבש ולא כתיתין יבשין. קשיא כתיתין אכתיתין. רישא קתני נותנין ע"ג המכה מוך יבש והוא כתיתין והדר תני ולא כתיתין יבשין ופרקינן לא קשיא הא בחדתי והא בעתיקי מוך יבש מותר שאין חשובין כרטיה. אבל כתיתין ישנין אסורין. ועלה אמר אביי ש"מ האי נקרא. פי' נקרא היא כתיתין והן סמרטוטין יבשים שיש עליהם טינוף זיעה ריעי. כדגרסינן בב"ק ליתו נקרא מקיקלתא כו': ת"ר ערלתו ודאי דוחה את השבת ולא ספק דוחה את השבת ולא אנדרוגינוס דוחה את השבת ר' יהודה אומר אנדרוגינוס דוחה את השבת. אמר מר ולא ספק דוחה את השבת לאתויי הא דתנו רבנן בן ז' מחללין עליו את השבת בן ח' אין מחללין עליו

את השבת ספק בן ח' אין מחללין עליו את השבת בן ח' הרי הוא כאבן ואסור לטלטלו אבל אמו שוחה עליו ומניקתו מפני הסכנה. (צריך לכתוב תשלום הברייתא כמות שהיא בתוספתא). אתמר רב אמר הלכה כת"ק דברייתא דאמר הא דתני ולא נולד כשהוא מהול דוחה את השבת שבית שמאי אומרים צריך להטיף ממנו דם ברית ובה"א אין צריך להטיף ממנו דם ברית ושמואל אמר הלכה כר' שמעון בן אלעזר שאמר לא נחלקו בית שמאי ובית הלל על הנולד כשהוא מהול שצריך להטיף ממנו דם ברית על מה נחלקו על גר שנתגייר כשהוא מהול שב"ש אומרים צריך להטיף ממנו דם ברית ובה"א אין צריך ובחול הוא שאין צריך ועל זה אמר שמואל הלכה כר"ש בן אלעזר והוא בחול ולא בשבת. ונחלקו עוד בזה רבה ורב יוסף רבה אמר חיישינן שמא ערלה כבושה היא וראינו דברי רבה שהן שוין בשבת דרב יוסף אמר ודאי ערלה כבושה היא

הגהות הב"ח

(א) גמ' מי אמר והוא סבר: (ב) רש"י ד"ה מפני הסכנה וכו' שחלב הרבה. נ"ב ובמס' יבמות דף פ פירש"י משום סכנת שניהם: (ג) תוס' ד"ה מפני הסכנה וכו' שמא תטלטל אותו. ולא ידענא מאי איריא כצ"ל ותיבת רשב"א נמחק: (ד) באד"ה אפי' לחלוב עצמה כצ"ל ותיבת היא נמחק:

מסורת הש"ס

א) [תוספתא פרק טו], ב) [לתמן עשה], ג) [תוספ' פט"ו], ד) יבמות ע. ב"ב כ., ה) [לעיל מב. יבמות כח.], ו) ב"ק לג. סוכה טו., ז) [צ"ל אמר רבה אמר ר' אסי כל שאמו וכו' וכן איתא בשאלתות פ' לך לך סי' ט וכ"ה ברי"ף והרא"ש], ח) [ב"ב קיז:], ט) [ברכות לו:], י) [צ"ל לגדול],

תורה אור השלם

א) דַּבֵּר אֶל בְּנֵי יִשְׂרָאֵל לֵאמֹר אִשָּׁה כִּי תַזְרִיעַ וְיָלְדָה זָכָר וְטָמְאָה שִׁבְעַת יָמִים כִּימֵי נִדַּת דְּוֹתָהּ תִּטְמָא: וּבַיּוֹם הַשְּׁמִינִי יִמּוֹל בְּשַׂר עָרְלָתוֹ: [ויקרא יב, ב-ג]

ליקוטי רש"י

ולא נולד בין השמשות. דתנן נולד בין השמשות נמול לעשרה כלומר לספק תשיעי בין השמשות של ערב שבת נמול לעשרה של יו"ט לאחר אותה שבת שאם עשירי הוא לאחר מצות מילה שלא בזמנה לא דחיא [סנהדרין] [חולין פד:]. **היכי** חיים לא אפשר ... **מפני הסכנה.** סכנת שניהם הבן והאם שלא יחלה מפני החלב [יבמות פ:].

רב נסים גאון

בזמנה דדאתיא מקל וחומר וגם זה פירשנו בפ' במה מדליקין: מילה דנכרתו עליה י"ג בריתות. מפורשין הן בתורה (בראשית יז) ואלו הן ואתנה בריתי אני הנה בריתי והקימותי את בריתי לברית עולם ואתה את בריתי תשמור והיתה בריתי בבשרכם לברית עולם את בריתי הפר והקימותי את בריתי לברית עולם ואת בריתי אקים את יצחק: ולא שאני לך בין חמין שהוחמו בשבת לבין חמין שהוחמו מערב שבת.

תמצא נשיאות ונתינות שבדבר זה ומה שנאמר עליו בפ' כירה (ד' לח) דתנן מעשה שעשו אנשי טבריא שהביאו סילון של צונן לתוך אמה של חמין ואמרו להם חכמים אם בשבת כחמין שהוחמו בשבת אסורין ברחיצה ובשתיה ... בן ח': הרי הוא כאבן. ... יצירה

ח"ש על רב נסים גאון: (א) פס הפרון והפר ... וכו'.

The Gemara returns to the subject of the Beis Shammai-Beis Hillel dispute, and the two Tannaic interpretations thereof:

אִיתְּמַר – **It was stated:** רַב אָמַר הֲלָכָה כְּתַנָּא קַמָּא – **Rav said** that **the law accords with the Tanna Kamma**'s interpretation of Beis Hillel's opinion,[16] וּשְׁמוּאֵל אָמַר הֲלָכָה כְּרַבִּי שִׁמְעוֹן בֶּן אֶלְעָזָר – **while Shmuel said** that **the law accords with R' Shimon ben Elazar**'s interpretation of the dispute.[17]

The Gemara records a related incident:

רַב אַדָּא בַּר אַהֲבָה אִתְיְלִיד לֵיהּ הַהוּא יְנוּקָא כְּשֶׁהוּא מָהוּל – A naturally **circumcised child was** once **born to Rav Adda bar Ahavah.** אַהַדְרֵיהּ אַתְלֵיסַר מְהוֹלָאֵי – On the eighth day after birth, which fell on the Sabbath, **[Rav Adda] went around to thirteen circumcisers,** attempting to enlist someone to cause covenantal blood to flow from the child,[18] עַד דְּשַׁוְיֵיהּ כְּרוּת שָׁפְכָה – **until he** himself performed the procedure and **rendered [his son] genitally mutilated.**[19] אָמַר – **[Rav Adda] said** to his colleagues: תֵּיתֵי לִי דַּעֲבַרִי אַדְּרַב – **[This tragedy] is coming to me,**[20] **for I transgressed** the ruling **of Rav.**[21] אָמַר לֵיהּ רַב נַחְמָן – **Rav Nachman said to him:** וְאַדִּשְׁמוּאֵל לֹא עָבַר – **And did** master **not transgress** the ruling **of Shmuel** as well?! אֵימַר דְּאָמַר שְׁמוּאֵל בְּחוֹל – For **one could say that Shmuel stated** his opinion **with regard to a weekday;**[22] בְּשַׁבָּת מִי אָמַר – however, **with regard to the Sabbath, did he state** it?![23]

The Gemara explains Rav Adda's thinking:

הוּא סָבַר וַדַּאי עָרְלָה כְּבוּשָׁה הִיא – But **[Rav Adda] held** that in R' Shimon Ben Elazar's opinion we assume that where the infant is born circumcised, **it is definitely a suppressed foreskin,** and so – since the obligation to circumcise is certain – a desecration of the Sabbath would be sanctioned by Shmuel (ruling in accordance with R' Shimon ben Elazar).

The Gemara now offers support for Rav Adda's understanding of Shmuel's (and R' Shimon ben Elazar's) opinion:

דְּאִיתְּמַר – **For it was stated:** רַבָּה אָמַר – **Rabbah said:** חָיְישִׁינַן שֶׁמָּא עָרְלָה כְּבוּשָׁה הִיא – In R' Shimon ben Elazar's ruling, **we are concerned** that **perhaps it is a suppressed foreskin.**[24] רַב יוֹסֵף אָמַר – However, **Rav Yosef said:** וַדַּאי עָרְלָה כְּבוּשָׁה הִיא – R' Shimon ben Elazar means that **it is definitely a suppressed foreskin.**[25]

Rav Yosef now offers evidence to support his opinion:

אָמַר רַב יוֹסֵף מְנָא אָמֵינָא לָהּ – **Rav Yosef**[26] **said** further: **From where do I say it?** דְּתַנְיָא – **For it was taught in a Baraisa:** רַבִּי אֱלִיעֶזֶר הַקַּפָּר אוֹמֵר – R' ELIEZER HAKAPPAR SAYS: לֹא נֶחְלְקוּ בֵּית שַׁמַּאי וּבֵית הִלֵּל עַל נוֹלַד כְּשֶׁהוּא מָהוּל – BEIS SHAMMAI AND BEIS HILLEL DO NOT DISAGREE OVER the basic law of ONE WHO WAS BORN CIRCUMCISED – שֶׁצָּרִיךְ לְהַטִּיף מִמֶּנּוּ דַּם בְּרִית – all agree THAT ONE MUST CAUSE COVENANTAL BLOOD TO FLOW FROM HIM. עַל מַה נֶּחְלְקוּ – OVER WHAT, then, DID THEY DISAGREE? לְחַלֵּל עָלָיו אֶת הַשַּׁבָּת – Over whether one is permitted TO DESECRATE THE SABBATH FOR [THE CHILD] by performing this procedure on Shabbos. בֵּית שַׁמַּאי אוֹמְרִים מְחַלְּלִין עָלָיו אֶת הַשַּׁבָּת – BEIS SHAMMAI SAY that WE DESECRATE THE SABBATH FOR HIM, וּבֵית הִלֵּל אוֹמְרִים אֵין מְחַלְּלִין עָלָיו אֶת הַשַּׁבָּת – WHILE BEIS HILLEL SAY that WE DO NOT DESECRATE THE SABBATH FOR HIM.

Rav Yosef now concludes his proof:

לָאו מִכְּלָל דְּתַנָּא קַמָּא סָבַר מְחַלְּלִין עָלָיו אֶת הַשַּׁבָּת – Does it **not** follow **by implication that the Tanna Kamma** of R' Eliezer HaKappar[27] **holds** that in the opinion of both Beis Hillel and Beis Shammai **we desecrate the Sabbath for [the infant],** which would correspond to my interpretation of R' Shimon ben Elazar's ruling?[28]

The Gemara asks:

וְדִילְמָא תַּנָּא קַמָּא דִּבְרֵי הַכֹּל אֵין מְחַלְּלִין קָאָמַר – **But perhaps the Tanna Kamma had stated** that in **the opinion of all we do not desecrate** the Sabbath for the child?[29]

Rav Yosef responds:

אִם כֵּן – But **if** this is **so,** רַבִּי אֱלִיעֶזֶר הַקַּפָּר טַעְמָא דְּבֵית שַׁמַּאי אָתָא

NOTES

by *Bach* §2). *Tosafos* wonder why the Baraisa uses the term סַכָּנָה, *danger,* since even the discomfort she is experiencing from the buildup of milk constitutes sufficient grounds for allowing her to nurse the baby. See also *Ritva MHK* ed.

Tosafos, citing *Ri,* rule that nowadays any infant may be moved, since we are no longer expert in determining the fetal birth month. Furthermore, contends *Ri,* even where an infant's eighth-month status is certain [e.g. the mother cohabited with her husband only once, and gave birth eight months later], the infant may nonetheless be moved and circumcised on the Sabbath so long as he exhibits no signs of immature hair and nail formation. [Indeed, *Ri* follows the opinion of Rebbi, who ruled in *Yevamos* (80b) that a baby born in the eighth month with mature hair and nail formation is actually a seventh-month baby that remained in the womb longer than necessary]. See also *Shiltei HaGiborim* here at length and *Chazon Ish, Even HaEzer* 115:4.

16. "The Tanna Kamma" refers to the first opinion of the Baraisa, where it was stated that Beis Hillel and Beis Shammai argue over whether one must cause covenantal blood to flow from a child born circumcised, and that Beis Hillel rule in the negative (*Rashi*).

17. According to R' Shimon ben Elazar, Beis Hillel agree that covenantal blood must be made to flow from a child born circumcised (and their dispute with Beis Shammai concerns the case of a circumcised convert).

18. Each of the *mohalim* refused him, however, on the grounds that even Beis Shammai would not permit this desecration of the Sabbath, since the existence of a suppressed foreskin was only a matter of doubt (*Rashi*).

19. By slicing off flesh from the child's member (*Rashi*).

20. I.e. I deserve it.

21. Rav ruled, in accordance with the Tanna Kamma's interpretation of Beis Hillel, that it is unnecessary to cause covenantal blood to flow from an infant born circumcised (*Rashi*). Rav Adda thus lamented that he performed an unsanctioned desecration of the Sabbath.

22. Rav Nachman argues: When Shmuel ruled, in accordance with R' Shimon ben Elazar's interpretation of Beis Hillel, that one must cause covenantal blood to flow from an infant born circumcised, it is reasonable to assume that Shmuel allows it only on a weekday [since the existence of a suppressed foreskin is only a *possibility*], when there is no desecration of the Sabbath.

23. Since in this case the obligation to circumcise is uncertain (*Rashi*), the circumciser would be performing a possible Sabbath desecration, an action that, presumably, Shmuel would not sanction.

24. Rabbah understands that when R' Shimon ben Elazar ruled that everyone requires the letting of covenantal blood for an infant born circumcised, he holds that it is only *suspected* that a foreskin exists and is suppressed, and so his ruling was perforce limited to the weekdays (where there can be no Sabbath desecration). Accordingly, we cannot apply his ruling to the Sabbath (*Rashi*).

25. According to Rav Yosef, R' Shimon ben Elazar's ruling is that we assume a *certain* suppressed foreskin, and so it would mean that both Beis Hillel and Beis Shammai require the letting-of-blood procedure even on the Sabbath (*Rashi*). It was this interpretation of R' Shimon ben Elazar's ruling that Shmuel endorsed, and that Rav Adda followed.

26. In the texts of *Rabbeinu Chananel, Rif, Ramban, Rashba* and *Ran,* the Gemara here states, "Rabbah said: From where do I know it?" See there for an elucidation of the Gemara according to this version.

27. This (the Tanna Kamma of R' Eliezer HaKappar) is a Tanna not encountered heretofore. However, Rav Yosef will attempt to buttress his interpretation by showing that this anonymous Tanna also holds the view that he, Rav Yosef, attributes to R' Shimon ben Elazar (*Rashi,* as explained by *Maharsha;* cf. *Ramban, Rashba, Chidushei HaRan* and *Ritva MHK* ed., who hold that the reference is to R' Shimon ben Elazar himself; but see *Tosafos,* who maintain that the reference is to the Tanna Kamma of the Baraisa at the top of the *amud*).

28. See note 25 above.

29. And R' Eliezer HaKappar is saying that in Beis Shammai's opinion we do desecrate the Sabbath.

א) [תוספתא פרק טו], ב) יבמות עב., ג) [תוספ' פט"ו], ד) יבמות עא: ב"ב כ., ה) [לעיל מב. יבמות כח. ב"ק לד. סוכה טו.], ו) [נ"ל אמר רבה אמר ר' אסי כל שאמו וכו' וכן איתא בשאלתות פ' לך לך סי' ט וכ"ה ברי"ף והרא"ש], ז) [ב"ב קיב.], ח) [ברכות לו:], ט) נ"ל דגדול ובדרך אם אינו ענין לשלא בזמנו שאף לודאי אינו דוחה, י) אפי' לחלוב בעצמה כצ"ל ותיבת היא נמחק.

לא א ב ג מיי' פ"א מהל' מילה הלכה יא סמג עשין כח טוש"ע א"ח סי' שלא סעי' ה וטוש"ע י"ד סי' רסו סעיף י וסעיף יג: לב ד מיי' שם הלכה ח סמג שם טוש"ע י"ד סי' רסג סעי' ד: לג ה מיי' וסמג שם ומיי' פי"ד מהל' איסורי ביאה הלכה יא טוש"ע י"ד סי' רסח סעי' א: לד ו מיי' פ"א מהל' מילה הלכה יד ופכ"ה מהל' שבת הלכה ז טוש"ע א"ח סי' של סעי' ז ח וי"ד סי' רסו סעי' יא בהגה:

ולא ספק דוחה את השבת ערלתו ודאי דוחה את השבת א ולא אנדרוגינוס דוחה את השבת רבי יהודה אומר אנדרוגינוס דוחה את השבת וענוש כרת ערלתו ודאי דוחה את השבת ב ולא נולד בין השמשות דוחה את השבת ערלתו ודאי דוחה את השבת ג ולא נולד כשהוא מהול דוחה את השבת שב"ש אומרים צריך להטיף ממנו דם ברית וב"ה אומרים אינו צריך ד א"ר שמעון בן אלעזר לא נחלקו ב"ש וב"ה ה על נולד כשהוא מהול שצריך להטיף ממנו דם ברית מפני שערלה כבושה היא על מה נחלקו על גר שנתגייר כשהוא מהול שבית שמאי אומרים ו צריך להטיף ממנו דם ברית ובה"א א"צ להטיף ממנו דם ברית: אמר מר ולא ספק דוחה את השבת לאתויי מאי לאתויי הא דתנו רבנן ז בן שבעה מחללין עליו את השבת ובן ח' אין מחללין עליו את השבת ספק בן ז' ספק בן ח' אין מחללין עליו את השבת ח בן שמונה הרי הוא כאבן ואסור לטלטלו אבל אמו שוחה ומניקתו מפני הסכנה איתמר רב אמר הלכה כת"ק ושמואל אמר הלכה כר"ש בן אלעזר רב אדא בר אהבה אתיליד ליה ההוא ינוקא כשהוא מהול אהדריה אתליסר מהולאי עד דשוייה כרות שפכה אמר תיתי לי דעברי אדרב אמר ליה רב נחמן ואדשמואל לא עבר אימר דאמר שמואל בחול בשבת מי אמר (א) הוא סבר ודאי ערלה כבושה היא דאיתמר רבה אמר חיישינן שמא ערלה כבושה היא רב יוסף אמר ודאי ערלה כבושה היא אמר רב יוסף מנא אמינא לה דתניא רבי אליעזר הקפר אומר לא נחלקו ב"ש וב"ה על נולד כשהוא מהול שצריך להטיף ממנו דם ברית על מה נחלקו לחלל עליו את השבת ב"ש אומרים מחללין עליו את השבת וב"ה אומרים אין מחללין עליו את השבת לאו מכלל דת"ק סבר מחללין עליו את השבת ודילמא ת"ק דברי הכל אין מחללין קאמר אם כן רבי אליעזר הקפר טעמא דב"ש אתא לאשמעינן דילמא ה"ק ט לא נחלקו ב"ש וב"ה בדבר זה: י אמר ר' אסי כל שאמו טמאה לידה נימול לשמונה וכל שאין אמו טמאה לידה אין נימול לשמנה שנאמר א אשה כי תזריע וילדה זכר וטמאה וגו' וביום השמיני ימול בשר ערלתו א"ל אביי דורות הראשונים יוכיחו שאין אמו טמאה לידה ונימול לשמנה א"ל י נתנה תורה ונתחדשה

רש"י

אנדרוגינוס. ספק הוא ונולד בין השמשות נמי ספק זמנו הוא ספק אינו זמנו וכן נולד מהול ספק שמא ערלה כבושה היא העור דבוק בבשר ולקמיה פריך ספק קמא לאתויי מאי הואיל ותני כל הני ספיקי: רבי יהודה אומר כו'. לקמיה יליף מילתיה: שב"ש אומרים צריך להטיף כו'. ואפילו הכי מודו דשבת לא דחי: שצריך להטיף. חיישינן שמא ערלה כבושה היא: על גר. דליכא שום ספק ערלה כגון ערבי מהול: בן ח' אין מחללין עליו. שהרי כמת הוא ואין מילתו מצוה ואי קשיא א"כ לאו חילול הוא שהרי הוא כמחתך בבשר מת לקמן נמי מוקי האי חילול במכשירי מילה ואליבא דר' אליעזר: מפני הסכנה. מפני שחלב הרבה (ב) בדדיה ומביאה לידי חולי: כת"ק. אליבא דב"ה דאמר א"צ להטיף ממנו דם ברית: אהדריה אתליסר מהולאי. שיטיפו ממנו דם ברית ולא רצו משום דשבת הואי ואפילו לב"ש ספק הוא ואין מחללין: עד דשוייה כרות שפכה. והוא עצמו מלו ועשאו כרות שפכה שחתך מן הגיד: אדרב. דאמר א"צ להטיף: בשבת מי אמר. הא ספיקא הוא: והוא סבר. רב אדא סבר דודאי ערלה כבושה היא ומחללינן: חיישינן. הא דאמר ר"ש בן אלעזר לדברי הכל צריך להטיף אספיקא קאמר ובחול שמא ערלה כבושה היא ולענין שבת נמי ודאי לא מחללינן: ודאי ערלה כבושה היא. ומחללינן: לאו מכלל דת"ק. דר' אליעזר הקפר סבר דברי הכל מחללין ואנא דאמרי כוותיה: ה"ג וממאי דילמא מכלל דת"ק סבר דברי הכל אין מחללין א"כ רבי אליעזר טעמא דב"ש אתא לאשמעינן כו'. א"כ דתנא לעיל מיניה אמר דברי הכל אין מחללין ר' אליעזר הקפר דאתא לאיפלוגי ולמימר דלאו דברי הכל הוא דהא לב"ש מחללין מאי רבותא אשמעינן דב"ש פליגי בה הא ב"ש במקום ב"ה אינה משנה (ס) ומשנינן דילמא הכי קאמר ר' אליעזר לת"ק דאמר בשבת לדברי הכל אין מחללין ופלוגתייהו בחול דלב"ה א"צ להטיף ממנו דם ברית הא ליתא דלא נחלקו בדבר זה אלא ודאי צריך ובשבת הוא דפליגי וטעמא דב"ה אתא לאשמעינן דבחול צריך ולאפוקי מת"ק דאמר לב"ה לא צריך: כל שאין אמו טמאה לידה. כגון יוצא דופן ונכרית שילדה ולמחר נתגיירה אין בנה ממתין עד שמנה אלא נימול מיד: דורות הראשונים. מאברהם עד מתן תורה שנתנה מילה ולא נהגו טומאה:

ונתחדשה

תוספות

ולא ספק דוחה את השבת. נראה לר"י דאסמכתא בעלמא הוא ולא איצטריך קרא להכי דהיכי תיסק אדעתין לחלל את השבת ולא ידענא אם הוא בר חיוב מילה או לא כדמפרש לקמן דספק נולד לז' או לח' ומשום נולד בין השמשות לא איצטריך נמי קרא למעוטי דתיבטל מצות מילה בשמיני מספיקא בשב ואל תעשה ואל יחלל שבת בידים מספק אלא נראה לר"י דעיקר האי קרא אתא לאנדרוגינוס שאינו דוחה שבת ונולד כשהוא מהול ומיהו לא מחד ערלתו נפקי דאין סברא לומר שקולים ויבואו שניהם וביום השמיני שהרי קראי כתיבי חד במילה בזמנה וביום השמיני ימול בשר ערלתו וחד במילה שלא בזמנה ט) דגדול וערל זכר אשר לא ימול בשר ערלתו (בראשית יז) א"כ קרא אתא לאנדרוגינוס ונולד כשהוא מהול מסברא ידעינן דאין צריך להטיף דם ברית לר"י. אי נמי עיקר קרא לנולד כשהוא מהול ולאנדרוגינוס לא צריך קרא דהא נפקא ליה לר' יהודה לקמן לאנדרוגינוס טעון מילה מדכתיב כל זכר ורבנן הוו דרשי לדרשה אחריתי:

לא נחלקו על נולד כשהוא מהול שצריך להטיף ממנו דם ברית כו' על מה נחלקו על גר שנתגייר. הכא משמע דיותר יש להצריך הטפה לנולד כשהוא מהול מלנתגייר כשהוא מהול דהא לנולד כ"ע מודו ובגר איכא פלוגתא וא"ת לקמן דפסיק רב הלכה כת"ק ומשמע דכוותיה קי"ל מדקאמר רב אדא בר אהבה תיתי לי דעברי אדרב וכיון דקי"ל כת"ק בנולד כשהוא מהול שאין צריך להטיף ממנו דם ברית כ"ש גר שנתגייר כשהוא מהול וה"ג לא פסקו כן אלא פסקו דקטן א"צ וגר צריך ובקטן ודאי כדין פסקו כשמועתנו ובגר נמי נראה לר"י שסמכו אההיא דיבמות דפרק החולץ (דף מו:) דתניא הרי שבא ואמר מלתי ולא טבלתי מטבילין אותו ומה בכך דברי רבי יהודה ור' יוסי אומר אין מטבילין ואת"ל דא"צ להטיף ממנו דם ברית בנתגייר כשהוא מהול לרבי יוסי אמאי אין מטבילין הרי הוא מהול לפנינו מאי נפקא מינה אם לא מלו אותו ב"ד לא יהא אלא ערבי מהול וגבעוני מהול אלא ודאי צריך להטיף ממנו דם ברית ולכך אין מטבילין דאינו גר עד שימול ויטבול ונראה לרשב"א לתת טעם בדבר שהרי הסברא הפוכה מסברא דשמעתין והיינו טעמא דבין קטן שנולד כשהוא מהול ובין גר שנתגייר כשהוא מהול דין הוא דשניהם היו טעונים הטפת דם ברית אי לאו דדרשינן הכא דקטן אין צריך להטיף ממנו משום דכתיב ערלתו ודוקא בקטן דגלי גלי בגר דלא גלי לא גלי ור"ח פסק איפכא מה"ג:

בן שמנה הרי הוא כאבן ואסור לטלטלו. נראה לר"י דעכשיו מותר לטלטל כל תינוקות שאין אנו בקיאין וכולם כמו ספק בן ח' ספק בן ט' ופעמים שהאשה מתעברת סמוך לטבילתה ופעמים שאינה מתעברת ומותר למולו בשבת ממ"נ כדאמרינן לקמן (דף קלו.) אפילו הוא בן שמנה ודאי כגון שלא בא על אשתו אלא פעם אחת ופירש וילדה לסוף ח' אפילו הכי נראה לר"י דמותר לטלטלו ולמולו בשבת אם אין ריעותא בשערו ובציפרניו כדאמר בפרק הערל (יבמות דף פ:) דאמרינן האי בר שבעה הוא ואישתהויי אישתהי: מפני הסכנה. סכנת חלב כשיש הרבה בדדין ולא חיישינן שמא תטלטל אותו ולא (ג) ידע רשב"א מאי איריא מפני הסכנה דאפילו לא יהא אלא צערא בעלמא מותר י) אפילו (ד) היא לחלוב עצמה ולהוציא חלב שבדדין אע"פ שהיא מלאכה שאינה צריכה לגופה דחמיר איסורא טפי מאיסור טלטול נראה דשרי מידי דהוה אמפיס מורסא דשרינן משום צערא: מכלל דת"ק סבר דה"ה מחללין. ר' אליעזר הקפר ור"ש בן אלעזר תרווייהו קיימי את"ק וה"ק ליה ר"א הקפר לר"ש בן אלעזר כך יש להשיב על דברי ת"ק אלא הכי אית לן למימר לא נחלקו כו' והשתא דייק שפיר מכלל דת"ק סבר וכו'. פירוש רשב"א:

כתנאי

הגהות הב"ח

(א) גמ' מי אמר והוא סבר: (ב) רש"י ד"ה מפני הסכנה וכו' שחלב הרבה. נ"ב ובמס' יבמות דף מ פירש"י מפני סכנת שניהם: (ג) תוס' ד"ה מפני הסכנה וכו' שמא תטלטל אותו. ולא ידענא מאי איריא כצ"ל ותיבת רשב"א נמחק: (ד) בא"ד אפי' לחלוב עצמה כצ"ל ותיבת היא נמחק:

תורה אור השלם

א) דַּבֵּר אֶל בְּנֵי יִשְׂרָאֵל לֵאמֹר אִשָּׁה כִּי תַזְרִיעַ וְיָלְדָה זָכָר וְטָמְאָה שִׁבְעַת יָמִים כִּימֵי נִדַּת דְּוֹתָהּ תִּטְמָא: וּבַיּוֹם הַשְּׁמִינִי יִמּוֹל בְּשַׂר עָרְלָתוֹ: [ויקרא יב, ב-ג]

ליקוטי רש"י

ולא נולד בין השמשות. דקטן נולד בין השמשות נמול לעשרה כלומר לספק תשיעי בין השמשות של ערב שבת נמול לעשרה של יו"ט לאחר אותה שבת שהוא עשירי ... [חולין פד:] ... מפני הסכנה ... [יבמות פ:].

רבינו חננאל

יאות איתבור ליה כתיובתיה דרב יהודה ורבה בר אבוה ... [illegible]

רב נסים גאון

בזמנה דאתיא מקל וחומר וגם זה פירשנו ... [illegible]

לְאַשְׁמְעִינַן – is R' Eliezer HaKappar then **coming to teach us the opinion of Beis Shammai?!** Obviously not![30]

The Gemara rejects this argument:

דִּילְמָא הָכִי קָאָמַר – **Perhaps [R' Eliezer HaKappar]** actually **said thus** to the Tanna Kamma: לֹא נֶחְלְקוּ בֵּית שַׁמַּאי וּבֵית הִלֵּל בְּדָבָר זֶה – **Beis Shammai and Beis Hillel never disagreed on this issue.**[31] Hence, Rav Yosef cannot support his interpretation of R' Shimon ben Elazar by citing the opinion of R' Eliezer HaKappar's Tanna Kamma. – ? –

The Gemara gives a rule for who must wait until the eighth day to be circumcised:

אָמַר רַבִּי אַסִּי – **R' Assi said:**[32] כֹּל שֶׁאִמּוֹ טְמֵאָה לֵידָה – **Any** newborn **whose mother becomes *tamei* due to childbirth** נִימּוֹל לִשְׁמוֹנָה – **is circumcised on the eighth** day, וְכֹל שֶׁאֵין אִמּוֹ טְמֵאָה לֵידָה – **while any** newborn **whose mother does not become *tamei* due to childbirth** אֵין נִימּוֹל לִשְׁמוֹנָה – **is not circumcised on the eighth day,** but rather on the first day;[33] שֶׁנֶּאֱמַר – **as [the verse] states:** "אִשָּׁה כִּי תַזְרִיעַ וְיָלְדָה זָכָר וְטָמְאָה וגו׳ וּבַיּוֹם הַשְּׁמִינִי יִמּוֹל בְּשַׂר עָרְלָתוֹ" – ***When a woman conceives and gives birth to a male, she shall be tamei etc., and on the eighth day, the flesh of his foreskin shall be circumcised.***[34] The verse links circumcision on the eighth day to the mother's becoming *tamei.*

Abaye challenges R' Assi's statement:

אָמַר לֵיהּ אַבַּיֵי – **Abaye said to him:** דּוֹרוֹת הָרִאשׁוֹנִים יוֹכִיחוּ – **The earlier generations,** from the time circumcision was commanded to Abraham until the day the Torah was given, **should demonstrate** otherwise, שֶׁאֵין אִמּוֹ טְמֵאָה לֵידָה – **since** in that era **[a newborn's] mother did not become *tamei* due to childbirth** וְנִימּוֹל לִשְׁמוֹנָה – **and** yet **he was circumcised on the eighth** day.[35] How, then, can R' Assi assert that only if the mother becomes *tamei* is circumcision mandated on the eighth day?

R' Assi responds:

אָמַר לֵיהּ – **He said to [Abaye]:** נִתְּנָה תוֹרָה – Once **the Torah was given**

NOTES

30. Rav Yosef argues as follows: If you say that the Tanna Kamma held that according to everyone we may not desecrate the Sabbath to circumcise the infant, and that R' Eliezer HaKappar came to dispute this and claim that Beis Shammai does sanction desecration, what then is the point of R' Eliezer HaKappar's statement? The established rule is that Beis Hillel's ruling prevails over any conflicting ruling by Beis Shammai. Hence, teaching Beis Shammai's contrary opinion in this case would serve no purpose. We may thus conclude that in the Tanna Kamma's (and R' Shimon ben Elazar's) view, Beis Hillel and Beis Shammai both hold that we do desecrate the Sabbath for the infant, as per Rav Yosef's understanding of that view [and that R' Eliezer HaKappar comes to argue that in the prevailing opinion of Beis Hillel, Sabbath desecration is prohibited] (*Rashi*).

31. The Gemara again argues that perhaps the Tanna Kamma never concurred with R' Shimon ben Elazar, as Rav Yosef interpreted him. Rather, the Tanna Kamma held, conversely, that *everyone prohibits* the letting-of-blood procedure on the Sabbath. Indeed, he holds that the dispute concerns whether it must be performed even on the weekdays, and Beis Hillel rule in the negative. It is against this interpretation that R' Eliezer HaKappar protested: Beis Shammai and Beis Hillel never disagreed on whether the procedure should be performed on the weekdays; all maintain that it surely must. Their dispute concerns the Sabbath, with Beis Hillel prohibiting its desecration and Beis Shammai allowing it. Accordingly, R' Eliezer HaKappar indeed comes to teach Beis Hillel's prevailing opinion, for the Tanna Kamma had stated that Beis Hillel do not require the letting of blood at any time, while R' Eliezer HaKappar contends that they require it on the weekdays (*Rashi*).

32. [Many Rishonim have the reading "Rabbah said in the name of R' Assi"; see *Rabbeinu Chananel, Rif* as emended by *Bach, Rosh, She'iltos D'Rav Achai Gaon, Lech Lecha;* cf. *Ramban;* see also *Dikdukei Soferim*).]

33. Ordinarily, a woman who gives birth becomes *tamei* for seven days for the birth of a boy and fourteen days for the birth of a girl (*Leviticus* 12:2-5). *Rashi* offers two examples of a woman who does not become *tamei* due to childbirth. The first is a woman who gives birth by Caesarean section. [She is not *tamei* because the Torah states: *When a woman conceives and gives birth ... she shall be tamei,* which the Gemara (*Niddah* 40a) understands to mean that *tumah* occurs only when she gives birth through the part of her body through which she conceived.] The second example is that of a non-Jewish woman who gave birth and then converted. She is not *tamei,* because she gave birth before she became Jewish, and the *tumah* of childbirth applies only to Jewish women. Thus, if she converted her child along with herself, the child would be a newborn whose mother is not *tamei* due to childbirth.

34. *Leviticus* 12:2,3.

35. In common with most other laws, the laws of *tumah* did not take effect until after the Torah was given at Mount Sinai. However, Abraham and his descendants were commanded to perform circumcision (*Genesis* 17:9-14).

ולא ספק דוחה את השבת ערלתו ודאי דוחה את השבת [א]ולא אנדרוגינוס דוחה את השבת רבי יהודה אומר אנדרוגינוס דוחה את השבת וענוש כרת ערלתו ודאי דוחה את השבת [ב]ולא נולד בין השמשות דוחה את השבת ערלתו ודאי דוחה את השבת [ג]ולא נולד כשהוא מהול דוחה את השבת שב"ש אומרים צריך להטיף ממנו דם ברית וב"ה אומרים אינו צריך [א]א"ר שמעון בן אלעזר לא נחלקו ב"ש וב"ה [ב][ד]על נולד כשהוא מהול שצריך להטיף ממנו דם ברית מפני שערלה כבושה היא על מה נחלקו על גר שנתגייר כשהוא מהול שבית שמאי אומרים [ה]צריך להטיף ממנו דם ברית ובה"א א"צ להטיף ממנו דם ברית: אמר מר ולא ספק דוחה את השבת לאתויי מאי לאתויי הא דתנו רבנן [ג][ו]בן שבעה מחללין עליו את השבת ובן ח' אין מחללין עליו את השבת ספק בן ז' ספק בן ח' אין מחללין עליו את השבת [ז]בן שמונה הרי הוא כאבן ואסור לטלטלו אבל אמו שוחה ומניקתו מפני הסכנה איתמר רב אמר הלכה כת"ק ושמואל אמר הלכה כר"ש בן אלעזר רב אדא בר אהבה אתיליד ליה ההוא ינוקא כשהוא מהול אהדריה אתליסר מהולאי עד דשוויה כרות שפכה אמר תיתי לי דעברי אדרב אמר ליה רב נחמן ואדשמואל לא עבר אימר דאמר שמואל בחול בשבת מי אמר [ד]הוא סבר ודאי ערלה כבושה היא דאיתמר רבה אמר חיישינן שמא ערלה כבושה היא רב יוסף אמר ודאי ערלה כבושה היא אמר רב יוסף מנא אמינא לה דתניא רבי אליעזר הקפר אומר לא נחלקו ב"ש וב"ה על נולד כשהוא מהול שצריך להטיף ממנו דם ברית על מה נחלקו לחלל עליו את השבת ב"ש אומרים מחללין עליו את השבת וב"ה אומרים אין מחללין עליו את השבת לאו מכלל דת"ק סבר מחללין עליו את השבת ודילמא ת"ק דברי הכל אין מחללין קאמר אם כן רבי אליעזר הקפר טעמא דב"ש אתא לאשמעינן דילמא ה"ק [ה]לא נחלקו ב"ש וב"ה בדבר זה: [י]אמר ר' אסי כל שאמו טמאה לידה נימול לשמונה וכל שאין אמו טמאה לידה אין נימול לשמונה שנאמר [א]אשה כי תזריע וילדה זכר וטמאה וגו' וביום השמיני ימול בשר ערלתו א"ל אביי דורות הראשונים יוכיחו שאין אמו טמאה לידה ונימול לשמונה א"ל [י]נתנה תורה ונתחדשה

רש"י

אנדרוגינוס. ספק הוא ונולד בין השמשות נמי ספק זמנו הוא ספק אינו זמנו וכן נולד מהול ספק שמא ערלה כבושה היא העור דבוק בבשר ולקמיה פריך ספק קמא לאתויי מאי הואיל ותני כל הני ספיקי: **רבי יהודה אומר כו'.** לקמיה יליף מילתיה: **שב"ש אומרים צריך להטיף כו'.** ואפילו הכי מודו דשבת לא דחי: **שצריך להטיף.** חיישינן שמא ערלה כבושה היא: **על גר.** דליכא שום ספק ערלה כגון ערבי מהול: **בן ח' אין מחללין עליו.** שהרי כמת הוא ואין מילתו מלוה ואי קשיא א"כ לאו חילול הוא שהרי הוא כמחתך בבשר מת לקמן נמי מוקי האי חילול במכשירי מילה ואליבא דר' אליעזר: **מפני הסכנה.** מפני שחלב הרבה (ג) בדדיה ומביאה לידי חולי: **כת"ק.** אליבא דב"ה דאמר א"צ להטיף ממנו דם ברית: **אהדריה אתליסר מהולאי.** שיטיפו ממנו דם ברית ולא רצו משום דשבת הואי ואפילו לב"ש ספק הוא ואין מחללין: **עד דשוויה כרות שפכה.** והוא עצמו מלו ועשאו כרות שפכה שחתך מן הגיד: **אדרב.** דאמר א"צ להטיף: **בשבת מי אמר.** הא ספיקא הוא: **והוא סבר.** רב אדא סבר דודאי ערלה כבושה היא ומחללינן: **חיישינן.** הא דאמר ר"ש בן אלעזר לדברי הכל צריך להטיף אספיקא קאמר ובחול שמא ערלה כבושה היא ולענין שבת נמי ודאי לא מחללינן: **ודאי ערלה כבושה היא.** ומחללינן: **לאו מכלל דת"ק.** דר' אליעזר הקפר סבר דברי הכל מחללין ואנא דאמרי כוותיה: ה"ג וממאי דילמא **מכלל דת"ק סבר דברי הכל אין מחללין א"כ רבי אליעזר טעמא דב"ש אתא לאשמעינן כו'.** א"כ דתנא לעיל מיניה אמר דברי הכל אין מחללין ר' אליעזר הקפר דאתא לאיפלוגי ולמימר דלאו דברי הכל הוא דהא לב"ש מחללין מאי רבותא אשמעינן דב"ש פליגי בה הא ב"ש במקום ב"ה אינה משנה [ח] ומשנינן דילמא הכי קאמר ר' אליעזר לת"ק דאמר בשבת לדברי הכל אין מחללין ופלוגתייהו בחול דלב"ה א"צ להטיף ממנו דם ברית הא ליתא דלא נחלקו בדבר זה אלא ודאי צריך ובשבת הוא דפליגי וטעמא דב"ה אתא לאשמעינן דבחול צריך ולאפוקי מת"ק דאמר לב"ה לא צריך: **כל שאין אמו טמאה לידה.** כגון יוצא דופן ונכרית שילדה ולאחר נתגיירה אין בנה ממתין עד שמנה אלא נימול מיד: **דורות הראשונים.** מאברהם עד מתן תורה שנתנה מילה ולא נהגו טומאה:

תוספות

ולא ספק דוחה את השבת. נראה לר"י דאסמכתא בעלמא הוא ולא איצטריך קרא להכי דהיכי תיסוק אדעתיה לחלל את השבת ולא ידענא אם הוא בר חיוב מילה או לא כדמפרש לקמן דספק נולד לז' או לח' ומשום נולד בין השמשות לא איצטריך נמי קרא דמוטב דתיבטל מצות מילה בשמיני מספיקא בשב ואל תעשה ואל יחלל שבת בידים מספק אלא נראה לר"י דעיקר האי קרא אתא לאנדרוגינוס שאינו דוחה שבת ונולד כשהוא מהול ומיהו לא מחד ערלתו נפקי דאין סברא לומר שקולים ויבואו שניהם אלא תרי קראי כתיבי חד במילה בזמנה וביום השמיני ימול בשר ערלתו וחד במילה שלא בזמנה [ט]דגדול וערל זכר אשר לא ימול בשר ערלתו (בראשית יז) א"נ קרא אתא לאנדרוגינוס ונולד כשהוא מהול מסברא ידעינן דאין צריך להטיף דם ברית ר"י. אי נמי עיקר קרא לנולד כשהוא מהול ולאנדרוגינוס לא צריך קרא דהא נפקא ליה לר' יהודה לקמן דאנדרוגינוס טעון מילה מדכתיב כל זכר ורבנן הוו דרשי לדרשה אחריתי:

לא נחלקו על נולד כשהוא מהול שצריך להטיף ממנו דם ברית כו' על מה נחלקו על גר שנתגייר. השתא משמע דיותר יש להצריך הטפה לנולד כשהוא מהול מלנתגייר כשהוא מהול דהא לנולד כ"ע מודו ובגר איכא פלוגתא וא"כ לקמן דפסיק רב הלכה כת"ק ומשמע דכוותיה קי"ל מדקאמר רב אדא בר אהבה תיתי לי דעברי אדרב וכיון דקי"ל כת"ק בנולד כשהוא מהול שאין צריך להטיף ממנו דם ברית כ"ש גר שנתגייר כשהוא מהול וה"ג לא פסקו כן אלא פסקו דקטן א"צ וגר צריך ובקטן ודאי כדין פסקו כשמועתנו ובגר נמי נראה לר"י שסמכו אההיא דיבמות דפרק החולץ (דף מו:) דתניא הרי שבא ואמר מלתי ולא טבלתי מטבילין אותו ומה בכך דברי רבי יהודה ור' יוסי אומר אין מטבילין ואת"ל דא"צ להטיף ממנו דם ברית בנתגייר כשהוא מהול לרבי יוסי אמאי אין מטבילין הרי הוא מהול לפנינו מאי נפקא מינה אם לא מלו אותו ב"ד לא יהא אלא ערבי מהול וגבעוני מהול אלא ודאי צריך להטיף ממנו דם ברית ולכך אין מטבילין דאינו גר עד שימול ויטבול ונראה לרשב"א לתת טעם בדבר שהרי הסברא הפוכה מסברא דשמעתין והיינו טעמא דבין קטן שנולד כשהוא מהול ובין גר שנתגייר כשהוא מהול דין הוא דשניהם היו טעונים הטפת דם ברית אי לאו דדרשינן הכא דקטן אין צריך להטיף ממנו משום דכתיב ערלתו ודוקא בקטן דגלי גלי בגר דלא גלי לא גלי ור"ח פסק איפכא מה"ג:

בן שמנה הרי הוא כאבן ואסור לטלטלו. נראה לר"י דעכשיו מותר לטלטל כל תינוקות שאין אנו בקיאין וכולם כמו ספק בן ח' ספק בן ט' ופעמים שהאשה מתעברת סמוך לטבילתה ופעמים שאינה מתעברת ומותר למולו בשבת ממ"נ כדאמרינן לקמן (דף קלו.) אפילו הוא בן שמנה ודאי כגון שלא בא על אשתו אלא פעם אחת ופירש וילדה לסוף ח' אפילו הכי נראה לר"י דמותר לטלטלו ולמולו בשבת אם אין ריעותא בשערו ובציפרניו כדאמר בפרק הערל (יבמות דף פ:) דאמרינן האי בר שבעה הוא ואישתהויי אישתהי:

מפני הסכנה. סכנת חלב כשיש הרבה בדדין ולא חיישינן שמא תטלטל אותו ולא (ג) ידע רשב"א מאי איריא מפני הסכנה דאפילו לא יהא אלא צערא בעלמא מותר [י] אפילו (ד) היא לחלוב עצמה ולהוציא חלב שבדדין אע"פ שהיא מלאכה שאינה צריכה לגופה דהמיר איסורא טפי מאיסור טלטול נראה דשרי מידי דהוה אמפיס מורסא דשרינן משום צערא:

מכלל דת"ק סבר ד"ה מחללין. ר' אליעזר הקפר ור"ש בן אלעזר תרווייהו קיימי את"ק וה"ק ליה ר"א הקפר לר"ש בן אלעזר לא כך יש להשיב על דברי ת"ק אלא הכי אית לן למימר לא נחלקו כו' והשתא דייק שפיר מכלל דת"ק סבר וכו'. פירוש רשב"א:

כתנאי

לא א ב ג מיי' פ"א מהל' מילה הלכה יא סמג עשין כח טוש"ע א"ח סי' שלא סעי' ה וטוש"ע י"ד סי' רסו סעיף ח וסעיף י:
לב ד מיי' שם הלכה א סמג שם טוש"ע י"ד סי' רסג סעי' ד:
לג ה מיי' וסמג שם ומיי' פי"ד מהל' איסורי ביאה הלכה ה טוש"ע י"ד סי' רסח סעי' א:
לד ו מיי' פ"א מהל' מילה הלכה יד ופכ"ה מהל' שבת הלכה ו טוש"ע א"ח סי' של סעי' ז ח וי"ד סי' רס"ו סעי' יא בהג"ה:

רבינו חננאל

יאות איתברר ליה כתירוציה דרב יהודה ורבה בר אבוה. דאי כתירוצי' דידיה דאוקמא למתניתין שאמרו חכמים מרחיצין ביום ראשון בשבת כדרכו ומזלפין ביום שלישי שחל להיות בשבת ר' אלעזר בן עזריה אומר אף מרחיצין ביום שלישי שחל להיות בשבת היה צריך לומר מפני שאמרו חכמים יום ג' שחל להיות בשבת מזלפין בא הוא ואמר מזלפין ואף מרחיצין אלא מכיון (כולא) [דלא] אמר כך שמעינן מינה שלא הזכירו חכמים ביום ג' שחל להיות בשבת לא רחיצה ולא זילוף. וממילא שמעינן דלית להו לרבנן ביום השלישי לא רחיצה ולא זילוף. ר' אלעזר בן עזריה אומר מרחיצין את המילה ביום השלישי שחל להיות בשבת שנאמר ויהי ביום השלישי בהיותם כואבים וכ"ש ביום ראשון וקיי"ל כר' אלעזר בן עזריה דאמר' א"ר אבהו א"ר יוחנן הלכה כר' אלעזר בן עזריה בין בחמין שהוחמו בשבת ובין חמין שהוחמו בע"ש. בין הרחצה כל גופו בין הרחצה מילה. מפני שסכנה היא לו: **גופא** אמר רב אין מונעין חמין ושמן מע"ג מכה בשבת ושמואל אמר נותנין חוץ למכה ושותת ויורד למכה. ואע"ג דקיי"ל רב ושמואל הלכה כרב באיסורי הכא הלכה כשמואל דתניא כוותיה. אין נותנין חמין ושמן ע"ג מכה בשבת אבל נותן חוץ למכה ושותת ויורד למכה. תני רב נותנין ע"ג מכה מוך יבש וספוג יבש אבל לא גמי יבש ולא כתיתין יבשין. קשיא כתיתין אכתיתין. רישא קתני נותנין ע"ג המכה מוך יבש והוא כתיתין והדר תני ולא כתיתין יבשין ופרקינן לא קשיא הא בחדתי והוא מוך יבש מותר שאין חושבין כרטיה. אבל כתיתין ישנין אסורין. ועלה אמר אביי ש"מ האי נקרא פי' נקרא היא כתיתין והן סמרטוטין יבשים שיש עליהם טינוף צואה רעיי'. כדגרסינן בע"ז ליתו נקרא מקיקלתא כו': ת"ר ערלתו ערלתו ודאי דוחה את השבת ולא ספק דוחה את השבת ערלתו ודאי דוחה את השבת ולא אנדרוגינוס דוחה את השבת וכו' אמר מר ולא ספק דוחה את השבת לאתויי הא דתנו רבנן בן ז' מחללין עליו את השבת בן ח' אין מחללין עליו

הגהות הב"ח

(א) גמ' מי אמר והוא סבר: (ב) רש"י ד"ה מפני הסכנה וכו' שחלב הרבה. נ"ב ובנמוקי יבמות דף פ פירש משום סכנת שניהם: (ג) תוס' ד"ה מפני הסכנה וכו' שמא תטלטל אותו. ולא ידענא מאי איריא כצ"ל ותיבת רשב"א נמחק: (ד) בא"ד אפי' לחלוב בעצמה כצ"ל ותיבת היא נמחק:

תורה אור השלם

א) דַּבֵּר אֶל בְּנֵי יִשְׂרָאֵל לֵאמֹר אִשָּׁה כִּי תַזְרִיעַ וְיָלְדָה זָכָר וְטָמְאָה שִׁבְעַת יָמִים כִּימֵי נִדַּת דְּוֹתָהּ תִּטְמָא: וּבַיּוֹם הַשְּׁמִינִי יִמּוֹל בְּשַׂר עָרְלָתוֹ: [ויקרא יב, ב-ג]

ליקוטי רש"י

ולא נולד בין השמשות. דקטן נולד בין השמשות נמול לתשעה כלומר לספק תשעי בין השמשות של ערב שבת נמול באחד בשבת של יו"ט לחיות אחר אותה שבת שהוא עשירי נמול לאחד עשר משום דמילה שלא בזמנה לא דחיא דנפקא לן מהוא לבדו הוא ולא מכשירין לבדו ולא מילה שלא בזמנה [בסנהדרין] [שבת כ"ד:] [חולין פד:]. **הרי הוא כאבן.** ע"פ אי אפשר למולו בשבת כהלא דשמא תשעה הוא והויא ליה מילה שלא בזמנה ואינה דוחה שבת ולריך להמתין עד לאחר השבת שהוא עשירי [לקמן קלו.]. **מפני הסכנה.** סכנת שניהם הבן והאם שלא ירבה חלב הדדין ויחלו וימות [יבמות פ:].

רב נסים גאון

בזמנה דאתיא מקל וחומר וגם זה פירשנו בפ' במה מדליקין: מילה דנכרתו עליה י"ג בריתות. מפורשין הן בתורה (בראשית יז) ואלו הן ואתנה בריתי ביני ובינך ואני הנה בריתי אתך והקימותי את בריתי לברית עולם ואתה את בריתי תשמור וזאת בריתי אשר תשמרו והיתה בריתי בבשרכם לברית עולם ואת בריתי הפר והקימותי את בריתי לברית עולם ואת בריתי אקים את יצחק (ה): ולא שאני לך בין חמין שהוחמו בשבת לחמין שהוחמו מערב שבת.

חי' על רב נסים גאון (א) פה חסרון וכפול ובלי סדרים. והמעיין במקורים ימלאם כמלואם וכסדרם:

ונתחדשה הלכה אני והא איתמר יוצא דופן א) ומי שיש לו שתי ערלות רב הונא ורב חייא בר רב חד אמר מחללין עליו את השבת וחד אמר א אין מחללין עד כאן לא פליגי אלא לחלל עליו את השבת ב אבל לשמנה ודאי מהלינן ליה ג) הא בהא תליא כתנאי יש יליד בית שנימול לאחד ויש יליד בית שנימול לשמנה יש מקנת כסף שנימול לאחד ויש מקנת כסף שנימול לשמנה יש מקנת כסף שנימול לא' ויש מקנת כסף שנימול לשמונה כיצד ג לקח שפחה מעוברת ואח"כ ילדה זהו מקנת כסף הנימול לשמנה לקח שפחה וולדה עמה זו היא מקנת כסף שנימול לאחד ויש יליד בית שנימול לשמנה ד כיצד לקח שפחה ונתעברה אצלו וילדה זהו יליד בית הנימול לשמנה רב חמא אומר ילדה ואח"כ הטבילה זהו יליד בית שנימול לאחד הטבילה ואחר כך ילדה זהו יליד בית הנימול לשמנה ותנא קמא לא שני ליה בין הטבילה ואח"כ ילדה בין ילדה ואח"כ הטבילה דאע"ג דאין אמו טמאה לידה נימול לשמנה ו) (אמר רבא) בשלמא לר' חמא משכחת לה יליד בית נימול לא' יליד בית נימול לח' מקנת כסף נימול לא' ומקנת כסף נימול לח' ילדה ואח"כ הטבילה זהו יליד בית שנימול לאחד הטבילה ואח"כ ילדה זהו יליד בית שנימול לח' מקנת כסף נימול לשמנה כגון שלקח שפחה מעוברת והטבילה ואח"כ ילדה מקנת כסף נימול לאחד כגון ה שלקח זה שפחה וזה עוברה אלא לת"ק בשלמא כולהו משכחת להו אלא יליד בית נימול לאחד היכי משכחת לה א"ר ירמיה בלוקח שפחה לעוברה ז) למ"ד קנין פירות לאו כקנין הגוף דמי אלא למ"ד קנין פירות כקנין הגוף דמי מאי איכא למימר אמר רב משרשיא בלוקח שפחה ע"מ שלא להטבילה ח) תניא ר"ש בן גמליאל אומר ה כל ששהה ל' יום באדם אינו נפל שנאמר א) ופדויו מבן חדש תפדה ו שמנת ימים בבהמה אינו נפל שנאמר ב) ומיום השמיני והלאה ירצה לקרבן וגו' הא לא שהה ספיקא הוי

מימהל

תוספות

כתנאי יש יליד בית כו'. תימה היכי משמע ליה מתוך הך ברייתא דרבי חמא תלי טעמא בטומאת לידה לעולם אימא לך דסבר יוצא דופן נימול לח' והאי דמצריך טבילה בשפחה משום דבענין אחר אינה תשובה גיורת עד שתטבול כדפסקינן ביבמות בפרק החולץ (דף מו.):

כגון שלקח זה שפחה וזה עוברה. פירש בקונטרס דהוי מצי למימר כגון שלקח שפחה מעוברת וילדה קודם טבילה אלא רבותא נקט דאפילו בטבילה ואח"כ ילדה משכחת לה מקנת כסף נימול לא' וקשה לר"י דא"כ ת"ק לעיל ה"ל למינקט נמי הך רבותא ואמאי קאמר (ג) מקנת כסף נימול כו' אפילו לקח מעוברת נמי אלא שלקח זה שפחה וזה עוברה אלא ודאי לקח זה שפחה וזה עוברה הוי שפיר דומיא דלכם וכגירסת שאילתות דרב אחאי. נראה לר"י דגרס כגון שלקח שפחה וולדה עמה מיהו תימה לר"י דהוה מצי למינקט רבותא אפילו בלא ולדה עמה כגון שלקח שפחה מעוברת וילדה קודם טבילה וי"ל דניחא ליה למינקט דקתני בברייתא במילתיה דת"ק ועוד אומר ר"י דמשום דהנך קראי נימול לאחד ונימול לשמונה דיליד בית ומקנת כסף כתיבי בפרשת לך לך הלכך ניחא לאשכוחינהו בכה"ג דשייך קודם מתן תורה דלא הוה טבילה ואע"ג דיליד בית נימול לא' לר' חמא לא משכחת לה אלא אחר מתן תורה בילדה ואח"כ טבלה מיהו כל מה שיכול לקיים לפני מתן תורה מקיים:

כגון שלקחה ע"מ שלא להטבילה. וכדמפר' ביבמות בפרק החולץ (דף מח.) דלוקח על מנת שלא לגיירו יכול להשהותו הרבה:

כל ששהה שלשים יום באדם וח' ימים בבהמה. אין שום דיום שמנה כלאחר שמנה דמוכחא לקמן דעבד להו עיגלא תילתא ביומא דשבעה וקאמר אי איתרמיתו עד לאורתא הוה אכלינן מיניה ויום שלשים כלפני שלשים דתנן בבכורות בפ' יש בכור לנחלה (דף מט.) ואפילו רבי עקיבא דפליג לא קאמר אלא דמספקא אם הוא כלפני שלשים או כלאחר שלשים ולענין אבילות אפילו ר"ע מודה דהוה כלפני שלשים משום דהלכה כדברי המיקל באבל:

מימהל

רש"י

ונתחדשה הלכה. דמי שאמו טמאה לידה נימול בח' ולא אחר: יוצא דופן. שנקרעת אמו: שתי ערלות. שני עורות זה על זה י) ואמרי לה שני גידין: אבל לשמנה ודאי מהלינן. ואע"ג דיוצא דופן אין אמו טמאה לידה: הא בהא תליא. וחילול שבת תלי במילה לח' דמי שנימול לח' דוחה שבת ומי שאינו נימול לח' אינו דוחה השבת דלא כתיב וביום השמיני דילפינן מיניה ואפילו בשבת בנימול לח' כתיב: כתנאי. הא דרב אסי: הא"ג הא מילתא בשאלתות דרב אחאי י) כיצד לקח שפחה (א) ואחר כך ילדה זהו מקנת כסף שנימול לשמונה לקח שפחה וולדה עמה זהו מקנת כסף שנימול לאחד לקח שפחה ונתעברה אצלו וילדה זהו יליד בית שנימול לח' רבי חמא אומר הטבילה ואחר כך ילדה זהו יליד בית שנימול לח' ילדה ואח"כ הטבילה זהו יליד בית שנימול לא' בשלמא לר' חמא משכחת לה יליד בית דקתני מקנת כסף שנימול לשמנה כגון שלקח שפחה ואחר כך ילדה יליד נימול לא' נמי כגון שלקח שפחה וולדה עמה אלא לת"ק כו'. ובספרים שלנו כתיב נימול לאחד נמי כגון שלקח זה שפחה וזה עוברה ונראה בעיני דהא דלא גריס בשאלתות כגון שלקח זה שפחה וזה עוברה משום דקשיא ליה מאי דוחקיה לאוקמיה בשני לקוחות ולשנויי גירסא דסיפא מרישא דקתני לקח שפחה וולדה זהו מקנת כסף שנימול לא': יש יליד בית שנימול לא'. דתרי קראי כתיבי ביליד בית ומקנת כסף חד כתיב ביה ח' וחד לא כתיב ביה ח' (בראשית יז) המול ימול יליד ביתך ומקנת כספך ולא מפרש ביה לח' ימים וכתיב (שם) ובן שמונת ימים ימול לכם כל זכר לדורותיכם יליד בית ומקנת כסף ומסתברא דהאי דמפרש ביה לשמנה היינו היכא דדמי לישראל מעליא שנולד בביתו של ישראל משקנאו לדומיא דלכם בענין דכתיב בההוא קרא ימול לכם כל זכר והדר יליד בית ומקנת כסף הלכך לקח שפחה מעוברת וילדה הרי זה מקנת כסף דגוף שלם הוא במעי אמו וקנאו שנימול לח' דדומיא דלכם הוא שנולד ברשותו של ישראל לקח שפחה וולדה עמה שכבר ילדתו ואע"פ שלא עברו עליו ח' ללידתו מלו מיד כדכתיב המול ימול וגו' דלאו דומיא דלכם הוא לקח שפחה ונתעברה אצלו לא הוי עובר מקנת כסף אלא יליד בית שנימול לח' דדומיא דלכם הוא ולקמיה מפרש יליד בית הנימול לאחד דליכא דת"ק: רבי חמא אומר. הטבילה לשם עבדות וחלה עליה שם תורת שפחת ישראל דנתחייבה בכל מצות שהאשה חייבת בהן והוא טמאה לידה זהו יליד בית שנימול לח': ילדה והטבילה זהו יליד בית שנימול לאחד. דכל שאין אמו טמאה לידה אין ממתינין לו לח' כרב אסי: בשלמא לרבי חמא. דשני בין הטבילה לילדה ואחר כך ילדה לילדה ואח"כ הטבילה: משכחת לה. כולהו יליד בית נימול לאחד ילדה ואח"כ הטבילה יליד בית נימול לח' הטבילה ואח"כ ילדה ושניהם בשנתעברה אצלו דלא הוי מקנת כסף. מקנת כסף נימול לח' כגון שלקח שפחה מעוברת וילדה לאחר שהטבילה. מקנת כסף הנימול לא' כגון שלקח זה שפחה וזה עוברה דכיון דאין לבעל העובר חלק באמו לאו דומיא דלכם הוא וה"ה נמי דמצי לפלוגי במקנת כסף בין ילדה ואחר כך הטבילה בין הטבילה ואחר כך ילדה ולמימר מקנת כסף נימול לא' כגון שלקח שפחה מעוברת ועוברה וילדה ואחר כך הטבילה אלא רבותא אשמעינן דאפילו בהטבילה ואח"כ ילדה משכחת לה והא דשני מקנת כסף נימול לא' לרבי חמא מלת"ק ולא אמר כגון שלקח שפחה וולדה עמה משום דאם כן ילדה קודם טבילה היא ומאי איריא נולד קודם שלקחה אפילו נולד משלקחה נמי לרבי חמא נימול לא': אלא יליד בית נימול לא' היכי משכחת לה. הא ודאי דומיא דלכם הוא הואיל ולאו בטומאת לידה תליא לדידיה: בלוקח שפחה לעוברה. ואפילו מישראל דהוי' טמאה לידה שכבר טבלה לאו דומיא דלכם הוא הואיל ואין לו חלק באמו: הניחא כו'. פלוגתא דר"ל ורבי יוחנן בבבא בתרא (דף קלו.): שלקחה על מנת שלא להטבילה. דלא שייכא בה תורת חיובא דמצות כלל דלאו דומיא דלכם הוא אבל לטומאת לידה לא חיישינן בילדה ואח"כ הטבילה: ופדויו. בבכור אדם כתיב: מבן חדש. מדתלי בהכי שמע מינה עכשיו נתברר שהוא בן קיימא ולא קודם לכן: הא לא שהה. שלשים יום באדם ובבהמה ח' ימים ספיקא הוי הש"ס פריך עלה:

מימהל

עין משפט נר מצוה

לה א מיי' שם הלכה יא טוש"ע א"ח סי' של סעיף ה וי"ד סי' רסו סעיף י:

לו ב מיי' שם הלכה ז סמג עשין כו טוש"ע י"ד סי' רסב סעיף ג וסימן רסו סעיף י:

לז ג ד מיי' שם הלכה ד ה סמג שם טוש"ע י"ד סי' רסו סעיף א:

לח ה מיי' שם הלכה יג ופ"א מהל' יבום וחליצה הלכה כב ופ"ב מהל' רוצח ושמירת נפש הלכה ו ופ"א מהל' אבל הלכה ו סמג עשין נא ועשין דרבנן ב טוש"ע י"ד סי' שמ סעיף ל וסי' שעג סעיף ד וסי' שעח סעיף ו וטוש"ע אה"ע סי' קנו סעיף ד:

לט ו מיי' פ"ד מהל' מאכלות אסורות הלכה ד (ופ"ג מהל' איסורי מזבח הלכה ח) סמג לאוין עה וקלג עשין קעח:

גליון הש"ס

גמ' שלקח זה שפחה וזה עוברה. עיין בשער המלך פי"ב מהל' נדה הלכה י'. ובקצות החושן סי' רע סעיף א. ובספר כתובה בדף יא בתד"ה א"ה: שם שמנת ימים בבהמה. עי' מנחות דף לז ע"א תד"ה שומע אני:

תורה אור השלם

א) וּפְדוּיָו מִבֶּן חֹדֶשׁ תִּפְדֶּה בְּעֶרְכְּךָ כֶּסֶף חֲמֵשֶׁת שְׁקָלִים בְּשֶׁקֶל הַקֹּדֶשׁ עֶשְׂרִים גֵּרָה הוּא: [במדבר יח, טז]

ב) שׁוֹר אוֹ כֶשֶׂב אוֹ עֵז כִּי יִוָּלֵד וְהָיָה שִׁבְעַת יָמִים תַּחַת אִמּוֹ וּמִיּוֹם הַשְּׁמִינִי וָהָלְאָה יֵרָצֶה לְקָרְבַּן אִשֶּׁה לַיָי: [ויקרא כב, כז]

רבינו חננאל

שמאי] אומרים מחללין ובה"א אין מחללין ודייק רבה מדברי ר' אליעזר הקפר מכלל דת"ק סבר דברי הכל אין מחללין ואמר רבה אנא דאמרי כת"ק לדברי הכל ואקשינן על הדין דוקיא דרבה א"ל ר' אליעזר הקפר טעמא דב"ש אתא לאשמעינן כלומר אם ת"ק אמר דברי הכל מחללין ור' אליעזר הקפר אמר כי ב"ה סבירא להו אין מחללין למה חלק על ת"ק. ת"ק אמר דברי הכל אין מחללין והוא עוד אמר כי ב"ה אין מחללין והלכה כמותם. לא בא אלא לפרש טעמא דב"ש מה הצורך לזה. והא בהדיא קיי"ל בכל מקום ב"ה אינה משנה פריק רבה דלמא ת"ק אמר לא נחלקו אלא בלהטיף ממנו דם ברית ור' אליעזר הקפר אמר לא נחלקו בזה אלא לחלל עליו את השבת נחלקו. ובקש רבה להעמיד דבריו כר"א אליבא דתנא [קמא] ולא נתברר אבל עמדו דבריו כב"ה אליבא דר' אליעזר הקפר ונמצאו דבריו ודברי רב שאמר הלכה כת"ק דבר אחד. וקיי"ל הלכתא כרב באיסורי. ועוד רבה ורב יוסף הלכתא כרבה בר משדה קנין ומחצה הלכך כוותייהו עבדינן וקיי"ל דנולד כשהוא מהול צריך להטיף ממנו דם ברית בחול שמא ערלה כבושה היא. ואם חל ח' שלו בשבת אין מחללין עליו את השבת וכן הלכה. ומעשה דרב אדא בר אהבה ברור הוא והזכירוהו בתלמוד א"י כלשון הזה. רב אדא בר אהבה איתיליד ליה חד בר (בן) [כין] ממסמס ביה מית רבי אבין אמר פצוע דכא נעשה ונתענה עליו ומת. גר שנתגייר כשהוא מהול אין לו תקנה אבל הוא בעצמו לא: אמר רבה אמר רב אסי כל שאמו טמאה לידה נימול לשמונה כו' מסתברא שלא בא רבה אלא למעט בן הנכרית שאין אמו טמאה לידה. אם יקנהו אין נימול לח' שבן בת ישראל ובן הגיורת ובן השפחה אמה טמאה לידה שכך שנינו בענין אשה כי תזריע בני ישראל בענין הזה. ואין הנכרים בענין הזה או בני ישראל אין לי אלא בני ישראל מניין לרבות את הגיורת ואת השפחה בין משוחררת ובין שאינה משוחררת ת"ל אשה כי תזריע וילדה זכר וטמאה גו' הא אפילו שפחה טמאה ומקשינן עלה וכל שאמו טמאה לידה נימול לשמונה ומי שאין אמו טמאה לידה אינו נימול לשמונה. והרי יוצא דופן שאין אמו טמאה לידה דתניא וילדה עד שתלד ממקום הולד פרט ליוצא דופן ר' שמעון אומר יוצא דופן הרי הוא כילוד וחייבין עליו קרבן ובלבד שהוא פטור מחמש סלעים ואתמר יוצא דופן ומי שיש לו ב' ערלות רב הונא ורב חייא בר רב חד אמר מחללין עליו את השבת וחד אמר אין מחללין עליו את השבת. עד כאן לא פליגי לחלל עליו את השבת אבל לשמונה ודאי מהלינן ליה. ופרקי' הא בהא תליא האומר מחללין עליו את השבת סבר נימול לח' והאומר אין מחללין סבר אינו נימול לשמונה ואמרי דדברי רבה כתנאי זה התנא שאמר לקח שפחה ועוברה עמה נימול לח'. פי' קנה שפחה גויה ועוברה נמצא זה העובר מקנת כסף וקודם שיטבלנה עודה בגיותה ילדתו כיון שיגיע ליום שמיני חייב למולו ואע"פ שילדתו בגיותה שאינה טמאה לידה ואמר התנא זהו מקנת כסף הנימול [לשמונה]. דלא כרבה ורב אחא אמר ילדה כו'. קיי"ל דכולהו תנאי מא"י אינון לפיכך קרי להו רבי בר מחלת דוכתי. ואע"ג דתנאי אינון קרי להו רב. רב אבא בהאשה שנפלו לה נכסים. ורב אבא נמי בג' שאכלו כאחד. ורב חמא בהדא דוכתא. ורב אחא אמר ילדה ואח"כ הטבילה מאחר שאין אמו טמאה לידה אינו נימול לשמונה אלא ליום אחד כרבה. וזהו שאמר רבה לרב חמא דבעי טבילה משכחת לה יליד בית נימול לשמונה כגון שהטבילה ואח"כ ילדה. מקנת כסף נימול לשמונה כגון שלקח שפחה ועוברה עמה. וגם זו הטבילה ואח"כ ילדה ומפני מה לא פירש בה טבילה כיון שההפרש מקודם לזה בין הטבילה ובין ילדה ואח"כ הטבילה. (מימי) [מין] לא שמעת לה לקח שפחה ועוברה עמה. זהו מקנת כסף שנימול לשמונה. לקח

מסורת הש"ס

א) [יבמות דף עב.], ב) [מגילה ו: נזיר יח: תמורה יח.], ג) ב"מ מ"ג, ד) ב"ק פח. ב"מ נו. ב"ב קלו. יבמ' לו: [גיטין מז: מח. ערכין כו.], ה) [יבמות מח: נדה מד: [תוספ' פס"ו]], ו) [עי' רש"י יבמות עב. ד"ה מי שיש לו], ז) [פרשת לך לך סימן טז].

הגהות הב"ח

(א) רש"י ד"ה ה"ג הא מילתא וכו' כיצד לקח שפחה מעוברת ואח"כ וכו' שנימול לשמונה כגון שלקח שפחה מעוברת והטבילה ואח"כ ילדה: (ב) תוס' ד"ה כגון שלקח זה וכו' רבותא ואמאי קאמר לקח שפחה וולדה עמה זו היא מקנת כסף שנימול לאחד אפילו לקח מעוברת נמי:

רב נסים גאון

יצירה לט' ויצירה לז' רב הונא אמר נולד לט' ובן לח' אינו חי: הניחא למאן דאמר קנין פירות [לאו] כקנין הגוף דמי אלא למאן דאמר קנין פירות (לאו) כקנין הגוף דמי. והמחלוקת היא על זה בין ר' יוחנן ובין ריש לקיש ותמצא מחלוקתם בהרבה מקומות מן התלמוד במס' גיטין בפרק השולח גט לאשתו (דף מז) איתמר המוכר שדהו לפירות ר' יוחנן אמר מביא וקורא ריש לקיש אמר מביא ואינו קורא ר' יוחנן אמר מביא וקורא קנין פירות כקנין הגוף דמי ריש לקיש אמר מביא ואינו קורא קנין פירות לאו כקנין הגוף דמי ובבבא בתרא בפרק יש נוחלין (קלו) מכר הבן בחיי האב וכן במס' יבמות בפרק החולץ (לו) כמו כן וזאת

ליקוטי רש"י

יוצא דופן. ע"י סם וכין הוא וכין אמו מין ומין לומר שאמר שמתה אמו הוציאוהו דקיי"ל במסכת נדה (דף מד.) הוא מית ברישא [חולין מג.]. שתי ערלות. ב' עורות זה על גבי זה [יבמות עב.]. אלא למ"ד קנין פירות. שיש לו לאלו הגוף קנוי לו דמי [ב"ב קלו:]. כל ששהה ל' יום. מ' ספק יום [יבמות לו:]. באדם אינו נפל. ופוטר את אמו מן החליצה [שם לו.] ואפילו לא כלו לו חדשי עיבור. שמנת ימים בבהמה. אין שחיטה מטהרתו עד שישהה שמונה ימים דשוב נפק ליה מכלל נפל דתניא רבן שמעון בן גמליאל אומר כל ששהה שלשים יום באדם אינו נפל ובבהמה שמונה ימים [ר"ה ז.]. ספיקא הוי. ומולגא ולא מחייבתא ודוקא אי מספקא לן אי כלו לו חדשיו אי לא אבל אי קים לן דכלו לו חדשיו תנן במסכת נדה (דף מג:) תינוק בן יומו פוטר מן הייבום [יבמות לו:].

וְנִתְחַדְּשָׁה הֲלָכָה – a new law went into effect, limiting the eighth-day rule to a child whose mother becomes *tamei* at birth. The structure of the law before the Torah was given is not relevant to the law today.

The Gemara challenges R' Assi's view:

אִינִי – Is this rule of R' Assi **indeed true? וְהָא אִיתְּמַר – But it has been stated: יוֹצֵא דוֹפֶן וּמִי שֶׁיֵּשׁ לוֹ שְׁתֵּי עָרְלוֹת** – Concerning **a child born by Caesarian section**[1] **or one that has two foreskins,**[2] **רַב הוּנָא וְרַב חִיָּיא בַּר רַב – Rav Huna and Rav Chiya bar Rav** are in dispute over the matter: **חַד אָמַר מְחַלְּלִין עָלָיו אֶת הַשַּׁבָּת – One said that we violate the Sabbath for him,** i.e. to circumcise him, **וְחַד אָמַר אֵין מְחַלְּלִין – and one said** that **we do not violate the Sabbath** to circumcise him.[3] **עַד כָּאן לֹא פְּלִיגֵי אֶלָּא לְחַלֵּל עָלָיו אֶת הַשַּׁבָּת** – Now **they argue only insofar as whether we** should **violate the Sabbath for him, אֲבָל לִשְׁמוֹנָה וַדַּאי מַהֲלִינַן לֵיהּ – but** both Rav Huna and Rav Chiya bar Rav agree that **we certainly circumcise him on the eighth** day.[4] We see from this that, although a child born by Caesarian section does not render his mother *tamei* due to childbirth,[5] he is still circumcised on the eighth day, contrary to R' Assi's view.[6] – ? –

The Gemara answers, in defense of R' Assi:

הָא בְּהָא תַּלְיָא – This law (circumcision on the Sabbath) **is dependent upon that law** (circumcision on the eighth day), because the Sabbath is violated only for a circumcision that is performed on the eighth day. Thus, the one who states that a child born by Caesarian section is not circumcised on the Sabbath holds this way because he is of the opinion that such a child is not circumcised on the eighth day, as R' Assi stated.[7]

The Gemara continues:

כְּתַנָּאֵי – R' Assi's ruling is the subject of a dispute **among Tannaim,** as we see in the following Baraisa, which discusses the circumcision of Canaanite slaves:[8] **יֵשׁ יְלִיד בַּיִת שֶׁנִּימוֹל לְאֶחָד – THERE IS A** slave **"BORN IN THE HOUSE" WHO IS CIRCUMCISED ON THE FIRST** day, **וְיֵשׁ יְלִיד בַּיִת שֶׁנִּימוֹל לִשְׁמֹנָה – AND THERE IS A** slave **"BORN IN THE HOUSE" WHO IS CIRCUMCISED ON THE EIGHTH** day.[9] **יֵשׁ מִקְנַת כֶּסֶף שֶׁנִּימוֹל לְאֶחָד – THERE IS A** slave **"PURCHASED WITH MONEY" WHO IS CIRCUMCISED ON THE FIRST** day, **וְיֵשׁ מִקְנַת כֶּסֶף שֶׁנִּימוֹל לִשְׁמוֹנָה – AND THERE IS A** slave **"PURCHASED WITH MONEY" WHO IS CIRCUMCISED ON THE EIGHTH** day. **יֵשׁ מִקְנַת כֶּסֶף שֶׁנִּימוֹל לְאֶחָד וְיֵשׁ מִקְנַת כֶּסֶף שֶׁנִּימוֹל לִשְׁמוֹנָה כֵּיצַד – THERE IS A SLAVE "PURCHASED WITH MONEY" WHO IS CIRCUMCISED ON THE FIRST** day **AND THERE IS A SLAVE "PURCHASED WITH MONEY" WHO IS CIRCUMCISED ON THE EIGHTH** day **– HOW SO? לָקַח שִׁפְחָה מְעוּבֶּרֶת וְאַחַר כָּךְ יָלְדָה – IF ONE BOUGHT A PREGNANT SLAVEWOMAN AND SHE LATER GAVE BIRTH** to a boy, **זֶהוּ מִקְנַת כֶּסֶף הַנִּימוֹל לִשְׁמוֹנָה – THIS IS A** slave **"PURCHASED WITH MONEY" WHO IS CIRCUMCISED ON THE EIGHTH** day. **לָקַח שִׁפְחָה וּוְלָדָהּ עִמָּהּ** – But **IF ONE BOUGHT A SLAVEWOMAN AND HER CHILD ALONG WITH HER, זוֹ הִיא מִקְנַת כֶּסֶף שֶׁנִּימוֹל לְאֶחָד – THIS** child **IS A** slave **"PURCHASED WITH MONEY" WHO IS CIRCUMCISED ON THE FIRST** day.[10]

וְיֵשׁ יְלִיד בַּיִת שֶׁנִּימוֹל לִשְׁמֹנָה כֵּיצַד – AND THERE IS A slave **"BORN IN THE HOUSE" WHO IS CIRCUMCISED ON THE EIGHTH** day **– HOW SO? לָקַח שִׁפְחָה וְנִתְעַבְּרָה אֶצְלוֹ וְיָלְדָה – IF ONE BOUGHT A SLAVEWOMAN AND SHE BECAME PREGNANT WHILE IN HIS POSSESSION AND THEN GAVE BIRTH, זֶהוּ יְלִיד בַּיִת שֶׁנִּימוֹל לִשְׁמֹנָה – THIS**

NOTES

1. Literally: "one who exits through the wall" of the stomach.

2. I.e. one growing on top of the other. Alternatively, a child born with two male organs (*Rashi;* see *Rashi, Yevamos* 72a; see also *Machatzis HaShekel* 331:4).

3. The Gemara will discuss why a child born by Caesarian section is not circumcised on the Sabbath according to this view. As for a child with two foreskins, *Meiri* explains (according to the second explanation cited in the previous note) that when a child is born with two male organs, one of them is considered his primary member and the other merely an extra appendage. But since the law of circumcision applies only to the primary one and we do not know which one that is, we cannot circumcise either of them on the Sabbath.

Meiri also quotes some commentators who reject the explanation that the Baraisa speaks of a single organ with two foreskins because in such a case there is no question that circumcision demands the removal of both. Hence, there should be universal agreement that the Sabbath is violated in this case. *Sfas Emes,* however, explains that the verse that teaches us to perform an eighth-day circumcision even on the Sabbath (the verse cited above by R' Assi) speaks of עָרְלָתוֹ, *his foreskin,* in the singular, implying that the permission to violate the Sabbath extends only to cutting a single foreskin, not two. Alternatively, the Torah's reference to the foreskin in the singular teaches that [as relates to the law of circumcision] a child has only one true foreskin, and since we do not know which of these two is the true foreskin, we cannot perform the circumcision on the Sabbath.

4. [For the only circumcision that ever overrides the Sabbath law is one performed on the eighth day. Thus, since they debate only whether the circumcision of such babies overrides the Sabbath, it seems evident that they both assume that the circumcision is performed on the eighth day.]

5. As explained above, 135a note 33.

6. *Sfas Emes* wonders why, if he is circumcised on the eighth day as the Gemara now assumes, anyone should hold that a child born by Caesarian section is not circumcised on the Sabbath. See *Meromei Sadeh* who suggests an answer, and discusses other aspects of the Gemara's question.

7. The Torah teaches the law that circumcision overrides the Sabbath in the verse וּבַיּוֹם הַשְּׁמִינִי יִמּוֹל בְּשַׂר עָרְלָתוֹ, *and on the eighth day the flesh of his foreskin shall be circumcised* (*Leviticus* 12:3; see above, 132a). Since that verse speaks of a child who is supposed to be circumcised on the eighth day, we can only derive from it that a circumcision mandated for the *eighth* day overrides the Sabbath, not any other circumcision (*Rashi*). Thus, even a circumcision that is *mandated* to be performed before the eighth day does not override the Sabbath!

8. The Torah (*Genesis* 17:12,13) requires a Jewish slaveholder to circumcise his Canaanite (i.e. non-Jewish) slaves. The Torah, in this regard, divides Canaanite slaves into two categories: יְלִיד בַּיִת, *one born in the house,* i.e. a child born to a slavewoman who is the property of a Jewish master, and a מִקְנַת כֶּסֶף, *one purchased with money.*

9. In *Genesis* 17:12 the Torah states that both a slave born in the house and a slave purchased with money are to be circumcised on the eighth day: . . . וּבֶן־שְׁמֹנַת יָמִים יִמּוֹל לָכֶם כָּל־זָכָר לְדֹרֹתֵיכֶם יְלִיד בָּיִת וּמִקְנַת־כֶּסֶף, *At the age of eight days every male shall be circumcised among you, throughout your generations — one who is born in the house or who is purchased with money . . .* However, in the very next verse, the Torah repeats the requirement to circumcise both types of slaves, this time without stipulating that they be circumcised on the eighth day: הִמּוֹל יִמּוֹל יְלִיד בֵּיתְךָ וּמִקְנַת כַּסְפֶּךָ, *He that is born in your house or purchased with your money shall surely be circumcised.* But why was it necessary for the Torah to repeat this requirement? The Sages therefore understood the repetition to be teaching that there are instances in which slave children of either category are circumcised even before the eighth day — i.e. on the first day (*Rashi* here and to the verse). See also *Maharsha* here, *Chasam Sofer,* and *Hagahos Mareh Kohen.*

10. Although the Torah does not state explicitly which slaves are to be circumcised before the eighth day, the verse that speaks of circumcising a slave on the eighth day begins by teaching the law for circumcision of a Jewish child on the eighth day: וּבֶן־שְׁמֹנַת יָמִים יִמּוֹל לָכֶם כָּל־זָכָר, *At the age of eight days every male among you shall be circumcised.* This indicates that the slave who is subject to circumcision on the eighth day is the one who is most similar to those *among you* (i.e. ordinary Jews) — namely, one who is *born* into a Jewish household, not one who was born into a gentile household and then purchased by a Jew. The latter is, by process of elimination, therefore subject to the rule of the other verse, namely, immediate circumcision (*Rashi*).

The Baraisa refers to a fetus growing in the womb at the time of his mother's purchase as "one who was purchased for money" because his body was already formed at the time of the purchase (*Rashi;* see *Chasam Sofer*).

ונתחדשה הלכה אני והא איתמר יוצא דופן ומי שיש לו שתי ערלות רב הונא ורב חייא בר רב חד אמר מחללין עליו את השבת וחד אמר אין מחללין עד כאן לא פליגי אלא לחלל עליו את השבת אבל לשמנה ודאי מהלינן ליה הא בהא תליא כתנאי יש יליד בית שנימול לאחד ויש יליד בית שנימול לשמנה יש מקנת כסף שנימול לאחד ויש מקנת כסף שנימול לשמנה יש מקנת כסף שנימול לא' ויש מקנת כסף שנימול לשמונה כיצד לקח שפחה מעוברת ואח"כ ילדה זהו מקנת כסף הנימול לשמונה לקח שפחה וולדה עמה זו היא מקנת כסף שנימול לאחד ויש יליד בית שנימול לשמנה כיצד לקח שפחה ונתעברה אצלו וילדה זהו יליד בית הנימול לשמנה רב חמא אומר ילדה ואח"כ הטבילה זהו יליד בית שנימול לאחד הטבילה ואחר כך ילדה זהו יליד בית הנימול לשמנה ותנא קמא לא שני ליה בין הטבילה ואח"כ ילדה בין ילדה ואח"כ הטבילה דאע"ג דאין אמו טמאה לידה נימול לשמנה (אמר רבא) בשלמא לר' חמא משכחת לה יליד בית נימול לא' יליד בית נימול לח' מקנת כסף נימול לא' ומקנת כסף נימול לח' ילדה ואח"כ הטבילה זהו יליד בית שנימול לאחד הטבילה ואח"כ ילדה זהו יליד בית שנימול לח' מקנת כסף נימול לשמנה כגון שלקח שפחה מעוברת והטבילה ואח"כ ילדה מקנת כסף נימול לאחד כגון שלקח זה שפחה וזה עוברה אלא לת"ק בשלמא כולהו משכחת להו אלא יליד בית נימול לאחד היכי משכחת לה א"ר ירמיה בלוקח שפחה לעוברה הניחא למ"ד קנין פירות לאו כקנין הגוף דמי אלא למ"ד קנין פירות כקנין הגוף דמי מאי איכא למימר אמר רב משרשיא בלוקח שפחה ע"מ שלא להטבילה תניא רשב"ג אומר כל ששהה ל' יום באדם אינו נפל שנאמר ופדויו מבן חדש תפדה שמנת ימים בבהמה אינו נפל שנאמר ומיום השמיני והלאה ירצה לקרבן וגו' הא לא שהה ספיקא הוי

מימהל

רש"י

ונתחדשה הלכה. דמי שאמו טמאה לידה נימול בח' ולא אחר: יוצא דופן. שנקרעת אמו: שתי ערלות. שני עורות זה על זה ואמרי לה שני גידין: אבל לשמנה ודאי מהלינן. ואע"ג דיולא דופן אין אמו טמאה לידה: הא בהא תליא. וחילול שבת תלי במילה לח' דמי שנימול לח' דוחה שבת ומי שאינו נימול לח' אינו דוחה השבת דכי כתיב וביום השמיני דילפינן מיניה ואפילו בשבת בנימול לח' כתיב: כתנאי. הא דרב אסי: ה"ג הא מילתא בשאלתות דרב אחאי כיצד לקח שפחה (א) ואחר כך ילדה זהו מקנת כסף שנימול לשמונה לקח שפחה וולדה עמה זהו מקנת כסף שנימול לאחד לקח שפחה ונתעברה אצלו וילדה זהו יליד בית שנימול לח' רבי חמא אומר הטבילה ואחר כך ילדה זהו יליד בית שנימול לח' ילדה ואח"כ הטבילה זהו יליד בית שנימול לא' בשלמא לר' חמא משכחת לה יליד בית כדקתני מקנת כסף שנימול לשמנה כגון שלקח שפחה ואחר כך ילדה נימול לא' נמי כגון שלקח שפחה וולדה עמה אלא לת"ק כו'. ובספרים שלנו כתיב נימול לאחד נמי כגון שלקח זה שפחה וזה עוברה ונראה בעיני דהא דלא גרים בשאלתות כגון שלקח זה שפחה וזה עוברה משום דקשיא ליה מאי דוחקיה לאוקמיה בשני לקוחות ולשנויי גירסא דסיפא מרישא דקתני לקח שפחה וולדה זהו מקנת כסף שנימול לא': יש יליד בית שנימול לא'. דתרי קראי כתיבי ביליד בית ומקנת כסף חד כתיב ביה ח' וחד לא כתיב ביה ח' (בראשית יז) המול ימול יליד ביתך ומקנת כספך ולא מפרש ביה לח' ימים וכתיב (שם) ובן שמונת ימים ימול לכם כל זכר לדורותיכם יליד בית ומקנת כסף ומסתברא דהאי דמפרש ביה לשמנה היינו היכא דדמי לישראל מעליא שנולד בביתו של ישראל משקנאו דדומיא דלכם בעינן דכתיב בההוא קרא ימול לכם כל זכר והדר יליד בית ומקנת כסף הלכך לקח שפחה מעוברת וילדה הרי זה מקנת כסף דגוף שלם הוא במעי אמו וקנאו שנימול לח' דדומיא דלכם הוא שנולד ברשותו של ישראל לקח שפחה וולדה עמה שכבר ילדתו ואע"פ שלא עברו עליו ח' ללידתו מלו מיד כדכתיב המול ימול וגו' דלאו דומיא דלכם הוא לקח שפחה ונתעברה אצלו לא הוי עובר מקנת כסף אלא יליד בית שנימול לח' דדומיא דלכם הוא ולקמיה מפרש יליד בית הנימול לאחד אליבא דת"ק: רבי חמא אומר. הטבילה לשם עבדות וחלה עליה שם תורת שפחת ישראל דנתחייבה בכל מצות שהאשה חייבת בהן והויא טמאה לידה זהו יליד בית שנימול לח': ילדה והטבילה זהו יליד בית שנימול לאחד. דכל שאין אמו טמאה לידה אין ממתינין לו לח' כרב אסי: בשלמא לרבי חמא. דשני בין הטבילה ואחר כך ילדה לילדה ואח"כ הטבילה: משכחת לה. כולהו יליד בית נימול לאחד ילדה ואח"כ הטבילה יליד בית נימול לח' הטבילה ואח"כ ילדה ושניהם בשנתעברה אצלו דלא הוי מקנת כסף. מקנת כסף נימול לח' כגון שלקח שפחה מעוברת וילדה לאחר שהטבילה. מקנת כסף הנימול לא' כגון שלקח זה שפחה וזה עוברה דכיון דאין לבעל העובר חלק באמו לאו דומיא דלכם הוא ה"ה נמי דמצי לפלוגי במקנת כסף בין ילדה ואחר כך הטבילה בין הטבילה ואחר כך ילדה ולמימר מקנת כסף נימול לח' כגון שלקח שפחה מעוברת ועוברה וילדה ואחר כך הטבילה אלא רבותא אשמעינן דאפילו בהטבילה ואח"כ ילדה משכחת לה והא דשני מקנת כסף נימול לא' לרבי חמא מלת"ק ולא אמר כגון שלקח שפחה וולדה עמה משום דאם כן ילדה קודם טבילה היא ומאי איריא נולד קודם שלקחה אפילו נולד משלקחה נמי לרבי חמא נימול לא': אלא יליד בית נימול לא' היכי משכחת לה. הא ודאי דומיא דלכם הוא הואיל ולאו בטומאת לידה תליא לדידיה: בלוקח שפחה לעוברה. ואפילו מישראל דהוי' טמאה לידה שכבר טבלה לאו דומיא דלכם הוא הואיל ואין לו חלק באמו: הניחא כו'. פלוגתא דר"ל ורבי יוחנן בבבא בתרא (דף קלו.): שלקחה על מנת שלא להטבילה. דלא חייכא בה תורת חיובא דמצות כלל דלאו דומיא דלכם הוא אבל לטומאת לידה לא חיישינן בילדה ואח"כ הטבילה: ופדויו. בבכור אדם כתיב: מבן חדש. מדתלי בהכי שמע מינה עכשיו נתברר שהוא בן קיימא ולא קודם לכן: הא לא שהה. שלשים יום באדם ובבהמה ח' ימים ספיקא הוי הש"ם פריך עלה:

מימהל

תוספות

כתנאי יש יליד בית כו'. תימה היכי משמע ליה מתוך הך ברייתא דרבי חמא תלי טעמא בטומאת לידה לעולם אימא לך לסבר יולא דופן נימול לח' והאי דמצריך טבילה בשפחה משום דבענין אחר אינה חשובה גיורת עד שתטבול כדנפקא לן ביבמות בפרק החולץ (דף מו.):

כגון שלקח זה שפחה וזה עוברה. פירש בקונטרס דהוי מצי למימר כגון שלקח שפחה מעוברת וילדה קודם טבילה אלא רבותא נקט דאפילו בטבלה ואח"כ ילדה משכחת לה במקנת כסף נימול לא' וקשה לר"י דא"כ ת"ק דלעיל ה"ל למינקט נמי הך רבותא ואמאי קאמר (ג) מקנת כסף נימול כו' אפילו לקח מעוברת נמי אלא שלקח זה שפחה וזה עוברה אלא ודאי לקח זה שפחה וזה עוברה הוי שפיר דומיא דלכם וכגירסת שאלתות דרב אחאי. נראה לר"י דגרס כגון שלקח שפחה וולדה עמה מיהו תימה לר"י דהוה מצי למינקט רבותא אפילו בלא ולדה עמה כגון שלקח שפחה מעוברת וילדה קודם טבילה וי"ל דניחא ליה למינקט דקתני בברייתא מילתיה דת"ק ועוד אומר ר"י משום דהנך קראי יליד בית ומקנת כסף כתיבי בפרשת לך לך הלכך ניחא לאשכוחינהו בכה"ג דשייך קודם מתן תורה דלא הוה טבילה ואע"ג דיליד בית נימול לח' לר' חמא לא משכחת לה אלא אחר מתן תורה בילדה ואח"כ טבלה מיהו כל מה שיכול לקיים לפני מתן תורה מקיים:

כגון שלקחה ע"מ שלא להטבילה. וכדמפר' ביבמות בפרק החולץ (דף מח.) דלקחה על מנת שלא לגיירו יכול להשהותו הרבה:

כל ששהה שלשים יום באדם וח' ימים בבהמה. אין שוין דיום שמנה כלאחר שמנה כדמוכח לקמן דעבד להו עיגלא תילתא ביומא דשבעה וקאמר אי איתרמינהו עד לאורתא הוה אכלינן מיניה ויום שלשים כלפני שלשים כדמוכח בבכורות בפ' יש בכור לנחלה (דף מט.) ואפילו רבי עקיבא דפליג לא קאמר אלא דמספקא אם הוא כלפני שלשים או כלאחר שלשים ולענין אבילות אפילו ר"ע מודה דהוה כלפני שלשים משום דהלכה כדברי המיקל באבל:

מימהל

הגהות הב"ח

רב נסים גאון

ליקוטי רש"י

גליון הש"ס

תורה אור

א) וּפְדוּיָו מִבֶּן חֹדֶשׁ תִּפְדֶּה בְּעֶרְכְּךָ כֶּסֶף חֲמֵשֶׁת שְׁקָלִים בְּשֶׁקֶל הַקֹּדֶשׁ עֶשְׂרִים גֵּרָה הוּא: [במדבר יח, טז]

ב) שׁוֹר אוֹ כֶשֶׂב אוֹ עֵז כִּי יִוָּלֵד וְהָיָה שִׁבְעַת יָמִים תַּחַת אִמּוֹ וּמִיּוֹם הַשְּׁמִינִי וָהָלְאָה יֵרָצֶה לְקָרְבַּן אִשֶּׁה לַיי: [ויקרא כב, כז]

רבינו חננאל

IS A slave "BORN IN THE HOUSE" WHO IS CIRCUMCISED ON THE EIGHTH day.

רַב חָמָא אוֹמֵר – RAV CHAMA[11] SAYS: יָלְדָה וְאַחַר כָּךְ הִטְבִּילָהּ – IF SHE GAVE BIRTH AND [THE MASTER] LATER IMMERSED HER in a *mikveh* for the purpose of rendering her a Canaanite slave-woman,[12] זֶהוּ יְלִיד בַּיִת שֶׁנִּימוֹל לְאֶחָד – THIS child IS A slave "BORN IN THE HOUSE" WHO IS CIRCUMCISED ON THE FIRST day. הִטְבִּילָהּ וְאַחַר כָּךְ יָלְדָה – However, IF HE IMMERSED HER in a *mikveh* AND SHE LATER GAVE BIRTH, זֶהוּ יְלִיד בַּיִת הַנִּימוֹל לִשְׁמֹנָה – THIS IS A slave "BORN IN THE HOUSE" WHO IS CIRCUMCISED ON THE EIGHTH day.[13] The reason for this distinction is that a slavewoman becomes subject to all the laws to which a Jewish woman is subject only after she has immersed in a *mikveh*. Therefore, if she gives birth *before* immersion, she is not *tamei* due to childbirth and so her son is circumcised on the first day. This conforms with R' Assi's view that a child whose mother is not *tamei* due to childbirth is circumcised on the first day.

The Gemara infers from Rav Chama's dissent that the Tanna Kamma disagrees with his distinction:

וְתַנָּא קַמָּא – **As for the Tanna Kamma,** לָא שָׁנֵי לֵיהּ – **it makes no difference** according **to him** בֵּין הִטְבִּילָהּ וְאַחַר כָּךְ יָלְדָה – **whether [the master] immersed [the slavewoman] and she gave birth later,** בֵּין יָלְדָה וְאַחַר כָּךְ הִטְבִּילָהּ – **or whether she gave birth** first **and [the master] later immersed her;** דְּאַף עַל גַּב דְּאֵין אִמּוֹ טְמֵאָה לֵידָה – **for although** in the latter case **[the child's] mother is not *tamei* due to childbirth,**[14] נִימוֹל לִשְׁמֹנָה – **he is** nonetheless **circumcised on the eighth** day – contrary to R' Assi's view. Thus, R' Assi's rule is the subject of a dispute between Rav Chama and the Tanna Kamma.

The Gemara now analyzes the Baraisa and looks to establish the case for each of its four laws:

(אָמַר רָבָא) בִּשְׁלָמָא לְרַבִּי חָמָא – **(Rava said:) Now according to Rav Chama** the Baraisa's rules **are understandable,** מַשְׁכַּחַת לָהּ יְלִיד בַּיִת נִימוֹל לְאֶחָד – for **[a case] can be found** in which **a** slave **"born in the house" is circumcised on the first** day יְלִיד בַּיִת נִימוֹל לִשְׁמֹנָה – **and a** slave **"born in the house" is circumcised on the eighth** day; מִקְנַת כֶּסֶף נִימוֹל לְאֶחָד – similarly, a case can be found in which **a** slave **"purchased with money" is circumcised on the first** day, וּמִקְנַת כֶּסֶף נִימוֹל לִשְׁמֹנָה – **and a** slave **"purchased with money" is circumcised on the eighth** day. The cases are as follows: יָלְדָה וְאַחַר כָּךְ הִטְבִּילָהּ – **If [a slavewoman]** conceived after she had been purchased by a Jewish master and **gave birth and [the master] later immersed her** in a *mikveh,* זֶהוּ יְלִיד בַּיִת שֶׁנִּימוֹל לְאֶחָד – **this** child **is a** slave **"born in the house" who is circumcised on the first** day, because the mother did not become *tamei* due to his birth, as explained above. הִטְבִּילָהּ וְאַחַר כָּךְ יָלְדָה – **If he immersed her** first **and she gave birth later,** זֶהוּ יְלִיד בַּיִת שֶׁנִּימוֹל לִשְׁמֹנָה – **this child is a** slave **"born in the house" who is circumcised on the eighth** day, since his mother did become *tamei* due to his birth.[15] מִקְנַת כֶּסֶף נִימוֹל לִשְׁמֹנָה – The case of **a** slave **"purchased with money" who is circumcised on the eighth** day occurs כְּגוֹן שֶׁלָּקַח שִׁפְחָה מְעוּבֶּרֶת וְהִטְבִּילָהּ וְאַחַר כָּךְ יָלְדָה – **in a case where [the master] purchased a pregnant slavewoman and immersed her** in a *mikveh,* **and she later gave birth.** Since she was pregnant at the time of purchase, her child is considered a slave "purchased with money"; and since she immersed prior to giving birth, she became subject to the laws of *tumah,* so that the child is one whose mother is *tamei* due to childbirth.[16] מִקְנַת כֶּסֶף נִימוֹל לְאֶחָד – The case of **a** slave **"purchased with money" who is circumcised on the first** day occurs כְּגוֹן שֶׁלָּקַח זֶה שִׁפְחָה וְזֶה עוּבָּרָהּ – **in a case where** a pregnant slavewoman was purchased by two people with **this one buying the slavewoman and this one** buying **her fetus.** Since circumcision on the eighth day is mandated for a slave child only when the circumstances of his birth are similar to those of a natural-born Jewish child,[17] a slave child born to a master who has no rights to the child's mother does not qualify.[18]

NOTES

11. This is one of three places in the Talmud where a Tanna is quested with the title "Rav" rather than "Rabbi," indicating that he was a Babylonian Tanna [who had not been to Eretz Yisrael and hence had not acquired the title of רַבִּי, *Rabbi*] (*Rabbeinu Chananel*).

12. For a non-Jew to acquire the status of a Canaanite slave [and the quasi-Jewish status to which this class is subject], he or she must undergo a conversion process similar to that of an ordinary convert. As part of this process, he or she must be immersed in a *mikveh* under the owner's direction (*Yevamos* 47b-48b; *Rambam, Isurei Biah* 13:11).

13. [Rav Chama agrees that the case of a slave "born in the house" is where the slavewoman became pregnant after the Jewish owner acquired her.] He disagrees, however, with the Tanna Kamma's blanket statement that her child is always circumcised on the eighth day. In his view, this is true only if she had already undergone immersion before giving birth, so that she became subject to the laws governing Jewish women and thus subject to the *tumah* of childbirth. If she gave birth before immersing, however, she was still a gentile at the time she gave birth and thus did not become *tamei* (*Rashi;* see *Tosafos* who question this proof).

14. Since she had not yet undergone the immersion necessary to convert her to the status of a Canaanite slave subject to the Torah's laws.

15. In both cases he is considered a slave "born in the house" because his mother did not conceive him until after she had become the property of a Jewish master (*Rashi*).

16. [The Gemara concluded above that Rav Chama subscribes to the view that a child is circumcised on the eighth day only if his mother is subject to childbirth *tumah.* Thus, she must have immersed before his birth for him to be circumcised on the eighth day. (In the Baraisa, Rav Chama makes this point in regard to a slave born in the house. The Gemara here states that the same is true according to him in regard to a purchased slave.)]

17. See above, note 10.

18. For he is not similar to those *"among you,"* in that the master has no connection to the child's mother (*Rashi*), unlike the father of a Jewish child who, even if he was not married to the mother, had at least a physical connection to her through which the child was conceived (cf. *Chidushei HaRan*). [See *Ketzos HaChoshen* 209:1 for a discussion concerning the validity of this type of purchase.]

[*Rashi* notes that the Gemara did not, strictly speaking, have to resort to a new case involving two owners to explain how a slave child purchased with money would be circumcised on the first day. The Gemara could simply have said that the case is where the master bought a pregnant slavewoman but did not immerse her until *after* she gave birth. Since she did not become *tamei* due to childbirth, her child is not circumcised on the eighth according to Rav Chama! The Gemara resorts to a new case of two owners, *Rashi* explains, because it wishes to teach that even where the child is born *after* its mother's immersion there is still a case in which Rav Chama agrees that he is circumcised immediately. (The Gemara is thus telling us that Rav Chama accepts the Tanna Kamma's rule concerning the similarity of a slave's birth to that of a Jewish child. Rav Chama disputes the Tanna Kamma only in regard to requiring yet *another* condition – that the child's mother be subject to childbirth *tumah.*)

Rashi also notes that the Gemara could have given the same case for Rav Chama as the Tanna Kamma gave in the Baraisa, namely, a slavewoman bought together with her already-born child! The Gemara did not do this because if the woman gave birth before her purchase, she had certainly not been immersed before giving birth (since she had not yet even been bought by a Jewish master; see *Minchas Chinuch* 2§15, Mechon Yerushalayim ed.). Accordingly, it would be irrelevant according to Rav Chama whether she gave birth before the purchase or afterwards, since even if she had given birth *after* her purchase the child would be circumcised on the first day as long as the mother had

ונתחדשה הלכה איני והא איתמר יוצא דופן ומי שיש לו שתי ערלות רב הונא ורב חייא בר רב חד אמר מחללין עליו את השבת וחד אמר אין מחללין עד כאן לא פליגי אלא לחלל עליו את השבת אבל לשמנה ודאי מהלינן ליה הא בהא תליא כתנאי יש יליד בית שנימול לאחד ויש יליד בית שנימול לשמנה יש מקנת כסף שנימול לאחד ויש מקנת כסף שנימול לשמנה יש מקנת כסף שנימול לא' ויש מקנת כסף שנימול לשמונה כיצד לקח שפחה מעוברת ואח"כ ילדה זהו מקנת כסף הנימול לשמונה לקח שפחה וולדה עמה זו היא מקנת כסף שנימול לאחד ויש יליד בית שנימול לשמנה כיצד לקח שפחה ונתעברה אצלו וילדה זהו יליד בית הנימול לשמונה רב חמא אומר ילדה ואח"כ הטבילה זהו יליד בית שנימול לאחד הטבילה ואחר כך ילדה זהו יליד בית הנימול לשמנה ותנא קמא לא שני ליה בין הטבילה ואח"כ ילדה בין ילדה ואח"כ הטבילה דאע"ג דאין אמו טמאה לידה נימול לשמנה (אמר רבא) בשלמא לר' חמא משכחת לה יליד בית נימול לא' יליד בית נימול לח' מקנת כסף נימול לא' ומקנת כסף נימול לח' ילדה ואח"כ הטבילה זהו יליד בית שנימול לאחד הטבילה ואח"כ ילדה זהו יליד בית שנימול לח' מקנת כסף נימול לשמנה כגון שלקח שפחה מעוברת והטבילה ואח"כ ילדה מקנת כסף נימול לאחד כגון שלקח זה שפחה וזה עוברה אלא לת"ק בשלמא כולהו משכחת להו אלא יליד בית נימול לאחד היכי משכחת לה א"ר ירמיה בלוקח שפחה לעוברה הניחא למ"ד קנין פירות לאו כקנין הגוף דמי אלא למ"ד קנין פירות כקנין הגוף דמי מאי איכא למימר אמר רב משרשיא בלוקח שפחה ע"מ שלא להטבילה תניא ר"ש בן גמליאל אומר כל ששהה ל' יום באדם אינו נפל שנאמר ופדויו מבן חדש תפדה שמנת ימים בבהמה אינו נפל שנאמר ומיום השמיני והלאה ירצה לקרבן וגו' הא לא שהה ספיקא הוי מימהל

רש"י

ונתחדשה הלכה. דמי שאמו טמאה לידה נימול בח' ולא אחר: יוצא דופן. שנקרעת אמו: שתי ערלות. שני עורות זה על זה ואמרי לה שני גידין: אבל לשמנה ודאי מהלינן. ואע"ג דיולא דופן אין אמו טמאה לידה: הא בהא תליא. וחילול שבת תלי במילה לח' דמי שנימול לח' דוחה שבת ומי שאינו נימול לח' אינו דוחה השבת דכי כתיב וביום השמיני דילפינן מיניה ואפילו בשבת בנימול לח' כתיב: כתנאי. הא דרב אסי: ה"ג הא מילתא בשאלתות דרב אחאי כילד לקח שפחה (א) ואחר כך ילדה זהו מקנת כסף שנימול לשמונה לקח שפחה וולדה עמה זהו מקנת כסף שנימול לאחד לקח שפחה ונתעברה אללו וילדה זהו יליד בית שנימול לח' רבי חמא אומר הטבילה ואחר כך ילדה זהו יליד בית שנימול לח' ילדה ואח"כ הטבילה זהו יליד בית שנימול לא' בשלמא לר' חמא משכחת לה יליד בית כדקתני מקנת כסף שנימול לשמנה כגון שלקח שפחה ואחר כך ילדה נימול לח' נמי כגון שלקח שפחה וולדה עמה אלא לת"ק כו'. ובספרים שלנו כתיב נימול לאחד נמי כגון שלקח זה שפחה וזה עוברה ונראה בעיני דהא דלא גרים בשאלתות כגון שלקח זה שפחה וזה עוברה משום דקשיא ליה מאי דוחקיה לאוקמיה בשני לקוחות ולשנויי גירסא דסיפא מרישא דקתני לקח שפחה וולדה זהו מקנת כסף שנימול לא': יש יליד בית שנימול לא'. דתרי קראי כתיבי ביליד בית ומקנת כסף חד כתיב ביה ח' וחד לא כתיב ביה ח' (בראשית יז) המול ימול יליד ביתך ומקנת כספך ולא מפרש ביה לח' ימים וכתיב (שם) ובן שמונת ימים ימול לכם כל זכר לדורותיכם יליד בית ומקנת כסף ומסתברא דהאי דמפרש ביה לשמנה היינו היכא דדמי לישראל מעליא שנולד בביתו של ישראל משקנאו דדומיא דלכם בעינן דכתיב בההוא קרא ימול לכם כל זכר והדר יליד בית ומקנת כסף הלכך לקח שפחה מעוברת וילדה הרי זה מקנת כסף דגוף שלם הוא במעי אמו וקנאו שנימול לח' דדומיא דלכם הוא שנולד ברשותו של ישראל לקח שפחה וולדה עמה שכבר ילדתו ואע"פ שלא עברו עליו ח' ללידתו מלו מיד כדכתיב המול ימול וגו' דלאו דומיא דלכם הוא לקח שפחה ונתעברה אללו לא הוי עובר מקנת כסף אלא יליד בית שנימול לח' דדומיא דלכם הוא ולקמיה מפרש יליד בית הנימול לאחד אליבא דת"ק: רבי חמא אומר. הטבילה לשם עבדות וחלה עליה שם תורת שפחת ישראל דנתחייבה בכל מלות שהאשה חייבת בהן והויא טמאה לידה זהו יליד בית שנימול לח': ילדה והטבילה זהו יליד בית שנימול לאחד. דכל שאין אמו טמאה לידה אין ממתינין לו לח' כרב אסי: בשלמא לרבי חמא. דשני בין הטבילה לילדה ואחר כך ילדה לילדה ואח"כ הטבילה: משכחת לה. כולהו יליד בית נימול לאחד ילדה ואח"כ הטבילה יליד בית נימול לח' הטבילה ושניהם בשנתעברה אללו דלא הוי מקנת כסף. מקנת כסף נימול לח' כגון שלקח שפחה מעוברת וילדה לאחר שהטבילה. מקנת כסף הנימול לא' כגון שלקח זה שפחה וזה עוברה דכיון דלאין לבעל העובר חלק באמו לאו דומיא דלכם הוא ה"ה נמי דמצי לפלוגי במקנת כסף בין ילדה ואחר כך הטבילה בין הטבילה ואחר כך ילדה ולמימר מקנת כסף נימול לא' כגון שלקח שפחה מעוברת ועוברה וילדה ואחר כך הטבילה אלא רבותא אשמעינן דאפילו בהטבילה ואח"כ ילדה משכחת לה והא דשני מקנת כסף נימול לא' לרבי חמא מלת"ק ולא אמר כגון שלקח שפחה וולדה עמה משום דאם כן ילדה קודם טבילה היא ומאי איריא נולד קודם שלקחה אפילו נולד משלקחה נמי לרבי חמא נימול לא': אלא יליד בית נימול לא' היכי משכחת לה. הא ודאי דומיא דלכם הוא הואיל ולאו בטומאת לידה תליא לדידיה: בלוקח שפחה לעוברה. ואפילו מישראל דהוי' טמאה לידה שכבר טבלה לאו דומיא דלכם הוא הואיל ואין לו חלק באמו: הניחא כו'. פלוגתא דר"ל ורבי יוחנן בבבא בתרא (דף קלו.): שלקחה על מנת שלא להטבילה. דלא שייכא בה תורת חיובא דמלות כלל דלאו דומיא דלכם הוא אבל לטומאת לידה לא חיישינן בילדה ואח"כ הטבילה: ופדויו. בבכור אדם כתיב: מבן חדש. מדתלי בהכי שמע מינה עכשיו נתברר שהוא בן קיימא ולא קודם לכן: הא לא שהה. שלשים יום באדם ובבהמה ח' ימים ספיקא הוי הש"ס פריך עלה: מימהל

תוספות

כתנאי יש יליד בית כו'. תימה היכי משמע ליה מתוך הך ברייתא דרבי חמא תלי טעמא בטומאת לידה לעולם אימא לך דסבר יולא דופן נימול לח' והאי דמצריך טבילה בשפחה משום דבעינן אחר אינה חשובה גיורת עד שתטבול כדנפקא לן ביבמות בפרק החולץ (דף מו.):

כגון שלקח זה שפחה וזה עוברה. פירש בקונטרס דהוי מצי למימר כגון שלקח שפחה מעוברת וילדה קודם טבילה אלא רבותא נקט דאפילו בטבלה ואח"כ ילדה משכחת לה מקנת כסף נימול לא' וקשה לר"י דלת"ק דלעיל ה"ל למינקט נמי הך רבותא ואמאי קאמר (ב) מקנת כסף נימול כו' אפילו לקח מעוברת נמי אלא שלקח זה שפחה וזה עוברה אלא ודאי לקח זה שפחה וזה עוברה הוי שפיר דומיא דלכם וכגירסת שאלתות דרב אחאי. נראה לר"י דגרס כגון שלקח שפחה וולדה עמה מיהו תימה לר"י דהוה מצי למינקט רבותא אפילו בלא ולדה עמה כגון שלקח שפחה מעוברת וילדה קודם טבילה וי"ל דניחא ליה למינקט כדקתני בברייתא במילתיה דת"ק ועוד אומר ר"י דמשום דהנך קראי נימול לאחד ונימול לשמונה דיליד בית ומקנת כסף כתיבי בפרשת לך לך הלכך ניחא לאשכוחינהו בכה"ג דשייך קודם מתן תורה דלא הוה טבילה ואע"ג דיליד בית נימול לח' לר' חמא לא משכחת לה אלא אחר מתן תורה בילדה ואח"כ טבלה מיהו כל מה שיכול לקיים לפני מתן תורה מקיים:

כגון שלקחה ע"מ שלא להטבילה. וכדמפר' ביבמות בפרק החולץ (דף מח.) דלקח על מנת שלא לגיירו יכול להשהותו הרבה:

כל ששהה שלשים יום באדם וח' ימים בבהמה. אין שוין דיום שמנה כלאחר שמנה כדמוכח לקמן דעבד להו עיגולא תילתא ביומא דשבעה וקאמר אי אימרמינהו עד לאורתא הוה אכלינן מיניה ויום שלשים כלפני שלשים כדמתן בבכורות בפ' יש בכור לנחלה (דף מט.) ואפילו רבי עקיבא דפליג לא קאמר אלא דמספקא אם הוא כלפני שלשים או כלאחר שלשים ולענין אבילות אפילו ר"ע מודה דהוה כלפני שלשים משום דהלכה כדברי המיקל באבל:

עין משפט נר מצוה

לה א מיי' שם הלכה יא טוש"ע י"ד סי' רסו סעיף ו:

לו ב מיי' שם הלכה ו סמג עשין כח טוש"ע י"ד סי' רסו סעיף ז:

לז ג ד מיי' שם הלכה ד סמג שם טוש"ע י"ד סי' רסו סעיף א:

לח ה מיי' שם הלכה יג ופ"א מהל' יבום וחליצה הלכה כג ופ"ב מהל' רוצח ושמירת נפש הלכה ו ופ"א מהל' אבל הלכה ו סמג עשין קלא ועשין דרבנן ב טוש"ע י"ד סי' שמ סעיף ל ושו"ע אה"ע סי' קנו סעיף ד:

לט ו מיי' פ"ד מהל' מעשה הקרבנות הלכה ד ופ"ב מהל' איסורי מזבח הלכה י סמג עשין קסח:

מסורת הש"ס

א) [יבמות דף עב.], ב) [מגילה ו: נזיר יט: תמורה יח.], ג) ר"מ מ"ז, ד) ב"ק פח. ב"מ לו. ב"ב נ. קלו. יבמות לו: [גיטין מז.], ה) ערכין כו:], ו) [יבמות שם ודף פ:] נדה מד: [תוספ' פט"ז], ז) [עי' רש"י יבמות עב. ד"ה בס שיש לו], ח) [פרשת לך לך סימן ט].

הגהות הב"ח

(א) רש"י ד"ה ה"ג הא מילתא וכו' כילד לקח שפחה מעוברת ואח"כ וכו' שנימול לשמונה כגון שלקח שפחה מעוברת והטבילה ואח"כ ילדה: (ב) תוס' ד"ה כגון שלקח וכו' הך רבותא ולמאי קאמר לקח שפחה וולדה עמה זו היא מקנת כסף שנימול לאחד אפילו מעוברת נמי:

רב נסים גאון

יצירה לט' ויצירה לז' רב הונא אמר נוצר לט' ונוצר לז' חי לח' אינו חי: הניחא למאן דאמר קנין פירות (לאו) כקנין הגוף דמי אלא למאן דאמר קנין פירות (לאו) כקנין הגוף דמי, ומחלוקת היא על זה בין ר' יוחנן ובין ריש לקיש ותמצא מחלוקתם בהרבה מקומות מן התלמוד במס' גיטין בפרק השולח גט לאשתו (דף מז) איתמר המוכר שדהו לפירות ר' יוחנן אמר מביא וקורא ריש לקיש אמר מביא ואינו קורא ר' יוחנן אמר מביא וקורא קנין פירות כקנין הגוף דמי ריש לקיש אמר מביא ואינו קורא קנין פירות לאו כקנין הגוף דמי ובבבא בתרא בפרק יש נוחלין (קלו) מכר הבן בחיי האב ובמס' יבמות בפרק החולץ (לו) כמו כן וזאת

ליקוטי רש"י

יוצא דופן. ע"י סם הוא וכבן אמו ואין לומר שלאחר שמתה אמו הוליאוהו דקיי"ל במסכת נדה (דף מד.) הוא מיית ברישא [חולין לח.]. שתי ערלות. ב' עורות זו על גבי זו [יבמות עב.]. אלא למ"ד קנין פירות. שיש לו בגוף הגוף קנוי לו [ב"ב קלו.]. כל ששהה שלשים יום. [יבמות לו.]. באדם אינו נפל. להכי נקט באדם דלאדם דמי נפל נקט לבהמה שנגמרה לורתו ולישתהי עד שמיני [שם פ:]. שמנת ימים בבהמה. אין שהיה מטהרתו עד שישהה שמונה ימים דשוב נפק ליה מכלל נפל דתניא רבן שמעון בן גמליאל אומר כל ששהה שלשים יום באדם אינו נפל ובבהמה שמונה ימים [ר"ה ז.]. ספיקא הוי. ומולנא ולא מחייבנא ודוקא אי מספקא לן אי כלו לו חדשיו אי לא אבל אי קים לן דכלו לו חדשיו תנן במסכת נדה (דף מג:) תינוק בן יומו פוטר מן הייבום [יבמות לו:].

גליון הש"ס

גמ' שלקח זה שפחה וזה עוברה. עיין בשער המלך פי"ב מהל' מילה הלכה י'. ובקונט' השוגן סי' רע סעיף ה'. ובספר כתובה בדף מ. א"ס: שם שמנת ימים בבהמה. עי' מנחות דף לז ע"א תד"ה שומע אני:

תורה אור השלם

א) וּפְדוּיָו מִבֶּן חֹדֶשׁ תִּפְדֶּה בְּעֶרְכְּךָ כֶּסֶף חֲמֵשֶׁת שְׁקָלִים בְּשֶׁקֶל הַקֹּדֶשׁ עֶשְׂרִים גֵּרָה הוּא: [במדבר יח, טז]

ב) שׁוֹר אוֹ כֶשֶׂב אוֹ עֵז כִּי יִוָּלֵד וְהָיָה שִׁבְעַת יָמִים תַּחַת אִמּוֹ וּמִיּוֹם הַשְּׁמִינִי וָהָלְאָה יֵרָצֶה לְקָרְבַּן אִשֶּׁה לַה': [ויקרא כב, כז]

רבינו חננאל

שמאי אומרים מחללין ובה"א אין מחללין ודייק רבה מדברי ר' אליעזר הקפר מכלל דת"ק סבר דברי הכל אין מחללין ואמר רבה אנא דאמרי כת"ק לדברי הכל ואקשינן על הדין דוקיא דרבה א"כ ר' אליעזר הקפר טעמא דב"ש אתא לאשמעינן כלומר אם ת"ק ור' אליעזר הקפר אמר כי ב"ה סבירא להו אין מחללין למה חלק על ת"ק. ת"ק אמר דברי הכל אין מחללין והוא עוד אמר כי ב"ה אין מחללין והלכה כמותם. לא בא אלא לפרש טעמא דב"ש מה הוצרך לזה. והא בהדיא קיי"ל ב"ש במקום ב"ה אינה משנה פריק רבה דלמא ת"ק אמר לא נחלקו אלא בלהטיף ממנו דם ברית ור' אליעזר הקפר אמר לא נחלקו בזה אלא לחלל עליו את השבת נחלקו. וביקש רבה להעמיד דבריו כד"ה אליבא דתנא [קמא] ולא נתברר אבל עמדו דבריו כב"ה אליבא דר' אליעזר הקפר ונמצאו דבריו ודברי רב שאמר הלכה כת"ק דבר אחד. וקיי"ל הלכתא כרב באיסורי. ועוד רבה ורב יוסף הלכתא כרבה בר משדה קנין ומחצה הלכך כוותייהו עבדינן וקיי"ל דנולד כשהוא מהול צריך להטיף ממנו דם ברית בחול שמא ערלה כבושה היא. ואם חל ח' שלו בשבת אין מחללין עליו את השבת וכן הלכה. ומעשה דרב אדא בר אהבה ברור הוא והזכירוהו בתלמוד א"י כלשון הזה. רב אדא בר אהבה איתליד ליה חד בר (בן) [כי] ממסמס ביה מית רבי אבין אמר פצוע דכא נעשה ונתענה עליו ומת. גר שנתגייר כשהוא מהול אין לו תקנה אבל הוא בעצמו לא: **אמר** רבה אמר רב אסי כל שאמו טמאה לידה נימול לשמונה כו' מסתברא שלא בא רבה אלא למעט בן הנכרית שאין אמו טמאה לידה. אם יקנהו אין נימול לח' שבן בת ישראל ובן הגיורת ובן השפחה אמה טמאה לידה שכך שנינו בענין אשה כי תזריע בני ישראל בענין הזה. ואין הנכרים בענין הזה או בני ישראל אין לי אלא בני ישראל מניין לרבות את הגיורת ואת השפחה בין משוחררת ובין שאינה משוחררת ת"ל אשה כי תזריע וילדה זכר וטמאה גו' הא אפילו שפחה טמאה ומקשינן עלה וכל שאמו טמאה לידה נימול לשמונה ומי שאין אמו טמאה לידה אינו נימול לשמונה. והרי יוצא דופן שאין אמו טמאה לידה דתניא וילדה עד שתלד ממקום הולד פרט ליוצא דופן ר' שמעון אומר יוצא דופן הרי הוא כילוד וחייבין עליו קרבן ובלבד שהוא פטור מחמש סלעים ואתמר יוצא דופן ומי שיש לו ב' ערלות רב הונא ורב חייא בר רב חד אמר מחללין עליו את השבת וחד אמר אין מחללין עליו את השבת. עד כאן לא פליגי לחלל עליו את השבת אבל ודאי לשמונה מהלינן ליה. ופרקי' הא בהא תליא האומר מחללין עליו את השבת סבר נימול לח' והאומר אין מחללין סבר אינו נימול לשמונה ואמרי דדברי רבה כתנאי זה התנא שאמר לקח שפחה ועוברה עמה נימול לח'. פי' קנה שפחה גויה ועוברה נמצא זה העובר מקנת כסף וקודם שיטבלנה עודה בגיותה ילדתו כיון שיגיע ליום שמיני חייב למולו ואע"פ שילדתו בגיותה שאינה טמאה לידה ואמר התנא זהו מקנת כסף הנימול [לשמונה]. דלא כרבה ורב אחא אמר ילדה כו'. קיי"ל דכולהו תנאי מא"י אינון לפיכך קרי להו רבי בר מתלת דוכתי. ואע"ג דתנאי אינון קרי להו רב. רב אבא בהאשה שנפלו לה נכסים. ורב אבא נמי בג' שאכלו כאחד. ורב חמא בהדא דוכתא. ורב אחא אמר ילדה ואח"כ הטבילה מאחר שאין אמו טמאה לידה אינו נימול לשמונה אלא ליום אחד כרבה. וזהו שאמר רבה לרב חמא דבעי טבילה משכחת לה יליד בית נימול לשמונה כגון שהטבילה ואח"כ ילדה. מקנת כסף נימול לשמונה כגון שלקח שפחה ועוברה עמה. וגם זו הטבילה ואח"כ ילדה ומפני מה לא פירש בה טבילה כיון שההפרש מקודם לזה בין הטבילה ואח"כ ילדה ובין ילדה ואח"כ הטבילה. (מימי) [מי] לא שמעת לה לקח שפחה ועוברה עמה. זהו מקנת כסף שנימול לשמונה. לקח

אֶלָּא לְתַנָּא קַמָּא – **According to the Tanna Kamma, however,** בִּשְׁלָמָא כּוּלְּהוּ מַשְׁכַּחַתְּ לְהוּ – **it is understandable** how **all [the other cases]** enumerated in the Baraisa **are to be found;** אֶלָּא יְלִיד בַּיִת נִימּוֹל לְאֶחָד הֵיכִי מַשְׁכַּחַתְּ לָהּ – **but how is there to be found a** case of a slave **"born in the house" who is circumcised on the first day?**[19]

The Gemara answers:

אָמַר רַבִּי יִרְמְיָה – **R' Yirmiyah said:** בְּלוֹקֵחַ שִׁפְחָה לְעוּבָּרָהּ – We find such a case **where [the master] buys a slavewoman for** the right to **her fetus.**[20] Since the master does not own the mother, the circumstances of this child's birth are dissimilar to those of a natural-born Jewish child, so that the slave child is circumcised on the first day.

The Gemara challenges R' Yirmiyah's answer:

הָנִיחָא לְמַאן דְּאָמַר קִנְיַן פֵּירוֹת לָאו כְּקִנְיַן הַגּוּף דָּמֵי – **This** answer **is acceptable according to the one who says** that **ownership of** the right to **the produce** of a property **is not tantamount to ownership of the essence** of the property.[21] Hence, although the master owns the child, he is not viewed as owning its mother. אֶלָּא לְמַאן דְּאָמַר קִנְיַן פֵּירוֹת כְּקִנְיַן הַגּוּף דָּמֵי – **However, according to the one who says** that **ownership of** the right to **the produce** of a property **is tantamount to ownership of the essence** of the property, מַאי אִיכָּא לְמֵימַר – **what is there to say?** Having acquired the right to the slavewoman's offspring, the owner is viewed as an owner of the slavewoman as well. Thus, when she conceives and gives birth, the circumstances of her child's birth *are* similar to those of an ordinary Jewish child and he should thus be circumcised on the eighth day. We therefore return to our previous difficulty: What is the case of a slave "born in the house" who is circumcised on the first day according to the Tanna Kamma?

The Gemara therefore suggests another answer:

אָמַר רַב מְשַׁרְשִׁיָּא – **Rav Mesharshiya said:** בְּלוֹקֵחַ שִׁפְחָה עַל מְנַת שֶׁלֹּא לְהַטְבִּילָהּ – The case is **where [a master] buys a slavewoman with the stipulation that he will not immerse her** in a *mikveh* to convert her to the legal status of a Canaanite slave. This slave later conceived and gave birth. Since she will never be subject to the laws that apply to Jewish women, the circumstances of her child's birth are dissimilar to those of a Jewish child, and the slave child is therefore not subject to circumcision on the eighth day.[22]

NOTES

not yet been immersed. Thus, to illustrate the case according to *Rav Chama,* the Gemara switches to another case.

Rashi does, however, note that according to the reading of our Gemara found in the *She'iltos* of *Rav Achai Gaon,* the Gemara does indeed give the same example for Rav Chama that the Tanna Kamma gave. Although the detail of the child having been born before the purchase is not strictly necessary according to Rav Chama (as we just explained), *Rav Achai Gaon* found this reading preferable because it would be unusual for the Gemara to change the case from the Tanna Kamma to Rav Chama simply for this reason (*Rashi*). *Tosafos,* who finds difficulty with *Rashi's* explanation, adopt *Rav Achai Gaon's* reading.]

19. [For the only case we found according to Rav Chama was one in which an unimmersed slavewoman conceived and gave birth while in her master's possession. Since she is not subject to childbirth *tumah,* Rav Chama rules that the child is circumcised immediately.] But the Tanna Kamma does not differentiate on the basis of immersion because he does not consider circumcision on the eighth day to be linked to childbirth *tumah* (*Rashi*). Thus, as long as the slavewoman conceived and gave birth after becoming the property of a Jewish master, her child would be circumcised on the eighth day whether or not she had immersed, since he is like those *among you* in that her master has legal connection to her (*Rashi*).

20. [I.e. he acquires a monetary interest in a slavewoman, whose sole benefit to him is the right to keep her offspring. The slavewoman herself, however, belongs in all other respects to someone else (e.g. in regard to her work and earnings).] The case may refer even to one in which she belongs to another Jewish master who previously immersed her, so that she is *tamei* due to childbirth. Nevertheless, her child is circumcised immediately because his master does not actually own the mother, only the right to her offspring (*Rashi*).

[R' Yirmiyah speaks of a case where this person acquired the right to the offspring *before* the woman became pregnant. Thus, the child is considered a יְלִיד בַּיִת, *slave born in his house,* i.e. possession. Had he acquired the rights to the fetus only *after* she had become pregnant, the child would be considered a מִקְנַת כֶּסֶף, *slave purchased with money,* as the Gemara said above.]

21. The Gemara in *Bava Basra* (136b) records a dispute in regard to a property that is owned by two people, one of whom holds the title to it and the other of whom owns the right to its production. R' Yochanan is of the opinion that the one who owns the right to the production is treated as its "owner" in regard to any Torah laws that pertain specifically to the "owner" of a property (see *Rashbam, Bava Basra* 50a ד"ה בקנין הגוף). Reish Lakish disputes this and rules that the title holder is treated as the owner, not the owner of the production. [According to Reish Lakish, therefore, the owner of the child in our case is *not* viewed as owning its mother, despite his right to her offspring.]

22. The fact that this child's mother is not subject to immersion and the obligation of mitzvos that comes thereby makes his condition utterly dissimilar to that of a Jewish child (*Rashi;* cf. *Chidushei HaRan*). [Although the Tanna Kamma holds that a child born to a slavewoman who has not *yet* immersed is circumcised on the eighth day (as the Gemara stated above), that child's circumstances are not fundamentally different from those *among you* because the slavewoman is subject to being immersed and will soon be immersed and become subject to Torah law. (Indeed, the master is under obligation to immerse her [see *Yevamos* 48b].) But where the master acquires her with the express stipulation that he will not immerse and convert her to the status of a Canaanite slave, he is not under obligation to do so (see ibid. 48b). Thus, her continued status as a gentile makes her child's condition significantly different from those "*among you,*" and the child is therefore not subject to the eighth-day rule.]

In Summary: There are two types of Canaanite slaves – a יְלִיד בַּיִת, *[slave] born in the [master's] house,* and a מִקְנַת כֶּסֶף, *[slave] purchased [by the master] with money.* Canaanite slaves must be circumcised by their Jewish master. However, the Torah teaches that with each of these types, there are some instances in which a slave child is circumcised at the age of eight days and others in which he is circumcised on the first day. There is a dispute between the Tanna Kamma and Rav Chama as to what factors determine this distinction. According to the Tanna Kamma there is only one factor – how closely the circumstances of the slave's birth resemble those *among you* [לָכֶם], i.e. Jewish children. Those whose circumstances are similar to those of a Jewish child are circumcised on the eighth day, while those whose circumstances are not similar are circumcised immediately. Rav Chama does not dispute this rule but adds an *additional* factor – the mother becoming subject to childbirth *tumah.* A child whose mother is not subject to *tumah* as a result of her childbirth is circumcised on the first day. The Tanna Kamma rejects this rule and maintains that he is circumcised on the eighth. The following distinctions emerge from this dispute:

(a) מִקְנַת כֶּסֶף, *purchased with money*: If a pregnant slavewoman was purchased by a Jewish master, her child (who is also considered purchased) is circumcised on the eighth day, according to the Tanna Kamma, whether she immersed in a *mikveh* before giving birth or not. According to Rav Chama, however, he is circumcised on the eighth day only if his mother was immersed in a *mikveh* before giving birth, so that she became subject to childbirth *tumah.* Otherwise, he is circumcised on the first day.

If a slavewoman is purchased together with her child immediately after giving birth, the child is circumcised on the first day according to all opinions because the circumstances of his birth are not similar to those *among you* – in that he was not born into a Jewish household. If a pregnant slavewoman was purchased by one Jewish master and her fetus by another, that child is also not circumcised on the eighth day because his circumstances are also different from those of a Jewish child – in that his master has no connection to his mother. (The Gemara states this according to Rav Chama but it would be true according to the Tanna Kamma as well, according to *Rashi;* cf. *Tosafos.*)

(b) יְלִיד בַּיִת, *born in the house* of a Jewish master: If a slavewoman did not

ונתחדשה הלכה איני והא איתמר יוצא דופן א) ומי שיש לו שתי ערלות רב הונא ורב חייא בר רב חד אמר מחללין עליו את השבת וחד אמר א אין מחללין עד כאן לא פליגי אלא לחלל עליו את השבת ב אבל לשמנה ודאי מהלינן ליה ג) הא בהא תליא כתנאי יש יליד בית שנימול לאחד ויש יליד בית שנימול לשמנה יש מקנת כסף שנימול לאחד ויש מקנת כסף שנימול לשמנה יש מקנת כסף שנימול לא' ויש מקנת כסף שנימול לשמונה כיצד ג לקח שפחה מעוברת ואח"כ ילדה זהו מקנת כסף הנימול לשמונה לקח שפחה וולדה עמה זו היא מקנת כסף שנימול לאחד ויש יליד בית שנימול לשמנה ד כיצד לקח שפחה ונתעברה אצלו וילדה זהו יליד בית הנימול לשמנה רב חמא אומר ילדה ואח"כ הטבילה זהו יליד בית שנימול לאחד הטבילה ואחר כך ילדה זהו יליד בית הנימול לשמנה ותנא קמא לא שני ליה בין הטבילה ואח"כ ילדה בין ילדה ואח"כ הטבילה דאע"ג דאין אמו טמאה לידה נימול לשמנה ג) (אמר רבא) בשלמא לר' חמא משכחת לה יליד בית נימול לא' יליד בית נימול לח' מקנת כסף נימול לא' ומקנת כסף נימול לח' ילדה ואח"כ הטבילה זהו יליד בית שנימול לאחד הטבילה ואח"כ ילדה זהו יליד בית שנימול לח' מקנת כסף נימול לשמנה כגון שלקח שפחה מעוברת והטבילה ואח"כ ילדה מקנת כסף נימול לאחד כגון ה שלקח זה שפחה וזה עוברה אלא לת"ק בשלמא כולהו משכחת להו אלא יליד בית נימול לאחד היכי משכחת לה א"ר ירמיה בלוקח שפחה לעוברה ז) למ"ד קנין פירות לאו כקנין הגוף דמי אלא למ"ד קנין פירות כקנין הגוף דמי מאי איכא למימר אמר רב משרשיא בלוקח שפחה ע"מ שלא להטבילה ה) תניא ר"ש בן גמליאל אומר ה כל ששהה ל' יום באדם אינו נפל שנאמר א) ופדויו מבן חדש תפדה * ו שמנת ימים בבהמה אינו נפל שנאמר ב) ומיום השמיני והלאה ירצה לקרבן וגו' הא לא שהה ספיקא הוי מימהל

רש"י

ונתחדשה הלכה. דמי שאמו טמאה לידה נימול בח' ולא אחר: יוצא דופן. שנקרעת אמו: שתי ערלות. שני עורות זה על זה [א] ואמרי לה שני גידין: אבל לשמנה ודאי מהלינן. ואע"ג דיוצא דופן אין אמו טמאה לידה: הא בהא תליא. וחילול שבת תלי במילה לח' דמי שנימול לח' דוחה שבת ומי שאינו נימול לח' אינו דוחה השבת דכי כתיב וביום השמיני דילפינן מיניה ואפילו בשבת בנימול לח' כתיב: כתנאי. הא דרב אסי: ה"ג הא מילתא בשאלתות דרב אחאי [ב] כיצד לקח שפחה (א) ואחר כך ילדה זהו מקנת כסף שנימול לשמונה לקח שפחה וולדה עמה זהו מקנת כסף שנימול לאחד לקח שפחה ונתעברה אצלו וילדה זהו יליד בית שנימול לח' רבי חמא אומר הטבילה ואחר כך ילדה זהו יליד בית שנימול לח' ילדה ואח"כ הטבילה זהו יליד בית שנימול לא' בשלמא לר' חמא משכחת לה יליד בית דקתני מקנת כסף שנימול לשמנה כגון שלקח שפחה ואחר כך ילדה זהו נמי כגון שלקח שפחה וולדה עמה אלא לת"ק כו'. ובספרים שלנו כתיב נימול לאחד נמי כגון שלקח זה שפחה וזה עוברה ונראה בעיני דהכא לא גרים בשאלתות כגון שלקח זה שפחה וזה עוברה משום דקשיא ליה מאי דוחקיה לאוקמיה בשני לקוחות ולשנויי גירסא דסיפא מרישא דקתני לקח שפחה וולדה זהו מקנת כסף שנימול לא': יש יליד בית שנימול לא'. דתרי קראי כתיבי יליד בית ומקנת כסף חד כתיב ביה ח' וחד לא כתיב ביה ח' (בראשית יז) המול ימול יליד ביתך ומקנת כספך ולא מפרש ביה לח' ימים וכתיב (שם) ובן שמונת ימים ימול לכם כל זכר לדורותיכם יליד בית ומקנת כסף ומסתברא דהאי דמפרש ביה לשמנה היינו היכא דדמי לישראל מעליא שנולד ברשותו של ישראל משקנאו דדומיא דלכם בעינן דכתיב בההוא קרא ימול לכם כל זכר והדר יליד בית ומקנת כסף הלכך לקח שפחה מעוברת וילדה הרי זה מקנת כסף דגוף שלם הוא במעי אמו וקנאו שנימול לח' דדומיא דלכם הוא שנולד ברשותו של ישראל לקח שפחה וולדה עמה שכבר ילדתו ואע"פ שלא עברו עליו ח' ללידתו מלו מיד כדכתיב המול ימול וגו' דלאו דומיא דלכם הוא לקח שפחה ונתעברה אצלו לא הוי עובר מקנת כסף אלא יליד בית שנימול לח' דדומיא דלכם הוא ולקמיה מפרש יליד בית הנימול לאחד אליבא דת"ק: רבי חמא אומר. הטבילה לשם עבדות וחלה עליה שם תורת שפחת ישראל דנתחייבה בכל מצות שהאשה חייבת בהן והויא טמאה לידה זהו יליד בית שנימול לח': ילדה והטבילה זהו יליד בית שנימול לאחד. דכל שאין אמו טמאה לידה אין ממתינין לו לח' כרב אסי: בשלמא לרבי חמא. דשני בין הטבילה לילדה ואחר כך ילדה לילדה ואח"כ הטבילה: משכחת לה. כולהו יליד בית נימול לאחד ילדה ואח"כ הטבילה יליד בית נימול לח' הטבילה ואח"כ ילדה ושניהם בשנתעברה אצלו דלא הוי מקנת כסף. מקנת כסף נימול לח' כגון שלקח שפחה מעוברת וילדה לאחר שהטבילה. מקנת כסף הנימול לא' כגון שלקח זה שפחה וזה עוברה דכיון דאין לבעל העובר חלק באמו לאו דומיא דלכם הוא ה"ה נמי דמצי לפלוגי במקנת כסף בין ילדה ואחר כך הטבילה בין הטבילה ואחר כך ילדה ולמימר מקנת כסף נימול לא' כגון שלקח שפחה מעוברת ועוברה וילדה ואחר כך הטבילה אלא רבותא אשמעינן דאפילו בהטבילה ואח"כ ילדה משכחת לה והא דשני מקנת כסף נימול לא' לרבי חמא מלת"ק ולא אמר כגון שלקח שפחה וולדה עמה משום דאם כן ילדה קודם טבילה היא ומאי איריא נולד קודם שלקחה אפילו נולד משלקחה נמי לרבי חמא נימול לא': אלא יליד בית נימול לא' היכי משכחת לה. הא ודאי דומיא דלכם הוא הואיל ולאו בטומאת לידה תליא לדידיה: בלוקח שפחה לעוברה. ואפילו מישראל דהוי' טמאה לידה שכבר טבלה לאו דומיא דלכם הוא הואיל ואין לו חלק באמו: הניחא כו'. פלוגתא דר"ל ורבי יוחנן בבבא בתרא (דף קלו.): שלקחה על מנת שלא להטבילה. דלא שייכא בה תורת חיובא דמצות כלל דלאו דומיא דלכם הוא אבל לטומאת לידה לא חיישינן בילדה ואח"כ הטבילה: ופדויו. בבכור אדם כתיב: מבן חדש. מדתלי בהכי שמע מינה עכשיו נתברר שהוא בן קיימא ולא קודם לכן: הא לא שהה. שלשים יום באדם ובבהמה ח' ימים ספיקא הוי הש"ס פריך עלה: מימהל

תוספות

כתנאי יש יליד בית כו'. תימה היכי משמע ליה מתוך הך ברייתא דרבי חמא תלי טעמא בטומאת לידה לעולם אימא לך דסבר יוצא דופן נימול לח' והאי דמצריך טבילה בשפחה משום דלענין אחר אינה חשובה גיורת עד שתטבול כדנפקא לן ביבמות בפרק החולץ (דף מו.):

כגון שלקח זה שפחה וזה עוברה. פירש בקונטרס דהוי מצי למימר כגון שלקח שפחה מעוברת וילדה קודם טבילה אלא רבותא נקט דאפילו בטבלה ואח"כ ילדה משכחת לה מקנת כסף נימול לא' וקשה לר"י דלת"ק לעיל ה"ל למינקט נמי הך רבותא ואמאי קאמר (ב) מקנת כסף נימול כו' אפילו לקח מעוברת נמי אלא שלקח זה שפחה וזה עוברה אלא ודאי לקח זה שפחה וזה עוברה הוי שפיר דומיא דלכם וכגירסת שאלתות דרב אחאי. נראה לר"י דגרס כגון שלקח שפחה וולדה עמה מיהו תימה לר"י דהוה מצי למינקט רבותא אפילו בלא ולדה עמה כגון שלקח שפחה מעוברת וילדה קודם טבילה וי"ל דניחא ליה למינקט דקתני בברייתא במילתיה דת"ק ועוד אומר ר"י דמשום דהכי קרא ימול לאחד וימול לשמונה דיליד בית ומקנת כסף כתיבי בפרשת לך לך הלכך ניחא לאשכוחינהו בכה"ג דשייך קודם מתן תורה דלא הוה טבילה ואע"ג דיליד בית נימול לח' לר' חמא לא משכחת לה אלא אחר מתן תורה בילדה ואח"כ טבלה מיהו כל מה שיכול לקיים לפני מתן תורה מקיים:

כגון שלקחה ע"מ שלא להטבילה. וכדמפר' ביבמות בפרק החולץ (דף מח:) דלקח על מנת שלא לגיירו יכול להשהותו הרבה:

כל ששהה שלשים יום באדם וח' ימים בבהמה. אינן שוין דיום שמנה כלאחר שמנה כדמוכח לקמן דעבד להו עיגלא תילתא ביומא דשבעה וקאמר אי איתרמיתו עד לאורתא הוה אכלינן מיניה ויום שלשים כלפני שלשים כדתנן בבכורות בפ' יש בכור לנחלה (דף מט.) ואפילו רבי עקיבא דפליג לא קאמר אלא דמספקא אם הוא כלפני שלשים או כלאחר שלשים ולענין אבילות אפילו ר"ע מודה דהוה כלפני שלשים משום דהלכה כדברי המיקל באבל: מימהל

עין משפט נר מצוה

לה א מיי' שם הלכה יא טוש"ע א"ח סי' שלא סעיף ה וי"ד סי' רסו סעיף יב:

לו ב מיי' שם הלכה ז סמג עשין כח טוש"ע י"ד סי' רסז סעיף ג וסימן רסו סעיף יב:

לז ג ד מיי' שם הלכה ח סמג שם טוש"ע י"ד סי' רסז סעיף ב:

לח ה מיי' שם הלכה יג וסי"א מהל' יבום וחליצה הלכה כב וכו"ע מהל' רוצח ושמירת נפש הלכה ו וסי"א מהל' אבל הלכה ו סמג עשין לו ועשין דרבנן ב טוש"ע י"ד סי' שמ סעיף ל וסי' שעד סעיף ח וטוש"ע אה"ע סי' קנו סעיף ד:

לט ו מיי' פ"ד מהל' מאכלות אסורות הלכה ד ופ"ג מהל' איסורי מזבח הלכה ח סמג לאוין שט וקלג עשין קמח:

גליון הש"ס

גמ' שלקח זה שפחה וזה עוברה. עיין בספר המלך פי"ב מהל' מילה הלכה י'. ובקונט' החושן סי' רנ סעיף א'. ובספר כתובה כדף מ"ג ע"א בהג"ה. רש"י ד"ה שמנת ימים בבהמה. עי' מנחות דף לו ע"ב תד"ה שומע אני:

תורה אור השלם

א) וּפְדוּיָו מִבֶּן חֹדֶשׁ תִּפְדֶּה בְּעֶרְכְּךָ כֶּסֶף חֲמֵשֶׁת שְׁקָלִים בְּשֶׁקֶל הַקֹּדֶשׁ עֶשְׂרִים גֵּרָה הוּא: [במדבר יח, טז]

ב) שׁוֹר אוֹ כֶשֶׂב אוֹ עֵז כִּי יִוָּלֵד וְהָיָה שִׁבְעַת יָמִים תַּחַת אִמּוֹ וּמִיּוֹם הַשְּׁמִינִי וָהָלְאָה יֵרָצֶה לְקָרְבַּן אִשֶּׁה לַייָ: [ויקרא כב, כז]

רבינו חננאל

שמאין אומרים מחללין ובה"א אין מחללין ודייק רבה מדברי ר' אליעזר הקפר מכלל דת"ק סבר דברי הכל אין מחללין ואמר רבה אנא דאמרי כת"ק לדברי הכל ואקשינן על הדין דוקיא דרבה א"כ ר' אליעזר הקפר טעמא דב"ש אתא לאשמעינן כלומר אם ת"ק אמר דברי הכל מחללין ור' אליעזר הקפר אמר כי ב"ה סבירא להו אין מחללין נמצא לא חלק על ת"ק. ת"ק אמר דברי הכל אין מחללין והוא עוד אמר כי ב"ה אין מחללין והלכה כמותם. לא בא אלא לפרש טעמא דב"ש מה הצורך לזה. והא בהדיא קיי"ל ב"ש במקום ב"ה אינה משנה פריק רבה דלמא ת"ק אמר לא נחלקו אלא בלהטיף ממנו דם ברית ור' אליעזר הקפר אמר לא נחלקו בזה אלא לחלל עליו את השבת נחלקו. וביקש רבה להעמיד דבריו כד"ה אליבא דתנא [קמא] ולא נתברר אבל עמדו דבריו כב"ה אליבא דר' אליעזר הקפר ונמצאו דבריו ודברי רב שאמר הלכה כת"ק דבר אחד. וקיי"ל הלכתא כרב באיסורי. ועוד רבה ורב יוסף הלכתא כרבה בר משדה קנין ומחצה הלכך כוותייהו עבדינן וקיי"ל דנולד כשהוא מהול צריך להטיף ממנו דם ברית בחול שמא ערלה כבושה היא. ואם חל ח' שלו בשבת אין מחללין עליו את השבת וכן הלכה. ומעשה דרב אדא בר אהבה ברור הוא והזכירוהו בתלמוד א"י כלשון הזה. רב אדא בר אהבה איתיליד ליה חד בר [בן] [כי] ממסמס ביה מית רבי אבין אמר פצוע דכא נעשה ונתענה עליו ומת. גר שנתגייר כשהוא מהול אין לו תקנה אבל הוא בעצמו לא: אמר רבה אמר רב אסי כל שאמו טמאה לידה נימול לשמונה כו' מסתברא שלא בא רבה אלא למעט בן הנכרית שאין אמו טמאה לידה. אם יקנהו אין נימול לח' שבן בת ישראל ובן הגיורת ובן השפחה אמה טמאה לידה שכך שנינו בענין אשה כי תזריע בני ישראל בענין לידה. ואין הנכרים בענין הזה או בני ישראל אין לי אלא בני ישראל מניין לרבות את הגיורת ואת השפחה בין משוחררת ובין שאינה משוחררת ת"ל אשה כי תזריע וילדה זכר וטמאה גו' הא אפילו שפחה טמאה ומקשינן עלה וכל שאמו טמאה לידה נימול לשמונה ומי שאין אמו טמאה לידה אינו נימול לשמונה. והרי יוצא דופן שאין אמו טמאה לידה דתניא וילדה עד שתלד ממקום הולד פרט ליוצא דופן ר' שמעון אומר יוצא דופן הרי הוא כילוד וחייבין עליו קרבן ובלבד שהוא פטור מחמש סלעים ואתמר יוצא דופן ומי שיש לו ב' ערלות רב הונא ורב חייא בר רב חד אמר מחללין עליו את השבת וחד אמר אין מחללין עליו את השבת. עד כאן לא פליגי לחלל עליו את השבת אבל ודאי לשמונה מהלינן ליה. ופרקי' הא בהא תליא האומר מחללין עליו את השבת סבר נימול לח' והאומר אין מחללין סבר אינו נימול לשמונה ואמרי דדברי רבה כתנאי זה התנא שאמר לקח שפחה ועוברה עמה נימול לח'. פי' קנה שפחה גויה ועוברה נמצא זה העובר מקנת כסף וקודם שיטבלנה עודה בגיותה ילדתו כיון שיגיע ליום שמיני חייב למולו ואע"פ שילדתו בגיותה שאינה טמאה לידה ואמר התנא זהו מקנת כסף הנימול [לשמונה]. דלא כרבה ורב אחא אמר ילדה כו'. קיי"ל דכולהו תנאי מאי"י אינון לפיכך קרי להו רבי בר מתלת דוכתי. ואע"ג דתנאי אינון קרי להו רב. רב אבא בהאשה שנפלו לה נכסים. ורב אבא נמי בג' שאכלו כאחד. ורב חמא בהדא דוכתא. ורב אחא אמר ילדה ואח"כ הטבילה מאחר שאין אמו טמאה לידה אינו נימול לשמונה אלא ליום אחד כרבה. וזהו שאמר רבה לרב חמא דבעי טבילה משכחת לה יליד בית נימול לשמונה כגון שהטבילה ואח"כ ילדה. מקנת כסף נימול לשמונה כגון שלקח שפחה ועוברה עמה. וגם זו הטבילה ואח"כ ילדה ומפני מה לא פירש בה טבילה כיון שהפרש מקודם לזה בין הטבילה ואח"כ ילדה ובין ילדה ואח"כ הטבילה. (מימי) [מי] לא שמעת לה לקח שפחה ועוברה עמה. זהו מקנת כסף שנימול לשמונה. לקח

מסורת הש"ס

א) [יבמות דף עב.], ב) [מגילה ו: נזיר יח: תמורה יח.], ג) [ר"מ מ"ז], ד) כ"ק סח: [כ"מ נו. ב"ב ג. קלו. יבמו' מו: גיטין מו: מח. ערכין כו:], ה) [יבמות שם ודף פ:] נדה מד: [תוספ' פסחים], ו) [ע' רש"י יבמות עב. ד"ה שם שיש לו], ז) [פרשת לך לך סימן טו].

הגהות הב"ח

(א) רש"י ד"ה ה"ג הא מילתא וכו' כיצד לקח שפחה מעוברת ואח"כ ילדה זהו מקנת כסף וכו' שנימול לשמונה כגון שלקח שפחה מעוברת והטבילה ואח"כ ילדה: (ב) תוס' ד"ה כגון שלקח זה וכו' רבותא ואמאי קאמר לקח שפחה וולדה עמה זו היא מקנת כסף שנימול לאחד אפילו מעוברת נמי:

רב נסים גאון

יצירה לט' ויצירה לז' רב הונא אמר נוצר לט' ונוצר לז' חי לח' אינו חי: הניחא למאן דאמר קנין פירות (לאו) כקנין הגוף דמי אלא למאן דאמר קנין פירות (לאו) כקנין הגוף דמי. ומחלוקת היה על זה בין ר' יוחנן ובין ריש לקיש ותמצא מחלוקתם בהרבה מקומות מן התלמוד במס' גיטין בפרק השולח גט לאשתו (דף מז) איתמר המוכר שדהו לפירות ר' יוחנן אמר מביא וקורא ריש לקיש אמר מביא ואינו קורא ר' יוחנן אמר מביא וקורא קנין פירות כקנין הגוף דמי ריש לקיש אמר מביא ואינו קורא קנין פירות לאו כקנין הגוף דמי ובבבא בתרא בפרק יש נוחלין (קלו) מכר הבן בחיי האב וכו' ובמס' יבמות בפרק החולץ (לו) כמו כן וזולת

ליקוטי רש"י

יוצא דופן. ע"י סם וכגון הוא וכגון ולא מיין ולא לומר שלאחר שמתה אמו הוציאוהו דקיי"ל במסכת נדה (דף מג.) הוא מיים כרישא [חולין נא.]. שתי ערלות. ב' עורות זו על גבי זו [יבמות עב.]. אלא למ"ד קנין פירות. שיש לו לאיש גוף הקרקע קנוי לו [רשב"ם ב"ב קלו.]. כל ששהה ל' יום. משנולד חי שלשים יום [יבמות לו:]. באדם אינו נפל. לאפי שלשים יום [שם פ:]. שמונה ימים שהה אין נפל [שם פ:]. אינו נפל. ופוטר את אמו מן החליצה [שם לו:]. ואפילו לא כלו לו חדשי עיבור דאמרינן לשבעה נגמרה צורתו ואישתהי עד שמיני [שם פ:]. שמנת ימים בבהמה. אין שחיטה מטהרתו עד ששהה שמונה ימים דשוב נפק ליה מכלל נפל דתניא רבן שמעון בן גמליאל אומר כל ששהה שלשים יום באדם אינו נפל ובבהמה שמונה ימים [ר"ה ז.]. ספיקא הוי. ומולגת ולא מתייבמת ודוקא אי מספקא לן אי כלו לו חדשיו אי לא אבל אי קים לן דכלו לו חדשיו תנן במסכת נדה (דף מג:) תינוק בן יומו פוטר מן הייבום [יבמות לו:].

The Gemara questions how circumcision can ever be performed on the Sabbath. The Gemara's question is based on a ruling in regard to נֵפֶל, *a non-viable birth*:

תַּנְיָא – **It was taught in a Baraisa:** רַבָּן שִׁמְעוֹן בֶּן גַּמְלִיאֵל אוֹמֵר – RABBAN SHIMON BEN GAMLIEL SAYS: כֹּל שֶׁשָּׁהָה שְׁלֹשִׁים יוֹם בָּאָדָם אֵינוֹ נֵפֶל – ANY HUMAN newborn THAT SURVIVES for THIRTY DAYS IS NOT suspected of being A NON-VIABLE CHILD,[23] שֶׁנֶּאֱמַר ,,וּפְדוּיָו מִבֶּן־חֹדֶשׁ תִּפְדֶּה" – FOR [THE VERSE] STATES in regard to the mitzvah of redeeming a firstborn child: ***THOSE [THAT ARE TO BE] REDEEMED, YOU SHALL REDEEM FROM THE AGE OF ONE MONTH.***[24] שְׁמוֹנַת יָמִים בִּבְהֵמָה אֵינוֹ נֵפֶל – By contrast, EIGHT DAYS IN in the case of AN ANIMAL demonstrates that it IS NOT A NON-VIABLE [ANIMAL], שֶׁנֶּאֱמַר ,,וּמִיּוֹם הַשְּׁמִינִי וָהָלְאָה יֵרָצֶה לְקָרְבַּן וגו' " – **for [the verse] states:** ***from the eighth day forward, it shall be acceptable for an offering*** **etc.**[25]

The Gemara questions this ruling:

הָא לֹא שָׁהָה סְפֵיקָא הָוֵי – **This implies** that **if [a child] did not** yet **survive** for thirty days, **it is** considered as **a** child of **uncertain** viability.

NOTES

become pregnant until after she was acquired by her Jewish master, her child is considered "born in the house." According to the Tanna Kamma, whether she immersed before giving birth or afterwards, the child is circumcised on the eighth day, because her *tumah* is *not* a factor in determining when he is circumcised. According to Rav Chama, however, if the slavewoman had not immersed before giving birth and so did not become *tamei,* the child is circumcised on the first day. According to the Tanna Kamma, the only cases in which a slave born in a Jewish household is circumcised on the first day is where the child belonged *at birth* to a different master than his mother (if we follow the view of Reish Lakish; see note 21) or where the mother was purchased with the stipulation that she not be immersed. Both of these situations make the child's birth dissimilar to that of those *among you*: in the first case because his master has no connection to his mother, and in the second case because his mother will never be subject to mitzvos. [Though the Gemara does not say so explicitly, Rav Chama would agree with the Tanna Kamma's rulings in these last two cases, since he does not dispute the Tanna Kamma's rule requiring similarity to those *among you.*]

This summary follows *Rashi's* reading of the Gemara; cf. *Tosafos.*

23. [A נֵפֶל, *non-viable child,* is a child which, even if it is born alive, is not able to survive due to its failure to have developed fully. Such a child is not subject to the laws that pertain to living children, e.g. redemption of a firstborn. The Baraisa teaches that when a newborn lives for thirty days, he is established to be a viable child and is now subject to all laws pertaining to children.]

24. *Numbers* 18:16. Since the Torah ties the mitzvah of redemption to the child's having reached the age of a month, we learn that it is at that age that the child is first established to be a viable being, not earlier (*Rashi;* cf. *Ran MHK* ed.; see also *Rashi* to *Bava Kamma* 11b and *Bechoros* 49a; see also *Yad David* [*Kamma*] and *Chasam Sofer* here).

25. *Leviticus* 22:27. The eight-day waiting period for an animal, however, differs from the thirty-day period prescribed for a human. The latter extends until the end of the thirtieth day, whereas the waiting period for an animal concludes at the end of the seventh (*Tosafos*).

מִימְהַל הֵיכִי מְהַלִינַן לֵיהּ – If so, **how can we circumcise [any child]** on the Sabbath when, if he is not viable, there is no obligation to circumcise him, and the circumcision is therefore a violation of the Sabbath?[1]

The Gemara answers:

אָמַר רַב אַדָּא בַּר אַהֲבָה – **Rav Adda bar Ahavah said:** מָלִין אותו מִמָּה נַפְשָׁךְ – **We circumcise it** because **however we consider the matter,** the Sabbath is not violated. אִם חַי הוּא שַׁפִּיר קָא מָהִיל – **If it is** in fact **a viable [child],**[2] then **it is proper for one to circumcise** it on the Sabbath; וְאִם לַאו מְחַתֵּךְ בְּבָשָׂר הוּא – **and if** it is **not, one is** merely **cutting meat** when he circumcises it, which does not violate the Sabbath.[3]

The Gemara challenges Rav Adda's explanation:

וְאֶלָּא הָא דְתַנְיָא – **But then that which was taught in the** following **Baraisa:** סָפֵק בֶּן שִׁבְעָה סָפֵק בֶּן שְׁמוֹנָה – If there is A QUESTION WHETHER IT IS A CHILD OF THE SEVENTH month (which is considered viable) OR A CHILD OF THE EIGHTH month (which is not deemed viable),[4] אֵין מְחַלְּלִין עָלָיו אֶת הַשַּׁבָּת – WE DO NOT VIOLATE THE SABBATH FOR IT (i.e. to circumcise it) – אַמַּאי – **why** indeed not? נִימְהֲלֵיהּ מִמָּה נַפְשָׁךְ – **We should circumcise [the child]** on the grounds that **however we consider the matter,** no violation of the Sabbath occurs. אִם חַי הוּא שַׁפִּיר קָא מָהִיל – **If it is** in fact **a viable [child],** then **it is proper for one to circumcise** it on the Sabbath; וְאִם לַאו מְחַתֵּךְ בְּבָשָׂר הוּא – **and if** it is **not,** then **one is merely cutting meat** when he circumcises it! – ? –

The Gemara answers:

אָמַר מַר בְּרֵיהּ דְּרָבִינָא – **Mar the son of Ravina said:** אֲנָא וְרַב נְחוּמִי בַּר זְכַרְיָה תַּרְגִּימְנָא – **I and Rav Nechumi bar Zecharyah interpreted** the Baraisa as follows: מִימְהִיל הָכִי נַמִּי מְהַלִינַן לֵיהּ – **Regarding circumcision, we do indeed circumcise it** on the Sabbath. לֹא נִצְרְכָה אֶלָּא לְמַכְשִׁירֵי מִילָה – As for the Baraisa, **it is needed only** to teach the law **for the preliminaries of circumcision,** וְאַלִּיבָּא דְּרַבִּי אֱלִיעֶזֶר – **and** this, **according to** the view of **R' Eliezer,** who permits violating the Sabbath even to prepare for the circumcision.[5] Our Baraisa teaches that R' Eliezer would agree that the preliminaries to the circumcision of such a child do not override the Sabbath, because of the doubt.[6]

In his answer to the question, Rav Adda bar Ahavah maintained that a child born in the eighth month of pregnancy is not only considered non-viable but is actually treated as if he were already dead. The Gemara now considers this premise:[7]

אָמַר אַבַּיֵי – **Abaye said:** כְּתַנָּאֵי – Whether a non-viable child is considered to be legally dead is a matter of dispute **among Tannaim,** as we find in the following Baraisa: ,,וְכִי יָמוּת מִן־הַבְּהֵמָה אֲשֶׁר־הִיא לָכֶם לְאָכְלָה" – When the verse states: *IF THERE SHOULD DIE FROM AMONG THE ANIMALS THAT ARE FOR YOU TO EAT, one who touches its carcass shall be tamei until evening,*[8] לְהָבִיא בֶּן שְׁמֹנָה שֶׁאֵין שְׁחִיטָתוֹ מְטַהַרְתּוֹ – it means TO BRING into the law of *tumah* AN OFFSPRING OF THE EIGHTH month, to teach THAT ITS SLAUGHTER DOES NOT RENDER IT *TAHOR.*[9] רַבִּי יוֹסֵי בְּרַבִּי יְהוּדָה וְרַבִּי אֶלְעָזָר בְּרַבִּי שִׁמְעוֹן אוֹמְרִים – R' YOSE THE SON OF R' YEHUDAH AND R' ELAZAR THE SON OF R' SHIMON SAY: שְׁחִיטָתוֹ מְטַהַרְתּוֹ – ITS SLAUGHTER DOES RENDER IT *TAHOR,* removing it from the category of *neveilah.* מַאי לַאו בְּהָא קָא מִיפַּלְגֵי – **Is it not that they argue regarding this** point: דְּמָר סָבַר חַי הוּא – **that one master** (R' Yose the son of R' Yehudah and R' Elazar the son of R' Shimon) **maintains** that **it is** legally considered **a living being** and its slaughter therefore removes it from the category of *neveilah,*[10]

NOTES

1. [Since there is a doubt about the viability of any child less than thirty days old, we should be forbidden to perform circumcision on the Sabbath because of the possibility of desecrating the Sabbath. Yet the Torah commands us to circumcise a child of eight days on the Sabbath!]

Our interpretation follows *Rashi,* according to whom Rabban Shimon ben Gamliel states his rule for all children [unless it is certain beyond any doubt that he was carried a full nine months; see Gemara below and note 6]. This is also the view of most Rishonim (see *Tosafos, Rashba, Ritva MHK* ed., *Ran;* cf. *Ramban*).

2. That is, a child that completed the months necessary for its full development (*Rashi*). [Thus, it is capable of living and is not a *nefel.* See further in note 6.]

3. [When one cuts fresh meat he also causes blood to ooze, yet this is permitted on the Sabbath because a wound is by definition something made in a living being. A *nefel* (non-viable child), however, is not legally considered a living being and wounding it is therefore not a *melachah.* (See General Introduction to *Pri Megadim, Hilchos Shabbos* ד״ה אגב, and *Minchas Chinuch,* Mitzvah 32 – *Mosach HaShabbos, Meleches Dash* §5, for further discussion of this point.)]

4. See above, 135a note 10-12.

5. Mishnah above, 130a.

6. [Rav Adda bar Ahavah's logic is effective only in regard to the *melachah* of making a wound, since if the child is considered dead, an incision in him is not considered a wound.] But there are other *melachos* involved in preparing for circumcision, e.g. burning wood to make a scalpel. Since the obligation to circumcise in this case is not definite, R' Eliezer does not permit performing these *melachos.*

Accordingly, the only case where R' Eliezer would permit violating the Sabbath to prepare for a circumcision is where it is absolutely certain that the child was carried the full nine months, e.g. where, after cohabiting with her husband, the mother did not again cohabit until she gave birth a full nine months later (*Rashi*). [Seemingly, we could be certain even if they separated for less than nine months. As long as they did not have relations for three months, by which time her pregnancy becomes visible, we can be certain as to the date on which she conceived. See *Avnei Nezer, Even HaEzer* 206:57 who discusses this problem.]

[Although it is possible for a fetus to complete its development in less than a full nine months and thereby be viable (see 135a note 10), it is impossible for us to *know* that it has done so unless it has been carried to full term. If it was not, or if we cannot be sure of whether it was because of our uncertainty as to the exact day on which she conceived, the child's status must be treated as questionable until it survives for thirty days.]

7. [Our explanation of the following discussion follows *Rashi;* cf. *Ramban* and *Ran* (*MHK* ed.).]

8. *Leviticus* 11:39. This is the verse that teaches the *tumah* of *neveilah* (an animal that dies without a valid *shechitah*).

9. [I.e. even though it is slaughtered properly, the *shechitah* is ineffective and it becomes a *neveilah.*] This verse is expounded in *Toras Kohanim* (*Shemini, Parshasa* 10) to teach a number of laws concerning which animal carcasses become a *neveilah.* The first phrase: וְכִי יָמוּת מִן־הַבְּהֵמָה, *If there should die from among the animals,* teaches that some animals do not become *tamei* at death. (The word מִן, *from,* is generally taken to be a limiting term.) This is understood to refer to the case of a *tereifah* (a kosher animal afflicted with a mortal defect) and to teach that though a *tereifah* cannot be rendered permissible to eat by being slaughtered [and thus ought to be considered a *neveilah*], its *shechitah* nonetheless removes it from the category of *neveilah* so that its carcass does *not* become a source of *tumah.* It follows from this that the verse is referring to a kosher animal (since *shechitah* can certainly not have any effect on a non-kosher animal). [It would therefore seem unnecessary for the verse to add אֲשֶׁר־הִיא לָכֶם לְאָכְלָה, *that is for you to eat.*] That phrase is therefore expounded to refer to two separate cases: אֲשֶׁר־הִיא לָכֶם, *that is for you,* refers to non-kosher animals, and teaches that these too became a *neveilah* at death, and the word לְאָכְלָה, *to eat,* refers to an eighth-month offspring of a kosher animal [which in cattle is assumed to be non-viable, as it is among humans]. It teaches that such an offspring is also *always* a *neveilah* when it dies – even when it dies through *shechitah* (*Rashi;* see there for further elaboration).

10. [Thus, they do not consider it logical for the word expounded by the Rabbis to be referring to this case, since there is no reason why *shechitah* should not be effective for it.]

[It should be noted that the term חַי here does not mean what it meant above in Rav Adda bar Ahavah's statement. There it referred to the child's physical status and meant that the child was *viable,* i.e. capable of living. Here, however, we speak of an eighth-month offspring, which is certainly not viable. Rather, the term is used here to denote the

מימהל היכי מהלינן ליה אמר רב אדא בר אהבה מלין אותו ממה נפשך אם חי הוא שפיר קא מהיל ואם לאו מחתך בבשר הוא ואלא הא דתניא ספק בן ז' ספק בן ח' אין מחללין עליו את השבת אמאי נימהליה ממה נפשך אם חי הוא שפיר קא מהיל ואם לאו מחתך בבשר הוא אמר מר בריה דרבינא אנא ורב נחומי בר זכריה תרגימנא מימהיל הכי נמי מהלינן ליה לא נצרכה אלא למכשירי מילה ואליבא דרבי אליעזר אמר אביי כתנאי וכי ימות מן הבהמה אשר היא לכם לאכלה להביא בן שמנה שאין שחיטתו מטהרתו רבי יוסי ברבי יהודה ור' אלעזר בר"ש אומרים שחיטתו מטהרתו מאי לאו בהא קא מיפלגי דמר סבר חי הוא ומ"ס מת הוא אמר רבא אי הכי אדמיפלגי לענין טומאה וטהרה ליפלגי לענין אכילה אלא דכולי עלמא מת הוא ורבי יוסי ברבי יהודה ורבי אלעזר ברבי שמעון סברי כטרפה טרפה לאו אף על גב דמתה היא שחיטתה מטהרתה הכא נמי לא שנא ורבנן לא דמי לטרפה טרפה היתה לה שעת הכושר האי לא היתה לה שעת הכושר וכ"ת טרפה מבטן מאי איכא למימר התם יש במינה שחיטה הכא אין במינה שחיטה איבעיא להו מי פליגי רבנן עליה דרבן שמעון בן גמליאל או לא אם תמצי לומר פליגי הלכה כמותו או אין הלכה כמותו ת"ש עגל שנולד ביום טוב שוחטין אותו בי"ט הכא במאי עסקינן דקים ליה בגוויה שכלו לו חדשיו ת"ש ושוין שאם נולד הוא ומומו עמו שזה מן המוכן ה"נ שכלו לו חדשיו ת"ש דאמר רב יהודה אמר שמואל הלכה כרבן שמעון בן גמליאל הלכה מכלל דפליגי ש"מ אמר אביי נפל מן הגג או אכלו ארי דברי הכל חי הוא כי פליגי שפיהק ומת מר סבר חי הוא ומר סבר מת הוא למאי נפקא מיניה לפטור מן הייבום נפל מן הגג או אכלו ארי דברי הכל חי הוא והא רב פפא ורב הונא בריה דרב יהושע איקלעו לבי בריה דרב אידי בר אבין ועביד להו עיגלא תילתא בימא דשבעא ואמרי ליה אי איתרחיתו ליה עד לאורתא הוה אכלינן מיניה השתא לא אכלינן מיניה אלא כשפיהק ומת דברי הכל מת הוא כי פליגי בנפל מן הגג ואכלו ארי מר סבר מת הוא ומר סבר חי הוא בריה דרב דימי בר יוסף אתיליד ליה ההוא ינוקא בגו תלתין יומין שכיב יתיב קמתאביל עילויה אמר ליה אבוה צוורוניתא קבעית למיכל אמר ליה קים לי ביה שכלו לו חדשיו רב אשי איקלע בי רב כהנא איתרע ביה מילתא בגו תלתין יומין חזייה דיתיב וקא מתאבל עילויה אמר ליה לא סבר ליה מר להא דאמר רב יהודה אמר שמואל הלכה כרבן שמעון בן גמליאל אמר ליה קים לי בגויה שכלו לו חדשיו איתמר מת בתוך שלשים ועמדה ונתקדשה אמר רבינא משמיה דרבא אם

רש"י

מימהל היכי מהלינן. שום קטן ביום השמיני בשבת דילמא נפל הוא ולא חזי למול ועושה חבורה שלא לשם מצוה: אם חי הוא. כלומר אם כלו לו חדשיו שפיר קא מהיל: מחתך בבשר. שחוטה הוא ולא חבורה היא: לא נצרכה. הא דקתני אין מחללין אלא לענין מכשירי מילה לרבי אליעזר דאמר דחו שבת ה"מ דקים ליה בגויה שכלו לו חדשיו שעברו ט' חדשים משמשה עד שילדתו ולא שמשה כל ימי עיבורה אבל ספק אין מכשיריו דוחין דילמא לאו בר מימהל הוא ומחלל שבת בעשותו פחמים וברזל: כתנאי. נפל גמור אם חשוב כמת דקאמר רב אדא בר אהבה דאינו אלא מחתך בבשר או לא והויא חבורה: לאכלה להביא בן ח'. דכוליה קרא דריש ליה בתורת כהנים מן הבהמה מקצת בהמה מטמאה ומקצת אינה מטמאה פרט לטרפה ששחטה ומדממעיט טרפה ששחטה מכלל דבטהורה קאי אשר היא לכם להביא בהמה טמאה לפי שפרשה ראשונה דכתיב בה לכל הבהמה אשר היא מפרסת פרסה ואינה מעלת גרה וגו' מוקי לה התם באבר מן החי הכתוב מדבר ופרשה זו במתה ודאי לאכלה להביא בן ח' חדשים שאף שחיטתו מיתה ומטמאה: מר סבר חי הוא. ולפיכך שחיטתו מטהרתו: לענין אכילה. אי מותר באכילה בשחיטתו אם לאו: טרפה. שחיטתה מטהרתה מלטמא כדפרישית: היתה לה שעת הכושר. לישחט וליטהר קודם שנטרפה: מי פליגי. למישרי ולד של בהמה בתוך ח' ימים: שוחטים אותו ביו"ט. ואינו מוקצה שהרי בין השמשות נמי היה מוכן אגב אמו מיהו שמעינן מינה דמותר לבו ביום: ושוין. רבי יהודה ורבי שמעון שנחלקו ברואין מומין ביו"ט במסכת ביצה שאם נולד היום הוא ומומו עמו שהוא מן המוכן ומותר לבקר מומו ביו"ט דלא דמי כמתקן ביו"ט דלא איתחזק באיסורא ומוקמינן לה התם כגון דיתבי דייני התם ורואהו בשעת לידה מיד: נפל מן הגג או אכלו ארי. שמת מחמת מיתה הבאה לו בתוך ל' ממקום אחר דברי הכל בחזקת כלו לו חדשיו קאי דאי לאו הכי מיתה לא הוה מת הילכך חי הוא ובאדם הוי ולד ופוטר את אמו מן החליצה וגבי בהמה נמי ולד בהמה ששחט בתוך ח' מותר באכילה דלא חזינא ביה ריעותא ורוב היולדות אינן מפילות: שפיהק. ביי"ר בלע"ז כלומר לאחר לידתו לא ראו בו אלא חיות מעט שפיהק ומת וגבי אדם קאי: ה"ג ועבדו (א) עגלא תילתא בימא דשבעא: איתרחיתו. מלשהותו עד אורתא שהוא ליל שמיני: הוה אכלינן מיניה. דמקצת היום ככולו כדכתיב (ויקרא כב) והיה שבעת ימים תחת אמו הא לילה חזי ומיהו מיום השמיני הוא דירצה דאורתא לאו בת הקרבה היא כדכתיב (שם ז) ביום צוותו להקריב אבל מכלל נפל נפקי ליה וחזי לאקדושי כדאמרינן בזבחים (דף יב.) לילה לקדושה יום להרצאה והלכך לענין חולין חזי מאורתא למשחטיה ומיכל אלמא מאן דס"ל כרשב"ג פליג במיתה הבאה לו ממקום אחר ואמר ספיקא הוא: שכיב בגו תלתין. ללידתו: צוורוניתא. מטעמים שמאכילין את האבל: קא בעית למיכל. לכך אתה מתאבל חנם: איתרע מילתא. אבילות: בגו תלתין יומין. ללידת הולד: מת הולד בתוך ל'. ללידתו ולא היה לאביו בן אלא הוא ונולד לאחר מיתת אביו ועל ידו היו פוטרין אמו מן החליצה אם היה בר קיימא: ועמדה ונתקדשה. לאחר זמן לפי שסבורה שאינה זקוקה ליבם:

תוספות

מימהל היכי מהלינן ליה. מכאן משמע דלא איירי רשב"ג בבן שמנה (ג) דוקא אלא בסתם ולדות וכן משמע לקמן דאמר ת"ש עגל שנולד בי"ט שוחטין אותו בי"ט ודחי דכלו לו חדשיו ואת"ל דלא איירי רשב"ג אלא בודאי בן שמנה הוה ליה לדחויי הכא בסתם ולדות ועוד דאמר לקמן נפל מן הגג ואכלו ארי דברי הכל חי הוא ואי בודאי בן ח' איירי היכי תיסק אדעתיה לומר ד"ה חי הוא וכולהו דלקמן נמי דמוקמינן דקים ליה בגוויה שכלו לו חדשיו וקשה לר"י מהא דאמרינן בפ' הערל (יבמות דף פ:) איזהו בן ח' כל שלא כלו לו חדשיו רבי אומר שערו וצפרניו מוכיחין עליו וכו' לדאמר דהאי בר שבעה הוא ואשתהויי אשתהי ופריך (ג) הא דעבד רבה תוספאה עובדא באשה שהלך בעלה למדינת הים ואשתהי עד תריסר ירחי שתא כמאן כרבי כיון דאיכא רשב"ג דאמר אשתהי דתני כל ששהה כו' כרבי עבד אלמא משמע בהדיא דבודאי בן ח' איירי מדמוכח מיניה דמשתהי כרבי ומנא ליה דילמא לעולם ס"ל דלא משתהי ובסתם ולדות איירי רשב"ג כדפרישית ואור"י דע"כ בודאי בן ח' נמי איירי דהא בתוספתא דמכילתין מיתני מילתיה דרשב"ג בתר מילתיה דרבנן ורבי דיבמות ואפלוגתייהו קאי דאיירי בבן ח' וא"ת ובשמעתין מנלן דבסתם ולדות ס"ל לרשב"ג הא לא שהה ספיקא הוי דילמא קסבר ולד מעליא הוי ולא איירי כלל בסתם ולדות אלא בודאי בן ח' ויש לומר דדייקינן מדקתני כל ששהה דכל משמע לרבות סתם דווקא שהה הא לא שהה ספיקא הוי והא דמבעיא לן לקמן אי פליגי רבנן עליה דרשב"ג היינו בסתם ולדות דבן ח' ודאי בהדיא קתני לה בתוספתא וא"ת והיכי פשיט לקמן מדאמר רב יהודה אמר שמואל הלכה כרשב"ג מכלל דפליגי בסתם ולדות תאמר דלעולם לא פליגי בסתם ולדות וכי פסיק רב יהודה כוותיה הנ"מ בודאי בן ח' וי"ל דא"כ ה"ל למיתני הלכה כר' (ד) דליכא למימר דלא קאמר הלכה כרבי משום דבעי הוכחת סימנין שערו וצפרניו אבל רשב"ג לא בעי דהא פשיטא דבן ח' שלא גמרו שערו וצפרניו לכ"ע לא חי ומדנקט רשב"ג ש"מ דבסתם ולדות איירי ופסק בכולא מילתא כוותיה והשתא נמי אין צריך לדקדק (ה) מכל דבלאו הכי יש להוכיח דבסתם ולדות איירי כמו שהוכחתי ר"י: צודניתא. גרס בערוך לשון לידה ומזונות:

עין משפט נר מצוה

לט א מיי' פ"א מהל' מילה הלכה יד סמג עשין כח טוש"ע י"ד סי' רסו סעיף יא בהג"ה:
מא ב ג ד מיי' פ"ב מהל' שאר אבות הטומאות הלכה ו:
מב ה ו מיי' פ"ב מהל' יום טוב הלכה ה סמג לאוין עה טוש"ע או"ח סי' תצח סעיף ח:
מג ז מיי' שם הלכה ד טוש"ע שם סעיף טו:
מד ח ט מיי' פ"א מהל' יבום הלכה ה סמג עשין נ טוש"ע אה"ע סי' קנו סעיף ב:
מה י מיי' פ"ד מהל' מאכלות אסורות הלכה ד סמג לאוין קלב טוש"ע י"ד סי' טו סעיף ג:
מו כ מיי' פ"א מהל' אבלות הלכה ו סמג עשין מד"ס ב טוש"ע י"ד סי' שעד סעיף ח [ברי"ף כאן וכמ"ש הרמב"ם לק' וכן ברא"ש כאן והכסף משנה לג]:

גליון הש"ס

גמ' ואם לאו מחתך בבשר הוא. עי' מ"ל פ' תקמו פ"ק יח. ועי' בירושלמי פ"ב דיבמות הלכה ו: שם הכא אין במינה שחיטה. עי' חולין עד ע"א תד"ה נפקא ליה: רש"י ד"ה לא נצרכה וכו' ט' חדשים משמשה. עי' תוס' ב"ק טו: ד"ה שפיהק ביי"ר בלע"ז. עי' נדה סג ע"א תד"ה מפסקת: ד"ה הוה אכלינן מיניה וכו' לילה לקדושה. ועי' בתוס' שם וזבחים יב ע"א ד"ה יום וכו'ע:

תורה אור השלם

א) וְכִי יָמוּת מִן הַבְּהֵמָה אֲשֶׁר הִיא לָכֶם לְאָכְלָה הַנֹּגֵעַ בְּנִבְלָתָהּ יִטְמָא עַד הָעָרֶב: [ויקרא יא, לט]

מסורת הש"ס

א) [לעיל קל.], ב) חולין נא:, ג) חולין שם ביצה כו:, ד) [לעיל קל.], ה) יבמות לו:, ו) [עי' תוס' בכורות מט. ד"ה מת ותוס' יבמות לו: ד"ה מת וכו' שכתבו דבל"י הכלה גורס בסוף שלשים], ז) [במו"ק כ: גרס רש"י לידותיה], ח) סעודת אבל כמו גירי' הערוך שהביא תוס' ד"ה צודניתא], ט) [צ"ל בסוף ע"פ עדות של תוס' יבמות ובכורות], י) [צ"ל ומי לאחר מיתת אביו], כ) [ר"ל מדקתני כל ששהה כו' ולא תני אם שהה כו' עברין], ל) [ונ"ל דלאו הכי מה לו רשב"ג להוסיף על מילתא דרבנן], מ) [ערך לד ג].

הגהות הב"ח

(א) רש"י ד"ה ה"ג ועביד להו עגלא תלתא: (ג) תוס' ד"ה מימהל וכו' בבן שמונה ודאי דוקא אלא: (ג) בא"ד ופריך אלא הא דעבד: (ד) בא"ד הוה ליה למיתני הלכה כרבי וכרשב"ג דליכא: (ה) בא"ד אין צריך לדקדק מכל כמו שהוכיח ר"י דבלאו הכי יש להוכיח דבסתם ולדות איירי הס"ד:

רב נסים גאון

וזאת אחת מג' הלכות כריש לקיש כמו שאמר רבא הלכתא כריש לקיש בהני תלת חדא הא אבל בכל מקום שיש מחלוקת בין ר' יוחנן וריש לקיש הלכה כר' יוחנן לבד מהני תלת: אמר אביי כתנאי לאכלה להביא בן ח' שאין שחיטתו מטהרתו עיקר דבר זה שנוי בתורת כהנים (ויקרא יא) וכי ימות מן הבהמה אשר היא לכם לאכלה וכי ימות הרי זו מיתה ודאי מן הבהמה יש מן הבהמה מטמאה ויש מן הבהמה שאין מטמאה פרט לטרפה ששחטה ונתבאר לנו בזה הכתוב בהמה [טרפה] ששחטה אינה מטמאה ונשאו ונתנו בדבר זה הרבה ואמרו באמצע הדברים בן ח' יוכיח שיש למינו שחיטה ואין שחיטתו מטהרתו ולאחר

ליקוטי רש"י

מחתך בבשר הוא. ואין חיוב אלא במוציא כמי מקלקל הוא [ערכין ז:]. טרפה היתה לה שעת הכושר. וכיון דכל עלה הוא פורת שחיטה לא שפקעה מיניה והויא בכלל שאר ולאו ונקר. לא היתה לה שעת הכושר. ליטהר מטומאתה ע"י שחיטה. יש במינה שחיטה. הלכך לא נפקא מכלל בקר ולאן אבל בן שמונה חי שנולד מבהמה חיה אין לנו במה לטהר אפי' נשחט לפי שאינו בכלל בקר ולאן [חולין עב:]. ושוין כו'. ר' יהודה ור' שמעון שאם נולד היום ומומו עמו שזה מן המוכן שאין בזה משום תקון ומשום דין שלא היתה בו חזקת איסור מעולם וכדמוקי לה לקמן כגון דיתבי דייני התם [ביצה כו:]. ושוין תנאי דפליגי במסכת ביצה (כו:) גבי בכור שנולד בו מום בי"ט ושוין דאפילו האוסר בנולד בו ביום מום משום דמוקצה היה בין השמשות מחמת איסור קדשים בחוץ אבל אם נולד היום ומומו עמו מוכן הוא שלא נאסר מעולם דהא במעי אמו היה מוכן אגב אמו ומותר דבכור אינו קדוש עד שיולד וכשנולד הרי מומו עמו וראוי לישחט בחוץ [חולין נא:]. פיהק. באליי"ר בלע"ז אין מלקוחיו פותח להוציא רוח הפה מלא כאדם שרוצה לישן או שעמד משינה ויש שדורשים נוטריקון פיהק פיו הקיס [ברכות כד.]. אישטריליי"ר בלע"ז [נדה סג. עי"ש בתוס']. עיגלא תילתא. שלישי לבטן שהוא משובח מפני שהבהמה בקטנותה אינה עדיין בכחה והולד ראשון ושני אינו בריא [לעיל יא. ועי"ש בב"ח]. שלישי לבטן ומובחר הוא [פסחים סח: וע"ע עירובין סג. סנהדרין סה: ובתוס' גיטין נו.]. מת בתוך שלשים. בן היבמה ונתקדשה לשוק בחזקת שפטורה משום בנה [יבמות לו:].

רבינו חננאל

זה שפחה וזהו עובר זהו יליד בית שנימול לאחד דברי הכל הוא. כי פליגי בילדה ואח"כ הטבילה ת"ק סבר גם זה יליד בית נימול לשמונה. ורב אחא סבר זה יליד בית נימול לאחד. ושאר השמועה פשוטה היא: תניא רשב"ג אומר כל ששהה באדם שלשים יום אינו נפל שנאמר ופדויו מבן חדש תפדה. שמונת ימים בבהמה אינו נפל שנאמר ומיום השמיני והלאה ירצה וגו'. הא שלא שהה ספק הוי וזה שאנו מלין כל קטן בן ח' ימים הלא אמר רשב"ג קודם ל' יום ספק נפל הוא ואין מחללין עליו את השבת ומלין אותו בן ח' ימים שמא נפל הוא. ופרקי' מלין אותו ממה נפשך אי חי הוא שפיר קא מהיל. ואי נפל הוא מחתך בבשר הוא ולא מלאכה היא ומקשינן אלא הא דתניא ספק בן ז' או בן ח' אין מחללין עליו את השבת אמאי (נימא) [נימהליה] ליה ממ"נ ופרקינן מימהל ה"נ ומהלינן ליה לא נצרכה אלא למכשירי מילה ואליבא דר' אליעזר ולית הלכתא הכי דשנויא היא ואשינויא לא סמכינן ואם יש להקשות עוד אי הכי אם המילה חיתוך בשר היא ואינה מלאכה אפילו מילה שאינה בזמנה יהא נימול בשבת מחתך בבשר הוא. ופירקו כי מילה דחי מלאכה היא כי מתקן הוא כי כיון שחותך הערלה מתקנו לאכול תרומה ולשחוט עליו אביו את הפסח: לאכלה להביא בן ח' שאין שחיטתו מטהרתו פי' זו בהמה גסה טהורה שיולדת לט' חדשים היא. ומיבעיא לן רשב"ג פליגי רבנן עליה אי לא ופשטינן דפליגי רבנן עליה והלכתא כוותיה דאמר רב יהודה אמר שמואל הלכה כרשב"ג ואי לא דפליגי הלכה למה. אמר אביי נפל מן הגג ואכלו אריה. דברי הכל כמו חי הוא. [כי] פליגי שפיהק ומת ומקשינן עליה מדרב פפא ורב הונא בריה דר' יהושע דאיקלעו לבי בריה דרב אידי בר אבין ועבד להו עיגלא תלתא ביומא דשבעא ואמר ליה אי אחרתו עד לאורתא הוה אכלינן מיניה. והרי זה נשחט ולא אכלו ממנו שאמרו כיון שלא שהה ח' ימים כנפל חשוב ואין שחיטתו מתירתו באכילה. והדר ביה ואמר אלא שפיהק ומת דברי הכל מת הוא כי פליגי בנפל מן הגג או אכלוה אריה ושמעינן מהאי מעשה דרב פפא ורב הונא בריה דרב יהושע שאם נשחט קודם ח' ימים אסור באכילה ואינו מותר אלא מלילי ח' והלאה (לקרבן) הלכך לילי שמיני מותר באכילה ולקרבן פסול. ואין כשר לקרבן אלא מיום השמיני והלאה וזה שאמר אביי. וכי ימות מן הבהמה אשר היא לכם לאכלה להביא בן שמונת ימים שאין שחיטתו מטהרתו. ר' יוסי בר יהודה ור' אלעזר בר' שמעון אומרים שחיטתו מטהרתו: ברייתא זו שנויה בתורת כהנים. לח' חדשים חלוקתם. דתני בהדיא במתניתא דבי ר' חייא

וּמַר סָבַר מֵת הוּא – **whereas the other master** (the Rabbis) **maintains** that **it is** legally considered **dead,** as Rav Adda bar Ahavah said, and its slaughter therefore has no legal effect on it.[11]

Rava refutes Abaye's contention:

אָמַר רָבָא – **Rava said:** אִי הָכִי – **If so,** that the dispute in the Baraisa concerns whether the eighth-month offspring is considered alive or not, אַדְמִיפַּלְגֵי לְעִנְיַן טוּמְאָה וְטָהֳרָה – then **rather than dispute the issue of *tumah* and *taharah,*** לִיפַּלְגֵי לְעִנְיַן אֲכִילָה – **let them dispute the issue of** whether slaughter permits **eating** the meat of the eighth-month offspring.[12] – ? –

Rava therefore explains the dispute in the Baraisa differently: אֶלָּא דְכוּלֵּי עָלְמָא מֵת הוּא – **Rather,** since they dispute only the issue of its *tumah,* **all** must **agree that [an eighth-month offspring] is** legally considered **dead,** as R' Adda bar Ahavah said. וְרַבִּי יוֹסֵי בְּרַבִּי יְהוּדָה וְרַבִּי אֶלְעָזָר בְּרַבִּי שִׁמְעוֹן סָבְרֵי כִּטְרֵפָה – **But R' Yose the son of R' Yehudah and R' Elazar the son of R' Shimon believe it is like a *tereifah.*** טְרֵפָה לָאו אַף עַל גַּב דְּמֵתָה הִיא שְׁחִיטָתָהּ מְטַהַרְתָּהּ – **Is it not** true that **even though a *tereifah* is considered** as if it were **dead, its slaughter** nonetheless **renders it *tahor,*** removing it from the category of *neveilah,* הָכָא נַמִּי לֹא שְׁנָא – **so too here,** in the case of an offspring of the eighth month, **it is no different.** Although it is legally considered dead, its slaughter removes it from the category of *neveilah.*[13] וְרַבָּנָן – **As for the Rabbis,** לֹא דָמֵי לִטְרֵפָה – they believe that **it is not analogous to** the case of ***tereifah*** for the following reason: טְרֵפָה הָיְתָה לָהּ שְׁעַת הַכּוֹשֶׁר – **A *tereifah* had a moment of fitness** when it could be slaughtered and eaten, before it became mortally wounded. Therefore, the Torah continues to consider slaughter effective for it even after it became a *tereifah* to the extent of rendering it *tahor* from the *tumah* of *neveilah.* הַאי לֹא הָיְתָה לָהּ שְׁעַת הַכּוֹשֶׁר – **This one** (the animal born in the eighth month), however, **never had a moment of fitness** to be slaughtered and eaten. Thus, you cannot assume that the Torah considered slaughter effective for it in any capacity.[14]

Rava notes and rejects a possible refutation of this argument: וְכִי תֵּימָא טְרֵפָה מִבֶּטֶן מַאי אִיכָּא לְמֵימַר – **And if you will say** in response: **What is there to say to** refute an analogy to an animal that became **a *tereifah* in the womb?** Such an animal was never fit to be slaughtered and eaten (since it was born a *tereifah*), and yet slaughtering it renders it *tahor* from the *tumah* of *neveilah*![15] By the same token, an animal born in the eighth month should be rendered *tahor* by being slaughtered. – ? –

Rava answers that there is nonetheless a distinction: הָתָם יֵשׁ בְּמִינָהּ שְׁחִיטָה – **There,** in the case of a born *tereifah,* although this animal was never fit to be slaughtered and eaten, **there are among its kind** animals that were once fit for **slaughter,** namely, those that were not born a *tereifah,* but which only become so later. הָכָא אֵין בְּמִינָהּ שְׁחִיטָה – Whereas **here,** in the case of an animal born in the eighth month, **there is not** even found **among its kind** an animal that was even fit for **slaughter,** since every animal born in the eighth month is non-viable and thus unfit to be slaughtered and eaten.[16]

The Gemara now returns to Rabban Shimon ben Gamliel's teaching that an animal is not assumed to be definitely viable until it is eight days old:[17]

אִיבַּעְיָא לְהוּ – **They inquired:** מִי פְּלִיגֵי רַבָּנָן עֲלֵיהּ דְּרַבָּן שִׁמְעוֹן בֶּן גַּמְלִיאֵל אוֹ לֹא – **Do the Rabbis argue with Rabban Shimon ben Gamliel or not?** אִם תִּמְצֵי לוֹמַר פְּלִיגֵי – **And if you will conclude and say that they** do **argue** with him, הֲלָכָה כְּמוֹתוֹ אוֹ אֵין הֲלָכָה כְּמוֹתוֹ – **is the law in accordance with him or is the law not in accordance with him?**

The Gemara tries to prove that the Rabbis do argue with Rabban Shimon ben Gamliel:

תָּא שְׁמַע – **Come, learn** the answer from the following Baraisa: עֵגֶל שֶׁנּוֹלַד בְּיוֹם טוֹב – A CALF THAT WAS BORN ON YOM TOV שׁוֹחֲטִין אוֹתוֹ בְּיוֹם טוֹב – MAY BE SLAUGHTERED ON YOM TOV and it is not considered *muktzeh.*[18] Hence, we see that a one-day-old animal may be slaughtered, and that the Rabbis of this Baraisa dispute Rabban Shimon ben Gamliel's view.[19]

The Gemara rejects the proof:

הָכָא בְּמַאי עַסְקִינַן – **With what** case **are we dealing here?** דְּקִים לֵיהּ בְּגַוֵּיהּ שֶׁכָּלוּ לוֹ חֳדָשָׁיו – With a situation **where he is certain that its months** of gestations **were completed,** i.e. where it is certain that it was carried to full term.[20] Even Rabban Shimon ben Gamliel agrees that a full-term animal is deemed viable immediately, and may be slaughtered on the first day of life.

The Gemara again tries to prove that the Rabbis argue with Rabban Shimon ben Gamliel:

תָּא שְׁמַע – **Come, learn** the answer from the following Baraisa, which deals with permitting a blemished *bechor* for slaughter on Yom Tov: וְשָׁוִין שֶׁאִם נוֹלַד הוּא וּמוּמוֹ עִמּוֹ – Although R' Yehudah and R' Shimon disagree whether a *bechor* may be examined for blemishes and permitted on Yom Tov,[21] THEY AGREE THAT IF THE

NOTES

offspring's legal status: Although it is a *nefel,* it is legally treated as alive as long as it still breathes. See *Ramban,* who notes this as a difficulty with *Rashi's* explanation.]

11. Even according to the view that an eight-month offspring is considered alive, it is still not subject to circumcision, due to its inability to survive for more than a few days. Nonetheless, the minimal life that it does possess suffices, in the case of an animal, to make *shechitah* effective for it (see *Tos. Rid* who discusses this and other aspects of this dual status).

12. [I.e. R' Yose the son of R' Yehudah and R' Elazar the son of R' Shimon should permit eating the meat as well, since the calf was legally alive in their opinion when it was slaughtered.]

13. [But, as with a *tereifah,* its *shechitah* is effective only in regard to removing its *tumah,* not in rendering it permissible to eat. See further in note 16.]

14. [I.e. you cannot derive from *tereifah* that *shechitah* is effective in rendering an eighth-month offspring *tahor* from the *tumah* of *neveilah.*]

15. [For the rule regarding the slaughter of a *tereifah* makes no distinction in regard to when the animal became a *tereifah.*]

16. [Rava has thus concluded that a *nefel* is considered legally dead according to all opinions, as Rav Adda bar Ahavah said, and the issue in the Baraisa is only whether *shechitah* is effective in rendering an eighth-month offspring *tahor* from the *tumah* of *neveilah* as it does with a *tereifah.* It should follow from this that just as there is no liability for wounding a *nefel* on the Sabbath, as Rav Adda bar Ahavah said, so too there should be no liability for wounding a *tereifah* on the Sabbath, for a *tereifah* is analogous to an eighth-month offspring, as Rava just said. But this is in fact not true, for the Gemara says in *Pesachim* 73a that one is liable for slaughtering a *tereifah* on the Sabbath. Thus, it is clear that a *tereifah* is considered a living being. How then can an eighth-month offspring be compared to it? Because of this question *Ramban* rejects *Rashi's* explanation in favor of *Rabbeinu Chananel's* (see also *Ran MHK* ed.). *Rashba,* however, defends *Rashi's* explanation; see there; see also *R' Akiva Eiger* and *Chazon Ish, Orach Chaim* 62:29.]

17. *Rashi; Ritva MHK* ed.

18. Objects that are not מוּכָן, *prepared* (i.e. available for use), before Yom Tov are *muktzeh.* However, an animal born on Yom Tov is considered prepared because it was part of its mother at the onset of Yom Tov and was thus suitable for food if its mother had been slaughtered (*Rashi,* from *Beitzah* 6a).

19. [For according to Rabban Shimon ben Gamliel, one could *not* slaughter and eat a day-old calf since it is possibly a *nefel.*]

20. See above, end of note 6.

21. A *bechor,* a firstborn kosher male animal, must be given to a Kohen,

מימהל היכי מהלינן ליה אמר רב אדא בר אהבה מלין אותו ממה נפשך אם חי הוא שפיר קא מהיל ואם לאו מחתך בבשר הוא ואלא הא דתניא ספק בן ז' ספק בן ח' אין מחללין עליו את השבת אמאי נימהליה ממה נפשך אם חי הוא שפיר קא מהיל ואם לאו מחתך בבשר הוא אמר מר בריה דרבינא אנא ורב נחומי בר זכריה תרגימנא מימהיל הכי נמי מהלינן ליה לא נצרכה אלא למכשירי מילה ואליבא דרבי אליעזר אמר אביי כתנאי וכי ימות מן הבהמה אשר היא לכם לאכלה להביא בן שמנה שאין שחיטתו מטהרתו רבי יוסי ברבי יהודה ור' אלעזר בר"ש אומרים שחיטתו מטהרתו מאי לאו בהא קא מיפלגי דמר סבר חי הוא ומ"ס מת הוא אמר רבא אי הכי אדמיפלגי לענין טומאה וטהרה ליפלגי לענין אכילה אלא דכולי עלמא מת הוא ורבי יוסי ברבי יהודה ורבי אלעזר ברבי שמעון סברי כטרפה טרפה לאו אף על גב דמתה היא שחיטתה מטהרתה הכא נמי לא שנא ורבנן לא דמי לטרפה טרפה היתה לה שעת הכושר האי לא היתה לה שעת הכושר וכ"ת טרפה מבטן מאי איכא למימר התם יש במינה שחיטה הכא אין במינה שחיטה איבעיא להו מי פליגי רבנן עליה דרבן שמעון בן גמליאל או לא אם תמצי לומר פליגי הלכה כמותו או אין הלכה כמותו ת"ש עגל שנולד ביום טוב שוחטין אותו בי"ט הכא במאי עסקינן דקים ליה בגוויה שכלו לו חדשיו ת"ש ושוין שאם נולד הוא ומומו עמו שזה מן המוכן ה"נ שכלו לו חדשיו ת"ש דאמר רב יהודה אמר שמואל הלכה כרבן שמעון בן גמליאל הלכה מכלל דפליגי ש"מ אמר אביי נפל מן הגג או אכלו ארי דברי הכל חי הוא כי פליגי שפיהק ומת מר סבר חי הוא ומר סבר מת הוא למאי נפקא מיניה לפטור מן הייבום נפל מן הגג או אכלו ארי דברי הכל חי הוא והא רב פפא ורב הונא בריה דרב יהושע איקלעו לבי בריה דרב אידי בר אבין ועביד להו עיגלא תילתא בימנא דשבעה ואמרי ליה אי איתרחיתו ליה עד לאורתא הוה אכלינן מיניה השתא לא אכלינן מיניה אלא כשפיהק ומת דברי הכל מת הוא כי פליגי בנפל מן הגג ואכלו ארי מר סבר מת הוא ומר סבר חי הוא בריה דרב דימי בר יוסף אתיליד ליה ההוא ינוקא בגו תלתין יומין שכיב יתיב קמתאביל עילויה אמר ליה אבוה צוורוניתא קבעית למיכל אמר ליה קים לי ביה שכלו לו חדשיו רב אשי איקלע בי רב כהנא איתרע ביה מילתא בגו תלתין יומין חזייה דיתיב וקא מתאבל עילויה אמר ליה לא סבר ליה מר להא דאמר רב יהודה אמר שמואל הלכה כרבן שמעון בן גמליאל אמר ליה קים לי בגויה שכלו לו חדשיו איתמר מת בתוך שלשים ועמדה ונתקדשה אמר רבינא משמיה דרבא
אם

רש"י

מימהל היכי מהלינן. שום קטן ביום השמיני בשבת דילמא נפל הוא ולא חזי למול ועושה חבורה שלא לשם מצוה. כלומר אם כלו לו חדשיו שפיר קא מהיל: מחתך בבשר. שמוטה הוא ולא חבורה היא: לא נצרכה. הא דקתני אין מחללין אלא לענין מכשירי מילה לרבי אליעזר דאמר דמו שבת ה"מ דקים ליה בגויה שכלו לו חדשיו שעברו ° ט' חדשים משמשה עד שילדתו ולא שמשה כל ימי עיבורה אבל ספק אין מכשיריו דוחין דילמא לאו בר מימהל הוא ומחלל שבת בעשותו פחמים ובכול: כתנאי. נפל גמור אם חשוב כמת כדקאמר רב אדא בר אהבה דאינו אלא מחתך בבשר או לא והויא חבורה: לאכלה להביא בן ח'. דכוליה קרא דריש ליה בתורת כהנים מן הבהמה מקצת בהמה מטמאה ומקצת אינה מטמאה פרט לטרפה ששחטה ומדממעטינן טרפה ששחטה ראשונה דטהורה קאי אשר היא לכם להביא בהמה טמאה לפי שפרשה ראשונה דכתיב בה לכל הבהמה אשר היא מפרסת פרסה ואיננה מעלת גרה וגו' מוקי לה התם באבר מן החי הכתוב מדבר ופרשה זו במתה ודאי לאכלה להביא בן ח' חדשים שאף שחיטתו מיתה ומטמאה: מר סבר חי הוא. לפיכך שחיטתו מטהרתו: לענין אכילה. אי מותר באכילה בשחיטתו מטהרתו: טרפה. שחיטתה מטהרתה מלטמא כדפרישית: היתה לה שעת הכושר. לישחט וליטהר קודם שנטרפה: מי פליגי. למישרי ולד של בהמה בתוך ח' ימים: שוחטים אותו ביו"ט. ולאו מוקצה שהרי בין השמשות נמי היה מוכן אגב אמו מיהו שמעינן מינה למותר לנו ביום: ושוין. רבי יהודה ורבי שמעון שנחלקו ברואין מומין ביו"ט במסכת ביצה שאם נולד היום הוא ומומו עמו שהוא מן המוכן ומותר לבקר מומו ביו"ט דלא דמי כמתקן ביו"ט דלא איתחזק באיסורא ומוקמינן לה התם כגון דיתבי דייני התם ורואהו בשעת לידה מיד: נפל מן הגג או אכלו ארי. שמת ממיתה הבאה לו בתוך ל' ממקום אחר דברי הכל בחזקת כלו לו חדשיו קאי דאי לאו הך מיתה לא הוה מת הילכך חי הוא ובאדם הוי ולד ופוטר את אמו מן החליצה וגבי בהמה נמי סתם ולד בהמה ששחטו בתוך ח' מותר באכילה דלא חזינא ביה ריעותא ורוב היולדות אינן מפילות: שפיהק. ° ביילי"ר בלע"ז כלומר לאחר לידתו לא ראו בו אלא חיות מעט שפיהק ומת וגבי אדם קאי: ה"ג ועבדו (א) עגלא תילתא בימנא דשבעה: איתרחיתו. מלשוחטו עד אורתא שהוא ליל שמיני: הוה אכלינן מיניה. דמקצת היום ככולו כדכתיב (ויקרא כב) והיה שבעת ימים תחת אמו הא לילה חזי ומיהו מיום השמיני הוא דירצה דאורתא לאו בת הקרבה היא כדכתיב (שם ז) ביום צוותו להקריב אבל מכלל נפל נפקי ליה וחזי לאקדושי כדאמרינן בזבחים (דף יב.) ° לילה לקדושה יום להרצאה והלכך לענין חולין חזי מאורתא למשחטיה ומיכל אלמא מאן דס"ל כרשב"ג פליג במיתה הבאה לו ממקום אחר ואמר ספיקא הוא: שכיב בגו תלתין. ללידתו: ° צוורוניתא. מטעמים שמאכילין את האבל: קא בעית למיכל. לכך אתה מתאבל חנם: איתרע מילתא. אבילות: בגו תלתין יומין. ללידת הולד: מת הולד ° בתוך ל'. ללידתו ולא היה לאביו בן אלא הוא ° ונולד לאחר מיתת אביו ועל ידו היו פוטרין אמו מן החליצה אם היה בר קיימא: ועמדה ונתקדשה. לאחר זמן לפי שסבורה שאינה זקוקה ליבם:
אם

תוספות

מימהל היכי מהלינן ליה. מכאן משמע דלא איירי רשב"ג בבן שמנה (ב) דוקא אלא בסתם ולדות וכן משמע לקמן דאמר ת"ש עגל שנולד בי"ט שוחטין אותו בי"ט ודחי דכלו לו חדשיו ואת"ל דלא איירי רשב"ג אלא בודאי בן שמנה הוה ליה לדחויי הב"ע בסתם ולדות ועוד אמר לקמן נפל מן הגג ואכלו ארי דברי הכל חי הוא ואי בודאי בן ח' איירי היכי תיסק אדעתיה לומר ד"ה חי הוא ובכולהו דלקמן נמי דמוקמינן דקים ליה בגוויה שכלו לו חדשיו וקשה לר"י מהא דאמרינן בפ' הערל (יבמות דף פ:) איזהו בן ח' כל שלא כלו לו חדשיו רבי אומר שערו וצפרניו מוכיחין עליו כו' דאמר האי בר שבעה הוא ואישתהויי אישתהי ופריך (ג) הא דעבד רבה תוספאה עובדא באשה שהלך בעלה למדינת הים ואישתהי עד תריסר ירחי שתא כמאן כרבי כיון דאיכא רשב"ג דאמר אישתהי ° דתני כל ששהה כו' כרבי עבד אלמא משמע בהדיא דבודאי בן ח' איירי מדמוכח מיניה דמשתהי כרבי ומנא ליה דילמא לעולם ס"ל דלא משתהי ובסתם ולדות איירי רשב"ג כדפרישית ואור"י דע"כ בודאי בן ח' נמי איירי דהא בתוספתא דמכילתין מיתני מילתיה דרשב"ג בתר מילתיה דרבנן ורבי דיבמות ואפלוגתייהו קאי דאיירי בבן ח' וא"ת ובשמעתין מנלן דבסתם ולדות ס"ל לרשב"ג הא לא שהה ספיקא הוי דילמא קסבר ולד מעליא הוי ולא איירי כלל בסתם ולדות אלא בודאי בן ח' ויש לומר דדייקינן מדקתני כל ששהה דכל משמע לרבות סתם דווקא שהה הא לא שהה ספיקא הוי והא דמבעיא לן לקמן אי פליגי רבנן עליה דרשב"ג היינו בסתם ולדות דבן ח' ודאי בהדיא קתני לה בתוספתא וא"ת והיכי פשיט לקמן מדאמר רב יהודה אמר שמואל הלכה כרשב"ג מכלל דפליגי בסתם ולדות תאמר דלעולם לא פליגי בסתם ולדות וכי פסיק רב יהודה כוותיה הנ"מ בודאי בן ח' וי"ל דא"כ ה"ל למיתני הלכה כר' (ד) דליכא למימר דלא קאמר הלכה כרבי משום דבעי הוכחת סימנין שערו וצפרניו אבל רשב"ג לא בעי דהא פשיטא דבן ח' שלא גמרו שערו וצפרניו לכ"ע לא חי ומדנקט רשב"ג ש"מ דבסתם ולדות איירי ופסק בכולא מילתא כוותיה והשתא נמי אין צריך לדקדק (ה) מכל דבלאו הכי יש להוכיח דבסתם ולדות איירי כמו שהוכחתי ° ר"י: צודניתא. גרס בערוך ° לשון לידה ומזונות:
ואם

מסורת הש"ס

א) [לעיל קלה.], ב) חולין נא:, ג) ביצה ו:, ד) חולין עט:, ה) ביצה כו:, ו) [לעיל קו: ושי"נ], ז) יבמות לו:, ח) [עי' תוס' בכורות מט. ד"ה מת ותוס' יבמות לו: ד"ה מת וכו' שכתבו דרש"י להכא גורס בשוק שלשים], ט) [במו"ק כז: גרס רש"י לדווים ופי' סעודת אבל כמו גירי ערוך שהביא תוס' ד"ה לגנות], י) [כנוק ע"פ עדות של תוס' יבמות ובכורות], כ) [עי' תוס' לקמן ...], ל) [ערך לד ב].

הגהות הב"ח

(א) רש"י ד"ה ה"ג ועביד להו עגלא תלתא: (ב) תוס' ד"ה מימהל וכו' בבן שמונה ודאי דוקא אלא: (ג) באד"ה ופריך אלא הא דעבד: (ד) באד"ה הוה ליה למיתני הלכה כרבי וכרשב"ג דליכא: (ה) באד"ה אין צריך לדקדק מכל כמו שהוכיח ר"י דבלאו הכי יש להוכיח דבסתם ולדות איירי הס"ד:

רב נסים גאון

וזאת אחת מג' הלכות כר"ל דקיש כמו שאמר רבא הלכתא כריש לקיש בהני תלת ותה אבל בכל מקום שיש מחלוקת בין ר' יוחנן וריש לקיש הלכה כר' יוחנן לבד מהני תלת: אמר אביי כתנאי לאכלה להביא בן ח' שאין שחיטתו מטהרתו עיקר דבר זה שנוי בתורת כהנים (ויקרא יא) וכי ימות מן הבהמה אשר היא לכם לאכלה וכי ימות הרי זו מיתה ודאי מן הבהמה יש מן הבהמה מטמאה ויש מן הבהמה שאין מטמאה פרט לטרפה ששחטה ונתבאר לנו בזה הכתוב בהמה [טרפה] ששחטה אינה מטמאה ונשאו ונתנו בדבר זה הרבה ואמרו באמצע הדברים בן ח' יוכיח שיש למינו שחיטה ואין שחיטתו מטהרתו ולאחר

ליקוטי רש"י

מחתך בבשר הוא. ואין מיוס אלא כמוכל כמי דמוליא דם [ערכין ז:]. טרפה היתה לה שעת הכושר. וכיון דאל עלה תורת שחיטה תו לא פקעה מיניה והויא בכלל שאר בהמה [חולין עב:]. לא היתה לה שעת הכושר. ליטהר מטומאתה ע"י שחיטה. יש במינה שחיטה. הלכך לא נפקא מכלל בקר ולאו אלא בן שמונה חי שנולד ... ושוין. ר' יהודה ור' שמעון שאם נולד היום הוא ומומו עמו שזה מן המוכן שאין בזה משום מקון

עין משפט נר מצוה

מ א מיי' פ"א מהל' מילה הלכה יד סמג עשין כח טוש"ע י"ד סי' רסו סעיף יא בהגה"ה:
מא ב ג ד מיי' פ"ב מהל' שאר אבות הטומאות הלכה ו:
מב ה ו מיי' פ"ב מהל' יום טוב הלכה ח סמג לאוין עה טוש"ע א"ח סי' תקיז סעיף ה:
מג ז מיי' שם הלכה ד טוש"ע שם סעיף ט:
מד ח ט מיי' פ"ב מהל' יבום הלכה ה סמג עשין נ טוש"ע אה"ע סי' קנו סעיף ד:
מה י מיי' פ"ה מהל' אבלות הלכה ו סמג עשין ב טוש"ע י"ד סי' שעד סעיף ח:
מו כ מיי' פ"א מהל' אבלות הלכה ז סמג עשין ב טוש"ע י"ד סי' שעד סעיף ח [וברי"ף כאן וכרא"ש כאן והטור סי' לג]:

גליון הש"ס

גמ' ואם לאו מחתך בבשר הוא. עי' מ"א סי' תקכו ס"ק יא. ועי' בירושלמי פ"ו דיבמות הלכה ז: שם הכא אין במינה שחיטה. עי' חולין עב ע"א תוד"ה נפקא ליה: רש"י ד"ה לא נצרכה וכו' חדשים משמשה. עי' מג"א סי' ... ד"ה שפיהק ביילי"ר בלעז. עי' נדה סג ע"א תוד"ה מפהקת: ד"ה הוה אכלינן מינה וכו' לילה לקדושה. ועי' בתוס' זבחים יב ע"א ד"ה יום ולי"ע:

תורה אור השלם

א) וְכִי יָמוּת מִן הַבְּהֵמָה אֲשֶׁר הִיא לָכֶם לְאָכְלָה הַנֹּגֵעַ בְּנִבְלָתָהּ יִטְמָא עַד הָעָרֶב: [ויקרא יא, לט]

רבינו חננאל

זה שפחה והוו עובר זהו יליד בית שנימול לאחד דברי הכל הוא. כי פליגי בילדה ואח"כ הטבילה ת"ק סבר גם זה יליד בית נימול לשמונה. ורב אחא סבר זה יליד בית נימול לאחד. ושאר השמועה פשוטה היא: תניא רשב"ג אומר כל ששהה באדם שלשים יום אינו נפל שנאמר ופדויו מבן חדש תפדה. שמונת ימים בבהמה אינו נפל שנאמר ומיום השמיני והלאה ירצה וגו'. הא לא שהה ספק הוי וזה שאנו מלין כל קטן בן ח' ... אמר רשב"ג קודם ל' יום ספק נפל הוא ואין מחללין עליו את השבת ומלין אותו בן ח' ימים שמא נפל הוא. ופרקי' מלין אותו ממה נפשך אם חי הוא שפיר קא מהיל. ואי נפל הוא מחתך בבשר הוא ולא מלאכה הוא ומקשינן אלא הא דתניא ספק בן ז' או בן ח' אין מחללין עליו את השבת אמאי [נימהליה] ליה ממ"נ ופרקינן מימהל ה"נ מהלינן ליה לא נצרכה אלא למכשירי מילה ואליבא דר' אליעזר ולית הלכתא כר' אליעזר

היא ואשינויא לא סמכינן ואם יש להקשות עוד אי הכי אם המילה חיתוך בשר היא ואינה מלאכה אפילו מילה שאינה בזמנה יהא נימול בשבת מחתך בבשר הוא. ופירקו כי מילה דחי מלאכה היא כי מתקן הוא כי כיון שחותך הערלה מתקנו לאכול תרומה ולשחוט עליו אביו את הפסח: לאכלה להביא בן ח' שאין שחיטתו מטהרתו ... טהורה שילדת לט' חדשים היא. ומיבעיא לן רשב"ג פליגי רבנן עליה אי לא ופשטינן דפליגי ... כוותיה דאמר רב יהודה אמר שמואל הלכה כרשב"ג ואי לא פליגי הלכה למה. אמר אביי נפל מן הגג ואכלו אריה דברי הכל חי הוא. [כי] פליגי שפיהק ומת מר סבר חי הוא ומר סבר מת הוא ... דרב אידי בר אבין ועבד להו עיגלא תלתא ביומא דשבעא ואמר ליה אי אחרתו עד לאורתא הוה אכלינן מיניה ...

דרב יהושע שאם נשחט קודם ח' ימים אסור באכילה ואינו מותר אלא מלילי ח' והלאה (לקרבן) הלכך לילי שמיני מותר באכילה ולקרבן פסול. ואין כשר לקרבן אלא מיום השמיני והלאה וזה שאמר אביי. וכי ימות מן הבהמה אשר היא לכם לאכלה להביא בן שמונת ימים שאין שחיטתו מטהרתו: ברייתא זו שנויה בתורת כהנים. לח' חדשים חלוקות. דתני בהדיא במתניתא דבי ר' חייא

ליקוטי רש"י (המשך)

... בו חזקת איסור מעולם וכדמוקי לה לקמן כגון דיתבי דייני התם [ביצה כו:]. ושוין תנאי דפליגי גבי בכור שנולד בו מום בי"ט ושוין דאפילו האוסר בנולד בו ביום מום משום דמוקצה היה בין השמשות ... בתוך אבל אם נולד היום ומומו עמו מוכן הוא שלא נאסר מעולם דהא במעי אמו היה מוכן אגב אמו ... קדוש עד שיולד וכשנולד הרי מומו עמו ולאוי לישחט בתוך [חולין נא:]. פיהק. באליי"ר בלע"ז ... רוח הפה מלא כאדם שרוצה לישון או שעמד משינה ויש שדורשים נוטריקון פיהק פיו הקים [ברכות ...] ... בלע"ז [נדה סג. עי"ש בתוס']. עיגלא תילתא. שליש לבטן שהוא משובח מפני שהבהמה בקטנותה אינה ... לאשון ושני אינו בריא [לעיל יא. וע"ש בב"ח]. שליש לבטן ומובחר הוא [פסחים סח: וע"ע עירובין סג. ... גיטין נו.]. מת בתוך שלשים. בן היבמה ונתקדשה לשוק בחזקת שפטורה משום בנה [יבמות לו:].

ANIMAL WAS BORN on Yom Tov **WITH ITS** permanent **BLEMISH,** שֶׁזֶּה מִן הַמּוּכָן – **THAT IT IS** considered to be **PREPARED,** and may be slaughtered that day. It appears, then, that the Rabbis argue with Rabban Shimon ben Gamliel and permit the consumption of a one-day-old animal.

The Gemara rejects this proof as well:

הָכָא נַמִּי שֶׁכָּלוּ לוֹ חֳדָשָׁיו – **Here too** we are dealing with a case **where** it is certain that **its months** of gestation **were completed.** Thus, even Rabban Shimon ben Gamliel would agree that it may be slaughtered immediately.

The Gemara resolves the question from an Amoraic statement:

תָּא שְׁמַע – **Come, learn** the answer from the following: דְּאָמַר רַב יְהוּדָה אָמַר שְׁמוּאֵל – **For Rav Yehudah said in the name of Shmuel:** הֲלָכָה כְּרַבָּן שִׁמְעוֹן בֶּן גַּמְלִיאֵל – **The law is in accordance with Rabban Shimon ben Gamliel.** הֲלָכָה מִכְּלָל דִּפְלִיגִי – The fact that he states that **the law** follows Rabban Shimon ben Gamliel **implies that [the Rabbis] disagree** with him! שְׁמַע מִינָּהּ – **Indeed, learn from this** that they disagree.

Abaye qualifies the dispute between Rabban Shimon ben Gamliel and the Rabbis:

אָמַר אַבַּיֵי – **Abaye said:** נָפַל מִן הַגַּג אוֹ אֲכָלוֹ אֲרִי – If **[a child]** younger than thirty days[22] **fell from a roof** and died, **or** it **was eaten by a lion,** i.e. it died of external causes, דִּבְרֵי הַכֹּל חַי הוּא – **all agree** (both Rabban Shimon ben Gamliel and the Rabbis) **that it is** assumed to have been **a viable [child].**[23] כִּי פְּלִיגֵי שֶׁפִּיהֵק וּמֵת – **In what** case **do they disagree? Where [the child] yawned and** then **died,** i.e. it exhibited only limited vitality after being born, for example, yawning and then dying.[24] מַר סָבַר חַי הוּא – **This master** (the Sages) **maintains that** we assume that **it was a viable [child]** despite its obvious frailty.[25] וּמַר סָבַר מֵת הוּא – Whereas **this master** (Rabban Shimon ben Gamliel) **maintains that** we suspect in such a case that **it was not a viable [child].**[26]

The Gemara asks:

לְמַאי נַפְקָא מִינֵּיהּ – Since the child is now dead, **what** practical **difference is there** whether we assume that it was once viable or not?

The Gemara answers:

לִפְטוֹר מִן הַיִּיבּוּם – The difference is whether **to exempt** its mother **from** the requirement of ***yibum.*** If we assume that the newborn was viable, its mother is exempt from the laws of *yibum*. If not, she is subject to this law.[27]

The Gemara questions Abaye's explanation of the dispute:

נָפַל מִן הַגַּג אוֹ אֲכָלוֹ אֲרִי – Can it be that **if [the child] fell from the roof** and died, **or** it **was eaten by a lion,** דִּבְרֵי הַכֹּל חַי הוּא – that **all agree that it is** assumed to have been **a viable [child]?** וְהָא רַב פַּפָּא וְרַב הוּנָא בְּרֵיהּ דְּרַב יְהוֹשֻׁעַ אִיקְלַעוּ לְבֵי בְּרֵיהּ דְּרַב אִידִי בַּר אָבִין – **But Rav Pappa and Rav Huna the son of Rav Yehoshua visited the home of the son of Rav Idi bar Avin,** וְעָבִיד לְהוּ עִיגְלָא תִּילְתָּא – **and he prepared for them a third**-born **calf**

NOTES

who in turn offers it as a sacrifice. If a *bechor* is blemished, it is no longer brought as a sacrifice; rather, it is given to a Kohen who may slaughter it anywhere for its meat. Before doing so, however, the blemish must be confirmed as such by an expert. The Mishnah (*Beitzah* 25b-26a) states that where a *bechor* appeared to have a blemish before Yom Tov, R' Yehudah permits the expert to examine it on Yom Tov, while R' Shimon forbids it on one of two grounds: (a) The examination is considered מְתַקֵּן, *repairing,* since it makes the animal permissible for ordinary use, and repairing is forbidden on Yom Tov; (b) the examination is the equivalent to adjudicating a lawsuit, which is forbidden on Yom Tov (*Rashi* ibid.). The Baraisa quoted here states that if the *bechor* was born with a blemish, R' Shimon agrees with R' Yehudah that the animal may be examined on Yom Tov by an expert and then slaughtered. The reason is that, having been born blemished, it was never established to be prohibited, and permitting it is thus not like "repairing" nor like adjudicating. The Gemara there adds that this is so only if the panel of experts actually saw the calf being born with its blemish, so that it was never assumed to be prohibited (*Rashi;* see Gemara there 26b).

22. [Who was not definitely known to have been full term.]

23. Since most births result in normal viable offspring and we have no evidence to suggest that this infant was atypical, all agree that we assume that it was viable (i.e. that it completed the period of gestation needed for its full development) and would have lived if not for these unfortunate occurrences.

This assumption has practical ramifications with regard to both human and animal offspring. In the case of a human infant, it would have the effect of exempting its mother from the requirement of *chalitzah* [in a case where the father died without leaving any other offspring], as the Gemara will explain below. With respect to animals it would mean that *shechitah* is effective in permitting its meat even within its first eight days (*Rashi*).

24. *Rashi.* [Since the infant's condition was never robust we suspect that it never completed its development and thus was never viable.]

[*Baal HaMaor* asserts that sickness is treated as an external cause of death, like falling from a roof. Thus, if an infant developed a discernible sickness and then died, we would attribute its death to the sickness and not to a lack of innate viability. This would seem to be *Rashi's* view as well, since he explains the point about yawning to be that the infant exhibited only weak signs of vitality from the very beginning (*Maharshal*). *Ramban* (in *Milchamos*), however, contends that contracting a sickness and dying within thirty days also gives rise to the suspicion that the infant was not viable (see also *Rabbeinu Yonah* cited by *Ran, MHK* ed. and *Rashba*). Abaye speaks of "yawning and dying" rather than sickness because sudden death is the most common demonstration of an infant's inability to sustain life.]

25. [For we assume even a weak infant to be from among the majority of newborns that are indeed viable. Its death, therefore, is assumed to have been caused by some unknown illness.]

26. [Literally: dead. The term מֵת is used here in a different sense then it was used above. There it referred to the child's legal status; here it refers to its physical status, i.e. its inability to survive. See note 10.]

The suspicion of non-viability is not because it died but simply because it showed such weak signs of vitality in the first place. Thus, even if it would have died of external causes, it would still be suspected of being a *nefel* according to Rabban Shimon ben Gamliel (*Teshuvos R' Akiva Eiger* §98; see end of next note).

27. If a man dies childless, the Torah (*Deuteronomy* 25:5-10) requires his brother to marry his widow. This union is referred to as *yibum*. If the brother does not wish to marry her, he must release her from her bond to him through a ceremony known as *chalitzah*.

The question of the infant's viability is relevant to a case where the husband dies and is survived by his widow and this one infant, who then dies within thirty days of birth. If we assume that the infant was viable, the widow is exempt from the laws of *yibum* and *chalitzah* for the husband was not childless at the time of his death. If, however, we suspect that the infant was not viable, then the widow would now be obligated to undergo *chalitzah*. [She would not, however, be allowed to *marry* her brother-in-law (*yibum*), for we only *suspect* that the infant was not viable but we do not know with certainty that this was the case, and marrying one's brother-in-law in the absence of a *mitzvah* of *yibum* is forbidden.]

[Where a newborn yawns and *dies,* there is only a practical difference to the dispute in the case of a human child. In the case of an animal, however, the only difference it ever makes whether we consider an animal less than eight days old viable or not is whether one may slaughter it and eat its meat, as *Rashi* explained above (see note 23). But where the animal yawned and *died,* it is in any case a *neveilah,* since it was never slaughtered. For this reason *Rashi* says (ד״ה שפיהק) that Abaye is discussing specifically the case of a human newborn, not an animal (see also *Ritva MHK* ed.; cf. *Hagahos R' Elazar Moshe Horowitz*). Rabban Shimon ben Gamliel, however, said his rule in regard to an animal as well (see Baraisa above). The practical consequence of his ruling would be where the animal yawned and was then *slaughtered.* For it is not how the newborn died that makes us suspect its non-viability, but simply the fact that it showed little vitality. Thus, even if it was slaughtered Rabban Shimon ben Gamliel would forbid its meat because of a doubt as to its viability (*Teshuvos R' Akiva Eiger* §98). Abaye, however, happened to be discussing the law in regard to humans (*Rashi*). He therefore spoke of a case in which the newborn yawned and *died.* For this reason the Gemara

מימהל היכי מהלינן ליה אמר רב אדא בר אהבה [א]מלין אותו ממה נפשך אם חי הוא שפיר קא מהיל ואם לאו מחתך בבשר הוא ואלא הא דתניא ספק בן ז' ספק בן ח' אין מחללין עליו את השבת אמאי נימהליה ממה נפשך אם חי הוא שפיר קא מהיל • ואם לאו מחתך בבשר הוא אמר מר בריה דרבינא אנא ורב נחומי בר זכריה תרגימנא מימהיל הכי נמי מהלינן ליה לא נצרכה אלא למכשירי מילה [ה]ואליבא דרבי אליעזר אמר אביי כתנאי [א]וכי ימות מן הבהמה אשר היא לכם לאכלה להביא [ב]בן שמנה שאין שחיטתו מטהרתו רבי יוסי ברבי יהודה ור' אלעזר בר"ש אומרים שחיטתו מטהרתו מאי לאו בהא קא מיפלגי דמר סבר חי הוא ומ"ס מת הוא אמר רבא אי הכי אדמיפלגי לענין טומאה וטהרה ליפלגו לענין אכילה אלא דכולי עלמא מת הוא ורבי יוסי ברבי יהודה ורבי אלעזר ברבי שמעון סברי כטרפה טרפה לאו [ג]אף על גב דמתה היא שחיטתה מטהרתה הכא נמי לא שנא ורבנן לא דמי לטרפה טרפה היתה לה שעת הכושר האי לא היתה לה שעת הכושר וכ"ת טרפה מבטן מאי איכא למימר התם יש במינה שחיטה • [ד]הכא אין במינה שחיטה איבעיא להו מי פליגי רבנן עליה דרבן שמעון בן גמליאל או לא אם תמצי לומר פליגי הלכה כמותו או אין הלכה כמותו ת"ש [ה]עגל שנולד ביום טוב שוחטין אותו בי"ט הכא במאי עסקינן [ו]דקים ליה בגוויה שכלו לו חדשיו ת"ש [ז]ושוין [ח]שאם נולד הוא ומומו עמו שזה מן המוכן ה"נ שכלו לו חדשיו ת"ש דאמר רב יהודה אמר שמואל [ט]הלכה כרבן שמעון בן גמליאל הלכה מכלל דפליגי ש"מ אמר אביי נפל מן הגג או אכלו ארי דברי הכל חי הוא כי פליגי שפיהק ומת מר סבר חי הוא ומר סבר מת הוא למאי נפקא מיניה לפטור מן הייבום נפל מן הגג או אכלו ארי דברי הכל חי הוא והא רב פפא ורב הונא בריה דרב יהושע איקלעו לבי בריה דרב אידי בר אבין ועביד להו עיגלא תילתא ביממא דשבעה ואמרי ליה אי איתרחיתו ליה עד לאורתא הוה אכלינן מיניה השתא לא אכלינן מיניה אלא כשפיהק ומת דברי הכל מת הוא כי פליגי בנפל מן הגג ואכלו ארי מר סבר מת הוא ומר סבר חי הוא בריה דרב דימי בר יוסף אתיליד ליה ההוא ינוקא בגו תלתין יומין שכיב יתיב קמתאביל עילויה אמר ליה אבוה צוורוניתא קבעית למיכל אמר ליה [כ]קים לי ביה שכלו לו חדשיו רב אשי איקלע בי רב כהנא איתרע ביה מילתא בגו תלתין יומין חזייה דיתיב וקא מתאבל עילויה אמר ליה לא סבר ליה מר להא דאמר רב יהודה אמר שמואל הלכה כרבן שמעון בן גמליאל אמר ליה קים לי בגויה שכלו לו חדשיו [ל]איתמר מת בתוך שלשים ועמדה ונתקדשה אמר רבינא משמיה דרבא אם

רש"י

מימהל היכי מהלינן. שום קטן ביום השמיני בשבת דילמא נפל הוא ולא חזי למול ועושה חבורה שלא לשם מלוה: אם חי הוא. כלומר אם כלו לו חדשיו שפיר קא מהיל: מחתך בבשר. שמוטה הוא ולא חבורה היא: לא נצרכה. הא דקתני אין מחללין אלא לענין מכשירי מילה לרבי אליעזר דאמר דחו שבת ה"מ דקים ליה בגויה שכלו לו חדשיו שעברו • ט' חדשים משמשה עד שילדתו ולא שמשה כל ימי עיבורה אבל ספק אין מכשיריו דוחין דילמא לאו בר מימהל הוא ומחלל שבת בעשותו פחמים וברזל: כתנאי. נפל גמור אם חשוב כמת כדקאמר רב אדא בר אהבה דאינו אלא מחתך בבשר או לא והויא חבורה: לאכלה להביא בן ח'. דכוליה קרא דריש ליה בתורת כהנים מן הבהמה מקצת בהמה מטמאה ומקצת אינה מטמאה פרט לטרפה ששחטה ומדממעיט טרפה ששחטה מכלל דבטהורה קאי אשר היא לכם להביא בהמה טמאה לפי שפרשה ראשונה דכתיב בה לכל הבהמה אשר היא מפרסת פרסה ואיננה מעלת גרה וגו' מוקי לה התם באבר מן החי הכתוב מדבר ופרשה זו בנבלה ודאי לאכלה להביא בן ח' חדשים שאף שחיטתו מיתה ומטמאה: מר סבר חי הוא. לפיכך שחיטתו מטהרתו: לענין אכילה. אי מותר באכילה בשחיטתו אם לאו: טרפה. שחיטתה מטהרתה מלטמא כדפרישית: היתה לה שעת הכושר. לישחט וליטהר קודם שנטרפה: מי פליגי. למישרי ולד של בהמה בתוך ח' ימים: שוחטים אותו ביו"ט. ואינו מוקצה שהרי בין השמשות נמי היה מוכן אגב אמו מיהו שמעינן מינה דמותר לנו ביום: ושוין. רבי יהודה ורבי שמעון שנחלקו ברואין מומין ביו"ט במסכת ביצה שאם נולד היום הוא ומומו עמו שהוא מן המוכן ומותר לבקר מומו ביו"ט דלא דמי כמתקן ביו"ט דלא איתחזק באיסורא ומוקמינן לה התם כגון דיתבי דייני התם ורואוהו בשעת לידה מיד: נפל מן הגג או אכלו ארי. שמת מחמת מיתה הבאה לו בתוך ל' ממקום אחר דברי הכל בחזקת כלו לו חדשיו קאי דאי לאו הך מיתה לא הוה מת הילכך חי הוא ובאדם הוי ולד ופוטר את אמו מן החליצה וגבי בהמה נמי סתם ולד בהמה ששחט בתוך ח' מותר באכילה דלא חזינא ביה ריעותא ורוב היולדות אינן מפילות: שפיהק. • ביילי"ר בלע"ז כלומר לאחר לידתו לא ראו בו אלא חיות מעט שפיהק ומת וגבי אדם קאי: ה"ג ועבדו (א) עגלא תילתא ביממא דשבעה: איתרחיתו. מלשוחטו עד אורתא שהוא ליל שמיני: הוה אכלינן מיניה. דמקצת היום ככולו כדכתיב (ויקרא כב) והיה שבעת ימים תחת אמו הא לילה חזי ומיהו מיום השמיני הוא דירצה לאורתא לאו בת הקרבה היא כדכתיב (שם ז) ביום צוותו להקריב אבל מכלל נפל נפקי ליה וחזי לאקדושי כדאמרינן בזבחים (דף יב.) • לילה לקדושה יום להרצאה והלכך לענין חולין חזי מאורתא למישחטיה ומיכל אלמא מאן דס"ל כרשב"ג פליג במיתה הבאה לו ממקום אחר ואמר ספיקא הוא: שכיב בגו תלתין. ללידתו: צוורוניתא. מטעמים שמאכילין את האבל: קא בעית למיכל. לכך אתה מתאבל חנם: איתרע מילתא. אבילות: בגו תלתין יומין. ללידת הולד: מת הולד [מ]בתוך ל'. ללידתו ולא היה לאביו בן אלא הוא [נ]ונולד לאחר מיתת אביו ועל ידו היו פוטרין אמו מן החליצה אם היה בר קיימא: ועמדה ונתקדשה. לאחר זמן לפי שסבורה שאינה זקוקה ליבם: ואם

תוספות

מימהל היכי מהלינן ליה. מכאן משמע דלא איירי רשב"ג בבן שמנה (ב) דוקא אלא בספק ולדות וכן משמע לקמן דאמר ת"ש עגל שנולד בי"ט שוחטין אותו בי"ט ודחי דכלו לו חדשיו ואת"ל דלא איירי רשב"ג אלא בודאי בן שמנה הוה ליה לדחויי הכ"ע בספק ולדות ועוד אמר לקמן נפל מן הגג ואכלו ארי דברי הכל חי הוא ואי בודאי בן ח' איירי היכי תיסק אדעתיה לומר ד"ה חי הוא ובכולהו דלקמן נמי דמוקמינן בדקים ליה בגוויה שכלו לו חדשיו וקשה לר"י מהא דאמרינן בפ' הערל (יבמות דף פ:) איזהו בן ח' כל שלא כלו לו חדשיו רבי אומר שערו וצפרניו מוכיחין עליו כו' דאמר האי בר שבעה הוא ואישתהוי אישתהי ופריך (ג) הא דעבד רבה תוספאה עובדא באשה שהלך בעלה למדינת הים ואישתהי עד תריסר ירחי שתא כמאן כרבי כיון דאיכא רשב"ג דאמר אישתהי [י]דתני כל ששהה כו' כרבי עבד אלמא משמע בהדיא דבודאי בן ח' איירי מדמוכח מיניה דמשתהי כרבי ומנא ליה דילמא לעולם ס"ל דלא משתהי ובספק ולדות איירי רשב"ג כדפרישית ואור"י דע"כ בודאי בן ח' נמי איירי דהא בתוספתא דמכילתין מיתני מילתיה דרשב"ג בתר מילתיה דרבנן ורבי דיבמות ואפלוגתייהו קאי דאיירי בבן ח' וא"ת ובשמעתין מנלן דבספק ולדות ס"ל לרשב"ג הא לא שהה ספיקא הוי דילמא קסבר ולד מעליא הוי ולא איירי כלל בספק ולדות אלא בודאי בן ח' ויש לומר דדייקינן מדקתני כל ששהה דכל משמע לרבות סתם דווקא שהה הא לא שהה ספיקא הוי והא דמבעיא לן לקמן אי פליגי רבנן עליה דרשב"ג היינו בספק ולדות דבן ח' ודאי בהדיא קתני לה בתוספתא וא"ת והיכי פשיט לקמן מדאמר רב יהודה אמר שמואל הלכה כרשב"ג מכלל דפליגי בספק ולדות תאמר דלעולם לא פליגי בספק ולדות וכי פסיק רב יהודה כוותיה הנ"מ בודאי בן ח' וי"ל דא"כ ה"ל למיתני הלכה כר' (ד) דליכא למימר דלא קאמר הלכה כרבי משום דבעי הוכחת סימנין שערו וצפרניו אבל רשב"ג לא בעי דהא פשיטא דבן ח' שלא גמרו שערו וצפרניו לכ"ע לא חי ומדנקט רשב"ג ש"מ דבספק ולדות איירי ופסק בכולא מילתא כוותיה והשתא נמי אין צריך לדקדק (ה) מכל דבלאו הכי יש להוכיח דבספק ולדות איירי כמו שהוכחתי [כ] ר"י: צוורוניתא. גרס בערוך [ל] לשון לידה ומזונות:

מסורת הש"ס

א) [לעיל קל.], ב) חולין נא: ביצה ו:, ג) חולין שם ביצה כו:, ד) [לעיל קו: וש"נ], ה) יבמות לו:, ו) [עי' תוס' בכורות מט. ד"ה מת ותוס' יבמות לו: ד"ה מת וכו' שכתבו דרש"י דהכא גורס בסוף שלשים], ז) [במו"ק כ: גרס רש"י לידונייס' ופי' סעודת אבל כמו גיר' הערוך שהביא תוס' הכא ד"ה צודניתא], ח) [צ"ל בסוף ע"פ עדות' של תוס' יבמות ובכורות], ט) [צ"ל ומי לאחר מיתת אביו], י) [צ"ל מדקתני כל ששהה ולא תני אם שהה כרבי עבדי], כ) [ור"ל דאי לאו הכי מה בא רשב"ג להוסיף על מילתא דרבי], ל) [ערך לד ג].

הגהות הב"ח

(א) רש"י ד"ה ה"ג ועביד להו עגלא תלתא: (ב) תוס' ד"ה מימהל וכו' בבן שמונה ודאי דוקא אלא: (ג) בא"ד ופריך אלא הא דעבד: (ד) בא"ד הוה ליה למיתני הלכה כרבי וכרשב"ג דליכא: (ה) בא"ד אין צריך לדקדק מכל כמו שהוכיח ר"י דבלאו הכי יש להוכיח דבספק ולדות איירי הס"ד:

רב נסים גאון

וזאת אחת מג' הלכות כריש לקיש כמו שאמר רבא הלכתא כריש לקיש בהני תלת חדא הא אבל בכל מקום שיש מחלוקת בין ר' יוחנן וריש לקיש הלכה כר' יוחנן לבד מהני תלת: אמר אביי כתנאי לאכלה להביא בן ח' שאין שחיטתו מטהרתו עיקר דבר זה שנוי בתורת כהנים (ויקרא יא) וכי ימות מן הבהמה אשר היא לכם לאכלה וכי ימות הרי זו מיתה ודאי מן הבהמה יש מן הבהמה מטמאה ויש מן הבהמה שאין מטמאה פרט לטרפה ששחטה ונתבאר לנו בזה הכתוב בהמה [טרפה] ששחטה אינה מטמאה ונשאו ונתנו בדבר זה הרבה ואמרו באמצע הדברים בן ח' יוכיח שיש למינו שחיטה ואין שחיטתו מטהרתו ולאחר

ליקוטי רש"י

מחתך בבשר הוא. ולאו מיזו אלא כמוכל כמי דמוליא דם [ערכין ז:]. טרפה היתה לה שעת הכושר. ...

עין משפט נר מצוה

מ א מיי' פ"א מהל' מילה הלכה יד סמג עשין כח טוש"ע י"ד סי' רסו סעיף יא בהג"ה:

מא ב ג ד מיי' פ"ב מהל' שאר אבות הטומאות הלכה ו:

מב ה ו מיי' פ"ב מהל' יום טוב הלכה א סמג לאוין עה טוש"ע א"ח סי' תצח סעיף ה:

מג ז מיי' שם הלכה ד טוש"ע שם סעיף ט:

מד ח ט מיי' פ"א מהל' יבום הלכה ה סמג עשין כ טוש"ע אה"ע סי' קנו סעיף ד:

מה י מיי' פ"ד מהל' מאכלות אסורות הלכה ד סמג לאוין עה וקלג טוש"ע י"ד סי' טו סעיף ב:

מו כ מיי' פ"א מהל' אבלות הלכה ז סמג עשין מד"ס ב טוש"ע י"ד סי' שעד סעיף ח [ברי"ף כאן ובפ"ג דמו"ק דף רל: וכן ברא"ש כאן והתם סי' לג]:

גליון הש"ס

גמ' ואם לאו מחתך בבשר הוא. עי' מ"א סי' תקכו ס"ק יא. ועי' בירושלמי פ"י דיבמות הלכה ז: שם הכא אין במינה שחיטה. עי' חולין עד ע"א מד"ה נפקא ליה: רש"י ד"ה לא נצרכה וכו' ט' חדשים משמשה. עי' חכ"צ סי' טו ס"ק טו: ד"ה שפיהק ביילי"ר בלע"ז. עי' נדה סג ע"א מד"ה מפהקת: ד"ה הוה אכלינן מיניה וכו' לילה לקדושה. ועי' בתוס' שם זבחים יב ע"א ד"ה יום ול"ע:

תורה אור השלם

א) וְכִי יָמוּת מִן הַבְּהֵמָה אֲשֶׁר הִיא לָכֶם לְאָכְלָה הַנֹּגֵעַ בְּנִבְלָתָהּ יִטְמָא עַד הָעָרֶב: [ויקרא יא, לט]

רבינו חננאל

זה שפחה וזהו עובר זהו יליד בית שנימול לאחד דברי הכל הוא. כי פליגי בילדה ואח"כ הטבילה ת"ק סבר גם זה יליד בית נימול לשמונה. ורב אחא סבר זה יליד בית נימול לאחד. ושאר השמועה פשוטה היא: תניא רשב"ג אומר כל ששהה באדם שלשים יום אינו נפל שנאמר ופדויו מבן חדש תפדה. שמונת ימים בבהמה אינו נפל שנאמר ומיום השמיני והלאה ירצה וגו'. הא לא שהה ספק הוי וזה שאנו מלין כל קטן בן ח' ימים הלא אמר רשב"ג קודם ל' יום ספק נפל הוא ואין מחללין עליו את השבת ומלין אותו בן ח' ימים שמא נפל הוא. ופרקי' מלין אותו ממה נפשך אי חי הוא שפיר קא מהיל. ואי נפל הוא מחתך בבשר הוא ולא מלאכה היא ומקשינן אלא הא דתניא ספק בן ז' או בן ח' אין מחללין עליו את השבת אמאי [נימהליה] (נימא) ליה ממ"נ ופרקינן מימהל ה"נ מהלינן ליה לא נצרכה אלא למכשירי מילה ואליבא דר' אליעזר ולית הלכתא הכי דשנוא

בִּימָמָא דִשְׁבְעָה – that was seven days old.[28] **וְאָמְרֵי לֵיהּ** – And they said to him: **אִי אִיתְרַחִיתוּ לֵיהּ עַד לְאוּרְתָּא הֲוָה אַכְלִינַן מִינֵּיהּ** – "Had you delayed slaughtering it until tonight (the beginning of its eighth day), we would have eaten from it.[29] **הַשְׁתָּא לֹא אַכְלִינַן מִינֵּיהּ** – Now, however, that you have slaughtered it before the eighth day, we will not eat from it," because an animal is not assumed to be definitely viable until its eighth day. Now, here is a case where the animal died an unnatural death – it was slaughtered – and yet the calf was suspected of being not viable. This contradicts Abaye's assertion that when a newborn dies an unnatural death, even Rabban Shimon ben Gamliel agrees that we assume it to have been viable.[30]

The Gemara therefore revises Abaye's qualification of the debate between Rabban Shimon ben Gamliel and the Sages: **אֶלָּא כְּשֶׁפִּיהֵק וּמֵת דִּבְרֵי הַכֹּל מֵת הוּא** – Rather, Abaye said as follows: Where [the child] yawned and died, all agree that we suspect that it was not viable. **כִּי פְּלִיגֵי בְּנָפַל מִן הַגַּג וַאֲכָלוֹ אֲרִי** – In what case do they disagree? Where [the child] fell from the roof and died, or was eaten by a lion, i.e. where it died from external causes. **מָר סָבַר מֵת הוּא** – This master (Rabban Shimon ben Gamliel) maintains that we suspect that it was not a viable [child],[31] **וּמָר סָבַר חַי הוּא** – whereas this master (the Sages) maintains that it is assumed to have been a viable [child] since we have no reason to believe to the contrary.

The Gemara cites a related incident: **בְּרֵיהּ דְּרַב דִּימִי בַּר יוֹסֵף אִתְיְלִיד לֵיהּ הַהוּא יְנוּקָא** – The son of Rav Dimi bar Yosef had a child born to him **בְּגוֹ תְּלָתִין יוֹמִין שְׁכִיב** – but it died within the first thirty days of its life. **יָתִיב קָמִתְאַבִּיל עִילָוֵיהּ** – He then sat and mourned for it. **אָמַר לֵיהּ אֲבוּהּ** – Thereupon, his father (Rav Dimi) said to him: **צְוּורוֹנִיתָא קָבָעִית לְמֵיכַל** – Do you wish to eat the traditional mourners' food?[32] There is no reason for you to mourn![33] **אָמַר לֵיהּ** – He said to [his father]: **קִים לִי בֵּיהּ שֶׁכָּלוּ לוֹ חֳדָשָׁיו** – I know for certain that its months of gestation were completed, i.e. that it was carried to full term and was thus born viable.[34]

A similar incident: **רַב אַשִׁי אִיקְלַע בֵּי רַב כַּהֲנָא** – Rav Ashi visited the home of Rav Kahana. **אִיתְרַע בֵּיהּ מִילְּתָא בְּגוֹ תְּלָתִין יוֹמִין** – During his visit, an unfortunate thing occurred to [Rav Kahana] (i.e. his child died) within thirty days of its birth. **חֲזְיֵיהּ דְּיָתִיב וְקָא מִתְאַבֵּל עִילָוֵיהּ** – [Rav Ashi] observed that [Rav Kahana] was sitting and mourning for it. **אָמַר לֵיהּ** – [Rav Ashi] said to [Rav Kahana]: **לֹא סָבַר לֵיהּ מָר לְהָא דְּאָמַר רַב יְהוּדָה אָמַר שְׁמוּאֵל** – Does the master not accept that which Rav Yehudah said in the name of Shmuel: **הֲלָכָה כְּרַבָּן שִׁמְעוֹן בֶּן גַּמְלִיאֵל** – The law is in accordance with the view of Rabban Shimon ben Gamliel who asserts that an infant that dies within thirty days of its birth is suspected of not having been viable? Hence, you are not obligated to mourn its death. **אָמַר לֵיהּ** – [Rav Kahana] said to [Rav Ashi]: **קִים לִי בְּגַוֵּיהּ שֶׁכָּלוּ לוֹ חֳדָשָׁיו** – I know for certain that its months of gestation were completed, i.e. that it was carried to full term.

The Gemara cites a related Amoraic dispute: **אִיתְּמַר** – It was stated: **מֵת בְּתוֹךְ שְׁלֹשִׁים** – If [an infant], who was the sole surviving issue of his dead father, died within[35] thirty days of his birth, **וְעָמְדָה וְנִתְקַדְּשָׁה** – and [his mother] went ahead and betrothed herself to a man,[36] **אָמַר רָבִינָא מִשְּׁמֵיהּ דְּרָבָא** – Ravina said in the name of Rava:

NOTES

gave a practical difference only in regard to humans (namely, *yibum*).]

28. Literally: on the seventh day; i.e. the calf was in only the seventh day of its life. [See above, 119b note 14, for an explanation of a "third-born calf; cf. *Chidushei HaRan.*"]

29. The verse in *Leviticus* 22:27 states: שׁוֹר אוֹ־כֶשֶׂב אוֹ־עֵז כִּי יִוָּלֵד וְהָיָה שִׁבְעַת יָמִים תַּחַת אִמּוֹ וּמִיּוֹם הַשְּׁמִינִי וָהָלְאָה יֵרָצֶה לְקָרְבַּן אִשֶּׁה לַה׳, *When an ox, sheep, or goat is born, for seven days it shall remain under its mother and from the eighth day and on it is acceptable as a fire offering to Hashem.* [This is the verse from which Rabban Shimon ben Gamliel derives that once an animal has lived into its eighth day, we assume that it is definitely viable.] By stating *"for seven days it shall remain under its mother,"* the verse implies that immediately following the conclusion of the seventh *day* – that very *night* – the animal is acceptable as a sacrifice, teaching in effect that we apply here the principle מִקְצָת הַיּוֹם כְּכוּלּוֹ, *a portion of a day is equivalent to a full day* (see *Ritva MHK* ed.; see *Minchas Chinuch*, Mitzvah 293:1,3). The reason the verse states that it is not fit for an offering until the eighth *day* is because there is a general prohibition against offering a sacrifice at night. Nonetheless, the verse does permit one to consecrate the animal on the night of the eighth (as taught in *Zevachim* 12a), making it clear that the animal is considered definitely viable as soon as the seventh day has ended and the eighth has begun. Therefore, as far as *chullin* is concerned, we would be permitted to slaughter and eat the animal as soon as night fell on the seventh day and the eighth day began, as Rav Pappa and Rav Huna the son of Rav Yehoshua said (*Rashi*).

30. Rather, it is clear from these two Amoraim that Rabban Shimon ben Gamliel considers the possibility of an animal being non-viable even if it died from external causes (*Rashi*).

The Gemara is not refuting Abaye from these Amoraim, for one Amora's position cannot refute another's. Rather, the Gemara is asserting that since it is unlikely that these Amoraim disagree with Abaye, we most likely are misquoting Abaye's qualification (*Rashba*).

31. [Although we generally follow the majority and most newborns are viable, Rabban Shimon ben Gamliel maintains that the law regarding newborns is exceptional, as derived from the verse cited by him above (135b). This teaches that we must be concerned for the minority of newborns that are not viable (*Yad David* to 135b, quoting *R' Zelig Auerbach;* see *Rashi* 135b ד״ה מבן חדש). Alternatively, Rabban Shimon ben Gamliel holds that we cannot ignore the sizable minority of infants that are not viable (*Tosafos, Yevamos* 36b ד״ה הא; cf. *Tosafos* there 119a ד״ה מחורתא and *Chullin* 11b ד״ה לרבי; see also *Tos. Rid* here).

32. Tasty foods traditionally served to a mourner [to ease his anguish] (*Rashi*).

33. Since the Gemara stated above that the halachah is in accordance with Rabban Shimon ben Gamliel's view, we must suspect that the infant was not viable (*Ritva MHK* ed.), and one is not obligated to mourn in cases of doubt (*Radvaz, Hil. Eivel* 1:6).

34. He knew this to be so because he had had relations with his wife a full nine months prior to the child's birth and had then abstained until its birth (*Rashi* above ד״ה לא נצרכא and responsum of *Rashi* cited by *Hagahos Maimoniyos, Hil. Eivel* 1:4; see note 6 above). Since it was certain that the child had been carried to full term, even Rabban Shimon ben Gamliel agrees that it is considered viable.

35. [See *Tosafos* (to *Yevamos* 36b ד״ה מת בתוך and to *Bechoros* 49a ד״ה מת ביום), who cite *Rashi's* reading of this Gemara as מֵת בְּסוֹף שְׁלֹשִׁים, *if he died "at the end" of thirty days,* or as: מֵת בְּיוֹם שְׁלֹשִׁים, *if he died "on" the thirtieth day,* and who discuss the ramifications of the variant reading.]

36. Since the infant died within thirty days, his status is subject to the dispute between Rabban Shimon ben Gamliel and the Sages. If he is deemed to have been viable, then his mother may remarry without first undergoing *chalitzah;* if he is deemd *not* to have been viable, then she must undergo *chalitzah* before she is free to remarry (see note 27).

In the case presently under discussion, the mother accepted *kiddushin* from a man without first undergoing *chalitzah,* thinking that the birth of her child had freed her from *yibum* (*Rashi*). She accepted the *kiddushin* some time after the death of her child (*Rashi,* as explained by *Chasam Sofer,* who is, however, at a loss to explain why *Rashi* specifies this; cf. *Leshon HaZahav*; see, however, *Aruch LaNer* to *Yevamos* 36b ד״ה בגמ׳ מת בתוך ל׳).

[*Rashi* (as his comments appear in our texts) also states that the child was born after his father died, but it is not clear why he specifies this either (see *Chasam Sofer* and *Leshon HaZahav*; see also *Aruch LaNer* loc. cit.). Another version of *Rashi* (cited in the margin of the Vilna edition) has it that the child *died* after his father died. This is, indeed, an essential element of this case, for a child must survive his father in order to exempt his mother from the *yibum* bond.]

מימהל היכי מהלינן ליה אמר רב אדא בר אהבה מלין אותו ממה נפשך אם חי הוא שפיר קא מהיל ואם לאו מחתך בבשר הוא ואלא הא דתניא ספק בן ז' ספק בן ח' אין מחללין עליו את השבת אמאי נימהליה ממה נפשך אם חי הוא שפיר קא מהיל ואם לאו מחתך בבשר הוא אמר מר בריה דרבינא אנא ורב נחומי בר זכריה תרגימנא מימהיל הכי נמי מהלינן ליה לא נצרכה אלא למכשירי מילה ואליבא דרבי אליעזר אמר אביי כתנאי וכי ימות מן הבהמה אשר היא לכם לאכלה להביא בן שמנה שאין שחיטתו מטהרתו רבי יוסי ברבי יהודה ור' אלעזר בר"ש אומרים שחיטתו מטהרתו מאי לאו בהא קא מיפלגי דמר סבר חי הוא ומ"ס מת הוא אמר רבא אי הכי אדמיפלגי לענין טומאה וטהרה ליפלגי לענין אכילה אלא דכולי עלמא מת הוא ורבי יוסי ברבי יהודה ורבי אלעזר ברבי שמעון סברי כטרפה טרפה לאו אף על גב דמתה היא שחיטתה מטהרתה הכא נמי לא שנא ורבנן לא דמי לטרפה טרפה היתה לה שעת הכושר האי לא היתה לה שעת הכושר וכ"ת טרפה מבטן מאי איכא למימר התם יש במינה שחיטה הכא אין במינה שחיטה איבעיא להו מי פליגי רבנן עליה דרבן שמעון בן גמליאל או לא אם תמצי לומר פליגי הלכה כמותו או אין הלכה כמותו ת"ש עגל שנולד ביום טוב שוחטין אותו בי"ט הכא במאי עסקינן דקים ליה בגוויה שכלו לו חדשיו ת"ש ושוין שאם נולד הוא ומומו עמו שזה מן המוכן ה"נ שכלו לו חדשיו ת"ש דאמר רב יהודה אמר שמואל הלכה כרבן שמעון בן גמליאל הלכה מכלל דפליגי ש"מ אמר אביי נפל מן הגג או אכלו ארי דברי הכל חי הוא כי פליגי שפיהק ומת מר סבר חי הוא ומר סבר מת הוא למאי נפקא מיניה לפטור מן הייבום נפל מן הגג או אכלו ארי דברי הכל חי הוא והא רב פפא ורב הונא בריה דרב יהושע איקלעו לבי בריה דרב אידי בר אבין ועביד להו עיגלא תילתא בימא דשבעה ואמרי ליה אי איתרחיתו ליה עד לאורתא הוה אכלינן מיניה השתא לא אכלינן מיניה אלא כשפיהק ומת דברי הכל מת הוא כי פליגי בנפל מן הגג ואכלו ארי מר סבר מת הוא ומר סבר חי הוא בריה דרב דימי בר יוסף אתיליד ליה ההוא ינוקא בגו תלתין יומין שכיב יתיב קמתאביל עילויה אמר ליה אבוה צוורוניתא קבעית למיכל אמר ליה קים לי ביה שכלו לו חדשיו רב אשי איקלע בי רב כהנא איתרע ביה מילתא בגו תלתין יומין חזייה דיתיב וקא מתאבל עילויה אמר ליה לא סבר ליה מר להא דאמר רב יהודה אמר שמואל הלכה כרבן שמעון בן גמליאל אמר ליה קים לי בגויה שכלו לו חדשיו איתמר מת בתוך שלשים ועמדה ונתקדשה אמר רבינא משמיה דרבא אם

רש"י

מימהל היכי מהלינן. שום קטן ביום השמיני ולא חזי למול ועושה חבורה שלא לשם מלוה: אם חי הוא. כלומר אם כלו לו חדשיו שפיר קא מהיל: מחתך בבשר. שמוטה הוא ולא חבורה היא: לא נצרכה. הא דקתני אין מחללין אלא לענין מכשירי מילה לרבי אליעזר דאמר דחו שבת ה"מ דקים ליה בגויה שכלו לו חדשיו שעברו ° ט' חדשים משמשה עד שילדתו ולא שמשה כל ימי עיבורה אבל ספק אין מכשיריו דוחין דילמא לאו בר מימהל הוא ומחלל שבת בעשותו פחמים וברזל: כתנאי. נפל גמור אם חשוב כמת כדקאמר רב אדא בר אהבה דאינו אלא מחתך בבשר או לא והויא חבורה: לאכלה להביא בן ח'. דכוליה קרא דריש ליה בתורת כהנים מן הבהמה מקצת בהמה מטמאה ומקצת אינה מטמאה פרט לטרפה ששחטה ומדממעיט טרפה ששחטה מכלל דבטהורה קאי אשר היא לכם להביא בהמה טמאה לפי שפרשה ראשונה דכתיב בה לכל הבהמה אשר היא מפרסת פרסה ואיננה מעלת גרה וגו' מוקי לה התם באבר מן החי הכתוב מדבר ופרשה זו במתה ודאי לאכלה להביא בן ח' חדשים שאף שחיטתו מיתה ומטמאה: מר סבר חי הוא. לפיכך שחיטתו מטהרתו: לענין אכילה. אי מותר באכילה בשחיטתו אם לאו: טרפה. שחיטתה מטהרתה מלטמא כדפרישית: היתה לה שעת הכושר. לישחט וליטהר קודם שנטרפה: מי פליגי. למישרי ולד של בהמה בתוך ח' ימים: שוחטים אותו ביו"ט. ואינו מוקצה שהרי בין השמשות נמי היה מוכן אגב אמו מיהו שמעינן מינה דמותר לבו ביום: ושוין. רבי יהודה ורבי שמעון שנחלקו ברואין מומין ביו"ט במסכת ביצה שאם נולד היום הוא ומומו עמו שהוא מן המוכן ומותר לבקר מומו ביו"ט דלא דמי כמתקן ביו"ט דלא איתחזק באיסורא ומוקמינן לה התם כגון דיתבי דייני התם ורלוהו בשעת לידה מיד: נפל מן הגג או אכלו ארי. שמת מחמת מיתה הבאה לו בתוך ל' ממקום אחר דברי הכל בחזקת כלו לו חדשיו קאי דאי לאו הך מיתה לא הוה מת הילכך חי הוא ובאדם הוי ולד ופוטר את אמו מן החליצה וגבי בהמה נמי סתם ולד בהמה ששחט בתוך ח' מותר באכילה דלא חזינא ביה ריעותא ורוב היולדות אינן מפילות: שפיהק. ° ביילי"ר בלע"ז כלומר לאחר לידתו לא ראו בו אלא חיות מעט שפיהק ומת וגבי אדם קאי: ה"ג ועבדו (א) עגלא תילתא בימא דשבעה: איתרחיתו. מלשהותו עד אורתא שהוא ליל שמיני: הוה אכלינן מיניה. דמקצת היום ככולו כדכתיב (ויקרא כב) והיה שבעת ימים תחת אמו הא לילה חזי ומיהו מיום השמיני הוא דירלה לאורתא לאו בת הקרבה היא כדכתיב (שם ז) ביום צוותו להקריב אבל מכלל נפל נפקי ליה וחזי לאקדושי כדאמרינן בזבחים (דף יב.) ° לילה לקודשה יום להרלאה והלכך לענין חולין חזי מאורתא למשחטיה ומיכל אלמא מאן דס"ל כרשב"ג פליג במיתה הבאה לו ממקום אחר ואמר ספיקא הוא: שכיב בגו תלתין. ללידתו: ° צוורוניתא. מטעמים שמאכלין את האבל: קא בעית למיכל. לכך אתה מתאבל כוס: איתרע מילתא. אבילות: בגו תלתין יומין. ללידת הולד: מת הולד ° בתוך ל'. ללידתו ולא היה לאביו בן אלא הוא ° ונולד לאחר מיתת אביו ועל ידו היו פוטרין אמו מן החליצה אם היה בר קיימא: ועמדה ונתקדשה. לאחר זמן לפי שסבורה שאינה זקוקה ליבם: אם

תוספות

מימהל היכי מהלינן ליה. מכאן משמע דלא איירי רשב"ג בבן שמנה (ג) דוקא אלא בספק ולדות וכן משמע לקמן דאמר ת"ש עגל שנולד בי"ט שוחטין אותו בי"ט ודחי דכלו לו חדשיו ואת"ל דלא איירי רשב"ג אלא בודאי בן שמנה הוה ליה לדחויי הב"ע בספק ולדות ועוד אמר לקמן נפל מן הגג ואכלו ארי דברי הכל חי הוא ואי לא איירי בן ח' איירי היכי מיסק אדעתיה לומר ד"ה חי הוא וכולהו לקמן נמי דמוקמינן דקים ליה בגווייה שכלו לו חדשיו וקשה לר"י מהא דאמרינן בפ' הערל (יבמות דף פ:) איזהו בן ח' כל שלא כלו לו חדשיו רבי אומר שערו וצפרניו מוכיחין עליו כו' דאמר האי בר שבעה הוא ואישתהויי אישתהי ופריך (ג) הא דעבד רבה תוספאה עובדא באשה שהלך בעלה למדינת הים ואישתהי עד תריסר ירחי שתא כמאן כרבי כיון דאיכא רשב"ג לאמר אישתהי ° דתני כל ששהה כו' כרבי עבד אלמא משמע בהדיא דבודאי בן ח' איירי מדמוכח מיניה דמשתהי כרבי ומנא ליה דילמא לעולם ס"ל דלא משתהי ובספק ולדות איירי רשב"ג כדפרישית ואור"י דע"כ בודאי בן ח' נמי איירי דהא בתוספתא דמכילתין מיתני מילתיה דרשב"ג בתר מילתיה דרבנן ורבי דיבמות ואפלוגתייהו קאי דאיירי בבן ח' וא"ת ובשמעתין מנלן דבספק ולדות ס"ל לרשב"ג הא לא שהה ספיקא הוי דילמא קסבר ולד מעליא הוי ולא איירי כלל בספק ולדות אלא בודאי בן ח' ויש לומר דדייקינן מדקתני כל ששהה דכל משמע לרבות סתם דווקא שהה הא לא שהה ספיקא הוי והא דמבעיא לן לקמן אי פליגי רבנן עליה דרשב"ג היינו בספק ולדות דבן ח' ודאי בהדיא קתני לה בתוספתא וא"ת והיכי פשיט לקמן מדאמר רב יהודה אמר שמואל הלכה כרשב"ג מכלל דפליגי בספק ולדות תאמר דלעולם לא פליגי בספק ולדות וכי פסיק רב יהודה כוותיה הנ"מ בודאי בן ח' וי"ל דא"כ ה"ל למיתני הלכה כר' (ד) דליכא למימר דלא קאמר הלכה כרבי משום דבעי הוכחת סימנין שערו וצפרניו אבל רשב"ג לא בעי דהא פשיטא דבן ח' שלא גמרו שערו וצפרניו לכ"ע לא חי ומדנקט רשב"ג ש"מ דבספק ולדות איירי ופסק בכולא מילתא כוותיה והשתא נמי אין צריך לדקדק (ה) מכל דבלאו הכי יש להוכיח דבספק ולדות איירי כמו שהוכחתי ר"י: צודניתא. גרס בערוך ° לשון לידה ומזונות: ואם

מסורת הש"ס

א) [לעיל קל.], ב) חולין נא: ביצה ו:, ג) חולין שם ביצה כו:, ד) [לעיל קו: וש"נ], ה) יבמות לו:, ו) [עי' תוס' בכורות מט. ד"ה מת ותוס' יבמות לו: ד"ה מת וכו' שכתבו דרש"י דהכא גורס בסוף שלשים], ז) [במו"ק כ: גרס רש"י לידוניים' ופי' סעודת אבל כמו גיר' הערוך שהביא תוס' הכא ד"ה לודניתא], ח) [נ"ל בסוף ע"פ עדות' של תוס' יבמות ובכורות], ט) [נ"ל ומי לאחר מיתת אביו], י) [ר"ל מדקתני כל ששהה ולא תני אם שהה כרבי עבדין], כ) [ור"ל דאי לאו הכי מה בא רשב"ג להוסיף על מילתא דרבי], ל) [ערך לד ג].

הגהות הב"ח

(א) רש"י ד"ה ה"ג ועביד להו עגלא תלתא: (ב) תום' ד"ה מימהל וכו' בבן שמונה ודאי דוקא אלא: (ג) בא"ד ופריך אלא הא דעבד: (ד) בא"ד הוה ליה למיתני הלכה כרבי וכרשב"ג דליכא: (ה) בא"ד אין צריך לדקדק מכל כמו שהוכיח ר"י דבלאו הכי יש להוכיח דבספק ולדות איירי הס"ד:

רב נסים גאון

וזאת אחת מג' הלכות כריש לקיש כמו שאמר רבא הלכתא כריש לקיש בהני תלת חדא הא אבל בכל מקום שיש מחלוקת בין ר' יוחנן וריש לקיש הלכה כר' יוחנן לבד מהני תלת: אמר אביי כתנאי לאכלה להביא בן ח' שאין שחיטתו מטהרתו עיקר דבר זה שנוי בתורת כהנים (ויקרא יא) וכי ימות מן הבהמה אשר היא לכם לאכלה וכי ימות הרי זו מיתה ודאי יש מן הבהמה מטמאה ויש מן הבהמה שאין מטמאה איזו זו טריפה ששחטה ונתבאר בזה הכתוב בהמה [טרפה] ששחטה אינה מטמאה ונשאו ונתנו בדבר זה הרבה ואמרו באמצע הדברים בן ח' יוכיח שיש למינו שחיטה ואין שחיטתו מטהרתו ולאחר

ליקוטי רש"י

מחתך בבשר הוא. ואין חיוב אלא במקלקל כמי למוציא דם [ערכין ז:]. טרפה היתה לה שעת הכושר.

עין משפט נר מצוה

מ א מיי' פ"א מהל' מילה הלכה יד סמג עשין כח טוש"ע י"ד סי' רסו סעיף יא בהגה"ה:

מא ב ג ד מיי' פ"ב מהל' שאר אבות הטומאות הלכה ו:

מב ה ו מיי' שם מהל' יום טוב הלכה ב סמג לאוין עה טוש"ע א"ח סי' תקו סעיף ג:

מג ז מיי' שם הלכה ד טוש"ע שם סעיף ע:

מד ח מיי' פ"א מהל' יבום הלכה ה סמג עשין נ טוש"ע א"ה סי' קנו סעיף ד:

מה י מיי' פ"ד מהל' מאכלות אסורות הלכה ד סמג לאוין קלא טוש"ע י"ד סי' טו סעיף ג:

מו כ מיי' פ"א מהל' אבלות הלכה ו סמג עשין מד"ס ג טוש"ע י"ד סי' שעד סעיף ח [ברי"ף ולבפ"ב דמו"ק דף ל:]. ובכל"ש כאן והקס סי' לג:

גליון הש"ס

גמ' ואם לאו מחתך בבשר הוא. עי' ח"א סי' חקקי דף קיה ע"ב ועי' בירושלמי פ"ו דיבמות הלכה ו: שם הבא אין במינה שחיטה. עי' חולין עד ע"א מד"ה נפקא ליה: רש"י ד"ה לא נצרכה וכו' ט' חדשים משמשה. עי' תוס' סי' טו סי' קג סי' טן: ד"ה שפיהק ביילי"ר בלע"ז. עי' נדה מד ע"ב תד"ה מפסקת: ד"ה הוה אכלינן מיניה וכו' לילה לקדושה. עי' כתוס' שם ונדה יג ע"א ד"ה יום ולי"ט:

תורה אור השלם

א) וְכִי יָמוּת מִן הַבְּהֵמָה אֲשֶׁר הִיא לָכֶם לְאָכְלָה הַנֹּגֵעַ בְּנִבְלָתָהּ יִטְמָא עַד הָעָרֶב: [ויקרא יא, לט]

רבינו חננאל

זה שפחה וזהו עובר זהו יליד בית שנימול לאחד דברי הכל הוא. כי פליגי בילדה ואח"כ הטבילה ת"ק סבר גם זה יליד בית נימול לשמונה. ורב אחא סבר זה יליד בית נימול לאחד. ושאר השמועה פשוטה היא: תניא רשב"ג אומר כל ששהה באדם שלשים יום אינו נפל שנאמר ופדויו מבן חדש תפדה. שמונת ימים בבהמה אינו נפל שנאמר ומיום השמיני והלאה ירצה וגו'. הא לא שהה ספק הוי וזה שאנו מלין כל קטן בן ח' ימים הלא אמר רשב"ג לא שהה תוך ל' יום ספק נפל הוא ואין מחללין עליו את השבת ומלין אותו בן ח' ימים שמא נפל הוא. ופרקי' מלין אותו ממה נפשך אם חי הוא שפיר קא מהיל. ואי נפל הוא מחתך בבשר הוא ולאו מלאכה הוא ואקשינן אלא הא דתניא ספק בן ז' או בן ח' אין מחללין עליו את השבת אמאי [נימהליה] ממה נפשך ופרקינן מימהל ה"נ מהלינן ליה כי לא נצרכה אלא למכשירי מילה ואליבא דר' אליעזר וליח הלכתא כר' אליעזר דשנויא

דרב יהושע שאם נשחט קודם ח' ימים אסור באכילה ואינו מותר אלא מליל ח' והלאה (לקרבן) הלכך לילי שמיני מותר באכילה ולקרבן פסול. ואין כשר לקרבן אלא מיום השמיני והלאה וזה שאמר אביי. וכי ימות מן הבהמה אשר היא לכם לאכלה להביא בן שמנה שאין שחיטתו מטהרתו: ברייתא זו שנויה בתורת כהנים. לח' חדשים חלוקתם. דתני בהדיא במתניתא דבי ר' חייא

אם אשת ישראל היא חולצת אם אשת כהן היא אינה חולצת ורב שרביא משמיה דרבא אמר אחת זו ואחת זו חולצת אמר ליה רבינא לרב שרביא באורתא אמר רבא הכי לצפרא הדר ביה אמר ליה שריתוה יהא רעוא דתשרו תרבא: ר' יהודה מתיר וכו': אמר רב שיזבי אמר רב חסדא לא לכל אמר רבי יהודה אנדרוגינוס זכר הוא שאם אתה אומר כן בערכין יערך ומנלן דלא מיערך דתניא הזכר ולא טומטום ואנדרוגינוס יכול לא יהא בערך איש אבל יהא בערך אשה תלמוד לומר הזכר ואם נקבה היא זכר ודאי נקבה ודאית ולא טומטום ואנדרוגינוס וסתם

רש"י

אם אשת ישראל היא. אם אינו כהן זה שנתקדשה לו ומותר בחלוצה: **חולצת.** מן הספק ואח"כ תנשא ואם כהן הוא שאם תחלוץ תהא אסורה לו סמכינן אדרבנן ואמרינן לאו נפל הוא ואינה חולצת: **לאורתא אמר רבא הכי.** כדקאמרת דאחת זו ואחת זו חולצת: **ולצפרא הדר ביה.** ואמר אשת כהן אינה חולצת: **אמר ליה.** רב שרביא לרבינא: **שריתוה.** בלא חליצה ועבריתו אדרבנן יהא רעוא דתשרון חלב בהכילה: **לא לכל אמר ר"י.** לא לכל דבר זכר הוא אלא לענין מילה בלבד דיליף ליה מריבויא דקרא לדלקמן: **שאם אתה אומר.** זכר הוא לכל דבר: **בערכין יערך.** האומר ערכו עלי יעריכוהו: **הזכר.** ה' יתירה קדריש וגבי נקבה דריש נמי יתירה ולא טומטום ואנדרוגינוס: והא

תוספות

ואם אשת כהן היא אינה חולצת. הקשה ה"ר משה מפונטייז ומה בכך הא אמרי' בפ"ב דיבמות (דף כ.) דספק חלוצה היכא דנכנסה שרי"ל דתנן התם אם קדמו וכנסו אין מוציאין מידם ואמרינן בגמ' תני שלא אפילו שניהם כהנים מ"ט חלוצה דרבנן ועל ספק חלוצה לא גזרו ואומר רבי דהכא דלאינה חולצת בשמעתין לא משום שאם חלצה (לא) יהא מחויב להוציאה אלא כיון דאפשר בלא חליצה מוטב שלא תחלוץ שלא הוציא לעז על בניה כעין שמצינו בפרק בתרא דיבמות (דף קיט.) דתנן האשה שהלך בעלה וצרתה למדינת הים ובאו ואמרו לה מת בעליך לא תנשא ולא תתייבם עד שתדע שמא מעוברת צרתה ואמר בגמ' ולעולם אמר זעירי ג' לעצמה ט' לחבירתה וחולצת ממ"נ פי' שאם נתעברה צרתה וילדה מותרת לשוק בלא חליצה ואם לא נתעברה הרי חליצה פוטרת ר' יוחנן אמר לעצמה ג' לחבירתה לעולם ופריך ותחלוץ ממ"נ ומשני גזירה שמא יהא ולד של קיימא ונמצא מצריכה כרוז לכהונה ולצרכה דילמא איכא דהוי בחליצה ולא הוה בהכרזה ואמרו קא שרו חלוצה לכהונה אלמא אנו מעגנין אשה זו לעולם משום טעמא דנמצא מצריכה כרוז לכהונה ולכך אין אנו מניחים לחלוץ וכל שכן הכא שיש לימנע יותר מחליצה ואיכא למיחש טפי שלא יאמרו קא שרו חלוצה לכהן. מ"ר: **ואם אשת כהן היא אינה חולצת.** דחי הוא אפילו כי לא שהה כרבנן כדאי' בהחולץ (יבמות דף לו: ושם) והא דאמרינן לעיל דהלכה כרשב"ג היינו דוקא באשת ישראל אבל באשת כהן לא קי"ל כוותיה להצריכה חליצה הואיל ואשת כהן היא. מ"ר: **דתניא** הזכר ולא טומטום ואנדרוגינוס. השתא משמע דדריש מלשון זכר ונקבה ולא מיתורא דה' דהזכר ואם נקבה דאם לא כן מאי קפריך בסמוך ומ"ש גבי מילה מאי קרא צריך במילה לרבות אנדרוגינוס והא אדרבה צריך מיעוט גבי ערכין למעוטי אנדרוגינוס אלא ע"כ לאו מיתורא דקרא ממעט ליה מערך איש ואשה אלא ממשמעות דזכר ונקבה הלכך צריך קרא במילה לרבות אנדרוגינוס וכ"מ נמי דגבי קידוש ממעט אנדרוגינוס בלא שום ייתור כדמוכח בפרק טרף בקלפי ביומא (דף מג. ושם) דאמר תנן התם הכל כשרים לקדש כו' ומפרש אשה מנלן אמר קרא ונתן ולא ונתנה כו' ומההיא טעמא דממעט אשה ממעט אנדרוגינוס וקשה לרבי דבנדה פרק המפלת (דף כח: ושם) מייתינן הך מילתא דערכין וקאמר טעמא דכתב רחמנא הזכר ואם נקבה הא מזכר ונקבה לחוד לא הוה ממעט להו אלמא מיתורא דואם וה' דהזכר קדריש ואומר רבי דודאי מיתורא קדריש כדמשמע התם והא דאיצטריך כל זכר גבי מילה לרבות אנדרוגינוס כי היכי דלא נילף מערכין ומשום הכי גבי קידוש לא צריך קרא למעט אנדרוגינוס דילפינן מערכין וממילה לא ילפינן דאית לן למילף מערכין לחומרא ופסול לקדש והא דאמר רב בהמפלת (גם זה שם) טומטום ואנדרוגינוס שראו לובן ואודם כאחת אין חייבין על ביאת מקדש ושורפין עליו את התרומה ונפקא ליה התם ביאת מקדש מדכתיב מזכר ועד נקבה תשלחו זכר ודאי נקבה ודאית ולא טומטום ואנדרוגינוס ופריך התם וכל היכא דכתיב זכר ונקבה למעוטי טומטום ואנדרוגינוס והתניא כו' דטעמא דכתב רחמנא הזכר ואם נקבה כו' והשתא מאי קפריך דבלא יתור נמי שפיר ממעט טומטום ואנדרוגינוס משום דילפינן מערכין וי"ל דכי גמרי מערכין לחומרא כמו גבי קידוש אבל לקולא לפוטרו מביאת מקדש כשראה לובן ואודם כאחת לא ילפינן מערכין אלא אדרבה ילפינן ממילה לחומרא לחייבו על ביאת מקדש מיהו קשה לרבי מהא דתני בבכורות בפרק אלו מומין (דף מב. ושם) הזכר ולא הנקבה כשהוא אומר למטה זכר שאין תלמוד לומר להוציא טומטום ואנדרוגינוס והשתא אמאי איצטריך קרא למעט טומטום ואנדרוגינוס תיפוק ליה משום דילפינן מערכין לחומרא דהיינו חומרא שאין קדושה חלה עליהם וצריך להביא קרבן אחר ובדוחק אומר ר"י דלאדרבה היא קולא שאם לא מצא אלא אנדרוגינוס יהא יושב ובטל כעין שמצינו גבי סוכה בפרק לולב הגזול (דף לו:) דתניא ר' יהודה אומר אין סוכה נוהגת אלא בד' מינים שבלולב והדין נותן ומה לולב שאינו בלילות כבימים כו' אמרו לו כל דין שאתה דן שתחילתו להחמיר וסופו להקל אינו דין לא מצא ד' מינין יהא יושב ובטל ומיהו לא דמיא שפיר להאי דהתם דלאי סופו להקל שאם לא ימצא ד' מינים כל ימי סוכה נמצא המצוה עוברת וא"א לעשותה עוד אפילו ימצא אחרי כן אבל גבי קרבן אם אינו מוצא עכשיו אלא אנדרוגינוס אחר זמן ימצא וא"כ תחילתו וסופו להחמיר הוא ועוד אומר רבי דהשתא קרא דהזכר גבי עולת נדבה הוא דכתיב ולא גבי חובה הלכך לא שייך התם יהא יושב ובטל כיון שאינו מחויב שום קרבן. מ"ר: **הזכר** ולא טומטום ואנדרוגינוס. בבכורות בפרק (א) אלו מומין (מב. ושם) אמר סמי מכאן טומטום דתנן התם טומטום ואנדרוגינוס אין שוחטין עליו לא במקדש ולא במדינה רבי ישמעאל אומר אין מום גדול מזה וחכ"א אינו בכור אלא נגזז ונעבד ואמר בגמ' אר"ח מחלוקת באנדרוגינוס אבל טומטום דברי הכל ספיקא הוא וקדוש מספיקא אמר ליה (ב) אלא מעתה בערכין יערך אלמה תניא הזכר ולא טומטום ואנדרוגינוס ומשני סמי מכאן טומטום ומשמע דהכי פריך אלמה תניא הזכר ולא טומטום (ג) וכיון דאמרת דספיקא היא אצטריך קרא למעוטי ספיקא ומאי קשיא דבשלמא בההיא סוגיא דלעיל דהתם פריך גבי אנדרוגינוס איצטריך קרא למעוטי ספיקא שפיר פריך שהרי אין סברא לומר שיהא ספק לפסוק דודאי ברור למקרא אם הוא זכר או נקבה ואם הוא אמת שהפסוק חושבו זכר למה ימעטנו שלא יהא קדוש לעולה ואם קרא חשיב ליה נקבה א"כ לכתוב למעטו (ד) [ו] אלא טומטום ודאי צריך קרא שיש מהן זכרים ויש מהן נקבות וכי האי גוונא שייך שפיר למקרא למעטו כיון שהוא ספק לנו אם הוא זכר או נקבה כעין שמצינו גבי מעשר בהמה דתנן בפ' בתרא דבכורות (דף נח:) ומייתי לה בפ"ק דב"מ (דף ו:) קפץ אחד מן המנויין לתוכן כולן פטורין ומפרש התם טעמא דעשירי וודאי אמר רחמנא ולא עשירי ספק וכן בנגעים ספק בהרת קדמה לשער לבן קדם לבהרת ונפקא לן בשלהי מסכת נזיר (דף סה.) דטהור מדכתיב לטהרו או לטמאו שפתח הכתוב תחילה בטהרה ונראה לר' דה"פ מילתא דרב חסדא אבל טומטום קדוש מספיקא משום דלכל כמה דמצינן לאוקמי קרא למעט אנדרוגינוס דממעטי להו רבנן מדכתיב הזכר כדדריש התם לעיל לית לן לאוקמי לקרא למעוטי טומטום משום דאם הוא זכר ודאי אין סברא למעוטי ואם הוא נקבה אין צריך קרא דהשתא פריך שפיר מערכין דלא הוה לן למעוטי טומטום כיון דאיכא לאוקמי קרא לאנדרוגינוס לית לן למעוטי טומטום מיניה דליכא למימר ואם נקבה לאנדרוגינוס לא איצטריך דככר מיעטוה מהזכר (ה) מ"מ הוה אמינא נהי דמעטיה קרא מערך איש מיהו לא גרע מאשה ויהא לו לכל הפחות ערך אשה הלכך לאנדרוגינוס נמי אצטריך ואם נקבה לפיכך הוצרכו לתרץ סמי מכאן טומטום והא דתני בפ"ק דחגיגה (דף ד. ושם) זכורך להוציא טומטום ואנדרוגינוס ולא פריך מינה בבכורות לרב חסדא ולישני סמי מכאן טומטום ונראה לר' משום דקרא יתירא (ו) למעט טומטום דתרי זכורך כתיבי והא דפריך בפ"ק דחגיגה בשלמא אנדרוגינוס איצטריך סד"א הואיל ואית ליה זכרות ליחייב קמ"ל דבריה הוא בפני עצמו אלא טומטום ספיקא הוא איצטריך קרא למעוטי ספיקא ומשני כשביליו מבחוץ ונראה לרבי דשפיר פריך דהתם ודאי לא הוה צריך קרא למעוטי טומטום דפשיטא בלא קרא דלא מייתי עולת ראייה דהיכי נעביד מספיקא לא מייתי על תנאי דאם נקבה הוא תהא עולת נדבה דהא עולת ראייה לא בעי סמיכה ואסור לסמוך משום עבודה בקדשים [ועולת נדבה בעי סמיכה] ואם לא יסמוך טוב שלא יביא כמו שמצינו גבי פסח בפסחים פרק האשה (דף פח:) דתניא חבורה שנתערבו עורות פסחיהן ונמצאה יבלת באחת מהן כולן יצאו לבית השריפה ופטורין מלעשות פסח שני כו' עד דפריך ונייתי מותר הפסח ומשני משום סמיכה דאילו מותר הפסח בעי סמיכה ואילו פסח לא בעי סמיכה אלמא משום סמיכה נמנעים מלעשות פסח כ"ש מלהביא עולת ראייה ובבכורות על מילתא דרב חסדא לא הוה מצי לשנויי כשביליו מבחוץ דכ"ש דלא הוה ליה לקרא למעוטיה. מ"ר. וקשה לי לרב חסדא אמאי ממעט רב בנדה טומטום

מסורת הש"ס

א) [יבמות לו: ליתא משרשיא], ב) בכורות מב. ערכין ד: נדה כח., ג) [שם כח.], ד) [דף קיט.], ה) [גי' רש"ל הא קל וחומר שלא שייך התם יושב ובטל ועוד סבר רבי כו' ולא גבי סוכה והוי סופו להחמיר כיון שאינו מחויב שום קרבן], ו) ס"א אלא טומטום ד"ל שספקותו חושבו לא זכר ולא נקבה דיש מהם זכרים כו'.

הגהות הב"ח

(א) תוס' ד"ה הזכר וכו' בבכורות בפרק אלו מומין וכו' אין לך מום גדול: (ב) בא"ד אמר ליה רבא אלא מעתה וכו': (ג) בא"ד דכיון דאמרת: (ד) בא"ד אלא טומטום דיש לומר שאין המקרא חושבו אלא זכר ולא נקבה דיש מהן זכרים: (ה) בא"ד מהזכר דמ"מ ה"א נמי: (ו) בא"ד דקרא יתירא אינה למעט:

רב נסים גאון

ולאחר כן אמרו לאכלה להביא בן ח' שאין שחיטתו מטהרתו כלומר בן ח' חדשים בבהמה גסה טהורה על דעת כמו שאמרו בפרק א' מסכת בכורות (דף) בבהמה גסה יולדת לט' חדשים] טהורה בחודש ח' הרי הוא כמת ולא תועיל בו השחיטה להוציאו מידי נבילה לענין הטומאה כמו שמעלת בטריפה מכאן הראיה שהקדמנו ממה שאמרו ויש מן הבהמה שאינה מטמאה פרט לטריפה

תורה אור השלם

א) וְהָיָה עֶרְכְּךָ הַזָּכָר מִבֶּן עֶשְׂרִים שָׁנָה וְעַד בֶּן שִׁשִּׁים שָׁנָה וְהָיָה עֶרְכְּךָ חֲמִשִּׁים שֶׁקֶל כֶּסֶף בְּשֶׁקֶל הַקֹּדֶשׁ: (ויקרא כז, ג)
ב) וְאִם נְקֵבָה הִוא וְהָיָה עֶרְכְּךָ שְׁלֹשִׁים שָׁקֶל: (ויקרא כז, ד)

ליקוטי רש"י

אם אשת ישראל היא. אם זה שקדשה ישראל הוא שאם תחלוץ לא תיאסר עליו מן הינם לאחר קדושין אלא מיאסר על בעלה חולצת. **אם אשת כהן היא.** ואם זה שקדשה כהן הוא שאם תחלוץ תיאסר עליו אינה חולצת ומקילין אולד [יבמות לו:]. **לצפרא הדר ביה.** ושמעתי מפיו שאינה חולצת [שם לז:]. **הזכר ולא טומטום.** והיה ערכך הזכר ומריבויא דה"א נפקא לן ולא טומטום [בכורות מב.]. **טומטום.** אטום אינו ניכר בו לא זכרות ולא נקבות וספק זכר ספק נקבה הוא [רשב"ם ב"ב קמ:]. **ואם נקבה.** מריבויא דאם נפקא לן ולא טומטום וכו' [בכורות שם ע"ש].

[מכאן שייך לדף קלז.] **וסתם ספרא.** תורת כהנים ר' יהודה היא הכי

עין משפט נר מצוה

מז א מיי' פ"כ מהל' יסוה"ב הלכה כא סמג עשין נ טוש"ע אה"ע סי' קסד סעיף ז:
מח ב מיי' פ"א מהל' ערכין הלכה ה:

רבינו חננאל

ודבי ר' אושעיא איזה בן ח' כל שלא יצאו לו חדשיו. ר' אומר סימנים ניכרין בו שערו וצפרניו שלא גמרו וכדרך שבן שמנה חדשים באדם נפל כך בן ח' בבהמה גסה וכן ד' בדקה נפל. רשב"ג אומר כל ששהה באדם ל' יום אינו נפל וכו'. והלכתא כת"ק דאמר בן שמנה אין שחיטתו מטהרתו אלא אמרינן מת היה ונבילה היא ומטמאה שאין שחיטה מועלת בנבילה דתנינן מתניתין סתמא כוותיה בפרק בהמה המקשה לילד ופירשנוהו שם. מי יש במינו שחיטה מי אין במינו שחיטה בן ח' חי אין שחיטתו מטהרתו. לפי שאין למינו שחיטה. וסוגיא דשמעתא שאין שחיטתו מטהרתו בפחות משמנה ימים אלא בדמוחזק לן שכלו חדשיו כגון שהיתה בהמה קשורה לו בביתו ט' חדשים לגסה וד' לדקה וילדה וברי לן שלא עלה [עליה] זכר בביתו וזה ששנינו במשנתנו סתם תינוק בן יום א' מטמא בזיבה. ומטמא בנגעים ומטמא בטמא מת. וזוקק ליבום ופוסל מן היבום ומאכיל בתרומה ופוסל בתרומה ונוחל ומנחיל וההורגו חייב והרי הוא לאביו ולאמו ולכל קרוביו כחתן שלם ואמרינן בגמרא למאי הלכתא אמר רב פפא לענין אבלות לימא מתניתין דלא כרשב"ג דתניא רשב"ג אומר כל ששהה באדם ל' יום אינו נפל הא לא שהה (ספק) ספיקא הוי. ומפרקינן דקים ליה ביה שכלו לו חדשיו. ודין כל השנוים במשנה זאת דינם אחד במוחזק לן ביה שכלו לו חדשיו ומיהא הוו (מיתא) [מתאבלין] באלי בריה דרב דימי בריה דרב יוסף ורב כהנא בינוקא דשכיב בגו תלתין יומין דהוו מוחזקין שכלו לו חדשיו: **אתמר** מת בתוך ל' ועמדה ונתקדשה אמר רבינא משמיה דרבא אם אשת ישראל היא חולצת אם אשת כהן היא אינה חולצת ורב שרביא משמיה דרבא אמר אחת זו ואחת זו חולצת. א"ל רבינא לרב שרביא באורתא אמר רבא הכי כי דאמרת לצפרא הדר ביה. א"ל יהא רעוא דתשרי תרבא כלומר עתה תאסר ואחר שעה תתירה. יהי רצון שתתיר אף החלב. והלכתא כרבינא משמא דרבא. והאמר רבינא והדר ביה רבא מההיא: **ר' יהודה** מתיר באנדרוגינוס פי' למולו בשבת אמר רב שיזבי אמר רב חסדא לא לכל ששחטה

קאמר בסנהדרין (פו.) והא בתורת כהנים היא דהא קרא בספר ויקרא כתיב [יומא מא.]. **לקדש.** לתת מים על האפר בכלי חרס [שם מג.]. לערב מים חיים באפר חטאת טעמייהו דרבנן ורבי יהודה מפרש במס' יומא בפרק טרף בקלפי (מג.) [ערכין ג.]. **ושכח ומל את של אחר השבת בשבת חייב.** דטעה בדבר מצוה ולא עשה מצוה הוא דעדיין לא הגיע זמנו ומודה ר' יהושע דמייב. **את של ערב שבת בשבת.** קסבור שהוא של שבת וזה של ערב שבת היה אתמול הוה לו שנהגם ומילה שלא בזמנה אינה דוחה את השבת הואיל ועבר זמנה יתמין עד למחר. **ר' אליעזר מחייב חטאת.** דלית ליה טועה בדבר מצוה ועשה מצוה פטור. **ורבי יהושע פוטר.** דטעה בדבר מצוה ועשה מצוה פטור ואף על גב דהאי לא היה לדעת שבת ועשה שלא כדת מכל מקום מצות מילה קיים [פסחים עב.]. **הכא טריד מצוה.** שהיה טרוד למול את של שבת כדי שלא יעבור זמנו [יבמות לד.]. **על מה נחלקו וכו'.** וקא סלקא דעתך השתא ברישא מחייב ר' מאיר כשמל את שניהם על ידי [שסבור] שנשניהן ככר הגיע זמנן ומל של שבת תחלה שזמנו היום ואחר כך מל את של אתמול ואף על גב דעשה מצוה כיון דלא רמיא עליה כתר דמהליה לשל שבת לאו טועה בדבר מצוה הוא ואמר שבת וההוא בשל לה דלא לקמר שמל את שניהם דהא לא טעי בהכי [ע"ש]. **השתא רבי יהושע סיפא דלא קא עביד מצוה.** דעדיין לא הגיע זמנו פטור רישא דעבד מצוה מחייב. **אמרי דבי ר' ינאי רישא כגון.** שנתחלף לו אתמול של שבת בערב שבת ומלו בערב שבת ועדיין לא נודע טעותו וסבור שזה העומד של שבת הוא ואף על גב דטריד ביה דרמיא מצוה עליה כפי מחשבתו וגם עשה מצוה אפילו הכי חייב משום דלא ניתנה שבת לידחות אלא של שבת וטעה בדבר מצוה ועשה מצוה פטור ואפילו לא עשה מצוה לר' מאיר פטור [פסחים שם].

אִם אֵשֶׁת יִשְׂרָאֵל הִיא – If she is the wife of an Israelite (i.e. the one from who she has accepted *kiddushin* is a non-Kohen, who is permitted to marry a divorcee or a woman who has undergone *chalitzah*), **חוֹלֶצֶת – she must undergo *chalitzah.*** [1] **אִם אֵשֶׁת כֹּהֵן הִיא – If,** however **she is the wife of a Kohen** (i.e. the one from whom she has accepted *kiddushin* is a Kohen, who is forbidden to marry a divorcee),[2] **אֵינָהּ חוֹלֶצֶת – she need not undergo *chalitzah.*** [3]

A differing report of Rava's position:

וְרַב שֵׁרֵבְיָא מִשְּׁמֵיהּ דְּרָבָא אָמַר – But Rav Sheravya in the name of Rava said: אַחַת זוֹ וְאַחַת זוֹ – Both in the case of **this one** who has accepted *kiddushin* from a non-Kohen **and** in the case of **that one** who has accepted *kiddushin* from a Kohen, the law is that **חוֹלֶצֶת – she must undergo *chalitzah.*** [4]

Ravina defends his lenient version of Rava's ruling:

אָמַר לֵיהּ רָבִינָא לְרַב שֵׁרֵבְיָא – Ravina said to Rav Sheravya: בְּאוּרְתָּא אָמַר רָבָא הָכִי – It is true that **at night Rava said so,** i.e. as you report, that she must undergo *chalitzah* even if she has accepted *kiddushin* from a Kohen. **לְצַפְרָא הָדַר בֵּיהּ –** However, **the following morning,** when you were not present, **he recanted** and ruled as I reported in his name, that she need *not* undergo *chalitzah* if she has accepted *kiddushin* from a Kohen.

Rav Sherevya, however, does not accept what Ravina reports as Rava's final decision, and retorts caustically:

אָמַר לֵיהּ – [Rav Sherevya] said to [Ravina]: שְׁרִיתוּהָ – You have ignored the ruling of Rabban Shimon ben Gamliel and **permitted her** to remarry without *chalitzah*!? **יְהֵא רַעֲוָא דְּתִשְׁרוּ תַּרְבָּא – May it be the** Divine **will that you will permit forbidden** animal **fats** to be eaten as well![5]

The Gemara now turns to the final ruling of the Mishnah, which states:

רַבִּי יְהוּדָה מַתִּיר וכו׳ – R' YEHUDAH PERMITS etc. [one to circumcise an androgyne on the Sabbath].

The Gemara elaborates R' Yehudah's view:

אָמַר רַב שִׁיזְבִי אָמַר רַב חִסְדָּא – Rav Shizvi said in the name of Rav Chisda: לֹא לַכֹּל אָמַר רַבִּי יְהוּדָה אַנְדְּרוֹגִינוֹס זָכָר הוּא – Not with respect to all matters did R' Yehudah say that **an androgyne is** considered a definite **male.**[6] **שֶׁאִם אַתָּה אוֹמֵר כֵּן – For if you say** that he did say **so** with respect to all matters, **בַּעֲרָכִין יַעֲרֵךְ –** then **with respect to *erech* vows,**[7] **[the androgyne] should have an *erech,*** i.e. if one vowed the *erech* of an androgyne, he should thereby become obligated to pay the Temple the *erech* of an equivalent male.[8] **וּמְנָלַן דְּלָא מִיעֲרַךְ – And from where** is it known **to us that an androgyne does not have an *erech,*** so that one who vows it does *not* thereby become obligated to pay anything? **דְּתַנְיָא – For it was taught in a Baraisa** in *Sifra*:[9] **,,הַזָּכָר" וְלֹא טוּמְטוּם וְאַנְדְּרוֹגִינוֹס –** The Torah states with regard to *erech* vows: ***THE MALE,***[10] from which we derive: **BUT NOT A *TUMTUM***[11] **OR ANDROGYNE. יָכוֹל לֹא יְהֵא בְּעֶרֶךְ אִישׁ – IT COULD BE** thought **THAT HE** [the *tumtum* or androgyne] **IS NOT** assessed **ACCORDING TO THE *ERECH* OF A MAN, אֲבָל יְהֵא בְּעֶרֶךְ אִשָּׁה – BUT HE IS** assessed **ACCORDING TO THE *ERECH* OF A WOMAN. תַּלְמוּד לוֹמַר ,,הַזָּכָר . . . וְאִם־נְקֵבָה הִוא" –** To dispel this notion **THE TORAH STATES *"THE" MALE . . . AND "IF" SHE IS A FEMALE,***[12] to teach that **זָכָר וַדַּאי נְקֵבָה וַדָּאִית –** only **A DEFINITE MALE** and **A DEFINITE FEMALE** are the proper subjects of an *erech* vow, **וְלֹא טוּמְטוּם וְאַנְדְּרוֹגִינוֹס – BUT NOT A *TUMTUM* OR *ANDROGYNE.***[13] This Baraisa states clearly that an androgyne is not treated as a definite male with regard to *erech* vows.

NOTES

1. The Gemara above (136a) has concluded that the halachah follows Rabban Shimon ben Gamliel, who considers a newborn that does not survive thirty days to be a child that is only questionably viable. In the present case, where such a child is the father's sole surviving issue, we consider the possibility that the child was *not* viable (and that his mother is, therefore, bound to her brother-in-law). And we do not, therefore, allow her to remarry without the benefit of *chalitzah* (to remove that bond) since her undergoing *chalitzah* will not in any way affect her permissibility to her new husband, from whom she has accepted *kiddushin* (see *Rashi;* see also *Aruch LaNer* to *Yevamos* 36b ד״ה שם אם אשת כהן היא, who discusses *Rashi's* comments here).

2. The Torah (*Leviticus* 21:7) prohibits a Kohen from marrying a divorcee. The Rabbis decreed that he also may not marry a woman who has undergone *chalitzah,* since *chalitzah* is akin to the divorce procedure in that it, too, severs the woman's marital bond (see *Kiddushin* 78a; cf. *Rashi* to *Makkos* 13a ד״ה גרושה and *Tosafos* there).

3. For were she to undergo *chalitzah* (even if only to account for the *possibility* that she is subject to the *yibum* bond), then – as a *chalutzah* (woman who has undergone *chalitzah*) – she would be Rabbinically forbidden to remain with her new husband, who is a Kohen (cf. *Tosafos* here; see also *Tos. HaRosh*). In order to preserve this new marriage, we dispense with the *chalitzah,* and rely instead on the view of the Sages above, who do *not* question the child's viability. In their view, she is simply the widow of a man who has died with issue, and she is permitted to marry a Kohen (*Rashi;* see *Yevamos* 36b-37a). And though the Gemara above has concluded that the halachah follows Rabban Shimon ben Gamliel's view, that conclusion is meant only as a stringency, and not as a definitive ruling [since the halachah should by rights follow the majority opinion] (see *Ritva* and *Nimukei Yosef* to *Yevamos* loc. cit.; see also *Tosafos* here, end of ד״ה ואם and *Rosh;* see also *Rosh* to *Yevamos,* end of 4:5).

4. For the halachah in this matter follows Rabban Shimon ben Gamliel's opinion in all its ramifications.

5. See *Hagahos Maharsham,* for an explanation of this strange statement; see also *Rabbeinu Chananel,* and see *Aruch LaNer* to *Yevamos* 37a ד״ה יהא רעוא. [See also *Ritva MHK* ed., who cites *Tosafos'* reading as: תַּרְבָּא, *a divorcee,* rather than תַּרְבָּא, *forbidden fats.*]

6. By ruling that an androgyne is circumcised even on the Sabbath, R' Yehudah would seem to hold that an androgyne is legally deemed to be a definite male. For if an androgyne would be of doubtful status (or classified as a third gender that is neither male nor female), his circumcision would not override the Sabbath prohibitions. Rav Shizvi in the name of Rav Chisda, however, now demonstrates that R' Yehudah's ruling in our Mishnah is specific to the case of circumcision. But with respect to other laws, R' Yehudah does *not* consider the androgyne to be a male (see 137a note 8).

7. An *erech* vow is a declaration by which a person vows to donate the *erech* [value] of some individual to the Temple. With regard to such vows, the Torah assigns a fixed *erech* (valuation), based on age and gender, for all people, regardless of an individual's actual "market" value. For example, if one vowed the *erech* of a male between the ages of five and twenty, he must give a fixed *erech* of twenty *shekels;* the fixed *erech* of a male between the ages of twenty and sixty is fifty *shekels* (see *Leviticus* 27:1-8).

8. Yet, the law is (as the Gemara will soon show) that one who vows the *erech* of an androgyne does not thereby become obligated to pay anything at all.

9. *Sifra* (or: *Toras Kohanim*) is a collection of Baraisos on the Book of *Leviticus.*

10. *Leviticus* 27:3. The verse in its entirety reads: וְהָיָה עֶרְכְּךָ הַזָּכָר מִבֶּן עֶשְׂרִים שָׁנָה וְעַד בֶּן־שִׁשִּׁים שָׁנָה וְהָיָה עֶרְכְּךָ חֲמִשִּׁים שֶׁקֶל כֶּסֶף בְּשֶׁקֶל הַקֹּדֶשׁ, *The erech valuation of the male shall be: for someone from twenty years to sixty years of age, the valuation shall be fifty silver shekels, in shekels of the Sanctuary.* The Baraisa is expounding the superfluous *hei* in the word הַזָּכָר, *"the" male* (*Rashi;* see *Tosafos* ד״ה דתניא).

11. A *tumtum* is a person born with the genitals covered by a thick membrane, and whose gender, therefore, is unknown.

12. The verse that states *the male* (cited in note 10) is followed immediately by the verse: וְאִם־נְקֵבָה הִוא וְהָיָה עֶרְכְּךָ שְׁלֹשִׁים שָׁקֶל, *And if she is a female, the valuation shall be thirty shekels.* The Baraisa now expounds both *"the" male* (as expounded above) and *"if" a female,* where the expression "and if" is superfluous (*Rashi*).

13. Thus, if someone vows to give the *erech* of a *tumtum* or androgyne, the vow does not take effect, and he owes nothing to the Temple.

וּסְתָם סִפְרָא רַבִּי יְהוּדָה – Now, an anonymous Baraisa in *Sifra* generally reflects the view of **R' Yehudah.** Thus we see that R' Yehudah does not regard an androgyne as a male with respect to *erech* vows.

The Gemara brings further proof that in general R' Yehudah does *not* treat androgynes as males:

אָמַר רַב נַחְמָן בַּר יִצְחָק – **Rav Nachman bar Yitzchak said:** אַף אֲנַן נַמִּי תְּנֵינָא – **We have also learned in a Mishnah** that R' Yehudah does not consider androgynes as male. For a Mishnah states:[1] הַכֹּל כְּשֵׁרִים לְקַדֵּשׁ – ALL ARE QUALIFIED TO PREPARE the "purification waters,"[2] חוּץ מֵחֵרֵשׁ שׁוֹטֶה וְקָטָן – EXCEPT FOR A DEAF-MUTE, A DERANGED PERSON OR A MINOR.[3] רַבִּי יְהוּדָה מַכְשִׁיר בְּקָטָן – R' YEHUDAH, however, QUALIFIES A MINOR,[4] וּפוֹסֵל בְּאִשָּׁה וְאַנְדְּרוֹגִינוֹס – BUT DISQUALIFIES A FEMALE[5] AND AN ANDROGYNE.[6] שְׁמַע מִינָּהּ – **Learn from this** Mishnah that R' Yehudah does not legally deem an androgyne to be a definite male.

The Gemara explains why R' Yehudah considers the androgyne a male only with respect to circumcision:

וּמַאי שְׁנָא מִילָה – **And what is different** about **circumcision** that causes the androgyne to be deemed a male specifically with respect to that context? מִשּׁוּם דִּכְתִיב ,,הִמּוֹל לָכֶם כָּל־זָכָר" – **Because it is written** in the Torah with respect to circumcision: ***Circumcise for you "all" your males.***[7] The inclusive word "all" serves to include androgynes as well.[8]

Mishnah As we have previously learned (132a), only a circumcision performed on the eighth day overrides the Sabbath prohibition against inflicting a wound, not one performed earlier or later. Our Mishnah discusses the liability of a person who inadvertently performed circumcision on the Sabbath upon a baby that was either less or more than eight days old:

מִי שֶׁהָיוּ לוֹ שְׁנֵי תִינוֹקוֹת – **One who had two infants** to circumcise, אֶחָד לָמוּל אַחַר הַשַּׁבָּת – **one to circumcise after the Sabbath** וְאֶחָד לָמוּל בְּשַׁבָּת – **and one to circumcise on the Sabbath,**[9] וְשָׁכַח וּמָל אֶת שֶׁל אַחַר הַשַּׁבָּת בְּשַׁבָּת – **and he forgot** which one was which **and circumcised the one due after the Sabbath on the Sabbath,**[10] חַיָּיב – **he is liable** to a *chatas* for having inadvertently desecrated the Sabbath.[11] אֶחָד לָמוּל בְּעֶרֶב שַׁבָּת – If he had two infants, **one to circumcise on Friday**[12] וְאֶחָד לָמוּל בְּשַׁבָּת – **and one to circumcise on the Sabbath,** וְשָׁכַח וּמָל אֶת שֶׁל עֶרֶב שַׁבָּת בְּשַׁבָּת – **and he forgot and circumcised the Friday one on the Sabbath:** רַבִּי אֱלִיעֶזֶר מְחַיֵּיב חַטָּאת – **R' Eliezer declares** him **liable** to **a** ***chatas,***[13] וְרַבִּי יְהוֹשֻׁעַ פּוֹטֵר – **and R' Yehoshua exempts** him.[14]

NOTES

1. *Parah* 5:4.

2. I.e. to mix the ashes of the *parah adumah* into spring water [as described in *Numbers* 19:17] (*Rashi;* see also *Rashi* to *Yoma* 43a ד״ה לקדש with *Tosafos* there).

3. The Gemara in *Yoma* (43a) presents the derivation for this law.

4. See *Yoma* ibid.

5. Women are disqualified, for the Torah states (*Numbers* 19:17): וְלָקְחוּ לַטָּמֵא מֵעֲפַר שְׂרֵפַת הַחַטָּאת וְנָתַן עָלָיו מַיִם חַיִּים אֶל־כֶּלִי, *And they shall take for the tamei from the ashes of the burning of the purification offering and "he" shall put spring water upon it in a vessel.* The particular use of the masculine singular וְנָתַן, *and "he" shall put,* (a shift from the plural *"they" shall take* used at the beginning of the verse) teaches that only a male, and not a female, may mix the "purification waters" (see *Rashi* and *Tosafos* to *Yoma* loc. cit.).

6. Because an androgyne is possibly [not a male but] a female (*Rashi* to *Yoma* loc. cit., from *Yevamos* 72b).

7. *Genesis* 17:10.

8. Thus, in the final analysis, R' Yehudah considers androgynes to be of doubtful gender. Therefore in regard to preparing the purification waters, which requires specifically a male, they are disqualified. With regard to *erech* vows, since androgynes are anomalous, they are not assigned the *erech* of men *or* women (as expounded above from *"the" male . . . and "if" a female*). With respect to circumcision, the word *"all" males* teaches that regardless of gender, all male genitalia require circumcision (*Tosafos* to *Bechoros* 42a, end of ד״ה אלמה; cf. *Tosafos* above, 136b ד״ה דתניא and *Chidushei HaRan*).

[The general status of an androgyne is a subject of dispute. Various possibilities are that an androgyne is: (a) a definite male; (b) possibly male and possibly female; (c) a third gender that is neither male or female; and (d) part male and part female. These possibilities emerge primarily from *Bikkurim* ch. 4 and *Yevamos* 81a ff., with the commentaries of the Rishonim thereon (see also *Kuntreis Acharon* of *Ramban,* printed at the end of *Chidushei HaRamban* to *Yevamos;* and *Raavad* to *Hil. Shofar* 2:2, and to *Hil. Terumos* 7:16 with *Radbaz* and *Kesef Mishneh*).]

9. For example, one was born the previous Sabbath and the other on Sunday.

10. I.e. he mixed up the infants and circumcised the infant that was supposed to be circumcised on Sunday on the Sabbath (see *Kereisos* 19b and *Rashi* there ד״ה תינוקות).

11. Since this child is less than eight days old, there is as yet no mitzvah to circumcise him. The circumciser has therefore made a wound in the child for no purpose and is thus liable (*Rashi;* see further in note 14).

[The *melachah* involved here is חוֹבֵל, *wounding* (a *toladah* of שׁוֹחֵט, *slaughtering*). Although this act of wounding is completely destructive (since it is not a valid circumcision), our Mishnah nonetheless considers him liable, for the Tanna of our Mishnah is R' Shimon who rules (see Gemara 106a) that wounding and burning are exceptions to the general rule for destructive acts (see *Kereisos* 19b). However, *Rambam* asserts in his *Commentary* (quoted in *Tos. Yom Tov* and explained in *Tos. R' Akiva)* that our Mishnah can conform even to the opinion of R' Yehudah who states (above) that completely destructive acts of burning and wounding are also exempt. For though the circumcision in this case was invalid because it was performed prematurely, the act of removing the foreskin was nevertheless constructive, since there is no longer any necessity to remove the foreskin (see *Tos. R' Akiva Eiger* and *Lechem Shamayim*).]

See *Kereisos* 19b for a discussion of why the circumciser is not exempt under the rule of מִתְעַסֵּק, *one who is preoccupied with doing another act* (see above, 72b note 2).

12. [I.e. he was born on Friday and should therefore have been circumcised before the Sabbath. For some reason, however, he was not circumcised on that day. Since the Sabbath is not his eighth day, he may not be circumcised then but must wait for Sunday.]

13. Although he performed a mitzvah of circumcision (since the infant is more than eight days old), he is nevertheless liable because the mitzvah of circumcising an infant more than eight days old does not override the Sabbath (*Rashi*).

14. Since he erred while attempting to perform a mitzvah (the circumcision of the infant born the previous Sabbath) and in the end he did, in fact, perform a mitzvah (the circumcision of the infant born the previous Friday), R' Yehoshua exempts him from a *chatas.* The Gemara will explain the reason for this. [In the first case of the Mishnah, however, R' Yehoshua agrees that he is liable, for although he erred while attempting to perform a mitzvah, he did not in the end perform a mitzvah – because the child he circumcised was *less* than eight days old and not yet eligible for circumcision.]

[For a discussion of the status of a circumcision made before the infant's eighth day, see *Yoreh Deah* 262:1 with commentators, as well as *Shaagas Aryeh,* §52 and §54, *Korban Nesanel* here §4, *Chasam Sofer* חידושי סוגיא דטעה בדבר מצוה, *Teshuvos Ksav Sofer, Orach Chaim* 35, and *Tz'lach* to *Pesachim* 72a.]

עין משפט נר מצוה

נ א מיי' פ"ו מהל' פרה הלכה ב סמג עשין רלב:

נא ב ג מיי' פ"ב מהל' שגגות הלכה ט:

נא ד מיי' פ"א מהל' מילה הלכה יב סמג עשין כח טוש"ע י"ד סי' רסב סעיף ט:

נב ה מיי' שם הלכה טו סמג שם טוש"ע י"ד סי' רסב סעיף ג:

נג ו ז מיי' פ"ב מהל' מילה הלכה ג ה סמג שם טוש"ע י"ד סי' רסד סעיף ה ו:

רבינו חננאל

א"ר יהודה אנדרוגינוס זכר הוא. שאם אי אתה אומר כן יערך ומנ"ל דלא מערך דתניא הזכר ולא טומטום ואנדרוגינוס כו' ופשוטה היא ומסקינן בה ומאי שנא גבי מילה דכתיב המול לכם כל זכר כל לרבות. ויש מי שאומר הלכתא כרבנן דאמרי ספק ואנדרוגינוס אין מחללין עליו את השבת ואין הלכה כר' יהודה ומדחזינן רב חסדא דריש לטעמיה דר' יהודה ש"מ הלכתא כוותיה: **מתניתין מי שהיו** לו ב' תינוקות אחד למול אחר השבת ואחד למול בשבת ושכח ומל את של אחר השבת בשבת חייב וכו' [ואמרינן בגמ'] רב הונא מתני חייב ורב יהודא מתני פטור פי' רב הונא מתני חייב דמוקים ליה למתניתין לר"ש דאמר ר"ש לא נחלקו ר' אליעזר (ור"ש) [ור' יהושע] על מי שהיו לו א) דקיי"ל סתם משנה ר' מאיר ובהא תנא דבי ר' חייא פליגי עליה ורב הונא דמוקים לה כר' שמעון כוותיה עבדינן וחלוקת ר' אליעזר ור' יהושע דברים ברורין הן. (שנים) ושניהם מע"ז למדוה דהא איתקשא כל התורה כולה לע"ז ר' אליעזר סבירא כע"ז מה ע"ז אמרה תורה לא תעבוד ואם תעבוד ע"ז בשגגה מכל מקום חייב חטאת. כן אמרה תורה בשבת. המחלל השבת בשגגה מ"מ חייב חטאת. ור' יהושע סבר התם לגבי ע"ז לא נתכוין לקיים המצוה הכא בשבת נתכוין לקיים מצות מילה. לפיכך פטור הוא והלכתא כר' יהושע וכדמתניתין ר' שמעון: **אחד** למול ערב שבת ואחד למול בשבת ושכח ומל את של שבת בע"ש ואת של ע"ש בשבת פטור כי מ"מ מצוה עשה. ואע"פ שמל בט'. אבל בזמן ששכח ומל את של אחר השבת בשבת כיון שלא עשה מצוה כי בו' מלו אפילו ר' יהושע מודה שחייב חטאת. וכן הלכה וכל היכא דפליג ר' אליעזר ור' יהושע הלכה כר' יהושע חוץ ממקומות ידועים. וזה אינו מהם. וכן רב הונא הלכתא כוותיה דשכיח גבי ריש גלותא וגרסינן הלכתא כוותין או הלכתא כוותייכו כו': **מתניתין קטן** נימול לשמונה לתשעה כו' קטן חולה אין מלין אותו עד שיבריא. אמר שמואל חלצתו חמה נותנין לו כל ז' להברותו כשמואל דאמר שחלצתו חמה שבעת ימים

רש"י

והא סתם ספרא הוא דבתורת כהנים תניא לה וסתם ספרא רבי יהודה: לקדש. מי חטאת לתת אפר על המים: מכשיר בקטן ופוסל באשה. טעמיה מפרש בסדר יומא בפ"ג: ובאנדרוגינוס. שמע מינה דלרבי יהודה כאשה משוי ליה: כל זכר. ריבויא הוא: מתני' ושכח ומל את של אחר השבת בשבת חייב. דטעה בדבר מצוה ולא עשה מצוה הוא ועבד ליה חבורה שלא לצורך והאי אפילו רבי יהושע מודה: אחד למול בשבת ואחד למול בע"ש ושכח ומל את של ע"ש בשבת ר"א מחייב חטאת. דמילה שלא בזמנה אינה דוחה שבת ואע"ג דטעה בדבר מצוה שהיה טרוד באותו של שבת ומתוך כך טעה בזה ואף בזה עשה מצוה שהרי ראוי הוא למול אלא שאינו דוחה שבת ס"ל לר"א טעה בדבר מצוה ועשה מצוה שיש בה חיוב חטאת חייב ורבי יהושע פוטר דס"ל טעה בדבר מצוה ועשה מצוה פטור: גמ' רב הונא מתני. במתניתין ברישא חייב לדברי הכל כדמתנינן לה לכן: ורב יהודה מתני ברישא פטור. דמוקי לה בשכח ומל את של ע"ש בשבת ופלוגתא היא בשל אחר השבת בשבת: שהוא חייב. דאע"ג דטריד במצוה וטעה בה כיון דלאו מצוה שעדיין לא הגיע זמנו למול חייב: אלא מע"ז. שהוקשו כל חטאות שבתורה לחטאת ע"ז דכתיב תורה אחת יהיה לכם וגו' בפרשת שלח לך אנשים גבי קרבן ע"ז: ור' יהושע התם. עובד עבודת כוכבים לא עשה מצוה: ה"ג רב יהודה מתני פטור דתניא אמר ר"מ לא נחלקו ר"א ורבי יהושע על שהיו לו שני תינוקות אחד למול ע"ש כו': ה"ג ורבי יהושע התם לא טריד במצוה הכא טריד במצוה. טרוד להתעסק במצוה גמורה שהרי אחד מהם זמנו היום וטרוד לבו למהר ולעשות ומתוך טרדו טעה ומל את זה שאין בו מצוה כלל: ושכח ומל של ע"ש בשבת שהוא חייב. לקמיה מפרש לה: דלא ניתנה שבת לידחות. שאין לו תינוק שיהא זמנו היום הלכך לא היה טרוד היום במצוה שלא היה מוטל עליו כלום לעשות ולא היה לו לטעות: מתני' נולד בין השמשות נימול לט'. שהרי ליום שמיני של אחר הוא נימול ושמא בין השמשות יום הוא ונימול לט': היה היום ע"ש. א"א למולו בשבת הבאה דשמא ט' הוא והויא ליה מילה שלא בזמנה ואינה דוחה שבת וצריך להמתין עד לאחר השבת שהוא עשירי: חל יו"ט להיות אחר השבת. אין מילה שלא בזמנה דוחה אותו ונימול לי"א: גמ' חלצתו חמה. נשלף ממנו החולי ויצא מגופו: דתני לודא. שם חכם: יום הבראתו כיום הולדו. ממתינין לו כיום הולדו: מאי לאו. יום הולדו דווקא קאמר דלא בעינן מעת לעת: לא. כיום הולדו דקתני למיתב ליה ז' מיהו עדיף יום הבראתו מהא דבעינן מעת לעת ומהא ליכא למשמע מידי: מתני' ציצין. רצועות של בשר שנשארו מן הערלה: עטרה. היא שפה גבוה המקפת את הגיד סביב וממנה משפע ויורד לראשו: ואינו אוכל בתרומה. אם כהן הוא דילפינן ביבמות (ד' ע.) שערל אסור בתרומה: ואם היה בעל בשר. שהיה שמן ונראה כשר שלמעלה מעלגלות לאחר שניטלה ערלה כולה כאילו אותו בשר חוזר וחופה את הגיד: מתקנו. ומשפע באיזמל מאותו עובי: מפני מראית העין. שלא יהא נראה כערל:

גמרא

(א) וסתם ספרא רבי יהודה אמר רב נחמן בר יצחק אף אנן נמי תנינא א הכל כשרים לקדש חוץ מחש"ו רבי יהודה מכשיר בקטן ופוסל באשה ואנדרוגינוס ש"מ ומאי שנא מילה משום דכתיב א המול לכם כל זכר: **מתני'** ג מי שהיו לו שני תינוקות אחד למול אחר השבת ואחד למול בשבת ושכח ומל את של אחר השבת בשבת חייב אחד למול בע"ש ואחד למול בשבת ושכח ומל את של ע"ש בשבת רבי אליעזר מחייב חטאת ורבי יהושע פוטר: **גמ'** רב הונא מתני חייב רב יהודה מתני פטור רב הונא מתני חייב דתניא אמר ר"ש בן אלעזר לא נחלקו רבי ד אליעזר ור' יהושע על מי שהיו לו ב' תינוקות אחד למול בשבת ואחד למול אחר השבת ושכח ומל את של אחר השבת בשבת שהוא חייב על מה נחלקו על מי שהיו לו ב' תינוקות א' למול בע"ש וא' למול בשבת ושכח ומל את של ע"ש בשבת שר' אליעזר מחייב חטאת ורבי יהושע פוטר ושניהם לא למדוה אלא מעבודת כוכבים ר' אליעזר סבר כעבודת כוכבים מה עבודת כוכבים אמר רחמנא לא תעביד וכי עביד מיחייב ה"נ לא שנא ורבי יהושע התם דלאו מצוה הכא מצוה רב יהודה מתני פטור דתניא א"ר מאיר ב לא נחלקו ר"א ורבי יהושע על מי שהיו לו ב' תינוקות אחד למול בע"ש ואחד למול בשבת ושכח ומל את של ע"ש בשבת שהוא פטור על מה נחלקו על מי שהיו לו ב' תינוקות אחד למול אחר השבת וא' למול בשבת ושכח ומל את של אחר השבת בשבת שר"א מחייב חטאת ורבי יהושע ג פוטר ושניהם לא למדוה אלא מעבודת כוכבים ר"א סבר כעבודת כוכבים מה עבודת כוכבים אמר רחמנא לא תעביד וכי עביד מיחייב ה"נ לא שנא ור' יהושע התם לא טריד מצוה הכא טריד מצוה ה תני ר' חייא אומר היה ר"מ לא נחלקו רבי ו אליעזר ורבי יהושע על מי שהיו לו ב' תינוקות א' למול בע"ש וא' למול בשבת ושכח ומל את של ע"ש בשבת שהוא חייב על מה נחלקו על מי שהיו לו ב' תינוקות א' למול אחר השבת וא' למול בשבת ושכח ומל של אחר השבת בשבת ז שר"א מחייב חטאת ור' יהושע פוטר השתא רבי יהושע סיפא דלא קא עביד מצוה פוטר רישא דקא עביד מצוה מחייב אמרי דבי ר' ינאי רישא כגון שקדם ומל של שבת בע"ש דלא ניתנה שבת לידחות סיפא ניתנה שבת לידחות א"ל רב אשי לרב כהנא רישא נמי ניתנה שבת לידחות לגבי תינוקות דעלמא להאי גברא מיהא לא איתיהיב: **מתני'** ח דקטן נימול לשמנה לתשעה ולעשרה ולאחד עשר ולי"ב לא פחות ולא יותר הא כיצד כדרכו לשמנה נולד לבין השמשות נימול לט' ביה"ש של ע"ש נימול לעשרה יו"ט לאחר השבת נימול לאחד עשר ב' ימים של ר"ה נימול לשנים עשר קטן החולה אין מוהלין אותו עד שיבריא: **גמ'** ט אמר שמואל ה חלצתו חמה נותנין לו כל ז' להברותו איבעיא להו מי בעינן מעת לעת ת"ש דתני י לודא יום הבראתו כיום הולדו מאי לאו מה יום הולדו לא בעינן מעת לעת אף יום הבראתו לא בעינן מעת לעת לא עדיף יום הבראתו מיום הולדו דאילו יום הולדו לא בעינן מעת לעת ואילו יום הבראתו בעינן מעת לעת: **מתני'** כ ו אלו הן ציצין המעכבין את המילה בשר החופה את רוב העטרה ואינו אוכל בתרומה ז ואם היה בעל בשר מתקנו מפני מראית העין

מל

תוספות

טומטום שראה לובן ואודם מביאה מקדש וכ"ש משום דאיכא קרא יתירא (ג) דדריש לה לטומטום דכתיב מזכר ועד נקבה תשלחו ואי למעוטי אנדרוגינוס גרידא לא ה"ל למיכתב אלא זכר לא הוא דאי לא כתב אלא זכר ה"א אשה לא מחייב בביאת מקדש מדכתיב זכר ולא כתיב אדם ושמא י"ל דלית ליה לרב דר"ח דאיכא אמורא נמי דפליג עליה בבכורות וא"ת ומאי איצטריך רב למעוטי אנדרוגינוס והא איהו ס"ל בפרק הערל ביבמות (דף פג.) דאנדרוגינוס ספיקא הוא (ג) ואיצטריך קרא למעוטי ספק מיהו הא לא קשיא דה"א כשראה לובן ואודם כאחת יתחייב ממ"נ אבל הא תימה כיון דסבר רב אנדרוגינוס ספיקא הוא אמאי קאמר רב מזכר ועד נקבה זכר ודאי נקבה ודאית ואם הוא זכר ימעט אותו מזכר ואם הוא נקבה ימעט אותו מנקבה ומיהו י"ל דמשום טומטום נקטיה דפעמים הוי זכר ופעמים הוי נקבה:

הזכר ולא טומטום ואנדרוגינוס. תימה לרבי דבפרק אלו מומין (בכורות דף מב.) גבי בכור מצריך הזכרים למעוטי טומטום ואנדרוגינוס משמע התם דמהזכר לחודיה לא הוה ממעט לה והכא ממעטין ליה מהזכר לחודיה:

מסורת הש"ס

א) [עירובין נו: וש"נ], ב) יומא מג. יבמות עב: ערכין ג. פרה פ"ה מ"ד, ג) פסחים עב. כריתות יט:, ד) [צ"ל אליעזר], ה) פסחים עב. ע"ש, ו) [צ"ל אליעזר], ז) [יבמות לג.], ח) ערכין ח:, ט) יבמות עא., י) ב"ז שם:, כ) יבמות מז: עא:, ל) [סנהדרין מו.]

הגהות הב"ח

(א) גמ' וסתם ספרא ר' יהודה. נ"ב ול"ע מן מס' נדה דף מו: (ב) תוס' ד"ה הזכר וכו' יתירא למעוטי לה לטומטום: (ג) בא"ד ספיקא הוא ומי איצטריך:

גליון הש"ס

מתני' ור' יהושע פוטר. עי' מנחות דף סד ע"א תד"ה ואפי' נתכפר:

תורה אור השלם

א) זֹאת בְּרִיתִי אֲשֶׁר תִּשְׁמְרוּ בֵּינִי וּבֵינֵיכֶם וּבֵין זַרְעֲךָ אַחֲרֶיךָ הִמּוֹל לָכֶם כָּל זָכָר: [בראשית יז, י]

רב נסים גאון

ששחטה ותמצא כמותה בשחיטת חולין (עב) בפרק בהמה המקשה לילד: אף אנן נמי תנינא הכל כשרין לקדש חוץ מחרש שוטה וקטן כו'. זו המשנה במס' פרה בפרק ה' ולענין קידוש מי חטאת נתכוונה. א) לומר שבעת שישארו ציצין המעכבין את המילה הרי הוא ערל עדיין ואם הוא כהן אסור לוכל בתרומה כמו שנינו במס' יבמות (דף ע) הערל וכל הטמאין לא יאכלו בתרומה והזכירו בתלמוד המחלוקת שהיתה בין ר' אליעזר ובין ר' עקיבא בתורת כהנים במה שכתוב (ויקרא כב) איש איש מזרע אהרן ומה שכתב (שם) תושב כהן ר' אליעזר גמר לערל בגזירה שוה לערל מפסח ור' עקיבא אמר איש איש לרבות את הערל: אבל

חשק שלמה על רב נסים גאון

א) זה לפרש את המשנה אלו הן ציצין כו':

ליקוטי רש"י

[התחלה בדף קלו:] נימול לט'. כלומר לספק תשיעי [חולין סד:]. ביה"ש של ע"ש. נולד בין השמשות של ערב שבת אינו נימול בשבת דשמא תשיעי הוא דבין השמשות ספק יום ספק לילה ואם לילה הוא נמצא שבת יום [תשיעי] ומילה שלא בזמנה אינה דוחה שבת ולא יו"ט [ערכין ח:].

יו"ט לאחר השבת. מל יו"ט להיות אחר אותה שבת שהוא עשירי נמול לאחד עשר משום דמילה שלא בזמנה לא דחיא לן מהוא לבדו הוא ולא מכשיריו לבדו ולא מילה שלא בזמנה (בסנהדרין) [בשבת כ"ד:] [חולין שם]. ב' ימים של ר"ה. ואם אלו שני ימים טובים של ר"ה אחר אותו שבת אינו נימול עד יום שלישי שהוא שנים עשר ללידתו [ערכין שם]. חלצתו חמה. שלפתו ניטלה מגופו החמה הוא החולי הקודמו חלצתו לשון חלץ מהם (הושע ה) [ברכות לד:]. שהיה חולה ונתחלחלה ונשתלפה ממנו חמה [יבמות עא.]. יום הבראתו כיום הולדו. צריך להמתין שמונה ימים [שם.]. עד ז' ימים לא מהלין ליה [שם.]. מאי לאו. הכי קאמר מה יום הולדו לא בעינן מעת לעת אף יום הבראה לא בעי מעת לעת. לא עדיף יום הבראתו כו'. והא דמגלה לודא הא אתא לאשמועינן שצריך להמתין עד ז' ימים שלמים [שם:]. ציצין. שיורי ערלה ובמתניתין מפרש אלו הן ציצין המעכבין ויש שאין מעכבין כגון בשר שאינה חופה רוב העטרה אלא מקצת [לעיל קלג:]. עטרה. סובב גבוה שסביב הגיד וממנה הגיד משפע ויורד לצד הנקב [שם מז:]. שלא מחך כל הערלה [לעיל קלג:].

חשק שלמה על רבינו חננאל

א) [נראה דצ"ל לא נחלקו ר"א ורי"ה על מי שהיו לו שני תינוקות אחד למול בשבת ואחד למול אחר השבת ושכח ומל את של אחר השבת בשבת שהוא חייב וכו'. ורב יהודה מתני פטור דמוקי לה כר"מ ור' יהושע דלמוקמי מתני' כר"מ משום דקיי"ל דסתם משנה ר"מ וכו']:

Gemara Our Mishnah states in its opening case that all agree that he is liable. The Gemara now records that there is an Amoraic dispute as to how the Mishnah's opening case should read:

רַב הוּנָא מַתְנֵי חַיָּיב – **Rav Huna taught** in the opening statement of **the Mishnah** that all agree that **he is liable.**[15] רַב יְהוּדָה מַתְנֵי פָּטוּר – **Rav Yehudah taught** in the opening statement of **the Mishnah** that all agree that **he is exempt.**[16]

The Gemara elaborates, starting with Rav Huna's reading:

רַב הוּנָא מַתְנֵי חַיָּיב – **Rav Huna taught** in the opening statement of the Mishnah that all agree that **he is liable,** דְּתַנְיָא – **for we learned in a Baraisa:** אָמַר רַבִּי שִׁמְעוֹן בֶּן אֶלְעָזָר – R' SHIMON BEN ELAZAR SAID: לֹא נֶחְלְקוּ רַבִּי אֱלִיעֶזֶר וְרַבִּי יְהוֹשֻׁעַ – R' ELIEZER AND R' YEHOSHUA DID NOT DISAGREE עַל מִי שֶׁהָיוּ לוֹ שְׁנֵי תִינוֹקוֹת – CONCERNING the case of SOMEONE WHO HAD TWO INFANTS, אֶחָד לָמוּל בְּשַׁבָּת וְאֶחָד לָמוּל אַחַר הַשַּׁבָּת – ONE TO CIRCUMCISE ON THE SABBATH AND ONE TO CIRCUMCISE AFTER THE SABBATH, וְשָׁכַח וּמָל אֶת שֶׁל אַחַר הַשַּׁבָּת בְּשַׁבָּת – AND HE FORGOT AND CIRCUMCISED THE ONE DUE AFTER THE SABBATH ON THE SABBATH, שֶׁהוּא חַיָּיב – THAT HE IS LIABLE.[17] עַל מַה נֶּחְלְקוּ – CONCERNING WHAT case DID THEY DISAGREE? עַל מִי שֶׁהָיוּ לוֹ שְׁנֵי תִינוֹקוֹת – CONCERNING the case of SOMEONE WHO HAD TWO INFANTS, אֶחָד לָמוּל בְּעֶרֶב שַׁבָּת וְאֶחָד לָמוּל בְּשַׁבָּת – ONE TO CIRCUMCISE ON FRIDAY AND ONE TO CIRCUMCISE ON THE SABBATH, וְשָׁכַח וּמָל אֶת שֶׁל עֶרֶב שַׁבָּת בְּשַׁבָּת – AND HE FORGOT AND CIRCUMCISED THE FRIDAY ONE ON THE SABBATH, שֶׁרַבִּי אֱלִיעֶזֶר מְחַיֵּיב חַטָּאת – FOR in this case R' ELIEZER DECLARES him LIABLE to A *CHATAS* וְרַבִּי יְהוֹשֻׁעַ פּוֹטֵר – AND R' YEHOSHUA EXEMPTS him.[18]

Rav Huna now explains the basis of the dispute according to this reading:

וּשְׁנֵיהֶם לֹא לְמֵדוּהָ אֶלָּא מֵעֲבוֹדַת כּוֹכָבִים – **And both [R' Eliezer and R' Yehoshua] derived [their respective opinions] only from** the *chatas* for **idolatry,** which serves as the model for *chatas* liability.[19] רַבִּי אֱלִיעֶזֶר סָבַר כַּעֲבוֹדַת כּוֹכָבִים – **R' Eliezer holds** that **this** case **is comparable to** the case of **idolatry:** מָה עֲבוֹדַת כּוֹכָבִים אָמַר רַחֲמָנָא לֹא תַעֲבִיד – **Just as in** the case of **idolatry the Merciful One said** in His Torah, **"You shall not do it,"** וְכִי עָבִיד מִיחַיֵּיב – **and when one does do** it inadvertently, **he is liable** to a *chatas,* הָכָא נַמִּי לֹא שְׁנָא – **here too,** in the case of a mistaken circumcision on the Sabbath, **it is no different** and he is liable.[20] וְרַבִּי יְהוֹשֻׁעַ – **And R' Yehoshua** holds that there is a distinction: הָתָם דְּלָאו מִצְוָה – **There** (in the case of idolatry) he is liable **because no mitzvah** is being performed, הָכָא מִצְוָה – whereas **here** (in the case of a mistaken circumcision on the Sabbath) **a mitzvah** is being performed. Hence, this case of circumcision does not conform to the *chatas* model of idolatry and he is therefore exempt.[21]

The Gemara now elaborates Rav Yehudah's reading of the Mishnah:

רַב יְהוּדָה מַתְנֵי פָּטוּר – **Rav Yehudah taught** in the opening statement of **the Mishnah** that all agree that **he is exempt,** דְּתַנְיָא – **for we learned in a Baraisa:** אָמַר רַבִּי מֵאִיר – R' MEIR SAID: לֹא נֶחְלְקוּ רַבִּי אֱלִיעֶזֶר וְרַבִּי יְהוֹשֻׁעַ – R' ELIEZER AND R' YEHOSHUA DID NOT DISAGREE עַל מִי שֶׁהָיוּ לוֹ שְׁנֵי תִינוֹקוֹת – CONCERNING the case of SOMEONE WHO HAD TWO INFANTS, אֶחָד לָמוּל בְּעֶרֶב שַׁבָּת וְאֶחָד לָמוּל בְּשַׁבָּת – ONE TO CIRCUMCISE ON FRIDAY AND ONE TO CIRCUMCISE ON THE SABBATH, וְשָׁכַח וּמָל אֶת שֶׁל עֶרֶב שַׁבָּת בְּשַׁבָּת – AND HE FORGOT AND CIRCUMCISED THE FRIDAY ONE ON THE SABBATH, שֶׁהוּא פָּטוּר – THAT HE IS EXEMPT.[22] עַל מַה נֶּחְלְקוּ – CONCERNING WHAT case DID THEY DISAGREE? עַל מִי שֶׁהָיוּ לוֹ שְׁנֵי תִינוֹקוֹת – CONCERNING the case of SOMEONE WHO HAD TWO INFANTS, אֶחָד לָמוּל אַחַר הַשַּׁבָּת וְאֶחָד לָמוּל בְּשַׁבָּת – ONE TO CIRCUMCISE AFTER THE SABBATH AND ONE TO CIRCUMCISE ON THE SABBATH, וְשָׁכַח וּמָל אֶת שֶׁל אַחַר הַשַּׁבָּת בְּשַׁבָּת – AND HE FORGOT AND CIRCUMCISED THE ONE DUE AFTER THE SABBATH ON THE SABBATH, שֶׁרַבִּי אֱלִיעֶזֶר מְחַיֵּיב חַטָּאת – FOR in this case R' ELIEZER DECLARES him LIABLE to A *CHATAS* וְרַבִּי יְהוֹשֻׁעַ פּוֹטֵר – AND R' YEHOSHUA EXEMPTS him.[23]

NOTES

15. Rav Huna's version of the Mishnah is exactly as we have it: The Mishnah begins by saying that where he mistakenly circumcised an after-Sabbath infant on the Sabbath all agree that he is *liable* to a *chatas* [since he did not actually perform a mitzvah] (*Rashi*). The point of contention between R' Eliezer and R' Yehoshua is where he circumcised a Friday child on the Sabbath – where his error did *result* in the performance of a mitzvah (see note 14).

16. Rav Yehudah had a different reading of the Mishnah and a completely different understanding of the dispute. According to his reading the Mishnah begins with a case in which both R' Eliezer and R' Yehoshua agree that the circumciser is *exempt.* According to his reading, the Mishnah first states that if there was a mix-up between a *Friday* infant and a Sabbath infant, everyone agrees that he is *exempt* [since he did in fact perform a mitzvah]. The Mishnah then goes on to state that the dispute between R' Eliezer and R' Yehoshua concerns the case where he mistakenly circumcised an *after*-Sabbath infant instead of the Sabbath one (*Rashi*). Although in this case he did not in the end perform a mitzvah, R' Yehoshua nevertheless exempts him because he erred while *attempting* to perform a mitzvah.

17. [Since his action did not result in the performance of a mitzvah; see note 14.]

18. Rav Huna's version is the reading found in our Mishnah. See note 14 for the explanation of the dispute.

19. The rules for *chatas* liability are derived from the *chatas* brought for the transgression of idolatry. This is indicated by the Torah when it says in regard to that *chatas* (*Numbers* 15:29): תּוֹרָה אַחַת יִהְיֶה לָכֶם לָעֹשֶׂה בִּשְׁגָגָה, *there shall be a single law for you, for one who acts with inadvertence* (*Rashi,* from Gemara above, 68b-69a; see 68b note 24 and 69a note 3).

20. [R' Eliezer considers the defining feature of idolatry to be the simple fact that one has transgressed a prohibition forbidden by the Torah under penalty of *kares* (see Gemara 69a).]

21. [According to R' Yehoshua the element of mitzvah contained in this act of circumcision is sufficient to remove it from the class of sins that resemble idolatry, where no element of mitzvah exists. Therefore, there is no source to make such an act liable to a *chatas.*]

[From the fact that our Mishnah teaches this in the context of one who has *two* infants to circumcise, it is evident that R' Yehoshua exempts him only because there was one infant that was supposed to be circumcised on the Sabbath and his error resulted from his concern to perform that mitzvah. Had there been just one infant to circumcise (a Friday baby), the circumciser would be liable since he would not then have been טָרוּד בִּדְבַר מִצְוָה, *occupied with performing a mitzvah,* that should be performed on the Sabbath (see *Rashi* to the Mishnah ד״ה אחד למול בשבת).] Indeed, the Gemara in *Pesachim* (72a) states that even where there are two infants, R' Yehoshua exempts him only if he erred and circumcised the Friday baby *before* circumcising the Sabbath baby. If he erred and circumcised the Friday baby *after* the Sabbath baby had been circumcised, R' Yehoshua would agree that he is liable, since at the time he circumcised the Friday baby he was no longer occupied with performing any mitzvah scheduled for the Sabbath. [Thus, according to this version of the dispute, R' Yehoshua exempts him only if he was both attempting to perform a mitzvah that should be performed that day *and* he actually did perform a mitzvah, albeit not one that should have been performed that day.]

22. [According to this version, since his actions resulted in the performance of a mitzvah even R' Eliezer concedes that he is exempt from a *chatas.*]

23. R' Eliezer declares him liable because no mitzvah was performed, since this infant is only seven days old. Therefore, even though he was busy attempting to perform a mitzvah, R' Eliezer rules him liable. R' Yehoshua rules him exempt because in his opinion, being occupied with attempting to perform a mitzvah exempts a person even if his action does not result in the performance of a mitzvah.]

והא סתם ספרא הוא דבתורת כהנים תניא לה וסתם ספרא רבי יהודה: לקדש. מי חטאת לתת אפר על המים: מכשיר בקטן ופוסל באשה. טעמיה מפרש בסדר יומא בפ"ג: ובאנדרוגינוס. שמע מינה דרבי יהודה כאשה משוי ליה: כל זכר. ריבויא הוא:

טומטום שרואה לובן ואודם מביאת מקדש וכ"ת משום דאיכא קרא ימירא (ג) דדריש לה לטומטום דכתיב מזכר ועד נקבה תשלחו ואי למעוטי אנדרוגינוס גרידא לא ה"ל למיכתב אלא זכר לא היא דאי לא כתב אלא זכר ה"א אשה לא מחייב' בביאת מקדש מדכתיב זכר ולא כתיב אדם ושמא י"ל דלית ליה לרב דר"מ דאיכא אמורא נמי דפליג עליה בבכורות וא"ת ומאי איצטריך רב למעוטי אנדרוגינוס והא איהו ס"ל בפרק הערל ביבמות (דף פג.) דאנדרוגינוס ספיקא הוא (ג) ואיצטריך קרא למעוטי ספק מיהו הא לא קשיא דה"א כשרואה לובן ואודם כאחת יתחייב ממ"נ אבל הא תימה כיון דסבר רב אנדרוגינוס ספיקא הוא אמאי קאמר רב מזכר ועד נקבה זכר ודאי נקבה ודאית ואם הוא זכר ימעט אותו מזכר ואם הוא נקבה ימעט אותו מנקבה ומיהו י"ל דמשום טומטום נקטיה דפעמים הוי זכר ופעמים הוי נקבה:

הזכר ולא טומטום ואנדרוגינוס. תימה לרבי דבפרק אלו מומין (בכורות דף מב.) גבי בכור מצריך הזכר הזכרים למעוטי טומטום ואנדרוגינוס משמע התם דמהזכר למודיה לא הוה ממעט לה והכא ממעטין ליה מהזכר למודיה:

(א) וסתם ספרא רבי יהודה אמר רב נחמן בר יצחק אף אנן נמי תנינא הכל כשרים לקדש חוץ מחש"ו רבי יהודה מכשיר בקטן ופוסל באשה ואנדרוגינוס ש"מ ומאי שנא מילה משום דכתיב המול לכם כל זכר: **מתני'** מי שהיו לו שני תינוקות אחד למול אחר השבת ואחד למול בשבת ושכח ומל את של אחר השבת בשבת חייב אחד למול בע"ש ואחד למול בשבת ושכח ומל את של ע"ש בשבת רבי אליעזר מחייב חטאת ורבי יהושע פוטר: **גמ'** רב הונא מתני חייב רב יהודה מתני פטור רב הונא מתני חייב דתניא אמר ר"ש בן אלעזר לא נחלקו רבי אליעזר ור' יהושע על מי שהיו לו ב' תינוקות אחד למול בשבת ואחד למול אחר השבת ושכח ומל את של אחר השבת בשבת שהוא חייב על מה נחלקו על מי שהיו לו ב' תינוקות א' למול בע"ש וא' למול בשבת ושכח ומל את של ע"ש בשבת שר' אליעזר מחייב חטאת ורבי יהושע פוטר ושניהם לא למדוה אלא מעבודת כוכבים ר' אליעזר סבר כעבודת כוכבים מה עבודת כוכבים אמר רחמנא לא תעביד וכי עביד מיחייב ה"נ לא שנא ורבי יהושע התם דלאו מצוה הכא מצוה רב יהודה מתני פטור דתניא א"ר מאיר לא נחלקו ר"א ורבי יהושע על מי שהיו לו ב' תינוקות אחד למול בע"ש ואחד למול בשבת ושכח ומל את של ע"ש בשבת שהוא פטור על מה נחלקו על מי שהיו לו ב' תינוקות א' למול אחר השבת וא' למול בשבת ושכח ומל את של אחר השבת בשבת שר"א מחייב חטאת ורבי יהושע פוטר ושניהם לא למדוה אלא מעבודת כוכבים ר"א סבר כעבודת כוכבים מה עבודת כוכבים אמר רחמנא לא תעביד וכי עביד מיחייב ה"נ לא שנא ור' יהושע התם לא טריד מצוה הכא טריד מצוה תני ר' חייא אומר היה ר"מ לא נחלקו רבי אליעזר ורבי יהושע על מי שהיו לו ב' תינוקות א' למול בע"ש וא' למול בשבת ושכח ומל את של ע"ש בשבת שהוא חייב על מה נחלקו על מי שהיו לו ב' תינוקות א' למול אחר השבת וא' למול בשבת ושכח ומל של אחר השבת בשבת שר"א מחייב חטאת ור' יהושע פוטר השתא רבי יהושע סיפא דלא קא עביד מצוה פוטר רישא דקא עביד מצוה מחייב אמרי דבי ר' ינאי רישא כגון שקדם ומל של שבת בע"ש דלא ניתנה שבת לידחות סיפא ניתנה שבת לידחות א"ל רב אשי לרב כהנא רישא נמי ניתנה שבת לידחות דעלמא להאי גברא מיהא לא איתיהיב: **מתני'** קטן נימול לשמנה לתשעה ולעשרה ולאחד עשר ולי"ב לא פחות ולא יותר הא כיצד כדרכו לשמנה נולד לבין השמשות נימול לט' ביה"ש של ע"ש נימול לעשרה יו"ט לאחר השבת נימול לאחד עשר ב' ימים של ר"ה נימול לשנים עשר קטן החולה אין מוהלין אותו עד שיבריא: **גמ'** אמר שמואל חלצתו חמה נותנין לו כל ז' להברותו איבעיא להו מי בעינן מעת לעת ת"ש דתני לודא יום הבראתו כיום הולדו מאי לאו מה יום הולדו לא בעינן מעת לעת אף יום הבראתו לא בעינן מעת לעת לא עדיף יום הבראתו מיום הולדו דאילו יום הולדו לא בעינן מעת לעת ואילו יום הבראתו בעינן מעת לעת: **מתני'** אלו הן ציצין המעכבין את המילה בשר החופה את רוב העטרה ואינו אוכל בתרומה ואם היה בעל בשר מתקנו מפני מראית העין

מל

מתני' ושכח ומל את של אחר השבת בשבת חייב. דטעה בדבר מצוה ולא עשה מצוה הוא ועבד ליה חבורה שלא לצורך והא אפילו רבי יהושע מודה: אחד למול בשבת ואחד למול בע"ש ושכח ומל את של ע"ש בשבת ר"א מחייב חטאת. דמילה שלא בזמנה אינה דוחה שבת ואע"ג דטעה בדבר מצוה שהיה טרוד באותו של שבת ומתוך כך טעה בזה ואף בזה עשה מצוה שהרי ראוי הוא למול אלא שאינו דוחה שבת ס"ל לר"א טעה בדבר מצוה ועשה מצוה שיש בה חיוב חטאת חייב ורבי יהושע פוטר דס"ל טעה בדבר מצוה ועשה מצוה פטור: **גמ'** רב הונא מתני. במתניתין ברישא חייב לדברי הכל כדתנינן לה אנן: ורב יהודה מתני ברישא פטור. דמוקי לה בשכח ומל את של ע"ש בשבת ופלוגתא היא בשל אחר השבת בשבת: שהוא חייב. דאע"ג דטריד במצוה וטעה בה כיון דלאו מצוה שעדיין לא הגיע זמנו למול חייב: אלא מע"ז. שהוקשו כל חטאות שבתורה לחטאת ע"ז דכתיב תורה אחת יהיה לכם וגו' בפרשת שלח לך אנשים גבי קרבן ע"ז: ור' יהושע התם. עובד עבודת כוכבים לא עשה מצוה: ה"ג רב יהודה מתני פטור דתניא אמר ר"מ לא נחלקו ר"א ורבי יהושע על שהיו לו שני תינוקות אחד למול ע"ש כו': ה"ג ורבי יהושע התם לא טריד במצוה הכא טריד במצוה. טרוד להתעסק במצוה גמורה שהרי אחד מהם זמנו היום וטרוד לבו למהר ולעשות ומתוך טרדו טעה ומל את זה שאין בו מצוה כלל: ושכח ומל של ע"ש בשבת שהוא חייב. לקמיה מתרץ לה: דלא ניתנה שבת לידחות. שאין לו תינוק שיהא זמנו היום הלכך לא היה טרוד היום במצוה שלא היה מוטל עליו כלום לעשות ולא היה לו לטעות: **מתני'** נולד בין השמשות נימול לט'. שהרי ליום שמיני של מחר הוא נימול ושמא בין השמשות יום הוא ונימול לט': היה היום ע"ש. א"א למולו בשבת הבאה דשמא ט' הוא והויא ליה מילה שלא בזמנה ואינה דוחה שבת וצריך להמתין עד לאחר השבת שהוא עשירי: חל יו"ט להיות אחר השבת. אין מילה שלא בזמנה דוחה אותו ונימול לי"א: **גמ'** חלצתו חמה. נשלף ממנו החולי ויצא מגופו: דתני לודא. שם חכם: יום הבראתו כיום הולדו. ממתינין לו כיום הולדו: מאי לאו. יום הולדו דווקא קאמר דלא בעינן מעת לעת: לא. כיום הולדו דקתני למיתב ליה ז' מיהו עדיף יום הבראתו מהא דבעינן מעת לעת ומהא ליכא למשמע מידי: **מתני'** ציצין. רצועות של בשר שנשארו מן הערלה: עטרה. היא שפה גבוה המקפת את הגיד סביב וממנה משפע ויורד לראשו: ואינו אוכל בתרומה. אם כהן הוא דילפינן ביבמות (ד' ע.) שערל אסור בתרומה: ואם היה בעל בשר. שהיה שמן ונראה בשר שלמעלה מערלתו לאחר שניטלה ערלה כולה כאלו אותו בשר חופה את הגיד: מתקנו. ומשפע באיזמל מאותו עובי: מפני מראית העין. שלא יהא נראה כערל:

פרע

מסורת הש"ס

א) [עירובין לו: וש"נ], ב) יומא מג. יבמות עב: ערכין ג. פרה פ"ה מ"ד, ג) פסחים עב. כריתות יט., ד) [צ"ל אליעזר], ה) פסחים עב. ע"ש, ו) [צ"ל אליעזר], ז) [יבמות לד.], ח) ערכין ח:, ט) יבמות עא. י) ג"ז שם, כ) יבמות מז: עב., ל) [סנהדרין סו.].

הגהות הב"ח

(א) גמ' וסתם ספרא ר' יהודה. נ"ב וע"ע מן מס' נדה דף מו: (ב) תוס' ד"ה הזכר וכו' ימירא למעוטי לה לטומטום: (ג) בא"ד ספיקא הוא וכי אילטריך:

גליון הש"ס

מתני' ור' יהושע פוטר. עי' מנחות דף סד ע"א תד"ה ואפי' נתכוון:

תורה אור השלם

א) זֹאת בְּרִיתִי אֲשֶׁר תִּשְׁמְרוּ בֵּינִי וּבֵינֵיכֶם וּבֵין זַרְעֲךָ אַחֲרֶיךָ הִמּוֹל לָכֶם כָּל זָכָר: [בראשית יז, י]

רב נסים גאון

ששחטה ומצא כמותה בשחיטת חולין (עב) בפרק בהמה המקשה לילד: אף אנן נמי תנינא הכל כשרין לקדש חוץ מחרש שוטה וקטן כו'. זו המשנה במס' פרה בפרק ה' ולענין קידוש מי חטאת נתכוונה. לומר שבעת שישארו ציצין המעכבין את המילה הרי הוא ערל עדיין ואם הוא כהן אסור לוכל בתרומה כמו ששנינו במס' יבמות (דף ע) הערל וכל הטמאין לא יאכלו בתרומה והזכיר התלמוד המחלוקת שהיתה בין ר' אליעזר ובין ר' עקיבא בתורת כהנים במה שכתוב (ויקרא כב) איש איש מזרע אהרן ומה (שם) תושב כהן ר' אליעזר גמר לערל בגזירה שוה לערל מפסח ור' עקיבא אמר איש איש לרבות את הערל: אבל

חשק שלמה על רב נסים גאון

א) נ"ה דפרק המשנה אלו הן ללין כו'.

ליקוטי רש"י

[ההתחלה בדף קלו:] נימול לט'. כלומר לספק תשיעי [חולין פד:]. ביה"ש של ע"ש. נולד בין השמשות של ערב שבת אינו נימול בשבת דשמא תשיעי הוא דבין השמשות ספק יום ולילה הוא ומשום ספק לא מחללינן שבת ואם יום הוא נמלא שבת יום תשיעי ומילה שלא בזמנה אינה דוחה שבת ולא יו"ט [ערכין ח:]. יו"ט לאחר השבת. חל יו"ט להיות אחר השבת

עין משפט נר מצוה

מט א מיי' פ"ו מהל' פרה הלכה ב סמג עשין רלג:

נ ב ג מיי' פ"ב מהל' שגגות הלכה ח:

נא ד מיי' פ"א מהל' מילה הלכה יב סמג עשין כח טוש"ע י"ד סי' רסב סעיף ה:

נב ה מיי' שם הלכה טו סמג שם טוש"ע י"ד סי' רסב סעיף ב:

נג ו ז מיי' פ"ב מהל' מילה הלכה ג ה סמג שם טוש"ע י"ד סי' רסד סעיף ה ו:

רבינו חננאל

א"ר יהודה אנדרוגינוס זכר הוא. שאם אי אתה אומר כך יערך ומנ"ל דלא מערך דתניא הזכר ולא טומטום ואנדרוגינוס כו' ופשוטה היא ומסקינן בה ומאי שנא גבי מילה דכתיב המול לכם כל זכר כל לרבות. ויש מי שאומר הלכתא כרבנן דאמרי ספק ואנדרוגינוס אין מחללין עליו את השבת ואין הלכה כר' יהודה ומדחזינן רב חסדא דריש לטעמיה דר' יהודה ש"מ דהלכתא כוותיה: מתניתין מי שהיו לו ב' תינוקות אחד למול אחר השבת ואחד למול בשבת ושכח ומל את של אחר השבת בשבת חייב כו' (ואמרינן בגמ') רב הונא מתני חייב ורב יהודה מתני פטור פי' רב הונא מתני חייב דמוקים ליה למתניתין לר"ש דאמר ר"ש לא נחלקו ר' אליעזר (ור"ש) [ור' יהושע] על מי שהיו לו (א) דקיי"ל סתם משנה ר' מאיר והדא תנא דבי ר' חייא פליגי עליה ורב הונא דמוקים לה כר' שמעון כוותיה דעבינן וחלוקת ר' אליעזר ור' יהושע דברים ברורין הן (שנים) ושניהם לא למדוה מע"ז למדו דהא איתקשא כל התורה כולה לע"ז ר' אליעזר סבירא כע"ז מה ע"ז אמרה תורה לא תעבוד ואם תעבוד ע"ז בשגגה מכל מקום חייב חטאת. כן אמרה תורה בשבת. המחלל שבת בשגגה מ"מ חייב חטאת. ור' יהושע סבר התם לגבי ע"ז לא נתכוין לקיום המצוה הכא בשבת נתכוין לקיים מצות מילה. לפיכך פטור הוא והלכתא כר' יהושע וכדמתניתין ר' שמעון לפי' אחד למול ערב שבת ואחד למול בשבת ושכח ומל את של שבת בע"ש ואת של ע"ש בשבת פטור כי מ"מ מצוה עשה. ואע"פ שמל בס'. אבל בזמן ששכח ומל את של אחר השבת ומל כיון שלא עשה מצוה כי בז' מלו אפילו ר' יהושע מודה שחייב חטאת. וכן הלכה וכל היכא דפליג ר' אליעזר ור' יהושע הלכה כר' יהושע חוץ ממקומות ידועים. וזה אינו מהם. וכן רב הונא הלכתא כוותיה דשכיח גבי ריש גלותא וגרסינן הלכתא כוותיה או הלכתא כוותיה כו': מתניתין קטן נימול לשמנה לתשעה כו' חולה אין מלין אותו עד שיבריא. אמר שמואל חלצתו חמה נותנין לו כל ז' להברותו והלכתא כשמואל דאיבעיא לן מאחר דשלצתה חמה כמה ימים

חשק שלמה על רבינו חננאל

א) נראה דלריך להוסיף כאן כמו מימיס שהיו לו שני תינוקות אחד למול בשבת ואחד למול לאחר השבת ושכח ומל את של אחר השבת בשבת שהוא חייב וכו' על מה נחלקו על מי שהיו לו שני תינוקות כו' סבור דמעיל אמר ר"מ וכו' והמדל ללוקמי מתני' כר"מ משום דקיי"ל דסתם משנה ר"מ וכו'.

ולא יו"ט [ערכין ח:]. ימים של ר"ה. שני ימים של ר"ה שהוא שבת ושלפני השבת שני ימים ויו"ט לאחר השבת. חל יו"ט לאחר השבת שאין מילה שלא בזמנה דוחה ולא יו"ט [שבת קל"ד:]. נולד בין השמשות של ערב שבת והשבת ספק ויום טוב לאחר השבת לכך מתינן עד לאחר שני ימים [חולין שם]. ב' ימים של ר"ה. ואם בין השמשות היה יום חמישי וחל ר"ה להיות אחר השבת ונמצא נימול בי"ב [ערכין שם]. חלצתו חמה. חלצתו חמה נשלף ממנו החולי ויצא מגופו [יבמות עא:]. עד שיבריא. לריך להמתין עד שיבריא לגמרי [ברכות לד:]. שהיה חולה ונתרפא ונחלש. ונשלפה ממנו חמה [יבמות עא:]. יום הבראתו כיום הולדו. לריך להמתין שבעה ימים [שם]. לעד ז' יומי לא מהלינן ליה [שם]. מאי לאו. הכי קאמר מה יום הולדו לא בעינן מעת לעת אף יום הבראתו לא בעי מעת לעת. לא עדיף יום הבראתו כו'. והא דתנא להודיע דאף יום הבראתו כיום הולדו הוא דלא אתא למימר אלא שלריך להמתין עד יום שמיני [שם]. ציצין. שיורי ערלה המעכבין את המילה שאם לא חתכן כאילו לא מל [חולין שם]. ציצין. שיורי ערלה וממעכבין ויש שאין מעכבין ואין בכולן קרא לפרש אלא מדרבנן הוא דאגמריה דעל כרחך מ ליהוי איכא המילה [לעיל קלג:]. רצועות של בשר שנשארו ושלא אחר קלקתן ותוכשר מעולים ורכים. מילת מראה מפני גופו נימול [שם מז:]. עטרה. שורה גבוה המקפת סביב הגיד שממנה משפע ויורד לצד הכובע [לעיל שם].

Rav Yehudah now explains the basis of the dispute according to this reading:

וּשְׁנֵיהֶם לֹא לְמָדוּהָ אֶלָּא מֵעֲבוֹדַת כּוֹכָבִים – And both [R' Eliezer and R' Yehoshua] derived [their respective opinions] only from the *chatas* for **idolatry,** which serves as the model for *chatas* liability.[24] **רַבִּי אֱלִיעֶזֶר סָבַר כַּעֲבוֹדַת כּוֹכָבִים – R' Eliezer holds** that **this** case of circumcision **is comparable to** the case of idolatry: **מָה עֲבוֹדַת כּוֹכָבִים אָמַר רַחֲמָנָא לֹא תַעֲבִיד – Just as** in the case of **idolatry the Merciful One said** in His Torah, **"You shall not do it," וְכִי עָבִיד מִיחַיֵּיב – and when one does do** it inadvertently **he is liable** to a *chatas,* **הָכָא נַמִּי לֹא שְׁנָא – here too,** in the case of a mistaken circumcision on the Sabbath, **it is no different** and he is liable.[25] **וְרַבִּי יְהוֹשֻׁעַ – And R' Yehoshua** holds that there is a distinction: **הָתָם לֹא טָרִיד מִצְוָה – There** (in the case of idolatry) **he is not occupied with** attempting to perform **a mitzvah, הָכָא טָרִיד מִצְוָה –** whereas **here** (in the case of a mistaken circumcision) **he is occupied with** attempting to perform **a mitzvah.**[26]

The Gemara presents another statement about the dispute between R' Eliezer and R' Yehoshua:

תָּנֵי רַבִּי חִיָּיא – R' Chiya taught the following **Baraisa: אוֹמֵר הָיָה רַבִּי מֵאִיר – R' MEIR WOULD SAY**[27] that **לֹא נֶחְלְקוּ רַבִּי אֱלִיעֶזֶר וְרַבִּי יְהוֹשֻׁעַ – R' ELIEZER AND R' YEHOSHUA DID NOT DISAGREE עַל מִי שֶׁהָיוּ לוֹ שְׁנֵי תִינוֹקוֹת – CONCERNING** the case of **SOMEONE WHO HAD TWO INFANTS, אֶחָד לָמוּל בְּעֶרֶב שַׁבָּת וְאֶחָד לָמוּל בְּשַׁבָּת – ONE TO CIRCUMCISE ON FRIDAY AND ONE TO CIRCUMCISE ON THE SABBATH, וְשָׁכַח וּמָל אֶת שֶׁל עֶרֶב שַׁבָּת בְּשַׁבָּת – AND HE FORGOT AND CIRCUMCISED THE FRIDAY ONE ON THE SABBATH, שֶׁהוּא חַיָּיב – THAT HE IS LIABLE. עַל מַה נֶּחְלְקוּ – CONCERNING WHAT** case **DID THEY DISAGREE? עַל מִי שֶׁהָיוּ לוֹ שְׁנֵי תִינוֹקוֹת – CONCERNING SOMEONE WHO HAD TWO INFANTS, אֶחָד לָמוּל אַחַר הַשַּׁבָּת וְאֶחָד לָמוּל בְּשַׁבָּת – ONE TO CIRCUMCISE AFTER THE SABBATH AND ONE TO CIRCUMCISE ON THE SABBATH, וְשָׁכַח וּמָל שֶׁל אַחַר הַשַּׁבָּת בְּשַׁבָּת – AND HE FORGOT AND CIRCUMCISED THE ONE DUE AFTER THE SABBATH ON THE SABBATH, שֶׁרַבִּי אֱלִיעֶזֶר מְחַיֵּיב חַטָּאת – FOR** in this case **R' ELIEZER DECLARES** him **LIABLE** to **A** ***CHATAS*** **וְרַבִּי יְהוֹשֻׁעַ פּוֹטֵר – AND R' YEHOSHUA EXEMPTS** him.

The Gemara questions the logic of this position:

הַשְׁתָּא רַבִּי יְהוֹשֻׁעַ סֵיפָא דְּלֹא קָא עָבִיד מִצְוָה פּוֹטֵר – Now if **R' Yehoshua exempts** from a *chatas* in **the latter case, where he did not** actually **perform a mitzvah** (because the infant he mistakenly circumcised was less than eight days old), **רֵישָׁא דְּקָא עָבִיד מִצְוָה מְחַיֵּיב –** then in **the first case, where he did perform a mitzvah** (because the infant he mistakenly circumcised had already passed its eighth day), can it be that **[R' Yehoshua] declares** him **liable?**[28]

The Gemara answers:

אָמְרֵי דְּבֵי רַבִּי יַנַּאי – The school of R' Yannai said in answer to this question: **רֵישָׁא כְּגוֹן שֶׁקָּדַם וּמָל שֶׁל שַׁבָּת בְּעֶרֶב שַׁבָּת – The first case** is dealing **with an instance in which he went ahead and circumcised the Sabbath [infant] on Friday,**[29] **דְּלֹא נִיתְּנָה שַׁבָּת לִידָּחוֹת – in which** case **the Sabbath is not** any longer **given to being overridden.**[30] Therefore, even though he performed a mitzvah when he circumcised the Friday infant on the Sabbath, he is nevertheless liable. **סֵיפָא נִיתְּנָה שַׁבָּת לִידָּחוֹת – In the latter case,** however, **the Sabbath is** still **given to being overridden,** since he has not yet circumcised the Sabbath infant.[31] Therefore, R' Yehoshua holds that he is exempt when he mistakenly circumcises the after-Sabbath infant on the Sabbath.

The distinction is questioned:

אָמַר לֵיהּ רַב אָשֵׁי לְרַב כַּהֲנָא – Rav Ashi said to Rav Kahana: רֵישָׁא נַמִּי נִיתְּנָה שַׁבָּת לִידָּחוֹת לְגַבֵּי תִּינוֹקוֹת דְּעָלְמָא – In **the first case too** (where he mistakenly circumcised the Friday infant on the Sabbath), **the Sabbath is given to being overridden in regard to** other **infants of the world** whose time for circumcision is on the Sabbath.[32] – ? –

Rav Kahana answers:

לְהַאי גַּבְרָא מִיהָא לֹא אִיתְּהִיב – In regard **to this person, however, it was not given** to being overridden and he is therefore liable.[33]

NOTES

24. See note 19.

25. [Although R' Eliezer does exempt him in the case where his action resulted in the performance of a mitzvah (i.e. where he circumcised a Friday baby on the Sabbath), R' Eliezer does not consider the mere *attempt* to perform a mitzvah a significant enough distinction to differentiate this case from the case of idolatry. Only the actual *performance* of a mitzvah removes the act from the ordinary *chatas* category.]

26. I.e. he was occupied in trying to perform a true mitzvah, namely, circumcising the infant that is supposed to be circumcised this Sabbath day. It was as a result of his preoccupation with this mitzvah that he mistakenly sinned by circumcising the infant whose circumcision was no mitzvah at all, namely, the after-Sabbath infant (*Rashi*). [According to R' Yehoshua since the *root* of his error was different from that of the standard model of *chatas,* this case is considered dissimilar to the model case (idolatry) and is therefore not subject to a *chatas.*]

27. [The Gemara will conclude that R' Chiya is not necessarily disputing the earlier Baraisa's quotation of R' Meir. He is merely amplifying what R' Meir would hold in a case not discussed in the previous Baraisa.]

28. [If merely being occupied with a mitzvah is sufficient to exempt an act from a *chatas* – even when he does not in the end perform a mitzvah – then surely where he also performs a mitzvah he should be exempt!]

29. [Not only did he mistakenly circumcise the Friday infant on the Sabbath, but he also mistakenly circumcised the Sabbath infant on Friday – i.e. he confused the two infants and circumcised each one on the day due for the other.]

30. Since the Sabbath infant was circumcised before the Sabbath, there was in truth no mitzvah to be concerned with on this Sabbath. He should therefore not have made the mistake (*Rashi*). [I.e. there was no *greater* reason for him to have erred in this case than in any other case of *chatas* liability. The reason R' Yehoshua exempts someone who is occupied in trying to perform a mitzvah is because the Torah's command that he, for example, engage in circumcision this day was a contributing factor in his mistake. Had he not been required to engage in this *melachah* activity, he would have avoided cutting any flesh on the Sabbath and would never have sinned. Since the mitzvah requirement contributed to his sinning, this case is different from the standard *chatas* case of idolatry and there is no *chatas* for it. Where, however, there is no mitzvah required of him this day, and it is merely that he *thinks* he is so obligated, the Torah's commandment did not place him in a situation where he was closer to sinning, because there was no commandment to perform any *melachah* this day. His mistake was simply the result of his confusion about the circumstances relating to this day. His error is thus no different from other errors that cause one to violate the Sabbath and be liable.]

31. [Since the second infant was not due to be circumcised until *after* the Sabbath, his confusing them did not result in his doing anything *before* the Sabbath.]

32. [I.e. the fact that there is a mitzvah to circumcise children on the Sabbath when that is their eighth day did contribute to his error. If not for this mitzvah, he would not have circumcised the Friday infant on the Sabbath despite his mistake about its age. Thus, we should still say that this is a case in which a mitzvah contributed to the transgression, making it dissimilar to idolatry and exempting it from a *chatas.*]

33. [The distinction between an error prompted by a mitzvah and one prompted by some other miscalculation is deemed significant only when this person himself was *required* to perform the mitzvah, and hence the *melachah,* on the Sabbath. It is the fact that he did an act that the Torah *required him* to do (albeit to the wrong child) that sets this error apart from other errors and exempts him from a *chatas.* A mistaken

עין משפט
נר מצוה

מט א מיי' פ"ו מהל' פרה הלכה ב סמג עשין רלג:
נ ב ג מיי' פ"ב מהל' שגגות הלכה ח:
נא ד מיי' פ"א מהל' מילה הלכה יב סמג עשין כח טוש"ע י"ד סי' רסו סעיף ח:
נב ה מיי' שם הלכה טז סמג שם טוש"ע י"ד סי' רסב סעיף ג:
נג ו ז מיי' פ"ב מהל' מילה הלכה ג ה סמג שם טוש"ע י"ד סי' רסד סעיף ה ו:

רבינו חננאל

א"ר יהודה אנדרוגינוס זכר הוא. שאם אי אתה אומר כך יערך ומנ"ל דלא מערך דתניא הזכר ולא טומטום ואנדרוגינוס כו' ופשוטה היא ומסקינן בה ומאי שנא גבי מילה דכתיב המול לכם כל זכר כל לרבות. ויש מי שאומר הלכתא כרבנן דאמרי ספק ואנדרוגינוס אין מחללין עליו את השבת ואין הלכה כר' יהודה ומדחזינן רב חסדא דריש לטעמיה דר' יהודה ש"מ הלכתא כוותיה: מתניתין מי שהיו לו ב' תינוקות אחד למול אחר השבת ואחד למול בשבת ושכח ומל את של אחר השבת בשבת חייב וכו' [ואמרינן בגמ'] רב הונא מתני חייב ורב יהודה מתני פטור פי' רב הונא מתני חייב דמוקים ליה למתניתין לר"ש דאמר ר"ש לא נחלקו ר' אליעזר (ור"ש) [ור' יהושע] על מי שהיו לו (א) דקיי"ל סתם משנה ר' מאיר והא תנא דבי ר' חייא פליגי עליה ורב הונא דמוקים לה כר' שמעון כוותיה עבדינן וחלוקת ר' אליעזר ור' יהושע דברים ברורין הן. (שנים) ושניהם מע"ז למדוה דהא איתקשא כל התורה כולה לע"ז ר' אליעזר סבירא כע"ז מה ע"ז אמרה תורה לא תעבוד ואם תעבוד ע"ז בשגגה מכל מקום חייב חטאת. כן אמרה תורה בשבת. המחלל השבת בשגגה מ"מ חייב חטאת. ור' יהושע סבר התם לגבי ע"ז לא נתכוין לקיים המצוה הכא בשבת נתכוין לקיים מצות מילה. לפיכך פטור הוא והלכתא כר' יהושע וכדמתניתין ר' שמעון: אחד למול ערב שבת ואחד למול בשבת ושכח ומל את של שבת בע"ש ואת של ע"ש בשבת פטור כי מ"מ מצוה עשה. ואע"פ שמל בט'. אבל בזמן ששכח ומל את של אחר השבת בשבת כיון שלא עשה מצוה כי בו' מלו אפילו ר' יהושע מודה שחייב חטאת. וכן הלכה וכל היכא דפליג ר' אליעזר ור' יהושע הלכה כר' יהושע חוץ ממקומות ידועים. וזה אינו מהם. וכן רב הונא הלכתא כוותיה דשכיח גבי ריש גלותא וגרסינן הלכתא כוותיה או הלכתא כוותייכו כו': מתניתין קטן נימול לשמנה לתשעה כו' קטן חולה אין מלין אותו עד שיבריא. אמר שמואל חלצתו חמה נותנין לו כל ז' להברותו והלכתא כשמואל דיהבינן ליה מאחר שחלצתו חמה שבעת ימים

חשק שלמה על רבינו חננאל
א) [נראה לענין דחסר פה כמה תיבות וכצ"ל על מי שהיו לו שני תינוקות אחד למול בשבת ואחד למול אחר השבת ושכח ומל של אחר השבת בשבת שהוא חייב וכו'. ורב יהודה מתני פטור דמוקי לה כר"מ וכו' ומהדר לאוקמי מתני' כר"מ משום דקיי"ל דסתם משנה ר"מ וכו']:

טומטום שראה לובן ואודם מביאת מקדש וכ"ת משום דאיכא קרא יתירא (ג) דדריש לה לטומטום דכתיב מזכר ועד נקבה תשלחו ואי למעוטי אנדרוגינוס גרידא לא ה"ל למיכתב אלא זכר לא היא דאי לא כתב אלא זכר א"כ ה"א אשה לא מחייב' בביאת מקדש מדכתיב זכר ולא כתיב אדם ושמא י"ל דלית ליה לרב דר"מ דאיכא אמורא נמי דפליג עליה בבכורות וא"ת ומאי איצטריך רב למעוטי אנדרוגינוס והא איהו ס"ל בפרק הערל ביבמות (דף פג.) דאנדרוגינוס ספיקא הוא (ג) ואיצטריך קרא למעוטי ספק מיהו הא לא קשיא דה"א כשראה לובן ואודם כאחת יתחייב ממ"נ אבל הא תימה כיון דסבר רב אנדרוגינוס ספיקא הוא מאי קאמר רב מזכר ועד נקבה זכר ודאי נקבה ודאית ואם הוא זכר ימעט אותו מזכר ואם הוא נקבה ימעט אותו מנקבה ומיהו י"ל דמשום טומטום נקטיה דפעמים הוי זכר ופעמים הוי נקבה:

הזכר ולא טומטום ואנדרוגינוס. תימה לרבי דבפרק אלו מומין (בכורות דף מב.) גבי בכור מצריך הזכר הזכרים למעוטי טומטום ואנדרוגינוס משמע הכא דמהזכר לחודיה לא הוה ממעטינן ליה והכא ממעטינן ליה מהזכר לחודיה:

(א) וסתם ספרא רבי יהודה אמר רב נחמן בר יצחק אף אנן נמי תנינא הכל כשרים לקדש חוץ מחש"ו רבי יהודה מכשיר בקטן ופוסל באשה ואנדרוגינוס ש"מ ומאי שנא מילה משום דכתיב המול לכם כל זכר: **מתני'** מי שהיו לו שני תינוקות אחד למול אחר השבת ואחד למול בשבת ושכח ומל את של אחר השבת בשבת חייב אחד למול בע"ש ואחד למול בשבת ושכח ומל את של ע"ש בשבת רבי אליעזר מחייב חטאת ורבי יהושע פוטר: **גמ'** רב הונא מתני חייב רב יהודה מתני פטור רב הונא מתני חייב דתניא אמר ר"ש בן אלעזר לא נחלקו רבי אליעזר ור' יהושע על מי שהיו לו ב' תינוקות אחד למול בשבת ואחד למול אחר השבת ושכח ומל את של אחר השבת בשבת שהוא חייב על מה נחלקו על מי שהיו לו ב' תינוקות א' למול בע"ש וא' למול בשבת ושכח ומל את של ע"ש בשבת שר' אליעזר מחייב חטאת ורבי יהושע פוטר ושניהם לא למדוה אלא מעבודת כוכבים ר' אליעזר סבר כעבודת כוכבים מה עבודת כוכבים אמר רחמנא לא תעביד וכי עביד מיחייב ה"נ לא שנא ורבי יהושע התם דלאו מצוה הכא מצוה רב יהודה מתני פטור דתניא א"ר מאיר לא נחלקו ר"א ורבי יהושע על מי שהיו לו ב' תינוקות אחד למול בע"ש ואחד למול בשבת ושכח ומל את של ע"ש בשבת שהוא פטור על מה נחלקו על מי שהיו לו ב' תינוקות אחד למול אחר השבת וא' למול בשבת ושכח ומל את של אחר השבת בשבת שר"א מחייב חטאת ורבי יהושע פוטר ושניהם לא למדוה אלא מעבודת כוכבים ר"א סבר כעבודת כוכבים מה עבודת כוכבים אמר רחמנא לא תעביד וכי עביד מיחייב ה"נ לא שנא ור' יהושע התם לא טריד מצוה הכא טריד מצוה תני ר' חייא אומר היה ר"מ לא נחלקו רבי אליעזר ורבי יהושע על מי שהיו לו ב' תינוקות א' למול בע"ש וא' למול בשבת ושכח ומל את של ע"ש בשבת שהוא חייב על מה נחלקו על מי שהיו לו ב' תינוקות א' למול אחר השבת וא' למול בשבת ושכח ומל את של אחר השבת בשבת שר"א מחייב חטאת ור' יהושע פוטר השתא רבי יהושע סיפא דלא קא עביד מצוה פוטר רישא דקא עביד מצוה מחייב אמרי דבי ר' ינאי רישא כגון שקדם ומל של שבת בע"ש דלא ניתנה שבת לידחות סיפא ניתנה שבת לידחות א"ל רב אשי לרב כהנא רישא נמי ניתנה שבת לידחות לגבי תינוקות דעלמא להאי גברא מיהא לא איתיהיב: **מתני'** קטן נימול לשמנה לתשעה ולעשרה ולאחד עשר ולי"ב לא פחות ולא יותר הא כיצד כדרכו לשמנה נולד לבין השמשות נימול לט' ביה"ש של ע"ש נימול לעשרה יו"ט לאחר השבת נימול לאחד עשר ב' ימים של ר"ה נימול לשנים עשר קטן החולה אין מוהלין אותו עד שיבריא: **גמ'** אמר שמואל חלצתו חמה נותנין לו כל ז' להברותו איבעיא להו מי בעינן מעת לעת ת"ש דתני לודא יום הבראתו כיום הולדו מאי לאו מה יום הולדו לא בעינן מעת לעת אף יום הבראתו לא בעינן מעת לעת לא עדיף יום הבראתו מיום הולדו דאילו יום הולדו לא בעינן מעת לעת ואילו יום הבראתו בעינן מעת לעת: **מתני'** אלו הן ציצין המעכבין את המילה בשר החופה את רוב העטרה ואינו אוכל בתרומה ואם היה בעל בשר מתקנו מפני מראית העין מל

והא סתם ספרא הוא דבתורת כהנים תניא לה וסתם ספרא רבי יהודה (ב): לקדש. מי חטאת לתת אפר על המים: מכשיר בקטן ופוסל באשה. טעמיה מפרש בסדר יומא בפ"ג: ובאנדרוגינוס. שמע מינה דרבי יהודה כאשה משוי ליה: כל זכר. ריבויא הוא:

מתני' ושכח ומל את של אחר השבת בשבת חייב. דטעה בדבר מצוה ולא עשה מצוה הוא ועבד ליה חבורה שלא לצורך והא אפילו רבי יהושע מודה: אחד למול בשבת ואחד למול בע"ש ושכח ומל את של ע"ש בשבת ר"א מחייב חטאת. דמילה שלא בזמנה אינה דוחה שבת ואע"ג דטעה בדבר מצוה שהיה טרוד באותו של שבת ומתוך כך טעה בזה ואף בזה עשה מצוה שהרי ראוי הוא למול אלא שאינו דוחה שבת קס"ל לר"א טעה בדבר מצוה ועשה מצוה שיש בה חיוב חטאת חייב ורבי יהושע פוטר דס"ל טעה בדבר מצוה ועשה מצוה פטור: **גמ'** רב הונא מתני. במתניתין ברישא חייב לדברי הכל כדתנינן לה אלן: ורב יהודה מתני ברישא פטור. דמוקי לה בשכח ומל את של ע"ש בשבת ופלוגתא היא בשל אחר השבת בשבת: שהוא חייב. דאע"ג דטריד במצוה וטעה בה כיון דלאו מצוה עבדיין לא הגיע זמנו למול חייב: אלא מע"ז. שהוקשו כל מצות שבתורה לחטאת ע"ז דכתיב תורה אחת יהיה לכם וגו' בפרשת שלח לך אנשים גבי קרבן ע"ז: ור' יהושע התם. עובד עבודת כוכבים לא עשה מצוה: ה"ג רב יהודה מתני פטור דתניא אמר ר"מ לא נחלקו ר"א ורבי יהושע על שהיו לו שני תינוקות אחד למול ע"ש כו': ה"ג ורבי יהושע התם לא טריד במצוה הכא טריד במצוה. טרוד להתעסק במצוה גמורה שהרי אחד מהם ומנו היום וטרוד לבו למהר ולעשות ומתוך טרדו טעה ומל את זה שאין בו מצוה כלל: ושכח ומל של ע"ש בשבת שהוא חייב. לקמיה מפרש לה: דלא ניתנה שבת לידחות. שאין לו תינוק שיהא זמנו היום הלכך לא היה טרוד היום במצוה שלא היה מוטל עליו כלום לעשות ולא היה לו לטעות: **מתני'** נולד בין השמשות נימול לט'. שהרי ליום שמיני של מחר הוא נימול ושמא בין השמשות יום הוא ונימול לט': היה היום ע"ש. א"א למולו בשבת הבאה דשמא לט' הוא והוי ליה מילה שלא בזמנה ואינה דוחה שבת וצריך להמתין עד לאחר השבת שהוא עשירי: חל יו"ט להיות אחר השבת. אין מילה שלא בזמנה דוחה אותו ונימול לי"א: **גמ'** חלצתו חמה. נשלף ממנו החולי ויצא מגופו: דתני לודא. שם חכם: יום הבראתו כיום הולדו. ממתינין לו כיום הולדו: מאי לאו. יום הולדו דווקא קאמר דלא בעינן מעת לעת: לא. כיום הולדו דקתני למיתב ליה ז' מיהו עדיף יום הבראתו מהא דבעינן מעת לעת ומהא ליכא למשמע מידי: **מתני'** ציצין. רצועות של בשר שנשארו מן הערלה: עטרה. היא שפה גבוה המקפת את הגיד סביב וממנה משפע ויורד לראשו: ואינו אוכל בתרומה. אם כהן הוא דילפינן ביבמות (ד' ע.) שערל אסור בתרומה: ואם היה בעל בשר. שהיה שמן ונראה בשר שלמעלה מערלתו לאחר שניטלה ערלה כולה כאילו אותו בשר חוזר וחופה את הגיד: מתקנו. ומשפע באיזמל מאותו עובי: מפני מראית העין. שלא יהא נראה כערל:

פרע

מסורת הש"ס

א) [עירובין לו: וש"נ], ב) יומא מג. יבמות עב: ערכין ג. פרה פ"ה מ"ד, ג) פסחים עב. כריתות יט., ד) [נ"ל אליעזר], ה) פסחים עב. ע"ש, ו) [נ"ל אליעזר], ז) [יבמות לד.], ח) ערכין ח:, ט) יבמות עא., י) ג"ז שם:, כ) יבמות מז: עה:, ל) [סנהדרין פו.].

הגהות הב"ח

(א) גמ' וסתם ספרא ר' יהודה. נ"ב וכ"ע מן מס' נדה דף מו: (ב) תוס' ד"ה הזכר וכו' יתירא למעוטי לה לטומטום: (ג) בא"ד ספיקא הוא וכי איצטריך:

גליון הש"ס

מתני' ור' יהושע פוטר. ע' מנחות דף סד ע"א מד"ה ואפי' נתכפר:

תורה אור השלם

א) זֹאת בְּרִיתִי אֲשֶׁר תִּשְׁמְרוּ בֵּינִי וּבֵינֵיכֶם וּבֵין זַרְעֲךָ אַחֲרֶיךָ הִמּוֹל לָכֶם כָּל זָכָר: [בראשית יז, י]

רב נסים גאון

ששחטה ותמצא כמותה בשחיטת חולין (עב) בפרק בהמה המקשה לילד: אף אנן נמי תנינא הכל כשרין לקדש חוץ מחרש שוטה וקטן כו'. זו המשנה במס' פרה בפרק ה' ולענין קידוש מי חטאת נתכונה. א) לומר שבעת שישארו ציצין המעכבין את המילה הרי הוא ערל עדיין ואם הוא כהן אסור לוכל בתרומה כמו ששנינו במס' יבמות (דף ע) הערל וכל הטמאין לא יאכלו בתרומה והזכירו בתלמוד המחלוקת שהיתה בין ר' אליעזר ובין ר' עקיבא בתורת כהנים במה שכתוב (ויקרא כב) איש איש מזרע אהרן ומה שכתוב (שם) תושב כהן ר' אליעזר גמר לערל בגזירה שוה לערל מפסח ור' עקיבא אמר איש איש לרבות את הערל: אבל

חשק שלמה על רב נסים גאון
א) זה לפרש את המשנה אלו הן ציצין כו':

ליקוטי רש"י

[ההתחלה בדף קלו:]
נימול לט'. כלומר לספק תשיעי [חולין פד:]. ביה"ש של ע"ש. נולד בין השמשות של ערב שבת אינו נימול בשבת דשמא תשיעי הוא לבין השמשות ספק יום ספק לילה ואם יום הוא נמצא שבת יום [תשיעי] ומילה שלא בזמנה אינה דוחה לא שבת ולא יו"ט [ערכין ח:]. יו"ט לאחר השבת. חל יו"ט להיות אחר אותה שבת שהוא עשירי נמול לאחד עשר משום דמילה שלא בזמנה לא דחיא דנפקא לן מהוא לבדו הוא ולא מכשיריו לבדו ולא מילה שלא בזמנה (סנהדרין) [בשבת כ"ד:] [חולין שם]. ב' ימים של ר"ה. ואם חלו שני ימים טובים של ר"ה אחר אותו שבת אינו נימול עד יום שלישי שהוא שנים עשר ללידתו [ערכין שם]. חלצתו חמה. שלפתו ניטלה מגופו החמה הוא החולי הקודחו חלצתו לשון חלץ מהם (הושע ה) [ברכות לד:]. שהיה חולה ונתרפא ונתחלצה ונשלפה ממנו חמה [יבמות עא.]. יום הבראתו כיום הולדו. צריך להמתין שמונה ימים [שם:]. לעד ז' יומי לא מהלינן ליה [שם]. מאי לאו. הכי קאמר מה יום הולדו לא בעינן מעת לעת אף יום הבראה לא בעי מעת לעת. לא עדיף יום הבראתו כו'. והא דתנא לודאה יום הבראתו כיום הולדו הא אתא לאשמועינן שצריך להמתין עד יום שמיני [שם:]. ציצין. שיורי ערלה ובמתניתין מפרש אלו הן ציצין המעכבין ויש שאין מעכבין כגון בשר שאינו חופה רוב העטרה אלא מיעוטה [לעיל קלג:]. חתיכות בשר שלא נפרעה המילה כהלכתה [יבמות מז:]. ציצין שנשתיירו שלא חתך כל הערלה [שם עא:]. עטרה. שורה גבוהה המקפת בגיד סביב וממנה הולך ומשפע מעלה ולמטה [שם מז:]. שורה גבוהה שסביב הגיד משפע ויורד לצד הקרקע ומשפע ויורד לצד הגוף [לעיל שם].

Mishnah The following Mishnah delineates various instances in which circumcision must be postponed until the ninth, tenth, eleventh, or twelfth day, because of a doubt as to whether the Sabbath was the child's eighth day:

קָטָן נִימּוֹל לִשְׁמֹנָה לְתִשְׁעָה וְלַעֲשָׂרָה וּלְאַחַד עָשָׂר וְלִשְׁנֵים עָשָׂר – **A child is** sometimes **circumcised on the eighth, ninth, tenth, eleventh, or twelfth** day, לֹא פָּחוֹת וְלֹא יוֹתֵר – **not earlier nor later.**[34] הָא כֵּיצַד – **How is this?** כְּדַרְכּוֹ לִשְׁמֹנָה – **In normal circumstances** a child is circumcised **on the eighth** day. נוֹלַד לְבֵין הַשְּׁמָשׁוֹת נִימּוֹל לְתִשְׁעָה – **If he was born during twilight, he is circumcised on the ninth.**[35] בֵּין הַשְּׁמָשׁוֹת שֶׁל עֶרֶב שַׁבָּת נִימּוֹל לַעֲשָׂרָה – If he was born during **twilight on the eve of the Sabbath, he is circumcised on the tenth.**[36] יוֹם טוֹב לְאַחַר הַשַּׁבָּת נִימּוֹל לְאַחַד עָשָׂר – **If,** in the previous case, **Yom Tov falls** on the day **after the Sabbath, he is circumcised on the eleventh.**[37] שְׁנֵי יָמִים שֶׁל רֹאשׁ הַשָּׁנָה נִימּוֹל לִשְׁנֵים עָשָׂר – **If the two days of Rosh Hashanah** fall immediately after the Sabbath, **he is circumcised on the twelfth.**[38] קָטָן הַחוֹלֶה אֵין מוֹהֲלִין אוֹתוֹ עַד שֶׁיַּבְרִיא – In the case of **a sick child, we do not circumcise him until he becomes healthy.**[39]

Gemara The Gemara discusses the last statement of the Mishnah:

אָמַר שְׁמוּאֵל – **Shmuel said:** חַלְצָתוֹ חַמָּה – Once **the fever has left him** נוֹתְנִין לוֹ כָּל שִׁבְעָה לְהַבְרוֹתוֹ – **we give him all of seven**

NOTES

assumption that what he did was permitted because the Torah required it of him is no different than any other mistaken assumption that leads one to do something forbidden. Every *chatas* liability results from some mistaken assumption that the act was permitted.]

In conclusion: According to R' Chiya, the dispute between R' Eliezer and R' Yehoshua is in the case where he circumcised an after-Sabbath child on the Sabbath. The basis of the dispute is whether being occupied with performing a required mitzvah exempts one from a *chatas* when he does not actually fulfill a mitzvah [טָעָה בִּדְבַר מִצְוָה וְלֹא עָשָׂה מִצְוָה]. In this, R' Chiya agrees with the earlier Baraisa's explanation of the dispute according to R' Meir. R' Chiya merely adds that even according to R' Meir, the dispute is only in a case where both infants are still awaiting circumcision. But if the Sabbath infant was mistakenly circumcised on Friday (so that there is no longer any mitzvah to be performed on the Sabbath), everyone would agree that one is liable for circumcising the other infant on the Sabbath (see further, *Shabbos Shel Mi*).

⊸§ **Summary:** According to *R' Shimon ben Elazar* and *Rav Huna,* the dispute between R' Eliezer and R' Yehoshua is whether, *being occupied with a required mitzvah, and actually performing a mitzvah* (though not the permitted one) [טָעָה בִּדְבַר מִצְוָה וְעָשָׂה מִצְוָה] exempts one from having to bring a *chatas* for his transgression. R' Yehoshua holds that it does exempt; R' Eliezer holds that it does not. But if one did not perform a mitzvah, both agree that one is liable.

According to *R' Meir* and *Rav Yehudah* all agree that if one was both occupied with a required mitzvah and he actually performed a mitzvah, then he is exempt. The dispute concerns a case where he was occupied with trying to perform a required mitzvah but did *not* in the end perform any mitzvah [טָעָה בִּדְבַר מִצְוָה וְלֹא עָשָׂה מִצְוָה]. R' Yehoshua exempts even in this case whereas R' Eliezer considers him liable.

R' Chiya points out that in the reverse case — where the person was not required to perform any mitzvah that day (though he mistakenly thought he was) but he did perform a mitzvah — he is nonetheless liable.

34. [I.e. there are circumstances in which even a perfectly healthy child is prevented by law from having its circumcision performed on his eighth day but rather has it postponed to one of these days. However, a circumcision is never advanced to before the eighth day nor postponed until after the twelfth day for reasons of law.]

35. [Twilight is the period of time between sunset and nightfall. (In regard to the length of twilight, see above, 35a, and *Tosafos* ibid. ד״ה תרי.) There is a legal question as to whether twilight should be judged the end of the preceding day or the beginning of the following night (see above, 34a). Therefore, if a child was born, for example, on Sunday between sunset and nightfall, we are uncertain whether to consider him born on Sunday or Monday.]

Since circumcision cannot take place before the eighth day, we must, because of this doubt, postpone the circumcision until the following Monday — the ninth day as counted from the day preceding the twilight [of which the twilight may actually be a part] (*Rashi*). Although by doing so we knowingly ignore the requirement to circumcise on the eighth day, it is better to perform the circumcision on the ninth day, when the circumcision is surely valid, than to perform it possibly prematurely, in which case the mitzvah has not been fulfilled at all (*Chidushei HaRan;* see *Sfas Emes*).

36. I.e. on Sunday. Since we are uncertain whether to count Friday or the Sabbath as the day of his birth, we cannot circumcise him either on the following Friday (because that may be only his seventh day) or the Sabbath (since if Friday is judged to be the day of his birth, the Sabbath would be the ninth day, and a postponed circumcision may not take place on the Sabbath). The circumcision must, therefore, be postponed until Sunday, which is the tenth day (*Rashi*).

[The *Yerushalmi* asks why we should not perform the circumcision during twilight of Friday. That way, if twilight is considered part of the previous day, then both the birth and the circumcision will have taken place on Friday. If twilight is considered the onset of the following night, then both the birth and circumcision will have taken place on the Sabbath. The *Yerushalmi* answers that the uncertainty in regard to twilight pertains to every moment of the duration of twilight. While one moment of twilight may be considered part of the previous day, the next moment may already be considered the onset of the night. Since it is virtually impossible to time the performance of circumcision to the exact moment of birth, we are afraid that the birth may have taken place at a time of twilight which is considered part of the previous day, while the circumcision will have been performed at a time of twilight which is possibly the onset of night, resulting in a circumcision after the eighth day.

The *Yerushalmi's* question and answer assume that a nighttime circumcision is valid. This is the subject of a great dispute among the *Poskim* — see *Yoreh Deah* 262:1 with *Beis Yosef, Taz* §2 and *Shach* §2. See also *Hagahos HaGra* 264:10 and *She'eilos Yavetz* 1:35.]

37. I.e. if the child was born during twilight on Friday night and Sunday is Yom Tov, it cannot be circumcised on Sunday because a postponed circumcision does not override Yom Tov any more than it does the Sabbath (see above, 24b; See also *Chullin* 84b). It is therefore postponed until Monday (the day following Yom Tov), which is the eleventh day (*Rashi*).

38. If the two days of Rosh Hashanah fall on Sunday and Monday, the circumcision cannot be made on Monday either, for a postponed circumcision does not override even the prohibitions of the second day. Thus, the circumcision must be delayed until Tuesday — the twelfth day.

[*Rambam* (*Milah* 1:15 and *Commentary,* as explained by *Kesef Mishneh*) deduces from the Mishnah's shift from Yom Tov in general to Rosh Hashanah specifically that this stringency applies only to the second day of Rosh Hashanah. The second day of Yom Tov observed in the Diaspora, however, is treated more leniently and a postponed circumcision would be allowed on that day (cf. *Teshuvos Chasam Sofer* §250 for a different explanation of *Rambam's* ruling). This is disputed by *Rosh* (Responsum §26, cited in *Tur Yoreh Deah* 266), who explains that the reason the Tanna speaks of Rosh Hashanah in this case is because he wished to give an example that was relevant to Eretz Yisrael, where the Mishnah was written. *Shulchan Aruch* rules according to *Rosh* (but see *Shach* §8 there). See further in *Ba'er Hetev, Hagahos R' Akiva Eiger* and *Pischei Teshuvah* there; see additionally, *Sefer HaBris* 266:4.]

39. I.e. even if he is not dangerously ill we postpone the circumcision for fear that [in his weakened condition] it might endanger his life (*Beis Yosef* from *Nimukei Yosef,* cited by *Shach, Yoreh Deah* 262:3).

מסורת הש"ס

א) [עירובין לו: וש"נ], ב) יומא מג. יבמות עב: ערכין ג. פרה פ"ה מ"ד, ג) פסחים עב. כריתות יט:, ד) [צ"ל אליעזר], ה) פסחים עב. ע"ש, ו) [צ"ל אליעזר], ז) [יבמות לד.], ח) ערכין ח:, ט) יבמות עא., י) ג"ז שם., כ) יבמות מז: עא:, ל) [סנהדרין פו.].

עין משפט נר מצוה

מט א מיי' פ"ו מהל' פרה הלכה ג סמג עשין רלג:

נ ב ג מיי' פ"ב מהל' שגגות הלכה ס:

נא ד מיי' פ"א מהל' מילה הלכה יב סמג עשין כח טוש"ע י"ד סי' רסו סעיף ס:

נב ה מיי' שם הלכה יח סמג שם טוש"ע י"ד סי' רסב סעיף ב:

נג ו ז מיי' פ"ב מהל' מילה הלכה ג ה סמג שם טוש"ע י"ד סי' רסד סעיף ה ו:

(א) וסתם ספרא רבי יהודה אמר רב נחמן בר יצחק אף אנן נמי תנינא ב) הכל כשרים לקדש חוץ מחש"ו רבי יהודה מכשיר בקטן ופוסל באשה ואנדרוגינוס ש"מ ומאי שנא מילה משום דכתיב א) המול לכם כל זכר: **מתני'** ג) מי שהיו לו שני תינוקות אחד למול אחר השבת ואחד למול בשבת ושכח ומל את של אחר השבת בשבת חייב אחד למול בע"ש ואחד למול בשבת ושכח ומל את של ע"ש בשבת רבי אליעזר מחייב חטאת ה) ורבי יהושע פוטר: **גמ'** רב הונא מתני חייב רב יהודה מתני פטור רב הונא מתני חייב דתניא אמר ר"ש בן אלעזר לא נחלקו רבי ו) אליעזר ור' יהושע על מי שהיו לו ב' תינוקות אחד למול בשבת ואחד למול אחר השבת ושכח ומל את של אחר השבת בשבת שהוא חייב על מה נחלקו על מי שהיו לו ב' תינוקות א' למול בע"ש וא' למול בשבת ושכח ומל את של ע"ש בשבת שר' אליעזר מחייב חטאת ורבי יהושע פוטר ושניהם לא למדוה אלא מעבודת כוכבים ר' אליעזר סבר כעבודת כוכבים מה עבודת כוכבים אמר רחמנא לא תעביד וכי עביד מיחייב ה"נ לא שנא ורבי יהושע התם דלאו מצוה הכא מצוה רב יהודה מתני פטור דתניא א"ר מאיר ג) לא נחלקו ר"א ורבי יהושע על מי שהיו לו ב' תינוקות אחד למול בע"ש ואחד למול בשבת ושכח ומל את של ע"ש בשבת שהוא פטור על מה נחלקו על מי שהיו לו ב' תינוקות אחד למול אחר השבת וא' למול בשבת ושכח ומל את של אחר השבת בשבת שר"א מחייב חטאת ורבי יהושע ג) פוטר ושניהם לא למדוה אלא מעבודת כוכבים ר"א סבר כעבודת כוכבים מה עבודת כוכבים אמר רחמנא לא תעביד וכי עביד מיחייב ה"נ לא שנא ור' יהושע התם לא טריד מצוה הכא טריד מצוה ח) תני ר' חייא אומר היה ר"מ לא נחלקו רבי ו) אלעזר ורבי יהושע על מי שהיו לו ב' תינוקות א' למול בע"ש וא' למול בשבת ושכח ומל את של ע"ש בשבת שהוא חייב על מה נחלקו על מי שהיו לו ב' תינוקות א' למול אחר השבת וא' למול בשבת ושכח ומל של אחר השבת בשבת י) שר"א מחייב חטאת ור' יהושע פוטר השתא רבי יהושע סיפא דלא קא עביד מצוה פוטר רישא דקא עביד מצוה מחייב אמרי דבי ר' ינאי רישא כגון שקדם ומל של שבת בע"ש דלא ניתנה שבת לידחות סיפא ניתנה שבת לידחות א"ל רב אשי לרב כהנא רישא נמי ניתנה שבת לידחות לגבי תינוקות דעלמא להאי גברא מיהא לא איתיהיב: **מתני'** ט) קטן נימול לשמנה לתשעה ולעשרה ולאחד עשר ולי"ב לא פחות ולא יותר הא כיצד כדרכו לשמנה נולד לבין השמשות נימול לט' ביה"ש של ע"ש נימול לעשרה יו"ט לאחר השבת נימול לאחד עשר ב' ימים של ר"ה נימול לשנים עשר קטן החולה אין מוהלין אותו עד שיבריא: **גמ'** י) אמר שמואל ה) חלצתו חמה נותנין לו כל ז' להברותו איבעיא להו מי בעינן מעת לעת ת"ש דתני ו) לודא יום הבראתו כיום הולדו מאי לאו מה יום הולדו לא בעינן מעת לעת אף יום הבראתו לא בעינן מעת לעת לא עדיף יום הבראתו מיום הולדו דאילו יום הולדו לא בעינן מעת לעת ואילו יום הבראתו בעינן מעת לעת: **מתני'** כ) אלו הן ציצין המעכבין את המילה בשר החופה את רוב העטרה ואינו אוכל בתרומה ו)ואם היה בעל בשר מתקנו מפני מראית העין

מל

רש"י

והא סתם ספרא הוא דבתורת כהנים תניא לה וסתם ספרא רבי יהודה: לקדש. מי חטאת לתת אפר על המים: מכשיר בקטן ופוסל באשה. טעמיה מפרש בסדר יומא בפ"ג: ובאנדרוגינוס. שמע מינה דרבי יהודה כאשה משוי ליה: כל זכר. ריבויא הוא:

מתני' ושכח ומל את של אחר השבת בשבת חייב. דטעה בדבר מצוה ולא עשה מצוה הוא ועבד ליה חבורה שלא לצורך והא אפילו רבי יהושע מודה: אחד למול בשבת ואחד למול בע"ש ושכח ומל את של ע"ש בשבת ר"א מחייב חטאת. דמילה שלא בזמנה אינה דוחה שבת ואע"ג דטעה בדבר מצוה שהיה טרוד באותו של שבת ומתוך כך טעה בזה ואף בזה עשה מצוה שהרי ראוי הוא למול אלא שאינו דוחה שבת ס"ל לר"א טעה בדבר מצוה ועשה מצוה שיש בה חיוב חטאת חייב ורבי יהושע פוטר דס"ל טעה בדבר מצוה ועשה מצוה פטור: **גמ'** רב הונא מתני. במתניתין ברישא חייב לדברי הכל כדמפרש לה לקמן: ורב יהודה מתני ברישא פטור. דמוקי לה בשכח ומל את של ע"ש בשבת ופלוגתא היא בשל אחר השבת בשבת: שהוא חייב. לר"א דטריד במצוה וטעה בה כיון דאותו מצוה שעדיין לא הגיע זמנו למול חייב: אלא מע"ז. שהוקשו כל מצות שבתורה לחטאת ע"ז דכתיב תורה אחת יהיה לכם וגו' בפרשת שלח לך אנשים גבי קרבן ע"ז: ור' יהושע התם. עובד עבודת כוכבים לא עשה מצוה: ה"נ רב יהודה מתני פטור דקאמר ר"מ לא נחלקו ר"א ורבי יהושע על שהיו לו שני תינוקות אחד למול ע"ש כו'. ה"נ ורבי יהושע התם לא טריד במצוה הכא טריד במצוה. טרוד להתעסק במצוה גמורה שהרי אחד מהם זמנו היום וטרוד לבו למהר ולעשות ומתוך טרדו טעה ומל את זה שאין בו מצוה כלל: ושכח ומל של ע"ש בשבת שהוא חייב. לקמיה מפרש לה: דלא ניתנה שבת לידחות. שאין לו תינוק שיהא זמנו היום הלכך לא היה טרוד היום במצוה שלא היה מוטל עליו כלום לעשות ולא היה לו לטעות: **מתני'** נולד בין השמשות נימול לט'. שהרי ליום שמיני של מחר הוא נימול ושמא בין השמשות יום הוא ונימול לט': היה היום ע"ש. א"א למולו בשבת הבאה דשמא ט' הוא והויא ליה מילה שלא בזמנה ואינה דוחה שבת וצריך להמתין עד לאחר השבת שהוא עשירי: חל יו"ט להיות אחר השבת. אין מילה שלא בזמנה דוחה אותו ונימול לי"א: **גמ'** חלצתו חמה. נשלף ממנו החולי ויצא מגופו: דתני לודא. שם חכם: יום הבראתו כיום הולדו. ממתינין לו כיום הולדו: מאי לאו. יום הולדו דווקא קאמר דלא בעינן מעת לעת: לא. כיום הולדו דקתני למיתב ליה ז' מיהו עדיף יום הבראתו מהא דבעינן מעת לעת ומהא ליכא למשמע מידי: **מתני'** ציצין. רצועות של בשר שנשארו מן הערלה: עטרה. היא שפה גבוה המקפת את הגיד סביב וממנה משפע ויורד לראשו: ואינו אוכל בתרומה. אם כהן הוא דילפינן ביבמות (ד' ע.) שערל אסור בתרומה: ואם היה בעל בשר. שהיה שמן ונראה בשר שלמעלה מערלתו לאחר שניטלה ערלה כולה כאילו אותו בשר חוזר וחופה את הגיד: מתקנו. ומשפע באיזמל מאותו עובי: מפני מראית העין. שלא יהא נראה כערל:

פרע

תוספות

טומטום שראה לובן ואודם מביאת מקדש וכ"ש משום דאיכא קרא יתירא (ג) דדריש לה לטומטום דכתיב מזכר ועד נקבה תשלחו ואי למעוטי אנדרוגינוס גרידא לא ה"ל למיכתב אלא זכר לא היה לא כתב אלא זכר א"כ ה"א אשה לא מחייב בביאת מקדש מדכתיב זכר ולא כתיב אדם ושמא י"ל דלית ליה לרב דר"מ דאיכא אמורא נמי דפליג עליה בבכורות וא"ת ומאי איצטריך רב למעוטי אנדרוגינוס והא איהו ס"ל בפרק הערל ביבמות (דף פג.) דאנדרוגינוס ספיקא הוא (ד) ואיצטריך קרא למעוטי ספק מיהו הא לא קשיא דה"א כשראה לובן ואודם כאחת יתחייב ממ"נ אבל הא תימה כיון דסבר רב אנדרוגינוס ספיקא הוא אמאי קאמר רב מזכר ועד נקבה זכר ודאי ונקבה ודאית ואם הוא זכר ימעט אותו מזכר ואם הוא נקבה ימעט אותו מנקבה ומיהו י"ל דמשום טומטום נקטיה דפעמים הוי זכר ופעמים הוי נקבה:

הזכר ולא טומטום ואנדרוגינוס. תימה לרבי דבפרק אלו מומין (בכורות דף מב.) גבי בכור מצריך הזכר הזכרים למעוטי טומטום ואנדרוגינוס משמע התם דמהזכר לחודיה לא הוה ממעטין לה והכא ממעטין ליה מהזכר לחודיה:

הגהות הב"ח

(א) גמ' וסתם ספרא ר' יהודה. נ"ב וע"ע מן מס' נדה דף מו: (ג) תום' ד"ה הזכר וכו' יתירא למעוטי לה לטומטום: (ד) בא"ד ספיקא הוא ומי איצטריך:

גליון הש"ס

מתני' ור' יהושע פוטר. ע' מנחות דף סד ע"א סד"ה ואפי' נתכפר:

תורה אור השלם

א) זֹאת בְּרִיתִי אֲשֶׁר תִּשְׁמְרוּ בֵּינִי וּבֵינֵיכֶם וּבֵין זַרְעֲךָ אַחֲרֶיךָ הִמּוֹל לָכֶם כָּל זָכָר: [בראשית יז, י]

רב נסים גאון

ששחטה ותמצא כמותה בשחיטת חולין (עב) בפרק בהמה המקשה לילד: אף אנן נמי תנינא הכל כשרין לקדש חוץ מחרש שוטה וקטן כו'. זו המשנה במס' פרה בפרק ה' ולענין קידוש מי חטאת נתכונה. א) לומר שבעת שישארו ציצין המעכבין את המילה הרי הוא ערל עדיין ואם הוא כהן אסור לוכל בתרומה כמו ששנינו במס' יבמות (דף ע) הערל וכל הטמאין לא יאכלו בתרומה והזכירו בתלמוד המחלוקת שהיתה בין ר' אליעזר ובין ר' עקיבא בתורת כהנים במה שכתוב (ויקרא כב) איש איש מזרע אהרן ומה שכתוב (שם) תושב כהן ר' אליעזר גמר לערל בגזירה שוה לערל מפסח ור' עקיבא אמר איש איש לרבות את הערל: אבל

חשק שלמה על רב נסים גאון

א) זה לפרש את המשנה אלו הן ציצין כו':

רבינו חננאל

א"ר יהודה אנדרוגינוס זכר הוא. שאם אי אתה אומר כך יערך ומנ"ל דלא מערך דתניא הזכר ולא טומטום ואנדרוגינוס כו' ופשוטה היא ומסקינן בה ומאי שנא גבי מילה דכתיב המול לכם כל זכר כל לרבות. ויש מי שאומר הלכתא כרבנן דאמרי ספק ואנדרוגינוס אין מחללין עליו את השבת ואין הלכה כר' יהודה ומדחזינן רב חסדא דריש לטעמיה דר' יהודה ש"מ הלכתא כוותיה: **מתניתין** מי שהיו לו ב' תינוקות אחד למול אחר השבת ואחד למול בשבת ושכח ומל את של אחר השבת בשבת חייב וכו' [ואמרינן בגמ'] רב הונא מתני חייב ורב יהודא מתני פטור פי' רב הונא מתני חייב דמוקים ליה למתניתין לר"ש דאמר ר"ש לא נחלקו ר' אליעזר (ור"ש) [ור' יהושע] על מי שהיו לו א) דקיי"ל סתם משנה ר' מאיר ובהא תנא דבי ר' חייא פליגי עליה ורב התא דמוקים לה כר' שמעון כוותיה עבדינן וחלוקת ר' אליעזר ור' יהושע דברים ברורין הן. (שנים) ושניהם מע"ז למדוה דהא איתקשא כל התורה כולה לע"ז ר' אליעזר סבירא כע"ז מה ע"ז אמרה תורה לא תעבוד ואם תעבוד ע"ז בשגגה מכל מקום חייב חטאת. כן אמרה תורה בשבת. המחלל השבת בשגגה מ"מ חייב חטאת. ור' יהושע סבר התם לגבי ע"ז לא נתכוין לקיים המצוה הכא בשבת נתכוין לקיים מצות מילה. לפיכך פטור הוא והלכתא כר' יהושע וכדמתניתין ר' שמעון: אחד למול ערב שבת ואחד למול בשבת ושכח ומל את של שבת בע"ש ואת של ע"ש בשבת פטור כי מ"מ מצוה עשה. ואע"פ שמל בט'. אבל בזמן ששכח ומל את של אחר השבת בשבת כיון שלא עשה מצוה כי בז' מלו אפילו ר' יהושע מודה שחייב חטאת. וכן הלכה וכל היכא דפליג ר' אליעזר ור' יהושע הלכה כר' יהושע חוץ ממקומות ידועים. וזה אינו מהם. וכן רב הונא הלכתא כוותיה דשיטה גבי ריש גלותא וגרסינן הלכתא כוותיה או הלכתא כוותיה כר': **מתניתין** קטן נימול לשמונה לתשעה כו' קטן חולה אין מלין אותו עד שיבריא. אמר שמואל חלצתו חמה נותנין לו כל ז' להברותו והלכתא כשמואל דיהבינן ליה מאחר שחלצתו [illegible]

חשק שלמה על רבינו חננאל

א) [נראה לעין דחסר פה כמה תיבות וצ"ל על מי שהיו לו שני תינוקות אחד למול אחר השבת ואחד למול בשבת ושכח ומל של אחר השבת בשבת שהוא חייב [illegible] סטור דתניא אמר ר"מ וכו' ומהדר לאוקמי מתני' כר"מ משום דקיי"ל [illegible]

ליקוטי רש"י

[ההתחלה בדף קלו:] נימול לט'. כלומר לספק תשיעי [חולין פד:]. ביה"ש של ע"ש. נולד בין השמשות של ערב שבת אינו נימול בשבת דשמא תשיעי הוא דבין השמשות ספק יום ספק לילה ואם יום הוא נמצא שבת יום [תשיעי] ומילה שלא בזמנה אינה דוחה לא שבת ולא יו"ט [ערכין ח:]. יו"ט לאחר השבת. חל יו"ט להיות אחר אותה שבת שהוא עשירי נמול לאחד עשר משום דמילה שלא בזמנה לא דחיא דנפקא לן מהוא לבדו הוא ולא מכשיריו לבדו ולא מילה שלא בזמנה (בסנהדרין) [בשבת כ"ד:] [חולין שם]. ב' ימים של ר"ה. ואם חלו שני ימים טובים של ר"ה אחר אותו שבת אינו נימול עד יום שלישי שהוא שנים עשר ללידתו [ערכין שם]. חלצתו חמה. שלפתו ניטלה מגופו החמה הוא החולי הקודמו חלצתו לשון חלץ מהם (הושע ה) [ברכות לד:]. שהיה חולה ונתרפא ונתחלחלה ונשתלפה ממנו חמה [יבמות עא.]. יום הבראתו כיום הולדו. צריך להמתין שמונה ימים [שם:]. לעד ז' יומי לא מהלינן ליה [שם.]. מאי לאו. הכי קאמר מה יום הולדו לא בעינן מעת לעת אף יום הבראה לא בעי מעת לעת. לא עדיף יום הבראתו כו'. והא דתנא לודאה יום הבראתו כיום הולדו הא לא להמתין עד יום שמיני [שם:]. ציצין. שיורי ערלה ובמתניתין מפרש אלו הן ציצין המעכבין ויש שאינן מעכבין כגון בשר שאינה חופה רוב העטרה אלא מיעוטה [לעיל קלג:]. חתיכות בשר שלא נפרעת המילה כהלכתה [יבמות מז:]. שלא חתך כל הערלה [שם עא:]. עטרה. שורה גבוהה המקפת בגיד סביב שממנה הגיד משפע מעלה ולמטה [שם מז:]. שורה גבוהה שסביב הגיד וממנה הולך ומשפע ויורד לצד הקרקע ומשפע ויורד לצד הגוף [לעיל קלג:].

days from the time of **his recovery** before circumcising him.[40]

An inquiry concerning Shmuel's statement:

אִיבַּעְיָא לְהוּ – They inquired: מִי בְּעִינַן מֵעֵת לְעֵת – Do we require an interval of seven **twenty-four hour periods?**[41]

The Gemara attempts to resolve this inquiry:

תָּא שְׁמַע – Come, learn the proof from the following Baraisa: **דְּתָנֵי לוּדָא – For Luda taught a Baraisa: יוֹם הַבְרָאָתוֹ כְּיוֹם הִוָּלְדוֹ – THE DAY OF HIS RECOVERY IS THE SAME AS THE DAY OF HIS BIRTH. מַאי לָאו – Is it not** that this comparison means to teach that **מַה יוֹם הִוָּלְדוֹ לֹא בְּעִינַן מֵעֵת לְעֵת – just as** in the case of **the day of his birth we do not require** an interval of seven **twenty-four-hour periods** before circumcising him,[42] **אַף יוֹם הַבְרָאָתוֹ לֹא בְּעִינַן מֵעֵת לְעֵת – so too** in the case of **the day of his recovery we do not require** an interval of seven **twenty-four-hour periods** before circumcising him? Rather, he can be circumcised on the morning of the eighth day following his recovery.

The Gemara rejects the proof:

לֹא – No, עָדִיף יוֹם הַבְרָאָתוֹ מִיּוֹם הִוָּלְדוֹ – the day of his recovery is equal to and even **greater** [i.e. treated more stringently] **than the day of his birth. דְּאִילּוּ יוֹם הִוָּלְדוֹ לֹא בְּעִינַן מֵעֵת לְעֵת – For with the day of his birth we do not require** seven **twenty-four-hour periods, וְאִילּוּ יוֹם הַבְרָאָתוֹ בְּעִינַן מֵעֵת לְעֵת – whereas with the day of his recovery we do require** seven **twenty-four-hour periods.**[43]

Mishnah **אֵלּוּ הֵן צִיצִין הַמְעַכְּבִין אֶת הַמִּילָה – These are the shreds that impede** the validity **of the circumcision:**[44] **בָּשָׂר הַחוֹפֶה אֶת רוֹב הָעֲטָרָה – flesh that covers the larger part of the corona.**[45] **וְאֵינוֹ אוֹכֵל בִּתְרוּמָה – And one** whose circumcision left him with such shreds **may not eat *terumah*.**[46] **וְאִם הָיָה בַּעַל בָּשָׂר – If [a child] was fleshy** and thus gave the appearance of being uncircumcised even after its foreskin was removed, **מְתַקְּנוֹ מִפְּנֵי מַרְאִית הָעַיִן – he should rectify it because of the appearance** of wrongdoing.[47]

NOTES

40. [I.e. we do not circumcise him until seven days have passed from the time the fever departed.]

This regulation applies only to children who suffer illnesses that affect their whole body. A child afflicted by an ailment that is limited to but one of his limbs does not require this waiting period and is circumcised as soon as he has recovered from his sickness (*Ran; Yoreh Deah* 262:2). [See *Teshuvos Binyan Tzion* (87) for a discussion of whether this seven-day waiting period is by Biblical or Rabbinical decree. From *Rosh* and *Ran* here it would seem that it is based on the medical concern that he may still possibly be too weak to survive the circumcision (see below, note 43).]

41. [Literally: from time to time. Although under normal circumstances a child is circumcised on the eighth day without having to wait seven twenty-four-hour periods, the Gemara held that in a case of an infant who was ill, the full seven-day interval may be necessary to insure the infant's full capacity to undergo circumcision.]

42. Rather, we apply the legal principle of מִקְצָת הַיּוֹם כְּכֻלּוֹ, *part of a day is equivalent to a full day,* and we consider the day of his birth up until nightfall as a complete twenty-four-hour period (see *Teshuvos Mahari Weil* §158).

43. Accordingly, the Baraisa's comparison only means to teach Shmuel's ruling – that a recovered infant must undergo a seven-day waiting period the same as a newborn [for we view the day of recovery as if the child had been born that day] (*Rashi;* see *Ritva MHK* ed.).

[Since the question is not resolved by the Gemara, we rule stringently and require a full seven days to elapse before circumcising the child, for it is a question of possible danger to the child to do it earlier (*Rosh*). Additionally, though the Gemara does not resolve the question here, the Gemara in *Yevamos* 71b reaches the conclusion that a recovered infant needs a waiting period of seven full days before undergoing circumcision (*Ran;* cf. *Korban Nesanel* §8). *Shulchan Aruch* (*Yoreh Deah* 262:2) follows this conclusion.]

44. These are the strips of foreskin (*Rashi*) that, if not removed during circumcision, render the circumcision invalid, pending their removal. (See Gemara above, 133b, for the law for shreds that are not critical to validity.)

45. I.e. the ridge surrounding the membrum, from which it tapers to a point (*Rashi*). Some define עֲטָרָה, *corona,* as the entire glans (see *Beis Yosef* and *Bach* to *Yoreh Deah* 264; for further discussion, see *Sefer HaBris* ch. 8 at length).

46. A Kohen may not eat *terumah* unless he is circumcised (*Rashi* from *Yevamos* 70a). [Even if he is uncircumcised for a valid reason (e.g. two of his older brothers died from circumcision), he may not eat *terumah.*] Any shreds remaining on a Kohen that invalidate the circumcision therefore disqualify that Kohen from eating *terumah.*

47. If as a result of the child's plumpness the excess flesh above the foreskin hangs down and appears to cover the corona after the foreskin is removed, the circumciser should trim away the excess flesh so that the child should not appear to be uncircumcised (*Rashi* as explained by *Nekudas HaKesef* to *Yoreh Deah* 264:6; cf. *Terumas HaDeshen* §264 who explains *Rashi* differently; see further, 137b note 7).

(א) וסתם ספרא רבי יהודה אמר רב נחמן בר יצחק אף אנן נמי תנינא הכל כשרים לקדש חוץ מחש"ו רבי יהודה מכשיר בקטן ופוסל באשה ואנדרוגינוס ש"מ ומאי שנא מילה משום דכתיב המול לכם כל זכר: **מתני'** מי שהיו לו שני תינוקות אחד למול אחר השבת ואחד למול בשבת ושכח ומל את של אחר השבת בשבת חייב אחד למול בע"ש ואחד למול בשבת ושכח ומל את של ע"ש בשבת רבי אליעזר מחייב חטאת ורבי יהושע פוטר: **גמ'** רב הונא מתני חייב רב יהודה מתני פטור רב הונא מתני חייב דתניא אמר ר"ש בן אלעזר לא נחלקו רבי אליעזר ור' יהושע על מי שהיו לו ב' תינוקות אחד למול בשבת ואחד למול אחר השבת ושכח ומל את של אחר השבת בשבת שהוא חייב על מה נחלקו על מי שהיו לו ב' תינוקות א' למול בע"ש וא' למול בשבת ושכח ומל את של ע"ש בשבת שר' אליעזר מחייב חטאת ורבי יהושע פוטר ושניהם לא למדוה אלא מעבודת כוכבים ר' אליעזר סבר כעבודת כוכבים מה עבודת כוכבים אמר רחמנא לא תעביד וכי עביד מיחייב ה"נ לא שנא ורבי יהושע התם דלאו מצוה הכא מצוה רב יהודה מתני פטור דתניא א"ר מאיר לא נחלקו ר"א ורבי יהושע על מי שהיו לו ב' תינוקות אחד למול בע"ש ואחד למול בשבת ושכח ומל את של ע"ש בשבת שהוא פטור על מה נחלקו על מי שהיו לו ב' תינוקות אחד למול אחר השבת וא' למול בשבת ושכח ומל את של אחר השבת בשבת שר"א מחייב חטאת ורבי יהושע פוטר ושניהם לא למדוה אלא מעבודת כוכבים ר"א סבר כעבודת כוכבים מה עבודת כוכבים אמר רחמנא לא תעביד וכי עביד מיחייב ה"נ לא שנא ור' יהושע התם לא טריד מצוה הכא טריד מצוה תני ר' חייא אומר היה ר"מ לא נחלקו רבי אלעזר ורבי יהושע על מי שהיו לו ב' תינוקות א' למול בע"ש וא' למול בשבת ושכח ומל את של ע"ש בשבת שהוא חייב על מה נחלקו על מי שהיו לו ב' תינוקות א' למול אחר השבת וא' למול בשבת ושכח ומל של אחר השבת בשבת שר"א מחייב חטאת ור' יהושע פוטר השתא רבי יהושע סיפא דלא קא עביד מצוה פוטר רישא דקא עביד מצוה מחייב אמרי דבי ר' ינאי רישא כגון שקדם ומל של שבת בע"ש דלא ניתנה שבת לידחות סיפא ניתנה שבת לידחות א"ל רב אשי לרב כהנא רישא נמי ניתנה שבת לידחות לגבי תינוקות דעלמא להאי גברא מיהא לא איתיהיב: **מתני'** קטן נימול לשמנה לתשעה ולעשרה ולאחד עשר ולי"ב לא פחות ולא יותר הא כיצד כדרכו לשמנה נולד לבין השמשות נימול לט' ביה"ש של ע"ש נימול לעשרה יו"ט לאחר השבת נימול לאחד עשר ב' ימים של ר"ה נימול לשנים עשר קטן החולה אין מוהלין אותו עד שיבריא: **גמ'** אמר שמואל חלצתו חמה נותנין לו כל ז' להברותו איבעיא להו מי בעינן מעת לעת ת"ש דתני לודא יום הבראתו כיום הולדו מאי לאו מה יום הולדו לא בעינן מעת לעת אף יום הבראתו לא בעינן מעת לעת לא עדיף יום הבראתו מיום הולדו דאילו יום הולדו לא בעינן מעת לעת ואילו יום הבראתו בעינן מעת לעת: **מתני'** אלו הן ציצין המעכבין את המילה בשר החופה את רוב העטרה ואינו אוכל בתרומה ואם היה בעל בשר מתקנו מפני מראית העין מל

רש"י

והא סתם ספרא הוא דבתורת כהנים תניא לה וסתם ספרא רבי יהודה: לקדש. מי שטמא לתת אפר על המים: מכשיר בקטן ופוסל באשה. טעמיה מפרש בסדר יומא בפ"ג: ובאנדרוגינוס. שמע מינה דרבי יהודה כאשה משוי ליה: כל זכר. ריבויא הוא: **מתני'** ושכח ומל את של אחר השבת בשבת חייב. דטעה בדבר מצוה ולא עשה מצוה הוא ועבד ליה סבורה שלא לצורך וקהא אפילו רבי יהושע מודה: אחד למול בשבת ואחד למול בע"ש ושכח ומל את של ע"ש בשבת ר"א מחייב חטאת. דמילה שלא בזמנה אינה דוחה שבת ואע"ג דטעה בדבר מצוה שהיה טרוד באותו של שבת ומתוך כך טעה בזה ואף בזה עשה מצוה שהרי ראוי הוא למול אלא שאינו דוחה שבת ס"ל לר"א טעה בדבר מצוה ועשה מצוה שיש בה חיוב חטאת חייב ורבי יהושע פוטר דס"ל טעה בדבר מצוה ועשה מצוה פטור: **גמ'** רב הונא מתני. במתניתין ברישא חייב לדברי הכל כדתנינן לה אנן: ורב יהודה מתני ברישא פטור. דמוקי לה בשכח ומל את של ע"ש בשבת ופלוגתא היא בשל אחר השבת בשבת: שהוא חייב. דאע"ג דטריד במצוה וטעה בה כיון דלאו מצוה שעדיין לא הגיע זמנו למול חייב: אלא מע"ז. שהוקשו כל חטאות שבתורה לחטאת ע"ז דכתיב תורה אחת יהיה לכם וגו' בפרשת שלח לך אנשים גבי קרבן ע"ז: ור' יהושע התם. עובד עבודת כוכבים לא עשה מצוה: ה"ג רב יהודה מתני פטור דתניא אמר ר"מ לא נחלקו ר"א ורבי יהושע על שהיו לו שני תינוקות אחד למול ע"ש כו': ה"ג ורבי יהושע התם לא טריד במצוה הכא טריד במצוה. טרוד להתעסק במצוה גמורה שהרי אחד מהם זמנו היום וטרוד לבו למהר ולעשות ומתוך טרדו טעה ומל את זה שאין בו מצוה כלל: ושכח ומל של ע"ש בשבת שהוא חייב. לקמיה מתרץ לה: דלא ניתנה שבת לידחות. שאין לו תינוק שיהא זמנו היום הלכך לא היה טרוד היום במצוה שלא היה מוטל עליו כלום לעשות ולא היה לו לטעות: **מתני'** נולד בין השמשות נימול לט'. שהרי ליום שמיני של מחר הוא נימול ושמא בין השמשות יום הוא ונימול לט': היה היום ע"ש. א"א למולו בשבת הבאה דשמא ט' הוא והויא ליה מילה שלא בזמנה ואינה דוחה שבת וצריך להמתין עד לאחר השבת שהוא עשירי: חל יו"ט להיות אחר השבת. אין מילה שלא בזמנה דוחה אותו ונימול לי"א: **גמ'** חלצתו חמה. נשלף ממנו החולי ויצא מגופו: דתני לודא. שם חכם: יום הבראתו כיום הולדו. ממתינין לו כיום הולדו: מאי לאו. יום הולדו דווקא קאמר דלא בעינן מעת לעת: לא. כיום הולדו דקתני למיתב ליה ז' מיהו עדיף יום הבראתו מהא דבעינן מעת לעת ומהא ליכא למשמע מידי: **מתני'** ציצין. רצועות של בשר שנשארו מן הערלה: עטרה. היא שפה גבוה המקפת את הגיד סביב וממנה משפע ויורד לראשו: ואינו אוכל בתרומה. אם כהן הוא דילפינן ביבמות (ד' ע.) שערל אסור בתרומה: ואם היה בעל בשר. שהיה שמן ונראה בשר שלמעלה מעורלתו לאחר שניטלה ערלה כולה כאילו אותו בשר חוזר וחופה את הגיד: מתקנו. ומשפע באיזמל מאותו עובי: מפני מראית העין. שלא יהא נראה כערל:

פרק

תוספות

טומטום שראה לובן ואודם מביאת מקדש וכ"ת משום דאיכא קרא יתירא (ג) דדריש לה לטומטום דכתיב מזכר ועד נקבה תשלחו ואי למעוטי אנדרוגינוס גרידא לא ה"ל למיכתב אלא זכר לא היא דאי לא כתב אלא זכר א"כ ה"א אשה לא מחייב' בביאת מקדש מדכתיב זכר ולא כתיב אדם ושמא י"ל דלית ליה לרב דר"ח דאיכא אמורא נמי דפליג עליה בבכורות וא"ת ומאי איצטריך רב למעוטי אנדרוגינוס והא איהו ס"ל בפרק הערל ביבמות (דף פג.) דאנדרוגינוס ספיקא הוא (ג) ואיצטריך קרא למעוטי ספק מיהו הא לא קשיא דה"א כשראה לובן ואודם כאחת יתחייב ממ"נ אבל הא תימה כיון דסבר רב אנדרוגינוס ספיקא הוא אמאי קאמר רב מזכר ועד נקבה זכר ודאי נקבה ודאית ואם הוא זכר ימעט אותו מזכר ואם הוא נקבה ימעט אותו מנקבה ומיהו י"ל דמשום טומטום נקטיה דפעמים הוי זכר ופעמים הוי נקבה:

הזכר ולא טומטום ואנדרוגינוס. תימה לרבי דבפרק אלו מומין (בכורות דף מב.) גבי בכור מצריך הזכר הזכרים למעוטי טומטום ואנדרוגינוס משמע התם דמהזכר לחודיה לא הוה ממעט לה והכא ממעטין ליה מהזכר לחודיה:

מל

מסורת הש"ס

א) [עירובין ט: וש"נ], ב) יומא מג. יבמות עב: ערכין ג. פרה פ"ה מ"ד, ג) פסחים עב. כריתות יט., ד) [צ"ל אליעזר], ה) פסחים עב. ע"ש, ו) [צ"ל אליעזר], ז) [יבמות לד.], ח) ערכין ח: ט) יבמות עא. י) ג"ז שם, כ) יבמות מז: עא:, ל) [סנהדרין פו.].

הגהות הב"ח

(א) גמ' וסתם ספרא ר' יהודה. נ"ב וכ"ש אם אנן מס' נדה דף מו: (ג) תוס' ד"ה הזכר וכו' יתירא למעוטי טומטום: (ד) בא"ד ספיקא הוא וכי איצטריך:

גליון הש"ס

מתני' ור' יהושע פוטר. עי' מנחות דף סד ע"א תד"ה ואפי' נתכוין:

תורה אור השלם

א) זֹאת בְּרִיתִי אֲשֶׁר תִּשְׁמְרוּ בֵּינִי וּבֵינֵיכֶם וּבֵין זַרְעֲךָ אַחֲרֶיךָ הִמּוֹל לָכֶם כָּל זָכָר: [בראשית יז, י]

רב נסים גאון

ששחטה ותמצא כמותה בשחיטת חולין (עב) בפרק בהמה המקשה לילד: אף אנן נמי תנינא הכל כשרין לקדש חוץ מחרש שוטה וקטן כו'. זו המשנה במס' פרה בפרק ה' ולענין קידוש מי חטאת נתכוונה. א) לומר שבעת ששיארו ציצין המעכבין את המילה הרי הוא ערל עדיין ואם הוא כהן אסור לו בתרומה כמו ששנינו במס' יבמות (דף ע) הערל וכל הטמאין לא יאכלו בתרומה והזכירו בתלמוד המחלוקת שהיתה בין ר' אליעזר ובין ר' עקיבא בתורת כהנים במה שכתוב (ויקרא כב) איש איש מזרע אהרן ומה שכתוב (שם) תושב כהן ר' אליעזר גמר לערל בגזירה שוה לערל מפסח ור' עקיבא אמר איש איש לרבות את הערל: אבל

חשק שלמה על רב נסים גאון

א) זה לפרש את המשנה אלו הן ציצין כו':

ליקוטי רש"י

[ההתחלה בדף קלו:] נימול לט'. כלומר לספק תשיעי [חולין פד:]. ביה"ש של ע"ש. נולד בין השמשות של ערב שבת אינו נימול בשבת הבאה דשמא תשיעי הוא ודוחין אותו ספק יום ספק לילה ואם יום הוא נולד הבאה שבת בזמנה אינה דוחה שבת

עין משפט נר מצוה

מט א מיי' פ"ו מהל' פרה הלכה ב סמג עשין רלג:
נ ב ג מיי' פ"ב מהל' שגגות הלכה ח:
נא ד מיי' פ"א מהל' מילה הלכה יב סמג עשין כח טוש"ע י"ד סי' רסו סעיף ח:
נב ה מיי' שם הלכה טו סמג שם טוש"ע י"ד סי' רסב סעיף ג:
נג ו ז מיי' פ"ב מהל' מילה הלכה ג ה סמג שם טוש"ע י"ד סי' רסד סעיף ה ו:

רבינו חננאל

א"ר יהודה אנדרוגינוס זכר הוא. שאם אי אתה אומר כך יערך ומנ"ל דלא מערך דתניא הזכר ולא טומטום ואנדרוגינוס כו' ופשוטה היא ומסקנן בה ומאי שנא גבי מילה דכתיב המול לכם כל זכר כל לרבות. ויש מי שאומר הלכתא כרבנן דאמרי ספק ואנדרוגינוס אין מחללין עליו את השבת ואין הלכה כר' יהודה ומדחזינן רב חסדא דריש לטעמיה דר' יהודה ש"מ הלכתא כוותיה: מתניתין מי שהיו לו ב' תינוקות אחד למול אחר השבת ואחד למול בשבת ושכח ומל את של אחר השבת בשבת חייב כו' [ואמרינן בגמ'] רב הונא מתני חייב רב יהודה מתני פטור פי' רב הונא מתני חייב דמוקים ליה למתניתין לר"ש דאמר ר"ש לא נחלקו ר' אליעזר (ור"ש) [ור' יהושע] על מי שהיו לו א') דקיי"ל סתם משנה ר' מאיר והבא תנא דבי ר' חייא פליגי עליה ורב הונא דמוקים לה כר' שמעון כוותיה עבדינן וחלוקת ר' אליעזר ור' יהושע דברים בהדרין הן. (שנים) ושניהם מע"ז למדוה דהא איתקשא כל התורה כולה לע"ז ר' אליעזר סבירא כע"ז מה ע"ז אמרה תורה לא תעבוד ואם תעבוד ע"ז בשגגה בכל מקום חייב חטאת. כן אמרה תורה לא תחלל השבת. המחלל השבת בשגגה מ"מ חייב חטאת. ור' יהושע סבר התם לגבי ע"ז לא נתכוין לקיים המצוה הכא בשבת נתכוין לקיים מצות מילה. לפיכך פטור הוא והלכתא כר' יהושע וכדמתניתין ר' שמעון. אחד למול ערב שבת ואחד למול בשבת ושכח ומל את של ערב שבת בשבת פטור כי מ"מ מצוה עשה. ואע"פ שמל בט'. אבל בזמן ששכח ומל את של אחר השבת בשבת כיון שלא עשה מצוה כי בו' מלו אפילו ר' יהושע מודה שחייב חטאת. וכן הלכה וכל היכא דפליג ר' אליעזר ור' יהושע הלכה כר' יהושע חוץ ממקומות ידועים. וזה אינו מהם. וכן רב הונא הלכתא כוותיה דשכיח גבי ריש גלותא וגרסינן הלכתא כוותיה או הלכתא כוותיה כר': מתניתין קטן נימול לשמנה לתשעה כו': קטן חולה אין מלין אותו עד שיבריא. אמר שמואל חלצתו חמה נותנין לו כל ז' להברותו הלכתא כשמואל דאיבעיין ליה מאחר שחלצתו חמה שבעת ימים

חשק שלמה על רבינו חננאל

א) נראה דצ"ל על מי שהיו לו ב' תינוקות אחד למול בשבת ואחד למול אחר השבת כו' שהוא חייב וכו'. ורב יהודה מתני פטור דמוקי לה כר"מ וכו' והחזר לדבריו ור' יהושע מתרי אמרי דקאמר ר"מ וכו': ב) נראה דצ"ל דהכא משום דקיי"ל דסתם משנה ר"מ.

ולא יו"ט [ערכין ח:]. יו"ט לאחר השבת. של יו"ט להיות לאחר שבת שהוא עשירי נמול לאחד עשר משום דמילה שלא בזמנה אינה דוחה יו"ט דכל מילה שלא בזמנה [שבת כ"ד] [חולין שם]. ב' ימים של ר"ה. ואם חלו שני ימים טובים של ר"ה אחר השבת נמול עד יום שלישי שהוא שנים עשר ללידתו [ערכין שם]. חלצתו חמה. שלפתו ניטלה [ערכין שם]. שהיה חולה ונתרפא (ברכות לד:). ימים [שם]. לעת [יבמות עא.]. יום הבראתו כיום הולדו. מאי לאו. ציצין. שיורי ערלה וממתינין עד יום שמיני [שם]. עטרה. חוזה גבוה שסביב הגיד ומשפע ויורד לצד הקרקע ומשפע ויורד לצד הגוף [לעיל קלו:].

מל ולא פרע את המילה כאילו לא מל: גמ' (א) אמר רבי אבינא א"ר ירמיה בר אבא אמר רב ב בשר החופה את רוב גובהה של עטרה: ואם היה בעל בשר וכו': אמר שמואל קטן המסורבל בבשר רואין אותו כ"ז שמתקשה ונראה מהול אינו צריך למול ואם לאו צריך למול במתניתא תנא ג) רשב"ג אומר ג קטן המסורבל בבשר רואין אותו כל זמן שמתקשה ואינו נראה מהול צריך למולו ואם לאו אינו צריך למולו מאי בינייהו איכא בינייהו נראה ואינו נראה: מל ולא פרע: ת"ר ד המל אומר אקב"ו על המילה אבי הבן אומר אקב"ו להכניסו בבריתו של אברהם אבינו העומדים (א) אומרים כשם שנכנס לברית כך יכנס לתורה לחופה ולמע"ט והמברך אומר אשר קידש ידיד מבטן חוק בשארו שם וצאצאיו חתם באות ברית קדש על כן בשכר זאת אל חי חלקנו (ג) צוה ה) להציל ידידות שארינו משחת למען בריתו אשר שם בבשרנו בא"י כורת הברית ה המל את הגרים אומר ברוך אתה ה' אלהינו מלך העולם אקב"ו על המילה והמברך אומר אקב"ו למול את הגרים ולהטיף מהם דם ברית שאילמלא דם ברית לא נתקיימו שמים וארץ שנאמר א) אם לא בריתי יומם ולילה חוקות שמים וארץ לא שמתי בא"י כורת הברית ו המל את העבדים אומר אקב"ו על המילה והמברך אומר אקב"ו למול את העבדים ולהטיף מהם דם ברית ז שאילמלא דם ברית חוקות שמים וארץ לא נתקיימו שנאמ' אם לא בריתי יומם ולילה חוקות שמים וארץ לא שמתי בא"י כורת הברית:

הדרן עלך רבי אליעזר דמילה

רבי אליעזר אומר תולין את המשמרת בי"ט ונותנין לתלויה בשבת וחכ"א ח אין תולין את המשמרת בי"ט ואין נותנין לתלויה בשבת אבל נותנין לתלויה ביו"ט: גמ' השתא ר"א אוסופי אהל עראי לא מוספינן למיעבד לכתחלה שרי מאי היא דתנן ו) פקק החלון ר"א אומר בזמן שקשור ותלוי פוקקין בו ואם לאו אין פוקקין בו וחכ"א בין כך ובין כך פוקקין בו ואמר רבה בר בר חנה א"ר יוחנן ז) הכל מודים שאין עושין אהל עראי בתחלה בי"ט ואין צ"ל בשבת לא נחלקו אלא להוסיף שר"א אומר אין מוסיפין בי"ט ואין צ"ל בשבת וחכ"א מוסיפין בשבת ואין צ"ל ביום טוב ר"א סבר לה כרבי יהודה דתניא ח) אין בין יום טוב לשבת אלא אוכל נפש בלבד רבי יהודה מתיר אף מכשירי אוכל נפש אימר דשמעינן ליה לר' יהודה במכשירין שאי אפשר לעשותם מערב יום טוב במכשירין שאפשר לעשותם מעיו"ט מי שמעת ליה דר"א עדיפא מדרבי יהודה: וחכ"א: איבעיא להו תלה מאי אמר רב יוסף תלה חייב חטאת א"ל אביי אלא מעתה תלה כוזא בסיכתא הכי נמי דמיחייב אלא

רש"י

פרע. גילה: גמ' רוב גובהה. לא תימא רוב העטרה דקתני מתני' רוב היקפה אלא אפילו רוב גובהה במקום אחד: קטן המסורבל בבשר. פלטר"י בלע"ז שמן ועב ולאחר שימול נראה כמכוסה: כל זמן שמתקשה. ומתוך הקישוי מתפשט בשרו. בדשמואל גרסינן ונראה מהול במתניתא גרסינן ואינו נראה מהול: איכא בינייהו נראה ואינו נראה. לשמואל נראה מהול הוא דאין צריך למולו הא נראה ואינו נראה צריך למתניתא אינו נראה הוא דצריך הא נראה ואינו נראה אינו צריך: אשר קידש ידיד מבטן. יצחק קרי ידיד על שם אהבה (בראשית כב): מבטן. דקודם שנולד נתקדש למצוה זו דכתיב (שם יז) אבל שרה אשתך וגו' והקימותי את בריתי אתו היינו מילה: בשארו. בבשרו: שם. חק של מילה: וצאצאיו. אחריו: חתם באות. זו של ברית קדש: צוה להציל ידידות שארינו משחת. מגיהנם דכתיב גם את בדם בריתך שלחתי אסיריך מבור אין מים בו (זכריה ט):

הדרן עלך ר' אליעזר דמילה

תולין את המשמרת. שמסננין בה שמרי יין ומותח פיה לכל צד בעגול ועשה כאהל על חלל הכלי שקורין אשטנד"א ואע"ג דעביד אהל שרי בי"ט כדמפרש בגמרא אבל בשבת מיהא לכתחילה לא אבל אם תלויה היא נותנין לתוכה שמרים ומסנן דאין דרך בורר בכך: גמ' פקק החלון. כגון ארובת הגג: אלא להוסיף. כגון פקק זה שאינו אלא תוספת עראי על האהל: סבר ליה כרבי יהודה. הלכך הכא שרי דמכשירי אוכל נפש הוא: שאי אפשר לעשותן מעי"ט. כגון שפוד שנרצם בי"ט: עדיפא. דקאמר דהוא שרי אפילו מכשירין שאפשר מעיו"ט: תלה כוזא בסיכתא. תלה כלי קטן במגוד: ה"נ דמיחייב. והכא מאי חיובא איכא באהל עראי בנין גמור לא הוי ומדרבנן הוא דמיתסר: אלא

תוספות

מל ולא פרע את המילה כאילו לא מל. תימה אמאי איצטריך למיתני הא כיון דכבר תנא דבשר החופה את רוב העטרה מעכב המילה וכי לא פרע עדיין רוב עטרה מכוסה: אבי הבן אומר כו'. רבינו שמואל גרים אבי הבן ברישא והדר המל אומר וכבר הנהיג לעשות כן לברך אבי הבן קודם המילה משום דלהכניסו להבא משמע כדאמרינן בפ"ק דפסחים (ד' ז. ושם) בלבער כ"ע לא פליגי דלהבא משמע ועוד ז) דכל המלות מברך עליהן עובר לעשייתן ור"ת החזיר המנהג לקדמותו וגרס המל ברישא והדר אבי הבן כמו שכתוב בכל הספרים וכן מוכח כולה סוגיא מדקאמר העומדים שם אומרים כשם שהכניסו לברית מכלל שכבר הכניסו ועוד דגבי גר דבסמוך גרס ברישא המל כו' והדר המברך אומר אקב"ו למול את הגרים ונראה הוא שזהו כנגד ברכת אבי הבן והשתא א"א לשנות הגירסא שיש בה אותה ברכה להטיף מהן דם ברית כו' ברוך כורת הברית משמע דכל זה הוא אחר המילה ועוד המברך מברך לעולם אחר המילה כמו במילת קטן והיינו דפסחים ה"פ בלבער כ"ע לא פליגי להבא משמע טפי מלשעבר ומיהו לשעבר נמי משמע כי פליגי בעל ביעור מר סבר דמשמע מעיקרא טפי מלהבא ומר סבר להבא נמי משמע כמו מעיקרא והא דאמרינן דכל המלות מברך עובר לעשייתן ה"מ כשהמברך עצמו עושה המלוה: ידיד מבטן. אומר ר"ת שהוא אברהם אבינו שנקרא ידיד שנאמר (ירמיה יא) מה לידידי בביתי כדדרשינן במנחות בפרק כל המנחות (ד' נג: ושם) ושלשת האבות נזכרים חוק בשארו שם הוא יצחק וצאצאיו חתם באות ברית קדש הוא יעקב וצאצאיו הוא ובניו כמו שתרגם יונתן הצאצאים והצפיעות בניא ובני בניא (ישעיה כב) כלומר יוצאי צאצאיו י): במצותיו וצונו למול את העבדים. שנאמר יליד בית ומקנת כסף (בראשית יז):

הדרן עלך ר' אליעזר דמילה

תולין. אבל נותנין לתלויה ביום טוב. וצריך לפרש ולומר שאם היה עושהו מאתמול לא היה טוב כל כך וחזק והא דתניא בפרקין דלעיל (ד' קלד. ושם) דאין מסננין את החרדל במסננת שלו בי"ט אם היה עושהו מאתמול לא היה מתקלקל: דרבי אליעזר עדיפא מדר"י. תימה ולר"א תיקשה ליה הנהו קראי דדריש בפ"ק דמגילה (ד' ז:) דקאמר ורבי יהודה כתיב הוא וכתיב לכם ולא קשיא כאן במכשירין שאפשר וכו' וכ"ת ר"א הוה דריש הוא לדרשה אחרינא א"כ מנ"ל התם דרבי יהודה הוה מפליג לימא דרבי יהודה הוה דריש ליה לדרשה אחריתי כר' אליעזר ונראה דבדאורייתא מודה ר' אליעזר דמכשירין דאפשר אסורים ט) וכי שרי להו הכא ה"מ באהל עראי דאינו אלא מדרבנן גזירה אטו אהל קבע כדאמרינן בבילה בפרק המביא (ד' לג:) מיהו קשה מנ"ל דעדיפא דילמא בהא מודה אפילו רבי יהודה: אלא

עין משפט נר מצוה

נד א מיי' פ"ג מהל' מילה הלכה ד סמג עשין כח טוש"ע י"ד סי' רסד סעיף ד:
נה ב מיי' שם הלכה ג טוש"ע שם סעי' ה:
נו ג מיי' שם הלכה ה טור וש"ע שם סעיף ט:
נז ד מיי' פ"ג מהל' מילה הלכה ג סמג שם טוש"ע י"ד סי' רסה סעיף א:
נח ה מיי' שם הלכה ד סמג שם טוש"ע י"ד סי' רסח סעיף ה:
נט ו מיי' שם הלכה ה סמג שם טוש"ע י"ד סי' רסז סעיף יג:
א ז מיי' פכ"ב מהל' שבת הלכה יח ופ"ד מהל' י"ט הלכה יז סמג לאוין סה טוש"ע א"ח סי' שטו סעי' ט וסי' שיט סעיף ט וסי' תקי סעיף ד:

תורה אור השלם

א) כֹּה אָמַר יְיָ אִם לֹא בְרִיתִי יוֹמָם וָלָיְלָה חֻקּוֹת שָׁמַיִם וָאָרֶץ לֹא שָׂמְתִּי: [ירמיה לג, כה]

רבינו חננאל

מעת לעת להבראותו. וזה מפורש ביבמות בפר' הערל וכל הטמאים: מתני' ואלו הן ציצין המעכבין את המילה. א"ר אבינא א"ר ירמיה בר אבא אמר רב בשר החופה את רוב גובהה של עטרה וכו' וכן הלכתא. ואם הוא בעל בשר מתקנו מפני מראית העין כלומר אע"פ שהציצין הללו אינן חופין את רוב גובהה של עטרה מתקנו מפני שלא יהא נראה כערלה. אמר שמואל קטן המסורבל בבשר רואין אותו כל זמן שמתקשה [ונראה מהול אין צריך למול במתניתא תנא רשב"א קטן המסורבל בבשר רואין אותו כ"ז שמתקשה] ואינו נראה מהול צריך למול ואמרי' מאי בינייהו איכא בינייהו [נראה] ואינו נראה צריך למול לרשב"ג דאמר ואינו נראה מהול כלל צריך למול אבל אם נראה ואינו נראה אינו צריך למול. פי' מסורבל מסובב בבשר כדכתיב מסורבלין בסרבליהון וכו'. מל ולא פרע את המילה וכו'. פי' מי שמל ולא פרע את המילה כלומר לא קרע את העור וגילה את העטרה כאילו לא מל:
הדרן עלך ר' אליעזר אם לא הביא. עז ותהלה לאל אבי. שית עזר גלילין. חלץ באזר והדלין. בפ' ר' אליעזר תולין:
ר' אליעזר אומר תולין את המשמרת ביו"ט וכו' ואקשי' עלה השתא ר' אליעזר להוסיף באהל עראי מחמיר ואמר אין מוסיפין לכתחלה (שאי) [מאי היא]. דתנן פקק החלון ר' אליעזר אומר בזמן שקשור ותלוי פוקקין בו כו' ופקק זה כגון מסך לסתום בו חללו של חלון ואמר רבה בר בר חנה א"ר יוחנן הכל מודים שאין עושין אהלי עראי בתחלה ביו"ט ואין צריך לומר בשבת לא נחלקו אלא להוסיף שר' אליעזר אומר אין מוסיפין ביו"ט ואין צ"ל בשבת וחכ"א מוסיפין בשבת ואין צ"ל ביו"ט ומפרקינן ר' אליעזר סבר לה כר' יהודה דתניא אין בין יו"ט לשבת אלא אוכל נפש בלבד. ר' יהודה אומר אף מכשירי אוכל נפש וזה שמתיר ר' אליעזר לעשות אהל לכתחלה ביו"ט לתלות המשמרת מפני שהוא מכשירי אוכל נפש כדי לשמר היין לשתות בשמחת יו"ט ונמצא ר' אליעזר מיקל מר' יהודה שר' יהודה אינו מתיר אלא במכשירין שאי אפשר לעשותן מעיו"ט אבל במכשירין שאפשר לעשותן מעיו"ט כגון שימור היין וכדומה לו אוסר ור' אליעזר מתיר אפילו בזה. ואין הלכה

מסורת הש"ס

א) יבמות דף מז: עב., ב) [תוספתא פרק טז], ג) [מנחות מב. תוספתא ברכות פ"ו כל הענין עד סופו], ד) הג"מ יעב"ץ ז"ל ניקד זה במירו"ק, ה) [נדרים לב.], ו) לעיל קכה: עירובין מד. סוכה כז:, ז) [תוספ' סוכה פ"א לעיל קכה. וש"נ], ח) [תוספ' מגילה פ"א] בילה כח. לו: מגילה ז: לעיל קכד., ט) [שם], י) [ועי' תוס' מנחות נג. ד"ה בן], כ) [עי' תוס' פסחים ז: ד"ה מה ראיה לשון].

הגהות הב"ח

(א) גמ' העומדין שם אומרים כשם שהכנסתו לברית כך תכניסהו לתור' כצ"ל וכן בתוס': (ג) שם חלקנו צורנו צוה:

ליקוטי רש"י

מל. את הערלה. ולא פרע. את העור המכסה ראש הגיד [לעיל קלג:]. רוב גובהה. של אותה שורה ולא תימא רוב היקיפה [יבמות מז:]. אע"ג דאין רוב הקיפה [שם עא:]. קטן המסורבל בבשר. המלובש בבשר כסרבל [קידושין עב.]. ולשון מלבוש הוא כמו כפיתו בסרבליהון (דניאל ג) [ע"ז ב:]. ולהטיף מהם דם ברית. הטפת דם ברית מלוה כדכתיב (זכריה ט) גם את בדם בריתך [לעיל קלד.]. בזמן שקשור. שם כל שעה [סוכה כז:]. ותלוי. שאינו נגרר בארץ שהחבל שהוא קשור בו אינו מגיע לארץ [לעיל קכה:]. פוקקין בו. כיון דמתוקן ועומד לכך אין זה לא בונה ולא מוסיף. ואם לאו אין פוקקין בו. דמוסיף הוא על סתימת אהל [סוכה שם]. דדמי לבונה שמוסיף על סתימת הבית ואף על פי שעראי הוא שהרי יחזור ויפתחנו [עירובין מד.]. דמיחזי כמוסיף על הבנין [לעיל שם]. הכל מודים. ר"א ומחלוקתו שנחלקו בתוספת אהל עראי גבי פקק חלון דאיכא למאן דאמר פוקקין בו ואף על גב דמוסיף על אהל עראי הוא מודים שאין עושין את כל האהל לכתחלה בשבת בפרק כל הכלים (קכה:) [עירובין פו:]. שאין עושין אהל עראי. לפרוס מחצלת על ארבע קונדסים להיות לו לאהל מן החמה ודוקא גג אבל מחילה לאו אהל הוא ושרי לפרסה לצניעות כדאמרינן עירובין (לג.) בעובדא דשמואל ופקק החלון דמתוקן משום דבנין קבוע הוא ומיחזי כמוסיף על הבנין [ע"ש במסורת וע"ש בתוס' וברש"י כאן]. אלא להוסיף. כגון שהיה מחצלת פרוסה עליהן וכרוכה ונשאר בה אויר ולמחר פושטה דומיא דפקק [לעיל שם]. דאפילו רבנן לא שרו אלא להוסיף כגון פקק חלון דתוספת בעלמא הוא [עירובין מד. ע"ש בתוס']. אין בין יום טוב לשבת. להיות מותר לכתחלה ביום טוב מה שאסור בשבת אבל לענין עונשין יש הרבה שזה בסקילה וזה בלאו גרידא [מגילה ז:]. מתיר אף מכשירי אוכל נפש. וטעמא משום דדריש יעשה לכם לכל צרכיכם [ביצה כח.]. שאי אפשר. כגון סכין שנפגמה ביום טוב. שאפשר. כגון סכין שנפגם מערב יום טוב [מגילה שם]. סיכתא. קבילי"א בלע"ז [עירובין ח.]. יתד [יומא ז:].

מָל וְלֹא פָּרַע אֶת הַמִּילָה כְּאִילוּ לֹא מָל – If he circumcised but did not uncover the circumcision,[1] it is as if he did not circumcise.[2]

Gemara The Mishnah stated that a circumcision is invalid if there remains "flesh that covers the larger part of the corona." The Gemara clarifies this term:

אָמַר רַבִּי אָבִינָא אָמַר רַבִּי יִרְמְיָה בַּר אַבָּא אָמַר רַב – R' Avina said in the name of R' Yirmiyah bar Abba who said in the name of Rav: בָּשָׂר הַחוֹפֶה אֶת רוֹב גּוֹבְהָהּ שֶׁל עֲטָרָה – This term refers even to **flesh** of the foreskin **that covers the larger part of** only **the** ***height*** **of the corona.**[3]

The Mishnah stated:

וְאִם הָיָה בַּעַל בָּשָׂר וכו' – AND IF [A CHILD] WAS FLESHY **etc.**

The Gemara cites a related ruling:

אָמַר שְׁמוּאֵל – Shmuel said: קָטָן הַמְסוּרְבָּל בְּבָשָׂר – An infant who is thickly coated with flesh,[4] **רוֹאִין אוֹתוֹ – we examine him** as follows: **כָּל זְמַן שֶׁמִּתְקַשֶּׁה וְנִרְאֶה מָהוּל** – If **when his membrum is erect**[5] **he appears circumcised, אֵינוֹ צָרִיךְ לָמוּל – one need not circumcise** him again. **וְאִם לַאו – But if not,**[6] **צָרִיךְ לָמוּל – one must circumcise** him again.[7]

The Gemara quotes a similar Baraisa:

בְּמַתְנִיתָא תָּנָא – It was taught in a Baraisa: רַבָּן שִׁמְעוֹן בֶּן גַּמְלִיאֵל אוֹמֵר – RABBAN SHIMON BEN GAMLIEL SAYS: קָטָן הַמְסוּרְבָּל בְּבָשָׂר – AN INFANT WHO IS THICKLY COATED WITH FLESH, רוֹאִין אוֹתוֹ – WE EXAMINE HIM as follows: כָּל זְמַן שֶׁמִּתְקַשֶּׁה וְאֵינוֹ נִרְאֶה מָהוּל – If WHEN THE MEMBRUM IS ERECT HE DOES NOT APPEAR CIRCUMCISED, צָרִיךְ לְמוּלוֹ – ONE MUST CIRCUMCISE HIM again. וְאִם לַאו – BUT IF NOT, אֵינוֹ צָרִיךְ לְמוּלוֹ – ONE NEED NOT CIRCUMCISE HIM again.

The Gemara notes a difference between Shmuel's statement and the Baraisa:

מַאי בֵּינַיְיהוּ – What is the difference **between them? אִיכָּא בֵּינַיְיהוּ נִרְאֶה וְאֵינוֹ נִרְאֶה – There is** a difference **between them** in a case **where** to some extent **he appears** circumcised, **but** to some extent **he does not appear** circumcised.[8]

The Gemara introduces the next discussion with a quote from the Mishnah:

מָל וְלֹא פָּרַע – If HE CIRCUMCISED BUT DID NOT UNCOVER the circumcision.

A Baraisa records the various blessings and prayers recited at a circumcision:

תָּנוּ רַבָּנָן – The Rabbis taught in a Baraisa: הַמָּל אוֹמֵר – THE CIRCUMCISER SAYS:[9] אֲשֶׁר קִדְּשָׁנוּ בְּמִצְוֹתָיו וְצִוָּנוּ עַל הַמִּילָה – "Blessed are You, Hashem, our God, King of the Universe, WHO HAS SANCTIFIED US WITH HIS COMMANDMENTS AND COMMANDED US REGARDING CIRCUMCISION."[10] אֲבִי הַבֵּן אוֹמֵר – THE FATHER OF THE CHILD SAYS:[11] אֲשֶׁר קִדְּשָׁנוּ בְּמִצְוֹתָיו וְצִוָּנוּ לְהַכְנִיסוֹ בִּבְרִיתוֹ

NOTES

1. I.e. he removed the foreskin but did not split the membrane underneath it and pull it back to expose the corona. This procedure is known as פְּרִיעָה, *periah.* [The requirement for *periah* is derived not from the laws of circumcision given to Abraham, but from *Joshua* 5:2 (*Yevamos* 71b, according to *Rashi's* first approach ibid.).]

[Here *Rashi* renders פָּרַע as *he uncovered* (the corona), whereas on 133a he explains it as meaning *he tore* (the membrane that covers the corona). For an explanation of this change, see *Hagahos R' Eliyahu Guttmacher* to תוד"ה מל; see also *Sfas Emes.*]

2. *Periah* must therefore be performed on the Sabbath even after the *mohel* has ceased to engage in the circumcision (*Rambam, Commentary to the Mishnah*).

Additionally, the Mishnah teaches that if one cut off the foreskin on the Sabbath, but neglected to perform *periah,* he is regarded as a desecrator of the Sabbath, since he inflicted a wound without performing a mitzvah (*Meiri; see Teshuvos Chasam Sofer, Yoreh Deah* §249; see also *Sefer HaBris* p. 204 §6).

3. Do not assume that the Mishnah deems the circumcision invalid only when the remaining foreskin covers the majority of the *circumference* of the corona. Rather, even if it covers only a narrow part of the circumference, as long as it covers the majority of the *height* of the corona, the circumcision is invalid (*Rashi,* according to *Yad HaKetanah, Hil. Milah* §30; see also *Bechor Shor*).

4. Flesh appears to cover the corona after the foreskin is removed (*Rashi;* see 137a note 21).

5. In this state, the flesh spreads outward (*Rashi*).

6. I.e. even when the membrum is erect, flesh covers the corona.

7. The circumcision is certainly valid under Biblical law, since the foreskin is removed. The Rabbis, however, decreed that the excess flesh must be cut away (*Rambam, Hil. Milah* 2:5; *Meiri; Taz, Yoreh Deah* 264:9).

The Mishnah stated: "If [the child] was fleshy, he should rectify it, because of appearance." Here, the Gemara uses a stronger expression: "one must circumcise." The difference in wording demonstrates that these are two distinct laws. The Mishnah refers to a case in which flesh droops over and covers the corona only when the membrum is limp. This excess flesh need be removed only for appearance's sake. At the time of the circumcision, the *mohel* may cut it away with his knife (see *Rashi* to 137a ד"ה מתקנו). After the circumcision, cutting is not necessary [rather, one should try, if possible, to bandage the flesh so that it will grow away from the corona (*Terumas HaDeshen* §264, cited by *Bach* §264 and *Rama* 264:6)]. The Gemara, however, speaks of a case in which the corona is covered even when the membrum is erect. In this case, it is obligatory to perform a second "circumcision." That is, one must cut away the excess flesh with a knife even after the initial circumcision has ended (*Rashi,* as explained by *Nekudas HaKesef* to *Yoreh Deah* 264:6; cf. *Terumas HaDeshen,* who explains *Rashi* differently; see also *Bach* and *Taz* §264:9).

8. I.e. when the membrum is erect, the corona is only partially exposed.

Both Shmuel and the Baraisa deal with only one case in specific terms. Shmuel specifies the case in which the child appears circumcised ("If when the membrum is erect he appears circumcised, one does not need to circumcise him again"), and then covers all other cases with a general statement ("but if not, etc."). This implies that the child must appear circumcised to avoid further cutting. In all other cases, including partial appearance of circumcision, a second incision *is* necessary. The Baraisa, on the other hand, specifies the case in which the child does *not* appear circumcised ("If when the membrum is erect he does not appear circumcised, one must circumcise him again; but if not, etc."). This formula implies that the child requires a second incision only if his circumcision is concealed. In every other case, including partial appearance of the circumcision, there is no such obligation (*Rashi*).

9. The general custom is that the *mohel* recites this blessing after he has begun to cut the foreskin (see *Aruch HaShulchan Yoreh Deah* 265:10; see, however, *Tevuas Shor* 19:5).

10. In a case where the circumciser is the father of the child, the Gemara (*Pesachim* 7b) discusses whether he too says עַל הַמִּילָה, *regarding the circumcision,* or לָמוּל [אֶת הַבֵּן], *to circumcise [the son]* (see *Rashi* ibid. 7b ד"ה והלכתא; *Rambam, Hil. Milah* 3:1; *Tur* and *Rama, Yoreh Deah* 265:2).

11. The order in which the Baraisa records the blessings implies that the father's blessing is recited after that of the *mohel.* This requires explanation in view of the rule (*Pesachim* 7b) that a blessing for a mitzvah should be recited before its performance.

One answer given is that this rule applies only when the person reciting the blessing is also the one performing the mitzvah (see *Raavad* to *Hil. Ishus* 3:23, who suggests why). Here the *mohel* performs the mitzvah, whereas the father recites the blessing (*Tosafos*).

An alternative solution is that this is not a blessing for a mitzvah [בִּרְכַּת הַמִּצְוָה]. Rather, it is a blessing of praise [בִּרְכַּת הַשֶּׁבַח] in which the father thanks God for having been given the opportunity to bring his son into the covenant of Abraham (see *Rashba, Ritva MHK* ed. and *Ran MHK* ed.; cf. *Tosafos* to *Pesachim* 7a ד"ה בלבער).

Yet another approach is that since the *periah* (which is essential to the validity of the circumcision) has not yet been performed, the blessing is

מל ולא פרע את המילה כאילו לא מל: **גמ'** אמר רבי אבינא א"ר ירמיה בר אבא אמר רב [ב] בשר החופה את רוב גובהה של עטרה: ואם היה בעל בשר וכו': אמר שמואל קטן המסורבל בבשר רואין אותו כ"ז שמתקשה ונראה מהול אינו צריך למול ואם לאו צריך למול במתניתא תנא רשב"ג אומר [ג] קטן המסורבל בבשר רואין אותו כל זמן שמתקשה ואינו נראה מהול צריך למולו ואם לאו אינו צריך למולו מאי בינייהו איכא בינייהו נראה ואינו נראה: מל ולא פרע: ת"ר [ד] המל אומר אקב"ו על המילה אבי הבן אומר אקב"ו להכניסו בבריתו של אברהם אבינו העומדים (א) אומרים כשם שנכנס לברית כך יכנס לתורה לחופה ולמע"ט והמברך אומר אשר קידש ידיד מבטן חוק בשארו שם וצאצאיו חתם באות ברית קדש על כן בשכר זאת אל חי חלקנו (ב) צורנו צוה להציל ידידות שארינו משחת למען בריתו אשר שם בבשרנו בא"י כורת הברית [ה] המל את הגרים אומר ברוך אתה ה' אלהינו מלך העולם אקב"ו על המילה והמברך אומר אקב"ו למול את הגרים ולהטיף מהם דם ברית שאילמלא דם ברית לא נתקיימו שמים וארץ שנאמר א) אם לא בריתי יומם ולילה חוקות שמים וארץ לא שמתי בא"י כורת הברית [ו] המל את העבדים אומר אקב"ו על המילה והמברך אומר אקב"ו למול את העבדים ולהטיף מהם דם ברית שאילמלא דם ברית לא נתקיימו שמים וארץ שנאמ' אם לא בריתי יומם ולילה חוקות שמים וארץ לא שמתי בא"י כורת הברית:

הדרן עלך רבי אליעזר דמילה

רבי אליעזר אומר תולין את המשמרת בי"ט ונותנין לתלויה בשבת וחכ"א [ז] אין תולין את המשמרת בי"ט ואין נותנין לתלויה בשבת אבל נותנין לתלויה ביו"ט: **גמ'** השתא ר"א אוסופי אהל עראי לא מוספינן למיעבד לכתחלה שרי מאי היא דתנן [ח] פקק החלון ר"א אומר בזמן שקשור ותלוי פוקקין בו ואם לאו אין פוקקין בו וחכ"א בין כך ובין כך פוקקין בו ואמר רבה בר בר חנה א"ר יוחנן [ט] הכל מודים שאין עושין אהל עראי בתחלה בי"ט ואין צ"ל בשבת לא נחלקו אלא להוסיף שר"א אומר אין מוסיפין בי"ט ואין צ"ל בשבת וחכ"א מוסיפין בשבת ואין צ"ל ביום טוב ר"א סבר לה כרבי יהודה דתניא [י] אין בין יום טוב לשבת אלא אוכל נפש בלבד רבי יהודה מתיר אף מכשירי אוכל נפש אימר דשמעינן ליה לר' יהודה במכשירין שאי אפשר לעשותם מערב יום טוב במכשירין שאפשר לעשותם מעיו"ט מי שמעת ליה דר"א עדיפא מדרבי יהודה: וחכ"א: איבעיא להו תלה מאי אמר רב יוסף תלה חייב חטאת א"ל אביי אלא מעתה תלה כוזא בסיכתא הכי נמי דמיחייב אלא

רש"י

פרע. גילה: **גמ' רוב גובהה.** לא תימא רוב העטרה דקתני מתני' רוב היקפה אלא אפילו רוב גובהה במקום אחד: **קטן המסורבל בבשר.** פלטר"י בלע"ז שמנן ועב ולאחר שנימול נראה כמכסהו: **כל זמן שמתקשה.** ומתוך הקישוי מתפשט בשרו. בדשמואל גרסינן ונראה מהול במתניתא גרסינן ואינו נראה מהול: **איכא בינייהו נראה ואינו נראה.** לשמואל נראה מהול הוא דאין צריך למולו הא נראה ואינו נראה צריך למתניתא אינו נראה הוא דצריך הא נראה ואינו נראה אינו צריך: **אשר קידש ידיד מבטן.** יצחק קרי ידיד על שם אשר אהבת (בראשית כב): **מבטן.** דקודם שנולד נתקדש למצוה זו דכתיב (שם יז) אבל שרה אשתך וגו' והקימותי את בריתי אתו היינו מילה: **בשארו.** בבשרו: **שם.** חק של מילה: **וצאצאיו.** אחריו: **חתם באות.** זו של ברית קדש: **צוה להציל ידידות שארינו משחת.** מגיהנם דכתיב גם את בדם בריתך שלחתי אסיריך מבור אין מים בו (זכריה ט):

הדרן עלך ר' אליעזר דמילה

תולין את המשמרת. שמסננין בה שמרי יין ומותח פיה לכל לד בעגול ונעשה כאהל על חלל הכלי שקורין אשטנד"א ואע"ג דעביד אהל שרי בי"ט כדמפרש בגמרא אבל בשבת מיתלא לכתחילה לא אבל אם תלויה היא נותנין לתוכה שמרים ומסנן דאין דרך בורר בכך: **גמ' פקק החלון.** כגון ארובת הגג: **אלא להוסיף.** כגון פקק זה שאינו אלא תוספת עראי על האהל: **סבר ליה כרבי יהודה.** הלכך הכא שרי דמכשירי אוכל נפש הוא: **שאי אפשר לעשותן מעי"ט.** כגון שפוד שנרצם בי"ט: **עדיפא.** חזקה דהוא שרי אפילו מכשירין שאפשר מעיו"ט: **תלה כוזא בסיכתא.** תלה כלי קטן במגוד: **ה"נ דמיחייב.** והכא מאי חיובא איכא באהל עראי בנין גמור לא הוי ומדרבנן הוא דמיתסר: אלא

תוספות

מל ולא פרע את המילה כאילו לא מל. תימה אמאי איצטריך למיתני האי כיון דכבר תנא דבשר החופה את רוב העטרה מעכב המילה וכי לא פרע עדיין רוב עטרה מכוסה: **אבי** הבן אומר כו'. רבינו שמואל גרים אבי הבן ברישא והדר המל ואומר וכבר הנהיג לעשות כן לברך אבי הבן קודם המילה משום דלהכניסו להבא משמע כדאמרינן בפ"ק דפסחים (ד' ז. ושם) בלבער כ"ע לא פליגי דלהבא משמע ועוד [ט] דכל המצות מברך עליהן עובר לעשייתן ור"ת החזיר המנהג לקדמותו וגרם המל ברישא והדר אבי הבן כמו שכתוב בכל הספרים וכן מוכח כולה סוגיא מדקאמר העומדים שם אומרים כשם שהכניסו לברית מכלל שכבר הכניסו ועוד דגבי גר דבסמוך גרם ברישא המל כו' והדר המברך אומר אקב"ו למול את הגרים ונראה הוא שזהו כנגד ברכת אבי הבן והתם א"א לשנות הגירסא שיש באותה ברכה להטיף מהן דם ברית כו' ברוך כורת הברית משמע דכל זה הוא אחר המילה ועוד דהמברך מברך לעולם אחר המילה כמו במילת קטן והיא דפסחים ה"פ בלבער כ"ע לא פליגי דלהבא משמע טפי מלשעבר ומיהו לשעבר נמי משמע כי פליגי בעל ביעור מר סבר דמשמע מעיקרא טפי מלהבא ומר סבר להבא נמי משמע כמו מעיקרא והא דאמרינן דכל המצות מברך עובר לעשייתן ה"מ כשהמברך עצמו עושה המצוה: **ידיד** מבטן. אומר ר"ת שהוא אברהם אבינו שנקרא ידיד שנאמר (ירמיה יא) מה לידידי בביתי כדדרשינן במנחות בפרק כל המנחות (ד' נג: ושם) ושלשת האבות נזכרים חוק בשארו שם הוא יצחק וצאצאיו חתם באות ברית קדש הוא יעקב וצאצאיו הוא ובניו כמו שתרגם יונתן הצאצאים והצפיעות בניא ובני בניא (ישעיה כב) כלומר יוצאי חלציו [י]: **במצותיו** וצונו למול את העבדים. שנאמר יליד בית ומקנת כסף (בראשית יז):

הדרן עלך ר' אליעזר דמילה

תולין. אבל נותנין לתלויה ביום טוב. וצריך לפרש ולומר שאם היה עושהו מאתמול לא היה טוב כל כך וחזק והא דתניא בפרקין דלעיל (ד' קלד. ושם) דאין מסננין את החרדל במסננת שלו בי"ט אם היה עושהו מאתמול לא היה מתקלקל: **דרבי** אליעזר עדיפא מדר"י. תימה ולר"א תיקשה ליה הנהו קראי דדריש בפ"ק דמגילה (ד' ז:) דקאמר ורבי יהודה כתיב הוא וכתיב לכם ולא קשיא כאן במכשירין שאפשר וכו' וכ"ת ר"א הוה דריש הוא לדרשה אחרינא א"כ מנ"ל התם דרבי יהודה הוה מפליג לימא דרבי יהודה הוה דריש ליה לדרשה אחריתי כר' אליעזר ונראה דבדאורייתא מודה ר' אליעזר דמכשירין דאפשר אסורים [כ] וכי שרי להו הכא ה"מ באהל עראי דאינו אלא מדרבנן גזירה אטו אהל קבע כדאמרינן בביצה בפרק המביא (ד' לג:) מיהו קשה מנ"ל דעדיפא דילמא בהא מודה אפילו רבי יהודה:

עין משפט נר מצוה

נד א מיי' פ"ב מהל' מילה הלכה ד סמג עשין כח טוש"ע י"ד סי' רסד סעיף ד:

נה ב מיי' שם הלכה ג טוש"ע שם סעי' ה:

נו ג מיי' שם הלכה ה טור וש"ע שם סעיף ו:

נז ד מיי' פ"ג מהל' מילה הלכה א סמג שם טוש"ע י"ד סי' רסה סעיף א:

נח ה מיי' שם הלכה ד סמג שם טוש"ע י"ד סי' רסח סעיף ה:

נט ו מיי' שם הלכה ה סמג שם טוש"ע י"ד סי' רסז סעיף יב:

א ז מיי' פכ"ב מהל' שבת הלכה יז ופ"ו מהל' יו"ט הלכה יז סמג לאוין סה טוש"ע או"ח סי' שטו סעי' ט וסי' שיט סעיף ט וסי' תקי סעיף ד:

תורה אור השלם

א) כֹּה אָמַר יְיָ אִם לֹא בְרִיתִי יוֹמָם וָלָיְלָה חֻקּוֹת שָׁמַיִם וָאָרֶץ לֹא שָׂמְתִּי: [ירמיה לג, כה]

רבינו חננאל

מעת לעת להבראותו. וזה מפורש ביבמות בפר' הערל וכל הטמאים: מתני' ואלו הן ציצין המעכבין את המילה. א"ר אבינא א"ר ירמיה בר אבא אמר רב בשר החופה את רוב גובהה של עטרה וכו' וכן הלכתא. ואם הוא בעל בשר מתקנו מפני מראית העין כלומר אע"פ שהציצין הללו אינן חופין רוב גובהה של עטרה מתקנו מפני שלא יהא נראה כערלה: אמר שמואל קטן המסורבל בבשר רואין אותו כל זמן שמתקשה [ונראה מהול אין צריך למול במתניתא תנא רשבג"א קטן המסורבל בבשר רואין אותו כ"ז שמתקשה] שאינו נראה מהול צריך למול ואמרי מאי ביניהם [נראה] ואינו נראה צריך למול לרשב"ג דאמר ואינו נראה מהול צריך למול אבל אם נראה ואינו נראה אינו צריך למול. פי' מסורבל בבשר כדכתי' כפיתו בסרבלתהון וכו'. מל ולא פרע את המילה וכו'. פי' מי שמל ולא פרע את המילה כלומר לא קרע את העור וגילה את העטרה כאלו לא מל:

הדרן עלך ר' אליעזר אם לא הביא.

עז ותהלה לאל אבי. שית עזר גללין. חלץ באזר וההלין. שבפ' ר' אליעזר תולין:

ר' אליעזר אומר תולין את המשמרת ביו"ט וכו' ואקשי' עלה השתא ר' אליעזר להוסיף באהל עראי מחמיר ואמר אין מוסיפין לכתחלה (שאי) [מאי היא]. דתנן פקק החלון ר' אליעזר אומר בזמן שקשור ותלוי פוקקין בו כו'. ופקק זה כגון מסך קטן לסתום בו חללו של חלון ואמר רבה בר בר חנה א"ר יוחנן הכל מודים שאין עושין אהלי עראי בתחלה ביו"ט ואין צריך לומר בשבת לא נחלקו אלא להוסיף שר' אליעזר אומר אין מוסיפין ביו"ט ואין צ"ל בשבת וחכ"א מוסיפין בשבת ואין צ"ל ביו"ט ומפרקינן לה כו' ר' אליעזר סבר לה כר' יהודה דתניא אין בין יו"ט לשבת אלא אוכל נפש בלבד. ר' יהודה אומר אף מכשירי אוכל נפש וזה שמתיר ר' אליעזר לעשות אהל לכתחלה ביו"ט לתלות המשמרת מפני שהוא מכשירי אוכל נפש כדי לשתות היין בשמחת יו"ט ומקשינן ר' יהודה אינו מתיר אלא במכשירין שאי אפשר לעשותן מעיו"ט אבל במכשירין שאפשר לעשותן מעיו"ט כגון שימור היין וכדומה לו אוסר ור' אליעזר מתיר אפילו בזה. ואין הלכה

מסורת הש"ס

א) יבמות דף מז: עא., ב) [תוספתא פרק טו], ג) [מנחות מב. תוספתא ברכות פ"ו כל הענין עד סופו], ד) הג"ה יעב"ץ ז"ל ניקד לזה כמהרי"ק, ה) [נדרים לב.], ו) לעיל קכה: עירובין מד. סוכה כז:, ז) [תוספ' סוכה פ"א לעיל קכה: וש"נ], ח) [תוספ' מגילה פ"א] ביצה כח. לו: מגילה ז:, לעיל ס: קכד. [שם], ט) [ועי' תוס' מנחות נג. ד"ה בן], י) [עי' תוס' דפסחים ז: ד"ה מה לאיה רשות].

הגהות הב"ח

(א) גמ' העומדין שם אומרים כשם שהכנסתו לברית כך תכניסהו לתור' כצ"ל וכמוס': (ב) שם חלקנו צורנו לוה:

ליקוטי רש"י

מל. את הערלה. ולא פרע. את העור המכסה ראש הגיד [לעיל קלג.]. רוב גובהה. של אותה שורה ולא תימא רוב היקיפה [יבמות מז:]. אע"ג דאין רוב הקיפה [שם עא.]. קטן המסורבל בבשר. המלובש בבשר כסרבל ולשון מלבוש הוא כמו כפיתו בסרבליהון (דניאל ג) [קידושין עב.]. ולהטיף מהם דם ברית. הטעם של מצוה לכתוב דכתיב (זכריה ט) גם את בדם בריתך [לעיל קלד.]. בזמן שקשור. שם כל שעה [סוכה כז:]. ותלוי. שאינו נגרר לארץ שהכל ניכר שהוא קשור בו אינו מגיע לארץ [לעיל קכה:]. פוקקין בו. כיון דמתוקן ועומד לכך אין זה לא בונה ולא מוסיף. ואם לאו אין פוקקין בו. סתימתו כאהל [סוכה שם]. דדמי לבונה שמוסיף על סתימת הבית ואף על פי שעראי הוא שהרי יחזור ויפתחנו [עירובין מד.]. דמיחזי כמוסיף על הבנין [לעיל קכה:]. הכל מודים. ר"א וחכמים שנחלקו במוספות אהל עראי כגון פקק חלון דלאיל לחלוק גם דמוסיף הוא ואף על פי שעראי הוא מודים שאין עושין אהל עראי לכתחלה בשבת בפרק כל הכלים [קכה:]. שאין עושין אהל עראי. לפרוס מחצלת על ארבע מחיצות או על ארבע קונדסים להיות לצל או מן החמה ודוקא גג אבל מחיצה לאו אהל הוא ושרי לפורסה לצניעות כדאמרינן עירובין [קב.] בעובדא דשמואל ופקק החלון דמתמיתין משום דבנין קבוע הוא ומיחזי במסורת [עירובין שם] ובר"ש כאן. אלא

אלא להוסיף. כגון שהיה מחצלת פרוסה עליהן וכרוכה ונשאר בה טפח ולמחר פושטה דומיא דפקק דמוסיף בעלמא הוא [לעיל שם]. דלאפילו רבנן לא שרו אלא להוסיף כגון פקק חלון דתוספת בעלמא הוא [עירובין מד. עי"ש בתוס']. אין בין יום טוב לשבת. להיות מותר לכתחלה ביום טוב מה שאסור בשבת אלא לענין עושין יש הא דהלכה זה בקפולה וכבולת כולו גדולה [מגילה ז:]. מתיר אף מכשירי אוכל נפש. וטעמא משום דדריש לכם לכל צרכיכם [ביצה כח.]. שאי אפשר. כגון סכין שנפגמה ביום טוב [יומא ז:]. סיכתא. קבילי"א בלע"ז [עירובין ח.].

שֶׁל אַבְרָהָם אָבִינוּ – "Blessed are You, Hashem, our God, King of the Universe, WHO HAS SANCTIFIED US WITH HIS COMMANDMENTS AND COMMANDED US TO BRING HIM INTO THE COVENANT OF ABRAHAM OUR FOREFATHER."[12] הָעוֹמְדִים[13] אוֹמְרִים – THOSE STANDING[14] there (i.e. the people present at the ceremony) PROCLAIM: כְּשֵׁם שֶׁנִּכְנַס לַבְּרִית כָּךְ יִכָּנֵס לְתוֹרָה לְחוּפָּה וּלְמַעֲשִׂים טוֹבִים – "JUST AS HE HAS ENTERED INTO THE COVENANT, SO MAY HE ENTER INTO THE study of TORAH, THE MARRIAGE CANOPY, AND the performance of GOOD DEEDS."[15] וְהַמְבָרֵךְ אוֹמֵר – AND THE ONE DESIGNATED TO RECITE THE BLESSING SAYS:[16] אֲשֶׁר קִידֵּשׁ יְדִיד מִבֶּטֶן – "Blessed are You, Hashem, Our God, King of the Universe, WHO HAS SANCTIFIED THE BELOVED ONE FROM THE WOMB,[17] חוֹק בִּשְׁאֵרוֹ שָׂם – PLACED the mark of THE DECREE IN HIS FLESH,[18] וְצֶאֱצָאָיו חָתַם בְּאוֹת בְּרִית קֹדֶשׁ – AND SEALED HIS OFFSPRING[19] WITH THE SIGN OF THE HOLY COVENANT. עַל כֵּן בִּשְׂכַר זֹאת אֵל חַי חֶלְקֵנוּ – THEREFORE, AS REWARD FOR THIS, O LIVING GOD, OUR PORTION, our Rock,[20] צַוֵּה לְהַצִּיל יְדִידוּת שְׁאֵרֵינוּ מִשַּׁחַת – GIVE THE COMMAND TO RESCUE THE BELOVED OF OUR FLESH[21] FROM DESTRUCTION,[22] לְמַעַן בְּרִיתוֹ אֲשֶׁר שָׂם בִּבְשָׂרֵנוּ – FOR THE SAKE OF HIS COVENANT THAT HE HAS PLACED IN OUR FLESH. בָּרוּךְ אַתָּה ה׳ כּוֹרֵת הַבְּרִית – BLESSED ARE YOU HASHEM, WHO ESTABLISHES THE COVENANT."

The blessings recited at the circumcision of a convert:[23] הַמָּל אֶת הַגֵּרִים אוֹמֵר – ONE WHO CIRCUMCISES CONVERTS SAYS: בָּרוּךְ אַתָּה ה׳ אֱלֹהֵינוּ מֶלֶךְ הָעוֹלָם אֲשֶׁר קִדְּשָׁנוּ בְּמִצְוֹתָיו וְצִוָּנוּ עַל הַמִּילָה – "BLESSED ARE YOU, HASHEM, OUR GOD, KING OF THE UNIVERSE, WHO HAS SANCTIFIED US WITH HIS COMMANDMENTS AND COMMANDED US REGARDING CIRCUMCISION." וְהַמְבָרֵךְ אוֹמֵר – AND THE ONE DESIGNATED[24] TO RECITE THE BLESSING SAYS: אֲשֶׁר קִדְּשָׁנוּ בְּמִצְוֹתָיו וְצִוָּנוּ לָמוּל אֶת הַגֵּרִים – "Blessed are You, Hashem, our God, King of the universe, WHO HAS SANCTIFIED US WITH HIS COMMANDMENTS AND COMMANDED US TO CIRCUMCISE THE CONVERTS,[25] וּלְהַטִּיף מֵהֶם דַּם בְּרִית – AND TO DRAW FROM THEM BLOOD OF THE COVENANT.[26] שֶׁאִילְמָלֵא דַּם בְּרִית לֹא נִתְקַיְּימוּ שָׁמַיִם וָאָרֶץ – FOR WITHOUT BLOOD OF THE COVENANT, HEAVEN AND EARTH WOULD NOT ENDURE, שֶׁנֶּאֱמַר – AS IT IS STATED:[27] "אִם־לֹא בְרִיתִי יוֹמָם וָלָיְלָה חֻקּוֹת שָׁמַיִם וָאָרֶץ לֹא־שָׂמְתִּי" – *IF NOT FOR MY COVENANT OF DAY AND NIGHT, THE STATUTES OF HEAVEN AND EARTH I WOULD NOT HAVE ESTABLISHED.*[28] בָּרוּךְ אַתָּה ה׳ כּוֹרֵת הַבְּרִית – BLESSED ARE YOU HASHEM, WHO

NOTES

regarded as being made before the performance (*Rosh, Meiri*).

[See *Tosafos,* who cite an opinion that the father should recite his blessing before that of the *mohel.*]

12. According to those who maintain that this is a blessing for a mitzvah (see previous note), it is difficult to understand why the Sages required this blessing in addition to the one made by the *mohel.* For various explanations, see *Hagahos Maimoniyos* (*Hil. Milah* 3:1 §3), *Bach, Yoreh Deah* §265, *Beis Yosef* ibid. and *Aruch HaShulchan* ibid. §8.

[Some authorities rule that the father also makes the blessing of שֶׁהֶחֱיָנוּ (*Rambam, Hil. Milah* 3:3). Others maintain that this blessing should be omitted in view of the baby's discomfort (*Meiri; Tosafos* to *Eruvin* 40b ד״ה דלמא; see *Tosafos* to *Succah* 46a ד״ה העושה).]

13. The text should include the word שָׁם, *there* (*Hagahos HaBach*).

14. From here it is evident that one must stand during a circumcision. This requirement is based on the verse (*II Kings* 23:3): וַיַּעֲמֹד כָּל־הָעָם בַּבְּרִית, *All the people stood to the covenant* (*Mordechai* §422; *Rama, Yoreh Deah* 265:1; cf. *Tur* ibid., who gives a different Scriptural source).

15. Many authorities have the reading כְּשֵׁם שֶׁהִכְנַסְתּוֹ . . . כָּךְ תַּכְנִיסֵהוּ, *Just as you have entered him ... so may you enter him,* which is a direct declaration to the father (*Rif; Tosafos; Rosh; Rambam, Hil. Milah* 3:2; *Tur* and *Shulchan Aruch, Yoreh Deah* 265:1; cf. *Meiri*). *Taz* (*Yoreh Deah* 265:2) rules that those at the ceremony who can actually see the father say כְּשֵׁם שֶׁהִכְנַסְתּוֹ, *just as you have entered him,* while those who do not see him make the indirect statement כְּשֵׁם שֶׁנִּכְנַס, *just as he has entered. Shach* (ibid. §13) prefers the indirect form כְּשֵׁם שֶׁנִּכְנַס, *just as he has entered,* because it is appropriate in all situations.

We bless the father that just as he has merited to circumcise this son, so may he merit to fulfill all the duties a father has toward his son — namely, to teach him Torah, to marry him off and to lead him on the right path (*Chidushei HaRan; Rabbeinu Manoach,* cited by *Beis Yosef, Yoreh Deah* §265).

We mention "marriage" before "good deeds" on the basis of a Baraisa quoted in *Kiddushin* (29a) which states: "A father is obligated with respect to his son, to circumcise him, to redeem him [if he is a firstborn], to teach him Torah, to take a wife for him and to teach him a profession." [A profession is equated with "good deeds," because a person who lacks a means of livelihood might resort to stealing (see Gemara ibid.).] The reason why the Baraisa lists a profession after marriage is that a person is not liable to Divine punishment [which a profession is designed to prevent] until he is twenty, whereas marriage is recommended (in *Pirkei Avos* 5:21) at the age of eighteen (*Abudraham,* cited by *Beis Yosef* ibid.; see, however, the objection raised by *Maadanei Yom Tov,* end of *Bechoros,* §6).

16. This blessing is not necessarily recited by the *mohel* (*Rambam, Hil. Milah* 3:3; *Tur* and *Shulchan Aruch, Yoreh Deah* 265:1). It may be recited by anyone whom the father, mother or *beis din* appoints (*Hagahos Yavetz*).

This blessing is recited over a cup of wine. The blessing on wine (בּוֹרֵא פְּרִי הַגָּפֶן, *Who creates the fruit of the vine*) is recited first (*Tur* and *Shulchan Aruch* ibid.).

17. This refers to Isaac, concerning whom it is said (*Genesis* 22:2): אֲשֶׁר־אָהַבְתָּ, *whom you love* (*Rashi*).

A year before Isaac's birth Abraham was told to circumcise his son (see *Genesis* 17:19). Thus, Isaac was sanctified for this mitzvah even before his birth (*Rashi*). Alternatively: Since Abraham circumcised himself a year before Isaac's birth, Isaac was conceived in holiness (*Abudraham; Iyun Yaakov*).

According to *Rabbeinu Tam,* the blessing mentions all three of our forefathers: *The beloved one* is Abraham; *his flesh* is Isaac; *his offspring* is Jacob (*Tosafos;* see *Rashba*).

18. Circumcision is unique in that it is the only mitzvah that is inseparable from the body of man, as opposed to other mitzvos, such as tefillin or *tzitzis,* which can be removed (*Maharsha*).

19. Those who descend from [Isaac] (*Rashi*), i.e. the Jewish people.

20. The text should read חֶלְקֵנוּ צוּרֵנוּ, *our Portion, our Rock* (as it is recorded in *Rif, Rosh* et al.).

21. יְדִידוּת שְׁאֵרֵינוּ, *beloved of our flesh,* apparently refers to the child. Some interpret it as signifying the soul [the aspect of man most beloved to God] which is within our "flesh," i.e. the physical body (*Taz, Yoreh Deah* 265:5; see *Maayan Beis HaSho'eivah* to *Genesis* 17:1).

22. This refers to Gehinnom [from which one can be saved in the merit of this mitzvah], as it is written (*Zechariah* 9:11): *Because of the blood of your covenant I have sent your prisoners from the pit* (*Rashi*).

Our translation follows *Shach* (*Yoreh Deah* 265:5), who reads צַוֵּה, *command* [imperative]. Others, though, read צִוָּה, *he commanded* [past tense] (*Hagahos Yavetz*). [The second version can be explained with the Midrash (*Tanchuma, Lech Lecha* §20), which states: God swore to Abraham that anyone who is circumcised will not descend to Gehinnom. See also *Eruvin* 19a, cited by *Maharsha.*]

23. Circumcision is one of the procedures required for conversion (*Kereisos* 9a).

24. By the *beis din* who supervised the conversion (*Hagahos Yavetz*).

25. Regarding the use of וְצִוָּנוּ, *and has commanded us,* in this context, see *Tos. HaRosh, Sfas Emes* and *Devar Avraham* 2:25 at length.

26. A convert who is already circumcised (or an infant that was born circumcised) still requires the procedure of הַטָּפַת דַּם בְּרִית, *drawing blood of the covenant* (see 135a note 4). Since many converts are in this position, the blessing for converts explicitly mentions this procedure (*Ramban's* first approach).

27. *Jeremiah* 33:25.

28. The "covenant of day and night" is the covenant of circumcision, which leaves its imprint on a person both day and night (*Tos. Yom Tov* to *Nedarim* 3:11).

The world was created to serve man. This purpose, however, can be truly fulfilled only when man is in his complete form. Thus, since man

עין משפט נר מצוה

נד א מיי' פ"ג מהל' מילה הלכה ד סמג עשין כח טוש"ע י"ד סי' רסד סעיף ד:

נה ב מיי' שם הלכה ג טוש"ע שם סעיף ה:

נו ג מיי' שם הלכה ה טור וש"ע שם סעיף ו:

נז ד מיי' פ"ג מהל' מילה הלכה ה סמג שם טוש"ע י"ד סי' רסה סעיף א:

נח ה מיי' שם הלכה ד סמג שם טוש"ע י"ד סי' רסח סעיף ה:

נט ו מיי' שם הלכה ה סמג שם טוש"ע י"ד סי' רסז סעיף יב:

א ז מיי' פכ"א מהל' שבת הלכה יז ופ"ג מהל' י"ט הלכה ח סמג לאוין סה עה טוש"ע א"ח סי' שטו סעיף ט וסי' שיט סעיף ט וסי' תקי סעיף ד:

תורה אור השלם

א) כֹּה אָמַר יְיָ אִם לֹא בְרִיתִי יוֹמָם וָלָיְלָה חֻקּוֹת שָׁמַיִם וָאָרֶץ לֹא שָׂמְתִּי: (ירמיה לג, כה)

רבינו חננאל

מעת לעת להבראותו. וזה מפורש ביבמות בפר' הערל וכל הטמאים: מתני' ואלו הן ציצין המעכבין את המילה. א"ר אבינא א"ר ירמיה בר אבא אמר רב בשר החופה את רוב גובהה של עטרה וכו' וכן הלכתא. ואם הוא בעל בשר מתקנו מפני מראית העין כלומר אע"פ שהציצין הללו אינן חופין רוב גובהה של עטרה מתקנו מפני שלא יהא נראה כערלה. אמר שמואל קטן המסורבל בבשר רואין אותו כל זמן שמתקשה [ונראה מהול אין צריך למול במתניתא] תנא רשב"א קטן המסורבל בבשר רואין אותו כ"ז שמתקשה שאינו נראה מהול צריך למול ואמרי' מאי בינייהו איכא בינייהו [נראה] ואינו נראה צריך למול לרשב"ג דאמר ואינו נראה מהול כלל צריך למול אבל אם נראה ואינו נראה אינו צריך למול. פי' מסורבל מסובב בבשר כדכתי' כפיתו סרבלתהון וכו'. מל ולא פרע את המילה וכו'. פי' מי שמל ולא פרע את המילה כלומר לא קרע את העור וגילה את העטרה כאלו לא מל:

הדרן עלך ר' אליעזר אם לא הביא. עז ותהלה לאל אבי. שית עזר גלילין. חלץ באזר והחלין. בפ' ר' אליעזר תולין:

ר' אליעזר אומר תולין את המשמרת ביו"ט וכו' ואקשי' עלה השתא ר' אליעזר להוסיף באהל עראי מחמיר ואמר אין מוסיפין לכתחלה (שאי) [מאי היא]. דתנן פקק החלון ר' אליעזר אומר בזמן שקשור ותלוי פוקקין בו כו' ופקק זה כגון מסך לסתום בו חללו של חלון ואמר רבה בר בר חנה א"ר יוחנן הכל מודים שאין עושין אהלי עראי בתחלה ביו"ט ואין צריך לומר בשבת לא נחלקו אלא להוסיף שר' אליעזר אומר אין מוסיפין ביו"ט ואין צ"ל בשבת וחכ"א מוסיפין בשבת ואין צ"ל ביו"ט ומפרקינן ר' אליעזר סבר לה כר' יהודה דתניא אין בין יו"ט לשבת אלא אוכל נפש בלבד. ר' יהודה אומר אף מכשירי אוכל נפש וזה שמתיר ר' אליעזר לעשות אהל לכתחלה ביו"ט לתלות המשמרת מפני שהוא מכשירי אוכל נפש כדי לשמר היין לשתות בשמחת יו"ט ונמצא ר' אליעזר מיקל מר' יהודה שר' יהודה אינו מתיר אלא במכשירין שאי אפשר לעשותן מעיו"ט אבל במכשירין שאפשר לעשותן מעיו"ט כגון שימור היין וכדומה לו אוסר ור' אליעזר מתיר אפילו בזה. ואין הלכה

תוספות

מל ולא פרע את המילה כאילו לא מל. תימה אמאי איצטריך למיתני הא כיון דבכל מנה את בשר החופה את רוב העטרה מעכב המילה וכי לא פרע עדיין רוב עטרה מכוסה: **אבי** הבן אומר כו'. רבינו שמואל גריס אבי הבן ברישא והדר המל ומכר הנהיג לעשות כן לברך אבי הבן קודם המילה משום דלהכניסו להבא משמע כדאמרינן בפ"ק דפסחים (ד' ז. ושם) בלבער כ"ע לא פליגי דלהבא משמע ועוד דכל המצות מברך עליהן עובר לעשייתן ור"ת החזיר המנהג לקדמותו וגרס המל ברישא והדר אבי הבן כמו שכתוב בכל הספרים וכן מוכח סוגיא מדקאמר העומדים שם אומרים כשם שהכניסו לברית מכלל שכבר הכניסו ועוד דגבי גר דבסמוך גרס ברישא המל כו' והדר המברך אומר אקב"ו למול את הגרים ונראה הוא שזהו כנגד ברכת אבי הבן והתם א"א לשנות הגירסא שיש באותה ברכה להטיף מהן דם ברית כו' ברוך כורת הברית משמע דכל זה הוא אחר המילה ועוד דהמברך מברך לעולם אחר המילה כמו במילת קטן והיא דפסחים ה"פ בלבער כ"ע לא פליגי דלהבא משמע טפי מלשעבר ומיהו לשעבר נמי משמע כי פליגי בעל ביעור מר סבר דמשמע מעיקרא טפי מלהבא ומר סבר להבא נמי משמע כמו מעיקרא והא דאמרינן דכל המצות מברך עובר לעשייתן ה"מ כשהמברך עצמו עושה המצוה: **ידיד** מבטן. אומר ר"ת שהוא אברהם אבינו שנקרא ידיד שנאמר (ירמיה יא) מה לידידי בביתי כדדרשינן במנחות בפרק כל המנחות (ד' נג: ושם) ושלשת האבות נזכרים חוק בשארו שם הוא יצחק וצאצאיו חתם באות ברית קדש הוא יעקב וצאצאיו הוא ובניו כמו שתרגם יונתן הצאצאים והצפיעות בניא ובני בניא (ישעיה כב) כלומר יוצאי חלציו: **במצותיו** וצונו למול את העבדים. שנאמר יליד בית ומקנת כסף (בראשית יז):

הדרן עלך ר' אליעזר דמילה

תולין. אבל נותנין לתלויה ביום טוב. וצריך לפרש ולומר שאם היה עושהו מאתמול לא היה טוב כל כך וחזק והא דתניא בפרקין לעיל (ד' קלד. ושם) דאין מסננין את החרדל במסננת שלו בי"ט אם היה עושהו מאתמול לא היה מתקלקל: **דרבי** אליעזר עדיפא מדר"י. תימה ולר"א תיקשה ליה הנהו קראי דדריש בפ"ק דמגילה (ד' ז:) דקאמר וכי יהודה כתיב הוא וכתיב לכם ולא קשיא כאן במכשירין שאפשר וכו' וכ"ת ר"א הוה דריש הוא לדרשה אחרינא א"כ מנ"ל התם דרבי יהודה הוה מפליג לימא דרבי יהודה הוה דריש ליה לדרשה אחריתי כר' אליעזר ונראה דבדאורייתא מודה ר' אליעזר דמכשירין דאפשר אסורים וכי שרי להו הכא ה"מ באהל עראי דלאו אלא מדרבנן גזירה אטו אהל קבע כדאמרינן בגילה בפרק המביא (ד' לג:) מיהו קשה מנ"ל דעדיפא דילמא בהא מודה אפילו רבי יהודה:

מל ולא פרע את המילה כאילו לא מל: **גמ'** אמר רבי אבינא א"ר ירמיה בר אבא אמר רב בשר החופה את רוב גובהה של עטרה: ואם היה בעל בשר וכו': אמר שמואל קטן המסורבל בבשר רואין אותו כ"ז שמתקשה ונראה מהול אינו צריך למול ואם לאו צריך למול במתניתא תנא רשב"ג אומר קטן המסורבל בבשר רואין אותו כל זמן שמתקשה ואינו נראה מהול צריך למולו ואם לאו אינו צריך למולו מאי בינייהו איכא בינייהו נראה ואינו נראה: מל ולא פרע: ת"ר המל אומר אקב"ו על המילה אבי הבן אומר אקב"ו להכניסו בבריתו של אברהם אבינו העומדים אומרים כשם שנכנס לברית כך יכנס לתורה לחופה ולמע"ט והמברך אומר אשר קידש ידיד מבטן חוק בשארו שם וצאצאיו חתם באות ברית קדש על כן בשכר זאת אל חי חלקנו צורנו צוה להציל ידידות שארינו משחת למען בריתו אשר שם בבשרנו בא"י כורת הברית המל את הגרים אומר ברוך אתה ה' אלהינו מלך העולם אקב"ו על המילה והמברך אומר אקב"ו למול את הגרים ולהטיף מהם דם ברית שאילמלא דם ברית לא נתקיימו שמים וארץ שנאמר אם לא בריתי יומם ולילה חוקות שמים וארץ לא שמתי בא"י כורת הברית המל את העבדים אומר אקב"ו על המילה והמברך אומר אקב"ו למול את העבדים ולהטיף מהם דם ברית שאילמלא דם ברית לא נתקיימו חוקות שמים וארץ שנאמר אם לא בריתי יומם ולילה חוקות שמים וארץ לא שמתי בא"י כורת הברית:

הדרן עלך רבי אליעזר דמילה

רבי אליעזר אומר תולין את המשמרת בי"ט ונותנין לתלויה בשבת וחכ"א אין תולין את המשמרת בי"ט ואין נותנין לתלויה בשבת אבל נותנין לתלויה ביו"ט: **גמ'** השתא ר"א אוסופי אהל עראי לא מוספינן למיעבד לכתחלה שרי מאי היא דתנן פקק החלון ר"א אומר בזמן שקשור ותלוי פוקקין בו ואם לאו אין פוקקין בו וחכ"א בין כך ובין כך פוקקין בו ואמר רבה בר בר חנה א"ר יוחנן הכל מודים שאין עושין אהל עראי בתחלה בי"ט ואין צ"ל בשבת לא נחלקו אלא להוסיף שר"א אומר אין מוסיפין בי"ט ואין צ"ל בשבת וחכ"א מוסיפין בשבת ואין צ"ל ביום טוב ר"א סבר לה כרבי יהודה דתניא אין בין יום טוב לשבת אלא אוכל נפש בלבד רבי יהודה מתיר אף מכשירי אוכל נפש אימר דשמעינן ליה לר' יהודה במכשירין שאי אפשר לעשותם מערב יום טוב במכשירין שאפשר לעשותם מעיו"ט מי שמעת ליה דר"א עדיפא מדרבי יהודה: וחכ"א: איבעיא להו תלה מאי אמר רב יוסף תלה חייב חטאת א"ל אביי אלא מעתה תלה כוזא בסיכתא הכי נמי דמיחייב אלא

רש"י

פרע. גילה: **גמ' רוב גובהה.** לא תימא רוב העטרה דקתני מתני' רוב היקיפה אלא אפילו רוב גובהה במקום אחד: **קטן המסורבל בבשר.** פלטר"י בלע"ז שמן ועב ולאחר שנימול נראה כמכוסהו: **כל זמן שמתקשה.** ומתוך הקישוי מתפשט בשרו. בדשמואל גרסינן ונראה מהול במתניתא גרסינן ואינו נראה מהול: **איכא בינייהו נראה ואינו נראה.** לשמואל נראה מהול הוא דאין צריך למולו הא נראה ואינו נראה צריך למתניתא אינו נראה הוא דצריך הא נראה ואינו נראה אינו צריך: **אשר קידש ידיד מבטן.** יצחק קרי ידיד על שם אשר אהבת (בראשית כב): **מבטן.** דקודם שנולד נתקדש למצוה זו דכתיב (שם יז) אבל שרה אשתך וגו' והקימותי את בריתי אתו היינו מילה: **בשארו.** בבשרו: **שם.** חק של מילה: **וצאצאיו.** אחריו: **חתם באות.** זו של ברית קדש: **צוה להציל ידידות שארינו משחת.** מגיהנם דכתיב גם את בדם בריתך שלחתי אסיריך מבור אין מים בו (זכריה ט):

הדרן עלך ר' אליעזר דמילה

תולין את המשמרת. שמסננין בה שמרי יין ומותח פיה לכל צד בעגול ונעשה כאהל על חלל הכלי שקורין אשטנד"א ולא"ג דעביד אהל שרי בי"ט כדמפרש בגמרא אבל בשבת מיהא לכתחילה לא אבל אם תלויה היא נותנין לתוכה שמרים ומסנן דאין דלך זורר בכך: **גמ' פקק החלון.** כגון ארובת הגג: **אלא להוסיף.** כגון פקק זה שאינו אלא תוספת ערלי על האהל: **סבר ליה כרבי יהודה.** הלכך הכא שרי דמכשירי אוכל נפש הוא: **שאי אפשר לעשותן מעי"ט.** כגון שפוד שנרצס בי"ט: **עדיפא.** חזקה דהוא שרי אפילו מכשירין שאפשר מעיו"ט: **תלה כוזא בסיכתא.** תלה כלי קטן במגוד: **ה"נ דמיחייב.** והכא מאי חיובא איכא באהל עראי בנין גמור לא הוי ומדרבנן הוא דמיתסר: אלא

מסורת הש"ס

א) יבמות דף מז: עא., ב) [תוספתא פרק טו], ג) [מנחות מג. תוספתא ברכות פ"ו כל הענין עד סופו], ד) הג"מ יעב"ץ ז"ל ניקד לזה במירי"ק, ה) [נדרים לב.], ו) לעיל קכה: עירובין מד. סוכה כז., ז) [תוספ' סוכה פ"א לעיל קכה: וש"נ], ח) [תוספ' מגילה פ"א] ביצה כח. לו: מגילה ז: לעיל ס: קכד., ט) [שם], י) [ועי' תוס' מנחות נג. ד"ה בן], כ) [עי' תוס' דפסחים קטו: ד"ה מה ראיה רשות].

הגהות הב"ח

(א) גמ' העומדין שם אומרים כשם שהכנסתו לברית כך תכניסהו לתור' כצ"ל וכן בתוס': (ב) שם חלקנו צורנו לוה:

ליקוטי רש"י

מל. את הערלה. **ולא פרע.** את העור המכסה ראש הגיד [לעיל קלג.]. **רוב גובהה.** של אותה שורה ולא תימא רוב היקיפה [יבמות מז:]. אע"ג דאין רוב הקיפה [שם עא.]. **קטן המסורבל בבשר.** המלובש בבשר כסרבל [קידושין עב.]. ולשון מלבוש הוא כמו כפיתו בסרבליהון (דניאל ג) [ע"ז ב:]. **ולהטיף מהם דם ברית.** הטפת דם ברית מלוה כדכתיב (זכריה ט) גם את בדם בריתך [לעיל קלד.]. **בזמן שקשור.** שם כל שעה [סוכה כז:]. **ותלוי.** שאינו נגרר בארץ שהמבדל שהוא קשור בו אינו מגיע לארץ [לעיל קכה:]. **פוקקין בו.** כיון דמתוקן ועומד לכך אין זה לא בונה ולא מוסיף. **ואם לאו אין פוקקין בו.** דמוסיף הוא על סתימת אהל [סוכה שם]. דדמי לבונה שמוסיף על סתימת הבית ואף על פי שערלי הוא שהרי יחזור ויפתחנו [עירובין מד.]. דמיחזי כמוסיף על הבנין [לעיל שם]. **הכל מודים.** ר"א ומחלוקתו שנחלקו בתוספת אהל ערלי גבי פקק חלון דליכא למאן דאמר פוקקין בו ואף על גב דמוסיף על אהל ערלי הוא מודים שאין עושין את כל האהל לכתחלה בשבת בפרק כל הכלים (קכה:) [עירובין פו:]. **שאין עושין אהל עראי.** לפרוס מחצלת על ארבע ממילות או על ארבע קונדסים להיות לל לאהל מן החמה ודוקא גג אבל מחילה לאו אהל הוא ושרי לפורסה לצניעות כדאמרינן עירובין (לד.) בעובדא דשמואל ופקק החלון דממעיטין משום דבנין קבוע הוא ומיחזי כמוסיף על הבנין [ע"ש במסורה"ש וע"ע בתוס' שם וברש"י כאן]. **אלא להוסיף.** כגון שהיה מחצלת פרוסה עליהן וכרוכה ונשאר בה אויר ולאחר פושטה דומיא דפקק דמוסיף בעלמא הוא [לעיל שם]. דאפילו רבנן לא שרו אלא להוסיף כגון פקק חלון דתוספת בעלמא הוא [עירובין מד. ע"ש בתוס']. **אין בין יום טוב לשבת.** להיות מותר לכתחלה ביום טוב מה שאסור בשבת אבל לענין עונשין יש הרבה שזה בסקילה וזה בלאו גרידא [מגילה ז:]. **מתיר אף מכשירי אוכל נפש.** וטעמא משום דדריש יעשה לכם לכל צרכיכם [ביצה כח.]. **שאי אפשר.** כגון סכין שנפגמה ביום טוב. **שאפשר.** כגון סכין שנפגם מערב יום טוב [מגילה שם]. **סיכתא.** קביליי"א בלע"ז [עירובין ח.]. יתד [יומא ז:].

ESTABLISHES THE COVENANT."[29]

The blessings recited at the circumcision of a Canaanite slave:[30]

הַמָּל אֶת הָעֲבָדִים אוֹמֵר – ONE WHO CIRCUMCISES SLAVES SAYS: **אֲשֶׁר קִדְּשָׁנוּ בְּמִצְוֹתָיו וְצִוָּנוּ עַל הַמִּילָה** – "Blessed are You, Hashem, Our God, King of the universe, WHO HAS SANCTIFIED US WITH HIS COMMANDMENTS AND COMMANDED US REGARDING CIRCUMCISION." **וְהַמְבָרֵךְ אוֹמֵר** – AND THE ONE DESIGNATED[31] TO RECITE THE BLESSING SAYS: **אֲשֶׁר קִדְּשָׁנוּ בְּמִצְוֹתָיו וְצִוָּנוּ לָמוּל אֶת הָעֲבָדִים** – "Blessed are You, Hashem, Our God, King of the Universe, WHO HAS SANCTIFIED US WITH HIS COMMANDMENTS AND COMMANDED US TO CIRCUMCISE THE SLAVES, **וּלְהַטִּיף מֵהֶם דַּם בְּרִית** – AND TO DRAW FROM THEM BLOOD OF THE COVENANT. **שֶׁאִילְמָלֵא דַּם בְּרִית חוּקוֹת שָׁמַיִם וָאָרֶץ לֹא נִתְקַיְּימוּ**[32] – FOR WITHOUT BLOOD OF THE COVENANT, HEAVEN AND EARTH WOULD NOT ENDURE, **שֶׁנֶּאֱמַר** – AS IT IS STATED: **,,אִם־לֹא בְרִיתִי יוֹמָם וָלָיְלָה חֻקּוֹת שָׁמַיִם וָאָרֶץ לֹא־שָׂמְתִּי''** – *IF NOT FOR MY COVENANT OF DAY AND NIGHT, THE STATUTES OF HEAVEN AND EARTH I WOULD NOT HAVE ESTABLISHED.* **בָּרוּךְ אַתָּה ה׳ כּוֹרֵת הַבְּרִית** – BLESSED ARE YOU HASHEM, WHO ESTABLISHES THE COVENANT."

הדרן עלך רבי אליעזר דמילה

WE SHALL RETURN TO YOU, R' ELIEZER D'MILAH

NOTES

attains completeness through circumcision (see *Genesis* 17:1), it can be said that the world endures because of the mitzvah of circumcision. (*Maharal* in *Chidushei Aggados* to *Nedarim* 31b). [See *Maharsha* ibid. ד״ה גדולה (ב).]

29. Based on an alternative text, some authorities rule that only one blessing is recited at the circumcision of a convert [or Canaanite slave (see below)]. The circumciser does not say the short blessing (עַל הַמִּילָה, *regarding the circumcision*). Rather, he recites only the longer blessing: לָמוּל אֶת הַגֵּרִים וּלְהַטִּיף מֵהֶם דַּם בְּרִית וכו׳, *to circumcise the converts and to draw from them blood of the covenant,* etc. (*Rif,* as understood by *Baal HaMaor, Ramban, Ran,* et al.; *Rambam, Hil. Milah* 3:4; cf. *Ritva MHK* ed., *Chidushei HaRan* and *Rosh*).

30. A Jew is required to circumcise his Canaanite slave, as stated in *Genesis* 17:12 (*Tosafos*).

31. By the master (*Hagahos Yavetz;* see *Shach, Yoreh Deah* 267:22).

32. [Other versions read here as above (concerning converts): שְׁאִילְמָלֵא דַּם בְּרִית לֹא נִתְקַיְּימוּ שָׁמַיִם וָאָרֶץ (see *Dikdukei Soferim*); our translation follows this reading.]

עין משפט נר מצוה

נד א מיי' פ"ב מהל' מילה הלכה ד סמג עשין כח טוש"ע י"ד סי' רסד סעיף ד:
נה ב מיי' שם הלכה ג טוש"ע שם סעי' ה:
נו ג מיי' שם הלכה ב טור וש"ע שם סעיף ו:
נז ד מיי' פ"ג מהל' מילה הלכה א סמג שם טוש"ע י"ד סי' רסה סעיף א:
נח ה מיי' שם הלכה ד סמג שם טוש"ע י"ד סי' רסח סעיף ה:
נט ו מיי' שם הלכה ה סמג שם טוש"ע י"ד סי' רסז סעיף יב:
א ז מיי' פכ"א מהל' שבת הלכה יז ופ"ג מהל' י"ט הלכה יז סמג לאוין סה טוש"ע א"ח סי' שטו סעי' ט וסי' שיט סעיף ט וסי' תקי סעיף ד:

תורה אור השלם

א) כה אמר יי אם לא בריתי יומם ולילה חקות שמים וארץ לא שמתי: [ירמיה לג, כה]

רבינו חננאל

מעת לעת להבראותו. וזה מפורש ביבמות בפר' הערל וכל השמאים: מתני' ואלו הן ציצין המעכבין את המילה. א"ר אבינא א"ר ירמיה בר אבא אמר רב בשר החופה את רוב גובהה של עטרה וכו' וכן הלכתא. ואם הוא בעל בשר מתקנו מפני מראית העין כלומר אע"פ שהציצין הללו אינן חופין את רוב גובהה של עטרה מתקנו מפני שלא יהא נראה כערלה: אמר שמואל קטן המסורבל בבשר רואין אותו כל זמן שמתקשה [ונראה מהול אין צריך למול ו]אם לאו צריך למול. תנא רשב"ג קטן המסורבל בבשר רואין אותו כ"ז שמתקשה [ש]אינו נראה מהול צריך למול ואמרי' מאי בינייהם איכא בינייהם [נראה] ואינו נראה צריך למול לרשב"ג דאמר ואינו נראה מהול כלל צריך למול אבל אם נראה ואינו נראה אינו צריך למול. פי' מסורבל מסובב בבשר כדכתי' כפיתו בסרבליהון וכו'. מל ולא פרע את המילה וכו'. פי' מי שמל ולא פרע את המילה כלומר לא קרע את העור וגילה את העטרה כאלו לא מל:

הדרן עלך ר' אליעזר אם לא הביא. עז ותהלה לאל אבי. שית עזר גלילין. חלץ באזר והחלין. בפ' ר' אליעזר תולין:

ר' אליעזר אומר תולין את המשמרת ביו"ט וכו' ואקשי' עלה השתא ר' אליעזר להוסיף באהל עראי מחמיר ואמר אין מוסיפין לכתחלה (שאי) [מאי היא]. דתנן פקק החלון ר' אליעזר אומר בזמן שקשור ותלוי פוקקין בו כר' וכו' ופקק זה כגון מסך לסתום בו חללו

מל ולא פרע את המילה כאילו לא מל:

גמ' (א) אמר רבי אבינא א"ר ירמיה בר אבא אמר רב בשר החופה את רוב גובהה של עטרה: ואם היה בעל בשר וכו': אמר שמואל קטן המסורבל בבשר רואין אותו כ"ז שמתקשה ונראה מהול אינו צריך למול ואם לאו צריך למול במתניתא תנא רשב"ג אומר קטן המסורבל בבשר רואין אותו כל זמן שמתקשה ואינו נראה מהול צריך למולו ואם לאו אינו צריך למולו מאי בינייהו איכא בינייהו נראה ואינו נראה: מל ולא פרע: ת"ר המל אומר אקב"ו על המילה אבי הבן אומר אקב"ו להכניסו בבריתו של אברהם אבינו העומדים (א) אומרים כשם שנכנס לברית כך יכנס לתורה לחופה ולמע"ט והמברך אומר אשר קידש ידיד מבטן חוק בשארו שם וצאצאיו חתם באות ברית קדש על כן בשכר זאת אל חי חלקנו (ב) צורנו צוה להציל ידידות שארינו משחת למען בריתו אשר שם בבשרנו בא"י כורת הברית המל את הגרים אומר ברוך אתה ה' אלהינו מלך העולם אקב"ו על המילה והמברך אומר אקב"ו למול את הגרים ולהטיף מהם דם ברית שאילמלא דם ברית לא נתקיימו שמים וארץ שנאמר א) אם לא בריתי יומם ולילה חוקות שמים וארץ לא שמתי בא"י כורת הברית המל את העבדים אומר אקב"ו על המילה והמברך אומר אקב"ו למול את העבדים ולהטיף מהם דם ברית שאילמלא דם ברית חוקות שמים וארץ לא נתקיימו שנאמ' אם לא בריתי יומם ולילה חוקות שמים וארץ לא שמתי בא"י כורת הברית:

הדרן עלך רבי אליעזר דמילה

רבי אליעזר אומר תולין את המשמרת בי"ט ונותנין לתלויה בשבת וחכ"א אין תולין את המשמרת בי"ט ואין נותנין לתלויה בשבת אבל נותנין לתלויה ביו"ט:

גמ' השתא ר"א אוסופי אהל עראי לא מוספינן למיעבד לכתחלה שרי מאי היא דתנן פקק החלון ר"א אומר בזמן שקשור ותלוי פוקקין בו ואם לאו אין פוקקין בו וחכ"א בין כך ובין כך פוקקין בו ואמר רבה בר בר חנה א"ר יוחנן הכל מודים שאין עושין אהל עראי בתחלה בי"ט ואין צ"ל בשבת לא נחלקו אלא להוסיף שר"א אומר אין מוסיפין בי"ט ואין צ"ל בשבת וחכ"א מוסיפין בשבת ואין צ"ל ביום טוב הכא סבר לה ר"א כרבי יהודה דתניא אין בין יום טוב לשבת אלא אוכל נפש בלבד רבי יהודה מתיר אף מכשירי אוכל נפש אימר דשמעינן ליה לר' יהודה במכשירין שאי אפשר לעשותם מערב יום טוב במכשירין שאפשר לעשותם מעיו"ט מי שמעת ליה דר"א עדיפא מדרבי יהודה: וחכ"א: איבעיא להו תלה מאי אמר רב יוסף תלה חייב חטאת א"ל אביי אלא מעתה תלה כוזא בסיכתא הכי נמי דמיחייב אלא

פרע. גילה: גמ' רוב גובהה. לא תימא רוב העטרה דקתני מתני' רוב היקפה אלא אפילו רוב גובהה במקום אחד: קטן המסורבל בבשר. פלטר"י בלע"ז שמן ועב ולאחר שנימול נראה כמכסהו: כל זמן שמתקשה. ומתוך הקישוי מתפשט בשרו. בדשמואל גרסינן ונראה מהול במתניתא גרסינן ואינו נראה מהול: איכא בינייהו נראה ואינו נראה. לשמואל נראה מהול הוא דאין צריך למולו הא נראה ואינו נראה צריך למתניתא אינו נראה הוא דצריך הא נראה ואינו נראה אינו צריך: אשר קידש ידיד מבטן. יצחק קרי ידיד על שם אשר אהבת (בראשית כב): מבטן. דקודם שנולד נתקדש למצוה זו דכתיב (שם יז) אבל שרה אשתך וגו' והקימותי את בריתי אתו היינו מילה: בשארו. בבשרו: שם. חק של מילה: וצאצאיו. אחריו: חתם באות. זו של ברית קדש: צוה להציל ידידות שארינו משחת. מגיהנם דכתיב גם את בדם בריתך שלחתי אסיריך מבור אין מים בו (זכריה ט):

הדרן עלך ר' אליעזר דמילה

תולין את המשמרת. שמסננין בה שמרי יין ומותח פיה לכל צד בעגול ונעשה כאהל על חלל הכלי שקורין אשטנד"א ואע"ג דעביד אהל שרי בי"ט כדמפרש בגמרא אבל בשבת מיתלא לכתחילה לא אבל אם תלויה היא נותנין לתוכה שמרים ומסנן דאין דרך בורר בכך: גמ' פקק החלון. כגון ארובת הגג: אלא להוסיף. כגון פקק זה שאינו אלא תוספת עראי על האהל: סבר ליה כרבי יהודה. הלכך הכא שרי דמכשירי אוכל נפש הוא: שאי אפשר לעשותן מעי"ט. כגון שפוד שנרצם בי"ט: עדיפא. חזקה דהוא שרי אפילו מכשירין שאפשר מעיו"ט: תלה כוזא בסיכתא. תלה כלי קטן במגוד: ה"נ דמיחייב. והכא מאי חיובא איכא באהל עראי בנין גמור לא הוי ומדרבנן הוא דמיתסר: אלא

מל ולא פרע את המילה כאילו לא מל. תימה אמאי איצטריך למיתני האי כיון דכבר תנא דבשר החופה את רוב העטרה מעכב המילה וכי לא פרע עדיין רוב עטרה מכוסה: אבי הבן אומר כו'. רבינו שמואל גרים אבי הבן ברישא והדר המל אומר וכבר הנהיג לעשות כן לברך אבי הבן קודם המילה משום דלהכניסו להבא משמע כדאמרינן בפ"ק דפסחים (ד' ז. ושם) בלבער כ"ע לא פליגי דלהבא משמע ועוד ט) דכל המצות מברך עליהן עובר לעשייתן ור"ת החזיר המנהג לקדמותו וגרס המל ברישא והדר אבי הבן כמו שכתוב בכל הספרים וכן מוכח כולה סוגיא מדקאמר העומדים שם אומרים כשם שהכניסו לברית מכלל שכבר הכניסו ועוד דגבי גר דבסמוך גרס ברישא המל כו' והדר המברך אומר אקב"ו למול את הגרים ונראה הוא שזהו כנגד ברכת אבי הבן והתם א"א לשנות הגירסא שיש באותה ברכה להטיף מהן דם ברית כו' ברוך כורת הברית משמע דכל זה הוא אחר המילה ועוד דהמברך מברך לעולם אחר המילה כמו במילת קטן והיא דפסחים ה"פ בלבער כ"ע לא פליגי דלהבא משמע טפי מלשעבר ומיהו לשעבר נמי משמע כי פליגי בעל ביעור מר סבר דמשמע מעיקרא טפי מלהבא ומר סבר להבא נמי משמע כמו מעיקרא והא דאמרינן דכל המצות מברך עובר לעשייתן ה"מ כשהמברך עצמו עושה המצוה: ידיד מבטן. אומר ר"ת שהוא אברהם אבינו שנקרא ידיד שנאמר (ירמיה יא) מה לידידי בביתי כדדרשינן במנחות בפרק כל המנחות (ד' נג: ושם) ושלשת האבות נזכרים חוק בשארו שם הוא יצחק וצאצאיו חתם באות ברית קדש הוא יעקב וצאצאיו הוא ובניו כמו שתרגם יונתן הצאצאים והצפיעות בניא ובני בניא (ישעיה כב) כלומר יוצאי צאצאיו י): במצותיו וצונו למול את העבדים. שנאמר יליד בית ומקנת כסף (בראשית יז):

הדרן עלך ר' אליעזר דמילה

תולין. אבל נותנין לתלויה ביום טוב. וצריך לפרש ולומר שאם היה עושהו מאתמול לא היה טוב כל כך וחזק והא דתניא בפרקין דלעיל (ד' קלד. ושם) דאין מסננין את החרדל במסננת שלו בי"ט אם היה עושהו מאתמול לא היה מתקלקל: דרבי אליעזר עדיפא מדר"י. תימה ולר"א תיקשה ליה הנהו קראי דדריש בפ"ק דמגילה (ד' ז:) דקאמר ורבי יהודה כתיב הוא וכתיב לכם ולא קשיא כאן במכשירין שאפשר וכו' וכ"ת ר"א הוה דריש הוא לדרשה אחרינא א"כ מנ"ל התם דרבי יהודה הוה מפליג לימא דרבי יהודה הוה דריש ליה לדרשה אחריתי כר' אליעזר ונראה דבדאורייתא מודה ר' אליעזר דמכשירין דאפשר אסורים כ) וכי שרי להו הכא ה"מ באהל עראי דאינו אלא מדרבנן גזירה אטו אהל קבע כדאמרינן בביצה בפרק המביא (ד' לג:) מיהו קשה מנ"ל דעדיפא דילמא בהא מודה אפילו רבי יהודה: אלא

מסורת הש"ס

א) יבמות דף מז: עא., ב) [תוספתא פרק טז], ג) [מנחות מב. תוספתא ברכות פ"ו כל הענין עד סופו], ד) הג"מ יעב"ץ ז"ל ניקד לוה בחיריק, ה) [נדרים לב.], ו) לעיל קכה: עירובין מד. סוכה טו:, ז) [תוספ' סוכה פ"א], ח) [תוספ' מגילה פ"א] ביצה כח. לו: מגילה ז: לעיל קכד., ט) [שם], י) [ועי' תוס' ד"ה בגן], כ) [עי' תוס' דפסחים סט: ד"ה מה ראיה רשות].

הגהות הב"ח

(א) גמ' העומדין שם אומרים כשם שהכנסתו לברית כך תכניסהו לתור' כצ"ל וכן בתוס': (ב) שם חלקנו צורנו צוה:

ליקוטי רש"י

מל. את הערלה. ולא פרע. את העור המכסה את הגיד [לעיל קלג.]. רוב גובהה. של אותה שורה ולא תימא רוב הקיפה [יבמות מז:]. ואע"ג דאין רוב הקיפה [שם עא.]. קטן המסורבל בבשר. המלובש בבשר כסרבל [קידושין עב.]. ולשון מלובש הוא כמו כפיתו בסרבליהון (דניאל ג) [ע"ז כו:]. ולהטיף מהם דם ברית. הטפת דם ברית מצוה דכתיב (זכריה ט) גם את בדם בריתך [לעיל קלד.]. בזמן שקשור. ותלוי. שאינו נגרר לארץ שמתוך שהוא קשור בו אינו מגיע לארץ [לעיל קכה:]. פוקקין בו. כיון דמתוקן ועומד לכך אין זה לא בונה ולא מוסיף. ואם לאו אין פוקקין בו. דמוסיף הוא על שתימת אהל [סוכה שם]. דדמי לבונה שמוסיף על סתימת הבית ואף על פי שעראי הוא שהרי עשוי ליטול ולפתחו [עירובין מד.]. דמיחזי כמוסיף על הבנין [לעיל שם]. הכל מודים. ר"א ורבנן דפליגי בתוספת אהל עראי גבי פקק חלון דאילו לאחר לאמר פוקקין בו ואף על גב דמוסיף על אהל עראי הוא מודים הכל שאין עושין אהל לכתחלה בשבת בפרק כל הכלים [עירובין קב.]. שאין עושין אהל עראי. לפרוס מחצלת על ארבע מחיצות או על ארבע קונדסים להיות צל לאהל מן החמה ודווקא גג אהל מילתא לאו אהל הוא אלא מחיצה ושרי לפורסה ולעשותה כדאמרינן עירובין (קב.) בעובדא דשמואל ודפקק החלון דמתמיהן משום דבנין קבוע הוא ומיחזי כמוסיף על הבנין [ע"ש מסוכה ע"ש בתוס' וברש"י כאן]. אלא

להוסיף. כגון שהיה מחצלת פרוסה עליהן וכרוכה ונשאר בה אויר ולאחר פושטה דומיא דפקק דמוסיף הוא בעלמא הוא [לעיל קכה:]. דאפילו רבנן לא שרו אלא להוסיף כגון פקק חלון דתוספת בעלמא הוא [עירובין קב.]. אין בין יום טוב לשבת. להיות מותר לכתחלה ביום טוב מה שאסור בשבת אלא לענין עונשין יש הרבה שזה בסקילה ובכרת וזה בלאו גרידא [מגילה ז:]. מתיר אף מכשירי אוכל נפש. וטעמא משום דדריש הוא לבדו יעשה לכם לכל צרכיכם [ביצה כח.]. שאי אפשר. כגון סכין שנפגמה ביום טוב. שאפשר. כגון סכין שנפגמה מערב יום טוב [מגילה שם]. סיכתא. קנבי"ל בלע"ז [עירובין ח.]. יתד [יומא ז:].

Chapter Twenty

Mishnah The first Mishnah of this chapter discusses the permissibility of performing certain labors on the Sabbath and Yom Tov in the preparation of food:

רַבִּי אֱלִיעֶזֶר אוֹמֵר – **R' Eliezer says:** תּוֹלִין אֶת הַמְשַׁמֶּרֶת בְּיוֹם טוֹב – **We may suspend a strainer on Yom Tov,**[1] but not on the Sabbath, וְנוֹתְנִין לַתְּלוּיָה בְּשַׁבָּת – **and we may pour into a suspended** strainer even **on the Sabbath,** and certainly on Yom Tov.[2]

וַחֲכָמִים אוֹמְרִים – **But the Sages say:** אֵין תּוֹלִין אֶת הַמְשַׁמֶּרֶת בְּיוֹם טוֹב – **We may not suspend a strainer on Yom Tov,** and certainly not on the Sabbath,[3] וְאֵין נוֹתְנִין לַתְּלוּיָה בְּשַׁבָּת – **and we may not pour into a suspended** strainer **on the Sabbath.**[4] אֲבָל נוֹתְנִין לַתְּלוּיָה בְּיוֹם טוֹב – **But we may pour into a suspended** strainer **on Yom Tov.**[5]

Gemara R' Eliezer permits the suspension of a strainer on Yom Tov, even though it involves the construction of a temporary tent. The Gemara notes that this does not conform with a position known to be held by R' Eliezer elsewhere:

הַשְׁתָּא רַבִּי אֱלִיעֶזֶר אוֹסוּפֵי אֹהֶל עֲרַאי לֹא מוֹסְפִינַן – **Now, if R' Eliezer** himself holds that **we do not even add a temporary tent** onto an existing tent on Yom Tov,[6] לְמֵיעֲבַד לְכַתְּחִלָּה שָׁרֵי – **would he** then **permit constructing** a temporary tent (i.e. suspending a strainer) **even initially,** as he seems to do in our Mishnah?

The Gemara cites its source for R' Eliezer's position with respect to adding a temporary tent:

מַאי הִיא – And **what is that** ruling in which he prohibited even temporarily adding to an existing tent on Yom Tov? דִּתְנַן – It is **that which we learned in a Mishnah:**[7] פְּקָק הַחַלּוֹן – Concerning A WINDOW SHUTTER –[8] רַבִּי אֱלִיעֶזֶר אוֹמֵר – R' ELIEZER SAYS: בִּזְמַן שֶׁקָּשׁוּר וְתָלוּי – WHEN IT IS ATTACHED to the building by a rope, AND the rope is so short that [THE SHUTTER] IS SUSPENDED in the air when not in place, פּוֹקְקִין בּוֹ – WE MAY SHUTTER the window WITH IT on the Sabbath and Yom Tov. וְאִם לָאו – HOWEVER, IF the shutter is NOT suspended in this manner, אֵין פּוֹקְקִין בּוֹ – WE MAY NOT SHUTTER the skylight window WITH IT. It is Rabbinically prohibited to do so even though the shutter is placed over the window only temporarily.[9]

וַחֲכָמִים אוֹמְרִים – BUT THE SAGES SAY: בֵּין כָּךְ וּבֵין כָּךְ פּוֹקְקִין בּוֹ – IN EITHER CASE, WE MAY SHUTTER the window WITH IT, because the addition to the structure is only temporary.

The Tannaic dispute is explained:

וְאָמַר רַבָּה בַּר בַּר חָנָה אָמַר רַבִּי יוֹחָנָן – **And Rabbah bar bar Chanah said in the name of R' Yochanan:** הַכֹּל מוֹדִים שֶׁאֵין עוֹשִׂין אֹהֶל עֲרַאי בַּתְּחִלָּה בְּיוֹם טוֹב – **All** [both R' Eliezer and the Sages] **agree that we may not erect** even **a temporary structure initially on Yom Tov,** וְאֵין צָרִיךְ לוֹמַר בְּשַׁבָּת – **and it need not be said** that this is forbidden **on the Sabbath.** לֹא נֶחְלְקוּ אֶלָּא לְהוֹסִיף – **They disagree only** whether one is permitted **to make** a temporary **addition** to an existing structure, such as in the case of a shutter.[10] שֶׁרַבִּי אֱלִיעֶזֶר אוֹמֵר אֵין מוֹסִיפִין בְּיוֹם טוֹב – **For** in such a case **R' Eliezer says: We may not** even **make** a temporary **addition** to a building **on Yom Tov,**

NOTES

1. The Mishnah refers to a strainer through which wine is poured to filter out its dregs. The strainer is similar to a porous sack whose bottom comes to a point. The bottom of the sack is placed into a container, and the sack's narrow opening is stretched tightly around the rim of the container. The wine is then poured through the strainer and into the container; the filtered wine enters the container, while the dregs remain behind in the strainer.

Although suspending (literally: hanging) such a strainer constitutes making a temporary tent, or *ohel*, an act normally prohibited even on Yom Tov as a *toladah* of the *melachah* of *building*, R' Eliezer permits it here on Yom Tov [if the strainer is to be used to strain wine for Yom Tov use], when there is a special dispensation granted for preparation of food (see Gemara below). On the Sabbath, however [where there is no such dispensation], R' Eliezer agrees that one may not suspend a strainer (*Rashi;* see *Mishnah Berurah* 315:36; see also next note).

2. When the strainer has already been suspended before the Sabbath, there is no question of construction. However, filtering the wine by pouring it through a strainer would seem to be a violation of the prohibition against *selecting* [בורר], which generally forbids one to sort inedible matter from food (see Mishnah above, 73a, and Gemara 73b-74b). Still, R' Eliezer holds that pouring wine through a strainer is permitted, for it is not the usual manner of selecting (*Rashi*). [*Rashi* does not explain why this method of selecting is considered unusual. *Ritva* (*MHK* ed.) suggests that R' Eliezer holds that since most selecting is usually done with the intent to store away the sorted food, not to consume it immediately (as is usually the case with filtered wine), it is permitted (see also *Ritva* to 74a ד״ה אמרוה and *Chidushei HaRan* to the Mishnah here; see also *Piskei HaRid,* and *Rashba* to 138a ד״ה איבעיא; see also below, 138a notes 21 and 22).] Thus, it is permitted even on the Sabbath to filter wine by pouring it through a strainer constructed *before* the Sabbath.

3. The Sages' position will be explained below, 138a note 1.

4. For the Sages dispute R' Eliezer, and consider filtering wine through a strainer as a *toladah* of either *selecting* or *sifting;* see Gemara below, 138a.

5. I.e. the Sages concur that if the strainer was suspended prior to Yom Tov, we may pour wine through it on Yom Tov. Straining wine is an *actual* preparation of food, which all agree is permissible on Yom Tov (see *Beur Halachah* to 510:4 ד״ה מותר; see also *Ritva MHK* ed.). *Suspending the strainer,* however, is regarded as a *preliminary* to the preparation of the food, and it is therefore prohibited according to the Sages.

[Now in truth even actual preparation of food is prohibited [at least Rabbinically] if it is of the sort that would have produced the same results had it been performed prior to Yom Tov (e.g. cooking itself is only permitted on Yom Tov because fresher food is more desirable). Thus, the Mishnah perforce deals with a case where straining the wine before Yom Tov would have adversely affected the wine's strength and taste (*Tosafos*; see *Rama* to *Orach Chaim* 495:1 and *Beur Halachah* to 510:3 ד״ה אין מסננין; see also *Meiri*).]

The halachah is in accordance with the Sages (see *Orach Chaim* 315:9, 319:9 and 510:4).

6. [The Gemara will cite the source for this shortly.] I.e. even where an existing *ohel* already covers an area, R' Eliezer prohibits adding a temporary *ohel* to cover any part of the area which remained uncovered.

7. Above, 125b.

8. E.g. a shutter that is used to cover a skylight (*Rashi;* see also above, 125b, and note 3 there).

9. According to R' Eliezer, even temporary construction such as placing an unattached shutter over a skylight window is Rabbinically prohibited, because of its similarity to building a permanent structure, which is Biblically prohibited (see further below, 138a note 1). He permits shuttering a skylight window, however, if the shutter is attached to the skylight and never rests on the ground, for it is then viewed as already part of the building, not as an addition to the building.

10. The shutter is considered only a temporary addition to the roof (*Rashi*).

עין משפט נר מצוה

נד א מיי' פ"ב מהל' מילה הלכה ד סמג עשין כח טוש"ע י"ד סי' רסד סעיף ד:
נה ב מיי' שם הלכה ג טוש"ע שם סעי' ה:
נו ג מיי' שם הלכה ה טור וש"ע שם סעיף ו:
נז ד מיי' פ"ג מהל' מילה הלכה א סמג שם טוש"ע י"ד סי' רסה סעיף א:
נח ה מיי' שם הלכה ד סמג שם טוש"ע י"ד סי' רסח סעיף ה:
נט ו מיי' שם הלכה ה סמג שם טוש"ע י"ד סי' רסו סעיף יב:
א ז מיי' פכ"א מהל' שבת הלכה יז ופ"ג מהל' י"ט הלכה יז סמג לאוין סה עה טוש"ע א"ח סי' שטו סעי' ט וסי' שיט סעיף ט וסי' תקי סעיף ד:

תורה אור השלם

א) כֹּה אָמַר יְיָ אִם לֹא בְרִיתִי יוֹמָם וָלָיְלָה חֻקּוֹת שָׁמַיִם וָאָרֶץ לֹא שָׂמְתִּי: [ירמיה לג, כה]

רבינו חננאל

מעת לעת להבראותו. וזה מפורש ביבמות בפר' הערל וכל הטמאים: מתני' ואלו הן ציצין המעכבין את המילה. א"ר אבינא א"ר ירמיה בר אבא אמר רב בשר החופה את רוב גובהה של עטרה וכו' וכן הלכתא. ואם הוא בעל בשר מתקנו מפני מראית העין כלומר אע"פ שהציצין הללו אינן חופין רוב גובהה של עטרה מתקנו מפני שלא יהא נראה כערלה: אמר שמואל קטן המסורבל בבשר רואין אותו כל זמן שמתקשה [ונראה מהול אין צריך למול במתניתא תנא רשבג"א קטן המסורבל בבשר רואין אותו כ"ז שמתקשה] שאינו נראה מהול צריך למול ואמרי' מאי בינייהם איכא בינייהם [נראה] ואינו נראה צריך למול לרשב"ג דאמר ואינו נראה מהול כלל צריך למול אבל אם נראה ואינו נראה אינו צריך למול. פי' מסורבל מסובב בבשר כדכתי' כפיתו סרבלתהון וכו'. מל ולא פרע את המילה וכו'. פי' מי שמל ולא פרע את המילה כלומר לא קרע את העור וגילה את העטרה כאלו לא מל:

הדרן עלך ר' אליעזר אם לא הביא. עז ותהלה לאל אבי. שית עזר גלילין. חלץ באזר וההלין. בפ' ר' אליעזר תולין:

ר' אליעזר אומר תולין את המשמרת ביו"ט וכו' ואקשי' עלה השתא ר' אליעזר להוסיף באהל עראי מחמיר ואמר אין מוסיפין לכתחלה (שאי) [מאי היא]. דתנן פקק החלון ר' אליעזר אומר בזמן שקשור ותלוי פוקקין בו כו' ופקק זה כגון מסך לסתום בו חללו של חלון ואמר רבה בר בר חנה א"ר יוחנן הכל מודים שאין עושין אהלי עראי בתחלה ביו"ט ואין צריך לומר בשבת לא נחלקו אלא להוסיף שר' אליעזר אומר אין מוסיפין ביו"ט ואין צ"ל בשבת וחכ"א מוסיפין בשבת ואין צ"ל ביו"ט ומפרקינן ר' אליעזר סבר לה כר' יהודה דתניא אין בין יו"ט לשבת אלא אוכל נפש בלבד. ר' יהודה אומר אף מכשירי אוכל נפש וזה שמתיר ר' אליעזר לעשות אהל לכתחלה ביו"ט לתלות המשמרת מפני שהוא מכשירי אוכל נפש כדי לשמר היין לשתות בשמחת יו"ט ונמצא ר' אליעזר מיקל מר' יהודה שר' יהודה אינו מתיר אלא במכשירין שאי אפשר לעשותן מעיו"ט אבל במכשירין שאפשר לעשותן מעיו"ט כגון שימור היין וכדומה לו אוסר ור' אליעזר מתיר אפילו בזה. ואין הלכה

גמרא

מל ולא פרע את המילה כאילו לא מל: **גמ'** אמר רבי אבינא א"ר ירמיה בר אבא אמר רב בשר החופה את רוב גובהה של עטרה: ואם היה בעל בשר וכו': אמר שמואל קטן המסורבל בבשר רואין אותו כ"ז שמתקשה ונראה מהול אינו צריך למול ואם לאו צריך למול במתניתא תנא רשב"ג אומר קטן המסורבל בבשר רואין אותו כל זמן שמתקשה ואינו נראה מהול צריך למולו ואם לאו אינו צריך למולו מאי בינייהו איכא בינייהו נראה ואינו נראה: מל ולא פרע: ת"ר המל אומר אקב"ו על המילה אבי הבן אומר אקב"ו להכניסו בבריתו של אברהם אבינו העומדים (א) אומרים כשם שנכנס לברית כך יכנס לתורה לחופה ולמע"ט והמברך אומר אשר קידש ידיד מבטן חוק בשארו שם וצאצאיו חתם באות ברית קדש על כן בשכר זאת אל חי חלקנו (ב) צוה להציל ידידות שארינו משחת למען בריתו אשר שם בבשרנו בא"י כורת הברית המל את הגרים אומר ברוך אתה ה' אלהינו מלך העולם אקב"ו על המילה והמברך אומר אקב"ו למול את הגרים ולהטיף מהם דם ברית שאילמלא דם ברית לא נתקיימו שמים וארץ שנאמר אם לא בריתי יומם ולילה חוקות שמים וארץ לא שמתי בא"י כורת הברית המל את העבדים אומר אקב"ו על המילה והמברך אומר אקב"ו למול את העבדים ולהטיף מהם דם ברית שאילמלא דם ברית חוקות שמים וארץ לא נתקיימו שנאמ' אם לא בריתי יומם ולילה חוקות שמים וארץ לא שמתי בא"י כורת הברית:

הדרן עלך רבי אליעזר דמילה

רבי אליעזר אומר תולין את המשמרת בי"ט ונותנין לתלויה בשבת וחכ"א אין תולין את המשמרת בי"ט ואין נותנין לתלויה בשבת אבל נותנין לתלויה ביו"ט: **גמ'** השתא ר"א אוסופי אהל עראי לא מוספינן למיעבד לכתחלה שרי מאי היא דתנן פקק החלון ר"א אומר בזמן שקשור ותלוי פוקקין בו ואם לאו אין פוקקין בו וחכ"א בין כך ובין כך פוקקין בו ואמר רבה בר בר חנה א"ר יוחנן הכל מודים שאין עושין אהל עראי בתחלה בי"ט ואין צ"ל בשבת לא נחלקו אלא להוסיף שר"א אומר אין מוסיפין בי"ט ואין צ"ל בשבת וחכ"א מוסיפין בשבת ואין צ"ל ביום טוב ר"א סבר לה כרבי יהודה דתניא אין בין יום טוב לשבת אלא אוכל נפש בלבד רבי יהודה מתיר אף מכשירי אוכל נפש אימר דשמעינן ליה לר' יהודה במכשירין שאי אפשר לעשותם מערב יום טוב במכשירין שאפשר לעשותם מעיו"ט מי שמעת ליה דר"א עדיפא מדרבי יהודה: וחכ"א: איבעיא להו תלה מאי אמר רב יוסף תלה חייב חטאת א"ל אביי אלא מעתה תלה כווא בסיכתא הכי נמי דמיחייב אלא

רש"י

פרע. גילה: **גמ'** רוב גובהה. לא תימא רוב העטרה דקתני מתני' רוב היקפה אלא אפילו רוב גובהה במקום אחד: קטן המסורבל בבשר. פלטר"י בלע"ז שמשן ועב ולאחר שימול נראה כמכוסה: כל זמן שמתקשה. ומתוך הקישוי מתפשט בשרו. בדשמואל גרסינן ונראה מהול בדמתניתא גרסינן ואינו נראה מהול: איכא בינייהו נראה ואינו נראה. לשמואל נראה מהול הוא דאין צריך למולו הא נראה ואינו נראה צריך לדמתניתא אינו נראה הוא דצריך הא נראה ואינו נראה אינו צריך: אשר קידש ידיד מבטן. יצחק קרי ידיד על שם אשר אהבת (בראשית כב): מבטן. דקודם שנולד נתקדש למצוה זו דכתיב (שם יז) אבל שרה אשתך וגו' והקימותי את בריתי אתו היינו מילה: בשארו. בבשרו: שם. חק של מילה: וצאצאיו. אחריו: חתם באות. זו של ברית קדש: צוה להציל ידידות שארינו משחת. מגיהנם דכתיב גם את בדם בריתך שלחתי אסיריך מבור אין מים בו (זכריה ט):

הדרן עלך ר' אליעזר דמילה

תולין את המשמרת. שמסננין בה שמרי יין ומותח פיה לכל צד בעגול ונעשה כאהל על חלל הכלי שקורין אשטנד"א ולע"ג דעביד אהל שרי בי"ט דמפרש בגמרא אבל בשבת מיהא לכתחלה לא אבל אם תלויה היא נותנין לתוכה שמרים ומסנן דאין דרך בורר בכך: **גמ'** פקק החלון. כגון ארובה הגג: אלא להוסיף. כגון פקק זה שאינו אלא תוספת עראי על האהל: סבר ליה כרבי יהודה. הלכך הכא שרי למכשירי אוכל נפש הוא: שאי אפשר לעשותן מעי"ט: עדיפא. חזקה דהוא שרי אפילו מכשירין שאפשר מעיו"ט: תלה כווא בסיכתא. תלה כלי קטן במגוד: ה"נ דמיחייב. והכא מאי חיובא איכא באהל עראי בנין גמור לא הוי ומדרבנן הוא דמיתסר: אלא

תוספות

מל ולא פרע את המילה כאילו לא מל. תימה אמאי איצטריך למיתני האי כיון דכבר תנא דבשר החופה את רוב העטרה מעכב המילה וכי לא פרע עדיין רוב עטרה מכוסה: **אבי** הבן אומר כו'. רבינו שמואל גרים אבי הבן ברישא והדר המל אומר וכבר הנהיג לעשות כן לברך אבי הבן קודם המילה משום להכניסו להבא משמע כדאמרינן בפ"ק דפסחים (ד' ז. ושם) בלבער כ"ע לא פליגי דלהבא משמע ועוד דכל המצות מברך עליהן עובר לעשייתן ור"ת החזיר המנהג לקדמותו וגרס המל ברישא והדר אבי הבן כמו שכתוב בכל הספרים וכן מוכח כולה סוגיא מדקאמר העומדים שם אומרים כשם שהכניסו לברית מכלל שכבר הכניסו ועוד דגבי גר דבסמוך גרס ברישא המל כו' והדר המברך אומר אקב"ו למול את הגרים ונראה הוא שזהו כנגד ברכת אבי הבן והתם א"א לשנות הגירסא שיש באותה ברכה להטיף מהן דם ברית כו' ברוך כורת הברית משמע דלכל זה הוא אחר המילה ועוד דהמברך מברך לעולם אחר המילה כמו במילת קטן והיינו דפסחים ה"פ בלבער כ"ע לא פליגי דלהבא משמע ומיהו לשעבר נמי משמע כי פליגי בעל ביעור מר סבר דמשמע מעיקרא עפי מלהבא ומר סבר להבא נמי משמע כמו מעיקרא והא דאמרינן דכל המצות מברך עובר לעשייתן ה"מ כשהמברך עצמו עושה המצוה: **ידיד** מבטן. אומר ר"ת שהוא אברהם אבינו שנקרא ידיד שנאמר (ירמיה יא) מה לידידי בביתי כדדרשינן במנחות בפרק כל המנחות (ד' נג: ושם) ושלשת האבות מזכיר חוק בשארו שם הוא יצחק וצאצאיו חתם באות ברית קדש הוא יעקב וצאצאיו הוא ובניו כמו שתרגם יונתן הצאצאים והצפיעות בניא ובני בניא (ישעיה כב) כלומר יוצאי חלציו: **במצותיו** וצונו למול את העבדים. שנאמר יליד בית ומקנת כסף (בראשית יז):

הדרן עלך ר' אליעזר דמילה

תולין. אבל נותנין לתלויה ביום טוב. וצריך לפרש ולומר שאם היה עושהו מאתמול לא היה טוב כל כך ומזה והא דתנן בפרקין דלעיל (ד' קלט. ושם) דאין מסננין את החרדל במסננת שלו בי"ט אם היה עושהו מאתמול לא היה מתקלקל: **דרבי** אליעזר עדיפא מדר"י. תימה ולר"א מיקשה ליה הנהו קראי דדריש בפ"ק דמגילה (ד' ז:) דקאמר ורבי יהודה כתיב הוא וכתיב לכם ולא קשיא כאן במכשירין שאפשר וכו' וכ"ת ר"א הוה דריש הוא לדרשה אחרינא א"כ מנ"ל התם דרבי יהודה הוה מפליג לימא דרבי יהודה הוה דריש ליה לדרשה אחרינא כר' אליעזר ונראה דבדאורייתא מודה ר' אליעזר דמכשירין דאפשר אסורים וכי שרי להו הכא ה"מ באהל עראי דאינו אלא מדרבנן גזירה אטו אהל קבע דאמרינן בביצה בפרק המביא (ד' לג:) מיהו קשה מנ"ל דעדיפא דילמא בהא מודה אפילו רבי יהודה:

מסורת הש"ס

א) יבמות דף מז: עא., ב) [תוספתא פרק טז], ג) [מנחות נג. תוספתא ברכות פ"ו כל הענין עד סופו], ד) הג"מ יעב"ץ ז"ל ניקד לזה במירי"ק, ה) [נדרים לב.], ו) לעיל קכה: עירובין מד. סוכה כו:, ז) [תוספ' סוכה פ"א לעיל קכה: וש"נ], ח) [תוספ' מגילה פ"א ביצה כח. לו: מגילה ז: לעיל ס: קכד.], ט) [שם], י) [ועי' תוס' מנחות נג. ד"ה בן], כ) [עי' תוס' דפסחים סח: ד"ה מה ראיה רשות].

הגהות הב"ח

(א) גמ' העומדין שם אומרים כשם שהכנסתו לברית כך תכניסהו לתור' כצ"ל וכן בתוס': (ב) שם חלקנו צורנו צוה:

ליקוטי רש"י

מל. את הערלה. ולא פרע. את העור המכסה ראש הגיד [לעיל קלג.]. רוב גובהה. של אותה שורה ולא תימא רוב היקיפה [יבמות מז:]. אע"ג דאין רוב הקיפה [שם עא:]. קטן המסורבל בבשר. המלובש בבשר כסרבל [קידושין עב.]. ולשון מלבוש הוא כמו כפיתו בסרבליהון (דניאל ג) [ע"ז ב:]. ולהטיף מהם דם ברית. הטפת דם ברית מצוה כדכתיב (זכריה ט) גם את בדם בריתך [לעיל קלד.]. בזמן שקשור. שם כל שעה [סוכה כז:]. ותלוי. שאינו נגרר בארץ שהכל שהוא קשור בו אינו מגיע לארץ [לעיל קכה:]. פוקקין בו. כיון דמתוקן ועומד לכך אין זה לא בונה ולא מוסיף. ואם לאו אין פוקקין בו. דמוסיף הוא על סתימת אהל [סוכה שם]. דדמי לבונה שמוסיף על סתימת הבית ואף על פי שערלאי הוא שהרי יחזור ויפתחנו [עירובין מד.]. דמיחזי כמוסיף על הבנין [לעיל שם]. הכל מודים. ר"א ומחלוקתו שנחלקו בתוספת אהל עראי גבי פקק חלון דאיכא למאן דאמר פוקקין בו ואף על גב דמוסיף על אהל עראי הוא מודים שאין עושין את כל האהל לכתחלה בשבת בפרק כל הכלים (קכה:) [עירובין פו:]. שאין עושין אהל עראי. לפרוס מחצלת על ארבע מחיצות או על ארבע קונדסים להיות כל לאהל מן החמה ודוקא גג אבל מחיצה לאו אהל הוא ושרי לפורסה לצניעות כדאמרינן עירובין (לד.) בעובדא דשמואל ופקק החלון דמתניתין משום דבנין קבוע הוא ומיחזי כמוסיף על הבנין [ע"ש במסוה"ש וע"ע בתוס' שם וברש"י כאן]. אלא להוסיף. כגון שהיה מחצלת פרוסה עליהן וכרוכה ונשאר בה אויר ולמחר פושטה דומיא דפקק דמוסיף בעלמא הוא [לעיל שם]. דאפילו רבנן לא שרו אלא להוסיף כגון פקק חלון דתוספת בעלמא הוא [עירובין מד. ע"ש בתוס']. אין בין יום טוב לשבת. להיות מותר לכתחלה ביום טוב מה שאסור בשבת אבל לענין עונשין יש הרבה שזה בסקילה ובכרת וזה בלאו גרידא [מגילה ז:]. מתיר אף מכשירי אוכל נפש. וטעמא משום דדריש יעשה לכם לכל צרכיכם [ביצה כח.]. שאי אפשר. כגון סכין שנפגמה ביום טוב. שאפשר. כגון סכין שנפגם מערב יום טוב [מגילה שם]. סיכתא. קביליי"א בלע"ז [עירובין ח.]. יתד [יומא ז:].

וְאֵין צָרִיךְ לוֹמַר בְּשַׁבָּת – **and it need not be said** that it is forbidden **on the Sabbath;** וַחֲכָמִים אוֹמְרִים מוֹסִיפִין בְּשַׁבָּת – **while the Sages say: We may make** a temporary **addition** to a building even **on the Sabbath** וְאֵין צָרִיךְ לוֹמַר בְּיוֹם טוֹב – **and it need not be said** that we may do so **on Yom Tov.**[11] This Mishnah clearly indicates that R' Eliezer prohibits even temporarily adding to an existing structure. How, then, can he permit here the construction of a strainer on Yom Tov, which creates a temporary tent *initially?*

The Gemara answers:

רַבִּי אֱלִיעֶזֶר סָבַר לָהּ כְּרַבִּי יְהוּדָה – **R' Eliezer ascribes to the opinion of R' Yehudah,** who would permit such labor on Yom Tov if it were performed in the process of preparation of food. דְּתַנְיָא – **For it was taught in a Baraisa:**[12] אֵין בֵּין יוֹם טוֹב לְשַׁבָּת – **THERE IS NO DIFFERENCE BETWEEN YOM TOV AND THE SABBATH,** אֶלָּא אוֹכֶל נֶפֶשׁ בִּלְבַד – **EXCEPT** in regard to **FOOD PREPARATION ALONE.**[13] רַבִּי יְהוּדָה מַתִּיר אַף מַכְשִׁירֵי אוֹכֶל נֶפֶשׁ – **R' YEHUDAH PERMITS EVEN** acts which are **PRELIMINARIES OF FOOD PREPARATION.**[14] Thus, R' Yehudah maintains that a labor which is a preliminary of food preparation, such as the placing of the strainer, would be permitted on Yom Tov; and R' Eliezer's ruling in our Mishnah is a reflection of his view.[15]

The Gemara objects:

אֵימַר דְּשָׁמְעִינַן לֵיהּ לְרַבִּי יְהוּדָה – But when can **we say that we heard R' Yehudah** permit such preliminary labors? בְּמַכְשִׁירִין שֶׁאִי אֶפְשָׁר לַעֲשׂוֹתָם מֵעֶרֶב יוֹם טוֹב – Only **concerning preliminaries which could** *not* **have been done before Yom Tov.**[16] בְּמַכְשִׁירִין שֶׁאֶפְשָׁר לַעֲשׂוֹתָם מֵעֶרֶב יוֹם טוֹב מִי שָׁמְעַתְּ לֵיהּ – **Concerning preliminaries which could have been done before Yom Tov,** however, **did you** ever **hear** that they are permitted **in his** opinion? Certainly not! Rather, he too agrees that such preliminaries must be performed before Yom Tov.[17] If so, R' Yehudah's opinion cannot explain R' Eliezer's ruling permitting the suspending of a strainer on Yom Tov, since this is a preliminary which *could* have been performed before Yom Tov. – ? –

The Gemara answers:

דְּרַבִּי אֱלִיעֶזֶר עֲדִיפָא מִדְּרַבִּי יְהוּדָה – Perforce, we must say that **[the view] of R' Eliezer is** indeed **greater** [i.e. is more permissive] **than that of R' Yehudah.** I.e. R' Eliezer is even more lenient than R' Yehudah, for he permits performing even preliminaries which *could* have been performed before Yom Tov.[18]

The Mishnah stated:

וַחֲכָמִים אוֹמְרִים – **AND THE SAGES SAID:** We may not suspend a strainer on Yom Tov, and it need not be said that it may not be suspended on the Sabbath. The Gemara discusses to what degree suspending a strainer is prohibited according to the Sages:

אִיבַּעְיָא לְהוּ – **They** (the scholars of the academy) **inquired:** תָּלָה מַאי – **If one** unlawfully **suspended** a strainer, **what** is the law according to the Sages? Is he Biblically or Rabbinically liable?[19] אָמַר רַב יוֹסֵף – **Rav Yosef said:** תָּלָה חַיָּיב חַטָּאת – **One who** unlawfully **suspended** a strainer **is liable to a *chatas*** offering.[20]

Rav Yosef's ruling is questioned:

אָמַר לֵיהּ אַבַּיֵי – **Abaye said to [Rav Yosef]:** אֶלָּא מֵעַתָּה תָּלָא כּוּזָא בְּסִיכְּתָא – **But now, if one were to suspend a jug from a peg,** הָכִי נַמִּי דְּמִיחַיַּיב – **would it also be so that he is liable?** Surely not! Why, then, should one be Biblically liable for the construction of a temporary structure such as a strainer?[21]

NOTES

a11. [Although R' Eliezer forbids adding a temporary *ohel* to an existing *ohel* both on the Sabbath and Yom Tov, his ruling is more novel in regard to Yom Tov (which, in terms of extent and punishment, is more lenient in the area of the prohibited *melachos*) than the Sabbath. Thus, he rules that "we may *not* make a temporary addition [even] on Yom Tov, and certainly not on the Sabbath." The Sages, however, permit such an addition on both days; thus, the greater novelty is that "we *may* make a temporary addition even on the *Sabbath* . . ."]

12. [This Baraisa includes R' Yehudah's disputing opinion, which is omitted from the Mishnah in *Megillah* 7b.]

13. I.e. most *melachos* forbidden on the Sabbath are forbidden on Yom Tov as well. The chief exception is *melachah* performed as part of food preparation, which is generally permitted on Yom Tov but not on the Sabbath. According to the Sages, this dispensation applies only to labor involved directly in preparing the food itself (e.g. slaughtering, cooking). Acts of labor involved in the preliminary stages of food preparation (e.g. sharpening a knife, preparing a spit for roasting meat) are forbidden even on Yom Tov.

14. According to R' Yehudah, even *melachos* performed as preliminaries to food preparation are permitted on Yom Tov.

15. Thus, while R' Eliezer holds that even temporarily *adding* to a structure (such as a skylight shutter) is prohibited on Yom Tov, even *initially* constructing an *ohel* required for the preliminary stages of food preparation (such as a strainer) is *permitted* on Yom Tov (see *Rashi*).

16. I.e. the repair of a spit which had become bent *after* the onset of Yom Tov is an example of a preliminary which could not have been done before Yom Tov (*Rashi*).

17. The Gemara now assumes that R' Yehudah would agree that a preliminary which *could* have been done before Yom Tov (such as repairing a spit which had become bent *before* Yom Tov) may not be performed on Yom Tov.

18. An apparent difficulty: The Gemara (*Megillah* 7b) states that R' Yehudah's distinction between preliminaries which *could* and *could not* have been done before Yom Tov is derived from Scriptural allusions. How, then, does R' Eliezer, who allows *melachos* performed as a preliminary of food preparation in all cases, deal with those allusions? *Tosafos* suggest that perhaps R' Eliezer agrees with R' Yehudah's distinction in regard to those *melachos* which are otherwise Biblically prohibited. But a *melachah* which is otherwise only Rabbinically prohibited, such as building a temporary *ohel* (e.g. a strainer), is permitted even if it is a preparation which could have been performed before Yom Tov (cf. *Netziv* in *Meromei Sadeh;* see also *Ritva MHK* ed., *Rashash*, and *Leshon HaZahav;* see also next note).

19. We have already established that R' Eliezer permits building a temporary *ohel* such as a strainer on Yom Tov because such temporary construction is normally only a Rabbinic prohibition [and it is therefore permitted on Yom Tov in the preliminary preparation of food] (see previous note). The Gemara now wonders if the Sages prohibit the suspending of the strainer even on Yom Tov because they maintain that it is a *Biblically* prohibited *melachah*, and thus one who suspended a strainer on the Sabbath would be Biblically liable to a *chatas.* Or do they agree that suspending a strainer is only Rabbinically prohibited (and would carry no Biblical liability on the Sabbath), but they nevertheless prohibit it on Yom Tov because they maintain that no preliminary of food preparation may be performed on Yom Tov? (see *Chidushei R' Akiva Eiger*).

20. Rav Yosef rules that suspending a strainer is a Biblical violation according to the Sages; thus, one who does so inadvertently on the Sabbath is liable to a *chatas* offering.

21. [Abaye does not choose this example because of its similarity to suspending a strainer. Rather, his meaning is that] just as one would surely not be liable for hanging a jug from a peg, which involves no construction at all, so too one should not be Biblically liable for spreading a strainer over a vessel. For by suspending a strainer he is not performing any permanent construction, but rather a mere temporary *ohel;* hence, it is unreasonable to assume that there is anything more than Rabbinic liability (*Rashi;* see *Menachem Meishiv Nefesh*; see also *Ritva MHK* ed.; cf. *Rashba* and *Chidushei HaRan*).

אֶלָּא אָמַר אַבַּיֵי – Rather, Abaye said: מִדְּרַבָּנָן הִיא – It is Rabbinically prohibited to suspend a strainer; the Rabbis prohibited this temporary construction **שֶׁלֹּא יַעֲשֶׂה כְּדֶרֶךְ שֶׁהוּא עוֹשֶׂה בְּחוֹל – so that one should not act in the manner in which he acts during the week.**[1]

Abaye codifies this and other rulings:

מַנְקִיט אַבַּיֵי חוּמְרֵי מַתְנְיָתָא וְתָנֵי – Abaye collected and **grouped** similar **rulings** found **in** separate **Baraisos, and taught** them together,[2] as follows: **הַגּוּד וְהַמְשַׁמֶּרֶת כִּילָּה וְכִסֵּא גַּלִּין – A leather bag**[3] **and a strainer, a canopy**[4] **and a chair of Galin,**[5] **לֹא יַעֲשֶׂה – one should not make** them on the Sabbath or Yom Tov. **וְאִם עָשָׂה פָּטוּר אֲבָל אָסוּר – And if one did make** them, **he is** Biblically **exempt, although it is** Rabbinically **prohibited** to do so.[6] **אֹהֶלֵי קֶבַע לֹא יַעֲשֶׂה – One should not make permanent tent**[7] on the Sabbath or Yom Tov, **וְאִם עָשָׂה חַיָּיב חַטָּאת – but if one did make** them, **he is liable to a *chatas* offering.**

אֲבָל מִטָּה וְכִסֵּא טְרַסְקָל וְאַסְלָא – But a bed, or a folding chair or a folding toilet seat – [8] **מוּתָּר לִנְטוֹתָן לְכַתְּחִילָּה – it is permitted to spread them out even initially.** [9]

The Mishnah continued, citing the Sages' opinion:

וְאֵין נוֹתְנִין לַתְּלוּיָה בְּשַׁבָּת – The Sages say: **AND WE MAY NOT POUR INTO A SUSPENDED** strainer **ON THE SABBATH.**

The Gemara inquires as to the penalty for straining on the Sabbath:

אִיבַּעְיָא לְהוּ – They inquired; שִׁימֵּר מַאי – If one unlawfully **strained** wine on the Sabbath, **what** is the law? Is he Biblically or Rabbinically liable?

אָמַר רַב כַּהֲנָא – Rav Kahana said: שִׁימֵּר חַיָּיב חַטָּאת – One who unlawfully **strained** wine on the Sabbath **is liable to a *chatas*** offering.[10]

Rav Kahana's view is challenged:

מַתְקִיף לָהּ רַב שֵׁשֶׁת – Rav Sheishess challenged [Rav Kahana's assertion]: מִי אִיכָּא מִידִי דְּרַבָּנָן מְחַיְּיבֵי חַטָּאת – But is there any case in which the Rabbis would hold a transgressor **liable to a *chatas* offering, וְרַבִּי אֱלִיעֶזֶר שָׁרֵי לְכַתְּחִילָּה – while R' Eliezer would allow** that very act **even initially?** Surely the two disputing opinions cannot be that far apart![11] Thus, since R' Eliezer *permits* straining on the Sabbath, the Sages cannot hold

NOTES

1. That is, the Sages prohibit the construction of the strainer *not* because it creates any sort of a tent, but rather because the Sages did not allow a person to suspend the strainer in the manner in which he is accustomed to do during the week (*Rashi* here and below, 139b ד״ה מערים).

⁂ עוּבְדָא דְחוֹל – *Weekday Activity:*

The Rabbis prohibited any activity that is in essence specifically a weekday activity. Obviously, this prohibition does not ban every activity customarily engaged in during the week; rather, the ban is limited to *activities which may lead to a melachah.* Although these activities do not in themselves resemble a *melachah,* they are part of a process leading up to a *melachah.* The Rabbis therefore prohibited them out of concern that a person engaging in a weekday routine would forget that it was the Sabbath and conclude the process by doing a *melachah.* Here, as well, assembling a strainer in and of itself does not resemble erecting an *ohel* to a degree that it would be even Rabbinically prohibited on that account. Rather, it is prohibited out of concern that one might actually come to strain wine on the Sabbath, a Biblically prohibited activity [see below] (see *Rashi, Rashba,* and *Korban Nesanel* here §1, and *Rambam, Hil. Shabbos* 21:17).

The Rishonim, however, reject this explanation on the basis of the Gemara above (137b), which had compared the suspending of a strainer to the temporary addition of a roof shutter, which R' Elazar clearly prohibited due to its similarity to erecting a full-fledged *ohel.* This implies that a strainer as well would be prohibited because it constitutes the construction of an *ohel,* and not because one might come to strain wine. They therefore explain that Abaye holds that the Rabbinic prohibition of constructing a strainer is based on the vague similarity of a strainer to a tent. According to them, the Rabbinic ban here of עוּבְדָא דְחוֹל, *weekday activity,* is based on the fact that the activity only *resembles* a *melachah*; i.e., since this activity only faintly resembles a *melachah,* it is indeed prohibited only because it is reminiscent of a *melachah.* Thus, although suspending a strainer is not really akin to erecting an *ohel* and is unlikely to be mistaken for it, it was banned because it is *reminiscent* of making a tent and is therefore deemed a "weekday activity" (*Chidushei HaRan*). See also *Ramban, Rashba* and *Ran* [*MHK* ed.] at length; see *Chazon Ish, Orach Chaim* 52:1, *Magen Avraham* 315:§11 with commentaries, and *Beur HaGra* to 315:9.

2. I.e. Abaye found these similar rulings in separate Baraisos, and combined them into categorized teachings, with all of those actions that are Rabbinically forbidden in one grouping, all of those Biblically forbidden in a second grouping, and all of those that are permitted in a third grouping (see *Rashi;* see also *Rashba*).

3. This wide-mouthed leather (i.e. hide) bag was closed with drawstrings; it was used by travelers to carry liquids such as wine or milk. When a traveler would stop for the night, he would hang up the bag by opening its very wide mouth and stretching it over stakes; the air circulating beneath and around the bag ensured that the contents would not spoil. The Baraisa teaches that one may not suspend the bag in this way on the Sabbath because of the temporary *ohel* that is constructed when the bag is stretched over the pegs (*Rashi;* see *Rashba* and *Ran MHK* ed.; see also *Beur HaGra* to *Orach Chaim* 315:5).

4. A כִּילָּה is an angled canopy which slopes down either side of a bed (see below, 138b note 1). The Baraisa discusses a canopy that has a horizontal roof that is at least a *tefach* in width [for if the roof of the canopy is less than a *tefach* wide, spreading it out would not be even Rabbinically prohibited] (*Rashi;* cf. *Rif,* who maintains that the canopy discussed here, which is only Rabbinically prohibited, must have a roof which is *less* than a *tefach* wide, for to spread out a canopy with a roof that is a *tefach* wide would be *Biblically* prohibited; see *Ran* to *Rif* fol. 56a-b; see also *Orach Chaim* 315:8 with *Mishnah Berurah* §35).

5. Residents of Galin would use sectional beds and chairs which could be completely disassembled and taken along to a new location, where they would reassemble them (*Rashi;* see next note).

6. Spreading the leather bag and the canopy are prohibited because these acts constitute erecting a temporary tent; assembling sectional beds is Rabbinically forbidden as well, lest one affix the sections tightly [with pegs], thus violating either the Biblical prohibition against *building* or the prohibition against *striking the final blow* (see *Rashi;* see also Gemara above, 47a-b and 138b note 18; cf. *Tosafos;* see also *Ramban* and *Rashba*). [As noted above, the construction of a strainer is prohibited for yet a third reason – it constitutes *weekday activity.*] See note 1.

7. See *Megadim Chadashim,* who discusses how long a tent must remain in place for it to be considered "permanent."

8. A מִטָּה refers to a simple bed that was often stood up on end or on its side when not in use. A כִּסֵּא טְרַסְקָל is a chair with a leather seat that can be folded up and placed out of the way when not in use. An אַסְלָא is similar to the chair, but it is constructed with a hole in the middle of the seat, allowing it to be used as a toilet. Abaye teaches that one may lower the bed into place and open the folding chairs on the Sabbath.

9. One may set a bed down upon its feet (even though by doing so the area under the bed now becomes covered) because by doing so one does not create the *ohel;* rather, one merely sets the preconstructed *ohel* (the bed) in its place. Additionally, he may unfold a chair, for since the chair is constructed in such a manner that it may be easily opened and closed, the chair is viewed as a preconstructed *ohel* even in its closed state (*Rashi, Mishnah Berurah* 315 §27; see *Sefer Meshivas Nefesh,* vol. I 7:3; cf. *Ritva MHK* ed.; see also *Noda BiYehudah Mahadura Tinyana, Orach Chaim,* end of §30; see also *Chazon Ish* 52:6).

See *Tosafos* and Rishonim at length, and *Shulchan Aruch, Orach Chaim* §315 with commentaries, for guidelines concerning when one is permitted to construct various types of temporary *ohalim* on the Sabbath and Yom Tov.

10. If he strained the wine thinking that doing so was permitted, or not realizing that it was the Sabbath, he is liable to a *chatas* offering to atone for the inadvertent desecration of the Sabbath.

11. [The Rishonim (see *Rashba, Ran MHK* ed.) note that although instances of such disputes can indeed be found (e.g. above, 113a, where the Sages permit the tying of a bow on the Sabbath while R' Yehudah holds that it is Biblically forbidden), Rav Sheishess' challenge is still a valid one; for although it occasionally happens that an individual Tanna

אלא אמר אביי מדרבנן היא שלא יעשה כדרך שהוא עושה בחול מנקיט אביי חומרי מתניתא ותני הגוד והמשמרת כילה וכסא גלין לא יעשה ואם עשה פטור אבל אסור אוהלי קבע לא יעשה ואם עשה חייב חטאת אבל מטה וכסא טרסקל ואסלא מותר לנטותן לכתחילה: ואין נותנין לתלויה בשבת: איבעיא להו שימר מאי אמר רב כהנא שימר חייב חטאת מתקיף לה רב ששת מי איכא מידי דרבנן מחייבי חטאת ורבי אליעזר שרי לכתחילה מתקיף לה רב יוסף אלמה לא הרי עיר של זהב דר"מ מחייב חטאת ורבי אליעזר שרי לכתחילה מאי היא דתניא לא תצא אשה בעיר של זהב ואם יצאה חייבת חטאת דברי ר"מ וחכמים אומרים לא תצא ואם יצאה פטורה ר"א אומר יוצאה אשה בעיר של זהב לכתחילה א"ל אביי מי סברת ר"א אדר"מ קאי דאמר חייבת חטאת אדרבנן קאי דאמרי פטור אבל אסור ואמר להו איהו מותר לכתחילה משום מאי מתרינן ביה רבה אמר משום בורר רבי זירא אמר משום מרקד אמר רבה כוותי דידי מסתברא מה דרכו של בורר נוטל אוכל ומניח הפסולת אף הכא נמי נוטל את האוכל ומניח את הפסולת אמר ר' זירא כוותי דידי מסתברא מה דרכו של מרקד פסולת מלמעלה ואוכל מלמטה אף הכא נמי פסולת מלמעלה ואוכל מלמטה תני רמי בר יחזקאל טלית כפולה לא יעשה ואם עשה פטור אבל אסור היה כרוך עליה חוט או משיחה מותר לנטותה לכתחילה בעא מיניה רב כהנא מרב כילה מהו א"ל אף מטה אסורה מטה מהו א"ל אף כילה מותרת כילה ומטה מהו א"ל כילה אסורה ומטה מותרת ולא קשיא הא דקאמר אף מטה אסורה בדקרמנאי הא דקאמר ליה אף כילה מותרת כדרמי בר יחזקאל כילה אסורה ומטה מותרת כדדידן אמר רב יוסף חזינא להו לכילי דבי רב הונא דמאורתא נגידו ומצפרא חביטא רמיא אמר רב משום רבי חייא וילון מותר לנטותו ומותר לפורקו ואמר שמואל משום רבי חייא כילת

רש"י

אלא אמר אביי מדרבנן. קאסרי לה חכמים דמתניתין דלא שבקינן ליה למיתליה למיעבד עובדא דחול: **מנקיט.** מלקיט: **חומרי מתניתא.** כללות של ברייתות: חומר קשר כלומר כללות שמצא בברייתות הגוד לבדה ומשמרת לבדה וכילה לבדה וכסא גלין לבדה ושנאן כולן הפטורין אבל אסורין בחומר אחד והמותרים לכתחילה בחומר אחד: **הגוד.** הוא עור של בהמה תפור ופיו רחב מאד ויש לו שנצים ועוברי דרכים ממלאין אותו יין או חלב במקום שתוקעין שם אהליהם ללון ושוטחין אותו ופיו מתוח ע"ג יתידות והרוח עוברת מתחתיו ומלמטן שלא יתקלקל היין והוי דומה לאהל לאחר שנמתח: **כילה.** שיש [א] בגגה טפח: **וכסא גלין.** כמו מטה גללניתא דכירה (לעיל דף מז:) והוא שם מקום ומפרקין מטותיהן וכשאותן וטוענין אותן עמהן וחוזרין ומחזירין אותן: **לא יעשה.** דאהל עראי ניהו וכסא גלין נמי גזירה שמא יתקע בחוזק: **אבל מטה.** שלנו המתוכרת ועומדת אם היתה זקופה או מוטה על צדיה מותר לנטותה ליישבה על רגליה ואע"ג דהשתא עביד אהל שרי דלא מידי עביד אלא ליתובה בעלמא: **כסא טרסקל.** כך שמו ובלעז פלודשטויי"ל ועליונו של עור ומקפלין אותו וכשמקפלין אותו סומכין אותו לכותל וכשרוצה לישב עליו נוטהו ויושב על ד' רגלים: **ואסלא.** עשוי כעין כסא טרסקל אבל עור הפרוש עליו נקוב לבית הכסא מותר לנטותו לכתחילה דהא עביד וקאי: **שימר.** נתן שמרים לתלויה וסינן: **חייבת חטאת.** דלאו תכשיט הוא אלא משוי: **פטור.** דתכשיט הוא ולכתחילה אסור דילמא שלפא ומחוי: **יוצאה אשה.** דמאן דרכה למיפק בעיר של זהב אשה חשובה ואשה חשובה לא שלפא ומחוי: **משום מאי מתרינן ביה.** למשמר: **משום בורר.** דהאי נמי בורר הוא: **כוותי דידי מסתברא.** דלאי אתרו ביה משום בורר התראה היא: **דנוטל אוכל ומניח פסולת.** ולרבה ה"ה נמי דלאי אתרו ביה משום מרקד הויא התראה אבל לרבי זירא לאי אתרו ביה משום בורר לאו התראה היא דלא דמי לבורר שהאוכל למטה ופסולת למעלה מה שאין כן בבורר קטנית שהפסולת למטה: **טלית כפולה לא יעשה.** לשטוח טליתו על גבי ארבע יתידות ליסן תחתיה וראשיו מתכפלין לכאן ולכאן לצד הארץ והויא ליה לכתלים להגן מן החמה דהוי אהלא: **כרך עליה.** מבעוד יום: **חוט או משיחה.** ונתנה על הנס שעל הקנוף כשהיא מכופלת וכרך עליה חוט למשכה בו לפורסה לכאן ולכאן מותר למושכה בו בשבת דמוסיף על אהל עראי הוא ואינו כעושה לכתחילה: **בדקרמנאי.** היינו גללניתא שפורקה ומחזירה והוא שם מקום לשון אחר קרמנאי מוכרי בגדי פשתן מוכרין עליהן: **כדרמי.** כרך עליה חוט: **כדידן.** מטה שהיתה זקופה והוא מושיבה על רגליה: **דמאורתא נגידו ומצפרא חביטא.** בלילי שבת ראיתים פרוסות ולבקר ראיתים מושלכים לארץ אלמא מותר לפורקה וה"נ מותר לנטותה: **וילון.** מסך שכנגד הפתח: **מותר לנטותו.** שאין אהל אלא מי שעשוי כעין גג:

תוספות

אלא אמר אביי מדרבנן. ואף על גב דתלא כווא בסיכתא אפילו איסור דרבנן ליכא במילי דרבנן שייך שפיר לחלק אבל אי במשמרת מדאורייתא אסור אין שייך לחלק. מ"ר: **כסא** גלין. לא כפי' הקונטרס מטה גללניתא דשלהי כירה ואסור משום שמא יתקע דכולה שמעתא איירי באיסור אהל אלא היינו [כעין] מטה שפורסין עליה עור ואסור משום אהל כשמושיב תחילה המטה ואחר כך פורס העור דהוי ממטה למעלה ואסור כדאיתא בביצה בפ' המביא כדי יין (ד' לג.) דפוריא אסור מלמטה למעלה. מ"ר: **כסא** טרסקל. יש בהן עור וכשרוצה לישב עליו נוטה העור ויושב על ד' רגלים כדפירש בקונטר' וכגון שהוא קבוע בכסא דאם לא כן היה אסור לנטותו כדאמר בפ' המביא (שם דף לב:) אמר רב יהודה האי מדורתא מלמעלה למטה שרי פירוש כשנותנין עצים מכאן ומכאן ונותנין עליהם עצים ארוכים ארכן לרחב של אלו ובמביא תחילה עצים שנותן למעלה ואחרי כן עצים שמכאן ומכאן אינו כן דרך עשיית אהל לעשות הגג תחילה ואחריו הדפנות ושרי וכה"ג קרי מלמעלה למטה מלמטה למעלה אסור וכן ביעתא פירוש כשנותנין ביצים ע"ג האסכלא שקורין גרדיי"ל וכשנותנין הביצים תחילה ואוחז בהן בידו עד שמביא הכלי תחתיהן שרי דהיינו מלמעלה למטה וכן קידרא שמושיבה על שתי חביות שצריך לאוחזה בידו ואחר כך לסדר תחתיה החביות וכן חביתא חביות שמסדרין באוצר ומושיבין אחת על גבי שתים וכן פוריא לפרוס העור תחילה באויר ואח"כ להביא המטה תחתיו ומיהו יש לפרש הך דשמעתא באינו קשור ומיירי כגון שעושה מלמעלה למטה אבל משמע דבכל ענין מיירי. מ"ר. וכל הנהו דאסרינן בביצה אומר ר"ת דדווקא דברים שיש להם מחיצה עד לארץ אבל להושיב הקדרה על טרפיד בי"ט שרי אפילו מלמטה למעלה להביא הטרפיד תחילה ואחר כך להושיב הקדרה וכן להושיב השולחן על גבי ספסלין וביעתא וקידרא וחביתא ופוריא י"ל שיש להם מחיצה. מ"ר: **מי** סברת דר' אליעזר קאי אדר"מ כו'. ° לא ידע רבי מאי קמשני [ס]: **מה** דרכו של בורר. לא תקשה אההיא דשלהי כלל גדול (לעיל דף עד.) כמו שפי' שם (בד"ה בורר ואוכל): **כרך** עליה חוט או משיחה מותר לנטותה. כגון ששייר בה טפח דבענין אחר לא הוה שרי כדאשכחן בפרק בתרא דעירובין (דף קב.) כרוך בודיא ושייר בה טפח למחר פושטת דמוסיף על אהל עראי הוא אי נמי כריכת חוט או משיחה מועלת בלא שייר בה טפח: **בעא** מיניה רב כהנא מרב כו'. ונראה לר"י ששאל לו סתם בכל כילות אם הם מותרות אמר ליה אפילו מטה יש מהן שאסורות הדר בעא אם כל מטות אסורות אמר ליה אף כילות מותרות אמר ליה כיון שאין אתה מחלק בשניהם מהו להשוותן כילה ומטה ובמקום שאסור בזה כנגדו אסור בזה א"ל כילה אסורה ומטה מותרת וכן יש לפרש ההיא דפרק אלו טרפות (חולין דף נג.) יש דרוסה לחתול א"ל אף לחולדה יש דרוסה לחולדה א"ל אף לחתול אין דרוסה לחתול ולחולדה יש דרוסה או אין להם דרוסה א"ל לחתול יש דרוסה ולחולדה אין דרוסה ומפרש התם דבגדיים וטלאים יש דרוסה לחתול ולא לחולדה ובאימרי רברבי אין דרוסה אפילו לחתול ובעופות יש דרוסה אפילו לחולדה ויש ליישב כעין שפירש הר"ר יצחק בן ר"מ (פי') התם שבשהיה עוסק באימרי שאלו אם יש דרוסה לחולדה וכן כולם. מ"ר: **אף** כילה מותרת כדרמי בר יחזקאל. הוה מצי למימר כי ההיא דשנינו בסמוך לכילי דבי רב הונא וי"ל כדרמי בר יחזקאל הוו:

שאין

מסורת הש"ס

א) [לקמן קמ.], ב) לעיל נא: תוספ' פ"ה, ג) עדיות פ"ב מ"ז, ד) [עי' תוס' לעיל עג: ד"ה משום ותוס' ב"ק ב. ד"ה ולרבי אליעזר], ה) עירובין קב., ו) [ל"ל ולרבה], ז) [עי' לעיל מז.], ח) [ע"ל פירוש דלא אם לא קאי אר"מ מ"מ הדבר תמוה איך יחלקו בסברות רחוקות כ"כ אם לא שלא ידע ר"מ מסברת ר"מ כלום וחזו טונת התוס'].

גליון הש"ס

גמ' דתניא לא תצא אשה. ע"ל קב ע"א: תוס' ד"ה מי סברת וכו' לא ידע. כעין זה לעיל קיט ע"ב תוס' ד"ה אלו היה וש"נ:

הגהות הגר"א

[א] רש"י ד"ה כילה שיש בגגה טפח. נ"ב אבל הרי"ף והרמב"ם כתבו דוקא שאין בגגה וב' סמוך לגגה טפח:

רב נסים גאון

פרק ר' אליעזר אומר תולין: אבל מטה כסא טרסקל ואסלא מותר לנטותן לכתחלה. משכחת לה בעירובין בפרק מבוי (דף י) מאי עור אסלא אמר רבה בר בר חנה אמר ר' יוחנן עור כסא של בית הכסא:

ליקוטי רש"י

שלא יעשה כו'. לא שבקינן רבנן למעבד עובדי דחול [לקמן קמ.]. עיר של זהב. כמין נוסק"א ומליירין בה כמין עיר [לעיל נז. ע"ש בתוס' סוטה מט: ובתוס' לעיל נט.]. כתי' ירושלים [נדרים נ.]. תכשיט של זהב שירושלים מצוירה בו [רש"י נדרים שם ועיין לעיל נט. בגמ']. וילון. כנגד הפתח לצניעות. מותר לנטותו. דלאו אהל הוא דלא קביעא הפתח אלא מה דרכו לינתן ולהסתלק כדלת בעלמא [עירובין קב.].

עין משפט נר מצוה

ב א ב מיי' פכ"א מהל' שבת הלכה ו ופכ"ב שם הלכה כח סמג לאוין סה טוש"ע א"ח סימן שטו סעיף ג ד ו ט:
ג ג מיי' פכ"ב שם הלכה כט:
ד ד מיי' שם הלכה כח סמג שם טוש"ע שם סעיף ה:
ה ה מיי' פ"ח מהל' שבת הלכה יד סמג שם:
ו ו מיי' שם הלכה יא ופכ"ב הלכה כח סמג שם:
ז ז ח מיי' פכ"ב מהל' שבת הלכה כט סמג שם טוש"ע א"ח סי' שטו סעיף ז:

רבינו חננאל

הלכה כר' אליעזר: מתני' וחכ"א אין תולין את המשמרת ביו"ט. איבעיא לן תלא מאי וסליקא חיובא מדרבנן (ובלבד) שלא יעשה כדרך שהוא עושה בחול. מנקיט אביי חומרי מתנייתא ותני הגוד והמשמרת כילה וכסא [גלין] לא יעשה ואם עשה פטור אבל אסור כלומר איסורא דרבנן. אהל קבוע לא יעשה ואם עשה חייב חטאת אבל המטה והכסא והטרסקל והאסלא מותר לנטותו בתחלה. פי' משמרת הא דאמרן והיא מסננת של יין. גוד הוא חמת מים. כלולב [וערבה] (הגוזל) (דף מח) משכיה דההוא גברא דעבדינן ליה גודא. ומלינן ביה מיא והולכי דרכים נועצים יתדות בארץ וקושרין (אותו) [אחת] זה בחוטין עבין ותולין אותו באלו היתידות להצטנן מימיו. כילה שיש בגגה טפח כסא גלין הוא של חוליות. טוענין עליו קרשים ויושבין עליו וכשעומדין פורקין אותו מטה כגון הא דידן ולא בורייא לן מלאכתה אלא דברים מוכיחין שהיא מטה (גליתא) [גללניתא]. והכרעים שמחזיר רפיין הן ולפיכך היא מותרת כדאמרינן (לעיל מז ע"ב) אם היה רפוי מותר. ולגבה היא עשויה במסמרים והיא זקופה ומרביצה לישן עליה הואיל ולגבה עשויה אינה חשובה כאהל וכן כסא לשבת בו וזה שאמר גורר אדם מטה וכסא וספסל שלשתן ענין אחד הן. טרסקל הוא קערה פשוטה כגון שלחן קטן וכדתניא ר' יוסי בר' יהודה נעץ קנה ברה"ר והניח בראשו טרסקל וזרק ונח על גביו גם זה לגביו עשוי לאכול בו. או לתת בו חפצים. אסלא הוא ספסל של ברזל. דתנן האסלא של המדרס וטמא מת (פרשה) [ופירושין] היא טמאה מדרס. והברזל טמא טמא מת. וספסל זה של ברזל. ועליו עור נטוי לישב עליו. ותנן עור האסלא והחלל שלו מצטרפין לטפח ואמרינן בתחלת עירובין מאי עור אסלא אמר רבה בר בר חנה א"ר יוחנן עור אסלא עור כסא של בית הכסא והוא שאמרנו ספסל של ברזל נטוי עליו עור נקוב באמצע כשיעור סיט הן חסר הן יתר וישב עליו אדם ותחתיו גרף כדי לקבל בו הרעי לפיכך נקרא כסא של בית הכסא אלו כולן מותר לנטותן בתחלה. ואין

נותנין לתלויה בשבת דתני ר' אליעזר דהוי ונותנין לתלויה בשבת סבר מותר לשמר בתחלה בשבת וחכמים אוסרין ואיבעיא לן אליבא דרבנן שימר מאי ואמר רב כהנא חייב חטאת ופר' שימור בשוגג חייב חטאת דלא אשכחן במזיד בשבת חייב חטאת. אלא כל שהוא בשבת בשוגג חייב חטאת במזיד חייב מיתה ועל זה הטעם אמרו משום מאי מתרינן ביה רבה אמר משום בורר ר' זירא אמר משום מרקד. סבר בורר ומרקד שניהן אבות מלאכות הן ובורר זירא: תאני רמי בר יחזקאל טלית כפולה לא יעשה ואם עשה פטור אבל אסור היה כרוך עליה חוט או משיחה מותר לנטותה לכתחילה. בעא מיניה רב כהנא מרב כילה מהו א"ל אף מטה אסורה ... כילה אסורה ומטה מותרת ... קבוע

that it is Biblically forbidden; rather, they must hold that it is prohibited by Rabbinic decree at the most!

The basis of Rav Sheishess' challenge to Rav Kahana is refuted: מַתְקִיף לָהּ רַב יוֹסֵף – **Rav Yosef challenged** Rav Sheishess' assertion: אַלְמָה לֹא – **But why** can there **not** be a dispute in which the disputants are so far apart? הֲרֵי עִיר שֶׁל זָהָב – **But there is** the dispute in the case of the ornament known as **a "city of gold,"**[12] דְּרַבִּי מֵאִיר מְחַיֵּיב חַטָּאת – **in which R' Meir holds a woman liable to a *chatas*** for wearing it in a public domain, וְרַבִּי אֱלִיעֶזֶר שָׁרֵי לְכַתְּחִילָּה – **while R' Eliezer allows it in the first place;** i.e. it is completely permitted.

The Gemara recounts that dispute:

מַאי הִיא – **And what is that case?** דְּתַנְיָא – **As it was taught in a Baraisa:**[13] לֹא תֵצֵא אִשָּׁה בְּעִיר שֶׁל זָהָב – A WOMAN MAY NOT GO OUT on the Sabbath while WEARING A "CITY OF GOLD." וְאִם יָצְאָה חַיֶּיבֶת חַטָּאת – AND IF SHE WENT OUT wearing it, SHE IS LIABLE TO A *CHATAS* offering.[14] דִּבְרֵי רַבִּי מֵאִיר – These are THE WORDS OF R' MEIR.

וַחֲכָמִים אוֹמְרִים – BUT THE SAGES SAY: לֹא תֵצֵא – SHE MAY NOT GO OUT wearing such an ornament on the Sabbath, וְאִם יָצְאָה פְּטוּרָה – BUT IF SHE DID GO OUT wearing it, SHE IS EXEMPT from a *chatas* offering.[15]

רַבִּי אֱלִיעֶזֶר אוֹמֵר – R' ELIEZER SAYS: יוֹצְאָה אִשָּׁה בְּעִיר שֶׁל זָהָב לְכַתְּחִילָּה – A WOMAN MAY GO OUT WEARING A "CITY OF GOLD" on the Sabbath even IN THE FIRST PLACE; i.e. it is completely permitted.[16]

Clearly, two of the disputants (R' Meir and R' Eliezer) are far apart in their views. Similarly, it is conceivable that R' Eliezer allows straining wine on the Sabbath while the Sages would hold one Biblically liable for doing so.

The Gemara suggests a distinction between our case and the case of the "city of gold":

אָמַר לֵיהּ אַבָּיֵי – **Abaye said to [Rav Yosef]** concerning the case of the "city of gold": מִי סָבְרַתְּ רַבִּי אֱלִיעֶזֶר אַדְּרַבִּי מֵאִיר קָאֵי דְּאָמַר חַיֶּיבֶת חַטָּאת – **Do you think that R' Eliezer** there **was addressing R' Meir, who held** that **she would be liable for a *chatas*?** No! אַדְּרַבָּנָן קָאֵי – Rather, **he was addressing the Sages,** דְּאָמְרֵי פָּטוּר אֲבָל אָסוּר – **who say that one is** Biblically **exempt** for wearing such an ornament outside, **but** doing so is Rabbinically **prohibited.** וְאָמַר לְהוּ אֵיהוּ מוּתָּר לְכַתְּחִילָּה – **And [R' Eliezer]** then **said to [the Sages]: It is permitted in the first place** for a woman to wear this ornament outside. Thus, R' Eliezer's opinion is to be contrasted not with R' Meir's opinion to the other extreme, but rather to the Sages' intermediate opinion.[17] In our dispute concerning straining, however, the Sages' very stringent opinion is stated in direct contrast to R' Eliezer's very lenient opinion.[18]

Having determined that straining on the Sabbath is Biblically prohibited, the Gemara now explains how a person about to commit that act could be warned:[19]

מִשּׁוּם מַאי מַתְרִינַן בֵּיהּ – **On account of which** *av melachah* **can we warn [a person]** who is about to strain wine on the Sabbath?[20] רַבָּה אָמַר מִשּׁוּם בּוֹרֵר – **Rabbah said:** He can be warned that straining is prohibited **on account of selecting.** רַבִּי זֵירָא אָמַר מִשּׁוּם מְרַקֵּד – **R' Zeira said:** He is only to be warned that straining is prohibited **on account of sifting.**

The disputants explain their opinions:

אָמַר רַבָּה – **Rabbah said:** כְּוָותִי דִּידִי מִסְתַּבְּרָא – **My opinion is the more reasonable one.** מַה דַּרְכּוֹ שֶׁל בּוֹרֵר נוֹטֵל אוֹכֶל וּמַנִּיחַ הַפְּסוֹלֶת – For **just as the normal manner of selecting** involves **taking the food and leaving the undesired matter** behind, אַף הָכָא נַמִּי נוֹטֵל אֶת הָאוֹכֶל וּמַנִּיחַ אֶת הַפְּסוֹלֶת – **so too here,** straining wine **takes the food and leaves the undesired matter** behind.[21]

NOTES

will Biblically forbid that which most Tannaim permit, an individual Tanna will seldom permit that which most Tannaim forbid Biblically.] Cf. *Chidushei HaRan;* see also *Sfas Emes.*

12. The Gemara above (59a) describes this as a golden ornament engraved with the likeness of the city of Jerusalem. According to *Rashi* (57a ד״ה עיר) it was a clasp, while according to *Tosafos* (59a ד״ה ולא) it was a tiara.

13. Above, 59b.

14. I.e. if she wore it outside thinking that doing so was permitted, or not realizing that it was the Sabbath, she is liable to a *chatas* offering to atone for the inadvertent desecration of the Sabbath.

R' Meir maintains that this "city of gold" is a burden rather than an ornament, and that wearing it is akin to carrying it; it is thus no different than carrying any other burden, which is Biblically prohibited (*Rashi,* from Gemara ibid.; see above, 59b note 5).

15. The Sages are of the opinion that wearing this ornament outside is only Rabbinically prohibited; accordingly, no liability to a *chatas* is incurred for an inadvertent transgression. They maintain that Biblically there is no difference between a "city of gold" ornament and any other ornament which may be worn outside on the Sabbath; it is, however, Rabbinically prohibited to wear it outside because a woman may remove it to show to a friend and come to carry it four *amos* in the *reshus harabim* (*Rashi,* from Gemara ibid.).

16. R' Eliezer concurs with the Sages that the "city of gold" is deemed an ornament and not a burden. In his opinion, however, there is no cause for concern that the woman will come to carry this ornament in the public domain. For only a distinguished woman who could afford such an ornament would wear it, and a distinguished woman is not likely to remove her ornaments and show them to others (*Rashi,* from Gemara ibid.). Thus, there was no reason to Rabbinically forbid wearing the "city of gold."

17. *Tosafos* remains unsatisfied with Abaye's distinction, for notwithstanding the Sages' "compromise" opinion, in the final analysis, R' Eliezer's and R' Meir's opinions remain very diverse! See *Tos. HaRosh* and bracketed marginal note in Vilna ed. of the *Shas* for possible solutions to this problem; see also *Hagahos R' Ronsburg, Sfas Emes* and *Leshon HaZahav.*

18. The halachah (see *Rambam, Hil. Shabbos* 8:14) follows Rav Kahana that straining wine on the Sabbath is Biblically prohibited. For Rav Yosef refuted Rav Sheishess' objection, showing that it *is* conceivable for the Sages and R' Eliezer to differ widely. And Abaye's attempt to deflect Rav Yosef's refutation is not conclusive (*Rashba;* see there, and see *Beur Halachah* to 510:4 ד״ה מותר).

19. For one to be held liable to court-imposed execution for intentional Sabbath desecration, he must have first been given a legal warning not to perform the prohibited labor. That warning must refer specifically to the *av melachah* being violated; a general warning against desecrating the Sabbath does not suffice. A warning not to perform a *toladah* of an *av melachah* must specify the *av melachah* under which that *toladah* falls, and not any other *av melachah.* [Whether a warning that specifies only the *toladah* itself is valid is a matter of dispute in the Rishonim; see *Tosafos* above, 73b ד״ה משום.]

[The explanation of the upcoming passage of the Gemara follows the view of *Rashi;* see below, note 22.]

20. We have learned that three *avos melachos* — זוֹרֶה, *winnowing,* בּוֹרֵר, *selecting,* and מְרַקֵּד, *sifting* — are essentially similar in that they accomplish one thing: the separation of undesired or inedible parts of food from the desired part of the food (see above, 73b,74a; see also *Eglei Tal, Boreir* §1). The Gemara now discusses which of these three *melachos* is violated when one filters wine by pouring it through a strainer.

21. When filtering wine, one "takes" the wine and leaves the dregs behind in the strainer. Thus, filtering wine is closely related to the *melachah* of *selecting,* and this *av melachah* can be mentioned when one is warned not to strain wine on the Sabbath.

[An apparent difficulty: The Gemara here seems to state that the forbidden form of *selecting* is performed by taking edible food and leaving over the undesired matter. The Rishonim ask, however, that the Gemara above (74a) clearly states that the prohibited act of *selecting* is

אלא אמר אביי א) מדרבנן היא שלא יעשה כדרך שהוא עושה בחול מנקיט אביי חומרי מתניתא ותני ב) הגוד והמשמרת כילה וכסא גלין לא יעשה ואם עשה פטור אבל אסור ג) אהלי קבע לא יעשה ואם עשה חייב חטאת ד) אבל מטה וכסא טרסקל ואסלא מותר לנטותן לכתחילה: ואין נותנין לתלויה בשבת: איבעיא להו שימר מאי אמר רב כהנא ה) שימר חייב חטאת מתקיף לה רב ששת מי איכא מידי דרבנן מחייבי חטאת ורבי אליעזר שרי לכתחילה מתקיף לה רב יוסף אלמה לא הרי עיר של זהב דר"מ מחייב חטאת ורבי אליעזר שרי לכתחילה מאי היא ו) דתניא לא תצא אשה בעיר של זהב ואם יצאה חייבת חטאת דברי ר"מ וחכמים אומרים לא תצא ואם יצאה פטורה ר"א אומר יוצאה אשה בעיר של זהב לכתחילה א"ל אביי מי סברת ר"א אדר"מ קאי דאמר חייבת חטאת אדרבנן קאי דאמרי פטור אבל אסור ואמר להו איהו מותר לכתחילה ז) משום מאי מתרינן ביה רבה אמר משום בורר רבי זירא אמר משום מרקד אמר רבה כוותי דידי מסתברא מה דרכו של בורר נוטל אוכל ומניח את הפסולת אף הכא נמי נוטל את האוכל ומניח את הפסולת אמר ר' זירא כוותי דידי מסתברא מה דרכו של מרקד פסולת מלמעלה ואוכל מלמטה אף הכא נמי פסולת מלמעלה ואוכל מלמטה תני רמי בר יחזקאל ז) טלית כפולה לא יעשה ואם עשה פטור אבל אסור היה כרוך עליה חוט או משיחה מותר לנטותה לכתחילה בעא מיניה רב כהנא מרב כילה מהו א"ל אף מטה אסורה מטה מהו א"ל אף כילה מותרת כילה ומטה מהו א"ל כילה אסורה ומטה מותרת ולא קשיא הא דקאמר אף מטה אסורה כדקרמנאי הא דקאמר ליה אף כילה מותרת כדרמי בר יחזקאל כילה אסורה ומטה מותרת כדדידן אמר רב יוסף חזינא להו לכילי דבי רב הונא דמאורתא נגידו ומצפרא חביטא רמיא ט) אמר רב משום רבי חייא ח) וילון מותר לנטותו ומותר לפורקו ואמר שמואל משום רבי חייא כילת

רש"י

אלא אמר אביי מדרבנן. קאסרי לה חכמים דמתמיהין דלא שבקינן ליה למיתליה למיעבד עובדא דחול: **מנקיט.** מלקט: **חומרי מתניתא.** כללות של ברייתות: חומר קשר כלומר כללות שמלא בברייתות בגוד לבדה ובמשמרת לבדה ובכילה לבדה ובכסא גלין לבדה ושנתן כולן הפטורין אבל אסורין בחומר אחד והמותרים לכתחילה בחומר אחד: **הגוד.** הוא עור של בהמה תפור ופיו רחב מאד ויש לו שנצים ועוברי דרכים ממלאין אותו יין או חלב במקום שמוקפין שם אהליהם ללון ושוטחין אותו ופיו פתוח ע"ג יתידות והרוח עוברת מתחתיו ומלמטן שלא יתקלקל היין והוי דומה לאהל לאחר שנמתח: **כילה.** שיש [א] בגגה טפח: **וכסא גלין.** כמו מטה גללניתא דכירה (לעיל דף מז:) והוא שם מקום ומפרקין מטותיהן וכשאותן וטוענין אותן עמהן וחוזרין ומחזירין אותן: **לא יעשה.** דאהל עראי ניהו וכסא גלין נמי גזרה שמא יתקע בתוקע: **אבל מטה.** שלנו המחוברת ועומדת אם היתה זקופה או מוטה על צדיה מותר לנטותה לישבה על רגליה ואע"ג דהשתא עביד אהל שרי דלא מידי עביד אלא ליתובא בעלמא: **כסא טרסקל.** כך שמו ובלעז פלודשטויי"ל ועליונו של עור ומקפלין אותו וכשמסלקין אותו סומכין אותו לכותל וכשרוצה לישב עליו נוטהו ויושב על ד' רגלים: **ואסלא.** עשוי כעין כסא טרסקל אבל עור הפרוש עליו נקוב לבית הכסא מותר לנטותו לכתחילה דהא עביד וקאי: **שימר.** נתן שמרים לתלויה וסינן: **חייבת חטאת.** דלאו תכשיט הוא אלא משוי: **פטור.** דתכשיט הוא ולכתחילה אסור דילמא שלפא ומחויא: **יוצאה אשה.** דמאן דרכה למיפק בעיר של זהב אשה חשובה ואשה חשובה לא שלפא ומחויא: **משום מאי מתרינן ביה.** למשמר: **משום בורר.** דהאי נמי בורר הוא: **כוותי דידי מסתברא.** דאי אתרו ביה משום בורר התראה היא: דנוטל אוכל ומניח פסולת. י) ולרבא ה"ה נמי דאי אתרו ביה משום מרקד הויא התראה אבל לרבי זירא אי אתרו ביה משום בורר לאו התראה היא דלא דמי לבורר שהאוכל למטה ופסולת למעלה מה שאין כן בבורר קטנית שהפסולת למטה: **טלית כפולה לא יעשה.** לשטוח טליתו על גבי ארבע יתידות לישן תחתיה וראשיו מתכפלין לכאן ולכאן לצד הארץ והויא ליה לכתלים להגן מן החמה דהוי אהלא: **כרך עליה.** מבעוד יום: **חוט או משיחה.** ונתנה על הנס שעל הקנוף כשהיא מכופלת וכרך עליה חוט למשכה בו לפורסה לכאן ולכאן מותר למושכה בו בשבת דמוסיף על אהל עראי הוא ואינו כעושה לכתחילה: **כדקרמנאי.** היינו גללניתא ו) שפורקה ומחזירה והוא שם מקום לשון אחר קרמנאי מוכרי בגדי פשתן מוכרין עליהן: **כדרמי.** כרך עליה חוט: **כדידן.** מטה שהיתה זקופה והוא מושיבה על רגליה: **דמאורתא נגידו ומצפרא חביטא.** בלילי שבת ראשיהם פרוקים ובבקר ראשיהם מושלכים לארץ אלמא מותר לפורקה וה"נ מותר לנטותה: **וילון.** מסך שכנגד הפתח: **מותר לנטותו.** שאין אהל אלא מי שעשוי כעין גג:

תוספות

אלא אמר אביי מדרבנן. ואף על גב דתלא כווא בסיכתא אפילו איסור דרבנן ליכא במילי דרבנן שייך שפיר לחלק אבל אי במשמרת מדאורייתא אסור אין שייך לחלק. מ"ר: **כסא גלין.** לא כפי' הקונטרס מטה גללניתא דשילהי כירה ואסור משום שמא יתקע דכולה שמעתא איירי באיסור אהל אלא היינו [כעין] מטה שפורסין עליה עור ואסור משום אהל כשמושיב תחילה המטה ואחר כך פורס העור דהוי ממטה למעלה ואסור כדאיתא בביצה בפ' המביא כדי יין (ד' לג.) דפוריא אסור מלמטה למעלה. מ"ר: **כסא טרסקל.** יש בהן עור וכשרוצה לישב עליו נוטה העור ויושב על ד' רגלים כדפירש בקונטר' וכגון שהוא קבוע בכסא דאם לא כן היה אסור לנטותו כדאמר בפ' המביא (שם דף לב:) אמר רב יהודה האי מדורתא מלמעלה למטה שרי פירוש כשנותנין עצים מכאן ומכאן ונותנין עליהם עצים ארוכים ארכן לרחב של אלו ובמביא תחילה עצים שנותן למעלה ואחרי כן עצים שמכאן ומכאן אינו כן דרך עשיית אהל לעשות הגג תחילה ואחריו הדפנות ושרי וכה"ג קרי מלמעלה למטה מלמטה למעלה אסור וכן ביעתא פירוש כשנותנין ביצים ע"ג האסכלא שקורין גרדיי"ל וכשנותנין הביצים תחילה ואוחז בהן בידו עד שמביא הכלי תחתיהן שרי דהיינו מלמעלה למטה וכן קידרא שמושיבה על שתי חביות שצריך לאוחזה בידו ואחר כך לסדר תחתיה החביות וכן חביתא חביות שמסדרין באוצר ומושיבין אחת על גבי שתים וכן פוריא לפרוס העור תחילה באויר ואח"כ להביא המטה תחתיו ומיהו יש לפרש הך דשמעתא באינו קשור ומיירי כגון שעושה מלמעלה למטה אבל משמע דבכל ענין מיירי. מ"ר. וכל הנהו דאסרינן בביצה אומר ר"ת דדווקא דברים שיש להם מחיצה עד לארץ אבל להושיב הקדרה על טרפיד בי"ט שרי אפילו מלמטה למעלה להביא הטרפיד תחילה ואחר כך להושיב הקדרה וכן להושיב השולחן על גבי ספסלין וביעתא וקידרא וחביתא ופוריא י"ל שיש להם מחיצה. מ"ר: **מי סברת דר' אליעזר קאי אדר"מ כו'.** ° לא ידע רבי מאי קמשני ח): **מה דרכו של בורר.** לא תקשה אההיא דשילהי כלל גדול (לעיל דף עד.) כמו שפי' שם (בד"ה בורר ואוכל): **כרך עליה חוט או משיחה מותר לנטותה.** כגון ששייר בה טפח דבענין אחר לא הוה שרי כדאשכחן בפרק בתרא דעירובין (דף קב.) כרוך בודיא ושייר בה טפח למחר פושטת דמוסיף על אהל עראי הוא אי נמי כריכת חוט או משיחה מועלת בלא שייר בה טפח: **בעא מיניה רב כהנא מרב כו'.** ונראה לר"י ששאל לו סתם בכל כילות אם הם מותרות אמר ליה אפילו מטה יש מהן שאסורות הדר בעא אם כל מטות אסורות אמר ליה אף כילות מותרות אמר ליה כיון שאין אתה מחלק בשניהם מהו להשותן כילה ומטה ובמקום שאסור בזה כנגדו אסור בזה א"ל כילה אסורה ומטה מותרת וכן יש לפרש ההיא דפרק אלו טרפות (חולין דף נג.) יש דרוסה לחתול לחתול אין דרוסה לחולדה או אין להם דרוסה א"ל לחתול יש דרוסה לחולדה אין דרוסה לחולדה יש דרוסה לחתול ולחולדה א"ל אף יש דרוסה לחתול ולא לחולדה ובאימרי רברבי אין דרוסה אפילו לחתול ובעופות יש דרוסה אפילו לחולדה ויש לגדיים וטלאים הר"ר יצחק בן ר"מ (פי') התם שכשהיה עוסק באימרי שאלו אם יש דרוסה לחולדה וכן כולם. מ"ר: **אף כילה מותרת כדרמי בר יחזקאל.** הוה מצי למימר כי היכא דשנינו בסמוך בכילי דבי רב הונא וי"ל דרמי בר יחזקאל הוו:

שאין

מסורת הש"ס

א) [לקמן קמ.], ב) לעיל מו: תוספ' פ"ה, ג) עדיות פ"ד מ"ג, ד) [ע' תוס' לעיל עג: ד"ה משום תופר], ה) ב"ק ג. ד"ה ולרבי אליעזר, ו) עירובין קב., ז) [צ"ל ולרבה], ח) [עי' לעיל מו:], ט) [צ"ל פירושו דלא אם לא קאי אר"מ מ"מ הדבר תמוה איך יחלקו בסברות רחוקות כ"כ אם לא שלא ידע ר"מ מסברת ר"מ כלום והוא טעות הסופר].

גליון הש"ס

גמ' דתניא לא תצא אשה. ע"ל קב ע"ב: תוס' ד"ה מי סברת וכו' לא ידע. כעין זה לעיל קיט ע"ב תוד"ה אלו היה וש"נ:

הגהות הגר"א

[א] רש"י ד"ה כילה שיש בגגה טפח. נ"ב אבל הרי"ף והרמב"ם כתבו דוקא שאין בגגה וכו' סמוך לגגה טפח:

רב נסים גאון

פרק כ' אליעזר אומר תולין: **אבל מטה וכסא טרסקל ואסלא מותר לנטותן לכתחילה.** משכחת לה בעירובין בפרק מבוי (דף י) מאי עור אסלא אמר רבה בר בר חנה אמר ר' יוחנן עור כסא של בית הכסא:

ליקוטי רש"י

שלא יעשה כו'. לא שבקינן ליה למעבד עובדי דחול [לקמן קמ.]. **עיר של זהב.** כמין טוטפת ומליינין בה כמין עיר [לעיל נז. ע"ע בתוס' סוטה מט:]. ירושלים של זהב. כתי נפש שמצויירת בכל עיניני ירושלים [נדרים נ.]. תכשיט הוא [לעיל נט: ועיין לעיל נט. וילון]. **וילון.** כנגד הפתח [לגיטות]. **מותר לנטותו.** דלאו אהל הוא דלא קביעא התם אלא דרך נוטין והסתלק כדלת בעלמא [עירובין קב.].

עין משפט נר מצוה

ב א ב מיי' פכ"ב מהל' שבת הלכה יט ופכ"ב שם הלכה כח סמג לאוין סה טוש"ע א"ח סימן שטו סעיף ג ד ו ט:
ג ג מיי' פכ"ב שם הלכה כו:
ד ד מיי' שם הלכה כח סמג שם טוש"ע א"ח שם סעיף ה:
ה ה מיי' פ"ח מהל' שבת הלכה יד סמג שם:
ו ו מיי' שם הלכה יא ופכ"ב הלכה יז סמג שם:
ז ז ח מיי' פכ"ב מהל' שבת הלכה כט סמג שם טוש"ע א"ח סי' שטו סעיף י:

רבינו חננאל

הלכה כר' אליעזר: **מתני' וחכ"א** אין תולין את המשמרת ביו"ט. איבעיא לן תלא מאי ופליקא חיובא מדרבנן [ובלבד] שלא יעש' כדרך שהוא עושה בחול. מנקיט אביי חומרי מתנייתא ותני הגוד והמשמרת כילה וכסא [גלין] לא יעשה ואם עשה פטור אבל אסור כלומר איסורא דרבנן. אהל קבוע לא יעשה ואם עשה חייב חטאת אבל המטה והכסא והטרסקל והאסלא מותר לנטותן בתחלה. פי' משמרת הא דאמרן והיא מסננת של יין. גוד הוא חמת מים. כלולב [וערבה] (הגזול) (דף מח) משכיה דההוא גברא דעבדינן ליה גודא. ומלינן ביה מיא והולכי דרכים נועצים יתידות בארץ וקושרין (אחת) [אותן] זה בחוטין עבין ותולין אותו באלו היתידות להצטנן מימיו. כילה שיש בגגה טפח כסא גלין הוא של חוליות. טוענין עליו קרשים ויושבין עליו וכשעומדין פורקין אותו מטה כגון הא דידן ולא ברירא לן מלאכתה אלא דברים מוכיחין שהיא מטה (גליתא) [גללניתא]. והכרעים שמחזיר רפוין הן ולפיכך היא מותרת כדאמרינן (לעיל מו ע"ב) אם היה רפוי מותר. ולגבה היא עשויה במסמרים והיא זקופה ומרביצה לישן עליה הואיל ולגבה עשויה אינה חשובה כאהל וכן כסא לשבת בו וזה שאמר גורר אדם מטה וכסא וספסל שלשתן טעם אחד הן. טרסקל הוא קערה פשוטה כגון שלחן קטן וכדתניא ר' יוסי בר' יהודה נעץ קנה ברה"י והניח בראשו טרסקל חורק ונח על גביו גם זה לגביו עשוי לאכול בו. או לתת בו חפצים. אסלא הוא ספסל של ברזל. דתנן האסלא טמא המדרס וטמא מת (פרשה) [ופירושו] היא טמאה מדרס. והברזל טמא מת. וספסל זה של ברזל. ועליו עור נטוי לישב עליו. ותנן עור האסלא וחלל שלו מצטרפין לטפח ואמרינן בתחלת עירובין מאי עור אסלא אמר רבה בר בר חנה א"ר יוחנן עור אסלא עור כסא של בית הכסא והוא שאמרנו ספסל של ברזל נטוי עליו עור נקוב באמצע כשיעור טיט חסר הן יתר וישב עליו אדם ותחתיו גרף כדי לקבל בו הרעי לפיכך נקרא עור כסא של בית הכסא אלו כולן מותר לנטותן בתחלה.

נותנין לתלויה בשבת דתני ר' אליעזר ונותנין לתלויה בשבת סבר מותר לשמר בתחלה בשבת וחכמים אוסרין ואיבעיא לן אליבא דרבנן שימר מאי ואמר רב כהנא חייב חטאת ופי' שימור בשוגג חייב חטאת במזיד בשבת חטאת. אלא כל שהוא בשבת בשוגג חייב חטאת כמזיד חייב מיתה ועל זה התשובה שאמרו משום מאי מתרינן ביה רבה אמר משום בורר ר' זירא אמר משום מרקד. סבר בורר ומרקד שניהן אבות מלאכות הן ובורר ומרקד כעין דבר אחד הן ולא נחלקו בשמותן אלא מפני שהיה במקדש ולמה [רבא] [רבה] ור' זירא אלא להודיע שאם התרו בו משום בורר אינו חייב ואליבא דר' זירא אם התרו בו משום בורר. והלכתא כר' זירא: תאני רמי בר יחזקאל טלית כפולה לא יעשה ואם עשה פטור אבל אסור. פי' אדם שקפל טלית וקשרה בין ב' כתלים והדביק קצות הטלית בארץ ונכנס לישן תחתיה בגגה כאמצע ושופעת ויורדת למטה כארץ כמלוא קומת אדם ברוחב טפח ולא בפחות משלשה הוי אהל עראי הוא. ומפני שאין בגגה טפח ולא בפחות משלשה טפחים מותרת ויש עליה חוטין מאתמול ונטה אותה מותר. והא דבעי רב כהנא מרב כילה מהו א"ל אף מטה אסורה מכלל שגם כילה אסורה פי' מטה קרמנאי. היא מטה של פרסים. וכן לטעמיה דאשכחנן בסוף כירה רב ושמואל דאמרי תרוייהו המחזיר מטה של פרסים בשבת חייב חטאת ומפרשינן בגמ' דהאי מטה של פרסים אלא אם יתקע לפי שמלבנותיה וכרעיה דחוקין ואינן נשלבין אלא אם יתקע בהן וכיון שתקע בהן חייב כולה כילה היא שיש בגגה טפח שמצינו באהלי טומאה טפח והנה נטה אהל קבוע

אָמַר רַבִּי זֵירָא – **R' Zeira said:** כְּוָותִי דִּידִי מִסְתַּבְּרָא – On the contrary, **my opinion is the more reasonable one.** מַה דַּרְכּוֹ שֶׁל מְרַקֵּד פְּסוֹלֶת מִלְמַעְלָה וְאוֹכֶל מִלְּמַטָּה – For **just as the normal manner of sifting** results in **the undesired matter** remaining **on top while the food** falls **below,** אַף הָכָא נַמִּי פְּסוֹלֶת מִלְמַעְלָה וְאוֹכֶל מִלְּמַטָּה – **so too here** straining wine results in **the undesired matter** (i.e. the dregs) remaining **on top** of the strainer **and the food** (i.e. the wine) **below.**[22]

The Gemara discusses other cases of temporary construction that are forbidden on the Sabbath and Yom Tov:

טַלִּית כְּפוּלָה – **Rami bar Yechezkel taught:** תָּנֵי רָמִי בַּר יְחֶזְקֵאל לֹא יַעֲשֶׂה – **One should not make** a tent formed by **a folded cloak,**[23] וְאִם עָשָׂה פָּטוּר אֲבָל אָסוּר – **and if one did make** it, **he is** Biblically **exempt although it is** Rabbinically **prohibited** to do so.[24]

הָיָה כָּרוּךְ עָלֶיהָ חוּט אוֹ מְשִׁיחָה – **If there was a string or rope tied around [the cloak]** before the onset of the Sabbath or Yom Tov, however, מוּתָּר לִנְטוֹתָהּ לְכַתְּחִילָּה – **it is permitted to spread out [the cloak]** and make such a tent **even initially.** [25]

The Gemara continues its discussion of actions forbidden because they involve erecting a temporary tent on the Sabbath:

בְּעָא מִינֵּיהּ רַב כַּהֲנָא מֵרַב – **Rav Kahana inquired of Rav:** כִּילָּה מַהוּ – **What is [the law]** concerning the spreading of **a canopy?**[26] May it be spread out on the Sabbath? אָמַר לֵיהּ – **[Rav] said to [Rav Kahana]:** אַף מִטָּה אֲסוּרָה – **Even** setting up **a bed may be prohibited.**

מִטָּה מַהוּ – Rav Kahana then inquired: **What is [the law]** concerning the setting up of **a bed?** אָמַר לֵיהּ – **[Rav] said to [Rav Kahana]:** אַף כִּילָּה מוּתֶּרֶת – **Even** spreading out **a canopy may be permitted.**

כִּילָּה וּמִטָּה מַהוּ – Rav Kahana then inquired: **What is** the law concerning **a canopy and a bed?** אָמַר לֵיהּ – **[Rav] said to [Rav Kahana]:** כִּילָּה אֲסוּרָה וּמִטָּה מוּתֶּרֶת – **A canopy is prohibited, but a bed is permitted.**

The Gemara explains these apparently contradictory rulings:

וְלֹא קַשְׁיָא – **And there is no difficulty** in reconciling Rav's rulings. הָא דְּקָאָמַר אַף מִטָּה אֲסוּרָה – For **that which [Rav] said, "even a bed may be prohibited,"** כְּדְקַרְמַנָּאֵי – **refers to** a sectional bed **similar to those of the Karmana'ei,**[27] which must be assembled. Its assembly is Rabbinically prohibited, lest he come to tightly affix the sections of the bed together.[28]

הָא דְּקָאָמַר לֵיהּ אַף כִּילָּה מוּתֶּרֶת – And **that which [Rav] said, "even a canopy may be permitted,"** כְּדְרָמִי בַּר יְחֶזְקֵאל – **refers to the teaching of Rami bar Yechezkel** that if there was a string or rope tied around the cloak and it was fastened to the frame before the Sabbath of Yom Tov, it is permitted to make a tent formed by a folded cloak; a canopy, too, would be permitted in a similar situation.

כִּילָּה אֲסוּרָה וּמִטָּה מוּתֶּרֶת – And that which Rav said, **"a canopy may be prohibited and a bed permitted,"** כְּדִידָן – **refers to our [beds and canopies].**[29]

The Gemara cites a related ruling:

אָמַר רַב יוֹסֵף – **Rav Yosef said:** חֲזֵינָא לְהוּ לְכִילֵּי דְּבֵי רַב הוּנָא – **I have seen the canopies of the house of Rav Huna,** דְּמֵאוּרְתָּא נְגִידוּ וּמִצַּפְרָא חֲבִיטָא רְמִיָא – and I saw **that in the evening** (i.e. Friday evening) **they were spread out, while on the next morning they were thrown down** to the ground. Apparently, they were allowed to collapse the canopies on the Sabbath, and by extension, we learn that they would have been allowed to spread out the canopies on the Sabbath.[30]

NOTES

primarily comprised of *removing inedible food from edible food, not* vice versa (see previous note)! *Tosafos* (to 74a ד״ה בורר ואוכל) answer that the Gemara there speaks of a case where there is more food than inedible matter; thus, one would normally *select* by removing the smaller quantity of inedible food. But our Gemara speaks of a case where there is a large quantity of dregs that contain only a small amount of wine; thus, it is normal to *select* by removing the small quantity of desirable wine. Cf. *Ritva* (*MHK* ed.); see also *Tosafos* to *Beitzah* 14b ד״ה הבורר ; see also *Ran* [*MHK* ed.] to 74a ד״ה היו לפניו and *Hagahos R' Simcha of Dessau* and *Tos. Rid* here.]

22. R' Zeira notes that there is a very basic distinction between *sifting* and *selecting*: In *sifting,* the inedible portions of the food remain above the tool used for sifting, while the edible portions fall below. In *selecting,* the edible portions of the food remain above, while the inedible portions fall through below. [*Rashi* notes that this is true in the prototypical case of *selecting,* which is the removal of refuse from legumes.] And since filtering wine results in the dregs of the wine remaining above, in the strainer, it can fall only under the *av melachah* of *sifting;* accordingly, *sifting* is the *av melachah* that should be mentioned when warning one not to filter wine on the Sabbath.

[*Rashi* notes that Rabbah does not dispute R' Zeira's argument that wine straining can fall under the category of *sifting,* and a warning specifying *sifting* would certainly be valid even in his opinion (for straining wine is indeed similar to both *melachos*). He maintains, however, that filtering wine is similar enough to *selecting* that a warning specifying *selecting* would be valid as well (*Rashi* ד״ה דנוטל, see *Sfas Emes;* cf. *Ritva MHK* ed., *Chidushei HaRan*, and *Tosafos* above, 73b ד״ה משום זורע; see also *Orach Chaim* 319:9 with *Beur Halachah* ד״ה משמרת).]

23. A person would spread a cloak over a framework consisting of four vertical stakes arranged in a square that were connected by four crossbars, and sleep underneath the resulting shelter. The Gemara refers to this arrangement as a טַלִּית כְּפוּלָה, *folded cloak,* because the sides of the cloak were כְּפוּלָה, *folded down;* i.e. the cloak, draped down on the sides, forming walls to shelter the person sleeping under the cloak from the heat of the sun (see *Rashi* and *Ritva MHK* ed.; cf. *Tos. Rid*).

24. This is prohibited only Rabbinically, because the *ohel* thus formed is only temporary in nature.

25. If the rolled-up cloak was attached to one of the crossbars before the Sabbath, and a rope was attached to it in such a way that one could easily draw the cloak back and forth over the frame, it is permitted to spread out the *ohel* over the frame on the Sabbath. For in such a case one is considered to be merely *adding* a temporary *ohel* onto an already existing *ohel* [which the Sages allow – see above, 137b] rather than constructing a new *ohel* (*Rashi, Meiri*).

[Now, normally there is deemed to be "an existing *ohel*" only when there is at least a *tefach* area that is already covered. In our case, however, the Gemara implies that the rolled-up cloak need not actually cover a *tefach* area to permit it to be spread out on the Sabbath; rather, the mere fact that the cloak is tied with the rope and can be easily drawn over the frame lets us view the rolled-up cloak as though it is partially covering the poles (see *Rabbeinu Yonah,* cited in *Rashba; Mishnah Berurah* 315 §37; see also *Tosafos* and *Rashba,* who cite differing views regarding this; see also *Magen Avraham* quoted by *Mishnah Berurah* ibid. and *Shaar HaTziyun* §45).

26. See above, note 4.

27. These were identical to the beds used by the residents of Galin [see above, note 5] (*Rashi*).

28. [See above, note 6.] Alternatively, these are collapsible beds upon which flax merchants would display and sell their products after assembling them (*Rashi*).

29. A normal bed would be preassembled and leaned against the wall until it was time to use it. Then, it would be set down on its legs (*Rashi*), an act permitted on the Sabbath (see above, notes 8 and 9). Construction of a typical canopy, on the other hand, is prohibited on the Sabbath [see further in Gemara below] (*Ritva MHK* ed.; see *Tosafos;* see also *Cheifetz Hashem* by *R' Chaim ibn Atar* for an explanation of the interchange between Rav and Rav Kahana according to *Rashi*).

30. The prohibitions against assembly and disassembly of an *ohel* are interdependent; an *ohel* which may be assembled on the Sabbath may be disassembled as well, and one which may not be assembled on the Sabbath may not be disassembled. Thus, since we see that the

אלא אמר אביי א) מדרבנן היא שלא יעשה כדרך שהוא עושה בחול מנקיט אביי חומרי מתניתא ותני ב הגוד והמשמרת כילה וכסא גלין לא יעשה ואם עשה פטור אבל אסור ג אהלי קבע לא יעשה ואם עשה חייב חטאת ד אבל מטה וכסא טרסקל ואסלא מותר לנטותן לכתחילה: ואין נותנין לתלויה בשבת: איבעיא להו שימר מאי אמר רב כהנא ה שימר חייב חטאת מתקיף לה רב ששת מי איכא מידי דרבנן מחייבי חטאת ורבי אליעזר שרי לכתחילה מתקיף לה רב יוסף אלמה לא הרי עיר של זהב דר"מ מחייב חטאת ורבי אליעזר שרי לכתחילה מאי היא ו דתניא ז) לא תצא אשה בעיר של זהב ואם יצאה חייבת חטאת דברי ר"מ וחכמים אומרים לא תצא ואם יצאה פטורה ח) ר"א אומר יוצאה אשה בעיר של זהב לכתחילה א"ל אביי מי סברת ר"א אדר"מ קאי דאמר חייבת חטאת אדרבנן קאי דאמרי פטור אבל אסור ואמר להו איהו מותר לכתחילה ט) משום מאי מתרינן ביה רבה אמר משום בורר רבי זירא אמר משום מרקד אמר רבה כוותי דידי מסתברא מה דרכו של בורר נוטל אוכל ומניח הפסולת אף הכא נמי נוטל את האוכל ומניח את הפסולת אמר ר' זירא כוותי דידי מסתברא מה דרכו של מרקד פסולת מלמעלה ואוכל מלמטה אף הכא נמי פסולת מלמעלה ואוכל מלמטה תני רמי בר יחזקאל ז טלית כפולה לא יעשה ואם עשה פטור אבל אסור היה כרוך עליה חוט או משיחה מותר לנטותה לכתחילה בעא מיניה רב כהנא מרב כילה מהו א"ל אסורה מטה מהו א"ל אף כילה מותרת כילה ומטה מהו א"ל כילה אסורה ומטה מותרת ולא קשיא הא דקאמר אף מטה אסורה כדקרמנאי הא דקאמר ליה אף כילה מותרת כדרמי בר יחזקאל כילה אסורה ומטה מותרת כדידן אמר רב יוסף חזינא להו לכילי דבי רב הונא דמאורתא נגידו ומצפרא חביטא רמיא ט) אמר רב משום רבי חייא ח וילון מותר לנטותו ומותר לפורקו ואמר שמואל משום רבי חייא כילת

רש"י

אלא אמר אביי מדרבנן. קאסרי לה חכמים דמתניתין דלא שבקינן ליה למיתליה למיעבד עובדא דחול: **מנקיט.** מלקיט: **חומרי מתנייתא.** כללות של ברייתות: חומר קשר כלומר כללות שמלא בברייתות בגוד לבדה ובמשמרת לבדה ובכילה לבדה ובכסא גלין לבדה ושנאן כולן הפטורין אבל אסורין בחומר אחד והמותרים לכתחילה בחומר אחד: **הגוד.** הוא עור של בהמה תפור ופיו רחב מאד ויש לו שנצים ועוברי דרכים ממלאין אותו יין או חלב במקום שתוקעין שם אהליהם ללון וטוענין אותו ופיו מתוח ע"ג יתידות והרוח עוברת מתחתיו ומנקבתו שלא יתקלקל היין והוי דומה לאהל עראי שנמתח: **כילה.** שיש [א] בגגה טפח: **וכסא גלין.** כמו מטה גללניתא דכירה (לעיל דף מז:) והוא שם מקום ומפרקין מטותיהן וכסאותן וטוענין אותן עמהן וחוזרין ומחזירין אותן: **לא יעשה.** דאהל עראי נינהו וכסא גלין נמי גזרה שמא יתקע בחוזק: **אבל מטה.** שלנו המסובכת ועומדת אם היתה זקופה או מוטה על לדיה מותר לנטותה לישבה על רגליה ואע"ג דהשתא עביד אהל שרי דלא מידי עביד אלא ליתובה בעלמא: **כסא טרסקל.** כך שמו ובלעז פלודשטויל"י ועליונו של עור ומקפלין אותו וכשמפשטין אותו סומכין אותו לכותל וכשרוצה לישב עליו נוטהו ויושב על ד' רגלים: **ואסלא.** עשוי כעין כסא טרסקל אבל עור הפרוס עליו נקוב לבית הכסא מותר לנטותו לכתחילה דהא עביד וקאי: **שימר.** נתן שמרים לתלויה וסינן: **חייבת חטאת.** דלאו תכשיט הוא אלא משוי: **פטור.** דתכשיט הוא ולכתחילה אסור דילמא שלפא ומחויא: **יוצאה אשה.** דמאן דרכה למיפק בעיר של זהב אשה חשובה ואשה חשובה לא שלפא ומחויא: **משום מאי מתרינן ביה.** למשמר: **משום בורר.** דהאי נמי בורר הוא: **כוותי דידי מסתברא.** דלאי אתרו ביה משום בורר התראה היא: **דנוטל אוכל ומניח פסולת.** י) ולרבא ה"ה נמי דלאי אתרו ביה משום מרקד הויא התראה אבל לרבי זירא אי אתרו ביה משום בורר לאו התראה היא דלא דמי לבורר שהאוכל למטה ופסולת למעלה מה שאין כן בבורר קטנית שהפסולת למטה: **טלית כפולה לא יעשה.** לשטוח טליתו על גבי ארבע יתידות ליישן תחתיה וראשיו מתכפלין לכאן ולכאן לצד הארץ והויא ליה כתלים להגן מן החמה דהוי אהלא: **כרוך עליה.** מבעוד יום: **חוט או משיחה.** ונתנה על הנס שעל הקנוף כשהיא מכופלת וכרך עליה חוט למשכה בו לפורסה לכאן ולכאן מותר למושכה בו בשבת דמוסיף על אהל עראי הוא ואינו כעושה לכתחילה: **כדקרמנאי.** היינו גללניתא י) שפורקה ומחזירה והוא שם מקום לשון אחר קרמנאי מוכרי בגדי פשתן מוכרין עליהן: **כדרמי.** כרך עליה חוט: **כדידן.** מטה שהיתה זקופה והוא מושיבה על רגליה: **דמאורתא נגידו ומצפרא חביטא.** בלילי שבת ראיתים פרוסות ולבקר ראיתים מושלכים לארץ אלמא מותר לפורקה וה"נ מותר לנטותה: **וילון.** מסך שכנגד הפתח: **מותר לנטותו.** שאין אהל אלא מי שעשוי כעין גג:

כילת

תוספות

אלא אמר אביי מדרבנן. ואף על גב דתלא כוזא בסיכתא אפילו איסור דרבנן ליכא במילי דרבנן שייך שפיר לחלק אבל אי במשמרת מדאורייתא אסור אין שייך לחלק. מ"ר: **כסא גלין.** לא כפי' הקונטרס מטה גללניתא דשילהי כירה ואסור משום שמא יתקע דכולה שמעתא איירי באיסור אהל אלא היינו [כעין] מטה שפורסין עליה עור ואסור משום אהל כשמושיב תחילה המטה ואחר כך פורס העור דהוי ממטה למעלה ואסור כדאיתא בבילה בפ' המביא כדי יין (ד' לג.) דפוריא אסור מלמטה למעלה. מ"ר: **כסא טרסקל.** יש בהן עור וכשרוצה לישב עליו נוטה העור ויושב על ד' רגלים כדפירש בקונטר' וכגון שהוא קבוע דאם לא כן היה אסור לנטותו כדאמר בפ' המביא (שם דף לג:) אמר רב יהודה האי מדורתא מלמעלה למטה שרי פירוש כשנותנין עלים מכאן ומכאן ונותנין עליהם עלים ארוכים ארכן לרחב של אלו ומביא תחילה עלים שנותן למעלה ואחרי כן עלים שמכאן ומכאן אינו כן דרך עשיית אהל לעשות הגג תחילה ואחריו הדפנות ושרי וכה"ג קרי מלמעלה למטה מלמטה למעלה אסור וכן ביעתא פירוש כשנותנין בילים ע"ג האסכלה שקורין גרדיי"ל וכשנותנין הבילים תחילה ואוחז בהן בידו עד שמביא הכלי שתחתיהן שרי דהיינו מלמעלה למטה וכן קידרא שמושיבה על שתי חביות שצריך לאוחזה בידו ואחר כך לסדר תחתיה החביות וכן חביתא חביות שמסדרין בלולר ומושיבין אחת על גבי שתים וכן פוריא לפרוס העור תחילה באויר ואח"כ להביא המטה תחתיו ומיהו יש לפרש הך דשמעתא באינו קשור ומיירי כגון שעושה מלמעלה למטה אבל משמע דבכל ענין מיירי. מ"ר. וכל הנהו דאסרינן בבילה אומר ר"ת דדווקא דברים שיש להם מחילה עד לארץ אבל להושיב הקדרה על טרפיד בי"ט שרי אפילו מלמטה למעלה להביא הטרפיד תחילה ואחר כך להושיב הקדרה וכן להושיב השולחן על גבי ספסלין וביעתא וקידרא וחביתא ופוריא י"ל שיש להם מחילה. מ"ר: **מי סברת דר' אליעזר קאי אדר"מ כו'.** לא ידע רבי מאי קמשני ס): **מה דרכו של בורר.** לא תקשה אההיא דשילהי כלל גדול (לעיל דף עד.) כמו שפי' שם (בד"ה בורר ואוכל): **כרך עליה חוט או משיחה מותר לנטותה.** כגון ששייר בה טפח דבענין אחר לא הוה שרי כדאשכחן בפרק בתרא דעירובין (דף קב.) כרוך בודיא ושייר בה טפח למחר פושטת דמוסיף על אהל עראי הוא אי נמי כריכת חוט או משיחה מועלת בלא שייר בה טפח: **בעא מיניה רב כהנא מרב כו'.** ונראה לר"י ששאל לו סתם בכל כילות אם הם מותרות אמר ליה אפילו מטה יש מהן שאסורות הדר בעא אם כל מטות אסורות אמר ליה אף כילות מותרות אמר ליה כיון שאין אתה מחלק בשניהם מהו להשוותן כילה ומטה ובמקום שאסור בזה כנגדו אסור בזה א"ל כילה אסורה ומטה מותרת וכן יש לפרש ההיא דפרק אלו טרפות (חולין דף נג.) יש דרוסה לחתול א"ל אף לחולדה יש דרוסה יש דרוסה לחולדה א"ל אף לחתול אין דרוסה לחתול ולחולדה יש דרוסה א"ל לחתול יש דרוסה ולחולדה אין דרוסה ומפרש התם דבגדיים וטלאים יש דרוסה לחתול ולא לחולדה ובאימרי רברבי אין דרוסה אפילו לחתול ובעופות יש דרוסה אפילו לחולדה ויש ליישב כעין שפירש הר"ר יצחק בן ר"מ (פי') התם שכשהיה עוסק באימרי שאלו אם יש דרוסה לחולדה וכן כולם. מ"ר: **אף כילה מותרת כדרמי בר יחזקאל.** הוה מצי למימר כי ההיא דשנינו בסמוך לכילי דבי רב הונא וי"ל דרמי בר יחזקאל הוו:

שאין

מסורת הש"ס

א) [לקמן קמ.], ב) לעיל נג: תוספ' פ"ה, ג) עדיות פ"ב מ"ז, ד) [ע' תוס' לעיל נג: ד"ה משום ותוס' ב"ק ...], ה) [ע' ערובין קב.], ו) ...[illegible], ז) [לעיל נט.], ח) [נ"ל פירושו דלא אם לא קאי אר"מ מ"מ הדבר תמוה איך יחלוקו בסברות רחוקות כ"כ אם לא שלא ידע ר"א מסברת ר"מ כלום וחוזר כוונת התוס'].

גליון הש"ס

גמ' דתניא לא תצא אשה. ע"ל סב ע"א: תוס' ד"ה מי סברת וכו' לא ידע. כעין זה לעיל קיח ע"ב תוד"ה אלו היו וש"נ:

הגהות הגר"א

[א] רש"י ד"ה כילה שיש בגגה טפח. נ"ב אבל הרי"ף והרמב"ם כתבו דוקא שאין בגגה וכו' סמוך לגגה טפח:

רב נסים גאון

פרק ר' אליעזר אומר תולין אבל מטה כסא טרסקל ואסלא מותר לנטותן לכתחילה. משכחת לה בעירובין בפרק מבוי (דף יו) מאי עור אסלא אמר רבה בר בר חנה אמר ר' יוחנן עור כסא של בית הכסא:

ליקוטי רש"י

שלא יעשה כו'. לא שבקוה רבנן למעבד עובדי דחול [לקמן קמ.]. עיר של זהב. כמין טסקא ומליירין בה כמין עיר [לעיל נט. ע"ש בתוס' סוטה מט: ובתוס' לעיל נט.]. כמי נסם שמצויירת בכל עניני ירושלים [נדרים נ.]. תכשיט של זהב שירושלים מצוייר בה [ר"ן נדרים שם ועיין לעיל נט. בגמ']. וילון. כנגד הפתח לצניעות. מותר לנטותו. דלאו אהל הוא דלא קביעא התם אלא כן דרכו ליכנס ולהסתלק כדלת בעלמא [עירובין קב.].

עין משפט נר מצוה

ב א ב מיי' פכ"ב מהל' שבת הלכה ל וסכ"ג הלכה ... סמג לאוין סה טוש"ע א"ח סימן שטו סעיף א ג ד ו ט:

ג ג מיי' פכ"ב שם הלכה ל:

ד ד מיי' שם הלכה כח סמג שם טוש"ע שם סעיף ה:

ה ה מיי' פכ"א מהל' שבת הלכה יד סמג שם:

ו ו מיי' שם הלכה יא ופכ"ח הלכה ח סמג שם:

ז ז ח מיי' פכ"ב מהל' שבת הלכה כט סמג שם טוש"ע א"ח סי' שטו סעיף י:

רבינו חננאל

הלכה כר' אליעזר: **מתני'** וחכ"א אין תולין את המשמרת ביו"ט. איבעיא לן תלא מאי וסליקא חיובא מדרבנן (וכלבד) שלא יעשי' כדרך שהוא עושה בחול. מנקיט אביי חומרי מתניתא ותני הגוד והמשמרת כילה וכסא [גלין] לא יעשה ואם עשה פטור אבל אסור כלומר איסורא דרבנן. אהל קבע לא יעשה ואם עשה חייב חטאת אבל המטה והכסא והטרסקל והאסלא מותר לנטותן בתחלה. פי' משמרת הא דאמרן היא מסננת של יין. גוד הוא חמת מים. בלולב [וערבה] (הגזול) (דף מה) משכיה דההוא גברא דעבדין ליה גודא. ותולין ביה מיא והולכי דרכים נועצים יתידות בארץ וקושרין (אותו) [אותם] בחוטין עבין ותולין אותו באלו היתידות להצטנן מימיו. כילה שיש בגגה טפח כסא גלין הוא של חוליות. טוענין עליו קרשים ויושבין עליו וכשעומדין פורקין אותו מטה כגון הא דידן ולא בריא לן מלאכתה אלא דברים מוכיחין שהיא מטה (גליתא) [גללניתא] והכרעים שמחזיר ופורין הן ולפיכך היא מותרת כדאמרינן (לעיל מו ע"ב) אם היה רפוי מותר. ולגבה היא עשויה במסמרים והיא זקופה ומרביצה לישן עליה הואיל ולגבה עשויה אינה חשובה כאהל וכן כסא לשבת בו וזה שאמר גורר אדם מטה וכסא וספסל שלשתן טעם אחד הן. טרסקל הוא קערה פשוטה כגון שלחן קטן וכדתניא ר' יוסי בר' יהודה נעץ קנה בהר"ר והניח בראשו טרסקל חורק ונח על גביו גם זה לגביו עשוי לאכול בו. או לתת בו חפצים. אסלא הוא ספסל של ברזל. דתנן האסלא טמא המדרס וטמא מת (פרשה) [ופירושו] עור היה טמאה מדרס. והברזל טמא טמא מת. וספסל זה של ברזל. ועליו עור נטוי לישב עליו. ותנן עור האסלא וחלל שלו מצטרפין לטפח ואמרינן בפרק עירובין מאי עור אסלא אמר רבה בר בר חנה א"ר יוחנן עור כסא של בית הכסא והוא שאמרנו ספסל של ברזל נטוי עליו עור נקוב באמצע כשיעור סיט הן חסר הן יתר ויושב עליו אדם ומתחתיו גרף כדי לקבל בו הרעי לפיכך נקרא עור כסא של בית הכסא אלו כולן מותר לנטותן בתחלה. ואין

נותנין לתלויה בשבת ר' אליעזר דתני ונותנין לתלויה בשבת בתחלה בשבת וחכמים אוסרין ואיבעיא לן אליבא דרבנן שימר מאי ואמר רב כהנא חייב חטאת ופי' שימור בשוגג חייב חטאת במזיד [illegible] בשבת. אלא כל שהוא עושה בשבת בשוגג חייב חטאת [illegible] משום מאי מתרינן ביה רבה אמר משום בורר ר' זירא אמר משום מרקד. סבר בורר ומרקד שניהן אבות מלאכות הן [illegible] ובורר ומרקד כעין דבר אחד הן ולא נחלקו בשמותן אלא מפני שהיה במקדש [illegible] זירא. **תאני** רמי בר יחזקאל טלית כפולה לא יעשה ואם עשה פטור אבל אסור. פי' אדם שקפל טלית וקשרה בין ב' כתלים [illegible] קומת אדם או ברוחב [illegible] כילה אסורה פי' מטה דקרמינא. היא מטה [illegible] אלא אם יתקע לפי שמלבנותיה וכרעיה דחוקין ואינן נשלפין אלא אם יתקע בהן וכיון שתקע בהן חייב כולה היא כילה שיש בגגה טפח או בפחות משלשה סמוך לגגה טפח. שמצינו באהלי טומאה טפח והגה נשה אהל

קבוע

The Gemara continues with two more rulings concerning the erection of a temporary tent:

אָמַר רַב מִשּׁוּם רַבִּי חִיָּיא – Rav said in the name of R' Chiya: וִילוֹן מוּתָּר לִנְטוֹתוֹ וּמוּתָּר לְפוֹרְקוֹ – A curtain may be hung and may be taken down on the Sabbath.[31]

A related ruling in the name of R' Chiya:

וְאָמַר שְׁמוּאֵל מִשּׁוּם רַבִּי חִיָּיא – And Shmuel said in the name of R' Chiya:

NOTES

household of Rav Huna would disassemble their canopies on the Sabbath, we may assume that they allowed the spreading out of such canopies as well (*Rashi, Meiri;* see also *Mishnah Berurah* 315:§38 with *Shaar HaTziyun* 46).

The Gemara does not explain why the spreading out of the canopies of Rav Huna's household was permitted. Perhaps the canopies were already in place and ropes were attached to them before the Sabbath, and they were permitted because they could easily be spread out, as Rami bar Yechezkel stated above (*Tosafos;* see also *Meiri* and *Sfas Emes*).

31. The curtain serves as a screen for an entranceway. It may be hung and taken down on the Sabbath because only rooflike structures are included in the general prohibition against making a temporary tent (*Rashi* here and above 125b ד״ה שאין עושין; cf. *Rashi* to *Eruvin* 102a ד״ה מותר לנטותו; see *Tosafos* above, 125b ד״ה הכל מודים, *Sfas Emes* here and *Shaar HaTziyun* 315:5).

אלא אמר אביי [א] מדרבנן היא שלא יעשה כדרך שהוא עושה בחול מנקיט אביי חומרי מתניתא ותני [ב] הגוד והמשמרת כילה וכסא גלין לא יעשה ואם עשה פטור אבל אסור [ג] אהלי קבע לא יעשה ואם עשה חייב חטאת [ד] אבל מטה וכסא טרסקל ואסלא מותר לנטותן לכתחילה: ואין נותנין לתלויה בשבת: איבעיא להו שימר מאי אמר רב כהנא [ה] שימר חייב חטאת מתקיף לה רב ששת מי איכא מידי דרבנן מחייבי חטאת ורבי אליעזר שרי לכתחילה מתקיף לה רב יוסף אלמה לא הרי עיר של זהב דר"מ מחייב חטאת ורבי אליעזר שרי לכתחילה מאי היא דתניא לא תצא אשה בעיר של זהב ואם יצאה חייבת חטאת דברי ר"מ וחכמים אומרים לא תצא ואם יצאה פטורה [ו] ר"א אומר יוצאה אשה בעיר של זהב לכתחילה א"ל אביי מי סברת ר"א אדר"מ קאי דאמר חייבת חטאת אדרבנן קאי דאמרי פטור אבל אסור ואמר להו איהו מותר לכתחילה [ז] משום מאי מתרינן ביה רבה אמר משום בורר רבי זירא אמר משום מרקד אמר רבה כוותי דידי מסתברא מה דרכו של בורר נוטל אוכל ומניח הפסולת אף הכא נמי נוטל את האוכל ומניח את הפסולת אמר ר' זירא כוותי דידי מסתברא מה דרכו של מרקד פסולת מלמעלה ואוכל מלמטה אף הכא נמי פסולת מלמעלה ואוכל מלמטה תני רמי בר יחזקאל [ז] טלית כפולה לא יעשה ואם עשה פטור אבל אסור היה כרוך עליה חוט או משיחה מותר לנטותה לכתחילה בעא מיניה רב כהנא מרב כילה מהו א"ל אף מטה אסורה מטה מהו א"ל אף כילה מותרת כילה ומטה מהו א"ל כילה אסורה ומטה מותרת ולא קשיא הא דקאמר אף מטה אסורה כדקרמנאי הא דקאמר ליה אף כילה מותרת כדרמי בר יחזקאל כילה אסורה ומטה מותרת כדידן אמר רב יוסף חזינא להו לכילי דבי רב הונא דמאורתא נגידו ומצפרא חביטא רמיא [ט] אמר רב משום רבי חייא [ח] וילון מותר לנטותו ומותר לפורקו ואמר שמואל משום רבי חייא כילת

רש"י

אלא אמר אביי מדרבנן. קאסרי לה חכמים דמתניתין דלא שבקינן ליה למיתליה למיעבד עובדא דחול: **מנקיט.** מלקיט: **חומרי מתנייתא.** כללות של ברייתות: חומר קשר כלומר כללות שמלא בברייתות בגוד לבדה ובמשמרת לבדה ובכילה לבדה ובכסא גלין לבדה ושנאן כולן כאן הפטורין אבל אסורין בחומר אחד והמותרים לכתחילה בחומר אחד: **הגוד.** הוא עור של בהמה תפור ופיו רחב מאד ויש לו שנצים ועוברי דרכים ממלאין אותו יין או חלב במקום שמוציאין שם אהליהם ללון ושוטחין אותו ופיו מתוח ע"ג יתידות והרוח עוברת מתחתיו ומלמטן שלא יתקלקל היין והוי דומה לאהל לאחר שנמתח: **כילה.** שיש [א] בגגה טפח: **וכסא גלין.** כמו מטה גללניתא דכירה (לעיל דף מז:) והוא שם מקום ומפרקין מטותיהן וכסאותן וטוענין אותן עמהן וחוזרין ומחזירין אותן: **לא יעשה.** דאהל ערלאי ניהו וכסא גלין נמי גזרה שמא יתקע בחוזק: **אבל מטה.** שלנו המחוברת ועומדת אם היתה זקופה או מוטה על לדיה מותר לנטותה לישבה על רגליה ואע"ג דהשתא עביד אהל שרי דלא מידי עביד אלא ליתובה בעלמא: **כסא טרסקל.** כך שמו ובלעז פלדשטויי"ל ועליונו של עור ומקפלין אותו וכשמסלקין אותו סומכין אותו לכותל וכשרוצה לישב עליו נוטהו ויושב על ד' רגלים: **ואסלא.** עשוי כעין כסא טרסקל אבל עור הפרוס עליו נקוב לבית הכסא מותר לנטותו לכתחילה דהא עביד וקאי: **שימר.** נתן שמרים לתלויה וסינן: **חייבת חטאת.** דלאו תכשיט הוא אלא משוי: **פטור.** דתכשיט הוא ולכתחילה אסור דילמא שלפא ומחויא: **יוצאה אשה.** דמאן דרכה למיפק בעיר של זהב אשה חשובה ואשה חשובה לא שלפא ומחויא: **משום מאי מתרינן ביה.** למשמר: **משום בורר.** דהאי נמי בורר הוא: **כוותי דידי מסתברא.** דלאו אתרו ביה משום בורר התראה היא: **דנוטל אוכל ומניח פסולת.** [י] ולרבה ה"ה נמי דלאו אתרו ביה משום מרקד הויא התראה אבל לרבי זירא לא אתרו ביה משום בורר לאו התראה היא דלא דמי לבורר שהאוכל למטה ופסולת למעלה מה שאין כן בבורר קטנית שהפסולת למטה: **טלית כפולה לא יעשה.** לשטוח טליתו על גבי ארבע יתידות ליישן תחתיה וראשיו מתכפלין לכאן ולכאן לצד הארץ והויא ליה לכתלים להגן מן החמה דהוי אהלא: **כרך עליה.** מבעוד יום: **חוט או משיחה.** ונתנה על הגם שעל הקנוף כשהיא מכופלת וכרך עליה חוט למשכה בו לפורסה לכאן ולכאן מותר למושכה בו בשבת דמוסיף על אהל עראי הוא ואינו כעושה לכתחילה: **כדקרמנאי.** היינו גללניתא [י] שפורקה ומחזירה והוא שם מקום לשון אחר קרמנאי מוכרי בגדי פשתן מוכרין עליהן: **כדרמי.** כרך עליה חוט: **כדידן.** מטה שהיתה זקופה והוא מושיבה על רגליה: **דמאורתא נגידו ומצפרא חביטא.** בלילי שבת ראיתים פרוסות ולבקר ראיתים מושלכים לארץ אלמא מותר לפורקה וה"נ מותר לנטותה: **וילון.** מסך שכנגד הפתח: **מותר לנטותו.** שאין אהל אלא מי שעשוי כעין גג:

תוספות

אלא אמר אביי מדרבנן. ואף על גב דתלא כוזא בסיכתא אפילו איסור דרבנן ליכא במילי דרבנן שייך שפיר לחלק אבל אי במשמרת מדאורייתא אסור אין שייך לחלק. מ"ר: **כסא גלין.** לא כפי' הקונטרס מטה גללניתא דשילהי כירה ואסור משום שמא יתקע דכולה שמעתא איירי באיסור אהל אלא היינו [כעין] מטה שפורסין עליה עור ואסור משום אהל כשמושיב תחילה המטה ואחר כך פורס העור דהוי ממטה למעלה ואסור כדאיתא בבילה בפ' המביא כדי יין (ד' לג.) דפוריא אסור מלמטה למעלה. מ"ר: **כסא טרסקל.** יש בהן עור וכשרוצה לישב עליו נוטה העור ויושב על ד' רגלים כדפירש בקונטר' וכגון שהוא קבוע בכסא דאם לא כן היה אסור לנטותו כדאמר בפ' המביא (שם דף לג:) אמר רב יהודה האי מדורתא מלמעלה למטה שרי פירוש כשנותנין עצים מכאן ומכאן ונותנין עליהם עצים ארוכים ארכן לרחב של אלו ובמביא תחילה עצים שנותן למעלה ואחרי כן עצים שמכאן ומכאן אינו כן דרך עשיית אהל לעשות הגג תחילה ואחריו הדפנות ושרי וכה"ג קרי מלמעלה למטה מלמטה למעלה אסור וכן ביעתא פירוש כשנותנין בילים ע"ג האסכלא שקורין גרדיי"ל וכשנותנין הבילים תחילה ואוחז בהן בידו עד שמביא הכלי תחתיהן שרי דהיינו מלמעלה למטה וכן קידרא שמושיבה על שתי חביות שצריך לאוחזה בידו ואחר כך לסדר תחתיה החביות וכן חביתא חביות שמסדרין באולר ומושיבין אחת על גבי שתים וכן פוריא לפרוס העור תחילה באויר ואח"כ להביא המטה תחתיו ומיהו יש לפרש הך דשמעתא באינו קשור ומיירי כגון שעושה מלמעלה למטה אבל משמע דבכל ענין מיירי. מ"ר. וכל הנהו דאסרינן בבילה אומר ר"ת דדווקא דברים שיש להם מחילה עד לארץ אבל להושיב הקדרה על טרפיד בי"ט שרי אפילו מלמטה למעלה להביא הטרפיד תחילה ואחר כך להושיב הקדרה וכן להושיב השולחן על גבי ספסלין וביעתא וקידרא וחביתא ופוריא י"ל שיש להם מחילה. מ"ר: **מי סברת דר' אליעזר קאי אדר"מ כו'.** לא ידע רבי מאי קמשני [ח]: **מה דרכו של בורר.** לא תקשה אההיא דשילהי כלל גדול (לעיל דף עד.) כמו שפי' שם (בד"ה בורר ואוכל): **כרך עליה חוט או משיחה מותר לנטותה.** כגון ששייר בה טפח דבענין אחר לא הוה שרי כדאשכחן בפרק בתרא דעירובין (דף קב.) כרוך בודיא ושייר בה טפח למחר פושטת דמוסיף על אהל עראי הוא אי נמי כריכת חוט או משיחה מועלת בלא שייר בה טפח: **בעא מיניה רב כהנא מרב כו'.** ונראה לר"י ששאל לו סתם בכל כילות אם הם מותרות אמר ליה אפילו מטה יש מהן שאסורות הדר בעא אם כל מטות אסורות אמר ליה אף כילות מותרות אמר ליה כיון שאין אתה מחלק בשניהם מהו להשוותן כילה ומטה ובמקום שאסור בזה כנגדו אסור בזה א"ל כילה אסורה ומטה מותרת וכן יש לפרש ההיא דפרק אלו טרפות (חולין דף נג.) יש דרוסה לחתול א"ל אף לחולדה יש דרוסה לחולדה א"ל אף לחתול אין דרוסה לחתול ולחולדה יש דרוסה או אין להם דרוסה א"ל לחתול יש דרוסה ולחולדה אין דרוסה ומפרש התם דבגדיים וטלאים יש דרוסה לחתול ולא לחולדה ובאימרי רברבי אין דרוסה אפילו לחתול ובעופות יש דרוסה אפילו לחולדה ויש ליישב כעין שפירש הר"ר יצחק בן ר"מ (פי') התם שכשהיה עוסק באימרי שאלו אם יש דרוסה לחולדה וכן כולם. מ"ר: **אף כילה מותרת כדרמי בר יחזקאל.** הוה מצי למימר כי ההיא דשנינו בסמוך לכילי דבי רב הונא וי"ל כדרמי בר יחזקאל הוו:

שאין

מסורת הש"ס

א) [לקמן קמ.], ב) לעיל נט: תוספ' פ"ה, ג) עדיות פ"ב מ"ז, ד) [ע' תוס' לעיל עג: ד"ה משום ותוס' ב"ק ב. ד"ה ולכי אליעזר], ה) עירובין קב., ו) [ע"ל ולרבה], ז) [עי' לעיל מז:], ח) [נ"ל פירוש דאף אם לא קאי אר"מ מ"מ הדבר תמוה איך יחלקו בסברות רחוקות כ"כ לא שלא ידע ר"ח מסברת ר"מ כלום והוא כוונת התוס'].

גליון הש"ס

גמ' דתניא לא תצא אשה. ע"ל סב ע"א: תוס' ד"ה מי סברת וכו' לא ידע. כעין זה לעיל קיט ע"ב תוד"ה אלו היה וש"נ:

הגהות הגר"א

[א] רש"י ד"ה כילה שיש בגגה טפח. נ"ב אבל הרי"ף והרמב"ם כתבו דוקא שאין בגגה וכו' סמוך לגגה טפח:

רב נסים גאון

פרק ר' אליעזר אומר תולין: אבל מטה כסא טרסקל ואסלא מותר לנטותן לכתחילה. משכחת לה בעירובין בפרק מבוי (דף י) מאי עור אסלא אמר רבה בר בר חנה אמר ר' יוחנן עור כסא של בית הכסא:

ליקוטי רש"י

שלא יעשה כו'. לא שבקינן רבנן למעבד עובדי דחול [לקמן קמ.]. עיר של זהב. כמין טוטפ"ת ומציירין בה כמין עיר [לעיל נז. ע"ש בתוס' לעיל נט.]. כתר נפש שמצויירת בכל עניני ירושלים [נדרים נ.]. תכשיט של זהב שירושלים מצוירת בה [ר"ן נדרים שם ועיין לעיל נט.]. וילון. כנגד הפתח לצניעות. מותר לנטותו. דלאו אהל דלא קביע התם אלא כל דרכו לינתן ולהסתלק כלה בעלמא [עירובין קב.].

עין משפט נר מצוה

ב א ב מיי' פכ"א מהל' שבת הלכה ט ופכ"ב שם הלכה כח סמג לאוין סה טוש"ע א"ח סימן שטו סעיף א ג ד ו ט:
ג ג מיי' פכ"ב שם הלכה כז:
ד ד מיי' שם הלכה כח סמג שם טוש"ע שם סעיף ה:
ה ה מיי' פי"ט מהל' שבת הלכה יד סמג שם:
ו ו מיי' שם הלכה יא ופכ"א הלכה יז סמג שם:
ז ז ח מיי' פכ"ב מהל' שבת הלכה כט סמג שם טוש"ע א"ח סי' שטו סעיף ו':

רבינו חננאל

הלכה כר' אליעזר: מתני' וחכ"א אין תולין את המשמרת ביו"ט. איבעיא לן תלא מאי וסליקא חיובא מדרבנן (ובלבד) שלא יעשה כדרך שהוא עושה בחול. מנקיט אביי חומרי מתנייתא ותני הגוד והמשמרת כילה וכסא [גלין] לא יעשה ואם עשה פטור אבל אסור כלומר איסורא דרבנן. אהל קבוע לא יעשה ואם עשה חייב חטאת אבל המטה והכסא והטרסקל והאסלא מותר לנטותן בתחלה. פי' משמרת הא דאמרן והיא מסננת של יין. גוד הוא חמת מים. כלולב [וערבה] (הגזול) (דף מח) משכיה דההוא בברא דעבדינן ליה גודא. ומלינן ביה מיא והולכי דרכים נועצים יתידות בארץ וקושרין (אחת) [אותו] זה בחוטין עבין ותולין אותו באלו היתידות להצטנן מימיו. כילה שיש בגגה טפח כסא גלין הוא של חוליות. טוענין עליו קרשים ויושבין עליו וכשעומדין פורקין אותו מטה כגון הא דידן ולא ברירא לן מלאכתה אלא דברים מוכיחין שהיא מטה (גליתא) [גללניתא]. והכרעים שמחזיר רפויין הן ולפיכך היא מותרת כדאמרינן (לעיל מז ע"ב) אם היה רפוי מותר. ולגבה היא עשויה במסמרים והיא זקופה ומרביצה לישן עליה הואיל ולגבה עשויה אינה חשובה כאהל ולכן כסא לשבת בו וזה שאמר גורר אדם מטה וכסא וספסל שלשתן טעם אחד הן. טרסקל הוא קערה פשוטה כגון שלחן קטן ובדתניא ר' יוסי בר' יהודה נעץ קנה בה"ר והניח בראשו טרסקל וזוק ונח על גביו גם זה לגביו עשוי לאכול בו. או לתת בו חפצים. אסלא הוא ספסל של ברזל. דתנן האסלא טמא מדרס וטמא מת (פרשה) [ופירושו] היא טמאה מדרס. והברזל טמא טמא מת. וספסל זה של ברזל. ועליו עור נטוי לישב עליו. ותנן עור האסלא וחלל שלו מצטרפין לטפח ואמרינן בתחלת עירובין מאי עור אסלא אמר רבה בר בר חנה א"ר יוחנן עור אסלא עור כסא של בית הכסא והוא שאמרנו ספסל של ברזל נטוי עליו עור נקוב באמצע כשיעור סיט הן חסר הן יתר וישב עליו אדם ותחתיו גרף כדי לקבל בו הרעי לפיכך נקרא עור כסא של בית הכסא אלו כולן מותר לנטותן בתחלה. ואין נותנין לתלויה בשבת ר' אליעזר דתני ונותנין לתלויה בשבת סבר מותר לשמר בתחלה בשבת וחכמים אוסרין ואיבעיא לן אליבא דרבנן שימר מאי ואמר רב כהנא חייב חטאת ופי' שימור בשוגג חייב חטאת דלא אשכחן במזיד בשבת חייב חטאת. אלא כל שהוא בשבת בשוגג חייב חטאת במזיד חייב מיתה ועל זה הטעם אמרו משום מאי מתרינן ביה רבה אמר משום בורר ר' זירא אמר משום מרקד. סבר בורר ומרקד שניהן אבות מלאכות הן ובורר ומרקד כעין דבר אחד הן ולא נחלקו בשמותן אלא מפני שהיה במקדש ולמה (רבא) [רבה] ור' זירא אלא להודיעך שאם התרו בו משום מרקד אליבא דרבה אינו חייב וכן אליבא דר' זירא אם התרו בו משום בורר. והלכתא כר' זירא: **תאני** רמי בר יחזקאל טלית כפול לא יעשה ואם עשה פטור אבל אסור. פי' אדם שקפל טלית וקשרה בין ב' כתלים והדביק קצוות הטלית בארץ ונכנס לישן תחתיה בגגה כאמצע ושופעת ויורדת למטה בארץ כמלוא קומת אדם ברוחב אהל עראי הוא. ומפני שאין בגגה טפח ולא בפחות משלשה לפיכך פטור אבל אסור. ואם היו עליה חוטין מאתמול ונטה אותה מותר. והא דבעי רב כהנא מרב כילה מהו א"ל אף מטה אסורה מכלל שגם כילה אסורה פי' מטה דקרמינא. היא מטה של פרסיים. ורב לטעמיה דאשכחינן בסוף כירה רב ושמואל דאמרי תרוייהו המחזיר מטה של פרסיים בשבת חייב חטאת ומסתברא דהאי מטה של פרסיים לא יתכן לו להחזירה אלא אם יתקע לפי שמלבנותיה וכרעיה דחוקין ואינן נשלבין אלא אם יתקע בהן וכיון שתקע בהן חייב כולה היא כילה שיש בגגה טפח או בפחות משלשה סמוך לגגה טפח. שמצינו באהלי טומאה טפח והנה נטה אהל קבוע

ח א מיי' פכ"ב מהל' שבת הלכה לג סמג לאוין סה טוש"ע א"ח סי' שטו סעיף יא:
ט ב ג מיי' פכ"ב מהל' שבת הלכה לא סמג שם טוש"ע א"ח סי' שא סעיף מ:
י ד מיי' שם טוש"ע שם סעיף יא:
יא ה ו מיי' שם הלכה לב סמג שם טוש"ע א"ח סי' שטו סעיף יב:
יב ז מיי' שם הלכה ו סמג שם טוש"ע א"ח סי' שח סעיף טו:
יג ח מיי' פ"א מהל' שאר אבות הטומאות הלכה ג:
יד ט מיי' פ"ה מהל' טומאת מת הלכה ו ופי"ג מהל' כלים הלכה א:

רבינו חננאל

תוספות

שאין בשיפועה טפח. הרבה יש תימה (ד) איך יתכן זה דא"כ למה הוא ראוי אם לכל השיפוע אין טפח ויש לפרש כגון שהסדין שפרוס על הכילה מונח על גבי קנים מרודים ולא פשטו הסדין היטב ומונח ונופל בין קנה לקנה כעין שורות דיש עכשיו בין כל קנה שיפוע ואין באותו שיפוע טפח ודוחק וי"מ שאין בשיפוע טפח בגובה י' דכשילא השיפוע טפח אין משם עד למטה גובה י' דלא חשיב אהל כדאשכחן בפ"ק דסוכה (דף י.) דכילה כי הך מותר לישן בסוכה דאמר רב יהודה אמר שמואל מותר לישן בכילת חתנים אע"פ שיש לה גג והוא שאינה י' טפחים ואין נראה לר"י דודאי נהי דגבי סוכה לא חשיב אהל וכן לגבי ק"ש כדאיתא התם (דף י:) מיהו לגבי שבת חשיב ואסירי שהרי משמרת וכיעתא וקידרא ותביתא אסירי משום אהל ולא משמע שיש בגובהן י' טפחים. מ"ר. ועוד קשה מדלקמן גבי כפיפה מצרית ובשם רבינו שמואל פי' דל"ג להאי לישנא כלל שיפועי אהלים כאהלים דמו דבסוף פ"ק דסוכה (דף יט:) מסקינן דשיפוע אהלים לאו כאהלים דמו ואי משום הא לא איריא דיש לפרש דהתם באין בשיפועו טפח והכא כשיש בשיפועו טפח:

הא דמהדק. פירש ר"ח שאינו נכפף דאז נראה כעין אהל דלא מהדק שהוא נכפף ואז אין נראה כעין אהל:

דבר ה' זה הקץ. דכתיב גבי גלות שבעים לכלות דבר ה' מפי ירמיה (עזרא א). מ"ר: ולישנא

רש"י

כילת חתנים. לא דמיא לשאר כילות שפרוסות על גבי קינוף שהיא לד' רגלים ויש לה גג דהוי אהל ושל חתנים על גבי נקליטין שאינם אלא שנים באמצעית המטה וקנה נתון עליהם והבגד נתון עליו ונופל לכאן ולכאן ואין לה גג הלכך לאו אהל הוא: בפחות מג'. שהיא הולכת ומתפשטת למטה: ולא אמרן אלא שאין בשיפועה טפח. שאין לה לצד זה ולצד זה (ג) נפשט למטה להתרחק טפח מכנגד אמצעיתו דהיינו שאין ברחבו למטה טפחיים וכילות חתנים אינה עשויה לישן מתחתיה: אבל נחתא מפוריא טפח. הוא טפח זה קיר לאהל והמטה נעשית לו גג: סיאנא. כובע של לבד פלטר"ן: אסור. לצאת בו בשבת ולקמיה מפרש ואזיל: הא דאית ביה טפח. שהוא מתפשט להלן מראשו טפח אסור משום אהל: אלא מעתה שרביב בגלימיה טפח. הניח טליתו על ראשו כדרך שהוא מתעטף (ג) והרחיקה להלן מראשו טפח: אלא. טעמא לאו משום אהל הוא אלא משום שלא יגביהנו הרוח מראשו ואתי לאתויי ארבע אמות הלכך מיהדק בראשו שפיר שרי לא מיהדק אסור: תרתי בשבת וחדא בתורה. שהיה רגיל לומר שני דברים משמו בהלכות שבת ואחת בתורה כדלקמן: גוד בכיסנא. גוד ברצועותיו ומונח על מקום קבוע שלו: מותר לנטותו בשבת. והא דאמרן לעיל פטור אבל אסור היכא דלא הוי מתוקן בכיסנין: בב' בני אדם. לא מימתח ליה שפיר: באדם אחד. ממתח ליה שפיר שמותחו על יתד זו וקושרו בה וחוזר ומותחו על יתד זו וקושרו בה כך פירשו רבותי וכן מצאתי בתשובת הגאונים ואיני יודע מהו: אידך. דשבת מאי היא: מירכותיה. פטפוטים שלה כעין רגלים: שמא יתקע. כשמחבר לה הרגל יתקענה בחוזק והוי בונה אבל (פ"ק) היכא דלא נשמטה אלא אחת לא חיים למתקע כולי האי: הפלא ופלא. סיפא דקרא ואבדה חכמת חכמיו: בכרם. על שם שהיו יושבין שורות שורות ככרם: זו הלכה. כדכתיב (דברים ה) [להגיד לכם] את דבר ה' דהיינו תורה: זו נבואה. כדכתיב (הושע א) דבר ה' אשר היה אל הושע: זה הקץ. לא ידענו מהיכא: בהדיא כתיב. ותורה שבכתב הרי כתובה ומונחת יקראו וילמדו: שהתנור תחלה. שנטמא מן האויר כדכתיב (ויקרא יא) אל תוכו והוא אחר ומטמא אוכלין שבתוכו מן האויר: כמאן דמלי טומאה. כשנפל השרץ באוירו דהא בלא נגיעה מטמא והלכך כמאן דמלי טומאה הוא ותהוי פת ראשונה:

גמרא

כילת חתנים מותר לנטותה ומותר לפורקה אמר רב ששת בריה דרב אידי לא אמרן אלא שאין בגגה טפח אבל יש בגגה טפח אסורה וכי אין בגגה טפח נמי לא אמרן אלא שאין בפחות משלשה סמוך לגגה טפח אבל יש בפחות משלשה סמוך לגגה טפח אסור [א]ולא אמרן אלא שאין בשיפועה טפח אבל יש בשיפועה טפח שפועי אהלים כאהלים דמו ולא אמרן אלא דלא נחית מפוריא טפח אבל נחית מפוריא טפח אסור: ואמר רב ששת בריה דרב אידי האי סיאנא שרי והאיתמר סיאנא אסור לא קשיא הא דאית ביה טפח הא דלית ביה טפח אלא מעתה שרביב בגלימא טפח ה"נ דמיחייב אלא לא קשיא הא דמיהדק הא דלא מיהדק שלח ליה רמי בר יחזקאל לרב הונא אימא לן איזי הנך מילי מעלייתא דאמרת לן משמיה דרב תרתי בשבת וחדא בתורה שלח ליה הא דתניא גוד בכיסנא מותר לנטותה בשבת אמר רב לא שנו אלא בב' בני אדם אבל באדם אחד אסור אמר אביי וכילה אפילו בי' בני אדם אסור אי אפשר דלא מימתחא פורתא אידך מאי היא דתניא כירה שנשמטה אחת מירכותיה מותר לטלטלה שתים אסור רב אמר אפילו אחד נמי אסור גזירה שמא יתקע תורה דאמר רב עתידה תורה שתשתכח מישראל שנאמר והפלא ה' את מכותך הפלאה זו איני יודע מהו כשהוא אומר לכן הנני יוסיף להפליא את העם הזה הפלא ופלא הוי אומר הפלאה זו תורה ת"ר כשנכנסו רבותינו לכרם ביבנה אמרו עתידה תורה שתשתכח מישראל שנאמר הנה ימים באים נאם ה' אלהים והשלחתי רעב בארץ לא רעב ללחם ולא צמא למים כי אם לשמוע את דברי ה' וכתיב ונעו מים עד ים ומצפון ועד מזרח ישוטטו לבקש את דבר ה' ולא ימצאו דבר ה' זו הלכה דבר ה' זה הקץ דבר ה' זו נבואה ומאי ישוטטו לבקש את דבר ה' אמרו עתידה אשה שתטול ככר של תרומה ותחזור בבתי כנסיות ובבתי מדרשות לידע אם טמאה היא ואם טהורה היא ואין מבין אם טהורה היא ואם טמאה היא בהדיא כתיב ביה מכל האוכל אשר יאכל אלא לידע אם ראשונה היא ואם שניה היא ואין מבין הא נמי מתניתין היא כדתנן השרץ שנמצא בתנור הפת שבתוכו שניה שהתנור תחילה מסתפקא להו הא דאמר ליה רב אדא בר אהבה לרבא ליחזייה האי תנורא כמאן דמלי טומאה ותיהוי פת ראשונה א"ל לא אמרינן ליחזייה האי תנורא כמאן דמלי טומאה דתניא יכול יהו כל הכלים מיטמאין באויר כלי חרס ת"ל כל אשר בתוכו יטמא מכל האוכל אשר יאכל אוכלין (א) מטמאין באויר כלי חרס ואין כלים מטמאין באויר כלי חרס תניא רבי שמעון בן יוחי אומר חס ושלום שתשתכח תורה מישראל שנאמר כי לא תשכח מפי זרעו אלא מה אני מקיים ישוטטו לבקש את דבר ה' ולא ימצאו הלכה

לא ס"ד. למיהוי כמאן דמלי טומאה: דתניא יכול יהו כל הכלים טמאים מאויר כלי חרס. שאם היה כלי אחר בתוכו שיטמא מחמת השרץ שבאויר החיצון או מחמת שיטמאנו אויר כלי החיצון שהוא טמא: תלמוד לומר כל אשר בתוכו יטמא. וסמיך ליה מכל האוכל אשר יאכל: אוכלין ומשקין שבתוכו טמאים ולא כלים שמע מינה תרתי חדא דלא אמרינן חזייה כמאן דמלי טומאה דאם כן אם כלי שטף הוא הפנימי שמטמא מגבו יהא טמא דהא נגע בטומאה אלא לא אמרינן חזייה כמאן דמלי טומאה ואוכלין ומשקין שבחיצון הוא דמטמאי מחמת הכלי שהכלי ראשון והם שניים אבל כלים לא דהואיל דאין טומאה זו באה אלא מחמת הכלי אשמעינן האי קרא שאין כלי שאינו אב הטומאה מטמא כלי:
הלכה

תורה אור השלם

א) וְהִפְלָא יְיָ אֶת מַכֹּתְךָ וְאֵת מַכּוֹת זַרְעֶךָ מַכּוֹת גְּדֹלֹת וְנֶאֱמָנוֹת וָחֳלָיִם רָעִים וְנֶאֱמָנִים: (דברים כח, נט)

ב) לָכֵן הִנְנִי יוֹסִף לְהַפְלִיא אֶת הָעָם הַזֶּה הַפְלֵא וָפֶלֶא וְאָבְדָה חָכְמַת חֲכָמָיו וּבִינַת נְבֹנָיו תִּסְתַּתָּר: (ישעיה כט, יד)

ג) הִנֵּה יָמִים בָּאִים נְאֻם אֲדֹנָי אֱלֹהִים וְהִשְׁלַחְתִּי רָעָב בָּאָרֶץ לֹא רָעָב לַלֶּחֶם וְלֹא צָמָא לַמַּיִם כִּי אִם לִשְׁמֹעַ אֵת דִּבְרֵי יְיָ: (עמוס ח, יא)

ד) וְנָעוּ מִיָּם עַד יָם וּמִצָּפוֹן וְעַד מִזְרָח יְשׁוֹטְטוּ לְבַקֵּשׁ אֶת דְּבַר יְיָ וְלֹא יִמְצָאוּ: (עמוס ח, יב)

ה) מִכָּל הָאֹכֶל אֲשֶׁר יֵאָכֵל אֲשֶׁר יָבוֹא עָלָיו מַיִם יִטְמָא וְכָל מַשְׁקֶה אֲשֶׁר יִשָּׁתֶה בְּכָל כְּלִי יִטְמָא: (ויקרא יא, לד)

ו) וְכָל כְּלִי חֶרֶשׂ אֲשֶׁר יִפֹּל מֵהֶם אֶל תּוֹכוֹ כֹּל אֲשֶׁר בְּתוֹכוֹ יִטְמָא וְאֹתוֹ תִשְׁבֹּרוּ: (ויקרא יא, לג)

ז) וְהָיָה כִּי תִמְצֶאןָ אֹתוֹ רָעוֹת רַבּוֹת וְצָרוֹת וְעָנְתָה הַשִּׁירָה הַזֹּאת לְפָנָיו לְעֵד כִּי לֹא תִשָּׁכַח מִפִּי זַרְעוֹ כִּי יָדַעְתִּי אֶת יִצְרוֹ אֲשֶׁר הוּא עֹשֶׂה הַיּוֹם בְּטֶרֶם אֲבִיאֶנּוּ אֶל הָאָרֶץ אֲשֶׁר נִשְׁבָּעְתִּי: (דברים לא, כא)

רב נסים גאון

כשנכנסו רבותינו לכרם ביבנה. כבר פירשו בברכות בגמ' דברי מערבא וכי כרם יש שם אלא אלו תלמידי חכמים שהם עשויים שורות שורות ככרם.

ליקוטי רש"י

כילת חתנים מותר לנטותה.

כִּילַּת חֲתָנִים מוּתָּר לְנָטוֹתָהּ וּמוּתָּר לְפוֹרְקָהּ – **The canopy of a bridal bed may be hung and may be taken down** on the Sabbath. Since it consists primarily of sloping sides without any significant horizontal section, it is not considered a tent.[1]

The Gemara qualifies this permit:

אָמַר רַב שֵׁשֶׁת בְּרֵיהּ דְּרַב אִידִי – **Rav Sheishess the son of Rav Idi said:** לֹא אֲמָרָן אֶלָּא שֶׁאֵין בְּגַגָּהּ טֶפַח – **This** ruling **was not said except where its roof** [i.e. the narrow horizontal section at the apex of the canopy] **is not a** ***tefach*** wide. אֲבָל יֵשׁ בְּגַגָּהּ טֶפַח אֲסוּרָה – **But if its roof is a** ***tefach*** wide, **it is forbidden** to hang the canopy or take it down on the Sabbath.[2]

Yet another qualification for this permit:

וְכִי אֵין בְּגַגָּהּ טֶפַח נַמִּי – **And even if its roof is not a** ***tefach*** wide, לֹא אֲמָרָן אֶלָּא שֶׁאֵין בְּפָחוֹת מִשְּׁלֹשָׁה סָמוּךְ לְגַגָּהּ טֶפַח – **this** ruling permitting the bridal canopy **was not said except where** the slope of the canopy is so steep that its width does **not** amount to **a** ***tefach*** **within three** ***tefachim*** **of the apex,** אֲבָל יֵשׁ בְּפָחוֹת מִשְּׁלֹשָׁה סָמוּךְ לְגַגָּהּ טֶפַח אָסוּר – **but** if the width of the canopy amounts to **a** ***tefach*** **within three** ***tefachim*** **of the apex, it is forbidden** to hang it or take it down on the Sabbath.[3]

Yet another qualification:

וְלֹא אֲמָרָן אֶלָּא שֶׁאֵין בְּשִׁיפּוּעָהּ טֶפַח – And even if the width of the canopy does not amount to a *tefach* within three *tefachim* of the apex, **this** ruling permitting a bridal canopy still **was not said except where there is not a** ***tefach*** **beneath its slope,** i.e. the horizontal distance between the foot of the slope and the top of the slope on either side is less than a *tefach.*[4] אֲבָל יֵשׁ בְּשִׁיפּוּעָהּ טֶפַח – **But if there is a** ***tefach*** **beneath its slope, it is forbidden** to hang it up and take it down on the Sabbath, שִׁפּוּעֵי אֹהָלִים כְּאֹהָלִים דָּמוּ – because **the sloping** sides **of canopies are** themselves **regarded as canopies,** i.e. they have the same status as the horizontal rooflike part of the canopy which the Rabbis prohibited when it is a *tefach* in width.[5]

Still another qualification for this permit:

וְלֹא אֲמָרָן אֶלָּא דְּלָא נָחֵית מִפּוּרְיָא טֶפַח – **And** even if there is not a *tefach* underneath its slope, **this** ruling permitting a bridal canopy **was not said except where** the bottom ends of the canopy **do not extend a** ***tefach*** **below** the bed. אֲבָל נָחֵית מִפּוּרְיָא טֶפַח אָסוּר – **But if** the ends of the canopy **extend a** ***tefach*** below the bed, **it is forbidden** to hang it up and take it down on the Sabbath.[6]

Another ruling from Rav Sheishess related to the erection of a temporary tent on the Sabbath:

וְאָמַר רַב שֵׁשֶׁת בְּרֵיהּ דְּרַב אִידִי – **And Rav Sheishess the son of Rav Idi** also **said:** הַאי סְיָאנָא שָׁרֵי – **This felt hat**[7] is permitted; i.e. it may be worn on the Sabbath.

The Gemara challenges this ruling from a Baraisa:

וְהָאִיתְּמַר סְיָאנָא אָסוּר – **But it was stated** in a Baraisa: Wearing **A FELT HAT IS PROHIBITED** on the Sabbath. — ? —

The Gemara answers:

לֹא קַשְׁיָא – This is **not a difficulty.** הָא דְּאִית בֵּיהּ טֶפַח – **This** Baraisa refers to a hat with a brim **that is a** ***tefach*** wide; since the brim juts out a *tefach,* it has the status of a tent. הָא דְּלֵית בֵּיהּ טֶפַח – Whereas **this** ruling of Rav Sheishess refers to a hat with a brim **that is not a** ***tefach*** wide, and therefore does not possess the status of a tent.

The Gemara rejects this answer:

אֶלָּא מֵעַתָּה שֶׁרְבִיב בִּגְלִימָא טֶפַח – **But now, if one were to extend one's cloak a** ***tefach*** beyond the front of one's head,[8] הָכִי נַמִּי דְּמִיחַיֵּיב – **would this too render him at all liable?!** Since this is

NOTES

1. Normal bed-canopies are spread over a frame connected to the four bedposts, forming a full-fledged roof above the bed. A bridal bed, however, has only two vertical poles — one attached to the middle of each end of the bed — and a third pole that extends across the top of the two vertical poles. A triangular canopy is formed by draping a curtain over this assembly. See diagram. R' Chiya permits the assembly of such a canopy, provided that an *ohel* which is a *tefach* in width is not formed. The Gemara now sets forth the criteria which determine whether or not such an *ohel* is formed.

2. For the horizontal width at the canopy's apex is deemed a tent if it is a *tefach* or more wide (*Rashi*).

3. See diagram. [By the principle of *lavud,* the roof of the canopy can be considered to be up to three *tefachim* lower than the actual apex. Therefore, if the canopy is one *tefach* wide within three *tefachim* of the apex, we regard the canopy as having a roof one *tefach* wide (*Chidushei HaRan*).]

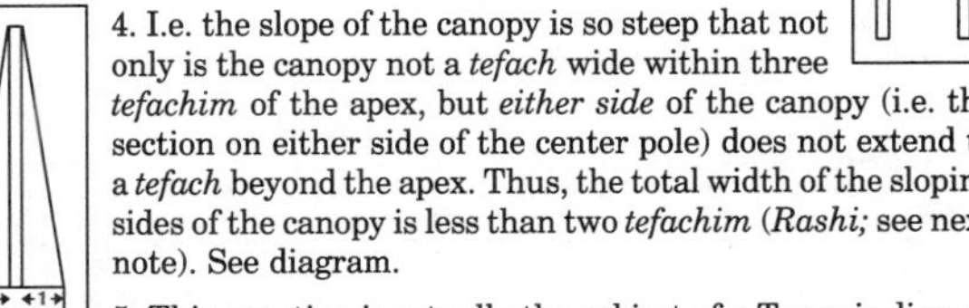

4. I.e. the slope of the canopy is so steep that not only is the canopy not a *tefach* wide within three *tefachim* of the apex, but *either side* of the canopy (i.e. the section on either side of the center pole) does not extend to a *tefach* beyond the apex. Thus, the total width of the sloping sides of the canopy is less than two *tefachim* (*Rashi;* see next note). See diagram.

5. This question is actually the subject of a Tannaic dispute between R' Eliezer and the Sages (*Succah* 19b). The opinion followed in the Gemara here is that of the Sages of the Mishnah cited there, who hold that a slanting projection can have the status of a horizontal one [for it is viewed as a roof rather than a wall] (see *Rashi* to *Eruvin* 102b), provided that it spans an area of at least one *tefach.* This, however, is not the prevailing opinion in the Gemara there (see *Tosafos* and *Meiri;* cf. *Rosh* §2 and *Korban Nesanel* §9); rather, the slanting projection is not viewed as a roof even where it overhangs an area of a *tefach.* For this reason, this third qualification is not cited by the *Rambam* and *Shulchan Aruch* 315:11; see also *Beur HaGra* there.

According to the outcome of this Gemara, the canopy of a bridal bed may not be erected unless the bed that it covers is less than three *tefachim* wide (for the canopy's horizontal segment must be narrower than one *tefach,* and the two sloping sides must each span less than a *tefach*). This is difficult to understand, for surely such a bed is far too narrow to be of any practical use! *Rashi* thus explains that one did not sleep under such a canopy; it was only used for decorative purposes (*Tur* 315; see *Menachem Meishiv Nefesh*). *Rashi* to *Eruvin* (102b ד״ה בשיפועה), however, proposes that the case under discussion is not of a bed which has only one canopy over it, but of a bed covered with two or three small canopies, each one less than three *tefachim* in width; see diagram (see *Tosafos* here for a similar explanation; see also *Sfas Emes*).

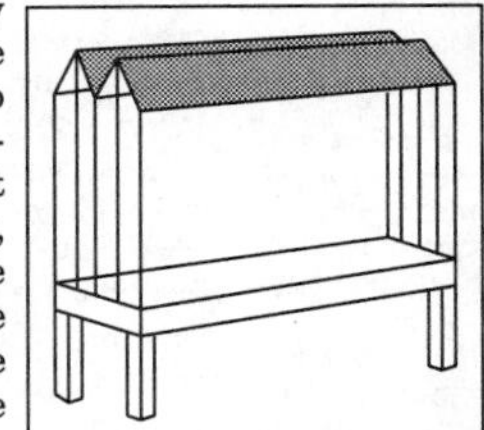

6. If the canopy hangs alongside the bed and extends to one *tefach* below the surface of the bed, then that *tefach* of cloth would be viewed as the walls and the bed itself as the roof of a tent surrounding the area under the bed (*Rashi;* see also *Re'ah,* cited in *Chidushei HaRan*).

Now, based on this ruling it should be forbidden for one to spread a cover across a bed, or a tablecloth across a table on the Sabbath, if the sides of the covering hang a *tefach* below the sides of the bed or table. The commentators, however, explain that the above ruling applies only in a case where the cloth was spread out to act as an *ohel* over the area below it. [In such a case, the bed within the canopy is viewed as a part of the *ohel.*] A sheet spread across a bed, however, was never placed there for the purpose of being a tent; thus, the bed below it would never be deemed an *ohel* (see *Rashba, Ran MHK* ed., *Mishnah Berurah* 315:§42; see also *Chidushei HaRan*). See also *Sfas Emes.*

7. This was a wide-brimmed felt hat that was worn by travelers to protect them from the sun or rain (*Chidushei HaRan*).

8. I.e. if he covers his head with his cloak and pulls the cloak forward, until it juts out a full *tefach* beyond the front of his head (*Rashi*).

עין משפט נר מצוה

ח א מיי' פכ"ב מהל' שבת הלכה ל טוש"ע א"ח סי' שטו סעיף יא:
ט ב ג מיי' פכ"ב מהל' שבת הלכה לא סמג שם טוש"ע א"ח סי' שא סעיף מ:
י ד מיי' שם טוש"ע שם סעיף מא:
יא ה ו מיי' שם הלכה לב סמג שם טוש"ע א"ח סי' שטו סעיף יב:
יב ז מיי' פכ"ו שם הלכה ו סמג שם טוש"ע שם סי' שח סעיף טז:
יג ח מיי' פי"א מהל' שאר אבות הטומאות הלכה ב:
יד ט מיי' פ"ה מהל' טומאת מת הלכה ו ופי"ג מהל' כלים הלכה א ב:

רבינו חננאל

קבוע וחייב חטאת במטה של פרסיים כדאמרן תוב בעא מיניה כילה מהו וא"ל אף מטה מותרת מכלל ששתיהן מותרות כילה שאין בגגה טפח ויש עליה חוטין קשורין מאתמול והוא כגון הטלית שאמר רמי בר יחזקאל ומטה היא גליתא מטה שהמחזירה אין צריך לתקע שמלבנותיה וכרעיה אינן דוחקות וברפיון נכנסין ויוצאין. תוב בעא מיניה כילה ומטה מהו. א"ל כילה אסורה ומטה מותרת. פי' כילה אסורה שיש בגגה טפח. ומטה מותרת כדידן. והיא מטה גליתא שהיו מחזירין אותה בשבת בבית רב חמא ומפורש בסוף פרק כירה. והני כילי דבי רב הונא ודבי רב פפא ורב הונא בריה דרב יהושע דהוו מאורתא נגידין ובצפרא חביטא רמיין. יש מי שאומרים משלבות היו בארץ שאסור לטלטלן בשבת ואנו קבלנו מרבותינו כי נטויות היו מע"ש ומשוכות למעלה כמין כפולות ובבקר הי' משפיעין ומשרבבין אותן למטה ונמצאו מוסיפין כחכמים שחולקין על ר' אליעזר ואומרים מוסיפין באהלי עראי בשבת ואין צ"ל ביו"ט וכדאמרינן בהמוצא תפילין הנהו דיכרי דהוו בי רב הונא דביממא בעי טולא ובליליא בעו אוירא אתו לקמיה דרב א"ל זיל כרוך (פוריא) [בודיא] ושייר בה טפח ולמחר פושטה דמוסיף על אהל עראי הוא ושפיר דמי. ובתרה א' הא שמעתא דשמואל כילת חתנים וכו' שמעינן מינה דכולהו חד טעמא אינון אמר רב משום ר' חייא וילון פי' פרוכת מותר לנטותו ומותר לפרקו וזה בזמן שכרוכין עליו ב' חוטין או משיחות דלא גרע מטלית כפולה כילת חתנים כדאמרן שאין בגגה טפח ולא בפחות מג' סמוך לגגה טפח וגם אינה יורדת למטה מן המטה טפח. צ"ע שבעין שמעתה זו בפרק מי שהחשיכו גרים: גמ' פעם אחת לא

תוספות

שאין בשיפועה טפח. הכא יש תימה (ד) היך יתקן זה דא"כ למה הוא דלאו אם לכל השיפוע אין טפח ויש לפרש כגון שהסדין פרוס על הכילה מונח על גבי קנים מרודים ולא פשטו הסדין היטב ומונח ונופל בין קנה לקנה כעין שורות דיש עכשיו בין כל קנה שיפוע ואין בכולו שיפוע טפח ודוחק וי"מ שאין בשיפוע טפח בגובה י' דכשיש השיפוע טפח אין משם עד למטה גובה י' דלא חשיב אהל דלאשכחן בפ"ק דסוכה (דף י.) דבכילה כי הך מותר לישן בסוכה דאמר רב יהודה אמר שמואל מותר לישן בכילת חתנים אע"פ שיש לה גג והוא שאינה י' טפחים ואין נראה לר"י דודאי נהי לגבי סוכה לא חשיב אהל וכן לגבי ק"ש כדאיתא התם (דף י:) מיהו לגבי שבת חשיב ואסירי שהרי משמרת וטעינתא וקידרא ותביתא אסירי משום אהל ולא משמע שיש בגובהן י' טפחים. מ"ר. ועוד קשה מלקמן גבי כפיפה מצרית ובגם רבינו שמואל פי' דל"ג להאי לישנא כלל שיפועי אהלים כאהלים דמו דבסוף פ"ק דסוכה (דף יט:) מסקינן דשיפועי אהלים לאו כאהלים דמו ואי משום הא לא איריא דיש לפרש דהתם בלאין בשיפועו טפח והכא כשיש בשיפועו טפח:

הא דמהדק. פירש ר"ח שאינו נכפף דלאו נראה כעין אהל דלא מהדק שהוא נכפף ולאו אין נראה כעין אהל:

דבר ה' זה הקץ. דכתיב גבי גלות שבעים לכלות דבר ה' מפי ירמיה (עזרא א). מ"ר: ולישלח

גמרא

[א] כילת חתנים מותר לנטותה ומותר לפורקה אמר רב ששת בריה דרב אידי [א] לא אמרן אלא שאין בגגה טפח אבל יש בגגה טפח אסורה וכי אין בגגה טפח נמי לא אמרן אלא שאין בפחות משלשה סמוך לגגה טפח אבל יש בפחות משלשה סמוך לגגה טפח אסור [ו]ולא אמרן אלא שאין בשיפועה טפח אבל יש בשיפועה טפח [ב] שפועי אהלים כאהלים דמו ולא אמרן אלא דלא נחית מפוריא טפח אבל נחית מפוריא טפח אסור: [ג] ואמר רב ששת בריה דרב אידי האי [ב] סיאנא שרי והאיתמר סיאנא אסור לא קשיא [ג] הא דאית ביה טפח הא דלית ביה טפח אלא מעתה שרביב בגלימא טפח ה"נ [ד] דמיחייב [ה] אלא לא קשיא [ד] הא דמיהדק הא דלא מיהדק שלח ליה רמי בר יחזקאל לרב הונא אימא לן איזי הנך מילי מעלייתא דאמרת לן משמיה דרב תרתי בשבת וחדא בתורה שלח ליה הא דתניא גוד בכיסנא מותר לנוטותה בשבת אמר רב לא שנו אלא [ה] בב' בני אדם אבל באדם אחד אסור אמר אביי [ו] וכילה אפילו בי' בני אדם אחד אסור אי אפשר דלא מימתחא פורתא אידך מאי היא דתניא [ו] כירה שנשמטה אחת מירכותיה מותר לטלטלה שתים אסור רב אמר אפילו [ז] חד נמי אסור גזירה שמא יתקע תורה דאמר רב עתידה תורה שתשתכח מישראל שנאמר [א] והפלא ה' את מכותך [ז] הפלאה זו איני יודע מהו כשהוא אומר [ב] לכן הנני יוסיף להפליא את העם הזה הפלא ופלא הוי אומר הפלאה זו תורה ת"ר [ח] כשנכנסו רבותינו לכרם ביבנה אמרו עתידה תורה שתשתכח מישראל שנאמר [ג] הנה ימים באים נאם ה' אלהים והשלחתי רעב בארץ לא רעב ללחם ולא צמא למים כי אם לשמוע את דברי ה' וכתיב [ד] ונעו מים עד ים ומצפון ועד מזרח ישוטטו לבקש את דבר ה' ולא ימצאו דבר ה' זו הלכה דבר ה' זה הקץ דבר ה' זו נבואה ומאי ישוטטו לבקש את דבר ה' אמרו עתידה אשה שתטול ככר של תרומה ותחזור בבתי כנסיות ובבתי מדרשות לידע אם טמאה היא ואם טהורה היא ואין מבין אם טהורה היא ואם טמאה היא בהדיא כתיב ביה [ה] מכל האוכל אשר יאכל אלא לידע אם ראשונה היא ואם שניה היא ואין מבין ° הא נמי מתניתין היא כדתנן [ט] [ח] השרץ שנמצא בתנור הפת שבתוכו שניה שהתנור תחילה מסתפקא להו הא דאמר ליה רב אדא בר אהבה לרבא ליחזייה האי תנורא כמאן דמלי טומאה ותיהוי פת ראשונה א"ל לא אמרינן ליחזייה האי תנורא כמאן דמלי טומאה [י] דתניא יכול יהו כל הכלים מיטמאין באויר כלי חרס ת"ל [ו] כל אשר בתוכו יטמא [ה] מכל האוכל אשר יאכל [ט] אוכלין (א) מטמאין באויר כלי חרס ואין כלים מטמאין באויר כלי חרס תניא רבי שמעון בן יוחי אומר חס ושלום שתשתכח תורה מישראל שנאמר [ז] כי לא תשכח מפי זרעו אלא מה אני מקיים ישוטטו לבקש את דבר ה' ולא ימצאו שלא ימצאו הלכה

רש"י

כילת חתנים. לא דמיא לשאר כילות ששאר כילות פרוסות על גבי קינוף שהיא לד' רגלים ויש לה גג דהוי אהל ושל חתנים על גבי נקליטין שאינם אלא שנים באמצעית המטה וקנה נתון עליהם והבגד נתון עליו ונופל לכאן ולכאן ואין לה גג טפח הלכך לאו אהל הוא: **בפחות מג'.** שהיא הולכת ומתפשטת למטה: **ולא אמרן אלא שאין בשיפועה טפח.** שאין כל צד וצד (ב) נפשט למטה להתרחק טפח מכנגד אמצעיתו דהיינו שאין ברחבו למטה טפחיים וכילת חתנים אינה עשויה לישן תחתיה: **אבל נחתא מפוריא טפח.** ההוא טפח הוה קיר לאהל והמטה נעשית לו גג: **סייאנא.** כובע של לבד פלטר"ץ: **אסור.** לצאת בו בשבת ולקמיה מפרש ואזיל: **הא דאית ביה טפח.** שהוא מתפשט להלן מראשו טפח אסור משום אהלא: **אלא מעתה שרביב בגלימיה טפח.** הניח טליתו על ראשו כדרך שהוא מתעטף (ג) והרחיקה להלן מראשו טפח: **אלא.** טעמא לאו משום אהל הוא אלא משום שלא יגביהנו הרוח מראשו ואתי לאתויי ארבע אמות הלכך מיהדק בראשו שפיר שרי לא מיהדק אסור: **תרתי בשבת וחדא בתורה.** שהיית רגיל לומר שני דברים משמו בהלכות שבת ואחת בתורה כדלקמן: **גוד בכיסנא.** גוד ברצועותיו ומונח על מקום קבוע שלו: **מותר לנטותו בשבת.** והא דאמרן לעיל פטור אבל אסור היכא דלא הוי מתוקן בכיסנין: **בב' בני אדם.** לא מימתח ליה שפיר: **באדם אחד.** ממתח ליה שפיר שמותחו על יתד זו וקושרו בה וחוזר ומותחו על זו וקושרו בה כך פירשו רבותי וכן מצאתי בתשובת הגאונים ואיני יודע מהו: **אידך.** דשבת מאי היא: **מירכותיה.** פטפוטים שלה כעין רגלים: **שמא יתקע.** כשמחבר לה הרגל יתקענה בחוזק והוי בונה אבל [ק] (ת"ק) היכא דלא נשמטה אלא אחת לא חייש למתקע כולי האי: **הפלא ופלא.** סיפא דקרא ואבדה חכמת חכמיו: **בכרם.** על שם שהיו יושבין שורות שורות ככרם: **זו הלכה.** כדכתיב (דברים ה) [להגיד לכם] את דבר ה' דהיינו תורה: **זו נבואה.** כדכתיב (הושע א) דבר ה' אשר היה אל הושע וגו': **זה הקץ.** ° לא ידענא מהיכא: **בהדיא כתיב.** ותורה שבכתב הרי כתובה ומונחת יקראו ויראו: **שהתנור תחלה.** שנטמא מן האויר כדכתיב (ויקרא יא) אל תוכו והוא חוזר ומטמא אוכלין שבתוכו מן האויר: **כמאן דמלי טומאה.** כשנפל השרץ באוירו דהא בלא נגיעה מטמא והלכך כמאן דמלי טומאה הוא ותהוי פת ראשונה: **לא ס"ד.** למיהוי כמאן דמלי טומאה: **דתניא יכול יהו כל הכלים טמאים מאויר כלי חרס.** שאם היה כלי אחר בתוכו שיטמא מחמת השרץ שבאויר החיצון או מחמת שיטמאנו אויר כלי החיצון שהוא טמא: **תלמוד לומר כל אשר בתוכו יטמא.** וסמיך ליה מכל האוכל אשר יאכל: אוכלין ומשקין שבתוכו טמאים ולא כלים שמע מינה תרתי חדא דלא אמרינן הוייה כמאן דמלי טומאה דאם כן אם כלי שטף הוא הפנימי שמטמא מגבו יהא טמא דהא נגע בטומאה אלא לא אמרינן הוייה כמאן דמלי טומאה ואוכלין ומשקין שבחילון הוא דמטמאי מחמת הכלי שהכלי ראשון והם שניים אבל כלים לא דהואיל דאין טומאה זו באה אלא מחמת הכלי אין כלי שאינו אב הטומאה מטמא כלי:

מסורת הש"ס

א) עירובין קב. ע"ש לעיל מה: ע"ש, ב) [סוכה יט:], ג) עירובין קב: ושם, ד) [נ"ל דאסור וכ"א בהרש"ש], ה) ר"ח ל"ג אלא, ו) [ערוך פי' כירה זו כלי מתכת הוא וכל זמן שמורת כלי עליה מותר לטלטלה לצורך מקומה לפיכך אם אחת מירכותיה נשמטה עדיין היא כלי שיכולה לעמוד בשלש אבל אם נטלו שתים בטלה מתורת כלי שאינה יכולה לעמוד בשתים], ז) [תמורה ג: מכות יג: ע"ש], ח) [תוספ' עדיות פ"א], ט) פסחים כ. כלים פ"ח מ"ה, י) פסחים כ., כ) עיין רש"ל.

הגהות הב"ח

(א) גמ' אוכלין ומשקין מטמאין באויר: (ב) רש"י ד"ה ולא אמרן וכו' לד ולד נמפשט למטה: (ג) ד"ה אלא מעתה וכו' מתעטף בה על ראשו והרחיקה: (ד) תוס' ד"ה שאין וכו' תימה. נ"ב ובעירובין דף קב מירך רש"י על זה כעין מירוץ שכתבו התוס' כאן:

גליון הש"ס

גמ' הא נמי מתני' היא. עי' חולין קי ע"א תוד"ה דתנן הככר: רש"י ד"ה זה כו' לא ידענא. עי' ברכות כה ע"ב רש"י ד"ה מאן שמעת ליה וש"נ:

הגהות הגר"א

[א] גמ' (ולא אמרן אלא שאין בשיפועה טפח אבל יש בש"ם שפועי אהלים כאהלים דמו). תא"מ וכ"ב הרמב"ם ל"ג לה (ועמ"ש רבינו בא"ח סי' שטו ס"ק כא):

רב נסים גאון

כשנכנסו רבותינו לכרם ביבנה. כבר פירשו בברכות בגמ' דבני מערבא וכי כרם שם אלא אלו תלמידי חכמים שהם עשוים שורות שורות ככרם.

תורה אור השלם

א) וְהִפְלָא יְיָ אֶת מַכֹּתְךָ וְאֵת מַכּוֹת זַרְעֶךָ מַכּוֹת גְּדֹלֹת וְנֶאֱמָנוֹת וָחֳלָיִם רָעִים וְנֶאֱמָנִים: [דברים כח, נט]

ב) לָכֵן הִנְנִי יוֹסִף לְהַפְלִיא אֶת הָעָם הַזֶּה הַפְלֵא וָפֶלֶא וְאָבְדָה חָכְמַת חֲכָמָיו וּבִינַת נְבֹנָיו תִּסְתַּתָּר: [ישעיה כט, יד]

ג) הִנֵּה יָמִים בָּאִים נְאֻם אֲדֹנָי אֱלֹהִים וְהִשְׁלַחְתִּי רָעָב בָּאָרֶץ לֹא רָעָב לַלֶּחֶם וְלֹא צָמָא לַמַּיִם כִּי אִם לִשְׁמֹעַ אֵת דִּבְרֵי יְיָ: [עמוס ח, יא]

ד) וְנָעוּ מִיָּם עַד יָם וּמִצָּפוֹן וְעַד מִזְרָח יְשׁוֹטְטוּ לְבַקֵּשׁ אֶת דְּבַר יְיָ וְלֹא יִמְצָאוּ: [עמוס ח, יב]

ה) מִכָּל הָאֹכֶל אֲשֶׁר יֵאָכֵל אֲשֶׁר יָבוֹא עָלָיו מַיִם יִטְמָא וְכָל מַשְׁקֶה אֲשֶׁר יִשָּׁתֶה בְּכָל כְּלִי יִטְמָא: [ויקרא יא, לד]

ו) וְכָל כְּלִי חֶרֶשׂ אֲשֶׁר יִפֹּל מֵהֶם אֶל תּוֹכוֹ כֹּל אֲשֶׁר בְּתוֹכוֹ יִטְמָא וְאֹתוֹ תִשְׁבֹּרוּ: [ויקרא יא, לג]

ז) וְהָיָה כִּי תִמְצֶאןָ אֹתוֹ רָעוֹת רַבּוֹת וְצָרוֹת וְעָנְתָה הַשִּׁירָה הַזֹּאת לְפָנָיו לְעֵד כִּי לֹא תִשָּׁכַח מִפִּי זַרְעוֹ כִּי יָדַעְתִּי אֶת יִצְרוֹ אֲשֶׁר הוּא עֹשֶׂה הַיּוֹם בְּטֶרֶם אֲבִיאֶנּוּ אֶל הָאָרֶץ אֲשֶׁר נִשְׁבָּעְתִּי: [דברים לא, כא]

רבינו חננאל (המשך)

נכנסו לנמל עד שתשכח אפי' על הארץ למה מניחין אותן ובין לצורך גופן ובין לצורך מקומן שרי. ואנו פירשנו מה שקבלנו. ולפי שהוא מלאכה שמים הזכרנו דברים הדברים הללו שאמרו מוטלת ומשולשת לארץ היו לא כתבנו הפירכא של הדברים הללו. וראינו סיוע על הטעם שהזכרנו כי קבלנוהו וסוגיין של דברים הללו בפרק המוצא תפלין שגורים רבותינו בענין תוספת אהלים. כלומר טעם אחד הן. ולולי כן הקושיא היא מקשה מהן: סיינא. כובע שמשימין בני אדם בראשיהם יוצא כמין פסל מן הראש כשיראה טפח הוא יתר. ואנן ראינוהו ...

ליקוטי רש"י

כילת חתנים מותר לנטותה. דהאי כילת חתנים יש לה גג טפח שנקליטין יוצאין לשני ראשי המטה באמצעית ... כילת חתנים. ... שאין בגגה טפח. ... בשיפועה. ... סיאנא שרי. ... הא דאית ביה טפח. ... אלא הא דמיהדק הא דלא מיהדק. ... גוד. ... גזירה שמא יתקע. ... והפלא ה' את מכותך. ...

not the case, we must conclude that a head covering that juts out from one's head is not deemed a tent.[9] Consequently, the contradiction between the Baraisa and Rav Sheishess' ruling cannot be resolved in this way. – ? –

The Gemara presents a different resolution of the contradiction:

אֶלָּא לֹא קַשְׁיָא – **Rather,** this is **not a difficulty** for the following reason: הָא דְּמִיהֲדָק – **This** ruling of Rav Sheishess refers to a hat **that is fitted tightly,** הָא דְּלֹא מִיהֲדַק – whereas **this** Baraisa refers to a hat **that is not fitted tightly.**[10] Since a loosely worn hat could fall off, the Rabbis prohibited wearing it in a public domain out of concern that one might come to carry it four *amos* in the public domain.

Yet another ruling related to the erection of a temporary tent on the Sabbath:

שְׁלַח לֵיהּ רָמִי בַּר יְחֶזְקֵאל לְרַב הוּנָא – **Rami bar Yechezkel sent** the following message **to Rav Huna:** אֵימָא לָן אֵיזִי הָנָךְ מִילֵּי מְעַלְּיָיתָא דְּאָמַרְתְּ לָן מִשְּׁמֵיהּ דְּרַב – **Tell us, my friend,**[11] **those excellent teachings that you told us in the name of Rav,** תַּרְתֵּי בְּשַׁבָּת וַחֲדָא בַּתּוֹרָה – **two concerning** the laws of **the Sabbath and one concerning the Torah** itself.[12] שְׁלַח לֵיהּ – **Rav Huna sent** the following **to [Rami bar Yechezkel]:** הָא דְּתַנְיָא גּוּד בְּכִיסְנָא מוּתָּר לְנַטּוֹתָהּ בְּשַׁבָּת – **Concerning that which was taught in a Baraisa,** IT IS PERMITTED TO HANG A LEATHER BAG BY ITS STRAPS ON THE SABBATH,[13] אָמַר רַב – **Rav said:** לֹא שָׁנוּ אֶלָּא בִּשְׁנֵי בְּנֵי אָדָם – **This was taught only** where it was being hung **by two people.** אֲבָל בְּאָדָם אֶחָד אָסוּר – **But it is forbidden for a single person** to hang it.[14]

A related ruling:

אָמַר אַבַּיֵי – **Abaye said:** וְכִילָּה אֲפִילּוּ בַּעֲשָׂרָה בְּנֵי אָדָם אָסוּר – **But a canopy may not be spread out even by ten people,** אִי אֶפְשָׁר דְּלֹא מִימַּתְחָא פּוּרְתָּא – **for it is impossible that even a small portion** of it **would not be spread** properly.[15]

The Gemara cites Rav's second ruling quoted by Rav Huna concerning the laws of the Sabbath:

אִידָךְ מַאי הִיא – **And what is the other** ruling? דְּתַנְיָא – It is **that which was taught in a Baraisa:** כִּירָה שֶׁנִּשְׁמְטָה אַחַת מִירַכּוֹתֶיהָ – AN OVEN WHICH HAD ONE OF ITS LEGS BROKEN OFF, מוּתָּר לְטַלְטְלָהּ – IT IS PERMITTED TO MOVE IT on the Sabbath.[16] שְׁתַּיִם – If it lost TWO of its legs, however, אָסוּר – IT IS PROHIBITED to move it.[17]

רַב אָמַר – **Rav said:** אֲפִילּוּ חַד נַמִּי אָסוּר – **Even** if it lost just **one** of its legs **it is also prohibited** to move it; גְּזֵירָה שֶׁמָּא יִתְקַע – for the Rabbis issued **a decree** forbidding this, **lest one come to affix it** tightly, which is an act akin to building.[18]

The Gemara cites Rav's last teaching quoted by Rav Huna concerning the Torah:

תּוֹרָה – **Concerning the Torah,** דְּאָמַר רַב – **for Rav said:** עֲתִידָה תּוֹרָה שֶׁתִּשְׁתַּכַּח מִיִּשְׂרָאֵל – **The Torah will eventually be forgotten from** the nation of **Israel,** שֶׁנֶּאֱמַר "וְהִפְלָא ה' אֶת־מַכֹּתְךָ" – **as it is stated:**[19] ***Then Hashem will make extraordinary*** (*ve'hifla*) ***your blows.*** הַפְלָאָה זוֹ אֵינִי יוֹדֵעַ מַהוּ – **I do not know what** suffering **is meant by** the term ***haflaah,*** until its meaning is clarified by another verse. כְּשֶׁהוּא אוֹמֵר "לָכֵן הִנְנִי יוֹסִף לְהַפְלִיא אֶת־הָעָם־הַזֶּה הַפְלֵא וָפֶלֶא" – **When Scripture states:**[20] ***Therefore, I will do extraordinary things among this people, exceedingly extraordinary*** (*haflei va'feleh*), *for the wisdom of their wise men shall perish,* הֱוֵי אוֹמֵר הַפְלָאָה זוֹ תּוֹרָה – **say, then, that** the suffering alluded to by the term ***haflaah*** **refers to the** forgetting of **Torah** wisdom.[21]

NOTES

9. For something which is worn as a garment is not considered a tent (*Shaar HaTziyun* 301:187; see also *Aruch HaShulchan* 301:110).

10. The Gemara explains that the reason to prohibit the wearing of such a hat is not due to the prohibition against constructing a tent, but rather because such a hat is liable to be blown off in the wind. Thus, the distinction is made that when the hat is tightly secured onto one's head he may wear it outside [Rav Sheishess] and when it is loosely placed on one's head he may not wear it outside [the Baraisa] (*Rashi;* see also *Rashi* to *Eruvin* 102b ד״ה אלא הא with *Rashash,* and *Shulchan Aruch* 301:41 with *Mishnah Berurah* who explains the parameters of this law; cf. *Rabbeinu Chananel* quoted by *Tosafos,* and *Shulchan Aruch* 301:40; see also *Chidushei HaRan* here).

11. See *Chochmas Shlomo* to *Bava Metzia* 70a; cf. *Rashbam* to *Genesis* 27:33.

12. Rav Huna was wont to repeat three teachings from his teacher, Rav. Two of these teachings were related to the laws of the Sabbath, while the third was an Aggadic teaching concerning Torah wisdom (*Rashi*).

13. [See above, 138a note 3, where this bag was described.] The Baraisa here permits mounting the leather bag by its straps in its reserved spot for the night by fastening it in place with stakes.

The Baraisa quoted by Abaye above on 138a, which *prohibited* mounting the leather bag by its straps onto its pegs, speaks of a case where the straps were not set into the bag [see further in next note] (*Rashi;* see *Ran;* cf. *Rashba, Chidushei HaRan* et al. for an alternate explanation of this passage).

14. Two people mounting the bag will generally not spread it tightly; thus, it is not considered even a temporary tent. A single person, however, will tie one end and then stretch out the bag before tying the second end; this will result in a more tightly drawn bag, which resembles a tent (*Rashi,* quoting his teachers; *Rashi* himself expresses uncertainty as to this explanation of this passage; see *Chochmas Manoach;* cf. *Rashba* and *Ran MHK* ed. and *Chidushei HaRan;* see also *Ritva MHK* ed.; see also *Shulchan Aruch* 315:12 with *Mishnah Berurah* §43-47). [Where the straps are *not* set into the bag, however, even two people will spread it tightly, and the Baraisa above forbids mounting the bag in this case (see previous note).]

15. Accordingly, it will always resemble a tent, and spreading it out is forbidden. Cf. *Ritva MHK* ed. and *Ran;* see also *Rambam, Hil. Shabbos* 22:32.

16. [An oven is a utensil normally used for a purpose forbidden on the Sabbath (baking); such utensils may generally be moved if the spot that they occupy must be used (צוֹרֶךְ מְקוֹמוֹ).] Although one of the legs is broken, the oven is still considered usable, for it can stand on the remaining three legs (see *Aruch* ד״ה כירה, cited in marginal gloss); thus, it may still be moved on the Sabbath.

17. Once the oven loses two of its legs, it cannot be used, for it is unable to stand on its two remaining legs; thus, it loses its status as a utensil, and may not be moved at all on the Sabbath (*Aruch* ibid., *Meiri;* cf. *Chidushei HaRan;* see also next note).

18. Rav states that although the oven with one broken leg is not *muktzeh,* the Rabbis prohibited one from handling it on the Sabbath for fear that one would attempt to repair it by reattaching the leg. Although reattaching the leg *loosely* poses no problem, the Rabbis were concerned that one might come to *tightly* affix the leg; this would be forbidden on account of the *melachah* of *building* (cf. *Rashi* to 47a ד״ה חייב חטאת, who says that this would be forbidden on account of the *melachah* of *striking the final blow*). The Tanna of the Baraisa held, however, that the Rabbis were concerned for this only if *two* legs would come off; if just one leg came off, there would not be enough reason for concern to warrant a Rabbinic decree (*Rashi,* based on our text of the Gemara; see *Chidushei HaRan* and *Shaar HaTziyun* 308:69, who explain why it would be possible to say that if two legs came off, the oven might *not* be *muktzeh;* cf. *Meiri;* see also *Cheifetz Hashem* for an explanation of *Rashi;* see also *Shulchan Aruch* 308:16 with *Mishnah Berurah* §68 and *Shaar HaTziyun* §68; cf. *Maharshal* for an alternative text and reading of our *Rashi*). [Rav was given the status of a Tanna in that he was able to dispute Tannaic rulings (רַב תַּנָּא הוּא וּפָלִיג).]

19. *Deuteronomy* 28:59.

20. *Isaiah* 29:14.

21. That verse, too, described "extraordinary" suffering, and then defined it in the verse's conclusion: וְאָבְדָה חָכְמַת חֲכָמָיו וּבִינַת נְבֹנָיו תִּסְתַּתָּר, *for the wisdom of their wise men shall perish* etc., which refers to the Torah

כילת חתנים מותר לנטותה ומותר לפורקה אמר רב ששת בריה דרב אידי לא אמרן אלא שאין בגגה טפח אבל יש בגגה טפח אסורה וכי אין בגגה טפח נמי לא אמרן אלא שאין בפחות משלשה סמוך לגגה טפח אבל יש בפחות משלשה סמוך לגגה טפח אסור ולא אמרן אלא שאין בשיפועה טפח אבל יש בשיפועה טפח שפועי אהלים כאהלים דמו ולא אמרן אלא דלא נחית מפוריא טפח אבל נחית מפוריא טפח אסור: ואמר רב ששת בריה דרב אידי האי סיאנא שרי והאיתמר סיאנא אסור לא קשיא הא דאית ביה טפח הא דלית ביה טפח אלא מעתה שרביב בגלימא טפח ה"נ דמיחייב אלא לא קשיא הא דמיהדק הא דלא מיהדק שלח ליה רמי בר יחזקאל לרב הונא אימא לן איזי הנך מילי מעלייתא דאמרת לן משמיה דרב תרתי בשבת וחדא בתורה שלח ליה הא דתניא גוד בכיסנא מותר לנטותה בשבת אמר רב לא שנו אלא בב' בני אדם אבל באדם אחד אסור אמר אביי וכילה אפילו בב' בני אדם אסור אי אפשר דלא מימתחא פורתא אידך מאי היא דתניא כירה שנשמטה אחת מירכותיה מותר לטלטלה שתים אסור רב אמר אפילו חד נמי אסור גזירה שמא יתקע תורה דאמר רב עתידה תורה שתשתכח מישראל שנאמר והפלא ה' את מכותך הפלאה זו איני יודע מהו כשהוא אומר לכן הנני יוסיף להפליא את העם הזה הפלא ופלא הוי אומר הפלאה זו תורה ת"ר כשנכנסו רבותינו לכרם ביבנה אמרו עתידה תורה שתשתכח מישראל שנאמר הנה ימים באים נאם ה' אלהים והשלחתי רעב בארץ לא רעב ללחם ולא צמא למים כי אם לשמוע את דברי ה' וכתיב ונעו מים עד ים ומצפון ועד מזרח ישוטטו לבקש את דבר ה' ולא ימצאו דבר ה' זו הלכה דבר ה' זה הקץ דבר ה' זו נבואה ומאי ישוטטו לבקש את דבר ה' אמרו עתידה אשה שתטול ככר של תרומה ותחזור בבתי כנסיות ובבתי מדרשות לידע אם טמאה היא ואם טהורה היא ואין מבין אם טהורה היא ואם טמאה היא בהדיא כתיב ביה מכל האוכל אשר יאכל אלא לידע אם ראשונה היא ואם שניה היא ואין מבין הא נמי מתניתין היא כדתנן השרץ שנמצא בתנור הפת שבתוכו שניה שהתנור תחילה מסתפקא להו הא דאמר ליה רב אדא בר אהבה לרבא ליחזייה האי תנורא כמאן דמלי טומאה ותיהוי פת ראשונה א"ל לא אמרינן ליחזייה האי תנורא כמאן דמלי טומאה דתניא יכול יהו כל הכלים מיטמאין באויר כלי חרם ת"ל כל אשר בתוכו יטמא מכל האוכל אשר יאכל אוכלין מטמאין באויר כלי חרם ואין כלים מטמאין באויר כלי חרם תניא רבי שמעון בן יוחי אומר חס ושלום שתשתכח תורה מישראל שנאמר כי לא תשכח מפי זרעו אלא מה אני מקיים ישוטטו לבקש את דבר ה' ולא ימצאו שלא ימצאו

הלכה

תוספות

שאין בשיפועה טפח. הלכה יש תימה איך יתכן זה דא"כ למה הוא רואה אם לכל השיפוע אין טפח ויש לפרש כגון שהסדין שפרוש על הכילה מונח על גבי קנים מרובים ולא פשטו הסדין היטב ומונח ונופל בין קנה לקנה כעין שורות דיש עכשיו בין כל קנה שיפוע ואין בכולו שיפוע טפח ודוחק וי"מ שאין בשיפוע טפח בגובה י' דכשלא השיפוע טפח אין מהם עד למטה גובה י' דלא חשיב אהל כדאשכחן בפ"ק דסוכה (דף י.) דכילה כי הך מותר לישן בסוכה דאמר רב יהודה אמר שמואל מותר לישן בכילת חתנים אע"פ שיש לה גג והוא שאינה י' טפחים ואין נראה לר"י דהלי נהי דגבי סוכה לא חשיב אהל וכן לגבי ק"ש כדאיתא התם (דף י:) מיהו לגבי שבת חשיב ואסירי שהרי משמרת וכיפתא וקילקלה ומכבתא אסירי משום אהל ולא משמע שיש בגובהן י' טפחים. מ"ר. ועוד קשה מדלקמן גבי כפיפה מצרית והסם רבינו שמואל פי' דל"ג להאי לישנא כלל שיפועי אהלים כאהלים דמו דבסוף פ"ק דסוכה (דף יט:) מסקינן דשיפוע אהלים לאו כאהלים דמו ואי משום הא לא איריא דיש לפרש דהתם דאין בשיפועו טפח והכא כשיש בשיפוע טפח:

הא דמהדק. פירש ר"ח שאינו נכפף דלאו נראה כעין אהל דלא מהדק שהוא נכפף ולאו אין נראה כעין אהל:

דבר ה' זה הקץ. דכתיב גבי גלות שבעים לכלות דבר ה' מפי ירמיה (עזרא א). מ"ר: ולישלח

רש"י

כילת חתנים. לא דמיא לשאר כילות שאר כילות פרוסות על גבי קינוף שהיא לד' רגלים ויש לה גג דהוי אהל ושל חתנים על גבי נקליטין שאינם אלא שנים באמצעית המטה וקנה נתון עליהם והבגד נתון עליו ונופל לכאן ולכאן ואין לה גג טפח הלכך לאו אהל הוא: בפחות מג'. שהיא הולכת ומתפשטת למטה: ולא אמרן אלא שאין בשיפועה טפח. שאין כל צד וצד נפשט למטה להתרחק טפח מכנגד מלמעלה דהיינו שאין ברחבו למטה טפחים וכילת חתנים אינה עשויה לישן תחתיה: אבל נחתא מפוריא טפח. ההוא טפח הוה קיר לאהל והמטה נעשית לו גג: סייאנא. כובע של לבד פלטר"ץ: אסור. לצאת בו בשבת ולקמיה מפרש ואזיל: הא דאית ביה טפח. שהוא מתפשט להלן מראשו טפח אסור משום אהלה: אלא מעתה שרביב בגלימיה טפח. הניח טליתו על ראשו דלכך שהוא מתפשט (ג) והרחיקה להלן מראשו טפח: אלא. טעמא לאו משום אהל הוא אלא משום שלא יגביהנו הרוח מראשו ואתי לאתויי ארבע אמות הלכך מיהדק בראשו שפיר שרי לא מיהדק אסור: תרתי בשבת וחדא בתורה. שהיית רגיל לומר שני דברים משמו בהלכות שבת ואחת בתורה דלקמן: גוד בכיסנא. גוד כלעותו ומונח על מקום קבוע שלו: מותר לנטותו בשבת. והא דאמרן לעיל פטור אבל אסור היכא דלא הוי מתוקן בכיסנין: בב' בני אדם. לא מימתח ליה שפיר: באדם אחד. ממתח ליה שפיר שמותחו על יתד זו וקושרו בה וחוזר ומותחו על זו וקושרו בה כך פירשו רבותי וכן מצאתי בתשובת הגאונים ואיני יודע מהו: אידך. דשבת מאי היא: מירכותיה. פטפוטים שלה כעין רגלים: שמא יתקע. כשמחבר לה הרגל יתקענה בחוזק והוי בונה אבל (ת"ק) היכא דלא נשמטה אלא אחת לא חייש למתקע כולי האי: הפלא ופלא. סיפא דקרא ואבדה חכמת חכמיו: בכרם. על שם שהיו יושבין שורות שורות ככרם: זו הלכה. כדכתיב (דברים ה) [להגיד לכם] את דבר ה' דהיינו תורה: זו נבואה. כדכתיב (הושע א) דבר ה' אשר היה אל הושע וגו': זה הקץ. לא ידענא מהיכא: בהדיא כתיב. ותורה שבכתב הרי כתובה ומונחת יקראו וידעו: שהתנור תחלה. שנטמא מן האויר כדכתיב (ויקרא יא) אל תוכו והוא חוזר ומטמא אוכלין שבתוכו מן האויר: כמאן דמלי טומאה. כשנפל השרץ באוירו דהא בלא נגיעה מטמא והלכך כמאן דמלי טומאה הוא ותהוי פת ראשונה:

לא ס"ד. למיהוי כמאן דמלי טומאה: דתניא יכול יהו כל הכלים טמאים מאויר כלי חרס. שאם היה כלי אחר בתוכו שיטמא מחמת אויר כלי חרס. שבאויר המיטמא או מחמת שיטמאהו אויר כלי המיטמא שהוא טמא: תלמוד לומר כל אשר בתוכו יטמא. וסמיך ליה מכל האוכל אשר יאכל: אוכלין ומשקין שבתוכו טמאים ולא כלים שמע מינה תרתי חדא דלא אמרינן חזייה כמאן דמלי טומאה דאם כן אם כלי שטף הוא הפנימי שמטמא מגבו יהא טמא דהא נגע בטומאה אלא לא אמרינן חזייה כמאן דמלי טומאה ואוכלין ומשקין שבכלי הוא דמטמאי מחמת הכלי שהכלי ראשון והם שניים אבל כלים לא דהוציא דאין טומאה זו באה אלא מחמת הכלי אשמעינן האי קרא שאין כלי שאינו אב הטומאה מטמא כלי:

מסורת הש"ס

א) ערכין קכ. ע"ש לעיל מה: ע"ש, ב) [סוכה יט:], ג) עירובין קב: ושם, ד) [ע"ל אהלות ומסקין כאלור], ה) ר"ח ל"ג אלא, ו) [ערוך פי' כירה זו כלי מתכת הולך וכל זמן שתולין על עליה מותר לטלטלה], ז) [תוספתא ידים פ"ב], ח) [מתוס' ר"ח דנשמטה], ט) [תוספ' עדיות פ"א], י) פסחים כ. כליס פ"ח מ"ה, כ) פסחים כ., ל) עיין רש"ל.

הגהות הב"ח

(א) גמ' אוכלין ומשקין מטמאין באויר כלי חרס: (ב) רש"י ד"ה ולא אמרן וכו' לד ולד מתפשט למטה: (ג) ד"ה אלא מעתה וכו' מתפשט בה על ראשו והרחיקה: (ד) תוס' ד"ה שאין וכו' שאין בגובה הד בין כל קנה שיפוע וכו':

גליון הש"ס

גמ' הא נמי מתניתין היא. עי' תולין קי ע"ח ובתוס' ד"ה האי פת ראשונה: רש"י ד"ה דר ב' ידענא. עי' ברכות כה ע"ב ברש"י ד"ה ולא שמעת ליה ונ"ל:

הגהות הגר"א

[א] גמ' (ולא אמרן אלא שאין בשיפועה טפח אבל יש בשיפוע טפח שפועי אהלים כאהלים דמו). תא"מ וג"ר הרמ"ם ל"ג לה ועמ"ש רבינו בא"ח סי' שטו ס"ק כז:

רב נסים גאון

כשנכנסו רבותינו לכרם ביבנה. כבר פירשו בברכות בגמ' דבני מערבא וכי כרם שם היה אלא תלמידי חכמים שהם עשוים שורות שורות ככרם.

תורה אור השלם

א) וְהִפְלָא יְיָ אֶת מַכֹּתְךָ וְאֵת מַכּוֹת זַרְעֶךָ מַכּוֹת גְּדֹלוֹת וְנֶאֱמָנוֹת וָחֳלָיִם רָעִים וְנֶאֱמָנִים: (דברים כח, נט)

ב) לָכֵן הִנְנִי יוֹסִף לְהַפְלִיא אֶת הָעָם הַזֶּה הַפְלֵא וָפֶלֶא וְאָבְדָה חָכְמַת חֲכָמָיו וּבִינַת נְבֹנָיו תִּסְתַּתָּר: (ישעיה כט, יד)

ג) הִנֵּה יָמִים בָּאִים נְאֻם אֲדֹנָי אֱלֹהִים וְהִשְׁלַחְתִּי רָעָב בָּאָרֶץ לֹא רָעָב לַלֶּחֶם וְלֹא צָמָא לַמַּיִם כִּי אִם לִשְׁמֹעַ אֵת דִּבְרֵי יְיָ: (עמוס ח, יא) ד) וְנָעוּ מִיָּם עַד יָם וּמִצָּפוֹן וְעַד מִזְרָח יְשׁוֹטְטוּ לְבַקֵּשׁ אֶת דְּבַר יְיָ וְלֹא יִמְצָאוּ: (עמוס ח, יב) ה) מִכָּל הָאֹכֶל אֲשֶׁר יֵאָכֵל אֲשֶׁר יָבוֹא עָלָיו מַיִם יִטְמָא וְכָל מַשְׁקֶה אֲשֶׁר יִשָּׁתֶה בְּכָל כְּלִי יִטְמָא: (ויקרא יא, לד) ו) וְכָל כְּלִי חֶרֶשׂ אֲשֶׁר יִפֹּל מֵהֶם אֶל תּוֹכוֹ כֹּל אֲשֶׁר בְּתוֹכוֹ יִטְמָא וְאֹתוֹ תִשְׁבֹּרוּ: (ויקרא יא, לג) ז) וְהָיָה כִּי תִמְצֶאןָ אֹתוֹ רָעוֹת רַבּוֹת וְצָרוֹת וְעָנְתָה הַשִּׁירָה הַזֹּאת לְפָנָיו לְעֵד כִּי לֹא תִשָּׁכַח מִפִּי זַרְעוֹ כִּי יָדַעְתִּי אֶת יִצְרוֹ אֲשֶׁר הוּא עֹשֶׂה הַיּוֹם בְּטֶרֶם אֲבִיאֶנּוּ אֶל הָאָרֶץ אֲשֶׁר נִשְׁבָּעְתִּי: (דברים לא, כא)

עין משפט נר מצוה

ח א מיי' פכ"ב מהל' שבת הלכה ל טוש"ע א"ח סי' שטו סעיף יא:

ט ב ג מיי' פכ"ב מהל' שבת הלכה לג סמג שם טוש"ע א"ח סי' שא סעיף מ:

י ד מיי' שם טוש"ע שם סעיף מא:

יא ה ו מיי' שם הלכה לב סמג שם טוש"ע א"ח סי' שטו סעיף יב:

יב ז מיי' פכ"ה שם הלכה ו סמג שם טוש"ע שם סי' שח סעיף טז:

יג ח מיי' פי"א מהל' שאר אבות הטומאות הלכה כ:

יד ט מיי' פ"ה מהל' טומאת מת הלכה ו ופי"ג מהל' כלים הלכה א:

רבינו חננאל

קבוע וחייב חטאת במטה של פרסים כדאמרן תוב בעא מיניה כילה מהו וא"ל אף מטה מותרת מכלל שעשיהן מותרות כילה שאין בגגה טפח ויש עליה חוטין קשורין מאחמול והוא כגון הטלית שאמר רמי בר יחזקאל ומטה היא גליתא מטה שהמחזירה אין צריך לתקע שמלבנותיה וכרעיה אינן דחוקות ובפירקן נכנסין ויוצאין. תוב בעא מיניה כילה ומטה מהו. א"ל כילה אסורה ומטה מותרת. פי' כילה אסורה שיש בגגה טפח. ומטה מותרת כדרך. והיא מטה גליתא שהיו מחזירין אותה בשבת בבית רב חמא ומפורש בסוף פרק כירה. והני כולי דבי רב הונא ודבי רב פפא ורב הונא בריה דרב יהושע הוו מאורתא נגידין ובצפרא חביטא רמיין. יש מי שאומרים שלבלת היו בארץ שאסור לטלטלן בשבת ואנו קבלנו מרבותינו כי נטויות היו מע"ש ומשוכות למעלה כמין כפולות ובבקר היו משפיעין ומשרבבין אותן למטה ונמצאו מוסיפין כחכמים שחולקין על ר' אליעזר ואומרים מוסיפין באהלי עראי בשבת ואין צ"ל ביו"ט וכדאמרינן במוצא תפילין הנהו דיכרי דהוו בי רב הונא דביממא בעי טולא ובליליא בעו אוירא אתו לקמיה דרב א"ל זיל כרוך (פוריא) [בודיא] ושייר בה טפח ולמחר פושטה דמוסיף על אהל עראי הוא ושפיר דמי. ובהדיא א' הא שמעתא דשמואל כילת חתנים וכו' שמעינן מינה דכולהו חד טעמא אינון אמר רב משום ר' חייא וילון פי' פרוכת מותר לנטותו ומותר לפרקו וזה בזמן שכרוכין עליו ב' חוטין או משיחות דלא גרע מטלית כפולה כילת חתנים כדאמרן שאין בגגה טפח ואין בפחות מג' סמוך לגגה טפח וגם אינה יורדת למטה מן המטה טפח. צ"ע שבעין שמועה זו בפרק מי שהוציאוהו ...

ליקוטי רש"י

כילת חתנים מותר לנטותה. דהסם כילה חתנים אין לה גג טפח שנקליטין יוצאין לנטי ראשי המטה באמצעיתה ...

מטה שאין ברחבה שני טפחים או ג' ...

[illegible]

The Gemara cites a Baraisa containing a similar teaching: תָּנוּ רַבָּנַן – **The Rabbis taught in a Baraisa:** כְּשֶׁנִּכְנְסוּ רַבּוֹתֵינוּ לַכֶּרֶם בְּיַבְנֶה אָמְרוּ – WHEN OUR RABBIS ENTERED THE VINEYARD IN YAVNEH,[22] THEY SAID: עֲתִידָה תּוֹרָה שֶׁתִּשְׁתַּכַּח מִיִּשְׂרָאֵל – THE TORAH WILL EVENTUALLY BE FORGOTTEN FROM the nation of ISRAEL, שֶׁנֶּאֱמַר ,,הִנֵּה יָמִים בָּאִים נְאֻם ה׳ אֱלֹהִים וְהִשְׁלַחְתִּי רָעָב בָּאָרֶץ – AS IT IS STATED:[23] *BEHOLD, DAYS ARE COMING, DECLARES HASHEM, THAT I WILL SEND A HUNGER INTO THE LAND,* לֹא־רָעָב לַלֶּחֶם וְלֹא־צָמָא לַמַּיִם כִּי אִם־לִשְׁמֹעַ אֵת דִּבְרֵי ה׳ '' – *NOT A HUNGER FOR BREAD AND NOT A THIRST FOR WATER, BUT TO HEAR THE WORDS OF HASHEM.* וּכְתִיב ,,וְנָעוּ מִיָּם עַד־יָם וּמִצָּפוֹן וְעַד־מִזְרָח יְשׁוֹטְטוּ לְבַקֵּשׁ אֶת־דְּבַר־ה׳ וְלֹא יִמְצָאוּ'' – AND IT IS WRITTEN in the next verse, in description of the search that will ensue, *AND THEY SHALL JOURNEY FROM SEA TO SEA AND FROM THE NORTH UNTO THE EAST, THEY SHALL WANDER TO SEEK THE WORD OF HASHEM, BUT SHALL NOT FIND IT.* ,,דְּבַר־ה׳ '' זוֹ הֲלָכָה – *THE WORD OF HASHEM,* THIS REFERS TO HALACHAH;[24] ,,דְּבַר־ה׳ '' זֶה הַקֵּץ – *THE WORD OF HASHEM,* THIS REFERS TO THE END OF THE EXILE;[25] ,,דְּבַר־ה׳ '' זוֹ נְבוּאָה – *THE WORD OF HASHEM,* THIS REFERS TO PROPHECY.[26] Thus, this Baraisa, too, states that the Torah will eventually be forgotten from Israel.

The Gemara examines the final verse cited in the Baraisa: וּמַאי ,,יְשׁוֹטְטוּ לְבַקֵּשׁ אֶת־דְּבַר־ה׳ '' – **And what** is meant by: *They shall wander to seek the word of Hashem?* אָמְרוּ עֲתִידָה אִשָּׁה שֶׁתִּטּוֹל כִּכָּר שֶׁל תְּרוּמָה – **[The Sages] said: A woman will eventually take a loaf of *terumah*** bread which had been in a *tamei* oven, וְתַחֲזוֹר בְּבָתֵּי כְנֵסִיּוֹת וּבְבָתֵּי מִדְרָשׁוֹת לֵידַע אִם טְמֵאָה הִיא וְאִם טְהוֹרָה הִיא – **and bring it to the houses of prayer and study halls to find out whether it is *tamei* or *tahor*,** וְאֵין מֵבִין – **and** there will be **none** who **will understand** Torah sufficiently to know the law.

The Gemara asks: אִם טְהוֹרָה הִיא וְאִם טְמֵאָה הִיא – Will there be no one to answer **whether the bread is *tamei* or *tahor*?** בְּהֶדְיָא כְּתִיב בֵּיהּ ,,מִכָּל־הָאֹכֶל אֲשֶׁר יֵאָכֵל'' – But **this is explicitly written** in Scripture:[27] ***From all foods which are eaten.*** Since it is in the Written Torah, it will surely not be forgotten![28] אֶלָּא לֵידַע אִם רִאשׁוֹנָה הִיא וְאִם שְׁנִיָּה הִיא – **Rather,** the woman will bring the bread to determine **whether it is** contaminated with **a first**-degree *tumah* **or a second**-degree *tumah,* וְאֵין מֵבִין – **and** there will be **none** who **will understand** Torah sufficiently to know the law.[29]

The Gemara asks again: הָא נַמִּי מַתְנִיתִין הִיא – **But that is also** taught explicitly in **a Mishnah,** כְּדִתְנַן – **as we learned in a Mishnah:**[30] הַשֶּׁרֶץ שֶׁנִּמְצָא בַּתַּנּוּר – If A SHERETZ IS FOUND IN AN OVEN, הַפַּת שֶׁבְּתוֹכוֹ שְׁנִיָּה – THE BREAD IN [THE OVEN] acquires a SECOND-degree *tumah,* שֶׁהַתַּנּוּר תְּחִילָּה – FOR THE OVEN had acquired a FIRST-degree *tumah.* The Mishnah clearly teaches that the oven's air-space acquires a first-degree *tumah* from the *sheretz,* and it in turn imparts a second-degree *tumah* to the food in the oven's air-space. What, then, could have been the woman's uncertainty?[31]

The Gemara explains the basis for the uncertainty in this case: מִסְתַּפְּקָא לְהוּ הָא דְּאָמַר לֵיהּ רַב אַדָּא בַּר אַהֲבָה לְרָבָא – **They will be uncertain** with regard to **that which Rav Adda bar Ahavah said to Rava** concerning the Mishnah's ruling: לֵיחְזְיֵיהּ הַאי תַּנּוּרָא כְּמַאן דְּמָלֵי טוּמְאָה – **Let us view this oven as though it is full of *tumah,*** וְתֶיהֱוֵי פַּת רִאשׁוֹנָה – **and let the bread become** contaminated with **a first**-degree *tumah*![32] The uncertainty will center around this challenge to the Mishnah's ruling.

The Gemara presents a defense of the Mishnah's ruling: אָמַר לֵיהּ – **[Rava] said to [Rav Adda bar Ahavah]:** לֹא אָמְרִינַן לֵיחְזְיֵיהּ הַאי תַּנּוּרָא כְּמַאן דְּמָלֵי טוּמְאָה – **We do not say that we view this oven as though it is full of *tumah,*** דְּתַנְיָא – **as it was**

NOTES

knowledge of the Sages (*Rashi;* see *Maharsha*).

See *Maharal, Tiferes Yisrael* ch. 56 for a lengthy dissertation explaining this chilling prediction; see also *Yad David [Basra]* and *Korban Nesanel* 4:70; cf. *Hagahos Maharsham.*

22. Yavneh was for a time the seat of the Sanhedrin (see *Rosh Hashanah* 31a,b and *Gittin* 56b), where the Torah scholars were arranged in rows [according to their level of scholarship] much as the grapevines in a vineyard are arranged (*Rashi*).

23. *Amos* 8:11,12.

24. The Torah [and its laws] is referred to as the word of Hashem in *Deuteronomy* 5:5: לְהַגִּיד לָכֶם אֶת־דְּבַר ה׳, *to relate the word of Hashem to you* (*Rashi;* cf. *Ritva MHK* ed.). This verse in *Amos* thus describes a time when people will be unable to find a person who possesses knowledge of halachah, as the Rabbis taught in the Baraisa. See also *Cheifetz Hashem.*

25. *Rashi* states that he is unaware of a source where the end of the exile is referred to as "the word of Hashem." *Tosafos* suggest that this is found in *Ezra* 1:1, which states: לִכְלוֹת דְּבַר־ה׳ מִפִּי יִרְמְיָה, *upon the conclusion of Hashem's word by the mouth of Yirmiyah,* which refers to the end of the seventy-year exile after the destruction of the First Temple (cf. *Eitz Yosef* in *Ein Yaakov*).

26. Prophecy is referred to as "the word of Hashem" in *Hosea* (1:1): דְּבַר־ה׳ אֲשֶׁר הָיָה אֶל־הוֹשֵׁעַ, *The word of Hashem that came to Hosea* [Hosea being one of the Twelve Prophets] (*Rashi*). [The verse thus foretells of the end of the period of prophecy, which occurred at the beginning of the Second Temple era.]

27. *Leviticus* 11:33 states: וְכָל־כְּלִי־חֶרֶשׂ אֲשֶׁר־יִפֹּל מֵהֶם אֶל־תּוֹכוֹ כֹּל אֲשֶׁר בְּתוֹכוֹ יִטְמָא . . ., *Any earthenware utensil into whose interior one of them* [i.e. a dead *sheretz*] *will fall, everything in it shall become tamei . . .*
And in verse 34 it is written: מִכָּל־הָאֹכֶל אֲשֶׁר יֵאָכֵל . . . יִטְמָא, *Of any food that is eaten . . . shall become tamei.* Thus, Scripture clearly rules that food inside an earthenware utensil (such as an oven) which already contained a dead *sheretz* is rendered *tamei,* although the food did not come into contact with the *sheretz.*

28. The prediction of the Torah being forgotten cannot refer to laws explicitly taught in the written Torah, for those laws are clearly written and can be referenced easily (*Rashi*).

29. A *sheretz* is itself an אַב הַטּוּמְאָה, *av hatumah* (literally: a father of *tumah;* i.e. a primary source of *tumah*). A person, object or food which contracts *tumah* directly from this *sheretz* becomes a רִאשׁוֹן לְטוּמְאָה, *first degree of* [acquired] *tumah,* or *rishon* for short. A *rishon* is able, in certain cases, to impart *tumah* to yet another object, which becomes a שֵׁנִי לְטוּמְאָה, *second degree of* [acquired] *tumah,* or *sheni* for short.

Thus, while the woman may indeed be certain that the bread is *tamei,* as Scripture clearly teaches, she, and the Torah scholars she will ask, will still be uncertain whether the bread is a *rishon* or a *sheni.* [The Gemara goes on to explain the nature of the uncertainty involved here.]

[The exact *tumah* status of the bread is of import in many areas, among them: A *rishon* imparts *tumah* to any food or beverage, while a *sheni* imparts *tumah* only to *terumah* and consecrated foods (*kodashim*).]

30. *Keilim* 8:5.

31. [The Gemara assumes that the prediction that the Torah would eventually be forgotten cannot refer to laws which would later be explicitly taught in a Mishnah, for scholars of any era would surely be well versed in the laws codified therein (see *Tosafos* to *Chullin* 110b ד״ה דתנן and *Ritva MHK* ed. here; cf. *Maharshal*).]

32. Scripture teaches (see *Leviticus* 11:33 [quoted above] and *Chullin* 24b) that a *sheretz* in the airspace of an earthenware vessel such as an oven renders the oven *tamei* even if the *sheretz* is not touching the inner walls of the oven. Rav Adda thus suggests: Let us interpret this as implying that the *sheretz* is viewed as if it fills the entire airspace and is touching the whole interior of the oven, thereby transmitting *tumah* to it. It would then follow that if a *sheretz* is in an oven along with a loaf of bread, the bread should acquire first-degree *tumah* just like the oven, for the primary *tumah* of the *sheretz* is viewed as filling the space, and it thus "touches" the bread, too, so to speak (see *Rashi* here and to *Pesachim* 20a ד״ה וליחזייה).

עין משפט נר מצוה

כילת חתנים מותר לנטותה ומותר לפורקה אמר רב ששת בריה דרב אידי לא אמרן אלא שאין בגגה טפח אבל יש בגגה טפח אסורה וכי אין בגגה טפח נמי לא אמרן אלא שאין בפחות משלשה סמוך לגגה טפח אבל יש בפחות משלשה סמוך לגגה טפח אסור ולא אמרן אלא שאין בשיפועה טפח אבל יש בשיפועה טפח שפועי אהלים כאהלים דמו ולא אמרן אלא דלא נחית מפוריא טפח אבל נחית מפוריא טפח אסור ואמר רב ששת בריה דרב אידי האי סיאנא שרי והאיתמר סיאנא אסור לא קשיא הא דאית ביה טפח הא דלית ביה טפח אלא מעתה שרביב בגלימא טפח ה"נ דמיחייב אלא לא קשיא הא דמיהדק הא דלא מיהדק שלח ליה רמי בר יחזקאל לרב הונא אימא לן איזי הנך מילי מעלייתא דאמרת לן משמיה דרב תרתי בשבת וחדא בתורה שלח ליה הא דתניא גוד בכיסנא מותר לנטותה בשבת אמר רב לא שנו אלא בב' בני אדם אבל באדם אחד אסור אמר אביי וכילה אפילו בי' בני אדם אסור אי אפשר דלא מימתחא פורתא אידך מאי היא דתניא כילה שנשמטה אחת מירכותיה מותר לטלטלה שתים אסור רב אמר אפילו אחד נמי אסור גזירה שמא יתקע תורה דאמר רב עתידה תורה שתשתכח מישראל שנאמר והפלא ה' את מכותך הפלאה זו איני יודע מהו כשהוא אומר לכן הנני יוסיף להפליא את העם הזה הפלא ופלא הוי אומר הפלאה זו תורה ת"ר כשנכנסו רבותינו לכרם ביבנה אמרו עתידה תורה שתשתכח מישראל שנאמר הנה ימים באים נאם ה' אלהים והשלחתי רעב בארץ לא רעב ללחם ולא צמא למים כי אם לשמוע את דברי ה' וכתיב ונעו מים עד ים ומצפון ועד מזרח ישוטטו לבקש את דבר ה' ולא ימצאו דבר ה' זו הלכה דבר ה' זה הקץ דבר ה' זו נבואה ומאי ישוטטו לבקש את דבר ה' אמרו עתידה אשה שתטול ככר של תרומה ותחזור בבתי כנסיות ובבתי מדרשות לידע אם טמאה היא ואם טהורה היא ואין מבין אם טהורה היא ואם טמאה היא בהדיא כתיב ביה מכל האוכל אשר יאכל אלא לידע אם ראשונה היא ואם שניה היא ואין מבין הא נמי מתניתין היא כדתנן השרץ שנמצא בתנור הפת שבתוכו שניה שהתנור תחילה מסתפקא להו הא דאמר ליה רב אדא בר אהבה לרבא ליחזייה האי תנורא כמאן דמלי טומאה ותיהוי פת ראשונה א"ל לא אמרינן ליחזייה האי תנורא כמאן דמלי טומאה דתניא יכול יהו כל הכלים מיטמאין באויר כלי חרס ת"ל כל אשר בתוכו יטמא מכל האוכל אשר יאכל אוכלין מטמאין באויר כלי חרס ואין כלים מטמאין באויר כלי חרס תניא רבי שמעון בן יוחי אומר חס ושלום שתשתכח תורה מישראל שנאמר כי לא תשכח מפי זרעו אלא מה אני מקיים ישוטטו לבקש את דבר ה' ולא ימצאו שלא ימצאו הלכה

רש"י

כילת חתנים. לא דמיא לשאר כילות שאר כילות פרוסות על גבי קינוף שהיא לד' רגלים ויש לה גג דהוי אהל ושל חתנים על גבי נקליטין שאינם אלא שנים באמצעית המטה וקנה נתון עליהם והבגד נתון עליו ונופל לכאן ולכאן ואין לה גג טפח הלכך לאו אהל הוא: **בפחות מג'.** שהיא הולכת ומתפשטת למטה: **ולא אמרן אלא שאין בשיפועה טפח.** שאין כל צד וצד (ב) נפשט למטה להתרחק טפח מכנגד אמצעיתו דהיינו שאין ברחבו למטה טפחיים וכילת חתנים אינה עשויה לישן תחתיה: **אבל נחתא מפוריא טפח.** ההוא טפח הוה קיר לאהל והמטה נעשית לו גג: **סייאנא.** כובע של לבד פלטר"ן: **אסור.** לצאת בו בשבת ולקמיה מפרש ואזיל: **הא דאית ביה טפח.** שהוא מתפשט להלן מראשו טפח אסור משום אהלא: **אלא מעתה שרביב בגלימיה טפח.** הניח טליתו על ראשו כדרך שהוא מתעטף (ג) והרחיקה להלן מראשו טפח: **אלא.** טעמא לאו משום אהל הוא אלא משום שלא יגביהנו הרוח מראשו ואתי לאתויי ארבע אמות הלכך מיהדק בראשו שפיר שרי לא מיהדק אסור: **תרתי בשבת וחדא בתורה.** שהיית רגיל לומר שני דברים משמו בהלכות שבת ואחת בתורה כדלקמן: **גוד בכיסנא.** גוד ברצועותיו ומונח על מקום קבוע שלו: **מותר לנטותו בשבת.** והא דאמרן לעיל פטור אבל אסור היכא דלא הוי מתוקן בכיסנין: **בב' בני אדם.** לא מימתח ליה שפיר: **באדם אחד.** ממתח ליה שפיר שמותחו על יתד זו וקושרו בה וחוזר ומותחו על זו וקושרו בה כך פירשו רבותי וכן מצאתי בתשובת הגאונים ואיני יודע מהו: **אידך.** דשבת מאי היא: **מירכותיה.** פטפוטים שלה כעין רגלים: **שמא יתקע.** כשמחבר לה הרגל יתקענה בחוזק והוי בונה אבל (ד) (ת"ק) היכא דלא נשמטה אלא אחת לא חייש למתקע כולי האי: **הפלא ופלא.** סיפא דקרא ואבדה חכמת חכמיו: **בכרם.** על שם שהיו יושבין שורות שורות ככרם: **זו הלכה.** כדכתיב (דברים ה) [להגיד לכם] את דבר ה' דהיינו תורה: **זו נבואה.** כדכתיב (הושע א) דבר ה' אשר היה אל הושע וגו': **זה הקץ.** לא ידענא מהיכא: **בהדיא כתיב.** ותורה שבכתב הרי כתובה ומונחת יקראו ויראו: **שהתנור תחלה.** שנטמא מן האויר כדכתיב (ויקרא יא) אל תוכו והוא חזר ומטמא אוכלין שבתוכו מן האויר: **כמאן דמלי טומאה.** כשנפל השרץ באוירו דהא בלא נגיעה מטמא והלכך כמאן דמלי טומאה הוא ותהוי פת ראשונה:

תוספות

שאין בשיפועה טפח. הרבה יש תימה (ד) איך יתכן זה דא"כ למה הוא ראוי אם לכל השיפוע אין טפח ויש לפרש כגון שהסדין שפרוש על הכילה מונח על גבי קנים מרודים ולא פשטו הסדין היטב ומונח ונופל בין קנה לקנה כעין שורות דיש עכשיו בין כל קנה שיפוע ואין באותו שיפוע טפח ודוחק וי"מ שאין בשיפוע טפח בגובה י' דכשילא השיפוע טפח אין חשש עד למטה גובה י' דלא חשיב אהל כדאשכחן בפ"ק דסוכה (דף י.) דכילה כי הך מותר לישן בסוכה דאמר רב יהודה אמר שמואל מותר לישן בכילת חתנים אע"פ שיש לה גג והוא שאינה י' טפחים ואין נראה לר"י דודאי נהי דגבי סוכה לא חשיב אהל וכן לגבי ק"ש כדאיתא התם (דף י:) מיהו לגבי שבת חשיב ואסירי שהרי משמרת וביעתא וקידרא וחביתא אסירי משום אהל ולא משמע שיש בגובהן י' טפחים. מ"ר. ועוד קשה מדלקמן גבי כפיפה מצרית ובשם רבינו שמואל פי' דל"ג להאי לישנא כלל שיפועי אהלים כאהלים דמו דבסוף פ"ק דסוכה (דף יט:) מסקינן דשיפוע אהלים לאו כאהלים דמו ואי משום הא לא איריא דיש לפרש דהתם באין בשיפועו טפח והכא כשיש בשיפועו טפח:

הא דמהדק. פירש ר"ח שאינו נכפף דאז נראה כעין אהל דלא מהדק שהוא נכפף ואז אין נראה כעין אהל:

דבר ה' זה הקץ. דכתיב גבי גלות שבעים לכלות דבר ה' מפי ירמיה (עזרא א). מ"ר: ולישנא

לא ס"ד. למיהוי כמאן דמלי טומאה: **דתניא יכול יהו כל הכלים מטמאים מאויר כלי חרס.** שאם היה כלי אחר בתוכו שיטמא מחמת השרץ שבאויר הכלי או מחמת שיטמאהו אויר כלי החיצון שהוא טמא: **תלמוד לומר כל אשר בתוכו יטמא.** וסמיך ליה מכל האוכל אשר יאכל: אוכלין ומשקין שבתוכו טמאים ולא כלים שמע מינה תרתי חדא דלא אמרינן מחזי כמאן דמלי טומאה דאם כן אם כלי שטף הוא הפנימי שמטמא מגבו יהא טמא דהא לא נגע בטומאה אלא לא אמרינן מחזי כמאן דמלי טומאה ואוכלין ומשקין שבכלי הוא דמטמאי מחמת הכלי שהכלי ראשון והם שניים אבל כלים לא דהואיל דאין טומאה זו באה אלא מחמת הכלי אשמעינן האי קרא שאין כלי שאינו אב הטומאה מטמא כלי:

רבינו חננאל

מסורת הש"ס

הגהות הב"ח

גליון הש"ס

הגהות הגר"א

רב נסים גאון

תורה אור השלם

ליקוטי רש"י

taught in a Baraisa: יָכוֹל יְהוּ כָּל הַכֵּלִים מִיטַּמְּאִין בַּאֲוִיר כְּלִי חֶרֶס – YOU MIGHT THINK THAT ALL UTENSILS SHOULD CONTRACT *TUMAH* IN THE AIRSPACE OF AN EARTHENWARE VESSEL;[33] תַּלְמוּד לוֹמַר ,,כֹּל אֲשֶׁר בְּתוֹכוֹ יִטְמָא . . . מִכָּל־הָאֹכֶל אֲשֶׁר יֵאָכֵל'' – SCRIPTURE THEREFORE STATES: *WHATEVER IS WITHIN IT SHALL BECOME TAMEI,* and states in the very next verse *FROM ALL FOOD THAT IS EATEN.* אוֹכָלִין מִטַּמְּאִין בַּאֲוִיר כְּלִי חֶרֶס – The juxtaposition of these two phrases teaches that only FOODS CONTRACT *TUMAH* IN THE AIRSPACE OF AN EARTHENWARE VESSEL, וְאֵין כֵּלִים מִטַּמְּאִין בַּאֲוִיר כְּלִי חֶרֶס – BUT UTENSILS DO NOT CONTRACT *TUMAH* IN THE AIRSPACE OF AN EARTHENWARE VESSEL.[34] If utensils do not contract *tumah* in this manner, it is apparent that we do *not* view the oven as though it is full of *tumah.* Thus, the Mishnah is correct in ruling the bread as a second-degree *tumah.*

Since the Mishnah's ruling was placed in doubt by Rav Adda's question, it is possible that it is in this matter that the later-day scholars would be uncertain.[35]

The Baraisa just cited stated that the Torah would eventually be forgotten by Israel. A disputing Tannaic opinion is cited: תַּנְיָא – **It was taught in a Baraisa:** רַבִּי שִׁמְעוֹן בֶּן יוֹחַי אוֹמֵר – R' SHIMON BEN YOCHAI SAYS: חַס וְשָׁלוֹם שֶׁתִּשְׁתַּכַּח תּוֹרָה מִיִּשְׂרָאֵל – HEAVEN FORBID THAT THE TORAH WOULD BE FORGOTTEN FROM ISRAEL! שֶׁנֶּאֱמַר ,,כִּי לֹא תִשָּׁכַח מִפִּי זַרְעוֹ'' – FOR IT IS STATED:[36] *FOR IT SHALL NOT BE FORGOTTEN FROM THE MOUTH OF [THE NATION'S] OFFSPRING.* אֶלָּא מָה אֲנִי מְקַיֵּים ,,יְשׁוֹטְטוּ לְבַקֵּשׁ אֶת־דְּבַר־ה' וְלֹא יִמְצָאוּ'' – BUT HOW, then, CAN I UPHOLD Amos' prophecy:[37] *THEY SHALL WANDER TO SEEK THE WORD OF HASHEM, BUT SHALL NOT FIND IT?* שֶׁלֹּא יִמְצְאוּ – This means THAT THEY WILL NOT FIND

NOTES

33. That is, you might think that another vessel that is inside an oven with a *sheretz* should become *tamei,* in one of two ways: either (a) directly from the *sheretz* suspended in the oven's airspace, which is viewed as "filling" the entire airspace [and it should become a *rishon*]; or (b) by way of the oven's airspace which had contracted *tumah* from the *sheretz* and then imparted the *tumah* to the vessel [and it should become a *sheni*] (*Rashi*).

34. The verse's implication that only *foods* inside an oven are rendered *tamei,* not vessels, tells us that a vessel will not acquire *tumah* in either of the two ways described in the previous note. For, as explained above, vessels would become *tamei* directly from the *sheretz* hanging in the oven's airspace only if the *tumah* were viewed as though filling the oven's interior space, thus "touching" the vessel as well. The verse thus teaches that this is not so, and in fact the *tumah* within the interior space of the oven is *not* viewed as filling that space. Rather, the fact that the dead *sheretz* transmits *tumah* to the earthenware oven is a law particular to earthenware vessels, for it is only in the case of earthenware vessels that *tumah* is imparted to them through their interior space without direct contact. Any other object within their interior can acquire *tumah* only from actual contact with the earthenware vessel. See further in *Maharsha.*

As for the vessel contracting *tumah* from the oven, that too will not occur. For the vessel would become *tamei* by way of the oven only if a vessel could contract *tumah* from another vessel that is a *rishon.* By stating in the next verse that *foods* will become *tamei* in this manner, the Torah is also teaching that a vessel would *not* become *tamei,* for only an *av hatumah* can convey *tumah* to vessels; a *rishon* will not convey *tumah* to vessels, only to food or drink (*Rashi*).

35. [See *Hagahos Yavetz,* who discusses when this prophecy (which foretold the uncertainty in the matter of the loaf of *terumah*) was fulfilled.]

36. *Deuteronomy* 31:21. [*Menachem Meishiv Nefesh* notes that the final letters of these five words can be combined to spell יוֹחַאי – an allusion to R' Shimon bar Yochai, who made this statement. See there.]

37. *Amos* 8:12.

הֲלָכָה בְּרוּרָה וּמִשְׁנָה בְּרוּרָה בְּמָקוֹם אֶחָד – CLEAR HALACHAH AND CLEAR TEACHINGS IN any ONE PLACE where they shall seek.[1]

The Gemara introduces a Baraisa which discusses a cause for Jewish suffering:

תַּנְיָא – **It was taught in a Baraisa:** רַבִּי יוֹסֵי בֶּן אֱלִישָׁע אוֹמֵר – R' YOSE BEN ELISHA SAYS: אִם רָאִיתָ דּוֹר שֶׁצָּרוֹת רַבּוֹת בָּאוֹת עָלָיו – IF YOU SEE A GENERATION UPON WHICH MANY TROUBLES COME, צֵא וּבְדוֹק בְּדַיָּינֵי יִשְׂרָאֵל – GO AND EXAMINE the deeds of THE JUDGES OF ISRAEL in that generation, שֶׁכָּל פּוּרְעָנוּת שֶׁבָּאָה לָעוֹלָם – FOR ALL MISFORTUNE THAT COMES TO THE WORLD לֹא בָּאָה אֶלָּא בִּשְׁבִיל דַּיָּינֵי יִשְׂרָאֵל – COMES ONLY ON ACCOUNT OF THE JUDGES OF ISRAEL.[2] שֶׁנֶּאֱמַר ,,שִׁמְעוּ־נָא זֹאת רָאשֵׁי בֵּית יַעֲקֹב וּקְצִינֵי בֵּית יִשְׂרָאֵל – AS IT IS STATED:[3] *HEAR THIS NOW, O HEADS OF THE HOUSE OF JACOB AND OFFICERS OF THE HOUSE OF ISRAEL,* הַמְתַעֲבִים מִשְׁפָּט וְאֵת כָּל־הַיְשָׁרָה יְעַקֵּשׁוּ – *WHO DETEST JUSTICE AND TWIST ALL THAT IS STRAIGHT;* בֹּנֶה צִיּוֹן בְּדָמִים וִירוּשָׁלַםִ בְּעַוְלָה – *WHO BUILD ZION WITH BLOOD AND JERUSALEM WITH INIQUITY.* רָאשֶׁיהָ בְּשֹׁחַד יִשְׁפֹּטוּ וְכֹהֲנֶיהָ בִּמְחִיר יוֹרוּ וּנְבִיאֶיהָ בְּכֶסֶף יִקְסֹמוּ – *HER HEADS JUDGE FOR BRIBES AND HER PRIESTS ISSUE RULINGS FOR A FEE AND HER PROPHETS DIVINE FOR MONEY,* וְעַל־ה׳ יִשָּׁעֵנוּ וגו׳ ״ – *YET THEY RELY ON HASHEM* etc. *saying, "Is not Hashem in our midst? Nothing bad will befall us!"*[4] רְשָׁעִים הֵן – THEY [the leaders, priests and prophets] ARE WICKED PEOPLE, אֶלָּא שֶׁתָּלוּ בִּטְחוֹנָם בְּמִי שֶׁאָמַר וְהָיָה הָעוֹלָם – BUT THEY PLACED THEIR TRUST IN THE ONE WHO SAID, "LET THE WORLD EXIST," arrogantly assuming that He would not punish them. לְפִיכָךְ מֵבִיא הַקָּדוֹשׁ בָּרוּךְ הוּא עֲלֵיהֶן שָׁלֹשׁ פּוּרְעָנִיּוֹת – THEREFORE, GOD BRINGS UPON THEM THREE PUNISHMENTS, כְּנֶגֶד שָׁלֹשׁ עֲבֵירוֹת שֶׁבִּידָם – CORRESPONDING TO THE THREE SINS IN THEIR HANDS,[5] שֶׁנֶּאֱמַר ,,לָכֵן בִּגְלַלְכֶם צִיּוֹן שָׂדֶה תֵחָרֵשׁ וִירוּשָׁלַםִ עִיִּין תִּהְיֶה וְהַר הַבַּיִת לְבָמוֹת יָעַר״ – AS THE VERSE STATES: *THEREFORE, BECAUSE OF YOU, ZION SHALL BE PLOWED AS A FIELD, AND JERUSALEM SHALL BECOME HEAPS OF RUINS, AND THE TEMPLE MOUNT [SHALL BE] AS THE HIGH PLACES OF THE FOREST.*[6]

The Gemara further demonstrates the negative impact of a corrupt judiciary:

וְאֵין הַקָּדוֹשׁ בָּרוּךְ הוּא מַשְׁרֶה שְׁכִינָתוֹ עַל יִשְׂרָאֵל – **And the Holy One, Blessed is He, will not rest his Divine Presence on Israel** עַד שֶׁיִּכְלוּ שׁוֹפְטִים וְשׁוֹטְרִים רָעִים מִיִּשְׂרָאֵל – **until corrupt judges and officers**[7] **cease from Israel.** שֶׁנֶּאֱמַר ,,וְאָשִׁיבָה יָדִי עָלַיִךְ וְאֶצְרֹף כַּבֹּר סִיגָיִךְ וְאָסִירָה כָּל־בְּדִילָיִךְ – **As it is stated:** ***I will turn My hand against you, I will clean away your dross as with soap and I will remove all your tin.***[8] וְאָשִׁיבָה שֹׁפְטַיִךְ כְּבָרִאשֹׁנָה וְיֹעֲצַיִךְ כְּבַתְּחִלָּה וגו׳ ״ – ***And I will restore your judges as in the first place, and your advisers as in the beginning* etc.;** *afterwards you will be called a city of righteousness, a faithful city.* This implies that the Divine Presence will rest among Israel only after the corrupt judiciary is removed and righteous judges are installed in its place.[9]

The Gemara cites a teaching based on the verse that follows the verse just cited:

אָמַר עוּלָּא – **Ulla said:** אֵין יְרוּשָׁלַיִם נִפְדָּה אֶלָּא בִּצְדָקָה – **Jerusalem**[10] **will not be redeemed except through charity,**[11] שֶׁנֶּאֱמַר ,,צִיּוֹן בְּמִשְׁפָּט תִּפָּדֶה וְשָׁבֶיהָ בִּצְדָקָה״ – **as it is stated:** ***Zion shall be redeemed through justice, and her returnees through charity.***[12]

NOTES

1. That is, there will not be a consensus of opinion about the reasons for many halachic rulings among Torah Sages, wherever they may be found, resulting in constant halachic disputes (*Rashi*, *Maharsha*; see also *Hagahos Yavetz*). "Clear halachah" refers to the reasonings behind the Mishnah's rulings, while "clear teachings" refers to the accurate text of the Mishnah itself. It may well be that this situation is also implied in the verse in *Deuteronomy*, for the root *haflaah* often connotes "separation" (see, for example, *Exodus* 9:4). Here as well, the extraordinary suffering visited on the Jews will come in the form of separation, i.e. halachic dispute, between Torah scholars (*Ben Yehoyada*).

In truth, this punishment carried with it a hidden benefit to the Jews, for the many halachic disputes force the Jews to toil ever harder to clarify the halachah, giving them the opportunity to earn the great reward such toil brings. Additionally, the disputes often force them to adopt stringencies in cases of doubt, which would serve them in good stead before the Heavenly Court (*Ben Yehoyada* ibid.).

2. Under normal circumstances, God's mercy protects the Jews from the full force of His punishment [even if they are unworthy]. But that is true only when His *Shechinah* (Divine Presence) is in their midst, such as when judges adjudicate properly, for then Scripture testifies that He rests among us (see below, note 9). When judges are corrupt and adjudge improperly, however, His Merciful Presence departs and we are left to His strict justice (*Iyun Yaakov;* see also *Maharal* in *Chidushei Aggados;* see also *Yad David [Basra]* and *Cheifetz Hashem*).

3. *Micah* 3:9-11.

4. For, as noted, the wicked leaders assumed that God was among them and His Presence would guarantee their safety from retribution for their sins (*Iyun Yaakov*).

5. The three sins were: (a) *Her heads judge for bribes*, (b) *her priests issue rulings for a fee*, and (c) *her prophets divine for money* (*Rashi*). [Thus, the end of the verse expounds upon the description of the corrupt heads and officers (*who detest justice and twist* etc.) by specifically stating *how* they do so.]

6. Ibid v. 12.

Maharal (in *Nesiv HaDin* ch. 2) explains that the three punishments – (a) *Zion shall be plowed as a field,* (b) *Jerusalem shall become heaps of ruins,* and (c) *the Temple Mount [shall be] as the high places of the forest,* – correspond measure for measure with the three sins, as follows: Their sin in the matter of adjudication (*her heads judge for bribes*) was punished with the devastation of the Temple Mount, the seat of the Sanhedrin, which was the nation's Highest Court. Their sin in the matter of Torah rulings (*her priests issue rulings for a fee*) was punished with the ruination of Jerusalem, which is the source of Torah wisdom. And their sin in the matter of prophecy (*her prophets divine for money*) was punished with the destruction of Zion, i.e. the Holy Temple, from whence the Divine Presence and prophecy emanated. See also *Chasam Sofer*.

7. Officials who enforce the law at the bidding of the judges (see *Rashi* to *Deuteronomy* 16:18 ד״ה ושוטרים).

8. *Isaiah* 1:25,26. [Tin is removed from silver that is being purified.]

9. *Rashi*. The resting of the Divine Presence is dependent on the presence of qualified judges, as it states (*Psalms* 82:1): *God stands among the Godly congregation,* which refers to the courts of law (*Maharal, Chidushei Aggados*).

[The first verse cited by the Gemara – *I will clean away your dross* etc. – also refers to the removal of corrupt judges, as will be explained by the Gemara below.]

10. The text possessed by the *Rambam* (*Hil. Matnos Aniyim* 10:1) and *Tur* (*Yoreh Deah* 247:1) reads יִשְׂרָאֵל, *Israel*, rather than יְרוּשָׁלַיִם, *Jerusalem* (see note 12).

11. This means that Jerusalem will be rebuilt in the merit of the mitzvah of charity (*Metzudos* to *Isaiah* 1:27; see also *Bava Basra* 10a). [Alternatively, it means that God will employ the attribute of רַחֲמִים, *mercy* or *charity* (as opposed to דִּין, *justice*), to allow for the rebuilding of Jerusalem.]

12. *Isaiah* 1:27.

Many commentators raise the following difficulty: The verse states that Zion [Jerusalem] itself will be redeemed with justice (only its returnees will be redeemed with charity). How, then, can the Gemara infer from it that Jerusalem itself will be redeemed with charity? See *Maharsha* to *Sanhedrin* 98a for his solution to this difficulty; see also *Ben Yehoyada* here and to *Bava Basra* ibid.; see also *Haggadah Simchas Yaabetz* by *R' David Cohen*, pp. 143-4. [Note that this problem does not arise according to the alternative text quoted in note 10.]

הלכה ברורה ומשנה ברורה במקום אחד: תניא רבי יוסי בן אלישע אומר אם ראית דור שצרות רבות באות עליו צא ובדוק בדייני ישראל [א] שכל פורענות שבאה לעולם לא באה אלא בשביל דייני ישראל שנאמר [א] שמעו נא זאת ראשי בית יעקב וקציני בית ישראל המתעבים משפט ואת כל הישרה יעקשו בונה ציון בדמים וירושלים בעולה ראשיה בשוחד ישפטו וכהניה במחיר יורו ונביאיה בכסף יקסומו ועל ה' ישענו וגו' [ב] רשעים הן אלא שתלו בטחונם במי שאמר והיה העולם לפיכך מביא הקב"ה עליהן ג' פורעניות כנגד ג' עבירות שבידם שנאמר [ב] לכן בגללכם ציון שדה תחרש וירושלים עיין תהיה והר הבית לבמות יער *ואין הקב"ה משרה שכינתו על ישראל עד שיכלו שופטים ושוטרים רעים מישראל שנאמר [ג] ואשיבה ידי עליך ואצרוף כבור סיגיך ואסירה כל בדיליך ואשיבה שופטיך כבראשונה ויועציך כבתחלה וגו' [ג] אמר עולא [ד] אין [ד] ירושלים נפדה אלא בצדקה שנאמר [ד] ציון במשפט תפדה ושביה בצדקה אמר רב פפא אי בטלי יהירי בטלי אמגושי אי בטלי דייני בטלי [ה] גזירפטי אי בטלי יהירי בטלי אמגושי דכתיב ואצרוף כבור סיגיך אי בטלי דייני בטלי גזירפטי דכתיב [ה] הסיר ה' משפטיך פנה אויבך אמר רבי מלאי משום ר"א בר' שמעון מ"ד [ו] שבר ה' מטה רשעים שבט מושלים שבר ה' מטה רשעים אלו הדיינין שנעשו מקל לחזניהם שבט מושלים אלו ת"ח שבמשפחות הדיינין מר זוטרא אמר אלו תלמידי חכמים שמלמדים הלכות ציבור לדייני בור אמר ר"א בן מלאי משום ר"ל מאי דכתיב [ז] כי כפיכם נגואלו בדם ואצבעותיכם בעון שפתותיכם דברו שקר לשונכם עולה תהגה כי כפיכם נגואלו בדם אלו הדיינין ואצבעותיכם בעון אלו סופרי הדיינין שפתותיכם דברו שקר אלו עורכי הדיינין לשונכם עולה תהגה אלו בעלי דינין ואמר רבי מלאי משום ר' יצחק מגדלאה מיום שפירש יוסף מאחיו לא טעם טעם יין דכתיב [ח] ולקדקד נזיר אחיו ר' יוסי בר' חנינא אמר אף הן לא טעמו טעם יין דכתיב [ט] וישתו וישכרו עמו מכלל דעד האידנא לא (הוה שיכרות) ואידך שיכרות הוא דלא הוה שתיה מיהא הוה ואמר רבי מלאי בשכר [י] וראך ושמח בלבו זכה לחשן המשפט על לבו: שלחו ליה בני בשכר ללוי כילה מהו כשותא בכרמא מהו מת בי"ט מהו אדאזיל נח נפשיה דלוי אמר שמואל לרב מנשיא אי חכימת שלח להו כילה חזרנו על כל צידי כילה ולא מצינו לה צד היתר ולישלח להו כדרמי בר יחזקאל לפי שאינן בני תורה כשותא בכרמא עירבובא ולישלח להו כדר"ט דתניא [ו] כישות ר' טרפון אומר אין כלאים בכרם וחכמים אומרים כלאים בכרם וקי"ל [ז] כל המיקל בארץ הלכה כמותו בחו"ל לפי שאינן בני תורה מכריז רב האי מאן דבעי למיזרע כשותא בכרמא ליזרע רב עמרם חסידא מנגיד עילויה רב משרשיא יהיב ליה פרוטה לתינוק נכרי וזרע ליה וליתן ליה לתינוק ישראל אתי למיסרך וליתן ליה לגדול נכרי אתי לאיחלופי בישראל מת שלח להו מת לא יתעסקו ביה לא יהודאין ולא ארמאין לא ביום טוב ראשון ולא ביום טוב שני איני והאמר רבי יהודה בר שילת אמר רבי אסי עובדא הוה בבי כנישתא דמעון ביום טוב הסמוך לשבת ולא

רש"י

הלכה ברורה. בטעמים שלא יהא בה מחלוקת: **ג' עבירות.** בשחד ישפוטו במחיר יורו ונביאיה בכסף יקסמו: **ג' פורעניות.** שדה תחרש עיין תהיה ולבמות יער: **ויועציך כבתחלה.** ואחר כך יקרא לך עיר הצדק לשרות בה שכינה: **אי בטלי יהירי.** ישראל המתייהרים בבלורית ובמלבושי יהירות כפרסים הללו: **בטלי אמגושי.** יבטלו מסיתים ומדיחים המשניאים אותנו: **סיגיך.** הם גסי הרוח שמגדלין עצמן לשון ישגה מאד (איוב ח) ואח"כ ואסירה כל בדיליך אלו אותם המבדילים שונאי ישראל מן הקב"ה בשקריהם ובפחזותם: **בטלי דייני.** רשעים מישראל שמטין דין: **בטלי.** מעל ישראל: **גזירפטי.** נוגשי שוטרי עובדי כוכבים: **שנעשו מקל לחזניהם.** לשמשיהן נותנין יד והווין להן לחוזק לומר לא אהיה שליח ואזמין את פלוני לב"ד אם לא תרבה שכר ואחר פסק דין לא ארדנו ליכנס למשכנו: **שבט מושלים.** מקל אגרופין של מושלים היינו דיינים רשעים שת"ח שבמשפחותם להם למקל ולאגרוף שעל ידיהם היו מעמידין אותן ומחפין עליהם ועושין סניגרון לדבריהם: **לדייני בור.** שבהבטחת אותן ת"ח מעמידין דייני בור לדון את כל הבא והרבה דינין שאין נמלכים בהן ומטין אותן: **כפיכם נגואלו בדם אלו הדיינין.** שכפיהן פשוטין לקבל שוחד ומטין את הדין ונוטלין ממון מן הבעלים שלא כדין ונותנו לשכנגדו והרי הוא כנוטל נשמתו: **סופרי הדיינין.** שכותבין שטרות של רמיה: **עורכי הדיינין.** מלמדין את בעלי דינין לטעון: **עמו.** מכלל דעד השתא לא: **זכה לחשן המשפט.** שכנגד הלב שהיה גדול ממנו וקודם למשה נגלית שכינה על אהרן כדכתיב (שמואל א ב) הנגלה נגליתי אל בית אביך ונאמרה לו נבואה של מצרים הכתובה ביחזקאל (כ) עד וימרו בי ואעפ"כ לא נתקנא בו בזאת: **בני בשכר.** שם מקום: **כילה מהו.** לנטותה בשבת: **כשותא.** הימלון שגדל על ההגא מהו בכרמא ירק הוא וכלאים בכרם או אילן הוא ואינו כלאים בכרם: **ולישלח להו.** לצד היתר בה: **כדרמי בר יחזקאל.** כרך עליה חוט או משיחה: **ומשני לפי שאינן בני תורה.** ומקילי טפי: **עירבובא.** כלאים: **וקי"ל.** בברכות בפרק כילד גבי ערלה וה"ה לכלאים שאף היא מצוה התלויה בארץ ואינה נוהגת מן התורה אלא בארץ: **יהיב פרוטה לתינוק נכרי.** קסבר בחוץ לארץ שרי ומיהו כל כמה דאפשר משני שלא ילמדו להקל: ולא

תוספות

ולישלח להו כר"ט. הא לא פריך לישלח להו כר' יאשיה דאמר אינו חייב עד שיזרע חטה ושעורה וחרצן במפולת יד דשמא הם לא שאלו כשותא בכרמא מהו אלא היכא שעשה כדין ליאסור כלאים ג' מינים כאחד ועוד שמא לא ס"ל כר' יאשיה ואע"ג דקי"ל כר' יאשיה בספ"ק דקדושין (דף לט.) א"ל לא נהריתו [^ס לא] קי"ל כר' יאשיה ואמר נמי בברכות פרק מי שמתו (דף כב.) נהוג עלמא כתלת סבי כר' אילעי בראשית הגז כרבי יאשיה בכלאים כר' יהודה בן בתירא בדברי תורה מיהו י"ל שלא היו סבורין כן דהא קאמר נמי נהוג כרבי יהודה בדברי תורה ואפ"ה פליגי עליה אמוראי טובא בשמעתא דהתם וקאמר נמי כרבי אילעי בראשית הגז דאמר אינו נוהג אלא בארץ ואפ"ה אמרינן בחולין בשילהי פ' הזרוע (דף קלו:) אמר רב חסדא האי טבחא דלא מפריש מתנתא ליהוי בשמתא דה' אלהי ישראל ואמר נמי דרבא קנים אטמא ואפילו רב נחמן גופיה דאמר נהוג עלמא כתלת סבי אמר התם דקנים גלימא וא"ת נהי דלא ס"ל כר' יאשיה מ"מ לישלח להו כרבי יאשיה דכל המיקל בארץ הלכה כמותו בחו"ל וי"ל דלא שייך למימר הכי אלא במין של איסור דהמתירו חושבו מין היתר בארץ הלכה כמותו בחו"ל אבל בדבר שאינו תלוי אלא בזריעה חטה ושעורה וחרצן במפולת יד בהא לא אמר הלכה כמותו בחו"ל. מ"ר:

רב עמרם חסידא מנגיד עלה רב משרשיא יהיב ליה פרוטה לנכרי כו'. קשיא לי אמאי הא אמרינן לעיל דהלכה כר"ט דמיקל בחו"ל וצריך לומר דבמקומם לא היו בני תורה:

וליתן ליה לתינוק ישראל. אומר רבי שקבלה הוא בידינו שזה המקשה רב אחא בר יעקב והיינו הא דאמר בעירובין בשילהי בכל מערבין (דף מ: ושם) גבי ברכת זמן על הכוס ביוה"כ דמפרש התם דלא אפשר דהיכי ליעביד כו' ליתביה לתינוק לית הלכתא כרב אחא בר יעקב דילמא אתי למיסרך ולא מלינו במקום אחר דאית ליה לרב אחא האי סברא וי"מ דהוא ההוא דפ' בתרא דנדה (דף סז:) דאתקין ביממא דתמניא משום גנבי ולא חיישינן לסרך בתה במקום צורך ולא נהירא דמאי שנא דנקיט טפי רב אחא בר יעקב מכל שאר אמוראי דהתם ועל ההיא דהתם אומר ר"ת שמותר ליתן לתינוק לשתות כוס של ברכה כי מיקלע מילה ביוה"כ ולא חיישינן דילמא אתי למיסרך כיון שאין זה מנהג [בקבוע] ולא דמי לכוס דיוה"כ דאי הוו יהבי ליה אתי למיסרך אף כשיהיה גדול כיון שעושין מנהג לשתות בכל שנה ושנה ביוה"כ:

י"ט

עין משפט נר מצוה

טו א מיי' פכ"ג מהל' סנהדרין הלכה ט סמג לאוין רו טוש"ע ח"מ סי' ט סעיף ג:

טז ב מיי' פ"ו מהל' מתנות עניים הלכה א סמג עשין קסב טוש"ע י"ד סי' רמז:

רבינו חננאל

ותהרי פת ראשונה הכא הוא מפורש בפסחים בסוף פ"א: והא שהשיב רב מנשיא לבני בי בשכר על הכילה ועל הכשות בכרם ועל המת ביו"ט כולן לאיסור לפי שאינן בני תורה. מהא שמעינן שאפילו דברים המותרים כגון אלו וכדומה להן המסורין לעם הארץ אין אדם רשאי להורות להן להתיר אלא יחמיר עליהן:

תורה אור השלם

א) שמעו נא זאת ראשי בית יעקב וקציני בית ישראל המתעבים משפט ואת כל הישרה יעקשו: בנה ציון בדמים וירושלים בעולה: ראשיה בשחד ישפטו וכהניה במחיר יורו ונביאיה בכסף יקסמו ועל יי ישענו לאמר הלוא יי בקרבנו לא תבוא עלינו רעה: [מיכה ג, ט-יא]

ב) לכן בגללכם ציון שדה תחרש וירושלים עיין תהיה והר הבית לבמות יער: [מיכה ג, יב]

ג) ואשיבה ידי עליך ואצרף כבר סיגיך ואסירה כל בדיליך: ואשיבה שפטיך כבראשנה ויעציך כבתחלה אחרי כן יקרא לך עיר הצדק קריה נאמנה: [ישעיה א, כה-כו]

ד) ציון במשפט תפדה ושביה בצדקה: [ישעיה א, כז]

ה) הסיר יי משפטיך פנה איבך מלך ישראל יי בקרבך לא תיראי רע עוד: [צפניה ג, טו]

ו) שבר יי מטה רשעים שבט משלים: [ישעיה יד, ה]

ז) כי כפיכם נגאלו בדם ואצבעותיכם בעון שפתותיכם דברו שקר לשונכם עולה תהגה: [ישעיה נט, ג]

ח) ברכת אביך גברו על ברכת הורי עד תאות גבעת עולם תהיין לראש יוסף ולקדקד נזיר אחיו: [בראשית מט, כו]

ט) וישא משאת מאת פניו אלהם ותרב משאת בנימן ממשאת כלם חמש ידות וישתו וישכרו עמו: [בראשית מג, לד]

י) ויחר אף יי במשה ויאמר הלא אהרן אחיך הלוי ידעתי כי דבר ידבר הוא וגם הנה הוא יצא לקראתך וראך ושמח בלבו: [שמות ד, יד]

מסורת הש"ס

א) [יבמות סג. ע"ש ב"ב ח. ע"ש], ב) [יומא ט:], ג) סנהדרין צח., ד) [נ"ל ישראל וכ"א ברמב"ם ובטור וע"ע מ"ש על הגליון סנהדרין צח.], ה) [ג' הערוך ערך גז ז' גאזי דפאפי פי' קריסי וסוטרי רשעים וכערך יהיר גרס גזירפטי פי' רשעים], ו) [תוספ' סוף פרק ג דכלאים], ז) ברכות לו., ח) [ע"ב בהרש"ש והריטב"א מתקן].

ליקוטי רש"י

לבן הבנוי. הוא אשר יוסיף להפילה פלא ותוסף על פלא כיסוי על כסוי אותם על אותם ומהו הפלא ופלא ואבדה חכמת חכמיו [ישעיה כט, יד]. **כשנכנסו רבותינו לכרם ביבנה.** כשנכנסו לכרם ביבנה והעידו כל אחד ואחד על אותו שבידו [לעיל עז.]. **לכרם.** על שם שהיו יושבים שורות שורות ככרם זה הנטוע שורות שורות [ברכות כג.]. זה בית המדרש שיושבין שורות שורות כך מפורש בירושלמי בברכות [לעיל לג:]. **דבר ה' זו נבואה.** שמפסקת מכס רוח הקדש [עמוס ח, יא]. **כל האוכל אשר יאכל.** מוסב על אשר בתוכו יטמא כל האוכל אשר יאכל אשר יבא עליו מים והוא בתוך כלי חרס טמא וכל משקה אשר ישתה בכל כלי והוא בתוך כלי חרס טמא [ויקרא יא, לג]. **השרץ שנמצא בתנור.** ולא נגע בפת ולא בתנור שאין כלי טומאה מטמא כלי חרס אלא מאוירו... **ואין כלים מטמאין מאויר כלי חרס.**

Having mentioned the elimination of corrupt judges, the Gemara elaborates upon this point:

אָמַר רַב פָּפָּא – **Rav Pappa said:** אִי בָּטְלֵי יְהִירֵי בָּטְלֵי אַמְגוּשֵׁי – **If the arrogant**[13] **disappear, the** ***amgushei***[14] **will disappear.** אִי בָּטְלֵי דַיָּינֵי בָּטְלֵי גְזִירְפָּטֵי – **If the** corrupt **judges disappear, the** ***gazirpatei***[15] **will disappear.**[16]

The Gemara cites Scriptural allusions for these teachings:

אִי בָּטְלֵי יְהִירֵי בָּטְלֵי אַמְגוּשֵׁי – **If the arrogant disappear, the** ***amgushei*** **will disappear,** דִּכְתִיב ,,וְאֶצְרֹף כַּבֹּר סִיגָיִךְ" – **as it is written:** ***I will clean away your dross as with soap,*** *and I will remove all your tin.*[17] אִי בָּטְלֵי דַיָּינֵי בָּטְלֵי גְזִירְפָּטֵי – **If the judges disappear, the** ***gazirpatei*** **will disappear,** דִּכְתִיב ,,הֵסִיר ה' מִשְׁפָּטַיִךְ פִּנָּה אֹיְבֵךְ" – **as it is written:** ***God had removed your judgments; He has turned away your enemy.***[18]

The Gemara cites further verses referring to the tragedy of a corrupt judiciary:

אָמַר רַבִּי מַלַּאי מִשּׁוּם רַבִּי אֶלְעָזָר בְּרַבִּי שִׁמְעוֹן – **R' Mallai said in the name of R' Elazar the son of R' Shimon:** מַאי דִּכְתִיב ,,שָׁבַר ה' מַטֵּה רְשָׁעִים שֵׁבֶט מֹשְׁלִים" – **What is meant by that which is written:**[19] ***Hashem has broken the staff of the wicked, the rod of the rulers?*** ,,שָׁבַר ה' מַטֵּה רְשָׁעִים" אֵלּוּ הַדַּיָּינִין שֶׁנַּעֲשׂוּ מַקֵּל לְחַזָּנֵיהֶם – ***Hashem has broken the staff of the wicked*** **– these are the judges who become a stick in** the hands of **their officers.**[20] ,,שֵׁבֶט מֹשְׁלִים" אֵלּוּ תַּלְמִידֵי חֲכָמִים שֶׁבְּמִשְׁפְּחוֹת הַדַּיָּינִין – ***The rod of the rulers,*** **these are the Torah scholars in the** extended **families of the** corrupt **judges.**[21]

Another explanation of this last phrase:

מַר זוּטְרָא אָמַר – **Mar Zutra said:** אֵלּוּ תַּלְמִידֵי חֲכָמִים שֶׁמְּלַמְּדִים הִלְכוֹת צִיבּוּר לְדַיָּינֵי בּוּר – **These are Torah scholars who teach general laws to unlearned judges,** who in turn adjudge incorrectly.[22]

Further verses referring to the tragedy of a corrupt judiciary:

אָמַר רַבִּי אֱלִיעֶזֶר בֶּן מַלַּאי מִשּׁוּם רֵישׁ לָקִישׁ – **R' Eliezer ben Mallai said in the name of Reish Lakish:** מַאי דִּכְתִיב ,,כִּי כַפֵּיכֶם נְגֹאֲלוּ בַדָּם וְאֶצְבְּעוֹתֵיכֶם בֶּעָוֹן – **What is** meant by **that which is written:**[23] ***For your hands are sullied with blood, and your fingers with sin;*** שִׂפְתוֹתֵיכֶם דִּבְּרוּ־שֶׁקֶר לְשׁוֹנְכֶם עַוְלָה תֶהְגֶּה" – ***your lips have spoken lies and your tongue mutters wickedness?***

,,כִּי כַפֵּיכֶם נְגֹאֲלוּ בַדָּם" אֵלּוּ הַדַּיָּינִין – ***For your hands are sullied with blood*** **– these are corrupt judges.**[24] ,,וְאֶצְבְּעוֹתֵיכֶם בֶּעָוֹן" אֵלּוּ סוֹפְרֵי הַדַּיָּינִין – ***And your fingers with sin*** **– these are the court scribes.**[25] ,,שִׂפְתוֹתֵיכֶם דִּבְּרוּ־שֶׁקֶר" אֵלּוּ עוֹרְכֵי הַדַּיָּינִין – ***Your lips have spoken lies*** **– these are the lawyers,** ,,לְשׁוֹנְכֶם עַוְלָה תֶהְגֶּה" אֵלּוּ בַּעֲלֵי דִינִין – ***And your tongue mutters wickedness*** **– these are the litigants.**[26]

Having cited one teaching of R' Mallai (and one of his son, R' Eliezer), the Gemara now cites two unrelated teachings issued by him:

וְאָמַר רַבִּי מַלַּאי מִשּׁוּם רַבִּי יִצְחָק מִגְדְּלָאָה – **And R' Mallai said in the name of R' Yitzchak Migdelaah:** מִיּוֹם שֶׁפֵּירַשׁ יוֹסֵף מֵאֶחָיו לֹא טָעַם טַעַם יַיִן – **From the day that Joseph was separated from his brothers, he did not drink wine,** דִּכְתִיב ,,וּלְקָדְקֹד נְזִיר אֶחָיו" – **as it is written:** ***And upon the head of the exile*** *(nezir)* ***from his brothers.***[27]

רַבִּי יוֹסֵי בְּרַבִּי חֲנִינָא אָמַר – **R' Yose the son of R' Chanina said:** אַף הֵן לֹא טָעֲמוּ טַעַם יַיִן – **They** [Joseph's brothers] **too did not drink wine** from the day they separated from him, דִּכְתִיב ,,וַיִּשְׁתּוּ וַיִּשְׁכְּרוּ עִמּוֹ" – **as it is stated:**[28] ***And they drank and became intoxicated with him.*** מִכְּלָל דְּעַד הָאִידָּנָא לֹא (הוה שיכרות) – **This** word *with him* **implies that until that time they did not** drink wine.[29]

NOTES

13. Arrogant people who sport long locks of hair in the manner of the idolaters (see *Rashi* to *Bava Kamma* 83a ד"ה המספר קומי and ד"ה מדרכי האמורי, and *Rashi* to *Avodah Zarah* 8a ד"ה בלוריתו), and wear grandiose clothing (*Rashi*; cf. *Yad Ramah* and *Maharsha* to *Sanhedrin* 98a).

14. Heretics who incite others to idolatry, causing us to be hated [before God] (see *Rashi* here and above, 75a ד"ה וחד; see Gemara there, which cites a view that they were sorcerers). [Some relate the *amgushei* to the magi – a priestly caste in ancient Persia.]

15. Idolatrous court officers who used physical force against the Jews (*Rashi*; cf. *Ritva MHK* ed.).

16. If there are no corrupt Jewish judges who rule incorrectly, there will be no hostile gentile court officials forcing the Jews to follow their edicts. This is a manifestation of מִדָּה כְּנֶגֶד מִדָּה, *measure for measure* – the deed is rewarded or punished in a manner that resembles and is commensurate with it (*Maharsha* to *Sanhedrin* ibid.). [This applies also to the next two groups mentioned in the Gemara – the arrogant and the *amgushei.*]

17. In Hebrew, the phonetically identical letters ס and שׂ are interchangeable, so that the word סִיגָיִךְ is read שָׂגָיִךְ, from the root שָׂגִי, meaning "big" (see, for example *Job* 8:7). [In Aramaic, as well, סַגִּי means "big."] Thus סִיגָיִךְ (*your dross*) is interpreted as referring to arrogant *people who make themselves great.* The verse then continues: וְאָסִירָה כָּל־בְּדִילָיִךְ. Now, בְּדִיל (*tin*) is similar to מוּבְדָּל, *separate,* and alludes to the *amgushei*, who *separate* Jews from their God by inciting them to idolatry with their lies and deception. The verse thus means: *When I clean away your arrogant ones, I will remove all the separatists* [i.e. the *amgushei*] (*Rashi*; see also *Ritva MHK* ed.).

18. *Zephaniah* 3:15. מִשְׁפָּטַיִךְ, *your judgments,* resembles שֹׁפְטַיִךְ, *your judges*. אֹיְבֵךְ, *your enemy,* signifies the *gazirpatei* (*Rashi* to *Sanhedrin* ibid.). Hence, the verse is interpreted: *When Hashem removes your* [corrupt] *judges, He will remove the gazirpatei*.

19. *Isaiah* 14:5.

20. A court officer might threaten the abandonment of his duties, crippling the court's effectiveness, if certain demands, such as a raise in his salary, are not met. The verse refers to judges who improperly accede to such demands, thereby becoming no more than tools in the hands of their corrupt officers (see *Rashi*).

21. The "rulers" refers to wicked judges whose family members, who are Torah scholars, are their "rods," i.e. their support. For the Torah scholars see to their appointment to the judiciary, and later cover up their mistakes and defend their decisions (*Rashi*).

22. An ignoramus might be appointed as a judge on the recommendation of a Torah scholar who taught him some general laws [believing that the judge would consult with the scholar before rendering decisions]. In fact, however, the judge will fail to do so, and as a result he will render incorrect decisions (*Rashi*, *Ritva MHK* ed.).

[Alternatively, the Torah scholars would teach an ignoramus the laws concerning interacting with the public, certainly a necessity for a judge. But they would not teach them the Torah laws upon which their rulings must be based (*Maharal*).]

23. Ibid. 59:3.

24. A corrupt judge who take a bribe will then rule in the favor of his benefactor, wrongly taking money away from the other disputant, which is akin to killing him (see *Bava Kamma* 119a). Thus, his hands (which took the bribe) are full of the blood of the wrongly obligated disputant (*Rashi*; see *Maharsha*).

25. These are court scribes who will prepare false documents [for a fee] (*Rashi*).

26. Lawyers will train their clients to [lie when stating their] claim (*Rashi*; see *Ritva MHK* ed.).

27. *Genesis* 49:26. While the word *nezir* in this verse is generally rendered "*exiled*" (i.e. separated) from his brothers (see *Rashi* and *Onkelos* there), R' Mallai expounds it as alluding to his adopting the practice of a Nazirite, who is prohibited from drinking wine (see *Numbers* ch. 6). See *Maharal* at length.

28. Ibid. 43:34.

29. That is, the word עִמּוֹ, *with him,* modifies the previous statement that they drank, implying that it was only now, with Joseph, that they drank, and not earlier.

This view maintains that all the brothers refrained from drinking

מסורת הש"ס

א) [יבמות סג. ע"ש ב"ב ח. ע"ש], ב) [יומא ט:], ג) סנהדרין לח., ד) [ל"ל ישראל וכ"א ברמב"ם ובטור וע"ע מ"ש על הגליון סנהדרין לח.], ה) [גיר' הערוך ערך גז ז' גאזי דפאטי פי' סריסי ושוטרי השרים ובערך יהיר גרס גזירפטי פי' רשעים], ו) [תוספ' סוף פרק ג דכלאים], ז) ברכות לו., ח) כ"ג הרש"ל והריעב"ץ מחקו.

עין משפט נר מצוה

טו א מיי' פכ"ג מהל' סנהדרין הלכה ט סמג לאוין רז טוש"ע ח"מ סי' ח סעיף ב:

טז ב מיי' פ"ו מהל' מתנות עניים הלכה א סמג עשין קסב טוש"ע י"ד סי' רמו:

רבינו חננאל

ותהדר פת ראשונה הכא הוא מפורש בפסחים בסוף פ"א: והא שהשיב רב מנשיא לבני בי בשכר על הכילה ועל הכשות בכרם ועל המת ביו"ט כולן לאיסור לפי שאינן בני תורה. מהא שמעינן שאפילו דברים המותרים כגון אלו וכדומה להן המסורין לעם הארץ אין אדם רשאי להורות להן להיתר אלא יחמיר עליהן:

הלכה ברורה ומשנה ברורה במקום אחד: תניא רבי יוסי בן אלישע אומר אם ראית דור שצרות רבות באות עליו צא ובדוק בדייני ישראל שכל פורענות שבאה לעולם לא באה אלא בשביל דייני ישראל שנאמר א) שמעו נא זאת ראשי בית יעקב וקציני בית ישראל המתעבים משפט ואת כל הישרה יעקשו בונה ציון בדמים וירושלים בעולה ראשיה בשוחד ישפטו וכהניה במחיר יורו ונביאיה בכסף יקסמו ועל ה' ישענו וגו' רשעים הן אלא שתלו בטחונם במי שאמר והיה העולם לפיכך מביא הקב"ה עליהן ג' פורעניות כנגד ג' עבירות שבידם שנאמר ב) לכן בגללכם ציון שדה תחרש וירושלים עיין תהיה והר הבית לבמות יער ואין הקב"ה משרה שכינתו על ישראל עד שיכלו שופטים ושוטרים רעים מישראל שנאמר ג) ואשיבה ידי עליך ואצרוף כבור סיגיך ואסירה כל בדיליך ואשיבה שופטיך כבראשונה ויועציך כבתחלה וגו' אמר עולא אין ירושלים נפדה אלא בצדקה שנאמר ד) ציון במשפט תפדה ושביה בצדקה אמר רב פפא אי בטלי יהירי בטלי אמגושי אי בטלי דייני בטלי גזירפטי אי בטלי יהירי בטלי אמגושי דכתיב ואצרוף כבור סיגיך אי בטלי דייני בטלי גזירפטי דכתיב ה) הסיר ה' משפטיך פנה אויבך אמר רבי מלאי משום ר"א בר' שמעון מ"ד ו) שבר ה' מטה רשעים שבט מושלים שבר ה' מטה רשעים אלו הדיינין שנעשו מקל לחזניהם שבט מושלים אלו ת"ח שבמשפחות הדיינין מר זוטרא אמר אלו תלמידי חכמים שמלמדים הלכות ציבור לדייני בור אמר ר"א בן מלאי משום ר"ל מאי דכתיב ז) כי כפיכם נגואלו בדם ואצבעותיכם בעון שפתותיכם דברו שקר לשונכם עולה תהגה כי כפיכם נגואלו בדם אלו הדיינין ואצבעותיכם בעון אלו סופרי הדיינין שפתותיכם דברו שקר אלו עורכי הדיינין לשונכם עולה תהגה אלו בעלי דינין ואמר רבי מלאי משום ר' יצחק מגדלאה מיום שפירש יוסף מאחיו לא טעם טעם יין דכתיב ח) ולקדקד נזיר אחיו ר' יוסי בר' חנינא אמר אף הן לא טעמו טעם יין דכתיב ט) וישתו וישכרו עמו מכלל דעד האידנא לא (הוה שיכרות) ואידך שיכרות הוא דלא הוה שתיה מיהא הוה ואמר רבי מלאי בשכר י) וראך ושמח בלבו זכה לחשן המשפט על לבו: שלחו ליה בני בשכר ללוי כילה מהו כשותא בכרמא מהו מת בי"ט מהו אדאזיל נח נפשיה דלוי אמר שמואל לרב מנשיא אי חכימת שלח להו כילה חזרנו על כל צידי כילה ולא מצינו לה צד היתר ולישלח להו כדרמי בר יחזקאל לפי שאינן בני תורה כשותא בכרמא עירובא ולישלח להו כדר"ט דתניא כישות ר' טרפון אומר אין כלאים בכרם וחכמים אומרים כלאים בכרם וקי"ל כל המיקל בארץ הלכה כמותו בחו"ל לפי שאינן בני תורה מכריז רב האי מאן דבעי למיזרע כשותא בכרמא ליזרע רב עמרם חסידא מנגיד עילויה רב משרשיא יהיב ליה פרוטה לתינוק נכרי וזרע ליה וליתן ליה לתינוק ישראל אתי למיסרך וליתן ליה לגדול נכרי אתי לאיחלופי בישראל מת שלח להו מת לא יתעסקו ביה לא יהודאין ולא ארמאין לא ביום טוב ראשון ולא ביום טוב שני איני והאמר רבי יהודה בר שילת אמר רבי אסי עובדא הוה בבי כנישתא דמעון ביום טוב הסמוך לשבת

ולא

רש"י

הלכה ברורה. בטעמים שלא יהא בה מחלוקת: ג' עבירות. בשחד ישפטו במחיר יורו ונביאיה בכסף יקסמו: ג' פורעניות. שדה תחרש עיין תהיה ולבמות יער: ויועציך כבתחלה. ואחר כך יקרא לך עיר הצדק לשרות בה שכינה: אי בטלי יהירי. ישראל מתייהרים בבלורית ובמלבושי יהירות כפרסים הללו: בטלי אמגושי. יבטלו מסיתים ומדיחים המשניאים אותנו: סיגיך. הם גסי הרוח שמגדלין עצמן לשון ישגה מאד (איוב ח) ואח"כ ואסירה כל בדיליך אלו אותם המבדילים שונאי ישראל מן הקב"ה בשקריהם ובפחזותם: בטלי דייני. רשעים מישראל שמטין דין: בטלי. מעל ישראל: גזירפטי. נוגשי שוטרי עובדי כוכבים: שנעשו מקל לחזניהם. לשמשיהן נותנין יד והויין להן לחוזק לומר לא אהיה שליח ואזמין את פלוני לב"ד אם לא תרבה שכר ואחר פסק דין לא ארדנו ליכנס למשכנו: שבט מושלים. מקל אגרופין של מושלים היינו דיינים רשעים שת"ח שבמשפחותם להם למקל ולאגרוף שעל ידיהם היו מעמידין אותן ומחפין עליהם ועושין סניגרון לדבריהם: לדייני בור. שבהבטחת אותן ת"ח מעמידין דייני בור לדון את כל הבא והרבה דינין שאין נמלכים בהן ומטין אותן: כפיכם נגואלו בדם אלו הדיינין. שכפיהן פשוטין לקבל שוחד ומטין את הדין ונוטלין ממון מן הבעלים שלא כדין ונותנו לשכנגדו והרי הוא כנוטל נשמתו: סופרי הדיינין. שכותבין שטרות של רמיה: עורכי הדיינין. מלמדין את בעלי דינין לטעון: עמו. מכלל דעד השתא לא: זכה לחשן המשפט. שכנגד הלב שהיה גדול ממנו וקודם למשה נגלית שכינה על אהרן כדכתיב (שמואל א ב) הנגלה נגליתי אל בית אביך ונאמרה לו נבואה של מצרים הכתובה ביחזקאל (כ) עד וימרו בי ואעפ"כ לא נתקנא בו בזאת: בני בשכר. שם מקום: כילה מהו. לנטותה בשבת: כשותא. הימלון שגדל על הגפא מהו בכרמא ירק הוא וכלאים בכרם או אילן הוא ואין כלאים בכרם: ולישלח להו. לא סיתר בה: כדרמי בר יחזקאל. כרך עליה חוט או משיחה: ומשני לפי שאינן בני תורה. ומקילי טפי: עירובא. כלאים: וקי"ל. בברכות בפרק כיצד גבי ערלה וה"ה לכלאים שאף היא מצוה התלויה בארץ ואינה נוהגת מן התורה אלא בארץ: יהיב פרוטה לתינוק נכרי. קסבר בחוץ לארץ שרי ומיהו כל כמה דאפשר משני שלא ילמדו להקל: ולא

תוספות

ולישלח להו כר"ט. הא לא פריך לישלח להו כר' יאשיה דאמר אינו חייב עד שיזרע חטה ושעורה וחרצן במפולת יד דשמא הם לא שאלו כשותא בכרמא מהו אלא היכא שעשה כדין איסור כלאים ג' מינים כאחד ועוד שמא לא ס"ל כר' יאשיה ואע"ג דקי"ל כר' יאשיה בספ"ק דקדושין (דף לט.) א"ל לא נהריתו [לא] קי"ל כר' יאשיה ואמר נמי בברכות פרק מי שמתו (דף כב.) נהוג עלמא כתלת סבי כר' אילעי בראשית הגז כרבי יאשיה בכלאים כר' יהודה בן בתירא בדברי תורה מיהו י"ל שלא היו סבורין כן דהא קאמר נמי נהוג כרבי יהודה בדברי תורה ואפ"ה פליגי עליה אמוראי טובא בשמעתא דהתם וקאמר נמי כרבי אילעי בראשית הגז דאמר אינו נוהג אלא בארץ ואפ"ה אמרינן בחולין בשילהי פ' הזרוע (דף קלו.) אמר רב חסדא האי טבחא דלא מפריש מתנתא ליהוי בשמתא דה' אלהי ישראל ואמר נמי דרבא קנים אטמא ואפילו רב נחמן גופיה דאמר נהוג עלמא כתלת סבי אמר התם דקנים גלימא וא"ת נהי דלא ס"ל כר' יאשיה מ"מ לישלח להו כרבי יאשיה דכל המיקל בארץ הלכה כמותו בחו"ל וי"ל דלא שייך למימר הכי אלא במין של איסור דהמתירו חושבו מין היתר בארץ הלכה כמותו בחו"ל אבל בדבר שאינו תלוי אלא בזריעה חטה ושעורה וחרצן במפולת יד בהא לא אמר הלכה כמותו בחו"ל. מ"ר:

רב עמרם חסידא מנגיד עלה רב משרשיא יהיב ליה פרוטה לנכרי כו'. קשיא לי אמאי הא אמרינן לעיל דהלכה כר"ט דמיקל בחו"ל וצריך לומר דבמקומם לא היו בני תורה:

וליתן ליה לתינוק ישראל. אומר רבי שקבלה הוא בידינו שזה המקשה רב אחא בר יעקב והיינו הא דאמר בעירובין בשילהי כל מערבין (דף מ: ושם) גבי ברכת זמן על הכוס ביוה"כ דמפרש התם דלא אפשר דהיכי ליעביד כו' ליתביה לתינוק לית הלכתא כרב אחא בר יעקב דילמא אתי למיסרך ולא מצינו במקום אחר דאית ליה לרב אחא האי סברא וי"מ דהוא ההוא דפ' בתרא דנדה (דף סז:) דאתקין בימא דתמניא משום גנבי ולא חיישינן לסרך בתה במקום צורך ולא נהירא דמאי שנא דנקיט טפי רב אחא בר יעקב מכל שאר אמוראי דהתם ועל ההיא דהתם אומר ר"ת שמותר ליתן לתינוק לשתות כוס של ברכה כי מיקלע מילה ביוה"כ ולא חיישינן דילמא אתי למיסרך כיון שאין זה מנהג [בקבוע] ולא דמי לכוס דיוה"כ דאי הוו יהבי ליה אתי למיסרך אף כשיהיה גדול כיון שעושין מנהג לשתות בכל שנה ושנה ביוה"כ: י"ט

תורה אור השלם

א) שִׁמְעוּ נָא זֹאת רָאשֵׁי בֵּית יַעֲקֹב וּקְצִינֵי בֵּית יִשְׂרָאֵל הַמְתַעֲבִים מִשְׁפָּט וְאֵת כָּל הַיְשָׁרָה יְעַקֵּשׁוּ: בֹּנֶה צִיּוֹן בְּדָמִים וִירוּשָׁלִַם בְּעַוְלָה: רָאשֶׁיהָ בְּשֹׁחַד יִשְׁפֹּטוּ וְכֹהֲנֶיהָ בִּמְחִיר יוֹרוּ וּנְבִיאֶיהָ בְּכֶסֶף יִקְסֹמוּ וְעַל יְיָ יִשָּׁעֵנוּ לֵאמֹר הֲלוֹא יְיָ בְּקִרְבֵּנוּ לֹא תָבוֹא עָלֵינוּ רָעָה: [מיכה ג, ט-יא]

ב) לָכֵן בִּגְלַלְכֶם צִיּוֹן שָׂדֶה תֵחָרֵשׁ וִירוּשָׁלִַם עִיִּין תִּהְיֶה וְהַר הַבַּיִת לְבָמוֹת יָעַר: [מיכה ג, יב]

ג) וְאָשִׁיבָה יָדִי עָלַיִךְ וְאֶצְרֹף כַּבֹּר סִיגָיִךְ וְאָסִירָה כָּל בְּדִילָיִךְ: וְאָשִׁיבָה שֹׁפְטַיִךְ כְּבָרִאשֹׁנָה וְיֹעֲצַיִךְ כְּבַתְּחִלָּה אַחֲרֵי כֵן יִקָּרֵא לָךְ עִיר הַצֶּדֶק קִרְיָה נֶאֱמָנָה: [ישעיה א, כה-כו]

ד) צִיּוֹן בְּמִשְׁפָּט תִּפָּדֶה וְשָׁבֶיהָ בִּצְדָקָה: [ישעיה א, כז]

ה) הֵסִיר יְיָ מִשְׁפָּטַיִךְ פִּנָּה אֹיְבֵךְ מֶלֶךְ יִשְׂרָאֵל יְיָ בְּקִרְבֵּךְ לֹא תִירְאִי רָע עוֹד: [צפניה ג, טו]

ו) שָׁבַר יְיָ מַטֵּה רְשָׁעִים שֵׁבֶט מֹשְׁלִים: [ישעיה יד, ה]

ז) כִּי כַפֵּיכֶם נְגֹאֲלוּ בַדָּם וְאֶצְבְּעוֹתֵיכֶם בֶּעָוֹן שִׂפְתוֹתֵיכֶם דִּבְּרוּ שֶׁקֶר לְשׁוֹנְכֶם עַוְלָה תֶהְגֶּה: [ישעיה נט, ג]

ח) בִּרְכֹת אָבִיךָ גָּבְרוּ עַל בִּרְכֹת הוֹרַי עַד תַּאֲוַת גִּבְעֹת עוֹלָם תִּהְיֶיןָ לְרֹאשׁ יוֹסֵף וּלְקָדְקֹד נְזִיר אֶחָיו: [בראשית מט, כו]

ט) וַיִּשָּׂא מַשְׂאֹת מֵאֵת פָּנָיו אֲלֵהֶם וַתֵּרֶב מַשְׂאַת בִּנְיָמִן מִמַּשְׂאֹת כֻּלָּם חָמֵשׁ יָדוֹת וַיִּשְׁתּוּ וַיִּשְׁכְּרוּ עִמּוֹ: [בראשית מג, לד]

י) וַיִּחַר אַף יְיָ בְּמֹשֶׁה וַיֹּאמֶר הֲלֹא אַהֲרֹן אָחִיךָ הַלֵּוִי יָדַעְתִּי כִּי דַבֵּר יְדַבֵּר הוּא וְגַם הִנֵּה הוּא יֹצֵא לִקְרָאתֶךָ וְרָאֲךָ וְשָׂמַח בְּלִבּוֹ: [שמות ד, יד]

ליקוטי רש"י

לכן הנני. הוא אשר יוסיף להפליא פלא ונוסף על פלא כיסוי על כסוי אוטם על אוטם ומהו הפלא ופלא ואבדה חכמת חכמיו [ישעיה כט, יד]. כשנכנסו רבותינו לכרם ביבנה. כשנכנסו לכרם ביבנה והעידו כל אחד ואחד על אותו שבידו [לעיל עז.]. לכרם. על שם שהיו יושבים שורות שורות ככרם זה הנטוע שורות שורות [ברכות סג:]. זה בית המדרש שיושבין שורות שורות ככרם כך מפורש בירושלמי בברכות [לעיל לג:]. דבר ה' זו נבואה. שמספוק מכם רוח הקדש [עמוס ח, יא]. מכל האוכל אשר יאכל. מוסב על מקרא העליון כל אשר בתוכו יטמא מכל האוכל אשר יאכל אשר יבא עליו מים והוא בתוך כלי חרס הטמא יטמא וכן כל משקה אשר ישתה בכל כלי והוא בתוך כלי חרס הטמא יטמא [ויקרא יא, לד]. השרץ שנמצא בתנור. ולא נגע בפת הפת שבתוכו שני לטומאה ואינו מטמאים חולין...

וְאִידָךְ – **And the other** Tanna (R' Mallai), who maintained that only Joseph refrained from drinking wine, not his brothers, explains that the phrase *with him* implies שִׁיכְּרוּת הוּא דְּלָא הֲוָה – that **there was no intoxication** among the brothers from the time they separated from Joseph, שְׁתִיָּה מִיהָא הֲוָה – **but there was drinking** of wine.[30]

Another teaching from R' Mallai:

וְאָמַר רַבִּי מַלַּאי – **And R' Mallai said:** בִּשְׂכַר ,,וְרָאֲךָ וְשָׂמַח בְּלִבּוֹ" – **In the merit of** that which God testified concerning Aaron:[31] ***And he will see you and he will rejoice in his heart,*** זָכָה לְחֹשֶׁן הַמִּשְׁפָּט עַל לִבּוֹ – **[Aaron] merited to** wear **the *Choshen Mishpat* upon his heart.**[32]

The Gemara returns to discuss, among other rulings, the laws of erecting an *ohel* on the Sabbath:

שָׁלְחוּ לֵיהּ בְּנֵי בַּשְׁכַּר לְלֵוִי – **The people of Bashkar sent** the following three queries **to Levi:** כִּילָה מַהוּ – Firstly, **what is the law concerning** the erection of **a canopy** on the Sabbath? כְּשׁוּתָא בְּכַרְמָא מַהוּ – Secondly, **what is the law concerning hops in a vineyard?** Does the mixture of hops and vines constitute *kilayim*?[33] מֵת בְּיוֹם טוֹב מַהוּ – And thirdly, **what is the law concerning** digging a grave for **a corpse on Yom Tov?**[34]

אַדְּאָזִיל נָח נַפְשֵׁיהּ דְּלֵוִי – **By the time [the messenger] arrived** with the queries, **Levi passed away.** אָמַר שְׁמוּאֵל לְרַב מְנַשְּׁיָא – **Shmuel said to Rav Menashya:** אִי חַכִּימַתְּ שְׁלַח לְהוּ – **If you are** sufficiently **wise,** and know the answers to their queries, **send** them **to them.**

Rav Menashya then ruled on each of the three queries, beginning with the first:

שְׁלַח לְהוּ – **[Rav Menashya] sent to them:** כִּילָה – Concerning **a canopy,** חֲזַרְנוּ עַל כָּל צִידֵּי כִּילָה – **I have reviewed all the** possible **considerations of** the status of **a canopy,** וְלֹא מָצִינוּ לָהּ צַד הֶיתֵּר – **and I have not found grounds to permit** its construction.

The Gemara asks:

וְלִישְׁלַח לְהוּ כִּדְרָמֵי בַּר יְחֶזְקֵאל – **But let him send to them** a permissible way to construct a canopy; viz. that a canopy may be constructed **as taught by Rami bar Yechezkel,** i.e. a canopy tied with a cord or rope.[35]

The Gemara answers:

לְפִי שֶׁאֵינָן בְּנֵי תוֹרָה – He did not send this information to them **because [Bashkarians] are not Torah scholars,** and they would likely adopt other, groundless leniencies, if they were informed of this legitimate leniency.

Rav Menashya rules on the second query:

כְּשׁוּתָא בְּכַרְמָא עִירְבוּבְיָא – Growing **hops in a vineyard constitutes *kilayim*.**

The Gemara asks:

וְלִישְׁלַח לְהוּ כְּדְרַבִּי טַרְפוֹן – **But let him send to them** that it is permitted, **as maintained by R' Tarfon,** דְּתַנְיָא – **as it was taught in a Baraisa:** כִּישׁוּת – Concerning HOPS, רַבִּי טַרְפוֹן אוֹמֵר – R' TARFON SAYS: אֵין כִּלְאַיִם בְּכֶרֶם – THEY DO NOT CONSTITUTE *KILAYIM* if they are planted IN A VINEYARD. וַחֲכָמִים אוֹמְרִים כִּלְאַיִם בְּכֶרֶם – BUT THE SAGES SAY: THEY DO CONSTITUTE *KILAYIM* if planted IN A VINEYARD.[36] וְקַיְימָא לָן כֹּל הַמֵּיקֵל בָּאָרֶץ הֲלָכָה כְּמוֹתוֹ בְּחוּץ לָאָרֶץ – **And we have established that whoever takes the** more **lenient** position in a dispute with regard to plantings **within Eretz** Yisrael, **the halachah follows him** concerning such planting **outside of Eretz** Yisrael.[37] Since R' Tarfon's is the lenient view, why did Rav Menashya not rule leniently in accordance with his view to the people of Bashkar, which is located outside of Eretz Yisrael?

The Gemara answers:

לְפִי שֶׁאֵינָן בְּנֵי תוֹרָה – In this case, too, R' Menashya chose not to rule leniently **because [Bashkarians] are not Torah scholars,** and they would likely adopt other groundless leniencies if they were informed of this legitimate leniency.

NOTES

wine, because it was through their desire for eating and drinking that they came to sell Joseph in the first place (see *Rashi* to *Genesis* 37:12). Still, Joseph was referred to as "the *nezir* of the brothers," implying he was unique among them, because as a prisoner and then as royalty only he would have found himself in situations where adhering to the vow would be most difficult (*Maharsha*; cf. *Eitz Yosef*).

[Joseph was certainly released from his vow not to drink wine upon seeing his brothers; the brothers, who did not yet recognize Joseph, were forced to partake of the wine out of respect for the monarchy (Joseph), and they had to seek legal release from their vow (*Maharsha*, *Rif* in *Ein Yaakov*; see also *Chasam Sofer*).]

30. The word *with him* thus modifies only the second word וַיִּשְׁכְּרוּ, *and they became intoxicated,* for while they had indeed drunk wine over the years, it was only now that they drank to such a degree that they became intoxicated.

31. *Exodus* 4:14. God was assuring Moses that his brother Aaron would not secretly envy him for being chosen as God's prime agent in delivering the Jews from Egypt. To the contrary, God said, Aaron's happiness for his brother would be complete and without blemish. Now, the prophecy (*Ezekiel* 20:7): *Every man, cast away the idols of his eyes, and with the idols of Egypt do not defile yourselves,* was delivered to the Jews in Egypt by Aaron well before God revealed himself to Moses at the burning bush, as God said to Eli HaKohen (*I Samuel* 2:27): *Did I not surely reveal myself to the house of your forefather* [Aaron] *while they were in Egypt?* Thus, Aaron might have justifiably been distressed that Moses, and not he, was chosen to lead the Jews from Egypt. Still, God told Moses that this was not the case (see *Rashi* and *Maharsha*).

32. [The *Choshen*, which was the breastplate worn by the Kohen Gadol (Aaron) that contained the *Urim VeTumim* (see Glossary), was worn upon the heart; Aaron merited this due to the fact that his joy over Moses' appointment as God's prime agent was truly heartfelt. See also *Ben Yehoyada* and *Chasam Sofer*.]

33. One of the varieties of *kilayim* (a forbidden mixture of plantings) is *kilei hakerem* – *kilayim* of the vineyard. Now, while planting certain vegetable, seeds or grains in a vineyard does constitute *kilei hakerem*, planting a tree in a vineyard does not. The people of Baskar had thus posed the following question: Are hops [which are various species of twining plants that are used in brewing and in the preparation of certain medicines] considered a vegetable, and planting them in a vineyard would therefore constitute *kilayim*, or are they considered produce of the tree upon which they grow, and planting them in a vineyard would not constitute *kilayim*? (*Rashi*; cf. *Ritva MHK* ed.).

34. I.e. is there any permitted way to dig a grave (which involves the Biblically prohibited labor of building or plowing – see below, 139b note 2) on Yom Tov?

35. See 138a note 25.

The Gemara does not ask that he should have suggested to them the case of the permitted bridal canopy (see above, 138b note 5), for the query of the Baskarians was limited to canopies with a roof that was a *tefach* wide (*Rashba*; see also *Ritva MHK* ed.).

36. Their dispute centers on whether hops are deemed a vegetable or a tree product, as explained above (see note 33).

37. There is a general rule that a mitzvah which centers upon the earth or its produce is Biblically applicable only in Eretz Yisrael, not outside of Eretz Yisrael (see *Kiddushin* 36b,37a). Still, there are some such mitzvos, *kilei hakerem* among them, which are Rabbinically applicable even outside of Eretz Yisrael. Our Gemara now cites the rule (see *Berachos* 36a) that wherever there is a dispute as to whether such a mitzvah applies at all in a specific case on the Biblical level within Eretz Yisrael, the lenient view in that dispute is followed outside Eretz Yisrael (where the mitzvah is of Rabbinic origin). Thus, since R' Tarfon rules leniently, exempting hops from the prohibition of *kilei hakerem* inside Eretz Yisrael, his view should have been advanced to the people of Bashkar, which is located outside of Eretz Yisrael.

הלכה ברורה ומשנה ברורה במקום אחד: תניא רבי יוסי בן אלישע אומר אם ראית דור שצרות רבות באות עליו צא ובדוק בדייני ישראל שכל פורענות שבאה לעולם לא באה אלא בשביל דייני ישראל שנאמר שמעו נא זאת ראשי בית יעקב וקציני בית ישראל המתעבים משפט ואת כל הישרה יעקשו בונה ציון בדמים וירושלים בעולה ראשיה בשוחד ישפוטו וכהניה במחיר יורו ונביאיה בכסף יקסמו ועל ה' ישענו וגו' רשעים הן אלא שתלו בטחונם במי שאמר והיה העולם לפיכך מביא הקב"ה עליהן ג' פורעניות כנגד ג' עבירות שבידם שנאמר לכן בגללכם ציון שדה תחרש וירושלים עיין תהיה והר הבית לבמות יער ואין הקב"ה משרה שכינתו על ישראל עד שיכלו שופטים ושוטרים רעים מישראל שנאמר ואשיבה ידי עליך ואצרוף כבור סיגיך ואסירה כל בדיליך ואשיבה שופטיך כבראשונה ויועציך כבתחלה וגו' אמר עולא אין ירושלים נפדה אלא בצדקה שנאמר ציון במשפט תפדה ושביה בצדקה אמר רב פפא אי בטלי יהירי בטלי אמגושי אי בטלי דייני בטלי גזירפטי אי בטלי יהירי בטלי אמגושי דכתיב ואצרוף כבור סיגיך ואסירה כל בדיליך אי בטלי דייני בטלי גזירפטי דכתיב הסיר ה' משפטיך פנה אויבך אמר רבי מלאי משום ר"א בר' שמעון מ"ד שבר ה' מטה רשעים שבט מושלים שבר ה' מטה רשעים אלו הדיינין שנעשו מקל לחזניהם שבט מושלים אלו ת"ח שבמשפחות הדיינין מר זוטרא אמר אלו תלמידי חכמים שמלמדים הלכות ציבור לדייני בור אמר ר"א בן מלאי משום ר"ל מאי דכתיב כי כפיכם נגואלו בדם ואצבעותיכם בעון שפתותיכם דברו שקר לשונכם עולה תהגה כי כפיכם נגואלו בדם אלו הדיינין ואצבעותיכם בעון אלו סופרי הדיינין שפתותיכם דברו שקר אלו עורכי הדיינין לשונכם עולה תהגה אלו בעלי דינין ואמר רבי מלאי משום ר' יצחק מגדלאה מיום שפירש יוסף מאחיו לא טעם טעם יין דכתיב ולקדקד נזיר אחיו ר' יוסי בר' חנינא אמר אף הן לא טעמו טעם יין דכתיב וישתו וישכרו עמו מכלל דעד האידנא לא (הוה שיכרות) ואידך שיכרות הוא דלא הוה שתיה מיהא הוה ואמר רבי מלאי בשכר וראך ושמח בלבו זכה לחשן המשפט על לבו: שלחו ליה בני בשכר ללוי כילה מהו כשותא בכרמא מהו מת בי"ט מהו אדאזיל נח נפשיה דלוי אמר שמואל לרב מנשיא אי חכמית שלח להו כילה חזרנו על כל צידי כילה ולא מצינו לה צד היתר ולישלח להו כדרמי בר יחזקאל לפי שאינן בני תורה כשותא בכרמא עירובבא ולישלח להו כדר"ט דתניא כישות ר' טרפון אומר אין כלאים בכרם וחכמים אומרים כלאים בכרם וקי"ל כל המיקל בארץ הלכה כמותו בחו"ל לפי שאינן בני תורה מכריז רב האי מאן דבעי למיזרע כשותא בכרמא ליזרע רב עמרם חסידא מנגיד עליה רב משרשיא יהיב ליה פרוטה לתינוק נכרי וזרע ליה וליתן ליה לתינוק ישראל אתי למיסרך וליתן ליה לגדול נכרי אתי לאיחלופי בישראל מת שלח להו מת לא יתעסקו ביה לא יהודאין ולא ארמאין לא ביום טוב ראשון ולא ביום טוב שני איני והאמר רבי יהודה בר שילת אמר רבי אסי עובדא הוה בבי כנישתא דמעון ביום טוב הסמוך לשבת ולא

רש"י

הלכה ברורה. בטעמים שלא יהא בה מחלוקת: ג' עבירות. בשמד ישפוטו במחיר יורו ונביאיה בכסף יקסמו: ג' פורעניות. שדה תחרש עיין תהיה ולבמות יער: ויועציך כבתחלה. ואחר כך יקרא לך עיר הצדק לשרות בה שכינה: אי בטלי יהירי. ישראל מתייהרים בגלוריות ובמלבושי יהירות כפרסים הללו: בטלי אמגושי. יבטלו מסיתים ומדיחים המשניאים אותנו: סיגיך. הם גסי הרוח שמגדלין עצמן לשון ישגה מאד (איוב ח) ואח"כ ואסירה כל בדיליך אלו אותם המבדילים שונאי ישראל מן הקב"ה בשקריהם ובפחזותם: בטלי דייני. רשעים מישראל שמטין דין: בטלי. מעל ישראל: גזירפטי. נוגשי שוטרי עובדי כוכבים שנעשו מקל לחזניהם. לשמשיהן נותנין יד והוין להן לחוק לומר לא אהיה שליח ואזמין את פלוני לב"ד אם לא תרבה שכר ואחר פסק דין לא ארדנו ליכנס למשכנו: שבט מושלים. מקל אגרופין של מושלים היינו דיינים רשעים שת"ח שבמשפחותם להם למקל ולאגרוף שעל ידיהם היו מעמידין אותן ומחפין עליהם ועושין סניגרון לדבריהם: לדייני בור. שבהבטחת אותן ת"ח מעמידין דייני בור לדון את כל הבא והרבה דינין שאין נמלכים בהן ומטין אותן: כפיכם נגואלו בדם אלו הדיינין. שכפיהן פשוטין לקבל שוחד ומטין את הדין ונוטלין ממון מן הבעלים שלא כדין ונותנו לשכנגדו והרי הוא כנוטל נשמתו: סופרי הדיינין. שכותבין שטרות של רמיה: עורכי הדיינין. מלמדין את בעלי דינין לטעון: עמו. מכלל דעד השתא לא: זכה לחשן המשפט. שכנגד הלב שהיה גדול ממנו וקודם למשה נגלית שכינה על אהרן כדכתיב (שמואל א ב) הנגלה נגליתי אל בית אביך ונאמרה לו נבואה של מצרים הכתובה ביחזקאל (כ) עד וימרו בי ואעפ"כ לא נתקנא בו בזאת: בני בשכר. שם מקום: כילה מהו. לנטותה בשבת: כשותא. הימלוני שגדל על ההגא מהו בכרמא ירק הוא וכלאים בכרם או אילן הוא ואינו כלאים בכרם: ולישלח להו. צד היתר בה: כדרמי בר יחזקאל. כרך עליה חוט או משיחה: ומשני לפי שאינן בני תורה. ומקילי טפי: עירבובא. כלאים: וקי"ל. בברכות בפרק כיצד גבי ערלה וה"ה לכלאים שאף היא מצוה התלויה בארץ ואינה נוהגת מן התורה אלא בארץ: יהיב פרוטה לתינוק נכרי. קסבר בחוץ לארץ שרי ומיהו כל כמה דאפשר משני שלא ילמדו להקל: ולא

תוספות

ולישלח להו כר"ט. הא לא פריך לישלח להו כר' יאשיה דאמר אינו חייב עד שיזרע חטה ושעורה וחרצן במפולת יד דשמא הם לא שאלו כשותא בכרמא מהו אלא היכא שעשה כדין איסור כלאים ג' מינים כאחד ועוד שמא לא ס"ל כר' יאשיה ואע"ג דקי"ל כר' יאשיה בספ"ק דקדושין (דף לט.) א"ל לא נהריתו [ס"א לא] קי"ל כר' יאשיה ואמר נמי בברכות פרק מי שמתו (דף כב.) נהוג עלמא כתלת סבי כר' אילעי בראשית הגז כרבי יאשיה בכלאים כר' יהודה בן בתירא בדברי תורה מיהו י"ל שלא היו סבורין כן דהא קאמר נמי נהוג כרבי יהודה בדברי תורה ואפ"ה פליגי עליה אמוראי טובא בשמעתא דהתם וקאמר נמי כרבי אילעי בראשית הגז דאמר אינו נוהג אלא בארץ ואפ"ה אמרינן בחולין בשילהי פ' הזרוע (דף קלו.) אמר רב חסדא האי טבחא דלא מפריש מתנתא ליהוי בשמתא דה' אלהי ישראל ואמר נמי דרבא קנים אטמא ואפילו רב נחמן גופיה דאמר נהוג עלמא כתלת סבי אמר התם דקנים גלימא וא"ת נהי דלא ס"ל כר' יאשיה מ"מ לישלח להו כרבי יאשיה דכל המיקל בארץ הלכה כמותו בחו"ל וי"ל דלא שייך למימר הכי אלא במין של איסור דהמתירו חושבו מין היתר בארץ הלכה כמותו בחו"ל אבל בדבר שאינו תלוי אלא בזריעה חטה ושעורה וחרצן במפולת יד בהא לא אמר הלכה כמותו בחו"ל. מ"ר:

רב עמרם חסידא מנגיד עלה רב משרשיא יהיב ליה פרוטה לנכרי כו'. קשיא לי אמאי הא אמרינן לעיל דהלכה כר"ט דמיקל בחו"ל וצריך לומר דבמקומם לא היו בני תורה:

וליתן ליה לתינוק ישראל. אומר רבי שקבלה הוא בידינו שזה המקשה רב אחא בר יעקב והיינו הא דאמר בעירובין בשילהי בכל מערבין (דף מ: ושם) גבי ברכת זמן על הכוס ביוה"כ דמפרש התם דלא אפשר דהיכי ליעביד כו' ליתביה לתינוק לית הלכתא כרב אחא בר יעקב דילמא אתי למיסרך ולא מצינו במקום אחר דאית ליה לרב אחא האי סברא וי"מ דהוא ההוא דפ' בתרא דנדה (דף סז:) דאתקין בימא דתמניא משום גנבי ולא חיישינן לסרך בתה במקום צורך ולא נהירא דמאי שנא דנקיט טפי רב אחא בר יעקב מכל שאר אמוראי דהתם ועל ההיא דהתם אומר ר"ת שמותר ליתן לתינוק לשתות כוס של ברכה כי מיקלע מילה ביוה"כ ולא חיישינן דילמא אתי למיסרך כיון שאין זה מנהג [בקבוע] ולא דמי לכוס דיוה"כ דלא הוו יהבי ליה אלא למיסרך אף כשיהיה גדול כיון שעושין מנהג לשתות בכל שנה ושנה ביוה"כ:

מסורת הש"ס

א) [יבמות סג. ע"ש ב"ב ח. ע"ש], ב) [יומא עז:], ג) סנהדרין לח., ד) [נ"ל ישראל וכ"א ברמב"ם וכפור ועי' מ"ש על גליון סנהדרין לח.], ה) [גי' הערוך ערך גז ז' גאזי דפאפי פי' קריסי ושוטרי השרים ועבדן יהיר גרם גזירפטי פי' רשעים], ו) [תוספ' סוף פרק ג דכלאים], ז) ברכות לו., ח) כ"כ הרש"ל והרי"ץ ממקו.

ליקוטי רש"י

לכן בגללכם. הוא אשר יוסף להכליא שלא ונוסף על שלא ליקוי על כפרי אותם ועל אותם ומהו הכלה ושלא ולפרה מכמת מכמיו [ישעיה כט, יד]. כשנכנסו לכרם ביבנה. כשנכנסו לכרם ביבנה והעידו כל אחד ואחד על אותו שבידו [לעיל עז.]. לכרם. על שם שהיו יושבים שורות שורות ככרם זה הנטוע שורות שורות [ברכות סג:]. זה בית המדרש שיושבין שורות שורות ככרם של מטרע בירושלמי בברכות [לעיל לג:]. דבר ה' זו נבואה. שמפסוק מכס רום הקודש [עמוס ח, יא].

עין משפט נר מצוה

טו א מיי' פכ"ג מהל' סנהדרין הלכה ט סמג לאוין רו טוש"מ סי' ח סעיף ג:

טז ב מיי' פ"ה מהל' מתנות עניים הלכה א סמג עשין קסב טוש"ע י"ד סי' רמז:

רבינו חננאל

ותהוי פת ראשונה הכא הוא מפורש בפסחים בסוף פ"א: וזה שהשיב רב מנשיא לבני בי בשכר על הכילה ועל הכשות בכרם ועל המת בי"ט כולן לאיסור לפי שאינן בני תורה. מהא שמעינן שאפילו דברים המותרים כגון אלו וכדומה להן המסורין לעם הארץ אין אדם רשאי להורות להן להיתר אלא יחמיר עליהן

תורה אור השלם

א) שמעו נא זאת ראשי בית יעקב וקציני בית ישראל המתעבים משפט ואת כל הישרה יעקשו: בנה ציון בדמים וירושלים בעולה: ראשיה בשחד ישפטו וכהניה במחיר יורו ונביאיה בכסף יקסמו ועל יי ישענו לאמר הלוא יי בקרבנו לא תבוא עלינו רעה: [מיכה ג, ט-יא]

ב) לכן בגללכם ציון שדה תחרש וירושלים עיין תהיה והר הבית לבמות יער: [מיכה ג, יב]

ג) ואשיבה ידי עליך ואצרף כבר סיגיך ואסירה כל בדיליך: ואשיבה שפטיך כבראשנה ויעציך כבתחלה אחרי כן יקרא לך עיר הצדק קריה נאמנה: [ישעיה א, כה-כו]

ד) ציון במשפט תפדה ושביה בצדקה: [ישעיה א, כז]

ה) הסיר יי משפטיך פנה איבך מלך ישראל יי בקרבך לא תיראי רע עוד: [צפניה ג, טו]

ו) שבר יי מטה רשעים שבט משלים: [ישעיה יד, ה]

ז) כי כפיכם נגאלו בדם ואצבעותיכם בעון שפתותיכם דברו שקר לשונכם עולה תהגה: [ישעיה נט, ג]

ח) ברכת אביך גברו על ברכת הורי עד תאות גבעת עולם תהיין לראש יוסף ולקדקד נזיר אחיו: [בראשית מט, כו]

ט) וישא משאת מאת פניו אלהם ותרב משאת בנימן ממשאת כלם חמש ידות וישתו וישכרו עמו: [בראשית מג, לד]

י) ויחר אף יי במשה ויאמר הלא אהרן אחיך הלוי ידעתי כי דבר ידבר הוא וגם הנה הוא יצא לקראתך וראך ושמח בלבו: [שמות ד, יד]

The Gemara digresses to cite opposing views concerning the planting of hops in a vineyard:

מַכְרִיז רַב – **Rav announced:** הַאי מַאן דְּבָעֵי לְמִיזְרַע כְּשׁוּתָא בְּכַרְמָא לִיזְרַע – **Whoever wishes to plant hops in a vineyard may plant** them. רַב עַמְרָם חֲסִידָא מְנַגֵּיד עִילָוֵיהּ – But **Rav Amram Chasida would penalize** one **with lashes for doing so.** רַב מְשַׁרְשִׁיָּא יָהִיב לֵיהּ פְּרוּטָה לְתִינוֹק נָכְרִי וְזָרַע לֵיהּ – **Rav Mesharshiya would give a** ***perutah*** **coin to a non-Jewish child and [the child] would plant** hops in a vineyard **for him.**[38]

The Gemara explains why Rav Mesharshiya went to such lengths:

וְלִיתֵּן לֵיהּ לְתִינוֹק יִשְׂרָאֵל – **But let him give** the *perutah* **to a Jewish child** to plant for him?

The Gemara answers:

אָתֵי לְמִיסְרַךְ – **The child might** come to **continue** to plant as such as an adult, not realizing that the act he had performed as a child was in fact inappropriate.

The Gemara persists:

וְלִיתֵּן לֵיהּ לְגָדוֹל נָכְרִי – **But let him give it to a non-Jewish adult?**

The Gemara answers:

אָתֵי לְאִיחַלּוּפֵי בְּיִשְׂרָאֵל – He was concerned that **[people]** observing this arrangement **might confuse him with a Jew,** and conclude that planting in this manner is totally permitted even for a Jew.

The Gemara cites Rav Menashya's ruling on the third query:

מֵת – Regarding **a corpse** that awaits burial on Yom Tov, שְׁלַח לְהוּ – **he sent to them:** מֵת לֹא יִתְעַסְּקוּ בֵּיהּ לֹא יְהוּדָאִין וְלֹא אַרְמָאִין – Concerning **a corpse, neither a Jew nor a non-Jew should be involved** in his burial, לֹא בְּיוֹם טוֹב רִאשׁוֹן וְלֹא בְּיוֹם טוֹב שֵׁנִי – **neither on the first Yom Tom** day, **nor on the second Yom Tov** day.

The Gemara asks:

אִינִי – **Is this indeed so?** וְהָאָמַר רַבִּי יְהוּדָה בַּר שִׁילַת אָמַר רַבִּי אַסִּי – **But R' Yehudah bar Shilas said in the name of R' Assi:** עוּבְדָּא הֲוָה בְּבֵי כְּנִישְׁתָּא דְּמָעוֹן בְּיוֹם טוֹב הַסָּמוּךְ לְשַׁבָּת – **There was an occurrence in the Synagogue of Maon on a Yom Tov adjoining to the Sabbath** of a corpse which needed to be buried,

NOTES

38. Rav, who lived outside of Eretz Yisrael, followed the view of R' Tarfon that planting hops in a vineyard is permitted. Rav Amram, however, prohibited it.

Rav Mesharshiya agreed that such planting is in essence permitted. However, in his view it is preferable to use alternative methods so that people should not learn to be generally lenient (*Rashi*; see *Ran MHK* ed. and *Ritva MHK* ed.).

Ram Amram and Rav Mesharshiya did not utilize R' Tarfon's lenient opinion because their neighbors were, similar to the people of Baskar, not Torah scholars (*Tosafos*). [See the Rishonim here for the parameters of the law that one should not have a child perform a forbidden act due to the concern that the child will continue to perform that forbidden act as an adult.]

הלכה ברורה ומשנה ברורה במקום אחד: תניא רבי יוסי בן אלישע אומר אם ראית דור שצרות רבות באות עליו צא ובדוק בדייני ישראל שכל פורענות שבאה לעולם לא באה אלא בשביל דייני ישראל שנאמר שמעו נא זאת ראשי בית יעקב וקציני בית ישראל המתעבים משפט ואת כל הישרה יעקשו בונה ציון בדמים וירושלים בעולה ראשיה בשוחד ישפוטו וכהניה במחיר יורו ונביאיה בכסף יקסומו ועל ה' ישענו וגו' רשעים הן אלא שתלו בטחונם במי שאמר והיה העולם לפיכך מביא הקב"ה עליהן ג' פורעניות כנגד ג' עבירות שבידם שנאמר לכן בגללכם ציון שדה תחרש וירושלים עיין תהיה והר הבית לבמות יער ואין הקב"ה משרה שכינתו על ישראל עד שיכלו שופטים ושוטרים רעים מישראל שנאמר ואשיבה ידי עליך ואצרוף כבור סיגיך ואסירה כל בדיליך ואשיבה שופטיך כבראשונה ויועציך כבתחלה וגו' אמר עולא אין ירושלים נפדה אלא בצדקה שנאמר ציון במשפט תפדה ושביה בצדקה אמר רב פפא אי בטלי יהירי בטלי אמגושי אי בטלי דייני בטלי גזירפטי אי בטלי יהירי בטלי אמגושי דכתיב ואצרוף כבור סיגיך אי בטלי דייני בטלי גזירפטי דכתיב הסיר ה' משפטיך פנה אויבך אמר רבי מלאי משום ר"א בר' שמעון מ"ד שבר ה' מטה רשעים שבט מושלים שבר ה' מטה רשעים אלו הדיינין שנעשו מקל לחזניהם שבט מושלים אלו ת"ח שבמשפחות הדיינין מר זוטרא אמר אלו תלמידי חכמים שמלמדים הלכות ציבור לדייני בור אמר ר"א בן מלאי משום ר"ל מאי דכתיב כי כפיכם נגואלו בדם ואצבעותיכם בעון שפתותיכם דברו שקר לשונכם עולה תהגה כי כפיכם נגואלו בדם אלו הדיינין ואצבעותיכם בעון אלו סופרי הדיינין שפתותיכם דברו שקר אלו עורכי הדיינין לשונכם עולה תהגה אלו בעלי דינין ואמר רבי מלאי משום ר' יצחק מגדלאה מיום שפירש יוסף מאחיו לא טעם טעם יין דכתיב ולקדקד נזיר אחיו ר' יוסי בר' חנינא אמר אף הן לא טעמו טעם יין דכתיב וישתו וישכרו עמו מכלל דעד האידנא לא (הוה שיכרות) ואידך שיכרות הוא דלא הוה שתיה מיהא הוה ואמר רבי מלאי בשכר וראך ושמח בלבו זכה לחשן המשפט על לבו: שלחו ליה בני בשכר ללוי כילה מהו כשותא בכרמא מהו מת בי"ט מהו אדאזיל נח נפשיה דלוי אמר שמואל לרב מנשיא אי חכימת שלח להו כילה חזרנו על כל צידי כילה ולא מצינו לה צד היתר ולישלח להו כדרמי בר יחזקאל לפי שאינן בני תורה כשותא בכרמא עירבובא ולישלח להו כדר"ט דתניא כישות ר' טרפון אומר אין כלאים בכרם וחכמים אומרים כלאים בכרם וקי"ל כל המיקל בארץ הלכה כמותו בחו"ל לפי שאינן בני תורה מכריז רב האי מאן דבעי למיזרע כשותא בכרמא ליזרע רב עמרם חסידא מנגיד עילויה רב משרשיא יהיב ליה פרוטה לתינוק נכרי וזרע ליה וליתן ליה לתינוק ישראל אתי למיסרך וליתן ליה לגדול נכרי אתי לאיחלופי בישראל מת שלח להו מת לא יתעסקו ביה לא יהודאין ולא ארמאין לא ביום טוב ראשון ולא ביום טוב שני איני והאמר רבי יהודה בר שילת אמר רבי אסי עובדא הוה בבי כנישתא דמעון ביום טוב הסמוך לשבת ולא

רש"י

הלכה ברורה. בטעמים שלא יהא בה מחלוקת: ג' עבירות. בשחד ישפוטו במחיר יורו ונביאיה בכסף יקסמו: ג' פורעניות. שדה תחרש עיין תהיה ולבמות יער: ויועציך כבתחלה. ואחר כך יקרא לך עיר הצדק לשרות בה שכינה: אי בטלי יהירי. ישראל המתיהרים בכלורית ומלבושי יהירות כפרסיים הללו: בטלי אמגושי. יבטלו מסיתים ומדיחים המשניאים אותנו: סיגיך. הם גסי הרוח שמגדלין עצמן ולשון שגה מאד (איוב ח) ואח"כ ואסירה כל בדיליך אלו אותם המבדילים שונאי ישראל מן הקב"ה בשקריהם ובפחזותם: בטלי דייני. רשעים מישראל מטה דין: בטלי. מעל ישראל: גזירפטי. נוגשי שוטרי עובדי כוכבים: שנעשו מקל לחזניהם. לשמשיהן נותנין יד והויין להן לחזוק לומר לא אהיה שליו ואזמין את פלוני לב"ד אם לא תרבה שכר ואחר פסק דין לא ארדנו ליכנס למשכנו: שבט מושלים. מקל אגרופין של מושלים היינו דיינים רשעים שת"ח שבמשפחותם להם למקל ולאגרוף שעל ידיהם היו מעמידין אותן ומחפין עליהם ועושין סניגרון לדבריהם: לדייני בור. שבהבטחתם אותן ת"ח מעמידין דייני בור לדון את כל הבא והרבה דינין שאין נמלכים בהן ומטין אותן: כפיכם נגואלו בדם אלו הדיינין. שכפיהן פשוטין לקבל שוחד ומטין את הדין ונוטלין ממון מן הבעלים שלא כדין ונותנו לשכנגדו והכי הוא כנוטל נשמתו: סופרי הדיינין. שכותבין שטרות של רמיה: עורכי הדיינין. מלמדין את בעלי דינין לטעון: עמו. מכלל דעד השתא לא: זכה לחשן המשפט. שכנגד הלב שהיה גדול ממנו וקודם למשה נגלית שכינה על אהרן כדכתיב (שמואל א ב) הנגלה נגליתי אל בית אביך ואמרה לו נבואה של מצרים הכתובה ביחזקאל (כ) עד וימרו בי ועאפ"כ לא נתקנא בו בזאת: בני בשכר. שם מקום: כילה מהו. לנטותה בשבת: כשותא. הימלון שגדל על ההגא מהו בכרמא ירק הוא וכלאים בכרם או אילן הוא ואינו כלאים בכרם: ולישלח להו. לד היתר בה: כדרמי בר יחזקאל. כך עליה חוט או משיחה: ומשני לפי שאינן בני תורה. ומקילי טפי: עירבובא. כלאים: וקי"ל. בברכות בפרק כילד גבי ערלה וה"ה לכלאים שאף היא מצוה התלויה בארץ ואינה נוהגת מן התורה אלא בארץ: יהיב פרוטה לתינוק נכרי. קסבר בחוץ לארץ שרי ומיהו כל כמה דאפשר משני שלא ילמדו להקל:

תוספות

ולישלח להו כר"ש. הא לא פריך לישלח להו כר' יאשיה דאמר אינו חייב עד שיזרע חטה ושעורה וחרצן במפולת יד דשמא הם לא שאלו כשותא בכרמא מהו אלא היכא שעשה כדין איסור כלאים כי מיניס כאחד ועוד שמא לא ס"ל כר' יאשיה ואע"ג דקי"ל כר' יאשיה בספ"ק דקדושין (דף לט.) א"ל לא נהרימו [מ] לאו קי"ל כר' יאשיה ואמר נמי בברכות פרק מי שמתו (דף כב.) נהוג עלמא כתלת סבי כר' אלעאי בראשית הגז כרבי יאשיה בכלאים כר' יהודה בן בתירה בדברי תורה מיהו י"ל שלא היו סבורין כן דהא קאמר נמי נהוג כרבי יהודה בן בתירה בדברי תורה ואפ"ה פליגי עליה אמוראי טובא בשמעתא דהתם וקאמר נמי כרבי אלעאי בראשית הגז דאמר אינו נוהג אלא בארץ ואפ"ה אמרינן בחולין בשילהי פ' הזרוע (דף קלז.) אמר רב חסדא האי טבחא דלא מפריש מתנתא ליהוי בשמתא דה' אלהי ישראל ואמר נמי דרבא קנים אטמא ואפילו רב נחמן גופיה דאמר נהוג עלמא כתלת סבי אמר התם דקנים גלימא וא"ת נהי דלא ס"ל כר' יאשיה מ"מ לישלח להו כרבי יאשיה דכל המיקל בארץ הלכה כמותו בחו"ל וי"ל דלא שייך למימר הכי אלא במין של איסור דהמחמירו אוסרו מין היתר בארץ הלכה כמותו בחו"ל אבל בדבר שאינו תלוי אלא בזריעה חטה ושעורה וחרצן במפולת יד בהא לא אמר הלכה כמותו בחו"ל. מ"ר:

רב עמרם חסידא מנגיד עלה רב משרשיא יהיב ליה פרוטה לנכרי כו'. קשיא לי אמאי הא אמרינן לעיל דהלכה כר"ט דמיקל בחו"ל ולריך לומר דבמקומות לא היו בני תורה:

וליתן ליה לתינוק ישראל. אומר רבי שקבלה הוא בידינו שזה המקשה רב אחא בר יעקב והיינו הא דאמר בעירובין בשילהי כל מערבין (דף מ: וסס) גבי ברכת זמן על הכוס ביוה"כ דמפרש התם דלא אפשר דהיכי ליעביד כו' ליתביה לתינוק לית הלכתא כרב אחא בר יעקב דילמא אתי למיסרך ולא מלינו במקום אחר דאית ליה לרב אחא האי סברא וי"מ דהוא ההוא דפ' בתרא דנדה (דף סו:) דאתקין ביממא דתמניא משום גנבי ולא חיישינן לסרך בתה במקום לורך ולא נהירא דמאי שנא דנקיט טפי רב אחא בר יעקב מכל שאר אמוראי דהתם ועל ההיא דהתם אומר ר"ת שמותר ליתן לתינוק לשתות כוס של ברכה כי מיקלע מילה ביוה"כ ולא חיישינן דילמא אתי למיסרך כיון שאין זה מנהג [בקבוע] ולא דמי לכוס דיוה"כ דאי הוו יהבי ליה אתי למיסרך אף כשיהיה גדול כיון שעושין מנהג לשתות בכל שנה ושנה ביוה"כ:

רבינו חננאל

ותהוי פת ראשונה הכא הוא מפורש בפסחים בסוף פ"א: וזה שהשיב רב מנשיא לבני בי בשכר על הכילה ועל הכשות בכרם ועל המת ביו"ט כולן לאיסור לפי שאינן בני תורה. מהא שמעינן שאפילו דברים המותרים כגון אלו וכדומה להן המסורין לעם הארץ אין אדם רשאי להורות להן להיתר אלא יחמיר עליהן:

עין משפט נר מצוה

טו א מיי' פכ"ג מהל' סנהדרין הלכה ט סמג לאוין רו טוש"ע ח"מ סי' ח סעיף ג:

טז ב מיי' פ"א מהל' מתנות עניים הלכה ה סמג עשין קסב טוש"ע י"ד סי' רמז:

מסורת הש"ס

א) [יבמות סג. ע"ש ב"ב ח. ע"ש], ב) [יומא ט:], ג) סנהדרין לח., ד) [צ"ל ישראל וכ"ל ברמב"ם ובטור וע"ע מ"ש על הגליון סנהדרין לח.], ה) [גי' הערוך ערך גז ו' גזזי דפאמי פי' קריסי ושוטרי השרים ובערך יהיר גרס גזירפטי פי' רשעים], ו) [תוספ' סוף פרק ג דכלאים], ז) ברכות לו., ח) כ"ג הרש"ל והריעב"ץ מחקו.

ליקוטי רש"י

לכן הנני. הוא אשר יוסיף לנפילה אלא ועוסף על אלה כיסוי על כסוי אותם על אותם ומהו הפלא ופלא ואבדה חכמת חכמיו [ישעיה כט, יד]. כשכנונו רבותינו לכרם ביבנה. כשכנסנו לכרם ביבנה וסעידו כל אחד ואחד על אותו שבידו [לעיל עז:]. לכרם. על שם שהיו יושבים שורות שורות כרם זה ונטוע שורות שורות [ברכות סג:].

תורה אור השלם

א) שִׁמְעוּ נָא זֹאת רָאשֵׁי בֵּית יַעֲקֹב וּקְצִינֵי בֵּית יִשְׂרָאֵל הַמְתַעֲבִים מִשְׁפָּט וְאֵת כָּל הַיְשָׁרָה יְעַקֵּשׁוּ: בֹּנֶה צִיּוֹן בְּדָמִים וִירוּשָׁלַיִם בְּעַוְלָה: רָאשֶׁיהָ בְּשֹׁחַד יִשְׁפֹּטוּ וְכֹהֲנֶיהָ בִּמְחִיר יוֹרוּ וּנְבִיאֶיהָ בְּכֶסֶף יִקְסֹמוּ וְעַל יְיָ יִשָּׁעֵנוּ לֵאמֹר הֲלוֹא יְיָ בְּקִרְבֵּנוּ לֹא תָבוֹא עָלֵינוּ רָעָה: [מיכה ג, ט-יא]

ב) לָכֵן בִּגְלַלְכֶם צִיּוֹן שָׂדֶה תֵחָרֵשׁ וִירוּשָׁלַיִם עִיִּין תִּהְיֶה וְהַר הַבַּיִת לְבָמוֹת יָעַר: [מיכה ג, יב]

ג) וְאָשִׁיבָה יָדִי עָלַיִךְ וְאֶצְרֹף כַּבֹּר סִיגָיִךְ וְאָסִירָה כָּל בְּדִילָיִךְ: וְאָשִׁיבָה שֹׁפְטַיִךְ כְּבָרִאשֹׁנָה וְיֹעֲצַיִךְ כְּבַתְּחִלָּה אַחֲרֵי כֵן יִקָּרֵא לָךְ עִיר הַצֶּדֶק קִרְיָה נֶאֱמָנָה: [ישעיה א, כה-כו]

ד) צִיּוֹן בְּמִשְׁפָּט תִּפָּדֶה וְשָׁבֶיהָ בִּצְדָקָה: [ישעיה א, כז]

ה) הֵסִיר יְיָ מִשְׁפָּטַיִךְ פִּנָּה אֹיְבֵךְ מֶלֶךְ יִשְׂרָאֵל יְיָ בְּקִרְבֵּךְ לֹא תִירְאִי רָע עוֹד: [צפניה ג, טו]

ו) שָׁבַר יְיָ מַטֵּה רְשָׁעִים שֵׁבֶט מֹשְׁלִים: [ישעיה יד, ה]

ז) כִּי כַפֵּיכֶם נְגֹאֲלוּ בַדָּם וְאֶצְבְּעוֹתֵיכֶם בֶּעָוֺן שִׂפְתוֹתֵיכֶם דִּבְּרוּ שֶׁקֶר לְשׁוֹנְכֶם עַוְלָה תֶהְגֶּה: [ישעיה נט, ג]

ח) בִּרְכֹת אָבִיךָ גָּבְרוּ עַל בִּרְכֹת הוֹרַי עַד תַּאֲוַת גִּבְעֹת עוֹלָם תִּהְיֶיןָ לְרֹאשׁ יוֹסֵף וּלְקָדְקֹד נְזִיר אֶחָיו: [בראשית מט, כו]

ט) וַיִּשָּׂא מַשְׂאֹת מֵאֵת פָּנָיו אֲלֵהֶם וַתֵּרֶב מַשְׂאַת בִּנְיָמִן מִמַּשְׂאֹת כֻּלָּם חָמֵשׁ יָדוֹת וַיִּשְׁתּוּ וַיִּשְׁכְּרוּ עִמּוֹ: [בראשית מג, לד]

י) וַיִּחַר אַף יְיָ בְּמֹשֶׁה וַיֹּאמֶר הֲלֹא אַהֲרֹן אָחִיךָ הַלֵּוִי יָדַעְתִּי כִּי דַבֵּר יְדַבֵּר הוּא וְגַם הִנֵּה הוּא יֹצֵא לִקְרָאתֶךָ וְרָאֲךָ וְשָׂמַח בְּלִבּוֹ: [שמות ד, יד]

ולא ידענא אי מלפניה אי מלאחריה ואתו לקמיה דרבי יוחנן ואמר להו יתעסקו ביה עממין (א) ואמר רבא מת בי"ט ראשון יתעסקו בו עממין ביום טוב שני יתעסקו בו ישראל ואפילו ביו"ט שני של ראש השנה מה שאין כן בביצה לפי שאינן בני תורה: א"ר אבין בר רב הונא אמר רב חמא בר גוריא מתעטף אדם בכילה ובכסכסיה ויוצא לרה"ר בשבת ואינו חושש מ"ש מדרב הונא דאמר רב הונא אמר רב היוצא בטלית שאינה מצוייצת כהלכתה בשבת חייב חטאת ציצית לגבי טלית חשיבי ולא בטלי הני לא חשיבי ובטלי אמר (א) רבה בר רב הונא מערים אדם על המשמרת ביו"ט לתלות בה רמונים ותולה בה שמרים אמר רב אשי והוא דתלה בה רמונים מאי שנא מהא דתניא מטילין שכר במועד לצורך המועד שלא לצורך המועד אסור אחד שכר תמרים ואחד שכר שעורים אע"פ שיש להן ישן מערים ושותה מן החדש התם לא מוכחא מילתא הכא מוכחא מילתא אמרו ליה רבנן לרב אשי חזי מר האי צורבא מרבנן ורב הונא ב"ר חיון שמיה ואמרי לה רב הונא בר חלוון שמיה דשקל ברא דתומא ומנח בברזא דדנא ואמר לאצנועיה קמיכוינא ואזיל ונאים במברא ועבר להך גיסא וסייר פירי ואמר אנא למינם קמיכוינא אמר להו הערמה קאמרת הערמה בדרבנן היא וצורבא מרבנן לא אתי למיעבד לכתחילה: **מתני'** נותנין מים ע"ג השמרים בשביל שיצולו ומסננין את היין [א] בסודרין ובכפיפה מצרית ונותנין ביצה במסננת של חרדל ועושין אנומלין בשבת ר' יהודה אומר בשבת בכוס ביו"ט בלגין ובמועד בחבית רבי צדוק אומר הכל לפי האורחין: **גמ'** אמר זעירי נותן אדם יין צלול ומים צלולין לתוך המשמרת בשבת ואינו חושש אבל עכורין לא מיתיבי רבן שמעון בן גמליאל אומר טורד אדם חבית של יין ביינה ושמריה ונותן לתוך המשמרת ואינו חושש תרגמה זעירי בין הגיתות שנו: מסננין את היין בסודרין: אמר רב שימי בר חייא ובלבד שלא יעשה גומא: ובכפיפה מצרית: אמר רב חייא בר אשי אמר רב ובלבד שלא יגביה מקרקעיתו של כלי טפח אמר רב האי פרונקא אפלגיה דכובא שרי אכוליה כובא אסור אמר רב פפא לא ניהדק איניש (ג) ציניתא בפומיה דכוזני דחביתא משום דמיחזי כמשמרת דבי רב פפא שאפו שיכרא ממנא למנא (ג) אמר ליה רב אחא מדיפתי לרבינא האיכא ניצוצות ניצוצות לבי רב פפא לא חשיבי: ונותנין ביצה במסננת: תני יעקב קרחה לפי

תוספות

יום טוב שני יתעסקו בו ישראל. ובכילה (ד' ו.) מסקינן בתר הך מילתא אמר רבינא האידנא דאיכא חברי חיישינן פירוש ולא יתעסקו בו ישראל פן יגלו עליהם חברי לעשות מלאכה ביו"ט כיון שרואין שעושין בשביל מת ומעשה היה והוליכו מת חוץ לתחום ביו"ט והלכו אחריו בסוסים להתעסק במת וכעס ר"ת אף על ההולכים ברגל בלא סוסים ושמע רבי דטעמו משום דמסיק רבינא האידנא דאיכא חברי ולדידן אע"ג דליכא למיחש יש לאסור כיון דמסיק הכי גם יש ליראה פן יגלו השרים להתעסק במלאכתן ולכתוב מה שהם רוצים ושלח להם ר"ת בני בשכר אינם בני תורה בני מליאון (ז) (אותה הענין) בני תורה:

ציצית חשיבי ולא בטלי. שאינם מבוטלין לפי שמחשובים הם בעיניו שדעתו ליתן בטלית ציצית רביעית כך פי' ר"ח: **הא לא חשיבי ובטלי** על זה סמך רבי להניח באבנטו רצועות התלויות בו ויש שקושרים בהם בתי שוקים דבטלי דלא חשיבי כולי האי: **מאי שנא מהא דתניא** כו'. פי' [וס"ל כרבי יוסי בר' יהודה דאמר מערימין] לעיל בפ' כל כתבי (דף קיז:):

תלא דבישרא כו'. לא כפירוש הקונטרס דפי' בשר מליח שתלו ליבשו דהל"ל הא בפרק מפנין דמה שייך הכא ועוד למה מזכיר תלא ועוד מוכח לעיל בפרק מפנין (דף קכח.) דדג מליח נמי חזי לאומצא ועוד דהכא בטלטול איירי ואמרינן לעיל דרב במוקצה לטלטל סבר לה כר"ש ונראה כפי' הערוך דמשום תלא נקטיה ובלא בשר אלא תלא דבשרא לא ממאים ושרי לטלטולי ושל דגים מאים והוי מוקצה מחמת מיאום והשתא אתי שפיר באיסור דתלא כעין כישא דירקא ור' פי' לנו דלתלא דבשרא רגיל להיות בו תורת כלי אבל של דגים לא ולא משום מוקצה מחמת מיאום דלא איירי שמעתין במוקצה מחמת מיאום. מ"ר: אבל

רש"י

ולא ידענא אי מלפניה. אם חל י"ט בע"ש ומת בו ביום ומפני שלא יוכלו להתעסק בו למחר התירו לקוברו ע"י עממים: **אי מלאחריה.** והוא מת בשבת ומפני שנשתהא כבר והיה מסריח התירו: **מת ביו"ט ראשון** כו'. מת שנשתהא כגון שמת בשבת ולמחר היה יו"ט: **מה שאין כן בביצה.** דאין ר"ה שוה לימים טובים של גליות דאילו ר"ה חמיר יו"ט שני דיליה ונולדה בזה אסורה בזה: **מתעטף אדם בכילה.** שהוא כסדין ומתעטף בה דרך מלבוש: **וכסכסיה.** רצועות התלויות בה ולא אמרינן הך רצועות לאו לצורך עיטוף נינהו והוה משאוי והוא שעתא שאין כיסכסין עשוין אלא לנטותה באהל: **חייב חטאת.** ואילו לא היתה מצויצת כלל לא מיחייב דהא לבושיה הוא אלמא הציציות הויין לו משאוי הואיל ואינן כמצותו אינן צריכין לה ומן הבגד ממש אינן דליחשבינן כוותיה: **חשיבי.** משום דשל תכלת הן ולא בטלי והוו בה משוי: **מערים אדם על המשמרת ביו"ט.** לרבנן דאמרי אין תולין את המשמרת ביום טוב ואוקימנא דטעמא לאו משום אהל אלא משום עובדא דחול מערים ותולה אותה לצורך רמונים דלאו עובדין דחול נינהו ומסנן בה שמרים הואיל ונתלית דהא אמרינן נותנין לתלויה ביו"ט: **והוא דתלי בה רמונים.** ברישא דמוכח מילתא דמעיקרא לאו לשמרים תלייה: **מטילין.** ברשי"ר בלע"ז: **במועד.** בחולו של מועד: **מערים ושותה מן החדש.** אלמא בלא שום הוכחה מותר להערים: **התם לאו מוכחא מילתא.** דמילתא דאיסורא הוא דהרואה אומר לצורך המועד הוא שאין הכל יודעין שיש לו מן הישן הכא מוכחא מילתא לאיסור דסתם תולה משמרת לשמרים הוא תולה ואי לא יהיב בה רימונים ברישא להצניע בעלמא כי יהיב בה שמרים מוכח דלהכי תלייה: **ברא דתומא.** גלע של שום: **ומנח בברזא דדנא.** מקום שיש בו נקב בחבית והיין יוצא [ב] ונותנו שם בשבת לסתום והוי כמתקן ומערים לכתחילה: **ואומר לאצנועיה.** להאי ברא דתומא מיכוינא ועוד עביד אחריתי אזל נאים במברא בספינה רחבה העשויה לעבור המים והיא של נכרי ויודע הוא שיעבירנה הנכרי לצד האחר: **וסייר פירי.** ומשמר שם פירות כרמו ונמצא שהנכרי מעבירו במים בשבת: **הערמה בדרבנן היא.** ה"ג הך הערמה לאו באיסורא דאורייתא הוא אלא באיסורא דרבנן דא"נ עביד ממש בלא הערמה אדרבנן הוא דעבר הלכך כיון דצורבא מרבנן הוא לא אחמירו עליה דהוא לא אתי למעבד לכתחילה להדיא בלא הערמה לעבור שם לפני הכל: **מתני' נותנין מים.** בשבת ע"ג שמרים הנתונים במשמרת מבעוד יום: **כדי שיצולו.** שיהו צלולין לזוב (ז) את היין מפני הקמחים שקורים יינ"ש: **בסודרין ובכפיפה מצרית.** העשויה מצורי דקל: **כפיפה.** סל: **ונותנין ביצה במסננת.** שהחרדל נתון בה להסתנן וקולטת את הפסולת ואף הביצה החלמון שלה נוטף ומסתנן עמו והוה ליה לחרדל למראה והחלבון שהוא קשור נשאר למעלה ורבינו הלוי פירש סימנה של ביצה לתוך תבשיל היא ולא לתוך חרדל הוא דשרי משום שינוי ויורד לתוך הקערה שהוא כלי שני ומתלבן התבשיל: **אינומלין.** פוסו"ן: **לגין.** גדול מכוס וקטן מחבית: **גמ' טורד.** מערבב: **בין הגיתות שנו.** שכל היינות עכורין ושותין אותן בשמריהם הלכך אין כאן תיקון דבלאו הכי משתתי: **שלא יעשה גומא.** מן הסודר בפי הכלי כי עובדא דחול אי נמי אתי לידי סחיטה: **שלא יגביה.** הכפיפה מקרקעית (ד) כלי התחתון טפח כמדת אהל: **פרונקא.** בגד שטוחין על גיגית יין לכסותה: **אפלגא דכובא שרי.** דלאו אוהלא הוי: **לא ניהדק איניש ציניתא בפומא דכוזני דחביתא.** כלי חרס קטן שמערין בו יין מחבית לא יתן בפיו קשין וקסמים בחזקה לפי שאין לך מסננת גדולה מזו: **שפו שיכרא.** כל היכא דתני לשון שפוי בנחת הוא והפסולת נשאר בשולי הכלי: **והאיכא ניצוצות.** קטנות הניסופות באחרונה מתוך הפסולת שקורין ברי"ש והנהו מוכחן דבורר הוא: **ניצוצות בי רב פפא לא חשיבי.** (ה) שחנוני מטיל שכר היה כדאמרינן בבבא מציעא (דף סה:) ובפסחים (דף קיג.) הלכך אינו מקפיד לניצוצות כל כך וכשמגיע לניצוצות משליך הן ופסולתן לחוץ ותחילת שפייתן (ו) מן הפסולת ניכר דלאו בורר הוא: לפי

עין משפט נר מצוה

יז א מיי' פ"א מהל' י"ט הלכה כג סמג לאוין עה טוש"ע א"ח סי' תקכו סעיף א:
יח ב מיי' שם טוש"ע שם סעיף ד:
יט ג מיי' פי"ט מהל' שבת הלכה כ סמג לאוין סה טוש"ע א"ח סי' שא סעיף לט:
כ ד מיי' שם טוש"ע שם סעיף לח וסי' יג סעיף א:
כא ה מיי' פ"ו מהל' י"ט הלכה יז סמג לאוין עה טוש"ע א"ח סי' תקיו סעיף ג:
כב ו מיי' פ"ז שם הלכה ח סמג שם טוש"ע שם סי' תקלג סעיף ב:
כג ז מיי' פכ"ג מהל' שבת הלכה ג טוש"ע שם סי' שיח סעיף יא:
כד ח טור א"ח סימן שלג:
כה ט מיי' פ"א מהל' שבת הלכה יד ופכ"א הלכה יז סמג שם טוש"ע א"ח סי' שיט סעיף ט:
כו י מיי' שם טוש"ע שם סעיף יג:
כז כ ל מ נ מיי' פ"ח מהל' שבת הלכה יז ופכ"א הלכה יז סמג שם טוש"ע שם סעיף י ויא:
כח ס מיי' פכ"ב הלכה לב טוש"ע שם סעיף יב:
כט פ מיי' שם סמג שם טוש"ע א"ח סי' שטו סעיף יג:
ל צ טוש"ע שם סימן שיט סעיף יג:
לא ק שם סעיף יד:

רבינו חננאל

לאיסור. וזה שאמר מתעטף אדם בכילה וכסכסיה ויוצא בה לרה"ר פי' כוסכיא חוטין ומשיחות שעליה. הלכה היא דקא מקשינן עלה מדרב הונא דאמר היוצא בטלית שאינה מצויצת כהלכתה כגון שתלה ציצית בג' כנפי הטלית והניח הרביעית אותן חוטי הציצית כיון שאינה מצויצת בד' כנפות שלה אינה חשובה ציצית דמצוה. וכהוציאו דעלמא הן חשובין והיוצא בה חייב חטאת ומפרקינן ציצית לגבי טלית חשיבי ולא בטלי רוצה בקיומן כי בדעתו שיתלה הרביעית וילבשנה. אבל כוסכיא לגבי כילה אינו צריך להן ובטלי: והא דאמר רבה בר בר חנה מערים אדם על המשמרת ביו"ט לתלות בה רמונים ותולה בה שמרים אליבא דרבנן שאוסרין לתלות ולשמר לכתחלה ואע"פ שהיא אסורה והוא דתלה לה רמונים כרב אשי ואע"ג דאמרינן מ"ש מהא דתניא מטילין שכר במועד וכו' התם בשכר מועד לא מוכחא מלתא הכא במשמרת מוכחא מילתא ולשמר הוא תולה ואם תלה בה רמונים אין ואי לא לא. והא דאמרו ליה לרב אשי חזי מר הונא בר חיון. ואמרי לה רב הונא בר חילון דהוה שקיל ברא דתומא ומנח בברזא דדנא פי' שהיה נוטל ראש שום ונותנו בנקב של חבית שיוצא ממנו היין ולא היה מספסף מאותה חבית אלא חבית שבאוצר והיה ראש השום וסותם הנקב להצניע ראש השום והיה אומר

מסורת הש"ס

א) ביצה ו. כב., ב) מנחות לו. ע"ש, ג) מו"ק יב:, ד) [גירסת הערוך ובכפיפה], ה) לעיל דף קלח., ו) ...

הגהות הב"ח

(א) גמ' לא חשיבי ובטלי אמר (רבה) תא"מ ונ"ב ס"א רבי אבין: (ב) שם לא ניהדק איניש (ציניתא): (ג) שם ממנא למנא...

גליון הש"ס

מתני' ומסננין את היין בסודרין. ע"ל קלט ע"א תוד"ה אלא מסוכריא: תוס' ד"ה תלא כו' ושל דגים מאים. ע"ל ...

הגהות הגר"א

[א] במשנה ומסננין את היין. נ"ב צלול... [ב] רש"י ד"ה ומנח בברזא דדנא כו' והיין יוצא כו'...

ליקוטי רש"י

[נדפס בדף קמ.]

וְלָא יָדְעֲנָא אִי מִלְּפָנֶיהָ אִי מִלְּאַחֲרֶיהָ – but I do not know whether the Yom Tov was **before [the Sabbath]** (i.e. on Friday), **or after [the Sabbath]** (i.e. on Sunday);[1] **וְאָתוּ לְקַמֵּיהּ דְּרַבִּי יוֹחָנָן – and they came before R' Yochanan** for a ruling. **וְאָמַר לְהוּ – And he said to them: יִתְעַסְּקוּ בֵּיהּ עֲמָמִין – Let** those of **the nations** (i.e. non-Jews) **involve themselves with it.**[2]

The Gemara cites a second similar ruling:

וְאָמַר רָבָא – And Rava said: מֵת – Concerning **a corpse** that awaits burial, the law is as follows:[3] **בְּיוֹם טוֹב רִאשׁוֹן יִתְעַסְּקוּ בּוֹ עֲמָמִין –** If burial occurs **on the first Yom Tov** day, those of **the nations should involve themselves with it; בְּיוֹם טוֹב שֵׁנִי יִתְעַסְּקוּ בּוֹ יִשְׂרָאֵל –** but if the burial occurs **on the second Yom Tov** day, **Jews should involve themselves with it.**[4] **וַאֲפִילוּ בְּיוֹם טוֹב שֵׁנִי שֶׁל רֹאשׁ הַשָּׁנָה – And** this rule applies **even on the second Yom Tov** day **of Rosh Hashanah, מַה שֶּׁאֵין כֵּן בְּבֵיצָה – which is not the case regarding an egg.**[5] Since it is established that a corpse may be buried on Yom Tov (either by a gentile or a Jew), why did Rav Menashya issue a blanket ruling prohibiting it?[6]

The Gemara answers:

לְפִי שֶׁאֵינָן בְּנֵי תוֹרָה – Because [Bashkarians] are not Torah scholars, and they would likely adopt other groundless leniencies if they were informed of this legitimate leniency.

Having mentioned the laws of erecting a canopy on the Sabbath, the Gemara digresses to discuss the wearing of a canopy cloth as a cloak in a public domain:

אָמַר רַב אָבִין בַּר רַב הוּנָא אָמַר רַב חָמָא בַּר גּוּרְיָא – Rav Avin bar Rav Huna said in the name of Rav Chama bar Gurya: מִתְעַטֵּף אָדָם בְּכִילָּה וּבְכַבְּסֶיהָ – A person may wrap himself in a canopy and its strings,[7] **וְיוֹצֵא לִרְשׁוּת הָרַבִּים בְּשַׁבָּת וְאֵינוֹ חוֹשֵׁשׁ – and go out into the public domain on the Sabbath without concern** that he will be liable for carrying the attached strings.[8]

The Gemara asks:

מַאי שְׁנָא מִדְּרַב הוּנָא – But what is the difference between this case and **that of Rav Huna? דְּאָמַר רַב הוּנָא אָמַר רַב – For Rav Huna said in the name of Rav: הַיּוֹצֵא בְּטַלִּית שֶׁאֵינָהּ מְצוּיֶּצֶת כְּהִילְכָתָהּ בְּשַׁבָּת – One who goes out** into the public domain **on the Sabbath wearing a cloak which is not equipped with *tzitzis* in the halachically correct** manner[9] **חַיָּיב חַטָּאת – is liable to a *chatas*** offering, for the *tzitzis* strings are viewed as a burden being carried.[10] Similarly, we should forbid the wearing of

NOTES

1. R' Assi was unsure of the precise nature of the inquiry. That is, the person may have died on a Yom Tov which fell on a Friday, in which case the body would remain unburied not only that day but through the next day (the Sabbath) as well, without a special dispensation [necessary so that the corpse would not decay]. Or, the person may have died on the Sabbath, and they came on Sunday, which was Yom Tov, to ask whether they were permitted to bury the *already* decaying corpse.

2. It is prohibited for a Jew to perform a burial under any circumstances [even if the corpse will decay — see *Rama*, *Orach Chaim* 526:1], because digging a grave transgresses a *melachah* (either *building* or *plowing*; see *Rashi* to 73b ד״ה פטור). However, since human dignity is involved, burial does override the Rabbinic prohibition of אֲמִירָה לְנָכְרִי, *telling a gentile [to perform a melachah]* (*Meiri* to *Beitzah* 6a; see also *Rashba* here). Therefore, R' Yochanan permitted instructing non-Jews to perform the burial on Yom Tov in either of the above two cases.

3. Rava discusses a case where the burial of the corpse is already (or definitely will be) delayed, such as when the person died on the Sabbath, and the first Yom Tov day fell on the following Sunday (*Rashi*; see next note; see also *Rashba, Ritva MHK* ed., and *Ran MHK* ed.).

4. If the corpse is being buried on the first day of Yom Tov, it must be buried by non-Jews, as explained above (see note 2). If, however, the burial is being performed on the *second* day of Yom Tov (e.g. in a case where the person died on Sabbath, which was the first day of Yom Tov), even Jews may perform the burial. For after the introduction of the fixed calendar, the observance of the second day of Yom Tov is only Rabbinic in origin (see *Beitzah* 4b); and with respect to the needs of a corpse, the Sages treated that day as a regular weekday, and allowed Jews to perform the burial. [See, however, below; see also *Orach Chaim* 526:4 with *Rama* as to whether this holds true even if non-Jews are readily available to perform the burial.]

Note that in *Rashi's* view the permit issued by Rava allowing non-Jews to bury the corpse on the first day of Yom Tov only applies to a case where the burial of the corpse is already delayed (see previous note). [*Rashi* apparently bases his opinion upon the fact that R' Yehudah bar Shilas saw fit to specify that the inquiry of the people of Maon was advanced concerning this sort of situation (see *Rashba*).] Many Rishonim, however (see *Ramban*, *Rashba*, *Ritva MHK* ed., et al.), favor the view of the Geonim, who maintain that according to Rava a corpse may be buried through a non-Jew on the first Yom Tov day even on a Yom Tov which falls midweek. The halachah follows this view; see *Orach Chaim* 526:1,4. For a discussion concerning the practice in our time, see *Beur Halachah* ad loc. ד״ה ואפילו and *Igros Moshe, Orach Chaim* III: §76. See also *Emes LeYaakov* at length for a discussion of *Rashi's* view here; see also below, note 6. [See *Maharsha* and *Leshon HaZahav*, who state that *Rashi's* qualification only refers to the permit of Rava allowing burial by non-Jews on the first day of Yom Tov — however, Jews may certainly bury a corpse on the second day of Yom Tov even if it falls midweek.]

There is also a dispute among the Rishonim if other Rabbinic prohibitions, such as moving the corpse to place it in the grave, are also waived for a Jew, or if we say that once a gentile will be digging the grave he should also attend to the entire burial. See *Ramban, Rashba, Rambam, Hil. Yom Tov* 1:23, and *Orach Chaim* 526:4; see also *Chidushei HaRan*.

5. The Sages distinguished between Rosh Hashanah and other festivals in the case of a newly laid egg, ruling that an egg laid on the first day of Rosh Hashanah is *prohibited* for consumption even on the second day, although an egg laid on the first day of any other Yom Tov is *permitted* on the second day. Regarding burial, however, the second day of Rosh Hashanah is accorded the same lenient treatment that the second day of the other festivals receive (*Rashi*; see *Beitzah* 4b-6a for why Rosh Hashanah is different than the other festivals).

6. An apparent difficulty: Since the permit issued by Rava only applied to cases where the burial of the corpse is already delayed [according to *Rashi* — see above, note 4], how can the Gemara ask that Rav Menashya should have sent a ruling to the people of Bashkar permitting burial of a corpse on Yom Tov? Their query did not indicate that the subject of their inquiry was a case of this sort! [According to the *Maharsha* cited above (in note 4), this difficulty does not arise, for burial on the *second* day of Yom Tov is permitted in any case.] *Rashba* answers that since their query left the circumstances of the case unclear, Rav Menashya should have specified that burial would be permitted in certain specific cases, instead of issuing a blanket prohibition (see also *Rashash*). [This difficulty obviously does not arise according to the view of the Geonim, who hold that Rava's permit concerning both days of Yom Tov applies even to a Yom Tov that falls midweek.]

7. A canopy consists of a wide cloth with strings sewn onto the sides which are used to tie the canopy to the bedposts (*Rashi*).

8. Rav Avin rules that one may wrap this cloth around himself as a cloak and walk out into the public domain; one need not be concerned that the attached strings, which perform no function when the cloth is being used as a cloak, are considered a burden which may not be carried four *amos* in the public domain (*Rashi*).

9. E.g. only three out of the four corners of the cloak were equipped with *tzitzis*.

10. [Had the cloak been equipped with *tzitzis* in the halachically correct manner, there would have been no question of carrying, for since the garment requires the strings, they are viewed as part of the garment. Thus, they are being worn, not carried (see *Rambam, Hil. Shabbos* 19:20). Furthermore,] had the cloak not been equipped with *tzitzis* at all, there would have been no question of carrying, for although the wearer of such a cloak transgresses the sin of wearing a four-cornered garment without *tzitzis*, the cloak remains a garment that is being "worn," not "carried." The halachically invalid *tzitzis*, however, perform no function for the cloak and are viewed not as part of the garment but rather as a burden. Carrying them four *amos* in the public domain is thus Biblically prohibited (*Rashi*).

עין משפט
נר מצוה

יז א מיי' פ"א מהל' י"ט הלכה כב סמג לאוין עה טוש"ע א"ח סי' תקכו סעיף ד:
יח ב מיי' שם טוש"ע שם סעיף ד:
יט ג מיי' פי"ט מהל' שבת הלכה כ סמג לאוין סה טוש"ע א"ח סי' שא סעיף לט:
כ ד מיי' שם טוש"ע שם סעיף לח וסי' יג סעיף ד:
כא ה מיי' פ"ג מהל' י"ט הלכה יא סמג לאוין עה טוש"ע א"ח סי' תקיז סעיף ד:
כב ו מיי' פ"ז הלכה ח סמג שם טוש"ע שם סי' תקלג סעיף ב:
כג ז מיי' פכ"א מהל' שבת הלכה ג טוש"ע שם סי' שיט סעיף יא:
כד ח טור א"ח סימן שלט:
כה ט מיי' פ"ח מהל' שבת הלכה יד ופכ"א הלכה יא סמג שם טוש"ע א"ח סי' שיט סעיף ט:
כו י מיי' פ"ח מהלכות י"ט הלכה יח סמג שם טוש"ע שם סעיף יד:
כז כ ל מ נ מיי' פ"ח מהל' שבת הלכה יד ופכ"א הלכה יז סמג לג טוש"ע שם סעיף י יא:
כח ס ע מיי' פכ"א שם הלכה יח טוש"ע שם סעיף יב:
כט פ מיי' שם סמג שם טוש"ע שם סעיף יג:
ל צ טוש"ע שם סימן שיט סעיף יג:
לא ק שם סעיף יד:

ולא ידענא אי מלפניה אי מלאחריה ואתו לקמיה דרבי יוחנן ואמר להו יתעסקו ביה עממין א) ואמר רבא א מת בי"ט ראשון יתעסקו בו עממין ב ביום טוב שני יתעסקו בו ישראל ואפילו ביו"ט שני של ראש השנה מה שאין כן בביצה לפי שאינן בני תורה: א"ר אבין בר רב הונא אמר רב חמא בר גוריא ג מתעטף אדם בכילה ובכסכסיה ויוצא לרה"ר בשבת ואינו חושש מ"ש מדרב הונא ד דאמר רב הונא אמר רב ה היוצא בטלית שאינה מצויצת כהלכתה בשבת חייב חטאת ציצית לגבי טלית חשיבי ולא בטלי הני לא חשיבי ובטלי אמר (א) רבה בר רב הונא ו מערים אדם על המשמרת ביו"ט לתלות בה רמונים ותולה בה שמרים אמר רב אשי והוא דתלה בה רמונים מאי שנא מהא דתניא ז ח מטילין שכר במועד לצורך המועד שלא לצורך המועד אסור אחד שכר תמרים ואחד שכר שעורים אע"פ שיש להן ישן מערים ושותה מן החדש התם לא מוכחא מילתא הכא מוכחא מילתא אמרו ליה רבנן לרב אשי חזי מר האי צורבא מרבנן ורב הונא ב"ר חיון שמיה ואמרי לה רב הונא בר חלוון שמיה ט דשקל ברא דתומא ומנח בברזא דדנא ואמר לאצנועיה קמיכוינא ואזיל י ונאים במברא ועבר להך גיסא וסייר פירי ואמר אנא למינם קמיכוינא אמר להו הערמה קאמרת הערמה דרבנן היא וצורבא מרבנן לא אתי למיעבד לכתחילה: **מתני'** כ נותנין מים ע"ג השמרים בשביל שיצולו ל ומסננין את היין [א] בסודרין ז) ובכפיפה מצרית מ ונותנין ביצה במסננת של חרדל ועושין אנומלין בשבת ר' יהודה אומר בשבת בכוס ביו"ט בלגין ובמועד בחבית רבי צדוק אומר הכל לפי האורחין: **גמ'** י) אמר זעירי נ נותן אדם יין צלול ומים צלולין לתוך המשמרת בשבת ואינו חושש אבל עכורין לא מיתיבי רבן שמעון בן גמליאל אומר טורד אדם חבית של יין ינה ושמריה ונותן לתוך המשמרת בשבת ואינו חושש תרגמה זעירי ס בין הגיתות שנו: ע מסננין את היין בסודרין: אמר רב שימי בר חייא ובלבד שלא יעשה גומא: פ ובכפיפה מצרית: אמר רב חייא בר אשי אמר רב צ ובלבד שלא יגביה מקרקעיתו של כלי טפח אמר ק רב האי פרונקא אפלגיה דכובא שרי אכוליה כובא אסור אמר רב פפא ר לא ניהדק איניש (ב) ש ציניתא בפומיה דכוזני דחביתא משום דמיחזי כמשמרת דבי רב פפא ת שאפו שיכרא ממנא למנא (ג) אמר ליה רב אחא מדפתי לרבינא האיכא ניצוצות ניצוצות לבי רב פפא לא חשיבי: ונותנין ביצה במסננת: תני יעקב קרחה לפי

רש"י

ולא ידענא אי מלפניה. אם חל י"ט בע"ש ומת בו ביום ומפני שלא יוכלו להתעסק בו למחר התירו לקוברו ע"י עממים: **אי מלאחריה.** והוא מת בשבת ומפני שנסתפק ככר והיה מסריח התירו: **מת ביו"ט ראשון כו'.** מת שנסתפק כגון שמת בשבת ולמחר היה יו"ט: **מה שאין כן בביצה.** דאין ר"ה שוה לימים טובים של גליות דאילו ר"ה אמיר יו"ט שני דיליה ונולדה בזה אסורה בזה: **מתעטף אדם בכילה.** שהוא כסדין ומתעטף בה דרך מלבוש: **ובכסכסיה.** רצועות התלויות בה ולא אמרינן הך רצועות לאו לצורך עיטוף נינהו והוה משאוי ההוא שעתא שאין כיסכסין עשויין אלא לנטותה באהל: **חייב חטאת.** ואילו לא היתה מצויצת כלל לא מיחייב דהא לבושיה הוא אלמא הציציות הויין לו משאוי הואיל ואינן כמצותו אינן צריכין לה ומן הבגד ממש אינן דליחשבינן כוותיה: **חשיבי.** משום דשל תכלת הן ולא בטלי והוו בה משוי: **מערים אדם על המשמרת ביו"ט.** לרבנן דאמרי אין תולין את המשמרת ביום טוב ואוקימנא דטעמא לאו משום אהל אלא משום עובדא דחול מערים ותולה אותה לצורך רמונים דלאו עובדין דחול נינהו ומסנן בה שמרים הואיל ונתלית דהא אמרינן נותנין לתלויה ביו"ט: **והוא דתלי בה רמונים.** ברישא דמוכח מילתא דמעיקרא לאו לשמרים תלייה: **מטילין.** ברשיי"ר בלע"ז: **במועד.** בחולו של מועד: **מערים ושותה מן החדש.** אלמא בלא שום הוכחה מותר להערים: **התם לאו מוכחא מילתא.** דמילתא דאיסורא הוא דהרואה אומר לצורך המועד הוא שאין הכל יודעין שיש לו מן הישן הכא מוכחא מילתא לאיסור דסתם תולה משמרת לשמרים הוא תולה ואי לא יהיב בה רימונים ברישא להצניע בעלמא כי יהיב בה שמרים מוכח דלהכי תלייה: **ברא דתומא.** צלע של שום: **ומנח בברזא דדנא.** מקום שיש בו נקב בחבית והיין יוצא [ב] נותנו שם בשבת לסתום והוי כמתקן ומערים לכתחילה: **ואומר לאצנועיה.** להאי ברא דתומא מיכוינא ועוד עביד אחריתי אזיל נאים במברא בספינה רחבה העשויה לעבור המים והיא של נכרי ויודע הוא שיעבירנו הנכרי לצד האחר: **וסייר פירי.** ומשמר שם פירות כרמו ונמצא שהנכרי מעבירו במים בשבת: **הערמה בדרבנן היא.** ה"ג הך הערמה לאו באיסורא דאורייתא הוא אלא באיסורא דרבנן דלא אתי למעבד ממש בלא הערמה דלרבנן הוא דעבד הלכך כיון דצורבא מרבנן הוא לא אחמירו עליה דהוא לא אתי למעבד לכתחילה להדיא בלא הערמה לעבור שם לפני הכל: **מתני' נותנין מים.** בשבת ע"ג שמרים הנתונים במשמרת מבעוד יום: **כדי שיצולו.** שיהו צלולין לזוב י) את היין מפני הקמחים שקורים יינ"ש: **בסודרין ובכפיפה מצרית.** העשויה מצורי דקל: **כפיפה.** סל: **ונותנין ביצה במסננת.** שהחרדל נתון בה להסתנן וקולטת את הפסולת ואף הבילה החלמון שלה נוטף ומסתנן עמו והוה ליה לחרדל למראה והחלבון שהוא קשור נשאר למעלה ורבינו הלוי פירש סינונה של בילה לתוך תבשיל היא ולא לתוך חרדל ובמסננת של חרדל הוא דשרי משום שינוי ויורד לתוך הקערה שהוא כלי שני ומתלבן התבשיל: **אינומלין.** פוסו"ן: לגין. גדול מכוס וקטן מחבית: **גמ' טורד.** מערבב: **בין הגיתות שנו.** שכל היינות עכורין ושותין אותן בשמריהם הלכך אין כאן תיקון דבלאו הכי משתתי: **שלא יעשה גומא.** מן הסודר בפי הכלי כי עובדא דחול אי נמי אתי לידי סחיטה: **שלא יגביה.** הכפיפה מקרקעית (ד) כלי התחתון טפח כמדת אהל: **פרונקא.** בגד שטוחין על גיגית יין לכסותה: **אפלגא דכובא שרי.** דלאו אוהלא הוי: **לא ניהדק איניש ציניתא בפומא דכוזני דחביתא.** כלי חרס קטן שמערין בו יין מחבית לא יתן בפיו קשין וקסמים בחוזקה לפי שאין לך מסננת גדולה מזו: **שפו שיכרא.** כל היכא דתני לשון שפוי בנחת הוא והפסולת נשאר בשולי הכלי: **והאיכא ניצוצות.** קטנות הנישופות באחרונה מתוך הפסולת שקורין ברייו"ש והנהו מוכחן דבורר הוא: **ניצוצות בי רב פפא לא חשיבי.** (ה) שהמוני מטיל שכר היה כדאמרינן בבבא מליעא (דף סה:) ובפסחים (דף קיג.) הלכך אינו מקפיד לניצוצות כל כך וכשמגיע לניצוצות משליך הן ופסולתן לחוץ ותחילת שפייתן (ו) מן הפסולת ניכר דלאו בורר הוא:
לפי

תוספות

יום טוב שני יתעסקו בו ישראל. ובבילה (ד' ו.) מסקינן בתר הך מילתא אמר רבינא האידנא דאיכא חברי חיישינן פירוש ולא יתעסקו בו ישראל פן ילוו עליהם חברי לעשות מלאכה ביו"ט כיון שרואין שעושין בשביל מת ומעשה היה והוליכו מת חוץ לתחום ביו"ט והלכו אחריו בסוסים להתעסק במת וכעס ר"ת אף על ההולכים ברגל בלא סוסים ושמע רבי דטעמו משום דמסיק רבינא האידנא דאיכא חברי ולדידן אע"ג דליכא למיחש יש לאסור כיון דמסיק הכי גם יש ליראה פן ילוו השרים להתעסק במלאכתן ולכתוב מה שהם רוצים ושלח להם ר"ת בני בשכר אינם בני תורה בני מליאון (ז) (אותה העיר) בני תורה ל):

ציצית חשיבי ולא בטלי. שאינם מבוטלין לפי שחשובים הם בעיניו שדעתו ליתן בטלית ציצית רביעית כך פי' ר"ח: **הא לא חשיבי ובטלי** על זה סמך רבי להניח באבנטו רצועות התלויות בו ויש שקושרים בהם בתי שוקים דבטלי דלא חשיבי כולי האי: **מאי** שנא מהא דתניא כו'. פי' [וס"ל כרבי יוסי בר' יהודה דאמר מערימין] לעיל בפ' כל כתבי (דף קיז:):

תלא ל) דבישרא כו'. לא כפירוש הקונטרס דפי' בשר מליח שתלו ליבשו דהל"ל הא בפרק מפנין דמה שייך הכא ועוד למה מזכיר תלא ועוד מוכח לעיל בפרק מפנין (דף קמח.) דדג מליח נמי חזי לאומצא ועוד דהכא בטלטול איירי ואמרינן לעיל דרב במוקצה לטלטל סבר לה כר"ש ונראה כפי' הערוך דמשום תלא נקטיה ובלא בשר אלא תלא דבשרא לא ממאיס ושרי לטלטולי ושל דגים מאיס והוי מוקצה מחמת מיאוס והשתא אתי שפיר באיסור דתלא כעין כישא דירקא ור' פי' לנו דתלא דבשרא רגיל להיות בו תורת כלי אבל של דגים לא ולא משום מוקצה מחמת מיאוס דלא איירי שמעתין במוקצה מחמת מיאוס. מ"ר:
אבל

מסורת הש"ס

א) ביצה ו. כב., ב) מנחות לז. ע"ש, ג) מו"ק יג:, ד) [גירסת הערוך ובכפיפה], ה) לעיל דף קלד., ו) שם קמ., ז) [גירס' הערוך רבא], ח) [עי' תוס' ביצה לב: ד"ה מלמטה למעלה], ט) גי' הערוך בערך נכת א' לא נהדק איניש לכאת לפומא דכוזינתא, י) כאן יש ערבוב דברים ע"י הסמכת נקודות המבדלים וצ"ל כך שיהיו צלולין לזוב את היין מפני הקמחים וכו' ועי' פירש"י לעיל קלד., כ) [וע' תוס' ביצה ו. ד"ה והאידנא], ל) [שייך לדף קמ.].

הגהות הב"ח

(א) גמ' לא חשיבי ובטלי אמר (רבה) תא"מ ונ"ב ס"א אבין: (ב) שם לא ניהדק איניש (ציניתא) תא"מ ונ"ב צבא: (ג) שם ממנא למנא בלבלא א"ל ר' אחא: (ד) רש"י ד"ה שלא יגביה וכו' מקרקעיתו של כלי: (ה) ד"ה ניצוצות וכו' לא חשיבי שהמוני ומטיל שכר היה כדאמרינן בב"מ. נ"ב ע"ש דף סה דקאמר רב פפא ערסא דידי שרי מ"ט שכרא שלי לא פסיד. ובפסחים דף קיג קאמרי מאי לכותך לבי קוריות וכו' אמר רב פפא אי לאו דרמאי שכרא לא איעתרי ולא מצינא אלא לגבי רב פפא קודי ופירש"י שתי לשונות: (ו) באד' ותחלת שפיתן שאין הפסולת ניכר לאו בורר הוא: (ז) תוס' ד"ה יום וכו' בני מליאון (אותה העיר) תא"מ ונ"ב הגה"ה הוא:

גליון הש"ס

מתני' ומסננין את היין בסודרין. עי' קיא תוס' ד"ה מהו מוקצייתא: תוס' ד"ה תלא בר' ושל דגים מאיס. עי' יע ע"ש תוס' ד"ה אני כרכי:

הגהות הגר"א

[א] במשנה ומסננין את היין. נ"ב בגלל כמ"ש בגמ'. וקאמר בסודרין לאפוקי משמרת דאסור. ומשמרת דגמרא ע"י פנו סודר כן פסק הרמב"ם. אבל הטור כתב דכ"ש במשמרת דמותר. וקאמר דמותר דמים בו שמי אסור משא"כ במשמרת לכ"ש בגמרא ומים כו'. והרשב"א פירש דקאמר סודרין דאפילו עבור מותר. (ועמ"ש רבינו בא"ח סי' שיט): [ב] רש"י ד"ה ומנח בברזא דדנא כו' והיין יוצא כו'. נ"ב והיין דוחק יוצא. (ועמ"ש רבינו בא"ח סי' שיב):

ליקוטי רש"י

[נדפס בדף קמ.]

רבינו חננאל

לאיסור. וזה שאמר מתעטף בכילה ובכסכסיה ויוצא בה לרה"ר פי' כוסכיא חוטין ומשיחות שעליה. הלכה היא דקא מקשינן עלה מדרב הונא דאמר היוצא בטלית שאינה מצויצת כהלכתה כגון שתלה ציצית בג' כנפי הטלית והניח הרביעית אותן חוטי הציצית כיון שאינה מצויצת בד' כנפות שלה אינה חשובה ציצית דמצוה. וכחוטין דעלמא הן חשובין והיוצא בה חייב חטאת ופרקינן ציצית לגבי טלית חשיבי ולא בטלי שלב האדם רוצה בקיומן כדי להטילן שיתלה הרביעית וילבשנה. אבל כוסכיא לגבי כילה אינו צריך להן ובטלי: והא דאמר רבה בר בר חנה מערים אדם על המשמרת בי"ט לתלות בה רמונים ותולה בה שמרים אליבא דרבנן שאוסרין לתלות ולשמר לכתחלה ואע"פ שהיא אסורה והוא דתלה לה רמונים כרב אשי ואע"ג דאמרינן מ"ש מהא דתניא מטילין שכר במועד וכו' התם בשכר במועד לא מוכחא מלתא הכא במשמרת מוכחא מילתא דשמר הוא תולה ואם תלה בה רמונים אין ואי לא לא. והא דאמרו ליה לרב אשי חזי מר האי צורבא מרבנן רב הונא בר חיון. ואמרי לה בר חילון דהוה שקיל ברא דתומא ומנח בברזא דדנא פי' שהיה נוטל ראש שום ונותנו בנקב של חבית שיצא ממנו היין והיה הנקב מתספק מאוחה חבית אלא חבית שבאוצר והיה הנקב בראש השום והיה אומר להצניע ראש השום אני הולך וישן במעברא וכו' אמר להו רב אשי הערמה מדרבנן היא והערמה לכתחלה ת"ח לא עבדי **ונותנין המים** על השמרים בשביל שיצלו אמר זעירי נותן אדם יין צלול ומים צלולין לתוך המשמרת בשבת ואינו חושש אבל עכורין לא. ואם בין הגתות הוא שעדיין היין תוסס ואינו צלול טורד אדם חבית ינה ושמריה בשבת ואינו חושש ואפילו אליבא דרבנן וליכא דפליג בהא ומסננין את היין בסודרין אמר רב שימי בר חייא ובלבד שלא יעשה גומא. פי' שלא ימשוך קצות הסודר למעלה וישאר כמו גומא באמצעיתו. ובכפיפה מצרית. ואמרינן משמיה דרב שלא יגביה מקרקעיתו של כלי טפח. וכל מקום שאמרו טפח כאהל חשוב ואין עושין אהלי עראי לכתחלה בשבת. פי' צבא הפך הקנקן והיו בו נקבים קטנים קטנים. לסנן בו היין כאשר יצוקהו לקנקן. אם יהיה זה הכיסוי בחצי פי הכלי אינו מסנן. ואם הוא כל הכלי הפה של כלי הרי הוא כמסננת ונראה כמשמר היין משמרת: רי"א פרונקא מטלית של בגד שעשאו לכסוי כובא בפונדקאות ... לא ניהדק צבתא בפומא דכוזא משום דמחזי כמשמרת. ... ונותנין ביצה במסננת של חרדל ...
לפי

a canopy outside, for the wearer is carrying the strings that are attached to the canopy.[11] – ? –

The Gemara answers:

צִיצִית לְגַבֵּי טַלִּית חֲשִׁיבֵי וְלֹא בָּטְלֵי – ***Tzitzis*, in relation to the cloak, are significant, and are** thus **not** rendered **subordinate** to the cloak; rather, they remain distinct. **הָנֵי לֹא חֲשִׁיבֵי וּבָטְלֵי** – **These** strings attached to the canopy, however, **are insignificant, and are** thus rendered **subordinate** to the cloak.[12]

The Sages ruled in the Mishnah above (137b) that suspending a strainer is prohibited both on the Sabbath and on Yom Tov. The Gemara now describes a manner in which suspending a strainer would be permitted:

אָמַר רַבָּה בַּר רַב הוּנָא – **Rabbah bar Rav Huna said:**[13] **מַעֲרִים אָדָם עַל הַמְשַׁמֶּרֶת בְּיוֹם טוֹב לִתְלוֹת בָּהּ רִמּוֹנִים** – **A person may employ a subterfuge with regard to** the erecting of **a strainer on Yom Tov**, by erecting it **to hold pomegranates, וְתוֹלֶה בָהּ שְׁמָרִים** – **and** once he has constructed it for that purpose, he may then **hold dregs in it**; that is, he may use it to strain wine.[14]

The Gemara qualifies this permit:

אָמַר רַב אַשִׁי – **Rav Ashi said: וְהוּא דְתָלָה בָהּ רִמּוֹנִים** – **But this** may be done **only if he** actually **holds pomegranates in it** first, to demonstrate positively that it was constructed originally for that purpose. [15]

The Gemara challenges this permit, citing a case where a subterfuge may be used without actually carrying out the ostensible intent beforehand:

מַאי שְׁנָא מֵהָא דְתַנְיָא – **But how does this differ from that which was learned in a Baraisa: מְטִילִין שֵׁכָר בַּמּוֹעֵד לְצוֹרֶךְ הַמּוֹעֵד** – **WE MAY BREW BEER ON** the intermediate days **OF THE FESTIVAL IF IT IS NEEDED FOR THE FESTIVAL. שֶׁלֹּא לְצוֹרֶךְ הַמּוֹעֵד אָסוּר** – But if it is **NOT NEEDED FOR THE FESTIVAL, IT IS FORBIDDEN** to do so. **אֶחָד שֵׁכָר תְּמָרִים וְאֶחָד שֵׁכָר שְׂעוֹרִים** – This is true regarding **BOTH DATE BEER AND BARLEY BEER.**[16] **אַף עַל פִּי שֶׁיֵּשׁ לָהֶן יָשָׁן מַעֲרִים וְשׁוֹתֶה מִן הֶחָדָשׁ** – **And EVEN THOUGH THEY HAVE OLDER** beer in stock, **THEY MAY** brew new beer and **EMPLOY A SUBTERFUGE BY DRINKING** exclusively **FROM THE NEW** stock.[17] Now, if one employs this subterfuge and brews new beer, it was never positively demonstrated that that beer was needed for Yom Tov. Nevertheless, employing this subterfuge is permitted by the Baraisa. Here, as well, the subterfuge should be permitted even if pomegranates were *not* actually held in the strainer.[18] – ? –

The Gemara answers:

הָתָם לֹא מוֹכְחָא מִילְּתָא – **There, it is not apparent** that a usually prohibited act was intended, for it is permitted to brew beer for Yom Tov. Thus, the subterfuge may be employed without any prior qualification. **הָכָא מוֹכְחָא מִילְּתָא** – **Here,** however, **it is apparent** that a usually prohibited act was intended, because it is generally prohibited to erect a strainer which is presumably for straining wine. Thus, one is only permitted to construct the strainer if he first demonstrates the purpose of its construction by using it to hold pomegranates.[19]

NOTES

11. For these strings perform no function for the cloak, and should thus be viewed as being "carried," not "worn," in the public domain (*Rashi*).

12. The *tzitzis* include strings of *techeiles* (strings treated with a costly bluish dye); thus, they are not deemed subordinate to the cloak to which they are attached, but rather remain an independent burden. Strings attached to the canopy being worn as a cloak, however, are made of inexpensive materials. They are thus rendered subordinate to the cloak, and take on the cloak's garment status (*Rashi*).

Alternatively, since the owner of the cloak no doubt wishes for the *tzitzis* already attached to the cloak to remain so that he may add *tzitzis* strings to the cloak's fourth corner, those *tzitzis* are significant on their own and not subordinate to the cloak. In our case, however, as long as the cloth is being used as a cloak, he has no use for the attached strings and they are therefore deemed insignificant (*Rabbeinu Chananel,* quoted by *Tosafos*; see *Chidushei HaRan* and *Ritva MHK* ed. at length; see also *Chasam Sofer*; see also *Chayei Adam, Hil. Shabbos* 56:13,14 with *Nishmas Adam*; also *Orach Chaim* 301:38,39 with *Mishnah Berurah* [see there §150]).

13. *Bach* cites editions that read: R' Avin bar Rav Huna [who taught as well the Gemara's previous ruling concerning one who wraps himself in a canopy cloth and walks in the public domain].

14. Rabbah suggests that one may circumvent the prohibition against a strainer by constructing one initially for the alternative purpose of storing pomegranates, and then using this already constructed strainer for straining wine (*Rashi*). [As has been explained above (138a, see there note 1), the Sages prohibited the construction of a strainer not because it constitutes erecting an *ohel*, but rather because it constitutes עוּבְדָא דְחוֹל, *weekday activity*, for constructing the strainer is the first step in the straining process. Consequently, constructing a strainer for a different purpose, such as to store pomegranates, does not constitute "weekday activity," and is permitted on Yom Tov (see *Rashi*).]

Now, we have learned that other Rishonim dispute *Rashi* and maintain that the prohibition against constructing a strainer *is* directly based on the prohibition against erecting an *ohel*. They explain that constructing a strainer to store pomegranates is not similarly prohibited because a strainer constructed to strain wine is drawn tightly over the vessel [and thus resembles an *ohel*], while one constructed to hold pomegranates is drawn loosely over the vessel (*Ramban* above, 138a; see also *Ran MHK* ed.). Alternatively, a distinction can be drawn between the two cases as follows: A strainer constructed to strain wine is built for the purpose of covering the vessel underneath the *ohel*, and is thus prohibited; while one constructed to hold pomegranates is built for the purpose of the area above the vessel [and therefore does not constitute an *ohel*] (*Rashba* to 138a, citing *Rabbeinu Yonah*). [Once the strainer is permissibly constructed, wine may be placed in it, as taught in the Mishnah.]

[Note that while in the Mishnah and the Gemara above the verb תוֹלֶה, *he suspends*, referred to the act of putting the strainer in place, in Rabbah's ruling here it refers to the placing of items into an already constructed strainer.]

15. [See the Rishonim cited in the previous note for how each of them understand Rav Ashi's qualification.]

16. Barley beer was especially difficult to brew (see *Mishnah Berurah* 533:4); the Baraisa teaches that it, too, may be brewed on the intermediate days of the festival if it is needed for the festival.

17. The Baraisa rules that while one may not brew beer during the intermediate festival days for use after the festival, one who has older beer already on hand can effectively circumvent this prohibition by brewing a new batch and drinking from that new batch. When this subterfuge is employed, one is permissibly brewing beer for festival use, all the while assuring himself of sufficient supplies of beer for after the festival.

18. The fact that one may brew new beer even when he has an older batch of beer on hand indicates that no demonstration of intent is necessary when employing a subterfuge of this nature. For while the new beer is being brewed, there is no indication that it is needed for use during the festival. And although it is drunk during the festival, this cannot be viewed as a demonstration of its having been needed for Yom Tov. Although R' Ashi's qualification stated that one must use the strainer for pomegranates *first* and only then use it to strain, drinking of the new beer *after* it has been brewed is sufficient, and therefore *later* use of the strainer for pomegranates should also suffice! See *Rashi* and *Ritva MHK* ed.

19. Rav Ashi answers that since refining beer on the intermediate days of the festival is permitted if it is done for use on the festival, an observer in the above case, unaware of the older beer in stock, would likely conclude that the new beer is for festival use. Thus, no obvious indication of an innocent intent is required [for he will not be suspected of wrongdoing in any case]. In the case of one who constructs a strainer, however, even if the person would later use it to hold pomegranates, an observer would most likely assume that it was made for its usual purpose of straining wine, and only later used for an alternative purpose. Therefore, ruled Rav Ashi, it must first be used to hold pomegranates and

יום טוב שני יתעסקו בו ישראל. ובבילה (ד' ו.) מסקינן בתר הך מילתא אמר רבינא האידנא דאיכא חברי חיישינן פירוש ולא יתעסקו בו ישראל פן יבואו עליהם חברי לעשות מלאכה ביו"ט כיון שרואין שעושין בשביל מת ומעשה היה והוליכו מת חוץ לתחום ביו"ט והלכו אחריו בסוסים להתעסק במת וכעס ר"ת אף על ההולכים ברגל בלא סוסים ושמע רבי דטעמו משום דמסיק רבינא האידנא דאיכא חברי ולדידן אע"ג דליכא למיחש יש לאסור כיון דמסיק הכי גם יש לירא פן יבואו השרים להתעסק במלאכתן ולכתוב מה שהם רוצים ושלא להם ר"ת בני בשכר אינם בני תורה בני מליאון (ז) (אותה העיר) בני תורה:

ציצית חשיבי ולא בטלי. שאינם מבוטלין לפי שמקושרים הם בעניינו שדעתו ליתן בטלית ציצית רביעית כך פי' ר"ח: **הא לא חשיבי** ובטלי על זה סמך רבי להניח באבנטו רצועות התלויות בו ויש שקושרים בהם בתי שוקים דבטלי דלא חשיבי כולי האי: **מאי שנא מהא דתניא** כו'. פי' [וס"ל כרבי יוסי בר' יהודה דאמר מערימין] לעיל בפ' כל כתבי (דף קיז:):

תלא דבישרא כו'. לא כפירוש הקונטרס דפי' בשר מליח שתלו ליבשו דהל"ל הא בפרק מפנין דמה שייך הכא ועוד למה מזכיר תלא ועוד מוכח לעיל בפרק מפנין (דף קכח.) דדג מליח נמי חזי לאומצא ועוד דהכא בטלטול איירי ואמרינן לעיל דרב במוקצה לטלטל סבר לה כר"ש ונראה כפי' הערוך דמשום תלא נקטיה ובלא בשר אלא תלא דבשרא לא ממאיס ושרי לטלטולי ° ושל דגים מאיס והוי מוקצה מחמת מיאוס והשתא אתי שפיר דאיסור דתלא כעין כישא דירקא ור' פי' לנו דתלא דבשרא רגיל להיות בו תורת כלי אבל של דגים לא ולא משום מוקצה מחמת מיאוס דלא איירי שמעתין במוקצה מחמת מיאוס. מ"ר: אבל

ולא ידענא אי מלפניה אי מלאחריה ואתו לקמיה דרבי יוחנן ואמר להו יתעסקו ביה עממין (א) ואמר רבא א מת ביו"ט ראשון יתעסקו בו עממין ב ביום טוב שני יתעסקו בו ישראל ואפילו ביו"ט שני של ראש השנה מה שאין כן בביצה לפי שאינן בני תורה: א"ר אבין בר רב הונא אמר רב חמא בר גוריא ג מתעטף אדם בבילה ובכסכסיה ויוצא לרה"ר בשבת ואינו חושש מ"ש מדרב הונא ד דאמר רב הונא אמר רב ה היוצא בטלית שאינה מצוייצת כהלכתה בשבת חייב חטאת ציצית לגבי טלית חשיבי ולא בטלי הני לא חשיבי ובטלי אמר (א) רבה בר רב הונא ו מערים אדם על המשמרת ביו"ט לתלות בה רמונים ותולה בה שמרים אמר רב אשי והוא דתלה בה רמונים מאי שנא מהא דתניא ז מטילין שכר במועד לצורך המועד שלא לצורך המועד אסור אחד שכר תמרים ואחד שכר שעורים אע"פ שיש להן ישן מערים ושותה מן החדש התם לא מוכחא מילתא הכא מוכחא מילתא אמרו ליה רבנן לרב אשי חזי מר האי צורבא מרבנן ורב הונא ב"ר חיון שמיה ואמרי לה רב הונא בר חלון שמיה ח דשקיל ברא דתומא ומנח בברזא דדנא ואמר לאצנועיה קמיכוינא ואזיל ט ונאים במברא ועבר להך גיסא וסייר פירי ואמר אנא למינם קמיכוינא אמר להו הערמה קאמרת הערמה בדרבנן היא וצורבא מרבנן לא אתי למיעבד לכתחילה: **מתני'** י נותנין מים ע"ג השמרים בשביל שיצולו כ ומסננין את היין [א] בסודרין ל ובכפיפה מצרית מ ונותנין ביצה במסננת של חרדל ועושין אנומלין בשבת ר' יהודה אומר בשבת בכוס ביו"ט בלגין ובמועד בחבית רבי צדוק אומר הכל לפי האורחין: **גמ'** נ אמר זעירי נותן אדם יין צלול ומים צלולין לתוך המשמרת בשבת ואינו חושש אבל עכורין לא מיתיבי רבן שמעון בן גמליאל אומר טורד אדם חבית של יין יינה ושמריה ונותן לתוך המשמרת ואינו חושש תרגמה זעירי ס בין הגיתות שנו: מסננין את היין בסודרין: אמר רב שימי בר חייא ע ובלבד שלא יעשה גומא: פ ובכפיפה מצרית: אמר רב חייא בר אשי אמר רב ע ובלבד שלא יגביה מקרקעיתו של כלי טפח אמר י רב פ האי ט פרונקא אפלגיה דכובא שרי אכוליה כובא אסור אמר רב פפא צ לא ניהדק איניש (ב) ט צינייתא בפומיה דכוזני דחביתא משום דמיחזי כמשמרת דבי רב פפא ק שאפו שיכרא ממנא למנא (ג) אמר ליה רב אחא מדיפתי לרבינא האיכא ניצוצות ניצוצות לבי רב פפא לא חשיבי: ונותנין ביצה במסננת: תני יעקב קרחה לפי

ולא ידענא אי מלפניה. אם חל י"ט בע"ש ומת בו ביום ומפני שלא יוכלו להתעסק בו למחר התירו לקוברו ע"י עממים: **אי מלאחריה.** והוא מת בשבת ומפני שנשתהה ככר והיה מסריח התירו: **מת ביו"ט ראשון כו'.** מת שנשתהה כגון שמת בשבת ולמחר היה יו"ט: **מה שאין כן בביצה.** דאין ר"ה שוה לימים טובים של גליות דאילו ר"ה אמיר יו"ט שני דיליה ונולדה בזה אסורה בזה: **מתעטף אדם בבילה.** שהוא כסדין ומתעטף בה דרך מלבוש: **ובכסכסיה.** רצועות התלויות בה ולא אמרינן הך רצועות לאו לצורך עיטוף נינהו והוה משאוי ההוא שעתא שאין כיסכסין עשויין אלא לנטותה באהל: **חייב חטאת.** ואילו לא היתה מצויצת כלל לא מיחייב דהא לבושיה הוא אלמא הציציות הוין לו משאוי הואיל ואינן כמצותו אינן צריכין לה ומן הבגד ממש אינן דליחשבינן כוותיה: **חשיבי.** משום דשל תכלת הן ולא בטלי והוו בה משוי: **מערים אדם על המשמרת ביו"ט.** לרבנן דאמרי אין תולין את המשמרת ביום טוב ואוקימנא דטעמא לאו משום אהל אלא משום עובדא דחול מערים ותולה אותה לצורך רמונים דלאו עובדין דחול נינהו ומסנן בה שמרים הואיל ונתלית דהא אמרינן נותנין לתלויה ביו"ט: **והוא דתלי בה רמונים.** ברישא דמוכח מילתא דמעיקרא לאו לשמרים תלייה: **מטילין.** ברשיי"ר בלע"ז: **במועד.** בחולו של מועד: **מערים ושותה מן החדש.** אלמא בלא שום הוכחה מותר להערים: **התם לאו מוכחא מילתא.** דמילתא דאיסורא הוא דהרואה אומר לצורך המועד הוא שאין הכל יודעין שיש לו מן הישן הכא מוכחא מילתא לאיסור דסתם תולה משמרת לשמרים הוא תולה ואי לא יהיב בה רימונים ברישא להצניע בעלמא כי יהיב בה שמרים מוכח דלהכי תלייה: **ברא דתומא.** ללע של שום: **ומנח בברזא דדנא.** מקום שיש בו נקב בחבית והיין יוצא [ב] נותנו שם בשבת לסתום והוי כמתקן ומערים לכתחילה: **ואומר לאצנועיה.** להאי ברא דתומא מיכוינא ועוד עביד אחריתי אזל נאים במברא בספינה רחבה העשויה לעבור המים והיא של נכרי ויודע הוא שיעבירנה הנכרי לצד האחר: **וסייר פירי.** ומשמר שם פירות כרמו ונמצא שהנכרי מעבירו במים בשבת: **הערמה בדרבנן היא.** ה"ג הך הערמה לאו באיסורא דאורייתא הוא אלא באיסורא דרבנן דא"נ עביד ממש בלא הערמה אדרבנן הוא דעבר הלכך כיון דצורבא מרבנן הוא לא אחמירו עליה דהוא לא אתי למעבד לכתחילה להדיא בלא הערמה לעבור שם לפני הכל: **מתני'** נותנין מים. בשבת ע"ג שמרים הנתונים במשמרת מבעוד יום: **כדי שיצולו.** שיהו צלולין לזוב' את היין מפני הקמחים שקורים ייי"ש: **בסודרין ובכפיפה מצרית.** העשויה מצורי דקל: **כפיפה.** סל: **ונותנין ביצה במסננת.** שהחרדל נתון בה להסתנן וקולטת את הפסולת ואף הבילה החלמון שלה נוטף ומסתנן עמו והוה ליה לחרדל למראה והחלבון שהוא קשור נשאר למעלה ורבינו הלוי פירש סינונה של בילה לתוך תבשיל היא ולא לתוך חרדל ובמסננת של חרדל הוא דשרי משום שינוי ויורד לתוך הקערה שהוא כלי שני ומתלבן התבשיל: **אינומלין.** פוסו"ן: **לגין.** גדול מכוס וקטן מחבית: **גמ'** טורד. מערבב: **בין הגתות שנו.** שכל היינות עכורין ושותין אותן בשמריהם הלכך אין כאן תיקון דבלאו הכי משתי: **שלא יעשה גומא.** מן הסודר בפי הכלי כי עובדא דחול אי נמי אתי לידי סחיטה: **שלא יגביה.** הכפיפה מקרקעית (ד) כלי התחתון טפח כמדת אהל: **פרונקא.** בגד שטוטחין על גיגית יין לכסותה: **אפלגא דכובא שרי.** דלאו אוהלא הוי: **לא ניהדק איניש צינייתא בפומא דכוזני דחביתא.** כלי חרס קטן שמערין בו יין מחבית לא יתן בפיו קשין וקסמים בחזקה לפי שאין לך מסננת גדולה מזו: **שפו שיכרא.** כל היכא דתני לשון שפוי בנחת הוא והפסולת נשאר בשולי הכלי: **והאיכא ניצוצות.** קטנות הנישופות באחרונה מתוך הפסולת שקורין ברי"ש והנהו מוכחן דבורר הוא: **ניצוצות בי רב פפא לא חשיבי.** (ה) שחנוני מטיל שכר היה כדאמרינן בבבא מליעא (דף סה.) ובפסחים (דף קיג.) הלכך אינו מקפיד לניצוצות כל כך וכשמגיע לניצוצות משליך הן ופסולתן לחוץ ותחילת שפייתן (ו) מן הפסולת ניכר דלאו בורר הוא: לפי

יז א מיי' פ"א מהל' יו"ט הלכה כב סמג לאוין עה טוש"ע א"ח סי' תקכו סעיף ד:
יח ב מיי' שם טוש"ע שם סעיף ד:
יט ג מיי' פי"ט מהל' שבת הלכה כ סמג לאוין סה טוש"ע א"ח סי' שא סעיף לג:
כ ד מיי' שם טוש"ע שם סעיף לח וסי' יג סעיף א:
כא ה מיי' פ"ג מהל' ציצית הלכה יח סמג לאוין עה טוש"ע א"ח סי' תקי סעיף ד:
כב ו מיי' פ"ו שם הלכה ח סמג שם טוש"ע שם סעיף ח:
כג ז מיי' פ"ז מהל' שבת הלכה ב טוש"ע א"ח סי' שיז סעיף יא:
כד ח טור א"ח סימן שלג:
כה ט מיי' פ"ח מהל' שבת הלכה יד ופכ"א הלכה יז סמג שם טוש"ע א"ח סי' שיט סעיף ט:
כו י מיי' פ"ח שם ופ"ג מהלכות יו"ט הלכה יז סמג שם טוש"ע שם סעיף טו:
כז כ ל מ נ מיי' פ"ח מהל' שבת הלכה יד ופכ"א הלכה יז סמג טוש"ע שם סעיף י ויא:
כח ס ע מיי' שם סמג שם הלכה לג טוש"ע שם סעיף יב:
כט פ מיי' שם סמג שם טוש"ע א"ח סי' שטו סעיף יג:
ל צ טוש"ע שם סימן שיט סעיף יג:
לא ק שם סעיף יד:

רבינו חננאל

לאיסור. וזה שאמר מתעטף אדם בבילה ובכסכסיה ויוצא בה לרה"ר פי' כוסכיא חוטין ומשיחות שעליה. הלכה היא דקא מקשינן עלה מדרב הונא דאמר היוצא בטלית שאינה מצוייצת כהלכתה בשבת כגון שתלה ציצית בב' כנפי הטלית והניח הרביעית אותן חוטי הציצית כיון שאינה מצויצת בד' כנפות שלה אינה חשובה ציצית למצוה. וכהוציא דעלמא הן חשובין והיוצא בהן חייב חטאת ופרקינן ציצית לגבי טלית חשיבי ולא בטלי שלב האדם רוצה בקיומן עד בדעתו שיתלה הרביעית וילבשנה. אבל כוסכיא לגבי בילה אינו צריך להן ובטלי: והא דאמר רבה בר רב הונא מערים אדם על המשמרת ביו"ט לתלות בה רמונים ותולה בה שמרים ואליבא דרבנן דאסורים לתלות ולשמר לכתחלה ואע"פ שהיא אסורה והוא דתלה לה רמונים כרב אשי ואע"ג דאמרינן מ"ש מהא דתניא מטילין שכר במועד וכו' התם שכר במועד לא מוכחא מילתא הכא במשמרת מוכחא מילתא ולשמר הוא תולה ואם תלה בה רמונים אין ואי לא לא. והא דאמרו ליה לרב אשי חזי מר רב הונא בר חיון ואמרי לה בר חילון דהוה שקיל ברא דתומיא ומנח בברזא דדנא פי' שהיה נוטל ראש שום ונותנו בנקב של חבית שיצא ממנו היין ולא היה מתפסק מאותה חבית אלא חבית שבאוצר והיה מערים וסותם הנקב בראש השום והיה אומר להצניע ראש השום אני צריך ועוד היה הולך

מסורת הש"ס

א) ביצה ו. כב., ב) מנחות לו. ע"ש, ג) מו"ק יב:, ד) [גירסת הערוך ובפספסיה], ה) לעיל דף קלה., ו) שם קטו., ז) [גירס' הערוך רבא], ח) [פי' תוס' ביצה לב: ד"ה מלמטה למעלה], ט) גי' הערוך בערך צנה א' לא נהדק איניש צננתא בפומא דכוזניתא, י) כאן עירוב דברים ע"פ חסרון נקודות המבדילות וכ"ל כדי שיצולו. שיהיו צלולין לזוב: את היין. מפני הקמחים כו' ועי' פירש"י בהרי"ף, כ) ע"ע תוס' ביצה ו. ד"ה והאידנא, ל) שייך לדף קמ:).

הגהות הב"ח

(א) גמ' לא חשיבי ובטלי אמר (רבה) תו"מ ונ"ב פ"ל ר' חבין: (ב) שם לא ניהדק איניש (ציניתא) תו"מ ונ"ב צינייתא: (ג) שם ממנא למנא א"ל רב אחא: (ד) רש"י ד"ה שלא יגביה וכו' מקרקעיתו של כלי: (ה) ד"ה ניצוצות וכו' לא חשיבי ומטיל ולשכר היה כדאמרינן בב"מ. נ"ב ע"ש דף סה דקאמר רב פפא עבדא דידי שרי מ"ט שכראי לא ספד. ובפסחים דף קיג קאמרי רשוט וכו' אמר רב פפא אי לאו דרמאי שכרא לא אעתרי: (ו) בא"ד ותחלת שפייתן שאין הפסולת ניכר דלאו בורר הוא: (ז) תוס' ד"ה יו"ט שני כו' בני מליאון (אותה העיר) תא"מ ונ"ב הגה"ה היא:

גליון הש"ס

מתני' ומסננין את היין בסודרין. ע"ל קיט ע"א תוד"ה האי מקבעיתא: תוס' ד"ה תלא בר' ודגים מאיס. ע"ל יט ע"ב תוד"ה הכי כלכי:

הגהות הגר"א

[א] משנה ומסננין את היין. נ"ב צלול כמ"ש בגמ'. וקאמר דסודרין לאו לאפוקי משמרת דאסור. ומשמרת דבגמרא מיירי בשמרים. היינו שחקן כן פסק הרמב"ם. אבל הטור כתב דכ"ש במשמרת למותר. וקאמר דמים כו'. והרא"ש והטור פסקו דקאמר סודרין לאפוקי עכור מותר. (ועמ"ש רבינו בא"ח סי' שיט): [ב] רש"י בד"ה ומנח בברזא דדנא כו' והיין יוצא כו'. נ"ב רבינו גורס דווקא יוצא. (ועמ"ש בא"ח סי' שיד).

ליקוטי רש"י

[נדפס בדף קמ.]

The Gemara cites another case of a subterfuge being employed to circumvent a prohibition:

אָמְרוּ לֵיהּ רַבָּנָן לְרַב אַשִׁי – Some students said to Rav Ashi: חֲזִי מַר הַאי צוּרְבָא מֵרַבָּנָן וְרַב הוּנָא בֶּן רַבִּי חִיּוּן שְׁמֵיהּ – **See, master, that young Torah scholar, and Rav Huna ben R' Chayun is his name,** וְאָמְרֵי לָהּ רַב הוּנָא בְּרַבִּי חַלְוָן שְׁמֵיהּ – **and some say, Rav Huna the son of R' Chalvan is his name,** דְּשָׁקַל בְּרָא דְתוּמָא וּמַנַּח בְּבִרְזָא דְדַנָּא – **who took a clove of garlic and placed it in the spigot of a barrel,** וְאָמַר לְאַצְנוּעֵיהּ קָמִיכַּוֵּינָא – **and said, "I intended to put it away,"** not to plug the spigot.[20]

The students reported that the scholar employed a subterfuge to circumvent a prohibition on yet another matter:

וְאָזִיל וְנָאִים בְּמַבְרָא וְעָבַר לְהַךְ גִּיסָא וְנָטַר פֵּירֵי – **And [the scholar] went to sleep in a ferryboat** on the Sabbath, **crossed to the other side** of the river, **and watched over his produce there;** וְאָמַר אֲנָא לְמֵינַם קָמִיכַּוֵּינָא – **and he said** in defense of his actions, **"I intended to sleep,"** not to cross the river.[21]

Rav Ashi responded in defense of the student:

אָמַר לְהוּ – **[Rav Ashi] said to them:** הַעֲרָמָה קָאָמְרַתְּ – **Are you saying** that he should not be allowed to use **a subterfuge?** הַעֲרָמָה בִּדְרַבָּנָן הִיא – But each of these **subterfuges were** employed **to circumvent a Rabbinic prohibition,** וְצוּרְבָא מֵרַבָּנָן לֹא אָתֵי לְמֵיעֲבַד לְכַתְּחִילָּה – **and a young Torah scholar would not come to** actually **transgress** the prohibition **in the first place.** Thus, he may employ such subterfuges.[22]

Mishnah

The previous Mishnah had taught that according to the Sages using a wine strainer is prohibited. Our Mishnah now delineates several similar activities which are permitted on the Sabbath:

נוֹתְנִין מַיִם עַל גַּב הַשְּׁמָרִים בִּשְׁבִיל שֶׁיִּצוֹלוּ – **We may pour water over wine dregs so that [the dregs] become cleared.**[23] וּמְסַנְּנִין אֶת הַיַּיִן בְּסוּדָרִין וּבִכְפִיפָה מִצְרִית – **And we may filter wine through cloths**[24] **or through a basket made of palm twigs.**[25]

וְנוֹתְנִין בֵּיצָה בִּמְסַנֶּנֶת שֶׁל חַרְדָּל – **And we may put an egg into a mustard strainer.**[26]

NOTES

then to strain wine, positively demonstrating that the strainer was initially constructed to hold pomegranates (*Rashi*, *Rashba*, *Ritva MHK* ed.).

20. The scholar used a clove of garlic to plug an open spigot in a barrel out of which wine was leaking. Plugging such a hole to stop the leaking is Rabbinically forbidden on the Sabbath, because it is similar to תִּקּוּן מָנָא, *fixing a vessel.* [There is no *Biblical* transgression for several reasons: Firstly, because the clove was inserted loosely and does not constitute an addition to the barrel; secondly, because one is not likely to intend to leave a food item there forever, and thus inserting the clove is not viewed as fixing the barrel; and thirdly, because a barrel is not usually plugged in this manner (*Ritva MHK* ed.). Inserting a *wooden* plug tightly, however, would be Biblically prohibited.] The scholar, wishing to plug the hole, circumvented the Rabbinic prohibition by claiming to have placed the garlic in the barrel merely to store it there (*Rashi*, as explained by *Beis Yosef* 314 ד״ה אסור ליתן; cf. *Bach* ad loc. ד״ה אסור ליתן; see also *Taz* 314:§10; see *Mishnah Berurah* ad loc. §47).

21. Setting sail not only on the Sabbath, but even within three days of the Sabbath, is Rabbinically prohibited (see above, 19a note 24 at length for the parameters of this ruling; see also *Orach Chaim* 248:3 for circumstances under which sailing on the Sabbath is permitted). The scholar here, who wished to cross the river to watch over his vineyard, circumvented this prohibition by going to sleep on the ferryboat — knowing full well that the ferry captain would eventually set sail — claiming that he wished nothing more than to sleep on the boat (*Rashi*).

22. A subterfuge may be employed only where one would have committed a *Rabbinic* prohibition had the subterfuge not been employed; it cannot be employed to allow what would otherwise be a Biblical prohibition. And even then, only a Torah scholar can be trusted not to eventually abandon the subterfuge and transgress the less stringent Rabbinic prohibitions outright (*Rashi*; see *Taz* 314:10, who discusses *Rashi's* comment here that the scholar will not come to transgress the prohibition *in public view*; cf. *Rambam, Hil. Shabbos* 23:3 with *Maggid Mishneh*).

[It is important to note that subterfuges in general cannot be derived one from another, for some subterfuges (such as these just mentioned in our Gemara) may be employed only by Torah scholars, while others may be employed by all people (see, for example, *Beitzah* 11b), and still others may not be employed at all [see, for example, above, 117b] (*Rosh*).]

23. Dregs left in a wine strainer (from straining done before the Sabbath) are certain to contain wine residue. This residue can be extracted [thus "clearing" the dregs] by pouring water over the dregs; the wine-water mixture then drains of its own from the solid dregs (*Rashi*). [Although by pouring water through the dregs which are in the strainer one is causing the water to mix with the dregs and then separate from them, this is not considered *sorting*, because the person pouring is not himself doing any sorting. He has merely poured water which itself needs no straining, and the mixture which is created is sorted by itself (see *Mishnah Berurah* 319:33). Furthermore, since the water and the dregs came together only in a situation where they could not remain together, i.e. in a strainer, they are never considered mixed (see *Ohr HaChamah*).]

Some understand the Mishnah to mean pouring water into dregs which are still in the bottom of a wine barrel. By soaking the dregs in water, whatever residue of wine that remains is absorbed by the water, giving it the flavor of wine. It is then drawn off and drunk on the Sabbath (*Chidushei HaRan*).

According to either explanation, the point of the Mishnah is that such actions are permitted because there is no sorting involved.

24. I.e. we may filter the wine to eliminate the funguslike mold which can collect there (*Rashi*; see also *Rashi* printed alongside *Rif*).

Now, wine can be grouped into three categories as regards its purity. The least pure is wine containing lees, which renders the wine almost undrinkable. A second level is wine containing a certain amount of impurities, which is somewhat drinkable, but will usually be filtered before it is drunk. A third level is clear wine which basically requires no further filtering.

Most Rishonim explain our Mishnah to be dealing with the middle category of wine. Filtering such wine using a wine strainer would be a Rabbinically prohibited form of sorting; our Mishnah teaches that using a simple cloth is a sufficient deviation to render the filtering permitted. [See *Ritva MHK* ed., who explains why we are not concerned that the cloth is being dyed, or laundered, by the wine.] Wine containing lees (such as that of the previous Mishnah), however, *may not* be filtered even using a cloth, while clear wine with negligible impurities *may* be filtered even through a wine strainer (see *Rashba*, *Ran MHK* ed., *Ritva MHK* ed.; see also *Beis Yosef* 319 ד״ה ויין או מים, who attributes this view to *Rashi* as well).

Alternatively, our Mishnah deals with *clear* wine (albeit containing some mold). Since it is already eminently drinkable as is, the filtering does not render it potable, and one may use even a *wine strainer* for this purpose. The Mishnah specifies the use of a cloth to teach only that there is no concern that one may come to transgress the *melachah* of סְחִיטָה, *squeezing* [providing that one uses cloths especially designated for this purpose] (see *Chidushei HaRan* and *Sfas Emes* who attribute this view to *Rashi*; see also *Beur Halachah* to 319:10 ד״ה קיסמין דקין). Others, however, maintain that one may not use a strainer even for clear wine which most people never bother to strain; for this reason the Mishnah specifies a cloth (*Rambam*, *Hil. Shabbos* 8:14). A strainer is prohibited apparently so that one may distinguish his Sabbath activities from his weekday ones (*Mishnah Berurah* 319:41).

25. The translation follows *Rashi,* who understands the word מִצְרִית as deriving from צוּרֵי הַדֶּקֶל, *palm twigs.* Alternatively, it is a basket made of reed or willows (see *Orach Chaim* 319:12).

26. I.e. we may add a raw egg to a strainer in which mustard has been strained. [The Mishnah is referring to mustard which is already lying at the bottom of a strainer from before the Sabbath, for mustard may not

ולא ידענא אי מלפניה אי מלאחריה ואתו לקמיה דרבי יוחנן ואמר להו יתעסקו ביה עממין א) ואמר רבא אמת ביו"ט ראשון יתעסקו בו עממין ביום טוב שני יתעסקו בו ישראל ואפילו ביו"ט שני של ראש השנה מה שאין כן בביצה לפי שאינן בני תורה: א"ר אבין בר רב הונא אמר רב חמא בר גוריא מתעטף אדם בכילה ובכסכסיה ויוצא לרה"ר בשבת ואינו חושש מ"ש מדרב הונא דאמר רב הונא אמר רב היוצא בטלית שאינה מצוייצת כהלכתה בשבת חייב חטאת ציצית לגבי טלית חשיבי ולא בטלי הני לא חשיבי ובטלי אמר (א) רבה בר רב הונא מערים אדם על המשמרת ביו"ט לתלות בה רמונים ותולה בה שמרים אמר רב אשי והוא דתלה בה רמונים מאי שנא מהא דתניא מטילין שכר במועד לצורך המועד שלא לצורך המועד אסור אחד שכר תמרים ואחד שכר שעורים אע"פ שיש להן ישן מערים ושותה מן החדש התם לא מוכחא מילתא הכא מוכחא מילתא אמרו ליה רבנן לרב אשי חזי מר האי צורבא מרבנן ורב הונא ב"ר חיון שמיה ואמרי לה רב הונא בר חלון שמיה דשקל בראך דתומא ומנח בברזא דדנא ואמר לאצנועיה קמיכוונא ואזיל ונאים במברא ועבר להך גיסא וסייר פירי ואמר אנא למינם קמיכוונא אמר להו הערמה קאמרת בדרבנן היא וצורבא מרבנן לא אתי למיעבד לכתחילה: **מתני'** נותנין מים ע"ג השמרים בשביל שיצולו ומסננין את היין [א] בסודרין ובכפיפה מצרית ונותנין ביצה במסננת של חרדל ועושין אנומלין בשבת ר' יהודה אומר בשבת בכוס ביו"ט בלגין ובמועד בחבית רבי צדוק אומר הכל לפי האורחין: **גמ'** אמר זעירי נותן אדם יין צלול ומים צלולין לתוך המשמרת בשבת ואינו חושש אבל עכורין לא מיתיבי רבן שמעון בן גמליאל אומר טורד אדם חבית של יין יינה ושמריה ונותן לתוך המשמרת ואינו חושש תרגמה זעירי בין הגיתות שנו: מסננין את היין בסודרין: אמר רב שימי בר חייא ובלבד שלא יעשה גומא: ובכפיפה מצרית: אמר רב חייא בר אשי אמר רב ובלבד שלא יגביה מקרקעיתו של כלי טפח אמר רב האי פרונקא אפלגיה דכובא שרי אכוליה כובא אסור אמר רב פפא לא ניהדק איניש (ב) ציניתא בפומיה דכוזני דחביתא משום דמיחזי כמשמרת דבי רב פפא שאפו שיכרא ממנא למנא (ג) אמר ליה רב אחא מדיפתי לרבינא האיכא ניצוצות לבי רב פפא לא חשיבי: ונותנין ביצה במסננת: תני יעקב קרחה לפי

תוספות

יום טוב שני יתעסקו בו ישראל. ובבילה (ד' ו.) מסקינן בתר הך מילתא אמר רבינא האידנא דאיכא חברי חיישינן פירוש ולא יתעסקו בו ישראל פן ילוו עליהם חברי לעשות מלאכה ביו"ט כיון שרואין שעושין בשביל מת ומעשה היה והוליכו מת חוץ לתחום ביו"ט והלכו אחריו בסוסים להתעסק במת וכעס ר"ת אף על ההולכים ברגל בלא סוסים ושמע רבי דטעמו משום דמסיק רבינא האידנא דאיכא חברי ולדידן אע"ג דליכא למיחש יש לאסור כיון דמסיק הכי גם יש ליראה פן ילוו השרים להתעסק במלאכתן ולכתוב מה שהם רוצים ושלא להם ר"ת בני שכר אינם בני תורה בני מליאון (ז) (לותה העיר) בני תורה:

ציצית חשיבי ולא בטלי. שאינם מבוטלין לפי שמקשטים הם בעיניו שדעתו ליתן בטלית ציצית רביעית כך פי' ר"ת: **הא לא חשיבי ובטלי** על זה סמך רבי להניח בלבנתו רצועות התלויות בו ויש שקושרים בהם בתי שוקים דבטלי דלא חשיבי כולי האי: **מאי שנא מהא דתניא כו'.** פי' [וס"ל כרבי יוסי בר' יהודה דאמר מערימין] לעיל בפ' כל כתבי (דף קיז:):

תלא דבישרא כו'. לא כפירוש הקונטרס דפי' בשר מליח שתלו ליבשו דהל"ל הא בפרק מפנין דמה שייך הכא ועוד למה מזכיר תלא ועוד מוכח לעיל בפרק מפנין (דף קכח.) דדג מליח נמי חזי לאומצא ועוד דהכא בטלטול איירי ואמרינן לעיל דרב במוקצה לטלטל סבר לה כר"ש ונראה כפי' הערוך דמשום תלא נקטיה ובלא בשר אלא תלא דבשרא לא ממאיס ושרי לטלטולי ושל דגים מאיס והוי מוקצה מחמת מיאוס והשתא אתי שפיר דאיסור דתלא כעין כישא דירקא ור' פי' לנו דתלא דבשרא רגיל להיות בו תורת כלי אבל של דגים לא ולא משום מוקצה מחמת מיאוס דלא איירי שמעתין במוקצה מחמת מיאוס. מ"ר: אבל

רש"י

ולא ידענא אי מלפניה. אם חל יו"ט בע"ש ומת בו ביום ומפני שלא יוכלו להתעסק בו למחר הסירו לקוברו ע"י עממים: **אי מלאחריה.** והוא מת בשבת ומפני שנסתפקה כבר והיא מסריח הסירו: **מת ביו"ט ראשון כו'.** מת שנסתפקה כגון שמת בשבת ולמחר היה יו"ט: **מה שאין כן בביצה.** דאין ר"ה שני לימים טובים של גליות דאילו ר"ה שני חמיר יו"ט שני דיליה ונולדה בזה אסורה בזה: **מתעטף אדם בכילה.** שהוא כסדין ומתעטף בה דרך מלבוש: **ובכסכסיה.** רצועות התלויות בה ולא אמרינן הך רצועות לאו לצורך עיטוף נינהו והוה משאוי הוא שעמא שאין מיסככין עשויין אלא לנטותה באהל: **חייב חטאת.** ואילו לא היתה מצויצת כלל לא מיחייב דהא לבושיה הוא אלמא הציציות הויין לו משאוי הואיל ואינן כמלותו אינן צריכין לה ומן הבגד ממש אינן דליחשבינן כוותיה: **חשיבי.** משום דשל תכלת הן ולא בטלי והוו בה משוי: **מערים אדם על המשמרת ביו"ט.** לרבנן דאמרי אין תולין את המשמרת ביום טוב ואוקימנא דטעמא לאו משום אהל אלא משום עובדא דחול מערים ותולה אותה לצורך רמונים דלאו עובדין דחול נינהו ומסנן בה שמרים הואיל ונתלית דהא אמרינן נותנין לתוכה ביו"ט: **והוא דתלי בה רמונים.** ברישא דמוכח מילתא דמעיקרא לאו לשמרים תלייה: **מטילין.** ברשי"ר בלע"ז: **במועד.** בחולו של מועד: **מערים ושותה מן החדש.** אלמא בלא שום הוכחה מותר להערים: **התם לאו מוכחא מילתא.** דמילתא דאיסורא הוא דהרואה אומר לצורך המועד הוא שאין הכל יודעין שיש לו מן הישן הכא מוכחא מילתא לאיסור דסתם תולה משמרת לשמרים הוא תולה ואי לא יהיב בה רימונים ברישא להצניע בעלמא כי יהיב בה שמרים מוכח דלהכי תלייה: **ברא דתומא.** צלע של שום: **ומנח בברזא דדנא.** מקום שיש בו נקב בחבית והיין יוצא [ב] נותנו שם בשבת לסתום והוי כמתקן ומערים לכתחילה: **ואומר לאצנועיה.** להאי ברא דתומא מיכוינא ועוד עביד אחריתי אזל נאים במברא בספינה רחבה העשויה לעבור המים והיא של נכרי ויודע הוא שיעבירנה הנכרי לצד האחר: **וסייר פירי.** ומשמר שם פירות כרמו ונמלא שהנכרי מעבירו במים בשבת: **הערמה בדרבנן היא.** ה"ג הך הערמה לאו באיסורא דאורייתא הוא אלא באיסורא דרבנן דא"נ עביד ממש בלא הערמה אדרבנן הוא דעבר הלכך כיון דצורבא מרבנן הוא לא אחמירו עליה דהוא לא אתי למעבד לכתחילה להדיא בלא הערמה לעבור שם לפני הכל: **מתני'** נותנין מים. בשבת ע"ג שמרים הנתונים במשמרת מבעוד יום: **כדי שיצולו.** שיהו צלולין לזוב את היין מפני הקמחים שקורים ייו"ש: **בסודרין ובכפיפה מצרית.** העשויה מלורי דקל: **כפיפה.** סל: **ונותנין ביצה במסננת.** שהחרדל נתון בה להסתנן וקולטת את הפסולת ואף הבילה החלמון שלה נוטף ומסתנן עמו והוה ליה לחרדל למראה והחלבון שהוא קשור נשאר למעלה ורבינו הלוי פירש סיננה של בילה לתוך תבשיל היא ולא לתוך חרדל ובמסננת של חרדל הוא דשרי משום שינוי ויורד לתוך הקערה שהוא כלי שני ומתלבן התבשיל: **אינומלין.** פוסו"ן: **לגין.** גדול מכוס וקטן מחבית: **גמ'** טורד. מערבב: **בין הגתות שנו.** שכל היינות עכורין ושותין אותן בשמריהם הלכך אין כאן תיקון דבלאו הכי משתתי: **שלא יעשה גומא.** מן הסודר בפי הכלי כי עובדא דחול אי נמי אתי לידי סחיטה: **שלא יגביה.** הכפיפה מקרקעית (ד) כלי התחתון טפח כמדת אהל: **פרונקא.** בגד שטוחין על גיגית יין לכסותה: **אפלגא דכובא שרי.** דלאו אוהלא הוי: **לא ניהדק איניש צינייתא בפומא דכוזני דחביתא.** כלי חרס קטן שמערין בו יין מחבית לא יתן בפיו קשין וקסמים בחזקה לפי שאין לך מסננת גדולה מזו: **שפו שיכרא.** כל היכא דתני לשון שפוי בנחת הוא והפסולת נשאר בשולי הכלי: **והאיכא ניצוצות.** קטנות הנישופות באחרונה מתוך הפסולת שקורין ברי"ש והגהה מוכחן לדורך הוא: **ניצוצות בי רב פפא לא חשיבי.** (ה) שמנוי מטיל שכר היה כדאמרינן בבבא מציעא (דף סה:) ובפסחים (דף קיג.) הלכך אינו מקפיד לניצוצות כל כך וכשמגיע לניצוצות משליך הן ופסולתן לחוץ ותחילת שפייתן (ו) מן הפסולת ניכר דלאו צורך הוא: לפי

עין משפט נר מצוה

יז א מיי' פ"א מהל' י"ט הלכה כב סמג לאוין עה טוש"ע א"ח סי' תקכו סעיף ד:
יח ב מיי' שם טוש"ע שם סעיף ד:
יט ג מיי' פי"ט מהל' שבת הלכה כ סמג לאוין סה טוש"ע א"ח סי' ש סעיף לג:
כ ד מיי' שם טוש"ע שם סעיף לה ובסי' יג סעיף א:
כא ה מיי' פ"ג מהל' י"ט הלכה יז סמג לאוין עה טוש"ע א"ח סי' תקי סעיף ד:
כב ו מיי' פ"ז שם הלכה ח סמג שם טוש"ע שם סי' תקלג סעיף ח:
כג ז מיי' פכ"א מהל' שבת הלכה ג טוש"ע שם סי' שיד סעיף יא:
כד ח טור א"ח סימן שלט:
כה ט מיי' פ"ח מהל' שבת הלכה יד ופכ"א הלכה יז סמג שם טוש"ע א"ח סי' שיט סעיף ט:
כו י מיי' פ"ח שם ופ"ג מהלכות י"ט הלכה יז סמג שם טוש"ע שם סעיף טו:
כז כ ל מ נ מיי' פ"ח מהל' שבת הלכה יד ופכ"א הלכה יז סמג שם טוש"ע שם סעיף יג ויא:
כח ס ע מיי' פכ"א שם הלכה לג טוש"ע שם סעיף יב:
כט פ מיי' שם סמג שם טוש"ע א"ח סי' שטו סעיף יג:
ל צ טוש"ע שם סימן שיט סעיף יג:
לא ק שם סעיף יד:

רבינו חננאל

לאיסור. וזה שאמר מתעטף אדם בכילה ובכסכסיא ויוצא בה לרה"ר כסכסיא חוטין ומשיחות שעליה. הלכה היא דקא מקשינן עלה מדרב הונא דאמר היוצא בטלית שאינה מצויצת כהלכתה כגון שתלה ציצית בג' כנפי הטלית והניח הרביעית אותן חוטי הציצית כיון שאינה מצויצת כהלכתה אינה חשובה ציצית דמצוה. וכחוטין דעלמא הן חשובין והוצאה הן חייב חטאת ופרקינן ציצית לגבי טלית חשיבי ולא בטלי שלא האדם רוצה בקיומן כי בדעתו שיתלה הרביעית וילבשנה. אבל כסכסיא לגבי כילה אינו צריך להן ובטלי: והא דאמר רבה בר רב הונא מערים אדם על המשמרת ביו"ט לתלות בה רמונים ותולה בה שמרים ואליבא דרבנן שאסורים לתלות ולשמר לכתחלה ואע"פ שהיא אסורה והוא דתלה לה רמונים כרב אשי ואע"ג דאמרינן מ"ש מהא דתניא מטילין שכר במועד וכו' התם שכר במועד לא מוכחא מלתא הכא מוכחא מלתא ולשמר הוא תולה ואם תלה בה רמונים אין ואי לא. והא דאמרו ליה לרב אשי על רב הונא בר חיון ואמרי לה בר חילון דהוה שקיל ברא דתומא ומנח בברזא דדנא פי' שהיה נוטל ראש שום ונותנו בנקב החבית שיוצא ממנו היין ולא היה מתכוון אלא חבית שבאוצר והיה ממשמש וסותם הנקב בראש השום והיה אומר להצניע ראש השום אני צריך ועוד היה הולך

ונותנין המים על השמרים בשביל שיצולו אמר להו רב אשי הערמה מדרבנן היא והערמה לכתחלה ת"ח לא עבדי אמר זעירי נותן אדם יין צלול ומים צלולין לתוך המשמרת בשבת ואינו חושש אבל עכורין לא. ואם בין הגתות הוא שעדיין היין תוסס טורד אדם חבית של יין יינה ושמריה בשבת ואינו חושש ואפילו אליבא דרבנן וליכא דפליג בהא ומסננין את היין בסודרין ובכפיפה מצרית אמר רב שימי בר חייא ובלבד שלא יעשה גומא. לפי

מסורת הש"ס

א) ביצה ו. כב., ב) מנחות לו. ע"ש, ג) מו"ק יב:, ד) [גירסת הערוך ובכפיפה], ה) לעיל דף קלז., ו) שם קנא., ז) [גיר' הערוך רבא], ח) [ע' תוס' ביצה לג: ד"ה מלמטה למעלה], ט) גי' הערוך בערך לבת א' יהדק איניש, י) כאן ערכו ועי' תוס' מו"ק יב:, כ) [ועי' תוס' ביצה ו. ד"ה והאידנא], ל) [שייך לדף קמ.].

הגהות הב"ח

(א) גמ' לא חשיבי ובטלי אמר (רבה) תא"מ ונ"ב ס"א ר' אבין: (ב) שם לא ניהדק איניש (ציניתא) תא"מ ונ"ב ס"א לבלמא: (ג) שם ממנא למנא אמר ליה ר' אחא: (ד) רש"י ד"ה שלא יגביה וכו' מקרקעיתו של כלי: (ה) ד"ה ניצוצות וכו' לא חשיבי שמנוי מטיל לשכר היה כדאמרינן ב"מ. נ"ב ע"ש דף סה דקאמר רב פפא טרשא דידי שרי מ"ש שכרי לא פסיד. ובפסחים דף קיג קאמר' ... (ו) בא"ד ומתחלת שפייתן.

גליון הש"ס

מתני' ומסננין את היין בסודרין. ע"ל קלט ע"א תוס' ד"ה האי מסוכרייתא: תוס' ד"ה תלא כו' ושל דגים מאיס. ע"ל יט ע"ב תוד"ה הני כרכי:

הגהות הגר"א

[א] במשנה ומסננין את היין. כצ"ל וכן לקמן כמ"ש בגמ' וקאמר בסודרין לאפוקי משמרת דאסור. [ב] רש"י ד"ה ומנח בברזא דדנא כו' והיין יוצא. כצ"ל.

ליקוטי רש"י

[נדפס בדף קמ.]

וְעוֹשִׂין אִנוּמְלִין בְּשַׁבָּת – **And we may make** ***innumlin*** **on the Sabbath.**[27] רַבִּי יְהוּדָה אוֹמֵר – **R' Yehudah says:** בְּשַׁבָּת בְּכוֹס – **On the Sabbath,** it may be made **in a cup;**[28] בְּיוֹם טוֹב בְּלָגִין – **on Yom Tov,** it may be made **in a bottle;**[29] וּבַמּוֹעֵד בְּחָבִית – **and on the** intermediate **festival** days, it may be made **in a barrel.**[30] רַבִּי צָדוֹק אוֹמֵר – **R' Tzadok says:** הַכֹּל לְפִי הָאוֹרְחִין – **Everything depends on the** number of **guests.**[31]

Gemara The Mishnah allowed the filtering of wine through a cloth. The Gemara cites a related ruling:

אָמַר זְעִירִי – **Zeiri said:** נוֹתֵן אָדָם יַיִן צָלוּל וּמַיִם צְלוּלִין לְתוֹךְ הַמְשַׁמֶּרֶת בְּשַׁבָּת וְאֵינוֹ חוֹשֵׁשׁ – **A person may place clear wine and clear water through a wine strainer on the Sabbath, and not be concerned** for Sabbath desecration.[32] אֲבָל עֲכוּרִין לֹא – **But murky wine may not** be placed through a wine strainer.[33]

The Gemara asks:

מֵיתִיבֵי – **They challenged** Zeiri's ruling from a Baraisa: רַבָּן שִׁמְעוֹן בֶּן גַּמְלִיאֵל אוֹמֵר – RABBAN SHIMON BEN GAMLIEL SAYS: טוֹרֵד אָדָם חָבִית שֶׁל יַיִן יֵינָהּ וּשְׁמָרֶיהָ – A PERSON MAY STIR A BARREL OF WINE, mixing together ITS WINE AND ITS LEES, וְנוֹתֵן לְתוֹךְ הַמְשַׁמֶּרֶת בְּשַׁבָּת וְאֵינוֹ חוֹשֵׁשׁ – AND PLACE IT INTO A WINE STRAINER ON THE SABBATH AND NOT BE CONCERNED for Sabbath desecration.[34] Apparently, even wine requiring some sort of straining may be filtered even through a wine strainer, unlike the ruling of Zeiri which prohibited using a wine strainer in such a case. – ? –

The Gemara answers:

תַּרְגְּמָה זְעִירִי – **Zeiri interpreted** Rabban Shimon ben Gamliel's ruling: בֵּין הַגִּיתּוֹת שָׁנוּ – **It was taught concerning** wine drunk **between the winepresses.**[35] It was only there that Rabban Shimon ben Gamliel permitted the use of a wine strainer; elsewhere, however, only clear wine, not murky wine, may be filtered through a wine strainer.

The Mishnah stated:

מְסַנְּנִין אֶת הַיַּיִן בְּסוּדָרִין – AND WE MAY FILTER WINE THROUGH CLOTHS.

The Gemara adds a caveat to this permit:

אָמַר רַב שִׁימִי בַּר חִיָּיא – **Rav Shimi bar Chiya said:** וּבִלְבַד שֶׁלֹּא יַעֲשֶׂה גּוּמָא – One may do so **provided that one** does **not make a hollow** in the cloth.[36]

The Mishnah continued:

וּבִכְפִיפָה מִצְרִית – OR THROUGH A BASKET MADE OF PALM TWIGS.

אָמַר רַב חִיָּיא בַּר אַשִׁי אָמַר רַב – **Rav Chiya bar Ashi said in the**

NOTES

be strained on the Sabbath (Gemara 134a).] It was customary to add egg yolk to mustard for coloring by cracking an egg over the mustard strainer. The thinner yolk would drain through the strainer, coloring the mustard as it passed through, while the more viscous egg white would remain above (*Rashi*). [The Gemara will explain why this is not Biblically prohibited as full-fledged straining.] Alternatively, the Mishnah discusses straining an egg yolk (as described above) into any cook*ing pot of food* for coloring; the Mishnah permits this only if it is done in a somewhat unusual manner, such as if a mustard strainer is used (*Rashi*, quoting *Rabbeinu HaLevi*; cf. *Meiri* and *Ritva MHK* ed. who reject this explanation for various reasons).

27. The Gemara (140a) will identify the composition of this beverage.

[Though a considerable amount of work is involved in making this mixture, and it is usually made for many days, it is still permissible (*Tiferes Yisrael*).] Some say that the Tanna Kamma allows unlimited making of *innumlin* (*Rambam's Commentary to Mishnah*), while others maintain that the Tanna Kamma's permit is now explained by R' Yehudah to have certain limits (*Chidushei HaRan*; see also *Rashash*).

28. On the Sabbath it may be made only by the cupful, because of the excessive toil involved in making large quantities.

29. A *log* is larger than a cup, but smaller than a barrel.

30. [During the intermediate days of the festival, even though certain forms of labor are prohibited, one is still permitted to toil more than on the festival itself.]

31. R' Tzadok means to be more lenient than R' Yehudah, allowing one to prepare at one time even a large quantity of *innumlin* even on the Sabbath to meet the needs of the guests. Alternatively, R' Tzadok means to be more stringent insofar as the festival is concerned; a barrelful of *innumlin* may be made on the intermediate days of the festival only if it is needed to meet the requirements of the guests (see *Sfas Emes*; see also *Rashash*). The halachah follows the Tanna Kamma, who apparently places no limits on the production of *innumlin* (see *Rambam's Commentary to the Mishnah* and *Chidushei HaRan*).

In any case, only mixing together the ingredients lightly is permitted. It is forbidden to stir it excessively and strain it, for that constitutes excessive and professional toil (*Mishnah Berurah* 321:69; see *Chidushei HaRan*).

32. Since the wine can be drunk as is without further straining, he has not done anything of legal significance (see Gemara above, 109a).

33. Darker wine, i.e. wine with impurities that is potable but which most people will filter before drinking, may not be placed in a wine strainer on the Sabbath; it may only be filtered through cloth. Zeiri maintains that the fact that most people will filter this somewhat potable wine indicates that its filtering represents an improvement, and straining it therefore would fall under the *melachah* of *sorting*. Thus, Zeiri's ruling parallels our Mishnah's second ruling – that wine of a medium level of purity may not be filtered using a wine strainer, but only through a simple cloth, which is a sufficient deviation to render the filtering permitted. See note 24.

34. [The Gemara is assuming that Rabban Shimon ben Gamliel cannot be discussing wine which is rendered completely undrinkable by its lees, since the previous Mishnah has taught that such wine may definitely *not* be filtered through a wine strainer, for that would constitute *selecting*. Rather,] he must be discussing wine which is technically potable as is, but which is filtered by most people first. Yet, Rabban Shimon ben Gamliel allows using even a wine strainer in such a case, apparently because he holds that since the wine is in fact potable, its filtering represents no great improvement, and its straining is permitted without any sort of deviation (*Ran MHK* ed.). This is in conflict with Zeiri, who ruled that only clear wine may be poured through a wine strainer on the Sabbath; murky wine may be strained only with a deviation (such as straining through a cloth).

The sage asking this question must have understood our Mishnah, which prohibits filtering through a wine strainer, as discussing completely undrinkable wine. For if the Mishnah was discussing somewhat drinkable wine, then Zeiri's ruling would exactly parallel that of our Mishnah (see previous note), and no difficulty would be posed from Rabban Shimon ben Gamliel! (*Ritva, Ran MHK* ed.).

35. Unlike wine drunk away from the press, freshly pressed wine drunk among the winepresses is *usually* drunk in its murkier, unfiltered state. Thus, filtering performed there is not viewed as having rendered the wine drinkable, and even a wine strainer may be used for that purpose (*Rashi*; cf. *Rambam, Hil. Shabbos* 8:14).

36. When spreading the cloth over the mouth of the container, one may not form a hollow in the cloth. (A hollow is made to direct the flow of the wine into the center of the container, rather than have it drip from all points of the cloth.) This is forbidden because of עוּבְדָּא דְחוֹל, *weekday activity,* i.e. because it appears as though he is performing straining, a form of *sorting* (see *Ritva MHK* ed. and *Meiri*). Alternatively, we are concerned lest one doing so might come to wring the wine from the gathered cloth (*Rashi*; see *Shabbos Shel Mi*). Rather, one must place the cloth flat over the mouth of the container [which does not appear to be straining, since the wine does not gather in the center of the cloth].

The hollow may, however, be allowed to form as a natural consequence of pouring the liquid through the cloth (*Tur* 319:11).

ולא ידענא אי מלפניה אי מלאחריה ואתו לקמיה דרבי יוחנן ואמר להו יתעסקו ביה עממין ואמר רבא מת ביו"ט ראשון יתעסקו בו עממין ביום טוב שני יתעסקו בו ישראל ואפילו ביו"ט שני של ראש השנה מה שאין כן בביצה לפי שאינן בני תורה: א"ר אבין בר רב הונא אמר רב חמא בר גוריא מתעטף אדם בכילה ובכסכסיה ויוצא לרה"ר בשבת ואינו חושש מ"ש מדרב הונא דאמר רב הונא אמר רב היוצא בטלית שאינה מצוייצת כהלכתה בשבת חייב חטאת ציצית לגבי טלית חשיבי ולא בטלי הני לא חשיבי ובטלי אמר (א) רבה בר רב הונא מערים אדם על המשמרת ביו"ט לתלות בה רמונים ותולה בה שמרים אמר רב אשי והוא דתלה בה רמונים מאי שנא מהא דתניא מטלין שכר במועד לצורך המועד שלא לצורך המועד אסור אחד שכר תמרים ואחד שכר שעורים אע"פ שיש להן ישן מערים ושותה מן החדש התם לא מוכחא מילתא הכא מוכחא מילתא אמרו ליה רבנן לרב אשי חזי מר האי צורבא מרבנן ורב הונא ב"ר חיון שמיה ואמרי לה רב הונא בר' חלון שמיה דשקל ברא דתומא ומנח בברזא דדנא ואמר לאצנועיה קמיכוינא ואזיל ונאים במברא ועבר להך גיסא וסייר פירי ואמר אנא למינם קמיכוינא אמר להו הערמה קאמרת הערמה בדרבנן היא וצורבא מרבנן לא אתי למיעבד לכתחילה: **מתני'** נותנין מים ע"ג השמרים בשביל שיצולו ומסננין את היין [א] בסודרין ובכפיפה מצרית ונותנין ביצה במסננת של חרדל ועושין אנומלין בשבת ר' יהודה אומר בשבת בכוס ביו"ט בלגין ובמועד בחבית רבי צדוק אומר הכל לפי האורחין: **גמ'** אמר זעירי נותן אדם יין צלול ומים צלולין לתוך המשמרת בשבת ואינו חושש אבל עכורין לא מיתיבי רבן שמעון בן גמליאל אומר טורד אדם חבית של יין יינה ושמריה ונותן לתוך המשמרת בשבת ואינו חושש תרגמה זעירי בין הגיתות שנו: ומסננין את היין בסודרין: אמר רב שימי בר חייא ובלבד שלא יעשה גומא: ובכפיפה מצרית: אמר רב חייא בר אשי אמר רב ובלבד שלא יגביה מקרקעיתו של כלי טפח אמר רב האי פרונקא אפלגיה דכובא שרי אכוליה כובא אסור אמר רב פפא לא ניהדק איניש (ג) ציניתא בפומיה דכוזני דחביתא משום דמיחזי כמשמרת דבי רב פפא שאפו שיכרא ממנא למנא (ג) אמר ליה רב אחא מדיפתי לרבינא האיכא ניצוצות ניצוצות לבי רב פפא לא חשיבי: ונותנין ביצה במסננת: תני יעקב קרחה לפי

יום טוב שני יתעסקו בו ישראל. ובכילה (ד' ו.) מסקינן בתר הך מילתא אמר רבינא האידנא דאיכא חברי חיישינן פירוש ולא יתעסקו בו ישראל פן ילוו עליהם חברי לעשות מלאכה ביו"ט כיון שרואין שעושין בשביל מת ומעשה היה והוליכו מת חוץ לתחום ביו"ט והלכו אחריו בסוסים להתעסק במת וכעס ר"ת אף על ההולכים ברגל בלא סוסים ושמע רבי דטעמו משום דמסיק רבינא האידנא דאיכא חברי ולדידן אע"ג דליכא למיחש יש לאסור כיון דמסיק הכי גם יש לירא פן ילוו השרים להתעסק במלאכתן ולכתוב מה שהם רוצים ושלא להם ר"ח בני בשכר אינם בני תורה בני מליאון (ז) (אותה העיר) בני תורה:

ציצית חשיבי ולא בטלי. שאינם מבוטלין לפי שמשובים הם בעיניו שדעתו ליתן בטלית ליצית רביעית כך פי' ר"ח: הא לא חשיבי ובטלי על זה סמך רבי להניח באבנטו רצועות התלויות בו ויש שקושרים בהם בתי שוקים דבטלי דלא חשיבי כולי האי: **מאי** שנא מהא דתניא כו'. פי' [וס"ל כרבי יוסי בר' יהודה דאמר מערימין] לעיל בפ' כל כתבי (דף קיז:):

תלא דבישרא כו'. לא כפירוש הקונטרס דפי' בשר מליח שתלו ליבשו דהל"ל הא בפרק מפנין דמה שייך הכא ועוד למה מזכיר תלא ועוד מוכח לעיל בפרק מפנין (דף קכח.) דדג מליח נמי חזי לאומלא ועוד דהכא בטלטול איירי ואמרינן לעיל דרב במוקצה לטלטל סבר לה כר"ש ונראה כפי' הערוך דמשום תלא נקטיה ובלא בשר אלא תלא דבשרא לא ממאיס ושרי לטלטולי ושל דגים לא ממאיס והוי מוקצה מחמת מיאוס והשתא אתי שפיר באיסור דתלא כעין כיפה דירקא וכו' פי' לנו לתלות דבשרא רגיל להיות בו תורת כלי אבל של דגים לא ולא משום מוקצה מחמת מיאוס דלא איירי במוקצה מחמת מיאוס. מ"ר: אבל

ולא ידענא אי מלפניה. אם חל י"ט בע"ש ומת בו ביום ומפני שלא יוכלו להתעסק בו למחר התירו לקוברו ע"י עממים: אי מלאחריה. והוא מת בשבת ומפני שנשתהא כבר והיה מסריח התירו: מת ביו"ט ראשון כו'. מת שנשתהא כגון שמת בשבת ולמחר היה יו"ט: מה שאין כן בביצה. דאין ר"ה שני לימים טובים של גליות דאלו ר"ה שני חמיר יו"ט שני דיליה וגולדה בזה אסורה בזה: מתעטף אדם בכילה. שהוא כסדין ומתעטף בה דרך מלבוש: ובכסכסיה. רצועות התלויות בה ולא אמרינן הך רצועות לאו לצורך עיטוף נינהו והוה משאוי ההוא שעתא שאין מיכסכסין עשוין אלא לנטותה באהל: חייב חטאת. ואילו לא היתה מצויצת כלל לא מיחייב דהא לבושיה הוא אלמא הציציות הוויין לו משאוי הואיל ואינן כמלבוש אינן צריכין לה ומן הבגד ממש אינן דליתכשיבין כוותיה: חשיבי. משום דשל תכלת הן ולא בטלי והוו בה משוי: מערים אדם על המשמרת ביו"ט. לרבנן דאמרי אין תולין את המשמרת ביום טוב ואוקימנא דטעמא לאו משום אהל אלא משום עובדא דחול מערים ותולה אותה לצורך רמונים דלאו עובדין דחול נינהו ומסנן בה שמרים הואיל ונתלית דהא אמרינן נותנין לתלויה ביו"ט: והוא דתלי בה רמונים. ברישא דמוכח מילתא דמעיקרא לאו לשמרים תלייה: מטילין. ברשי"ר בלע"ז: במועד. בחולו של מועד: מערים ושותה מן החדש. אלמא בלא שום הוכחה מותר להערים: התם לאו מוכחא מילתא. דמילתא דאיסורא הוא דהרואה אומר לצורך המועד הוא שאין הכל יודעין שיש לו מן הישן הכא מוכחא מילתא לאיסור דסתם תולה משמרת לשמרים הוא תולה ואי לא יהיב בה רימונים ברישא להניע בעלמא כי יהיב בה שמרים מוכח דלהכי תלייה: ברא דתומא. גלע של שום: ומנח בברזא דדנא. מקום שיש בו נקב בחבית והיין יוצא [ב] נותנו שם בשבת לסתום והוי כמתקן ומערים לכתחילה: ואומר לאצנועיה. להאי ברא דתומא מיכוינא ועוד עביד אחריתי אזל נאים במברא בספינה רחבה העשויה לעבור המים והיא של נכרי ויודע הוא שיעבירנה הנכרי לצד האחר: וסייר פירי. ומשמר שם פירות כרמו ונמצא שהנכרי מעבירו במים בשבת: הערמה בדרבנן היא. ה"ג הך הערמה לאו באיסורא דאורייתא הוא אלא באיסורא דרבנן דא"נ עביד ממש בלא הערמה אדרבנן הוא דעבר הלכך כיון דצורבא מרבנן הוא לא אחמירו עליה דהוא לא אתי למעבד לכתחילה להדיא בלא הערמה לעבור שם לפני הכל: **מתני'** נותנין מים. בשבת ע"ג שמרים הנתונים במשמרת מבעוד יום: כדי שיצולו. שיהו צלולין לזוב אֶת היין מפני הקמחים שקורים ייר"ש: בסודרין ובכפיפה מצרית. העשויה מצורי דקל: כפיפה. סל: ונותנין ביצה במסננת. שהחרדל נתון בה להסתנן וקולטת את הפסולת ואף הבילה החלמון שלה נוטף ומסתנן עמו והוה ליה לחרדל למראה והחלבון שהוא קשור נשאר למעלה ורבינו הלוי פירש סיגונה של בילה לתוך תבשיל היא ולא לתוך חרדל ובמסננת של חרדל הוא דשרי משום שינוי ויורד לתוך הקערה שהוא כלי שני ומתלבן התבשיל: אינומלין. פוסו"ן: לגין. גדול מכוס וקטן מחבית: **גמ'** טורד. מערבב: בין הגתות שנו. שכל היינות עכורין ושותין אותן בשמריהם הלכך אין כאן תיקון דבלאו הכי משתתי: שלא יעשה גומא. מן הסודר בפי הכלי כי עובדא דחול אי נמי אתי לידי סחיטה: שלא יגביה. הכפיפה מקרקעית (ד) כלי התחתון טפח כמדת אהל: פרונקא. בגד שפוטחין על גיגית יין לכסותה: אפלגא דכובא שרי. דלאו אוהלא הוי: לא ניהדק איניש ציניתא בפומא דכוזני דחביתא. כלי חרס קטן שמערין בו יין מחבית לא יתן בפיו קשין וקסמים בחזקה לפי שאין לך מסננת גדולה מזו: שפו שיכרא. כל היכא דתני לשון שפוי בנחת הוא והפסולת נשאר בשולי הכלי: והאיכא ניצוצות. קטנות הניסופות באחרונה מתוך הפסולת שקורין ברי"ש והנהו מוכחן דבורר הוא: ניצוצות בי רב פפא לא חשיבי. (ה) שחנוני מטיל שכר היה כדאמרינן בבבא מליעא (דף סה:) ובפסחים (דף קיג.) הלכך אינו מקפיד לניצוצות כל כך וכשמגיע לניצוצות משליך הן ופסולתן לחוץ ותחילת שפייתן (ו) מן הפסולת ניכר דלאו בורר הוא: לפי

רבינו חננאל

לאיסור. וזה שאמר מתעטף אדם בכילה ובכסכיא ויוצא בה לרה"ר פי' כוסכיא חוטין ומשיחות שעליה. הלכה היא דקא מקשינן עלה מדרב הונא דאמר היוצא בטלית שאינה מצויצת כהלכתה כגון שתלה ציצית בב' כנפי הטלית והניח הרביעית אותן חוטי הציצית כיון שאינה מצוייצת בד' כנפות שלה אינה חשובה ציצית דמצוה. והחוטין דעלמא הן חשובין והיוצא בה חייב חטאת ופרקינן ציצית לגבי טלית חשיבי ולא בטלי שלב האדם רוצה בקיומן כי בדעתו שיתלה הרביעית וילבשנה. אבל כוסכיא לגבי כילה אינו צריך להן ובטלי: והא דאמר רבה בר בר חנה מערים אדם על המשמרת ביו"ט לתלות בה רמונים ותולה בה שמרים אליבא דרבנן שאוסרים לתלות משמרת לכתחלה ואע"פ שהיא אסורה והוא דתלה לה רמונים כרב אשי ואע"ג דאמרינן מ"ש מהא דתניא מטילין שכר במועד וכו' התם בשכר במועד לא מוכחא מלתא הכא במשמרת מוכחא מילתא ולשמר הוא תולה ואם תלה בה רמונים אין ואי לא לא. והא דאמרו ליה לרב אשי על רב הונא בר חיון. ואמרי לה בר חילון דהוה שקיל ברא דתומיא ומנח בבירזא דדנא פי' שהיה נוטל ראש שום ונותנו בנקב של חבית שיוצא ממנו היין ולא היה מסתפק מאותה חבית אלא חבית שבאוצר והיה מערים וסותם הנקב בראש השום והיה אומר להצניע ראש השום אני צריך ועוד היה הולך וישן במעברא וכו' אמר להו רב אשי הערמה מדרבנן היא והערמה לכתחלה ת"ח לא עבדי **ונותנין המים** על השמרים בשביל שיצלו אמר זעירי נותן אדם יין צלול ומים צלולין לתוך המשמרת בשבת ואינו חושש אבל עכורין לא. ואם בין הגתות הוא שעדיין היין תוסס ואינו צלול טורד אדם חבית יינה ושמריה בשבת ואינו חושש ואפילו אליבא דרבנן וליכא דפליג בהא ומסננין את היין בסודרין אמר רב שימי בר חייא ובלבד שלא יעשה גומא. פי' שלא ימשוך קצות הסודר למעלה וישאר כמו גומא באמצעיתו. ובכפיפה מצרית. ואמרינן משמיה דרב שלא יגביה מקרקעיתו של כלי טפח. שכן מצינו באהלי טומאה טפח: וכל מקום שיש בו חלל טפח כאהל חשוב ואין עושין אהלי עראי לכתחלה בשבת: פי' כסוי כדי שיכוסו בהן כפי הקנקן ויש בו נקבים קטנים. פרונקא. פי' כסוי של בגד שעושים לכסוי החבית בצד השפת של הכובא כבר הוא משום אהל עשוי אמר...

עין משפט נר מצוה

יז א מיי' פ"א מהל' י"ט הלכה כב סמג לאוין עה טוש"ע א"ח סי' תקטו סעיף ו:
יח ב מיי' שם טוש"ע שם סעיף ד:
יט ג מיי' פי"ט מהל' שבת הלכה כ סמג לאוין סה טוש"ע א"ח סי' שא סעיף לט:
כ ד מיי' שם טוש"ע שם סעיף לח וסי' יג סעיף א:
כא ה מיי' פ"ד מהל' י"ט הלכה כ סמג לאוין עה טוש"ע א"ח סי' תקי סעיף ז:
כב ו מיי' פ"ז מהל' י"ט הלכה ח סמג שם טוש"ע א"ח סי' תקלג סעיף ג:
כג ז מיי' פכ"א מהל' שבת הלכה ו טוש"ע שם סי' שיז סעיף יא:
כד ח טור א"ח סימן שלט:
כה ט מיי' פ"ח מהל' שבת הלכה יד ופכ"א הלכה יז סמג שם טוש"ע א"ח סי' שיט סעיף ט:
כו י מיי' פ"ח שם ופ"ג מהלכות יו"ט הלכה יז סמג שם טוש"ע שם סעיף טו:
כז כ ל מ נ מיי' פכ"ב מהל' שבת הלכה יד ופכ"א הלכה יז סמג שם טוש"ע שם סעיף י ויא:
כח ס מיי' שם הלכה לג טוש"ע שם סעיף יג:
כט ע מיי' שם סמג שם טוש"ע שם סי' שטו סעיף יג:
ל צ טוש"ע שם סימן שטו סעיף יב:
לא ק שם סעיף יב:

מסורת הש"ס

א) ביצה ו. כב. ב) מנחות לו. ע"ש, ג) מו"ק יב. ד) [גירסת הערוך ובפסיפה], ה) לעיל דף קלד. ו) שם קמ. ז) [גי' הערוך רבא], ח) [עי' תוס' ביצה לב: ד"ה מלמטה למעלה], ט) גי' הערוך בערך גמא ב' לא נהדק אינש בגמא לפומא דכוזניתא, י) כאן יש ערבוב דברים ע"י מסרון נקודות המבדילות וצ"ל כדי שיצולו. שיהו צלולין לזוב: את היין. מפני הקמחים וכו'. ועי' פירש"י להרי"ף, כ) [וע"ע תוס' ביצה ו. ד"ה והאידנא], ל) [שייך לדף קמ.].

הגהות הב"ח

(א) גמ' לא חשיבי ובטלי אמר (רבה) תו"מ ונ"ב פ"א ר' אבין: (ב) שם לא ניהדק איניש (ציניתא) תו"מ ונ"ב פ"א בגמא: (ג) שם ממנא למנא נ"ב פ"א ר' אחא: (ד) רש"י ד"ה שלא יגביה וכו' מקרקעיתו של כלי: (ה) ד"ה ניצוצות וכו' לא חשיבי שמוכר ומטיל לשכר היה כדאמרינן בב"מ. נ"ב ע"ש דף סה דקאמר רב פפא שכרא דידי שרי מ"ש שכרא לא פסקי. ובפסחים דף קיג קאמר' מאי דאמרינן לגבי סחורה וכו' אמר רב פפא אי לאו דרמאי שכרא לא איעתרי מאי משמע ובו'. ובפס"ק דנדה קס"ל רבא לרב פפא עודי ופירש"י שם סגולתו: (ו) באד ותחלת שפייתן שאין הפסולת ניכר לאו בורר הוא: (ז) תוס' ד"ה יו"ט שני בני מליאון (אותה העיר) תא"מ ונ"ב הגה"ה היא:

גליון הש"ס

מתני' ומסננין את היין בסודרין. ע"ל קיא ע"א תוד"ה האי מסוכריתא: תוס' ד"ה תלא וכו' דבשרא לא מאיס. ע"ל יע ע"ב תוד"ה הני כרכי:

הגהות הגר"א

[א] במשנה ומסננין את היין. נ"ב צלול כמ"ש בגמ'. ואם עכור בסודרין לאפוקי משמרת דאסור. ומשמרת דגמרא היינו סודר בפי כלי כמ"ש ספק הרמב"ם. אבל הטור כתב דכ"ש במשמרת דמותר. וקאמר דמותר דכים אין קודר אלא כמשמרת כמ"ש בגמרא ומים כו'. והכוונה פירש דקאמר סודרין דלפילו עכור מותר. (ועמ"ש רבינו בלו"ח ס"ש שיט): [ב] רש"י בד"ה ומנח בברזא דדנא כו' והיין יוצא כו'. נ"ב והיין דווקא יוצא. (ועמ"ש רבינו בא"ח ס"ש שיד):

ליקוטי רש"י

[נדפס בדף קמ.]

name of Rav: **וּבִלְבַד שֶׁלֹּא יַגְבִּיהַּ מִקַּרְקָעִיתוֹ שֶׁל כְּלִי טֶפַח** – One may do so **provided that** the bottom of **[the basket] not rise a** ***tefach*** **above the floor of the container** into which the wine is draining.[37]

A related ruling:

אָמַר רַב – **Rav said:** **הַאי פְּרוֹנְקָא** – **That rag** which is used to cover a barrel, **אַפַּלְגֵיהּ דְּכוּבָא שָׁרֵי** – **it is permitted** to place it **on half the barrel**'s opening, **אַכּוּלֵּיהּ כּוּבָא אָסוּר** – but **it is forbidden** to place it **on the barrel's entire** opening.[38]

A ruling related to wine filtering:

אָמַר רַב פָּפָּא – **Rav Pappa said:** **לֹא נִיהֲדַק אִינִישׁ צִינִיָּיתָא בְּפוּמֵיהּ דְּכוּוזֵי דְחָבִיתָא** – **A person should not pack straw and wood chips in the mouth of a barrel-jug,**[39] **מִשּׁוּם דְּמֵיחֲזֵי כִּמְשַׁמֶּרֶת** – **because it appears as a wine strainer.**[40]

Another ruling related to wine filtering:

דְּבֵי רַב פָּפָּא שָׁאפוּ שִׁיכְרָא מִמָּנָא לְמָנָא – **In the house of Rav Pappa, they would pour beer slowly from vessel to vessel** so as to separate the beer from its dregs.[41] **אָמַר לֵיהּ רַב אַחָא מִדִּיפְתִּי לְרָבִינָא** – **Rav Acha of Difti said to Ravina:** **הָאִיכָּא נִיצוֹצוֹת** – **But there are drippings** which pour out at the end from amid the dregs. Why is that not considered sorting?[42]

Ravina answered:

נִיצוֹצוֹת לְבֵי רַב פָּפָּא לֹא חֲשִׁיבִי – **Drippings to the household of Rav Pappa were insignificant,** i.e. he did not bother to collect the drippings from among the dregs.[43]

The Mishnah continued:

וְנוֹתְנִין בֵּיצָה בִּמְסַנֶּנֶת – **AND WE MAY PUT AN EGG INTO A [MUSTARD] STRAINER.** The Gemara explains why this is permitted:[44]

תָּנֵי יַעֲקֹב קַרְחָה – **Yaakov Karchah taught:**

NOTES

37. Rav warns that one should not leave a space of a *tefach* (the space which renders a covering above it an *ohel*) between the basket suspended over the container and the floor of the container, lest one unlawfully form an *ohel* (*Rashi, Rambam, Hil. Shabbos* 22:33, *Rabbeinu Chananel*). According to this explanation, one must be careful not to do so even when filtering through cloths (*Ritva MHK* ed.; see *Taz* 319:11). Cf. *Rashba*, *Ran MHK* ed. See also *Orach Chaim* 319:12 with *Mishnah Berurah* §49 and *Beur Halachah* ד״ה ויזהר and ד״ה הכפיפה.

38. Completely covering the mouth of an upright barrel creates an *ohel*. Thus, one may cover a barrel only halfway (*Rashi*). Of course, this is a problem only if there is a space of a *tefach* between the covering and the liquid in the barrel, as explained in the previous note (*Rashba*, in explanation of *Rashi*; see also *Taz* 315:11). And while it is certainly permitted to cover a bottle with its cover on the Sabbath even if it is not full, that is because a bottle's mouth is generally narrower than a barrel's (*Tosafos* to *Beitzah* 33a ד״ה מלמטה, *Orach Chaim* 315:13 with *Mishnah Berurah* §48).

Many Rishonim, however, disagree and maintain that the prohibition against erecting and dismantling an *ohel* does not apply to any vessel coverings at all. Covering the barrel is prohibited here because a wine strainer is constructed in that manner (and it appears as if he intends to strain), while covering it halfway would be an unusual manner to construct a strainer (*Ritva MHK* ed. quoting *Raavad*; see also *Rashba*).

39. [A wine barrel would often have] an accompanying jug which would be used to decant and dispense the wine (*Rashi*). One could filter wine without the bother of using a separate strainer by simply packing the filled jug's mouth tightly with straw or the like, so that the wine would be automatically filtered when poured (see *Meiri*). Rav Pappa thus warns that one should not prepare a jug *even before the Sabbath* for such use on the Sabbath (*Chidushei HaRan*). [Packing the mouth of the jug *loosely*, however, is permitted (*Ran MHK* ed.).]

40. [The straw-and-wood-chips mixture appears as a wine strainer, because although it will not catch the wine lees,] it does serve to filter out [the larger pieces of dirt and debris in the wine] as effectively as a wine strainer does (*Rashi*, as explained by *Eliyahu Rabbah* 319:22, *Ran MHK* ed.; see. *Magen Avraham* 319:14 with *Machatzis HaShekel* there; see also *Beur Halachah* 319:13 ד״ה בחוזקה). [The Gemara discusses murky wine which requires some filtering, for clear wine may be filtered even through a wine strainer (*Meiri*, *Mishnah Berurah* 319:50).]

41. Beer dregs would settle to the bottom of the brewing vessel. Rav Pappa's household would pour the beer slowly into another vessel, leaving the dregs behind at the bottom of the first vessel. This was permitted because the dregs were not visible while the beer was being poured; the pouring therefore does not have the appearance of *sorting* (*Rashi* ד״ה שפו and ד״ה ניצוצות).

42. The last drops of beer poured out from the brewing vessel were mixed together with the now visible dregs. Thus, when one carefully drains those last drops, he is clearly separating – performing the *melachah* of *sorting*! (*Rashi*).

43. Rav Pappa was a beer merchant; his household [for whom beer was plentiful] had no interest in the last few drops mixed with the dregs, and discarded them outright (*Rashi*).

44. The Gemara will deal with the question of why this is not prohibited as a form of *sorting*, for the yolk part of the egg, which is being used, is being separated from the albumen, which is being discarded. See further below, 140a note 1.

לְפִי שֶׁאֵין עוֹשִׂין אוֹתָהּ אֶלָּא לְגָוֶון – **Because we do not perform this** separating of an egg **except for coloring** purposes. Thus, one who separates an egg while coloring mustard has not performed the *melachah* of *sorting*.[1]

The Gemara now discusses other potential pitfalls in the preparation of mustard and other foods:

אִיתְּמַר – **It was stated:** חַרְדָּל שֶׁלָּשׁוֹ מֵעֶרֶב שַׁבָּת – **Mustard which was kneaded from before the Sabbath,**[2] לְמָחָר – concerning its further processing **on the following day** [i.e. on the Sabbath], אָמַר רַב – **Rav said:** מְמַחוּ בִּכְלִי אֲבָל לֹא בְּיָד – **One may steep it** by mixing liquid into it **with a utensil, but not by hand.**[3]

אָמַר לֵיהּ שְׁמוּאֵל – **Shmuel said to [Rav]:** בְּיָד – Is it prohibited to mix it **by hand?** אַטּוּ כָּל יוֹמָא מְמַחוּ לֵיהּ בְּיָד – **But does one steep it** by mixing liquid into it **by hand on any** other **day?** Surely not! מַאֲכַל חֲמוֹרִים הוּא – **Is it the fodder of donkeys** that one would knead it in such a manner?

אֶלָּא אָמַר שְׁמוּאֵל – **Rather, Shmuel said:** מְמַחוּ בְּיָד וְאֵינוֹ מְמַחוּ בִּכְלִי – **One may steep it** by mixing liquid into it **with one's hand, but not with a utensil.**[4]

Another recorded dispute in this matter:

אִתְּמַר – **It was stated:** רַבִּי אֶלְעָזָר אָמַר – **R' Elazar said:** Concerning steeping mustard by mixing liquid into it on the Sabbath – אֶחָד זֶה וְאֶחָד זֶה אָסוּר – **both that** [mixing by hand] **and that** [mixing with a utensil] **are prohibited.** וְרַבִּי יוֹחָנָן אָמַר – **And R' Yochanan said:** אֶחָד זֶה וְאֶחָד זֶה מוּתָּר – **Both that** [mixing by hand] **and that** [mixing with a utensil] **are permitted.**[5]

אַבַּיֵי וְרָבָא דְּאָמְרֵי תַּרְוַיְיהוּ – **And Abaye and Rava both said:** אֵין הֲלָכָה כְּרַבִּי יוֹחָנָן – **The halachah does not follow R' Yochanan,** but rather R' Elazar.

קָם רַבִּי יוֹחָנָן בְּשִׁיטָּתֵיהּ דְּרַבִּי אֶלְעָזָר – **R' Yochanan** subsequently **took up R' Elazar's view,** prohibiting mixing liquid into mustard in any manner, קָם רַבִּי אֶלְעָזָר בְּשִׁיטָּתֵיהּ דִּשְׁמוּאֵל – **and R' Elazar** subsequently **took up Shmuel's view,** prohibiting mixing liquid into mustard with a utensil, but permitting it by hand.

אַבַּיֵי וְרָבָא דְּאָמְרֵי תַּרְוַיְיהוּ – **And Abaye and Rava** then **both said:** הֲלָכָה כְּרַבִּי יוֹחָנָן – **The halachah follows R' Yochanan,** who now prohibits mixing liquid into mustard in any manner.[6]

The Gemara cites several instances where Amoraim acted stringently in this matter:

אִימֵּיהּ דְּאַבַּיֵי עֲבַדָא לֵיהּ וְלֹא אֲכַל – **Abaye's mother**[7] once **prepared for him** mustard by mixing liquid into it on the Sabbath **and he did not eat it.**[8]

דְּבֵיתְהוּ דִּזְעֵירָא עֲבַדָא לֵיהּ לְרַב חִיָּיא בַּר אַשִׁי וְלֹא אָכִיל – **The wife of Ze'ira** once **prepared [mustard] for Rav Chiya bar Ashi** by mixing liquid into it on the Sabbath, **and he did not eat it.** אָמְרָה לֵיהּ – **She said to him:** לְרַבָּךְ עֲבִידִי לֵיהּ וְאָכַל וְאַתְּ לֹא אָכְלַתְּ – **I have prepared** it in this fashion **for your teacher** [Ze'ira] **and he has eaten** it, **and you will not eat** it?!

אָמַר רָבָא בַּר שַׁבָּא – **Rava bar Shabba said:** הֲוָה קָאֵימְנָא קַמֵּיהּ דְּרָבִינָא – **I was once standing before Ravina,** וּבְחַשִׁי לֵיהּ בְּשׁוּפְתָּא דְּתוּמָא וְאָכַל – **and I stirred it for him with a center stalk of garlic,**[9] **and he ate it.**

The halachah is recorded:

אָמַר מַר זוּטְרָא – **Mar Zutra said:** לֵית הִלְכְתָא כְּכָל הָנֵי שְׁמַעְתָּתָא – **The halachah does not follow any of these teachings,**[10] אֶלָּא כִּי הָא דְּאִתְּמַר – **but rather it accords with that which was stated:**[11] חַרְדָּל שֶׁלָּשׁוֹ מֵעֶרֶב שַׁבָּת – **Mustard which was mixed from before the Sabbath,** לְמָחָר מְמַחוּ בֵּין בְּיָד בֵּין בִּכְלִי – **the following day** [i.e. the Sabbath] **one may steep** the mustard by mixing liquid into it **both by hand and with a utensil.**

NOTES

1. Although the yolk goes through the strainer while the albumen remains above, putting the egg in the strainer is not forbidden under the *melachah* of *sorting*. This is because both parts of the egg are foods; neither one is considered refuse. Although separating one food from another can sometimes be forbidden as *sorting*, this is only when they are separated so that they can be eaten separately. In the case of this Mishnah, however, since the person is separating the egg only to be able to use the yolk for coloring the mustard, and the albumen is not actually refuse, the separation is not considered *sorting*. However, one may *not* strain the yolk from the albumen if he is doing so in order to eat only one of them, for this would indeed be considered *sorting* (*Rashi*, *Tur* §319 as explained by *Bach*; cf. *Magen Avraham* 319:16 as explained by *Machatzis HaShekel*).

[There is no concern for the *melachah* of *dyeing*, for this *melachah* does not apply in the case of foodstuffs; see *Orach Chaim* 320:19; see, however, *Mishnah Berurah* there §56.]

2. [Lit. from the eve of the Sabbath.] The mustard seeds were combined into one mass before the Sabbath by way of the moisture contained in them (*Mishnah Berurah* 321:58; see *Beur Halachah* there ד״ה יכול לערבו). The Gemara now discusses how one may further steep the mass on the Sabbath by mixing it with water or wine added at that time (*Rashi*). [If the mustard had not been mixed *at all* before the Sabbath, even merely adding liquid on the Sabbath would certainly be prohibited, for during the initial addition of liquid to the mustard some extent of kneading will certainly be performed (see *Aruch HaShulchan* 321:23).]

[From the Gemara's upcoming discussion, which discusses the method that one should use in mixing the mass, it seems that merely adding a liquid to a solid mass without mixing it does not in itself constitute the act of kneading. (Although some liquid was added to the mass before the Sabbath, it is still considered a solid, and when additional liquid is added to it, this could be considered *kneading*.) This is indeed the view of the first opinion cited by *Shulchan Aruch, Orach Chaim* 321:15,16. There is another view, however, which maintains that the mere act of adding a liquid to a mass constitutes kneading. According to this view, our Gemara discusses a case where liquid was already added to the mustard before the Sabbath; on the Sabbath *additional* liquid was added and the ingredients were then mixed together (see *Ritva MHK* ed., and *Shulchan Aruch* 321:16 with *Mishnah Berurah* §64-68).]

3. Kneading by hand yields a better mix of mustard than kneading with a utensil does. Thus, one who wishes to knead the mustard on the Sabbath must use a utensil, as this is considered kneading in an irregular manner (*Rashi*).

4. Although kneading by hand mixes the mustard better, generally people will use a utensil to prepare food that is intended for human consumption. Thus, mixing it by hand is permitted on the Sabbath, for it represents a deviation from the normal method, while mixing it with a utensil is prohibited (*Rashi*).

5. The Gemara will explain shortly under what conditions this would indeed be permitted.

6. [See *Sfas Emes*, who explains why Abaye and Rava ruled in accordance with R' Yochanan once he took up the view of R' Elazar, even though they did not rule in accordance with R' Elazar initially, and merely ruled against R' Yochanan's more inclusive permit.]

7. [Abaye's mother died when Abaye was born; the Gemara here refers to his nurse (see *Kiddushin* 31b).]

8. Abaye (and Rav Chiya bar Ashi below) apparently follow the view that one may not derive benefit from the product of a Sabbath desecration even if that desecration was an unwitting one (see *Milchamos Hashem* to *Rif*, fol. 17a; *Orach Chaim* 318:1 with *Mishnah Berurah* §7 and *Beur Halachah* ד״ה מבשל; cf. *Sfas Emes*).

9. See *Rashi*. Cf. *Rashi* to *Avodah Zarah* 28b ד״ה וליתי and *Hagahos HaBach* there; cf. *Megadim Chadashim*, who explains *Rashi* as being consistent with his comments there.

10. This is not to be taken literally (*see Tosafos, Kesubos* 54a ד״ה ולית), for the final ruling about to be cited was indeed originally suggested by R' Yochanan before he reconsidered his opinion (*Shabbos Shel Mi*; cf. *Sfas Emes*). [Rather, the Gemara means that the halachah does not accord with any of the *final* positions cited above.]

11. The Gemara will now quote three nearly identical rulings. In all three, the permitted method of kneading such foods on the Sabbath (after an initial processing before the Sabbath) is taught.

לפי שאין עושין אותה אלא לגוון איתמר חרדל שלשו מע"ש למחר אמר רב ממחו בכלי אבל לא ביד א"ל שמואל ביד אטו כל יומא ממחו ליה ביד מאכל חמורים הוא אלא אמר שמואל ממחו ביד ואינו ממחו בכלי אתמר ר"א אמר אחד זה ואחד זה אסור ורבי יוחנן אמר אחד זה ואחד זה מותר אביי ורבא דאמרי תרוייהו אין הלכה כרבי יוחנן קם רבי יוחנן בשיטתיה דר"א קם רבי אלעזר בשיטתיה דשמואל אביי ורבא דאמרי תרוייהו הלכה כרבי יוחנן אימיה דאביי עבדא ליה ולא אכל דביתהו דזעירא עבדא ליה לרב חייא בר אשי ולא אכיל א"ל לרבך עבידי ליה ואכל ואת לא אכלת אמר רבא בר בר שבא הוה קאימנא קמיה דרבינא ובחשי ליה בשופתא דתומא ואכל אמר מר זוטרא לית הלכתא ככל הני שמעתתא אלא כי הא דאתמר חרדל שלשו מע"ש למחר ממחו בין ביד בין בכלי ונותן לתוכו דבש ולא יטרוף אלא מערב שחליים ששחקן מע"ש למחר נותן לתוכן שמן וחומץ וממשיך לתוכן אמיתא ולא יטרוף אלא מערב שום שריסקו מע"ש למחר נותן לתוכו פול וגריסין ולא ישחוק אלא מערב וממשיך את אמיתא לתוכן מאי אמיתא נינייא אמר אביי ש"מ האי נינייא מעליא לתחלי: ועושין אנומלין בשבת: ת"ר עושין אנומלין בשבת ואין עושין אלונטית ואיזו היא אנומלין ואיזו היא אלונטית אנומלין יין ודבש ופלפלין אלונטית יין ישן ומים צלולין ואפרסמון דעבדי לבי מסותא למיקר אמר רב יוסף זימנא חדא עלית בתר מר עוקבא לבי באני כי נפקי אתאי אשקיין חמרא חד כסא וחשי מבינתא דראשי ועד טופרא דכרעי ואי אשקיין כסא אחרינא הואי מסתפינא דלמא מנכו לי מזכותא דעלמא דאתי והא מר עוקבא דשתי כל יומא שאני מר עוקבא דדש ביה: **מתני'** אין שורין את החילתית בפושרין אבל נותן לתוך החומץ ואין שולין את הכרשינין ולא שפין אותן אבל נותן לתוך הכברה או לתוך הכלכלה אין כוברין את התבן בכברה ולא יתננו על גבי מקום גבוה בשביל שירד המוץ אבל נוטל הוא בכברה ונותן לתוך האיבוס: **גמ'** איבעיא להו שרה מאי תרגמא רב אדא נרשאה קמיה דרב יוסף שרה חייב חטאת א"ל אביי אלא מעתה שרה אומצא במיא הכי נמי דמיחייב אלא אמר אביי מדרבנן שלא יעשה כדרך שהוא עושה בחול בעא מיניה רבי יוחנן מר ינאי מהו לשרות את החילתית בצונן א"ל אסור והא אנן תנן אין שורין את החילתית בפושרין הא בצונן מותר א"ל א"כ מה בין לי ולך מתניתין יחידאה היא דתניא אין שורין את החילתית לא בחמין ולא בצונן רבי יוסי אומר בחמין אסור בצונן מותר למאי עבדי ליה ליוקרא דליבא רב אחא בר יוסף חש ביוקרא דליבא אתא לקמיה דמר עוקבא א"ל זיל שתי תלתא תיקלי חילתתא בתלתא יומי אזל אישתי חמשא בשבת ומעלי שבת לצפרא אזל שאל בי מדרשא אמרו ליה תנא דבי רב אדא ואמרי לה תנא דבי מר בר רב אדא שותה אדם קב או קביים ואינו חושש אמר להו לשתות לא קמיבעיא לי כי קא מיבעיא לי לשרות מאי אמר להו רב חייא בר אבין בדידי הוה עובדא ואתאי שאילתיה לרב אדא בר אהבה ולא הוה בידיה אתאי שאילתיה לרב הונא ואמר הכי קאמר רב שורה בצונן ומניח בחמה כמאן דשרי אפילו למאן דאסר ה"מ היכא דלא אישתי כלל אבל הכא כיון דאישתי חמשא ומעלי שבתא אי לא שתי בשבת מיסתכן מיסתמיך ואזיל רב אחא בר יוסף אכתפיה דרב נחמן בר יצחק בר אחתיה א"ל כי מטינן לבי רב ספרא עיילינא כי מטו עייליה בעא מיניה מהו לכסכוסי כיתניתא בשבתא לרכוכי כיתניתא קא מיכוין ושפיר דמי או דילמא לאולודי חיורא קמיכוין ואסיר א"ל לרכוכי קא מיכוין ושפיר דמי כי נפק אתא א"ל מאי בעא מר מיניה א"ל בעי מיניה מהו לכסכוסי כיתניתא בשבתא ואמר לי שפיר דמי ותבעי ליה למר סודרא לא קא מיבעיא לי דבעי מרב הונא ופשיט לי ותיפשיט ליה למר מסודרא א"ל התם מיחזי כי אולודי חיורא הכא לא מיחזי כאולודי חיורא אמר רב חסדא האי כיתניתא

משלפו

רש"י

לפי שאין עושין (א) אלא לגוון. למראה שהאלמון יפה לגוון ולא האלבון הלכך אידי ואידי אוכל הוא ואין כאן ברירת פסולת מאוכל: ממחו. דישטיפדי"ר בלע"ז במים או ביין: ממחו בכלי. משמע זהו שינוי שלו: ואינו ממחו ביד. דממחו ליה שפיר טפי: אלא אמר שמואל ממחו ביד. שאין זה דרכו בחול: קם ר' יוחנן בשיטתיה דר"א. חזר בו ואסר: אביי ורבא דאמרי תרוייהו הלכה כר' יוחנן. דאסר: לרבך. לזעירי: בשופתא דתומא. אמצעי של שום: ולא יטרוף. כדרך שטורפין ביצים בקערה בכף דרך טריפה שמכה בכח: שחליים. כרישין והיו שוחקין אותם במים: ממשיך. נותן: אמיתא. מינט"א בלע"ז: מעליא לתחלי. לערב עם שחליים: ואין עושין אלונטית. שאינה למשקה כמא אלא לצנן לאחר המרחץ ודוגמת רפואה: וחשי מבינתא דרישא. הרגשתי בלינתו משערת ראשי עד צפרני רגלי: מנכו לי מזכיותי. אם הייתי ניצול ממנו שלא אמות: שתי כל יומא. ולא היה מזיקו: דדש ביה. רגיל בו: מתני' חילתית. אלטי"ש בלשון ישמעאל ובלע"ז לזרי"א ושורין אותו בפושרין ושותין אותן המים לרפואה: אבל נותן. החלתית: בתוך החומץ. ומטבל בו מאכלו ולקמיה מפרש אמאי אין שורין: ואין שולין את הכרשינין. מליף עליהם מים בכלי לברור פסולתן כדתנן במסכת ביצה (דף יד:) אף מדיח ושולה: ולא שפין אותן. ביד להסיר פסולת דהוה ליה בורר: אבל נותן לתוך הכברה. ואע"פ דפעמים שהפסולת נופל דרך נקבי הכברה ונמצא נתברר מאליו: תבן. הוא שעושין מן הקש מחתכין אותו במוריגין ועושה כל זנב (ב) השבולת תבן: מוץ. הוא מזקן השבולת העליון ואינו ראוי למאכל וכוברין אותו (ג) בכברין שיפול המוץ: אבל נוטל (ד) בכברה. ליתן בתוך האבוס ואע"פ שהמוץ נופל ° מאליו כר"ש דאמר דבר שאין מתכוין מותר: גמ' שרה. חילתית בפושרין מאי: אומצא. בשר חי: שלא יעשה כו'. לא שבקוה רבנן למעבד עובדי דחול: אם כן. דלא ידענא לפרושי מתני' טפי מינך מה בין לי ולך: מתניתין יחידאה היא. ור' יוסי אמרה אבל לרבנן אף בצונן אסור: ליוקרא דליבא. שלבו כבד עליו: תלתא תקלי חילתתא. משקל ג' זהובים: שאיל בי מדרשא. מה יעשה בשבת: לשתות לא קמיבעיא לי. דבלאו רפואה משקה הוא ותנן כל המשקין שותה (לעיל דף קט:): לשרות. דתנן מתניתין אין שורין: כמאן דשרי. בעיא הוא הך דרב לימא כרבי יוסי דשרי בצונן אבל לרבנן אסור: עיילינא. הכניסני ואיש זקן היה: לכסכוסי כיתניתא. חלוק כתונת של פשתן שנתכבסה והרי היא קשה ומשפשפה בין שתי ידיו והיא מתרככה ואף הליבון שלה מאהיל על ידי השפשוף: אולודי חיורא. הליבון מאהיל: התם מיחזי כאולודי חיורא. שמקפיד על ליבונו ולוהרו של סודר יותר מכיתונא:

משלפה

עין משפט נר מצוה

לב א מיי' פ"ח מהל' שבת הל' יד ופכ"ב הלכה יג סמג לאוין סה טוש"ע א"ח סי' שכא סעיף טו:
לג ב ג מיי' פכ"ב שם טוש"ע שם סעיף יח:
לד ד מיי' שם טוש"ע שם סעיף יז:
לה ה מיי' פ"ד מהל' דעות הלכה יג:
לו ו מיי' פכ"ב מהל' שבת הלכה ז סמג לאוין סה טוש"ע א"ח סי' שכא סעיף יט:
לז ז (מיי' פ"ח מהל' שבת) סמג לאוין סה טוש"ע א"ח סי' שיט סעיף ט:
לח ח מיי' פכ"א שם הלכה לג סמג שם טוש"ע שם סי' שכח סעיף מ:
לט ט י כ מיי' פכ"א שם הלכה כב ופכ"ב הל' ז סמג שם טוש"ע א"ח סי' שכח סעיף יח:
מ ל מ מיי' פכ"ב שם הלכה יח סמג שם טוש"ע א"ח סי' שב סעיף ה:

רבינו חננאל

לפי שאין עושין אותה אלא לגוון. פי' לצבעו להתראות בו גוונא של ביצה מאכל המרס. פי' זה המאכל ממורס הוא כדתנן (נתן) [נטל] את הדם ונתנו לממרס בו על הרובד הרביעי וי"א מאכל חמורים הוא כלומר אינו מאכל ב"א אלא מאכל חמורים הוא: חרדל שלשו מע"ש חלקו עליו רב ושמואל ור' יוחנן ור' אלעזר ודבריהן פשוטין הן ומר זוטרא דהוא בתרא אמר לית הלכתא ככל הני שמעתתא אלא כי הא דתניא חרדל שלשו מע"ש למחר מניחו בין ביד בין בכלי ונותן לתוכו דבש ולא יטרוף אלא מערב. שום שריסקו מע"ש למחר נותן לתוכו פול או גריסין ולא ישחוק אלא מערב. וממשיך את האמיתה לתוכה מאי אמיתה נגחה. אנומלין יין ושמן ודבש ופלפלין אלונתית יין ישן ומים צלולין ואפרסמון: אין שורין את החלתית בפושרין אבל נותן לתוך החומץ ומיבעיא לן שרה מאי. ומסקנא שרה אמר אביי איסורא מדרבנן וא"ר יוחנן מתניתין יחידאה היא והוא ר' יוסי אבל חכ"א בין בחמין בין בצונן אסור וסוגיא דשמעתא אם שרה מאתמול לשתות חלתית בשבת מותר. אבל לשרותו אסור אפילו בצונן. ואם שרה קודם השבת ועכשיו בשבת חושש אם לא ישתה מסתכן מותר לו לשרות בתוכו ולהניחה בחמה: לכסכוסי כיתונתא. פי' לרכוכי קא מיכוון ושרי או דלמא לאולודי וכו'. פי' לקבץ מקצת הבגד של פשתים לתוך ידו לשופו מפני שרוחצין הבגד ומתייבש בשמש או ברוח עומד אנסו פי' קשה ורוצה לרככו נותן הבגד לתוך ידיו ומוליך ומביא ידיו עד שיעשה הבגד ההוא כמו קפולין קטנים כמין קמטין כי הא דא"ר זירא בפ' חבית (דף קמז:) מאי מרבב בגגון א) כסכוסי מאני דמתחזי כחדתי וכי הא דתנן בפ' האשה שהיא עושה צרכיה: צריכה לכסכס ג' פעמים על כל דבר ודבר ואמרינן בגמ' בעי ר' ירמיה אמטויי חד ואיתויי [חד] או דלמא אמטויי [חד] ואיתויי [תרתי] תיקו: וכן עוד מפורש בתלמוד א"י בענין מוליך ומביא שבלולב. מהא שמעינן דכיסכוס כעין שפשוף הוא ומתקבץ הבגד [illegible] [illegible] מכסכסו מבפנים. (ומרדכי) [ומדקדק] להאי כיתונתא. שמעינן מנה דסודרא ליתיה כתיתנתא ולא יתכן לומר שהוא צמר שאם הוא צמר איך אומר לו היה לך ללמד משתים מצמר. והדבר רחוק ביניהם ואינה אלא צמר גפן שזה קרוב לזה ופשט

חשק שלמה על רבינו חננאל א) לפנינו בגמ' איתא שם ליתא בגליונות.

מסורת הש"ס

א) [עיין קידושין לט:], ב) [ע' תוס' כתובות נד. ד"ה לית], ג) [לעיל קכח.], ד) ע"ז ל., ה) [שם לאיתא אלונתית אבל בערוך גרס כגי' שלפנינו], ו) [לעיל קלד.], ז) [חולי' קלז:], ח) [תוספ' פי"ז], ט) פ"א לאיסורא.

הגהות הב"ח

(א) רש"י ד"ה לפי שאין עושין אותה אלא: (ב) ד"ה תבן וכו' כל זנב השבלים תבן: (ג) ד"ה מוץ וכו' בכברה כדי שיפול: (ד) ד"ה אבל נוטל הוא בכברה ונותן לתוך האבוס:

גליון הש"ס

גמ' אמר מר זוטרא לית הלכתא ככל הני שמעתתא. עיין כתובות דף נד ע"א תוס' ד"ה לית הלכתא: רש"י ד"ה אבל נוטל וכו' נופל מאליו כר"ש. עיין לעיל דף נד ע"א ברש"י ד"ה כלאים דכלאים:

רב נסים גאון

אין שורין את הכרשינין. גרסי' בגמ' דבני מערבא תני אין שורין את הכרשינים משום בורר ולא שפין אותן משום דש אין כוברין את התבן משום מרקד. גורפין מלפני הפטם ומסלקין לצדדין מפני הרעי בגמ' דבני מערבא גרסי מה שהפטם אוכל ומותיר הרעי אוכל:

ליקוטי רש"י

ואמר רבא מת ביום טוב ראשון כו'. מת המוטל לקבור אם יום טוב ראשון הוא וכו'. מה שאין כן בביצה. לענין ביצה לא הקלו ביום טוב שני דראש השנה להשוות של גליות דאלו ראש השנה נולדה בזה אסורה בזה [ביצה ו.]. דקדושה אחת הן ולא הקלו ביום טוב שני של ראש השנה אלא לענין מת בלבד [שם כב:]. מערים ושותה מן החדש. שיכול לומר לצורך המועד הטילו [מו"ק יב:]. בראה דתומא. בן השום בלע של שום [תענית כה.]. כפיפה מצרית. סל של נצרי דקל ודדים שגדלין סביב הדקל [סוטה יד.]. סל נצרים של ערבה [ב"ב כב.]. ונותנין ביצה במסננת של חרדל. ומסננה בתוכו לייפות מראיתו לא מיחזי כבורר שכולה יוצאה דרך המסננת ואין מעמיד שם פסולת [לעיל קלד. ע"ש בהגהות ר' שמחה מרעסויא]. ובלבד שלא יגביה כו' טפח. אלא טפח אהל הוא [סוכה טז.].
[ע"כ שייך לדף קלט:].

אימיה דאביי. אומנתו [לעיל קלד.]. עושין אנומלין. בשבת שהוא לשתות. ואין עושין אלונטית. שהוא לרפואה להצטנן כשיוצאין מבית המרחץ [לעיל קלד.]. ומים צלולין. שנשלכו ועמדו בכלי או יומים להיות צלולין ושופין העליונים בנחת במסננת [ע"ז ל.]. חלתית. מין פירי הוא שקורין לזר"א בלע"ז [שם לה:]. מה בין לי ולך. אם איני יודע פירושה של משנתינו יותר ממך מה אני גדול ממך [חולין קלז:]. לכסכוסי. לשפשף [נדה סב.].

וְנוֹתֵן לְתוֹכוֹ דְּבַשׁ – **And one may** also **add honey into it.** וְלֹא יִטְרוֹף אֶלָּא מְעָרֵב – **But one should not beat the mixture, but merely stir it.**[12]

Two related rulings:

שַׁחֲלַיִים שֶׁשְּׁחָקָן מֵעֶרֶב שַׁבָּת – **Cress which was chopped from before the Sabbath,** לְמָחָר נוֹתֵן לְתוֹכָן שֶׁמֶן וְחוֹמֶץ – **the following day one may add into [the choppings] oil and vinegar,** וּמַמְשִׁיךְ לְתוֹכָן אַמִּיתָא – **and then add** ***amisa*** **into [the mixture].** וְלֹא יִטְרוֹף אֶלָּא מְעָרֵב – **But one should not beat** the mixture, **merely stir it.**

שׁוּם שֶׁרִיסְּקוֹ מֵעֶרֶב שַׁבָּת – **Garlic which was ground up** from **before the Sabbath,** לְמָחָר נוֹתֵן לְתוֹכוֹ פּוֹל וּגְרִיסִין – **the following day one may add into it beans or split beans.** וְלֹא יִשְׁחוֹק אֶלָּא מְעָרֵב – **But one should not pound**[13] the mixture, **but merely stir** it.

The Gemara identifies one of the ingredients just mentioned:

וּמַמְשִׁיךְ אֶת אַמִּיתָא לְתוֹכָן – The Amora had said: **and then add** ***amisa*** **into [the mixture].** מַאי אַמִּיתָא – **What is** ***amisa*?** נִינְיָיא – **Mint.** אָמַר אַבַּיֵי – **Abaye said:** שְׁמַע מִינָּה הַאי נִינְיָיא מְעַלְּיָא לְתַחְלֵי – **Learn from here that** the addition of **mint is beneficial to a cress dish**; i.e it improves the flavor.[14]

The Mishnah continued:

וְעוֹשִׂין אִנּוֹמְלִין בְּשַׁבָּת – AND WE MAY MAKE *INNOMLIN* ON THE SABBATH.

The Gemara cites a Baraisa that identifies the ingredients of this beverage:

תָּנוּ רַבָּנָן – **The Rabbis taught** in a Baraisa: עוֹשִׂין אִנּוֹמְלִין בְּשַׁבָּת וְאֵין עוֹשִׂין אֲלוּנְטִית – WE MAY MAKE *INNOMLIN* ON THE SABBATH, BUT WE MAY NOT MAKE *ALUNTIS* on the Sabbath. וְאֵיזוֹ הִיא אִנּוֹמְלִין וְאֵיזוֹ הִיא אֲלוּנְטִית – AND WHAT IS THIS *INNOMLIN* AND WHAT IS THIS *ALUNTIS*? אִנּוֹמְלִין יַיִן וּדְבַשׁ וּפִלְפְּלִין – *INNOMLIN* IS WINE mixed WITH HONEY AND PEPPER. אֲלוּנְטִית יַיִן יָשָׁן וּמַיִם צְלוּלִין וַאֲפַרְסְמוֹן – *ALUNTIS* IS OLD WINE,[15] mixed WITH CLEAR WATER AND BALSAM, דְּעָבְדִי לְבֵי מַסּוּתָא לְמֵיקַר – WHICH IS MADE TO COOL OFF THOSE WHO USE THE BATHHOUSE.[16]

The Gemara recounts a related incident:

אָמַר רַב יוֹסֵף – **Rav Yosef said:** זִימְנָא חֲדָא עָלִית בָּתַר מַר עוּקְבָא לְבֵי בָּאנֵי – **One time I went after Mar Ukva into a bathhouse.** כִּי נָפְקִי אַתְאֵי אַשְׁקְיַין חַמְרָא חַד כָּסָא – **When I came out** of the bathhouse, **he brought me one cup of wine**[17] **to drink,** וְחָשַׁי מִבִּינִתָא דְּרֵאשִׁי וְעַד טוּפְרָא דְּכַרְעַי – **and I felt its** cooling effect **from the hair on my head down to the nails of my feet.** וְאִי אַשְׁקְיַין כָּסָא אַחֲרִינָא הֲוַאי מִסְתְּפִינָא דִּלְמָא מְנַכּוּ לִי מִזְּכוּתָא דְּעָלְמָא דְּאָתֵי – **And if he had given me a second cup to drink, I would be nervous that [the Heavenly Court] would deduct from my merits** awaiting reward **in the World to Come.**[18]

The Gemara asks:

וְהָא מַר עוּקְבָא דְּשָׁתֵי כָּל יוֹמָא – **But there is Mar Ukva who drinks** *aluntis* **daily.** Obviously, then it does not have such a strong chilling effect!

The Gemara answers:

שָׁאנִי מַר עוּקְבָא דְּרָשׁ בֵּיהּ – **Mar Ukva is different, for he was accustomed to drinking it.** Thus, it did not affect him so greatly.

Mishnah

The next Mishnah continues to enumerate types of prohibited and permitted activities performed in food preparation:

אֵין שׁוֹרִין אֶת הַחִילְתִּית בְּפוֹשְׁרִין – **We may not soak asafetida**[19] **in warm water,**[20] אֲבָל נוֹתֵן לְתוֹךְ הַחוֹמֶץ – **but** one **may put it in vinegar.**[21]

וְאֵין שׁוֹלִין אֶת הַכַּרְשִׁינִין וְלֹא שָׁפִין אוֹתָן – **We may not make** the refuse of **vetches float,**[22] **nor may we rub them;**[23]

NOTES

12. The Biblically prohibited *melachah* of kneading as it applies to mustard would include employing the usual *forceful beating action* used when beating an egg. Mixing liquid into mustard (or any of the foods soon to be taught) with *gentle stirring action,* however, is not a form of kneading for these items, and is permitted (see *Mishnah Berurah* 321:58; see, however, note 2 above). [Since it is not kneading at all, it is permitted whether performed by hand or with a utensil.]

13. [The law cited in *Shulchan Aruch* states that one may not *beat* the mixture (as stated regarding cress above). See *Mishnah Berurah* 321:60, who notes that according to our text there is also a possibility that one who pounds this mixture is liable on account of *grinding*; see *Chazon Ish* 58:9.]

14. Abaye apparently gleaned this from the fact that all the above mixtures were allowed only because they improved the food. Apparently, then, mint represents an improvement in the cress as well (*Ohr HaChamah*).

15. This is defined elsewhere (*Bava Basra* 98a) as wine that is two years old (i.e. wine from the previous season, that is now in its second year).

16. This beverage is used primarily not to quench one's thirst, but rather to help one recover from the fatiguing effect of the heat of a bathhouse. Since healthy people do not usually partake of this concoction, it is apparent that one's intention in drinking it is for medicinal purposes. That being the case, the Rabbinic injunction against the use of medications on the Sabbath applies [and it may not be consumed even if it was prepared before the Sabbath] (*Rashi*, see *Mishnah Berurah* 321:70).

17. [*Maharshal* deletes the word חַמְרָא, *wine*, from the text, as it is obvious from the Gemara that follows that the drink mentioned here was an *aluntis* mixture rather than simply wine.]

18. Rav Yosef felt that the wine's chilling effect was severe enough to bring him close to death. Being saved from this fate would require that he "use up" some of the reward earned through his good deeds, which would otherwise have been preserved for his reward in the World to Come (*Rashi*). Alternatively, Rav Yosef exclaimed that drinking the wine gave him much pleasure, and, had he had a second cup, the pleasure would have been so great that it would have been deemed as though he had received a portion of his reward in the World to Come (*Maharshal, Aruch* [ע' חש [ב']).

19. [A gum resin having a bitter, acrid taste and obnoxious odor, obtained from the roots of any of several plants of the genus *Ferula* (see *HaTzome'ach VeHaChai BaMishnah*, by *Y. Feliks*.]

20. [The asafetida would dissolve somewhat in the warm water.] The resulting liquid would then be drunk for therapeutic purposes (*Rashi*). The Gemara will explain why this is prohibited (see below, note 29).

21. I.e. one may add asafetida to vinegar and dip his food into it (*Rashi*). Since healthy people partake of this condiment, it is not apparent that one who eats it intends to do so for medicinal purposes. That being the case, the Rabbinic injunction against the use of medications on the Sabbath does not apply (*Meiri*). Accordingly, it is permissible to do so even if one's intent is, indeed, for therapeutic purposes (*Beur Halachah* to *Orach Chaim* 321:18 ד"ה פתו).

22. Vetch is a species of beans used for cattle fodder. We may not pour water over these beans to make the refuse mixed into them float to the top (*Rashi*), for doing so constitutes *sorting*.

[In some editions of the Mishnah, the text reads as אין שורין, *we may not soak* ... Before feeding vetch to the cattle, the beans were often soaked in water to soften them. According to this version as well, this separates the refuse from the food, by having the beans sink to the bottom, and doing so constitutes *sorting*. See also *Beitzah* 14b and *Shaar HaTziyun* 319:21.]

23. I.e. we may not rub vetch by hand to remove the refuse. This too is prohibited as *sorting* (*Rashi*). [*Sorting* is permitted only when one extracts the usable part of the mixture while leaving behind the refuse; and even this is permitted only when done by hand for immediate use (see *Mishnah Berurah,* beginning of §319 for the parameters of this law). To remove the refuse while leaving behind the usable part, however, is forbidden even if it is done by hand. See above, 74a.]

לפי שאין עושין (א) אלא לגוון. למראה שהחלמון יפה לגוון ולא החלבון הלכך אידי ואידי אוכל הוא ואין כאן ברירת פסולת מאוכל: ממחו. דיסטיפי"ר בלע"ז במים או ביין: ממחו בכלי. משמע זהו שינוי שלו: ואינו ממחו ביד. דממחו ליה שפיר טפי: אלא אמר שמואל ממחו ביד. שאין זה דרכו בחול: קם ר' יוחנן בשיטתיה דר"א. חזר בו ואסר: אביי ורבא דאמרי תרוייהו הלכה כר' יוחנן. דאסר: לרבך. לזעירי: בשופתא דתומא. אמעצי של שום: ולא יטרוף. כדרך שטורפין ביצים בקערה בכף לדך טריפה שמכה בכח: שחליים. כרישין והיו שוחקין אותם במים: ממשיך. נותן: אמיתא. מינט"א בלע"ז: מעליא לתחלי. לערב עם שחליים: ואין עושין אלונטית. שאינה למשקה אלא לצנן לאחר המרחץ ודוגמת רפואה: וחשי מבינתא דרישא. הרגשתי בגידים ששערת נמשכה לאחר עד לצפרני רגלי: מנכו לי מזכיותי. אם הייתי ניזול ממנו שלא אמות: שתי כל יומא. ולא היה מזיקו: דדש ביה. רגיל בו: מתני' חילתית. חלטי"ט בלשון ישמעאל ובלע"ז לזר"א ושורין אותו בפושרין ושותין אותן המים לרפואה: אבל נותן. בתוך החומץ. ומטבל בו מאכלו ולקמיה מפרש אמאי אין שורין: ואין שולין את הכרשינין. מציף עליהם מים בכלי לברור פסולתן כדתנן במסכת ביצה (דף יד:) אף מדיח ושולה: ולא שפין אותן. ביד להסיר פסולת דהוה ליה בורר: אבל נותן לתוך הכברה. ואע"פ דפעמים שהפסולת נופל דרך נקבי הכברה ונמצא נברר מאליו: תבן. הוא שעושין מן הקש מחתכין אותו במוריגין ועושה כל זנב (ב) השבולת תבן: מוץ. הוא מזקן השבולת העליון ואינו ראוי למאכל וכוברין אותו (ג) בכברה כדי שיפול המוץ: אבל נוטל (ד) בכברה. ליתן בתוך האבוס ואע"פ שהמוץ נופל * מאליו כר"ש דאמר דבר שאין מתכוין מותר: גמ' שרה. חילתית בפושרין מאי: אומצא. בשר חי: שלא יעשה כו'. לא שנקוה רבנן למעבד עובדי דחול: אם כן. דלא ידענא לפרושי מתני' טפי מינך מה בין לי ולך: מתניתין יחידאה היא. ור' יוסי אמרה אבל לרבנן אף בצונן אסור: ליוקרא דליבא. שלבו כבד עליו: תלתא תקלי חילתתא. משקל ג' זהובים: שאיל בי מדרשא. מה יעשה בשבת: לשתות לא קמיבעיא לי. דבלאו רפואה משקה הוא ותנן כל המשקין שותה (לעיל דף קט:): לשרות. דתנן מתניתין אין שורין: כמאן דשרי. בעיא הוא הך דרב לימא כרבי יוסי דשרי בצונן אבל לרבנן אסור: עיילינא. הכניסני ואיש זקן היה: לכסכוסי כיתניתא. חלוק כתונת של פשתן שנתכבסה והרי היא קשה ומשפשפה בין שתי ידיו והיא מתרככה ואף הליבון שלה מהליל על ידי השפשוף: אולודי חיורא. הליבון מהליל: התם מיחזי כאולודי חיורא. שמקפיד על ליבונו ולוהרו של סודר יותר מכיתונא:
משלפה

לפי שאין עושין אותה אלא לגוון איתמר חרדל שלשו מע"ש למחר אמר רב ממחו בכלי אבל לא ביד א"ל שמואל ביד אטו כל יומא ממחו ליה ביד מאכל חמורים הוא אלא אמר שמואל ממחו ביד ואינו ממחו בכלי אתמר ר"א אמר אחד זה ואחד זה אסור ורבי יוחנן אמר אחד זה ואחד זה מותר אביי ורבא דאמרי תרוייהו אין הלכה כרבי יוחנן קם רבי יוחנן בשיטתיה דר"א קם רבי אלעזר בשיטתיה דשמואל אביי ורבא דאמרי תרוייהו הלכה כרבי יוחנן א) אימיה דאביי עבדא ליה ולא אכל דביתהו דזעירא עבדא ליה לרב חייא בר אשי ולא אכיל א"ל לרבך עבידי ליה ואכל ואת לא אכלת אמר רבא בר שבא הוה קאימנא קמיה דרבינא ובחשי ליה בשופתא דתומא ואכל * אמר מר זוטרא ג) לית הלכתא ככל הני שמעתתא אלא כי הא דאתמר א חרדל שלשו מע"ש למחר ממחו בין ביד בין בכלי ונותן לתוכו דבש ולא יטרוף אלא מערב ב שחליים ששחקן מע"ש למחר נותן לתוכן שמן וחומץ וממשיך לתוכן אמיתא ולא יטרוף אלא מערב ג שום שריסקו מע"ש למחר נותן לתוכו פול וגריסין ולא ישחוק אלא מערב וממשיך את אמיתא לתוכן ד) מאי אמיתא נינייא אמר אביי ש"מ האי נינייא מעליא לתחלי: ועושין אנומלין בשבת: ה) ת"ר ד עושין אנומלין בשבת ואין עושין ה) אלונטית ואיזו היא אנומלין ואיזו היא אלונטית אנומלין יין ודבש ופלפלין אלונטית יין ישן ומים צלולין ואפרסמון דעבדי לבי מסותא למיקר אמר רב יוסף זימנא חדא עלית בתר מר עוקבא לבי באני כי נפקי אתאי אשקיין ו) חמרא חד כסא וחשי מבינתא דראשי ועד טופרא דכרעי ואי אשקיין כסא אחרינא הואי מסתפינא דלמא מנכו לי מזכותא דעלמא דאתי והא מר עוקבא דשתי כל יומא שאני מר עוקבא דדש ביה: **מתני'** אין שורין את החילתית בפושרין ו אבל נותן לתוך החומץ ז ואין שולין את הכרשינין ולא שפין אותן אבל נותן לתוך הכברה או לתוך הכלכלה ח אין כוברין את התבן בכברה ולא יתננו על גבי מקום גבוה בשביל שירד המוץ אבל נוטל הוא בכברה ונותן לתוך האיבוס: **גמ'** איבעיא להו שרה מאי תרגמא רב אדא נרשאה קמיה דרב יוסף שרה חייב חטאת א"ל אביי אלא מעתה שרה אומצא במיא הכי נמי דמיחייב אלא אמר אביי ז) מדרבנן שלא יעשה כדרך שהוא עושה בחול בעא מיניה רבי יוחנן מר' ינאי מהו לשרות את החלתית בצונן א"ל אסור והא אנן תנן אין שורין את החלתית בפושרין הא בצונן מותר א"ל ח) א"כ מה בין לי ולך מתניתין יחידאה היא דתניא ט) ט אין שורין את החלתית לא בחמין ולא בצונן רבי יוסי אומר בחמין אסור בצונן מותר למאי עבדי ליה ליוקרא דליבא רב אחא בר יוסף חש ביוקרא דליבא אתא לקמיה דמר עוקבא א"ל זיל שתי תלתא תיקלי חילתתא בתלתא יומי אזל אישתי חמשא בשבת ומעלי שבת לצפרא אזל שאל בי מדרשא אמרו ליה תנא דבי רב אדא ואמרי לה תנא דבי מר בר רב אדא י שותה אדם קב או קביים ואינו חושש אמר להו לשתות לא קמיבעיא לי כי קא מיבעיא לי לשרות מאי אמר להו רב חייא בר אבין בדידי הוה עובדא ואתאי שאילתיה לרב אדא בר אהבה ולא הוה בידיה אתאי שאילתיה לרב הונא ואמר הכי קאמר רב שורה בצונן ומניח בחמה כמאן דשרי כ אפילו למאן דאסר ה"מ היכא דלא אישתי כלל אבל הכא כיון דאישתי חמשא ומעלי שבתא אי לא שתי בשבת מיסתכן מיסתמיך ואזיל רב אחא בר יוסף אכתפיה דרב נחמן בר יצחק בר אחתיה א"ל כי מטינן לבי רב ספרא עיילינא כי מטו עייליה בעא מיניה מהו לכסכוסי כיתניתא בשבתא לרכוכי קא מיכוין ושפיר דמי או דילמא לאולודי חיורא קא מיכוין ואסיר א"ל י) לרכוכי קא מיכוין ושפיר דמי כי נפק אתא א"ל מאי בעא מר מיניה א"ל בעי מיניה מהו לכסכוסי כיתניתא בשבתא ואמר לי שפיר דמי ותבעי ליה למר סודרא סודרא לא קא מיבעיא לי דבעי מרב הונא ופשיט לי ט) ותיפשיט ליה למר מסודרא א"ל מ) התם מיחזי כי אולודי חיורא הכא לא מיחזי כאולודי חיורא אמר רב חסדא האי כיתניתא
משלפו

מסורת הש"ס

א) [עיין קדושין לא:], ב) [ע' תוס' כתובות נד. ד"ה לית], ג) [לעיל קכח.], ד) ע"ז ל., ה) [שם איתא אלונתית אבל בערוך גרס כגי' שלפנינו], ו) [לעיל קלח.], ז) [חולי' קלד:], ח) [תוספ' פי"ז], ט) ס"א לאיסורא.

הגהות הב"ח

(א) רש"י ד"ה לפי שאין עושין אותה אלא: (ב) ד"ה תבן וכו' כל זנב השבלים תבן: (ג) ד"ה מוץ וכו' בכברה כדי שיפול: (ד) ד"ה אבל נוטל הוא בכברה ונותן לתוך האבוס:

גליון הש"ס

גמ' אמר מר זוטרא לית הלכתא ככל הני שמעתתא. עיין כתובות דף נד ע"א תוס' ד"ה לית הלכתא: רש"י ד"ה אבל נוטל וכו' נופל מאליו כר"ש. עיין לעיל דף נד ע"א ברש"י ד"ה כלאים דחבלים:

רב נסים גאון

אין שורין את הכרשינין. גרסי' בגמ' דבני מערבא תני אין שורין את הכרשינים משום בורר ולא שפין אותן משום דש אין כוברין את התבן משום מרקד. גורפין מלפני הפטם ומסלקין לצדדין מפני הרעי בגמ' דבני מערבא גרסי מה שהפטם אוכל ומותיר הרעי אוכל:

ליקוטי רש"י

ואמר רבא מת ביום טוב ראשון כו'. מת המוטל לקבור אם יום טוב ראשון הוא וכו'. מה שאין כן בביצה. לענין ביצה לא הקלו ביום טוב שני דראש השנה להשוות לשל גליות דאלו ראש השנה נולדה בזה אסורה בזה [ביצה ו.]. דקדושה אחת הן ולא הקלו ביום טוב שני של ראש השנה אלא לענין מת בלבד [שם כב:]. מערים ושותה מן החדש. שיכול לומר לצורך המועד הטילו [מו"ק יב:]. ברא דתומא. בן השום צלע של שום [תענית כה.]. כפיפה מצרית. סל של נצרי דקל ורדים שגדלין סביב הדקל [סוטה יד.]. סל נצרים של ערבה [ב"ב כב.]. ונותנין ביצה במסננת של חרדל. ומסננה בתוכו לייפות מראיתו לא מיחזי כבורר שכולה יוצאה דרך המסננת ואין משתייר שם פסולת [לעיל קלד. ע"ש בהגהות ר' שמחה מדעסויא]. ובלבד שלא יגביה כו' טפח. חלל טפח אהל הוא [סוכה טז.].
[ע"כ שייך לדף קלט:].

אימיה דאביי. אומנתו [לעיל קלד.]. עושין אנומלין. בשבת שהוא לשתות. ואין עושין אלונטית. שהוא לרפואה להצטנן כשיוצאין מבית המרחץ כמפרש. ומים צלולין. שנשאבו ועמדו בכלי יום או יומים להיות צלולין וצופין העליונים בנחת במסננת [ע"ז ל.]. חלתית. מין פירי הוא שקורין לזר"א בלע"ז [שם לה:]. מה בין לי ולך. אם איני יודע פירושה של משנתינו יותר ממך מה אני גדול ממך [חולין קלז:]. לכסכוסי. לשפשף [נדה סב.].

עין משפט נר מצוה

לב א מיי' פ"ח מהל' שבת הל' יד ופכ"ב הלכה יג סמג לאוין סה טוש"ע א"ח סי' שכא סעיף טו:
לג ב ג מיי' פכ"ב שם טוש"ע שם סעיף טז:
לד ד מיי' שם טוש"ע שם סעיף יז:
לה ה מיי' פ"ד מהל' דעות הלכה יז:
לו ו מיי' פכ"ב מהל' שבת הלכה ז סמג לאוין סה טוש"ע א"ח סי' שכא סעיף יח:
לז ז (מיי' פ"ח מהל' שבת) סמג לאוין סה טוש"ע א"ח סי' שיט סעיף מ:
לח ח מיי' פכ"א שם הלכה לג סמג שם טוש"ע א"ח סי' שכד סעיף א:
לט ט י כ מיי' פכ"א שם הלכה כב ופכ"ב שם הל' ז סמג שם טוש"ע א"ח סי' שכא סעיף יט:
מ ל מ מיי' פכ"ב שם הלכה יח סמג שם טוש"ע א"ח סי' שב סעיף ה:

רבינו חננאל

לפי שאין עושין אותה אלא לגוון. פי' לצבעו להתראות בו גוונא של ביצה מאכל המרס. פי' זה המאכל ממורס הוא כדתנן (נתן) [נטל] את הדם ונתנו לממרס בו על הרובד הרביעי וי"א מאכל חמורים הוא כלומר אינו מאכל ב"א אלא מאכל חמורים הוא: חרדל שלשו מע"ש חלקו עליו רב ושמואל ור' יוחנן ור' אלעזר ודבריהן פשוטין הן ומר זוטרא דהוא בתרא אמר לית הלכתא ככל הני שמעתתא אלא כי הא דתניא חרדל שלשו מע"ש למחר מניחו בין ביד בין בכלי ונותן לתוכו דבש ולא יטרוף אלא מערב. שום שריסקו מע"ש למחר נותן לתוכו פול או גריסין ולא ישחוק אלא מערב. וממשיך את האמיתה לתוכה מאי אמיתה נגחה. אנומלין יין ושמן ודבש ופלפלין אלונתית יין ישן ומים צלולין ואפרסמון: אין שורין את החלתית בפושרין אבל נותן לתוך החומץ ומיבעיא לן שרה מאי. ומסקנא שרה אמר אביי איסורא מדרבנן וא"ר יוחנן מתניתין יחידאה היא והוא ר' יוסי אבל חכ"א בין בחמין בין בצונן אסור וסוגיא דשמעתא אם שרה מאתמול לשתות חלתית בשבת מותר. אבל לשרותו אסור אפילו בצונן. ואם שרה קודם השבת ועכשיו בשבת חושש אם לא ישתה מסתכן מותר לו לשרות בתוכו ולהניחה בחמה: לכסכוסי כיתונתא. פי' לרכוכי קא מיכוון ושרי או דלמא לאולודי וכו'. פי' לקבץ מקצת הבגד של פשתים לתוך ידו לשופו מפני שרוחצין הבגד ומתייבש בשמש או ברוח עומד אנסו פי' קשה ורוצה לרככו נותן הבגד לתוך ידיו ומוליך ומביא ידיו עד שיעשה הבגד ההוא כמו קפולין קטנים כמין קמטין כי הא דא"ר זירא בפ' חבית (דף קמז) מאי מרוב כגון א) כסכוסי מאני דמתחזי כמרוב וכי הא דתנן בפ' האשה שהיא עושה צרכיה: צריכה לכסכס ג' פעמים על כל דבר ודבר ואמרי' בגמ' בעי ר' ירמיה אמטויי חד ואיתויי [חד] או דלמא אמטויי [חד] ואיתויי [תרתי] תיקו: וכן עוד מפורש בתלמוד א"י בענין מוליך ומביא שבלולב. מהא שמעינן דכיסכוס כעין שפשוף הוא ומתקבץ הבגד פי' יתכמש ותראה קמטין קמטין וכשלובשו מתפשט וכדאמרינן אמר רב כהנא ואיתימא רב יהודה טיט שעל בגדו מכסכסו מבפנים. (ומרקי) [ומדקרי] להאי כיתונתא. שמעינן מנה דסודרא ליתיה כתינתא ולא יתכן לומר שהוא צמר שאם הוא צמר איך אומר לו היה לך ללמוד פשתים מצמר. והדבר רחוק ביניהם ואינה אלא צמר גפן שזה קרוב לזה ופשט

חשק שלמה על רבינו חננאל א) לפנינו בגמ' איתא שם כיסו בבלייתא:

אֲבָל נוֹתֵן לְתוֹךְ הַכְּבָרָה אוֹ לְתוֹךְ הַכַּלְכָּלָה – **but** one **may put them into a sieve or into a basket.**[24] אֵין כּוֹבְרִין אֶת הַתֶּבֶן בִּכְבָרָה – **We may not sift straw**[25] **with a sieve,** וְלֹא יִתְּנֶנּוּ עַל גַּבֵּי מָקוֹם גָּבוֹהַּ בִּשְׁבִיל שֶׁיֵּרֵד הַמּוֹץ – **nor may we put it on a high place so that the chaff will drop** from it;[26] אֲבָל נוֹטֵל הוּא בִּכְבָרָה וְנוֹתֵן לְתוֹךְ הָאֵיבוּס – **but one may take it in a sieve and pour it into the feeding trough.**[27]

Gemara The Gemara discusses the level of the Mishnah's prohibition against soaking asafetida in warm water on the Sabbath:

אִיבַּעְיָא לְהוּ – **They inquired:** שָׁרָה מַאי – **If one soaked** asafetida in warm water, **what** is the law? Is he Biblically liable, or is it only Rabbinically prohibited?

The Gemara answers:

תַּרְגְּמָא רַב אַדָּא נַרְשָׁאָה קַמֵּיהּ דְּרַב יוֹסֵף – **Rav Adda Narshaah interpreted** this law **before Rav Yosef:** שָׁרָה חַיָּיב חַטָּאת – **If one soaked** asafetida unwittingly on the Sabbath, **he is liable to a *chatas*;** i.e. it is Biblically prohibited. אֲמַר לֵיהּ אַבָּיֵי – **Abaye said to [Rav Adda]:** אֶלָּא מֵעַתָּה שָׁרָה אוּמְצָא בְּמַיָּא הָכִי נַמִּי דְּמִיחַיֵּיב – **But now, if one soaked raw meat in water, would he be liable in this case as well?** Certainly not! Why, then, should he be liable for soaking asafetida?[28]

Abaye gives his opinion:

אֶלָּא אָמַר אַבָּיֵי – **Rather, Abaye said:** מִדְּרַבָּנָן שֶׁלֹּא יַעֲשֶׂה כְּדֶרֶךְ שֶׁהוּא עוֹשֶׂה בְּחוֹל – It is **Rabbinically** prohibited, **so that one should not act in the manner which he acts during the week.**[29]

The Gemara explores further the prohibition against soaking asafetida:

בְּעָא מִינֵּיהּ רַבִּי יוֹחָנָן מֵרַבִּי יַנַּאי – **R' Yochanan queried of R' Yannai:** מַהוּ לִשְׁרוֹת אֶת הַחִלְתִּית בְּצוֹנֵן – **What is the law concerning soaking asafetida in cold water?**[30] אֲמַר לֵיהּ אָסוּר – **[Rav Yannai] said to [R' Yochanan]: It is prohibited.**

R' Yochanan asked:

וְהָא אֲנַן תְּנַן – **But we learned in our Mishnah:** אֵין שׁוֹרִין אֶת הַחִלְתִּית בְּפוֹשְׁרִין – WE MAY NOT SOAK ASAFETIDA IN WARM WATER. הָא בְּצוֹנֵן מוּתָּר – **This implies** that soaking it **in cold water is permitted!**[31]

R' Yannai responds:

אֲמַר לֵיהּ – **[R' Yannai] said to [R' Yochanan]:** אִם כֵּן מָה בֵּין לִי וְלָךְ – **If it is so** that I cannot resolve a difficulty that you have raised from a Mishnah, **what difference is there between me and you?**[32] מַתְנִיתִין יְחִידָאָה הִיא – Our Mishnah cannot be cited as a proof, for **our Mishnah is** reflective of the opinion **of an individual,** דְּתַנְיָא – **as it was taught in a Baraisa:** אֵין שׁוֹרִין אֶת הַחִלְתִּית לֹא בְּחַמִּין וְלֹא בְּצוֹנֵן – WE MAY NOT SOAK ASAFETIDA NEITHER IN HOT WATER NOR IN COLD WATER. רַבִּי יוֹסֵי אוֹמֵר – R' YOSE SAYS: בְּחַמִּין אָסוּר בְּצוֹנֵן מוּתָּר – IN HOT WATER IT IS PROHIBITED to soak asafetida; IN COLD WATER, however, IT IS PERMITTED. The unattributed view of the Tanna Kamma, however, is the majority, and thus prevailing, opinion.

The Gemara explains what the asafetida mixture was used to treat:

לְמַאי עָבְדֵי לֵיהּ – **For what** condition was **[the asafetida mixture] made?** לְיוֹקְרָא דְּלִיבָּא – **For heaviness of the heart.**[33]

The Gemara cites a case where this medication was used to treat this condition:

רַב אַחָא בַּר יוֹסֵף חָשׁ בְּיוֹקְרָא דְּלִיבָּא – **Rav Acha bar Yosef suffered from heaviness of the heart.** אֲתָא לְקַמֵּיהּ דְּמָר עוּקְבָא – **He came before Mar Ukva.** אֲמַר לֵיהּ – **[Mar Ukva] told [Rav Acha bar Yosef]:** זִיל שְׁתֵי תְּלָתָא תִּיקְלֵי חִילְתָּתָא בִּתְלָתָא יוֹמֵי – **Go drink three gold [*dinars'*] weights of asafetida** potion **over the course of three days.** אֲזַל אִישְׁתִּי חַמְשָׁא בְּשַׁבָּת וּמַעֲלֵי שַׁבָּת – **He**

NOTES

24. I.e. one may put the beans into a sieve or basket for storage, even though the refuse will sometimes fall through the holes of the sieve, and the food will therefore be sorted (*Rashi*). Since by putting them into the sieve he has no intention of sorting them, and it is not inevitable that they will be sorted, it is permissible (*Mishnah Berurah* 319:30 and *Beur Halachah* there). [To put the beans into a sieve in order to sort them, however, is certainly prohibited.]

25. I.e. the stalks of cut grain that have been chopped up by means of a threshing-sledge (see *Rashi*; see also *Shabbos Shel Mi*, and above, 36b note 2).

26. I.e. one may not place a sieve containing straw on a high place, so that the inedible chaff will fall through the holes, leaving behind clean straw that can be used as fodder for livestock. This constitutes *sifting*, and is prohibited (*Rashi, Rambam, Hil. Shabbos* 21:32; see *Shaar HaTziyun* 324:1).

Others explain that one may not put the straw on a high place so that the chaff will blow away, leaving only the edible parts behind. [This would be a *toladah* of the *melachah* of *sorting*] (*Meiri*; see also *Chidushei HaRan*).

27. I.e. he may scoop the straw up with a sieve and pour it into an animal's feeding trough. Although some chaff will thereby be eliminated when it falls through the holes in the sieve, it is permissible, since he does not intend to sort the straw, and it is not inevitable that sorting will occur (*Rashi*; *Rambam, Hil. Shabbos* 21:32; cf. *Sfas Emes*).

28. There is no real prohibition that could apply in the case of soaking raw meat, and so there is no real comparison between the cases of soaking raw meat and soaking asafetida. Abaye chose this case as a form of hyperbole, declaring that soaking asafetida should be prohibited as much as soaking raw meat (*Ritva MHK* ed.).

[Perhaps Rav Adda and Rav Yosef held that soaking the asafetida in warm water carries a Biblical liability because that is the final step in its preparation, much as pouring hot water over certain types of fish (see below, 145b), or placing an egg next to a kettle causing it to become just slightly cooked [see above, 39a] (*Chasam Sofer*, Machon Chasam Sofer ed.).]

29. The Rabbis prohibit us from performing certain actions which we do during the week (*Rashi*; see above, 138a note 1 and General Introduction).

While the Gemara explains that the Rabbis prohibited soaking asafetida because of עוּבְדָא דְחוֹל, *weekday activity*, *Meiri* and *Chidushei HaRan* (and *Shulchan Aruch, Orach Chaim* 321:18) state that it is included in the Rabbinic prohibition against making medications on the Sabbath. Perhaps the Gemara adds the reason of *weekday activity* to teach that it is forbidden to soak the asafetida even for non-medicinal uses, i.e. for a beverage (see *Beur Halachah* to *Shulchan Aruch* ibid. ד״ה שהוא; see also *Chidushei Basra,* who discusses these opinions in light of the Gemara below). See also note 34.

[It is also possible that it is considered a weekday activity for this very reason – because this mixture was *usually* prepared for medicinal use only, and therefore one who prepares it appears as one who is preparing a medication, and not as one who is preparing a beverage. See above, 138a note 1.]

30. [Since it is generally soaked in warm water, perhaps soaking it in cold water is not reminiscent of a weekday activity.]

31. [See *Menachem Meishiv Nefesh*, *Yad David [Basra]*, and *Shabbos Shel Mi*, who inquire as to why R' Yochanan asked the question of R' Yannai if he himself had deduced the answer from the Mishnah.]

32. [R' Yannai was greater than R' Yochanan in scholarship. Thus,] R' Yannai countered to R' Yochanan that he stated his position fully aware of the possible refutation from our Mishnah – "For if I were unable to explain our Mishnah properly," says R' Yannai, then "what difference would there be between me and you," i.e what would my superior scholarship avail me? (see *Rashi* here and to *Chullin* 137b; see *Meromei Sadeh,* who explains the dispute between R' Yannai and R' Yochanan).

33. A type of chest pain (*Meiri*). [This obviously refers to a non-life threatening condition, since in situations where a life is endangered, even Biblical prohibitions may be violated.]

לפי שאין עושין (א) אלא לגוון. למראה שהחלמון יפה לגוון ולא להלבון הלכך אידי ואידי אוכל הוא ואין כאן ברירת פסולת מאוכל: ממחו. דיסטמפי"ר בלע"ז כמים או ביין: ממחו בכלי. משמע זהו שינוי שלו: ואינו ממחו ביד. דממחו ליה שפיר טפי: אלא אמר שמואל ממחו ביד. שאין זה דרכו בחול: קם ר' יוחנן בשיטתיה דר"א. חזר בו והסכים: אביי ורבא דאמרי הלכה כר' יוחנן. דלאסור: לרבך. לזעירי: בשופתא דתומא. אמלעי של שום: ולא יטרוף. כלך שטורפין ביצים בקערה בכף לכך טריפה שמכה בכח: שחליים. כרישין והיו שוחקין אותם כמים: ממשיך. נותן: אמיתא. מינט"א בלע"ז: מעליא לתחלי. לערב עם שחליים: ואין עושין אלונטית. שאינה למשקה אלא לצנן לאחר המרחץ ודוגמת רפואה: וחשי מבינתא דרישא. הרגשתי בגידתו משערת ראשי עד צפרני רגלי: מנכו לי מזכיותי. אם הייתי ניצול ממנו שלא אמות: שתי כל יומא. ולא היה מזיקו: דדש ביה. רגיל בו: מתני' חילתית. אלטנ"ש בלשון ישמעאל ובלע"ז לזרי"א ושורין אותו בפושרין ושותין אותן המים לרפואה: אבל נותן. החלתית: בתוך החומץ. ומתבל בו מאכלו ולקמיה מפרש אמאי אין שורין: ואין שולין את הכרשינין. מליף עליהם מים בכלי לברור פסולתן כדתנן במסכת ביצה (דף יד:) אף מדיח ושולה: ולא שפין אותן. ביד להסיר פסולת דהוה ליה בורר: אבל נותן לתוך הכברה. ואע"פ דפעמים שהפסולת נופל דרך נקבי הכברה ונמצא נברר מאליו: תבן. הוא שעושין מן הקש מחתכין אותו במוריגין ועושה כל זנב (ב) השבולת תבן: מוץ. הוא מוזקין השבולת העליון ואינו ראוי למאכל וכוברין אותו (ג) בכברה כדי שיפול המוץ: אבל נוטל (ד) בכברה. ליתן בתוך האבוס ואע"פ שהמוץ נופל מאליו כר"ש דאמר דבר שאין מתכוין מותר: גמ' שרה. חילתית בפושרין מאי: אומצא. בשר חי: שלא יעשה כו'. לא שבקוה רבנן למעבד עובדי דחול: אם כן. דלא ידענא לפרושי מתני' טפי מינך מה בין לי ולך: מתניתין יחידאה היא. ור' יוסי אמרה אבל לרבנן אף בצונן אסור: ליוקרא דליבא. שלבו כבד עליו: תלתא תקלי חילתתא. משקל ג' זהובים: שאיל בי מדרשא. מה יעשה בשבת: לשתות לא קמיבעיא לי. דבלאו רפואה משקה הוא ותנן כל המשקין שותה (לעיל דף קט:): לשרות. דתנן מתניתין אין שורין: כמאן דשרי. בעילא הוא הך דרב לימא כרבי יוסי דשרי בצונן אבל לרבנן אסור: עייליה. הכניסני ואיש זקן היה: לכסכוסי כיתניתא. חלוק כתונת של פשתן שנתכבסה והרי היא קשה ומשפשפה בין שתי ידיו והיא מתרככת ואף הלובן שלה מגהיל על ידי השפשוף: אולודי חיורא. הלובן מגהיל: התם מיחזי כאולודי חיורא. שמקפיד על ליבונו ולובשו של סודר יותר מכתונתו:

לפי שאין עושין אותה אלא לגוון איתמר חרדל שלשו מע"ש למחר רב ממחו בכלי אבל לא ביד א"ל שמואל ביד אמטו כל יומא ממחו ליה ביד מאכל חמורים הוא אלא אמר שמואל ממחו ביד ואינו ממחו בכלי אתמר ר"א אמר אחד זה ואחד זה אסור ורבי יוחנן אמר אחד זה ואחד זה מותר אביי ורבא דאמרי תרוייהו אין הלכה כרבי יוחנן קם רבי יוחנן בשיטתיה דר"א קם רבי אלעזר בשיטתיה דשמואל אביי ורבא דאמרי תרוייהו הלכה כרבי יוחנן (א) אימיה דאביי עבדא ליה ולא אכל דביתהו דזעירא עבדא ליה לרב חייא בר אשי ולא אכיל א"ל לרבך עבידי ליה ואכל ואת לא אכלת אמר רבא בר שבא הוה קאימנא קמיה דרבינא ובחשי ליה בשופתא דתומא ואכל אמר מר זוטרא (ב) לית הלכתא ככל הני שמעתתא אלא כי הא דאתמר חרדל שלשו מע"ש למחר ממחו בין ביד בין בכלי ונותן לתוכו דבש ולא יטרוף אלא מערב שחליים ששחקן מע"ש למחר נותן לתוכן שמן והחומץ וממשיך לתוכן אמיתא ולא יטרוף אלא מערב שום שריסקו מע"ש למחר נותן לתוכו פול וגריסין ולא ישחוק אלא מערב וממשיך את אמיתא לתוכן (ג) מאי אמיתא נינייא אמר אביי ש"מ האי נינייא מעליא לתחלי: ועושין אנומלין בשבת: (ד) ת"ר עושין אנומלין בשבת ואין עושין (ה) אלונטית ואיזו היא אנומלין ואיזו היא אלונטית אנומלין יין ודבש ופלפלין אלונטית יין ישן ומים צלולין ואפרסמון דעבדי לבי מסותא למיקר אמר

רב יוסף זימנא חדא עלית בתר מר עוקבא לבי באני כי נפקי אתאי אשקיין (ח) חמרא חד כסא וחשי מבינתא דראשי ועד טופרא דכרעי ואי אשקיין כסא אחרינא הואי מסתפינא דלמא מנכו לי מזכותא דעלמא דאתי והא מר עוקבא דשתי כל יומא שאני מר עוקבא דדש ביה: מתני' אין שורין את החילתית בפושרין אבל נותן לתוך החומץ ואין שולין את הכרשינין ולא שפין אותן אבל נותן לתוך הכברה או לתוך הכלכלה אין כוברין את התבן בכברה ולא יתננו על גבי מקום גבוה בשביל שירד המוץ אבל נוטל הוא בכברה ונותן לתוך האיבוס: גמ' איבעיא להו שרה מאי תרגמא רב אדא נרשאה קמיה דרב יוסף שרה חייב חטאת א"ל אביי אלא מעתה שרה אומצא במיא הכי נמי דמיחייב אלא אמר אביי (ט) מדרבנן שלא יעשה כדרך שהוא עושה בחול בעא מיניה רבי יוחנן מר' ינאי מהו לשרות את החלתית בצונן א"ל אסור והא אנן תנן אין שורין את החלתית בפושרין הא בצונן מותר א"ל א"כ מה בין לי ולך מתניתין יחידאה היא דתניא אין שורין את החילתית לא בחמין ולא בצונן רבי יוסי אומר בחמין אסור בצונן מותר למאי עבדי ליה ליוקרא דליבא רב אחא בר יוסף חש ביוקרא דליבא אתא לקמיה דמר עוקבא א"ל זיל שתי תלתא תיקלי חילתתא בתלתא יומי אזל אישתי חמשא בשבת ומעלי שבת לצפרא אזל שאל בי מדרשא אמרו ליה תנא דבי רב אדא ואמרי לה תנא דבי מר בר רב אדא שותה אדם קב או קביים ואינו חושש אמר להו לשתות לא קמיבעיא לי כי קא מיבעיא לי לשרות מאי אמר להו רב חייא בר אבין בדידי הוה עובדא ואתאי שאילתיה לרב אדא בר אהבה ולא הוה בידיה אתאי שאילתיה לרב הונא ואמר הכי קאמר רב שורה בצונן ומניח בחמה אפילו למאן דאסר כמאן דשרי ה"מ היכא דלא אישתי כלל אבל הכא כיון דאישתי חמשא ומעלי שבתא אי לא שתי בשבתא מיסתכן מיסתמיך ואזיל רב אחא בר יוסף אכתפיה דרב נחמן בר יצחק בר אחתיה א"ל כי מטינן לבי רב ספרא עיילינא כי מטו עייליה בעא מיניה מהו לכסכוסי כיתניתא בשבתא לרכוכי כיתניתא קא מיכוין ושפיר דמי או דילמא לאולודי חיורא קמיכוין ואסיר א"ל לרכוכי קא מיכוין ושפיר דמי כי נפק אתא א"ל בעא מר מיניה א"ל מאי בעי מיניה מהו לכסכוסי כיתניתא בשבתא ואמר לי שפיר דמי ותבעי ליה למר סודרא סודרא לא קא מיבעיא לי דבעי מרב הונא ופשיט לי ותיפשיט ליה למר מסודרא א"ל התם מיחזי כי אולודי חיורא הכא לא מיחזי כאולודי חיורא אמר רב חסדא האי כיתניתא משלפו

עין משפט נר מצוה

לב א מיי' פ"ח מהל' שבת הל' יד ופכ"ב הלכה יב סמג לאוין סה טוש"ע א"ח סי' שכא סעיף טו:
לג ב ג מיי' פכ"ב שם טוש"ע שם סעיף טז:
לד ד מיי' שם טוש"ע שם סעיף יז:
לה ה מיי' פ"ד מהל' דעות הלכה יח:
לו ו מיי' פכ"ב מהל' שבת הלכה ז סמג לאוין סה טוש"ע א"ח סי' שכא סעיף יח:
לז ז (מיי' פ"ח מהל' שבת) סמג לאוין סה טוש"ע א"ח סי' שיט סעיף ח:
לח ח מיי' פכ"א שם הלכה לג סמג שם טוש"ע א"ח סי' שכד סעיף א:
לט ט י כ מיי' פכ"א שם הלכה כב ופכ"ב שם הל' ז סמג שם טוש"ע א"ח סי' שכא סעיף יח:
מ ל מ מיי' פכ"ב שם הלכה יח סמג שם טוש"ע א"ח סי' שב סעיף ה:

רבינו חננאל

לפי שאין עושין אותה אלא לגוון. פי' לצבעו להתראות בו גוונא של ביצה מאכל המרס. פי' זה המאכל ממורס הוא כדתנן (נתן) [נטל] את הדם ונתנו לממרס בו על הרובד הרביעי וי"א מאכל חמורים הוא כלומר אינו מאכל ב"א אלא מאכל חמורים הוא: חרדל שלשו מע"ש חלקו עליו רב ושמואל ור' יוחנן ור' אלעזר ודבריהן פשוטין הן ומר זוטרא דהוא בתרא אמר לית הלכתא ככל הני שמעתתא אלא כי הא דתניא חרדל שלשו מע"ש למחר מניחו בין ביד בין בכלי ונותן לתוכו דבש ולא יטרוף אלא מערב. שום שריסקו מע"ש למחר נותן לתוכו פול או גריסין ולא ישחוק אלא מערב. וממשיך את האמיתה לתוכה מאי אמיתה נגחה. אנומלין יין ושמן ודבש ופלפלין אלונתית יין ישן ומים צלולין ואפרסמון: אין שורין את החלתית בפושרין אבל נותן לתוך החומץ ומיבעיא לן שרה מאי. ומסקנא שרה אמר אביי איסורא מדרבנן וא"ר יוחנן מתניתין יחידאה היא והוא ר' יוסי אבל חכ"א בין בחמין בין בצונן אסור וסוגיא דשמעתא אם שרה מאתמול לשתות חלתית בשבת מותר. אבל לשרותו אסור אפילו בצונן. ואם שרה קודם השבת ועכשיו בשבת חושש אם לא ישתה מסתכן מותר לו לשרות בתוכו ולהניחה בחמה: לכסכוסי כיתונתא. פי' לרכוכי קא מיכוון ושרי או דלמא לאולודי וכו'. פי' לקבץ מקצת הבגד של פשתים לתוך ידו לשופו מפני שרוחצין הבגד ומתייבש בשמש או ברוח עומד אנסו פי' קשה ורוצה לרככו נותן הבגד לתוך ידיו ומוליך ומביא ידיו עד שיעשה הבגד ההוא כמו קפולין קטנים כמין קמטין כי הא דא"ר זירא בפ' חבית (דף קמז) מאי מרזב כגון (א) כסכוסי מאני דמתחזי כמרזב וכי הא דתנן בפ' האשה שהיא עושה צרכיה: צריכה לכסכס ג' פעמים על כל דבר ודבר ואמרי' בגמ' בעי ר' ירמיה אמטויי חד ואיתויי [חד] או דלמא אמטויי [חד] ואיתויי [תרתי] תיקו: וכן עוד מפורש בתלמוד א"י בענין מוליך ומביא שבלולב. מהא שמעינן דכיסכוס כעין שפשוף הוא ומתקבץ הבגד פי' יתכמש ונראה קמטין קמטין וכשלובשו מתפשט וכדאמרינן אמר רב כהנא ואיתימא רב יהודה טיט שעל בגדו מכסכסו מבפנים. (ומרקדי) [ומדקרי] להאי כיתונתא. שמעינן מנה דסודרא ליתיה כתינתא ולא יתכן לומר שהוא צמר שאם הוא צמר איך אומר לו היה לך ללמוד פשתים מצמר. והדבר רחוק ביניהם ואינה אלא צמר גפן שזה קרוב לזה ופשט

חשק שלמה על רבינו חננאל א) לפנינו בגמ' ליתא שם מיכו בבלייתא:

מסורת הש"ס

א) [עיין קדושין לא:], ב) [ע' תוס' כתובות נד. ד"ה לית], ג) [לעיל קכח.], ד) ע"ז ל., ה) [שם איתא אלונתית אבל בערוך גרס כגי' שלפנינו], ו) [לעיל קלח.], ז) [תולי' קלד:], ח) [תוספ' פי"ז], ט) ס"א לאיסורא.

הגהות הב"ח

(א) רש"י ד"ה לפי שאין עושין אותה אלא: (ב) ד"ה תבן וכו' כל זנב השבלים תבן: (ג) ד"ה מוץ וכו' בכברה כדי שיפול: (ד) ד"ה אבל נוטל הוא בכברה ונותן לתוך האבוס:

גליון הש"ס

גמ' אמר מר זוטרא לית הלכתא ככל הני שמעתתא. עיין כתובות דף נד ע"א תוס' ד"ה לית הלכתא: רש"י ד"ה אבל נוטל וכו' נופל מאליו כר"ש. עיין לעיל דף נד ע"א ברש"י ד"ה כלאים דמכלים:

רב נסים גאון

אין שורין את הכרשינין. גרסי' בגמ' דבני מערבא תני אין שורין את הכרשינים משום בורר ולא שפין אותן משום דש אין כוברין את התבן משום מרקד. גורפין מלפני הפטם ומסלקין לצדדין מפני הרעי בגמ' דבני מערבא גרסי מה שהפטם אוכל ומותיר הרעי אוכל:

ליקוטי רש"י

ואמר רבא מת ביום טוב ראשון כו'. מת המוטל לקבור אם יום טוב ראשון הוא וכו'. מה שאין כן בביצה. לענין ביצה לא הקלו ביום טוב שני דראש השנה להשוות לשל גליות דאלו ראש השנה נולדה בזה אסורה בזה [ביצה ו.]. דקדושה אחת הן ולא הקלו ביום טוב שני של ראש השנה אלא לענין מת בלבד [שם כב:]. מערים ושותה מן החדש. שיכול לומר לצורך המועד הטילו [מו"ק יב:]. ברא דתומא. בן השום ללע של שום [תענית כה.]. כפיפה מצרית. סל של נצרי דקל זרדים שגדלין סביב הדקל [סוטה יד.]. סל נצרים של ערבה [ב"ב כב.]. ונותנין ביצה במסננת של חרדל. ומסננה בתוכו לייפות מראיתו לא מיחזי כבורר שכולה יוצאה דרך המסננת ואין משתייר שם פסולת [לעיל קלד. ע"ש בהגהות ר' שמחה מדעסויא]. ובלבד שלא יגביה כו' טפח. חלל טפח אהל הוא [סוכה טז.]. [ע"כ שייך לדף קלט:].

אימיה דאביי. אומנתו [לעיל קלד.]. עושין אנומלין. בשבת שהוא לשתות. ואין עושין אלונטית. שהוא לרפואה להצטנן כשיוצאין מבית המרחץ כדמפרש. ומים צלולין. שנשאבו ועמדו בכלי יום או יומים להיות צלולין וטופין העליונים בנחת במסננת [ע"ז ל.]. חלתית. מין פירי הוא שקורין לזר"א בלע"ז [שם לה:]. מה בין לי ולך. אם איני יודע פירושה של משנתינו יותר ממך מה אני גדול ממך [חולין קלז:]. לכסכוסי. לשפשף [נדה סב.].

went and drank a dose on the fifth day of the week (Thursday) **and on Erev Shabbos** (Friday). לְצַפְרָא אָזַל שָׁאַל בֵּי מִדְרְשָׁא – **The following day he went and asked in the study hall** concerning whether he was permitted to take his third dose. אָמְרוּ לֵיהּ – **[The students] told him:** תָּנָא דְבֵי רַב אַדָּא וְאָמְרֵי לָהּ תָּנָא דְבֵי מַר בַּר רַב אַדָּא – **It was taught in the academy of Rav Adda, and some say it was taught in the academy of Mar bar Rav Adda:** שׁוֹתֶה אָדָם קַב אוֹ קַבַּיִים וְאֵינוֹ חוֹשֵׁשׁ – **A person may drink a** ***kav*** **or two** ***kavs*** of asafetida potion **and not be concerned** for Sabbath violation.[34] Therefore, you (Rav Acha bar Yosef) are certainly permitted to take your third dose!

Rav Acha bar Yosef clarifies his question:

אָמַר לְהוּ – **[Rav Acha bar Yosef] said to them:** לִשְׁתּוֹת לֹא קָמִיבַּעְיָא לִי – **I was not unsure** whether I was permitted **to drink** it, for that I know I certainly may do. כִּי קָא מִיבַּעְיָא לִי לִשְׁרוֹת מַאי – **Rather, my uncertainty was: What is** the ruling **concerning soaking** asafetida on the Sabbath? Is it prohibited even in my case on account of it being a weekday activity?[35]

The question is resolved:

אָמַר לְהוּ רַב חִיָּיא בַּר אָבִין – **Rav Chiya bar Avin said to [Rav Acha bar Yosef]:** בְּדִידִי הֲוָה עוּבְדָא – **A similar incident happened to me,** i.e. I found myself in a similar situation, וְאָתַאי שְׁאֵילְתֵּיהּ לְרַב אַדָּא בַּר אַהֲבָה – **and I went and asked Rav Adda bar Ahavah,** וְלָא הֲוָה בִּידֵיהּ – **and it was not in his hand,** i.e. he was unsure of the halachah. אָתַאי שְׁאֵילְתֵּיהּ לְרַב הוּנָא וְאָמַר – **I then went and asked Rav Huna, and he said:** הָכִי קָאָמַר רַב – **This is what Rav said:** שׁוֹרֶה בְּצוֹנֵן וּמַנִּיחַ בַּחַמָּה – **One may soak** asafetida **in cold water and leave it in the sun** to become warm.

The Gemara asks:

כְּמַאן דְּשָׁרֵי – Did Rav permit this only **in accordance with the one** (R' Yose) **who permits** soaking asafetida in cold water in the Baraisa cited previously?[36]

The Gemara answers:

אֲפִילוּ לְמַאן דְּאָסַר – Rav permitted this **even according to the one who prohibits** soaking asafetida in cold water (i.e. the Tanna Kamma cited in the Baraisa previously). הָנֵי מִילֵּי הֵיכָא דְּלָא אִישְׁתִּי כְּלָל – For **those words** of the Tanna Kamma were said only **where one had not begun drinking** the medication **at all,** prohibiting one from soaking asafetida on the Sabbath. אֲבָל כֵּיוָן דְּאִישְׁתִּי חֲמִשָּׁא וּמַעֲלֵי שַׁבְּתָא – **But** in our cases, **since he began to drink** the asafetida **on the fifth** day of the week (Thursday) **and on erev Shabbos** (Friday), אִי לָא שָׁתֵי בְּשַׁבָּת מִסְתַּכֵּן – **if he were not to drink it on the Sabbath** as well, **he would be in mortal danger,** as a dangerous relapse might result. Thus, Rav allowed one to soak the asafetida, for any prohibition is overriden in a life-threatening situation.[37]

The Gemara recounts another incident involving Rav Acha bar Yosef:

מִיסְתְּמֵיךְ וְאָזִיל רַב אַחָא בַּר יוֹסֵף אַכַּתְפֵּיהּ דְּרַב נַחְמָן בַּר יִצְחָק בַּר אַחְתֵּיהּ – Once, **Rav Acha bar Yosef was walking while leaning on the shoulder of his nephew Rav Nachman bar Yitzchak.**[38] אָמַר לֵיהּ – **[Rav Acha bar Yosef] said to [Rav Nachman bar Yitzchak]:** כִּי מָטֵינָא לְבֵי רַב סַפְרָא עַיְילִינָא – **When we reach the house of Rav Safra, bring me in.** כִּי מְטוּ עַיְילֵיהּ – **When they reached there, he brought him in.** בְּעָא מִינֵּיהּ – **[Rav Acha bar Yosef] then inquired of [Rav Safra]:** מַהוּ לְכַסְכּוּסֵי כִּיתָּנִיתָא בְּשַׁבְּתָא – **What is [the law]** concerning whether one is permitted **to rub a** freshly cleaned **linen shirt on the Sabbath?** לְרַכּוּכֵי כִּיתָּנִיתָא קָא מִיכַּוֵּין וְשַׁפִּיר דָּמֵי – Do we say that **he intends merely to soften the linen shirt, and** therefore **he may do so,** אוֹ דִילְמָא לְאוֹלוּדֵי חִיוָּרָא קָמִיכַּוֵּין וְאָסוּר – **or perhaps, he intends to make [the shirt] brighter, and thus it is prohibited?**[39] אָמַר לֵיהּ – **[Rav Safra] said to him:** לְרַכּוּכֵי כִּיתָּנִיתָא קָא מִיכַּוֵּין וְשַׁפִּיר דָּמֵי – **He intends** merely **to soften the linen shirt, and he may do so.** כִּי נְפַק – **When [Rav Acha bar Yosef] left** Rav Safra's house, אָתָא אָמַר לֵיהּ – **[Rav Nachman bar Yitzchak] came and said to [Rav Acha bar Yosef]:** מַאי בְּעָא מַר מִינֵּיהּ – **What did the master ask of [Rav Safra]?** אָמַר לֵיהּ – **[Rav Acha bar Yosef] said to [Rav Nachman bar Yitzchak]:** בְּעַי מִינֵּיהּ מַהוּ לְכַסְכּוּסֵי כִּיתָּנִיתָא בְּשַׁבְּתָא – **I inquired: What is [the law]** concerning whether one is permitted **to rub a** freshly cleaned **linen shirt on the Sabbath?** וְאָמַר לִי שַׁפִּיר דָּמֵי – **And he said to me, "One may do so."**

Rav Nachman bar Yitzchak asked Rav Acha bar Yosef:

וְתִבְּעֵי לֵיהּ לְמַר סוּדָרָא – **But master should have posed [his query] concerning a** linen **kerchief,** which also receives both benefits when rubbed!

Rav Acha bar Yosef responds:

סוּדָרָא לָא קָא מִיבַּעְיָא לִי – **I had no question concerning** whether one may rub **a** linen **kerchief,** דִּבְעַי מֵרַב הוּנָא וּפְשַׁיט לִי [לְאִיסּוּרָא] – **because I already inquired concerning it to Rav Huna, and he resolved it for me** [ruling that it is prohibited].[40]

Rav Nachman bar Yitzchak asked Rav Acha bar Yosef:

וְתִיפְשׁוֹט לֵיהּ לְמַר מִסּוּדָרָא – **Then let master resolve** his question concerning clothes **from** Rav Huna's ruling concerning **a** linen **kerchief.** Why did you bother to ask the query in regard to a shirt when you had already been told that doing so to a kerchief is prohibited?

NOTES

34. For although the asafetida potion is usually taken as a medication, it is also drunk by healthy people as a beverage. Thus, drinking it is not prohibited as are other beverages taken strictly as medicine (*Ritva MHK* ed.; see *Mishnah Berurah* 321:72; see *Chidushei Basra*).

35. For, as our Mishnah teaches, one may not soak asafetida on the Sabbath (*Rashi*).

36. [If this were the case, then Rav's ruling would be of no practical consequence, for the halachah is in accordance with the Tanna Kamma, as stated above!]

37. I.e. although this "heavy heart" condition is non-life-threatening at its outset, if its treatment is interrupted a life-threatening condition can result. See *Ritva MHK* ed. for another approach.

Where possible, however, Rav instructed that the soaking be performed in a manner *least* reminiscent of a weekday activity, i.e. soaking it with cold water and warming it in the sun. But had that option not been available, Rav would have allowed soaking the asafetida even in warm water (*Ritva MHK* ed.; see *Mishnah Berurah* ibid. §75; cf. *Chasam Sofer* [Machon Chasam Sofer ed.]; see also *Emes LeYaakov,* in explanation of *Rambam's* position).

38. Rav Acha bar Yosef was an elderly man (*Rashi*) and he required assistance when walking.

39. Freshly laundered linen is stiff and uncomfortable against the skin. Rubbing the fabric vigorously between one's hands softens the fabric (this is permitted on the Sabbath); at the same time, however, it enhances the effect of earlier laundering by causing the fabric to brighten further [which, if performed with that intention, would be prohibited as a form of laundering] (*Rashi*).

The issue is not each individual's intent when rubbing the fabric, for if it was so we would rule after determining the intent of each individual. Rather, *everyone* rubs freshly laundered fabric for mainly one purpose. Our Gemara now wishes to determine whether that purpose is softening or brightening. If it is done for the purpose of softening, then the act is not considered an act of laundering, and it is permitted (see *Ritva MHK* ed.; see also *Gilyon Maharsha* and *Yad David [Basra]*).

40. We have added here the marginal emendation לְאִיסּוּרָא, *to be prohibited,* based on *Rashi* below. See following note; see also *Rosh* and *Dikdukei Soferim.*

לפי שאין עושין אותה אלא לגוון איתמר חרדל שלשו מע"ש למחר אמר רב ממחו בכלי אבל לא ביד א"ל שמואל ביד אטו כל יומא ממחו ליה ביד מאכל חמורים הוא אלא אמר שמואל ממחו ביד ואינו ממחו בכלי אתמר ר"א אמר אחד זה ואחד זה אסור ורבי יוחנן אמר אחד זה ואחד זה מותר אביי ורבא דאמרי תרוייהו אין הלכה כרבי יוחנן קם רבי יוחנן בשיטתיה דר"א קם רבי אלעזר בשיטתיה דשמואל אביי ורבא דאמרי תרוייהו הלכה כרבי יוחנן (א) אימיה דאביי עבדא ליה ולא אכל דביתהו דזעירא עבדא ליה לרב חייא בר אשי ולא אכיל א"ל לרבך עבידי ליה ואכל ואת לא אכלת אמר רבא בר שבא הוה קאימנא קמיה דרבינא ובחשי ליה בשופתא דתומא ואכל ° אמר מר זוטרא ג) לית הלכתא ככל הני שמעתתא אלא כי הא דאתמר א חרדל שלשו מע"ש למחר ממחו בין ביד בין בכלי ונותן לתוכו דבש ולא יטרוף אלא מערב ב שחליים ששחקן מע"ש למחר נותן לתוכן שמן וחומץ וממשיך לתוכן אמיתא ולא יטרוף אלא מערב ג שום שריסקו מע"ש למחר נותן לתוכו פול וגריסין ולא ישחוק אלא מערב וממשיך את אמיתא לתוכן ג) מאי אמיתא נינייא אמר אביי ש"מ האי נינייא מעליא לתחלי: ד) ת"ר ד עושין אנומלין בשבת ואין עושין ה) אלונטית ואיזו היא אנומלין ואיזו היא אלונטית אנומלין יין ודבש ופלפלין אלונטית יין ישן ומים צלולין ואפרסמון דעבדי לבי מסותא למיקר אמר רב יוסף זימנא חדא עלית בתר מר עוקבא לבי באני כי נפקי אתאי אשקיין ו) חמרא חד כסא וחשי מבינתא דראשי ועד טופרא דכרעי ואי אשקיין כסא אחרינא הואי מסתפינא דלמא מנכו לי מזכותא דעלמא דאתי והא מר עוקבא דשתי כל יומא שאני מר עוקבא דדש ביה: **מתני'** אין שורין את החילתית בפושרין ו אבל נותן לתוך החומץ ז ואין שולין את הכרשינין ולא שפין אותן אבל נותן לתוך הכברה או לתוך הכלכלה ח אין כוברין את התבן בכברה ולא יתננו על גבי מקום גבוה בשביל שירד המוץ אבל נוטל הוא בכברה ונותן לתוך האיבוס: **גמ'** איבעיא להו שרה מאי תרגמא רב אדא נרשאה קמיה דרב יוסף שרה חייב חטאת א"ל אביי אלא מעתה שרה אומצא במיא הכי נמי דמיחייב אלא אמר אביי ז) מדרבנן שלא יעשה כדרך שהוא עושה בחול בעא מיניה רבי יוחנן מר' ינאי מהו לשרות את החילתית בצונן א"ל אסור והא אנן תנן אין שורין את החילתית בפושרין הא בצונן מותר א"ל ח) א"כ מה בין לי ולך מתניתין יחידאה היא דתניא ט ט) אין שורין את החילתית לא בחמין ולא בצונן רבי יוסי אומר בחמין אסור בצונן מותר למאי עבדי ליה ליוקרא דליבא רב אחא בר יוסף חש ביוקרא דליבא אתא לקמיה דמר עוקבא א"ל זיל שתי תלתא תיקלי חילתתא בתלתא יומי אזל אישתי חמשא בשבת ומעלי שבת לצפרא אזל שאל בי מדרשא אמרו ליה תנא דבי רב אדא ואמרי לה תנא דבי מר בר רב אדא י שותה אדם קב או קביים ואינו חושש אמר להו לשתות לא קמיבעיא לי כי קא מיבעיא לי לשרות מאי אמר להו רב חייא בר אבין בדידי הוה עובדא ואתאי שאילתיה לרב אדא בר אהבה ולא הוה בידיה אתאי שאילתיה לרב הונא ואמר הכי קאמר רב שורה בצונן ומניח בחמה כמאן דשרי כ אפילו למאן דאסר ה"מ היכא דלא אישתי כלל אבל הכא כיון דאישתי חמשא ומעלי שבתא אי לא שתי בשבת מיסתכן מיסתמיך ואזיל רב אחא בר יוסף אכתפיה דרב נחמן בר יצחק בר אחתיה א"ל כי מטינן לבי רב ספרא עיילינא כי מטו עייליה בעא מיניה מהו לכסכוסי כיתניתא בשבתא לרכוכי קא מיכוין ושפיר דמי או דילמא לאולודי חיורא קמיכוין ואסיר א"ל לרכוכי קא מיכוין ושפיר דמי כי נפק אתא א"ל מאי בעא מר מיניה א"ל בעי מיניה מהו לכסכוסי כיתניתא בשבתא ואמר לי שפיר דמי ותבעי ליה למר סודרא סודרא לא קא מיבעיא לי דבעי מרב הונא ופשיט לי ותיפשיט ליה למר מסודרא א"ל התם מיחזי כי אולודי חיורא הכא לא מיחזי כאולודי חיורא אמר רב חסדא האי כיתניתא

משלפו

רש"י

לפי שאין עושין (א) **אלא לגוון.** למראה שהחלמון יפה לגוון ולא החלבון הלכך אידי ואידי אוכל הוא ואין כאן ברירת פסולת מאוכל: **ממחו.** דיסטיפדי"ר בלע"ז במים או ביין: **ממחו בכלי.** משמע זהו שינוי שלו: **ואינו ממחו ביד.** דממחו ליה שפיר טפי: **אלא אמר שמואל ממחו ביד.** שאין זה דרכו בחול: **קם ר' יוחנן בשיטתיה דר"א.** חזר בו ואסר: **אביי ורבא דאמרי תרוייהו הלכה כר' יוחנן.** דאסר: **לרבך.** לזעירי: **בשופתא דתומא.** אמלעי של שום: **ולא יטרוף.** כדרך שטורפין ביצים בקערה בכף דרך טריפה שמכה בכח: **שחליים.** כרשין והיו שוחקין אותם במים: **ממשיך. נותן: אמיתא.** מינט"א בלע"ז: **מעליא לתחלי.** לערב עם שחליים: **ואין עושין אלונטית.** שאינה למשקה אלא לצנן לאחר המרחץ ודוגמת רפואה: **וחשי מבינתא דרישא.** הרגשתי בצינתו משערת ראשי עד צפרני רגלי: **מנכו לי מזכיותי.** אם הייתי ניזול ממנו שלא אמות: **שתי כל יומא.** ולא היה מזיקו: **דדש ביה.** רגיל בו: **מתני' חילתית.** חלטי"ת בלשון ישמעאל ובלע"ז לזרי"א ושורין אותו בפושרין ושותין אותן המים לרפואה: **אבל נותן.** החלתית: **בתוך החומץ.** ומטבל בו מאכלו ולקמיה מפרש אמאי אין שורין: **ואין שולין את הכרשינין.** מציף עליהם מים בכלי לברור פסולתן כדתנן במסכת ביצה (דף יד:) אף מדיח ושולה: **ולא שפין אותן.** ביד להסיר פסולת דהוה ליה בורר: **אבל נותן לתוך הכברה.** ואע"פ דפעמים שהפסולת נופל דרך נקבי הכברה ונמצא נתברר מאליו: **תבן.** הוא שעושין מן הקש מחתכין אותו במוריגין ועושה כל זנב (ב) השבולת תבן: **מוץ.** הוא מוקן השבולת העליון ואינו ראוי למאכל וכוברין אותו (ג) בכברין שיפול המוץ: **אבל נוטל** (ד) **בכברה.** ליתן בתוך האבוס ואע"פ שהמוץ נופל ° מאליו כר"ש דאמר דבר שאין מתכוין מותר: **גמ' שרה.** חילתית בפושרין מאי: **אומצא.** בשר חי: **שלא יעשה כו'.** לא שבקוה רבנן למעבד עובדי דחול: **אם כן.** דלא ידענא לפרושי מתני' טפי מינך מה בין לי ולך: **מתניתין יחידאה היא.** ור' יוסי אמרה אבל לרבנן אף בצונן אסור: **ליוקרא דליבא.** שלבו כבד עליו: **תלתא תקלי חילתתא.** משקל ג' זהובים: **שאיל בי מדרשא.** מה יעשה בשבת: **לשתות לא קמיבעיא לי.** דבלאו רפואה משקה הוא ותנן כל המשקין שותה (לעיל דף קט:): **לשרות.** דתנן מתניתין אין שורין: **כמאן דשרי.** בעיא הוא הך דרב לימא כרבי יוסי דשרי בצונן אבל לרבנן אסור: **עיילינא.** הכניסני ואיש זקן היה: **לכסכוסי כיתניתא.** חלוק כתונת של פשתן שנתכבסה והרי היא קשה ומשפשפה בין שתי ידיו והיא מתרככה ואף הליבון שלה מאהיל על ידי השפשוף: **אולודי חיורא.** הליבון מאהיל: **התם מיחזי כאולודי חיורא.** שמקפיד על ליבונו וזוהרו של סודר יותר מכיתונא:

משלפא

אימיה דאביי. לומנתו [לעיל קלד.] **עושין אנומלין.** בשבת שהוא לשתות. **ואין עושין אלונטית.** שהוא לרפואה להכניס לאלונטית מים צלולין. שנשלכו ועמדו בכלי יום או יומים להיות צלולין ושופין העליונים כשלוחין מים המתוקן למקפלת. **ומים צלולין.** ... **חלתית.** מן פירי הוא שקורין לזרי"א בלע"ז [שם לה:] **מה בין לי ולך.** אם איני יודע פירושה של משנתנו יותר ממך מה אני גדול ממך [חולין קלז:] **לכסכוסי.** לשפשף [נדה סב.]

לתוך ידיו ומוליך ומביא ידיו עד שיעשה הבגד ההוא כמו קפולין קטנים כמין קמטין כי הא דא"ר זירא בפ' חבית (דף קמו.) מאי ארבא כגון (א) כסכוסי ומתחזי כרבה וכי הא דתנן בפ' האשה שהיא עושה צרכיה: צריכה לכסכס ג' פעמים על כל דבר ודבר ואמרינן בגמ' בעי ר' ירמיה אמטויי [חד] ואיתויי [חד] או דלמא אמטויי [חד] ואיתויי [תרתי] תיקו: וכן עוד מפורש בתלמוד א"י בענין מוליך ומביא שבלולב. מהא שמעינן דכיסכוס כעין שפשוף הוא ומתקבץ הבגד פי' יתכבס ונראה קמטין קמטין וכשלובשו מתפשט וכדאמרינן בפ' חבית אמר רב כהנא ואיתימא רב יהודה טיט שעל בגדו מכסכס מבפנים. (ומדקרי) [ומדרקי] להאי כיתונתא. שמעינן מנה דסודרא ליתיה כתינתא ולא יתכן לומר שהוא צמר שאם הוא צמר איך אומר לו היה לך ללמוד פשתים מצמר. והדבר רחוק ביניהם ואינה אלא צמר גפן שזה קרוב לזה ופשט

חשק שלמה על רבינו חננאל (א) לפנינו בגמ' ליתא שם הך כיצד כבליתא:

עין משפט נר מצוה

לב א מיי' פ"ח מהל' שבת הל' יד ופכ"ב הלכה יג סמג לאוין סה טוש"ע א"ח סי' שכא סעיף טו:

לג ב ג מיי' פכ"ב שם טוש"ע שם סעיף טז:

לד ד מיי' שם טוש"ע שם סעיף יז:

לה ה מיי' פ"ד מהל' דעות הלכה יח:

לו ו מיי' פכ"ב מהל' שבת הלכה ז סמג לאוין סה טוש"ע א"ח סי' שכא סעיף יח:

לז ז (מיי' פ"ח מהל' שבת) סמג לאוין סה טוש"ע א"ח סי' שיט סעיף ח:

לח ח מיי' פכ"א שם הלכה לג סמג שם טוש"ע א"ח סי' שכד סעיף א:

לט ט י כ מיי' פכ"א שם הלכה כב ופכ"ב שם הל' ז סמג שם טוש"ע א"ח סי' שכא סעיף יח:

מ ל מ מיי' פכ"ב שם הלכה יח סמג שם טוש"ע א"ח סי' שב סעיף ה:

רבינו חננאל

לפי שאין עושין אותה אלא לגוון. פי' לצבעו להתראות בו גוונא של ביצה מאכל המרס. פי' זה המאכל ממורס הוא כדתנן (נתן) [נטל] את הדם ונתנו לממרס בו על הרובד הרביעי וי"א מאכל חמורים הוא כלומר אינו מאכל ב"א אלא מאכל חמורים הוא: חרדל שלשו מע"ש חלקו עליו רב ושמואל ור' יוחנן ור' אלעזר ודבריהן פשוטין הן ומר זוטרא דהוא בתרא אמר לית הלכתא ככל הני שמעתתא אלא כי הא דתניא חרדל שלשו מע"ש למחר מניחו בין ביד בין בכלי ונותן לתוכו דבש ולא יטרוף אלא מערב. שום שריסקו מע"ש למחר נותן לתוכו פול או גריסין ולא ישחוק אלא מערב. וממשיך את האמיתה לתוכה מאי אמיתה נגחה. אנומלין יין ושמן ודבש ופלפלין אלונתית יין ישן ומים צלולין ואפרסמון: אין שורין את החלתית בפושרין אבל נותן לתוך החומץ ומיבעיא לן שרה מאי. ומסקנא שרה אמר אביי איסורא מדרבנן וא"ר יוחנן מתניתין יחידאה היא והוא ר' יוסי אבל חכ"א בין בחמין בין בצונן אסור וסוגיא דשמעתא אם שרה מאתמול לשתות חלתית בשבת מותר. אבל לשרותו אסור אפילו בצונן. ואם שרה קודם השבת ועכשיו בשבת חושש אם לא ישתה מסתכן מותר לו לשרות בתוכו ולהניחה בחמה: לכסכוסי כיתונתא. פי' לרכוכי קא מיכוון ושרי או דלמא לאולודי וכו'. פי' לקבץ מקצת הבגד של פשתים לתוך ידו לשופו מפני שרוחצין הבגד ומתייבש בשמש או ברוח עומד אנסו פי' קשה ורוצה לרככו נותן הבגד

מסורת הש"ס

א) [עיין קדושין לא:], ב) [ע' תוס' כתובות נד. ד"ה לית], ג) [לעיל קכח.], ד) ע"ז ל., ה) [שם איתא אלונתית אבל בערוך גרס כגי' שלפנינו], ו) [לעיל קלח.], ז) [חולי' קלז:], ח) [תוספ' פי"ז], ט) ס"א לאיסורא.

הגהות הב"ח

(א) רש"י ד"ה לפי שאין עושין אותה אלא: (ב) ד"ה תבן וכו' כל זנב השבלים תבן: (ג) ד"ה מוץ וכו' בכברה כדי שיפול: (ד) ד"ה אבל נוטל הוא בכברה ונותן לתוך האבוס:

גליון הש"ס

גמ' אמר מר זוטרא לית הלכתא ככל הני שמעתתא. עיין כתובות דף נד ע"א תוס' ד"ה לית הלכתא: רש"י ד"ה אבל נוטל וכו' נופל מאליו כר"ש. עיין לעיל דף נד ע"א ברש"י ד"ה כלאים דמבלים:

רב נסים גאון

אין שורין את הכרשינין. גרסי' בגמ' דבני מערבא תני אין שורין את הכרשינים משום בורר ולא שפין אותן משום דש אין כוברין את התבן משום מרקד. גורפין מלפני הפטם ומסלקין לצדדין מפני הרעי בגמ' דבני מערבא גרסי מה שהפטם אוכל ומותיר הרעי אוכל:

ליקוטי רש"י

ואמר רבא מת ביום טוב ראשון כו'. מת המוטל לקבור אם יום טוב ראשון הוא וכו'. מה שאין כן בביצה. לענין ביצה לא הקלו ביום טוב שני דראש השנה להשוות לשל גליות דאלו ראש השנה נולדה בזה אסורה בזה [ביצה ו.]. דקדושה אחת הן ולא הקלו ביום טוב שני של ראש השנה אלא לענין מת בלבד [שם כב:]. מערים ושותה מן החדש. שיכול לומר לצורך המועד הטילו [מו"ק יב:]. בררא דתומא. בן השום לגע של שום [תענית כה.]. כפיפה מצרית. סל של נצרי דקל ודדים שגדלין סביב הדקל [סוטה יד.]. של נצרים של ערבה [ב"ב כב.]. ונותנין ביצה במסננת של חרדל. ומסננה בתוכו לייפות מראיתו לא מחזי כבורר שכולה יוצאה דרך המסננת ואין משתייר שם פסולת [לעיל קלט: ע"ש בהגהות ר' שמחה מדסוי"א]. ובלבד שלא יגביה כבר טפח. מלל טפח אהל הוא [סוכה טו.]

[ע"כ שייך לדף קלט:]

Rav Acha bar Yosef responds:

אָמַר לֵיהּ – **[Rav Acha bar Yosef] said to [Rav Nachman bar Yitzchak]:** הָתָם מֵיחֲזֵי כִּי אוּלוּדֵי חִיוָּרָא – **There** in the case of a kerchief **it appears as though he intends to make it brighter,** and thus Rav Huna prohibited rubbing it. הָכָא לָא מֵיחֲזֵי כְּאוּלוּדֵי חִיוָּרָא – While **here** in the case of the clothes **it does not appear as though he intends to make it brighter,** and rubbing it might very well have been permitted.[41] This was in fact the case, as Rav Safra permitted rubbing the shirt.

The Gemara cited a ruling concerning the handling of freshly laundered garments. The Gemara now digresses to discuss such garments relative to a case where the Rabbinic decree of *muktzeh* may apply:

אָמַר רַב חִסְדָּא – **Rav Chisda said:** הַאי כִּיתָּנִיתָא – **That** freshly laundered **linen shirt,**

NOTES

41. One is far more meticulous about the cleanliness and brightness of his kerchief, which is worn as a highly visible head-covering, than his shirt, which is covered by his outer garments. Thus, we can assume that one rubs his shirt for the purpose of softening it, while one rubs his kerchief to enhance its brightness (*Rashi*, *Meiri*, *Chidushei HaRan*). [Nevertheless, one may not rub a shirt with the specific intent of brightening it (*Mishnah Berurah* 302:24).]

It is clear from *Rashi* that Rav Huna ruled that rubbing a freshly laundered kerchief is prohibited (see previous note). This is also the view of *Rambam* (*Hil. Shabbos* 22:17) and *Shulchan Aruch* (*Orach Chaim* 302:5). See, however, *Raavad* (to *Rambam* ibid.) and *Baal HaMaor* quoted in *Ran MHK* ed. et al., who dispute this view based on the text of the Gemara which appears in the Vilna *Shas*, in which Rav Huna is not quoted as ruling that rubbing a freshly laundered kerchief is prohibited; see there for a different interpretation of this passage.

According to the Gemara's conclusion that one rubs a kerchief with the intention of brightening it, rubbing a kerchief of any composition, whether linen or cotton or wool, is prohibited (*Beur Halachah* to 302:5 ד״ה דינן).

לפי שאין עושין (א) אלא לגוון. למראה שהחלמון יפה לגוון ולא החלבון הלכך אידי ואידי אוכל הוא ואין כאן ברירת פסולת מאוכל: ממחו. דיסטיפנ"ר בלע"ז במים או ביין: ממחו בכלי. משמע זהו שינוי שלו: ואינו ממחה ביד. דממחו ליה שפיר טפי: אלא אמר שמואל ממחו ביד. שאין זה דרכו כמלו: קם ר' יוחנן בשיטתיה דר"א. חזר בו ואסר: אביי ורבא דאמרי תרוייהו הלכה כר' יוחנן. לאסור: לרבך. לזעירי: בשופתא דתומא. אמצעי של שום: ולא יטרוף. כדרך שטורפין ביצים בקערה בכף לכך טריפה שמכה בכח: שחליים. כרישין והיו שוחקין אותם במים: ממשיך. נותן: אמיתא. מינט"א בלע"ז: מעליא לתחלי. לערב עם שחליים: ואין עושין אלונטית. שאינה למשקה אלא לצנן לאחר המרחץ ודוגמת רפואה: וחשי מבינתא דרישא. הרגשתי בצינתו משערת ראשי עד לפרסי רגלי: מנכו לי מזכיותי. אם הייתי ניזול ממנו שלא אמות: שתי כל יומא. ולא היה מזיקו: דדש ביה. רגיל בו: מתני' חילתית. חלטי"ט בלע"ז ובלע"ז לזר"א ושורין אותו בפושרין ושותין אותו המים לרפואה: אבל נותן. החלתית: בתוך החומץ. ומטבל בו מאכלו ולקמיה מפרש אמאי אין שורין: ואין שולין את הכרשינין. מציף עליהם מים בכלי לבורר פסולתן כדתנן במסכת ביצה (דף יד:) אף מדיח ושולה: ולא שפין אותן. ביד להסיר פסולת דהוה ליה בורר: אבל נותן לתוך הכברה. ואע"פ לפעמים שהפסולת נופל דרך נקבי הכברה ונמצא נתברר מאליו: תבן. הוא שעושין מן הקש מחתכין אותו במוריגין ועושה כל זנב (ב) השבולת תבן: מוץ. הוא מוזקן השבולת העליון ואינו ראוי למאכל וכוברין אותו (ג) בכברין שיפול המוץ: אבל נוטל (ד) בכברה. ליתן בתוך האבוס ואע"פ שהמוץ נופל ° מאליו כר"ש דאמר דבר שאין מתכוין מותר: גמ' שרה. חילתית בפושרין מאי: אומצא. בשר חי: שלא יעשה כו'. לא שבקוה רבנן למעבד עובדי דחול: אם כן. דלא ידענא לפרושי מתני' טפי מינך מה בין לי ולך: מתניתין יחידאה היא. ור' יוסי אמרה אבל לרבנן אף בצונן אסור: ליוקרא דליבא. שלבו כבד עליו: תלתא תקלי חילתתא. משקל ג' זהובים: שאיל בי מדרשא. מה יעשה בשבת: לשתות לא קמיבעיא לי. דבלאו רפואה משקה הוא ותנן כל המשקין שותה (לעיל דף קט:): לשרות. דתנן מתניתין אין שורין: כמאן דשרי. בעיא הוא הך דרב לימא כרבי יוסי דשרי בצונן אבל לרבנן אסור: עיילינא. הכניסני ואיש זקן היה: לכסכוסי כיתניתא. חלוק כתונת של פשתן שנתכבסה והרי היא קשה ומשפשפה בין שתי ידיו והיא מתרככה ואף הליבון שלה מאהיל על ידי השפשוף: אולודי חיורא. הליבון מאהיל: התם מיחזי כאולודי חיורא. שמקפיד על ליבונו ולוהרו של סודר יותר מכיתונא: משלפא

לפי שאין עושין אותה אלא לגוון איתמר חרדל שלשו מע"ש למחר אמר רב ממחו בכלי אבל לא ביד א"ל שמואל ביד אטו כל יומא ממחו ליה ביד מאכל חמורים הוא אלא אמר שמואל ממחו ביד ואינו ממחו בכלי אתמר ר"א אמר אחד זה ואחד זה אסור ורבי יוחנן אמר אחד זה ואחד זה מותר אביי ורבא דאמרי תרוייהו אין הלכה כרבי יוחנן קם רבי יוחנן בשיטתיה דר"א קם רבי אלעזר בשיטתיה דשמואל אביי ורבא דאמרי תרוייהו הלכה כרבי יוחנן [א]אימיה דאביי עבדא ליה ולא אכל דביתהו דזעירא עבדא ליה לרב חייא בר אשי ולא אכיל א"ל לרבך עבידי ליה ואכל ואת לא אכלת אמר רבא בר בר שבא הוה קאימנא קמיה דרבינא ובחשי ליה בשופתא דתומא ואכל • אמר מר זוטרא [ג]לית הלכתא ככל הני שמעתתא אלא כי הא דאתמר [א]חרדל שלשו מע"ש למחר ממחו בין ביד בין בכלי ונותן לתוכו דבש ולא יטרוף אלא מערב [ב]שחליים ששחקן מע"ש למחר נותן לתוכן שמן וחומץ וממשיך לתוכן אמיתא ולא יטרוף אלא מערב [ג]שום שריסקו מע"ש למחר נותן לתוכו פול וגריסין ולא ישחוק אלא מערב וממשיך את אמיתא לתוכן [ג]מאי אמיתא נינייא אמר אביי ש"מ האי נינייא מעליא לתחלי: ועושין אנומלין בשבת: [ה]ת"ר [ד]עושין אנומלין בשבת ואין עושין [ה]אלונטית ואיזו היא אנומלין ואיזו היא אלונטית אנומלין יין ודבש ופלפלין אלונטית יין ישן ומים צלולין ואפרסמון דעבדי לבי מסותא למיקר אמר רב יוסף זימנא חדא עלית בתר מר עוקבא לבי באני כי נפקי אתאי אשקיין [ה]חמרא חד כסא וחשי מבינתא דראשי ועד טופרא דכרעי ואי אשקיין כסא אחרינא הואי מסתפינא דלמא מנכו לי מזכותא דעלמא דאתי והא מר עוקבא דשתי כל יומא שאני מר עוקבא דדש ביה: מתני' אין שורין את החילתית בפושרין [י]אבל נותן לתוך החומץ [ז]ואין שולין את הכרשינין ולא שפין אותן אבל נותן לתוך הכברה או לתוך הכלכלה [ח]אין כוברין את התבן בכברה ולא יתננו על גבי מקום גבוה בשביל שירד המוץ אבל נוטל הוא בכברה ונותן לתוך האיבוס: גמ' איבעיא להו שרה מאי תרגמא רב אדא נרשאה קמיה דרב יוסף שרה חייב חטאת א"ל אביי אלא מעתה שרה אומצא במיא הכי נמי דמיחייב אלא אמר אביי [י]מדרבנן שלא יעשה כדרך שהוא עושה בחול בעא מיניה רבי יוחנן מר' ינאי מהו לשרות את החלתית בצונן א"ל אסור והא אנן תנן אין שורין את החלתית בפושרין הא בצונן מותר א"ל [י]א"כ מה בין לי ולך מתניתין יחידאה היא דתניא [ט]אין שורין את החלתית לא בחמין ולא בצונן רבי יוסי אומר בחמין אסור בצונן מותר למאי עבדי ליה ליוקרא דליבא רב אחא בר יוסף חש ביוקרא דליבא אתא לקמיה דמר עוקבא א"ל זיל שתי תלתא תיקלי חילתתא בתלתא יומי אזל אישתי חמשא בשבת ומעלי שבת לצפרא אזל שאל בי מדרשא אמרו ליה תנא דבי רב אדא ואמרי לה תנא דבי מר בר רב אדא [י]שותה אדם קב או קביים ואינו חושש אמר להו לשתות לא קמיבעיא לי כי קא מיבעיא לי לשרות מאי אמר להו רב חייא בר אבין בדידי הוה עובדא ואתאי שאילתיה לרב אדא בר אהבה ולא הוה בידיה אתאי שאילתיה לרב הונא ואמר הכי קאמר רב שורה בצונן ומניח בחמה כמאן דשרי [כ]אפילו למאן דאסר ה"מ היכא דלא אישתי כלל אבל הכא כיון דאישתי חמשא ומעלי שבתא אי לא שתי בשבת מיסתכן מיסתמיך ואזיל רב אחא בר יוסף אכתפיה דרב נחמן בר יצחק בר אחתיה א"ל כי מטינן לבי רב ספרא עיילינא כי מטו עייליה בעא מיניה מהו לכסכוסי כיתניתא בשבתא לרכוכי כיתניתא קא מיכוין ושפיר דמי או דילמא לאולודי חיורא קמיכוין ואסיר א"ל [י]לרכוכי קא מיכוין ושפיר דמי כי נפק אתא א"ל מאי בעא מר מיניה מהו לכסכוסי כיתניתא בשבתא ואמר לי שפיר דמי ותבעי ליה למר סודרא סודרא לא קא מיבעיא לי דבעי מרב הונא ופשיט לי [ט]ותיפשיט ליה למר מסודרא א"ל [מ]התם מיחזי כי אולודי חיורא הכא לא מיחזי כאולודי חיורא אמר רב חסדא האי כיתניתא משלפו

[לעיל קלד.]. אימיה דאביי. אומנתו. עושין אנומלין. בשבת שהוא לשתות. ואין עושין אלונטית. שהוא לרפואה להצטנן כשיוצאין מבית המרחץ כדמפרש. ומים צלולין. שנשלנו ועמדו בכלי יום או יומים להיות צלולין וטופין [ע"ז ל.]. חלתית. מין פירי הוא שקורין לזר"א בלע"ז [שם לה:]. מה בין לי ולך. אם איני יודע פירושה של משנתינו יותר ממך מה אני גדול ממך [חולין קלז:]. לכסכוסי. לשפשף [נדה סב.].

מסורת הש"ס

א) [עיין קדושין לא:], ב) [ע' תוס' כתובות נד. ד"ה לית], ג) [לעיל קכח.], ד) ע"ז ל., ה) [שם איתא אלונתית אבל בערוך גרס כגי' שלפנינו], ו) [לעיל קלח.], ז) [חולי' קלז:], ח) [תוספ' פי"ז], ט) ס"א לאיסורא.

הגהות הב"ח

(א) רש"י ד"ה לפי שאין עושין אותה אלא: (ב) ד"ה תבן וכו' כל זנב השבלים תבן: (ג) ד"ה מוץ וכו' בכברה כדי שיפול: (ד) ד"ה אבל נוטל הוא בכברה ונותן לתוך האבוס:

גליון הש"ס

גמ' אמר מר זוטרא לית הלכתא ככל הני שמעתתא. עיין כתובות דף נד ע"א תוס' ד"ה לית הלכתא: רש"י ד"ה אבל נוטל וכו' נופל מאליו כר"ש. עיין לעיל דף נד ע"א ברש"י ד"ה כלאים דמכלים:

רב נסים גאון

אין שורין את הכרשינין. גרסי' בגמ' דבני מערבא תני אין שורין את הכרשינים משום בורר ולא שפין אותן משום דש אין כוברין את התבן משום מרקד. גורפין מלפני הפטם ומסלקין לצדדין מפני הרעי בגמ' דבני מערבא גרסי מה שהפטם אוכל ומותיר הרעי אוכל:

ליקוטי רש"י

ואמר רבא מת ביום טוב ראשון כו'. מת המוטל לקבור אם יום טוב ראשון הוא וכו'. מה שאין כן בביצה. לענין ביצה לא הקלו ביום טוב שני דראש השנה להשוות לשל גליות דאלו ראש השנה נולדה בזה אסורה בזה [ביצה ו.]. דקדושה אחת הן ולא הקלו ביום טוב שני של ראש השנה אלא לענין מת בלבד [שם כב:]. מערים ושותה מן החדש. שיכול לומר לצורך המועד הטילו [מו"ק יב:]. ברא דתומא. בן השום לגע של שום [תענית כה.]. כפיפה מצרית. כל נצרי דקל וורדים שגדלין סביב הדקל [סוטה יד.]. כל נצרים של ערבה [ב"ב כב.]. ונותנין ביצה במסננת של חרדל. ומסננת בתוכו לייפות מראיתו לא מיחזי כבורר שכולה יוצאה דרך המסננת ואין מפשיר שם פסולת [לעיל קלט:]. עי"ש בהגהות ר' שמחה מרגליות. ובלבד שלא יגביה כרי מפסח. ללא טפח אלא הוא [סוכה טו.]. [ע"כ שייך לדף קלט:]

עין משפט נר מצוה

לב א מיי' פ"ח מהל' שבת הל' יד ופכ"ב הלכה יב סמג לאוין סה טוש"ע א"ח סי' שכא סעיף טו:
לג ב ג מיי' שם טוש"ע שם סעיף טז:
לד ד מיי' שם טוש"ע שם סעיף יז:
לה ה מיי' פ"ד מהל' דעות הלכה יז:
לו ו מיי' פכ"ב מהל' שבת הלכה ז סמג לאוין סה טוש"ע א"ח סי' שכא סעיף יח:
לז ז (מיי' פכ"א מהל' שבת) סמג לאוין סה טוש"ע א"ח סי' שיט סעיף ח:
לח ח מיי' פכ"א שם הלכה לב סמג שם טוש"ע א"ח סי' שכ סעיף ה:
לט ט י כ מיי' פכ"א שם הלכה כג ופכ"ב שם הל' ו סמג שם טוש"ע א"ח סי' שכא סעיף יט:
מ ל מ מיי' פכ"ב שם הלכה יז סמג שם טוש"ע א"ח סי' שב סעיף ה:

רבינו חננאל

לפי שאין עושין אותה אלא לגוון. פי' לצבעו להתראות בו גוונא של ביצה מאכל המרס. פי' זה המאכל ממורס הוא כדתנן (נתן) [נטל] את הדם ונתנו לממרס בו על הרובד הרביעי וי"א מאכל חמורים הוא כלומר אינו מאכל ב"א אלא מאכל חמורים הוא: חרדל שלשו מע"ש חלקו עליו רב ושמואל ור' יוחנן ור' אלעזר ודבריהן פשוטין הן ומר זוטרא דהוא בתרא אמר לית הלכתא ככל הני שמעתתא אלא כי הא דתניא חרדל שלשו מע"ש למחר מניחו בין ביד בין בכלי ונותן לתוכו דבש ולא יטרוף אלא מערב. שום שריסקו מע"ש למחר נותן לתוכו פול או גריסין ולא ישחוק אלא מערב. וממשיך את האמיתה לתוכה מאי אמיתה נגחה. אנומלין יין ושמן ודבש ופלפלין אלונתית יין ישן ומים צלולין ואפרסמון: אין שורין את החלתית בפושרין אבל נותן לתוך החומץ ומיבעיא לן שרה מאי. ומסקנא שרה אמר אביי איסורא מדרבנן וא"ר יוחנן מתניתין יחידאה היא והוא ר' יוסי אבל חכ"א בין בחמין בין בצונן אסור וסוגיא דשמעתא אם שרה מאתמול לשתות חלתית בשבת מותר. אבל לשרותו אסור אפילו בצונן. ואם שרה קודם השבת ועכשיו בשבת חושש אם לא ישתה מסתכן מותר לו לשרות בתוכו ולהניחה בחמה: לכסכוסי כיתונתא. פי' לרכוכי קא מיכוון ושרי או דלמא לאולודי וכו'. פי' לקבץ מקצת הבגד של פשתים לתוך ידו לשופו מפני שרוחצין הבגד ומתייבש בשמש או ברוח עומד אנסו פי' קשה ורוצה לרככו נותן הבגד לתוך ידיו ומוליך ומביא ידיו עד שיעשה הבגד ההוא כמו קפולין קטנים כמין קמטין כי הא דא"ר זירא בפ' חבית (דף קמז) מאי מרזב כגון (א) כסכוסי מאני דמתחזי כמרזב וכי הא דתנן בפ' האשה שהיא עושה צרכיה: צריכה לכסכס ג' פעמים על כל דבר ודבר ואמרי' בגמ' בעי ר' ירמיה אמטויי חד ואיתויי [חד] או דלמא אמטויי [חד] ואיתויי [תרתי] תיקו: וכן עוד מפורש בתלמוד א"י בענין מוליך ומביא שבלולב. מהא שמעינן דכיסכוס כעין שפשוף הוא ומתקבץ הבגד פי' יתכמש ונראה קמטין קמטין וכשלובשו מתפשט וכדאמרינן אמר רב כהנא ואיתימא רב יהודה טיט שעל בגדו מכסכסו מבפנים. (ומרקדי) [ומדקרי] להאי כיתונתא. שמעינן מנה דסודרא ליתיה כתינתא ולא יתכן לומר שהוא צמר שאם הוא צמר איך אומר לו היה לך ללמוד פשתים מצמר. והדבר רחוק ביניהם ואינה אלא צמר גפן שזה קרוב לזה ופשט

חשק שלמה על רבינו חננאל (א) לפנינו בגמ' איתא שם מינו כנלייתא:

עין משפט
נר מצוה

מא א ב מיי' פכ"ה מהל' שבת הל' יח סמג לאוין סה טוש"ע א"ח סי' שח סעיף טז:
מב ג מיי' פכ"ו מהל' שבת הל' טז סמג שם טוש"ע שם סעיף כז וכח:
מג ד מיי' פ"ז מהל' ברכות הלכה ג:
מד ה ו מיי' פכ"ו מהל' שבת הלכה יט סמג לאוין סה טוש"ע א"ח סי' שכד סעיף טו:
מה ז מיי' שם טוש"ע שם סעיף יד:

רבינו חננאל

רב חסדא דלרכוכי מיכוון ושרי. אמר רב חסדא הא כיתניתא משלפה לדילא מקניא: פי' למשוך הבגד ששוטחו בקנה להנגב ונעשה נגוב וישאר הקנה במקומו. ולא מטלטלין מותר אבל למשוך הקנה מן הבגד ולטלטלו בשבת אסור שהקנה אינו כלי להטלטל בחצר. אמר רבא ואם כלי קיואי מותר. פי' אם הוא הבגד שטוח בכלי האורג וכלי האורג נקראין כלי קיואי כדאמרינן בפרק ואלו קשרים שחייבין עליהן. אתמר אמר רב נחמן אמר שמואל כלי קיואי מותר לטלטלו בשבת ואפי' כובד העליון וכובד התחתון אבל לא את העמודים ותוב בעא מיניה ר' יוחנן מרבי יהודה בר ליואי כלי קיואי כגון כובד העליון וכובד התחתון כו'. האי תלא דבשרא פי' יתד של עץ עשוי לתלות בו בשר ופעמים שתולין בו זולתו [שרי לטלטולי] אבל העץ שתולין בו דגים. כיון שהדגים ריחם רע וקשה אין תולין בו דבר אחר ומסיחין דעתן ממנו ומוקצה מחמת מיאוס הוא ואסור: **מדנהר** אבא. שם מקום הוא: **ציפיתא** חדתא. פי' מחצלת חדשה בורא בחדא ידא. כגון אבן שאין לה דמים ולא צורך. ומפני שהסתירה מהן נתייקרה בעיניהם ופייסוהו להראותה להן: **מתני' אין שולין** את הכרשינין ולא שפין כו' גורפין מלפני הפטם ומסלקין לצדדים כו'. פי' גורפין המאכל של בהמה מלפני הפטם ומאכל שאר בהמות מסלקין לצדדין דברי ר' דוסיא חכמים אוסרין ואיבעיא לן רבנן ארישא פליגי והיא גורפין [או] אסיפא פליגי והוא שמסלקין לצדדין ואמרינן ת"ש וחכ"א אחד זה ואחד זה לא יסלקנו לצדדין. ש"מ רבנן אתרווייהו פליגי. אמר רב חסדא מחלוקת באבוס של כלי ואפי' בזה חכמים אוסרין אבל באבוס של קרקע דברי הכל אסור לגרוף:

אבל באיבום של קרקע דברי הכל אסור. אע"ג דמרבנן שרינן לרבי שמעון (לעיל דף כט.) הכא רגילות הוא להתכוין לאשויי גומות ומיישינן טפי שמא יתכוין הקס

משלפו לדידה מקניא שרי קניא ממנה אסור אמר רבא (א) ואם כלי קיואי הוא מותר אמר רב חסדא האי כישתא דירקא אי חזיא למאכל בהמה שרי לטלטולי ואי לא אסיר אמר רב חייא בר אשי אמר רב האי תליא דבשרא שרי לטלטולי דכוורי אסיר אמר רב קטינא העומד באמצע המטה כאילו עומד בכריסה של אשה ולאו מילתא היא ואמר רב חסדא בר בי רב דזבין ירקא ליזבין אריכא כישא כי כישא ואורכא ממילא ואמר רב חסדא בר בי רב דזבין קניא ליזבין אריכא טונא כי טונא ואורכא ממילא ואמר רב חסדא בר בי רב [ד] דלא נפישא ליה ריפתא] לא ליכול ירקא משום דגריר ואמר רב חסדא אנא לא בעניותי אכלי ירקא ולא בעתירותי אכלי ירקא בעניותי משום דגריר בעתירותי דאמינא היכא דעייל ירקא ליעול בשרא וכוורי (א) ואמר רב חסדא בר בי רב דלא נפישא ליה ריפתא לא ליבצע בצועי ואמר רב חסדא בר בי רב דלא נפישא ליה ריפתא לא ליבצע מ"ט דלא עביד בעין יפה ואמר רב חסדא אנא מעיקרא לא הואי בצענא עד דשדאי ידי בכולי מנא ואשכחי [ביה כל צרכי] ואמר רב חסדא האי מאן דאפשר ליה למיכל נהמא דשערי ואכל דחיטי קעבר משום א בל תשחית ואמר רב פפא האי מאן דאפשר למישתי שיכרא ושתי חמרא עובר משום בל תשחית ולאו מילתא היא בל תשחית דגופא עדיף ואמר רב חסדא בר בי רב דלית ליה משחא נימשי במיא דחריצי ואמר רב חסדא בר בי רב דזבין אומצא ליזבין אונקא דאית ביה תלתא מיני בישרא וא"ר חסדא בר בי רב דזבין כיתוניתא ליזבן מדנהר אבא וניחוורה כל תלתין יומין דמפטיא ליה תריסר ירחי שתא ואנא ערבא מאי כיתוניתא כיתא נאה וא"ר חסדא בר בי רב לא ליתיב אציפתא חדתא דמכליא מאניה וא"ר חסדא בר בי רב לא לישדר מאניה לאושפיזיה לחוורינהו ליה דלאו אורח ארעא דילמא חזי ביה מידי ואתי למגניא אמר להו רב חסדא לבנתיה תיהוי צניעתן באפי גברייכו לא תיכלון נהמא באפי גברייכו לא תיכלון ירקא בליליא לא תיכלון תמרי בליליא ולא תשתון שיכרא בליליא ולא תיפנון היכא דמפני גברייכו וכי קא קארי אבבא איניש לא תימרון מנו אלא מני נקיט מרגניתא בחדא ידיה וכורא בחדא ידיה מרגניתא אחוי להו וכורא לא אחוי להו עד דמיצטערן והדר אחוי להו: אין שולין את הכרשינין: מתני' דלא כי האי תנא דתניא ר"א בן יעקב אומר אין משגיחין בכברה כל עיקר: **מתני'** גורפין מלפני הפטם ומסלקין לצדדין מפני הרעי דברי רבי דוסא וחכמים אוסרין נוטלין מלפני בהמה זו ונותנין לפני בהמה זו בשבת: **גמ'** איבעיא להו רבנן ארישא פליגי או אסיפא פליגי או אתרווייהו פליגי ת"ש דתניא וחכמים אומרים ה אחד זה ואחד זה לא יסלקנו לצדדין אמר רב חסדא מחלוקת באיבום של קרקע אבל באיבום של כלי דברי הכל מותר ואיבום של קרקע מי איכא למאן דשרי הא קא משוי גומות אלא אי איתמר הכי איתמר א"ר חסדא ו מחלוקת באיבום של כלי אבל באיבום של קרקע דברי הכל אסור: ונוטלין מלפני בהמה: תנא חדא נוטלין מלפני בהמה שפיה יפה ונותנין לפני בהמה שפיה רע ותניא אידך נוטלין מלפני בהמה שפיה רע ונותנין לפני בהמה שפיה יפה אמר אביי ז אידי ואידי מקמי חמרא לקמי תורא שקלינן מקמי תורא לקמי חמרא לא שקלינן והא דקתני נוטל מלפני בהמה שפיה יפה בחמור דלית ליה רירי ונותנין לפני בהמה שפיה רע בפרה

משלפא לדידה מקניא. כששוטחין אותה לנגבה תוחבים קנה מבית יד לבית יד וכשנוטלה בשבת ישלפנה מן הקנה ולא הקנה ממנה דלא חזי לטלטולי להסקה קאי: ואם כלי קיואי היא. קנה של אורגים דתורת כלי עליו שרי: תליא דבשרא. בשר מליח התלוי לייבשו ומלא החבל קרי תליא: שרי. דנאכל חי באומצא: דכוורי. אין נאכלין חיין: באמצע מטה. שאיש ואשתו רגילין בה לישן: כאילו עומד כו'. דמהרהר: לזבין אריכא. אגודה ארוכה של כרוב ארוך ושל כרישין ארוכים: כישא כי כישא. שכל אגודות הגנין שוות בעובין שלכולן מדה אחת לתבל שהוא אגוד בו: ואורכא ממילא. כלומר ארכו של זה שהוא ארוך מחבירו הוא משתכר בו: קניא. חבילי קנים לעצים: לא ליכול ירקא. ירק חי (ב) כרישין לירפו"ל ושאלייס: משום דגריר ליבא. ומאכילו לחם הרבה ואין לו: לא ליבצע בצועי. מורשיליונ"ש בלע"ז לא יאכל עכשיו מעט פת שימלא לו ולאחר שעה מעט מפני שאין לו דרך שביעה אלא יצרף ויאכל יחד: מעיקרא. קודם שנתעשרתי: עד דשדאי ידי בכולא מנא. כשהייתי ממשמש בסל ומוצא בו פת הרבה הייתי מברך המוציא: דלית ליה משחא. שהיו סכין ידיהן שמן קודם מים אחרונים להעביר את הזוהמא: במיא דחריצי. הנקוים יחד וגדל עליהם ירקרוקית עבה ונוחה כשמן: אונקא. צואר: תלתא מיני בשרא. יטעום בו ג' מיני מטעמים שמן וכחוש וגיד הצואר: מדנהר אבא. מאותו מקום שפשתנו יפה: דמפטיא ליה תריסר ירחי שתא ואנא ערבא. אני ערב בדבר שתתקיים לו שנה שלימה ותפטיהו שלא יצטרך לקנות חלוק: כיתא נאה. כת נאה ראויה להושיב בעליה בכת נאה: אציפתא חדתא. מחצלת חדשה של גמי לח ולחלוחית הגמי מבלה הבגדים: לאושפיזא. לפונדקית שלו לא ישלח חלוקו ללבן: דילמא חזיא בהו. קרי ומגניא עליה: לא תיכלון נהמא באפי גברייכו. פעמים תאכל הרבה ותתגנה עליו: לא תיכלון ירקא בלילה. מפני ריח הפה: שיכרא ותמרי. משלשלין ומביאין לידי הפחה: היכא דמפני גברייכו. בגילוי בפניהם בשדות ואפילו שלא בפניהם שמכיר מקומו ומקומכם ונמאסת' לו בזוכרו: לא תימרון מנו. מי הוא לשון זכר לא תרגילו לשונכם לדבר עם זכרים: אלא מני. מי היא: נקיט מרגניתא בחדא ידיה וכורא בחדא ידיה. כשבעליך ממשמש ביך להתאוות ליך לתשמיש ואוחז הדדים בידו אחת והאחרת עד אותו מקום: מרגניתא אחוין ליה. הדדין המציאי לו שתתרבה תאותו ומקום תשמיש אל תמציאי לו מהר כדי שיתרבה תאותו וחיבתו ויצטער הדר אחוי ליה: כורא. לשון כור נורפין (לעיל דף עח.) לשון אחר כור לשון בור שוחה: מתניתין. דקתני אבל נותנין לתוך הכברה: **מתני'** גורפין מלפני הפטם. שור שמפטמין אותו גורפין אבוס שלפניו בשבת לתת לתוכו התבן והשעורין ולא יתערב בהן עפרורית ויקוץ במאכלו: ומסלקין תבן (ג) שלפניו לצדדין כשהוא רב כדי שלא ידרסנו ברעי: וחכמים אוסרים. מפרש בגמרא אהיא: ונוטלין מלפני בהמה זו. שעורין ותבן ונותנין לפני זו ולא אמרינן טלטול דלא חזי הוא אלא ודאי חזי הוא דאין בהמה קצה במאכל הניטל מלפני חבירתה: **גמ'** ארישא פליגי. אגורפין ואסרי לגרוף משום דפעמים שהאבוס של קרקע וקא מכוין לאשויי גומות שלא יפלו השעורים לתוכו: או אסיפא פליגי. ומשום דלא חזי שיש בו (ד) שנמאס במדרס רגליו: תא שמע. דאתרווייהו פליגי: אחד זה ואחד זה. אחד גריפת האבוס ואחד תבן שלפניו לא יסלקנו לצדדין: של קרקע. כעין שעושין גדר קטן לפני בהמה ונותנין מאכל לפנים ממנו דאיכא למיחש לאשויי גומות: מחלוקת באבום של כלי. וגזרו רבנן גזרה אטו של קרקע: שפיה יפה. לקמיה מפרש: אידי ואידי. שתיהן המשניות סבירא להו: מקמי חמרא לקמי תורא שקלינן. שאינו מטיל רירין ואין מה שלפניו נמאס וראוי לתתו לפני שור: מקמי תורא לקמי חמרא לא שקלינן.
דאית

מסורת הש"ס

א) [לעיל קיג.], ב) [בערוך איתא הוצא], ג) [עי' תוס' לעיל קלט: ד"ה תלא], ד) [עי' תוס' עירובין נה: ד"ה כל עיר וכו' נראה דלא גרסי להנך ד' תיבות], ה) ברכות מו:, ו) [לעיל קכט.], ז) [גירס' אחרינא ופירושו עי' בערוך ערך בור א'], ח) צ"ל וכו'.

הגהות הב"ח

(א) גמ' דלא נפישא ליה ריפתא (לא ליבצע וכו' יפה) תא"מ ונ"ב ס"א לא ליבצע בצועי והשאר נמחק. והכי משמע מפירש"י: (ב) רש"י ד"ה לא ליכול ירקא ירק חי. נ"ב עיין פרק כילד מעברין בדף נה במ"ש התוס' בד"ה כל עיר: (ג) ד"ה ומסלקין תבן מלפניו לצדדין: (ד) ד"ה או אסיפא וכו' שיש בו מה שנמאס:

תורה אור השלם

א) כִּי תָצוּר אֶל עִיר יָמִים רַבִּים לְהִלָּחֵם עָלֶיהָ לְתָפְשָׂהּ לֹא תַשְׁחִית אֶת עֵצָהּ לִנְדֹּחַ עָלָיו גַּרְזֶן כִּי מִמֶּנּוּ תֹאכֵל וְאֹתוֹ לֹא תִכְרֹת כִּי הָאָדָם עֵץ הַשָּׂדֶה לָבֹא מִפָּנֶיךָ בַּמָּצוֹר: [דברים כ, יט]

ליקוטי רש"י

דכוורי. דגים [תענית כד.]. **כישא**. אגודה שלרך הירק להיות מחולק באגודות וכל האגודות הן שוות [קידושין נב:]. **דגריר**. ממשיך את הלב לתאות רעבון [יומא פג:]. **חריצי**. מקום כנוס מים גדל עליהם כמין ירקרוקת [לעיל כ:].

מִשְׁלְפוּ לְדִידָהּ מִקַּנְיָא שְׁרֵי – **to remove it from its rod is permitted,** קַנְיָא מִמֶּנָּה אָסוּר – but to slip **the rod out of [the shirt] is prohibited.**[1]

This prohibition is qualified:

אָמַר רָבָא – **Rava said:** וְאִם כְּלִי קִיוּאֵי הוּא מוּתָּר – **But if it is a weaver's rod, it is permitted** to slip the rod out of the shirt.[2]

Yet another halachah concerning *muktzeh* from Rav Chisda:

אָמַר רַב חִסְדָּא – **Rav Chisda said:** הַאי כִּישְׁתָּא דְיַרְקָא – **This bunch of herbs,** אִי חַזְיָא לְמַאֲכַל בְּהֵמָה שְׁרֵי לְטַלְטוּלֵי – **if they are fit for animal consumption, it is permitted to move them;** וְאִי לֹא אָסִיר – **but if not, it is prohibited to move them.**[3]

A related halachah:

אָמַר רַב חִיָּיא בַּר אַשִׁי אָמַר רַב – **Rav Chiya bar Ashi said in the name of Rav:** הַאי תַּלְיָא דְבִשְׂרָא שְׁרֵי לְטַלְטוּלֵי – **This string of** animal **meat**[4] **is permitted to be moved,** since it is fit to be eaten as is, without cooking. דְּכְווֹרֵי אָסִיר – But a string **of** raw **fish is forbidden** to be moved since it cannot be eaten as is.[5]

The Gemara now digresses to discuss many practical and moral issues pertinent to a Torah student and the public in general:[6]

אָמַר רַב קְטִינָא – **Rav Ketina said:** הָעוֹמֵד בְּאֶמְצַע הַמִּטָּה כְּאִילּוּ עוֹמֵד בִּבְרֵיסָהּ שֶׁל אִשָּׁה – **One who stays in the middle of a** married couple's **bed is considered to be standing on the** very **stomach of a woman.**[7]

Rav Ketina rejects this teaching:

וְלָאו מִילְּתָא הִיא – **But there is** actually **no problem** in doing so.[8]

A series of practical suggestions:

וְאָמַר רַב חִסְדָּא – **And Rav Chisda said:** בַּר בֵּי רַב דְּזָבִין יַרְקָא לִיזְבִּין אֲרִיכָא – **A Torah scholar who buys** a bunch of **vegetables should buy** a bundle that contains **longer** herbs. כִּישָׁא כִּי כִּישָׁא – For **one bunch is** as thick **as the next bunch,** וְאוֹרְכָּא מִמֵּילָא – **and the** added **length** of the longer vegetables represents an **automatic** benefit over shorter bunches.[9]

A similar thought:

וְאָמַר רַב חִסְדָּא – **And Rav Chisda said:** בַּר בֵּי רַב דְּזָבִין קַנְיָא לִיזְבִּין אֲרִיכָא – **A Torah scholar who buys** a bundle of **reeds should buy** a bundle containing **longer** reeds. טוּנָא כִּי טוּנָא – For **one bundle is** as thick **as the next bundle,** וְאוֹרְכָּא מִמֵּילָא – **and the** added **length** of one bundle represents an **automatic** benefit over a shorter bundle.

Another piece of advice:

וְאָמַר רַב חִסְדָּא – **And Rav Chisda said:** בַּר בֵּי רַב – **A Torah scholar** [דְּלָא נְפִישָׁא לֵיהּ רִיפְתָּא – **who does not have much bread]** לֹא לֵיכוּל יַרְקָא – **should not eat herbs,** מִשּׁוּם דְּגָרִיר – **because they whet one's appetite,** and he does not have enough bread to satisfy that appetite.[10]

A similar thought:

וְאָמַר רַב חִסְדָּא – **And Rav Chisda said:** אֲנָא לֹא בַּעֲנִיּוּתִי אָכְלִי יַרְקָא – **I myself did not eat herbs when I was poor,** וְלָא בַּעֲתִירוּתִי אָכְלִי יַרְקָא – **nor did I eat herbs when I was wealthy.**

NOTES

1. In Talmudic times, the practice was to spread a freshly laundered shirt to dry by inserting a long rod through the two sleeves. Now, it was not the norm to set aside rods for this purpose; rather, rods which would later be used for firewood were used (see *Mishnah Berurah* 308:65). Thus, such rods are not deemed utensils, and fall into the category of מוּקְצֶה מֵחֲמַת גופו, items that are *inherently muktzeh*. Therefore, such a rod may not be moved directly. However, in a case in which one's primary motive is to move a non-*muktzeh* item, one may *indirectly* move a *muktzeh* item (see above, 44a note 2 and 123a note 2). Accordingly, one may slip a shirt (a non-*muktzeh* item) from a drying rod (a *muktzeh* item) even though the rod is indirectly moved about. One may *not,* however, remove the drying rod from the shirt [because in doing so one directly moves a *muktzeh* item, which is never permitted (*Rashi*)]. See, however, *Mishnah Berurah* 308:16.

2. A weaver's rod is indeed viewed as a utensil, and may be moved about if its place is needed [צוֹרֶךְ מְקוֹמוֹ] (see *Rashi* to 113a ד״ה מותר לטלטלן and *Tosafos* to 122b ד״ה רחת). Thus, if it is used for drying, one may directly remove the rod from the shirt (*Rashi*).

3. Only food fit for animal or human consumption may be moved on the Sabbath; see below, 143a.

The *Aruch* (ע׳ הץ) had another version of this ruling which read הָאי הוּצָא דְיַרְקָא, *those leaves of herbs. Rambam* (*Hil. Shabbos* 26:19), apparently following this version of the text, explains this as referring to foul-smelling leaves which would be מוּקְצֶה מֵחֲמַת מיאוס, *muktzeh by dint of repugnance,* unless they had some redeeming value in being fit for animal consumption. [All agree that the leaves are not fit for human consumption.]

4. Salted meat was commonly hung from a string, called a תַּלְיָא, to allow it to dry out (see *Rashi*).

5. This ruling mirrors that which we have learned above (128a) that a food which is generally consumed by humans but is not fit to be eaten in its present state is *muktzeh* (*Ritva MHK* ed.).

According to *Rashi,* this ruling focuses on the *muktzeh* status of the animal and fish meats, basing it on whether they may be eaten as is. *Tosafos* (printed on 139b ד״ה תלא) ask, among other questions, that according to this explanation, the Gemara need not have bothered to mention the *string* holding the meats. They therefore explain (see also *Rashba* and *Ritva MHK* ed.) the Gemara as teaching that the string commonly used to hold animal meat was reused again and again, and thus earned the status of a utensil, which is not *muktzeh.* Strings used to hold fish, however, which would become somewhat repulsive and be discarded after one use, would never earn the status of a utensil, and thus are *muktzeh.* [For possible defenses of *Rashi,* see *Chasam Sofer* and *Maginei Shlomo.*]

Tosafos (ibid.) also cite *Aruch* who (see also *Rambam, Hil. Shabbos* 26:19) explains that the Gemara distinguishes between the string used to hold meat which does not become repugnant (and is thus not *muktzeh)* and the string used to hold fish which does become repulsive and is actually מוּקְצֶה מֵחֲמַת מיאוס, *muktzeh by dint of repugnance.* [According to *Aruch* and the *Rambam,* both this case and the previous one deal with this category of *muktzeh;* see above, note 3.]

6. The Gemara will now set forth many points of advice, most of them from Rav Chisda, in areas ranging from commerce to eating habits to hygiene, to name just a few. The fact that it is unusual for the Gemara to speak of some of these matters, and the fact that Rav Chisda addresses specifically a בַּר בֵּי רַב, *a Torah scholar,* in many of the cases, lead the commentators, chiefly the *Chasam Sofer* and *Maharal (Chidushei Aggados),* to interpret many of the points as allegorically referring to moral and ethical issues which relate to Torah scholars.

[As a bridge between the previous rulings and the upcoming Gemara,] *Rashash* suggests that the attribution of the ruling that is to follow should read אָמַר רַב חִסְדָּא אָמַר רַב קְטִינָא, *Rav Chisda said in the name of Rav Ketina* (a common citation in the Gemara). [Thus, the Gemara followed Rav Chisda's ruling concerning the *muktzeh* status of a bunch of herbs with one of his other teachings.]

7. One standing upon the bed will inevitably give thought to intimate relations with women (*Rashi*).

8. See *Megadim Chadashim.*

9. The Gemara refers to stalks of vegetables such as cabbage or leeks, which are sold in bunches. The bunches are tied with strings of uniform length, and they are all priced alike. But while the bunches will generally have the same thickness (for that is dictated by the length of the string), they may vary in length. A bunch with longer pieces, therefore, will offer greater value, because the extra length comes at no extra cost (*Rashi;* cf. *Chasam Sofer* [Machon Chasam Sofer ed.]).

10. This refers to raw herbs such as leek, chervil and cress (*Rashi*). [These herbs must be avoided only when raw; when they are cooked they are actually the *preferred* food for Torah scholars since they satisfy one's hunger easily at little cost (*Tosafos* to *Eruvin* 55b ד״ה כל עיר).]

[Apparently, *Tosafos'* (ibid.) text of our Gemara did not include the phrase דְּלָא נְפִישָׁא לֵיהּ רִיפְתָּא, *who does not have much bread,* for they explain that the herbs are to be avoided because eating them would require the scholar to expend money unnecessarily to buy enough bread to satisfy the now whetted appetite. Indeed, *Dikdukei Soferim* also omits this line, as does *Rashbam* to *Pesachim* 107b ד״ה בירקא. See also *Maharal, Chidushei Aggados.*]

משלפא לדידה מקניא. כששוטחין אותה לגבה תוחבים קנה מבית יד לבית יד וכשנוטלה בשבת ישלפנה מן הקנה ולא הקנה ממנה דלא חזי לטלטולי להסקה קאי: ואם כלי קיואי היא. קנה של אורגים דתורת כלי עליו שרי: תליא דבשרא. בשר מליח התלוי לייבשו ומלא המבל קרי תליא: שרי. דנאכל חי באומצא: דכוורי. אין נאכלין חיין: באמצע מטה. שאיש ואשתו רגילין בה לישן: כאילו עומד כו'. דמהרהר: ליזבין אריכא. אגודה ארוכה של כרוב ארוך ושל כרישין ארוכים: כישא כי כישא. שכל אגודות הגנין שוות בעובין שלכולן מדה אחת לחבל שהוא אגוד בו: ואורכא ממילא. כלומר ארכו של זה שהוא ארוך מחבירו הוא משתכר בו: קניא. חבילי קנים לעצים: לא ליכול ירקא. ירק חי (ג) כרישין לירפו"ל ושחליים: משום דגריר ליבא. ומאכילו לחם הרבה ואין לו: לא ליבצע בצועי. מורשיליונ"ש בלע"ז לא יאכל עכשיו מעט פת שימלא לו ולאחר שעה מעט מפני שאין לו דרך שביעה אלא יצרף ויאכל יחד: מעיקרא. קודם שנתעשרתי: עד דשדאי ידי בכולא מנא. כשהייתי ממשש בסל ומוצא בו פת הרבה הייתי מברך המוציא: דלית ליה משחא. שהיו סכין ידיהן שמן קודם מים אחרונים להעביר את הזוהמא: במיא דחריצי. הנקוים יחד וגדל עליהם ירקרוקית עבה ונוחה כשמן: אונקא. צואר: תלתא מיני בשרא. יטעום בו ג' מיני מטעמים שמן וכחוש וגיד הצואר: מדנהר אבא. מאותו מקום שפשתנו יפה: דמפטיא ליה תריסר ירחי שתא ואנא ערבא. אני ערב בדבר שתתקיים לו שנה שלימה ותפטיהו שלא יצטרך לקנות חלוק: כיתא נאה. כת נאה ראויה להושיב בעליה בכת נאה: אציפתא חדתא. מחצלת חדשה של גמי לח ולחלוחית הגמי מבלה הבגדים: לאושפיזא. לפונדקית שלו לא ישלח חלוקו ללבן: דילמא חזיא בהו. קרי ומגניא עליה: לא תיכלון נהמא באפי גברייכו. פעמים תאכל הרבה ותתגנה עליו: לא תיכלון ירקא בלילה. מפני ריח הפה: שיכרא ותמרי. משלשלין ומביאין לידי הפחה: היכא דמפני גברייכו. בגילוי בפניהם בשדות ואפילו שלא בפניהם שמכיר מקומו ומקומכם ונמאסת' לו בזוכרו: לא תימרון מנו. מי הוא לשון זכר לא תרגילו לשונכם לדבר עם זכרים: אלא מני. מי היא: נקיט מרגניתא בחדא ידיה וכורא בחדא ידיה. כשבעליך ממשמש בין להתאוות לך לתשמיש ואוחז הדדים בידו אחת והאחרת עד אותו מקום: מרגניתא אחוין ליה. הדדין המליאי לו שתתרבה תאותו ומקום תשמיש אל תמליאי לו מהר כדי שיתרבה תאותו ויכתו ויצטער הדר אחוי ליה: כורא. לשון כור נורפין (לעיל דף עת.) לשון אחר כור לשון בור שוחה: מתניתין. דקתני אבל נותנין לתוך הכברה: מתני' גורפין מלפני הפטם. שור שמפטמין אותו גורפין אבוס שלפניו בשבת לתת לתוכו התבן והשעורין ולא יתערב בהן עפרורית ויקוץ במאכלו: ומסלקין תבן (ג) שלפניו לצדדין כשהוא רב כדי שלא ידרסנו ברעי: וחכמים אוסרים. מפרש בגמרא אהיא: ונוטלין מלפני בהמה זו. שעורין ותבן ונותנין לפני זו ולא אמרינן טלטול דלא חזי הוא אלא ודאי חזי הוא דאין בהמה קצה במאכל הניטל מלפני חבירתה: גמ' ארישא פליגי. אגורפין ואסרי לגרוף משום דפעמים שהאבוס של קרקע וקא מכוין לאשויי גומות שלא יפלו השעורים לתוכו: או אסיפא פליגי. ומשום דלא חזי שיש בו (ד) שנמאס במדרס רגליו: דאתרוייהו פליגי: תא שמע. אחד זה ואחד זה. אחד גריפת האבוס ואחד תבן שלפניו לא יסלקנו לצדדין: של קרקע. כעין שעושין גדר קטן לפני בהמה ונותנין מאכל לפנים ממנו דאיכא למיחש לאשויי גומות: מחלוקת באבוס של כלי. וגזרו רבנן גזרה אטו של קרקע: שפיה יפה. לקמיה מפרש: אידי ואידי. שתיהן המשניות סבירא להו: מקמי חמרא לקמי תורא שקלינן. שאינו מטיל רירין ואין מה שלפניו נמאס וראוי לתתו לפני שור: מקמי תורא לקמי חמרא לא שקלינן.

דלית

אבל באיבום של קרקע דברי הכל אסור. אע"ג דמרבן שרינן לרבי שמעון (לעיל דף לה.) הכא רגילות הוא להתכוין לאשווי גומות וחיישינן טפי שמא יתכוין: הקש

משלפו לדידה מקניא שרי קניא ממנה אסור אמר רבא (א) ואם כלי קיואי הוא מותר אמר רב חסדא האי כישתא דירקא אי חזיא למאכל בהמה שרי לטלטולי ואי לא אסיר אמר רב חייא בר אשי אמר רב האי תליא דבשרא שרי לטלטולי דכוורי אסיר

אמר רב קטינא העומד באמצע המטה כאילו עומד בבריסה של אשה ולאו מילתא היא ואמר רב חסדא בר בי רב דזבין ירקא ליזבין אריכא כישא כי כישא ואורכא ממילא ואמר רב חסדא בר בי רב דזבין קניא ליזבין אריכא טונא כי טונא ואורכא ממילא ואמר רב חסדא בר בי רב [דלא נפישא ליה ריפתא] לא ליכול ירקא משום דגריר ואמר רב חסדא אנא לא בעניותי אכלי ירקא ולא בעתירותי אכלי ירקא בעניותי משום דגריר בעתירותי דאמינא היכא דעייל ירקא ליעול בשרא וכוורי (א) ואמר רב חסדא בר בי רב דלא נפישא ליה ריפתא לא ליבצע בצועי ואמר רב חסדא בר בי רב דלא נפישא ליה ריפתא לא ליבצע מ"ט דלא עביד בעין יפה ואמר רב חסדא אנא מעיקרא לא הואי בצענא עד דשדאי ידי בכולי מנא ואשכחי [ביה כל צרכי] ואמר רב חסדא האי מאן דאפשר ליה למיכל נהמא דשערי ואכל דחיטי קעבר משום בל תשחית ואמר רב פפא האי מאן דאפשר למישתי שיכרא ושתי חמרא עובר משום בל תשחית ולאו מילתא היא בל תשחית דגופא עדיף ואמר רב חסדא בר בי רב דלית ליה משחא נימשי במיא דחריצי ואמר רב חסדא בר בי רב דזבין אומצא ליזבין אונקא דאית ביה תלתא מיני בישרא וא"ר חסדא בר בי רב דזבין כיתוניתא ליזבין מדנהר אבא וניחוורה כל תלתין יומין דמפטיא ליה תריסר ירחי שתא ואנא ערבא מאי כיתוניתא כיתא נאה וא"ר חסדא בר בי רב לא ליתיב אציפתא חדתא דמכליא מאניה וא"ר חסדא בר בי רב לא לישדר מאניה לאושפיזיה לחוורי ליה דלאו אורח ארעא דילמא חזי ביה מידי ואתי למגניא אמר להו רב חסדא לבנתיה תיהוי צניעתן באפי גברייכו לא תיכלון נהמא באפי גברייכו לא תיכלון ירקא בליליא לא תיכלון תמרי בליליא ולא תשתון שיכרא בליליא ולא תיפנון היכא דמפני גברייכו וכי קא קארי אבבא איניש לא תימרון מנו אלא מני נקיט מרגניתא בחדא ידיה וכורא בחדא ידיה מרגניתא אחוי להו וכורא לא אחוי להו עד דמיצטערן והדר אחוי להו: אין שולין את הכרשינין: מתני' דלא כי האי תנא דתניא ר"א בן יעקב אומר אין משגיחין בכברה כל עיקר: מתני' גורפין מלפני הפטם ומסלקין לצדדין מפני הרעי דברי רבי דוסא וחכמים אוסרין נוטלין מלפני בהמה זו ונותנין לפני בהמה זו בשבת: גמ' איבעיא להו רבנן ארישא פליגי או אסיפא פליגי או אתרוייהו פליגי ת"ש דתניא וחכמים אומרים אחד זה ואחד זה לא יסלקנו לצדדין אמר רב חסדא מחלוקת באיבום של קרקע אבל באיבום של כלי דברי הכל מותר ואיבום של קרקע מי איכא למאן דשרי הא קא משוי גומות אלא אי איתמר הכי איתמר א"ר חסדא מחלוקת באיבום של כלי אבל באיבום של קרקע דברי הכל אסור: ונוטלין מלפני בהמה: תנא חדא נוטלין מלפני בהמה שפיה יפה ונותנין לפני בהמה שפיה רע ותניא אידך נוטלין מלפני בהמה שפיה רע ונותנין לפני בהמה שפיה יפה אמר אביי אידי ואידי מקמי חמרא לקמי תורא שקלינן מקמי תורא לקמי חמרא לא שקלינן והא דקתני נוטל מלפני בהמה שפיה יפה בחמור דלית ליה רירי ונותנין לפני בהמה שפיה רע בפרה

מסורת הש"ס

א) [לעיל קיג.], ב) [בערוך איתא הוצא], ג) [עי' תוס' לעיל קלט: ד"ה הלא], ד) [עי' תוס' עירובין נה: ד"ה כל עיר וכו' נראה דלא גרסי להנך ד' תיבות], ה) ברכות מו:, ו) [לעיל קכט.], ז) [גירס' אחרינא ופירושו עי' בערוך ערך בור א'], ח) ל"ל וכרי.

עין משפט נר מצוה

מא א ב מיי' פכ"ה מהל' שבת הל' יח סמג לאוין סה טוש"ע א"ח סי' שח סעיף טז:

מב ג מיי' פכ"ו מהל' שבת הל' טז סמג שם טוש"ע שם סעיף כז וכח:

מג ד מיי' פ"ז מהל' ברכות הלכה ג:

מד ה ו מיי' פכ"ו מהל' שבת הלכה יט סמג לאוין סה טוש"ע א"ח סי' שכד סעיף טו:

מה ז מיי' שם טוש"ע שם סעיף יד:

רבינו חננאל

רב חסדא דלרכוכי מיכוון ושרי. אמר רב חסדא הא כיתניתא משלפה לדילא מקניא: פי' למשוך הבגד ששוטחו בקנה להנגב ונעשה נגוב וישאר הקנה במקומו. ולא מטלטלין מותר אבל למשוך הקנה מן הבגד ולטלטלו בשבת אסור שהקנה אינו כלי להטלטל בחצר. אמר רבא ואם כלי קיואי מותר. פי' אם הוא הבגד שטוח בכלי האורג וכלי האורג נקראין כלי קיואי כדאמרינן בפרק ואלו קשרים שחייבין עליהן. אתמר אמר רב נחמן אמר שמואל כלי קיואי מותר לטלטלו בשבת ואפי' כובד העליון וכובד התחתון אבל לא את העמודים ותוב בעא מיניה ר' יוחנן מרבי יהודה בר ליואי כלי קיואי כגון כובד העליון וכובד התחתון כו'. האי תלא דבשרא פי' יתד של עץ עשוי לתלות בו בשר ופעמים שתולין בו זולתו [שרי לטלטולי] אבל העץ שתולין בו דגים. כיון שהדגים ריחם רע וקשה אין תולין בו דבר אחר ומסיחין דעתן ממנו ומוקצה מחמת מיאוס הוא ואסור: מדנהר אבא. שם מקום הוא: ציפיתא חדתא. פי' מחצלת חדשה בזרא בחדא ידא. כגון אבן שאין לה דמים ולא צורך. ומפני שהסתירה מהן נתייקרה בעיניהם ופייסוהו להראותה להן: מתני' אין שולין את הכרשינין ולא שפין כו' גורפין מלפני הפטם ומסלקין לצדדים כו'. פי' גורפין המאכל של בהמה מלפני הפטם ומאכל שאר בהמות מסלקין לצדדין דברי ר' דוסיא חכמים אוסרין ואיבעיא לן רבנן ארישא פליגי והיא גורפין [או] אסיפא פליגי והוא שמסלקין לצדדין ואמרינן ת"ש וחכ"א אחד זה ואחד זה לא יסלקנו לצדדין. ש"מ רבנן אתרווייהו פליגי. אמר רב חסדא מחלוקת באבוס של כלי ואפי' בזה חכמים אוסרין אבל באבוס של קרקע דברי הכל אסור לגרוף:

הגהות הב"ח

(א) גמ' דלא נפישא ליה ריפתא (לא ליבצע וכו' יפה) תא"מ ונ"ב ס"א לא ליבלע בלועי והשאר נמחק. והכי משמע מפירש"י: (ב) רש"י ד"ה לא ליכול ירקא ירק חי. נ"ב עיין פרק כילד מעברין בדף נה במ"ש התוס' בד"ה כל עיר: (ג) ד"ה ומסלקין תבן מלפניו לצדדין: (ד) ד"ה או אסיפא וכו' שיש בו מה שנמאס:

תורה אור השלם

א) כִּי תָצוּר אֶל עִיר יָמִים רַבִּים לְהִלָּחֵם עָלֶיהָ לְתָפְשָׂהּ לֹא תַשְׁחִית אֶת עֵצָהּ לִנְדֹּחַ עָלָיו גַּרְזֶן כִּי מִמֶּנּוּ תֹאכֵל וְאֹתוֹ לֹא תִכְרֹת כִּי הָאָדָם עֵץ הַשָּׂדֶה לָבֹא מִפָּנֶיךָ בַּמָּצוֹר: [דברים כ, יט]

ליקוטי רש"י

דכוורי. דגים [תענית כד.]. כישא. אגודה שדרך הירק להיות ממסלק באגודות וכל האגודות הן שוות [קידושין נב:]. דגריר. ממשיך את הלב לתאות רעבון [יומא פג:]. חריצי. מקום כנוס מים גדל עליהם כמין ירקרוקת [לעיל כ:].

בַּעֲנִיּוּתִי מִשּׁוּם דְּגָרִיר – **When I was poor** I did not eat herbs **because they whet one's appetite,** and I did not have enough bread to satisfy that appetite. בַּעֲתִירוּתִי – **When I was wealthy** I did not eat herbs דַּאֲמִינָא הֵיכָא דְּעָיֵיל יַרְקָא לֵיעוּל בִּשְׂרָא וְכַוּוֹרֵי – **because I said,** "In the place **where herbs can enter, let meat and fish enter** instead."[11]

Another piece of advice for the poor Torah scholar:

וְאָמַר רַב חִסְדָּא – **And Rav Chisda said:** בַּר בֵּי רַב דְּלָא נְפִישָׁא לֵיהּ רִיפְתָּא לָא לִיבְצַע בְּצוּעֵי – **A Torah scholar who does not have much bread should not divide** his bread **into many** small **pieces,** and eat many small meals; rather, he should save his bread until he has enough for a satisfying meal.[12]

A related teaching:[13]

וְאָמַר רַב חִסְדָּא – **And Rav Chisda said:** בַּר בֵּי רַב דְּלָא נְפִישָׁא לֵיהּ רִיפְתָּא לָא לִיבְצַע – **A Torah scholar who does not have much bread should not** make the blessing over it and **divide** the bread for those partaking in a meal together. מַאי טַעְמָא – **What is the reason** for this? דְּלָא עָבֵיד בְּעַיִן יָפָה – **Because** there is a possibility that **he will not apportion the bread generously.**[14]]

A related teaching:

וְאָמַר רַב חִסְדָּא – **And Rav Chisda said:** אֲנָא מֵעִיקָּרָא לָא הֲוַאי בָּצַעְנָא – **I myself, originally** when I was poor, **would not break bread** עַד דְּשָׁדַאי יָדִי בְּכוּלֵּי מָנָא – **unless I had first examined the entire basket** of bread **with my hand**[15] [וְאַשְׁכְּחִי בֵּיהּ כָּל צָרְכִּי – **and found** that **there** was **enough for my needs** for the meal].

Another teaching:

וְאָמַר רַב חִסְדָּא – **And Rav Chisda said:** הַאי מַאן דְּאֶפְשָׁר לֵיהּ לְמֵיכַל נַהֲמָא דְשַׂעֲרֵי וְאָכַל דְּחִיטֵּי – **Any person who is able to eat barley bread and instead eats** bread made **of wheat** קָעָבַר מִשּׁוּם בַּל תַּשְׁחִית – **transgresses the sin of** ***"You shall not destroy."***[16] וְאָמַר רַב פָּפָּא – **And Rav Pappa said:** הַאי מַאן דְּאֶפְשָׁר לְמִישְׁתֵּי שִׁיכְרָא וְשָׁתֵי חַמְרָא – **Any person who is able to drink beer and instead drinks wine** עוֹבֵר מִשּׁוּם בַּל תַּשְׁחִית – **transgresses the sin of** ***"You shall not destroy."***[17]

The Gemara concludes:

וְלָאו מִילְּתָא הִיא – **But there is actually no problem** in doing so, בַּל תַּשְׁחִית דְּגוּפָא עָדִיף – for seeking to avoid transgressing the sin of **"You shall not destroy" with regard to one's body is a greater** consideration.[18]

Another teaching:

וְאָמַר רַב חִסְדָּא – **And Rav Chisda said:** בַּר בֵּי רַב דְּלֵית לֵיהּ מִשְׁחָא – **A Torah scholar who does not have oil** with which to clean his soiled hands after a meal[19] נִימְשֵׁי בְּמַיָּא דַּחֲרִיצֵי – **should wash with** the stagnant oil-like **water** which is found **in pits.**[20]

Another teaching:

וְאָמַר רַב חִסְדָּא – **And Rav Chisda said:** בַּר בֵּי רַב דְּזָבֵין אוּמְצָא לִיזְבִּין אוּנְקָא – **A Torah scholar who buys meat should buy neck meat,** דְּאִית בֵּיהּ תְּלָתָא מִינֵי בִּישְׂרָא – **for there is in it** the taste of **three types of meat.**[21]

Another teaching:

וְאָמַר רַב חִסְדָּא – **And Rav Chisda said:** בַּר בֵּי רַב דְּזָבֵין כִּיתּוּנִיתָא לִיזְבַּן מִדְּנְהַר אַבָּא – **A Torah scholar who buys** a **linen** garment **should buy** it **from** the area of **Nehar Abba.**[22] וְנִיחַוְּורָהּ כָּל תְּלָתִין יוֹמִין – **And he should clean it every thirty days,** דְּמִפַּסְּיָא לֵיהּ תְּרֵיסַר יַרְחֵי שַׁתָּא – **so that it will fill his** need for a garment **for a full twelve months.** וַאֲנָא עַרְבָא – **And I will be a guarantor to this.**[23]

NOTES

11. Rav Chisda teaches here that one should be careful to manage his household in a manner commensurate with his means. Thus, when he was poor he would not allow herbs in his house, to assure that he would not later be forced to spend beyond his means to buy additional bread. And when he became wealthy, he did not eat herbs because he was able to afford a richer diet (*Meiri;* cf. *Megadim Chadashim* and *Ben Yehoyada;* see also below, note 16).

12. A scholar who has but a small amount of bread should not eat it at once and then later eat another small piece that comes his way. Rather, he should wait until he is able to accumulate enough small pieces to eat together and satisfy himself (*Rashi;* see *Chasam Sofer*).

13. It would seem that *Rashi*'s text did not include Rav Chisda's next teaching (*Hagahos HaBach*). This is even more evident from the *Maharsha,* who explains Rav Chisda's previous teaching as teaching the same lesson as the very next teaching in our text. See also *Dikdukei Soferim.*

14. The Gemara elsewhere (*Berachos* 46a) teaches that the one to whom the meal belongs should make the *berachah* over the bread and divide it for those partaking in the meal, because he will surely apportion the bread most generously. But where all the participants are partners in the meal, or if all are guests, then the greatest among them should apportion the bread. Rav Chisda thus teaches here that if the greatest Torah scholar among them was poor, he should not divide the bread, for due to his poverty it is possible that he will not be as generous as he should be (*Chasam Sofer,* see there).

15. [Literally: until I threw my hand through the entire utensil.]

16. Scripture (*Deuteronomy* 20:19) warns a battling Jewish army that they may not needlessly destroy fruit-bearing trees. By extension, this prohibits any indiscriminate waste of food or resources. Rav Chisda applies it in our cases as follows: If a poor person, who should be limiting his expenses by buying lower quality barley bread, instead indulges in more expensive wheat bread, he "wastes" the extra money spent on this indulgence (*Meiri*). [R' Chisda applies this stricture only to a poor person; a person who can afford the more expensive wheat bread is certainly entitled to purchase it. Indeed, R' Chisda himself stated above that once he became wealthy he would eat fish and wine rather than herbs (see *Megadim Chadashim*). See also *Sfas Emes* for another explanation.]

Rav Chisda did not address this segment to Torah scholars only, for since it involves a Torah prohibition, the warning applies equally to all (*Maharsha;* cf. *Chasam Sofer* and *Megadim Chadashim*).

17. Rav Pappa similarly teaches that a poor person, who should be limiting his expenses by buying beer and instead indulges in more expensive wine, "wastes" the extra money spent on this indulgence. See *Maharsha* and *Rashash;* see also *Maharal.*

18. Wheat bread and wine are healthier for the body than barley bread and beer. Thus, the added expense incurred in the poor person acquiring these is justified, and cannot be decried as a waste of money.

See *Dikdukei Soferim,* which states that some versions of the Gemara do not include this conclusion, leaving Rav Chisda's and Rav Pappa's teachings standing.

19. Before washing מַיִם אַחֲרוֹנִים (the water with which one washes his hands before reciting the blessings after a meal), one would first cleanse his hands of the greasy remnants of his meal by rubbing them with a light oil (*Rashi,* see *Drishah* 181:1, and *Megadim Chadashim*).

Rav Chisda thus advises a Torah scholar who cannot afford such oil not to forsake this practice, and substitute an oil-like water.

20. This still water develops a thick green algaelike growth, making it smooth as oil (*Rashi*).

21. That cut of meat contains fatty meat, lean meat and the tough sinews of the neck (*Rashi,* see *Megadim Chadashim;* cf. *Chasam Sofer;* see *Chullin* 90b).

Maharal (*Chidushei Aggados*) explains that the last two teachings provide an insight into God's bountiful kindness. For since most luxuries are beyond the means of a poor person, God sees to it that there is always an inexpensive substitute that mimics each and every luxury. Thus, He provides a certain type of water to substitute for oil, and a certain type of meat from which a poor person will enjoy a variety of tastes that only one who could afford many different cuts of meat would otherwise enjoy.

22. For the linen produced there is of exceptional quality (*Rashi*).

23. Rav Chisda personally guaranteed that if his regimen of cleaning the shirt every thirty days were followed, it would last for a full year (*Rashi;* see *Menachem Meishiv Nefesh;* cf. *Chasam Sofer*). But if it were to be

עין משפט
נר מצוה

מא א ב מיי' פכ"ה מהל' שבת הל' יח סמג לאוין סה טוש"ע א"ח סי' שח סעיף מז:
מב ג מיי' פכ"ו מהל' שבת הל' טו סמג שם טוש"ע שם סעיף כח וכח:
מג ד מיי' פ"ו מהל' ברכות הלכה ג:
מד ה ו מיי' פכ"ו מהל' שבת הלכה יט סמג לאוין סה טוש"ע א"ח סי' שכד סעיף טו:
מה ז מיי' שם טוש"ע שם סעיף יד:

אבל באיבום של קרקע דברי הכל אסור. אע"ג דמרכן שרינן לרבי שמעון (לעיל דף נה.) הכא רגילות הוא להתכוין לאשווי גומות וחיישינן טפי שמא יתכוין:

הקש

משלפו לדידה מקניא שרי קניא ממנה אסור אמר רבא ואם כלי קיואי הוא מותר אמר רב חסדא האי כישתא דירקא אי חזיא למאכל בהמה שרי לטלטולי ואי לא אסיר אמר רב חייא בר אשי אמר רב האי תליא דבשרא שרי לטלטולי דכוורי אסיר

אמר רב קטינא העומד באמצע המטה כאילו עומד בכריסה של אשה ולאו מילתא היא ואמר רב חסדא בר בי רב דזבין ירקא ליזבין אריכא כישא כי כישא ואורכא ממילא ואמר רב חסדא בר בי רב דזבין קניא ליזבין אריכא טונא כי טונא ואורכא ממילא ואמר רב חסדא בר בי רב [דלא נפישא ליה ריפתא] לא ליכול ירקא משום דגריר ואמר רב חסדא אנא לא בעניותי אכלי ירקא ולא בעתירותי אכלי ירקא בעניותי משום דגריר בעתירותי דאמינא היכא דעייל ירקא ליעול בשרא וכוורי (א) ואמר רב חסדא בר בי רב דלא נפישא ליה ריפתא לא ליבצע בצועי ואמר רב חסדא בר בי רב דלא נפישא ליה ריפתא לא ליבצע מ"ט דלא עביד בעין יפה ואמר רב חסדא אנא מעיקרא לא הואי בצענא עד דשדאי ידי בכולי מנא ואשכחי [ביה כל צרכי] ואמר רב חסדא האי מאן דאפשר ליה למיכל נהמא דשערי ואכל דחיטי קעבר משום בל תשחית ואמר רב פפא האי מאן דאפשר למישתי שיכרא ושתי חמרא עובר משום בל תשחית ולאו מילתא היא בל תשחית דגופא עדיף ואמר רב חסדא בר בי רב דלית ליה משחא נימשי במיא דחריצי ואמר רב חסדא בר בי רב דזבין אומצא ליזבין אונקא דאית ביה תלתא מיני בישרא וא"ר חסדא בר בי רב דזבין כיתוניתא ליזבן מדנהר אבא וניחוורה כל תלתין יומין דמפטיא ליה תריסר ירחי שתא ואנא ערבא מאי כיתוניתא כיתא נאה וא"ר חסדא בר בי רב לא ליתיב אציפתא חדתא דמכליא מאניה וא"ר חסדא בר בי רב לא לישדר מאניה לאושפיזיה לחווריה ליה דלאו אורח ארעא דילמא חזי ביה מידי ואתי למגניא אמר להו רב חסדא לבנתיה תיהוי צניעתן באפי גברייכו לא תיכלון נהמא באפי גברייכו לא תיכלון ירקא בליליא לא תיכלון תמרי בליליא ולא תשתון שיכרא בליליא ולא תיפנון היכא דמפני גברייכו וכי קא קארי אבבא איניש לא תימרון מנו אלא מני נקיט מרגניתא בחדא ידיה וכורא בחדא ידיה מרגניתא אחוי להו וכורא לא אחוי להו עד דמיצטערן והדר אחוי להו: אין שולין את הכרשינין: מתני' דלא כי האי תנא דתניא ר"א בן יעקב אומר אין משגיחין בכברה כל עיקר: **מתני'** גורפין מלפני הפטם ומסלקין לצדדין מפני הרעי דברי רבי דוסא וחכמים אוסרין נוטלין מלפני בהמה זו ונותנין לפני בהמה זו בשבת: **גמ'** איבעיא להו רבנן ארישא פליגי או אסיפא פליגי או אתרוייהו פליגי ת"ש דתניא וחכמים אומרים אחד זה ואחד זה לא יסלקנו לצדדין אמר רב חסדא מחלוקת באיבום של קרקע אבל באיבום של כלי דברי הכל מותר ואיבום של קרקע מי איכא למאן דשרי הא קא משוי גומות אלא אי איתמר הכי איתמר א"ר חסדא מחלוקת באיבום של כלי אבל באיבום של קרקע דברי הכל אסור: ונוטלין מלפני בהמה: תנא חדא נוטלין מלפני בהמה שפיה יפה ונותנין לפני בהמה שפיה רע ותניא אידך נוטלין מלפני בהמה שפיה רע ונותנין לפני בהמה שפיה יפה אמר אביי אידי ואידי מקמי חמרא לקמי תורא שקלינן מקמי תורא לקמי חמרא לא שקלינן והא דקתני נוטל מלפני בהמה שפיה יפה בחמור דלית ליה רירי ונותנין לפני בהמה שפיה רע בפרה

משלפא לדידה מקניא. כששוטחין אותה לנגבה תוחבים קנה מבית יד לבית יד וכשנוטלה בשבת ישלפנה מן הקנה ולא הקנה ממנה דלא חזי לטלטולי להסקה קאי: ואם כלי קיואי היא. קנה של אורגים דתורת כלי עליו שרי: תליא דבשרא. בשר מליח התלוי לייבשו ומלא הסבל קרי תליא: שרי. דנאכל חי באומצא: דכוורי. אין נאכלין חיין: באמצע מטה. שאיש ואשתו רגילין בה לישן: כאילו עומד כו' למהרהר: ליזבין אריכא. אגודה ארוכה של כרוב ארוך ושל כרישין ארוכים: כישא כי כישא. שכל אגודות הגנין שוות בעוביין שלכולן מדה אחת לחבל שהוא אגוד בו: ואורכא ממילא. כלומר ארכו של זה שהוא ארוך מחבירו הוא משתכר בו: קניא. חבילי קנים לעצים: לא ליכול ירקא. ירק חי (ב) כרישין לירפו"ל ושחליים: משום דגריר ליבא. ומאכילו לחם הרבה ואין לו: לא ליבצע בצועי. מורסיליונ"ט בלע"ז לא יאכל עכשיו מעט פת שימלא לו ולאחר שעה מעט מפני שאין לו דרך שביעה אלא יצרף ויאכל יחד: מעיקרא. קודם שנתעשרתי: עד דשדאי ידי בכולא מנא. כשהייתי ממשמש בסל ומוצא בו פת הרבה הייתי מברך המוציא: דלית ליה משחא. שהיו סכין ידיהן שמן קודם מים אחרונים להעביר את הזוהמא: במיא דחריצי. הנקוים יחד וגדל עליהם ירקרוקית עבה ונוחה כשמן: אונקא. צואר: תלתא מיני בשרא. יטעום בו ג' מיני מטעמים שמן וכחוש וגיד הצואר: מדנהר אבא. מאותו מקום שפשתנו יפה: דמפטיא ליה תריסר ירחי שתא ואנא ערבא. אני ערב בדבר שתתקיים לו שנה שלימה ותפטירהו שלא יצטרך לקנות חלוק: כיתא נאה. כת נאה ראויה להושיב בעליה בכת נאה: אציפתא חדתא. מחצלת חדשה של גמי לח ולחלוחית הגמי מבלה הבגדים: לאושפיזא. לפונדקית שלו לא ישלח חלוקו ללבן: דילמא חזיא בהו. קרי ומגנא עליה: לא תיכלון נהמא באפי גברייכו. פעמים תאכל הרבה ותתגנה עליו: לא תיכלון ירקא בלילה. מפני ריח הפה: שיכרא ותמרי. משלשלין ומביאין לידי הפחה: היכא דמפני גברייכו. בגילוי בפניהם בשדות ואפילו שלא בפניהם שמכיר מקומו ומקומכם ונמאסת' לו בזוכרו: לא תימרון מנו. מי הוא לשון זכר לא תרגילו לשונכם לדבר עם זכרים: אלא מני. מי היא: נקיט מרגניתא בחדא ידיה וכורא בחדא ידיה. כשבעליך ממשמש בין להתאוות לך לתשמיש ואוחז הדדים בידו אחת והאחרת עד אותו מקום: מרגניתא אחוין ליה. הדדין המגיאי לו שתתרבה תאותו ומקום תשמיש אל תמציאי לו מהר כדי שיתרבה תאותו וחיבתו וילטער הדר אחוי ליה: כורא. לשון כור גורפין (לעיל דף עח.) לשון אחר בור לשון בור שוחה: מתניתין. דקתני אבל נותנין לתוך הכברה: מתני' גורפין מלפני הפטם. שור שמפטמין אותו גורפין אבוס שלפניו בשבת לתת לתוכו התבן והשעורין ולא יתערב בהן עפרורית ויקוץ במאכלו: ומסלקין תבן (ג) שלפניו לצדדין כשהוא רב כדי שלא ידרסנו ברעי: וחכמים אוסרים. מפרש בגמרא היא: ונוטלין מלפני בהמה זו. שעורין ותבן ונותנין לפני זו ולא אמרינן טלטול דלא חזי הוא אלא ודאי חזי הוא דאין בהמה קצה במאכל הניטל מלפני חבירתה: גמ' ארישא פליגי. אגורפין ואסרי לגרוף משום דפעמים שהאבוס של קרקע וקא מכוין לאשווי גומות שלא יפלו השעורים לתוכו: או אסיפא פליגי. ומשום דלא חזי שיש בו (ד) שנמאס במדרס רגליו: תא שמע. דאתרוייהו פליגי: אחד זה ואחד זה. אחד גריפת האבוס ואחד תבן שלפניו לא יסלקנו לצדדין: של קרקע. כעין שעושין גדר קטן לפני בהמה ונותנין מאכל לפנים ממנו דאיכא למיחש לאשווי גומות: מחלוקת באבוס של כלי. וגזרו רבנן גזירה אטו של קרקע: שפיה יפה. לקמיה מפרש: אידי ואידי. שתיהן המשניות סבירא להו: מקמי חמרא לקמי תורא שקלינן. שאינו מטיל רירין ואין מה שלפניו נמאס ורואי לתתו לפני שור: מקמי תורא לקמי חמרא לא שקלינן.

מסורת הש"ס

א) [לעיל קיג.], ב) [בערוך איתא הוצא], ג) [עי' תוס' לעיל קלט: ד"ה תלא], ד) [עי' תוס' עירובין נה: ד"ה כל עיר וכו' נראה דלא גרסי להנך ד' מיתות], ה) ברכות מו:, ו) [לעיל קכט.], ז) [גירס' אחרינא ופירושו עי' בערוך ערך כור א'], ח) ל"ל וכר'.

הגהות הב"ח

(א) גמ' דלא נפישא ליה ריפתא (לא ליבלע וכו' יפה) תא"מ ונ"ב ס"א לא ליבלע בלועי והשאר נמחק. והכי משמע מפירש"י: (ב) רש"י ד"ה לא ליכול ירקא ירק חי. נ"ב עיין פרק כילד מעברין בדף נה בהתוס' בד"ה כל עיר: (ג) ד"ה ומסלקין תבן מלפניו לצדדין: (ד) ד"ה או אסיפא וכו' שיש בו מה שנמאס:

תורה אור השלם

א) כִּי תָצוּר אֶל עִיר יָמִים רַבִּים לְהִלָּחֵם עָלֶיהָ לְתָפְשָׂהּ לֹא תַשְׁחִית אֶת עֵצָהּ לִנְדֹּחַ עָלָיו גַּרְזֶן כִּי מִמֶּנּוּ תֹאכֵל וְאֹתוֹ לֹא תִכְרֹת כִּי הָאָדָם עֵץ הַשָּׂדֶה לָבֹא מִפָּנֶיךָ בַּמָּצוֹר: [דברים כ, יט]

ליקוטי רש"י

דכוורי. לדגים [תענית כד.]. כישא. אגודה שדרך הירק להיות מתחלק באגודות וכל האגודות הן שוות [קידושין נב:]. דגריר. ממשיך את הלב לתאות רעבון [יומא פג:]. חריצי. מקום כנוס מים גדל עליהם כמין ירקרוקת [לעיל כ:].

רבינו חננאל

רב חסדא דלרכובי מיכוון ושרי. אמר רב חסדא הא כיתניתא משלפה לדילא מקניא: פי' למשוך הבגד ששוטחו בקנה להנגב ונעשה נגוב וישאר הקנה במקומו. ולא מטלטלין מותר אבל למשוך הקנה מן הבגד ולטלטלו בשבת אסור שהקנה אינו כלי להטלטל בחצר. אמר רבא ואם כלי קיואי מותר. פי' אם הוא הבגד שטוח בכלי האורג וכלי האורג נקראין כלי קיואי כדאמרינן בפרק ואלו קשרים שחייבין עליהן. אתמר אמר רב נחמן אמר שמואל כלי קיואי מותר לטלטלו בשבת ואפי' כובד העליון וכובד התחתון אבל לא את העמודים ותוב בעא מיניה ר' יוחנן מרבי יהודה בר ליואי כלי קיואי כגון כובד העליון וכובד התחתון כו'. האי תלא דבשרא פי' יתד של עץ עשוי לתלות בו בשר ופעמים שתולין בו זולתו [שרי לטלטולין] אבל העץ שתולין בו דגים. כיון שהדגים ריחם רע וקשה אין תולין בו דבר אחר ומסיחין דעתן ממנו ומוקצה מחמת מיאוס הוא ואסור: מדנהר אבא. שם מקום הוא: ציפיתא חדתא. פי' מחצלת חדשה בורא בחדא ידא. כגון אבן שאין לה דמים ולא צורך. ומפני שהסתירה מהן נתיקרה בעיניהם ופייסוהו להראותה להן: מתני' אין שולין את הכרשינין ולא שפין כו' גורפין מלפני הפטם ומסלקין לצדדים כו'. פי' גורפין המאכל של בהמה מלפני הפטם ומאכל שאר בהמות מסלקין לצדדין דברי ר' דוסיא חכמים אוסרין ואיבעיא לן רבנן ארישא פליגי והיא גורפין [או] אסיפא פליגי והוא שמסלקין לצדדין ואמרינן ת"ש וחכ"א אחד זה ואחד זה לא יסלקנו לצדדין. ש"מ רבנן אתרווייהו פליגי. אמר רב חסדא מחלוקת באבוס של כלי ואפי' בזה חכמים אוסרין אבל באבוס של קרקע דברי הכל אסור לגרוף:

The Gemara interjects the root of the word *kisonisa*: מַאי כִּיתּוּנִיתָא – **What is** the root of the word ***kisonisa*****?** כִּיתָא נָאָה – **Fine fellowship,**[24] i.e. the quality of the shirt declares that its wearer is fit to be part of good company.

Further instruction to a Torah scholar about his clothes: וְאָמַר רַב חִסְדָּא – **And Rav Chisda said:** בַּר בֵּי רַב לֹא לֵיתִיב אַצִּיפְּתָא חַדְתָּא – **A Torah scholar should not sit on a new hemp mat,** דִּמְכַלְיָא מָאנֵיהּ – **because it ruins his clothing.**[25]

Further instruction to a Torah scholar about his clothes: וְאָמַר רַב חִסְדָּא – **And Rav Chisda said:** בַּר בֵּי רַב לֹא לִישַׁדַּר מָאנֵיהּ לְאוּשְׁפִּיזְיהּ לְחַוּוֹרֵיהּ לֵיהּ – **A Torah scholar should not send his tunic to his hostess to be cleaned for him** דְּלָאו אוֹרַח אַרְעָא – **for it is not proper,** דִּילְמָא חָזֵי בֵּיהּ מִידֵי וְאָתֵי לְמִגְנְיָא – **lest she see something on it and** he will **come to be repulsive to her.**[26]

The Gemara now presents the advice which Rav Chisda would give his daughters regarding proper behavior with their husbands: אָמַר לְהוּ רַב חִסְדָּא לִבְנָתֵיהּ – **Rav Chisda said to his daughters:** תֶּיהֱוֵי צְנִיעָתָן בְּאַפֵּי גַּבְרַיְיכוּ – **You should be modest before your husband:** לֹא תֵּיכְלוּן נַהֲמָא בְּאַפֵּי גַּבְרַיְיכוּ – **You should not eat bread in your husbands' presence.**[27] לֹא תֵּיכְלוּן יַרְקָא בְּלֵילְיָא – **You should not eat herbs at night.**[28] לֹא תֵּיכְלוּן תַּמְרֵי בְּלֵילְיָא – **You should not eat dates at night,** וְלֹא תִשְׁתּוּן שִׁיכְרָא בְּלֵילְיָא – **nor should you drink beer at night.**[29] וְלֹא תִּיפַּנּוּן הֵיכָא דְּמִפַּנֵּי גַּבְרַיְיכוּ – **And you should not relieve yourselves where your husbands relieve themselves.**[30] וְכִי קָא קָארֵי אַבָּבָא אִינִישׁ – **And when a man is knocking at the door** of your home, לֹא תֵּימְרוּן מַנּוּ – **do not say "who is it"** using the masculine form, אֶלָּא מַנִּי – **but rather "who is it"** using the feminine form.[31]

Rav Chisda then instructed his daughters in how they should act during intimate relations with their husbands: נָקִיט מַרְגָּנִיתָא בְּחַדָא יְדֵיהּ וְכוּרָא בְּחַדָא יְדֵיהּ – When in the course of cohabitation, **[the husbands] will hold your pearl in one hand and the kiln in one hand.**[32] מַרְגָּנִיתָא אַחְוֵי לְהוּ – **You,** however, **should offer them the pearl,** וְכוּרָא לֹא אַחְוֵי לְהוּ עַד דְּמִיצְטַעֲרָן – **but the kiln you should not offer them until they are tormented,** וַהֲדַר אַחְוֵי לְהוּ – **and** only **then should you offer it to them.**[33]

The Mishnah continued: אֵין שׁוֹלִין אֶת הַכַּרְשִׁינִין – WE MAY NOT MAKE VETCHES FLOAT **etc.** [but one may put them into a sieve or into a basket].

The Gemara addresses the Mishnah's permit to place the vetches into a sieve: מַתְנִיתִין דְּלֹא כִּי הַאי תַּנָּא – The ruling of **our Mishnah** does **not** accord with the view of **this** other **Tanna,** דְּתַנְיָא – **for we learned in a Baraisa:** רַבִּי אֱלִיעֶזֶר בֶּן יַעֲקֹב אוֹמֵר – **R' ELIEZER BEN YAAKOV SAYS:** אֵין מַשְׁגִּיחִין בִּכְבָרָה כָּל עִיקָּר – **WE MAY NOT USE A SIEVE AT ALL.**[34]

Mishnah The Mishnah continues to discuss how food for an animal may be moved about: גּוֹרְפִין מִלִּפְנֵי הַפְּטָם – **We may sweep out** a feeding trough **from before a stall ox,**[35] וּמְסַלְּקִין לַצְּדָדִין מִפְּנֵי הָרְעִי – **and we may move** excess fodder **to the sides** of the stall **because of the excrement.**[36] דִּבְרֵי רַבִּי דוֹסָא – These are **the words of R' Dosa.** וַחֲכָמִים אוֹסְרִין – **But the Sages prohibit it.**[37]

NOTES

cleaned more often, it would not last the year (*Meiri*).

Rav Chisda urged Torah scholars to wear respectable clothing as befitting the honor of the Torah in which they are immersed. And here as well, Rav Chisda shows that God provides a means through which even one of little means can obtain fine clothing. For one can purchase an initially expensive linen garment, but, by preserving it through a strict cleaning regimen, actually *save* money over the year, for if he cleans it properly he will not require another linen garment. Rav Chisda "guaranteed" that such a purchase will result in a net gain, not a loss (*Maharal*).

24. That is, the word כִּיתּוּנִיתָא is a compound word derived from the words כִּיתָא נָאָה, which mean "fine fellowship."

25. The residual moisture in a brand new hemp mat ruins the clothes which comes into contact with it (*Rashi;* cf. *Chasam Sofer*). Rav Chisda thus continues with the theme begun in the previous teaching: that Torah scholars should take care that their clothes befit the dignity of their Torah studies (*Maharal*).

26. Perhaps the hostess will see on it stains from a seminal emission, from which she will be repulsed (*Rashi*). This, as well, represents advice that a scholar should take care to protect his own honor, and thereby the honor of the Torah (*Maharal*).

27. Because on occasion you will eat more than you should, and he will be repulsed by that (*Rashi;* see *Ben Yehoyada*).

28. Because it will give your breath an unpleasant odor (*Rashi*).

29. Each of these will cause diarrhea and flatulence (*Rashi*).

30. That is, if you are both in a field, your husbands will be repulsed if they were to see you voiding yourselves before them. Furthermore, instructed Rav Chisda, if you relieve yourselves in the same place that your husbands use [some traces of elimination may remain visible, and] they may [see them and] be repulsed (see *Rashi*).

31. In Hebrew and Aramaic, the question "who is it" can be said in either a masculine form (מַנּוּ, מִי הוּא) or in the feminine form (מַנִּי, מִי הִיא). Rav Chisda, wishing to impress upon his daughters the importance of minimizing conversations with men, told them that even when answering a door, they should call out as though a woman was surely knocking, so as not to become accustomed to using the form of address that would be used in conversation with a man (see *Rashi*).

32. Rav Chisda here teaches his daughters, using very delicate language, the ideal way for them to play their part in intimate relations with their husbands. In referring to their female anatomy, he used the word "pearl" to refer to their breasts, and the word "kiln" to refer to their private parts. Alternatively, the reading is בּוּרָא which means *pit* (*Rashi;* cf. *Ritva MHK* ed.).

[Perhaps a womb is described as a "kiln," such as that which is used to refine precious metals, because a woman's womb receives the male's seed and refines it into a child.]

33. Rav Chisda taught them that when a man engages in foreplay to arouse desire for intercourse, he holds his wife's breasts with one hand and extends his other hand toward her private parts. Rav Chisda advised his daughters, however, to initially offer only their "pearl" to their husbands to arouse their passion, but to delay in offering their "kiln." This temporary denial would lead to heightened desire and affection (*Rashi,* see *Chidushei HaRan;* cf. *Meiri;* see *Chidushei R' Elazar Moshe Horowitz;* see also *Meromei Sadeh*).

This advice was intended to bring about a stronger ejaculation, one more capable of producing children (*Maharal;* see *Rambam* [*Hil. Ishus* 15:18] with *Lechem Mishneh, Maaseh Rokeach* and *Birkei Yosef* to *Even HaEzer* 25:3).

34. The halachah follows the view of the Tanna of our Mishnah (*Chidushei HaRan*; see *Keren Orah*).

35. [A stall ox is an ox that is being fattened for slaughter.] The Mishnah teaches that we may sweep out the cinders and dirt from its feeding trough on the Sabbath so that they will not become mingled with the ox's food, thereby causing the food to be revolting to the ox (*Rashi*).

36. When there is too much straw and fodder before the ox, we may move it aside, lest the ox tread upon the fodder with his feet and soil it with his excrement that is there (*Rashi*).

Others translate the word רְעִי as *a pasture ox.* In their view, the second ruling of the Mishnah teaches that in the case of a pasture ox, which is not as particular as a stall ox, the refuse in the trough may not be swept out completely, just pushed to the side (*Meiri, Ritva MHK* ed., *Chidushei HaRan;* see *Maharatz Chayes,* and *Megadim Chadashim* at length).

37. The Gemara below will explain in which case or cases R' Dosa and the Sages disagree, and the rationale for the Sages' position.

אבל באיבום של קרקע דברי הכל אסור. אע"ג דמרכן שרינן לרבי שמעון (לעיל דף לה.) הכא רגילות הוא להתכוין לאשווי גומות ומיישינן טפי שמא יתכוין: הקש

א משלפו לדידה מקניא שרי קניא ממנה אסור אמר רבא (א) ב ואם כלי קיואי הוא מותר אמר רב חסדא ג האי ג כישתא דירקא אי חזיא למאכל בהמה שרי לטלטולי ואי לא אסיר אמר רב חייא בר אשי אמר רב האי ד תליא דבשרא שרי לטלטולי דכוורי אסיר

אמר רב קטינא העומד באמצע המטה כאילו עומד בבריסה של אשה ולאו מילתא היא ואמר רב חסדא בר בי רב דזבין ירקא ליזבין אריכא כישא כי כישא ואורכא ממילא ואמר רב חסדא בר בי רב דזבין קניא ליזבין אריכא טונא כי טונא ואורכא ממילא ואמר רב חסדא בר בי רב [ד דלא נפישא ליה ריפתא] לא ליכול ירקא משום דגריר ואמר רב חסדא אנא לא בעניותי אכלי ירקא ולא בעתירותי אכלי ירקא בעניותי משום דגריר בעתירותי דאמינא היכא דעייל ירקא ליעול בשרא וכוורי (א) ואמר רב חסדא בר בי רב דלא נפישא ליה ריפתא לא ליבצע בצועי ואמר רב חסדא בר בי רב דלא נפישא ליה ריפתא ה לא ליבצע מ"ט ו דלא עביד בעין יפה ואמר רב חסדא אנא מעיקרא לא הואי בצענא עד דשדאי ידי בכולי מנא ואשכחי [ביה כל צרכי] ואמר רב חסדא האי מאן דאפשר ליה למיכל נהמא דשערי ואכל דחיטי קעבר משום א בל תשחית ואמר רב פפא האי מאן דאפשר למישתי שיכרא ושתי חמרא עובר משום בל תשחית ולאו מילתא היא ו בל תשחית דגופא עדיף ואמר רב חסדא בר בי רב דלית ליה משחא נימשי במיא דהחריצי ואמר רב חסדא בר בי רב דזבין אומצא ליזבין אונקא דאית ביה תלתא מיני בישרא וא"ר חסדא בר בי רב דזבין כיתוניתא ליזבן מדנהר אבא וניחוורה כל תלתין יומין דמפטיא ליה תריסר ירחי שתא ואנא ערבא מאי כיתוניתא כיתא נאה וא"ר חסדא בר בי רב לא ליתיב אציפתא חדתא דמכליא מאניה וא"ר חסדא בר בי רב לא לישדר מאניה לאושפיזיה לחוורויה ליה דלאו אורח ארעא דילמא חזי ביה מידי ואתי למגניא אמר להו רב חסדא לבנתיה תיהוי צניעתן באפי גברייכו לא תיכלון נהמא באפי גברייכו לא תיכלון ירקא בליליא לא תיכלון תמרי בליליא ולא תשתון שיכרא בליליא ולא תיפנון היכא דמפני גברייכו וכי קא קארי אבבא איניש לא תימרון מנו אלא מני נקיט ז מרגניתא בחדא ידיה וכורא בחדא ידיה מרגניתא אחוי להו וכורא לא אחוי להו עד דמיצטער והדר אחוי להו: אין שולין את הכרשינין: ח מתני' דלא כי האי תנא דתניא ר"א בן יעקב אומר אין משגיחין בכברה כל עיקר:

מתני' גורפין מלפני הפטם ומסלקין לצדדין מפני הרעי דברי רבי דוסא וחכמים אוסרין נוטלין מלפני בהמה זו ונותנין לפני בהמה זו בשבת: **גמ'** איבעיא להו רבנן ארישא פליגי או אסיפא פליגי או אתרוייהו פליגי ת"ש דתניא וחכמים אומרים ה אחד זה ואחד זה לא יסלקנו לצדדין אמר רב חסדא מחלוקת באיבום של כלי אבל באיבום של קרקע דברי הכל מותר ואיבום של קרקע מי איכא למאן דשרי הא קא משוי גומות אלא אי איתמר הכי איתמר א"ר חסדא ו מחלוקת באיבום של כלי אבל באיבום של קרקע דברי הכל אסור: ונוטלין מלפני בהמה: תנא חדא נוטלין מלפני בהמה שפיה יפה ונותנין לפני בהמה שפיה רע ותניא אידך נוטלין מלפני בהמה שפיה רע ונותנין לפני בהמה שפיה יפה אמר אביי ז אידי ואידי מקמי חמרא לקמי תורא שקלינן מקמי תורא לקמי חמרא לא שקלינן והא דקתני נוטל מלפני בהמה שפיה יפה בחמור דלית ליה רירי ונותנין לפני בהמה שפיה רע בפרה

משלפא לדידה מקניא. כששוטחין אותה לגגבה תוחבים קנה תבית יד לבית יד וכשנוטלה בשבת ישלפנה מן הקנה ולא הקנה ממנה דלא חזי לטלטולי להסקה קאי: **ואם כלי קיואי היא.** קנה של אורגים דתורת כלי עליו שרי: **תליא דבשרא.** בשר מליח התלוי לייבשו ומלא התבל קרי תליא: **שרי.** דנאכל חי באומצא: **דכוורי.** אין נאכלין חיין: **באמצע מטה.** שאיש ואשתו רגילין בה לישן: **כאילו עומד כו'.** דמהרהר: **ליזבין אריכא.** אגודה ארוכה של כרוב ארוך ושל כרישין ארוכים: **כישא כי כישא.** שכל אגודות הגנין שוות בעובין שלכולן מדה אחת לחבל שהוא אגוד בו: **ואורכא ממילא.** כלומר ארכו של זה שהוא ארוך מחבירו הוא משתכר בו: **קניא.** חבילי קנים לעצים: **לא ליכול ירקא.** ירק חי (ב) כרישין לירפו"ל ושחליים: **משום דגריר ליבא.** ומאכילו לחם הרבה ואין לו: **לא ליבצע בצועי.** מורסיליונ"ט בלע"ז לא יאכל עכשיו מעט פת שימלא לו ולאחר שעה מעט מפני שאין לו דרך שביעה אלא יצרף ויאכל יחד: **מעיקרא.** קודם שנתעשרתי: **עד דשדאי ידי בכולא מנא.** כשהייתי ממשמש בסל ומוצא בו פת הרבה הייתי מברך המוציא: **דלית ליה משחא.** שהיו סכין ידיהן שמן קודם מים אחרונים להעביר את הזוהמא: **במיא דהחריצי.** הנקוים יחד וגדל עליהם ירקרוקית עבה ונוחה כשמן: **אונקא.** צואר: **תלתא מיני בשרא.** יטעום בו ג' מיני מטעמים שמן וכחוש וגיד הצואר: **מדנהר אבא.** מאותו מקום שפשתנו יפה: **דמפטיא ליה תריסר ירחי שתא ואנא ערבא.** אני ערב בדבר שתתקיים לו שנה שלימה ותפטיהו שלא יצטרך לקנות חלוק: **כיתא נאה.** כת נאה ראויה להושיב בעליה בכת נאה: **אציפתא חדתא.** מחצלת חדשה של גמי לח ולחלוחית הגמי מבלה הבגדים: **לאושפיזא.** לפונדקית שלו לא ישלח חלוקו ללבן: **דילמא חזיא בהו.** קרי ומגניא עליה: **לא תיכלון נהמא באפי גברייכו.** פעמים תאכל הרבה ותתגנה עליו: **לא תיכלון ירקא בלילה.** מפני ריח הפה: **שיכרא ותמרי.** משלשלין ומביאין לידי הפחה: **היכא דמפני גברייכו.** בגילוי בפניהם בשדות ואפילו שלא בפניהם שמכיר מקומו ומקומכם ונמאסת' לו בזוכרו: **לא תימרון מנו.** מי הוא לשון זכר לא תרגילו לשונכם לדבר עם זכרים: **אלא מני.** מי היא: **נקיט מרגניתא בחדא ידיה וכורא בחדא ידיה.** כשבעליך ממשמש בך להתאוות לך לתשמיש ואוחז הדדים בידו אחת והאחרת עד אותו מקום: **מרגניתא אחוין ליה.** הדדין המאיאי לו שתתרבה תאותו ומקום תשמיש אל תמציאי לו מהר כדי שיתרבה תאותו ויחבתו ויצטער הדר אחוי ליה: **כורא.** לשון כור צורפין (לעיל דף עח.) לשון אחר כור לשון בור שוחה: **מתניתין.** דקתני אבל נותנין לתוך הכברה: **מתני' גורפין מלפני הפטם.** שור שמפטמין אותו גורפין אבוס שלפניו בשבת לתת לתוכו התבן והשעורין ולא יתערב בהן עפרורית ויקוץ במאכלו: **ומסלקין** תבן (ג) שלפניו לצדדין כשהוא רב כדי שלא ידרסנו ברעי: **וחכמים אוסרים.** מפרש בגמרא אהיא: **ונוטלין מלפני בהמה זו.** שעורין ותבן ונותנין לפני זו ולא אמרינן טלטול דלא חזי הוא אלא ודאי חזי הוא דאין בהמה קצה במאכל הניטל מלפני חבירתה: **גמ' ארישא פליגי.** אגורפין ואסרי לגרוף משום דפעמים שהאבוס של קרקע וקא מכוין לאשווי גומות שלא יפלו השעורים לתוכו: **או אסיפא פליגי.** ומשום דלא חזי שיש בו (ד) שנמאס במדרס רגליו: **תא שמע.** דאתרוייהו פליגי: **אחד זה ואחד זה.** אחד גריפת האבוס ואחד תבן שלפניו לא יסלקנו לצדדין: **של קרקע.** כעין שעושין גדר קטן לפני בהמה ונותנין מאכל לפנים ממנו דאיכא למיחש לאשווי גומות: **מחלוקת באבוס של כלי.** וגזרו רבנן גזרה אטו של קרקע: **שפיה יפה.** לקמיה מפרש: **אידי ואידי.** שתיהן המשניות סבירא להו: **מקמי חמרא לקמי תורא שקלינן.** שאינו מטיל רירין ואין מה שלפניו נמאס ולאו לתוך לפני שור: **מקמי תורא לקמי חמרא לא שקלינן.**

דלית

עין משפט נר מצוה

מא א ב מיי' פכ"ה מהל' שבת הל' יח סמג לאוין סה טוש"ע א"ח סי' שח סעיף מח:

מב ג מיי' פכ"ו מהל' שבת הל' טו סמג שם טוש"ע שם סעיף כ וכח:

מג ד מיי' פ"ז מהל' ברכות הלכה ג:

מד ה ו מיי' פכ"ו מהל' שבת הלכה יט סמג לאוין סה טוש"ע א"ח סי' שכד סעיף טו:

מה ז מיי' שם טוש"ע שם סעיף יד:

רבינו חננאל

רב חסדא דלרכוכי מיכוון ושרי. אמר רב חסדא הא כיתניתא משלפה לדילא מקניא: פי' למשוך הבגד ששוטחו בקנה להנגב ונעשה נגוב וישאר הקנה במקומו. ולא מטלטלין מותר אבל למשוך הקנה מן הבגד ולטלטלו בשבת אסור שהקנה אינו כלי להטלטל בחצר. אמר רבא ואם כלי קיואי מותר. פי' אם הוא הבגד שטוח בכלי האורג וכלי האורג נקראין כלי קיואי כדאמרינן בפרק ואלו קשרים שחייבין עליהן. אתמר אמר רב נחמן אמר שמואל כלי קיואי מותר לטלטלו בשבת ואפי' כובד העליון וכובד התחתון אבל לא את העמודים ותוב בעא מיניה ר' יוחנן מרבי יהודה בר ליואי כלי קיואי כגון כובד העליון וכובד התחתון כו'. האי תלא דבשרא פי' יתד של עץ עשוי לתלות בו בשר ופעמים שתולין בו זולתו [שרי לטלטולי] אבל העץ שתולין בו דגים. כיון שהדגים ריחם רע וקשה אין תולין בו דבר אחר ומסיחין דעתן ממנו ומוקצה מחמת מיאוס הוא ואסור: **מדנהר אבא.** שם מקום הוא: **ציפיתא** חדתא. פי' מחצלת חדשה בורא בחדא ידא. כגון אבן שאין לה דמים ולא צורך. ומפני שהסתירה מהן נתייקרה בעיניהם ופייסוהו להראותה להן: **מתני' אין שולין** את הכרשינין ולא שפין כו' גורפין מלפני הפטם ומסלקין לצדדים כו'. פי' גורפין המאכל של בהמה מלפני הפטם ומאכל שאר בהמות מסלקין לצדדין דברי ר' דוסיא חכמים אוסרין ואיבעיא לן רבנן ארישא פליגי והיא גורפין [או] אסיפא פליגי והוא שמסלקין לצדדין ואמרינן ת"ש וחכ"א אחד זה ואחד זה לא יסלקנו לצדדין. ש"מ רבנן אתרווייהו פליגי. אמר רב חסדא מחלוקת באבוס של כלי ואפי' בזה חכמים אוסרין אבל באבוס של קרקע דברי הכל אסור לגרוף:

מסורת הש"ס

א) [לעיל קיג.], ב) [בערוך איתא הוצא], ג) [עי' תוס' לעיל קלט: ד"ה חלא], ד) [עי' תוס' עירובין נה: ד"ה כל עיר וכו' ונראה דלא גרסי להנך ד' תיבות], ה) ברכות מו:, ו) [לעיל קכט.], ז) [גירס' אחרינא ופירושו עי' בערוך ערך כור א'], ח) צ"ל וכרי.

הגהות הב"ח

(א) גמ' דלא נפישא ליה ריפתא (לא ליבצע וכו' יפה) תא"מ ונ"ב ס"א לא ליבצע בצועי והשאר נמחק. והכי משמע מפירש"י: (ב) רש"י ד"ה לא ליכול ירקא ירק חי. נ"ב עיין פרק כיצד מברכין דף מד בתוס' בד"ה כל עיר: (ג) ד"ה ומסלקין תבן שלפניו לצדדין: (ד) ד"ה או אסיפא וכו' שיש בו מה שנמאס:

תורה אור השלם

א) כִּי תָצוּר אֶל עִיר יָמִים רַבִּים לְהִלָּחֵם עָלֶיהָ לְתָפְשָׂהּ לֹא תַשְׁחִית אֶת עֵצָהּ לִנְדֹּחַ עָלָיו גַּרְזֶן כִּי מִמֶּנּוּ תֹאכֵל וְאֹתוֹ לֹא תִכְרֹת כִּי הָאָדָם עֵץ הַשָּׂדֶה לָבֹא מִפָּנֶיךָ בַּמָּצוֹר: [דברים כ, יט]

ליקוטי רש"י

דכוורי. דגים [תענית כו:]. כישא. אגודה שדרך הירק להיות מתקשר באגודות וכל האגודות הן שוות [קידושין נב:]. דגריר. ממשיך דהלב לתאות רעבון [יומא פג:]. חריצי. מקום כנוס מים גדל עליהם כמין ירקרוקת [לעיל כ:].

נוֹטְלִין מִלִּפְנֵי בְהֵמָה זוֹ וְנוֹתְנִין לִפְנֵי בְהֵמָה זוֹ בְּשַׁבָּת – We may take feed **from before this animal and place it before this** other **animal on the Sabbath.**[38]

Gemara

The Gemara seeks to identify the case that is the subject of the dispute between R' Dosa and the Sages:

אִיבַּעְיָא לְהוּ – They [the students of the academy] inquired: רַבָּנָן אַרֵישָׁא פְּלִיגֵי – Do the Sages dispute the Mishnah's **first clause** and prohibit us to clean out a trough,[39] **אוֹ אַסֵּיפָא פְּלִיגֵי – or do they dispute the** Mishnah's **latter clause** and prohibit us to move feed to the side,[40] **אוֹ אַתַּרְוַיְיהוּ פְּלִיגֵי – or do they dispute both** rulings and prohibit both?[41]

The Gemara answers:

תָּא שְׁמַע – Come, learn an answer, **דְּתַנְיָא – for it was taught in a Baraisa** as follows: **וַחֲכָמִים אוֹמְרִים – BUT THE SAGES SAY: אֶחָד זֶה וְאֶחָד זֶה לֹא יְסַלְּקֶנּוּ לַצְּדָדִין – BOTH THIS** (dirt in a trough) **AND THIS** (feed before it becomes ruined) **MAY NOT BE MOVED TO THE SIDE.** Clearly, then, the Sages dispute R' Dosa in both of the Mishnah's clauses.

The Gemara explains the first dispute between R' Dosa and the Sages:

אָמַר רַב חִסְדָּא – Rav Chisda said: מַחֲלוֹקֶת בְּאֵיבוּס שֶׁל קַרְקַע – The dispute between R' Dosa and the Sages **concerns a trough** whose floor is made **of earth;**[42] R' Dosa permits one to sweep it out while the Sages prohibit it. **אֲבָל בְּאֵיבוּס שֶׁל כְּלִי דִּבְרֵי הַכֹּל מוּתָּר – But in a** case of a **trough which is a utensil, all agree that it is permitted** to sweep it out.

The Gemara asks:

וְאֵיבוּס שֶׁל קַרְקַע מִי אִיכָּא לְמַאן דְּשָׁרֵי – But does anyone permit sweeping out a trough whose floor is made **of earth? הָא קָא מַשְׁוֵי גּוּמוֹת – Why,** there is definitely the concern that **he will** probably **even out crevices,** which is a Biblical violation! **אֶלָּא אִי אִיתְּמַר הָכִי אִיתְּמַר – Rather, if [an explanation]** of the dispute **was said, this is what was said: אָמַר רַב חִסְדָּא – Rav Chisda said: מַחֲלוֹקֶת בְּאֵיבוּס שֶׁל כְּלִי – The dispute** between R' Dosa and the Sages **concerns a trough which is a utensil;** R' Dosa permits one to sweep it out while the Sages prohibit it. **אֲבָל בְּאֵיבוּס שֶׁל קַרְקַע דִּבְרֵי הַכֹּל אָסוּר – But in a** case of a **trough** whose floor is made **of earth, all agree that it is prohibited** to sweep it out.[43]

The Mishnah continued:

וְנוֹטְלִין מִלִּפְנֵי בְהֵמָה – AND WE MAY TAKE feed **FROM BEFORE [THIS] ANIMAL** and place it before this other animal on the Sabbath.

The Gemara cites a pair of related Baraisos:

תָּנָא חֲדָא – One Baraisa taught: נוֹטְלִין מִלִּפְנֵי בְהֵמָה שֶׁפִּיהָ יָפֶה – WE MAY TAKE feed **FROM BEFORE THIS ANIMAL WHICH HAS A FINE MOUTH, וְנוֹתְנִין לִפְנֵי בְהֵמָה שֶׁפִּיהָ רַע – AND PLACE IT BEFORE AN ANIMAL WITH A POOR MOUTH.**[44] **וְתַנְיָא אִידָךְ – And it was taught** in another Baraisa: **נוֹטְלִין מִלִּפְנֵי בְהֵמָה שֶׁפִּיהָ רַע – WE MAY TAKE** feed **FROM BEFORE THIS ANIMAL WHICH HAS A POOR MOUTH, וְנוֹתְנִין לִפְנֵי בְהֵמָה שֶׁפִּיהָ יָפֶה – AND PLACE IT BEFORE AN ANIMAL WITH A FINE MOUTH.**

The Gemara immediately explains these two Baraisos:

אָמַר אַבַּיֵי – Abaye said: אִידִי וְאִידִי – Both this Baraisa **and that** Baraisa maintain **מַקַּמֵּי חֲמָרָא לְקַמֵּי תּוֹרָא שָׁקְלִינַן – that we may take** feed **from before a donkey to place before an ox, מִקַּמֵּי תּוֹרָא לְקַמֵּי חֲמָרָא לֹא שָׁקְלִינַן – but we may not take** feed **from before an ox to place before a donkey.**[45]

Abaye continues, explaining the phraseology of each Baraisa:

וְהָא דְּקָתָנֵי – And when the first **Baraisa taught: נוֹטֵל מִלִּפְנֵי בְהֵמָה שֶׁפִּיהָ יָפֶה – WE MAY TAKE** feed **FROM BEFORE THIS ANIMAL WHICH HAS A FINE MOUTH, בַּחֲמוֹר דְּלֵית לֵיהּ רִירֵי – it referred to a donkey, which does not drool** into its feed; it is thus said to have a "fine" mouth. **וְנוֹתְנִין לִפְנֵי בְהֵמָה שֶׁפִּיהָ רַע – And when** the Baraisa taught: **AND PLACE IT BEFORE AN ANIMAL WITH A POOR MOUTH, בְּפָרָה – it referred to an ox,**[46]

NOTES

38. I.e. we may take away feed from before one animal and place it before another. Since one animal will eat the leftovers of another, moving the feed from one trough to another is a useful activity and therefore permissible (*Rashi*); it is not considered an excessive exertion, which is sometimes forbidden on the Sabbath (see *Meiri* and see also below, 155a). *Yerushalmi* explains the Mishnah as referring to two animals of the same breed, such as two oxen or two donkeys, for they will eat each other's leftovers (see *Ben Uri*); the Gemara below will discuss other cases.

39. One will sometimes sweep a feeding-trough that has an earthen floor (see below, note 43) with the added intent to smooth loose earth into any crevices in the trough floor, so as to prevent wheat kernels from falling there. Doing so is Biblically prohibited as a form of *building* (see *Tosafos;* see also above, 95a). According to this interpretation of the dispute between R' Dosa and the Sages, the issue in question is whether there is a concern that one will come to level the floor of the trough; see below, notes 42-43.

40. And they prohibit moving the feed because there is surely mixed therein some feed which was already trampled and rendered unusable, and thus *muktzeh* (*Rashi;* cf. *Meiri*).

[For explanations of why sweeping dirt from the trough presents no problem of *muktzeh,* while moving unusable feed does present this problem, see *Sfas Emes* and *Ohr HaChamah.*]

41. For the unrelated reasons enumerated in the two previous notes.

42. I.e. the trough was simply a low enclosure that was built on the ground within which the feed was placed (*Rashi;* see next note).

43. Thus, both R' Dosa and the Sages agree that one may not sweep out a feeding-trough that has an earthen floor. This is prohibited because while doing so one may come to intentionally even out any irregularities in the floor, violating the *melachah* of *building* (see *Rashi* and *Tosafos;* cf. *Ran* fol. 58b and *Hagagos HaBach* there §9). The Mishnah, however, is discussing a trough which is a utensil [i.e. its floor is one piece with its walls, in which the Biblically prohibited *melachah* cannot take place, since there is no earthen floor to even out]. The Sages would prohibit sweeping out even such a trough for fear that people would fail to distinguish between a trough that is a utensil and an earthen-floored trough. R' Dosa sees no reason to prohibit it, for he does not subscribe to this concern (see *Rashi*).

44. These terms will be defined in the Gemara below.

45. Although the two Baraisos seem to be saying two different laws, Abaye explains that both of them are really teaching the same thing: that it is permitted to take food from a donkey to put before an ox [but not vice versa]. The Gemara will explain how both Baraisos state this law, each using different terminology to say the same thing. See also *Meiri.*

46. [Literally: to a cow.]

דְּאִית לָהּ רִירֵי – **which drools** into its feed. Its mouth is thus "poor" in that it emits something repulsive. The Baraisa's ruling is thus understood: Since the donkey does not drool into his feed, his leftovers are not *muktzeh* and may be placed before an ox. But an ox's leftovers are ruined by its drool and thus rendered *muktzeh,* and may not be placed before a donkey. וְהָא דְּקָתָנֵי נוֹטְלִין מִלִּפְנֵי בְהֵמָה שֶׁפִּיהָ רַע – **And when the second Baraisa teaches: WE MAY TAKE** feed **FROM BEFORE THIS ANIMAL WHICH HAS A POOR MOUTH,** בַּחֲמוֹר דְּלֹא דָּיֵיק וְאָכִיל – **it refers to a donkey, which is not a discriminating eater.**[1] Its mouth is referred to as "poor" because it will eat even virtually inedible thorns and thistles. וְנוֹתְנִין לִפְנֵי בְהֵמָה שֶׁפִּיהָ יָפֶה – And when that Baraisa taught: **AND PLACE IT BEFORE AN ANIMAL WITH A FINE MOUTH,** בְּפָרָה דְּדָיְיקָא וְאָכְלָה – **it refers to an ox, which is a discriminating eater.** Its mouth is referred to as "fine" in that it will take in only unsullied foods. In the final analysis, however, both Baraisos are teaching the same ruling: We may move the leftovers of a donkey and place them before an ox, but not vice versa.[2]

Mishnah The next Mishnah first deals with the proper methods of moving *muktzeh* items when this is permitted:

הַקַּשׁ שֶׁעַל גַּבֵּי הַמִּטָּה – **Straw that is on a bed,**[3] לֹא יְנַעְנְעֶנּוּ בְיָדוֹ – **one may not move it with his hand,**[4] אֶלָּא מְנַעְנְעוֹ בְגוּפוֹ – **but he may move it with his body.**[5] וְאִם הָיָה מַאֲכַל בְּהֵמָה – **And if [the straw] was animal feed,**[6] אוֹ שֶׁהָיָה עָלָיו כַּר אוֹ סָדִין – **or if there was a pillow or sheet on it** from before the beginning of the Sabbath, מְנַעְנְעוֹ בְיָדוֹ – **he may move [the straw]** even **with his hand.**[7]

The Mishnah now deals with an unrelated Sabbath law:

מַכְבֵּשׁ שֶׁל בַּעֲלֵי בָתִּים מַתִּירִין – **We may release a householder's press**[8] to remove a garment held therein,[9] אֲבָל לֹא כוֹבְשִׁין – **but we may not** initially **press it down** on a garment on the Sabbath.[10] וְשֶׁל כּוֹבְסִין לֹא יִגַּע בּוֹ – **And we may not touch a launderer's** press, even to release it.[11] רַבִּי יְהוּדָה אוֹמֵר – **R' Yehudah says:** אִם הָיָה מוּתָּר מֵעֶרֶב שַׁבָּת – **If it was** partially **released from before the Sabbath,**[12] מַתִּיר אֶת כּוּלּוֹ וְשׁוֹמְטוֹ – **one may release it completely** on the Sabbath **and remove [the garment]** held therein.

NOTES

1. *Rashi;* cf. *Rashash.*

2. Thus, the first Baraisa refers to a donkey as an animal with a fine mouth, because it does not drool into its food, and the second Baraisa refers to it as an animal that has a poor mouth because it is not a discriminating eater (*Rashi*). [The second Baraisa adds the additional point that an ox will eat a donkey's leftovers, *even though an ox is a discriminating eater,* because the donkey does not drool into its feed. And a donkey will *not* eat an ox's leftovers, *even though a donkey is a less discriminating eater,* since the ox surely drooled into it (see *Ohr HaChamah*). One ox, however, will eat the leftovers of another ox, and the fact that another ox ate from it will not deter it.]

3. Straw is usually used for kindling. Since this is a use forbidden on the Sabbath, the straw is *muktzeh* (*Ritva MHK* ed.). In this case, a person wishes to move the straw about in order to fluff it up, making it softer and more comfortable to lie on (*Rashi, Rosh* [3:19]; cf. *Ran* [fol. 20b, to Gemara 43b]; see also *Ohr HaChamah*).

4. Since it is *muktzeh,* one may not move it with his hand (*Rashi*).

5. I.e. [while lying down on the bed] he may shift his shoulders, causing the straw to move. Since he moves the straw in an unusual fashion (with his body rather than his hands) it is regarded as טִלְטוּל מִן הַצַּד, *an indirect movement of muktzeh,* which is permissible (*Rashi*).

An apparent difficulty: The halachah is that indirect movement of *muktzeh* is permitted only when it is done for the sake of a non-*muktzeh* object, e.g. to facilitate the use of a non-*muktzeh* object. It is, however, prohibited to move a *muktzeh* object even indirectly for the sake of the *muktzeh* object itself, i.e. to utilize or protect the *muktzeh* object. In our Mishnah (as explained by *Rashi;* cf. *Ran* cited in note 3), where the straw is being moved to make the straw itself into a more comfortable mattress, one is moving the *muktzeh* object to better utilize the *muktzeh* object itself. This, as explained above, should be prohibited even through indirect movement!

To resolve this difficulty, *Rosh* (3:19; see *Orach Chaim* 311:8 and *Magen Avraham* 311:24 with *Machatzis HaShekel*) distinguishes between טִלְטוּל מִן הַצַּד, *indirect movement* (during which a *muktzeh* object is moved indirectly by directly moving a non-*muktzeh* object with one's hands), and an even less direct means of moving a *muktzeh* object known as טִלְטוּל בְּגוּפוֹ, *moving muktzeh with one's body,* in which any movement of the *muktzeh* item is performed by way of any part of the body other than one's hands. Such movement, explains *Rosh,* has even more lenient rules than indirect movement of *muktzeh.* While the latter is permitted only for the sake of a non-*muktzeh* object, the former is permitted even for the sake of a *muktzeh* object. [According to this explanation, when *Rashi* refers to טִלְטוּל מִן הַצַּד, *indirect movement of muktzeh,* when explaining the reason why moving the straw is permitted in the case of the Mishnah, he means to say that it is permitted because it is טִלְטוּל בְּגוּף, *moving muktzeh with one's body.*]

[This is the origin of the custom permitting the movement of *muktzeh* with one's foot (see notes of *R' Akiva Eiger* on *Magen Avraham* 279:9 who places certain restrictions on this rule). Cf. *Chazon Ish* 47:12-14; but see also the *Hagahos* of *R' Shlomo Zalman Auerbach* in *Shemiras Shabbos KeHilchasah* p. 558.]

6. I.e. if the straw had been designated for use as animal fodder prior to the Sabbath, it is not *muktzeh.*

7. By placing a pillow or a sheet over the straw, the person indicates his intention to use it as a mattress. Thus, it is no longer set aside for kindling but acquires the status of a utensil (mattress), and it is not *muktzeh* (*Rashi;* see also *Mishnah Berurah* 311:33).

This special designation is required only in places where straw is usually used for kindling. In countries where straw is usually used for fodder or bedding, it is not *muktzeh* even if it was not specifically designated as such (*Magen Avraham* 308:53).

8. The press was composed of two long, heavy boards. Garments were laid out on the lower board, and the upper one was then lowered upon them to press them. To secure the press, four posts were set at the four corners of the lower boards. The posts passed through four corresponding holes in the upper boards, and the upper boards would move up and down along these posts. When the upper board was pressed down into place, pegs were inserted into specially placed holes in the posts, and they would hold the upper boards down (*Rashi*).

9. I.e. we may release the press [by removing the holding pegs] to remove the garments for Sabbath wear (*Rashi*).

10. Pressing the garments prepares them for use after the Sabbath (*Rashi*) for they would not be ready for use on the Sabbath. Thus, pressing it down would constitute preparation for the upcoming week. [Since the pressing was achieved through pressure alone without added heat, the boards needed to be held in place for some time.] Cf. *Meiri;* see also *Rashash* and *Sfas Emes.*

11. Since this press is made to shape and form creases in clothing, its boards are pressed together very tightly. Releasing it is therefore (Rabbinically) considered akin to *demolishing* (*Rashi;* see *Hagahos R' Simchah of Dessau,* but see *Yerushalmi,* cited by *Ben Uri*).

Some Rishonim rule that even if the press is already released, one may not handle it. Since it is used for professional work, and may be damaged by using it for other purposes, it is regarded as *muktzeh due to fear of monetary loss* (*Rambam, Hil. Shabbos* 26:12). This accords well with the Mishnah's language "we may not touch it," for *any* contact with it is prohibited. [For how *Rashi* might explain this phrase, see next note.]

12. I.e. if it was partially undone before the Sabbath, one may release it completely on the Sabbath, even though it was still partially fastened (see also *Meiri*).

[There is a question whether the Tanna Kamma is in dispute with R' Yehudah in this case. If the Tanna Kamma prohibited opening a press

דאית לה רירי והא דקתני נוטלין מלפני בהמה שפיה רע בחמור דלא דייק ואכיל ונותנין לפני בהמה שפיה יפה בפרה דדייקא ואכלה: מתני׳ (א) הקש שעל גבי המטה לא ינענענו בידו אלא מנענעו בגופו ואם היה מאכל בהמה או שהיה עליו כר או סדין מנענעו בידו ב מכבש של בעלי בתים מתירין אבל לא כובשין ושל כובסין לא יגע בו ר' יהודה אומר אם היה מותר מע"ש מתיר את כולו ושומטו: גמ׳ ג) אמר רב נחמן האי פוגלא מלמעלה למטה שרי מלמטה למעלה אסיר אמר רב אדא בר אבא אמרי בי רב תנינא דלא כרב נחמן הקש שע"ג המטה לא ינענענו בידו אבל מנענעו בגופו ואם היה מאכל בהמה או שהיה עליו כר או סדין מנענעו בידו ש"מ ג טלטול מן הצד לא שמיה טלטול ש"מ אמר רב ד) יהודה הני פלפלי מידק חדא חדא בקתא דסכינא שרי תרתי אסיר רבא אמר ד כיון דמשני אפילו טובא נמי ו) אמר רב יהודה ה מאן דסחי במיא לינגיב נפשיה ברישא והדר ליסליק דילמא אתי לאתויי ד' אמות בכרמלית אי הכי כי קא נחית נמי קא דחי כחו ד' אמות ואסיר ז) כחו בכרמלית לא גזרו אמר אביי ואיתימא רב יהודה טיט שע"ג רגלו מקנחו בקרקע ואין מקנחו בכותל אמר רבא מ"ט בכותל לא משום דמיחזי כבונה הא בנין חקלאה הוא אלא אמר רבא ו מקנחו בכותל ואין מקנחו בקרקע דילמא אתי לאשוויי גומות איתמר מר בריה דרבינא אמר אחד זה ואחד זה אסור רב פפא אמר אחד זה ואחד זה מותר למר בריה דרבינא במאי מקנחי ליה מקנחי ליה בקורה ז) אמר רבא (א) ז לא ליתיב איניש אפומיה דליחייא דילמא מיגנדרא ליה חפץ ואתי לאתויי ואמר רבא ח לא ליצדד איניש כובא (ג) דילמא אתי לאשוויי גומות ואמר רבא ט לא ליהדוק איניש אודרא בפומא דשישא • דילמא אתי לידי סחיטה אמר רב כהנא י טיט שע"ג בגדו מכסכסו מבפנים ואין מכסכסו מבחוץ מיתיבי טיט שע"ג מנעלו מגררו בגב סכין [א] ושעל בגדו מגררו בצפורן ובלבד שלא יכסכם מאי לאו שלא יכסכם כלל לא שלא יכסכם מבחוץ אלא מבפנים א"ר אבהו א"ר אלעזר אמר ר' ינאי מגררין מנעל חדש אבל לא ישן

במה

רש"י

דאית לה רירי. ואמאיס והא דקרי לה הכא פיה יפה והכא פיה רע למפרע ואזיל פיה יפה דלית ליה רירי פיה רע דלא דייק ואכיל שאוכל קוצים וברקנים: מתני׳ הקש שעל המטה. וסתמא להסקה ומוקצה הוא ובא לשכב עליו ומנענעו כדי שיהא לף ורך לשכב: לא ינענענו בידו. דמוקצה הוא: אבל מנענעו בגופו. בכתפיו וטלטול מן הצד הוא דלא שמיה טלטול: או שהיה עליו כר או סדין. דגלי דעתיה דאקצייה לשכיבה מעתה תורת כלי עליו: מכבש. פירש"י שני לווחים ארוכים וכבדים וסודרין בגדים על התחתון ומורידין העליון עליו וכובשים את הבגדים על ידי יתדות שיש עמודים קבועין מנוקבין בארבע הפיאות של התחתונות והעליונה מנוקבת בארבע זוויותיה ועולה ויורדת בעמודים וכפי מה שהוא רוצה לכבוש מורידה ותוחב יתד בנקב העמוד ואינה יכולה לעלות: מתירין. את המכבש שנוטל את היתד והוא ניתר דהיינו צורך שבת שנוטל את הכלים: אבל לא כובשין. דהיינו צורך חול: ושל כובסין לא יגע בו. מפני שהוא עשוי לתקן הבגדים ותוחבו בחזקה ומיהדק והתרה שלו דומה לסתירה: גמ׳ האי פוגלא. כגון שטומנין בקרקע להתקיים בשבת לחלוף מלמעלה למטה שרי אם היה ראשה מלמעלה ועוקרה מלמטה ומוליכה מראשה העבה תחילה ועוקרה נמשך אחריה מותר לפי שהגומא רחבה מלמעלה ואין מזיזין הקרקע כשהוא שומטה אבל אם מוליכה מלמטה למעלה שתחתונה נתון למעלה וראש עליונה שהוא נתון למטה והוא שומטה מקופה לראשה אסור לפי שהגומא קצרה מלמעלה וכשהוא מוליכה מזיז העפר ומטלטלו ואע"ג דטלטול מן הצד הוא שמיה טלטול ואסור: תנינא דלא כר"נ. דאילו ממתניתין שמעינן דלא שמיה טלטול דקתני מנענעו בגופו: מידק. דייק: חדא חדא. לאו טוחן הוא אלא כלאחר יד: דקמשני. שלא כרחים ושלא במדוכה: לאתויי ד' אמות. מים שעליו: קא דחי כחו. את המים ד' אמות: אחד זה ואחד זה אסור. זה משום בונה וזה משום אשווי גומות: אחד זה ואחד זה מותר. אין לדבר מתכוין בכך וקי"ל כר"ש: בקורה. בעץ המוטל על הקרקע (ג): אפומא דליחייא. של מבוי דליכא הכירא: אודרא. מוכין שסותמין בהן פי הפך: שישא. פך: מכסכסו. משפשפו: מבפנים. דלא מוכחא מילתא לאיתחזויי כמלבן • ומלבן ממש לא הוי דאין נותן שם מים: כסכוס דמי למכבס: אבל לא ישן. שקולפו והוי ממחק:

תוספות

הקש שע"ג המטה. בריש פרק כירה (דף לו:) פי' מה הוא קש: הני פלפלי מידק חדא כו'. פירש ר"ח ט) בשאלתות דרב אחאי בפרשת אמור אל הכהנים מפרש דבי"ט מיירי וקשה לר' דהוה ליה לפרש בהדיא כיון דבמכילתין לא מיירי אלא בשבת ועוד היכי אסר רב יהודה כולי האי בפלפלין הא אפילו מלח שרינא בפ"ק דביצה (ד' יד.) במדוך של עץ אלא נראה לרבי דהכא בשבת איירי ואגב דאיירי בטלטול ע"י שינוי מייתי ליה הכא וכולה שמעתא נמי מייתי מילי דשבת טובא אע"ג דלא שייכן הכא כולי האי אבל בי"ט נראה לר"י דשרי בלא שינוי אפי' במדוך של אבן כשאר תבלין דתנן בפ"ק דביצה (שם) ב"ה אומר תבלין נדוכין במדוך של אבן והמלח במדוך של עץ ואמרי' בגמרא דכ"ע מלח בעי שינוי מ"ט רב הונא ורב חסדא חד אמר כל הקדרות כולן צריכות מלח ואין כל הקדרות צריכות תבלין וחד אמר כולן מפיגין טעמן ומלח אין מפיגה טעמה מאי בינייהו איכא בינייהו דידע מאי בעי בשולי (ד) אי נמי מוריקא פירוש מוריקא אינה מפיגה טעמה ולמ"ד משום הפגת טעם אסור ולמ"ד משום כל הקדרות כו' שרי א"כ פלפלין דהכא נמי שרי דאין כל הקדרות צריכות פלפלין וא"כ (ס"א ואי נמי) למ"ד נמי משום הפגת טעם פלפלין שרו דצריך לומר נמי שמפיגים טעמם מדלא קאמר איכא בינייהו פלפלין ומיהו אומר רבי דאין זה דקדוק שצריך לפרש שם בע"א דקשיא למ"ד דשרי מוריקא משום דאין כל הקדרות צריכות מוריקא א"כ יהא מותר לקוצרו ולתולשו מן המחובר אע"כ צריך לפרש יש בו הפגת טעם ולא כשאר תבלין להכי שרי למ"ד אין כל הקדרות כו' כיון דאיכא נמי קצת הפגת טעמא והשתא אתי שפיר לקוצר אסור והשתא אין ראיה להתיר פלפלין דשמא אין בהם הפגת טעם כלל ומיהו אומר ר"י דע"כ הם מפיגין טעמם דתנן בפ"ב דביצה (ד' כג.) ג' דברים רבי אלעזר בן עזריה מתיר וחכמים אוסרין שוחקין את הפלפלין ברחים שלהן והיכי הוה שרי רבי אלעזר בן עזריה אי לא מפיגין טעמא ואין סברא לומר דבהא פליגי רבי אלעזר בן עזריה ורבנן דמר סבר דמפיגין טעמא ומר סבר אין מפיגין טעמא אלא מדשרי ר' אלעזר בן עזריה ש"מ דמפיגין טעמא ורבנן דאסרי משום דברחים שלהם מיחזי טפי כי עובדא דחול ועוד תניא בהדיא בתוספתא דביצה בתר פלוגתא דבית שמאי ובית הלל הפלפלין כתבלין על כן נראה לר"י דמותר לכתוש פלפלין ביום טוב אפילו במדוך של אבן ומיהו היכא דידע מאי קדרה בעי בשולי אסור במדוך של אבן דלא ידענא כמאן הלכתא ואזלינן לחומרא ולא שייך למימר בשל סופרים הלך אחר המיקל היכא דאם הוא קולא בדבר אחד חומרא הוא בדבר אחר מיהו במדוך של עץ ממ"נ שרי אפי' במדוכה של אבן כעין שלנו שקורין מורטי"ר כיון שהמדוך של עץ דלא אסרינן התם היכא דידע מאי קדרה בעי בשולי אלא בלא שינוי ושומין הנדוכים בי"ט נראה לר"י דשרי אפי' ידע מאי קדרה בעי בשולי לפי שמפיגין טעמן יותר מדאי ושרי מידי דהוי אשוחט ומבשל דשרי לכ"ע אפילו יודע מאי קדרה בעי בשולי דנראה הוא דהפגת טעם היינו שתש כח התבלין ואינם חדין כל כך ויכול לתקן הדבר כשמרבה התבלין אבל הפגת טעם שומין אין יכול לתקן מידי דהוה אשוחט ואופה ומבשל וגם רוח רעה שורה עליהן [נדה יז.] אם דכן מערב י"ט (ה) אפילו במדוך של אבן או של ברזל שרי ועוד דאין נראה שיהו בכלל תבלין דלא מיקרי תבלין אלא ירקות כעין כמון אבל שומין ובצלים אינם בכלל תבלין ט):

דילמא אתי לאשוויי גומות. אע"ג דרבא ס"ל בסוף פ"ב דביצה (ד' כג.) בדבר שאין מתכוין כר"ש גזרינן הכא כשיהא עסוק לקנח רגלו ישכח שבת ויתכוין לאשוויי גומות כעין שמצינו בפ' בתרא דעירובין (ד' קד.) דנשים המשחקות באגוזים ובתפוחים אסור דילמא אתי לאשוויי גומות כלומר במתכוין שמשכחת שבת מחמת שחוק שלהן: אודרא אפומא דשישא. פי' בפ' ח' שרצים (לעיל ד' קיא:) [בד"ה האי מסוכרייתא שם ע"א]:

במנעל

מסורת הש"ס

א) לעיל נ., ב) [לעיל דף מג: קכג.], ד) [ברא"ש ביצה פ"א סי' כה איתא רב הונא], ה) [נ"ל ואמר], ו) [לעיל קג. קמז.], ז) לקמן קמח:, ח) ביצה ל., ח) [נ"ל וכן בשאלתות], ט) [וע"ע תוס' ביצה יד. ד"ה בית הלל].

הגהות הב"ח

(א) גמ' אמר רבא (לא ליתיב איניש) תא"מ ונ"ב גי' אלפסי לא לישתמש איניש וע"ל בדף קמח: (ב) שם כובא בארעא דילמא: (ג) רש"י ד"ה בקורה וכו' הקרקע הס"ד ואח"כ מ"ה לא ליצדד לא ליצדדנה להושיבה הס"ד: (ד) תוס' ד"ה הני וכו' מאי בעי בשולים. למ"ד משום כל הקדרות כו' אסור ולמ"ד משום הפגת טעם שרי אי נמי מוריקא וכו' א"כ פלפלין לא הוי בכל הקדרות: (ה) בא"ד מערב יו"ט הלכך אפי' במדוך:

גליון הש"ס

גמ' דילמא אתי לידי סחיטה. עיין לקמן דף קמה ע"א תוס' ד"ה כבשים: רש"י ד"ה מכבשים וכו' ומלבן ממש לא הוי דאין נותן שם מים. עיין לקמן דף קמו ריש ע"ב ברש"י ד"ה מיג מטפח ול"ע:

הגהות הגר"א

[א] גמ' ושעל בגדו מגררו בצפורן. נ"ב וכ"ש בגב סכין:

ליקוטי רש"י

הקש. שממיה לטינא קאי לבנים או להסקה ומוקצה הוא ולא יהב דעתיה עליה לשכב עליו ובא לשכב עליו והולך ומנענעו לשכיבה שלא יהא נכזר וקשה. לא ינענענו בידו. שאסור לטלטלו. אלא מנענעו בגופו. כלאחר יד. או שהיה עליו כר או סדין. שהקצה עליו מבעוד יום ואף על פי שלא יחדו לכך ולא חישב עליו [לעיל נ.]. פוגלא. כגון שטמניה בארץ ונתגלה ראשו. מלמעלה למטה שרי. אם היה העליון שלה למעלה ומושכו. מלמטה למעלה אסור. שמזיז עפר לפי שהגומא קצרה מלמעלה והוה ליה טלטול מן הצד. קתא. בית יד הסכין [שבועות מג:]. קתא. בית יד [לקמן קמח.]. אפומיה דליחייא. לפי שאינו ניכר כל כך בין מבוי לרשות הרבים [לקמן קמח.]. דליחייא. לחי המבוי בשבת. דילמא מיגנדרא ליה חפץ. ואתי לאתויי. מסך המתגלגל חוץ לארבע אמות [לקמן שם]. מתוך שאינו במבוי מקורה להכיר שזה רשות הרבים וזה רשות היחיד ומביאו [ביצה שם]. כובא. גיגית [ב"מ כה.]. לאשוויי גומות. דמלאכה הוא בשבת דהוי בונה [עירובין קד.]. מכסכסו. משפשף לזה על זה [שם]. בין שתי ידיו לדבר המכבס בגדים שכופף לזה עם זה ומשפשף ומוליך ומביא [נדה סב.].

עין משפט נר מצוה

מו א מיי' פכ"ה מהל' שבת הלכה כב סמג לאוין סה טוש"ע או"ח סי' שיא סעיף ח:
מז ב מיי' פכ"ו שם הל' יג סמג שם טוש"ע או"ח סי' שב סעיף ד:
מח ג מיי' פכ"ה שם הל' יד טו סמג שם טוש"ע או"ח סי' שיא סעיף ח:
מט ד מיי' פכ"א שם הלכה כ סמג שם טוש"ע או"ח סי' שכא סעיף ז:
נ ה מיי' פט"ו שם הל' כב סמג שם טוש"ע או"ח סימן שכו סעיף ז:
נא ו מיי' פכ"א שם הל' ב סמג שם טוש"ע או"ח סימן שב סעיף ו:
נב ז מיי' פי"ז שם הל' יז טוש"ע או"ח סי' שסה סעיף ה:
נג ח טוש"ע או"ח סי' שלז סעיף ד:
נד ט מיי' פכ"ב שם הלכה טו סמג שם טוש"ע שם סי' שכ סעיף טז:
נה י מיי' פכ"ב שם הלכה יז סמג שם טוש"ע או"ח סי' שב סעיף ז:

רבינו חננאל

הקש שע"ג המטה לא ינענעו בידו אבל מנענעו בגופו: אמר רב נחמן האי פוגלא מלמעלה למטה שרי ממטה למעלה אסור. יש מי שאומרים לא יגררה ויש מי שאומרים מותר לגררה ממעלה וכבר פירשנו דברי רב נחמן בפרק כל הכלים. אמר רב יהודה [הני] פלפלי [מידק] חדא חדא בקתא דסכינא שרי למידק. פי' ביו"ט אבל בלדכן אסור דהא אין מפיגין טעמן והוה ליה למידק מעיו"ט. רבא אמר כיון דמשני אפי' טובא והלכתא כרבא ביו"ט ויש מי שמתיר כי האי גוונא אפי' בשבת: טיט שע"ג רגליו הלכתא כמר בריה דרבנא דאסר בין בקרקע ובין בכותל ולא שרי אלא בקורה בלבד. ואמר רבא לא לצדד איניש כובא בארעא דלא אתו לאשויי גומות ואמר רבא לא ליהדוק איניש אודרא בפומא דשישא דילמא אתו לידי סחיטה. פי' לא ידחוק אדם מוכין שרויין בפי אשישה שמא יבא לידי סחיטה טיט שעל בגדו מכסכסו מבפנים ואין מכסכסו מבחוץ או מגררו בצפורן כססו כבר פירשנוהו למעלה. וכל אלו שאמר רבא אסור אחד בשבת ואחד ביו"ט לא שנא וגירור

רב נסים גאון

טיט שעל גבי מנעל איכא חספא דרבא משכחת לה בפרק כל הכלים ניטלין בשבת (דף קכב) רבא הוה קאזיל בריסתקא במחוזא איתווס מסאניה בטינא אתא שמעיה שקל חספא וקא מכפר ליה:

Gemara The Gemara cites a *muktzeh*-related ruling that it will proceed to challenge from our Mishnah:

אָמַר רַב נַחְמָן – **Rav Nachman said:** הַאי פּוּגְלָא – **Concerning this radish** that had been plucked and then buried in the ground to ripen, but is partially exposed, מִלְמַעְלָה לְמַטָּה שְׁרֵי – if it is lying **right side up, it is permitted** to grasp the exposed part and lift the radish out of the ground, מִלְּמַטָּה לְמַעְלָה אָסִיר – but if it is **upside down, it is forbidden.**[13]

It is apparent that Rav Nachman forbids even the indirect movement of *muktzeh.* The Gemara challenges this view from our Mishnah:

אָמַר רַב אַדָּא בַּר (אַבָּא) [אַהֲבָה][14] – **Rav Adda bar Ahavah said:** אָמְרֵי בֵּי רַב – **The scholars of the academy said:** תְּנֵינָא דְּלָא כְּרַב נַחְמָן – **We have already learned a Mishnah that is not in accord with Rav Nachman:** הַקַּשׁ שֶׁעַל גַּבֵּי הַמִּטָּה לֹא יְנַעְנְעוֹ בְּיָדוֹ – STRAW THAT IS ON A BED, ONE MAY NOT MOVE IT WITH HIS HAND, אֲבָל מְנַעְנְעוֹ בְגוּפוֹ – BUT HE MAY MOVE IT WITH HIS BODY. וְאִם הָיָה מַאֲכַל בְּהֵמָה – AND IF THE STRAW WAS ANIMAL FEED, אוֹ שֶׁהָיָה עָלָיו כַּר אוֹ סָדִין – OR IF THERE WAS A PILLOW OR SHEET ON IT, מְנַעְנְעוֹ בְּיָדוֹ – HE MAY MOVE [THE STRAW] even WITH HIS HAND. שְׁמַע מִינָּהּ טִלְטוּל מִן הַצַּד לָא שְׁמֵיהּ טִלְטוּל – **Learn from here that moving** an item **indirectly is not deemed moving** with respect to the laws of *muktzeh,* and is therefore permitted. This refutes Rav Nachman's ruling that one may not indirectly move earth which is *muktzeh.*

The Gemara concludes:

שְׁמַע מִינָּהּ – Indeed, **learn from here;** R' Nachman's view is refuted.[15]

Pursuant to its mention of the permit to move *muktzeh* in an unusual manner, the Gemara now describes another *melachah* that is permitted when performed in an unusual manner:[16]

אָמַר רַב יְהוּדָה – **Rav Yehudah said:** הָנֵי פִּלְפְּלֵי מֵידָק חֲדָא חֲדָא בְּקַתָּא דְסַכִּינָא שְׁרֵי – **Crushing these peppers one at a time with the handle of a knife is permitted.** תַּרְתֵּי אָסִיר – But crushing **two** at a time **is prohibited.**[17]

A disputing opinion:

רָבָא אָמַר – **Rava said:** כֵּיוָן דְּמִשַּׁנֵּי – **Since he has deviated** from the normal method of crushing by using the handle of a knife,[18] אֲפִילּוּ טוּבָא נַמִּי – he may crush **even many at a time.**[19]

Another ruling from Rav Yehudah:

[וְ]אָמַר רַב יְהוּדָה – **[And] Rav Yehudah said:** מַאן דְּסָחֵי בְּמַיָּא – **One who was bathing in** a stream of **water**[20] and wishes to exit the water לִינַגֵּיב נַפְשֵׁיהּ בְּרֵישָׁא וְהָדַר לִיסְּלֵיק – **should dry himself first and then go out,**[21] דִּילְמָא אָתֵי לְאַתּוּיֵי אַרְבַּע אַמּוֹת בְּכַרְמְלִית – **lest he come to carry** the water upon his body **four *amos* in a *karmelis.***[22]

NOTES

because it is akin to *demolishing* (as explained by *Rashi*), it is possible that he would concur with R' Yehudah in such a case, since opening a partially opened press does not constitute *demolishing* (*Rabbeinu Yerucham* 12:13; *Eliyah Rabbah* 302:11). Others, however, explain that the Tanna Kamma prohibits opening the press completely even when it is already partially open, lest one come to open it when it is completely closed (*Chidushei HaRan, Maggid Mishneh, Hil. Shabbos* 26:12, *Magen Avraham* 302:7). See *Orach Chaim* 302:4 with *Mishnah Berurah* §21 and *Shaar HaTziyun* §25 and 26. [According to the latter view, the Sages may have intended to stress that "we may not touch" a launderer's press under *any circumstances,* even if it is partially opened (see also *Aruch HaShulchan* 302:14).]

[According to *Rambam,* who explains that the Tanna Kamma regards the launderer's press as *muktzeh* (see previous note), R' Yehudah obviously differs with the Tanna Kamma, since there is no reason to permit handling a press which is *muktzeh* just because it is already partially open.]

Even should the Tanna Kamma dispute R' Yehudah, all agree that when the press is completely open, and it is possible to remove the garments without moving the press at all, one is permitted to remove them (*Mishnah Berurah* ibid., citing *R' Akiva Eiger*).

13. A radish was inserted in the ground before the Sabbath so that it would be preserved there. [Since the radish had already been plucked, the *melachah* of *harvesting* is not applicable, and the only issue is that of moving the *muktzeh* earth.] Now, the top of a radish is wider than its bottom. Therefore, if the radish was buried right side up and its top is exposed, one can grasp the wide top and lift the narrower bottom from the hole without moving the earth at all. However, if it was buried upside down with only the narrow bottom exposed, one who lifts it will automatically lift some earth that is resting on the wider top. Although this would merely constitute indirect movement of the earth, for it is the radish that is moving the earth, and not the person, Rav Nachman forbids it (*Rashi;* see *Tosafos* above, 123a ד״ה האי פוגלא).

14. [Emendation follows *Dikdukei Soferim.*]

15. An apparent difficulty: We have learned that moving an object with one's *body* (טִלְטוּל בְּגוּפוֹ) is more lenient than indirect movement, i.e. moving a non-*muktzeh* object with one's *hand* to move a *muktzeh* object [טִלְטוּל מִן הַצַּד] (see note 5). If so, how can the Gemara prove that the indirect movement of earth caused by pulling a radish from the ground with one's hand should be permitted from our Mishnah which allows moving straw with one's *body*? The answer is that with respect to the various levels of the moving of *muktzeh,* indirect movement of dirt performed *for the sake of a non-muktzeh object* (e.g. a radish) is equivalent to moving straw with one's body *for the sake of the muktzeh object* [i.e. the straw] (see *Beis Yosef* to 311:8).

16. See *Tosafos.*

17. Crushing any produce into very small pieces is prohibited as a form of the *melachah* of *grinding.* According to Rav Yehudah, crushing produce would be permitted where one deviates from the normal way of doing so in two ways: (a) He performs the crushing in a highly irregular manner, *and* (b) he crushes no more than one pepper at a time.

There is a view in the Rishonim that this ruling was stated concerning Yom Tov, but all forms of crushing would be prohibited on Shabbos (*Rabbeinu Chananel* and *She'iltos DeRav Achai Gaon,* cited by *Tosafos*). Most Rishonim, however, maintain that Rav Yehudah permitted this on the Sabbath; on Yom Tov, even normal crushing would be permitted in most cases (see *Tosafos* at length). This is the view of the *Shulchan Aruch* (*Orach Chaim* 321:7) as well.

18. And not with millstones or a mortar (*Rashi*). [*Rashi* implies that we require, in addition to the irregularity of crushing with the handle of a knife (and not with millstones or a pestle), that it be ground into a plate or on a table (and not in a mortar), because grinding in a mortar is viewed as *weekday activity* (*Mishnah Berurah* ibid. §25; cf. *Magen Avraham* ibid. §9).

[This stands in contrast with the general rule that *melachos* remain Rabbinically prohibited when performed in an irregular manner. The Sages made an exception in the case of grinding with a handle since they viewed this as a *highly* irregular manner of doing the act (see *Beis Yosef* 321 ד״ה כתב האגור).]

19. As long as they are needed for that Sabbath (*Mishnah Berurah* 321:24; see also below, 145a note 28).

20. [It is technically permitted to bathe or enter a body of water on the Sabbath, provided that the water was not warmed. Practically speaking, however, many *poskim* advise, for a number of reasons, that one not do so (*Mishnah Berurah* 326:21, *Aruch HaShulchan* 326:9).]

21. I.e. he should not come onto dry land until he dries himself off from the water that is on his body. Alternatively, when he alights upon dry land, he should continue no further until he dries himself off (see *Chidushei HaRan;* see *Mishnah Berurah* 326:22 and *Shaar HaTziyun* §10; cf. *Meiri*).

22. The area alongside the sea is usually a *karmelis* [as is the sea itself] (see *Mishnah Berurah* 301:176). Thus, walking there while still wet is prohibited, lest one come to walk more than four *amos* with the water upon his body. See *Chidushei HaRan;* see also *Pri Megadim* (cited by *Mishnah Berurah* 326:22).

[Note that one may walk in a public domain while it is raining, even though one carries the rainwater upon his body. This is because the water accumulating on one's body will not reach the amount required for liability (*Orach Chaim* 326:7 with *Mishnah Berurah* §23). In addition, one who becomes wet in a downpour is incapable of avoiding

דאית לה רירי והא דקתני נוטלין מלפני בהמה שפיה רע בחמור דלא דייק ואכיל ונותנין לפני בהמה שפיה יפה בפרה דדייקא ואכלה: **מתני׳** הקש שעל גבי המטה לא ינענעו בידו אלא מנענעו בגופו ואם היה מאכל בהמה או שהיה עליו כר או סדין מנענעו בידו מכבש של בעלי בתים מתירין אבל לא כובשין ושל כובסין לא יגע בו ר׳ יהודה אומר אם היה מותר מע"ש מתיר את כולו ושומטו: **גמ׳** אמר רב נחמן האי פוגלא מלמעלה למטה שרי מלמטה למעלה אסיר אמר רב אדא בר אבא אמרי בי רב תנינא דלא כרב נחמן הקש שע"ג המטה לא ינענעו בידו אבל מנענעו בגופו ואם היה מאכל בהמה או שהיה עליו כר או סדין מנענעו בידו ש"מ טלטול מן הצד לא שמיה טלטול ש"מ אמר רב יהודה הני פלפלי מידק חדא חדא בקתא דסכינא שרי תרתי אסיר רבא אמר כיון דמשני אפילו טובא נמי אמר רב יהודה מאן דסחי במיא לינגיב נפשיה והדר ליסליק דילמא אתי לאתויי ד׳ אמות בכרמלית אי הכי כי קא נחית נמי קא דחי כחו ד׳ אמות ואסיר כחו בכרמלית לא גזרו אמר אביי ואיתימא רב יהודה טיט שע"ג רגלו מקנחו בקרקע ואין מקנחו בכותל אמר רבא מ"ט בכותל לא משום דמיחזי כבונה הא בנין חקלאה הוא אלא אמר רבא מקנחו בכותל ואין מקנחו בקרקע דילמא אתי לאשווי גומות איתמר מר בריה דרבינא אמר אחד זה ואחד זה אסור רב פפא אמר אחד זה ואחד זה מותר למר בריה דרבינא במאי מקנחי ליה מקנחי ליה בקורה אמר רבא לא ליתיב איניש אפומיה דליחייא דילמא מיגנדרא ליה חפץ ואתי לאתויי ואמר רבא לא ליצדד איניש כובא דילמא אתי לאשווי גומות ואמר רבא לא ליהדוק איניש אודרא בפומא דשישא דילמא אתי לידי סחיטה אמר רב כהנא טיט שע"ג בגדו מכסכסו מבפנים ואין מכסכסו מבחוץ מיתיבי טיט שע"ג מנעלו מגררו בגב סכין [א] ושעל בגדו מגררו בצפורן ובלבד שלא יכסכס מאי לאו שלא יכסכס כלל לא שלא יכסכס מבחוץ אלא מבפנים א"ר אבהו א"ר אלעזר אמר ר׳ ינאי מגררין מנעל חדש אבל לא ישן במה

רש"י

דאית לה רירי. ולימלאים והא דקרי לה רע כדמפרש ואזיל פיה יפה דלית ליה רירי פיה רע דלא דייק ואכיל שאוכל קוצים ודרקים: **מתני׳** הקש שעל המטה. וסתמא להסקה ומוקצה הוא וכא לשכב עליו ומנענעו כדי שיהא נח ורך לשכב: **לא ינענעו בידו.** דמוקצה הוא: **אבל מנענעו בגופו.** בכתפיו וטלטול מן הצד הוא דלא שמיה טלטול: **או שהיה עליו כר או סדין.** דגלי דעתיה דאקלייה לשכיבה מעתה תורת כלי עליו: **מכבש.** פריש"א שני לווחים ארוכים וכבדים וסודרין בגדים על התחתון ומורידין העליון עליו וכובשים את הבגדים על ידי יתדות שיש עמודים קבועין מנוקבין בארבע הפיאות של התחתונות והעליונה מנוקבת בארבע זויותיה ועולה ויורדת בעמודים וכפי מה שהוא רוצה לכבוש מורידה ותוחב יתד בנקב העמוד ואינה יכולה לעלות: **מתירין.** את המכבש שנוטל את היתד והוא ניתר דהיינו צורך שבת שנוטל את הכלים: **אבל לא כובשין.** דהיינו צורך חול: **ושל כובסין לא יגע בו.** מפני שהוא עשוי לתקן הבגדים ותוחבו בחזקה ומיהדק והתרה שלו דומה לסתירה: **גמ׳ האי פוגלא.** כגון שטומנין בקרקע להתקיים כשבא לחלצו מלמעלה למטה שרי אם היה ראשה מלמעלה ועוקצה מלמטה ושולפה מראשה העבה תחילה ועוקצה נמשך אחריה מותר לפי שהגומא רחבה מלמעלה ואין מזיזין הקרקע כשהוא שומטה אבל אם שולפה מלמטה למעלה שתחתונה נתון למעלה וראש עליונה שהוא עב נתון למטה והוא שומטה מסופה לראשה אסור לפי שהגומא קצרה מלמעלה וכשהוא שולפה מזיז העפר ומטלטלו ואע"ג דטלטול מן הצד הוא שמיה טלטול ואסור: **תנינא דלא כר"נ.** דאילו ממתניתין שמעינן דלא שמיה טלטול דקתני מנענעו בגופו: **מידק.** דייק: **חדא חדא.** לאו טוחן הוא אלא כלאחר יד: **דקמשני.** שלא בריחים ושלא במדוכה: **לאתויי ד׳ אמות.** מים שעליו: **קא דחי כחו.** את המים ד׳ אמות: **אחד זה ואחד זה אסור.** זה משום בונה וזה משום אשווי גומות: **אחד זה ואחד זה מותר.** אין דרך מתכוין בכך וקי"ל כר"ש: **בקורה.** בעץ המוטל על הקרקע (ג): **אפומא דליחייא.** של מבוי ליכא הכירא: **אודרא.** מוכין שסותמין בהן פי הפך: **שישא.** פך: **מכסכסו.** משפשפו: **מבפנים.** דלא מוכחא מילתא לאיתחזויי כמלבן ° ומלבן ממש לא הוי דאין נותן שם מים: כסכוס דמי למכבס: **אבל לא ישן.** שקולפו והוי ממחק:

תוספות

הקש שע"ג המטה. בריש פרק כירה (דף לו:) פי׳ מה הוא קש: **הני פלפלי מידק חדא כו׳.** פירש ר"ח בשלשלות דרב אחאי בפרשת אמור אל הכהנים מפרש דבי"ט מיירי וקשה לר"י דהוה ליה לפרש בהדיא כיון דבמכילתין לא מיירי אלא בשבת ועוד היכי אסר רב יהודה כולי האי בפלפלין הא אפילו מלח שריא בפ"ק דביצה (ד׳ יד.) במדוך של עץ אלא נראה לרבי דהכא בשבת איירי ואגב דאיירי בטלטול ע"י שינוי מייתי ליה הכא ובכולה שמעתא נמי מייתי מילי דשבת טובא אע"ג דלא שייכן הכא כולי האי אבל בי"ט נראה לר"י דשרי בלא שינוי אפי׳ במדוך של אבן כשאר תבלין דתנן בפ"ק דביצה (שם) ב"ה אומר תבלין נדוכין במדוך של אבן והמלח במדוך של עץ ואמרי׳ בגמרא דכ"ע מלח בעי שינוי מ"ט רב הונא ורב חסדא חד אמר כל הקדרות כולן צריכות מלח ואין כל הקדרות צריכות תבלין וחד אמר כולן מפיגין טעמן ומלח אין מפיגה טעמא מאי בינייהו איכא בינייהו דידע מאי בעי בשולי (ד) אי נמי מוריקא פירוש מוריקא אינה מפיגה טעמא למ"ד משום הפגת טעם אסור ולמ"ד משום כל הקדרות כו׳ שרי א"כ פלפלין דהכא נמי שרי דאין כל הקדרות צריכות פלפלין וא"כ (ס"א ואי נמי) למ"ד נמי משום הפגת טעם פלפלין שרו דצריך לומר נמי שמפיגים טעמם מדלא קאמר איכא בינייהו פלפלין ומיהו אומר רבי דאין זה דקדוק שצריך לפרש שם בע"א דקשיא למ"ד דשרי מוריקא משום דאין כל הקדרות צריכות מוריקא א"כ יהא מותר לקוצרו ולחותכו מן המחובר אע"כ צריך לפרש יש בו הפגת טעם ולא כשאר תבלין להכי שרי למ"ד אין כל הקדרות כו׳ כיון דאיכא נמי קצת הפגת טעמא והשתא אתי שפיר דלקצור אסור ומהשתא אין ראיה להתיר פלפלין דשמא אין בהם הפגת טעם כלל ומיהו אומר ר"י דע"כ הם מפיגין טעמם דתנן בפ"ב דביצה (ד׳ כג.) ג׳ דברים רבי אלעזר בן עזריה מתיר וחכמים אוסרין שוחקין את הפלפלין ברחים שלהן והיכי הוה שרי רבי אלעזר בן עזריה אי לא מפיגין טעמא ואין סברא לומר דהא פליגי רבי אלעזר בן עזריה ורבנן דמר סבר דמפיגין טעמא ומר סבר אין מפיגין טעמא אלא מדשרי ר׳ אלעזר בן עזריה ש"מ דמפיגין טעמא ורבנן דאסרי משום דברחים שלהם מיחזי טפי כי עובדא דחול ועוד תניא בהדיא בתוספתא דביצה בתר פלוגתא דבית שמאי ובית הלל הפלפלין כתבלין על כן נראה לר"י דמותר לכתוש פלפלין ביום טוב אפילו במדוך של אבן ומיהו היכא דידע מאי קדרה בעי בשולי אסור במדוך של אבן דלא ידענא כמאן הלכתא ואזלינן לחומרא ולא שייך למימר בשל סופרים הלך אחר המיקל היכא דאם הוא קולא בדבר אחד חומרא הוא בדבר אחר מיהו במדוך של עץ ממ"נ שרי אפי׳ במדוכה של אבן כעין שלנו שקורין מורטיי"ר כיון שהמדוך של עץ דלא אסרינן התם היכא דידע מאי קדרה בעי בשולי אלא בלא שינוי ושומין הנדוכים בי"ט נראה לר"י דשרי אפי׳ ידע מאי קדרה בעי בשולי לפי שמפיגין טעמן יותר מדאי ושרי מידי דהוי אשוחט ומבשל דשרי לכ"ע אפילו יודע מאי קדרה בעי בשולי דנראה הוא דהפגת טעם היינו שתש כח התבלין ואינם חדין כל כך ויכול לתקן הדבר כשמרבה התבלין אבל הפגת טעם שומין אין יכול לתקן מידי דהוה אשוחט ואופה ומבשל וגם רוח רעה שורה עליהן [נדה יז.] אם דכן מערב י"ט (ה) אפילו במדוך של אבן או של ברזל שרי ועוד דאין נראה שיהו בכלל תבלין דלא מיקרי תבלין אלא ירקות כעין כמון אבל שומין ובצלים אינם בכלל תבלין (ט): **דילמא אתי לאשווי גומות.** אע"ג דרבא ס"ל בסוף פ"ב דביצה (ד׳ כג.) בדבר שאין מתכוין כר"ש גזרינן הכא כשיהא עסוק לקנח רגלו ישכח שבת ויתכוין לאשווי גומות כעין שמצינו בפ׳ בתרא דעירובין (ד׳ קד.) דנשים המשחקות באגוזים ובתפוחים אסור דילמא אתי לאשווי גומות כלומר במתכוין שמשכחת שבת מחמת שחוק שלהן: **אודרא אפומא דשישא.** פי׳ בפ׳ ח׳ שרצים (לעיל קיא:) [בד"ה האי מסוכריית׳ שם ע"ש]:

במנעל

עין משפט נר מצוה

מו א מיי׳ פכ"ה מהל׳ שבת הלכה כב סמג לאוין סה טוש"ע או"ח סי׳ שיא סעיף ח:
מז ב מיי׳ פכ"א שם הל׳ יב סמג שם טוש"ע או"ח סי׳ שכ סעיף י:
מח ג מיי׳ פכ"ה שם הל׳ יד טוש"ע או"ח סי׳ שיא סעיף ח:
מט ד מיי׳ פכ"א שם הלכה כ סמג שם טוש"ע או"ח סי׳ שכא סעיף ז:
נ ה מיי׳ פכ"א שם הל׳ כב סמג שם טוש"ע או"ח סימן שכו סעיף ז:
נא ו מיי׳ פכ"א שם הל׳ ב סמג שם טוש"ע או"ח סימן שכ סעיף ו:
נב ז מיי׳ פי"ד שם הל׳ יז טוש"ע או"ח סי׳ שכח סעיף ה:
נג ח טוש"ע או"ח סי׳ שלג סעיף ה:
נד ט מיי׳ פכ"ב שם הלכה טו סמג שם טוש"ע או"ח סי׳ שב סעיף ו:
נה י מיי׳ פכ"ב שם הלכה יז סמג שם טוש"ע או"ח סי׳ שב סעיף ז:

רבינו חננאל

הקש שע"ג המטה לא ינענעו בידו אבל מנענעו בגופו: אמר רב נחמן האי פוגלא מלמעלה למטה שרי ממטה למעלה אסור. יש מי שאומרים לא לגרדה ויש מי שאומרים מותר לגרדה ממעלה וכבר פירשנו דברי רב נחמן בפרק כל הכלים. אמר רב יהודה [הני] פלפלי [מידק] חדא חדא בקתא דסכינא שרי למידק. פי׳ ביו"ט אבל בלדוכן אסור דהא אין מפיגין טעמן והוה ליה למידק מעיו"ט. רבא אמר כיון דמשני אפי׳ טובא והלכתא כרבא ביו"ט ויש מי שמתיר כי האי גונא אפי׳ בשבת: טיט שע"ג רגליו הלכתא כמר בריה דרבנא דאסר בין בקרקע ובין בכותל ולא שרי אלא בקורה בלבד. ואמר רבא לא לצדד איניש כובא בארעא דלא אתו לאשווי גומות ואמר רבא לא ליהדוק איניש אודרא בפומא דשישא דלמא אתו לידי סחיטה. פי׳ לא ידחוק אדם מוכין שרויין בפי אשישא שמא יבא לידי סחיטה טיט שעל בגדו מכסכסו מבפנים ואין מכסכסו מבחוץ או מגררו בצפורן כססכו כבר פירשנוהו למעלה. וכל אלו שאמר רבא אסור אחד בשבת ואחד ביו"ט לא שנא וגירוד

רב נסים גאון

טיט שעל גבי מנעל איכא חספא דרבא משכחת לה בפרק כל הכלים ניטלין בשבת (דף קכב) רבא הוה קאזיל בריסתקא דמחוזא איתווס מסאניה בטינא אתא שמעיה שקל חספא וקא מכפר ליה:

מסורת הש"ס

א) לעיל כ., ב) לעיל קכג., ג) [לעיל דף מג: קכג.], ד) [ברא"ש ביצה פ"א סי׳ כא איתא רב הונא], ה) [ל"ל ואמר], ו) [לעיל קא.], ז) לקמן קמח: ביצה ל., ח) [ל"ל וכן בשלשלות], ט) [וע"ע תוס׳ ביצה יד. ד"ה בית הלל].

הגהות הב"ח

(א) גמ׳ אמר רבא לא ליצדד איניש וכו׳ תא"מ וכ"ב גי׳ אלפסי לא לישתמש איניש וע"ל בדף קמח: (ב) שם כוכא בארעא דילמא: (ג) רש"י ד"ה בקורה וכו׳ הקרקע הס"ד ואח"כ מ"ה לא ליצדד לא ידחנו להושיבה הס"ד: (ד) תוס׳ ד"ה הני וכו׳ מאי בעי בשוליה. למ"ד משום כל הקדרות כו׳ אסור ולמ"ד משום הפגת טעם שרי אי נמי מוריקא וכו׳ א"כ פלפלין כל הקדרות: (ה) בא"ד מערב י"ט הלכך אפי׳ במדוך:

גליון הש"ס

גמ׳ דילמא אתי לידי סחיטה. עיין לקמן דף קמח ע"א תוס׳ ד"ה כבשים: רש"י ד"ה מבפנים וכו׳ ומלבן לא הוי דאין נותן שם מים. עיין לקמן דף קמו ע"א ברש"י ד"ה חייב חטאת וצ"ע:

הגהות הגר"א

[א] גמ׳ ושעל בגדו מגררו בצפורן. נ"ב וכ"ש בגב סכין:

ליקוטי רש"י

הקש. סתמיה לטינא קאי לצבעים או להסקה ומוקצה הוא ואם היה נתון על המטה ולא לשכב עליו וכא בשבת לשכב עליו ומוכך לנענעו ולשוטחו לשכיבה לא יטלנו לכור וקשה. לא ינענעו בידו. שאסור לטלטלו. אלא מנענעו בגופו. כלאחר יד. או שהיה עליו כר או סדין. ששכב עליו מבעוד יום ואף על פי שלא יחדו לכך ולא חישב עליו [לעיל נ.]. פוגלא. כגון תלוש שטמנו בקרקע ונתגלה ראשו. מלמעלה למטה שרי. אם היה העליון שלה למעלה והקלר למטה וכשהוא שולפה מולה מעליון שלה לתחתון שלה ורוחב הנקב למעלה מותר ליטלה שלשה נתוך לעפר כלל שכבר נתגלה ראשו. מלמטה למעלה אסור. שמוח עפר לפי שהגומא קלרה מלמעלה ורוחב הנקב למטה ואף על גב דטלטול עפר מן הצד הוא שלותו אלותו ממש בידו [שם קכג.]. מן הצד. כלאחר יד [שם מג:]. בקתא. בית יד [שבועות מג.]. אפומיה דליחייא. לפי שאין היכר כל כך בין מבוי לרשות הרבים [לקמן קמח.]. דליחייא. לחי המתיר מבוי בשבת. דילמא מיגנדרא ליה חפץ. כרשות הרבים חוץ ללחי [ביצה ל.]. ואתי לאתויי. חפץ המתגלגל תוך ארבע אמות [לקמן שם]. מתוך שאינו במבוי מקורה להכיר שזה רשות הרבים וזה רשות היחיד ומביאו [ביצה שם]. כובא. גיגית [ב"מ כה.]. לאשווי גומות. למלאכה הוא בשבת דהוי כבנין [עירובין קד.]. מכסכסו. משפשף לזה על לזו [שם] זה כדרך המכבס בגדים מוזה הבגד בשתי ידיו ומשפשף [זבחים צד:]. בין שתי ידיו לדרך כיבוס בגדים שכופל לזו עם לזו ומשפשף ומולין ומביא [נדה סב.].

In this ruling Rav Yehudah raises the concern that one might transport seawater four *amos* in a *karmelis* upon exiting the sea.

The Gemara asks:

אִי הָכִי – If it is so that this is prohibited, **כִּי קָא נָחִית נַמִּי קָא דָּחֵי כֹּחוֹ אַרְבַּע אַמּוֹת וְאָסִיר – then when he enters** the water **as well, his force** of entry **pushes** the water away for a distance of **four *amos*** in the sea, which is also a *karmelis*. This too, then, should be prohibited.

The Gemara answers:

כֹּחוֹ בְּכַרְמְלִית לֹא גָּזְרוּ – The Sages did not decree a prohibition against transferring through **one's force in** regard to **a *karmelis*.** That is, they did not prohibit using one's force to bring about the transfer of an object a distance of four *amos* in a *karmelis*. Thus, the indirect transfer of seawater a distance of four *amos* is permitted.

The Gemara cites another Sabbath ruling:

אָמַר אַבַּיֵי וְאִיתֵימָא רַב יְהוּדָה – Abaye, and some say Rav Yehudah, said: טִיט שֶׁעַל גַּבֵּי רַגְלוֹ – Clay which is on one's foot,[23] **מְקַנְּחוֹ בַּקַּרְקַע וְאֵין מְקַנְּחוֹ בַּכּוֹתֶל – he may scrape it off onto the ground, but he may not scrape it off onto a wall.**

This ruling is challenged:

אָמַר רָבָא – Rava said: מַאי טַעְמָא בַּכּוֹתֶל לֹא – For what reason do you say that one may **not** scrape it off **onto a wall? מִשּׁוּם דְּמֶיחֱזֵי כְּבוֹנֶה –** Apparently, **because it appears as though he is *building*** by applying a layer of clay to the wall.[24] **הָא בִּנְיַן חַקְלָאָה הוּא – But this is the building of a peasant,** i.e. it is but a crude form of building. We surely would not prohibit scraping clay off one's foot on account of this![25]

Rava offers his own ruling:

אֶלָּא אָמַר רָבָא – Rather, Rava said: מְקַנְּחוֹ בַּכּוֹתֶל וְאֵין מְקַנְּחוֹ בַּקַּרְקַע – He may scrape it off onto a wall, but he may not scrape it off onto the ground, דִּילְמָא אָתֵי לְאַשְׁוּוּיֵי גּוּמוֹת – lest he come to level out holes in the ground with the clay that he is scraping off.[26]

The Gemara cites a dispute in this matter:

אִיתְּמַר – It was stated concerning this question: **מַר בְּרֵיהּ דְּרָבִינָא אָמַר – Mar the son of Ravina, said: אֶחָד זֶה וְאֶחָד זֶה אָסוּר – Both this** [scraping clay onto a wall] **and this** [scraping clay onto the ground] **are prohibited.**[27] **רַב פַּפָּא אָמַר – Rav Pappa said: אֶחָד זֶה וְאֶחָד זֶה מוּתָּר – Both this** [scraping clay onto a wall] **and this** [scraping clay onto the ground] **are permitted.**[28]

The Gemara asks:

לְמַר בְּרֵיהּ דְּרָבִינָא בְּמַאי מְקַנַּחֵי לֵיהּ – According to Mar the son of Ravina, in what way may one scrape [clay] off his foot?

The Gemara answers:

מְקַנַּחֵי לֵיהּ בְּקוֹרָה – He may scrape off the clay onto a beam, for this will result in neither the leveling of holes, nor *building*.[29]

Another Sabbath ruling:

אָמַר רָבָא – Rava said: לֹא לֵיתִיב אִינִישׁ אַפּוּמֵּיהּ דְּלֶיחְיָיא – A person may not sit at the edge of a *lechi* on the Sabbath,[30] **דִּילְמָא מִיגַּנְדְּרָא לֵיהּ חֵפֶץ וְאָתֵי לְאַתּוּיֵי – because an object might roll** beyond the *lechi* **and he might come to carry it** back.[31]

Another ruling by Rava:

וְאָמַר רָבָא – And Rava said: לֹא לִיצַדֵּד אִינִישׁ כּוּבָּא – One may not rock a barrel back and forth on the ground to make it sit well, **דִּילְמָא אָתֵי לְאַשְׁוּוּיֵי גּוּמוֹת – lest he come to level holes** in the ground.[32]

Yet another Sabbath ruling issued by Rava:

וְאָמַר רָבָא – And Rava said: לֹא לִיהֲדוֹק אִינִישׁ אוּדְרָא בְּפוּמָּא דְּשִׁישָׁא – One may not pack wet **flocking into the mouth of a jug,**[33] **דִּילְמָא אָתֵי לִידֵי סְחִיטָה – lest he come to squeeze**

NOTES

carrying the water, and is thus considered an אָנוּס, one who *unavoidably* carried water (see *Aruch HaShulchan* 326:8).]

23. Or one's shoe (*Rama* 302:6; see below; see also *Mishnah Berurah* 302:26 and *Beur Halachah* there ד״ה או על מנעליו).

24. [In earlier times, houses built with stone or bricks were often coated with a layer of clay.]

25. Only a peasant would use simple clay to coat the house; most people, however, used a specialized lime. Since coating with clay is an irregular form of building (and thus only Rabbinically prohibited), it should be permitted completely in this case, where it is a דָּבָר שֶׁאֵינוֹ מִתְכַּוֵּן, *an unintended act* (*Chidushei HaRan;* see note 28).

26. Uneven ground will remove clay better than smooth ground [as the lip of a ripple in the ground can be used to scrape off the mud]. We must therefore be concerned that one will seek out uneven terrain and scrape off the clay there, thus leveling the ground (*Ramban;* cf. *Chidushei HaRan*).

27. In one case, because it appears that he is building, and in the other case, lest he come to level holes in the ground (*Rashi*).

28. Because in the first case the person is not deemed to be *building,* since this is an irregular form of building (see above, note 25); and, in the second case, because any leveling which may occur is deemed to be a דָּבָר שֶׁאֵינוֹ מִתְכַּוֵּן, *an unintended act,* and Rav Pappa follows the view of R' Shimon, who says that one is not liable for such an act (see *Rashi* and *Mishnah Berurah* 302:28; cf. *Chidushei HaRan;* see also above, 29b; *Beitzah* 23b). Even this view will admit, however, that the very area in which he is scraping the clay may not contain a hole, for in that case he will certainly level the hole (*Mishnah Berurah* ibid.).

Now, it is clear from the Gemara elsewhere (*Beitzah* 23a) that Rava too agrees with R' Shimon in this matter. Still, Rava prohibits scraping clay off one's foot on the ground, because we are concerned that one will seek out uneven terrain to scrape off the clay, and then forget the Sabbath entirely and *intentionally* level holes in the ground (*Tosafos, Ramban, Rashba*). Cf. *Tos. Rid.*

29. Or, he may scrape it off on a stone. In addition, one may scrape it off on a wall made of wood [which is not usually coated with a layer of clay] (*Mishnah Berurah* 302:27).

The Rishonim are at odds as to whom the halachah follows, with some prohibiting all cases, others permitting all cases and yet others distinguishing between scraping onto a wall and scraping onto the ground. See *Rashba, Ran MHK* ed. and *Orach Chaim* 302:6 with *Mishnah Berurah.*

30. According to Rabbinic decree, one may not carry in an alleyway (*mavoi*) which has three walls and a fourth side open to the public domain, unless a minimal correction is placed on the side that is open to the public domain. This correction may take the form of a לֶחִי, *sidepost,* or קוֹרָה, *crossbeam.* The area of the alleyway within these corrections is a private domain; beyond the alleyway is a public domain. Carrying between the two areas is Biblically prohibited. [See above, 117a note 10.]

31. Since the alleyway has no roof, it is not readily apparent to one sitting alongside the *lechi* that he is sitting in a private domain, and he may mistakenly believe that he is sitting in the adjacent public domain. Therefore, he might unwittingly bring in an article which rolled outside the alleyway within four *amos* to where he is sitting alongside the *lechi,* thereby performing the *melachah* of *transferring* from the public domain to the private domain (*Rashi* below, 148b, and to *Beitzah* 30a; see *Shulchan Aruch* 365:5 with *Mishnah Berurah*; see also *Meiri*).

32. It was common practice to rock a full barrel back and forth, thus flattening the ground below it so that the barrel would sit steady in its place. Thus, rocking a barrel in this manner is prohibited under any circumstances, lest one come to do so on uneven ground and thereby level the ground there, or lest he come to level the ground with his hands so that the barrel will sit properly (*Ramban, Rashba, Meiri;* cf. *Orach Chaim* 337:4 with *Tos. Shabbos, Mishnah Berurah* §20 and *Shaar HaTziyun* §16).

33. Only wet flocking may not be packed into the jug's opening, for the reasons to be explained below; dry flocking *may* be squeezed into the opening of a jug (see *Beur Halachah* to 320:16 ד״ה להדק).

דאית לה רירי והא דקתני נוטלין מלפני בהמה שפיה רע בחמור דלא דייק ואכיל ונותנין לפני בהמה שפיה יפה בפרה דדייקא ואכלה: **מתני'** א הקש שעל גבי המטה לא ינענענו בידו אלא מנענעו בגופו ואם היה מאכל בהמה או שהיה עליו כר או סדין מנענעו בידו ב מכבש של בעלי בתים מתירין אבל לא כובשין ושל כובסין לא יגע בו ר' יהודה אומר אם היה מותר מע"ש מתיר את כולו ושומטו: **גמ'** ג אמר רב נחמן האי פוגלא מלמעלה למטה שרי מלמטה למעלה אסיר אמר רב אדא בר אבא אמרי בי רב תנינא דלא כרב נחמן הקש שע"ג המטה לא ינענענו בידו אבל מנענעו בגופו ואם היה מאכל בהמה או שהיה עליו כר או סדין מנענעו בידו ש"מ ד טלטול מן הצד לא שמיה טלטול ש"מ אמר רב ה יהודה הני פלפלי מידק חדא חדא בקתא דסכינא שרי תרתי אסיר רבא אמר ו כיון דמשני אפילו טובא נמי ז אמר רב יהודה ח מאן דסחי במיא לינגיב נפשיה ברישא והדר ליסליק דילמא אתי לאתויי ד' אמות בכרמלית אי הכי כי קא נחית נמי קא דחי כחו ד' אמות ואסיר ט כחו בכרמלית לא גזרו אמר אביי ואיתימא רב יהודה טיט שע"ג רגלו מקנחו בקרקע ואין מקנחו בכותל אמר רבא מ"ט בכותל לא משום דמיחזי כבונה הא בנין חקלאה הוא אלא אמר רבא י מקנחו בכותל ואין מקנחו בקרקע דילמא אתי לאשוויי גומות איתמר מר בריה דרבינא אמר אחד זה ואחד זה אסור רב פפא אמר אחד זה ואחד זה מותר למר בריה דרבינא במאי מקנחי ליה בקורה כ אמר רבא (א) ל לא ליתיב איניש אפומיה דליחייא דילמא מיגנדרא ליה חפץ ואתי לאתויי ואמר רבא מ לא ליצדד איניש כובא (ג) דילמא אתי לאשוויי גומות ואמר רבא נ לא ליהדוק איניש אודרא בפומא דשישא ס דילמא אתי לידי סחיטה אמר רב כהנא ע טיט שע"ג בגדו מכסכסו מבפנים ואין מכסכסו מבחוץ מיתיבי טיט שע"ג מנעלו מגררו בגב סכין [א] ושעל בגדו מגררו בצפורן ובלבד שלא יכסכס מאי לאו שלא יכסכס כלל לא שלא יכסכס מבחוץ אלא מבפנים א"ר אבהו א"ר אלעזר אמר ר' ינאי מגררין מנעל חדש אבל לא ישן

במה

רש"י

דאית לה רירי. ולימאלם והא דקרי לה הכא פיה יפה והכא פיה רע כדמפרש ואזיל פיה יפה דלית ליה רירי פיה רע דלא דייק ואכיל שאוכל קוצים וברקנים: **מתני' הקש שעל המטה.** וקסמא להסקה ומוקצה הוא ובא לשכב עליו ומנענעו כדי שיהא נח ורך לשכב: **לא ינענענו בידו.** דמוקצה הוא: **אבל מנענעו בגופו.** בכתפיו ובמתניו מן הצד הוא דלא שמיה טלטול: **או שהיה עליו כר או סדין.** דגלי דעתיה דאקצייה לשכיבה מעתה תורת כלי עליו: **מכבש.** פירש"י שני לווחים ארוכים וכבדים וסודרין בגדים על התחתון ומורידין העליון עליו וכובשים את הבגדים על ידי יתדות שיש עמודים קבועין מנוקבין בארבע הפיאות של התחתונה והעליונה מנוקבת בארבע זויותיה ועולה ויורדת בעמודים וכפי מה שהוא רוצה לכבוש מורידה ותוחב יתד בנקב העמוד ואינה יכולה לעלות: **מתירין.** את המכבש שנוטל את היתד והוא ניתר דהיינו צורך שבת שנוטל את הכלים: **אבל לא כובשין.** דהיינו צורך חול: **ושל כובסין לא יגע בו.** מפני שהוא עשוי לתקן הבגדים ותוחבו בחוזקה ומיהדק והתרה שלו דומה לסתירה: **גמ' האי פוגלא.** כגון שטומנין בקרקע להתקיים כשבא לתלוש מלמעלה למטה שרי אם היה ראשה מלמעלה ועוקצה מלמטה ושולה מראשה העבה תחילה ועוקצה נמשך אחריה מותר לפי שהגומא רחבה מלמעלה ואין מזיזין הקרקע כשהוא שומטה אבל אם שולה מלמטה למעלה שמתחתונה נתון למעלה וראש עליונה שהוא עב נתון למטה והוא שומטה מסופה לראשה אסור לפי שהגומא קצרה מלמעלה וכשהוא שולה מזיז העפר ומטלטלו ואע"ג דטלטול מן הצד הוא שמיה טלטול ואסור: **תנינא דלא כר"נ.** דאילו ממתניתין שמעינן דלא שמיה טלטול דקתני מנענעו בגופו: **מידק.** דייק: **חדא חדא.** לאו טוחן הוא אלא כלאחר יד: **דקמשני.** שלא ברחים ושלא במדוכה: **לאתויי ד' אמות.** מים שעליו: **קא דחי כחו.** את המים ד' אמות: **אחד זה ואחד זה אסור.** זה משום בונה וזה משום אשויי גומות: **אחד זה ואחד זה מותר.** אין דרך מתכוין בכך וקי"ל כר"ש: **בקורה.** בעץ המוטל על הקרקע (ג): **אפומא דלחייא.** של מבוי דליכא היכרא: **אודרא.** מוכין שסותמין בהן פי הפך: **שישא.** פך: **מכסכסו.** משפשפו: **מבפנים.** דלא מוכחא מילתא לאיתחזויי כמלבן ומלבן ממש לא הוי דאין נותן שם מים: כסכוס דמי למכבס: **אבל לא ישן.** שקולפו והוי ממחק:

תוספות

הקש שע"ג המטה. בריש פרק כירה (דף לו:) פי' מה הוא קש: **הני פלפלי מידק חדא כו'.** פירש ר"ח ה בשאלתות דרב אחאי בפרשת אמור אל הכהנים מפרש דבי"ט מיירי וקשה לר' דהוה ליה לפרש בהדיא כיון דבמכילתין לא מיירי אלא בשבת ועוד היכי אסר רב יהודה כולי האי בפלפלין הא אפילו מלח שרינא בפ"ק דביצה (ד' יד.) במדוך של עץ אלא נראה לרבי דהכא בשבת איירי ואגב דאיירי בטלטול ע"י שינוי מייתי ליה הכא ובכולה שמעתא נמי מייתי מילי דשבת טובא אע"ג דלא שייכן הכא כולי האי אבל בי"ט נראה לר"י דשרי בלא שינוי אפי' במדוך של אבן כשאר תבלין דתנן בפ"ק דביצה (שם) ב"ה אומר תבלין נדוכין במדוך של אבן והמלח במדוך של עץ ואמרי' בגמרא דכ"ע מלח בעי שינוי מ"ט רב הונא ורב חסדא חד אמר כל הקדרות כולן צריכות מלח ואין כל הקדרות צריכות תבלין וחד אמר כולן מפיגין טעמן ומלח אין מפיגה טעמא מאי בינייהו איכא בינייהו דידע מאי בעי בשולי (ד) אי נמי מוריקא פירוש מוריקא אינה מפיגה טעמא למ"ד משום הפגת טעם אסור ולמ"ד משום כל הקדרות כו' שרי א"כ פלפלין דהכא נמי שרי דאין כל הקדרות צריכות פלפלין וא"כ (ס"א ואי נמי) למ"ד נמי משום הפגת טעם פלפלין שרו דצריך לומר נמי שמפיגים טעמם מדלא קאמר איכא בינייהו פלפלין ומיהו אומר רבי דאין זה דקדוק שצריך לפרש שם בע"א דקשיא למ"ד דשרי מוריקא משום דאין כל הקדרות צריכות מוריקא א"כ יהא מותר לקוצרו ולחותכו מן המחובר אע"כ צריך לפרש יש בו הפגת טעם ולא כשאר תבלין להכי שרי למ"ד אין כל הקדרות כו' כיון דאיכא נמי קצת הפגת טעמא והשתא אתי שפיר דלקצור אסור ומהשתא אין ראיה להתיר פלפלין דשמא אין בהם הפגת טעם כלל ומיהו אומר ר"י דע"כ הם מפיגין טעמם דתנן בפ"ב דביצה (ד' כג.) ג' דברים רבי אלעזר בן עזריה מתיר וחכמים אוסרין שוחקין את הפלפלין ברחים שלהן והיכי הוה שרי רבי אלעזר בן עזריה אי לא מפיגין טעמא ואין סברא לומר דבהא פליגי רבי אלעזר בן עזריה ורבנן דמר סבר דמפיגין טעמא ומר סבר אין מפיגין טעמא אלא מדשרי ר' אלעזר בן עזריה ש"מ דמפיגין טעמא ורבנן דאסרי משום דברחים שלהם מיחזי טפי כי עובדא דחול ועוד תניא בהדיא בתוספתא דביצה בתר פלוגתא דבית שמאי ובית הלל הפלפלין כתבלין על כן נראה לר"י דמותר לכתוש פלפלין ביום טוב אפילו במדוך של אבן ומיהו היכא דידע מאי קדרה בעי בשולי אסור במדוך של אבן דלא ידענא כמאן הלכתא ואזלינן לחומרא ולא שייך למימר בשל סופרים הלך אחר המיקל היכא דאם הוא קולא בדבר אחד חומרא הוא בדבר אחר מיהו במדוך של עץ ממ"נ שרי אפי' במדוכה של אבן כעין שלנו שקורין מורטי"ר כיון שהמדוך של עץ דלא אסרינן התם היכא דידע מאי קדרה בעי בשולי אלא בלא שינוי ושומין הנדוכים בי"ט נראה לר"י דשרי אפי' ידע מאי קדרה בעי בשולי לפי שמפיגין טעמן יותר מדאי ושרי מידי דהוי אשוחט ומבשל דשרי לכ"ע אפילו יודע מאי קדרה בעי בשולי דנראה הוא דהפגת טעם היינו שפג כח התבלין ואינם חדין כל כך ויכול לתקן הדבר כשמרבה התבלין אבל הפגת טעם שומין אין יכול לתקן מידי דהוה אשוחט ואופה ומבשל וגם רוח רעה שורה עליהן [נדה יז.] אם דכן מערב י"ט (ה) אפילו לשל אבן או בכרוש שרי ועוד דאין נראה להוסיף עליו בכלל תבלין דלא מיקרי תבלין אלא ירקות כעין כמון אבל שומין ובצלים אינם בכלל תבלין: **דילמא אתי לאשוויי גומות.** אע"ג דרבה לרבה ס"ל בסוף פ"ב דביצה (ד' כג.) בדבר שאין מתכוין כר"ש גזרינן הכא כשהוא עסוק לנקות רגלו ישכח שבת ויתכוין לאשוויי גומות כעין שמצינו בפ' במה מדליקין (שבת כט:) דנקיש המשחקות באגוזים ותפוחים אסור דילמא אתי לאשוויי גומות כלומר במתכוין שמשכחת שבת מחמת שחוק שלהן: **אודרא אפומא דשישא.** פי' בפ' ח' שרצים (לעיל ד' קיא:) [בד"ה האי מסוכריא שם ע"א]:

מסורת הש"ס

א) לעיל ג., ב) לעיל קכג., ג) לעיל דף מג: קכג., ד) [כרמ"ש פ"ב כל אימת רב הונא], ה) [צ"ל ואמר], ו) לעיל קמ., ז) לקמן קמח., ח) [צ"ל וכן בשאלתות], ט) [וע"ע תוס' ביצה יד. ד"ה בית הלל].

הגהות הב"ח

(א) גמ' אמר רבא לא ליתיב איניש אפומיה דליחייא וכו' [...]: (ב) שם כובא בארעא דילמא: (ג) רש"י ד"ה בקורה [...]: (ד) תוס' ד"ה הני וכו' מאי בעי בשולי [...]: (ה) בא"ד מערב יו"ט הלכך אפי' במדוך:

גליון הש"ס

גמ' דילמא אתי לידי סחיטה. עיין לקמן דף קמה ע"א תוס' ד"ה כבסים. רש"י ד"ה מבפנים וכו' ומלבן ממש לא הוי דאין נותן שם מים. עיין לקמן דף קמז ע"ב רש"י ד"ה מייט סעלח וכו':

הגהות הגר"א

[א] גמ' ושעל בגדו מגררו בצפורן. נ"ב וכ"ש בגב סכין:

ליקוטי רש"י

הקש. מתמיה לנטילה קאי ללבנים או להסקה ומוקצה הוא ואם היה נתון על המטה ולא לשכב עליו ובא בשבת לשכב עליו והוצרך לנענעו ולשוטחו לשכיבה שלא יהא צבור וקשה. לא ינענענו בידו. שאסור לטלטלו. אלא מנענעו בגופו. כלאחר יד. או שהיה עליו כר או סדין. שכבר עליו מבעוד יום ואף על פי שלא יחדו לכך ולא חשב עליו [לעיל נ.]. פוגלא. כגון שטומנין בקרקע ומגלה ראשו. מלמעלה למטה שרי. אם היה העליון שלה למעלה והקצר למטה וכשהוא שולפה מתחתון שלה ורוחב הגומא למעלה מותר דליכא טלטול לעפר כלל שהרי נתגלה ראשו. מלמטה למעלה אסור. שמזיז עפר לפי שהגומא קצרה מלמעלה ורוחב הגומא למטה והוי על גב דטלטול עפר מן הצד הוא שאינו מוחזו [...]. מן הצד. כלאחר יד [שם מג:]. קתא. בית יד [שם מג.]. אפומיה דליחייא. לפי שיכול לכך על בין מבוי לרשות הרבים [לקמן קמח.]. דליחייא. לחי המבוי במבוי בשבת. דילמא מיגנדרא ליה חפץ. ברשות הרבים חוץ ללחי [ביצה ל.]. ואתי לאתויי. חפץ המתגלגל חוץ ארבע אמות [לקמן שם]. מתוך שאינו במבוי מקורה להכיר שזה רשות הרבים וזה רשות היחיד ומביאו [ביצה שם]. כובא. גיגית [ב"מ כה.]. לאשוויי גומות. דמלאכה הוא בשבת דהוי כבנין [עירובין קד.]. מכסכסו. משפשף לזה על לזה [שם]. זה כדרך המכבס בגדים שאוחז הבגד בשתי ידיו ומשפשף ומוליך ומביא [נדה סב.].

רבינו חננאל

הקש שע"ג המטה לא ינענענו בידו אבל מנענעו בגופו: אמר רב נחמן האי פוגלא מלמעלה למטה שרי ממטה למעלה אסור. יש מי שאומרים לא יגררה ויש מי שאומרים מותר לגררה ממעלה וכבר פירשנו דברי רב נחמן בפרק כל הכלים. אמר רב יהודה [הני] פלפלי [מידק] חדא חדא בקתא דסכינא שרי למידק. פי' ביו"ט אבל בלדכן אסור דהא אין מפיגין טעמן והוה ליה למידק מעיו"ט. רבא אמר כיון דמשני אפי' טובא והלכתא כרבא ביו"ט ויש מי שמתיר כל האי גוונא אפי' בשבת: טיט שע"ג רגליו הלכתא כמר בריה דרבינא דאסר בין בקרקע ובין בכותל ולא שרי אלא בקורה בלבד. ואמר רבא לא לצדד איניש כובא בארעא דלא אתו לאשווי גומות ואמר רבא לא ליהדוק איניש אודרא בפומיה דשישא דלמא אתו לידי סחיטה. פי' לא יהדוק אדם מוכין שרוין בפי אשישא שמא יבא לידי סחיטה. טיט שעל בגדו מכסכסו מבפנים ואין מכסכסו מבחוץ. מכסכסו כבר פירשנוהו למעלה. וכל אלו שאמר רבא אסור אחד בשבת ואחד ביו"ט לא שנא וגירוד

רב נסים גאון

טיט שעל גבי מנעל איכא חספא דרבא משכחת לה בפרק כל הכלים ניטלין בשבת (דף קכד) רבא הוה קאזיל בריסתקא דמחוזא איתוס מסאניה בטינא אתא שמעיה שקל חספא וקא מכפר ליה:

עין משפט נר מצוה

מו א מיי' פכ"ה מהל' שבת הלכה כב סמג לאוין סה טוש"ע או"ח סי' שח סעיף מ:

מז ב מיי' פכ"ב שם הל' יג סמג שם טוש"ע או"ח סי' שב סעיף ד:

מח ג מיי' פכ"א שם הל' יג טור סמג שם טוש"ע או"ח סי' שיא סעיף ח:

מט ד מיי' פכ"א שם הלכה כ סמג שם טוש"ע או"ח סי' שכא סעיף ז:

נ ה מיי' פט"ו שם הל' כב סמג שם טוש"ע או"ח סימן שכו סעיף ז:

נא ו מיי' פכ"א שם הל' ג סמג שם טוש"ע או"ח סימן שב סעיף ו:

נב ז מיי' פי"ח שם הל' יח טוש"ע או"ח סי' שמה סעיף ה:

נג ח טוש"ע או"ח סי' שלו סעיף ד:

נד ט מיי' פכ"ב שם הלכה טו סמג שם טוש"ע או"ח סי' שכ סעיף טז:

נה י מיי' פכ"ב שם הלכה יז סמג שם טוש"ע או"ח סי' שב סעיף ז:

liquid out of the cloth.[34]

Another Sabbath ruling:

אָמַר רַב כָּהֲנָא – And Rav Kahana said: טִיט שֶׁעַל גַּבֵּי בִּגְדוֹ – **Clay which is on one's garment,** מְכַסְכְּסוֹ מִבִּפְנִים וְאֵין מְכַסְכְּסוֹ מִבַּחוּץ – **one may rub the** garment **from the inside, but he may not rub it from the outside.**[35]

The Gemara asks:

מֵיתִיבֵי – **They challenged this** ruling **from a Baraisa:** טִיט שֶׁעַל גַּבֵּי מִנְעָלוֹ מְגָרְרוֹ בְּגַב סַכִּין – CLAY WHICH IS ON ONE'S SHOE, ONE MAY SCRAPE IT OFF WITH THE BACK OF A KNIFE.[36] וְשֶׁעַל בִּגְדוֹ מְגָרְרוֹ בְּצִפּוֹרֶן – AND THAT WHICH IS ON ONE'S GARMENT, HE MAY SCRATCH IT OFF WITH A FINGERNAIL,[37] וּבִלְבַד שֶׁלֹּא יְכַסְכֵּס – AS LONG AS HE DOES NOT RUB the garment, because this resembles the forbidden *melachah* of *whitening*.

The Gemara develops the challenge:

מַאי לָאו שֶׁלֹּא יְכַסְכֵּס כְּלָל – Does this Baraisa **not mean** to teach **that he may not rub** the clothing **at all,** both on the inside and on the outside? This refutes Rav Kahana's ruling that rubbing from the inside is permitted! – ? –

The Gemara answers:

לֹא – **No.** The Baraisa does not mean to prohibit rubbing in all cases; rather, שֶׁלֹּא יְכַסְכֵּס מִבַּחוּץ אֶלָּא מִבִּפְנִים – it means to rule **that one should not rub from the outside** of the garment, **but only from the inside.**[38]

The Gemara returns to a discussion concerning scraping clay off a shoe:

אָמַר רַבִּי אַבָּהוּ אָמַר רַבִּי אֶלְעָזָר אָמַר רַבִּי יַנַּאי – **R' Abahu said in the name of R' Elazar who said in the name of R' Yannai:** מְגָרְרִין מִנְעָל חָדָשׁ אֲבָל לֹא יָשָׁן – **We may scrape** clay off **a new shoe, but not off an old shoe.**[39]

NOTES

34. Squeezing liquid out of a cloth on the Sabbath involves the *melachah* of מְלַבֵּן, *whitening* [i.e. laundering], since the passage of the liquid through the cloth cleans it out somewhat. And even according to the view that whitening is prohibited only when *water* is squeezed out of the garment (see *Tosafos* to 111b, middle of ד״ה האי), squeezing the liquid absorbed in the flocking into the jug is prohibited on account of מְפָרֵק, *extracting* [a derivative of the primary category דָּשׁ, *threshing*], for squeezing the cloth serves to detach the liquid from where it is absorbed in the cloth (*Mishnah Berurah* 320:44, see there with *Shaar HaTziyun* §49).

35. The *melachah* of *whitening* includes putting water onto a stained garment. Improving the garment's appearance by rubbing it would not transgress the Biblical form of *whitening,* for he is only removing the clay adhering to the garment, and vestiges of the stain remain (see *Meromei Sadeh*); but it is still Rabbinically prohibited. Rav Kahana teaches here that one may rub the stain indirectly from the inside, i.e. from the underside of the stain, because it is not obvious that he is rubbing it to clean it, and thus it does not *resemble* whitening; it is thus not prohibited even Rabbinically (see *Rashi;* see *Chidushei Basra;* cf. *Re'ah,* cited by *Chidushei HaRan*).

36. [He may not, however, use the knife blade or a fingernail – see below, note 39.]

37. And certainly with the back of a knife (*Hagahos HaGra*), and perhaps even with the blade of a knife (*Mishnah Berurah* §34).

38. This permit to rub the shirt's underside allows only the removal of dirt; rubbing a shirt to *brighten its appearance* is prohibited even if one only rubs it from its underside [see Gemara above, 140a] (*Mishnah Berurah* 302:32).

Some explain our Gemara as discussing only *damp* clay adhering to a garment. In their view, one would be prohibited from scratching off dried-up clay from a garment on account of the *melachah* of *grinding* (*Orach Chaim* 302:7, see *Mishnah Berurah* §36 and *Beur Halachah* ד״ה דהוי).

39. Because by doing so one peels off a thin layer of leather, thereby performing the *melachah* of מְמַחֵק, *smoothing out* (*Rashi*).

דאית לה רירי והא דקתני נוטלין מלפני בהמה שפיה רע בחמור דלא דייק ואכיל ונותנין לפני בהמה שפיה יפה בפרה דדייקא ואכלה: **מתני׳** הקש שעל גבי המטה לא ינענענו בידו אלא מנענעו בגופו ואם היה מאכל בהמה או שהיה עליו כר או סדין מנענעו בידו מכבש של בעלי בתים מתירין אבל לא כובשין ושל כובסין לא יגע בו ר׳ יהודה אומר אם היה מותר מע"ש מתיר את כולו ושומטו: **גמ׳** אמר רב נחמן האי פוגלא מלמעלה למטה שרי מלמטה למעלה אסיר אמר רב אדא בר אבא אמרי בי רב תנינא דלא כרב נחמן הקש שע"ג המטה לא ינענענו בידו אבל מנענעו בגופו ואם היה מאכל בהמה או שהיה עליו כר או סדין מנענעו בידו ש"מ טלטול מן הצד לא שמיה טלטול ש"מ אמר רב יהודה הני פלפלי מידק חדא חדא בקתא דסכינא שרי תרתי אסיר רבא אמר כיון דמשני אפילו טובא נמי אמר רב יהודה מאן דסחי במיא לינגיב נפשיה ברישא והדר ליסליק דילמא אתי לאתויי ד׳ אמות בכרמלית אי הכי כי קא נחית נמי קא דחי כחו ד׳ אמות ואסיר כחו בכרמלית לא גזרו אמר אביי ואיתימא רב יהודה טיט שע"ג רגלו מקנחו בקרקע ואין מקנחו בכותל אמר רבא מ"ט בכותל לא משום דמיחזי כבונה הא בנין חקלאה הוא אלא אמר רבא מקנחו בכותל ואין מקנחו בקרקע דילמא אתי לאשוויי גומות איתמר מר בריה דרבינא אמר אחד זה ואחד זה אסור רב פפא אמר אחד זה ואחד זה מותר למר בריה דרבינא במאי מקנחי ליה מקנחי ליה בקורה אמר רבא (א) לא ליתיב איניש אפומיה דליחייא דילמא מיגנדרא ליה חפץ ואתי לאתויי ואמר רבא לא ליצדד איניש כובא (ב) דילמא אתי לאשוויי גומות ואמר רבא לא ליהדוק איניש אודרא בפומא דשישא דילמא אתי לידי סחיטה אמר רב כהנא טיט שע"ג בגדו מכסכסו מבפנים ואין מכסכסו מבחוץ מיתיבי טיט שע"ג מנעלו מגררו בגב סכין [א] ושעל בגדו מגררו בצפורן ובלבד שלא יכסכס מאי לאו שלא יכסכס כלל לא שלא יכסכס מבחוץ אלא מבפנים א"ר אבהו א"ר אלעזר אמר ר׳ ינאי מגררין מנעל חדש אבל לא ישן

במה

רש"י

דאית לה רירי. ולימאים והא דקרי לה הכא פיה יפה והכא פיה רע לדמפרש ואזיל פיה יפה דלית ליה רירי פיה רע דלא דייק ואכיל שאוכל קוצים וברקנים: **מתני׳ הקש שעל המטה.** וסתמא להסקה ומוקצה הוא ובא לשכב עליו ומנענעו כדי שיהא רך לשכב: **לא ינענענו בידו.** דמוקצה הוא: **אבל מנענעו בגופו.** בכתפיו ובגופו טלטול מן הצד הוא דלא שמיה טלטול: **או שהיה עליו כר או סדין.** דגלי דעתיה דלהקלייה לשכיבה מעתה תורת כלי עליו: **מכבש.** פרים"א שני לווחים ארוכים וכבדים וסודרין בגדים על התחתון ומורידין העליון עליו וכובשים את הבגדים על ידי יתדות שיש עמודים קבועין מנוקבין בארבע הפיאות של התחתונות והעליונה מנוקבת בארבע זוויותיה ועולה ויורדת בעמודים וכפי מה שהוא רוצה לכבוש מורידה ותוחב יתד בנקב העמוד ואינה יכולה לעלות: **מתירין.** את המכבש שנוטל את היתד והוא נימר דהיינו צורך שבת שנוטל את הכלים: **אבל לא כובשין.** דהיינו צורך חול: **ושל כובסין לא יגע בו.** מפני שהוא עשוי לתקן הבגדים ותוחבו בחוזקה ומיהדק והתרה שלו דומה לסתירה: **גמ׳ האי פוגלא.** כגון שטומנין בקרקע להתקיים כשבא לחלצו מלמעלה למטה שרי אם היה ראשה מלמעלה ועוקצה מלמטה ותולשה מראשה העבה תחילה ועוקצה נמשך אחריה מותר לפי שהגומא רחבה מלמעלה ואין מזיז הקרקע כשהוא שומטה אבל אם תולשה מלמטה למעלה שהתחתונה נתון למעלה וראש עליונה שהוא עב נתון למטה והוא שומטה מסופה לראשה אסור לפי שהגומא קצרה מלמעלה וכשהוא תולשה מזיז העפר ומטלטלו ואע"ג דטלטול מן הצד הוא שמיה טלטול ואסור: **תנינא דלא כר"נ.** דאילו ממתניתין שמעינן דלא שמיה טלטול דקתני מנענעו בגופו: **מידק.** דייק: **חדא חדא.** לאו טוחן הוא אלא כלאחר יד: **דקמשני.** שלא ברחים ושלא במדוכה: **לאתויי ד׳ אמות.** מים שעליו: **קא דחי כחו.** את המים ד׳ אמות: **אחד זה ואחד זה אסור.** זה משום בונה וזה משום אשויי גומות: **אחד זה ואחד זה מותר.** אין דרך מתכוין בכך וקי"ל כר"ש: **בקורה.** בעץ המוטל על הקרקע (ג): **אפומא דלחייא.** של מבוי דליכא היכרא: **אודרא.** מוכין שסותמין בהן פי הפך: **שישא.** פך: **מכסכסו.** משפשפו: **מבפנים.** דלא מוכחא מילתא לאיתחזויי כמלבן ומלבן ממש לא הוי דאין נותן שם מים: כסכוס דמי למכבס: **אבל לא ישן.** שקולפו והוי ממחק:

תוספות

הקש שע"ג המטה. בריש פרק כירה (דף לו:) פי׳ מה הוא קש: **הני** פלפלי מידק חדא כו׳. פירש ר"ח בשאלתות דרב אחאי בפרשת אמור אל הכהנים מפרש דבי"ט מיירי וקשה לר׳ דהוה ליה לפרש בהדיא כיון דבמכילתין לא מיירי אלא בשבת ועוד היכי אסר רב יהודה כולי האי בפלפלין הא אפילו מלח שרינא בפ"ק דביצה (ד׳ יד.) במדוך של עץ אלא נראה לרבי דהכא בשבת איירי ואגב דאיירי בטלטול ע"י שינוי מייתי ליה הכא ובכולה שמעתא נמי מייתי מילי דשבת טובא אע"ג דלא שייכן הכא כולי האי אבל בי"ט נראה לר"י דשרי בלא שינוי אפי׳ במדוך של אבן כשאר תבלין דתנן בפ"ק דביצה (שם) ב"ה אומר תבלין נדוכין במדוך של אבן והמלח במדוך של עץ ואמרי׳ בגמרא דכ"ע מלח בעי שינוי מ"ט רב הונא ורב חסדא חד אמר כל הקדרות כולן צריכות מלח ואין כל הקדרות צריכות תבלין וחד אמר כולן מפיגין טעמן ומלח אין מפיגה טעמא מאי בינייהו איכא בינייהו דידע מאי בעי בשולי (ד) אי נמי מוריקא פירוש מוריקא אינה מפיגה טעמא למ"ד משום הפגת טעם אסור ולמ"ד משום כל הקדרות כו׳ שרי א"כ פלפלין דהכא נמי שרי דאין כל הקדרות צריכות פלפלין וא"כ (ס"א ואי נמי) למ"ד נמי משום הפגת טעם פלפלין שרו דצריך לומר נמי שמפיגים טעמם מדלא קאמר איכא בינייהו פלפלין ומיהו אומר רבי דאין זה דקדוק שצריך לפרש שם בע"א דקשיא למ"ד דשרי מוריקא משום דאין כל הקדרות צריכות מוריקא א"כ יהא מותר לקולרו ולחותכו מן המחובר אע"כ צריך לפרש יש בו הפגת טעם ולא כשאר תבלין להכי שרי למ"ד אין כל הקדרות כו׳ כיון דאיכא נמי קלת הפגת טעמא והשתא אתי שפיר דלקלור אסור ומהשתא אין ראיה להתיר פלפלין דשמא אין בהם הפגת טעם כלל ומיהו אומר ר"י דע"כ הם מפיגין טעמם דתנן בפ"ב דביצה (ד׳ כג.) ג׳ דברים רבי אלעזר בן עזריה מתיר וחכמים אוסרין שוחקין את הפלפלין ברחים שלהן והיכי הוה שרי רבי אלעזר בן עזריה אי לא מפיגין טעמא ואין סברא לומר דבהא פליגי רבי אלעזר בן עזריה ורבנן דמר סבר דמפיגין טעמא ומר סבר אין מפיגין טעמא אלא מדשרי ר׳ אלעזר בן עזריה ש"מ דמפיגין טעמא ורבנן דאסרי משום דברחים שלהם מיחזי טפי כי עובדא דחול ועוד תניא בהדיא בתוספתא דביצה בתר פלוגתא דבית שמאי ובית הלל הפלפלין כתבלין על כן נראה לר"י דמותר לכתוש פלפלין ביום טוב אפילו במדוך של אבן ומיהו היכא דידע מאי קדרה בעי בשולי אסור במדוך של אבן דלא ידענא כמאן הלכתא ואזלינן לחומרא ולא שייך למימר בשל סופרים הלך אחר המיקל היכא דלאו הוא קולא בדבר אחד חומרא הוא בדבר אחר מיהו במדוך של עץ ממ"נ שרי אפי׳ במדוכה של אבן כעין שלנו שקורין מורטי"ר כיון שהמדוך של עץ דלא אסרינן התם היכא דידע מאי קדרה בעי בשולי אלא בלא שינוי ושומין הנדוכים בי"ט נראה לר"י דשרי אפי׳ ידע מאי קדרה בעי בשולי לפי שמפיגין טעמן יותר מדאי ושרי מידי דהוי אשוחט ומבשל דשרי לכ"ע אפילו יודע מאי קדרה בעי בשולי דנראה הוא דהפגת טעם היינו שתש כח התבלין ואינם חדין כל כך ויכול לתקן הדבר כשמרבה התבלין אבל הפגת טעם שומין אין יכול לתקן מידי דהוה אשוחט ואופה ומבשל וגם רוח רעה שורה עליהן [נדה יז.] אם דכן מערב י"ט (ה) אפילו במדוך של אבן או של ברזל שרי ועוד דאין נראה שיהו בכלל תבלין דלא מיקרי תבלין אלא ירקות כעין כמון אבל שומין ובצלים אינם בכלל תבלין (ט): **דילמא** אתי לאשוויי גומות. אע"ג דרבא ס"ל בסוף פ"ב דביצה (ד׳ כג.) בדבר שאין מתכוין כר"ש גזרינן הכא כשיהא עסוק לקנח רגלו ישכח שבת ויתכוין לאשויי גומות כעין שמלינו בפ׳ בתרא דעירובין (ד׳ קד.) דנשים המשחקות באגוזים ובתפוחים אסור דילמא אתי לאשויי גומות כלומר במתכוין שמשכחת שבת מחמת שחוק שלהן: **אודרא** אפומא דשישא. פי׳ בפ׳ ח׳ שרצים (לעיל ד׳ קיא:) [בד"ה האי מסוכרייתא שם ע"א]:

במנעל

מסורת הש"ס

א) לעיל נ., ב) לעיל קכג., ג) [לעיל דף מג: קכג.], ד) [ברא"ש ובי"ף ליתא רב הונא], ה) [צ"ל ואמר], ו) [לעיל קח.], ז) לקמן קמח: ביצה ג., ח) [צ"ל וכן בשאלתות], ט) [וע"ע תוס׳ ביצה יד. ד"ה בית הלל].

הגהות הב"ח

(א) גמ׳ אמר רבא לא ליתיב איניש. תא"מ ונ"ב ג"י אלפסי לא ליתמשמש איניש וע"ל בדף קמח: (ב) שם כובא בארעא דילמא: (ג) רש"י ד"ה בקורה וכו׳ הקרקע הס"ד ואח"כ מ"ה לא ליצדד וכו׳ לדגלהו להוציאה הס"ד: (ד) תוס׳ ד"ה הני וכו׳ מאי בעי בשולים. למ"ד משום כל הקדרות כו׳ אסור ולמ"ד משום מוריקא וכו׳ א"כ פלפלין נמי שרי הכא נמי אין כל הקדרות: (ה) בא"ד מערב יו"ט הלכך אפי׳ במדוך:

גליון הש"ס

גמ׳ דילמא אתי לידי סחיטה. עיין לקמן דף קמז ע"א תוס׳ ד"ה כבסים: רש"י ד"ה ומלבן ממש לא הוי דאין נותן שם מים. עיין לקמן דף קמח ע"א ברש"י ד"ה סייג תעלת וצ"ע:

הגהות הגר"א

[א] גמ׳ ושעל בגדו מגררו בצפורן. נ"ב וכ"ה בגב סכין:

ליקוטי רש"י

הקש. שממיה לטינא קאי ללבנים או לתקנה לו לבוקה הוא ואם היה נתון על המטה ולא לשכב עליו ובא בשבת לשכב עליו והולך לנענעו ולשוטתו לשכיבה שלא יהא צבור וקשה. לא ינענענו בידו. שאסור לטלטלו. אלא מנענעו בגופו. כלאחר יד. או שהיה עליו כר או סדין. שכבר שכב עליו מבעוד יום ואף על פי שלא יחדו לכך ולא חישב עליו [לעיל נ.]. פוגלא. כגון שטומנין בארץ ומגלה ראשו. מלמעלה למטה שרי. אם היה העליון שלה למעלה והקלר למטה וכשהוא שולפה תולה מעלין שלה דקרוב לתתון נלה ורוחב הגומא למעלה מותר לפיכך טלטול לעפר כלל שהרי נתגלה ראשו. מלמטה למעלה אסור. שמזיז עפר לפי שהגומא קלרה מלמעלה ורוחב קלרה מלמעלה והוי על גב דטלטול עפר מן הלד הוא שאינו אוחז אותו ממש בידו [שם קכג.]. מן הצד. כלאחר יד [מג.]. בקתא. בית יד [שבועות מג:]. אפומיה דליחייא. לפי שאין ניכר כל כך בין מבוי לרשות הרבים [לקמן קמח:]. דליחייא. לחי העומד במבוי בשבת. דילמא מיגנדרא ליה חפץ. ברשות לחי [ביצה ל.]. ואתי לאתויי. ספק המתגלגל תוך ארבע אמות [לקמן שם]. מתוך שאינו במבוי מקורה להכיר שזה רשות הרבים וזה רשות היחיד ומביאו [ביצה שם]. כובא. גיגית [ב"מ כה.]. לאשוויי גומות. דמלאכה הוא בשבת דהוי בנין [עירובין קד.]. מכסכסו. משפשף לדו זה על לדו [שלו] זה כדרך המכבס בגדים אוחז הבגד בשתי ידיו ומשפשף [זבחים צד:]. בין שתי ידיו כדרך כיבוס בגדים שכופל לדו עם לדו ומשפשף ומוליך ומביא [נדה סב.].

עין משפט נר מצוה

מו א מיי׳ פכ"ה מהל׳ שבת הלכה כב סמג לאוין סה טוש"ע או"ח סי׳ שח סעיף מ:
מז ב מיי׳ שם הל׳ יב סמג שם טוש"ע או"ח סי׳ שב סעיף ד:
מח ג מיי׳ פכ"ה שם הל׳ יד טו סמג שם טוש"ע או"ח סי׳ שיא סעיף ח:
מט ד מיי׳ פכ"א הלכה ב סמג שם טוש"ע או"ח סי׳ שכא סעיף ח:
נ ה מיי׳ פכ"ו שם הל׳ כב סמג שם טוש"ע או"ח סימן שכו סעיף ז:
נא ו מיי׳ פכ"ה שם הל׳ ג סמג שם טוש"ע או"ח סימן שכו סעיף ו:
נב ז מיי׳ פי"ז שם הל׳ יז טוש"ע או"ח סי׳ שסה סעיף ה:
נג ח טוש"ע או"ח סי׳ שלו סעיף ד:
נד ט מיי׳ פכ"ב שם הלכה טו סמג שם טוש"ע או"ח סי׳ שב סעיף ט:
נה י מיי׳ פכ"ב שם הלכה יז סמג שם טוש"ע או"ח סי׳ שב סעיף ז:

רבינו חננאל

הקש שע"ג המטה לא ינענענו בידו אבל מנענעו בגופו: אמר רב נחמן האי פוגלא מלמעלה למטה שרי מלמטה למעלה אסור. יש מי שאומרים לא יגרה ויש מי שאומרים מותר לגררה ממעלה וכבר פירשנו דברי רב נחמן בפרק כל הכלים. אמר רב יהודה [הני] פלפלי [מידק] חדא חדא בקתא דסכינא שרי למידק. פי׳ ביו"ט אבל בלדכן אסור דהא אין מפיגין טעמן והוה ליה למידק מעיו"ט. רבא אמר כיון דמשני אפי׳ טובא והלכתא כרבא ביו"ט ויש מי שמתיר כי האי גוונא אפי׳ בשבת: טיט שע"ג רגלו הלכתא כמר בריה דרבנא דאסר בין בקרקע ובין בכותל ולא שרי אלא בקורה בלבד. ואמר רבא לא לצדד איניש כובא בארעא דלא אתו לאשווי גומות ואמר רבא לא ליהדוק איניש אודרא בפומיה דשישא דלמא אתו לידי סחיטה. פי׳ לא ידחוק אדם מוכין שרויין בפי אשישה שמא יבא לידי סחיטה. טיט שעל בגדו מכסכסו מבפנים ואין מכסכסו מבחוץ או מגררו בצפורן כסכוס כבר פירשנוהו למעלה. וכל אלו שאמר רבא אסור אחד בשבת ואחד ביו"ט לא שנא וגידור

רב נסים גאון

טיט שעל גבי מנעל איכא חספא דרבא משכחת לה בפרק כל הכלים ניטלין בשבת (דף קכד) רבא הוה קאזיל ברסתקא דמחוזא איתוס מסאניה בטינא אתא שמעיה שקל חספא וקא מכפר ליה:

במה מגררו א"ר אבהו בגב סכין א"ל ההוא סבא סמי דידך מקמי הא דתני רבי חייא אין מגררין לא מנעל חדש ולא מנעל ישן ולא יסוך את רגלו שמן והוא בתוך המנעל או בתוך הסנדל אבל סך את רגלו שמן ומניח בתוך המנעל או בתוך הסנדל וסך כל גופו שמן ומתעגל ע"ג קטבליא ואינו חושש אמר רב חסדא לא שנו אלא לצחצחו אבל לעבדו אסור לעבדו פשיטא ותו לצחצחו מי איכא מאן דשרי אלא אי איתמר הכי איתמר אמר רב חסדא לא שנו אלא שיעור לצחצחו אבל שיעור לעבדו אסור ת"ר לא יצא קטן במנעל גדול אבל יוצא הוא בחלוק גדול ולא תצא אשה במנעל מרופט ולא תחלוץ בו ואם חלצה חליצתה כשרה ואין יוצאין במנעל חדש באיזה מנעל אמרו במנעל של אשה תני בר קפרא ל"ש אלא שלא יצאה בו שעה אחת מבעוד יום אבל יצאה בו מע"ש מותר תני חדא שומטין מנעל מעל גבי אימום ותניא אידך אין שומטין לא קשיא הא ר' אליעזר הא רבנן דתנן מנעל שעל גבי אימום רבי אליעזר מטהר וחכמים מטמאים הניחא לרבא דאמר דבר שמלאכתו לאיסור בין לצורך גופו בין לצורך מקומו מותר שפיר אלא לאביי דאמר לצורך גופו מותר לצורך מקומו אסור מאי איכא למימר הכא במאי עסקינן ברפוי דתניא רבי יהודה אומר אם היה רפוי מותר טעמא דרפוי הא לא רפוי לא הניחא לאביי דאמר דבר שמלאכתו לאיסור לצורך גופו מותר לצורך מקומו אסור שפיר אלא לרבא דאמר בין לצורך גופו בין לצורך מקומו מותר מאי איריא רפוי אפי' לא רפוי נמי ההיא דרבי יהודה משום דרבי אליעזר הוא דתניא ר' יהודה אומר משום רבי אליעזר אם היה רפוי מותר:

הדרן עלך תולין

נוטל אדם את בנו והאבן בידו וכלכלה והאבן בתוכה ומטלטלין תרומה טמאה עם הטהורה ועם החולין רבי יהודה אומר אף מעלין את המדומע באחד ומאה: **גמ'** אמר רבא הוציא תינוק חי וכים תלוי בצוארו חייב משום כים תינוק מת וכים תלוי לו בצוארו פטור תינוק חי וכים תלוי לו בצוארו חייב משום כים וליחייב נמי משום תינוק רבא כרבי נתן סבירא ליה דאמר חי נושא את עצמו וליבטל כים לגבי תינוק מי לא תנן את החי במטה פטור אף על המטה שהמטה טפילה לו מטה לגבי חי מבטלי ליה כים לגבי תינוק לא מבטלי ליה תינוק מת וכים תלוי לו בצוארו פטור וליחייב משום תינוק רבא כר"ש ס"ל דאמר כל מלאכה שא"צ לגופה פטור עליה תנן נוטל אדם את בנו והאבן בידו אמרי דבי רבי ינאי בתינוק שיש לו גיעגועין על אביו אי הכי מאי

תוספות

במנעל מרופט כו' ואם חלצה חליצתה כשרה. וא"ת אמאי גזרינן בפרק מצות חליצה (יבמות דף קג.) מנעל אטו מנעל מרופט כיון דליעבד חליצתה כשרה ואומר ר"י דגזרינן אטו מרופט יותר מדאי שאינו חופה רוב רגלו דאם חלצה בו אין חליצתה כשרה.

ההיא דרבי יהודה משום דרבי אליעזר היא. מכאן ראיה דרבי יהודה שרי דבר שמלאכתו לאיסור לצורך גופו ולצורך מקומו כמו שפירשתי בסוף פרק במה מדליקין (דף לו: ד"ה הא ר"י):

הדרן עלך תולין

נוטל. רבא כרבי נתן ס"ל. פירש' בפ' המלניע (א) (לעיל ד' לג:):

תינוק מת וכים תלוי בצוארו פטור. דאגב מרריה מבטיל ליה לכים א"נ תינוק חי הוא לריך לכים לטייל בו התינוק אבל תינוק מת מה לריך לכים והוי מלאכה שאינה לריכה לגופה (ג) ופטור שלא הוליאה לצורך המוליאין: **אי** הכי מאי איריא אבן אפי' דינר נמי. אי אמרת בשלמא דתרוייהו מבטל להו בין אבן ובין דינר ואין כאן טלטול מוקצה כלל היינו דנקט אבן משום דאי נפיל לא אתי אבוה לאתויי אבל דינר אי נפיל אתי אבוה לאתויי אלא אי אמרינן דתרוייהו לא בטלי ואפ"ה שרינן איסור מוקצה כשמטלטל התינוק עם האבן משום גיעגועין בדינר נמי ליסתרי לא שייך למימר דילמא אתי אבוה לאתויי דמאי נפקא לן מינה דהשתא נמי דאיכא איסור מוקצה שרינן ליה משום גיעגועין ומשני דאע"פ שיש איסור מוקצה כשמטלטל התינוק עם האבן ושרינן ליה משום גיעגועין מיהו יש לנו להחמיר במוקצה יותר כשמטלטלו בידים משמטלטלו אגב תינוק אף על גב דבההיא שעתא נמי איכא מוקצה הלכך גזרינן דילמא נפיל בדינר ואתי אבוה לאתויי. כך פירש רבינו שמואל:
ונשלינהו

רש"י

במה מגררו. למחק: והוא בתוך המנעל. מפני שהמנעל נהנה ממנו ומלאה מעבדו: מתעגל. מתגלגל: קטבליא. עור שלוק שעושין ממנו משטחות לשלחן ולמטות: אלא לצחצחו. לא שנו דמותר לסוך שמן לרגלו ונותנו בתוך המנעל אלא שמתכוין לצחצחו מי שרי. במתכוין הא איכא למיגזר אטו לעבדו: שיעור לצחצחו. שלא היה כ"כ שמן הניסוך לעור מגופו כדי לעבד לעור אלא לצחצחו ומיהו איהו אפי' לצחצחו לא מתכוין: לא יצא. אדם קטן במנעל שהוא גדול לו משום דנופל מרגלו ואתי לאתויי: אבל יוצא בחלוק גדול. דלא נפיל מיניה ולמישלף ולאתויי לא חיישינן דלא שכיח ערום בשוק: מרופט. קרוע מלמעלה דגנאי הוא לה וכי מיחזי עלה שלפה ומייתי לה: ולא תחלוץ בו. לכתחילה דלאו נעל מעליא הוא: במנעל חדש. כדמפרש ואזיל שלא יצאה בו מבעוד יום ובאשה קיימינן דאשה מקפדת אם אינו מכוון למדת רגלה אבל יצאה בו כבר הסירה בו למכוון הוא לה או אינה מקפדת: אימום. פורמ"ש: ר' אליעזר מטהר. אלמא לאו כלי הוא ובשבת נמי אסור לטלטלו: הניחא לרבא דאמר. בפ' כל הכלים דבר שמלאכתו לאיסור בין שהוא לריך להשתמש בגופו של כלי בין שאינו לריך אלא למקומו מותר לטלטלו מאחר שתורת כלי עליו שפיר איכא לאוקומי להא דתני שומטין כרבנן דכיון דכלי הוא ואימום נמי כלי הוא ואף על גב דמלאכתו דאימום לאיסור לתקן מנעלין מטלטלין להאי אימום משום לורך מקומו דהיינו מנעל שהאימום נתון לתוכו: אלא לאביי. נהי נמי דמנעל שעל האימום לרבנן כלי הוא אימום מיהא מלאכתו לאיסור הוא וזה ששומט ממנו את המנעל אינו לריך לגופו של אימום והיכי מטלטל ליה: ברפוי. שהמנעל נשמט מאליו וא"ל לטלטל האימום: הא לאו רפוי לא. וע"כ טעמא משום דאימום אסור לטלטל לצורך מקומו: ה"ג ההיא רבי יהודה משום רבי אליעזר הוא. כי אמרה ליה ר' יהודה לההוא דמפליג בין רפוי לשאינו רפוי אליבא דרבי אליעזר אמר דאמר מנעל שעל האימום לאו גמר כלי הוא כל זמן שמחוסר הולאה ולענין שבת נמי אסור לטלטלו משום דלאו כלי הוא ואשמעינן דרפוי לאו מחוסר הולאה הוא ומותר לטלטלו דאילו לרבנן אף על גב דאין רפוי מותר דטעמא דשאין רפוי אסור לרבי יהודה לאו משום אימום הוא אלא משום מנעל גופיה:

הדרן עלך תולין

נוטל. והאבן בידו. בשלר ולא אמרי' דמטלטל לאבן: עם הטהורה. אגב הטהורה ואגב חולין אבל טמאה באפי נפשה לאו בת טלטול היא: אף מעלין את המדומע. סאה תרומה שנפלה לק' של חולין דקי"ל דעולה מותר להעלותו לסאה תרומה מהן בשבת ויהיו החולין מותרין ולא אמרינן מתקן הוא ובגמרא מפרש טעמא: גמ' חייב משום כים. ולא משום תינוק כדמפרש ואזיל משום כים מיהו חייב ולא אמרינן איהו לא מפיק ליה אלא תינוק קא מפיק ליה ולקמיה פריך לה ממתניתין: פטור. לגמרי כדמפרש ואזיל: מטה לגבי חי מבטל לה. להיות טפילה לו שהרי לריך לה: מלאכה שאינה צריכה לגופה. ומוליא מת לקוברו מלאכה שא"ל לגופה היא כדאמר בהמלניע (ו) וכים שהיה תלוי בלוארו לשחק בו אגב מרריה מבטל ליה לגבי תינוק שמת ולא חשיב ליה ההיא שעתא: והאבן בידו. מדשרי ליה בטלטול בשלר ש"מ לאו כמאן דנקיט לה איהו לאבן דמי ולגבי כים היכי מחייבת ליה: בתינוק שיש לו גיעגועין על אביו. שאם לא יטלנו יחלה ולא העמידו טלטול שלא בידים במקום סכנה ואע"ג דלאו סכנת נפש גמורה אלא סכנת חולי:
אתי

וקאמר רבי שמעון פטור על הולאה זו שבלרכו לא היתה באה אליו ולא היה לריך לה [חגיגה י:] לקוברו אינו לריך לגופה דהולאה ולא למת אלא לפנות ביתו והולאה הלריכה לגופה כגון שהוא אמר [לעיל עג:] געגועין. כרמור"ט מגעגע עליו ואינו יכול ליפרד ממנו [שם סו:]

עין משפט נר מצוה

נו א מיי' פכ"ג מהלכות שבת הלכה יח סמג שם טוש"ע או"ח סי' שכ סעיף ט:
נז ב ג ד מיי' (שם הל' יח) ופכ"ב הלכה כב סמג שם טוש"ע או"ח סי' שכז סעיף ד:
נח ה מיי' פי"ט שם הל' טו סמג שם טוש"ע או"ח סי' שא סעיף ז:
נט ו מיי' וסמג שם טוש"ע או"ח סי' שב סעיף יג:
ס ז מיי' פ"ד מהל' יבום הלכה יט סמג עשין נב טוש"ע אה"ע סי' קסט סעיף מ:
סא ח מיי' פי"ט מהל' שבת הלכה טו סמג לאוין סה טוש"ע או"ח סי' שא סעיף יג:
סב ט מיי' פכ"ו מהל' שבת הלכה יב סמג שם טוש"ע או"ח סי' שח סעיף יד:
סג י מיי' פכ"ד מהלכות כלים הלכה ה:
א כ מיי' פכ"ה מהלכות שבת הלכה כ סמג שם טוש"ע או"ח סי' שט סעיף א:
ב ל מיי' פי"ח מהלכות שבת הלכה יז:
ג מ מיי' פכ"ה שם הל' יט סמג שם טוש"ע או"ח סי' שט סעיף ב:

רבינו חננאל

וגרסי' מנעל הלכה כדתני ר' חייא אין מגררין לא מנעל חדש ולא מנעל ישן. ולא יסוך רגלו שמן והוא בתוך המנעל או בתוך הסנדל. אבל סך את רגלו בשמן ומניחה בתוך המנעל או בתוך הסנדל וסך כל גופו שמן ומתעגל ע"ג קטבליא. פי' ספרה. ואינו חושש ואמר רב חסדא לא שנו אלא אם נתן שמן מעט שיעור לצחצחו אבל שיעור לעבדו אסור. [אבל] לצחצחו אסור וכ"ש לעבדו. וכן הלכה: ת"ר לא יצא קטן במנעל גדול אבל יוצא הוא בחלוק גדול. פי' של אדם גדול ולא תצא אשה במנעל מרופט רפוי שמשתרבב מן הרגל כמו שאמור אם יטעום עבדך את אשר אכל ואת אשר אשתה מיכן [ואמר לקמן] (קלב) ששפחותיהן של זקנים מתרפסות ואין יכול לקפרן שפחותיו לטעום החן המאכל וכן עוד לא תצא אשה במנעל חדש בשבת אא"כ יצאה בו שעה אחת מבע"י: תני חדא שומטין מנעל מע"ג האימום בשבת. אימום זה דפוס של מנעל ואליבא דרבנן שאומרין מנעל שע"ג אימום כלי הוא ומקבל טומאה. ותניא אידך אין שומטין הא לרבי אליעזר דאמר מנעל ע"ג אימום אינו כלי ואינו מקבל טומאה דתנן בסדר טהרות בבא בתרא פ' סנדל עמקי וכיס של שנצות מנעל על האמום ר' אליעזר מטהר וחכמים מטמאין. פי' ר' אליעזר מטהר סבר מנעל על האמום אינו כלי לפיכך אינו מטמא ובשבת אסור לשומטו וחכמים שמטמאין סברי מנעל על האמום כבר נגמרה מלאכתו וכלי הוא לקבל טומאה. וכיון שהוא כלי מותר לשומטו בשבת והלכה כחכמים ואקשינן עלה הניחא לרבא דאמר דבר שמלאכתו לאיסור כגון האימום וכיוצא בו מכלי אומנות מלאכה בין לצורך מקומו מותר לטלטלו שפיר לטעמייהו דרבנן דסברי שומטין מנעל מעל אמום בשבת אלא (לאבין) [לרבא] דאמר לצורך גופו בלבד שרי אמום מאי לצורך גופו איכא דשומטין ומפרקינן הכא במאי עסקינן ברפוי כלומר מנעל זה רפוי הוא על האמום ואינו צריך להגביהו אלא מושך המנעל מעליו ונשאר האמום במקומו דתניא ר' יהודה אומר אם היה רפוי מותר וחזרנו להקשות על זה הפירוק לרבא ופשוטה היא ופריק רבא הא ר' יהודה משום ר' אליעזר היא כלומר אפילו ר' אליעזר שאמר אין שומטין סבר הני מילי כשהוא מהודק דצריך לטלטוליה ולאשמוטיה אבל אם היה רפוי שמושך המנעל והאמום נשאר במקומו מותר לשומטו אבל חכמים סבירא להו אע"פ שאינו רפוי אלא מהודק אם אינו לצורך גופו מותר לטלטלו לצורך מקומו:

הדרן עלך רבי אליעזר אומר תולין

פרק כא נוטל אדם את בנו והאבן בידו כו'. אמר רבא הוציא תינוק חי וכים תלוי לו בצוארו חייב משום כים תינוק מת וכים תלוי לו בצוארו פטור. פי' תינוק מת לקברו והכיס עמו כדאמר ריש לקיש וסנדלים

מסורת הש"ס

א) [תוספ' פ"ד], ב) כלים פכ"ו מ"ד [סנהדרין סח.], ג) [ע"ל אימום וכן הוא בערוך ובמשנה דכלים ובמפרשים שעליו], ד) [לעיל קכג.], ה) [לעיל קמ:], ו) לעיל מז., ז) לעיל לג. [עירובין קג.] יומא סו:, ח) עירובין לג: לעיל צג:, ט) [לעיל קמ: וש"נ], י) [דף לו:].

הגהות הב"ח

(א) תוס' ד"ה נוטל וכו' בפ' המלניע. נ"ב דף לד (ב) [illegible] (ג) ד"ה תינוק וכו' שאינו לריכה לגופה אי נמי אפי' לריך לו פטור שלא הוליא:

גליון הש"ס

גמ' ולא יסוך את רגלו שמן. וכן איתא בירושלמי פס"ח דשביעית לענין שמן שביעית:

רב נסים גאון

תני בר קפרא לא שנו אלא שלא יצאת בו שעה אחת מבעוד יום. בגמ' דבני מערבא בפרק במה אשה יוצאה (הלכה ב) ובפרק כל ישראל יש להם חלק (הלכה א) גרסי כמה שיעורו והכין גרסי לא ילבש אדם מנעלים

ליקוטי רש"י

מרופט. מנוקב קרוע מלמעלה [יבמות קב:]. אימום. [illegible]

בַּמֶּה מְגָרְרוֹ – And **with what can one scrape [a new shoe]?**[1] אָמַר רַבִּי אַבָּהוּ – **R' Abahu said:** בְּגַב סַכִּין – **With the back of a knife.**[1]

This opinion is rejected:

אָמַר לֵיהּ הַהוּא סָבָא – **This certain elder said to [R' Abahu]:** סַמֵּי דִּידָךְ מִקַּמֵּי הָא דְּתָנֵי רַבִּי חִיָּיא – **Delete your [ruling] in favor of that** ruling found **in a Baraisa taught by Rav Chiya:** אֵין מְגָרְרִין לֹא מִנְעָל חָדָשׁ וְלֹא מִנְעָל יָשָׁן – **We may not scrape neither a new shoe nor an old shoe.**[2] וְלֹא יָסוּךְ אֶת רַגְלוֹ שֶׁמֶן וְהוּא בְּתוֹךְ הַמִּנְעָל אוֹ בְּתוֹךְ הַסַּנְדָּל – **And one may not anoint his foot with oil while it is inside a shoe or sandal.**[3] אֲבָל סָךְ אֶת רַגְלוֹ שֶׁמֶן וּמַנִּיחַ בְּתוֹךְ הַמִּנְעָל – **But one may anoint his foot with oil** וְסָךְ **and then place it in his shoe** אוֹ בְּתוֹךְ הַסַּנְדָּל **or sandal;**[4] כָּל גּוּפוֹ שֶׁמֶן וּמִתְעַגֵּל עַל גַּבֵּי קְטַבְלִיָא – **and one may anoint his entire body with oil and then roll around atop a leather sheet,**[5] וְאֵינוֹ חוֹשֵׁשׁ – **and he need not be concerned for Sabbath desecration** in either of these last two cases.

This last ruling is qualified:

אָמַר רַב חִסְדָּא – **Rav Chisda said:** לֹא שָׁנוּ אֶלָּא לְצַחְצְחוֹ – **This** permit to indirectly oil shoe leather **was taught only** in a case where one's intent was **to polish**[6] the shoe's leather. אֲבָל לְעַבְּדוֹ אָסוּר – **But** if one's intent was **to tan** the leather, **it is prohibited.**[7]

The Gemara asks:

לְעַבְּדוֹ פְּשִׁיטָא – But if one's intent was **to tan** the leather, **it is obvious** that it is prohibited! Why was it necessary for Rav Chisda to point this out? וְתוּ – **And furthermore,** לְצַחְצְחוֹ מִי אִיכָּא מַאן דְּשָׁרֵי – **is there anyone who allows** one to apply oil with intent **to polish** leather? Even that should be prohibited![8]

The Gemara thus retracts its original understanding, and declares that one may not even indirectly oil shoe leather on the Sabbath even if his intent was only to polish it; one may insert his oiled foot into a leather shoe only if he applied the oil to benefit his *foot*, without any other intention. The Gemara restates Rav Chisda's qualification as applying to that permit:

אֶלָּא אִי אִיתְּמַר הָכִי אִיתְּמַר – **Rather, if** Rav Chisda's qualification **was said, this** is how it **was said:** אָמַר רַב חִסְדָּא – **Rav Chisda said:** לֹא שָׁנוּ אֶלָּא שִׁיעוּר לְצַחְצְחוֹ – **This** permit **was taught only** where oil **in an amount** sufficient only **to polish** the leather was transferred to the shoe. אֲבָל שִׁיעוּר לְעַבְּדוֹ אָסוּר – **But** if oil **in an amount** sufficient **to tan** the leather was transferred, even if he never intended to even polish it, **it is prohibited.**[9]

The Gemara states a series of rulings concerning shoes on the Sabbath:

תָּנוּ רַבָּנָן – **The Rabbis taught in a Baraisa:** לֹא יֵצֵא קָטָן בְּמִנְעָל גָּדוֹל – A SMALL PERSON SHOULD NOT GO OUT into a public domain WEARING A LARGE-size SHOE,[10] אֲבָל יוֹצֵא הוּא בְּחָלוּק גָּדוֹל – BUT HE MAY GO OUT WEARING A LARGE-size SHIRT.[11] וְלֹא תֵּצֵא אִשָּׁה בְּמִנְעָל מְרוּפָּט – AND A WOMAN SHOULD NOT GO OUT into the public domain WEARING A TORN SHOE,[12] וְלֹא תַּחֲלוֹץ בּוֹ – AND SHE SHOULD NOT PERFORM *CHALITZAH* WITH [A TORN SHOE].[13] וְאִם חָלְצָה חֲלִיצָתָהּ כְּשֵׁרָה – BUT IF SHE PERFORMED *CHALITZAH* WITH IT, THE *CHALITZAH* IS VALID.[14]

NOTES

1. *Rashi*. According to R' Abahu, one is permitted to scrape a new shoe in this manner, because its leather is tougher and will not be affected by the back of a knife (see next note).

[See *Yad David [Kamma]* and *Shabbos Shel Mi*, who discuss how *Rashi* knew that R' Abahu permits only the scraping of a new shoe.]

2. Because even the back of a knife will peel off a new shoe's upper layer, *smoothing* its leather (*Orach Chaim* 302:8; see also *Chidushei HaRan*). [Only a metallic surface such as a knife will surely peel off a layer of leather. Non-metallic surfaces, such as a wooden beam or a rock, will not necessarily peel off a layer, and may be used to scrape clay off a shoe, as above (141a) (*Mishnah Berurah* 302:26).]

Because of this ruling, some discourage the use of entryway mats made of metal, because rubbing one's shoes on such a mat transgresses the prohibition discussed here. However, if the metal surface upon which the shoe is rubbed is thick and wide (as opposed to the back of a knife, which is very narrow), it is possible that one may use such a mat. Furthermore, one may use even a mat in which narrow slivers of metal come into contact with the shoe, as long as one takes care to scrape the shoe gently, or if the clay is very moist [and thus needs only light rubbing] (*Mishnah Berurah* 302:26 and 38).

3. One of the thirty-nine *melachos* is מְעַבֵּד, *tanning* [animal hide]. This *melachah* includes salting or working other substances into hide [thus transforming it into a stronger and more durable material (leather)]. *Tolados* of this *melachah* include hardening hide by rubbing it or stamping on it, or softening it by stretching it. It is also forbidden to rub oil into it, for this too softens the hide. Because of this, pouring oil over a shoe is [at least] Rabbinically prohibited, and some forbid this on both old and new shoes. Therefore, it is prohibited for one to pour oil over his foot for pleasure while wearing a shoe, since he will simultaneously be oiling the shoe leather (see *Mishnah Berurah* 327:12).

4. Because at the time one anoints his foot with the oil, it does not come into contact with the shoe (ibid. §14). The shoe would later become oiled only as a consequence of the natural act of inserting the foot into the shoe. [The Gemara will shortly explain why this is permitted.]

5. A long wide sheet of leather used for tablecoths or bedsheets (*Rashi*). [In this case too, the oil was not poured onto the leather directly (see also *Chidushei HaRan*).]

6. [This does *not* refer to the "polishing" of shoes that is commonly done nowadays; such polishing can actually involve several Biblical prohibitions. See *Mishnah Berurah* 326:16.]

7. Now, while *tanning* leather is a *melachah* on the Sabbath, merely *polishing* it [with oil] is not. Rav Chisda taught that the leniency allowing the indirect oiling of shoe leather on the Sabbath can be utilized only where the intent is to polish the leather (*Rashi*). [Smearing oil directly on the shoe to polish it would still be prohibited, lest one come to oil the leather for the purpose of tanning it. Where one intends to *tan* the leather, even indirectly oiling the leather is prohibited.]

8. I.e. it should be Rabbinically forbidden, lest one come to oil shoe leather for the purpose of *tanning* it (*Rashi*).

9. The amount of oil applied to shoe leather to polish it is less than the amount needed to tan it. Rav Chisda teaches that one may apply oil to his foot (for the benefit of his foot) and insert it into a shoe only if the amount transferred to the shoe would be enough to polish the leather, and no more (*Rashi*). If there is enough oil to tan the leather, then he may not apply it in any case. Furthermore, even if there is not enough oil to tan the leather, he is forbidden to oil the shoe even if he *intends* to polish it (*Chidushei HaRan MHK* ed., *Ritva MHK* ed., *Milchamos* and *Baal HaMaor*; see also *Chidushei HaRan*). See also *Shulchan Aruch* 327:4.

10. For it will likely slip off his foot, and he may come to carry it four *amos* in a public domain (*Rashi*).

11. An ill-fitting shirt may be worn, because it is unlikely that the shirt will slip off his body. Nor is he likely to remove it [due to its ill fit], since he surely will not leave himself unclothed in the public domain (*Rashi*).

12. I.e. a shoe whose visible section (i.e. the upper) is torn. Since she will be embarrassed to be seen wearing such a shoe, we are concerned that she may remove it and carry the shoe home through the public domain (*Rashi*). [A man, however, is not so particular – see *Shulchan Aruch* 303:13.]

13. *Chalitzah* is a ceremony performed in a Jewish court through which a widow whose husband died childless is released from her bond to her late husband's brother, allowing her to marry another. Part of the ceremony includes her removing a shoe from the foot of the brother (the *yavam*). The Baraisa teaches that a torn shoe should preferably not be used, since it is not a full-fledged shoe (*Rashi*; cf. *Meiri*).

14. [Our Baraisa discusses a slightly torn shoe; using a completely torn [or even mostly torn – *Ritva MHK* ed.] shoe, however, would indeed render the *chalitzah* invalid (*Tosafos*).

במה מגררו א"ר אבהו בגב סכין א"ל ההוא סבא סמי דידך מקמי הא דתני רבי חייא א) אין מגררין לא מנעל חדש ולא מנעל ישן ב) ולא יסוך את רגלו שמן והוא בתוך המנעל או בתוך הסנדל אבל סך את רגלו שמן ומניחה בתוך המנעל או בתוך הסנדל וסך כל גופו שמן ומתעגל ע"ג קטבליא ואינו חושש אמר רב חסדא לא שנו אלא לצחצחו אבל לעבדו אסור לעבדו פשיטא ג) ותו לצחצחו מי איכא מאן דשרי אלא אי איתמר הכי איתמר אמר רב חסדא ד) לא שנו אלא שיעור לצחצחו אבל שיעור לעבדו אסור ת"ר ה) לא יצא קטן במנעל גדול אבל יוצא הוא בחלוק גדול ו) ולא תצא אשה במנעל מרופט ולא תחלוץ בו ז) ואם חלצה חליצתה כשרה ואין יוצאין במנעל חדש באיזה מנעל אמרו במנעל של אשה תני בר קפרא ל"ש אלא ח) שלא יצאה בו שעה אחת מבעוד יום אבל יצאה בו מע"ש מותר תני חדא ט) שומטין מנעל מעל גבי אימום ותניא אידך אין שומטין לא קשיא הא ר' אליעזר הא רבנן י) דתנן מנעל שעל גבי כ) אימום רבי אליעזר מטהר ל) וחכמים מטמאים הניחא לרבא מ) דאמר דבר שמלאכתו לאיסור בין לצורך גופו בין לצורך מקומו מותר שפיר אלא לאביי דאמר נ) לצורך גופו מותר לצורך מקומו אסור מאי איכא למימר הכא במאי עסקינן ברפוי דתניא רבי יהודה אומר אם היה רפוי מותר טעמא דרפוי הא לא רפוי לא הניחא לאביי דאמר דבר שמלאכתו לאיסור לצורך גופו מותר לצורך מקומו אסור שפיר אלא לרבא דאמר בין לצורך גופו בין לצורך מקומו מותר מאי איריא רפוי אפי' לא רפוי נמי ההיא דרבי יהודה משום דרבי אליעזר הוא דתניא ר' יהודה אומר משום רבי אליעזר אם היה רפוי מותר:

הדרן עלך תולין

נוטל ס) אדם את בנו והאבן בידו וכלכלה והאבן בתוכה ומטלטלין תרומה טמאה עם הטהורה ועם החולין רבי יהודה אומר אף מעלין את המדומע באחד ומאה: **גמ'** אמר רבא ע) הוציא תינוק חי וכיס תלוי בצוארו חייב משום כיס תינוק מת וכיס תלוי לו בצוארו פטור תינוק חי וכיס תלוי לו בצוארו חייב משום כיס וליחייב נמי משום תינוק רבא כרבי נתן סבירא ליה פ) דאמר חי נושא את עצמו וליבטל כיס לגבי תינוק מי לא תנן צ) את החי במטה פטור אף על המטה שהמטה טפילה לו מטה לגבי חי מבטלי ליה כיס לגבי תינוק לא מבטלי ליה תינוק מת וכיס תלוי לו בצוארו פטור וליחייב משום תינוק רבא כר"ש ס"ל דאמר ק) כל מלאכה שא"צ לגופה פטור עליה תנן נוטל אדם את בנו והאבן בידו אמרי דבי רבי ינאי ר) בתינוק שיש לו געגועין על אביו אי הכי מאי

רש"י

במה מגררו. לחדש: והוא בתוך המנעל. מפני שהמנעל נהנה ממנו ונמלא מעבדו: מתעגל. מתגלגל: קטבליא. עור שלוק שעושין ממנו משטחות לשלחן ולמטה: אלא לצחצחו. לא שנו דמותר לסוך שמן לרגלו ונותנו בתוך המנעל אלא שמתכוין לצחצחו למנעל: ולצחצחו מי שרי. במתכוין הא איכא למיגזר אטו לעבדו: שיעור לצחצחו. שלא היה כ"כ שמן הנישוף מגופו כדי לעבד עור אלא לצחצחו ומיהו איהו אפי' לצחצח לא מתכוין: לא יצא. אדם קטן במנעל שהוא גדול לו משום דנופל מרגלו ואתי לאתויי: אבל יוצא בחלוק גדול. דלא נפיל מיניה ולמישלף ואתויי לא חיישינן דלא קפי ערום בשוק: מרופט. קרוע מלמעלה דגנאי הוא לה וכי חייכי עלה שלפה ומייתי לה: ולא תחלוץ בו. לכתחילה דלאו נעל מעליא הוא: במנעל חדש. כדמפרש ואזיל שלא יצאה בו מבעוד יום ובאשה קיימינן דאשה מקפדת אם אינו מכוון למדת רגלה אבל יצאה בו כבר הכירה בו דמכוון הוא לה או אינה מקפדת: אימום. פורמ"ה: ר' אליעזר מטהר. אלמא לאו כלי הוא ובשבת נמי אסור לטלטלו: הניחא לרבא דאמר. בפ' כל הכלים דבר שמלאכתו לאיסור בין שהוא צריך להשתמש בגופו של כלי בין שאינו צריך אלא למקומו מותר לטלטלו מאחר שתורת כלי עליו שפיר איכא לאוקומי להא דתני שומטין כרבנן דכיון דכלי הוא ואימום נמי כלי הוא ואף על גב דמלאכתו דאימום לאיסור לתקן מנעלים מטלטלין להאי אימום משום לורך מקומו דהיינו מנעל שהאימום נתון לתוכו: אלא לאביי. נהי נמי דמנעל שעל האימום לרבנן כלי הוא אימום מיהא מלאכתו לאיסור הוא וזה ששומט ממנו את המנעל אינו צריך לגופו של אימום והיכי מטלטל ליה: ברפוי. שהמנעל נשמט מאליו ולא טלטל האימום: הא לאו רפוי לא. וע"כ טעמא משום דאימום אסור לטלטל לצורך מקומו: ה"ג ההיא דרבי יהודה משום רבי אליעזר הוא. כי אמרה ליה ר' יהודה להההיא דמפליג בין רפוי לשאינו רפוי אליבא דרבי אליעזר אמר דאמר מנעל שעל האימום לאו גמר כלי הוא כל זמן שמחוסר הוצאה ולענין שבת נמי אסור לטלטלו משום דלאו כלי הוא ואשמעינן דרפוי לאו מחוסר הוצאה הוא ומותר לטלטלו דאילו לרבנן אף על גב דלאין רפוי מותר דטעמא דשאין רפוי אסור לרבי יהודה לאו משום אימום הוא אלא משום מנעל גופיה:

הדרן עלך תולין

נוטל. והאבן בידו. בחצר ולא אמרי' דמטלטל לאבן: עם הטהורה. אגב הטהורה ואגב חולין אבל טמאה באפי נפשה לאו בת טלטול היא: אף מעלין את המדומע. סאה תרומה שנפלה לק' של חולין דקי"ל דעולה מותר להעלותו לסאה תרומה מהן בשבת ויהיו החולין מותרין ולא אמרינן מתקן הוא ובגמרא מפרש טעמא: גמ' חייב משום כיס. ולא משום תינוק כדמפרש ואזיל משום כיס מיהו חייב ולא אמרינן איהו לא מפיק ליה אלא תינוק קא מפיק ליה ולקמיה פריך לה ממתניתין: פטור. לגמרי כדמפרש ואזיל: מטה לגבי חי מבטל לה. להיות טפילה לו שהרי צריך לה: מלאכה שאינה צריכה לגופה. ומוציא מת לקוברו מלאכה שא"צ לגופה היא כדאמר בהמצניע י) וכיס שהיה תלוי בצוארו לשחק בו אגב מרריה מבטל ליה לגבי תינוק שמת ולא חשיב ליה ההיא שעתא: והאבן בידו. מדשרי ליה בטלטול בחצר ש"מ לאו כמאן דנקיט לה איהו לאבן דמי ולגבי כיס היכי מחייבת ליה: בתינוק שיש לו געגועין על אביו. שאם לא יטלנו יחלה ולא העמידו טלטול שלא בידים במקום סכנה ואע"ג דלאו סכנת נפש גמורה אלא סכנת חולי:

אתי

וקאמר רבי שמעון פטור על הוצאה זו שברצונו לא היתה באה אליו ולא היה צריך לה [חגיגה י.]. כמו הוצאת המת לקוברו אינו צריך לגופה דהוצאה ולא למת אלא לפנות ביתו והוצאה הצריכה לגופה כגון שהוא צריך לו למקום אחר [לעיל עג:] געגועין. ברמור"ט מגעגע עליו ואינו יכול ליפרד ממנו [שם סו:].

תוספות

במנעל מרופט כו' ואם חלצה חליצתה כשרה. וא"ת אמאי גזרינן בפרק מצות חליצה (יבמות דף קב.) מנעל אטו מנעל מרופט כיון דלדיעבד חליצתה כשרה ואומר ר"י דגזרינן אטו מרופט יותר מדאי שאינו חופה רוב רגלו דאם חלצה בו אין חליצתה כשרה.

ההיא דרבי יהודה משום דרבי אליעזר היא. מכאן ראיה דרבי יהודה שרי דבר שמלאכתו לאיסור לצורך גופו ולצורך מקומו כמו שפירשתי בסוף פרק במה מדליקין (דף מו: ד"ה הא ר"י):

הדרן עלך תולין

נוטל. רבא כרבי נתן ס"ל. פירש' בפ' המצניע (א) (לעיל ד' צד.):

תינוק מת וכיס תלוי בצוארו פטור. דאגב מרריה מבטיל ליה לכיס אע"ג דתינוק חי הוא צריך לכים לטייל בו התינוק אבל תינוק מת מה צריך לכים והוי מלאכה שאינה צריכה לגופה (ב) ופטור שלא הוליא כדרך המוליאין: **אי הכי מאי איריא אבן אפי' דינר נמי.** אי אמרת בשלמא דתרוייהו מבטל להו בין אבן ובין דינר ואין כאן טלטול מוקצה כלל היינו דנקט אבן משום דאי נפיל לא אתי אבוה לאתויי אבל דינר אי נפיל אתי אבוה לאתויי לא אלא אי אמרינן דתרוייהו לא בטלי ואפ"ה שרינן איסור מוקצה כשמטלטל התינוק עם האבן משום געגועין בדינר נמי ליסתרי דלא שייך למימר דילמא אתי אבוה לאתויי דמאי נפקא לן מינה דהשתא נמי דאיכא איסור מוקצה שרינן ליה משום געגועין ומשני דלא"פ שיש איסור מוקצה כשמטלטל התינוק עם האבן ושרינן ליה משום געגועין מיהו יש לנו להחמיר במוקצה יותר כשמטלטלו בידים משמטלטלו אגב תינוק אף על גב דבההיא שעתא נמי איכא מוקצה הלכך גזרינן דילמא נפיל בדינר ואתי אבוה לאתויי. כך פירש רבינו שמואל: ונשלחינהו

הגהות הב"ח

(א) תוס' ד"ה נוטל וכו' בפ' המצניע. נ"ב דף צד בד"ה אבל אדם: (ב) ד"ה תינוק וכו' שאינה צריכה לגופה אי נמי אפי' צריך לו פטור שלא הוליא:

גליון הש"ס

גמ' ולא יסוך את רגלו שמן. וכן איתא בירושלמי פס"ח דשביעית לענין שמן שביעית:

רב נסים גאון

תני בר קפרא לא שנו אלא שלא יצאת בו שעה אחת מבעוד יום. במס' דבני מערבא בפרק במה אשה יוצאה (הלכה ב) ובפרק כל ישראל יש להם חלק (הלכה א) גרסי כמה שיעורו והכין גרסי לא ילבש אדם מנעלים

ליקוטי רש"י

מרופט. מנוקב קרוע מלמעלה [יבמות קב.]. אימום. אימום שלהם של עור היה כעין דפוס ועושין המנעל מתוכו ועור ופיו ספור והיו עושין המנעלים לאימום כמו שעושין הרלענין שלנו בדפוס של עץ. רבי אליעזר מטהר וחכמים מטמאים. חכמים אומרין הואיל ואינו מחוסר אלא להוציא האימום שהדיוט יכול לשלוף מעל האימום כבר שם כלי עליו וטמא ור' אליעזר מטהר שעדיין לא נגמרה מלאכתו [סנהדרין סח.]. בין לצורך גופו. אם צריך בשבת לגופו [למלאכה] אחרת של היתר מותר [לעיל קכג.]. אלא לאביי דאמר. דבר שמלאכתו לאיסור לצורך גופו הוא דשרי אבל לצורך מקומו לא [שם קכד.]. חי נושא את עצמו. ואין זו לא הוצאה ולא משוי שבת ולפוטרה [לעיל צד.]. ויומא סו:. דלא מיתסר אלא מדרבנן [עירובין קג.]. את החי במטה. ומי לא מיחייב על הולאתו דהוא מקיל עלמו ונושא עלמו [לעיל צד:]. פטור אף על המטה. החולה ופטור על המטה דקיימא לן מי נושא את עצמו [עירובין לו:]. מלאכה שא"צ לגופה וכו'. וכל מלאכה שאינה צריכה (לגופה) אלא לתקן עליו ... לגופה וכו' לא אמר לה ... לר' שמעון ... ורבי שמעון ... גבי מוציא את המת ... לקוברו בשבת (שם לג:).

רבינו חננאל

וגירוד מנעל הלכה כדתני ר' חייא אין מגררין לא מנעל חדש ולא מנעל ישן. ולא יסוך רגלו שמן והוא בתוך המנעל או בתוך הסנדל. אבל סך את רגלו בשמן ומניחה בתוך המנעל או בתוך הסנדל וסך כל גופו שמן ומתעגל ע"ג קטבליא. פי' סדינה. ואינו חושש ואמר רב חסדא לא שנו אלא אם נתן שמן מעט שיעור לצחצחו אבל שיעור לעבדו אסור. [אבל] לצחצחו אסור וכ"ש לעבדו. וכן הלכה: ת"ר לא יצא קטן במנעל גדול אבל יוצא הוא בחלוק גדול. פי' של אדם גדול ולא תצא אשה במנעל מרופט רפוי שמשתרבב מן הרגל כמו שאמור אם יטעום עבדך את אשר אכל ואת אשר אשתה מיכן [ואמר לקמן] (קלב) ששפתותיהן של זקנים מתרפטות ואין יכול לקפוץ שפתותיו לטעום החך המאכל וכן עוד לא תצא אשה במנעל חדש בשבת אא"כ יצאה בו שעה אחת מבע"י: תני חדא שומטין מנעל מע"ג האימום בשבת. אימום זה דפוס של מנעל ואליבא דרבנן שאומרין מנעל שע"ג אימום כלי הוא ומקבל טומאה. ותניא אידך אין שומטין הא לרבי אליעזר דאמר מנעל ע"ג אימום אינו כלי ואינו מקבל טומאה דתנן בסדר טהרות בבא בתרא פ' סנדל עמקי וכיס של שנצות מנעל על האמום ר' אליעזר מטהר וחכמים מטמאין. פי' ר' אליעזר מטהר סבר מנעל על האמום אינו כלי לפיכך אינו מטמא ובשבת אסור לשומטו וחכמים שמטמאין סברי מנעל על האמום כבר נגמרה מלאכתו וכלי הוא לקבל טומאה. וכיון שהוא כלי מותר לשומטו בשבת הלכה כחכמים ואקשינן עלה הניחא לרבא דאמר דבר שמלאכתו לאיסור כגון האימום וכיוצא בו מכלי אומנות מלאכה בין לצורך מקומו מותר לטלטלו שפיר לטעמייהו דרבנן דסברי שומטין מנעל מעל אמום בשבת אלא (לאבין) [לרבא] דאמר לצורך גופו בלבד שרי אמום מאי לצורך גופו איכא דשומטין ומפרקינן הכא במאי עסקינן ברפוי כלומר מנעל זה רפוי הוא על האמום ואינו צריך להגביהו אלא מושך המנעל מעליו ונשאר האמום במקומו דתניא ר' יהודה אומר אם היה רפוי מותר וחזרנו להקשות על זה הפירוק לרבא ופשוטה היא ופריק רבא הא ר' יהודה משום ר' אליעזר היא כלומר אפילו ר' אליעזר שאמר אין שומטין סבר הני מילי כשהוא מהודק דצריך לטלטוליה ולאשמוטיה אבל אם היה רפוי שמושך המנעל והאמום נשאר במקומו מותר לשומטו אבל חכמים סבירא להו אע"פ שאינו רפוי אלא מהודק אם אינו לצורך גופו מותר לטלטלו לצורך מקומו:

הדרן עלך רבי אליעזר אומר תולין

פרק כא נוטל אדם את בנו והאבן בידו כו'. אמר רבא הוציא תינוק חי וכיס תלוי לו בצוארו חייב משום כיס תינוק מת וכיס תלוי לו בצוארו פטור. פי' תינוק מת לקברו והכיס עמו כדאמר ריש לקיש וסנדלים

וְאֵין יוֹצְאִין בְּמִנְעָל חָדָשׁ – AND WE MAY NOT GO OUT WITH A NEW SHOE on the Sabbath.

The Gemara clarifies this last ruling:

בְּאֵיזֶה מִנְעָל אָמְרוּ – **Concerning what shoe did [the Rabbis] state this** last ruling? בְּמִנְעָל שֶׁל אִשָּׁה – **Concerning a woman's shoe.**[15]

This ruling is qualified:

תָּנֵי בַּר קַפָּרָא – **Bar Kappara taught in a Baraisa:** לֹא שָׁנוּ אֶלָּא שֶׁלֹּא יָצְאָה בּוֹ שָׁעָה אַחַת מִבְּעוֹד יוֹם – THIS WAS TAUGHT ONLY WHERE THE WOMAN DID NOT GO OUT WEARING IT FOR A WHILE[16] BEFORE THE SABBATH, אֲבָל יָצְאָה בּוֹ מֵעֶרֶב שַׁבָּת מוּתָּר – BUT WHERE THE WOMAN WENT OUT WEARING IT for a while BEFORE THE SABBATH, IT IS PERMITTED for her to wear it outside on the Sabbath.[17]

The Gemara cites two Baraisos that apparently teach contradictory rulings concerning shoes on the Sabbath:

תָּנֵי חֲדָא – **One Baraisa taught:** שׁוֹמְטִין מִנְעָל מֵעַל אִימוּס – WE MAY SLIP A SHOE OFF THE SHOE-FORM on the Sabbath.[18] וְתַנְיָא אִידָךְ – **And another Baraisa taught:** אֵין שׁוֹמְטִין – WE MAY *NOT* SLIP a shoe off the shoe-form on the Sabbath. – ? –

The Gemara reconciles the two Baraisos:

לֹא קַשְׁיָא – **There is no difficulty.** הָא רַבִּי אֱלִיעֶזֶר הָא רַבָּנָן – **This** Baraisa follows the view of **R' Eliezer,** while **this** Baraisa follows the view of **the Rabbis,** דִּתְנַן – **as we learned in a Mishnah:**[19] מִנְעָל שֶׁעַל גַּבֵּי אִימוּס – A SHOE THAT IS ON THE SHOE-FORM, רַבִּי אֱלִיעֶזֶר מְטַהֵר וַחֲכָמִים מְטַמְּאִים – R' ELIEZER RULES IT *TAHOR*, i.e. it is not susceptible to *tumah*, WHILE THE SAGES RENDER IT *TAMEI*, i.e. it is susceptible to *tumah*. Now, their dispute hinges on whether a shoe is considered a utensil before it has been removed from the shoe-form. Our two Baraisos differ in this matter, as well, with the first Baraisa ruling in accord with the Sages that the shoe is a utensil (and thus *may* be removed on the Sabbath), and the second Baraisa ruling in accord with R' Eliezer that it is not a utensil (and thus it may *not* be removed on the Sabbath).

According to this interpretation, the first Baraisa allows the removal of the shoe based on the opinion of the Sages that such a shoe is already viewed as a utensil. The Gemara now notes that this should possibly be forbidden for another reason:

הָנִיחָא לְרָבָא דְּאָמַר דָּבָר שֶׁמְּלַאכְתּוֹ לְאִיסּוּר בֵּין לְצוֹרֶךְ גּוּפוֹ בֵּין לְצוֹרֶךְ מְקוֹמוֹ מוּתָּר – **This is understandable according to Rava who states that** moving **something that is used** primarily **for prohibited work**[20] **is permitted both for the sake of its use and for the sake of its place,**[21] שַׁפִּיר – for according to his view **it is good** that the first Baraisa allowed moving the shoe-form for the sake of its place, i.e. the shoe.[22] אֶלָּא לְאַבָּיֵי דְּאָמַר לְצוֹרֶךְ גּוּפוֹ מוּתָּר – **But according to Abaye, who states that** taking something that is used primarily for prohibited work **for the sake of its use is permitted,** לְצוֹרֶךְ מְקוֹמוֹ אָסוּר – but taking it **for the sake of its place is prohibited,**[23] מַאי אִיכָּא לְמֵימַר – **what is there to say?** How could the Baraisa have allowed moving the shoe-form for the sake of its place, i.e. the shoe?[24]

The Gemara answers:

הָכָא בְּמַאי עַסְקִינַן – **Here, with what** manner of **case are we dealing?** בְּרָפוּי – **Where** the shoe was fastened **loosely** upon the shoe-form. In such a case, one is permitted to remove the shoe, because it can be slipped off without moving the shoe-form at all.[25]

The Gemara cites a Baraisa in support of this interpretation:

דְּתַנְיָא – And this is indeed **as it was taught in a Baraisa:** רַבִּי יְהוּדָה אוֹמֵר – R' YEHUDAH SAYS: אִם הָיָה רָפוּי מוּתָּר – IF [THE SHOE] was LOOSELY fastened upon the shoe-form, IT IS PERMITTED to remove the shoe from it.

The Gemara attempts to support Abaye's position from the Baraisa just cited:

טַעְמָא דְּרָפוּי – **The reason** R' Yehudah permits removing the shoe **is because it** was fastened **loosely** upon the shoe-form. הָא לֹא רָפוּי לֹא – **This implies** that had [the shoe] **not** been fastened **loosely,** but held tightly, he would not have allowed removing the shoe. הָנִיחָא לְאַבָּיֵי דְּאָמַר דָּבָר שֶׁמְּלַאכְתּוֹ לְאִיסּוּר לְצוֹרֶךְ גּוּפוֹ מוּתָּר לְצוֹרֶךְ מְקוֹמוֹ אָסוּר שַׁפִּיר – Now, **this is understandable according to Abaye, who states that** moving **something that is used primarily for prohibited work for the sake of its use is permitted, but moving it for the sake of its place is prohibited** – for according to his view **it is good** that R' Yehudah limited the permit to where the shoe was loose, and the shoe-form did not need to be moved at all. אֶלָּא לְרָבָא דְּאָמַר בֵּין לְצוֹרֶךְ גּוּפוֹ בֵּין לְצוֹרֶךְ מְקוֹמוֹ מוּתָּר – **But according to Rava, who states** that moving something used primarily for prohibited work **is permitted both for the sake of its use and for the sake of its place,**

NOTES

15. A woman is very particular that her shoe fit her foot precisely. Thus, we are concerned that if she were to wear a new shoe, she might come to remove it in the public domain after finding that it is too large or too small (*Rashi*). Nor will the prospect of walking in the street without shoes deter her, because she will be wearing stockings that will protect her feet (*Chidushei HaRan*).

16. Literally: one hour.

17. If she wore the shoes before the Sabbath, she has already determined that they fit well; there is then no concern that she will be particular about their fit and remove them on the Sabbath (*Rashi;* see *Yerushalmi*, cited in *Megadim Chadashim*, who discusses how long the shoes must have been worn).

18. A shoe-form was an oblong leather skin shaped like a foot upon which shoemakers would craft shoes.

19. *Keilim* 26:4. The law is that an unfinished utensil is not susceptible to *tumah*. R' Eliezer maintained that a shoe is not considered "finished" until its crafting is completed with its removal from the shoe-form (see *Rashi* below ד"ה ההיא). Thus, while on the shoe-form, it is not susceptible to *tumah* even if the rest of the shoemaking process has been completed. The Sages, however, maintain that since removing the shoe from the form does not require skilled labor, a shoe that is otherwise complete is considered "finished" and is susceptible to *tumah* even while it is on the form.

20. A shoe-form, which is used in the crafting of shoes, is an example of *a forbidden-use utensil* [כְּלִי שֶׁמְּלַאכְתּוֹ לְאִיסּוּר].

21. According to Rava, a forbidden-use utensil (e.g. a hammer) may be moved for the sake of its permitted use (e.g. to crack nuts) or for the sake of its place (i.e. to use its place on a table). This is permitted because, unlike stones and the like which are *inherently muktzeh* (מוּקְצֶה מֵחֲמַת גּוּפוֹ), it is a full-fledged utensil (*Rashi;* see Gemara above, 123b, 124a). [The Gemara is assuming that the shoe cannot be removed without moving the shoe-form.]

22. Since one needs the place where the shoe-form rests inside the shoe for another purpose, i.e. to place one's foot therein, one is permitted to remove the shoe-form from the shoe for the sake of its place (*Rashi*).

23. Abaye maintains that such a utensil may be taken for the sake of using it for a task that is permitted on the Sabbath, but *not* for the sake of vacating its place (*Rashi;* see next note).

24. While it is true that the shoe itself is a utensil and not *muktzeh*, removing the shoe should be prohibited because in doing so one will inevitably move the shoe-form; this is prohibited, for it is being moved not for its own sake, but for the sake of the shoe which it occupies (*Rashi*).

25. A shoe that is tightly fastened upon the shoe-form, however, may indeed not be moved at all.

במה מגררו א"ר אבהו בגב סכין א"ל ההוא סבא סמי דידך מקמי הא דתני רבי חייא א אין מגררין לא מנעל חדש ולא מנעל ישן ב ולא יסוך את רגלו שמן והוא בתוך המנעל או בתוך הסנדל אבל סך את רגלו שמן ומניח בתוך המנעל או בתוך הסנדל וסך כל גופו שמן ומתעגל ע"ג קטבליא ואינו חושש אמר רב חסדא לא שנו אלא לצחצחו אבל לעבדו אסור לעבדו פשיטא ג ותו לצחצחו מי איכא מאן דשרי אלא אי איתמר הכי איתמר אמר רב חסדא ד לא שנו אלא שיעור לצחצחו אבל שיעור לעבדו אסור ת"ר ה לא יצא קטן במנעל גדול אבל יוצא הוא בחלוק גדול ו ולא תצא אשה במנעל מרופט ולא תחלוץ בו ז ואם חלצה חליצתה כשרה ואין יוצאין במנעל חדש באיזה מנעל אמרו במנעל של אשה תני בר קפרא ל"ש אלא ח שלא יצאה בו שעה אחת מבעוד יום אבל יצאה בו מע"ש מותר תני חדא ט שומטין מנעל מעל גבי אימום ותניא אידך אין שומטין לא קשיא הא ר' אליעזר הא רבנן י דתנן ג מנעל שעל גבי אימום רבי אליעזר מטהר וחכמים מטמאים הניחא לרבא ד דאמר דבר שמלאכתו לאיסור בין לצורך גופו בין לצורך מקומו מותר שפיר אלא לאביי דאמר ה לצורך גופו מותר לצורך מקומו אסור מאי איכא למימר הכא במאי עסקינן ברפוי דתניא רבי יהודה אומר אם היה רפוי מותר טעמא דרפוי הא לא רפוי לא הניחא לאביי דאמר דבר שמלאכתו לאיסור לצורך גופו מותר לצורך מקומו אסור שפיר אלא לרבא דאמר בין לצורך גופו בין לצורך מקומו מותר מאי איריא רפוי אפי' לא רפוי נמי ההיא דרבי יהודה משום דרבי אליעזר הוא דתניא ר' יהודה אומר משום רבי אליעזר אם היה רפוי מותר:

הדרן עלך תולין

נוטל אדם את בנו והאבן בידו וכלכלה והאבן בתוכה ומטלטלין תרומה טמאה עם הטהורה ועם החולין רבי יהודה אומר אף מעלין את המדומע באחד ומאה: **גמ'** אמר רבא הוציא תינוק חי וכיס תלוי בצוארו חייב משום כיס תינוק מת וכיס תלוי לו בצוארו פטור תינוק חי וכיס תלוי לו בצוארו חייב משום כיס וליחייב נמי משום תינוק רבא כרבי נתן סבירא ליה דאמר חי נושא את עצמו וליבטל כיס לגבי תינוק מי לא תנן את החי במטה פטור אף על המטה שהמטה טפילה לו מטה לגבי חי מבטלי ליה כיס לגבי תינוק לא מבטלי ליה תינוק מת וכיס תלוי לו בצוארו פטור וליחייב משום תינוק רבא כר"ש ס"ל דאמר כל מלאכה שא"צ לגופה פטור עליה תנן נוטל אדם את בנו והאבן בידו אמרי דבי רבי ינאי בתינוק שיש לו געגועין על אביו אי הכי מאי

רש"י

במה מגררו. לגלח: **והוא בתוך המנעל.** מפני שהמנעל נהנה ממנו ונמלא מעבדו: **מתעגל.** מתגלגל: **קטבליא.** עור שלוק שעושין ממנו משטוחות לשלחן ולמטה: **אלא לצחצחו.** לא שנו דמותר לסוך שמן לרגלו ונותנו בתוך המנעל אלא שמתכוין לצחצחו למנעל: **ולצחצחו מי שרי.** במתכוין הא איכא למיגזר אטו לעבדו: **שיעור לצחצחו.** שלא היה כ"כ שמן הניסוך לעור מגופו כדי לעבד לעור אלא לצחצחו ומיהו איהו אפי' לצחצח לא מתכוין: **לא יצא.** אדם קטן במנעל שהוא גדול לו משום דנופל מרגלו ואתי לאתויי: **אבל יוצא בחלוק גדול.** דלא נפיל מיניה ולמישלף ולאתויי לא חיישינן דלא קאי ערום בשוק: **מרופט.** קרוע מלמעלה דגנאי הוא לה וכי חייכי עלה שלפה ומייתי לה: **ולא תחלוץ בו.** לכתחילה דלאו נעל מעליא הוא: **במנעל חדש.** כדמפרש ואזיל שלא יצאה בו מבעוד יום ובאשה קיימינן דאשה מקפדת אם אינו מכוון למדת רגלה אבל יצאה בו כבר הסירה בו דמכוון הוא לה או אינה מקפדת: **אימום.** פורמ"ה: **ר' אליעזר מטהר.** אלמא לאו כלי הוא ובשבת נמי אסור לטלטלו: **הניחא לרבא דאמר.** בפ' כל הכלים דבר שמלאכתו לאיסור בין שהוא צריך להשתמש בגופו של כלי בין שאינו צריך אלא למקומו מותר לטלטלו מאחר שתורת כלי עליו שפיר איכא לאוקומי להא דתני שומטין כרבנן דכיון דכלי הוא ואימום נמי כלי הוא ואף על גב דמלאכתו דאימום לאיסור לתקן מנעלין מטלטלין להאי אימום משום צורך מקומו דהיינו מנעל שהאימום נתון לתוכו: **אלא לאביי.** נהי נמי דמנעל שעל האימום לרבנן כלי הוא אימום מיהא מלאכתו לאיסור הוא וזה ששומט ממנו את המנעל אינו צריך לגופו של אימום והיכי מטלטל ליה: **ברפוי.** שהמנעל נשמט מאליו וא"צ לטלטל האימום: **הא לאו רפוי לא.** וע"כ טעמא משום דאימום אסור לטלטל לצורך מקומו: **ה"ג ההיא רבי יהודה משום רבי אליעזר הוא.** כי אמרה ליה ר' יהודה להאי דמפליג בין רפוי לשאינו רפוי אליבא דרבי אליעזר אמר דאמר מנעל שעל האימום לאו גמר כלי הוא כל זמן שמחוסר הוצאה ולענין שבת נמי אסור לטלטלו משום דלאו כלי הוא ואשמעינן דרפוי לאו מחוסר הוצאה הוא ומותר לטלטלו דאילו לרבנן אף על גב דאין רפוי מותר דטעמא דשאין רפוי אסור לרבי יהודה לאו משום אימום הוא אלא משום מנעל גופיה:

הדרן עלך תולין

נוטל. והאבן בידו. בחצר ולא אמרי' דמטלטל לאבן: **עם הטהורה.** אגב הטהורה ואגב חולין אבל טמאה באפי נפשה לאו בת טלטול היא: **אף מעלין את המדומע.** סאה תרומה שנפלה לק' של חולין דקי"ל דעולה מותר להעלותו לסאה תרומה מהן בשבת ויהיו החולין מותרין ולא אמרינן מתקן הוא ובגמרא מפרש טעמא: **גמ' חייב משום כיס.** ולא משום תינוק כדמפרש ואזיל משום כיס מיהו חייב ולא אמרינן איהו לא מפיק ליה אלא תינוק קא מפיק ליה ולקמיה פריך לה ממתניתין: **פטור.** לגמרי כדמפרש ואזיל: **מטה לגבי חי מבטל לה.** להיות טפילה לו שהרי צריך לה: **מלאכה שאינה צריכה לגופה.** ומוציא מת לקוברו מלאכה שא"צ לגופה היא כדאמר בהמצניע ו) וכיס שהיה תלוי בצוארו לשחק בו אגב מרריה מבטל ליה לגבי תינוק שמת ולא חשיב ליה ההיא שעתא: **והאבן בידו.** מדשרי ליה בטלטול בחצר ש"מ לאו כמאן דנקיט לה איהו לאבן דמי ולגבי כיס היכי מחייבת ליה: **בתינוק שיש לו געגועין על אביו.** שאם לא יטלנו יחלה ולא העמידו טלטול שלא בידים במקום סכנה ואע"ג דלאו סכנת נפש גמורה אלא סכנת חולי:

אתי

תוספות

במנעל מרופט כו' ואם חלצה חליצתה כשרה. וא"ת אמאי גזרינן בפרק מצות חליצה (יבמות דף קב.) מנעל אטו מנעל מרופט כיון דלדיעבד חליצתה כשרה ואומר ר"י דגזרינן אטו מרופט יותר מדאי שאינו חופה רוב רגלו דאם חלצה בו אין חליצתה כשרה.

מ"ר: **ההיא** דרבי יהודה משום דרבי אליעזר היא. מכאן ראיה דרבי יהודה שרי דבר שמלאכתו לאיסור לצורך גופו ולצורך מקומו כמו שפירשתי בסוף פרק במה מדליקין (דף לו: ד"ה הא ר"י):

הדרן עלך תולין

נוטל. רבא כרבי נתן ס"ל. פירש' בפ' המצניע (א) (לעיל ד' צג:):

תינוק מת וכיס תלוי בצוארו פטור. דאגב מרריה מבטיל ליה לכיס א"נ תינוק מי הוא צריך לכיס לטייל בו התינוק אבל תינוק מת מה צריך לכיס והוי מלאכה שאינה צריכה לגופה (ב) ופטור שלא הוציא כדרך המוציאין: **אי הכי מאי איריא אבן אפי'** דינר נמי. אי אמרת בשלמא דמתניתין מבטל להו בין אבן ובין דינר ואין כאן טלטול מוקצה כלל היינו דנקט אבן משום דאי נפיל לא אתי אבוה לאתויי אבל דינר אי נפיל אתי אבוה לאתויי לא אלא אי אמרינן דמתרוייהו לא בטלי ואפ"ה שרינן איסור מוקצה כשמטלטל התינוק עם האבן משום געגועין בדינר נמי ליסתרי לא שייך למימר דילמא אתי אבוה לאתויי דמאי נפקא לן מינה דהשתא נמי דאיכא איסור מוקצה שרינן ליה משום געגועין ומשני דאע"פ שיש איסור מוקצה כשמטלטל התינוק עם האבן ושרינן ליה משום געגועין מיהו יש לנו להחמיר במוקצה יותר כשמטלטלו בידים משמטלטלו אגב תינוק אף על גב דבהשתא נמי איכא מוקצה הלכך גזרינן דילמא נפיל בדינר ואתי אבוה לאתויי. כך פירש רבינו שמואל: ושלימו

עין משפט נר מצוה

נו א מיי' פכ"ו מהלכות שבת הלכה יט סמג שם טוש"ע או"ח סי' שכז סעיף ט:

נז ב ג ד מיי' (שם הל' יח) ופכ"ג הלכה י סמג שם טוש"ע או"ח סי' שכג סעיף ז:

נח ה מיי' פי"ט שם הל' טו סמג שם טוש"ע או"ח סי' שא סעיף ז:

נט ו מיי' ומסג שם טוש"ע או"ח סי' שג סעיף יג:

ס ז מיי' פ"ד מהל' יבום הלכה יט סמג עשין נג טוש"ע אה"ע סי' קסט סעיף טז [קטן]:

סא ח מיי' פי"ט מהל' שבת הלכה טו סמג לאוין סה טוש"ע או"ח סי' שג סעיף יג:

סב ט מיי' פכ"ו מהל' שבת הל' יב סמג שם טוש"ע או"ח סי' שח סעיף יד:

סג י מיי' פכ"ד מהלכות כלים הלכה ה:

א כ מיי' פכ"ה מהלכות שבת הלכה ו סמג לאוין סה טוש"ע או"ח סי' שט סעיף א:

ב ל מיי' פכ"ה מהלכות שבת הלכה יז:

ג מ מיי' פכ"ה שם הל' כו סמג שם טוש"ע או"ח סי' שט סעיף א:

רבינו חננאל

וגירוד מנעל הלכה כדתני ר' חייא אין מגררין לא מנעל חדש ולא מנעל ישן. ולא יסוך רגלו שמן והוא בתוך המנעל או בתוך הסנדל. אבל סך את רגלו בשמן ומניחה בתוך המנעל או בתוך הסנדל וסך כל גופו שמן ומתעגל ע"ג קטבליא. פי' ספרה. ואינו חושש ואמר רב חסדא לא שנו אלא אם נתן שמן מעט שיעור לצחצחו אבל שיעור לעבדו אסור. [אבל] לצחצחו אסור וכ"ש לעבדו. וכן הלכה: ת"ר לא יצא קטן במנעל גדול אבל יוצא הוא בחלוק גדול. פי' של אדם גדול ולא תצא אשה במנעל מרופט רפוי שמשתרבב מן הרגל כמו שאמור בו יטעום עבדך את אשר אכל ואת אשר אשתה מיכן [ואמר לקמן] (קלב) ששפחותיהן של זקנים מתרפטות ואין יכול לקפוץ שפחותיו לטעום החק המאכל וכן עוד לא תצא אשה במנעל חדש בשבת אא"כ יצאה בו שעה אחת מבעו"י: תני חדא שומטין מנעל מע"ג האימום בשבת. אימום זה דפוס של מנעל ואליבא דרבנן שאומרין מנעל שע"ג אימום כלי הוא ומקבל טומאה. ותניא אידך אין שומטין הא לרבי אליעזר דאמר מנעל ע"ג אימום אינו כלי ואינו מקבל טומאה דתנן בסדר טהרות בבא בתרא פ' סנדל עמקי וכיס של שנצות מנעל על האמום ר' אליעזר מטהר וחכמים מטמאין. פי' ר' אליעזר מטהר סבר מנעל על האמום אינו כלי לפיכך אינו מטמא ובשבת אסור לשומטו וחכמים שמטמאין סברי מנעל על האמום כבר נגמרה מלאכתו וכלי הוא לקבל טומאה. וכיון שהוא כלי מותר לשומטו בשבת והלכה כחכמים ואקשינן עלה הניחא לרבא דאמר דבר שמלאכתו לאיסור כגון האימום וכיוצא בו מכלי אומנות מלאכה בין לצורך מקומו מותר לטלטלו שפיר לטעמייהו דרבנן דסברי שומטין מנעל מעל אמום בשבת אלא (לאבין) [לרבא] דאמר לצורך גופו בלבד שרי אמום מאי לצורך גופו איכא דשומטין ומפרקינן הכא במאי עסקינן ברפוי כלומר מנעל זה רפוי הוא על האמום ואינו צריך להגביהו אלא מושך המנעל מעליו ונשאר האמום במקומו דתניא ר' יהודה אומר אם היה רפוי מותר וחזרנו להקשות על זה הפירוק לרבא ופשוטה היא ופריק רבא הא ר' יהודה משום ר' אליעזר היא כלומר אפילו ר' אליעזר שאמר אין שומטין סבר הני מילי כשהוא מהודק דצריך לטלטוליה ולאשמוטיה אבל אם היה רפוי שמושך המנעל והאמום נשאר במקומו מותר לשומטו אבל חכמים סבירא להו אע"פ שאינו רפוי אלא מהודק אם אינו לצורך גופו מותר לטלטלו לצורך מקומו:

הדרן עלך רבי אליעזר אומר תולין

פרק כא נוטל אדם את בנו והאבן בידו כו'. אמר רבא הוציא תינוק חי וכיס תלוי לו בצוארו חייב משום כיס תינוק מת וכיס תלוי לו בצוארו פטור. פי' תינוק מת לקברו והכיס עמו כדאמר ריש לקיש וסנדלים

מסורת הש"ס

א) [תוספ' פ"ד], ב) כלים פכ"ו מ"ד [סנהדרין סח.], ג) [נ"ל אימום וכן הוא בערוך ובמשנה דכלים ובמפרשים שעליו], ד) לעיל קכב., ה) [לעיל קכג.], ו) לעיל צג., ז) לעיל צג: [עירובין קג.] יומא סו., ח) עירובין קג:, ט) [לעיל קה: וש"נ], י) [דף לג.]

הגהות הב"ח

(א) תוס' ד"ה נוטל וכו' בפ' המצניע. נ"ב דף צג ע"ב: (ב) ד"ה תינוק וכו' אבל תינוק מת מה צריך לכיס לגופה אי נמי אפי' צריך לו פטור שלא הוציא:

גליון הש"ס

גמ' ולא יסוך את רגלו שמן. וכן איתא בירושלמי פפ"ח דשביעית לענין שמן שביעית:

רב נסים גאון

תני בר קפרא לא שנו אלא שלא יצאה בו שעה אחת מבעוד יום. בגמ' דבני מערבא בפרק במה אשה יוצאה (הלכה ב) ובפרק כל ישראל יש להם חלק (הלכה א) גרסי כמה שיעורו והכין גרסי לא ילבש אדם מנעלים

ליקוטי רש"י

מרופט. מנוקב קרוע מלמעלה [יבמות קב.]. אימום. אימום שלהם של עור היה כעין מנעל וממולא מתוכו שער ופיו סתור ובו היו עושין המנעלים כמו שעושין הרלענין שלנו בדפוס של עץ. רבי אליעזר מטהר וחכמים מטמאים. חכמים אומרין הואיל ואינו חסר מלאכה אלא שצריך לשומטו מעל האימום כבר שם כלי עליו ומקבל טומאה ור' אליעזר מטהר שעדיין לא נגמרה מלאכתו [סנהדרין סח.]. בין לצורך גופו. כגון קורנס לפצוע בו אגוזים. בין לצורך מקומו. שצריך למקומו [לעיל קכב:]. אלא לאביי דאמר לצורך גופו אין לצורך מקומו לא. דלא מיתסר אלא מדרבנן [עירובין קג.]. את החי במטה. ומי שלא הוציא את החי מתחייב הואיל והחי נושא את עצמו. פטור אף על המטה. הואיל והמטה טפלה לו [לעיל צג:]. מלאכה שא"צ לגופה. וכל מלאכה שאינה צריכה לגופה ולא לתקן דבר אלא לסלק מעליו היזק דברים שאינה צריכה לגופה דבר שלא בא לו ולא היה צריך לה הלכך לאו מלאכת מחשבת היא לר' שמעון [לעיל שם]. ורבי שמעון אמר מילתיה גבי מוציא את המת במטה לקוברו בשבת (שבת צג:) וקאמר רבי שמעון פטור על הוצאה זו שברצונו לא היתה באה אליו ולא היה צריך לה [חגיגה י.]. כמו מוציא את המת לקוברו אינו צריך לגופה דהוצאה ולא למת אלא לפנות ביתו והוצאה הצריכה לגופה כגון שהוא צריך לחפץ זה במקום אחר [לעיל עג:]. געגועין. ברמור"ט מגעגע עליו ואינו יכול ליפרד ממנו [שם סו:].

מַאי אִירְיָא רָפוּי – **why did [R' Yehudah] teach** that removing the shoe is permitted where the shoe was **loose?** אֲפִילוּ לֹא רָפוּי נַמִי – **Even if it was not loose,** it should **also** be permitted to move the shoe-form for the sake of the shoe!

Rava answers that R' Yehudah limited the permit for an entirely different reason:

הַהִיא דְּרַבִּי יְהוּדָה מִשּׁוּם דְּרַבִּי אֱלִיעֶזֶר הוּא – **That** Baraisa, which cited **R' Yehudah** as saying that the shoe must be loose, **was** R' Yehudah speaking **in the name of R' Eliezer,** who maintained that a shoe, before it is removed from a shoe-form, is itself not a utensil and may not be moved. Thus, it was necessary from the perspective of the shoe that the shoe be loose, so that even R' Eliezer may agree that it is a utensil.[26]

דְּתַנְיָא – **As it was taught in a Baraisa:** רַבִּי יְהוּדָה אוֹמֵר מִשּׁוּם רַבִּי אֱלִיעֶזֶר – R' YEHUDAH SAID IN THE NAME OF R' ELIEZER: אִם הָיָה רָפוּי מוּתָּר – IF [THE SHOE] WAS fastened LOOSELY upon the shoe-form, IT IS PERMITTED to take the shoe off the shoe-form, because the shoe is then viewed as a utensil.

הדרן עלך תולין

WE SHALL RETURN TO YOU, TOLIN

NOTES

26. As explained above (note 19), R' Eliezer maintains that a shoe is not considered "finished" until it is removed from the shoe-form. Thus, such a shoe is not susceptible to *tumah*, and it is *muktzeh*. R' Yehudah teaches us here that R' Eliezer would agree that a shoe fastened loosely upon the shoe-form is indeed considered "finished," because it is deemed not to be lacking removal from the shoe-form. [According to this, it would have been possible to resolve the conflicting Baraisos quoted above as both reflecting the view of R' Eliezer, with the first Baraisa dealing with a loosely fastened shoe, and the second Baraisa dealing with a tightly held shoe (see *Maharsha* and *Rashash*).]

This is all true only according to R' Eliezer, who maintains that a shoe gripped tightly onto the shoe-form is not a utensil and therefore *muktzeh*. The Sages, however, who maintain that a shoe held tightly on a shoe-form is a utensil, would allow removing such a shoe on the Sabbath, for the shoe (which is a utensil) may be moved, and the shoe-form may be moved for the purpose of its place (see *Rashi*).

In summation: Abaye and Rava dispute for what reason R' Yehudah allowed the removal of a shoe from a shoe-form only where the shoe was loosely upon the shoe-form. According to Abaye, this is because removing a shoe gripping the shoe-form tightly would necessarily move the *muktzeh* shoe-form, which is prohibited. According to Rava, R' Yehudah follows the opinion of R' Eliezer who would deem *muktzeh* a shoe gripping the shoe-form tightly.

במנעל מרופט כו' ואם חלצה חליצתה כשרה. וא"ת אמאי גזרינן בפרק מצות חליצה (יבמות דף קג.) מנעל אטו מנעל מרופט כיון דדיעבד חליצתה כשרה ואומר ר"י דגזרינן אטו מרופט יותר מדאי שאינו חופה רוב רגלו דאם חלצה בו אין חליצתה כשרה.

ההיא דרבי יהודה משום דרבי אליעזר היא. מכאן ראיה דרבי יהודה שרי דבר שמלאכתו לאיסור לצורך גופו ולצורך מקומו כמו שפירשתי בסוף פרק במה מדליקין (דף לו: ד"ה הא ר"י):

הדרן עלך תולין

נוטל. רבא כרבי נתן ס"ל. פירש' בפ' המצניע (א) (לעיל ד' צג.):

תינוק מת וכים תלוי בצוארו פטור. דאגב מרריה מבטיל ליה לכים א"נ תינוק חי הוא צריך לכים לטייל בו התינוק אבל תינוק מת מה צריך לכים והוי מלאכה שאינה צריכה לגופה (ב) ופטור שלא הוציא כדרך המוציאין: **אי** הכי מאי איריא אבן אפי' דינר נמי. אי אמרת בשלמא דתרוייהו מבטל להו בין אבן ובין דינר ואין כאן טלטול מוקצה כלל היינו דנקט אבן משום דאי נפיל לא אתי אבוה לאתויי אבל דינר אי נפיל אתי אבוה לאתויי לא אלא אי אמרינן דתרוייהו לא בטלי ואפ"ה שרינן איסור מוקצה כשמטלטל התינוק עם האבן משום גיעגועין בדינר נמי לישתרי דלא שייך למימר דילמא אתי אבוה לאתויי דמאי נפקא לן מינה דהשתא נמי דאיכא איסור מוקצה שרינן ליה משום גיעגועין ומשני דאע"פ שיש איסור מוקצה כשמטלטל התינוק עם האבן ושרינן ליה משום גיעגועין מיהו יש לנו להחמיר במוקצה יותר כשמטלטלו בידים משמטלטלו אגב תינוק אף על גב דההיא שעתא נמי איכא מוקצה הלכך גזרינן דילמא נפיל דינר ואתי אבוה לאתויי. כך פירש רבינו שמואל: ונשדיהו

במה מגררו א"ר אבהו בגב סכין א"ל ההוא סבא שמי דידך מקמי הא דתני רבי חייא אין מגררין לא מנעל חדש ולא מנעל ישן ולא יסוך את רגלו שמן והוא בתוך המנעל או בתוך הסנדל אבל סך את רגלו שמן ומניח בתוך המנעל או בתוך הסנדל וסך כל גופו שמן ומתעגל ע"ג קטבליא ואינו חושש אמר רב חסדא לא שנו אלא לצחצחו אבל לעבדו אסור לעבדו פשיטא ותו לצחצחו מי איכא מאן דשרי אלא אי איתמר הכי איתמר אמר רב חסדא לא שנו אלא שיעור לצחצחו אבל שיעור לעבדו אסור ת"ר לא יצא קטן במנעל גדול אבל יוצא הוא בחלוק גדול ולא תצא אשה במנעל מרופט ולא תחלוץ בו ואם חלצה חליצתה כשרה ואין יוצאין במנעל חדש באיזה מנעל אמרו במנעל של אשה תני בר קפרא ל"ש אלא שלא יצאה בו שעה אחת מבעוד יום אבל יצאה בו מע"ש מותר תני חדא שומטין מנעל מעל גבי אימום ותניא אידך אין שומטין לא קשיא הא ר' אליעזר הא רבנן דתנן מנעל שעל גבי אימום רבי אליעזר מטהר וחכמים מטמאים הניחא לרבא דאמר דבר שמלאכתו לאיסור בין לצורך גופו בין לצורך מקומו מותר שפיר אלא לאביי דאמר לצורך גופו מותר לצורך מקומו אסור מאי איכא למימר הכא במאי עסקינן ברפוי דתניא רבי יהודה אומר אם היה רפוי מותר טעמא דרפוי הא לא רפוי לא הניחא לאביי דאמר דבר שמלאכתו לאיסור לצורך גופו מותר לצורך מקומו אסור שפיר אלא לרבא דאמר בין לצורך גופו בין לצורך מקומו מותר מאי איריא רפוי אפי' לא רפוי נמי ההיא דרבי יהודה משום דרבי אליעזר הוא דתניא ר' יהודה אומר משום רבי אליעזר אם היה רפוי מותר:

הדרן עלך תולין

נוטל אדם את בנו והאבן בידו וכלכלה והאבן בתוכה ומטלטלין תרומה טמאה עם הטהורה ועם החולין רבי יהודה אומר אף מעלין את המדומע באחד ומאה: **גמ'** אמר רבא הוציא תינוק חי וכים תלוי בצוארו חייב משום כים תינוק מת וכים תלוי לו בצוארו פטור תינוק חי וכים תלוי לו בצוארו חייב משום כים וליחייב נמי משום תינוק רבא כרבי נתן סבירא ליה דאמר חי נושא את עצמו וליבטל כים לגבי תינוק מי לא תנן את החי במטה פטור אף על המטה שהמטה טפילה לו מטה לגבי חי מבטלי ליה כים לגבי תינוק לא מבטלי ליה תינוק מת וכים תלוי לו בצוארו פטור וליחייב משום תינוק רבא כר"ש ס"ל דאמר כל מלאכה שא"צ לגופה פטור עליה תנן נוטל אדם את בנו והאבן בידו אמרי דבי רבי ינאי בתינוק שיש לו גיעגועין על אביו אי הכי מאי

במה מגררו. למלטש: והוא בתוך המנעל. מפני שהמנעל נהנה ממנו ונמלא מעבדו: מתעגל. מתגלגל: קטבליא. עור שלוק שעושין ממנו משטוחות לשלחן ולמטה: אלא לצחצחו. לא שנו דמותר לסוך שמן לרגלו ונותנו בתוך המנעל אלא שמתכוין לצחצחו למנעל: ולצחצחו מי שרי. במתכוין הא איכא למיגזר אטו לעבדו: שיעור לצחצחו. שלא היה כ"כ שמן הניסוך לעור מגופו כדי לעבד לעור אלא לצחצחו ומיהו איהו אפי' לצחצח לא מתכוין: לא יצא. אדם קטן במנעל שהוא גדול לו משום דנופל מרגלו ואתי לאתויי: אבל יוצא בחלוק גדול. דלא נפיל מיניה ולמישלף ואתויי לא חיישינן דלא קאי ערום בשוק: מרופט. קרוע מלמעלה דגנאי הוא לה וכי חייכי עלה שלפה ומייתי לה: ולא תחלוץ בו. לכתחילה דלאו נעל מעליא הוא: במנעל חדש. כדמפרש ואזיל שלא יצאה בו מבעוד יום ובאשה קיימינן דאשה מקפדת אם אינו מכוון למדת רגלה אבל יצאה בו כבר הכירה בו דמכוון הוא לה או אינה מקפדת: אימום. פורמ"ה: ר' אליעזר מטהר. אלמא לאו כלי הוא ובשבת נמי אסור לטלטלו: הניחא לרבא דאמר. בפ' כל הכלים דבר שמלאכתו לאיסור בין שהוא צריך להשתמש בגופו של כלי בין שאינו צריך אלא למקומו מותר לטלטלו מאחר שתורת כלי עליו שפיר איכא לאוקומי להא דתני שומטין כרבנן דכיון דכלי הוא ואימום נמי כלי הוא ואף על גב דמלאכתו דאימום לאיסור לתקן מנעלין מטלטלין להאי אימום משום צורך מקומו דהיינו מנעל שהאימום נתון לתוכו: אלא לאביי. נהי נמי דמנעל שעל האימום לרבנן כלי הוא אימום מיהא מלאכתו לאיסור הוא וזה ששומט ממנו את המנעל אינו צריך לגופו של אימום והיכי מטלטל ליה: ברפוי. שהמנעל נשמט מאליו וא"צ לטלטל האימום: הא לאו רפוי לא. וע"כ טעמא משום דאימום אסור לטלטל לצורך מקומו: ה"ג ההיא רבי יהודה משום רבי אליעזר הוא. כי אמרה ליה ר' יהודה להאי דמפליג בין רפוי לשאינו רפוי אליבא דרבי אליעזר אמר דאמר מנעל שעל האימום לאו גמר כלי הוא כל זמן שמחוסר הוצאה ולענין שבת נמי אסור לטלטלו משום דלאו כלי הוא ואשמעינן דרפוי לאו מחוסר הוצאה הוא ומותר לטלטלו דאילו לרבנן אף על גב דאין רפוי מותר דטעמא דשאין רפוי אסור לרבי יהודה לאו משום אימום הוא אלא משום מנעל גופיה:

הדרן עלך תולין

נוטל. והאבן בידו. בחצר ולא אמרי' דמטלטל לאבן: עם הטהורה. אגב הטהורה ואגב חולין אבל טמאה באפי נפשה לאו בת טלטול היא: אף מעלין את המדומע. סאה תרומה שנפלה לק' של חולין דקי"ל דעולה מותר להעלותו לסאה תרומה מהן בשבת ויהיו החולין מותרין ולא אמרינן מתקן הוא ובגמרא מפרש טעמא: גמ' חייב משום כים. ולא משום תינוק כדמפרש ואזיל משום כים מיהו חייב ולא אמרינן איהו לא מפיק ליה אלא תינוק קא מפיק ליה ולקמיה פריך לה ממתניתין: פטור. לגמרי כדמפרש ואזיל: מטה לגבי חי מבטל לה. להיות טפילה לו שהרי צריך לה: מלאכה שאינה צריכה לגופה. ומוציא מת לקוברו מלאכה שא"צ לגופה היא כדאמר בהמצניע וכים שהיה תלוי בצוארו לשחק בו אגב מרריה מבטל ליה לגבי תינוק שמת ולא חשיב ליה ההיא שעתא: והאבן בידו. מדשרי ליה בטלטול בחצר ש"מ לאו כמאן דנקיט לה איהו לאבן דמי ולגבי כים היכי מחייבת ליה: בתינוק שיש לו גיעגועין על אביו. שאם לא יטלנו יחלה ולא העמידו טלטול שלא בידים במקום סכנה ואע"ג דלאו סכנת נפש גמורה אלא סכנת חולי: אתי

וקאמר רבי שמעון פטור על הוצאה זו שברצונו לא היתה באה אליו ולא היה צריך לה [חגיגה י.] לקוברו אינו צריך לגופה דהוצאה ולא למת אלא לפנות בימו והוצאה הצריכה לגופה כגון שהוצא אחר [לעיל עג:] געגועין. ברמור"ט מגעגע עליו ואינו יכול ליפרד ממנו [שם סו:]

עין משפט נר מצוה

נו א מיי' פכ"ד מהלכות שבת הלכה יג סמג שם טוש"ע או"ח סי' שכ סעיף מ:
נז ב ג ד מיי' (שם הל' יח) ופכ"ב הלכה י סמג שם טוש"ע או"ח סי' שכו סעיף ז:
נח ה מיי' פי"ט שם הל' טו סמג שם טוש"ע או"ח סי' שא סעיף ז:
נט ו מיי' שם וסמג שם טוש"ע או"ח סי' שג סעיף יג:
ס ז מיי' פ"ג מהל' יבום הלכה יט סמג עשין נג טוש"ע אה"ע סי' קסט סעיף יג:
סא ח מיי' פי"ט מהל' שבת הלכה יב סמג לאוין סה טוש"ע או"ח סי' שא סעיף יג:
סב ט מיי' פכ"ו מהל' שבת הלכה יג סמג שם טוש"ע או"ח שם סעיף יז:
סג י מיי' פכ"ד מהלכות כלים הלכה ה:
א כ מיי' פכ"ה מהלכות שבת הלכה כ סמג לאוין סה טוש"ע או"ח סי' שט סעיף א:
ב ל מיי' פי"ח מהלכות שבת הלכה ז:
ג מ מיי' פכ"ה שם הל' טו סמג שם טוש"ע או"ח סי' שט סעיף ג:

רבינו חננאל

וגירוד מנעל הלכה כדתני ר' חייא אין מגררין לא מנעל חדש ולא מנעל ישן. ולא יסוך רגלו שמן והוא בתוך המנעל או בתוך הסנדל. אבל סך את רגלו בשמן ומניחה בתוך המנעל או בתוך הסנדל וסך כל גופו שמן ומתעגל ע"ג קטבליא. פי' ספרה. ואינו חושש ואמר רב חסדא לא שנו אלא מע"ש נתן שמן מעט שיעור לצחצחו אבל שיעור לעבדו אסור. [אבל] לצחצחו אסור וכ"ש לעבדו. וכן הלכה: ת"ר לא יצא קטן במנעל גדול אבל יוצא הוא בחלוק גדול. פי' של אדם גדול ולא תצא אשה במנעל מרופט רפוי שמשתרבב מן הרגל כמו שאמור אם יטעום עבדך את אשר אכל ואת אשר אשתה מיכן [נאמר לקמן] (קלב) ששפחותיהן של זקנים מתרפטות ואין יכול לקפוץ שפחותיו לשום החק המאכל וכן עוד לא תצא אשה במנעל חדש בשבת אא"כ יצאה בו שעה אחת מבע"י: תני חדא שומטין מנעל מע"ג האימום בשבת. פי' הוא דפוס של מנעל ואליבא דרבנן שאומרים מנעל שע"ג אימום מקבל טומאה. ותניא אידך אין שומטין הא לרבי אליעזר דאמר מנעל ע"ג אימום אינו כלי ואינו מקבל טומאה דתנן בסדר טהרות בבא קמא פ' סנדל עמקי וכיס של שנצות מנעל שע"ג האמום ר' אליעזר מטהר וחכמים מטמאין. פי' ר' אליעזר מטהר סבר מנעל על האמום אינו כלי לכך אינו מקבל טומאה ובשבת אסור לשומטו וחכמים שמטמאין סברי דעל האמום כבר נגמרה מלאכתו וכלי הוא לקבל טומאה. וכיון שהוא כלי מותר לשומטו בשבת והלכה כחכמים ואקשינן הלא הניחא לרבא דאמר דבר שמלאכתו לאיסור

כגון האימום וכיוצא בו מכלי אומנות מלאכה בין לצורך מקומו מותר לטלטלו שפיר לטעמייהו דרבנן דסברי שומטין מנעל מעל אמום בשבת אלא (לאבין) [לרבא] דאמר לצורך גופו בלבד שרי אמום מאי לצורך גופו איכא דשומטין הכא במאי עסקינן ברפוי כלומר מנעל זה רפוי הוא על האמום ואינו צריך להגביהו אלא מושך המנעל מעליו ונשאר האמום במקומו דתניא ר' יהודה אומר אם היה רפוי מותר וחזרנו להקשות על זה הפירוק לרבא ופשוטה היא ופריק רבא הא ר' יהודה משום ר' אליעזר היא כלומר אפילו ר' אליעזר שאמר אין שומטין סבר הני מילי כשהוא מהודק דצריך לטלטוליה ולאשמוטיה אבל אם היה רפוי שמושך המנעל והאמום נשאר במקומו מותר לשומטו אבל חכמים סבירא להו אע"פ שאינו רפוי אלא מהודק אם אינו לצורך גופו מותר לטלטלו לצורך מקומו:

הדרן עלך רבי אליעזר אומר תולין

פרק כא נוטל אדם את בנו והאבן בידו כו'. אמר רבא הוציא תינוק חי וכיס תלוי לו בצוארו חייב משום כיס תינוק מת וכיס תלוי לו בצוארו פטור. פי' תינוק מת לקברו והכיס עמו כדאמר ריש לקיש וסנדלים

מסורת הש"ס

א) [תוספ' פי"ד], ב) כלים פכ"ו מ"ד [סנהדרין סח.], ג) [נ"ל אימום וכן הוא בערוך ובמשנה דכלים ובמפרשים שעלין], ד) לעיל קכג., ה) [לעיל קכ.], ו) לעיל לד., ז) [עירובין קג.] יומא סו:, ח) עירובין קג: לעיל צג:, ט) [לעיל קה: וש"נ], י) [דף לד:].

הגהות הב"ח

(א) תוס' ד"ה נוטל וכו' בפ' המצניע. נ"ב דף צד בד"ה אבל אדם: (ב) ד"ה תינוק וכו' אינה צריכה לגופה אי נמי אפי' צריך לו פטור שלא הוציא:

גליון הש"ס

גמ' ולא יסוך את רגלו שמן. וכן איתא בירושלמי ספ"ח דשביעית לענין שמן שביעית:

רב נסים גאון

תני בר קפרא לא שנו אלא שלא יצאת בו שעה אחת מבעוד יום. בגמ' דבני מערבא בפרק במה אשה יוצאה (הלכה ב) ובפרק כל ישראל יש להם חלק (הלכה א) גרסי כמה שיעורו והכין גרסי לא ילבש אדם מנעלים

ליקוטי רש"י

מרופט. מנוקב קרוע מלמעלה [יבמות קב.]. אימום. אימום שלהם של עור היה כעין אבן ממולא ומתוך שער ופיו תפור.

Chapter Twenty-one

Mishnah This chapter deals with exceptions to the ban on moving *muktzeh*:[1] נוֹטֵל אָדָם אֶת בְּנוֹ וְהָאֶבֶן בְּיָדוֹ – **A person may take his son** in his arms even **when there is a stone in [the son's] hand,**[2] וְכַלְכָּלָה וְהָאֶבֶן בְּתוֹכָהּ – **or a basket** even **when there is a stone in it.**[3] וּמְטַלְטְלִין תְּרוּמָה טְמֵאָה עִם הַטְּהוֹרָה – **Similarly, we may move *terumah* that is *tamei* together with that which is *tahor*,** וְעִם הַחוּלִּין – **or together with *chullin*.**[4]

רַבִּי יְהוּדָה אוֹמֵר – **R' Yehudah says:** אַף מַעֲלִין אֶת הַמְדוּמָּע בְּאֶחָד וּמֵאָה – **We may also remove one part** of *terumah* **from a mixture with one hundred parts** of *chullin*.[5]

Gemara The Mishnah taught that a father is not restricted from lifting his child even though there is a *muktzeh* object in the child's hand. The Gemara cites a ruling which deals with a similar case but relates to the *melachah* of transferring between domains:

אָמַר רָבָא – **Rava said:** הוֹצִיא תִּינוֹק חַי וְכִיס תָּלוּי בְּצַוָּארוֹ – **If one took out a live child** to a public domain **with a pouch suspended from its neck,** חַיָּיב מִשּׁוּם כִּיס – **he is liable on account of** taking out **the pouch.**[6] תִּינוֹק מֵת וְכִיס תָּלוּי לוֹ בְּצַוָּארוֹ פָּטוּר – If one took out **a dead child with a pouch suspended from its neck, he is** entirely **exempt.**

The first part of Rava's ruling is repeated and analyzed:

תִּינוֹק חַי וְכִיס תָּלוּי לוֹ בְּצַוָּארוֹ חַיָּיב מִשּׁוּם כִּיס – If one took out **a live child with a pouch suspended from its neck, he is liable on account of the pouch.** וְלִיחַיֵּיב נַמִּי מִשּׁוּם תִּינוֹק – **But let him be liable on account of the child as well.**[7] – ? –

The Gemara answers:

רָבָא כְּרַבִּי נָתָן סְבִירָא לֵיהּ – **Rava concurs with R' Nassan,** דְּאָמַר חַי נוֹשֵׂא אֶת עַצְמוֹ – **who said** that **a living creature supports its own weight.** Thus, one is exempt for carrying out a live person.[8]

The Gemara asks from a different perspective:

וְלִיבָּטֵל כִּיס לְגַבֵּי תִּינוֹק – **Then let the pouch be** viewed as **an accessory to the child,** and let the transporter be exempt on account of the pouch as well! מִי לֹא תְּנַן – **Did we not learn in a Mishnah:**[9] אֶת הַחַי בְּמִטָּה – If one carries out A LIVE PERSON IN A BED, פָּטוּר אַף עַל הַמִּטָּה – HE IS EXEMPT for the entire act, EVEN FOR taking out THE BED, שֶׁהַמִּטָּה טְפֵילָה לוֹ – BECAUSE THE BED IS SECONDARY TO [THE PERSON] being carried on it?[10] Here, too, the person should be exempt even for carrying out the pouch, because it is secondary to the child from whose neck it is suspended. – ? –

NOTES

1. *Meiri.*

2. I.e. he may lift the child in a courtyard in which one is permitted to carry on the Sabbath. Although the child is holding a *muktzeh* stone which he refuses to drop, the father is permitted to lift the child, and is not regarded as handling the stone itself (*Rashi*). The Gemara will further clarify this ruling.

3. The Gemara (142a) will explain why the basket is not considered a *base to muktzeh.*

4. [I.e. together with unconsecrated food.] *Terumah* that is *tamei* may not be eaten even by a Kohen. Since the only thing for which it may be used is kindling – which is forbidden on the Sabbath – it is completely unusable on the Sabbath, and is consequently deemed *inherently muktzeh.* Our Mishnah teaches, however, that one may carry such *terumah* in a container that also has in it *terumah* that is *tahor* or *chullin* (*Rashi*). Although this container is a base to both *muktzeh* (*terumah* that is *tamei*) and non-*muktzeh* (*terumah* that is *tahor,* or *chullin*), since the non-*muktzeh* is the more valuable, the base may be moved (see 142a note 7).

5. This ruling is unrelated to the subject of *muktzeh,* but is included here incidentally, since the Mishnah touched upon the case of *terumah* that is in a container with *chullin* (cf. *Ohr Gadol, Sfas Emes*).

If *terumah* becomes mixed with *chullin,* the entire mixture receives the stringency of *terumah,* i.e. it may be eaten only by a Kohen. However, if one measure of *terumah* becomes mixed with one hundred or more measures of *chullin,* the *terumah* becomes nullified and the mixture may be eaten by anyone. Although it no longer has any sanctity, one part must be removed to avoid depriving the Kohanim of their due (*Terumos* 4:7; see also *Orlah* 2:1).

R' Yehudah maintains that one may remove the measure of *terumah* from the mixture on the Sabbath, even though the remaining food thereby becomes permitted for consumption. In his opinion, this act is not considered a prohibited "repair" to the remaining food. The Gemara (142a) will clarify this point (*Rashi*).

6. But not on account of taking out the child. The Gemara will shortly explain why this is so.

Now, since the person is liable on account of the pouch, it is evident that although he does not carry it with his own hands we view him, and not the child, as the one carrying it. The Gemara will point out below that this apparently contradicts our Mishnah, which permits lifting a child who is holding a *muktzeh* stone, presumably because the child, not the adult, is the one considered to be carrying the stone (*Rashi*). [The pouch we are dealing with is an empty one that the child plays with (see *Chidushei R' Elazar Moshe Horowitz* and *Rashi* below ד״ה מלאכה שאינה צריכה לגופה).]

7. Although the person who carried both objects out together can be held liable to only one *chatas* offering for his act of transferring, his liability can devolve either on account of the pouch or on account of the child. Thus, if he would carry out a child who did *not* have a pouch suspended from its neck, he would also be liable. Why does Rava state that the liability is specifically on account of the pouch? (*Ritva MHK* ed.; see there for an alternative explanation).

8. The Gemara above (94a) cited the view of R' Nassan that one is not liable for carrying out a living creature, because the living creature aids in its own transport. The one being carried holds on and instinctively balances himself, in effect lightening the burden for the person transporting him (see 94a note 7 for further explanation as to why this is reason to exempt the perpetrator).

[Actually, Rava stated above (94a) that the Sages dispute R' Nassan's ruling only in regard to transporting animals, but they concede that a human being aids in his own transport. It is therefore difficult to understand the Gemara's presumption that Rava's ruling here accords specifically with the view of R' Nassan. Some commentators explain that the Sages concede to R' Nassan only in regard to adults or older children who can walk at least with assistance. They consider a small child who can only be dragged analogous to an animal in the regard that he does not aid in his own transport. Only R' Nassan maintains that even a small child carries himself. Since Rava was presumably dealing with a small child – because it was common to hang pouches from the necks of small children – he must have stated his ruling in accordance with the opinion of R' Nassan (*Ramban, Rashba, Ran MHK* ed., *Ritva MHK* ed.; see also *Tosafos* to 94a ד״ה אבל and *Mishnah Berurah* 308:154; cf. *Chidushei HaRan*). However, *Rashi* (142a ד״ה פטור, cited there in note 5) attributes specifically to R' Nassan even a ruling exempting a person who carried out an *adult.* This matter, therefore, requires further study (*Leshon HaZahav* to 142a; see there for a possible explanation of *Rashi's* view; cf. *Rashi* to 128b ד״ה דמקפיא נפשא).]

9. Above, 93b.

10. [The bed was not transported for its own sake, but merely as a means of holding the person. As such, it was merely an accessory that is deemed subordinate to the person. Since there is no liability for carrying out the primary object, as the person supports his own weight, there can be no liability for carrying out the accessory.]

במה מגררו א"ר אבהו בגב סכין א"ל ההוא סבא סמי דידך מקמי הא דתני רבי חייא אין מגררין לא מנעל חדש ולא מנעל ישן ולא יסוך את רגלו שמן והוא בתוך המנעל או בתוך הסנדל אבל סך את רגלו שמן ומניח בתוך המנעל או בתוך הסנדל וסך כל גופו שמן ומתעגל ע"ג קטבליא ואינו חושש אמר רב חסדא לא שנו אלא לצחצחו אבל לעבדו אסור לעבדו פשיטא ותו לצחצחו מי איכא מאן דשרי אלא אי איתמר הכי איתמר אמר רב חסדא לא שנו אלא שיעור לצחצחו אבל שיעור לעבדו אסור ת"ר לא יצא קטן במנעל גדול אבל יוצא הוא בחלוק גדול ולא תצא אשה במנעל מרופט ולא תחלוץ בו ואם חלצה חליצתה כשרה ואין יוצאין במנעל חדש באיזה מנעל אמרו במנעל של אשה תני בר קפרא ל"ש אלא שלא יצאה בו שעה אחת מבעוד יום אבל יצאה בו מע"ש מותר תני חדא שומטין מנעל מעל גבי אימום ותניא אידך אין שומטין לא קשיא הא ר' אליעזר הא רבנן דתנן מנעל שעל גבי אימום רבי אליעזר מטהר וחכמים מטמאים הניחא לרבא דאמר דבר שמלאכתו לאיסור בין לצורך גופו בין לצורך מקומו מותר שפיר אלא לאביי דאמר לצורך גופו מותר לצורך מקומו אסור מאי איכא למימר הכא במאי עסקינן ברפוי דתניא רבי יהודה אומר אם היה רפוי מותר טעמא דרפוי הא לא רפוי לא הניחא לאביי דאמר דבר שמלאכתו לאיסור לצורך גופו מותר לצורך מקומו אסור שפיר אלא לרבא דאמר בין לצורך גופו בין לצורך מקומו מותר מאי איריא רפוי אפי' לא רפוי נמי ההיא דרבי יהודה משום דרבי אליעזר הוא דתניא ר' יהודה אומר משום רבי אליעזר אם היה רפוי מותר:

הדרן עלך תולין

נוטל אדם את בנו והאבן בידו וכלכלה והאבן בתוכה ומטלטלין תרומה טמאה עם הטהורה ועם החולין רבי יהודה אומר אף מעלין את המדומע באחד ומאה: **גמ'** אמר רבא הוציא תינוק חי וכיס תלוי בצוארו חייב משום כיס תינוק מת וכיס תלוי לו בצוארו פטור תינוק חי וכיס תלוי לו בצוארו חייב משום כיס וליחייב נמי משום תינוק רבא כרבי נתן סבירא ליה דאמר חי נושא את עצמו וליבטל כיס לגבי תינוק מי לא תנן את החי במטה פטור אף על המטה שהמטה טפילה לו מטה לגבי חי מבטלי ליה כיס לגבי תינוק לא מבטלי ליה תינוק מת וכיס תלוי לו בצוארו פטור וליחייב משום תינוק רבא כר"ש ס"ל דאמר כל מלאכה שא"צ לגופה פטור עליה תנן נוטל אדם את בנו והאבן בידו אמרי דבי רבי ינאי בתינוק שיש לו געגועין על אביו אי הכי מאי

רש"י

במה מגררו. לטיט: **והוא בתוך המנעל.** מפני שהמנעל נהנה ממנו ונמלא מעבדו: **מתעגל.** מתגלגל: **קטבליא.** עור שלוק שעושין ממנו משטחות לשלחן ולמטה: **אלא לצחצחו.** לא שנו דמותר לסוך שמן לרגלו ונותנו בתוך המנעל אלא שמתכוין לצחצחו למנעל: **ולצחצחו מי שרי.** במתכוין הא איכא למיגזר אטו לעבדו: **שיעור לצחצחו.** שלא היה כ"כ שמן הנישוף לעור מגופו כדי לעבד לעור אלא לצחצחו ומיהו איהו אפי' לצחצח לא מתכוין: **לא יצא.** אדם קטן במנעל שהוא גדול לו משום דנופל מרגלו ואתי לאתויי: **אבל יוצא בחלוק גדול.** דלא נפיל מיניה ולמישלף ואתויי לא חיישינן דלא קאי ערום בשוק: **מרופט.** קרוע מלמעלה דגנאי הוא לה וכי חייכי עלה שלפה ומייתי לה: **ולא תחלוץ בו.** לכתחילה דלאו נעל מעליא הוא: **במנעל חדש.** כדמפרש ואזיל שלא יצאה בו מבעוד יום ובאשה קיימינן דאשה מקפדת אם אינו מכוון למדת רגלה אבל יצאה בו כבר הכירה בו דמכוון הוא לה או אינה מקפדת: **אימום.** פורמ"ה: **ר' אליעזר מטהר.** אלמא לאו כלי הוא ובשבת נמי אסור לטלטלו: **הניחא לרבא דאמר.** בפ' כל הכלים דבר שמלאכתו לאיסור בין שהוא צריך להשתמש בגופו של כלי בין שאינו צריך אלא למקומו מותר לטלטלו מאחר שתורת כלי עליו שפיר איכא לאוקומי להא דתני שומטין כרבנן דכיון דכלי הוא ואימום נמי כלי הוא ואף על גב דמלאכתו דאימום לאיסור לתקן מנעלין מטלטלין להאי אימום משום צורך מקומו דהיינו מנעל שהאימום נתון לתוכו: **אלא לאביי.** נהי נמי דמנעל שעל האימום לרבנן כלי הוא אימום מיהא מלאכתו לאיסור הוא וזה ששומט ממנו את המנעל אינו צריך לגופו של אימום והיכי מטלטל ליה: **ברפוי.** שהמנעל נשמט מאליו וא"צ לטלטל האימום: **הא לאו רפוי לא.** וע"כ טעמא משום דאימום אסור לטלטל לצורך מקומו: **ה"ג ההיא רבי יהודה משום רבי אליעזר הוא.** כי אמרה ליה ר' יהודה לההוא דמפליג בין רפוי לשאינו רפוי אליבא דרבי אליעזר אמר דאמר מנעל שעל האימום לאו גמר כלי הוא כל זמן שמחוסר הוצאה ולענין שבת נמי אסור לטלטלו משום דלאו כלי הוא ואשמעינן דרפוי לאו מחוסר הוצאה הוא ומותר לטלטלו דאילו לרבנן אף על גב דאין רפוי מותר דטעמא דשאין רפוי אסור לרבי יהודה לאו משום אימום הוא אלא משום מנעל גופיה:

הדרן עלך תולין

נוטל. והאבן בידו. בשאר ולא אמרי' דמטלטל לאבן: **עם הטהורה.** אגב הטהורה ואגב חולין אבל טמאה באפי נפשה לאו בת טלטול היא: **אף מעלין את המדומע.** סאה תרומה שנפלה לק' של חולין דקי"ל דעולה מותר להעלותו לסאה תרומה מהן בשבת ויהיו החולין מותרין ולא אמרינן מתקן הוא ובגמרא מפרש טעמא: **גמ' חייב משום כיס.** ולא משום תינוק כדמפרש ואזיל משום כיס מיהו חייב ולא אמרינן איהו לא מפיק ליה אלא תינוק קא מפיק ליה ולקמיה פריך לה ממתניתין: **פטור.** לגמרי כדמפרש ואזיל: **מטה לגבי חי מבטל לה.** להיות טפילה לו שהרי צריך לה: **מלאכה שאינה צריכה לגופה.** ומוציא מת לקוברו מלאכה שא"צ לגופה היא כדאמר בהמצניע וכיס שהיה תלוי בצוארו לשחק בו אגב מרריה מבטל ליה לגבי תינוק שמת ולא חשיב ליה ההיא שעתא: **והאבן בידו.** מדשרי ליה בטלטול בשאר ש"מ לאו כמאן דנקיט לה איהו לאבן דמי ולגבי כיס היכי מחייבת ליה: **בתינוק שיש לו געגועין על אביו.** שאם לא יטלנו יחלה ולא העמידו טלטול שלא בידים במקום סכנה ואע"ג דלאו סכנת נפש גמורה אלא סכנת חולי:

אלא

תוספות

במנעל מרופט כו' ואם חלצה חליצתה כשרה. וא"ת אמאי גזרינן בפרק מצות חליצה (יבמות דף קג.) מנעל אטו מנעל מרופט כיון דדיעבד חליצתה כשרה ואומר ר"י דגזרינן אטו מרופט יותר מדאי שאינו חופה רוב רגלו דאם חלצה בו אין חליצתה כשרה.

ההיא דרבי יהודה משום דרבי אליעזר היא. מכאן ראיה דרבי יהודה שרי דבר שמלאכתו לאיסור לצורך גופו ולצורך מקומו כמו שפירשתי בסוף פרק במה מדליקין (דף לו: ד"ה הא ר"י):

הדרן עלך תולין

נוטל. רבא כרבי נתן ס"ל. פירש' בפ' המצניע (א) (לעיל ד' צד.):

תינוק מת וכיס תלוי בצוארו פטור. דאגב מרריה מבטיל ליה לכיס א"נ תינוק חי הוא צריך לכיס לטייל בו התינוק אבל תינוק מת מה צריך לכיס והוי מלאכה שאינה צריכה לגופה (ב) ופטור שלא הוציא כדרך המוציאין: **אי** הכי מאי איריא אבן אפי' דינר נמי. אי אמרת בשלמא דתרוייהו מבטל להו בין אבן ובין דינר ואין כאן טלטול מוקצה כלל היינו דנקט אבן משום דאי נפיל לא אתי אבוה לאתויי אבל דינר אי נפיל אתי אבוה לאתויי לא אלא אי אמרינן דתרוייהו לא בטלי ואפ"ה שרינן איסור מוקצה כשמטלטל התינוק עם האבן משום געגועין בדינר נמי לישתרי דלא שייך למימר דילמא אתי אבוה לאתויי דמאי נפקא לן מינה דהשתא נמי דאיכא איסור מוקצה שרינן ליה משום געגועין ומשני דאע"פ שיש איסור מוקצה כשמטלטל התינוק עם האבן ושרינן ליה משום געגועין מיהו יש לנו להחמיר במוקצה יותר כשמטלטלו בידים משמטלטלו אגב תינוק אף על גב דבההיא שעתא נמי איכא מוקצה הלכך גזרינן דילמא נפיל בדינר ואתי אבוה לאתויי. כך פירש רבינו שמואל:

ונשדינהו

עין משפט נר מצוה

נו א מיי' פכ"ב מהלכות שבת הלכה כה סמג שם טוש"ע או"ח סי' שכ סעיף ח:
נז ב ג ד מיי' (שם הל' יח) ופכ"ב הלכה י סמג שם טוש"ע או"ח סי' שכז סעיף ד:
נח ה מיי' פי"ט שם הל' טו סמג שם טוש"ע או"ח סי' שא סעיף ז:
נט ו מיי' ושמג שם טוש"ע או"ח סי' שב סעיף יג:
ס ז מיי' פי"ח מהל' יבום הלכה יט סמג עשין כב טוש"ע אה"ע סימן קסט סעיף לג:
סא ח מיי' פי"ט מהל' שבת הלכה טו סמג לאוין סה טוש"ע או"ח סי' שא סעיף יב:
סב ט מיי' פכ"ו מהל' שבת הלכה יב סמג שם טוש"ע או"ח סי' שח סעיף יז:
סג י מיי' פכ"א מהלכות כלים הלכה ה:
א כ מיי' פכ"ה מהלכות שבת הלכה כז סמג לאוין סה טוש"ע או"ח סי' שט סעיף א:
ב ל מיי' פי"ח מהלכות שבת הלכה כז:
ג מ מיי' פכ"ה שם הל' כח סמג שם טוש"ע או"ח סי' שט סעיף א:

רבינו חננאל

וגירוד מנעל הלכה כדתני ר' חייא אין מגררין לא מנעל חדש ולא מנעל ישן. ולא יסוך רגלו שמן והוא בתוך המנעל או בתוך הסנדל. אבל סך את רגלו בשמן ומניחה בתוך המנעל או בתוך הסנדל וסך כל גופו שמן ומתעגל ע"ג קטבליא. פי' ספרה. ואינו חושש ואמר רב חסדא לא שנו אלא אם נתן שמן מעט שיעור לצחצחו אבל שיעור לעבדו אסור. [אבל] לצחצחו אסור וכ"ש לעבדו. וכן הלכה: ת"ר לא יצא קטן במנעל גדול אבל יוצא הוא בחלוק גדול. פי' של אדם גדול ולא תצא אשה במנעל מרופט רפוי שמשתרבב מן הרגל כמו שאמור אם יטעום עבדך את אשר אכל ואת אשר אשתה מיכן [ואמר לקמן] (קלב) ששפתותיו מתרפטות ואין יכול לקפוץ שפתותיו לטעום החך המאכל וכן עוד לא תצא אשה במנעל חדש בשבת אא"כ יצאה בו שעה אחת מבע"י: תני חדא שומטין מנעל מע"ג האימום בשבת. אימום זה דפוס של מנעל ואליבא דרבנן שאומרין מנעל שע"ג אימום כלי הוא ומקבל טומאה. ותניא אידך אין שומטין הא לרבי אליעזר דאמר מנעל ע"ג אימום אינו כלי ואינו מקבל טומאה דתנן בסדר טהרות בבא בתרא פ' סנדל עמקי וכיס של שנצות מנעל על האמום ר' אליעזר מטהר וחכמים מטמאין. פי' ר' אליעזר מטהר סבר מנעל על האמום אינו כלי לפיכך אינו מטמא ובשבת אסור לשומטו וחכמים שמטמאין סברי מנעל על האמום כבר נגמרה מלאכתו וכלי הוא לקבל טומאה. וכיון שהוא כלי מותר לשומטו בשבת והלכה כחכמים ואקשינן עלה הניחא לרבא דאמר דבר שמלאכתו לאיסור כגון האימום וכיוצא בו מכלי אומנות מלאכה בין לצורך גופו בין לצורך מקומו מותר לטלטל שפיר לטעמייהו דרבנן דסברי שומטין מנעל מעל אמום בשבת אלא לאביי [לרבא] דאמר לצורך גופו בלבד שרי אמום מאי לצורך גופו איכא דשומטין ומפרקינן הכא במאי עסקינן ברפוי כלומר מנעל שהוא רפוי על האמום ואינו צריך להגביהו אלא מושך המנעל מעליו ונשאר האמום במקומו דא"ר יהודה אם היה רפוי מותר וחזרנו להקשות על זה הפירוק לרבא ופשוטה היא ופריק רבא הא ר' יהודה משום ר' אליעזר היא כלומר אפילו ר' אליעזר שאמר אין שומטין סבר הני מילי כשהוא מהודק דצריך לטלטולי' ולאשמוטיה אבל אם היה רפוי מושך המנעל והאמום נשאר במקומו מותר לשומטו אבל חכמים סבירא להו אע"פ שאינו רפוי אלא מהודק אם אינו לצורך גופו מותר לטלטלו לצורך מקומו:

הדרן עלך רבי אליעזר אומר תולין

פרק כא נוטל אדם את בנו והאבן בידו כו'. אמר רבא הוציא תינוק חי וכיס תלוי לו בצוארו חייב משום כיס תינוק מת וכיס תלוי לו בצוארו פטור. פי' תינוק מת לקברו והכיס עמו כדאמר ריש לקיש וסנדלים

מסורת הש"ס

א) [תוספ' פי"ד], ב) כלים פכ"ו מ"ד [סנהדרין סח.], ג) [נ"ל אימום וכן הוא בערוך ובמשנה דכלים ובמפרשים שעלין], ד) לעיל קכד., ה) [לעיל קכ.], ו) לעיל מז., ז) לעיל לד. [עירובין קג.] יומא סו:, ח) עירובין לז: לעיל לג:, ט) [לעיל קג: וש"נ], י) [דף לד:].

הגהות הב"ח

(א) תוס' ד"ה נוטל וכו' בפ' המצניע. נ"ב דף לד בד"ה אבל אדם: (ב) ד"ה תינוק וכו' שאינה צריכה לגופה אי נמי אפי' צריך לו פטור שלא הוציא:

גליון הש"ס

גמ' ולא יסוך את רגלו שמן. וכן איתא בירושלמי ספ"ח דשביעית לענין שמן שביעית:

רב נסים גאון

תני בר קפרא לא שנו אלא שלא יצאת בו שעה אחת מבעוד יום. בגמ' דבני מערבא בפרק מצות חליצה (הלכה ב) ובפרק כל ישראל יש להם חלק (הלכה א) גרסי כמה שיעורו וחכין גרסי לא ילבש אדם מנעלים

ליקוטי רש"י

מרופט. מנוקב קרוע מלמעלה [יבמות קג.]. אימום. אימום שלהם של עור היה כעין מנעל וממולא מתוכו שער וגמי תפור וגו היו עושין המנעלים כמו שעושין הרגלים שלנו דפוס של עץ. רבי אליעזר מטהר וחכמים מטמאים. חכמים אומרין הואיל ואינו מחוסר מלאכה הכריה אומן שהרי יכול לפקע מן האימום ככבר כלי עליו וטמא ור' אליעזר מטהר שעדיין לא נגמרה מלאכתו [סנהדרין סח.]. בין לצורך גופו. בשבת צריך לגופו [למלאכה] המותרת של היתר מותר [לעיל קכב.]. אלא לאביי דאמר. דבר שמלאכתו לאיסור לצורך גופו הוא דשרי להשתמש ביה אבל לא לצורך מקומו ואע"ג לצורך למקומו לא [שם קכד:]. חי נושא את עצמו הוא. ואין בו אלא משום שבות ופלוגתא במסכת שבת (לג.) [יומא סו:]. דלא מיקטר אלא מדרבנן [עירובין קג.]. את החי במטה. ומי לא מיחייב על הולאתו דהוא מקיל עצמו ונושא עצמו [לעיל צג:]. פטור אף על המטה. הואיל ופטור על החי דקיימא לן חי נושא את עצמו [עירובין צד:]. מלאכה שא"צ לגופה וכו'. וכל מלאכה שאינה צריכה (לגופה) אלא לסלקה מעליו הוי מלאכה שאינה צריכה לגופה דברצונו לא באה לו ולא היה צריך לה הלכך לאו מלאכת מחשבת היא לר' שמעון [לעיל שם]. ורבי שמעון אמר מלאכה גבי מוציא את המת במטה לקוברו בשבת [צג:]

וקאמר רבי שמעון פטור על הוצאה זו שברצונו לא היתה באה אליו ולא היה צריך לה [חגיגה י.] כמו מוציא את המת לקוברו אינו צריך לגופו הוצאה ולא למת אלא לפנות ביתו והוצאה הצריכה לגופה כגון שהוא צריך לחפץ זה במקום אחר [לעיל עג:] געגועין. כדמתרגמינן מגעגע עליו ואינו יכול ליפרד ממנו [שם סו:]

The Gemara answers:

מִטָּה לְגַבֵּי חַי מְבַטְּלֵי לֵיהּ – **A bed is considered an accessory to a live person** who is lying upon it, because it is servicing him. כִּיס לְגַבֵּי תִּינוֹק לֹא מְבַטְּלֵי לֵיהּ – However, **a pouch is not considered an accessory to a child** from whose neck it is suspended, because it is not servicing him, but is an extraneous object that he is using as a toy.

The Gemara now repeats and analyzes the second part of Rava's ruling:

תִּינוֹק מֵת וְכִיס תָּלוּי לוֹ בְּצַוָּארוֹ פָּטוּר – If one took out **a dead child with a pouch suspended from its neck, he is** entirely **exempt.** וְלִיחַיַּיב מִשּׁוּם תִּינוֹק – **But let him be liable on account of the child.**[11] – ? –

The Gemara answers:

רָבָא כְּרַבִּי שִׁמְעוֹן סְבִירָא לֵיהּ – **Rava concurs with R' Shimon,** דְּאָמַר כָּל מְלָאכָה שֶׁאֵינָהּ צְרִיכָה לְגוּפָהּ פָּטוּר עָלֶיהָ – **who says** that **one is exempt for** performing **any labor not needed for its defined purpose,** and carrying out a dead child is in this category of labor.[12]

Having clarified Rava's ruling, the Gemara challenges it on the basis of our Mishnah:

תְּנַן – **We learned in our Mishnah:** נוֹטֵל אָדָם אֶת בְּנוֹ וְהָאֶבֶן בְּיָדוֹ – A PERSON MAY TAKE HIS SON in his arms even WHEN THERE IS A STONE IN HIS HAND. Thus, we see that one who carries his son is not deemed to be carrying the stone that is in his hand. This would seem to contradict Rava's ruling that one who takes out a live child with a pouch suspended from its neck is liable on account of the pouch.[13] – ? –

The Gemara answers:

אָמְרֵי דְּבֵי רַבִּי יַנַּאי – **It was said in the academy of R' Yannai:** בְּתִינוֹק שֶׁיֵּשׁ לוֹ גִּיעְגּוּעִין עַל אָבִיו – The Mishnah is dealing **with a child that longs for its father.** Since the child is in danger of becoming ill if the father does not lift it, the Rabbis waived the *muktzeh* restriction for this case. Ordinarily, however, one who carries a person who is holding something is subject to the restrictions associated with carrying the object itself.[14]

The Gemara asks:

אִי הָכִי – **If so,** that the Mishnah's rule represents a special dispensation on account of the possibility of illness,

NOTES

11. [In this case, the principle that a living creature carries itself obviously does not apply. The corpse is like any other inanimate object, for whose transfer one should be liable.]

12. It is a general principle of Sabbath law that a labor must serve a constructive purpose to qualify as a *melachah*. However, throughout this tractate, R' Shimon and R' Yehudah dispute whether the Torah recognizes only certain specific purposes in such a regard. According to R' Yehudah, a labor done for *any* constructive purpose is considered a *melachah* and one is liable for its performance. According to R' Shimon, though, a labor is considered a Biblically prohibited *melachah* only if it is done for the creative purpose inherent in the labor itself, not if it is performed for some external reason, such as in reaction to an undesirable situation.

In the case of transferring, R' Shimon considers the act as meeting the criteria for prohibited *melachah* only if the perpetrator needs the object in the domain to which he is carrying it. One who removes a corpse to the public domain is not involved in such a creative act, but merely seeks to rid his house of the corpse. Even if one removes the corpse for burial, the act is of no benefit to the perpetrator, but benefits only the corpse itself. According to R' Shimon, this does not fulfill the defined purpose of the *melachah,* and the perpetrator is therefore exempt (see 93b note 34 and 94b note 1 for further elaboration). Rava follows R' Shimon's opinion in this regard.

Rava also exempts the father for carrying out the pouch that is around the dead child's neck, because in his intense grief the father is likely to bury the pouch, which was the child's toy during its lifetime, along with the child. Thus, at this time, the father does not view the pouch as a significant object in its own right, but as part of the child's burial shrouds. As such, it is deemed to be servicing the dead child and is an accessory to it (*Rashi,* as explained by *Ritva MHK* ed.; *Tos. Rid*).

[Alternatively, the father is exempt for carrying out the pouch because the child no longer has any use for it, and thus, its transfer to a different domain is deemed *a labor not needed for its defined purpose.* Furthermore, the father did not carry the pouch outside in the usual manner (i.e. around his own neck) (*Tosafos,* as emended by *Bach, Tos. HaRosh;* see *Maharsha*).]

13. I.e. we may extrapolate from the law of *muktzeh* to the law of *transferring* that one who carries a person who is holding something is not viewed as carrying that object (see *Rashi*).

14. Although the child's *life* is not endangered, for this case of possible minor illness the Rabbis relaxed their restriction against moving *muktzeh* without touching it (*Rashi; cf. Meiri, Tos. Rid, Ritva MHK* ed.). [The Rabbis did not require the father to force the child to drop the stone, since this would add to the child's distress (*Tosafos* to 142a, first ד״ה ונשדינהו).]

One might ask: We have learned that טִלְטוּל מִן הַצַּד, *indirect movement* of *muktzeh,* is permitted when it is done for the sake of a non-*muktzeh* object (see above, 44a note 2 and below, 142 note 2). Accordingly, why is a dispensation necessary in our case? It should be permitted to lift the child simply on the basis of the necessity to calm it, since one is moving the *muktzeh* stone indirectly for the benefit of a non-*muktzeh* object (i.e. the child)!? One possible answer is that in our case the father is deemed to be moving the stone *directly,* since it is usual to lift a child who has something in its hand. Nevertheless, since the father is not taking the stone in his own hand, the Rabbis granted the dispensation for the sake of precluding possible illness (*R' Shlomo Zalman Auerbach,* quoted in *Shemiras Shabbos KeHilchasah* ch. 22 note 99, based on *Ran* and *Mishnah Berurah* 309:1,3; see also *Pri Megadim – Eishel Avraham* 309:1; cf. *Chazon Ish* 47:2; see *Tosafos* to 142a [ד״ה ונשדינהו [א׳ with *Chidushei R' Akiva Eiger,* and see *He'ir Yosef*).

מַאי אִירְיָא אֶבֶן – **what is the** Mishnah's **point in** teaching specifically about a child holding **a stone?** אֲפִילּוּ דִּינָר נַמִּי – The same principle can be applied **even** if the child is holding **a *dinar*** coin **as well!** אַלְּמָה אָמַר רָבָא – **Why,** then, **did Rava say:** לֹא שָׁנוּ אֶלָּא אֶבֶן – **They taught** that one is permitted to lift his child **only** concerning a case where the child is holding **a stone,** אֲבָל דִּינָר אָסוּר – **but** when the child is holding **a *dinar* it is forbidden** to lift him?[1]

The Gemara answers:

אֶבֶן – When the child is holding **a stone,** אִי נָפְלָה לֵהּ לֹא אָתֵי אֲבוּהּ לְאַיְתוּיֵי – **if it should fall** from his hand, **his father will not come to carry it** himself. Therefore, we allow the father to lift his child. דִּינָר – However, when the child is holding **a *dinar*,** אִי נָפֵיל אָתֵי אֲבוּהּ לְאַתּוּיֵי – **if it should fall** from his hand, **his father will come to carry it** himself. Due to this concern, we do not allow him to lift the child even when the child is distressed.[2]

The Gemara cites a Baraisa in support of Rava's opinion that one who carries another person who is holding an object is regarded as carrying that object himself:

תַּנְיָא כְּוָותֵיהּ דְּרָבָא – **A Baraisa was taught in accordance with Rava:** הַמּוֹצִיא כֵּלָיו מְקוּפָּלִים וּמוּנָּחִים עַל כְּתֵפוֹ – ONE WHO CARRIES OUT HIS CLOTHES FOLDED AND RESTING UPON HIS SHOULDER, וְסַנְדְּלָיו וְטַבְּעוֹתָיו בְּיָדוֹ – WITH HIS SANDALS AND HIS RINGS held IN HIS HAND, חַיָּיב – IS LIABLE. וְאִם הָיָה מְלוּבָּשׁ בָּהֶם – BUT IF HE went outside while he WAS CLOTHED IN THEM, פָּטוּר – HE IS EXEMPT.[3] הַמּוֹצִיא אָדָם וְכֵלָיו עָלָיו – ONE WHO CARRIES OUT A PERSON WHO IS WEARING HIS CLOTHES, וְסַנְדְּלָיו בְּרַגְלָיו וְטַבְּעוֹתָיו בְּיָדָיו – WITH HIS SANDALS ON HIS FEET AND HIS RINGS ON HIS HANDS,[4] פָּטוּר – IS entirely EXEMPT.[5] וְאִילּוּ הוֹצִיאָן כְּמוֹת שֶׁהֵן – BUT IF HE HAD CARRIED [THE CLOTHES] OUT AS THEY ARE, i.e. folded upon the shoulder of the one being carried, with his shoes and rings held in his hand, חַיָּיב – [THE CARRIER] WOULD BE LIABLE on account of the clothes. This accords with Rava's opinion that one who carries another person who is holding an object is regarded as carrying that object himself.

The Mishnah stated:

כַּלְכָּלָה וְהָאֶבֶן בְּתוֹכָהּ – Or A BASKET even WHEN THERE IS A STONE IN IT.

The Gemara asks:

וְאַמַּאי – **But why** should one be allowed to carry the basket? תֶּיהֱוֵי כַּלְכָּלָה בָּסִיס לְדָבָר הָאָסוּר – Since there is a *muktzeh* stone in it, **the basket should be** considered **a base to a forbidden object** and should itself be deemed *muktzeh*.[6] – ? –

The Gemara answers:

אָמַר רַבָּה בַּר בַּר חָנָה אָמַר רַבִּי יוֹחָנָן – **Rabbah bar bar Chanah said in the name of R' Yochanan:** הָכָא בְּכַלְכָּלָה מְלֵאָה פֵּירוֹת עָסְקִינָן – **Here, we are dealing with a basket that is filled with produce** but contains a stone as well. Thus, the basket is primarily a base to permitted matter (the produce).[7]

Although the previous answer explains why the basket itself is not *muktzeh*, it fails to explain why one may move it *while* the stone is inside it and thereby move the stone as well. The Gemara therefore asks:

וְלִישַׁדְּיִנְהוּ לְפֵירֵי וְנִישַׁדֵּי לְאֶבֶן – **But let him spill the produce and the stone** to the ground, וְנִינְקְטִינְהוּ בְּיָדַיִם – **and** then **collect the produce by hand** and return it to the basket, thus enabling himself to move the basket and produce without moving the stone. Why do we allow the person to move the stone as well?

The Gemara answers:

כִּדְרַבִּי אִלְעַאי אָמַר רַב – It is **as R' Il'ai said in the name of Rav** below, concerning a similar case: בְּפֵירוֹת הַמִּיטַּנְּפִין – We are dealing **with produce that** readily **becomes soiled** and ruined. הָכָא נַמִּי בְּפֵירוֹת הַמִּיטַּנְּפִין – **Here too,** we are dealing **with produce that** readily **becomes soiled** and ruined if it is dumped upon the ground. Thus, spilling the contents of the basket onto the ground is not an option.[8]

NOTES

1. The distinction between the two cases would be understandable if we would say that one who lifts a child is *not* deemed to be carrying that which is in the child's hand. Although the lifting itself would not violate the law of *muktzeh* in either case, there would be reason to prohibit it when the child is holding a coin (or another valuable *muktzeh* item), due to the concern that if he drops the coin the father will come to pick it up and thus handle *muktzeh* directly. But since you say that lifting the child is itself a violation of *muktzeh* law but a dispensation was granted to preclude the possibility of illness, why should we forbid lifting the child when he is holding a coin? Even if he drops it and the father picks it up, we can rely upon the dispensation for handling *muktzeh* to preclude illness (*Tosafos* to 141b ד״ה אי הכי; cf. *Ramban; see Rashba, Ritva MHK* ed. and *Chazon Ish* 47:3).

2. I.e. we do not rely on the dispensation for minor illness when there is the concern that the father might come to actually take a *muktzeh* item in his own hand. Since the child's life is not at stake, we permit only the lesser violation of carrying a child who is holding a *muktzeh* item in *his* hand (ibid.).

The Gemara has concluded that although there is ample basis to permit the act of lifting a child who is holding a coin, we prohibit this due to the concern that the father might come to take the coin in his own hand. It follows that other acts that are permissible in their own right must nevertheless be prohibited where this concern exists. Thus, it is even forbidden to hold the hand of a *walking* child who is carrying a coin in his other hand, lest he drop the coin and the father come to pick it up (*Rashi;* cf. *Ramban;* see also *Beur Halachah* to 309:1 ד״ה ויש אומרים and *Megillas Sefer* 44:19).

3. Because a person's clothes are accessories to him (*Rashi*).

4. The Baraisa's usage of the plural בְּיָדָיו, *his hands,* in this clause, as opposed to the singular בְּיָדוֹ, *his hand,* which it employed above, indicates that in this case it means the person was wearing the rings *on* his hands, i.e. on his fingers (*Rashi;* see *Maharam* and *Rashash*).

5. He is exempt on account of the clothes since they are accessories to the person wearing them, and he is exempt on account of the person in accordance with R' Nassan's opinion that a living being carries himself (*Rashi;* see 141b note 8).

6. An otherwise non-*muktzeh* object upon which a *muktzeh* item has been placed becomes a בָּסִיס לְדָבָר הָאָסוּר, *a base to a forbidden [muktzeh] object,* and is itself rendered *muktzeh.* Thus, it should be forbidden to move not only the stone but even the basket itself (*Rashi*).

[A non-*muktzeh* object does not become classified as a *base to muktzeh* unless the *muktzeh* object was placed upon it *intentionally.* However, there is no indication that our Mishnah is dealing with a case where the stone was left in the basket intentionally. Thus, the Gemara does not mean to ask a definite question, but rather to explore the possibilities, as follows: *If* the stone was placed there intentionally, let the basket be considered a *base to muktzeh.* And if it was *not* placed there intentionally, another difficulty applies, as will be pointed out after the initial question is deflected (*Rashba;* cf. *Raavad* quoted by *Chidushei HaRan* and *Ritva MHK* ed.; see also *Meiri* here and *Rashba* to *Beitzah* 2a).]

7. Since the produce is more valuable than the stone, the basket is viewed as a base to it, rather than to the stone. And [as the Gemara will go on to explain,] since it is permitted to carry the basket and produce, it is permitted also to carry the stone along with them (*Rashi, Mishnah Berurah* 309:9; see *Rashba* and *Ritva MHK* ed.).

8. The Mishnah is dealing with a basket that is filled with delicate produce, such as ripe figs, berries or grapes (*Rashi*). Since it is unfeasible to dump the contents and remove the stone, one may move the basket and produce together with the stone (see *Rambam, Hil. Shabbos* 25:16 and *Chazon Ish* 47:22; see also *Chidushei R' Akiva Eiger,* who deals at length with related issues). One is not required to remove the produce from the basket and carry it to its destination by hand, because on the way it might fall and be ruined (*Tosafos,* second ד״ה ונשדינהו and ד״ה הכא נמי; *Mishnah Berurah* 309:9).

If the basket contains a variety that would not be damaged when spilled upon the ground, one must indeed empty the basket, replace only the produce and carry it without the stone (see *Orach Chaim* 309:3 with *Mishnah Berurah* §11).

מאי איריא אבן אפילו דינר נמי אלמה אמר רבא [א]לא שנו אלא אבן אבל דינר אסור אבן אי נפלה לה לא אתי אבוה לאיתויי דינר אי נפיל אתי אבוה לאתויי תניא כוותיה דרבא [ב]המוציא כליו מקופלים ומונחים על כתפו וסנדליו וטבעותיו בידו חייב ואם היה מלובש בהן פטור [ג]המוציא אדם וכליו עליו וסנדליו ברגליו וטבעותיו בידיו פטור ואילו הוציאן כמות שהן חייב: כלכלה והאבן בתוכה: ואמאי תיהוי כלכלה בסים לדבר האסור אמר רבה בר בר חנה אמר ר' יוחנן הכא בכלכלה מלאה פירות עסקינן ולישדינהו לפירי ונישדי לאבן [ד]ונינקטינהו בידים כדרבי אלעי אמר רב בפירות המיטנפין [ה]ה"נ בפירות המיטנפין ולינערינהו נעורי [א] אמר רב חייא בר אשי אמר רבא [ו]הכא בכלכלה פחותה עסקינן דאבן גופה נעשית דופן לכלכלה: [ז]מטלטלין תרומה וכו': אמר רב חסדא לא שנו [ח]אלא שטהורה למטה וטמאה למעלה אבל טהורה למעלה וטמאה למטה שקיל ליה לטהורה ושביק ליה לטמאה וכי טהורה למטה נמי לישדינהו ולינקטינהו אמר רבי אלעי אמר רב [ט]בפירות המיטנפין עסקינן מיתיבי מטלטלין תרומה טמאה עם הטהורה ועם החולין בין שטהורה למעלה וטמאה למטה בין שטמאה למעלה וטהורה למטה תיובתא דרב חסדא אמר לך רב חסדא [י]מתניתין לצורך גופו ברייתא לצורך מקומו מאי דוחקיה דרב חסדא לאוקמי מתניתין לצורך גופו אמר רבא מתני' כוותיה דייקא דקתני סיפא מעות שעל הכר מנער את הכר והן נופלות ואמר רבה בר בר חנה אמר רבי יוחנן לא שנו אלא לצורך גופו אבל לצורך מקומו מטלטלו ועודן עליו ומדסיפא לצורך גופו רישא נמי לצורך גופו: רבי יהודה אומר אף מעלין וכו': ואמאי [כ]הא קא מתקן רבי יהודה כר' אליעזר סבירא ליה דאמר תרומה בעינא מחתא [ב]דתנן סאה תרומה שנפלה לפחות ממאה ונדמעו ונפל מן המדומע למקום אחר רבי אליעזר אומר מדמעת כתרומת ודאי וחכמים אומרים [ל]אין המדומע מדמע אלא לפי חשבון אימר דשמעת ליה לחומרא לקולא מי שמעת ליה אלא הוא דאמר כר"ש כדתנן [ג] [מ]סאה תרומה שנפלה למאה ולא הספיק להגביה עד שנפלה אחרת הרי זו אסורה ור"ש מתיר וממאי דילמא התם בהא קמיפלגי דתנא קמא סבר אע"ג דנפלו בזה אחר זה כמאן דנפל בבת אחת דמי והא לחמשין נפלה והא לחמשין נפלה ור"ש סבר קמייתא בטיל במאה והא תיבטיל במאה וחד אלא הוא דאמר כרבי שמעון בן אלעזר דתניא ר' שמעון בן אלעזר אומר [ד]נותן עיניו בצד זה ואוכל מצד אחר ומי סבר ליה כוותיה

והא

אתי לאתויי. וטעמא לאו משום טלטול הוא דאפילו לאוחזו בידו והתינוק מהלך ברגליו אסר ליה רבא דילמא נפיל ואתי לאתויי וכיון דלאו סכנת נפש היא לא שרו ביה טלטול: תניא כוותיה דרבא. דכי נקט לה עליון כמאן דאפקא תחתון גופיה דמי ומיחייב: וסנדליו וטבעותיו בידיו. בקומצו שלא כדרך מלבוש: המוציא אדם וכליו עליו. מלובש בהן: וטבעותיו בידיו. באצבעותיו מדלא תנא בידו כדנקט רישא: פטור. דבגדיו בטלי לגביה ועליו הוא פטור כרבי נתן: ואילו הוציאן כמות שהן. שהיה אותו עליון אחוז בהן ולא מלובש חייב הנושא והיינו כרבא: תיהוי כלכלה בסים. והיא עצמה תיאסר: מליאה פירות. דעיקר נעשית בסים לפירות הלכך אבן מיטלטלת אגב כלי ופירות שהוא מותר: ונינקטינהו בידים. ילקטם מעל הארץ בידיו ויחזירם לכלכלה ויטלטלם ולמה התירו אבן לטלטל אגב כלי ופירות: בפירות המיטנפין. בפירות מבושלין ורכין מאד כגון תאנים ותותים וענבים שאם ישליכם לארץ יטנפו: ולנערינהו נעורי. עד שיסתלקו הפירות מן האבן לתוך הכלכלה לצדדין וישליך האבן לבדה בנעורתה: פחותה. שנפחית דופנה או שוליה: וטמאה למעלה. והוא צריך לטהורה ואינו יכול ליטול הטמאה בידים לפי שהיא מוקצה לפיכך יטלטל הכל עד השלחן וישליך הכל עליו ויטול הטהורה: לישדינהו. לארץ כולן: ולינקטינהו. לטהורה ביד ויחזירנה לכלכלה: מתני' לצורך גופו. שצריך לטהורה לגופה לאוכלה הלכך אי לאו דטהורה למטה לא שרו ליה לטלטולי לטמאה אלא שקיל לטהורה וממטי לה לשלחן: ברייתא לצורך מקומו. שצריך למקום הכלי וע"כ כולו הוא צריך לסלקו משם ושרו ליה רבנן לטלטל האי אטו האי: ומאי דוחקיה כו'. דאיצטריך למימר לא שנו אלא שהטמאה למעלה לשבקי כדקס"ד בין שטמאה למעלה בין שטמאה למטה ולוקמי בצריך למקומו: אלא לצורך גופו. שצריך לכר לשכב עליו שם ולא לסלקו לפיכך לא התירו לו ליטלו עם המעות אלא מנערו במקומו אבל צריך למקום הכר מטלטל הכל ביחד: ומדסיפא כו' רישא נמי לצורך גופו. הלכך אי הוה טהורה למעלה לא הוי שרי ליה לטלטולי טמאה כדקתני גבי מעות מנערו ונופלות ומטלטל היתרא לחודיה: הא קמתקן. שמביאה לידי היתר ונגזר ביה אטו תיקון שע"י מלאכה: כר"א דאמר תרומה. הואיל וניתנה להעלות אחת שירצה בעינא מחתא כאילו מונחת לבדה ואינה מעורבת הלכך לא קמתקן מידי: מדמעת. זה שנפרד משם ואוסר צ"ט של חולין כאילו היא תרומה ודאי: וחכ"א אין המדומע מדמע. חולין אחרים אלא לפי חשבון התרומה שבמדומע כגון אם תחילתו נדמע ס' של חולין ע"י סאה תרומה וחזרה סאה ממנו ונפלה לתוך אחרים לא חשבינן תרומה אלא ס' שבסאה זו ומדמע עד צ"ט שכנגדו ואם יש חולין יותר מק' כנגדו עולה: אימר דשמעת ליה. לר"א דאמר תרומה כמאן דמחתא בעינא: לחומרא. לדמעה כתרומה ודאי: לקולא. דלא ליהוי המעלה אותה בשבת כמתקן: מי אמר. הא ודאי מתקן הוא ע"כ: הוא דאמר. רבי יהודה דמתני' כרבי שמעון דאמר לקולא נמי כמאן דמחתא בעינא דמיא: למאה. וראויה להעלותה ויתכשרו החולין: עד שנפלה אחרת. ועכשיו אין בה חולין כדי להעלותה באחד וק': ר"ש מתיר. קס"ד משום דס"ל קמייתא כמאן דמחתא בעינא דמיא ונמצאת אחרונה זו נופלת בתוך ק' של חולין: בטל בק'. והוו להו ככולהו חולין ומיהו כיון דצריך להעלותה ע"כ המעלה מתקנו: נותן עיניו. במדומע בצד זה להעלותו לתרומה ואוכל בצד אחר הלכך הואיל ובלא העלאה מתחיל ואוכל אין תיקון בהעלאתו:

והא

ונשדינהו לפירי ונשדייה לאבן. ואם תאמר גבי קטן נמי נשדייה לאבן מידו ואמאי שרי לטלטולי עם האבן וי"ל אם ישליכו מידו יצעק התינוק ויבכה וא"ת מ"מ דלא שרינן לטלטל תינוק אלא כשיש לו געגועין תיבטל אבן אגב תינוק כמו שהיא בטלה אגב כלכלה מלאה פירות וי"ל דאינו צריך כל כך טלטול התינוק וא"ת אפילו אין הכלכלה מלאה פירות תיבטל האבן אגבה כי היכי דבטלי בפ"ב דביצה (דף כא:) שיורי הכוס אגב הכוס אי לאו דאיסורי הנאה נינהו וי"ל שאני שיורי דגריעי יותר מדאי ובטלו טפי וכן צ"ל מתוך שמעתא גופה דביצה כמו שפירשתי לעיל בסוף כירה (דף מו. בד"ה הוה):

ונשדינהו לפירי ונשדייה לאבן כו'. וא"ת מכל מקום נינקטינהו לפירי בידים וניתיב האבן בכלכלה והא אמרינן לקמן לא שנו אלא שטהורה למטה וטמאה למעלה אבל טהורה למעלה וטמאה למטה שקיל לה לטהורה ושביק לה לטמאה והיינו על כרחך בידיו דאי זריק לה בכלי א"כ גם בטמאה למעלה יכול לזורקה בכלי אלא שמע מינה דשקיל לה בידיו וא"כ הכי נמי לישקלינהו לפירי בידיו וי"ל דמיירי שפי הכלכלה צר הוא ואינו יכול להכניס שם ידיו אי נמי י"ל דההיא דלקמן מיירי בתרומה שהיא בכלים קטנים בתוך הקופה שאין דרך להניח טמאה וטהורה ביחד אלא בכלים זה בפני עצמו וזה בפ"ע ולהכי מצי שקיל לטהורה שהיא למעלה בידיו אבל כלכלה דהכא אין כאן כלים ולא מצי נקיט להו בידיו פן יפול לארץ והשתא לא צריכא לשינויא קמא דפירות המיטנפין דהא כיון דאבן עצמה הוי דופן לכלכלה אפי' הוי שדי לפירות ולאבן והדר שקיל לפירי ושבק לאבן לא הוי ליה במאי לאנחינהו כיון שהכלכלה פחותה [ה] שהאבן נעשה לה דופן. והא דלא קאמר אלא לפי שלא הוחזר אמורא לעיל. א"נ השתא יש להעמיד נמי בפירות המיטנפין דאל"כ טול להשליך הסל בקרקע ולהוליך בכלכלה מעט מעט כמה שתוכל להחזיק עד מקום הפחת. מ"ר:

הכא נמי בפירות המיטנפין. וא"ת אכתי יטלם בידו ויניחם בתוך כלי אחר או על גבי טבלא או ע"ג סודר כדמוכח בסמוך גבי תרומה דאמר רב חסדא לא שנו אלא שטהורה למטה וטמאה למעלה אבל טהורה למעלה וטמאה למטה שקיל לטהורה ושביק הטמאה ואע"ג דמוקמינן נמי בפירות המיטנפין וי"ל דהתם מיירי כגון שטהורה מונחת בסלים קטנים בפני עצמה וכן הטמאה ואותם סלים מונחים בתוך כלי אחד גדול והיו סלים של טהורה למעלה מסלים של טמאה דיכול ליקח סלי טהורה ולהניחם ע"ג קרקע אבל אם מונחת זו על גב זו בלא שום כלי כי הכא שהפירות מונחים ביחד בהא ודאי לא אמר שביק לה לטמאה ושקיל לה לטהורה. מ"ר:

שנפלה לפחות מק' חולין. מכאן משמע דתרומה עולה באחד ומאה עם האיסור ורש"י לא פירש כן בפרק גיד הנשה (חולין דף צט:) גבי כל איסורין שבתורה במאה דלפירו' שיטתו לא אתי' מסקנא הכי [ו]:

מסורת הש"ס

א) ס"א אלא, ב) תרומות פ"ה מ"ו תמורה יב. ע"ש, ג) תרומות פ"ה מ"ח, ד) בכורות נט. [ע"ש תוס' ד"ה במחשבה ותוס' מנחות נה. ד"ה במחשבה], ה) בקצת ספרים פתוחה, ו) [ועי' תוס' חולין צט: ד"ה לא].

רב נסים גאון

וסנדלים חדשים אלא אם כן הילך בהן מבעוד יום כמה יהא הילוכן בני ביתיה דבר קפרא אמרין (מן דבית רבא דבר קפרא אמרין) מן דבית רבה דבר קפרא עד בית רבה דר' הושעיא צפראי אמרין מכניסתא דבבלאי עד דרתיה דר' חמא בר חנינא טבראי אמרין מן סדרא רבה עד חנותיה דר' הושעיא: הניחא לרבא דאמר דבר שמלאכתו לאיסור בין לצורך גופו בין לצורך מקומו מותר שפיר אלא לאביי דאמר דבר שמלאכתו לאיסור לצורך גופו מותר לצורך מקומו אסור מאי איכא למימר. ומשכחת עיקר דיליה בפרק כל הכלים ניטלין בשבת (דף קכג): פרק כא נוטל אדם את בנו ר' יהושע אומר אף מעלין את המדומע באחד ומאה. פירושו שבעת שיפול חלק אחד תרומה בצ"ט חלקים חולין כולן אסורין לישראל וימכרו לכהן ואם יפול חלק במאה חלקים מוציאין

ליקוטי רש"י

על כתפו. שאינו לבוש בהן. וסנדליו וטבעותיו בידו. אחוז בידו טבעותיו דומיא דסנדליו [סוכה ה:]. שאין מלובשין בו דרך מלבוש דומיא דכליו על כתפיו [עירובין ד.]. חייב. דאינו מכשיט אלא בזמן שלובשו דרך מלבוש [לעיל נח.]. אמר ר' יוחנן לא שנו. דמנערה ואינו מטלטלה בעודן עליה. אלא לצורך גופו. של כר לשכב עליו הלכך בניעור סגיא ושדי ליה באחרייהו. אבל לצורך מקומו. של כר מטלטלו עם המעות למקום אחר [לקמן ע"ב]. מדמעת כתרומות ודאי. שאם נפלה סאה מן הדימוע למקום אחר ואין שם מאה סאין לבד סאה זו כולן אסורין שאני אומר סאה [של תרומה] שנפלה לתוך הדימוע היא סאה שעלתה וחזרה ונפלה לתוך האחרים. אלא לפי חשבון. לפי מה שיש תרומה בסאה זו של דימוע בעינן מאה שיעורין מן החולין אבל מאה סאין לא בעינן כגון אם נפלה תחילה סאה של תרומה לתוך עשרים וארבע סאין של חולין נדמעו ועכשיו כל סאה וסאה שיש שם הוי אחד מכ"ד שבו תרומה והיינו לוג תרומה בכל סאה וסאה אם חזרה ונפלה סאה מאותו דימוע לתוך חולין אחרים אם יש שם שבעים ושבעה לוגין אחרים של חולין מצטרפין עם עשרים [ושלשה] לוגין חולין שבסאה זו ומבטלין את לוג התרומה [תמורה יב.]. סאה תרומה שנפלה למאה. שיש בחולין מאה ואחד [ב]תרומה [ו]דינה לבטל בכך דנפקא לן בספרי מקראי מכל חלבו את מקדשו ממנו שאם נפל בתוכו הרי הוא מקדשו ובתרומת מעשר משמעי קרא שהיא אחד ממאה וקאמר שאם חזרה לתוך התשעים ותשעה מקדשתן מכאן אמרו תרומה במאה עם האסור אסורה במאה והיא מותרת [חולין צט.].

עין משפט
נר מצוה

ד א מיי' וסמג שם וטוש"ע שם:
ה ב ג מיי' פי"ח מהל' שבת הלכה יח ופי"ט הלכה יט:
ו ד טוש"ע א"ח סי' שלה סעיף ה:
ז ה מיי' פכ"ה שם הל' טו טוש"ע א"ח סי' שט סעיף ג:
ח ו מיי' שם טוש"ע שם סעיף ב:
ט ז ח ט י מיי' שם הלכה כ:
י כ (מיי' פכ"ג שם הלכה ט והלכה טו):
יא ל מיי' פי"ג מהל' תרומות הל' ג:
יב מ שם הלכה י:

רבינו חננאל

פוטר היה ר' שמעון במוציא את המת לקברו והלכתא כרבא דקאי כר' שמעון דסבר כל מלאכה שאינה צריכה לגופה פטור עליה. ובפרק יציאות השבת אוקימנא להא דתני זב שיצא בכיס שלו בשבת פטור כר' שמעון דסבר מלאכה שאינה צריכה לגופה פטור ולא תימא מלאכה צריכה לגופה כגון מר לעשות טס וס"ת להגיהו אלא אפי' מר לחפור בו וס"ת לקרות בו מלאכה צריכה לגופה היא וכי לא פטר ר' שמעון אלא מלאכה שאינה צריכה לגופה אבל מלאכה שצריכה לגופה אפי' ר' שמעון מחייב ותניא כרבא המוציא כלים מקופלין ומונחין לו על כתפו וסנדליו וטבעתו בידו חייב. ואם היה מלובש בהן פטור. המוציא אדם וכליו וסנדליו ברגליו וטבעתו בידו פטור. שאלו הרציא כמות שהן חייב והלכתא כוותיה: מתני' מטלטלין תרומה טמאה עם הטהור' אוקמה רב חסדא למתניתין הא בשטהורה למטה וטמאה למעלה ואותבוה הא מטלטלין תרומה טמאה עם הטהורה ועם החולין בין טהורה למטה וטמאה למעלה ובין טהורה למעלה וטמאה למטה. ופרקה רב חסדא מתני' לצורך גופו כדי לאכלו. שאינו מותר לו לטלטל אלא הראוי לו לאכילה. ובברייתא לצורך מקומו שצריך לפנות המקום לבית המדרש או לאורחים שמותר לו לטלטל לצורך מקומו. אפילו מה שאינו ראוי לאכילה. ואמרינן מאי דוחקיה דרב חסדא לאוקימנא למתני' לצורך גופו אמר רבא מתניתא קשיתיה דקתני סיפא מעות שעל הכר נוער את הכר והן נופלות ואוקימנא ר' יוחנן לצורך גופו דאי לצורך מקומו אפי' עודן עליו מטלטלן ואמר רב חסדא לא מוקמינן מתניתין בתרי טעמי ומדסיפא לצורך גופו רישא נמי לצורך גופו: פיסקא דמתני' ר' יהודה אומר אף מעלין את המדומע באחד ומאה. פי' מדומע תרומה שנפלה בחולין ודימעה מעלין אותה אם יש שם מאה ואחד.

The Gemara persists:

וְלִינַעֲרִינְהוּ נִעוּרֵי – But let him shake [the basket and its contents] until the stone falls out, leaving only the produce behind.[9] – ? –

The Gemara therefore provides an alternative answer:

אָמַר רַב חִיָּיא בַּר אַשִׁי אָמַר רָבָא – Rav Chiya bar Ashi said in the name of Rava: הָכָא בְּכַלְכָּלָה פְּחוּתָה עָסְקִינַן – Here, we are dealing with a punctured basket, דְּאֶבֶן גּוּפָהּ נַעֲשֵׂית דּוֹפֶן לְכַלְכָּלָה – in which the stone itself became part of the basket wall by filling the hole. Since the stone is part of the basket structure, it is not *muktzeh* at all.[10]

The Mishnah continued:

מְטַלְטְלִין תְּרוּמָה וכו׳ – WE MAY MOVE *TERUMAH* etc. [that is *tamei* together with that which is *tahor* or together with *chullin*].

This ruling is qualified:

אָמַר רַב חִסְדָּא – Rav Chisda said: לֹא שָׁנוּ אֶלָּא שֶׁטְּהוֹרָה לְמַטָּה וּטְמֵאָה לְמַעְלָה – They taught this only concerning a case where the *tahor [terumah]* is on bottom of a basket and the *tamei [terumah]* is on top of it, אֲבָל טְהוֹרָה לְמַעְלָה וּטְמֵאָה לְמַטָּה – but if the *tahor [terumah]* is on top and the *tamei [terumah]* on bottom, שָׁקִיל לֵיהּ לַטְּהוֹרָה וְשָׁבֵיק לֵיהּ לַטְּמֵאָה – one must take the *tahor [terumah]* out of the basket and carry it by itself, and leave the *tamei [terumah]* behind in the basket.[11]

The Gemara asks:

וְכִי טְהוֹרָה לְמַטָּה נַמִּי – But even if the *tahor [terumah]* is on bottom, לִישְׁדִּינְהוּ וְלִינַקְטִינְהוּ – let him spill [all the *terumah*] to the ground, and then collect [the *tahor terumah*] and return it to the basket, thus alleviating the need to move the *tamei terumah*. – ? –

The Gemara answers:

אָמַר רַבִּי אִלְעַי אָמַר רַב – R' Il'ai said in the name of Rav: בְּפֵירוֹת הַמִּיטַּנְּפִין עָסְקִינַן – We are dealing with produce that readily becomes soiled and ruined. Thus, spilling it to the ground is not a viable option.[12]

Rav Chisda's qualification is challenged:

מֵיתִיבֵי – They challenged Rav Chisda on the basis of the following Baraisa: מְטַלְטְלִין תְּרוּמָה טְמֵאָה עִם הַטְּהוֹרָה וְעִם הַחוּלִּין – WE MAY MOVE *TERUMAH* THAT IS *TAMEI* TOGETHER WITH THAT WHICH IS *TAHOR*, OR TOGETHER WITH *CHULLIN*, בֵּין שֶׁטְּהוֹרָה לְמַעְלָה וּטְמֵאָה לְמַטָּה – WHETHER THE *TAHOR [TERUMAH]* or *chullin* IS ON TOP AND THE *TAMEI [TERUMAH]* IS ON BOTTOM, בֵּין שֶׁטְּמֵאָה לְמַעְלָה וּטְהוֹרָה לְמַטָּה – OR THE *TAMEI [TERUMAH]* IS ON TOP AND THE *TAHOR [TERUMAH]* or *chullin* IS ON BOTTOM. תְּיוּבְתָּא דְּרַב חִסְדָּא – This would seem to be a refutation of Rav Chisda. – ? –

The Gemara answers:

אָמַר לָךְ רַב חִסְדָּא – Rav Chisda will tell you: מַתְנִיתִין לְצוֹרֶךְ גּוּפוֹ – Our Mishnah is dealing with a case where one needs to move the *tahor terumah* for the sake of its use, i.e. to eat it. In that case, it is permitted to move the *tamei terumah* along with it only when no other option is viable. בָּרַיְיתָא לְצוֹרֶךְ מְקוֹמוֹ – The Baraisa, however, is dealing with a case where one needs to move it for the sake of its place. In that case, the entire basket may be moved, because removing the *tahor terumah* and leaving the basket behind will not accomplish the purpose of freeing up the place it occupies.[13]

The Gemara concedes that this distinction is valid, but nevertheless questions Rav Chisda's interpretation of the Mishnah:

מַאי דּוּחְקֵיהּ דְּרַב חִסְדָּא לְאוֹקְמֵי מַתְנִיתִין לְצוֹרֶךְ גּוּפוֹ – What compelled Rav Chisda to interpret our Mishnah as dealing with a case where one needs to move the *tahor terumah* for the sake of its use, and thus to limit the scope of its permit to a situation where the *tahor terumah* is on bottom? Why not interpret it as dealing with a case where one needs to move it for the sake of its place, so that its ruling would apply even to a situation where the *tahor terumah* is on top?

The Gemara answers:

אָמַר רָבָא – Rava said: מַתְנִיתִין כְּוָותֵיהּ דַּיְיקָא – Our Mishnah reads more precisely as interpreted by [Rav Chisda], דְּקָתָנֵי סֵיפָא – for it teaches in its latter clause:[14] מָעוֹת שֶׁעַל הַכַּר מְנַעֵר אֶת הַכַּר וְהֵן נוֹפְלוֹת – MONEY THAT IS ON A PILLOW – ONE MAY SHAKE THE PILLOW SO THAT IT FALLS OFF. וְאָמַר רַבָּה בַּר בַּר חָנָה אָמַר רַבִּי יוֹחָנָן – And Rabbah bar bar Chanah said in the name of R' Yochanan: לֹא שָׁנוּ אֶלָּא לְצוֹרֶךְ גּוּפוֹ – They taught that one must shake the money off the pillow only concerning a case

NOTES

9. Even if the produce is of a delicate variety, let the person maneuver the basket so that the produce slips aside and the stone remains on top, and then tilt it so that only the stone falls to the ground (*Rashi;* see *Chazon Ish* 47:15 and *Megillas Sefer* 44:20).

10. The explanation follows *Orach Chaim* 309:2; see *Mishnah Berurah* ad loc. §6 and *Aruch HaShulchan* §3. Cf. *Tosafos,* second ד״ה ונשדינהו, *Ritva MHK* ed., *Chidushei HaRan* and *Meiri.*

The Gemara has apparently conceded that the Mishnah cannot be explained as dealing with a basket containing delicate produce and a stone, for in such a case the basket must be maneuvered until only the stone falls out. Rather, the Mishnah must be discussing a case where the stone became part of the basket structure. Indeed, some texts of our Gemara read אֶלָּא אָמַר רַב חִיָּיא בַּר אַשִׁי, *Rather, Rav Chiya bar Ashi said,* implying a complete departure from the Gemara's previous explanation (see *Mesoras HaShas* and *Tosafos,* second ד״ה ונשדינהו).

However, *Rambam* (*Hil. Shabbos* 25:16) and *Shulchan Aruch* (309:2-3) cite both explanations as halachically viable. That is, one may move the basket with the stone in it if *either* the stone has become part of the basket structure *or* the basket also contains delicate produce. Thus, Rav Chiya bar Ashi's explanation does not represent a rejection of the previous one, but rather an alternative answer. Apparently, *Rambam's* text did not incude the question וְלִינַעֲרִינְהוּ נִעוּרֵי, *But let him shake [the basket and its contents]* until the stone falls out (*Maggid Mishneh* ad loc.; see also *Tos. Yom Tov* to our Mishnah and *Rashash*).

11. Since the *tamei terumah* is *muktzeh,* one cannot handle it by itself. Thus, when it is lying on top of the *tahor terumah,* there is no option but to carry the entire basket to the table, spill its contents there [so as not to handle the *tamei terumah*] and select the *tahor terumah* for consumption (*Rashi;* see *Meiri*). But when the *tahor terumah* is on top, there is no basis to permit carrying the basket with the *tamei terumah.* Rather, one must remove the *tahor terumah* and carry it separately, leaving the *tamei terumah* behind.

However, this requirement pertains only when the *tahor terumah* is in an individual container within the large basket. If it is lying loosely in the basket, one is not required to remove it and carry it by hand [lest it fall on the ground] (*Tosafos* ד״ה הכא נמי).

[The references to moving *tamei terumah* together with *tahor terumah* apply equally to moving *tamei terumah* together with *chullin.*]

12. Unlike the previous case, the Gemara does not ask that we should require the person to shake the basket until only the *tamei terumah* falls out. This is because when a basket contains small containers of produce it is impossible to spill out the *tamei* produce without also spilling some *tahor* produce. However, when it contains produce and a stone, it is possible to maneuver the basket so that only the stone should fall out (*Meiri*).

13. It is ordinarily forbidden to move an inherently *muktzeh* object for the sake of its place. Only a כְּלִי שֶׁמְּלַאכְתּוֹ לְאִיסּוּר, a *forbidden-use utensil,* which is subject to lesser restrictions, qualifies for this dispensation (see Introduction to Chapter Seventeen). However, when the *muktzeh* object is in a basket together with a non-*muktzeh* object that is more valuable, one is allowed to move the entire basket for the sake of its place (see *Rashi*).

14. Below, 142b.

מסורת הש"ס

א) ס"א אלא, ב) תרומות פ"ה מ"ו תמורה יב. ע"ש, ג) תרומות פ"ה מ"ה, ד) בכורות נט. [ע"ש תוס' ד"ה במשכנה ותוס' מנחות נב. ד"ה במשכנה], ה) בקצת ספרים ליתא, ו) [ועי' תוס' חולין לט: ד"ה לא].

מאי איריא אבן אפילו דינר נמי אלמה אמר רבא [א]לא שנו אלא אבן אבל דינר אסור אבן אי נפלה לה לא אתי אבוה לאיתויי דינר אי נפיל אתי אבוה לאתויי תניא כוותיה דרבא [ב]המוציא כליו מקופלים ומונחים על כתפו וסנדליו וטבעותיו בידו חייב ואם היה מלובש בהן פטור [ג]המוציא אדם וכליו עליו וסנדליו ברגליו וטבעותיו בידיו פטור ואילו הוציאן כמות שהן חייב: כלכלה והאבן בתוכה: ואמאי תיהוי כלכלה בסיס לדבר האסור אמר רבה בר בר חנה אמר ר' יוחנן הכא בכלכלה מלאה פירות עסקינן ולישדינהו לפירי ונישדי לאבן [ד]ונינקטינהו בידים כדרבי אלעי אמר רב בפירות המיטנפין [ה]ה"נ בפירות המיטנפין ולינערינהו נעורי [א] אמר רב חייא בר אשי אמר רבא [ו]הכא בכלכלה פחותה עסקינן דאבן גופה נעשית דופן לכלכלה: [ז]מטלטלין תרומה וכו': אמר רב חסדא לא שנו [ח]אלא שטהורה למטה וטמאה למעלה אבל טהורה למעלה וטמאה למטה שקיל ליה לטהורה ושביק ליה לטמאה וכי טהורה למטה נמי לישדינהו ולינקטינהו אמר רבי אלעי אמר רב [ט]בפירות המיטנפין עסקינן מיתיבי מטלטלין תרומה טמאה עם הטהורה ועם החולין בין שטהורה למעלה וטמאה למטה בין שטמאה למעלה וטהורה למטה תיובתא דרב חסדא אמר לך רב חסדא [י]מתניתין לצורך גופו ברייתא לצורך מקומו מאי דוחקיה דרב חסדא לאוקמי מתניתין לצורך גופו אמר רבא מתני' כוותיה דייקא דקתני סיפא מעות שעל הכר מנער את הכר והן נופלות ואמר רבה בר בר חנה אמר רבי יוחנן לא שנו אלא לצורך גופו אבל לצורך מקומו מטלטלו ועודן עליו ומדסיפא לצורך גופו רישא נמי לצורך גופו: רבי יהודה אומר אף מעלין וכו': ואמאי [כ]הא קא מתקן רבי יהודה כר' אליעזר סבירא ליה דאמר תרומה בעינא מחתא [ב]דתנן סאה תרומה שנפלה לפחות ממאה ונדמעו ונפל מן המדומע למקום אחר רבי אליעזר אומר מדמעת כתרומת ודאי וחכמים אומרים [ל]אין המדומע מדמע אלא לפי חשבון אימר דשמעת ליה לחומרא לקולא מי שמעת ליה אלא הוא דאמר כר"ש כדתנן [ג][מ]סאה תרומה שנפלה למאה ולא הספיק להגביה עד שנפלה אחרת הרי זו אסורה ור"ש מתיר וממאי דילמא התם בהא קמיפלגי דתנא קמא סבר אע"ג דנפלו בזה אחר זה כמאן דנפל בבת אחת דמי והא לחמשין נפלה והא לחמשין נפלה ור"ש סבר קמייתא בטיל במאה והא תיבטיל במאה וחד אלא הוא דאמר כרבי שמעון בן אלעזר דתניא ר' שמעון בן אלעזר אומר [ד]נותן עיניו בצד זה ואוכל מצד אחר ומי סבר ליה כוותיה והא

רש"י

אתי לאתויי. וטעמא לאו משום טלטול הוא דאפילו לאוחזו בידו והתינוק מהלך ברגליו אסר ליה רבא דילמא נפיל ואתי לאתויי וכיון דלאו סכנת נפש היא לא שרו ביה טלטול: תניא כוותיה דרבא. דכי נקטן לה עליון כמאן דאפקא תחתון גופיה דמי ומיחייב: וסנדליו וטבעותיו בידו. בקומצו שלא כדרך מלבוש: המוציא אדם וכליו עליו. מלובש בהן: וטבעותיו בידיו. באצבעותיו מדלא תנא בידו כדנקט רישא: פטור. דבגדיו בטלי לגביה ועליו הוא פטור כרבי נתן: ואילו הוציאן כמות שהן. שהיה אותו עליון אחוז בהן ולא מלובש חייב הנושא והיינו כרבא: תיהוי כלכלה בסיס. והיא עצמה תיאסר: מליאה פירות. דעיקר נעשית בסיס לפירות הלכך אבן מיטלטלת אגב כלי ופירות שהוא מותר: ונינקטינהו בידים. ילקטם מעל הארץ בידיו ויחזירם לכלכלה ויטלטלם ולמה התירו אבן לטלטל אגב כלי ופירות: בפירות המיטנפין. בפירות מבושלין ורכין מאד כגון תאנים וענבים שאם ישליכם לארץ יטנפו: ולנערינהו נעורי. עד שיסתלקו הפירות מן האבן לתוך הכלכלה לצדדין וישליך האבן לבדה בנעורתה: פחותה. שנפחתת דופנה או שוליה: וטמאה למעלה. והוא צריך לטהורה ואינו יכול ליטול הטמאה בידים לפי שהיא מוקצה לפיכך יטלטל הכל עד השלחן וישליך הכל עליו ויטול הטהורה: לישדינהו. לארץ כולן: ולינקטינהו. לטהורה ביד ויחזירנה לכלכלה: מתני' לצורך גופו. שצריך לטהורה לגופה לאוכלה הלכך אי לאו דטהורה למטה לא שרו ליה לטלטולי לטמאה אלא שקיל לטהורה וממטי לה לשלחן: ברייתא לצורך מקומו. שצריך למקום הכלי וע"כ כולו הוא צריך לסלקו משם ושרו ליה רבנן לטלטל האי אטו האי: ומאי דוחקיה כו'. דאיצטריך למימר לא שנו אלא שהטמאה למעלה לשבקי דקס"ד בין שטמאה למעלה בין שטמאה למטה ולוקמי בצריך למקומו: אלא לצורך גופו. שצריך לכר לשכב עליו שם ולא לסלקו לפיכך לא התירו לו ליטלו עם המעות אלא מנערו במקומו אבל צריך למקום הכר מטלטל הכל ביחד: ומדסיפא כו' רישא נמי לצורך גופו. הלכך אי הוה טהורה למעלה לא הוה שרי ליה לטלטולי טמאה דקתני גבי מעות מנערו ונופלות ומטלטל היתרא לחודיה: הא קמתקן. שמביאה לידי היתר ונגזר ביה אטו תיקון שע"י מלאכה: כר"א דאמר תרומה. הואיל וניתנה להעלות אחת שירבה בעינא מחתא כאילו מונחת לבדה ואינה מעורבת הלכך לא קמתקן מידי: מדמעת. זה שנפלה משם ואוסר כ"ש של חולין כאילו היא תרומה ודאי: וחכ"א אין המדומע מדמע. חולין אחרים אלא לפי חשבון התרומה שבמדומע כגון אם תחילתו נדמע ק' של חולין ע"י סאה תרומה וחזרה סאה ממנו ונפלה לתוך אחרים לא חשבינן תרומה אלא ק' שבסאה זו וחולין עד ל"ט שכנגדו ואם יש חולין יותר מק' כנגדו עולה: אימר דשמעת ליה. לר"א דאמר תרומה כמאן דמחתא בעינא: לחומרא. למעטה כתרומה ודאי: לקולא. דלא ליהוי המעלה אותה בשבת כמתקן: מי אמר. הא ודאי מתקן הוא ע"כ: הוא דאמר. רבי יהודה דמתני' כרבי שמעון דאמר לקולא נמי כמאן דמחתא בעינא דמיא: למאה. ורמאיה להעלותה ויתכשרו החולין: עד שנפלה אחרת. ועכשיו אין בה חולין כדי להעלותה באחד וק': ר"ש מתיר. קס"ד משום דס"ל קמייתא כמאן דמחתא בעינא דמיא ונמצאת אחרונה זו נופלת בתוך ק' של חולין: בזה אחר זה. והוו להו כולהו חולין ומיהו כיון דצריך להעלותה ע"כ המעלה מתקנו: נותן עיניו. במדומע בצד זה להעלותו לתרומה ואוכל בצד אחר הלכך הוא אוכל ובלא העלאה ממחיל ואוכל אין תיקון בהעלאתו:

והא

תוספות

ונשדינהו לפירי ונשדייה לאבן. ואם תאמר גבי קטן נמי נשדייה לאבן מידו ואמאי שרי לטלטולי עם האבן וי"ל אם ישליכו מידו יצעק התינוק ויבכה וא"ת מ"ש דלא שרינן לטלטל תינוק אלא כשיש לו געגועין ניבטל אבן אגב תינוק כמו שהיא בטלה אגב כלכלה מלאה פירות וי"ל דאינו צריך כל כך טלטול התינוק וא"ת אפילו אין הכלכלה מלאה פירות תיבטל האבן אגבה כי היכי דבטלי בפ"ב דביצה (דף כא:) שיורי הכוס אגב הכוס אי לאו דאיסורי הנאה נינהו וי"ל שאני שיורי דגרעי יותר מדאי ובטלו טפי וכן צ"ל מתוך שמעתא גופה דביצה כמו שפירשתי לעיל בסוף כירה (דף מג: בד"ה הוה):

ונשדינהו לפירי ונשדייה לאבן כו'. וא"ת מכל מקום לינקטינהו לפירי בידים ויניח האבן בכלכלה והא אמרינן לקמן לא שנו אלא שטהורה למטה וטמאה למעלה אבל טהורה למעלה וטמאה למטה שקיל לה לטהורה ושביק לה לטמאה והיינו על כרחך בידיו דאי זריק לה בכלי א"כ גם בטמאה למעלה יכול לזורקה בכלי אלא שמע מינה דשקיל לה בידיו וא"כ הכי נמי לישקלינהו לפירי בידיו וי"ל דמיירי שפי הכלכלה צר הוא ואינו יכול להכניס שם ידיו אי נמי י"ל דהיא דלקמן מיירי בתרומה שהיא בכלים קטנים בתוך הקופה שאין דרך להניח טמאה וטהורה ביחד אלא בכלים זה בפני עצמו וזה בפ"ע ולהכי מצי שקיל לטהורה שהיא למעלה בידיו אבל כלכלה דהכא אין כאן כלים ולא מצי נקיט להו בידיו פן יפול לארץ והשתא לא נריכא לשינויא קמא דפירות המיטנפין דהא כיון דאבן עצמה הוי דופן לכלכלה אפי' הוי שדי לפירות ולאבן והדר שקיל לפירי ושבק לאבן לא הוי ליה במאי לאנחינהו כיון שהכלכלה פחותה [ה] שהאבן נעשה לה דופן. והא דלא קאמר אלא לפי שלא החכר אמורא לעיל. א"נ השתא יש להעמיד נמי בפירות המיטנפין דאל"כ נוכל להשליך הכל בקרקע ולהוליך בכלכלה מעט מעט כמה שתוכל להחזיק עד מקום הפחת. מ"ר:

הכא נמי בפירות המיטנפין. וא"ת אכתי יטלם בידו ויניחם בתוך כלי אחר או על גבי טבלא או ע"ג סודר כדמוכח בסמוך גבי תרומה דאמר רב חסדא לא שנו אלא שטהורה למטה וטמאה למעלה אבל טהורה למעלה וטמאה למטה שקיל לטהורה ושביק הטמאה ולא"ג דמוקמינן נמי בפירות המיטנפין וי"ל דהתם איירי כגון שטהורה מונחת בכלים קטנים בפני עצמה וכן הטמאה ואותם סלים מונחים בתוך כלי אחד גדול והיו סלים של טהורה למעלה מסלים של טמאה דיכול ליקח סלי טהורה ולהכניס ע"ג קרקע אבל אם מונחת זו על גב זו בלא שום כלי כי הכא שהפירות מונחים ביחד בהא ודאי לא אמר שביק לה לטמאה ושקיל לה לטהורה. מ"ר:

שנפלה לפחות מק' חולין. מכאן משמע דתרומה עולה באחד ומאה עם האיסור ורש"י לא פירש כן בפרק גיד הנשה (חולין דף צט:) גבי כל איסורין שבתורה במאה דלפירושו שיטתו לא אתי מסקנא הכי:

עין משפט נר מצוה

ד א מיי' וסמג שם וטוש"ע שם:
ה ב ג מיי' פי"ח מהל' שבת הלכה טז ופי"ט הלכה יט:
ו ד טוש"ע א"ח סי' שלה סעיף ה:
ז ה מיי' פכ"ה שם הל' טו טוש"ע א"ח סי' שט סעיף ג:
ח ו מיי' שם טוש"ע שם סעיף ב:
ט ז ח ט י מיי' שם הלכה כ:
י כ (מיי' פכ"ג שם הלכה ט והלכה טו):
יא ל מיי' פי"ג מהל' תרומות הל' ג:
יב מ שם הלכה י:

רבינו חננאל

פטור היה ר' שמעון במוציא את המת לקברו והלכתא כרבא דקאי כר' שמעון דסבר כל מלאכה שאינה צריכה לגופה פטור עליה. ובפרק יציאות השבת אוקימנא להא דתני זב שיצא בכיס שלו בשבת פטור כר' שמעון דסבר מלאכה שאינה צריכה לגופה פטור ולא תימא מלאכה צריכה לגופה כגון מר לעשות טס וס"ת להגיהו אלא אפי' מר לחפור בו וס"ת לקרות בו מלאכה צריכה לגופה היא וכי לא פטר ר' שמעון אלא מלאכה שאינה צריכה לגופה אבל מלאכה שצריכה לגופה אפי' ר' שמעון מחייב ותניא כרבא המוציא כלים מקופלין ומונחין לו על כתפו וסנדליו וטבעתו בידו חייב. ואם היה מלובש בהן פטור. המוציא אדם וכליו וסנדליו ברגליו וטבעתו בידו פטור. שאלו הוציא כמות שהן חייב והלכתא כוותיה: **מתני'** מטלטלין תרומה טמאה עם הטהור' אוקמה רב חסדא למתניתין הא בשטהורה למטה וטמאה למעלה ואותבוה הא מטלטלין תרומה טמאה עם הטהורה ועם החולין בין טהורה למטה וטמאה למעלה ובין טהורה למעלה וטמאה למטה. ופרקה רב חסדא מתני' לצורך גופו כדי לאכלו. שאינו מותר לו לטלטלו אלא הראוי לו לאכילה. ובריית' לצורך מקומו שצריך לפנות המקום לבית המדרש או לאורחים שמותר לו לטלטל לצורך מקומו. אפילו מה שאינו ראוי לאכילה. ואמרינן מאי דוחקיה דרב חסדא לאוקימנא למתני' לצורך גופו אמר רבא מתניתא קשיתיה דקתני סיפא מעות שעל הכר נוער את הכר והן נופלות ואוקימנא ר' יוחנן לצורך גופו אבל לצורך מקומו אפי' עודן עליו מטלטלן ואמר רב חסדא לא מוקמינן מתניתין בתרי טעמי ומדסיפא לצורך גופו רישא נמי לצורך גופו: **פיסקא** דמתני' ר' יהודה אומר אף מעלין את המדומע באחד ומאה. פי' מדומע תרומה שנפלה בחולין ודימעה מעלין אותה באחד אם יש שם מאה ואחד.

רב נסים גאון

וסנדלים חדשים אלא אם כן הילך בהן מבעוד יום כמה יהא הולכין בני ביתיה רבה בר קפרא אמרין מן דבית רבה דבר קפרא עד בית רבה דר' הושעיא צפראי אמרין מכניסתא דבבלאי עד דרתיה דר' חמא בר חנינא טבראי אמרין מן סדרא רבה עד חנותיה דר' הושעיא: הניחא לרבא דאמר דבר שמלאכתו לאיסור בין לצורך גופו בין לצורך מקומו מותר שפיר אלא לאביי דאמר דבר שמלאכתו לאיסור לצורך גופו מותר לצורך מקומו אסור מאי איכא למימר. ומשכחת עיקר דיליה בפרק כל הכלים ניטלין בשבת (דף קכב:) פרק כא נוטל אדם את בנו ר' יהושע אומר אף מעלין את המדומע באחד ומאה. פירוש שבעת שיפול חלק אחד תרומה בצ"ט חלקים חולין כולן אסורין לישראל וימכרו לכהן ואם יפול חלק במאה חלקים מוציאין

ליקוטי רש"י

על כתפו. שאינו לבוש בהן. וסנדליו וטבעותיו בידו. אוחזן בידו שכשנתון דומיא דסנדליו [סוכה ה:]. שאינן מלובשין בו דרך מלבוש דומיא דכליו על כתפיו [עירובין ד.]. חייב. דאינו מכשיר אלא מתון מלובשין דרך מלבוש [לעיל נח.]. אמר ר' יוחנן לא שנו. למתניתין ואינו מטלטלו בעודן עליו. אלא לצורך גופו. של כר לשכב עליו הלכך בניעור סגיא ושדי להו במחייהו. אבל לצורך מקומו. של כר מטלטלו עם המעות למקום אחר [לקמן קנ:]. מדמעת כתרומת ודאי. שאם נפלה סאה מן הדימוע למקום אחר ואין שם מאה סאין לבד סאה זו כולן אסורין שאני אומר סאה [של תרומה] שנפלה לתוך הדימוע היא סאה שנטלה ונפלה לתוך האחרים. אלא לפי חשבון. לפי מה שיש תרומה בסאה זו של דימוע [illegible] סאה ותוך כנגדה אבל מאה סאין לא בעינן [illegible] [תמורה יב.]. סאה תרומה שנפלה למאה. שיש כולין מאה ואחד [ג]תרומה [ו]דינה לבטל בכך דנפקא לן בספרי מקראי מכל חלבו את מקדשו ממנו מה שאתה מרים ממנו אם נפל לתוכו הרי הוא מקדשו ובתרומת מעשר משמעי קרא שהיא אחד ממאה וקאמר שאם הורה לתוך התשעים ותשעה מקדשתן מכאן אמרו תרומה במאה עם האיסור אסורה [illegible] [חולין צט.].

where the pillow is needed **for the sake of its use,** אֲבָל לְצוֹרֶךְ מְקוֹמוֹ – **but** when one needs to move it **for the sake of its place,** מְטַלְטְלוֹ וְעוֹדָן עָלָיו – one may move it to a different location **while [the money] is on it.**[15] וּמִדְּסֵיפָא לְצוֹרֶךְ גּוּפוֹ – **And since the** Mishnah's **latter clause** deals with a case where one needs to move the pillow **for the sake of its use,** רֵישָׁא נַמִּי לְצוֹרֶךְ גּוּפוֹ – it is reasonable to say that **the first clause similarly** deals with a case where one needs to move the *tahor terumah* **for the sake of its use.** Rav Chisda therefore stated that the permit to move the basket with the *tamei terumah* inside it is limited to a situation where the *tahor terumah* is on bottom and cannot be retrieved separately.[16]

The Mishnah continued:
רַבִּי יְהוּדָה אוֹמֵר אַף מַעֲלִין וכו׳ – **R' YEHUDAH SAYS: WE MAY ALSO REMOVE etc.** [one part of *terumah* from a mixture with one hundred parts of *chullin*].

The Gemara asks:
וְאַמַּאי – **But why** is this permitted? הָא קָא מְתַקֵּן – **Why, one is "repairing"** the mixture by rendering it fit for consumption.[17] – ? –

The Gemara answers:
רַבִּי יְהוּדָה כְּרַבִּי אֱלִיעֶזֶר סְבִירָא לֵיהּ – **R' Yehudah concurs with R' Eliezer,** דְּאָמַר תְּרוּמָה בְּעֵינָא מַחְתָּא – **who said** that **the *terumah*** part of such a mixture is regarded as though it **is lying separately** within the mixture. Thus, we do not consider the separation of the *terumah* to be a true "repair."[18] דִּתְנַן – **For we learned in a Mishnah:**[19] סְאָה תְרוּמָה שֶׁנָּפְלָה לְפָחוֹת מִמֵּאָה וְנִדְמְעוּ – **IF A *SE'AH* OF *TERUMAH* FELL INTO LESS THAN ONE HUNDRED** *se'ah* of *chullin,* **THUS BECOMING A FORBIDDEN MIXTURE,**[20] וְנָפַל מִן הַמְדוּמָּע לְמָקוֹם אַחֵר – **AND SOME OF THAT FORBIDDEN MIXTURE FELL INTO ANOTHER PLACE** containing less than one hundred *se'ah* of *chullin,* רַבִּי אֱלִיעֶזֶר אוֹמֵר – **R' ELIEZER SAYS:** מְדַמַּעַת כִּתְרוּמַת וַדַּאי – **[THE PART THAT FELL IN] CREATES A** new **FORBIDDEN MIXTURE AS** though it were **CERTAIN *TERUMAH*.**[21] וַחֲכָמִים אוֹמְרִים אֵין הַמְדוּמָּע מְדַמֵּעַ אֶלָּא לְפִי חֶשְׁבּוֹן – **BUT THE SAGES SAY:** Produce of **A FORBIDDEN MIXTURE WILL CREATE A** new **FORBIDDEN MIXTURE ONLY ACCORDING TO THE CALCULATION** of how much *terumah* it actually ought to contain.[22] Thus, we see that according to R' Eliezer *terumah* in a mixture is regarded as though it is distinctly defined. Therefore, we do not consider its separation from the mixture to be a true repair.

The Gemara rejects this explanation:
אֵימַר דִּשְׁמַעְתְּ לֵיהּ – **When did you hear [R' Eliezer]** state that *terumah* in a mixture is regarded as distinct? לְחוּמְרָא – It is only insofar as this leads **to a stringency,** such as *prohibiting* a second mixture when a portion of the original mixture fell into it as if it were *terumah.* לְקוּלָּא מִי שְׁמַעְתְּ לֵיהּ – **Did you hear [R' Eliezer]** maintain his opinion even where it leads **to a leniency,** such as allowing the removal of the "*terumah*" from a mixture on the Sabbath?[23]

The Gemara concedes and therefore suggests an alternate source for its thesis that the removal of the portion is permitted because the *terumah* is viewed as distinct:
אֶלָּא הוּא דְּאָמַר כְּרַבִּי שִׁמְעוֹן – **Rather, [R' Yehudah] concurs with R' Shimon,** who follows the previous reasoning even to effect a leniency. כִּדְתְנַן – **As we learned in a Mishnah:**[24] סְאָה תְרוּמָה שֶׁנָּפְלָה לְמֵאָה – **IF A *SE'AH* OF *TERUMAH* FELL INTO ONE HUNDRED** *se'ah* of *chullin,* וְלֹא הִסְפִּיק לְהַגְבִּיהָהּ עַד שֶׁנָּפְלָה אַחֶרֶת – **AND ONE DID NOT HAVE THE OPPORTUNITY TO REMOVE [A *SE'AH*]** and rectify the mixture **BEFORE ANOTHER** *se'ah* of *terumah* **FELL IN,** הֲרֵי זוֹ אֲסוּרָה – **[THE MIXTURE] IS FORBIDDEN** on the basis of the two *se'ah* of *terumah* that it now contains;[25] וְרַבִּי שִׁמְעוֹן מַתִּיר – **BUT R' SHIMON PERMITS** the mixture.[26] Apparently, R' Shimon views the first *se'ah* of *terumah* as distinct and separate even before it is removed. Consequently, the second *se'ah* is deemed to have fallen into one hundred *se'ah* of *chullin* that are *alongside* one *se'ah* of *terumah.* And since it fell into one hundred

NOTES

15. When one merely needs to use the pillow to rest upon, the Rabbis did not allow moving it while the money is on it, but required that the money be shaken off. However, if one needs to make the place occupied by the pillow available for another use, they allowed moving it along with the money that is on it, since shaking the money off will interfere with the objective (see *Rashi;* see *Ritva MHK* ed. and *Orach Chaim* 309:5). Thus, the ruling of the Mishnah below is limited to a case in which one seeks to move the pillow for the sake of its use.

16. But if the *tahor terumah* is on top, one must remove it and carry it separately. This is similar to the rule stated in the latter clause, that where it is possible to take the pillow without taking the money (i.e. where shaking it off is an option) one may not carry the money along with the pillow unnecessarily (*Rashi*).

17. Since consumption of the mixture is prohibited until the one part is removed, its removal in effect repairs the produce. This should be prohibited, as it bears similarity to repairing a damaged utensil [which is a Biblically prohibited *melachah*] (*Rashi*). [Indeed, a Mishnah (*Beitzah* 36b teaches) that tithing produce on the Sabbath is prohibited for this very reason!]

18. R' Eliezer maintains that since one is allowed to separate from the mixture a portion which represents the *terumah* that fell in (thus permitting consumption of the remainder), even before its removal we view the mixture not as a true mixture, but as one hundred portions of defined *chullin* and one *separate* portion of *terumah.* Consequently, the *chullin* was never actually forbidden and the removal of the "*terumah*" from it does not truly repair it (*Rashi;* see also *Rav* to our Mishnah).

19. *Terumos* 5:6.

20. [A mixture of one part *terumah* in *less* than one hundred parts of *chullin* is forbidden for consumption by non-Kohanim, since the *terumah* retains its identity within the mixture. Only when the *terumah* has become nullified by being mixed with one hundred or more parts of *chullin,* thus losing its identity, may a non-Kohen arbitrarily remove one part to protect the Kohanim's property rights and eat the remainder.]

21. R' Eliezer maintains that the *terumah* portion of the original mixture is regarded as a defined cohesive unit rather than as scattered throughout the mixture. Accordingly, when a *se'ah* of the first mixture is transplanted into a second container of *chullin,* the law considers the possibility that this portion consisted entirely of the lost *se'ah* of *terumah* [even though this is statistically unlikely] (see *Temurah* 12a). Thus, unless the second mixture contained a full one hundred *se'ah* of *chullin,* it too will be prohibited (*Rashi;* see also *Tos. Rid*).

22. That is, we calculate the ratio of *terumah* to *chullin* in the original mixture and presume that the portion which fell into the second container consisted of a mixture of *terumah* and *chullin* in that ratio. Thus, the *chullin* in the second container need measure only one hundred times as much as the *terumah segment* of that which fell in in order for it to be permissible to non-Kohanim. For example, if originally one *se'ah* of *terumah* fell into fifty-nine *se'ah* of *chullin,* a *se'ah* extracted from that mixture is viewed as only one-sixtieth *terumah.* Should that *se'ah* fall into another quantity of *chullin,* the new mixture will be prohibited only if it contains less than one hundred times one-sixtieth of a *se'ah* of *chullin* (*Rashi;* see *Tosafos* ד״ה שנפלה and *Maharsha;* see also *Chasam Sofer* [*Machon Chasam Sofer* ed.] and *Tos. R' Akiva Eiger* to *Terumos* 5:6).

23. For, by removing the one portion, a person certainly repairs the mixture [since none of it may be consumed until the portion is physically removed] (*Rashi*).

24. *Terumos* 5:8.

25. [Since the ratio of *terumah* to *chullin* in the mixture is now one to fifty, the mixture can no longer be rectified by the removal of a portion.]

26. [I.e. he allows removing two *se'ah* to rectify the mixture.]

מאי איריא אבן אפילו דינר נמי אלמה אמר רבא לא שנו אלא אבן אבל דינר אסור אבן אי נפלה לה לא אתי אבוה לאיתויי דינר אי נפיל אתי אבוה לאתויי תניא כוותיה דרבא המוציא כליו מקופלים ומונחים על כתפו וסנדליו וטבעותיו בידו חייב ואם היה מלובש בהן פטור המוציא אדם וכליו עליו וסנדליו ברגליו וטבעותיו בידיו פטור ואילו הוציאן כמות שהן חייב: כלכלה והאבן בתוכה: ואמאי תיהוי כלכלה בסיס לדבר האסור אמר רבה בר בר חנה אמר ר' יוחנן הכא בכלכלה מלאה פירות עסקינן ולישדינהו לפירי ונישדי לאבן ולינקטינהו בידים כדרבי אלעי אמר רב בפירות המיטנפין ה"נ בפירות המיטנפין ולינערינהו נעורי אמר רב חייא בר אשי אמר רבא הכא בכלכלה פחותה עסקינן דאבן גופה נעשית דופן לכלכלה: מטלטלין תרומה וכו': אמר רב חסדא לא שנו אלא שטהורה למטה וטמאה למעלה אבל טהורה למעלה וטמאה למטה שקיל ליה לטהורה ושביק ליה לטמאה וכי טהורה למטה נמי לישדינהו ולינקטינהו אמר רבי אלעי אמר רב בפירות המיטנפין עסקינן מיתיבי מטלטלין תרומה טמאה עם הטהורה ועם החולין בין שטהורה למעלה וטמאה למטה בין שטמאה למעלה וטהורה למטה תיובתא דרב חסדא אמר לך רב חסדא מתניתין לצורך גופו ברייתא לצורך מקומו מאי דוחקיה דרב חסדא לאוקמי מתניתין לצורך גופו אמר רבא מתני' כוותיה דייקא דקתני סיפא מעות שעל הכר מנער את הכר והן נופלות ואמר רבה בר בר חנה אמר רבי יוחנן לא שנו אלא לצורך גופו אבל לצורך מקומו מטלטלו ועודן עליו ומדסיפא לצורך גופו רישא נמי לצורך גופו: רבי יהודה אומר אף מעלין וכו': ואמאי הא קא מתקן רבי יהודה כר' אליעזר סבירא ליה דאמר תרומה בעינא מחתא דתנן סאה תרומה שנפלה לפחות ממאה ונדמעו ונפל מן המדומע למקום אחר רבי אליעזר אומר מדמעת כתרומה ודאי וחכמים אומרים אין המדומע מדמע אלא לפי חשבון אימר דשמעת ליה לחומרא לקולא מי שמעת ליה אלא הוא דאמר כר"ש דתנן סאה תרומה שנפלה למאה ולא הספיק להגביה עד שנפלה אחרת הרי זו אסורה ור"ש מתיר וממאי דילמא התם בהא קמיפלגי דתנא קמא סבר אע"ג דנפלו בזה אחר זה כמאן דנפל בבת אחת דמי והא לחמשין נפלה והא לחמשין נפלה ור"ש סבר קמייתא בטיל במאה והא תיבטיל במאה וחד אלא הוא דאמר כרבי שמעון בן אלעזר דתניא ר' שמעון בן אלעזר אומר נותן עיניו בצד זה ואוכל מצד אחר ומי סבר ליה כוותיה והא

רש"י

אתי לאתויי. וטעמא לאו משום טלטול הוא דאפילו לאוחזו בידו והתינוק מהלך ברגליו אסר ליה רבה דילמא נפיל ואתי לאתויי וכיון דלאו סכנת נפש היא לא שרו ביה טלטול: תניא כוותיה דרבא. דכי נקט לה עליון כמאן דאפקה תחתון גופיה דמי ומיחייב: וסנדליו וטבעותיו בידו. בקומלו שלא כדרך מלבוש: המוציא אדם וכליו עליו. מלובש בהן: וטבעותיו בידיו. באצבעותיו מדלא תנא בידו כדנקט רישא: פטור. דבגדיו בטלי לגביה ועליו הוא פטור כרבי נתן: ואילו הוציאן כמות שהן. שהיה אותו עליון אוחז בהן ולא מלובש חייב הנושא והיינו כרבא: תיהוי כלכלה בסיס. והיא עצמה מיאסר: מליאה פירות. דעיקר נעשית בסיס לפירות הלכך אבן מיטלטלת אגב כלי ופירות שהוא מותר: ונינקטינהו בידים. ילקטם מעל הארץ בידיו ויחזירם בכלכלה ויטלטלם ואינה תחזירו אבן טלטול אגב כלי ופירות: בפירות המיטנפין. בפירות מבושלין ורכין מאד כגון תאנים ותותים וענבים שאם ישליכם לארץ יטנפו: ולנערינהו נעורי. עד שיתמלקו הפירות מן האבן לתוך הכלכלה לצדדין וישליך האבן לבדה בנעורתה: פחותה. שנפחת דופנה או שוליה: וטמאה למעלה. והוא צריך לטהורה ואינו יכול ליטול הטמאה בידים לפי שהיא מוקצה לפיכך יטלטל הכל עד השלחן וישליך הכל עליו ויטול הטהורה: לישדינהו. לארץ כולן: ולינקטינהו. לטהורה ביד ויחזירנה לכלכלה: מתני' לצורך גופו. שצריך לטהורה לגופה לאוכלה הלכך אי לאו דטהורה למטה לא שרו ליה לטלטולי לטמאה אלא שקיל לטהורה וממטי לה לשלחן: ברייתא לצורך מקומו. שצריך למקום הכלי וע"כ כולו הוא צריך לסלקו משם ושרו ליה רבנן לטלטל האי אטו האי: ומאי דוחקיה כו'. דאיצטריך למימר לא שנו אלא שהטמאה למעלה לשבקי דקדק"ד בין שטמאה למעלה בין שטמאה למטה ולוקמי בצריך למקומו: אלא לצורך גופו. שצריך לכר לשכב עליו שם ולא לסלקו לפיכך לא התירו לו ליטלו עם המעות אלא מנערו במקומו אבל צריך למקום הכר מטלטל הכל ביחד: ומדסיפא כו' רישא נמי לצורך גופו. הלכך אי הוה טהורה למעלה לא הוי שרי ליה לטלטולי טמאה כדקתני גבי מעות מנערו ונופלות ומטלטל הכר היתרא לחודיה: הא קמתקן. שמביאה לידי היתר ונגזר ביה אטו תיקון שע"י מלאכה: כר"א דאמר תרומה. הואיל וניתנה להעלות אחת שירצה בעינה מחתא כאילו מונחת לבדה ואינה מעורבת הלכך לא קמתקן מידי: מדמעת. זה שנפרד משם ואוסר ל"ט של חולין כאילו היא תרומה ודאי: וחכ"א אין המדומע מדמע. חולין אחרים אלא לפי חשבון התרומה שבמדומע כגון אם תחילתו נדמע ק' של חולין ע"י סאה תרומה וחזרה סאה ממנו ונפלה לתוך אחרים לא חשבינן תרומה אלא ק' שבסאה זו ומדמע עד ל"ט שכנגדו ואם יש חולין יותר מק' כנגדו עולה: אימר דשמעת ליה. לר"א דאמר תרומה כמאן דמחתא בעינה: לחומרא. לדמעה כתרומה ודאי: לקולא. דלא ליהוי המעלה אותה בשבת כמתקן: מי אמר. הא ודאי מתקן הוא ע"כ: הוא דאמר. רבי יהודה דמתני' כרבי שמעון דאמר לקולא נמי כמאן דמחתא בעינא דמיא: למאה. וראויה להעלותה ויתכשרו החולין: עד שנפלה אחרת. ועכשיו אין בה חולין כדי להעלותה באחד וק': ר"ש מתיר. קס"ד משום דס"ל קמייתא כמאן דמחתא בעינה דמיא ונמצאת אחרונה זו נופלת בתוך ק' של חולין: בטל בק'. והוו להו כולהו חולין ומיהו כיון דצריך להעלותה ע"כ המעלה מתקנו: נותן עיניו. במדומע בצד זה להעלותו לתרומה ואוכל בצד אחר הלכך הואיל ואוכל אין תיקון בהעלאתו: והא

תוספות

ונשדינהו לפירי ונשדייה לאבן. ואם תאמר גבי קטן נמי נשדייה לאבן מידו ואמאי שרי לטלטולי עם האבן וי"ל אם ישליכו מידו יצעק התינוק ויבכה וא"ת מ"מ דלא שרינן לטלטל תינוק אלא כשיש לו געגועין תיבטל אבן אגב תינוק כמו שהיא בטלה אגב כלכלה מלאה פירות וי"ל דאינו צריך כל כך טלטול התינוק וא"ת אפילו אין הכלכלה מלאה פירות תיבטל האבן אגבה כי היכי דבטלי בפ"ב דבילה (דף כא:) שיורי הכוס אגב הכוס אי לאו דאיסורי הנאה נינהו וי"ל שאני שיורי דגריעי יותר מדאי ובטלו טפי וכן צ"ל מתוך שמעתא גופה דבילה כמו שפירשתי לעיל בסוף כירה (דף מז. בד"ה הוה):

ונשדינהו לפירי ונשדייה לאבן כו'. וא"ת מכל מקום נינקטינהו לפירי בידים ויניח האבן בכלכלה והא אמרינן לקמן לא שנו אלא שטהורה למטה וטמאה למעלה אבל טהורה למעלה וטמאה למטה שקיל לה לטהורה ושביק לה לטמאה והיינו על כרחך בידיו דאי זריק לה בכלי א"כ גם בטמאה למעלה יכול לזורקה בכלי אלא שמע מינה דשקיל לה בידיו וא"כ הכי נמי לישקלינהו לפירי בידיו וי"ל דמיירי שפי הכלכלה צר הוא ואינו יכול להכניס שם ידיו אי נמי י"ל דהסיא דלקמן מיירי בתרומה שהיא בכלים קטנים בתוך הקופה שאין דרך להניח טמאה וטהורה ביחד אלא בכלים זה בפני עצמו וזה בפ"ע והכי מצי שקיל לטהורה שהיא למעלה בידיו אבל כלכלה דהכא אין כאן כלים ולא מצי נקיט להו בידיו פן יפול לארץ והשתא לא צריכא לשינויא קמא דפירות המיטנפין דהא כיון דאבן עצמה הוי דופן לכלכלה אפי' הוי שדי לפירות ולאבן והדר שקיל לפירי ושבק לאבן לא הוי ליה במאי לאנחינהו כיון שהכלכלה פחותה שהאבן נעשה לה דופן. והא דלא קאמר אלא לפי שלא החזר אמורא לעיל. א"נ השתא יש להעמיד נמי בפירות המיטנפין דאל"כ נוכל להשליך הסל בקרקע ולהוליך בכלכלה מעט מעט כמה שתוכל להחזיק עד מקום הפחת. מ"ר:

הכא נמי בפירות המיטנפין. וא"ת אכתי יטלם בידו ויניחם בתוך כלי אחר או על גבי טבלא או ע"ג סודר כדמוכח בסמוך גבי תרומה דאמר רב חסדא לא שנו אלא שטהורה למטה וטמאה למעלה אבל טהורה למעלה וטמאה למטה שקיל לטהורה ושביק הטמאה ואע"ג דמוקמינן נמי בפירות המיטנפין וי"ל דהתם מיירי כגון שטהורה מונחת בסלים קטנים בפני עצמה וכן הטמאה ואותם סלים מונחים בתוך כלי אחד גדול והיו סלים של טהורה למעלה מסלים של טמאה דיכול ליקח סלי טהורה ולהניחם ע"ג קרקע אבל אם מונחת זו על גב זו בלא שום כלי כי הכא שהפירות מונחים ביחד בהא ודאי לא אמר שביק לה לטמאה ושקיל לה לטהורה. מ"ר:

שנפלה לפחות מק' חולין. מכאן משמע דתרומה עולה באחד ומאה עם האיסור ורש"י לא פירש כן בפרק גיד הנשה (חולין דף צט:) גבי כל איסורין שבתורה במאה דלפירו' שיטתו לא אתי' מסקנא הכי:

ד א מיי' וסמג שם וטוש"ע שם:
ה ב ג מיי' פי"ט מהל' שבת הלכה יז ופי"ט הלכה יט:
ו ד טוש"ע א"ח סי' שלה סעיף ה:
ז ה מיי' פכ"ה שם הל' טו טוש"ע א"ח סי' שט סעיף ג:
ח ו מיי' שם טוש"ע שם סעיף ב:
ט ז ח ט י מיי' שם הלכה כ:
י כ (מיי' פכ"ג שם הלכה ט והלכה טו):
יא ל מיי' פי"ג מהל' תרומות הל' ג:
יב מ שם הלכה י:

רבינו חננאל

פוטר היה ר' שמעון במוציא את המת לקברו והלכתא כרבא דקאי כר' שמעון דסבר כל מלאכה שאינה צריכה לגופה פטור עליה. ובפרק יציאות השבת אוקימנא להא דתני זב שיצא בכיס שלו בשבת פטור כר' שמעון דסבר מלאכה שאינה צריכה לגופה פטור ולא תימא מלאכה צריכה לגופה כגון מר לעשות טס וס"ת להגיהו אלא אפי' מר לחפור בו וס"ת לקרות בו מלאכה צריכה לגופה היא וכי לא פטר ר' שמעון אלא מלאכה שאינה צריכה לגופה אבל מלאכה שצריכה לגופה אפי' ר' שמעון מחייב ותניא כרבא המוציא כלים מקופלין ומונחין לו על כתפו וסנדליו וטבעתו בידו חייב. ואם היה מלובש בהן פטור. המוציא אדם וכליו וסנדליו ברגליו וטבעתו בידו פטור. שאלו הוציא כמות שהן חייב והלכתא כוותיה: **מתני'** מטלטלין תרומה טמאה עם הטהור' אוקמה רב חסדא למתניתין הא בשטהורה למטה וטמאה למעלה ואותבוה הא מטלטלין תרומה טמאה עם הטהורה ועם החולין בין טהורה למטה וטמאה למעלה ובין טהורה למעלה וטמאה למטה. ופרקה רב חסדא מתני' לצורך גופו כדי לאכלו. שאינו מותר לו לטלטלו אלא הראוי לו לאכילה. ובריתא לצורך מקומו שצריך לפנות המקום לבית המדרש או לאורחים שמותר לו לטלטל לצורך מקומו. אפילו מה שאינו ראוי לאכילה. ואמרינן מאי דוחקיה דרב חסדא לאוקימנא למתני' לצורך גופו אמר רבא מתניתא קשיתיה דקתני סיפא מעות שעל הכר נוער את הכר והן נופלות ואוקימנא ר' יוחנן לצורך גופו דאי לצורך מקומו אפי' עודן עליו מטלטלן ואמר רב חסדא לא מוקמינן מתניתין בתרי טעמי ומדסיפא לצורך גופו רישא נמי לצורך גופו: **פיסקא** דמתני' ר' יהודה אומר אף מעלין את המדומע באחד ומאה. פי' מדומע תרומה שנפלה בחולין ודימעה מעלין אותה אם יש שם מאה ואחד.

א) ס"א אלא, ב) תרומות פ"ה מ"ו תמורה יב. ע"ש, ג) תרומות פ"ה מ"ט, ד) בכורות כב. [ע"ש תוס' ד"ה כמחשבה ותוס' מנחות כג. ד"ה כמחשבה], ה) בקצת ספרים פחותה, ו) [ועי' תוס' חולין לט: ד"ה לא].

רב נסים גאון

וסנדלים חדשים אלא אם כן הילך בהן מבעוד יום כמה יהא הילוכן בני ביתיה דבר קפרא אמרין (מן דבית רבא דבר קפרא אמרין) מן דבית רבה דבר קפרא עד בית רבה דר' הושעיא צפראי אמרין מכביתא דבבלאי עד דרתיה דר' חמא בר חנינא טבראי אמרין מן סדרא רבה עד חנותיה דר' הושעיא: הניחא לרבא דאמר דבר שמלאכתו לאיסור בין לצורך גופו בין לצורך מקומו מותר שפיר אלא לאביי דאמר דבר שמלאכתו לאיסור לצורך גופו מותר לצורך מקומו אסור מאי איכא למימר. ומשכחת עיקר דיליה בפרק כל הכלים ניטלין בשבת (דף קכג:) פרק כא נוטל אדם את בנו ר' יהושע אומר אף מעלין את המדומע באחד ומאה. פירוש שבעת שיפול חלק אחד תרומה בצ"ט חלקים חולין כולן אסורין לישראל ויאכלו לכהן ואם יפול חלק במאה חלקים מוציאין

ליקוטי רש"י

על כתפו. שאינו לבוש כהן. וסנדליו וטבעותיו בידו. אחוזין בידו טבעותיו דומיא דסנדליו [סוכה ה:]. שאינן מלובשין כן דרך מלבוש דומיא דכליו על כתפו [עירובין ד.]. חייב. דאינו מכשיט אלא כמין שלובשו דרך מלבוש [לעיל נח.]. אמר ר' יוחנן לא שנו. למעגרה ואינו מטלטלה בעודן עליה. אלא לצורך גופו. של כר לשכב עליו הלכך בניעור סגיא ושדי ליה במטרתייה. אבל לצורך מקומו. של כר מטלטלו עם המעות לצורך מקום אחר [לקמן ע"ב]. מדמעת. כתרומות ודאי. שאם נפלה סאה מן הדימוע למקום אחר אם יש מאה סאין לבד סאה זו כולן אסורין שאני אומר סאה [של תרומה] שנפלה לתוך הדימוע היא סאה שעלתה ונפלה לתוך האחרים. אלא לפי חשבון. לפי מה שיש תרומה בסאה זו של דימוע כגון אם היה הסאה שיעורין מן החולין אבל מאה סאין לא כגון אם נפלה סאה זו של תרומה לתוך עשרים וארבע סאין של חולין נתמעט ונעשו של סאה וסאה שיש בה הוי אחד מכ"ד שנו תרומה והוי לוג תרומה בכל סאה וסאה אותו דימוע שנפלה לתוך חולין אם יש שם ששה ושבעה לוגין חולין מלבדה [לבדה] מעלה אותו לוג של תרומה [תמורה יב.]. סאה תרומה שנפלה למאה. שיש בחולין מאה ואחד [נ]תרומה [ו]דינה לבטל בכך דנפקא [ל]ן מספרי מכל חלבו את מקדשו ממנו שאם נפל [illegible] בתוכו הרי הוא מקדשו

וכתרומות מעשר משמעי קרא שהיא אחד ממאה וקאמר שאם חזרה לתוך השמנים ומשמע מקדשהן מכאן אמרו תרומה במאה עם האסור אסורה במאה והיא מותרת [חולין צט.].

se'ah of *chullin,* it does not prohibit the mixture. Thus, we see that R' Shimon follows the reasoning that the *terumah* portion of the mixture is viewed as distinct, even when this leads to a leniency.

The Gemara rejects this explanation as well:

וּמִמַּאי – But on what basis do you presume that this is R' Shimon's reasoning? **דִּילְמָא הָתָם בְּהָא קָמִיפַּלְגֵי – Perhaps there it is in this** issue **that they** (the Tanna Kamma and R' Shimon) **disagree: דְּתַנָּא קַמָּא סָבַר – The Tanna Kamma maintains** that **אַף עַל גַּב דְּנָפְלוּ בָּזֶה אַחַר זֶה – even though [the two *se'ah* of *terumah*] fell** into the *chullin* **separately, כְּמַאן דְּנָפַל בְּבַת אַחַת דָּמֵי – it is as though they fell** in **together,** since the first *se'ah* was still there when the second *se'ah* fell in. **וְהָא לְחַמְשִׁין נָפְלָה וְהָא לְחַמְשִׁין נָפְלָה – Thus,** in effect, **this [*se'ah*] fell into fifty** *se'ah* of *chullin* **and this [*se'ah*] fell into fifty** *se'ah* of *chullin,* and the mixture is therefore forbidden.[27] **וְרַבִּי שִׁמְעוֹן סָבַר – But R' Shimon maintains** that **קַמַּיְיתָא בָּטִיל בְּמֵאָה – the first** *se'ah* of *terumah* **was nullified by** the **one hundred** *se'ah* of *chullin* when it fell in, producing a mixture totaling one hundred and one *se'ah* of permitted food, **וְהָא תִּיבְטִיל בְּמֵאָה וְחַד – and this** second *se'ah* of *terumah* **can be nullified by** the **one hundred and one** *se'ah* of permitted food when it falls in.[28] However, R' Shimon concedes that the *terumah* is not considered distinct within the mixture, and consequently, its removal is a repair that is prohibited on the Sabbath. **– ? –**

The Gemara concedes and therefore gives another explanation for why R' Yehudah allows removing one portion from the mixture on the Sabbath:

אֶלָּא הוּא דְּאָמַר כְּרַבִּי שִׁמְעוֹן בֶּן אֶלְעָזָר – Rather, [R' Yehudah] stated his opinion **in accordance with** that of **R' Shimon ben Elazar. דְּתַנְיָא – For it was taught in a Baraisa: רַבִּי שִׁמְעוֹן בֶּן אֶלְעָזָר אוֹמֵר – R' SHIMON BEN ELAZAR SAYS: נוֹתֵן עֵינָיו בְּצַד זֶה – ONE MAY DIRECT HIS EYES AT THIS SIDE** of a mixture containing one part of *terumah* and one hundred parts of *chullin,* deciding that he will eventually remove a portion from here, **וְאוֹכֵל מִצַּד אַחֵר – AND EAT FROM THE OTHER SIDE** even before he actually removes the required portion.[29] R' Yehudah follows this opinion and rules that since one is allowed to eat from the mixture without physically removing one portion, its physical removal on the Sabbath is not a forbidden repair.[30]

Presumably, since R' Yehudah's ruling is based upon the opinion of R' Shimon ben Elazar, the latter must concur with it. The Gemara therefore asks:

וּמִי סָבַר לֵיהּ כְּוָותֵיהּ – But does [R' Shimon ben Elazar] agree with [R' Yehudah]?

NOTES

27. Technically, the first *se'ah* is nullified as soon as it falls into the one hundred *se'ah* of *chullin.* However, since a *se'ah* must be removed for the mixture to be permitted and it was not yet removed, the first *se'ah* is regarded as still extant. It therefore combines with the second *se'ah* to make the mixture forbidden (*Meleches Shlomo* to *Terumos* 5:8, from *Yerushalmi*).

28. R' Shimon holds that since the person was aware that the first *se'ah* of *terumah* fell in and he intended to remove a *se'ah* to rectify the mixture, it is as though the *se'ah* has already been removed in the regard that it cannot combine with the second one to make the mixture forbidden (*Rav* and *Meleches Shlomo* ibid.).

29. R' Shimon ben Elazar maintains that the physical removal of one portion is not a prerequisite to eating from the mixture. It is sufficient to mentally designate a portion for removal (see *Tosafos* to *Gittin* 31a, *Menachos* 55a and *Bechoros* 59a ד"ה במחשבה).

30. Since it is *possible* to rectify the mixture without a physical act, the rectification is not a forbidden repair. [It does not resemble the physical *melachah* of repairing a utensil.] Therefore, even if one rectifies it through a physical act (i.e. by removing a portion without first designating it mentally) his action is not in the category of forbidden repairs (*Rashi* here and to 142b).

מסורת הש"ס

א) פ"א אלא, ב) תרומות פ"ה מ"ז תמורה יב. ע"ש, ג) תרומות פ"ה מ"ש, ד) בכורות נט. [ע"ש תוס' ד"ה כמחשבה ותוס' מנחות נה. ד"ה כמחשבה], ה) בקצת ספרים פחותה, ו) [ועי' תוס' חולין נט: ד"ה לא].

עין משפט נר מצוה

ד א מיי' וסמג שם וטוש"ע שם:
ה ב ג מיי' פ"ח מהל' שבת הלכה יז ופי"ג הלכה יט:
ו ד טוש"ע א"ח סי' שלה סעיף ה:
ז ה מיי' פכ"ה שם הל' טז טוש"ע א"ח סי' שט סעיף ג:
ח ו מיי' שם טוש"ע שם סעיף ב:
ט ז ח ט מיי' שם הלכה כ:
י כ (מיי' פכ"ב שם הלכה ט והלכה טו):
יא ל מיי' פי"ג מהל' תרומות הל' ג:
יב מ שם הלכה י:

גמרא

מאי איריא אבן אפילו דינר נמי אלמה אמר רבא לא שנו אלא אבן אבל דינר אסור אבן אי נפלה לה לא אתי אבוה לאיתויי דינר אי נפיל אתי אבוה לאתויי תניא כוותיה דרבא המוציא כליו מקופלים ומונחים על כתפו וסנדליו וטבעותיו בידו חייב ואם היה מלובש בהן פטור המוציא אדם וכליו עליו וסנדליו ברגליו וטבעותיו בידיו פטור ואילו הוציאן כמות שהן חייב: כלכלה והאבן בתוכה: ואמאי תיהוי כלכלה בסיס לדבר האסור אמר רבה בר בר חנה אמר ר' יוחנן הכא בכלכלה מלאה פירות עסקינן ולישדינהו לפירי ונישדי לאבן ונינקטינהו בידים כדרבי אלעי אמר רב בפירות המיטנפין ה"נ בפירות המיטנפין ולינערינהו נעורי אמר רב חייא בר אשי אמר רבא הכא בכלכלה פחותה עסקינן דאבן גופה נעשית דופן לכלכלה: מטלטלין תרומה וכו': אמר רב חסדא לא שנו אלא שטהורה למטה וטמאה למעלה אבל טהורה למעלה וטמאה למטה שקיל ליה לטהורה ושביק ליה לטמאה וכי טהורה למטה נמי לישדינהו ולינקטינהו אמר רבי אלעי אמר רב בפירות המיטנפין עסקינן מיתיבי מטלטלין תרומה טמאה עם הטהורה ועם החולין בין שטהורה למעלה וטמאה למטה בין שטמאה למעלה וטהורה למטה תיובתא דרב חסדא אמר לך רב חסדא מתניתין לצורך גופו ברייתא לצורך מקומו מאי דוחקיה דרב חסדא לאוקמי מתניתין לצורך גופו אמר רבא מתני' כוותיה דייקא דקתני סיפא מעות שעל הכר מנער את הכר והן נופלות ואמר רבה בר בר חנה אמר רבי יוחנן לא שנו אלא לצורך גופו אבל לצורך מקומו מטלטלו ועודן עליו ומדסיפא לצורך גופו רישא נמי לצורך גופו: רבי יהודה אומר אף מעלין וכו': ואמאי הא קא מתקן רבי יהודה כר' אליעזר סבירא ליה דאמר תרומה בעינא מחתא דתנן סאה תרומה שנפלה לפחות ממאה ונדמעו ונפל מן המדומע למקום אחר רבי אליעזר אומר מדמעת כתרומת ודאי וחכמים אומרים אין המדומע מדמע אלא לפי חשבון אימר דשמעת ליה לחומרא לקולא מי שמעת ליה אלא הוא דאמר כר"ש כדתנן סאה תרומה שנפלה למאה ולא הספיק להגביה עד שנפלה אחרת הרי זו אסורה ור"ש מתיר וממאי דילמא התם בהא קמיפלגי דתנא קמא סבר אע"ג דנפלו בזה אחר זה כמאן דנפל בבת אחת דמי והא לחמשין נפלה והא לחמשין נפלה ור"ש סבר קמייתא בטיל במאה והא תיבטיל במאה וחד אלא הוא דאמר כרבי שמעון בן אלעזר דתניא ר' שמעון בן אלעזר אומר נותן עיניו בצד זה ואוכל מצד אחר ומי סבר ליה כוותיה והא

רש"י

אתי לאתויי. וטעמא לאו משום טלטול הוא דאפילו לאוחזו בידו והתינוק מהלך ברגליו אסר ליה רבה דילמא נפיל ואתי לאתויי וכיון דלאו סכנת נפש היא לא שרו ביה טלטול: תניא כוותיה דרבא. דכי נקטו לה עליון כמאן דאפקא מתחתון גופיה דמי ומחייב: וסנדליו וטבעותיו בידיו. בקומתו שלא כדרך מלבוש: המוציא אדם וכליו עליו. מלובש בהן: וטבעותיו בידיו. באצבעותיו מדלא תנא בידו כדנקט רישא: פטור. דבגדיו בטלי לגביה ועליו הוא פטור כרבי נתן: ואילו הוציאן כמות שהן. שהיה אותו עליון אחוז בהן ולא מלובש חייב הנושא והיינו כרבה: תיהוי כלכלה בסיס. והיא עצמה תיאסר: מליאה פירות. דעיקר נעשית בסיס לפירות הלכך אבן מיטלטלא אגב כלי ופירות שהוא מותר: ונינקטינהו בידים. ילקטם מעל הארץ בידיו ויחזירם לכלכלה ויטלטלם ולמה התירו אבן לטלטל אגב כלי ופירות: בפירות המיטנפין. בפירות מבושלין ורכין מאד כגון תאנים ותותים וענבים שאם ישליכם לארץ יטנפו: ולנערינהו נעורי. עד שיפלו הפירות מן האבן מתוך הכלכלה לצדדין וישליך האבן לבדה בנעורתה: פחותה. שנפחת דופנה או שוליה: וטמאה למעלה. והוא צריך לטהורה ואינו יכול ליטול הטמאה בידים לפי שהיא מוקצה לפיכך יטלטל הכל עד השלחן וישליך הכל עליו ויטול הטהורה: לישדינהו. לארץ כולן: ולינקטינהו. לטהורה ביד ויחזירנה לכלכלה: מתני' לצורך גופו. שצריך לטהורה לגופה לאוכלה הלכך אי לאו לטהורה למטה לא שרו ליה לטלטולי לטמאה אלא שקיל לטהורה וממטי לה לשלחן: ברייתא לצורך מקומו. שצריך למקום הכלי וע"כ כולו הוא צריך לסלקו משם ושרו ליה רבנן לטלטל האי אטו האי: ומאי דוחקיה כו'. דאיצטריך למימר לא שנו אלא שהטמאה למעלה לשבקי לקרא כדקס"ד בין שטמאה למעלה בין שטמאה למטה ולוקמי בצריך למקומו: אלא לצורך גופו. שצריך לכר לשכב עליו שם ולא לסלקו לפיכך לא התירו לו ליטלו עם המעות אלא מנערו במקומו אבל צריך למקום הכר מטלטל הכל ביחד: ומדסיפא כו' רישא נמי לצורך גופו. הלכך אי הוה טהורה למעלה לא הוי שרי ליה לטלטולי טמאה כדקתני גבי מעות מנערו ונופלות ומטלטל היתרא לחודיה: הא קמתקן. שמגביהה לידי היתר ונגזר ביה אטו תיקון שע"י מלאכה: כר"א דאמר תרומה. הואיל ונימוחה להעלות אחת שילה בעינא מחמת כאילו מונחת לבדה ואינה מעורבת הלכך לא קמתקן מידי: מדמעת. זה שנפרד משם ואוסר ל"ט של חולין כאילו היא תרומה ודאי: וחכ"א אין המדומע מדמע. חולין אחרים אלא לפי חשבון התרומה שבמדומע כגון אם תחילתו נדמע ק' של חולין ע"י סאה תרומה וחזרה סאה ממנו ונפלה לתוך אחרים לא חשבינן תרומה אלא ק' שבסאה זו ומדמע עד ל"ט שכנגדו ואם יש חולין יותר מק' כנגדו עולה: אימר דשמעת ליה. לר"א דאמר תרומה כמאן דמחתא בעינא: לחומרא. לדמעה כתרומה ודאי: לקולא. דלא ליהוי המעלה אותה בשבת כמתקן: מי אמר. הא ודאי מתקן הוא ע"כ: הוא דאמר. רבי יהודה דמתני' כרבי שמעון דאמר לקולא נמי כמאן דמחתא בעינא דמיא: למאה. וראויה להעלותה ויתכשרו החולין: עד שנפלה אחרת. ועכשיו אין בה חולין כדי להעלותה באחד וק': ר"ש מתיר. קס"ד משום דס"ל קמייתא כמאן דמחתא בעינא דמיא ונתלת אחרונה זו ונופלת בתוך ק' של חולין: בטל בק'. והוו להו כולהו חולין ומיהו כיון דצריך להעלותה ע"כ המעלה מתקנו: נותן עיניו. במדומע בצד זה להעלותו לתרומה ואוכל בצד אחר הלכך הואיל ובלא העלאה מתחיל ואוכל אין תיקון בהעלאתו:

תוספות

ונשדינהו לפירי ונשדייה לאבן. ואם תאמר גבי קטן נמי נשדייה לאבן מידו ואמאי שרי לטלטולי עם האבן וי"ל אם ישליכו מידו יצעק התינוק ויבכה וא"ת מ"מ דלא שרינן לטלטל תינוק אלא כשיש לו געגועין תיבטל אבן אגב תינוק כמו שהיא בטלה אגב כלכלה מלאה פירות וי"ל דאינו צריך כל כך טלטול התינוק וא"ת אפילו אין הכלכלה מלאה פירות תיבטל האבן אגבה כי היכי דבטלי בפ"ב דבילה (דף כא:) שיורי הכוס אגב הכוס אי לאו דאיסורי הנאה נינהו וי"ל שאני שיורי דגריעי יותר מדאי ובטלו טפי וכן צ"ל מתוך שמעתא גופה דבילה כמו שפירשתי לעיל בסוף כירה (דף מו. בד"ה הוה):

ונשדינהו לפירי ונשדייה לאבן כו'. וא"ת מכל מקום ניקנטינהו לפירי בידים וינח האבן בכלכלה והא אמרינן לקמן לא שנו אלא שטהורה למטה וטמאה למעלה אבל טהורה למעלה וטמאה למטה שקיל לה לטהורה ושביק לה לטמאה והיינו על כרחך בידיו דאי זריק לה בכלי א"כ גם בטמאה למעלה יכול לזורקה בכלי אלא שמע מינה דשקיל לה בידיו וא"כ הכי נמי ליםקלינהו לפירי בידיו וי"ל דמיירי שפי הכלכלה צר הוא ואינו יכול להכניס שם ידיו אי נמי י"ל דההיא דלקמן מיירי בתרומה שהיא בכלים קטנים בתוך הקופה שאין דרך להניח טמאה וטהורה ביחד אלא בכלים זה בפני עצמו וזה בפ"ע ולהכי מצי שקיל לטהורה שהיא למעלה בידיו אבל כלכלה דהכא אין כאן כלים ולא מצי נקיט להו בידיו פן יפול לארץ והשתא לא נריכנא לשינויא קמא דפירות המיטנפין דהא כיון דאבן עצמה הוי דופן לכלכלה אפי' הוי שדי לפירות ולאבן והדר שקיל לפירי ושבק לאבן לא הוי ליה במאי לאנחינהו כיון שהכלכלה פחותה שהאבן נעשה לה דופן. והא דלא קאמר אלא לפי שלא החכר אמורא לעיל. א"נ השתא יש להעמיד נמי בפירות המיטנפין דאל"כ יוכל להשליך הסל בקרקע ולהוליך בכלכלה מעט מעט כמה שיוכל להחזיק עד מקום הפחת. מ"ר:

הכא נמי בפירות המיטנפין. וא"ת אכתי יטלם בידו ויניחם בתוך כלי אחר או על גבי טבלא או ע"ג סודר כדמוכח בסמוך גבי תרומה דאמר רב חסדא לא שנו אלא שטהורה למטה וטמאה למעלה אבל טהורה למעלה וטמאה למטה שקיל לטהורה ושביק הטמאה ואע"ג דמוקמינן נמי בפירות המיטנפין וי"ל דהתם מיירי כגון שטהורה מונחת בסלים קטנים בפני עצמה וכן הטמאה ואותם סלים מונחים בתוך כלי אחד גדול והיו סלים של טהורה למעלה מסלים של טמאה דיכול ליקח סלי טהורה ולהניחם ע"ג קרקע אבל אם מונחת זו על גב זו בלא שום כלי כי הכא שהפירות מונחים ביחד בהא ודאי לא אמר שביק לה לטמאה ושקיל לה לטהורה. מ"ר:

שנפלה לפחות מק' חולין. מכאן משמע דתרומה עולה באחד ומאה עם האיסור ורש"י לא פירש כן בפרק גיד הנשה (חולין דף צט:) גבי כל איסורין שבתורה במאה דלפירו' שיטתו לא אתי' מסקנא הכי:

רבינו חננאל

פוטר היה ר' שמעון במוציא את המת לקברו והלכתא כרבא דקאי כר' שמעון דסבר כל מלאכה שאינה צריכה לגופה פטור עליה. ובפרק יציאות השבת אוקימנא להא דתני זב שיצא בכיס שלו בשבת פטור כר' שמעון דסבר מלאכה שאינה צריכה לגופה פטור ולא תימא מלאכה צריכה לגופה כגון מר לעשות טס וס"ת להגיהו אלא אפי' מר לחפור בו וס"ת לקרות בו מלאכה צריכה לגופה היא וכי לא פטר ר' שמעון אלא מלאכה שאינה צריכה לגופה אבל מלאכה שצריכה לגופה אפי' ר' שמעון מחייב ותניא כרבא המוציא כלים מקופלין ומונחין לו על כתפו וסנדליו וטבעתו בידו חייב. ואם היה מלובש בהן פטור. המוציא אדם וכליו וסנדליו ברגליו וטבעתו בידו פטור. שאלו הוציא כמות שהן חייב והלכתא כוותיה: מתני' מטלטלין תרומה טמאה עם הטהור' אוקמה רב חסדא למתניתין הא בשטהורה למטה וטמאה למעלה ואותבה הא מטלטלין תרומה טמאה עם הטהורה ועם החולין בין טהורה למטה וטמאה למעלה ובין טהורה למעלה וטמאה למטה. ופרקה רב חסדא מתני' לצורך גופו כדי לאכלו. שאינו מותר לו לטלטלו אלא הראוי לו לאכילה. וברייתא לצורך מקומו שצריך לפנות המקום לבית המדרש או לאורחים שמותר לו לטלטל לצורך מקומו. אפילו מה שאינו ראוי לאכילה. ואמרינן מאי דוחקיה דרב חסדא לאוקימנא למתני' לצורך גופו אמר רבא מתניתא קשיתיה דקתני סיפא מעות שעל הכר נוער את הכר והן נופלות ואוקימנא ר' יוחנן לצורך גופו דאי לצורך מקומו אפי' עודן עליו מטלטלן ואמר רב חסדא לא מוקמינן מתניתין בתרי טעמי ומדסיפא לצורך גופו רישא נמי לצורך גופו: פיסקא דמתני' ר' יהודה אומר אף מעלין את המדומע באחד ומאה. פי' מדומע תרומה שנפלה בחולין ודימעה מעלין אותה אם יש שם מאה ואחד.

רב נסים גאון

וסנדלים חדשים אלא אם כן הילך בהן מבעוד יום כמה יהא הילוכן בני ביתיה דבר קפרא אמרין (מן דבית רבא דבר קפרא אמרין) מן דבית רבה דבר קפרא עד בית רבה דר' הושעיא צפראי אמרין מכניסתא דבבלאי עד דרתיה דר' חמא בר חנינא טבראי אמרין מן סדרא רבה עד חנותיה דר' הושעיא: הניחא לרבא דאמר דבר שמלאכתו לאיסור בין לצורך גופו בין לצורך מקומו מותר שפיר אלא לאביי דאמר דבר שמלאכתו לאיסור לצורך גופו מותר לצורך מקומו אסור מאי איכא למימר. ומשכחת עיקר דיליה בפרק כל הכלים ניטלין בשבת (דף קכג:) פרק כא נוטל אדם את בנו ר' יהושע אומר אף מעלין את המדומע באחד ומאה. פירושו שבעת שיפול חלק אחד תרומה בצ"ט חלקים חולין כולן אסורין לישראל וימכרו לכהן ואם יפול חלק במאה חלקים מרציאין

ליקוטי רש"י

על כתפו. שאינו לבוש בהן. וסנדליו וטבעותיו בידו. אוחזן בידו טבעותיו דומיא דסנדליו [סוכה ה:]. שאינן מלובשין בו דרך מלבוש דומיא דכליו על כתפיו [עירובין ד.]. חייב. דאינו מכסיא אלא כמאן שלובשו דרך מלבוש [לעיל נח.]. אמר ר' יוחנן לא שנו. דמנערה ואינו מטלטלה בעודן עליה. אלא לצורך גופו. של כר לשכב עליו הלכך בניעור סגיא ושדי ליה באתריה. אבל לצורך מקומו. של כר מטלטלו עם המעות למקום אחר [לקמן ע"ב]. מדמעת כתרומת ודאי. שאם נפלה סאה מן הדימוע למקום אחר ואין שם מאה סאין לבד סאה זו כולן אסורין שאני אומר סאה [של תרומה] שנפלה לתוך הדימוע היא סאה שעלתה וחזרה ונפלה לתוך האחרים. אלא לפי חשבון. לפי מה שיש תרומה בסאה זו של דימוע בעינן מאה שיעורין מן החולין אבל מאה סאין לא בעינן כגון אם נפלה תחילה סאה של תרומה לתוך עשרים וארבע סאין של חולין נדמעו ועכשיו כל סאה וסאה שיש בו הוי אחד מכ"ד שבו תרומה והיינו לוג תרומה בכל סאה וסאה אם חזרה ונפלה סאה מאותו דימוע לתוך חולין אחרים אם יש שם שבעים ושבעה לוגין אחרים של חולין מלטרפין עם עשרים [ושלשה] לוגין חולין שבסאה זו ומבטלין את לוג התרומה [תמורה יב.]. סאה תרומה שנפלה למאה. שיש כחולין מאה ואחד [כ]תרומה [ו]דינה לבטל בכך דנפקא לן בספרי מקרא מכל חלבו את מקדשו ממנו שאם נפל כמוכו הרי הוא מקדשו ובתרומת מעשר משתעי קרא שהיא אחד ממאה וקאמר שאם חזרה לתוך התשעים ותשעה מקדשתן מכאן אמרו תרומה במאה עם האסור אסורה במאה והיא מותרת [חולין צט.].

והא מיפליג פליג עילויה דתניא רבי יהודה אומר מעלין את המדומע באחד ומאה רבי שמעון בן אלעזר אומר נותן עיניו בצד זה ואוכל מצד אחר דרבי יהודה עדיפא מדר"ש בן אלעזר: **מתני׳** האבן שע"פ החבית מטה על צדה והיא נופלת היתה בין החביות מגביה ומטה על צדה והיא נופלת מעות שעל הכר מנער את הכר והן נופלות היתה עליו לשלשת מקנחה בסמרטוט היתה של עור נותנין עליה מים עד שתכלה: **גמ׳** אמר רב הונא אמר רב לא שנו אלא בשוכח אבל במניח נעשה בסיס לדבר האסור: [היתה בין החביות כו׳]: מאן תנא דכל היכא דאיכא איסורא והיתרא בהיתרא טרחינן באיסורא לא טרחינן אמר רבה בר בר חנה אמר רבי יוחנן רשב"ג היא דתנן הבורר קטנית ביו"ט ב"ש אומרים בורר אוכל ואוכל וב"ה אומרים בורר כדרכו בחיקו ובתמחוי ותניא אמר רשב"ג במה דברים אמורים שהאוכל מרובה על הפסולת אבל פסולת מרובה על האוכל דברי הכל בורר אוכל והא הכא דכי אוכל מרובה על הפסולת דמי הכא נמי כיון דאי בעי למישקל לא משתקיל ליה יין עד דשקיל לה (א) לאבן כפסולת מרובה על האוכל דמי: היתה בין החביות מגביה: תניא רבי יוסי אומר היתה החבית מונחת באוצר או שהיו כלי זכוכית מונחין תחתיה מגביה למקום אחר ומטה על צדה והיא נופלת ונוטל הימנה מה שצריך לו ומחזירה למקומה: מעות שעל הכר: אמר רב חייא בר אשי אמר רב לא שנו אלא בשוכח אבל במניח נעשה בסיס לדבר האסור אמר רבה בר בר חנה אמר ר׳ יוחנן לא שנו אלא לצורך גופו אבל לצורך מקומו מטלטלו ועודן עליו וכן תני חייא בר רב מדיפתי לא שנו אלא לצורך גופו אבל לצורך מקומו מטלטלו ועודן עליו: מעות שעל הכר מנער וכו׳: א"ר אושעיא שכח ארנקי בחצר מניח עליה ככר או תינוק ומטלטלה אמר רב יצחק שכח לבינה בחצר מניח עליה ככר או תינוק ומטלטלה אמר רבי יהודה בר שילא אמר ר׳ אסי פעם אחת שכחו דסקיא מלאה מעות בסרטיא ובאו ושאלו את ר׳ יוחנן ואמר להן הניחו עליה ככר או תינוק וטלטלוה אמר מר זוטרא הלכתא ככל הני שמעתתא בשוכח רב אשי אמר אפילו שכח נמי [לא] ולא אמרו ככר או תינוק אלא למת בלבד אביי מנח כפא אכיפי רבא מנח סכינא אבר יונה ומטלטלה אמר רב יוסף כמה חריפא שמעתתא דדרדקי אימר דאמור רבנן בשוכח לכתחילה מי אמור אמר אביי אי לאו דאדם חשוב אנא כפא אכיפי למה לי הא חזו למיזגא עלייהו אמר רבא אנא אי לאו דאדם חשוב אנא אבר יונה למה לי הא חזי לי לאומצא טעמא דחזי לאומצא הא לא חזי לאומצא לא למימרא דרבא כרבי יהודה סבירא ליה והאמר רבא לשמעיה טווי לי בר אווזא ושדי מיעיה לשונרא

התם

רש"י

מתני׳ מטה על צדה. מטה חבית על צדה אם צריך ליטול מן היין והאבן נופלת ולא יטלנה בידים: **היתה בין החביות.** וירא שלא תפול האבן על החביות וישברם: **מגביה.** לחבית כולה ומסלקה מבין החביות ושם מטה על צדה: **לשלשת.** שום דבר מיאוס כגון רוק או צואה: **מקנחה בסמרטוט.** ולא יתן עליה מים דסתם כר של בגד הוא וכגד שרייתו במים הוא כבוסו: **היתה.** לשלשת זו על כר של עור דלאו בר כיבוס הוא: **נותן עליה מים עד שתכלה.** ומיהו כיבוס ממש לא (ב) דהואיל וסתם כרים וכסתות רכים ניינהו שייך למימר בהו כיבוס בעורות רכין ומיהו שרייתן לא זהו כבוסן וכן מפורש בזבחים בפרק דם חטאת: **גמ׳ לא שנו.** מטה על צדה: **אלא בשכח.** שכח האבן עליה בין השמשות ולא מדעת: **נעשה חבית בסיס לדבר האסור.** ואסור לטלטלה שאף החבית מוקצה: **מאן תנא.** דמתניתין דקתני מגביה ומטה על צדה דאית ליה דכי טרח מטרח בחבית דהוי היתרא ולא יטול האבן ממש דהוי איסורא ואע"ג דהשתא נמי אבן מטלטל בהדי חבית: **רבן שמעון.** אליבא דבית הלל: **בורר אוכל ואוכל.** המאכל יטול והפסולת ישאר בכלי: **בורר כדרכו.** נוטל פסולת ומניח אוכל אם ירצה: **כשהאוכל מרובה על הפסולת.** דלאי שקיל אוכל מפיש בטרחא: **דברי הכל בורר אוכל.** דבהיתרא טרח ולא באיסורא ופרכינן והא הכא דמתניתין דאוכל מרובה על הפסולת וכי מגביה האבן עם החבית טרח טפי והוה (ג) למשקל פסולת כר"ש: **כיון דאי בעי למשקל.** לכולי יין מן החבית לא משתקיל ליה יין שבשוליה עד דשקיל ומגבה לאבן לחבית כפסולת מרובה דמי דאי בתחלתו לא מגבה לה לחבית סוף סוף מיבעי ליה לאגבוהה מו לחבית הלכך הוה ליה מפיש בטרחא: ה"ג לא משתקיל ליה (ד) עד דשקיל לה ול"ג עד דשקיל לה לאבן: **היתה החבית מונחת באוצר.** כלומר במקום מכונס שאוצרין שם חביות הרבה ודואג שמא יטלה ותפול האבן על החבית שאצלה: **לא שנו.** דמנער: **נעשה.** הכר בסיס למעות ואף הכר אסור בטלטול: **לא שנו.** דמנערה ואינו מטלטלה בעודן עליה: **אלא שצריך לגופו.** של כר לשכב עליו הלכך בניעור סגיא ושדי ליה באחריניהו: **אבל צריך למקומו.** של כר מטלטלו עם המעות למקום אחר: **דסקיא מלאה מעות** גרסינן: **בסרטיא.** רה"ר: **הניחו עליה ככר או תינוק.** לאישתרי לטלטלה אגבייהו תוך ד׳ אמות וטלטלוה פחות פחות מד׳ אמות או במחילה של בני אדם כדאמרי׳ בעירובין (דף מג:): **בשוכח.** אבל במניח מבעוד יום (יום) שבת לא התירו לו לטלטלו ע"י ככר או תינוק: **אלא למת.** משום כבוד הבריות כשמוטל בחמה: **אביי מנח כפא אכיפי.** מניח תרווד על העומרים לטלטלן אגב תרווד: **אבר יונה.** חי [בלא] מלים: **חריפא שמעתתא דדרדקי.** סבורים הם שהם חריפים: **אימר דאמור רבנן.** בארנקי ודסקיא מניח עליה ככר או תינוק בשכחה ובמקום התורפה ומשום הפסד ממון: **אמר אביי.** אנא שפיר מטלטלנא כיפי ואפילו בלא תרווד: **אי לאו דאדם חשוב אנא.** ואנא מחמיר על עצמי שלא ילמדו ממני להקל באסורין: **כפא אכיפי למה לי.** בלאו כפא נמי שרי לטלטולינהו דהא חזו למיזגא עלייהו: **לאומצא.** לאוכלו חי בשבת שיש בני אדם שדעתן יפה ואוכלים בשר חי וקרו לה אומצא: **הא לא חזי לאומצא לא.** ואע"ג דחזו לשונרא דאמרינן מוכן לאדם לא הוי מוכן לכלבים: **כר׳ יהודה.** במסכת ביצה (דף ו:): **טווי לי בר אווזא.** ביום טוב: **ושדי מיעיה לשונרא.** אלמא מטלטל להו משום שונרא ואע"ג דהאידנא לא חזי לאדם דלאו אורח ארעא למיכלא ביום טוב ומיהו מאתמול לאדם הוו קיימי:

התם

תוספות

שאוכל מרובה על הפסולת. פי׳ בקונטרס משום דהשתא הוי טרחא יתירא למישקליה לאוכל ואינו נראה לר"י דאי משום טרחא הוי מאי קאמרי בסמוך הכא נמי כיון דאי בעי למישקל לא מישתקיל ליה עד דשקיל ליה לאבן כפסולת מרובה על האוכל דמי היכי הוי משום האי טעמא כפסולת מרובה על האוכל ולכך הוצרך ר"י לפרש דל"ג עד דשקיל ליה לאבן על כן נראה לר"ת דטעמא משום דכי אוכל מרובה על הפסולת הוה פסולת כבטל לגבי רובו ומותר ליטול מן האוכל ולזורקו אבל פסולת מרובה על האוכל לא בטיל ליה פסולת (ה) לגבי אוכל והשתא אתי שפיר גירסת הספרים דגבי חבית נמי כיון דאי בעי למישקל לא משתקיל ליה (ה) עד דשקיל ליה לאבן כפסולת מרובה על האוכל דמי דכיון שאין יכול כלל ליטול מן היין בלא נטילת האבן לא חשיב כבטיל לגבי האוכל כיון שהאוכל אינו ניכר כלל ואינו יכול ליטול הימנו כשהאבן על פי החבית. מ"ר. והא דמוקי לה בפ"ק דביצה (ד׳ יד: ושם) כגון דנפיש בטורחא חוטר בשיעורא האוכל קאי ולא אפסולת ולפירש"י קאי אפסולת ולא אאוכל [וע"כ לא יכרור הפסולת דנפיש בטירחא]:

לא שנו אלא בשכח. וא"ת תרתי דרב למה לי וי"ל חדא מכלל חבירתה איתמר והא לא תקשה תרתי מתני׳ למה לי דהוה אמינא אבן ודאי שרי בשכח שנראה טפי ככיסוי החבית אבל מעות שעל גבי הכר אפילו בשכח ה"א דאסיר:

התם

והא מיפליג פליג עילויה. ואמר כיון דאפשר ליה למיעבד עונג שבת בכה"ג ליתן עיניו בצד זה ולאכול בצד אחר אין מעלין: **דרבי יהודה עדיפא.** מיקל טפי פורתא ואמר כיון דיכול ליתן (עליו) עיניו בצד זה ולאכול בצד זה לא הוי מתקן בהעלאתו ומעלין:

עין משפט נר מצוה

יג א מיי׳ פכ"א מהל׳ שבת הל׳ יז טוש"ע א"ח סי׳ שט סעיף ד:

יד ב מיי׳ פכ"ה שם הל׳ יח טוש"ע א"ח סי׳ שב סעיף ט:

טו ג מיי׳ פכ"ה שם הלכה יז טוש"ע א"ח סי׳ שט סעיף ד:

טז ד ה מיי׳ פ"ג מהל׳ י"ט הל׳ טו סמג לאוין עה טוש"ע א"ח סי׳ תקי סעיף ג:

יז ו מיי׳ פכ"ה מהל׳ שבת הלכה יז טוש"ע א"ח סי׳ שט סעיף ה:

יח ז מיי׳ פכ"ה שם הלכה כא סמג שם טוש"ע א"ח סי׳ שיא סעיף ה:

רבינו חננאל

ואקשינן אמאי והא קא מתקן טיבלא ונמצא עושה מעשה בשבת ופרקי׳ ר׳ יהודה דאמר כי מעלין את המדומע כר׳ אליעזר סבירא ליה דאמר תרומה בעינא מחתא. פי׳ תרומה שנפלה בחולין אין מחשבין אותה שנתערבה בכל החולין אלא כאילו נתונה במקום אחד היא וכשנוטל ממאה ואחד סאין סאה אנן אומרין כי היא היא התרומה. אבל שאר החולין מתוקנין היו מקודם. ולא היה אסור אלא זו הסאה שנטלה במקום התרומה שנפלה בלבד. דתנן סאה של תרומה שנפלה לפחות ממאה ונדמעו ונפל מן המדומע למקום אחד. ר׳ אליעזר אומר מדומע כתרומה ודאי. פי׳ סאה תרומה שנפלה לתוך חמשים סאין חולין ועוד נפלה מאלו החמשים ואחד סאין סאה אחת לששים סאה חולין ר׳ אליעזר סבר הכל אסור חמשים הראשונים וששים האחרונים שאני אומר הסאה של תרומה עצמה היא שנפלה בששים האחרונים לפי שאין המדומע עולה אלא בא׳ ומאה ואין באחד מהן מאה בעת נפילתה בהן וחכ"א אין המדומע מדמע אלא לפי חשבון פי׳ סאה שנפלה לחמשים סאין ונפלה מאלו החמשים סאין לפחות מחמשים מדמעת אבל אם נפלה סאה לששים סאין עולה לפי שאילו היתה סאה במאה סאין ואחת היתה עולה וחזרנו עוד להקשות אימור דשמעת ליה לר׳ אליעזר שמחשב מכלל נ"א סאין הללו הסאה האחת שנפלה לס׳ סאין אחרות תרומה כולה. ומדמעת עד מאה ואחת לחומרא לקולא לתקן בשבת מי שמעת ליה ולא עמדה ופירקנן פירוק אחר והוא ר׳ יהודה סבר לה כר׳ שמעון דתנן סאה של תרומה שנפלה למאה חולין ונדמעו ולא הספיק להגביהה עד שנפלה האחרת הרי זו אסורה ור׳ שמעון מתיר ת"ק סבר כיון שלא הגביהה נמצא שנפלו ב׳ סאין למאה סאין ואין עולין כי פחות ממאה הן. ור׳ שמעון סבר מאותה העת שנפלה סאה תרומה למאה חולין הותרו המאה. ונשארו חולין בהכשרין. וסאה אחת בתוכן תרומה התרומה היא אסורה בלבד וכשנפלה אחר כן עוד סאה אחרת תרומה עליהן על מאה חולין נפלה ועולה כר׳ ופרקי׳ לה ודברים פשוטין הן. והדרנן ומוקמינן ר׳ יהודה דמתני׳ כר׳ שמעון בן אלעזר דאמר נותן עיניו בצד זה כלומר מחשב להוציא התרומה מצד זה ואוכל מצד אחר ש"מ כי התרומה מחתא במקום אחד. ואקשינן וכי ר׳ יהודה כר׳ שמעון בן אלעזר סבירא ליה והא מפלג פליג עליה דתניא ר׳ יהודה אומר מעלין את המדומע באחד ומאה ר׳ שמעון אומר נותן עיניו בצד זה ואוכל מצד זה ומפרקי׳ דר׳ יהודה עדיפא שר׳ יהודה מתיר אפי׳ להעלותה ור׳ שמעון אינו מתיר להעלותה אלא לתת עיניו בצד זה ולאכול מצד זה. ותרווייהו סבירא להו סאה תרומה שנפלה למאה חולין בעת שנפלה למאה מותרין הן ובתקונן הן ואין צריכין תיקון אלא סילוק סאה אחת מהן בלבד במקום התרומה: **פיסקא** האבן שעל

מסורת הש"ס

א) [תוספתא פרק טו], ב) [לעיל קכה:], ג) זבחים צד., ד) [פי׳ צואת תרנגולים. ערוך], ה) [לעיל קכה: ע"ש], ו) ביצה יד:, ז) ג"ז שם ע"ש, ח) [לעיל ל: מג:], ט) [לעיל נא. וש"נ], י) ביצה לג., כ) נ"ל לגבי אוכל והאוכל לא בטל לגבי פסולת משום דחשיב וע"כ בורר את האוכל והשתא כו׳, ל) נ"ל אאוכל קאי שהאוכל נפיש בטרחא ואפ"ה בורר אוכל הואיל חוטר בשיעורא ולא בטל ליה פסולת.

הגהות הב"ח

(א) גמ׳ דשקיל לה כפסולת כצ"ל ותיבת לאבן נמחק: (ב) רש"י ד"ה נותן וכו׳ כיבוס ממש לא דהואיל: (ג) ד"ה דברי הכל וכו׳ והוה ליה למשקל: (ד) ד"ה ה"ג לא משתקיל ליה יין עד: (ה) תוס׳ ד"ה שאוכל וכו׳ לא משתקיל ליה יין עד:

גליון הש"ס

גמ׳ מאן תנא דכל היכא דאיכא איסורא והיתרא. עיין לעיל דף נא ע"ב תוס׳ ד"ה אינו נוטל:

רב נסים גאון

מוציאין חלק אחד והשאר מותר לישראל ותמצא עיקר דבר זה בסיפרי מכל חלבו את מקדשו ממנו שאם נפל לתוכו הרי זה מקדשו מיכן אמרו תרומה עולה באחד ומאה אין לי אלא תרומה טהורה ותמצא במשנת תרומות ותוספות תרומות מזה הענין הרבה ועיקרו מה שהזכרנו׳ ובגמ׳ דערלה בפרק ב׳ (ירושלמי שם הלכה א) מניין שהן עולין אמר ר׳ יונה כתיב (במדבר יח) מכל חלבו את מקדשו ממנו דבר שאתה מרים ממנו שאם יפול לתוכו הרי זה מקדשו וכמה הוא אחד ממאה ואיתא נמי בפרק ד׳ דתרומות התרומה צריך להרים כמה שהוא במשנה במסכת ערלה בראש פרק ב׳ התרומה ותרומת מעשר של דמאי מצטרפין זה עם זה ואינו צריך להרים וכו׳ וטעמו של דבר לפי שהתרומות והחלה והביכורים הם נכסי כהן וצריך להרים תרומה ויתנה ואם לא ירים ויתן לו הרי זה גוזל ממונו ואין להם בעלים שראויין להם לפיכך אינו צריך להרים

ליקוטי רש"י

האבן שע"פ החבית. והולך ליטול מן היין שבתוכה [לעיל קכה:]. **היתה עליו לשלשת.** היתה על הכר של בגד גיעול של רוק או של צואה מקנחו בסמרטוט בשבת ואינו נותן עליה מים לכלותה [ו]להעבירה מפני שהוא מכבס וכיבוס אב מלאכה הוא [ד]הייני מלבן ואם היתה לשלשת זו על כר של עור נותן עליה מים עד שתכלה בשטיפת מים ומיהו שפשופי בידים לא [זבחים צד.]. **בשוכח.** האבן עליה שלא במתכוין. **אבל במניח נעשה.** החבית בסיס לאבן שהיא דבר האיסור [לעיל שם]. **תמחוי.** קערה גדולה [ביצה יב:]. **במה דברים אמורים.** דשרו בית הלל ליטול פסולת ממש ולהשליך. בזמן שטורח האוכל מרובה על של פסולת הוא דקא אמרי בית הלל נוטל פסולת דמעוטי בטרחא עדיף אבל אם טורח הפסולת מרובה על של האוכל דברי הכל כו׳ [שם יד:]. **אלא לצורך גופו.** שצריך לכר לשכב עליו שם ולא לסלקו לפיכך לא התירו לו ליטלו עם המעות אלא מנערו במקומו אבל צריך למקום הכר מטלטל הכל ביחד [לעיל ע"א]. **דסקיא.** שק של עור סקורזין טשינ"א [כתובות צו.]. מרצוף גדול של עור [ברכות יח.]. **סרטיא.** מסילה שהולכין בה מעיר לעיר [לעיל ו.]. **אלא למת.** מת המוטל בחמה ויש לחוש שמא ימהר להסריח [שם מג:]. **דאדם חשוב אנא.** שהרואה אותו שהוא מיקל עומד ומיקל יותר [שם נא.]. **ושדי מיעיה לשונרא.** השלך בני מעים לחתול ולרבי יהודה אסור לטלטלו ולתתו לחתול דמאתמול מוכן לאדם היה ולא לכלבים דקאמר אם לא היתה נבילה מערב שבת אסורה [ביצה לג.].

וְהָא מִיפְלִיג פָּלִיג עִילָוֵיהּ – Why, he disputes the ruling of [R' Yehudah]! דְּתַנְיָא – For it was taught in a Baraisa: רַבִּי יְהוּדָה אוֹמֵר – R' YEHUDAH SAYS: מַעֲלִין אֶת הַמְּדוּמָּע בְּאֶחָד וּמֵאָה – WE MAY REMOVE ONE PART of *terumah* FROM A MIXTURE WITH ONE HUNDRED PARTS of *chullin* on the Sabbath. רַבִּי שִׁמְעוֹן בֶּן אֶלְעָזָר אוֹמֵר – R' SHIMON BEN ELAZAR SAYS: נוֹתֵן עֵינָיו בְּצַד זֶה וְאוֹכֵל מִצַּד אַחֵר – ONE MAY DIRECT HIS EYES AT THIS SIDE of the mixture, deciding that he will eventually remove a portion from here, AND EAT FROM THE OTHER SIDE without actually removing the required portion. However, one may not physically remove it on the Sabbath.[1] How can you say that R' Yehudah's ruling is based on R' Shimon ben Elazar's view?

The Gemara answers:

דְּרַבִּי יְהוּדָה עֲדִיפָא מִדְּרַבִּי שִׁמְעוֹן בֶּן אֶלְעָזָר – **R' Yehudah's** view is **even more** lenient **than that of R' Shimon ben Elazar.** R' Shimon ben Elazar holds that one may rectify the mixture on the Sabbath by mentally designating a portion for removal, but not by physically removing a portion. However, R' Yehudah maintains that since the mixture can be rectified through mental designation, even the physical removal of a portion is permitted.

Mishnah The Mishnah next discusses the indirect movement of *muktzeh*: הָאֶבֶן שֶׁעַל פִּי הֶחָבִית – **A stone that is on the opening of a cask** – מַטֶּה עַל צִדָּהּ וְהִיא נוֹפֶלֶת – **one may tilt [the cask] on its side so that [the stone] falls off.**[2] הָיְתָה בֵּין הֶחָבִיּוֹת – **If [the cask] was among other casks** which might break if the stone would fall against them, מַגְבִּיהָהּ וּמַטֶּה עַל צִדָּהּ וְהִיא נוֹפֶלֶת – **one may lift [the cask]** as is, remove it to a safe area, **and** there **tilt it on its side so that [the stone] falls off.**[3]

מָעוֹת שֶׁעַל הַכַּר – **Money that is on a pillow** – מְנַעֵר אֶת הַכַּר וְהֵן נוֹפְלוֹת – **one may shake the pillow so that it falls off.**[4]

Having mentioned a law concerning a pillow, the Mishnah digresses to discuss other Sabbath laws concerning pillows: הָיְתָה עָלָיו לִשְׁלֶשֶׁת – **If there was filth on [the pillow]** which one wishes to clean on the Sabbath, מְקַנְּחָהּ בִּסְמַרְטוּט – **he may wipe it off with a rag,** but may not rinse it with water.[5] הָיְתָה שֶׁל עוֹר – **If [the pillow] was made of leather,** נוֹתְנִין עָלֶיהָ מַיִם עַד שֶׁתִּכְלֶה – **we may pour water on it until [the filth] disappears.**[6]

Gemara The Gemara qualifies the Mishnah's opening rule:

אָמַר רַב הוּנָא אָמַר רַב – **Rav Huna said in the name of Rav:** לֹא שָׁנוּ אֶלָּא בְּשׁוֹכֵחַ – **They taught** that one may tilt the cask to remove a stone **only** concerning a case **where one forgot** the stone upon the cask, אֲבָל בְּמַנִּיחַ – **but** in a case **where one left** it there intentionally before the Sabbath, נַעֲשָׂה בָּסִיס לְדָבָר הָאָסוּר – **[the cask] has become a base to a forbidden object** and may not be moved at all.[7]

The Mishnah continued:

[הָיְתָה בֵּין הֶחָבִיּוֹת כו׳ – IF IT WAS AMONG OTHER CASKS, one may lift the cask as is, remove it to a safe area **etc.**]

The Gemara analyzes this ruling:

מַאן תַּנָּא דְּכָל הֵיכָא דְּאִיכָּא אִיסּוּרָא וְהֶיתֵּרָא – **Who is the Tanna** of our Mishnah who maintains **that wherever there is** a choice between handling a **prohibited** object **and** handling a **permitted** object, בְּהֶיתֵּרָא טָרְחִינַן בְּאִסּוּרָא לֹא טָרְחִינַן – **one should work with the permitted** object, **not the prohibited**

NOTES

1. R' Shimon ben Elazar maintains that since the produce can be made available for Sabbath enjoyment by merely gazing at it and designating a portion for removal, we do not allow the physical removal of the portion on the Sabbath [for the physical removal does somewhat resemble a repair] (*Rashi*).

2. I.e. if a stone is covering the mouth of a cask from which one wishes to draw wine, one may not remove the *muktzeh* stone with his hands, but may tilt the cask so that the stone falls off (*Rashi*). This indirect movement of *muktzeh* is permissible only when it is done for the sake of a non-*muktzeh* object, e.g. to enable one to draw wine from the cask. However, if the intent would be to protect the stone (or the money in the Mishnah's next case) from theft or the like, even tilting the cask to remove the *muktzeh* would be prohibited (see *Mishnah Berurah* 309:14 with *Shaar HaTziyun* §17).

3. Although this is permitted when necessary, it is preferable when feasible to remove the *muktzeh* object by merely tilting the non-*muktzeh* object, rather than carrying it with the *muktzeh* on it (see *Mishnah Berurah* 309:17, and *Chazon Ish* §156.

Upon reaching an area where one can slide the stone off the cask without causing any damage, one must do so immediately and not carry the cask any further unnecessarily (*Rashi,* as understood by *R' Akiva Eiger;* however, *R' Akiva Eiger* wonders why we do not apply to this case the rule stated above, 124a note 20, that once permission is granted to move a *muktzeh* object one may take it to any convenient location; see also 143a end of note 13).

4. If one needs to use the non-*muktzeh* pillow, he may indirectly remove the *muktzeh* money (Gemara). This ruling is essentially identical to the Mishnah's first ruling. Nevertheless, one might have thought that only a stone which is upon a cask may be shaken off because it appears like a non-*muktzeh* lid, whereas money that is on a pillow, which is obviously *muktzeh,* may not be moved even indirectly. The Mishnah therefore teaches that even money may be shaken off (*Tosafos* ד״ה לא שנו; see *Tos. HaRosh* and *Meromei Sadeh*).

5. One may not rinse off filth [such as spittle, excrement (*Rashi*) or bird droppings (*Aruch*)] from a cloth pillow on the Sabbath, because soaking cloth is tantamount to laundering it (*Rashi*) and laundering is a *toladah* of the *melachah* of לִיבּוּן, *whitening* (see 141a note 34).

One may wipe the filth off the pillow with a damp rag, but one must be careful to do so gently, so as not to wring out any water from the rag (*Orach Chaim* 302:9; see below, 143a).

6. The rule that soaking is tantamount to washing applies only to absorbent fabric, not to leather. Thus, one may rinse the leather pillow with water (see *Avnei Nezer* 157:2 and *Beur Halachah* to 302:9 ד״ה אין סחיטה בעור). Nevertheless, since a pillow is made of soft leather, one may not *scrub* it to remove the stain, for that would be a violation of the prohibition against laundering (*Rashi,* from *Zevachim* 94a,b).

7. If at *bein hashemashos* (the onset of the Sabbath) the stone was inadvertently allowed to remain upon the cask, the cask is not deemed a *base to muktzeh* (*Rashi*). That is to say, even if the stone was originally placed there intentionally, since its owner did not intend to leave it there for the Sabbath, it is deemed to have been *forgotten* there (see *Mishnah Berurah* 309:18 with *Shaar HaTziyun* §20).

However, if the stone was left on the cask with intent that it remain there for the Sabbath, the cask is rendered a *base to muktzeh* and is itself subject to the *muktzeh* restrictions. Thus, it may not even be tilted (see *Rashi;* see also *Tosafos* to 123a ד״ה האי פוגלא and *Meiri* here). [This pertains to a case where the stone was placed there for storage. If it was placed on the cask in the capacity of a lid, a different rule applies, as explained above, 125b note 8.]

Many commentators ask: Even if the stone was placed on the cask intentionally, the cask should not become a *base to muktzeh.* Since it contains wine, which is more valuable than the stone, it should be deemed a base to the non-*muktzeh* wine, rather than the *muktzeh* stone!? (see 142a note 7). The commonly cited answer is that whereas the lower walls of the cask which surround the wine support both the wine and the stone, the upper walls (above the wine level) and the mouth of the cask support only the stone, and it is they that become a *base to muktzeh* (*Beur Halachah* to 309:4 ד״ה ואם; cf. *Aruch HaShulchan* 309:10).

עין משפט
נר מצוה

יג א מיי' פכ"ה מהל' שבת הל' יז טוש"ע א"ח סי' שט סעיף ד:
יד ב מיי' פכ"ב שם הל' יח טוש"ע א"ח סי' שב סעיף ט:
טו ג מיי' פכ"ה שם הלכה יז טוש"ע א"ח סי' שט סעיף ד:
טז ד ה מיי' פ"ג מהל' י"ט הל' טו סמג לאוין עה טוש"ע א"ח סי' תקי סעיף ב:
יז ו מיי' פכ"ה מהל' שבת הלכה יז טוש"ע א"ח סי' שט סעיף ה:
יח ז מיי' פכ"ו שם הלכה כא סמג שם טוש"ע א"ח סי' שיא סעיף ה:

רבינו חננאל

ואקשינן אמאי והא קא מתקן טיבלא תמצא עושה מעשה בשבת ופרקי' ר' יהודה דאמר כי מעלין את המדומע כר' אליעזר סבירא ליה דאמר תרומה בעינא מחתא. פי' תרומה שנפלה בחולין אין מחשבין אותה שנתערבה בכל החולין אלא כאילו נתונה במקום אחד היא וכשנוטל ממאה ואחד סאין סאה אנן אומרין כי היא היא התרומה. אבל שאר החולין מתוקנין היו מקודם. ולא היה אסור אלא זו הסאה שנוטלה במקום התרומה שנפלה בלבד. דתנן סאה של תרומה שנפלה לפחות ממאה ונדמעו ונפל מן המדומע למקום אחד. ר' אליעזר אומר מדומע כתרומה ודאי. פי' סאה תרומה שנפלה לתוך חמשים סאין חולין ועוד נפלה מאלו החמשים ואחד סאין סאה אחת לששים סאה חולין ר' אליעזר סבר הכל אסור חמשים הראשונים וששים האחרונים שאני אומר הסאה של תרומה עצמה היא שנפלה בששים האחרונים לפי שאין המדומע עולה אלא בא' ומאה ואין באחד מהן פחות מסאה שנפלה בהן וחכ"א אין המדומע מדמע אלא לפי חשבון פי' סאה שנפלה לתוך סאין ונפלה מאלו החמשים סאין לפחות מחמשים מדמעת אבל אם נפלה סאה לששים סאין עולה לפי שאילו היתה סאה במאה סאין ואחת היתה עולה וחוזרו עוד להקשות אימור דשמעת ליה לר' אליעזר שמחשב מכלל נ"א סאין הללו הסאה האחת שנפלה לס' סאין אחרות תרומה כולה. ומדמעת עד מאה לחומרא לקולא לתקן בשבת מי שמעת ליה ולא עמד ופירקינן הכי אמר והוא ר' יהודה סבר לה כר' שמעון בן אלעזר דתנן סאה של תרומה שנפלה למאה חולין ונדמעו ולא הספיק להגביהה עד שנפלה האחרת הרי זו אסורה ור' שמעון מתיר מ"ט ר"ש סבר כיון שלא הגביה נמצא שנפלו ב' סאין למאה סאין ואין עולין כי פחות ממאה הן. ור' שמעון סבר תרומה הנעה בתוכן סאה תרומה למאה חולין הותרו המאה. ונשארו חולין בהכשרן. וסאה אחת בתוכן תרומה התרומה היא אסורה בלבד וכשנפלה סאה אחרת תרומה עוד סאה אחרת תרומה

שאוכל מרובה על הפסולת. פי' בקונטרס משום דהשתא הוי טרחא יתירא למישקליה לאוכל ואינו נראה לר"י דאי משום טרחא הוי מאי קאמרי בסמוך הכא נמי כיון דאי בעי למישקל לא מישתקיל ליה עד דשקיל ליה לאבן כפסולת מרובה על האוכל דמי היכי הוי משום האי טעמא כפסולת מרובה על האוכל ולכך הוצרך רש"י לפרש דל"ג עד דשקיל ליה לאבן על כן נראה לר"ת דטעמא משום דכי אוכל מרובה על הפסולת הוה פסולת כבטל לגבי רובו ומותר ליטלו מן האוכל ולזורקו אבל פסולת מרובה על האוכל לא בטיל ליה פסולת [ס] לגבי אוכל והשתא אתי שפיר גירסת הספרים דגבי חבית נמי כיון דאי בעי למישקל לא משתקיל ליה (ה) עד דשקיל ליה לאבן כפסולת מרובה על האוכל דמי דכיון שאין יכול כלל ליטול מן היין בלא נטילת האבן לא חשיב כבטיל לגבי האוכל כיון שהאוכל אינו ניכר כלל ואינו יכול ליטול הימנו כשהאבן על פי החבית. מ"ר. והא דמוקי לה בספ"ק דבילה (ד' יד: ושם) כגון דנפיש בטרחא וזוטר בשיעורא [ל] אאוכל קאי ולא אפסולת ולפירש"י קאי אפסולת ולא אאוכל [וע"כ לא יברור הפסולת דנפיש בטירחא]:

לא שנו אלא בשכח. וא"ת תרתי דרב למה לי וי"ל חדא מכלל חבירתה איתמר והא לא תקשה תרתי מתני' למה לי דהוה אמינא אבן ודאי שרי בשכח שנראה טפי ככיסוי החבית אבל מעות שעל גבי הכר אפילו בשכח ה"א דאסיר:

התם

והא מיפליג פליג עילויה דתניא [א] רבי יהודה אומר מעלין את המדומע באחד ומאה רבי שמעון בן אלעזר אומר נותן עיניו בצד זה ואוכל מצד אחר דרבי יהודה עדיפא מדר"ש בן אלעזר: **מתני'** [ג] האבן שע"פ החבית מטה על צדה והיא נופלת היתה בין החביות מגביה ומטה על צדה והיא נופלת מעות שעל הכר מנער את הכר והן נופלות [ב] היתה עליו [ד] לשלשת מקנחה בסמרטוט היתה של עור נותנין עליה מים עד שתכלה: **גמ'** אמר רב הונא אמר רב [ה] לא שנו אלא בשוכח אבל במניח נעשה בסיס לדבר האסור: [היתה בין החביות כו']: [ו] מאן תנא דכל היכא דאיכא איסורא והיתרא בהיתרא טרחינן באיסורא לא טרחינן אמר רבה בר בר חנה אמר רבי יוחנן רשב"ג היא דתנן [ז] הבורר קטנית ביו"ט ב"ש אומרים בורר אוכל ואוכל וב"ה אומרים [ד] בורר כדרכו בחיקו ובתמחוי [ח] ותניא אמר רשב"ג [ה] במה דברים אמורים שהאוכל מרובה על הפסולת אבל פסולת מרובה על האוכל דברי הכל בורר אוכל והא הכא דכי אוכל מרובה על הפסולת דמי הכא נמי כיון דאי בעי למישקל לא משתקיל ליה יין עד דשקיל לה (א) לאבן כפסולת מרובה על האוכל דמי: היתה בין החביות מגביה: תניא רבי יוסי אומר היתה החבית מונחת באוצר או שהיו כלי זכוכית מונחין תחתיה מגביה למקום אחר ומטה על צדה והיא נופלת ונוטל הימנה מה שצריך לו ומחזירה למקומה: מעות שעל הכר: אמר רב חייא בר אשי אמר רב לא שנו אלא בשוכח אבל במניח נעשה בסיס לדבר האסור אמר רבה בר בר חנה אמר ר' יוחנן [ט] לא שנו אלא לצורך גופו אבל לצורך מקומו מטלטלו ועודן עליו וכן תני חייא בר רב מדיפתי לא שנו אלא לצורך גופו אבל לצורך מקומו מטלטלו ועודן עליו: מעות שעל הכר מנער וכו': א"ר אושעיא שכח ארנקי בחצר מניח עליה ככר או תינוק ומטלטלה אמר רב יצחק שכח לבינה בחצר מניח עליה ככר או תינוק ומטלטלה אמר רבי יהודה בר שילא אמר ר' אסי פעם אחת שכחו דסקיא מלאה מעות בסרטיא ובאו ושאלו את ר' יוחנן ואמר להן הניחו עליה ככר או תינוק וטלטלוה אמר מר זוטרא הלכתא ככל הני שמעתתא בשוכח רב אשי אמר אפילו שכח נמי [לא] [י] ולא אמרו [כ] ככר או תינוק אלא למת בלבד אביי מנח כפא אכיפי רבא מנח סכינא אבר יונה ומטלטלה אמר רב יוסף כמה חריפא שמעתתא דרדקי אימר דאמור רבנן בשוכח לכתחילה מי אמור אמר אביי אי לאו [ל] דאדם חשוב אנא כפא אכיפי למה לי הא חזו למיזגא עליהו אמר רבא אנא אי לאו דאדם חשוב אנא סכינא אבר יונה למה לי הא חזי לי לאומצא טעמא דחזי לאומצא הא לא חזי לאומצא לא [מ] למימרא דרבא כרבי יהודה סבירא ליה והאמר רבא לשמעיה טווי לי בר אווזא ושדי מיעיה לשונרא

התם

והא מיפליג פליג עילויה. ואמר כיון דאפשר ליה למיעבד עונג שבת בכה"ג ליתן עיניו בצד זה ולאכול בצד אחר אין מעלין: דרבי יהודה עדיפא. מיקל טפי פורתא ואמר כיון דיכול ליתן (עליו) עיניו בצד זה ולאכול בצד זה לא הוי מתקן בהעלאתו ומעלין: **מתני'** מטה על צדה. מטה חבית על צדה אם צריך ליטול מן היין והאבן נופלת ולא יטלנה בידים: היתה בין החביות. וירא שלא תפול האבן על החביות וישברם: מגביה. לחבית כולה ומסלקה מבין החביות ושם מטה על צדה: לשלשת. שום דבר מיאוס כגון רוק או צואה: מקנחה בסמרטוט. ולא יתן עליה מים דהשתא כר של בגד הוא ובגד שרייתו במים הוא כבוסו: היתה. לשלשת זו על כר של עור דלאו בר כיבוס הוא: נותן עליה מים עד שתכלה. ומיהו כיבוס ממש לא (ב) והואיל וסתם כרים וכסתות רכים נינהו שייך למימר בהו כיבוס בעורות רכין ומיהו שרייתן לא זהו כבוסן וכן מפורש בזבחים בפרק דם חטאת: **גמ'** לא שנו. מטה על צדה דחבית: אלא בשכח. ששכח האבן עליה בין השמשות ולא מדעת: נעשה חבית בסיס לדבר האסור. ואסור להטותה שאף החבית מוקצה: מאן תנא. דמתניתין דקתני מגביה ומטה על צדה דאית ליה דכי טרח מטרח בחבית דהוי היתרא ולא יטול האבן ממש דהוי איסורא ואע"ג דהשתא נמי אבן מטלטל בהדי חבית: רבן שמעון. אליבא דבית הלל: בורר אוכל ואוכל. המאכל יטול והפסולת ישאר בכלי: בורר כדרכו. נוטל פסולת ומניח אוכל אם ירצה: כשהאוכל מרובה על הפסולת. דלאי שקיל אוכל מפיש בטרחא: דברי הכל בורר אוכל. דבהיתירא טרח ולא באיסורא ופרכינן והא הכא דמתניתין דאוכל מרובה על הפסולת וכי מגביה האבן עם החבית טרח טפי והוה (ג) למשקל פסולת כר"ש: כיון דאי בעי למשקל. לכולי יין מן החבית לא משתקיל ליה יין שבשוליה עד דשקיל ומגבה לה לחבית כפסולת מרובה דמי דאי בתחלתו לא מגבה לה לחבית סוף סוף מיבעי ליה לאגבוהה תו לחבית הלכך הוה ליה מפיש בטרחא: ה"ג לא משתקיל ליה (ד) עד דשקיל לה ול"ג עד דשקיל לה לאבן: היתה החבית מונחת באוצר. כלומר במקום מכונס שאוצרין שם חביות הרבה ודואג שמא יטלה ותפול האבן על החבית שאלה: לא שנו. למנער: נעשה. הכר בסיס למעות ואף הכר אסור בטלטול: לא שנו. דמנערה ואינו מטלטלה בעודן עליה: אלא שצריך לגופו. של כר לשכב

עליו הלכך בניעור סגיא ושדי ליה באתרייהו: אבל צריך למקומו. של כר מטלטלו עם המעות למקום אחר: דסקיא מלאה מעות גרסינן: בסרטיא. רה"ר: הניחו עליה ככר או תינוק. דליפשרי לטלטלה אגבייהו תוך ד' אמות וטלטלה פחות פחות מד' אמות או במחילה של בני אדם כדאמרי' בעירובין (דף מג:): בשוכח. אבל במניח מדעת מערב (יום) שבת לא התירו לו לטלטלה ע"י ככר או תינוק: אלא למת. משום כבוד הבריות כשמוטל בחמה: אביי מנח כפא אכיפי. מניח תרווד על העומרים לטלטלן אגב תרווד: אבר יונה. מי [בלא] מלים: חריפא שמעתתא דרדקי. תנוקות הם שהם מרפים: אימר דאמור רבנן. בארנקי ודסקיא מניח עליה ככר או תינוק בשכחה ובמקום התורפה ומשום הפסד ממון: אמר אביי. אנא שפיר מטלטלנא כיפי ואפילו בלא תרווד: דאדם חשוב אנא. ואנא מחמיר על עצמי שלא ילמדו ממני להקל באסורין: כפא אכיפי למה לי. בלאו כפא נמי שרי לטלטלינהו דהא חזו למיזגא עלייהו: לאומצא. לאכלו חי בשבת שיש בני אדם שדעתן יפה ואוכלים בשר חי וקרו לה אומצא: הא לא חזי לאומצא לא. ואע"ג דחזו לשונרא דלמאכל מוכן לאדם לא הוי מוכן לכלבים: כר' יהודה. במסכת ביצה (דף ו:): טווי לי בר אווזא. ביום טוב: ושדי מיעיה לשונרא. אלמא מטלטל להו משום שונרא ואע"ג דהאידנא לא חזי לאדם דלאו אורח ארעא למיכלינהו ביום טוב ומיהו מאתמול לאדם הוו קיימי:

התם

מסורת הש"ס

א) [תוספתא פרק טו], ב) [לעיל קכה:], ג) זבחים צד., ד) [פי' צואת תרנגולים. ערוך], ה) [לעיל קכה: ע"ש], ו) ביצה יד:, ז) ג"ז שם ע"ש, ח) [לעיל ל: מג:], ט) [לעיל נא. וש"נ], י) ביצה לג., כ) צ"ל לגבי אוכל והאוכל לא בטל לגבי פסולת משום דחשיב וע"כ בורר את האוכל והשתא כו', ל) צ"ל אאוכל קאי שהאוכל נפיש בטרחא ואפ"ה בורר אוכל הואיל חוטר בשיעורא ולא בטל ליה פסולת.

הגהות הב"ח

(א) גמ' דשקיל לה כפסולת כצ"ל ותיבת לאבן נמחק: (ב) רש"י ד"ה נותן וכו' כיבוס ממש לא להואיל: (ג) ד"ה דברי הכל וכו' והוה ליה למשקל: (ד) ד"ה ה"ג לא משתקיל ליה יין עד: (ה) תוס' ד"ה שאוכל וכו' לא משתקיל ליה יין עד:

גליון הש"ס

גמ' מאן תנא דכל היכא דאיכא איסורא והיתרא. עיין לעיל דף נא ע"ב תוס' ד"ה אינו נוטל:

רב נסים גאון

מוציאין חלק אחד והשאר מותר לישראל ותמצא עיקר דבר זה בסיפרי מכל חלבו את מקדשו ממנו שאם נפל לתוכו הרי זה מקדשו מיכן אמרו תרומה עולה באחד ומאה אין לי אלא תרומה טהורה ותמצא במשנת תרומות ותוספות תרומות מזה הענין הרבה ועיקרו מה שהזכרנו' ובגמ' דערלה בפרק ב' (ירושלמי שם הלכה א) מניין שהן עולין אמר ר' יונה כתיב (במדבר יח) מכל חלבו את מקדשו ממנו דבר שאתה מרים ממנו שאם יפול לתוכו הרי זה מקדשו וכמה הוא אחד ממאה ואיתא נמי בפרק ד' דתרומות התרומה צריך להרים כמה שהוא במשנה במסכת ערלה בראש פרק ב' התרומה ותרומת מעשר של דמאי מצטרפין זה עם זה ואינו צריך להרים וכו' וטעמו של דבר לפי שהתרומות והחלה והביכורים הם נכסי כהן וצריך להרים תרומה ויתנה ואם לא ירים ויתן לו הרי זה גוזל ממנו ואין להם בעלים שראויין להם לפיכך אינו צריך להרים

ליקוטי רש"י

האבן שע"פ החבית. והולך ליטול מן היין [לעיל קכה:]. היתה עליו לשלשת. היתה על הכר של בגד גיעול של רוק או של צואה מקנחה בסמרטוט ולא יתן עליה מים דהוי כיבוס ואינו נותן עליה מים לכלותה [ו]לסטפה מפני שהוא מכבס [זבחים צד.]

מלבן ולא היתה לשלשת זו על כר של עור נותן עליה מים עד שתכלה כשטיפת מים ומיהו משפשפו בידים לא [זבחים צד.]. בשוכח. האבן לא נעשה בסיס לא נעשית החבית בסיס לאבן אבל במניח נעשה. החבית בסיס לאבן [לעיל קכה:]. תמחוי. קערה גדולה [ביצה יב:]. במה דברים אמורים. דשרו בית הלל ליטול פסולת ממש ולהשליך. כשהאוכל מרובה על הפסולת הוא דקא אמרי בית הלל נוטל פסולת דמעוטי עדיף אבל אם היתה הפסולת מרובה על האוכל דברי הכל בורר אוכל ומניח את הפסולת [שם יד:]. אלא לצורך גופו. שצריך לכר לישב עליו או לשכב עליו לא יטלטלנו עם המעות אלא מנערו כמקומו ואח"כ יטלנו [לעיל נא.]. דסקיא. שק של עור לפיכך לא יטלטלו בידים [לעיל מד:]. סרטיא. מהלך גדול של עיר [ברכות יח.]. מרבלה. דרך רחבה [כתובות צג.]. שקורין טשכ"ה. אלא למת. מת המוטל בחמה ויש לחוש שמא יסריח [שם מג:]. דאדם חשוב אנא. שמסתכלין בי להקל וכל חשוב יותר מעט. ושדי מיעיה לשונרא. הלכך בני מעים של אווז אסור לטלטלו ולתתו לחתול דלמאכל מוכן לאדם היה ולא לכלבים דקאמר אם לא היתה נבילה מערב שבת אסורה [ביצה לג.].

עליהן על מאה חולין נפלה ר' יהודה אומר נותן עיניו בצד זה ואוכל מצד אחר ש"מ כי התרומה מחתא במקום אחד. ואקשינן וכי ר' יהודה כר' שמעון בן אלעזר סבירא ליה והא מפלג פליג עליה דתניא ר' יהודה אומר מעלין את המדומע באחד ומאה ר' שמעון אומר נותן עיניו בצד זה ואוכל מצד זה ומפרקי' דר' יהודה עדיפא שר' יהודה מתיר אפי' להעלותה ור' שמעון אינו מתיר להעלותה אלא לתת עיניו בצד זה ולאכול מצד זה. והתרומה שנפלה לתוך מאה חולין תקנתן הן ואין צריכין תיקון אחר אלא סילוק סאה אחת מהן בלבד במקום התרומה: פיסקא האבן שעל

one?[8] אָמַר רַבָּה בַּר בַּר חָנָה אָמַר רַבִּי יוֹחָנָן – **Rabbah bar bar Chanah said in the name of R' Yochanan:** רַבָּן שִׁמְעוֹן בֶּן גַּמְלִיאֵל הִיא – **[The Mishnah] is** reflective of the opinion of **Rabban Shimon ben Gamliel.** דִּתְנַן – **For we learned in a Mishnah:**[9] הַבּוֹרֵר קִטְנִית בְּיוֹם טוֹב – ONE WHO wishes to SEPARATE LEGUMES from a mixture containing impurities ON YOM TOV[10] – בֵּית שַׁמַּאי אוֹמְרִים – BEIS SHAMMAI SAY: בּוֹרֵר אוֹכֵל וְאוֹכֵל – HE MUST SELECT THE FOOD from the impurities AND EAT it.[11] וּבֵית הִלֵּל אוֹמְרִים – BUT BEIS HILLEL SAY: בּוֹרֵר כְּדַרְכּוֹ – If he wishes, HE MAY SELECT IN THE USUAL MANNER, by taking the impurities from the food, בְּחֵיקוֹ וּבְתַמְחוּי – IN HIS LAP OR WITH A LARGE PLATE.[12] וְתַנְיָא – **And it was taught in a Baraisa:** אָמַר רַבָּן שִׁמְעוֹן בֶּן גַּמְלִיאֵל – RABBAN SHIMON BEN GAMLIEL SAID: בַּמֶּה דְּבָרִים אֲמוּרִים – IN WHAT case WERE THESE WORDS SAID, i.e. when do Beis Hillel say that the impurities may be removed from the food? שֶׁהָאוֹכֶל מְרוּבֶּה עַל הַפְּסוֹלֶת – Only WHEN THE FOOD IS MORE THAN THE IMPURITIES, such that taking the *muktzeh* impurities from the food is the method that involves the least effort. אֲבָל פְּסוֹלֶת מְרוּבָּה עַל הָאוֹכֶל – BUT if THE IMPURITIES ARE MORE THAN THE FOOD, דִּבְרֵי הַכֹּל בּוֹרֵר אוֹכֶל – ALL AGREE THAT HE must SELECT THE FOOD and leave the impurities.[13] It is thus Rabban Shimon ben Gamliel who holds that where there is a choice between handling either a *muktzeh* object or a permitted object, one should handle the permitted object.

The Gemara asks:

וְהָא הָכָא דְּכִי אוֹכֶל מְרוּבֶּה עַל הַפְּסוֹלֶת דָּמֵי – **But here,** in our Mishnah, **[the case] is analogous to** one in which **the food is more than the impurities,** since more effort is expended in moving the permitted cask than in moving the stone alone. In such a case, even Rabban Shimon ben Gamliel concedes that one may handle the *muktzeh* object so as to minimize the effort. Why, then, does our Mishnah require lifting the cask?

The Gemara answers:

הָכָא נַמִּי – **Here, as well,** כֵּיוָן דְּאִי בָּעֵי לְמִישְׁקַל – **since if one wishes to take out** all the wine from the cask, לֹא מִשְׁתַּקִּיל לֵיהּ יַיִן עַד דְּשָׁקִיל לָהּ (לאבן) – **the wine** at its bottom **will not come out unless he lifts [the cask]**[14] from the ground and turns it over, כִּפְסוֹלֶת מְרוּבָּה עַל הָאוֹכֶל דָּמֵי – **[the case] is analogous to** one in which **the impurities are more than the food.** For since at some point the entire cask will have to be lifted from the ground, more effort is expended in removing the stone by itself, and later lifting the cask to empty it, than in lifting the cask, moving it to an area where the stone can be shaken off and immediately pouring out the wine.[15]

The Mishnah continued:

הָיְתָה בֵּין הֶחָבִיּוֹת מַגְבִּיהָהּ – IF IT WAS AMONG other CASKS, ONE MAY LIFT [THE CASK] as is, remove it to a safe area and there tilt it on its side so that the stone falls off.

The Gemara cites a Baraisa that elaborates on this ruling:

תַּנְיָא – **It was taught in a Baraisa:** רַבִּי יוֹסֵי אוֹמֵר – R' YOSE SAYS: הָיְתָה הֶחָבִית מוּנַּחַת בָּאוֹצָר – IF THE CASK WAS RESTING IN A STOREROOM with other casks, אוֹ שֶׁהָיוּ כְּלֵי זְכוּכִית מוּנָּחִין תַּחְתֶּיהָ – OR THERE WERE GLASS VESSELS RESTING NEARBY,[16] and the other casks or the glass vessels might break if the stone were to fall against them, מַגְבִּיהָהּ לְמָקוֹם אַחֵר וּמַטֶּה עַל צִדָּהּ וְהִיא נוֹפֶלֶת – ONE MAY LIFT and carry [THE CASK] TO ANOTHER AREA AND TILT IT ON ITS SIDE SO THAT [THE STONE] FALLS off there, וְנוֹטֵל הֵימֶנָּה מַה שֶּׁצָּרִיךְ לוֹ – TAKE FROM IT WHATEVER amount of wine HE NEEDS, וּמַחֲזִירָהּ לִמְקוֹמָהּ – AND RETURN [THE CASK] TO ITS PLACE.

NOTES

8. The Tanna of our Mishnah rules that one must not lift the stone with his hands and carry it away, but must carry it by means of the cask. Thus, although the stone is being moved in any case, the Tanna considers it preferable to handle only the non-*muktzeh* directly. Whose opinion does he follow? (*Rashi*).

9. *Beitzah* 14b.

10. The impurities that are commonly mixed with legumes, such as earth and straw, are *muktzeh,* since they are not fit for consumption even by animals (see *Rashba, Ritva MHK* ed. and *Rashi* to *Beitzah* 14b ד״ה מי איכי מאן דשרי). Thus, there are two issues to be dealt with here – firstly, the prohibition of בּוֹרֵר, i.e. *selecting* desired substances from undesired substances or vice versa; and secondly, that of handling *muktzeh.*

11. But he may not select the impurities from the food because, according to Beis Shammai, בּוֹרֵר, *selecting,* is prohibited on Yom Tov, as it is on the Sabbath. Even on the Sabbath, however, selecting is permitted when three conditions are met: (a) One takes the desired substance from the undesired substance, (b) by hand, and (c) immediately before the desired substance is to be used (see above, 74a). Accordingly, Beis Shammai rule that on Yom Tov one must take the desired substance from the mixture, just as he must do on the Sabbath (*Rosh Yosef* to *Beitzah* 14b). [Similarly, according to Beis Shammai, on Yom Tov one must select by hand, immediately before the desired substance is to be used.]

12. He may spread a sheet on his lap to create a wide surface on which he spreads the mixture, and tilt the sheet in a manner such that the legumes, which are round (e.g. peas), roll away from the impurities. Or, he spreads the mixture over a wide plate, and then gently shakes the plate, at a slight angle, so that the legumes roll to its lower end (see *Bach, Orach Chaim* 319 ד״ה ומש״כ בורר בידו; cf. *Beis Yosef* ad loc.).

According to Beis Hillel, selecting is permitted on Yom Tov because it is a labor that may be performed in the preparation of food [אֹכֶל נֶפֶשׁ]. Thus, a person may even select the impurities from the food, and may use the utensils mentioned here (*Ritva MHK* ed.; see *Maggid Mishneh* to *Hil. Yom Tov* 3:15 ד״ה וכן, *Mishnah Berurah* 510:7 and *Beur Halachah* ad loc. ד״ה אם רוצה). [However, even Beis Hillel forbid selecting with a sieve or any other utensil that is normally used to separate large quantities (see *Beitzah* 14b and *Rashi* to *Beitzah* 12b ד״ה אבל).]

In addition to their lenient view concerning selecting on Yom Tov, Beis Hillel maintain that the law of *muktzeh* does not restrict a person from even handling the impurities in order to remove them from the mixture. Their reasoning is that discarding a *muktzeh* object that impedes one's enjoyment of a food item is regarded as an act of rectifying the food, rather than an act of "taking" the *muktzeh* (see *Ramban, Rashba, Ritva MHK* ed. and *Chazon Ish* 47:15; cf. *Re'ah,* cited by *Chidushei HaRan*).

According to the Mishnah's report of Beis Hillel's view, Beis Hillel allow removing the impurities from the mixture even where the impurities are of a greater quantity than the food. They express no preference for handling the non-*muktzeh.* The Gemara will now cite a variant report (*Ritva MHK* ed.).

13. According to Rabban Shimon ben Gamliel, Beis Hillel allow handling the *muktzeh* impurities only when this serves to reduce the effort involved in the selection. When no benefit will be realized by the handling of *muktzeh,* we revert back to the general preference against handling *muktzeh,* and one must take the permitted object (*Rashi;* cf. *Mishnah Berurah* 510:8).

Our Mishnah's case is analogous to the one just discussed, for in our case the *muktzeh* stone impedes one's access to the wine in the cask. Thus, according to the first report of Beis Hillel's view, one should be allowed to handle the stone directly in order to discard it. According to Rabban Shimon ben Gamliel's report, however, one must remove it by handling the non-*muktzeh* cask rather than the *muktzeh* stone (*Ramban, Rashba, Ritva MHK* ed.; cf. *Tosafos* ד״ה שאוכל).

14. Our explanation follows *Rashi,* who remarks that accordingly the word לאבן must be deleted from the text. Cf. *Tosafos* ד״ה שאוכל, who favor a different explanation, which preserves the reading עַד דְּשָׁקִיל לָהּ לְאֶבֶן.

15. *Rashi.* [In notes 12 and 13, we followed *Ramban's* explanation of the views of Beis Hillel and Rabban Shimon ben Gamliel because *Ramban's* explanation and reading here parallel *Rashi's. Rashi's* own explanation of Beis Hillel and Rabban Shimon ben Gamliel is very brief. See *R' Akiva Eiger,* who discusses a difficulty inherent in *Rashi's* words and concludes that they require intense analysis.]

16. Literally: underneath it.

עין משפט נר מצוה

יג א מיי' פכ"ה מהל' שבת הל' יז טוש"ע א"ח סי' שט סעיף ד:

יד ב מיי' פכ"ב שם הל' יח טוש"ע א"ח סי' שיט סעיף ט:

טו ג מיי' פכ"ה שם הלכה יז טוש"ע א"ח סי' שט סעיף ד:

טז ד ה מיי' פ"ג מהל' י"ט הל' טו סמג לאוין עה טוש"ע א"ח סי' תקי סעיף ב:

יז ו מיי' פכ"ה מהל' שבת הלכה יז טוש"ע א"ח סי' שט סעיף ה:

יח ז מיי' פכ"ה שם הלכה כא סמג שם טוש"ע א"ח סי' שיא סעיף ה:

שאוכל מרובה על הפסולת. פי' בקונטרס משום דהשתא הוי טרחא יתירא למישקליה לאוכל ואינו נראה לר"י דאי משום טרחא הוי מאי קאמרי בסמוך הכא נמי כיון דאי בעי למישקל לא מישתקיל ליה עד דשקיל ליה לאבן כפסולת מרובה על האוכל דמי היכי הוי משום האי טעמא כפסולת מרובה על האוכל ולכך הוצרך רש"י לפרש דל"ג עד דשקיל ליה לאבן על כן נראה לר"ת דטעמא משום דכי אוכל מרובה על הפסולת הוה פסולת כבטל לגבי רובו ומותר ליטלו מן האוכל ולזורקו אבל פסולת מרובה על האוכל לא בטיל ליה פסולת[כ] לגבי אוכל והשתא אתי שפיר גירסת הספרים דגבי חבית נמי כיון דאי בעי למישקל לא משתקיל ליה (ה) עד דשקיל ליה לאבן כפסולת מרובה על האוכל דמי דכיון שאין יכול כלל ליטול מן היין בלא נטילת האבן לא חשיב כבטיל לגבי האוכל כיון שהאוכל אינו ניכר כלל ואינו יכול ליטול הימנו כשהאבן על פי החבית. מ"ר. והא דמוקי לה בפ"ק דביצה (ד' יד: ושם) כגון דנפיש בטרחא חוטר בשיעורא[ל] דאוכל קאי ולא אפסולת ולפירש"י קאי אפסולת ולא אאוכל [וע"כ לא יברור הפסולת דנפיש בטירחא]:

לא שנו אלא בשכח. וא"ת תרתי דרב למה לי וי"ל חדא מכלל חבירתה איתמר והא לא תקשה תרתי מתני' למה לי דהוה אמינא אבן ודאי שרי בשכח שנראה טפי ככיסוי החבית אבל מעות שעל גבי הכר אפילו בשכח ה"א דאסיר:

והא מיפליג פליג עילויה דתניא [א] רבי יהודה אומר מעלין את המדומע באחד ומאה רבי שמעון בן אלעזר אומר נותן עיניו בצד זה ואוכל מצד אחר דרבי יהודה עדיפא מדר"ש בן אלעזר: **מתני'** [ב] האבן שע"פ החבית מטה על צדה והיא נופלת היתה בין החביות מגביה ומטה על צדה והיא נופלת מעות שעל הכר מנער את הכר והן נופלות [ג] היתה עליו [ד] לשלשת מקנחה בסמרטוט היתה של עור נותנין עליה מים עד שתכלה: **גמ'** אמר רב הונא אמר רב [ה] לא שנו אלא בשוכח אבל במניח נעשה בסיס לדבר האסור: [היתה בין החביות כו']: מאן תנא דכל היכא דאיכא איסורא והיתרא בהיתרא טרחינן באיסורא לא טרחינן אמר רבה בר בר חנה אמר רבי יוחנן רשב"ג היא דתנן [ו] הבורר קטנית ביו"ט ב"ש אומרים בורר אוכל ואוכל וב"ה אומרים [ז] בורר כדרכו בחיקו ובתמחוי ותניא אמר רשב"ג במה דברים אמורים שהאוכל מרובה על הפסולת אבל פסולת מרובה על האוכל דברי הכל בורר אוכל והא הכא דכי אוכל מרובה על הפסולת דמי הכא נמי כיון דאי בעי למישקל לא משתקיל ליה יין עד דשקיל לה (א) לאבן כפסולת מרובה על האוכל דמי: היתה בין החביות מגביה: תניא רבי יוסי אומר היתה החבית מונחת באוצר או שהיו כלי זכוכית מונחין תחתיה מגביה למקום אחר ומטה על צדה והיא נופלת ונוטל הימנה מה שצריך לו ומחזירה למקומה: מעות שעל הכר: אמר רב חייא בר אשי אמר רב לא שנו אלא בשוכח אבל במניח נעשה בסיס לדבר האסור אמר רבה בר בר חנה אמר ר' יוחנן [ח] לא שנו אלא לצורך גופו אבל לצורך מקומו מטלטלו ועודן עליו וכן תני חייא בר רב מדיפתי לא שנו אלא לצורך גופו אבל לצורך מקומו מטלטלו ועודן עליו: מעות שעל הכר מנער וכו': א"ר אושעיא שכח ארנקי בחצר מניח עליה ככר או תינוק ומטלטלה אמר רב יצחק שכח לבינה בחצר מניח עליה ככר או תינוק ומטלטלה אמר רבי יהודה בר שילא אמר ר' אסי פעם אחת שכחו דסקיא מלאה מעות בסרטיא ובאו ושאלו את ר' יוחנן ואמר להן הניחו עליה ככר או תינוק וטלטלוה אמר מר זוטרא הלכתא ככל הני שמעתתא בשוכח רב אשי אמר אפילו שכח נמי [לא] [ט] ולא אמרו ככר או תינוק אלא למת בלבד אביי מנח כפא אכיפי רבא מנח סכינא אבר יונה ומטלטלה אמר רב יוסף כמה חריפא שמעתתא דדרדקי אימר דאמור רבנן בשוכח לכתחילה מי אמור אמר אביי אי לאו [י] דאדם חשוב אנא כפא אכיפי למה לי הא חזו למיזגא עלייהו אמר רבא אנא אי לאו דאדם חשוב אנא סכינא אבר יונה למה לי הא חזי לי לאומצא טעמא דחזי לאומצא הא לא חזי לאומצא לא [י] למימרא דרבא כרבי יהודה סבירא ליה והאמר רבא לשמעיה טווי לי בר אווזא ושדי מיעיה לשונרא התם

והא מיפליג פליג עילויה. ואמר כיון דאפשר ליה למיעבד עונג שבת בכה"ג ליתן עיניו בצד זה ולאכול בצד אחר אין מעלין: דרבי יהודה עדיפא. מיקל טפי פורתא ואמר כיון דיכול ליתן (עליו) עיניו בצד זה ולאכול בצד זה לא הוי מתקן בהעלאתו ומעלין: **מתני'** מטה על צדה. מטה חבית על צדה אם צריך ליטול מן היין והאבן נופלת ולא יטלנה בידים: היתה בין החביות. וירא שלא תפול האבן על החביות וישברם: מגביה. לחבית כולה ומסלקה מבין החביות ושם מטה על צדה: לשלשת. שום דבר מיאוס כגון רוק או צואה: מקנחה בסמרטוט. ולא יתן עליה מים דסתם כר של בגד הוא ונגד שרייתו במים הוא כבוסו: היתה. לשלשת זו על כר של עור דלאו בר כיבוס הוא: נותן עליה מים עד שתכלה. ומיהו כיבוס ממש לא (ב) והואיל ואסור כרים וכסתות רכים נינהו שייך למימר בהו כיבוס בעורות רכין ומיהו שרייתן לא זהו כבוסן וכן מפורש בזבחים בפרק דם חטאת: **גמ'** לא שנו. מטה על צדה לחבית: אלא בשכח. ששכח האבן עליה בין השמשות ולא מדעת: נעשה חבית בסיס לדבר האסור. ואסור לטלטלה שאף החבית מוקצה: מאן תנא. דמתניתין דקתני מגביה ומטה על צדה דאית ליה דכי טרח מטרח בחבית דהוי היתרא ולא יטול האבן ממש דהוי איסורא ואע"ג דהשתא נמי אבן מטלטל בהדי חבית: רבן שמעון. אליבא דבית הלל: בורר אוכל ואוכל. המאכל יטול והפסולת ישאר בכלי: בורר כדרכו. נוטל פסולת ומניח אוכל אם ירצה: כשהאוכל מרובה על הפסולת. דאי שקיל אוכל מפיש בטרחא: דברי הכל בורר אוכל. דבהיתרא טרח ולא באיסורא ופרכינן והא הכא דמתניתין דאוכל מרובה על הפסולת וכי מגביה האבן עם החבית טרח טפי והוה (ג) למשקל פסולת כר"ש: כיון דאי בעי למשקל. לכולי יין מן החבית לא משתקיל ליה יין שבשוליה עד דשקיל ומגבה לה לחבית כפסולת מרובה דמי דאי בתחלתו לא מגבה לה לחבית סוף סוף מיבעי ליה לאגבוהה או לחבית הלכך הוה ליה מפיש בטרחא: ה"ג לא משתקל ליה (ד) עד דשקיל לה ול"ג עד דשקיל לה לאבן: היתה החבית מונחת באוצר. כלומר במקום מכונס שאוצרין שם חביות הרבה ודואג שמא יטלה ותפול האבן על החבית שאצלה: לא שנו. דמנער: נעשה. הכר בסיס למעות ואף הכר אסור בטלטול: לא שנו. דמנערה ואינו מטלטלה בעודן עליה: אלא שצריך לגופו. של כר לשכב עליו הלכך בניעור סגיא ושדי ליה באתרייהו: אבל צריך למקומו. של כר מטלטלו עם המעות למקום אחר: דסקיא מלאה מעות גרסינן: בסרטיא. רה"ר: הניחו עליה ככר או תינוק. לישתרי לטלטלה אגבייהו תוך ד' אמות וטלטלוה פחות פחות מד' אמות או במחילה של בני אדם כדאמרי' בעירובין (דף מג:): בשוכח. אבל במניח מדעת מערב (יום) שבת לא התירו לו לטלטלה ע"י ככר או תינוק: אלא למת. משום כבוד הבריות כשמוטל בחמה: אביי מנח כפא אכיפי. מניח תרווד על העומרים לטלטלן אגב תרווד: אבר יונה. חי [בלא] מליח: חריפא שמעתתא דדרדקי. סבורים הם שהם חריפים: אימר דאמור רבנן. בארנקי ודסקיא מניח עליה ככר או תינוק בשכחה ובמקום התורפה ומשום הפסד ממון: אמר אביי. אנא שפיר מטלטלנא כיפי ואפילו בלא תרווד: אי לאו דאדם חשוב אנא. ואנא מחמיר על עצמי שלא ילמדו ממני להקל באסורין: כפא אכיפי למה לי. בלאו כפא נמי שרי לטלטלינהו דהא חזו למיזגא עלייהו: לאומצא. לאוכלו חי בשבת שיש בני אדם שדעתן יפה ואוכלים בשר חי וקרו לה אומצא: הא לא חזי לאומצא לא. ואע"ג דחזו לשונרא דאמרינן מוכן לאדם לא הוי מוכן לכלבים: כר' יהודה. במסכת ביצה (דף ו:): טווי לי בר אווזא. ביום טוב: ושדי מיעיה לשונרא. אלמא מטלטל להו משום שונרא ואע"ג דהאידנא לא חזי לאדם דלאו אורח ארעא למיכלא ביום טוב ומיהו מאתמול לאדם הוו קיימי:

רבינו חננאל

ואקשינן אמאי והא קא מתקן טיבלא תמצא עושה מעשה בשבת ופרקי' ר' יהודה דאמר כי מעלין את המדומע כר' אליעזר סבירא ליה דאמר תרומה בעינא מחתא. פי' תרומה שנפלה בחולין אין מחשבין אותה שנתערבה בכל החולין אלא כאילו נתונה במקום אחד היא וכשנוטל ממאה ואחד סאין סאה אנן אומרין כי היא היא התרומה. אבל שאר החולין מתוקנין היו מקודם. ולא היה אסור אלא זו הסאה שנטלה במקום התרומה שנפלה בלבד. דתנן סאה של תרומה שנפלה לפחות ממאה ונדמעו ונפל מן המדומע למקום אחד. ר' אליעזר אומר מדומע כתרומה ודאי. פי' סאה תרומה שנפלה לתוך חמשים סאין חולין ועוד נפלה מאלו החמשים ואחד סאין סאה אחת לששים סאה חולין ר' אליעזר סבר הכל אסור חמשים הראשונים וששים האחרונים שאני אומר הסאה של תרומה עצמה היא שנפלה בששים האחרונים לפי שאין המדומע עולה אלא בא' ומאה ואין באחד מהן מאה בעת שנפלה בהן וחכ"א אין המדומע מדמע אלא לפי חשבון פי' סאה שנפלה לחמשים סאין ונפלה מאלו החמשים סאין לפחות מחמשים מדמעת או אם נפלה לששים סאין עולה לפי שאילו היתה סאה במאה סאין ואחת היתה עולה וחזרנו עוד להקשות איסור דשמעת ליה לר' אליעזר שמחשב מכלל נ"א סאין הללו הסאה האחת שנפלה לס' סאין אחרות תרומה כולה. ומדמעת עד מאה ואחת לחומרא לקולא לתקן בשבת כי שמעת ליה לא עמדה ופירקן פירוק אחר והוא ר' יהודה סבר לה כר' שמעון דתנן סאה של תרומה שנפלה למאה חולין ונדמעו ולא הספיק להגביהה עד שנפלה האחרת הרי זו אסורה ור' שמעון מתיר ת"ק סבר כיון שלא הגביהה נמצא שנפלו ב' סאין למאה סאין ואין עולין כי פחות ממאה הן. ור' שמעון סבר מאותה העת שנפלה סאה תרומה למאה חולין הותרו המאה. ונשארו חולין בהכשרן. וסאה אחת בתוכן תרומה התרומה היא אסורה בלבד וכשנפלה אחר כן עוד סאה אחרת תרומה עליהן על מאה חולין נפלה ועולה כו' ופרקי' לה ודברים פשוטין הן. והדרנן ומוקמינן ר' יהודה דמתני' כר' שמעון בן אלעזר דאמר נותן עיניו בצד זה כלומר מחשב להוציא התרומה מצד זה ואוכל מצד אחר ש"מ כי התרומה מחתא במקום אחד. ואקשינן וכי ר' יהודה כר' שמעון בן אלעזר סבירא ליה והא מפלג פליג עליה דתניא ר' יהודה אומר מעלין את המדומע באחד ומאה ר' שמעון אומר נותן עיניו בצד זה ואוכל מצד זה ומפרקי' דר' יהודה עדיפא שר' יהודה מתיר אפי' להעלותה ור' שמעון אינו מתיר להעלותה אלא לתת עיניו בצד זה ולאכול מצד זה. ותרוויהו סבירא להו סאה תרומה שנפלה למאה חולין בעת שנפלה למאה מותרין הן ובתקונן הן ואין צריכין תיקון אלא סילוק סאה אחת מהן בלבד במקום התרומה: **פיסקא** האבן שעל

מסורת הש"ס

א) [תוספתא פרק טו], ב) [לעיל קכה:], ג) זבחים צד., ד) [פי' מרגלית, ערוך], ה) [לעיל קכה: ע"ש], ו) ביצה יד:, ז) ג"ז שם ע"ש, ח) [לעיל מג.], ט) [לעיל נא: וש"נ], י) ביצה לג:, כ) נ"ל לגבי אוכל והאוכל לגבי פסולת משום דחשיב והשתא ה"ג נמי כו', ל) נ"ל לאוכל קאי שהאוכל נפיש בטרחא ואפ"ה בורר אוכל הואיל וחוטר בשיעורא ולא בטל ליה פסולת.

הגהות הב"ח

(א) גמ' דשקיל לה כפסולת כצ"ל ותיבת לאבן נמחק: (ב) רש"י ד"ה נותן וכו' כיבוס ממש לא הואיל: (ג) ד"ה דברי הכל וכו' והוה ליה למשקל: (ד) ד"ה לא משתקיל ליה יין עד: (ה) תוס' ד"ה שאוכל וכו' לא משתקיל ליה יין עד:

גליון הש"ס

גמ' מאן תנא דכל היכא דאיכא איסורא והיתרא. עיין לעיל דף נא ע"ב תוס' ד"ה ואינו נוטל:

רב נסים גאון

מוציאין חלק אחד והשאר מותר לישראל ותמצא עיקר דבר זה בספרי מכל חלבו את מקדשו ממנו שאם נפל לתוכו הרי זה מקדשו מיכן אמרו תרומה עולה באחד ומאה ואין לי אלא תרומה טהורה ותמצא במשנת תרומות ותוספות תרומות וזה הענין הרבה ועיקרו מה שהזכרנו ובגמ' דערלה בפרק ב' (ירושלמי שם הלכה א) מניין שהן עולין אמר ר' יונה כתיב (במדבר יח) מכל חלבו את מקדשו ממנו מדבר שאתה מרים ממנו שאם יפול לתוכו הרי זה מקדשו וכמה הוא אחד ממאה ואיתא נמי בפרק ד' דתרומות התרומה צריך להרים כמה שהוא במשנה במסכת ערלה בראש פרק ב' התרומה ותרומת מעשר של דמאי מצטרפין זה עם זה ואינו צריך להרים וכו' וטעמו של דבר שהתרומות והחלה והביכורים הם נכסי כהן וצריך להרים ויתנו לו הרי זה גזל ממנו ואין להם בעלים שראוין להם לפיכך אינו צריך להרים

ליקוטי רש"י

האבן שע"פ החבית. והולך ליטול מן היין שבתוכה [לעיל קכה:]. היתה עליו לשלשת. ליחה של רוק או של צואה כגון גיעול של רוק או של צואה מקנחה בסמרטוט בשבת ואינו נותן עליה מים שהוא מלבנו ולכבסו ושריה זהו כבוסו [ו]היינו מלאכה מלבן ואם היתה לשלשת זו על כר של עור נותן עליה מים עד שתכלה בשטיפת מים ומיהו שפשוף בידים לא [זבחים צד.]. בשוכח. האבן עליה שלא במתכוין. אבל במניח נעשה. החבית בסיס לאבן שהיא דבר האסור [לעיל קכה:]. תמחוי. קערה גדולה [ביצה יב:]. במה דברים אמורים. דשרו בית הלל ליטול פסולת ממש ולהשליך. בזמן שהאוכל מרובה על של פסולת הוא דקא אמרי בית הלל נוטל פסולת דמעוטי בטרחא עדיף אבל אם פסולת מרובה על של האוכל דברי הכל כו' [שם יד:]. אלא לצורך גופו. שצריך לכר לשכב עליו שם ולא לטלטלו עם המעות אלא מנערו במקומו אבל צריך למקום הכר מטלטל הכל ביחד [לעיל ע"א]. דסקיא. שק של עור שקורין טשי"א [כתובות צו.]. מרצוף גדול של עור [ברכות יח.]. סרטיא. מסילה שהולכין בה מעיר לעיר. אלא למת. מת המוטל בחמה ויש לחוש שמא יסריח [שם מג:]. דאדם חשוב אנא. שהרואה אותו שהוא מיקל עומד ומיקל יותר [שם נא.]. ושדי מיעיה לשונרא. הפלך בני מעים לחתול ולרבי יהודה אסור לטלטלו מוכן לאדם היה ולא לכלבים דקאמר אם לא היתה נבילה מערב שבת אסורה [ביצה לג.].

The Mishnah continued:

מָעוֹת שֶׁעַל הַכַּר – MONEY THAT IS ON A PILLOW – one may shake the pillow so that it falls off.

The Gemara qualifies this rule:

אָמַר רַב חִיָּיא בַּר אַשִׁי אָמַר רַב – **Rav Chiya bar Ashi said in the name of Rav:** לֹא שָׁנוּ אֶלָּא בְּשׁוֹכֵחַ – **They taught** that one may shake the pillow **only** concerning a case **where one forgot** the money upon it, אֲבָל בְּמַנִּיחַ – **but if one left** the money upon it intentionally before the Sabbath, נַעֲשָׂה בָּסִיס לְדָבָר הָאָסוּר – **[the pillow] has become a base to a forbidden object,** and may not even be shaken.[17]

The Mishnah's ruling is further qualified:

אָמַר רַבָּה בַּר בַּר חָנָה אָמַר רַבִּי יוֹחָנָן – **Rabbah bar bar Chanah said in the name of R' Yochanan:** לֹא שָׁנוּ אֶלָּא לְצוֹרֶךְ גופו – **They taught** that one is *required* to shake the money off the pillow **only** concerning a case **where** the pillow is needed **for the sake of its use,** אֲבָל לְצוֹרֶךְ מְקוֹמוֹ – **but** when one needs to move it **for the sake of its place,** מְטַלְטְלוֹ וְעוֹדֶן עָלָיו – **one may move it while [the money] is on it.**[18] וְכֵן תָּנֵי חִיָּיא בַּר רַב מִדִּיפְתִּי – **And so, too, did Chiya bar Rav of Difti teach a Baraisa:** לֹא שָׁנוּ אֶלָּא לְצוֹרֶךְ גופו – THEY TAUGHT this ONLY concerning a case where the pillow is needed FOR THE SAKE OF ITS USE, אֲבָל לְצוֹרֶךְ מְקוֹמוֹ – BUT when one needs to move it FOR THE SAKE OF ITS PLACE, מְטַלְטְלוֹ וְעוֹדֶן עָלָיו – ONE MAY MOVE IT WHILE [THE MONEY] IS ON IT.

The Mishnah stated:

מָעוֹת שֶׁעַל הַכַּר מְנַעֵר וכו׳ – MONEY THAT IS ON A PILLOW – ONE MAY SHAKE **etc.** [the pillow so that it falls off].

The Gemara introduces another means of moving *muktzeh*:

אָמַר רַבִּי אוֹשַׁעְיָא – **R' Oshaya said:** שָׁכַח אַרְנָקִי בְּחָצֵר – **If one forgot a purse** containing money **in a courtyard** where it is unprotected, מַנִּיחַ עָלֶיהָ כִּכָּר אוֹ תִּינוֹק וּמְטַלְטְלָהּ – **he may place a loaf of bread or a young child upon it, and move it** to a protected area.[19]

A similar ruling:

אָמַר רַב יִצְחָק – **Rav Yitzchak said:** שָׁכַח לְבֵינָה בְּחָצֵר – **If one forgot a brick in a courtyard** where it is unprotected,[20] מַנִּיחַ עָלֶיהָ כִּכָּר אוֹ תִּינוֹק וּמְטַלְטְלָהּ – **he may place a loaf of bread or a young child upon it, and move it.**

A related incident is cited:

אָמַר רַבִּי יְהוּדָה בַּר שִׁילָא אָמַר רַבִּי אַסִּי – **R' Yehudah bar Shila said in the name of R' Assi:** פַּעַם אַחַת שָׁכְחוּ דִּסְקְיָא מְלֵאָה מָעוֹת בִּסְרַטְיָא – It **once** occurred that **they forgot a pouch filled with money in a public thoroughfare,** וּבָאוּ וְשָׁאֲלוּ אֶת רַבִּי יוֹחָנָן – **and they came and inquired of R' Yochanan** whether they were allowed to move it. וְאָמַר לָהֶן – **And he said to them:** הַנִּיחוּ עָלֶיהָ כִּכָּר אוֹ תִּינוֹק וְטַלְטְלוּהָ – **Place a loaf of bread or a young child upon it, and move it.**[21]

The previous rulings are qualified:

אָמַר מָר זוּטְרָא – **Mar Zutra said:** הִלְכְתָא כְּכָל הָנֵי שְׁמַעְתָּתָא בְּשׁוֹכֵחַ – **The halachah follows all these teachings** only **when** the *muktzeh* object was **forgotten** in an unprotected area. If it was left there intentionally, this tactic may not be utilized to move it.[22]

According to all the previous opinions, any *muktzeh* object may be moved when a non-*muktzeh* object is placed on it. A dissenting opinion is now cited:

רַב אַשִׁי אָמַר – **Rav Ashi said:** אֲפִילּוּ שָׁכַח נַמִּי [לֹא] – **Even** if one **forgot** the *muktzeh* object in an unprotected area, he may **also** [not] utilize this tactic to move it. וְלֹא אָמְרוּ כִּכָּר אוֹ תִּינוֹק – **They did not state** the dispensation for moving *muktzeh* by placing **a loaf of bread or a young child** upon it, אֶלָּא לְמֵת בִּלְבַד – **except for** the purpose of moving **a corpse alone.**[23]

The Gemara cites incidents in which Amoraim relied upon the previous dispensation to move objects other than a corpse:

אַבַּיֵּי מַנַּח כַּבָּא אַכִּיפֵי – **Abaye placed a spoon on sheaves of grain** and then moved them. רָבָא מַנַּח סַכִּינָא אַבְּבַר יוֹנָה וּמְטַלְטְלָהּ – **Rava placed a knife on** raw **dove** meat **and** then **moved it.**[24]

These practices are questioned:

אָמַר רַב יוֹסֵף – **Rav Yosef said:** כַּמָּה חֲרִיפָא שְׁמַעְתָּתָא דְּדַרְדְּקֵי –

NOTES

17. This is identical with Rav's qualification of the Mishnah's first clause (see note 7). Actually, Rav taught the qualification only once, and his students applied it to each of the Mishnah's clauses (*Tosafos*).

18. See 142a note 15.

19. The purse is a *base to muktzeh*. To preclude loss of the money inside it, the Rabbis granted a dispensation allowing one to move the purse while a loaf of bread or infant is on it (*Rashi* below ד״ה אימור דאמר רבנן). The basis for this dispensation is that whenever a non-*muktzeh* item is carried upon a *muktzeh* item, the *muktzeh* is regarded as an accessory (like a tray or base) to the non-*muktzeh*. Thus, the *muktzeh* purse is considered secondary to the non-*muktzeh* bread or infant that is resting upon it, and one is deemed to be primarily moving the bread or infant. A loaf of bread and an infant are mentioned merely as examples (presumably because they are lightweight and usually available). Any other non-*muktzeh* item will do equally well (*Ritva MHK* ed. above, 43b; see also *Chasam Sofer* and *Chazon Ish* 47:23, and see *Ramban* and *Rashba* to 143a).

20. A brick is *inherently muktzeh* (*Mishnah Berurah* 308:74).

21. The purse was lying in a public domain, where carrying is forbidden, whether an item is *muktzeh* or not. However, once a non-*muktzeh* object was placed on the pouch, it would be permissible to move it to a more secure area within the public domain by carrying it less than four *amos* at a time (see below, 153b; cf. *Ritva MHK* ed.). Alternatively, a private domain could be created around it by lining up people so that their bodies would form an enclosure. It would then be permissible to carry the purse anywhere within the enclosure (*Rashi;* see *Eruvin* 43b).

These two methods of moving things in the public domain are normally forbidden Rabbinically. However, a special dispensation was granted for this case of monetary loss. The Rabbis feared that if they did not waive their decrees in this case a person distraught about the possible loss of his money might come to carry it four *amos* outright and thus violate Biblical law (see *Ritva MHK* ed.; see also below, 153a, *Orach Chaim* 266:1-8 and 405:4; see *Sfas Emes*).

22. [The dispensation for moving a *muktzeh* object upon which a loaf of bread or a child was placed may be relied upon only when the *muktzeh* was left in an unprotected area inadvertently.]

23. This mode of transporting *muktzeh* represents a special leniency declared by the Sages expressly for the purpose of preserving human dignity. It applies only in cases where the physical integrity of a corpse is threatened if it should remain in the same place throughout the Sabbath, such as if it is outside exposed to the sun (*Rashi;* see *Ritva MHK* ed. and *Chazon Ish* ibid.).

[The halachah follows this view (see *Orach Chaim* 311:5). Nevertheless, there is an opinion that our Gemara means to exclude only objects that are completely *muktzeh* (e.g. money) from this dispensation. A corpse is the only completely *muktzeh* object that may be moved on the basis of placing a non-*muktzeh* item upon it. However, this tactic may be utilized when necessary to move a forbidden-use utensil (כְּלִי שֶׁמְּלַאכְתּוֹ לְאִיסוּר), which has a limited *muktzeh* status [as taught above, 123b-124a] (*Teshuvos HaRosh* 22:8, cited in *Orach Chaim* 308:5; see also *Teshuvos R' Akiva Eiger* §22; and see 123a note 2, where it was explained that *Rashi* seems to accept this view). The halachic consensus, however, is that our Gemara is to be understood literally as limiting the applicability of this dispensation *exclusively* to moving a corpse (*Mishnah Berurah* 308:26).]

24. Sheaves of grain and raw meat would seem to be classified as *inherently muktzeh* because they are not fit for consumption in their current state (see below).

והא מיפליג פליג עילויה דתניא רבי יהודה אומר מעלין את המדומע באחד ומאה רבי שמעון בן אלעזר אומר נותן עיניו בצד זה ואוכל מצד אחר דרבי יהודה עדיפא מדר"ש בן אלעזר: **מתני'** האבן שע"פ החבית מטה על צדה והיא נופלת היתה בין החביות מגביה ומטה על צדה והיא נופלת מעות שעל הכר מנער את הכר והן נופלות היתה עליו לשלשת מקנחה בסמרטוט היתה של עור נותנין עליה מים עד שתכלה: **גמ'** אמר רב הונא אמר רב לא שנו אלא בשוכח אבל במניח נעשה בסיס לדבר האסור: [היתה בין החביות כו']: מאן תנא דכל היכא דאיכא איסורא והיתרא בהיתרא טרחינן באיסורא לא טרחינן אמר רבה בר בר חנה אמר רבי יוחנן רשב"ג היא דתנן הבורר קטנית ביו"ט ב"ש אומרים בורר אוכל ואוכל וב"ה אומרים בורר כדרכו בחיקו ובתמחוי ותניא אמר רשב"ג במה דברים אמורים שהאוכל מרובה על הפסולת אבל פסולת מרובה על האוכל דברי הכל בורר אוכל והא הכא דכי אוכל מרובה על הפסולת דמי הכא נמי כיון דאי בעי למישקל לא משתקיל ליה יין עד דשקיל לה (א) לאבן כפסולת מרובה על האוכל דמי: היתה בין החביות מגביה: תניא רבי יוסי אומר היתה החבית מונחת באוצר או שהיו כלי זכוכית מונחין תחתיה מגביה למקום אחר ומטה על צדה והיא נופלת ונוטל הימנה מה שצריך לו ומחזירה למקומה: מעות שעל הכר: אמר רב חייא בר אשי אמר רב לא שנו אלא בשוכח אבל במניח נעשה בסיס לדבר האסור אמר רבה בר בר חנה אמר ר' יוחנן לא שנו אלא לצורך גופו אבל לצורך מקומו מטלטלו ועודן עליו וכן תני חייא בר רב מדיפתי לא שנו אלא לצורך גופו אבל לצורך מקומו מטלטלו ועודן עליו: מעות שעל הכר מנער וכו': א"ר אושעיא שכח ארנקי בחצר מניח עליה ככר או תינוק ומטלטלה אמר רב יצחק שכח לבינה בחצר מניח עליה ככר או תינוק ומטלטלה אמר רבי יהודה בר שילא אמר ר' אסי פעם אחת שכחו דסקיא מלאה מעות בסרטיא ובאו ושאלו את ר' יוחנן ואמר להן הניחו עליה ככר או תינוק וטלטלוה אמר מר זוטרא הלכתא ככל הני שמעתתא בשוכח רב אשי אמר אפילו שכח נמי [לא] ולא אמרו ככר או תינוק אלא למת בלבד אביי מנח כפא אכיפי רבא מנח סכינא אבר יונה ומטלטלה אמר רב יוסף כמה חריפא שמעתתא דדרדקי אימר דאמור רבנן בשוכח לכתחילה מי אמור אמר אביי אי לאו דאדם חשוב אנא כפא אכיפי למה לי הא חזו למיזגא עלייהו אמר רבא אנא אי לאו דאדם חשוב אנא סכינא אבר יונה למה לי הא חזי לי לאומצא טעמא דחזי לאומצא הא לא חזי לאומצא לא למימרא דרבא כרבי יהודה סבירא ליה והאמר רבא לשמעיה טווי לי בר אווזא ושדי מיעיה לשונרא
התם

רש"י

והא מיפליג פליג עילויה. ואמר כיון דאפשר ליה למיעבד עונג שבת כבכה"ג ליתן עיניו בצד זה ולאכול בצד אחר אין מעלין: **דרבי יהודה עדיפא.** מיקל טפי פורתא ואמר כיון דיכול ליתן (עליו) עיניו בצד זה ולאכול בצד זה לא הוי מתקן בהעלאתו ומעלין: **מתני' מטה על צדה.** מטה חבית על לדה אם צריך ליטול מן היין והאבן נופלת ולא יטלנה בידים: **היתה בין החביות.** וירא שלא תפול האבן על החביות וישברם: **מגביה.** לחבית כולה ומסלקה מבין החביות ושם מטה על לדה: **לשלשת.** שום דבר מיאוס כגון רוק או צואה: **מקנחה בסמרטוט.** ולא יתן עליה מים דקסס כר של בגד הוא ובגד שריתו במים הוא כבוסו: **היתה.** לשלשת זו על כר של עור דלאו בר כיבוס הוא: **נותן עליה מים עד שתכלה.** ומיהו כיבוס ממש לא (ג) והוליל וקסס כרים וכסתות רכים ניניהו שייך למימר בהו כיבוס בעורות רכין ומיהו שריינן לא זהו כבוסן וכן מפורש בזבחים בפרק דם חטאת: **גמ' לא שנו.** מטה על לדה לחבית: **אלא בשכח.** ששכח האבן עליה בין השמשות ולא מדעת: **נעשה חבית בסיס לדבר האסור.** ואסור להטותה שאף החבית מוקלה: **מאן תנא.** דמתניתין דקתני מגביה ומטה על לדה דאית ליה דכי טרח מטרח בחבית דהוי היתרא ולא יטול האבן ממש דהוי איסורא ואע"ג דהשתא נמי אבן מטלטל בהדי חבית: **רבן שמעון.** אליבא דבית הלל: **בורר אוכל ואוכל.** המאכל יטול והפסולת ישאר בכלי: **בורר כדרכו.** נוטל פסולת ומניח אוכל אם ירלה: **כשהאוכל מרובה על הפסולת.** דאי שקיל אוכל מפיש בטרחא: **דברי הכל בורר אוכל.** דבהיתירא טרח ולא באיסורא ופרכינן והא הכא דמתניתין דאוכל מרובה על הפסולת וכי מגביה האבן עם החבית טרח טפי והוה (ג) למשקל פסולת כר"ש: **כיון דאי בעי למשקל.** לכולי יין מן החבית לא משתקיל ליה יין שבשוליה עד דשקיל ומגבה לה לחבית כפסולת מרובה דמי דאי בתחלתו לא מגבה לה לחבית סוף סוף מיבעי ליה לאגבוהה תו לחבית הלכך הוה ליה מפיש בטרחא: **ה"ג לא משתקל ליה (ד) עד דשקיל לה** ול"ג עד דשקיל לה לאבן: **היתה החבית מונחת באוצר.** כלומר במקום מכונס שאוצרין שם חביות הרבה ודואג שמא יטלה ותפול האבן על החבית שאצלה: **לא שנו.** דמנער: **נעשה.** הכר בסיס למעות ואף הכר אסור בטלטול: **לא שנו.** דמנערה ואינו מטלטלה בעודן עליה: **אלא שצריך לגופו.** של כר לשכב עליו הלכך בניעור סגיא ושדי ליה באתרייהו: **אבל צריך למקומו.** של כר מטלטלו עם המעות למקום אחר: **דסקיא מלאה מעות** גרסינן: **בסרטיא.** רה"ר: **הניחו עליה ככר או תינוק.** דלישתרי לטלטלה אגבייהו תוך ד' אמות וטלטלוה פחות פחות מד' אמות או במחילה של בני אדם כדאמרי' בעירובין (דף מג:): **בשוכח.** אבל במניח מדעת מערב (יום) שבת לא התירו לו לטלטלה ע"י ככר או תינוק: **אלא למת.** משום כבוד הבריות כשמוטל בחמה: **אביי מנח כפא אכיפי.** מניח תרווד על העומרים לטלטלן אגב תרווד: **אבר יונה.** חי [בלא] מליח: **חריפא שמעתתא דדרדקי.** סבורים הם שהם חריפים: **אימר דאמור רבנן.** בארנקי ודסקיא מניח עליה ככר או תינוק בשכחה ובמקום התורפה ומשום הפסד ממון: **אמר אביי.** אנא שפיר מטלטלנא כיפי ואפילו בלא תרווד: **אי לאו דאדם חשוב אנא.** ואנא מחמיר על עצמי שלא ילמדו ממני להקל באסורין: **כפא אכיפי למה לי.** בלאו כפא נמי שרי לטלטלינהו דהא חזו למיזגא עלייהו: **לאומצא.** לאוכלו חי בשבת שיש בני אדם שדעתן יפה ואוכלים בשר חי וקרו לה אומצא: **הא לא חזי לאומצא לא.** ואע"ג דחזו לשונרא דאמרינן מוכן לאדם לא הוי מוכן לכלבים: **כר' יהודה.** במסכת ביצה (דף ו:): **טווי לי בר אווזא.** ביום טוב: **ושדי מיעיה לשונרא.** אלמא מטלטל להו משום שונרא ואע"ג דהאידנא לא חזי לאדם דלאו אורח ארעא למיכלא ביום טוב ומיהו מאתמול לאדם הוו קיימי:

תוספות

שאוכל מרובה על הפסולת. פי' בקונטרס משום דהשתא הוי טרחא יתירא למישקליה לאוכל ולאו נראה לר"י דלאי משום טרחא הוי מאי קאמרי בסמוך דהכא נמי כיון דאי בעי למישקל לא משתקיל ליה עד דשקיל ליה לאבן כפסולת מרובה על האוכל דמי היכי הוי משום האי טעמא כפסולת מרובה על האוכל ולכך הוצרך רש"י לפרש דל"ג עד דשקיל ליה לאבן על כן נראה לר"ת דטעמא משום דכי אוכל מרובה על הפסולת הוה פסולת כבטל לגבי רובו ומותר ליטלו מן האוכל ולזורקו אבל פסולת מרובה על האוכל לא בטיל ליה פסולת לגבי אוכל והשתא אתי שפיר גירסת הספרים דגבי חבית נמי כיון דאי בעי למישקל לא משתקיל ליה (ה) עד דשקיל ליה לאבן כפסולת מרובה על האוכל דמי דכיון שאין יכול כלל ליטול מן היין בלא נטילת האבן לא חשיב כבטיל לגבי האוכל כיון שהאוכל אינו ניכר כלל ואינו יכול ליטול הימנו כשהאבן על פי החבית. מ"ר. והא דמוקי לה בפ"ק דביצה (ד' יד: ושם) כגון דנפיש בטירחא חוטר בשיעורא דאוכל קאי ולא אפסולת ולפירש"י קאי אפסולת ולא אאוכל [וע"כ לא יברור הפסולת דנפיש בטירחא]:

לא שנו אלא בשכח. וא"ת תרתי דרב למה לי וי"ל חדא מכלל חבירתה איתמר והא לא תקשה תרתי מתני' למה לי דהוה אמינא אבן ודאי שרי בשכח שנראה טפי ככיסוי החבית אבל מעות שעל גבי הכר אפילו בשכח ה"א דאסיר:

עין משפט נר מצוה

יג א מיי' פכ"ה מהל' שבת הל' יח טוש"ע א"ח סי' שט סעיף ד:
יד ב מיי' פכ"ג שם הל' יח טוש"ע א"ח סי' שב סעיף ט:
טו ג מיי' פכ"ה שם הלכה יח טוש"ע א"ח סי' שט סעיף ד:
טז ד ה מיי' פ"ג מהל' י"ט הל' טו סמג לאוין עה טוש"ע א"ח סי' תקי סעיף ג:
יז ו מיי' פכ"ה מהל' שבת הלכה יח טוש"ע א"ח סי' שט סעיף ה:
יח ז מיי' פכ"ו שם הלכה כא סמג שם טוש"ע א"ח סי' שיא סעיף ה:

רבינו חננאל

ואקשינן אמאי והא קא מתקן טיבלא תמצא עושה מעשה בשבת ופרקי' ר' יהודה דאמר כי מעלין את המדומע כר' אליעזר סבירא ליה דאמר תרומה בעינא מחתא. פי' תרומה שנפלה בחולין אין מחשבין אותה שנתערבה בכל החולין אלא כאילו נתונה במקום אחד היא וכשנוטל ממאה ואחד סאין סאה אנן אומרין כי היא היא התרומה. אבל שאר החולין מתוקנין היו מקודם. ולא היה אסור אלא זו הסאה שנוטלה במקום התרומה שנפלה בלבד. דתנן סאה של תרומה שנפלה לפחות ממאה ונדמעו ונפל מן המדומע למקום אחד. ר' אליעזר אומר מדומע כתרומה ודאי. פי' סאה תרומה שנפלה לתוך חמשים סאין חולין ועוד נפלה מאלו החמשים ואחד סאין סאה אחת לששים סאה חולין ר' אליעזר סבר הכל אסור חמשים הראשונים וששים האחרונים שאני אומר הסאה של תרומה עצמה היא שנפלה בששים האחרונים לפי שאין המדומע עולה אלא בא' ומאה ואין באחד מהן מאה בעת נפילתה בהן וחכ"א אין המדומע מדמע אלא לפי חשבון פי' סאה שנפלה לחמשים סאין ונפלה מאלו החמשים סאין לפחות מחמשים מדמעת אבל אם נפלה סאה לששים סאין עולה לפי שאילו היתה סאה במאה סאין ואחת היתה עולה וחזרנו עוד להקשות אימור דשמעת ליה לר' אליעזר שמחשב מכלל נ"א סאין הללו הסאה האחת שנפלה לס' סאין אחרות תרומה כולה. ומדמעת עד מאה ואחת לחומרא לקולא לתקן בשבת מי שמעת ליה ולא עמדה ופירקנן פירוק אחר והוא ר' יהודה סבר לה כר' שמעון דתנן סאה של תרומה שנפלה למאה חולין ונדמעו ולא הספיק להגביהה עד שנפלה האחרת הרי זו אסורה ור' שמעון מתיר ת"ק סבר כיון שלא הגביהה נמצא שנפלו ב' סאין למאה סאין ואין עולין כי פחות ממאה הן. ור' שמעון סבר מאותה העת שנפלה סאה תרומה למאה חולין הותרו המאה. ונשארו חולין בהכשרן. וסאה אחת בתוכן תרומה התרומה היא אסורה בלבד וכשנפלה אחר כן עוד סאה אחרת תרומה עליהן על מאה חולין נפלה ועולה כו' ופרקי' לה הדברים פשוטין הן. והדרנן ומוקמינן ר' יהודה דמתני' כר' שמעון בן אלעזר דאמר נותן עיניו בצד זה כלומר מחשב להוציא התרומה מצד זה ואוכל מצד אחר ש"מ כי התרומה מחתא במקום אחד. ואקשינן וכי ר' יהודה כר' שמעון בן אלעזר סבירא ליה והא מפלג פליג עליה דתניא ר' יהודה אומר מעלין את המדומע באחד ומאה ר' שמעון אומר נותן עיניו בצד זה ואוכל מצד זה ומפרקי' דר' יהודה עדיפא שר' יהודה מתיר אפי' להעלותה ור' שמעון אינו מתיר להעלותה אלא לתת עיניו בצד זה ולאכול מצד זה. ותרווייהו סבירא להו סאה תרומה שנפלה למאה חולין בעת שנפלה למאה מותרין הן ובתקונן הן ואין צריכין תיקון אלא סילוק סאה אחת מהן בלבד במקום התרומה: **פיסקא** האבן שעל

מסורת הש"ס

א) [תוספתא פרק טו], ב) [לעיל קכה:], ג) זבחים לב., ד) [פי' בלשון ערבי תרנגולת. ערוך], ה) [לעיל קכה: ע"ש], ו) ביצה יד:, ז) ג"ז שם ע"ש, ח) [לעיל ל: מג:], ט) [לעיל נא. וש"נ], י) ביצה לג., כ) ל"ל אוכל והאוכל לא בטיל לגבי פסולת משום דהשתא לא אוכל קאי דנפיש בטירחא ובורר אוכל הוא והשתא כו', ל) ל"ל לאוכל קאי שהאוכל נפיש בטירחא ואפ"ה בורר אוכל הואיל חוטר בשיעורא ולא בטיל ליה פסולת.

הגהות הב"ח

(א) גמ' דשקיל לה לאבן כפסולת כל"ל ותיבת ליה נמחק: (ב) רש"י ד"ה נותן וכו' כיבוס ממש לא הוא והוליל: (ג) ד"ה דברי הכל וכו' והוה ליה למשקל: (ד) ד"ה ה"ג לא משתקיל ליה יין עד: (ה) תוס' ד"ה שאוכל וכו' לא משתקיל ליה יין עד:

גליון הש"ס

גמ' מאן תנא דכל היכא דאיכא איסורא והיתרא. עיין לעיל דף נא ע"ב תוס' ד"ה אינו נוטל:

רב נסים גאון

מוציאין חלק אחד לישראל והשאר מותר לישראל ותמצא עיקר דבר זה בסיפרי מכל חלבו את מקדשו ממנו שאם נפל לתוכו הרי זה מקדשו מיכן אמרו תרומה עולה באחד ומאה אין לא אלא תרומה טהורה ותמצא במשנת תרומות ותוספות תרומה מזה הענין הרבה ועיקרו מה שהזכרנו ובגמ' דערלה בפרק ב' (ירושלמי שם הלכה א') מניין שהן עולין אמר ר' יונה כתיב (במדבר יח) מכל חלבו את מקדשו ממנו דבר שאתה מרים ממנו שאם יפול לתוכו הרי זה מקדשו וכמה הוא אחד מאה ואיתא נמי בפרק ד' דתרומות התרומה צריך להרים כמה שהוא במשנה במסכת ערלה בראש פרק ב' התרומה ותרומת מעשר של דמאי מצטרפין זה עם זה ואינו צריך להרים והשבטו של דבר לפי שהתרומות והחלה והביכורים הם נכסי כהן וצריך להרים תרומה ויתנה לו ואם לא ירים ויתן לו הרי זה גוזל ממונו ואין להם בעלים שראויין להם לפיכך אינו צריך להרים

ליקוטי רש"י

האבן שע"פ החבית. והולכך ליטול מן היין שבתוכה [לעיל קכה:]. **היתה עליו לשלשת.** היתה על כר של בגד גיעול של רוק או צואה מקנחו בסמרטוט בשבת לכלוכה [ו]להעבירו מפני שהוא מגכם ובכיבוס לא מלבן ואם היתה לשלשת זו על כר של עור נותן עליה מים עד שתכלה בשטיפת מים ומיהו שפשוף בידים לא [זבחים צד.]. **בשוכח.** האבן עליה שלא במתכוין. **אבל במניח נעשה.** החבית בסיס לאבן שהיא דבר האיסור [לעיל שם]. **תמחוי.** קערה גדולה [ביצה יב:]. **במה דברים אמורים.** דשרו בית הלל ליטול פסולת ממש כשהאוכל מרובה על של פסולת הוא דקא אמרי בית הלל נוטל פסולת דמעוטי בטרחא עדיף אבל אם על של האוכל דברי הכל כו' [שם יד:]. **אלא לצורך גופו.** שצריך לכר לשכב עליו שם ולא לכלו ליטלו עם המעות אלא מנערו במקומו אבל צריך למקום הכר מטלטל הכל ביחד [לעיל ע"א]. שקורין טשי"א [כתובות צו.]. מרצוף גדול של עור [ברכות יח.]. **סרטיא.** מסילה שהולכין בה מעיר [לעיל ...].

למת. מת המוטל בחמה ויש לחוש שמא יתחיל להסריח [שם מג:]. **דאדם חשוב אנא.** שהרואה אותו שהוא מיקל עומד ומיקל יותר [שם נא.]. **ושדי מיעיה לשונרא.** השלך בני מעיים לחתול ולרבי יהודה אסור לטלטלו מוכן לאדם היה ולא לכלבים דקאמר אם לא היתה נבילה מערב שבת אסורה [ביצה לג.].

How sharp the teaching of these **youngsters** appears to be![25] אֵימַר דְּאָמוּר רַבָּנַן – But actually, they have erred, for **when did the Rabbis say** that a *muktzeh* item may be moved by placing a non-*muktzeh* object upon it? בְּשׁוֹכֵחַ – Only concerning a case **where one *forgets*** the *muktzeh* object in an unprotected place and it stands to be lost if left there. לְכַתְּחִילָּה מִי אָמוּר – **Did they say** that this stratagem may be employed to move something **in the first place?**[26] Certainly not! Therefore, Abaye and Rava were wrong in utilizing this stratagem to move sheaves and dove meat that were lying in their usual places.

Abaye and Rava defend their actions:

אָמַר אַבַּיֵי – **Abaye said:** אִי לָאו דְּאָדָם חָשׁוּב אֲנָא – **If not** for the fact **that I am a distinguished person** whom people emulate, כַּפָּא אַכִּיפֵי לָמָּה לִי – **why do I** even **need** to place **a spoon on the sheaves** before moving them? הָא חֲזוּ לְמִיזְגָא עֲלַיְיהוּ – **Why, they are fit to recline upon,** and are thus not *muktzeh* at all![27] I placed the spoon upon them before moving them merely as an added stringency.[28]

אָמַר רָבָא – **Rava said:** אֲנָא אִי לָאו דְּאָדָם חָשׁוּב אֲנָא – **I,** too, **if not** for the fact **that I am a distinguished person** whom people emulate, סַכִּינָא אַבַּר יוֹנָה לָמָּה לִי – **why do I** even **need** to place **a knife on the** raw **dove** meat before moving it? הָא חֲזוּ לִי לְאוּמְצָא – **Why, it is fit for me** to eat **while raw,** and is thus not *muktzeh* at all! I placed the knife on it before moving it merely as an added stringency.[29]

The Gemara analyzes Rava's response:

טַעְמָא דַּחֲזוּ לְאוּמְצָא – **The reason** Rava maintained that he was allowed to move the raw meat **is that it was fit** to be eaten **while** it is **raw meat.** הָא לֹא חֲזוּ לְאוּמְצָא לֹא – This implies that if, **however,** it were **not fit** to be eaten **while raw meat,** one would **not** be allowed to move it. Rather, it would be considered *muktzeh* even though it was fit for consumption by animals. לְמֵימְרָא דְּרָבָא כְּרַבִּי יְהוּדָה סְבִירָא לֵיהּ – Is this **to say that Rava concurs with R' Yehudah,** who subscribes to a broad application of *muktzeh* law?[30] וְהָאָמַר רָבָא לְשַׁמָּעֵיהּ – **But Rava told his attendant** on Yom Tov: טְוֵוי לִי בַּר אַוָּזָא – **Roast a goose for me,** וּשְׁדֵי מֵיעֵיהּ לְשׁוּנְרָא – **and throw its intestines to the cat!** This follows the opinion of R' Shimon, who holds that food which on Yom Tov became suitable only for animals may be fed to them.[31] – ? –

NOTES

25. I.e. they think that they are sharp in utilizing this stratagem to transport otherwise *muktzeh* items (*Rashi*).

26. I.e. even the Rabbis who allowed moving any *muktzeh* object when a non-*muktzeh* object is resting upon it granted this dispensation only for the sake of avoiding an unforeseen monetary loss. Nobody sanctions the utilization of this tactic for the mere sake of convenience! In these cases, then, where the sheaves and dove meat were in their usual place and there was no danger of their being lost, there was absolutely no basis to allow moving them by placing a non-*muktzeh* item on them (*Rashi, Ritva MHK* ed.).

Rav Yosef could have further objected that the dispensation is in fact applicable only to the case of a corpse (*Ritva MHK* ed., *Chidushei HaRan*).

27. Since the sheaves have the practical function of being used to rest upon, and they are commonly utilized in this capacity, they are classified as non-*muktzeh* utensils (see 124b note 25).

28. It behooves a person of my standing to act with a superior degree of stringency, lest people [who think that sheaves are *muktzeh*] misconstrue my actions and allow themselves to move that which is actually forbidden (*Rashi;* see *Sfas Emes* and *Shabbos Shel Mi*).

29. People who were not finicky used to sometimes eat raw meat. Thus, it is considered a non-*muktzeh* food item (*Rashi;* see *Mishnah Berurah* 308:125 for a discussion of whether this pertains only to poultry, which is relatively tender, or even to beef).

Abaye and Rava concede that any truly *muktzeh* object (other than a corpse) may not be moved simply because a non-*muktzeh* object was placed upon it, as Rav Ashi stated above (*Chidushei HaRan*).

30. R' Yehudah and R' Shimon have a wide-ranging dispute concerning the extent of the *muktzeh* prohibitions, with R' Yehudah adopting a more stringent attitude (see 126b note 28). One of R' Yehudah's rulings is that "something which was prepared for humans is not considered prepared for animals." That is, if at the onset of the Sabbath or Yom Tov an item was designated as human food, it is considered *muktzeh* in regard to use as animal feed. Its suitability for humans causes it to be set aside from utilization for feeding animals; hence, it was not "prepared" for this purpose (see Mishnah 156b and *Beitzah* 6b). And since consumption by animals is not a legitimate use for human food, if a food item is inedible on the Sabbath (e.g. it requires cooking), it will be considered inherently *muktzeh* even though it can be eaten in its current form by animals (see *Rashi* ד״ה ושדי). [R' Shimon, however, holds that human food is considered prepared even for animals, and by extension, human food that is fit for consumption by animals is non-*muktzeh*.]

Now, if Rava followed R' Shimon's opinion, he could have said that the raw dove meat was not *muktzeh* because it was fit for consumption by animals. Since he resorted to the defense that it was suitable for the [minority of] humans who eat raw meat, it would seem that he follows R' Yehudah's stringent opinion that human food which is fit only for animals is *muktzeh* (*Rashi;* cf. *Baal HaMaor, Rashba, Ritva MHK* ed.; see 128a note 38).

31. The goose [which included the intestines] had generally been designated for human consumption at the start of Yom Tov. However, the intestines [once they are separate from the goose] are no longer considered human food on Yom Tov, since people do not usually eat them at a holiday meal, when they have better food (*Rashi,* as explained by *Tosafos* to *Beitzah* 33a ד״ה ושדי). Since the status of the intestines changed on Yom Tov from human food to animal food, they are considered *nolad* (literally: just born, i.e. a new entity), a category that is considered *muktzeh* according to R' Yehudah (*Maharsha* to 143a; see 124b notes 22 and 24 for a fuller explanation of *nolad*). Since Rava allowed his attendant to throw the intestines to the cat, he apparently follows the lenient view of R' Shimon regarding *muktzeh.* R' Shimon considers *nolad* non-*muktzeh* (see 143a note 14).

The Gemara answers that Rava can follow R' Yehudah's opinion:

הָתָם – **There,** he allowed the intestines to be thrown to a cat because בֵּיוָן דְמַסְרַח – **since they would spoil** if left over until the next day, דַּעְתֵּיהּ עִילָוֵיהּ מֵאֶתְמוֹל – **he had intended the previous day** (i.e. before Yom Tov) **to** use **them** as animal feed.[1]

The Gemara corroborates its answer:

הָכִי נַמִי מִסְתַּבְּרָא דְּרָבָא כְּרַבִּי יְהוּדָה סְבִירָא לֵיהּ – **It is indeed reasonable** to say **that Rava concurs with R' Yehudah,** דְּדָרַשׁ רָבָא – **for Rava lectured:** אִשָּׁה לֹא תִכָּנֵס לְבֵית הָעֵצִים לִיטּוֹל מֵהֶן אוּד – **A woman may not enter a woodshed to take** a piece of wood for use as **a poker** with which to stir up coals;[2] וְאוּד שֶׁנִּשְׁבַּר אָסוּר לְהַסִּיקוֹ בְּיוֹם טוֹב – **and a** wooden **poker that broke** on Yom Tov **may not be kindled on Yom Tov,** לְפִי שֶׁמַּסִּיקִין בְּכֵלִים – **because one may fuel** a fire **with** undamaged **utensils** on Yom Tov, וְאֵין מַסִּיקִין בְּשִׁבְרֵי כֵלִים – **but one may not fuel** a fire **with fragments of utensils** that broke on Yom Tov.[3]

שְׁמַע מִינַּהּ – Indeed, **learn from this** that Rava follows the opinion of R' Yehudah with regard to *muktzeh*.

Mishnah

The Mishnah cites a dispute concerning the permissibility of removing *muktzeh* remnants from a table:

בֵּית שַׁמַּאי אוֹמְרִים – **Beis Shammai say:** מַעֲבִירִין מֵעַל הַשֻּׁלְחָן עֲצָמוֹת וּקְלִיפִּין – **We may remove bones and husks from the table** by hand. וּבֵית הִלֵּל אוֹמְרִים – **But Beis Hillel say:** מְסַלֵּק אֶת הַטַּבְלָא כּוּלָּהּ וּמְנַעֲרָהּ – **One must take up the entire table board**[4] **and shake it** clean, and not handle the bones and husks directly.[5]

The Mishnah continues:

מַעֲבִירִין (מלפני) [מֵעַל] הַשֻּׁלְחָן – **We may remove from the table**[6] by hand פֵּירוּרִין פָּחוֹת מִכְּזַיִת – **crumbs** that are **smaller than a** ***kezayis,*** וְשֶׂעָר שֶׁל אֲפוּנִין וּשְׂעַר עֲדָשִׁים – **as well as pea pods and lentil pods,** מִפְּנֵי שֶׁהוּא מַאֲכַל בְּהֵמָה – **because they are** fit for use as **animal fodder.**[7]

Having set forth several *muktzeh* laws related to clearing off a table, the Mishnah continues with another law concerning this subject:

סְפוֹג – **A sponge** – אִם יֵשׁ לוֹ עוֹר בֵּית אֲחִיזָה מְקַנְּחִין בּוֹ – **if it has a leather handle, we may wipe** a table **with it** even when it is damp, וְאִם לָאו אֵין מְקַנְּחִין בּוֹ – **but if not, we may not wipe** a table **with it** when it is damp.[8]

NOTES

1. He knew he would not need them for his own use on Yom Tov. Since keeping them for after Yom Tov would cause them to spoil, he already intended beforehand that after the goose was slaughtered he would throw them to a cat. Thus, they were prepared for animal consumption before Yom Tov (*Rashi;* cf. *Tosafos* to 29a ד״ה אכלן and to *Beitzah* 33a ד״ה ושדי; *Rashba*, *Ritva MHK* ed.).

2. This follows the opinion of R' Yehudah, who holds that wood is generally set aside for kindling, and may not be taken up to be used as a utensil; it is considered *muktzeh* regarding all uses other than kindling (*Rashi;* see *Beitzah* 33a; see *Rashba* there and *Rashi* to *Beitzah* 33b ד״ה לא יטול for further explanation of this rule).

3. A stick which had been designated as a poker before Yom Tov is a non-*muktzeh* utensil; therefore, it may be used for any purpose, even for kindling. When it breaks, however, it is no longer fit for its designated function, but is newly classified as firewood. Since it has turned into a new entity on Yom Tov, it has the status of *nolad.* One is accordingly forbidden to use it even for kindling.

This ruling is a direct quote of R' Yehudah's opinion in this matter – an opinion that is disputed by R' Shimon (see 124b note 24; see also note 14 below). Clearly Rava concurs with R' Yehudah's broad application of the law of *muktzeh* (*Rashi*).

4. This is a large board placed under a small table to catch the crumbs (*Rambam, Commentary*). Alternatively, this is a board placed on the table; the modern-day equivalent would be a breadboard or tablecloth (*Mishnah Berurah* 308:115).

5. The Mishnah refers to bones and nutshells that are too hard to be eaten even by animals. Beis Shammai permit taking these off the table by hand because they do not accept the *muktzeh* prohibition [as pertaining to this case. They concur with R' Shimon's narrow application of *muktzeh* law, according to which these bones and husks may be removed by hand.] Beis Hillel, however, concur with R' Yehudah's broad application of *muktzeh,* and therefore forbid handling the bones or shells directly (see below). They allow only handling the table board, which is a non-*muktzeh* utensil, and shaking the undesirable matter off it (*Rashi;* see *Mishnah Berurah* 308:115; see also *Rashba*). [For a discussion of whether one must tilt the board in its place to remove the dirt, or one may carry it to a proper disposal area, see *Ramban* and *Rashba* to the Gemara, *Chasam Sofer* cited at end of note 13, *Sfas Emes* and *Beur Halachah* to 308:27 ד״ה מנער.]

Tosafos and other Rishonim object to *Rashi's* explanation of Beis Shammai as allowing the handling of hard bones and nutshells that are unfit for use as animal fodder, since even R' Shimon agrees that such scraps are inherently *muktzeh,* like stones. (This would seem to emerge clearly from the Mishnah's next ruling – see note 7.) Rather, *Tosafos* contend, the Mishnah is dealing with soft bones and fruit peels, which *can* be fed to animals (see *Rashash*).

However, *Pnei Yehoshua* (*Beitzah* 2a to *Tosafos* ד״ה מגביהין) defends *Rashi's* view by noting that since in its next clause the Mishnah specifies that certain items may be moved because they are fit for animals, and it omits this point here, the implication is that this clause deals with bones and shells that are unfit for animals (cf. *Tos. Rid*). The basis of Beis Shammai's permit to remove them from the table is that the Rabbis granted a dispensation allowing the removal of repulsive *muktzeh* items from one's presence [and when bones or husks accumulate on the table they become repulsive (*Mishnah Berurah* ibid.; see note 23)]. Beis Hillel do not dispute the dispensation. Nevertheless, following R' Yehudah's stringent approach to *muktzeh,* they hold that since it is possible to alleviate the discomfort without handling the *muktzeh* directly, i.e. by removing the table board and shaking it clean, one may not remove the *muktzeh* by hand (see also *Maginei Shlomo* and *Chasam Sofer*).

The Gemara will revise the respective positions of Beis Shammai and Beis Hillel.

6. Our emendation of the text follows *Rashi;* see *Bach.*

7. Although people do not generally eat crumbs that are smaller than a *kezayis* or the pods of legumes, these are not *muktzeh* because they are suitable for consumption by animals (*Rashi*). The Gemara will explain that this ruling follows R' Shimon's lenient opinion concerning *muktzeh* (see note 14).

8. Wringing water out of wet cloth is a *toladah* of the *melachah* of מְלַבֵּן, *whitening*. This prohibition also applies to wringing water out of a sponge (*Rambam, Hil. Shabbos* 22:15). Others explain that wringing water out of a sponge is a *toladah* of דָּשׁ, *threshing* [for extracting liquid from a fabric is similar to extracting grain from its husk. However, this applies only if the liquid is salvaged for use] (*Tosafos* above, 111a-b ד״ה האי מסוכרייתא דנזייתא; see *Beur Halachah* to 320:18 ד״ה יש מי שמתיר). When one grasps a wet sponge with his bare hand, water is likely to be squeezed out between his fingers. [Since the water will be used to facilitate cleaning the table, the squeezing is prohibited even according to the view of *Tosafos* that was just cited.] The Mishnah therefore permits using only a sponge that has a handle (*Rashi*). This ruling will be clarified in the Gemara (see notes 15-16).

התם כיון דמסרח דעתיה עילויה מאתמול הכי נמי מסתברא דרבא כר' יהודה סבירא ליה [א]דדרש רבא [א]אשה לא תכנס לבית העצים ליטול מהן אוד ואוד שנשבר אסור להסיקו ביום טוב לפי [ב]שמסיקין בכלים ואין מסיקין בשברי כלים שמע מינה:

מתני' ב"ש אומרים [ד][ב]מעבירין מעל השלחן עצמות וקליפין וב"ה אומרים [ה]מסלק את הטבלא כולה ומנערה מעבירין (א) מלפני השלחן פירורין פחות מכזית ושער של אפונין ושער עדשים מפני שהוא מאכל בהמה [ג]ספוג אם יש לו עור בית אחיזה מקנחין בו ואם לאו אין מקנחין בו (ב) [ו](וחכמים אומרים) בין כך ובין כך [ז]ניטל בשבת ואינו מקבל טומאה:

גמ' [ח]אמר רב נחמן אנו אין לנו אלא ב"ש כרבי יהודה וב"ה כרבי שמעון: מעבירין (ג) מלפני השלחן פירורין: מסייע ליה לר' יוחנן [ט]דאמר רבי יוחנן [ד]פירורין שאין בהן כזית אסור לאבדן ביד: שער של אפונין: מני ר"ש היא דלית ליה מוקצה אימא סיפא ספוג אם יש לו עור בית אחיזה מקנחין בו ואם לאו אין מקנחין בו אתאן לר' יהודה דאמר דבר שאין מתכוין אסור בהא אפילו ר"ש מודה [י]דאביי ורבא דאמרי תרוייהו מודה ר"ש בפסיק רישיה ולא ימות [ה]הני גרעינין דתמרי ארמייתא שרו לטלטולינהו הואיל וחזיין אגב אמן ודפרסייתא אסור שמואל מטלטל להו אגב ריפתא: (שרנ"ם שפ"ז סימן): שמואל לטעמיה [כ]דאמר שמואל [ו]עושה אדם כל צרכו בפת [ל]רבה מטלטל להו אגב לקנא דמיא רב הונא בריה דרב יהושע עביד להו כגרף של ריעי א"ל רב אשי לאמימר [מ][ז]וכי עושין גרף של ריעי לכתחילה רב ששת זריק להו בלישניה רב פפא זריק להו אחורי המטה [נ]אמרו עליו על רבי זכריה בן אבקולס [ח]שהיה מחזיר פניו אחורי המטה וזורקן:

הדרן עלך נוטל אדם את בנו

רש"י

התם כיון דמסרח. מעייל אי מלגע ליה עד אורתא: מאתמול דעתיה עליה. לשורגא ובין השמשות נמי מוכן לבהמה הוא: אוד. פורגו"ן דסתם עצים להסקה ניתנו ולא לטלטול כלי: ואוד שנשבר. ביו"ט: בשברי כלים. שנשברו היום דהוו להו נולד: ש"מ. דכרבי יהודה סבירא ליה דאית ליה מוקצה:

מתני' מעבירין. בידים מעל השלחן: עצמות. קשין שאינן ראויין לכלב: וקליפין. של אגוזים דלית להו לב"ש מוקצה: וב"ה אומרים מסלק את הטבלא. שיש תורת כלי עליה אבל לא יטלטל הקליפין בידים כרבי יהודה: מעבירין מעל השלחן. סתמא היא: פירורין פחות מכזית. וכ"ש כזית כדמפרש טעמא שהם מאכל בהמה: ושער של אפונין. שרביטין של קטנית שהקטנית גדל בהם: אפונין. ייש"ש: עור בית אחיזה. [בית אחיזה] של עור שיאחזנו בו: מקנחין בו. טבלא: אין מקנחין בו. שכשאוחזו נסחט בין אצבעותיו: ניטל בשבת. כשהוא נגוב: ואינו מקבל טומאה. דאינו לא כלי עץ ולא בגד ולא שק ולא מתכת: גמ' אנו אין לנו. אין אנו סומכין על משנתינו כמות שהיא שנויה אלא מוחלפת שיטתה וב"ש כרבי יהודה כו': אסור לאבדן ביד. מדקתני מעבירין בידים ולא זריק להו: דלית ליה מוקצה. דאי ר' יהודה מאתמול לאו לבהמה קיימי שהרי האוכל היה עמהן והיום לוקח מהם: שאין מתכוין. שאין מתכוין לסחוט: גרעינין. של תמרים והם לבהמה: ארמייתא. תמרים רעים הם ומאכילין התמרים עצמן לבהמה הלכך אגב אימייהו לבהמה נמי קיימי: פרסייתא. תמרים טובים הם ואין מאכילין אותן לבהמה: כל צרכו. משתמש בו ואין כאן משום בזיון וממחהו בתבשיל: לקנא דמיא. ספל של מים: גרף של ריעי. נוכרן לפניו כשאוכל התמרים עד שנמאסות בעיניו ונוטלין אותן מפניו כגרף של ריעי ונותנן לבהמה: זריק להו בלישני'. אל עבר השלחן: אחורי המטה. שהוא מיסב עליה:

הדרן עלך נוטל

תוספות

התם כיון דמסרח. ומתקלקל ואין ראוי למאכל אדם מאתמול דעתיה עילויה ליתנו לבהמה אע"ג דבשער של אפונין ושל עדשים אסרינן לרבי יהודה אע"ג דחזו למאכל בהמה וכן גרעינין דלעיל בפרק במה מדליקין (דף כט.) דאמרינן לרבי יהודה אכלן אין מסיקין בגרעינין מ"מ הכא שרי כדפי' התם: ליטול מהן אוד. נראה לר"ת כפירוש ה"ג דאסירי משום תיקוני מנא דלפירו' זה (ד) דאע"ג דלא מתקצא ליה גזרינן שלא יבא לידי תיקון כלי: עצמות וקליפין. לא כפירוש הקונטרס דפירש אפילו קשין ואין ראויין לאכילת כלבים [ס]דהאי תנא אמרינן בגמרא דכרבי שמעון סבירא ליה ור"ש בעי לכל הפחות ראויות למאכל בהמה דקתני מעבירין מעל השלחן פירורין כו' מפני שהוא מאכל בהמה ומוקמינן בגמרא כוותיה: אנו אין לנו אלא ב"ש כר"י כו'. במסכת עדיות לא מיתניא בהדי קולי ב"ש וחומרי ב"ה והיינו כרב נחמן והא דלא מייתי סייעתא מהתם משום דמאי אולמא דהא מהא: פירורין שאין בהן כזית אסור לאבדן ביד. פי' בקונט' מדקתני מעבירין ולא קתני זורקין וקשה לרבי דברישא נמי קתני מגביהין מעל השלחן עצמות וקליפין ולא קתני זורקין אע"פ שמותר לאבדן ביד ועוד דאמרינן בברכות בריש אלו דברים (דף נב:) וב"ה אומרים אם שמש ת"ח הוא נוטל פירורין שיש בהן כזית ומניח פירורין שאין בהן כזית ומסייע ליה לר' יוחנן דאמר פירורין שאין בהן כזית מותר לאבדן ביד ואי אפשר ליגרס התם אסור [ע]ונראה לר' דהכא גרסי' מותר ודייק מדאצטריך למיתני מפני שהוא מאכל בהמה דהיינו משמע דלא חזי לאדם והוו כשאר מאכל בהמה ומותר לאבדן. מ"ר: ואם לאו אין מקנחין בו. אית ספרים דגרסי וחכ"א בין כך ובין כך מקנחין בו ולא יתכן דאמר בגמרא דבאין לו עור בית אחיזה אפילו ר"ש מודה דאסור משום דפסיק רישיה הוא וה"ר יצחק מדנפירא גרס בין כך ובין כך אין מקנחין בו כרבי יהודה דאמר דבר שאין מתכוין אסור ואין נראה לר"י דהא בגמרא משמע דברישא מודה ר' יהודה (ה) דאמר אימא סיפא ספוג אם יש לו עור בית אחיזה מקנחין בו ואם לאו אין מקנחין בו אתאן לרבי יהודה אם כן בין כך ובין כך אין מקנחין בו לא רבי יהודה ולא ר' שמעון אלא ודאי לא גרסינן ליה כלל. מ"ר: שמואל מטלטל להו אגב ריפתא. אף על גב דכר"ש סבירא ליה דשרי לקמן בפרק בתרא (דף קנו:) נבלה שנתנבלה בשבת מיהו מחמיר היה משום דהוה אדם חשוב כאביי ורבא דלעיל. ר"ת: רבא מטלטל להו אגב לקנא דמיא. ואם תאמר והא רבא סבר לעיל כר"י דאית ליה מוקצה ואנוחי לקנא דמיא היכי שרי לכתחילה ויש לומר דשני לן בין היכא דאפשר למיעבד האי טלטול מאתמול להיכא דלא אפשר דכיפין ובר יונה היו מאתמול בידו והיה יכול לטלטלם אבל הני גרעיני תמרה לא אפשר ושרי אפילו לרבי יהודה ואף לאדם חשוב דאמר בביצה פרק יו"ט (דף כא:) דאמר ליה אביי לרב יוסף הני סופלי לחיותא היכי שדינן ביומא טבא לרבי יוסי דאמר לכם ולא לכלבים חזיין להסקה כו' בשבת מאי איכא למימר מטלטלין להו אגב ריפתא כדשמואל אלמא דאפילו רב יוסף דלא בעי למישרי לעיל אגב כפא וסכינא אפילו דבר הראוי לאדם שרי התם גרעיני תמרה אגב ריפתא:

הדרן עלך נוטל אדם את בנו

עין משפט נר מצוה

יט א מיי' פ"ד מהל' י"ט הלכה יב סמג לאוין עה טוש"ע א"ח סי' תקז סעיף ג:

כ ב מיי' פכ"ו מהלכות שבת הלכה טז סמג לאוין סה טוש"ע א"ח סי' שח סעיף כז:

כא ג מיי' פכ"ב שם הלכה טו סמג שם טוש"ע א"ח סי' שכ סעיף יז:

כב ד מיי' פ"ז מהל' ברכות הלכה ט טוש"ע א"ח סי' קפ סעיף ד:

כג ה מיי' פכ"ה מהל' שבת הלכה יג סמג לאוין סה טוש"ע א"ח סי' שח סעיף לב:

כד ו מיי' פ"ז מהלכות ברכות הל' ט טוש"ע א"ח סי' קעא סעיף ב:

כה ז מיי' פכ"ו מהל' שבת הלכה יג סמג לאוין סה טוש"ע א"ח סי' שח סעיף כז:

כו ח מיי' פכ"ו שם הל' יח טוש"ע שם סעיף ל:

מסורת הש"ס

א) ביצה לג. ושם, ב) (שם לב.) לעיל כט: וקכד:, ג) לקמן קנו. [ביצה ב. תוספ' פ"ו ממחי מליפכא ע"ש], ד) פ"ח מגביהין, ה) [ע' תוס' ביצה ב. ד"ה וכ"ת], ו) פ"ז ל"ג, ז) כ"א מקנחין בו וניטל, ח) [לקמן קנו. ע"ש ביצה ב.], ט) ברכות נב: ע"ש, י) לעיל עה. קג. קיא: קח. קלג., כ) [ביצה לג:], ל) כתובות כה: [ביצה לו.], מ) [ביצה כא: ד"ה רבא], נ) [ביצה לו:], ס) [תוספ' פי"ז], ע) [ע' תוס' ביצה ב. ד"ה מגביהין], פ) [ע' תוס' מנחות ד"ה ולימא ודוחק לאמרי דזהו מסוגיות הפוסקים].

הגהות הב"ח

(א) במשנה מעבירין מעל השלחן פירורין: (ב) שם מקנחין בו (וחכ"א וכו' עד סופה) תא"מ וגי' רש"י ותוספות ולפסי' לא גרסי וחכ"א אבל מפי' המשניות להרמב"ם משמע דגרס לה: (ג) גמ' מעבירין מעל השלחן פירורין: (ד) תוס' ד"ה ליטול וכו' לפירוש זה אע"ג: (ה) ד"ה ואם וכו' מודה ר' יהודה דאמרינן אימא:

רבינו חננאל

פי' החבית מטה על צדה והיא נופלת. אמר רב הונא אמר רב לא שנו אלא בשוכח אבל במניח נעשה בסיס לדבר האסור. פי' נעשית החבית בסיס לאבן ואסור להטות החבית כלל. והלכתא כוותיה דרבא דר' אמי אמר ר' יוחנן קאי כוותיה. בפרק כל הכלים: היתה בין החביות מגביה ומטה על צדה כו'. תניא (א') ר' יוסי אומר היתה החבית מונחת באוצר או שהיו כלי זכוכית מונחין תחתיה מגביהה למקום אחר ומטה על צדה ונוטל מה שצריך לו ומחזירה למקומה. מעות שעל הכר נמי אוקמה משמ' דרב בשוכח אבל במניח נעשה הכר בסיס למעות ואסור אפילו לנערן ואמר רבה משמיה דר' יוחנן לא שנו אלא לצורך גופו כגון שצריך (סבר) לישב עליו אבל אם הוא צריך למקומו מטלטלו ועודן עליו. וכן תני חייא בר רב מדפתי היה ההוא דא"ר הושעיא שכח ארנקי בחצר ור' יצחק דאמר שכח לבינה בחצר ויהודה בר שילא דאמר שכחו דסקיא מלאה מעות בסטין ואמרו שמניח עליה ככר או תינוק ומטלטלו ואמר מר זוטרא הלכתא ככל הני שמעתתא בשכח ולית הלכתא כוותייהו אלא הלכתא כרב אשי דהוא בתראה דאמר לא אמרו ככר או תינוק אלא למת בלבד. אביי מנח כפא פי' תרווד אכיפי הן כגון כיפה של צמר ורבא מנח סכינא אבר יונה והוא מליח אבל היה מבושל והיה מטלטל בן יונה אגב סכינא אמר שאלו מותרין לטלטלן בשבת דתניא בראשונה היו אומרים ג' כלים

רב נסים גאון

להרים: רבא כר' נתן סבירא ליה דאמר חי נושא את עצמו. עיקר דבריו של ר' נתן בפרק המצניע (דף צד) דתנן ר' נתן אומר על שהוציא חייב על החיים פטור מפני שהחי נושא את עצמו. רבא כר' שמעון סבירא ליה דאמר מלאכה שאינה צריכה לגופה פטור עליה ועיקר דבריו של ר' שמעון גם בפרק המצניע (דף צג) דתנן וכן כזית מן המת וכעדשה מן השרץ חייב ור' שמעון פוטר וגרסי' בגמ' אמר רבה אמר ר' יוחנן ורב יוסף אמר ריש לקיש פוטר היה ר' שמעון אף במוציא את המת לקוברו וכבר פירשנו זה בפרק יציאות השבת: הכי נמי מסתברא דרבא כר' יהודה סבירא ליה דדרש רבא אשה לא תכנס לבין העצים ליטול מהן אוד ואוד שנשבר ביום טוב אסור להסיקו לפי שמסיקין בכלים ואין מסיקין בשברי כלים והא שוה לדברי ר' יהודה שאמר במשנה בפ' במה מדליקין (דף כט) ואין מסיקין בשברי כלים דברי ר' יהודה הואיל וסבירא ליה כוותיה בנולד במוקצה נמי דתנן בסוף מסכתא (לקמן דף קנו) ר' יהודה אומר אם לא היתה נבילה מערב שבת אסורה לפי שאינה מן המוכן

(וחכמים אומרים) בֵּין כָּךְ וּבֵין כָּךְ נִיטָּל בְּשַׁבָּת – **In either case, it may be taken on the Sabbath** when it is dry,[9] וְאֵינוֹ מְקַבֵּל טוּמְאָה – **and it is not susceptible to *tumah*.**[10]

Gemara The Mishnah cited Beis Shammai as taking a lenient stand concerning *muktzeh*, allowing one to handle bones and husks directly, and Beis Hillel as taking a stringent stand in this regard. The Gemara reports a version of the Mishnah that reverses their opinions:

אָמַר רַב נַחְמָן – **Rav Nachman said:** אָנוּ אֵין לָנוּ אֶלָּא בֵּית שַׁמַּאי כְּרַבִּי יְהוּדָה – **We have no** reliance on this version of the Mishnah, **but rather,** on the following version, which I heard from my masters:[11] **Beis Shammai** rule **like R' Yehudah,** who applies *muktzeh* broadly, and they prohibit the direct handling of bones and husks, וּבֵית הִלֵּל כְּרַבִּי שִׁמְעוֹן – **while Beis Hillel** rule **like R' Shimon** who does not apply *muktzeh* broadly, and they permit this practice. Thus, the Mishnah should read that Beis Shammai say one must take up the entire table board and shake it clean, whereas Beis Hillel say we may remove bones and husks from the table by hand.[12]

The Mishnah continued:

מַעֲבִירִין (מלפני) [מֵעַל] הַשֻּׁלְחָן פֵּירוּרִין – **WE MAY REMOVE FROM THE TABLE CRUMBS** that are smaller than a *kezayis.*

The Gemara draws an inference from the Mishnah:

מְסַיֵּיע לֵיהּ לְרַבִּי יוֹחָנָן – This Mishnah is **a support to R' Yochanan,** דְּאָמַר רַבִּי יוֹחָנָן – **for R' Yochanan said:** פֵּירוּרִין שֶׁאֵין בָּהֶן כְּזַיִת אָסוּר לְאַבְּדָן בַּיָּד – Even **crumbs that are smaller than a *kezayis* may not be destroyed manually.** Rather, they must be treated in a manner befitting food remnants. The Mishnah supports this rule, since it implies that the crumbs may be removed from the table but may not be discarded.[13]

The Mishnah continued:

שֶׁעָר שֶׁל אֲפוּנִין – We may remove from the table . . . **PEA PODS** and lentil pods, because they are fit for use as animal fodder.

The Gemara analyzes this ruling and contrasts it with the Mishnah's later ruling:

מַנִּי – **Who is [the Tanna]** whose opinion this reflects? רַבִּי שִׁמְעוֹן הִיא דְּלֵית לֵיהּ מוּקְצֶה – **[The ruling] is** reflective of the opinion of **R' Shimon, who does not accept** a broad application of ***muktzeh.*** According to R' Yehudah, however, the pods are *muktzeh*.[14] אֵימָא סֵיפָא – But **consider the latter clause** of the Mishnah: סְפוֹג – **A SPONGE** – אִם יֵשׁ לוֹ בֵּית אֲחִיזָה מְקַנְּחִין בּוֹ – **IF IT HAS A** leather **HANDLE, WE MAY WIPE** a table **WITH IT.** וְאִם לָאו אֵין מְקַנְּחִין בּוֹ – **BUT IF NOT, WE MAY NOT WIPE** a table **WITH IT.** Presumably, the reason this is forbidden is that while grasping the sponge one might inadvertently squeeze out some water. אֲתָאן לְרַבִּי יְהוּדָה – In this segment of the Mishnah, **we have arrived at** the opinion of **R' Yehudah,** דְּאָמַר דָּבָר שֶׁאֵין מִתְכַּוֵּין אָסוּר – **who said** that **something that is unintended is prohibited.** R' Shimon, however, permits doing an act that might unintentionally result in the violation of a prohibition.[15] How could the Mishnah have stated two consecutive rulings that reflect the views of conflicting Tannaim?

NOTES

9. [Although we may not wipe with a wet sponge that has no handle,] since a sponge is a utensil it may be moved about on the Sabbath when it is dry [and no concern for wringing exists] (*Rashi*). However, since the primary function of a bare sponge [i.e. wiping a table while wet] is prohibited on the Sabbath, the sponge is classified as a כְּלִי שֶׁמְּלַאכְתּוֹ לְאִיסּוּר (a forbidden-use utensil). As we learned above (124a), this type of utensil may be moved only for the sake of its use in a permissible capacity or for the sake of its place (*Ritva MHK* ed.; *Pri Megadim – Eishel Avraham* 320:22; *Chasam Sofer; cf. Sfas Emes*).

[*Rashi's* text did not include the words וַחֲכָמִים אוֹמְרִים. See *Bach* and *Tosafos* ד״ה ואם לאו; cf. *Rambam, Commentary.*]

10. *Tumah* contamination of utensils is limited by the Torah to garments, metal utensils, leather goods, and wooden utensils (see *Numbers* 31:20,22). Since a sponge does not fit into any of these categories, it is not susceptible to *tumah* (*Rashi*).

11. *Rashi* to *Beitzah* 2a.

12. Rav Nachman's revised version of the dispute appears in Tosefta (17:4). It is further substantiated by the Mishnahs in Tractate *Eduyos* (Chs.4,5), in which the instances that Beis Hillel's rulings are more stringent than those of Beis Shammai are enumerated. Our Mishnah is conspicuously absent, implying that here, too, Beis Hillel rule leniently regarding *muktzeh* while Beis Shammai rule stringently, as is true in the vast majority of cases (see *Tosafos* ד״ה אנו אין לנו and *Chasam Sofer*).

13. Since the Mishnah stated מַעֲבִירִין, *We may remove* crumbs that are smaller than a *kezayis,* rather than זוֹרְקִין, *We may throw* the crumbs off the table, it implies that the crumbs must not be discarded indiscriminately (*Rashi,* as explained by *Tosafos* ד״ה פירורין).

Tosafos reject this explanation for two reasons. Firstly, the Mishnah used the phrase מַעֲבִירִין even in its first clause concerning husks and bones, which may certainly be discarded indiscriminately. Moreover, the text of the parallel Gemara in Tractate *Berachos* (52b) has R' Yochanan *allowing* the discarding of crumbs that are smaller than a *kezayis* – and the correctness of that reading is borne out by the Gemara's discussion there! *Tosafos* therefore emend the text here to match the reading in *Berachos.* They explain our Gemara as meaning that since the Mishnah describes the small crumbs as animal fodder, it supports R' Yochanan's ruling that such crumbs *may* be discarded, like anything else that is unfit for human consumption.

Numerous commentators explain that according to *Rashi* R' Yochanan taught *two* rulings. In Tractate *Berachos* he taught that small crumbs *may* be destroyed, and here he taught that they may *not* be destroyed. The intent is that it is permissible to discard small crumbs in an area where they will not be stepped on, but it is forbidden to discard them where they will be stepped on, for it is improper to treat edible remnants with such disregard. Our Gemara means that since the Mishnah states that small crumbs may be *removed* from the table, it implies that they should not be swept off the table to the floor, since people might step on them there. Rather, they should be taken to a location where they can be disposed of properly. In the first clause, where the Mishnah stated that bones and husks may be *removed* from the table, it meant to imply that they *need not* be discarded immediately, but may be carried to a trash bin. [Although the permit to move them is based on their repulsiveness, once moving them one is allowed to carry them to a convenient disposal area – see note 23 and 124a note 20] (*Chasam Sofer;* see also *Magen Avraham* 180:3 and *Maginei Shlomo;* see *Beur Halachah* cited in note 5). [*Rashi's* words here (ד״ה אסור לאבדן ביד) seem to support this interpretation.]

14. Since the pea pods were part of the produce, and thus deemed human food at the onset of the Sabbath, and by being separated from the edible peas they have become designated as animal fodder during the Sabbath, they fall under the category of *nolad* (see note 3 and 142b note 31). R' Yehudah, who includes *nolad* in the class of items that are *muktzeh,* would prohibit handling the pods. Thus, the Mishnah follows the opinion of R' Shimon, who does not classify *nolad* as *muktzeh* (see *Rashi* and *Mishnah Berurah* 495:17).

15. When a person performs a permissible act and as a result a second, forbidden act also takes place, this second act is classified as דָּבָר שֶׁאֵין מִתְכַּוֵּין, *something that is unintended.* The person was *aware* that the prohibited act might occur but he did not *intend* for it to occur. Consider, for example, the case of dragging a heavy bench across an unpaved courtyard, where one might thereby create a furrow in the ground – an action that would qualify as a *toladah* of either *plowing* or *building* (see 73b). R' Yehudah prohibits the performance of the permitted act (dragging the bench), since it might result in the performance of the forbidden labor (creating the furrow). R' Shimon, however, allows the person to perform the permitted act as long as he does not intend to do the forbidden labor (see above, 29b, 41b).

In our case, as well, the person performs a permissible act of wiping a table with a damp sponge. He does not intend to squeeze water out of the sponge (*Rashi*), but only to wipe away the surface dirt. Since the

התם כיון דמסרח דעתיה עילויה מאתמול הכי נמי מסתברא דרבא כר' יהודה סבירא ליה א דדרש רבא אשה לא תכנס לבית העצים ליטול מהן אוד ואוד שנשבר אסור להסיקו ביום טוב לפי ב שמסיקין בכלים ואין מסיקין בשברי כלים שמע מינה: **מתני'** ג ב"ש אומרים ד מעבירין מעל השלחן עצמות וקליפין וב"ה אומרים ה מסלק את הטבלא כולה ומנערה מעבירין (א) מלפני השלחן פירורין פחות מכזית ושער של אפונין ושער עדשים מפני שהוא מאכל בהמה ג ספוג אם יש לו עור בית אחיזה מקנחין בו ואם לאו אין מקנחין בו (ב) ו (וחכמים אומרים) בין כך ובין כך ניטל בשבת ואינו מקבל טומאה: **גמ'** ז אמר רב נחמן אנו אין לנו אלא ב"ש כרבי יהודה וב"ה כרבי שמעון: מעבירין (ג) מלפני השלחן פירורין: מסייע ליה לר' יוחנן ד דאמר רבי יוחנן פירורין שאין בהן כזית אסור לאבדן ביד: שער של אפונין: מני ר"ש היא דלית ליה מוקצה אימא סיפא ספוג אם יש לו בית אחיזה מקנחין בו ואם לאו אין מקנחין בו אתאן לר' יהודה דאמר דבר שאין מתכוין אסור בהא אפילו ר"ש מודה ח דאביי ורבא דאמרי תרוייהו מודה ר"ש בפסיק רישיה ולא ימות ה הני גרעינין דתמרי ארמייתא שרו לטלטולינהו הואיל וחזיין אגב אמן ודפרסייתא אסור שמואל מטלטל להו אגב ריפתא: (שרנ"ם שפ"ז סימן): שמואל לטעמיה ט דאמר שמואל ו עושה אדם כל צרכו בפת י רבה מטלטל להו אגב לקנא דמיא רב הונא בריה דרב יהושע עביד להו כגרף של ריעי א"ל רב אשי לאמימר מ ז וכי עושין גרף של ריעי לכתחילה רב ששת זריק להו בלישניה רב פפא זריק להו אחורי המטה י אמרו עליו על רבי זכריה בן אבקולם ח שהיה מחזיר פניו אחורי המטה וזורקן:

הדרן עלך נוטל אדם את בנו

רש"י

התם כיון דמסרח. מעיקרא לא מלגע ליה עד אורתא: **מאתמול דעתיה עליה.** לשורלה ובין השמשות נמי מוכן לבהמה הוה: **אוד.** פורגו"ן דקסם עלים להסקה ניתנו ולא לטלטול כלי: **ואוד שנשבר.** ביו"ט: **בשברי כלים.** שנשברו היום דהוו להו נולד: **ש"מ.** דכרבי יהודה סבירא ליה דלית ליה מוקלה: **מתני' מעבירין.** בידים מעל השלחן: **עצמות.** קשין שאין ראוין לכלב: **וקליפין.** של אגוזים דלית להו לב"ש מוקלה: **וב"ה אומרים מסלק את הטבלא.** שיש תורת כלי עליה אבל לא יטלטל הקליפין בידים כרבי יהודה: **מעבירין מעל השלחן.** סתמא היא: **פירורין פחות מכזית.** וכ"ש כזית דלמפרע טעמא שהם מאכל בהמה: **ושער של אפונין.** שרביטין של קטנית שקטניות גדל בהם: **אפונין.** יש"ש: **עור בית אחיזה.** [בית אחיזה] של עור שיאחזנו בו: **מקנחין בו.** טבלא. שכשאוחזו נסחט בין אלבעותיו: **ניטל בשבת.** כשהוא נגוב: **ואינו מקבל טומאה.** דלאו לא כלי עץ ולא בגד ולא שק ולא מתכת: **גמ' אנו אין לנו.** אין אנו סומכין על משנתינו כמות שהיא שנויה אלא מוחלפת שיטתה וב"ש כרבי יהודה כו': **אסור לאבדן ביד.** מדקתני מעבירין בידים ולא זריק להו: **מוקלה.** דלאי ר' יהודה מאתמול לאו לבהמה קיימי שהרי האוכל היה עמהן והיום לוקח מהם: **שאין מתכוין.** לסחוט: **גרעינין.** של תמרים והם לבהמה: **ארמייתא.** תמרים רעים הם ומאכילין התמרים עלמן לבהמה הלכך אגב אימיהו לבהמה נמי קיימי: **פרסייתא.** תמרים טובים הם ואין מאכילין אותן לבהמה: **כל צרכו.** משתמש בו ואין כאן משום בזיון וממחהו בתבשיל: **לקנא דמיא.** ספל של מים: **גרף של ריעי.** לוברן לפניו כשאוכל התמרים עד שנמאסות בעיניו ונוטלין אותן מפניו כגרף של ריעי ונותנן לבהמה: **זריק להו בלישניה.** אל עבר השלחן: **אחורי המטה.** שהוא מיסב עליה:

הדרן עלך נוטל

תוספות

התם כיון דמסרח. ומתקלקל ואין ראוי למאכל אדם מאתמול דעתיה עילויה ליתנו לבהמה אע"ג דבשער של אפונין ושל עדשים אסרינן לרבי יהודה אע"ג דחזו למאכל בהמה וכן גרעינין לעיל בפרק במה מדליקין (דף כט.) דאמרינן לרבי יהודה אבלן אין מסיקין בגרעינין מ"מ הכא שרי כדפי' התם: **ליטול** מהן אוד. נראה לר"ת כפירוש ה"ג דאסירי משום תיקוני מנא דלפירו' זה (ד) דאע"ג דלא מתקלא ליה גזרינן שלא יבא לידי תיקון כלי: **עצמות** וקליפין. לא כפירוש הקונטרס דפירש אפילו קשין ואין ראוין לאכילת כלבים ס) דהאי תנא אמרינן בגמרא דכרבי שמעון סבירא ליה ור"ש בעי לכל הפחות ראויות למאכל בהמה דקתני מעבירין מעל השלחן פירורין כו' מפני שהוא מאכל בהמה ומוקמינן בגמרא כוותיה: **אנו** אין לנו אלא ב"ש כר"י כו'. במסכת עדיות לא מיתניא בהדי קולי ב"ש וחומרי ב"ה והיינו כרב נחמן והא דלא מייתי סייעתא מהתם משום דמאי אולמא דהא מהא: **פירורין** שאין בהן כזית אסור לאבדן ביד. פי' בקונט' מדקתני מעבירין ולא קתני זורקין וקשה לרבי דברישא נמי קתני מגביהין מעל השלחן עצמות וקליפין ולא קתני זורקין אע"פ שמותר לאבדן ביד ועוד דאמרינן בברכות בריש אלו דברים (דף נב:) וב"ה אומרים אם שמש ת"ח הוא נוטל פירורין שיש בהן כזית ומניח פירורין שאין בהן כזית ומסייע ליה לר' יוחנן דאמר פירורין שאין בהן כזית מותר לאבדן ביד ואי אפשר ליגרס התם אסור י) ונראה לר' דהכא גרסי' מותר ודייק מדאצטריך למיתני מפני שהוא מאכל בהמה דהיינו משמע דלא חזי לאדם והוו כשאר מאכל בהמה ומותר לאבדן. מ"ר: **ואם** לאו אין מקנחין בו. אית ספרים דגרסי וחכ"א בין כך ובין כך מקנחין בו ולא יתכן דאמר בגמרא דבאין לו עור בית אחיזה אפילו ר"ש מודה דאסור משום דפסיק רישיה הוא וה"ר יצחק מדנפירא גרס בין כך ובין כך אין מקנחין בו כרבי יהודה דאמר דבר שאין מתכוין אסור ואין נראה לר"י דהא בגמרא משמע דברישא מודה ר' יהודה (ה) דאמר אימא סיפא ספוג אם יש לו עור בית אחיזה מקנחין בו ואם לאו אין מקנחין בו אתאן לרבי יהודה אם כן בין כך ובין כך אין מקנחין בו לא רבי יהודה ולא ר' שמעון אלא ודאי לא גרסינן ליה כלל. מ"ר: **שמואל** מטלטל להו אגב ריפתא. אף על גב דכר"ש סבירא ליה דשרי לקמן בפרק בתרא (דף קנו:) נבלה שנתנבלה בשבת מיהו מחמיר היה משום דהוה אדם חשוב כאביי ורבא דלעיל. ר"ת: **רבא** מטלטל להו אגב לקנא דמיא. ואם תאמר והא רבא סבר לעיל כר"י דאית ליה מוקצה ואנוחי לקנא דמיא היכי שרי לכתחילה ויש לומר דשני לן בין היכא דאפשר למיעבד האי טלטול מאתמול להיכא דלא אפשר דכיפין ובר יונה היו מאתמול בידו והיה יכול לטלטלם אבל הני גרעיני תמרה לא אפשר ושרי אפילו לרבי יהודה ואף לאדם חשוב דאמר בביצה פרק יו"ט (דף כא:) דאמר ליה אביי לרב יוסף הני סופלי לחיותא היכי שדינן ביומא טבא לרבי יוסי דאמר לכס ולא לכלבים חזיין להסקה כו' בשבת מאי איכא למימר מטלטלין להו אגב ריפתא כדשמואל אלמא דאפילו רב יוסף דלא בעי למישרי לעיל אגב כפא וסכינא אפילו דבר הראוי לאדם שרי התם גרעיני תמרה אגב ריפתא:

הדרן עלך נוטל אדם את בנו

מסורת הש"ס

א) ביצה לג. ושם, ב) [שם לב:], לעיל כט: וקכד:, ג) לקמן קמז. [ביצה ב. תוספ' פי"ח], ד) [ער' תוס' ביצה ב.], ה) מגביהין, ו) [עי' תוס'], ז) נ"ל מקנחין בו וכו', ח) לקמן קמז. ע"ש, ט) לעיל עה. כתובות ו. בכורות כה. [ביצה לו.], י) ברכות נ: לעיל ג: ביצה כא:, כ) [ג"ל רבא עי' תוס' ד"ה רבא], ל) [ביצה שם. לו:], מ) [תוספ' פי"ז], נ) [עי' תוס' ביצה ב.], ס) [עי' תוס' מנחות נח:]

הגהות הב"ח

(א) במשנה מעבירין מעל השלחן פירורין: (ב) שם מקנחין בו (וחכ"א) תא"מ וכ"כ רש"י ותוספות ולפניהם לא גרסי וחכ"א אבל מפי' המשניות משמע דגרס להרמב"ם: (ג) גמ' מעבירין מעל השלחן פירורין: (ד) תוס' ד"ה ליטול וכו' דלפירוש זה אע"ג: (ה) ד"ה ואם לאו וכו' מודה ר' יהודה דאמרינן אימא:

רב נסים גאון

להרים: **רבא** כר' נתן סבירא ליה דאמר חי נושא את עצמו. עיקר דבריו של ר' נתן בפרק המצניע (דף צד) ר' נתן אומר על השוחט חייב על החיים פטור מפני שהחי נושא את עצמו. רבא כר' שמעון סבירא ליה דאמר מלאכה שאינה צריכה לגופה פטור עליה ועיקר דבריו של ר' שמעון גם בפרק המצניע (דף צג) דתנן וכן כזית מן המת וכעדשה מן השרץ חייב ור' שמעון פוטר וגרסי' בגמ' אמר רבה אמר ר' יוחנן ורב יוסף אמר ר' שמעון בן לקיש פוטר היה ר' שמעון אף במוציא את המת לקוברו וכבר פירשנו זה בפרק יציאות השבת: **הכי נמי** מסתברא דרבא כר' יהודה סבירא ליה דדרש רבא אשה לא תכנס לבין העצים ליטול מהן אוד ואוד שנשבר ביום טוב אסור להסיקו לפי שמסיקים בכלים ואין מסיקין בשברי כלים וזה שוה לדברי ר' יהודה שאמר במשנה בפ' במה מדליקין (ד' כט) ואין מסיקין בשברי כלים דברי ר' יהודה הואיל וסבירא ליה כוותיה בנולד במוקצה נמי דתנן בסוף מסכתא (לקמן דף קנו) ר' יהודה אומר אם לא היתה נבלה מערב שבת אסורה לפי שאינה מן המוכן כר' יהודה סבירא ליה ולכך אמר סכינא אבר יונה למה לי הא חזי לאומצא דדייקא מינה הא לא חזי לאומצא לא וכמו שאמר בתחילת מסכת יום טוב (דף ב) דאית ליה מוקצה אית ליה נולד ודלית ליה מוקצה לית ליה נולד כי הכלל עיקר אחד חוזר והיא ההכנה: **אמר** רב נחמן אנו אין לנו אלא בית שמאי כרבי יהודה ובית הלל כרבי שמעון וכן אמרו עוד מני ר' שמעון היא דלית ליה מוקצה ועיקר דברי רבי יהודה ור' שמעון בפרק כירה וכבר פירשנו למעלה. אתאן לרבי יהודה דאמר דבר שאין מתכוין אסור עיקר דבריו של ר' יהודה במשנה במסכת בכורות (דף לג) ובמס' יום טוב (דף כג) וכבר פירשנו דבריו גם במס' זו בפ' כירה: **סליק פרק נוטל**

עין משפט נר מצוה

יט א מיי' פכ"ו מהל' שבת הלכה יח סמג לאוין סה טוש"ע א"ח סי' שח סעיף ג:
כ ב מיי' פכ"ה מהלכות שבת הלכה טו סמג לאוין סה טוש"ע א"ח סי' שח סעיף כז:
כא ג מיי' פכ"ב שם הלכה טו סמג שם טוש"ע א"ח סי' שכ סעיף יז:
כב ד מיי' פ"ז מהל' ברכות הלכה יא טוש"ע א"ח סי' קפ סעיף ד:
כג ה מיי' פכ"ו מהל' שבת הלכה טו סמג לאוין סה טוש"ע א"ח סי' שח סעיף לב:
כד ו מיי' פ"ז מהלכות ברכות הל' ט טוש"ע א"ח סי' קעא סעיף א:
כה ז מיי' פכ"ה מהל' שבת הלכה כד ופכ"ו הלכה יג סמג לאוין סה טוש"ע א"ח סי' שח סעיף לג:
כו ח מיי' פכ"ו שם הל' ט טוש"ע שם סעיף ל:

רבינו חננאל

פי' החבית מטה על צדה והיא נופלת. אמר רב הונא אמר רב לא שנו אלא בשוכח אבל במניח נעשה בסיס לדבר האסור. פי' נעשית החבית בין לאבן ואסור להטות החבית כלל. והלכתא כוותיה דרבא דר' אמי אמר ר' יוחנן קאי כוותיה. בפרק כל הכלים: היתה בין החביות מגביהה ומטה על צדה כו'. תנא (א') ר' יוסי אומר אם היתה החבית מונחת באוצר או שהיו כלי זכוכית מונחין תחתיה מגביהה למקום אחר ומטה על צדה ונוטל מה שצריך לו ומחזירה למקומה. מעות שעל הכר נמי אוקמה משמי' דרב בשוכח אבל במניח נעשה הכר בסיס למעות ואסור אפילו לנערן ואמר רבה משמיה דר' יוחנן לא שנו אלא לצורך גופו כגון שצריך (סבר) לישב עליו אבל אם הוא צריך למקומו מטלטלין ועודן עליו. וכן רבי חייא בר רב מדפתי והא דר' הושעיא שכח ארנקי בחצר ור' יצחק דאמר שכח לבינה בחצר ויהודה בר שילא דאמר שכחו דסקיא מלאה מעות בסטן ואמרו שמניח עליה ככר או תינוק ומטלטלו ואמר מר זוטרא הלכתא ככל הני שמעתתא בשכח ולית הלכתא כוותייהו אלא בשוכח. כרב אשי דהוא בתראה דאמר לא אמרו ככר או תינוק אלא למת בלבד. אביי מנח כפא פי' תרווד אכיפי הן כגון כיפה של צמר ורבא מנח סכינא אבר יונה והוא מליח אבל היה מבושל והיה מטלטל בן יונה אגב סכינא אמר שאלו מותרין לטלטלן בשבת דתניא בראשונה היו אומרים ג' כלים מותרין בשבת מקצוע של דבילה וזומלוסטרין וסכין קטנה שע"ג השולחן וכפה היא זומליסטרון כדתנן ניטלה כיפה טמאה משום מזלג. ואקשינן על רבה טעמא דחזי לאומצא הא לא חזי לאומצא לא דהא מוקצה הוא כלומר כר' יהודה סבירא ליה ולא כר' שמעון דאי ר' שמעון לית ליה מוקצה אלא אפילו בשר תפוח שרי לטלטוליה וכל בשר אחר בין חי בין מליח. ותוב אקשינן עליה ומי סבר לה רבא כר' יהודה והא א"ל רבא לשמעיה טוי לי בר אווזא ביו"ט ושדי מיעיא לשונרא כר' שמעון דאי כר' יהודה הא אמר כל דבר שאינו מוכן לאכילה אסור לטלטלו ואפילו בהמה לא היה מתיר לבודקה אלא באשפה שאם תמצא טריפה יניחנה באשפה. ומסקנא דשמעתא דרבה כר' יהודה ס"ל ופשוטה היא: **מתני'** בה"א מגביהין מעל השולחן עצמות וקליפין וכו'. אמר רב נחמן אנו אין לנו אלא ב"ש כר' יהודה וב"ה כר' שמעון מעבירין מעל גבי השלחן פירורין פחות מכזית מסייע ליה לר' יוחנן דאמר פירורין שאין בהן כזית מותר לאבדן ביד. ספוג אם יש לו עור בית אחיזה מקנחין בו ואם לאו אין מקנחין בו אפילו לר' שמעון דהא אי אפשר שלא לסחוט באחוז בספוג אלא אם יש לו עור בית אחיזה. גרעינין דתמרי. ארמי ארמייתא שרי לטלטולי הואיל וחזיין על גב אימן. פי' רכים הן ונאכלין עם התמרים עצמן. דפרסייתא שמואל מטלטלינהו ואגב ריפתא וכו' שמעתא: **הדרן עלך נוטל אדם**

ליקוטי רש"י

כיון דמסרח. אם יניחם לצורך מחר והיום לא היה צריך להם מאתמול דעתיה עלוייהו להשליכם לבהמות. **אוד.** עץ לעשות אוד למטר פורגי"ן בלע"ז וטעמא משום דלא נתנו אלא להסיק אלא אם ... יום [ביצה לג.]. **שמסיקין בכלים.** ביום טוב שהרי ראוין לטלטל ויטלטל ויתנם לתוך האור [לעיל ...] נמי ניניהו ומטלטלן נמי להסיקן [ביצה לב.]. **ואין מסיקין בשברי כלים.** דהוו להו מוקצין ולא חזו ... שנשברו ביו"ט דהשתא לא חזי לטלטול ולאו משום דחזו להסקה מאתמול לא להכי קיימי [ביצה שם]. ... מעל השלחן עצמות שאינן ראוין לאכילה וקליפי אגוזים ולא חיישינן למוקצה. **ובית הלל אומרים.** אין מטלטלין אותן בידים שמוקצה הן. **מסלק את הטבלא.** שיש תורת כלי עליה ומנערה. **אמר רב נחמן אנו אין לנו.** ... לפי שמוחלפת שיטתה אלא כך שמעתי מרבותינו דבית שמאי כרבי יהודה ומחמרי ובית הלל כרבי שמעון [שם ב.]. **אפילו ר"ש.** דאמר במסכת שבת (מא:) דבר שאין מתכוין מותר [בכורות כה.]. **מודה ר' שמעון בפסיק רישיה** ... כלומר אחתוך ראש בהמה זו בשבת ואיני רוצה שתמות דמתכוין חשיב ליה וכי אמרינן דבר שאין מתכוין מותר כגון היכא דאפשר ליה בלא איסור כגון גורר אדם מטה כסא וספסל ובלבד שלא ... ואף על גב דליכא למיחש דלמא עביד חריץ כיון דלא מתכוין להכי ואפשר לגרירה בלא חריץ כי עביד נמי חריץ דהוי מלאכה גמורה לא מיחייב אבל היכא דודאי עביד מודי [סוכה לג:]. **ארמייתא.** דאין מתבשלות יפה ואין ... ומשתייר בגרעיניהן וחזו לאדם. **ודפרסייתא.** תמרים טובים ומתבשלים יפה וכל אוכל שלהם נפרש מעל גרעיניהן ואין הגרעינין ראוין (לטלטל) [לאכול] [לעיל כט. ע"ש ברש"ש]. **עושה אדם כל צרכו בפת.** ומטלטל על ידי ... בזיון דאוכלין [ביצה כא:]. כל צורכו בין תשמיש בין לפרר אותה ולמחות בתבשיל רותח [לעיל נ:]. **כגרף של ריעי.** שמותר לטלטלו ולפנותו לאשפה מחמת מאוס כדאמרינן בפרק בתרא (ביצה לו:) [ביצה שם]. **גרף.** כלי חרס ... גרף ועביט כלי חרס הן אלא של רעי קרוי גרף ושל מימי רגלים קרוי עביט [ביצה לו:]. **וכי עושין גרף של ריעי לכתחילה.** נהי דכי איתיה קמן מסלקינן ליה אבל לאתויי קמן או למיזל אנן לגביה כי היכי דנמאס עלן ונסלקיה מי שרי [שם כא:]. וכי מותר לגרום שיהא הדבר מאוס לו כדי שיוליכנו [שם לו:].

The Gemara answers:

בְּהָא – In this case of wiping a table with a sponge that has no handle, **אֲפִילוּ רַבִּי שִׁמְעוֹן מוֹדֶה – even R' Shimon concedes** that it is prohibited, **דְּאַבַּיֵי וְרָבָא דְּאָמְרֵי תַּרְוַיְיהוּ – for Abaye and Rava both said: מוֹדֶה רַבִּי שִׁמְעוֹן בִּפְסִיק רֵישֵׁיהּ וְלֹא יָמוּת – R' Shimon agrees** that an act is forbidden **where its forbidden consequence is inevitable.**[16]

The Gemara discusses the *muktzeh* status of another item that is normally used as fodder:

הָנֵי גַּרְעִינִין דְּתַמְרֵי אֲרַמְיָיתָא – The pits of Aramean dates, which are commonly fed to animals – **שְׁרוּ לְטַלְטוּלִינְהוּ – it is permitted to move them** on the Sabbath, **הוֹאִיל וַחֲזִיין אַגַּב אִמָּן – since they were fit** for use as fodder **along with their mothers,** i.e. the dates themselves, at the onset of the Sabbath.[17] **וּדְפַרְסִיָּיתָא אָסוּר – But** the pits **of Persian [dates] may not** be moved on the Sabbath, since at the onset of the Sabbath the dates, including the pits, had been set aside for human consumption.[18]

The Gemara cites a permissible method of removing *muktzeh* pits from one's presence:

שְׁמוּאֵל מְטַלְטֵל לְהוּ אַגַּב רִיפְתָּא – Shmuel would move them on top of a piece of **bread.**[19]

A memory aid is provided:

(שרנ״ם שפ״ז סִימָן – SHaRNaM SHaPaZ is a mnemonic for the names of several sages who devised permissible ways of discarding date pits.)[20]

The Gemara digresses to explain how Shmuel could have used bread for a purpose other than eating:

שְׁמוּאֵל לְטַעְמֵיהּ – Shmuel followed his own reasoning, דְּאָמַר שְׁמוּאֵל – for Shmuel said: עוֹשֶׂה אָדָם כָּל צְרָכָיו בְּפַת – A person may use bread for all his needs. Thus, one may use bread even to transport date pits.[21]

The Gemara now cites the methods by which other Sages discarded date pits:

רַבָּה מְטַלְטֵל לְהוּ אַגַּב לַקְנָא דְּמַיָּא – Rabbah would move them along with a bucket of water.[22] **רַב הוּנָא בְּרֵיהּ דְּרַב יְהוֹשֻׁעַ עָבִיד לְהוּ כִּגְרָף שֶׁל רְעִי – Rav Huna the son of Rav Yehoshua would** pile them up to **make them** repulsive like **a vessel of excrement.** He then relied upon the dispensation for removing a vessel of excrement from one's presence.[23]

The latter practice is rejected:

אָמַר לֵיהּ רַב אַשִׁי לְאַמֵימָר – Rav Ashi said to Ameimar:[24]

NOTES

wringing is an *unintended* consequence of the act, R' Shimon would permit wiping the table. Thus, in forbidding this act, the Mishnah follows the opinion of R' Yehudah.

16. Literally: its head is cut off and it should not die? Although R' Shimon holds that one incurs no liability for a forbidden labor performed unintentionally while one was engaged in a permitted activity, he concedes that liability does occur when the forbidden labor is an inevitable consequence of the permitted action. Hence, if someone cuts off the head of a living creature on the Sabbath, he has violated the prohibition against taking a life on the Sabbath – even if he declares that he does not intend for the creature to die. Since its death is inevitable, he is considered to have taken the creature's life intentionally, and he has transgressed even according to R' Shimon (*Rashi* to *Succah* 33b; *Rambam, Hil. Shabbos* 1:6).

Here, too, since water will surely be extracted when one grasps a sponge with his bare hand, the person is considered to have squeezed out the water intentionally. Thus, if the sponge has no handle, even R' Shimon forbids using it to wipe a table (*Rashi;* see also *Rambam, Hil. Shabbos* 22:15). However, if it has a handle, no water will be wrung out when one grasps it, and it is even possible to wipe a table lightly with it and not wring out water. Therefore, its use is permitted (*Magen Avraham* 320:19; *Mishnah Berurah* 320:47,55; see *Chasam Sofer* to 143b).

Raavad (*Hil. Shabbos* ibid.) objects to this explanation, contending that even if a sponge has a handle the water will inevitably be squeezed out when one wipes the table with it. He therefore explains that a sponge that has a handle is viewed as the equivalent of a bottle of water [since it, too, has been made into a utensil designated to hold water] from which one may empty the contents. A sponge without a handle is, however, viewed as the equivalent of a garment, which may not be wrung out on the Sabbath.

17. Aramean dates were of poor quality and the dates themselves were normally used as fodder (cf. *Rashi* to 29a ד״ה בארמיתא). Thus, at the onset of the Sabbath the dates, including their pits, were prepared for the use of animals. If the pits were separated from the fruit on the Sabbath, they remain fit for the purpose for which they had been prepared. Accordingly, they are not *nolad* and may be moved (*Rashi*). That is, they may be moved even according to R' Yehudah, who considers *nolad* to be *muktzeh* (see *Tosafos* ד״ה שמואל).

18. Persian dates were of superior quality and were reserved for human consumption. At the onset of the Sabbath, therefore, the dates, including their pits, were prepared for the use of humans. Since, according to R' Yehudah, something that was prepared for humans is not considered prepared for animals (see 142b note 30), when the pits are separated from the fruit on the Sabbath and become designated as animal fodder, they are considered *nolad*. Thus, according to R' Yehudah, it is forbidden to move the pits on the Sabbath (see *Rashi* and *Tosafos* ibid.; see *Rashi* above, 29a, for an alternative explanation of the nature of Aramean and Persian dates; see also *Meromei Sadeh*). [See *Ramban, Rashba* and *Ritva MHK* ed., who explain the Gemara's rule as pertaining even according to R' Shimon's opinion. See also *Orach Chaim* 308:30, and see *Beur Halachah* there ד״ה גרעיני תמרים for a discussion concerning the pits of other fruits.]

19. I.e. when removing the pits from his mouth, he would place them on a piece of bread, and he would then carry the bread with the pits on it [to the trash bin, where he would discard the pits] (*Re'ah* to *Beitzah* 21b; see also *Rashba* there). Thus, he avoided handling the pits directly. Now, we shall learn (below, 156b) that Shmuel actually concurs with R' Shimon, according to whom date pits are not *muktzeh* at all (as explained in the previous notes). Nevertheless, since he was a distinguished person, he acted with an added degree of stringency, like Abaye and Rava (above, 142b) (*Tosafos;* see *Orach Chaim* 308:30; cf. *Ramban* et al.).

20. שרנ״ם שפ״ז = ש, **Sh**muel; ר, **R**abbah; נ, Rav Hu**n**a the son of Rav Yehoshua; מ, A**m**eimar; ש, Rav **Sh**eishess; פ, Rav **P**appa; ז, R' **Z**echaryah ben Avkulas. Shmuel's method of moving the pits was just cited. The methods of the other sages will be cited shortly.

21. One need not be concerned that he is treating the bread with disregard by using it for purposes other than eating or by crumbling it into a cooked dish (*Rashi*; see *Rashi* to *Berachos* 50b). However, it is forbidden to use bread or any other food in a manner that might make it repulsive and completely inedible. It is also forbidden to throw [bread or] foods that might thereby be spoiled (see above, 50b, and *Orach Chaim* 171:1 with *Mishnah Berurah*).

22. I.e. he would initially toss them in the bucket, and he would then remove the entire bucket.

Tosafos and some Rishonim have the reading: *Rava* would move them along with a bucket of water (cf. *Rif, Rosh*). The Rishonim ask: Since we concluded above that Rava follows R' Yehudah's opinion concerning *muktzeh* (see note 3), he should not have been allowed to put the pits in the pail in the first place. Furthermore, he should not have been allowed to move the pail with the pits inside it. See *Tosafos* ד״ה רבא, *Ramban* et al. for various resolutions of this difficulty.

23. A special dispensation from the *muktzeh* law was granted for removing items such as a commode from one's presence, to alleviate discomfort (see *Beitzah* 36b). Rav Huna the son of R' Yehoshua, when eating dates, would pile up the pits until there were so many that they were repulsive to him. He would then take advantage of the dispensation for removing repulsive items. Once carrying the pits, he would proceed to offer them to his animals as fodder (*Rashi;* see end of note 13 and *Hagahos R' Akiva Eiger* to *Orach Chaim* 325:11).

24. [Apparently, Ameimar also relied upon this dispensation. This would explain the inclusion of Ameimar in the mnemonic provided above.]

התם כיון דמסרח דעתיה עילויה מאתמול הכי נמי מסתברא דרבא כר' יהודה סבירא ליה דדרש רבא אשה לא תכנס לבית העצים ליטול מהן אוד ואוד שנשבר אסור להסיקו ביום טוב לפי שמסיקין בכלים ואין מסיקין בשברי כלים שמע מינה: **מתני'** ב"ש אומרים מעבירין מעל השלחן עצמות וקליפין וב"ה אומרים מסלק את הטבלא כולה ומנערה מעבירין (א) מלפני השלחן פירורין פחות מכזית ושער של אפונין ושער עדשים מפני שהוא מאכל בהמה ספוג אם יש לו עור בית אחיזה מקנחין בו ואם לאו אין מקנחין בו (ב) (וחכמים אומרים) בין כך ובין כך נוטל בשבת ואינו מקבל טומאה: **גמ'** אמר רב נחמן אנו אין לנו אלא ב"ש כרבי יהודה וב"ה כרבי שמעון: מעבירין (ג) מלפני השלחן פירורין: מסייע ליה לר' יוחנן דאמר רבי יוחנן פירורין שאין בהן כזית אסור לאבדן ביד: שער של אפונין: מני ר"ש היא דלית ליה מוקצה אימא סיפא ספוג אם יש לו בית אחיזה מקנחין בו ואם לאו אין מקנחין בו אתאן לר' יהודה דאמר דבר שאין מתכוין אסור בהא אפילו ר"ש מודה דאביי ורבא דאמרי תרוייהו מודה ר"ש בפסיק רישיה ולא ימות הני גרעינין דתמרי ארמייתא שרו לטלטולינהו הואיל וחזיין אגב אמן ודפרסייתא אסור שמואל מטלטל להו אגב ריפתא: (שרנ"ם שפ"ז סימן): שמואל לטעמיה דאמר שמואל עושה אדם כל צרכו בפת רבה מטלטל להו אגב לקנא דמיא רב הונא בריה דרב יהושע עביד להו כגרף של ריעי א"ל רב אשי לאמימר וכי עושין גרף של ריעי לכתחילה רב ששת זריק להו בלישניה רב פפא זריק להו אחורי המטה אמרו עליו על רבי זכריה בן אבקולם שהיה מחזיר פניו אחורי המטה וזורקן:

הדרן עלך נוטל אדם את בנו

רש"י

התם כיון דמסרח. מעיילא לי מלגע ליה עד אורתא: מאתמול דעתיה עליה. לשורגא ובין השמשות נמי מוכן לבהמה הוה: אוד. פורגו"ן דקסס עלים להסקה ניתנו ולא לטלטול כלי: ואוד שנשבר. ביו"ט: בשברי כלים. שנשברו היום דהוו להו נולד: ש"מ. דכרבי יהודה סבירא ליה דאית ליה מוקצה: **מתני'** מעבירין. בידים מעל השלחן: עצמות. קשין שאין ראויין לכלב: וקליפין. של אגוזים דלית להו לב"ש מוקצה: וב"ה אומרים מסלק את הטבלא. שיש תורת כלי עליה אבל לא יטלטל הקליפין בידים כרבי יהודה: מעבירין מעל השלחן. קמתא היא: פירורין פחות מכזית. וכ"ש כזית כדמפרש טעמא שהם מאכל בהמה: ושער של אפונין. שרביטין של קטנית שהקטנית גדל בהם: אפונין. יש"ש: עור בית אחיזה. [בית אחיזה] של עור שיאחזנו בו: מקנחין בו. טבלא: אין מקנחין בו. שכשאוחזו נסחט בין אצבעותיו: נוטל בשבת. כשהוא נגוב: ואינו מקבל טומאה. דאינו לא כלי עץ ולא בגד ולא שק ולא מתכת: **גמ'** אנו אין לנו. אין אנו סומכין על משנתינו כמות ששנויה אלא מוחלפת שיטתה וב"ש כרבי יהודה כו': אסור לאבדן ביד. מדקתני מעבירין בידים ולא זריק להו: דלית ליה מוקצה. דלר' יהודה מאתמול לאו לבהמה קיימי שהרי האוכל היה עומד והיום לוקח מהם: שאין מתכוין. שאין מתכוין לסחוט: גרעינין. של תמרים והם לבהמה: ארמייתא. תמרים רעים הם ומאכילין התמרים עצמן לבהמה הלכך אגב אימיהו לבהמה נמי קיימי: פרסייתא. תמרים טובים הם ואין מאכילין אותן לבהמה: כל צרכו. משתמש בו ואין כאן משום בזיון ומתמהה כמבשל: לקנא דמיא. ספל של מים: גרף של ריעי. זורקן לפניו כשאוכל התמרים עד שנמאסות בעיניו ונוטלן אותן מפניו כגרף של ריעי ונותנן לבהמה: זריק להו בלישני'. אל עבר השלחן: אחורי המטה. שהוא מיסב עליה:

הדרן עלך נוטל

תוספות

התם כיון דמסרחא. ומתקלקל ואין ראוי למאכל אדם מאתמול דעתיה עילויה ליתנו לבהמה אע"ג דבשער של אפונין ושל עדשים אסרינן לרבי יהודה אע"ג דחזו למאכל בהמה וכן גרעינין דלעיל בפרק במה מדליקין (דף כט.) דאמרינן לרבי יהודה אכלן אין מסיקין בגרעינין מ"מ הכא שרי כדפי' התם: **ליטול** מהן אוד. נראה לר"ת כפירוש ה"ג דאסירי משום תיקוני מנא דלפירו' זה (ד) דאע"ג דלא מתקלא ליה גזרינן שלא יבא לידי תיקון כלי: **עצמות** וקליפין. לא כפירוש הקונטרס דפירש אפילו קשין ואין ראויין לאכילת כלבים דהאי תנא אמרינן בגמרא דכרבי שמעון סבירא ליה ור"ש בעי לכל הפחות ראויות למאכל בהמה דקתני מעבירין מעל השלחן פירורין כו' מפני שהוא מאכל בהמה ומוקמינן בגמרא כוותיה: **אנו** אין לנו אלא ב"ש כר"י כו'. במסכת עדיות לא מיתניא בהדי קולי ב"ש וחומרי ב"ה והיינו כרב נחמן והא דלא מייתי סייעתא מהתם משום דמאי אולמא דהא מהא: **פירורין** שאין בהן כזית אסור לאבדן ביד. פי' בקונט' מדקתני מעבירין ולא קתני זורקין וקשה לרבי דברישא נמי קתני מגביהין מעל השלחן עצמות וקליפין ולא קתני זורקין אע"פ שמותר לאבדן ביד ועוד דאמרינן בברכות בריש אלו דברים (דף נב:) וב"ה אומרים אם שמש ת"ח הוא נוטל פירורין שיש בהן כזית ומניח פירורין שאין בהן כזית ומסייע ליה לר' יוחנן דאמר פירורין שאין בהן כזית מותר לאבדן ביד ואי אפשר ליגרס התם אסור ונראה לר' דהכא גרסי' מותר ודייק מדאצטריך למיתני מפני שהוא מאכל בהמה דהיינו משמע דלא חזי לאדם והוו כשאר מאכל בהמה ומותר לאבדן. מ"ר: **ואם** לאו אין מקנחין בו. אית ספרים דגרסי וחכ"א בין כך ובין כך מקנחין בו ולא יתכן דאמר בגמרא דבאין לו עור בית אחיזה אפילו ר"ש מודה דאסור משום דפסיק רישיה הוא וה"ר יצחק מדנפירא גרס בין כך ובין כך אין מקנחין בו כרבי יהודה דאמר דבר שאין מתכוין אסור ואין נראה לר"י דהא בגמרא משמע דברישא מודה ר' יהודה (ה) דאמר אימא סיפא ספוג אם יש לו עור בית אחיזה מקנחין בו ואם לאו אין מקנחין בו אתאן לרבי יהודה אם כן בין כך ובין כך אין מקנחין בו לא רבי יהודה ולא ר' שמעון אלא ודאי לא גרסינן ליה כלל. מ"ר: **שמואל** מטלטל להו אגב ריפתא. אף על גב דכר"ש סבירא ליה דשרי לקמן בפרק בתרא (דף קנז.) נבלה שנתנבלה בשבת מיהו מחמיר היה משום דהוה אדם חשוב כאביי ורבא דלעיל. ר"ת: **רבא** מטלטל להו אגב לקנא דמיא. ואם תאמר והא רבא סבר לעיל כר"י דלית ליה מוקצה ואנוחי לקנא דמיא היכי שרי לכתחילה ויש לומר דשני לן בין היכא דאפשר למיעבד האי טלטול מאתמול להיכא דלא אפשר דליפתן וכר יונה היו מאתמול בידו והיה יכול לטלטלם אבל הני גרעיני תמרה לא אפשר ושרי אפילו לרבי יהודה ואף לאדם חשוב דאמר בביצה פרק יו"ט (דף כא:) דאמר ליה אביי לרב יוסף הני קופלי לחיותא היכי שדינן ביומא טבא לרבי יוסי דאמר לכם ולא לכלבים חזיין להסקה כו' בשבת מאי איכא למימר מטלטלין להו אגב ריפתא כדשמואל אלמא דאפילו רב יוסף דלא בעי למישרי לעיל אגב כפא וסכינא אפילו דבר הראוי לאדם שרי התם גרעיני תמרה אגב ריפתא:

עין משפט נר מצוה

יט א מיי' פ"ד מהל' י"ט הלכה יא סמג לאוין עה טוש"ע א"ח סי' תקז סעיף ג:
כ ב מיי' פכ"ו מהלכות שבת הלכה טו סמג לאוין סה טוש"ע א"ח סי' שח סעיף כז:
כא ג מיי' פכ"ב שם הלכה טו סמג שם טוש"ע א"ח סי' שכ סעיף יז:
כב ד מיי' פ"ז מהל' ברכות הלכה ט טוש"ע א"ח סי' קפ סעיף ד:
כג ה מיי' פכ"ו מהל' שבת הלכה טו סמג לאוין סה טוש"ע א"ח סי' שח סעיף ל:
כד ו מיי' פ"ז מהלכות ברכות הל' ט טוש"ע א"ח סי' קעא סעיף א:
כה ז מיי' פכ"ה מהל' שבת הל' ג וכ"ו הלכה יג סמג לאוין סה טוש"ע א"ח סי' שח סעיף לו:
כו ח מיי' פכ"ו שם הל' טו טוש"ע א"ח סי' קעא סעיף ג:

מסורת הש"ס

א) ביצה לג. ושם, ב) [שם לב:] לעיל כט:, ג) לקמן קנז. [ביצה ב. תוספ' פ"ד מגביהין], ה) [עי' תוס' לעיל קג. ד"ה ...], ו) ברכות נב: מקנחין בו ... כז) ... ברכות כה. ... לעיל ... ביצה לו. ... כתובות ... פסחים ... רבא עי' תוס' כתובות ו. ד"ה ... ביצה כא. ... תוס' מנחות נג. ד"ה ... דאמרי דהוו מסוגיות הסוגיות.

הגהות הב"ח

(א) במשנה מעבירין מעל השלחן פירורין: (ב) שם מקנחין בו (וחכ"א) תא"מ וכ"נ רש"י ותוספות ולקמיה לא גרסי וחכ"א אבל מפרי המשנה: (ג) גמ' מעבירין מעל השלחן פירורין. נ"ב: (ד) תוס' ד"ה ליטול וכו' דלפירוש זה לאע"ג: (ה) ד"ה ואם לאו וכו' מודה ר' יהודה דלאמרינן אימא:

רבינו חננאל

פי' החבית מטה על צדה והיא נופלת. אמר רב הונא אמר רב לא שנו אלא בשוכח אבל במניח נעשה בסיס לדבר האסור. פי' נעשית החבית בסיס לאבן ואסור להטות החבית כלל. והלכתא כוותיה דרבא דר' אמי אמר ר' יוחנן קאי כוותיה. בפרק כל הכלים. היתה בין החביות מגביה מטה על צדה כו'. תניא (א') ר' יוסי אומר היתה החבית מונחת באוצר או שהיו כלי זכוכית מונחין תחתיה מגביהה למקום אחר ומטה על צדה ונוטל מה שצריך לו ומחזירה למקומה. מעות שעל הכר נמי אוקמה משמ' דרב בשוכח אבל במניח נעשה הכר בסיס למעות ואסור אפילו לנערן ואמר רבה משמיה דר' יוחנן לא שנו אלא לצורך גופו כגון שצריך (סבר) לישב עליו אבל אם הוא צריך למקומו מטלטלין ועודן עליו. וכן תני אביי בר בר מדפתי הא דא"ר הושעיא שכח ארנקי בחצר ור' יצחק דאמר שכח לבינה בחצר ויהודה בר שילא דאמר שכחו דסקיא מלאה מעות ואמרו שמניח עליה ככר או תינוק ומטלטלו ואמר זוטרא הלכתא ככל הני שמעתתא בשכח ולית הלכתא כוותיהו אלא הלכתא כרב אשי דהוא בתראה דאמר לא אמרו ככר או תינוק אלא למת בלבד. אביי מנח כפא אכיפי הן כגון כיפה של צמר ורבא מנח סכינא אבר יונה והוא מליח אבל היה מבושל והיה מטלטל בן יונה אגב סכינא אמר שאלו מותרין לטלטל בשבת דתניא בראשונה היו אומרים ג' כלים מותרין בשבת מקצוע של דבילה וזומלסטרין וסכין קטנה שע"ג השולחן וכפה היא זומליסטרין כדתנן נוטלה כיפה טמאה משום מזלג. ואקשינן על רבה טעמא דחזי לאומצא הא לא חזי לאומצא לא הא מוקצה הוא כלומר כר' יהודה סבירא ליה הא כר' שמעון לית ליה מוקצה ואפילו בשר תפוח שרי לטלטוליה וכל בשר אחר בין חי בין מליח. ותוב אקשינן עליה ומי סבר לה רבא כר' יהודה והא א"ל רבא לשמעיה טוי לי בר אווזא ושדי מעייא לשונרא כר' שמעון דאי כר' יהודה הא אמר כל דבר שאינו מוכן לאכילה אסור לטלטלו ואפילו בהמה לא היה מתיר לבודקה אלא באשה שאם תמצא טריפה יניחנה באשפה. ומסקנא דשמעתתא דרבא כר' יהודה ס"ל ופשוטה היא: מתני' ב"ה אומרים מגביהין מעל השולחן עצמות וקליפין כו'. אמר רב נחמן אנו אין לנו אלא ב"ש כר' יהודה וב"ה כר' שמעון: מעבירין מעל גבי השלחן פירורין פחות מכזית מסייע ליה לר' יוחנן דאמר פירורין שאין בהן כזית מותר לאבדן ביד. ספוג אם יש לו עור בית אחיזה מקנחין בו ואם לאו אין מקנחין בו אפילו לר' שמעון דהא אי אפשר שלא לסחוט. גרעינין דתמרי ארמייתא שרו לטלטולינהו אגב אמן ונאכלין עם התמרים עצמן. דפרסייתא שמואל מטלטל להו אגב ריפתא ורבא אגב לקנא דמיא וכו' שמעתתא:

הדרן עלך נוטל אדם

רב נסים גאון

להרים: רבא כר' נתן סבירא ליה דאמר חי נושא את עצמו. עיקר דבריו של ר' נתן בפרק המצניע (דף צד) ר' נתן אומר על השחוטין חייב על החיים פטור מפני שהחי נושא את עצמו. רבא כר' שמעון סבירא ליה דאמר מלאכה שאינה צריכה לגופה פטור עליה ועיקר דבריו של ר' שמעון גם בפרק המצניע (דף צג) דתנן וכן כזית מן המת וכעדשה מן השרץ חייב ור' שמעון פוטר וגרסי' בגמ' אמר רבה אמר ר' יוחנן ורב יוסף אמר ריש לקיש פוטר היה ר' שמעון אף במוציא את המת לקוברו וכבר פירשנו זה בפרק יציאות השבת: הכי נמי מסתברא דרבא כר' יהודה סבירא ליה דדרש רבא אשה לא תכנס לבית העצים ליטול מהן אוד אוד שנשבר ביום טוב אסור להסיקו לפי שמסיקין בכלים ואין מסיקין בשברי כלים וזה הוא לדברי ר' יהודה שאמר במשנה בפ' במה מדליקין (ד' כט) ואין מסיקין בשברי כלים דברי ר' יהודה הואיל וסבירא ליה כוותיה בנולד במוקצה נמי דתנן בסוף מסכת (לקמן קנו) ר' יהודה אומר אם לא היתה נבילה מערב שבת אסורה לפי שאינה מן המוכן כר' יהודה סבירא ליה ולכך אמר סכינא אבר יונה למה לי הא חזי לאומצא ודייקא מינה הא לא חזי לאומצא לא וכמו שאמר בתחלת מסכת יום טוב (דף ב) דאית ליה מוקצה אית ליה נולד ודלית ליה מוקצה לית ליה נולד כי הכלל עיקר אחד חוזר והיא ההכנה: אמר רב נחמן אנו אין לנו אלא בית שמאי כרבי יהודה ובית הלל כרבי שמעון וכן אמרו עוד מני ר' שמעון היא דלית ליה מוקצה ועיקר דברי רבי יהודה ור' שמעון בפרק כירה (דף מד) ולקמן בפרק מי שהחשיך (דף קנו) אתאן לר' יהודה דאמר דבר שאין מתכוין אסור עיקר דבריו של ר' יהודה במסכת בכורות (דף לד) ובמס' יום טוב (דף כג) וכבר פירשנו דבריו בפ' כירה:

סליק פרק נוטל

ליקוטי רש"י

כיון דמסרח. אם יגיע לערב לא יהא ראוי לאדם הלכך מאתמול דעתיה עלויה להאכילו לבהמה. אוד. עץ לעשות אוד להפך בו את הגחלים ולמוכר ... ואוד שנשבר. ביו"ט ... שמסיקין בכלים. ביום טוב שלם ... ואין מסיקין בשברי כלים. שנשברו היום ... מעבירין. בכלי ... מסלק את הטבלא. שיש תורת כלי עליה ... ובית הלל אומרים. אבל לא יטלטל הקליפין בידים ... פחות מכזית. ... אסור לאבדן ביד ... בפסיק רישיה ולא ימות. ... ארמייתא. ... דפרסייתא. ... עושה אדם כל צרכו בפת. ... כגרף של ריעי. ... זריק להו בלישניה. ... אחורי המטה. ...

וְכִי עוֹשִׂין גְּרָף שֶׁל רְעִי לְכַתְּחִילָּה – **But may we purposefully create** a situation similar to **a vessel of excrement?** No! And by making a pile of pits, the conditions of this dispensation are being purposefully created.[25] – ? –

The Gemara cites the practice of sages who sought to completely avoid the necessity to move the pits after their removal:[26] רַב שֵׁשֶׁת זָרֵיק לְהוּ בְּלִישָּׁנֵיהּ – **Rav Sheishess would toss them** beyond the table **with his tongue.**[27] רַב פָּפָּא זָרֵיק לְהוּ אֲחוֹרֵי הַמִּטָּה – **Rav Pappa would toss them behind the couch** upon which he was reclining. אָמְרוּ עָלָיו עַל רַבִּי זְכַרְיָה בֶּן אַבְקוּלָס – **They said about R' Zecharyah ben Avkulas** שֶׁהָיָה מְחַזִּיר פָּנָיו אֲחוֹרֵי הַמִּטָּה וְזוֹרְקָן – **that he would turn his face behind the couch** upon which he was reclining **and toss [the pits]** there.[28]

הדרן עלך נוטל

WE SHALL RETURN TO YOU, NOTEIL

NOTES

25. Although a repulsive object may be removed if it happens to be in one's proximity, one may not purposely create it in order to become nauseated by it and be permitted to remove it (*Rashi* to *Beitzah* 21b).

26. These Sages concurred with Rav Ashi that one may not purposely create a "vessel of excrement." See *Meiri.*

27. Rav Sheishess did not handle the pits with his hands at all; rather, he spit them beyond the table [where they could remain out of sight] (see *Rashi*).

28. That is, he would toss them there with his tongue (*Meiri; Minchas Bikkurim* to Tosefta 17:4; cf. *Megadim Chadashim*).

התם כיון דמסרחא דעתיה עילויה מאתמול הכי נמי מסתברא דרבא כר' יהודה סבירא ליה דדרש רבא אשה לא תכנס לבית העצים ליטול מהן אוד ואוד שנשבר אסור להסיקו ביום טוב לפי שמסיקין בכלים ואין מסיקין בשברי כלים שמע מינה: **מתני'** ב"ש אומרים מעבירין מעל השלחן עצמות וקליפין וב"ה אומרים מסלק את הטבלא כולה ומנערה מעבירין (א) מלפני השלחן פירורין פחות מכזית ושער של אפונין ושער עדשים מפני שהוא מאכל בהמה ספוג אם יש לו עור בית אחיזה מקנחין בו ואם לאו אין מקנחין בו (ב) (וחכמים אומרים) בין כך ובין כך ניטל בשבת ואינו מקבל טומאה: **גמ'** אמר רב נחמן אנו אין לנו אלא ב"ש כרבי יהודה וב"ה כרבי שמעון: מעבירין (ג) מלפני השלחן פירורין: מסייע ליה לר' יוחנן דאמר רבי יוחנן פירורין שאין בהן כזית אסור לאבדן ביד: שער של אפונין: מני ר"ש היא דלית ליה מוקצה אימא סיפא ספוג אם יש לו עור בית אחיזה מקנחין בו ואם לאו אין מקנחין בו אתאן לר' יהודה דאמר דבר שאין מתכוין אסור בהא אפילו ר"ש מודה דאביי ורבא דאמרי תרוייהו מודה ר"ש בפסיק רישיה ולא ימות הני גרעינין דתמרי ארמייתא שרו לטלטלינהו הואיל וחזיין אגב אמן ודפרסייתא אסור שמואל מטלטל להו אגב ריפתא: (שרנ"ם שפ"ז סימן): שמואל לטעמיה דאמר שמואל עושה אדם כל צרכו בפת רבה מטלטל להו אגב לקנא דמיא רב הונא בריה דרב יהושע עביד להו כגרף של ריעי א"ל רב אשי לאמימר וכי עושין גרף של ריעי לכתחילה רב ששת זריק להו בלישניה רב פפא זריק להו אחורי המטה אמרו עליו על רבי זכריה בן אבקולם שהיה מחזיר פניו אחורי המטה וזורקן:

הדרן עלך נוטל אדם את בנו

רש"י

התם כיון דמסרחא. מעיקרא לא מלגע ליה עד אורתא: **מאתמול דעתיה עליה.** לשורקא ובין השמשות נמי מוכן לבהמה הוה: **אוד.** פורגו"ן דקסם עלים להסקה ניתנו ולא לטלטול כלי: **ואוד שנשבר.** ביו"ט: **בשברי כלים.** שנשברו היום דהוו להו נולד: **ש"מ.** דכרבי יהודה סבירא ליה דאית ליה מוקצה: **מתני' מעבירין.** בידים מעל השלחן: **עצמות.** קשין שאינן ראוין לכלב: **וקליפין.** של אגוזים דלית להו לב"ש מוקצה: **וב"ה אומרים מסלק את הטבלא.** שיש תורת כלי עליה אבל לא יטלטל הקליפין בידים כרבי יהודה: **מעבירין מעל השלחן.** סתמא היא: **פירורין פחות מכזית.** וכ"ש כזית דלמפרש טעמא שהם מאכל בהמה: **ושער של אפונין.** שרביטין של קטנית שהקטנית גדל בהם: **אפונין.** יש"ם: **עור בית אחיזה.** [בית אחיזה] של עור שיאחזו בו: **מקנחין בו.** טבלא: **אין מקנחין בו.** שכשאוחזו נסחט בין אצבעותיו: **ניטל בשבת.** כשהוא נגוב: **ואינו מקבל טומאה.** דאינו לא כלי עץ ולא בגד ולא שק ולא מתכת: **גמ' אנו אין לנו.** אין אנו סומכין על משנתינו כמות שהיא שנויה אלא מוחלפת שיטתה וב"ש כרבי יהודה כו': **אסור לאבדן ביד.** מדקתני מעבירין בידים ולא זריק להו: **דלית ליה מוקצה.** דאי ר' יהודה מאתמול לאו לבהמה קיימי שהרי האוכל היה עמהן והיום לוקח מהם: **שאין מתכוין.** שאין מתכוין לסחוט: **גרעינין.** של תמרים והם לבהמה: **ארמייתא.** תמרים רעים הם ומאכילין התמרים עצמן לבהמה הלכך אגב אימייהו לבהמה נמי קיימי: **פרסייתא.** תמרים טובים הם ואין מאכילין אותן לבהמה: **כל צרכו.** משתמש בו ואין כאן משום בזיון וממחהו בתבשיל: **לקנא דמיא.** כלי של מים: **גרף של ריעי.** נוכרן לפניו כשהוכל התמרים על שמנקשות בעיניו ונוטלין אותן מפניו כגרף של ריעי ונותן לבהמה: **זריק להו בלישניה.** אל עבר השלחן: **אחורי המטה.** שהוא מיסב עליה:

הדרן עלך נוטל

תוספות

התם כיון דמסרחא. ומתקלקל ואין ראוי למאכל אדם מאתמול דעתיה עילויה ליתנו לבהמה אע"ג דבשער של אפונין ושל עדשים אסרינן לרבי יהודה אע"ג דחזו למאכל בהמה וכן גרעינין לעיל בפרק במה מדליקין (דף כט.) דאמרינן לרבי יהודה אכלן אין מסיקין בגרעינין מ"מ הכא שרי כדפי' התם: **ליטול** מהן אוד. נראה לר"ת כפירוש ה"ג דאסירי משום תיקוני מנא דלפירו' זה (ד) דלע"ג דלא מתקלקל ליה גזרינן שלא יבא לידי תיקון כלי: **עצמות** וקליפין. לא כפירוש הקונטרס דפירש אפילו קשין ואין ראוין לאכילת כלבים (ו) דהאי תנא לא אמרינן בגמרא דכרבי שמעון סבירא ליה ור"ש בעי לכל הפחות ראויות למאכל בהמה דקתני מעבירין מעל השלחן פירורין כו' מפני שהוא מאכל בהמה ומוקמינן בגמרא כוותיה:

אנו אין לנו אלא ב"ש כר"י כו'. במסכת עדיות לא מיתניא בהדי קולי ב"ש ומחומרי ב"ה והיינו כרב נחמן והא דלא מייתי סייעתא מהתם משום דמאי אולמא דהאי מהאי:

פירורין שאין בהן כזית אסור לאבדן ביד. פי' בקונט' מדקתני מעבירין ולא קתני זורקין וקשה לרבי דברישא נמי קתני מגביהין מעל השלחן עצמות וקליפין ולא קתני זורקין אע"פ שמותר לאבדן ביד ועוד דאמרינן בברכות בריש אלו דברים (דף נב:) וב"ה אומרים אם שמש ת"ח הוא נוטל פירורין שיש בהן כזית ומניח פירורין שאין בהן כזית ומסייע ליה לר' יוחנן דאמר פירורין שאין בהן כזית מותר לאבדן ביד ואי אפשר ליגרס התם אסור ונראה לר"י דהכא גרסי' מותר ודייק מדאצטריך למיתני מפני שהוא מאכל בהמה דהיינו משמע דלא חזו לאדם והוו כשאר מאכל בהמה ומותר לאבדן. מ"ר:

ואם לאו אין מקנחין בו. אית ספרים דגרסי וחכ"א בין כך ובין כך מקנחין בו ולא יתכן דאמר בגמרא דבאין לו עור בית אחיזה אפילו ר"ש מודה דאסור משום דפסיק רישיה הוא וה"ר יצחק מדנפירא גרס בין כך ובין כך אין מקנחין בו כרבי יהודה דאמר דבר שאין מתכוין אסור ואין נראה לר"י דהא בגמרא משמע דברישא מודה ר' יהודה (ה) דאמר אימא סיפא ספוג אם יש לו עור בית אחיזה מקנחין בו ואם לאו אין מקנחין בו אתאן לרבי יהודה אם כן בין כך ובין כך אין מקנחין בו לא רבי יהודה ולא ר' שמעון אלא ודאי לא גרסינן ליה כלל. מ"ר:

שמואל מטלטל להו אגב ריפתא. אף על גב דכר"ש סבירא ליה דשרי לקמן בפרק בתרא (דף קנו:) נבלה שנתנבלה בשבת מיהו מחמיר היה משום דהוה אדם חשוב כאביי ורבא דלעיל. ר"ת:

רבא מטלטל להו אגב לקנא דמיא. ואם תאמר והא רבא סבר לעיל כר"י דאית ליה מוקצה ואנוחי לקנא דמיא היכי שרי לכתחילה ויש לומר דשני לן בין היכא דאפשר למיעבד האי טלטול מאתמול להיכא דלא אפשר דכיפין ובר יונה היו מאתמול בידו והיה יכול לטלטלם אבל הני גרעיני תמרה לא אפשר ושרי אפילו לרבי יהודה ואף לאדם חשוב דאמר בביצה פרק יו"ט (דף כא:) דאמר ליה אביי לרב יוסף הני סופלי לחיותא היכי שדינן ביומא טבא לרבי יוסי דאמר לכס ולא לכלבים חזיין להסקה כו' בשבת מאי איכא למימר מטלטלין להו אגב ריפתא כדשמואל אלמא דאפילו רב יוסף דלא בעי למישרי לעיל אגב כפא וסכינא אפילו דבר הראוי לאדם שרי התם גרעיני תמרה אגב ריפתא:

הדרן עלך נוטל אדם את בנו

מסורת הש"ס

א) ביצה לג. ושם, ב) [שם לב.], ג) לעיל כט: כט. וקכד:, ג) לקמן קנו., [ביצה ב. תוספ' פ"ו] מתני' איסכא ע"ש], ד) [מגביהין], ה) [ע' תוס' ביצה ב: ד"ה ור"ה], ו) ס"א [לא], ז) ס"א מקנחין, ח) לקמן קמו. ע"ש ביצה ב., ט) ברכות נב:, י) לעיל קנו. קיא: קג. וקלג., כ) ביצה כא:, ל) [ביצה לו:], מ) [ביצה שם. לו:], נ) [תוספ' פי"ו], ס) [ע' תוס' מגילה כ. ד"ה מגבהין], ע) [ע' תוס' מנחות נח: ד"ה ואלה לאמרי דהכי מסוגיות הפוסקים].

הגהות הב"ח

(א) במשנה מעבירין מעל השלחן פירורין: (ב) שם מקנחין בו (וחכ"א) תא"מ ונ"ב רש"י ותוספות ולאפסי לא גרסי וחכ"א בגל מפרי המשניות להרמב"ם משמע דגרס לה: (ג) גמ' מעבירין מעל השלחן פירורין: (ד) תוס' ד"ה ליטול וכו' דלפירוש זה אע"ג: (ה) ד"ה ואם לאו וכו' מודה ר' יהודה דאמרינן אימא:

עין משפט נר מצוה

יט א מיי' פ"ד מהל' יו"ט הלכה יא סמג לאוין עה טוש"ע א"ח סי' תקז סעיף ג:
כ ב מיי' פכ"ו מהלכות שבת הלכה טו סמג לאוין סה טוש"ע א"ח סי' שח סעיף כז:
כא ג מיי' פכ"ב שם הלכה טו סמג שם טוש"ע א"ח סי' שם סעיף יח:
כב ד מיי' פ"ז מהל' ברכות הלכה יא טוש"ע א"ח סי' קפ סעיף ד:
כג ה מיי' פכ"ו מהל' שבת הלכה טז סמג לאוין סה טוש"ע א"ח סי' שח סעיף ל:
כד ו מיי' פ"ו מהלכות ברכות הל' טו טוש"ע א"ח סי' קעא סעיף ב:
כה ז מיי' פכ"ה מהל' שבת הל' כ ופכ"ו הלכה יג סמג לאוין סה טוש"ע א"ח סי' שח סעיף לו:
כו ח מיי' פכ"ו שם הל' טז טוש"ע שם סעיף ל:

רבינו חננאל

פי' החבית מטה על צדה והיא נופלת. אמר רב הונא אמר רב לא שנו אלא בשוכח אבל במניח נעשה בסיס לדבר האסור. פי' נעשת החבית כַּן לאבן ואסור להטות החבית כלל. והלכתא כוותיה דרבא דר' אמי אמר ר' יוחנן קאי כוותיה. בפרק כל הכלים: **היתה** בין החביות מגביהה מטה על צדה כו'. תניא (א') ר' יוסי אומר היתה החבית מונחת באוצר או שהיו כלי זכוכית מונחין תחתיה מגביהה למקום אחד ומטה על צדה ונוטל מה שצריך לו ומחזירה למקומה. מעות שעל הכר נמי אוקמוה משמ' דרב בשוכח אבל במניח נעשת הכר בסיס למעות ואסור אפילו לנערן ואמר רבה משמיה דר' יוחנן לא שנו אלא לצורך גופו כגון שצריך (סבר) לישב עליו אבל אם הוא צריך למקומו מטלטלין ועודן עליו. וכן תני חייא בר רב מדפתי והא דא"ר הושעיא שכח ארנקי בחצר ור' יצחק דאמר שכח לבינה בחצר ויהודה בר שילא דאמר שכחו דסקיא מלאה מעות בסטין ואמרו שמניח עליה ככר או תינוק ומטלטלו ואמר מר זוטרא הלכתא ככל הני שמעתתא בשכח ולית הלכתא כוותייהו אלא הלכתא כרב אשי דהוא בתראה דאמר לא אמרו ככר או תינוק אלא למת בלבד. אביי מנח כפא פי' תרווד אכיפי הן כגון כיפה של צמר ורבא מנח סכינא אבר יונה והוא מליח אבל היה מבושל והיה מטלטל בן יונה אגב סכינא אמר שאלו מותרין לטלטלן בשבת דתניא בראשונה היו אומרים ג' כלים מותרין בשבת מקצוע של דבילה וזומלוסטרין וסכין קטנה שע"ג השולחן וכפה היא זומליסטרון כדתנן ניטלה כיפה טמאה משום מזלג. ואקשינן על רבה טעמא דחזי לאומצא הא לא חזי לאומצא לא דהא מוקצה הוא כלומר כר' יהודה סבירא ליה ולא כר' שמעון דאי ר' שמעון לית ליה מוקצה אלא אפילו בשר תפוח שרי לטלטוליה וכל בשר אחר בין חי בין מליח. ותוב אקשינן עליה ומי סבר לה רבא כר' יהודה והא א"ל רבא לשמעיה טוי לי בר אווזא ביו"ט ושדי מיעיא לשונרא כר' שמעון דאי כר' יהודה הא אמר כל דבר שאינו מוכן לאכילה אסור לטלטלו ואפילו בהמה לא היה מתיר לבודקה אלא באשפה שאם תמצא טריפה יניחנה באשפה. ומסקנא דשמעתא דרבה כר' יהודה ס"ל ופשוטה היא: **מתני'** בה"א מגביהין מעל השולחן עצמות וקליפין וכו'. אמר רב נחמן אנו אין לנו אלא ב"ש כר' יהודה וב"ה כר' שמעון מעבירין מעל גבי השלחן פירורין פחות מכזית מסייע ליה לר' יוחנן דאמר פירורין שאין בהן כזית מותר לאבדן ביד. ספוג אם יש לו עור בית אחיזה מקנחין בו ואם לאו אין מקנחין בו אפילו לר' שמעון דהא אי אפשר שלא לסחוט באחוז בספוג אלא אם יש לו עור בית אחיזה. גרעינין דתמרי. ארמי ארמייתא שרי לטלטולי הואיל וחזיין על גב אימן. פי' רכים הן ונאכלין עם התמרים עצמן. דפרסייתא שמואל מטלטלינהו ואגב ריפתא וכו' שמעתא:

הדרן עלך נוטל אדם

רב נסים גאון

להרים: **רבא** כר' נתן סבירא ליה דאמר חי נושא את עצמו. עיקר דבריו של ר' נתן בפרק המצניע (דף צד) דתנן ר' נתן אומר על השחוטין חייב על החיים פטור מפני שהחי נושא את עצמו. רבא כר' שמעון סבירא ליה דאמר מלאכה שאינה צריכה לגופה פטור עליה ועיקר דבריו של ר' שמעון גם בפרק המצניע (דף צג) דתנן וכן כזית מן המת וכעדשה מן השרץ חייב ור' שמעון פוטר וגרסי' בגמ' אמר רבה אמר ר' יוחנן ורב יוסף אמר ריש לקיש פוטר היה ר' שמעון אף במוציא את המת לקוברו וכבר פירשנו זה בפרק יציאות השבת: **הכי** נמי מסתברא דרבא כר' יהודה סבירא ליה דדרש רבא אשה לא תכנס לבין העצים ליטול מהן אוד אוד שנשבר ביום טוב אסור להסיקו לפי שמסיקים בכלים ואין מסיקין בשברי כלים וזה שוה לדברי ר' יהודה שאמר במשנה בפ' במה מדליקין (ד' כט) ואין מסיקין בשברי כלים דברי ר' יהודה הואיל וסבירא ליה כוותיה בנולד במוקצה נמי דתנן בסוף מסכתא (לקמן דף קנו) ר' יהודה אומר אם לא היתה נבילה מערב שבת אסורה לפי שאינה מן המוכן כר' יהודה סבירא ליה ולכך אמר סכינא אבר יונה למה לי הא חזי לאומצא דדייקת מינה הא לא חזי לאומצא לא וכמו שאמר בתחילת מסכת יום טוב (דף ב) דאית ליה מוקצה אית ליה נולד ודלית ליה מוקצה לית ליה נולד כי הכלל עיקר אחד חוזר והיא ההכנה: **אמר** רב נחמן אנו אין לנו אלא בית שמאי כרבי יהודה ובית הלל כרבי שמעון וכן אמרו עוד מני ר' שמעון היא דלית ליה מוקצה ועיקר דברי רבי יהודה ור' שמעון בפרק כירה (דף מד) וכבר פירשנו למעלה. אתאן לרבי יהודה דאמר דבר שאין מתכוין אסור עיקר דבריו של ר' יהודה במשנה במסכת בכורות (דף לג) ובמס' יום טוב (דף כג) וכבר פירשנו דבריו גם במס' זו בפ' כירה:

סליק פרק נוטל

ליקוטי רש"י

כיון דמסרחא. אם יניחם לצורך מחר והיום לא היה צריך להם מאתמול דעתיה עלוייהו להשליכם לחמור. **אוד.** עץ לעשות אוד לתנור פורגי"ן בלע"ז וטעמא משום דלא נתנו אלא להסיק אלא אם כן נעשה כלי מבעוד יום [ביצה לג.]. **שמסיקין בכלים.** ביום טוב שהרי ראוין לטלטל ויטלטל ויתנם לתוך האור [לעיל קכד:]. דהני טלטול נמי ניהו ומטלטלן נמי להסיקן [ביצה לב.]. **ואין מסיקין בשברי כלים.** דהוו להו מוקצין ולא חזו לטלטול [לעיל שם]. שנשברו ביו"ט דהשתא לא חזי לטלטול ולאו משום דחזו להסקה אתמול לא להכי קיימי [ביצה שם]. **מעבירין.** בשבת מעל השלחן עצמות שאינן ראוין לאכילה וקליפי אגוזים ולא חיישינן למוקצה. **ובית הלל אומרים.** אין מטלטלין אותן בידים שמוקצה הן. **מסלק את הטבלא.** שיש תורת כלי עליה ומנערה. **אמר רב נחמן אנו אין לנו.** בשיטת משנה זו לפי שמוחלפת שיטתה אלא כך שמעתי מרבותינו דבית שמאי כרבי יהודה ומחמרי ובית הלל כרבי שמעון [שם ב.]. **אפילו ר"ש.** דאמר במסכת שבת (מא:) דבר שאין מתכוין מותר [בכורות כה.]. **מודה ר' שמעון בפסיק רישיה ולא ימות.** כאומר אחתוך ראש בהמה זו בשבת ואיני רוצה שתמות דכיון דאי אפשר שלא תמות כמתכוין חשיב ליה וכי אמרינן דבר שאין מתכוין מותר כגון היכא דאפשר ליה בלא איסור כגון גורר אדם מטה כסא וספסל ובלבד שלא יתכוין לעשות חריץ ואף על גב דאיכא למיחש דלמא עביד חריץ כיון דלא מתכוין להכי ואפשר לגרירה בלא חריץ כי עביד נמי חריץ דהוי מלאכה גמורה לא מיחייב אבל היכא דודאי עביד מודי [סוכה לג:]. **ארמייתא.** דאין מתבשלות יפה ואין האוכל נפרש מהן ומשייר בגרעיניהן וחזו לאדם. **ודפרסייתא.** תמרים טובים ומתבשלים יפה וכל אוכל שלהם נפרש מעל גרעיניהן ואין הגרעינין ראוין (לטלטל) [לאכול] [לעיל כט. ע"ש ברש"ש]. **עושה אדם כל צרכו בפת.** ומטלטל על ידי הפת ולא חיישינן לבזיון דאוכלין [ביצה כא:]. כל צורכו בין תשמיש בין לפרר אותה ולמחות בתבשיל רותח [לעיל נ:]. **כגרף של ריעי.** שמותר לטלטלו ולפנותו לאשפה מחמת מאוס כדאמרינן בפרק בתרא (ביצה לו:) [ביצה שם]. **גרף.** כלי חרס המוכן לכך [לעיל מז.]. גרף ועביט כלי חרס הן אלא של רעי קרוי גרף ושל מימי רגלים קרוי עביט [ביצה לו:]. **וכי עושין גרף של ריעי לכתחילה.** נהי דכי איתיה קמן מסלקינן ליה אבל לאתויי קמן או למיזל אנן לגביה כי היכי דנמאס עלן ונסלקיה מי שרי [שם כא:]. וכי מותר לגרום שיהא הדבר מאוס לו כדי שיוציאנו [שם לו:].

עין משפט נר מצוה

א א ב מיי' פכ"ב מהל' שבת הלכה כט סמג לאוין סה טוש"ע א"ח סי' שלה סעיף א:
ב ג מיי' שם פכ"א הל' יא טוש"ע שם סעיף ה:
ג ד ה ו מיי' פכ"א מהל' שבת הלכה יב סמג שם טוש"ע א"ח סי' שכ סעיף א:
ד ז מיי' פ"י מהלכות טומאת אוכלין הל' ד:
ה ח שם הל' ה ופ"ט מהל' משכב ומושב הלכה טז:

רבינו חננאל

חבית שנשברה מצילין הימנה מזון ג' סעודות וכו' תנא לא יספוג ביין בכפיו ולא יטפח בשמן ביד כדרך שהוא עושה בחול. לא יטפח כדאמרינן בכל מקום טופח ע"מ להטפיח וכדתנן בפרק החובל בחבירו וכו'. מעשה באחד שפרע ראשה של אשה כו' עד שמרה עומדת על פתח חצירה ושיבר הפך בפניה. ובה כאיסר שמן. גילתה ראשה והיתה מטפחת ומנחת על ראשה וכו': ת"ר נתפזרו לו פירות בחצירו מלקט על יד על יד ואוכל. אבל לא לתוך הסל ולא לתוך הקופה שלא יעשה כדרך שהוא עושה בחול וכו' וחלקו רב יהודה אמר שמואל ורב ועולא כל חד וחד מעמיד חלוקת ר' יהודה וחכמים ור' יוחנן אמר הלכה כר' יהודה בשאר פירות ואין הלכה כמותו בזיתים וענבים. א"ר אבא אמר רב יהודה אמר שמואל מודה היה רבי יהודה לחכמים בזיתים וענבים ומודים חכמים לרבי יהודה בשאר פירות. ובמאי פליגי בתותים ורמונים דתניא זיתים שמשך מהן שמן וענבים שמשך מהן יין והכניסן בין לאוכלין בין למשקין היוצא מהן אסור. תותים שמשך מהן מים ורמונים שמשך מהן יין והכניסן לאוכלין היוצא מהן מותר למשקין ולסתם היוצא מהן אסור דברי ר' יהודה וחכ"א בין לאוכלין בין למשקין היוצא מהן אסור. נמצאת חלוקת ר' יהודה וחכמים בתותים ורמונים ובה א"ר יוחנן הלכה כר' יהודה בשאר פירות וכיון שפסק ר' יוחנן הלכה כר' יהודה הוצרכנו לברר דבריו ולפיכך אמרינן וסבר ר' יהודה סתם אסור והתנן

תוספות

חבית. ובלבד שלא יספוג. אפילו יש לו עור בית אחיזה דליכא משום סחיטה אסור כדמפרש בגמרא שלא יעשה כדרך שעושה בחול: **מלקט** על יד ואוכל. נראה דלה"ג ואוכל מדקתני סיפא אבל לא לתוך הסל ולא לתוך הקופה משמע הנך דווקא אסירי משום עובדא דחול אבל לתוך ו) כפו שרי: **ורבי** יוחנן אמר הלכה כרבי יהודה בשאר פירות. בריש מסכת ביצה (דף ג. ושם) רבי יוחנן רמי דר' יהודה אדר' יהודה תנן ר"י אומר אם לאוכלין היוצא מהן מותר אם למשקין כו' אלמא כל לאוכלין אוכלא דאיפרת הוא ורמינהו ועוד אמר ר"י מתנה אדם על הכלכלה של פירות ביו"ט ראשון ואוכלה בשני וכן ביצה שנולדה בראשון אוכלה בשני בשני אין בראשון לא ואמר רבי יוחנן מוחלפת השיטה וצריך לומר דהכא דמתנה אדם מחליף דאי מתני' מחליף אם כן במאי דנקט הכא ר' יהודה הוה ליה למינקט רבנן וה"ל למימר הלכה כרבנן בשאר פירות. מ"ר. ז) ולי נראה דאפילו אפיך מתני' אתי שפיר כעין שמצינו בב"ק בפרק הגוזל קמא (דף צו:) דתנן גזל בהמה והכחישה עבדים והזקינו משלם כשעת הגזילה ר"מ אומר בעבדים אומר לו הרי שלך לפניך ואמר בגמרא אמר רבי חנינא בר אבדימי אמר רב הלכה כר"מ ופריך ורב שביק רבנן ועביד כר"מ כו' עד דמסיק דרב מתניתין איפכא מתני' אלמא אע"ג שהיה שונה במתניתין וחכ"א בעבדים אומר לו הרי שלך לפניך וה"ל למימר השתא הלכה כחכמים אפ"ה נקט ר"מ לפי מה שהאחרים שונין המשנה ה"נ נקט רבי יוחנן רבי יהודה בשמעתין וכן נמי מצינו בשילהי פ"ק דסוכה (דף יט:) דתנן העושה סוכתו כמין צריף ר"א פוסל וחכמים מכשירין ואמרינן בגמרא אביי אשכחיה לרב יוסף דגני בכילת חתנים בסוכה א"ל כמאן כר"א א"ל שבקת רבנן ועבדת כר"א אמר ליה ברייתא איפכא תניא השתא היה לו להשיב רב יוסף כרבנן ולא כר"א כיון דאיהו איפכא תני אלא כן דרך הש"ס בכל מקום. נראה לי:

הלכה כר' יהודה בשאר פירות. אע"ג דבריש ביצה (ד' ג.) גזר ר' יוחנן ביצה שנולדה ביו"ט משום משקין שזבו והכא לא גזר בשאר פירות י"ל דשייך טפי לגזור בביצה לפי שהיא עומדת ליסחט מן התרנגולת י) ודרך לגומעה חיה אבל שאר פירות אין עומדים ליסחט כלל. מ"ר:

שמשך מהן שמן כו'. פי' בקונט' שמשך זב מאליהן כמו נהרות המושכין ולפירושו צריך לומר הכניסן בין לאוכלין כו' היינו הכניסן מתחילתן ואין הלשון משמע כן ועוד קשה לר"י דאי משך מאליו קאמר גבי תותים שמשך מהם מים ה"ל למימר שמשכו או שנמשכו דמים בכל מקום לשון רבים ועוד קשה לר"י אם כן הך ברייתא הוה תיובתא דרב ורבי יוחנן דאמרי לעיל חלוק היה רבי יהודה בזיתים וענבים דהכא משמע דבזיתים וענבים מודה אלא נראה לר"י דמשך דאדם קאי וסחטן תחילה ושוב הכניסן דהשתא לרב ורבי יוחנן דסברי חלוק היה רבי יהודה בזיתים וענבים נקט דוקא משך דאיכא למיחש טפי דילמא יהיב דעתיה לסחוט משקה אחר שהכניסו נמי לאכילה מאחר שסחטן תחילה להוציא מהן משקה הא לא משך לא ולשמואל דאמר מודה רבי יהודה בזיתים וענבים נקט משך משום רבותא דתותים ורמונים דאפילו משך הכניסן לאוכלין היוצא מהן מותר. מ"ר: **חלב** האשה מטמא לרצון ושלא לרצון. והא דתנן במסכת מכשירין (פ"א) כל משקה שתחילתו לרצון אף על פי שאין סופו לרצון או שסופו לרצון אף על פי שאין תחלתו לרצון מכשיר לא דמי רצון דהתם לרצון דהכא דהתם איירי בשעת נפילתן על הזרעים שיהא לרצון דבעינן יותן דומיא דכי יתן מה יתן דניחא ליה אף יותן דניחא ליה אבל הכא איירי בשעת פרישה מן האשה או מן הבהמה: **לרצון** ושלא לרצון. כדמפרש בסמוך טעמא משום דדם מגפתה טמא וחלב ודם חד הוא דדם נעכר ונעשה חלב ולא צריכין למה שפי' בקונט' משום דאיקרי משקה שנאמר ותפתח את נאד החלב ותשקהו ונראה לר"י דהא דאיצטריך לפרש האי טעמא בפ' דם נדה (נדה דף נה:) גבי חלב האשה הנ"מ לרבי עקיבא דשמעתין דלית ליה טעמא ט) דפרישה או למאן דלית ליה דם נעכר ונעשה חלב אבל לרבנן דשמעתין לא צריך (ד) כדפרישית לחלב האשה אלא דוקא לטמא חלב בהמה לרצון. ט) מ"ר:
מחמיר

משנה

חבית א שנשברה מצילין הימנה מזון שלש סעודות ואומר לאחרים באו והצילו לכם ובלבד שלא יספוג א) אין סוחטין את הפירות להוציא מהן משקין ואם יצאו מעצמן אסורין ר' יהודה אומר אם לאוכלין היוצא מהן מותר ואם למשקין היוצא מהן אסור ב) חלות דבש שריסקן מע"ש ויצאו מעצמן אסורין (א) ורבי אליעזר מתיר: **גמ'** תנא לא יספוג ביין ולא יטפח בשמן שלא יעשה כדרך שהוא עושה בחול ת"ר ג נתפזרו לו פירות בחצר מלקט על יד על יד ואוכל אבל לא לתוך הסל ולא לתוך הקופה שלא יעשה כדרך שהוא עושה בחול: אין סוחטין את הפירות: ג) אמר רב יהודה אמר שמואל מודה היה רבי יהודה לחכמים בזיתים וענבים מ"ט כיון דלסחיטה נינהו יהיב דעתיה ועולא אמר רב חלוק היה ר' יהודה אף בזיתים וענבים ורבי יוחנן אמר הלכה כרבי יהודה בשאר פירות ואין הלכה כרבי יהודה בזיתים וענבים אמר רבה אמר רב יהודה אמר שמואל מודה היה רבי יהודה לחכמים בזיתים וענבים ד ומודים חכמים לרבי יהודה בשאר פירות א"ל רבי ירמיה לרבי אבא אלא במאי פליגי א"ל לכי תשכח אמר רב נחמן בר יצחק מסתברא בתותים ורמונים פליגי דתניא ה זיתים שמשך מהן שמן וענבים שמשך מהן יין והכניסן בין לאוכל בין למשקין היוצא מהן אסור ו תותים שמשך מהן מים ורמונים שמשך מהן יין והכניסן לאוכלין היוצא מהן מותר למשקין ולסתם היוצא מהן אסור דברי רבי יהודה וחכמים אומרים בין לאוכלין בין למשקין היוצא מהן אסור וסבר רבי יהודה סתם אסור ז) והתנן ז חלב האשה מטמא לרצון ושלא לרצון חלב בהמה אינו מטמא אלא לרצון אמר ר' עקיבא קל וחומר הוא ומה חלב האשה שאינו מיוחד אלא לקטנים מטמא לרצון ושלא לרצון חלב הבהמה שמיוחד בין לקטנים בין לגדולים אינו דין שיטמא בין לרצון ובין שלא לרצון אמרו לו אם טמא חלב האשה שלא לרצון ח שדם מגפתה טמא יטמא חלב הבהמה שלא

רש"י

חבית. מצילין הימנה מזון ג' סעודות. ואפילו בכלים הרבה דאילו בחד מנא אמרי' בכל כתבי הקדש (לעיל דף קכ.) דכמה דבעי מציל: לכם. כל אחד מזון ג' סעודות: ובלבד שלא יספוג. שלא ישים ספוג במקום היין לחזור ולהטיפו בכלי גזירה שמא יסחוט: אין סוחטין את הפירות. דהוי ליה מפרק (ב) תולדה דדישה: אסורין. גזירה שמא יסחוט לכתחילה: רבי יהודה אומר אם לאוכלין. הם מכונסין אותם פירות היוצא מהן מותר דלא ניחא ליה במה שזבו וליכא למגזר בהן שמא יסחוט: ואם למשקין. מכונסין אסורין דניחא ליה במאי דנפקא מינייהו ומתקיימא מחשבתו ואיכא למגזר שמא יסחוט והכי אמרי' בביצה לטעמא דמשקין שזבו אסורין משום שמא יסחוט הוא: חלות דבש. מאחר שמרוסקין הדבש זב מאליו מתוך השעוה ואין דרך לסוחטו הלכך רבי אליעזר מתיר וחכמים אוסרין גזירה אטו שאין מרוסקין דילמא מרסק להו (ג): גמ' ויטפח. מכניס בו כפו והשמן נדבק בה ומקנחו בשפת הכלי ומסרה משום עובדין דחול: מודה ר' יהודה בזיתים. דאע"ג דהכניסן לאוכלין היוצא מהן אסור דמין לרובן לסחיטה קיימי כי אתו לידי משקה יהיב דעתיה למיהוי ניחא ליה בהכי: אפי' בזיתים וענבים. הואיל והכי לאוכלין כנסן: מסתברא בתותים ורמונים פליגי. דאיכא דבעו להו למשקין הלכך משוו להו רבנן כזיתים וענבים ור' יהודה פליג עלייהו אבל שאר פירות ליכא דבעי להו למשקין הלכך מודו רבנן בהם: שמשך. זב מאליהן כמו נהרות המושכין (לעיל דף קכח.): והכניסן. מתחילתן בין לאוכלין בין למשקין כו' דרמונים קרי יין משום דלאים להו קיוהא: וחכ"א כו'. והא דנקט רב נחמן לישנא דמסתברא ולא אמר בהדיא דבתותים ורמונים פליגי משום דאיכא למימר פליגי בתותים ורמונים וה"ה לשאר פירות ולהודיעך כחו דרבי יהודה נקט להו ואי משום ברייתא דלקמן דשמעינן מינה דמודים חכמים לרבי יהודה בשאר פירות לאו בהדיא שמעינן לה דאיכא למימר רבי יהודה היא דפרכינן עלה: וסבר רבי יהודה סתם. שלא פירש לאוכל ולא למשקה הוי המשקה הזב מהן אסור: והתנן חלב האשה מטמא. מכשיר: לרצון ושלא לרצון. בין שילא ממנה לרצון בין שילא שלא לרצון שהחלב קרוי משקה שנאמר ותפתח את נאד החלב ותשקהו (שופטים ד): חלב הבהמה אינו מטמא אלא אם כן יצא לרצון. ואי לא לא חשיב משקה ואם נגע בו שרץ אינו מקבל טומאה וטעמא מפרש לקמיה:
שדם

מסורת הש"ס

א) ביצה ג. חולין יד., ב) לעיל יט: חולין יד:, ג) מכשירין פ"ו מ"ה כריתות יג., ה) [נספקי תוספות ליתא כמותו], ו) [עיין תוס' ביצה ג. ד"ה ר"י אמר], ז) כ"א ועוד וכ"ל לא אמרי רק משאר פירות גם מוחים ועגבים אבל מתותים ורמונים ליתו מוכר כלום דעתו משא"כ ר' יהודה דאמר בפי' תותים ורמונים אם הכניסן לאוכלין היוצא מהן מותר והן דומין לביצה ואפ"ה וע"כ דגרסינן אסור בביצה וע"כ רמי ליה אהדדי במסכת עירובין לג. ובמס' ביצה והוכחנו פשוט שאין להגיה כלום וצ"ל הדרך לגומעה ור"ל ליישב לדף אם עומדת לסחוט ומ"מ לא צריך עוד תקון ואינו רואי לדחות למשקין הוא אבל אינו שום תקון אם ר"י אמר והדרך כו', ח) ע"י דפריכם, ט) [ועי' תוס' נדה יט: ד"ה כמיב הכא].

הגהות הב"ח

(א) במשנה ור"א מתיר. נ"ב ר' אלעזר גרסי'. עי' בפירש"י בפ"ק דשבת דף יט ריש ע"ב: (ב) רש"י ד"ה אין סוחטין וכו' מפרק דהוא תולדה: (ג) ד"ה חלות וכו' להו הס"ד ואח"כ מ"ה ולא יטפח: (ד) תוס' ד"ה לרצון וכו' לא צריך לחלב האשה כדפי' אלא:

ליקוטי רש"י

אין סוחטין את הפירות. וסחיטת פירות תולדה דדש היא שמפרקן מתוך זג שלהן כמפרק תבואה מקש שלה [ביצה ג.]. סחיטה אב מלאכה היא [חולין יד: ע"ש במסורה"ש]. **ואם יצאו מעצמן אסורין.** בו ביום גזרה שמא יסחוט. **אם לאוכלין.** הן מכונסין הפירות הללו היוצא מהן מותר בו ביום דכיון דלא ניחא ליה בהני משקין ליכא למגזר שמא יסחוט. היוצא מהן אוכלא דאפרת הוא ואינו בכלל גזירת משקין שזבו [ביצה שם]. אם היו עומדין לאכילה ולא לסחוט היוצא מהם מותר דכיון דלא ניחא ליה ליכא למיגזר אי שרית להו בשמייה ביום אתי לסחוט דהא לאו להכי קיימי. **ואם למשקין.** הואיל ונתקיימה מחשבתו אי שרית להו כשזבו איכא למיגזר בהו שמא יסחוט דהא לנהכי קיימי [חולין שם]. **חלות דבש.** הכוורת לאחר שעשאה פירות ויצאו הנחילין לוקחין את הדבש והוא עשוי חלות חלות ויש בו כ' חלות או עשרים זה בצד זה משעוה ודבש מעורב יחד [רשב"ם ב"ב פ.]. שהכוורת רודה ועשויין כמין חלות של שעוה והדבש בתוכן. **שריסקן.** כותשן. **אסורין.** לאותו שבת באכילה. **ורבי [אלעזר].** הוא ר' אלעזר בן שמוע סתם ר' אלעזר של משנה וברייתא מתיר. דבש לאחר שזב מן החלות נמי אוכלא הוא הלכך ליכא למיגזר ביה שמא יסחוט משמתסך דלא שייכא ביה סחיטה [לעיל יט: ועיין כאן ברש"ש]. **מודה היה רבי יהודה לחכמים** בזיתים וענבים. שאפילו הכניסן לאכילה הואיל ורוב בני אדם סוחטין אותם האי נמי ממליך עלייהו ואי שרית למשקין שזבו מהן אתי למיסחט. כיון דלסחיטה נינהו. כיון דלהכי קיימי סתם ענבים. יהיב דעתיה. עלייהו למשקין וכי הוו משקין הוה ליה נתקיימה מחשבתו וגזרה שמא יסחוט. חלוק היה ר' יהודה. ומתיר [חולין שם]. מגפתה. לשון (תהלים לא) פן תגוף באבן רגלך [שם לה:].

Chapter Twenty-two

Mishnah חָבִית שֶׁנִּשְׁבְּרָה – Concerning a wine **cask that has broken:** מַצִּילִין הֵימֶנָּה מְזוֹן שָׁלֹשׁ סְעוּדוֹת – **We may save from it** on the Sabbath enough **provisions for three meals,**[1] וְאוֹמֵר לַאֲחֵרִים בֹּאוּ וְהַצִּילוּ לָכֶם – **and one may say to others: Come and save** some of the wine **for yourselves;**[2] וּבִלְבַד שֶׁלֹּא יִסְפּוֹג – **but provided that one does not sponge up** the spilled wine,[3] since one may be led to squeeze it from the sponge, which is forbidden.[4]

Having mentioned the prohibition against squeezing out liquid, the Mishnah records a related law: אֵין סוֹחֲטִין אֶת הַפֵּירוֹת לְהוֹצִיא מֵהֶן מַשְׁקִין – **We may not squeeze fruits** on the Sabbath **to extract liquid from them.**[5] וְאִם יָצְאוּ מֵעַצְמָן אֲסוּרִין – **And** even **if [the liquids] oozed** from the fruits on the Sabbath **of their own accord, they are prohibited** for consumption on that Sabbath[6] by Rabbinic decree. For the Rabbis feared that permitting this liquid might lead one to squeeze the fruits, which is forbidden.[7] רַבִּי יְהוּדָה אוֹמֵר – But **R' Yehudah says:** אִם לְאוֹכָלִין הַיּוֹצֵא מֵהֶן מוּתָּר – **If** one originally stored the fruits **for food** (i.e. for eating), **[the liquid] that oozes from them is permitted,** for since one does not intend these fruits for squeezing, he will not be led to squeeze them.[8] וְאִם לְמַשְׁקִין הַיּוֹצֵא מֵהֶן אָסוּר – **But if** one originally stored the fruits **for liquid** (i.e. for squeezing), **[the liquid] that oozes from them is prohibited,** lest using it lead one to squeeze the fruits.[9]

A similar case:

חַלּוֹת דְּבַשׁ שֶׁרִיסְּקָן מֵעֶרֶב שַׁבָּת וְיָצְאוּ מֵעַצְמָן אֲסוּרִין – If **honeycombs were chopped before the Sabbath, and [honey]** then **oozed** from them on the Sabbath **of its own accord, it is prohibited** for consumption on that Sabbath. וְרַבִּי [אֶלְעָזָר] (אליעזר) מַתִּיר – **But R' Elazar permits** one to consume it.[10]

Gemara The Gemara cites a Baraisa that discusses the prohibition against sponging up spilled liquid:

תָּנָא – A Baraisa **taught:** לֹא יִסְפּוֹג בְּיַיִן – ONE SHOULD NOT SPONGE UP spilled WINE on the Sabbath, lest one come to squeeze the wine from the sponge.[11] וְלֹא יָטַפַּח בְּשֶׁמֶן – AND ONE SHOULD NOT MOISTEN one's hand WITH spilled OIL on the Sabbath in order to return it to its vessel, שֶׁלֹּא יַעֲשֶׂה כְּדֶרֶךְ שֶׁהוּא עוֹשֶׂה בְּחוֹל – SO THAT ONE WILL NOT DO on the Sabbath AS ONE DOES ON THE WEEKDAY.[12]

The Gemara mentions another weekday activity:

תָּנוּ רַבָּנָן – **Our Rabbis taught:** נִתְפַּזְּרוּ לוֹ פֵּירוֹת בֶּחָצֵר – IF ONE'S FRUITS BECAME SCATTERED IN A COURTYARD, מְלַקֵּט עַל יָד

NOTES

1. The Rabbis prohibited one to rescue more than is needed for the Sabbath, lest one come, in his panic to save his wine, to transport additional vessels through the public domain, in violation of the Sabbath (see above, 117b). Alternatively, they feared that in one's eagerness to save *all* his wine, one might come to repair the cask, which is prohibited (*Rama, Orach Chaim* 335:1; see *Tosafos* to 117b ד״ה הא דתניא for further reasons for this decree). They therefore limited the amount one might save to provisions for the three Sabbath meals. However, this stricture applies only to rescue performed with more than one vessel. If one is employing only a single vessel, he may save as much wine as he pleases (see above, 120a). Thus, our Mishnah is discussing one using a number of vessels; nonetheless, he is permitted to rescue sufficient provisions for three meals (*Rashi*).

[The above decree applies to a cask that has developed a serious break and is swiftly losing its contents. If, however, the cask is only slightly cracked and is leaking at a slow rate, one may save as much wine as he wishes. For since one does not panic over a slow leak, there is no danger that one might be led to violate the Sabbath (see *Tosafos* ibid.).]

[When the Mishnah states that one may save enough for three meals, it refers to a wine cask that broke with the onset of the Sabbath, before any of the three Sabbath meals took place. However, if the cask broke after one or two meals were already eaten, one may save only enough wine for the meals that remain (*Shabbos Shel Mi,* from 117b; see *Mishnah Berurah* 335:2).]

2. I.e. enough for your three Sabbath meals (*Rashi*).

3. I.e. provided that one does not lay a sponge upon the wine to soak it up, so that he can later let the sponge drip into a vessel, lest he come to squeeze [the wine from the sponge into the vessel] (*Rashi;* see *Rashash; Shabbos Shel Mi*).

4. See below, 145a notes 22 and 29.

5. This is a prohibition against squeezing fruits by hand (*Shulchan Aruch HaRav, Orach Chaim* קונטרס אחרון 510:1), an act forbidden under the Biblical prohibition of מְפָרֵק, *extracting.* This prohibition is a *toladah* of דָּשׁ, *threshing,* whereby one extracts grain from its outer covering (*Rashi*). Extracting the liquid from the fruit is analogous to extracting the grains from the husks (*Rashi* to *Beitzah* 3a ד״ה שמא יסחוט). [Thus, one who squeezes fruit for its juice will be liable to a *chatas* if he does so inadvertently, and to *kares* and to death by stoning if deliberately. However, one is liable only if one squeezes out a measure of liquid equal to the volume of a dried fig (*Rambam, Shabbos* 7:7; 8:10). Not every act of squeezing falls under this prohibition, nor is one prohibited to squeeze *every* type of fruit. Rather, the squeezing of certain fruits, as well as certain acts of squeezing, are prohibited only by Rabbinic decree, while others are entirely permissible! (see below, 144b, especially notes 1, 11, 22, and 34; and see 145a, especially notes 21, 22, 27, 29).]

[It is forbidden as well for one to press fruit by means of a utensil, such as a winepress or an olive-press. However, this act (known as דְּרִיכָה) falls under the category of the *av melachah* of *threshing,* and not under the *toladah* of *extracting* (*Shulchan Aruch HaRav* ibid.).]

6. See *Rashi* to 19b ד״ה אסורין.

7. *Rashi;* see *Rashi* to *Beitzah* 3a ד״ה משום וד״ה ואם; cf. *Ramban, Ritva* (*MHK* ed.) et al.; see also below, 145a.

8. For since he intends these fruits for eating, he derives no particular satisfaction from the juice that flows from them. He is therefore unlikely to inadvertently take a fruit into his hand and squeeze it (*Rashi*).

9. For since the liquid that oozes from the fruit is in accord with his original intention when he stored them, he looks upon it with satisfaction. We therefore fear that he might heedlessly take a fruit in hand and squeeze it for its juice (*Rashi*).

10. Once a honeycomb has been chopped, it is not the usual practice to then squeeze it, since the honey will flow from it on its own. R' Elazar therefore permits eating the honey, for there is no danger that one might squeeze the honeycomb. But the Sages forbid the honey, lest one erroneously infer from here that it is permissible to derive honey from *unchopped* honeycombs by squeezing them on the Sabbath (*Rashi;* see *Rashash;* see *Eglei Tal* דש 42:3).

[Emendation of "R' Eliezer" to "R' Elazar" follows *Bach* et al., and is implicit in *Rashi* to 19b ד״ה ורבי אלעזר אומר.]

11. *Rashi* to the Mishnah, as explained by *Ritva MHK* ed. and *Maharshal;* see above, note 3; cf. *Tosafos; Rambam, Shabbos* 22:16; *Shabbos Shel Mi;* see *Shiltei HaGiborim.*

12. I.e. one may not put his palm into spilled oil so that it will stick to his palm, and then wipe the oil off on the edge of a vessel, for, as a weekday activity, this act will detract from the aura of the Sabbath (*Rashi;* cf. *Rambam* ibid.). [Activities forbidden because of עוּבְדָא דְחוֹל, *weekday activity,* fall into three categories (see General Introduction). One of these categories is that of weekday activities that will detract from the aura of the Sabbath.]

חבית *שנשברה מצילין הימנה מזון שלש סעודות ואומר לאחרים באו והצילו לכם ובלבד שלא יספוג (א) אין סוחטין את הפירות להוציא מהן משקין ואם יצאו מעצמן אסורין ר' יהודה אומר אם לאוכלין היוצא מהן מותר ואם למשקין היוצא מהן אסור (ב) חלות דבש שריסקן מע"ש ויצאו מעצמן אסורין (ג) ורבי אליעזר מתיר: **גמ'** תנא לא ב יספוג ביין ולא יטפח בשמן שלא יעשה כדרך שהוא עושה בחול ת"ר ג נתפזרו לו פירות בחצר מלקט על יד על יד ואוכל אבל לא לתוך הסל ולא לתוך הקופה שלא יעשה כדרך שהוא עושה בחול: **אין סוחטין את הפירות:** ד אמר רב יהודה אמר שמואל מודה היה רבי יהודה לחכמים בזיתים וענבים מ"ט כיון דלסחיטה ניתנו יהיב דעתיה ועולא אמר רב חלוק היה ר' יהודה אף בזיתים וענבים ורבי יוחנן אמר הלכה כרבי יהודה בשאר פירות ואין הלכה כרבי יהודה בזיתים וענבים אמר רבה אמר רב יהודה אמר שמואל מודה היה רבי יהודה לחכמים בזיתים וענבים ו ומודים חכמים לרבי יהודה בשאר פירות א"ל רבי ירמיה לרבי אבא אלא במאי פליגי א"ל לכי תשכח אמר רב נחמן בר יצחק מסתברא בתותים ורמונים פליגי דתניא ה זיתים שמשך מהן שמן וענבים שמשך מהן יין והכניסן בין לאוכל בין למשקין היוצא מהן אסור ו תותים שמשך מהן מים ורמונים שמשך מהן יין והכניסן לאוכלין היוצא מהן מותר למשקין ולסתם היוצא מהן אסור דברי רבי יהודה וחכמים אומרים בין לאוכלין בין למשקין היוצא מהן אסור וסבר רבי יהודה סתם אסור (ד) והתנן ז חלב האשה מטמא לרצון ושלא לרצון חלב בהמה אינו מטמא אלא לרצון אמר ר' עקיבא קל וחומר הוא ומה חלב האשה שאינו מיוחד אלא לקטנים מטמא לרצון ושלא לרצון חלב הבהמה שמיוחד בין לקטנים בין לגדולים אינו דין שיטמא בין לרצון ובין שלא לרצון אמרו לו אם טמא חלב האשה שלא לרצון ח שדם מגפתה טמא יטמא חלב הבהמה שלא

רש"י

חבית. מצילין הימנה מזון ג' סעודות. ואפילו בכלים הרבה דאילו בחד מנא אמרי' בכל כתבי הקדש (לעיל דף קכ.) דכמה דבעי מציל: **לכם.** כל אחד מזון ג' סעודות: **ובלבד שלא יספוג.** שלא ישים ספוג במקום היין לחזור ולהטיפו בכלי גזירה שמא יסחוט: **אין סוחטין את הפירות.** דהוה ליה מפרק (ג) תולדה דדישה: **אסורין.** גזירה שמא יסחוט לכתחילה: **רבי יהודה אומר אם לאוכלין.** הם מכונסין אותם פירות היוצא מהן מותר דלא ניחא ליה במה שזבו וליכא למגזר בהן שמא יסחוט: **ואם למשקין.** מכונסין אסורין דניחא ליה במאי דנפקא מינייהו ונתקיימה מחשבתו ואיכא למיגזר שמא יסחוט והכי אמרי' בביצה דטעמא דמשקין שזבו משום שמא יסחוט הוא: **חלות דבש.** מאחר שמרוסקין הדבש זב מאליו מתוך השעוה ואין דרך לסוחטו הלכך רבי אליעזר מתיר וחכמים אוסרין גזירה אטו שאינן מרוסקין דילמא מרסק להו (ג): **גמ' ויטפח.** מכניס בו כפו והשמן נדבק בה ומקנחו בשפת הכלי ואסרוה משום עובדין דחול: **מודה ר' יהודה בזיתים.** דאע"ג דהכניסן לאוכלין היוצא מהן אסור דכיון דרובן לסחיטה קיימי כי אתו לידי משקה יהיב דעתיה למיהוי ניחא ליה בהכי: **אפי' בזיתים וענבים.** הואיל והני לאוכלין נכנסו: **מסתברא בתותים ורמונים פליגי.** דאיכא דבעו להו למשקין הלכך משוו להו רבנן כזיתים וענבים ור' יהודה פליג עלייהו אבל שאר פירות דליכא דבעי להו למשקין הלכך מודו רבנן בהם: **שמשך.** זב מאליהן כמו נהרות המושכין (לעיל דף קכב.): **והכניסן.** מתחילתן בין לאוכלין בין למשקין כו' ברמונים קרי יין משום דאית להו קיוהא: **וחכ"א כו'.** והא דנקט רב נחמן לישנא דמסתברא ולא אמר בהדיא דבתותים ורמונים פליגי משום דאיכא למימר פליגי בתותים ורמונים וה"ה לשאר פירות ולהודיעך כחו דרבי יהודה נקט להו ולאו משום ברייתא דלקמן דשמעינן מינה דמודים חכמים לרבי יהודה בשאר פירות לאו בהדיא שמעינן לה דאיכא למימר רבי יהודה היא כדפרכינן עלה: **וסבר רבי יהודה סתם.** שלא פירש לאוכל ולא למשקה הוי המשקה הזב מהן אסור: **והתנן חלב האשה מטמא.** מכשיר: **לרצון ושלא לרצון.** בין שיצא ממנה לרצון בין שיצא שלא לרצון שהחלב קרוי משקה שנאמר ותפתח את נאד החלב ותשקהו (שופטים ד): **חלב הבהמה אינו מטמא אלא אם כן יצא לרצון.** ואי לא לא חשיב משקה ואם נגע בו שרץ אינו מקבל טומאה וטעמא מפרש לקמיה: שדם

תוספות

חבית. ובלבד שלא יספוג. אפילו יש לו עוד בית אחיזה דליכא חשש סחיטה אסור כדמפרש בגמרא שלא יעשה כדרך שעושה בחול: **מלקט** על יד על יד ואוכל. נראה דל"ג ואוכל מדקתני סיפא אבל לא לתוך הסל ולא לתוך הקופה משמע הכא דווקא אסירי משום עובדא דחול אבל לתוך (א) כפו שרי: **ורבי** יוחנן אמר הלכה כרבי יהודה בשאר פירות. בריש מסכת ביצה (דף ג. ושם) רבי יוחנן רמי דר' יהודה אדר' יהודה תנן ר"י אומר אם לאוכלין היוצא מהן מותר אם למשקין כו' אלמא כל לאוכלין אוכלא דאפרת הוא ורמינהו ועוד אמר ר"י מתנה אדם על הכלכלה של פירות ביו"ט ראשון ואוכלה בשני וכן ביצה שנולדה בראשון אוכלה בשני בשני אין בראשון לא ואמר רבי יוחנן מוחלפת השיטה וצריך לומר דההיא דמתנה אדם מחליף דאי מתני' מחליף אם כן במאי דנקט הכא ר' יהודה הוה ליה למינקט רבנן וה"ל למימר הלכה כרבנן בשאר פירות. מ"ר. (ו) ולי נראה דאפילו אפיך מתני' אתי שפיר כעין שמצינו בב"ק בפרק הגוזל קמא (דף צו:) דתנן גזל בהמה והזקינה עבדים והזקינו משלם כשעת הגזלה ר"מ אומר בעבדים אומר לו הרי שלך לפניך ואמר בגמרא אמר רבי חנינא בר אבדימי אמר רב הלכה כר"מ ופריך ורב שביק רבנן ועביד כר"מ כו' עד דמסיק דרב מתניתין איפכא אתנא' אלמא אע"פ שהיה שונה במתניתין וחכ"א בעבדים אומר לו הרי שלך לפניך וה"ל למימר השתא הלכה כחכמים אפ"ה נקט ר"מ לפי מה שהאחרים שונין המשנה ה"נ נקט רבי יוחנן רבי יהודה בשמעתין וכן נמי מצינו בשילהי פ"ק דסוכה (דף יט:) דתנן העושה סוכתו כמין צריף ר"א פוסל וחכמים מכשירין ואמרינן בגמרא אביי אשכחיה לרב יוסף דגני בכילת חתנים בסוכה א"ל כמאן כר"א א"ל שבקת רבנן ועבדת כר"א אמר ליה ברייתא איפכא תניא השתא היה לו להשיב רב יוסף כרבנן ולא כר"א כיון דלדידיה איפכא תני אלא כן דרך הש"ס בכל מקום. נראה לי: **הלכה** כר' יהודה בשאר פירות. אע"ג דבריש ביצה (ד' ג.) גזר ר' יוחנן ביצה שנולדה ביו"ט משום משקין שזבו והכא לא גזר בשאר פירות י"ל דשייך טפי לגזור בביצה לפי שהיא עומדת ליסחט מן התרנגולת (י) ודרך לגומעה חיה אבל שאר פירות אין עומדים ליסחט כלל. מ"ר: **שמשך** מהן שמן כו'. פי' בקונט' שמשך זב מאליהן כמו נהרות המושכין ולפירושו צריך לומר הכניסן בין לאוכלין כו' היינו הכניסן מתחילתן ואין הלשון משמע כן ועוד קשה לר"י דאי משך מאליו קאמר גבי תותים שמשך מהם מים ה"ל למימר שמשכו או שנמשכו דמים בכל מקום לשון רבים ועוד קשה לר"י אם כן הך ברייתא הוה תיובתא דרב ורבי יוחנן דאמרי לעיל חלוק היה רבי יהודה בזיתים וענבים דהכא משמע דבזיתים וענבים מודה אלא נראה לר"י דמשך אאדם קאי וסחטן תחילה ושוב הכניסן דהשתא לרב ורבי יוחנן דסברי חלוק היה רבי יהודה בזיתים וענבים נקט דוקא משך דאיכא למיחש טפי דילמא יהיב דעתיה לסחוט משקה אחר שהכניסו נמי לאכילה מאחר שסחטן תחילה להוציא מהן משקה הא לא משך לא ולשמואל דאמר מודה רבי יהודה בזיתים וענבים נקט משך משום רבותא דתותים ורמונים דאפילו משך הכניסן לאוכלין היוצא מהן מותר. מ"ר: **חלב** האשה מטמא לרצון ושלא לרצון. והא דתנן במסכת מכשירין (פ"א) כל משקה שתחילתו לרצון אף על פי שאין סופו לרצון או שסופו לרצון אף על פי שאין תחלתו לרצון מכשיר לא דמי רצון דהתם לרצון דהכא דהתם מיירי בשעת נפילתן על הזרעים שיהא לרצון דבעינן יותן דומיא דכי יתן מה יתן דניחא ליה אף יותן דניחא ליה אבל הכא מיירי בשעת פרישה מן האשה או מן הבהמה: **לרצון** ושלא לרצון. כדמפרש בסמוך טעמא משום דדם מגפתה טמא וחלב ודם חד הוא דדם נעכר ונעשה חלב ולא צריכין למה שפי' בקונט' משום דאיקרי משקה שנאמר ותפתח את נאד החלב ותשקהו ונראה לר"י דהא דאיצטריך לפרש האי טעמא בפ' דם נדה (נדה דף נה:) גבי חלב האשה הנ"מ לרבי עקיבא דשמעתין דלית ליה טעמא (ל) דפרישה או למאן דלית ליה דם נעכר ונעשה חלב אבל לרבנן דשמעתין לא צריך (ד) כדפרישית לחלב האשה אלא דוקא לטמא חלב בהמה לרצון. (מ) מ"ר:

מחמיר

עין משפט נר מצוה

א א ב מיי' פכ"ב מהל' שבת הלכה טו סמג לאוין סה טוש"ע א"ח סי' שלה סעיף א:
ב ג מיי' שם פכ"א הל' יא טוש"ע שם סעיף ה:
ג ד ה ו מיי' פכ"א מהל' שבת הלכה יב סמג שם טוש"ע א"ח סי' שכ סעיף א:
ד ז מיי' פ"י מהלכות טומאת אוכלין הל' ד:
ה ח שם הל' ה ופ"א מהל' משכב ומושב הלכה טו:

רבינו חננאל

חבית שנשברה מצילין הימנה מזון ג' סעודות וכו' תנא לא יספוג ביין בכפיו ולא יטפח בשמן ביד כדרך שהוא עושה בחול. לא יטפח כדאמרינן בכל מקום טופח ע"מ להטפיח וכדתנן בפרק החובל בחבירו וכו'. מעשה באחד שפרע ראשה של אשה כו' עד שמרה עומדת על פתח חצירה ושיבר הפך בפניה. ובה כאיסר שמן. גילתה ראשה והיתה מטפחת ומנחת על ראשה וכו': ת"ר נתפזרו לו פירות בחצירו מלקט על יד על יד ואוכל. אבל לא לתוך הסל ולא לתוך הקופה שלא יעשה כדרך שהוא עושה בחול וכו' וחלקו רב יהודה אמר שמואל ורב ועולא כל חד וחד מעמיד חלוקת ר' יהודה וחכמים ור' יוחנן אמר הלכה כר' יהודה בשאר פירות ואין הלכה כמותו בזיתים וענבים. א"ר אבא אמר רב יהודה אמר שמואל מודה היה רבי יהודה לחכמים בזיתים וענבים ומודים חכמים לרבי יהודה בשאר פירות. ובמאי פליגי בתותים ורמונים דתניא זיתים שמשך מהן שמן וענבים שמשך מהן יין והכניסן בין לאוכלין בין למשקין היוצא מהן אסור. תותים שמשך מהן מים ורמונים שמשך מהן יין והכניסן לאוכלין היוצא מהן מותר למשקין ולסתם היוצא מהן אסור דברי ר' יהודה וחכ"א בין לאוכלין בין למשקין היוצא מהן אסור. נמצאת חלוקת ר' יהודה וחכמים בתותים ורמונים ובה א"ר יוחנן הלכה כר' יהודה בשאר פירות וכיון שפסק ר' יוחנן הלכה כר' יהודה הוצרכנו לברר דבריו ולפיכך אמרינן וסבר ר' יהודה סתם אסור והתנן

מסורת הש"ס

א) ביצה ג. חולין יד., ב) לעיל יט., ג) חולין יד., ד) מכשירין פ"ו מ"ח כריתות יג., ה) [בכמקון תוספות איתא כמותו], ו) [עיין תוס' ביצה ג. ד"ה ר"י אמר], ז) נ"א ועוד ור"י לא איירי רק משאר פירות גם מזיתים וענבים אבל מתותים ורמונים ליכא מוכר כלום דעמו משא"כ ר' יהודה דאמר כפי' תותים ורמונים אם הכניסן לאוכלין היוצא מהן מותר והן דומין לביצה ואפ"ה ס"ל דבראשון אסור בביצה וע"כ רמי ליה אהדדי במסכת עירובין לט. ובמס' ביצה והיותר פשוט שאין להגיה כלום וצ"ל והדרך לגומעה ור"ל לישב לדף אם עומדת לסחיטה ומ"מ צריך עוד תיקון ואינו ראוי לדמות למשקין שזבו שא"צ שום תקון ע"ז אמר והדרך כו', ח) י"ג דפריסית, ט) [ועי' תוס' נדה יט: ד"ה כמיב הכא].

הגהות הב"ח

(א) במשנה ור"א מתיר. נ"ב ר' אלעזר גרסי'. עי' בפירש"י בפ"ק דשבת דף יט ריש ע"ב: (ב) רש"י ד"ה אין סוחטין וכו' מפרק דהוא תולדה: (ג) ד"ה חלות וכו' להו הס"ד ואח"כ מ"ה ולא יטפח: (ד) תוס' ד"ה לרצון וכו' לא צריך לחלב האשה כדפי' אלא:

ליקוטי רש"י

אין סוחטין את הפירות. וסחיטת פירות תולדה דדש היא שמפרקן מתוך זג שלהן כמפרק תבואה מקש שלה [ביצה ג.]. סחיטה אב מלאכה היא [חולין יד: ע"ש במסורש"י]. **ואם יצאו מעצמן אסורין.** בו ביום גזרה שמא יסחוט. **אם לאוכלין.** הן מכונסין הפירות הללו היוצא מהן מותר בו ביום דכיון דלא ניחא ליה בהכי משקין ליכא למגזר שמא יסחוט. היוצא מהן אוכלא דאפרת הוא ואינו בכלל גזרת משקין שזבו [ביצה שם]. אם היו עומדין לאכילה ולא לסחוט היוצא מהם מותר דכיון דלא ניחא ליה ליכא למיגזר אי שרית להו בשמיה היום אתי לסחוט דהא לאו להכי קיימי. **ואם למשקין.** הואיל ונתקיימה מחשבתו אי שרית להו כשזבו איכא למיגזר בהו שמא יסחוט דהא להכי קיימי [חולין שם]. **חלות דבש.** הכוורת דאמר שעשאה פירות ויצאו הנחילין לוקחין את הדבש והוא עשוי חלות חלות ויש בו י' חלות או עשרים זה בצד זה מסוגר והדבש מעורב יחד [רשב"ם ב"ב פ.]. שהכוורת רודה ועשויין כמין חלות של שעוה והדבש בתוכן. **שריסקן.** כתתן. **אסורין.** לאוכלן שבת באכילה. **ורבי אליעזר.** הוא ר' אלעזר בן שמוע שהם ר' אלעזר של משנה ובריית' מתיר. דבא לאמר שזב מן החלות נמי אוכלא הוא הלכך ליכא למיגזר ביה שמא יסחוט משמשכן דלא שייכא ביה סחיטה [לעיל יט: ועיין כאן ברש"ש]. **מודה היה רבי יהודה לחכמים**

בזיתים וענבים. שאפילו הכניסן לאכילה הואיל ורוב בני אדם סוחטין אותם האי נמי ממליך עלייהו ואי שרית למשקין שזבו מהן אתי למיסחט. כיון דלסחיטה ניתנו. כיון דלהכי קיימי סתם ענבים. יהיב דעתיה. עלייהו למשקין וכי הוו משקין הוה ליה נתקיימה מחשבתו וגזרה שמא יסחוט. חלוק היה ר' יהודה. ומתיר [חולין שם]. מגפתה. לשון (תהלים לא) פן תגוף באבן רגלך [שם לה:].

עַל יָד וְאוֹכֵל – ONE MAY GATHER them A LITTLE AT A TIME AND EAT them as one gathers them, אֲבָל לֹא לְתוֹךְ הַסַּל וְלֹא לְתוֹךְ הַקּוּפָּה – BUT one should NOT gather them INTO A BASKET OR INTO A BOX, שֶׁלֹּא יַעֲשֶׂה כְּדֶרֶךְ שֶׁהוּא עוֹשֶׂה בְּחוֹל – SO THAT ONE WILL NOT DO on the Sabbath AS ONE DOES ON THE WEEKDAY.[13]

The Mishnah stated:
אֵין סוֹחֲטִין אֶת הַפֵּירוֹת – WE MAY NOT SQUEEZE FRUITS [on the Sabbath to extract liquid from them].

In the Mishnah, the Sages and R' Yehudah dispute the permissibility of liquid that oozed from fruits on the Sabbath. The Gemara records several Amoraic opinions regarding their dispute:
אָמַר רַב יְהוּדָה אָמַר שְׁמוּאֵל – **Rav Yehudah stated in the name of Shmuel:** מוֹדֶה הָיָה רַבִּי יְהוּדָה לַחֲכָמִים בְּזֵיתִים וַעֲנָבִים – **R' Yehudah** in fact **agreed with the Sages in** the case of liquid that oozed from **olives or grapes** on the Sabbath. He admits that even if the olives and grapes were stored for eating, the juice that flowed from them is prohibited. מַאי טַעְמָא – **What is the reason** for this? כֵּיוָן דִּלְסְחִיטָה נִינְהוּ יָהִיב דַּעְתֵּיהּ – For **since** most **[olives and grapes] are** designated **for squeezing, one will** often **change one's mind**[14] upon seeing juice flow from them,[15] and will designate for squeezing fruits that were originally stored for eating. We therefore fear that allowing one to use the juice of these fruits could lead one to unthinkingly squeeze them on the Sabbath.

A divergent opinion regarding this dispute:
וְעוּלָּא אָמַר רַב – **But Ulla said in the name of Rav:** חָלוּק הָיָה רַבִּי יְהוּדָה אַף בְּזֵיתִים וַעֲנָבִים – **R' Yehudah disagreed** with the Sages **even in** the case of liquid that oozed from **olives or grapes.**[16] Thus, R' Yehudah holds that the liquid they exude is prohibited only if they were stored for squeezing; but if they were stored for eating, it is permissible.

A third Amoraic statement:
וְרַבִּי יוֹחָנָן אָמַר – **And R' Yochanan said:** הֲלָכָה כְּרַבִּי יְהוּדָה בִּשְׁאָר פֵּירוֹת – **The halachah follows R' Yehudah in** the case of liquid that oozed from **other** sorts of **fruit** on the Sabbath. If the fruits were stored for eating, one may consume the liquid. וְאֵין הֲלָכָה כְּרַבִּי יְהוּדָה בְּזֵיתִים וַעֲנָבִים – **But the halachah does not follow R' Yehudah in** the case of liquid that oozed from **olives and grapes.** Even if the olives and grapes were stored for eating, one may not consume the liquid they exuded.[17]

A fourth statement:
אָמַר רַבָּה אָמַר רַב יְהוּדָה אָמַר שְׁמוּאֵל – **Rabbah said in the name of Rav Yehudah, who said in the name of Shmuel:** מוֹדֶה הָיָה רַבִּי יְהוּדָה לַחֲכָמִים בְּזֵיתִים וַעֲנָבִים – **R' Yehudah agreed with the Sages in** the case of liquid that oozed from **olives or grapes** on the Sabbath.[18] וּמוֹדִים חֲכָמִים לְרַבִּי יְהוּדָה בִּשְׁאָר פֵּירוֹת – **And the Sages agree with R' Yehudah in** the case of liquid that oozed from **other** sorts of **fruit.**[19]

The Gemara asks:
אָמַר לֵיהּ רַבִּי יִרְמְיָה לְרַבִּי אַבָּא – **R' Yirmiyah said to R' Abba:** אֶלָּא בְּמַאי פְּלִיגִי – **But** then **in what** case **do they disagree?**

R' Abba answered:
אָמַר לֵיהּ – **He said to him:** לְכִי תִשְׁכַּח – **When** you will study the matter, **you will find** in what case they disagree.[20]

Rav Nachman bar Yitzchak gives the case in which they disagree:
אָמַר רַב נַחְמָן בַּר יִצְחָק – **Rav Nachman bar Yitzchak said:** מִסְתַּבְּרָא בְּתוּתִים וְרִמּוֹנִים פְּלִיגִי – **It is probable that they disagree in** the case of liquid that oozed from **mulberries and pomegranates.**[21] דְּתַנְיָא – **For it has been taught in a Baraisa:** זֵיתִים שֶׁמָּשַׁךְ מֵהֶם שֶׁמֶן וַעֲנָבִים שֶׁמָּשַׁךְ מֵהֶן יַיִן – Concerning OLIVES FROM WHICH OIL OOZED on the Sabbath, AND GRAPES FROM WHICH WINE OOZED on the Sabbath: וְהִכְנִיסָן בֵּין לְאוֹכֵל בֵּין לְמַשְׁקִין – WHETHER ONE had originally STORED THEM FOR FOOD OR WHETHER one had stored them FOR LIQUID,[22] הַיּוֹצֵא מֵהֶן אָסוּר – [THE LIQUID] THAT OOZED FROM THEM IS PROHIBITED for consumption.

NOTES

13. The Rishonim explain this law in several ways. *Ramban* states that the case concerns fruit that became mixed with the dirt and pebbles commonly found in courtyards. Although one who picks the fruit from the dirt is not in violation of the *melachah* of בורר, *selecting,* [either because the pieces of fruit are large (*Ramban;* see *Terumas HaDeshen* §57) or because one plans to eat them immediately (*Mishnah Berurah* 335:17)] one is forbidden to do so and then place the fruit into a receptacle, as this would *resemble* the act of selecting [for storage], which is prohibited. If one eats the fruit as he gathers it, however, the gathering does not resemble selecting and is therefore permissible. [According to *Ramban,* this act is an example of a weekday activity prohibited because it *resembles* a *melachah* (see General Introduction).] Other Rishonim explain that the case concerns fruits that were widely scattered throughout the courtyard. One is prohibited to collect the fruits and place them into a receptacle because gathering fruits for storage is an activity generally reserved for the weekdays (*Rashba; Ritva MHK* ed., second explanation). [One is permitted, however, to gather the fruit a little at a time for immediate consumption, as this act is *not* deemed a weekday activity. According to these Rishonim, this is a weekday activity prohibited because of *detraction from the aura of the Sabbath* (see General Introduction).] *Tosafos* and *Rosh* maintain that the Baraisa's injunction against placing the fruit into receptacles implies that to gather it into one's lap or garment is permissible, even if one intends to eventually store the fruit and not to eat it immediately. They therefore emend the Baraisa, removing the word וְאוֹכֵל, *and eat* [them] (see, however, *Beur HaGra* to *Orach Chaim* 335:5 and *Beur Halachah* ibid.). Finally, *Rambam* (*Shabbos* 21:11) prohibits this act because it is a weekday activity that could lead one to violation of the *melachah* of מְעַמֵּר, *gathering together* (this is a third category of weekday activity – see General Introduction). [*Hagahos Maimoniyos* (ibid. §8) questions *Rambam* on the grounds that gathering is forbidden only if it is performed in the place that the fruits were grown; for a lengthy discussion of this issue, see *Eglei Tal* מעמר §2 and §10; see also *Rambam, Shabbos* 8:6 with *Kesef Mishneh.*]

14. [Literally: put one's mind (to using them for squeezing).]

15. For since the majority of olives and grapes are designated for squeezing, one will look with satisfaction upon oil or juice that oozes from them even if he originally intended them for eating (*Rashi*).

16. For although most olives and grapes are indeed designated for squeezing, since these particular ones were designated for eating [we do not fear that one will inadvertently squeeze them on the Sabbath. One is therefore permitted to consume the liquid they exude] (*Rashi*).

17. [Since R' Yochanan gives the halachah for both the case of liquid that oozed from olives and grapes, and for that of liquid that oozed from other sorts of fruits, it is clear that he holds that the dispute concerned both these sorts of liquid. He is thus in opposition to Shmuel, who is quoted above as saying that R' Yehudah agrees with the Sages in the case of liquid that oozed from olives and grapes, and below as saying that the Sages agree with R' Yehudah in the case of liquid that oozed from other sorts of fruit (see *Tosafos* ד"ה שמשך).]

18. [I.e. that even if the olives and grapes were stored for eating, the juice they exude is prohibited.]

19. [Regarding what exactly the Sages and R' Yehudah hold in the case of liquid that oozed from other sorts of fruit, see below 144b note 8.]

20. *Chidushei HaRan.*

21. The Sages hold that since mulberries and pomegranates are designated for squeezing by some people, their law is identical to that of olives and grapes. Therefore, even if they are stored for eating, the juice that oozes from them is forbidden, lest one be led to unthinkingly take them in hand and squeeze them. R' Yehudah disagrees [for since mulberries and pomegranates, unlike olives and grapes, are not universally used for squeezing, we do not suspect that one who originally stored them for eating will change his mind and come to squeeze them]. With regard to other sorts of fruit, however, the Sages agree with R' Yehudah, since no one at all designates them for squeezing (*Rashi*; see *Mishnah Berurah* 320:8,9).

22. *Rashi;* cf. *Tosafos;* see *Tosafos* to 144a ד"ה תותים; see *Hagahos R' Elazar Moshe Horowitz.*

עין משפט
נר מצוה

א א ב מיי' פכ"ב מהל' שבת הלכה טז סמג לאוין סה טוש"ע א"ח סי' שלה סעיף א:
ב ג מיי' שם פכ"א הל' יא טוש"ע שם סעיף ה:
ג ד ה ו מיי' פכ"א מהל' שבת הלכה יב סמג שם טוש"ע א"ח סי' שכ סעיף א:
ד ז מיי' פ"י מהלכות טומאת אוכלין הל' ד:
ה ח שם הל' ה ופ"א מהל' משכב ומושב הלכה טז:

מסורת הש"ס

א) ביצה ג. חולין יד:, ב) לעיל יט:, ג) חולין יד:, ד) מכשירין פ"ו מ"ח כריתות יג., ה) [נפסקי תוספות איתא כתותן], ו) [עיין תוס' ביצה ג. ד"ה ר"י אמר], ז) נ"א ועוד ור"י לא איירי רק משאר פירות גם מזיתים וענבים אבל מתותים ורמונים אינו מזכיר כלום דעתו משא"כ ר' יהודה דאמר בפי' תותים ורמונים אם הכניסן לאוכלין היוצא מהן מותר והן דומין לביצה ואפ"ה ס"ל דבראשון אסור בביצה וע"כ רמי ליה אהדדי במסכת עירובין לט. וכמש' ביצה והיותר פשוט שאין להגיה כלום וצ"ל ודרך לגומעה ור"ל לייסב דאף אם עומדת לסחיטה ומ"מ צריך עוד תיקון ואינו ראוי לדמות למשקין שזבו שא"צ שום תקון ע"ז אמר ודרך כו', ח) י"ג דפריסית, ט) [ועי' תוס' נדה יט: ד"ה כתיב הכא].

הגהות הב"ח

(א) במשנה ור"א מתיר. נ"ב ר' אלעזר גרסי'. עי' בפירש"י בפ"ק דשבת דף יט ע"ב: (ב) רש"י ד"ה אין סוחטין וכו' מפרק דהוא תולדה: (ג) ד"ה חלות וכו' להו הס"ד ואח"כ מ"ה ולא יטפח: (ד) תוס' ד"ה לרצון וכו' לא צריך לחלב האשה כדפי' אלא:

ליקוטי רש"י

אין סוחטין את הפירות. וסחיטת פירות תולדה דדש היא שמפרקן מתוך זג שלהן כמפרק תבואה מקש שלה [ביצה ג.]. סחיטה אב מלאכה היא [חולין יד: ע"ש במסוה"ש]. ואם יצאו מעצמן אסורין. בו ביום גזרה שמא יסחוט. אם לאוכלין. הן מכונסין הפירות הללו היוצא מהן מותר בו ביום דכיון דלא ניחא ליה בהני משקין ליכא למגזר שמא יסחוט. היוצא מהן אוכלא דאפרת הוא ואינו בכלל גזירת משקין שזבו [ביצה שם]. אם היו עומדין לאכילה ולא לסחוט היוצא מהם מותר דכיון דלא ניחא ליה ליכא למיגזר אי שרית להו דשמייה הייס אתי לסחוט דהא לאו להכי קיימי. ואם למשקין. הואיל ונתקיימה מחשבתו אי שרית להו כשזבו איכא למיגזר בהו שמא יסחוט דהא להכי קיימי [חולין שם]. חלות דבש. הכוורת לאחר שעשתה פירות ויצאו הנחילין לוקחין את הדבש והוא עשוי חלות חלות ויש בו י' חלות או עשרים זה בצד זה משעוה ודבש מעורב יחד [רשב"ם ב"ב פ.]. שהכוורת רודה ועשוין כמין חלות של שעוה והדבש בתוכן. שריסקן. כותתן. אסורין. לאותו שבת באכילה. ורבי [אלעזר]. הוא ר' אלעזר בן שמוע סתם ר' אלעזר של משנה וברייתא מתיר. דבש לאחר שזב מן החלות נמי אוכלא הוא הלכך ליכא למיגזר ביה שמא יסחוט משמשך דלא שייכא ביה סחיטה [לעיל יט: ועיין כאן ברש"ש]. מודה היה רבי יהודה לחכמים

חבית. ובלבד שלא יספוג. אפילו יש לו עור בית אחיזה דליכא משום סחיטה אסור כדמפרש בגמרא שלא יעשה כדרך שעושה בחול: מלקט על יד על יד ואוכל. נראה דלר"ג ואוכל מדקתני סיפא אבל לא לתוך הסל ולא לתוך הקופה משמע הך דווקא אסירי משום עובדא דחול אבל לתוך ט) כפו שרי: ורבי יוחנן אמר הלכה כרבי יהודה בשאר פירות. בריש מסכת ביצה (דף ג. ושם) רבי יוחנן רמי דר' יהודה אדר' יהודה תנן ר"י אומר אם לאוכלין היוצא מהן מותר אם למשקין כו' אלמא כל לאוכלין אוכלא דאפרת הוא ורמינהו ועוד אמר ר"י מתנה אדם על הכלכלה של פירות ביו"ט ראשון ואוכלה בשני וכן ביצה שנולדה בראשון אוכלה בשני אלמא אין ברירה לא ואמר רבי יוחנן מוחלפת השיטה וצריך לומר דהיינו מתני' מחליף אם כן במאי דנקט הכא ר' יהודה הוה ליה למינקט רבנן וה"ל למימר הלכה כרבנן בשאר פירות. מ"ר. י) ולי נראה דאפילו אפיך מתני' אתי שפיר כעין שמצינו בב"ק בפרק הגוזל קמא (דף צו:) דתנן גזל בהמה והכחישה עבדים והזקינו משלם כשעת הגזלה ר"מ אומר בעבדים אומר לו הרי שלך לפניך ואמר בגמרא אמר רבי חנינא בר אבדימי אמר רב הלכה כר"מ ופריך ורב שביק רבנן ועביד כר"מ כו' עד דמסיק דרב מתניתין איפכא תנא' אלמא אע"פ שהיה שונה במתניתין וחכ"א בעבדים אומר לו הרי שלך לפניך וה"ל למימר הלכה כחכמים אפ"ה נקט ר"מ לפי מה שהאחרים שונין המשנה ה"נ נקט רבי יוחנן רבי יהודה בשמעתין וכן נמי מצינו בשילהי פ"ק דסוכה (דף יט.) דתנן העושה סוכתו כמין צריף ר"א פוסל וחכמים מכשירין ואמרינן בגמרא אביי אשכחיה לרב יוסף דגני בכילת חתנים בסוכה א"ל כמאן כר"א א"ל שבקת רבנן ועבדת כר"א אמר ליה ברייתא איפכא תניא השתא היה לו להשיב רב יוסף כרבנן ולא כר"א כיון דלדידיה איפכא תני אלא כן דרך הש"ס בכל מקום. נראה לי:

הלכה כר' יהודה בשאר פירות. אע"ג דבריש ביצה (ד' ג.) גזר ר' יוחנן ביצה שנולדה ביו"ט משום משקין שזבו והכא לא גזר בשאר פירות י"ל דשייך טפי לגזור בביצה לפי שהיא עומדת ליסחט מן התרנגולת ז) ודרך לגומעה היא אבל שאר פירות אין עומדים ליסחט כלל. מ"ר:

שמשך מהן שמן כו'. פי' בקונט' שמשך זב מאליהן כמו נהרות המושכין ולפירושו צריך לומר הכניסן בין לאוכלין כו' היינו הכניסן מתחילתן ואין הלשון משמע כן ועוד קשה לר"י דאי משך מאליו קאמר גבי תותים שמשך מהם מים ה"ל למימר שמשכו או שנמשכו דמים בכל מקום לשון רבים ועוד קשה לר"י אם כן הך ברייתא הויא תיובתא דרב ורבי יוחנן דאמרי לעיל חלוק היה רבי יהודה בזיתים וענבים דהכא משמע דבזיתים וענבים מודה אלא נראה לר"י דמשך אאדם קאי וסחטן תחילה ושוב הכניסן דהשתא לרב ורבי יוחנן דסברי חלוק היה רבי יהודה בזיתים וענבים נקט דוקא משך דאיכא למיחש טפי דילמא יהיב דעתיה לסחוט משקה אחר שהכניסו נמי לאכילה מאחר שסחטן תחילה להוציא מהן משקה הא לא משך לא ולשמואל דאמר מודה רבי יהודה בזיתים וענבים נקט משך משום רבותא דתותים ורמונים דאפילו משך הכניסן לאוכלין היוצא מהן מותר. מ"ר:

חלב האשה מטמא לרצון ושלא לרצון. והא דתנן במסכת מכשירין (פ"ו) כל משקה שתחילתו לרצון אף על פי שאין סופו לרצון או שסופו לרצון אף על פי שאין תחלתו לרצון מכשיר לא דמי רצון דהתם לרצון דהכא דהתם מיירי בשעת נפילתן על הזרעים שיהא לרצון דבעינן יותן דומיא דכי יתן מה יתן דניחא ליה אף יותן דניחא ליה אבל הכא מיירי בשעת פרישה מן האשה או מן הבהמה:

לרצון ושלא לרצון. כדמפרש בסמוך טעמא משום דדם מגפתה טמא וחלב ודם חד הוא דדם נעכר ונעשה חלב ולא צריכין למה שפי' בקונט' משום דאיקרי משקה שנאמר ותפתח את נאד החלב ותשקהו ונראה לר"י דהא דאיצטריך לפרש האי טעמא בפ' דם נדה (נדה דף נה:) גבי חלב האשה הנ"מ לרבי עקיבא דשמעתין דלית ליה טעמא ח) דפרישה או למאן דלית ליה דם נעכר ונעשה חלב אבל לרבנן דשמעתין לא צריך (ד) כדפרישית לחלב האשה אלא דוקא לטמא חלב בהמה לרצון. ט) מ"ר:

מחמיר

חבית אשנשברה מצילין הימנה מזון שלש סעודות ואומר לאחרים באו והצילו לכם ובלבד שלא יספוג א אין סוחטין את הפירות להוציא מהן משקין ואם יצאו מעצמן אסורין ר' יהודה אומר אם לאוכלין היוצא מהן מותר ואם למשקין היוצא מהן אסור ב חלות דבש שריסקן מע"ש ויצאו מעצמן אסורין (א) ורבי אליעזר מתיר: גמ' תנא לא ג יספוג ביין ולא יטפח בשמן שלא יעשה כדרך שהוא עושה בחול ת"ר ג נתפזרו לו פירות בחצר מלקט על יד על יד ואוכל אבל לא לתוך הסל ולא לתוך הקופה שלא יעשה כדרך שהוא עושה בחול: אין סוחטין את הפירות: ג אמר רב יהודה אמר שמואל מודה היה רבי יהודה לחכמים בזיתים וענבים מ"ט כיון דלסחיטה נינהו יהיב דעתיה ועולא אמר רב חלוק היה ר' יהודה אף בזיתים וענבים ורבי יוחנן אמר הלכה כרבי יהודה בשאר פירות ואין הלכה כרבי יהודה בזיתים וענבים אמר רבה אמר רב יהודה אמר שמואל מודה היה רבי יהודה לחכמים בזיתים וענבים ד ומודים חכמים לרבי יהודה בשאר פירות א"ל רבי ירמיה לרבי אבא אלא במאי פליגי א"ל לכי תשכח אמר רב נחמן בר יצחק מסתברא בתותים ורמונים פליגי דתניא ה זיתים שמשך מהן שמן וענבים שמשך מהן יין והכניסן בין לאוכל בין למשקין היוצא מהן אסור ו תותים שמשך מהן מים ורמונים שמשך מהן יין והכניסן לאוכלין היוצא מהן מותר למשקין ולסתם היוצא מהן אסור דברי רבי יהודה וחכמים אומרים בין לאוכלין בין למשקין היוצא מהן אסור וסבר רבי יהודה סתם אסור ז והתנן ז חלב האשה מטמא לרצון ושלא לרצון חלב בהמה אינו מטמא אלא לרצון אמר ר' עקיבא קל וחומר הוא ומה חלב האשה שאינו מיוחד אלא לקטנים מטמא לרצון ושלא לרצון חלב הבהמה שמיוחד בין לקטנים בין לגדולים אינו דין שיטמא בין לרצון ובין שלא לרצון אמרו לו אם טמא חלב האשה שלא לרצון ח שדם מגפתה טמא יטמא חלב הבהמה שלא

חבית. מצילין הימנה מזון ג' סעודות. ואפילו בכלים הרבה דאילו בחד מנא אמרי' בכל כתבי הקדש (לעיל דף קכ.) דכמה דבעי מציל: לכם. כל אחד מזון ג' סעודות: ובלבד שלא יספוג. שלא ישים ספוג במקום היין לחזור ולהטיפו בכלי גזירה שמא יסחוט: אין סוחטין את הפירות. דהוה ליה מפרק (ב) תולדה דדישה: אסורין. גזירה שמא יסחוט לכתחילה: רבי יהודה אומר אם לאוכלין. הם מכונסין אותם פירות היוצא מהן מותר דלא ניחא ליה במה שזבו וליכא למגזר בהן שמא יסחוט: ואם למשקין. מכונסין אסורין דניחא ליה במאי דנפקא מינייהו ונתקיימה מחשבתו ואיכא למיגזר שמא יסחוט והכי אמרי' בביצה דטעמא דמשקין שזבו משום שמא יסחוט הוא: חלות דבש. מאחר שמרוסקין הדבש זב מאליו מתוך השעוה ואין דרך לסוחטו הלכך רבי אליעזר מתיר וחכמים אוסרין גזירה אטו שאינן מרוסקין דילמא מרסק להו (ג): גמ' ויטפח. מכניס בו כפו והשמן נדבק בה ומקנחו בשפת הכלי ואסרוה משום עובדין דחול: מודה ר' יהודה בזיתים. דאע"ג דהכניסן לאוכלין היוצא מהן אסור דכיון דרובן לסחיטה קיימי כי אתו לידי משקה יהיב דעתיה למיהוי ניחא ליה בהכי: אפי' בזיתים וענבים. הואיל והני לאוכלין נכנסו: מסתברא בתותים ורמונים פליגי. דאיכא דבעו להו לאוכל ואיכא דבעו להו למשקין הלכך משוו להו רבנן כזיתים וענבים ור' יהודה פליג עלייהו אבל שאר פירות ליכא דבעי להו למשקין הלכך מודו רבנן בהם: שמשך. זב מאליהן כמו נהרות המושכין (לעיל דף קכא.): והכניסן. מתחילתן בין לאוכלין בין למשקין כו' דרמונים קרי יין משום דאית להו קיוהא: וחכ"א כו'. והא דנקט רב נחמן לישנא דמסתברא ולא אמר בהדיא משום דאיכא למימר פליגי בתותים ורמונים וה"ה לשאר פירות ולהודיעך כחו דרבי יהודה נקט להו ולאו משום ברייתא דלקמן דשמעינן מינה דמודים חכמים לרבי יהודה בשאר פירות לאו בהדיא שמעינן לה דאיכא למימר רבי יהודה היא כדפרכינן עלה: וסבר רבי יהודה סתם. שלא פירש לאוכל ולא למשקה הוי המשקה הזב מהן אסור: והתנן חלב האשה מטמא. מכשיר: לרצון ושלא לרצון. בין שיצא ממנה לרצון בין שיצא שלא לרצון שהחלב קרוי משקה שנאמר ותפתח את נאד החלב ותשקהו (שופטים ד): חלב הבהמה אינו מטמא אלא אם כן יצא לרצון. ואי לא לא חשיב משקה ואם נגע בו שרץ אינו מקבל טומאה וטעמא מפרש לקמיה:

שדם

בזיתים וענבים. שאפילו הכניסן לאכילה הואיל ורוב בני אדם סוחטין אותם הא נמי ממליך עלייהו ואי שרית למשקין שזבו מהן אתי למיסחט. כיון דלסחיטה נינהו. כיון דלהכי קיימי סתם ענבים. יהיב דעתיה. עלייהו למשקין וכי הוו משקין הוה ליה נתקיימה מחשבתו וגזרה שמא יסחוט. חלוק היה ר' יהודה. ומתיר [חולין שם]. מגפתה. לשון (תהלים לא) פן תגוף באבן רגלך [שם לה:].

רבינו חננאל

חבית שנשברה מצילין הימנה מזון ג' סעודות וכו' תנא לא יספוג ביין בכפיו ולא יטפח בשמן ביד כדרך שהוא עושה בחול. לא יטפח כדאמרינן בכל מקום טופח ע"מ להטפיח וכדתנן בפרק החובל בחבירו וכו'. מעשה באחד שפרע ראשה של אשה כו' עד שמרה עומדת על פתח חצירה ושיבר הפך בפניה. ובה כאיסר שמן. גילתה ראשה והיתה מטפחת ומנחת על ראשה וכו': ת"ר נתפזרו לו פירות בחצירו מלקט על יד על יד ואוכל. אבל לא לתוך הסל ולא לתוך הקופה שלא יעשה כדרך שהוא עושה בחול וכו' וחלקו רב יהודה אמר שמואל ורב ועולא כל חד וחד מעמיד חלוקת ר' יהודה וחכמים ור' יוחנן אמר הלכה כר' יהודה בשאר פירות ואין הלכה כמותו בזיתים וענבים. א"ר אבא אמר רב יהודה אמר שמואל מודה היה רבי יהודה לחכמים בזיתים וענבים ומודים חכמים לרבי יהודה בשאר פירות. ובמאי פליגי בתותים ורמונים דתניא זיתים שמשך מהן שמן וענבים שמשך מהן יין והכניסן בין לאוכלין בין למשקין היוצא מהן אסור. תותים שמשך מהן מים ורמונים שמשך מהן יין והכניסן לאוכלין היוצא מהן מותר למשקין ולסתם היוצא מהן אסור דברי ר' יהודה וחכ"א בין לאוכלין בין למשקין היוצא מהן אסור. נמצאת חלוקת ר' יהודה וחכמים בתותים ורמונים ובה א"ר יוחנן הלכה כר' יהודה בשאר פירות וכיון שפסק ר' יוחנן הלכה כר' יהודה הוצרכנו לברר דבריו ולפיכך אמרינן וסבר ר' יהודה סתם אסור והתנן

תותים שֶׁמָּשַׁךְ מֵהֶן מַיִם וְרִמּוֹנִים שֶׁמָּשַׁךְ מֵהֶן יַיִן – However, in a case of **MULBERRIES FROM WHICH LIQUID OOZED, OR POMEGRANATES FROM WHICH WINE**[23] **OOZED** – וְהִכְנִיסָן לְאוּכָלִין – **IF ONE** had originally **STORED THEM FOR EATING,** הַיּוֹצֵא מֵהֶן מוּתָּר – **[THE LIQUID] THAT OOZED FROM THEM IS PERMISSIBLE** for consumption. לְמַשְׁקִין וְלִסְתָם – But if one had stored them **FOR LIQUID** [i.e. for squeezing], **OR FOR NO STATED PURPOSE,**[24] הַיּוֹצֵא מֵהֶן אָסוּר – **[THE LIQUID] THAT OOZED FROM THEM IS PROHIBITED.**[25] דִּבְרֵי רַבִּי יְהוּדָה – **THESE ARE THE WORDS OF R' YEHUDAH.** וַחֲכָמִים אוֹמְרִים – **BUT THE SAGES SAY:** בֵּין לְאוּכָלִין בֵּין לְמַשְׁקִין הַיּוֹצֵא מֵהֶן אָסוּר – **WHETHER** one had originally stored them **FOR FOOD, OR WHETHER** one had stored them **FOR LIQUID, [THE LIQUID] THAT OOZED FROM THEM IS PROHIBITED.**

We see from this Baraisa that R' Yehudah's disagreement with the Sages concerns liquid that oozed on the Sabbath from mulberries or pomegranates. R' Yehudah holds that if the fruits were originally stored for eating, the liquid is permissible for consumption; the Sages prohibit it even in this case.[26]

The Gemara will now focus on one point in R' Yehudah's ruling in this Baraisa, and will demonstrate that it is in apparent contradiction with a ruling set forth in a Mishnah elsewhere. The Gemara accordingly asks:

וְסָבַר רַבִּי יְהוּדָה סְתָם אָסוּר – **But** then **does R' Yehudah** truly **hold that** when one stored mulberries or pomegranates for **no stated purpose it is forbidden** to consume the juice that oozes from them on the Sabbath?[27] וְהָתְנַן – **But we have learned** otherwise in the following Mishnah:[28] חֲלֵב הָאִשָּׁה מְטַמֵּא לְרָצוֹן וְשֶׁלֹּא לְרָצוֹן – **THE MILK OF A WOMAN WILL CAUSE SUSCEPTIBILITY TO** ***TUMAH*** whether its emergence is **TO** one's **SATISFACTION**[29] **OR** is **NOT TO** one's **SATISFACTION,**[30] for it is legally considered a beverage in either case. חֲלֵב בְּהֵמָה אֵינוֹ מְטַמֵּא אֶלָּא לְרָצוֹן – But **THE MILK OF AN ANIMAL WILL ONLY CAUSE SUSCEPTIBILITY TO** ***TUMAH*** if its emergence is **TO** one's **SATISFACTION,**[31] since only in that case does it have legal status as a beverage.[32] This is the opinion of the Sages. אָמַר רַבִּי עֲקִיבָא – **R' AKIVA** disputed the Sages, and **SAID:** קַל וָחוֹמֶר הוּא – But **IT IS** known through the following ***KAL VACHOMER*** that animal milk is equivalent to human milk in this regard – that even if one was not satisfied with its emergence, it is nonetheless considered a beverage, and will cause susceptibility to *tumah*! וּמַה חֲלֵב הָאִשָּׁה – **FOR IF** we find in the case of **THE MILK OF A WOMAN,** שֶׁאֵינוֹ מְיוּחָד אֶלָּא לִקְטַנִּים – **WHICH IS INTENDED ONLY FOR CHILDREN,**[33] מְטַמֵּא לְרָצוֹן וְשֶׁלֹּא לְרָצוֹן – that it **WILL CAUSE SUSCEPTIBILITY TO** ***TUMAH*** whether its emergence was **TO** one's **SATISFACTION OR** was **NOT TO** one's **SATISFACTION,** חֲלֵב הַבְּהֵמָה – then in the case of **ANIMAL MILK,** שֶׁמְּיוּחָד בֵּין לִקְטַנִּים בֵּין לִגְדוֹלִים – **WHICH IS INTENDED FOR BOTH CHILDREN AND ADULTS,** אֵינוֹ דִין שֶׁיְּטַמֵּא בֵּין לְרָצוֹן וּבֵין שֶׁלֹּא לְרָצוֹן – **IS IT NOT LOGICAL THAT IT SHOULD CAUSE SUSCEPTIBILITY TO** ***TUMAH*** irregardless of **WHETHER** its emergence was **TO** one's **SATISFACTION OR WHETHER** it was **NOT TO** one's

NOTES

23. The Gemara refers to pomegranate juice as "wine" because of its sharp taste (*Rashi*).

24. I.e. he does not say whether he wishes these fruits to be for eating or for squeezing (*Rashi*).

25. [If the fruits were stored for squeezing, the liquid is prohibited because of the fear that one may squeeze the fruits. If they were not explicitly designated for any specific purpose, they are assumed to be designated for squeezing; their juice is therefore prohibited.]

26. *Rashi* wonders why Rav Nachman bar Yitzchak said only that it is *probable* that the disagreement concerns mulberries and pomegranates when the Baraisa appears to state *explicitly* that this is the case in which they disagree! *Rashi* explains that the Baraisa might be citing the case of mulberries and pomegranates simply to demonstrate *R' Yehudah's* most extreme position – that even the juice of mulberries and pomegranates is permissible, so long as they are intended for eating. The Sages, however, might dispute R' Yehudah even with regard to the juice of other fruits! Rav Nachman bar Yitzchak is therefore careful to note that the juice of mulberries or pomegranates is only the *probable* subject of this dispute (*Rashi*).

[The Gemara below (144a-b) does prove from yet another Baraisa that the Sages agree with R' Yehudah in regard to liquid exuded by other sorts of fruits. However, R' Nachman bar Yitzchak suspects that that Baraisa might actually represent only the view of R' Yehudah, as the Gemara there suggests (*Rashi*).]

27. [As is stated in the Baraisa just cited.]

28. *Machshirin* 6:8. The conclusion of the Gemara's question comes below on 144a.

29. I.e. milk that one was desirous of having emerge, such as milk intentionally expressed – either by the woman herself (*Rambam* and *Rav* to *Machshirin* ibid.), or by a nursing child, who intends to remove the milk (*Rashi* to *Kereisos* 13a ד״ה בין לרצון). [However, it is not *necessary* for the milk to be removed intentionally; rather, even milk that emerged by accident, but whose emergence was looked upon with satisfaction, will be deemed a beverage, and will generate susceptibility to *tumah.*]

30. I.e. milk that emerges without one's being particularly desirous that it do so, such as milk that dripped from the breast without the woman intending it to (*Rambam* and *Rav* ibid.), or milk suckled by a child who does not wish to nurse [but is only doing so reflexively] (*Rashi* ibid.).

31. Such as in the case of one who deliberately milks the animal to obtain the milk. However, if one is not particularly desirous of having the milk emerge, such as in a case in which it drips from the animal's udder (see *Rashi* to 144a ד״ה שהחולב), or where one milks the animal in sport, with no intention of using the milk (*Rambam* ibid.), it is not deemed a beverage, and thus will not cause susceptibility to *tumah*.

32. The Torah states that food becomes susceptible to *tumah* through contact with water or with any other liquid that falls under the category of a מַשְׁקֶה, literally: a beverage (see *Leviticus* 11:34 and 11:38 with *Toras Kohanim;* see Tosefta, *Shabbos* 9:14). [This susceptibility is known as הֶכְשֵׁר, or "preparation" for *tumah.*] The six other liquids that are referred to in various Scriptural verses as "beverages" [although some are obviously unsuitable for drinking] are wine, blood, oil, milk, dew and bee's honey (see Tosefta ibid.). Thus, these liquids will cause food to become susceptible to *tumah* (*Machshirin* 6:4). The verse that calls milk a beverage is one in *Judges* 4:19, which tells of a woman named Yael who gave a drink of milk to the Canaanite general Sisera. The verse reads, in pertinent part: וַתִּפְתַּח אֶת־נֹאד הֶחָלָב וַתַּשְׁקֵהוּ, *and she opened the flask of milk, and she gave him to drink*. The word וַתַּשְׁקֵהוּ (*and she gave him to drink*), which derives from the term מַשְׁקֶה, teaches that milk is legally regarded as a beverage. This is true both of milk from a woman and milk from an animal (*Rashi;* see *Niddah* 55b; cf. *Tosafos;* see *Chasam Sofer*).

This Mishnah differentiates between a woman's milk and an animal's milk in that it accords legal beverage status to a woman's milk even if it is extracted unintentionally, while it witholds such status from animal milk that was extracted unintentionally. The reason that the emergence of animal milk must be to its owner's satisfaction is because of a verse in *Leviticus* (11:38) that teaches that these seven liquids will cause *tumah* susceptibility *only* if the owner of the food is content with its being wet (see *Bava Metzia* 22b and *Kiddushin* 59b). The same is true with regard to the beverage status of these liquids; they are legally regarded as beverages *only* if their owner was satisfied with their coming into being (*Rashi* to *Kereisos* 13a ד״ה בין לרצון; cf. *Tosafos* here; see *Maharsha;* see *Baal HaMaor*). Accordingly, if animal milk emerged unintentionally, it is not deemed a legal beverage, and thus will neither cause susceptibility to *tumah* nor become *tamei* itself [as only liquid with beverage status is itself subject to contamination with *tumah* – see *Rambam* to *Machshirin* ibid.; *Tumas Ochalin* 1:4,15:1; cf. *Raavad* there] (*Rashi;* see *Ishei Yisrael;* see *Chazon Ish, Machshirin* 7:6). The Baraisa will explain shortly why this rule does not apply to a woman's milk.

33. [Since it is generally consumed only by infants.]

חבית

מתני׳ חבית אשנשברה מצילין הימנה מזון שלש סעודות ואומר לאחרים באו והצילו לכם ובלבד שלא יספוג (א) אין סוחטין את הפירות להוציא מהן משקין ואם יצאו מעצמן אסורין ר' יהודה אומר אם לאוכלין היוצא מהן מותר ואם למשקין היוצא מהן אסור ג) חלות דבש שריסקן מע"ש ויצאו מעצמן אסורין (א) ורבי אליעזר מתיר: **גמ'** תנא לא ביספוג ביין ולא יטפח בשמן שלא יעשה כדרך שהוא עושה בחול ת"ר גנתפזרו לו פירות בחצר מלקט על יד על יד ואוכל אבל לא לתוך הסל ולא לתוך הקופה שלא יעשה כדרך שהוא עושה בחול: אין סוחטין את הפירות: גאמר רב יהודה אמר שמואל מודה היה רבי יהודה לחכמים בזיתים וענבים מ"ט כיון דלסחיטה נינהו יהיב דעתיה ועולא אמר רב חלוק היה ר' יהודה אף בזיתים וענבים ורבי יוחנן אמר הלכה כרבי יהודה בשאר פירות ואין הלכה כרבי יהודה בזיתים וענבים אמר רבה אמר רב יהודה אמר שמואל מודה היה רבי יהודה לחכמים בזיתים וענבים דומודים חכמים לרבי יהודה בשאר פירות א"ל רבי ירמיה לרבי אבא אלא במאי פליגי א"ל לכי תשכח אמר רב נחמן בר יצחק מסתברא בתותים ורמונים פליגי דתניא הזיתים שמשך מהן שמן וענבים שמשך מהן יין והכניסן בין לאוכל בין למשקין היוצא מהן אסור ותותים שמשך מהן מים ורמונים שמשך מהן יין והכניסן לאוכלין היוצא מהן מותר למשקין ולסתם היוצא מהן אסור דברי רבי יהודה וחכמים אומרים בין לאוכלין בין למשקין היוצא מהן אסור וסבר רבי יהודה סתם אסור ז) והתנן זחלב האשה מטמא לרצון ושלא לרצון חלב בהמה אינו מטמא אלא לרצון אמר ר' עקיבא קל וחומר הוא ומה חלב האשה שאינו מיוחד אלא לקטנים מטמא לרצון ושלא לרצון חלב הבהמה שמיוחד בין לקטנים בין לגדולים אינו דין שיטמא בין לרצון ובין שלא לרצון אמרו לו אם טמא חלב האשה שלא לרצון חשדם מגפתה טמא יטמא חלב הבהמה שלא

רש"י

מצילין הימנה מזון ג' סעודות. ואפילו בכלים הרבה דאילו בחד מנא אמרי' בכל כתבי הקדש (לעיל דף קכ.) דכמה דבעי מציל: לכם. כל אחד מזון ג' סעודות: ובלבד שלא יספוג. שלא ישים ספוג במקום היין לחזור ולהטיפו בכלי גזירה שמא יסחוט: אין סוחטין את הפירות. דהוה ליה מפרק (ב) תולדה דדישה: אסורין. גזירה שמא יסחוט לכתחלה: רבי יהודה אומר אם לאוכלין. הם מכונסין אותם פירות היוצא מהן מותר דלא ניחא ליה במה שזבו וליכא למגזר בהן שמא יסחוט: ואם למשקין. מכונסין אסורין דניחא ליה במאי דנפקא מינייהו ונתקיימה מחשבתו ואיכא למיגזר שמא יסחוט והכי אמרי' בביצה דטעמא דמשקין שזבו משום שמא יסחוט הוא: חלות דבש. מאחר שמרוסקין הדבש זב מאליו מתוך השעוה ואין דרך לסוחטו הלכך רבי אליעזר מתיר וחכמים אוסרין גזירה אטו שאינן מרוסקין דילמא מרסק להו (ג): גמ' ויטפח. מכניס בו כפו והשמן נדבק בה ומקנחו בשפת הכלי ואסרוה משום עובדין דחול: מודה ר' יהודה בזיתים. דאע"ג דהכניסן לאוכלין היוצא מהן אסור דכיון דרובן לסחיטה קיימי כי אתו לידי משקה יהיב דעתיה למיהוי ניחא ליה בהכי: אפי' בזיתים וענבים. הואיל והני לאוכלין כנסינהו: מסתברא בתותים ורמונים פליגי. דאיכא דבעו להו למשקין הלכך משוו להו רבנן כזיתים וענבים ור' יהודה פליג עלייהו אבל שאר פירות ליכא דבעי להו למשקין הלכך מודו רבנן בהם: שמשך. זב מאליהן כמו נהרות המושכין (לעיל דף קכא.): והכניסן. מתחילתן בין לאוכלין בין למשקין כו' דרמונים קרי יין משום דאית להו קיוהא: וחכ"א כו'. והא דנקט רב נחמן לישנא דמסתברא ולא אמר בהדיא דבתותים ורמונים פליגי משום דאיכא למימר פליגי בתותים ורמונים וה"ה לשאר פירות ולהודיעך כחו דרבי יהודה נקט להו ואי משום ברייתא דלקמן דשמעינן מינה דמודים חכמים לרבי יהודה בשאר פירות לאו בהדיא שמעינן לה דאיכא למימר רבי יהודה היא כדפרכינן עלה: וסבר רבי יהודה סתם. שלא פירש לאוכל ולא למשקה הוי המשקה הזב מהן אסור: והתנן חלב האשה מטמא. מכשיר: לרצון ושלא לרצון. בין שיצא ממנה לרצון בין שיצא שלא לרצון שהחלב קרוי משקה שנאמר ותפתח את נאד החלב ותשקהו (שופטים ד): חלב הבהמה אינו מטמא אלא אם כן יצא לרצון. ואי לא לא חשיב משקה ואם נגע בו שרץ אינו מקבל טומאה וטעמא מפרש לקמיה: שדם

תוספות

חבית. ובלבד שלא יספוג. אפילו יש לו עור בית אחיזה דליכא חשש סחיטה אסור כדמפרש בגמרא שלא יעשה כדרך שעושה בחול: מלקט על יד על יד ואוכל. נראה דל"ג ואוכל מדקתני סיפא אבל לא לתוך הסל ולא לתוך הקופה משמע הנך דווקא אסירי משום עובדא דחול אבל לתוך ה) כפו שרי: ורבי יוחנן אמר הלכה כרבי יהודה בשאר פירות. בריש מסכת ביצה (דף ג. ושם) רבי יוחנן רמי דר' יהודה אדרבי יהודה תנן ר"י אומר אם לאוכלין היוצא מהן מותר אם למשקין כו' אלמא כל לאוכלין אוכלא דאיפרת הוא ורמינהו ועוד אמר ר"י מתנה אדם על הכלכלה של פירות ביו"ט ראשון ואוכלה בשני וכן ביצה שנולדה בראשון אוכלה בשני בשני אין בראשון לא ואמר רבי יוחנן מוחלפת השיטה וצריך לומר דההיא דמתנה אדם מחליף דאי מתני' מחליף אם כן במאי דנקט הכא ר' יהודה הוה ליה למינקט רבנן וה"ל למימר הלכה כרבנן בשאר פירות. מ"ר. י) ולי נראה דאפילו אפיך מתני' אתי שפיר כעין שמצינו בב"ק בפרק הגוזל קמא (דף צו:) דתנן גזל בהמה והוכחשה עבדים והזקינו משלם כשעת הגזלה ר"מ אומר בעבדים אומר לו הרי שלך לפניך ואמר בגמרא אמר רבי חנינא בר אבדימי אמר רב הלכה כר"מ ופריך ורב שביק רבנן ועביד כר"מ כו' עד דמסיק דרב מתניתין איפכא אתנא' אלמא אע"פ שהיה שונה במתניתין וחכ"א בעבדים אומר לו הרי שלך לפניך וה"ל למימר השתא הלכה כחכמים אפ"ה נקט ר"מ לפי מה שהאחרים שונין המשנה ה"נ נקט רבי יוחנן רבי יהודה בשמעתין וכן נמי מצינו בשילהי פ"ק דסוכה (דף יט:) דתנן העושה סוכתו כמין צריף ר"א פוסל וחכמים מכשירין ואמרינן בגמרא אביי אשכחיה לרב יוסף דגני בכילת חתנים בסוכה א"ל כמאן כר"א א"ל שבקת רבנן ועבדת כר"א אמר ליה ברייתא איפכא תניא השתא היה לו להשיב רב יוסף כרבנן ולא כר"א כיון דאיהו איפכא תני אלא כן דרך הש"ס בכל מקום. נראה לי: הלכה כר' יהודה בשאר פירות. אע"ג דבריש ביצה (ד' ג.) גזר ר' יוחנן ביצה שנולדה ביו"ט משום משקין שזבו והכא לא גזר בשאר פירות י"ל דשייך טפי לגזור בביצה לפי שהיא עומדת ליסחט מן התרנגולת ט) ודרך לגומעה חיה אבל שאר פירות אין עומדים ליסחט כלל. מ"ר: שמשך מהן שמן כו'. פי' בקונט' שמשך זב מאליהן כמו נהרות המושכין ולפירושו צריך לומר הכניסן בין לאוכלין כו' היינו הכניסן מתחילתן ואין הלשון משמע כן ועוד קשה לר"י דאי משך מאליו קאמר גבי תותים שמשך מהם מים ה"ל למימר שמשכו או שנמשכו דמים בכל מקום לשון רבים ועוד קשה לר"י אם כן הך ברייתא הוה תיובתא דרב ורבי יוחנן דאמרי לעיל חלוק היה רבי יהודה בזיתים וענבים דהכא משמע דבזיתים וענבים מודה אלא נראה לר"י דמשך אאדם קאי וסחטן תחילה ושוב הכניסן דהשתא לרב ורבי יוחנן דסברי חלוק היה רבי יהודה בזיתים וענבים נקט דוקא משך דאיכא למימר טפי דילמא יהיב דעתיה לסחוט משקה אחר שהכניסו נמי לאכילה מאחר שסחטן תחילה להוציא מהן משקה הא לא משך לא ולשמואל דאמר מודה רבי יהודה בזיתים וענבים נקט משך משום רבותא דתותים ורמונים דאפילו משך והכניסן לאוכלין היוצא מהן מותר. מ"ר: חלב האשה מטמא לרצון ושלא לרצון. והא דתנן במסכת מכשירין (פ"א) כל משקה שתחילתו לרצון או שסופו לרצון אף על פי שאין סופו לרצון אף על פי שאין תחלתו לרצון מכשיר לא דמי רצון דהתם לרצון דהכא דהתם מיירי בשעת נפילתן על הזרעים שיהא לרצון דבעינן יותן דומיא דכי יתן מה יתן דניחא ליה אף יותן דניחא ליה אבל הכא מיירי בשעת פרישה מן האשה או מן הבהמה: לרצון ושלא לרצון. כדמפרש בסמוך טעמא משום דדם מגפתה טמא וחלב ודם חד הוא דדם נעכר ונעשה חלב ולא צריכין למה שפי' בקונט' משום דאיקרי משקה שנאמר ותפתח את נאד החלב ותשקהו ונראה לר"י דהא דאיצטריך לפרש האי טעמא דלית ליה טעמא דכפ' דם נדה (דף נה:) גבי חלב האשה הכ"מ לרבי עקיבא דשמעתין דלית ליה טעמא ט) דפרישה או למאן דלית ליה דם נעכר ונעשה חלב אבל לרבנן דשמעתין לא צריך (ד) כדפרישית לחלב האשה אלא דוקא לטמא חלב בהמה לרצון. מ"ר:

עין משפט נר מצוה

א א ב מיי' פכ"א מהל' שבת הלכה טו סמג לאוין סה טוש"ע א"ח סי' שלה סעיף א:
ב ג מיי' שם פכ"א הל' יא טוש"ע שם סעיף ה:
ג ד ה ו מיי' פכ"א מהל' שבת הלכה יב סמג שם טוש"ע א"ח סי' שכ סעיף א:
ד ז מיי' פ"י מהלכות טומאת אוכלין הל' ד:
ה ח שם הל' ה ופ"א מהל' משכב ומושב הלכה טו:

רבינו חננאל

חבית שנשברה מצילין הימנה מזון ג' סעודות וכו' תנא לא יספוג ביין בכפיו ולא יטפח בשמן ביד כדרך שהוא עושה בחול. לא יטפח כדאמרינן בכל מקום טופח ע"מ להטפיח וכדתנן בפרק החובל בחבירו וכו'. מעשה באחד שפרע ראשה של אשה כו' עד שמרה עומדת על פתח חצירה ושיבר הפך בפניה. ובה כאיסר שמן. גילתה ראשה והיתה מטפחת ומנחת על ראשה וכו': ת"ר נתפזרו לו פירות בחצירו מלקט על יד על יד ואוכל. אבל לא לתוך הסל ולא לתוך הקופה שלא יעשה כדרך שהוא עושה בחול וכו' וחלקו רב יהודה אמר שמואל ועולא כל חד וחד מעמיד חלוקת ר' יהודה וחכמים ור' יוחנן אמר הלכה כר' יהודה בשאר פירות ואין הלכה כמותו בזיתים וענבים. א"ר אבא אמר רב יהודה אמר שמואל מודה היה רבי יהודה לחכמים בזיתים וענבים ומודים חכמים לרבי יהודה בשאר פירות. ובמאי פליגי בתותים ורמונים דתניא זיתים שמשך מהן שמן וענבים שמשך מהן יין והכניסן בין לאוכלין בין למשקין היוצא מהן אסור. תותים שמשך מהן מים ורמונים שמשך מהן יין והכניסן לאוכלין היוצא מהן מותר למשקין ולסתם היוצא מהן אסור. דברי ר' יהודה וחכמים אומרים בין לאוכלין בין למשקין היוצא מהן אסור. נמצאת חלוקת ר' יהודה וחכמים בתותים ורמונים ובה א"ר יוחנן הלכה כר' יהודה בשאר פירות וכיון דאמרינן הלכה כר' יהודה הוצרכנו לברר דבריו ולפיכך אמרינן וסבר ר' יהודה סתם אסור והתנן

מסורת הש"ס

א) ביצה ג. חולין יד:, ב) לעיל יט:, ג) חולין יד:, ד) מכשירין פ"ו מ"ח כריתות יג., ה) [בתוספתא גם זיתים ועוד], ו) [עיין תוס' ביצה ג. ד"ה ר"י אמר], ז) נ"א ועוד ור"י לא אייתי רק משאר פירות גם זיתים וענבים אבל מתותים ורמונים ליתו מידי כלום דעתו משמע, ח) [ע"ש], ט) [ועי' תוס' נדה יד.], י) [עי' תוס' מ"ק יג: ד"ה כמאן כו'].

הגהות הב"ח

(א) במשנה ור"א מתיר. נ"ב ר' אלעזר גרסי' ע' פירש"י בפ"ק דשבת דף יט ריש ע"ב: (ב) רש"י ד"ה אין סוחטין וכו' מפרק הוא תולדה: (ג) ד"ה חלות וכו' להו הס"ד ואח"כ מ"ה ולא יטפח: (ד) תוס' ד"ה לרצון וכו' לא צריך לחלב האשה כדפרישית אלא:

ליקוטי רש"י

אין סוחטין את הפירות. וסחיטת פירות תולדה דדש היא שמפרקן מתוך זג שלהן כמפרק תבואה מקש שלה [ביצה ג.]. סחיטה אב מלאכה היא [חולין יד: ע"ש במסורש"ש]. ואם יצאו מעצמן אסורין. גו ביום גזרה שמא יסחוט. אם לאוכלין. כן מכונסין הפירות הללו היוצא מהן מותר גו ביום דכיון דלא ניחא ליה בהני משקין ליכא למיגזר שמא יסחוט. היוצא מהן אסור דלאו אוכלא הוא ולאו בכלל גזירת משקין שזבו [ביצה שם]. אם היו עומדין לאכילה ולא למשוך היוצא מהן מותר דכיון דלא ניחא ליה לא אתי לאימגזר ואי שרית להו ליכא למיחש הא לא לאכלי קיימי. ואם למשקין. הואיל ונתקיימה מחשבתו אי שרית להו אתי למיגזר בהו שמא יסחוט [חולין שם]. חלות דבש. הכוורת לאחר שעוממה פירות לוקחין אותו הדבש והוא עשוי חלות חלות ויש בו ד' חלות או ג' זה כל זה משעוה והדבש מעורב יחד [רשב"ם ב"ב ס.]. שהכוורת רודה ומשין כמין חלות של שעוה והדבש בתוכן. שריסקן. כותשן. אסורין. לאוכלו שבת לאלילה. ורבי אלעזר. הוא ר' אלעזר בן שמוע סתם ר' אלעזר במשנה ובריתא. מתיר. דבש לאחר שזב מן החלות הוי אוכלא הוא הכא לאו משקין הלכך ליכא למיגזר ביה שמא יסחוט [לעיל יט:]. מודה היה רבי יהודה לחכמים בזיתים וענבים. שאפילו הכניסן לאכילה הואיל ורוב בני אדם סוחטין אותם הוי נמי ממלך עלייהו ואי שרית למשקין שזבו מהן אתי למיסחט. כיון דלסחיטה נינהו. כיון דלהכי קיימי אפי' כנסן לאכלן. יהיב דעתיה. עלייהו למשקין וכי הוו משקין הוה ליה נתקיימה מחשבתו וגזרה שמא יסחוט. חלוק היה ר' יהודה. ומחמיר [חולין שם]. מגפתה. לשון (תהלים לא) מן מגוף בלבן רגלך [שם לה:].

SATISFACTION?[34] אָמְרוּ לוֹ – [THE SAGES] SAID TO HIM: אִם טִמֵּא חֲלֵב הָאִשָּׁה שֶׁלֹּא לְרָצוֹן – What comparison can be made between the milk of a woman and the milk of an animal? For IF [THE TORAH] DESIGNATED as A CAUSE OF SUSCEPTIBILITY TO *TUMAH* THE MILK OF A WOMAN that did NOT emerge TO one's SATISFACTION, שֶׁדַּם מַגֵּפָתָהּ טָמֵא – INSOFAR AS THE BLOOD OF HER WOUND CAUSES SUSCEPTIBILITY TO *TUMAH*, יְטַמֵּא חֲלֵב הַבְּהֵמָה – WILL IT likewise DESIGNATE as A CAUSE OF SUSCEPTIBILITY TO *TUMAH* THE MILK OF AN ANIMAL

NOTES

34. [R' Akiva argues that if women's milk, which is not a universal drink, is nonetheless considered a beverage even when it was extracted unintentionally, then it follows that animal milk, which *is* a universal drink, will certainly be considered a beverage even when its emergence was unintended!]

שֶׁלֹּא לְרָצוֹן – that did **NOT** emerge **TO** one's **SATISFACTION,** שֶׁדָּם מְגֵפָתָהּ טָהוֹר – **WHEN THE BLOOD OF ITS WOUND DOES NOT CAUSE SUSCEPTIBILITY TO *TUMAH*?** Certainly not! For the only reason that a woman's milk that emerged unintentionally is legally considered a beverage is because it is like the blood of her wound, which has beverage status even though she is not generally desirous of its coming forth. The blood of an animal's wound, by contrast, is not considered a beverage altogether. Its milk will therefore not be considered a beverage unless its owner is content with its having come forth.[1] אָמַר לָהֶן – **[R' AKIVA] SAID TO THEM:** מַחְמִיר אֲנִי בְּחָלָב מִבְּדָם – With regard to causing susceptibility to *tumah,* **I CONSIDER** the law of **MILK TO BE MORE STRINGENT THAN** the law of **BLOOD.** שֶׁהַחוֹלֵב לִרְפוּאָה טָמֵא – **FOR IF ONE MILKS** an animal **FOR THERAPEUTIC REASONS, [THE MILK] WILL CAUSE SUSCEPTIBILITY TO *TUMAH;***[2] וְהַמַּקִּיז לִרְפוּאָה טָהוֹר – **BUT IF ONE BLEEDS** an animal **FOR THERAPEUTIC REASONS, [THE BLOOD] WILL NOT CAUSE SUSCEPTIBILITY TO *TUMAH!***[3] We see that the law of milk is more stringent than that of blood. Likewise with regard to milk that came out unintentionally, I treat the milk of an animal more stringently than I do its blood, and therefore rule that although an animal's blood does not cause susceptibility to *tumah,* its milk will, even if its emergence was not to its owner's satisfaction.[4] אָמְרוּ לוֹ – **[THE SAGES] SAID TO [R' AKIVA]:** סַלֵּי זֵיתִים וַעֲנָבִים יוֹכִיחוּ – The law of liquid that flowed from **BASKETS OF OLIVES OR GRAPES WILL DEMONSTRATE** that liquids that come forth unintentionally cannot be compared to liquids that come forth to the satisfaction of their owner. שֶׁהַמַּשְׁקִין הַיּוֹצְאִין מֵהֶן – **FOR** this is the law regarding **THE LIQUIDS THAT OOZE FROM [THESE BASKETS]:** לְרָצוֹן טְמֵאִין – If their coming forth is **TO** the owner's **SATISFACTION, THEY WILL CAUSE SUSCEPTIBILITY TO *TUMAH,*** as they are then deemed as beverages. שֶׁלֹּא לְרָצוֹן טְהוֹרִים – But if their coming forth is **NOT TO** his **SATISFACTION, THEY WILL NOT CAUSE SUSCEPTIBILITY TO *TUMAH,*** since they are then not legally considered beverages.[5] We see that the legal character of liquids is dependent upon whether they emerged to their owner's satisfaction – if they did not, they are not legally deemed beverages. Accordingly, animal milk extracted unintentionally is not regarded as a beverage, and thus cannot generate susceptibility to *tumah.*[6]

The Gemara makes an assumption regarding this Mishnah:

מַאי לָאו לְרָצוֹן דְּנִיחָא לֵיהּ – Now, **does not** the Mishnah's term **"to** the owner's **satisfaction"** mean **that [the owner of the fruit] is satisfied** that the liquids are oozing from the fruit, שֶׁלֹּא לְרָצוֹן בִּסְתָמָא – and the term **"not to his satisfaction"** mean **that he makes no** explicit **statement** either way?[7]

NOTES

1. Blood that flows from one's wound is one of the seven "beverages" that render food susceptible to *tumah.* This is derived in *Niddah* 55b from one of the verses in Bilaam's second set of prophecies concerning the Jews. The verse states (*Numbers* 23:24): וְדַם־חֲלָלִים יִשְׁתֶּה, *and the blood of the slain it will drink.* Allegorically, this verse concerns the capture by the Jewish people of the treasure of their enemies (*Targum Onkelos* and *Ibn Ezra* ad loc.). Literally, it speaks of a lion, which drinks the blood of its human prey. Now, by speaking of "drinking" the blood of the slain, the Torah classifies the blood of a dead human as a "beverage" – i.e. a liquid capable of generating susceptibility to *tumah.* This classification applies as well to blood that flows from one's wound, for since a person's blood contains his very life force (see *Deuteronomy* 12:23), the loss of any of it from a wound constitutes some small measure of death (see *Niddah* ibid.). One who bleeds from a wound is thus considered in some degree to have been "slain," and his blood, like the blood of one who actually was slain, is legally regarded as a beverage. Now one does not generally look with satisfaction upon blood that flows from one's wound – nonetheless, the Torah classifies it as a beverage! We see that although the attainment of beverage status generally requires an owner to regard the liquid's coming into being with satisfaction (see 143b note 31), this is not so in the case of blood. Rather, blood will render food susceptible to *tumah* even if it did *not* issue forth to one's satisfaction.

This verse in *Numbers* speaks of blood from a *human's* wound; the blood from an *animal's* wound, however – whether from an ordinary wound or from a death wound – is not regarded as a beverage at all, and thus will not *ever* generate susceptibility to *tumah* (*Rashi;* cf. *Rashi* to *Chullin* 35b; see *Tosafos* there ד״ה דם המת; see our note 32 there). The Sages employ this difference between human blood and animal blood to counter R' Akiva's attempt to derive the law of animal milk from that of women's milk. For [say the Sages] the only reason women's milk extracted unintentionally generates susceptibility is because milk is in reality a product of blood (see *Niddah* 9a) – thus, just as a woman's blood that emerges unintended is regarded as a beverage, so too is its product, milk, regarded as a beverage even if it emerges unintended. But an animal's blood is not regarded as a beverage altogether! Since its milk is therefore subject to the usual rules governing beverage status, it will not generate susceptibility to *tumah* unless it emerges to the satisfaction of its owner (*Rashi;* cf. *Tosafos; Rash* to *Machshirin* 6:8; see *Chasam Sofer; Shabbos Shel Mi*).

[Although blood from a slain animal or from an animal's wound does not generate susceptibility to *tumah,* the blood of an animal's *shechitah* (ritual slaughtering) *will* generate such susceptibility. This is derived from a verse (*Deuteronomy* 12:16) that equates *shechitah* blood with water – itself the primary liquid identified (in *Leviticus* 11:34,38) as causing food to become susceptible to *tumah* (*Rashi;* see *Chullin* 35b).]

2. Since one is satisfied to have it come out (*Rashi*).

3. Since animal blood is not regarded as a beverage [as was explained in note 1] (*Rashi*).

4. R' Akiva's rejoinder is based upon his conviction that with regard to a liquid's beverage status, there is no reason to differentiate between whether its owner was or was not satisfied with its coming into being. [Although it might appear from R' Akiva's first remark to the Sages (on 143b) that he does recognize this differentiation, it is not so. For R' Akiva was simply attempting to show with that statement that even according to the *Sages'* reasoning, it would be logical to extend beverage status to animal milk that issued forth unintentionally. He himself, however, does not agree with their reasoning (see *Shabbos Shel Mi* to 143b ד״ה פיסקא).] Accordingly, R' Akiva is at a loss to understand why the Sages will not accord beverage status to animal milk that emerged unintended. He therefore assumes that their reason is connected to the fact that an animal's *blood* is not a beverage – just as its blood is not a beverage, so too is the milk that derives from the blood not a beverage. R' Akiva rebuts this argument by demonstrating that the law of milk is more stringent than that of blood. For while milk extracted from an animal for healing purposes is considered a beverage, blood extracted for the same reason is not! Evidently, the law of an animal's milk cannot be derived from that of its blood. Thus, even if the milk's emergence was not to its owner's satisfaction, it should be capable of generating susceptibility to *tumah.* (*Rashi;* cf. *Tosafos;* see *Shabbos Shel Mi* ibid.). The Sages will now prove that there *is* a difference between liquid that emerged in accordance with one's desire and that which did not.

5. [The Gemara will shortly expound upon the meaning in this context of the phrases "to the owner's satisfaction" and "not to his satisfaction."]

6. [The milk of a *woman,* however, will generate susceptibility even if its emergence was accidental, since it shares the law of the blood of her wound.]

The Sages are proving from the law of liquid that oozes from baskets of olives or grapes that as regards beverage status there *is* a difference between liquids that emerge to the satisfaction of their owner, and those that do not (*Rashi*). R' Akiva's proof of the stringency of milk over blood is thus irrelevant, since the Sages' reasoning in ruling animal milk that dripped out unintended as incapable of generating *tumah* susceptibility is dependent not upon the law of animal blood, as R' Akiva assumed, but upon their conviction that beverage status is limited to liquids whose owner is content with their having come forth (*Shabbos Shel Mi* ibid.).

[Our Gemara ends its citation of the Mishnah in *Machshirin* here, since the introduction of the law of liquid that oozes from olives or grapes was its sole purpose in citing this Mishnah; however, the Mishnah in fact continues with R' Akiva's rebuttal of the Sages' proof, and then with a further exchange between them.]

7. [At this point the Gemara assumes that the term "to his satisfaction" implies an *explicit* statement of satisfaction. If the owner says nothing,

שלא לרצון [א] שדם מגפתה טהור אמר להן מחמיר אני בחלב מבדם שהחולב לרפואה טמא [ב] והמקיז לרפואה טהור אמרו לו סלי זיתים וענבים יוכיחו [ג] שהמשקין היוצאין מהן לרצון טמאין שלא לרצון טהורים מאי לאו לרצון דניחא ליה שלא לרצון בסתמא ומה זיתים וענבים דבני סחיטה נינהו שלא לרצון ולא כלום תותים ורמונים דלאו בני סחיטה נינהו לא כ"ש לא לרצון בסתמא שלא לרצון דגלי אדעתיה דאמר לא ניחא לי ואיבעית אימא שאני סלי זיתים וענבים כיון דלאיבוד קיימי מעיקרא אפקורי מפקרי להו אשכחן ר' יהודה דמודי לרבנן בזיתים ובענבים רבנן דמודו ליה לרבי יהודה בשאר פירות מנלן דתניא סוחטין בפגעין

רש"י

א) שדם מגפתה. של אשה אם נגף רגלה או ידה וכל חבורה שיצא ממנה דם כדאמר בפרק דם הנדה (נדה דף נה:) דם חללים דהיינו דם הרוג קרוי משקה שנאמר ודם חללים ישתה ודם מגפתו מפרש התם דדם חללים הוי דמה לי קטליה כוליה מה לי קטליה פלגא וחלב כדם מגפתו דדם נעכר ונעשה חלב ודם מגפתה סתמיה שלא לרצון הוא וטמא: יטמא חלב הבהמה שלא לרצון. בתמיה שהרי דם מגפתה טהור דבהמה לאו בכלל חללי הוא ומיהו דם שחיטה מכשר משום דאיתקש למים דכתיב (דברים יב) על הארץ תשפכנו כמים: ב) מחמיר אני בחלב. לטמאו אף שלא לרצון מבדם: שהחולב. לרפואת הבהמה שלא יזיקנה חלבה טמא דהא לרצון הוא והמקיז דם לבהמתו לרפואה טהור דדם מגפתה היא והואיל והחולב לרפואה טמא אף הנוטף שלא לרצון טמא: אמרו לו. אינו דומה שלא לרצון ליוצא לרצון שהרי סלי זיתים וענבים יוכיחו שהמשקה כו': שלא לרצון בסתמא. וקתני טהורין דלא חשיב משקה אי רבי יהודה קאמר לה קשיא ואי רבנן קאמרי כל שכן טהורין לרבי יהודה דהא מידי דלרבנן משקה הוא לרבי יהודה לאו משקה הוא וכ"ש מידי דלרבנן לאו משקה והשתא ומה זיתים וענבים כו' והוא הדין מצי למירמי נמי זיתים וענבים אזיתים וענבים דקתני לעיל דמודה בהו רבי יהודה דאף לאוכלין היוצא מהן אסור אלא הא אלימא ליה לאקשויי דתותים ורמונים דלאו בני סחיטה נינהו קתני לעיל דסתם אסור והכא קתני דאפי' זיתים וענבים סתמא לאו למשקה: דגלי דעתיה. בהדיא ואמר לא ניחא לי והוי גילוי דעתא טפי מהכניסו לאוכלין: ואיבעית אימא שאני סלי זיתים וענבים וכו'. ודווקא נקט סלין שהמשקה הנוטף מהן נופל לארץ והולך לאיבוד הלכך סתמא לא ניחא ליה: אפקורי מפקיר. לההוא משקה אבל שאר כלים אפילו תותים ורמונים אימא לך סתמא למשקה: בפגעין

תוספות

מחמיר אני בחלב מבדם שהחולב לרפואה טמא והמקיז לרפואה טהור. א"כ מאי דמטמאין חלב האשה לא מחמת דם הוא דדם נעכר ונעשה חלב דא"כ חולב לרפואה טהור כמו דם אלא ודאי משום דכתיב ותפתח את נאד החלב ואומר רבי דבחנם נקט חולב לרפואה דהכי נמי הו"מ להשיב לרבנן מחלב בהמה גופה שדמה טהור (א) וחלבה טמא א"כ החלב אינו טמא מחמת דם אלא משום דכתיב ותפתח את נאד החלב וא"כ שלא לרצון נמי מהאי טעמא יהא טמא. מ"ר: סלי זיתים וענבים יוכיחו שמשקה היוצא מהן לרצון טמא שלא לרצון טהור. בשילהי מסכת מכשירין מסיים לא אם אמרת בסלי זיתים וענבים שהרי תחילתו אוכל וסופו משקה תאמרו בחלב שתחילתו וסופו משקה: מאי לאו לרצון דניחא ליה ושלא לרצון בסתמא. ולרצון ושלא לרצון דגבי חלב אשה ליכא למימר דמיירי בשלא לרצון בסתמא ודווקא בסתמא אבל אמר לא ניחא לי אינו מטמא דהא לפי מה שפירשתי הטעם משום דם מגפתה אפי' אמר לא ניחא לי נמי מטמא אלא משמע דשלא לרצון דקתני בכולהו באשה ובהמה וזיתים וענבים איירי בכל ענין בין מסתמא בין אמר לא ניחא לי: תותים ורימונים דלאו בני סחיטה נינהו. תימה לי מאי קשה דילמא הא דתניא לעיל גבי תותים ורמונים למשקין ולסתם היוצא מהן אסור הכ"מ במשך דוקא והכא בלא משך איירי הלכך שלא לרצון דהיינו בסתמא לא חשיב משקה: לא לרצון בסתמא ושלא לרצון דגלי דעתיה דאמר לא ניחא לי. (ב) דתניא התם בכריתות פרק אמרו לו (דף יג.) התירו (ג) לו למגע טמא מת להניק את בנה ובנה טהור ופריך בנה אמאי טהור כיון דינק חלב איטמי ליה מחלב וכי תימא לא איתכשר איתכשר בטיפה המלוכלכת ע"פ הדד ואע"ג דחלב אשה משקה הוא ואין צריך הכשר [משמע ליה] דמה שהוא בפי התינוק שהתינוק יונק חשיב כאוכל וצריך הכשר לפי שזהו מאכלו של תינוק וקאמר דלאיתכשר בטיפה המלוכלכת בפי הדד דהוי משקה כשתם חלב דלאו לאוכל בעי ליה ומשני רב נחמן אמר רבה בר אבוה (ד) בתקיפה אחת שלא הניח טיפה המלוכלכת ע"פ הדד אמר רבא שתי תשובות בדבר חדא דקא זקיף ליה לפומיה דינוקא דמלא חלבא ועוד מקום חלב מעין הוא דהא תנן חלב האשה מטמא לרצון ושלא לרצון מאי היא לאו ניחא ליה וקתני מטמא פי' אלמא חשיבא כמעין מדמטמאה שלא לרצון וכיון דחשוב כמעין גם בפי התינוק נמי יהא חשוב כמשקה כמו שאם היה מעין ואין צריך הכשר כך צריך לפרש דאל"ל דלאו מזכיר מעין אלא כלומר דכמשקה חשיב א"כ מאי צריך למימר שלא לרצון מאי היא כו' דמדקתני לרצון מטמא הו"מ למיפרך אלמא לרצון חשיב כי משקה ואשה דמניקה את בנה לרצון הוא אלא אמר רבא כו' עד ולרבא מקום חלב מעין הוא ולא צריך הכשר והתנן האשה שנטף חלב מדדיה ונפל לאויר התנור התנור טמא וקשיא לן במאי איתכשר ואמר ר' יוחנן בטיפה המלוכלכת ע"פ הדד והשתא קשה לר"י מאי קאמר במאי איתכשר דמדבעי הכשר אלמא אוכל חשיב ליה וא"כ איך יטמא אוכל את התנור והא אין אוכל מטמא כלי ואומר ר"י דה"פ וקשיא לן במאי איתכשר כלומר לא מבעיא שאין התנור טמא אלא חלב הנוטף מדדיה גופה אמאי יהא טמא הא לא איתכשר ומשני בטיפה המלוכלכת ע"פ הדד ואותה טיפה עצמה המלוכלכת ע"פ הדד מטמא התנור שהיא חשובה משקה ומשקה מטמאה כלי כדאמרינן בפ' קמא דמכילתין (דף יג:) והשתא פריך שפיר לרבא דאמר דאפילו אמר לא ניחא לי מטמא חלב האשה דחשיב משקה והכא חשיב ליה אוכל אבל לר"נ אמר רבה בר אבוה אתי שפיר דהכא דאמר לא ניחא לי ודאי חשיב ליה אוכל ונטף חלב מדדיה חשיב לא ניחא ליה כיון שהוא נופל לאויר תנור ואזיל לאיבוד דודאי לא ניחא ליה ועוד פריך התם לרבא מדתניא ט' משקין בזב הזיעה וליחה סרוחה והריעי טהורים מכלום דמעת עינו ודם מגפתו וחלב האשה מטמא טומאת משקין ברביעית רוקו חוטו ומימי רגליו מטמא טומאה חמורה בכל שהוא ואי אמרת מקום חלב מעין הוא חלב האשה נמי יטמא טומאה חמורה בכל שהוא כזובו ורוקו וקשה לרבי מאי קפריך לעולם מעין הוא ואפ"ה לא יטמא טומאה חמורה משום דבעינן דומיא דרוק דאיתא בנדה (ד' נו.) מה רוק שמתגלגל ויוצא וחוזר ונבלע אף כל שמתגלגל ויוצא וחוזר ונבלע יצא חלב שבאשה שמתגלגל ויוצא ואינו חוזר ונבלע ותימה הוא לומר דמה שהוא חוזר ונבלע גרם לו ליחשב כמעין ומכל מקום ודאי כן הוא וצריך לומר דמה שהיה חושבו רבא כמעין להיות חשיב משקה בפי התינוק היינו משום דסלקא דעתיה שחוזר ונבלע ומייתי ראיה מן המשנה דחוזר ונבלע הוא מדקתני מטמא שלא לרצון דהיינו אמר לא ניחא לי א"כ חוזר ונבלע הוא דאי לאו הכי אם אמר לא ניחא ליה לא יהיה מטמא והשתא פריך ליה מהכא דאינו חוזר ונבלע אלמא מקום חלב האשה לאו מעין הוא ופריך אי הכי קשה הא דקתני מטמא שלא לרצון ומשני מי סברת שלא לרצון דלא ניחא ליה לא שלא לרצון בסתמא דדעתיה לתינוק קרובה גבי חלב אבל אמר לא ניחא ליה טהור והיה חלב הנוטף מדדיה ונפל לתוך התנור כאומר לא ניחא ליה חשיב דודאי לא ניחא ליה כיון שהלך לאיבוד והא דקאמר שלא לרצון בסתמא היינו כשנופל בקערה שאינו הולך לאיבוד דמהני טעמא דדעתיה דתינוק קרובה גבי חלב לאחשוביה אז כמשקה ובפי התינוק לעולם כאוכל חשיב והשתא קשה לר"י חדא דבשמעתא מסקינן איפכא לרצון בסתמא ושלא לרצון דאמר לא ניחא ליה ודומיא דהך דזיתים וענבים הוי ההוא דחלב האשה דאי לאו הכי לא שייך למימר יוכיחו וכ"ת ס"ל כאיבעית אימא דאמר שאני סלי זיתים וענבים כיון דלאיבוד קיימא אפקורי מפקר להו אכתי קשה דדומיא דהכי אית לן למימר בחלב האשה דאזיל לאיבוד וא"כ היינו באומר לא ניחא ליה והתם מטמא דוקא סתמא אבל לא ניחא ליה טהור ועוד קשה לרבי מאי קאמר התם אלא קשה הא מתני' וקאמר נמי מי סברת שלא לרצון לא ניחא ליה וקאמר דלא ניחא (ה) טהור ואמאי והא טעמא שלא לרצון טמא היינו משום דחשיב דם מגפתו דדם נעכר ונעשה חלב כדפי' לעיל וא"כ גם שלא ניחא ליה נמי יהא טמא. מ"ר:

מי

מסורת הש"ס

א) שייך לעמוד הקודם, ב) ע"ב.

הגהות הב"ח

(א) תוס' ד"ה מחמיר וכו' שדמה טהור. נ"ב ובתוספות יו"ט סוף מס' מכשירין מתרץ קושיא זו דנאמת דם בהמה לשתיה מכשיר כמו חלב שהוא לשתיה ע"כ מוכרח לומר מדם הקזה והחולב לרפוא' ע"ש: (ב) ד"ה לא לרצון וכו' לא ניחא לי תניא כצ"ל ואות ד' נמחק: (ג) בא"ד התירו לה למגע טמא מת: (ד) בא"ד אמר רבה בר אבוה שינק בתקיפה: (ה) בא"ד וקאמר דלא ניחא ליה טהור:

עין משפט נר מצוה

ו א ב מיי' פ"י מהלכות טומאת אוכלין הל"ג:
ז ג מיי' פ"א שם הלכה ג ופ"י הלכה יב:

רבינו חננאל

והתנן במס' מכשירין אמרו לו זיתים וענבים יוכיחו שהמשקין היוצא מהן לרצון טמאין פי' מקבלין טומאה. מפני שהן משקין והמשקין אין צריכין הכשר ושלא לרצון טהורין כלומר אוכלין הן. וכיון שלא הוכשרו אינן מטמאין. ובאנו להעמיד משנה זו לרצון דניחא ליה. שלא לרצון בסתמא להודיע כי אפילו זיתים וענבים דבני סחיט' נינהו סתמא אוכל הן. וכ"ש תותים ורמונים. ואמרינן לא. פי' לרצון דמתניתין בסתמא. וכל סתם משקה הוא חשוב. ופי' שלא לרצון דגלי אדעתא בפי' שאין רצונו להוציא מהן משקין. (איכא) [איבעיא] תימא שאני סלי זיתים וענבים כיון שהסלין לאו בני קיבול משקה הן דבר ידוע הוא שכל משקה השותת מהן לעפר והולך וזהו לאיבוד כאילו מעיקרא הפקירן וכשאינן חשובין ולפיכך הן טהורין. תוב אתינן לפרושי דרבנן מודו לי' לר' יהודה בשאר פירות מהא דתניא סוחטין בפגעים. יש מי שאומר ספיגיל ובפרישין ובעוזרדין אבל לא ברמונים. ואוקימנא אפילו תימא רבנן כיון דלא בני סחיטה נינהו אפילו לכתחלה. ושל בית מנשיא היו סוחטין בחול ברמונים ועושין ממנו יין של רמונים כלומר שהרמונים בני סחיטה נינהו כזיתים וענבים ואסור לסוחטן בשבת. אמר רב נחמן הלכה כשל בית מנשיא בן מנחם. ואמרינן וכי מנשיא תנא הוא. ואוקימנא האי תנא

Based on this assumption, the Gemara concludes its question regarding R' Yehudah's opinion concerning the juice of mulberries and pomegranates stored for no stated purpose:

וּמָה זֵיתִים וַעֲנָבִים – Now **if** in the case of **olives or grapes,** **דִּבְנֵי סְחִיטָה נִינְהוּ** – **which are** generally designated **for squeezing,** **שֶׁלֹּא לְרָצוֹן וְלֹא כְלוּם** – the liquid that oozed from them **not to** the owner's **satisfaction** [i.e. without the owner stating his intent] **is** regarded as **[no beverage] at all,** since we assume that the owner is dissatisfied with its emergence, **תּוּתִים וְרִמּוֹנִים** – then in the case of **mulberries or pomegranates,** **דְּלָאו בְּנֵי סְחִיטָה נִינְהוּ** – **which are not** generally designated **for squeezing,** **לֹא כָּל שֶׁכֵּן** – **is it not** certainly **true** that the liquid that oozed from them without the owner stating his intent will not be considered a legal beverage? For in that case we may certainly assume that the owner is not satisfied with the liquid! But the aforecited Baraisa stated in the name of R' Yehudah that if one stores mulberries and pomegranates without stating what they are to be used for, the juice that oozes from them is prohibited for consumption, since we assume that the owner *will* be satisfied with the emergence of liquid from these fruits, and may consequently be led to squeeze them. But this assumption is in contradiction to this Mishnah's ruling![8]

The Gemara resolves the contradiction:

לֹא לְרָצוֹן בִּסְתָמָא – **No,** what the Mishnah's term **"to** the owner's **satisfaction"** means **is that [the owner of the fruit] makes no statement** regarding his intent; **שֶׁלֹּא לְרָצוֹן דְּגַלֵּי אַדַּעְתֵּיהּ** – while the term **"not to** his **satisfaction"** means that **he** explicitly **revealed his intent,** **דְּאָמַר** – **inasmuch as he** clearly **stated:** **לֹא נִיחָא לִי** – **I do not find it satisfactory** that this liquid oozes out. The Mishnah is thus ruling that if the owner gives no indication of his wishes for the fruit, we in fact *do* assume his satisfaction – the juice the fruit exudes will accordingly be considered a beverage. This Mishnah is thus in perfect accord with the Baraisa cited above.[9]

The Gemara resolves the contradiction in another manner:

וְאִיבָּעִית אֵימָא שָׁאנֵי סַלֵּי זֵיתִים וַעֲנָבִים – **Or if you wish you may say** that liquid that oozes from **olives or grapes** that are placed **in baskets** (the Mishnah's case) **is different,** **כֵּיוָן דִּלְאִיבּוּד קָיְימֵי** **מֵעִיקָּרָא אַפְקוּרֵי מַפְקְרֵי לְהוּ** – for **since it stands to** seep through the holes in the baskets and **be lost, [the owners,]** by placing the fruits in baskets, **are** clearly **abandoning [the juice] from the start** – therefore, even without an explicit statement of dissatisfaction with the oozing of the juice, we may assume that the owners are not particularly satisfied with it. The Baraisa, however, deals with a case of fruit placed in sealed containers, in which there is no reason to presume dissatisfaction. In that case we indeed assume that, there being no indication to the contrary, the owner is in fact satisfied with the emergence of the juice.[10]

The Gemara now returns to the comment made above in the name of Shmuel, namely, that R' Yehudah agrees with the Sages in the case of liquid that oozes from olives or grapes, while the Sages agree with R' Yehudah in the case of liquid that oozes from other sorts of fruits. The Gemara therefore asks:

אַשְׁכְּחַן רַבִּי יְהוּדָה דְּמוֹדֵי לְרַבָּנַן בְּזֵיתִים וּבַעֲנָבִים – **We have** indeed **found** a source that says **that R' Yehudah agrees with the Rabbis** [i.e. the Sages] **regarding** liquid that oozed from **olives and grapes.**[11] **רַבָּנַן דְּמוֹדוּ לֵיהּ לְרַבִּי יְהוּדָה בִּשְׁאָר פֵּירוֹת מְנָלַן** – But **from where do we know that the Rabbis agree with R' Yehudah regarding** liquid that oozed from **other** sorts of **fruits?**

The Gemara answers:

דְּתַנְיָא – **For it has been taught** in a Baraisa: **סוֹחֲטִין** – **WE MAY SQUEEZE**

NOTES

he is assumed to be *dissatisfied* – thus, the emergence of the liquid is "not to his satisfaction."]

8. *Rashi* notes that the validity of this question does not depend upon whether the Mishnah in *Machshirin* follows the opinion of R' Yehudah. Rather, even if the Mishnah is in accordance with the Sages [i.e. those who dispute R' Yehudah in *our* Mishnah], it will still represent a contradiction to the Baraisa's statement. For consider: The Sages of our Mishnah take a more stringent position than does R' Yehudah regarding assuming an owner's satisfaction with liquid that oozes from fruit (see below for how this is known). It thus follows that in any case in which the Sages assume an owner's *dissatisfaction* with the oozing liquid, R' Yehudah will *certainly* assume that he is dissatisfied with it. Accordingly, if the Sages rule that one is assumed to be dissatisfied with the liquid that flows from baskets of olives or grapes, R' Yehudah will rule likewise. But the Baraisa states that R' Yehudah assumes the owner's *satisfaction* in the case of mulberries or pomegranates stored for no stated purpose! Thus, even if this Mishnah follows the opinion of the Sages, it *still* contradicts the Baraisa. [We know that the Sages rule more stringently than R' Yehudah on the issue of an owner's satisfaction with oozing liquid from their position concerning liquid that oozed from pomegranates and mulberries stored for eating. They assume that the owner is satisfied with its emergence, and consequently suspect that he may come to squeeze the fruit, while R' Yehudah assumes that he is *not* particularly satisfied to have it emerge.]

Rashi notes further that the Gemara, instead of pointing out the contradiction to the Baraisa's statement regarding mulberries and pomegranates, could just as well have pointed out the contradiction to its statement regarding olives and grapes. For both R' Yehudah and the Sages prohibit liquid that oozed from olives or grapes stored for eating, since we assume that the owner is satisfied with its emergence. But in this Mishnah we assume that even if the olives and grapes were *not* explicitly stored for eating [but for no stated reason at all], we assume that the owner will *not* be satisfied with the liquid that flows from them! *Rashi* explains that the reason the Gemara focuses specifically on the case of mulberries and pomegranates is because it wishes to draw the contradiction as sharply as possible. It therefore contrasts a case in which an owner is assumed to be satisfied with liquid that oozes from fruit *not* usually designated for squeezing with a case in which he is assumed *not* to be satisfied with liquid that oozes from fruit that *is* generally designated for squeezing (*Rashi;* cf. *Ramban; Ritva MHK* ed. et al.).

9. [Since both the Mishnah and the Baraisa can rule that we may assume one's satisfaction with liquid that oozed from mulberries or pomegranates that were stored for no stated purpose.]

[If, however, one states explicitly that he is not pleased to have liquid flow from the fruit, we can be sure that he does not regard the oozing liquid with any sort of satisfaction – it accordingly will not be considered a beverage. Now this might seem a contradiction to the Baraisa's ruling regarding olives or grapes stored for eating – for in that case, although one certainly does not desire their liquid, both R' Yehudah and the Sages assume that one will change his mind and look upon the liquid with satisfaction once it appears. Yet in this Mishnah we assume no such change of heart!] *Rashi* explains that a person's explicit *statement* of dissatisfaction is a better indicator of his true desire than his mere *intention* based on storing it for eating; we therefore do not assume that one who verbally articulates his dissatisfaction with the liquid will change his mind upon seeing it ooze from the fruit (*Rashi*).

10. [According to this explanation, the term "not to his satisfaction" in the Mishnah in fact means that the owner made no explicit statement concerning his intention, as the Gemara assumed at first. Nonetheless, we may assume that he does not regard the juice with any particular satisfaction, since he is abandoning it for lost by placing the fruit into baskets.]

Although the Gemara on 17a rules that juice that flows from grapes that were picked into baskets will cause *tumah* susceptibility by Rabbinic decree, that law applies only to grapes that were originally picked for squeezing. In our case, however, the fruit was intended for no particular purpose at all. The owner's placing it into baskets is thus a sign that he derives no satisfaction from the fact that it has emerged (*Baal HaMaor;* see also glosses of *R' Simchah MiDessau*).

11. [Namely, the Baraisa cited above, 143b.]

שלא לרצון [א]שדם מגפתה טהור אמר להן מחמיר אני בחלב מבדם שהחולב לרפואה טמא [ב]והמקיז לרפואה טהור אמרו לו סלי זיתים וענבים יוכיחו [ג]שהמשקין היוצאין מהן לרצון טמאין שלא לרצון טהורים מאי לאו לרצון דניחא ליה שלא לרצון בסתמא ומה זיתים וענבים דבני סחיטה נינהו שלא לרצון ולא כלום תותים ורמונים דלאו בני סחיטה נינהו לא כ"ש לא לרצון בסתמא שלא לרצון דגלי אדעתיה דאמר לא ניחא לי ואיבעית אימא שאני סלי זיתים וענבים כיון דלאיבוד קיימי מעיקרא אפקורי מפקרי להו אשכחן ר' יהודה דמודי לרבנן בזיתים ובענבים רבנן דמודו ליה לרבי יהודה בשאר פירות מנלן דתניא סוחטין בפגעין

רש"י

א) שדם מגפתה. של אשה אם נגף רגלה או ידה וכל תבורה שילא ממנה דם כדאמר בפרק דם הנדה (נדה דף נה:) דם חללים דהיינו דם הרוג קרוי משקה שנאמר ודם חללים ישתה ודם מגפתו מפרש התם דדם חללים הוי דמה לי קטליה כוליה מה לי קטליה פלגא וחלב כדם מגפתו דדם נעכר ונעשה חלב ודם מגפתה סתמיה שלא לרצון הוא וטמא: יטמא חלב הבהמה שלא לרצון. בתמיה שהרי דם מגפתה טהור דבהמה לאו בכלל חלל הוא ומיהו דם שחיטה מכשר משום דאיתקש למים דכתיב (דברים יב) על הארץ תשפכנו כמים: ב) מחמיר אני בחלב. לטמאו אף שלא לרצון מבדם: שהחולב. לרפואת הבהמה שלא יזיקנה חלבה טמא דהא לרצון הוא והמקיז דם לבהמתו לרפואה טהור דדם מגפתה היא והואיל והחולב לרפואה טמא אף הנוטף שלא לרצון טמא: אמרו לו. אינו דומה שלא לרצון ליוצא לרצון שהרי סלי זיתים וענבים יוכיחו שהמשקה כו': שלא לרצון בסתמא. וקתני טהורין דלא חשיב משקה אי רבי יהודה קאמר לה קשיא ואי רבנן קאמרי כל שכן טהורין לרבי יהודה דהא מידי דלרבנן משקה הוא לרבי יהודה לאו משקה הוא וכ"ש מידי דלרבנן לאו משקה והשתא ומה זיתים וענבים כו' והוא הדין מצי למירמי נמי זיתים וענבים אזיתים וענבים דקתני לעיל דמודה בהו רבי יהודה דאף לאוכלין היוצא מהן אסור אלא הא אלימא ליה לאקשויי דתותים ורמונים דלאו בני סחיטה נינהו קתני לעיל דסתם אסור והכא קתני דאפי' זיתים וענבים סתמא לאו למשקה: דגלי דעתיה. בהדיא ואמר לא ניחא לי והוי גילוי דעתא טפי מהכניסו לאוכלין: ואיבעית אימא שאני סלי זיתים וענבים וכו'. ודווקא נקט סלין שהמשקה הנוטף מהן נופל לארץ והולך לאיבוד הלכך סתמא לא ניחא ליה: אפקורי מפקיר. לההוא משקה אבל שאר כלים אפילו תותים ורמונים אימא לך סתמא למשקה: בפגעין

תוספות

מחמיר אני בחלב מבדם שהחולב לרפואה טמא והמקיז לרפואה טהור. א"כ מאי דמטמינן חלב האשה לא מחמת דם הוא דדם נעכר ונעשה חלב דא"כ חולב לרפואה טהור כמו דם אלא ודאי משום דכתיב ותפתח את נאד החלב ואומר רבי דבתנס נקט חולב לרפואה דהכי נמי הו"מ להשיב לרבנן מחלב בהמה גופה שדמה טהור (א) וחלבה טמא א"כ החלב אינו טמא מחמת דם אלא משום דכתיב ותפתח את נאד החלב וא"כ שלא לרצון נמי מהאי טעמא יהא טמא. מ"ר: סלי זיתים וענבים יוכיחו שמשקה היוצא מהן לרצון טמא שלא לרצון טהור. בשילהי מסכת מכשירין מסיים לא אם אמרת בסלי זיתים וענבים שהרי תחילתו אוכל וסופו משקה תאמרו בחלב שתחילתו וסופו משקה: מאי לאו לרצון דניחא ליה ושלא לרצון בסתמא. ולרצון ושלא לרצון דגבי חלב אשה ליכא למימר דמיירי בשלא לרצון בסתמא ודווקא בסתמא אבל אמר לא ניחא לי אינו מטמא דהא לפי מה שפירשתי הטעם משום דם מגפתה אפי' אמר לא ניחא לי נמי מטמא אלא משמע דשלא לרצון דקתני בכולהו באשה ובהמה וזיתים וענבים מיירי בכל ענין בין מסתמא בין אמר לא ניחא לי: תותים ורימונים דלאו בני סחיטה נינהו. תימה לי מאי קשה דילמא הא דתניא לעיל גבי תותים ורמונים למשקין ולסתם היוצא מהן אסור הנ"מ במשך דוקא והכא בלא משך איירי הלכך שלא לרצון דהיינו בסתמא לא חשיב משקה: לא לרצון בסתמא ושלא לרצון דגלי דעתיה דאמר לא ניחא לי. (ב) דתניא התם בכריתות פרק אמרו לו (דף יג.) התירו (ג) לו למגע טמא מת להניק את בנה ובנה טהור ופריך בנה אמאי טהור כיון דינק חלב איטמי ליה מחלב וכי תימא לא איתכשר איתכשר בטיפה המלוכלכת ע"פ הדד ואע"ג דחלב אשה משקה הוא ואין צריך הכשר [משמע ליה] דמה שהוא בפי התינוק שהתינוק יונק חשיב כאוכל וצריך הכשר לפי שזהו מאכלו של תינוק וקאמר דאיתכשר בטיפה המלוכלכת בפי הדד דהוי משקה כסתם חלב דלאו לאוכל בעי ליה ומשני רב נחמן אמר רבה בר אבוה (ד) בתקיפה אחת שלא הניח טיפה המלוכלכת ע"פ הדד ומקשה רבא שתי תשובות בדבר חדא דקא חזין ליה לפומיה דינוקא דמלא חלבא ועוד מקום חלב מעין הוא דהא תנן חלב האשה מטמא לרצון ושלא לרצון מאי היא דלא ניחא ליה וקתני מטמא פי' אלמא חשיבא כמעין מדמטמא שלא לרצון וכיון דחשוב כמעין גם בפי התינוק נמי יהא חשוב כמשקה כמו שאם היה מעין ואין צריך הכשר כך צריך לפרש דאע"ג דאינו מזכיר מעין אלא כלומר דכמשקה חשיב א"כ מאי צריך למימר שלא לרצון מאי היא כו' דמדקתני לרצון מטמא הו"מ למיפרך אלמא לרצון חשיב כי משקה ואשה דמניקה את בנה לרצון הוא אלא אמר רבא כו' עד ולרבא מקום חלב מעין הוא ולא צריך הכשר והתנן האשה שנטף חלב מדדיה ונפל לאויר התנור התנור טמא וקשיא לן במאי איתכשר ואמר ר' יוחנן בטיפה המלוכלכת ע"פ הדד והשתא קשה לר"י מאי קאמר במאי איתכשר דמדבעי הכשר אלמא אוכל חשיב ליה וא"כ איך יטמא אוכל את התנור והא אין אוכל מטמא כלי ואומר ר"י דה"פ וקשיא לן במאי איתכשר כלומר לא מבעיא שאין התנור טמא אלא חלב הנוטף מדדיה גופה אמאי יהא טמא הא לא איתכשר ומשני בטיפה המלוכלכת ע"פ הדד ואותה טיפה עצמה המלוכלכת ע"פ הדד מטמא התנור שהיא חשובה משקה ומשקה מטמא כלי כדאמרינן בפ' קמא דמכילתין (דף יג:) והשתא פריך שפיר לרבא דאמר דאפילו אמר לא ניחא לי מטמא חלב האשה דחשיב משקה והכא חשיב ליה אוכל אבל לר"נ אמר רבה בר אבוה אתי שפיר דהכא דאמר לא ניחא לי ודאי חשיב ליה אוכל ונטף חלב מדדיה חשיב לא ניחא ליה כיון שהוא נופל לאויר תנור ואזיל לאיבוד דודאי לא ניחא ליה ועוד פריך התם לרבא מדתניא ט' משקין זוב הזיעה וליחה סרוחה והריעי טהורים מכלום דמעת עינו ודם מגפתו וחלב האשה מטמא טומאת משקין ברביעית רוקו חוטו ומימי רגליו מטמא טומאה חמורה בכל שהוא ואי אמרת מקום חלב מעין הוא חלב האשה נמי יטמא טומאה חמורה בכל שהוא כזובו ורוקו וקשה לרבי מאי קפריך לעולם מעין הוא ואפ"ה לא יטמא טומאה חמורה משום דבעינן דומיא דרוק כדאיתא בנדה (ד' נו.) מה רוק שמתגלגל ויוצא וחוזר ונבלע אף כל שמתגלגל ויוצא וחוזר ונבלע יצא חלב שבאשה שמתגלגל ויוצא ואינו חוזר ונבלע ותימה הוא לומר דמה שהוא חוזר ונבלע גרם לו ליחשב כמעין ומכל מקום ודאי כן הוא וצריך לומר דמה שהיה חושבו רבא כמעין להיות חשיב משקה בפי התינוק היינו משום דסלקא דעתיה שחוזר ונבלע ומייתי ראיה מן המשנה דחוזר ונבלע הוא מדקתני מטמא שלא לרצון דהיינו אמר לא ניחא לי א"כ חוזר ונבלע הוא דאי לאו הכי אם אמר לא ניחא ליה לא יהיה מטמא והשתא פריך ליה מהכא דאינו חוזר ונבלע אלמא מקום חלב האשה לאו מעין הוא ופריך אי הכי קשה הא דקתני מטמא שלא לרצון ומשני מי סברת שלא לרצון דלא ניחא ליה לא שלא לרצון בסתמא דלדעתיה דתינוק קרובה גבי חלב אבל אמר לא ניחא ליה טהור והשתא דנטף חלב מדדיה ונפל לתוך התנור כאומר לא ניחא ליה חשיב דודאי לא ניחא ליה כיון שהלך לאיבוד והא דקאמר שלא לרצון בסתמא היינו כשנופל בקערה שאינו הולך לאיבוד דמהני טעמא דלדעתיה דתינוק קרובה גבי חלב לאחשובה או משקה ובפי התינוק לעולם כאוכל חשיב והשתא קשה לר"י חדא דבשמעתא מסקינן איפכא לרצון בסתמא ושלא לרצון דאמר לא ניחא ליה ודומיא דהכי דזיתים וענבים הוי ההוא דחלב האשה דאי לאו הכי לא שייך למימר יוכיחו וכ"ת ס"ל כאיבעית אימא דאמר שאני סלי זיתים וענבים כיון דלאיבוד קיימא אפקורי מפקר להו אכתי קשה דדומיא דהכי איכא לן למימר בחלב האשה דאזיל לאיבוד וא"כ היינו כאומר לא ניחא ליה והתם מטמא דוקא סתמא אבל לא ניחא ליה טהור ועוד קשה לר"י מאי קאמר התם אלא קשה הא מתני' וקאמר נמי מי סברת שלא לרצון לא ניחא ליה וקאמר דלא ניחא ליה (ה) טהור ואמאי והא טעמא שלא לרצון טמא היינו משום דחשיב דם מגפתו דדם נעכר ונעשה חלב כדפי' לעיל וא"כ גם אמר לא ניחא ליה נמי יהא טמא. מ"ר:

מי

מסורת הש"ס

א) שייך לעמוד הקודם, ב) ע"ב.

הגהות הב"ח

(א) תוס' ד"ה מחמיר וכו' שדמה טהור. נ"ב ובתוספות יו"ט סוף מס' מכשירין מתרץ קושיא זו דבאמת דם בהמה לשתיה מכשיר כמו חלב שהוא לשתיה ע"כ מוכרח לומר מדם הקזה והמולב לרפוא' ע"ש: (ב) ד"ה לא לרצון וכו' לא ניחא לי תניא כצ"ל ואות ד' נמחק: (ג) בא"ד התירו לה למגע טמא מת: (ד) בא"ד אמר רבה בר אבוה שינק בתקיפה: (ה) בא"ד וקאמר דלא ניחא ליה טהור:

עין משפט נר מצוה

ו א ב מיי' פ"י מהלכות טומאת אוכלין הל"ג:
ז ג מיי' פ"א שם הלכה ג ופ"י הלכה יב:

רבינו חננאל

והתנן במס' מכשירין אמרו לו זיתים וענבים יוכיחו שהמשקין היוצא מהן לרצון טמאין פי' מקבלין טומאה. מפני שהן משקין והמשקין אין צריכין הכשר ושלא לרצון טהורין כלומר אוכלין הן. וכיון שלא הוכשרו אינן מטמאין. ובאנו להעמיד משנה זו לרצון דניחא ליה. שלא לרצון בסתמא להודיע כי אפילו זיתים וענבים דבני סחיט' נינהו סתמא אוכל הן. וכ"ש תותים ורמונים. ואמרינן לא. פי' לרצון דמתניתין בסתמא. וכל סתם משקה הוא חשוב. ופי' שלא לרצון דגלי אדעתא בפי' שאין רצונו להוציא מהן משקין. (איכא) [איבעיא] תימא שאני סלי זיתים וענבים כיון שהסלין לאו בני קיבול משקה הן דבר ידוע הוא שכל משקה השותת מהן לעפר והולך וזהו לאיבוד כאילו מעיקרא הפקירן וכשאינן חשובין ולפיכך הן טהורין. תוב אתינן לפרושי דרבנן מודו לי' לר' יהודה בשאר פירות מהא דתניא סוחטין בפגעים. יש מי שאומר ספיגיל ובפרישין ובעוזרדין אבל לא ברמונים. ואוקימנא אפילו תימא רבנן כיון דלא בני סחיטה נינהו אפילו לכתחלה. ושל בית מנשיא היו סוחטין בחול ברמונים ועושין ממנו יין של רמונים כלומר שהרמונים בני סחיטה נינהו כזיתים וענבים ואסור לסוחטן בשבת. אמר רב נחמן הלכה כשל בית מנשיא בן מנחם. ואמרינן וכי מנשיא תנא הוא. ואוקימנא האי תנא

בפגעין ובפרישין ובעוזרדין אבל לא ברמונים ושל בית מנשיא בר מנחם היו סוחטין ברמונים וממאי דרבנן היא דילמא ר׳ יהודה היא ותהוי נמי ר׳ יהודה אימר דשמעת ליה לר׳ יהודה יצאו מעצמן סוחטן לכתחילה מי שמעת ליה אלא מאי אית לך למימר כיון דלאו בני סחיטה נינהו אפילו לכתחילה אפילו תימא רבנן כיון דלאו בני סחיטה נינהו אפילו לכתחילה ש״מ רבנן היא ש״מ של בית מנשיא בר מנחם היו סוחטין ברמונים אמר רב נחמן הלכה כשל בית מנשיא בר מנחם א״ל רבא לרב נחמן מנשיא בן מנחם תנא הוא וכי תימא הלכה כי האי תנא דסבר לה כשל מנשיא בן מנחם ומשום דסבר כמנשיא בן מנחם הלכה כמותו מנשיא בן מנחם הוי ה) רובא דעלמא אין דתנן ו) המקיים קוצים בכרם ר״א אומר קדש וחכ״א א אינו מקדש אלא דבר שכמוהו מקיימין וא״ר חנינא מ״ט דרבי ג) אליעזר שכן בערביא מקיימין קוצי שדות לגמליהם מידי איריא דערביא אתרא הכא בטלה דעתו אצל כל אדם אלא היינו טעמא כדרב חסדא דאמר רב חסדא תרדין שסחטן ונתנן במקוה פוסלין את המקוה בשינוי מראה והא לאו בני סחיטה נינהו אלא מאי אית לך למימר כיון דאחשבינהו הוה להו משקה ה״נ כיון דאחשבינהו הוה להו משקה רב פפא אמר משום דהוי דבר שאין עושין ממנו מקוה לכתחילה ב וכל דבר שאין עושין ממנו מקוה לכתחילה פוסל את המקוה בשינוי מראה ז) תנן התם ג נפל לתוכו יין או חומץ ומוהל ושינה מראיו פסול מאן תנא דמוהל משקה הוא אמר אביי רבי יעקב היא ח) דתניא ר׳ יעקב אומר ד מוהל הרי הוא כמשקה ומה טעם אמרו מוהל היוצא בתחלה טהור לפי שאינו רוצה בקיומו ר״ש אומר מוהל אינו כמשקה ומה טעם אמרו מוהל היוצא מעיקול בית הבד טמא לפי שאי אפשר לו בלא ציחצוחי שמן מאי בינייהו איכא בינייהו דאתי בתר איצצתא רבא אמר משום דהוי דבר שאין עושין הימנו מקוה ופוסל את המקוה בשינוי מראה אמר רב יהודה אמר שמואל ה סוחט אדם אשכול של ענבים לתוך הקדרה אבל לא לתוך הקערה אמר רב חסדא מדברי רבינו נלמד ט) ו חולב אדם עז לתוך הקדרה אבל לא לתוך הקערה ז אלמא קסבר משקה הבא לאוכל אוכל הוא מתיב רמי בר חמא י) ח זב שחולב את העז החלב טמא ואי אמרת משקה הבא לאוכלין אוכל הוא במאי איתכשר כ) כדאמר ר׳ יוחנן בטיפה המלוכלכת ע״פ הדד הכא נמי בטיפה המלוכלכת ע״פ הדד מתיב רבינא ל) ט טמא מת שסחט זיתים וענבים
כביצה

רש״י

בפגעין. פרוש״ש בלע״ז ולהוציא מימיהן לשתות: ובפרישין. קוידונ״ץ: ובעוזרדין. קורמ״ש דלאו אורחייהו בהכי ואין כאן משום דם: אבל לא ברמונים. דאורחייהו בהכי: ושל בית מנשיא. היו רגילין לסחוט רמונים בחול אלמא איכא דסחיט להו הלכך בשבת אסור: אלא מאי אית לך למימר. לר׳ יהודה כיון דלאו בני סחיטה כו׳ וכי היכי דלרבי יהודה שרי לכתחילה מהאי טעמא מהשתא אפי׳ תימא רבנן ושרו ליה מהאי טעמא: מנשיא תנא הוא. בתמיה וכי איהו פליג למימר דבשבת אסור דתימא הלכתא כוותיה והא לא הוזכר אלא לדברי התנא לראיה דהאי תנא הוא סבר כוותיה: וכ״ת. הא דאמר הלכה כשל בית מנשיא ה״ק הלכה כהאי תנא דאסר ברימונים הואיל וקאי מנשיא כוותיה דסוחטין רימונים בחול אלמא בני סחיטה נינהו: הוי רובא דעלמא. דמשום איהו למודיה נשוי דרך לרמונים לסחיטה: קוצים. קרדונ״ש: מקדש. את התבואה משום כלאים דזריעה הוא: ואמר רבי חנינא כו׳. אלמא משום חד מקום דלאחשבינהו משוינן להו דבר חשוב: אתרא. הוא ותשיבות לרבים הוי חשיבותא: הכא. חד גברא למודיה הוא נימא בטלה דעתו: אלא היינו טעמא. דרב נחמן דאמר הלכה אין סוחטין: כרב חסדא. אע״ג דלעלמא לא חשיב כיון דלאחשיב איהו הוי לדידיה משקה והכי מפרש רב נחמן לבריתא דלעיל סוחטין בפגעין ובפרישין למתק הפרי ולא לצורך המשקה אבל לא ברימונים ואפילו למתקן (א) דשל בית מנשיא היו סוחטין בחול לצורך משקה הלכך בשבת אסור אפי׳ למתק הואיל ואיכא חד דעביד לשם משקה ולא משום דמנשיא רובא דעלמא אלא חיישינן אי שרית ליה למתק אתי למעבד לשום משקה וכיון דאיהו מחשב ליה הוי משקה ומיחייב אבל בפגעין ליכא (ב) למיחש דלאין אדם עושה אותו למשקה: בשינוי מראה. לא בשלשת לוגין דלא הוזכרו שלש לוגין אלא במים שאובין אבל שאר משקין לא פסלי אלא א״כ נשתנה מראה המקוה על ידיהן: רב פפא אמר. טעמא דתרדין לאו משום חשיבותא דלאחשבינהו הוא ולעולם לאו משקה נינהו והא דמפסיל משום דכל דבר שאין עושין ממנו מקוה שאינו מים או שלג או ברד פוסל את המקוה בשינוי מראה: נפל לתוכו. של מקוה יין או חומץ או מוהל והוא כמין מים חב מן הזיתים וג׳ מינים יש בו כשטוענן מתחילה במעטן להתחמם ולהתבשל מאליהן מוהל זב מהן והוא צלול כמים ולאחר שעמדו ימים ודקקו זה את זה חוזר מוהל לזוב מהן והוא קרוב להיות כשמן ולאחר שעלרן להוציא שמנן בבית הבד ומשתהה התפוח של גפת בעקלים שהוא אגוד בהן בבית הבד חוזר מוהל וזב מהן: מאן תנא דמוהל משקה הוא. קס״ד דלאין מקוה נפסל אלא על ידי משקה ואפילו בשינוי מראה: בתחילה. בתחילת טעינתן של זיתים: מעקול בית הבד. לאחר שנסחט שמנו או לפני סחיטתו: מאי בינייהו. במאי פליגי הואיל ותרוייהו מודו דמוהל היוצא בתחילה טהור והיוצא מעקל בית הבד טמא באיזה מוהל נחלקו דלמר הוי משקה וטמא ולמר לא הוי משקה וטהור: דאתי בתר איצצתא. לאחר שהתחילו להתחמם ודקקו זה את זה ונשתהה הכומר ימים: רבא אמר. קמייתא דקתני מוהל פוסל מקוה דברי הכל הוא ומשום דהוי כו׳: לתוך הקדרה. של תבשיל לתקנו דמוכחא מילתא דלאו למשקה בעי ליה אלא לאוכל ° ואין זה דרך פריקתו והוי כמפריד אוכל מאוכל: אבל לא לתוך הקערה. דזמנין דלמשקה קאי ואף על גב דבקערה לא שתי איניש לא מוכחא מילתא ואיכא איסור: אלמא. מדקאמר סוחט לתוך הקדרה קסבר כו׳: החלב טמא. שהזב מטמא כל דבר במשא והרי היסטו הקילוה ולא קמפליג בין לתוך הקדרה בין לתוך הכוס: ואי אמרת אוכל הוא. הא אין אוכל מקבל טומאה שלא בהכשר והאי במאי איתכשר: כדאמר רבי יוחנן. במסכת כריתות גבי האשה שנטף חלב מדדיה: בטיפה המלוכלכת על פי הדד. טיפה ראשונה מלכלכת בה פי הדד בדעת ונוחה ליחלב וההיא הוי משקה כשתם חלב דלא לאוכל בעי ליה: טמא מת שסחט זיתים וענבים
כבילה

תוספות

מי דמי ערביא אתרא הוא. הו״מ למיפרך הניחא לרבי אליעזר לרבנן מאי איכא למימר אלא פריך דאפילו לרבי אליעזר לא ניחא ומה שקשה מאנשי הוצל דפרק המצניע (לעיל דף צב:) פירשתי שם (ד״ה ואת״ל): ה״נ כיון דאחשביה הוו להו משקה. תמיהה ס״ד דסוחטין בפגעין כו׳ היינו סחיטה ממש אבל השתא אי אפשר לומר דהא פשיטא דאסור דכיון דלאחשביה הוה להו משקה אלא סוחטין דקתני היינו בליל״ר בלע״ז למתק הפרי כדפי׳ בקונטרס: אמר אביי ר׳ יעקב היא. קשה לי לימא דהאי מוהל דקתני היינו במוהל היוצא מעקול בית הבד ודברי הכל וכי תימא מדקתני מוהל סתמא משמע דבכל מוהל איירי לא היא דע״כ אפי׳ לרבי יעקב לא איירי בכל מוהל דהא מודה דמוהל היוצא בתחלה טהור וי״ל דמוהל היוצא מעקול בית הבד לא הוה קרינן ליה מוהל סתם כיון דאי אפשר לו בלא צחצוחי שמן:

חולב אדם עז כו׳. נראה לר״ת דהיינו דווקא בי״ט דחזיא בהמה לאכילה הוי כמו אוכלא דאיפרת אבל בשבת לא חזיא לשחיטה כמו דם שיצא שבהמה היא כפסולת וכשחולב הוי כנוטל אוכל מתוך פסולת וכן משמע בבה״ג דבי״ט איירי ומיהו סחיטת זיתים וענבים דשרי לעיל לתוך הקדירה היינו אפי׳ בשבת כיון דאשכול חזיא לאכילה:
כבילה

ליקוטי רש״י (המשך)

הסיטו של זב מכאן למדנו זב שהסיט את הטהור טמא שלא מצינו בכל התורה טומאה המסטת טהרה שלא אם כן נשא טהור את הטמא והכא הוא דבזב הוא דגלי רחמנא [נדה מג.]. ואי אמרת משקה הבא לאוכלין אוכל הוא במאי איתכשר. שאין אוכל מוכשר ומתוקן לקבל טומאה עד שיבאו עליו מים פעם אחת ומשבאו עליו מים פעם אחת מקבל טומאה לעולם ואפילו נגוב והיין והשמן וכל הנקרא משקה מכשיר זרעים לטומאה כמים שכך יש לדרוש המקרא אשר יבא עליו מים או כל משקה אשר ישתה בכל כלי יטמא האוכל [ויקרא יא, לד]. האי חלב ולאו כו׳ תורת משקה דמשקה הבא לאוכל כאוכל דמי במסכת שבת בפרק חבית שנשברה הלכך בעי הכשר. בטיפה המלוכלכת על פי הדד. כלומר בטפה שפי הדד מלוכלך בו דההיא ודאי מכשר לשאר החלב דרך שם דהא [האי] לא קיימא לאכילה מיטק [כריתות יג.].

רבינו חננאל (המשך)

לתוך הקערה שהוא ודאי משקה. ומפני מה לא פירק פירוק זה לגבי חולב עז חדא מתרי תלתא טעמא קאמר. א״ר ירמיה כתנאי. המחלק בענבים לא הוכשר. פי׳ מחלק משפשף פעמים שמתמצה בהן משקין. ומחליקן בו. ולפיכך א״ר יהודה הוכשר שכך משקה גמור הוא. ות״ק אמר משקה הבא לאוכל הוא וכאוכל הוא חשוב ואינו מכשיר ובא רב הונא ופירש כי התנאין החולקין במחלק במחליק בענבים פליגי במשקה העומד לצחצחו ואלו החולקין במפצע זיתים בידים מסואבות פליגי. במשקה העומד לאיבוד. א״ר זירא א״ר חייא בר אשי אמר רב סוחט אדם אשכול של ענבים לתוך הקדירה אבל לא לתוך הקערה וכן פירושו כל דבר הנסחט בקדירה הוא אוכל ומותר ולתוך הקערה משקה ואסור. זולתי הדג שאפילו סחיטתו בקערה שרי. והא דאתמר כבשים שסחטן אמר רב לגופן מותר וכו׳. דברים פשוטין הן. ואין צריכין לפנים ולא לפני פנים. אמנם צריכין אנו לברר כמי ההלכה. לפיכך אנו מזכירין דברי כולן:

עין משפט נר מצוה

ח א מיי׳ פ״ה מהלכות כלאים הל״ח טוש״ע יו״ד סימן רלו סעיף יד:
ט ב מיי׳ פ״ז מהלכות מקוואות הלכה א סמג עשין רמח:
י ג מיי׳ שם והלכה ט סמג שם טוש״ע יו״ד סימן רא סעיף כה:
יא ד מיי׳ פ״י מהלכות טומאת אוכלין הלכה יג ופי״א הלכה ו:
יב ה מיי׳ פ״ח מהלכות שבת הל״י סמג לאוין סה טור שו״ע או״ח סימן שכ סעיף ד:
יג ו ז מיי׳ שם וסמג שם טור שו״ע או״ח סימן תקה:
יד ח ט מיי׳ פ״ע מהל׳ טומאת אוכלין הל״ג:

גליון הש״ס

רש״י ד״ה לתוך הקדירה וכו׳ ואין זה דרך פריקתו. עיין לעיל דף עג ע״ב תוספות ד״ה מפרק:

רבינו חננאל

דאמר סוחטין בפגעין ובפרישין ובעוזרדין אבל לא ברמונים וסבר לה כמנשיא בן מנחם שסוחט בחול ברמונים להוציא מהן מים וכן כמו זיתים וענבי׳ וקיי״ל כוותיה ואקשינן וכי מנשיא הוה רובא לעלמא. ומהדרינן אין. כי הא דתנן המקיים קוצים בכרם וכו׳ ואוקימנא אע״פ שאין דרך בני אדם לקיים קוצים בכרם כיון שבערביא מקיימין קידש הכא נמי אע״פ שאין דרך בני אדם לסחוט רמונים בחול כיון שסוחטין של בית מנשיא בחול בשבת אסור לסחוט ודחינן ערביא מקום בני אדם רבים ומנשיא אדם אחד הוא ובטלה דעתו אצל [כל] בני אדם ואתינן לטעמא אחריתי אלא האי תנא כטעמיה דרב חסדא דאמר תרדין שסחטן ונתנן למקוה פסלו המקוה בשנוי מראה וכיון שהזכרנו פסולות המקוה אמרינן. תנן התם [נפל] לתוכו יין ומוהל כו׳ פי׳ מוהל המים היוצאים מעוקל בית הבד עת שטוען קורות בית הבד על הזיתים הטחונין והוא מי הזיתים ויש בהן צחצוחי שמן: איצצאי דוחק. כדגרסינן בפרק המפקיד (דף מ ע״א) אמר ר׳ יהודה אמר שמואל סוחט אדם אשכול של ענבים בתוך הקדירה אבל לא לתוך הקערה. אמר רב חסדא מדברי רבינו נלמד חולב אדם עז לתוך הקדירה אבל לא לתוך הקערה אלמא קא סבר משקה הבא לאוכל אוכל הוא. ואותביה רמי [בר חמא] זב שחלב עז החלב טמא. כלומר (טמא) [שטימא אותה] הזב בנגיעתו. וא״ת אוכל הוא במאי אתכשר ופרקינן כר׳ יוחנן דאמר איתכשר בטפה המלוכלכת על פי הדד שנפסלה מאוכל והיא מכשרת במשקה ואותיב רבינא טמא מת שסחט זיתים וענבי׳ וכו׳ ופרקינן בסוחט

מסורת הש״ס

א) [לעיל לב. ושם נסמן], ב) כלאים פ״ה מ״ח ב״ב קנו:, ג) [ל״ל אליעזר], ד) מקוואות פ״ז מ״ד, ה) תוספ׳ דטהרות פרק י, ו) [ע״ל תוס׳ עג: ד״ה מפרק וכו׳], ז) טהרות פ״ג מ״ג, ח) כריתות יג. ט) פסחים לג:, י) טהרות פ״ג מ״ג.

הגהות הב״ח

(א) רש״י ד״ה כרב חסדא וכו׳ ואפילו למתקן הואיל דשל בית וכו׳: (ב) בא״ד למיחש להכי דאין אדם:

רב נסים גאון

פכ״ב רבא אמר משום דהוה דבר שאין עושין ממנו מקוה לכתחילה וכל דבר שאין עושין ממנו מקוה לכתחילה פוסל את המקוה בשינוי מראה. עיקר דיליה בתורת כהנים מקוה מים לא מקוה כל המשקין כולן פרט לשנפל בתוכו מי כבשין ומי צבעין ושינו את מראיו ובתוספתא טבול יום (פרק א) חומר במשקין שאין להן טהרת הגוף ואין להן טהרה מטומאתן ואינן טהורין בגוף ופוסלין את המקוה בשינוי מראה מה שאין כן במים: כדאמר ר׳ יוחנן בטיפה על פי הדד. משכחת לה במס׳ כריתות בפרק אמרו לו אכלת חלב (דף יג) ולרבא מקום חלב מעין הוא ולא צריך הכשר והתנן האשה שחלב מדדיה ונפל לאויר תנור תנור טמא וקשיא לן במאי איתכשר ואמר ר׳ יוחנן בטיפה מלוכלכת ע״פ הדד:

ליקוטי רש״י

המקיים קוצים בכרם. דכה״ג אשמעינן במסכת כלאים [illegible] כלאים בכרם [illegible] כלאים דאפילו מקיים לוקה [illegible] במועד קטן (ג:) [illegible] [ושבים ב״ב קנו:]. ר״א אומר קדש. משום כלאי הכרם דכתיב פן תקדש המלאה [illegible] (סוטה מג.). שכן בערביא כו׳. ורבנן סבר רובא דעלמא אלו שאין מקיימין שדות [ושבים שם]. שאי אפשר לו בלא ציחצוחי שמן. ושמן מיקרי משקה דכתיב (ישעיה כה) משתה שמנים [חולין קיד.]. היוצא מעיקול בית הבד. ועקל בית הבד עשוי כמין קופה מסורגת [מגלרז] ואחרי כתישת הזיתים נותן הגפת לתוכו עקל ומניח עליו [הקורה] ומכביד להוציא המשקה הנשאר [ע״ז עה.]. איצצתא. דוחק [ב״מ מ.]. זב שחולב את העז החלב טמא. דכתיב וכל אשר יגע בו הזב וגו׳ [illegible]

בְּפַגְעִין וּבִפְרִישִׁין וּבְעוּזְרְדִין – PLUMS, QUINCES OR SORB-APPLES on the Sabbath in order to drink their juice, since these fruits are not generally designated for squeezing.[1] אֲבָל לֹא בְּרִמּוֹנִים – BUT we may NOT squeeze POMEGRANATES on the Sabbath in order to drink their juice, since pomegranates are generally designated for squeezing.[2]

The Baraisa supports the notion that pomegranates are used for squeezing:

וְשֶׁל בֵּית מְנַשְׁיָא בַּר מְנַחֵם הָיוּ סוֹחֲטִין בְּרִמּוֹנִים – AND the members OF THE HOUSEHOLD OF MENASHYA BAR MENACHEM WOULD SQUEEZE POMEGRANATES during the weekdays. We see that there are those who customarily squeeze these fruits; one is therefore prohibited to do so on the Sabbath.[3]

We see from this Baraisa that in the case of other sorts of fruit, one is permitted even to deliberately squeeze them for their juice – one is thus certainly permitted to use the juice that oozes from them of its own accord.

The Gemara asks:

וּמִמַּאי דְּרַבָּנָן הִיא – **But from where** do you know **that this** ruling **is** the opinion of **the Rabbis** (i.e. the Sages)? דִּילְמָא רַבִּי יְהוּדָה הִיא – **Perhaps it is** only the opinion of **R' Yehudah!**

The Gemara answers:

וְתֶהֱוֵי נַמִּי רַבִּי יְהוּדָה – **But let it be R' Yehudah's** opinion! Even if it is, the Baraisa will still constitute proof that the Rabbis agree with R' Yehudah in the case of other sorts of fruit. אֵימַר דִּשְׁמַעַתְּ לֵיהּ לְרַבִּי יְהוּדָה – For what **can you say you have heard** said **of R' Yehudah** in our Mishnah – יָצְאוּ מֵעַצְמָן – only that liquids that **oozed** from the fruits **of their own accord** are permitted for consumption.[4] סוֹחֲטִין לְכַתְּחִילָּה מִי שְׁמַעַתְּ לֵיהּ – But with regard to **initially squeezing** the fruits on the Sabbath, **have you** then **heard** it said in our Mishnah **of [R' Yehudah]** that he permits this? No, you have not![5] אֶלָּא מַאי אִית לָךְ לְמֵימַר – **What then must you say?**[6] כֵּיוָן דְּלָאו בְּנֵי סְחִיטָה נִינְהוּ – That **since** these fruits **are not** generally designated **for squeezing,** אֲפִילּוּ לְכַתְּחִילָּה – R' Yehudah permits one **even** to **initially** squeeze them on the Sabbath! אֲפִילּוּ תֵּימָא רַבָּנָן – Accordingly, **you can even say** that the ruling is that of **the Rabbis.** כֵּיוָן דְּלָאו בְּנֵי סְחִיטָה נִינְהוּ – For the Rabbis will no doubt agree that **since [these fruits] are not** generally designated **for squeezing,** אֲפִילּוּ לְכַתְּחִילָּה – one is permitted **even** to **initially** squeeze them on the Sabbath![7] שְׁמַע מִינָּהּ רַבָּנָן הִיא – One may **learn from this** reasoning **that this** ruling **is** the opinion of **the Rabbis** as well as that of R' Yehudah.

The Gemara concludes:

שְׁמַע מִינָּהּ – Indeed, one may **learn** this **from this** reasoning. This Baraisa thus constitutes proof that with regard to fruits other than olives, grapes, mulberries and pomegranates, the Rabbis and R' Yehudah agree that one is permitted even to squeeze them on the Sabbath for their juice, and certainly to make use of juice that flows from them of its own accord.[8]

The aforecited Baraisa stated:

שֶׁל בֵּית מְנַשְׁיָא בַּר מְנַחֵם הָיוּ סוֹחֲטִין בְּרִמּוֹנִים – The members OF THE HOUSEHOLD OF MENASHYA BAR MENACHEM WOULD SQUEEZE POMEGRANATES [during the weekdays].

Rav Nachman comments on this statement:

אָמַר רַב נַחְמָן – **Rav Nachman said:** הֲלָכָה כְּשֶׁל בֵּית מְנַשְׁיָא בַּר מְנַחֵם – The halachah follows the members **of the household of Menashya bar Menachem.** One is therefore prohibited to squeeze pomegranates on the Sabbath.

The Gemara asks:

אָמַר לֵיהּ רָבָא לְרַב נַחְמָן – **Rava said to Rav Nachman:** מְנַשְׁיָא בֶּן מְנַחֵם תַּנָּא הוּא – **Is** then **Menashya ben Menachem a disputant**[9] in this Baraisa? But his practice is merely cited in *support* of the Tanna who prohibits squeezing pomegranates![10] Why do you say that the halachah follows Menashya?

Rava continues:

וְכִי תֵּימָא הֲלָכָה כִּי הַאי תַּנָּא דִּסְבַר לָהּ כְּשֶׁל מְנַשְׁיָא בֶּן מְנַחֵם – **And if you will say** that all you mean is that **the halachah follows this Tanna who** prohibits squeezing pomegranates ***because*** **[his**

NOTES

1. The act of squeezing them is therefore not included in the *melachah* of דָּשׁ, *threshing,* and is therefore permissible (*Rashi*). For the *melachah* of *threshing* is defined as an act in which one category of object is extracted from within a *different* category of object that conceals it. [This definition is derived from the act of threshing, in which a food – the kernel – is extracted from a non-food – its husk.] It follows, then, that squeezing liquid from fruits is prohibited under the *melachah* of *threshing* only if the liquid is a beverage [i.e. something generally used for drinking], since only in that case will the squeezing represent the extraction of one category of object – the beverage – from a different category of object – the food that covers it. However, if the liquid extracted is not one generally used for drinking, it itself is legally regarded as a food! One who squeezes it out would therefore not be in violation of the *melachah* of *threshing,* since he has merely extracted one sort of food from another (*Rashi* below ד״ה לתוך הקדירה; see *Tosafos* to 73b ד״ה מפרק; see *Shulchan Aruch HaRav, Orach Chaim* 305:28). The Baraisa therefore rules that since it is not common practice to squeeze plums, quinces and sorb-apples for their juice, their juice is legally regarded as a food. One will therefore be permitted to squeeze these fruits on the Sabbath (*Rashi,* as explained by *Eglei Tal* דש §16).

2. It is common practice to squeeze pomegranates for the purpose of drinking their juice (*Rashi*). [Since their juice is therefore considered a beverage, one who squeezes it out will be liable for the *melachah* of מְפָרֵק, *extraction* (a *toladah* of threshing).]

3. [The Baraisa cites the case of Menashya's household as an example of the many people who regularly squeeze pomegranates to obtain juice (see *Beis Yosef* §320). The fact that there are large numbers of people who regularly squeeze pomegranates for their juice establishes pomegranates as fruits designated for squeezing; since their juice is therefore considered a beverage, its extraction is prohibited.]

4. [R' Yehudah said this with regard to mulberries or pomegranates stored for eating, as the Gemara explained above (143b).]

5. [For our Mishnah says only that he permits the juice that oozes from the fruits, but not that he permits one to actually squeeze the fruits!]

6. [I.e. what then must you say to explain why in the case of plums, quinces, and sorb-apples R' Yehudah permits one to deliberately squeeze them?]

7. [For the only disagreement between the Rabbis and R' Yehudah was whether the juice that oozes from the fruit will cause one to squeeze it. They are in agreement, though, regarding the laws governing which fruits may be squeezed.]

8. [The following point should be noted. When the Gemara states on 143b that the Sages agree with R' Yehudah regarding liquid that oozed from other sorts of fruit, it implies that they too differentiate between fruits stored for eating and those stored for squeezing, just as R' Yehudah does. But this Baraisa does not differentiate in this manner at all! It would appear that whether the plums, quinces and sorb-apples were stored for eating *or* for squeezing, they may be squeezed on the Sabbath! *Chazon Ish* (*Orach Chaim* 55:2) explains (in a similar context) that the language of the Gemara on 143b was in fact imprecise; what was meant was that in the case of other sorts of fruit, the Sages will even *go beyond* the ruling of R' Yehudah in his case – they thus permit even the deliberate squeezing of the fruits, *and* they do not differentiate between whether the fruits were originally stored for eating or for squeezing (see *Sfas Emes* for further discussion).]

9. [Literally: a Tanna.]

10. By ruling according to Menashya bar Menachem, Rav Nachman implies that Menashya is a disputant in the Baraisa. But in fact there is no dispute. Rather, Menashya's practice [which establishes pomegranates as a fruit designated for squeezing] is cited in *support* of the Tanna who prohibits one to squeeze pomegranates (*Rashi*).

ח א מיי' פ"ה מהלכות כלאים הל"ח טוש"ע יו"ד סימן רלו סעיף יג:
ט ב מיי' פ"ו מהלכות מקוואות הלכה ח סמג עשין רמח:
י ג מיי' שם והלכה ט סמג שם טוש"ע יו"ד סימן רא סעיף כה:
יא ד מיי' פ"י מהלכות טומאת אוכלין הלכה יג ופ"א הלכה ו:
יב ה מיי' פ"ח מהלכות שבת הל"י סמג לאוין סה טור שו"ע או"ח סימן שכ סעיף ד:
יג ו ז מיי' שם וסמג שם טור שו"ע או"ח סימן שכ סעיף ד:
יד ח ט מיי' פ"ט מהל' טומאת אוכלין הל"ב:

גליון הש"ס

רש"י ד"ה לתוך הקדירה וכו' ואין זה דרך פריקתו. עיין לעיל דף עג ע"ב תוספות ד"ה מפרק:

רבינו חננאל

דאמר סוחטין בפגעין ובפרישין ובעוזרדין אבל לא ברמונים וסבר לה כמנשיא בן מנחם שסוחט בחול ברמונים להוציא מהן מים וכן כמו זיתים וענבי' וקיי"ל כוותיה ואקשינן וכי מנשיא הוה רובא לעלמא. ומהדרינן אין. כי הא דתנן המקיים קוצים בכרם וכו' ואוקימנא אע"פ שאין דרך בני אדם לקיים קוצים בכרם כיון שבערביא מקיימין קידש הכא נמי אע"פ שאין דרך בני אדם לסחוט רמונים בחול כיון שסוחטין של בית מנשיא בחול בשבת אסור לסחוט ודחינן ערביא מקום בני אדם רבים ומנשיא אדם אחד הוא ובטלה דעתו אצל [כל] בני אדם ואתינן לטעמא אחריתי אלא האי תנא כטעמיה דרב חסדא דאמר תרדין שסחטן ונתנן למקוה פסלו המקוה בשנוי מראה וכיון שהזכרנו פסולות המקוה אמרינן. תנן התם [נפל] לתוכו יין ומוהל כו' פי' מוהל המים היוצאים מעוקל בית הבד עת שטוענן קורות בית הבד על הזיתים הטחונין והוא מי הזיתים ויש בהן צחצוחי שמן: איצצאי דוחק. כדגרסינן בפרק המפקיד (דף מ ע"א) אמר ר' יהודה אמר שמואל סוחט אדם אשכול של ענבים בתוך הקדירה אבל לא לתוך הקערה. אמר רב חסדא מדברי רבינו נלמד חולב אדם עז לתוך הקדירה אבל לא לתוך הקערה. ואותביה רמי [בר חמא] זב שחלב את העז החלב טמא. כלומר (טמא) [שטימא אותה] הזב בנגיעתו. וא"ת אוכל הוא במאי אתכשר ופרקינן כר' יוחנן דאמר איתכשר בטפה המלוכלכת על פי הדד שנפסלה מאוכל והיא מכשרת לחלב ואותיב רבינא טמא מת שסחט זיתים וענבי' וכו'

תוספות

מי דמי ערביא אתרא הוא. הו"מ למיפרך הניחא לרבי אליעזר לרבנן מאי איכא למימר אלא פריך דאפילו לרבי אליעזר לא ניחא ומה שקשה מאנשי הוצל דפרק המצניע (לעיל דף צב:) פירשתי שם (ד"ה ואמ"ע): **ה"נ** כיון דאחשביה הוו להו משקה. תמיה ס"ד דסוחטין בפגעין כו' היינו סחיטה ממש אבל השתא אי אפשר לומר דהא פשיטא דאסור דכיון דאחשביה הוה להו משקה אלא סוחטין דקתני היינו בלילא"ר בלע"ז למתק הפרי כדפי' בקונטרס: **אמר** אביי ר' יעקב היא. קשה לי לימא דהאי מוהל דקתני היינו במוהל היוצא מעקול בית הבד ודברי הכל וכי תימא מדקתני מוהל סתמא משמע דבכל מוהל איירי לא היא דע"כ אפי' לרבי יעקב לא איירי בכל מוהל דהא מודה דמוהל היוצא בתחלה טהור וי"ל דמוהל היוצא מעקול בית הבד לא הוה קרינן ליה מוהל סתם כיון דאי אפשר לו בלא צחצוחי שמן: **חולב** אדם עז כו'. נראה לר"ת דהיינו דווקא ביו"ט דמותר בהמה לאכילה הוי כמו אוכלא דאיפרת אבל בשבת לא חזיא לשחיטה כמו דם שחיטה שבבהמה היא כפסולת וכשחולב הוי כבורר אוכל מתוך פסולת וכן משמע בבה"ג דבי"ט איירי ומיהו סחיטת זיתים וענבים דשרי לעיל לתוך הקדירה היינו אפי' בשבת כיון דלאכול חזיא לאכילה:

גמרא

בפגעין ובפרישין ובעוזרדין אבל לא ברמונים ושל בית מנשיא בר מנחם היו סוחטין ברמונים וממאי דרבנן היא דילמא ר' יהודה היא ותהוי נמי ר' יהודה אימר דשמעת ליה לר' יהודה יצאו מעצמן סוחטין לכתחילה מי שמעת ליה אלא מאי אית לך למימר כיון דלאו בני סחיטה נינהו אפילו לכתחלה אפילו תימא רבנן כיון דלאו בני סחיטה נינהו אפילו לכתחילה ש"מ רבנן היא ש"מ של בית מנשיא בר מנחם היו סוחטין ברמונים אמר רב נחמן הלכה כשל בית מנשיא בר מנחם א"ל רבא לרב נחמן מנשיא בן מנחם תנא הוא וכי תימא הלכה כי האי תנא דסבר לה כשל מנשיא בן מנחם ומשום דסבר כמנשיא בן מנחם הלכה כמותו מנשיא בן מנחם הוי רובא דעלמא אין דתנן המקיים קוצים בכרם ר"א אומר קדש וחכ"א אינו מקדש אלא דבר שכמוהו מקיימין וא"ר חנינא מ"ט דרבי אליעזר שכן בערביא מקיימין קוצי שדות לגמליהם מידי איריא דערביא אתרא הכא בטלה דעתו אצל כל אדם אלא היינו טעמא כדרב חסדא דאמר רב חסדא תרדין שסחטן ונתנן במקוה פוסלין את המקוה בשינוי מראה והא לאו בני סחיטה נינהו אלא מאי אית לך למימר כיון דאחשבינהו הוה להו משקה ה"נ כיון דאחשבינהו הוה להו משקה רב פפא אמר משום דהוי דבר שאין עושין ממנו מקוה וכל דבר שאין עושין ממנו מקוה לכתחילה פוסל את המקוה בשינוי מראה תנן התם נפל לתוכו יין או חומץ ומוחל ושינה מראיו פסול מאן תנא דמוחל משקה הוא אמר אביי רבי יעקב היא דתניא ר' יעקב אומר מוחל הרי הוא כמשקה ומה טעם אמרו מוחל היוצא בתחלה טהור לפי שאינו רוצה בקיומו ר"ש אומר מוחל אינו כמשקה ומה טעם אמרו מוחל היוצא מעיקול בית הבד טמא לפי שאי אפשר לו בלא ציחצוחי שמן מאי בינייהו איכא בינייהו דאתי בתר איצצתא רבא אמר משום דהוי דבר שאין עושין הימנו מקוה ופוסל את המקוה בשינוי מראה אמר רב יהודה אמר שמואל סוחט אדם אשכול של ענבים לתוך הקדרה אבל לא לתוך הקערה אמר רב חסדא מדברי רבינו נלמד חולב אדם עז לתוך הקדרה אבל לא לתוך הקערה אלמא קסבר משקה הבא לאוכל אוכל הוא מתיב רמי בר חמא זב שחולב את העז החלב טמא ואי אמרת משקה הבא לאוכלין אוכל הוא במאי איתכשר כדאמר ר' יוחנן בטיפה המלוכלכת ע"פ הדד הכא נמי בטיפה המלוכלכת ע"פ הדד מתיב רבינא טמא מת שסחט זיתים וענבים כביצה

רש"י

בפגעין. פרוס"ש בלע"ז והוציא מימיהן לשתות: ובפרישין. קוידונ"ץ: ובעוזרדין. קורמ"ש דלאו אורחייהו בהכי ואין כאן משום דש: אבל לא ברמונים. דאורחייהו בהכי: ושל בית מנשיא. היו רגילין לסחוט רמונים בחול אלמא איכא דסחיט להו הלכך בשבת אסור: אלא מאי אית לך למימר. לר' יהודה כיון דלאו בני סחיטה כו' וכי היכי דלרבי יהודה שרי לכתחילה מהאי טעמא מהשתא אפי' תימא רבנן ושרו ליה מהאי טעמא: מנשיא תנא הוא. בתמיה וכי איהו פליג למימר דבשבת אסור דתימא הלכתא כוותיה והא לא הוזכר אלא לדברי התנא לראיה דהאי תנא הוא סבר כוותיה: וכ"ת. הא דאמר הלכה כשל בית מנשיא ה"ק הלכה כהאי תנא דאסר ברימונים הואיל וקאי מנשיא כוותיה דסוחטין רימונים בחול אלמא בני סחיטה נינהו: הוי רובא דעלמא. דמשום איהו נמודיה נשוו דרך רמונים לסחיטה: קוצים. קרדונ"ש: מקדש. את התבואה משום כלאים דזריעה הוא: ואמר רבי חנינא כו'. אלמא משום חד מקום דאחשבינהו משוינן להו דבר חשוב: אתרא. הוא וחשיבי דרבים הוו חשיבותא: הכא. חד גברא הוא ולדידיה הוא לימא בטלה דעתו: אלא היינו טעמא. דרב נחמן דאמר הלכה אין סוחטין: כרב חסדא. אע"ג דלעלמא לא חשיב כיון דאחשיב איהו הוי לדידיה משקה והכי מפרש רב נחמן לברייתא דלעיל סוחטין בפגעין ובפרישין למתק הפרי ולא לצורך המשקה אבל לא ברימונים ואפילו למתקן (א) דשל בית מנשיא היו סוחטין בחול לצורך משקה הלכך בשבת אסור אפי' למתק הואיל ואיכא חד דעביד לשם משקה ולא משום דמנשיא רובא דעלמא אלא חיישינן אי שרית ליה למתק אתי למעבד לשום משקה וכיון דאיהו מחשב ליה הוי משקה ומיחייב אבל בפגעין ליכא (ב) למיחש דאין אדם עושה אותו למשקה: בשינוי מראה. לא בשלשת לוגין דלא הוזכרו שלש לוגין אלא במים שאובין אבל שאר משקין לא פסלי אא"כ נשתנה מראה המקוה על ידיהן: רב פפא אמר. טעמא דתרדין לאו משום חשיבותא דאחשבינהו הוא ולעולם לאו משקה נינהו והא דמפסיל משום דכל דבר שאין עושין ממנו מקוה שאינו מים או שלג או ברד פוסל את המקוה בשינוי מראה: נפל לתוכו. של מקוה יין או חומץ או מוהל והוא כמין מים זב מן הזיתים וג' מינים יש בו כשטוענן מתחילה במעטן להתחמם ולהתבשל מאליהן מוהל זב מהן והוא צלול כמים ולאחר שעמדו ימים ודחקו זה את זה חוזר מוהל לזוב מהן והוא קרוב להיות כשמן ולאחר שעגלן להוציא שמנן בבית הבד ומשהה התפוח של גפת בעקלים שהוא אגוד בהן בבית הבד חוזר מוהל וזב מהן: מאן תנא דמוהל משקה הוא. קס"ד דאין מקוה נפסל אלא על ידי משקה ואפילו בשינוי מראה: בתחילה. בתחילת טעינתן של זיתים: מעקול בית הבד. לאחר שנסחט שמנו או לפני סחיטתו: מאי בינייהו. במאי פליגי הואיל ותרוייהו מודו דמוהל היוצא בתחילה טהור והיוצא מעקל בית הבד טמא באיזה מוהל נחלקו דלמר הוי משקה וטמא ולמר לא הוי משקה וטהור: דאתי בתר איצצתא. לאחר שהתחילו להתחמם ודחקו זה את זה ונשתהה הכומר ימים: רבא אמר. קמייתא דקתני מוהל פוסל מקוה דברי הכל הוא ומשום דהוי כו': לתוך הקדרה. של תבשיל לתקנו דמוכחא מילתא דלאו למשקה בעי ליה אלא לאוכל ° ואין זה דרך פריקתו והוי כמפריד אוכל מאוכל: אבל לא לתוך הקערה. דזמנין דלמשקה קאי ואף על גב דבקערה לא שתי איניש לא מוכחא מילתא ואיכא איסור: אלמא. מדקאמר סוחט לתוך הקדרה קסבר כו': החלב טמא. שהזב מטמא כל דבר במשא והרי היסט הקילות ולא קמפליג בין לתוך הקדרה בין לתוך הכוס: ואי אמרת אוכל הוא. הא אין אוכל מקבל טומאה שלא בהכשר והאי במאי איתכשר: כדאמר רבי יוחנן. במסכת כריתות גבי האשה שנטף חלב מדדיה: בטיפה המלוכלכת על פי הדד. טיפה ראשונה מלכלכת בה פי הדד בדעת ונוחה ליחלב וההיא הוי משקה כשאר חלב דלא לאוכל בעי ליה: טמא מת שסחט זיתים וענבים כביצה

הסיטו של זב מכאן למדנו זב שהסיט את הטהור טמא שלא מצינו בכל התורה טומאה המסטת אלא כן נשא טהור את הטמא והכא זב הוא דגלי רחמנא [נדה מג.]. ואי אמרת משקה הבא לאוכלין אוכל הוא במאי איתכשר. שאין אוכל מוכשר ומתוקן לקבל טומאה עד שיבאו עליו מים פעם אחת ומשבא מקבל טומאה לעולם ואפילו נגוב והיין והשמן וכל הנקרא משקה מכשיר זרעים לטומאה כמים אשר יבא עליו מים או כל משקה אשר ישתה בכל כלי יטמא האוכל [ויקרא יא, לד]. האי חלב ולאו תורת משקה למשקה הבא לאוכל כאוכל דמי במסכת שבת בפרק חבית שנשברה הלכך בעי הכ... בטיפה המלוכלכת על פי הדד. כלומר בטפה שפי הדד מלוכלך בו דההיא ודאי מכשר לשא... דהא [האי] לא קיימא לאכילת תינוק [כריתות יג.].

רבינו חננאל (המשך)

... הקערה שהוא ודאי משקה. ומפני מה לא פירק פירוק זה לגבי חולב עז חדא מתרי תלתא טעמא ... תנאי. המחלק בענבים לא הוכשר. פי' מחלק משפשף פעמים שמתמצה בהן משקין. ומחליקן בו. ... ה הוכשר שכך משקה גמור הוא. ות"ק אמר משקה הבא לאוכל הוא וכאוכל הוא חשוב ואינו ... ופירש כי התנאין החולקין במחליק בענבים פליגי במשקה העומד לצחצחו ואלו החולקין ... מסואבות פליגי. במשקה העומד לאיבוד. א"ר זירא א"ר חייא בר אשי אמר רב סוחט אדם אשכול של ... אבל לא לתוך הקערה וכן פירושו כל דבר הנסחט בקדירה הוא אוכל ומותר ולתוך הקערה משקה ... דג שאפילו סחיטתו בקערה שרי. והא דאתמר כבשים שסחטן אמר רב לגופן מותר וכו'. דברים ... יכין לפנים ולא לפני פנים. אמנם צריכין אנו לברר כמי ההלכה. לפיכך אנו מזכירין דברי כולן:

מסורת הש"ס

א) [לעיל נב. ושם נסמן], ב) כלאים פ"ה מ"ח ב"ב קנו., ג) [ע"ל אלעזר], ד) מקואות פ"ז מ"ד, ה) תוספ' דטהרות פרק י, ו) [ע"ל תוס' עג: ד"ה מפרק וכו'], ז) טהרות פ"ג מ"א, ח) כריתות יג. פסחים לג:, ט) טהרות פ"ג מ"ג.

הגהות הב"ח

(א) רש"י ד"ה כרב חסדא וכו' ואפילו למתקן הואיל דשל בית וכו': (ב) בא"ד למיחש להכי דאין אדם:

רב נסים גאון

פכ"ב רבא אמר משום דהוה דבר שאין עושין ממנו מקוה לכתחלה וכל דבר שאין עושין ממנו מקוה לכתחילה פוסל את המקוה בשינוי מראה. עיקר דיליה בתורת כהנים מקוה מים לא מקוה כל המשקין כולן פרט לשנפל בתוכו מי כבשים ומי צבעין ושינו את מראיו ובתוספתא טבול יום (פרק א) חומר במשקין שאין להן טהרה הגוף ואין להן טהרה מטומאתן ואינן טהורין בגוף ופוסלין את המקוה בשינוי מראה מה שאין כן במים: כדאמר ר' יוחנן בטיפה על פי הדד משכחת לה במס' כריתות בפרק אמרו לו (דף יג) ולדבא מקום חלב מעין הוא ולא צריך הכשר והתנן האשה שחלב מדדיה לתוך תנור טמא וקשיא לן במאי איתכשר ואמר ר' יוחנן בטיפה המלוכלכת על פי הדד:

ליקוטי רש"י

המקיים קוצים בכרם. דכה"ג אשמן במסכת כלאים דמאכל בהמה לא כלאים בכרם משום לא תזרע כרמך כלאים ואפילו מקיים קוצה דדרך שדך לא. [רשב"ם ב"ב קנו:]. ר"א אומר קדש. משום כלאי הכרם דכתיב פן תקדש המלאה הזרע [סוטה מג.]. שכן בערביא כו'. ורבנן סברי רובא דעלמא לאו אינון מקיימין שדות לגמליהון [רשב"ם שם]. שאי אפשר לו בלא ציחצוחי שמן. ושמן לעולם משקה דכתיב (ישעיה כה) משתה שמנים [חולין קיז.]. היוצא מעיקול בית הבד. עקול בית הבד עשוי כמין קופה מקורעת [כמלגזים] ולאחר סחיטת הזיתים נותן הגפת לתוכו עקל ונותן עליו [קורה] ומכבידו להוציא המשקה הנבלע [ע"ז עה.]. איצצתא. דוחק [ב"מ מ.]. זב שחולב את העז החלב טמא. דכתיב אשר יגע בו הזב וגו' והיסט קרא לא ... והנוגע בבשר הזב ...

ruling] is in accordance with the practice of the household **of Menashya ben Menachem** that establishes pomegranates as fruit designated for squeezing[11] – וּמִשּׁוּם דְּסָבַר כִּמְנַשְּׁיָא בֶּן מְנַחֵם הֲלָכָה כְּמוֹתוֹ – **but** then can you say that just **because [this Tanna] is in accordance with Menashya ben Menachem the halachah follows him?** But the practice of Menashya's household alone is not sufficient reason to establish pomegranates as being designated for squeezing! מְנַשְּׁיָא בֶּן מְנַחֵם הָוֵי רוּבָּא דְּעָלְמָא – For **is Menashya ben Menachem the majority of the world** that we should set the standard for the proper use of pomegranates according to his custom? How can you say that the prohibition against squeezing pomegranates is based on the practice of a single individual?[12]

The Gemara answers:

אִין – **Yes,** with regard to establishing the legal character of a fruit, the practice of even a single individual has significance. דִּתְנַן – **For we have learned in a Mishnah:**[13] הַמְקַיֵּים קוֹצִים בַּכֶּרֶם – IF ONE MAINTAINS THISTLES IN A VINEYARD, רַבִּי (אליעזר) [אֶלְעָזָר] אוֹמֵר – R' ELAZAR[14] SAYS: קִדֵּשׁ – HE HAS RENDERED the grapevines FORBIDDEN for benefit.[15] וַחֲכָמִים אוֹמְרִים – BUT THE SAGES SAY: אֵינוֹ מְקַדֵּשׁ אֶלָּא דָּבָר שֶׁכְּמוֹהוּ מְקַיְּימִין – [NO SPECIES] RENDERS a vineyard FORBIDDEN EXCEPT ONE WHOSE LIKE IS usually MAINTAINED by people in their fields. Since people do not normally cultivate thistles, they do not render a vineyard forbidden.

R' Chanina explains R' Elazar's position:

וְאָמַר רַבִּי חֲנִינָא – **And R' Chanina said:** מַאי טַעְמָא דְּרַבִּי (אליעזר) [אֶלְעָזָר] – **What is R' Elazar's reason** for ruling that thistles will render a vineyard forbidden? שֶׁכֵּן בַּעֲרַבְיָא מְקַיְּימִין קוֹצֵי שָׂדוֹת לִגְמַלֵּיהֶם – **For in Arabia [people] maintain field thistles for their camels** to eat.[16] We thus see that if even the inhabitants of only a single place use a given item in a particular manner, their practice will set the standard for what is *universally* regarded as proper use of that item. Likewise with regard to Menashya bar Menachem; although he is but a single individual, his practice will cause pomegranates to be universally regarded as being designated for squeezing.

The Gemara challenges this proof:

מִידֵּי אִירְיָא – **Is this any proof?** דַּעֲרַבְיָא אַתְרָא – **Arabia is a place,** and boasts many inhabitants. The fact that so large a public maintains thistles in its fields is indeed good reason to consider thistles a commonly cultivated plant. הָכָא בָּטְלָה דַּעְתּוֹ אֵצֶל כָּל אָדָם – **Here,** however [i.e. in the case of Menashya bar Menachem], since he is a mere individual, **his opinion** concerning the squeezing of pomegranates **is negated by** that of **all other men!** Rava's challenge to Rav Nachman thus returns – how can he say that the prohibition to squeeze pomegranates is based on nothing other than the practice of Menashya bar Menachem?[17]

Due to Rava's challenge, the Gemara will now give an entirely different explanation of Rav Nachman's understanding of why the Baraisa cited the practice of Menashya bar Menachem. The basis for this understanding is Rav Nachman's adoption of a novel means of establishing a liquid's beverage status, which he deduces from a statement made by R' Chisda:

אֶלָּא הַיְינוּ טַעְמָא כִּדְרַב חִסְדָּא – **Rather, this is the reasoning** underlying Rav Nachman's ruling – it is **in accordance with** a statement made by **Rav Chisda.** דְּאָמַר רַב חִסְדָּא – **For Rav Chisda said:** תְּרָדִין שֶׁסְּחָטָן וּנְתָנָן בְּמִקְוֶה – Concerning **beets that one squeezed and** whose juice one **placed into a *mikveh:*** פּוֹסְלִין אֶת הַמִּקְוֶה בְּשִׁינּוּי מַרְאֶה – **[The juice] will invalidate the *mikveh* by** causing **a change in the appearance** of the water.[18]

The Gemara notes:

וְהָא לָאו בְּנֵי סְחִיטָה נִינְהוּ – **Now** since **beets are not** generally **designated for squeezing,** their juice is not considered a beverage. A *mikveh,* however, can only be invalidated by a liquid that possesses beverage status.[19]

The Gemara therefore concludes:

אֶלָּא מַאי אִית לָךְ לְמֵימַר – **What then must you say?** כֵּיוָן דְּאַחְשְׁבִינְהוּ הָוֵה לְהוּ מַשְׁקֶה – That **since** when one squeezes the beets for their juice, **he gives [the juice] significance, it is** regarded as **a beverage** despite the fact that most people would not recognize it as such.[20] הָכָא נַמִּי – **Here too** with regard to

NOTES

11. [And thus as fruit that it is forbidden to squeeze on the Sabbath.] Rava now suggests that what Rav Nachman is saying is that the Baraisa [is not merely giving the case of Menashya's household as an *example* of people who squeeze pomegranates (see note 3), but rather] considers the custom of this particular family to be the *reason* that squeezing pomegranates is prohibited. For the Baraisa holds that there need not be a large public that customarily squeezes a given fruit for it to be considered designated for squeezing. Rather, even the practice of a *single* individual suffices to establish a fruit as designated for such use. Thus, since the members of Menashya's household squeeze pomegranates, they are regarded as fruit designated for squeezing (*Rashi*).

12. Having suggested a possible interpretation of Rav Nachman's statement, Rava now questions it. For how can the legal status of a fruit possibly be established by the practice of a mere individual?! (*Rashi*).

13. *Kilayim* 5:8.

14. Emendation of R' Eliezer to R' Elazar follows *Mesoras HaShas,* and *Rashash* from *Tosafos, Bava Basra* 156a-b ד״ה רבי אלעזר אומר.

15. [The Torah commands (*Deuteronomy* 22:9): לֹא־תִזְרַע כַּרְמְךָ כִּלְאָיִם פֶּן־תִּקְדַּשׁ הַמְלֵאָה הַזֶּרַע אֲשֶׁר תִּזְרָע וּתְבוּאַת הַכָּרֶם, *You shall not sow your vineyard with disparate species, lest it become forbidden the fullness of the seed that you will sow and the produce of the vineyard,* thus rendering forbidden the produce of a grapevine or vineyard in whose vicinity other sorts of plants were sown. The phrase *that you will sow* teaches that the prohibition is only against mixing in plants that people will normally sow.] R' Elazar holds that thistles are in the category of plants that are normally sown (*Rashi;* see *Kilayim* ibid. with commentaries).

16. Thus, although people do not cultivate thistles in most areas, they are nonetheless considered plants that it is normal to maintain, since there is one region in which they are cultivated. They therefore will render the grapes forbidden (*Rashi*).

17. See *Tosafos* for an alternative challenge that the Gemara could have raised; see also *Tosafos* above, 92b ד״ה ואת״ל.

18. [A *mikveh* is valid only if filled with water; other liquids are not suitable for *mikveh* use. Moreover, the *mikveh* must retain the *appearance* of water. Therefore, if one pours into a *mikveh* a liquid that will change its color, the *mikveh* is rendered invalid (see *Mikvaos* 7:3,4 and *Toras Kohanim* to *Leviticus* 11:36).] It makes no difference how much foreign liquid is added – even a tiny amount will invalidate the *mikveh,* as long as it alters the water's color. [This stands in contrast to the law of מַיִם שְׁאוּבִים, *drawn water,* which will only invalidate a *mikveh* if it measures at least three *lugin*] (*Rashi*).

[The Rishonim debate the origin of this law. Some say it is of Rabbinic origin (although supported by a Biblical verse [*Leviticus* ibid.]). The Rabbis feared that allowing immersion in a mixture of water and other liquids might lead people to immerse in a *mikveh* consisting *entirely* of other liquids. They therefore decreed that a *mikveh* identifiably mixed with a foreign liquid is invalid (*Baalei HaNefesh L'HaRaavad, Shaar HaMayim;* see also *Tiferes Yisrael* to *Mikvaos* ibid. §32). Others hold that a *mikveh* whose color was changed by adding other liquids is in fact invalid by Biblical law (*Shitah Mekubetzes, Zevachim* 78b [השמטות]; *Kiryas Sefer* to *Hil. Mikvaos* 7:9; *Mishnah Acharonah* to *Mikvaos* ibid.).]

19. [It is important to note that the designation מַשְׁקֶה, *beverage,* has a different meaning here than it did above (143b note 32), when it was introduced to describe the liquids that cause susceptibility to *tumah.* Here it refers to any liquid meant for drinking; above it refers to the six liquids explicitly described by the Torah as "beverages," some of which are not even suitable for drinking (see *Chazon Ish, Orach Chaim* 55:4).]

20. For by squeezing the juice from the beets for the purpose of drinking it he demonstrates his regard for it. To him it is therefore a beverage (*Rashi*).

בפגעין ובפרישין ובעוזרדין אבל לא ברמונים ושל בית מנשיא בר מנחם היו סוחטין ברמונים וממאי דרבנן היא דילמא ר' יהודה היא ותהוי נמי ר' יהודה אימר דשמעת ליה לר' יהודה יצאו מעצמן סוחטין לכתחילה מי שמעת ליה אלא מאי אית לך למימר כיון דלאו בני סחיטה נינהו אפילו לכתחילה אפילו תימא רבנן כיון דלאו בני סחיטה נינהו אפילו לכתחילה ש"מ רבנן היא ש"מ של בית מנשיא בר מנחם היו סוחטין ברמונים אמר רב נחמן הלכה כשל בית מנשיא בר מנחם א"ל רבא לרב נחמן מנשיא בן מנחם תנא הוא וכי תימא הלכה כי האי תנא דסבר לה כשל מנשיא בן מנחם ומשום דסבר כמנשיא בן מנחם הלכה כמותו מנשיא בן מנחם הוי [א] רובא דעלמא אין דתנן [ז] המקיים קוצים בכרם ר"א אומר קדש וחכ"א [א] אינו מקדש אלא דבר שכמוהו מקיימין וא"ר חנינא מ"ט דרבי [ג] אליעזר שכן בערביא מקיימין קוצי שדות לגמליהם מידי איריא דערביא אתרא הכא בטלה דעתו אצל כל אדם אלא היינו טעמא כדרב חסדא דאמר רב חסדא תרדין שסחטן ונתנן במקוה פוסלין את המקוה בשינוי מראה והא לאו בני סחיטה נינהו אלא מאי אית לך למימר כיון דאחשבינהו הוה להו משקה ה"נ כיון דאחשבינהו הוה להו משקה רב פפא אמר משום דהוי דבר שאין עושין ממנו מקוה לכתחילה [ב] וכל דבר שאין עושין ממנו מקוה לכתחילה פוסל את המקוה בשינוי מראה [ד] תנן התם [ג] נפל לתוכו יין או חומץ ומוחל ושינה מראיו פסול מאן תנא דמוחל משקה הוא אמר אביי רבי יעקב היא [ה] דתניא ר' יעקב אומר [ו] מוחל הרי הוא כמשקה ומה טעם אמרו מוחל היוצא בתחלה טהור לפי שאינו רוצה בקיומו ר"ש אומר מוחל אינו כמשקה ומה טעם אמרו מוחל היוצא מעיקול בית הבד טמא לפי שאי אפשר לו בלא ציחצוחי שמן מאי בינייהו איכא בינייהו דאתי בתר איצצתא רבא אמר משום דהוי דבר שאין עושין הימנו מקוה ופוסל את המקוה בשינוי מראה אמר רב יהודה אמר שמואל [ה] סוחט אדם אשכול של ענבים לתוך הקדרה אבל לא לתוך הקערה אמר רב חסדא מדברי רבינו נלמד [ז] [ו] חולב אדם עז לתוך הקדרה אבל לא לתוך הקערה [ז] אלמא קסבר משקה הבא לאוכל אוכל הוא מתיב רמי בר חמא [ח] [ח] זב שחולב את העז החלב טמא ואי אמרת משקה הבא לאוכלין אוכל הוא במאי איתכשר [ט] כדאמר ר' יוחנן בטיפה המלוכלכת ע"פ הדד הכא נמי בטיפה המלוכלכת ע"פ הדד מתיב רבינא [י] [ט] טמא מת שסחט זיתים וענבים

כביצה

בפגעין. פרונ"ש בלע"ז ולהוציא מימיהן לשתות: ובפרישין. קוידונ"ן: ובעוזרדין. קורמ"ש דלאו אורחייהו בהכי ואין כאן משום לש: אבל לא ברמונים. דאורחייהו בהכי: ושל בית מנשיא. היו רגילין לסחוט רמונים בחול אלמא איכא דסחיט להו הלכך בשבת אסור: אלא מאי אית לך למימר. לר' יהודה כיון דלאו בני סחיטה כו' וכי היכי דלרבי יהודה שרי לכתחילה מהאי טעמא מהשתא אפי' תימא רבנן ושרו ליה מהאי טעמא: מנשיא תנא הוא. בתמיה וכי איהו פליג למימר דבשבת אסור דתימא הלכתא כוותיה והא לא הוזכר אלא לדברי התנא לראיה דהאי תנא הוא סבר כוותיה: וכ"ת. הא דאמר הלכה כשל בית מנשיא ה"ק הלכה כהאי תנא דאסר ברימונים הואיל וקאי מנשיא כוותיה דסוחטין רימונים בחול אלמא בני סחיטה נינהו: הוי רובא דעלמא. דמשום איהו לחודיה נשוי דרך רמונים לסחיטה: קוצים. קרדונ"ש: מקדש. את התבואה משום כלאים דזריעה הוא: ואמר רבי חנינא כו'. אלמא משום חד מקום דאחשבינהו משוין להו דבר חשוב: אתרא. הוא וחשיבות דרבים הוי חשיבותא: הכא. חד גברא לחודיה הוא נימא בטלה דעתו: אלא היינו טעמא. דרב נחמן דאמר הלכה אין סוחטין: כרב חסדא. אע"ג דלעלמא לא חשיב כיון דאחשיב איהו הוי לדידיה משקה והכי מפרש רב נחמן לברייתא דלעיל סוחטין בפגעין ובפרישין למתק הפרי ולא לצורך המשקה אבל לא ברימונים ואפילו למתקן (א) דשל בית מנשיא היו סוחטין בחול לצורך משקה הלכך בשבת אסור אפי' למתק הואיל ואיכא חד דעביד לשם משקה ולא משום דמנשיא רובא דעלמא אלא חיישינן אי שרית ליה למתק אתי למעבד לשום משקה וכיון דאיהו מחשב ליה הוי משקה ומיחייב אבל בפגעין ליכא (ב) למיחש דאין אדם עושה אותו למשקה: בשינוי מראה. לא בשלשת לוגין דלא הוזכרו שלש לוגין אלא במים שאובין אבל שאר משקין לא פסלי אא"כ נשתנה מראה המקוה על ידיהן: רב פפא אמר. טעמא דתרדין לאו משום חשיבותא דאחשבינהו הוא ולעולם לאו משקה נינהו והא דמפסיל משום דכל דבר שאין עושין ממנו מקוה שאינו מים או שלג או ברד פוסל את המקוה בשינוי מראה: נפל לתוכו. של מקוה יין או חומץ או מוחל והוא כמין מים זב מן הזיתים וג' מינים יש בו כשטוענן מתחילה במעטן להתחמם ולהתבשל מאליהן מוחל זב מהן והוא צלול כמים ולאחר שעמדו ימים ודקקו זה את זה חוזר מוחל לזוב מהן והוא קרוב להיות כשמן ולאחר שעצרן להוציא שמנן בבית הבד ומשההה התפוח של גפת בעקלים שהוא אגוד בהן בבית הבד חוזר מוחל זב מהן: מאן תנא דמוחל משקה הוא. קס"ד דאין מקוה נפסל אלא על ידי משקה ואפילו בשינוי מראה: בתחילה. בתחילת טעינתן של זיתים: מעקול בית הבד. לאחר שנסחט שמנו או לפני סחיטתו: מאי בינייהו. במאי פליגי הואיל ותרוייהו מודו דמוחל היוצא בתחילה טהור והיוצא מעקל בית הבד טמא באיזה מוחל נחלקו דלמר הוי משקה וטמא ולמר לא הוי משקה וטהור: דאתי בתר איצצתא. לאחר שהתחילו להתחמם ודקקו זה את זה ונשהה הכומר ימים: רבא אמר. קמייתא דקתני מוחל פוסל מקוה דברי הכל הוא ומשום דהוי כו': לתוך הקדרה. של תבשיל לתקנו דמוכחא מילתא דלאו למשקה בעי ליה אלא לאוכל ° ואין זה דרך פריקתו והוי כמפריד אוכל מאוכל: אבל לא לתוך הקערה. דזמנין דלמשקה קאי ואף על גב דבקערה לא שתי איניש לא מוכחא מילתא ואיכא איסור: אלמא. מדקאמר סוחט לתוך הקדרה קסבר כו': החלב טמא. שהזב מטמא כל דבר במשא והרי הסיט הקילוח ולא קמפליג בין לתוך הקדרה בין לתוך הכוס: ואי אמרת אוכל הוא. הא אין אוכל מקבל טומאה שלא בהכשר והאי במאי איתכשר: כדאמר רבי יוחנן. במסכת כריתות גבי האשה שנטף חלב מדדיה: בטיפה המלוכלכת על פי הדד. טיפה ראשונה מלכלכת בה פי הדד בדעת ונוחה ליחלב והיא הוי משקה כשסחט חלב דלא לאוכל בעי ליה: טמא מת שסחט זיתים וענבים

כביצה

מי דמי ערביא אתרא הוא. הו"מ למיפרך לרבי אליעזר לרבנן מאי איכא למימר אלא פריך דאפילו לרבי אליעזר לא ניחא ומה שקשה מאנשי הוצל דפרק המצניע (לעיל דף צב:) פירשתי שם (ד"ה ואמ"ל): ה"נ כיון דאחשביה הוו להו משקה. תימה ס"ד דסוחטין בפגעין כו' היינו סחיטה ממש אבל השתא אי אפשר לומר דהא פשיטא דאסור דכיון דאחשביה הוה להו משקה אלא סוחטין דקתני היינו בליל"ר בלע"ז למתק הפרי כדפי' בקונטרס: אמר אביי ר' יעקב היא. קשה לי לימא דהאי מוחל דקתני היינו במוחל היוצא מעקול בית הבד ודברי הכל וכי תימא מדקתני מוחל סתמא משמע דבכל מוחל איירי לא היא דע"כ אפי' לרבי יעקב לא איירי בכל מוחל דהא מודה דמוחל היוצא בתחילה טהור י"ל דמוחל היוצא מעקול בית הבד לא הוה קרינן ליה מוחל סתם כיון דאי אפשר לו בלא לחלוחי שמן: חולב אדם עז כו'. נראה לר"ת דהיינו דווקא בי"ט דחזיא בהמה לאכילה הוי כמו אוכלא דאיפרת אבל בשבת לא חזיא לשחיטה כמו דש חשיבא שהבהמה היא כפסולת וכשחולב הוי כנוטל אוכל מתוך פסולת וכן משמע בבה"ג דבי"ט איירי ומיהו סחיטת זיתים וענבים דשרי לעיל לתוך הקדירה היינו אפי' בשבת כיון דאשכול חזיא לאכילה:

כביצה

עין משפט נר מצוה

ח א מיי' פ"ה מהלכות כלאים הל"ה סמג לאוין רפ טוש"ע יו"ד סימן רצו סעיף יד:

ט ב מיי' פ"ז מהלכות מקוואות הלכה ב סמג עשין רמח:

י ג מיי' שם והלכה ט סמג שם טוש"ע יו"ד סימן רא סעיף כה:

יא ד מיי' פ"ז מהלכות טומאת אוכלין הלכה יג ופי"א הלכה ו:

יב ה מיי' פ"ח מהלכות שבת הל"י סמג לאוין סה טור ש"ע או"ח סימן שכ סעיף ז:

יג ו ז מיי' שם וסמג שם טור ש"ע או"ח סימן שכח:

יד ח ט מיי' פ"ט מהל' טומאת אוכלין הל"ב:

גליון הש"ס

רש"י ד"ה לתוך הקדרה וכו' ואין זה דרך פריקתו. עיין לעיל דף עג ע"ב תוספות ד"ה מפרק:

רבינו חננאל

דאמר סוחטין בפגעין ובפרישין ובעוזרדין אבל לא ברמונים וסבר לה כמנשיא בן מנחם שסוחט בחול ברמונים להוציא מהן מים וכן כמו זיתים וענבי' וקיי"ל כוותיה ואקשינן וכי מנשיא הוה רובא לעלמא. ומהדרינן אין. כי הא דתנן המקיים קוצים בכרם וכו' ואוקימנא אע"פ שאין דרך בני אדם לקיים קוצים בכרם כיון שבערביא מקיימין קודש הכא נמי אע"פ שאין דרך בני אדם לסחוט רמונים בחול כיון שסוחטין של בית מנשיא בחול בשבת אסור לסחוט ודחינן ערביא מקום רבים ומנשיא אדם אחד הוא ובטלה דעתו אצל [כל] בני אדם ואתינן לטעמא אחריני אלא האי תנא כטעמיה דרב חסדא דאמר תרדין שסחטן ונתנן למקוה פסלו המקוה בשינוי מראה וכיון שהזכרנו פסולת המקוה אמרינן. תנן התם [נפל] לתוכו יין ומוחל כו' פי' מוחל המים היוצאים מעוקל בית הבד עד שטוענן קורות בית הבד על הזיתים הטחונין והוא מי הזיתים ויש בהן צחצוחי שמן: איצצאי דוחק. כדגרסינן בפרק המפקיד (דף מ ע"א) אמר ר' יהודה אמר שמואל סוחט אדם אשכול של ענבים בידים בתוך הקדירה אבל לא לתוך הקערה. אמר רב חסדא מדברי רבינו נלמד חולב אדם עז לתוך הקדירה אבל לא לתוך הקערה אלמא קא סבר משקה הבא לאוכל אוכל הוא. ואותיבה רמי [בר חמא] זב שחלב את העז החלב טמא. כלומר (טמא) [שטימא אותה] הזב בגבינתו. וא"ת אוכל הוא במאי אתכשר ופרקינן כר' יוחנן דאמר אוכשר בטפה המלוכלכת על פי הדד שנפסלה מאוכל והיא מכשרת ואותיב רבינא טמא מת שסחט זיתים וענבי' וכו' ופרקינן בסוחט לתוך הקערה שהוא ודאי משקה. ומפני מה לא פירק פירוק זה לגבי חולב עז חדא מתרי תלתא טעמא ... כתנאי. המחלק בענבים לא הוכשר. פי' מחלק משפשף פעמים שמתמצה בהן משקין. ומחליקן בו. ... הודה הוכשר שכך משקה גמור הוא. ות"ק אמר משקה הבא לאוכל הוא וכאוכל הוא חשוב ואינו ... ופירש כי התנאין החולקין במחלק במחליק בענבים פליגי במשקה העומד לצחצחו ואלו החולקין ... מסואבות פליגי. במשקה העומד לאיבוד. א"ר זירא א"ר חייא בר אשי אמר רב סוחט אדם אשכול של ... אבל לא לתוך הקערה וכן פירשו כל דבר הנסחט בקדירה הוא אוכל ומותר ולתוך הקערה משקה הוא ואסור. זולתי הרב שאפילו סחיטתו בקערה שרי. והא דאמרתו כבשים שסחטן אמר רב לגופן מותר וכו'. דברים פשוטין הן. ואין צריכין לפנים ולא לפני פנים. אמנם צריכין אנו לברר כמי ההלכה. לפיכך אנו מזכירין דברי כולן:

מסורת הש"ס

א) [לעיל לב. ושם נסמן], ב) כלאים פ"ה מ"ח ב"ב קנו., ג) [ב"א אליעזר], ד) מקוואות פ"ז מ"ד, ה) תוספ' דטהרות פרק י, ו) [ע"ל תוס' עג: ד"ה מפרק וכו'], ז) טהרות פ"ג מ"ג, ח) כריתות יג, ט) טהרות פ"ג מ"ג, י) פסחים לג., כ) טהרות פ"ג מ"ג.

הגהות הב"ח

(א) רש"י ד"ה כרב חסדא וכו' ואפילו למתקן הואיל דשל בית וכו': (ב) בא"ד למיחש להכי דאין אדם:

רב נסים גאון

פכ"ב רבא אמר משום דהוה דבר שאין עושין ממנו מקוה לכתחילה וכל דבר שאין עושין ממנו מקוה לכתחילה פוסל את המקוה בשינוי מראה. עיקר דיליה בתורת כהנים מקוה מים לא מקוה כל המשקין כולן פרט לשנפל בתוכו מי כבשים ומי צבעין ושינו את מראיו ובתוספתא טבול יום (פרק א) חומר במשקין בשרץ להן טהרה הגוף ואין להן טהרה מטומאתן ואינן טהורין בגוף ופוסלין את המקוה בשינוי מראה מה שאין כן במים: כדאמר ר' יוחנן בטיפה על פי הדד. משכחת לה במס' כריתות בפרק אמרו לו אכלת חלב (דף יג) ולרבא מקום חלב מעין הוא ולא צריך הכשר והתנן האשה שחלב מדדיה ונפל לאויר תנור התנור טמא וקשיא לן במאי איתכשר ואמר ר' יוחנן בטיפה מלוכלכת ע"פ הדד:

ליקוטי רש"י

המקיים קוצים בכרם. דכס"ג במסכת כלאים דמאכל בהמה הוי כלאים בכרם משום לא תזרע כרמך כלאים ואפילו מקיים לוקה דדרשי' במועד קטן (ב:) כלאים שדך לא. [רשב"ם ב"ב קנו.]. ר"א אומר קדש. משום כלאי הכרם דכתיב פן תקדש המלאה הזרע [סוטה מג:]. שכן בערביא כו'. ולכבד בהר רוצה לקיים קוצים בכרמו מקיימין שדות לגמליהן [רשב"ם שם]. שאי אפשר לו בלא צחצוחי שמן. ושמן איקרי משקה דכתיב (ישעיה כה) משתה שמנים [חולין קיד:]. היוצא מעיקול בית הבד. ועקל בית הבד עשוי כמין קופה מסורגת [מצלה] ואחרי מקימת הזיתים טוען הגפת בכלתו עקל ומניח עליו [קורה] ומכבידין להוציא המשקה הנשאר [ע"ז עה.]. איצצתא. דוחק [ב"מ מ.]. זב שחולב את העז החלב טמא. דכתיב וכל אשר יגע בו הזב וגו' והסיט קרי להו למגע לאיפרוך הלכה למשה.

סחיטו של זב מכאן למדו זב שהסיט את הטהור טמא שלא מצינו בכל התורה טומאה המסיטת שלא ... כן נשא טהור את הטמא והכא בזב הוא דגלי רחמנא [נדה מג.]. ואי אמרת משקה הבא לאוכלין אוכל הוא במאי איתכשר. שאין אוכל מוכשר ומתוקן לקבל טומאה עד שיבאו עליו מים פעם אחת ומשנבאו ... מקבל טומאה לעולם ואפילו נגוב והיין והשמן וכל הנקרא משקה מכשיר זרעים לטומאה כמים ... אשר יבא עליו מים או כל משקה אשר ישתה בכל כלי יטמא האוכל [ויקרא יא, לד]. האי חלב ולאו ... תורת משקה דמשקה הבא לאוכל כאוכל דמי במסכת שבת בפרק חבית שנשברה הלכך בעי הכשר. כדאמר ר' יוחנן בטיפה המלוכלכת על פי הדד. כלומר כשנסחב הטיפה מן הדד מלוכלכת על פי הדד ... דהא [האי] לא קיימא לאכילת תינוק [כריתות יג.].

one who squeezes fruit for their juice – **כֵּיוָן דְּאַחְשְׁבִינְהוּ הָוָה לְהוּ מַשְׁקֶה – since** by doing so **he gives [the juice] significance** as a beverage, **it is** regarded as **a beverage,** and thus will render him liable if he squeezes it out on the Sabbath.

We see that even if a given fruit is not used by the majority of the world for its liquid, one who does squeeze it for its juice on the Sabbath will nonetheless be liable for doing so, since his action, by demonstrating his regard for the liquid that is extracted, lends significance to it. One is accordingly prohibited from squeezing fruit for the purpose of drinking the liquid that will be extracted. Accordingly, when the Baraisa permits one to squeeze plums, quinces and sorb-apples it perforce does not permit one to do so for the purpose of obtaining their juice, for squeezing for this reason would render the juice a beverage, which is prohibited! Evidently, then, the Baraisa is only sanctioning the squeezing of these fruits for the purpose of sweetening them, since in that case the squeezing does not demonstrate regard for the liquid, and therefore does not render it a beverage. Now, since the Baraisa's ruling regarding the plums, quinces and sorb-apples concerns squeezing for the purpose of sweetening, it follows that its ruling regarding pomegranates also concerns squeezing for the purpose of sweetening. Thus, the Baraisa is prohibiting one to squeeze pomegranates even in order to sweeten them! The source of this prohibition is a Rabbinic decree. The Rabbis feared that allowing one to squeeze pomegranates for the purposes of sweetening them might lead one to squeeze them for their juice. The basis for their suspicion was the fact that there are individuals, such as the members of the household of Menashya bar Menachem, who squeeze pomegranates for juice on a regular basis.[21] Thus, when Rav Nachman states that the halachah follows Menashya, he means only to rule in accordance with this decree. Rava's challenge is thus resolved.[22]

Rav Pappa objects to the above explanation of Rav Chisda's statement regarding beet juice in a *mikveh:*

רַב פָּפָּא אָמַר – Rav Pappa said: מִשּׁוּם דְּהָוֵי דָּבָר שֶׁאֵין עוֹשִׂין מִמֶּנּוּ מִקְוֶה לְכַתְּחִילָּה – The reason beet juice invalidates a *mikveh* is not because it is regarded as a beverage, but **because it is a substance from which one may not initially make a *mikveh,* וְכָל דָּבָר שֶׁאֵין עוֹשִׂין מִמֶּנּוּ מִקְוֶה לְכַתְּחִילָּה – and any substance from which one may not initially make a *mikveh* פּוֹסֵל אֶת הַמִּקְוֶה בְּשִׁינּוּי מַרְאֶה – will invalidate the *mikveh*** by causing **a change in the appearance** of the water. It is not necessary for the substance to be a legal beverage.[23]

Having cited this dispute regarding what sort of substance will invalidate a *mikveh* through altering its color, the Gemara cites an identical dispute between two other Amoraim:

תְּנַן הָתָם – We have learned in a Mishnah **there:**[24] **נָפַל לְתוֹכוֹ יַיִן אוֹ חוֹמֶץ וּמוֹחַל וְשִׁנָּה מַרְאָיו – IF WINE OR VINEGAR OR OLIVE-WATER FELL INTO [THE *MIKVEH*] AND CHANGED ITS APPEARANCE, פָּסוּל – IT IS INVALID.**

The Gemara assumes that only a liquid with legal beverage status will invalidate a *mikveh* in this manner, and accordingly asks:

מַאן תַּנָּא דְּמוֹחַל מַשְׁקֶה הוּא – Who is the Tanna who holds **that olive-water is** regarded as **a beverage?**[25]

The Gemara answers:

אָמַר אַבַּיֵי – Abaye said: רַבִּי יַעֲקֹב הִיא – It is R' Yaakov. דְּתַנְיָא – For it has been taught in a Baraisa: רַבִּי יַעֲקֹב אוֹמֵר – R' YAAKOV SAYS: מוֹחַל הֲרֵי הוּא כְּמַשְׁקֶה – OLIVE-WATER IS LIKE A BEVERAGE, and is therefore susceptible to *tumah.*[26] **וּמָה טַעַם אָמְרוּ מוֹחַל הַיּוֹצֵא בַּתְּחִלָּה טָהוֹר – WHAT THEN IS THE REASON THEY SAID** that **THE OLIVE-WATER THAT COMES OUT** of the olives **AT THE BEGINNING** of the pressing process[27] **IS NOT SUSCEPTIBLE TO *TUMAH*? לְפִי שֶׁאֵינוֹ רוֹצֶה בְּקִיּוּמוֹ – BECAUSE** in the case of this sort of olive-water, **[THE OWNER] DOES NOT DESIRE ITS EXISTENCE.** It therefore cannot be considered a beverage.[28]

NOTES

21. With regard to plums, quinces and sorb-apples, however, the Rabbis do not suspect that allowing one to squeeze them for the purpose of sweetening them will lead one to squeeze them for their juice, since there is no one at all who squeezes these fruits in order to obtain their juice (*Rashi*).

22. [For according to this explanation, the Baraisa does not cite Menashya bar Menachem's practice in order to establish pomegranates as fruit designated for squeezing, but only in order to set forth the basis of the Rabbis' fear that allowing the sweetening of pomegranates through squeezing could lead one to squeeze them for their juice. Thus, Rava's challenge to Rav Nachman's ruling is answered.]

According to this explanation, the Baraisa permits squeezing plums, quinces, and sorb-apples in order to sweeten them, but not in order to obtain their juice, since squeezing for juice renders the juice a beverage; it prohibits one to squeeze pomegranates even in order to sweeten them because of the suspicion, based on Menashya's practice, that one will come to squeeze them for their juice (*Rashi; Tosafos;* cf. *Rif; Ramban; Rashba* et al.; see *Beis Yosef, Orach Chaim* §320:1; *Beur HaGra* ibid. §1; *Beur Halachah* ibid. ד״ה מותר לסוחטן; see also *Eglei Tal* דש 29:2,3).

[Rav Nachman interpreted Rav Chisda's statement regarding beet juice in a *mikveh* as saying that the act of squeezing makes the juice into a beverage. We will shortly see, however, that his interpretation of Rav Chisda's statement is in fact subject to dispute.]

[With regard to whether the Baraisa according to the present understanding can still serve as proof that the Sages agree with R' Yehudah in the case of liquid that oozes from other sorts of fruit, see *Chasam Sofer; Chazon Ish, Orach Chaim* 55:1.]

23. Rav Pappa holds that Rav Chisda's reason for ruling that beet juice invalidates a *mikveh* is not that one who squeezes beets renders their juice a beverage [as Rav Nachman assumed]. For in fact one's regard for a liquid does not confer beverage status upon it [as only that which is commonly used for drinking can be deemed a beverage]! Rather, the *mikveh* is invalidated because beet juice is a substance from which a *mikveh* may not be made, and any such substance will invalidate a *mikveh* even if it is not legally a beverage (*Rashi*). [Thus, Rav Pappa shows that Rav Chisda's statement need not be construed as saying that squeezing a fruit for juice renders the juice a beverage. He accordingly does not explain the Baraisa as discussing squeezing performed for the purpose of sweetening, and therefore disputes Rav Nachman as to the Baraisa's point in citing the practice of Menashya bar Menachem. He holds that the Baraisa is discussing squeezing for the purpose of obtaining juice, and merely cites Menashya's custom as an example of a practice followed by many (see notes 3 and 11). Since there is thus a large public that squeezes pomegranates, their juice is deemed a beverage, and may not be extracted (*Rashi,* as explained by *Beis Yosef* ibid.; see *Rashi* above ד״ה אבל לא ברימונים; cf. *Beur HaGra* ibid.; cf. *Rashba* et al.).]

24. *Mikvaos* 7:3.

25. In the process of pressing olives, various secretions, known as olive-water [מוֹחַל], ooze from the olives. There are three distinct types of olive-water, each of which emerge at different stages of the process. The olives are first placed into a large vat [called a מַעֲטָן], in which their proximity to one another causes them to generate heat and thereby ripen. At this point, they exude liquid that is as thin and clear as water. After the olives have spent several days in the vat, their weight upon one another draws forth a more viscous fluid, nearly similar to actual olive oil. [The olives are then tied into a sort of netting (an עיקול), and placed under a beam or heavy stone that presses out the oil.] After the pressing, the mass of pulp remains in the netting for a time, and a third type of olive-water oozes from it.

The Gemara assumes that only a beverage can invalidate a *mikveh,* and therefore inquires after the identity of the Tanna who holds that olive-water is regarded as such (*Rashi*).

26. See 143b note 32.

27. [I.e. when the olives are first placed into the vat (see previous note).]

28. [For with regard to acquiring *tumah,* a liquid is generally considered a beverage only if its owner is satisfied that it has come into being, as was explained above, 143b note 32.]

בפגעין ובפרישין ובעוזרדין אבל לא ברמונים ושל בית מנשיא בר מנחם היו סוחטין ברמונים וממאי דרבנן היא דילמא ר' יהודה היא ותהוי נמי ר' יהודה אימר דשמעת ליה לר' יהודה יצאו מעצמן סוחטין לכתחילה מי שמעת ליה אלא מאי אית לך למימר כיון דלאו בני סחיטה נינהו אפילו לכתחלה אפילו תימא רבנן כיון דלאו בני סחיטה נינהו אפילו לכתחילה ש"מ רבנן היא ש"מ של בית מנשיא בר מנחם היו סוחטין ברמונים אמר רב נחמן הלכה כשל בית מנשיא בר מנחם א"ל רבא לרב נחמן מנשיא בן מנחם תנא הוא וכי תימא הלכה כי האי תנא דסבר לה כשל מנשיא בן מנחם ומשום דסבר כמנשיא בן מנחם הלכה כמותו מנשיא בן מנחם הוי רובא דעלמא אין דתנן המקיים קוצים בכרם ר"א אומר קדש וחכ"א אינו מקדש אלא דבר שכמוהו מקיימין וא"ר חנינא מ"ט דרבי אליעזר שכן בערביא מקיימין קוצי שדות לגמליהם מידי איריא דערביא אתרא הכא בטלה דעתו אצל כל אדם אלא היינו טעמא כדרב חסדא דאמר רב חסדא תרדין שסחטן ונתנן במקוה פוסלין את המקוה בשינוי מראה והא לאו בני סחיטה נינהו אלא מאי אית לך למימר ה"נ כיון דאחשבינהו הוה להו משקה הכא נמי כיון דאחשבינהו הוה להו משקה רב פפא אמר משום דהוי דבר שאין עושין ממנו מקוה וכל דבר שאין עושין ממנו מקוה לכתחילה פוסל את המקוה בשינוי מראה תנן התם נפל לתוכו יין או חומץ ומוחל ושינה מראיו פסול מאן תנא דמוחל משקה הוא אמר אביי רבי יעקב היא דתניא ר' יעקב אומר מוחל הרי הוא כמשקה ומה טעם אמרו מוחל היוצא בתחלה טהור לפי שאינו רוצה בקיומו ר"ש אומר מוחל אינו כמשקה ומה טעם אמרו מוחל היוצא מעיקול בית הבד טמא לפי שאי אפשר לו בלא ציחצוחי שמן מאי בינייהו איכא בינייהו דאתי בתר איצצתא רבא אמר משום דהוי דבר שאין עושין הימנו מקוה ופוסל את המקוה בשינוי מראה אמר רב יהודה אמר שמואל סוחט אדם אשכול של ענבים לתוך הקדרה אבל לא לתוך הקערה אמר רב חסדא מדברי רבינו נלמד חולב אדם עז לתוך הקדרה אבל לא לתוך הקערה אלמא קסבר משקה הבא לאוכל אוכל הוא מתיב רמי בר חמא זב שחולב את העז החלב טמא ואי אמרת משקה הבא לאוכלין אוכל הוא במאי איתכשר כדאמר ר' יוחנן בטיפה המלוכלכת ע"פ הדד הכא נמי בטיפה המלוכלכת ע"פ הדד מתיב רבינא טמא מת שסחט זיתים וענבים כביצה

רש"י

בפגעין. פרו"ש בלע"ז ולהוציא מימיהן לשתות: ובפרישין. קוידונ"ן: ובעוזרדין. קורמ"ש דלאו אורחייהו בהכי ואין כאן משום דש: אבל לא ברמונים. דאורחייהו בהכי: ושל בית מנשיא. היו רגילין לסחוט רמונים בחול אלמא איכא דסחיט להו הלכך בשבת אסור: אלא מאי אית לך למימר. לר' יהודה כיון דלאו בני סחיטה כו' וכי היכי דלרבי יהודה שרי לכתחילה מהאי טעמא מהשתא אפי' תימא רבנן ושרו ליה מהאי טעמא: מנשיא תנא הוא. בתמיה וכי איהו פליג למימר דבשבת אסור דתימא הלכתא כוותיה והא לא הזכר אלא לדברי התנא לראיה דהאי תנא הוא סבר כוותיה: וכ"ת. הא דאמר הלכה כשל בית מנשיא ה"ק הלכה כהאי תנא דאסר ברימונים הואיל וקאי מנשיא כוותיה דסוחטין רימונים בחול אלמא בני סחיטה נינהו: הוי רובא דעלמא. למשום איהו לאודויי נשוי לדך רמונים לסחיטה: קוצים. קרדונ"ש: מקדש. את התבואה משום כלאים דזריעה הוא: ואמר רבי חנינא כו'. אלמא משום חד מקום דאחשבינהו משוין להו דבר חשוב: אתרא. הוא ותשובת דרבים הוי חשיבותא: הכא. חד גברא למודיה הוא ודאי בטלה דעתו: אלא היינו טעמא. דרב נחמן דאמר הלכה אין סוחטין: כרב חסדא. אע"ג דלעלמא לא חשיב כיון דאחשיב איהו הוי לדידיה משקה והכי מפרש רב נחמן לברייתא דלעיל סוחטין בפגעין ובפרישין למתק הפרי ולא לצורך המשקה אבל לא ברמונים ואפילו למתקן (א) דשל בית מנשיא היו סוחטין בחול לצורך משקה הלכך בשבת אסור אפי' למתק הואיל ואיכא חד דעביד לשם משקה ולא משום דמנשיא רובא דעלמא אלא חיישינן אי שרית ליה למתק אתי למעבד לשם משקה וכיון דאיהו מחשב ליה הוי משקה ומיחייב אבל בפגעין ליכא (ב) למיחש דאין אדם עושה אותו למשקה: בשינוי מראה. לא בשלשת לוגין דלא הוזכרו שלשה לוגין אלא במים שאובין אבל שאר משקין לא פסלי אא"כ נשתנה מראה המקוה על ידיהן: רב פפא אמר. טעמא דתרדין לאו משום חשיבותא דאחשבינהו הוא ולעולם לאו משקה נינהו והא דמפסיל משום דכל דבר שאין עושין ממנו מקוה שאינו מים או שלג או ברד פוסל את המקוה בשינוי מראה: נפל לתוכו. של מקוה יין או חומץ או מוחל והוא כמין מים זב מן הזיתים וג' מינים יש בו כשטוענן מתחילה במעטן להתחמם ולהתבשל מאליהן מוחל זב מהן והוא צלול כמים ולאחר שעמדו ימים ודחקו זה את זה חוזר מוחל לזוב מהן והוא קרוב להיות כשמן ולאחר שעכרן להוציא שמנן בבית הבד ומשתהה התפוח של גפת בעקלים שהוא אגוד בהן בבית הבד חוזר מוחל וזב מהן: מאן תנא דמוחל משקה הוא. קס"ד דאין מקוה נפסל אלא על ידי משקה ואפילו בשינוי מראה: בתחילה. בתחילת טעינתן של זיתים: מעקול בית הבד. לאחר שנסחט שמנו או לפני סחיטתו: מאי בינייהו. במאי פליגי הואיל ותרוייהו מודו דמוחל היוצא בתחילה טהור והיוצא מעקל בית הבד טמא באיזה מוחל נחלקו דלמר הוי משקה וטמא ולמר לא הוי משקה וטהור: דאתי בתר איצצתא. לאחר שהתחילו להתחמם ודחקו זה את זה ונשתהה הכומר ימים: רבא אמר. קמייתא דקתני מוחל פוסל מקוה דברי הכל הוא ומשום דהוי כו': לתוך הקדרה. של תבשיל לתקנו דמוכחא מילתא דלאו למשקה בעי ליה אלא לאוכל ° ואין זה דרך פריקתו והוי כמפריד אוכל מאוכל: אבל לא לתוך הקערה. דזמנין דלמשקה קאי ואף על גב דבקערה לא שתי אינשי לא מוכחא מילתא ואיכא איסור: אלמא. מדקאמר סוחט לתוך הקדרה קסבר כו': החלב טמא. שהזב מטמא כל דבר במשא והרי היסט הקילוח ולא קמפליג בין לתוך הקדרה בין לתוך הכוס: ואי אמרת אוכל הוא. הא אין אוכל מקבל טומאה שלא בהכשר והאי במאי איתכשר: כדאמר רבי יוחנן. במסכת כריתות גבי האשה שנטף חלב מדדיה: בטיפה המלוכלכת על פי הדד. טיפה ראשונה מלכלכת בה פי הדד בדעת ונוחה ליחלב וההיא הוי משקה כסתם חלב דלא לאוכל בעי ליה: טמא מת שסחט זיתים וענבים כבילה

תוספות

מי דמי ערביא אתרא הוא. הו"מ למיפרך הניחא לרבי אליעזר לרבנן מאי איכא למימר אלא פריך דאפילו לרבי אליעזר לא ניחא ומה שקשה מאנשי הוצל דפרק המצניע (לעיל דף צב:) פירשתי שם (ד"ה ואמ"ל): ה"נ כיון דאחשביה הוו להו משקה. תחילה ס"ד דסוחטין בפגעין כו' היינו סחיטה ממש אבל השתא אי אפשר לומר דהא פשיטא דאסור דכיון דאחשביה הוה להו משקה אלא סוחטין דקתני היינו בליל"ר בלע"ז למתק הפרי כדפי' בקונטרס: אמר אביי ר' יעקב היא. קשה לי לימא דהאי מוחל דקתני היינו במוחל היוצא מעקול בית הבד ודברי הכל וכי תימא מדקתני מוחל סתמא משמע דבכל מוחל איירי לא היא דע"כ אפי' לרבי יעקב לא איירי בכל מוחל דהא מודה דמוחל היוצא בתחלה טהור וי"ל דמוחל היוצא מעקול בית הבד לא הוה קרינן ליה מוחל סתם כיון דאי אפשר לו בלא צחצוחי שמן: חולב אדם עז כו'. נראה לר"ת דהיינו דווקא בי"ט דחזיא בהמה לאכילה הוי כמו אוכלא דאיפרת אבל בשבת לא חזיא לשחיטה כמו דם חשיבה שהבהמה היא כפסולת וכשחולב הוי כבורר אוכל מתוך פסולת וכן משמע בבה"ג דבי"ט איירי ומיהו סחיטת זיתים וענבים דשרי לעיל לתוך הקדירה היינו אפי' בשבת כיון דאשכול חזיא לאכילה:

עין משפט נר מצוה

ח א מיי' פ"ה מהלכות כלאים הל"ח טוש"ע יו"ד סימן רצו סעיף יז:
ט ב מיי' פ"ז מהלכות מקוואות הלכה א סמג עשין רמח:
י ג מיי' שם והלכה ט סמג שם טוש"ע יו"ד סימן רא סעיף כה:
יא ד מיי' פ"י מהלכות טומאת אוכלין הלכה יג ופי"א הלכה ו:
יב ה מיי' פ"ח מהלכות שבת הל"י סמג לאוין סה טור שו"ע או"ח סימן שכ סעיף ד:
יג ו ז מיי' שם וסמג שם טור שו"ע או"ח סימן תקה:
יד ח ט מיי' פ"ט מהל' טומאת אוכלין הל"ב:

גליון הש"ס

רש"י ד"ה לתוך הקדירה וכו' ואין זה דרך פריקתו. עיין לעיל דף עג ע"ב תוספות ד"ה מפרק:

רבינו חננאל

דאמר סוחטין בפגעין ובפרישין ובעוזרדין אבל לא ברמונים וסבר לה כמנשיא בן מנחם שסוחט בחול ברמונים להוציא מהן מים וכן כמו זיתים וענבי' וקיי"ל כוותיה ואקשינן וכי מנשיא הוה רובא לעלמא. ומהדרינן אין. כי הא דתנן המקיים קוצים בכרם וכו' ואוקימנא אע"פ שאין דרך בני אדם לקיים קוצים בכרם כיון שבערביא מקיימין קידש הכא נמי אע"פ שאין דרך בני אדם לסחוט רמונים בחול כיון שסוחטין של בית מנשיא בחול בשבת אסור לסחוט ודחינן ערביא מקום בני אדם רבים ומנשיא אדם אחד הוא ובטלה דעתו אצל [כל] בני אדם ואתינן לטעמא אחריתי אלא האי תנא כטעמיה דרב חסדא דאמר תרדין שסחטן ונתנן למקוה פסלו המקוה בשנוי מראה וכיון שהזכרנו פסולות המקוה אמרינן. תנן התם [נפל] לתוכו יין ומוהל כו' פי' מוהל המים היוצאים מעוקל בית הבד עת שטוען קורות בית הבד על הזיתים הטחונין והוא מי הזיתים ויש בהן צחצוחי שמן: איצצאי דוחק. כדגרסינן בפרק המפקיד (דף מ ע"א) אמר ר' יהודה אמר שמואל סוחט אדם אשכול של ענבים בתוך הקדירה אבל לא לתוך הקערה. אמר רב חסדא מדברי רבינו נלמד חולב אדם עז לתוך הקדירה אבל לא לתוך הקערה אלמא קא סבר משקה הבא לאוכל אוכל הוא. ואותביה רמי [בר חמא] זב שחלב עז החלב טמא. כלומר (טמא) [שטימא אותה] הזב בנגיעתו. וא"ת אוכל הוא במאי אתכשר ופרקינן כר' יוחנן דאמר איתכשר בטפה המלוכלכת על פי הדד שנפסלה מאוכל והיא מכשרת במשקה ואותיב רבינא טמא מת שסחט זיתים וענבי' וכו' ופרקינן בסוחט לתוך הקערה שהוא ודאי משקה. ומפני מה לא פירק פירוק זה לגבי חולב עז חדא מתרי תלתא טעמא קאמר. א"ר ירמיה כתנאי. המחלק בענבים לא הוכשר. פי' מחלק משפשף פעמים שמתמצה בהן משקין. ומחליקן בו. ולפיכך אמר ר' יהודה הוכשר שכך משקה גמור הוא. ות"ק אמר משקה הבא לאוכל הוא וכאוכל הוא חשוב ואינו מכשיר ובא רב הונא ופירש כי התנאין החולקין במחלק במחליק בענבים פליגי במשקה העומד לצחצחו ואלו החולקין במפצע זיתים בידים מסואבות פליגי. במשקה העומד לאיבוד. א"ר זירא א"ר חייא בר אשי אמר רב סוחט אדם אשכול של ענבים לתוך הקדרה אבל לא לתוך הקערה וכן פירושו כל דבר הנסחט בקדירה הוא אוכל ומותר ולתוך הקערה משקה הוא ואסור. זולתי הדג שאפילו סחיטתו בקערה שרי. והא דאתמר כבשים שסחטן אמר רב לגופן מותר וכו'. דברים פשוטין הן. ואין צריכין לפנים ולא לפני פנים. אמנם צריכין אנו לברר כמי ההלכה. לפיכך אנו מזכירין דברי כולן:

מסורת הש"ס

א) [לעיל לג. וש"נ], ב) כלאים פ"ה מ"ח ב"ב קנו:, ג) [ע"ל אלעזר], ד) מקואות פ"ז מ"ד, ה) תוספ' דטהרות פרק י', ו) [ע"ל קמג: ד"ה מפרק וכו'], ז) טהרות פ"ג מ"א, ח) כריתות יג., ט) פסחים לג:, י) טהרות פ"ג מ"ג.

הגהות הב"ח

(א) רש"י ד"ה כרב חסדא וכו' ואפילו למתקן הואיל דשל בית וכו': (ב) בא"ד למיחש להכי דאין אדם:

רב נסים גאון

פכ"ב רבא אמר משום דהוה דבר שאין עושין ממנו מקוה לכתחלה וכל דבר שאין עושין ממנו מקוה לכתחלה פוסל את המקוה בשינוי מראה. עיקר דיליה בתורת כהנים מקוה מים לא מקוה כל המשקין כולן פרט לשופך בתוכו מי כבשים ומי צבעים ושינו את מראיו ובתוספתא טבול יום (פרק א) חומר במשקין שאין להן טהרת הגוף ואין להן טהרה מטומאתן ואינן טהורין בגוף ופוסלין את המקוה בשינוי מראה מה שאין כן במים: כדאמר ר' יוחנן בטיפה המלוכלכת על פי הדד. משכחת לה במס' כריתות בפרק אמרו לו מקום חלב מעין הוא ולא צריך הכשר והתנן האשה שחלב מדדיה ונטף לאויר תנור טמא וקשיא לן במאי איתכשר ואמר ר' יוחנן בטיפה מלוכלכת ע"פ הדד:

ליקוטי רש"י

המקיים קוצים בכרם. דכ"ג אשמען במסכת כלאים דמלהל במקום שאין כלאים בכרם משום לא תזרע כרמך כלאים ואפילו מקיים לוקה דכתיב כלאים שדך לא. [רשב"ם ב"ב קנו:]. ר"א אומר קדש. משום כלאים דכתיב פן תקדש המלאה הזרע [סוטה מג.]. שכן בערביא כו'. ולכן גבי קוצים רוצה דעלמא אלי שאינן מקיימין שדות לגמליהן [רשב"ם שם]. שאי אפשר לו בלא ציחצוחי שמן. ושמן איקרי משקה דכתיב (ישעיה כה) משתה שמנים [חולין קיד.]. היוצא מעיקול בית הבד. ועקל של בית הבד עשוין כמין קופה מקורעת [כמלגדה] ולאחר סחיטת הזיתים נותן קופה על הגפת ועקל נותנים עליו [קורה] ומכבידין להוציא המשקה הנבלע [ע"ז עה.]. איצצתא. דוחק [ב"מ]. זב שחולב את העז החלב טמא. דכתיב וכל אשר יגע בו הזב וגו' והאי קרא לאו למגע אלימא ליה דהא כתיב הסיטו של זב מכאן למדנו זב שהסיט את הטהור טמא שלא מצינו בכל התורה טומאה המסטת כן נשא טהור את הטמא והכא בזב הוא דגלי רחמנא [נדה מג.]. ואי אמרת משקה הבא לאוכלין אוכל הוא במאי איתכשר. שאין אוכל מוכשר ומתוקן לקבל טומאה עד שיבאו עליו מים פעם אחת ומשבאו עליו פעם אחת מקבל טומאה לעולם ואפילו נגוב והיין והשמן וכל הנקרא משקה מכשיר זרעים לטומאה כמים דכתיב אשר יבא עליו מים או כל משקה אשר ישתה בכל כלי יטמא האוכל [ויקרא יא, לד]. האי חלב ולאו תורת משקה דמשקה הבא לאוכל כאוכל דמי במסכת שבת בפרק חבית שנשברה הלכך בעי הכשר: בטיפה המלוכלכת על פי הדד. כלומר בטפה שפי הדד מלוכלך בו דההיא ודאי מכשר לשאר דהא [האי] לא קיימא לאכילת תינוק [כריתות יג.].

רַבִּי שִׁמְעוֹן אוֹמֵר – R' SHIMON SAYS: מוֹחַל אֵינוֹ כְּמַשְׁקֶה – OLIVE-WATER IS NOT LIKE A BEVERAGE, and therefore will not be susceptible to *tumah*. וּמַה טַּעַם אָמְרוּ מוֹחַל הַיּוֹצֵא מֵעִיקּוּל בֵּית הַבַּד טָמֵא – WHAT THEN IS THE REASON THEY SAID that THE OLIVE-WATER THAT FLOWS FROM THE NETTING OF THE OLIVE PRESS[29] IS SUSCEPTIBLE TO *TUMAH*? לְפִי שֶׁאִי אֶפְשָׁר לוֹ בְּלֹא צִיחְצוּחֵי שֶׁמֶן – BECAUSE IT IS IMPOSSIBLE FOR [THIS SORT OF OLIVE-WATER] to be WITHOUT TRACES OF actual OIL, which, as a full-fledged beverage, will certainly be susceptible to *tumah*. The water itself, however, is not deemed a beverage.

We see that with the exception of the water that emerges at the beginning of the pressing process, R' Yaakov holds that all olive-water is considered a beverage. It thus must be he who rules that olive-water will invalidate a *mikveh* by changing its color.

The Gemara asks:

מַאי בֵּינַיְיהוּ – But **what** practical difference **is** there **between [R' Yaakov and R' Shimon]?** Both seem to agree that the olive-water that comes out at the beginning is not susceptible to *tumah*, while that which flows from the netting is![30]

The Gemara answers:

אִיכָּא בֵּינַיְיהוּ דְּאָתֵי בָּתַר אִיצְצְתָּא – **The** difference **between them is** regarding the olive-water **that comes** out **after** the **pressure** of the olives upon one another.[31] This water is not actual oil, but is yet something whose existence is desirable to its owner. R' Yaakov and R' Shimon disagree as to whether it has beverage status.[32]

Rava disagrees with the above explanation of why olive-water invalidates a *mikveh:*

רָבָא אָמַר – **Rava said:** מִשּׁוּם דְּהָוֵי דָּבָר שֶׁאֵין עוֹשִׂין הֵימֶנּוּ מִקְוֶה – The reason olive-water invalidates the *mikveh* is not because it is a legal beverage, but **because it is a substance from which one may not make a *mikveh;*** וּפוֹסֵל אֶת הַמִּקְוֶה בְּשִׁינּוּי מַרְאֶה – it therefore **invalidates the *mikveh*** by causing **a change in the appearance** of the water. A liquid need not be a legal beverage in order to cause such invalidation.[33]

The Gemara cites an Amoraic ruling regarding squeezing grapes on the Sabbath:

אָמַר רַב יְהוּדָה אָמַר שְׁמוּאֵל – **Rav Yehudah said in the name of Shmuel:** סוֹחֵט אָדָם אֶשְׁכּוֹל שֶׁל עֲנָבִים לְתוֹךְ הַקְּדֵרָה – **A person may squeeze a cluster of grapes into a pot** of food on the Sabbath, אֲבָל לֹא לְתוֹךְ הַקְּעָרָה – **but not into a bowl.**[34]

The Gemara draws an inference from Shmuel's statement:

אָמַר רַב חִסְדָּא – **Rav Chisda said:** מִדִּבְרֵי רַבֵּינוּ נִלְמַד – **We can learn from the words of our teacher** that חוֹלֵב אָדָם עֵז לְתוֹךְ הַקְּדֵרָה – **one may milk a goat into a pot,** אֲבָל לֹא לְתוֹךְ הַקְּעָרָה – **but not into a bowl.**[35]

NOTES

29. I.e. the liquid that oozes from the mass after it has been pressed, or [shortly] before it is to be pressed (*Rashi;* see *Rashash*).

30. For although R' Yaakov and R' Shimon may disagree as to the beverage status of each of these two sorts of olive-water, they are in perfect agreement with regard to their susceptibility to *tumah.* For both hold that the early olive-water is not susceptible, while the final one is. With regard to what sort of olive-water, then, do they agree, with R' Yaakov holding that its beverage status renders it susceptible to *tumah,* and R' Shimon holding that since it is not a beverage it is insusceptible to *tumah*? (*Rashi*).

31. [I.e. the second sort of olive-water enumerated in note 25.]

32. [*Tosafos* ask: Why does Abaye assume that the Mishnah discussing invalidation of a *mikveh* speaks of this type of olive-water, and thus represents only the opinion of R' Yaakov? Perhaps it speaks of the final olive-water that runs from the netting, and is in accordance with both R' Yaakov and R' Shimon! *Tosafos* answer that the Mishnah would not refer to this final liquid by the unqualified term "olive-water," since it consists in fact of a mixture of olive-water and oil (see *Chasam Sofer; Chidushei R' Akiva Eiger; Sfas Emes.*]

33. The Mishnah is thus in accordance with both R' Yaakov and R' Shimon [since even liquid without beverage status will invalidate a *mikveh*] (*Rashi; Chidushei HaRan*).

34. As explained above (note 1), the act of squeezing fruits is prohibited on the Sabbath only if it entails extracting a beverage from a food, since the *melachah* of דָּשׁ, *threshing,* demands the removal of one category of object from another (*Rashi; Tosafos* 73b ד״ה מפרק). Accordingly, Shmuel permits one to squeeze grapes directly into a pot of food to improve the food's flavor. For since the juice of these grapes is designated to be used as food, it is legally regarded not as a beverage, as grape juice usually is, but as a food! Thus, one who squeezes it out is merely extracting one sort of food from another, and is not in violation of *threshing* (*Rashi*). There need not actually be food in the pot; rather, one's mere *intention* to mix the juice with food suffices to render it a food. However, one is prohibited to squeeze the grapes into an empty *bowl* even if one intends to use their juice for food. For since a bowl is occasionally used to store liquid for drinking, its use might suggest to an onlooker that he is squeezing the grapes to obtain their juice, in violation of the Sabbath! This act is therefore forbidden by Rabbinic decree, as an activity that gives the *appearance* of wrongdoing [מַרְאִית הָעַיִן] (*Rashi,* as understood by *Tos. Rid; Radvaz* §686; *Eglei Tal* דש §18; see also *Rashi* 145a ד״ה הבא; cf. *Tos. Rid; Ritva MHK* ed.; *Rashba* et al.). [One would be permitted, however, to squeeze the grapes into a bowl filled with food, since in that case it is evident that the juice is being used in food.]

Alternatively, one is permitted to squeeze grapes into a pot according to Shmuel *only* when there is actually food inside the pot, for only then is their juice deemed a food. One's mere *intention* to later combine the juice with food does not suffice to effect its transformation from beverage to food. One is therefore prohibited to squeeze grapes on the Sabbath unless one does so directly into food (see *Mishnah Berurah* 320:18; *Chazon Ish, Orach Chaim* 55:6). This applies to squeezing done into a pot; one is prohibited, however, to squeeze grapes into a bowl *even* if it contains food! For since bowls are occasionally used for drinking, the Rabbis forbade one to squeeze grapes into them under all circumstances (*Rashi,* as understood by *Meiri;* see *Beur Halachah* 320:4 ד״ה לתוך).

[It is important to realize that this rule assigning food status to a beverage that is or will be mixed into food applies only to a beverage that was designated for such use from its first moment of existence, such as fruit juice squeezed directly into food. However, if one squeezes the fruit without plans to combine its juice with food, neither his later decision to do so, nor the actual act of mixing will transform the juice from a beverage into a food! (*Chasam Sofer* to 145a; *Chazon Ish* ibid.).]

[Note that according to this ruling, when the Mishnah states that one is prohibited from squeezing fruits on the Sabbath, it refers to one who squeezes them into a bowl, not into a pot (*Rashba; Ritva MHK* ed. to 143b et al.).]

35. The act of milking an animal, like that of squeezing fruit, falls into the category of מְפָרֵק, *extracting* (a *toladah* of threshing), since drawing the milk from the teat is analogous to extracting the kernel from its husk. Rav Chisda rules that just as when one squeezes grapes into food, the squeezings are considered a food, so too with regard to milking into food – the milk is not deemed a beverage, but a food. One who milks into food is thus merely extracting one sort of food from another, and may therefore do so on the Sabbath (*Rif; Ramban; Rashba; Ritva MHK* ed.).

[*Rabbeinu Tam* (cited in *Tosafos*) asks: How is milking a goat on the Sabbath comparable to squeezing grapes? In the case of grapes, both the grapes and the juice are edible; one is thus extracting one food from another. But a goat cannot be considered a food on the Sabbath, since on that day its slaughter is forbidden! Thus, one who milks it on the Sabbath is in effect extracting a food – the milk – from a non-food – the goat. This act should accordingly fall into the category of מְפָרֵק, *extracting! Rabbeinu Tam* therefore concludes that Rav Chisda is only permitting milking into food on a festival day (Yom Tov); since slaughter is permissible on a festival, the goat will be considered a food on that day! However, others maintain that since the goat can be slaughtered and eaten after the Sabbath, it is deemed a food even during the Sabbath (*Ramban; Rashba;* see there and in *Ran* for further reasons to permit this act on the Sabbath).]

עין משפט
נר מצוה

ח א מיי' פ"ה מהלכות כלאים הל"ח טוש"ע יו"ד סימן רלו סעיף יד:
ט ב מיי' פ"ז מהלכות מקוואות הלכה א סמג עשין רמח:
י ג מיי' שם והלכה ט סמג שם טוש"ע יו"ד סימן רא סעיף כה:
יא ד מיי' פ"י מהלכות טומאת אוכלין הלכה יג ופי"א הלכה ו:
יב ה מיי' פ"ח מהלכות שבת הל"י סמג לאוין סה טור שו"ע או"ח סימן שכ סעיף ד:
יג ו ז מיי' שם וסמג שם טור שו"ע או"ח סימן תקה:
יד ח ט מיי' פ"ט מהל' טומאת אוכלין הל"ב:

גליון הש"ס

רש"י ד"ה לתוך הקדירה וכו' ואין זה דרך פריקתו. עיין לעיל דף עג ע"ב תוספות ד"ה מפרק:

רבינו חננאל

דאמר סוחטין בפגעין ובפרישין ובעוזרדין אבל לא ברמונים וסבר לה כמנשיא בן מנחם שסוחט בחול ברמונים להוציא מהן מים וכן כמו זיתים וענבי' וקיי"ל כוותיה ואקשינן וכי מנשיא הוה רובא לעלמא. ומהדרינן אין. כי הא דתנן המקיים קוצים בכרם וכו' ואוקימנא אע"פ שאין דרך בני אדם לקיים קוצים בכרם כיון שבערביא מקיימין קידש הכא נמי אע"פ שאין דרך בני אדם לסחוט רמונים בחול כיון שסוחטין של בית מנשיא בחול בשבת אסור לסחוט ודחינן ערביא מקום בני אדם רבים ומנשיא אדם אחד הוא ובטלה דעתו אצל [כל] בני אדם ואתינן לטעמא אחריתי אלא האי תנא כטעמיה דרב חסדא דאמר תרדין שסחטן ונתנן למקוה פסלו המקוה בשנוי מראה וכיון שהזכרנו פסולות המקוה אמרינן. תנן התם [נפל] לתוכו יין ומוהל כו' פי' מוהל המים היוצאים מעוקל בית הבד עת שטוען קורות בית הבד על הזיתים הטחונין והוא מי הזיתים ויש בהן צחצוחי שמן: איצצאי דוחק. כדגרסינן בפרק המפקיד (דף מ ע"א) אמר ר' יהודה אמר שמואל סוחט אדם אשכול של ענבים בתוך הקדירה אבל לא לתוך הקערה. אמר רב חסדא מדברי רבינו נלמד חולב אדם עז לתוך הקדירה אבל לא לתוך הקערה אלמא קא סבר משקה הבא לאוכל אוכל הוא. ואותביה רמי [בר חמא] זב שחלב עז החלב טמא. כלומר (טמא) [שטימא אותה] הזב בנגיעתו. וא"ת אוכל הוא במאי אתכשר ופרקינן כר' יוחנן דאמר איתכשר בטפה המלוכלכת על פי הדד שנפסלה מאוכל והיא מכשרת במשקה ואותיב רבינא טמא מת שסחט זיתים וענבי' וכו'

ופרקינן בסוחט לתוך הקערה שהוא ודאי משקה. ומפני מה לא פירק פירוק זה לגבי חולב עז חדא מתרי תלתא טעמא קאמר. א"ר ירמיה כתנאי. המחלק בענבים לא הוכשר. פי' מחלק משפשף פעמים שמתמצה בהן משקין. ומחליקן בו. ולפיכך אמר ר' יהודה הוכשר שכך משקה גמור הוא. ות"ק אמר משקה הבא לאוכל הוא וכאוכל הוא חשוב ואינו מכשיר ובא רב הונא ופירש כי התנאין החולקין במחלק בענבים פליגי במשקה העומד לצחצחו ואלו החולקין במפצע זיתים בידים מסואבות פליגי. במשקה העומד לאיבוד. א"ר זירא א"ר חייא בר אשי אמר רב סוחט אדם אשכול של ענבים לתוך הקדרה אבל לא לתוך הקערה וכן פירושו כל דבר הנסחט בקדירה הוא אוכל ומותר ולתוך הקערה משקה הוא ואסור. זולתי הדג שאפילו סחיטתו בקערה שרי. והא דאתמר כבשים שסחטן אמר רב לגופן מותר וכו'. דברים פשוטין הן. ואין צריכין לפנים ולא לפני פנים. אמנם צריכין אנו לברר כמי ההלכה. לפיכך אנו מזכירין דברי כולן:

מי דמי ערביא אתרא הוא. הו"מ למיפרך היכא לרבי אליעזר לרבנן מאי איכא למימר אלא פריך דאפילו לרבי אליעזר לא ניחא ומה שקשה מהנהו דהולך דפרק המצניע (לעיל דף צג:) פירשתי שם (ד"ה ואם"ל):

ה"נ כיון דאחשביה הוו להו משקה. תימה לר"י דסוחטין בפגעין כו' היינו סחיטה ממש אבל השתא אי אפשר לומר דהא פשיטא דאסור דכיון דאחשביה הוה להו משקה אלא סוחטין דקתני היינו בליי"ר בלע"ז למתק הפרי כדפי' בקונטרס:

אמר אביי ר' יעקב היא. קשה לי לימא דהאי מוהל דקתני היינו במוהל היוצא מעקול בית הבד ודברי הכל וכי תימא מדקתני מוהל סתמא משמע דבכל מוהל איירי לא היא דע"כ אפי' לרבי יעקב לא איירי בכל מוהל דהא מודה דמוהל היוצא בתחילה טהור וי"ל דמוהל היוצא מעקול בית הבד לא הוה קרינן ליה מוהל סתם כיון דאי אפשר לו בלא צחצוחי שמן:

חולב אדם עז כו'. נראה לר"ת דהיינו דווקא בי"ט דחזיא בהמה לאכילה הוי כמו אוכלא דאיפרת אבל בשבת לא חזיא לשחיטה כמו דם חשיבא שהבהמה היא כפסולת וכשחולב הוי כנוטל אוכל מתוך פסולת וכן משמע בבה"ג דבי"ט איירי ומיהו סחיטת זיתים וענבים דשרי לעיל לתוך הקדירה היינו אפי' בשבת כיון דלאכול חזיא לאכילה:

בפגעין ובפרישין ובעוזרדין אבל לא ברמונים ושל בית מנשיא בר מנחם היו סוחטין ברמונים וממאי דרבנן היא דילמא ר' יהודה היא ותהוי נמי ר' יהודה אימר דשמעת ליה לר' יהודה יצאו מעצמן סוחטין לכתחילה מי שמעת ליה אלא מאי אית לך למימר כיון דלאו בני סחיטה נינהו אפילו לכתחילה אפילו תימא רבנן כיון דלאו בני סחיטה נינהו אפילו לכתחילה ש"מ רבנן היא ש"מ של בית מנשיא בר מנחם היו סוחטין ברמונים אמר רב נחמן הלכה כשל בית מנשיא בר מנחם א"ל רבא לרב נחמן מנשיא בן מנחם תנא הוא וכי תימא הלכה כי האי תנא דסבר לה כשל מנשיא בן מנחם ומשום דסבר כמנשיא בן מנחם הלכה כמותו מנשיא בן מנחם הוי רובא דעלמא אין דתנן המקיים קוצים בכרם ר"א אומר קדש וחכ"א אינו מקדש אלא דבר שכמוהו מקיימין וא"ר חנינא מ"ט דרבי אליעזר שכן בערביא מקיימין קוצי שדות לגמליהם מידי איריא דערביא אתרא הכא בטלה דעתו אצל כל אדם אלא היינו טעמא כדרב חסדא דאמר רב חסדא תרדין שסחטן ונתנן במקוה פוסלין את המקוה בשינוי מראה והא לאו בני סחיטה נינהו אלא מאי אית לך למימר כיון דאחשבינהו הוה להו משקה ה"נ כיון דאחשבינהו הוה להו משקה אמר רב פפא אמר משום דהוי דבר שאין עושין ממנו מקוה לכתחילה וכל דבר שאין עושין ממנו מקוה לכתחילה פוסל את המקוה בשינוי מראה תנן התם נפל לתוכו יין או חומץ ומוהל ושינה מראיו פסול מאן תנא דמוהל משקה הוא אמר אביי רבי יעקב היא דתניא ר' יעקב אומר מוהל הרי הוא כמשקה ומה טעם אמרו מוהל היוצא בתחלה טהור לפי שאינו רוצה בקיומו ר"ש אומר מוהל אינו כמשקה ומה טעם אמרו מוהל היוצא מעיקול בית הבד טמא לפי שאי אפשר לו בלא ציחצוחי שמן מאי בינייהו איכא בינייהו דאתי בתר איצצתא רבא אמר משום דהוי דבר שאין עושין הימנו מקוה ופוסל את המקוה בשינוי מראה אמר רב יהודה אמר שמואל סוחט אדם אשכול של ענבים לתוך הקדרה אבל לא לתוך הקערה אמר רב חסדא מדברי רבינו נלמד חולב אדם עז לתוך הקדרה אבל לא לתוך הקערה אלמא קסבר משקה הבא לאוכל אוכל הוא מתיב רמי בר חמא זב שחולב את העז החלב טמא ואי אמרת משקה הבא לאוכלין אוכל הוא במאי איתכשר כדאמר ר' יוחנן בטיפה המלוכלכת ע"פ הדד הכא נמי בטיפה המלוכלכת ע"פ הדד מתיב רבינא טמא מת שסחט זיתים וענבים
כבילה

בפגעין. פרונ"ש בלע"ז ולהוציא מימיהן לשתות: ובפרישין. קוידונ"ץ: ובעוזרדין. קורמ"ש דלאו לורכייהו בהכי ואין כאן משום לש: אבל לא ברמונים. דלורכייהו בהכי: ושל בית מנשיא. היו רגילין לסחוט רמונים בחול אלמא איכא דסחיט להו הלכך בשבת אסור: אלא מאי אית לך למימר. לר' יהודה כיון דלאו בני סחיטה כו' וכי היכי דלרבי יהודה שרי לכתחילה מהאי טעמא מהשתא אפי' תימא רבנן ושרו ליה מהאי טעמא: מנשיא תנא הוא. בתמיה וכי איהו פליג למימר דבשבת אסור דתימא הלכתא כוותיה והא לא הוזכר אלא לדברי התנא לראיה דהאי תנא הוא סבר כוותיה: וכ"ת. הא דאמר הלכה כשל בית מנשיא ה"ק הלכה כהאי תנא דאסר ברימונים הואיל וקאי מנשיא כוותיה דסוחטין רימונים בחול אלמא בני סחיטה נינהו: הוי רובא דעלמא. דמשום איהו לחודיה נשוי דרך רמונים לסחיטה: קוצים. קרדו"ס: מקדש. את התבואה משום כלאים דזריעה הוא: ואמר רבי חנינא כו'. אלמא משום חד מקום דאחשבינהו משוינן להו דבר חשוב: אתרא. הוא וחשיבות דרבים הוי חשיבות: הכא. חד גברא לחודיה הוא וגמה בטלה דעתו: אלא היינו טעמא. דרב נחמן דאמר הלכה אין סוחטין: כרב חסדא. אע"ג דלעלמא לא חשיב כיון דאחשיב איהו הוי לדידיה משקה והכי מפרש רב נחמן לברייתא דלעיל סוחטין בפגעין ובפרישין למתק הפרי ולא לצורך המשקה אבל לא ברימונים ואפילו למתקן (א) דשל בית מנשיא היו סוחטין בחול לצורך משקה הלכך בשבת אסור אפי' למתק הואיל ואיכא חד דעביד לשם משקה ולא משום דמנשיא רובא דעלמא אלא חיישינן אי שרית ליה למתק אתי למעבד לשם משקה וכיון דלאיהו מחשב ליה הוי משקה ומיחייב אבל בפגעין ליכא (ג) למיחש דלאין אדם עושה אותו למשקה: בשינוי מראה. לא בשלשה לוגין דלא הוזכרו שלשה לוגין אלא במים שאובין אבל שאר משקין לא פסלי אא"כ נשתנה מראה המקוה על ידיהן: רב פפא אמר. טעמא דתרדין לאו משום חשיבותא דאחשבינהו הוא ולעולם לאו משקה נינהו והא דמפסיל משום דכל דבר שאין עושין ממנו מקוה שאינו מים שלא בא דרך מים

פוסל את המקוה בשינוי מראה: נפל לתוכו. של מקוה יין או חומץ או מוהל והוא כמין מים חב מן הזיתים וג' מינים יש בו כשטוענין מתחילה במעטן להתחמם ולהתבשל מוציאין מוהל זה מהן והוא צלול כמים ולאחר שעמדו ימים ודחקו זה את זה מוהל זב מהן והוא קרוב להיות כשמן ולאחר שנעלכו להוציא שמן מהן ומשהם התפוח של גפת שבעקולים שהוא אגוד בהן בבית הבד אחר מוהל זב מהן: מאן תנא דמוהל משקה הוא. קס"ד דלאין מקוה נפסל אלא על ידי משקה ואפילו בשינוי מראה: בתחילה. בתחילת טעינתן של זיתים: מעקול בית הבד. לאחר שנסחט שמנו או לפני סחיטתו: מאי בינייהו. במאי פליגי הואיל ותרוייהו מודו דמוהל היוצא בתחילה טהור והיוצא מעקל בית הבד טמא: דאתי בתר איצצתא. לאחר שהתחילו להתחמם ודחקו זה את זה ונשתהה הכומר ימים: רבא אמר. קמייתא דקתני מוהל פוסל מקוה דברי הכל הוא ומשום דהוי כו': לתוך הקדרה. של תבשיל דמוכחא מילתא דלאו למשקה בעי ליה אלא לאוכל ואין זה דרך פריקתו והוי כמפריד אוכל מאוכל: אבל לא לתוך הקערה. דזמנין דלמשקה קאי ואף על גב דבקערה לא שתי איניש לא מוכחא מילתא ואיכא איסור: אלמא. מדקאמר סוחט לתוך הקדרה קסבר כו': החלב טמא. שהזב מטמא כל דבר במשא והרי היסט הקילוח ולא קמפליג בין לתוך הקדרה בין לתוך הכוס: ואי אמרת אוכל הוא. הא אין אוכל מקבל טומאה שלא בהכשר והאי במאי איתכשר: כדאמר רבי יוחנן. במסכת כריתות גבי האשה שנטף חלב מדדיה: בטיפה המלוכלכת על פי הדד. טיפה ראשונה מלכלכת בה פי הדד בדעת ונוחה ליחלב וההיא הוי משקה כשהוא חלב דלא לאוכל בעי ליה: טמא מת שסחט זיתים וענבים
כבילה

מסורת הש"ס

א) [לעיל לב. ושם נסמן], ב) כלאים פ"ה מ"ח ב"ב קנו., ג) [ג"ל אליעזר], ד) מקוואות פ"ז מ"ה, ה) תוספ' דטהרות פרק י, ו) [ע"ל תוס' עג: ד"ה מפרק וכו'], ז) טהרות פ"ג מ"ג, ח) כריתות יג. פסחים לג:, ט) טהרות פ"ג מ"ג.

הגהות הב"ח

(א) רש"י ד"ה כרב חסדא וכו' ואפילו למתקן הואיל דשל בית וכו': (ג) באד"ה למיחש להכי דלאין אדם:

רב נסים גאון

פכ"ב רבא אמר משום דהוה דבר שאין עושין ממנו מקוה לכתחילה וכל דבר שאין עושין ממנו מקוה לכתחילה פוסל את המקוה בשינוי מראה. עיקר דיליה בתורת כהנים מקוה מים לא מקוה כל המשקין כולן פרט לשנפל בתוכו מי כבשין ומי צבעין ושינו את מראיו ובתוספתא טבול יום (פרק א) חומר במשקין שאין להן טהרת הגוף ואין להן טהרה מטומאתן ואינן טהורין בגוף ופוסלין את המקוה בשינוי מראה מה שאין כן במים: כדאמר ר' יוחנן בטיפה על פי הדד. משכחת לה במס' כריתות בפרק אמרו לו אכלת חלב (דף יג) ולרבא מקום חלב מעין הוא ולא צריך הכשר והתנן האשה שחלב מדדיה ונפל לאויר תנור תנור טמא וקשיא לן במאי איתכשר ואמר ר' יוחנן בטיפה מלוכלכת ע"פ הדד:

ליקוטי רש"י

המקיים קוצים בכרם. דכה"ג אשכחן במסכת כלאים דמהלל בהמה הוי כלאים בכרם משום לא תזרע כרמך כלאים ואפילו מקיים לוקה דדרשי במועד קטן (ג:) כלאים שדך לא. [רשב"ם ב"ב קנו:]. ר"א אומר קדש. משום כלאי הכרם דכתיב פן תקדש המלאה הזרע [סוטה מג:]. שכן בערביא כו'. ורבנן בתר רובא דעלמא אזלי שאין מקיימין שדות לגמליהן [רשב"ם שם]. שאי אפשר לו בלא ציחצוחי שמן. וסתמן ליקרי משקה דכתיב (ישעיה כה) משתה שמנים [חולין קיד.]. היוצא מעיקול בית הבד. ועקל בית הבד עשוין כמין קופה מסורגת [כמלודה] ומשרי סחיטת הזיתים טוען הגפת בלתוך עקל ומניח עליו [קורה] ומכבידו להוליא המשקה הנשאר [עי"ז עה.]. איצצתא. דוחק [ב"מ מ.]. זב שחולב את העז החלב טמא. דכתיב וכל אשר יגע בו הזב וגו' והאי קרא לאו למגע אילטריך דהא כתיב והנוגע בבשר הזב אלא זה הסיטו של זב מכאן למדו זב שהסיט את הטהור טמא שלא מצינו בכל התורה טומאה המסטת טהרה שמטמאה אלא אם כן נשא טהור את הטמא והכא כזב הוא דגלי רחמנא [נדה מג.]. ואי אמרת משקה הבא לאוכלין אוכל הוא במאי איתכשר. שאין אוכל מוכשר ומתוקן לקבל טומאה עד שיבאו עליו מים פעם אחת ומשבאו עליו מים פעם אחת מקבל טומאה לעולם ואפילו נגוב והיין והשמן וכל הנקרא משקה מכשיר זרעים לטומאה כמים שכך יש לדרוש המקרא אשר יבא עליו מים או כל משקה אשר ישתה בכל כלי יטמא האוכל [ויקרא יא, לד]. והאי חלב ולאו טמא הוא דחלב אין בו תורת משקה דמשקה הבא לאוכל כאוכל דמי במסכת שבת בפרק חבית שנשברה הלכך בעי הכשר. כדאמר ר' יוחנן בטיפה המלוכלכת על פי הדד. כלומר בטפה שפי הדד מלוכלך בו דההיא ודאי מכשר לשאר החלב היוצא דרך שם דהא [האין] לא קיימא לאכילה מינוק [כריתות יג.].

The Gemara returns to Shmuel's ruling:[36]

אַלְמָא קָסָבַר מַשְׁקֶה הַבָּא לְאוֹכֶל אוֹכֶל הוּא – **We see that [Shmuel] holds that a beverage extracted for** use in **food,** such as one squeezed into a pot, **is itself** regarded as **a food.** One is therefore permitted to squeeze it out, since one is only prohibited to squeeze out liquids if they possess legal beverage status.[37]

The Gemara objects to Shmuel's principle:

מְתִיב רָמִי בַּר חָמָא – **Rami bar Chama challenged** Shmuel on the basis of the following Mishnah:[38] זָב שֶׁחוֹלֵב אֶת הָעֵז הֶחָלָב טָמֵא – If A *ZAV* MILKS A GOAT, THE MILK IS *TAMEI*.[39] Now since this Mishnah does not differentiate between whether the *zav* milked the goat into a pot or into a bowl, it implies that the milk will be *tamei* in either case. וְאִי אָמְרַת מַשְׁקֶה הַבָּא לְאוֹכָלִין אוֹכֶל הוּא – **But if you say** that **a beverage extracted for** use in **food is itself** regarded as **a food,** then when the milking is done into a pot, the milk is a food and accordingly cannot acquire *tumah* without first being made susceptible to it[40] – בְּמַאי אִיתְכַּשַׁר – but **with what does it become susceptible?** It was not brought into contact with any beverage! Since the Mishnah nonetheless rules it *tamei*, it evidently holds that a beverage extracted for use in food is not considered a food, but a beverage![41] – ? –

The Gemara answers:

כִּדְאָמַר רַבִּי יוֹחָנָן – No, the explanation is **as R' Yochanan** once **said**[42] regarding the milk of a *tamei* woman: בְּטִיפָּה הַמְלוּכְלֶכֶת עַל פִּי הַדַּד – It is made susceptible to *tumah* through contact **with the drop** of milk **that is smeared upon the opening of the nipple,** which is considered a beverage.[43] הָכָא נַמִּי – **Here too** [in the case of goat milk], בְּטִיפָּה הַמְלוּכְלֶכֶת עַל פִּי הַדַּד – it is made susceptible to *tumah* through contact **with the drop of milk that is smeared upon the opening of the nipple.**[44] Shmuel's principle thus stands.

The Gemara challenges Shmuel again:

מְתִיב רָבִינָא – **Ravina challenged** him from the next segment of this Mishnah, which states: טְמֵא מֵת שֶׁסָּחַט זֵיתִים וַעֲנָבִים – In the case of ONE CONTAMINATED WITH CORPSE *TUMAH* WHO SQUEEZED OLIVES OR GRAPES:

NOTES

36. *Rashi;* cf. *Sfas Emes.*

37. See above, note 34.

38. *Tohoros* 3:3.

39. [A *zav* is a male contaminated through discharge of a particular sort of urethral emission (described in *Leviticus* 15:3 and *Niddah* 35b).] The law is that a *zav* [or a *zavah, niddah,* or woman after childbirth] will generate *tumas heset* (a form of *tumah* unique to a *zav*) in any item whose weight he supports (see above, 83b). In the act of milking, one supports the weight of the milk while directing its stream – thus, when this act is performed by a *zav,* the milk becomes *tamei* [even though the *zav* does not come into direct contact with it] (*Rashi*). [See above, 83a notes 13,19-23 for a lengthy discussion regarding the various forms of *tumas heset.*]

40. See above, 143b note 32.

41. [It thus can be contaminated by the *zav,* since beverages need not be specially rendered susceptible in order to acquire *tumah.*]

42. In *Kereisos* 13a.

43. The Gemara there deals with a Mishnah (*Keilim* 8:11) that states that if milk drips from the breast of a *niddah* into an earthenware stove, it [being *tamei* through contact with the *niddah*] will contaminate the stove. Now, although a woman's milk is normally regarded as a beverage (see above, 143b-144a), since in this case it will surely be lost, it is as though she stated explicitly that she is dissatisfied with its emergence. It accordingly is not classified as a beverage, but as a food (*Tosafos* 144a ד״ה לא). The Gemara there therefore inquires as to how this "food" became susceptible to *tumah,* to which R' Yochanan answers that it was made susceptible through contact with the first drop of the woman's milk, which a woman will deliberately smear upon her nipple in order to facilitate nursing. Since the woman desires the emergence of this first drop of milk, it is considered a beverage, and thus will make the milk that follows susceptible to *tumah* (*Rashi;* cf. *Rashi* to *Kereisos* ibid. ד״ה הא איתכשר וד״ה לפומיה; see *Chazon Ish, Orach Chaim* 55:7).

44. [For one who milks a goat will smear the first drop of milk upon the opening of the udder to facilitate milking. This drop, which like all other milk is deemed a beverage, will render the milk that follows susceptible to *tumah.* It therefore will become *tamei* through being supported by the *zav.*]

כְּבֵיצָה מְכֻוֶּנֶת טָהוֹר – If the olives or grapes squeezed are PRECISELY EQUIVALENT in volume TO AN EGG, then although they themselves are *tamei,*[1] [THE LIQUID EXTRACTED] from them WILL NOT BE CONTAMINATED by them. For immediately upon being squeezed, the fruit is reduced to less than the volume of an egg, and food of less than an egg-volume cannot generate *tumah.*[2] הָא יוֹתֵר מִכְּבֵיצָה טָמֵא – **This implies that** if the fruits squeezed are **greater** in volume **than an egg, [the liquid extracted]** from them **will be contaminated** by them![3] Now since this Mishnah does not differentiate between whether the fruit was squeezed into a pot or into a bowl, the implication is that the liquid will be contaminated in either case! וְאִי אָמְרַתְּ מַשְׁקֶה הַבָּא לְאוֹכֶל אוֹכֶל הוּא – **But if you say** that **a beverage that is extracted for** use in **food is itself** regarded as **a food,** then when the squeezing is done into a pot, the juice is a food and accordingly will not acquire *tumah* without first being made susceptible – בְּמַאי אִיתְכְּשַׁר – but **with what does it become susceptible?** It was not brought into contact with any beverage! Since the Mishnah nonetheless rules it *tamei,* it evidently holds that a beverage extracted for use in food is not a food, but a beverage! – ? –

The Gemara answers:

הוּא מוֹתִיב לָהּ וְהוּא מְפָרֵק לָהּ – **[Ravina] asked [this question], and he answered it** as well: בְּסוֹחֵט לְתוֹךְ הַקְּעָרָה – The Mishnah speaks only about the case of **one who squeezes** the fruit **into a bowl.** Thus, the juice is not deemed a food, but a beverage, and can therefore acquire *tumah* without first being made susceptible.[4]

The Gemara suggests that Shmuel's principle is the subject of a Tannaic dispute:

אָמַר רַבִּי יִרְמְיָה – **R' Yirmiyah said:** כְּתַנָּאֵי – The question of whether a beverage extracted for use in food is to be regarded as a food is a matter **of** dispute between **Tannaim.** For we have learned in a Mishnah elsewhere:[5] הַמְחַלִּיק בַּעֲנָבִים – If [A BAKER] RUBS his loaves WITH GRAPES so that the juice will give them a shiny crust, לֹא הוּכְשַׁר – [THE GRAPES] DO NOT BECOME SUSCEPTIBLE to *tumah* through contact with the juice that emerges from them.[6] רַבִּי יְהוּדָה אוֹמֵר – R' YEHUDAH SAYS: הוּכְשַׁר – THEY DO BECOME SUSCEPTIBLE to *tumah* thereby. מַאי לָאו בְּהָא קָמִיפַּלְגִי – Now, **is it not in this** issue **that they disagree?** מַר סָבַר מַשְׁקֶה הַבָּא לְאוֹכֶל אוֹכֶל הוּא – **The** one **master** (the Tanna Kamma) **holds that a beverage that is extracted for** use in **food is itself** regarded as **a food.** The juice of these grapes is therefore considered a food, since it is being extracted for use on the loaves. It thus cannot render the grapes susceptible to *tumah.*[7] וּמַר סָבַר לָאו אוֹכֶל הוּא – **But the** other **master** (R' Yehudah) **holds** that such a beverage **is not** regarded as **a food,** but as a beverage; it therefore *will* generate susceptibility to *tumah*![8] We thus see that Shmuel's principle is actually a matter of Tannaic dispute.

Rav Pappa disagrees:

אָמַר רַב פָּפָּא – **Rav Pappa said:** דְּכוּלֵּי עָלְמָא מַשְׁקֶה הַבָּא לְאוֹכֶל לָאו אוֹכֶל הוּא – No! **All** (i.e. the Tanna Kamma and R' Yehudah) **agree that a beverage that is extracted for** use in **food is not** regarded as **a food.**[9] Thus, the juice rubbed upon the loaves is certainly not a food. וְהָכָא בְּמַשְׁקֶה הַבָּא לְאִיבּוּד קָמִיפַּלְגִי – **However, they disagree here with** regard to the law **of a beverage that is extracted** only **to be discarded.**[10] מַר סָבַר מַשְׁקֶה הוּא – The one **master** (R' Yehudah) **holds that [a beverage meant to be discarded] is** legally regarded as **a beverage.** Thus, although the juice of these grapes is slated for burning, it is nonetheless a beverage, and will therefore render the grapes susceptible to *tumah.* וּמַר סָבַר לָאו מַשְׁקֶה הוּא – **But** the other **master** (i.e. the Tanna Kamma) **holds that [a beverage meant to be discarded] is not** regarded as **a beverage.** Thus, since this juice is destined for burning, it is not a beverage, and therefore does not cause the grapes to become susceptible to *tumah.* וּבִפְלוּגְתָּא דְהָנֵי תַּנָּאֵי – **And** this disagreement between the Tanna Kamma and R' Yehudah is bound up **in** another **dispute of Tannaim.** דְּתַנְיָא – **For it has been taught in a Baraisa:** הַמְפַצֵּעַ בְּזֵיתִים בְּיָדַיִם מְסוֹאָבוֹת – If ONE BRUISES OLIVES[11] WITH UNCLEAN HANDS,[12] הוּכְשַׁר – THEY BECOME SUSCEPTIBLE to *tumah* through contact with the oil that drips from them.[13] This is true if the reason he bruises them is in order

NOTES

1. Through contact with the *tamei* person who is squeezing them (*Rashi*).

2. See *Rashi* to *Pesachim* 33b ד״ה בכביצה. This Mishnah speaks of a case in which the person performing the squeezing does not come into contact with the liquid, and thus does not render it *tamei.* Although he does contaminate the fruit itself through contact, the fruit will not transmit *tumah* to its juice. For since the fruit before it is squeezed measures no more than one egg-volume, it is reduced in the first instant of squeezing to less than an egg-volume – a size incapable of generating *tumah.* However, if the person would come into contact with even the most minute drop of the liquid itself, he would render it *tamei,* since beverages are subject to *tumah* whatever their quantity (*Rashi*). [For why the liquid did not become *tamei* while it was still a part of the fruit, see *Pesachim* 33b; see also *Tosafos.*]

[The Mishnah's ruling holds true for one contaminated with any sort of contact-generated *tumah* (e.g. *tumas meis, tumas sheretz*). The reason the Mishnah singles out one contaminated with corpse *tumah* (*tumas meis*) is in order to contrast this law with the law [mentioned further on in this same Mishnah] of a *zav* who squeezes this same volume of olives or grapes. In the case of a *zav,* the juice *will* become *tamei,* since *tumas heset* does not require that the *zav* touch the juice directly, but only that he support its weight. Now, of all the types of contact-generated *tumah,* only *tumas meis* is equivalent to *zav tumah* in its ability to render articles *tamei* as an *av hatumah* can (literally: father of *tumah*). Other sorts of contact-generated *tumah,* by contrast, generate *tumah* of only a lesser degree. Thus, the Mishnah mentions one contaminated with corpse *tumah* to show that although he can generate *tumah* to the degree of *av,* he cannot render the juice *tamei,* unlike a *zav,* who can (*Rashi*).]

3. Although the Gemara derives this implication from the quoted part of the Mishnah, it is in fact stated explicitly later in the same Mishnah (see *Rashash*).

4. For why the Gemara did not give this answer to its previous challenge to Shmuel (144b), see *Rabbeinu Chananel* and *Rashba.*

5. *Maasros* 1:8.

6. *Rashi,* as explained by *Maharshal* and *Chasam Sofer;* cf. *Mesoras HaShas;* see *Rashash.*

7. [Since only a liquid with beverage status can generate susceptibility to *tumah* (see above, 143b note 32).]

8. [Since the juice of grapes is one of the seven beverages that render foods susceptible to *tumah* (see 143b ibid.).]

9. *Rashi;* cf. reading of *Ramban* and *Rashba.*

10. Which this juice is, since it is meant to be heated and evaporated in the oven (*Rashi*).

11. This is done in order to soften the olives, so that they will become sweet (*Rashi* here and to 50b ד״ה לפצוע זיתים).

12. The Rabbis decreed that with regard to contaminating *terumah* or sacrificial foods (*kodashim*), one's hands possess imposed *tumah* of a *sheni* degree (see above, 14a note 32 and *Chullin* 33a note 21 for the reason underlying this decree). The hands' ability to contaminate *kodashim* is removed by immersing them in a *mikveh;* their ability to contaminate *terumah* is removed by rinsing them with water from a vessel (see Mishnah, *Chagigah* 18b). Hands that are neither immersed nor rinsed (i.e. unclean hands) will invalidate any *terumah* or *kodashim* with which they come into contact.

13. [Thus, if the olives are of *terumah* his unclean hands will contaminate them! (but see *Rashash*).]

[The reason the olives become susceptible is that since his purpose in bruising them is to improve their flavor,] he is pleased if olive oil comes out in the process, as it adds flavor to the olives. [The oil is therefore

א) מעשרות פ"א מ"ט, ב) פ"ח לר"ג, ג) יבמות פח: ודף קכב. בכורות לו. מו:, ד) ל"ל והענבים וא"ר, ה) בפת שלוש כמו פירות ובשבט הוכשר, ו) רש"ל ועי' מהרש"א.

טו א מיי' פי"א מהלכות טומאת אוכלין הל"ד:
טז ב טוש"ע או"ח סימן של סעיף ט:
יז ג מיי' פ"ח מהלכות שבת הל"ג ופכ"א הל' יג סמג לאוין סה טוש"ע או"ח שם סעיף ז:
יח ד מיי' פ"ח שם הל"ב ופכ"א הלכה יב:
יט ה מיי' פי"ז מהלכות גרושין הלי"ג סמג עשין נ טור ש"ע אה"ע סימן יז סעיף ג:

כביצה מכוונת טהור הא יותר מכביצה טמא ואי אמרת משקה הבא לאוכל אוכל הוא במאי איתכשר הוא מותיב לה והוא מפרק לה בסוחט לתוך הקערה א"ר ירמיה כתנאי א) המחליק בענבים לא הוכשר רבי יהודה אומר הוכשר מאי לאו בהא קמיפלגי מ"ס משקה הבא לאוכל אוכל הוא ומ"ס לאו אוכל הוא אמר רב פפא דכולי עלמא משקה הבא לאוכל לאו אוכל הוא [א] והכא במשקה הבא לאיבוד קמיפלגי מר סבר משקה הוא ומ"ס לאו משקה הוא ובפלוגתא דהני תנאי דתניא א המפצע בזיתים בידים מסואבות הוכשר לסופתן במלח לא הוכשר לידע אם הגיעו זיתיו למסוק אם לאו לא הוכשר רבי יהודה אומר הוכשר מאי לאו בהא קמיפלגי דמ"ס משקה העומד לאיבוד משקה הוא ומ"ס לאו משקה הוא אמר רב הונא בריה דרב יהושע הני תנאי במשקה העומד לאיבוד פליגי והנך תנאי במשקה העומד לצחצחו קמיפלגי א"ר זירא אמר רב חייא בר אשי אמר רב סוחט אדם אשכול של ענבים לתוך הקדרה אבל לא לתוך הקערה ב ודג לצירו אפילו לתוך הקערה יתיב רב דימי וקאמר לה להא שמעתא א"ל אביי לרב דימי אתון משמיה דרב מתניתון ולא קשיא לכו אנן משמיה דשמואל מתנינן לה וקשיא לן מי אמר שמואל דג לצירו אפי' לתוך הקערה והאיתמר כבשים שסחטן אמר רב לגופן מותר למימיהן פטור אבל אסור ושלקות בין לגופן בין למימיהן מותר ושמואל אמר אחד כבשים ואחד ° שלקות לגופן מותר למימיהן פטור אבל אסור א"ל האלהים א) עיני ראו ולא זר ג) (כלו כליותי בחקי וגו') מפומיה דר' ירמיה שמיע לי ור' ירמיה מר' זירא ור' זירא מרב חייא בר אשי ורב חייא בר אשי מרב: גופא כבשים שסחטן אמר רב לגופן מותר למימיהן פטור אבל אסור ושלקות בין לגופן בין למימיהן מותר ושמואל אמר ג אחד זה ואחד זה לגופן מותר למימיהן פטור אבל אסור ורבי יוחנן אמר אחד כבשים ואחד שלקות לגופן מותר למימיהן חייב חטאת מיתיבי סוחטין כבשים בשבת לצורך השבת אבל לא למוצ"ש וזיתים וענבים לא יסחוט ואם סחט חייב חטאת קשיא לרב קשיא לשמואל קשיא לר' יוחנן רב מתרץ לטעמיה שמואל מתרץ לטעמיה ר' יוחנן מתרץ לטעמיה סוחטין כבשים בשבת לצורך השבת אבל לא למוצ"ש בד"א לגופן אבל למימיהן פטור אבל אסור ושלקות בין לגופן בין למימיהן מותר וזיתים וענבים לא יסחוט ואם סחטן חייב חטאת שמואל מתרץ לטעמיה סוחטין כבשים בשבת לצורך השבת הוא הדין לשלקות בד"א לגופן אבל למימיהן פטור אבל אסור וזיתים וענבים לא יסחוט ואם סחט חייב חטאת ר' יוחנן מתרץ לטעמיה סוחטין כבשים בשבת לצורך השבת אבל לא למוצ"ש אחד כבשים ואחד שלקות בד"א לגופן אבל למימיהן לא יסחוט ואם סחט נעשה כמי שסחט זיתים וענבים וחייב חטאת אמר רב חייא בר אשי אמר רב ד) דבר תורה אינו חייב אלא על דריסת זיתים וענבים בלבד וכן תני דבי מנשה דבר תורה אינו חייב אלא על דריסת זיתים וענבים בלבד ג) ואין עד מפי עד כשר אלא

רש"י

כביצה מכוונת טהור. משנה היא במסכת טהרות ומפרש בה בהדיא ובלבד שלא יגע במשקה שאינו נוגע אלא באוכל וכיון דכבילה מכוונת הוא לכי סחיט טיפה קמייתא חסר ליה מכבילה ואין האוכל אע"פ שהוא טמא מטמא המשקה שאין אוכל מטמא אחרים בפחות מכבילה אבל אם היה נוגע במשקה איטמי ליה משקה מטיפה ראשונה שהמשקה מקבל טומאה בכל שהוא וה"נ תני בה בהדיא יותר מכבילה טמא שכיון שיצאה טיפה ראשונה נטמאה בכבילה וטמא מת דווקא נקט שאינו מטמא בהיסט וה"ה לטמא שרץ וכל טמאי מגע וטמא מת לרבותא נקט דהוי אב הטומאה משום דקתני סיפא אבל זב שסוחט זיתים וענבים אפי' גרגיר יחידי טמא שכיון שיצאה טיפה ראשונה נטמא המשקה במשא הזב: ואי אמרת כו'. דקס"ד אפי' סוחט לתוך הקדירה: כתנאי. משקה הבא לאוכל אוכל הוא או משקה הוא: המחליק בענבים. נחתום המחליק פני ככרותיו בענבים שסוחט המשקה על הככר: הוכשר. האוכל ד) הענבים הוכשרו: הבא. לצורך אוכל כגון שסחטן לשם הפת: ה"ג דכ"ע משקה הבא לאוכל לאו אוכל הוא. אלא משקה הוא והיינו טעמא דמ"ד לא הוכשר שמתחילה נסחט אדעתא דאזיל לאיבוד שהאור שואבו ושורפו: המפצע בזיתים. בלע"ז כדי שיהיו רכין: הוכשר. דניחא ליה במשקה דטייף עלייהו שמתוך כך הם מרכים טעם: לסופתן במלח. שמתוך שהן קשין אין המלח נדבק בהן ומפצעם לרככן מבחוץ מעט: לא הוכשר. דלא מכוין למשקה דידהו דליעקר: לידע אם הגיעו זיתיו למסוק. צריך הוא לראות אם שומנו נוח לצאת מיהו המשקה אזיל לאיבוד: הני תנאי. דמפצע ודאי במשקה העומד לאיבוד פליגי כדאמרי' אבל תנאי דמחליק לאו בעומד לאיבוד פליגי דלאו לאיבוד אזל שהרי לנאות האוכל נתנו והרי מנאנו אלא במשקה העומד לנאנאו לאוכל קא מיפלגי דא"נ משקה הבא לאוכל משקה הוא ה"מ היכא דקא שריף ליה א"נ שטר ביה ריפתא דתורת משקה עביד אבל לנאנאו פליגי: ודג לצירו. סחיטת דג להוציא צירו לאו משקה הוא אלא אוכלין: כבשין. ירק חי כבוש ביין וחומץ: לגופו. אם לאכול הכבשים סוחטן ממשקה הנף עליהן והנבלע בהן מותר לכתחילה דלא מפרק הוא הואיל ולאו למשקה הוא צריך: פטור. שאין זה מפרק שאין המשקה הזה יוצא מן הכבשים שלא גדל בתוכן אבל אסור אטו זיתים וענבים: שלקות. אפילו למימיהן לאו משקה נינהו אלא אוכל: למימיהן פטור אבל אסור. והא שלקות דומיא דדג לצירן הוא ולא שרי ליה שמואל לכתחילה: עיני ראו ולא זר. הא דבעינא למימר לך דמשמיה דרב איתמר: סוחטין כבשין. ולא מפליג בין לגופן בין למימיהן ושרי לכתחילה וקשיא לכולהו דליכא בהו דשרי כבשין למימיהן לכתחילה: דבר תורה. כלומר אסרה תורה סחיטה דהויא מלאכה ודריכת זיתים וענבים הוא דהויא מלאכה אבל שאר דריכות לאו אורחייהו בהכי ולאו מלאכה נינהו:

לעדות

תוספות

כביצה מכוונת טהור. פי' בקונטרס שאע"פ שהאוכל טמא אינו מטמא את המשקה שאין אוכל מטמא בפחות מכבילה והאי טעמא לא ניחא אלא למ"ד בפרק כל שעה (פסחים דף לג: ושם) משקים מיפקד פקידי אבל למ"ד התם מיבלע בליעי טמאים המשקין מאליהן כיון שנגע באוכל ה) [ומשני התם דבמתני' איירי בענבים שלא הוכשרו לאימת מתכשרי לכי סחיט להו וכי סחיט להו בציר שעוריה והשתא לפי' רש"י מה בכך] מיד כשיצאה הטיפה ראשונה (א) נטמאה הואיל ואוכל מקבל טומאה בכל שהוא ומה שהקשה ר"ת לפירו' פי' לעיל בריש המצניע (דף לא.):

דכ"ע משקה הבא לאוכל לאו אוכל הוא. לא מצינן למימר דכ"ע אוכל הוא (ב) א"כ מ"ט דמ"ד הוכשר:

אם הגיעו זיתיו למסוק כו'. מה שקשה ליה לרב נחמן דמפרש בפ"ק (דף יז.) דגזרו לבצור בטהרה משום דפעמים שאדם הולך כו' שם פירשתי. [בד"ה גוזרי]:

כבשים שסחטן לגופן מותר למימיהן פטור אבל אסור. רב לטעמיה דאמר לקמן דבר תורה אינו חייב אלא על דריכת זיתים וענבים ולפירוש הקונטרס דפי' משום דאתי המשקה מעלמא קשה לרבי אמאי גזרו להדוקי אודרא אפומא דשישא בשלהי תולין (לעיל דף קמא.) שמא יסחוט הא אפילו סחיט ליכא איסור דאורייתא מיהו י"ל דהתם רבא דקאמר לה וס"ל כר' יוחנן דמחייב חטאת: **ורבי** יוחנן אמר אחד כבשין ואחד שלקות לגופן מותר למימיהן חייב חטאת. ובדג לצירו נמי הוה מחייב ר' יוחנן חטאת לתוך הקערה דדג לצירו מדמינן לשלקות בכולה שמעתיה דפריך מדשמואל דשלקות אההיא דדג לצירו ופי' ר"ח דהלכה כר' יוחנן דקיי"ל כוותיה לגבי רב ושמואל ושמעינן ממילתא דר"י שאסור לסחוט כבשים ושלקות למימיהן ואם סחט חייב חטאת ולא הפריש בסחיטה בין קדירה לקער' אלא הכל אסור מתוך אלו דברים מתברר שאין הלכה לא כשמואל ולא כרב שאמרו סוחט אדם אשכול של ענבים לתוך הקדירה ויש שמעמידין דברי רב ושמואל ביו"ט מדדייק רב חסדא מדברי שמואל כן ואין לנו להדורי אפריכי ולאפוקי שמעתא מדוכתיה אלא ודאי בשבת קאמרי רב ושמואל ואין הלכה כמותן לא בשבת ולא ביו"ט ע"כ פי' ר"ח ומה שדקדק מדלא מפליג ר' יוחנן משמע דמיירי אפילו לתוך הקדירה אין זה דיוק דהא רב ושמואל נמי אסרי סתמא בכבשים (ג) למימיהן ואע"ג דשרו לסחוט בהדיא אשכול של ענבים לתוך הקדירה ומה שדחה דברי המעמידין דברי רב ושמואל ביו"ט אומר ר"ת שהדין עמו אבל דברי רב חסדא ביום טוב כדפירשתי לעיל:

בהמה

רבינו חננאל

גופא כבשים שסחטן כגון ירקות וראשי לפתות וכרוב וכל הדומה להן. אמר רב לגופן מותר כלומר לסחטן כדי להסיר מימיהן ולאכלן מותר. אבל אם כוונתו למימיהן והוא צריך להן פטור אבל אסור. ושלקות כגון ירקות וכדומה להן שלקן מקודם השבת ונשארו מימיהן בהן וכן דגים מלוחין בין לגופן בין למימיהן מותר. ושמואל אמר אחד כבשים ואחד שלקות לגופן מותר למימיהן פטור אבל אסור ור' יוחנן אמר אחד כבשים ואחד שלקות לגופן מותר למימיהן חייב חטאת ומותיבנן עלייהו סוחטין כבשים בשבת לצורך השבת אבל לא למוצ"ש. זיתים וענבים לא יסחוט ואם סחט חייב חטאת קשיא לרב וקשיא לשמואל וקשיא לר' יוחנן וכל אחד מהן מתרץ מתניתא דא לטעמיה דבריהן פשוטין הן אבל אנחנו כותבין תירוץ טעמא דר' יוחנן דהלכתא כוותיה דקיי"ל כל היכא דפליגי רב ושמואל ור' יוחנן הלכה כר' יוחנן. ולפיכך מדקדקין בדבריו להעמיד הלכה על בוריה. ר' יוחנן מתרץ לטעמיה סוחטין כבשים בשבת לצורך השבת. אבל לא למוצ"ש ואחד כבשים ואחד שלקות לגופן אבל למימיהן לא יסחוט ואם סחט נעשה כמי שסחט זיתים וענבים וחייב חטאת. ולא הפריש בסחיטתן למימיהן בין קדירה לקערה אלא הכל אסור. דהא סחיטת זיתים וענבים בין לקדירה ובין לקערה הן למימיהן צריך. וא"ר יוחנן שהסוחט כבשים ושלקות למימיהן כסוחט זיתים וענבים וחייב חטאת. ומתוך אלו הדברים מתברר שאין הלכה לא כשמואל ולא כרב שאומ' סוחט אדם אשכול של ענבים לתוך הקדירה אבל לא לתוך הקערה. ויש שמעמידי דברי (רבינו) רב ושמואל ביו"ט. מדדייק רב חסדא מדברי שמואל. ואמר מדברי רבינו נלמד חולב אדם עז לתוך הקדירה אבל לא לתוך הקערה כדי לקיים דבריהם להיות הלכה ואינן דבריהם נכונים שאפילו ביו"ט כל אילו אסורין ולינק בפיו מן הבהמה ביו"ט אסור וכ"ש לחלוב כדגרסינן בסוף פרק חרש (שנשא) פקחת. אבא שאול אומר ונוהגין היינו שיונקין מן הבהמה טהורה ביו"ט ואקשינן עליה היכי דמי אי דאיכא סכנה אפילו בשבת שרי אי דליכא סכנה אפילו ביו"ט אסור. ומפרקי' לא צריכא דאית בה צערא (וסברא) [ונקסבר] מפרק כלאחר יד הוא. שבת

הגהות הב"ח

(א) תוס' ד"ה כביצה וכו' הטיפה ראשונה הוכשר האוכל ואוכל וכו' כדאיתא במכשירין. נ"ב דף לא ע"ב ד"ה אי לענין וכו': (ב) ד"ה דכ"ע וכו' דל"כ מ"ט: (ג) ד"ה ור' יוחנן וכו' אסרי סתמא בכבשים ובשלקות למימיהן:

גליון הש"ס

גמ' שלקות לגופן מותר למימיהן. עי' לעיל דף עג ע"ב תוס' ד"ה וצריך לעצים:

הגהות הגר"א

[א] גמ' משקה הבא לאוכל לאו אוכל הוא. נ"ב גירסת הגאונים אוכל הוא, עי' רשב"א ובר"ן ע"ש:

תורה אור השלם

א) אֲשֶׁר אֲנִי אֶחֱזֶה לִּי וְעֵינַי רָאוּ וְלֹא זָר כָּלוּ כִלְיֹתַי בְּחֵקִי: [איוב יט, כז]

ליקוטי רש"י

כביצה מכוונת וכו'. אוכל ומשקה מקבל טומאה בכל שהן אבל אין מטמאין אחרים אלא אוכל כביצה ומשקה ברביעית והכי תניא בתורת כהנים מכל האוכל מלמד שמטמא בכל שהוא יכול יטמא לאחרים בכל שהוא תלמוד לומר אשר יאכל אוכל הנאכל בבת אחת והיינו כביצה כדאמרינן בפרק יום הכפורים (יומא פ.) אין בית הבליעה מחזקת יותר מביצת תרנגולת ... [illegible] בעי כביצה. טהור. ובמסכת טהרות מיתניא במכבשים טהרות ובלבד שלא יגע במשקה ... [illegible] מאי הכא ... [illegible]

דאיסור סקילה הוא גזור רבנן. י"ט דאיסור לאו לא גזור רבנן. הנה אפי' לינק ביו"ט לא התירו אלא במקום שיש צער כ"ש לחלוב במקום שאין צער שודאי אסור. ואין לנו להדורי אפירכי ולאפוקי שמעתא מדוכתא אלא ודאי זה שאומר סוחט אדם לתוך הקדירה אבל לא לתוך הקערה בשבת אמרו. ושאמר רב חסדא ביו"ט הוא ואין הלכה כמותם לא בשבת ולא ביו"ט וכך קיבלנו מרבותינו והא דתנא דבי מנשה דבר תורה אינו חייב אלא על דריכת זיתים וענבים בלבד. לא קשיא הא דר' יוחנן ... [illegible] ושאר פירות דזולתי זיתים וענבים סלקא שמעתא כר' יהודה דאמר לאוכלין היוצא מהן מותר למשקין

לי ושמי מימיהם מים ... [illegible]

to sweeten them. לְסוּפְתָן בְּמֶלַח – However, if he bruises them IN ORDER TO DIP THEM INTO SALT,[14] לֹא הוּכְשַׁר – THEY DO NOT BECOME SUSCEPTIBLE.[15] לֵידַע אִם הִגִּיעוּ זֵיתָיו לְמָסוֹק אִם לָאו – Likewise, if he bruises them IN ORDER TO KNOW WHETHER OR NOT HIS OLIVES HAVE ARRIVED AT the stage when they are ready TO BE PICKED, לֹא הוּכְשַׁר – THEY DO NOT BECOME SUSCEPTIBLE.[16] רַבִּי יְהוּדָה אוֹמֵר – R' YEHUDAH SAYS: הוּכְשַׁר – Even if he bruises them in order to check whether they are ready to be picked, THEY DO BECOME SUSCEPTIBLE to *tumah* through contact with the oil that drips from them. מַאי לָאו בְּהָא קָמִיפְלְגֵי – Now, **is it not in this** issue **that they disagree?** דְּמָר סָבַר מַשְׁקֶה הָעוֹמֵד לְאִיבּוּד מַשְׁקֶה הוּא – **For** the one **master** (R' Yehudah) **holds that a beverage meant to be discarded is** regarded as **a beverage;** he therefore rules that the oil extracted from olives while checking them for ripeness will render them susceptible to *tumah.* וּמָר סָבַר לָאו מַשְׁקֶה הוּא – **But** the other **master** (the Tanna Kamma) **holds that [a beverage meant to be discarded] is not** regarded as **a beverage;** accordingly, this oil does not render the olives susceptible.

We thus see that the Tannaic dispute regarding grape juice rubbed onto a baker's loaves is identical to the one regarding the oil that oozes from bruised olives.

The Gemara takes issue with Rav Pappa's understanding of the dispute regarding juice rubbed onto a baker's loaves:

אָמַר רַב הוּנָא בְּרֵיהּ דְּרַב יְהוֹשֻׁעַ – **Rav Huna the son of Rav Yehoshua said:** הָנֵי תַּנָּאֵי בְּמַשְׁקֶה הָעוֹמֵד לְאִיבּוּד פְּלִיגֵי – **These Tannaim** that dispute the law of oil that drips from bruised olives **are** indeed **disagreeing about** whether **a beverage meant to be discarded** is regarded as a beverage. וְהָנָךְ תַּנָּאֵי בְּמַשְׁקֶה הָעוֹמֵד לְצַחְצְחוֹ קָמִיפְלְגֵי – **But those Tannaim** that dispute the law of juice rubbed on a baker's loaves **are disagreeing about** whether **a beverage meant to lend a sheen** to food is regarded as a beverage.[17] They by no means consider such juice a beverage meant to be discarded![18]

The Gemara now again cites the principle set forth by Shmuel, but this time in Rav's name:

אָמַר רַבִּי זֵירָא אָמַר רַב חִיָּיא בַּר אַשִׁי אָמַר רַב – **R' Zeira said in the name of Rav Chiya bar Ashi, who said in the name of Rav:** סוֹחֵט אָדָם אֶשְׁכּוֹל שֶׁל עֲנָבִים לְתוֹךְ הַקְּדֵרָה – **A person may squeeze a cluster of grapes into a pot** of food on the Sabbath, אֲבָל לֹא לְתוֹךְ הַקְּעָרָה – **but not into a bowl.** וְדָג לְצִירוֹ אֲפִילּוּ לְתוֹךְ הַקְּעָרָה – **However, a fish** may be squeezed **for its brine, even into a bowl.**[19]

The Gemara discusses this teaching:

יָתִיב רַב דִּימִי וְקָאָמַר לָהּ לְהָא שְׁמַעְתָּא – **Rav Dimi was sitting, and he repeated this teaching.** אָמַר לֵיהּ אַבָּיֵי לְרַב דִּימִי – **Abaye said to Rav Dimi:** אַתּוּן מִשְּׁמֵיהּ דְּרַב מַתְנִיתוּן וְלֹא קַשְׁיָא לְכוּ – **You teach** this ruling **in the name of Rav, and it** therefore **presents no difficulty for you.** אֲנַן מִשְּׁמֵיהּ דִּשְׁמוּאֵל מַתְנִינַן לַהּ וְקַשְׁיָא לַן – But **we teach [this ruling] in the name of Shmuel, and it** therefore **presents a difficulty for us!** מִי אָמַר שְׁמוּאֵל דָּג לְצִירוֹ אֲפִילּוּ לְתוֹךְ הַקְּעָרָה – **For did Shmuel** truly **say: A fish** may be squeezed **for its brine, even into a bowl?** וְהָאִיתְּמַר – **But it has been stated:** כְּבָשִׁים שֶׁסְּחָטָן – Concerning **the squeezing of pickled vegetables:**[20] אָמַר רַב – **Rav said:** לְגוּפָן – If one wishes to squeeze them **for themselves** [i.e. in order to make them ready to eat], מוּתָּר – **one is permitted** to do so.[21] לְמֵימֵיהֶן – But if one wishes to squeeze them **for their liquid,** פָּטוּר אֲבָל אָסוּר – **one is exempt** from penalty on the Biblical level, **but [the act] is prohibited** by Rabbinic decree.[22] וּשְׁלָקוֹת – **But** with regard to **boiled vegetables:** בֵּין לְגוּפָן בֵּין לְמֵימֵיהֶן – **Whether** one wishes to squeeze them **for themselves, or whether for their liquid,** מוּתָּר – **one is permitted** to do so.[23] וּשְׁמוּאֵל אָמַר – **But Shmuel**

NOTES

considered a beverage and will render food susceptible to *tumah*] (*Rashi*; see *Sfas Emes*).

14. When the olives are hard, the salt will not adhere to them; he therefore bruises them in order to soften them a bit (*Rashi*).

15. For since he has no desire in this case for the oil to come out, it is not considered a beverage if it does come out (*Rashi;* see 143b note 32).

16. In this case, he seeks to determine whether the oil is ready to flow from the olives. He therefore bruises the olives enough to allow a little oil to ooze from them. However, although he desired the emergence of this oil, it is not regarded as a beverage, since it is extracted only to be discarded. [It therefore will not generate susceptibility in the olives] (*Rashi*).

17. For even if a beverage extracted for use in food retains its beverage status, perhaps that is only true of beverages consumed in liquid form — i.e. either while mixed with food, or by having bread dipped into them and eaten. Since such consumption is a legitimate "beverage" use, a liquid consumed in this manner will be considered a beverage *even* when combined with food. But if the beverage is evaporated, and remains only in the form of a shiny crust, perhaps it will indeed be considered a food! Rav Huna sees this question as the issue engaging these Tannaim. R' Yehudah holds that a beverage used to lend a sheen to a crust is a beverage; he accordingly rules the grapes susceptible to *tumah.* The Tanna Kamma, however, does not consider this a true beverage use; the juice is therefore a food and will not render the grapes susceptible (*Rashi;* see *Maharsha* and *Hagahos R' Yaakov Emden*).

18. For since the juice is smeared onto the loaves for a purpose, and it in fact accomplishes that purpose, it cannot be considered a substance meant to be discarded! (*Rashi*).

19. Fish brine is not regarded as a beverage but as a food (*Rashi*). [One is therefore permitted to squeeze it from the fish, as one is merely extracting one food from another.]

20. This refers to raw vegetables pickled in wine or vinegar (*Rashi*).

21. Thus, one who wishes to eat the pickled vegetables is permitted to squeeze them to remove the wine or vinegar that coats them or that is absorbed within them. For the *melachah* of *threshing* and, by extension, that of *extracting,* applies only to cases in which one desires the extraction of an item for its own sake [such as in the case of a kernel extracted from its husk] (*Rashi; Tosafos* to 73b ד"ה וצריך לעצים).

22. The reason one who squeezes these vegetables in order to obtain their liquid is exempt from penalty is because the *melachah* of *threshing,* and likewise of *extracting,* applies only to cases in which the item being extracted came into existence while within its covering [just as kernels grow inside their husks]. But the liquid being extracted from the pickled vegetables did not originally grow there, but was introduced from without! [One is therefore not liable for squeezing it out] (*Rashi;* cf. *Tosafos*). The Rabbis nonetheless forbade one to squeeze these vegetables, lest one be led to squeeze olives or grapes, whose squeezing is prohibited by Biblical law (*Rashi*).

[*Ritva* (*MHK* ed.) challenges *Rashi's* explanation on the basis of our Mishnah, which states that one is prohibited to sponge up spilled wine by Rabbinic decree, lest one be led to squeeze out the sponge. But according to *Rashi,* squeezing out a sponge is permissible by Biblical law, since the wine did not come into existence while inside the sponge! (See *Tosafos* and *Ritva* for a similar challenge from the Gemara (141a) that prohibits stuffing a rag into a barrel spigot because of the danger of squeezing out wine.) *Sfas Emes* suggests (based on *Rosh*) that the liquid is required to have grown within the item *only* in the case of fruits and vegetables; one who extracts liquid from other items, however, such as rags and sponges, will be liable even if the liquid did not grow within them (see *Sfas Emes* for further discussion).]

[*Tosafos* and *Ritva* (*MHK* ed.) do not agree that the *melachah* of *extracting* applies only to items that grew within their covering. They hold that the reason Rav exempts one who squeezes pickled or boiled vegetables from Biblical penalty is because the liquid absorbed in these vegetables is not regarded as a beverage, since these items are not normally squeezed for their juice (as Rav himself states below; see note 29).]

23. Rav holds that [since people do not generally squeeze boiled vegetables,] the liquid they contain is viewed not as a beverage, but as a food. One is therefore permitted to squeeze the vegetables for the purpose of obtaining the liquid [as he is merely extracting one food from another] (*Rashi*). The liquid contained in pickled vegetables, by contrast, is regarded as a beverage, since such vegetables are commonly squeezed

מסורת הש"ס

א) מעשרות פ"א מ"ס, ב) פ"א ל"ג, ג) יבמות מו: ודף קכב. בכורות לו. מו:, ד) ל"ל הענבים ולאחר כמה שנלוס כמי פירות ונכבשו הוכשר, ה) רש"ל ועי' מהרש"ל.

הגהות הב"ח

(א) תוס' ד"ה כבילה וכו' הטיפה ראשונה הוכשר הואיל ואוכל וכו' ברים המלניע. נ"ב דף לג לף ד"ה אי לענין וכו': (ב) ד"ה דכ"ע וכו' דא"כ מ"ט: (ג) ד"ה ור' יוחנן וכו' אסרי סתמא בכבשים ושלקות למימיהן:

גליון הש"ס

גמ' שלקות לגופן מותר למימיהן. עי' לעיל קמג ע"ב תוס' ד"ה ולריך לעיין:

הגהות הגר"א

[א] גמ' משקה הבא לאוכל לאו אוכל הוא. נ"ב גירסת הגאונים אוכל הוא. עי' רשב"א וכ"כ הרי"ף ע"ש.

תורה אור השלם

א) אֲשֶׁר אֲנִי אֶחֱזֶה לִּי וְעֵינַי רָאוּ וְלֹא זָר כָּלוּ כִלְיֹתַי בְּחֵקִי: [איוב יט, כז]

ליקוטי רש"י

כביצה מכוונת וכו'. אוכל ומשקה מקבל טומאה בכל שהן אבל אין מטמא אחרים אלא אוכל כביצה ומשקה ברביעית והכי תניא בתורת כהנים מכל האוכל אשר יאכל מלמד שמטמא בכל שהוא יכול יטמא לאחרים בכל שהוא תלמוד לומר אשר יאכל אוכל הנאכל בבת אחת והיינו כביצה כדאמרינן בפרק יום הכפורים (יומא פ.) אין בית הבליעה מחזקת יותר מביצת תרנגולת ואמר שמעתי דאף לקבל טומאה בעי כביצה. טהור. ובמשקה מיירי במסכת טהרות ובלבד שלא יגע במשקה ובגון שדרכו בכשיעור כלל עד שאין מטמאין שאין כאן מטמא משקה אלא האוכל שנגע במשקה קודם לכן כדים שהוא לא מכר אלא משקה משקה והמשקה נוגעין בזגין ככר מפר שיעור כביצה ויותר מכביצה כל דהו קתני המסלך כל שהוא משום שילאה טפה ראשונה נטמאה המשקה בכבילה שעדיין היה האוכל כביצה אף על גב דלאו משקה הנבלע באוכל מקבל את שיעורו דכתובות מכן הכס טובא והמכוונות (נד:) נמי מיתי לה בגמרא כביצה אוכלין שכניסו בכמה והמכונוס לאו ופיגול ונותר זור והניקן בגגמסים ותפמו טמאין וחייבין עליהן משום פיגול ונותר ומלב ואף על גב דגגמסים הנבלעין במוגו אלא לבד ושפי מיניהו כיון שלאו המתקבל בהדו דלוקה לא:

רש"י

כביצה מכוונת טהור. משנה היא במסכת טהרות ומפרש בה בהדיא ובלבד שלא יגע במשקה שאינו נוגע אלא באוכל וכיון דכבילה מכוונת הוא לכי סחיט טיפה קמייתא חסר ליה מכבילה ואין האוכל אע"פ שהוא טמא מטמא המשקה שאין אוכל מטמא אחרים בפחות מכבילה אבל אם היה נוגע במשקה איטמי ליה משקה מטיפה ראשונה שהמשקה מקבל טומאה בכל שהוא וה"נ תני בה בהדיא יותר מכבילה טמא שכיון שילאה טיפה ראשונה נטמאה בכבילה וטמא מת דווקא נקט שאינו מטמא בהיסט וה"ה לטמא שרץ וכל טמאי מגע וטמא מת לרבותא נקט דהוי אב הטומאה משום דקתני סיפא אבל זב שסוחט זיתים וענבים אפי' גרגיר יחידי טמא שכיון שילאה טיפה ראשונה נטמא המשקה במשא הזב: ואי אמרת כו'. דקס"ד אפי' סוחט לתוך הקדירה: כתנאי. משקה הבא לאוכל אוכל הוא או משקה הוא: המחליק בענבים. נחתום המחליק פני ככרותיו בענבים שסוחט המשקה על הככר: הוכשר. האוכל ד) הענבים הוכשרו: הבא. לצורך אוכל כגון שסחטן לשם הפת: ה"ג דכ"ע משקה הבא לאוכל לאו אוכל הוא. אלא משקה הוא והיינו טעמא דמ"ד לא הוכשר שמתחילה נסחט אדעתא דאזיל לאיבוד שהאור שואבו ושורפו: המפצע בזיתים. בלע"ז כדי שיהיו רכין: הוכשר. דניחא ליה במשקה דטייף עלייהו שמתוך כך הס מרכים טעם: לסופתן במלח. שמתוך שהן קשין אין המלח נדבק בהן ומפצעם לרככן מבחוץ מעט: לא הוכשר. דלא מכוין למשקה דידהו דליעקר: לידע אם הגיעו זיתיו למסוק. צריך הוא לראות אם שומנו נוח לצאת מיהו המשקה אזיל לאיבוד: הני תנאי. דמפצע ודאי במשקה העומד לאיבוד פליגי כדאמרי' אבל תנאי דמחליק לאו בעומד לאיבוד פליגי דלאו לאיבוד אזל שהרי לנאת האוכל נתנו והרי מנאנאו אלא במשקה העומד לנאנאו לאוכל קא מיפלגי דא"נ משקה הבא לאוכל משקה הוא ה"מ היכא דקא צריך ליה א"נ שטר ביה ריפתא דתורת משקה עביד אבל לנאנאו פליגי: ודג לצירו. סחיטת דג להוציא צירו לאו משקה הוא אלא אוכלין: כבשין. ירק חי כבוש ביין וחומץ: לגופו. אם לאכול הכבשים סוחטן ממשקה הצף עליהן והנבלע בהן מותר לכתחילה דלא מפרק הוא הואיל ולאו למשקה הוא צריך: פטור. שאין זה מפרק שאין המשקה הזה יוצא מן הכבשים שלא גדל בתוכן אבל אסור אטו זיתים וענבים: שלקות. אפילו למימיהן לאו משקה נינהו אלא אוכל: למימיהן פטור אבל אסור. והא שלקות דומיא דדג לצירן הוא ולא שרי ליה שמואל לכתחילה: עיני ראו ולא זר. הא דבעינא למימר לך דמשמיה דרב איתמר: סוחטין כבשין. ולא מפליג בין לגופן בין למימיהן ושרי לכתחילה וקשיא לכולהו דליכא בהו דשרי כבשין למימיהן לכתחילה: דבר תורה. כלומר אסרה תורה מלאכה ודריכת זיתים וענבים הוא דהויא מלאכה אבל שאר דריכות לאו אורחייהו בהכי ולאו מלאכה נינהו:

לעדות

תוספות

כביצה מכוונת טהור. פי' בקונטרס שאע"פ שהאוכל טמא אינו מטמא את המשקה שאין אוכל מטמא בפחות מכבילה והאי טעמא לא ניחא אלא למ"ד בפרק כל שעה (פסחים דף לג: ושם) משקים מיפקד פקידי אבל למ"ד התם מיבלע בליעי טמאים המשקין מאליהן כיון שנגע באוכל ה) [ומשני התם דבמתני' מיירי בענבים שלא הוכשרו לאימת מתכשרי לכי סחיט להו וכי סחיט להו בליר שעוריה והשתא לפי' רש"י מה בכך] מיד כשילאה הטיפה ראשונה (א) נטמאה הואיל ואוכל מקבל טומאה בכל שהוא ומה שהקשה ר"ת לפירו' פי' לעיל בריש המלניע (דף לא.):

דכ"ע משקה הבא לאוכל לאו אוכל הוא. לא מלינן למימר דכ"ע אוכל הוא (ב) א"כ מ"ט דמ"ד הוכשר:

אם הגיעו זיתיו למסוק כו'. מה שקשה ליה לרב נחמן דמפרש בפ"ק (דף יז.) דגזרו לבלור בטהרה משום דפעמים שאדם הולך כו' שם פירשתי. [בד"ה גחרמי]:

כבשים שסחטן לגופן מותר למימיהן פטור אבל אסור. רב לטעמיה דאמר לקמן דבר תורה אינו חייב אלא על דריכת זיתים וענבים ולפירוש הקונטרס דפי' משום דאתי המשקה מעלמא קשה לרבי אמאי גזרו להדוקי אודרא אפומא דשישא בשלהי תולין (לעיל דף קמא.) שמא יסחוט הא אפילו סחיט ליכא איסור דאורייתא מיהו י"ל דהתם רבא דקאמר לה וס"ל כר' יוחנן דמחייב חטאת:

ורבי יוחנן אמר אחד כבשין ואחד שלקות לגופן מותר למימיהן חייב חטאת. ובדג לצירו נמי הוה מחייב ר' יוחנן חטאת לתוך הקערה דדג לצירו מדמינן לשלקות בסוגיא שמעתיה דפריך מדשמואל דשלקות אההיא דדג לצירו ופי' ר"ח דהלכה כר' יוחנן דקיי"ל כוותיה לגבי רב ושמואל ושמעינן ממילתא דר"י שאסור לסחוט כבשים ושלקות למימיהן ואם סחט חייב חטאת ולא הפריש בסחיטה בין קדירה לקער' אלא הכל אסור מתוך אלו דברים מתברר שאין הלכה לא כשמואל ולא כרב שאמרו סוחט אדם אשכול של ענבים לתוך הקדירה ויש שמעמידין דברי רב ושמואל ביו"ט מדדייק רב חסדא מדברי שמואל כן ואין לנו להדורי אפריכי ולאפוקי שמעתא מדוכתיה אלא ודאי בשבת קאמרי רב ושמואל ואין הלכה כמותן לא בשבת ולא ביו"ט ע"כ פי' ר"ח ומה שדקדק מדלא מפליג ר' יוחנן משמע דמיירי אפילו לתוך הקדירה אין זה דיוק דהא רב ושמואל נמי אסרי סתמא בכבשים (ג) למימיהן ולא"ג דשרו לסחוט בהדיא אשכול של ענבים לתוך הקדירה ומה שדחה דברי המעמידין דברי רב ושמואל ביו"ט אומר ר"ת שהדין עמו אבל דברי רב חסדא ביום טוב כדפירשתי לעיל:

בהמה

גמרא

כביצה מכוונת טהור הא יותר מכביצה טמא ואי אמרת משקה הבא לאוכל אוכל הוא במאי איתכשר הוא מותיב לה והוא מפרק לה בסוחט לתוך הקערה א"ר ירמיה כתנאי [א] המחליק בענבים לא הוכשר רבי יהודה אומר הוכשר מאי לאו בהא קמיפלגי מ"ס משקה הבא לאוכל אוכל הוא ומ"ס לאו אוכל הוא אמר רב פפא דכולי עלמא [א] משקה הבא לאוכל לאו אוכל הוא והכא במשקה הבא לאיבוד קמיפלגי מר סבר משקה הוא ומ"ס לאו משקה הוא ובפלוגתא דהני תנאי דתניא [א] המפצע בזיתים בידים מסואבות הוכשר לסופתן במלח לא הוכשר לידע אם הגיעו זיתיו למסוק אם לאו לא הוכשר רבי יהודה אומר הוכשר מאי לאו בהא קמיפלגי דמ"ס משקה העומד לאיבוד משקה הוא ומ"ס לאו משקה הוא אמר רב הונא בריה דרב יהושע הני תנאי במשקה העומד לאיבוד פליגי והנך תנאי במשקה העומד לצחצחו קמיפלגי א"ר זירא אמר רב חייא בר אשי אמר רב סוחט אדם אשכול של ענבים לתוך הקדרה אבל לא לתוך הקערה [ב] ודג לצירו אפילו לתוך הקערה יתיב רב דימי וקאמר לה להא שמעתא א"ל אביי לרב דימי אתון משמיה דרב מתניתון ולא קשיא לכו אנן משמיה דשמואל מתנינן לה וקשיא לן מי אמר שמואל דג לצירו אפי' לתוך הקערה והאיתמר כבשים שסחטן אמר רב לגופן מותר למימיהן פטור אבל אסור ושלקות בין לגופן בין למימיהן מותר ושמואל אמר כבשים ואחד שלקות לגופן מותר למימיהן פטור אבל אסור א"ל האלהים [א] עיני ראו ולא זר [ג] (כלו כליותי בחקי וגו') מפומיה דר' ירמיה שמיע לי ור' ירמיה מר' זירא ור' זירא מרב חייא בר אשי ורב חייא בר אשי מרב: גופא כבשים שסחטן אמר רב לגופן מותר למימיהן פטור אבל אסור ושלקות בין לגופן בין למימיהן מותר ושמואל אמר [ג] אחד זה ואחד זה לגופן מותר למימיהן פטור אבל אסור ורבי יוחנן אמר אחד כבשים ואחד שלקות לגופן מותר למימיהן חייב חטאת מיתיבי סוחטין כבשים בשבת לצורך השבת אבל לא למוצ"ש וזיתים וענבים לא יסחוט ואם סחט חייב חטאת קשיא לרב קשיא לשמואל קשיא לר' יוחנן רב מתרץ לטעמיה שמואל מתרץ לטעמיה ר' יוחנן מתרץ לטעמיה רב מתרץ לטעמיה סוחטין כבשים בשבת לצורך השבת אבל לא למוצ"ש בד"א לגופן אבל למימיהן פטור אבל אסור ושלקות בין לגופן בין למימיהן מותר וזיתים וענבים לא יסחוט ואם סחט חייב חטאת שמואל מתרץ לטעמיה סוחטין כבשים בשבת לצורך השבת הוא הדין לשלקות בד"א לגופן אבל למימיהן פטור אבל אסור וזיתים וענבים לא יסחוט ואם סחט חייב חטאת ר' יוחנן מתרץ לטעמיה סוחטין כבשים לצורך השבת אבל לא למוצ"ש אחד כבשים ואחד שלקות בד"א לגופן אבל למימיהן לא יסחוט ואם סחט נעשה כמי שסחט זיתים וענבים וחייב חטאת אמר רב חייא בר אשי אמר רב [ד] דבר תורה אינו חייב אלא על דריסת זיתים וענבים בלבד וכן תני דבי מנשה דבר תורה אינו חייב אלא על דריסת זיתים וענבים בלבד [ג] [ה] ואין עד מפי עד כשר אלא

עין משפט נר מצוה

טו א מיי' פ"י מהלכות טומאת אוכלין הל"ד:
טז ב טוש"ע או"ח סימן שכ סעיף ח:
יז ג מיי' פ"ח מהלכות שבת הלי"א ופכ"א הל' יב סמג לאוין סה טוש"ע או"ח סי' שכ סעיף ז:
יח ד מיי' פ"ח שם הל"י ופכ"א הלכה יב:
יט ה מיי' פי"א מהלכות גרושין הלכ"ט סמג עשין נ טור ש"ע אה"ע סימן יז סעיף ג:

רבינו חננאל

גופא כבשים שסחטן כגון ירקות וראשי לפתות וכרוב וכל הדומה להן. אמר רב לגופן מותר כלומר סחטן להסיר מימיהן ולאכלן מותר. אבל אם כוונתו למימיהן והוא צריך פטור אבל אסור. ושלקות כגון ירקות וכדומה להן שלקן מקודם השבת ונשארו מימיהן בהן וכן דגים מלוחין בין לגופן בין למימיהן מותר. ושמואל אמר אחד כבשים ואחד שלקות לגופן מותר למימיהן פטור אבל אסור ור' יוחנן אמר אחד כבשים וא' שלקות לגופן מותר למימיהן חייב חטאת ומותבינן עלייהו סוחטין כבשים בשבת לצורך השבת אבל לא למוצ"ש. זיתים וענבים לא יסחוט ואם סחט חייב חטאת קשיא לרב וקשיא לשמואל וקשיא לר' יוחנן וכל אחד מהן מתרץ מתניתא דא לטעמיה ודבריהם פשוטין הן אבל אנחנו כותבין תירוץ טעמא דר' יוחנן דהלכתא כוותיה דקיי"ל כל היכא דפליגי רב ושמואל ור' יוחנן הלכה כר' יוחנן. ולפיכך מדקדקין בדבריו להעמיד הלכה על בוריו. ר' יוחנן מתרץ לטעמיה סוחטין כבשים בשבת לצורך השבת. אבל לא למוצ"ש ואחד כבשים ואחד שלקות לגופן אבל למימיהן לא יסחוט ואם סחט נעשה כמי שסחט זיתים וענבים וחייב חטאת. ולא הפריש בסחיטתן למימיהן בין קדירה לקערה אלא הכל אסור. דהא סחיטה זיתים וענבים בין לקדירה ובין לקערה למימיהן הוא צריך. וא"ר יוחנן שהסוחט כבשים ושלקות למימיהן כסוחט זיתים וענבים וחייב חטאת. ומתוך אלו הדברים מתברר שאין הלכה לא כשמואל ולא כרב שאומ' סוחט אדם אשכול של ענבים לתוך הקדירה אבל לא לתוך הקערה. ויש שמעמידי דברי (רבינו) רב ושמואל ביו"ט. מדדייק רב חסדא מדברי שמואל. ואמר מדברי רבינו נלמד חולב אדם עז לתוך הקדירה אבל לא לתוך הקערה כדי לקיים דבריהם להיות הלכה ואינן דבריהם נכונים שאפילו ביו"ט כל אלו אסורין ולינק בפיו מן הבהמה ביו"ט אסור וכ"ש לחלוב כדגרסינן בסוף פרק חרש [שנשא] פקחת. אבא שאול אומר ונוהגין היינו שיונקין מן הבהמה טהורה ביו"ט ואקשינן עליה היכי דמי אי דאיכא סכנה אפילו בשבת שרי אי דליכא סכנה אפילו ביו"ט אסור. ומפרקי' לא צריכא דאית בה צערא (וסברא) [וקסבר] מפרק כלאחר יד הוא. שבת

חשק שלמה / חדושי

ואנרי מכם הוא קומח במשה ולה ולן לאוכליה. אלא כבש מחייב. טומאה: מטומס ויפגל, ונתבא כין כפי רבי' הכל לף לבסוף להגוינן לכס שהוא אי שולין והגבו למה הא לס מטומאת בכיבה. טהור מטמאת בהיסטפ ו ולמה לף לכנוף פלולת מכ שמת מתכמה זו מסכתות לשביתה מלולה. גל ז למטומאת האוכלין מטומאת האם לאוכל מטומא שני כולם אין מטמא טומאה של מוכל בקי"ש בשרוף מנמח את כדו נוחס מלא מוכן.

דאיסור סקילה הוא גזור רבנן. י"ט דאיסור לאו לא גזור רבנן. הנה אפי' לינק ביו"ט לא התירו אלא במקום שיש צער כ"ש לחלוב במקום שאין צער שהוא אסור. ואין לנו להדורי אפירכי ולאפוקי שמעתא מדוכתא אלא ודאי זה שאומר סוחט אדם לתוך הקדירה אבל לא לתוך הקערה בשבת אמרו. ושאמר רב חסדא ביו"ט הוא ואין הלכה כמותן לא בשבת ולא ביו"ט וכן קיבלנו מרבותינו וכן הלכה ואם הדבר ידוע הוא שמה בשבת אלא על דריכת זיתים וענבים בלבד. לא קשיא הא דר' יוחנן ז) ושאר פירות זולתי זיתים וענבים סלקא שמעתא כר' יהודה דאמר לאוכלין היוצא מהן מותר למשקין

said: אֶחָד כְּבָשִׁים וְאֶחָד שְׁלָקוֹת – Concerning **both pickled and boiled vegetables:** לְגוּפָן מוּתָּר – If one wishes to squeeze them **for themselves, one is permitted** to do so; לְמֵימֵיהֶן פָּטוּר אֲבָל אָסוּר – but if he wishes to squeeze them **for their liquid, one is exempt** from penalty, **but [the act] is prohibited** by Rabbinic decree.[24] Now, the law concerning fish brine is equivalent to that concerning the liquid contained in boiled vegetables. Why then does Shmuel permit squeezing a fish for its brine, yet prohibit squeezing boiled vegetables for their liquid? The fact that we teach the law of fish brine in the name of Shmuel thus presents a difficulty for us!

Rav Dimi replies:

אָמַר לֵיהּ – **[Rav Dimi] said to him:** הָאֱלֹהִים – **By God!** "עֵינַי רָאוּ וְלֹא־זָר" (כלו כליתי בחקי וגו׳) – ***My eyes saw, and not a stranger's!***[25] מִפּוּמֵיהּ דְּרַבִּי יִרְמְיָה שְׁמִיעַ לִי – For I myself **heard** this ruling **from the mouth of R' Yirmiyah,** וְרַבִּי יִרְמְיָה מֵרַבִּי זֵירָא – **and R' Yirmiyah from R' Zeira,** וְרַבִּי זֵירָא מֵרַב חִיָּיא בַּר אַשִׁי – **and R' Zeira from Rav Chiya bar Ashi,** וְרַב חִיָּיא בַּר אַשִׁי מֵרַב – **and Rav Chiya bar Ashi** heard it directly **from Rav!** I can therefore testify that it was in fact not Shmuel who taught the law of squeezing a fish for its brine, but Rav! This ruling thus does not represent a contradiction to Shmuel's ruling concerning boiled vegetables.

The Gemara now returns to discuss in greater detail the dispute between Rav and Shmuel regarding squeezing pickled or boiled vegetables:

גּוּפָא – **The text itself** stated: כְּבָשִׁים שֶׁסְּחָטָן – Concerning **the squeezing of pickled vegetables:** אָמַר רַב – **Rav said:** לְגוּפָן – If one wishes to squeeze them **for themselves** [i.e. in order to make them ready to eat], מוּתָּר – **one is permitted** to do so. לְמֵימֵיהֶן – But if one wishes to squeeze them **for their liquid,** פָּטוּר אֲבָל אָסוּר – **one is exempt** from penalty on the Biblical level, **but [the act] is prohibited** by Rabbinic decree. וּשְׁלָקוֹת – **But** with regard to **boiled vegetables:** בֵּין לְגוּפָן בֵּין לְמֵימֵיהֶן – **Whether** one wishes to squeeze them **for themselves, or whether for their liquid,** מוּתָּר – **one is permitted** to do so. וּשְׁמוּאֵל אָמַר – **But Shmuel said:** אֶחָד זֶה וְאֶחָד זֶה – Concerning **both these and those** [i.e. both pickled and boiled vegetables]: לְגוּפָן מוּתָּר – If one wishes to squeeze them **for themselves, he is permitted** to do so; לְמֵימֵיהֶן פָּטוּר אֲבָל אָסוּר – but if he wishes to squeeze them **for their liquid, one is exempt** from penalty on the Biblical level, **but [the act] is prohibited** by Rabbinic decree.

The Gemara introduces a third opinion:

רַבִּי יוֹחָנָן אָמַר – **R' Yochanan said:** אֶחָד כְּבָשִׁים וְאֶחָד שְׁלָקוֹת – Concerning **both pickled and boiled vegetables:** לְגוּפָן מוּתָּר – If one wishes to squeeze them **for themselves, one is permitted** to do so.[26] לְמֵימֵיהֶן חַיָּיב חַטָּאת – But if he squeezes them **for their liquid, one is liable to a *chatas*** for doing so.[27]

The Gemara challenges the opinions of all these three Amoraim:

מֵיתִיבֵי – **They challenged** the rulings of Rav, Shmuel and R' Yochanan on the basis of the following Baraisa: סוֹחֲטִין כְּבָשִׁים בְּשַׁבָּת לְצוֹרֶךְ הַשַּׁבָּת – WE MAY SQUEEZE PICKLED VEGETABLES ON THE SABBATH FOR USE ON THE SABBATH, אֲבָל לֹא לְמוֹצָאֵי שַׁבָּת – BUT NOT FOR use after THE DEPARTURE OF THE SABBATH.[28] וְזֵיתִים וַעֲנָבִים – BUT with regard to squeezing OLIVES OR GRAPES, לֹא יִסְחוֹט – ONE MAY NOT SQUEEZE them on the Sabbath at all. וְאִם סָחַט – AND IF ONE DID SQUEEZE them on the Sabbath, חַיָּיב חַטָּאת – ONE IS LIABLE TO A *CHATAS*. Now, this Baraisa does not distinguish between one who squeezes pickled vegetables in order to obtain their liquid and one who does so in order to render them fit to eat, but states simply that squeezing them is permissible. This implies that one is even permitted to squeeze these vegetables for their liquid. But Rav, Shmuel and R' Yochanan all state the opposite! קַשְׁיָא לְרַב – Thus, this Baraisa represents **a difficulty for Rav,** קַשְׁיָא לִשְׁמוּאֵל – **a difficulty for Shmuel** קַשְׁיָא לְרַבִּי יוֹחָנָן – and **a difficulty for R' Yochanan!**

The Gemara answers:

רַב מְתָרֵץ לְטַעְמֵיהּ – **Rav resolves** the difficulty **according to his opinion,** שְׁמוּאֵל מְתָרֵץ לְטַעְמֵיהּ – **Shmuel resolves** the difficulty **according to his opinion** רַבִּי יוֹחָנָן מְתָרֵץ לְטַעְמֵיהּ – and **R' Yochanan resolves** the difficulty **according to his opinion.**

The Gemara elaborates:

רַב מְתָרֵץ לְטַעְמֵיהּ – **Rav resolves** the difficulty **according to his opinion** by emending the Baraisa in this manner: סוֹחֲטִין כְּבָשִׁים בְּשַׁבָּת לְצוֹרֶךְ הַשַּׁבָּת אֲבָל לֹא לְמוֹצָאֵי שַׁבָּת – WE MAY SQUEEZE PICKLED VEGETABLES ON THE SABBATH FOR USE ON THE SABBATH, BUT NOT FOR use after THE DEPARTURE OF THE SABBATH. בַּמֶּה דְּבָרִים אֲמוּרִים – WHEN ARE THESE WORDS SAID? לְגוּפָן – With regard to squeezing the vegetables FOR THEMSELVES. אֲבָל לְמֵימֵיהֶן – BUT with regard to squeezing them FOR THEIR LIQUID, פָּטוּר אֲבָל אָסוּר – ONE IS EXEMPT from penalty on the Biblical level, BUT [THE ACT] IS PROHIBITED by Rabbinic decree. וּשְׁלָקוֹת – BUT with regard to BOILED VEGETABLES, בֵּין לְגוּפָן בֵּין לְמֵימֵיהֶן מוּתָּר – WHETHER one wishes to squeeze them FOR THEMSELVES OR WHETHER FOR THEIR JUICE, HE IS PERMITTED to do so. וְזֵיתִים וַעֲנָבִים – BUT with regard to squeezing OLIVES OR GRAPES, לֹא יִסְחוֹט – ONE MAY NOT SQUEEZE them on the Sabbath at all. וְאִם סָחַט חַיָּיב חַטָּאת – AND IF ONE DID SQUEEZE them on the Sabbath, HE IS LIABLE TO A *CHATAS*.

שְׁמוּאֵל מְתָרֵץ לְטַעְמֵיהּ – **Shmuel resolves** the difficulty **according to his opinion,** by emending the Baraisa in this manner: סוֹחֲטִין כְּבָשִׁים בְּשַׁבָּת לְצוֹרֶךְ הַשַּׁבָּת – WE MAY SQUEEZE PICKLED VEGETABLES ON THE SABBATH FOR USE ON THE SABBATH. הוּא הַדִּין לִשְׁלָקוֹת – THE SAME APPLIES TO BOILED VEGETABLES! בַּמֶּה דְּבָרִים אֲמוּרִים – WHEN ARE THESE WORDS SAID? לְגוּפָן – With regard to squeezing the vegetables FOR THEMSELVES. אֲבָל לְמֵימֵיהֶן – BUT with regard to squeezing them FOR THEIR LIQUID, פָּטוּר אֲבָל אָסוּר – ONE IS EXEMPT from penalty for doing so, BUT [THE ACT] IS PROHIBITED by Rabbinic law. וְזֵיתִים וַעֲנָבִים – BUT with regard to squeezing OLIVES OR GRAPES, לֹא יִסְחוֹט – ONE MAY NOT SQUEEZE them on the Sabbath at all.

NOTES

for their juices (see *Rashi* ד״ה פטור, and *Tosafos* ד״ה כבשים). [The Rabbis therefore prohibited one to squeeze it out, lest one be led thereby to squeeze juice from grapes or olives.]

24. [Shmuel views both pickled *and* boiled vegetables as items that it is usual to squeeze. He therefore regards the liquid contained in either of these vegetables as a beverage, and thus rules that one is prohibited by Rabbinic decree from squeezing it out, lest one come to squeeze juice from grapes or olives.]

25. *Job* 19:27. [Rav Dimi, in asserting the veracity of his account, couched his response in the words of this verse.]

26. See above, note 21, for why this is so.

27. [R' Yochanan holds that one is liable for squeezing out even a beverage that did not originally come into existence within the fruit (see note 22).] He holds further that both pickled and boiled vegetables are items that it is usual to squeeze [as does Shmuel] (*Beur Halachah* to 320:7 ד״ה ולר״ח; see *Chazon Ish, Orach Chaim* 55:4). Since the juice of these vegetables is accordingly deemed a beverage, one who squeezes it out will be liable. [For an entirely divergent explanation of R' Yochanan's position, see *Rabbeinu Chananel* with *Tosafos;* see also *Sfas Emes; Shevisas HaShabbos* p. 44a; *Ben Uri.*]

28. [Because of the prohibition against preparing on the Sabbath for the weekdays (see above, 113a note 29).]

כביצה מכוונת טהור הא יותר מכביצה טמא ואי אמרת משקה הבא לאוכל אוכל הוא במאי איתכשר הוא מותיב לה והוא מפרק לה בסוחט לתוך הקערה א"ר ירמיה כתנאי המחליק בענבים לא הוכשר רבי יהודה אומר הוכשר מאי לאו בהא קמיפלגי מ"ס משקה הבא לאוכל אוכל הוא ומ"ס לאו אוכל הוא אמר רב פפא דכולי עלמא [א] משקה הבא לאוכל לאו אוכל הוא והכא במשקה הבא לאיבוד קמיפלגי מר סבר משקה הוא ומ"ס לאו משקה הוא ובפלוגתא דהני תנאי דתניא המפצע בזיתים בידים מסואבות הוכשר לסופתן במלח לא הוכשר לידע אם הגיעו זיתיו למסוק אם לאו לא הוכשר רבי יהודה אומר הוכשר מאי לאו בהא קמיפלגי דמ"ס משקה העומד לאיבוד משקה הוא ומ"ס לאו משקה הוא אמר רב הונא בריה דרב יהושע הני תנאי במשקה העומד לאיבוד פליגי והנך תנאי במשקה העומד לצחצחו קמיפלגי א"ר זירא אמר רב חייא בר אשי אמר רב סוחט אדם אשכול של ענבים לתוך הקדרה אבל לא לתוך הקערה ודג לצירו אפילו לתוך הקערה יתיב רב דימי וקאמר לה להא שמעתא א"ל אביי לרב דימי אתון משמיה דרב מתניתון ולא קשיא לכו אנן משמיה דשמואל מתנינן לה וקשיא לן מי אמר שמואל דג לצירו אפי' לתוך הקערה והאיתמר כבשים שסחטן אמר רב לגופן מותר למימיהן פטור אבל אסור ושלקות בין לגופן בין למימיהן מותר ושמואל אמר אחד כבשים ואחד שלקות לגופן מותר למימיהן פטור אבל אסור א"ל האלהים א) עיני ראו ולא זר (כלו כליותי בחקי וגו') מפומיה דר' ירמיה שמיע לי ור' ירמיה מר' זירא ור' זירא מרב חייא בר אשי ורב חייא בר אשי מרב: גופא כבשים שסחטן אמר רב לגופן מותר למימיהן פטור אבל אסור ושלקות בין לגופן בין למימיהן מותר ושמואל אמר אחד זה ואחד זה לגופן מותר למימיהן פטור אבל אסור ורבי יוחנן אמר אחד כבשים ואחד שלקות לגופן מותר למימיהן חייב חטאת מיתיבי סוחטין כבשים בשבת לצורך השבת אבל לא למוצ"ש וזיתים וענבים לא יסחוט ואם סחט חייב חטאת קשיא לרב קשיא לשמואל קשיא לר' יוחנן רב מתרץ לטעמיה שמואל מתרץ לטעמיה ר' יוחנן מתרץ לטעמיה רב מתרץ לטעמיה סוחטין כבשים בשבת לצורך השבת אבל לא למוצ"ש בד"א לגופן אבל למימיהן פטור אבל אסור ושלקות בין לגופן בין למימיהן מותר וזיתים וענבים לא יסחוט ואם סחטן חייב חטאת שמואל מתרץ לטעמיה סוחטין כבשים בשבת לצורך השבת הוא הדין לשלקות בד"א לגופן אבל למימיהן פטור אבל אסור וזיתים וענבים לא יסחוט ואם סחט חייב חטאת ר' יוחנן מתרץ לטעמיה סוחטין כבשים בשבת לצורך השבת אבל לא למוצ"ש אחד כבשים ואחד שלקות בד"א לגופן אבל למימיהן לא יסחוט ואם סחט נעשה כמי שסחט זיתים וענבים וחייב חטאת אמר רב חייא בר אשי אמר רב ד) דבר תורה אינו חייב אלא על דריסת זיתים וענבים בלבד וכן תני דבי מנשה דבר תורה אינו חייב אלא על דריסת זיתים וענבים בלבד ה) ואין עד מפי עד כשר אלא

רש"י

כביצה מכוונת טהור. משנה היא במסכת טהרות ומפרש בה בהדיא ובלבד שלא יגע במשקה שאינו נוגע אלא באוכל וכיון דכביצה מכוונת הוא לכי סחיט טיפה קמייתא חסר ליה מכביצה ואין האוכל אע"פ שהוא טמא מטמא המשקה שאין אוכל מטמא אחרים בפחות מכביצה אבל אם היה נוגע במשקה איטמי ליה משקה מטיפה ראשונה שהמשקה מקבל טומאה בכל שהוא וה"נ תני בה בהדיא יותר מכביצה טמא שכיון שיצאה טיפה ראשונה נטמאה בכביצה וטמא מת דווקא נקט שאינו מטמא בהיסט וה"ה לטמא שרץ וכל טמאי מגע וטמא מת לרבותא נקט דהוי אב הטומאה משום דקתני סיפא אבל זב שסוחט זיתים וענבים אפי' גרגיר יחידי טמא שכיון שיצאה טיפה ראשונה נטמא המשקה במשא הזב: ואי אמרת כו'. דקס"ד אפי' סוחט לתוך הקדירה: כתנאי. משקה הבא לאוכל אוכל הוא או משקה הוא: המחליק בענבים. נחתום המחליק פני ככרותיו בענבים שסוחט המשקה על הככר: הוכשר. האוכל ד) הענבים הוכשרו: הבא. לצורך אוכל כגון שסחטן לשם הפת: ה"ג דכ"ע משקה הבא לאוכל לאו אוכל הוא. אלא משקה הוא והיינו טעמא דמ"ד לא הוכשר שמתחילה נסחט אדעתא דאזיל לאיבוד שהאור שואבו ושורפו: המפצע בזיתים. בגלוסקא"ר כדי שיהיו רכין: הוכשר. דניחא ליה במשקה דטייף עלייהו שמתוך כך הם מרכים טעם: לסופתן במלח. שמתוך שהן קשין אין המלח נדבק בהן ומפצעם לרככן מבחוץ מעט: לא הוכשר. דלא מכוין למשקה דידהו דליעקר: לידע אם הגיעו זיתיו למסוק. צריך הוא לראות אם שומנו נוח לצאת מיהו המשקה אזיל לאיבוד: הני תנאי. דמפצע ודאי במשקה העומד לאיבוד פליגי כדאמרי' אבל תנאי דמחליק לאו בעומד לאיבוד פליגי דלאו לאיבוד אזל שהרי לצחצח האוכל נתנו והרי מצחצחו אלא במשקה העומד לצחצחו לאוכל קא מיפלגי דה"נ משקה הבא לאוכל משקה הוא ה"מ היכא דקא שריף ליה א"נ שטר ביה ריפתא דתורת משקה עביד אבל לצחצחו פליגי: ודג לצירו. סחיטת דג להוציא צירו לאו משקה הוא אלא אוכלין: כבשין. ירק חי כבוש ביין וחומץ: לגופו. אם לאכול הכבשים סוחטן ממשקה הצף עליהן והנבלע בהן מותר לכתחילה דלא מפרק הוא הואיל ולאו למשקה הוא צריך: פטור. שאין זה מפרק שאין המשקה הזה יוצא מן הכבשים שלא גדל בתוכן אבל אסור אטו זיתים וענבים: שלקות. אפילו למימיהן לאו משקה נינהו אלא אוכל: למימיהן פטור אבל אסור. והא שלקות דומיא דדג לצירן הוא ולא שרי ליה שמואל לכתחילה: עיני ראו ולא זר. הא דבעינא למימר לך דמשמיה דרב איתמר: סוחטין כבשין. ולא מפליג בין לגופן בין למימיהן ושרי לכתחילה וקשיא לכולהו דהא שרי כבשין למימיהן לכתחילה: דבר תורה. כלומר אסרה תורה מלאכה ודריכת זיתים וענבים הוא דהויא מלאכה אבל שאר דריכות לאו אורחייהו בהכי ולאו מלאכה נינהו: לעדות

תוספות

כביצה מכוונת טהור. פי' בקונטרס שאע"פ שהאוכל טמא אינו מטמא את המשקה שאין אוכל מטמא בפחות מכביצה והאי טעמא לא ניחא אלא למ"ד בפרק כל שעה (פסחים דף לג: ושם) משקים מיפקד פקידי אבל למ"ד התם מיבלע בליעי טמאים המשקין מאליהן כיון שנגע באוכל ה) [ומשני התם דבמתני' איירי בענבים שלא הוכשרו לאימת מתכשרי לכי סחיט להו וכי סחיט להו בציר שעוריה והשתא לפי' רש"י מה בכך] מיד כשיצאה הטיפה ראשונה (א) נטמאה הואיל ואוכל מקבל טומאה בכל שהוא ומה שהקשה ר"ת לפירו' פי' לעיל בריש המצניע (דף צא.): דכ"ע משקה הבא לאוכל לאו אוכל הוא. לא מצינן למימר דכ"ע אוכל הוא (ב) א"כ מ"ט דמ"ד הוכשר: אם הגיעו זיתיו למסוק כו'. מה שקשה ליה לרב נחמן דמפרש בפ"ק (דף יז.) דגזרו לבצור בטהרה משום דפעמים שאדם הולך כו' שם פירשתי. [בד"ה גחרני]: כבשים שסחטן לגופן מותר למימיהן פטור אבל אסור. רב לטעמיה דאמר לקמן דבר תורה אינו חייב אלא על דריכת זיתים וענבים ולפירוש הקונטרס דפי' משום דאתי המשקה מעלמא קשה לרבי אמאי גזרו להדוקי אודרא אפומא דשישא בשלהי תולין (לעיל דף קמא.) שמא יסחוט הא אפילו סחיט ליכא איסור דאורייתא מיהו י"ל דהתם רבא דקאמר לה וס"ל כר' יוחנן דמחייב חטאת: ורבי יוחנן אמר אחד כבשין ואחד שלקות לגופן מותר למימיהן חייב חטאת. ובדג לצירו נמי הוה מחייב ר' יוחנן חטאת לתוך הקערה דדג לצירו מדמינן לשלקות בכולה שמעתיה דפריך מדשמואל דשלקות אההיא דדג לצירו ופי' ר"ח דהלכה כר' יוחנן דקיי"ל כוותיה לגבי רב ושמואל ושמעינן ממילתא דר"י שאסור לסחוט כבשים ושלקות למימיהן ואם סחט חייב חטאת ולא הפריש בסחיטה בין קדירה לקער' אלא הכל אסור מתוך אלו דברים מתברר שאין הלכה לא כשמואל ולא כרב שאמרו סוחט אדם אשכול של ענבים לתוך הקדירה ויש שמעמידין דברי רב ושמואל ביו"ט מדדייק רב חסדא מדברי שמואל כן ואין לנו להדורי אפריכי ולאפוקי שמעתא מדוכתיה אלא ודאי בשבת קאמרי רב ושמואל ואין הלכה כמותן לא בשבת ולא ביו"ט ע"כ פי' ר"ח ומה שדקדק מדלא מפליג ר' יוחנן משמע דמיירי אפילו לתוך הקדירה אין זה דיוק דהא רב ושמואל נמי אסרי סתמא בכבשים (ג) למימיהן ואע"ג דשרו לסחוט בהדיא אשכול של ענבים לתוך הקדירה ומה שדחה דברי המעמידין דברי רב ושמואל ביו"ט אומר ר"ת שהדין עמו אבל דברי רב חסדא ביום טוב כדפירשתי לעיל: בהמה

רבינו חננאל

גופא כבשים שסחטן כגון ירקות וראשי לפתות וכרוב וכל הדומה להן. אמר רב לגופן מותר כלומר סחטן להסיר מימיהן ולאכלן מותר. אבל אם כוונתו למימיהן והוא צירן פטור אבל אסור. ושלקות כגון ירקות וכדומה להן שלקן מקודם השבת ונשארו מימיהן בהן וכן דגים מלוחין בין לגופו בין למימיהן מותר. ושמואל אמר אחד כבשים ואחד שלקות לגופן מותר למימיהן פטור אבל אסור ור' יוחנן אמר אחד כבשים וא' שלקות לגופן מותר למימיהן חייב חטאת ומותבינן עלייהו סוחטין כבשים בשבת לצורך השבת אבל לא למוצ"ש. זיתים וענבים לא יסחוט ואם סחט חייב חטאת קשיא לרב וקשיא לשמואל וקשיא לר' יוחנן וכל אחד מהן מתרץ מתניתא דא לטעמיה ודבריהן פשוטין הן אבל אנחנו כותבין תירוץ. טעמא דר' יוחנן דהלכתא כוותיה דקיי"ל כל היכא דפליגי רב ושמואל ור' יוחנן הלכה כר' יוחנן. ולפיכך מדקדקין בדבריו להעמיד הלכה על בוריו. ר' יוחנן מתרץ לטעמיה סוחטין כבשים בשבת לצורך השבת. אבל לא למוצ"ש ואחד כבשים ואחד שלקות לגופן אבל למימיהן לא יסחוט ואם סחט נעשה כמי שסחט זיתים וענבים וחייב חטאת. ולא הפריש בסחיטתן למימיהן בין קדירה לקערה אלא הכל אסור. דהא סחיטת זיתים וענבים בין לקדירה ובין לקערה למימיהן הוא צריך. וא"ר יוחנן שהסוחט כבשים ושלקות למימיהן כסוחט זיתים וענבים וחייב חטאת. ומתוך אלו הדברים מתברר שאין הלכה לא כשמואל ולא כרב שאומ' סוחט אדם אשכול של ענבים לתוך הקדירה אבל לא לתוך הקערה. ויש שמעמיד דברי (רבינו) רב ושמואל ביו"ט. מדדייק רב חסדא מדברי שמואל. ואמר מדברי רבינו נלמד חולב אדם עז לתוך הקדירה אבל לא לתוך הקערה כדי לקיים דבריהם להיות הלכה ואינן דבריהם נכונים שאפילו ביו"ט כל אילו אסורין ולינק בפיו מן הבהמה ביו"ט אסור וכ"ש לחלוב כדגרסינן בסוף פרק חרש [שנשא] פקחת. אבא שאול אומר נוהגין היינו שיונקין מן בהמה טהורה ביו"ט ואקשינן עליה היכי דמי אי דאיכא סכנה אפילו בשבת שרי אי דליכא סכנה אפילו ביו"ט אסור. ומפרקי' לא צריכא דאית בה צערא (וסברא) [וקסבר] מפרק כלאחר יד הוא. שבת דאיסור סקילה הוא גזור רבנן. י"ט דאיסור לאו לא גזור רבנן. הנה אפי' לינק ביו"ט לא התירו אלא במקום שיש צער כ"ש לחלוב במקום שאין צער שודאי אסור. ואין לנו להדורי אפירכי ולאפוקי שמעתא מדוכתא אלא ודאי זה שאומר סוחט אדם לתוך הקדירה אבל לא לתוך הקערה בשבת אמרו. ושאמר רב חסדא ביו"ט הוא ואין הלכה כמותם לא בשבת ולא ביו"ט וכך קיבלנו מרבותינו והא דתנא דבי מנשה דבר תורה אינו חייב אלא על דריכת זיתים וענבים בלבד. לא קשיא הא דר' יוחנן א) ושאר פירות זולתי זיתים וענבים סלקא שמעתא כר' יהודה דאמר לאוכלין היוצא מהן מותר למשקין

חשק שלמה על רבינו חננאל א) [נראה דר"ל דתנא דבי מנשה לא כו' למעט רק שאר פירות אבל לא כבשים ושלקות. אך לשונו צריכה תיקון קצת. ועי' ברי"ף כאן]:

ליקוטי רש"י

...פטור אפילו הכי כל כמה דבגווה נינהו משלמי לשיעוריה וטמא מת דוקא נקט שאינו מטמא ... שרץ וכל טומאת מגע וכו' ... [פסחים לג:]. האלהים. שבועה [סנהדרין עב.]. שלקות. כל ירק שלוק [ברכות לח:].

עין משפט נר מצוה

טו א מיי' פי"א מהלכות טומאת אוכלין הל' ד:
טז ב טוש"ע או"ח סימן שכ סעיף א:
יז ג מיי' פ"ח מהלכות שבת הל' י ופכ"א הל' יג סמג לאוין סה טוש"ע או"ח שם סעיף ז:
יח ד מיי' פ"ח שם הל' י ופכ"א הלכה יב:
יט ה מיי' פי"ג מהלכות גרושין הלכה כט סמג עשין נ טור שו"ע אה"ע סימן יז סעיף ג:

מסורת הש"ס

א) מעשרות פ"א מ"ח, ב) פ"א מ"ד, ג) יבמות מז: ודף קכב. כתובות ל. מו:, ד) ל"ל והענבים ולמ"ד ..., ה) רש"ל ועי' מהרש"א.

הגהות הב"ח

(א) תוס' ד"ה כביצה וכו' הטיפה ראשונה הוכשר הואיל ואוכל וכו' בריש המצניע. נ"ב דף לא ע"ב לא לענין וע"ש: (ב) ד"ה דכ"ע וכו' דא"כ מ"ט: (ג) ד"ה ור' יוחנן וכו' אסרי סתמא בכבשים ובשלקות למימיהן:

גליון הש"ס

גמ' שלקות לגופן מותר למימיהן. עי' לעיל ... תוס' ד"ה ...

הגהות הגר"א

[א] גמ' משקה הבא לאוכל לאו אוכל הוא. נ"ב גירסת הגאונים אוכל הוא. עי' רש"א וכ"כ הרי"ף ע"ש:

תורה אור השלם

א) אֲשֶׁר אֲנִי אֶחֱזֶה לִּי וְעֵינַי רָאוּ וְלֹא זָר כָּלוּ כִלְיֹתַי בְּחֵקִי: [איוב יט, כז]

וְאִם סָחַט חַיָּיב חַטָּאת – AND IF ONE DID SQUEEZE them on the Sabbath, HE IS LIABLE TO A *CHATAS.*

רַבִּי יוֹחָנָן מְתָרֵץ לְטַעְמֵיהּ – **R' Yochanan resolves** the difficulty **according to his opinion,** by emending the Baraisa in this manner: סוֹחֲטִין כְּבָשִׁים בְּשַׁבָּת לְצוֹרֶךְ הַשַּׁבָּת אֲבָל לֹא לְמוֹצָאֵי שַׁבָּת – WE MAY SQUEEZE PICKLED VEGETABLES ON THE SABBATH FOR USE ON THE SABBATH, BUT NOT FOR use after THE DEPARTURE OF THE SABBATH. אֶחָד כְּבָשִׁים וְאֶחָד שְׁלָקוֹת – This applies BOTH to PICKLED VEGETABLES AND TO BOILED VEGETABLES! בַּמֶּה דְּבָרִים אֲמוּרִים – WHEN ARE THESE WORDS SAID? לְגוּפָן – With regard to squeezing the vegetables FOR THEMSELVES. אֲבָל לְמֵימֵיהֶן – BUT with regard to squeezing them FOR THEIR LIQUID, לֹא יִסְחוֹט – ONE MAY NOT SQUEEZE them on the Sabbath. וְאִם סָחַט – AND IF ONE DID SQUEEZE them for their liquid, נַעֲשָׂה כְּמִי שֶׁסָּחַט זֵיתִים וַעֲנָבִים וְחַיָּיב חַטָּאת – HE IS REGARDED AS ONE WHO SQUEEZED OLIVES OR GRAPES for their liquid, AND IS thus LIABLE TO A *CHATAS.* Thus, each of these three Amoraim resolves the difficulty in accordance with his own ruling.

The Gemara presents yet another of Rav's statements regarding squeezing performed on the Sabbath:

אָמַר רַב חִיָּיא בַּר אַשִׁי אָמַר רַב – **Rav Chiya bar Ashi said in the name of Rav:** דְּבַר תּוֹרָה – **It is a Torah principle** that אֵינוֹ חַיָּיב אֶלָּא עַל דְּרִיסַת זֵיתִים וַעֲנָבִים בִּלְבַד – **one is liable only for the pressing of olives or grapes.**[29]

The Gemara supports this statement with a Baraisa:

וְכֵן תָּנֵי דְּבֵי מְנַשֶּׁה – **And this was taught as well** in a Baraisa **in the academy of Menasheh:** דְּבַר תּוֹרָה אֵינוֹ חַיָּיב אֶלָּא עַל דְּרִיסַת זֵיתִים וַעֲנָבִים בִּלְבַד – IT IS A TORAH PRINCIPLE THAT ONE IS LIABLE ONLY FOR THE PRESSING OF OLIVES OR GRAPES.

This Baraisa continues with an unrelated topic:

וְאֵין עֵד מִפִּי עֵד כָּשֵׁר – AND A WITNESS who acquired his information FROM THE MOUTH OF A second WITNESS IS NOT a VALID witness

NOTES

29. For it is a Torah principle that one is liable on the Sabbath *only* for *melachah* performed in its *usual* manner, which as regards the act of squeezing fruit is defined as squeezing a beverage from a food. One is therefore liable for squeezing olives and grapes, for since it is common practice to do so, their juice is legally regarded as a beverage. One is not liable, however, for squeezing other fruits, since it is not common practice to squeeze these fruits for their juice (*Rashi,* as explained by *Eglei Tal* דש §16; cf. explanation of *Pri Megadim* ibid.).

[*Ritva* (*MHK* ed.) questions Rav's statement on two counts. On 143b he points out that our Mishnah states that one is prohibited by Rabbinic decree to sponge up spilled wine, lest one be led to squeeze out the sponge. But according to Rav one is permitted by Biblical law to squeeze out a sponge, since only squeezing olives or grapes is prohibited! For various answers to this question, see *Ritva* there; *Rosh* and *Meiri* here. And in our Gemara he notes that Rav's statement seems to contradict the Mishnah's ruling against consuming the juice that oozes from mulberries and pomegranates (see Gemara 143b). For the reason to prohibit consumption of these liquids is to prevent one from squeezing them – but according to Rav it is permissible to squeeze them! See *Ritva MHK* ed. and *Pri Megadim* (*Eishel Avraham,* Introduction to §320) for an answer to this question.]

כביצה מכוונת טהור הא יותר מכביצה טמא ואי אמרת משקה הבא לאוכל אוכל הוא במאי איתכשר הוא מותיב לה והוא מפרק לה בסוחט לתוך הקערה א"ר ירמיה כתנאי המחליק בענבים לא הוכשר רבי יהודה אומר הוכשר מאי לאו בהא קמיפלגי מ"ס משקה הבא לאוכל אוכל הוא ומ"ס לאו אוכל הוא אמר רב פפא דכולי עלמא [א] משקה הבא לאוכל לאו אוכל הוא והכא במשקה הבא לאיבוד קמיפלגי מר סבר משקה הוא ומ"ס לאו משקה הוא ובפלוגתא דהני תנאי דתניא המפצע בזיתים בידים מסואבות הוכשר לסופתן במלח לא הוכשר לידע אם הגיעו זיתיו למסוק לא הוכשר רבי יהודה אומר הוכשר מאי לאו בהא קמיפלגי דמ"ס משקה העומד לאיבוד משקה הוא ומ"ס לאו משקה הוא אמר רב הונא בריה דרב יהושע הני תנאי במשקה העומד לאיבוד פליגי והנך תנאי במשקה העומד לצחצחו קמיפלגי א"ר זירא אמר רב חייא בר אשי אמר רב סוחט אדם אשכול של ענבים לתוך הקדרה אבל לא לתוך הקערה ודג לצירו אפילו לתוך הקערה יתיב רב דימי וקאמר לה להא שמעתא א"ל אביי לרב דימי אתון משמיה דרב מתניתון ולא קשיא לכו אנן משמיה דשמואל מתנינן לה וקשיא לן מי אמר שמואל דג לצירו אפי' לתוך הקערה והאיתמר כבשים שסחטן אמר רב לגופן מותר למימיהן פטור אבל אסור ושלקות בין לגופן בין למימיהן מותר ושמואל אמר אחד כבשים ואחד שלקות לגופן מותר למימיהן פטור אבל אסור א"ל האלהים א עיני ראו ולא זר (כלו כליותי בחקי וגו') מפומיה דר' ירמיה שמיע לי ור' ירמיה מר' זירא ור' זירא מרב חייא בר אשי ורב חייא בר אשי מרב: גופא כבשים שסחטן אמר רב לגופן מותר למימיהן פטור אבל אסור ושלקות בין לגופן בין למימיהן מותר ושמואל אמר אחד זה ואחד זה לגופן מותר למימיהן פטור אבל אסור ורבי יוחנן אמר אחד כבשים ואחד שלקות לגופן מותר למימיהן חייב חטאת מיתיבי סוחטין כבשים בשבת לצורך השבת אבל לא למוצ"ש וזיתים וענבים לא יסחוט ואם סחט חייב חטאת קשיא לרב קשיא לשמואל קשיא לר' יוחנן רב מתרץ לטעמיה שמואל מתרץ לטעמיה ר' יוחנן מתרץ לטעמיה רב מתרץ לטעמיה סוחטין כבשים בשבת לצורך השבת אבל לא למוצ"ש בד"א לגופן אבל למימיהן פטור אבל אסור וזיתים וענבים לא יסחוט ואם סחט חייב חטאת שמואל מתרץ לטעמיה סוחטין כבשים בשבת לצורך השבת והוא הדין לשלקות בד"א לגופן אבל למימיהן פטור אבל אסור וזיתים וענבים לא יסחוט ואם סחט חייב חטאת ר' יוחנן מתרץ לטעמיה סוחטין כבשים בשבת לצורך השבת אבל לא למוצ"ש בד"א לגופן אבל למימיהן לא יסחוט ואם סחט נעשה כמי שסחט זיתים וענבים וחייב חטאת אמר רב חייא בר אשי אמר רב דבר תורה אינו חייב אלא על דריסת זיתים וענבים בלבד וכן תני דבי מנשה דבר תורה אינו חייב אלא על דריסת זיתים וענבים בלבד ואין עד מפי עד כשר אלא

רש"י

כביצה מכוונת טהור. משנה היא במסכת טהרות ומפרש בה בהדיא ובלבד שלא יגע במשקה שאינו נוגע אלא באוכל וכיון דכביצה מכוונת הוא לכי סחיט טיפה קמייתא חסר ליה מכביצה ואין האוכל אע"פ שהוא טמא מטמא המשקה שאין אוכל מטמא אחרים בפחות מכביצה אבל אם היה נוגע במשקה איטמי ליה משקה מטיפה ראשונה שהמשקה מקבל טומאה בכל שהוא וה"נ תני בה בהדיא יותר מכביצה טמא שכיון שיצאה טיפה ראשונה נטמאה בכביצה וטומאת מת דווקא נקט שאינו מטמא בהיסט וה"ה לטמא שרץ וכל טמאי מגע וטומאת מת לרבותא נקט דהוי אב הטומאה משום דקתני סיפא אבל זב שסוחט זיתים וענבים אפי' גרגיר יחידי טמא שכיון שיצאה טיפה ראשונה נטמאה המשקה במשא הזב: ואי אמרת כו'. דקס"ד אפי' סוחט לתוך הקדירה: כתנאי. משקה הבא לאוכל אוכל הוא או משקה הוא: המחליק בענבים. נחמוס המחליק פני כרכומיו בענבים שסוחט המשקה על הככר: הוכשר. האוכל הענבים הוכשרו: הבא. לצורך אוכל כגון שסחטן לשם הפת: ה"ג דכ"ע משקה הבא לאוכל לאו אוכל הוא. אלא משקה הוא והיינו טעמא דמ"ד לא הוכשר שמתחילה נסחט לדעתא דאזיל לאיבוד שהאוכל בולעו ושורפו: המפצע בזיתים. בגלוסקי"ר כדי שיהיו רכין להוכשר. דכיון ליה במשקה דטייף עלייהו שמתוך כך הם מרכים טעם: לסופתן במלח. שמתוך שהן קשין אין המלח נדבק בהן ומפצעם לרככן במתוק מעט: לא הוכשר. דלא מכוין למשקה דידהו לעיקר: לידע אם הגיעו זיתיו למסוק. צריך הוא לראות אם שומנו נוח לצאת מיהו המשקה אזיל לאיבוד: הני תנאי. המפצע והאי משקה העומד לאיבוד פליגי כדאמרי' אבל תנאי דמחליק לאו בעומד לאיבוד פליגי דלאו לאיבוד אזיל שהרי לצחצח האוכל נתנו והרי מלאכתו אלא במשקה העומד לצחצחו לאוכל קא מיפלגי דה"ג משקה הבא לאוכל משקה הוא ה"מ היכא דקא שריך ליה א"נ שטר ביה ריפתא דתורת משקה עביד אבל לצחצחו פליגי: ודג לצירו. סחיטת דג להוציא צירו לאו משקה הוא אלא מוהל: כבשין. ירק כבוש ביין ובחומץ: לגופו. אם לאכול הכבשים סוחטן ממשקה הנספג עליהן והנבלע בהן מותר לכתחילה דלא מפרק הוא דלא ולאו משקה הוא צריך: פטור. שאין זה מפרק שאין המשקה הזה יוצא מן הכבשים שלא גדל בתוכן אבל אסור אטו זיתים וענבים: שלקות. אפילו למימיהן לאו משקה נינהו אלא אוכל: למימיהן פטור אבל אסור. והא שלקות דומיא דדג לצירו הוא ולא שרי ליה שמואל לכתחילה: עיני ראו ולא זר. הא דבעינא למימר לך דמשמיה דרב איתמר: סוחטין כבשין. ולא מפליג בין גופן בין למימיהן ושרי לכתחילה וקשיא לכולהו דהא שרי כבשין למימיהן לכתחילה: דבר תורה. כלומר אסרה תורה מלאכה ודריכת זיתים וענבים הוא דהויא מלאכה אבל שאר דריכות לאו תולדותיהו נינהו ולאו מלאכה נינהו: לעדות

תוספות

כביצה מכוונת טהור. פי' בקונטרס שאע"פ שהאוכל טמא אינו מטמא את המשקה שאין אוכל מטמא בפחות מכביצה והאי טעמא לא ניחא אלא למ"ד בפרק כל שעה (פסחים דף לג: ושם) משקים מיפקד פקידי אבל למ"ד התם מיבלע בליעי טמאים המשקין מאליהן כיון שנגע באוכל [ומשני התם דבמתני' מיירי בענבים שלא הוכשרו לאימת מתכשרי לכי סחיט להו וכי סחיט להו בציר שעוריה והשתא לפי' רש"י מה בכך] מיד כשיצאה הטיפה ראשונה (א) נטמאה הואיל ואוכל מקבל טומאה בכל שהוא ומה שהקשה ר"ת לפירו' פי' לעיל בריש המצניע (דף צא.): דכ"ע משקה הבא לאוכל לאו אוכל הוא. לא מצינן למימר דכ"ע אוכל הוא (ב) א"כ מ"ט דמ"ד הוכשר: אם הגיעו זיתיו למסוק כו'. מה שקשה ליה לרב נחמן דמפרש בפ"ק (דף יז.) דגזרו לבצור בטהרה משום דפעמים שאדם הולך כו' שם פירשתי. [בד"ה גחרי]: כבשים שסחטן לגופן מותר למימיהן פטור אבל אסור. רב לטעמיה דאמר לקמן דבר תורה אינו חייב אלא על דריכת זיתים וענבים ולפירוש הקונטרס דפי' משום דאתי המשקה מעלמא קשה לרבי אמאי גזרו להדוקי אודרא אפומא דשישא בשלהי תולין (לעיל דף קמא.) שמא יסחוט הא אפילו סחיט ליכא איסור דאורייתא מיהו י"ל דהתם רבא דקאמר לה וס"ל כר' יוחנן דמחייב חטאת: ורבי יוחנן אמר אחד כבשין ואחד שלקות לגופן מותר למימיהן חייב חטאת. ובדג לצירו נמי הוה מחייב ר' יוחנן חטאת לתוך הקערה דדג לצירו מדמינן לשלקות בכולה שמעתיה דפריך מדשמואל דשלקות אההיא דדג לצירו ופי' ר"ח דהלכה כר' יוחנן דקי"ל כוותיה לגבי רב ושמואל ושמעינן ממילתא דר"י שאסור לסחוט כבשים ושלקות למימיהן ואם סחט חייב חטאת ולא הפריש בסחיטה בין קדירה לקער' אלא הכל אסור מתוך אלו דברים מתברר שאין הלכה לא כשמואל ולא כרב שאמרו סוחט אדם אשכול של ענבים לתוך הקדירה ויש שמעמידין דברי רב ושמואל ביו"ט מדדייק רב חסדא מדברי שמואל כן ואין לנו להדורי אפריכי ולאפוקי שמעתא מדוכתיה אלא ודאי בשבת קאמרי רב ושמואל ואין הלכה כמותן לא בשבת ולא ביו"ט ע"כ פי' ר"ח ומה שדקדק מדלא מפליג ר' יוחנן משמע דמיירי אפילו לתוך הקדירה אין זה דיוק דהא רב ושמואל נמי אסרי סתמא בכבשים (ג) למימיהן ואע"ג דשרו לסחוט בהדיא אשכול של ענבים לתוך הקדירה ומה שדחה דברי המעמידין דברי רב ושמואל ביו"ט אומר ר"ת שהדין עמו אבל דברי רב חסדא ביום טוב כדפירשתי לעיל: בהמה

רבינו חננאל

גופא כבשים שסחטן כגון ירקות וראשי לפתות וכרוב וכל הדומה להן. אמר רב לגופן מותר כלומר סחטן להסיר מימיהן ולאכלן מותר. אבל אם כוונתו למימיהן והוא צירן פטור אבל אסור. ושלקות כגון ירקות וכדומה להן שלקן מקודם השבת ונשארו מימיהן בהן וכן דגים מלוחין בין לגופו בין למימיהן מותר. ושמואל אמר אחד כבשים ואחד שלקות לגופן מותר למימיהן פטור אבל אסור ור' יוחנן אמר אחד כבשים וא' שלקות לגופן מותר למימיהן חייב חטאת ומותבינן עלייהו סוחטין כבשים בשבת לצורך השבת אבל לא למוצ"ש. זיתים וענבים לא יסחוט ואם סחט חייב חטאת קשיא לרב וקשיא לשמואל וקשיא לר' יוחנן וכל אחד מהן מתרץ מתניתא דא לטעמיה ודבריהן פשוטין הן אבל אנחנו כותבין תירוץ. טעמא דר' יוחנן דהלכתא כוותיה דקיי"ל כל היכא דפליגי רב ושמואל ור' יוחנן הלכה כר' יוחנן. ולפיכך מדקדקין בדבריו להעמיד הלכה על בוריו. ר' יוחנן מתרץ לטעמיה סוחטין כבשים בשבת לצורך השבת. אבל לא למוצ"ש ואחד כבשים ואחד שלקות לגופן אבל למימיהן לא יסחוט ואם סחט נעשה כמי שסחט זיתים וענבים וחייב חטאת. ולא הפריש בסחיטתן למימיהן בין קדירה לקערה אלא הכל אסור. דהא סחיטת זיתים וענבים בין לקדירה ובין לקערה למימיהן הוא צריך. וא"ר יוחנן שהסוחט כבשים ושלקות למימיהן כסוחט זיתים וענבים וחייב חטאת. ומתוך אלו הדברים מתברר שאין הלכה לא כשמואל ולא כרב שאומ' סוחט אדם אשכול של ענבים לתוך הקדירה אבל לא לתוך הקערה. ויש שמעמיד דברי (רבינו) רב ושמואל ביו"ט. מדרייק רב חסדא מדברי שמואל. ואמר מדברי רבינו נלמד חולב אדם עז לתוך הקדירה אבל לא לתוך הקערה כדי לקיים דבריהם להיות הלכה ואינן דבריהם נכונים שאפילו ביו"ט כל אילו אסורין ולינק בפיו מן הבהמה ביו"ט אסור וכ"ש לחלוב כדגרסינן בסוף פרק חרש [שנשא] פקחת. אבא שאול אמר נוהגין היינו שיונקין מן בהמה טהורה ביו"ט ואקשינן עליה היכי דמי אי דאיכא סכנה אפילו בשבת שרי אי דליכא סכנה אפילו ביו"ט אסור. ואוקימנא לא צריכא דאית בה צערא (וסברא) [וקסבר] מפרק כלאחר יד הוא. שבת דאיסור סקילה הוא גזור רבנן. י"ט דאיסור לאו לא גזור רבנן. הנה אפי' לינק ביו"ט לא התירו אלא במקום שיש צער כ"ש לחלוב במקום שאין צער שודאי אסור. ואין לנו להדורי אפריכי ולאפוקי שמעתא מדוכתא אלא ודאי זה שאמר רב חסדא

עין משפט נר מצוה

טו א מיי' פי"א מהלכות טומאת אוכלין הל' ד':
טז ב טוש"ע או"ח סימן של סעיף ח:
יז ג מיי' פ"ח מהלכות שבת הל' ו ופכ"א הל' יג סמג לאוין סה טוש"ע או"ח שם סעיף ו:
יח ד מיי' פ"ח שם הל' ו ופכ"א הלכה יג:
יט ה מיי' פי"ז מהלכות גרושין הל' ט סמג עשין נ טור שו"ע אה"ע סימן יז סעיף ג:

מסורת הש"ס

א) מעשרות פ"א מ"ח, ב) פ"א נ"ג, ג) יבמות פו: ודף קכב. בכורות לו. מו., ד) נ"ל והענבים ואיירי בפת שנילוש במי פירות ועכשיו הוכשר, ה) רש"ל ועי' מהרש"א.

הגהות הב"ח

(א) תוס' ד"ה כביצה וכו' הטיפה ראשונה הוכשר הואיל ואוכל וכו' בריש המצניע. נ"ב דף צא ד"ה לא לענין וא"ש: (ב) ד"ה דכ"ע וכו' דא"כ מ"ט: (ג) ד"ה ור' יוחנן וכו' אסרי סתמא בכבשים ובשלקות למימיהן:

גליון הש"ס

גמ' שלקות לגופן מותר למימיהן. עי' לעיל דף קט ע"ב תוס' ד"ה ולריך לעיין:

הגהות הגר"א

[א] גמ' משקה הבא לאוכל לאו אוכל הוא. נ"ב גירסת הגאונים אוכל הוא. עי' רשב"א וכ"כ הרי"ף ע"ש:

תורה אור השלם

א) אֲשֶׁר אֲנִי אֶחֱזֶה לִּי וְעֵינַי רָאוּ וְלֹא זָר כָּלוּ כִלְיֹתַי בְּחֵקִי: [איוב יט, כז]

ליקוטי רש"י

כביצה מכוונת וכו'.

עין משפט נר מצוה

כ א מיי' פ"ב מהלכות בכורות הלכה טו סמג עשין ריא טוש"ע יו"ד סימן שיד סעיף ה:

כא ב מיי' פכ"א מהל' שבת הלכה טז טור שו"ע או"ח סימן רנג סעיף ה וסי' שכ סעיף ג:

כב ג מיי' פכ"ב שם הלכה ח סמג לאוין סה טוש"ע או"ח סימן שיח סעיף ד:

כג ד מיי' פ"כ מהלכות סנהדרין הלכה ז סמג עשין כז טור שו"ע חו"מ סימן י סעיף א:

רבינו חננאל

למשקין היוצא מהן אסור. והא דתניא סוחטין בפגעים ובפרישין ובעוזרדין אבל לא ברמונים דשל בית מנשיא בן מנחם היו סוחטין ברמונים אמר רב נחמן הלכה כשל בית מנשיא בן מנחם וסלקא שמעתא דאסור לסחוט ברמונים בשבת והא דתני אין עד מפי עד כשר אלא לעדות אשה בלבד. אוקימנא לעדות שהאשה כשרה לה והלכתא עד מפי עד כשר לבכור. פי' עד מפי עד נאמן להעיד על בכור בהמה טהורה שזה המום שיש בו אפי' שראוי לבוא בידי אדם הוא לא נפל בו מידי אדם ובזו העדות החכם מתירו להאכל במומו וכ"ש בעדות גדולה מזו. ומפורש כך בבכורות פ' כל פסולי המוקדשי'. וסלקא שמעתא התם דהלכתא כרשב"ג דאמר אפילו בנו ובתו נאמנים ויש מי שאומר כי עד מפי עד נאמן בבכור אדם וטעות הוא בידו: **חלות** דבש שריסקן מע"ש ויצאו מעצמן אסורין ור' אלעזר מתיר. כי אתא רב הושעיא מנהרדעא אתא ואייתי מתניתא בידיה זיתים וענבים שריסקן מע"ש ויצאו מעצמן אסורים. ור' אלעזר ור"ש מתירין. והא מתניתא מסייעא נמי לר' יוחנן: **מתני'** כל שבא בחמין מלפני השבת וכו'. ומיבעיא לן כגון מאי. ואמר רב ספרא כגון תרנגולתא דר' אסא שהיתה מלוחה ביותר וכשמבקשין לאוכלה שורין אותה במים חמין. אמר רב ספרא כגון זו התרנגולת אם הובאה בחמין מלפני השבת מותר לשרותה בחמין בשבת ולאוכלה. ואם לאו אסור לשרותה ומותר להדיחה והמליח הישן וקולייס האיספנין

רב נסים גאון

ואין עד מפי עד כשר אלא לעדות אשה בלבד כשאמר כי מת בעלה התירוה בית דין לינשא ואע"פ שהמועט העתיק דבר זה מזולתו וכמו שביארו דבר זה בפרק אשה שהלך בעלה וצרתה (דף קכב) והוחזקו להיות משיאין עד מפי עד וכו': **עד** מפי עד בבכור מהו. עיקר דיליה במסכת בכורות בפרק כל פסולי המוקדשין (דף לה) דתניא ר' יהושע בן קפוסאי אומר בכור בי כהן צריך ב' מן השוק להעיד עליו רבן שמעון בן גמליאל אומר אפילו בנו ובתו ואמרו הלכתא כרבן שמעון ודוקא בנו ובתו אבל אשתו לא מאי טעמא אשתו כגופו דמיא ועוד אמרו איבעיא להו עד מפי עד מהו לעדות בכור אמר ליה תני אלא לעדות אשה כשירה לו וכבר נתברר לנו שבתו כשירה והואיל ואשה כשירה לעדות בכור עד מפי עד נמי כשר לעדות בכור וכן פסקה ההלכה וזה שאמרו בבכור בהמה אבל בבכור אדם לא. גרסינן בפרק י' יוחסין (דף עד) ג' נאמנין על הבכור חיה ואמו ואביו חיה לאלתר אמו כל ז' אביו לעולם: **כגון** תרנגולתיה דר' אבא. כך פירשה אדונינו האיי גאון ז"ל תרנגולת שמבשלין אותה ומוציאין אותה מהמרק וממלאין אותה בתבלין וכשרוצה לאכול ממנה שורין אותה במים חמים ואוכלים אותה כאילו היא חמה:

סליק פרק חבית

בהמה בגימטריא. אסמכתא בעלמא היא דנ"ב נפקא לן בלאו גימטריא כדפי' בקונטרס:

אלא לעדות אשה בלבד א) איבעיא להו עד מפי עד לעדות בכור מהו רב אמי אסיר ורב אסי שרי א"ל רב אמי לרב אסי והא תנא דבי מנשיא אין עד מפי עד כשר אלא לעדות אשה בלבד אימא לעדות שהאשה כשרה לה בלבד רב יימר אכשר עד מפי עד לבכור קרי עליה מרימר יימר שרי בוכרא א והלכתא עד מפי עד כשר לבכור: חלות דבש: כי אתא רב הושעיא מנהרדעא ב) אתא ואייתי מתניתא בידיה זיתים וענבים שריסקן מע"ש ויצאו מעצמן אסורין ג ור"א ור"ש מתירין אמר רב יוסף גברא יתירא אתא לאשמעינן א"ל אביי טובא קמ"ל דאי ממתניתין הוה אמינא התם הוא דמעיקרא אוכלא ולבסוף אוכלא אבל הכא דמעיקרא אוכלא ולבסוף משקה אימא לא קמ"ל: **מתני'** ג כל שבא בחמין מערב שבת שורין אותו בחמין בשבת וכל שלא בא בחמין מערב שבת מדיחין אותו בחמין בשבת חוץ מן המליח הישן ד) (ודגים מלוחין קטנים) ה) וקולייס האיספנין שהדחתן זו היא גמר מלאכתן: **גמ'** כגון מאי אמר רב ספרא כגון תרנגולתא דר' אבא ואמר רב ספרא זימנא חדא איקלעית להתם ואוכלן מיניה ואי לא רבי אבא דאשקיין חמרא בר תלתא טרפי איתנסי רבי יוחנן רייק מכותח דבבלאי אמר רב יוסף ולירוק אנן מתרנגולתא דרבי אבא ועוד אמר רב גזא זימנא חדא איקלעית להתם ועבדית כותח דבבלאי שאילו מיניה ו) כל בריחי מערבא: כל שלא בא בחמין וכו': הדיה מאי אמר רב יוסף הדיה חייב חטאת אמר מר בריה דרבינא אף אנן נמי תנינא חוץ ממליח ישן וקולייס האיספנין שהדחתן זו היא גמר מלאכתן שמע מינה יתיב רבי חייא בר אבא ורבי אסי קמיה דרבי יוחנן ויתיב רבי יוחנן וקא מנמנם אמר ליה רבי חייא בר אבא לרבי אסי מפני מה עופות שבבבל שמנים א"ל כלך למדבר עזה ואראך שמנים מהן מפני מה מועדים שבבבל שמחים מפני שהן עניים מפני מה ת"ח שבבבל מצויינין לפי שאינן בני תורה מפני מה עובדי כוכבים מזוהמי' מפני שאוכלין שקצי' ורמשי' ז) איתער בהו רבי יוחנן אמר להו דרדקי לא כך אמרתי לכם א אמור לחכמה אחותי את ח) אם ברור לך הדבר כאחותך שהיא אסורה לך אומרהו ואם לאו לא תאמרהו אמרו ליה ולימא לן מר איזה מהן מפני מה עופות שבבבל שמנים מפני שלא גלו שנאמר ב שאנן מואב מנעוריו ושקט הוא אל שמריו ובגולה לא הלך והכא מנלן דגלו דתניא ט) רבי יהודה אומר נ"ב שנה לא עבר איש ביהודה שנאמר ג על ההרים אשא בכי ונהי וגו' מעוף השמים ועד בהמה נדדו הלכו בהמ"ה בגימטריא חמשין ותרתין הוו א"ר יעקב א"ר יוחנן כולן חזרו חוץ מקולייס האיספנין י) דאמר רב הני מדרי דבבל מהדרי מיא לעין עיטם והאי כיון דלא שריר שדריה לא מצי סליק מפני מה מועדים שבבבל שמחים מפני שלא היו באותה קללה דכתיב ד והשבתי כל משושה חגה חדשה ושבתה וכל מועדה וכתיב ה חדשיכם ומועדיכם שנאה נפשי היו עלי לטורח כ) מאי היו עלי לטורח א"ר אלעזר אמר הקב"ה לא דיין לישראל שחוטאין לפני אלא שמטריחין אותי לידע איזו גזירה קשה אביא עליהן א"ר יצחק אין לך כל רגל ורגל שלא באתה בולשת לציפורי ואמר רבי חנינא אין לך כל רגל ורגל שלא בא לטבריה אגמון וקמטון ובעל זמורה מפני מה ת"ח שבבבל מצויינין לפי שאינן (א) בני מקומן דאמרי אינשי במתא שמאי בלא מתא תותבאי ו הבאים ישרש יעקב יציץ ופרח ישראל תני רב יוסף אלו תלמידי חכמים שבבבל שעושין ציצין ופרחים לתורה מפני מה עובדי כוכבים מזוהמין שלא עמדו על הר סיני שבשעה

שבא

רש"י

לעדות אשה. לומר לאשה מת בעליך דאקילו בה רבנן משום עיגונא וכל דמקדש אדעתא דרבנן מ) מקדש ואפקועי רבנן לקדושין מיניה: **לעדות בכור.** בכור ביד כהן כשנתנו ישראל לו שלם ואירע לו בו מום קי"ל בבכורות (דף לה.) נחשדו כהנים להטיל מום בבכור ואין נאמן לומר מום זה נפל בו מאליו וצריך להביא עדים ואמרינן התם דאשה כשרה לעדות זו: **אימא לעדות שהאשה כשרה לה.** והאי נמי כשרה לה: **גברא יתירא.** ר"ש דמתני' ר"א תנן בה: **אתא לאשמעינן.** בתמיה כלומר מה בא ללמדנו אם לא זאת: **מתני' כל שבא בחמין.** כלומר שנתבשל: **שורין אותו בחמין.** כדי שיהא נמוח: **וכל שלא בא בחמין.** כגון בשר יבש שאוכלין אותו חי ע"י הדחק: **מדיחין אותו.** ולא אמרי' זהו בישולו אבל לא שורין: **חוץ מן המליח ישן.** דג מליח של שנה שעברה: **וקולייס האיספנין.** שם דג שאוכלין אותו מחמת מלחו ע"י הדחה בחמין והכך אפילו הדחה נמי לא שזהו גמר מלאכתן והוי בשול: **גמ' כגון מאי.** הוי בא בחמין שחוזרין ושורין אותו בחמין: **תרנגולתיה דר' אבא.** מבשלה ושורה אותה ימים רבים בחמין למחות מאליה ואוכלה לרפואה: **בר תלתא טרפי.** בן ג' שנים: **איתנסי.** הייתי נאנס להקיא מחמת מיאוס: **רייק.** רוקק מכותחא דבבלאי כשנזכרו שהיה מאוס בעיניו: **אמר רב יוסף כו'.** קשה היה בעיניו שנמאסין בני בבל על בני ארץ ישראל אמר אנו נמי יש לנו לרוק מתרנגולתיה דר' אבא שהם אוכלים: **ועוד כותח.** אינו מאוס כל כך בעיני אלא בני מערבא: **דהא אמר רב גזא כו'.** ושאלו מיניה אותו כותח: **בריחי.** חולים: **הדיה.** קולייס מאי: **חייב חטאת.** דהוי בישול: **מפני מה עופות שבבבל שמנים.** משל א"י: **כלך.** לכה לך אלא שקיצר הלשון: **למדבר עזה.** והיא מא"י: **מועדים שבבבל שמחים.** רגילים לשמוח במועדים יותר מא"י: **מפני שהם עניים.** וכל השנה אין להם שמחה במאכל ומשתה ואין להם מרגוע ממלאכה לפיכך במועדים כל שמחתם: **מצויינין.** מצויינין עצמן בלבושים נאים: **מצויינין.** מקושטין: **שאינן בני תורה.** כל כך לכבדם ככבני ארץ ישראל מחמת תורתם מכבדים אותם מחמת לבושיהן שנראין חשובים: **דרדקי.** תינוקות בחורים שלא הגיעו לסברא: **מפני שלא גלו.** העופות כמו אותן של א"י כדאמרינן לקמן: **שאנן מואב מנעוריו וגו'.** סיפיה דקרא על כן עמד טעמו בו אלמא הגולין מפיגין טעמן ושמנן: **נ"ב שנה.** משגלו בימי צדקיה בחרבות ירושלים עד שנפקדו בימי כורש ואז עלו מהם לייסד את הבית י"ח שנים קודם גמר הבנין שהיה לסוף ע' שנה בשנת שתים לדריוש כדאמרי' במגילה (דף יא:): **וכולן חזרו.** הבהמות ועופות ואף הדגים חוץ מן קולייס האספנין וכולן חזרו דהא עד בהמה כתיב ומכלל דמכאן ואילך הדור חוץ מקולייס כדמפרש: **הני מדרי דבבל מהדרי מיא לעין עיטם.** מדרונות שבבבל מחזירין מים הנשפכים בהן לעין עיטם שהוא מקום גבוה שבא"י שאותו מעיין מביא מים לבית טבילת כה"ג ביוה"כ דמתוקן בחומת עזרה על גבי שער המים כדאמרינן בסדר יומא (דף לא.) עין עיטם גבוה מקרקע העזרה כ"ג אמות והיאך מחזירין שיש בפרת סילונות וסולמות למטה מן הקרקע (הים) ודרך אותן סולמות חוזרין המים לא"י וחוזרין ונובעין במעיינות והדגים חזרו דרך אותן סולמות שנוחים להעלותן יותר מדרך פרת עצמו: **והאי.** קולייס האספנין: **כיון דלא שריר שדריה.** אין קשה שדרה שלו: **לטבריה.** לבא ולהטיל עליהם עול ולא שמתכוונין לבטלן משמחת הרגל אבל הקללה גרמה לכך: **קומטין.** נ) לשון לעז הוא שלטון: **בולשת.** חיל המלך: **ליפורי וטבריא** מא"י: **שאינן במקומם.** שמא"י גלו לשם והגולה למקום נכרי מצוין עצמו במלבושים שיהא חשוב: **במתא שמאי.** בעירי איני צריך להתכבד אלא בשמי שאני ניכר בו: **בלא מתא.** במקום שאינה עירי: **תותבאי.** כבודי תלוי בשמלתי שמלתו מתרגמינן תותביה (שמות כב): **ציצין.** למחין: **הבאים.** אותן של יעקב שיבאו לבבל ישרשו ויעשו ציצין ופרחים לתורה וסייעתא אתיא לר' יוחנן דטעמא דמצויינין לאו לפי שאינן בני תורה כדרבי אסי אלא לפי שאינן במקומן:

כשבא

מסורת הש"ס

א) בכורות דף לו. ע"ש, ב) לעיל יט:, ג) לעיל לט., ד) כ"א ל"ג, ה) [דג שבמקומות האספניא ושמו בלשון הקודש שיבוטא ערוך ערך אספנן], ו) [עי' לעיל כא.], ז) ב"ב טז:, ח) סנהדרין ז:, ט) [יומא נד.], י) בכורות מד:, כ) [מגילה לא:], ל) [ועי' שבות יעקב חלק ב' סימן קטן], מ) [יבמות צ:], נ) לשון קומטוס כמו קומוס ולשון רומי הוא עי' רש"י סוטה יד ד"ה גסטרא.

הגהות הב"ח

(א) גמרא לפי שאינן במקומן כצ"ל ותיבת בני נמחק:

תורה אור השלם

א) אֱמֹר לַחָכְמָה אֲחֹתִי אָתְּ וּמֹדָע לַבִּינָה תִקְרָא: [משלי ז, ד]

ב) שַׁאֲנַן מוֹאָב מִנְּעוּרָיו וְשֹׁקֵט הוּא אֶל שְׁמָרָיו וְלֹא הוּרַק מִכְּלִי אֶל כֶּלִי וּבַגּוֹלָה לֹא הָלָךְ עַל כֵּן עָמַד טַעְמוֹ בּוֹ וְרֵיחוֹ לֹא נָמָר: [ירמיה מח, יא]

ג) עַל הֶהָרִים אֶשָּׂא בְכִי וָנֶהִי וְעַל נְאוֹת מִדְבָּר קִינָה כִּי נִצְּתוּ מִבְּלִי אִישׁ עֹבֵר וְלֹא שָׁמְעוּ קוֹל מִקְנֶה מֵעוֹף הַשָּׁמַיִם וְעַד בְּהֵמָה נָדְדוּ הָלָכוּ: [ירמיה ט, ט]

ד) וְהִשְׁבַּתִּי כָּל מְשׂוֹשָׂהּ חַגָּהּ חָדְשָׁהּ וְשַׁבַּתָּהּ וְכֹל מוֹעֲדָהּ: [הושע ב, יג]

ה) חָדְשֵׁיכֶם וּמוֹעֲדֵיכֶם שָׂנְאָה נַפְשִׁי הָיוּ עָלַי לָטֹרַח נִלְאֵיתִי נְשֹׂא: [ישעיה א, יד]

ו) הַבָּאִים יַשְׁרֵשׁ יַעֲקֹב יָצִיץ וּפָרַח יִשְׂרָאֵל וּמָלְאוּ פְנֵי תֵבֵל תְּנוּבָה: [ישעיה כז, ו]

ליקוטי רש"י

לעדות אשה. שמת בעלה במדינת הים. **לעדות בכור.** להעיד שלא הטיל בו מום בכוונה. **אימא לעדות שהאשה כשרה.** ובעדות בכור נמי אשה כשרה דאמרינן הלכתא כרבן שמעון ואפי' בנו. **יימר שרי בוכרא.** יימר המתיר בכורות לשון יימר [בכורות לו.]. **התם דמעיקרא הוא אוכלא ולבסוף אוכלא.** דבש לאחר שזב מן החלות נמי אוכלא הוא הלכך ליכא למיגזר ביה משום דלא שייכי ביה סחיטה. **אבל הכא.** זיתים וענבים דמעיקרא אוכלא והשתא משקה איכא למיגזר שמא יסחוט ותדע מסחטן הוא ודאי סחיטה היא [לעיל יט.]. **כל שבא בחמין.** ככר. **מדיחין.** שאין זה גמר מלאכתו אבל לא שורין. **וקולייס האיספנין.** דג שקורין טוניי"א [שם לט.] ורך ונאכל כמו שהוא חי אלא שנותנין עליו חמין וזה בשולו כדתנן במסכת שבת שהדחתו זו היא גמר מלאכתו [ביצה טז.]. **בר תלתא טרפי.** בן שלש שנים שטענה אמו מסנקלט שלשה עלין חדשין [לעיל קכט.]. **כותח דבבלאי.** ... חמץ כדאמרינן באלו עוברין ואינו עשוי לאכול יחד אלא לטבול בו ואינו כלה עד זמן מרובה [שם ...] כדמפרש באלו עוברין (פסחים מב.) דיהבו ביה עיפושי פת ונסיובי דחלבא מסג"א בלע"ז [ע"ז ל:]. **שהדחתן זו היא גמר מלאכתן.** מדקרי ליה גמר מלאכתו שמע מינה וזהו בישולו וחייב [לעיל לט.]. **תלמידי חכמים שבבבל מצויינין.** דומים למלאכי השרת לבושים לבנים ועטופים כמלאכי השרת וכתיב (יחזקאל ט) והאיש לבוש הבדים ... אמרינן בבמה מדליקין (שבת כה:) על רבי יהודה שהיה מתעטף ויושב בסדינים המצויינין ודומה ...

(כ:) נמי אמרינן מאן מלאכי השרת רבנן ואמאי קרי להו מלאכי השרת משום דמצויינין כמלאכי השרת במלבושים נאים [קידושין עב.]. **אמור לחכמה אחותי את.** שתהא בקי בה כאחותך שאסורה לך [שם ל:]. **נ"ב שנה.** ... בגלות צדקיהו עד פקידת כורש ... לגלות יהויקים היתה הפקידה כמו ששנינו במגילה (יא:) ושמונה עשרה שנה היה מכיבוש יהויקים עד חרבות ירושלים ... **על ההרים.** על חורבן ההרים ... **נדדו הלכו.** ... [ירמיה ט, ט]. **הני מדרי דבבל.** מקומות מדרון שבבבל. **מהדרי מיא לעין עיטם.** שהו כ"ג טובל ביוה"כ כדאמרי' במסכת יומא בפרק ג' (לא.) [בכורות מד:]. [המשך בדף קמו.]

אֶלָּא לְעֵדוּת אִשָּׁה בִּלְבַד – EXCEPT with regard TO offering TESTIMONY concerning the marital staus OF A WOMAN.[1]

The Gemara presents a related inquiry:

אִיבַּעְיָא לְהוּ – **They inquired:** **עֵד מִפִּי עֵד לְעֵדוּת בְּכוֹר מַהוּ** – **What is [the law]** with regard to whether **a witness** who acquired his information **from the mouth of a** second **witness** is believed **to** offer **testimony** concerning the blemishes **of a firstborn** animal? Does the Kohen become permitted to use the blemished animal on the basis of such testimony or not?[2]

The Gemara records a disagreement regarding this question: **רַב אַמִּי אָסִיר** – **Rav Ami prohibits** the Kohen to make use of the animal on the basis of such testimony, **וְרַב אַסִּי שָׁרֵי** – **but Rav Assi permits** him to do so. **אָמַר לֵיהּ רַב אַמִּי לְרַב אַסִּי** – **Rav Ami asked Rav Assi:** **וְהָא תָּנָא דְּבֵי מְנַשְּׁיָא** – **But [a Baraisa] was taught in the academy of Menashya** [i.e. Menasheh]: **אֵין עֵד מִפִּי עֵד כָּשֵׁר אֶלָּא לְעֵדוּת אִשָּׁה בִּלְבַד** – A WITNESS who acquired his information FROM THE MOUTH OF A second WITNESS IS NOT a VALID witness EXCEPT with regard TO offering TESTIMONY concerning the marital status OF A WOMAN. This implies that with regard to any other legal question, such a witness is not believed! How then can Rav Assi say that we accept his testimony concerning the blemish of a firstborn animal?

The Gemara therefore interprets the Baraisa differently: **אֵימָא לְעֵדוּת שֶׁהָאִשָּׁה כְּשֵׁרָה לָהּ בִּלְבַד** – **Say** rather that what the Baraisa means is that the only testimony for which such a witness is valid is **testimony for which a woman** too **is valid.**[3] Thus, just as a woman may bear witness concerning the blemish of a firstborn animal, so too may one who acquired his information from another.

The Gemara relates:

רַב יֵימַר אַכְשַׁר עֵד מִפִּי עֵד לִבְכוֹר – **Rav Yeimar validated** the testimony of **a witness** who acquired his information **from the mouth of a** second **witness** in a case **regarding** the blemishes of **a firstborn** animal, **קָרֵי עֲלֵיהּ מְרֵימַר** – whereupon **Mereimar** disparagingly[4] **referred to him** as **יֵימַר שָׁרֵי בּוּכְרָא** – **Yeimar, the Permitter of the Firstborn.**

The Gemara rules:

וְהִלְכְתָא – **And the halachah is** that **עֵד מִפִּי עֵד כָּשֵׁר לִבְכוֹר** – **a witness** who acquires his testimony **from the mouth of a** second **witness** is considered a **valid** witness **to** testify about the blemishes of **a firstborn** animal.

The Mishnah stated:

חַלּוֹת דְּבַשׁ – If HONEYCOMBS [were chopped before the Sabbath, and honey then oozed from the chopped combs on the Sabbath of its own accord, it is forbidden for consumption on that Sabbath. But R' Elazar permits one to consume it].

The Gemara relates:

כִּי אֲתָא רַב הוֹשַׁעְיָא מִנְּהַרְדְּעָא – **When Rav Hoshaya came from Nehardea,** **אֲתָא וְאַיְיתֵי מַתְנִיתָא בִּידֵיהּ** – **he came and brought a Baraisa with him:** **זֵיתִים וַעֲנָבִים שֶׁרִיסְּקָן מֵעֶרֶב שַׁבָּת וְיָצְאוּ מֵעַצְמָן אֲסוּרִין** – If OLIVES OR GRAPES WERE CHOPPED BEFORE THE SABBATH, AND [THEIR JUICE] then OOZED from them on the Sabbath OF ITS OWN ACCORD, IT IS FORBIDDEN for consumption on that Sabbath. **וְרַבִּי אֶלְעָזָר וְרַבִּי שִׁמְעוֹן מַתִּירִין** – BUT R' ELAZAR AND R' SHIMON PERMIT one to consume it.

The Gemara asks:

אָמַר רַב יוֹסֵף – **Rav Yosef said:** **גַּבְרָא יְתֵירָא אֲתָא לְאַשְׁמְעִינַן** – **Did [Rav Hoshaya] merely come to inform us** that there is **an additional man** [i.e. R' Shimon] who joins R' Elazar in his dissent? What else does this Baraisa teach us that the Mishnah does not?![5]

The Gemara answers:

אָמַר לֵיהּ אַבַּיֵי – **Abaye said to him:** **טוּבָא קָא מַשְׁמַע לָן** – **It informs us of much** that the Mishnah does not! **דְּאִי מִמַּתְנִיתִין** – **For if** we would only have learned of this dispute **from the Mishnah,** **הֲוָה אָמֵינָא** – **I would have said** that **הָתָם הוּא** – **it is** only **there** in the case of crushed honeycombs that R' Elazar permits consumption of the honey, **דְּמֵעִיקָּרָא אוּכְלָא וּלְבַסּוֹף אוּכְלָא** – **since [the honey] is a food in the beginning** [before it is extracted from the honeycomb] **and** remains **a food in the end** [after it oozes from the comb]. **אֲבָל הָכָא** – **But here** in the case of crushed olives and grapes, **דְּמֵעִיקָּרָא אוּכְלָא וּלְבַסּוֹף מַשְׁקֶה אֵימָא לֹא** – **where [the juice] is a food in the beginning, but a beverage in the end,** perhaps R' Elazar will **not** permit its consumption! **קָא מַשְׁמַע לָן** – This Baraisa therefore **informs us** that even in the case of crushed olives or crushed grapes, R' Elazar permits consumption of the liquid that oozes from them on the Sabbath.[6]

NOTES

1. For if a witness testifies that another informed him of the death overseas of a woman's husband, we accept his testimony, and the woman is permitted to remarry. Although such testimony is Biblically invalid, the Rabbis, fearing that the woman would be left an *agunah* (a woman permanently restrained from remarrying), ruled that it be accepted in this case. Now the Rabbis do not have the power to contravene Biblical law; however, every Jewish marriage is conditional upon the will of the Rabbis (see *Yevamos* 90b; *Gittin* 33a; *Bava Basra* 48b). They employed this jurisdiction over marriages to rule retroactively invalid any marriage in which a witness gives hearsay testimony of the overseas death of the husband. Thus, hearsay testimony is accepted in this case (*Rashi;* see *Tosafos* to *Yevamos* 88a ד״ה מתוך with *Gilyon HaShas; Teshuvos HaRashba* §1162; *Chasam Sofer; Rashash*).

2. The Torah mandates that one give the male firstborn (*bechor*) of one's kosher domesticated animals (*beheimah*) to a Kohen, who must offer them as sacrifices in the Temple (see *Exodus* 13:2; *Deuteronomy* 15:19). After throwing the blood and burning the sacrificial portions of such an animal upon the Altar, the Kohen may consume its meat. If a *bechor* develops a disqualifying blemish, it cannot be brought as a sacrifice, but becomes the property of the Kohen, who may consume it as he pleases (*Rambam, Bechoros* 1:1,2,3). However, this is true only if the blemish develops on its own; if the Kohen deliberately causes the blemish [in order to gain full ownership of the animal], he is penalized by being forbidden to use it (*Bechoros* 34a; *Rambam* ibid. 2:7). Now, there were unscrupulous Kohanim who would deliberately inflict blemishes upon such animals and then claim that they developed of their own accord. The Mishnah in *Bechoros* (35a) therefore rules that a Kohen is not believed to say that a blemish occurred on its own, but must produce witnesses who support his claim. Certain leniencies, though, were allowed for this "testimony" (see there 35a,b). The Gemara thus inquires as to whether these witnesses must have firsthand knowledge of the development of the blemish, or if they may give hearsay testimony (*Rashi;* see *Rashi* to *Sanhedrin* 30b ד״ה בעדות בכור and *Tosafos* there).

3. [For the Baraisa's statement, חוּץ מֵעֵדוּת אִשָּׁה בִּלְבַד, translates literally as, *except for the testimony of a woman.* In its challenge, the Gemara understood this as a reference to testimony *concerning* a woman, i.e. testimony that allows her to remarry. The Gemara now explains the statement as referring to testimony *offered* by a woman, which is valid in only a few limited instances. The Baraisa is teaching that hearsay testimony is equivalent to the testimony of a woman – where one is valid, the other is as well.] Thus, Rav Assi permits hearsay testimony in the case of a firstborn, since that is a case in which a woman's testimony would be valid (*Rashi;* see *Bechoros* ibid.).

4. *Rashi* to *Bechoros* 36a ד״ה יימר שרי בוכרא.

5. [Although the Baraisa discusses olives and grapes and the Mishnah honeycombs, the disputes they set forth by each are identical!] Rav Yosef accordingly wonders whether Rav Hoshaya's only purpose in teaching this Baraisa was to demonstrate that R' Shimon agrees to R' Elazar (*Rashi*).

6. It has been explained above (see 144b note 1) that the acts of דָּשׁ, *threshing,* and מְפָרֵק, *extracting,* are prohibited as *melachos* only if their performance effects a change in an object's classification [such as in the threshing of a kernel of grain, which before being threshed is classified as a non-food, but which after threshing falls into the category of a food].

לעדות אשה. לומר לאשה מת בעליך דאקילו בה רבנן משום עיגונא וכל דמקדש אדעתא דרבנן מקדש ואפקועי רבנן לקדושין מיניה: לעדות בכור. בכור ביד כהן כשנתנו ישראל לו שלם ואירע לו בו מום קי"ל בבכורות (דף לה.) נחשדו כהנים להטיל מום בבכור ואין נאמן לומר מום זה נפל בו מאליו וצריך להביא עדים ואמרינן התם דאשה כשרה לעדות זו: אימא לעדות שהאשה כשרה לה. והאי נמי כשרה לה: גברא יתירא. ר"ש דמתני' ר"א תנן בה: אתא לאשמעינן. בתמיה כלומר מה בא ללמדנו אם לא זאת:

בהמה בגימטריא. אסמכתא בעלמא היא דנ"ב נפקא לן בלאו גימטריא כדפי' בקונטרס: שוכר

אלא לעדות אשה בלבד איבעיא להו עד מפי עד לעדות בכור מהו רב אמי אסיר ורב אסי שרי א"ל רב אמי לרב אסי והא תנא דבי מנשיא אין עד מפי עד כשר אלא לעדות אשה בלבד אימא לעדות שהאשה כשרה לה בלבד רב יימר אכשר עד מפי עד לבכור קרי עליה מרימר יימר שרי בוכרא והלכתא עד מפי עד כשר לבכור: חלות דבש: כי אתא רב הושעיא מנהרדעא אתא ואייתי מתניתא בידיה זיתים וענבים שריסקן מע"ש ויצאו מעצמן אסורין ור"א ור"ש מתירין אמר רב יוסף גברא יתירא אתא לאשמעינן א"ל אביי טובא קמ"ל דאי ממתניתין הוה אמינא התם הוא דמעיקרא אוכלא ולבסוף אוכלא אבל הכא דמעיקרא אוכלא ולבסוף משקה אימא לא קמ"ל: **מתני'** כל שבא בחמין מערב שבת שורין אותו בחמין בשבת וכל שלא בא בחמין מערב שבת מדיחין אותו בחמין בשבת חוץ מן המליח הישן (ודגים מלוחין קטנים) וקוליים האיספנין שהדחתן זו היא גמר מלאכתן: **גמ'** כגון מאי אמר רב ספרא כגון תרנגולתא דר' אבא ואמר רב ספרא זימנא חדא איקלעית להתם ואוכלן מיניה ואי לא רבי אבא דאשקיין חמרא בר תלתא טרפי איתנסי רבי יוחנן רייק מכותח דבבלאי אמר רב יוסף ולירוק אנן מתרנגולתא דרבי אבא ועוד אמר רב גזא זימנא חדא איקלעית להתם ועבדית כותח דבבלאי שאילו מיניה כל בריחי מערבא: כל שלא בא בחמין וכו': הדיח מאי אמר רב יוסף הדיח חייב חטאת אמר מר בריה דרבינא אף אנן נמי תנינא חוץ ממליח ישן וקוליים האיספנין שהדחתן זו היא גמר מלאכתן שמע מינה יתיב רבי חייא בר אבא ורבי אסי קמיה דרבי יוחנן ויתיב רבי יוחנן וקא מנמנם אמר ליה רבי חייא בר אבא לרבי אסי מפני מה עופות שבבבל שמנים א"ל כלך למדבר עזה ואראך שמנים מהן מפני מה מועדים שבבבל שמחים מפני שהן עניים מפני מה ת"ח שבבבל מצויינין לפי שאינן בני תורה מפני מה עובדי כוכבים מזוהמי' מפני שאוכלין שקצי' ורמשי' איתער בהו רבי יוחנן אמר להו דרדקי לא כך אמרתי לכם אמור לחכמה אחותי את אם ברור לך הדבר כאחותך שהיא אסורה לך אומרהו ואם לאו לא תאמרהו אמרו ליה ולימא לן מר איזה מהן מפני מה עופות שבבבל שמנים מפני שלא גלו שנאמר שאנן מואב מנעוריו ושקט הוא אל שמריו ובגולה לא הלך והכא מנלן דגלו דתניא רבי יהודה אומר נ"ב שנה לא עבר איש ביהודה שנאמר על ההרים אשא בכי ונהי וגו' מעוף השמים ועד בהמה נדדו הלכו בהמ"ה בגימטריא חמשין ותרתין הוו א"ר יעקב א"ר יוחנן כולן חזרו חוץ מקוליים האיספנין דאמר רב הני מדרי דבבל מהדרי מיא לעין עיטם והאי כיון דלא שריר שדריה לא מצי סליק מפני מה מועדים שבבבל שמחים מפני שלא היו באותה קללה דכתיב והשבתי כל משושה חגה חדשה ושבתה וכל מועדה וכתיב חדשיכם ומועדיכם שנאה נפשי היו עלי לטורח מאי היו עלי לטורח א"ר אלעזר אמר הקב"ה לא דיין לישראל שחוטאין לפני אלא שמטריחין אותי לידע איזו גזירה קשה אביא עליהן א"ר יצחק אין לך כל רגל ורגל שלא באתה בולשת לציפורי ואמר רבי חנינא אין לך כל רגל ורגל שלא בא לטבריה אגמון וקמטון ובעל זמורה מפני מה ת"ח שבבבל מצויינין לפי שאינן (א) בני מקומן דאמרי אינשי במתא שמאי בלא מתא תותבאי הבאים ישרש יעקב יציץ ופרח ישראל תני רב יוסף אלו תלמידי חכמים שבבבל שעושין ציצין ופרחים לתורה מפני מה עובדי כוכבים מזוהמין שלא עמדו על הר סיני שבשעה

שבא

רבינו חננאל

למשקין היוצא מהן אסור. והא דתניא סוחטין בפגעים ובפרישין ובעוזרדין אבל לא ברמונים דשל בית מנשיא בן מנחם היו סוחטין ברמונים אמר רב נחמן הלכה כשל בית מנשיא בן מנחם וסלקא שמעתא דאסור לסחוט ברמונים בשבת והא דתניא אין עד מפי עד כשר אלא לעדות אשה בלבד. אוקימנא לעדות שהאשה כשרה לה והלכתא עד מפי עד כשר לבכור.

רב נסים גאון

ואין עד מפי עד כשר אלא לעדות אשה בלבד כשאמר כי מת בעלה התירוה בית דין לינשא...

הגהות הב"ח

(א) גמרא לפי שאינן במקומן נ"ב ותיבת בני נמחק:

תורה אור השלם

א) אֱמֹר לַחָכְמָה אֲחֹתִי אָתְּ וּמֹדָע לַבִּינָה תִקְרָא: [משלי ז, ד]

ב) שַׁאֲנַן מוֹאָב מִנְּעוּרָיו וְשֹׁקֵט הוּא אֶל שְׁמָרָיו וְלֹא הוּרַק מִכְּלִי אֶל כֶּלִי וּבַגּוֹלָה לֹא הָלָךְ עַל כֵּן עָמַד טַעְמוֹ בּוֹ וְרֵיחוֹ לֹא נָמָר: [ירמיה מח, יא]

ג) עַל הֶהָרִים אֶשָּׂא בְכִי וָנֶהִי וְעַל נְאוֹת מִדְבָּר קִינָה כִּי נִצְּתוּ מִבְּלִי אִישׁ עֹבֵר וְלֹא שָׁמְעוּ קוֹל מִקְנֶה מֵעוֹף הַשָּׁמַיִם וְעַד בְּהֵמָה נָדְדוּ הָלָכוּ: [ירמיה ט, ט]

ד) וְהִשְׁבַּתִּי כָּל מְשׂוֹשָׂהּ חַגָּהּ חָדְשָׁהּ וְשַׁבַּתָּהּ וְכֹל מוֹעֲדָהּ: [הושע ב, יג]

ה) חָדְשֵׁיכֶם וּמוֹעֲדֵיכֶם שָׂנְאָה נַפְשִׁי הָיוּ עָלַי לָטֹרַח נִלְאֵיתִי נְשֹׂא: [ישעיה א, יד]

ו) הַבָּאִים יַשְׁרֵשׁ יַעֲקֹב יָצִיץ וּפָרַח יִשְׂרָאֵל וּמָלְאוּ פְנֵי תֵבֵל תְּנוּבָה: [ישעיה כז, ו]

ליקוטי רש"י

לעדות אשה. שמת בעלה כמדינת הים. לעדות בכור. להעיד שלא הטיל בו מום זה בכוונה. אימא לעדות שהאשה כשרה...

Mishnah כֹּל שֶׁבָּא בְחַמִּין מֵעֶרֶב שַׁבָּת – **Anything that was placed into hot water** [i.e. that was cooked] **before the Sabbath,** שׁוֹרִין אוֹתוֹ בְחַמִּין בְּשַׁבָּת – **we may soak in hot water on the Sabbath.**[7] וְכֹל שֶׁלֹּא בָא בְחַמִּין מֵעֶרֶב שַׁבָּת – **And anything that was not placed into hot water before the Sabbath,**[8] מְדִיחִין אוֹתוֹ בְחַמִּין בְּשַׁבָּת – **we may rinse** only **with hot water on the Sabbath,**[9] חוּץ מִן הַמָּלִיחַ הַיָּשָׁן (ודגים מלוחים קטנים) – **except for an aged salted fish,** וְקוּלְיָיס הָאִיסְפָּנִין – **or a** salted **Spanish mackerel,** which we may not even rinse with hot water on the Sabbath. שֶׁהֲדָחָתָן זוֹ הִיא גְּמַר מְלַאכְתָּן – **For their rinsing completes their preparation;** it is therefore prohibited as an act of cooking.[10]

Gemara The Gemara wonders what sort of food it is that is further soaked in hot water after having already been cooked:

כְּגוֹן מַאי – **Such as what?**

The Gemara answers:

אָמַר רַב סַפְרָא – **Rav Safra said:** כְּגוֹן תַּרְנְגוֹלְתָּא דְּרַבִּי אַבָּא – **Such as the hen of R' Abba,** which he would customarily soak for many days after cooking it, until it would dissolve of its own accord.[11]

Rav Safra relates an incident concerning this dish:

וְאָמַר רַב סַפְרָא – **And Rav Safra said:** זִימְנָא חֲדָא אִיקְּלַעִית לְהָתָם – **One time I happened to go there** [i.e. to R' Abba's home in Eretz Yisrael], וְאוֹכְלַן מִינֵּיהּ – **and he fed us of [this dish],** וְאִי לָא רַבִּי אַבָּא דְּאַשְׁקְיַין חַמְרָא בַּר תְּלָתָא טַרְפֵי – **and had R' Abba not given me three-year-old wine to drink,** אִיתְנְסִי – **I would have been compelled** to vomit in disgust at eating it!

The Gemara records R' Yochanan's opinion regarding a popular Babylonian dish:

רַבִּי יוֹחָנָן רָיֵיק מִכּוּתָּח דְּבַבְלָאֵי – **R' Yochanan,** who was from Eretz Yisrael, **would spit upon** remembering **the** revolting flavor of **Babylonian *kutach*.**[12]

Rav Yosef, who was from Babylonia, was troubled by the apparent contempt with which the Jews of Eretz Yisrael viewed the Jews of Babylonia.[13] The Gemara records his response to R' Yochanan's custom:

אָמַר רַב יוֹסֵף – **Rav Yosef said:** וְלֵירוֹק אֲנַן מִתַּרְנְגוֹלְתָּא דְּרַבִּי אַבָּא – **But we** Babylonians too **might** have good reason to **spit upon** remembering the repulsiveness of **the hen of R' Abba!**[14] וְעוֹד – **And furthermore,** others of Eretz Yisrael do not consider the Babylonian *kutach* to be repulsive, as is evident from an incident that occurred with Rav Gaza. אָמַר רַב גָּזָא – For **Rav Gaza said:** זִימְנָא חֲדָא אִיקְּלַעִית לְהָתָם – **One time I happened**

NOTES

One is therefore permitted on the Biblical level to squeeze chopped honeycombs on the Sabbath, since no change in the honey's character results – it is a food while within the comb, and remains one after being squeezed from it. In the case of chopped olives or grapes, by contrast, since the juice within the fruit only becomes a beverage upon being extracted from the fruit, one would be prohibited to squeeze it out (see above, 19a,b, and 19b note 10). One might assume that R' Elazar accordingly differentiates between the honey that oozes from chopped combs and the juice that flows from chopped fruit. In the case of honey, there is no reason to prohibit using it, since one is in any case permitted to squeeze the combs (see *Magen Avraham* 321:16). But in the case of juice, since one is forbidden to squeeze the olives or grapes, even R' Elazar will prohibit its use, since one might come thereby to squeeze the fruit, in violation of the Sabbath! The Baraisa introduced by Rav Hoshaya, however, teaches that R' Elazar's ruling applies even to the juice of chopped olives or grapes. Although one is prohibited to squeeze these fruits, we do not suspect that allowing consumption of their juice will lend one to do so. For it is not the usual practice to squeeze fruits that were previously chopped, since the juice will flow from them on its own. R' Elazar therefore permits one to make use of the juice. The Sages, however, prohibit the juice, lest one erroneously infer from its permissibility that it is permissible as well to derive juice from *unchopped* fruits by squeezing them on the Sabbath (see *Rashi* to 19b and to 143b).

[The Gemara's designation of honey as a food is imprecise, since it is fact a beverage. However, the Gemara here does not concern itself with precision on this point, since it merely wishes to point out that the character of honey, whether it is a food or a beverage, does not change with its extraction (see *Rash* to *Okatzin* 3:11 and *Teshuvos Chasam Sofer, Orach Chaim* §45; but cf. *Magen Avraham* 158:7).]

7. In order that it will become soft and dissolve (*Rashi*). [One may even soak the item in hot water that is in its primary vessel (כְּלִי רִאשׁוֹן – the vessel in which it was heated). For although water in a primary vessel will generally cook food that is placed into it, since this item is completely cooked, additional heating will not cook it further. One may not, however, place the item into a pot that is upon a fire, since this is prohibited by Rabbinic law as an act of *chazarah,* or *returning* a food to the fire (see *Mishnah Berurah* 318:33).]

8. Such as dried meat, which *in extremis* can be eaten raw (*Rashi*).

9. [For since this sort of food can be eaten raw,] we do not view the act of rinsing it in hot water as a form of cooking [unlike the two foods described below, whose rinsing is their "cooking"]. One is therefore permitted to rinse this sort of food, but not to soak it. [For since it was not previously cooked, soaking it will cause it to become so, and thus constitutes a prohibited act of cooking] (*Rashi*).

[According to some, one is only permitted to rinse these sorts of foods with water from a secondary vessel (כְּלִי שֵׁנִי – the vessel into which the water was transferred from the primary vessel). Water from a primary vessel, however, may not be used, since it accomplishes a limited degree of cooking even through rinsing. However, others hold that rinsing never effects cooking, and therefore permit rinsing the food even with water from a primary vessel (see *Tosafos* to 39a ד״ה כל שבא and *Mishnah Berurah* ibid. §35). Now, on the Biblical level, one is only prohibited to soak this sort of food in a *primary* vessel, since only in that case will soaking cook a food. However, the Rabbis prohibit even soaking in a secondary vessel, for since the water is hot, it resembles actual cooking (see *Tosafos* ibid. and *Mishnah Berurah* ibid. §34).]

10. An aged salted fish is a fish salted [at least] a year previously. Both this fish and a salted Spanish mackerel, because of their salt, must be rinsed in hot water in order to be fit for consumption. Since rinsing is all these fishes require to become ready to eat, it is considered their "cooking" and is thus prohibited (*Rashi* here and to *Beitzah* 16b; but see *Beur Halachah* to 318:4 ד״ה והדחתן at length for an alternative explanation of this prohibition). [One is prohibited even to rinse these foods with hot water from a secondary vessel (see *Mishnah Berurah* ibid. §36). This law applies not only to these salted fish, but to any sort of food that requires rinsing in hot water to render it edible. The rinsing of such a food is deemed to be cooking, and is therefore prohibited (*Mishnah Berurah* ibid. §39; see *Beur Halachah* ibid. ד״ה וקולייס).]

[Throughout this Mishnah, the term *hot water* refers to water that is *yad soledes bo* – i.e. heated to a degree that one's hand recoils when it comes into contact with it (see *Mishnah Berurah* ibid. §34; see *Beur Halachah* ibid. ד״ה היא גמר מלאכתן).]

[Our translation of קוּלְיָיס הָאִיסְפָּנִין as Spanish mackerel is in accordance with *Rashi* to 39a, who identifies this fish in Old French as a טוּנִינָא, or *tonine* [translated by *Targum HaLaaz* as a tunny, or tuna], and *Aruch* ע׳ אספנן, who states that it is a fish found in Spanish waters. Tuna and mackerel are both members of the scombroid family of fish – hence, Spanish mackerel. However, see *Aruch* ibid. for an alternative translation; see also *Yerushalmi, Taanis* 4:6. See also *Beur Halachah* ibid. ד״ה חוץ, who maintains that *Rashi* is actually unsure whether this fish is in fact a *tonine.*]

11. R' Abba would prepare this dish for medicinal reasons (*Rashi*). [See *Rav Nissim Gaon* and *Rabbeinu Chananel* for alternative descriptions of the preparation involved.]

12. [*Kutach* is a sauce or dip made of breadcrumbs and whey.]

13. [The Jews of Eretz Yisrael were known to dislike the Jews of Babylonia (see *Yoma* 66b).]

14. A dish popular among the inhabitants of Eretz Yisrael (*Rashi*).

עין משפט נר מצוה

כ א מיי' פ"ג מהלכות בכורות הלכה טו סמג עשין ריא טוש"ע יו"ד סימן שיד סעיף ה:

כא ב מיי' פכ"א מהל' שבת הלכה טז טור שו"ע או"ח סימן רנג סעיף ה וסי' שכ סעיף ג:

כב ג מיי' פכ"ב שם הלכה ח סמג לאוין סה טוש"ע או"ח סימן שיח סעיף ד:

כג ד מיי' פ"כ מהלכות סנהדרין הלכה ז סמג עשין מ טור שו"ע חו"מ סימן י סעיף א:

גמרא

בהמה בגימטריא. אסמכתא בעלמא היא דנ"ב נפקא לן בלאו גימטריא כדפי' בקונטרס שוכר

אלא לעדות אשה בלבד איבעיא להו עד מפי עד לעדות בכור מהו רב אמי אסיר ורב אסי שרי א"ל רב אמי לרב אסי והא תנא דבי מנשיא אין עד מפי עד כשר אלא לעדות אשה בלבד אימא לעדות שהאשה כשרה לה בלבד רב יימר אכשר עד מפי עד לבכור קרי עליה מרימר יימר שרי בוכרא והלכתא עד מפי עד כשר לבכור: חלות דבש: כי אתא רב הושעיא מנהרדעא אתא ואייתי מתניתא בידיה זיתים וענבים שריסקן מע"ש ויצאו מעצמן אסורין ר"א ור"ש מתירין אמר רב יוסף גברא יתירא אתא לאשמעינן א"ל אביי טובא קמ"ל דאי ממתניתין הוה אמינא התם הוא דמעיקרא אוכלא ולבסוף אוכלא אבל הכא דמעיקרא אוכלא ולבסוף משקה אימא לא קמ"ל: **מתני'** כל שבא בחמין מערב שבת שורין אותו בחמין בשבת וכל שלא בא בחמין מערב שבת מדיחין אותו בחמין בשבת חוץ מן המליח הישן (ודגים מלוחין קטנים) וקוליים האיספנין שהדחתן זו היא גמר מלאכתן: **גמ'** כגון מאי אמר רב ספרא כגון תרנגולתא דר' אבא ואמר רב ספרא זימנא חדא איקלעית להתם ואוכלן מיניה ואי לא רבי אבא דאשקיין חמרא בר תלתא טרפי איתנסי רבי יוחנן רייק מכותח דבבלאי אמר רב יוסף ולירוק אנן מתרנגולתא דרבי אבא ועוד אמר רב גזא זימנא חדא איקלעית להתם ועבדית כותח דבבלאי שאילו מיניה כל בריחי מערבא: כל שלא בא בחמין וכו': הדיח מאי אמר רב יוסף הדיח חייב חטאת אמר מר בריה דרבינא אף אנן נמי תנינא חוץ ממליח ישן וקוליים האיספנין שהדחתן זו היא גמר מלאכתן שמע מינה יתיב רבי חייא בר אבא ורבי אסי קמיה דרבי יוחנן ויתיב רבי יוחנן וקא מנמנם אמר ליה רבי חייא בר אבא לרבי אסי מפני מה עופות שבבבל שמנים א"ל כלך למדבר עזה ואראך שמנים מהן מפני מה מועדים שבבבל שמחים מפני שהן עניים מפני מה ת"ח שבבבל מצויינין לפי שאינן בני תורה מפני מה עובדי כוכבים מזוהמי' מפני שאוכלין שקצי' ורמשי' איתער בהו רבי יוחנן אמר להו דרדקי לא כך אמרתי לכם אמור לחכמה אחותי את אם ברור לך הדבר כאחותך שהיא אסורה לך אומרהו ואם לאו לא תאמרהו אמרו ליה ולימא לן מר איזה מהן מפני מה עופות שבבבל שמנים מפני שלא גלו שנאמר שאנן מואב מנעוריו ושקט הוא אל שמריו ובגולה לא הלך והכא מנלן דגלו דתניא רבי יהודה אומר נ"ב שנה לא עבר איש ביהודה שנאמר על ההרים אשא בכי ונהי וגו' מעוף השמים ועד בהמה נדדו הלכו בהמ"ה בגימטריא חמשין ותרתין הוו א"ר יעקב א"ר יוחנן כולן חזרו חוץ מקוליים האיספנין דאמר רב הני מדרי דבבל מהדרי מיא לעין עיטם והאי כיון דלא שריר שדריה לא מצי סליק מפני מה מועדים שבבבל שמחים מפני שלא היו באותה קללה דכתיב והשבתי כל משושה חגה חדשה ושבתה וכל מועדה וכתיב חדשיכם ומועדיכם שנאה נפשי היו עלי לטורח מאי היו עלי לטורח א"ר אלעזר אמר הקב"ה לא דיין לישראל שחוטאין לפני אלא שמטריחין אותי לידע איזו גזירה קשה אביא עליהן א"ר יצחק אין לך כל רגל ורגל שלא באתה בולשת לציפורי ואמר רבי חנינא אין לך כל רגל ורגל שלא בא לטבריה אגמון וקמטון ובעל זמורה מפני מה ת"ח שבבבל מצויינין לפי שאינן (א) בני מקומן דאמרי אינשי במתא שמאי בלא מתא תותבאי הבאים ישרש יעקב יציץ ופרח ישראל תני רב יוסף אלו תלמידי חכמים שבבבל שעושין ציצין ופרחים לתורה מפני מה עובדי כוכבים מזוהמין שלא עמדו על הר סיני שבשעה שבא

רש"י

לעדות אשה. לומר לאשה מת בעליך דאקילו בה רבנן משום עיגונא וכל דמקדש אדעתא דרבנן מקדש ואפקועי רבנן לקדושין מיניה: **לעדות בכור.** בכור ביד כהן כשנתנו ישראל לו שלם ואירע לו בו מום קי"ל בבכורות (דף לה.) נחשדו כהנים להטיל מום בבכור ואין נאמן לומר מום זה נפל בו מאליו וצריך להביא עדים ואמרינן התם דאשה כשרה לעדות זו: **אימא לעדות שהאשה כשרה לה.** והאי נמי כשרה לה: **גברא יתירא.** ר"ש דמתני' ר"א תנן בה: **אתא לאשמעינן.** בתמיה כלומר מה בא ללמדנו הא לא זהו: **מתני' כל שבא בחמין.** כלומר שנתבשל: **שורין אותו בחמין.** כדי שיהא נמוח: **וכל שלא בא בחמין.** כגון בשר יבש שאוכלין אותו חי ע"י הדחק: **מדיחין אותו.** ולא אמרי' זהו בישולו אבל לא שורין: **חוץ מן המליח ישן.** דג מליח של שנה שעברה: **וקוליים האיספנין.** שם דג שאוכלין אותו מחמת מלחו ע"י הדחה בחמין והכך אפילו הדחה נמי לא שזהו גמר מלאכתן והוי בשול: **גמ' כגון מאי.** הוי בא בחמין שחוזרין ושורין אותו בחמין: **תרנגולתיה דר' אבא.** מבשלה ושורה אותה ימים רבים בחמין למחות מאליה ואוכלה לרפואה: **בר תלתא טרפי.** בן ג' שנים: **איתנסי.** הייתי נאנס להקיא מחמת מיאוס: **רייק.** רוקק מכותחא דבבלאי כשזוכרו שהיה מאוס בעיניו: **אמר רב יוסף כו'.** קשה היה בעיניו שנמאסין בני בבל על בני ארץ ישראל אמר אנו נמי יש לנו לרוק מתרנגולתיה דר' אבא שהם אוכלים: **ועוד כותח.** אינו מאוס כל כך בעיני שאר בני מערבא: **דהא אמר רב גזא כו'.** ושאילו מיניה אותו כותח: **בריחי.** חולים: **הדיח.** קוליים מאי: **חייב חטאת.** דהוי בישול: **מפני מה עופות שבבבל שמנים.** משל הוא: **כלך.** לכה לך אלא שקיל הלכון: **למדבר עזה.** והיא מא"י: **מועדים שבבבל שמחים.** רגילים לשמוח במועדים יותר מא"י: **מפני שהם עניים.** וכל השנה אין להם שמחה במאכל ומשתה ואין להם מרגוע ממלאכה לפיכך במועדים כל שמחתם: **מצויינין.** מליינין עצמן בלבושים נאים: **מצויינין.** מקושטין: **שאינן בני תורה.** כל כך לכבדם כבני ארץ ישראל מחמת תורתם מכבדים אותם מחמת לבושין שנראין חשובים: **דרדקי.** בחורים שלא הגיעו לסברא: **מפני שלא גלו.** העופות כמו אותן של א"י כדאמרינן לקמן: **שאנן מואב מנעוריו וגו'.** סיפיה דקרא על כן עמד טעמו בו אלמא הגולין מפיגין טעמן ושמנן: **נ"ב שנה.** משגלו בימי צדקיה בחרבות ירושלים עד שנפקדו בימי כורש ואז עלו מהם לייסד את הבית י"ח שנים קודם גמר הבנין שהיה לסוף ע' שנה בשנת שתים לדריוש כדאמרי' במגילה (דף יא:): **וכולן חזרו.** הבהמות ועופות ואף הדגים חוץ מן קוליים האספנין וכולן חזרו דהא עד בהמה כתיב ומכלל דמכאן ואילך הדור חוץ מקוליים כדמפרש: **הני מדרי דבבל מהדרי מיא לעין עיטם.** מדרונות שבבבל מחזירין מים הנשפכים בהן לעין עיטם שבא"י שאותו מעיין מביא מים לבית טבילת כה"ג ביוה"כ דמתוקן בחומת עזרה על גבי שער המים כדאמרינן בסדר יומא (דף לא.) עין עיטם גבוה מקרקע העזרה כ"ג אמות והיאך מחזירין שיש בפרת סילונות וסולמות למטה מן הקרקע (הים) ודרך אותן סולמות חוזרין המים לא"י וחוזרין ונובעין במעיינות והדגים חוזרו דרך אותן סולמות שנוחים להעלותן יותר מדרך פרת עצמו: **והאי.** קוליים האספנין: **כיון דלא שריר שדריה.** אין קשה שדרה שלו: **לטבריה.** לבוז ולהטיל עליהם עול ולא שמתכוונין לבטלן משמחת הרגל אבל הקללה גרמה לכך: **קומטין.** לשון לעז הוא שלטון: **בולשת.** חיל המלך: **ליפורי וטבריה** מא"י: **שאינן במקומם.** שמא"י גלו לשם והגולה למקום נכרי מליין עצמו במלבושים שיהא חשוב: **במתא שמאי.** בעירי איני צריך להתכבד אלא בשמי שאני ניכר בו: **בלא מתא.** במקום שאינה עירי: **תותבאי.** כבודי תלוי בשמלתי שמלתו מתרגמינן תותביה (שמות כב): **ציצין.** למחין: **הבאים.** אותן של יעקב שיבאו לבבל ישרשו ויעשו ציצין ופרחים לתורה וסייעתא אתיא לר' יוחנן דטעמא דמצויינין לאו לפי שאינן בני תורה כדרבי אסי אלא לפי שאינן במקומן: כשבא

תוספות

בהמה בגימטריא. אסמכתא בעלמא היא דנ"ב נפקא לן בלאו גימטריא כדפי' בקונטרס:

רבינו חננאל

למשקין היוצא מהן אסור. והא דתניא סוחטין בפגעים ובפרישין ובעוזרדין אבל לא ברמונים דשל בית מנשיא בן מנחם היו סוחטין ברמונים אמר רב נחמן הלכה כשל בית מנשיא בן מנחם וסלקא שמעתא דאסור לסחוט ברמונים בשבת והא דתני אין עד מפי עד כשר אלא לעדות אשה בלבד. אוקימנא לעדות שהאשה כשרה לה והלכתא עד מפי עד כשר לבכור. פי' עד מפי עד נאמן להעיד על בכור בהמה טהורה שזה המום שיש בו אפי' שראוי לבוא בידי אדם הוא לא נפל בו מידי אדם ובזו העדות החכם מתירו להאכל במומו וכ"ש בעדות גדולה מזו. ומפורש כך בבכורות פ' כל פסולי המוקדשי'. וסלקא שמעתא התם דהלכתא כרשב"ג דאמר אפילו בנו ובתו נאמנים ויש מי שאומר כי עד מפי עד נאמן בבכור אדם וטעות הוא בידו: **חלות** דבש שריסקן מע"ש ויצאו מעצמן אסורין ור' אלעזר מתיר. כי אתא רב הושעיא מנהרדעא אתא ואייתי מתניתא בידיה זיתים וענבים שריסקן מע"ש ויצאו מעצמן אסורים. ור' אלעזר ור"ש מתירין. והא מתניתא מסייעא נמי לר' יוחנן: **מתני'** כל שבא בחמין מלפני השבת וכו'. ומיבעיא לן כגון מאי. ואמר רב ספרא כגון תרנגולתא דר' אסא שהיתה מלוחה ביותר וכשמבקשין לאוכלה שורין אותה במים חמין. אמר רב ספרא כגון זו התרנגולת אם הובאה בחמין מלפני השבת מותר לשרותה בחמין בשבת ולאוכלה. ואם לאו אסור לשרותה ומותר להדיחה והמליח הישן וקולייס האיספנין

רב נסים גאון

ואין עד מפי עד כשר אלא לעדות אשה בלבד כשאמר כי מת בעלה התירוה בית דין לינשא ואע"פ שהמועט העתיק דבר זה מזולתו וכמו שביארו דבר זה בפרק אשה שהלך בעלה וצרתה (דף קכב) והוחזקו להיות משיאין עד מפי עד וכו': **עד** מפי עד בבכור מהו. עיקר דיליה במסכת בכורות בפרק כל פסולי המוקדשין (דף לה) דתניא ר' יהושע בן קפוסאי אומר בכור בי כהן צריך ב' מן השוק להעיד עליו רבן שמעון בן גמליאל אומר אפילו בנו ובתו ואמרו הלכתא כרבן שמעון ודוקא בנו ובתו אבל אשתו לא מאי טעמא אשתו כגופו דמיא ועוד אמרו איבעיא להו עד מפי עד מהו לעדות בכור אמר ליה תני אלא לעדות אשה כשירה לו וכבר נתברר לנו שבתו כשירה והואיל ואשה כשירה לעדות בכור עד מפי עד נמי כשר לעדות בכור וכן פסקה ההלכה וזה שאמרו בבכור בהמה אבל בבכור אדם לא. גרסינן בפרק י' יוחסין (דף עד) ג' נאמנין על הבכור חיה ואמו ואביו חיה לאלתר אמו כל ז' אביו לעולם: **כגון** תרנגלתיה דר' אבא. כך פירשה אדוננו האיי גאון ז"ל תרנגולת שמבשלין אותה ומוציאין אותה מהמרק וממלאין אותה בתבלין וכשרוצה לאכול ממנה שורין אותה במים חמים ואוכלים אותה כאילו היא חמה: **סליק פרק חבית**

מסורת הש"ס

א) בכורות דף לו. ע"ש, ב) לעיל יט:, ג) לעיל לט., ד) נ"א ל"ג, ה) [דג שבמקומות האספניא ושמו בלשון הקודש שיבוטא ערוך ערך אספן], ו) [ע' לעיל כח.], ז) ב"ב טז:, ח) סנהדרין ז:, ט) [יומא נד.], י) בכורות מד:, כ) [מגילה לא:], ל) [וע' שבות יעקב חלק ב' סימן קטן], מ) [יבמות ל:], נ) לשון קומטוס כמו קומוס ולשון רומי הוא ע' רש"י סוטה יד ד"ה גסטרא.

הגהות הב"ח

(א) גמרא לפי שאינן במקומן כצ"ל ותיבת בני נמחק:

תורה אור השלם

א) אֱמֹר לַחָכְמָה אֲחֹתִי אָתְּ וּמֹדָע לַבִּינָה תִקְרָא: [משלי ז, ד]

ב) שַׁאֲנַן מוֹאָב מִנְּעוּרָיו וְשֹׁקֵט הוּא אֶל שְׁמָרָיו וְלֹא הוּרַק מִכְּלִי אֶל כֶּלִי וּבַגּוֹלָה לֹא הָלָךְ עַל כֵּן עָמַד טַעְמוֹ בּוֹ וְרֵיחוֹ לֹא נָמָר: [ירמיה מח, יא]

ג) עַל הֶהָרִים אֶשָּׂא בְכִי וָנֶהִי וְעַל נְאוֹת מִדְבָּר קִינָה כִּי נִצְּתוּ מִבְּלִי אִישׁ עֹבֵר וְלֹא שָׁמְעוּ קוֹל מִקְנֶה מֵעוֹף הַשָּׁמַיִם וְעַד בְּהֵמָה נָדְדוּ הָלָכוּ: [ירמיה ט, ט]

ד) וְהִשְׁבַּתִּי כָּל מְשׂוֹשָׂהּ חַגָּהּ חָדְשָׁהּ וְשַׁבַּתָּהּ וְכֹל מוֹעֲדָהּ: [הושע ב, יג]

ה) חָדְשֵׁיכֶם וּמוֹעֲדֵיכֶם שָׂנְאָה נַפְשִׁי הָיוּ עָלַי לָטֹרַח נִלְאֵיתִי נְשֹׂא: [ישעיה א, יד]

ו) הַבָּאִים יַשְׁרֵשׁ יַעֲקֹב יָצִיץ וּפָרַח יִשְׂרָאֵל וּמָלְאוּ פְנֵי תֵבֵל תְּנוּבָה: [ישעיה כז, ו]

ליקוטי רש"י

לעדות אשה. שמת בעלה במדינת הים. **לעדות בכור.** להעיד שלא הטיל בו מום זה בכוונה. **אימא לעדות שהאשה כשרה.** ובעדות בכור נמי אשה כשרה דאמרינן הלכתא כרבן שמעון ואפי' בתו. **יימר שרי בוכרא.** יימר המתיר בכורות לשון גנאי [בכורות לו.]. **התם הוא דמעיקרא אוכלא ולבסוף אוכלא.** דבש לאחר שזב מן החלות נמי אוכלא הוא הלכך ליכא למיגזר ביה שמא יסחוט משתמשך דלא שייכי ביה סחיטה. **אבל הכא.** זיתים וענבים דמתני' דמעיקרא אוכלא והשתא משקה איכא למיגזר שמא יסחוט משמשתך דהא ודאי סחיטה היא [לעיל יט:]. **כל שבא בחמין.** כל מלוח שבא בחמין מערב שבת שורין ושורין אותו בחמין בשבת ואין בו משום מיקון שהרי נתקן ככר. **מדיחין.** שאין זה גמר מלאכתו אבל לא שורין. **וקוליים האיספנין.** דג שקורין טוניי"א [ביצה טז:] וכך ונאכל כמו שהוא חי אלא שטומנין עליו חמין וזה בשולו כדתנן במסכת שבת שהדחתו זו היא גמר מלאכתן. **בר תלתא טרפי.** בן שלש שנים שטעונה אמו משנקלט שלשה עלין חדשין [לעיל קכט.]. **כותח דבבלאי.** ממן כדאמרינן באלו עוברין ואינו עשוי לאכול יחד אלא לטבול בו ואינו כלה עד זמן מרובה [שם קנח.] כדמפרש באלו עוברין (פסחים מב.) דיהבו ביה עיפושי פת ונסיובי דחלבא משג"א בלע"ז [ע"ז לח:]. **שהדחתן זו היא גמר מלאכתן.** מדקרי ליה גמר מלאכתו שמע מינה זהו בישולו וחייב [לעיל לט.]. **תלמידי חכמים שבבבל מצויינין.** דומים למלאכי השרת לבושים לבנים ועטופים כמלאכי השרת וכתיב (יחזקאל ט) והאיש לבוש הבדים ואמרינן בבמה מדליקין (שבת כה:) על רבי יהודה שהיה מתעטף ויושב בסדינים המצויינין ודומה למלאך (כ:) נמי אמרינן מאן מלאכי מלאכי השרת רבנן ואמאי קרי להו מלאכי השרת משום דמצויינין כמלאכי השרת במלבושים נאים [קידושין עב.]. **אמור לחכמה אחותי את.** שתהא נקי בה כאחותך שאסורה לך [שם ל:]. **נ"ב שנה.** היא מחרבות ירושלים עד פקידת כורש שעלו בגלות לבנות הבית שהרי לסוף שבעים לגלות יהויקים היתה הפקידה כמו ששנינו במגילה (יא:) ושמונה עשרה שנה היה מכיבוש יהויקים עד חרבות ירושלים דאמר מר גלו בשבע גלו בשמונה גלו בשמונה עשרה ופירושו גלה יכניה בשבע לכיבוש יהויקים שהוא שמונה לנבוכדנצר גלו צדקיהו וגלותו בחרבות ירושלים בשמונה עשר לכיבוש יהויקים שהוא תשע עשרה לנבוכדנצר דאמר מר שנה ראשונה כיבש נינוה שניה כיבש יהויקים נד.]. **על ההרים.** על חורבן ההרים. **נדדו הלכו.** סופן לילך. חמשים ושתים שנה לא עבר איש ביהודה מגלות צדקיהו עד פקודת כורש מלך פרס חמשים ושתים שנה היו ורמז לדבר ועד בהמה חשבונה בגימטריא נ"ב והם [ירמיה ט, ט]. **הני מדרי דבבל.** מקומות מדרון שבבבל. **מהדרי מיא לעין עיטם.** שבו כ"ג טובל ביוה"כ כדאמרי' במסכת יומא בפרק ג' (לא.) [בכורות מד:]. [המשך בדף קמו.]

to go there [i.e. to Eretz Yisrael], וְעָבְדִית כּוּתָּח דְּבַבְלָאֵי – **and I prepared Babylonian *kutach*.** שְׁאִילוּ מִינֵּיהּ כָּל בְּרִיחֵי מַעֲרָבָא – The fact is that **all the sick of the West** [i.e. Eretz Israel] then **begged** some of **[that *kutach*] from [Rav Gaza].** Evidently, they did not find it as unpalatable as R' Yochanan did.

The Mishnah stated:

[וְ]כֹל שֶׁלֹּא בָּא בְּחַמִּין וכו׳ – AND ANYTHING THAT WAS NOT PLACED INTO HOT WATER etc. [before the Sabbath, we may rinse with hot water on the Sabbath, except for an aged salted fish or a salted Spanish mackerel].

The Gemara asks:

הֱדִיחָהּ מַאי – If **one rinsed** a Spanish mackerel with hot water on the Sabbath, **what** is the law?

The Gemara answers:

אָמַר רַב יוֹסֵף – **Rav Yosef said:** הֱדִיחָהּ חַיָּיב חַטָּאת – **If one rinsed** it, **he is liable to a *chatas*,** for this act is one of cooking under Biblical law.

The Gemara shows proof that this act violates a Biblical prohibition:

אָמַר מַר בְּרֵיהּ דְּרָבִינָא – **Mar the son of Ravina said:** אַף אֲנַן נַמִּי תְּנֵינָא – **We too have learned this in our Mishnah as well,** which states: חוּץ מִמָּלִיחַ יָשָׁן וְקוֹלְיָיס הָאִיסְפָּנִין – And anything that was not placed into hot water before the Sabbath, we may rinse with hot water on the Sabbath, EXCEPT FOR AN AGED SALTED FISH OR A SPANISH MACKEREL, which may not be rinsed on the Sabbath. שֶׁהֲדָחָתָן זוֹ הִיא גְּמַר מְלַאכְתָּן – FOR THEIR RINSING COMPLETES THEIR PREPARATION; it is therefore considered an act of cooking under Biblical law.

The Gemara concludes:

שְׁמַע מִינַּהּ – We may indeed **learn from this** Mishnah that one who rinses such a fish on the Sabbath violates a Biblical prohibition; he is therefore liable to a *chatas*.

Having mentioned a ruling concerning the Spanish mackerel, the Gemara wishes to teach us something further regarding this fish. It therefore relates the following incident.

יָתִיב רַבִּי חִיָּיא בַּר אַבָּא וְרַבִּי אַסִּי קַמֵּיהּ דְּרַבִּי יוֹחָנָן – **R' Chiya bar Abba and R' Assi were sitting before R' Yochanan,** וְיָתִיב רַבִּי יוֹחָנָן וְקָא מְנַמְנֵם – **and R' Yochanan was sitting and was dozing.** אָמַר לֵיהּ רַבִּי חִיָּיא בַּר אַבָּא לְרַבִּי אַסִּי – **R' Chiya bar Abba said to R' Assi:** מִפְּנֵי מָה עוֹפוֹת שֶׁבְּבָבֶל שְׁמֵנִים – **Why are the birds in Babylonia fatter** than those in Eretz Yisrael? אָמַר לֵיהּ – **[R' Assi] said to him:** כַּלֵּךְ לְמִדְבַּר עַזָּה וְאַרְאֲךָ שְׁמֵנִים מֵהֶן – **Go to the Gaza Desert**[15] **and I will show you** birds that are **fatter than them!**

R' Chiya bar Abba asks further:

מִפְּנֵי מָה מוֹעֲדִים שֶׁבְּבָבֶל שְׂמֵחִים – **Why are the festivals in Babylonia more joyous** than those in Eretz Yisrael?[16]

R' Assi answers:

מִפְּנֵי שֶׁהֵן עֲנִיִּים – **Because they** [the Babylonian Jews] **are poor,** and all their rejoicing is reserved for the festivals.[17]

Another question:

מִפְּנֵי מָה תַּלְמִידֵי חֲכָמִים שֶׁבְּבָבֶל מְצוּיָּנִין – **Why are the Torah scholars of Babylonia adorned** with beautiful clothing, while those of Eretz Yisrael are not?[18]

R' Assi again answers:

לְפִי שֶׁאֵינָן בְּנֵי תוֹרָה – **Because [the Babylonians] are not Torah scholars** of the caliber of those in Eretz Yisrael. They therefore must adorn themselves in order to elicit proper honor from the populace.[19]

R' Chiya bar Abba's final question:

מִפְּנֵי מָה עוֹבְדֵי כוֹכָבִים מְזוֹהָמִים – **Why are idolaters impure?**[20]

R' Assi answers:

מִפְּנֵי שֶׁאוֹכְלִין שְׁקָצִים וּרְמָשִׂים – **Because they eat abominable creatures and crawling creatures.**[21]

R' Yochanan objects:

אִיתְּעַר בְּהוּ רַבִּי יוֹחָנָן – **R' Yochanan awoke to [these questions and answers].** אָמַר לְהוּ – **He said to them:** דַּרְדַּקֵּי – **Children!**[22] לֹא כָּךְ אָמַרְתִּי לָכֶם – **Have I not said to you thus?** "אֱמֹר לַחָכְמָה אֲחֹתִי אָתְּ" – When the verse states: ***Say to wisdom: You are my sister,***[23] it teaches that אִם בָּרוּר לְךָ הַדָּבָר כַּאֲחוֹתְךָ שֶׁהִיא אֲסוּרָה לְךָ אוֹמְרֵהוּ – **if a matter** of law **is as clear to you as** the fact that **your sister is forbidden to you, you may repeat it;** וְאִם לָאו לֹא תֹאמְרֵהוּ – **but if not, you may not repeat it!**[24] Why then do you speak of these matters, which are not clear to you at all!

R' Chiya bar Abba and R' Assi reply:

אָמְרוּ לֵיהּ – **They said to him:** וְלֵימָא לָן מַר אֵיזֶה מֵהֶן – **Let the master tell us** the answers to **some of these** questions.

R' Yochanan does so:

מִפְּנֵי מָה עוֹפוֹת שֶׁבְּבָבֶל שְׁמֵנִים – **Why are the birds in Babylonia fatter** than those in Eretz Yisrael? מִפְּנֵי שֶׁלֹּא גָּלוּ – **Because** unlike the birds of Eretz Yisrael, **they were not exiled.** They thus did not lose their fatness. שֶׁנֶּאֱמַר – **For it is stated** regarding those who were never exiled: "שַׁאֲנַן מוֹאָב מִנְּעוּרָיו וְשֹׁקֵט הוּא אֶל־שְׁמָרָיו . . . וּבַגּוֹלָה לֹא הָלָךְ" – ***Moav has been tranquil from its youth, and it rests quiet upon its lees . . . and into exile it has not gone;*** *therefore its flavor has remained and its aroma has*

NOTES

15. Which is in Eretz Yisrael (*Rashi;* see *Maharsha,* cited in note 26).

16. I.e. why are the Jews of Babylonia more joyful on the festivals than the Jews of Eretz Yisrael? (*Rashi*).

17. All year, because of their poverty, they derive no joy from food or drink, nor do they relax from their labors; all their joy is therefore reserved for the festivals (*Rashi;* but see *Rashi* to *Sanhedrin* 101a ד״ה שנוי וסת).

18. The scholars of Babylonia would adorn themselves with fine clothing, while those of Eretz Yisrael would not do so (*Rashi*).

19. The scholars of Eretz Yisrael are so great in Torah that they are respected for their Torah. Those of Babylonia, however, are of a lesser caliber; they therefore must dress importantly, so that the populace will show them honor (*Rashi;* see *Chidushei R' Elazar Moshe Horowitz*). The Babylonian scholars did not seek this honor for themselves, but for the Torah they personified, which would otherwise have gone unrecognized by the common folk (*Pri Tzaddik* vol. 2, p. 111).

20. The term מְזוֹהָם refers in this context to a spiritual impurity (see below, 146a note 1; *Maharsha, Yevamos* 103b).

21. *Shekatzim,* "abominable creatures" include all creatures referred to by the Torah as abominable (see, for example, *Leviticus* 11:10,13,23). These include unkosher fish and sea creatures such as seals, frogs, and the like; unkosher birds; insects such as flies, bees and mosquitoes; reptiles and rodents; and perhaps even unkosher wild and domesticated beasts. *Remasim,* "crawling creatures," are creatures that reproduce spontaneously, e.g. from dung or rotting carcasses. This includes also those that spawn from fruits and other foods. Once they emerge to crawl upon the earth, they are prohibited (*Tos. Yom Tov* to *Makkos* 3:2). R' Chiya bar Abba attributed the spiritual impurity of idolaters to their consumption of these creatures. Regarding the impurity engendered in Jews who partake of these foods, see *Toras Kohanim* and *Rashi* to *Leviticus* 11:43; *Yoma* 39a).

22. R' Yochanan referred to them as boys who have not yet reached the age of reason (*Rashi*).

23. *Proverbs* 7:4.

24. This implies that the exchange between R' Assi and R' Chiya bar Abba had ramifications in practical halachah; see *Ben Yehoyada* for what these ramifications might be (for discussion of R' Yochanan's dictum, see *Maharal, Chidushei Aggados; Beur HaGra* to *Proverbs* 22:12).

לעדות אשה. לומר לאשה מת בעליך דאפילו בה רבנן משום עיגונא וכל דמקדש אדעתא דרבנן [ל] מקדש [מ] ואפקועי רבנן לקדושין מיניה: לעדות בכור. בכור ביד כהן כשנתנו ישראל לו שלם ואירע לו בו מום קי"ל בבכורות (דף לה.) נחשדו הכהנים להטיל מום בבכור ואין נאמן לומר מום זה נפל בו מאליו וצריך להביא עדים ואמרינן התם דאשה כשרה לעדות זו: אימא לעדות שהאשה כשרה לה. והאי נמי כשרה לה: גברא יתירא. ר"ש דמתני' ר"א תנן בה: אתא לאשמעינן. בתמיה כלומר מה בא ללמדנו אם לא זאת: מתני' כל שבא בחמין. כלומר שנתבשל: שורין אותו בחמין. כדי שיהא נמוח: וכל שלא בא בחמין. כגון בשר יבש שאוכלין אותו חי ע"י הדחק: מדיחין אותו. ולא אמרי' זהו בישולו אבל לא שורין: חוץ מן המליח ישן. דג מליח של שנה שעברה: וקוליים האיספנין. שם דג שאוכלין אותו מחמת מלחו ע"י הדחה בחמין והכך אפילו הדחה נמי לא שזהו גמר מלאכתן והוי בשול: גמ' כגון מאי. הוי בא בחמין שמחזירין ושורין אותו בחמין: תרנגולתיה דר' אבא. מבשלה ושורה אותה ימים רבים בחמין למחות מאליה ואוכלה לרפואה: בר תלתא טרפי. בן ג' שנים: אתונסי. הייתי נאנס להקיא מחמת מיאום: רייק. רוקק מכותחא דבבלאי כשזוכרו שהיה מאוס בעיניו: אמר רב יוסף כו'. קשה היה בעיניו שנמאסין בני בבל על ארץ ישראל אמר אנו נמי יש לנו לרוק מתרנגולתיה דר' אבא שהם אוכלים: ועוד כותח. אינו מאוס כל כך בעיני שאר בני מערבא: דהא אמר רב גזא כו'. ושאלו מיניה אותו כותח: בריחי. חולים: הדיח. קוליס מאי: חייב חטאת. דהוי בישול: מפני מה עופות שבבבל שמנים. משל א"י: כלך. לכה לך אלא שקילך הלשון: למדבר עזה. והיא מא"י: מועדים שבבבל שמחים. רגילים לשמוח במועדים יותר מא"י: מפני שהם עניים. וכל השנה אין להם שמחה במאכל ומשתה ואין להם מרגוע ממלאכה לפיכך במועדים כל שמחתם: מצויינין. מליינין עצמן בלבושים נאים: מצויינין. מקושטין: שאינן בני תורה. כל כך לכבדם כבני ארץ ישראל מחמת תורתם מכבדים אותם מחמת לבושיהן שהלבוש מכבדם: דרדקי. תנוקות שלא הגיעו לסברא: מפני שלא גלו. העופות כמו אותן של א"י כדאמרינן לקמן: שאנן מואב מנעוריו וגו'. סיפיה דקרא על כן עמד טעמו בו אלמא הגולין מפיגין טעמן ושמנן: נ"ב שנה. משגלו בימי צדקיה מחרבות ירושלים עד שנפקדו בימי כורש ואז עלו מהם לייסד את הבית י"ח שנים קודם גמר הבנין שהיה לסוף ע' שנה בשנת שתים לדריוש כדאמרי' במגילה (דף יא:): וכולן חזרו. הבהמות והעופות ואף הדגים חוץ מן קוליים האספנין וכולן חזרו דהא עד בהמה כתיב ומכלל למכאן ואילך הדור חוץ מקוליים למפרע: הני מדרי דבבל מהדרי מיא לעין עיטם. מדרונות שבבבל מחזירין מים הנשפכים בהן לעין עיטם שהוא מקום גבוה שבא"י שאותו מעיין מביא מים לבית טבילת כה"ג ביוה"כ למתוקן בחומת עזרה על גבי שער המים כדאמרינן בסדר יומא (דף לא.) עין עיטם גבוה מקרקע העזרה כ"ג אמות והיאך מחזירין שיש בפרת סילונות וסולמות למטה מן הקרקע (הים) ודרך אותן סולמות חוזרין המים לא"י וחוזרין ונובעין במעיינות והדגים חזרו דרך אותן סולמות שנוחים להעלותן יותר מדרך פרת עצמו: והאי. קוליים האספנין: כיון דלא שריר שדריה. אין קשה שדרה שלו: לטבריה. לנוח ולהטיל עליהם עול ולא שמתכוונין לבטלן משמחת הרגל אבל הקללה גרמה לכך: קומטין. [נ] לשון לעז הוא שלטון: בולשת. חיל המלך: ציפורי וטבריה מא"י: שאינן במקומם. שמא"י גלו לשם והגולה למקום נכרי מליין עצמו במלבושים שיהא חשוב: במתא שמאי. בעירי איני צריך להתכבד אלא בשמי שאני ניכר בו: בלא מתא. במקום שאינה עירי: תותבאי. כבודי תלוי בשמלתי שמלתו מתרגמינן תותביה (שמות כב): ציצין. למחין: הבאים. אותן של יעקב שיבאו לבבל ישרשו ויעשו ציצין ופרחים לתורה וסייעתא אתיא לר' יוחנן דטעמא דמצויינין לאו לפי שאינן בני תורה כדרבי אסי אלא לפי שאינן במקומן:

כשבא

בהמה בגימטריא. אסמכתא בעלמא היא דנ"ב נפקא לן בלאו גימטריא כדפי' בקונטרס: שוכר

אלא לעדות אשה בלבד [א] איבעיא להו עד מפי עד לעדות בכור מהו רב אמי אסיר ורב אסי שרי א"ל רב אמי לרב אסי והא תנא דבי מנשיא אין עד מפי עד כשר אלא לעדות אשה בלבד אימא לעדות שהאשה כשרה לה בלבד רב יימר אכשר עד מפי עד לבכור קרי עליה מרימר יימר שרי בוכרא [א] והלכתא עד מפי עד כשר לבכור: חלות דבש: כי אתא רב הושעיא מנהרדעא [ב] אתא ואייתי מתניתא בידיה זיתים וענבים שריסקן מע"ש ויצאו מעצמן אסורין [ג] ור"א ור"ש מתירין אמר רב יוסף גברא יתירא אתא לאשמעינן א"ל אביי טובא קמ"ל דאי ממתניתין הוה אמינא התם הוא דמעיקרא אוכלא ולבסוף אוכלא אבל הכא דמעיקרא אוכלא ולבסוף משקה אימא לא קמ"ל: מתני' [ד] כל שבא בחמין מערב שבת שורין אותו בחמין בשבת וכל שלא בא בחמין מערב שבת מדיחין אותו בחמין בשבת חוץ מן המליח הישן [ה] (ודגים מלוחין קטנים) [ו] וקוליים האיספנין שהדחתן זו היא גמר מלאכתן: גמ' כגון מאי אמר רב ספרא כגון תרנגולתא דר' אבא ואמר רב ספרא זימנא חדא איקלעית להתם ואוכלן מיניה ואי לא רבי אבא דאשקיין חמרא בר תלתא טרפי איתנסי רבי יוחנן רייק מכותחא דבבלאי אמר רב יוסף ולירוק אנן מתרנגולתא דרבי אבא ועוד אמר רב גזא זימנא חדא איקלעית להתם ועבדית כותח דבבלאי שאילו מיניה [ז] כל בריחי מערבא: כל שלא בא בחמין וכו': הדיח מאי אמר רב יוסף הדיח חייב חטאת אמר מר בריה דרבינא אף אנן נמי תנינא חוץ ממליח ישן וקוליים האיספנין שהדחתן זו היא גמר מלאכתן שמע מינה יתיב רבי חייא בר אבא ורבי אסי קמיה דרבי יוחנן ויתיב רבי יוחנן וקא מנמנם אמר ליה רבי חייא בר אבא לרבי אסי מפני מה עופות שבבבל שמנים א"ל כלך למדבר עזה ואראך שמנים מהן מפני מה מועדים שבבבל שמחים מפני שהן עניים מפני מה ת"ח שבבבל מצויינין לפי שאינן בני תורה מפני מה עובדי כוכבים מזוהמי' מפני שאוכלין שקצי' ורמשי' [ח] איתער בהו רבי יוחנן אמר להו דרדקי לא כך אמרתי לכם [א] אמור לחכמה אחותי את [ט] אם ברור לך הדבר כאחותך שהיא אסורה לך אומרהו ואם לאו לא תאמרהו אמרו ליה ולימא לן מר איזה מהן מפני מה עופות שבבבל שמנים מפני שלא גלו שנאמר [ב] שאנן מואב מנעוריו ושקט הוא אל שמריו ובגולה לא הלך והכא מנלן דגלו דתניא [י] רבי יהודה אומר נ"ב שנה לא עבר איש ביהודה שנאמר [ג] על ההרים אשא בכי ונהי וגו' מעוף השמים ועד בהמה נדדו הלכו בהמה בגימטריא חמשין ותרתין הוו א"ר יעקב א"ר יוחנן כולן חזרו חוץ מקוליים האיספנין [כ] דאמר רב הני מדרי דבבל מהדרי מיא לעין עיטם והאי כיון דלא שריר שדריה לא מצי סליק מפני מה מועדים שבבבל שמחים מפני שלא היו באותה קללה דכתיב [ד] והשבתי כל משושה חגה חדשה ושבתה וכל מועדה וכתיב [ה] חדשיכם ומועדיכם שנאה נפשי היו עלי לטורח [ל] מאי היו עלי לטורח א"ר אלעזר אמר הקב"ה לא דיין לישראל שחוטאין לפני אלא שמטריחין אותי לידע איזו גזירה קשה אביא עליהן א"ר יצחק אין לך כל רגל ורגל שלא באתה בולשת לציפורי ואמר רבי חנינא אין לך כל רגל ורגל שלא בא לטבריה אגמון וקמטון ובעל זמורה מפני מה ת"ח שבבבל מצויינין לפי שאינן (א) בני מקומן דאמרי אינשי במתא שמאי בלא מתא תותבאי [מ] הבאים ישרש יעקב יציץ ופרח ישראל תני רב יוסף אלו תלמידי חכמים שבבבל שעושין ציצין ופרחים לתורה מפני מה עובדי כוכבים מזוהמין שלא עמדו על הר סיני שבשעה

שבא

עין משפט נר מצוה

כ א מיי' פ"ב מהלכות בכורות הלכה טו סמג עשין ריא טוש"ע יו"ד סימן שיד סעיף ה:

כא ב מיי' פכ"א מהל' שבת הלכה טו טור שו"ע או"ח סימן רנג סעיף ה וסי' שכ סעיף ג:

כב ג מיי' פכ"ב שם הלכה ח סמג לאוין סה טוש"ע או"ח סימן שיח סעיף ד:

כג ד מיי' פ"ב מהלכות סנהדרין הלכה ז סמג עשין מ טור שו"ע חו"מ סימן י סעיף א:

רבינו חננאל

למשקין היוצא מהן אסור. והא דתניא סוחטין בפגעים ובפרישין ובעוזרדין אבל לא ברמונים דשל בית מנשיא בן מנחם היו סוחטין ברמונים אמר רב נחמן הלכה כשל בית מנשיא בן מנחם וסלקא שמעתא דאסור לסחוט ברמונים בשבת והא דתני אין עד מפי עד כשר אלא לעדות אשה בלבד. אוקימנא לעדות שהאשה כשרה לה והלכתא עד מפי עד כשר לבכור. פי' עד מפי עד נאמן להעיד על בכור בהמה טהורה שזה המום שיש בו אפי' שראוי לבוא בידי אדם הוא לא נפל בו מידי אדם ובזו העדות החכם מתירו להאכל במומו וכ"ש בעדות גדולה מזו. ומפורש כך בבכורות פ' כל פסולי המוקדשי'. וסלקא שמעתא התם דהלכתא כרשב"ג דאמר אפילו בנו ובתו נאמנים ויש מי שאומר כי עד מפי עד נאמן בבכור אדם וטעות הוא בידו: חלות דבש שריסקן מע"ש ויצאו מעצמן אסורין ור' אלעזר מתיר. כי אתא רב הושעיא מנהרדעא אתא ואייתי מתניתא בידיה זיתים וענבים שריסקן מע"ש ויצאו מעצמן אסורים. ור' אלעזר ור"ש מתירין. והא מתניתא מסייעא ליה לר' יוחנן. מתני' כל שבא בחמין מלפני השבת וכו'. ומיבעיא לן כגון מאי. ואמר רב ספרא כגון תרנגולתא דר' אבא שהיתה מלוחה ביותר וכשמבקשין לאוכלה שורין אותה במים חמין. ואמר רב ספרא כגון זו התרנגולת אם הובאה בחמין מלפני השבת מותר לשרותה בחמין בשבת ולאוכלה. ואם לאו אסור לשרותה ומותר להדיחה חוץ מן המליח הישן וקוליים האיספנין

רב נסים גאון

ואין עד מפי עד כשר אלא לעדות אשה בלבד כשאמר כי מת בעלה התירוה בית דין לינשא ואע"פ שהמועט העתיק דבר זה מזולתו וכמו שביארו דבר זה בפרק אשה שהלך בעלה וצרתה (דף קכב) והוחזקו להיות משיאין עד מפי עד וכו': עד מפי עד בבכור מהו. עיקר דיליה במסכת בכורות בפרק כל פסולי המוקדשין (דף לה) דתניא ר' יהושע בן קפוסאי אומר בכור בי כהן צריך ב' מן השוק להעיד עליו רבן שמעון בן גמליאל אומר אפילו בנו ובתו ואמרו הלכתא כרבן שמעון ודוקא בנו ובתו אבל אשתו לא מאי טעמא אשתו כגופו דמיא ועוד אמרו איבעיא להו עד מפי עד מהו לעדות בכור אמר ליה תני אלא לעדות אשה כשירה לו וכבר נתברר לנו שבתו כשירה והואיל ואשה כשירה לעדות בכור וכן פסקה ההלכה וזה שאמרו בבכור בהמה אבל בבכור אדם לא. גרסינן בפרק י' יוחסין (דף עד) ג' נאמנין על הבכור חיה ואמו ואביו חיה לאלתר אמו כל ז' אביו לעולם: כגון תרנגולתיה דר' אבא. כך פירשה אדוננו האיי גאון ז"ל תרנגולת שמבשלין אותה ומוציאין אותה מהמרק וממלאין אותה בתבלין וכשרוצה לאכול ממנה שורין אותה במים חמים ואוכלים אותה כאילו היא חמה: סליק פרק חבית

מסורת הש"ס

א) בכורות דף לו. ע"ש, ב) לעיל יט:, ג) לעיל לט., ד) כ"א ל"ג, ה) [דג שבמקומות האספניא ושמו בלשון הקודש שיבוטא ערוך ערך אספן], ו) [עי' לעיל כא.], ז) ב"ב טז:, ח) סנהדרין ז:, ט) [יומא נד.], י) בכורות מד:, כ) [מגילה לא:], ל) [ועי' שבות יעקב חלק ב' סימן קטו], מ) [יבמות ל:], נ) לשון קומטוס כמו קומוס ולשון רומי הוא עי' רש"י סוטה יד ד"ה גסטרא.

הגהות הב"ח

(א) גמרא לפי שאין במקומן כל"ל ותיבת בני נמחק:

תורה אור השלם

א) אֱמֹר לַחָכְמָה אֲחֹתִי אָתְּ וּמֹדָע לַבִּינָה תִקְרָא: [משלי ז, ד]

ב) שַׁאֲנַן מוֹאָב מִנְּעוּרָיו וְשֹׁקֵט הוּא אֶל שְׁמָרָיו וְלֹא הוּרַק מִכְּלִי אֶל כֶּלִי וּבַגּוֹלָה לֹא הָלָךְ עַל כֵּן עָמַד טַעְמוֹ בּוֹ וְרֵיחוֹ לֹא נָמָר: [ירמיה מח, יא]

ג) עַל הֶהָרִים אֶשָּׂא בְכִי וָנֶהִי וְעַל נְאוֹת מִדְבָּר קִינָה כִּי נִצְּתוּ מִבְּלִי אִישׁ עֹבֵר וְלֹא שָׁמְעוּ קוֹל מִקְנֶה מֵעוֹף הַשָּׁמַיִם וְעַד בְּהֵמָה נָדְדוּ הָלָכוּ: [ירמיה ט, ט]

ד) וְהִשְׁבַּתִּי כָּל מְשׂוֹשָׂהּ חַגָּהּ חָדְשָׁהּ וְשַׁבַּתָּהּ וְכֹל מוֹעֲדָהּ: [הושע ב, יג]

ה) חָדְשֵׁיכֶם וּמוֹעֲדֵיכֶם שָׂנְאָה נַפְשִׁי הָיוּ עָלַי לָטֹרַח נִלְאֵיתִי נְשֹׂא: [ישעיה א, יד]

ו) הַבָּאִים יַשְׁרֵשׁ יַעֲקֹב יָצִיץ וּפָרַח יִשְׂרָאֵל וּמָלְאוּ פְנֵי תֵבֵל תְּנוּבָה: [ישעיה כז, ו]

ליקוטי רש"י

לעדות אשה. שמת בעלה במדינת הים. לעדות בכור. להעיד שלא הטיל בו מום זה בכוונה. אימא לעדות שהאשה כשרה. ובעדות בכור נמי אשה כשרה דאמרינן הלכתא כרבן שמעון ואפי' בתו. יימר שרי בוכרא. יימר המתיר בכורות לו. [בכורות לו.] התם הוא דמעיקרא אוכלא ולבסוף אוכלא. דכא לאמר שוב מן החלות נמי אוכלא הוא אלא הכך ליכא למיגזר שמא יסחוט משקה דלא שייך ביה סחיטה. אבל הכא. זיתים וענבים דמתני' דמעיקרא אוכלא והשתא משקה איכא למיגזר שמא יסחוט משמחשך דהא ודאי סחיטה היא [לעיל יט:]. כל שבא בחמין. כל מלוח שבא בחמין מערב שבת שורין ושורין אותו בחמין בשבת ואין בו משום תיקון שהרי נתקן כבר. מדיחין. שאין זה גמר מלאכתו אבל לא שורין. וקוליים האיספנין. דג שקורין טונינ"א [שם לט.]. דג מליח הוא רך ונאכל כמו שהוא חי אלא שנותנין עליו חמין וזה בשולו כדתנן במסכת שבת שהדחתו זו היא גמר מלאכתו [ביצה טז:]. בר תלתא טרפי. בן שלש שנים שטענה אמו משנקלט שלשה עלין חדשין [לעיל קכט.]. כותח דבבלאי. נותנין בו חמץ כדאמרינן באלו עוברין ואינו עשוי לאכול יחד אלא לטבול בו ואינו כלה עד זמן מרובה [שם יט.]. חזק הוא כחומץ כדמפרש באלו עוברין (פסחים מב.) דיהבו ביה עיפושי פת ונסיובי דחלבא מעג"א בלע"ז [ע"ז לו:]. שהדחתן זו היא גמר מלאכתן. מדקרי ליה גמר מלאכתו שמע מינה זהו בישולו וחייב [לעיל לט.]. תלמידי חכמים שבבבל מצויינין. דומים למלאכי השרת לבושים לבנים ועטופים כמלאכי השרת וכתיב (יחזקאל ט) והאיש לבוש הבדים והכי נמי אמרינן בבמה מדליקין (שבת כה:) על רבי יהודה שהיה מתעטף ויושב בסדינים המצויינין ודומה למלאך ה' ובנדרים (כ:) נמי אמרינן מאן מלאכי השרת רבנן ואמאי קרי להו מלאכי השרת משום דמצויינין כמלאכי השרת במלבושים נאים [קידושין עב.]. אמור לחכמה אחותי את. שתהא בקי בה כאחותך שאסורה לך [שם ל:]. נ"ב שנה. היה מחרבות ירושלים בגלות צדקיהו עד פקידת כורש שעלו לבנות הבית שהרי לסוף שבעים לגלות יהויקים היתה הפקידה כמו ששנינו במגילה (יא:) ושמונה עשרה שנה היה מכיבוש יהויקים עד חרבות ירושלים דאמר מר גלו בשבע גלו בשמונה גלו בשמונה עשרה גלו בתשע עשרה ופירושו גלה יכניה בשבע לכיבוש יהויקים שהוא שמונה לנבוכדנצר גלו צדקיהו וגלותו בחרבות ירושלים בשמונה עשר לכיבוש יהויקים שהוא תשע עשרה לנבוכדנצר דאמר מר שנה ראשונה כיבש נינוה שניה עלה וכיבש יהויקים [יומא נד.]. על ההרים. על חורבן ההרים. נדדו הלכו. סופן לילך. חמשים ושתים שנה לא עבר איש ביהודה מגלות צדקיהו עד פקודת כורש מלך פרס חמשים ושתים שנה היו ורמז לדבר ועד בהמה חשבונה בגימטריא נ"ב והחשבון מכוון במס' מגיל' [ירמיה ט, ט]. הני מדרי דבבל. מקומות מדרון שבבבל. מהדרי מיא לעין עיטם. שנו כ"ג טובל ביוה"כ כדאמרי' במסכת יומא בפרק ג' (לא.) [בכורות מד:]. [המשך בדף קמו.]

not changed.[25] We see that exile undermines the existence of those who suffer it. Thus, the birds of Eretz Yisrael, who suffered exile, are not as fat as those of Babylonia, who did not.[26]

The Gemara asks:

וְהָכָא מְנָלַן דְּגָלוּ – But from where do we know that [the birds] here in Eretz Israel **were** once **exiled?**

The Gemara answers:

דְּתַנְיָא – For it has been taught in a Baraisa: רַבִּי יְהוּדָה אוֹמֵר – R' YEHUDAH SAYS: חֲמִישִּׁים וּשְׁתַּיִם שָׁנָה לֹא עָבַר אִישׁ בִּיהוּדָה – For FIFTY-TWO YEARS of exile NO MAN PASSED THROUGH JUDEA.[27] שֶׁנֶּאֱמַר – FOR IT IS STATED regarding the Babylonian exile: ,,עַל־הֶהָרִים אֶשָּׂא בְכִי וָנֶהִי וגו׳ מֵעוֹף הַשָּׁמַיִם וְעַד־בְּהֵמָה נָדְדוּ הָלָכוּ'' – *UPON THE* [destruction of the] *HILLS I WILL RAISE UP WEEPING AND WAILING ... FROM THE BIRD OF THE HEAVENS UNTIL THE BEAST, [ALL] HAVE WANDERED AND GONE.*[28] בְּהֵמָ״ה בְּגִימַטְרִיָּא חַמְשִׁין וְתַרְתֵּין הָווּ – The word BEAST (*beheimah*) HAS A NUMERICAL VALUE OF FIFTY-TWO, which alludes to the fact that the abandonment of Eretz Yisrael lasted fifty-two years.[29] We see from this Baraisa that the birds and animals also went into exile.[30]

The Gemara interjects:

אָמַר רַבִּי יַעֲקֹב אָמַר רַבִּי יוֹחָנָן – R' Yaakov said in the name of R' Yochanan: כּוּלָּן חָזְרוּ חוּץ מִקּוֹלְיָיס הָאִיסְפָּנִין – **All** the beasts **returned** to Eretz Yisrael **except for the Spanish mackerel.**[31] **דְּאָמַר רַב – For Rav said:** הָנֵי מַדְרֵי דְּבָבֶל מְהַדְרֵי מַיָּא לְעֵין עֵיטָם – **The slopes of Babylonia return water to Ein Eitam.**[32] Thus, the exiled fishes must have returned to Eretz Yisrael by this route.[33] **וְהַאי – But this** fish [i.e. the Spanish mackerel], **כֵּיוָן דְּלָא שְׁרִיר שִׁדְרֵיהּ – since its backbone is not firm** enough to swim this route,[34] **לָא מָצֵי סָלִיק – could not ascend** from Babylonia to Eretz Yisrael.

R' Yochanan continues:

מִפְּנֵי מָה מוֹעֲדִים שֶׁבְּבָבֶל שְׂמֵחִים – Why are the festivals in Babylonia more joyous than those in Eretz Yisrael? **מִפְּנֵי שֶׁלֹּא הָיוּ בְּאוֹתָהּ קְלָלָה – Because [the Babylonians] were not** included **in that curse** that lessened the joy of the festivals. **דִּכְתִיב – For it is written** regarding the punishment that would befall the Jewish nation: ,,וְהִשְׁבַּתִּי כָּל־מְשׂוֹשָׂהּ חַגָּהּ חָדְשָׁהּ וְשַׁבַּתָּהּ וְכֹל מוֹעֲדָהּ'' – ***And I shall end all her joy – her festivals, her new months, her Sabbaths, and all her festivals.***[35] **וּכְתִיב – And it is written:** ,,חָדְשֵׁיכֶם וּמוֹעֲדֵיכֶם שָׂנְאָה נַפְשִׁי הָיוּ עָלַי לָטֹרַח'' – ***Your new months and your holidays My soul hates; they have become a burden to Me.***[36] These verses were addressed the Jews in Eretz Yisrael. Thus, their joy on the festivals was lessened. The Babylonian Jews, however, did not suffer from this curse.

Having mentioned the latter verse, the Gemara asks:

מַאי ,,הָיוּ עָלַי לָטֹרַח'' – What is meant by the words, ***they have become a burden to Me?***

The Gemara answers:

אָמַר רַבִּי אֶלְעָזָר – R' Elazar said: אָמַר הַקָּדוֹשׁ בָּרוּךְ הוּא – **The Holy One, Blessed be He, said:** לֹא דַּיָּין לְיִשְׂרָאֵל שֶׁחוֹטְאִין לְפָנַי – **It is not enough for Israel that they sin before Me,** אֶלָּא שֶׁמַּטְרִיחִין אוֹתִי לֵידַע אֵיזוֹ גְּזֵירָה קָשָׁה אָבִיא עֲלֵיהֶן – **but they** also **burden Me to know which harsh decree I should bring upon them!**[37]

The Gemara demonstrates the frequency of harsh decrees during the festivals:

אָמַר רַבִּי יִצְחָק – R' Yitzchak said: אֵין לְךָ כָּל רֶגֶל וָרֶגֶל שֶׁלֹּא בָּאתָה בּוֹלֶשֶׁת לְצִיפּוֹרִי – **There was never a festival** during **which a troop did not come to Tzippori** to plunder. **וְאָמַר רַבִּי חֲנִינָא – And R' Chanina said:** אֵין לְךָ כָּל רֶגֶל וָרֶגֶל שֶׁלֹּא בָּא לִטְבֶרְיָה אֶגְמוֹן וְקַמְטוֹן וּבַעַל זְמוֹרָה – **There was never a festival** during **which a**

NOTES

25. *Jeremiah* 48:11. This verse equates the nation of Moav with a bottle of wine that was never moved from its place. The lees of such wine settle to the bottom and the taste and the aroma of the wine are preserved. Likewise did this nation, at that time not yet exiled, retain its original strength (*Rashi*).

26. Although the Gaza Desert was a part of Eretz Yisrael, its birds were nonetheless as fat as those of Babylonia. For since the Gaza had reverted to Philistine control before the Babylonian exile, its denizens were not exiled (*Hagahos R' Yaakov Emden;* see *Maharsha*).

27. These were the fifty-two years that passed from the exile in the days of King Zedekiah until the time that Cyrus king of Persia gave the Jews permission to return and rebuild the Temple. At that point, some of the exiles returned and began work on the Second Temple. It was completed eighteen years later, in the second year of the reign of Darius, seventy years after the beginning of the exile. The calculation by which this number is reached is given in *Megillah* 11b (*Rashi*).

28. *Jeremiah* 9:9.

29. [The letter ב has a numerical value of 2; ה, 5; מ, 40; and ה, 5, for a total of 52. Thus, the verse says that the exile will last "until בְּהֵמָה," i.e. until the passage of fifty-two years.] The verse in its entirety reads: *Upon the* [destruction of the] *hills I will raise up weeping and wailing, and upon the huts of the pasturelands, a lament. For they have become desolate, with no man to pass, and they have not heard the sound of beasts. From the bird of the heavens until the beast, [all] have wandered and gone.* Now, having stated that the sound of beasts is not heard, the verse need not state further that the beasts are gone. The Baraisa accordingly expounds the second mention of beasts for its numerical value (*Maharsha;* see there for a second explanation; see *Maharal, Chidushei Aggados;* see *Pesach Einayim* of the *Chidah*). *Tosafos* explain that the fifty-two year figure could have been arrived at without this exposition, as it is in fact calculated in Tractate *Megillah* (ibid.); the Baraisa only presents the exposition as an אַסְמַכְתָּא, *a Scriptural support* for this calculation.

30. See *Ben Yehoyada* for an explanation of why the Gemara found it necessary to cite the Baraisa instead of deriving the exile of the birds directly from the verse.

31. R' Yochanan deduces from the phrase "until the beast" that the exile lasted only *until* fifty-two years had passed; afterwards, the animals and birds, as well as the fish, returned. Only the Spanish mackerel remained in exile, for reasons the Gemara will now explain (*Rashi*).

[Although the verse expounded by the Baraisa makes no mention of the exile of the fish, R' Yochanan knows of it from a verse in *Hosea* 4:3, which states explicitly that the fish too will be displaced (*Hagahos R' Yaakov Emden* from *Kiddushin* 13a; see *Maharsha*).]

32. The water that runs down the Babylonian slopes flows into the Euphrates River, and from there flows to Ein Eitam and to other springs in Eretz Yisrael by means of underground channels and streams that lead from the Euphrates to Eretz Yisrael. The exiled fish returned by means of these underground channels.

Ein Eitam is a spring on a ridge at the border between the tribal portions of Judah and Benjamin, close to the Temple Mount. This spring marks the highest point in Eretz Yisrael, and supplied water to the *mikveh* used by the Kohen Gadol on Yom Kippur. This *mikveh* was installed on the wall of the Temple Courtyard, above the Water Gate (see *Yoma* 31a) [and was filled from Ein Eitam by means of a pipe] (*Rashi*).

33. Since this was an easier route than swimming back up the Euphrates [against the current – see above, 66b] (*Rashi;* see *Tosafos, Bechoros* 44b ד״ה לא ישחין).

34. [Which demands that the fish swim from a country of low elevation – Babylonia – to one of high elevation – Eretz Yisrael (see *Rashi*).]

35. *Hosea* 2:13.

36. *Isaiah* 1:14.

37. [*Maharsha* relates this statement of R' Elazar to the rejoicing of the Babylonians during the festivals; see there, where he connects it to the statement of R' Yitzchak that follows, as well.]

עין משפט
נר מצוה

כ א מיי' פ"ג מהלכות בכורות הלכה טו סמג עשין ריא טוש"ע יו"ד סימן שיד סעיף ה:

כא ב מיי' פכ"א מהל' שבת הלכה טז טור שו"ע או"ח סימן רנג סעיף ה וסי' שכ סעיף ג:

כב ג מיי' פכ"ג שם הלכה ח סמג לאוין סה טוש"ע או"ח סימן שיח סעיף ד:

כג ד מיי' פ"כ מהלכות סנהדרין הלכה ז סמג עשין ס טור שו"ע חו"מ סימן י סעיף א:

רבינו חננאל

למשקין היוצא מהן אסור. והא דתניא סוחטין בפגעים ובפרישין ובעוזרדין אבל לא ברמונים דשל בית מנשיא בן מנחם היו סוחטין ברמונים אמר רב נחמן הלכה כשל בית מנשיא בן מנחם וסלקא שמעתא דאסור לסחוט ברמונים בשבת והא דתני אין עד מפי עד כשר אלא לעדות אשה בלבד. אוקימנא לעדות שהאשה כשרה לה והלכתא עד מפי עד כשר לבכור. פי' עד מפי עד נאמן להעיד על בכור בהמה טהורה שזה המום שיש בו אפי' שראוי לבוא בידי אדם הוא לא נפל בו מידי אדם ובזו העדות החכם מתירו להאכל במומו וכ"ש בעדות גדולה מזו. ומפורש כך בבכורות פ' כל פסולי המוקדשי'. וסלקא שמעתא התם דהלכתא כרשב"ג דאמר אפילו בנו ובתו נאמנים ויש מי שאומר כי עד מפי עד נאמן בבכור אדם וטעות הוא בידו: חלות דבש שריסקן מע"ש ויצאו מעצמן אסורין ור' אלעזר מתיר. כי אתא רב הושעיא מנהרדעא אתא ואייתי מתניתא בידיה זיתים וענבים שריסקן מע"ש ויצאו מעצמן אסורים. ור' אלעזר ור"ש מתירין. והא מתניתא מסייעא נמי לר' יוחנן: מתני' כל שבא בחמין מלפני השבת וכו'. ומיבעיא לן כגון מאי. ואמר רב ספרא כגון תרנגולתא דר' אסא שהיתה מלוחה ביותר וכשמבקשין לאוכלה שורין אותה במים חמין. אמר רב ספרא כגון זו התרנגולת אם הובאה בחמין מלפני השבת מותר לשרותה בחמין בשבת ולאוכלה. ואם לאו אסור לשרותה ומותר להדיחה והמליח הישן וקולייס האיספנין

רב נסים גאון

ואין עד מפי עד כשר אלא לעדות אשה בלבד כשאמר כי מת בעלה התירוה בית דין לינשא ואע"פ שהמועט העתיק דבר זה מזולתו וכמו שביארו דבר זה בפרק אשה שהלך בעלה וצרתה (דף קכב) והוחזקו להיות משיאין עד מפי עד וכו': עד מפי עד בבכור מהו. עיקר דיליה במסכת בכורות בפרק כל פסולי המוקדשין (דף לה) דתניא ר' יהושע בן קפוסאי אומר בכור בי כהן צריך ב' מן השוק להעיד עליו רבן שמעון בן גמליאל אומר אפילו בנו ובתו ואמרו הלכתא כרבן שמעון ודוקא בנו ובתו אבל אשתו לא מאי טעמא אשתו כגופו דמיא ועוד אמרו איבעיא להו עד מפי עד מהו לעדות בכור אמר ליה תני אלא לעדות אשה כשירה לו וכבר נתברר לנו שבתו כשירה והואיל ואשה כשירה לעדות בכור עד מפי עד נמי כשר לעדות בכור וכן פסקה ההלכה וזה שאמרו בבכור בהמה אבל בבכור אדם לא. גרסינן בפרק י' יוחסין (דף עד) ג' נאמנין על הבכור חיה ואמו ואביו חיה לאלתר אמו כל ז' אביו לעולם: כגון תרנגלתיה דר' אבא. כך פירשה אדוננו האיי גאון ז"ל תרנגולת שמבשלין אותה ומוציאין אותה מהמרק וממלאין אותה בתבלין וכשרוצה לאכול ממנה שורין אותה במים חמים ואוכלים אותה כאילו היא חמה: סליק פרק חבית

בהמה בגימטריא. אסמכתא בעלמא היא דנ"ב נפקא לן בלאו גימטריא כדפי' בקונטרס: שובר

אלא לעדות אשה בלבד ה) איבעיא להו עד מפי עד לעדות בכור מהו רב אמי אסיר ורב אסי שרי א"ל רב אמי לרב אסי והא תנא דבי מנשיא אין עד מפי עד כשר אלא לעדות אשה בלבד אימא לעדות שהאשה כשרה לה בלבד רב ייסר אכשר עד מפי עד לבכור קרי עליה מרימר ייסר שרי בוכרא א והלכתא עד מפי עד כשר לבכור: חלות דבש: כי אתא רב הושעיא מנהרדעא ב) אתא ואייתי מתניתא בידיה זיתים וענבים שריסקן מע"ש ויצאו מעצמן אסורין ג ור"א ור"ש מתירין אמר רב יוסף גברא יתירא אתא לאשמעינן א"ל אביי טובא קמ"ל דאי ממתניתין הוה אמינא התם הוא דמעיקרא אוכלא ולבסוף אוכלא אבל הכא דמעיקרא אוכלא ולבסוף משקה אימא לא קמ"ל: **מתני'** ג כל שבא בחמין מערב שבת שורין אותו בחמין בשבת וכל שלא בא בחמין מערב שבת מדיחין אותו בחמין בשבת חוץ מן המליח הישן ז) (ודגים מלוחין קטנים) ח) וקולייס האיספנין שהדחתן זו היא גמר מלאכתן: **גמ'** כגון מאי אמר רב ספרא כגון תרנגולתא דר' אבא ואמר רב ספרא זימנא חדא איקלעית להתם ואוכלן מיניה ואי לא רבי אבא דאשקיין חמרא בר תלתא טרפי איתנסי רבי יוחנן רייק מכותחא דבבלאי אמר רב יוסף ולירוק אנן מתרנגולתא דרבי אבא ועוד אמר רב גזא זימנא חדא איקלעית להתם ועבדית כותח דבבלאי שאילו מיניה י) כל בריחי מערבא: כל שלא בא בחמין וכו': הדיח מאי אמר רב יוסף הדיח חייב חטאת אמר מר בריה דרבינא אף אנן נמי תנינא חוץ ממליח ישן וקולייס האיספנין שהדחתן זו היא גמר מלאכתן שמע מינה יתיב רבי חייא בר אבא ורבי אסי קמיה דרבי יוחנן ויתיב רבי יוחנן וקא מנמנם אמר ליה רבי חייא בר אבא לרבי אסי מפני מה עופות שבבבל שמנים א"ל כלך למדבר עזה ואראך שמנים מהן מפני מה מועדים שבבבל שמחים מפני שהן עניים מפני מה ת"ח שבבבל מצויינין לפי שאינן בני תורה מפני מה עובדי כוכבים מזוהמי' מפני שאוכלין שקצי' ורמשי' איתער בהו רבי יוחנן אמר להו דרדקי לא כך אמרתי לכם א) אמור לחכמה אחותי את ט) אם ברור לך הדבר כאחותך שהיא אסורה לך אומרהו ואם לאו לא תאמרהו אמרו ליה ולימא לן מר איזה מהן מפני מה עופות שבבבל שמנים מפני שלא גלו שנאמר ב) שאנן מואב מנעוריו ושקט הוא אל שמריו ובגולה לא הלך והכא מנלן דגלו דתניא יא) רבי יהודה אומר נ"ב שנה לא עבר איש ביהודה שנאמר ג) על ההרים אשא בכי ונהי וגו' מעוף השמים ועד בהמה נדדו הלכו בהמ"ה בגימטריא חמשין ותרתין הוו א"ר יעקב א"ר יוחנן כולן חזרו חוץ מקולייס האיספנין דאמר רב הני מדרי דבבל מהדרי מיא לעין עיטם והאי כיון דלא שריר שדריה לא מצי סליק מפני מה מועדים שבבבל שמחים מפני שלא היו באותה קללה דכתיב ד) והשבתי כל משושה חגה חדשה ושבתה וכל מועדה וכתיב ה) חדשיכם ומועדיכם שנאה נפשי היו עלי לטורח מאי היו עלי לטורח א"ר אלעזר אמר הקב"ה לא דיין לישראל שחוטאין לפני אלא שמטריחין אותי לידע איזו גזירה קשה אביא עליהן א"ר יצחק אין לך כל רגל ורגל שלא באתה בולשת לציפורי ואמר רבי חנינא אין לך כל רגל ורגל שלא בא לטבריה אגמון וקמטון ובעל זמורה מפני מה ת"ח שבבבל מצויינין לפי שאינן (א) בני מקומן דאמרי אינשי במתא שמאי בלא מתא תותבאי ו) הבאים ישרש יעקב יציץ ופרח ישראל תני רב יוסף אלו תלמידי חכמים שבבבל שעושין ציצין ופרחים לתורה מפני מה עובדי כוכבים מזוהמין שלא עמדו על הר סיני שבשעה
שבא

לעדות אשה. לומר לאשה מת בעליך דאקילו בה רבנן משום עיגונא וכל דמקדש אדעתא דרבנן מקדש ואפקועי רבנן לקדושין מיניה: לעדות בכור. בכור ביד כהן כשנתנו ישראל לו שלם ואירע לו בו מום קי"ל בבכורות (דף לה.) נחשדו כהנים להטיל מום בבכור ואין נאמן לומר מום זה נפל בו מאליו וצריך להביא עדים ואמרינן התם דאשה כשרה לעדות זו: אימא לעדות שהאשה כשרה לה. והאי נמי כשרה לה: גברא יתירא. ר"ש דמתני' ר"א תנן כה: אתא לאשמעינן. בתמיה כלומר מה בא ללמדנו אם לא זאת: מתני' כל שבא בחמין. כלומר שנתבשל: שורין אותו בחמין. כדי שיהא נמוח: וכל שלא בא בחמין. כגון בשר יבש שאוכלין אותו חי ע"י הדחק: מדיחין אותו. ולא אמרי' זהו בישוליה אבל לא שורין: חוץ מן המליח ישן. דג מליח של שנה שעברה: וקולייס האיספנין. שם דג שאוכלין אותו מחמת מלחו ע"י הדחה בחמין והכך אפילו הדחה נמי לא שזהו גמר מלאכתן והוי בשול: גמ' כגון מאי. הוי בא בחמין שמחזרין ושורין אותו בחמין: תרנגולתיה דר' אבא. מבשלה ושורה אותה ימים רבים בחמין למחות מאליה ואוכלה לרפואה: בר תלתא טרפי. בן ג' שנים: אתונסי. הייתי נאנס להקיא מחמת מיאום: רייק. רוקק מכותחא דבבלאי כשזוכרו שהיה מאוס בעיניו: אמר רב יוסף כו'. קשה היה בעיניו שנמאסין בני בבל על בני ארץ ישראל אמר אנו נמי יש לנו לרוק מתרנגולתיה דר' אבא שהם אוכלים: ועוד כותח. אינו מאוס כל כך בעיני שאר בני מערבא: דהא אמר רב גזא כו'. ושאילו מיניה אותו כותח: בריחי. חולים: הדיח. קוליים מאי: חייב חטאת. דהוי בישול: מפני מה עופות שבבבל שמנים. משל א"י: כלך. לכה לך אלא שקיצר הלשון: למדבר עזה. והיא מא"י: מועדים שבבבל שמחים. רגילים לשמוח במועדים יותר מא"י: מפני שהם עניים. וכל השנה אין להם שמחה במאכל ומשתה ואין להם מרגוע ממלאכה לפיכך במועדים כל שמחתם: מצויינין. מליינין עלמן בלבושים נאים: מצויינין. מקושטין: שאינן בני תורה. כל כך לכבדם כבני ארץ ישראל מחמת תורתם מכבדים אותם מחמת לבושיהן שנראין חשובים: דרדקי. בחורים שלא הגיעו לסברא: מפני שלא גלו. העופות כמו אותן של א"י כדאמרינן לקמן: שאנן מואב מנעוריו וגו'. סיפיה דקרא על כן עמד טעמו בו אלמא הגולין מפיגין טעמן ושמנן: נ"ב שנה. משגלו בימי לדקיה בחרבות ירושלים עד שנפקדו בימי כורש ואז עלו מהם לייסד את הבית י"ח שנים קודם גמר הבנין שהיא לסוף ע' שנה בשנת שתים לדריוש כדאמרי' במגילה (דף יא:): וכולן חזרו. הבהמות ועופות ואף הדגים חוץ מן קוליים האספנין וכולן חזרו דהא עד בהמה כתיב ומכלל דמכאן ואילך הדור חוץ מקוליים כדמפרש: הני מדרי דבבל מהדרי מיא לעין עיטם. מדרונות שבבבל מחזירין מים הנשפכים בהן לעין עיטם שהוא מקום גבוה שבא"י שאותו מעיין מביא מים לבית טבילת כה"ג ביוה"כ דמתוקן בחומת עזרה על גבי שער המים כדאמרינן בסדר יומא (דף לא.) עין עיטם גבוה מקרקע העזרה כ"ג אמות והיאך מחזירין שיש בפרת סילונות וסולמות למטה מן הקרקע (הים) ודרך אותן סולמות חוזרין המים לא"י וחוזרין ונובעין במעיינות והדגים חזרו דרך אותן סולמות שנוחים להעלותן יותר מדרך פרת עלמו: והאי. קוליים האספנין: כיון דלא שריר שדריה. אין קשה שדרה שלו: לטבריה. לבוז ולהטיל עליהם עול ולא שמתכוונין לבטלן משמחת הרגל אבל הקללה גרמה לכך: קומטין. לשון לעז הוא שלטון: בולשת. חיל המלך: ציפורי וטבריא מא"י: שאינן במקומם. שמא"י גלו לשם והגולה למקום נכרי מליין עלמו במלבושים שיהא חשוב: במתא שמאי. בעירי איני לריך להתכבד אלא בשמי שאני ניכר בו: בלא מתא. במקום שאינה עירי: תותבאי. כבודי תלוי בשמלתי שמלתו מתרגמינן תותביה (שמות כב): ציצין. למחין: הבאים. אותן של יעקב שיבאו לבבל ישרשו ויעשו ליצין ופרחים לתורה וסייעתא אתיא לר' יוחנן דטעמא דמצויינין לאו לפי שאינן בני תורה כדרבי אסי אלא לפי שאינן במקומן:
כשבא

מסורת הש"ס

א) בכורות דף לו. ע"ש, ב) לעיל יט:, ג) לעיל לט:, ד) נ"א לי"ג, ה) [דג שבמקומות האספניא ושמו בלשון הקודש שיבוטא ערוך ערך אספנן], ו) [ע' לעיל כח.], ז) ב"ב טז:, ח) סנהדרין ז:, ט) [יומא נד.], י) בכורות מד:, כ) [מגילה לא:], ל) [ועי' שבות יעקב חלק ב' סימן קטן], מ) [יבמות ל:], נ) לשון קומטוס כמו קומוס ולשון רומי הוא עי' רש"י סוטה יד ד"ה גסטרא.

הגהות הב"ח

(א) גמרא לפי שאינן במקומן כל"ל ותיבת בני נמחק:

תורה אור השלם

א) אֱמֹר לַחָכְמָה אֲחֹתִי אָתְּ וּמֹדָע לַבִּינָה תִקְרָא: [משלי ז, ד]

ב) שַׁאֲנַן מוֹאָב מִנְּעוּרָיו וְשֹׁקֵט הוּא אֶל שְׁמָרָיו וְלֹא הוּרַק מִכְּלִי אֶל כֶּלִי וּבַגּוֹלָה לֹא הָלָךְ עַל כֵּן עָמַד טַעְמוֹ בּוֹ וְרֵיחוֹ לֹא נָמָר: [ירמיה מח, יא]

ג) עַל הֶהָרִים אֶשָּׂא בְכִי וָנֶהִי וְעַל נְאוֹת מִדְבָּר קִינָה כִּי נִצְּתוּ מִבְּלִי אִישׁ עֹבֵר וְלֹא שָׁמְעוּ קוֹל מִקְנֶה מֵעוֹף הַשָּׁמַיִם וְעַד בְּהֵמָה נָדְדוּ הָלָכוּ: [ירמיה ט, ט]

ד) וְהִשְׁבַּתִּי כָּל מְשׂוֹשָׂהּ חַגָּהּ חָדְשָׁהּ וְשַׁבַּתָּהּ וְכֹל מוֹעֲדָהּ: [הושע ב, יג]

ה) חָדְשֵׁיכֶם וּמוֹעֲדֵיכֶם שָׂנְאָה נַפְשִׁי הָיוּ עָלַי לָטֹרַח נִלְאֵיתִי נְשֹׂא: [ישעיה א, יד]

ו) הַבָּאִים יַשְׁרֵשׁ יַעֲקֹב יָצִיץ וּפָרַח יִשְׂרָאֵל וּמָלְאוּ פְנֵי תֵבֵל תְּנוּבָה: [ישעיה כז, ו]

ליקוטי רש"י

לעדות אשה. שמת בעלה במדינת הים. לעדות בכור. להעיד שלא הטיל בו מום זה בכוונה. אימא לעדות שהאשה כשרה. ובעדות בכור נמי אשה כשרה דאמרינן הלכתא כרבן שמעון ואפי' בתו. יימר שרי בוכרא. יימר המתיר בכורות לשון גנאי [בכורות לו.]. התם הוא דמעיקרא אוכלא ולבסוף אוכלא. דבש לאחר שזב מן החלות נמי אוכלא הוא הלכך ליכא למיגזר ביה שמא יסחוט משמשך דלא שייכי ביה סחיטה. אבל הכא. זיתים וענבים דמתני' דמעיקרא אוכלא והשתא משקה איכא למיגזר שמא יסחוט משמשך דהא ודאי סחיטה היא [לעיל יט:]. כל שבא בחמין. כל מלוח שבא בחמין מערב שבת מותר ושורין אותו בחמין בשבת ואין בו משום תיקון שהרי נתקן ...

כבר. מדיחין. שאין זה גמר מלאכתו אבל לא שורין. וקולייס האיספנין. דג שקורין טוני"א ... ורך ונאכל כמו שהוא חי אלא שנותנין עליו חמין וזה בשולו כדתנן במסכת שבת שהדחתו זו היא גמר מלאכתן ... בר תלתא טרפי. בן שלש שנים שטענה אמו משנקלט שלשה עלין חדשין [לעיל קכט.]. כותח ... חמץ כדאמרינן באלו עוברין ואינו עשוי לאכול יחד אלא לטבול בו ואינו כלה עד זמן מרובה [שם ...] כדמפרש באלו עוברין (פסחים מב.) דיהבו ביה עיפושי פת ונסיובי דחלבא מסג"א בלע"ז [ע"ז ל:]. ... גמר מלאכתן. מדקרי ליה גמר מלאכתו שמע מינה זהו בישולו וחייב [לעיל לט.]. תלמידי ... מצויינין. דומים למלאכי השרת לבושים לבנים ועטופים כמלאכי השרת וכתיב (יחזקאל ט) והאיש ... אמרינן בבמה מדליקין (שבת כה:) על רבי יהודה שהיה מתעטף ויושב בסדינים המצויינין ודומה ...

(כ:) נמי אמרינן מאן מלאכי השרת רבנן ואמאי קרי להו מלאכי השרת משום דמצויינין כמלאכי השרת במלבושים נאים [קידושין עב.]. אמור לחכמה אחותי את. שתהא בקי בה כאחותך שאסורה לך [שם ל:]. נ"ב שנה. ... בגלות לדקיהו עד פקידת כורש שעלו לבנות הבית שהרי לסוף שבעים לגלות יהויקים היתה הפקידה כמו ששנינו במגילה (יא:) ושמונה עשרה שנה היה מכיבוש יהויקים עד חרבות ירושלים דאמר מר גלו בשבע גלו בשמונה ... בתשע עשרה ופירושו גלה יכניה בשבע לכיבוש יהויקים שהוא שמונה לנבוכדנצר גלו לדקיהו וגלותו בחרבות ירושלים בשמונה עשר לכיבוש יהויקים שהוא תשע עשרה לנבוכדנצר דאמר מר שנה ראשונה כיבש נינוה שניה עלה ... נד.]. על ההרים. על חורבן ההרים. נדדו הלכו. סופן לילך. חמשים ושתים שנה לא עבר איש ביהודה מגלות לדקיהו עד פקודת כורש מלך פרס חמשים ושתים שנה היו ורמז לדבר ועד בהמה חשבונה בגימטריא נ"ב ... [ירמיה ט, ט]. הני מדרי דבבל. מקומות מדרון שבבבל. מהדרי מיא לעין עיטם. שהו כ"ג טובל ביוה"כ כדאמרי' במסכת יומא בפרק ג' (לא.) [בכורות מד:]. [המשך בדף קמו.]

governor, a ruler or an official[38] **did not come to Tiberias** to plunder or to impose taxes.[39]

R' Yochanan continues:

מִפְּנֵי מָה תַּלְמִידֵי חֲכָמִים שֶׁבְּבָבֶל מְצוּיָּנִין – Why are the Torah scholars of Babylonia adorned with beautiful clothing, while those of Eretz Yisrael are not? **לְפִי שֶׁאֵינָן בְּנֵי מְקוֹמָן – Because [the Babylonians] are not native to their locale,**[40] and they therefore find it necessary to distinguish themselves through their garments. **דְּאָמְרֵי אִינְשֵׁי – For,** as **people say: בְּמָתָא שְׁמַאי** – "When **in** my own **city, my name** is enough;[41] **בְּלֹא מָתָא תוֹתְבַאי** – when **in a city not** my own, I must rely on **my clothing.**"[42]

The Gemara cites a verse in support of R' Yochanan's explanation:

"הַבָּאִים יַשְׁרֵשׁ יַעֲקֹב יָצִיץ וּפָרַח יִשְׂרָאֵל" – *Those of Jacob who come will take root; they will bud and show blossom – Israel.*[43] **תָּנֵי רַב יוֹסֵף – Rav Yosef taught: אֵלּוּ תַּלְמִידֵי חֲכָמִים שֶׁבְּבָבֶל – These are the Torah scholars of Babylonia, שֶׁעוֹשִׂין צִיצִין וּפְרָחִים לַתּוֹרָה – who make buds and blossoms for the Torah.**[44] We thus see that the scholars of Babylonia were indeed great in Torah! Perforce, the reason they adorn themselves is because they find themselves in a strange place, as R' Yochanan explained.

R' Yochanan continues:

מִפְּנֵי מָה עוֹבְדֵי כוֹכָבִים מְזוֹהָמִין – Why are the idolaters impure? שֶׁלֹּא עָמְדוּ עַל הַר סִינַי – Because they did not stand at Mount Sinai to accept the Torah.

R' Yochanan explains:

שֶׁבְּשָׁעָה – For at the moment

NOTES

38. *Maharatz Chayes* explains that a בַּעַל זְמוֹרָה is a Roman elector, who customarily goes in public with a garland before him. Such officials were thus called בַּעֲלֵי זְמוֹרָה, or *masters of the garland* (cf. *Maharshal*).

39. The Romans did not deliberately send these troops and officials to mar the joy of the festivals; however, they invariably arrived at these times as a result of the curse (*Rashi*).

40. Having been exiled to Babylonia (*Rashi*).

41. In my own city, I am accorded honor because of my name [and reputation], which are known (*Rashi*). Thus, the Torah scholars of Eretz Yisrael, who were in their own "city," did not distinguish themselves by their dress.

42. One in a strange city must distinguish himself by his dress to be accorded honor. The Babylonians therefore adorned themselves with beautiful clothing (*Rashi;* see *R' Tzaddok HaKohen's Sichas Malachei HaShareis* pp. 8,9 for an in-depth discussion of this Gemara; see also *Pri Tzaddik* ibid.).

43. *Isaiah* 27:6.

44. Thus, the verse is saying that those of Jacob who come to Babylonia will make buds and blossoms for the Torah [by expounding the verses to derive various novel teachings] (*Rashi;* see *Maharal, Chidushei Aggados*).

שֶׁבָּא נָחָשׁ עַל חַוָּה – that the primal **serpent seduced Eve,** **הֵטִיל בָּהּ זוּהֲמָא** – **he cast impurity into her,**[1] which she then passed on to future generations of men. **יִשְׂרָאֵל שֶׁעָמְדוּ עַל הַר סִינַי פָּסְקָה זוּהֲמָתָן** – In the case of **Israel, who stood at Mount Sinai** to accept the Torah, **their impurity was removed,**[2] and they were returned to their original uncontaminated state. Thus, they are today free of impurity. **עוֹבְדֵי כוֹכָבִים שֶׁלֹּא עָמְדוּ עַל הַר סִינַי לֹא פָּסְקָה זוּהֲמָתָן** – In the case of **idolaters,** however, **who did not stand at Mount Sinai, their impurity was not removed.** It thus persists to this day.

The Gemara asks:

אָמַר לֵיהּ רַב אַחָא בְּרֵיהּ דְּרָבָא לְרַב אַשִׁי – **Rav Acha the son of Rava said to Rav Ashi:** **גֵּרִים מַאי** – **What about converts,** who did not stand at Mount Sinai?[3] **אָמַר לֵיהּ** – **He said to him:** **אַף עַל גַּב דְּאִינְהוּ לֹא הָווּ מַזָּלַיְיהוּ הָווּ** – **Even though they** themselves **were not** there, **their *mazals* were** there.[4] **דִּכְתִיב** – **For it is written** in a verse that identifies those with whom the covenant of Sinai was made: **"אֶת־אֲשֶׁר יֶשְׁנוֹ פֹּה עִמָּנוּ עֹמֵד הַיּוֹם לִפְנֵי ה' אֱלֹהֵינוּ וְאֵת אֲשֶׁר אֵינֶנּוּ פֹּה וגו'"** – ***those who are standing here with us today before Hashem our God, and those who are not here*** **etc.** *with us today.*[5] This teaches that even those who would only later join the Jewish nation were present in some form at the Revelation at Sinai. Their presence there caused their impurity to be removed.

The Gemara cites a dissenting opinion:

וּפְלִיגָא דְּרַבִּי אַבָּא בַּר כַּהֲנָא – **And this** [i.e. R' Yochanan's statement] **is contrary to** the opinion of **R' Abba bar Kahana;** **דְּאָמַר רַבִּי אַבָּא בַּר כַּהֲנָא** – **for R' Abba bar Kahana said:** **עַד שְׁלֹשָׁה דוֹרוֹת לֹא פָּסְקָה זוּהֲמָא מֵאֲבוֹתֵינוּ** – **Not until three generations** had passed **was the impurity** introduced into Eve by the serpent **removed from our forefathers.** **אַבְרָהָם הוֹלִיד אֶת יִשְׁמָעֵאל** – For we see that **Abraham sired Ishmael,** a product of his impurity, **יִצְחָק הוֹלִיד אֶת עֵשָׂו** – while **Isaac sired Esau,** a product of his impurity. **יַעֲקֹב הוֹלִיד שְׁנֵים עָשָׂר שְׁבָטִים** – But **Jacob sired the twelve tribes,** **שֶׁלֹּא הָיָה בָּהֶן שׁוּם דוֹפִי** – **in whom there was no abberation** – all were free of the serpent's contamination. Thus, R' Abba bar Kahana holds that the Jews were freed of impurity with the birth of Jacob, long before the Revelation at Sinai.[6]

Mishnah **שׁוֹבֵר אָדָם אֶת הֶחָבִית לֶאֱכוֹל הֵימֶנָּה גְּרוֹגָרוֹת** – **A person may break** open **a cask** in order **to eat dried figs from it,**[7] **וּבִלְבַד שֶׁלֹּא יִתְכַּוֵּין לַעֲשׂוֹת כְּלִי** – **provided that he does not intend to make a vessel;**[8] **וְאֵין נוֹקְבִין מְגוּפָה שֶׁל חָבִית** – **and one may not perforate the bung of a cask.** **דִּבְרֵי רַבִּי יְהוּדָה** – These are **the words of R' Yehudah;**[9] **וַחֲכָמִים מַתִּירִין** – **however, the Sages**

NOTES

1. When the Torah records Eve's words regarding her beguilement into eating from the Tree of Knowledge, it employs a term that connotes sexual relations. For the word הִשִּׁיאַנִי – from the verse הַנָּחָשׁ הִשִּׁיאַנִי, *the serpent deceived me* (*Genesis* 3:13) – shares the root of the word נִישׂוּאִין, *marriage.* The Torah thus teaches that when the serpent convinced Eve to eat, it "coupled" with her (*Rashi;* see *Sefer HaPardes,* quoted in *Shaarei Zohar; Ben Yehoyada;* see also *Maharal, Chidushei Aggados,* here and to *Yevamos* 63a). With this act, the serpent cast impurity into Eve. *Maharsha* (to *Yevamos* 103b) explains that Man, who is formed in God's image, was created free of all spiritual contamination. By causing Eve to sin, the serpent injected into Man the spiritual impurity that is at the root of all sin.

2. As were all their impairments, both spiritual and physical. For at the moment of the Revelation, all who were at Sinai were imbued with holiness and purity; even the blind and the lame [as well as those deaf and dumb] were healed of their physical defects (*Rashi,* from *Sifrei;* see *Rashi* to *Avodah Zarah* 22b ד״ה ישראל שעמדו, who derives this from *Song of Songs* 4:7; see also *Rashi* to *Exodus* 20:15).

3. How is their impurity removed from them? (*Rashi*). [The Gemara does not ask this question regarding the children of those who stood at Mount Sinai because it assumes [based on the verse cited in the Gemara below] that the souls of *all* Jews were present at the Revelation at Sinai. It wonders, though, regarding converts, whose souls were not at Sinai (*Maharsha*). Alternatively, the Gemara assumes that those who were at Sinai passed their sanctity on to their offspring (*Sfas Emes*).]

4. A מַזָּל, *mazal,* is a person's angel, who advocates his cause in the Heavenly Court (*Rashi* to 53b ד״ה מזליה). The Gemara now realizes that although the souls of converts were not at Sinai, their angels were; this sufficed to remove the impurity from them [upon their conversion] (*Maharsha;* see also *Shevuos* 39a).

5. *Deuteronomy* 29:14.

6. [But see *R' Tzaddok HaKohen's Yisrael Kedoshim* (p. 112), where he explains that these two opinions are not in actual disagreement, but only discuss two stages in the removal of the impurity.]

7. E.g. he breaks the barrel open with a knife or a sword (*Rashi*). Although making an opening in a cask can sometimes qualify as a *melachah* [e.g. מַכֶּה בְּפַטִּישׁ, *striking the final blow;* see next note], here it is permitted because the act is purely destructive [i.e. the hole he is making is not an improvement to the vessel; rather, he is ruining the cask to get to the figs] (see *Rashi;* see *Ran* to *Rif* and *Igros Moshe, Orach Chaim* I §122, *Chazon Ish* to *Orach Chaim* 51:8; cf. *Sfas Emes*).

Ran and others ask that the Mishnah earlier (105b) seems to indicate that purely destructive acts are at least Rabinically prohibited on the Sabbath. They therefore explain that although destructive acts are usually so prohibited, where they are necessary for the Sabbath, as for example, to reach food, the Rabbis permitted them (see *Igros Moshe* ibid.; see *Beur Halachah* to 314:1 ד״ה אסור).

[*Tosafos* and others note that this Mishnah seems to be contradicted by another Mishnah on *Eruvin* 34b. There the Tanna discusses the placing of the food of an *eruv techumim.* As a general rule, in order for such an *eruv* to be valid, one must be able to retrieve and eat on the Sabbath the food that one has placed at the site of the *eruv.* In consequence of this stipulation, the Mishnah there states that if one locked his food in a locker at the site and then lost the key, the *eruv* is invalid. According to the ruling of our Mishnah, however, the *eruv* should have still been valid, since one is permitted to retrieve the food by breaking open the locker.

To answer this question, *Tosafos* suggest that indeed, one is Rabbinically forbidden to break open a good utensil, for it was feared that one will in the process intend to fashion a proper opening (see below). Our Mishnah, however, refers specifically to a cask previously broken and glued back together. Since it is an inferior container, we need not fear that he will break it open in such a way as to fashion a proper opening (see also *Rosh*).

For an alternative solution to this difficulty, see *Ran.*]

8. I.e. provided he does not try to make a proper, symmetrical, opening for the cask (*Rashi*). [If he indeed makes such an opening, he would transgress at least a Rabbinic injunction (*Taz* to *Orach Chaim* 314:1); see below.]

Making a new opening in a container is considered putting the finishing touch on the utensil, and is therefore prohibited under the *melachah* of מַכֶּה בְּפַטִּישׁ, *striking the final blow* (see *Rashi* to 48a ד״ה חייב חטאת; see also *Rambam, Hil. Shabbos* 23:1; *Ran,* however, writes that the *melachah* is that of בּוֹנֶה, *building*). As we shall soon see, it is Biblically prohibited to make such an opening only if the hole serves both to allow things in the container to come out, and things outside to come in. Nonetheless, fashioning an opening that serves only one of these functions is Rabbinically prohibited (see Gemara below and *Rambam* ad loc.).

9. The מְגוּפָה, *bung,* was a clay stopper molded to the mouth of the cask. R' Yehudah maintains that it is forbidden to make a hole in the bung, for in so doing he is making a proper opening to the cask [and thereby transgresses the *melachah* of *striking the final blow;* see previous note]. If he wishes to open the cask on the Sabbath, he should instead do so by removing the entire bung. In so doing, he merely reopens a previously made opening, which is not a transgression since he has not fashioned anything new (see *Ran* ד״ה ושוין and Gemara below).

שבא נחש על חוה הטיל בה זוהמא ישראל שעמדו על הר סיני פסקה זוהמתן עובדי כוכבי' שלא עמדו על הר סיני לא פסקה זוהמתן א"ל רב אחא בריה דרבא לרב אשי גרים מאי א"ל אע"ג דאינהו לא הוו מזליהו הוו דכתיב א את אשר ישנו פה עמנו עומד היום לפני ה' אלהינו ואת אשר איננו פה וגו' ופליגא דר' אבא בר כהנא דא"ר אבא בר כהנא עד שלשה דורות לא פסקה זוהמא מאבותינו אברהם הוליד את ישמעאל יצחק הוליד את עשו יעקב הוליד י"ב שבטים שלא היה בהן שום דופי: **מתני'** שובר אדם את החבית לאכול הימנה גרוגרות ובלבד שלא יתכוין לעשות כלי ואין נוקבין מגופה של חבית דברי ר' יהודה וחכמים מתירין ולא יקבנה מצדה ואם היתה נקובה לא יתן עליה שעוה מפני שהוא ממרח אמר ר' יהודה מעשה בא לפני רבן יוחנן בן זכאי בערב ואמר חוששני לו מחטאת: **גמ'** א"ר אושעיא ל"ש אלא דרוסות אבל מפורדות לא ומפורדות לא מיתיבי ר' שמעון בן גמליאל אומר מביא אדם את החבית של יין ומתיז ראשה בסייף ומניחה לפני האורחים בשבת ואינו חושש ההיא רבנן היא (א) מתני' רבי נחמיה היא ומאי דוחקיה דרבי אושעיא לאוקמי מתניתין כרבי נחמיה ובדרוסות לוקמה במפורדות ורבנן אמר רבא מתני' קשיתיה מאי איריא דתני גרוגרות ליתני פירות אלא ש"מ בדרוסות תניא חדא חותלות של גרוגרות ושל תמרים מתיר ומפקיע וחותך ותניא אידך מתיר אבל לא מפקיע ולא חותך לא קשיא הא רבנן הא ר' נחמיה דתניא ר' נחמיה אומר אפי' תרווד ואפילו טלית ואפילו סכין אין ניטלין אלא לצורך תשמישן [א] בעו מיניה מרב ששת מהו למיברז חביתא בבורטיא בשבתא לפיתחא קמיכוין ואסיר או דילמא לעין יפה קמיכוין ושרי א"ל לפיתחא קא מכוין ואסור מיתיבי רשב"ג אומר מביא אדם חבית של יין ומתיז ראשה בסייף התם ודאי לעין יפה קמיכוין הכא אם איתא דלעין יפה קמיכוין לפתוחי מיפתח: אין נוקבין מגופה וכו': אמר רב הונא מחלוקת למעלה אבל מן הצד דברי הכל אסור והיינו דקתני לא יקבנה מצדה ורב חסדא אמר מחלוקת מן הצד אבל על גבה דברי הכל מותר והא דקתני לא יקבנה מצדה התם בגופה דחבית תנו רבנן אין נוקבין נקב חדש בשבת ואם בא להוסיף מוסיף ויש אומרים אין מוסיפין ושוין שנוקבין (ג) נקב ישן לכתחילה ותנא קמא מאי שנא מנקב חדש דלא דקא מתקן פיתחא אוסופי נמי קא מתקן פיתחא אמר רבה דבר תורה כל פתח שאינו עשוי להכנים ולהוציא אינו פתח ורבנן הוא דגזור משום לול של תרנגולין דעביד לעיולי אוירא ולאפוקי הבלא ואם בא להוסיף מוסיף אוסופי ודאי בלול של תרנגולים לא אתי לאוסופי

משום

רש"י

כשבא נחש על חוה. כשנתן לה עצה לאכול מן העץ בא עליה דכתיב (בראשית ג) הנחש השיאני לשון נשואין: **גרים מאי.** שלא היו על הר סיני מהיכן פסקה זוהמא: **מזלייהו הוו.** בסיני וכל שעמדו על הר סיני נתקדשו ונטהרו ונתרפאו מכל מום ואף עורים ופסחים שהיו בישראל כדתניא בספרי: **ופליגא.** הא דאמרן דלא פסקה זוהמא עד סיני: **מתני' שובר אדם חבית.** מליאה גרוגרות בסכין או בסייף לאכול ממנה גרוגרות דאין במקלקל שום איסור בשבת: **ובלבד שלא יתכוין לעשות כלי.** לנוקבה יפה בפתח נאה: **אין נוקבין מגופה.** הדבוקה (ג) בפה החבית לעשות נקב אלא נוטל את כולה אבל כי נקיב לה מתקן פתחא: **וחכמים מתירין.** דאין דרך פתח לחבית בכך: **ולא יקבנה מצידה.** בגמרא מפרש לה: **שהוא ממרח.** ויש כאן משום ממחק: **בערב.** מדינה: **מחטאת.** שמא מירח השעוה לדובקה בדופני הכלי סביב הנקב: **גמ' לא שנו.** דשובר החבית ומטלטל הסייף לכך: **אלא בדרוסות.** שהגרוגרות דרוסות בעיגול ותוכפן ממנו בקורדום או בסייף ואידי דמטלטל סייף לחתוך גרוגרות תבר ביה נמי לחבית: **אבל מפורדות.** שא"צ לחתכן לא יטלטל סייף לשבור החבית (ד) דמתני' ר' נחמיה דאמר אין כלי ניטל אלא לתשמיש המיוחד לו כדמוקי לקמן: **ואינו חושש.** ואע"ג דיין לאו למתחכיה קאי: **רבנן היא.** דפליגי אדר' נחמיה ואמרי כל הכלים ניטלים לצורך ושלא לצורך: **חותלות.** כלי של כפות תמרים ועושין כמין סלים ונותנים לתוכן תמרים רעים להתבשל: **מתיר.** אם הכסוי קשור בחבל: **אבל לא מפקיע.** קורע שרשרות החבל בכלי: **ולא חותך.** דאין כלי ניטל שלא לצורך תשמישו וסכין אינו עשוי לכך: **למיברז.** לתחוב פויינדור"א בלע"ז: **בבורטיא.** ברומח שלה בחוזת דופניה לנקוב: **לעין יפה.** להרחיב מוצא היין בנקב גדול מאלא נקיב ליה כדרך הנוקבין נקב עגול ויפה: **התם ודאי לעין יפה קמיכוין.** שמרחיב פיה למטה ממגופתה דקתני מתיז את ראשה שפת פיה: **לפתוחי מיפתח.** יטול מגופתה: **למעלה.** בראש המגופה התם הוא דשרו רבנן דלאו אורחא למיעבד פתחא התם אלא נוטל כל המגופה: **אבל מצדה.** זמנין דעבדי לה משום פתחא ואינו רוצה לפותחה למעלה שלא יפול עפר או פסולת ביין: **היינו דקתני ולא יקבנה מצדה.** ואמגופה קאי ודברי הכל: **מחלוקת מן הצד.** התם הוא דקאסר רבי יהודה משום דאיכא דעבדי ליה פתחא: **אין נוקבין נקב חדש.** בכלי: **נקב ישן.** שנסתם לכי חוזר ופותח לאו כעושה פתח הוא שהרי עשוי ועומד וסתימתו לאו כלום: **אוסופי נמי קמתקן פתחא.** שמרחיבו ויש כאן משום גמר מלאכה: **הבלא.** סרחון שלא ימותו התרנגולין: **ואם בא להוסיף מוסיף.** ולא גזרינן דילמא אתי לאוסופי בלול של תרנגולין דלא מוסיף איניש עליה:

משום

תוספות

שובר אדם את החבית לאכול הימנה גרוגרות. בגמרא מוקי לה בדרוסות לרבי נחמיה אבל לרבנן דרבי נחמיה שרי אפילו מפורדות ותימה לרבי מהא דתנן בפרק בכל מערבין (עירובין דף לד: ושם) גבי עירוב נתנו במגדל ונעל בפניו ואבד המפתח הרי זה עירוב ופריך בגמרא אמאי הוא במקום אחד ועירובו במקום אחר הוא ומשני רב ושמואל דאמרי תרווייהו הכא במגדל של (ה) בנין עסקינן ור"מ היא כו' ואמאי מבעי ליה לאוקמא הכי ומעיקרא נמי מאי קאמר והלא יכול לשבר ולפתוח את המגדל וליטול את העירוב כי היכי דהכא שרי לשבר החבית וליטול הגרוגרות ואם באת לחלק בין נטילת העירוב לנטילת הגרוגרות א"כ קשה היכי מוקי לה התם כר' מאיר ונראה דהתם אסור לשבר את המגדל והכא דשרי לשבר את החבית משום דמיירי במוסתקי כדמוקי לה בביצה פרק המביא כדי יין (דף לג: ושם) ומפ' רש"י התם דהיינו חבית שבורה ומדבקין שבריה בשרף של עץ שעושה ממנו זפת וקורין ריישנ"א ומש"ה דוקא חבית שרי דמחמת גריעותו לא חיים עליה וליכא למיחש שמא יתכוין לעשות כלי וכן כולה שמעתא דהכא במוסתקי ואע"ג דהתם בביצה לא מוקמינן הכי אלא לר"א דפריך ולית ליה לר"א הא דתנן שובר אדם את החבית כו' ועלה משני מתני' במוסתקי מ"מ אפילו לרבנן מיבעי לאוקמי הכי דרבנן לא פליגי אדר"א דקאמר לא יקטמנו פי' לא יקטום את ההדס להריח בו אלא משום דאיהו סבירא ליה דבקטימת קיסם חייב חטאת כשקוטמו לחצות בו שיניו וא"כ אי לא מוקמינן לה במוסתקי עליהו איכא למיפרך ולית להו הא דתנן כו' הלכך מיבעי לן למימר דאליבא דכולהו מיירי מתניתין במוסתקי והשתא אתיא שמעתא שפיר. מ"ר. ובגמ' ירושלמי בפרק בכל מערבין מגלאי הדא דתימא במגדל של אבן אבל במגדל של עץ נעשה כשובר החבית לאכול ממנה גרוגרות:

מתיר ומפקיע וחותך. אומר רבי מההיא דעירובין (דף לד:) יש ללמוד דהא דאמרינן (ביצה דף לא:) חותמות שבכלים מתיר ומפקיע וחותך היינו כגון דקטיר במיתנא אבל פותחת של עץ ושל מתכת אסור לשבר ולהפקיע מדקשיא ליה התם אמאי הוא במקום אחד ועירובו במקום אחר דפשיטא ליה שאינו יכול להפקיע הפותחת וליטול העירוב אע"פ שסתם מגדל שבכל הש"ס הוא כלי כמו הלד גבי לבית ולפור למגדל וכי ההיא דבריש כל הכלים (לעיל קכב:) ובמסקנא נמי לא בעי לאוקומי אלא בקטיר במיתנא דהיינו דוקא חותמות שבכלים אבל דבר שהוא חזק כעין פותחת לא הוה שרי ת"ק. מ"ר:

הא רבנן והא ר' נחמיה. תימה לי אמאי לא מוקי תרווייהו כר' נחמיה והא דקתני מתיר מפקיע וחותך ביו"ט והא דקתני מתיר אבל לא מפקיע וחותך בשבת דאיכא תנא דס"ל הכי אליבא דר' נחמיה בביצה בפ' המביא כדי יין (לג:) וי"ל דניחא ליה למימר הדא כרבנן מדנימא תרווייהו כר' נחמיה:

משום

מסורת הש"ס

א) ע"ז כב: יבמות קג:, ב) ביצה לג:, ג) ס"א ר' יוסי מתיר, ד) [לעיל קכא.], ה) עירובין לה. ביצה לב. [תוספתא פט"ו], ו) [לעיל קב:], ז) [לעיל קכא. פירש"י שם מקום], ח) [וע"ע תוס' עירובין לה: ד"ה בעי סכינא].

הגהות הב"ח

(א) גמ' ההיא רבנן היא מתניתין: (ב) שם בנקב ישן: (ג) רש"י ד"ה אין נוקבין וכו' הדבוקה בפי החבית: (ד) ד"ה אבל מפורדות וכו' החבית הס"ד ואח"כ מ"ה ואינו חושש וכו' קאי הס"ד ואח"כ מ"ה ההיא רבנן הוא וכו' ושלא לצורך הס"ד ואח"כ מ"ה מתני' ר' נחמיה היא דאמר אין כלי וכו' לקמן הס"ד ואח"כ מ"ה חותלות וכו' תמרים ועשוין כמין סלים: (ה) תוס' ד"ה שובר וכו' במגדל של לבנים עסקינן:

הגהות הגר"א

[א] גמרא בעו מיני' מרב ששת מהו למיברז. נ"ב ר"ל במקום שנקב אסור אם ברומח מותר. טור:

ליקוטי רש"י

עין עיטם. נראה בעיני שהוא מעין מי נפתוח האמור שם (יהושע טו, ט) אחר עליית ההר אשר על פני גיא בן הינום אשר לא נכתב ירידה ביניהם [זבחים נד:]. ממנו באה אמת המים לבית טבילת שער המים שעל החומה ולפי עניין המקראות נראה לי שהוא מעין מי נפתוח האמור בספר יהושע (טו) שמשם הגבול משפע ויורד למזרח ולמערב והוא [הגבוה] בכל ארץ ישראל וכו' גבוה מקרקע עזרה עשרים ושלש אמות כמדת גובה שער המים וכנין כלי של שלש אמות מלמעלה להחזיק ארבעים סאה שאי אפשר למים לעלות להר שהוא גבוה ממקום שנובעין שם [יומא לא.]. **בולשת.** חיילות גיים הבא לעיר על שם שמחפשין ובולשין את העיר קרי לה בולשת [לעיל מא.]. בולשת חיל שמחפשין ובוחין כדמתרגמינן (בראשית מד) ויחפש ובלש [נדה יג.]. [ע"כ שייך לדף קמה:].

ישראל שעמדו על הר סיני. ונתקנו מכל מום כדכתיב (שה"ש ד) כולך יפה רעיתי ומום אין בך [ע"ז כב:]. **שובר אדם את החבית.** מגופה שיש בה גרוגרות ואוכל ובלבד שלא יתכוין ליפות השבירה להיות לה לפה שתהא עוד כלי. **את החבית.** כי מגילה ההיא דמותר במוסתקי חבית שבורה שמדבקין שבריה בשרף של עץ שקורין שף שעושין הימנו זפת וקורין אותו ריישינ"א ודימו דומה לריח לבונה ובלשון ערבי קורין אותו מוסתקי"י ומדבקין בו קערות חרס הנשברים כך אמר לי רבי שמואל המכונה חסיד מן ברכשטי"א וכיון דרעועה היא ליכא למגזר בה שלא יתכוון לעשות כלי [ביצה לג: ועיין כאן בתוס']. **בערב.** מקום. **חוששני לו מחטאת.** איני יודע אם חייב אם לאו ומספקא לי לומר חייב חטאת הוא [לעיל קכא.]. **מפקיע.** המבל לפתור עבותו וגדילתו [ביצה לא:]. **אלא לצורך תשמישן.** ועיקר תשמישו של סכין לא לחתוך מכלים הוא אלא לאכל בשר ואוכלין [עירובין לה.]. **לול של תרנגולין.** בית קטן שמגדלין בו תרנגולין [ב"ב יא:]. של עץ הוא וכסוס ומנקבו שיצא הריח של צואה ולא יזיק להו [לעיל קב:].

עין משפט נר מצוה

כד א מיי' פכ"ג מהל' שבת הלכה ב סמג לאוין סה טוש"ע או"ח סימן שיד סעיף א:

כה ב מיי' שם טוש"ע שם סעיף ו:

כו ג מיי' שם הלכה יא טוש"ע שם סעיף יא:

כז ד שם סעיף א:

כח ה ו ז מיי' שם הל' ג טור שו"ע שם סעיף ו:

כט ח ט מיי' שם הל"א טוש"ע שם סעיף א:

ל י מיי' שם הל"א ופ"י הלכה טו סמג שם:

גליון הש"ס

גמרא מהו למיברז חביתא. ע"ל דף מח ע"ב תוס' ד"ה וכי מה בין:

תורה אור השלם

א) כִּי אֶת אֲשֶׁר יֶשְׁנוֹ פֹּה עִמָּנוּ עֹמֵד הַיּוֹם לִפְנֵי יְיָ אֱלֹהֵינוּ וְאֵת אֲשֶׁר אֵינֶנּוּ פֹּה עִמָּנוּ הַיּוֹם: [דברים כט, יד]

רבינו חננאל

אם לא הביאם בחמין מלפני השבת אפילו להדיחן בשבת אסור ואם עבר והדיחן חייב חטאת שגמר מלאכה. פי' מכותא מכותתא היא. ויש מי שאומר כותא כותחא היא בדיחי במערבא חולים שבמערב: **מתני'** שובר אדם את החבית לאכול ממנה גרוגרות כו'. א"ר הושעיא לא ששובר את החבית לאכול ממנה גרוגרות אלא דרוסות אבל מפורדות אינו שובר החבית אלא מוציא גרוגרות ואוכל ואינו שובר. ואוקימנא למתניתין כר' נחמיה. מדקתני גרוגרות ולא קתני פירות. והא דתניא רשב"ג אומר מביא אדם חבית של יין ומתיז ראשה בסייף ומניחה לפני האורחים בשבת ואינו חושש לרבנן. וכן הא דתני חותלות של תמרים ושל גרוגרות ומתיר ומפקיע וחותך לרבנן והא דתני מתיר אבל לא מפקיע ולא חותך ר' נחמיה דאמר אפילו תרווד ואפילו טלית אין ניטלין אלא לצורך תשמישן: **בעו** מיניה דרב ששת מהו למיברז חביתא בבורטיא. פי' לנקוב חבית ברומח. ויש שאומר במקדח ומסקנא לפיתחא קא מיכוין ואסיר: **פיס'** אין נוקבין מגופה של החבית. פי' מגופה כסוי החבית דברי ר' יהודה וחכמים מתירין והלכה כחכמים. והני מילי שיהא הנקב בגג הכסוי אבל לנקב נקב בצד הכסוי אסור כדתנן לא יקבנה מצדה שהוא דברי הכל. וכרב הונא דהלכתא כוותיה. דהוא לגביה דרב חסדא רבו וליתא לדרב חסדא: **ת"ר** אין נוקבין נקב חדש בשבת. ואם בא להוסיף מוסיף ואקשינן עלה למה אסור לנקוב נקב חדש שנמצא מתקן פתח גם בהוסיפו בנקב ומרחיבו נמצא מתקן פתח. ולמה מותר ופריק רבא מן התורה כל פתח שאינו עשוי להכניס ולהוציא אינו חשוב פתח. ואלו הנקבים כולן אין מכניסין בהן אלא להוציא הן עשויין בלבד ומותרין. ורבנן גזרו על כל נקב מפני שלא יפתחו נקב בבית התרנגולין והוא הנקרא לול של תרנגולים כדכתיב ובלולים יעלו. וזה לול של תרנגולים עשוי להכניס רוח ולהוציא בהמות והוא כמין פתח ואסור. ומפני שהוא פתח גמור אסור מן התורה. גזרו על כל נקב אבל ההרחבה שאין אדם מרחיב בלול של תרנגולים כי מתיירא אם מרחיב הלול יכנס ממנו הנחש ויזיק אותן. וכיון שאין דרך בני אדם להרחיב בלול של תרנגולים לא גזרו בהרחבה כל נקב וזהו טעם ת"ק.

permit it.[10] וְלֹא יְקַבְּנָה מִצִּדָּהּ – **And** everyone agrees that **one may not perforate it in its side.**[11] וְאִם הָיְתָה נְקוּבָה – Now, **if [the cask] was** already **perforated** and one wished to plug the hole, **he may not place** לֹא יִתֵּן עָלֶיהָ שַׁעֲוָה **wax upon it,** מִפְּנֵי שֶׁהוּא מְמָרֵחַ – **because he** thereby **smooths it.**[12] אָמַר רַבִּי יְהוּדָה – **R' Yehudah said:** מַעֲשֶׂה בָּא לִפְנֵי רַבָּן יוֹחָנָן בֶּן זַכַּאי בַּעֲרָב – **An incident** involving one who placed wax to plug a hole once **came before R' Yochanan ben Zakkai in** the town of **Arab,**[13] וְאָמַר – **and he said:** חוֹשְׁשַׁנִי לוֹ מֵחַטָּאת – **I fear on his account** that he may be liable **for a *chatas* offering.**[14]

Gemara The Gemara qualifies our Mishnah's first ruling: אָמַר רַבִּי אוֹשַׁעְיָא – **R' Oshaya said:** לֹא שָׁנוּ אֶלָּא דְּרוּסוֹת – **[The Mishnah's permit]** to break open a barrel, and in particular, to handle a sword or knife for this purpose, **was taught only** with reference to a cask full of **pressed [figs].**[15] In that case, the person will need the knife or sword anyway to cut apart the fig-cakes after removing them, and he is therefore permitted to handle the cutting implement even to break the cask. אֲבָל מְפוֹרָדוֹת לֹא – **But** to break apart a cask of **loose [figs],** one may **not** handle a knife or sword on the Sabbath.[16]

This interpretation is questioned:

וּמְפוֹרָדוֹת לֹא – **But** is it really so that regarding **loose [figs],** the permit does **not** apply? מֵיתִיבֵי – **They challenged this,** citing the following Baraisa: רַבָּן שִׁמְעוֹן בֶּן גַּמְלִיאֵל אוֹמֵר – RABBAN SHIMON BEN GAMLIEL SAYS: מֵבִיא אָדָם אֶת הֶחָבִית שֶׁל יַיִן – A PERSON MAY BRING A CASK OF WINE וּמַתִּיז רֹאשָׁהּ בְּסַיִיף – AND SEVER ITS TOP WITH A SWORD וּמַנִּיחָהּ לִפְנֵי הָאוֹרְחִים בְּשַׁבָּת – AND PLACE IT BEFORE his GUESTS ON THE SABBATH, וְאֵינוֹ חוֹשֵׁשׁ – AND HE NEED NOT BE CONCERNED that he may have desecrated the Sabbath.[17] Evidently, then, it is permissible to use a sword to puncture a cask even when one will not be using the same implement to cut apart the produce in the cask! – ? –

The Gemara replies:

הַהִיא רַבָּנָן מַתְנִיתִין רַבִּי נְחֶמְיָה הִיא – **That** Baraisa **reflects** the view of **the Sages,** whereas **our Mishnah reflects** the view of **R' Nechemyah.**[18]

The Gemara asks:

וּמַאי דוּחֲקֵיהּ דְּרַבִּי אוֹשַׁעְיָא לְאוֹקְמֵי מַתְנִיתִין כְּרַבִּי נְחֶמְיָה – **And what forced R' Oshaya to construe our Mishnah according** to the view of **R' Nechemyah,** וּבִדְרוּסוֹת – **and as dealing with pressed [figs]** in particular? לוֹקְמָהּ בִּמְפוֹרָדוֹת וְרַבָּנָן – **Let him interpret it as dealing** even **with loose [figs], and** as following even **the Sages!**[19] – ? –

The Gemara answers:

אָמַר רָבָא מַתְנִיתִין קַשִׁיתֵיהּ – **Rava said:** The wording of **our Mishnah posed a difficulty for him.** מַאי אִירְיָא דְּתָנֵי גְּרוֹגָרוֹת – **Why did [the Mishnah] teach** that the cask contained **figs** in particular? לִיתְנֵי פֵּירוֹת – **Let it** instead **teach** that it contained **"produce"** of any kind. אֶלָּא שְׁמַע מִינָּהּ בִּדְרוּסוֹת – **Rather, we can infer from here** that the Mishnah is dealing **with pressed produce,**[20] something that needs to be cut apart in order to be consumed.

The Gemara cites another instance of contradictory rulings that can be resolved by attributing one ruling to R' Nechemyah and the other to the Sages:

תַּנְיָא חֲדָא – **One Baraisa teaches:** חוֹתָלוֹת שֶׁל גְּרוֹגָרוֹת וְשֶׁל תְּמָרִים מַתִּיר – ONE MAY UNTIE ropes binding BASKETS OF DRIED FIGS OR DATES,[21] וּמְפַקִּיעַ וְחוֹתֵךְ – or HE MAY UNRAVEL these ropes OR CUT them.[22] וְתַנְיָא אִידָךְ – However, another Baraisa

NOTES

10. The Sages argue that perforating the bung is not the customary way of making an opening in a cask (*Rashi*). Doing so thus does not "put the finishing touch" on the utensil, and is therefore permissible on the Sabbath.

11. The Gemara will explain what is meant by this (*Rashi*).

12. In order to make the wax fill the hole and adhere properly to the cask, one must smooth the wax. מְמָרֵחַ, *smoothing,* is a forbidden labor on the Sabbath, being a *toladah* of *smoothing hides* (*Rashi*).

13. A certain town in the Galilee region. The Jerusalem Talmud (*Shabbos* 16:8) records that R' Yochanan resided there for eighteen years. See above, 121a note 28.

14. He feared that perhaps the person had smoothed out the wax, and was therefore liable to a *chatas* (*Rashi*).

15. [In Talmudic times, dried figs were often pressed into rounded cakes and then stored in barrels.]

16. As the Gemara soon makes clear, R' Oshaya perceives our Mishnah as reflecting the view of R' Nechemyah. R' Nechemyah adopts a particularly stringent interpretation of *muktzeh* law, under which an implement may be handled on the Sabbath only if one is using it for its specialized purpose; i.e. the purpose it normally serves [אֵין כְּלִי נִיטָל אֶלָּא לְתַשְׁמִישׁ הַמְיוּחָד לוֹ]. For example, according to R' Nechemyah, one may handle a knife to cut fig-cakes, for this is how knives are normally employed; one may not, however, use a knife to crack nuts, for knives are not generally used for this purpose.

R' Oshaya proposes, then, that our Mishnah teaches the following: One may use a sword to break a cask filled with caked figs, for since one is permitted to handle a sword to cut the fig-cakes [a "usual" use of the implement], he is also permitted to first break the cask with it. If, however, the figs inside are loose [in which case there will be no need to cut them], one is not permitted to break the cask with a sword, for this, in itself, is not a normative use of the implement (see *Rashi*).

17. Even though wine obviously does not need to be cut before being served (*Rashi*), one may handle a sword to break open the top of the cask. If so, the same should apply to handling a sword to break into a cask of loose figs.

18. The Sages adopt a less restrictive position on the issue of *muktzeh,* holding that one may use an instrument for any permissible activity on the Sabbath, even if this is not its specialized purpose. [Indeed, the Sages assert that even a utensil whose specialized use is forbidden on the Sabbath (e.g. a hammer, usually used for building) may be used for other, permitted uses (e.g. to crack nuts); see *Mishnah Berurah* 314:24.] Hence, in their view, handling a sword to break a cask is permissible, even though this is not how swords are generally used.

Our Mishnah, by contrast, reflects the view of R' Nechemyah, who states that implements may be handled only for their specialized purpose (see above, note 16).

19. If we were to explain our Mishnah as reflecting the Sages' view, there would be no need to restrict it to a case of pressed figs only. Why did R' Oshaya instead opt to see R' Nechemyah as our Mishnah's author?

20. [By speaking of dried figs in particular, the Mishnah implies that it is concerned with a quality unique to this specific type of produce. Now, figs are distinctive in that they are a type of produce that can be pressed into cakes. Hence, the Mishnah seems to indicate that it is only to retrieve *this* kind of produce that one may cut into a cask; one may not do so for other kinds of produce. The Mishnah must therefore reflect R' Nechemyah's position.]

21. חוֹתָלוֹת are closed baskets woven from palm leaves. Dates would often be placed in these baskets, where they would be left to ripen. The Baraisa teaches that if the lid of the basket is tied closed with rope, one may untie the rope (*Rashi*). Although untying a permanent knot is a forbidden labor on the Sabbath, the Baraisa is apparently referring to a very temporary kind of knot, which one is permitted to untie (see *Rashi* to *Beitzah* 31b ד״ה מתיר).

22. One may use an implement to unravel or cut the strands of the rope (*Rashi;* see *Beur Halachah* to 314:8 ד״ה חותלות). Either of these acts degrade the quality of the rope. This is not, however, a violation of the *melachah* of סוֹתֵר, *demolishing,* since the rope is not completely destroyed (*Mishnah Berurah* to 314:31).

א) ע"ז כב: יבמות קג:, ב) בילה לג., ג) ק"ש ר' יוסי שם, ד) לעיל קכא., ה) עירובין לג. בילה לג. [תוספתא פט"ו], ו) לעיל קג:, ז) לעיל קכא. פירש"י שם מקום, ח) [וע"ע תוס' עירובין לה: ד"ה בעי סכינא].

הגהות הב"ח

(א) גמ' ההיא רבנן היא ממתניתין: (ב) שם בנקב ישן: (ג) רש"י ד"ה אין נוקבין וכו' הדבוקה על החבית: (ד) ד"ה אבל מפורדות וכו' החבית הס"ד ואח"כ מ"ה ואינו חושש וכו' קאי הס"ד ואח"כ מ"ה רבנן היא וכו' ושלא לצורך הס"ד ואח"כ מ"ה מתני' ר' נחמיה היא דאמר אין כלי וכו' לקמן הס"ד ואח"כ מ"ה חותלות וכו' תמרים ועושין כמין סלים: (ה) תוס' ד"ה שובר וכו' במגדל של לבנים עסקינן:

הגהות הגר"א

[א] גמרא בעו מיני' מרב ששת מהו למיברז. נ"ב ר"ל במקום שנקב אסור אם ברומח מותר. טור:

ליקוטי רש"י

עין עיטם. נראה בעיני שהוא מעין מי נפתוח האמור שם (יהושע טו, ט) אשר עליה ההר אשר על פני גיא בן הינום אשר לא נכתב ירידה בינתיים [זבחים נד:]. ממנו באה אמת המים לבית עולת שער המים שעל החומה ולפי ענין המקראות נראה לי שהוא מעין מי נפתוח האמור בספר יהושע (טו) שמשם הגבול משפע ויורד למערב והולך [הגבוה] בכל ארץ ישראל וכו' גבוה מקרקע עזרה עשרים ושלש אמות כמות שהוא גבוה שער המים ומקורין כלי של שלא אמות למלמעלה להסמיך להלכה שיש כאן שלשה סמוכים שאסור למים לעלות לשער שהוא גבוה ממקום שנעשין שם [יומא לא.]. בולשת. חיילות גייס הבא לעיר על שם שמחפשין ובולשים את העיר קרי לה בולשת [לעיל מא.]. בולשת חיל שמחפשין ובוחנין כמתרגמינן (בראשית לא) ויחפש ובלש [נדה יג.]. [ע"כ שייך לדף קמה:]

ישראל שעמדו על הר סיני. ונתקנו מכל מום שנאמר (שה"ש ד) כלך יפה רעיתי ומום אין בך [ע"ז כב:]. שובר אדם את החבית. מגופה שיש בה גרוגרות ואוכל ובלבד שלא יתכוין ליפות השבירה להיות לה לפה שתהא עוד כלי. את החבית. כי מגילה הוא לומר במוסתקי חבית שבורה שמדבקין שבריה בשרף של עץ שקורין לשף ששופין ויועסן ועשין זפת וקורין אותו ריישנ"א ויהיה דומה לרים לבונה ולבלגן ערבי קורין אותו מוסתקי ומדבקין בו קצוצות חרס הנשברים כך אמר לי רבי שמואל המכונה מסיק מן ברכתא ויין דרעועה היא ליכא למגזר בה שלא יתכוין לעשות כלי [ביצה לג:].

א) שבא נחש על חוה הטיל בה זוהמא ישראל שעמדו על הר סיני פסקה זוהמתן עובדי כוכבי' שלא עמדו על הר סיני לא פסקה זוהמתן א"ל רב אחא בריה דרבא לרב אשי גרים מאי א"ל אע"ג דאינהו לא הוו מזלייהו הוו דכתיב א) את אשר ישנו פה עמנו עומד היום לפני ה' אלהינו ואת אשר איננו פה וגו' ופליגא דר' אבא בר כהנא דא"ר אבא בר כהנא עד שלשה דורות לא פסקה זוהמא מאבותינו אברהם הוליד את ישמעאל יצחק הוליד את עשו יעקב הוליד י"ב שבטים שלא היה בהן שום דופי: **מתני'** ג) א שובר אדם את החבית לאכול הימנה גרוגרות ובלבד שלא יתכוין לעשות כלי ואין נוקבין מגופה של חבית דברי ר' יהודה ג) וחכמים ב מתירין ולא יקבנה מצדה ואם ג היתה נקובה לא יתן עליה שעוה מפני שהוא ממרח אמר ר' יהודה ד) מעשה בא לפני רבן יוחנן בן זכאי בערב ואמר חוששני לו מחטאת: **גמ'** א"ר אושעיא ל"ש אלא דרוסות אבל מפורדות לא ומפורדות לא מיתיבי ר' שמעון בן גמליאל אומר מביא אדם את החבית של יין ומתיז ראשה בסייף ומניחה לפני האורחים בשבת ואינו חושש ההיא רבנן (א) מתני' רבי נחמיה היא ומאי דוחקיה דרבי אושעיא לאוקמי מתניתין כרבי נחמיה ורבנן לוקמה במפורדות ובדרוסות אמר רבא מתני' קשיתיה מאי איריא דתני גרוגרות ליתני פירות אלא ש"מ בדרוסות תניא חדא ד חותלות של גרוגרות ושל תמרים מתיר ומפקיע וחותך ותניא אידך מתיר אבל לא מפקיע ולא חותך לא קשיא הא רבנן הא ר' נחמיה ה) דתניא ר' נחמיה אומר אפי' תרווד ואפילו טלית ואפילו סכין אין ניטלין אלא לצורך תשמישן [א] בעו מיניה מרב ששת ו מהו למיברז חביתא בבורטיא בשבתא לפיתחא קמיכוין ואסיר או דילמא לעין יפה קמיכוין ושרי א"ל ז לפיתחא קא מכוין ואסיר מיתיבי רשב"ג אומר ח מביא אדם חבית של יין ומתיז ראשה בסייף התם ודאי לעין יפה קמיכוין הכא אם איתא דלעין יפה קמיכוין לפתוחי מיפתח: אין נוקבין מגופה וכו': אמר רב הונא מחלוקת למעלה ט אבל מן הצד דברי הכל אסור והיינו דקתני לא יקבנה מצדה ורב חסדא אמר מחלוקת מן הצד אבל על גבה דברי הכל מותר והא דקתני לא יקבנה מצדה התם בגופה דחבית תנו רבנן ח) אין נוקבין נקב חדש בשבת ואם בא להוסיף מוסיף ויש אומרים ט) אין מוסיפין ושוין שנוקבין (ב) נקב ישן לכתחילה ותנא קמא מאי שנא מנקב חדש דלא דקא מתקן פיתחא אוסופי נמי קא מתקן פיתחא אמר רבה י) דבר תורה כל פתח שאינו עשוי להכנים ולהוציא אינו פתח ורבנן הוא דגזור משום לול של תרנגולין י) דעביד לעיולי אוירא ולאפוקי הבלא ואם בא להוסיף מוסיף אוסופי ודאי בלול של תרנגולים לא אתי לאוסופי

משום

כשבא נחש על חוה. כשנתן לה עצה לאכול מן העץ בא עליה דכתיב (בראשית ג) הנחש השיאני לשון נשואין: **גרים מאי.** שלא היו על הר סיני מהיכן פסקה זוהמא: **מזלייהו הוו.** בסיני וכל שעמדו על הר סיני נתקדשו ונטהרו ונתרפאו מכל מום ואף עורים ופסחים שהיו בישראל כדתניא בספרי: **ופליגא.** הא דאמרן דלא פסקה זוהמא עד סיני: **מתני' שובר אדם חבית.** מליאה גרוגרות בסכין או בסייף לאכול ממנה גרוגרות דאין במקלקל שום איסור בשבת: **ובלבד שלא יתכוין לעשות כלי.** לנוקבה יפה בפתח נאה: **אין נוקבין מגופה.** הדבוקה (ג) בפה החבית לעשות נקב אלא נוטל את כולה אבל כי נקיב לה מתקן פתחא: **וחכמים מתירין.** דאין דרך פתח לחבית בכך: **ולא יקבנה מצידה.** בגמרא מפרש לה: **שהוא ממרח.** ויש כאן משום ממחק: **בערב.** מדינה י): **מחטאת.** שמא מירח השעוה לדובקה בדופני הכלי סביב הנקב: **גמ' לא שנו.** דשובר החבית ומטלטל הסייף לכך: **אלא בדרוסות.** שהגרוגרות דרוסות בעיגול וחותכין ממנו בקורדוס או בסייף ואיידי דמטלטל סייף לחתוך גרוגרות תבר ביה נמי לחבית: **אבל מפורדות.** שא"צ לחתכן לא יטלטל סייף לשבור החבית (ד) דמתני' ר' נחמיה דאמר אין כלי ניטל אלא לתשמיש המיוחד לו כדמוקי לקמן: **ואינו חושש.** ואע"ג דיין לאו למחתכיה קאי: **רבנן היא.** דפליגי אדר' נחמיה ואמרי כל הכלים ניטלים לצורך ושלא לצורך: **חותלות.** כלי של כפות תמרים ועושין כמין סלים ונותנים לתוכן תמרים רעים להתבשל: **מתיר.** את הכסוי קשור בחבל: **אבל לא מפקיע.** סותר שרשרות החבל בכלי: **ולא חותך.** דאין כלי ניטל אלא לצורך תשמישו וסכין אינו עשוי לכך: **למיברז.** לתחוב פויינדור"א בלע"ז: **בבורטיא.** ברומח לתוחבו בדופניה לנקוב: **לעין יפה.** להרחיב מולא היין בנקב גדול מדלא נקיב ליה כדרך הנוקבין נקב עגול ויפה: **התם ודאי לעין יפה קמיכוין.** שמרחיב פיה למטה ממגופתה כדקתני מתיז את ראשה שפת פיה: **לפתוחי מיפתח.** יטול מגופתה: **למעלה.** בראש המגופה התם הוא דשרו רבנן דלאו אורחא למיעבד פתחא התם אלא נוטל כל המגופה: **אבל מצדה.** זמנין דעבדי לה משום פתחא ואינו רוצה לפותחה למעלה שלא יפול עפר או פסולת ביין: **היינו דקתני ולא יקבנה מצדה.** ואמגופה קאי ודברי הכל: **מחלוקת מן הצד.** התם הוא דקאסר רבי יהודה משום דאיכא דעבדי ליה פתחא: **אין נוקבין נקב חדש.** בכלי: **נקב ישן.** שנסתם דכי חוזר ופותח לאו כעושה פתח הוא שהרי עשוי ועומד וסתימתו לאו כלום: **אוסופי נמי קמתקן פתחא.** שמרחיבו ויש כאן משום גמר מלאכה: **הבלא.** סרחון שלא ימותו התרנגולין: **ואם בא להוסיף מוסיף.** ולא גזרינן דילמא אתי לאוסופי בלול של תרנגולין דלא מוסיף איניש עליה:

משום

שובר אדם את החבית לאכול הימנה גרוגרות. בגמרא מוקי לה בדרוסות לרבי נחמיה אבל לרבנן דרבי נחמיה שרי אפילו מפורדות ותימה לרבי מהא דתנן בפרק בכל מערבין (עירובין דף לד: ושם) נתנו במגדל ונעל בפניו ואבד המפתח הרי זה עירוב ופריך בגמרא אמאי הוא במקום אחד ועירובו במקום אחר הוא ומשני רב ושמואל דאמרי תרוייהו הכא במגדל של (ה) בנין עסקינן ור"מ היא כו' ואמאי מבעי ליה לאוקמא הכי ומעיקרא נמי מאי קאמר והלא יכול לשבר ולפתוח את המגדל וליטול את העירוב כי היכי דהכא שרי לשבר החבית וליטול הגרוגרות ואם באת לחלק בין נטילת העירוב לנטילת הגרוגרות א"כ קשה היכי מוקי לה התם כר' מאיר ונראה דהתם אסור לשבר את המגדל והכא דשרי לשבר את החבית משום דמיירי במוסתקי כדמוקי לה בביצה פרק המביא כדי יין (דף לג: ושם) ומפ' רש"י התם דהיינו חבית שבורה ומדבקין שבריה בשרף של עץ שעושה ממנו זפת וקורין ריישנ"א ומש"ה דוקא חבית שרי דמחמת גריעותו לא חייס עליה וליכא למיחש שמא יתכוין לעשות כלי וכן כולה שמעתא דהכא במוסתקי ואע"ג דהתם בביצה לא מוקמינן הכי אלא לר"א דפריך ולית ליה לר"א הא דתנן שובר אדם את החבית כו' ועלה משני מתני' במוסתקי מ"מ אפילו לרבנן מיבעי לאוקמי הכי דרבנן לא פליגי אדר"א דקאמר לא יקטמנו פי' לא יקטום את ההדס להריח בו אלא משום דאיהו סבירא ליה דבקטימת קיסם חייב חטאת כשקוטמו לחצות בו שיניו וא"כ אי לא מוקמינן לה במוסתקי עלייהו איכא למיפרך ולית להו הא דתנן כו' הלכך מיבעי לן למימר דאליבא דכולהו מיירי מתניתין במוסתקי והשתא אתיא שמעתא שפיר. מ"ר. ובגמ' ירושלמי בפרק בכל מערבין מצאתי הדא דתימא במגדל של אבן אבל במגדל של עץ נעשה כשובר החבית לאכול ממנה גרוגרות:

מתיר ומפקיע וחותך. אומר רבי מהא דעירובין (דף לד:) יש ללמוד דהא דאמרינן (ביצה דף לג:) חותמות שבכלים מתיר ומפקיע וחותך היינו כגון דקטיר במיתנא אבל פותחת של עץ ושל מתכת אסור לשבר ולהפקיע מדקשיא ליה התם אמאי הוא במקום אחד ועירובו במקום אחר דפשיטא ליה שאינו יכול להפקיע הפותחת וליטול העירוב אע"פ שסתם מגדל שבכל הש"ס הוא כלי כמו הלך לבי לבית ולפור למגדל וכי ההיא דבריש כל הכלים (לעיל קכב:) ובמסקנא נמי לא בעי לאוקומי אלא בקטיר במיתנא דהיינו דוקא חותמות שבכלים אבל דבר שהוא חזק כעין פותחת לא הוה שרי ת"ק. מ"ר ם):

הא רבנן והא ר' נחמיה. תימה לי אמאי לא מוקי תרוייהו כר' נחמיה והא דקתני מתיר מפקיע וחותך ביו"ט והא דקתני מתיר אבל לא מפקיע וחותך בשבת דאיכא תנא דס"ל הכי אליבא דר' נחמיה בביצה בפ' המביא כדי יין (לג:) י"ל דניחא ליה למימר חדא כרבנן מדניחא תרוייהו כר' נחמיה:

משום

כד א מיי' פכ"ג מהל' שבת הלכה ג סמג לאוין סה טוש"ע או"ח סימן שיד סעיף א:
כה ב מיי' שם טוש"ע שם סעיף ו:
כו ג מיי' שם הלכה יא טוש"ע שם סעיף יא:
כז ד שם סעיף ח:
כח ה ו ז מיי' שם הל' ב טור שו"ע שם סעיף ד:
כט ח ט מיי' שם הל"א טוש"ע שם סעיף א:
ל י מיי' שם הל"א ופ"י הלכה טו סמג שם:

גליון הש"ס

גמרא מהו למיברז חביתא. ע"ל דף מח ע"ב תוס' ד"ה וכי מה בין:

תורה אור השלם

א) כִּי אֶת אֲשֶׁר יֶשְׁנוֹ פֹּה עִמָּנוּ עֹמֵד הַיּוֹם לִפְנֵי יְיָ אֱלֹהֵינוּ וְאֵת אֲשֶׁר אֵינֶנּוּ פֹּה עִמָּנוּ הַיּוֹם: [דברים כט, יד]

רבינו חננאל

אם לא הביאם בחמין מלפני השבת אפילו להדיחן בשבת אסור ואם עבר הדיחן חייב חטאת שגומר מלאכה. פי' מכותו מכותא היא. ויש מי שאומר כותא כותחא היא בדיחו במערבא חולים שבמערב: מתני' שובר אדם את החבית לאכול ממנה גרוגרות. א"ר הושעיא לא ששובר את החבית לאכול ממנה גרוגרות אלא דרוסות אבל מפורדות אינו שובר החבית אלא מוציא גרוגרות ואוכל ואינו שובר. ואוקימנא למתניתין כר' נחמיה. מדקתני גרוגרות ולא קתני פירות. והא דתניא רשב"ג אומר מביא אדם חבית של יין ומתיז ראשה בסייף ומניחה לפני האורחים בשבת ואינו חושש לרבנן. וכן הא דתני חותלות של תמרים ושל גרוגרות ומתיר ומפקיע וחותך לרבנן והא דתני מתיר אבל לא מפקיע ולא חותך ר' נחמיה דאמר אפילו תרווד ואפילו טלית אין ניטלין אלא לצורך תשמישן. בעו מיניה מרב ששת מהו למיברז חביתא בבורטיא. פי' לנקוב חבית ברומח. ויש שאומר במקדח ומסקנא לפיתחא קא מיכוין ואסיר: פיס' אין נוקבין מגופה של החבית. פי' מגופה כסוי החבית דברי ר' יהודה וחכמים מתירין והלכה כחכמים. והני מילי שיהא הנקב בגג הכסוי אבל לנקב נקב בצד הכסוי אסור כדתנן לא יקבנה מצדה שהוא מדברי הכל. וכרב הונא דהלכתא כוותיה. דהוא לגביה דרב חסדא רבו וליתא לדרב חסדא: ת"ר אין נוקבין נקב חדש בשבת. ואם בא להוסיף מוסיף ואקשינן עלה למה אסור לנקוב נקב חדש שנמצא מתקן פתח גם בהוסיפו בנקב ומרחיבו נמצא מתקן פתח. ולמה מותר ופריק רבא מן התורה כל פתח שאינו עשוי להכניס ולהוציא אינו חשוב פתח. ואלו הנקבים כולן אין מכניסין בהן אלא הן עשויין בלבד ומותרין. ורבנן גזרו על כל נקב מפני שלא יפתחו נקב בבית התרנגולין והוא הנקרא לול של תרנגולים כדכתיב ובלולים יעלו. וזה לול של תרנגולים עשוי להכניס רוח ולהוציא בהמות והוא כמין פתח ואסור גמור אסור מן התורה. גזרו על כל נקב אבל ההרחבה שאין אדם מרחיב בלול של תרנגולים כי מתייר יכנס ממנו הנחש ויזיק אותן. וכיון שאין דרך בני אדם להרחיב בלול של תרנגולים לא גזרו בהרחבת כל נקב וזהו טעם ת"ק.

לג: ועיין כאן בתוס']. בערב. מקום. חוששני לו מחטאת. איני יודע אם חייב אם לאו ומוספני לומר חייב חטאת הוא [לעיל קכא.]. מפקיע. סותר [ביצה לג:]. אלא לצורך תשמישן. ועיקר תשמישו של סכין לא למתוך מאכלים הוא [לקמן לג:]. לול של תרנגולין. בית קטן שמגדלין בו תרנגולין [ב"ב יא:]. של עץ הוא ופתוח ומנקבו שילא הריח של רעה ולא יזיק להו [לעיל קב:].

רי"א

teaches: מַתִּיר אֲבָל לֹא מְפַקִּיעַ וְלֹא חוֹתֵךְ – HE MAY UNTIE the ropes,[23] BUT HE MAY NOT UNRAVEL OR CUT them.[24] Now, it would appear that these teachings are contradictory. לֹא קַשְׁיָא הָא רַבָּנָן הָא רַבִּי נְחֶמְיָה – However, **there is no difficulty,** because **this** first one represents **the** view of **the Sages,** while **this** latter one represents the view of **R' Nechemyah.**

The Gemara elaborates R' Nechemyah's view:

דְּתַנְיָא – **For it was taught in a Baraisa:** רַבִּי נְחֶמְיָה אוֹמֵר – R' NECHEMYAH SAYS: אֲפִילּוּ תַּרְווָד וַאֲפִילּוּ טַלִּית וַאֲפִילּוּ סַכִּין – EVEN A SPOON, A CLOAK OR A KNIFE אֵין נִיטָּלִין אֶלָּא לְצוֹרֶךְ תַּשְׁמִישָׁן – MAY BE HANDLED on the Sabbath ONLY FOR THEIR specialized USE.

The Mishnah had stated that one may sever [with a knife or sword] the top of a cask on the Sabbath, so long as he does not intend to make a proper opening. The Gemara poses a related query:

בָּעוּ מִינֵּיהּ מֵרַב שֵׁשֶׁת – **They inquired of Rav Sheishess:** מַהוּ לְמִיבְרַז חָבִיתָא בְּבוּרְטְיָא בְּשַׁבְּתָא – **What** about **thrusting** into the side of **a cask with a spear on the Sabbath?** Is one permitted to open a cask in this way or not?

The Gemara amplifies the two sides of the question:

לְפִיתְחָא קָמְכַוֵּין וַאֲסִיר – Do we say that **[the person] intends to** make **a** new **opening** in the cask, **and** therefore his act is **forbidden;**[25] אוֹ דִילְמָא לְעַיִן יָפָה קָמִיכַּוֵּין וּשְׁרֵי – **or perhaps** we say that **he intends** only **to** allow the wine to flow out **generously, and** his act is therefore **permitted?**[26]

R' Sheishess replies:

אָמַר לְהוּ – **[R' Sheishess] said to them:** לְפִיתְחָא קָא מִכַּוֵּין וַאֲסִיר – It can be presumed that **he intends to** make **an opening, and** therefore it is **forbidden.**

The ruling is questioned:

מֵיתִיבֵי – **They challenged [the ruling of Rav Sheishess] from** the previously cited **Baraisa,** which states: רַבָּן שִׁמְעוֹן בֶּן גַּמְלִיאֵל אוֹמֵר – RABBAN SHIMON BEN GAMLIEL SAYS: מֵבִיא אָדָם חָבִית שֶׁל יַיִן – A PERSON MAY BRING A CASK OF WINE וּמַתִּיז רֹאשָׁהּ בְּסַיִיף – AND SEVER ITS TOP WITH A SWORD.[27] If severing with a sword is permitted, why should puncturing with a spear be forbidden?

The Gemara answers:

הָתָם וַדַּאי לְעַיִן יָפָה קָמִיכַּוֵּין – **There,** in the case of the sword, **it is certain that he intends** only to facilitate **a generous [flow]** of wine.[28] הָכָא אִם אִיתָא דִּלְעַיִן יָפָה קָמִיכַּוֵּין – **Here,** however, in the case of the spear, **if it were** so **that he intends** only **to** facilitate **a generous [flow],** לִפְתּוּחֵי מִיפְתַּח – **let him** simply **open** the cask by taking off the bung![29] Rather, since he instead uses his spear to puncture a new hole, it is evident that he intends to create yet another opening for the cask.

The Gemara quotes the next part of the Mishnah:

אֵין נוֹקְבִין מְגוּפָה וכו׳ – ONE MAY NOT PERFORATE THE BUNG of a cask, **etc.;** [these are the words of R' Yehudah].

The Mishnah went on to say that the Sages permit this; yet both the Sages and R' Yehudah agree that one may not "perforate it in its side." The Gemara now explains this ambiguous phrase:

אָמַר רַב הוּנָא – **Rav Huna said:** מַחֲלוֹקֶת לְמַעְלָה – **The dispute** between R' Yehudah and the Sages **concerns** making a hole **in the top** of the bung; אֲבָל מִן הַצַּד דִּבְרֵי הַכֹּל אָסוּר – **but** as for making a hole **in the side** of the bung, **everyone agrees** that this is **forbidden.**[30] וְהַיְינוּ דְּקָתָנֵי – And this, indeed, **is what** the Mishnah means when **it teaches** in the name of both Tannaim: לֹא יִקְבְּנָהּ מִצִּדָּהּ – "and ONE MAY NOT PERFORATE IT IN ITS SIDE."[31]

Another Amora, however, explains the Mishnah differently:

וְרַב חִסְדָּא אָמַר – **However, Rav Chisda said:** מַחֲלוֹקֶת מִן הַצַּד – **The dispute** between the Tannaim concerns perforating **the side** of the bung;[32] אֲבָל עַל גַּבָּהּ דִּבְרֵי הַכֹּל מוּתָּר – **but** as for **the top** of the bung, **everyone agrees** that making a hole there is **permitted.** וְהָא דְּקָתָנֵי לֹא יִקְבְּנָהּ מִצִּדָּהּ – And as for **that which [the Mishnah] teaches:** [According to everyone,] ONE MAY NOT PERFORATE IT IN ITS SIDE, הָתָם בְּגוּפָהּ דְּחָבִית – **there** it refers to making a hole **in the body of the cask,** not in the cap.[33]

From the above discussion it is clear that perforating the body of a cask is forbidden according to all Tannaim. The Gemara now discusses this law in greater detail:

תָּנוּ רַבָּנָן – **The Rabbis taught in a Baraisa:** אֵין נוֹקְבִין נֶקֶב חָדָשׁ בְּשַׁבָּת – ONE MAY NOT MAKE A NEW HOLE in a vessel ON THE SABBATH; וְאִם בָּא לְהוֹסִיף מוֹסִיף – HOWEVER, IF ONE COMES merely TO ENLARGE an already existing hole, HE MAY ENLARGE it. וְיֵשׁ אוֹמְרִים אֵין מוֹסִיפִין – AND SOME SAY that ONE MAY NOT ENLARGE a hole. וְשָׁוִין שֶׁנּוֹקְבִין נֶקֶב יָשָׁן לְכַתְּחִילָּה – BUT ALL

NOTES

23. [Presumably by hand; see following note.]

24. I.e. he may not use an implement [such as a knife] to do these things, for one may handle an implement on the Sabbath only for its specialized purpose, and a knife is not usually used for these things (*Rashi;* and see *Rashi* to *Eruvin* 35a ד״ה אלא לצורך תשמישן and to *Beitzah* 32a ד״ה הא מני ר׳ נחמיה היא.)

25. As explained above (note 8), making a new opening in a container is prohibited on the Sabbath, because this is considered putting the finishing touch on the utensil.

26. I.e. his intent is not to perfect the container by making a new opening in it; rather, he is trying to make a gesture of generosity to his guests by making a large breach in the container through which wine will flow abundantly (see *Rambam* to *Hil. Shabbos* 23:2; see *Rashi*). [Had he been trying primarily to improve the cask by making another opening, he presumably would have taken pains to create a round, symmetrical hole. The rough, jagged opening created by a spear seems less suited to this purpose (*Rashi*).]

27. It would seem from here that one who makes a rough, gaping hole in a container [by chopping off the top of the cask] is not seen as making a new opening for the cask. On the contrary, if anything, we say his intent is to show generosity to his guests by creating a wide breach, even at the expense of the integrity of his container. Why, then, should puncturing the side of a container with a spear be treated any differently?

28. This is clear because he chops off the body of the cask below the cap, thus making a wider opening than if he had simply removed the cap. [The Baraisa states that he "severs its top"; i.e. he chops off the entire upper portion of the barrel] (*Rashi*).

29. [Opening the bung is permitted on the Sabbath (since this does not create a new opening; it merely reopens an existing one), and this would indeed allow the wine to flow out even more generously than through the smaller spearhole. Hence, if the person chose to puncture the cask with a spear, it seems he intended not just to create a more generous flow of wine; rather, he wished to improve the jar by making a useful opening.]

30. I.e. the Tannaic dispute concerns making a hole in the top of the bung — an unusual place to make a hole, since if one wished the cask to be open in that place, he should merely remove the bung (*Rashi*). As for making a hole in the side of the bung, however, everyone agrees that this is forbidden, for some people prefer to make this sort of perforation, and an opening there is therefore seen as an improvement to the utensil. [An opening in the side of the bung can be advantageous, since this will create a spout to dispense the wine, but will not allow dirt to fall inside, as would occur if the bung were simply removed (*Rashi*).]

31. I.e. one may not peforate *the bung* in its side (*Rashi*).

32. Since some people have the practice to make a spout on the side of the bung, R' Yehudah deems this an improvement to the cask and forbids it (*Rashi*). [The Sages, however, permit it, for the general practice is not to perforate the side of the bung.]

33. [Making a spout in the body of the cask is universally recognized as an improvement to the cask.]

שבא נחש על חוה הטיל בה זוהמא ישראל שעמדו על הר סיני פסקה זוהמתן עובדי כוכבים שלא עמדו על הר סיני לא פסקה זוהמתן א"ל רב אחא בריה דרבא לרב אשי גרים מאי א"ל אע"ג דאינהו לא הוו מזלייהו הוו דכתיב א) את אשר ישנו פה עמנו עומד היום לפני ה' אלהינו ואת אשר איננו פה וגו' ופליגא דר' אבא בר כהנא דא"ר אבא בר כהנא עד שלשה דורות לא פסקה זוהמא מאבותינו אברהם הוליד את ישמעאל יצחק הוליד את עשו יעקב הוליד י"ב שבטים שלא היה בהן שום דופי:

מתני' שובר אדם את החבית לאכול הימנה גרוגרות ובלבד שלא יתכוין לעשות כלי ואין נוקבין מגופה של חבית דברי ר' יהודה וחכמים מתירין ולא יקבנה מצדה ואם היתה נקובה לא יתן עליה שעוה מפני שהוא ממרח אמר ר' יהודה מעשה בא לפני רבן יוחנן בן זכאי בערב ואמר חוששני לו מחטאת:

גמ' א"ר אושעיא ל"ש אלא דרוסות אבל מפורדות לא ומפורדות לא מיתיבי ר' שמעון בן גמליאל אומר מביא אדם את החבית של יין ומתיז ראשה בסייף ומניחה לפני האורחים בשבת ואינו חושש ההיא רבנן (א) מתני' רבי נחמיה היא ומאי דוחקיה דרבי אושעיא לאוקמי מתניתין כרבי נחמיה ובדרוסות לוקמה במפורדות ורבנן אמר רבא מתני' קשיתיה מאי איריא דתני גרוגרות ליתני פירות אלא ש"מ בדרוסות תניא חדא חותלות של גרוגרות ושל תמרים מתיר ומפקיע וחותך ותניא אידך מתיר אבל לא מפקיע ולא חותך לא קשיא הא רבנן הא ר' נחמיה דתניא ר' נחמיה אומר אפי' תרווד ואפילו טלית ואפילו סכין אין ניטלין אלא לצורך תשמישן [א] בעו מיניה מרב ששת מהו למיברז חביתא בבורטיא בשבתא לפיתחא קמיכוין ואסיר או דילמא לעין יפה קמיכוין ושרי א"ל לפיתחא קא מכוין ואסיר מיתיבי רשב"ג אומר מביא אדם חבית של יין ומתיז ראשה בסייף התם ודאי לעין יפה קמיכוין הכא אם איתא דלעין יפה קמיכוין לפתוחי מיפתח: אין נוקבין מגופה וכו': אמר רב הונא מחלוקת למעלה אבל מן הצד דברי הכל אסור והיינו דקתני לא יקבנה מצדה ורב חסדא אמר מחלוקת מן הצד אבל על גבה דברי הכל מותר והא דקתני לא יקבנה מצדה התם בגופה דחבית תנו רבנן אין נוקבין נקב חדש בשבת ואם בא להוסיף מוסיף ויש אומרים אין מוסיפין ושוין שנוקבין (ב) נקב ישן לכתחילה ותנא קמא מאי שנא מנקב חדש דלא דקא מתקן פיתחא אוסופי נמי קא מתקן פיתחא אמר רבה דבר תורה כל פתח שאינו עשוי להכנים ולהוציא אינו פתח ורבנן הוא דגזור משום לול של תרנגולין דעביד לעיולי אוירא ולאפוקי הבלא ואם בא להוסיף מוסיף ודאי בלול של תרנגולים לא אתי לאוסופי משום

רש"י

כשבא נחש על חוה. כשנתן לה עלה לאכול מן העץ בא עליה דכתיב (בראשית ג) הנחש השיאני לשון נשואין: **גרים מאי.** שלא היו על הר סיני מהיכן פסקה זוהמא: **מזלייהו הוו.** בסיני וכל שעמדו על הר סיני נתקדשו ונטהרו ונתרפאו מכל מום ואף עורים ופסחים שהיו בישראל כדתניא בספרי: **ופליגא.** הא דאמרן דלא פסקה זוהמא עד סיני: **מתני' שובר אדם חבית.** מליאה גרוגרות בסכין או בסייף לאכול ממנה גרוגרות דאין במקלקל שום איסור בשבת: **ובלבד שלא יתכוין לעשות כלי.** לנוקבה יפה כפתח נאה: **אין נוקבין מגופה.** הדבוקה (ג) בפה החבית לעשות נקב אלא נוטל את כולה אבל כי נקיב לה מתקן פתחא: **וחכמים מתירין.** דאין דרך פתח לחבית בכך: **ולא יקבנה מצידה.** בגמרא מפרש לה: **שהוא ממרח.** ויש כאן משום ממחק: **בערב.** מדינה: **מחטאת.** שמא מירח השעוה לדובקה בדופני הכלי סביב הנקב: **גמ' לא שנו.** דשובר החבית ומטלטל הסייף לכך: **אלא בדרוסות.** שהגרוגרות דרוסות בעיגול וחותכין ממנו בקורדום או בסייף ואיידי דמטלטל סייף לחתוך גרוגרות תבר ביה נמי לחבית: **אבל מפורדות.** שא"צ לחתכן לא יטלטל סייף לשבור החבית (ד) דמתני' ר' נחמיה דאמר אין כלי ניטל אלא לתשמיש המיוחד לו כדמוקי לקמן: **ואינו חושש.** ואע"ג דיין לאו למחתכיה קאי: **רבנן היא.** דפליגי אדר' נחמיה ואמרי כל הכלים ניטלים לצורך ושלא לצורך: **חותלות.** כלי של כפות תמרים ועושין כמין סלים ונותנים לתוכן תמרים רעים להתבשל: **מתיר.** אם הכסוי קשור בחבל: **אבל לא מפקיע.** סותר שרשרות החבל בכלי: **ולא חותך.** דאין כלי ניטל אלא לצורך תשמישו וסכין אינו עשוי לכך: **למיברז.** לתחוב פויינדור"א בלע"ז: **בבורטיא.** ברומח לתוחבו בדופניה לנקוב: **לעין יפה.** להרחיב מוצא היין בנקב גדול מדלא נקיב ליה כדרך הנוקבין נקב עגול ויפה: **התם ודאי לעין יפה קמיכוין.** שמרחיב פיה למטה ממגופתה כדקתני מתיז את ראשה שפת פיה: **לפתוחי מיפתח.** יטול מגופתה: **למעלה.** בראש המגופה התם הוא דשרו רבנן דלאו אורחא למיעבד פתחא התם אלא נוטל כל המגופה: **אבל מצדה.** זמנין דעבדי לה משום פתחא ואינו רוצה לפותחה למעלה שלא יפול עפר או פסולת ביין: **היינו דקתני ולא יקבנה מצדה.** ואמגופה קאי ודברי הכל: **מחלוקת מן הצד.** התם הוא דקאסר רבי יהודה משום דאיכא דעבדי ליה פתחא: **אין נוקבין נקב חדש.** בכלי: **נקב ישן.** שנסתם דכי חוזר ופותחו לאו כעושה פתח הוא שהרי עשוי ועומד וסתימתו לאו כלום: **אוסופי נמי קמתקן פתחא.** שמרחיבו ויש כאן משום גמר מלאכה: **הבלא.** סרחון שלא ימותו התרנגולין: **ואם בא להוסיף מוסיף.** ולא גזרינן דילמא אתי לאוסופי בלול של תרנגולין דלא מוסיף איניש עליה:

משום

תוספות

שובר אדם את החבית לאכול הימנה גרוגרות. בגמרא מוקי לה בדרוסות לרבי נחמיה אבל לרבנן דרבי נחמיה שרי אפילו מפורדות ותימה לרבי מהא דתנן בפרק בכל מערבין (עירובין דף לד: ושם) גבי עירוב נתנו במגדל ונעל בפניו ואבד המפתח הרי זה עירוב ופריך בגמרא אמאי הוא במקום אחד ועירובו במקום אחר הוא ומשני רב ושמואל דאמרי תרווייהו הכא במגדל של (ה) בנין עסקינן ור"מ היא כו' ואמאי מבעי ליה לאוקמא הכי ומעיקרא נמי מאי קאמר והלא יכול לשבר ולפתוח את המגדל וליטול את העירוב כי היכי דהכא שרי לשבר החבית וליטול הגרוגרות ואם באת לחלק בין נטילת העירוב לנטילת הגרוגרות א"כ קשה היכי מוקי לה התם כר' מאיר ונראה דהתם אסור לשבר את המגדל והכא דשרי לשבר את החבית משום דמיירי במוסתקי כדמוקי לה בביצה פרק המביא כדי יין (דף לג: ושם) ומפ' רש"י התם דהיינו חבית שבורה ומדבקין שבריה בשרף של עץ שעושה ממנו זפת וקורין ריישנ"א ומש"ה דוקא חבית שרי דמחמת גריעותו לא חיים עליה וליכא למיחש שמא יתכוין לעשות כלי וכן כולה שמעתא דהכא במוסתקי ואע"ג דהתם בביצה לא מוקמינן הכי אלא לר"א דפריך ולית ליה לר"א הא דתנן שובר אדם את החבית כו' ועלה משני מתני' במוסתקי מ"מ אפילו לרבנן מיבעי לאוקמי הכי דרבנן לא פליגי אדר"א דקאמר לא יקטמנו פי' לא יקטום את ההדס להריח בו אלא משום דלאיהו סבירא ליה דבקטימת קיסם חייב חטאת כשקוטמו לחצות בו שיניו וא"כ אי לא מוקמינן לה במוסתקי עלייהו איכא למיפרך ולית להו הא דתנן כו' הלכך מיבעי לן למימר דאליבא דכולהו מיירי מתניתין במוסתקי והשתא אתיא שמעתא שפיר. מ"ר. ובגמ' ירושלמי בפרק בכל מערבין מצאתי הדא דתימא במגדל של אבן אבל במגדל של עץ נעשה כשובר החבית לאכול ממנה גרוגרות:

מתיר ומפקיע וחותך. אומר רבי מהא דעירובין (דף לד:) יש ללמוד דהא דאמרינן (ביצה דף לג:) חותמות שבכלים מתיר ומפקיע וחותך היינו כגון דקטיר במיתנא אבל פותחת של עץ ושל מתכת אסור לשבר ולהפקיע מדקשיא ליה התם אמאי הוא במקום אחד ועירובו במקום אחר דפשיטא ליה שאינו יכול להפקיע הפותחת וליטול העירוב אע"פ שסתם מגדל שבכל הש"ס הוא כלי כמו הלך לבית ולפור למגדל ומי הסיא דבריש כל הכלים (לעיל קכב:) ובמסקנא נמי לא בעי לאוקומי אלא בקטיר במיתנא דהיינו דוקא חותמות שבכלים אבל דבר שהוא חזק כעין פותחת לא הוה שרי. מ"ר:

הא רבנן והא ר' נחמיה. תימה לי אמאי לא מוקי תרווייהו כר' נחמיה והא דקתני מתיר מפקיע וחותך ביו"ט והא דקתני מתיר אבל לא מפקיע וחותך בשבת דליכא תנא דס"ל הכי אליבא דר' נחמיה בביצה בפ' המביא כדי יין (לג:) י"ל דניחא ליה למימר חדא כרבנן מדנימא תרווייהו כר' נחמיה:

משום

מסורת הש"ס

א) ע"ז כב:, יבמות קג:, ב) ביצה לג:, ג) ס"א ר' יוסי מתיר, ד) [לעיל קכח.], ה) עירובין לה., ביצה לג. [תוספתא פט"ו], ו) [לעיל קב:] [לעיל קכא. פירש"י שם מקום], ח) [וע"ע תוס' עירובין לה: ד"ה בעי סכינא].

הגהות הב"ח

(א) גמ' ההיא רבנן היא מתניתין: (ב) שם בנקב ישן: (ג) רש"י ד"ה אין נוקבין וכו' הדבוקה בפי החבית: (ד) ד"ה אבל מפורדות וכו' החבית הס"ד ואח"כ מ"ה ואינו חושש וכו' ואח"כ ד"ה רבנן היא וכו' ושלא לצורך הס"ד ואח"כ מ"ה מתני' ר' נחמיה היא דאמר אין כלי וכו' לקמן הס"ד ואח"כ מ"ה חותלות וכו' תמרים ועושין כמין סלים: (ה) תוס' ד"ה שובר וכו' במגדל של לבנים עסקינן:

הגהות הגר"א

[א] גמרא בעו מיני' מרב ששת מהו למיברז. נ"ב ר"ל במקום שנקב אסור אם ברומח מותר. טור.

ליקוטי רש"י

עין עיטם. נראה בעיני שהוא מעין מי נפתוח האמור בס' (יהושע טו, ט) ואשר עליה הכר אשר על פי גיא בן הינום אשר לא נכתב ירידה בינתיים [זבחים נד:]. ישראל שעמדו על הר סיני. ונתקנו מכל מום כדכתיב (שה"ש ד) כולך יפה רעיתי ומום אין בך [ע"ז כב:]. שובר אדם את החבית. ואוכל ובלבד שלא יתכוין לעשות כלי. את החבית. כי מוקי לה במוסתקי חבית שבורה ומדבקין שבריה בשרף של עץ שקורין אותו רייסינ"א ודבק. מוסתקי ומדבקין בו קערות חרס הנשברים ... יתכוון לעשות כלי [ביצה לג: ועיין כאן בתוס']. **בערב.** מקום. **חוששני לו מחטאת.** איני יודע אם חייב אם לאו ומשמשני לומר חייב חטאת הוא [לעיל קכא.]. **מפקיע.** המבל לסתור עבותו וגדילתו [ביצה לא:]. **אלא לצורך תשמישן.** ועיקר תשמישו של סכין לא לחתוך מכלים הוא אלא לחם ובשר ואוכלין [עירובין לה.]. **לול של תרנגולין.** בית קטן שמגדלין בו תרנגולין [ב"ב יא:]. של עץ הוא וסתום ומנקבו שיצא הריח של צואה ולא יזיק להו [לעיל קב:].

עין משפט נר מצוה

כד א מיי' פכ"ג מהל' שבת הלכה ג סמג לאוין סה טוש"ע או"ח סימן שיד סעיף א:
כה ב מיי' שם טוש"ע שם סעיף ו:
כו ג מיי' שם הלכה ב טוש"ע שם סעיף יא:
כז ד שם סעיף יב:
כח ה ו ז מיי' שם הל' ג טור שו"ע שם סעיף ז:
כט ח ט מיי' שם הל"א טוש"ע שם סעיף ט:
ל י מיי' שם הל"א ופכ"ו הלכה טו סמג שם:

גליון הש"ס

גמרא מהו למיברז חביתא. ע"ל דף מח ע"ב תוס' ד"ה וכי מה בין:

תורה אור השלם

א) כִּי אֶת אֲשֶׁר יֶשְׁנוֹ פֹּה עִמָּנוּ עֹמֵד הַיּוֹם לִפְנֵי יְיָ אֱלֹהֵינוּ וְאֵת אֲשֶׁר אֵינֶנּוּ פֹּה עִמָּנוּ הַיּוֹם: [דברים כט, יד]

רבינו חננאל

אם לא הביאם בחמין מלפני השבת אפילו להדיחן בשבת אסור ואם עבר והדיחן חייב חטאת שגמר מלאכה. פי' מכותא מכותתא היא. ויש מי שאומר כותא כותחא היא בדיחי במערבא חולים שבמערב: מתני' שובר אדם את החבית לאכול ממנה גרוגרות כו'. א"ר הושעיא לא שנו אלא דרוסות אבל מפורדות אינו שובר החבית אלא מוציא גרוגרות ואוכל ואינו שובר. ואוקימנא למתניתין כר' נחמיה. מדקתני גרוגרות ולא קתני פירות. והא דתניא רשב"ג אומר מביא אדם חבית של יין ומתיז ראשה בסייף ומניחה לפני האורחים בשבת ואינו חושש לרבנן. וכן הא דתני חותלות של תמרים ושל גרוגרות ומתיר ומפקיע וחותך לרבנן והא דתני מתיר אבל לא מפקיע ולא חותך ר' נחמיה דאמר אפילו תרווד ואפילו טלית ואפילו סכין אין ניטלין אלא לצורך תשמישן: בעו מיניה מרב ששת מהו למיברז חביתא בבורטיא. פי' לנקוב חבית ברומח. ויש שאומר במקדח ומסקנא לפיתחא קא מיכוין ואסיר: פיס' אין נוקבין מגופה של החבית. פי' מגופה כסוי החבית דברי ר' יהודה וחכמים מתירין והלכה כחכמים. והני מילי שיהא הנקב בגג הכסוי אבל לנקוב נקב בצד הכסוי אסור כדתנן לא יקבנה מצדה שהוא ממרח דברי הכל. וכרב הונא דהלכתא כוותיה. דהוא לגביה דרב חסדא רבו וליתא לדרב חסדא: ת"ר אין נוקבין נקב חדש בשבת. ואם בא להוסיף מוסיף ואקשינן עלה למה אסור לנקוב נקב חדש שנמצא מתקן פתח גם בהוסיפו בנקב ומרחיבו נמצא מתקן פתח. ולמה מותר ופריק רבא מן התורה כל פתח שאינו עשוי להכניס ולהוציא אינו חשוב פתח. ואלו הנקבים כולן אין מכניסין בהן אלא להוציא הן עשויין בלבד ומותרין. ורבנן גזרו על כל נקב מפני שלא יפתחו נקב בבית התרנגולין והוא הנקרא לול של תרנגולים כדכתיב ובלולים יעלו. וזה לול של תרנגולים עשוי להכניס רוח ולהוציא בהמות והוא כמין פתח ואסור. ומפני שהוא פתח גמור אסור מן התורה. גזרו על כל נקב אבל ההרחבה שאין אדם מרחיב בלול של תרנגולים כי מתיירא אם מרחיב הלול יכנס ממנו הנחש ויזיק אותן. וכיון שאין דרך בני אדם להרחיב בלול של תרנגולים לא גזרו בהרחבת כל נקב וזהו טעם ת"ק.

וי"א

AGREE THAT IT IS ALTOGETHER PERMISSIBLE TO REOPEN AN OLD HOLE.[34]

The Gemara questions why the first Tanna permits enlarging an existing hole:

וְתַנָּא קַמָּא – **Now,** according to the **Tanna Kamma,** מַאי שְׁנָא מִנֶּקֶב חָדָשׁ דְּלֹא – **why may one not** make **a new hole** on the Sabbath? דְּקָא מְתַקֵּן פִּיתְחָא – **Because** in so doing, **one is fashioning an opening** in the vessel, which in effect finishes off construction of the vessel. But the same can be said for enlarging an opening, too! אוֹסוּפֵי נַמִּי קָא מְתַקֵּן פִּיתְחָא – In **enlarging** an existing hole, **one is also fashioning an opening** in the vessel![35]

The Gemara replies:

אָמַר רַבָּה – **Rabbah said:** דְּבַר תּוֹרָה כָּל פֶּתַח שֶׁאֵינוֹ עָשׂוּי לְהַכְנִיס וּלְהוֹצִיא – Actually, as a **matter** of **Biblical** law, **any opening that is not made for** the purpose of **bringing** things **in as well as taking** things **out** אֵינוֹ פֶּתַח – **is not** deemed **a** true **opening,** and one is not liable for its creation.[36] וְרַבָּנָן הוּא דִּגְזוּר מִשּׁוּם לוּל שֶׁל תַּרְנְגוֹלִין – **And it is the Rabbis who decreed** against creating other kinds of openings,[37] **on account of** the case of the **chicken coop,** דְּעָבִיד לְעַיּוּלֵי אֲוִירָא וּלְאַפּוּקֵי הֶבְלָא – in which a hole **is made to bring air in and take** harmful **vapors out.**[38] וְאִם בָּא לְהוֹסִיף מוֹסִיף – Hence, the Tanna Kamma rightfully rules AND IF ONE COMES TO ENLARGE an already existing hole, HE MAY ENLARGE it; אוֹסוּפֵי וַדַּאי – for **certainly** as far as **enlarging** is concerned, בְּלוּל שֶׁל תַּרְנְגוֹלִים לֹא אָתֵי לְאוֹסוּפֵי – **no one will come to enlarge** the hole **in a chicken coop,**

NOTES

34. I.e. reopening a hole that has been sealed or plugged is not considered making an opening in the vessel. The opening is already there, and the fact that it has been plugged is not legally significant (*Rashi*).

35. I.e. in widening an existing hole, one further improves the vessel (see *Rashi*), and his act should therfore be prohibited under the *melachah* of *striking the final blow* (see *Rashi* above, 48a ד״ה חייב חטאת).

36. I.e. on the level of Biblical law, only the creation of a "two-way" opening is deemed to perfect a vessel. Making an opening only for the purpose of one-way transfer [e.g. an opening solely intended to allow wine to flow out of a cask] is not Biblically prohibited.

37. I.e. openings whose purpose is to facilitate only one-way transfer.

38. The purpose of a hole in a chicken coop is twofold: It allows air to enter the coop, and potentially lethal vapors to escape (*Rashi*). Many people, however, are unaware of this second purpose, and tend to assume that the hole's only function is to allow air to enter (see *Tosafos* to 146b ד״ה משום ריחא). Thus, in order to prevent people from unwittingly transgressing the Sabbath by making holes in their chicken coops, the Sages prohibited the creation of *all* openings, even those clearly intended for one-way transfer [e.g. spouts made in wine casks].

שבא נחש על חוה הטיל בה זוהמא ישראל שעמדו על הר סיני פסקה זוהמתן עובדי כוכבי' שלא עמדו על הר סיני לא פסקה זוהמתן א"ל רב אחא בריה דרבא לרב אשי גרים מאי א"ל אע"ג דאינהו לא הוו מזלייהו הוו דכתיב א) את אשר ישנו פה עמנו עומד היום לפני ה' אלהינו ואת אשר איננו פה וגו' ופליגא דר' אבא בר כהנא דא"ר אבא בר כהנא עד שלשה דורות לא פסקה זוהמא מאבותינו אברהם הוליד את ישמעאל יצחק הוליד את עשו יעקב הוליד י"ב שבטים שלא היה בהן שום דופי:

מתני' א שובר אדם את החבית לאכול הימנה גרוגרות ובלבד שלא יתכוין לעשות כלי ואין נוקבין מגופה של חבית דברי ר' יהודה ג) וחכמים ב מתירין ולא יקבנה מצדה ואם ג היתה נקובה לא יתן עליה שעוה מפני שהוא ממרח אמר ר' יהודה ד) מעשה בא לפני רבן יוחנן בן זכאי בערב ואמר חוששני לו מחטאת:

גמ' א"ר אושעיא ל"ש אלא דרוסות אבל מפורדות לא ומפורדות לא מיתיבי ר' שמעון בן גמליאל אומר מביא אדם את החבית של יין ומתיז ראשה בסייף ומניחה לפני האורחים בשבת ואינו חושש ההיא רבנן (א) מתני' רבי נחמיה היא ומאי דוחקיה דרבי אושעיא לאוקמי מתניתין כרבי נחמיה ובדרוסות לוקמה במפורדות ורבנן אמר רבא מתני' קשיתיה מאי איריא דתני גרוגרות ליתני פירות אלא ש"מ בדרוסות תניא חדא ד חותלות של גרוגרות ושל תמרים מתיר ומפקיע וחותך ותניא אידך מתיר אבל לא מפקיע ולא חותך לא קשיא הא רבנן הא ר' נחמיה ה) דתניא ר' נחמיה אומר אפי' תרווד ואפילו טלית ואפילו סכין אין ניטלין אלא לצורך תשמישן [א] בעו מיניה מרב ששת ו מהו למיברז חביתא בבורטיא בשבתא לפיתחא קמיכוין ואסיר או דילמא לעין יפה קמיכוין ושרי א"ל ה) לפיתחא קא מכוין ואסיר מיתיבי רשב"ג אומר ז מביא אדם חבית של יין ומתיז ראשה בסייף התם ודאי לעין יפה קמיכוין הכא אם איתא דלעין יפה קמיכוין לפתוחי מיפתח: אין נוקבין מגופה וכו': אמר רב הונא מחלוקת למעלה ז אבל מן הצד דברי הכל אסור והיינו דקתני לא יקבנה מצדה ורב חסדא אמר מחלוקת מן הצד אבל על גבה דברי הכל מותר והא דקתני לא יקבנה מצדה התם בגופה דחבית תנו רבנן ח אין נוקבין נקב חדש בשבת ואם בא להוסיף מוסיף ויש אומרים ט אין מוסיפין ושוין שנוקבין (ג) נקב ישן לכתחילה ותנא קמא מאי שנא מנקב חדש דלא דקא מתקן פיתחא אוספוי נמי קא מתקן פיתחא אמר רבה י דבר תורה כל פתח שאינו עשוי להכנים ולהוציא אינו פתח ורבנן הוא דגזור משום לול של תרנגולין ו) דעביד לעיולי אוירא ולאפוקי הבלא ואם בא להוסיף מוסיף ודאי אוספוי בלול של תרנגולים לא אתי לאוסופי משום

רש"י

כשבא נחש על חוה. כשנתן לה עצה לאכול מן העץ בא עליה דכתיב (בראשית ג) הנחש השיאני לשון נשואין: גרים מאי. שלא היו על הר סיני מיסכן פסקה זוהמא: מזלייהו הוו. בסיני וכל שעמדו על הר סיני נתקדשו ונטהרו ונתרפאו מכל מום ואף עורים ופסחים שהיו בישראל כדאיתא בספרי: ופליגא. הא דאמרן דלא פסקה זוהמא עד סיני: מתני' שובר אדם חבית. מליאה גרוגרות בסכין או בסייף לאכול ממנה גרוגרות דאין מקלקל שום איסור בשבת: ובלבד שלא יתכוין לעשות כלי. לנוקבה יפה בפתח נאה: אין נוקבין מגופה. הדבוקה (ג) בפה החבית לעשות נקב אלא נוטל את כולה אבל כי נקיב לה מתקן פתחא: וחכמים מתירין. דאין דרך פתח לחבית בכך: ולא יקבנה מצידה. בגמרא מפרש לה: שהוא ממרח. ויש כאן משום ממחק: בערב. מדינה ז): מחטאת. שמא מירח השעוה לדובקה בדופני הכלי סביב הנקב: גמ' לא שנו. דשובר החבית ומטלטל הסייף לכך: אלא בדרוסות. שהגרוגרות דרוסות בעיגול וחותכין ממנו בקורדום או בסייף ואיידי דמטלטל סייף לחתוך גרוגרות תבר ביה נמי לחבית: אבל מפורדות. שא"צ לחתכן לא יטלטל סייף לשבור החבית (ד) דמתני' ר' נחמיה היא דאמר אין כלי ניטל אלא לתשמיש המיוחד לו כדמוקי לקמן: ואינו חושש. ואע"ג דיין לאו למתחכיה קאי: רבנן היא. דפליגי אדר' נחמיה ואמרי כל הכלים ניטלים לצורך ושלא לצורך: חותלות. כלי של כפות תמרים ועושין כמין סלים ונותנים לתוכן תמרים רעים להתבשל: מתיר. את הכסוי קשור בחבל: אבל לא מפקיע. סותר שרשרות החבל בכלי: ולא חותך. דאין כלי ניטל אלא לצורך תשמישו וסכין אינו עשוי לכך: למיברז. לתקוב פוינדור"א בלע"ז: בבורטיא. ברומח לתוחבו בדופניה לנקוב: לעין יפה. להרחיב מוצא היין בנקב גדול מדלא נקיב ליה כדרך הנוקבין נקב עגול ויפה: התם ודאי לעין יפה קמיכוין. שמרחיב פיה למטה ממגופתה כדקתני מתיז את ראשה ספת פיה: לפתוחי מיפתח. יטול מגופתה: למעלה. בראש המגופה התם הוא דשרו רבנן דלאו אורחא למיעבד פתחא התם אלא נוטל כל המגופה: אבל מצדה. זמנין דעבדי לה משום פתחא ואינו רוצה לפותחה למעלה שלא יפול עפר או פסולת ביין: היינו דקתני ולא יקבנה מצדה. ולמגופה קאי ודברי הכל: מחלוקת מן הצד. התם הוא דקאמר רבי יהודה משום דאיכא דעבדי ליה פתחא: אין נוקבין נקב חדש. בכלי: נקב ישן. שנסתם דכי חוזר ופותחו לאו כעושה פתח הוא שהרי עשוי ועומד וסתימתו לאו כלום: אוסופי נמי קמתקן פתחא. שמרחיבו ויש כאן משום גמר מלאכה: הבלא. סרחון שלא ימותו התרנגולין: ואם בא להוסיף מוסיף. ולא גזרינן דילמא אתי לאוסופי בלול של תרנגולין דלא מוסיף איסור עליה: משום

תוספות

שובר אדם את החבית לאכול הימנה גרוגרות. בגמרא מוקי לה בדרוסות לרבי נחמיה אבל לרבנן דרבי נחמיה שרי אפילו מפורדות ותימה לרבי מהא דתנן בפרק בכל מערבין (עירובין דף לד: ושם) גבי עירוב נתנו במגדל ונעל בפניו ואבד המפתח הרי זה עירוב ופריך בגמרא אמאי הוא במקום אחד ועירובו במקום אחר הוא ומשני רב ושמואל דאמרי תרווייהו הכא במגדל של (ה) בנין עסקינן ור"מ היא כו' ואמאי מבעי ליה לאוקמא הכי ומעיקרא נמי מאי קאמר והלא יכול לשבר ולפתוח את המגדל וליטול את העירוב כי היכי דהכא שרי לשבר החבית וליטול הגרוגרות ואם באת לחלק בין נטילת העירוב לנטילת הגרוגרות א"כ קשה היכי מוקי לה התם כר' מאיר ונראה דהתם אסור לשבר את המגדל והכא דשרי לשבר את החבית משום דמיירי במוסתקי כדמוקי לה בביצה פרק המביא כדי יין (דף לג: ושם) ומפ' רש"י התם דהיינו חבית שבורה ומדבקין שבריה בשרף של עץ שעושה ממנו זפת וקורין רייש"א ומש"ה דוקא חבית שרי דממתא גריעותו לא חיים עליה וליכא למיחש שמא יתכוין לעשות כלי וכן כולה שמעתא דהכא במוסתקי ואע"ג דהתם בביצה לא מוקמינן הכי אלא לר"א דפריך וליה ליה לר"א הא דתנן שובר אדם את החבית כו' ועלה משני מתני' במוסתקי מ"מ אפילו לרבנן מיבעי לאוקמי הכי דרבנן לא פליגי אדר"א דקאמר לא יקטמנו פי' לא יקטום את ההדס להריח בו אלא משום דלאו סבירא ליה דבקטימת קיסם חייב חטאת כשקוטמו לחצות בו שיניו וא"כ אי לא מוקמינן לה במוסתקי עלייהו איכא למיפרך וליה להו הא דתנן כו' הלכך מיבעי לן למימר דאליבא דכולהו מיירי מתניתין במוסתקי והשתא אתיא שמעתא שפיר. מ"ר. ובגמ' ירושלמי בפרק בכל מערבין מצאתי הדא דתימא במגדל של אבן אבל במגדל של עץ נעשה כשובר החבית לאכול ממנה גרוגרות:

מתיר ומפקיע וחותך. אומר רבי מההיא דעירובין (דף לד:) יש ללמוד דהא דאמרינן (ביצה דף לא:) חותלות שבכלים מתיר ומפקיע וחותך היינו כגון דקטיר במיתנא אבל פותחת של עץ ושל מתכת אסור לשבר ולהפקיע מדקשיא ליה התם אמאי הוא במקום אחד ועירובו במקום אחר דפשיטא ליה שאינו יכול להפקיע הפותחת וליטול העירוב אע"פ שהתם מגדל שבכלל הש"ס הוא כלי כמו הלל בי לבית ולפור למגדל וכי הביא דבריס כל הכלים (לעיל קכב:) ובמסקנא נמי לא בעי לאוקומי אלא בקטיר במיתנא דהיינו דוקא חותמות שבכלים אבל דבר שהוא חזק כעין פותחת לא הוה שרי מ"ק. מ"ר:

הא רבנן והא ר' נחמיה. תימה לי אמאי לא מוקי תרווייהו כר' נחמיה והא דקתני מתיר מפקיע וחותך ביו"ט והא דקתני מתיר אבל לא מפקיע וחותך בשבת דאיכא תנא דס"ל דהכי אליבא דר' נחמיה בביצה בפ' המביא כדי יין (לג:) י"ל דניחא ליה למימר חדא כרבנן מדנימא תרווייהו כר' נחמיה: משום

מסורת הש"ס

א) ע"ז כב: יבמות קג:, ב) ביצה לג:, ג) ס"א ר' יוסי מתיר, ד) [לעיל קכא.], ה) עירובין לה. ביצה לג. [תוספתא פט"ו], ו) [לעיל קב:], ז) [לעיל קכא. פירש"י שם מקום], ח) [וע"ע תוס' עירובין לה: ד"ה בעי סכינא].

הגהות הב"ח

(א) גמ' ההיא רבנן היא מתניתין: (ב) שם בנקב ישן: (ג) רש"י ד"ה אין נוקבין וכו' הדבוקה בפי החבית: (ד) ד"ה אבל מפורדות וכו' החבית הס"ד ואח"כ מ"ה ואינו חושש וכו' קאי הס"ד ואח"כ מ"ה ההיא רבנן הוא וכו' ושלא לצורך הס"ד ואח"כ מ"ה מתני' ר' נחמיה היא דאמר אין כלי וכו' לקמן הס"ד ואח"כ מ"ה חותלות וכו' תמרים ועשוין כמין סלים: (ה) תוס' ד"ה שובר וכו' במגדל של לבנים עסקינן:

הגהות הגר"א

[א] גמרא בעו מיני' מרב ששת מהו למיברז. נ"ב ר"ל במקום שנקב אסור אם ברומח מותר. טור:

ליקוטי רש"י

עין עיטם. נראה בעיני שהוא מעין מי נפתוח האמור שם (יהושע טו, ט) אחר עליית ההר אשר על פני גיא בן הינום אשר שם נכתב ירידה בינתיים [זבחים נד:]. ממנו באה אמת המים לבית טבילת שער המים שעל החומה ולפי ענין המקראות נראה לי שהוא מעיין מי נפתוח האמור בספר יהושע (טו) שמשם הגבול משפע ויורד למזרח ולמערב והוא [הגבוה] בכל ארץ ישראל [ובו] גובה מקרקע עזרה עשרים ושלש אמות ושלא גובה שער המים ובנין כלי של שלש אמות להחזיק מרבעים אמה שאי אפשר למים לעלות להר גובה מקום שנובעין שם [יומא לא.]. בולשת. חיילות גייס הבא לעיר על שם שמחפשין ובולשין את העיר קרי לה בולשת [לעיל מא.]. בולשת חיל שמחפשין ובוחנין כדמתרגמינן (בראשית לא) ויחפש ובלש [נדה יג.]. [ע"כ שייך לדף קמה:].

ישראל שעמדו על הר סיני. ונתקנו מכל מום כדכתיב (שה"ש ד) כולך יפה רעיתי ומום אין בך [ע"ז כב:]. שובר אדם את החבית. מגופה שיש בה גרוגרות ואוכל ובלבד שלא יתכוין ליפות שבירתה להיות לה נאה שראוי עוד לכלי. את החבית. כי תניא היא למותר במוסתקי חבית שבורה ומדבקין שבריה בשרף של עץ שקורין זפת שעושין הימנו זפת וקורין אותו רייש"א ודומה לזיפות לבונה ולזפת ובלשון ערבי קורין אותו מוסתקי ומדבקין בו קערות חרס המשברים כך אמר לי רבי שמואל המכונה חסיד מן הריינוס [ביצה לג:]. וכיון דרעועה היא ליכא למגזר בה שלא יתכוין לעשות כלי [ביצה לג: ועיין כאן בתוס']. בערב. מקום. חוששני לו מחטאת. איני יודע אם חייב אם לאו וחוששני לומר חייב חטאת הוא [לעיל קכא.]. מפקיע. החבל לסתור עבותו וגדילתו [ביצה לא:]. אלא לצורך תשמישן. ועיקר תשמישו של סכין לא לחתוך חבלים הוא אלא לחם ובשר ואוכלין [עירובין לה.]. לול של תרנגולין. בית קטן שמגדלין בו תרנגולין [ב"ב יא:]. של עץ הוא וסתום ומנקבו שיצא הריח של צואה ולא יזיק להו [לעיל קב:].

עין משפט נר מצוה

כד א מיי' פכ"ג מהל' שבת הלכה ב סמג לאוין סה טוש"ע או"ח סימן שיד סעיף א:
כה ב מיי' שם טוש"ע שם סעיף ו:
כו ג מיי' שם הלכה יא טוש"ע שם סעיף יא:
כז ד שם סעיף ח:
כח ה ו ז מיי' שם פכ"ג הל' ג טור שו"ע שם סעיף ט:
כט ח ט מיי' שם הל"א טוש"ע שם סעיף א:
ל י מיי' שם הל"א ופ"י הלכה טז סמג שם:

גליון הש"ס

גמרא מהו למיברז חביתא. ע"ל דף מח ע"ב תוס' ד"ה וכי מה בין:

תורה אור השלם

א) כִּי אֶת אֲשֶׁר יֶשְׁנוֹ פֹּה עִמָּנוּ עֹמֵד הַיּוֹם לִפְנֵי יְיָ אֱלֹהֵינוּ וְאֵת אֲשֶׁר אֵינֶנּוּ פֹּה עִמָּנוּ הַיּוֹם: [דברים כט, יד]

רבינו חננאל

אם לא הביאם בחמין מלפני השבת אפילו להדיחן בשבת אסור ואם עבר והדיחן חייב חטאת שגמר מלאכה. פי' מכותא מכותתא היא. ויש מי שאומר כותא כותחא היא בדיחי במערבא חולים שבמערב: מתני' שובר אדם את החבית לאכול ממנה גרוגרות כו'. א"ר הושעיא לא ששובר את החבית לאכול ממנה גרוגרות אלא דרוסות אבל מפורדות אינו שובר החבית אלא מוציא גרוגרות ואוכל ואינו שובר. ואוקימנא למתניתין כר' נחמיה. מדקתני גרוגרות ולא קתני פירות. והא דתניא רשב"ג אומר מביא אדם חבית של יין ומתיז ראשה בסייף ומניחה לפני האורחים בשבת ואינו חושש לרבנן. וכן הא דתני חותלות של תמרים ושל גרוגרות ומתיר ומפקיע וחותך לרבנן והא דתני מתיר אבל לא מפקיע ולא חותך ר' נחמיה דאמר אפילו תרווד ואפילו טלית אין ניטלין אלא לצורך תשמישן: בעו מיניה דרב ששת מהו למיברז חביתא בבורטיא. פי' לנקוב חבית ברומח. ויש שאומר במקדח ומסקנא לפיתחא קא מיכוין ואסירי: פיס' אין נוקבין מגופה של החבית. פי' מגופה כסוי החבית דברי ר' יהודה וחכמים מתירין והלכה כחכמים. והני מילי שיהא הנקב בגג הכסוי אבל לנקב נקב בצד הכסוי אסור כדתנן לא יקבנה מצדה שהוא דברי הכל. וכרב הונא דהלכתא כוותיה. דהוא לגביה דרב חסדא רבו וליתא לדרב חסדא: ת"ר אין נוקבין נקב חדש בשבת. ואם בא להוסיף מוסיף ואקשינן עלה למה אסור לנקוב נקב חדש שנמצא מתקן פתח גם בהוסיפו מתקן ומרחיבו נמצא מתקן פתח. ולמה מותר ופריק רבא מן התורה כל פתח שאינו עשוי להכניס ולהוציא אינו חשוב פתח. ואלו הנקבים כולן אין מכניסין בהן אלא להוציא הן עשויין בלבד ומותרין. ורבנן גזרו על כל נקב מפני שלא יפתחו נקב בבית התרנגולין והוא הנקרא לול של תרנגולים כדכתיב ובלולים יעלו. וזה לול של תרנגולים עשוי להכניס רוח ולהוציא בהמות והוא כמין פתח ואסור משום פתח גמור אסור מן התורה. גזרו על כל נקב אבל ההרחבה שאין אדם מרחיב בלול של תרנגולים כי מחייהו יכנס ממנו הנחש ויזיק אותן. וכיון שאין דרך בני אדם להרחיב בלול של תרנגולים לא גזרו בהרחבת כל נקב וזהו טעם ת"ק.

רי"א

משום ריחשא ור"א אין מוסיפים זימנין דלא תקניה מעיקרא ואתי לארוחי ביה דרש רב נחמן משום רבי יוחנן הלכה כיש אומרים: א ושוין שנוקבין נקב ישן לכתחלה: אמר רב יהודה אמר שמואל לא שנו אלא במקום העשוי לשמר אבל לחזק אסור היכי דמי לשמר היכי דמי לחזק · א"ר חסדא למעלה מן היין זהו לשמר למטה מן היין זהו לחזק (א) רבא אמר ב למטה מן היין נמי זהו לשמר והיכי דמי לחזק כגון שניקבה למטה מן השמרים א"ל אביי לרבא תניא דמסייע לך ג בית סתום יש לו ארבע אמות פרץ את פצימיו אין לו ד' אמות ד בית סתום אינו מטמא כל סביביו פרץ את פצימיו מטמא כל סביביו גובתא רב אסר ושמואל שרי ה מחתך לכתחלה דכ"ע לא פליגי דאסור אהדורי דכ"ע לא פליגי דשרי כי פליגי דחתיכה ולא מתקנא מאן דאסר גזרינן דילמא אתי למיחתך לכתחלה ומאן דשרי ו לא גזרינן כתנאי אין חותכין שפופרת ביו"ט וא"צ לומר בשבת נפלה (אין) מחזירין אותה בשבת ואין צריך לומר ביו"ט ור' יאשיה מיקל ר' יאשיה אהייא אילימא ארישא הא קמתקן מנא אלא אסיפא ת"ק נמי מישרא קשרי אלא דחתיכה ולא מתקנא איכא בינייהו מ"ס גזרינן ומ"ס לא גזרינן דרש רב שישא בריה דרב אידי משמיה דר' יוחנן הלכה כר' יאשיה: ואם היתה נקובה וכו': מישחא רב אסר ושמואל שרי מאן דאסר ז גזרינן משום שעוה ומאן דשרי לא גזרינן אמר ליה רב שמואל בר בר חנה לרב יוסף בפירוש אמרת לן משמיה דרב מישחא שרי אמר טבות רישבא אמר שמואל האי טרפא דאסא אסור מ"ט רב יימר מדפתי אמר גזירה משום מרזב רב אשי אמר ח גזירה שמא יקטום מאי בינייהו [א] איכא בינייהו דקטים ומנחי בי סדיא רב אסר ושמואל ט שרי ברכין דכולי עלמא לא פליגי דשרי י בקשין דכ"ע לא פליגי דאסור כי פליגי במיצעי מאן דאסר מיחזי כמשוי ומאן דשרי לא מיחזי כמשוי והא דרב לאו כ בפירוש איתמר אלא מכללא איתמר דרב איקלע לההוא אתרא דלא הוה ליה רווחא נפק יתיב בכרמלית אייתו ליה בי סדיא לא יתיב מאן דחזא סבר משום דבי סדיא אסור ולא היא דרב אכרוזי מכריז בי סדיא שרי · ומשום כבוד רבותינו לא ישב עליו ומאן נינהו רב כהנא ורב אסי: מתני' ל נותנין תבשיל לתוך הבור בשביל שיהא שמור ואת המים היפים ברעים בשביל שיצננו ואת הצונן בחמה בשביל שיחמו מ מי שנשרו כליו בדרך במים מהלך בהן ואינו חושש הגיע לחצר החיצונה שוטחן בחמה [ב] אבל לא כנגד העם: גמ' פשיטא מהו דתימא ניגזור משום אשוויי גומות קא משמע לן: ואת המים היפים ברעים: פשיטא סיפא איצטריכא ליה ואת הצונן בחמה הא נמי פשיטא מהו דתימא ניגזור דילמא אתי לאטמוני ברמץ קמ"ל: ' מי שנשרו וכו': י) אמר רב יהודה אמר רב ס כל מקום שאסרו חכמים מפני מראית העין אפילו בחדרי חדרים אסור תנן שוטחן בחמה אבל לא כנגד העם תנאי היא דתניא שוטחן בחמה אבל לא כנגד העם ר"א ור"ש ע אוסרין אמר רב הונא

המנער

רש"י

משום ריחשא. שלא יכנס בו שרץ כגון ז) נמייה וחולדה שממיתים את התרנגולים: זימנין דלא תקניה מעיקרא. שיהא כדי להוציא הכל ולהכניס את האויר: לא שנו. דנוקבין: אלא במקום. דסתימה זו לא נעשית אלא לשמור ריח היין שלא יצא ויתקלקל וכיון דלאו סתימה מעלייתא עבדי לה לאו כלום הוא: לחזק. שיחזק הכלי שלא יצא יינו הואיל וסתימה מעלייתא היא כי הדר נקיב לה הוי כפותח לכתחלה: למטה מן היין נמי לשמר הוא. כיון דלאו כובד היין נשען עליו סגי ליה בסתימה כל דהו: למטה מן השמרים. אבל שוליו שכל כובד היין נשען שם: תניא דמסייע לך. דלא פקע שם פתח מיניה אלא בסתימה מעלייתא: בית סתום יש לו ד"א. קיי"ל בבבא בתרא חצר מתחלקת לפי פתחיה לפי פתח הבתים הפתוחין לה אם באו לחלק את החצר בין שנים שהיה לזה בית שפתוחין לו לחצר שני פתחים ולזה בית שפתוחין לו לחצר ד' פתחים נוטל לכל פתח ארבע אמות בחצר נגד פתחו למדת רוחב פתחו והשאר חולקין בשוה ואם נסתם אחד מהם קודם חלוקת החצר ולא פירץ את פצימיו אלא סתם בין שני הפצימין אינו מפסיד [דין] פתחו בכך פירץ את פצימיו ואח"כ סתמו פקע שם פתח מיניה: בית סתום. והמת בתוכו אינו מטמא סביביו: פרץ פצימיו. וסתמו נעשה קבר ומטמא סביביו ד"א כדאמר בסוטה (ד' מד.) מת תופס ד"א לטומאה וגזרה דרבנן שמא יאהיל ולא יבין: גובתא. לתקוע קנה חלול בנקב החבית שילא היין דרך הקנה: מחתך. רונגיי"ר לתקנה למדת הנקב: אהדורי. אם נפלה: ולא מתקנא. לא ניתנה בנקב לידע אם למדתו היא: אי לימא ארישא. לחותכה ולשפותה: משחא. שמן עב: אסור. למרחו: טרפא דאסא. לתת עלה של הדס בנקב החבית שהעלה עשוי כמרזב והיין זב דרך שם: גזירה משום מרזב. שמא יכין מרזב: שמא יקטום. העלה מן הענף וכיון דקטמיה הוה ליה כמתקן כלי כדתניא במסכת ביצה (דף לג:) לחצות בו שיניו לא יקטמנו ואם קטמו חייב חטאת: בי סדיא. לבדין שקורין פלטר"ש ועשויין לקפלן תחתיו במקום הכר או הכסת: רב אסר. להביאו דרך מלבוש דרך רשות הרבים כשהוא מעוטף בו: ברכין. שדרכן להתחמם בהן: דשרו. דמלבוש הן: ולא הוה ליה רווחא. בבית למקום מושבם של תלמידים: ומשום כבוד רבותינו. שלא היה להן דבר לישב עליו ויושבין על גבי קרקע: רב כהנא ורב אסי. תלמידי חברים היו לו ח): מתני' לתוך הבור. שאין בו מים: שיהא שמור. שלא יסריח מחמת החום: ואת המים היפים ברעים. כלי מלא מים יפים לתוך מקוה מים רעים להשתמר (ג) שיצונו ולא יחמו: מי שנשרו. שנפלו למים בשבת: לחצר החיצונה. הסמוכה למבוא העיר בתוך העיר שהוא מקום משתמר: שוטחן בחמה. ליבשן: אבל לא כנגד העם. שיחשדוהו שכבסן: גמ' פשיטא. דנותנין תבשיל לתוך הבור: גומות. שבקרקע הבור שיהו שוין להושיב הקדרה:

המנער

תוספות

משום ריחשא. ואטו פתחא אחרינא דליכא למיחש לריחשא לא גזרינן דדוקא אטו לול של תרנגולין גזרינן דלא מסקי אינשי אדעתייהו שיהא עשוי להכניס ולהוציא:

פרץ פצימיו מטמא כל סביביו. פי' בקונטרס כל סביביו ד' אמות כקבר ואין נראה לזקיני הרב ר' שמשון זצ"ל דכיון דמסיימי מחילתא ולית לן למיחש שמא יעלה על הבית ויאהיל עליו ולא ידע לית לן למימר דמטמא ד' אמות כל סביביו כדמוכח בסוטה פרק משוח מלחמה (ד' מד.) גבי חצר הקבר העומד בתוכה טהור הני מילי חצר הקבר דמסיימא מחילתא אבל מת בעלמא תפיס ומשמע דבמת נמי היכא דמסיימא לא נטמא כל סביביו ד' אמות אלא נראה לו דהכי פי' זיזין באותו בית שבולטין מחוץ לבית מכל צד ויש בהם פותח טפח בכל אחד אם הבית סתום ועדיין נראית בו צורת הפתח אינו מטמא שסתמו של מת עומד לצאת דרך הפתח פרץ פצימיו וחזר ובנאו כשאר כותל ולא נותר בו כלל פתח מטמא כל סביביו דכל חד וחד איכא לספוקי דילמא דרך אותו מקום יצא מן הבית מיהו לאו פירכא היא כולי האי מה שהקשה לפירוש הקונטרס די"ל שלא חלקו חכמים במת ועוד נראה דלא קשה כלל לפי' הקונטרס דבית נמי לא מסיימי מחילתא שהוא מטמא הנוגע בכתלים אפילו לא יעלה על גביו כקבר שמטמא במגע אפילו מן הצד כדתניא בספרי בפרשת פרה אדומה או בקבר זה קבר סתום או אינו אלא קבר פתוח אמרת ק"ו ומה אהל שמקבל טומאה אינו מטמא מכל צדדין כשהוא פתוח קבר שאינו מקבל טומאה אינו דין שלא יטמא מכל צדדין כשהוא פתוח אלמא כשהוא סתום מטמא אף הנוגע מן הצד:

הלכה כרבי יאשיה. הלכך מותר לתת לכתחילה גובתא שקורין רזי"ל בחבית: משום מרזב. פי' הרב פור"ת שלא יבוא ליתן על גגו מרזב וקשה דבגובתא נמי נגזר אלא נראה לרבי כפי' הקונט' שלא יתקן מרזב לייט שיפול היין בתוכו וילך למרחוק דכשלוקח עלה של הדס ומקפלו כעין מרזב נראה כעושה מרזב אבל בגובתא שאינו עושה בו שום מעשה לא גזרינן. מ"ר:

אייתי ליה בי סדיא. בי מילעי הוה דאי לאו הכי היכי איתמר מכללא: מי שנשרו כליו במים. בדרך גרסינן ט) לשון נפילה לא כפי' הקונטרס לעיל בפרק במה אשה (דף סה.) שנשרו במי גשמים דהא אמרינן בביצה בפרק משילין (דף לה:) מאן דתני מנשירין לא משתבש כדתנן מי שנשרו כליו במים בדרך אלמא לשון נפילה הוא. י) מ"ר:

המנער

עין משפט נר מצוה

לא א ב מיי' פכ"ג מהלכות שבת הל"ח סמג לאוין סה טוש"ע או"ח סימן שיד סעיף ב:
לב ג מיי' פ"ב מהלכות שכנים הל"ט טוש"ע חו"מ סימן קעב סעיף ז:
לג ד מיי' פ"ט מהלכות טומאת מת הל"א:
לד ה ו מיי' פכ"ג מהל' שבת הלכה ו סמג לאוין סה טוש"ע או"ח סימן שיד סעיף ה:
לה ז מיי' שם הלכה יא סמג שם טור ש"ע שם סעיף יא:
לו ח שם סעיף ח:
לז ט י מיי' פי"ט מהל' שבת הלכה יז סמג שם טוש"ע או"ח סימן שא סעיף לה:
לח כ מיי' פכ"ב מהל' שבת הלכה ו טור או"ח סימן שיח:
לט ל מ נ מיי' שם הל"כ סמג לאוין סה טור ש"ע או"ח סימן שא סעיף מה:

רבינו חננאל

רי"א אין מוסיפין דזמנין דלא תקניה מעיקרא ואתי לארוחי ביה הלכתא כוותיה דדרש רב נחמן בר רב חסדא משמיה דר' יוחנן הלכה כרי"א. ושוין שנוקבין נקב ישן לכתחלה ואמר רב יהודה משמיה דשמואל אינו מותר לפתוח נקב ישן אלא במקום העשוי לשמר פי' להוציא היין מן השמרים אבל לחזק אסור פי' היה נקב בחבית וסתמו שלא יהא שותת. וחולק רב חסדא ורבה והלכתא כרבה דתניא מסייעתו ואלו דברי רבה רבה אמר למטה מן היין נמי זהו לשמר ומותר לפותחו והיכי דמי לחזק כגון שנקבה למטה מן השמרים המוכחא מלתא שאין אדם עושה נקב בקרקעיתה של חבית להוציא יין ולא לשמר. עשאו מפני כשמפנה החבית הופכה על פיה. וזה הנקב כיון שסתמו נעשה סתום. זה הגופה של חבית ובעל מלחיות נקב בו וחשוב כפתח בית הנסתם בפירוק פצימין שנתלק ממנו דין פתח לגמרי. גובתא שהיא שפופרת של קנה או של עצים שנותנין בנקב החבית או ביד הנוד של יין להיות מושכין ממנו יין מן החבית או מן הנוד. רב אסר ושמואל שרי ואוקימנא חלוקתן בשפופרת חתוכה ואינה מתוקנת להכניסה לנקב אבל לחתוך דברי הכל אסור. ואם היא חתוכה ומתוקנת דברי הכל מותר להחזירה בנקב החבית או בנוד למשוך ממנה יין. והעמדנו עוד חלוקת רב ושמואל כתנאי. דתניא אין חותכין שפופרת ביו"ט ואין צ"ל בשבת. נפלה מחזירין בשבת. ואין צ"ל ביו"ט. ור' יאשיה מיקל ודייק' עלה ר' יאשיה אהייא מיקל אילימא ארישא שאמר ת"ק אין חותכין כלומר אין חותכין מקנה גדול חתיכה לעשות' שפופרת בהא ר' יאשיה מיקל הא קא מתקן כלי בשבת אלא שאמר ת"ק נפלה מחזירין אותה. בהא לימא ר' יאשיה מיקל מי החמיר שיאמר בזה מיקל הלא בזה גם ת"ק מותר קאמר. ותריצנא אלא לאו דחתיכה ולא מתקנה איכא בינייהו וכך הציעה. אין עושין שפופרת ביו"ט ואין צ"ל בשבת. ואפי' חתכה ולא מתקנה אסור אבל אם היתה כבר בחבית ונפלה מחזירין אותה בשבת ואין צ"ל ביו"ט ור' יאשיה מיקל בחתיכה ולא מתקנה נמצאו דברי רב כת"ק ודברי שמואל כר' יאשיה והלכה כר' יאשיה ודרש רב שישא בריה דרב אידי משמא דר' יוחנן הלכתא כר' יאשיה וזה שאמר חתכה ולא מתקנה לאו שצריכה תיקון כלי כגון סכין וכדומה לו אלא תיקון ביד בלבד. ואם צריכה תיקון בסכין או זולתו סכין כלי אחר אסורה. ואם היתה החבית נקובה לא יתן עליה שעוה מפני שממרח. כלומר סותם כדאמרינן התם לענין חבית שניקבה וסתמה שמרים כר' מורח מן הצדדין. וכיון דר' יהודה דמתניתין וריב"ז ורב ושמואל אמרי ש"מ שאסור לתת שעוה בחבית. וכן משחא. רב אסר גזירה במשחא אטו שעוה. והלכתא כוותיה: טרפא דאסא. פי' עלה הדס שנותנין על הנקב של חבית להיות מקלח בו היין ולא יהיה שותת בדופני החבית. לדברי הכל אסור ליטול עלה של הדס בשבת ולשומו בנקב של חבית כמרזב. ואפילו רב אשי לא התיר אלא שאם היה הנקב מושך ממנו א) אבל לתתו לכתחלה אוסר: בי סדיא רב אסר ושמואל שרי אין זה מקומו אלא בשביל שהזכיר השמועות שחלקו בהן רב אסר ושמואל שרי נסבה בגררא. ופשוטה היא. כסת זו שחלקו בה כסת בינונית לא דקה ולא קשה. ומסקינן בה אפילו זו מותר לטלטלה: נותנין תבשיל בתוך הבור בשביל שיהא שמור. פי' בור זה אין בו מים ונותן התבשיל בקרקעיתו מהו דתימא לגזור דלמא אתי לאשויי גומות קמ"ל דלא גזרינן. ואת המים היפים ברעים פשיטא ואת הצונן בחמין פשיטא מהו דתימא לגזור דלמא אתי לאשויי גומות ב) ברמץ קמ"ל דלא גזרינן: מתני' מי שנשרו כליו בדרך כו'. אמר רב יהודה אמר רב כל מקום שאסרו חכמים מפני מראית העין אפילו בחדרי חדרים אסור. איני והא תנן שוטחן בחמה אבל לא כנגד העם ואוקימנא

חשק שלמה על רבינו חננאל א) נראה דל"ל מונח בנקב מותר למשוך ממנו: ב) אינו מובן. ואולי צ"ל דלמא אתי לאטמוני ברמץ וכדאיתא בגמ':

מסורת הש"ס

א) [פי' להוציא היין מן השמרים. ערוך ערך חזק ע"ש], ב) ב"ב יב., ג) [ברכות ט. וש"נ], ד) [לעיל לט., ה) ביצה לה:, ו) לעיל סד: ביצה ט. ע"ז יב., ז) עי' לעיל לט: רש"י ד"ה קטנה ושם משמע שנמייה וחולדה חיות הן, ח) [בדליפא סנהדרין לו:], ט) ר"ל דגרסי' הנו"ן דנשרו בקמץ לשון נפילה דאלו הנו"ן בחירק הוי לשון שריה. רש"ל, י) [ועי' תוס' ביצה לה: ד"ה מי שנשרו].

הגהות הב"ח

(א) גמ' רבא אמר למטה וכו' א"ל אביי לרבא: (ג) רש"י ד"ה ואת המים וכו' להשתמר שיצוננו ולא יחמו:

גליון הש"ס

גמ' אמר ר"ח למעלה מן היין זהו לשמר. גי' הרי"ף למעלה מן היין זהו לחזק למטה מן היין זהו לשמר רבה אמר למעלה וכו': שם ומשום כבוד רבותינו לא ישב. עי' שבועות דף מ ע"ב תוס' ד"ה הוה יתיב:

הגהות הגר"א

[א] גמ' איכא בינייהו דקטים ומנחי. נ"ב פי' שהוא קטום ויש עוד הרבה קטומים טור. ח"ש ומנמי. אבל גירסת הרי"ף והרא"ש וש"פ ומנח: [ב] שם שוטחן בחמה. נ"ב דווקא בחמה (ועמ"ש רבינו בא"ח סימן ש"א ס"ק מ"ה):

ליקוטי רש"י

בית סתום. שלא פרץ פצימיו. כשסתם פתחו לא סלק מזוזתו (ומשקופו ומפתן) דגלי דעתיה דלא סליק ממנה כל עיקר לפותחו לאחר זמן [ב"ב יא:]. שהיה לו פתח לחצר וסתמו. יש לו ד' אמות. בחלוקת החצר אם באו לחלוק כאילו הוא פתוח [שם יב.]. אמות. בחצר שלפני החצר אם באו לחלוק כאילו הוא פתוח ופתח והשלח והמכן ברחבו הפתח ואפילו הוא רחב עשר אמות נוטל ארבע אמות במכן וכנגד כל רחבו לפרק משאו [סוכה ז:]. אינו מטמא סביביו. אלא כנגד הפתח אם מת בתוכו. פרץ את פצימיו. הרי הוא קבר ומכוחם סביבות קברו ד' אמות כדי שלא יקרבו עושי טהרות עד הקבר ויאהילו ולאו לדעתייהו [ב"ב שם]. מטמא כל סביביו. חכמים גזרו שיהא המת תופס ומטמא את הכנסת בארבע אמותיו כדי שלא יגיעו אוכלי טהרות לקרוב לו ויאהילו ולאו לדעתייהו [סוטה מד.]. בפירוש אמרת לן משמיה דרב. לפני חלייך קודם ששכחת תלמודך [לעיל נט:]. טבות רישבא. לייד עופות כמו אין פורשין רשתים ליונים (ב"ק עט:) טבות שם אדם [תענית י.].

[המשך בדף קמז.]

מִשּׁוּם רִיחֲשָׁא – **because of** the threat of **creeping things.**[1]

Having explained why the Tanna Kamma permits the expansion of an existing opening, the Gemara questions why the other Tanna forbids it:

וְיֵשׁ אוֹמְרִים אֵין מוֹסִיפִים – Why, then, do SOME others SAY ONE MAY NOT ENLARGE a hole on the Sabbath? זִימְנִין דְּלָא תַקְנֵיה מֵעִיקָּרָא – They assert: **Sometimes one does not properly adjust** the size of **[the chicken coop's opening] when** he **originally** builds it, וְאָתֵי לְאַרְוָחֵי בֵּיהּ – **and** therefore, **he** might later **come to enlarge it.**[2] If he were to do so on the Sabbath, he would transgress a Biblical prohibition; therefore, the Sages prohibited the enlargement of *any* hole on the Sabbath.[3]

A ruling is issued on this Tannaic dispute:

דָּרַשׁ רַב נַחְמָן מִשּׁוּם רַבִּי יוֹחָנָן – **Rav Nachman lectured in the name of R' Yochanan:** הֲלָכָה כְּיֵשׁ אוֹמְרִים – **The law follows** the **"some who say"**; i.e. by Rabbinic decree, one may not expand any existing hole on the Sabbath.

The Gemara elaborates on the last teaching of the earlier-cited Baraisa:

וְשָׁוִין שֶׁנּוֹקְבִין נֶקֶב יָשָׁן לְכַתְּחִלָּה – The Baraisa had stated: BUT ALL AGREE THAT IT IS ALTOGETHER PERMISSIBLE TO REOPEN AN OLD HOLE. אָמַר רַב יְהוּדָה אָמַר שְׁמוּאֵל – Concerning this, **Rav Yehudah said in the name of Shmuel:** לֹא שָׁנוּ אֶלָּא בְּמָקוֹם הֶעָשׂוּי לְשַׁמֵּר – **They taught this** [that one may reopen a plugged hole] **only** if the plug was **in a place where it was meant to preserve** the aroma of the wine.[4] אֲבָל לְחַזֵּק – **But** if it was in a place where it was meant **to strengthen** the cask,[5] אָסוּר – it is **forbidden** to remove the plug.

The Gemara seeks to clarify this:

הֵיכִי דָּמֵי לְשַׁמֵּר – **What is an example** of a plug whose purpose is **"to preserve,"** הֵיכִי דָּמֵי לְחַזֵּק – **and what is an example** of a plug meant **"to strengthen"?**

The Gemara responds:

אָמַר רַב חִסְדָּא – **Rav Chisda said:** לְמַעְלָה מִן הַיַּיִן – If the plugged hole is **above the** level of **the wine** in the cask, זֶהוּ לְשַׁמֵּר – **this is** a plug meant only **"to preserve"** the wine's aroma. לְמַטָּה מִן הַיַּיִן – If, however, it is **below** the surface of **the wine,** זֶהוּ לְחַזֵּק – **this is** a plug meant **"to strengthen"** the cask.[6]

Another Amora gives a different view:

רָבָא אָמַר – However, **Rava said:** לְמַטָּה מִן הַיַּיִן נַמִּי זֶהוּ לְשַׁמֵּר – When the plugged hole is **below** the surface of **the wine, this too is** a plug meant just **"to preserve."**[7] וְהֵיכִי דָּמֵי לְחַזֵּק – **And what is an example** of a plug meant **"to strengthen"?** כְּגוֹן שֶׁנִּיקְּבָה לְמַטָּה מִן הַשְּׁמָרִים – A case **where, for example, the cask had been punctured** at the very bottom, just **below** the level of **the dregs,** and it was here that the cask had been plugged.[8]

Abaye lends support to Rava's position:

אָמַר לֵיהּ אַבַּיֵי לְרָבָא – **Abaye said to Rava:** תַּנְיָא דִּמְסַיַּיע לָךְ – **A Baraisa taught a ruling that supports you:** בַּיִת סָתוּם – The owner of A HOUSE whose entrance to a courtyard was SEALED יֵשׁ לוֹ אַרְבַּע אַמּוֹת – IS ENTITLED TO FOUR *AMOS* in front of the entrance when the courtyard is divided, as if the entrance were still open.[9] פָּרַץ אֶת פְּצִימָיו – If, however, HE TORE DOWN THE [DOOR'S] FRAME[10] when he sealed the entrance, אֵין לוֹ אַרְבַּע אַמּוֹת – HE IS NOT ENTITLED TO FOUR *AMOS,* for when the frame was removed the entrance ceased to exist, and the owner lost his right to this area in the courtyard.

The Baraisa continues:

בַּיִת סָתוּם – Likewise, A HOUSE with a corpse inside whose entrance is SEALED אֵינוֹ מְטַמֵּא כָּל סְבִיבָיו – DOES NOT RENDER *TAMEI* one who approaches within four *amos* of it from ALL SIDES.[11] פָּרַץ אֶת פְּצִימָיו – If, however, ONE TORE DOWN THE FRAME OF [THE DOOR] and thereby sealed the house permanently, מְטַמֵּא כָּל סְבִיבָיו – [THE HOUSE] DOES RENDER *TAMEI* anyone who approaches within four *amos* of it from ALL SIDES, for the house is accorded the status of a closed grave.[12] Now, in both these cases, we see that an opening loses its status as such only when it has been permanently and completely sealed off. This supports Rava's claim that only the strongest of all seals [i.e. a plug in the very bottom of a cask] legally eliminates the opening it had plugged.

Having discussed enlarging the openings of casks on the Sabbath, the Gemara considers the permissibility of other ways of enhancing openings on the Sabbath:

גּוּבְתָּא – As concerns placing **a spigot** in an existing hole in a wine

NOTES

1. An enlarged hole would allow predators such as rats and weasels to enter the coop (*Rashi*). As such, even if one were to mistakenly reason that enlarging an opening in a chicken coop were permissible, few people would in practice ever wish to do such a thing. This being the case, there was no need to decree against enlarging one-way openings, and the position of the Tanna Kamma is that no such decree was in fact made (see *Tosafos* ד״ה משום ריחשא).

2. He may not have made the hole large enough to admit an adequate amount of fresh air and release the vapors (*Rashi*).

3. I.e. even a hole intended only for one-way use.

4. I.e. the hole was plugged only to keep the vapors in the cask from escaping, which in turn preserves the quality of the wine. Now, strong, durable plugs were not needed to merely preserve an aroma, and in fact, the plugs used for this purpose were generally quite flimsy. Thus, this plug is not judged to "erase" the existing hole; rather, even while plugged, the cask is considered a perforated vessel, and reopening the hole is therefore permissible (*Rashi;* for an alternative explanation of these points, see *Rif* and *Ran*).

5. I.e. the plug was intended to ensure that wine did not flow out of the hole in the cask. Presumably, this sort of plug creates a full and complete seal, and therefore, from a legal standpoint, it erases the existence of the perforation. Removing this type of plug is therefore forbidden, as it is tantamount to making a new hole (*Rashi*).

6. [The placement of the latter plug makes clear that its purpose is to keep the wine from flowing out of the cask.]

7. Since the plug is not at the very bottom of the cask, where the entire weight of the wine exerts pressure on it, a strong plug is not necessary (*Rashi*). [Thus, although this plug obviously ensures that wine does not escape, still, since it is a relatively insubstantial plug, it is tantamount to a plug meant just to "preserve."]

8. Since the entire weight of the wine exerts pressure on this sort of plug, it must of necessity be a strong one (*Rashi*). Thus, reopening the hole is like creating a new opening.

9. The Gemara in *Bava Basra* (11a) teaches that whenever a courtyard is divided among the residents of the houses that open into it, each resident is automatically awarded rights to the four *amos* immediately adjacent to any entrance leading from his house into the courtyard. The rest of the courtyard is then divided equally among the residents. This Baraisa teaches that a resident retains rights to this area even if his entrance was sealed at the time the courtyard is divided (*Rashi*).

10. I.e. the doorposts, lintel and threshold (*Rashi* to *Bava Basra* 11b ד״ה שלא פרץ).

11. See next note.

12. The Sages imposed *tumah* on anyone who approaches within four *amos* of a grave, so that people who handle food that they wish to maintain in a state of *taharah* would not inadvertently stand over the grave itself and become *Scripturally* unclean (see *Sotah* 44a). As long as a house has an entrance, even one that is sealed, it is not considered a "grave." If the house is sealed and the door frame removed, however, the house is considered a large, closed tomb, and it renders *tamei* anyone who approaches within four *amos* of it on any side (see *Rashi*; cf. *Tosafos*).

גמרא

משום ריחשא ור"א אין מוסיפים זימנין דלא תקניה מעיקרא ואתי לארוחי ביה דרש רב נחמן משום רבי יוחנן הלכה כיש אומרים: [א] ושוין שנוקבין נקב ישן לכתחלה: אמר רב יהודה אמר שמואל לא שנו אלא במקום העשוי לשמר אבל לחזק אסור היכי דמי לשמר היכי דמי לחזק · א"ר חסדא למעלה מן היין זהו לשמר למטה מן היין זהו לחזק (א) רבא אמר [ב] למטה מן היין נמי זהו לשמר והיכי דמי לחזק כגון שניקבה למטה מן השמרים א"ל אביי לרבא תניא דמסייע לך [ג] בית סתום יש לו ארבע אמות פרץ את פצימיו אין לו ד' אמות [ד] בית סתום אינו מטמא כל סביביו פרץ את פצימיו מטמא כל סביביו גובתא רב אסר ושמואל שרי [ה] מחתך לכתחלה דכ"ע לא פליגי דאסור אהדורי דכ"ע לא פליגי דשרי כי פליגי דחתיכה ולא מתקנא מאן דאסר גזרינן דילמא אתי למיחתך לכתחלה ומאן דשרי [ו] לא גזרינן כתנאי אין חותכין שפופרת ביו"ט וא"צ לומר בשבת נפלה (אין) מחזירין אותה בשבת ואין צריך לומר ביו"ט ור' יאשיה מיקל ר' יאשיה אהייא אילימא ארישא הא קמתקן מנא אלא אסיפא ת"ק נמי מישרא קשרי אלא דחתיכה ולא מתקנא איכא בינייהו מ"ס גזרינן ומ"ס לא גזרינן דרש רב שישא בריה דרב אידי משמיה דר' יוחנן הלכה כר' יאשיה: ואם היתה נקובה וכו': מישחא רב אסר ושמואל שרי מאן דאסר [ז] גזרינן משום שעוה ומאן דשרי לא גזרינן אמר ליה רב שמואל בר בר חנה לרב יוסף בפירוש אמרת לן משמיה דרב מישחא שרי אמר טבות רישבא אמר שמואל האי טרפא דאסא אסור מ"ט רב יימר מדפתי אמר גזירה משום מרזב רב אשי אמר [ח] גזירה שמא יקטום מאי בינייהו [א] איכא בינייהו דקטים ומנחי בי סדיא רב אסר ושמואל [ט] שרי ברכין דכולי עלמא לא פליגי דשרי [י] בקשין דכ"ע לא פליגי דאסור כי פליגי במיצעי מאן דאסר מיחזי כמשוי ומאן דשרי לא מיחזי כמשוי והא דרב לאו [ג] בפירוש איתמר אלא מכללא איתמר דרב איקלע לההוא אתרא דלא הוה ליה רווחא נפק יתיב בכרמלית אייתו ליה בי סדיא לא יתיב מאן דחזא סבר משום דבי סדיא אסור ולא היא דרב אכרוזי מכריז בי סדיא שרי [ד] ומשום כבוד רבותינו לא ישב עליו ומאן נינהו רב כהנא ורב אסי: **מתני'** [ה] נותנין תבשיל לתוך הבור בשביל שיהא שמור ואת המים היפים ברעים בשביל שיצננו ואת הצונן בחמה בשביל שיחמו [ו] מי שנשרו כליו בדרך במים מהלך בהן ואינו חושש הגיע לחצר החיצונה שוטחן בחמה [ב] אבל לא כנגד העם: **גמ'** פשיטא מהו דתימא ניגזור משום אשווי גומות קא משמע לן: ואת המים היפים ברעים: פשיטא סיפא איצטריכא ליה ואת הצונן בחמה הא נמי פשיטא מהו דתימא ניגזור דילמא אתי לאטמוני ברמץ קמ"ל: [ז] מי שנשרו וכו': [י] אמר רב יהודה אמר רב [כ] כל מקום שאסרו חכמים מפני מראית העין אפילו בחדרי חדרים אסור תנן שוטחן בחמה אבל לא כנגד העם תנאי היא דתניא שוטחן בחמה אבל לא כנגד העם ר"א ור"ש [ל] אוסרין אמר רב הונא

המנער

רש"י

משום ריחשא. שלא יכנס בו שרץ כגון [ז] נמייה וחולדה שממיתים את התרנגולים: זימנין דלא תקניה מעיקרא. שיהא כדי להוציא הבל ולהכנים את האויר: לא שנו. דנוקבין: אלא במקום. דסתימה זו לא נעשית אלא לשמור ריח היין שלא יצא ויתקלקל וכיון דלאו סתימה מעלייתא עבדי לה לאו כלום הוא: לחזק. שיחזק הכלי שלא יצא יינו הואיל וסתימה מעלייתא היא כי הדר נקיב לה הוי כפותח לכתחלה: למטה מן היין נמי לשמר הוא. כיון דלאו כובד היין נשען עליו סגי ליה בסתימה כל דהו: למטה מן השמרים. אצל שוליו שכל כובד היין נשען שם: תניא דמסייע לך. דלא פקע שם פתח מיניה אלא בסתימה מעלייתא: בית סתום יש לו ד"א. קיי"ל בבבא בתרא חצר מתחלקת לפי פתחיה לפי פתח הבתים הפתוחין לה אם באו לחלק את החצר בין שנים שהיה לזה בית שפתוחין לו לחצר שני פתחים ולזה בית שפתוחין לו לחצר ד' פתחים נוטל לכל פתח ארבע אמות בחצר נגד פתחו למדת רוחב פתחו והשאר חולקין בשוה ואם נסתם אחד מהם קודם חלוקת החצר ולא פירץ את פצימיו אלא סתם בין שני הפצימין אינו מפסיד [דין] פתחו בכך פירץ את פצימיו ואח"כ סתמו פקע שם פתח מיניה: בית סתום. והמת בתוכו אינו מטמא סביביו: פרץ פצימיו. וסתמו נעשה קבר ומטמא סביביו ד"א כדאמר בסוטה (ד' מד.) מת תופס ד"א לטומאה וגזרה דרבנן שמא יאהיל ולא יבין: גובתא. לתקוע קנה חלול בנקב החבית שיצא היין דרך הקנה: מחתך. רונגי"ר לתקנה למדת הנקב: אהדורי. אם נפלה: ולא מתקנא. לא ניתנה בנקב לידע אם למדתו היא: אי לימא ארישא. לחותכה ולשפותה: משחא. שמן עב: אסור. למרחו: טרפא דאסא. לתת עלה של הדס בנקב החבית שהעלה עשוי כמרזב והיין זב דרך שם: גזירה משום מרזב. שמא יכין מרזב: שמא יקטום. העלה מן הענף וכיון דקטמיה הוה ליה כמתקן כלי כדתניא במסכת ביצה (דף לג:) לחצות בו שיניו לא יקטמנו ואם קטמו חייב חטאת: בי סדיא. לבדין שקורין פלטר"ש ועשויין לקפלן תחתיו במקום הכר או הכסת: רב אסר. להביאו דרך מלבוש דרך רשות הרבים כשהוא מעוטף בו: ברכין. שדרכן להתחמם בהן: דשרו. דמלבוש הן: ולא הוה ליה רווחא. בבית למקום מושבם של תלמידים: ומשום כבוד רבותינו. שלא היה להן דבר לישב עליו ויושבין על גבי קרקע: רב כהנא ורב אסי. תלמידי חברים היו לו [ח]: **מתני'** לתוך הבור. שאין בו מים: שיהא שמור. שלא יקריח מחמת החום: ואת המים היפים ברעים. כלי מלא מים יפים לתוך מקוה מים רעים להשתמר (ב) שיצוננו ולא יחמו: מי שנשרו. שנפלו למים בשבת: לחצר החיצונה. הסמוכה למבוי העיר בתוך העיר שהוא מקום משתמר: שוטחן בחמה. ליבשן: אבל לא כנגד העם. שיחשדוהו שכבסן: **גמ'** פשיטא. דנותנין תבשיל לתוך הבור: גומות. שבקרקע הבור שיהו שוין להושיב הקדרה:

המנער

תוספות

משום ריחשא. ואטו פתחא אחרינא ליכא למיחש לריחשא לא גזרינן דדוקא אטו לול של תרנגולין גזרינן דלא מסקי אינשי אדעתייהו שיהא עשוי להכניס ולהוציא:

פרץ פצימיו מטמא כל סביביו. פי' בקונטרס כל סביביו ד' אמות כקבר ואין נראה לזקיני הרב ר' שמשון זצ"ל דכיון דמסיימי מחילתא ולית לן למיחש שמא יעלה על הבית ויאהיל עליו ולא ידע לית לן למימר דמטמא ד' אמות כל סביביו כדמוכח בסוטה פרק משוח מלחמה (ד' מד.) גבי חצר הקבר העומד בתוכה טהור הני מילי חצר הקבר דמסיימא מחילתא אבל מת בעלמא תפיס ומשמע דבמת נמי היכא דמסיימא לא נטמא כל סביביו ד' אמות אלא נראה לו דהכי פי' דזין באותו בית שבולטין מחוץ לבית מכל צד ויש בהם פותח טפח בכל אחד אם הבית סתום ועדיין נראית בו צורת הפתח אינו מטמא שסתמו של מת עומד לצאת דרך הפתח פרץ פצימיו וחזר ובנאו כשאר כותל ולא נותר בו כלל פתח מטמא כל סביביו דכל חד וחד איכא לספוקי דילמא דרך אותו מקום יצא מן הבית מיהו לאו פירכא היא כולי האי מה שהקשה לפירוש הקונטרס די"ל שלא חלקו חכמים במת ועוד נראה דלא קשה כלל לפי' הקונטרס דבית נמי לא מסיימי מחילתא שהוא מטמא הנוגע בכתלים אפילו לא יעלה על גביו כקבר שמטמא במגע אפילו מן הצד כדתניא בספרי בפרשת פרה אדומה או בקבר זה קבר סתום או אינו אלא קבר פתוח אמרת ק"ו ומה אהל שמקבל טומאה אינו מטמא מכל צדדין כשהוא פתוח קבר שאינו מקבל טומאה אינו דין שלא יטמא מכל צדדין כשהוא פתוח אלמא כשהוא סתום מטמא אף הנוגע מן הצד:

הלכה כרבי יאשיה. הלכך מותר לתת לכתחילה גובתא שקורין רזיי"ל בחבית: משום מרזב. פי' הרב פור"ת שלא יבוא ליתן על גגו מרזב וקשה דבגובתא נמי נגזור אלא נראה לרבי כפי' הקונט' שלא יתקן מרזב ליינו שיפול היין בתוכו וילך למרחוק דכשלוקח עלה של הדס ומקפלו כעין מרזב נראה כעושה מרזב אבל בגובתא שאינו עושה בו שום מעשה לא גזרינן. מ"ר:

אייתי ליה בי סדיא. בי מילעי הוה דאי לאו הכי היכי איתמר מכללא: מי שנשרו כליו במים. בדרך גרסינן [ט] לשון נפילה לא כפי' הקונטרס לעיל בפרק במה אשה (דף סה.) שנשרו במי גשמים דהא אמרינן בביצה בפרק משילין (דף לה:) מאן דתני מנגבין לא משתבש דקתני מי שנשרו כליו במים בדרך אלמא לשון נפילה הוא. [י] מ"ר:

עין משפט נר מצוה

לא א ב מיי' פכ"ג מהלכות שבת הל"א סמג לאוין סה טוש"ע או"ח סימן שיד סעיף יא:
לב ג ד מיי' פ"ה מהלכות שכנים הל"ו טוש"ע חו"מ סימן קעג סעיף ז:
לג ד מיי' פ"ה מהל' טומאת מת הל"ג:
לד ה ו מיי' פכ"ג מהל' שבת הלכה ו סמג לאוין סה טוש"ע או"ח סימן שיד סעיף ט:
לה ז מיי' שם הלכה יא סמג שם טוש"ע שם סעיף יא:
לו ח שם סעיף ה:
לז ט י מיי' פי"ט מהל' שבת הלכה יח טוש"ע או"ח סימן שא סעיף לה:
לח כ מיי' פכ"ב מהל' שבת הלכה ט טור או"ח סימן שיח:
לט ל מ נ מיי' שם הל"כ סמג לאוין סה טור שו"ע או"ח סימן שא סעיף מה:

רבינו חננאל

ור"א אין מוסיפין דזמנין דלא תקניה מעיקרא ואתי לארוחי ביה הלכתא כוותיה דדרש רב נחמן בר רב חסדא משמיה דר' יוחנן הלכה כי"א. ושוין שנוקבין בנקב ישן לכתחלה ואמר רב יהודה משמיה דשמואל אינו מותר לפתוח נקב ישן אלא במקום העשוי לשמר פי' להוציא היין מן השמרים אבל לחזק אסור פי' היה נקב בחבית וסתמו שלא יהא שותת. וחלקו רב חסדא ורבה והלכתא כרבה דתניא מסייעתו ואלו דברי רבה רבה אמר למטה מן היין נמי זהו לשמר ומותר לפותחו והיכי דמי לחזק כגון שנקבה למטה מן השמרים דמוכחא מלתא שאין אדם עושה נקב בקרקעיתא של חבית להוציא יין ולא לשמר. עשאו מפני כשמפנה החבית הופכה על פיה. וזה הנקב כיון שסתמו נעשה סתום. זה בגופה של חבית ובטל מלהיות נקב בו וחשוב כפתח בית הנסתם בפירוץ פצימין שנסתלק ממנו דין פתח לגמרי. גובתא שהיא שפופרת של קנה או של עצים שנותנין בנקב החבית או ביד הנוד של יין להיות מושכין ממנו יין מן החבית או מן הנוד. רב אסר ושמואל שרי ואוקימנא חלוקתן בשפופרת חתוכה ואינה מתוקנת להכניסה לנקב אבל לחתוך דברי הכל אסור. ואם היא חתוכה ומתוקנת דברי הכל מותר להחזירה בנקב החבית או בנוד למשוך ממנה יין. והעמדנו עוד חלוקת רב ושמואל כתנאי. דתניא אין חותכין שפופרת ביו"ט ואין צ"ל בשבת. נפלה מחזירין בשבת. ואין צ"ל ביו"ט. ור' יאשיה מיקל ודייקי' עלה ר' יאשיה אהייא מיקל אילימא ארישא שאמר ת"ק אין חותכין כלומר אין חותכין מקנה גדול חתיכה לעשות' שפופרת בהא ר' יאשיה מיקל הא קא מתקן כלי בשבת אלא שאמר ת"ק נפלה מחזירין אותה. בהא לימא ר' יאשיה מיקל מי החמיר שיאמר בזה מיקל הלא בזה גם ת"ק מותר קאמר. ותריצנא אלא לאו דחתיכה ולא מתקנה איכא בינייהו וכך הציעה.

מסורת הש"ס

א) [פי' להוציא היין מן השמרים. ערוך ערך חזק ע"ש], ב) [ב"ב יב.], ג) [בכורות נו: וש"נ], ד) לעיל לט., ה) ביצה לה: ו) לעיל סד: ביצה ט. ע"ז יב., ז) עי' לעיל נא: רש"י ד"ה קטנה ושם תקן שמעתתא נמייה וחולדה חיות הן, ח) [כתובות סנהדרין לו:], ט) ר"ל דגרסי' הערוך דנשרו בקמץ לשון נפילה דאלו הערוך מפרש הוי לשון שריה. רש"ל, י) [עי' תוס' ביצה לה: ד"ה מי שנשרו].

הגהות הב"ח

(א) גמ' רבה אמר למטה וכו' א"ל אביי לרבא: (ב) רש"י ד"ה ואת המים וכו' להשתמר שיצוננו ולא יחמו:

גליון הש"ס

גמ' אמר ר"ח למעלה מן היין זהו לשמר. ע' הרי"ף למעלה מן היין זהו לחזק למטה מן היין זהו לשמר רבה אמר למעלה וכו': שם ומשום כבוד רבותינו לא ישב. עי' שבועות דף מו ע"א תוס' ד"ה הוה יתיב:

הגהות הגר"א

[א] גמ' איכא בינייהו דקטים ומנחי. נ"ב שהוא קטום ויש עוד הרבה קטומים טורח. וא"ש ומנחי. אבל גירסת הרי"ף והרא"ש והרמב"ם [illegible]: [ב] שם שוטחן בחמה. נ"ב דוקא (ועמ"ש רבינו בהגהות או"ח סימן ש"א ס"ק ק"ה):

ליקוטי רש"י

בית סתום. שלא פרץ פצימיו. כשנסתם סתמו אלא מחוץ [ומקפתו] דבלי דעתיה לא סילק נפשיה וסופו לפותחו לאחר זמן [ב"ב יב.]. [illegible] ד' אמות. כשחולקין החצר [illegible] אמות מחצר כנגד פתחו [שם יב.]. [illegible] מטמא סביביו. שלא כנגד הפתח אלא סתומה. פרץ את פצימיו. הרי הוא כקבר וחכמים טימאו את סביביו כל סביביו משום שלא יקרבו אצלו [illegible] [ב"ב שם]. מטמא כל סביביו. חכמים גזרו שיהא המת מטמא בכל סביביו כל מקום שלא יאהלו עליו [ב"ב שם]. [illegible] [המשך בדף קמו:]

אין עושין שפופרת ביו"ט ואין צ"ל בשבת. ואפי' חתכה ולא מתקנה אסור אבל אם היתה כבר בחבית ונפלה מחזירין אותה בשבת ואין צ"ל ביו"ט ור' יאשיה מיקל בחתיכה ולא מתקנה נמצאו דברי רב כת"ק ודברי שמואל כר' יאשיה והלכה כר' יאשיה [illegible] ואם היתה החבית נקובה לא יתן עליה שעוה מפני שממרח. [illegible] טרפא דאסא. [illegible] בי סדיא [illegible] רב אסר ושמואל שרי [illegible] מתני' נותנין תבשיל לתוך הבור [illegible] מי שנשרו כליו בדרך במים [illegible] אבל לא כנגד העם [illegible] ואוקימנא

חשק שלמה על רבינו חננאל א) נראה דל"ל מותר [illegible]

cask,[13] רַב אָסַר – **Rav forbids it,** וּשְׁמוּאֵל שָׁרֵי – **but Shmuel permits it.**

The Gemara defines their dispute more precisely:

מְחַתֵּךְ לְכַתְּחִלָּה – **Initially cutting** a reed to serve as a spigot,[14] דְּכוּלֵּי עָלְמָא לֹא פְּלִיגֵי דְּאָסוּר – **everyone agrees is forbidden.** אַהֲדוּרֵי – And **putting** an already trimmed reed **back** into the barrel after it has fallen out, דְּכוּלֵּי עָלְמָא לֹא פְּלִיגֵי דְּשָׁרֵי – **everyone agrees is permissible.** כִּי פְּלִיגֵי דַּחֲתִיכָה וְלֹא מְתַקְּנָא – **Where they disagree is** concerning a reed **that has** already **been cut** to serve as a spigot, **but has not been perfectly trimmed.**[15] מַאן דְּאָסַר – **The one who forbids** placing the spigot in the hole holds גָּזְרִינַן דִּלְמָא אָתֵי לְמִיחְתַּךְ לְכַתְּחִלָּה – that **[the Rabbis] issued a decree** forbidding this **lest one come to cut [the reed] in the first place.**[16] וּמַאן דְּשָׁרֵי – **And the one who permits** it maintains that לֹא גָּזְרִינַן – **[the Rabbis] did not issue** such **a decree.**

The Gemara observes that this Amoraic dispute apparently mirrors a Tannaic dispute:

כְּתַנָּאֵי – **It is like** the following dispute between **Tannaim:** אֵין חוֹתְכִין שְׁפוֹפֶרֶת בְּיוֹם טוֹב – ON YOM TOV, WE MAY NOT CUT A TUBE to serve as a spigot for a cask, וְאֵין צָרִיךְ לוֹמַר בְּשַׁבָּת – AND IT GOES WITHOUT SAYING that this is forbidden ON THE SABBATH.[17] נָפְלָה (אין) מַחֲזִירִין אוֹתָהּ בְּשַׁבָּת – If, however, the tube FELL out of its hole in the cask, WE MAY RETURN IT to its place ON THE SABBATH, וְאֵין צָרִיךְ לוֹמַר בְּיוֹם טוֹב – AND IT GOES WITHOUT SAYING that we may do so ON YOM TOV. וְרַבִּי יֹאשִׁיָּה מֵיקֵל – AND R' YOSHIYAH RULES LENIENTLY here.

The Gemara clarifies R' Yoshiyah's position:

רַבִּי יֹאשִׁיָּה אַהֲיָיא – **Concerning which** part of the Baraisa did **R' Yoshiyah** state his leniency? אִילֵימָא אַרֵישָׁא – **If you say** he stated it **concerning the beginning** of the Baraisa, i.e. he permits trimming the spigot to fit the hole, הָא קָמְתַקֵּן מָנָא – **surely** this constitutes **perfecting a vessel,** and it is inconceivable that R' Yoshiyah would permit it. אֶלָּא אַסֵּיפָא – **Rather,** we will say that R' Yoshiyah stated his leniency **concerning the end** of the Baraisa; i.e. he permits putting the spigot back into the hole if it falls out. This, however, gives rise to a difficulty, תַּנָּא קַמָּא נַמִי מִישְׁרָא קָשָׁרֵי – for **the Tanna Kamma also permits** putting the spigot back! What, then, is the difference between them? אֶלָּא דַּחֲתִיכָה וְלֹא מְתַקְּנָא אִיכָּא בֵּינַיְיהוּ – **Rather,** it must be **that the difference between them** arises in a case **where [the tube] has** already **been cut** to serve as a spigot, **but has not** yet **been perfectly trimmed.** מַר סָבַר גָּזְרִינַן – **One master,** the Tanna Kamma, **holds** that **[the Sages] issued a decree** forbidding the placement of the tube in the hole,[18] וּמַר סָבַר לֹא גָּזְרִינַן – **whereas** the other **master,** R' Yoshiyah, **holds** that **[the Sages] did not issue** such **a decree.** We thus find that the dispute between Rav and Shmuel is indeed mirrored by a Tannaic dispute.

The Gemara concludes:

דָּרַשׁ רַב שִׁישָׁא בְּרֵיהּ דְּרַב אִידִי מִשְּׁמֵיהּ דְּרַבִּי יוֹחָנָן – **Rav Shisha the son of Rav Idi lectured in the name of R' Yochanan** הֲלָכָה כְּרַבִּי יֹאשִׁיָּה – that **the halachah** in this matter **follows the** view of **R' Yoshiyah;** i.e. one may place a tube in a barrel for use as a spigot, even if it has not yet been trimmed to perfectly fit the hole.

The Gemara quotes the next part of the Mishnah as a preface to its new discussion:

וְאִם הָיְתָה נְקוּבָה וכו' – NOW, IF [THE CASK] WAS already PERFORATED, etc. [and one wished to plug the hole, he may not place wax upon it].[19]

The Gemara discusses a related law:

מִישְׁחָא – Regarding the use of **thick oil** to plug a cask, רַב אָסַר – **Rav prohibits** this on the Sabbath, וּשְׁמוּאֵל שָׁרֵי – **whereas Shmuel permits** it.

The dispute is explained:

מַאן דְּאָסַר גָּזְרִינַן מִשּׁוּם שַׁעֲוָה – **The one who prohibits** it maintains that **[the Sages] issued a decree** against using oil in this way **because of wax.**[20] וּמַאן דְּשָׁרֵי לֹא גָּזְרִינַן – **And the one who permits** it maintains that **[the Sages] did not issue** such **a decree.**

The Gemara cites a different report of Rav's position on this matter:

אָמַר לֵיהּ רַב שְׁמוּאֵל בַּר בַּר חָנָה לְרַב יוֹסֵף – **Rav Shmuel bar bar Chanah said to Rav Yosef:** בְּפֵירוּשׁ אָמַרְתְּ לָן מִשְּׁמֵיהּ דְּרַב מִישְׁחָא שָׁרֵי – **You explicitly told us in the name of Rav that** using **thick oil** in this way **is permitted.**

The Gemara discusses another law relating to the extraction of wine from a cask on the Sabbath:

אָמַר טָבוּת רִישְׁבָּא אָמַר שְׁמוּאֵל – **Tavus Rishba**[21] **said in the name of Shmuel:** הַאי טַרְפָּא דְּאָסָא אָסוּר – **That** practice of placing a **myrtle leaf** into the hole in a cask **is forbidden.**[22]

The Gemara explains the basis for this prohibition:

מַאי טַעְמָא – **What is the reason** for this? רַב יֵימַר מִדִּפְתִּי אָמַר –

NOTES

13. I.e. inserting a hollow reed into a hole in the cask so that wine will flow out, as through a spigot (*Rashi*).

14. I.e. trimming it so that it perfectly fits the hole (*Rashi*). [This would qualify as perfecting a vessel, and would be prohibited under the labor of *striking the final blow.*]

15. I.e. the reed was cut to length before the Sabbath, but the person did not place it in the hole to see whether it fits perfectly or needs trimming (*Rashi*).

16. I.e. one may find that the reed does not fit perfectly, and he would be tempted to trim it in violation of the Sabbath (see *Rambam, Hil. Shabbos* 23:6; see also *Mishnah Berurah* to 314:5).

17. [The restrictions on Sabbath labor are greater than those that apply on Yom Tov. E.g. certain *melachos,* such as those needed for the preparation of food, are permitted on Yom Tov but forbidden on the Sabbath.]

18. [I.e. the only time the Tanna Kamma permitted placing the tube in the hole was when the tube had once been in there and had fallen out. When the tube had *never* been in the hole – and it was therefore unknown whether it fits there perfectly or requires trimming – the Tanna Kamma does not permit its placement.]

19. For he would most likely smear the wax in order to make it adhere properly to the cask. He would then transgress the forbidden labor of מְמָרֵחַ, *smoothing,* a *toladah* of מְמַחֵק, *smoothing hides* (*Rashi* to 146a ד״ה שהוא ממרח).

20. I.e. smearing oil, even thick oil, does not constitute the forbidden labor of *smoothing* [for the consistency of oil is too thin for this labor to apply]. Nevertheless, the Sages prohibited smearing thick oil, since its consistency is close to that of wax (see *Mishnah Berurah* to 314:11).

21. The person's given name was Tavus. *Rashi* earlier (17b ד״ה רישבא) states that the appellation *Rishba* (from נִשְׁבִּין, *nets*) was given to him because he was a hunter, spreading nets to trap game (cf. *Aruch,* ערך רשבא).

22. A myrtle leaf is naturally curved, so that when it is placed in a hole in a wine cask, wine would flow down it as if down a gutter (*Rashi*). It is in this connection that the Gemara states that placing a myrtle leaf to direct the flow of wine from a cask is prohibited on the Sabbath.

[*Tosafos* (ד״ה משום מרזב) seems to understand that the leaf was not naturally shaped like a gutter, but that it was common practice for people to slightly fold the leaves to take on a gutter-like shape. According to *Tosafos,* it is this practice of folding the leaf that the Gemara prohibits.]

לא א ב מיי' פכ"ג מהלכות שבת הל"א סמג לאוין סה טוש"ע או"ח סימן שיד סעיף ג:
לב ג מיי' פכ"ג מהלכות שבת הל"ו סמג שם טוש"ע או"ח סימן שיד סעיף ז:
לג ד מיי' פי"ט מהלכות טומאת מת הל"א:
לד ה ו מיי' פכ"ג מהל' שבת הלכה ו סמג לאוין סה טוש"ע או"ח סימן שיד סעיף ה:
לה ז מיי' שם טוש"ע שם סעיף יא:
לו ח שם סעיף ה:
לז ט י מיי' פכ"ב מהל' שבת הלכה יז סמג שם טוש"ע או"ח סימן שא סעיף לה:
לח כ מיי' פכ"ב מהל' שבת הלכה כ טור או"ח סימן שיח:
לט ל מ נ ס מיי' שם הל"כ סמג לאוין סה טור שו"ע או"ח סימן שא סעיף מה:

משום ריחשא ווי"א אין מוסיפים זימנין דלא תקניה מעיקרא ואתי לארוחי ביה דרש רב נחמן משום רבי יוחנן הלכה כיש אומרים: א ושוין שנוקבין נקב ישן לכתחלה: אמר רב יהודה אמר שמואל לא שנו אלא במקום העשוי לשמר אבל לחזק אסור היכי דמי לשמר היכי דמי לחזק ב א"ר חסדא למעלה מן היין זהו לשמר למטה מן היין זהו לחזק (א) רבא אמר ג למטה מן היין נמי זהו לשמר והיכי דמי לחזק כגון שניקבה למטה מן השמרים א"ל אביי לרבא תניא דמסייע לך ד בית סתום יש לו ארבע אמות פרץ את פצימיו אין לו ד' אמות ה בית סתום אינו מטמא כל סביביו פרץ את פצימיו מטמא כל סביביו גובתא רב אסר ושמואל שרי ו מחתך לכתחלה דכ"ע לא פליגי דאסור אהדורי דכ"ע לא פליגי דשרי כי פליגי דחתיכה ולא מתקנא מאן דאסר גזרינן דילמא אתי למיחתך לכתחלה ומאן דשרי ז לא גזרינן כתנאי אין חותכין שפופרת ביו"ט וא"צ לומר בשבת נפלה (אין) מחזירין אותה בשבת ואין צריך לומר ביו"ט ור' יאשיה מיקל ר' יאשיה אהייא אילימא ארישא הא קמתקן מנא אלא אסיפא ת"ק נמי מישרא קשרי אלא דחתיכה ולא מתקנא איכא בינייהו מ"ס גזרינן ומ"ס לא גזרינן דרש רב שישא בריה דרב אידי משמיה דר' יוחנן הלכה כר' יאשיה: ואם היתה נקובה וכו': מישחא רב אסר ושמואל שרי מאן דאסר ח גזרינן משום שעוה ומאן דשרי לא גזרינן אמר ליה רב שמואל בר בר חנה לרב יוסף בפירוש אמרת לן משמיה דרב מישחא שרי אמר טבות רישבא אמר שמואל האי טרפא דאסא אסור מ"ט רב יימר מדפתי אמר גזירה משום מרזב רב אשי אמר ט גזירה שמא יקטום מאי בינייהו [א] איכא בינייהו דקטים ומנחי בי סדיא רב אסר ושמואל י שרי ברכין דכולי עלמא לא פליגי דשרי כ בקשין דכ"ע לא פליגי דאסור כי פליגי במיצעי מאן דאסר מיחזי כמשוי ומאן דשרי לא מיחזי כמשוי והא דרב לאו ל בפירוש איתמר אלא מכללא איתמר דרב איקלע להההוא אתרא דלא הוה ליה רווחא נפק יתיב בכרמלית אייתו ליה בי סדיא לא יתיב מאן דחזא סבר משום דבי סדיא אסור ולא היא דרב אכרוזי מכרזי בי סדיא שרי מ ומשום כבוד רבותינו לא ישב עליו ומאן נינהו רב כהנא ורב אסי: **מתני'** נ נותנין תבשיל לתוך הבור בשביל שיהא שמור ואת המים היפים ברעים בשביל שיצננו ואת הצונן בחמה בשביל שיחמו ס מי שנשרו כליו בדרך במים מהלך בהן ואינו חושש הגיע לחצר החיצונה שוטחן בחמה [ב] אבל לא כנגד העם: **גמ'** פשיטא מהו דתימא ניגזר משום אשווי גומות קא משמע לן: ואת המים היפים ברעים: פשיטא סיפא איצטריכא ליה ואת הצונן בחמה הא נמי פשיטא מהו דתימא ניגזור דילמא אתי לאטמוני ברמץ קמ"ל: י מי שנשרו וכו': אמר רב יהודה אמר רב ס כל מקום שאסרו חכמים מפני מראית העין אפילו בחדרי חדרים אסור תנן שוטחן בחמה אבל לא כנגד העם תנאי היא דתניא שוטחן בחמה אבל לא כנגד העם ר"א ור"ש נ אוסרין אמר רב הונא

המנער

רש"י

משום ריחשא. שלא יכנס בו שרץ כגון ז) נמייה וחולדה שממיתים את התרנגולים: זימנין דלא תקניה מעיקרא. שיהא כדי להוציא הכל ולהכניס את האויר: לא שנו. דנוקבין: אלא במקום. דסתימה זו לא נעשית אלא לשמור ריח היין שלא יצא ויתקלקל וכיון דלאו סתימה מעלייתא עבדי לה לאו כלום הוא: לחזק. שיחזק הכלי שלא יצא יינו הואיל וסתימה מעלייתא היא כי הדר נקיב לה הוי כפותח לכתחלה: למטה מן היין נמי לשמר הוא. כיון דלאו כובד היין נשען עליו סגי ליה בסתימה כל דהו: למטה מן השמרים. אבל שוליו שכל כובד היין נשען שם: תניא דמסייע לך. דלא פקע שם פתח מיניה אלא בסתימה מעלייתא: בית סתום יש לו ד"א. קיי"ל בבבא בתרא חצר מתחלקת לפי פתחיה לפי פתח הבתים הפתוחין לה אם באו לחלק את החצר בין שנים שהיה לזה בית שפתוחין לו לחצר שני פתחים ולזה בית שפתוחין לו לחצר ד' פתחים נוטל לכל פתח ארבע אמות בחצר נגד פתחו למדת רוחב פתחו והשאר חולקין בשוה ואם נסתם אחד מהם קודם חלוקת החצר ולא פירץ את פצימיו אלא סתם בין שני הפצימין אינו מפסיד [דין] פתחו בכך פירץ את פצימיו ואח"כ סתמו פקע שם פתח מיניה: בית סתום. והמת בתוכו אינו מטמא סביביו: פרץ פצימיו. וסתמו נעשה קבר ומטמא סביביו ד"א כדאמר בסוטה (ד' מד.) מת תופס ד"א לטומאה וגזרה דרבנן שמא יאהיל ולא יבין: גובתא. לתקוע קנה חלול בנקב החבית שילא היין דרך הקנה: מחתך. רונגי"ר לתקנה למדת הנקב: אהדורי. אם נפלה: ולא מתקנא. לא ניתנה בנקב לידע אם למדתו היא: אי לימא ארישא. לחותכה ולשפותה: משחא. שמן עב: אסור. למרחו: טרפא דאסא. לתת עלה של הדס בנקב החבית שהעלה עשוי כמרזב והיין זב דרך שם: גזירה משום מרזב. שמא יכין מרזב: שמא יקטום. העלה מן הענף וכיון דקטמיה הוה ליה כמתקן כלי כדתניא במסכת בילה (דף לג:) לחלות בו שיניו לא יקטמנו ואם קטמו חייב חטאת: בי סדיא. לבדין שקורין פלטר"ש ועשויין לקפלן תחתיו במקום הכר או הכסת: רב אסר. להביאו דרך מלבוש דרך רשות הרבים כשהוא מעוטף בו: ברכין. שדרכן להתחמם בהן: דשרו. דמלבוש הן: ולא הוה ליה רווחא. בבית למקום מושבם של תלמידים: ומשום כבוד רבותינו. שלא היה להן דבר לישב עליו ויושבין על גבי קרקע: רב כהנא ורב אסי. תלמידי חברים היו לו ס): **מתני'** לתוך הבור. שאין בו מים: שיהא שמור. שלא יסריח מחמת החום: ואת המים היפים ברעים. כלי מלא מים יפים לתוך מקוה מים רעים להשתמר (ב) שילטנו ולא יחמו: מי שנשרו. שנפלו למים בשבת: לחצר החיצונה. הסמוכה למבוא העיר בתוך העיר שהוא מקום משתמר: שוטחן בחמה. ליבשן: אבל לא כנגד העם. שיחשדוהו שכבסן: **גמ'** פשיטא. דנותנין תבשיל לתוך הבור: גומות. שבקרקע הבור שיהו שוין להושיב הקדרה:

המנער

תוספות

משום ריחשא. ואטו פתחא אחרינא דליכא למיחש לריחשא לא גזרינן דדוקא אטו לול של תרנגולין גזרינן דלא מסקי אינשי אדעתייהו שיהא עשוי להכניס ולהוציא:

פרץ פצימיו מטמא כל סביביו. פי' בקונטרס כל סביביו ד' אמות כקבר ואין נראה לנקיי הרב ר' שמשון זצ"ל דכיון דמסיימי מחילתא וליח לן למיחש שמא יעלה על הבית ויאהיל עליו ולא ידע לית לן למימר דמטמא ד' אמות כל סביביו כדמוכח בסוטה פרק משוח מלחמה (ד' מד.) גבי חצר הקבר העומד בתוכה טהור הכי מילי חצר הקבר דמסיימא מחילתא אבל מת בעלמא תפיס ומשמע דכמת נמי היכא דמסיימא לא נטמא כל סביביו ד' אמות אלא נראה לו דהכי פי' זזין באותו בית שבולטין מתוך לבית מכל צד ויש בהם פותח טפח בכל אחד אם הבית סתום ועדיין נראית בו צורת הפתח אינו מטמא שסתמו של מת עומד לצאת דרך הפתח פרץ פצימיו וחזר ובנאו כשאר כותל ולא נותר בו כלל פתח מטמא כל סביביו דכל חד וחד איכא לספוקי דילמא דרך אותו מקום יצא מן הבית מיהו לאו פירכא היא כולי האי מה שהקשה לפירוש הקונטרס דר"ל שלא חלקו חכמים במת ועוד נראה דלא קשה כלל לפי' הקונטרס דבית נמי לא מסיימי מחילתא שהוא מטמא הנוגע בכתלים אפילו לא יעלה על גביו כקבר שמטמא במגע אפילו מן הצד כדתניא בספרי בפרשת פרה אדומה או בקבר זה קבר סתום או אינו אלא קבר פתוח אמרת ק"ו ומה אהל שמקבל טומאה אינו מטמא מכל צדדין כשהוא פתוח קבר שאינו מקבל טומאה אינו דין שלא יטמא מכל צדדין כשהוא פתוח אלמא כשהוא סתום מטמא אף הנוגע מן הצד:

הלכה כרבי יאשיה. הלכך מותר לתת לכתחלה גובתא שקורין רוזי"ל בחבית: **משום** מרזב. פי' הרב פור"ת שלא יבוא ליתן על גגו מרזב וקשה דבגובתא נמי נגזר אלא נראה לרבי כפי' הקונט' שלא יתקן מרזב ליינו שיפול היין בתוכו וילך למרחוק דבשלוקת עלה של הדס ומקפלו כעין מרזב נראה כעושה מרזב אבל בגובתא שאינו עושה בו שום מעשה לא גזרינן. מ"ר:

איתי ליה בי סדיא. בי מילעי הוה דלאו הכי היכי ליתמר מכללא: **מי** שנשרו כליו במים. בדרך גרסינן ט) לשון נפילה לא כפי' הקונטרס לעיל בפרק במה אשה (דף סה.) שנשרו במי גשמים דהא אמרינן בבילה בפרק משילין (דף לט:) מאן דתני מנשירין לא משתבש כלומר מי שנשרו כליו במים בדרך אלמא לשון נפילה הוא. מ"ר:

המנער

רבינו חננאל

וי"א אין מוסיפין דזמנין דלא תקניה מעיקרא ואתי לארוחי ביה הלכתא כוותיה דדרש רב נחמן בר רב חסדא משמיה דר' יוחנן הלכה כי"א. ושוין שנוקבין בנקב ישן לכתחלה ואמר רב יהודה משמיה דשמואל אינו מותר לפתוח נקב ישן אלא במקום העשוי לשמר פי' להוציא היין מן השמרים אבל לחזק אסור פי' היה נקב בחבית וסתמו שלא יהא שותת. וחלקו רב חסדא ורבה והלכתא כרבה דתניא מסייעתו ואלו דברי רבה רבה אמר למטה מן היין נמי זהו לשמר ומותר לפותחו והיכי דמי לחזק כגון שנקבה למטה מן השמרים דמוכחא מלתא שאין אדם עושה נקב בקרקעיתא של חבית להוציא יין ולא לשמר. עשאו מפני כשמפנה החבית הופכה על פיה. וזה הנקב כיון שסתמו נעשה סתום. זה בגופה של חבית ובטל מלהיות נקב בו וחשוב כפתח בית הנסתם בפירוץ פצימין שנסתלק ממנו דין פתח לגמרי. גובתא שהיא שפופרת של קנה או של עצים שנותנין בנקב החבית או ביד הנוד של יין להיות מושכין ממנו יין מן החבית או מן הנוד. רב אסר ושמואל שרי ואוקימנא חלוקתן בשפופרת חתוכה ואינה מתוקנת להכניסה לנקב אבל לחתוך דברי הכל אסור. ואם היא חתוכה ומתוקנת דברי הכל מותר להחזירה בנקב החבית או בנוד למשוך ממנה יין. והעמדנו עוד חלוקת רב ושמואל כתנאי. דתניא אין חותכין שפופרת ביו"ט ואין צ"ל בשבת. נפלה מחזירין בשבת. ואין צ"ל ביו"ט. ור' יאשיה מיקל ודייקי' עלה ר' יאשיה אהייא מיקל אילימא ארישא שאמר ת"ק אין חותכין כלומר אין חותכין מקנה גדול חתיכה לעשות' שפופרת בהא ר' יאשיה מיקל הא קא מתקן כלי בשבת אלא שאמר ת"ק נפלה מחזירין אותה. בהא לימא ר' יאשיה מיקל מי החמיר שיאמר בזה מיקל הלא בזה גם ת"ק מותר קאמר. ותריצנא אלא לאו דחתיכה ולא מתקנה איכא בינייהו וכך הציעה. אין עושין שפופרת ביו"ט ואין צ"ל בשבת. ואפי' חתכה ולא מתקנה אסור אבל אם היתה כבר בחבית ונפלה מחזירין אותה בשבת ואין צ"ל ביו"ט ור' יאשיה מיקל בחתיכה ולא מתקנה נמצאו דברי רב כת"ק ודברי שמואל כר' יאשיה והלכה כר' יאשיה ודרש רב שישא בריה דרב אידי משמא דר' יוחנן הלכתא כר' יאשיה וזה שאמר חתכה ולא מתקנה לאו שצריכה תיקון כלי כגון סכין וכדומה לו אלא תיקון ביד בלבד. ואם צריכה תיקון בסכין או זולתו סכין כלי אחר אסורה. ואם היתה החבית נקובה לא יתן עליה שעוה מפני שממרח. כלומר סותם כדאמרינן התם לענין חבית שניקבה וסתמה שמרים כו' מורח מן הצדדין. וכיון דר' יהודה דמתניתין וריב"ז ורב ושמואל אמרי ש"מ שאסור לתת שעוה בחבית. וכן משחא. רב אסר גזירה במשחא אטו שעוה. והלכתא כוותיה: טרפא דאסא. פי' עלה הדס שנותנין על הנקב של חבית להיות מקלח בו היין ולא יהיה שותת בדופני החבית. לדברי הכל אסור ליטול עלה של הדס בשבת ולשומו בנקב של חבית כמרזב. ואפילו רב אשי לא התיר אלא שאם היה הנקב מושך ממנו א) אבל לתתו לכתחלה אוסר: בי סדיא רב אסר ושמואל שרי אין זה מקומו אלא בשביל שהזכיר השמועות שחלקו בהן רב אסר ושמואל שרי נסבה בגררא. ופשוטה היא. כסת זו שחלקו בה כסת בינונית לא דקה ולא קשה. ומסקינן בה אפילו זו מותר לטלטלה: נותנין תבשיל בתוך הבור בשביל שיהא שמור. פי' בור זה אין בו מים ונותן התבשיל בקרקעיתו מהו דתימא לגזור דלמא אתי לאשויי גומות קמ"ל דלא גזרינן. ואת המים היפים ברעים פשיטא ואת הצונן בחמין פשיטא מהו דתימא לגזור דלמא אתי לאשויי גומות ב) ברמץ קמ"ל דלא גזרינן: מתני' מי שנשרו כליו בדרך כו'. אמר רב יהודה אמר רב כל מקום שאסרו חכמים מפני מראית העין אפילו בחדרי חדרים אסור. איני והא תנן שוטחן בחמה אבל לא כנגד העם ואוקימנא

חשק שלמה על רבינו חננאל א) נראה דצ"ל מותר בנקב מותר למשוך ממנו: ב) אינו מובן. ואולי צ"ל דלמא אתי לאטמוני ברמץ וכדאיתא בגמ':

מסורת הש"ס

א) [פי' להוציא היין את השמרים. ערוך ערך חזק ע"ש], ב) כ"ב יב., ג) [ברכות ט. וש"נ], ד) לעיל לט., ה) בילה ט. ע"ש, ו) לעיל סד: בילה ט. ע"ז יב., ז) עי' לעיל נה: רש"י ד"ה קטנה וכו' ומשמע שנמייה וחולדה מיות הן, ח) [כדאיתא סנהדרין לו:], ט) נ"ל דגרסינן לשון נפילה דלאו הנ"ין במהרק הוי לשון שריה. רש"י, י) [ועי' תוס' בילה ט.: ד"ה מי שנשרו].

הגהות הב"ח

(א) גמ' רבא אמר למטה וכו' א"ל אביי לרבא: (ב) רש"י ד"ה ואת המים וכו' להשתמר שיצננו ולא יחמו:

גליון הש"ס

גמ' אמר ר"ח למעלה מן היין זהו לשמר. ג' הרי"ף למעלה מן היין זהו לחזק למטה מן היין זהו לשמר רבה אמר למעלה וכו': שם ומשום כבוד רבותינו לא ישב. עי' שבועות דף מז ע"א תוס' ד"ה הוה יתיב:

הגהות הגר"א

[א] גמ' איכא בינייהו דקטים ומנח. נ"ב פי' שכבר קטמו קודם עוד הרבה קטמו קוטמים טוב. וח"ש ומנח. אבל גורסת הרי"ף והרא"ש וש"פ ומנח: [ב] שם שוטחן בחמה. נ"ב דווקא (ועמ"ש רבינו באו"ח סימן ש"א ס"ק ק"ס):

ליקוטי רש"י

בית סתום. שלא פרץ פצימיו. כשנסתם הפתח לא סלק מזוזתו [ומשקופו] ומפתנו דגלי דעתיה דלא לפותחו לאחר זמן [ב"ב יא.]. שהיה לו פתח לחצר ויש לו ד' אמות. כשחולקין החצר אם באו לחלוק כאילו הוא פתוח [שם]. פרץ את פצימיו. מטמא כל סביביו. [סוטה מד.]. בפירוש אמרת לן משמיה דרב. לפני תלמודך [לעיל נט:]. טבות רישבא. ליד עופות כמו אין פורסין רשתות ליונים (ב"ק עט:) טבות שם אדם [תענית י.].

[המשך בדף קמז.]

Rav Yeimar of Difti said: גְּזֵירָה מִשּׁוּם מַרְזֵב – **A decree** was issued **because of** making a **gutter.**[23]

Another Amora gives a different reason for the decree:

רַב אַשִׁי אָמַר – **Rav Ashi said:** גְּזֵירָה שֶׁמָּא יִקְטוֹם – **A decree** was issued **lest one pluck** the leaf.[24]

The Gemara inquires:

מַאי בֵּינַיְיהוּ – **What is** the practical difference **between these** two views?

The Gemara replies:

אִיכָּא בֵּינַיְיהוּ – There is indeed **a difference between them;** דִּקְטִים וּמַנְחִי – it arises in a case **where [leaves] have** already **been plucked and placed** in readiness before the onset of the Sabbath.[25]

The Gemara begins a new discussion:[26]

בֵּי סַדְיָא – Concerning **felt padding,** רַב אָסַר – **Rav prohibits** one to wrap himself with this cloth and transport it through a public domain, וּשְׁמוּאֵל שָׁרֵי – **and Shmuel permits** this.[27]

The Gemara clarifies the parameters of the dispute:

בְּרַכִּין – Concerning lengths of **soft** felt, דְּכוּלֵּי עָלְמָא לֹא פְּלִיגֵי דְּשָׁרֵי – **everyone agrees that it is permissible** to transport it in this way.[28] בְּקָשִׁין – And **concerning** lengths of **stiff** felt, דְּכוּלֵּי עָלְמָא לֹא פְּלִיגֵי דְּאָסוּר – **everyone agrees that** its transport in this way **is prohibited.**[29] כִּי פְּלִיגֵי בְּמִיצְעֵי – **Where they disagree is concerning** cloth of **an intermediate** texture. מַאן דְּאָסַר מֶיחֱזֵי כְּמַשּׂוֹי – **The one who prohibits** (Rav) argues that someone wrapped in cloth of an intermediate texture **looks like** he is carrying **a burden,** not like he is wearing clothing. וּמַאן דְּשָׁרֵי לֹא מֶיחֱזֵי כְּמַשּׂוֹי – **And the one who permits,** (Shmuel) maintains that it **does not look like** he is carrying **a burden;** rather, he indeed appears to be wearing clothing.

The Gemara notes that Rav's opinion in this matter was gleaned through an inference:

וְהָא דְּרַב לָאו בְּפֵירוּשׁ אִיתְּמַר – And that **which Rav** purportedly ruled here **was not stated explicitly** by him, אֶלָּא מִכְּלָלָא אִיתְּמַר – **but rather was stated as an inference** by someone who observed his behavior. The incident through which Rav's ruling was inferred occurred as follows: דְּרַב אִיקְלַע לְהַהוּא אַתְרָא דְּלָא הֲוָה לֵיהּ רַוְוחָא – It once happened **that Rav came to a certain place where there was not** enough **room** for everyone to sit, נָפַק יָתִיב בְּכַרְמְלִית – so **he** left the house and **sat in an** adjacent *karmelis.*[30] אַיְיתוּ לֵיהּ בֵּי סַדְיָא – The students then **brought him** some lengths of **felt padding** to sit upon, לֹא יָתִיב – but he **did not sit** upon them, but rather seated himself directly upon the ground.

The Gemara continues:

מַאן דְּחָזָא סָבַר – Now, someone who observed Rav do this **concluded** מִשּׁוּם דְּבֵי סַדְיָא אָסוּר – that the reason Rav did not sit on the material was **because** he maintained that carrying **felt padding** from domain to domain **is forbidden,** even if one wears it like a robe.[31] וְלֹא הִיא – **However, it is not** actually **so.** דְּרַב אַכְרוּזֵי מַכְרִיז בֵּי סַדְיָא שָׁרֵי – **For,** indeed, it is on record that **Rav publicly declared** the wearing of **felt padding** to be **permissible,**[32] וּמִשּׁוּם כְּבוֹד רַבּוֹתֵינוּ לֹא יָשַׁב עָלָיו – **and it was** only **out of deference for** the other **Rabbis that he did not sit upon it.**[33]

The Gemara inquires:

וּמַאן נִינְהוּ – **And who were these** other rabbis to whom Rav wished to show deference?

The Gemara replies:

רַב כָּהֲנָא וְרַב אַסִּי – They were **Rav Kahana and Rav Assi.**[34]

NOTES

23. If the use of a leaf in this manner was permitted on the Sabbath, people might presume that they are also permitted to fashion an artificial gutter-like vessel, through which wine could be made to flow from the cask (*Rashi,* as interpreted by *Tosafos* ד״ה משום מרזב). The latter practice would surely constitute a transgression of the Sabbath, and therefore the Sages prohibited even the use of a leaf in this way.

It is noteworthy that a decree was established only against the practice of placing a leaf in the hole of a wine cask, but not, as we have seen above (according to Shmuel, at least), against placing a hollow reed in the hole to serve as a spigot. Addressing this point, *Tosafos* (ד״ה משום מרזב) explain that the Sages were concerned only about the case of the leaf, for there one physically improves the leaf (folding it slightly to shape it like a gutter) before placing it in the hole (see above, note 22). Were this permitted, people might reason that actively building an artificial gutter is also permissible, so the Sages banned the practice. The hollowed reed, however, is *naturally* shaped like a spigot, and no human act is required to make it take that shape. There was thus no fear that the use of a reed might lead people to assume that the *active creation* of a similar utensil was permissible.

24. Plucking a leaf from a (detached) branch for this purpose would constitute the creation of a vessel (מְתַקֵּן כְּלִי) and would be prohibited under the labor of *striking the final blow* (*Rashi,* from *Beitzah* 33b; see *Kesef Mishneh* to *Hil. Shabbos* 23:6; *Beis Yosef, Orach Chaim* 314:5).

25. According to Rav Ashi, if one plucked leaves before the Sabbath, he may put one in the hole on the Sabbath, for there is no danger that he might pluck another leaf. But according to Rav Yeimar, even if the person has a number of leaves already prepared, he still may not put one in the hole, since this appears as if he has created a gutter (*Tur* to *Orach Chaim* 314; cf. *Rabbeinu Chananel;* see *Beur Halachah* to 314:5 ד״ה במקום). See *Shaar HaTziyun* §23, who discusses how many leaves must be prepared.

26. The Gemara now embarks on an unrelated topic. Earlier, we had a dispute between Rav and Shmuel (concerning the case of the spigot) and the following discussion was therefore appended as another example of a dispute between Rav and Shmuel in Sabbath law (*Rabbeinu Chananel*).

27. The reference is to lengths of felt cloth. These were commonly folded and used in place of a pillow as a seat cushion (*Rashi*). According to Shmuel, these lengths of felt qualify as clothing when a person wraps himself in them and "wears" them – and thus, transporting them through a public domain in this way is permissible. According to Rav, however, one wrapped in felt *looks like* he is carrying a burden (not wearing clothes). Thus, the Rabbis decreed against transporting felt in this way, since it appears like a transgression of the *melachah* of *carrying* (see *Rambam, Hil Shabbos* 19:17).

28. It is not unusual to wrap oneself in soft felt to keep warm (*Rashi*). Thus, one wrapped in this kind of felt surely appears to be "wearing clothing."

29. Since people do not normally wrap themselves in such stiff material, a person wrapped in this kind of cloth does not appear to be wearing it. Rather, it seems as if he is carrying a burden.

30. A *karmelis* is an area into which it is Rabbinically prohibited to transport items from a private or public domain. Likewise, it is Rabbinically prohibited to traverse four *amos* in a *karmelis* while carrying something.

31. The observer thought that Rav refused to sit on it because it had been impermissibly carried from a private domain. [It was apparently clear that the padding that had been carried for Rav was of intermediate stiffness (*Tosafos; Rosh*).]

32. [Rav had once announced that it is permissible to wear felt padding of intermediate stiffness into a public domain.]

33. There were other rabbis present who did not have cushions and were sitting on the ground. Thus, out of respect for them, Rav declined the cushion and sat on the ground along with them (*Rashi*).

34. These were students of Rav who had advanced to the point that Rav considered them colleagues (*Rashi;* see also *Rashi* to *Sanhedrin* 36b ד״ה כי קאמר רב) [and therefore, they merited the title with which our Gemara refers to them: רַבּוֹתֵינוּ, *our Rabbis*] (cf. *Tosafos* to *Shevuos* 47a, ד״ה הוה and to *Bava Basra* 34a [ד״ה הוה [ב׳).

עין משפט נר מצוה

לא א ב מיי' פכ"ג מהלכות שבת הל"א סמג לאוין סה טוש"ע או"ח סימן שיד סעיף ג:
לב ג מיי' פ"ג מהלכות שכנים הל"ז טוש"ע חו"מ סימן קעג סעיף ז:
לג ד מיי' פ"ו מהלכות טומאת מת הל"א:
לד ה ו מיי' פכ"ג מהל' שבת הלכה ו סמג לאוין סה טוש"ע או"ח סימן שיד סעיף ה:
לה ז מיי' שם הלכה יא סמג שם טור שו"ע שם סעיף יא:
לו ח שם סעיף ה:
לז ט י מיי' פי"ט מהל' שבת הלכה יז סמג שם טוש"ע או"ח סימן שא סעיף לה:
לח כ מיי' פכ"ב מהל' שבת הלכה ט טור או"ח סימן שיח:
לט ל מ נ מיי' שם הל"כ סמג לאוין סה טור שו"ע או"ח סימן שא סעיף מה:

רבינו חננאל

וי"א אין מוסיפין דזמנין דלא תקניה מעיקרא ואתי לארוחי ביה הלכתא כוותיה דדרש רב נחמן בר רב חסדא משמיה דר' יוחנן הלכה כי"א. ושוין שנוקבין בנקב ישן לכתחלה ואמר רב יהודה משמיה דשמואל אינו מותר לפתוח נקב ישן אלא במקום העשוי לשמר פי' להוציא היין מן השמרים אבל לחזק אסור פי' היה נקב בחבית וסתמו שלא יהא שותת. וחלקו רב חסדא ורבה והלכתא כרבה דתניא מסייעתו ואלו דברי רבה רבה אמר למטה מן היין נמי זהו לשמר ומותר לפותחו והיכי דמי לחזק כגון שנקבה למטה מן השמרים דמוכחא מלתא שאין אדם עושה נקב בקרקעיתא של חבית להוציא יין ולא לשמר. עשאו מפני כשמפנה החבית הופכה על פיה. וזה הנקב כיון שסתמו נעשה סתום. זה בגופה של חבית ובטל מלהיות נקב בו וחשוב כפתח בית הנסתם בפירוץ פצימין שנסתלק ממנו דין פתח לגמרי. גובתא שהיא שפופרת של קנה או של עצים שנותנין בנקב החבית או ביד הנוד של יין להיות מושכין ממנו יין מן החבית או מן הנוד. רב אסר ושמואל שרי ורווקמא חלוקתן בשפופרת חתוכה ואינה מתוקנת להכניסה לנקב אבל לא לחתוך דברי הכל אסור. ואם היא חתוכה ומתוקנת דברי הכל מותר להחזירה בנקב החבית או בנוד למשוך ממנה יין. העמדנו עוד חלוקת רב ושמואל כתנאי. דתניא אין חותכין שפופרת ביו"ט ואין צ"ל בשבת. נפלה אין מחזירין בשבת. ואין צ"ל ביו"ט. ור' יאשיה מיקל ודייק עלה ר' יאשיה אהיא אילימא ארישא שאמר ת"ק אין חותכין מכלל דר' יאשיה אמר חותכין אין חותכין מקנה גדול חתיכה לעשות שפופרת בהא ר' יאשיה לא קא מתקן כלי בשבת אלא שאמר ת"ק נפלה אין מחזירין אותה. בהא לימא ר' יאשיה מיקל מי החזיר שאמר בזה מיקל הלא בזה גם ת"ק מותר קאמר. ותריצנא אלא לאו דחתיכה ולא מתקנה איכא בינייהו וכך הציעה.

א) [פי' להוציא היין מן השמרי'. ערוך ערך חזק ע"ש], ב) ב"ב יב, ג) [ברכו' ט. וש"נ], ד) לעיל לט., ה) ביצה לה:, ו) לעיל סד: ביצה ט. ע"ז יב., ז) עי' לעיל נא: רש"י ד"ה קטנה ושם משמע שנמייה וחולדה חיות הן, ח) [כדאיתא סנהדרין לו:], ט) ר"ל דגרסי' הט"ן דנשרו בקמץ לשון נפילה דאלו הט"ן בחירק הוי לשון שרייה. רש"א, י) [ועי' תוס' ביצה לה: ד"ה מי שנשרו].

הגהות הב"ח

(א) גמ' רבה אמר למטה וכו' א"ל אביי לרבה: (ב) רש"י ד"ה ואת המים וכו' להשתמר שילטננו ולא יחמו:

גליון הש"ס

גמ' אמר ר"ח למעלה מן היין זהו לשמר. ג' הרי"ף למעלה מן היין זהו לחזק למטה מן היין זהו לשמר רבה אמר למעלה וכו': שם ומשום כבוד רבותינו לא ישב. עי' שבועות דף מז ע"א תוס' ד"ה הוה יתיב:

הגהות הגר"א

[א] גמ' איכא בינייהו דקטים ומנח. נ"ב פי' שהוא קטוס ויש עוד הרבה קטומים טור. ח"ש ומנחי. אבל גירסת הרי"ף והרא"ש וש"פ ומנח: [ב] שם שוטחן בחמה. נ"ב דווקא (ועמ"ש רבינו באו"ח סימן ש"א ס"ק ק"ה):

ליקוטי רש"י

בית סתום. שלא פרץ פצימיו. כשנכנס פתחו לא סלק מזוזתו [ומשקופו ומפתן] דגלי דעתיה דלא סילק נפשיה ומשקופו לפתוחו לאחר זמן [ב"ב יא:]. שהיה לו ד' אמות. בחלוקת החצר אם בא לחלוק החצר לפי פתחיו [שם יב.]. ופרץ את פצימיו. והלכה ופתח לחוץ ופתח מבית לבית הרי הוא כפתח סתום. אינו מטמא סביביו. אלא כנגד הפתח. פרץ את פצימיו. הרי הוא כקבר ומכסהו מאהלו לד' אמות כל צד שלא יקרבו לו שיהו טמאים עד טהרתם [ב"ב שם]. מטמא כל סביביו. חכמים גזרו שיהא המת מטמא הכנגבו כלאחר ד' אמות ועושה סביבו עדי שלא יאהילו עליו וכו' [שם]. ... [ליקוטי רש"י ממשיך בדף קמז.]

תוספות

משום ריחשא. ולאו פתחא מעלייתא דליכא למיחש לריחשא לא גזרינן דודאי לאו לנוי של תרנגולין גזרינן דלא מסקי אינשי אדעתייהו שיהא עשוי להכניס ולהוציא:

פורץ פצימיו מטמא כל סביביו. פי' בקונטרס כל סביביו ד' אמות כקבר ואין נראה לזקיני הרב ר' שמשון זצ"ל דכיון דמסיימי מתניתא ולית לן למיחש שמא יעלה על הבית ויאהיל עליו ולא ידע לית לן למימר דמטמא ד' אמות כל סביביו כדמוכח בסוטה בפרק משוח מלחמה (ד' מד.) גבי חצר הקבר העומד בתוכה טהור הני מילי חצר הקבר דמסיימא מילתא אבל מת בעלמא תפיס ומשמע דבמת נמי היכא דמסיימא לא נטמא כל סביביו ד' אמות אלא נראה לו דהכי פי' זיזין באותו בית שבולטין מתוך לבית מכל צד ויש בהם פותח טפח בכל אחד אם הבית סתום ועדיין נראלים בו צורת הפתח אינו מטמא שסתמו של מת עומד לצאת דרך הפתח פרץ פצימיו וחזר ובנאו כשאר כותל ולא נותר בו כלל פתח מטמא כל סביביו דכל חד וחד איכא לספוקי דילמא דרך אותו מקום יצא מן הבית מיהו לאו פירכא היא כולי האי מה שהקשה לפירוש הקונטרס די"ל שלא חלקו חכמים במת ועוד נראה דלא קשה כלל לפי' הקונטרס דבית נמי לא מסיימי מילתא שהוא מטמא הנוגע בכתלים אפילו לא יעלה על גביו כקבר שמטמא במגע אפילו מן הצד כדתניא בספרי בפרשת פרה אדומה או בקבר זה קבר סתום או אינו אלא קבר פתוח אמרת ק"ו ומה אהל שמקבל טומאה אינו מטמא מכל לצדדין כשהוא פתוח קבר שאינו מקבל טומאה אינו דין שלא יטמא מכל לצדדין כשהוא פתוח אלא כשהוא סתום מטמא אף הנוגע מן הצד:

הלכה כרבי יאשיה. הלכך מותר לתת לכתחלה גובתא שקורין רזי"ל בחבית: **משום** מרזב. פי' הרב פור"ת שלא יבוא ליתן על גגו מרזב וקשה דבגובתא נמי נגזר אלא נראה לרבי כפי' הקונט' שלא יתקן מרזב ליינו שיפול היין בתוכו וילך למרחוק דכשלוקח עלה של הדס ומקפלו כעין מרזב נראה כעושה מרזב אבל בגובתא שאינו עושה בו שום מעשה לא גזרינן. מ"ר:

אייתי ליה בי סדיא. בי מילעי הוה דלאי לאו הכי היכי איתמר מכללא: **מי** שנשרו כליו במים. בדרך גרסינן ט) לשון נפילה לא כפי' הקונטרס לעיל בפרק במה אשה (דף סה.) שנשרו כמו גשמים דהא אמרינן בביצה בפרק משילין (דף לה:) מאן דתני מנשירין לא משתבש כדתנן מי שנשרו כליו במים בדרך אלמא לשון נפילה הוא. מ"ר:

המנער

גמרא

משום ריחשא וי"א אין מוספים זימנין דלא תקניה מעיקרא ואתי לארוחי ביה דרש רב נחמן משום רבי יוחנן הלכה כיש אומרים: א ושוין שנוקבין נקב ישן לכתחלה: אמר רב יהודה אמר שמואל לא שנו אלא במקום העשוי לשמר אבל לחזק אסור היכי דמי לשמר היכי דמי לחזק ב) א"ר חסדא למעלה מן היין זהו לשמר למטה מן היין זהו לחזק (א) רבא אמר ג למטה מן היין נמי זהו לשמר והיכי דמי לחזק כגון שניקבה למטה מן השמרים א"ל אביי לרבא תניא דמסייע לך ג) ב בית סתום יש לו ארבע אמות פרץ את פצימיו אין לו ד' אמות ד בית סתום אינו מטמא כל סביביו פרץ את פצימיו מטמא כל סביביו גובתא רב אסר ושמואל שרי ה מחתך לכתחלה דכ"ע לא פליגי דאסור אהדורי דכ"ע לא פליגי דשרי כי פליגי דחתיכה ולא מתקנא מאן דאסר גזרינן דילמא אתי למיחתך לכתחלה ומאן דשרי ו לא גזרינן כתנאי אין חותכין שפופרת ביו"ט וא"צ לומר בשבת נפלה (אין) מחזירין אותה בשבת ואין צריך לומר ביו"ט ור' יאשיה מיקל ר' יאשיה אהייא אילימא ארישא הא קמתקן מנא אלא אסיפא ת"ק נמי מישרא קשרי אלא דחתיכה ולא מתקנא איכא בינייהו מ"ס גזרינן ומ"ס לא גזרינן דרש רב שישא בריה דרב אידי משמיה דר' יוחנן הלכה כר' יאשיה: ואם היתה נקובה וכו': מישחא רב אסר ושמואל שרי מאן דאסר ז גזרינן משום שעוה ומאן דשרי לא גזרינן אמר ליה רב שמואל בר בר חנה לרב יוסף בפירוש אמרת לן משמיה דרב מישחא שרי אמר טבות ריש[ב]א אמר שמואל האי טרפא דאסא אסור מ"ט רב ייִמר מדפתי אמר גזירה משום מרזב רב אשי אמר ח גזירה שמא יקטום מאי בינייהו [א] איכא בינייהו דקטים ומנחי בי סדיא רב אסר ושמואל ט שרי ברכין דכולי עלמא לא פליגי דשרי י בקשין דכ"ע לא פליגי דאסור כי פליגי במיצעי מאן דאסר מיחזי כמשוי ומאן דשרי לא מיחזי כמשוי והא דרב לאו ג) בפירוש איתמר אלא מכללא איתמר דרב איקלע לההוא אתרא דלא הוה ליה רווחא נפק יתיב בכרמלית אייתו ליה בי סדיא לא יתיב מאן דחזא סבר משום דבי סדיא אסור ולא היא דרב אכרוזי מכריז בי סדיא שרי ה ומשום כבוד רבותינו לא ישב עליו ומאן נינהו רב כהנא ורב אסי: **מתני'** ד) כ נותנין תבשיל לתוך הבור בשביל שיהא שמור ואת המים היפים ברעים בשביל שיצננו ואת הצונן בחמה בשביל שיחמו ה) מי שנשרו כליו בדרך במים מהלך בהן ואינו חושש הגיע לחצר החיצונה שוטחן בחמה [ב] אבל לא כנגד העם: **גמ'** פשיטא מהו דתימא ניגזר משום אשווי גומות קא משמע לן: ואת המים היפים ברעים: פשיטא סיפא איצטריכא ליה ואת הצונן בחמה הא נמי פשיטא מהו דתימא ניגזור דילמא אתי לאטמוני ברמץ קמ"ל: ו) מי שנשרו וכו': ז) אמר רב יהודה אמר רב ח כל מקום שאסרו חכמים מפני מראית העין אפילו בחדרי חדרים אסור תנן שוטחן בחמה אבל לא כנגד העם תנאי היא דתניא שוטחן בחמה אבל לא כנגד העם ר"א ור"ש ט אוסרין אמר רב הונא

המנער

רש"י

משום ריחשא. שלא יכנס בו שרץ כגון ז) נמייה וחולדה שממיתים את התרנגולים: זימנין דלא תקניה מעיקרא. שיהא כדי להוציא הבל ולהכניס את האויר: לא שנו. דנוקבין: אלא במקום. דסתימה זו לא נעשית אלא לשמור ריח היין שלא יצא ויתקלקל וכיון דלאו סתימה מעלייתא עבדי לה לאו כלום הוא: לחזק. שיחזק הכלי שלא יצא יינו הוא וסתימה מעלייתא היא כי הדר נקיב לה הוי כפותח לכתחלה: למטה מן היין נמי לשמר הוא. כיון דלאו כובד היין נשען עליו סגי ליה בסתימה כל דהו: למטה מן השמרים. אלא שוליו שכל כובד היין נשען שם: תניא דמסייע לך. דלא פקע שם פתח מיניה אלא בסתימה מעלייתא: בית סתום יש לו ד"א. קיי"ל בבבא בתרא חצר מתחלקת לפי פתחיה לפי פתח הבתים הפתוחין לה אם באו לחלק את החצר בין שני שותפין שיש לזה בית שפתוחין לו לחצר שני פתחים ולזה בית שפתוחין לו לחצר ד' פתחים נוטל לכל פתח ארבע אמות בחצר נגד פתחו למדת רוחב פתחו והשאר חולקין בשוה ואם נסתם אחד מהם קודם חלוקת החצר ולא פירק את פצימיו אלא סתם בין שני הפצימין אינו מפסיד [דין] פתחו בכך פירק את פצימיו וא"כ סתמו פקע שם פתח מיניה: בית סתום. והמת בתוכו אינו מטמא סביביו: פרץ פצימיו. וסתמו נעשה קבר ומטמא סביביו ד"א כדאמר בסוטה (ד' מד.) מת תופס ד"א לטומאה וגזרה דרבנן שמא יאהיל ולא ידע: גובתא. למתקע קנה חלול בנקב החבית שילא היין דרך הקנה: מחתך. לתקנה למדת הנקב: אהדורי. אם נפלה: ולא מתקנא. לא ניתקנה בנקב לידע אם למדתו היא: אי לימא ארישא. אם לחותכה ולשפותה: מישחא. שמן עב: אסור. למרחו: טרפא דאסא. לתת עלה של הדס בנקב החבית שהעלה עשוי כמרזב והיין זב לדרך שם: גזירה משום מרזב. שמא יכין מרזב: שמא יקטום. העלה מן הענף וכיון דקטמיה הוה ליה כמתקן כלי כדתניא במסכת ביצה (דף לג:) לחלות בו שיניו ולא יקטמנו ואם קטמו חייב חטאת: בי סדיא. כר. לגבון שקורין פלטר"ש ועשוין לקפלן תחתיו במקום הכר או הכסת: רב אסר. להביאו לדרך מלבוש לדרך לשום הכרים כשהוא מעוטף בו: ברכין. שדרכן להתעטף בהן: דשרו. דמלבוש הן: ולאו הוה ליה רווחא. בבית למקום מושבם של תלמידים: ומשום כבוד רבותינו. שלא היה להן דבר לישב עליו ויושבין על גבי קרקע: רב כהנא ורב אסי. תלמידי חברים היו לו ט): **מתני'** לתוך הבור. שאין בו מים: שיהא שמור. שלא יסריח מחמת החום: ואת המים היפים ברעים. כלי מלא מים יפים לתוך מקוה מים רעים להשתמר (ב) שילונו ולא יחמו: מי שנשרו. שנפלו למים בשבת: לחצר החיצונה. הסמוכה למבוא העיר בתוך העיר שהוא מקום משתמר: שוטחן בחמה. ליבשן: אבל לא כנגד העם. שיחשדוהו שכבסן: **גמ'** פשיטא. דנותנין תבשיל לתוך הבור: גומות. שבקרקע הבור שיהו שוין להושיב הקדרה:

המנער

רבינו חננאל (המשך)

אין עושין שפופרת ביו"ט ואין צ"ל בשבת. ואפי' חתוכה ולא מתקנה אסור אבל אם היתה כבר בחבית ונפלה מחזירין אותה בשבת ואין צ"ל ביו"ט ור' יאשיה מיקל בחתיכה ולא מתקנה נמצאו דברי רב כת"ק ודברי שמואל כר' יאשיה והלכה כר' יאשיה כדדרש רב שישא בריה דרב אידי משמא דר' יוחנן הלכתא כר' יאשיה. ומנא תימרא דתניא תיקון כלי כגון סכין ובדומה לו אלא תיקון ביד בלבד. ואם צריכה תיקון בסכין או זולתו סכין כלי אחר אסורה. ואם היתה החבית נקובה לא יתן עליה שעוה מפני שהוא ממרח. כלומר סותם כדאמרינן התם לענין חבית שניקבה וסתמה שמרים כו' מורח מן הצדדין וכן דר' יהודה דמתניתין וריב"ז ורב ושמואל אמרי ש"מ שאסור לתת שעוה בחבית. וכן משחא. רב אסר גזירה משום שעוה. ולהלכתא כוותיה. **טרפא** דאסא. פי' עלה הדס שנותנין על הנקב של חבית להיות מקלח בו היין ולא יהיה שותת בדופני החבית. לדברי הכל אסור ליטול עלה של הדס בשבת ולשומו בנקב של חבית כמרזב. ואפילו רב אשי הנקב משום דקטים. וכן פליגי רב ושמואל בבי סדיא. ברכין ושפיר אפי' כר שהוא רך כבגד מלבוש אבל מה שהוא קשה כגון כרים מלאים נוצות ובדומה להן וכיוצא בהן אסור. אבל אם לא מקבל לגיר משמע שהוא מותר לטלטלה: **מתני'** נותנין תבשיל לתוך הבור שיהא שמור. **גמ'** פשיטא. מהו דתימא נגזור כי תימא. וחיישינן לאשווי גומות קמ"ל דלא גזרינן. **מתני'** מי שנשרו כליו בדרך במים שוטחן בחמה אבל לא כנגד העם. אמר רב יהודה אמר רב כל מקום שאסרו חכמים מפני מראית העין אפילו בחדרי חדרים אסור. איני והא תנן שוטחן בחמה אבל לא כנגד העם ואוקימנא

חשק שלמה על רבינו חננאל א) נראה דל"ל טוהם בנקב מותר למשוך ממנו: ב) אינו מובן. ואולי צ"ל דלמא אתי לאטמוני ברמץ ודלגינהו הגמ':

Mishnah נוֹתְנִים תַּבְשִׁיל לְתוֹךְ הַבּוֹר בִּשְׁבִיל שֶׁיְּהֵא שָׁמוּר – **One may place a cooked dish in a** cool, dry **pit in order that it may be preserved,**[35] וְאֶת הַמַּיִם הַיָּפִים בָּרָעִים בִּשְׁבִיל שֶׁיִּצֹּנּוּ – **and** one may put **good water into stale water in order that it cool off,**[36] וְאֶת הַצּוֹנֵן בַּחַמָּה בִּשְׁבִיל שֶׁיֵּחַמּוּ – **and** one may put **cold water in the sun in order that it become warm.**[37]

מִי שֶׁנָּשְׁרוּ כֵלָיו בַּדֶּרֶךְ בְּמַיִם – **One whose** outer **garments fell in water while traveling** מְהַלֵּךְ בָּהֶן וְאֵינוֹ חוֹשֵׁשׁ – **may** continue to **walk in them and need not fear** that people will suspect him of having laundered his clothes on the Sabbath.[38] הִגִּיעַ לֶחָצֵר הַחִיצוֹנָה – When **he arrives at the outermost courtyard,**[39] שׁוֹטְחָן בַּחַמָּה – **he may spread them out in the sun** in order to dry them, אֲבָל לֹא כְּנֶגֶד הָעָם – **but** he may **not** do so **in front of people.**[40]

Gemara The Mishnah had stated that one may place a cooked dish in a cool, dry pit in order to preserve it. The Gemara questions the necessity to even teach this:

פְּשִׁיטָא – **This is obvious;** why must it even be stated?

The Gemara responds:

מַהוּ דְּתֵימָא – Were it not for the Mishnah's teaching, **you might have said** that נִיגְזַר משום אַשְׁוּוּיֵי גּוּמוֹת – **[the Sages] would** have decreed against this practice **because of** the fear that **one will smooth out depressions** in the bottom of the pit in order to place the dish on level ground.[41] קָא מַשְׁמַע לָן – **[The Mishnah]** therefore **informs us** that no such decree was made.

The Gemara cites the next part of the Mishnah:

וְאֶת הַמַּיִם הַיָּפִים בָּרָעִים – AND one may put GOOD WATER INTO STALE water to cool it off.

The Gemara exclaims:

פְּשִׁיטָא – **This,** too, **is obvious!** Why would there be any reason to forbid this practice?

The Gemara replies that the teaching is indeed obvious, but was included as a preface to the next point the Mishnah makes:

סֵיפָא אִיצְטְרִיכָא לֵיהּ – **The second clause of the Mishnah,** which makes the converse point, is the **necessary** one. It states: וְאֶת הַצּוֹנֵן בַּחַמָּה – AND one may put COLD WATER IN THE SUN in order that it will become warm.

The Gemara objects further:

הָא נַמִּי פְּשִׁיטָא – But **this** second teaching **is also obvious!** Why might one think that warming something in the sun is impermissible?[42]

The Gemara replies:

מַהוּ דְּתֵימָא – **You might have said:** נִיגְזוֹר דִּילְמָא אָתֵי לְאַטְמוּנֵי בְּרֶמֶץ – **We ought to make a decree** prohibiting the placement of water in the sun **lest one come to** perform the similar act of **burying** food **in warm ashes,** the latter being clearly prohibited.[43] קָא מַשְׁמַע לָן – **[The Mishnah]** therefore **teaches us** that no such decree was made.

The Gemara quotes the next part of the Mishnah:

מִי שֶׁנָּשְׁרוּ וכו׳ – ONE WHOSE [GARMENTS] FELL in the water while traveling, **etc.** [may walk in them, and need not fear].

The Gemara cites an Amoraic ruling apparently inconsistent with our Mishnah:

אָמַר רַב יְהוּדָה אָמַר רַב – **Rav Yehudah said** the following **in the name of Rav:** כָּל מָקוֹם שֶׁאָסְרוּ חֲכָמִים מִפְּנֵי מַרְאִית הָעַיִן – Wherever the Sages **prohibited** an act **because** they were concerned it might give **the appearance of wrongdoing,** אֲפִילּוּ בְּחַדְרֵי חֲדָרִים אָסוּר – **the act is prohibited even in one's most private chambers.**[44] תְּנַן – **We learned,** however, **in our Mishnah:** שׁוֹטְחָן בַּחַמָּה – HE MAY SPREAD THEM OUT IN THE SUN in order to dry them, אֲבָל לֹא כְּנֶגֶד הָעָם – BUT he may NOT do so IN FRONT OF PEOPLE. Now, why does the Mishnah permit spreading out the clothes in private, if in public this is forbidden because of the appearance of wrongdoing? Evidently, private performance of such an act *is* permissible, contrary to Rav's teaching! – ? –

The Gemara replies:

תַּנָּאֵי הִיא – In fact, **[this point] is** the subject of **a Tannaic dispute,** דְּתַנְיָא – for it was taught in a Baraisa: שׁוֹטְחָן בַּחַמָּה – HE MAY SPREAD THEM OUT IN THE SUN, אֲבָל לֹא כְּנֶגֶד הָעָם – BUT NOT IN FRONT OF PEOPLE. רַבִּי אֶלְעָזָר וְרַבִּי שִׁמְעוֹן אוֹסְרִין – However, R' ELAZAR AND R' SHIMON RULE THAT THIS IS PROHIBITED even in a secluded area. Rav, then, rules in accord with R' Elazar and R' Shimon, who prohibit spreading out the clothes even in private.[45]

The Gemara cites a ruling concerning the cleaning of a garment:

אָמַר רַב הוּנָא – **Rav Huna said:**

NOTES

35. The Mishnah refers to a cistern without water in it (*Rashi*). [This is in contrast to the following part of the Mishnah, where something is placed inside a pit of water.] If left out in the sun, the food would soon spoil (*Rashi*).

36. I.e. he puts a container of warm, fresh water into a pit of cool, brackish water (see *Rashi*). *Meiri* explains that in the summer, a common practice was to take clear warm water from the rivers and submerge it in pits of cold, stale water or saltwater to cool it off.

The Gemara will explain why these two rulings, which appear obviously true, were included in the Mishnah.

37. Cooking is prohibited by the Torah only if the source of heat is fire or some derivative of fire. Warming by the heat of the sun therefore does not constitute the Biblical labor of *cooking* (see *Rashi* to 39a ד״ה דשרי).

38. [Washing clothes is a violation of the *melachah* of מְלַבֵּן, *whitening.*]

[Additionally, he need not fear that he will come to wring the water out of them, a *toladah* of *whitening* (see *Rambam, Hil. Shabbos* 22:20). Although the following Mishnah (147a) teaches that one may not carry a wet towel in his hand because he may come to wring out the water, still, in our case, out of respect for human dignity the Sages did not require a person to go without his clothing or even shed one item of his apparel (see *Sfas Emes*).]

39. I.e. he arrives at the first courtyard on the outskirts of the city, the first place he may safely leave his garments (*Rashi*).

40. I.e. he may not spread out his clothes in a public place lest people suspect him of having laundered them on the Sabbath (*Rashi*).

41. This would either constitute the forbidden labor of בּוֹנֶה, *building,* or חוֹרֵשׁ, *plowing* (see above, 73b, and *Rashi* ad loc. ד״ה בבית).

42. As explained above (note 37), it is clear that the labor of cooking does not apply when the source of heat being used is the sun.

43. Warming food by surrounding it with hot ashes indeed constitutes cooking, for hot ash is a תּוֹלֶדֶת הָאוּר, *derivative of fire* (see above, note 37, and *Rashi* to 39a ד״ה דאסיר and ד״ה שמא יטמין ברמץ).

44. Literally: in rooms of rooms.

Such Rabbinic decrees apply even in one's private quarters because of the apprehension that one will unknowingly be observed. Alternatively, there is the concern that if one is permitted to perform the act privately, ultimately one might perform it in public (*Ran* to *Beitzah* 9a; cf. *Mishnah Berurah* 301:165).

This stringency applies only where the concern is for the appearance of a Biblical violation (e.g. the case discussed here: laundering clothes). A decree that is made to avoid the appearance of a violation of Rabbinic law does not apply in a private room where one would not normally be seen (*Tosafos* to *Kesubos* 60a, *Magen Avraham* 301:56, *Mishnah Berurah* 301:165 with *Beur Halachah;* cf. *Ran* to *Beitzah* 9a).

45. Thus, Rav rules in accord with R' Elazar and R' Shimon, who prohibit spreading out the clothes even in private (*Rashi* to 65a ד״ה אבל and ד״ה אוסרין).

הַמְנַעֵר טַלִּיתוֹ בְּשַׁבָּת – **One who shakes out his cloak on the Sabbath** so as to clean it חַיָּיב חַטָּאת – **is liable to a** ***chatas.***[1]

The Gemara qualifies the ruling:

וְלֹא אָמְרָן אֶלָּא בְּחַדְתֵּי – **And we said this only as regards new [garments];**[2] אֲבָל בְּעַתִּיקֵי – **but with** regard to **old ones,** לֵית לָן בָּהּ – **we have no** objection to shaking them out. וְלֹא אָמְרָן אֶלָּא בְּאוּכָּמֵי – **And** furthermore, **we said this only as regards black [garments];**[3] אֲבָל בְּחִיוָּרֵי וְסוּמָּקֵי – **but as regards white or red** ones, לֵית לָן בָּהּ – **we have no** objection to shaking them out. וְהוּא דְּקָפִיד עֲלַיְיהוּ – **And [the above] applies when [the owner]** of the garment **is particular about it;** but if he generally wears these clothes even when they have not been shaken out, he does not transgress the Sabbath if he indeed shakes them.[4]

The Gemara cites an incident that confirms this last point:[5]

עוּלָּא אִיקְּלַע לְפוּמְבְּדִיתָא – It once happened that **Ulla came to the** city of **Pumbedisa,** חֲזָא רַבָּנָן דְּקָא מְנַפְּצֵי גְּלִימַיְיהוּ – and **he observed that the** local **scholars were shaking out their coats** on the Sabbath.[6] אָמַר קָמְחַלְּלִין רַבָּנָן שַׁבְּתָא – **He** then **exclaimed: The rabbis are desecrating the Sabbath!** אָמַר לְהוּ רַב יְהוּדָה – But **Rav Yehudah,** dean of the Pumbedisa academy, **said to [the scholars]:** נְפוּצֵי לֵיהּ בְּאַפֵּיהּ – **Shake [your coats] out to his face;** i.e. pay no mind to Ulla's objections, אֲנַן לָא קָפְדִינַן מִידֵי – for **we are not particular** about this **at all.** In our locale, we have no compunctions about wearing an unshaken cloak on a weekday, and therefore, if we indeed shake these garments to beautify them on the Sabbath, we commit no transgression.[7]

The Gemara relates a similar incident:

אַבָּיֵי הֲוָה קָאֵי קַמֵּיהּ דְּרַב יוֹסֵף – **Abaye** was once **standing before Rav Yosef,** his teacher, אָמַר לֵיהּ – and **[Rav Yosef] said to him:** הַב לִי כּוּמְתַאי – **"Give me my cap."** חֲזָא דְּאִיכָּא טַלָּא עֲלֵיהּ – **[Abaye] saw,** however, **that there was** some **dew** that had settled **upon it,** הֲוָה קָמְחַסֵּם לְמֵיתְבָהּ לֵיהּ – and **he was reluctant to give it to him.**[8] אָמַר לֵיהּ – **[Rav Yosef]** perceived this and **said to [Abaye]:** נְפוּץ שְׁדֵי אֲנַן לָא קָפְדִינַן מִידֵי – **Shake it out; throw** off the dew! **We are not particular at all** about wearing a garment that has dew on it.

A related discussion:[9]

אָמַר רַב יִצְחָק בַּר יוֹסֵף אָמַר רַבִּי יוֹחָנָן – **Rav Yitzchak bar Yosef said** the following **in the name of R' Yochanan:** הַיּוֹצֵא בְּטַלִּית מְקוּפֶּלֶת מוּנַּחַת לוֹ עַל כְּתֵיפוֹ בְּשַׁבָּת – If **one goes out** from a private to a public domain **on the Sabbath with a folded cloak resting on his shoulder,**[10] חַיָּיב חַטָּאת – **he is liable to a** ***chatas.***[11]

R' Yochanan's statement is buttressed by a Baraisa:

תַּנְיָא נַמִּי הָכִי – And **so it was also taught in a Baraisa:** סוֹחֲרֵי כְּסוּת הַיּוֹצְאִים – CLOTHING MERCHANTS WHO GO OUT into a public domain בְּטַלִּיתוֹת מְקוּפָּלוֹת וּמוּנָּחוֹת עַל כְּתֵיפָן בְּשַׁבָּת – WITH CLOAKS FOLDED AND RESTING ON THEIR SHOULDERS ON THE SABBATH חַיָּיבִין חַטָּאת – ARE LIABLE TO A *CHATAS.* וְלֹא סוֹחֲרֵי כְּסוּת בִּלְבַד אָמְרוּ – AND THIS APPLIES NOT JUST TO CLOTHING MERCHANTS, אֶלָּא כָּל אָדָם – BUT indeed to ALL PEOPLE; אֶלָּא שֶׁדַּרְכָּן שֶׁל מוֹכְרִין לָצֵאת כָּךְ – HOWEVER, we speak of merchants in

NOTES

1. I.e. he shakes the dust off his cloak (*Rashi*). In doing so, he makes the garment cleaner, and performs a *toladah* of the labor of laundering [מְלַבֵּן, *whitening*].

Tosafos dispute *Rashi* (see *Shaar HaTziyun* 302:7, arguing that legally speaking one cannot "launder" without the use of water (see also *Ritva MHK* ed.). They therefore assert that in our case dew had been on the person's cloak, and it was to remove these droplets that the person shook the garment (see also *Rosh* and *Ran;* see also *Mishnah Berurah* to 302:1; for an entirely different intepretation of our Gemara, see *Rambam, Hil. Shabbos* 10:18).

[Elsewhere, *Rashi* too states that water is required for the labor of laundering (see *Rashi* to 141a ד״ה מכבנים; see also *Gilyon HaShas* here). He states this, however, concerning a garment that has been soiled by mud, where simply rubbing the caked mud off the garment will not remove the underlying stain. In the case of a garment that is simply dusty, though, rubbing or shaking *can* clean it effectively, and this is therefore prohibited as an act of *laundering* (*Beur Halachah* to *Orach Chaim* 302:41 ד״ה והוא שמקפיד).]

2. There is some question as to what "new" means in this context. *Beis Yosef* suggests that the intent is to garments that have not yet been washed a first time. He notes, however, that *Rambam* (*Hil. Shabbos* 10:18) appears to maintain that even garments that were worn (and washed) a few times can be considered "new" as long as their appearance is still fresh and clean (*Beis Yosef* to *Orach Chaim* 302:1).

3. Dust is clearly apparent on a black garment, and most people would not don a cloak of this color without first removing its dust (*Rashi*). The removal of this dust is thus an act of *laundering* (see following note).

4. Whereas washing a garment in water is without question a violation of *laundering,* the shaking of a cloak is classified as such only if the owner considers the act an important improvement to his garment. If, during the week, he would wear the cloak without its being shaken, then shaking it on the Sabbath (to make the garment look its finest in honor of the day) is not deemed a significant enough act to qualify as *laundering* (*Beis Yosef* 302:1 and *Sfas Emes;* cf. *Maggid Mishneh* to *Rambam* loc. cit.).

The consideration of the owner's mindset is, indeed, also the reason the item must be black in color and new, for only in these cases is the owner presumed to be particular about wearing the garment free of dust. When the garment is older or is of a different color, he is not presumed to be particular about this, and therefore, his shaking the garment is permissible (*Beur Halachah* to 302:1).

[*Beur Halachah* adds that likewise, even if the garment *is* new and black, if that particular owner happens not to care about wearing the garment with dust on it, he too would be permitted to shake it (see also Gemara below). Similarly, if the garment is white or red and the owner *is* particular about it, he may not shake it out on the Sabbath.]

5. The following incident will prove that when one is not particular about the dust on his garment, it is entirely permissible for him to shake the dust off on the Sabbath [i.e. there is not even a Rabbinic prohibition against doing so] (*Mishnah Berurah* to 302:2).

6. The coats were black in color (*Rashi*), and, apparently, were also new.

7. See above, note 4.

8. Abaye was uncertain whether Rav Yosef was particular about wearing the cap with dew on it. If he was, it would be impermissible to shake the dew off, yet it would also not be respectful to hand him the cap with the dew on it. He was therefore reluctant to give the cap to him (*Sfas Emes;* see *Rashi*).

9. Since the Mishnah mentioned the law of one whose clothes fell into water on the road, the Gemara mentions the following law about folding a cloak onto one's shoulders, for in such a situation one might wish to raise his cloak onto his shoulders to keep it from getting wet (*Tosafos* ד״ה היוצא).

10. The Gemara refers to a large four-cornered garment similar in size and dimension to the *tallis* used during prayer today (*Aruch HaShulchan* 301:89; see also *Shulchan Aruch* 301:31). In Talmudic times, this garment was a normal part of daily attire (*Ritva MHK* ed.). It was generally worn draped over the head and shoulders in such a way that most of one's body would be covered by it; the sides of the cloak would flow down one's arms, and the end of the cloak would extend down one's back towards the floor (see *Rashi* and *Aruch HaShulchan* ad loc.). Here, though, the Gemara discusses a case where the cloak was not worn in this manner. Instead of allowing the cloak to drape behind him, the person lifted the back end of the garment onto his shoulders, in effect folding the cloak in half width-wise (*Rashi*). His purpose in doing so was presumably to guard against the end of the cloak touching the ground and becoming soiled or ripped (see *Shulchan Aruch* ad loc.).

11. Since this is not the normal way the cloak is worn, the person is deemed to be *carrying* the garment rather than wearing it (see *Rashi* here and above, 58a ד״ה חייב חטאת), and carrying from a private to a public domain is prohibited on the Sabbath (see above, 2a).

א המנער טליתו בשבת חייב חטאת ולא אמרן אלא בחדתי אבל בעתיקי לית לן בה ולא אמרן אלא באוכמי אבל בחיורי וסומקי לית לן בה והוא דקפיד עלייהו עולא איקלע לפומבדיתא חזא רבנן דקא מנפצי גלימייהו אמר קמחללין רבנן שבתא אמר להו רב יהודה נפוצי ליה באפיה אנן לא קפדינן מידי אביי הוה קאי קמיה דרב יוסף א"ל הב לי כומתאי [חזא דאיכא] טלא עליה הוה קמחסם למיתבה ליה א"ל נפוץ שדי אנן לא קפדינן מידי אמר רב יצחק בר יוסף א"ר יוחנן ב היוצא בטלית מקופלת מונחת לו על כתיפו בשבת חייב חטאת תנ"ה סוחרי כסות היוצאים בטליתות מקופלות ומונחות על כתיפן בשבת חייבין חטאת ולא סוחרי כסות בלבד אמרו אלא כל אדם אלא שדרכן של מוכרין לצאת כך וחנוני ג היוצא במעות הצרורין לו בסדינו חייב חטאת ולא חנוני בלבד אמרו אלא כל אדם אלא שדרכו של חנוני לצאת כך והרטנין יוצאין בסודרין [א] שעל כתיפן ולא רטנין בלבד אמרו אלא כל אדם אלא שדרכן של רטנין לצאת בכך א"ר יהודה מעשה בהורקנוס בנו של רבי אליעזר בן הורקנוס שיצא בסודר שעל כתיפו בשבת אלא שנימא כרוכה לו באצבעו וכשבא הדבר לפני חכמים אמרו ד אפילו אין נימא כרוכה לו באצבעו דרש רב נחמן בר רב חסדא משמיה דרב חסדא הלכה אע"פ שאין נימא כרוכה לו באצבעותיו עולא איקלע לבי אסי בר היני בעו מיניה מהו לעשות מרזב בשבת אמר להו הכי אמר רבי אלעי אסור לעשות מרזב בשבת מאי מרזב אמר ר' זירא כיסי בבלייתא ר' ירמיה הוה יתיב קמיה דר' זירא א"ל הכי מאי א"ל אסור והכי מאי א"ל אסור אמר רב פפא ה נקוט האי כללא בידך כל אדעתא דלכנופי [ב] אסור כל דלהתנאות שרי כי הא דרב שישא בריה דרב אידי מתנאה בסדינו הוה כי אתא רב דימי אמר פעם אחת יצא רבי לשדה והיו שני צידי טליתו מונחין על כתיפו אמר לפניו יהושע בן זירוז בן חמיו של רבי מאיר בזו לא חייב ר' מאיר חטאת אמר ליה דקדק רבי מאיר עד כאן שלשל רבי טליתו כי אתא רבין אמר לא יהושע בן זירוז הוה אלא יהושע בן כפוסאי היה חתנו של ר' עקיבא אמר בזו לא חייב ר' עקיבא חטאת אמר לו דקדק ר"ע עד כאן שלשל רבי טליתו כי אתא רב שמואל בר רב יהודה אמר נשאל איתמר: **מתני'** הרוחץ במי מערה ובמי טבריא ונסתפג אפילו בעשר אלונטיאות לא יביאם בידו אבל עשרה בני אדם מסתפגין באלונטית אחת פניהם ידיהם ורגליהם ומביאין אותן בידן סכין וממשמשין אבל לא מתעמלין ולא מתגררין אין יורדין לקורדימא ואין עושין אפיקטויזין ואין מעצבין את הקטן ואין מחזירין את השבר מי שנפרקה ידו ורגלו לא יטרפם בצונן אבל רוחץ הוא כדרכו ואם נתרפא נתרפא: **גמ'** קתני מי מערה דומיא דמי טבריא מה מי טבריא חמין אף מי מערה חמין הרוחץ דיעבד אין לכתחילה לא מכלל דלהשתטף

רש"י

המנער טליתו. מן העפר: חייב חטאת. דזהו ליבונה: אלא באוכמי. שהאבק מקלקל מראיתה וקפיד עליה: והוא דקפיד עלייהו. ללובשן עד שינערם: קמחללי (א) שבתא. וגלימי אוכמי הוו: לא קפדינן. לא איכפת לן אם יש עליה אבק הלכך לאו ליבון הוא: כומתאי. כובעי: הוה קא מחסם. לשון לא תחסום (דברים כה): למיתבא ליה. שצריך לנער הטל מעליה: בטלית מקופלת. לאחר שנתנה על ראשו הגביה שיפוליה על כתפיו: חייב חטאת. שאין זה דרך מלבוש: והרטנין. על שם מקום: נימא כרוכה על אצבעו. שלא יפול מכתפיו: בר היני: מרזב. מפרש לקמיה: כיסוי בבלייתא. שמסלקין בגדיהם מן הארץ כשהן ארוכין וכופלין אותן כלפי מעלה פרונצ"ש ומחזיקין אותן [ג] ע"י חוטין והיינו כמין כיס וכמו מרזב: אסור. משום תקוני מנא: הכי מאי. קולט חלוקו (בפניו) בענין אחד ושואלו כגון זה מרזב הוא או לא וחוזר וקולטו בענין אחר ושואלו: לכנופי. שיהא מתוקן תמיד להעמיד קיפולו לעולם: להתנאות. לפי שעה: מתנאה בסדינו. אחר שנתעטף היה מתקנו על גופו ומיישבו ובחול קאמר כלומר אלמא דאורחיה בהכי וה"ה לשבת: שני צידי טליתו. שבימינו ובשמאלו לצד הקרקע: בן זירוז בזו לא חייב ר"מ חטאת. בתמיה דאין זה דרך מלבוש אלא דרך משוי: דקדק ר"מ ע"כ. בתמיה לחייב חטאת בדבר הדומה להיות מותר כזה שאינה מקופלת ואחוריה נופלין למטה מכתפיו אלא שצידיה היו מונחין על כתפו: שלשל. הורידה למטה שקבל דבריו: נשאל איתמר. לא אירע מעשה זה לרבי אלא שאלו לפניו מהו לצאת בו ובקש להתיר עד שאמרו לפניו משום רבי מאיר חייב חטאת דאיהו סבר הואיל ואינה מקופלת שהרי אחוריה היו נופלין למטה מן כתפיו אלא שצידיה היו מונחים על כתפיו הוה סבר דרך מלבוש הוא: **מתני'** מי מערה. מי מקוה מקורה (ב) שהוא חם ואין חומו יוצא ודוקא חמין נקט ומש"ה קתני הרוחץ דיעבד: ונסתפג. וקינח: אפי' בעשר אלונטיות. סדינין שמקנחין בהן וסיפג בהן זה אחר זה ורבותא היא דלא נפישי מיא בכל חד אפ"ה לא יביאם בידו בתוך ביתו אפי' ע"י עירוב שמא ישכח ויסחט בבואו: אבל עשרה בני אדם. הואיל ומרובין הן מדכרי אהדדי: מסתפגין באלונטית אחת. והיינו נמי רבותא דחדא אלונטית לעשרה (ג) נפישא ביה מיא אפילו הכי מביאין אותה בידים: פניהם ידיהם ורגליהם. אורחא דמילתא נקט וה"ה לכל גופם: סכין. שמן בשבת: וממשמשין. ביד על כל הגוף להנאה: אבל לא מתעמלין. לשפשף בכח: ולא מתגררין. גרסינן במגררת שקורין אשטריל"א דהוי עובדא דחול: לקורדימא. שם הנהר ובגמ' מפרש טעמא: אפיקטויזין. להקיא: ואין מעצבין את הקטן. לשון ידיך עלבוני (איוב י) שמתקנים ומיישבין עצמותיו וחוליות שדרתו כמדת גלמו ובגמרא אמר טעמא: ואין מחזירין את השבר. עצם שנשבר. כל רפואה אסורה משום שחיקת סממנין: נפרקה. אלוישי"ר בלעז שילא העצם מפרק שלו: לא יטרפם. לשון ביצים טרופות בקערה (חולין דף סד.):

תוספות

המנער טליתו. פי' ר"ח מן הטל שעליו דהיינו ליבון וליבון חייב חטאת וכן משמע דהוי דומיא דכומתא דרב יוסף אבל בניעור מן העפר כדפירש בקונטרס אין נראה שיהא שייך ליבון:

היוצא בטלית מקופלת. איידי דאיירינן במי שנשרו כליו בדרך שאז דרך הוא לקפל טליתו נקטיה הכא:

הרטנין. רטנין כמו הרהטנין (הערוך פי' הרלים): **מהו** לעשות מרזב. נראה לרבי דלענין איסור הוצאה איירי כמו טלית של ד' כנפו' ולוקח שני צידי רוחב טליתו של צד ימינו ונותן על כתף השמאלית ואינו פושטו על כתף אלא מקופל ומונח על כתפו והיינו דקאמר מאי מרזב כיסי בבלייתא שקורין פרונלדר"ה דכשהוא מונח כמו שפירשתי יש בו כיסים מרובים וכל כיסא וכיסא נראה כמין מרזב ומיבעיא ליה אי איכא איסור הוצאה בכך כיון שאינה דרך מלבוש והיינו דקאמר כל אדעתא לכנופי אסור דהיינו כמו שפירשתי ששני צידי הימין מקובצים ומונחים על כתף השמאלית שיכול לילך במהרה ולא יכביד עליו טליתו אדעתא דלהתנאות שפיר דמי והיינו כשאין צידי טליתו מקובצין אלא צד אחד מונחת על כתפו אצל צוארו וצד האחר נופל על שכמו עד הזרוע ואין בו שום כיסוי והיינו שלשל רבי טליתו דבסמוך שלשל אותו כמו שפירשתי כעין להתנאות והיינו דרך מלבוש וכן פירש בערוך ערך מרזב אסור לעשות מרזב בשבת פירוש כשיעטוף אדם טליתו ויקפיל שני קצותיו כעין דרך קיפול ויניחנה על שכמו השמאלית ויחזור ויקפל שאר הטלית שבצד הימין ויניחנה בכתפו רק מה שפירש שקורין מרזב מה שטליתו מושפלת מהנה ומהנה וחלל כנגד השדרה דנראה כמין מרזב אינו נראה לרבי דא"כ מאי קאמר בתר הכי מאי מרזב כיסי בבלייתא אלא אינו עשוי כעין כיסא. מ"ר:

אף מי מערה חמין. (ד) שהוחמו באור דאי בחמי טבריא שרי לכתחילה כדאמר בפרק כירה (ד' מ. ושם) והניחו להן חמי טבריא ובפרק שמונה שרצים (ד' קט. ושם:) ל:

דיעבד אין. אמי מערה קאי ולא תנא במתני' חמי טבריא אלא למידק אף מי מערה חמין ל: דתניא

מסורת הש"ס

א) לעיל נח, ב) [תוספתא פ"ו], ג) פ"א היוצאין וכן גי' ר"ח, ד) [יומא ג. מגילה כג:], ה) פ"א בבני מעיים, ו) נ"א לפלוזמא, ז) לעיל קכג., ח) פ"א טובל, ט) [עי' תוס' חולין טו: ד"ה המבשל ועי' תוס' סוטה ב. ד"ה המקנא דיעבד], י) [בערך רטן וכיס שם הרלים יוצאין בסודר שעל כתפיהן מקובץ ולא מקופל בשביל שלא יעכבו לרוץ], כ) עי' רש"א וכו', ל) [ועי' תוספות לעיל קט. ד"ה רוחצין ותוס' חולין טו: ד"ה אלא נורך].

הגהות הב"ח

(א) רש"י ד"ה קמחללי רבנן שבתא. (ב) ד"ה מי מערה וכו' מקורה שהוא חם ואין חומו: (ג) ד"ה מסתפגין וכו' אלונטית לעשר' בני אדם נפישא: (ד) תוס' ד"ה אף מי מערה חמין כחמין שהוחמו וכו' ובפ' שמונה שרצים והא דקאמר דיעבד אין אמי והד"א:

גליון הש"ס

רש"י ד"ה חייב חטאת. דזהו דליבונה. עיין לעיל דף קמא ע"א רש"י ד"ה מכבסים ול"ע:

הגהות הגר"א

[א] גמרא יוצאין בסודרין שעל כתפן. נ"ב פי' אפילו מקופל. וח"ש רטנין ר"ל הרלים. ערוך פי' הרלים. [ב] שם כל אדעתא דלכנופי. נ"ב פי' הרמב"ם שלא יקרעו או שלא יתלכלכו: [ג] רש"י ד"ה כסוי בבלייתא ומחזיקין אותן. נ"ב אבל הרמב"ם כתב אפילו בידו או על כתפו:

ליקוטי רש"י

גזירה שמא יקנוס. ונמצא עושה כלי וחייב משום מכה בפטיש [לעיל קכה:]. דהמס כלי משוי ליה ואיכא איסורא דאורייתא [ביצה לג:]. בחמה. בשמש. בשביל שיחמו. דאין דרך בישול בכך ומחמה באור לא מיחלפא לגזור בה אטו הא [לעיל לט:]. מי שנשרו כליו בדרך. במי גשמים [שם מה. ועי' בתוס' כאן ובהגה"ש שם]. מהלך בהן. ואין חוששין ... וכן מתנגבין והולכין ואינו חושש שיסחטו [ביצה לה:]. שוטחן בחמה. והן נוגבין מאליהן. אבל לא כנגד העם. שלא יאמרו כבסן בשבת [שם ט.]. אשוויי גומות. דמלאכה הוא באשוויי גומות כבנין [עירובין קד.]. רמץ. אפר חם וכן שמו בלשון ערבי [חולין ח.]. גחלים ואפר בוערים [נדה מט:]. אפר המעורב בגחלים [לעיל לד:]. כל מקום שאסרו חכמים. דבר המותר ואסרוהו. מפני מראית העין. שכרואהו חושדו בדבר עבירה [ע"ז יב.]. שלא יחשדוהו לאיסור [לעיל סד:]. **אפילו בחדרי חדרים אסור.** במקום שאין אדם רואהו אסרוהו [ע"ז שם]. **תנן שוטחן בחמה אבל לא כנגד העם.** אלמא מידי דמשום מראית העין מותר במקום צנוע [ביצה שם]. [ע"כ שייך לדף קמו:].

מחסם. לשון (דברים כה) לא תחסום מגמגם [חולין נ.]. **חייב חטאת.** דליכא מכסיא אלא בזמן שלובשו דרך מלבוש [לעיל נח.]. **מי טבריא.** חמי טבריא. מעיינות רותחין [פסחים מא.]. **אלונטית.** בגד שמסתפגין בו כשיוצאין מבית המרחץ [עירובין פז:]. **אפיקטויזין.** הקאה גומיטא בלע"ז כך מצאתי [לעיל יב.]. להקיא והוא בנוטריקון אפיק טפי זין מזון שאוכל יותר מדאי מוציא ומקיא [סוכה מ:]. **ואין עושין אפיקטויזין.** להקיא שותה משקים ומקיא ולא לרפואה אלא להריק את מעיו שיוכל לאכול ולשתות [היום] הרבה כדאמרינן בפרק חבית ואף על גב דלא גזור בה משום שחיקת סממנין דהא לאו לרפואה היא אסור משום דמתקן גברא [לעיל קכג:]. כסם דדמי לרפואה וגזירה משום שחיקת סממנין אבל ביד להכניס יד לתוך גרונו עד שיקיא מותר [לקמן ע"ב עי"ש בגה"ש].

עין משפט נר מצוה

מ א מיי' פ"י מהלכות שבת הלכה כד סמג לאוין סה טוש"ע או"ח סימן שב סעיף א:
מא ב מיי' פי"ט שם הל' יט סמג שם טור שו"ע או"ח סימן שא סעיף כט:
מב ג שם סעיף לא לב:
מג ד מיי' פכ"א שם הל"ד טור שו"ע שם סעיף לד:
מד ה שם סעיף לא:
מה ו מיי' פכ"ב שם הלכה כ טור שו"ע או"ח סימן שכו סעיף א:

רבינו חננאל

ואוקימנא ליה כתנאי: **אמר** רב הונא המנער טליתו בשבת חייב חטאת. פי' המנער כדכתיב התנערי מעפר וכדגרסינן התם ומנערה אחת לשלשים. אם יש אבק בבגד חדש שחור ומקפיד עליו. או אם יש עליו דבר טינוף אוסר רב הונא לנפצו. אבל אם הוא בגד ישן או לבן או אדום ולא קפיד עלייהו שרי וכן הלכה. וזה שראה עולא לרבנן דהוו נפצי גלימייהו ואמר הני מחללי שבתא. רבנן דפומבדיתא במלבושין דלא קפדי עלייהו הוו נפצי. (אמתא) [כומתא] הוא כמין כובע של ראש במקום סודר כדאמרינן בפרק השולח גט לאשתו האי אמתא דהוה שכיב מרה אתת בכת קמיה. ואמרה ליה עד אימת תיתעבד ותזיל ההיא אמתא שקל כומתיה ושדא בה אמר ליה קני הא וקני נפשיך. כלומר קני נפשיך בחליפין. וי"א כומתא הוא כגון כאן דומה לגביע והוה באותו הטמנ' טינוף. והוה אביי מהסס. כלומר מתיירא כדאמרינן התם חזייה דהוה קא מהסס. א"ל רב יוסף לאביי נפרץ שדי אנן לא קפדינן מידי: היוצא בטלית מקופלת ומונחת לו על כתפו כגון אלו מוכרי כסות שמקפלין ומפשילין אותן על כתפייהו. אתמר משמיה דר' יוחנן חייב חטאת ותניא כוותיה והכי הלכתא וכן נמי היוצא וצרורין לו בסדינו מעות חייב חטאת אבל הרטנין שהם הרצים יוצאין בסודר שעל כתפיהן. ולא אלו בלבד אלא כל אדם. והנכון להיות כרוך בצוארו. או נימא כרוכה לו באצבעו. כהורקנוס בר' אליעזר. ואע"ג דאמר משמא דר' יוחנן הלכה אע"פ שאין נימא כרוכה לו על אצבעו: **עולא** איקלע לבי אסי בר (חני) [היני] בעא מיניה מהו לעשות מרזב בשבת א"ל הכי אמר ר' אלעזר אסור. כך קבלנו מרבותינו שיש בידם קבלה כי מרזב זה כשיתעטף אדם טליתו ויקפל ב' קצותיה כמין כרך קיפול ויניחה על כתפו השמאלית ויחזור ויקפל שאר הטלית המשולש בצידו הימין מניחה בכתפו הימין ונמצאת טליתו מקופלת מהנה ומהנה ומופשלת על כתפיו וחלל כנגד השדרה ונראה כמין מרזב. וכענין זה היה קשר (כישי) [כישא] בבלייתא שהיו קושרין ב' כריכות וקורין אותה כישא וכיסכוסי מאני א). וי"א זולתי פירוש זה. אבל חובה עלינו לומר בלשון רבותינו ומה שקיבלנוה בתראה עבדינן ואמר כללא כל אדעתא לכנופי אסור. כל להתנאות שפיר דמי וכדרב שישא בר מתנאה בסדינין כי אתא רב דימי אמר פעם אחת יצא רבי לשדה והיו ב' צידי טליתו מונחין הטלית כרוכה ומופשלת לו לאחוריו. אמר לפניו יהושע בן זירוז בן חמיו של ר"מ בזו לא חייב זה המעשה דומה לרטנין שיוצאין בסודרין בסדינין מקובצין ולא משולשין על כתפיהן ור' מאיר חטאת ב) אי לא אסורה מדרבנן. א"ל ר' דקדק ר"מ עד כאן שלשל רבי טליתו: **מתני'** הרוחץ

חשק שלמה על רבינו חננאל

א) עיין בערוך ערך מרזב א': ב) [אולי צ"ל אלמא דאסורה מדרבנן. ואפשר דרבינו מפרש בזו לא חייב ר"מ חטאת בניחותא דחטאת לא היה מחייב רק הוי אוסר מדרבנן ול"ע בזה]:

גמ'

particular because **IT IS THE PRACTICE OF MERCHANTS TO GO OUT IN THIS MANNER.**[12]

The Baraisa continues:

וְחֶנְוָנִי הַיּוֹצֵא בְּמָעוֹת הַצְּרוּרִין לוֹ בִּסְדִינוֹ – LIKEWISE, A SHOPKEEPER WHO GOES OUT into a public domain **WITH COINS TIED TO HIS GARMENT** **חַיָּיב חַטָּאת – IS LIABLE TO A *CHATAS*.**[13] **וְלֹא חֶנְוָנִי בִּלְבַד אָמְרוּ – AND THIS APPLIES NOT JUST TO A SHOPKEEPER,** **אֶלָּא כָּל אָדָם – BUT** indeed **TO ALL PEOPLE;** **אֶלָּא שֶׁדַּרְכּוֹ שֶׁל חֶנְוָנִי לָצֵאת כָּךְ – HOWEVER,** we speak of shopkeepers because it is the **PRACTICE OF STOREKEEPERS TO GO OUT IN THIS MANNER.**

The Baraisa concludes:

וְהָרַטָּנִין יוֹצְאִין בְּסוּדָרִין שֶׁעַל כְּתֵיפָן – BUT RATTANITES[14] **MAY GO OUT WITH KERCHIEFS** folded **ON THEIR SHOULDERS,**[15] **וְלֹא רַטָּנִין בִּלְבַד אָמְרוּ – AND THIS APPLIES NOT JUST FOR RATTANITES,** **אֶלָּא כָּל אָדָם – BUT** indeed to **ALL PEOPLE;** **אֶלָּא שֶׁדַּרְכָּן שֶׁל רַטָּנִין לָצֵאת בְּכָךְ – HOWEVER,** we speak of Rattanites because **IT IS THE WAY OF RATTANITES TO GO OUT IN THIS MANNER.**

The Baraisa continues with an anecdote about the wearing of kerchiefs on the Sabbath:

אָמַר רַבִּי יְהוּדָה – R' YEHUDAH SAID: **מַעֲשֶׂה בְּהוּרְקָנוֹס בְּנוֹ שֶׁל רַבִּי אֱלִיעֶזֶר בֶּן הוּרְקָנוֹס – IT IS TOLD OF HURKANOS, SON OF R' ELIEZER BEN HURKANOS,** **שֶׁיָּצָא בְּסוּדָר שֶׁעַל כְּתֵיפוֹ בְּשַׁבָּת – THAT HE** once **WENT OUT WITH THE KERCHIEF ON HIS SHOULDER** into a public domain **ON THE SABBATH;** **אֶלָּא שֶׁנִּימָא כְּרוּכָה לוֹ בְּאֶצְבָּעוֹ – HOWEVER,** as a protective measure, he saw to it that **THERE WAS A THREAD WRAPPED AROUND HIS FINGER** through which he could hold onto the kerchief and ensure it would not fall.[16] **וּכְשֶׁבָּא הַדָּבָר לִפְנֵי חֲכָמִים אָמְרוּ – AND WHEN THE MATTER CAME BEFORE THE SAGES, THEY SAID:** **אֲפִילוּ אֵין נִימָא כְּרוּכָה לוֹ בְּאֶצְבָּעוֹ – EVEN IF THERE HAD BEEN NO THREAD WRAPPED AROUND HIS FINGER,** his act still would have been permissible.

A ruling is handed down in connection with this Baraisa:

דָּרַשׁ רַב נַחְמָן בַּר רַב חִסְדָּא מִשְּׁמֵיהּ דְּרַב חִסְדָּא – Rav Nachman bar Rav Chisda lectured in the name of Rav Chisda: **הֲלָכָה אַף עַל פִּי שֶׁאֵין נִימָא כְּרוּכָה לוֹ בְּאֶצְבְּעוֹתָיו – The law is** that **even if there is no thread wrapped around one's fingers,** it is permissible to walk in a public domain with a kerchief folded on one's shoulders.

The Gemara returns to discuss the various ways a cloak may be worn on the Sabbath:

עוּלָּא אִיקְּלַע לְבֵי אַסִּי בַּר הִינִי – Ulla once **visited the academy of Assi bar Hini.** **בָּעוּ מִינֵּיהּ – There, [the students] inquired of him:** **מַהוּ לַעֲשׂוֹת מַרְזֵב בְּשַׁבָּת – What** of **making a "gutter" on the Sabbath?**[17] Is this permissible, or not? **אָמַר לְהוּ – He replied to them:** **הָכִי אָמַר רַבִּי אִלְעַאי – Thus said R' Il'ai:** **אָסוּר לַעֲשׂוֹת מַרְזֵב בְּשַׁבָּת – It is forbidden to make a "gutter" on the Sabbath.**

The Gemara questions:

מַאי מַרְזֵב – What is meant by **a "gutter"?**

An explanation is given::

אָמַר רַבִּי זֵירָא – R' Zeira said: **כִּיסֵי בַּבְלָיָתָא –** "Gutters" refers to **Babylonian pockets.**[18]

The Gemara relates how an Amora attempted to clarify the particulars of this law:

רַבִּי יִרְמְיָה הֲוָה יָתִיב קַמֵּיהּ דְּרַבִּי זֵירָא – R' Yirmiyah was once **sitting before R' Zeira,** attempting to learn from him the types of "gutters" that were impermissible to make on the Sabbath. **אָמַר לֵיהּ –** R' Yirmiyah formed a certain kind of ruffle in his cloak, and **he said to [R' Zeira]:** **הָכִי מַאי –** "If one folds it **thus, what** is the law?" **אָמַר לֵיהּ אָסוּר – [R' Zeira] replied to him:** "That is **forbidden."** **וְהָכִי מַאי –** R' Yirmiyah then formed a different kind of ruffle, and asked him: **"And thus, what** is the law?" **אָמַר לֵיהּ אָסוּר –** Whereupon **[R' Zeira]** again **replied:** "It is **forbidden."**

Rav Pappa explains a governing principle behind this law:

אָמַר רַב פָּפָּא – Rav Pappa said: **נְקוֹט הַאי כְּלָלָא בִּידָךְ – Take this general rule in your hand:** **כֹּל אַדַּעְתָּא דְּלִכְנוּפֵי –** Any time one makes a fold **with the intent of gathering up** the garment,[19] **אָסוּר – [the act] is forbidden.** **כֹּל דִּלְהִתְנָאוֹת –** And **any** time one makes a fold simply **to make [the garment] more attractive,**[20] **שְׁרֵי – [the act] is permissible;** **כִּי הָא דְּרַב שִׁישָׁא בְּרֵיהּ**

NOTES

12. [They generally keep the cloaks they are selling folded on their shoulders to keep them from becoming soiled.]

13. He is deemed to be carrying the coins, not "wearing" them, and he is therefore liable.

Aruch HaShulchan (301:98) asserts that it is indeed obvious that one is "carrying" (as opposed to "wearing") the coins. Rather, the main point of the Baraisa is that one is liable even though this is an unusual method of carrying. In general, one transports coins in a purse; he does not wrap them in his clothes. Nevertheless, since there are some people who *do* regularly transport coins this way [shopkeepers, as the Baraisa proceeds to explain], the practice is deemed normative, and one is liable for it.

[The implication of the Baraisa is that if one is in a private domain, where the *melachah* of הוֹצָאָה, *transferring,* is not a consideration, one *may* carry coins in this manner. As to why it is not prohibited to move the coins because they are *muktzeh,* see *Rama* to 301:32 with *Beur HaGra;* see also *Mishnah Berurah* ad loc.]

14. *Rashi* states that רַטָּן is the name of a place. *Tosafos,* however, suggests that the word is related to הָרַהֲטָנִין, *those who hurry,* and *Aruch* (*Erech* רטן) translates the term as הָרָצִים, *those who run* [e.g. messengers] (see also *Rabbeinu Chananel* and *Meiri*).

15. The kerchief mentioned here was a long but narrow garment that could be worn over the head and draped over the back and shoulders. It was customarily worn by messengers, and was designed not to hang down far in the back so as to allow the messengers to run quickly while wearing it. Since it was the practice of the messengers to wear the end of the kerchief folded back up onto their shoulders [to allow them even greater mobility] this is considered a normative way to wear this garment, and one so attired is therefore permitted to traverse a public domain (*Meiri;* see also *Mishnah Berurah* 301:127).

16. Apparently, he was concerned that if it fell off he might instinctively pick it up and carry it, thereby desecrating the Sabbath (see *Tosafos* to 147b ד״ה צריך לקשר).

17. In this context, "a gutter" refers to a particular way of wearing a cloak. The Gemara defines the term more precisely below (see following note).

18. In Talmudic times, people wearing particularly long cloaks or robes would ensure that the bottom of the garment did not drag on the floor by pulling up a section of the garment and creating a ruffle. The folds would then be fastened in place with threads that had been sewn into the garment specifically for this purpose (*Rashi,* with *Meiri;* see also *Rashi* to *Beitzah* 23a ד״ה אי קטורא בידי). Each of these folds resembled a kind of gutter, or pocket — hence the term "Babylonian pockets."

Forming these ruffles and fastening them into place on the Sabbath is ruled to be putting the finishing touch on a garment, and is therefore prohibited under the category of מַכֶּה בְּפַטִּישׁ, *striking the final blow* (see *Rashi*).

Others, however, adopt an entirely different interpretation of our Gemara, under which a מַרְזֵב is a cloak whose sides — the area normally draped over one's arms — are arranged in folds so that they rest on one's shoulders. Under this interpretation, the *melachah* in question is not *striking the final blow* but *transferring.* For details of this approach, see *Rif* and *Aruch* (*Erech* מרזב); see also *Rambam* (*Hil. Shabbos* 19:19; cf. *Tosafos* ד״ה מהו לעשות מרזב).

19. I.e. he wishes the ruffle to remain a permanent feature of the garment (*Rashi;* cf. *Rambam, Hil. Shabbos* 19:18).

20. I.e. he intends the folds to remain in place only for a certain designated time, after which he will unfurl them (*Rashi*).

Rambam (loc. cit.), however, takes an entirely different view of this

המנער טליתו בשבת חייב חטאת ולא אמרן אלא בחדתי אבל בעתיקי לית לן בה ולא אמרן אלא באוכמי אבל בחיורי וסומקי לית לן בה והוא דקפיד עלייהו עולא איקלע לפומבדיתא חזא רבנן דקא מנפצי גלימייהו אמר קמחללין רבנן שבתא אמר להו רב יהודה נפוצי ליה באפיה אנן לא קפדינן מידי אביי הוה קאי קמיה דרב יוסף א"ל הב לי כומתאי [חזא דאיכא] טלא עליה הוה קמחסם למיתבה ליה א"ל נפוץ שדי אנן לא קפדינן מידי אמר רב יצחק בר יוסף א"ר יוחנן **היוצא** בטלית מקופלת מונחת לו על כתיפו בשבת חייב חטאת תנ"ה סוחרי כסות היוצאים בטליתות מקופלות ומונחות על כתיפן בשבת חייבין חטאת ולא סוחרי כסות בלבד אמרו אלא כל אדם אלא שדרכן של מוכרין לצאת כך וחנוני היוצא במעות הצרורין לו בסדינו חייב חטאת ולא חנוני בלבד אמרו אלא כל אדם אלא שדרכו של חנוני לצאת כך והרטנין יוצאין בסודרין [א] שעל כתיפן ולא רטנין בלבד אמרו אלא כל אדם אלא שדרכן של רטנין לצאת בכך א"ר יהודה מעשה בהורקנוס בנו של רבי אליעזר בן הורקנוס שיצא בסודר שעל כתיפו בשבת אלא שנימא כרוכה לו באצבעו וכשבא הדבר לפני חכמים אמרו אפילו אין נימא כרוכה לו באצבעו דרש רב נחמן בר רב חסדא משמיה דרב חסדא הלכה אע"פ שאין נימא כרוכה לו באצבעותיו עולא איקלע לבי אסי בר היני בעו מיניה מהו לעשות מרזב בשבת אמר להו הכי אמר רבי אלעי אסור לעשות מרזב בשבת מאי מרזב אמר ר' זירא כיסי בבלייתא ר' ירמיה הוה יתיב קמיה דר' זירא א"ל הכי מאי א"ל אסור והכי מאי א"ל אסור אמר רב פפא נקוט האי כללא בידך כל אדעתא דלכנופי [ב] אסור כל דלהתנאות שרי כי הא דרב שישא בריה דרב אידי מתנאה בסדינו הוה כי אתא רב דימי אמר פעם אחת יצא רבי לשדה והיו שני צידי טליתו מונחין על כתיפו אמר לפניו יהושע בן זירוז בן חמיו של רבי מאיר בזו לא חייב ר' מאיר חטאת אמר ליה דקדק רבי מאיר עד כאן שלשל רבי טליתו כי אתא רבין אמר לא יהושע בן זירוז הוה אלא יהושע בן כפוסאי היה חתנו של ר' עקיבא אמר בזו לא חייב ר' עקיבא חטאת אמר לו דקדק ר"ע עד כאן שלשל רבי טליתו כי אתא רב שמואל בר רב יהודה אמר נשאל איתמר: **מתני'** הרוחץ במי מערה ובמי טבריא ונסתפג אפילו בעשר אלונטיאות לא יביאם בידו אבל עשרה בני אדם מסתפגין באלונטית אחת פניהם ידיהם ורגליהם ומביאין אותן בידן סכין וממשמשין אבל לא מתעמלין ולא מתגררין אין יורדין לקורדימא ואין עושין אפיקטויזין ואין מעצבין את הקטן ואין מחזירין את השבר מי שנפרקה ידו ורגלו לא יטרפם בצונן אבל רוחץ הוא כדרכו ואם נתרפא נתרפא: **גמ'** קתני מי מערה דומיא דמי טבריא מה מי טבריא חמין אף מי מערה חמין הרוחץ דיעבד אין לכתחילה לא מכלל דלהשתטף

רש"י

המנער טליתו. מן העפר: חייב חטאת. דזהו ליבונה: **אלא באוכמי**. שהאבק מקלקל מראיתה וקפיד עליה: והוא דקפיד עלייהו. ללובשן על סינער: קמחללי (א) שבתא. וגלימי אוכמי הוו: לא קפדינן. לא איכפת לן אם יש עליה אבק הלכך לאו ליבון הוא: כומתאי. כובעי: הוה קא מחסם. לשון לא תחסום (דברים כה): למיתבא ליה. שצריך לנער הטל מעליה: בטלית מקופלת. לאחר שנתנה על ראשו הגביה שיפוליה על כתפיו: חייב חטאת. שאין זה דרך מלבוש: והרטנין. על שם מקום: נימא כרוכה על אצבעו. שלא יפול מכתפיו: כר היינו: מרזב. מפרש לקמיה: כיסוי בבלייתא. שמסלקין בגדיהם מן הארץ כשהן ארוכין וכופלין אותן כלפי מעלה פרוגל"ר ומחזיקין אותן [ג] ע"י חוטין והיינו כמין כיס וכמו מרזב: אסור. משום תקוני מנא: הכי מאי. קולט חלוקו (בפניו) בענין אחד ושאלו כגון זה מרזב או לא וחזר וקולטו בענין אחר ושאלו: לכנופי. שיהא מתוקן תמיד להעמיד קיפולו לעולם: להתנאות. לפי שעה: מתנאה בסדינו. אחר שנתעטף היה מתקנו על גופו ומיישבו ובחול קאמר כלומר אלמא לאו לאורמיה בהכי וה"ה לשבת: שני צידי טליתו. שבימינו ושבשמאלו לצד הקרקע: בן זירוז בזו לא חייב ר"מ חטאת. בתמיה דלאין זה דרך מלבוש אלא דרך משוי: דקדק ר"מ ע"כ. בתמיה לחייב חטאת בדבר הדומה להיות מותר כזה שאינה מקופלת ואחוריה נופלין למטה מכתפיו אלא שצידיה היו מונחין על כתפו: שלשל. הורידה למטה שקבל דבריו: נשאל איתמר. לא אירע מעשה זה לרבי אלא שאלו לפניו מהו לצאת בו ובקש להתיר עד שאמרו לפניו משום רבי מאיר חייב חטאת דלאיהו סבר הואיל ואינה מקופלת שהרי אחוריה היו נופלין למטה מן כתפיו אלא שצידיה היו מונחים על כתפיו הוה סבר דרך מלבוש הוא: **מתני'** מי מערה. מי מקוה מקורה (ב) שהוא חם ואין חומו יולא ודוקא חמין נקט ומש"ה קתני הרוחץ דיעבד: ונסתפג. וקינח: **אפי' בעשר אלונטיות**. סדינין שמקנחין בהן וסיפג בהן זה אחר זה ורבותא היא דלא נפישי מיא בכל חד אפ"ה לא יביאם בידו בתוך ביתו אפי' ע"י עירוב שמא ישכח ויסחט בכולו: **אבל עשרה בני אדם**. הואיל ומרובין הן מדכרי אהדדי: מסתפגין באלונטית אחת. והיינו נמי רבותא דחדא אלונטית לעשרה (ג) נפישא ביה מיא אפילו הכי מביאין אותה בידים: פניהם ידיהם ורגליהם. אורחא דמילתא נקט וה"ה לכל גופס: סכין. שמן בשבת: וממשמשין. ביד על כל הגוף להנאה: **אבל לא מתעמלין**. לשפשף בכח: **ולא מתגררין**. גרסינן במגררת שקורין אשטריי"לא דהוי עובדא דחול: **לקורדימא**. שם הנהר ובגמ' מפרש טעמא: **אפיקטויזין**. להקיא: **ואין מעצבין את הקטן**. לשון ידיך עלבוני (איוב י) שמתקנים ומיישבין עצמותיו וחוליות שדרתו כמדת גלמו ובגמרא אמר טעמא: **ואין מחזירין את השבר**. עצם שנשבר. כל רפואה אסורה משום שחיקת סמנין: **נפרקה**. אלוישי"ר בלעז שיצא העצם מפרק שלו: **לא יטרפם**. לשון בילים טרופות בקערה (חולין דף סד.):

תוספות

המנער טליתו. פי' ר"ח מן הטל שעליו דהיינו כיבוס וליבון חייב חטאת וכן משמע דהוי דומיא דכומתא דרב יוסף אבל בניעור מן העפר כדפירש בקונטרס אין נראה שיהא שייך ליבון:

היוצא בטלית מקופלת. איידי דאיירינן במי שנשרו כליו בדרך שאז דרך הוא לקפל טליתו נקטיה הכא:

הרטנין. רטנין כמו הרהטנין [י] (הערוך פי' הרלים): **מהו** לעשות מרזב. נראה לרבי דלענין איסור הולאה איירי כמו טלית של ד' כנפו' ולוקח שני לידי רוחב טליתו של לד ימינו ונותן על כתף השמאלית ואינו פושטו על כתף אלא מקופל ומונח על כתפו והיינו דקאמר מאי מרזב כיסי בבלייתא שקורין פרונלדר"ה דכשהוא מונח כמו שפירשתי יש בו כיסים מרובים וכל כיסא וכיסא נראה כמין מרזב ומיבעיא ליה אי איכא איסור הולאה בכך כיון שאינה דרך מלבוש והיינו דקאמר כל אדעתא לכנופי אסור דהיינו כמו שפירשתי ששני לידי הימין מקובלים ומונחים על כתף השמאלית שיכול לילך במהרה ולא יכביד עליו טליתו אדעתא דלהתנאות שפיר דמי והיינו כשאין לידי טליתו מקובלין אלא לד אחד מונחת על כתפו אלל לוארו ולד האחר נופל על שכמו עד הזרוע ואין בו שום כיסוי והיינו שלשל רבי טליתו דבסמוך שלשל אותו כמו שפירשתי כעין להתנאות והיינו דרך מלבוש וכן פירש בערוך ערך מרזב אסור לעשות מרזב בשבת פירוש כשיעטוף אדם טליתו ויקפיל שני קלותיו כעין דרך קיפול ויניחנה על שכמו השמאלית ויחזור ויקפל שאר הטלית שבלד הימין ויניחנה בכתפו רק מה שפירש שקורין מרזב מה שטליתו מושפלת מהנה ומהנה וחלל כנגד השדרה דנראה כמין מרזב אינו נראה לרבי דא"כ מאי קאמר בתר הכי מאי מרזב כיסי בבלייתא הלא אינו עשוי כעין כיסא. מ"ר:

אף מי מערה חמין. (ד) שהוחמו באור דאי בחמי טבריא שרי לכתחילה כדאמר בפרק כירה (ד' מ. ושם) והכיתו להן חמי טבריא ובפרק שמונה שרצים (ד' קח. ושם:):

דיעבד אין. אמי מערה קאי ולא תנא במתני' חמי טבריא אלא למידק אף מי מערה חמין:

עין משפט נר מצוה

מ א מיי' פ"ט מהלכות שבת הלכה יח סמג לאוין סה טוש"ע או"ח סימן שב סעיף א:

מא ב מיי' פי"ט שם הל' יט סמג שם טור שו"ע או"ח סימן שא סעיף כט:

מב ג שם סעיף לב לג:

מג ד מיי' שם טור שו"ע שם סעיף לד:

מד ה שם סעיף לג:

מה ו מיי' פכ"א שם הלכה כ טור שו"ע או"ח סימן שכו סעיף א:

רבינו חננאל

ואוקימנא ליה דרב כתנאי: אמר רב הונא המנער טליתו בשבת חייב חטאת. פי' המנער כדכתיב התנערי מעפר וכדגרסינן התם ומנערה אחת לשלשים. אם יש אבק בבגד חדש שחור ומקפיד עליו. או אם יש עליו דבר טינוף אוסר רב הונא לנפצו. אבל אם הוא בגד ישן או לבן או אדום ולא קפיד עליה שרי וכן הלכה. וזה שראה עולא לרבנן דהוו נפצי גלימייהו ואמר הני מחללי שבתא. רבנן דפומבדיתא במלבושין דלא קפדי עלייהו הוו נפצי. (אמתא) [כומתא] הוא כמין כובע של ראש במקום סודר כדאמרינן בפרק השולח גט לאשתו האי אמתא דהוה שכיב מרע אחת בכת קמיה. ואמרה ליה עד אימת תיתעבד וחזיל ההיא אמתא שקל כומתיה ושדא בה אמר ליה קני הא וקני נפשיך. כלומר קני נפשיך בחליפין. רי"א כומתא הוא כגון כאן דומה לגביע והוה אותו הטמני טינוף. והוה אביי מהסם. כלומר מתירא כדאמרינן התם חזייה דהוה קא מהסס. א"ל רב יוסף לאביי נפוץ שדי אנן לא קפדינן מידי: היוצא בטלית מקופלת ומונחת לו על כתפו כגון אלו מוכרי כסות שמקפלין ומפשילין אותן על כתפיהם. אתמר משמיה דר' יוחנן חייב חטאת ותניא כוותיה והכי הלכתא וכן נמי היוצא וצרורין לו בסדינו מעות חייב חטאת אבל הרטנין שהם הרצים יוצאין בסודר שעל כתפיהן. ולא אלו בלבד אלא כל אדם. והנכון להיות כרוך בצווארו. או נימא כרוכה לו באצבעו. כהורקנוס בר' אליעזר. ואע"ג דאמר משמא דר' יוחנן הלכה אע"פ שאין נימא כרוכה לו על אצבעו: עולא איקלע לבי אסי בר (חני) [היני] בעא מיניה מהו לעשות מרזב בשבת א"ל הכי אמר ר' אלעזר אסור. כך קבלנו מרבותינו שיש בידם קבלה כי מרזב זה כשיתעטף אדם טליתו ויקפל ב' קצוותיה כמין כרך קיפול ויניחה על כתפו השמאלית ויחזור ויקפל שאר הטלית המשולש בצידו הימין מניחה בכתפו הימין ונמצאת טליתו מקופלת מהנה ומהנה ומופשלת על כתפיו וחלל כנגד השדרה ונראה כמין מרזב. וכענין זה היה קשר (כישי) [כישא] בבלייתא שהיו קושרין ב' כריכות וקורין אותה כישא וכיסכוסי מאני א). וי"א זולתי פירוש זה. אבל חובה עלינו לומר בלשון רבותינו ומה שקיבלנוהו. וכרב פפא שהוא בתראה עבדינן ואמר כללא כל אדעתא לכנופי אסור. כל להתנאות שפיר דמי וכדרב שישא בריה דרב אידי שהיה מתנאה בסדינין כי אתא רב דימי אמר פעם אחת יצא רבי לשדה והיו ב' צידי טליתו מונחין לו על כתפו ושאר הטלית כרוכה ומופשלת לו לאחוריו. אמר לפניו יהושע בן זירוז בן חמיו של ר"מ בזו לא חייב ר"מ חטאת. כלומר זה המעשה דומה לרטנין שיוצאין בסודרין בסדינין מקובצין ולא משולשין על כתפיהן ור' מאיר לא היה בזה מחייב חטאת ב) אי לא אסורה מדרבנן. א"ל ר' דקדק ר"מ עד כאן שלשל רבי טליתו: מתני' הרוחץ במי מערה כו'. אוקימנא

חשק שלמה על רבינו חננאל א) עיין בערוך ערך מרזב א': ב) [אולי צ"ל אלמא דאסורה מדרבנן. ואפשר דרבינו מפרש בזו לא חייב ר"מ חטאת בניחותא דחטאת לא היה מחייב רק הוי אוסר מדרבנן וצ"ע בזה]:

מסורת הש"ס

א) לעיל נח., ב) [תוספתא פ"ו], ג) פ"א היוצאין וכו' גי' ר"ח, ד) [יומא כ. מגילה כג:], ה) פ"א בבני מעיים, ו) נ"א לפלומא, ז) לעיל קכג., ח) פ"א טובל, ט) [עי' תוס' חולין ג. סד"ה המניח ועי' תוס' סוטה ב. ד"ה המקנא דיעבד], י) [בערוך רטנן ופיים שם הרלים יולאין בסודר שעל כתפיהן מקובץ ולא משולש בשביל שלא יעכבו לרוץ], כ) עי' רש"א ורש"ל, ל) [ועי' תוספות לעיל קנ. ד"ה רוחלין ותוס' חולין טו: ד"ה אלא גזר].

הגהות הב"ח

(א) רש"י ד"ה קמחללי רבנן שבתא: (ב) ד"ה מי מערה וכו' מקורה שהוסס ואין חומו: (ג) ד"ה מסתפגין וכו' אלונטית לעשרה כמי נפישה: (ד) תוס' ד"ה אף מי מערה חמין שהוחמו וכו' ובפ' שמונה שרצים והא דקאמר דיעבד אין אמי והה"א:

גליון הש"ס

רש"י ד"ה חייב חטאת. דזהו ליבונה. עיין לעיל דף קמא ע"א רש"י ד"ה מנפסם וצ"ע:

הגהות הגר"א

[א] גמרא יוצאין בסודרין שעל כתפן. נ"ב פי' אפילו מקופל. וח"ש רטנין ר"ל הרלים. ערוך ורמב"ם: [ב] שם כל אדעתא דלכנופי. נ"ב פי' הרמב"ם שלא יקרעו או שלא יתלכלכו: [ג] רש"י ד"ה כיסי בבלייתא ומחזיקין אותן. נ"ב אבל הרמב"ם כתב אפילו בידו או על כתפו:

ליקוטי רש"י

גזירה שמא יקבום. ונמלא עושה כלי וחייב משום מכה בפטיש [לעיל קכה:]. דהפס כלי משוי ליה ואיכא איסורא דאורייתא [ביצה לג:]. בחמה. בשמש. בשביל שיחומו. דאין דרך בישולו בכך ותחה כאור לא מיחלפא לגיזור לא אלחנו הא [לעיל לט.]. מי שנשרו כליו בדרך. במי גשמים [שם כה. ועי' בתוס' כאן והבהגר"א שם]. מהלך בהן. וכן מתעגגנין והולכין ולא חיישינן שיסחטום שמכבסן [ביצה לה:]. שוטחן בחמה. וכן נוגבין מאליהן. אבל לא כנגד העם. שלא יאמרו כבסן בשבת [שם ט.]. אשוויי גומות. דמלאכה הוא בשבת דהוי כבנין [עירובין קד.]. רמיץ. אפר חם וכך שמו בלשון ערבי [חולין ח.]. גחלים ואפר בוערים [נדה מט:]. אפר המעורב בגחלים [לעיל לד:]. כל מקום שאסרו חכמים. דבר המותר ואסרוהו. מפני מראית העין. שהרואהו חושדו בדבר עבירה [ע"ז יב.]. שלא יחשדוהו באיסור [לעיל סד:]. אפילו בחדרי חדרים אסור. במקום שאין אדם רואה אסרוהו [ע"ז שם]. תנן שוטחן בחמה אבל לא כנגד העם. אלמא מידי דמשום מראית העין מותר במקום לנוע [ביצה שם]. [ע"כ שייך לדף קמו:].

מחסם. לשון (דברים כה) לא תחסום מגמגם [חולין נ.]. חייב חטאת. דלאו תכשיט אלא בזמן שלובשו דרך מלבוש [לעיל נח.]. מי טבריא. חמי טבריא. מעיינות רותחין [פסחים מא.]. אלונטית. בגד שמסתפגין בו כשיוצאין מבית המרחץ [עירובין פז:]. אפיקטויזין. הקאה גומיטא בלע"ז כך מלאתי [לעיל יב.]. להקיא והוא בנוטריקון אפיק טפי זין מזון האוכל יותר מדאי מוליא ומקיא [סוכה מ:]. ואין עושין אפיקטויזין. להקיא שותה משקים ומקיא ולא לרפואה אלא להריק את מעיו שיוכל לאכול ולשתות [היום] הרבה כדאמרינן בפרק חבית ואף על גב דלא גזור בה משום שחיקת סממנין דהא לאו לרפואה היא אסור משום דמתקן גברא [לעיל קכג:]. בכם דדמי לרפואה וגזירה משום שחיקת סמנין אבל ביד להכניס יד לתוך גרונו עד שיקיא מותר [לקמן ע"ב בגה"ש].

כִּדְרַב אִידִי – an example of the latter being **the case of Rav Shisha the son of Rav Idi,** דְּמִתְנָאֶה בִּסְדִינוֹ הֲוָה – **who used to beautify his cloak** by arranging its folds after he had donned it.[21]

The Gemara above stated that one may not traverse a public domain with a folded cloak on his shoulders. The Gemara now relates an incident pertaining to this:

כִּי אֲתָא רַב דִּימִי אָמַר – **When Rav Dimi came** from the Land of Israel to Babylonia **he said:** פַּעַם אַחַת יָצָא רַבִּי לַשָּׂדֶה – **One time, Rebbi went out into a field** on the Sabbath, וְהָיוּ שְׁנֵי צִידֵּי טַלִּיתוֹ מוּנָּחִין עַל כְּתֵיפוֹ – **and the two sides of his cloak were resting on his shoulders.**[22] אָמַר לְפָנָיו יְהוֹשֻׁעַ בֶּן זֵירוּז בֶּן חָמִיו שֶׁל רַבִּי מֵאִיר – Seeing this, **Yehoshua ben Zeiruz, the son of R' Meir's father-in-law, said to [Rebbi]:** בְּזוֹ לֹא חִיֵּיב רַבִּי מֵאִיר חַטָּאת – **For** an act of **this** sort, **did R' Meir not hold one liable to a** ***chatas*****?**[23] אָמַר לֵיהּ – **[Rebbi]** then **replied to him:** דִּקְדֵּק רַבִּי מֵאִיר עַד כָּאן – **Was R' Meir** really **that exacting** on the matter?[24] שִׁלְשֵׁל רַבִּי טַלִּיתוֹ – Nevertheless, he accepted R' Yehoshua's words, and **Rebbe** then **unfurled his cloak** from upon his shoulder.[25]

Another Amora provides a different version of the episode: כִּי אֲתָא רָבִין אָמַר – **When Ravin came** from the Land of Israel to Babylonia, **he said:** לֹא יְהוֹשֻׁעַ בֶּן זֵירוּז הֲוָה – In fact, **it was not Yehoshua ben Zeiruz** who accosted Rebbi, אֶלָּא יְהוֹשֻׁעַ בֶּן כְּפוּסַאי הָיָה חַתְנוֹ שֶׁל רַבִּי עֲקִיבָא – **rather, it was Yehoshua ben Kefusai, the son-in-law of R' Akiva.** Furthermore, this person did not report a ruling in the name of R' Meir; rather, אָמַר בְּזוֹ לֹא חִיֵּיב רַבִּי עֲקִיבָא חַטָּאת – what **he said** was: **For** an act of **this** sort, **did R' Akiva not hold one liable to a** ***chatas*****?** אָמַר לוֹ – Whereupon **[Rebbi] replied to him:** דִּקְדֵּק רַבִּי עֲקִיבָא עַד כָּאן – **Was R' Akiva** really **that exacting** on the matter? שִׁלְשֵׁל רַבִּי טַלִּיתוֹ – And then, accepting R' Yehoshua's words, **Rebbe unfurled his cloak.**

The Gemara presents another variation of the story: כִּי אֲתָא רַב שְׁמוּאֵל בַּר רַב יְהוּדָה אָמַר – **When Rav Shmuel bar Rav Yehudah came** from the Land of Israel to Babylonia **he said:** נִשְׁאַל אִיתְּמַר – **It was reported** that **[Rebbi] was** ***asked*** about wearing one's cloak in this manner; it was not so that Rebbi himself had been wearing his cloak this way.[26]

Mishnah The Mishnah now discusses bathing and drying oneself on the Sabbath:[27] הָרוֹחֵץ בְּמֵי מְעָרָה וּבְמֵי טְבֶרְיָא – **One who bathes in the water of a cave**[28] **or in the waters of** the **Tiberias** hot springs, וְנִסְתַּפֵּג אֲפִילוּ בְּעֶשֶׂר אֲלוּנְטִיאוֹת – **and dried himself even with ten towels,** לֹא יְבִיאֵם בְּיָדוֹ – **may not carry [the towels]** home **in his hand.**[29] אֲבָל עֲשָׂרָה בְּנֵי אָדָם מִסְתַּפְּגִין בַּאֲלוּנְטִית אַחַת – **However, ten people may dry themselves with one towel;** פְּנֵיהֶם יְדֵיהֶם וְרַגְלֵיהֶם – drying **their faces, their hands, and their**

NOTES

discussion. He asserts that the Gemara is speaking of the ways in which the sides of a cloak may be folded onto one's shoulders, and the permissibility of traversing a public domain while wearing a cloak in this fashion. When the folds are made "to gather" (לְכַנּוּפֵי) the cloak up so it will not drag on the ground or rip, then the person is deemed to be carrying the garment and he may not traverse a public domain. But when the folds are made "to beautify" (לְהִתְנָאוֹת) the appearance of the garment, the person is said to be wearing the cloak, and he may indeed walk with the cloak in the public domain.

21. I.e. this was his daily practice during the week (*Rashi*). Evidently, then, the folds he made were only meant to be of a temporary nature (for he made them anew each day), and it was therefore permissible for him to make these folds on the Sabbath too.

22. He took the two sides of his cloak – the area normally draped over one's arms – and folded them back towards him, so that the right edge of the cloak rested on his right shoulder, and the left edge on his left shoulder (*Rashi*). [This is distinguished from the case of the "folded cloak" described at the beginning of the Gemara's discussion, where the *back* edge of the garment was lifted so that it rested on one's shoulders (see *Rashi* below ד״ה נשאל איתמר).]

23. R' Yehoshuah presumed that this was not a normative way to wear a cloak, and thus, legally speaking, Rebbi would be deemed to be carrying it (*Rashi*).

24. I.e. granted that R' Meir holds one liable when the cloak is folded from behind, but when just the *sides* of the cloak are resting on the shoulders (while in the back, the full length of the cloak hangs down), would he also ascribe liability? The latter seems like a far more normative way of wearing the garment! (*Rashi;* see also *Ritva*).

25. [As a practical matter, the permissibility of traversing a public domain in these varying modes of dress depends upon the prevalent custom of dress in a given locale. In Rebbi's time and in his locale, this was not deemed a normative way to wear a cloak. In other times or locales, however, the same may not apply (see *Rama* to 301:31).]

26. I.e. Rebbi had been asked about walking in a public domain while wearing a cloak in this manner, and his first inclination was to permit this [since the back of the cloak had not been folded]. He was told, however, that R' Meir forbade the act, and he then deferred to R' Meir's ruling (*Rashi*).

27. The Rabbis prohibited bathing in hot water on the Sabbath even if it was heated before the Sabbath. This was prohibited because the bathhouse attendants would often heat the water on the Sabbath and claim that it had been heated before the Sabbath. Initially, even bathing in the water of thermal springs was prohibited. When the Rabbis saw that people could not endure a total ban on hot-water bathing, they lifted the ban on bathing in thermal springs (see above, 40a).

28. For the purpose of bathing, water would sometimes be heated by fire and placed in an enclosed, roofed area, such as a pit inside a cave. [The roof of the cave would prevent the heat from dissipating] (*Rashi; Rashba;* see also *Rosh* cf. *Rif*).

By phrasing the case as *one who bathes* . . . (rather than "one *may* bathe . . ."), the Mishnah indicates that the bathing itself is prohibited and that we are dealing only with the aftermath of an act which should not have taken place. This is because bathing on the Sabbath in water heated even before the Sabbath is Rabbinically prohibited (*Rashi;* see above, note 27, and below, note 41).

29. Although he barely wet any of the towels (since he used ten of them), still, he may not carry them home with him, for fear that he will forget and wring them out on the way home, a violation of the Sabbath. [Squeezing water out of a towel, or any garment, constitutes an act of כִּבּוּס, *laundering,* a *toladah* of the *melachah* of מְלַבֵּן, *whitening*.] The Mishnah speaks of a locale where the person would otherwise be permitted to carry [e.g. the town was enclosed by a wall, and all the houses in the town were joined together in an *eruvei chatzeiros*] (see *Rashi*).

[Although the word נִסְתַּפֵּג, *and he dried himself,* is used in the past tense, it is not meant to imply that one is not permitted to dry himself in the first place (*Ran*). On the contrary, since the Mishnah will explicitly state below that ten people may dry themselves with one towel it follows that one person may certainly do so. The reason this is permitted can be explained as follows:

There are generally two reasons why wetting fabrics might be prohibited on the Sabbath: (a) for fear the person will wring them out, and (b) because soaking a fabric is tantamount to washing it (see above, 142b, and *Rashi* ad loc. ד״ה מקנחה). As far as the first consideration is concerned, since it is only Rabbinic in nature, the Rabbis did not forbid it in this case, because they felt that such a measure could not endure. Since it was necessary to permit some bathing (see above, note 27), and it is customary for all bathers to dry themselves, no one would heed such a prohibition (*Ran*).

As regards the second consideration, soaking a fabric is not regarded as tantamount to washing it unless it was originally soiled. Therefore, one may dry himself with a clean towel and thus avoid this prohibition (*Rama* to 302:9). [Others, however, prohibit soaking even a clean garment. Nevertheless, even they agree that one may dry himself with a towel since he is soiling the towel, rather than washing it (*Rama* ad loc.; see also *Mishnah Berurah* there §48).]

המנער טליתו. מן העפר: **חייב חטאת.** דזהו ליבונה: **אלא באוכמי.** שהאבק מקלקל מראיתה וקפיד עליה: **והוא דקפיד עלייהו.** ללובשן עד שינערם: **קמחללי** (א) **שבתא.** וגלימי אוכמי הוו: **לא קפדינן.** לא איכפת לן אם יש עליה אבק הלכך לאו ליבון הוא: **כומתאי.** כובעי: **הוה קא מחסם.** לשון לא תחסום (דברים כה): **למיתבא ליה.** שצריך לנער הטל מעליה: **בטלית מקופלת.** לאחר שנתנה על ראשו הגביה שיפוליה על כתפיו: **חייב חטאת.** שאין זה דרך מלבוש: **והרטנין.** על שם מקום: **נימא כרוכה על אצבעו.** שלא יפול מכתפיו: **בר היני: מרזב.** מפרש לקמיה: **כיסוי בבלייתא.** שמסלקין בגדיהם מן הארץ כשהן ארוכין וכופלין אותן כלפי מעלה פרונצי"ש ומחזיקין אותן [ג] ע"י חוטין והיינו כמין כיס וכמו מרזב: **אסור.** משום תקוני מנא: **הכי מאי.** קולט חלוקו (בפניו) בענין אחד ושואלו כגון זה מרזב או לא וחוזר וקולטו בענין אחר ושואלו: **לכנופי.** שיהא מתוקן תמיד להעמיד קיפולו לעולם: **להתנאות.** לפי שעה: **מתנאה בסדינו.** אחר שנתעטף היה מתקנו על גופו ומיישבו ובחול קאמר כלומר אלמא דאורחיה בהכי וה"ה לשבת: **שני צידי טליתו.** שבימינו ובשמאלו לצד הקרקע: **בן זירוז בזו לא חייב ר"מ חטאת.** בתמיה דאין זה דרך מלבוש אלא דרך משוי: **דקדק ר"מ ע"כ.** בתמיה לחייב חטאת בדבר הדומה להיות מותר כזה שאינה מקופלת ואחוריה נופלין למטה מכתפיו אלא שלידיה היו מונחין על כתפו: **שלשל.** הורידה למטה שקבל דבריו: **נשאל איתמר.** לא אירע מעשה זה לרבי אלא שאלו לפניו מהו לצאת בו ובקש להתיר עד שאמרו לפניו משום רבי מאיר חייב חטאת דאיהו סבר הואיל ואינה מקופלת שהרי אחוריה היו נופלין למטה מן כתפיו אלא שלידיה היו מונחים על כתפיו הוה סבר דרך מלבוש הוא: **מתני' מי מערה.** מי מקוה מקורה (ב) שהוא חם ואין חומו יולא ודוקא חמין נקט ומש"ה קתני הרוחץ דיעבד: **ונסתפג.** וקינח: **אפי' בעשר אלונטיות.** סדינין שמקנחין בהן וסיפג בהן זה אחר זה ורבותא היא דלא נפישי מיא בכל חד אפ"ה לא יביאם בידו בתוך ביתו אפי' ע"י עירוב שמא ישכח ויסחט בבואו: **אבל עשרה בני אדם.** הואיל ומרובין הן מדכרי אהדדי: **מסתפגין באלונטית אחת.** והיינו נמי רבותא דחדא אלונטית לעשרה (ג) נפישא ביה מיא אפילו הכי מביאין אותה בידים: **פניהם ידיהם ורגליהם.** אורחא דמילתא נקט וה"ה לכל גופם: **סכין.** שמן בשבת: **וממשמשין.** ביד על כל הגוף להנאה: **אבל לא מתעמלין.** לשפשף בכח: **ולא מתגררין.** גרסינן במגררת שקורין אשטרייל"א דהוי עובדא דחול: **לקורדימא.** שם הנהר וגמ' מפרש טעמא: **אפיקטויזין.** להקיא: **ואין מעצבין את הקטן.** לשון ידיך עצבוני (איוב י) שמתקנים ומיישבין עצמותיו וחוליות שדרתו כמדת גלמו ובגמרא אמר טעמא: **ואין מחזירין את השבר.** עלם שנשבר. כל רפואה אסורה משום שחיקת סמנין: **נפרקה.** אלוייש"ר בלעז שילא העלם ממקום מפרק שלו: **לא יטרפם.** לשון ביליס טרופות בקערה (חולין דף סד.):

המנער טליתו בשבת חייב חטאת ולא אמרן אלא בחדתי אבל בעתיקי לית לן בה ולא אמרן אלא באוכמי אבל בחיורי וסומקי לית לן בה והוא דקפיד עלייהו עולא איקלע לפומבדיתא חזא רבנן דקא מנפצי גלימייהו אמר קמחללין רבנן שבתא אמר להו רב יהודה נפוצי ליה באפיה אנן לא קפדינן מידי אביי הוה קאי קמיה דרב יוסף א"ל הב לי כומתאי [חזא דאיכא] טלא עליה הוה קמחסם למיתבה ליה א"ל נפוץ שדי אנן לא קפדינן מידי אמר רב יצחק בר יוסף א"ר יוחנן היוצא בטלית מקופלת מונחת לו על כתיפו בשבת חייב חטאת תנ"ה סוחרי כסות היוצאים בטליתות מקופלות ומונחות על כתיפן בשבת חייבין חטאת ולא סוחרי כסות בלבד אמרו אלא כל אדם אלא שדרכן של מוכרין לצאת כך וחנוני היוצא במעות הצרורין לו בסדינו חייב חטאת ולא חנוני בלבד אמרו אלא כל אדם אלא שדרכו של חנוני לצאת כך והרטנין יוצאין בסודרין [א] שעל כתיפן ולא רטנין בלבד אמרו אלא כל אדם אלא שדרכן של רטנין לצאת בכך א"ר יהודה מעשה בהורקנוס בנו של רבי אליעזר בן הורקנוס שיצא בסודר שעל כתיפו בשבת אלא שנימא כרוכה לו באצבעו וכשבא הדבר לפני חכמים אמרו אפילו אין נימא כרוכה לו באצבעו דרש רב נחמן בר רב חסדא משמיה דרב חסדא הלכה אע"פ שאין נימא כרוכה לו באצבעותיו עולא איקלע לבי אסי בר היני בעו מיניה מהו לעשות מרזב בשבת אמר להו הכי אמר רבי אלעי אסור לעשות מרזב בשבת מאי מרזב אמר ר' זירא כיסי בבלייתא ר' ירמיה הוה יתיב קמיה דר' זירא א"ל הכי מאי א"ל אסור והכי מאי א"ל אסור אמר רב פפא נקוט האי כללא בידך כל אדעתא דלכנופי [ב] אסור כל דלהתנאות שרי כי הא דרב שישא בריה דרב אידי מתנאה בסדינו הוה כי אתא רב דימי אמר פעם אחת יצא רבי לשדה והיו שני צידי טליתו מונחין על כתיפו אמר לפניו יהושע בן זירוז בן חמיו של רבי מאיר בזו לא חייב ר' מאיר חטאת אמר ליה דקדק רבי מאיר עד כאן שלשל רבי טליתו כי אתא רבין אמר לא יהושע בן זירוז הוה אלא יהושע בן כפוסאי היה חתנו של ר' עקיבא אמר בזו לא חייב ר' עקיבא חטאת אמר לו דקדק ר"ע עד כאן שלשל רבי טליתו כי אתא רב שמואל בר רב יהודה אמר נשאל איתמר: **מתני'** הרוחץ במי מערה ובמי טבריא ונסתפג אפילו בעשר אלונטיאות לא יביאם בידו אבל עשרה בני אדם מסתפגין באלונטית אחת פניהם ידיהם ורגליהם ומביאין אותן בידן סכין וממשמשין אבל לא מתעמלין ולא מתגררין אין יורדין לקורדימא ואין עושין אפיקטויזין ואין מעצבין את הקטן ואין מחזירין את השבר מי שנפרקה ידו ורגלו לא יטרפם בצונן אבל רוחץ הוא כדרכו ואם נתרפא נתרפא: **גמ'** קתני מי מערה דומיא דמי טבריא מה מי טבריא חמין אף מי מערה חמין הרוחץ דיעבד אין לכתחילה לא מכלל דלהשתטף

המנער טליתו. פי' ר"ח מן הטל שעליו דהיינו כיבוס וליבון חייב חטאת וכן משמע דהוי דומיא דכומתא דרב יוסף אבל בניעור מן העפר דפירש בקונטרס אין נראה שיהא שייך ליבון: **היוצא** בטלית מקופלת. איידי דאיירינן במי שנשרו כליו בדרך שאז דרך הוא לקפל טליתו נקטיה הכא: **הרטנין.** רטנין כמו הרהטנין (הערוך פי' הרלים): **מהו** לעשות מרזב. נראה לרבי דלענין איסור הוצאה איירי כמו טלית של ד' כנפות ולוקח שני לידי רוחב טליתו של לד ימינו ונותן על כתף השמאלית ואינו פושטו על כתף אלא מקופל ומונח על כתפו והיינו דקאמר מאי מרזב כיסי בבלייתא שקורין פרונלדר"ה דכשהוא מונח כמו שפירשתי יש בו כיסים מרובים וכל כיסא וכיסא נראה כמין מרזב ומיבעיא ליה אי איכא איסור הוצאה בכך כיון שאינה דרך מלבוש והיינו דקאמר כל אדעתא לכנופי אסור דהיינו כמו שפירשתי ששני לידי הימין מקובלים ומונחים על כתף השמאלית שיכול לילך במהרה ולא יכביד עליו טליתו אדעתא דלהתנאות שפיר דמי והיינו כשאין לידי טליתו מקובלין אלא לד אחד מונחת על כתפו אבל לוארו ולד האחר נופל על שכמו עד הזרוע ואין בו שום כיסוי והיינו שלשל רבי טליתו דבסמוך שלשל אותו כמו שפירשתי כעין להתנאות והיינו דרך מלבוש וכן פירש בערוך ערך מרזב אסור לעשות מרזב בשבת פירוש כשיעטוף אדם טליתו ויקפיל שני קלותיו כעין דרך קיפול ויניחנה על שכמו השמאלית ויחזור ויקפל שאר הטלית שבלד הימין ויניחנה בכתפו רק מה שפירש שקורין מרזב מה שטליתו מושפלת מהנה ומהנה וחלל כנגד השדרה דנראה כמין מרזב אינו נראה לרבי דא"כ מאי קאמר בתר הכי מאי מרזב כיסי בבלייתא הלא אינו עשוי כעין כיסא. מ"ר:

אף מי מערה חמין. (ד) שהוחמו באור דאי בחמי טבריא שרי לכתחילה כדאמר בפרק כירה (ד' מ. ושם) והניחו להן חמי טבריא ובפרק שמונה שרצים (ד' קט. ושם:):

דיעבד אין. אמי מערה קאי ולא תנא במתני' חמי טבריא אלא למידק אף מי מערה חמין: דתניא

עין משפט נר מצוה

מ א מיי' פי"ט מהלכות שבת הלכה יט סמג לאוין סה טוש"ע או"ח סימן שא סעיף ח: מא ב מיי' פכ"ב שם הל' יט סמג שם טור שו"ע או"ח סימן שא סעיף כג: מב ג שם סעיף לב לג: מג ד מיי' פכ"ב שם טור שו"ע שם סעיף לד: מד ה שם סעיף לה: מה ו מיי' פכ"ב שם הלכה כ טור שו"ע או"ח סימן שכו סעיף א:

רבינו חננאל

הגהות הב"ח

גליון הש"ס

הגהות הגר"א

ליקוטי רש"י

חשק שלמה על רבינו חננאל

feet,[30] **וּמְבִיאִין אוֹתָן בְּיָדָן – and they may carry [the towel]** home **in their hands.**[31]

The Mishnah discusses various other laws:

סָכִין וּמְמַשְׁמְשִׁין – On the Sabbath, **we may apply oil** to the skin **and massage** the body by hand;[32] **אֲבָל לֹא מִתְעַמְּלִין – but we may not massage vigorously,**[33] **וְלֹא מִתְגָּרְרִין – nor may we scrape** the skin.[34] **אֵין יוֹרְדִין לְקוֹרְדִימָא – We may not go down to the Kurdima** River on the Sabbath,[35] **וְאֵין עוֹשִׂין אַפִּיקְטְוִיזִין – nor may we take an emetic** to induce vomiting.[36] **וְאֵין מְעַצְּבִין אֶת הַקָּטָן – We may not straighten the** limbs of an **infant,**[37] **וְאֵין מַחֲזִירִין אֶת הַשֶּׁבֶר – nor may we set a broken bone.**[38] **מִי שֶׁנִּפְרְקָה יָדוֹ וְרַגְלוֹ – If one's hand or foot became dislocated, לֹא יִטְרְפֵם בְּצוֹנֵן – he may not massage them with cold water,**[39] **אֲבָל רוֹחֵץ הוּא כְּדַרְכּוֹ – but he may bathe according to his usual manner, וְאִם נִתְרַפֵּא נִתְרַפֵּא – and if he is healed** thereby, **he is healed.**

Gemara

The Gemara analyzes the first part of the Mishnah:

קָתָנֵי מֵי מְעָרָה – [The Mishnah] teaches the case of **cave waters דּוּמְיָא דְּמֵי טְבֶרְיָא – together with, and thus comparable to,** the case of **the waters of Tiberias'** hot springs. This leads to the following analogy: **מַה מֵּי טְבֶרְיָא חַמִּין – Just as the waters of Tiberias'** hot springs **are hot, אַף מֵי מְעָרָה חַמִּין – so** it must be that **the cave waters** about which the Mishnah speaks are **hot** as well.[40] **הָרוֹחֵץ** – Now, with reference to these cave waters, the Mishnah uses the expression: ONE WHO BATHES [in them . . .]. **דִּיעֲבַד אֵין לְכַתְּחִילָּה לֹא – This indicates** that **yes, after the fact** of his having bathed and dried himself, he may not carry the towels, etc., but **in the first place** he ought **not** to have bathed in these waters.[41] **מִכְּלָל – This,** in turn, **implies**

NOTES

30. They may even dry their whole body with the same towel. The Mishnah mentions faces, hands and feet only because it is more usual for many people to use a common towel for their face, hands and feet than for their whole body (*Rashi; see Hagahos R' Elazar Moshe Horowitz*).

31. Since many people are involved together, if one of them forgets that the towel may not be wrung out on the Sabbath, he will undoubtedly be reminded by the others. The ban against carrying the towel home therefore does not apply (*Rashi*).

32. [In Mishnaic times, it was common practice to rub olive oil into the skin to keep it soft. This was often done prior to a hand massage of the body (see Gemara, 147b).]

33. This is forbidden since it resembles a weekday activity (*Tos. Yom Tov; see Rashi*).

Alternatively, the Mishnah means that we may not pummel our body with force until we perspire, or we may not vigorously flex our muscles to cause perspiration. This would be forbidden as part of the general ban on using curatives on the Sabbath (see *Rambam, Hil. Shabbos* 21:28; *Shulchan Aruch* 327:2 with *Mishnah Berurah*).

34. I.e. one may not scrape the skin with a strigil, an instrument of metal, ivory or horn used, in olden times, to scrape the skin at the bath. This, too, is prohibited as a weekday type activity (*Rashi;* see also *Rambam, Hil. Shabbos* 21:30).

35. The Gemara below (147b) will explain the reason for this (*Rashi*).

36. The term אַפִּיקְטְוִיזִין – referring to a substance that can induce vomiting – is a contraction of three Aramaic words: אַפִּיק, *take out,* טְפֵי, *extra,* זוּן, *food* (*Aruch; Meiri*).

37. I.e. if one of the vertebrae becomes dislocated, it may not be reset on the Sabbath (*Rashi*). So long as it is not a dire emergency, this must wait until the next day (see *Rama* to 328:17 and *Tiferes Yisrael*).

38. These prohibitions derive from the general ban against administering medicine on the Sabbath, which was put in place to prevent people from pulverizing substances (e.g. herbs) to create medicine on the Sabbath [a violation of the *melachah* of טוֹחֵן, *grinding*] (*Rashi* here and to above, 53b ד"ה גוזרה). [The Gemara below (148a), however, will rule that it is indeed permitted to set a broken bone on the Sabbath.]

39. I.e. he may not rub vigorously with cold water (*Tur* 328) [since this is obviously being done for therapeutic purposes]. Others explain: He may not bathe the affected limbs alone, since it is then obviously a therapeutic measure, but he may bathe his entire body, thereby bathing the affected limbs as well (*Meiri*).

40. I.e. the water was heated manually before the Sabbath and placed in a pit in the cave where one could immerse in it (see above, note 28).

41. [Had the Mishnah held bathing in these waters to be permissible, it ought to have begun by stating: "One may bathe . . .".]

Tosafos state that the after-the-fact phraseology (indicating that the act is in the first place impermissible) is focused particularly on the case of bathing in [hot] cave waters. As mentioned above (note 27), bathing in Tiberian hot springs is entirely permitted. [Indeed, the only reason the case of the Tiberian hot springs was included in the Mishnah was to convey that the immediately following case, cave waters, involves water that is hot as well (*Tosafos;* see also *Ritva*).].

המנער טליתו. מן העפר: חייב חטאת. ° דזהו ליבונה: אלא באוכמי. שהאבק מקלקל מראיהם וקפיד עליה: והוא דקפיד עלייהו. ללובנן עד שינערם: קמחללי (א) שבתא. וגלימי אוכמי הוו: לא קפדינן. לא איכפת לן אם יש עליה אבק הלכך לאו ליבון הוא: כומתאי. כובעי: הוה קא מחסם. לשון לא תחסום (דברים כה): למיתבא ליה. שצריך לנער הטל מעליה: בטלית מקופלת. לאחר שנתנה על ראשו הגביה שיפוליה על כתפיו: חייב חטאת. שאין זה דרך מלבוש: והרטנין. על שם מקום: נימא כרוכה על אצבעו. שלא יפול מכתפיו: בר היני: מרזב. מפרש לקמיה: כיסוי בבלייתא. שמסלקין בגדיהם מן הארץ כשהן ארוכין וכופלין אותן כלפי מעלה פרונ"ש ומחזיקין אותן [ג] ע"י חוטין והיינו כמין כיס וכמו מרזב: אסור. משום תקוני מנא: הכי מאי. קולט חלוקו (בפניו) בענין אחד ושואלו כגון זה מרזב או לא וחוזר וקולטו בענין אחר ושואלו: לכנופי. שיהא מתוקן תמיד להעמיד קיפולו לעולם: להתנאות. לפי שעה: מתנאה בסדינו. אחר שנתעטף היה מתקנו על גופו ומיישבו ובהול קאמר כלומר אלמא לאורחיה בהכי וה"ה לשבת: שני צידי טליתו. שבימינו ובשמאלו לצד הקרקע: בן זירוז בזו לא חייב ר"מ חטאת. בתמיה דאין זה דרך מלבוש אלא דרך משוי: דקדק ר"מ ע"כ. בתמיה לחייב חטאת בדבר הדומה להיות מותר הוא שאינה מקופלת ואחוריה נופלין למטה מכתפיו אלא שלידיה היו מונחין על כתפיו: שלשל. הורידה למטה שקבל דבריו: נשאל איתמר. לא אירע מעשה זה לרבי אלא שאלו לפניו מהו לצאת בו ובקש להתיר עד שאמרו לפניו משום רבי מאיר חייב חטאת דאיהו סבר הואיל ואינה מקופלת שהרי אחוריה היו נופלין למטה מן כתפיו אלא שלידיה היו מונחים על כתפיו הוה סבר דרך מלבוש הוא: מתני' מי מערה. מי מקוה מקורה (ב) שהוא חם ואין חומו יוצא ודוקא חמין נקט ומש"ה קתני הרוחץ דיעבד: ונסתפג. וקינח: אפי' בעשר אלונטיות. סדינין שמקנחין בהן וסיפג בהן זה אחר זה ורבותא היא דלא נפישי מיא בכל חד אפ"ה לא יביאם בידו בתוך ביתו אפי' ע"י עירוב שמא ישכח ויסחטם בבואו: אבל עשרה בני אדם. הואיל ומרובין הן מדכרי אהדדי: מסתפגין באלונטית אחת. והיינו נמי רבותא דמדלא אלונטית לעשרה (ג) נפישיה ביה מיא אפילו הכי מבילין אותה בידים. אורחא למילתא נקט וה"ה לכל גופס: סכין. שמן בשבת: וממשמשין. ביד על כל הגוף להנאה: אבל לא מתעמלין. לשפשף בכח: ולא מתגררין. גרסינן במגררת שקורין אשטריי"א דהוי עובדא דחול: לקורדימא. שם הנהר ובגמ' מפרש טעמא: אפיקטויזין. להקיא: ואין מעצבין את הקטן. לשון ידיך עצבוני (איוב י) שמתקנים ומיישבין עצמותיו וחוליות שדרתו כמדת צלמו ובגמרא אמר טעמא: ואין מחזירין את השבר. עצם שנשבר. כל רפואה אסורה משום שחיקת סמנין: נפרקה. אלוייש"ר בלעז שיצא העצם מפרק שלו: לא יטרפם. לשון בילים טרופות בקערה (חולין דף סד.):

א **המנער** טליתו בשבת חייב חטאת ולא אמרן אלא בחדתי אבל בעתיקי לית לן בה ולא אמרן אלא באוכמי אבל בחיורי וסומקי לית לן בה והוא דקפיד עלייהו עולא איקלע לפומבדיתא חזא רבנן דקא מנפצי גלימייהו אמר קמחללין רבנן שבתא אמר להו רב יהודה נפוצי ליה באפיה אנן לא קפדינן מידי אביי הוה קאי קמיה דרב יוסף א"ל הב לי כומתאי [חזא דאיכא] טלא עליה הוה קמחסם למיתבה ליה א"ל נפוץ שדי אנן לא קפדינן מידי אמר רב יצחק בר יוסף א"ר יוחנן ב היוצא בטלית מקופלת מונחת לו על כתיפו בשבת חייב חטאת תנ"ה סוחרי כסות היוצאים בטליתות מקופלות ומונחות על כתיפן בשבת חייבין חטאת ולא סוחרי כסות בלבד אמרו אלא כל אדם אלא שדרכן של מוכרין לצאת כך וחנוני ג היוצא במעות הצרורין לו בסדינו חייב חטאת ולא חנוני בלבד אמרו אלא כל אדם אלא שדרכו של חנוני לצאת כך ג) והרטנין יוצאין בסודרין [א] שעל כתיפן ולא רטנין בלבד אמרו אלא כל אדם אלא שדרכן של רטנין לצאת בכך א"ר יהודה מעשה בהורקנוס בנו של רבי אליעזר בן הורקנוס שיצא בסודר שעל כתיפו בשבת אלא שנימא כרוכה לו באצבעו וכשבא הדבר לפני חכמים אמרו ד אפילו אין נימא כרוכה לו באצבעו דרש רב נחמן בר רב חסדא משמיה דרב חסדא הלכה אע"פ שאין נימא כרוכה לו באצבעותיו עולא איקלע לבי אסי בר היני בעו מיניה מהו לעשות מרזב בשבת אמר להו הכי אמר רבי אלעי אסור לעשות מרזב בשבת מאי מרזב אמר ר' זירא כיסי בבלייתא ר' ירמיה הוה יתיב קמיה דר' זירא א"ל הכי מאי א"ל אסור והכי מאי א"ל אסור אמר רב פפא ה) נקוט האי כללא בידך כל אדעתא דלכנופי [ו]אסור כל דלהתנאות שרי כי הא דרב שישא בריה דרב אידי מתנאה בסדינו הוה כי אתא רב דימי אמר פעם אחת יצא רבי לשדה והיו שני צידי טליתו מונחין על כתיפו אמר לפניו יהושע בן זירוז בן חמיו של רבי מאיר בזו לא חייב ר' מאיר חטאת אמר ליה דקדק רבי מאיר עד כאן שלשל רבי טליתו כי אתא רבין אמר לא יהושע בן זירוז הוה אלא יהושע בן כפוסאי היה חתנו של ר' עקיבא אמר בזו לא חייב ר' עקיבא חטאת אמר לו דקדק ר"ע עד כאן שלשל רבי טליתו כי אתא רב שמואל בר רב יהודה אמר נשאל איתמר: **מתני'** הרוחץ במי מערה ובמי טבריא ונסתפג אפילו בעשר אלונטיאות לא יביאם בידו אבל עשרה בני אדם מסתפגין באלונטית אחת פניהם ידיהם ורגליהם ומביאין אותן בידן סכין וממשמשין ס) אבל לא מתעמלין ולא מתגררין אין יורדין י) לקורדימא י) ואין עושין אפיקטויזין ואין מעצבין את הקטן ואין מחזירין את השבר מי שנפרקה ידו ורגלו לא יטרפם בצונן אבל פ) רוחץ הוא כדרכו ואם נתרפא נתרפא: **גמ'** קתני מי מערה דומיא דמי טבריא מה מי טבריא חמין אף מי מערה חמין ט) י הרוחץ דיעבד אין לכתחילה לא מכלל דלהשתטף

המנער טליתו. פי' ר"ח מן הטל שעליו דהיינו כיבוס וליבון חייב חטאת וכן משמע דהוי דומיא דכומתא דרב יוסף אבל בניעור מן העפר כדפירש בקונטרס אין נראה שיהא שייך ליבון: **היוצא** בטלית מקופלת. איידי דאיירינן במי שנשרו כליו בדרך שאז דרך הוא לקפל טליתו נקטיה הכא: **הרטנין.** רטנין כמו הרהטנין י) (הערוך פי' הרצים): **מהו** לעשות מרזב. נראה לרבי דלענין איסור הוצאה איירי כמו טלית של ד' כנפו' ולוקח שני צידי רוחב טליתו של צד ימינו ונותן על כתף השמאלית ואינו פושטו על כתף אלא מקופל ומונח על כתפו והיינו דקאמר מאי מרזב כיסי בבלייתא שקורין פרונגלד"ה דכשהוא מונח כמו שפירשתי יש בו כיסים מרובים וכל כיסא וכיסא נראה כמין מרזב ומיבעיא ליה אי איכא איסור הוצאה בכך כיון שאינה דרך מלבוש והיינו דקאמר כל אדעתא לכנופי אסור דהיינו כמו שפירשתי ששני צידי הימין מקובלים ומונחים על כתף השמאלית שיכול לילך במהרה ולא יכביד עליו טליתו אדעתא דלהתנאות שפיר דמי והיינו כשאין צידי טליתו מקובלין אלא צד אחד מונחת על כתפו אבל צוארו וצד האחר נופל על שכמו עד הזרוע ואין בו שום כיסוי והיינו שלשל רבי טליתו דבסמוך שלשל אותו כמו שפירשתי כעין להתנאות והיינו דרך מלבוש וכן פירש בערוך ערך מרזב אסור לעשות מרזב בשבת פירוש כשיעטוף אדם טליתו ויקפיל שני קצותיו כעין דרך קיפול ויניחנה על שכמו השמאלית ויחזור ויקפל שאר הטלית שבצד הימין ויניחנה בכתפו רק מה שפירש שקורין מרזב מה שטליתו מושפלת מהנה ומהנה וחלל כנגד השדרה דנראה כמין מרזב אינו נראה לרבי דלא ה"ל מאי קאמר בתר הכי מאי מרזב כיסי בבלייתא הלא אינו עשוי כעין כיסא. מ"ר:

אף מי מערה חמין. (ד) שהוחמו באור דלאו בחמי טבריא שרי לכתחילה כדאמר בפרק כירה (ד' מ. ושם) והיינו לכן חמי טבריא ובפרק שמונה שרצים (ד' קח. ושם):

דיעבד אין. אמי מערה קאי ולא תנא במתני' חמי טבריא אלא למידק אף מי מערה חמין ו):

דמתניא

רבינו חננאל

ואוקימנא ליה דרב כתנאי: אמר רב הונא המנער טליתו בשבת חייב חטאת. פי' המנער כדכתיב התנערי מעפר וכדגרסינן התם ומנערה אחת לשלשים. אם יש אבק בבגד חדש שחור ומקפיד עליו. או אם יש עליו דבר טינוף אוסר רב הונא לנפצו. אבל אם הוא בגד ישן או לבן או אדום ולא קפיד עלייהו שרי וכן הלכה. וזה שראה עולא לרבנן דהוו נפצי גלימייהו ואמר הני מחללי שבתא. רבנן דפומבדיתא במלבושין דלא קפדי עלייהו הוו נפצי. (אמתא) [כומתא] הוא כמין כובע של ראש במקום סודר כדאמרינן בפרק השולח גט לאשתו האי אמתא דהוה שכיב מרה אתת בכת קמיה. ואמרה ליה עד אימת תיתעבד ותזיל ההיא אמתא שקל כומתיה ושדא בה אמר ליה קני הא וקני נפשיך. כלומר קני נפשיך בחליפין. וי"א כומתא הוא כגון כאן דומה לגביע והוה באותו הטמנ' טינוף. והוה אביי מהסם. כלומר מתירא כדאמרינן התם חזייה דהוה קא מהסם. א"ל רב יוסף לאביי נפרץ שדי אנן לא קפדינן מידי: היוצא בטלית מקופלת ומונחת לו על כתפו כגון אלו מוכרי כסות שמקפלין ומפשילין אותן על כתפייהו. אתמר משמיה דר' יוחנן חייב חטאת ותניא כוותיה והכי הלכתא וכן נמי היוצא וצרורין לו בסדינו מעות חייב חטאת אבל הרטנין שהם הרצים יוצאין בסודר שעל כתפיהן. ולא אלו בלבד אלא כל אדם. והנכון להיות כרוך בצוארו. או נימא כרוכה לו באצבעו. כהורקנוס בר' אליעזר. ואע"ג דאמר משמא דר' יוחנן הלכה אע"פ שאין נימא כרוכה לו על אצבעו: עולא איקלע לבי אסי בר (חני) [היני] בעא מיניה מהו לעשות מרזב בשבת א"ל הכי אמר ר' אלעזר אסור. כך קבלנו מרבותינו שיש בידם קבלה כי מרזב זה כשיתעטף אדם טליתו ויקפל ב' קצותיה כמין כרך קיפול ויניחה על כתפו השמאלית ויחזור ויקפל שאר הטלית המשולשל בצידו הימין מניחה בכתפו הימין ונמצאת טליתו מקופלת מהנה ומהנה ומופשלת על כתפיו וחלל כנגד השדרה ונראה כמין מרזב. וכענין זה היה קשר (כישי) [כישא] בבלייתא שהיו קושרין ב' כריכות וקורין אותה כישא וכיסכוסי מאני א). וי"א זולתי פירוש זה. אבל חובה עלינו לומר בלשון רבותינו ומה שקיבלנוהו. וכרב פפא שהוא בתראה עבדינן ואמר כללא כל אדעתא לכנופי אסור. כל להתנאות שפיר דמי וכדרב שישא בריה דרב אידי שהיה מתנאה בסדינין כי אתא רב דימי אמר פעם אחת יצא רבי לשדה והיו ב' צידי טליתו מונחין לו על כתפו ושאר הטלית כרוכה ומופשלת לו לאחוריו. אמר לפניו יהושע בן זירוז בן חמיו של ר"מ בזו לא חייב ר"מ חטאת. כלומר זה המעשה דומה לרטנין שיוצאין בסודרין בסדינין מקובצין ולא משולשין על כתפיהן ור' מאיר לא היה בזה מחייב חטאת ג) אי לא אסורה מדרבנן. א"ל ר' דקדק ר"מ עד כאן שלשל רבי טליתו: מתני' הרוחץ במי מערה כו'. אוקימנא

חשק שלמה על רבינו חננאל א) עיין בערוך ערך מרזב א': ב) [אולי צ"ל אלמא דלאסורה מדרבנן. ואפשר דרבינו מפרש בזו לא חייב ר"מ חטאת בניחותא דמטלת לא היה מחייב רק הוי אוסר מדרבנן וצ"ע בזה]:

ליקוטי רש"י

[לעיל סד:]. אפילו בחדרי חדרים אסור. במקום שאין אדם רואה אסרוהו [ע"ז שם]. תנן שוטחן בחמה אבל לא כנגד העם. אלמא מידי דמשום מראית העין מותר במקום צנוע [ביצה שם]. [ע"כ שייך לדף קמו:]. ... (דברים כה) לא תחסום מגמגם [חולין ג.]. חייב חטאת. דאינו מכסיע אלא בזמן שלובשו דרך מלבוש [לעיל נח.]. מי טבריא. מי טבריא. מעיינות רותחין [פסחים מא.]. אלונטית. בגד שמסתפגין בו כשיוצאין מבית המרחץ [עירובין פח:]. אפיקטויזין. הקאה גומיטא בלע"ז כך מצאתי [לעיל יב.]. להקיא והוא בנוטריקון אפיק טפי זין מזון ... ומקיא [סוכה מ:]. ואין עושין אפיקטויזין. להקיא שותה משקים ומקיא ולא לרפואה אלא ... כל לאכול ולשתות [היום] הרבה כדאמרינן בפרק חבית ואף על גב דלא גזור בה משום שחיקת ... רפואה היא אסור משום דמתקן גברא [לעיל קכג:]. בכם דדמי לרפואה וגזירה משום שחיקת סמנין אבל ביד להכנים יד לתוך גרונו עד שיקיא מותר [לקמן ע"ב ע"ש בגה"ש].

עין משפט נר מצוה

מו א ב מיי' פכ"ב מהל' שבת הלכה יט טור שו"ע או"ח סימן שא סעיף מח:
מז ג ד מיי' פי"ט שם הלכה יט סמג לאוין סה טוש"ע שם סעיף לד:
מח ה ו מיי' פכ"א מהל' שבת הלכה כח סמג שם טוש"ע או"ח סימן שכו סעיף ג:
מט ז מיי' וסמג שם טוש"ע שם וסימן שכח סעיף מב:
נ ח מיי' שם:
נא ט מיי' שם הלכה ל טוש"ע או"ח סימן שכח סעיף ג:
נב י מיי' שם הלכה כט טוש"ע או"ח סי' שא סעיף מו בהג"ה:
נג כ ל מיי' שם הלכה לא סמג שם טוש"ע או"ח סי' שכח סעיף לט:
נד מ מיי' וסמג שם טור שו"ע או"ח סימן של סעיף י:
נה נ מיי' פכ"ב שם הלכה כו:

דתניא א"ר כשהיינו למדין תורה כו'. מסתמא יחידי היה שלא היה אלא אחד מתלמידיו עמו כשהיה רוחץ כדתניא במקום שנהגו (פסחים דף נא.) שלא ירחוץ תלמיד עם רבו ואם היה רבו צריך לו מותר ומסתמא ר"ש לא היה צריך אלא לאחד כשהיה רוחץ וכשהיו שנים לביתם היה התלמיד נושא האלונטית בפני עצמה שר"ש לא היה נושא עמו דהא ס"ל שיחיד מותר להביאה ולא חיישינן לסחיטה והא דקאמר היינו ר"ל כל אחד ואחד בפני עצמו כשהיה מגיע יומו לשמש רבו ולעיל בפ' כירה (דף מ:) גרסינן מעשה בתלמיד של ר' מאיר שנכנס אחריו לבית המרחץ ויש ספרים דגרסי תלמידיו ואינו ובכל הספרים גרסי לקמן בפרק שואל (דף קנא.) תלמודו. מ"ר:

צריך לקשר שני ראשיה למטה. בגיטין בפ' הניזקין (דף נט.) מפרש דסכניתא הוא בגד דק דאמרינן סוכני ומומר כי אמגוזא ופלגא דאמגוזא ומשום הכי צריך לקשר שני ראשיה למטה שלא יפריחנו מעליו הרוח ואתי לאתויי או משום דנראה כעין משוי לפי שהוא דק מאד ואינו נראה מלבוש אא"כ נראה קשור:

אין מעצבין את הקטן. פירשנו [בריש כל הכלים] (ד' קכ"ג. ד"ה אסוכי)

הדרן עלך חבית

דלהשתטף כל גופו אפי' לכתחילה שפיר דמי מני ר"ש היא דתניא לא ישתטף אדם בין בחמין בין בצונן דברי ר"מ ר"ש מתיר ר' יהודה אומר בחמין אסור בצונן מותר: ונסתפג אפילו בעשר אלונטיות: רישא רבותא קמ"ל וסיפא רבותא קמ"ל רישא רבותא קמ"ל דאפילו הני דלא נפישי בהו מיא כיון דחד הוא אתי לידי סחיטה וסיפא רבותא קמ"ל אפילו הני דנפישי בהו מיא כיון דרבים נינהו מדכרי אהדדי: ת"ר מסתפג אדם באלונטית ומניחה בחלון ולא ימסרנה לאוליירין מפני שחשודים על אותו דבר רבי שמעון אומר מסתפג באלונטית אחת ומביאה בידו לתוך ביתו אמר ליה אביי לרב יוסף הלכתא מאי אמר ליה הא ר' שמעון הא רבי הא שמואל הא ר' יוחנן ר' שמעון הא דאמרן רבי דתניא אמר רבי כשהיינו למדין תורה אצל ר' שמעון בתקוע היינו מעלין שמן ואלונטית מחצר לגג ומגג לקרפף עד שהיינו מגיעין אצל מעין שהיינו רוחצין בו שמואל דאמר רב יהודה אמר שמואל מסתפג אדם באלונטית ומביאה בידו לתוך ביתו ר' יוחנן דאמר ר' חייא בר אבא א"ר יוחנן הלכה מסתפג אדם באלונטית ומביאה בידו לתוך ביתו ומי א"ר יוחנן הכי והא"ר יוחנן הלכה כסתם משנה ותנן ונסתפג אפילו בעשר אלונטיות לא יביאם בידו ההוא כבן חכינאי מתני לה א"ר חייא בר אבא אר"י האוליירין מביאין בלרי נשים לבי בני ובלבד שיתכסה בהן ראשן ורובן סכיניתא (א) צריך לקשר ב' ראשיה למטה א"ר חייא בר אבא א"ר יוחנן למטה מכתפיים אמר להו רבא לבני מחוזא כי מעבריתו מאני לבני חילא שרביבו בהו למטה מכתפיים: סכין וממשמשין: ת"ר סכין וממשמשין בבני מעיים בשבת ובלבד שלא יעשה כדרך שהוא עושה בחול היכי עביד ר' חמא בר חנינא אמר סך ואח"כ ממשמש ר' יוחנן אמר סך וממשמש בבת אחת: אבל לא מתעמלין: א"ר חייא בר אבא א"ר יוחנן אסור לעמוד בקרקעיתה של דיומסת מפני שמעמלת ומרפא אמר ר' יהודה אמר רב כל ימיה של דיומסת עשרים ואחד יום ועצרת מן המנין איבעיא להו עצרת (בתחלה) להאי גיסא או להאי גיסא ת"ש דאמר שמואל כולהו שקייני מדיבחא ועד עצרתא מעלו דילמא התם הוא דכמה דקריר עלמא מעלי אבל הכא משום הבלא הוא כיון דחמים עלמא טפי מעלי אמר רבי חלבו חמרא דפרוגייתא ומיא דדיומסת קיפחו עשרת השבטים מישראל רבי אלעזר בן ערך איקלע להתם אימשיך בתרייהו איעקר תלמודיה כי הדר אתא קם למיקרי בספרא בעא למיקרא החדש הזה לכם אמר החרש היה לבם בעו רבנן רחמי עליה והדר תלמודיה והיינו דתנן ר' נהוראי אומר הוי גולה למקום תורה ואל תאמר שהיא תבא אחריך שחבריך יקיימוה בידך ואל בינתך אל תשען תנא לא ר' נהוראי שמו אלא ר' נחמיה שמו ואמרי לה ר' אלעזר בן ערך שמו ולמה נקרא שמו ר' נהוראי שמנהיר עיני חכמים בהלכה: אבל לא מתגררין: ת"ר אין גוררין במגררת בשבת רשב"ג אומר אם היו רגליו מלוכלכות בטיט ובצואה גורר כדרכו ואינו חושש רב שמואל בר יהודה עבדא ליה אימיה מגררתא דכספא: אין יורדין לקורדימא וכו': מאי טעמא משום פיקא: ואין עושין אפיקטויזין בשבת: אמר רבה בר בר חנה אמר רבי יוחנן לא שנו אלא בסם אבל ביד מותר תניא רבי נחמיה אומר אף בחול אסור מפני הפסד אוכלין: ואין מעצבין את הקטן: אמר רבה בר בר חנה אמר ר' יוחנן לפופי ינוקא בשבתא שפיר דמי והאנן תנן אין מעצבין התם בחומרי שדרה דמיחזי כבונה: ואין מחזירין את השבר: אמר רבי חנא בגדתאה אמר שמואל הלכה

גמ' דלהשתטף. שופכן על גופו דלאו דרך רחיצה היא שרי לכתחילה אפי' בחמין: סיפא. אבל עשרה בני אדם כו': ומניחה בחלון. הסמוכה לכותל המרחץ: לאוליירין. בלנים: על אותו דבר. סחיטה: הא רבי והא ר"ש כו'. הרי כל אלו שמתירין: מחצר לגג כו'. ר"ש לטעמיה דאמר בעירובין (דף צא.) אחד גגות ואחד חצירות ואחד קרפיפות כולן רשות אחת הן לטלטל מזה לזה ואפילו של בעלים הרבה: עד שהיינו מגיעין כו'. ומסתמא לא היו מניחין אותה על המעין במקום הפקר: כבן חכינאי מתני לה. דברי בן חכינאי מסיים בה ולאו סתמא: האוליירין. בלנין: מביאין בלרי נשים. סדינים שהנשים מסתפגין בהם מותר להביאן דרך מלבוש לבית המרחץ: סכיניתא. סודר גדול [א] שתולה לו בין כתפיו ולאשו עטוף בו: צריך לקשור שני ראשיה. זה בזה שלא תפול מראשו: כי מעבריתו מאני לבני חילא. כשתביאו בגדי העובדי כוכבי' בני החיל המוטלי' עליכם לשמשן ואתם מביאים להם בשבת דרך רשות הרבים: שרביבו בהו למטה מכתפיים. שלא יהיו שוליהם מונחים בכתפיכם אלא משולי' למטה שיהא נראה לבוש: סך ואח"כ ממשמש. [דקסבר] בחול ממשמש ואחר כך סך: דיומסית. שם נהר שמימיו מלוחים: שמעמלת. מחממת: ומרפא. שהטיט מלוח: כל ימיה. ימי רפואתה: להאי גיסא כו'. מתחלת הימים או בסוף: שקייני. משקין לרפואה: מדבחא לעצרת. אלמא עצרת בסוף: חמרא דפרוגיתא. שם מדינה שיינה משובח: קפחו עשרת השבטים. שהיו בעלי הנאה ועסוקים בכך ולא היו עוסקים בתורה ואלו לתרבות רעה: להתם. לפרוגיתא ודיומסת: אימשיך בתרייהו. אחר היין והרחיצה: איעקר תלמודיה. נעקר תלמודו ושכחו: החרש היה לבם: הוי גולה למקום תורה. אם מ"מ אתה אל תשב אלא במקום מ"מ חכרך ולא תאמר תלמידים הם יבואו אלי ודי לי בכך למה אהיה גולה: שחבריך יקיימוה בידך. שתהא רגיל אצלם ותשאנה מסכת אחת והם אחרת תשמענה והאל סדורה בפיך ואל תשכחנה מהרה: ואל בינתך אל תשען. לומר חכם גדול אני חוכתן לא אשכח וכשאחזור פרק זה או מסכת זו לא תשכחנה מהרה ממני: מגררת. אסטריג"ל ואדם מגרר בה: מגררתא דכספא. לשבת: משום פיקא. טיט של אותו נהר מחליק ובגדי האדם משורין במים כשהוא נופל ואתי לידי סחיטה: אלא בסם. דדמי לרפואה וגזירה משום שחיקת סממנין: אבל ביד. להכניס יד לתוך גרונו עד שיקיא מותר: מפני הפסד אוכלין. שמעיו ממהוך כך הוא רעב וחוזר ואוכל: לפופי. אונמלוטי"ל כמו שעושין לקטן שמיישבין אבריו ולא יתעקם: בחומרי שדרה. חוליות של שדרה שנתפרקה אחת מהן ולאחר זמן קמייריהו לאו ביום לידה (ב) אמר' (לעיל דף קכט:) כל האמור בפ' תוכחה דיחזקאל עושין לחיה בשבת: הלכה

מסורת הש"ס

א) לעיל לט:, ב) עירובין פח. ע"ש, ג) [חשודין לסוחטה ונותנין אותה לאחרים. ערוך ע"ש], ד) עירובין לא. [מנחות עב.], ה) [לעיל מו. וש"נ], ו) [עי' פירש"י עירובין סג. ד"ה מחלא וברש"י פסחים ה. ד"ה מחלא וברש"י ב"מ נט. עוד שם עו. ד"ה אוכלפא דמחלא], ז) סנהדרין קא., ח) [פסחים דף מב:], ט) אדר"נ ספי"ד, י) אבות פ"ד משנה י"ד, כ) עירובין יג: ע"ש, ל) [תוספ' פי"ז], מ) [לעיל סו: ע"ש], נ) [עמ"ש רש"י ברכות נד: וע"ע פרש"י ביבמות סו. ד"ה בגדתאה], ס) [ובישעיה כח א גרס ומיא דדורמסקית וכן גרס רד"ק שם], ע) [בגיטין אי' סוכני ומומא], פ) [שייך לעיל במשנה].

הגהות הב"ח

(א) גמרא סכניתא אמר ר' אבין בר רב חסדא א"ר יוחנן צריך לקשר שני וכו' ואמר ר' חייא: (ב) רש"י ד"ה בחומרי וכו' ביום לידה הא אמרינן. נ"ב סוף פ' מפנין ע"ש ברש"י שפי' לפופי הוא על ידי חגורות ופסקיאות:

גליון הש"ס

גמ' אמר החרש היה לבם. עי' דבר נחמד בקרניים בליקוטים שבסוף הספר: רש"י ד"ה אלא בסם וכו' משום שחיקת סמנין. ע"ל דף קכג ע"ב ברש"י ד"ה אפיקטויזין:

הגהות הגר"א

[א] רש"י ד"ה סוכניתא סודר גדול. נ"ב אבל הרמב"ם פי' קטן שאין מכסה ראשו ורובו:

תורה אור השלם

א) הַחֹדֶשׁ הַזֶּה לָכֶם רֹאשׁ חֳדָשִׁים רִאשׁוֹן הוּא לָכֶם לְחָדְשֵׁי הַשָּׁנָה: (שמות יב, ב)

ליקוטי רש"י

להשתטף. שוטף על גופו ומסתפג. לא ישתטף. בשבת. בין בחמין. ואפילו הוחמו מערב שבת. ר' שמעון מתיר. להשתטף כל גופו בחמין שהוחמו מערב שבת [לעיל לט:]. רישא רבותא קמ"ל. דלא נפישי מיא בכל חד ואפילו הכי לא יביאם לתוך ביתו ואפילו על ידי עירוב שמא ישכח ויסחטנו בכולו. וסיפא רבותא קמ"ל. דמלא אלונטית לעשרה [בני אדם נפישין בה מיא ואפילו הכי מביאין אותה בידים] [לעיל ע"א].

[המשך בדף קמח.]

רבינו חננאל

אוקימנא למתני' הרוחץ בחמין דיעבד אבל לכתחלה לרחוץ בחמין אסור. ולהשתטף בחמין נמי אפי' כל גופו מותר כר"ש דתניא לא ישתטף אדם בין בחמין בין בצונן דברי ר"מ. ור"ש מתיר. ר' יהודה אומר בחמין אסור ובצונן מותר. אע"פ דתנינן סתמא כר"ש לית הלכתא כוותיה דהא בפירוש נמי תנינן סתמא כוותיה (לעיל דף לח). מעשה שעשו אנשי טבריא כו' א) (ואע"ג דאמר עולא הלכה כאנשי טבריא הא אמר ליה רב נחמן תברינהו לסילונייהו אנשי טבריא) ואוקימנא כר"ש. ופסקי' בגמרי' אמר רבה בר בר חנה א"ר יוחנן הלכה כרבי יהודה ודקדק רב יוסף על רבה בר בר חנה וא"ל בפירוש שמיעא לך דהלכתא כר' יהודה או מכללא אמרתיה. א"ל בפירוש שמיעא ליה. וכיון דפסק ר' יוחנן בפירוש הלכה כר' יהודה כוותיה עבדינן: ומסתפג אפי' בעשר אלונטיות ולא יביאם בידו ואע"פ שאין בהם מים מרובין. דכיון דחד הוא דלמא אתי למעבד סחיטה. אבל אם היו ב"א הרבה אפילו אם מסתפגין כולן באלונטית אחת והיא שרויה במים כיון דרבים נינהו מדכרי אהדדי ולא אתו לידי סחיטה. ומותר להביאה בידים בחצר או מן הגג וכדומה לו מקום שמותר לו לטלטל. אוליירין השמשים בני אדם הנכנסים במרחץ והן חשודין בזמה שמא יסחטו לנטיות זו בשבת דרש. א"ל אביי לרב יוסף הלכתא מאי כי הא דא"ר חייא בר אבא א"ר יוחנן הלכה מסתפג אדם באלונטית ומביאה בידו לתוך ביתו. ומקשינן עלה הא"ר יוחנן הלכה כסתם משנה ותנן מסתפג אדם אפילו בעשר אלונטיות ולא יביאם בידו. ומפרקי' מתני' ר' יוחנן לא אמר לה סתמא. אלא כבן חכינאי מתני לה. בתלמוד א"י בפ' כירה ר' חנינא בן עקיבא התיר הבאת לנטיות: סכינתא: א"ר אבין בר רב חסדא א"ר יוחנן צריך לקשר ב' ראשיה למטה. א"ר חייא בר אבא א"ר יוחנן למטה מכתפים. וכן זה שאמר רבא לבני מחוזא כי מעבריתו מני דבני חילא שרביבו להו למטה מכתפים. שלא להראות שהם בכתף: בלרין קן של נשים כשמביאין להן האוליירין במרחץ לא התירו אלא עד שיתכסה בהן ראשו ורובו: סכין וממשמשין הלכתא כר' יוחנן דאמר סך וממשמש בבת אחת והוא משמש ביד בקלות. אבל לא מתעמלין. פי' פושטין ומקפלין זרועותיהם לפניהן ולאחוריהן ע"ג ירכותיהן ומתחממין ומזיעין והוא כמין מעשה רפואה ואסור. וכן אסור לעמוד בשבת בקרקעיתה של דיומסת מפני שמעמלת ומרפאה: חמרא דפרוגתא יין של פרוגיתא והוא שם מקום ומיא דרמיסת גם הוא שם מקום. כלומר יין של פרוגיתא ומיא של דיומסת טובים הם וערבין ונמשך לב שותה אותן בהן ואינו רוצה להניחם ומתאחר שם ואותן מקומות אין בהן בני תורה והמתאחר שם זמן הרבה מתקפח ושכח תלמודו. אבל לא מתגרדין. גירוד זה הוא חיכוך בכלי כי הא דתנן רבנן אין גורדין במגרת בשבת רשבג"א אם היו רגליו מלוכלכות בטיט ובצואה גורד כדרכו ואינו חושש. רב שמואל בר יהודה עבדא ליה אמיה מגרדתא דכספא להתחכך בה: אין יורדין לקירומא. ס"א לפילומא פי' בקעה ויש שם מים ותחתיו טיט כמו טפל. ואם יבקע ויטבע בו אינו יכול לעלות עד שמתקבצין הרבה ב"א ומעלין אותו משם. יש מי שאומרים הרוחץ באותה בקעה מצטנן ואותן המים משלשלין בני מעיו ג). וזה פי' ביקא. פי' אפיקטוריזין קיא. אמר רבה בר בר חנה א"ר יוחנן לא שנו אלא בסם שהוא אסור אבל ביד מותר. ואין מעצבין את הקטן כו'. פי' מושכין אבריו של קטן ומיישב בידו חוליות של שדרה אחת על חברתה וזהו עיצוב מלשון עצבון: לפופי ינוקא לחבר אבריו של תינוק. וכדתרגם ויחבר ולפיף: ואין מחזירין את השבר אמר רב הונא בגדתאה אמר שמואל מחזירין

חשק שלמה על רבינו חננאל א) לכאורה נראה דממיבת ואע"ג עד תברינהו לסילונייהו אנשי טבריא שייך להלן אחר מיבות כוותיה עבדינן ודו"ק: ב) עיין ערוך ערך פלם א':

דִּלְהִשְׁתַּטֵּף כָּל גּוּפוֹ – **that** if he does not actually immerse in the cave waters, but merely **rinses** (i.e. showers) **his whole body** with them, אֲפִילוּ לְכַתְּחִילָּה שַׁפִּיר דָּמֵי – then **even initially it is fine** for him to do this.[1]

Having isolated the Mishnah's position on this point, the Gemara asks:

מַנִּי – **Who,** then, is the author of our Mishnah? Which Tanna allows rinsing one's body with heated water on the Sabbath?

The Gemara replies:

רַבִּי שִׁמְעוֹן הִיא – **[Our Mishnah] reflects** the view of **R' Shimon,** דְּתַנְיָא – **for it was taught in a Baraisa:** לֹא יִשְׁתַּטֵּף אָדָם בֵּין בְּחַמִּין בֵּין בְּצוֹנֵן – ONE MAY NOT RINSE HIS ENTIRE BODY WITH EITHER HOT OR COLD WATER on the Sabbath. דִּבְרֵי רַבִּי מֵאִיר – These are THE WORDS OF R' MEIR.[2] רַבִּי שִׁמְעוֹן מַתִּיר – R' SHIMON, however, PERMITS rinsing the entire body with either hot water that was heated before the Sabbath or cold water.[3] רַבִּי יְהוּדָה אוֹמֵר – R' YEHUDAH SAYS: בְּחַמִּין אָסוּר – Rinsing the entire body WITH HOT water is FORBIDDEN, בְּצוֹנֵן מוּתָּר – but rinsing it WITH COLD water is PERMITTED.[4] Our Mishnah thus reflects R' Shimon's view.

The Gemara elaborates on a further section of the Mishnah:

וְנִסְתַּפֵּג אֲפִילוּ בְּעֶשֶׂר אֲלוּנְטִיּוֹת – The Mishnah stated: One who bathes . . . AND DRIED HIMSELF EVEN WITH TEN TOWELS, may not carry the towels home in his hand.

The Gemara comments:

רֵישָׁא רְבוּתָא קָא מַשְׁמַע לָן – **The first part** of the Mishnah **informs us of a novelty,** וְסֵיפָא רְבוּתָא קָא מַשְׁמַע לָן – **and the second part** of the Mishnah also **informs us of a novelty.**

The Gemara explains how this is so:

רֵישָׁא רְבוּתָא קָא מַשְׁמַע לָן – **The first part,** which speaks of a single person who dried himself with ten towels, **informs us of** the following **novelty:** דַּאֲפִילוּ הָנֵי דְּלָא נְפִישֵׁי בְּהוּ מַיָּא – **That even these** towels, **which do not have much water in them** at all,[5] the person may not bring them home, כֵּיוָן דְּחַד הוּא – for **since he is** but **one** lone person, אָתֵי לִידֵי סְחִיטָה – he may forget and **come to squeeze** water out of the towels, inadvertently violating the Sabbath.

The Gemara continues:

וְסֵיפָא רְבוּתָא קָא מַשְׁמַע לָן – **And** likewise, **the second part** of the Mishnah, which speaks of many people who dried themselves with a common towel, **informs us of** the following **novelty:** אֲפִילוּ הָנֵי דִּנְפִישֵׁי בְּהוּ מַיָּא – That **even these** people, **who** between them **have much water** upon their bodies, and consequently, the towel they use will doubtless become saturated, כֵּיוָן דְּרַבִּים נִינְהוּ – still, **since they are a group** of people, מַדְכְּרֵי אַהֲדָדֵי – **they will** certainly **remind one another** not to squeeze out the towel, and they are therefore permitted to carry it home.

A Baraisa is quoted, introducing an opposing Tannaic view on these matters:

תָּנוּ רַבָּנָן – **Our Rabbis taught in a Baraisa:** מִסְתַּפֵּג אָדָם בַּאֲלוּנְטִית וּמַנִּיחָהּ בַּחַלּוֹן – A PERSON MAY DRY HIMSELF WITH A TOWEL AND LEAVE IT IN THE bathhouse WINDOW,[6] וְלֹא יִמְסְרֶנָּה לְאוֹלְיָירִין – BUT HE MAY NOT GIVE IT TO THE BATHHOUSE ATTENDANTS, מִפְּנֵי שֶׁחֲשׁוּדִים עַל אוֹתוֹ דָּבָר – BECAUSE THEY ARE CONSIDERED SUSPECT IN THAT REGARD; i.e. of wringing the towels out on the Sabbath.[7] רַבִּי שִׁמְעוֹן אוֹמֵר – R' SHIMON SAYS: מִסְתַּפֵּג בַּאֲלוּנְטִית אַחַת – HE MAY DRY HIMSELF, even WITH only ONE TOWEL, וּמְבִיאָהּ בְּיָדוֹ לְתוֹךְ בֵּיתוֹ – AND then CARRY [THE TOWEL] HOME IN HIS HAND.[8]

The Gemara seeks a decision on the Tannaic dispute recorded here:

אָמַר לֵיהּ אַבָּיֵי לְרַב יוֹסֵף – **Abaye said to Rav Yosef:** הִלְכְתָא מַאי – **What,** then, **is the law?** As a practical matter, is a lone person permitted to carry the towel home or not?

Rav Yosef responds:

אָמַר לֵיהּ – **He replied to [Abaye]:** הָא רַבִּי שִׁמְעוֹן הָא רַבִּי – **Here is R' Shimon, here is Rebbe;** הָא שְׁמוּאֵל הָא רַבִּי יוֹחָנָן – **here is Shmuel, here is R' Yochanan;** all these Sages have permitted the practice; thus, it is to be allowed.

The Gemara proceeds to demonstrate that each of these Sages indeed takes such a position:

רַבִּי שִׁמְעוֹן – As for **R' Shimon,** הָא דַּאֲמָרָן – it is clear from the Baraisa **that we** just **quoted** that he permits a lone person to carry his towel home.

NOTES

1. *Ritva* (*MHK* ed.) gives this summary of the Gemara's inference: Clearly, the main purpose of the first part of the Mishnah is to teach a law about the carrying of towels. As such, it need not have specified cave waters or Tiberian waters at all; it could have merely stated: *One who bathes and dries himself with even ten towels* . . . Since, however, the Mishnah *does* mention these particular sources, it seems that the Tanna wishes to convey a secondary teaching concerning them. What, then, is the nature of this teaching?

At first glance, the intended secondary teaching would seem to be that bathing in cave waters or Tiberian waters is not initially permitted. [The word הָרוֹחֵץ, indicating an after-the-fact situation, implies that such bathing is initially forbidden.] This, however, cannot be, for we know that bathing in Tiberian waters is altogether permissible (above, 40a); and as for waters heated manually before the Sabbath [cave waters], it is obvious that one certainly may not bathe in them on the Sabbath, and the Mishnah would have no need to teach this. It must be, then, that the teaching lies in an inference to be drawn from the Mishnah's language. That is, it is only *bathing* [הָרוֹחֵץ] in cave waters that is impermissible; rinsing oneself in these waters, however, would be permitted. This, indeed, is a novelty, for as the Gemara proceeds to demonstrate, only R' Shimon allows such rinsing, whereas other Tannaim do not.

2. All Tannaim of the Baraisa agree that bathing on the Sabbath in water heated before the Sabbath is Rabbinically prohibited. Their dispute concerns showering on the Sabbath. In the view of R' Meir, rinsing or showering the entire body is quite similar to bathing, and he thus maintains that the prohibition against bathing in hot water was extended even to rinsing. As an added stringency, it was extended even to rinsing with cold water (see *Tosafos* to 39b ד״ה והא and *Pnei Yehoshua* to *Rashi* ad loc. ד״ה בכלי).

3. R' Shimon maintains that rinsing is not the ordinary method of bathing, and thus, he asserts this was not included in the ban on the latter. He therefore permits showering even with hot water (*Rashi;* see *Beis Yosef* to 326).

4. [R' Yehudah extends the injunction to rinsing with water heated before the Sabbath, but not to rinsing with cold water.]

5. Owing to the fact that so many were used (*Rashi*).

6. The Baraisa discusses bathing on the Sabbath in cold water in a bathhouse (*Rashi* to *Eruvin* 88a ד״ה מסתפג אדם), which is permitted. Nowadays, however, it is the custom not to bathe one's entire body on the Sabbath even with cold water (see *Mishnah Berurah* 326:21).

Bathhouses would typically have small locker-type storage areas called חַלּוֹנוֹת, *windows* (see *Tohoros* 7:7 with *Rav;* see *Rashi* here). According to this Tanna, a bather must leave his towel in one of these lockers and he may not carry it home, for fear that he may forget and wring out the towel while walking.

7. The attendants were often ignorant of Sabbath law (*Rav* to *Tohoros* 7:7). They had an interest in wringing out the towels, for they could then give them to other bathers (*Aruch,* ע׳ אליירין).

8. Even though the towel may be quite wet, R' Shimon is not concerned that the person will forget and wring it out. Clearly, R' Shimon speaks of a case where the *melachah* of carrying is not an issue [e.g. an *eruv* had been made in the town; see above, 147a note 29].

עין משפט
נר מצוה

מו א ב מיי' פכ"ב מהל' שבת הלכה יט טור שו"ע או"ח סימן שא סעיף מח:
מז ג ד מיי' פי"ט שם הלכה יט סמג לאוין סה טוש"ע שם סעיף לד:
מח ה ו מיי' פכ"א מהל' שבת הלכה כח סמג שם טוש"ע או"ח סימן שכו סעיף ג:
מט ז מיי' וסמג שם טוש"ע שם וסימן שכח סעיף מג:
נ ח מיי' שם:
נא ט מיי' שם הלכה ל טוש"ע או"ח סימן שכח סעיף ג:
נב י מיי' שם הלכה כט טוש"ע או"ח סי' שא סעיף מו בהג"ה:
נג כ ל מיי' שם הלכה לא סמג שם טוש"ע או"ח סי' שכח סעיף לט:
נד מ מיי' וסמג שם טור שו"ע או"ח סימן של סעיף י:
נה נ מיי' פכ"ב שם הלכה כו:

רבינו חננאל

אוקימנא למתני' הרוחץ בחמין דיעבד אבל לכתחלה לרחוץ בחמין אסור. ולהשתטף בחמין נמי אפי' כל גופו מותר כר"ש דתניא לא ישתטף אדם בין בחמין בין בצונן דברי ר"מ. ור"ש מתיר. ר' יהודה אומר בחמין אסור ובצונן מותר. אע"פ דתנינן סתמא כר"ש לית הלכתא כוותיה דהא בפירוש נמי תנינן סתמא כוותיה (לעיל דף לח). מעשה שעשו אנשי טבריא כו' א) (ואע"ג דאמר עולא הלכה כאנשי טבריא הא אמר ליה רב נחמן תברינהו לסילונייהו אנשי טבריא) ואוקימנא כר"ש. ופסקי' בגמרי' אמר רבה בר בר חנה א"ר יוחנן הלכה כרבי יהודה ודקדק רב יוסף על רבה בר בר חנה וא"ל בפירוש שמיעא לך דהלכתא כר' יהודה או מכללא אמרתיה. א"ל בפירוש שמיעא ליה. וכיון דפסק ר' יוחנן בפירוש הלכה כר' יהודה כוותיה עבדינן: ומסתפג אפי' בעשר אלונטיות ולא יביאם בידו ואע"פ שאין בהם מים מרובין. דכיון דחד הוא. דלמא מינשי ועביד סחיטה. אבל אם היו בי"א הרבה אלא אם מסתפגין כולן באלונטית אחת והיא שרוי' במים כיון דרבים נינהו מדכרי אהדדי ולא אתו לידי סחיטה. ומותר להביאה בידים בחצר או מן הגג וכדומה לו ממקום שמותר לו לטלטל: אוליירין הם השמשים בני אדם הנכנסין במרחץ והן חשודין בזמה שמא ישמאו לגנטיות זו בשכבת זרע. א"ל אביי לרב יוסף והלכתא מאי כר' הלכתא כי הא דא"ר חייא בר רבה א"ר יוחנן הלכה מסתפג אדם באלונטית ומביאה בידו לתוך ביתו. ומקשינן עלה הא"ר יוחנן הלכה כסתם משנה ותנן מסתפג אדם אפילו בעשר אלונטיות ולא יביאם בידו. ומפרקי' מתני' ר' יוחנן לא תאני לה סתמא. אלא כבן חכינאי מתני לה.

מסורת הש"ס

א) [לעיל לט:], ב) עירובין פח. ע"ש, ג) [תוספתא פ"ז], ד) עירובין ע"ש, ה) עירובין ע"ש, [מנחות עב.], ו) [לעיל מו. וש"נ], ז) פ"ק ערכין... ד"ה מחוח וכו' כ"מ עג. ...], ח) [פסחים דף מג:], ט) [מדר"ש פ"ו...], י) [תוספ' פי"ז], כ) [לעיל סו: ע"ש], ל) [עמ"ש רש"י ברכות נד: ...], מ) ונ"א ... ד"ה בגדתאה, נ) [ניתוקי... סוכה... (כפי' שם), ע) [גיטין א'... (לעיל מ...)], פ) [שייך לעיל במשנה].

דתניא א"ר כשהיינו למדין תורה כו'. מסתמא יחידי היה שלא היה אלא אחד מתלמידיו עמו כשהיה רוחץ כדתניא במקום שנהגו (פסחים דף נא.) שלא ירחוץ תלמיד עם רבו ואם היה רבו צריך לו מותר ומסתמא ר"ש לא היה צריך אלא לאחד כשהיה רוחץ וכשהיו שבים לביתם היה התלמיד נושא האלונטית בפני עצמה שר"ש לא היה נושא עמו דהא ס"ל שיחיד מותר להביאה ולא חיישינן לסחיטה והא דקאמר היינו ר"ל כל אחד ואחד בפני עצמו כשהיה מגיע יומו לשמש רבו ולעיל בפ' כירה (דף מ:) גרסינן מעשה בתלמיד של ר' מאיר שנכנס אחריו לבית המרחץ ויש ספרים דגרסי תלמידיו ואינו ובכל הספרים גרסי לקמן בפרק שואל (דף קנא:) תלמידו. מ"ר:

צריך לקשר שני ראשיה למטה. בגיטין בפ' הניזקין (דף נט.) מפרש דסכניתא הוא בגד דק דאמרינן ע) סוכני וזומר כי אמגוזא ופלגא דאמגוזא ומשום הכי צריך לקשר שני ראשיה למטה שלא יפריחנו מעליו הרוח ואתי לאתויי או משום דנראה כעין משוי לפי שהוא דק מאד ואינו נראה מלבוש אא"כ נראה קשור: פ) אין מעצבין את הקטן. פירשנו [בריש כל הכלים] (ד' קכ"ג, ד"ה אלוסי):

הדרן עלך חבית

דלהשתטף כל גופו אפי' לכתחילה שפיר דמי מני ר"ש היא א) דתניא לא ישתטף אדם בין בחמין בין בצונן דברי ר"מ ר"ש מתיר ר' יהודה אומר בחמין אסור בצונן מותר: ונסתפג אפילו בעשר אלונטיות: רישא רבותא קמ"ל וסיפא רבותא קמ"ל רישא רבותא קמ"ל דאפילו הני דלא נפישי בהו מיא כיון דחד הוא אתי לידי סחיטה וסיפא רבותא קמ"ל אפילו הני דנפישי בהו מיא כיון דרבים נינהו מדכרי אהדדי: ב) תנו רבנן מסתפג אדם באלונטית ומניחה בחלון א ולא ימסרנה לאוליירין מפני שחשודים ג) על אותו דבר רבי שמעון אומר מסתפג באלונטית אחת ומביאה בידו לתוך ביתו אמר ליה אביי לרב יוסף הלכתא מאי אמר ליה הא ר' שמעון הא רבי הא שמואל הא ר' יוחנן ר' שמעון הא דאמרן רבי ד) דתניא אמר רבי כשהיינו למדין תורה אצל ר' שמעון בתקוע היינו מעלין שמן ואלונטית מחצר לגג ומגג לקרפף עד שהיינו מגיעין אצל מעין שהיינו רוחצין בו שמואל דאמר רב יהודה אמר שמואל מסתפג אדם באלונטית ומביאה בידו לתוך ביתו ר' יוחנן דאמר ר' חייא בר אבא א"ר יוחנן ה) הלכה מסתפג אדם באלונטית ומביאה בידו לתוך ביתו ומי א"ר יוחנן הכי והא"ר יוחנן ו) הלכה כסתם משנה ותנן ונסתפג אפילו בעשר אלונטיות לא יביאם בידו ההוא כבן חכינאי מתני לה א"ר חייא בר אבא אר"י ז) האוליירין מביאין בלרי נשים לבי בני ובלבד שיתכסה בהן ראשן ורובן ח) סכניתא (א) צריך לקשר ב' ראשיה למטה א"ר חייא בר אבא א"ר יוחנן למטה מכתפיים אמר להו רבא לבני ט) מחוזא כי מעבריתו מאני לבני חילא שרביבו בהו למטה מכתפים: סכין וממשמשין: י) ת"ר סכין וממשמשין בבני מעיים בשבת ובלבד שלא יעשה כדרך שהוא עושה בחול היכי עביד ר' חמא בר חנינא אמר סך ואח"כ ממשמש ר' יוחנן אמר כ) סך וממשמש בבת אחת: אבל לא מתעמלין: א"ר חייא בר אבא א"ר יוחנן ל) אסור לעמוד בקרקעיתה של דיומסת מפני שמעמלת ומרפא אמר ר' יהודה אמר רב כל ימיה של דיומסת עשרים ואחד יום ועצרת מן המנין איבעיא להו עצרת (בתחלה) להאי גיסא או להאי גיסא ת"ש דאמר שמואל כולהו שקייני מ) מדיבחא ועד עצרתא מעלו דילמא התם הוא דכמה דקריר עלמא מעלי אבל הכא משום הבלא הוא כיון דחמים עלמא טפי מעלי אמר רבי חלבו חמרא דפרוגייתא ומיא דדיומסת קיפחו עשרת השבטים מישראל רבי אלעזר בן ערך איקלע להתם נ) אימשיך בתרייהו איעקר תלמודיה כי הדר אתא קם למיקרי בספרא בעא למיקרא א) החדש הזה לכם אמר החרש היה לבם בעו רבנן רחמי עליה והדר תלמודיה והיינו דתנן ס) ר' נהוראי אומר הוי גולה למקום תורה ואל תאמר שהיא תבא אחריך שחבריך יקיימוה בידך ואל בינתך אל תשען ע) תנא לא ר' נהוראי שמו אלא ר' נחמיה שמו ואמרי לה ר' אלעזר בן ערך שמו ולמה נקרא שמו ר' נהוראי שמנהיר עיני חכמים בהלכה: אבל לא מתגררין: ת"ר פ) אין גוררין במגררת בשבת רשב"ג אומר צ) אם היו רגליו מלוכלכות בטיט ובצואה גורר כדרכו ואינו חושש רב שמואל בר יהודה עבדא ליה אימיה מגררתא דכספא: אין יורדין לקורדימא וכו': מאי טעמא ק) משום פיקא: ואין עושין אפיקטויזין בשבת: אמר רבה בר בר חנה אמר רבי יוחנן ר) לא שנו אלא בסם אבל ביד מותר תניא רבי נחמיה אומר ש) אף בחול אסור מפני הפסד אוכלין: ואין מעצבין את הקטן: אמר רבה בר בר חנה אמר ר' יוחנן (ה) ת) לפופי ינוקא בשבת שפיר דמי והאנן תנן אין מעצבין התם א) בחומרי שדרה דמיחזי כבונה: ואין מחזירין את השבר: אמר רבי חנא ב) בגדתאה אמר שמואל הלכה

גמ' דלהשתטף. שופכן על גופו דלאו דרך רחיצה היא שרי לכתחילה אפי' בחמין: סיפא. אבל עשרה בני אדם כו': ומניחה בחלון. הסמוכה לכותל המרחץ: לאוליירין. בלנים: על אותו דבר. סחיטה: הא רבי והא ר"ש כו'. הרי כל אלו שמתירין: מחצר לגג כו'. ר"ש לטעמיה דאמר בעירובין (דף עד.) אחד גגות אחד חצירות וא' קרפיפות כולן רשות אחת הן לטלטל מזה לזה ואפילו של בעלים הרבה: עד שהיינו מגיעין כו'. ומסתמא לא היו מניחין אותה על המעין במקום הפקר: כבן חכינאי מתני לה. דברי בן חכינאי מסיים בה ולאו סתמא: האוליירין. בלנין: מביאין בלרי נשים. סדינים שהנשים מסתפגין בהם מותר להביאן דרך מלבוש לבית המרחץ: סכניתא. סודר גדול [א] שתלוי לו בין כתפיו וראשו עטוף בו: צריך לקשור שני ראשיה. זה בזה שלא תפול מראשו: כי מעבריתו מאני לבני חילא. כשתביאו בגדי העובדי כוכבי' בני החיל המוטלי' עליכם לשמשן ואתם מביאים להם בשבת דרך רשות הרבים: שרביבו בהו למטה מכתפיים. שלא יהיו שוליהם מונחים בכתפיכם אלא משוכי' למטה שיהא נראה לבוש: סך ואח"כ ממשמש. [דקסבר] בחול ממשמש ואחר כך סך: דיומסית[פ]. שם נהר שמימיו מלוחים: שמעמלת. מחממת: ומרפא. שהטיט מלוח: כל ימיה. ימי רפואתה: להאי גיסא כו'. מתחלת הימים או בסוף: שקייני. משקין לרפואה: מדבחא לעצרת. אלמא עצרת בסוף: חמרא דפרוגיתא. שם מדינה שיינה משובח: קפחו עשרת השבטים. שהיו בעלי הנאה ועסוקים בכך ולא היו עוסקים בתורה ויצאו לתרבות רעה: להתם. לפרוגיתא ודיומסית: אימשיך בתרייהו. אחר היין והרחיצה: איעקר תלמודיה. נעקר תלמודו ושכחו: החרש היה לבם: הוי גולה למקום תורה. אם ת"ח אתה אל תשב אלא במקום ת"ח חברך ואל תאמר תלמידים הם יבואו אלי ודי לי בכך למה אהיה גולה: שחביריך יקיימוה בידך. שתהא רגיל אצלם וכשתשנה מסכת אחת והם אחרת תשמענה ותהא סדורה בפיך ואל תשתכח הימנה: ואל בינתך אל תשען. לומר חכם גדול אני וזכרן וכשאחזור פרק זה או מסכת זו לא תשתכח חברתה ממני: מגררת. אשטריי"ל ואדם מגרר בה: מגירתא דכספא. לשבת: משום פיקא. טיט של אותו נהר מחליק ובגדי האדם נישורין במים כשהוא נופל ואתי לידי סחיטה: אלא בסם. דדמי לרפואה וגזירה ° משום שחיקת סמנין: אבל ביד. להכניס יד לתוך גרונו עד שיקיא מותר: מפני הפסד אוכלין. שבמעיו ומתוך כך הוא רעב וחוזר ואוכל: לפופי. אונמלוטי"א כמו שעושי' לקטן שיתיישבו אבריו ולא יתעקם: בחומרי שדרה. חוליות של שדרה שנתפרקה אחת מהן ולאחר זמן קמיירי דאי ביום לידה (ג) אמרי' (לעיל דף קכט:) כל האמור בפ' תוכחה דיחזקאל עושין לחיה בשבת:
הלכה

הגהות הב"ח

(א) גמרא סכניתא אמר ר' אבין בר רב חסדא א"ר יוחנן צריך לקשר שני ראשיה למטה ואמר ר' חייא: (ב) רש"י ד"ה כמותרי וכו' ביום לידה הא אמרינן. נ"ב סוף פ' מפנין הוא על ידי ספרי לפופי הוא על ידי חגורות ופסיקיות:

גליון הש"ס

גמ' אמר החרש היה לבם. עי' דבר נחמד בקרניס לגליקוטיס שבסוף הספר: רש"י ד"ה אלא בסם וכו' משום שחיקת סמנין. ע"ל דף קכב ע"ב ברש"י ד"ה אפיקטוויזין:

הגהות הגר"א

[א] רש"י ד"ה סוכניתא סודר גדול. נ"ב אבל הרמב"ם פי' קטן שאין מכסה ראשו ורובו:

תורה אור השלם

א) הַחֹדֶשׁ הַזֶּה לָכֶם רֹאשׁ חֳדָשִׁים רִאשׁוֹן הוּא לָכֶם לְחָדְשֵׁי הַשָּׁנָה: [שמות יב, ב]

ליקוטי רש"י

להשתטף. שוטפן על גופו ומשתטף. לא ישתטף. אפי' בצונן בין בחמין. ואפילו הוטמו בחול. רבי שמעון מתיר. להשתטף כל גופו בשבת בחמין שהוחמו מערב שבת [לעיל לט:]. רישא רבותא קמ"ל. דלא נפיש מים בכל אחד מהני לא יביאם בידו כמוך ליחוש לשמא יסחוט לפי שאינו על ידי עירוב שיש שמא יסחוט וכשום שעה. וסיפא רבותא קמ"ל. דמדה אלונטיות לעשרה [בני אדם נפישין] ביה מיא אפילו הכי מביאין אותה בידים [לעיל ע"א].

[המשך בדף קמח.]

בפ' כירה ר' חנניה בן עקיבא התיר הבאת לונטיות: סכינתאי א"ר אבין בר רב חסדא א"ר יוחנן צריך לקשר ב' ראשיה למטה. א"ר חייא בר אבא א"ר יוחנן למטה מכתפים. וכן זה שאמר רבא לבני מחוזא כי מעבריתו מאני דבני חילא שרביבו להו למטה מכתפים. שלא להראות משא בכתף: בלרין נשים לבי בני. פי' דהא קן של נשים כשמביאין להן האוליירין במרחץ לא התירו אלא עד שיתכסה בהן ראשו ורובו: סכין וממשמשין הלכתא כר' יוחנן דאמר סך וממשמש בבת אחת והוא משמש ביד בקלות. אבל לא מתעמלין. פי' פושטין ומקפלין זרועותיהם לפניהן ולאחריהן וכן רגליהן ע"ג ירכותיהן ומתחממין ומזיעין והוא כמין מעשה רפואה וכן אסור לעמוד בקרקעיתה של דיומסת מפני שמעמלת ומרפאה: חמרא דפרוגתא יין של פרוגיתא ומיא של דיומסת טובים הם וערבין ונמשך לב שותה להניחם ולתאחר שם ואותן מקומות אין בהן בני תורה והמתאחר שם זמן הרבה מתקפת ושכח תלמודו. אבל לא מתגרדין. גירוד זה הוא חיכוך בכלי כי הא דתנן רבנן אין גורדין במגרת בשבת רשב"ג א"א אם היו רגליו מלוכלכות בטיט ובצואה גורר כדרכו ואינו חושש. רב שמואל בר יהודה עבדא ליה אמיה מגרדתא דכספא להתחכך בה: אין יורדין לקירומא. ס"א לפילומא פי' בקעה ויש שם מים ותחתיו טיט כמו טפל. ואם יבקע ויטבע בו אינו יכול לעלות עד שמתקנחין הרבה בגדים לעבור עליהם. ואע"פ שאין מים שבה והיו שם שאין מלבושן רב ואין עושין אפיקטויזין קיא. פי' אפיקטויזין קיא. אמר רבה בר בר חנה א"ר יוחנן לא שנו אלא בסם שהוא אסור אבל ביד מותר. ואין מעצבין את הקטן כו'. פי' מרשכין אבריו של קטן ומיישב בידו חוליות של שדרה אחת על חברתה וזהו עיצוב מלשון עצבון ידיך. וכתרגום ויחבר ולפיף: לפופי ינוקא לחבר אברים של תינוק: ואין מחזירין את השבר. אמר רב הונא בגדתאה אמר שמואל מחזירין

חשק שלמה על רבינו חננאל א) לכאורה נראה דחסר כאן... ב) עיין ערוך ערך פלט ח':

The Gemara continues:

רַבִּי דְּתַנְיָא – And **Rebbi** agrees to this too, **for it was taught** in a Baraisa: אָמַר רַבִּי – REBBI SAID: כְּשֶׁהָיִינוּ לְמֵדִין תּוֹרָה אֵצֶל רַבִּי שִׁמְעוֹן בִּתְקוֹעַ – WHEN WE WERE STUDYING TORAH UNDER R' SHIMON IN the city of TEKOA, הָיִינוּ מַעֲלִין שֶׁמֶן וַאֲלוּנְטִית מֵחָצֵר לַגַּג – WE WOULD CARRY OIL AND TOWELS FROM COURTYARD TO ROOF וּמִגַּג לְקַרְפֵּף – AND FROM ROOF TO *KARPAF*[9] עַד שֶׁהָיִינוּ מַגִּיעִין אֵצֶל מַעְיָן שֶׁהָיִינוּ רוֹחֲצִין בּוֹ – UNTIL WE WOULD REACH THE SPRING IN WHICH WE WOULD BATHE.[10]

The Gemara cites evidence concerning the next of the Sages listed:

שְׁמוּאֵל – It can be shown that **Shmuel** permits a lone person to carry his wet towel, דְּאָמַר רַב יְהוּדָה אָמַר שְׁמוּאֵל – **for** it is known that **Rav Yehudah said** the following **in the name of Shmuel:** מִסְתַּפֵּג אָדָם בַּאֲלוּנְטִית – **A person may dry himself with a towel** וּמְבִיאָהּ בְּיָדוֹ לְתוֹךְ בֵּיתוֹ – and then **carry it home in his hand.**

The Gemara concludes:

רַבִּי יוֹחָנָן – And **R' Yochanan** likewise subscribes to this, דְּאָמַר רַבִּי חִיָּיא בַּר אַבָּא אָמַר רַבִּי יוֹחָנָן – **for** we know that **R' Chiya bar Abba said** the following **in the name of R' Yochanan:** הֲלָכָה מִסְתַּפֵּג אָדָם בַּאֲלוּנְטִית – **The law** is that **a person may dry himself with a towel** וּמְבִיאָהּ בְּיָדוֹ לְתוֹךְ בֵּיתוֹ – and then **carry it home in his hand.**

The Gemara challenges this last point:

וּמִי אָמַר רַבִּי יוֹחָנָן הָכִי – **But did R' Yochanan** really **say this?** וְהָאָמַר רַבִּי יוֹחָנָן – **But R' Yochanan** himself **said** that הֲלָכָה כִּסְתָם מִשְׁנָה – **the halachah** always **follows an anonymous Mishnah!** וּתְנַן – **And** indeed, **we learned** the following anonymous teaching **in our Mishnah:** וְנִסְתַּפֵּג אֲפִילּוּ בְּעֶשֶׂר אֲלוּנְטִיּוֹת – One who bathes ... AND DRIED HIMSELF EVEN WITH TEN TOWELS לֹא יְבִיאֵם בְּיָדוֹ – MAY NOT CARRY THE TOWELS home IN HIS HAND!

The Gemara resolves the difficulty:

הַהוּא כְּבֶן חֲכִינַאי מַתְנֵי לָהּ – **That** particular **teaching [R' Yochanan] attributes to Ben Chachinai.**[11]

The Gemara cites another teaching reported by R' Chiya in the name of R' Yochanan:[12]

אָמַר רַבִּי חִיָּיא בַּר אַבָּא אָמַר רַבִּי יוֹחָנָן – **R' Chiya bar Abba said** the following **in the name of R' Yochanan:** הָאוֹלְיָירִין מְבִיאִין בַּלָּרֵי נָשִׁים לְבֵי בָנֵי – **The bathhouse attendants may bring the womens' towels to the bathhouse** on the Sabbath,[13] וּבִלְבַד שֶׁיִּתְכַּסֶּה בָּהֶן רֹאשָׁן וְרוּבָּן – **provided that [the attendants] cover their heads and most of their bodies** with the towels while walking **with them.**[14]

The Gemara adds:

סְכַנִיתָא – As for someone wearing a ***sechanisa,***[15] if he wishes to traverse a public domain צָרִיךְ לְקַשֵּׁר שְׁנֵי רָאשֶׁיהָ לְמַטָּה – he **must tie the two ends [of the garment]** together **below,** so that it will not fall off his head.[16]

The Gemara explains what is meant by the term "below":

אָמַר רַבִּי חִיָּיא בַּר אַבָּא אָמַר רַבִּי יוֹחָנָן – **R' Chiya bar Abba said in the name of R' Yochanan:** לְמַטָּה מִכְּתֵפַיִים – "Below," in this context, means **below the shoulders.**

Another teaching on this topic:

אָמַר לְהוּ רָבָא לִבְנֵי מְחוֹזָא – **Rava told the citizens of Mechoza:**[17] כִּי מַעַבְרִיתוּ מָאנֵי לִבְנֵי חֵילָא – **When you bring garments to the soldiers** on the Sabbath, שַׁרְבִּיבוּ בְּהוּ לְמַטָּה מִכְּתֵפַיִים – **let [the ends of the garments] hang down below** your **shoulders.**[18]

NOTES

9. [A *karpaf* is an enclosed area not designated for residential purposes.]

On the Sabbath, when it is forbidden to carry these items through the public street, R' Shimon's students would chart a course through this series of contiguous private domains which enabled them to carry these bath items to the spring without passing through a public domain or *karmelis*. This is in accordance with R' Shimon's stated position (*Eruvin* 74a; see also above 130b) that adjoining roofs, courtyards, and *karpafs* are considered as a single private domain [with respect to Sabbath law], even if they are owned by several different people (*Rashi*). [Other Tannaim reckon these areas as separate domains, and therefore rule that carrying from one to the other violates Rabbinic law (see *Eruvin* 89a).]

10. Presumably, they did not leave the towel unguarded at the spring, where anyone could take it (*Rashi*). Rather, they must have carried it home with them. Apparently, then, Rebbi, who related this story concerning his own experiences, maintains that a lone person may carry his wet towel home with him.

[*Tosafos* explains that, clearly, R' Shimon was not accompanied by a *group* of disciples when he bathed. This is because it is generally forbidden for a disciple to accompany his teacher to the bathhouse (where he will be seen unclothed) unless his teacher needs the student to attend him (*Pesachim* 51a), and presumably, R' Shimon would not have needed more than one attendant. The attending disciple would then have carried the towel home himself (cf. *Rashba*).]

11. I.e. according to R' Yochanan, our Mishnah's teaching [that it is forbidden for one to carry home the towels] is not unattributed, but ends with the phrase: "These are the words of Ben Chachinai" (*Rashi*). [Thus, R' Yochanan is not bound to rule in accordance with this particular Tannaic view, as it is merely the position of an *individual* Tanna.]

12. [The following teaching is primarily related to the previous discussion of the Gemara (147a) concerning the distinction between "wearing" and "carrying" clothing in a public domain.]

13. I.e. to facilitate their bathing in a permissible fashion, e.g. in cold water baths (see *Piskei HaRid* and above, note 6). As mentioned above, bathing in heated water is not permitted, even if the water was heated prior to the Sabbath.

14. I.e as long as they wear the towels like clothing, draping them over their heads and shoulders like a cloak (see above, 147a), the attendants may traverse a public domain, and they are not deemed to have carried the towels (*Rashi*).

Rambam (*Hil. Shabbos* 19:19), however, seems to understand that they need not actually drape the towels at all. Rather, as long as the towels are *large enough* to cover the head and most of the body, they need not hang behind the person, but may be folded back onto his shoulders (see *Kesef Mishneh* ad loc., and *Beis Yosef* to *Orach Chaim* 301 ד״ה הבלנים; cf. *Derishah* §18-19 there).

[The emphasis of the Gemara seems to be on *bringing* the towels to the bathhouse. *Bach* (to *Orach Chaim,* loc. cit.) infers from this that once the towels have been used, they may not be taken *out* of the bathhouse, even if one wears them like clothing.]

15. A *sechanisa* is a kind of kerchief, usually wrapped over the head as one leaves the bathhouse [to protect one's wet hair from the elements] (*Maggid Mishneh* to *Rambam, Hil. Shabbos* 19:19; see *Ritva MHK* ed.; see also *Rashi*).

16. That is, the two ends which hang down over the shoulders (*Rashi*) must be tied. This is done to prevent the garment from falling off, in which case one might unthinkingly pick it up and carry it. *Tosafos* adds that this requirement applies specifically to a *sechanisa,* which is a very lightweight garment, easily prone to blowing away in the wind. Heavier cloaks need not be tied in this way (see *Tosafos* for alternative explanations of this requirement as well).

Others give different explanations of a *sechanisa* and its function. For some of these intepretations, see *Rambam* loc. cit., and *Meiri;* see also *Ritva MHK* ed.

17. The city in which Rava lived (*Rashi* to *Bava Metzia* 59a ד״ה מחוזא).

18. When gentile troops were stationed in a town, the local residents were often pressed into their service. This sometimes involved bringing the soldiers' clothing to them through a public domain (*Ran*). Rava told the townsfolk that if they were required to do this on the Sabbath, they should not carry the clothing folded back upon their shoulders [a manner of "carrying" garments]; rather, they should don the cloaks as if they were wearing them. That is, [they should put the cloaks over their heads, and] let the ends of the garment hang down below their shoulders (*Rashi*).

עין משפט נר מצוה

מו א ב מיי' פכ"ב מהל' שבת הלכה יט טור שו"ע או"ח סימן שא סעיף מח:
מז ג ד מיי' פי"ט שם הלכה יט סמג לאוין סה טוש"ע שם סעיף לד:
מח ה ו מיי' פכ"א מהל' שבת הלכה כח סמג שם טוש"ע או"ח סימן שכו סעיף ג:
מט ז מיי' וסמג שם טוש"ע שם וסימן שכח סעיף מג:
נ ח מיי' שם:
נא ט מיי' שם הלכה ל טוש"ע או"ח סימן שכח סעיף ג:
נב י מיי' שם הלכה כט טוש"ע או"ח סי' שא סעיף מו בהג"ה:
נג כ ל מיי' שם הלכה לא סמג שם טוש"ע או"ח סי' שכח סעיף לט:
נד מ מיי' וסמג שם טור שו"ע או"ח סימן של סעיף י':
נה נ מיי' פכ"ב שם הלכה כו:

רבינו חננאל

אוקימנא למתני' הרוחץ בחמין דיעבד אבל לכתחלה לרחוץ בחמין אסור. ולהשתטף בחמין נמי אפי' כל גופו מותר כר"ש דתניא לא ישתטף אדם בין בחמין בין בצונן דברי ר"מ. ור"ש מתיר. ר' יהודה אומר בחמין אסור ובצונן מותר. אע"פ דתנינן סתמא כר"ש לית הלכתא כוותיה דהא בפירוש נמי תנינן סתמא כוותיה (לעיל דף לח). מעשה שעשו אנשי טבריא כו' א) (ואע"ג דאמר עולא הלכה כאנשי טבריא הא אמר ליה רב נחמן תברינהו לסילוניהו אנשי טבריא) ואוקימנא כר"ש. ופסקי' בגמרי' אמר רבה בר בר חנה א"ר יוחנן הלכה כרבי יהודה ודקדק רב יוסף על רבה בר בר חנה וא"ל בפירוש שמיעא לך דהלכתא כר' יהודה או מכללא אמרתיה. א"ל בפירוש שמיעא ליה. וכיון דפסק ר' יוחנן בפירוש הלכה כר' יהודה כוותיה עבדינן: ומסתפג אפי' בעשר אלונטיות ולא יביאם בידו ואע"פ שאין בהם מים מרובין. דכיון דחד הוא. דלמא מינשי ועביד סחיטה. אבל אם היו ב"א הרבה אפילו אם מסתפגין כולן באלונטית אחת והיא שרוי' במים כיון דרבים נינהו מדכרי אהדדי ולא אתו לידי סחיטה. ומותר להביאה בידים בחצר או מן הגג וכדומה לו מקום שמותר לו לטלטל: אוליירין הם השמשים בני אדם הנכנסין במרחץ והן חשודין בזמה שמא יטמאו לתטיות זו בשכבת זרעם. א"ל אביי לרב יוסף והלכתא מאי כו' והלכתא כי הא דא"ר חייא בר רבה א"ר יוחנן הלכה מסתפג אדם באלונטית ומביאה בידו לתוך ביתו. ומקשינן עלה הא"ר יוחנן הלכה כסתם משנה ותנן מסתפג אדם אפילו בעשר אלונטיות ולא יביאם בידו. ומפרקי' מתני' ר' יוחנן לא תאני לה סתמא. אלא כבן חכינאי מתני לה. בתלמוד א"י בפ' כירה ר' חנניה בן עקיבא התיר הבאת לנטיות: **סכינתאי** א"ר אבין בר רב חסדא א"ר יוחנן צריך לקשר ב' ראשיה למטה. א"ר חייא בר אבא א"ר יוחנן למטה מכתפים. וכן זה שאמר רבא לבני מחוזא כי מעבריתו מני דבני חילא שרביבו להו למטה מכתפים. שלא להראות משא בכתף: בלרין נשים לבי בני. פי' דהא קן של נשים כשמביאין להן האוליירין במרחץ לא התירו אלא עד שיתכסה בהן ראשו ורובו: **סכין** כר' יוחנן דאמר סך וממשמש בבת אחת והוא משמוש ביד בקלות. אבל לא מתעמלין. פי' פושטין ומקפלין זרועותיהם לפניהן ולאחריהן וכן רגליהן ע"ג ירכותיהן ומתחממין ומזיעין והוא כמין מעשה רפואה ואסור. וכן אסור לעמוד בשבת בקרקעיתה של דיומסת מפני שמעמלת ומרפאה: חמרא דפרוגתא יין של פרוגיתא והוא שם מקום ומיא דרמיסת גם הוא שם מקום. כלומר יין של פרגיתא ומיא של דיומסת טובים הם וערבין ונמשך לב שותה אחריהם להניחם ומתאחר שם ואותן מקומות אין בהן בני תורה והמתאחר שם זמן הרבה מתקפת ושכח תלמודו. אבל לא מתגרדין. גירוד זה הוא חיכוך בכלי כי הא דתנן רבנן אין גורדין במגרת בשבת רשב"ג אומר אם היו רגליו מלוכלכות בטיט ובצואה גורד כדרכו ואינו חושש. רב שמואל בר יהודה עבדא ליה אמיה מגרדתא דכספא להתחכך בה: **אין** יורדין לקירומא. ס"א לפילומא פי' בקעה ויש שם מים ותחתיו טיט כמו טפל. ואם יבקע ויטבע בו אינו יכול לעלות עד שיבאו ב"א ומעלין אותו משם. יש מי שאומרים הרוחץ באותה בקעה מצטנן ואותן המים משלשלין בני מעיו ג). וזה פי' ביקא. פי' אפיקטויזין קיא. אמר רבה בר בר חנה א"ר יוחנן לא שנו אלא בסם שהוא אסור אבל ביד מותר. פי' מושכין אבריו של קטן ומיישב בידו חוליות של שזירה אחת על חברתה וזהו עיצוב מלשון עצבן: **לפופי** ינוקא לחבר אברים של תינוק. וכדתרגם ויחבר ולפיף: **ואין** מחזירין את השבר אמר רב הונא בגדתאה אמר שמואל מחזירין

תוספות

דתניא א"ר כשהיינו למדין תורה כו'. מסתמא יחידי היה שלא היה אלא אחד מתלמידיו עמו כשהיה רוחץ כדתניא במקום שנהגו (פסחים דף נא.) שלא ירחוץ תלמיד עם רבו ואם היה רבו צריך לו מותר ומסתמא ר"ש לא היה צריך אלא לאחד כשהיה רוחץ וכשהיו שנים לביתם היה התלמיד נושא האלונטית בפני עצמה שר"ש לא היה נושא עמו דהא ס"ל שיחיד מותר להביאה ולא חיישינן לסחיטה והא דקאמר היינו ר"ל כל אחד ואחד בפני עצמו כשהיה מגיע יומו לשמש רבו ולעיל בפ' כירה (דף מ:) גרסינן מעשה בתלמיד של ר' מאיר שנכנס אחריו לבית המרחץ ויש ספרים דגרסי תלמידיו ואינו ובכל הספרים גרסי לקמן בפרק שואל (דף קנא:) תלמידו. מ"ר:

צריך לקשר שני ראשיה למטה. בגיטין בפ' המזקין (דף נז.) מפרש דסכניתא הוא כנגד דק דלמריין ס) סוכני וחומר כי אמגוזא ופלגא דאמגוזא ומשום הכי צריך לקשר שני ראשיה למטה שלא יפריחנו מעליו הרוח ואתי לאתויי או משום דנראה כעין משוי לפי שהוא דק מאד ואינו נראה מלבוש אא"כ נראה קשור:

פ) **אין** מעצבין את הקטן. פירשנו [בריש כל הכלים (ד' קכ"ג. ד"ה אסוכי)]:

הדרן עלך חבית

גמרא

דלהשתטף כל גופו אפי' לכתחילה שפיר דמי מני ר"ש היא דתניא לא ישתטף אדם בין בחמין בין בצונן דברי ר"מ ר"ש מתיר ר' יהודה אומר בחמין אסור בצונן מותר: ונסתפג אפילו בעשר אלונטיות: רישא רבותא קמ"ל וסיפא רבותא קמ"ל רישא רבותא קמ"ל דאפילו הני דלא נפישי בהו מיא כיון דחד הוא אתי לידי סחיטה וסיפא רבותא קמ"ל אפילו הני דנפישי בהו מיא כיון דרבים נינהו מדכרי אהדדי: תנו רבנן מסתפג אדם באלונטית ומניחה בחלון ולא ימסרנה לאוליירין מפני שחשודים על אותו דבר רבי שמעון אומר מסתפג באלונטית אחת ומביאה בידו לתוך ביתו אמר ליה אביי לרב יוסף הלכתא מאי אמר ליה הא ר' שמעון הא רבי הא שמואל הא ר' יוחנן ר' שמעון הא דאמרן רבי דתניא אמר רבי כשהיינו למדין תורה אצל ר' שמעון בתקוע היינו מעלין שמן ואלונטית מחצר לגג ומגג לקרפף עד שהיינו מגיעין אצל מעין שהיינו רוחצין בו שמואל דאמר רב יהודה אמר שמואל מסתפג אדם באלונטית ומביאה בידו לתוך ביתו ר' יוחנן דאמר ר' חייא בר אבא א"ר יוחנן הלכה מסתפג אדם באלונטית ומביאה בידו לתוך ביתו ומי א"ר יוחנן הכי והא"ר יוחנן הלכה כסתם משנה ותנן ונסתפג אפילו בעשר אלונטיות לא יביאם בידו ההוא כבן חכינאי מתני לה א"ר חייא בר אבא אר"י האוליירין מביאין בלרי נשים לבי בני ובלבד שיתכסה בהן ראשן ורובן סכניתא (א) צריך לקשר ב' ראשיה למטה א"ר חייא בר אבא א"ר יוחנן למטה מכתפיים אמר להו רבא לבני מחוזא כי מעבריתו מאני לבני חילא שרביבו בהו למטה מכתפיים: סכין וממשמשין: ת"ר סכין וממשמשין בבני מעיים בשבת ובלבד שלא יעשה כדרך שהוא עושה בחול היכי עביד ר' חמא בר חנינא אמר סך ואח"כ ממשמש ר' יוחנן אמר סך וממשמש בבת אחת: אבל לא מתעמלין: א"ר חייא בר אבא א"ר יוחנן אסור לעמוד בקרקעיתה של דיומסת מפני שמעמלת ומרפא אמר ר' יהודה אמר רב כל ימיה של דיומסת עשרים ואחד יום ועצרת מן המנין איבעיא להו עצרת (בתחלה) להאי גיסא או להאי גיסא ת"ש דאמר שמואל כולהו שקייני מדיבחא ועד עצרתא מעלו דילמא התם הוא דכמה דקריר עלמא מעלי אבל הכא משום הבלא הוא כיון דחמים עלמא טפי מעלי אמר רבי חלבו חמרא דפרוגייתא ומיא דדיומסת קיפחו עשרת השבטים מישראל רבי אלעזר בן ערך איקלע להתם אימשיך בתרייהו איעקר תלמודיה כי הדר אתא קם למיקרי בספרא בעא למיקרא החדש הזה לכם אמר החרש היה לבם בעו רבנן רחמי עליה והדר תלמודיה והיינו דתנן ר' נהוראי אומר הוי גולה למקום תורה ואל תאמר שהיא תבא אחריך שחבריך יקיימוה בידך ואל בינתך אל תשען תנא לא ר' נהוראי שמו אלא ר' נחמיה שמו ואמרי לה ר' אלעזר בן ערך שמו ולמה נקרא שמו ר' נהוראי שמנהיר עיני חכמים בהלכה: אבל לא מתגרדין: ת"ר אין גוררין במגררת בשבת רשב"ג אומר אם היו רגליו מלוכלכות בטיט ובצואה גורר כדרכו ואינו חושש רב שמואל בר יהודה עבדא ליה אימיה מגררתא דכספא: אין יורדין לקורדימא וכו': מאי טעמא משום פיקא: ואין עושין אפיקטויזין בשבת: אמר רבה בר בר חנה אמר רבי יוחנן לא שנו אלא בסם אבל ביד מותר תניא רבי נחמיה אומר אף בחול אסור מפני הפסד אוכלין: ואין מעצבין את הקטן: אמר רבה בר בר חנה אמר ר' יוחנן לפופי ינוקא בשבת שפיר דמי והאנן תנן אין מעצבין התם בחומרי שדרה דמיחזי כבונה: ואין מחזירין את השבר: אמר רבי חנא בגדתאה אמר שמואל הלכה

רש"י

גמ' דלהשתטף. שופכן על גופו דלאו דרך רחיצה היא שרי לכתחילה אפי' בחמין: סיפא. אבל עשרה בני אדם כו': ומניחה בחלון. הסמוכה לכותל המרחץ: לאוליירין. בלנים: על אותו דבר. סחיטה: הא רבי והא ר"ש כו'. הרי כל אלו שמתירין: מחצר לגג כו'. ר"ש לטעמיה דאמר בעירובין (דף עד.) אחד גגות אחד חצירות וא' קרפיפות כולן רשות אחת הן לטלטל מזה לזה ואפילו של בעלים הרבה: עד שהיינו מגיעין כו'. ומסתמא לא היו מניחין אותה על המעין במקום הפקר: כבן חכינאי מתני לה. דברי בן חכינאי מסיים בה ולאו סתמא: האוליירין. בלנין: מביאין בלרי נשים. סדינים שהנשים מסתפגין בהם מותר להביאן דרך מלבוש לבית המרחץ: סכניתא. סודר גדול [א] שתלוי לו בין כתפיו וראשו עטוף בו: צריך לקשור שני ראשיה. זה בזה שלא תפול מראשו: כי מעבריתו מאני לבני חילא. כשתביאו בגדי העובדי כוכבי' בני החיל המוטלי' עליכם לשמשן ואתם מביאים להם בשבת דרך רשות הרבים: שרביבו בהו למטה מכתפיים. שלא יהיו שוליהם מונחים בכתפיכם אלא משוכי' למטה שיהא נראה לבוש: סך ואח"כ ממשמש. [דקסבר] בחול ממשמש ואחר כך סך: דיומסית[ס]. שם נהר שמימיו מלוחים: שמעמלת. מחממת: ומרפא. שהטיט מלוח: כל ימיה. ימי רפואתה: להאי גיסא כו'. מתחלת הימים או בסוף: שקייני. משקין לרפואה: מדבחא לעצרת. אלמא עצרת בסוף: חמרא דפרוגיתא. שם מדינה שיינה משובח: קפחו עשרת השבטים. שהיו בעלי הנאה ועסוקים בכך ולא היו עוסקים בתורה ויצאו לתרבות רעה: להתם. לפרוגיתא ודיומסית: אימשיך בתרייהו. אחר היין והרחיצה: איעקר תלמודיה. נעקר תלמודו ושכחו: החרש היה לבם: הוי גולה למקום תורה. אם ת"ח אתה אל תשב אלא במקום ת"ח חברך ואל תאמר תלמידים הם יבואו אלי ודי לי בכך למה אהיה גולה: שחביריך יקיימוה בידך. שתהא רגיל אצלם וכשתשנה מסכת אחת והם אחרת תשמענה ותהא סדורה בפיך ואל תשתכח הימנה: ואל בינתך אל תשען. לומר חכם גדול אני וחכרן וכשאחזור פרק זה או מסכת זו לא תשתכח תגרתה ממני: מגררת. אשטריי"ל ואדם מגרד בה: מגירתא דכספא. לשבת: משום פיקא. טיט של אותו נהר מחליק ובגדי האדם נישורין במים כשהוא נופל ואתי לידי סחיטה: אלא בסם. דדמי לרפואה וגזירה ° משום שחיקת סמנין: אבל ביד. להכניס יד לתוך גרונו עד שיקיא מותר: מפני הפסד אוכלין. שבמעיו ומתוך כך הוא רעב וחוזר ואוכל: לפופי. אונמלוטי"א כמו שעושי' לקטן שיתיישבו אבריו ולא יתעקם: בחומרי שדרה. חוליות של שדרה שנתפרקה אחת מהן ולאחר זמן קמיירי דאי ביום לידה (ג) אמרי' (לעיל דף קכט:) כל האמור בפ' מוכתה דיחזקאל עושין לחיה בשבת:

הלכה

(המשך בדף קמח.)

מסורת הש"ס

א) לעיל לט:, ב) עירובין פה. ע"ש, ג) [חשודין לסוחטה ונותנין אותה לאחרים. ערוך ע"ש], ד) עירובין לא. [מנחות עב.], ה) [לעיל מו. וש"נ], ו) [עי' פירש"י עירובין סג. ד"ה מחוא וברש"י פסחים ה. ד"ה מחוא וברש"י ב"מ נג. עוד שם עז. ד"ה אוכלתא דמחוא], ז) סנהדרין קא., ח) [פסחים דף מב:], ט) אדר"נ ספי"ד, י) אבות פ"ד משנה י"ד, כ) עירובין יג: ע"ש, ל) [תוספ' פי"ז], מ) [לעיל סו: ע"ש], נ) [עמ"ש רש"י ברכות כד: וע"ע פרש"י ביבמות סז. ד"ה בגדתאה], ס) [וכישעיה כח א גרס ומיא דדורמסקית וכן גרס רד"ק שם], ע) [בגיטין אי' סוכני וחומש], פ) [שייך לעיל במשנה].

הגהות הב"ח

(א) גמרא סכניתא אמר ר' אבין בר רב חסדא א"ר יוחנן צריך לקשר שני וכו' ואמר ר' חייא: (ג) רש"י ד"ה בחומרי וכו' ביום לידה הא אמרינן. נ"ב סוף פ' מפנין ע"ש וברש"י שפי' דלפופי הוא על ידי חגורות ופסיקיאות:

גליון הש"ס

גמ' אמר החרש היה לבם. עי' דבר נחמד בקרנים בליקוטים שבסוף הספר: רש"י ד"ה אלא בסם וכו' משום שחיקת סמנין. ע"ל דף קכג ע"ב ברש"י ד"ה אפיקטויזין:

הגהות הגר"א

[א] רש"י ד"ה סוכניתא סודר גדול. נ"ב אבל הרמב"ם פי' קטן שאין מכסה ראשו ורובו:

תורה אור השלם

א) הַחֹדֶשׁ הַזֶּה לָכֶם רֹאשׁ חֳדָשִׁים רִאשׁוֹן הוּא לָכֶם לְחָדְשֵׁי הַשָּׁנָה: [שמות יב, ב]

ליקוטי רש"י

להשתטף. שטוחן על גופו ומשתטף. **לא ישתטף.** בשבת. בין בחמין. ואפילו חוממו בחול. ר' שמעון מתיר. להשתטף כל גופו בשבת בחמין שהוחמו מערב שבת [לעיל לט:]. **רישא רבותא קמ"ל.** דלא נפישי מיא בכל חד אפילו הכי לא יביאם בידו כתוך בימו אפילו על ידי עירוב שמא ישכח ויסחט בבואו. **וסיפא רבותא קמ"ל.** דמדלא אלונטית לעשרה [בני אדם נפישן] ביה מיא אפילו הכי מביאין אותה בידים [לעיל ע"א]. [המשך בדף קמח.]

חשק שלמה על רבינו חננאל א) לכאורה נראה דממימא ואע"ג עד תברינהו לסילוניהו אנשי טבריא שייך להלן אמר מינות כוותיה עבדינן ודו"ק: ג) עיין ערוך ערך פלס א':

The Gemara quotes the next part of the Mishnah:

סָכִין וּמְמַשְׁמְשִׁין – On the Sabbath, WE MAY APPLY OIL to the skin AND MASSAGE the body by hand.

A Baraisa elaborates further:

תָּנוּ רַבָּנָן – The Rabbis taught in a Baraisa: סָכִין וּמְמַשְׁמְשִׁין בִּבְנֵי מֵעַיִים בְּשַׁבָּת – WE MAY APPLY OIL to the skin AND MASSAGE THE INTESTINAL AREA ON THE SABBATH, וּבִלְבַד שֶׁלֹּא יַעֲשֶׂה כְּדֶרֶךְ שֶׁהוּא עוֹשֶׂה בְּחוֹל – JUST SO LONG AS ONE DOES NOT DO IT THE WAY HE usually DOES IT ON A WEEKDAY.[19]

The Gemara inquires:

הֵיכִי עָבִיד – How, then, should one do it? What qualifies as performing a massage in a different way than usual?

The Gemara replies:

רַבִּי חָמָא בַּר חֲנִינָא אָמַר – R' Chama bar Chanina said: סָךְ וְאַחַר כָּךְ מְמַשְׁמֵשׁ – Let him first rub in the oil and afterwards massage the skin.[20] רַבִּי יוֹחָנָן אָמַר – However, R' Yochanan said: סָךְ וּמְמַשְׁמֵשׁ בְּבַת אַחַת – Let him rub in the oil and massage the skin simultaneously.[21]

The Gemara quotes the next part of the Mishnah:

אֲבָל לֹא מִתְעַמְּלִין – But we may not massage vigorously.

A related law:

אָמַר רַבִּי חִיָּיא בַּר אַבָּא אָמַר רַבִּי יוֹחָנָן – R' Chiya bar Abba said in the name of R' Yochanan: אָסוּר לַעֲמוֹד בְּקַרְקָעִיתָהּ שֶׁל דְּיוֹמְסֶת – On the Sabbath, it is forbidden to stand in the mud of the Diomses River[22] מִפְּנֵי שֶׁמְּעַמֶּלֶת וּמְרַפָּא – because it invigorates and heals the body.[23]

The Gemara provides some more information about this river:

אָמַר רַב יְהוּדָה אָמַר רַב – Rav Yehudah said the following in the name of Rav: כָּל יָמֶיהָ שֶׁל דְּיוֹמְסֶת עֶשְׂרִים וְאֶחָד יוֹם – The days in which the Diomses River possesses this therapeutic power, all in all, are twenty-one days, וַעֲצֶרֶת מִן הַמִּנְיָן – and the holiday of Shavuos is included in this count.

Presumably, Rav means that Shavuos marks either the beginning or the end of the season in which standing in the river can be especially healthful.[24] The Gemara therefore questions:

אִבַּעְיָא לְהוּ – They inquired: עֲצֶרֶת (בתחלה) לְהַאי גִּיסָא אוֹ לְהַאי גִּיסָא – Does Shavuos mark this side [the beginning] of the twenty-one day period, or does it mark that side [the end] of it?

The Gemara seeks to resolve the question:

תָּא שְׁמַע – Come, learn a proof that the holiday marks the end of the period. דְּאָמַר שְׁמוּאֵל – For Shmuel said: כּוּלְהוּ שִׁקְיָינֵי מִדִּיבְחָא וְעַד עֲצַרְתָּא מַעֲלוּ – All these kinds of healing drinks are at their best from Passover[25] until Shavuos.[26]

The Gemara rejects the proof:

דִּילְמָא הָתָם הוּא דְּכַמָּה דְּקָרִיר עָלְמָא מַעֲלֵי – Perhaps there, with regard to the therapeutic drinks mentioned by Shmuel, it is the case that the cooler the weather of the world is, the more effective the drinks are.[27] אֲבָל הָכָא מִשּׁוּם הַבְלָא הוּא – But here, in the case of the mud of the Diomses, the healing comes on account of the vapors rising from the hot earth. כֵּיוָן דְּחָמִים עָלְמָא טְפֵי מַעֲלֵי – Thus, it may be that when the climate of the world is warmer, [the mud] is more effective.

The Gemara relates an Aggadic tradition pertaining to the Diomses river:

אָמַר רַבִּי חֶלְבּוֹ – R' Chelbo said: חַמְרָא דפרוגי(י)תא וּמַיָּא דְּדְיוֹמְסֶת – The wine of Prugisa[28] and the water of the Diomses קִיפְּחוּ עֲשֶׂרֶת הַשְּׁבָטִים מִיִּשְׂרָאֵל – deprived Israel of the Ten Tribes.[29]

The Gemara tells of a Tanna who was likewise enticed by the waters of the Diomses:

רַבִּי אֶלְעָזָר בֶּן עֲרָךְ אִיקְּלַע לְהָתָם – R' Elazar ben Arach once came to that region [i.e. the area of Prugisa and the Diomses]. אִימְּשִׁיךְ בָּתְרַיְיהוּ – He became attracted to these worldly delights,[30] אִיעַקַּר תַּלְמוּדֵיהּ – and all his Torah knowledge became erased from his mind.[31] כִּי הֲדַר – When he later returned from that region, אָתָא קָם לְמִיקְרֵי בְּסִפְרָא – he came and got up to read from the Torah scroll. בְּעָא לְמִקְרָא ,,הַחֹדֶשׁ הַזֶּה לָכֶם'' – He had wanted to read the verse that begins: *This month shall be for you [the first of months].*[32] אֲמַר הַחֵרֵשׁ הָיָה לִבָּם – But instead, he said: "Was their heart silent?"[33] בְּעוּ רַבָּנָן רַחֲמֵי עֲלֵיהּ – Realizing that their colleague had forgotten his Torah knowledge, the Sages beseeched God to have mercy upon

NOTES

19. Otherwise, it is Rabbinically forbidden as an עוּבְדָּא דְחוֹל, *a weekday activity* (see *Rashi* to 147a ד״ה ולא מתגררין).

20. On the weekday, one usually first massages the skin and afterwards rubs in the oil (*Rashi*).

21. R' Yochanan holds that during the week there was no particular order: One might rub the oil in first, or massage the skin first. It was not the custom, however, to perform these acts simultaneously, so R' Yochanan allows their simultaneous performance on the Sabbath (see *Mishnah Berurah* to 327 §6).

22. A certain river whose waters were especially salty (*Rashi;* see *Rashi* to *Isaiah* 28:1 for a somewhat different version of the river's name). The river was apparently located near the Judean city of *Emaos* (see *Avos DeRabbi Nassan,* end of ch. 14; *Koheles Rabbah* 7:7; *Talmud Yerushalmi, Sheviis,* 9:2).

23. The river warms the body, and its salty mud is therapeutic (*Rashi*).

24. [I.e. Rav means that Shavuos is just barely included in the count.]

25. *Rashi* to *Pesachim* 42b ד״ה מדבחא. Literally, דִּבְחָא means *sacrifice.* [Presumably, Passover gets this name from the *pesach* offering, a sacrifice bearing the same name as the holiday.]

26. [Shmuel presumably refers to a number of healthful brews mentioned by the Gemara earlier in this tractate (110a). The Gemara there mentions that these brews should be imbibed in the early spring, between Passover and Shavuos. The Gemara surmises that the same period would be the most healthful time of year to benefit from the Diomses River.]

27. That is, they are most effective in the relatively cool springtime.

28. A country that produces wine of exceptional quality (*Rashi*). [Emendation to פרוגיתא follows *Dikdukei Soferim.*]

29. The Ten Tribes of the Northern Kingdom of Israel were exiled by Assyria, and, in effect, became lost from the Jewish people (see *II Kings* 15:29, 17:23 and *Rashi* to ibid. 17:1). The Gemara identifies the sin which precipitated their exile as an excessive involvement in material pleasures, signified by the wine of Prugisa and the water of the Diomses (see *Maharal*). Becoming involved in these pursuits, they forsook the Torah and adopted alien life-styles (*Rashi*).

30. [I.e. to the superior wine of Prugisa and the soothing waters of the Diomses (*Rashi*).]

31. *Koheles Rabbah* (7:7, Vilna Edition) tells an expanded version of this story. It relates that R' Elazar ben Arach was one of the five principal students of R' Yochanan ben Zakkai during the Roman siege of Jerusalem. When R' Yochanan died, his students re-established their academy in the city of Yavneh; however, R' Elazar ben Arach did not follow them. Instead, he settled in his wife's city, the beautiful town of Emaos, near the pleasing waters of the Diomses, and waited for the other students to join him there. As R' Elazar was the most exceptional of R' Yochanan ben Zakkai's students, his wife convinced him that it was not befitting for him to follow them; instead, the other students must come to him. In the end, the other students remained in Yavneh, and R' Elazar stayed in Emaos, until — isolated and alone — he began to forget the Torah he had learned.

32. *Exodus* 12:2.

33. He did not actually forget so much that he no longer knew how to read. Rather, he unintentionally mispronounced the words, mistaking the ד, ז, כ for the similar letters ר, י, ב. His colleagues then interpreted the resulting phrase [הַחֵרֵשׁ הָיָה לִבָּם, *was their heart silent*] as an oblique sign that he had forgotten much of his Torah learning (*Maharal;* see *Maharsha*).

עין משפט
נר מצוה

מו א ב מיי' פכ"ב מהל' שבת הלכה יט טור שו"ע או"ח סימן שא סעיף מח:
מז ג ד מיי' פי"ט שם הלכה יט סמג לאוין סה טוש"ע שם סעיף לד:
מח ה ו מיי' פכ"א מהל' שבת הלכה כח סמג שם טוש"ע או"ח סימן שכח סעיף ג:
מט ז מיי' וסמג שם טוש"ע שם וסימן שכח סעיף מב:
נ ח מיי' שם:
נא ט מיי' שם הלכה ל טוש"ע או"ח סימן שכ סעיף ג:
נב י מיי' שם הלכה כט טוש"ע או"ח סי' שא סעיף מו בהג"ה:
נג כ ל מיי' שם הלכה לא סמג שם טוש"ע או"ח סי' שכח סעיף לט:
נד מ מיי' וסמג שם טור שו"ע או"ח סימן של סעיף י:
נה נ מיי' פכ"ב שם הלכה כו:

רבינו חננאל

אוקימנא למתני' הרוחץ בחמין דיעבד אבל לכתחלה לרחוץ בחמין אסור. ולהשתטף בחמין נמי אפי' כל גופו מותר כר"ש דתניא לא ישתטף אדם בין בחמין בין בצונן דברי ר"מ. ור"ש מתיר. ר' יהודה אומר בחמין אסור ובצונן מותר. אע"פ דתנינן סתמא כר"ש לית הלכתא כוותיה דהא בפירוש נמי תנינן סתמא כוותיה (לעיל דף לח). מעשה שעשו אנשי טבריא כו' א) (ואע"ג דאמר עולא הלכה כאנשי טבריא הא אמר ליה רב נחמן תברינהו לסילונייהו אנשי טבריא) ואוקימנא כר"ש. ופסקי' בגמרי' אמר רבה בר בר חנה א"ר יוחנן הלכה כרבי יהודה ודקדק רב יוסף על רבה בר בר חנה וא"ל בפירוש שמיעא לך דהלכתא כר' יהודה או מכללא אמרתיה. א"ל בפירוש שמיעא ליה. וכיון דפסק ר' יוחנן בפירוש הלכה כר' יהודה כוותיה עבדינן. ומסתפג אפי' בעשר אלונטיות ולא יביאם בידו ואע"פ שאין בהם מים מרובין. דכיון דחד הוא. דלמא מינשי ועביד סחיטה. אבל אם היו ב"א הרבה אפילו אם מסתפגין כולן באלונטית אחת היא שרי' כיון דרבים נינהו מדכרי אהדדי ולא אתו לידי סחיטה. ומותר להביאה בידים בחצר או מן הגג וכדומה לו מקום שמותר לו לטלטל: אוליירין הם השמשים בני אדם הנכנסים במרחץ והן חשודין בזמה שמא יסחטו לאלונטיות. א"ל אביי לרב יוסף הלכתא מאי כו' א"ר יוחנן הלכה מסתפג אדם באלונטית ומביאה בידו לתוך ביתו. והקשינן עלה הא"ר יוחנן הלכה כסתם משנה ותנן מסתפג אדם אפילו בעשר אלונטיות ולא יביאם בידו. ומפרקי' מתני' ר' יוחנן לא תאני לה סתמא. אלא כבן חכינאי מתני

תוספות

דתניא א"ר כשהיינו למדין תורה כו'. מסתמא יחידי היה שלא היה אלא אחד מתלמידיו עמו כשהיה רוחץ כדתניא במקום שנהגו (פסחים דף נא.) שלא ירחוץ תלמיד עם רבו ואם היה רבו צריך לו מותר ומסתמא ר"ש לא היה צריך אלא לאחד כשהיה רוחץ וכשהיו שנים לביתם היה התלמיד נושא האלונטית בפני עצמה שר"ש לא היה נושא עמו דהא ס"ל שיחיד מותר להביאה ולא חיישינן לסחיטה והא דקאמר היינו ר"ל כל אחד ואחד בפני עצמו כשהיה מגיע יומו לשמש רבו ולעיל בפ' כירה (דף מ:) גרסינן מעשה בתלמיד של ר' מאיר שנכנס אחריו לבית המרחץ ויש ספרים דגרסי תלמידיו ואיננו ובכל הספרים גרסי לקמן בפרק שואל (דף קנא:) תלמידו. מ"ר:

צריך לקשר שני ראשיה למטה. בגיטין בפ' הניזקין (דף נט.) מפרש דסכניתא הוא בגד דק דאמרינן ע) סוכני ותומר כי אמגוזא ופלגא דאמגוזא ומשום הכי צריך לקשר שני ראשיה למטה שלא יפריחנו מעליו הרוח ואתי לאתויי או משום דנראה כעין משוי לפי שהוא דק מאד ואינו נראה מלבוש אא"כ נראה קשור:

פ) **אין** מעצבין את הקטן. פירשנו [בריש כל הכלים] (ד' קכ"ג. ד"ה אסוכי):

הדרן עלך חבית

גמרא

דלהשתטף כל גופו אפי' לכתחילה שפיר דמי מני ר"ש היא דתניא לא ישתטף אדם בין בחמין בין בצונן דברי ר"מ ר"ש מתיר ר' יהודה אומר בחמין אסור בצונן מותר: ונסתפג אפילו בעשר אלונטיות: רישא רבותא קמ"ל וסיפא רבותא קמ"ל רישא רבותא קמ"ל דאפילו הני דלא נפישי בהו מיא כיון דחד הוא אתי לידי סחיטה וסיפא רבותא קמ"ל אפילו הני דנפישי בהו מיא כיון דרבים נינהו מדכרי אהדדי: תנו רבנן מסתפג אדם באלונטית ומניחה בחלון ולא ימסרנה לאוליירין מפני שחשודים על אותו דבר רבי שמעון אומר מסתפג באלונטית אחת ומביאה בידו לתוך ביתו אמר ליה אביי לרב יוסף הלכתא מאי אמר ליה הא ר' שמעון הא רבי הא שמואל הא ר' יוחנן ר' שמעון הא דאמרן רבי דתניא אמר רבי כשהיינו למדין תורה אצל ר' שמעון בתקוע היינו מעלין שמן ואלונטית מחצר לגג ומגג לקרפף עד שהיינו מגיעין אצל מעין שהיינו רוחצין בו שמואל דאמר רב יהודה אמר שמואל מסתפג אדם באלונטית ומביאה בידו לתוך ביתו ר' יוחנן דאמר ר' חייא בר אבא א"ר יוחנן הלכה מסתפג אדם באלונטית ומביאה בידו לתוך ביתו ומי א"ר יוחנן הכי והא"ר יוחנן הלכה כסתם משנה ותנן ונסתפג אפילו בעשר אלונטיות לא יביאם בידו ההוא כבן חכינאי מתני לה א"ר חייא בר אבא אר"י האוליירין מביאין בלרי נשים לבי בני ובלבד שיתכסה בהן ראשון ורובן (א) סכניתא צריך לקשר ב' ראשיה למטה א"ר חייא בר אבא א"ר יוחנן למטה מכתפיים אמר להו רבא לבני מחוזא כי מעבריתו מאני לבני חילא שרביבו בהו למטה מכתפיים: סכין וממשמשין: ת"ר סכין וממשמשין בבני מעיים בשבת ובלבד שלא יעשה כדרך שהוא עושה בחול היכי עביד ר' חמא בר חנינא אמר סך ואח"כ ממשמש ר' יוחנן אמר סך וממשמש בבת אחת: אבל לא מתעמלין: א"ר חייא בר אבא א"ר יוחנן אסור לעמוד בקרקעיתה של דיומסת מפני שמעמלת ומרפא אמר ר' יהודה אמר רב כל ימיה של דיומסת עשרים ואחד יום ועצרת מן המנין איבעיא להו עצרת (בתחלה) להאי גיסא או להאי גיסא ת"ש דאמר שמואל כולהו שקייני מדיבחא ועד עצרתא מעלו דילמא התם הוא דכמה דקריר עלמא מעלי אבל הכא משום הבלא הוא כיון דחמים עלמא טפי מעלי אמר רבי חלבו חמרא דפרוגייתא ומיא דדיומסת קיפחו עשרת השבטים מישראל רבי אלעזר בן ערך איקלע להתם אימשיך בתרייהו איעקר תלמודיה כי הדר אתא קם למיקרי בספרא בעא למיקרא א) החדש הזה לכם ° אמר החרש היה לבם בעו רבנן רחמי עליה והדר תלמודיה והיינו דתנן ר' נהוראי אומר הוי גולה למקום תורה ואל תאמר שהיא תבא אחריך שחבריך יקיימוה בידך ואל בינתך אל תשען תנא לא ר' נהוראי שמו אלא ר' נחמיה שמו ואמרי לה ר' אלעזר בן ערך שמו ולמה נקרא שמו ר' נהוראי שמנהיר עיני חכמים בהלכה: אבל לא מתגררין: ת"ר אין גוררין במגררת בשבת רשב"ג אומר אם היו רגליו מלוכלכות בטיט ובצואה גורר כדרכו ואינו חושש רב שמואל בר יהודה עבדא ליה אימיה מגררתא דכספא: אין יורדין לקורדימא וכו': מאי טעמא משום פיקא: ואין עושין אפיקטויזין בשבת: אמר רבה בר בר חנה אמר רבי יוחנן לא שנו אלא בסם אבל ביד מותר תניא רבי נחמיה אומר אף בחול אסור מפני הפסד אוכלין: ואין מעצבין את הקטן: אמר רבה בר בר חנה אמר ר' יוחנן לפופי ינוקא בשבת שפיר דמי והאנן תנן אין מעצבין התם בחומרי שדרה דמיחזי כבונה: ואין מחזירין את השבר: אמר רבי חנא בגדתאה אמר שמואל
הלכה

רש"י

גמ' דלהשתטף. שופכן על גופו דלאו דרך רחיצה היא שרי לכתחילה אפי' בחמין: סיפא. אבל עשרה בני אדם כו': ומניחה בחלון. הסמוכה לכותל המרחץ: לאוליירין. בלנים: על אותו דבר. סחיטה: הא רבי והא ר"ש כו'. הרי כל אלו שמתירין: מחצר לגג כו'. ר"ש לטעמיה דאמר בעירובין (דף עד.) אחד גגות אחד חצירות וא' קרפיפות כולן רשות אחת הן לטלטל מזה לזה ואפילו של בעלים הרבה: עד שהיינו מגיעין כו'. ומסתמא לא היו מניחין אותה על המעין במקום הפקר: כבן חכינאי מתני לה. דברי בן חכינאי מסיים בה ולאו סתמא: האוליירין. בלנין: מביאין בלרי נשים. סדינים שהנשים מסתפגין בהם מותר להביאן דרך מלבוש לבית המרחץ: סכניתא. סודר גדול [א] שתלוי לו בין כתפיו וראשו עטוף בו: צריך לקשור שני ראשיה. זה בזה שלא תפול מראשו: כי מעבריתו מאני לבני חילא. כשתביאו בגדי העובדי כוכבי' בני החיל המוטלי' עליכם לשמשן ואתם מביאים להם בשבת דרך רשות הרבים: שרביבו בהו למטה מכתפיים. שלא יהיו שוליהם מונחים בכתפיכם אלא משוכי' למטה שיהא נראה לבוש: סך ואח"כ ממשמש. [דקסבר] בחול ממשמש ואחר כך סך: דיומסית[ס]. שם נהר שמימיו מלוחים: שמעמלת. מחממת: ומרפא. שהטיט מלוח: כל ימיה. ימי רפואתה: להאי גיסא כו'. מתחלת הימים או בסוף: שקייני. משקין לרפואה: מדבחא לעצרת. אלמא עצרת בסוף: חמרא דפרוגיתא. שם מדינה שיינה משובח: קפחו עשרת השבטים. שהיו בעלי הנאה ועסוקים בכך ולא היו עוסקים בתורה ויצאו לתרבות רעה: להתם. לפרוגיתא ודיומסית: אימשיך בתרייהו. אחר היין והרחיצה: איעקר תלמודיה. נעקר תלמודו ושכחו: החרש היה לבם: הוי גולה למקום תורה. אם ת"ח אתה אל תשב אלא במקום ת"ח חברך ואל תאמר תלמידים הם יבואו אלי ודי לי בכך למה אהיה גולה: שחבריך יקיימוה בידך. שתהא רגיל אצלם וכשתשנה מסכת אחת והם אחרת תשמענה ותהא סדורה בפיך ואל תשתכח הימנה: ואל בינתך אל תשען. לומר חכם גדול אני וזכרן וכשאחזור פרק זה או מסכת זו לא תשתכח חברתה ממני: מגררת. אשטריי"ל ואדם מגרר בה: מגירתא דכספא. לשבת: משום פיקא. טיט של אותו נהר מחליק ובגדי האדם נישורין במים כשהוא נופל ואתי לידי סחיטה: אלא בסם. דדמי לרפואה וגזירה ° משום שחיקת סמנין: אבל ביד. להכניס יד לתוך גרונו עד שיקיא מותר: מפני הפסד אוכלין. שבמעיו ומתוך כך הוא רעב וחוזר ואוכל: לפופי. אונמלוטי"א כמו שעושי' לקטן שיתיישבו אבריו ולא יתעקם: בחומרי שדרה. חוליות של שדרה שנתפרקה אחת מהן ולאחר זמן קמיירי דלאו ביום לידה (ב) דאמרי' (לעיל דף קכט:) כל האמור בפ' תוכחה דיחזקאל עושין לחיה בשבת:
הלכה

מסורת הש"ס

א) [לעיל לט:], ב) עירובין פח. ע"ש, ג) [חשודין] לסוחטה וגונבין אותה לאחרים. ערוך ע"ש], ד) עירובין ע"ש, ה) [מנחות עב.], ו) [לעיל מו. וש"נ], ז) [פי' פירש"י עירובין סב. ד"ה מחוח וכרש"י ב"מ נט. עוד שם נט. ד"ה מולכלת דמחוזא], ח) [פסחים דף מב:], ט) [גיטין נט.], י) [מוספתא פי"ז], כ) [לעיל נט:], ל) [עמ"ש רש"י], מ) [עי' ערוך], נ) [ד"ה גנדתאה], ס) [וכשיטה כת"י], ע) [גיטין לז. וע"ש], פ) [שייך לעיל במשנה]

הגהות הב"ח

(א) גמרא סכניתא אמר ר' אבין בר רב חסדא א"ר יוחנן צריך לקשר שני וכו' ואמר ר' חייא: (ב) רש"י ד"ה בחומרי וכו' ביום לידה דאמרינן. נ"ב סוף פ' מפנין ע"ש כרש"י שפי' דלפופי הוא על ידי חגורות ופסיקיאות:

גליון הש"ס

גמ' אמר החרש היה לבם. עי' דבר נחמד בקרנים בליקוטים שבסוף הספר: רש"י ד"ה אלא בסם וכו' משום שחיקת סממנין. ע"ל דף קכג ע"ב תוס' ד"ה אפיקטויזין:

הגהות הגר"א

[א] רש"י ד"ה סכניתא סודר גדול. נ"ב ע"ל הכרמלא פי' קטן שאין מכסה ראשו ורובו:

תורה אור השלם

א) הַחֹדֶשׁ הַזֶּה לָכֶם רֹאשׁ חֳדָשִׁים רִאשׁוֹן הוּא לָכֶם לְחָדְשֵׁי הַשָּׁנָה: [שמות יב, ב]

ליקוטי רש"י

להשתטף. שוטף על גופו [לעיל לט:]. לא ישתטף. בשבת. בין בחמין. ואפילו הוחמו בחול. ר' שמעון מתיר. להשתטף כל גופו בשבת בחמין שהוחמו מערב שבת [לעיל לט:]. רישא רבותא קמ"ל. דלא נפישי מיא בכל הני לא יביאם בידו כמון וכו' ... וסיפא רבותא קמ"ל. דקתני אלונטית אחת [בני אדם נסיפין] ... [המשך בדף קמח.]

מ"ל. בתלמוד א"י בפ' כירה ר' חנניה בן עקיבא התיר הבאת לונטיות: סכינתאי א"ר אבין בר רב חסדא א"ר יוחנן צריך לקשר ב' ראשיה למטה. א"ר חייא בר אבא א"ר יוחנן למטה מכתפים. וכן זה שאמר רבא לבני מחוזא כי מעבריתו מני דבני חילא שרביבו להו למטה מכתפים. שלא להראות משא בכתף: בלרין נשים לבי בני. פי' דהא קן של נשים כשמביאין להן האוליירין במרחץ לא התירו אלא עד שיתכסה בהן ראשו ורובו: סכין וממשמשין כר' יוחנן דאמר סך וממשמש בבת אחת והוא משמוש ביד בקלות. אבל לא מתעמלין. פי' פושטין ומקפלין זרועותיהם לפניהן ולאחריהן וכן רגליהן ע"ג ירכותיהן ומתחממין ומזיעין והוא כמין מעשה רפואה ואסור. וכן אסור לעמוד בשבת בקרקעיתה של דיומסת מפני שמעמלת ומרפאה: חמרא דפרוגתא יין של פרוגיתא והוא שם מקום ומיא דדמיסת גם הוא שם מקום. כלומר יין של פרגיתא ומיא של דיומסת טובים הם וערבין ונמשך לב שותה להניחם ומתאחר שם ואותן מקומות אין בהן בני תורה והמתאחר שם זמן הרבה מתקפח ושכח תלמודו. אבל לא מתגרדין. גירוד זה הוא חיכוך בכלי כי הא דתנן רבנן אין גורדין במגרת בשבת רשבג"א אם היו רגליו מלוכלכות בטיט ובצואה גורד כדרכו ואינו חושש. רב שמואל בר יהודה עבדא ליה אמיה מגרדתא דכספא להתחכך בה: **אין** יורדין לקירומא. ס"א לפילומא פי' בקעה ויש שם מים ותחתיו טיט כמו טפל. ואם יבקע ויטבע בו אינו יכול לעלות עד שיבואו ב"א ומעלין אותו משם. יש מי שאומרים הרוחץ באותה בקעה מצטנן ואותן המים משלשלין בני מעיו ג). וזה פי' ביקא. פי' אפיקטויזין קיא. אמר רבה בר בר חנה א"ר יוחנן לא שנו אלא בסם שהוא אסור אבל ביד מותר. ואין מעצבין את הקטן כו'. פי' מושכין אבריו של קטן ומיישב בידו חוליות של שדרה אחת על חברתה וזהו עיצוב מלשון עצבון: **לפופי** ינוקא לחבר אברים של תינוק. וכדתרגם ויחבר ולפיף: **ואין** מחזירין את השבר אמר רב הונא מחזירין

חשק שלמה על רבינו חננאל א) לכאורה נראה דמחיקת ואע"ג עד תברינהו לסילונייהו אנשי טבריא שייך להלן אחר מלות כוותיה עבדינן ודו"ק: ג) עיין ערוך ערך פלס א':

him, וְהָדַר תַּלְמוּדֵיהּ – and **his Torah knowledge returned** to him.

The Gemara concludes:

וְהַיְינוּ דִּתְנַן – **And this** story concerning R' Elazar ben Arach illustrates **that which we learned in the** following **Mishnah:**[34] רַבִּי נְהוֹרַאי אוֹמֵר – R' NEHORAI SAYS: הֱוֵי גּוֹלֶה לִמְקוֹם תּוֹרָה – EXILE YOURSELF TO A PLACE OF TORAH, וְאַל תֹּאמַר שֶׁהִיא תָּבֹא אַחֲרֶיךָ – AND DO NOT presume to SAY THAT [THE TORAH] WILL COME AFTER YOU,[35] שֶׁחֲבֵרֶיךָ יְקַיְּימוּהָ בְּיָדְךָ – FOR IT IS YOUR COLLEAGUES WHO WILL CAUSE IT TO REMAIN WITH YOU; וְאֶל בִּינָתְךָ אַל תִּשָּׁעֵן – AND DO NOT RELY ON YOUR OWN UNDERSTANDING.[36]

The Gemara concludes:

תָּנָא – **It was taught** in a Baraisa: לֹא רַבִּי נְהוֹרַאי שְׁמוֹ – In fact, [THE TANNA] who taught this WAS NOT NAMED R' NEHORAI, אֶלָּא רַבִּי נְחֶמְיָה שְׁמוֹ – RATHER, R' NECHEMYAH WAS HIS NAME. וְאָמְרֵי לָהּ רַבִּי אֶלְעָזָר בֶּן עֲרָךְ שְׁמוֹ – AND SOME SAY HIS NAME WAS R' ELAZAR BEN ARACH, the very person who had isolated himself near the Diomses River. וְלָמָּה נִקְרָא שְׁמוֹ רַבִּי נְהוֹרַאי – AND WHY, then, IS HE CALLED "R' NEHORAI"? שֶׁמַּנְהִיר עֵינֵי חֲכָמִים בַּהֲלָכָה – BECAUSE HE ILLUMINATED *[manhir]* THE EYES OF THE SAGES IN matters of HALACHAH.[37]

The Gemara quotes the next part of the Mishnah:

אֲבָל לֹא מִתְגָּרְרִין – BUT WE MAY NOT SCRAPE the skin.

A related Baraisa:

תָּנוּ רַבָּנָן – **The Rabbis taught in a Baraisa:** אֵין גּוֹרְרִין בְּמַגְרֶרֶת בְּשַׁבָּת – WE MAY NOT SCRAPE the skin WITH A STRIGIL[38] ON THE SABBATH. רַבָּן שִׁמְעוֹן בֶּן גַּמְלִיאֵל אוֹמֵר – However, RABBAN SHIMON BEN GAMLIEL SAYS: אִם הָיוּ רַגְלָיו מְלוּכְלָכוֹת בְּטִיט וּבְצוֹאָה – IF ONE'S LEGS ARE SOILED WITH MUD OR EXCREMENT, גּוֹרֵר כְּדַרְכּוֹ – HE MAY SCRAPE his skin AS HE USUALLY DOES on the weekday וְאֵינוֹ חוֹשֵׁשׁ – AND HE NEED NOT BE CONCERNED that this violates any prohibition.[39]

The Gemara adds:

רַב שְׁמוּאֵל בַּר יְהוּדָה עָבְדָא לֵיהּ אִימֵּיהּ מַגְרַרְתָּא דְּכַסְפָּא – **The mother of Rav Shmuel bar Yehudah made him a silver strigil** especially for use on the Sabbath.[40]

The Gemara elaborates on the next part of the Mishnah:

אֵין יוֹרְדִין לְקוֹרְדִימָא וכו׳ – The Mishnah had stated: WE MAY NOT GO DOWN TO THE KURDIMA River on the Sabbath. מַאי טַעְמָא – **What is the reason** for this? מִשּׁוּם פִּיקָא – It is **because of** the danger of **slipping.**[41]

The Mishnah further stated:

וְאֵין עוֹשִׂין אַפִּיקְטְוִיזִין בְּשַׁבָּת – NOR MAY WE TAKE AN EMETIC ON THE SABBATH.

The Gemara qualifies this:

אָמַר רַבָּה בַּר בַּר חָנָה אָמַר רַבִּי יוֹחָנָן – **Rabbah bar bar Chanah said in the name of R' Yochanan:** לֹא שָׁנוּ אֶלָּא בְּסַם – **This was taught only with** reference to using some sort of **herb** to induce vomiting.[42] אֲבָל בְּיָד מוּתָּר – **But** inducing vomiting **by hand** [e.g. to thrust one's finger down his throat] **is permitted** on the Sabbath.

A related Baraisa:

תַּנְיָא – **It was taught in a Baraisa:** רַבִּי נְחֶמְיָה אוֹמֵר – R' NECHEMYAH SAID: אַף בְּחוֹל אָסוּר – EVEN ON A WEEKDAY IT IS FORBIDDEN to induce vomiting מִפְּנֵי הֶפְסֵד אוֹכָלִין – BECAUSE of the consideration of WASTING FOOD.[43]

The Gemara quotes the next part of the Mishnah:

וְאֵין מְעַצְּבִין אֶת הַקָּטָן – AND WE MAY NOT STRAIGHTEN the limbs of AN INFANT.

A related law:

אָמַר רַבָּה בַּר בַּר חָנָה אָמַר רַבִּי יוֹחָנָן – **Rabbah bar bar Chanah said in the name of R' Yochanan:** לְפוּפֵּי יְנוּקָא בְּשַׁבָּת שַׁפִּיר דָּמֵי – **Wrapping an infant on the Sabbath is permitted.**[44]

The Gemara objects to this on the basis of our Mishnah's statement:

וְהָאֲנַן תְּנַן אֵין מְעַצְּבִין – **But we learned in our Mishnah:** WE MAY NOT STRAIGHTEN the limbs of an infant! – ? –

The Gemara answers:

הָתָם בְּחוּמְרֵי שִׁדְרָה – **There,** in our Mishnah, we are speaking **of**

NOTES

34. *Avos* 4:14.

35. I.e. if you are a Torah scholar, see to it that, at all costs, you settle among your colleagues. Do not be tempted to say: These other scholars are my students; let them come to me. Rather, settle amongst them even if you are the one who must move (*Rashi*).

[The Gemara's citation of this Mishnah in connection with R' Elazar ben Arach's behavior seems to parallel the expanded version of this story cited in *Koheles Rabbah* (see above, note 31).]

36. When one lives in isolation, his ability to retain Torah knowledge is diminished, for as he learns and concentrates upon a new tractate, he will naturally begin to forget the tractate he previously studied. When in the company of other scholars, however, his ability to remember is greatly enhanced. For while he studies a certain tractate, a different sage may be studying a tractate he previously mastered. Thus, by discussing issues with his colleagues, he can refresh his memory of that which he previously learned (*Rashi*).

37. The name Nehorai derives from the Aramaic root נְהַר, *to shine* or *illuminate.* Elsewhere (*Avos* 2:8), the Mishnah praises R' Elazar ben Arach as a virtual wellspring of Torah, and it further states that his wisdom outweighed the wisdom of all his colleagues (see above, note 31). Nevertheless, he was unable to maintain his lofty stature in isolation from his colleagues.

38. See above, 147a note 34.

39. During the week, scraping the skin was generally performed to provide physical relief. When, however, one scrapes his skin to remove mud or excrement, he clearly intends to cleanse himself, a different purpose altogether. In these cases, then, scraping no longer qualifies as a weekday activity, and it is deemed permissible (based on *Tur* 327; see *Mishnah Berurah* 327:11).

40. Since this particular utensil was made especially for use on the Sabbath, when one scraped with it, he was not deemed to be performing a standard weekday activity (see *Tur* §327).

41. The banks of this river abounded with very slippery spots where one was likely to fall and soak his clothes. He would, therefore, be placing himself in a position where he would be likely to wring out his drenched garments (*Rashi;* see also *Rama* to *Orach Chaim* 301:46). For alternative explanations, see *Rif, Rabbeinu Chananel* and *Rambam* (*Hil. Shabbos* 21:29).

42. Ingesting a potion of some sort to induce vomiting is similar to taking medicine, and is thus forbidden by Rabbinic decree (*Rashi;* see above, 147a note 38).

43. In Roman and other pagan cultures, it was the practice to induce vomiting after one had eaten gluttonously, so that he could then eat even more. This is considered a waste of food, and is thus forbidden (see *Rashi,* and *Mishnah Berurah* 328:123); moreover the practice is despicable, entirely unbefitting a Holy People (*Ramban*). If, however, he induces vomiting so as to relieve discomfort from overeating, this is permissible [during the week] (*Rif; Rosh; Shulchan Aruch* 328:39).

44. An infant's bones, which are soft, are often bent because of the forceful contractions it experiences during birth. The custom was to swaddle the infant tightly in cloths, securing them with a belt, thus straightening its bent limbs (*Rashi* to above, 66b ד״ה לפופי; see also *Rashi* here).

דלהשתטף כל גופו אפי' לכתחילה שפיר דמי מני ר"ש היא דתניא לא ישתטף אדם בין בחמין בין בצונן דברי ר"מ ר"ש מתיר ר' יהודה אומר בחמין אסור בצונן מותר: ונסתפג אפילו בעשר אלונטיות: רישא רבותא קמ"ל וסיפא רבותא קמ"ל רישא רבותא קמ"ל דאפילו הני דלא נפישי בהו מיא כיון דחד הוא אתי לידי סחיטה וסיפא רבותא קמ"ל אפילו הני דנפישי בהו מיא כיון דרבים נינהו מדכרי אהדדי: ת"ר מסתפג אדם באלונטית ומניחה בחלון ולא ימסרנה לאוליירין מפני שחשודים על אותו דבר רבי שמעון אומר מסתפג באלונטית אחת ומביאה בידו לתוך ביתו אמר ליה אביי לרב יוסף הלכתא מאי אמר ליה הא ר' שמעון הא רבי הא שמואל הא ר' יוחנן ר' שמעון הא דאמרן רבי דתניא אמר רבי כשהיינו למדין תורה אצל ר' שמעון בתקוע היינו מעלין שמן ואלונטית מחצר לגג ומגג לקרפף עד שהיינו מגיעין אצל מעין שהיינו רוחצין בו שמואל דאמר רב יהודה אמר שמואל מסתפג אדם באלונטית ומביאה בידו לתוך ביתו ר' יוחנן דאמר ר' חייא בר אבא א"ר יוחנן הלכה מסתפג אדם באלונטית ומביאה בידו לתוך ביתו ומי א"ר יוחנן הכי והא"ר יוחנן הלכה כסתם משנה ותנן ונסתפג אפילו בעשר אלונטיות לא יביאם בידו ההוא כבן חכינאי מתני לה א"ר חייא בר אבא אר"י האוליירין מביאין בלרי נשים לבי בני ובלבד שיתכסה בהן ראשן ורובן סכניתא (א) צריך לקשר ב' ראשיה למטה א"ר חייא בר אבא א"ר יוחנן למטה מכתפיים אמר להו רבא לבני מחוזא כי מעבריתו מאני לבני חילא שרביבו בהו למטה מכתפיים: סכין וממשמשין: ת"ר סכין וממשמשין בבני מעיים בשבת ובלבד שלא יעשה כדרך שהוא עושה בחול היכי עביד ר' חמא בר חנינא אמר סך ואח"כ ממשמש ר' יוחנן אמר סך וממשמש בבת אחת: אבל לא מתעמלין: א"ר חייא בר אבא א"ר יוחנן אסור לעמוד בקרקעיתה של דיומסת מפני שמעמלת ומרפא אמר ר' יהודה אמר רב כל ימיה של דיומסת עשרים ואחד יום ועצרת מן המנין איבעיא להו עצרת (בתחלה) להאי גיסא או להאי גיסא ת"ש דאמר שמואל כולהו שקייני מדיבחא ועד עצרתא מעלו דילמא התם הוא דכמה דקריר עלמא מעלי אבל הכא משום הבלא הוא כיון דחמים עלמא טפי מעלי אמר רבי חלבו חמרא דפרוגייתא ומיא דדיומסת קיפחו עשרת השבטים מישראל רבי אלעזר בן ערך איקלע להתם אימשיך בתרייהו איעקר תלמודיה כי הדר אתא קם למיקרי בספרא בעא למיקרא א החדש הזה לכם אמר החרש היה לבם בעו רבנן רחמי עליה והדר תלמודיה והיינו דתנן ר' נהוראי אומר הוי גולה למקום תורה ואל תאמר שהיא תבא אחריך שחבריך יקיימוה בידך ואל בינתך אל תשען תנא לא ר' נהוראי שמו אלא ר' נחמיה שמו ואמרי לה ר' אלעזר בן ערך שמו ולמה נקרא שמו ר' נהוראי שמנהיר עיני חכמים בהלכה: אבל לא מתגררין: ת"ר אין גוררין במגררת בשבת רשב"ג אומר אם היו רגליו מלוכלכות בטיט ובצואה גורר כדרכו ואינו חושש רב שמואל בר יהודה עבדא ליה אימיה מגרדתא דכספא: אין יורדין לקורדימא וכו': מאי טעמא משום פיקא: ואין עושין אפיקטויזין בשבת: אמר רבה בר בר חנה אמר רבי יוחנן לא שנו אלא בסם אבל ביד מותר תניא רבי נחמיה אומר אף בחול אסור מפני הפסד אוכלין: ואין מעצבין את הקטן: אמר רבה בר בר חנה אמר ר' יוחנן לפופי ינוקא בשבת שפיר דמי והאנן תנן אין מעצבין התם בחומרי שדרה דמיחזי כבונה: ואין מחזירין את השבר: אמר רבי חנא בגדתאה אמר שמואל הלכה

תוספות

דתניא א"ר כשהיינו למדין תורה כו'. מסתמא יחידי היה שלא היה אלא אחד מתלמידיו עמו כשהיה רוחץ כדתניא במקום שנהגו (פסחים דף נא.) שלא ירחוץ תלמיד עם רבו ואם היה רבו צריך לו מותר ומסתמא ר"ש לא היה צריך אלא לאחד כשהיה רוחץ וכשהיו שבים לביתם היה התלמיד נושא האלונטית בפני עצמה שר"ש לא היה נושא עמו דהא ס"ל שיחיד מותר להביאה ולא חיישינן לסחיטה והא דקאמר היינו ר"ל כל אחד ואחד בפני עצמו כשהיה מגיע יומו לשמש רבו ולעיל בפ' כירה (דף מ:) גרסינן מעשה בתלמיד של ר' מאיר שנכנס אחריו לבית המרחץ ויש ספרים דגרסי תלמידיו ואינו ובכל הספרים גרסי לקמן בפרק שואל (דף קנא:) תלמידו. מ"ר:

צריך לקשר שני ראשיה למטה. בגיטין בפ' הנזקין (דף נט.) מפרש דסכניתא הוא בגד דק דאמרינן סוכני ותומר כי אמגוזא ופלגא דאמגוזא ומשום הכי צריך לקשר שני ראשיה למטה שלא יפריחנו מעליו הרוח ואתי לאתויי או משום דנראה כעין משוי לפי שהוא דק מאד ואינו נראה מלבוש אא"כ נראה קשור:

אין מעצבין את הקטן. פירשנו [בריש כל הכלים (ד' קכ"ג. ד"ה אסוטי)]:

הדרן עלך חבית

רש"י

גמ' דלהשתטף. שופכן על גופו דלאו דרך רחיצה היא שרי לכתחילה אפי' בחמין: סיפא. אבל עשרה בני אדם כו': ומניחה בחלון. הסמוכה לכותל המרחץ: לאוליירין. בלנים: על אותו דבר. סחיטה: הא רבי והא ר"ש כו'. הרי כל אלו שמתירין: מחצר לגג כו'. ר"ש לטעמיה דאמר בעירובין (דף עד.) אחד גגות אחד חצירות וא' קרפיפות כולן רשות אחת הן לטלטל מזה לזה ואפילו של בעלים הרבה: עד שהיינו מגיעין כו'. ומסתמא לא היו מניחין אותה על המעין במקום הפקר: כבן חכינאי מתני לה. דברי בן חכינאי מסיים בה ולאו סתמא: האוליירין. בלנין: מביאין בלרי נשים. סדינים שהנשים מסתפגין בהם מותר להביאן דרך מלבוש לבית המרחץ: סכניתא. סודר גדול [א] שתלוי לו בין כתפיו וראשו עטוף בו: צריך לקשור שני ראשיה. זה בזה שלא תפול מראשו: כי מעבריתו מאני לבני חילא. כשתביאו בגדי העובדי כוכבי' בני החיל המוטלי' עליכם לשמשן ואתם מביאים להם בשבת דרך רשות הרבים: שרביבו בהו למטה מכתפיים. שלא יהיו שוליהם מונחים בכתפיכם אלא משוכי' למטה שיהא נראה לבוש: סך ואח"כ ממשמש. [דקסבר] בחול ממשמש ואחר כך סך: דיומסית. שם נהר שמימיו מלוחים: שמעמלת. מחממת: ומרפא. שהטיט מלוח: כל ימיה. ימי רפואתה: להאי גיסא כו'. מתחלת הימים או בסוף: שקייני. משקין לרפואה: מדבחא לעצרת. אלמא עצרת בסוף: חמרא דפרוגיתא. שם מדינה שיינה משובח: קפחו עשרת השבטים. שהיו בעלי הנאה ועסוקים בכך ולא היו עוסקים בתורה ויצאו לתרבות רעה: להתם. לפרוגיתא ודיומסית: אימשיך בתרייהו. אחר היין והרחיצה: איעקר תלמודיה. נעקר תלמודו ושכחו: החרש היה לבם: הוי גולה למקום תורה. אם ת"ח אתה אל תשב אלא במקום ת"ח חברך ואל תאמר תלמידים הם יבואו אלי ודי לי בכך למה אהיה גולה: שחביריך יקיימוה בידך. שתהא רגיל אצלם וכשתשנה מסכת אחת והם אחרת תשמענה ותהא סדורה בפיך ואל תשכח הימנה: ואל בינתך אל תשען. לומר חכם גדול אני וזכרן וכשאחזור פרק זה או מסכת זו לא תשתכח חברתה ממני: מגררת. אשטריי"ל ואדם מגרר בה: מגירתא דכספא. לשבת: משום פיקא. טיט של אותו נהר מחליק ובגדי האדם נישורין במים כשהוא נופל ואתי לידי סחיטה: אלא בסם. דדמי לרפואה וגזירה ° משום שחיקת סמנין: אבל ביד. להכניס יד לתוך גרונו עד שיקיא מותר: מפני הפסד אוכלין. שבמעיו ומתוך כך הוא רעב וחוזר ואוכל: לפופי. אונמלוטי"א כמו שעושי' לקטן שיתיישבו אבריו ולא יתעקם: בחומרי שדרה. חוליות של שדרה שנתפרקה אחת מהן ולאחר זמן קמיירי דאי ביום לידה (ג) אמרי' (לעיל דף קכט:) כל האמור בפ' תוכחה דיחזקאל עושין לחיה בשבת:

עין משפט נר מצוה

מו א ב מיי' פכ"ב מהל' שבת הלכה יט טור שו"ע או"ח סימן שא סעיף מח:
מז ג ד מיי' פי"ט שם הלכה יג סמג לאוין סה טוש"ע שם סעיף לד:
מח ה ו מיי' פכ"ב מהל' שבת הלכה כח סמג שם טוש"ע או"ח סימן שכח סעיף כ:
מט ז מיי' וסמג שם טוש"ע שם וסימן שכח סעיף מג:
נ ח מיי' שם:
נא ט מיי' שם הלכה ל טוש"ע או"ח סימן שכח סעיף ג:
נב י מיי' שם הלכה כט טוש"ע או"ח סי' שכח סעיף מו בהג"ה:
נג כ ל מיי' שם הלכה לא סמג שם טוש"ע או"ח סי' שכח סעיף לג:
נד מ מיי' וסמג שם טוש"ע או"ח סימן של סעיף י:
נה נ מיי' פכ"ב שם הלכה כו:

רבינו חננאל

אוקימנא למתני' הרוחץ בחמין דיעבד אבל לכתחלה לרחוץ בחמין אסור. ולהשתטף בחמין נמי אפי' כל גופו מותר כר"ש דתניא לא ישתטף אדם בין בחמין בין בצונן דברי ר"מ. ור"ש מתיר. ר' יהודה אומר בחמין אסור ובצונן מותר. אע"פ דתנינן סתמא כר"ש לית הלכתא כוותיה דהא בפירוש נמי תנינן סתמא כוותיה (לעיל דף לח). מעשה שעשו אנשי טבריא כו' (א) (ואע"ג דאמר עולא הלכה כאנשי טבריא הא אמר ליה רב נחמן תברינהו לסילונייהו אנשי טבריא) ואוקימנא כר"ש. ופסקי' בגמרי' אמר רבה בר בר חנה א"ר יוחנן הלכה כרבי יהודה ודקדק רב יוסף על רבה בר בר חנה וא"ל בפירוש שמיעא לך דהלכתא כר' יהודה או מכללא אמרתיה. א"ל בפירוש שמיעא ליה. וכיון דפסק ר' יוחנן בפירוש הלכה כר' יהודה כוותיה עבדינן: ומסתפג אפי' בעשר אלונטיות ולא יביאם בידו ואע"פ שאין בהם מים מרובין. דכיון דחד הוא. דלמא מינשי ועביד סחיטה. אבל אם היו ב"א הרבה אפילו אם מסתפגין כולן באלונטית אחת והיא שורי' במים כיון דרבים נינהו מדכרי אהדדי ולא אתו לידי סחיטה. ומותר להביאה בידים בחצר או מן הגג וכדומה לו מקום שמותר לו לטלטל: אוליירין הם השמשים בני אדם הנכנסין במרחץ והן חשודין בזמה שמא יטמאו לונטיות זו בשכבת זרעם. א"ל אביי לרב יוסף והלכתא מאי כו' והלכתא כי הא דא"ר חייא בר רבה א"ר יוחנן הלכה מסתפג אדם באלונטית ומביאה בידו לתוך ביתו. ומקשינן עלה הא"ר יוחנן הלכה כסתם משנה ותנן מסתפג אדם אפילו בעשר אלונטיות ולא יביאם בידו. ומפרקי' מתני' ר' יוחנן לא תאני לה סתמא. אלא כבן חכינאי מתני לה. בתלמוד א"י בפ' כירה ר' חנניה בן עקיבא התיר הבאת לונטיות: סכינתאי א"ר אבין בר רב חסדא א"ר יוחנן צריך לקשר ב' ראשיה למטה. א"ר חייא בר אבא א"ר יוחנן למטה מכתפים. וכן זה שאמר רבא לבני מחוזא כי מעבריתו מני דבני חילא שרביבו להו למטה מכתפים. שלא להראות משא בכתף: בלרין נשים לבי בני. פי' דהא קן של נשים כשמביאין להן האוליירין במרחץ לא התירו אלא עד שיתכסה בהן ראשו ורובו: סכין וממשמשין והלכתא כר' יוחנן דאמר סך וממשמש בבת אחת והוא משמוש ביד בקלות. אבל לא מתעמלין. פי' פושטין ומקפלין זרועותיהם לפניהן ולאחריהן וכן רגליהן ע"ג ירכותיהן ומתחממין ומזיעין והוא כמין מעשה רפואה ואסור. וכן אסור לעמוד בשבת בקרקעיתה של דיומסת מפני שמעמלת ומרפאה: חמרא דפרוגתא יין של פרוגיתא והוא שם מקום ומיא דרמיסת גם הוא שם מקום. כלומר יין של פרגיתא ומיא של דיומסת טובים הם וערבין ונמשך לב שותה אותן בהן ואינו רוצה להניחם ומתאחר שם ואותן מקומות אין בהן בני תורה ומתאחר שם זמן הרבה מתקפח ושכח תלמודו. אבל לא מתגרדין. גירוד זה הוא חיכוך בכלי כי הא דתנן רבנן אין גורדין במגרת בשבת רשבג"א אם היו רגליו מלוכלכות בטיט ובצואה גורד כדרכו ואינו חושש. רב שמואל בר יהודה עבדא ליה אימיה מגרדתא דכספא להתחכך בה: אין יורדין לקירומא. ס"א לפילומא פי' בקעה ויש שם מים ותחתיו טיט כמו טפל. ואם יבקע ויטבע בו אינו יכול לעלות עד שמתקבצין הרבה ב"א ומעלין אותו משם. יש מי שאומרים הרוחץ באותה בקעה מצטנן ואותן המים משלשלין בני מעיו ג). וזה פי' ביקא. פי' אפיקטויזין קיא. אמר רבה בר בר חנה א"ר יוחנן לא שנו אלא בסם שהוא אסור אבל ביד מותר. ואין מעצבין את הקטן כו'. פי' מושכין אבריו של קטן ומיישב בידו חוליות של שזירה אחת על חברתה וזהו עיצוב מלשון עצבון: לפופי ינוקא לחבר אברים של תינוק. וכדתרגם ויחבר ולפיף: ואין מחזירין את השבר אמר רב הונא בגדתאה אמר שמואל מחזירין

מסורת הש"ס

א) לעיל לט:, ב) עירובין פח. ע"ש, ג) [חשודין לסוחטה ונותנין אותה לאחרים. ערוך ע"ש], ד) עירובין לא. [מנחות עב.], ה) [לעיל מ. וש"נ], ו) [עי' פירש"י עירובין סג. ד"ה מחוח וכרש"י פסחים ה. ד"ה מחוח וכרש"י ב"מ נט. עוד שם עז. ד"ה אוכלפא דמחוחא], ז) סנהדרין קא., ח) [פסחים דף מב:], ט) אדר"נ ספי"ד, י) אבות פ"ד משנה י"ד, כ) עירובין יג: ע"ש, ל) [תוספ' פי"ז], מ) [לעיל סו: ע"ש], נ) [עמ"ש רש"י ברכות נד: וע"ע פרש"י ביבמות סז. ד"ה בגדתאה], ס) [ובישעיה כח א גרס ומיא דדורמסקית וכן גרס רד"ק שם], ע) [בגיטין אי' סוכני וחומץ], פ) [שייך לעיל במשנה].

הגהות הב"ח

(א) גמרא סכניתא אמר ר' אבין בר רב חסדא א"ר יוחנן צריך לקשר שני וכו' ואמר ר' חייא: (ב) רש"י ד"ה בחומרי וכו' ביום לידה הא אמרינן. נ"ב סוף פ' מפנין ע"ש ברש"י שפי' דלפופי הוא על ידי מגורות ופסיקאות:

גליון הש"ס

גמ' אמר החרש היה לבם. עי' דבר נחמד בקרנים בליקוטים שבסוף הספר: רש"י ד"ה אלא בסם וכו' משום שחיקת סמנין. ע"ל דף קכג. ע"ב ברש"י ד"ה אפיקטויזין:

הגהות הגר"א

[א] רש"י ד"ה סוכניתא סודר גדול. נ"ב אבל הרמב"ם פי' קטן שאין מכסה ראשו ורובו:

תורה אור השלם

א) הַחֹדֶשׁ הַזֶּה לָכֶם רֹאשׁ חֳדָשִׁים רִאשׁוֹן הוּא לָכֶם לְחָדְשֵׁי הַשָּׁנָה: [שמות יב, ב]

ליקוטי רש"י

להשתטף. שונתן על גופו ומשתטף. לא ישתטף. בשבת. בין בחמין. ואפילו הוחמו כחול. ר' שמעון מתיר. להשתטף כל גופו בשבת בחמין שהוחמו מערב שבת [לעיל לט:]. רישא רבותא קמ"ל. דלא נפישי מיא בכל חד אפילו הכי לא יביאם בידו לתוך ביתו אפילו על ידי עירוב שמא ישכח ויסחט בבואו. וסיפא רבותא קמ"ל. דהלא אלונטית לעשרה [בני אדם נפישן] ביה מיא אפילו הכי מביאין אותה בידים [לעיל ע"א].

[המשך בדף קמח.]

חשק שלמה על רבינו חננאל א) לכאורה נראה דממיבת ולאע"ג עד תברינהו לסילונייהו אנשי טבריא שייך להלן אחר תיבות כוותיה עבדינן ודו"ק: ג) עיין ערוך ערך פלס א':

aligning **the spinal vertebrae;**[45] **דְּמֵיחֲזֵי כְּבוֹנֶה** – this is Rabbinically forbidden **because it has the appearance of building,** one of the Biblically prohibited categories of labor. Wrapping the infant, however, does not even have this appearance, and therefore it is permissible.

The Gemara quotes the next part of the Mishnah:

וְאֵין מְחַזִּירִין אֶת הַשֶּׁבֶר – NOR MAY WE SET A BROKEN BONE.

The Gemara quotes Shmuel on this topic:

אָמַר רַבִּי חָנָא בַּגְדָּתָאָה אָמַר שְׁמוּאֵל – **R' Chana from Baghdad**[46] **said** the following **in the name of Shmuel:**

NOTES

45. I.e. the Mishnah's prohibition is limited to realigning a vertebrum that has slipped from its proper place in the spine. So long as the case is not an emergency, this procedure must wait until the Sabbath has concluded (see *Mishnah Berurah* to 330 §23).

This prohibition, however, applies only after some time has elapsed since the birth. On the day the child is actually born, any Rabbinic law may be violated to make the infant more comfortable (*Rashi* from 129b; see *Mishnah Berurah* ibid.). [Indeed, it goes without saying that if the child is truly in danger, even Biblical prohibitions are disregarded.]

46. *Rashi* to *Berachos* 54b. Alternatively, the expression בַּגְדָּתָאָה indicates that he was a master of Aggadah (*Rashi* to *Yevamos* 67a; see also *Succah* 52b and *Rashi* there ד״ה אמר רב ששת).

הֲלָכָה מְחֲזִירִין אֶת הַשֶּׁבֶר – **The law** is that **we may** indeed **set a broken bone.**[1]

A related episode:

רַבָּה בַּר בַּר חָנָה אִיקְּלַע לְפוּמְבְּדִיתָא – **Rabbah bar bar Chanah,** a scholar who resided in Eretz Yisrael, once **came** to visit **Pumbedisa.** לֹא עַל לְפִירְקֵיהּ דְּרַב יְהוּדָה – However, while there, **he did not go to** attend **the lecture** given by **Rav Yehudah,** the head of the local academy. שַׁדְרֵיהּ לְאַדָּא דַּיָּילָא – Seeking to draw his presence, **[Rav Yehudah] sent Adda,** his **attendant,** to Shmuel, אָמַר לֵיהּ זִיל גַּרְבֵּיהּ – and **instructed him: "Go, confiscate [his cloak]** until he comes."[2] אָזִיל גַּרְבֵּיהּ – So **[the official] went and confiscated [his cloak].** אֲתָא אַשְׁכְּחֵיהּ דְּקָא דָּרִישׁ אֵין מְחֲזִירִין אֶת הַשֶּׁבֶר – Rabbah bar bar Chanah then **came** to the lecture, **and found [Rav Yehudah] expounding** that **we may not set a broken bone on the Sabbath.** אָמַר לֵיהּ – Hearing this, **[Rabbah bar bar Chanah] said to [Rav Yehudah]:** הָכִי אָמַר רַב חָנָא בַּגְדָּתָאָה אָמַר שְׁמוּאֵל – **So said Rav Chana from Baghdad in the name of Shmuel:** הֲלָכָה מְחֲזִירִין אֶת הַשֶּׁבֶר – **The law** is that **we may** indeed **set a broken bone.** אָמַר לֵיהּ – **[Rav Yehudah] replied to him:** הָא חָנָא דִּידָן וְהָא שְׁמוּאֵל דִּידָן – **Behold, Chana is ours and Shmuel is ours** [i.e. they both reside here in Babylonia]; וְלָא שְׁמִיעַ לִי – **and** yet, until you came and related this to me, **I had not heard it!** וְלָאו בְּדִינָא גְּרַבְתִּיךְ – **Now, was it not right that I had [your garment] confiscated?**[3]

The next part of the Mishnah is quoted:

מִי שֶׁנִּפְרְקָה יָדוֹ כו׳ – IF ONE'S HAND or foot became dislocated, he may not massage them in cold water, **etc.**

A pertinent episode:

רַב אַוְיָא הֲוָה יָתִיב קַמֵּיהּ דְּרַב יוֹסֵף – **Rav Avya was** once **sitting in the presence of Rav Yosef,** his teacher. שַׁנְיָא לֵיהּ יְדֵיהּ – It was the Sabbath, and **[Rav Avya's] hand had become dislocated.** He was seeking to determine the type of therapies he might be permitted to practice, אָמַר לֵיהּ – so he demonstrated various therapeutic practices and **said to [Rav Yosef]:** הָכִי מַאי – If one does it **so, what** is the law? Is this permitted? אָסוּר – Rav Yosef replied to him: That would be **forbidden.** וְהָכִי מַאי – So he demonstrated a different practice and said: **And** if one does it **so, what** is the law? אָמַר לֵיהּ אָסוּר – Again, **[Rav Yosef] told him:** It is **forbidden.** אַדְּהָכִי אִיתְּפַח יְדֵיהּ – **In the course of** performing **these** demonstrations, **[Rav Avya's] hand became healed.** אָמַר לֵיהּ – Rav Yosef then **said to him:** מַאי תִּבָּעֵי לָךְ – **What had been your question?** Why had you even thought that any such therapy might be permitted? הָא תְּנַן – **Was it not** explicitly **taught in the Mishnah:** מִי שֶׁנִּפְרְקָה יָדוֹ אוֹ רַגְלוֹ לֹא יִטְרְפֵם בְּצוֹנֵן – IF ONE'S HAND OR FOOT BECAME DISLOCATED, HE MAY NOT MASSAGE THEM IN COLD WATER, אֲבָל רוֹחֵץ כְּדַרְכּוֹ וְאִם נִתְרַפֵּא נִתְרַפֵּא – BUT HE MAY BATHE ACCORDING TO HIS USUAL MANNER, AND IF IT BECOMES HEALED thereby, IT BECOMES HEALED?[4] אָמַר לֵיהּ – **[Rav Avya] replied to him:** וְלָא תְּנַן – **But** in that same Mishnah, **was it not** also **taught:** אֵין מְחֲזִירִין אֶת הַשֶּׁבֶר – WE MAY NOT SET A BROKEN BONE, וְאָמַר רַב חָנָא בַּגְדָּתָאָה אָמַר שְׁמוּאֵל – **and** yet, we know that **R' Chana from Baghdad has said in the name of Shmuel:** הֲלָכָה מְחֲזִירִין אֶת הַשֶּׁבֶר – **The law** is that **we may** indeed **set a broken bone.** Now, if that part of the Mishnah was emended, perhaps this part of the Mishnah is to be emended also! אָמַר לֵיהּ – **[Rav Yosef] replied to him:** כּוּלְּהוּ בַּחֲדָא מְחִיתָא מְחִיתַנְהוּ – All the parts of the Mishnah you have **woven in the same weave?**[5] Certainly not! הֵיכָא דְּאִיתְּמַר אִיתְּמַר – Rather, where **[an emendation] was stated,** there **it was stated;** הֵיכָא דְּלָא אִיתְּמַר לָא אִיתְּמַר – and **where [an emendation] was not stated,** it **was not stated,** and none can be presumed.[6]

הדרן עלך חבית

WE SHALL RETURN TO YOU, CHAVIS

NOTES

1. I.e. in Shmuel's version of the Mishnah, the text reads: "we *may* set a broken bone" (*Rashi*). The reason for the permit is that a broken bone endangers the entire limb if it is not set immediately (*Ritva MHK* ed.; see *Mishnah Berurah* 328:47).

2. [This translation follows *Rashi. Aruch,* though, quotes *Rabbeinu Chananel* as rendering זִיל גַּרְבֵּיהּ, *go, bring him;* i.e. force him to attend.]

Rav Yehudah strongly desired that Rabbah bar bar Chanah attend his lectures, for since he was a prominent scholar from Eretz Yisrael, Rav Yehudah wished to hear from him what he and the scholars of that land had to teach about the subjects being studied at his academy (*Glosses* of *HaBoneh* to *Ein Yaakov*).

3. Had you you not come, we would not have learned this from you! (*Rashi*).

4. [I.e. the Mishnah indicates that any type of massage or therapy is forbidden if it is clear and obvious that the intent of the act is purely medicinal.]

[Rav Yosef was not questioning the *actions* of Rav Avya, who had done nothing improper, but was merely showing the various therapies to Rav Yosef, and this caused the healing (see *Rabbeinu Chananel*). Rather, Rav Yosef asked why Rav Avya *inquired* as to the permissibility of the therapy, when the Mishnah clearly indicates that it is forbidden.]

5. See *Rashi* here and to *Chullin* 58b ד״ה חדא.

6. [Although the Mishnah rules that massaging a dislocated bone in cold water is forbidden, *Shulchan Aruch* rules that manually resetting the dislocated bone in its joint is indeed permitted (328:47). *Mishnah Berurah* (citing *Sefer Atzei Shitim*) explains this by suggesting that massaging is prohibited only when the dislocation is a minor one; when the dislocation is complete, it is permitted even to reset the bone, since not to do so immediately would endanger the entire limb (cf. *Magen Avraham,* as cited in *Mishnah Berurah* ad loc.).]

מסורת הש"ס

א) [ברכות כד. וש"נ], ב) רש"ל מ"ז, ג) [לעיל קכח: וש"נ] ביצה ל. ע"ש, ד) [עי' פרש"י חולין נח:], ה) [ועי' תוספות שם ד"ה טלית].

הגהות הב"ח

(א) גמ' לא יטרפם בצונן (אבל רוחץ). תא"מ ונ"ב ס"א אבל טובל: (ב) תוס' ד"ה שואל וכו' דסתם שאלה נמי ל' יום: (ג) בא"ד היה חייב להחזיר אלא דעבידי: (ד) ד"ה אתקין וכו' דלאמר בסמוך הא קא מפשי בהילוכא:

ליקוטי רש"י

מפתפג אדם. ביום טוב ובשבת אם רמן בלונן מתפפג באלונטית ואין חוששין שמא יסחוט. ומביאה בידו. ואין חוששין שמא ישכח ויסחוט [עירובין פח.]. היינו מעלין שמן. לסוך בו. ואלונטית. להסתפג בה [שם צא.]. מחצר לגג וכו'. ודברי שמעון לטעמיה דאמר בעירובין (פט.) אחד גגות ואחד חצירות רשות אחת להן לכלים ששבתו בתוכן [מנחות עב.]. מחצר לגג ומגג וכו'. ר' שמעון מיקל מכולם ואמר חצירות וגגות וקרפיפות שאינן יותר מבית סאתים הואיל וכולם אין משמשין מיוחד ומדיר רשות אחת הן ומטלטלין מזה לזה אפילו מחצר של רבים לחצר רבים בלא עירוב ולית ליה לר' שמעון עירובי חצירות אלא משום דירת כלי הבית [עירובין פט. הובא בהמשך לרש"י כאן]. דג' מחלוקות הן בעירובין בפרק כל גגות לדברי ר' מאיר גגין רשות לעצמן ומטלטלין מזה לזה ואפילו של בעלים הרבה וחצרות רשות לעצמן לטלטל מזו לזו בלא עירוב כלים ששבתו בתוכם אבל לא מגגין לחצרות וקרפיפות רשות לעצמן ולדברי חכמים גגין וחצרות רשות אחת וקרפיפות רשות אחת ולדברי ר' שמעון כולן רשות אחת חוץ מן הבתים [לעיל קל:]. הלכה כסתם משנה. רבי הוא סדר המשנה וכשראה דברי חכם ויישרו בעיניו שנאן סתם ולא הזכיר שם אומרו עליהן כדי שלא יהו שנויה מפי יחיד ונראין כאילו נשנו מפי המרובים ויעשו כמותן [ביצה ב:]. בי בני. בית המרחץ [ברכות ס.]. מחוזא. עיר שהיה רבא דר בתוכה כך שמה [ב"מ נט.]. ומשמשין בבני מעיים. של חולה בשבת ואין בכך משום רפואה דקיכה איתקש לשתיה. סך ואחר כך ממשמש. הוי שנוי דבחול דרך למשמש ואחר כך לסוך [סנהדרין קא.].

גמרא

הלכה מחזירין את השבר רבה בר בר חנה איקלע לפומבדיתא לא על לפירקיה דרב יהודה שדריה לאדא דיילא א"ל זיל גרביה אזיל גרביה אתא אשכחיה דקא דריש אין מחזירין את השבר א"ל הכי אמר רב חנא בגדתאה אמר שמואל הלכה מחזירין את השבר א"ל הא חנא דידן והא שמואל דידן ולא שמיע לי ולאו בדינא גרבתיך: מי שנפרקה ידו כו': רב אויא הוה יתיב קמיה דרב יוסף שניא ליה ידיה א"ל הכי מאי אסור והכי מאי א"ל אסור אדהכי איתפח ידיה א"ל מאי תיבעי לך הא תנן מי שנפרקה ידו או רגלו לא יטרפם בצונן (א) אבל רוחץ כדרכו ואם נתרפא נתרפא א"ל ולא תנן אין מחזירין את השבר ואמר רב חנא בגדתאה אמר שמואל הלכה מחזירין את השבר אמר ליה כולהו בחדא מחיתא מחיתנהו היכא דאיתמר איתמר היכא דלא איתמר לא איתמר:

הדרן עלך חבית

שואל אדם מחבירו כדי יין וכדי שמן ובלבד שלא יאמר לו הלויני וכן האשה מחבירתה ככרות ואם אינו מאמינו מניח טליתו אצלו ועושה עמו חשבון לאחר שבת וכן ערב פסח בירושלים שחל להיות בשבת מניח טליתו אצלו ונוטל את פסחו ועושה עמו חשבון לאחר יום טוב: **גמ'** א"ל רבא בר רב חנן לאביי מאי שנא השאילני ומאי שנא הלויני אמר ליה השאילני לא אתי למיכתב הלויני אתי למיכתב והא כיון דבחול זימנין דבעי למימר ליה הלויני וא"ל השאילני ולא קפיד עילויה ואתי למיכתב בשבת נמי אתי למיכתב א"ל (בחול דלא שנא כי א"ל הלויני ל"ש כי א"ל השאילני לא קפדינן עילויה אתי למיכתב) בשבת כיון דהשאילני הוא דשרו ליה רבנן הלויני לא שרו ליה מינכרא מילתא ולא אתי למיכתב א"ל רבא בר רב חנן לאביי מכדי אמרו רבנן כל מילי דיום טוב כמה דאפשר לשנויי משנינן הני נשי דמליין חצביהו מיא מ"ט לא משנין משום דלא אפשר היכי לעבדי דמליין בחצבא רבא לימלו בחצבא זוטא הא קא מפשו בהילוכא דמליין בחצבא זוטא לימלו בחצבא רבא קא מפשו במשוי ניפרום

רש"י

הלכה מחזירין את השבר. קבלה ליה לשמואל מחזירין תנן: **אדא דיילא.** מנשטר"ל ממונה: **גרביה.** קם נגדו עד שילך: **אתא.** רבה אשכחיה לרב יהודה כו': **הא חנא דידן.** ממקומנו הוא ולא שמענו זאת מפיו עד הנה: **ולאו בדינא גרבתיך.** במחמיה שהלו לא באת לא למדנו: **שניא ליה ידיה.** נשמטית ידו ממקומה אשולשיי"ר בלע"ז: **הכי מאי.** היה עושה בענינים הרבה ושואל: **בחדא מחיתא מחיתנהו.** בארינה אחת ארגנהו (ד): **היכא דאיתמר.** דמתניתין לאו דוקא תנן איתמר:

הדרן עלך חבית

שואל. שלא יאמר הלויני. מפרש בגמרא: **שחל להיות בשבת.** ולא מכר מע"ש לקנות: **לאחר יו"ט.** ליום שלישי: **גמ' הלויני** משמע לזמן מרובה וקיי"ל במסכת מכות (דף ג:) סתם הלואה ל' יום ואתי מלוה זה לכתוב על פנקסו כך וכך הלויתי כדי שלא ישכח: **א"ל וכיון** דבחול נמי זימנין דבעי למימר הלויני ואמר השאילני: **ולא קפיד עליה.** והויא הלואה: **בשבת נמי.** כי אמר השאילני סבר דהלואה היא ואתי למכתב ומאי היכר איכא. ה"ג א"ל בשבת כיון דהשאילני שרו ליה רבנן הלויני לא שרו ליה מינכרא מילתא ולא אתי למכתב: **אמרו רבנן.** במסכת ביצה: **כל כמה דאפשר לשנויי משנינן.** דאמרינן המביא כדי יין לא יביאם בסל ובקופה כו': בכתפא

תוספות

שואל אדם מחבירו כדי יין וכדי שמן ובלבד שלא יאמר לו הלויני. פירש רש"י טעמא משום דסתם הלואה ל' יום לזמן מרובה יותר משאלה ואתי למיכתב וקשה לר"ת דסתם שאלה (ג) ל' יום כדאמר במנחות בהתכלת (דף מד.) טלית שאולה כל ל' יום פטורה מן הציצית ואמרינן נמי התם הדר בפונדקי בא"י והשוכר בית בחו"ל כל ל' יום פטור מן המזוזה אלמא דסתם שאלה ל' יום איתא והכי פטורה כל ל' יום דאמר שאלה היא אבל מכאן ואילך נראה כמו שלו ומיהו יכול לומר לרש"י לאו משום דלא מתבע ליה לדינא בתוך ל' יום שאין צריך להחזיר דודאי היה חייב להחזיר (ג) לעבידי איניש דמשאלי פחות משלשים יום אבל טפי לא משאלי הלכך עד ל' יום אמרי אינשי שאולה היא ור"י פירש לנו דהיינו טעמא דשאלה לפי שהיא חוזרת בעין לא אתי למיכתב אבל לשון הלואה אינו חוזר בעין ואתי למיכתב ואע"ג דכי שאיל מיניה כדי יין וכדי שמן לא הדרי בעין מ"מ מתוך שמזכיר לו לשון שאלה זכור הוא ולא אתי למיכתב. מ"ר וכן פירש ה"ר פורת:

אתקין רבא במחוזא דדרו בדוחקא כו'. ברוב ספרים אינו כתוב כאן ולא בפירוש רש"י וברים המביא כדי יין (ביצה דף ל. ושם) נראה שהוא מקומו וזה לשון פירוש הקונטרס בביצה דדרו בדוחקא משוי שאדם יחיד נושא בחול על כתיפו בטורח אם בא לשאתו לצורך יום טוב ביו"ט כגון חבית או שק מלא פירות ישאנו ביו"ט בדיגלא עתר שקורין פורק"א כדרך נושאי מלח למכור מפני שצריך לשנות וכשמשנה ישנה להקל משאו ולא להרבות טורח ביו"ט ועתר זה נוח לשאת בו משא כבד וכשנושא בו חבית הנישאת בכתף ישנה להקל דדרו בדיגלא משוי חבית גדולה שרגילה לשאת בדיגלא לידרו באגרא ישאהו ביו"ט בב' בני אדם במוט על כתפים דהיינו נמי שינוי להקל דדרו באגרא במוט על כתפים לידרו ביו"ט אותו משוי באכפא במוט בידים משום שינוי ואפילו אינו להקל מ"מ שינוי הוא ואינו מרבה טורח בשינוי דדרו באכפא ניפרום סודרא קל הוא ואינו מכביד ושינוי בעלמא הוא ולהכנע עד כאן לשונו ומשמע מתוך פירושו דכל אלה משוי אחד להם בשוה ואין זה נושא יותר אלא שנושא משאו בענין אחר ממה שהיה רגיל וזה דחקו שאם נפרש שכל אלו ממעטים משאם מאשר היו רגילים לשאת קשיא הא דאמר בסמוך (ד) מפשי בהילוכא משמע מפירושא דאגרא נושאים שני בני אדם שפיר במוט בשנים ויש בו משוי שני בני אדם שנושאים כל מה שרגילין לשאת בדיגלא ודיגלא היא משוי שני בני אדם כדמשמע בבבא מציעא בס"פ השוכר את האומנים (דף פג.) וקשיא לר' דהתם משמע נמי דאגרא אין בו משוי לשני בני אדם דאמר התם דדרו באגרא ואיתבר משלם פלגא מ"ט נפיש לחד חוטר לתרי ודמי לפשיעה ודמי לאונס בדיגלא משלם כולה משמע דלא הוי זוטר לתרי נראה דאגרא לשום אדם אינו נראה עובדא דחול כמו דיגלא ומשום הכי דדרו בדיגלא לידרו באגרא ואע"פ שמפיש בהילוכא יכול לשנות כיון שאינו נראה כל כך עובדא דחול והשתא אתי שפיר דדרו באגרא לידרו באכפא אע"פ שבודאי מרבה במשאוי הוא בנושא בידים המוט מכשנושאו על כתיפו מ"מ כיון שאינו נראה עובדא דחול כמו אגרא יכול לעשות כעין שמצינו גבי בהמה מסוכנת דתנן בבילה (דף כה.) שחטה בשדה לא יביאנה במוט אלא מביאה בידו אברים אברים ותנן נמי (דף כט: ושם) בהמביא כדי יין לא יביאם בסל ובקופה אלא מביא הוא על כתפיו או לפניו אלמא הני אע"ג דמפשי בהילוכא כיון שאינו עושה כל כך כדרך שעושה בחול יש לו לשנות והיא דבסמוך דמליין בחצבא זוטא ודמליין בחצבא רבה תרוייהו עובדא דחול ובענין שנושאים זה נושאים זה הלכך אין לו לשנות לא להקל ולא להכביד כדפי' טעמא והיא דלעיל בריש מפנין (דף קכו.) לא שייכא עובדא דחול שאינו מטלטל אלא בבית מזוית לזוית. מ"ר. והיא דשחטה בשדה פירש בריש מפנין (ג"ז שם) בע"א וכמו שפירש כאן עיקר ועוד קשה לי לפי' הקונטרס דדרו באכפא אמאי ניפרום סודרא עליה הוה ליה למימר לידרו באגרא כיון שאינו משנה להכביד יותר מאכפא כמו שמשמע נמי מתוך פירושו ולפירוש רבי אתי שפיר:

ניפרום

עין משפט נר מצוה

נו א טוש"ע או"ח סימן שכח סעיף מז:

נז ב שם סעיף ל:

א ג ד מיי' פכ"ג מהל' שבת הלכה יב סמג לאוין סה טור שו"ע או"ח סימן שז סעיף יא:

ב ה מיי' פ"ה מהלכות י"ט הלכה א ב סמג לאוין עה טוש"ע או"ח סימן תקי סעיף ח:

ג ו מיי' שם טוש"ע שם סעיף י וסימן שכג סעיף ה:

גליון הש"ס

מתני' שואל אדם מחבירו. עי' בירושלמי פ"ח דשביעית על מ"ד הובא בר"ש שם:

רבינו חננאל

מחזירין את השבר. רבה בר בר חנה לא על (פי') לפירקי' דרב יהודה שדריה לאדא דייאלא א"ל זיל גרד ביה אזל גרביה. פירוש א) משכיהו והביאהו מלשון פרץ נחל מעם גר כלומר הבריחהו. כדגרסינן בפרק בנות כותים נדות מעריסתן. שילא בר אבינא עבד עובדא כרב. כי קא ניחא נפשיה דרב. א"ל לרב אמי זיל צניעיה ואי לא צאית גרדיה הוא סבר גרדיה א"ל ופי' הכהו וכו': מי שנפרקה ידו או רגלו פי' שף מבוכניה לא יטרפן בצונן אבל רוחץ כדרכו ואם נתרפא נתרפא ורב אויא דשניא ליה ידיה והיה אומר לרב יוסף ומראה בידו אם יעשה בידו כך או כך מותר או אסור עד שהיה מראה לו כדי שיראהו מה שהתירו חכמים חזרה ידו למקומה ונתרפא:

הדרן עלך חבית

פרק כ"ג שואל אדם מחבירו כדי יין וכדי שמן ובלבד שלא יאמר לו הלויני כו'. ואוקימנא דחיישינן שמא יכתוב ב) וכן שאם יאמר לו הלויני גוערין בו ואומרים לו אסור לומר כן ביום שבת לשון הלואה מינכרא מלתא ולא אתי למכתב וכיון שהזכיר א"ל רבא בר רב חנן לאביי נסיב

חשק שלמה על רבינו חננאל

א) עיין בערוך השלם ערך גרב א': ב) אינו מובן לכאורה. ואולי דהיה לו גיר' הספרים בגמרא המוסגר במאי לגנה והובא במי' הרשב"א כאן. ומפרש רבינו דהחלוק הוא דבשבת כיון שאם אומר הלוני קפדינן עלוסי יש לו היכירא ולא אתי למכתב מלשון שאלה וכו' ודו"ק:

מדיבחא ועד עצרתא. מפסח ועד עלרת [פסחים מב:]. **הוי גולה למקום תורה.** למקום שהרב שם. **ואל תאמר שהיא תבא אחריך.** יבא לכאן ואלמוד לפניו. **שחבריך יקיימוה בידך.** שכל ספקות שיש לך יאמרו לך. נ"א שאם תולך לשם תלמידים בני תורה המתחברים עמך ישאו ויתנו עמך שם בהלכה ותבינה כדאמרי' (ירמיה נ, לו) חרב אל הבדים וגו'. **ואל בינתך אל תשען.** אל תאמר איני צריך ללכת לרב אלא מעצמי יכול אני לירד לעומקה. נ"א שלא תהא עצל לשאול בדבר כל אוזך לשמוע הכל מפיו ואמר כך הבין בתשובתו כדאמרי' (ברכות סג:) הם ואח"כ כתת [אבות פ"ד מי"ג]. **לפופי.** לכורכו בבגדים וקושרו בחגורה רחבה ומתייסבין פרקי אבריו שהן רכין ונשמטין בחבלי הלידה וקורין אנמלטוויי"ר בלע"ז [לעיל סו:]. מלפפין אנמליין בלע"ז ולאו היינו אסוקי יעקא דאמרן לעיל בפרק כל הכלים (קכג.) דהא שמעינן ליה לרב נחמן דאסר אלא לפופי בעלמא כמו שעושין בחגורות ופסיקיאות [שם קכט:]. **בגדתאה.** שם עירו בגדד היא עיר המשובה שבבבל משחרבה בבל [ברכות נד:]. בעל אגדה ל"א שם מקום שהוא בבבל ששמו בגדד [יבמות סז.]. עיר שבבבל ושמה בגדא בפסק סדרו של רב שרירא גאון היא נזכרת [כתובות ז:]. למן בגדד עיר שעולה בה וכשדי רב שרירא היא נזכרת [רשב"ם ב"ב קמב:]. [ע"כ שייך לדף קמז:]

לאדא דיילא. שמש לרבנן [נדה כד:]. ע"ש בב"ח. **אדא.** שם הוא. **דיילא.** שמש [ב"ק קיט:]. שוטר [יומא יח.]. **בחדא מחיתא מחיתנהו.** וכי מליגה אחת ארגתם לכולם יחד עובד אחד ממיקון דכור קרו לו איניש מחמד דאייריש מחרה (שמות [למ'] במרגם) ... **דמליין חצבייהו מיא.** שואבות מים מן הנהר [ביצה כט.]. **מ"ט לא משנין.** דנכאל למעשה דמול ... **קא מפשו במשוי.** ... לאו דוקא מתעסקות ... שם ל.

Chapter Twenty-Three

Mishnah Financial dealings are generally forbidden on the Sabbath and Yom Tov.[1] The Mishnah discusses an exception to this rule:

שׁוֹאֵל אָדָם מֵחֲבֵירוֹ כַּדֵּי יַיִן וְכַדֵּי שֶׁמֶן – A person may borrow pitchers of wine or pitchers of oil from his friend on the Sabbath, **וּבִלְבַד שֶׁלֹּא יֹאמַר לוֹ הַלְוֵינִי – provided that he does not say to him "*halveini* [i.e. lend me]."**[2] **וְכֵן הָאִשָּׁה מֵחֲבֵירְתָּהּ כִּכָּרוֹת – In the same manner, a woman** may borrow **loaves** of bread **from her friend.**[3] **וְאִם אֵינוֹ מַאֲמִינוֹ – And if [the lender] does not trust him, מַנִּיחַ טַלִּיתוֹ אֶצְלוֹ – [the borrower] may leave his cloak with [the lender]**[4] **וְעוֹשֶׂה עִמּוֹ חֶשְׁבּוֹן לְאַחַר שַׁבָּת – and make a reckoning with him after the Sabbath.**[5] **וְכֵן עֶרֶב פֶּסַח בִּירוּשָׁלַיִם שֶׁחָל לִהְיוֹת בְּשַׁבָּת – So too, in Jerusalem,** when **the day before Pesach falls on the Sabbath,**[6] **מַנִּיחַ טַלִּיתוֹ אֶצְלוֹ – he** (i.e. the purchaser of a *pesach* offering) **may leave his cloak with [the seller], וְנוֹטֵל אֶת פִּסְחוֹ – take his *pesach* offering, וְעוֹשֶׂה עִמּוֹ חֶשְׁבּוֹן לְאַחַר יוֹם טוֹב – and make a reckoning with [the seller] after Yom Tov.**[7]

Gemara By specifying that one may not say *halveini* ("lend me"), the Mishnah implies that the expression *hashileini* (which is used to mean "lend me" in a different context) is permitted.[8] The Gemara seeks the explanation of this distinction:

אָמַר לֵיהּ רָבָא בַּר רַב חָנָן לְאַבַּיֵי – Rava bar Rav Chanan asked Abaye: מַאי שְׁנָא הַשְׁאִילֵנִי וּמַאי שְׁנָא הַלְוֵינִי – What is the difference between *hashileini* and *halveini*? That is, why does the Mishnah prohibit *halveini,* but permit *hashileini*?

Abaye answers Rava bar Rav Chanan:

אָמַר לֵיהּ – He said to him: הַשְׁאִילֵנִי – If the borrower says **"*hashileini,*" לֹא אָתֵי לְמִיכְתַּב – [the lender] will not come to write** the loan down in his ledger, because this term signifies a loan of minimal duration.[9] **הַלְוֵינִי** – However, if the borrower says **"*halveini,*" אָתֵי לְמִיכְתַּב – [the lender] will come to write** the loan down, since this expression connotes a loan of longer duration.[10]

Rava bar Rav Chanan questions Abaye's explanation:

וְהָא כֵּיוָן דִּבְחוֹל זִימְנִין דְּבָעֵי לְמֵימַר לֵיהּ הַלְוֵינִי – But since on weekdays, there are times when [the borrower] wants to say to [the lender] "*halveini,*"[11] **וְאָמַר לֵיהּ ,,הַשְׁאִילֵנִי" – but** instead **he says to him "*hashileini,*" וְלָא קָפֵיד עִילָוֵיהּ – yet [the lender] is not particular with him** (i.e. he allows the borrower to withhold repayment for a substantial period, as though he had said "*halveini*"),[12] **וְאָתֵי לְמִיכְתַּב – and [the lender]** therefore **comes to write** the loan down in his ledger, **בְּשַׁבָּת נַמִּי אָתֵי לְמִיכְתַּב** – thus, let us be afraid that **on the Sabbath, too, [the lender] will come to write** the loan down even if the borrower says "*hashileini.*"[13] – ? –

NOTES

1. There are two possible reasons for this prohibition: (a) Scripture states (*Isaiah* 58:13): מִמְּצוֹא חֶפְצְךָ וְדַבֵּר דָּבָר, [honor the Sabbath by refraining] *from pursuing your business and discussing the forbidden* [literally: speaking words] (see below, 150a note 8). (b) One who engages in commerce might draw up a contract, thus performing the *melachah* of כְּתִיבָה, *writing* (*Rashi* to *Beitzah* 37a ד״ה משום מקח וממכר; see *Ramban, Hil. Shabbos,* 23:12-18 and 24:1-2; see also *Ramban* to *Leviticus* 23:24 and *Maggid Mishneh* ibid. 21:1).

2. The Gemara will explain this (*Rashi*).

The Rabbis permitted borrowing on the Sabbath and Yom Tov (in the prescribed manner), so that people would not lack the items they need for their enjoyment of the Sabbath or Yom Tov (*Rashba* ד״ה אמר ליה השאילני; see *Shabbos Shel Mi;* see also *Mishnah Berurah* 307:45,46).

The parties to the loan understand that the borrower will repay wine and oil *or* their value in money (see Gemara below, 148b, and note 21 there).

3. See *Ritva* (*MHK* ed.), who gives two reasons why the Mishnah added this clause; cf. *Tos. Yom Tov.*

4. When leaving the cloak with the lender, he may not say, "Here is security" (*Meiri*). Such a statement, indicative as it is of a commercial transaction, represents weekday activity [עוּבְדָּא דְחוֹל] (*Rama, Orach Chaim* 307:11).

5. After the Sabbath they may reckon the precise amount owed (*Tiferes Yisrael*). This, however, may not be done on the Sabbath itself, for it falls under the prohibition of וְדַבֵּר דָּבָר, *speaking words* [see below, 150a-b] (*Meiri*).

6. I.e. the first night of Pesach falls on a Saturday night. In such a case, the *pesach* offering is offered that Sabbath afternoon. If someone forgot to acquire a lamb for his offering before the Sabbath (*Rashi*), or if he lost his animal (*Meiri*), he must buy one on the Sabbath itself.

7. That is, on Monday (see *Rashi*). [Just as one may not make a reckoning on the Sabbath, he may not do so on Yom Tov. Therefore, he must wait until after the first day of Pesach – i.e. until Monday, the first day of Chol HaMoed.]

See *Ritva* (*MHK* ed.) for an explanation of why the Mishnah included this case.

8. In Hebrew, there are two verbs which mean to borrow, שאל and לוה. The former refers to the loan of items which are *returned*, such as household utensils. The latter refers to the loan of items which are *replaced* or *repaid* rather than returned, such as food and money. [In the cases of the Mishnah, where one borrows consumable items (e.g. wine, oil, loaves) that will be replaced or repaid, the verb הַלְוֵינִי, *halveini,* (from לוה) would be appropriate.]

9. As explained above, הַשְׁאִילֵנִי, *hashileini,* (from שאל) denotes the loan of an item that is returned intact, rather than replaced. In such a case, the lender may demand the item's return at any time (*Rashi,* as explained by *Tosafos, Rashba, Ritva* et al.; cf. *Tosafos*). [Unless the lender specifies otherwise, it is understood that he is lending the item only until he asks for it back, since it deteriorates over time (*Sfas Emes*).] Hence, although the term *hashileini* does not strictly apply in the cases of the Mishnah (see previous note), its use is the equivalent of stipulating that the lender may request repayment at any time. Since the lender has this right, he is unlikely to make a record of the loan for fear that he will forget about it.

10. The term הַלְוֵינִי, *halveini,* refers to a loan of money or other items that will be replaced. A loan of this nature is for a period of thirty days, unless specified otherwise at the time of the loan. Since this verb connotes a loan of such long duration, the Rabbis feared that a lender, responding to a request of *halveini,* would make a note of the loan so as not to forget about it (*Rashi*). [He would thus perform the Biblically forbidden *melachah* of כְּתִיבָה, *writing.*]

Obviously, these differences apply only in Hebrew. In languages in which both types of borrowing are expressed in the same way, one must use an expression that does not signify borrowing, such as "Give me" (*Ran MHK* ed.; *Meiri;* see *Rashba;* see also *Mishnah Berurah* 307:44).

11. I.e. in a case such as ours, where the loaned item will be replaced or repaid [see note 8] (*Ritva MHK* ed. et al.).

12. Since the loan is of an item that will be replaced or repaid, the lender realizes that the loan is for a substantial period, regardless of the borrower's choice of words.

13. Although according to their strict definitions *halveini* and *hashileini* are different in meaning, people sometimes confuse one word with the other. In common usage *hashileini* might be used, like *halveini,* to mean a long-term loan. Hence, it is still difficult to understand why the Rabbis distinguished between these two expressions: If *halveini* could lead to writing, then so could *hashileini*!

א הלכה מחזירין את השבר רבה בר בר חנה איקלע לפומבדיתא לא על לפירקיה דרב יהודה שדריה לאדא דיילא א"ל זיל גרביה אזיל גרביה אתא אשכחיה דקא דריש אין מחזירין את השבר א"ל הכי אמר רב חנא בגדתאה אמר שמואל הלכה מחזירין את השבר א"ל הא חנא דידן והא שמואל דידן ולא שמיע לי ולאו בדינא גרבתיך: מי שנפרקה ידו כו': רב אויא הוה יתיב קמיה דרב יוסף שניא ליה ידיה א"ל הכי מאי אסור והכי מאי א"ל אסור אדהכי איתפח ידיה א"ל מאי תיבעי לך הא תנן ב מי שנפרקה ידו או רגלו לא יטרפם בצונן אבל (א) רוחץ כדרכו ואם נתרפא נתרפא א"ל ולא תנן אין מחזירין את השבר ואמר רב חנא בגדתאה אמר שמואל הלכה מחזירין את השבר אמר ליה ה) כולהו בחדא מחיתא מחיתנהו היכא דאיתמר איתמר היכא דלא איתמר לא איתמר:

הדרן עלך חבית

שואל • ג אדם מחבירו כדי יין וכדי שמן ובלבד שלא יאמר לו ד הלויני וכן האשה מחבירתה ככרות ואם אינו מאמינו מניח טליתו אצלו ועושה עמו חשבון לאחר שבת וכן ערב פסח בירושלים שחל להיות בשבת מניח טליתו אצלו ונוטל את פסחו ועושה עמו חשבון לאחר יום טוב: **גמ'** א"ל רבא בר רב חנן לאביי מאי שנא השאילני ומאי שנא הלויני אמר ליה השאילני לא אתי למיכתב הלויני אתי למיכתב והא כיון דבחול זמנין דבעי למימר ליה הלויני וא"ל השאילני ולא קפיד עילויה ואתי למיכתב בשבת נמי אתי למיכתב א"ל ו) (בחול דלא שנא כי א"ל הלויני ל"ש כי א"ל השאילני לא קפדינן עילויה אתי למיכתב) בשבת כיון דהשאילני הוא דשרו ליה רבנן הלויני לא שרו ליה מינכרא מילתא ולא אתי למיכתב ז א"ל רבא בר רב חנן לאביי מכדי אמרו רבנן ה כל מילי דיום טוב כמה דאפשר לשנויי משנינן הני נשי דמליין חצבייהו מיא מ"ט לא משנין ו משום דלא אפשר היכי לעבדי דמליין בחצבא רבא לימלו בחצבא זוטא הא קא מפשו בהילוכא דמליין בחצבא זוטא לימלו בחצבא רבא קא מפשו במשוי

ניפרום

רש"י

הלכה מחזירין את השבר. סבירא ליה לשמואל מחזירין תנן: אדא דיילא. מנשטר"ל ממונה: גרביה. קח בגדו עד שיבא: אתא. רבה אשכחיה לרב יהודה כו': הא חנא דידן. ממקומנו הוא ולא שמענו זאת מפיו עד הנה: ולאו בדינא גרבתיך. בתמיה שאילו לא באת לא למדנו: שניא ליה ידיה. נשתנית ידו ממקומה אשולשיי"ר בלע"ז: הכי מאי. היה עושה בענינים הרבה ושואל: בחדא מחיתא מחיתנהו. באריגה אחת ארגתו[ד]: היכא דאיתמר. דמתניתין לאו דוקא תנן איתמר:

הדרן עלך חבית

שואל. שלא יאמר הלויני. מפרש בגמרא: שחל להיות בשבת. ולא נזכר מע"ש לקנות: לאחר יו"ט. ליום שלישי: גמ' הלויני משמע לזמן מרובה וקיי"ל במסכת מכות (דף ג:) סתם הלואה ל' יום ואתי מלוה זה לכתוב על פנקסו כך וכך הלויתי כדי שלא ישכח: א"ל וכיון דבחול נמי זימנין דבעי למימר הלויני ואמר השאילני: ולא קפיד עליה. והויא הלואה: בשבת נמי. כי אמר השאילני סבר דהלואה היא ואתי למכתב ומאי היכר איכא: ה"ג א"ל בשבת כיון דהשאילני שרו ליה רבנן הלויני לא שרו ליה מינכרא מילתא ולא אתי למכתב: אמרו רבנן. במסכת ביצה: כל כמה דאפשר לשנויי משנינן. דאמרינן המביא כדי יין לא יביאם בסל ובקופה כו': בנכתמא

תוספות

שואל אדם מחבירו כדי יין וכדי שמן ובלבד שלא יאמר לו הלויני. פירש רש"י טעמא משום דסתם הלואה ל' יום ולפי שהוא לזמן מרובה יותר משאלה אתי למיכתב וקשה לר"ת דסתם שאלה (ב) ל' יום כדאמר במנחות בהתכלת (דף מד.[ה]) טלית שאולה כל ל' יום פטורה מן הציצית ואמרינן נמי התם הדר באכסני' בא"י והשוכר בית בחו"ל כל ל' יום פטור מן המזוזה מכאן ואילך חייב במזוזה אלמא דסתם שאלה ל' יום איתא ולהכי פטורה כל ל' יום דאמר שאולה היא אבל מכאן ואילך נראה כמו שלו ומיהו יכול לומר לרש"י לאו משום דאי מתבע ליה לדינא בתוך ל' יום שאין צריך להחזיר דודאי היה חייב להחזיר (ג) דעבידי אינשי דמשאלי פחות משלשים יום אבל טפי לא משאלי הלכך עד ל' יום אמרי אינשי שאולה היא ור"י פירש לנו דהיינו טעמא בשאלה לפי שהיא חוזרת בעין לא אתי למיכתב אבל לשון הלואה אינו חוזר בעין ואתי למיכתב ואע"ג דכי שאיל מיניה כדי יין וכדי שמן לא הדרי בעין מ"מ מתוך שמזכיר לו לשון שאלה זכור הוא ולא אתי למיכתב. מ"ר וכן פירש ה"ר פורת:

אתקין רבא במחוזא דדרו בדוחקא כו'. ברוב ספרים אינו כתוב כאן ולא בפירוש רש"י ובריש המביא כדי יין (ביצה דף ל. ושם) נראה שהוא מקומו וזה לשון פירוש הקונטרס בביצה דדרו בדוחקא משוי שאדם יחיד נושא בחול על כתיפו בטורח אם בא לשאתו לצורך יום טוב ביו"ט כגון חבית או שק מלא פירות ישאנו ביו"ט בדיגלא עתר שקורין פורק"א כלומר נושאי מלא למכור מפני שצריך לשנות וכשמשנה ישנה להקל משאו ולא להרבות טורח ביו"ט ועתר זה נוח לשאת בו משא כבד וכשנושא בו חבית הנישאת בכתף ישנה להקל דדרו בדיגלא משוי חבית גדולה שרגילה לשאת בדיגלא לידרו באגרא ישאהו ביו"ט בב' בני אדם במוט על כתפים דהיינו נמי שינוי להקל דדרו באגרא במוט על כתפים לידרו ביו"ט אותו משוי באכפא במוט בידים משום שינוי ואפילו אינו להקל מ"מ שינוי הוא ואינו מרבה טורח בשינוי דדרו באכפא ניפרוס סודרא קל הוא ואינו מכביד ושינוי בעלמא הוא ולהכנע עד כאן לשונו ומשמע מתוך פירושו דכל אלה משוי אחד להם בשוה ואין זה נושא יותר אלא שנושא משאו בענין אחר ממה שהיה רגיל וזה דחקו שאם נפרש שכל אלו ממעטים משאם מאשר היו רגילים לשאת קשיא הא דאמר בסמוך (ד) מפשי בהילוכא משמע מפירושא דאגרא נושאים שני בני אדם שפיר במוט בשנים ויש בו משוי שני בני אדם שנושאים כל מה שרגילין לשאת בדיגלא ודיגלא היא משוי שני בני אדם כדמשמע בבבא מציעא בס"פ השוכר את האומנים (דף פג.) וקשיא לר' דהתם משמע נמי דאגרא אין בו משוי לשני בני אדם דאמר התם דדרו באגרא ואיתבר משלם פלגא מ"ט נפיש לחד וזוטר לתרי ודמי לפשיעה ודמי לאונס בדיגלא משלם כולה משמע דלא הוי זוטר לתרי נראה דאגרא לשום אדם אינו נראה עובדא דחול כמו דיגלא ומשום הכי דדרו בדיגלא לידרו באגרא ואע"פ שמפיש בהילוכא יכול לשנות כיון שאינו נראה כל כך עובדא דחול והשתא אתי שפיר דדרו באגרא לידרו באכפא אע"פ שבודאי מרבה במשאוי הוא בנושא בידים המוט מכשנושאו על כתיפו מ"מ כיון שאינו נראה עובדא דחול כמו אגרא יכול לעשות כעין שמצינו גבי בהמה מסוכנת דתנן בביצה (דף כה.) שחטה בשדה לא יביאנה במוט אלא מביאה בידו אברים אברים ותנן נמי (דף כט: ושם) בהמביא כדי יין לא יביאם בסל ובקופה אלא מביא הוא על כתפיו או לפניו אלמא הני אע"ג דמפשי בהילוכא כיון שאינו עושה כל כך כדרך שעושה בחול יש לו לשנות והיא דבסמוך דמליין בחצבא זוטא ודמליין בחצבא רבה תרווייהו עובדא דחול וכענין שנושאים זה הלכך אין לו לשנות לא להקל ולא להכביד כדפי' טעמא וההיא דלעיל בריש מפנין (דף קכ.) לא שייכא עובדא דחול שאינו מטלטל אלא בבית מזוית לזוית. מ"ר. וההיא דשחטה בשדה פירש בריש מפנין (ג"ז שם) בע"א וכמו שפירש כאן עיקר ועוד קשה לי לפי' הקונטרס דדרו באכפא אמאי ניפרוס סודרא עליה הוה ליה למימר לידרו באגרא כיון שאינו משנה להכביד יותר מאכפא כמו שמשמע נמי מתוך פירושו ולפירוש רבי אתי שפיר:

ניפרום

מסורת הש"ס

א) [ברכות כד. וש"נ], ב) רש"ל מ"ז, ג) [לעיל קמה. וש"נ] ביצה ל. ע"ש, ד) [עי' פרש"י חולין נח:], ה) [ועי' תוספות שם ד"ה טלית].

הגהות הב"ח

(א) גמ' לא יטרפם בצונן (אבל רוחץ) תא"מ ונ"ב ס"א אבל טובל: (ב) תוס' ד"ה שואל וכו' דסתם שאלה נמי ל' יום: (ג) בא"ד היה חייב להחזיר אלא דעבידי: (ד) ד"ה דדרו וכו' דאמר בסמוך הא קא מפשי בהילוכא:

ליקוטי רש"י

מסוכן אדם. ביום טוב ובשבת אם רחץ בצונן מסתפג באלונטית ואין חוששין שמא יסחוט. ומביאה בידו. ואין חוששין שמא יסחוט [עירובין פח.]. היינו מעלין שמן. לתוך בו. ואלונטית. להסתפג בה [שם צא.]. מחצר לגג וכו'. ר' שמעון לטעמיה דאמר בעירובין (פט.) אחד גגות ואחד חצירות [illegible] רשות אחת הן [illegible] הלכה בכתם משנה [illegible] מחוזא. [illegible] ומשמשין בבני מעיים [illegible] כך [illegible] קא.].

עין משפט נר מצוה

נו א טוש"ע או"ח סימן שכח סעיף מז:

נז ב שם סעיף לג:

א ג ד מיי' פכ"ג מהל' שבת הלכה יב סמג לאוין סה טור שו"ע או"ח סימן שז סעיף יא:

ב ה מיי' פ"ה מהלכות י"ט הלכה ד ג סמג לאוין עה טוש"ע או"ח סימן תקי סעיף ח:

ג ו מיי' שם טוש"ע שם סעיף י וסימן שכא סעיף ה:

גליון הש"ס

מתני' שואל אדם מחבירו. עי' בירושלמי פ"ח דשביעית ה"ד הובא בר"ש שם:

רבינו חננאל

מחזירין את השבר. רבה בר בר חנה אזל (פי') לפירקי' דרב יהודה שדריה לאדא דיילא א"ל זיל גרד ביה א"ל גרביה. פירוש א) משכיבה והביאהו מלשון פרק נחל מעם גר כלומר הבריחהו. כדגרסינן בפרק בנות כותים נדות מעריסתן. שילא בר אבינא עבד עובדא כרב. כי קא ניחא נפשיה דרב. א"ל לרב אמי זיל צעייה ואי לא צאית גרדיה הוא סבר גרדיה א"ל ופי' הכהו וכו': מי שנפרקה ידו או רגלו פי' שף מבוכניה לא יטרפן בצונן אבל רוחץ כדרכו ואם נתרפא נתרפא ורב אויא דשניא ליה ידיה והיה אומר לרב יוסף ומראה בידו אם יעשה בידו כך או כך מותר או אסור עד שהיה מראה לו כדי שיראוהו חכמים שהחזיר ידו למקומה ונתרפא.

הדרן עלך חבית

פרק כ"ג שואל אדם מחבירו כדי יין וכדי שמן ובלבד שלא יאמר לו הלויני כו'. ואוקימנא דחיישינן שמא יכתוב ב) וכן שאם יאמר לו הלויני גוערין בו ואומרים לו אסור לומר כן ביום שבת לשון הלואה מינכרא מלתא ולא אתי למכתב וכיון שהזכיר א"ל רבא בר רב חנן לאביי נסיב

חשק שלמה על רבינו חננאל

א) עיין בערוך הערך גרב ג': ב) אינו מובן לכאורה. ואולי דסיה לו גיר' הספרים בגמרא [illegible] הרשב"א כאן. ותפרש רבינו [illegible] שאם אומר הלויני קפידין עלויה [illegible] ולא אתי למכתב מלשון שאלה וכו' ודו"ק:

מדיבחא ועד עצרתא. מפסח ועד עצרת [פסחים מב:]. הוי גולה למקום תורה. למקום שהרב שם. ואל תאמר שהיא תבא אחריך. יבא לכאן ואלמוד לפניו. שחבריך יקיימוה בידך. שכל ספקות שיש לך יאמרו לך. [illegible]

לאדא דיילא. [illegible] אדא. שם האיש. דיילא. [illegible] בחדא מחיתא מחיתנהו. [illegible] חצבייהו. [illegible] דמליין חצבייהו מיא. [illegible] מ"ט לא משנין. [illegible] מפשו במשוי. [illegible]

Abaye defends his explanation:

אָמַר לֵיהּ – **He said to [Rava bar Rav Chanan]:** (בְּחוֹל דְּלֹא שְׁנָא כִּי אָמַר לֵיהּ הַלְוֵינִי לָא שְׁנָא כִּי אָמַר לֵיהּ הַשְׁאִילֵנִי – **On weekdays, whether [the borrower] says to [the lender] "*halveini*" or "*hashileini,*"** לָא קָפְדִינַן עִילָּוֵיהּ – **we are not particular with him** [i.e. we realize that he seeks a loan of substantial duration, although this is not necessarily indicated by his choice of words], אָתֵי לְמִיכְתַּב – **and thus [the lender] will come to write** the loan down.) בְּשַׁבָּת – **On the Sabbath,** however, כֵּיוָן דְּהַשְׁאִילֵנִי הוּא דְּשָׁרוּ לֵיהּ רַבָּנָן – **since it is** only **"*hashileini*" that the Rabbis permitted him** to say, הַלְוֵינִי לָא שָׁרוּ לֵיהּ – **and they did not permit him** to say **"*halveini,*"** מִינְכְּרָא מִילְתָא – when he says "*hashileini,*" **it is evident** that he means a loan of minimal duration, וְלָא אָתֵי לְמִיכְתַּב – **and [the lender] will not come to write** it down.[14]

Having presented one exchange between Rava bar Rav Chanan and Abaye, the Gemara records another:

אָמַר לֵיהּ רָבָא בַּר רַב חָנָן לְאַבַּיֵּי – **Rava bar Rav Chanan said to Abaye:** מִכְּדִי – **Now,** let us see: אָמְרוּ רַבָּנָן כָּל מִילֵּי דְּיוֹם טוֹב – **The Rabbis said** that in **all matters of Yom Tov** (i.e. all activities performed on Yom Tov), כַּמָּה דְּאֶפְשָׁר לְשַׁנּוּיֵי מְשַׁנֵּינַן – **however much it is possible to deviate** from the normal manner of performing the activity, **we should deviate.**[15] הָנֵי נָשֵׁי דְּמַלְיָין חַצְבַּיְיהוּ מַיָּא – Therefore, **those women who fill their buckets with water** from the river on Yom Tov and carry them home, מַאי טַעְמָא לֹא מְשַׁנִּין – **why do they not deviate** from their usual manner of carrying water?

Abaye answers:

מִשּׁוּם דְּלֹא אֶפְשָׁר – The women may carry in the normal manner **because it is not possible** for them to deviate. הֵיכִי לֶעֱבְדֵי – **What should they do?** דְּמַלְיָין בְּחַצְבָּא רַבָּא – If you will suggest that **those who draw** water **with a large bucket** לִימְלוֹ בְּחַצְבָּא זוּטָא – **should** deviate and **draw with a small bucket,** הָא קָא מַפְּשׁוּ בְּהִילוּכָא – **this would increase** their **walking** and is consequently not a valid deviation![16] דְּמַלְיָין בְּחַצְבָּא זוּטָא – If you will suggest that **those who draw** water **with a small bucket** לִימְלוֹ בְּחַצְבָּא רַבָּא – **should** deviate and **draw with a large bucket,** קָא מַפְּשׁוּ בְּמַשּׂוֹי – **this would increase the load!**

NOTES

14. On the Sabbath, when the lender hears *hashileini* (instead of *halveini,* which is more appropriate for a loan of this nature), he will not attribute the error to the borrower's inaccuracy. Rather, he will realize that the borrower chose this word because *halveini* is forbidden. The lender also presumably knows that the reason why *halveini* is forbidden is that it signifies a long-term loan. Thus, *hashileini* will signal to him that the loan is of minimal duration (see *Ritva MHK* ed. et al.).

15. This rule is derived from the Mishnah in *Beitzah* 29b: "One who brings pitchers of wine from place to place may not bring them in a basket or box, but he may bring them on his shoulder or [in his hand] in front of himself etc." (*Rashi*).

16. If they use a smaller bucket to draw the water, they would have to make more trips to the river to bring the same amount of water that they could carry in a single trip using the large bucket. Optimally, the deviation should lessen the effort expended on Yom Tov; at the very least, it should not make it more difficult. A deviation which causes extra effort to be expended is not valid.

Tosafos point out that the very deviation proposed by the Mishnah in *Beitzah* 29b (see previous note) involves a decrease in the load and consequently an increase in the number of trips. *Tosafos* answer that since the use of a basket or box bears greater resemblance to a weekday activity than does carrying on one's shoulder, one must use the latter method although the number of trips is thereby increased. Here, however, carrying in a large bucket and carrying in a smaller bucket equally resemble a weekday activity. Hence, using a smaller bucket would only make the situation worse, by increasing the amount of walking (see *Maharsha, Shabbos Shel Mi;* see also *Tos. Yom Tov* ibid.).

הלכה מחזירין את השבר רבה בר בר חנה איקלע לפומבדיתא לא על לפירקיה דרב יהודה שדריה לאדא דיילא א"ל זיל גרביה אזיל גרביה אתא אשכחיה דקא דריש אין מחזירין את השבר א"ל הכי אמר רב חנא בגדתאה אמר שמואל הלכה מחזירין את השבר א"ל הא חנא דידן והא שמואל דידן ולא שמיע לי ולאו בדינא גרבתיך: מי שנפרקה ידו כו': רב אויא הוה יתיב קמיה דרב יוסף שניא ליה ידיה א"ל הכי מאי אסור והכי מאי א"ל אסור אדהכי איתפח ידיה א"ל מאי תיבעי לך הא תנן מי שנפרקה ידו או רגלו לא יטרפם בצונן אבל רוחץ כדרכו ואם נתרפא נתרפא א"ל ולא תנן אין מחזירין את השבר ואמר רב חנא בגדתאה אמר שמואל הלכה מחזירין את השבר א"ל כולהו בחדא מחיתא מחיתנהו היכא דאיתמר איתמר היכא דלא איתמר לא איתמר:

הדרן עלך חבית

שואל אדם מחבירו כדי יין וכדי שמן ובלבד שלא יאמר לו הלויני וכן האשה מחבירתה ככרות ואם אינו מאמינו מניח טליתו אצלו ועושה עמו חשבון לאחר שבת וכן ערב פסח בירושלים שחל להיות בשבת מניח טליתו אצלו ונוטל את פסחו ועושה עמו חשבון לאחר יום טוב: **גמ'** א"ל רבא בר רב חנן לאביי מאי שנא השאילני ומאי שנא הלויני אמר ליה השאילני לא אתי למיכתב הלויני אתי למיכתב והא כיון דבחול זימנין דבעי למימר ליה הלויני וא"ל השאילני ולא קפיד עילויה ואתי למיכתב בשבת נמי אתי למיכתב א"ל (בחול דלא שנא כי א"ל הלויני ל"ש כי א"ל השאילני לא קפדינן עילויה אתי למיכתב) בשבת כיון דהשאילני הוא דשרו ליה רבנן הלויני לא שרו ליה מינכרא מילתא ולא אתי למיכתב א"ל רבא בר רב חנן לאביי מכדי אמרו רבנן כל מילי דיום טוב כמה דאפשר לשנויי משנינן הני נשי דמליין חצבייהו מיא מ"ט לא משנין משום דלא אפשר היכי לעבדי דמליין בחצבא רבא לימלו בחצבא זוטא הא קא מפשו בהילוכא דמליין בחצבא זוטא לימלו בחצבא רבא קא מפשו במשוי ניפרום

רש"י

הלכה מחזירין את השבר. סבירא ליה לשמואל מחזירין תנן: אדא דיילא. מנשטר"ל ממונה: גרביה. קח בגדו עד שיבא: אתא. רבה אשכחיה לרב יהודה כו': הא חנא דידן. ממקומנו הוא ולא שמענו זאת מפיו עד הנה: ולאו בדינא גרבתיך. בתמיה שאילו לא באת לא למדנו: שניא ליה ידיה. נשמטה ידו ממקומה אשולטיי"ר בלע"ז: הכי מאי. היה עושה בענייני הרבה ושואל: בחדא מחיתא מחיתנהו. כאריגה אחת ארגתו: היכא דאיתמר. דמתניתין לאו דוקא תנן איתמר:

הדרן עלך חבית

שואל. שלא יאמר הלויני. מפרש בגמרא: שחל להיות בשבת. ולא נזכר מע"ש לקנות: לאחר יו"ט. ליום שלישי: **גמ'** הלויני משמע לזמן מרובה וקיי"ל במסכת מכות (דף ג:) סתם הלואה ל' יום ואתי מלוה זה לכתוב על פנקסו כך וכך הלויתי כדי שלא ישכח: **א"ל** וכיון דבחול נמי זימנין דבעי למימר הלויני ואמר השאילני: **ולא קפיד עליה.** והויא הלואה: בשבת נמי. כי אמר השאילני סבר דהלואה היא ואתי למכתב ומאי היכר איכא: ה"ג א"ל בשבת כיון דהשאילני שרו ליה רבנן הלויני לא שרו ליה מינכרא מילתא ולא אתי למכתב: **אמרו רבנן.** במסכת ביצה: **כל כמה דאפשר לשנויי משנינן.** דאמרינן המביא כדי יין לא יביאם בסל ובקופה כו': בנכתמא

תוספות

שואל אדם מחבירו כדי יין וכדי שמן ובלבד שלא יאמר לו הלויני. פירש רש"י טעמא משום דסתם הלואה ל' יום ולפי שהוא לזמן מרובה יותר משאלה אתי למיכתב וקשה לר"ת דסתם שאלה (נ) ל' יום כדאמר במנחות בהתכלת (דף מד.) טלית שאולה כל ל' יום פטורה מן הציצית ואמרינן נמי התם הדר בתוספתא באכסני' בא"י והשוכר בית בחו"ל כל ל' יום פטור מן המזוזה מכאן ואילך חייב במזוזה אלמא דסתם שאלה ל' יום איתא והכי פטורה כל ל' יום דאמר שאולה היא אבל מכאן ואילך נראה כמו שלו ומיהו יכול לומר לרש"י לאו משום דאי מתבע ליה לדינא בתוך ל' יום שאין צריך להחזיר דודאי היה חייב להחזיר (ג) דעבידי אינשי דמשאלי פחות משלשים יום אבל טפי לא משאלי הלכך עד ל' יום אמרי אינשי שאולה היא ור"י פירש לנו דהיינו טעמא דשאלה לפי שהיא חוזרת בעין לא אתי למיכתב אבל לשון הלואה אינו חוזר בעין ואתי למיכתב ואע"ג דכי שאיל מיניה כדי יין וכדי שמן לא הדרי בעין מ"מ מתוך שמוכיר לו לשון שאלה זכור הוא ולא אתי למיכתב. מ"ר וכן פירש ה"ר פורת:

אתקין רבא במחוזא דדרו בדוחקא כו'. ברוב ספרים אינו כתוב כאן ולא בפירוש רש"י וכיון המביא כדי יין (ביצה דף ל. ושם) נראה שהוא מקומו וזה לשון פירוש הקונטרס בביצה דדרו בדוחקא משוי שאדם יחיד נושא בחול על כתיפו בטורח אם לא נשאהו לצורך יום טוב ביו"ט כגון חבית או שק מלא פירות ישאהו ביו"ט בדיגלא עתר שקורין פורק"א בלע"ז כדרך נושאי מלא למכור מפני שצריך לשנות וכשמשנה ישנה להקל משאו ולא להרבות טורח ביו"ט ועתר זה יום לנשאת בו משא כבד וכשנושא בו חבית המשאת בכתף ישנה להקל דדרו בדיגלא משוי חבית גדולה שרגילה לשאת בדיגלא לידרו באגרא ישאהו ביו"ט בב' בני אדם במוט על כתפים דהיינו נמי שינוי להקל דדרו באגרא במוט על כתפים לידרו ביו"ט אותו משוי באכפא במוט בידים משום שינוי ואפילו אינו להקל מ"מ שינוי הוא ואינו מרבה טורח בשינוי דדרו באכפא ניפרום סודרא קל הוא ואינו מכביד ושינוי בעלמא הוא והגנע עד כאן לשונו ומשמע מתוך פירושו דכל אלה משוי אחד להם בשוה ואין זה נושא יותר אלא שנושא משאו בענין אחר ממה שהיה רגיל וזה דחקו שאם נפרש שכל אלו ממעטים משאם מאשר היו רגילים לשאת קשיא הא דאמר בסמוך (ד) מפשי בהילוכא משמע מפירושא דאגרא נושאים שני בני אדם שפיר במוט בשנים ויש בו משוי שני בני אדם שנושאים כל מה שרגילין לשאת בדיגלא ודיגלא היא משוי שני בני אדם כדמשמע בבבא מציעא בפ"ק השוכר את האומנים (דף פג.) וקשיא לר' דהתם משמע נמי דאגרא אין בו משוי לשני בני אדם דאמר התם דדרו באגרא ואיתבר משלם פלגא מ"ט נפיש לחד וזוטר לתרי ודמי לפשיעה ודמי לאונס בדיגלא משלם כולה משמע דלא הוי זוטר לתרי נראה דאגרא לשום אדם אינו נראה עובדא דחול כמו דיגלא ומשום הכי דדרו בדיגלא לידרו באגרא ואע"פ שמפיש בהילוכא יכול לשנות כיון שאינו נראה כל כך עובדא דחול והשתא אתי שפיר דדרו באגרא לידרו באכפא אע"פ שבודאי מרבה במשאוי הוא בנושא בידים המוט מכשנושאו על כתיפו מ"מ כיון שאינו נראה עובדא דחול כמו אגרא יכול לעשות כעין שמצינו גבי בהמה מסוכנת דתנן בבילה (דף כה.) שחטה בשדה לא יביאנה במוט אלא מביאה בידו אברים אברים ותנן נמי (דף כט: ושם) המביא כדי יין לא יביאם בסל ובקופה אלא מביא הוא על כתפיו או לפניו אלמא הני אע"ג דמפשי בהילוכא כיון שאינו עושה כל כך כדרך שעושה בחול יש לו לשנות והיא דבסמוך דמליין בחצבא זוטא ודמליין בחצבא רבה תרווייהו עובדא דחול וכענין שנושאים זה נושאים זה הלכך אין לו לשנות לא להקל ולא להכביד כדפי' טעמא וההיא דלעיל בריש מפנין (דף קכח.) לא שייכא עובדא דחול שאינו מטלטל אלא בבית מזוית לזוית. מ"ר. וההיא דשחטה בשדה פירש בריש מפנין (ג"ז שם) בע"א וכמו שפירש כאן עיקר ועוד קשה לי לפי' הקונטרס דדרו באכפא אמאי ניפרום סודרא עליה הוה ליה למימר לידרו באגרא כיון שאינו משנה להכביד יותר מאכפא כמו שמשמע נמי מתוך פירושו ולפירוש רבי אתי שפיר:

מסורת הש"ס

א) [כריתות כד. וש"נ], ב) רש"ל מ"ז, ג) [לעיל קמה: ושם], ד) [עי' פרש"י חולין נח:], ה) [ועי' תוספות שם ד"ה עלים].

הגהות הב"ח

(א) גמ' לא יטרפם בצונן (אבל רוחץ) תא"מ ונ"ב ס"א אבל רוחץ כדרכו: (ב) תוס' ד"ה שואל וכו' דסתם שאלה נמי ל' יום: (ג) באד"ה היה חייב להחזיר אלא דעבידי: (ד) ד"ה אתקין וכו' דאמר בסמוך הא קא מפשי בהילוכא:

ליקוטי רש"י

מפתחבר אדם. כיום טוב ובשבת אם רגיל בכלום ממכבר בתנועות ואינו חושש שמא יתקעו. ומביא בידו. ואינו חושש שמא ישכח ויתקנו [עירובין פח.]. היינו מעלין ביצה. לשון קנו. ואלונטית. להסתפג בה [שם צא.]. מחצר לגג וכו'. וכרי שאין לנעמידה לאמר לעירובין (שם.) אחד גגות ואלירות רשות אחת הן לכלים ששבתו בתוכן [מנחות פג.]. מחצר לגג ומגג וכו'. ר' שמעון מיקל מכולם ואמר אלירות וגגות וקרפיפות שאין יותר מבית סאתים הואיל וכולם אין משמשין מיוחד ומדיר רשות אחת הן ומטלטלין מזה לזה אפילו כלים ששבתו בזה או בזה ואף על פי שלא עירבו ולית ליה לר' אלא משום היסר כלי הבית [עירובין פט. הובא בהמשך לרש"י כאן]. דג' מחלוקות לו לגבי אלירות וגגות לר' מאיר גגין רשות לעלמן ומטלטלין מזה לזה ואפילו על פי שלא עירבו ולר' יהודה רשות לעלמן וגגות לא וקרפיפות ולא עירבו שלא מגגין לגגות רשות לעלמן וקרפיפות ולדברי מכמים רשות אחת ולדברי ר' שמעון כולן רשות אחת הן כל הכמים [לעיל קל:]. הלכה כסתם משנה. רבי הוא סדר המשנה ובשרה דברי מכם ושנאו ולא הזכיר שם אומרו והלכין כדברי שנוי מפי יחיד ובלא טעם נשנה מפי המרובים ויעשו כמותן [ביצה ב:]. בי בני. בית המרחץ [ברכות ס.]. מחוזא. עיר שהיה רבא דר בתוכה בס [ב"מ נט.]. וממשמשין בבני מעיים. של תולה כפשמ ואין בכך משום רפואה דמיירי אימקש לשמיה. דר ואוחר כך ממשמש. חוי שנוי דכמול דרך למשמש ולאמר כך לנון [סנהדרין קא.].

עין משפט נר מצוה

גו א טוש"ע או"ח סימן שכח סעיף מז:
גז ב שם סעיף לו:
א ג ד מיי' פכ"ג מהל' שבת הלכה יב סמג לאוין סה טוש"ע או"ח סימן שז סעיף יא:
ב ה מיי' פ"ה מהלכות י"ט הלכה ג סמג לאוין עה טוש"ע או"ח סימן תקי סעיף ט:
ג ו מיי' שם טוש"ע שם סעיף י ובסימן שכג סעיף ה:

גליון הש"ס

מתני' שואל אדם מחבירו. עי' ירושלמי פ"ח דשביעית על מ"ד הוכא בר"ש שם:

רבינו חננאל

מחזירין את השבר. רבה בר בר חנה לא על (פי') לפירקיה דרב יהודה שדריה לאדא דיילא א"ל זיל גרד ביה אזל גרביה. פירוש א) משכוה והביאהו מלשון פרק נחל מעם גר כלומר הבריחוהו. כדגרסינן בפרק בנות כותים נדות מעריסתן. שילא בר אבינא עבד עובדא כרב. כי קא ניחא נפשיה דרב. א"ל לרב אמי זיל צניעיה ואי לא צאית גרדיה הוא סבר גרדיה א"ל ופי' ההוא וכו': מי שנפרקה ידו או רגלו פי' שף מבורכיה לא יטרפם בצונן אבל רוחץ כדרכו ואם נתרפא נתרפא ורב אויא דשניא ליה ידיה והיה אומר לרב יוסף ומראה בידו אם יעשה בידו כך או כך מותר או אסור עד שהיה מראה לו כדי שיראוהו מה שהתחירו חכמים חזרה ידו למקומה ונתרפא.

הדרן עלך חבית

פרק כ"ג שואל אדם מחבירו כדי יין וכדי שמן ובלבד שלא יאמר לו הלויני כו'. ואוקימנא דחיישינן שמא יכתוב ג) וכן שאם יאמר לו הלויני גוערין בו ואומרים לו אסור לומר כן ביום שבת שלשון הלואה מינכרא מלתא ולא אתי למכתב וכיון שהזכיר א"ל רבא בר רב חנן לאביי נסיב

חשק שלמה על רבינו חננאל

א) עיין בערוך השלם ערך גרב א': ב) אינו מובן לכאורה. ואולי דהיה לו גי' הספרים בגמרא דמסוגר במלי לבנה והובא בפי' הרשב"א כאן. ומפרש רבינו דהסלוק הוא דבשבת כיון שאם אומר הלוי קפדינן עלויה יש לו היכירא ולא אתי למכתב מלשון שאלה וכו' ודו"ק:

א) מדיהא ועד עצרתא. מפסח ועד עלרת [פסחים מב:]. הוי גולה למקום תורה. למקום שהרב שם. ואל תאמר שהיא תבא אחריך. יבא לכאן ואלמוד לפניו. שחבריך יקיימוה בידך. שכל ספקות שיש לך יאמרו לך. נ"א שאם תוליך לשם תלמידים עמך ישאו ויתנו עמך שם בהלכה ותבינה כדאמרי' (ירמיה נ, לו) חרב אל הבדים וגו'. ואל בינתך אל תשען. אל תאמר איני צריך ללכת לרב אלא מעצמי יכול אני לירד לעומקה. נ"א שלא תהא עצל לשאול כדבר כל מה שבלבך אלא הט אונך לשמוע הכל מפיו ואחר כך הבין במשובתו כדאמרי' (ברכות סג:) הם ואח"כ כתת [אבות פ"ד מי"ג]. לפופי. לכורכו בבגדים וקושרו במגורה רפה ומתיישבין פרקי אבריו שהן רכין ונשמטין בחבלי הלידה וקורין אנמלטוייי"ר בלע"ז [לעיל סו:]. מלפפין היינו אסוכי יונקא דאמרינן לעיל בפרק כל הכלים (קכג.) דהא שמעינן ליה לרב נחמן דאסר אלא לפופי בעלמא כמו שעושין במגורות ופסיקיאות [שם קכט:]. בגדתאה. שם עירו בגדד היא עיר החשובה שבבבל מתחרבה בבל [ברכות נו:]. בעל אגדה ל"ש מקום שהוא בבבל ששמו בגדד [יבמות סז.]. עיר שבבבל ושמה בגדת בפסק סדרו של רב שרירא גאון היא מוכרת [כתובות ז:]. דמן בגדד עיר שנולד בה ובכתבי רב שרירא היא מוכרת [רשב"ם ב"ב קמב:]. [ע"כ שייך לדף קמז:].

לאדא דיילא. שמש דרבנן ולאו שמו [נדה כד: ע"ש בב"ח]. אדא. שם האיש. דיילא. שמש דרבנן [ב"ק קיט.]. שוטר [יומא יח.]. בחדא מחיתא מחיתנהו. וכי כאריגה אחת ארגתם לכולם לשון (שמות לט בתרגום) עובד מחי דמיקון דגור קרו לו אינשי אריגה שמקדר את דבריו [חולין נח:]. דמליין חצבייהו מיא. שואבות מים מן הנהר [ביצה ל.]. חצבייהו. חבית, כד של חרס שואבין בו המים [סוכה כט.]. מ"ט לא משנין. דנראה כמעשה דחול לשאת משאות [ביצה כט:]. קא מפשו במשוי. וכשהוא משנה ישנה להקל משאו ולא להרבות טורח ביום טוב [שם ל.].

ניפרום סודרא אתי לידי סחיטה נכסייה
בנבתמא זימנין דמיפסק ואתי למקטריה הלכך
לא אפשר וא"ל רבא בר רב חנן לאביי תנן
לא מספקין ולא מטפחין ולא מרקדין ביו"ט
וקא חזינן דעבדין ולא אמרינן להו ולא מידי
ולטעמיך הא דאמר רבא לא ליתיב איניש
אפומא דלחייא דילמא מיגנדר ליה חפץ
ואתי לאיתויי והא קא חזינן (א) נמי דמותבי
חצבי ויתבן אפומא דמבואה ולא אמרינן
להו ולא מידי אלא הנח לישראל מוטב
שיהו שוגגין ואל יהו מזידין סבור מינה
הנ"מ בדרבנן אבל בדאורייתא לא ולא היא
ל"ש בדרבנן ול"ש בדאורייתא דהא תוספת
דיוה"כ דאורייתא היא וקא חזינן להו דקאכלי
ושתו עד שתחשך ולא אמרי' להו ולא מידי:
וכן אשה מחבירתה ככרות: בשבת הוא
דאסיר אבל בחול שפיר דמי לימא מתני'
דלא כהלל דתנן וכן היה הלל אומר לא
תלוה אשה ככר לחבירתה עד שתעשינה
דמים שמא יוקרו חטין ונמצאו באות לידי
רבית אפילו תימא הלל הא באתרא דקייץ
דמיה הא באתרא דלא קייץ דמיה: ואם אינו
מאמינו: איתמר הלוואת יו"ט רב יוסף אמר
לא ניתנה ליתבע ורבה אמר ניתנה ליתבע
רב יוסף אמר לא ניתנה ליתבע דאי אמרת
ניתנה ליתבע אתי למיכתב רבה אמר ניתנה ליתבע דאי אמרת לא ניתנה לא
יהיב ליה ואתי לאימנועי משמחת יו"ט תנן אם אינו מאמינו מניח טליתו
אצלו אי אמרת בשלמא לא ניתנה ליתבע משום הכי מניח טליתו אצלו
ועושה עמו חשבון לאחר שבת אלא אי אמרת ניתנה ליתבע אמאי מניח
טליתו אצלו ליתן ליה ולתבעיה אמר לא בעינא דליקום בדינא ודיינא מתיב
רב אידי בר אבין השוחט את הפרה וחילקה בראש השנה אם היה חדש
מעובר משמט ואם לאו אינו משמט ואי לא ניתנה ליתבע מאי משמט
שאני התם דאיגלאי מילתא דחול הוא ת"ש מסיפא אם לאו אינו משמט
אי אמרת בשלמא ניתנה ליתבע היינו דקתני אינו משמט אלא אי אמרת
לא ניתנה ליתבע (ב) אמאי אינו משמט דאי יהיב ליה שקיל מכלל דרישא
אי יהיב ליה לא שקיל רישא צריך למימר ליה משמט אני סיפא לא צריך
למימר ליה משמט אני כדתנן המחזיר חוב בשביעית יאמר לו משמט
אני ואם אמר לו אעפ"כ יקבל ממנו משום שנאמר וזה דבר השמטה רב
אויא שקיל משכונא רבה בר עולא מערים איערומי: וכן ערב פסח: א"ר
יוחנן מקדיש אדם פסחו בשבת וחגיגתו ביו"ט נימא מסייע ליה וכן ערב
פסח בירושלים שחל להיות בשבת מניח טליתו אצלו ונוטל את פסחו ועושה
עמו חשבון לאחר יו"ט הכא במאי עסקינן בממנה אחרים עמו על פסחו
דמעיקרא מיקדש וקאי והא אנן תנן אין נמנין על הבהמה בתחילה ביו"ט
שאני הכא כיון דרגיל אצלו כמאן דאימני ביה מעיקרא דמי והא תני
רבי הושעיא הולך אדם אצל רועה הרגיל אצלו ונותן לו טלה לפסחו
ומקדישו ויוצא בו התם נמי כיון דרגיל אצלו אקדושי (ג) ליה מעיקרא והא
מקדיש קתני הקדש עילוי מדרבנן ומי אמר ר' יוחנן הכי והא אמר ר'
יוחנן הלכה כסתם משנה ותנן לא מקדישין ולא מעריכין ולא מחרימין
ולא מגביהין תרומות ומעשרות כל אלו ביו"ט אמרו ק"ו בשבת לא קשיא
כאן בחובות שקבוע להן זמן כאן בחובות שאין קבוע להן זמן: **מתני'** מונה
אדם את אורחיו ואת פרפרותיו מפיו אבל לא מן הכתב ומפיס עם
בניו ועם בני ביתו על השולחן ובלבד שלא יתכוין לעשות מנה גדולה
כנגד מנה קטנה ומטילין חלשין על הקדשים ביו"ט אבל לא על המנות:
גמ'

רש"י

בנבתמא. כיסוי: זימנין דמיפסק כו'. כיון דמצרכת ליה כיסוי קטר ליה בכד וזימנין דמיפסק ואתי למקטריה והיא קשר של קיימא דאסור מדאורייתא: ואתי לידי סחיטה. ודקאמר במסכת ביצה ניפרום סודרא עלויה כו' (ד) [התם] בדבר יבש קא מיירי: אין מספקין. כף אל כף משום אבל: מטפחין. על הלב: מרקדין. לשמחה וטעמא מפרש במסכת ביצה שמא יתקן כלי שיר: אפומא דלחייא. לפי שאין ניכר כל כך בין מבוי לרה"ר: ואתי לאתויי. חפץ המתגלגל תוך ד' אמות: ומגנדר אצליהן ומייתין ליה ל"ג: בשבת הוא דאסור. לומר הלויני משום מכתב: הא בחול שרי. ולא חיישינן לרבית ואף על גב דבלשון הלואה קאמר ליה: באתרא דקייץ דמיהו. דככרות לא אתי לידי רבית שאם יוקירו יתן דמיהן: לא ניתנה ליתבע. בב"ד שאין ב"ד נזקקין לה לעולם: בדינא ודיינא. לא לבא לדין ולא לברור דיין ולהטריח את עצמו: השוחט את הפרה וחילקה בראש השנה. של מוצאי שביעית ללוקחים בהקפה וקיי"ל שביעית משמטת בסופה דכתיב מקץ: אם היה חדש. אלול מעובר ועשו ראש השנה שני ימים משמט דיום טוב ראשון של סוף שביעית היה ונמצאת זו הלואת שביעית ואם לאו הויא לה הלואת מוצאי שביעית ואינו משמט: ל"ג אי אמרת בשלמא כו' ה"ג ואם לא ניתנה ליתבע מאי משמט. הואיל ואין ב"ד נזקקין לכופו שמוטה היא ועומדת: דחול הוא. שהרי חדש מעובר ולא הוי יו"ט עד למחר הלכך אי לאו דשביעית הוה גבי: ואם לאו אינו משמט. אלמא ניתנה ליתבע ומשני מאי אינו משמט דאי יהיב ליה שקיל: מכלל דרישא אי יהיב ליה לא שקיל. בתמיה: רישא. דהלואת שביעית היא אי נמי יהיב ליה לוה צריך למימר ליה מלוה משמט אני: (ה) ואם אמר. לוה אעפ"כ איני חפץ שישמטו יקבל ממנו: דבר השמטה. אפילו מקבל חובו יזכיר לו שמיטה בדבורו: שקיל משכונא. בשעת הלואה מהלואת יו"ט: מערים איערומי. לאחר י"ט לוקח ממנו שום חפץ ומעכבו: פסחו בשבת. אם חל י"ד בשבת: וחגיגתו ביו"ט. ביום הקרבתה מותר להקדיש ואע"ג דתנן אלו הן משום שבות אין מקדישין הני כיון דהקרבתן דוחה קדושתן דוחה: בממנה אחרים עמו. כדכתיב (שמות יב) במכסת נפשות: על פסחו. שהיה קדוש ועומד מאתמול: אקדושי. מקדיש ליה רועה מע"ש שהרי יודע שזה סומך עליו: עילוי. מעלה בעלמא שיקדישו בעלים: הא. דקתני אין מקדישין בחובות שאין קבוע להן זמן קאי שאין הקרבתן דוחה שבת: מתני' פרפרותיו. מיני מעדנים: אבל לא מן הכתב. אם כתב מע"ש כך וכך אורחים פלוני ופלוני זמנתי כדי שלא ישכחם לא יקרא באותו כתב בשבת ובגמ' מפרש טעמא: מפיס. לשון פייס מטיל פייס לחלק מי מגיע כל מנה ומנה: ובלבד שלא יתכוין לעשות כו'. שיהו המנות שוות ולא תהא אחת גדולה ואחת קטנה לזכות בגדולה הזוכה ע"פ הגורל והמתחייב ע"פ הגורל לקטנה יטלנה ובגמ' מפרש טעמא: חלשים. גורלות: על הקדשים. בין הכהנים: אבל לא על המנות. בגמרא מפרש:

תוספות

ניפרום סודרא עליה אתי למסחטיה. מכאן מייתי ר"ת ראיה דביין ושמן לא שייכא סחיטה לעיל בשלהי שמונה שרצים (דף קיא. בד"ה הא מסוכרייתא) פירשתי: **לא** מספקין ולא מטפחין. לא כפי' הקונטרס משום דא"כ מאי איריא ביו"ט אפי' בחול המועד נמי אסור כדתנן במועד קטן פרק בתרא (דף כח:) נשים במועד מענות אבל לא מטפחות אלא נראה לרבי משום שמחה רגילין לספק ולטפח בהשמעת קול ואסור שמא יתקן כלי שיר כדמפרש בהמוצא תפילין (עירובין דף קד.): **וכן** היה הלל אומר. כרבנן דפליגי עליה באיזהו נשך (ב"מ ד' עה.) וקי"ל: **רבה** אמר ניתנה ליתבע. הלכה כרבה לגבי רב יוסף: ורב אויא ורבה בר עולא ממרי אנפשייהו כ"ה בס"ל:

דאי אמרת ניתנה ליתבע אתי למיכתב. אע"פ שמוכר לו לשון שאלה: **דאיגלאי** מילתא דבחול הויא. ורב יוסף לא איירי אלא בשבת ויו"ט ודאי:

והא אנן תנן אין נימנין כו'. פירש ה"ר פורת בשם רבינו שמואל דל"ג ליה חדא דמה שייך להקשות מנמנין של רשות לנמנין של מלוה ועוד דמפרש התם בביצה פרק אין צדין (דף כט:) מאי אין נמנין אין פוסקין דמים בתחילה לבהמה ביו"ט הרי אני עמך בסלע הריני עמך בשתים אבל אומר לו הריני עמך לשליש ולרביע: ולמ"ד

עין משפט נר מצוה

ד א מיי' פכ"ג מהלכות שבת הלכה ב סמג לאוין סה טוש"ע או"ח סימן שלט סעיף ג וסימן תקכד סעיף א:
ה ב מיי' פ"ג מהלכות שביתת עשור הלכה ז סמג לאוין סה ועשין לב טור ושו"ע או"ח סימן תרח סעיף ב:
ו ג מיי' פ"ו מהלכות מלוה ולוה הלכה ב סמג לאוין קצג טוש"ע יו"ד סימן קסב סעיף א:
ז ד שם סעיף ג:
ח ה מיי' פ"ד מהלכות י"ט הלכה כה טוש"ע או"ח סימן תקכה סעיף א:
ט ו מיי' פ"ט מהלכות שמיטה ויובל הלכה כח סמג עשין קמב:
י ז מיי' שם הלכה כט סמג לאוין רעא טור ושו"ע חו"מ סימן סז סעיף לו:
יא ח מיי' פכ"ג מהלכ' שבת הלכה יד ופ"א מהלכות קרבן פסח הלכה יח סמג עשין רכג:
יב ט מיי' פ"ד מהלכות י"ט הלכה יט סמג לאוין עה טוש"ע או"ח סימן תקכז סעיף א:
יג י מיי' פכ"ג מהלכות שבת הלכה יד סמג לאוין סה ועה טוש"ע או"ח סימן שכג וסימן תקכד סעיף א:

רבינו חננאל

להא. דא"ל תנן לא מספקין ולא מרקדין ולא מטפחין. בגדרא. ופשוטה היא. ומיפרשא נמי בגמ' דהמביא כדי יין במס' יו"ט וכן שואלת אשה מחברתה ככרות. ודייקינן מינה בשבת הוא דאסור מכלל דבחול שרי מתניתין דלא כהלל כו' ומסקינן בה אפילו תימא כהלל באתרא דקייצי דמי. ואם אינו מאמינו מניח טליתו אצלו ועושה עמו חשבון לאחר שבת. אתמר הלואת יו"ט רב יוסף אמר לא ניתנה ליתבע ורבה אמר ניתנה ליתבע ואתינן למיגמר מן מתניתין תנן ואם אינו מאמינו מניח טליתו אצלו כו' ולא גמרינן מינה דלא מיפרשא בהדיא כחד מינייהו ומותבינן לרב יוסף מהא דתנן השוחט את הפרה וחילקה בראש השנה אם היה חדש מעובר משמט. פי' אם היה אלול מעובר נמצא יום לקיחתו חלק מן הפרה יום חול שר"ה מחר הוא וכיון שנושה בו דמי בשר הפרה שלקח מאתמול דכיון שנכנסה שנה שביעית משמטת לדברי רבא ניחא כי נתנה ליתבע ומלוה נושה בו וכשנכנסת שביעית משמטת אלא לרב יוסף דאמר לא נתנה ליתבע אמאי צריך לי למיתנא משמטת בלאו הכי פטור הוא מלשלם. ואפילו בשאר שני שבוע דהא לא ניתנה ליתבע. ופריק רב יוסף שאני התם דכיון דאיגלאי מלתא דחול היא (ניתנה ליתבע דהא מלוה דחול היא) ואנן לא קאימנא אלא בהלואת יו"ט ואסיקנא למשמע מסיפא אם לאו אינו משמט לרבא דאמר ניתנה ליתבע דתובעו ונפרע ממנו [ניחא] אלא לרב יוסף דאמר לא נתנה ליתבע קשיא כיון דתני אינו משמט הוא משמע דתובעו ונפרע ממנו ואינו יכול לומר לו כי השביעית השמיטתו ופריק רב יוסף לעולם לא נתנה ליתבע והמלוה אינו יכול ליתבע אלא אם יביא הלה ויפרענו אינו צריך לומר משמט אני. ואקשינן עליה מכלל דרישא אי יהיב ליה מעצמו לא שקיל. ופריק רב יוסף המחזיר לו צריך שיאמר לו משמט אני. דהא נושה בו מלוה. אבל ספק שאינו נושה בו מלוה אם יבא אינו צריך לומר לו משמט אני אלא יקבל כדתנן המחזיר חוב בשביעית צריך שיאמר משמט אני. ואם אמר לו אעפ"כ יקבל ממנו משום שנאמר וזה דבר השמטה. ומפורש ענין זה בפ' השולח גט לאשתו. וראינו רבותינו שהיו

מסורת הש"ס

א) ביצה ל. וש"נ, ב) [ע"ש], ג) לעיל קמח. ביצה ל., ד) [ב"ב ס:], ה) [עי' תוס' ב"מ עה.], ו) [ביצה ל:], ז) גיטין לז:, ח) [גיטין לז: ע"ש], ט) פסחים סו:, י) ביצה לו:, כ) [עי' תוס' פסחים סו:], ל) ביצה כט:, מ) [לעיל קמט.].

הגהות הב"ח

(א) גמ' והא קא חזינן נמי דמותבי חצביהו וכו' הנח להן לישראל: (ב) שם מאי אינו משמט דאי יהיב ליה: (ג) שם אקדושי מקדיש ליה מעיקרא: (ד) רש"י ד"ה ואתי לידי סחיטה וכו' סודרא עלויה כו' בעין ושמן קמיירי: (ה) ד"ה ואם אמר לו אם אמר לו לוה אעפ"כ כו' והד"א:

תורה אור השלם

א) וְזֶה דְּבַר הַשְּׁמִטָּה שָׁמוֹט כָּל בַּעַל מַשֵּׁה יָדוֹ אֲשֶׁר יַשֶּׁה בְּרֵעֵהוּ לֹא יִגֹּשׂ אֶת רֵעֵהוּ וְאֶת אָחִיו כִּי קָרָא שְׁמִטָּה לַיָי: [דברים טו, ב]

ליקוטי רש"י

ניפרום סודרא. קל הוא ואינו מכבד ושנוי [בעלמא הוא]. אתי לידי סחיטה. שטופה במים. נכסייה בנבתמא. כסוי של עץ העשוי לכדין. זימנין דמיפסק. שצריך לקושרו שלא יפול לכדך וזמנין דמפסק בהכלוכה ואתי למקטריה וקשר העשוי להתקיים אב מלאכה הוא. לא מספקין. משום שיר [ביצה ל.]. כגון לשמחה ולשיר ובגמרא מפרש גזרה שמא יתקן כלי שיר דקא עביד מנא [שם לו:]. אפומא דלחייא. לחי המתיר מבוי בשבת. דילמא מיגנדר ליה חפץ. מתגלגל החפץ מידו לחוץ. ואתי לאיתויי. מתוך שאינו במבוי מקורה להכיר שזה רשות הרבים וזה רשות היחיד ומביאו. ולא אמרינן להו ולא מידי. ואף על גב דעברן אדרבנן דאמור לא ליתיב ואינהו יתבן. הנח לישראל. בדבר שהרגילו בו ולא יחזרו בהם [שם ל.]. מוטב שיהו שוגגין. שאינם סבורים שיש איסור בדבר [רשב"ם ב"ב ס:]. ואל יהו מזידין. לעבור כשידעו ולא ינימו בכך. הני מילי. דהנח להם לישראל. בדרבנן. היכא דארגילו למעבר אדרבנן כי הנך דמטפחין והנך דיתבן אפומא דלחיא. תוספת דיום הכפורים. שצריך להתחיל ולהתענות מבעוד יום דאורייתא היא דנפקא לן (יומא פא:) מועניתם את נפשותיכם בתשעה. דקאכלי ושתו עד שתחשך. גרס ולא גרס משתכה [ביצה שם]. המחזיר חוב בשביעית. בזמן שהשביעית נוהגת ועברה עליו שביעית ואח"כ החזירו ולא שהחזירו בשביעית עצמה דא"כ לא הוה צריך למימר משמט אני דקי"ל אין שביעית משמטת אלא בסופה. יאמר לו. צריך המלוה שיאמר לו משמט אני. ואם אמר לו אע"פ כן. אני רוצה להחזירו לך. שנאמר וזה דבר השמטה. צריך לומר דיבור של שמיטה [גיטין לז:]. פסחו בשבת. ליכא למימר ביום טוב דאין פסח קרב ביום טוב וחגיגה ליכא למימר בשבת [פסחים סו.]. הלכה כסתם משנה. רבי הוא סדר המשנה וכשראה דברי חכם וישרו בעיניו שנאן סתם ולא הזכיר שם אומרו עליהן כדי שלא יהו שנויה מפי יחיד ונראין כאילו נשנו מפי המרובים ויעשו כמותן [ביצה ב:]. לא מקדישין. הקדשות. ולא מעריכין. ערכי עלי ונותן כפי שנים כמו שכתוב בפרשת ערכין (ויקרא כז). ולא מחרימין. הרי בהמה זו חרם וסתם חרמים לבדק הבית [שם לו:]. לא מקדישין ולא מעריכין וכו'. [גזירה] משום מקח וממכר דלמקח וממכר דמו שמוציא מרשותו ומקח וממכר אסור מן המקרא דכתיב ממצוא חפצך ודבר דבר (ישעיה נח) אי נמי מקח וממכר אתי לידי כתיבה שטרי מכירה ואם תאמר הויא לה גזרה לגזרה כולה חדא גזרה היא [שם לז.]. ולא מגביהין תרומות ומעשרות. איסור שבות דרבנן היא כדתנן במשילין (ביצה לו.) אלו הן משום שבות של מלוה אין מגביהין תרומות ומעשרות דמיחזי כמתקן [גיטין נד.]. בחובות שקבוע להן זמן. לכו ביום שפיר דמי דהואיל ונשחטין היום יכול להקדישן היום [פסחים סו:].

נִיפְרוֹס סוּדָרָא – If you will suggest that **they spread a kerchief** over the bucket, אָתֵי לִידֵי סְחִיטָה – the kerchief may become soaked with the water and **one might come to** perform the forbidden act of **squeezing.**[1] נְכַסְיֵיהּ בְּנַכְתְּמָא – If you will suggest that **they cover [the bucket] with a lid,**[2] זִימְנִין דְּמִיפְּסֵק וְאָתֵי לְמִקְטְרֵיהּ – there are **times when [the cord]** attaching the lid to the bucket[3] **breaks and one might come to tie it.**[4] הִלְכָּךְ לֹא אֶפְשָׁר – **Therefore, it is not possible** to deviate, and the women may carry in the normal manner.

The Gemara presents a third exchange between Rava bar Rav Chanan and Abaye:

וְאָמַר לֵיהּ רָבָא בַּר רַב חָנָן לְאַבַּיֵי – **And Rava bar Rav Chanan said to Abaye:** תְּנַן – **We learned in a Mishnah:**[5] לֹא מְסַפְּקִין וְלֹא מְטַפְּחִין וְלֹא מְרַקְּדִין בְּיוֹם טוֹב – WE MAY NOT CLAP HANDS, NOR BEAT CHESTS[6] NOR DANCE ON YOM TOV.[7] וְקָא חָזֵינַן דְּעָבְדִין – **But we see [that people] do** these things, וְלָא אָמְרִינַן לְהוּ וְלָא מִידֵּי – **and** yet **we tell them no** words of rebuke! – ? –

Abaye responds by showing that the lack of protest against a common practice does not necessarily indicate that the practice is permitted:

וּלְטַעְמִיךְ – **And according to your reasoning,** which postulates that it is incumbent upon the Rabbis to protest any violation of the law, how do you explain our lack of protest against non-compliance with הָא דְּאָמַר רָבָא – **that which Rava**[8] **said:** לֹא לֵיתִיב אִינִישׁ אַפּוּמָא דְלֶחְיָיא – **A person may not sit at the edge of** an alleyway by the ***lechi*** on the Sabbath,[9] דִּילְמָא מִיגַּנְדַּר לֵיהּ חֵפֶץ – because **an object might roll** away **from him** into the main thoroughfare, וְאָתֵי לְאַיְתוּיֵי – **and he might come to carry** it back?[10] וְהָא קָא חָזֵינַן נַמֵּי דְּמוֹתְבֵי חַצְבֵי – **Yet we still**[11] **see [women] place their buckets** וְיָתְבָן אַפּוּמָא דִּמְבוֹאָה – **and sit** on them **at the edge of the alleyway,** וְלָא אָמְרִינַן לְהוּ וְלָא מִידֵּי – **and we tell them no** words of rebuke![12]

Abaye now explains why we do not protest in both instances:

אֶלָּא הַנַּח לְיִשְׂרָאֵל – **Rather, let the Jews** continue in their practice since they will not change their ways, even if rebuked.[13] מוּטָב שֶׁיְּהוּ שׁוֹגְגִין וְאַל יְהוּ מְזִידִין – **It is preferable that they be unintentional [violators], and not be deliberate [violators].**[14]

The Gemara qualifies this principle:

סְבוּר מִינָּהּ הָנֵי מִילֵּי – **They thought**[15] that **these words** – that we should refrain from rebuking someone who will not listen – apply only בִּדְרַבָּנָן – **with** regard to **Rabbinic** law;[16] אֲבָל בִּדְאוֹרַיְיתָא לֹא – **but with** regard to **Biblical** law, it is **not** so; i.e. we must rebuke violators of Biblical law in all instances. וְלָא הִיא – **But this is not** correct. לֹא שְׁנָא בִּדְרַבָּנָן וְלֹא שְׁנָא בִּדְאוֹרַיְיתָא – **There is no difference between Rabbinic and Biblical** law; in both cases we do not rebuke violators who will not listen. דְּהָא תּוֹסֶפֶת דְּיוֹם הַכִּפּוּרִים דְּאוֹרַיְיתָא הִיא – This can be proven, **for the extension of** the **Yom Kippur** fast is required according to **Biblical** law.[17] וְקָא חָזֵינַן לְהוּ דְּקָאָכְלֵי וְשָׁתוּ עַד שֶׁתֶּחְשַׁךְ

NOTES

1. Squeezing out a wet cloth involves the Biblical labor of מְלַבֵּן, *whitening* (i.e. cleaning), because the water cleans the cloth as it passes through it.

According to our version of *Rashi's* text (cf. *Hagahos HaBach*), it states that using a kerchief is an acceptable deviation if one covers dry goods (e.g. fruit) with it. This implies that the *melachah* of מְלַבֵּן, *whitening,* applies to all liquids – even those other than water (e.g. wine or oil). *Tosafos,* however, maintain that it does not apply to such liquids, since they do not clean effectively (see *Maharsha* and *Shabbos Shel Mi;* see *Tosafos* to 111a ד״ה האי at length).

2. A נַכְתְּמָא is a wooden lid used for buckets (*Rashi* to *Beitzah* 30a).

3. Since a lid is required by halachah, they will surely tie it to the bucket (*Rashi*).

4. The knot would be a permanent one, which is Biblically forbidden (*Rashi*).

5. *Beitzah* 36b.

6. *Rashi.* However, *Rashi* to *Beitzah* (30a, 36b) translates מְסַפְּקִין as *slapping one's thigh,* and מְטַפְּחִין as *clapping.* [The Gemara in *Moed Katan* 27b (cited by *Rashash*) relates ספד (similar to ספק) to the chest and טפח to the hand.]

It is forbidden to clap hands or beat one's chest as an expression of mourning [on Yom Tov] (*Rashi*). In fact, this is forbidden on Chol HaMoed as well (*Moed Katan* 28b). When the Mishnah states that these activities are prohibited on Yom Tov, it does not necessarily mean that they are all permitted on Chol HaMoed (see *Tosafos* and *Maginei Shlomo*).

Clapping and slapping are [also] forbidden as accompaniment to song, lest one come to adjust a musical instrument (see *Rashi* to *Beitzah* 30a). This would be forbidden under the *melachah* of מַכֶּה בְּפַטִּישׁ, *striking the final blow.* [In such circumstances, the prohibition applies only on Yom Tov (see *Tosafos*).]

7. Dancing is forbidden lest it lead to the adjustment of a musical instrument (*Rashi,* from *Beitzah* 36b; see previous note).

8. [A marginal gloss emends the text to read רַבָּה, *Rabbah.* See, however, the marginal gloss to *Beitzah* 30a ד״ה צ״ל רבה.]

9. According to Rabbinic decree, one may not carry in an alleyway which has three walls unless an adjustment is made at the open fourth side. This adjustment may take the form of a לֶחִי, *sidepost,* or קוֹרָה, *crossbeam.*

10. Since the alleyway has no roof, it is not easy to tell where the alleyway [private domain] ends and the main thoroughfare [public domain] begins (*Rashi* to *Beitzah* 30a). Therefore, someone might unwittingly bring an article from outside the alleyway to inside it, thus performing the *melachah* of הוֹצָאָה, *transferring.* Even if the article was within four *amos* of the *mavoi* [and hence he would not be liable for transporting it four *amos* in a public domain], he would still have committed a Biblical violation (*Rashi,* as explained by *Menachem Meishiv Nefesh*).

11. The text should read נָשֵׁי, *women* [as in *Beitzah* 30a], instead of נַמִּי, *still* (*Hagahos HaBach*)

12. The commentators ask why Abaye mentioned this case. What point does it make that was not already made by the previous one (of clapping etc. on Yom Tov)? *Ritva* (*MHK* ed.) answers that Abaye sought to refute Rava bar Rav Chanan's premise that it is obligatory to protest all forms of wrongdoing. The fact that the Rabbis do not protest clapping on Yom Tov does not necessarily disprove this premise, because one could argue that the prohibition against clapping no longer applied in their times [when it was less common for people to adjust musical instruments (see note 6; see also *Tosafos* to *Beitzah* 30a ד״ה תנן)]. The prohibition against sitting at the entrance of a *mavoi,* however, was as relevant in their time as when it was promulgated. Hence, the fact that *this* behavior is not protested does prove that there are instances in which protest is inappropriate.

13. A practice to which the masses are accustomed is difficult to stop (*Ritva MHK* ed.; see *Rashi* to *Beitzah* 30a ד״ה הנח להם).

14. Since they will not abstain from sitting at the entrance of the alleyway even when told of the prohibition, it is better not to rebuke them. It is preferable to let them do so under the erroneous impression that what they are doing is permitted than for them to do so knowing it is prohibited; a deliberate violation of the law is worse than a violation due to error. [See note 19 for further elaboration on this rule.]

15. [This is indeed the Gemara's initial assumption in *Beitzah* 30a.]

16. I.e. in a case where people had become accustomed to violate a Rabbinic law, such as the prohibitions against clapping and sitting at the entrance of a *mavoi* (*Rashi* to *Beitzah* 30a).

17. The Torah states (*Leviticus* 23:32): *You shall afflict yourselves on the ninth of the month.* But Yom Kippur actually begins on the tenth day of Tishrei. This verse is therefore understood to require the fast to be started while it is still the day of the ninth, before nightfall of the tenth (see *Yoma* 81b). This extension need be only of minimal duration (*Ran* to *Beitzah* folio 16b סד״ה תנן; *Shulchan Aruch, Orach Chaim* 608:1; see, however, *Mishnah Berurah* ibid. end of §2; cf. *Tosafos* to *Beitzah* 30a ד״ה דהא).

ניפרום סודרא אתי לידי סחיטה נכסייה בנכתמא זימנין דמיפסק ואתי למקטריה הלכך לא אפשר וא"ל רבא בר רב חנן לאביי תנן לא מספקין ולא מטפחין ולא מרקדין ביו"ט וקא חזינן דעבדין ולא אמרינן להו ולא מידי ולטעמיך הא דאמר רבא לא ליתיב איניש אפומא דלחייא דילמא מיגנדר ליה חפץ ואתי לאיתויי והא קא חזינן (א) נמי דמותבי חצבי ויתבן אפומא דמבואה ולא אמרינן להו ולא מידי אלא הנח לישראל מוטב שיהו שוגגין ואל יהו מזידין סבור מינה הנ"מ בדרבנן אבל בדאורייתא לא ולא היא ל"ש בדרבנן ול"ש בדאורייתא דהא תוספת דיוה"כ דאורייתא היא וקא חזינן להו דקאכלי ושתו עד שתחשך ולא אמרי' להו ולא מידי: וכן אשה מחבירתה ככרות: בשבת הוא דאסיר אבל בחול שפיר דמי לימא מתני' דלא כהלל דתנן וכן היה הלל אומר לא תלוה אשה ככר לחבירתה עד שתעשינה דמים שמא יוקרו חטין ונמצאו באות לידי רבית אפילו תימא הלל הא באתרא דקיץ דמיה הא באתרא דלא קיץ דמיה: ואם אינו מאמינו: איתמר הלוואת יו"ט רב יוסף אמר לא ניתנה ליתבע ורבה אמר ניתנה ליתבע רב יוסף אמר לא ניתנה ליתבע דאי אמרת ניתנה ליתבע אתי למיכתב רבה אמר ניתנה ליתבע דאי אמרת לא ניתנה ליתבע לא יהיב ליה ואתי לאימנועי משמחת יו"ט תנן אם אינו מאמינו מניח טליתו אצלו אי אמרת בשלמא לא ניתנה ליתבע משום הכי מניח טליתו אצלו ועושה עמו חשבון לאחר שבת אלא אי אמרת ניתנה ליתבע אמאי מניח טליתו אצלו ליתן ליה ולתבעיה אמר לא בעינא דליקום בדינא ודיינא מתיב רב אידי בר אבין השוחט את הפרה וחילקה בראש השנה אם היה חדש מעובר משמט ואם לאו אינו משמט ואי לא ניתנה ליתבע מאי משמט שאני התם דאיגלאי מילתא דחול הוא ת"ש מסיפא אם לאו אינו משמט אי אמרת בשלמא ניתנה ליתבע היינו דקתני אינו משמט אלא אי אמרת לא ניתנה ליתבע (ב) אמאי אינו משמט דאי יהיב ליה שקיל מכלל דרישא אי יהיב ליה לא שקיל רישא צריך למימר ליה משמט אני כדתנן המחזיר חוב בשביעית יאמר לו משמט אני ואם אמר לו אעפ"כ יקבל ממנו משום שנאמר וזה דבר השמטה רב אויא שקיל משכונא רבה בר עולא מערים איערומי: וכן ערב פסח: א"ר יוחנן מקדיש אדם פסחו בשבת וחגיגתו ביו"ט נימא מסייע ליה וכן ערב פסח בירושלים שחל להיות בשבת מניח טליתו אצלו ונוטל את פסחו ועושה עמו חשבון לאחר יו"ט הכא במאי עסקינן בממנה אחרים עמו על פסחו דמעיקרא מיקדש וקאי והא אנן תנן אין נמנין על הבהמה בתחילה ביו"ט שאני הכא כיון דרגיל אצלו כמאן דאימני ביה מעיקרא דמי והא תני רבי הושעיא הולך אדם אצל רועה הרגיל אצלו ונותן לו טלה לפסחו ומקדישו ויוצא בו התם נמי כיון דרגיל אצלו אקדושי (ג) ליה מעיקרא והא מקדיש קתני הקדש עילוי מדרבנן ומי אמר ר' יוחנן הכי והא אמר ר' יוחנן הלכה כסתם משנה ותנן לא מקדישין ולא מעריכין ולא מחרימין ולא מגביהין תרומות ומעשרות כל אלו ביו"ט אמרו ק"ו בשבת לא קשיא כאן בחובות שקבוע להן זמן כאן בחובות שאין קבוע להן זמן: **מתני'** מונה אדם את אורחיו ואת פרפרותיו מפיו אבל לא מן הכתב ומפיס אדם עם בניו ועם בני ביתו על השולחן ובלבד שלא יתכוין לעשות מנה גדולה כנגד מנה קטנה ומטילין חלשין על הקדשים ביו"ט אבל לא על המנות: **גמ'**

רש"י

בנכתמא. כיסוי: זימנין דמיפסק כו'. כיון דמלכלך ליה כיסוי קטר ליה בכל וזימנין דמיפסק ואתי למקטריה והוא קשר של קיימא דאסור מדאורייתא: ואתי לידי סחיטה. ודקאמר במסכת ביצה (ד) [התם] בדבר יבש קא מיירי: ניפרום סודרא עלויה כו'. אין מספקין. כף אל כף משום אבל: מטפחין. על הלב: מרקדין. לשמחה וטעמא מפרש במסכת ביצה שמא יתקן כלי שיר: אפומא דלחייא. לפי שאין ניכר כל כך בין מבוי לרה"ר: ואתי לאתויי. חפץ המתגלגל תוך ד' אמות: ומגנדר מלבישן ומייתין ליה ל"ג: בשבת הוא דאסור. לומר הלוני משום מכתב: הא בחול שרי. ולא חיישינן לרבית ואף על גב דבלשון הלואה קאמר ליה: באתרא דקייץ דמייהו. דבכרות לא אתי לידי רבית שהרי יוקירו יתן דמיהן: לא ניתנה ליתבע. בב"ד מזקקין לה לעולם: בדינא ודיינא. לא לבא לדין ולא לברור דיין ולהטריח את עצמו: השוחט את הפרה וחילקה בראש השנה. של מוצאי שביעית ללוקחים והקפה וקיי"ל שביעית משמטת בסופה דכתיב מקץ: אם היה חדש. אלול מעובר ועשו ראש השנה שני ימים משמט דיום טוב ראשון של סוף שביעית היה ונמצאת זו הלואה שביעית ואם לאו הויא לה הלואה מוצאי שביעית ואינו משמטו: ל"ג אי אמרת בשלמא כו' ה"ג ואם לא ניתנה ליתבע מאי משמט. הואיל ואין ב"ד מזקקין לכופו שמוטה היא ועומדת: דחול הוא. שהרי חדש מעובר ולא הוי יו"ט עד למחר הלכך אי לאו דשביעית הוא הוה גבי: ואם לאו אינו משמט. אלמא ניתנה ליתבע ומשני מאי אינו משמט דאי יהיב ליה שקיל: מכלל דרישא אי יהיב ליה לא שקיל. בתמיה: רישא. דהלואה שביעית היא אי נמי יהיב ליה לוה צריך למימר ליה מלוה משמט אני: (ה) ואם אמר. לוה אע"פ כן אני חפץ שיקבל ממנו: דבר השמטה. אפילו מקבל הוא צריך לזכור לו שמיטה בדבורו: שקיל משכונא. בשעת הלואה מהלואות יו"ט: מערים איערומי. לאחר יו"ט לוקח ממנו שום חפץ ומעכבו: פסחו בשבת. אם חל י"ד בשבת: וחגיגתו ביו"ט. ביום הקרבתה מותר להקדיש ולא"ג דתנן אלו הן משום שבות אין מקדישין הני כיון דהקרבתן דוחה קדושתן דוחה: בממנה אחרים עמו. כדכתיב (שמות יב) במכסת נפשות: על פסחו. שהיה קדוש ועומד מאתמול: אקדושי. מקדיש ליה רועה מע"ש שהרי יודע שזה סומך עליו: עילוי. מעלה בעלמא שיקדישו בעלים: הא. דקתני אין מקדישין בחובות שאין קבוע להן זמן קאי שאין הקרבתן דוחה שבת: מתני' פרפרותיו. מיני מעדנים: אבל לא מן הכתב. אם כתב מע"ש כך וכך אורחים פלוני ופלוני זמנתי כדי שלא ישכחם לא יקרא באותו כתב בשבת ובגמ' מפרש טעמא: מפיס. לשון פיים מטיל פיים לחלק מי מגיע כל מנה ומנה: ובלבד שלא יתכוין לעשות כו'. שיהו המנות שוות ולא תהא אחת גדולה ואחת קטנה לזכות בגדולה הזוכה ע"פ הגורל והמתחייב ע"פ הגורל לקטנה יטלנה ובגמ' מפרש טעמא: חלשים. גורלות: על הקדשים. בין הכהנים: אבל לא על המנות. בגמרא מפרש:

תוספות

ניפרום סודרא עליה אתי לאסחוטיה. מכאן מייתי ר"ת ראיה דביין ושמן לא שייכא סחיטה לעיל בשלהי שמונה שרצים (דף קיא. בד"ה האי מסוכריתא) פירש"י: לא מספקין ולא מטפחין. לא כפי' הקונטרס משום דא"כ מאי איריא ביו"ט אפי' בחול המועד נמי אסור כדתנן במועד קטן פרק בתרא (דף כח:) נשים במועד מענות אבל לא מטפחות אלא נראה לרבי משום שמחה רגילין לספק ולטפח בהשמעת קול ואסור שמא יתקן כלי שיר כדמפרש בהמוצא תפילין (עירובין דף קד.): וכן היה הלל אומר. כרבנן דפליגי עליה באיזהו נשך (ב"מ ד' עה.) וקי"ל:

רבה אמר ניתנה ליתבע. הלכה כרבה לגבי רב יוסף: ורב אויא ורבה בר עולא מחמרי אנפשייהו כ"ה בס"ל:

דאי אמרת ניתנה ליתבע אתי למיכתב. אע"פ שמזכיר לו לשון שאלה:

דאיגלאי מילתא דבחול הויא. ורב יוסף לא מיירי אלא בשבת ויו"ט ודאי:

והא אנן תנן אין נימנין כו'. פירש ה"ר פורת בשם רבינו שמואל דל"ג ליה חדא דמה שייך להקשות מנמנין של רשות של מלוה ועוד דמפרש התם בביצה פרק אין צדין (דף כח.) מאי אין נמנין אין פוסקין דמים בתחילה לבהמה ביו"ט הרי אני עמך בסלע הריני עמך בשתים אבל אומר לו הריני עמך לשליש ולרביע: ולמ"ד

עין משפט נר מצוה

ד א מיי' פכ"ג מהלכות שבת הלכה ה סמג לאוין עה טוש"ע או"ח סימן שלט סעיף ג וסימן תקכד סעיף א:
ה ב מיי' פ"א מהלכות שביתת עשור הלכה ז סמג לאוין סה וסט טור ושו"ע או"ח סימן תרח סעיף ב:
ו ג מיי' פ"י מהלכות מלוה ולוה הלכה ב סמג לאוין קצג טוש"ע יו"ד סימן קסב סעיף א:
ז ד שם סעיף ג:
ח ה מיי' פ"ד מהלכות י"ט הלכה כה טוש"ע או"ח סימן תקכה סעיף א:
ט ו מיי' פ"ט מהלכות שמיטה ויובל הלכה ה סמג עשין קמט:
י ז מיי' שם הלכה כח סמג לאוין רעא טור ושו"ע חו"מ סימן סז סעיף לו:
יא ח מיי' פכ"ג מהלכו' שבת הלכה יד ופ"א מהלכות קרבן פסח הל"ט סמג עשין רכג:
יב ט מיי' פ"ד מהלכות י"ט הלכה יט סמג לאוין עה טוש"ע או"ח סימן תק סעיף א:
יג י מיי' פכ"ג מהלכות שבת הלכה יד סמג לאוין סה ועה טור ש"ע או"ח סימן שלט סעיף ד וסימן תקכד סעיף א:

רבינו חננאל

להא. דא"ל תנן לא מספקין ולא מרקדין ולא מטפחין. בגדרא. ופשוטה היא. ומיפרשא נמי בגמ' דהמביא כדי יין במס' יו"ט וכן שואלת אשה מחברתה ככרות. ודייקינן מינה בשבת הוא דאסור מכלל דבחול שרי מתניתין דלא כהלל כו' ומסקינן בה אפילו תימא כהלל באתרא דקייצי דמי. ואם אינו מאמינו מניח טליתו אצלו ועושה עמו חשבון לאחר שבת. אתמר הלואת יו"ט רב יוסף אמר לא נתנה ליתבע רבא אמר ניתנה ליתבע ואתינן למיגמר מן מתניתין תנן ואם אינו מאמינו מניח טליתו אצלו כו' ולא גמרינן מינה דלא מיפרשא בהדיא כחד מינייהו ומותבינן לרב יוסף מהא דתנן השוחט את הפרה וחילקה בראש השנה אם היה חדש מעובר משמט. פי' אם היה אלול מעובר נמצא יום לקיחתו חלק מן הפרה יום חול שר"ה מחר הוא וכיון שנושה בו דמי בשר הפרה שלקח מאתמול דכיון שנכנסה שנה שביעית משמטת לדברי רבא ניחא כי נתנה ליתבע ומלוה נושה בו וכשנכנסת שביעית משמטת אלא לרב יוסף דאמר לא נתנה ליתבע אמאי צריך למיתנא משמטת בלאו הכי פטור הוא מלשלם. ואפילו בשאר שני שבוע דהא לא ניתנה ליתבע. ופריק רב יוסף שאני התם דכיון דאיגלאי מלתא דחול היא (ניתנה ליתבע דהא מלוה דחול היא) ואנן לא קאימנא אלא הלואת יו"ט ואסיקנא למשמע מסיפא ואם לאו אינו משמט לרבא דאמר ניתנה ליתבע דתובעו ונפרע ממנו [ניחא] אלא לרב יוסף דאמר לא ניתנה ליתבע קשיא כיון דתני אינו משמט הלא משמע דתובעו ונפרע ממנו ואינו יכול לומר לו כי השביעית השמיטתו ופריק רב יוסף לעולם לא נתנה ליתבע והמלוה אינו יכול ליתבע אלא אם יביא הלוה ויפרענו יקבל ואינו צריך לומר משמט אני. ואקשינן עליה מכלל דרישא אי יהיב ליה מעצמו לא שקיל. ופריק רב יוסף ואמר רישא אם מחזיר לו צריך שיאמר לו משמט אני. דהא נושה בו מלוה. אבל ספק שאינו נושה בו מלוה אם יבא לחשבון אינו צריך לומר לו משמט אני אלא יקבל כדתנן המחזיר חוב בשביעית צריך שיאמר משמט אני. ואם אמר לו אעפ"כ יקבל ממנו משום שנאמר וזה דבר השמטה. ומפורש ענין זה בפ' השולח גט לאשתו. וראינו רבותינו שהיו

מסורת הש"ס

א) ביצה ל. וד' לו:, ב) [ל"ל רבה], ג) לעיל קמח. ביצה ל., ד) [ב"ב ס: ועי' תוס' לעיל נה. ד"ה ואע"ג ותוס' ב"ב ס: ד"ה מוטב ותוס' ע"ז ד. ד"ה שהי'], ה) [ביצה ל. ע"ש], ו) ב"מ עה., ז) [גי' רב אלפס והרא"ש ורבא], ח) שביעית פ"י משנה ב, ט) ג"ז שם [מ"ח גיטין לז:], י) נ"א רבא, כ) פסחים סו: [ועי' תוספות חגיגה ח. ד"ה משום ותוס' בכורות נח. ד"ה ואי], ל) ביצה מ., מ) [לעיל מו. וש"נ], נ) פסחים סו: ביצה לו:, ס) [עיין תוס' לקמן קמט:].

הגהות הב"ח

(א) גמ' והא קא חזינן נשי דמותבי אלבייהו וכו' הנח להן לישראל: (ב) שם מאי אינו משמט דאי יהיב ליה: (ג) שם אקדושי מקדיש ליה מעיקרא: (ד) רש"י ד"ה ואתא לידי סחיטה וכו' סודרא עלויה כו' ביין ושמן קמיירי: (ה) ד"ה רישא וכו' משמט אני ואם אמר לו הלוה אעפ"כ כצ"ל והד"א:

תורה אור השלם

א) וְזֶה דְּבַר הַשְּׁמִטָּה שָׁמוֹט כָּל בַּעַל מַשֵּׁה יָדוֹ אֲשֶׁר יַשֶּׁה בְּרֵעֵהוּ לֹא יִגֹּשׂ אֶת רֵעֵהוּ וְאֶת אָחִיו כִּי קָרָא שְׁמִטָּה לַייָ: [דברים טו, ב]

ליקוטי רש"י

ניפרום סודרא. קל הוא ואינו מכביד ושנוי [בעלמא הוא ולהצניע]. אתי לידי סחיטה. שנשרה במים. נכסייה בנכתמא. כסוי של עץ העשוי לכדין. זימנין דמיפסק. שצריך לקושרו שלא יפול בדרך חיישינן דמפסיק בהליכתו ואתי למקטריה וקשר העשוי להתקיין אב מלאכה הוא. לא מטפחין. משום שיר או משום אבל. מטפחין. ידיו זו לזו. מספקין. כף על ירך. מרקדין. ברגל וכולם נאסרו משום שבות גזרה שמא יתקן כלי שיר בפרק משילין (ביצה לו:) [ביצה ל.]. ברגל וכולן לשמחה ולשיר ובגמרא מפרש גזרה שמא יתקן כנגדן כלי שיר דקא עביד מנא [שם לו:]. אפומא דלחייא. לחי המתיר במבוי בשבת. דילמא מיגנדר ליה חפץ. ברשות הרבים חוץ ללחי. ואתי לאיתויי. מתוך שאינו במבוי מקורה להכיר שזה רשות הרבים וזה רשות היחיד ומביאו. ולא אמרינן להו ולא מידי. ואף על גב דעברן אדרבנן דאסור לא לימיב ואינהו יתבן. הנח לישראל. בדבר שהרגילו בו ולא יחזרו בהם [שם ל.]. מוטב שיהו שוגגין. שאינם סבורים שיש איסור בדבר [רשב"ם ב"ב ס:]. ואל יהו מזידין. לעבור כשידעו ולא יניחו בכך. הני מילי. דהנח להם לישראל. בדרבנן. היכא דלרגילו למעבר אדרבנן כי הנך דמטפחין והנך דיתבן אפומא דלחיא. תוספת דיום הכפורים. שצריך להתחיל ולהתענות מבעוד יום דאורייתא היא דנפקא לן (יומא פא:) מועניתם את נפשותיכם בתשעה. דקאכלי ושתו עד שתחשך. גרם ולא גרם משחשכה [ביצה שם]. המחזיר חוב בשביעית. בזמן שהשביעית נוהגת ועברה עליו שביעית ואח"כ המחזירו ולא שהחזירו בשביעית עצמה דא"כ לא הוה צריך למימר משמט אני דקי"ל אין שביעית משמטת אלא בסופה. יאמר לו. צריך המלוה שיאמר לו משמט אני. ואם אמר לו אע"פ כן. אני רוצה להחזירו לך. שנאמר וזה דבר השמטה. צריך לומר דיבור של שמיטה [גיטין לז:]. פסחו בשבת. ליכא למימר ביום טוב דאין פסח קרב ביום טוב וחגיגה ליכא למימר בשבת [פסחים סו:]. הלכה כסתם משנה. רבי הוא סדר המשנה וכשראה דברי חכם וישרו בעיניו שנאן סתם ולא הזכיר שם אומרו עליהן כדי שלא יהו שנויה מפי יחיד ונראין כאילו נשנו מפי המרובים ויעשו כמותן [ביצה ב:]. לא מקדישין. הקדשות. ולא מעריכין. ערכך עלי ונותן כפי שנים כמו שכתוב בפרשת ערכין (ויקרא כז). ולא מחרימין. הרי בהמה זו חרם וסתם חרמים לבדק הבית [שם לו:]. לא מקדישין ולא מעריכין וכו'. [גזירה] משום מקח וממכר דלמקח וממכר דמו שמוציא מרשותו לרשות הקדש ומקח וממכר אסור מן המקרא דכתיב ממצוא חפצך ודבר דבר (ישעיה נח) אי נמי מקח וממכר אתי לידי כתיבה שטרי מכירה ואם מאמר הוא לא גזרה לגזרה כולה חדא גזרה היא [שם לז.]. ולא מגביהין תרומות ומעשרות. איסור שבות דרבנן היא כדתנן במשילין (ביצה לו.) אלו הן משום שבות של מצוה אין מגביהין תרומות ומעשרות דמיחזי כמתקן [גיטין נד.]. בחובות שקבוע להן זמן. לגו ביום שפיר דמי דהואיל ונשחטין היום יכול להקדישן היום [פסחים סו:].

– **Yet we see [people] eat and drink until dark**[18] without starting their fast early, וְלָא אַמְרִינַן לְהוּ וְלָא מִידִי – **and we do not say to them any** words of rebuke! We see from this that even with regard to Biblical law we do not rebuke people when they will not listen.[19]

The Gemara discusses the next ruling in our Mishnah:

וְכֵן אִשָּׁה מֵחֲבֵירְתָּהּ כִּכָּרוֹת – IN THE SAME MANNER, A WOMAN may borrow LOAVES of bread FROM HER FRIEND [provided that she does not say, *"halveini"*]. בְּשַׁבָּת הוּא דַּאֲסִיר – The Mishnah implies that **it is on the Sabbath that it is forbidden** to borrow loaves if she says, *"halveini,"* אֲבָל בְּחוֹל – **but on weekdays** שַׁפִּיר דָּמֵי – **it is all right.**[20] לֵימָא מַתְנִיתִין דְּלֹא כְּהִלֵּל – **Shall we say that our Mishnah does not follow Hillel?** דִּתְנַן – **For we have learned in a Mishnah:** וְכֵן הָיָה הִלֵּל אוֹמֵר – AND SIMILARLY HILLEL USED TO SAY: לֹא תַּלְוֶה אִשָּׁה כִּכָּר לַחֲבֵירְתָּהּ – A WOMAN MAY NOT LEND A LOAF TO HER FRIEND to be repaid with another loaf עַד שֶׁתַּעֲשֶׂינָּה דָּמִים – UNLESS SHE ASSESSES ITS VALUE at the time of the loan. שֶׁמָּא יוּקְרוּ חִטִּין – For PERHAPS WHEAT WILL BECOME MORE EXPENSIVE, וְנִמְצְאוּ בָּאוֹת לִידֵי רִבִּית – AND as a result [THE PARTIES] WILL BE FOUND TO HAVE COME TO a violation of the laws of INTEREST.[21]

The Gemara reconciles our Mishnah with the view of Hillel:

אֲפִילוּ תֵּימָא הִלֵּל – **You can even say** that our Mishnah agrees with **Hillel.** הָא – **This** (i.e. our Mishnah, which permits lending loaves even without assessing their value) בְּאַתְרָא דְּקִיץ דְּמֵיהּ – refers **to a place where the price of [a loaf] is fixed;**[22] הָא – whereas **this** (i.e. Hillel's ruling, which prohibits lending loaves without monetary assessment) בְּאַתְרָא דְּלָא קִיץ דְּמֵיהּ – refers **to a place where the price of [a loaf] is not fixed.**

The Mishnah stated:

וְאִם אֵינוֹ מַאֲמִינוֹ – AND IF [THE LENDER] DOES NOT TRUST HIM, the borrower may leave his cloak with the lender and make a reckoning with him after the Sabbath.

The Gemara discusses whether a loan that was made in the permissible manner[23] on the Sabbath or Yom Tov is reclaimable in court:

אִיתְּמַר – **It was stated:** הַלְוָאַת יוֹם טוֹב – Regarding **a loan** made **on Yom Tov,**[24] רַב יוֹסֵף אָמַר – **Rav Yosef says:** לֹא נִיתְּנָה לִיתָּבַע – **It is not reclaimable** in court.[25] וְרַבָּה אָמַר –

NOTES

18. I.e. until the beginning of *bein hashemashos* (see *Ran* ibid. and *Beur Halachah* ibid. ד״ה עד). [Many Rishonim define *bein hashemashos* as the period between sunset and the appearance of stars (see *Mishnah Berurah* ibid. §2 and 261:23).]

The period of *bein hashemashos* is of questionable status. It is not clear whether it belongs to the day or to the night. As a rule, in matters of doubt regarding Biblical law, we follow the more stringent course. According to some authorities, this rule itself is of Biblical status. Hence, in their view, one is Biblically obligated to start the fast of Yom Kippur [proper] at the beginning of *bein hashemashos.* The extension required by the Torah thus begins a short time before *bein hashemashos* (*Ran* ibid. and *Shulchan Aruch* ibid.; cf. *Tosafos* ibid.; see also *Chasam Sofer*).

19. *Baal HaItur* maintains that this rule applies only to Biblical laws which are not explicitly stated in the Torah. When a law is explicitly stated, the Gemara's original qualification applies and one must rebuke a transgressor (cited by *Rashba* to *Beitzah* 30a, *Rosh* ibid., *Ran* ibid. and *Rama, Orach Chaim* 608:2; see, however, *Tosafos* above, 55a ד״ה ואע״ג; see also *Yad David* [*Basra*], *Chasam Sofer* and *Teshuvos Ksav Sofer, Orach Chaim* §57 ד״ה ובש״מ).

In addition, if there is any possibility that the violator might be affected by rebuke and mend his ways, we must rebuke him even for a Rabbinic prohibition (*Ritva MHK* ed. here; *Rif* and *Rosh* to *Beitzah* ibid.; *Tosafos* above, 55a; see note 13; see also *Mishnah Berurah* 608:3 with *Shaar HaTziyun*).

20. The Mishnah prohibits her from saying הַלְוִינִי, *halveini,* on the Sabbath out of fear that it may lead the lender to write a note, which would be a violation of the Sabbath laws. This implies that when writing is not forbidden (i.e. weekdays), she *may* say, *"halveini."*

21. *Bava Metzia* 75a. The Torah prohibits רִבִּית, prearranged interest payments on loans. The Rabbis extended this prohibition to various other situations, including סְאָה בִּסְאָה, "a *se'ah* for a *se'ah*" ("a bushel for a bushel") – a loan of a commodity for repayment of the same amount in kind. The Rabbis feared that in the time between the loan and the repayment the price of the produce might increase and the *se'ah* repaid would then be worth more than the *se'ah* lent, which would mean that the borrower could be paying interest to the lender. Of course, there is no question here of Biblical interest, because the interest was not prearranged; on the contrary, they arranged for the same amount to be returned – a *se'ah* for a *se'ah*. The Rabbis, though, forbade such a loan as part of their policy of forbidding *any* transaction that involves (or *may* involve) the payment to the lender of more than he lent. Since the value of the produce *may* increase by the time the borrower repays the lender, the Rabbis forbade the transaction. [One may, however, lend merchandise with the stipulation to be paid *money* in return. In such a case, there is no problem of interest, for even if the price of the commodity increases in the interim, the borrower repays only the original value.]

The extent of the Rabbinical prohibition of "a *se'ah* for a *se'ah*" is the subject of a dispute between Hillel and the Sages. Hillel holds that the prohibition applies even to small loans of food (e.g. loaves) to a neighbor, whereas the Sages maintain that it does not apply in such a case since people are generally not particular about price differences of such small amounts. The Gemara here notes that our Mishnah seems to follow the Sages, since it implies that a woman is permitted to borrow loaves from her friend on a weekday.

The following difficulty must be addressed: The Gemara draws an *inference* from our Mishnah to show that it contradicts Hillel ["on the Sabbath it is forbidden (if she says, *"halveini"*), but on a weekday it is permitted"]. Why did the Gemara not say that the Mishnah *itself* is at odds with Hillel's view, for it states, "a woman may borrow loaves from her friend [even on the Sabbath provided she does *not* say, *"halveini"*]. The Rishonim answer that in a case where the borrower does not say, *"halveini,"* one could argue that Hillel's ruling does not apply. Since such a loan is of only short duration (see 148a note 9), there is little chance of an increase in the price of wheat in the interim. It is only in a case of *halveini,* where the loan is for a substantial period, the wheat might appreciate and the repayment would thus constitute interest (*Ramban, Rashba* et al.).

[The Gemara poses a contradiction between our Mishnah and Hillel's rule only in the case of a woman lending loaves to her neighbor. Why did it not pose the very same contradiction regarding the Mishnah's first case of lending wine and oil? One answer given is that when one lends wine or oil, it is understood that the borrower could pay back money. Hence, there is no problem of interest, because if the price of wine or oil increases, the borrower will simply pay back its original value in money. In the case of loaves, however, the borrower is unlikely to pay back money, for since homemade loaves vary in size and weight, it is virtually impossible to recall their original value. Therefore, unless their value is assessed at the time of the loan (as Hillel suggests), the borrower is sure to pay back loaves. [The parties are assumedly not particular about the relative small difference in the loaves' size.] This could lead to interest if the price of wheat increases significantly (*Tos. R' Akiva Eiger,* based on *Rashba*).]

22. In a locale where the authorities set a fixed price for loaves of bread, that price is known. The parties to the loan are thus aware of the value of the borrowed loaves. Hence, even if no special assessment is made, Hillel would agree that the loan is permitted, because if the price of wheat increases, the borrower will pay the loaves' original value in money (*Rashba; Ran MHK* ed.; see *Rashi*).

23. I.e. the borrower said, *"hashileini,"* as opposed to *"halveini"* (see Gemara above, 148a).

24. The same applies to the Sabbath, as is evident from the continuation of the passage (*Shabbos Shel Mi;* cf. *Chasam Sofer*).

25. [Literally: it is not given to be claimed.] The courts will not get involved in the matter (*Rashi*). The lender's only recourse is to personally request payment from the borrower (see *Rashba, Ritva MHK* ed. and *Ran MHK* ed.; see, however, *Rabbeinu Chananel* and *Keren Orah*).

ניפרום סודרא אתי לידי סחיטה נכסייה בנכתמא זימנין דמיפסק ואתי למקטריה הלכך לא אפשר וא"ל רבא בר רב חנן לאביי תנן לא מספקין ולא מטפחין ולא מרקדין ביו"ט וקא חזינן דעבדין ולא אמרינן להו ולא מידי ולטעמיך הא דאמר רבא לא ליתיב איניש אפומא דלחייא דילמא מיגנדר ליה חפץ ואתי לאיתויי והא קא חזינן נמי דמותבי חצבי ויתבן אפומא דמבואה ולא אמרינן להו ולא מידי אלא הנח לישראל מוטב שיהו שוגגין ואל יהו מזידין סבור מינה הנ"מ בדרבנן אבל בדאורייתא לא ולא היא ל"ש בדרבנן ול"ש בדאורייתא דהא תוספת דיוה"כ דאורייתא היא וקא חזינן להו דאכלי ושתו עד שתחשך ולא אמרי' להו ולא מידי: וכן אשה מחבירתה ככרות: בשבת הוא דאסיר אבל בחול שפיר דמי לימא מתני' דלא כהלל דתנן וכן היה הלל אומר לא תלוה אשה ככר לחבירתה עד שתעשינה דמים שמא יוקרו חטין ונמצאו באות לידי רבית אפילו תימא הלל הא באתרא דקיץ דמיה הא באתרא דלא קייץ דמיה: ואם אינו מאמינו: איתמר הלוואת יו"ט רב יוסף אמר לא ניתנה ליתבע ורבה אמר ניתנה ליתבע רב יוסף אמר לא ניתנה ליתבע דאי אמרת ניתנה ליתבע אתי למיכתב רבה אמר ניתנה ליתבע דאי אמרת לא ניתנה ליתבע לא יהיב ליה ואתי לאימנועי משמחת יו"ט תנן אם אינו מאמינו מניח טליתו אצלו אי אמרת בשלמא לא ניתנה ליתבע משום הכי מניח טליתו אצלו ועושה עמו חשבון לאחר שבת אלא אי אמרת ניתנה ליתבע אמאי מניח טליתו אצלו ליתן ליה ולתבעיה אמר לא בעינא דליקום בדינא ודיינא מתיב רב אידי בר אבין השוחט את הפרה וחילקה בראש השנה אם היה חדש מעובר משמט ואם לאו אינו משמט ואי לא ניתנה ליתבע מאי משמט שאני התם דאיגלאי מילתא דחול הוא ת"ש מסיפא אם לאו אינו משמט אי אמרת בשלמא ניתנה ליתבע היינו דקתני אינו משמט אלא אי אמרת לא ניתנה ליתבע (ב) אמאי אינו משמט דאי יהיב ליה שקיל מכלל דרישא אי יהיב ליה לא שקיל רישא צריך למימר ליה משמט אני סיפא לא צריך למימר ליה משמט אני כדתנן המחזיר חוב בשביעית יאמר לו משמט אני ואם אמר לו אעפ"כ יקבל ממנו משום שנאמר וזה דבר השמטה רב אויא שקיל משכונא רבה בר עולא מערים איערומי: וכן ערב פסח: א"ר יוחנן מקדיש אדם פסחו בשבת וחגיגתו ביו"ט נימא מסייע ליה וכן ערב פסח בירושלים שחל להיות בשבת מניח טליתו אצלו ונוטל את פסחו ועושה עמו חשבון לאחר יו"ט הכא במאי עסקינן בממנה אחרים עמו על פסחו דמעיקרא מיקדש וקאי והא אנן תנן אין נמנין על הבהמה בתחילה ביו"ט שאני הכא כיון דרגיל אצלו כמאן דאימני ביה מעיקרא דמי והא תני רבי הושעיא הולך אדם אצל רועה הרגיל אצלו ונותן לו טלה לפסחו ומקדישו ויוצא בו התם נמי כיון דרגיל אצלו אקדושי (ג) ליה מעיקרא והא מקדיש קתני הקדש עילוי מדרבנן ומי אמר ר' יוחנן הכי והא אמר ר' יוחנן הלכה כסתם משנה ותנן לא מקדישין ולא מעריכין ולא מחרימין ולא מגביהין תרומות ומעשרות כל אלו ביו"ט אמרו ק"ו בשבת לא קשיא כאן בחובות שקבוע להן זמן כאן בחובות שאין קבוע להן זמן: **מתני'** מונה אדם את אורחיו ואת פרפרותיו מפיו אבל לא מן הכתב ומפיס עם בניו ועם בני ביתו על השולחן ובלבד שלא יתכוין לעשות מנה גדולה כנגד מנה קטנה ומטילין חלשין על הקדשים ביו"ט אבל לא על המנות: גמ'

תוספות

ניפרום סודרא עליה אתי למסחטיה. מכאן מייתי ר"ת ראיה דבשמן לא שייכא סחיטה לעיל בשלהי שמונה שרצים (דף קיא. בד"ה הא מסוכרייתא) פירשתי: **לא** מספקין ולא מטפחין. לא כפי' הקונטרס משום דלא מיחזי אירלא ביו"ט אפי' בחול המועד נמי אסור כדתנן במועד קטן פרק בתרא (דף כח:) נשים במועד מענות אבל לא מטפחות אלא נראה לרבי משום שמתה רגילין לספק ולטפח בהשמעת קול ואסור שמא יתקן כלי שיר כדמפרש בהמוצא תפילין (עירובין דף קד.): **וכן** היה הלל אומר. כרבנן דפליגי עליה באיזהו נשך (ב"מ ד' עה.) וקי"ל:

רבה אמר ניתנה ליתבע. הלכה כרבה לגבי רב יוסף: ורב אויא ורבה בר עולא מחמרי אנפשייהו כ"כ בה"ג:

דאי אמרת ניתנה ליתבע אתי למיכתב. אע"פ שמזכיר לו לשון שאלה:

דאיגלאי מילתא דבחול הויא. ורב יוסף לא מיירי אלא בשבת ויו"ט ודאי:

והא אנן תנן אין נימנין כו'. פירש ה"ר פורת בשם רבינו שמואל דל"ג ליה חדא דמה שייך להקשות מנמנין של רשות לנמנין של מצוה ועוד דמפרש התם בביצה פרק אין צדין (דף כז:) מאי אין נמנין אין פוסקין דמים בתחילה לבהמה ביו"ט הרי אני עמך בסלע הריני עמך בשתים אבל אומר לו הריני עמך לשליש ולרביע: ולמ"ד

רש"י

בנכתמא. כיסוי: זימנין דמיפסק כו'. כיון דמגלגלת ליה כיסוי קטר ליה בכד וזימנין דמיפסק ואתי למקטריה והיא קשר של קיימא דאסור מדאורייתא: ואתי לידי סחיטה. ניפרום סודרא עלויה כו' (ד) [והכא] בדבר יבש קא מיירי: אין מספקין. כף אל כף משום אבל: מטפחין. על הלב: מרקדין. לשמחה וטעמא מפרש במסכת ביצה שמא יתקן כלי שיר: אפומא דלחייא. לפי שאין ניכר כל כך בין מבוי לרה"ר: ואתי לאתויי. חפץ המתגלגל תוך ד' אמות: ומגנדר מלפניהן ומייתין ליה לג"ג: בשבת הוא דאסור. לומר הלויני משום מכמכ: הא בחול שרי. ולא חיישינן לרבית ואף על גב דבלשון הלואה קאמר ליה: באתרא דקייץ דמייהו. דככרות לא אתי לידי רבית שאם יוקירו יתן דמיהן: לא ניתנה ליתבע. בב"ד שאין ב"ד מזקקין לה לעולם: בדינא ודיינא. לא לבא לדין ולא לברור דיין ולהטריח את עצמו: השוחט את הפרה וחילקה בראש השנה. של מוצאי שביעית ללוקחים בהקפה וקיי"ל שביעית משמטת בסופה דכתיב מקץ: אם היה חדש. אלול מעובר ועשו ראש השנה שני ימים משמט דיום טוב ראשון של סוף שביעית היה ונמצא זו הלואת שביעית ואם לאו הויא לה הלואת מוצאי שביעית ואינו משמט: ל"ג אי לאו אי אמרת בשלמא כו' ה"ג ואם לא ניתנה ליתבע מאי משמט. הואיל ואין ב"ד מזקקין לכופו שמוטה היא ועומדת: דחול הוא. שהרי חדש מעובר ולא הוי יו"ט עד למחר הלכך אי לאו דשביעית הוא הוה גבי: ואם לאו אינו משמט. אלמא ניתנה ליתבע ומשני מאי אינו משמט דאי יהיב ליה שקיל: מכלל דרישא אי יהיב ליה לא שקיל. בתמיה: רישא. דהלואת שביעית היא אי נמי יהיב ליה לוה צריך למימר משמט אני: (ה) ואם אמר. לוה אעפ"כ: אינו חפץ שישמטנו יקבל ממנו: דבר השמטה. אפילו מקבל מנו יזכיר לו שמיטה בדבורו: שקיל משכונא. בשעת הלואה מהלואת יו"ט: מערים איערומי. לאחר י"ט לוקח ממנו שום חפץ ומעכבו: פסחו בשבת. אם חל י"ד בשבת: וחגיגתו ביו"ט. ביום הקרבתה מותר להקדיש ואע"ג דתנן אלו הן משום שבות אין מקדישין הני כיון דהקרבתן דוחה קודשתן דוחה: בממנה אחרים עמו. כדכתיב (שמות יב) במכסת נפשות: על פסחו. שהיה קדוש ועומד מאתמול: אקדושי. מקדיש ליה רועה מע"ש שהרי יודע שזה סומך עליו: עילוי. מעלה בעלמא שמקדישו בעלים: הא. דקתני אין מקדישין בחובות שאין קבוע להן זמן קאי שאין הקרבתן דוחה שבת: מתני' פרפרותיו. מיני מעדנים: אבל לא מן הכתב. אם כתב מע"ש כך וכך אורחים פלוני ופלוני זמנתי כדי שלא ישכחם לא יקרא באותו כתב בשבת ובגמ' מפרש טעמא: מפיס. לשון פיים מטיל פייס לחלק מי מגיע כל מנה ומנה: ובלבד שלא יתכוין לעשות כו'. שיהו המנות שוות ולא תהא אחת גדולה ואחת קטנה לזכות בגדולה הזוכה ע"פ הגורל והמתחייב ע"פ הגורל לקטנה יטלנה ובגמ' מפרש טעמא: חלשים. גורלות: על הקדשים. בין הכהנים: אבל לא על המנות. בגמרא מפרש:

עין משפט נר מצוה

ד א מיי' פכ"ג מהלכות שבת הלכה ה סמג לאוין סה טוש"ע או"ח סימן שלט סעיף ג וסימן תקכד סעיף א:

ה ב מיי' פ"א מהלכות שביתת עשור הלכה ז סמג לאוין סה ועשין לב טוש"ע או"ח סימן תרח סעיף ב:

ו ג מיי' פ"י מהלכות מלוה ולוה הלכה ב סמג לאוין קלג טוש"ע יו"ד סימן קסב סעיף ב:

ז ד שם סעיף ג:

ח ה מיי' פ"ד מהלכות שבת הלכה כ טוש"ע או"ח סימן תקכה סעיף א:

ט ו מיי' פ"ט מהלכות שמיטה ויובל הלכה ה סמג עשין קמנו:

י ז מיי' שם הלכה כח סמג לאוין רעא טור וש"ע חו"מ סימן סז סעיף לו:

יא ח מיי' פכ"ג מהלכות שבת הלכה יד ופ"ד מהלכות קרבן פסח הלכה ד סמג עשין רכג:

יב ט מיי' פ"ד מהלכות יו"ט הלכה יט סמג לאוין עה טוש"ע או"ח סימן תקכד:

יג י מיי' פכ"ג מהלכות שבת הלכה יד סמג לאוין סה ועה טור ש"ע או"ח סימן שלט סעיף ד וסימן תקכד סעיף א:

רבינו חננאל

להא. דא"ל תנן לא מספקין ולא מרקדין ולא מטפחין. בגדרא. ופשוטה היא. ומיפרשא נמי בגמ' דהמביא כדי יין במס' יו"ט וכן שואלת אשה מחברתה ככרות. ודייקינן מינה בשבת הוא דאסור מכלל דבחול שרי מתניתין דלא כהלל כו' ומסקינן בה אפילו תימא כהלל באתרא דקייצי דמי. ואם אינו מאמינו מניח טליתו אצלו ועושה עמו חשבון לאחר שבת. אתמר הלואת יו"ט רב יוסף אמר לא נתנה ליתבע רבא אמר ניתנה ליתבע ואתינן למיגמר מן מתניתין תנן ואם אינו מאמינו מניח טליתו אצלו כו' ולא גמרינן מינה דלא מיפרשא בהדיא כחד מינייהו ומותבינן לרב יוסף מהא דתנן השוחט את הפרה וחילקה בראש השנה אם היה חדש מעובר משמט. פי' אם היה אלול מעובר נמצא יום לקיחתו חלק מן הפרה יום חול שר"ה מחר הוא וכיון שנושה בו דמי בשר הפרה שלקח מאתמול דכיון שנכנסה שנה שביעית משמטת לדברי רבא ניחא כי נתנה ליתבע ומלוה נושה בו וכשנכנסת שביעית משמטת אלא לרב יוסף דאמר לא נתנה ליתבע אמאי צריך למיתנא משמטת בלאו הכי פטור הוא מלשלם. ואפילו בשאר שני שבוע דהא לא ניתנה ליתבע. ופריק רב יוסף שאני התם דכיון דאיגלאי מלתא דחול היא (ניתנה ליתבע דהא מלוה דחול היא) ואנן לא קאימנא אלא הלואת יו"ט ואסיקנא למשמע מסיפא ואם לאו אינו משמט לרבא דאמר ניתנה ליתבע דתובעו ונפרע ממנו [ניחא] אלא לרב יוסף דאמר לא ניתנה ליתבע קשיא כיון דתני אינו משמט הלא משמע דתובע ונפרע ממנו ואינו יכול לומר לו כי השביעית השמיטתו ופריק רב יוסף לעולם לא נתנה ליתבע והמלוה אינו יכול ליתבע אלא אם יביא הלוה ויפרענו יקבל ואינו צריך לומר משמט אני. ואקשינן עליה מכלל דרישא אי יהיב ליה מעצמו לא שקיל. ופריק רב יוסף רישא [המחזיר] לו צריך שיאמר לו משמט אני. דהא נושה בו מלוה. אבל ספק שאינו נושה בו מלוה אם יבא לחשבון אינו צריך לומר לו משמט אני אלא יקבל כדתנן המחזיר חוב בשביעית צריך שיאמר משמט אני. ואם אמר לו אעפ"כ יקבל ממנו משום שנאמר וזה דבר השמטה. ומפורש ענין זה בפ' השולח גט לאשתו. וראינו רבותינו שהיו

מסורת הש"ס

א) ביצה ל. וד' לו:, ב) [נ"ל רבה], ג) לעיל קמא. ביצה ל., ד) [ב"ב ס: ועי' תוס' לעיל נה. ד"ה ואע"ג ותוס' ב"ב ס. ד"ה מוטב ותוס' ע"ז ד. ד"ה שרי], ה) [ביצה ל. ע"ש], ו) ב"מ עה., ז) [גי' רב אלפס והרא"ש ורבא], ח) שביעית פ"י משנה ב, ט) ג"ז שם [ב"מ גיטין לז:], י) ר"ל רבא, כ) פסחים סו: [ועי' תוספות מגילה ח. ד"ה ואין], ל) ביצה לו:, מ) [לעיל מו. וש"נ], נ) פסחים סו: ביצה לו:, ס) [עיין תוס' לקמן קמט.].

הגהות הב"ח

(א) גמ' והא קא חזינן נמי דמותבי חצביהון וכו' הנח להן לישראל: (ב) שם מאי אינו משמט דאי יהיב ליה: (ג) שם אקדושי ליה מעיקרא: (ד) רש"י ד"ה ואתי לידי סחיטה וכו' סודרא עלויה כו' כיון דשמן קמיירי: (ה) ד"ה רישא וכו' דהלואה שביעית היא אמר לו הלוה אעפ"כ כו' והד"א:

תורה אור השלם

א) וְזֶה דְּבַר הַשְּׁמִטָּה שָׁמוֹט כָּל בַּעַל מַשֵּׁה יָדוֹ אֲשֶׁר יַשֶּׁה בְּרֵעֵהוּ לֹא יִגֹּשׂ אֶת רֵעֵהוּ וְאֶת אָחִיו כִּי קָרָא שְׁמִטָּה לַיְיָ: [דברים טו, ב]

ליקוטי רש"י

ניפרום סודרא. קל הוא ואינו מכביד ושנוי [בעלמא הוא ולהצניע]. אתי לידי סחיטה. שנשרה במים. נכסייה בנכתמא. כסוי של עץ העשוי לכדין. זימנין דמיפסק. שצריך לקושרו שלא יפול בדרך וזמנין דמפסיק בהליכתו ואתי למקטריה וקשר העשוי להתקין אב מלאכה הוא. לא מטפחין. משום שיר או משום אבל. מטפחין. ידיו זו לזו. מספקין. כף על ירך. מרקדין. ברגל וכולם נאסרו משום שבות גזרה שמא יתקן כלי שיר בפרק משילין (ביצה לו:) [ביצה ל.]. ברגל וכולן לשמחה ולשיר ובגמרא מפרש גזרה שמא יתקן כנגדן כלי שיר דקא עביד מנא [שם לו:]. אפומא דלחייא. לחי המתיר במבוי בשבת. דילמא מיגנדר ליה חפץ. ברשות הרבים חוץ ללחי. ואתי לאיתויי. מתוך שאינו במבוי מקורה להכיר שזה רשות הרבים וזה רשות היחיד ומביאו. ולא אמרינן להו ולא מידי. ואף על גב דעברן אדרבנן דאמור לא ליתיב ואינהו יתבן. הנח לישראל. בדבר שהרגילו בו ולא יחזרו בהם [שם ל.]. מוטב שיהו שוגגין. שאינם סבורים שיש איסור בדבר [רשב"ם ב"ב ס:]. ואל יהו מזידין. לעבור כשידעו ולא ימנעו בכך. הני מילי. דהנח להם לישראל. בדרבנן. היכא דלא רגילו למעבר אדרבנן כי הנך דמטפחין והנך דיתבן אפומא דלחיא. תוספת דיום הכפורים. שצריך להתחיל ולהתענות מבעוד יום דאורייתא היא דנפקא לן (יומא פא:) מועניתם את נפשותיכם בתשעה. דקאכלי ושתו עד שתחשך. [...] ולא גרם משמשכה [ביצה שם]. המחזיר חוב בשביעית. בזמן שהשביעית נוהגת ועברה עליו שביעית שהחזירו בשביעית עצמה דא"כ לא הוה צריך למימר משמט אני דקי"ל אין שביעית משמטת אלא בסופה. יאמר לו. צריך המלוה שיאמר לו משמט אני. ואם אמר לו אע"פ כן. אני רוצה להחזירו לך. שנאמר וזה דבר השמטה. צריך לומר דיבור של שמיטה [גיטין לז:]. פסחו בשבת. ליכא למימר ביום טוב דאין פסח קרב ביום טוב וחגיגה ליכא למימר בשבת [...]. הלכה כסתם משנה. רבי הוא סדר המשנה וכשראה דברי חכם וישרו בעיניו שנאן סתם ולא הזכיר שם אומרו עליהן כדי שלא יהו שנויה מפי יחיד ונראין כאילו נשנו מפי המרובים ויעשו כמותן [ביצה ב:]. לא מקדישין. הקדשות. ולא מעריכין. ערכך עלי ונותן כפי שנים כמו שכתוב בפרשת ערכין (ויקרא כז). ולא מחרימין. הרי בהמה זו חרם וסתם חרמים לבדק הבית [שם לו:]. לא מקדישין ולא מעריכין וכו'. [גזירה] משום מקח וממכר דלמקח וממכר דמו שמוציא מרשותו לרשות הקדש [...] וממכר אסור מן המקרא דכתיב ממצוא חפצך ודבר דבר (ישעיה נח) אי נמי מקח וממכר אתי לידי כתיבה שטרי מכירה ואם תאמר הויא לה גזרה לגזרה כולה חדא גזרה היא [שם לז.]. ולא מגביהין תרומות ומעשרות. איסור [...] היא כדתנן במשילין (ביצה לו.) אלו הן משום שבות של מצוה אין מגביהין תרומות ומעשרות דמיחזי כמתקן [גיטין נד.]. בחובות שקבוע להן זמן. לבו ביום שפיר דמי דהואיל ונשחטין היום יכול להקדישן היום [פסחים סו:].

But Rabbah[26] **says:** נִיתְּנָה לִיתָּבַע – **It is reclaimable** in court.

The Gemara explains the two sides of the dispute:

רַב יוֹסֵף אָמַר לֹא נִיתְּנָה לִיתָּבַע – **Rav Yosef says that it is not reclaimable** in court דְּאִי אָמְרַתְּ נִיתְּנָה לִיתָּבַע – **because if you say** that **it is reclaimable,** אָתֵי לְמִיכְתַּב – **[the lender] will come to write** a record of the loan on Yom Tov.[27] רַבָּה אָמַר נִיתְּנָה לִיתָּבַע – **Rabbah says** that **it is reclaimable** in court, דְּאִי אָמְרַתְּ לֹא נִיתְּנָה – **because if you say** that **it is not** reclaimable, לֹא יָהִיב לֵיהּ – **[the lender] will not give** anything **to [the borrower]** in the first place,[28] וְאָתֵי לְאִימְּנוּעֵי מִשִּׂמְחַת יוֹם טוֹב – **and [the borrower] will come to be prevented from enjoying Yom Tov.**[29]

The Gemara attempts a proof from our Mishnah:

תְּנַן – **We learned in** our **Mishnah:** אִם אֵינוֹ מַאֲמִינוֹ מַנִּיחַ טַלִּיתוֹ אֶצְלוֹ – IF [THE LENDER] DOES NOT TRUST HIM, [THE BORROWER] MAY LEAVE HIS CLOAK WITH [THE LENDER]. אִי אָמְרַתְּ בִּשְׁלָמָא לֹא נִיתְּנָה לִיתָּבַע – Now, **this is understandable if you say** that **it** (i.e. a loan made on Yom Tov) **is not reclaimable** in court; מִשּׁוּם הָכִי מַנִּיחַ טַלִּיתוֹ אֶצְלוֹ – **that is why [the borrower] would leave his cloak with [the lender]** וְעוֹשֶׂה עִמּוֹ חֶשְׁבּוֹן לְאַחַר שַׁבָּת – **and make a reckoning with him after the Sabbath.**[30] אֶלָּא אִי אָמְרַתְּ נִיתְּנָה לִיתָּבַע – **But if you say** that **[the loan]** *is* **reclaimable** in court, אַמַּאי מַנִּיחַ טַלִּיתוֹ אֶצְלוֹ – **why would [the borrower] leave his cloak with [the lender]?** לִיתֵּן לֵיהּ – **Let [the lender] give [the borrower]** whatever he needs, without taking a security in return, וְלִתְבְּעֵיהּ – **and,** if the borrower refuses to repay, **let [the lender] claim** payment from **him** in court!

The Gemara deflects the proof by arguing that even if the loan *is* reclaimable in court, the lender would want a security for the following reason:

אָמַר – **[The lender] might say:** לֹא בְּעֵינָא דְּלֵיקוּם בְּדִינָא וְדַיָּינָא – **"I do not want to become involved with litigation and judges."**[31]

The Gemara challenges Rav Yosef's opinion that a loan made on Yom Tov is not reclaimable in court:

מָתִיב רַב אִידִי בַּר אָבִין – **Rav Idi bar Avin challenged** it from the following Mishnah:[32] הַשּׁוֹחֵט אֶת הַפָּרָה וְחִילְּקָהּ בְּרֹאשׁ הַשָּׁנָה – Regarding ONE WHO SLAUGHTERS A COW AND APPORTIONS IT out to his friends[33] ON the ROSH HASHANAH after the *shemittah* year,[34] and they thus become obligated to pay him the price of their portions: אִם הָיָה חֹדֶשׁ מְעוּבָּר – IF THE preceding MONTH of Elul WAS FULL (i.e. it lasted thirty days), in which case that day belonged to the preceding (*shemittah*) year, מְשַׁמֵּט – *SHEMITTAH* CANCELS their debt.[35] וְאִם לָאו – BUT IF Elul was NOT full (i.e. it lasted only twenty-nine days), in which case that day belonged to the next year, אֵינוֹ מְשַׁמֵּט – *SHEMITTAH* DOES NOT CANCEL the debt. וְאִי לֹא נִיתְּנָה לִיתָּבַע – **Now, if [a loan made on Yom Tov] is not reclaimable** in court, מַאי מְשַׁמֵּט – **what** does the Mishnah mean when it states that if Elul was full *SHEMITTAH* CANCELS the debt? The debt is canceled in any event![36]

NOTES

26. Some authorities emend the text to read רָבָא, *Rava* [a student of Rav Yosef], instead of רַבָּה, *Rabbah* [Rav Yosef's teacher]. This emendation has bearing on the question of whose opinion is accepted as authoritative (see *Rashba* et al.).

27. If the lender has recourse in the courts, he will make a record of the loan lest he forget about it by the time he is able to summon the borrower to court. On the other hand, if the loan is not recoverable through the courts, the lender can only rely on the borrower's word that he will pay back immediately. In such a case, the lender has little reason to make a record of the loan.

The preceding distinction applies where the borrower says, "*hashileini,*" which signifies a short-term loan. If he says, "*halveini,*" which connotes a loan of longer duration, the lender will make a note of the loan in any event (even if he cannot claim it through the courts) so that he will remember to personally request payment from the borrower when it becomes due (see *Ritva MHK* ed.; see also *Ramban, Rashba, Ran MHK* ed. and *Shabbos Shel Mi*).

28. Because he will be afraid that the borrower might not want to pay him back (*Chidushei HaRan*).

29. [If one is unable to borrow on Yom Tov, one might come to lack the items needed for enjoyment of the festival.

In fact, no reason is required to explain why a legitimate loan is claimable in court. Rabbah presented this explanation only as a counterweight to Rav Yosef's argument that the loan should *not* be claimable in court lest the lender make a note of it (*Rashba; Sfas Emes*).

30. The lender needs the cloak as a security, for without it he would have no protection should the borrower refuse to pay.

31. He wishes to avoid the bother of going to court and selecting a judge (*Rashi*).

It seems that the lender is not afraid that once the borrower is brought to court he will deny the loan. The lender only wishes to avoid having to take him to court in the first place (*Ritva MHK* ed.; cf. *Chidushei HaRan;* see *Sfas Emes*).

32. *Sheviis* 10:2.

33. A group of people agreed to buy a cow for the purpose of slaughtering it for its meat. One of them bought the cow (or gave his own), slaughtered it, and gave out the portions (*Rav* ibid.).

34. The Torah mandates that every seventh year be designated as the *shemittah* year. Outstanding loans are automatically canceled at the end of this year (see *Deuteronomy* 15:1,2). The event described here occurred on the first day (Rosh Hashanah) of the year after *shemittah*.

35. Since Elul — the last month of the *shemittah* year — had thirty days, the day presumed to have been Rosh Hashanah of the next year was in fact the thirtieth day of Elul (see below for explanation). In that case the debt was incurred on the last day of the *shemittah* year, and since *shemittah* cancels debts at its conclusion (*Sifrei* to *Deuteronomy* 15:1, *Arachin* 28b), the debt is canceled (*Rav* to Mishnah there). [Actually, most Tannaim maintain that a purchase made on credit is not affected by *shemittah.* If this Mishnah follows their view, it speaks of a purchase that was immediately converted into a regular loan (see *Ritva MHK* ed., *Ran MHK* ed., *Meiri* and *Chasam Sofer*).]

The first day of the Jewish month (Rosh Chodesh) may occur on either the thirtieth day from the previous Rosh Chodesh (and that thirtieth day is not day thirty of the previous month, but day one of the new month), or the thirty-first. If it occurs on the thirtieth, the previous month (containing twenty-nine days) is said to have been חָסֵר, *deficient*; if it occurs on the thirty-first, the previous month (containing thirty days) is said to be מְעֻבָּר, *full.* In Mishnaic times, the determination was made by the Sanhedrin, based on the availability of witnesses attesting to a sighting of the new moon and various other factors. Because Rosh Chodesh was determined each month separately, on the thirtieth day of a month people would have to await the Sanhedrin's designation to know whether the day was really the thirtieth day of the month past or the first day of the following month. This posed a special problem for the holiday of Rosh Hashanah, which falls on the first day of the month of Tishrei. Nevertheless, the thirtieth day of Elul was always observed as Rosh Hashanah because of the probability that Elul would be deficient, making the thirtieth day Rosh Hashanah. If, however, the Sanhedrin designated the thirty-first day Rosh Hashanah (see *Beitzah* 6a), it would transpire that the day which had been observed as Rosh Hashanah actually belonged to the previous year.

36. Since the court does not enforce payment of the debt, it is already canceled (*Rashi*).

The Rishonim raise the following difficulty with *Rashi's* explanation: In the case of a loan canceled by *shemittah,* the law is that if the debtor offers payment, the creditor must declare that he relinquishes it (see Gemara below). A loan made on Yom Tov, though, is viable as far as the debtor and creditor are concerned; it is only the court that does not get involved (see note 25). Thus, the fact that *shemittah* cancels the loan does have a significant practical consequence. [In light of this difficulty, the Rishonim (*Ramban, Rashba, Ritva MHK* ed. et al.) adopt a different explanation of the Gemara based on an alternative text.]

In defense of *Rashi,* it may be argued that the Gemara currently understands the term מְשַׁמֵּט, *shemittah cancels,* to mean only that the lender has no power to *force* the borrower to pay. He may, however, accept any payment (see *Chidushei HaRan* ד״ה מכלל; see also *Ritva MHK* ed., *Meromei Sadeh* and *Yad David* [*Kamma*]).

עין משפט נר מצוה

ד א מיי' פכ"ג מהלכות שבת הלכה ה סמג לאוין סה טוש"ע או"ח סימן שלט סעיף ג וסימן תקכד סעיף א:
ה ב מיי' פ"א מהלכות שביתת עשור הלכה ז סמג לאוין סה וטור ושו"ע או"ח סימן תרח סעיף ג:
ו ג מיי' פי"א מהלכות מלוה ולוה הלכה ב סמג לאוין קצג טוש"ע יו"ד סימן קסב סעיף ג:
ז ד שם סעיף ג:
ח ה מיי' פ"ד מהלכות יו"ט הלכה כ טוש"ע או"ח סימן תקכה סעיף א:
ט ו מיי' פ"ט מהלכות שמיטה ויובל הלכה ה סמג עשין קמח:
י ז מיי' שם הלכה כח סמג לאוין רעא טור ושו"ע חו"מ סימן סז סעיף לו:
יא ח מיי' פכ"ג מהלכו' שבת הלכה יד ופ"א מהלכות קרבן פסח הלי"ט סמג עשין רכג:
יב ט מיי' פ"ד מהלכות יו"ט הלכה יט סמג לאוין עה טוש"ע או"ח סימן תקו סעיף א:
יג י מיי' פכ"ג מהלכות שבת הלכה יד סמג לאוין סה ועה טור ש"ע או"ח סימן שלט סעיף ד וסימן תקכד סעיף א:

רבינו חננאל

להא. דא"ל תנן לא מספקין ולא מרקדין ולא מטפחין. בגדרא. ופשוטה היא. ומיפרשא נמי בגמ' דהמביא כדי יין במס' יו"ט וכן שואלת אשה מחברתה ככרות. ודייקינן מינה בשבת הוא דאסור מכלל דבחול שרי מתניתין דלא כהלל כו' ומסקינן בה אפילו תימא כהלל באתרא דקייצי דמי. ואם אינו מאמינו מניח טליתו אצלו ועושה עמו חשבון לאחר שבת. אתמר הלואת יו"ט רב יוסף אמר לא נתנה ליתבע רבא אמר ניתנה ליתבע ואתינן למיגמר מן מתניתין תנן ואם אינו מאמינו מניח טליתו אצלו כו' ולא גמרינן מינה דלא מיפרשא בהדיא כחד מינייהו ומותבינן לרב יוסף מהא דתנן השוחט את הפרה וחילקה בראש השנה אם היה חדש מעובר משמט. פי' אם היה אלול מעובר נמצא יום לקיחתו חלק מן הפרה יום חול שר"ה מחר הוא וכיון שנושה בו דמי בשר הפרה שלקח מאתמול דכיון שנכנסה שנה שביעית משמטת לדברי רבא ניחא כי נתנה ליתבע ומלוה נושה בו וכשנכנסת שביעית משמטת אלא לרב יוסף דאמר לא נתנה ליתבע אמאי צריך למיתנא משמטת בלאו הכי פטור הוא מלשלם. ואפילו בשאר שני שבוע דהא לא ניתנה ליתבע. ופריק רב יוסף שאני התם דכיון דאיגלאי מלתא דחול היא (ניתנה ליתבע דהא מלוה דחול היא) ואנן לא קאימנא אלא הלואת יו"ט ואסיקנא למשמע מסיפא ואם לאו אינו משמט לרבא דאמר ניתנה ליתבע דתובעו ונפרע ממנו [ניחא] אלא לרב יוסף דאמר לא ניתנה ליתבע קשיא כיון דתני אינו משמט הלא משמע דתובע ונפרע ממנו ואינו יכול לומר לו כי השביעית השמיטתו ופריק רב יוסף לעולם לא נתנה ליתבע והמלוה אינו יכול ליתבע אלא אם יביא הלה ויפרענו יקבל ואינו צריך לומר משמט אני. ואקשינן עליה מכלל דרישא אי יהיב ליה מעצמו לא שקיל. ופריק רב יוסף ואמר רישא אם מחזיר לו צריך שיאמר לו משמט אני. דהא נושה בו מלוה. אבל ספק שאינו נושה בו מלוה אם יבא לחשבון אינו צריך לומר לו משמט אני אלא יקבל כדתנן המחזיר חוב בשביעית צריך שיאמר משמט אני. ואם אמר לו אעפ"כ יקבל ממנו משום שנאמר וזה דבר השמטה.

תוספות

ניפרוס סודרא עליה אתי למסחטיה. מכאן מייתי ר"ת ראיה דביין ושמן לא שייכא סחיטה לעיל בשלהי שמונה שרצים (דף קיא. בד"ה הא מסוכרייתא) פירשתי: **לא** מספקין ולא מטפחין. לא כפי' הקונטרס משום דא"כ מאי איריא ביו"ט אפי' בחול המועד נמי אסור כדתנן במועד קטן פרק בתרא (דף כח:) נשים במועד מענות אבל לא מטפחות אלא נראה לרבי משום שמחה רגילין לספק ולטפח בהשמעת קול ואסור שמא יתקן כלי שיר כדמפרש בהמוצא תפילין (עירובין דף קד.): **וכן** היה הלל אומר. כרבנן דפליגי עליה באיזהו נשך (ב"מ ד' עה.) וקי"ל: **רבה** אמר ניתנה ליתבע. הלכה כרבה לגבי רב יוסף: ורב אויא ורבה בר עולא מחמרי אנפשייהו כ"ה בס"א: **דאי** אמרת ניתנה ליתבע אתי למיכתב. אע"פ שמזכיר לו לשון שאלה: **דאיגלאי** מילתא דבחול הויא. ורב יוסף לא איירי אלא בשבת ויו"ט ודאי: **והא** אנן תנן אין נימנין כו'. פירש ה"ר פורת בשם רבינו שמואל דל"ג ליה חדא דמה שייך להקשות מנמנין של רשות לנמנין של מצוה ועוד דמפרש התם בביצה פרק אין צדין (דף כז:) מאי אין נמנין אין פוסקין דמים בתחילה לבהמה ביו"ט הרי אני עמך בסלע הריני עמך בשתים אבל אומר לו הריני עמך לשליש ולרביע: ולמ"ד

ניפרוס סודרא אתי לידי סחיטה נכסייה בנכתמא זימנין דמיפסק ואתי למקטריה הלכך לא אפשר וא"ל רבא בר רב חנן לאביי תנן לא מספקין ולא מטפחין ולא מרקדין ביו"ט וקא חזינן דעבדין ולא אמרינן להו ולא מידי ולטעמיך הא דאמר רבא לא ליתיב איניש אפומא דלחייא דילמא מיגנדר ליה חפץ ואתי לאיתויי והא קא חזינן נמי דמותבי חצבי ויתבן אפומא דמבואה ולא אמרינן להו ולא מידי אלא הנח לישראל מוטב שיהו שוגגין ואל יהו מזידין סבור מינה הנ"מ בדרבנן אבל בדאורייתא לא ולא היא ל"ש בדרבנן ול"ש בדאורייתא דהא תוספת דיוה"כ דאורייתא היא וקא חזינן להו דקאכלי ושתו עד שתחשך ולא אמרי' להו ולא מידי: וכן אשה מחבירתה ככרות: בשבת הוא דאסיר אבל בחול שפיר דמי לימא מתני' דלא כהלל דתנן וכן היה הלל אומר לא תלוה אשה ככר לחבירתה עד שתעשינה דמים שמא יוקרו חטין ונמצאו באות לידי רבית אפילו תימא הלל הא באתרא דקייץ דמיה הא באתרא דלא קייץ דמיה: ואם אינו מאמינו: איתמר הלוואת יו"ט רב יוסף אמר לא ניתנה ליתבע ורבה אמר ניתנה ליתבע רב יוסף אמר לא ניתנה ליתבע דאי אמרת ניתנה ליתבע אתי למיכתב רבה אמר ניתנה ליתבע דאי אמרת לא ניתנה ליתבע לא יהיב ליה ואתי לאימנועי משמחת יו"ט תנן אם אינו מאמינו מניח טליתו אצלו אי אמרת בשלמא לא ניתנה ליתבע משום הכי מניח טליתו אצלו ועושה עמו חשבון לאחר שבת אלא אי אמרת ניתנה ליתבע אמאי מניח טליתו אצלו ליתן ליה ולתבעיה אמר לא בעינא דליקום בדינא ודיינא מתיב רב אידי בר אבין השוחט את הפרה וחילקה בראש השנה אם היה חדש מעובר משמט ואם לאו אינו משמט ואי לא ניתנה ליתבע מאי משמט שאני התם דאיגלאי מילתא דחול הוא ת"ש מסיפא אם לאו אינו משמט אי אמרת בשלמא ניתנה ליתבע היינו דקתני אינו משמט אלא אי אמרת לא ניתנה ליתבע (ג) אמאי אינו משמט דאי יהיב ליה שקיל מכלל דרישא אי יהיב ליה לא שקיל רישא צריך למימר ליה משמט אני סיפא לא צריך למימר ליה משמט אני כדתנן המחזיר חוב בשביעית יאמר לו משמט אני ואם אמר לו אעפ"כ יקבל ממנו משום שנאמר וזה דבר השמטה רב אויא שקיל משכונא רבה בר עולא מערים איערומי: וכן ערב פסח: א"ר יוחנן מקדיש אדם פסחו בשבת וחגיגתו ביו"ט נימא מסייע ליה וכן ערב פסח בירושלים שחל להיות בשבת מניח טליתו אצלו ונוטל את פסחו ועושה עמו חשבון לאחר יו"ט הכא במאי עסקינן בממנה אחרים עמו על פסחו דמעיקרא מיקדש וקאי והא אנן תנן אין נמנין על הבהמה בתחילה ביו"ט שאני הכא כיון דרגיל אצלו כמאן דאימני ביה מעיקרא דמי והא תני רבי הושעיא הולך אדם אצל רועה הרגיל אצלו ונותן לו טלה לפסחו ומקדישו ויוצא בו התם נמי כיון דרגיל אצלו אקדושי (ג) ליה מעיקרא והא מקדיש קתני הקדש עילוי מדרבנן ומי אמר ר' יוחנן הכי והא אמר ר' יוחנן הלכה כסתם משנה ותנן לא מקדישין ולא מעריכין ולא מחרימין ולא מגביהין תרומות ומעשרות כל אלו ביו"ט אמרו ק"ו בשבת לא קשיא כאן בחובות שקבוע להן זמן כאן בחובות שאין קבוע להן זמן: **מתני'** מונה אדם את אורחיו ואת פרפרותיו מפיו אבל לא מן הכתב מפיס אדם עם בניו ועם בני ביתו על השולחן ובלבד שלא יתכוין לעשות מנה גדולה כנגד מנה קטנה ומטילין חלשין על הקדשים ביו"ט אבל לא על המנות: גמ'

רש"י

בנכתמא. כיסוי: זימנין דמיפסק כו'. כיון דמצרכת ליה כיסוי קטר ליה בכד וזימנין דמיפסק ואתי למקטריה והיא קשר של קיימא דאסור מדאורייתא: ואתי לידי סחיטה. ודקאמר במסכת ביצה ניפרוס סודרא עלויה כו' (ד) [התם] בדבר יבש קא מיירי: אין מספקין. כף אל כף משום אבל: מטפחין. כף על הלב: מרקדין. לשמחה וטעמא מפרש במסכת ביצה שמא יתקן כלי שיר: אפומא דלחייא. לפי שאין ניכר כל כך בין מבוי לרה"ר: ואתי לאתויי. חפץ המתגלגל חוץ לד' אמות: ומגנדר אלביהן ומייתין ליה ל"ג: בשבת הוא דאסור. לומר הלויני משום מכתב: הא בחול שרי. ולא חיישינן לרבית ואף על גב דבלשון הלואה קאמר ליה: באתרא דקייץ דמייהו. דככרות לא אתי לידי רבית שאם יוקירו יתן דמיהן: לא ניתנה ליתבע. בב"ד שאין ב"ד נזקקין לה לעולם: בדינא ודיינא. לא לבא לדין ולא לברור דיין ולהטריח את עצמו: השוחט את הפרה וחילקה בראש השנה. של מוצאי שביעית ללוקחים בהקפה וקי"ל שביעית משמטת בסופה דכתיב מקץ: אם היה חדש. אלול מעובר ועשו ראש השנה שני ימים משמטת דיום טוב ראשון של סוף שביעית היה ונמצאת זו הלואת שביעית ואם לאו הויא לה הלואת מוצאי שביעית ואינו משמט: ל"ג אי לאו אי אמרת בשלמא כו' ה"ג ואם לא ניתנה ליתבע מאי משמט. הואיל ואין ב"ד נזקקין לכופו שמוטה היא ועומדת: דחול הוא. שהרי חדש מעובר ולא היה יו"ט עד למחר הלכך אי לאו דשביעית הוה הוה גבי: ואם לאו אינו משמט. אלמא ניתנה ליתבע ומשני מאי אינו משמט דאי יהיב ליה שקיל: מכלל דרישא אי יהיב ליה לא שקיל. בתמיה: רישא. דהלואת שביעית היא אי נמי יהיב ליה לוה צריך למימר ליה מלוה משמט אני: (ה) ואם אמר. לוה אעפ"כ איני חפץ שישמטו יקבל ממנו: דבר השמטה. אפילו מקבל מהם יזכיר לו שמיטה בדבורו: שקיל משכונא. בשעת הלואה מהלואת יו"ט: מערים איערומי. לאחר יו"ט לוקח ממנו שום חפץ ומעכבו: פסחו בשבת. בערב פסח שחל בשבת: וחגיגתו ביו"ט. ביום הקרבתה מותר להקדיש ואע"ג דתנן אלו הן משום שבות אין מקדישין הני כיון דהקרבתן דוחה קדושתן דוחה: בממנה אחרים עמו. כדכתיב (שמות יב) במכסת נפשות: על פסחו. שהיה קדוש ועומד מאתמול: אקדושי. מקדיש ליה רועה מע"ש שהרי יודע שזה סומך עליו: עילוי. מעלה בעלמא שיקדישו בעלים: הא. דקתני אין מקדישין בחובות שאין קבוע להן זמן קאי שאין הקרבתן דוחה שבת: מתני' פרפרותיו. מיני מעדנים: אבל לא מן הכתב. אם כתב מע"ש כך וכך אורחים פלוני ופלוני זמנתי כדי שלא ישכחם לא יקרא באותו כתב בשבת ובגמ' מפרש טעמא: מפיס. לשון פייס מטיל פייס לחלק מי מגיע כל מנה ומנה: ובלבד שלא יתכוין לעשות כו'. שיהו המנות שוות ולא תהא אחת גדולה ואחת קטנה לזכות בגדולה הזוכה ע"פ הגורל והמתחייב ע"פ הגורל לקטנה יטלנה ובגמ' מפרש טעמא: חלשים. גורלות: על הקדשים. בין הכהנים: אבל לא על המנות. בגמרא מפרש: גמ'

מסורת הש"ס

א) ביצה ל. וד' לו:, ב) [נ"ל רבה], ג) לעיל קמא. ביצה ל., ד) [ב"ב ס: ועי' תוס' לעיל נה. ד"ה ואע"ג ותוס' ב"ב ס: ד"ה מוטב ותוס' ע"ז ז. ד"ה שרי], ה) [ביצה ל. ע"ש], ו) ב"מ עה., ז) [גי' רב אלפס והרא"ש ורבא], ח) שביעית פ"י משנה ב, ט) ג"ז שם [מ"ח גיטין לז:], י) נ"א רבא, כ) פסחים סו: [ועי' תוספות חגיגה ח. ד"ה משום ותוס' בכורות נח. ד"ה ואין], ל) ביצה מ:, מ) [לעיל מו. וש"נ], נ) פסחים סו: ביצה לו:, ס) [עיין תוס' לקמן קמט:].

הגהות הב"ח

(א) גמ' והא קא חזינן נמי דמותבי אלביהו וכו' הנח להן לישראל: (ב) שם מאי אינו משמט דאי יהיב ליה: (ג) שם אקדושי מקדיש ליה מעיקרא: (ד) רש"י ד"ה ואתא לידי סחיטה וכו' סודרא עלויה כו' ביין ושמן קמיירי: (ה) ד"ה רישא וכו' משמט אני ואם אמר לו הלוה אעפ"כ כצ"ל והד"א:

תורה אור השלם

א) וְזֶה דְּבַר הַשְּׁמִטָּה שָׁמוֹט כָּל בַּעַל מַשֵּׁה יָדוֹ אֲשֶׁר יַשֶּׁה בְּרֵעֵהוּ לֹא יִגֹּשׂ אֶת רֵעֵהוּ וְאֶת אָחִיו כִּי קָרָא שְׁמִטָּה לַייָ: [דברים טו, ב]

ליקוטי רש"י

ניפרוס סודרא. קל הוא ואינו מכביד ושוני [בעלמא הוא ולהלניע]. אתי לידי סחיטה. שנשרה במים. נכסייה בנכתמא. כסוי של עץ העשוי לכדין. זימנין דמיפסק. שצריך לקושרו שלא יפול בדרך וזמנין דמפסיק בהליכתו ואתי למקטריה וקשר העשוי להתקיים אב מלאכה הוא. לא מספקין. משום שיר או משום אבל. מספקין. ידיו זו לזו. מספקין. כף על ירך. מרקדין. ברגל וכולם נאסרו משום שבות גזרה שמא יתקן כלי שיר בפרק משילין (ביצה לו:) [ביצה ל.]. ברגל וכולן לשמחה ולשיר ובגמרא מפרש גזרה שמא יתקן כגנגן כלי שיר דקא עביד מנא [שם לו:]. אפומא דלחייא. לחי המתיר במבוי בשבת. דילמא מיגנדר ליה חפץ. ברשות הרבים חוץ ללחי. ואתי לאיתויי. מתוך שאינו במבוי מקורה להכיר שזה רשות הרבים וזה רשות היחיד ומביאו. ולא אמרינן להו ולא מידי. ואף על גב דעברן אדרבנן דלאמור להו לא ליעביד ולאינהו יתכן. הנח לישראל. בדבר שהרגילו בו ולא יחזרו בהם [שם ל.]. מוטב שיהו שוגגין. שאינם סבורים שיש איסור בדבר [רשב"ם ב"ב ס:]. ואל יהו מזידין. לעבור כשידעו ולא יניחו בכך. הני מילי. להנח להם לישראל. בדרבנן. היכא

דארגילו למעבר אדרבנן כי הנך דמטפחין והנך דיתבן אפומא דלחיא. תוספת דיום הכפורים. שצריך להוסיף מחול על הקדש מבעוד יום דאורייתא היא דנפקא לן (יומא פא.) מועניתם את נפשותיכם בתשעה. דקאכלי ושתו עד שתחשך. ולא גרס משתשכה [ביצה שם]. המחזיר חוב בשביעית. בזמן שהשביעית נוהגת ועברה עליו שביעית שהחזירו בשביעית עצמה דא"כ לא הוה צריך למימר משמט אני דקי"ל אין שביעית משמטת אלא בסופה.

The Gemara answers:

שָׁאנֵי הָתָם – **It is different in that case,** דְּאִיגַּלַּאי מִילְּתָא דְּחוֹל הוּא – **because it transpired that** the day the debt was contracted **was a weekday,** and not Yom Tov.[37]

The Gemara attempts another proof:

תָּא שְׁמַע מִסֵּיפָא – **Come, learn** a proof **from the last part** of that Mishnah: אִם לָאו אֵינוֹ מְשַׁמֵּט – IF Elul was NOT full (and thus the day of the debt belonged to the year after *shemittah*), *SHEMITTAH* DOES NOT CANCEL the debt. אִי אָמְרַתְּ בִּשְׁלָמָא נִיתְּנָה לִיתָּבַע – Now, **this is understandable if you say** that **[a loan made on Yom Tov] is reclaimable** in court; הַיְינוּ דְּקָתָנֵי אֵינוֹ מְשַׁמֵּט – **that is** the meaning of **what the Mishnah states:** *SHEMITTAH* DOES NOT CANCEL, i.e. the debt remains fully reclaimable. אֶלָּא אִי אָמְרַתְּ לֹא נִיתְּנָה לִיתָּבַע – **But if you say** that such a loan is **not reclaimable** in court, אַמַּאי אֵינוֹ מְשַׁמֵּט – **what**[38] does the Mishnah mean when it states: *SHEMITTAH* DOES NOT CANCEL the debt?[39]

The Gemara answers:

דְּאִי יָהֵיב לֵיהּ – The Mishnah means **that if [the debtor] gives [the creditor]** payment, שָׁקֵיל – **[the creditor] may take** it.[40]

The Gemara counters:

מִכְּלָל דְּרֵישָׁא – **That implies that in the** Mishnah's **first case** (i.e. where the debt *was* canceled by *shemittah*), אִי יָהֵיב לֵיהּ – **if [the debtor] gives [the creditor]** payment, לֹא שָׁקֵיל – **[the creditor] may not take** it! But if the debtor is willing to pay, why may the creditor not accept?[41]

The Gemara answers:

רֵישָׁא – In **the first case** of the Mishnah (i.e. where *shemittah* canceled the debt), צָרִיךְ לְמֵימַר לֵיהּ מְשַׁמֵּט אֲנִי – **[the creditor] must say to [the debtor]** who wishes to pay him: **"I relinquish** the debt." סֵיפָא – But in **the last** case of the Mishnah (i.e. where *shemittah* did not cancel the debt), לֹא צָרִיךְ לְמֵימַר לֵיהּ מְשַׁמֵּט אֲנִי – **[the creditor] does not need to say to [the debtor]: "I relinquish** the debt."

The Gemara cites the source for the law that a creditor must refuse payment of a debt canceled by *shemittah*:

כְּדִתְנַן – It is **as we learned in a Mishnah:**[42] הַמַּחֲזִיר חוֹב בַּשְּׁבִיעִית – IF ONE REPAYS A DEBT DURING *SHEVIIS*,[43] יֹאמַר לוֹ מְשַׁמֵּט אֲנִי – [THE CREDITOR] SHOULD SAY TO HIM: "I RELINQUISH the debt." וְאִם אָמַר לוֹ אַף עַל פִּי כֵן – AND IF [THE DEBTOR] REPLIED TO HIM: "EVEN SO, I wish to return the money to you," יְקַבֵּל מִמֶּנּוּ – [THE CREDITOR] MAY ACCEPT the money FROM HIM, מִשּׁוּם שֶׁנֶּאֱמַר ,,וְזֶה דְּבַר הַשְּׁמִטָּה'' – FOR IT IS STATED: *AND THIS IS THE "STATEMENT" OF THE RELINQUISHMENT*.[44]

The Gemara describes how two Amoraim used to assure that loans they made on Yom Tov would be repaid:

רַב אַוְיָא שָׁקֵיל מַשְׁכּוֹנָא – **Rav Avya would take collateral** when the loan was made. רַבָּה בַּר עוּלָּא מַעֲרִים אִיעֲרוּמֵי – **Rabbah bar Ulla would employ a subterfuge.**[45]

The Mishnah stated:

וְכֵן עֶרֶב פֶּסַח – SO TOO, when THE DAY BEFORE PESACH falls on the Sabbath, the purchaser of a *pesach* offering may leave his cloak with the seller, take his *pesach* offering, and make a reckoning with the seller after Yom Tov.

A related ruling:

אָמַר רַבִּי יוֹחָנָן – **R' Yochanan said:** מַקְדִּישׁ אָדָם פִּסְחוֹ בְּשַׁבָּת – **A person may consecrate his** ***pesach*** **offering on the Sabbath**[46] וַחֲגִיגָתוֹ בְּיוֹם טוֹב – **and his** ***chagigah*** **offering on Yom Tov.**[47]

The Gemara derives support for this ruling from our Mishnah:

נֵימָא מְסַיֵּיעַ לֵיהּ – **Let us say** that **[the following] supports [R' Yochanan]:** וְכֵן עֶרֶב פֶּסַח בִּירוּשָׁלַיִם שֶׁחָל לִהְיוֹת בְּשַׁבָּת – SO TOO, IN JERUSALEM, when THE DAY BEFORE PESACH FALLS ON THE SABBATH, מַנִּיחַ טַלִּיתוֹ אֶצְלוֹ – HE [the purchaser of a *pesach* offering] MAY LEAVE HIS CLOAK WITH [THE SELLER], וְנוֹטֵל אֶת פִּסְחוֹ – TAKE HIS *PESACH* OFFERING, וְעוֹשֶׂה עִמּוֹ חֶשְׁבּוֹן לְאַחַר יוֹם טוֹב – AND MAKE A RECKONING WITH [THE SELLER] AFTER YOM TOV. Our

NOTES

37. The day observed as Rosh Hashanah was actually not Rosh Hashanah, but the last day of the previous year (see note 35).

Although that day was treated as Rosh Hashanah, its real status was not certain. Rav Yosef's ruling that loans made on Yom Tov are not reclaimable in court applies to a day that is certainly Yom Tov (*Tosafos;* see *Rashba, Ritva MHK* ed. and *Keren Orah*).

38. Translation follows *Hagahos HaBach,* who reads here מַאי, *what,* in place of אַמַּאי, *why* (see, however, *Menachem Meishiv Nefesh*).

39. By saying אֵינוֹ מְשַׁמֵּט, *shemittah does not cancel,* the Mishnah implies that the debt is collectible in court (*Rashi*).

40. The Gemara is answering that in fact the debt *is* canceled with regard to the courts (because it was incurred on Yom Tov). When the Mishnah says, אֵינוֹ מְשַׁמֵּט, *shemittah does not cancel,* it does not mean that the debt is reclaimable in court. Rather, it means that the creditor is not required to refuse the payment, as he is required to do in the case of loans that *are* canceled by *shemittah.* (The last point is elaborated upon below.)

41. At this point in its argument, the Gemara does not yet "know" that a creditor must relinquish payment of debts canceled by *shemittah* if the borrower wishes to repay them (*Chidushei HaRan*).

42. *Sheviis* 10:8.

43. I.e. during the era in history when the laws of *sheviis* (i.e. *shemittah*) are in force. This cannot mean literally "during *sheviis,*" because loans are canceled only at the *end* of *sheviis* (*Rashi* to *Gittin* 37b). Alternatively, בַּשְּׁבִיעִית means after *shemittah* has passed (*Meiri*).

[*Rashi* implies that there are periods when *shemittah's* cancellation of loans does not apply even under Rabbinic law (see *Raavad* on *Rif, Gittin* folio 19a; cf. *Rashi* ibid. 36a ד״ה בשביעית; see also *Geresh Yerachim* and *Tiferes Yaakov* to *Gittin* 37b).]

44. *Deuteronomy* 15:2. Although the simple rendering of the verse is *and this is the matter of the relinquishment,* the Torah's use of the word דָּבָר, which has the root meaning of *speaking,* indicates that the lender is obligated to *say* that he relinquishes the debt when the borrower comes to return it (see *Rashi*).

45. After Yom Tov, Rabbah bar Ulla would take some article from the debtor and keep it [as payment of the loan] (*Rashi*).

Some Rishonim explain that Rabbah bar Ulla would ask the debtor to lend him something, and when the debtor would seek repayment, Rabbah bar Ulla would tell him that he should keep the items he had borrowed earlier on Yom Tov (*Rabbeinu Chananel, Rif, Rosh, Meiri;* see *Ritva MHK* ed.).

It seems that R' Avya and Rabbah bar Ulla resorted to these tactics because the halachah is that loans made on Yom Tov are not reclaimable in court (see *Rif*). On the other hand, it could be argued that such loans *are* reclaimable in court and that these Amoraim accepted an extra-legal stringency upon themselves (see *Tosafos, Rashba* and *Ran MHK* ed.).

46. R' Yochanan is speaking of a case where Pesach begins on a Saturday night. In such a case the *pesach* offering must be brought on the preceding afternoon, i.e. on the Sabbath. R' Yochanan teaches here that if one had not designated an animal as his *pesach* offering before the Sabbath, he may do so on the Sabbath itself (see *Shabbos Shel Mi*).

47. Every adult Jewish male is required to bring a *chagigah* (festival offering) on the first day of Pesach, Shavuos and Succos (see *Leviticus* 23:41 and *Chagigah* 9a). [R' Yochanan specifies Yom Tov in the case of the *chagigah,* and the Sabbath in the case of the *pesach,* because the *chagigah* is brought on Yom Tov whereas the *pesach* is always brought before Yom Tov.]

As the Gemara shall state below, R' Yochanan's permit applies only to a sacrifice that must be offered that particular day (see *Rashi*).

[R' Yochanan is teaching us that] even though it is ordinarily forbidden by Rabbinic decree to consecrate something on the Sabbath or Yom Tov (Mishnah, *Beitzah* 36b) in the present case it is permitted. For since the actual offering of the sacrifice overrides the Sabbath or Yom Tov, its consecration does as well (*Rashi*).

ד א מיי' פכ"ג מהלכות שבת הלכה ה סמג לאוין סה טוש"ע או"ח סימן שלט סעיף ג וסימן תקכד סעיף א:

ה ב מיי' פ"א מהלכות שביתת עשור הלכה ו סמג לאוין קמ וטוש"ע או"ח סימן תרח סעיף ב:

ו ג מיי' פ"י מהלכות מלוה ולוה הלכה ה סמג לאוין קלג טוש"ע יו"ד סימן קסב סעיף א:

ז ד שם סעיף ג:

ח ה מיי' פ"ד מהלכות יו"ט הלכה כה טוש"ע או"ח סימן תקכז סעיף א:

ט ו מיי' פ"ט מהלכות שמיטה ויובל הלכה ה סמג עשין קמח:

י ז מיי' שם הלכה כח סמג לאוין רעא טור וש"ע חו"מ סימן סז סעיף לו:

יא ח מיי' פכ"ג מהלכות שבת הלכה יד ופ"א מהלכות קרבן פסח הלכה ט סמג עשין רכג:

יב ט מיי' פ"ט מהלכות יו"ט הלכה יט סמג לאוין עה טוש"ע או"ח סימן תקכד סעיף א:

יג י מיי' פכ"ג מהלכות שבת הלכה יד סמג לאוין סה ועה טור ש"ע או"ח סימן שלט סעיף ד וסימן תקכד סעיף א:

רבינו חננאל

להא. דא"ל תנן לא מספקין ולא מרקדין ולא מטפחין. בגדרא. ופשוטה היא. ומיפרשא נמי בגמ' דהמביא כדי יין במס' יו"ט וכן שואלת אשה מחברתה ככרות. ודייקינן מינה בשבת הוא דאסור מכלל דבחול שרי מתניתין דלא כהלל כו' ומסקינן בה אפילו תימא כהלל באתרא דקייצי דמי. ואם אינו מאמינו מניח טליתו אצלו ועושה עמו חשבון לאחר שבת. אתמר הלואת יו"ט רב יוסף אמר לא נתנה ליתבע רבא אמר ניתנה ליתבע ואתינן למיגמר מן מתניתין תנן ואם אינו מאמינו מניח טליתו אצלו כו' ולא גמרינן מינה דלא מיפרשא בהדיא כחד מינייהו ומותבינן לרב יוסף מהא דתנן השוחט את הפרה וחילקה בראש השנה אם היה חדש מעובר משמט. פי' אם היה אלול מעובר נמצא יום לקיחתו חלק מן הפרה יום חול שר"ה מחר הוא וכיון שנושה בו דמי בשר הפרה שלקח מאתמול דכיון שנכנסה שנה שביעית משמטת לדברי רבא ניחא כי נתנה ליתבע ומלוה נושה בו וכשנכנסת שביעית משמטת אלא לרב יוסף דאמר לא נתנה ליתבע אמאי צריך למיתנא משמטת בלאו הכי פטור הוא מלשלם. ואפילו בשאר שני שבוע דהא לא ניתנה ליתבע. ופריק רב יוסף שאני התם דכיון דאיגלאי מלתא דחול היא (ניתנה ליתבע דהא מלוה דחול היא) ואנן לא קאימנא אלא הלואת יו"ט ואסיקנא למשמע מסיפא ואם לאו אינו משמט לרבא דאמר ניתנה ליתבע דתובעו ונפרע ממנו [ניחא] אלא לרב יוסף דאמר לא ניתנה ליתבע קשיא כיון דתני אינו משמט הלא משמע דתובע ונפרע ממנו ואינו יכול לומר לו כי השביעית השמיטתו ופריק רב יוסף לעולם לא נתנה ליתבע והמלוה אינו יכול ליתבע אלא אם יביא הלה ויפרענו יקבל ואינו צריך לומר משמט אני. ואקשינן עליה מכלל דרישא אי יהיב ליה מעצמו לא שקיל. ופריק רב יוסף ואמר רישא אם מחזיר לו צריך שיאמר לו משמט אני. דהא נושה בו מלוה. אבל ספק שאינו נושה בו מלוה אם יבא לחשבון אינו צריך לומר לו משמט אני אלא יקבל כדתנן המחזיר חוב בשביעית צריך שיאמר משמט אני. ואם אמר לו אעפ"כ יקבל ממנו משום שנאמר וזה דבר השמטה. ומפורש ענין זה בפ' השולח גט לאשתו. וראינו רבותינו שהיו

תוספות

ניפרוס סודרא עליה אתי למסחטיה. מכאן מייתי ר"ת ראיה דכיון ושמן לא שייכא סחיטה לעיל בשלהי שמונה שרצים (דף קיא. בד"ה הני מקורזלתא) פירשתי: **לא** מספקין ולא מטפחין. לא כפי' הקונטרס משום דא"כ מאי איריא ביו"ט אפי' בחול המועד נמי אסור כדתנן במועד קטן פרק בתרא (דף כח:) נשים במועד מענות אבל לא מטפחות אלא נראה לרבי משום שמחה רגילין לספק ולטפח בהשמעת קול ואסור שמא יתקן כלי שיר כדמפרש בהמולא תפילין (עירובין דף קד.): **וכן** היה הלל אומר. כרבנן דפליגי עליה באיזהו נשך (ב"מ דף עה.) וקי"ל:

רבה אמר ניתנה ליתבע. הלכה כרבה לגבי רב יוסף: ורב אויא ורבה בר עולא מחמרי אנפשייהו כ"ה בס"א:

דאי אמרת ניתנה ליתבע אתי למיכתב. אע"פ שמזכיר לו לשון שאלה:

דאיגלאי מילתא דבחול הויא. ורב יוסף לא מיירי אלא בשבת ויו"ט ודאי:

והא אנן תנן אין נימנין כו'. פירש ה"ר פורת בשם רבינו שמואל דל"ג ליה חדא דמה שייך להקשות מנמנין של רשות לנמנין של מצוה ועוד דמפרש התם בבילה פרק אין לדין (דף כז:) מאי אין נמנין אין פוסקין דמים בתחילה לבהמה ביו"ט הרי אני עמך בסלע הריני עמך בשתים אבל אומר לו הריני עמך לשליש ולרביע: ולמ"ד

גמרא

ניפרוס סודרא אתי לידי סחיטה נכסייה בנבתמא זימנין דמיפסק ואתי למקטריה הלכך לא אפשר וא"ל רבא בר רב חנן לאביי תנן [א] לא מספקין ולא מטפחין ולא מרקדין ביו"ט וקא חזינן דעבדין ולא אמרינן להו ולא מידי ולטעמיך הא דאמר [ב] רבא [ג] לא ליתיב איניש אפומא דלחייא דילמא מיגנדר ליה חפץ ואתי לאיתויי והא קא חזינן (א) נמי דמותבי חצבי ויתבן אפומא דמבואה ולא אמרינן להו ולא מידי אלא הנח לישראל [ד] מוטב שיהו שוגגין ואל יהו מזידין [ה] סבור מינה הנ"מ בדרבנן אבל בדאורייתא לא [ו] ולא היא ל"ש בדרבנן ול"ש בדאורייתא דהא תוספת דיוה"כ דאורייתא היא וקא חזינן להו דאכלי ושתו עד שתחשך ולא אמרי' להו ולא מידי: וכן אשה מחבירתה ככרות: בשבת הוא דאסיר אבל בחול שפיר דמי לימא מתני' דלא כהלל דתנן [ז] וכן היה הלל אומר [ח] לא תלוה אשה ככר לחבירתה עד שתעשינה דמים שמא יוקירו חטין ונמצאו באות לידי רבית אפילו תימא הלל [ט] הא באתרא דקייץ דמיה הא באתרא דלא קייץ דמיה: ואם אינו מאמינו: איתמר הלוואת יו"ט רב יוסף אמר לא ניתנה ליתבע [י] ורבה אמר [כ] ניתנה ליתבע רב יוסף אמר לא ניתנה ליתבע דאי אמרת ניתנה ליתבע אתי למיכתב רבה אמר ניתנה ליתבע דאי אמרת לא ניתנה לא יהיב ליה ואתי לאימנועי משמחת יו"ט תנן אם אינו מאמינו מניח טליתו אצלו אי אמרת בשלמא לא ניתנה ליתבע משום הכי מניח טליתו אצלו ועושה עמו חשבון לאחר שבת אלא אי אמרת ניתנה ליתבע אמאי מניח טליתו אצלו ליתן ליה ולתבעיה אמר לא בעינא דליקום בדינא ודיינא מתיב רב אידי בר אבין [ל] השוחט את הפרה וחילקה בראש השנה אם היה חדש מעובר משמט ואם לאו אינו משמט ואי לא ניתנה ליתבע מאי משמט שאני התם דאיגלאי מילתא דחול הוא ת"ש מסיפא אם לאו אינו משמט אי אמרת בשלמא ניתנה ליתבע היינו דקתני אינו משמט אלא אי אמרת לא ניתנה ליתבע (ב) אמאי אינו משמט דאי יהיב ליה שקיל מכלל דרישא אי יהיב ליה לא שקיל אי רישא צריך למימר ליה משמט אני סיפא לא צריך למימר ליה משמט אני כדתנן [מ] המחזיר חוב בשביעית יאמר לו משמט אני ואם אמר לו אעפ"כ יקבל ממנו משום שנאמר [א] וזה דבר השמטה רב אויא שקיל משכונא [נ] רבה בר עולא מערים איערומי: וכן ערב פסח: א"ר יוחנן [ס] מקדיש אדם פסחו בשבת וחגיגתו ביו"ט נימא מסייע ליה וכן ערב פסח בירושלים שחל להיות בשבת מניח טליתו אצלו ונוטל את פסחו ועושה עמו חשבון לאחר יו"ט הכא במאי עסקינן בממנה אחרים עמו על פסחו דמעיקרא מיקדש וקאי והא אנן תנן [ע] אין נמנין על הבהמה בתחילה ביו"ט שאני הכא כיון דרגיל אצלו כמאן דאימני ביה מעיקרא דמי והא תני רבי הושעיא הולך אדם אצל רועה הרגיל אצלו ונותן לו טלה לפסחו ומקדישו ויוצא בו התם נמי כיון דרגיל אצלו אקדושי (ג) ליה מעיקרא והא מקדיש קתני הקדש עילוי מדרבנן ומי אמר ר' יוחנן הכי [פ] והא אמר ר' יוחנן הלכה כסתם משנה ותנן [צ] לא מקדישין ולא מעריכין ולא מחרימין ולא מגביהין תרומות ומעשרות כל אלו ביו"ט אמרו ק"ו בשבת לא קשיא כאן בחובות שקבוע להן זמן כאן בחובות שאין קבוע להן זמן:

מתני' מונה אדם את אורחיו ואת פרפרותיו מפיו אבל לא מן הכתב מפיס אדם עם בניו ועם בני ביתו על השולחן ובלבד שלא יתכוין לעשות מנה גדולה כנגד מנה קטנה [ק] ומטילין חלשין על הקדשים ביו"ט אבל לא על המנות:

גמ'

רש"י

בנבתמא. כיסוי: **זימנין דמיפסק כו'.** כיון דמצרכת ליה כיסוי קטר ליה בכד וזימנין דמיפסק ואתי למקטריה והיא קשר של קיימא דאסור מדאורייתא: **ואתי לידי סחיטה.** ודקאמר במסכת בילה ניפרוס סודרא עלויה כו' (ד) [התם] בדבר יבש קא מיירי: **אין מספקין.** כף אל כף משום אבל: **מטפחין.** על הלב: **מרקדין.** לשמחה וטעמא מפרש במסכת בילה שמא יתקן כלי שיר: **אפומא דלחייא.** לפי שאין ניכר כל כך בין מבוי לרה"ר: **ואתי לאתויי.** חפץ המתגלגל תוך ד' אמות: ומגנדר מלבייהו ומייתין ליה ל"ג: **בשבת הוא דאסור.** לומר הלויני משום ממכח: **הא בחול שרי.** ולא חיישינן לרבית ואף על גב דבלשון הלואה קאמר ליה: **באתרא דקייץ דמייהו.** דככרות לא אתי לידי רבית שאם יוקירו יתן דמיהן: **לא ניתנה ליתבע.** בב"ד שאין ב"ד נזקקין לה לעולם: **בדינא ודיינא.** לא לבא לדין ולא לברור דיין ולהטריח את עלמו: **השוחט את הפרה וחילקה בראש השנה.** של מולאי שביעית ללוקחים ובהקפה וקיי"ל שביעית משמטת בסופה דכתיב מקן: **אם היה חדש.** אלול מעובר ועשו ראש השנה שני ימים משמט דיום טוב ראשון של סוף שביעית היה ונמלאת זו הלואת שביעית ואם לאו הויא לה הלואת מולאי שביעית ואינו משמט: ל"ג אי אמרת בשלמא כו' ה"ג **ואם לא ניתנה ליתבע מאי משמט.** הואיל ואין ב"ד נזקקין לכופו שמוטה היא ועומדת: **דחול הוא.** שהרי חדש מעובר ולא הוי יו"ט עד למחר הלכך אי לאו דשביעית הוא הוה גבי: **ואם לאו אינו משמט.** אלמא ניתנה ליתבע ומשני מאי אינו משמט דאי יהיב ליה שקיל: **מכלל דרישא אי יהיב ליה לא שקיל.** בתמיה: **רישא.** דהלואת שביעית היא אי נמי יהיב ליה לוה לריך למימר ליה מלוה משמט אני: (ה) **ואם אמר.** לוה אעפ"כ איני חפץ שישמטו יקבל ממנו: **דבר השמטה.** אפילו מקבל חובו יזכיר לו שמיטה בדבורו: **שקיל משכונא.** בשעת הלואה מהלואת יו"ט: **מערים איערומי.** לאחר י"ט לוקח ממנו שום חפץ ומעכבו: **פסחו בשבת.** אם חל י"ד בשבת: **וחגיגתו ביו"ט.** ביום הקרבתה מותר להקדיש ואע"ג דתנן אלו הן משום שבות אין מקדישין הני כיון דהקרבתן דוחה קדושתן דוחה: **בממנה אחרים עמו.** כדכתיב (שמות יב) במכסת נפשות: **על פסחו.** שהיה קדוש ועומד מאתמול: **אקדושי.** מקדיש ליה רועה מע"ש שהרי יודע שזה סומך עליו: **עילוי.** מעלה בעלמא שיקדישו בעלים: **הא.** דקתני אין מקדישין בחובות שאין קבוע להן זמן קאי שאין הקרבתן דוחה שבת: **מתני' פרפרותיו.** מיני מעדנים: **אבל לא מן הכתב.** אם כתב מע"ש כך וכך אורחים פלוני ופלוני זמנתי כדי שלא ישכחם לא יקרא באותו כתב בשבת ובגמ' מפרש טעמא: **מפיס.** לשון פיים מטיל פיים לחלק מי מגיע כל מנה ומנה: **ובלבד שלא יתכוין לעשות כו'.** שיהו המנות שוות ולא תהא אחת גדולה ואחת קטנה לזכות בגדולה הזוכה ע"פ הגורל והמתחייב ע"פ הגורל לקטנה יטלנה ובגמ' מפרש טעמא: **חלשים.** גורלות: **על הקדשים.** בין הכהנים: **אבל לא על המנות.** בגמרא מפרש: גמ'

מסורת הש"ס

א) בילה ל. ע"ש, ב) [נ"ל רבה], ג) לעיל קמח. בילה ל, ד) [ב"ב ס: ועי' תוס' לעיל נה. ד"ה ואע"ג ותוס' ב"ב ס: ד"ה מוטב ותוס' ע"ז ד. ד"ה סורי], ה) [בילה ל. ע"ש], ו) ר"ה עה. ז) [גי' רב אלפס והרא"ש ורבאן], ח) שביעית פ"י משנה ב, ט) ג"ז שם [ב"מ גיטין לו:], י) ר"ה רבא, כ) פסחים סו: [ועי' תוספות מגילה ב. ד"ה ואלו ותוס' בכורות נח. ד"ה ואלו], ל) בילה כ:, מ) [לעיל מו. ופ"ט], נ) פסחים סו: בילה לו:, ס) [עיין תוס' לקמן קמט:].

הגהות הב"ח

(א) גמ' והא קא חזינן נמי דמותבי חלביהו וכו' כמו להן לישראל: (ב) שם מאי אינו משמט דאי יהיב ליה: (ג) שם אקדושי ליה מעיקרא: (ד) רש"י ד"ה ואתי לידי סחיטה כו' סודרא עלויה כו' כיון דשמן קמיירי: (ה) ד"ה רישא וכו' משמט אני ואם אמר לו הלוה אעפ"כ כצ"ל והד"א:

תורה אור השלם

א) וְזֶה דְּבַר הַשְּׁמִטָּה שָׁמוֹט כָּל בַּעַל מַשֵּׁה יָדוֹ אֲשֶׁר יַשֶּׁה בְּרֵעֵהוּ לֹא יִגֹּשׂ אֶת רֵעֵהוּ וְאֶת אָחִיו כִּי קָרָא שְׁמִטָּה לַייָ: (דברים טו, ב)

ליקוטי רש"י

ניפרוס סודרא. קל הוא ואינו מכביד וטוני [בעלמא הוא ולהגלות]. **אתי לידי סחיטה.** שנסרה המים. **נכסייה בנבתמא.** כסוי של עץ העשוי לכדין. **זימנין דמיפסק.** שלריך לקושרו שלא יפול ונבדק זימנין דמיפסק בהליכתה ואתי למקטריה וקשר העשוי להתקיים של מלאכה הוא. **לא מספקין.** משום שיר או משום אבל. **מטפחין.** ידיו זו בזו. **מספקין.** כף על כף. **מרקדין.** ברגל וכולם נאסרו משום שבות גזרה שמא יתקן כלי שיר בפרק משילין (ביצה ל.). ברגל וכולן לשמחה ושיר [illegible] מפרש בפרק גזרה שמא יתקן כנגנן כלי שיר דקא עביד מנא [שם לו:]. **אפומא דלחייא.** למי המחיר במבוי בשבת. **דילמא מיגנדר ליה חפץ.** נראה מתוך הכרים חוץ לחי. **ואתי לאיתויי.** [illegible] **מוטב שיהו שוגגין.** שאינם סבורים שיש איסור בדבר [שבת ב"ב ס:]. **ואל יהו מזידין.** שאחר שנודיעם לא ימנעו [illegible]

דלרגילו למעבר אדרבנן כי הנך דמטפחין והנך דיתבן אפומא דלחיא. **תוספת דיום הכפורים.** של[illegible] מבעוד יום דאורייתא היא דנפקא לן (יומא פא:) מועניתם את נפשותיכם בתשעה. **דקאכלי ושתו** [illegible] ולא גרס משחשכה [ביצה שם]. **המחזיר חוב בשביעית.** בזמן שהשביעית נוהגת ועברה עליו שביעית [illegible] שהחזירו בשביעית עלמה דא"כ לא הוה לריך למימר משמט אני דקי"ל אין שביעית משמטת אלא בס[illegible] המלוה שיאמר לו משמט אני. **ואם אמר לו אע"פ כן.** אני רולה להחזירו לך. **שנאמר וזה דבר** [illegible] דיבור של שמיטה [גיטין לז:]. **פסחו בשבת.** ליכא למימר ביום טוב דאין פסח קרב ביום טוב וחגי[illegible]

[פסחים סו:]. **הלכה כסתם משנה.** רבי הוא סדר המשנה וכשראה דברי חכם וישרו בעיניו שנאן סתם ולא הזכיר שם אומרו עליהן כדי שלא יהו שנויה מפי יחיד ונראין כאילו נשנו מפי המרובים ויעשו כמותן [ביצה ב:]. **לא מקדישין** [illegible] **מעריכין.** ערכך עלי ונותן כפי שנים כמו שכתוב בפרשת ערכין (ויקרא כז). **ולא מחרימין.** הרי בהמה זו חרם וסתם חרמים לבדק הבית [שם לו:]. **לא מקדישין ולא מעריכין וכו'.** [גזירה] משום מקח וממכר דלמקח וממכר דמו מרשותו לרשות הקדש ומקח וממכר אסור מן המקרא דכתיב ממצוא חפצך ודבר דבר (ישעיה נח) אי נמי מקח וממכר אתי לידי כתיבה שטרי מכירה ואם תאמר הויא לה גזירה לגזירה כולה חדא גזירה היא [שם לז.]. **ולא מגביהין תרומות** ומעשרות. משום שבות של מלוה אין מגביהין תרומות ומעשרות דמיחזי כמתקן [גיטין נד.]. **בחובות שקבוע להן זמן.** לבו ביום שפיר דמי דהואיל ונשחטין היום יכול להקדישן היום [פסחים סו:].

Mishnah evidently permits one to consecrate a *pesach* offering on the Sabbath.

The Gemara deflects the proof from our Mishnah by limiting it to a particular case:

הָכָא בְּמַאי עַסְקִינַן – What are we dealing with here? בִּמְמַנֶּה אֲחֵרִים עִמּוֹ עַל פִּסְחוֹ – We are possibly dealing **with one who enrolls others along with himself** to share **in his *pesach* offering,** דְּמֵעִיקָּרָא מִיקְדַּשׁ וְקָאֵי – **so that** already **from before** the Sabbath the animal **stood consecrated.**[48] Since the Mishnah possibly speaks of this case (i.e. an animal consecrated before the Sabbath), it does not prove R' Yochanan's ruling that one may consecrate a *pesach* offering on the Sabbath itself.

The Gemara asks:

וְהָא אֲנַן תְּנַן – But we learned in a Mishnah:[49] אֵין נִמְנִין עַל הַבְּהֵמָה בַּתְּחִילָּה בְּיוֹם טוֹב – [PEOPLE] MAY NOT BE ENROLLED INITIALLY into a group TO purchase the meat of AN ANIMAL ON YOM TOV.[50] Thus, we see that it is forbidden to purchase an animal (or a share in one) on Yom Tov or the Sabbath.[51] – ? –

The Gemara answers:

שָׁאנֵי הָכָא – This case (i.e. where someone enrolls in a group that owns a *pesach* offering) **is different** from that of the aforementioned Mishnah. **כֵּיוָן דְּרָגִיל אֶצְלוֹ – Since [the person seeking to enroll] was accustomed to** do so with **[a member of this group]** in previous years,[52] כְּמַאן דְּאִימְנֵי בֵּיהּ מֵעִיקָּרָא דָּמֵי – **he is considered as one who was** already **enrolled from before** the Sabbath.[53]

The Gemara has argued that our Mishnah can be interpreted in accordance with the position that one may *not* consecrate a *pesach* offering on the Sabbath. This position is now challenged:

וְהָא תָּנֵי רַבִּי הוֹשַׁעְיָא – But R' Hoshaya has taught the following Baraisa: הוֹלֵךְ אָדָם אֵצֶל רוֹעֶה הָרָגִיל אֶצְלוֹ – A PERSON MAY GO on the Sabbath TO A SHEPHERD WHO IS ACCUSTOMED TO HIM (i.e. a shepherd who has sold him animals frequently in the past), וְנוֹתֵן לוֹ טָלֶה לְפִסְחוֹ – AND [THE SHEPHERD] MAY GIVE HIM A LAMB FOR HIS *PESACH* OFFERING. וּמַקְדִּישׁוֹ וְיוֹצֵא בּוֹ – [THE PURCHASER] MAY then CONSECRATE [THE LAMB] AND FULFILL HIS OBLIGATION WITH IT. This Baraisa states explicitly that one may consecrate an animal as a *pesach* offering on the Sabbath.

The Gemara rejects this proof as well:

הָתָם נַמִּי – In that case, too, כֵּיוָן דְּרָגִיל אֶצְלוֹ – **since [the shepherd] was accustomed to him** (which means that he had sold him animals for his *pesach* offerings in previous years), אַקְדּוּשֵׁי [מַקְדִּישׁ] לֵיהּ מֵעִיקָּרָא – **[the shepherd]** already **consecrated [that lamb] for him from before** the Sabbath.[54] Thus, no consecration took place on the Sabbath.

The Gemara challenges this interpretation of R' Hoshaya's Baraisa:

וְהָא מַקְדִּישׁ קָתָנֵי – But the Baraisa explicitly **states:** HE (i.e. the purchaser) CONSECRATES the animal!

The Gemara answers:

הֶקְדֵּשׁ עִילּוּי מִדְּרַבָּנַן – The Baraisa is possibly referring to **a consecration** that is only **a Rabbinic elevation** of the animal's status.[55]

The Gemara notes a seeming contradiction in R' Yochanan's stated positions:

וּמִי אָמַר רַבִּי יוֹחָנָן הָכִי – Did R' Yochanan actually say this (viz. that one may consecrate offerings on the Sabbath and Yom Tov)? **וְהָא אָמַר רַבִּי יוֹחָנָן – But R' Yochanan has said:** הֲלָכָה כִּסְתָם מִשְׁנָה – **The halachah follows** the view stated in **an anonymous Mishnah,** וּתְנַן – **and we learned in an** anonymous **Mishnah:** לֹא מַקְדִּישִׁין וְלֹא מַעֲרִיכִין וְלֹא מַחֲרִימִין – WE MAY NOT CONSECRATE;[56] NOR MAKE *ERECH* VOWS;[57] NOR MAKE A *CHEREM*;[58] וְלֹא מַגְבִּיהִין תְּרוּמוֹת וּמַעַשְׂרוֹת – NOR SEPARATE

NOTES

48. That is, the Mishnah refers to a person who seeks to join a group that had already (before the Sabbath) acquired and consecrated a *pesach* offering. [The *pesach* offering may be eaten only by those "registered" on it prior to its slaughter, as derived from the verse (*Exodus* 12:4): בְּמִכְסַת נְפָשֹׁת, *according to the number of people.*] When he approached the group on the Sabbath and asked them to include him, they requested payment. Since one may not pay on the Sabbath, he left his cloak with them as a security.

49. *Beitzah* 27b.

50. In Mishnaic times [and even until recently, before the advent of refrigeration], it was a standard practice not to slaughter an animal unless there were advance commitments to purchase all or most of the animal's meat. Commonly, several people would approach a butcher as a group to purchase an animal from him, and have him slaughter it and divide the meat among them. The Mishnah teaches that a group purchase of an animal may not be arranged on Yom Tov (and, by implication, certainly not on the Sabbath, whose prohibitions are more stringent). The reason for the Mishnah's ruling is that this violates the general prohibition against transacting business on Yom Tov (see *Rashi* ibid. ד״ה אין פוסקים). [Individual purchase is also forbidden; the Mishnah, however, illustrates the operative laws according to the prevalent method of group purchase.]

51. [Therefore, how could the Gemara have interpreted our Mishnah as referring to one who bought a share in a *pesach* offering on the Sabbath?]

[It is difficult to understand why the Gemara did not pose a direct contradiction between our Mishnah and this Mishnah from *Beitzah*. For regardless of how our Mishnah is interpreted (i.e. whether it refers to an animal consecrated on or before the Sabbath), it apparently sanctions the *sale* of an animal on the Sabbath, whereas the Mishnah in *Beitzah* prohibits such a sale.] *Tosafos* raise a different problem with the Gemara: In point of fact, there is no contradiction at all between the two Mishnahs, for these two reasons: (a) Our Mishnah refers to a person who must purchase an animal to fulfill a mitzvah, whereas the Mishnah in *Beitzah* speaks of one who makes a discretionary purchase. (b) The prohibition of the Mishnah in *Beitzah* is explained by the Gemara (ibid.) as applying only where the parties mention a price. In the case of our Mishnah, however, they do not discuss the price until after Yom Tov. In view of these difficulties, *Tosafos* conclude that our version of the Gemara's text is not accurate. The words וְהָא אֲנַן תְּנַן, *But we learned in a Mishnah,* through מֵעִיקָּרָא דָּמֵי, *as . . . from before,* should be deleted. [*Meiri* also reports that these words do not appear in authoritative versions of the text.]

52. [The Gemara is currently suggesting that this is the case to which our Mishnah refers.]

53. Knowing that he would ask to join them, the group had already allotted him a share. Thus, our Mishnah refers to a "sale" made before the Sabbath.

54. For the shepherd knew that this person would be relying on him (*Rashi*). [Emendation follows *Hagahos HaBach. Rashi* also seems to have the word מַקְדִּישׁ in his text.]

55. The Rabbis required a person who is going to offer an animal to verbally consecrate it even if it was already consecrated by someone else (see *Rashi* and *Ritva MHK* ed.; see also *Tos. Rid*). [Since the *actual* consecration took effect before the Sabbath, this Baraisa does not prove that one may consecrate offerings on the Sabbath.]

56. It is forbidden to designate an animal for sacrifice, or to donate an object to the Temple treasury on the Sabbath or Yom Tov.

57. The Torah (*Leviticus* 27:1-8) states that if a person pledges the value of a certain person (עֶרְכְּךָ עָלַי) [or his own value (עֶרְכִּי עָלַי)], he must donate to the Temple treasury the amount established by the Torah as the valuation for a person of that particular age [and gender] (*Rashi* to *Beitzah* 36b ד״ה מעריכין).

58. A person may pronounce an object which he owns as *cherem* (set aside for priestly or Temple use). When he does not specify the exact nature of the *cherem*, it becomes the property of the Temple treasury (*Rashi* ibid. ד״ה ולא מחרימין).

The Rabbis banned these activities because they resemble commercial transactions insofar as the ownership of an object is transferred from an individual to that of the Temple treasury (Gemara to *Beitzah* 37a with *Rashi* ibid.).

עין משפט נר מצוה

ד א מיי' פכ"ג מהלכות שבת הלכה ה סמג לאוין סה טוש"ע או"ח סימן שלט סעיף ג וסימן תקכד סעיף א:

ה ב מיי' פ"ג מהלכות שביתת עשור הלכה ז סמג לאוין סה וטור ושו"ע או"ח סימן תרח סעיף ג:

ו ג מיי' פ"י מהלכות מלוה ולוה הלכה ב סמג לאוין קלג טוש"ע יו"ד סימן קסב סעיף א:

ז ד שם סעיף ג:

ח ה מיי' פ"ד מהלכות י"ט הלכה כה סמג לאוין עה טוש"ע או"ח סימן תקכה סעיף א:

ט ו מיי' פ"ט מהלכות שמיטה ויובל הלכה ה סמג עשין קמט:

י ז מיי' שם הלכה כח סמג לאוין רעא טור ושו"ע חו"מ סימן סז סעיף לו:

יא ח מיי' פכ"ג מהלכות שבת הלכה יד ופ"ד מהלכות קרבן פסח הלכה יח סמג עשין רכג:

יב ט מיי' פ"ד מהלכות י"ט הלכה יט סמג לאוין עה טוש"ע או"ח סימן תקכד סעיף א:

יג י מיי' פכ"ג מהלכות שבת הלכה יד סמג לאוין סה ועה טור ש"ע או"ח סימן שכג סעיף ד וסימן תקכד סעיף א:

רבינו חננאל

להא. דא"ל תנן לא מספקין ולא מרקדין ולא מטפחין. בגדרא. ופשוטה היא. ומיפרש נמי בגמ' דהמביא ככדי יין במס' יו"ט וכן שואלת אשה מחברתה ככרות. ודייקינן מינה בשבת הוא דאסור מכלל דבחול שרי מתניתין דלא כהלל כו' ומסקינן בה אפילו תימא הלל באתרא דקייצי דמי. ואם אינו מאמינו מניח טליתו אצלו ועושה עמו חשבון לאחר שבת. אתמר הלואת יו"ט רב יוסף אמר לא נתנה ליתבע רבא אמר ניתנה ליתבע. ואותבינן למימר מן מתניתין תנן ואם אינו מאמינו מניח טליתו אצלו כו' ולא גמרינן מינה דלא מיפרשא בהדיא כחד מינייהו ומותבינן לרב יוסף מהא דתנן השוחט את הפרה וחילקה בראש השנה אם היה חדש מעובר משמט. פי' אם היה אלול מעובר נמצא יום לקיחתו חלק מן הפרה יום חול שריה מחר הוא וכיון שנושה בו דמי בשר הפרה שלקח מאתמול דכיון שנכנסה שנה שביעית משמטת לדברי רבא ניחא כי נתנה ליתבע ומלוה נושה בו וכשנכנסת שביעית משמטת אלא לרב יוסף דאמר לא נתנה ליתבע אמאי צריך למיתנא משמטת בלאו הכי פטור הוא. ואפילו בשאר שני שבוע דהא לא ניתנה ליתבע. ופריק רב יוסף שאני התם דכיון דאיגלאי מלתא דחול היא (ניתנה ליתבע דהא מלוה דחול היא) ואם לאו אינו משמט אלא הלואת יו"ט ואסיקנא למשמע מסיפא ואם לאו אינו משמט לרבא דאמר ניתנה ליתבע דתובעו ונפרע ממנו [ניחא] אלא לרב יוסף דאמר לא ניתנה ליתבע קשיא כיון דתני אינו משמט הא לאו משמע דתובעו ונפרע ממנו ואינו יכול לומר לו כי השביעית השמיטתו ופריק רב יוסף לעולם לא נתנה ליתבע והמלוה אינו יכול ליתבע אלא אם יביא הלוה ויפרעהו קבל ואינו צריך לומר לו משמט אני. ואקשינן עליה מכלל דרישא אי יהיב ליה מעצמו לא שקיל. ופריק רב יוסף ואמר רישא אם אחר המחזיר לו צריך שיאמר לו משמט אני. דהא נושה בו מלוה. אבל ספק שאינו נושה בו מלוה אם יבא לחשבון אינו צריך לומר לו משמט אני אלא לא יקבל כדתנן המחזיר חוב בשביעית צריך שיאמר משמט אני. ואם אמר לו אעפ"כ יקבל ממנו משום שנאמר וזה דבר השמטה. ומפורש ענין זה בפ' השולח גט לאשתו. ואוקימנא רבוותינו שהיו

מסורת הש"ס

א) ביצה ל. וד' לו: ב) [נ"ל רבה], ג) לעיל קמא. ביצה ל., ד) [נ"ב ם: ועי' תוס' לעיל נה. ד"ה ולעוג ותוס' ב"ק ס: ד"ה מוטב ותוס' ע"ז ד. ד"ה שסרי], ה) [ביצה ל. ע"ש], ו) ב"מ עה., ז) [גי' רב אלפס והרא"ש ורבא], ח) שביעית פ"י משנה ב, ט) ג"ז ס: [מ"ח גיטין לו:], י) נ"ל רבא, כ) פסחים סו: [ועי' תוספות חגיגה ח. ד"ה משום ותוס' כתובות נח. ד"ה ואין], ל) ביצה לו:, מ) [לעיל מו. וש"נ], נ) פסחים סו: ביצה לו:, ס) [עיין תוס' לקמן קמט.].

הגהות הב"ח

(א) גמ' והא קא חזינן נמי דמותבי אלבייהו וכו' הנח להן לישראל: (ב) שם מאי אינו משמט דאי יהיב ליה: (ג) שם אקדושי מקדיש ליה מעיקרא: (ד) רש"י ד"ה ואתי לידי סחיטה וכו' סודרא עלויה כו' בזמן ושמן קמיירי: (ה) ד"ה רישא וכו' משמט אני ואם אמר לו אעפ"כ כדי להוה אעפ"כ כל"ל והד"א:

תורה אור השלם

א) וְזֶה דְּבַר הַשְּׁמִטָּה שָׁמוֹט כָּל בַּעַל מַשֵּׁה יָדוֹ אֲשֶׁר יַשֶּׁה בְּרֵעֵהוּ לֹא יִגֹּשׂ אֶת רֵעֵהוּ וְאֶת אָחִיו כִּי קָרָא שְׁמִטָּה לַייָ: [דברים טו, ב]

ליקוטי רש"י

ניפרום סודרא. קל הוא ואינו מכביד ועשוי [כעטרא הוא ולכבוע]. אתי לידי סחיטה. שמעה במים. נכסיה בנכתמא. כסוי של כן העשוי לכדין. זימנין דמיפסק. שלריך לקושרו שלא יפול. ולידך תמיכון למפסקיה בכסלי ולאתי למקטריה וקשר העשוי להתקיים לא מלאכה הוא. לא מספקין. משום שיר ידיו זו לזו. מספקין. כף על ירך. מרקדין. ברגל וכולם משום שבות גזרה שמא יתקן כלי שיר בפרק משילין [ביצה לו:]. [ביצה ל.]. ברגל ובלון לשמחה ולשיר ובכשרה מפרש גזרה שמא יתקן כגבון כלי שיר דקא עביד מנא [שם לו:]. אפומא דלחייא. לחי המתיר מבוי בכשבת. דילמא מיגנדר ליה חפץ. מתגלגל בכותים חוץ ללחי. ואתי לאתויי. מתוך שאינו נמצוי ומצוי מקורה להפקר שם רשות הרבים מבני רשות היחיד ומביאו. ולא אמרינן להו ולא מידי. ולף על גב דעבדין לאיסורא לא מחינן. הנח להן לישראל. כדבר שאין לו לא יחיר כסס [שם ל.]. מוטב שיהו שוגגין. שאינם סבורים שיש איסור בדבר. ואל יהו מזידין. שעכשו כשהנו אין אנו משגיחין ולא ימנו מלשה. הנח מילי. דלא אמרינן לישראל. בדרבנן.

נִיפְרוֹם סודרא עליה אתי למסחטיה. מכאן מייתי ר"ת ראיה דביין ושמן לא שייכא סחיטה לעיל בשלהי שמונה שרצים (דף קיא. בד"ה האי מסוכרייתא) פירשתי: **לא** מספקין ולא מטפחין. לא כפי' הקונטרס משום דא"כ מאי איריא ביו"ט אפי' בחול המועד נמי אסור כדתנן במועד קטן פרק בתרא (דף כח:) נשים במועד מענות אבל לא מטפחות אלא נראה לרבי משום שמחה רגילין לספק ולטפח בהשמעת קול ואסור שמא יתקן כלי שיר כדמפרש בהמולא תפילין (עירובין דף קד.): **וכן** היה הלל אומר. כרבנן דפליגי עליה באיזהו נשך (ב"מ ד' עה.) וקי"ל:

רבה אמר ניתנה ליתבע. הלכה כרבה לגבי רב יוסף: ורב אויא ורבה בר עולא מחמרי אנפשייהו כ"ה בס"א:

דאי אמרת ניתנה ליתבע אתי למיכתב. אע"פ שמזכיר לו לשון שאלה:

דאיגלאי מילתא דבחול הויא. ורב יוסף לא מיירי אלא בשבת ויו"ט ודאי:

והא אנן תנן אין נמנין כו'. פירש ה"ר פורת בשם רבינו שמואל דל"ג ליה חדא דמה שייך להקשות מנמנין של רשות לנמנין של מלוה ועוד דמפרש התם בביצה פרק אין לדין (דף כז:) מאי אין נמנין אין פוסקין דמים בתחילה לבהמה ביו"ט הרי אני עמך בסלע הריני עמך בשתים אבל אומר לו הריני עמך לשליש ולרביע: ולמ"ד

בנכתמא. כיסוי: זימנין דמיפסק כו'. כיון דמלרכת ליה כיסוי קטר ליה בכד וזימנין דמיפסק ואתי למקטריה והיא קשר של קיימא דאסור מדאורייתא: ואתי לידי סחיטה. ודקאמר במסכת ביצה ניפרוס סודרא עלויה כו' (ד) [התם] בדבר יבש קא מיירי: אין מספקין. כף אל כף משום אבל: מטפחין. על הלב: מרקדין. לשמחה וטעמא מפרש במסכת ביצה שמא יתקן כלי שיר: אפומא דלחייא. לפי שאין ניכר כל כך בין מבוי לרה"ר: ואתי לאתויי. חפץ המתגלגל חוץ לד' אמות: ומגנדר אלביהן ומייתין ליה ל"ג: בשבת הוא דאסור. לומר הלויני משום מקח: הא בחול שרי. ולא חיישינן לרבית ואף על גב דבלשון הלואה קאמר ליה: באתרא דקייץ דמייהו. דככרות לא אתי לידי רבית שאם יוקירו יתן דמיהן: לא ניתנה ליתבע. בב"ד שאין ב"ד מזקקין לה לעולם: בדינא ודיינא. לא לבא לדין ולא לברור דיין ולהטריח את עצמו: השוחט את הפרה וחילקה בראש השנה. של מוצאי שביעית ללוקחים בהקפה וקיי"ל שביעית משמטת בסופה דכתיב מקץ: אם היה חדש. אלול מעובר ועשו ראש השנה שני ימים משמט דיום טוב ראשון של סוף שביעית היה ונמצאת זו הלואת שביעית ואם לאו הויא לה הלואת מוצאי שביעית ואינו משמט: ל"ג אי אמרת בשלמא כו' ה"ג ואם לא ניתנה ליתבע מאי משמט. הואיל ואין ב"ד מזקקין לכופו שמוטה היא ועומדת: דחול הוא. שהרי חדש מעובר ולא הוי יו"ט עד למחר הלכך אי לאו דשביעית הוא הוה גבי: ואם לאו אינו משמט. אלמא ניתנה ליתבע ומשני מאי אינו משמט דאי יהיב ליה שקיל: מכלל דרישא אי יהיב ליה לא שקיל. בתמיה: רישא. דהלואת שביעית היא אי נמי יהיב ליה לוה צריך למימר ליה מלוה משמט אני: (ה) ואם אמר. לוה אעפ"כ אני חפץ שיקבל ממנו: דבר השמטה. אפילו מקבל מוכו יזכיר לו שמיטה בדבורו: שקיל משכונא. בשעת הלואה מהלואת יו"ט: מערים איערומי. לאחר י"ט לוקח ממנו שום חפץ ומעכבו: פסחו בשבת. אם חל י"ד בשבת: וחגיגתו ביו"ט. ביום הקרבתה מותר להקדיש ואע"ג דתנן אלו הן משום שבות אין מקדישין הכי כיון דהקרבתן דוחה קדושתן דוחה: בממנה אחרים עמו. כדכתיב (שמות יב) במכסת נפשות: על פסחו. שהיה קדוש ועומד מאתמול: אקדושי. מקדיש ליה רועה מע"ש שהרי יודע שזה סומך עליו: עילוי. מעלה בעלמא שיקדישו בעלים: הא. דקתני אין מקדישין בחובות שאין קבוע להן זמן קאי שאין הקרבתן דוחה שבת: **מתני'** פרפרותיו. מיני מעדנים: אבל לא מן הכתב. אם כתב מע"ש כך וכך אורחים פלוני ופלוני זמנתי כדי שלא ישכחם לא יקרא באותו כתב בשבת ובגמ' מפרש טעמא: מפיס. לשון פיים מטיל פיים לחלק מי מגיע כל מנה ומנה: ובלבד שלא יתכוין לעשות כו'. שיהו המנות שוות ולא תהא אחת גדולה ואחת קטנה לזכות בגדולה הזוכה ע"פ הגורל והמתמיה ע"פ הגורל לקטנה יטלנה ובגמ' מפרש טעמא: חלשים. גורלות: על הקדשים. בין הכהנים: אבל לא על המנות. בגמרא מפרש:

ניפרום סודרא אתי לידי סחיטה נכסיה בנכתמא זימנין דמיפסק ואתי למקטריה הלכך לא אפשר וא"ל רבא בר רב חנן לאביי תנן [א] לא מספקין ולא מטפחין ולא מרקדין ביו"ט וקא חזינן דעבדין ולא אמרינן להו ולא מידי ולטעמיך הא דאמר [ב] רבא לא ליתיב איניש אפומא דלחייא דילמא מיגנדר ליה חפץ ואתי לאיתויי והא קא חזינן (א) נמי דמותבי חצבי ויתבן אפומא דמבואה ולא אמרינן להו ולא מידי אלא הנח להן לישראל [ג] מוטב שיהו שוגגין ואל יהו מזידין [ד] סבור מינה הנ"מ בדרבנן אבל בדאורייתא לא ולא היא ל"ש בדרבנן ול"ש בדאורייתא דהא תוספת דיוה"כ דאורייתא היא וקא חזינן להו דאכלי ושתו עד שתחשך ולא אמרי' להו ולא מידי: וכן אשה מחבירתה ככרות: בשבת הוא דאסיר אבל בחול שפיר דמי לימא מתני' דלא כהלל דתנן [ה] וכן היה הלל אומר לא תלוה אשה ככר לחבירתה עד שתעשינה דמים שמא יוקרו חטין ונמצאו באות לידי רבית אפילו תימא הלל [ו] הא באתרא דקייץ דמיה הא באתרא דלא קייץ דמיה: ואם אינו מאמינו: איתמר הלוואת יו"ט רב יוסף אמר לא ניתנה ליתבע [ז] ורבה אמר [ח] ניתנה ליתבע רב יוסף אמר לא ניתנה ליתבע דאי אמרת ניתנה ליתבע אתי למיכתב רבה אמר ניתנה ליתבע דאי אמרת לא ניתנה לא יהיב ליה ואתי לאימנועי משמחת יו"ט תנן אם אינו מאמינו מניח טליתו אצלו אי אמרת בשלמא לא ניתנה ליתבע משום הכי מניח טליתו אצלו ועושה עמו חשבון לאחר שבת אלא אי אמרת ניתנה ליתבע אמאי מניח טליתו אצלו ליתן ליה ולתבעיה אמר לא בעינא דליקום בדינא ודיינא מתיב רב אידי בר אבין [ט] השוחט את הפרה וחילקה בראש השנה אם היה חדש מעובר משמט ואם לאו אינו משמט ואי לא ניתנה ליתבע מאי משמט שאני התם דאיגלאי מילתא דחול הוא ת"ש מסיפא אם לאו אינו משמט אי אמרת בשלמא ניתנה ליתבע היינו דקתני אינו משמט אלא אי אמרת לא ניתנה ליתבע (ב) אמאי אינו משמט דאי יהיב ליה שקיל מכלל דרישא אי יהיב ליה לא שקיל רישא צריך למימר ליה משמט אני סיפא לא צריך למימר ליה משמט אני כדתנן [י] המחזיר חוב בשביעית יאמר לו משמט אני ואם אמר לו אעפ"כ יקבל ממנו משום שנאמר [א] וזה דבר השמטה רב אויא שקיל משכונא [כ] רבה בר עולא מערים איערומי: וכן ערב פסח: א"ר יוחנן [ל] מקדיש אדם פסחו בשבת וחגיגתו ביו"ט נימא מסייע ליה וכן ערב פסח בירושלים שחל להיות בשבת מניח טליתו אצלו ונוטל את פסחו ועושה עמו חשבון לאחר יו"ט הכא במאי עסקינן בממנה אחרים עמו על פסחו דמעיקרא מיקדש וקאי והא אנן תנן [מ] אין נמנין על הבהמה בתחילה ביו"ט שאני הכא כיון דרגיל אצלו כמאן דאימני ביה מעיקרא דמי והא תני רבי הושעיא הולך אדם אצל רועה הרגיל אצלו ונותן לו טלה לפסחו ומקדישו ויוצא בו התם נמי כיון דרגיל אצלו אקדושי (ג) ליה מעיקרא והא מקדיש קתני הקדש עילוי מדרבנן ומי אמר ר' יוחנן הכי והא אמר ר' יוחנן הלכה כסתם משנה ותנן [נ] לא מקדישין ולא מעריכין ולא מחרימין ולא מגביהין תרומות ומעשרות כל אלו ביו"ט אמרו ק"ו בשבת לא קשיא כאן בחובות שקבוע להן זמן כאן בחובות שאין קבוע להן זמן: **מתני'** מונה אדם את אורחיו ואת פרפרותיו מפיו אבל לא מן הכתב ומפיס עם בניו ועם בני ביתו על השולחן ובלבד שלא יתכוין לעשות מנה גדולה כנגד מנה קטנה [ס] ומטילין חלשין על הקדשים ביו"ט אבל לא על המנות:

גמ'

דלרבנן למעבר אדרבנן כי הנך דמטפחין וסנך דיתבו אפומא דלחיא. תוספת דיום הכפורים. שלריך להתחיל ולהתענות מבעוד יום לאורייתא היא דנפקא לן (יומא פא:) מועינתם את נפשותיכם בתשעה לחודש. דקאכלי ושתו עד שתחשך. גרס ולא גרס מחשכה. המחזיר חוב בשביעית. ממון שהשביעית נוהגת עליו לשמט וכמשך לו לשביעית שמשמטת בסופה [ביצה שם]. המחזיר חוב בשביעית. שהחזירו לוה למלוה לאחר שביעית שעברה עליו שביעית. יאמר לו. מלוה משמט אני ולא אקבלנו ממך אלא בתורת מתנה וכו' דלא כהוא נריך דלא למימר משמט אני אלא אם כן אמר לו. ואם אמר לו. ולוה מלוה דרש ליה דעבד אם כן (גיטין לז:). ואם אמר לו אע"פ כן. אני רולה לתכרי לך דלי יקבל ממנו. שנאמר וזה דבר השמטה. לימד שדיבור של שמיטה [גיטין לז:]. פסחו בשבת. גרכה לומר כיום טוב לה בשבת. ליכא למימר כיום טוב ושבתות ביום טוב ולא דבר רשות. ויהא מקדיש לצורך היום [פסחים סו:]. הלכה כסתם משנה. כי הוא סדר רבי המשנה וכשראה דברי חכם וישרו בעיניו שנאן סתם ולא הזכיר שם אומרו כדי שלא יהו נראין כיחיד ויעשו כמותן [ביצה ב:]. לא מקדישין. הקדשות. ולא מעריכין. ערכין שלי עליו נערך לגבוה (ויקרא כז). לא מחרימין. לכוהן לכהן (שם כז). וכל חרמי בלאו חרם בהקדש וכחרם דהרים סתם חרמים לכהנים. נמצא בחרם הכהנים [ערכין כח:]. הן לא מגביהין תרומות ומעשרות. ליכלו לה נגורה סוכה וקצ בכלי זה. גורות מקח ממכר יו"ט דהני משום שבות ואכורין (שם לו:). כל אלו. דבר מקח וממכר הוא מכוה מקדים הולם (ויקרא נז): ולא מגביהין תרומות ומעשרות. כיכור לרשום הקדש ומקח וממכר דכתיב ממצוא חפצך וגו' (ישעיה נח) שלא נמי משום מקח וממכר יש ללכת יודע להפרידשן [ביצה כז:]. ולא מגביהין תרומות ומעשרות. אימור שבות דרבנן היא לדמתם בשבת (ביצה לו:) ואלו הן משום שבות דמי דמולול ומעשרת כלו מגביהין תרומות ומעשרות לתקן [גיטין נד.] בחובות שקבוע להן זמן. לגו כגון פסח שבותו דמיפכין הן דקדוש שמיו יכול להקדישן ביום [פסחים סו:].

***TERUMAH* OR TITHES.**[59] כָּל אֵלּוּ בְּיוֹם טוֹב אָמְרוּ – **ALL THESE** prohibitions **WERE PROMULGATED FOR YOM TOV;** קַל וָחוֹמֶר בְּשַׁבָּת – **CERTAINLY,** they apply **TO THE SABBATH.** This anonymous Mishnah prohibits the consecration of anything on the Sabbath or Yom Tov. How, then, can R' Yochanan say that the law follows anonymous Mishnahs, and yet rule that one may consecrate offerings on the Sabbath and Yom Tov?

The Gemara resolves the contradiction:

לֹא קַשְׁיָא – **There is no difficulty.** כָּאן בְּחוֹבוֹת שֶׁקָּבוּעַ לָהֶן זְמַן – **Here** (i.e. R' Yochanan's permit to consecrate offerings on the Sabbath and Yom Tov) the reference is **to obligatory [offerings] that have a fixed time.**[60] כָּאן בְּחוֹבוֹת שֶׁאֵין קָבוּעַ לָהֶן זְמַן – **Here** (i.e. the Mishnah's prohibition against consecrating on the Sabbath or Yom Tov) the reference is **to obligatory [offerings] that do *not* have a fixed time.**[61]

Mishnah מוֹנֶה אָדָם אֶת אוֹרְחָיו וְאֶת פַּרְפְּרוֹתָיו מִפִּיו – **A person may count his guests**[62] **and delicacies**[63] **orally,** אֲבָל לֹא מִן הַכְּתָב – **but not from a written note.**[64] מֵפִיס אָדָם עִם בָּנָיו וְעִם בְּנֵי בֵיתוֹ עַל הַשּׁוּלְחָן – **A person may cast lots with his children and members of his household** for portions of food **at the table,** וּבִלְבַד שֶׁלֹּא יִתְכַּוֵּין לַעֲשׂוֹת מָנָה גְדוֹלָה כְּנֶגֶד מָנָה קְטַנָּה – **provided that he does not intend to wager a large portion against a small portion.**[65] וּמְטִילִין חֲלָשִׁין עַל הַקֳּדָשִׁים בְּיוֹם טוֹב – **And [Kohanim] may cast lots for sacrifices on Yom Tov,** אֲבָל לֹא עַל הַמָּנוֹת – **but not for portions.**[66]

NOTES

59. By separating *terumos* and *maasros* from food, one renders it permitted for eating. Hence, this is a violation of the prohibition against מְתַקֵּן, "*repairing*" (see *Rashi* ibid. ד״ה תני רב יוסף). Furthermore, since one thereby elevates the status of the separated portions, this is forbidden on account of its similarity to consecrating (*Meiri*).

60. The *pesach* must be offered on the fourteenth of Nissan, even if that day is a Sabbath. Similarly, the *chagigah* must be offered on Yom Tov. The obligation to bring these offerings overrides the various prohibitions of the day (e.g. slaughtering on the Sabbath). Since the Torah waived its prohibitions for the sake of these sacrifices, the Rabbis waived their prohibition against consecrating them (see *Rashi; cf. Tos. Rid;* see *Sfas Emes;* see also *Yad David* [*Basra*]).

61. Since the offering of such sacrifices (e.g. *chatas*) does not override the Sabbath and Yom Tov prohibitions, the Rabbinic prohibition of consecrating them on the Sabbath and Yom Tov remains in force.

62. I.e. he may count the number of guests he wishes to invite in order to know how many loaves of bread he will need (*Meiri*).

63. I.e. the number of delicacies (e.g. portions of dessert) he must serve to his guests (*Meiri*).

64. He may count his guests from memory, but not from a guest list prepared before the Sabbath. The Gemara (below, 149a) will discuss why this is prohibited (*Rashi*).

It is forbidden to read from the list even if one reads silently and does not recite the words out loud (*Rashba* et al.; cf. first opinion cited by *Rashba*).

65. The portions must be equal [in value]. He may not cast lots for unequal portions of food, the winner being awarded the larger portion, and the loser receiving the smaller. The Gemara (149b) will explain this rule (*Rashi*).

Lots are appropriate even to allocate equal portions because the people present might have a preference for a certain type of portion [e.g. the thigh of the meat, as opposed to the neck] (*Meiri*).

66. The Gemara (149b) will explain this (*Rashi*).

The Mishnah taught that there are circumstances in which one may not read a list on the Sabbath. The Gemara cites two reasons for this prohibition:

מַאי טַעְמָא – What is the reason? **רַב בִּיבִי אָמַר – Rav Bivi says:** גְּזֵירָה שֶׁמָּא יִמְחוֹק – This is a Rabbinic **decree** that was enacted **lest one erase** something from the list.[1] **אַבַּיֵי אָמַר – Abaye says:** גְּזֵירָה שֶׁמָּא יִקְרָא בִּשְׁטָרֵי הֶדְיוֹטוֹת – It is a Rabbinic **decree** that was enacted **lest one read common documents.**[2]

The Gemara seeks the practical difference between these two reasons:

מַאי בֵּינַיְיהוּ – What is the difference **between them?**

The Gemara answers:

אִיכָּא בֵּינַיְיהוּ דִּכְתַב אַכּוֹתֶל וּמִידְלֵי – There would be a difference **between them** in a case **where he wrote** the list **high up on a wall.**[3] **לְמַאן דְּאָמַר שֶׁמָּא יִמְחוֹק – According to the one** [Rav Bivi] **who says** that the prohibition was enacted **lest one erase** from the list, **לֹא חַיְישִׁינָן – we are not concerned** that he might do so in this case, since the list is too high up for him to reach and erase. **וּלְמַאן דְּאָמַר שֶׁמָּא יִקְרָא – But according to the one** [Abaye] **who says** that the prohibition was enacted **lest one read** common documents, **חַיְישִׁינָן – we are concerned** even in this case that he will come to do so. This scenario, therefore, represents the practical difference between the opinions of Rav Bivi and Abaye – Rav Bivi would permit reading a list written high up on a wall, whereas Abaye would forbid reading such a list.

The Gemara challenges the preceding analysis:

וּלְמַאן דְּאָמַר שֶׁמָּא יִמְחוֹק – But even **according to the one** [Rav Bivi] **who says** that the prohibition was enacted **lest one erase** from the list, **נֵיחוּשׁ שֶׁמָּא יִקְרָא – we should** also **be concerned lest one read** common documents![4] **וְתוּ – Furthermore,** **לֵיחוּשׁ שֶׁמָּא יִמְחוֹק לֹא חַיְישִׁינָן – are we not concerned lest one erase** even from a list that is high up? **וְהָתַנְיָא – Why, it was taught** in a Mishnah:[5] **לֹא יִקְרָא לְאוֹר הַנֵּר – ONE MAY NOT READ BY THE LIGHT OF A LAMP** on the Sabbath, lest he tilt the lamp.[6] **וְאָמַר רַבָּה – And Rabbah said**[7] that **אֲפִילוּ גָּבוֹהַּ שְׁתֵּי קוֹמוֹת – even** if the lamp is **twice the height of a man** above the ground, **אֲפִילוּ גָּבוֹהַּ שְׁתֵּי מַרְדְּעוֹת** – and **even** if it is at **the height of two ox-goads,**[8] **אֲפִילוּ עֲשָׂרָה בָּתִּים זֶה עַל גַּבֵּי זֶה** – and **even** if it is at the height of **ten houses one atop the other,** **לֹא יִקְרָא – one may** still **not read** by its light. Although, in these cases, there is no concern that he will tilt the lamp, the prohibition applies nevertheless.[9] Hence, in our case too, although the list is beyond reach, the ban against reading it (lest he erase it) should still apply. – ? –

Having argued that even Rav Bivi would agree that it is forbidden to read a list written high up on a wall, the Gemara presents a different analysis of the dispute between Rav Bivi and Abaye:

אֶלָּא אִיכָּא בֵּינַיְיהוּ – Rather, there would be a difference **between them** in a case **דִּכְתַב אַכּוֹתֶל וּמִיתַּתֵּי – where he wrote** the list **low down**[10] **on the wall.** **לְמַאן דְּאָמַר שֶׁמָּא יִמְחוֹק – According to the one** [Rav Bivi] **who says** that the prohibition to read from a list was enacted **lest one erase** from it, **חַיְישִׁינָן – we are concerned** that he will do so in this case as well. **לְמַאן דְּאָמַר שֶׁמָּא יִקְרָא** – But **according to the one** [Abaye] **who says** that the prohibition was enacted **lest he read** common documents, **לֹא חַיְישִׁינָן – we are not concerned** that he might do so in this case, **גּוּדָא בִּשְׁטָרָא לֹא מִיחַלַּף** – because the law for **a wall will not be confused with** that of **a**

NOTES

1. If the host sees that he has not prepared sufficient food for all his guests, he will regret having invited so many. He might then delete some names from the list so that his servant will not summon them (*Rashi;* see also *Meiri*).

Even if he does erase from the list, he would be guilty only of a Rabbinic transgression. Under Biblical law, erasing is not forbidden unless one's purpose is to make space for writing (see Mishnah above, 73a). Nevertheless, since erasing is frequent, the Rabbis deemed it necessary to prevent it in any form (see *Ritva MHK* ed.; cf. *Chasam Sofer*).

2. *Shetarei hedyotos* (common documents) are business-related writings, such as loan documents, deeds of sale, etc. (*Rashi* here, *Tosafos* to 116b). To read materials of this nature on the Sabbath or Yom Tov is forbidden under the rubric of מִמְּצוֹא חֶפְצְךָ, *from pursuing your business,* which includes all matters of commerce (*Rosh*).

Ritva (*MHK* ed.) and *Rambam* (*Hil. Shabbos* 23:19, as explained by *Maggid Mishneh*) include social letters as well as business documents in the category of *shetarei hedyotos.* This would also appear to be the view of *Rashi* as it is stated on 116b ד״ה שטרי הדיוטות (cf. *Tosafos* ibid.; see *Rashba, Shiltei HaGiborim, Hagahos R' Elazar Horowitz* ibid., *Chasam Sofer* and *Meromei Sadeh*). This approach can be explained with *Meiri's* definition of *shetarei hedyotos* – namely, any text whose reading is of no real benefit and fulfills no need related to the Sabbath or Yom Tov (see also *Chidushei HaRan*). Several reasons have been offered as to why one may not read such materials on the Sabbath: (a) Since they serve no purpose, they are treated as a form of *muktzeh* (*Meiri; Chidushei HaRan*). (b) If one reads them, one might feel as though it is a weekday and come to erase from them (*Rambam, Hil. Shabbos* 23:19; *Meiri; Ran* folio 43b). (c) One might write a response (*Chidushei HaRan*).

Although the prohibition of *shetarei hedyotos* is itself only a Rabbinic decree, the Rabbis forbade reading other materials (such as the guest list of our Mishnah), lest one come to read *shetarei hedyotos* (see *Ritva MHK* ed.). The scope of this secondary ban is discussed below, in note 33.

3. The list is too high to be easily erased but low enough to be read (see *Rashi* as emended by *Hagahos HaBach* §1 and *Menachem Meishiv Nefesh*). It is written on the wall in ink [rather than engraved] (*Rashi;* see continuation of the Gemara; see also *Shabbos Shel Mi*).

4. [It is certainly reasonable to fear that reading the list might lead to reading *shetarei hedyotos.* Therefore, although Rav Bivi said only "lest one erase," we can assume that he is also concerned "lest one read" (see *Tos. Rid* and *Rashash*). He would consequently prohibit reading a list even if it is high up on a wall.

[At this point the Gemara maintains that according to both Abaye and Rav Bivi the decree was enacted for fear that one might read *shetarei hedyotos.* Their disagreement is only that in Rav Bivi's opinion it was *also* enacted to prevent erasing, whereas Abaye does not regard this additional factor.]

5. Above, 11a.

6. It frequently occurs that the oil in a lamp draws away from the wick, causing the light to grow dim. This is usually rectified by tilting the lamp, thereby moving the oil toward the wick. On the Sabbath, however, this is forbidden, since it would constitute the *melachah* of מַבְעִיר, *kindling.* The Sages thus prohibited one from reading by lamplight, lest one inadvertently tilt the lamp to provide more light (*Rashi* ibid. ד״ה ולא יקרא).

7. Above, 12b.

8. [In those times, ox-goads were of a specific length and sometimes used as units of measure (see, for example, *Shevuos* 48a).]

9. In many cases where the Sages banned a certain activity for fear that it might lead to a transgression, they applied the ban in *all* circumstances, even those in which there is no risk of the transgression occurring. This principle is known as לֹא פָּלוּג, *they did not differentiate.* Some Rishonim explain that the Sages were worried that if they failed to apply the preventive measure even in circumstances where it is not needed, people might come to disregard it where it *is* needed (see *Ramban* below ד״ה הכא במראה; *Rabbeinu Perachyah* to 12b; cf. *Chidushei HaRan*).

The Gemara assumes that just as this stringency was applied in the case of reading by lamplight, so too was it applied in the case of reading a list. [However, it does not necessarily apply to decrees unrelated to the Sabbath (see *Rashi* below ד״ה דרבה cited in note 22).]

10. I.e. within reach (*Rashi*).

גמ' מ"ט רב ביבי אמר גזירה שמא ימחוק אביי אמר א גזירה שמא יקרא בשטרי הדיוטות מאי בינייהו א"ב דכתב אכותל ומידלי למ"ד שמא ימחוק לא חיישינן ולמ"ד שמא יקרא חיישינן ולמ"ד שמא ימחוק ניחוש שמא יקרא ותו לשמא ימחוק לא חיישינן ו) והתניא ז) לא יקרא לאור הנר ואמר רבה אפי' גבוה שתי קומות אפי' גבוה שתי מרדעות אפי' עשרה בתים זה ע"ג זה לא יקרא אלא איכא בינייהו דכתב אכותל ומיתתי למאן דאמר שמא ימחוק חיישינן למ"ד שמא יקרא לא חיישינן גודא בשטרא לא מיחלף ולמ"ד שמא יקרא ליחוש שמא ימחוק אלא איכא בינייהו דחייק אטבלא ואפינקס למ"ד שמא ימחוק לא חיישינן למ"ד שמא יקרא חיישינן ולמ"ד שמא ימחוק ליחוש שמא יקרא וכ"ת טבלא ופינקס בשטרא לא מיחלף והתניא ח) מונה אדם כמה מבפנים וכמה מבחוץ וכמה מנות עתיד להניח לפניהם ב מכתב שעל גבי הכותל אבל לא מכתב שעל גבי טבלא ופינקס היכי דמי אילימא דכתיב מיכתב מ"ש הכא ומ"ש הכא אלא לאו דחייק וקתני מכתב שעל גבי הכותל אבל לא מכתב שע"ג טבלא ופינקס אלא לעולם דכתב אכותל ומידלי ודקא קשיא לך דרבה דרבה תנאי היא דתניא ג מונה אדם את אורחיו ואת פרפרותיו מפיו אבל לא מן הכתב ר' אחא מתיר מכתב שעל גבי הכותל היכי דמי אילימא דכתיב מתתא ליחוש שמא ימחוק אלא לאו דכתב ומידלי וש"מ דרבה תנאי היא ש"מ והני תנאי כהני תנאי דתניא ט) ד אין רואין במראה בשבת י) רבי מאיר מתיר במראה הקבוע בכותל מ"ש הקבוע בכותל דאדהכי והכי מדכר והכי מדכר שאינו קבוע נמי אדהכי והכי מדכר הכא במראה של מתכת עסקינן וכדרב נחמן אמר רבה בר אבוה דא"ר נחמן אמר רבה בר אבוה ה מפני מה אמרו מראה של מתכת אסורה מפני י) שאדם עשוי להשיר בה נימין המדולדלין תנו רבנן • ס) ו כתב המהלך תחת הצורה ותחת הדיוקנאות אסור לקרותו בשבת ז ודיוקנא עצמה אף בחול אסור להסתכל בה משום שנאמר א) אל תפנו אל האלילים מאי תלמודא אמר רבי חנין אל תפנו אל מדעתכם: מפיס אדם עם בניו וכו': עם בניו ועם בני ביתו אין ועם אחר לא מאי טעמא כדרב יהודה אמר שמואל ס) דאמר רב יהודה אמר שמואל ח בני חבורה המקפידין זה על זה עוברין משום מדה ומשום משקל ומשום מנין ומשום לווין ופורעין ביו"ט וכדברי

רש"י

גמ' מ"ט. אבל לא מן הכתב: שמא ימחוק. מן האורחין שיהיה שלא הכין להם כל צרכם ויתחרט שזימן יותר מן הראוי וימחוק מן הכתב כדי שלא יקראם השמש: כל הני שמא יקרא בשטרי הדיוטות של מקח וממכר קאמר (א): דכתב. מנינא אכותל בדיו: ומידלי. שאינו מגיע לשם למחוק: (אפילו גבוה שאינו מגיע לשם למחוק): אפילו גבוה. שאינו מגיע שם להטות הנר אסור דהואיל ונמוך אסור גבוה נמי אסור שלא תחלוק: ומיתתי. שנמוך ויכול להגיע שם ולמחוק: ולמ"ד שמא יקרא. היכא דליכא למיחש לשמא יקרא ליחוש לשמא ימחוק: דחייק. בסכין בתוך העץ בטבלא שאין נוחה למחוק ולהכי מדכר וליכא למיחש למחוק: גודא. כותל: פינקס. כעין לוחות של סוחרים: כמה בפנים וכמה בחוץ. את מי ומי מושיב בפנים במקום המכובד ואת מי ומי מושיב בחוץ שאינו כל כך ספונין: אבל לא מכתב שעל גבי טבלא ופינקס. דגודא בשטרא לא מיחלף אבל טבלא ופינקס מיחלף: דכתיב מיכתב. כתב של דיו: אלא לעולם דכתב אכותל ומידלי. שאינו יכול למחוק ולשמא יקרא לא חיישינן דגודא בשטרא לא מיחלף ודקשיא לך דאע"ג דמידלי ליתסרי כדרבה דאמר גבי נר אפילו י' בתים: דרבה תנאי היא. דאיכא דחייש לשלא תחלוק באיסור שבת דרבנן ואיכא דמפליג: ליחוש לשמא ימחוק. דהא ר' אחא כותל דוקא נקט ואי מתתי מה לי כותל מה לי אגרת: אין רואין במראה. מירושלמי"ר לפי שכשרואה במראה אינו נמנע אם תלה לתקן שערות ראשו וזקנו הלכך חיישי' שמא יראה נימין המדולדלות שאינן שוות עם שאר השער ויגלחן: דאדהכי והכי. שילך להביא תער או מספרים: מדכר. שהוא שבת: של מתכת. שאינו צריך להביא מספרים שהיא עצמה מגלחת השער: כתב המהלך תחת הצורה ותחת הדיוקנאות. כגון בני אדם המציירים בכותל חיות משונות או דיוקנות של בני אדם של מעשים כגון מלחמת דוד וגלית וכותבין תחתיה זו צורת חיה פלונית וזו דיוקנית פלוני ופלונית: אסור לקרותו בשבת. שמא יקרא בשטרי הדיוטות: אל מדעתכם. אל אשר אתם עושי' מדעת לבבכם ואלו שלכם. אלילים לשון חלול: עם בניו ובני ביתו אין עם אחר לא. מחלק מנה ומפיס על המנות: משום לווין ופורעין. לגזור בהו רבנן שמא יכתוב: המקפידין. שאין מוחלים ומוותרין זה לזה:

תוספות

ולמ"ד שמא ימחוק ליחוש שמא יקרא. ולא מסיק אדעתיה גודא בשטרא לא מיחלף: בשטרי הדיוטות. פי' בקונט' של מקח וממכר ולעיל בפרק כל כתבי (דף קטז: ושם) פירש איגרות השלוחות למלוה מסכן: אלא איכא בינייהו דכתיב אכותל ומתתאי. ולא ידענא אמאי נקט מתתאי כיון דס"ד דכ"ע אית להו דרבה: אילימא דכתיב מיכתב מ"ש הכא מ"ש הכא. פירוש תרוייהו יהא אסור שמא ימחוק: לעולם דכתב אכותל ומידלי ודקשיא לך דרבה דרבה תנאי היא. לפירוש הקונטרס ז"ל דהשתא דמוקי לה דכתיב אכותל ומידלי למ"ד שמא ימחוק איכא דאית ליה דרבה ולמ"ד שמא יקרא לית ליה דרבה והשתא מיבעיא לן למימר דבדרבה פליגי תנאי כי היכי דפליגי אמוראי דהכא ובריית' קמייתא מיתוקמא שפיר דכתיב מכתב אכותל ומידלי דכולהו אמוראי גודא בשטרא לא מיחלף וקשה לפירוש זה דהשתא לא הוה פלוגתייהו כדהוה מוקמת לה מעיקרא למאן דאמר שמא ימחוק לא חיישינן למאן דאמר שמא יקרא חיישי' וה"ר פורת פירש דאביי ורב ביבי תרוייהו לית להו דרבה דפליגי בכתב אכותל ומידלי למאן דאמר שמא ימחוק לא חיישינן כיון דמידלי ולית לן דרבה ולשמא יקרא נמי לא חייש קסבר גודא בשטרא לא מיחלף ולמ"ד שמא יקרא חייש דקסבר גודא בשטרא מיחלף ואביי לא הוה מוקי פלוגתייהו דרבי אחא ורבנן (ב) כרבה דא"כ ר' אחא ע"כ לית ליה דאביי דשרי בכותל אלמא קסבר גודא בשטרא לא מיחלף וא"כ כמאן סבירא ליה דאפילו רבנן לא פליגי עליה דר' אחא אלא משום דאית להו דרבה וגזרינן שמא ימחוק אלא הוה מפרש אביי דכ"ע לית להו דרבה ולא חיישינן לשמא ימחוק במידלי ובגודא בשטרא מיחלף פליגי והא דקאמר ש"מ דרבה תנאי היא הו"מ למימר ודאי לכ"ע לית להו דרבה כדמפרש לאביי אלא דלא מצי למוכח הא בהדיא ולהכי קאמר דתנאי היא וליכא לאקשויי לרבה והא לא מצי למימר דפליגי (ג) בחייק מיחק רבי אחא ורבנן ובגודא בשטרא מיחלף פליגי אבל כ"ע אית להו דרבה משום דסברא הוא כיון דחייק ואיתא נמי בכותל פשיטא דהא לא הוי אמרי רבנן דגודא בשטרא מיחלף וצריך לאוקמא השתא ברייתא דלעיל דחייק מיחק למאן דסבר גודא בשטרא מיחלף וקשה קצת לפירוש זה דה"ל למימר דכ"ע (ד) לית להו דרבה ואביי ורב ביבי בגודא אי מיחלף בשטרא פליגי: ודיוקני עצמה אף בחול אסור. נראה דבשויה לשם עבודת גלולים אמר אבל (ה) לנוי מותר כדמשמע מבנן של קדושים דלא הוו מסתכלי בצורתא דזוזא (ע"ז דף נ.) מכלל דאחריני הוו מסתכלי: בני חבורה המקפידין זה על זה עוברין משום משקל ומשום מדה ומשום מנין. פירוש לפי שמקפידין זה על זה עוברין אפילו על מה שאין שאר בני אדם עוברין משום מדה כדאמרינן בביצה (דף כט.) יכול אדם לומר לחבירו מלא לי כלי זה אבל לא במדה פירוש כלי שמודדין בו אסור דדמי למקח וממכר והם כיון שהם מקפידים כל כלים הוי לגבייהו מדה לפי שמקפידין לידע שיעורו לשלם להם הכלי וכן משקל ששוקלים ומכוונים זה כנגד זה ביד ואמרינן בביצה אין משגיחין במאזנים ביום טוב ומשום מנין כדאמר בביצה (דף כט:) הולך אדם אצל חנוני הרגיל אצלו ואומר לו תן לי כו' ובלבד שלא יזכיר לו סכום מקח שאם היו נותנים מאה אגוזים בדינר ולקח כבר תשעים לא יאמר לו תן לי עשרים אגוזים שאתחייב לך עשרה אגוזים שנראה שעושה להשלים הדינר אבל יכול לומר לו תן לי כ' אגוזים סתם ובבני חבורה המקפידים אסור שיבא לידי איסור שיחזרו להשלים וכדברי (ו) בית הלל אף משום רבית דכשהם מחזירין זה לזה הם מקפידים מה ששוות יותר וקשה לפירוש

עין משפט נר מצוה

יד א ב ג מיי' פכ"ג מהלכות שבת הלכ"ט סמג לאוין סה טור שו"ע או"ח סימן שז סעיף יג:
טו ד ה מיי' פכ"ג מהל' שבת הלכה יד סמג שם טור שו"ע או"ח סימן שז סעיף יג:
טז ו מיי' פכ"ב שם הלכה יג סמג שם טור שו"ע או"ח סימן שז סעיף טו:
יז ז מיי' פ"ב מהלכות ע"ז הלכה ב סמג לאוין יד טוש"ע יו"ד סי' קמא סעיף טו:
יח ח מיי' פ"ז מהלכות גניבה הלכה י סמג לאוין קנ (אבל הפוסקים השמיטו מטעם שכ' הב"י באו"ח סוף סי' תקי"ז):

רבינו חננאל

מעמידין השמועה זו כרב יוסף. חדא (דרבה) [דרבא] לגבי רב יוסף תלמיד הוא ועוד סוגיא דשמעתא רובה כרב יוסף ריהטא ועוד מדחינן רב אויא מקבל משכונא מכלל שאם אין בידו משכון אינו יכול ליתבע. ותוב רבא בר עולא מיקום אירעומי כלומר לא היה תובעו בהדיא אלא היה אומר לו הלויני וכאשר יתן לך ויבאו המעות לידו אומר לו יש לי אצלך הלואת יו"ט נשתלמתי אתם מכלל כי הלואת יו"ט כי האי גוונא יתכן אבל בהדיא לא ניתנה ליתבע וראינו תשובה לגאון ופסק כרבא. ואמר רבא בתרא הוא. וקיי"ל דהלכתא כבתראי הדעת נוטה: וכן ערב פסחים בירושלים כר' א"ר יוחנן מקדיש אדם פסחו בשבת וחגיגתו ביו"ט נימא מסייעא ליה וכן ערב פסח כר' ופשוטה היא. הא דתני ר' הושעיא ומקדיש אוקמינא. הקדיש עלוי מדרבנן ואקשינן עלה והא תנא דאמר הלכה כסתם משנה ותנן אין מקדישין ואין מעריכין ואין מחרימין ומפרקינן הא דא"ר יוחנן מקדיש בשבת בחובות הקבוע להן זמן. כגון פסח שאם לא יעשנו היום אינו יכול לעשותו למחר והיא מצוה עוברת והא דתנן אין מקדישין בשבת ולא ביום טוב בחובות שאין קבוע להן זמן. מונה אדם את אורחיו ואת פרפרותיו מפיו אבל לא מן הכתב מ"ט ואמרינן מן הכתב מ"ט לא. רב ביבי אמר גזירה שמא ימחוק ואביי אמר גזירה שמא יקרא בשטרי הדיוטות ופירושו כיון שיראה אדם כתוב כמה אורחים צריך להביא כמה פרפרות אצלו אף הוא אומר מותר לקרוא בשטרי הדיוטות מאי בינייהו דכתיב אכותל במקום גבוה שאינו יכול למחוק דרב ביבי בכי האי גוונא שרי. ואביי אסר. ואקשינן על רב ביבי והתנן לא יקרא לאור הנר ואמר רבה אפילו גבוה ב' קומות או ב' מרדעות ואפילו עשרה בתים זה ע"ג זה לא יקרא. והא הכא דליכא למיחש אלא שמא יטה ואפי' גבוה כמה אמר (רבא) [רבה] חיישינן ואסור. ואע"ג דסלקא כתנאי הלכתא (כרבא) [כרבה] דסתם מתניתין כוותיה ולא חיישינן אמחלוקות דברייתא וחזרנו להביא טעם אחר לומר כי אינם חלוקים אלא אם הוא הכתב בכותל נמוך שמגעת לה ויכול למחוק דלרב ביבי אסור כטעמיה ולאביי שרי דכותל בשטר לא מיחלף. ואקשינן על אביי וליחוש שמא ימחוק הואיל והכותל נמוך הוא וגם זה הטעם נדחה ואתינן לאוקמי פלוגתיה בכתב דחייק אטבלא ופנקס וגם זה נדחה. וחזרנו על הטעם הראשון דכתוב אכותל ומידלי. לרב ביבי מותר ולאביי אסור. וזה שהקשינו לרב ביבי מדברי רבה שאסר אפילו גבוה כמה. אמר לך רב ביבי דרבה תנאי היא ואנא דאמרי כתנא דשרי. דתניא מונה אדם את אורחיו ואת פרפרותיו מפיו אבל לא מן הכתב. ר' אחא מתיר מן הכתב שעל גבי הכותל ואוקימנא דכתוב אכותל ומידלי. ואמרינן הני תנאי כי הני תנאי כלומר ר' אחא ות"ק חולקין במחלוקת ר' ות"ק דיליה דלר' אחא א) צחצוח הסיג מן המראה הוא מוחק לפיכך קתני אין רואין במראה ור' מתיר במראה הקבועה בכותל כת"ק דר' אחא ודמיא להא דאמרינן בכלל גדול (דף עה) דשף בין העמודים [חייב] משום ב) מוחק דומה למוחק כתב. ותלמוד א"י השף את העור ע"ג העמוד ר' אחא בשם ר' יהודה בן לוי משום מוחק ואקשינן עלה מ"ש מראה הקבועה בכותל דאדהכי והכי מדכר. ולא פירש מהו שיזכור וימנע. יש מי שאומר כי נאסר הראיה במראה בשבת שמא יראה כי עלה בו כעין חלודה (וכעין חלודה) בזה המראה ויצחצחנו בשבת ונמצא מתקן מנא. גם בהיות המראה למטה במקום נמוך עד שיתעסק להביא סכין כדי לצחצחו יזכור ששבת הוא וימנע ונדחה זה הטעם. ועמד כר"נ דאמר מפני מה מראה של מתכת אסורה מפני שאדם עשוי להשיר בה נימין המדולדלות ור' שמתיר אומר כיון שהיא גבוה לא גזרינן. ות"ק סבר גזרינן: ת"ר כתב של תחת הצורה של תחת דיוקני. פי' דיוקני צורת אדם והכתב שתחתיו אסור לקרותו בשבת ולא גרע משטרי הדיוטות דאסור בשבת. ודיוקני עצמה אסורה. אפילו בחול כטעמיה: מפיס אדם עם בניו ועם כו' פי' מפיס אדם מלשון פיוס כההיא דאמרי מי מפיס. וכמו שאמר על השכר (פסחים קז) מיסרו ומפיס. בניו ובני ביתו

חשק שלמה על רבינו חננאל א) לכאורה לפני גי' היה צ"ל להיפך דר' אחא כרבי. ואולי דגירסתו היה להיפך ובהעתקה נעתק בטעות וצ"ע: ב) לפנינו שם בגמ' איתא משום ממחק וצ"ע:

מסורת הש"ס

א) נ"ל והתנן, ב) לעיל יא., ג) [שם דף יב:], ד) [תוספתא פרק יז], ה) [תוספ' פי"ח], ו) [ברכות איתא דרבי מתיר וכו' וכן בבעל המאור ובמלחמות. אבל בהרא"ש אי' ר' יהודה מתיר וכו'], ז) [עי' תוס' ע"ז כט. ד"ה המספפר], ח) [תוספ' פי"ח], ט) ב"מ עה., י) וגלגם כמספפרים כל"י רש"ל, כ) [וע"ע תוספות ע"ז נ. ד"ה ר"ג], ל) [דף כג.].

הגהות הב"ח

(א) רש"י ד"ה כל הני וכו' וממכר קאמר. הס"ד ואח"כ מ"ה למ"ד שמא יקרא חיישינן ואפי' גבוה: (ב) תום' ד"ה לעולם וכו' דר' אחא ורבנן כדרבה ודר' אחא דלא"כ: (ג) בא"ד והא לא מצי למימר דפליגי ר' אחא ורבנן בחייק מיחק ובגודא בשטרא: (ד) בא"ד וקשה קצת לפי' זה דה"ל למימר דכ"ע לאביי ורב ביבי לית להו דרבה וכגודא: (ה) ד"ה ודיוקנא וכו' אבל לנוי מותר. נ"ב וע' בתוס' ר"פ כל הצלמים: (ו) ד"ה בני וכו' שיחזרו להשלים ובדברי הלל אף:

גליון הש"ס

גמ' אין רואין במראה בשבת. עי' ע"ז דף כט ע"א תוס' ד"ה המספפר: שם כתב המהלך תחת הצורה. עי' לעיל דף קטו ע"א תוס' ד"ה וכ"ש בשטרי:

תורה אור השלם

א) אַל תִּפְנוּ אֶל הָאֱלִילִם וֵאלֹהֵי מַסֵּכָה לֹא תַעֲשׂוּ לָכֶם אֲנִי יְיָ אֱלֹהֵיכֶם: [ויקרא יט, ד]

ליקוטי רש"י

בשטרי הדיוטות. כגון של משכנות או איגרות השלוחות למלוה מסכן [לעיל קטז: ועי' בתוס' כאן ושם]. לא יקרא לאור הנר. בספר שמא יטה הנר להביא השמן קרוב לפתילה שידלק יפה ונמצא מבעיר בשבת [שם יא.]. אפילו גבוה. דליכא למיחש לאטויי כיון דגזור לא פלוג למיגזר [שם יב:]. מרדעות. מלמד הבקר [שבועות מח.]. מלמד הוא דרבן, מרדע כדמתרגמינן בלע"ז [שופטים ג, לא]. בני חבורה. הוכלין בבית אחד לסעודת עצמו. המקפידין זה על זה. שאין מוחלין על דבר מועט ומקפידין להלוות זה את זה במדה במשקל ובמנין. עוברין. בשבתות ובימים טובים. ומשום לווין ופורעין. דתנן במסכת שבת (קמח.) ובלבד שלא יאמר לו הלויני והתם מפרש טעמא שמא יכתוב [ב"מ עה.].

document.[11] Thus, Rav Bivi would forbid reading such a list, whereas Abaye would allow it.[12]

The Gemara challenges this analysis as well:

וּלְמַאן דְּאָמַר שֶׁמָּא יִקְרָא – But even **according to the one** [Abaye] **who says** that the prohibition to read from a list was enacted **lest he read** common documents, **לֵיחוּשׁ שֶׁמָּא יִמְחוֹק – one should** also **be concerned lest he erase** from the list.[13] Hence, Abaye too would prohibit reading even a list that is on a wall. – ? –

In light of this difficulty, the Gemara isolates a different case as the one in which Rav Bivi and Abaye would disagree:

אֶלָּא אִיכָּא בֵּינַיְיהוּ – Rather, there would be a difference **between them** in a case **דְּחַיְּיק אַטַּבְלָא וְאַפִּינְקָס – where he engraved** the list **on a board or on a tablet.**[14] **לְמַאן דְּאָמַר שֶׁמָּא יִמְחוֹק – According to the one** [Rav Bivi] **who says** that the prohibition was enacted **lest he erase, לֹא חָיְישִׁינַן – we are not concerned** that he might erase in this case, since the writing is engraved.[15] **לְמַאן דְּאָמַר שֶׁמָּא יִקְרָא – According to the one** [Abaye] **who says** that it was enacted **lest he read** common documents, **חָיְישִׁינַן – we are concerned** even in this case that he might come to do so. Thus, Rav Bivi would permit reading an engraved list, whereas Abaye would forbid it.[16]

The Gemara asks:

וּלְמַאן דְּאָמַר שֶׁמָּא יִמְחוֹק – But according to the one [Rav Bivi] **who says** that the prohibition to read from a list was enacted **lest he erase** from it, **לֵיחוּשׁ שֶׁמָּא יִקְרָא – one should** also **be concerned lest he read** common documents. **וְכִי תֵּימָא טַבְלָא וּפִינְקָס בִּשְׁטָרָא לֹא מִיחַלַּף – And if you say** that the law for **a board or tablet will not be confused with** that of **a document** (i.e. reading from a board or tablet will not lead to reading from [paper] documents),[17] **וְהָתַנְיָא – but it was taught in a Baraisa** to the contrary: **מוֹנֶה אָדָם כַּמָּה מִבִּפְנִים וְכַמָּה מִבַּחוּץ – A PERSON MAY COUNT HOW MANY** of his guests he wishes to sit **INSIDE AND HOW MANY OUTSIDE,**[18] **וְכַמָּה מָנוֹת עָתִיד לְהָנִיחַ לִפְנֵיהֶם – AND HOW MANY PORTIONS HE IS GOING TO PLACE BEFORE THEM, מִכְּתָב שֶׁעַל גַּבֵּי הַכּוֹתֶל** – by reading **FROM [A LIST] WRITTEN ON A WALL, אֲבָל לֹא מִכְּתָב שֶׁעַל גַּבֵּי טַבְלָא וּפִינְקָס – BUT NOT FROM [A LIST] WRITTEN ON A BOARD OR TABLET. הֵיכִי דָּמֵי –** Now, **what are the circumstances** to which the Baraisa refers? **אִילֵימָא דִּכְתִיב מִיכְתַּב – If you say that [the list] was written** in ink, **מַאי שְׁנָא הָכָא וּמַאי שְׁנָא הָכָא – what is the difference between this** (i.e. a list on a wall) **and that** (i.e. a list on a tablet)? Both should be prohibited![19] **אֶלָּא לָאו דְּחַיְּיק – Rather,** the Baraisa **surely** means **that he** ***engraved*** the list on the wall or tablet. **וְקָתָנֵי מִכְּתָב שֶׁעַל גַּבֵּי הַכּוֹתֶל – And the Baraisa teaches** that one may read **from [an engraved list] written on a wall, אֲבָל לֹא מִכְּתָב שֶׁעַל גַּבֵּי טַבְלָא וּפִינְקָס – but not from one written on a board or tablet.** The Baraisa prohibits reading from a board or tablet even if it is engraved. This proves that we *are* afraid that reading from a board or tablet might lead to reading from [paper] documents.[20] – ? –

In light of this difficulty, the Gemara reverts to its original suggestion regarding the practical difference between Rav Bivi and Abaye:

אֶלָּא לְעוֹלָם – Rather, the difference between them is **indeed** in a case **דִּכְתַב אַכּוֹתֶל וּמִידְלֵי – where he wrote** the list **high up on the wall. וּדְקָא קַשְׁיָא לָךְ דְּרַבָּה – And the difficulty you had** on the basis **of Rabbah's** ruling[21] can be resolved as follows: **דְּרַבָּה תַּנָּאֵי הִיא – Rabbah's** ruling **is** actually the subject of a dispute between **Tannaim,**[22] **דְּתַנְיָא – for it was taught in a Baraisa:**

NOTES

11. [Literally: is not exchanged.] A wall that contains writing is clearly different from a sheet of paper or parchment that contains writing. A person would not automatically assume that just because he is allowed to read from a wall, he may also read from paper or parchment. [The rule of לֹא פָּלוּג, *they did not differentiate,* is not relevant here, because writing on a wall and writing on paper are regarded as two distinct categories (see note 31, second paragraph).]

It is difficult to understand why the Gemara specifies a case in which the writing is "low" (i.e. within reach). The Gemara has just accepted the argument that it makes no difference whether the list is written low down on the wall or high up. The Gemara could therefore have remained with its original case of a list written high up (*Tosafos*). Some Rishonim answer that had the Gemara here specified a list written high on a wall, one might have thought that only such writing would not be regarded as similar to writing on paper. A text written low on a wall, however, might indeed be associated with a text written on paper, and Abaye would consequently forbid one to read from it. The Gemara therefore deliberately mentions a list written *low* on the wall to teach that Abaye permits even this (*Rashba; Ritva MHK* ed.; *Tos. HaRosh; Ran MHK* ed.).

12. [The Gemara's current scenario is essentially the same as its original one (see previous note). The only change is that the attribution of the opinions has been reversed.]

13. [Although Abaye stated only "lest he read," he would surely agree that we should be concerned "lest he erase."

According to this assumption, there does not appear to be any dispute between Rav Bivi and Abaye. Both agree that the decree was enacted to prevent erasing *and* to prevent reading *shetarei hedyotos*. It shall be explained below that the dispute is about the *scope* of one of these concerns.]

14. A פִּינְקָס, *tablet,* is a ledger used by merchants that consisted of tablets coated with wax, upon which they would write with a stylus (*Rashi* to 104b [ד״ה על שני לוחי פנקס [א). [A טַבְלָא, *board,* is made of wood (see *Rashi* [ד״ה דחייק

15. Engraved lettering is not easy to erase. Thus, before he succeeds in doing so, he will realize [that it is forbidden] (*Rashi*).

16. For Abaye holds that even a tablet would be confused with a paper document. Rav Bivi, however, opines that people would distinguish between these materials. This, then, is the point of contention between Rav Bivi and Abaye. Although both agree that we are concerned lest one read *shetarei hedyotos,* Abaye extends this concern even to tablets, whereas Rav Bivi limits it to paper (see *Tos. Rid*).

17. As Rav Bivi's opinion was explained in the previous note.

18. A seat inside [a building] is more prestigious than one outside (*Rashi*).

19. The Baraisa should prohibit reading in both cases, since as far as regular writing (in ink) is concerned, the likelihood that one will erase it is the same whether it is on a wall or a tablet (*Tosafos*). [Accordingly, although we are not afraid that one who reads a list on a wall will come to read *shetarei hedyotos* (see note 11), he should still be forbidden to do so lest he *erase* from the list.]

20. By interpreting the Baraisa as referring to an *engraved* list, the Gemara eliminates the possibility that the reader will erase it (see note 15). The only remaining concern is that he will come to read *shetarei hedyotos.* The Baraisa therefore permits reading from a wall (see note 11), but it nevertheless forbids reading from a tablet, because even reading a tablet might lead to reading *shetarei hedyotos.* Since Rav Bivi does not have the authority to dispute a Baraisa, he too surely agrees that one may not read an engraved tablet. It has thus been shown that both Rav Bivi and Abaye would prohibit reading even a list engraved on a tablet. The original question is therefore reinstated: What is the practical difference between the positions of Rav Bivi and Abaye?

21. When this scenario was originally proposed, the Gemara refuted it on the basis of Rabbah's principle that Rabbinic decrees are not subject to exceptions (see note 9). The Gemara argued that according to this principle the decree against reading a guest list, which was promulgated lest one erase it, should apply even if the list is beyond reach and unlikely to be erased. Therefore, even if the list is written high up on the wall, both Rav Bivi and Abaye would agree that one may not read from it.

In point of fact, the Gemara above raised another objection. To wit, even Rav Bivi, who said "lest one erase," agrees that we are also concerned lest one read *shetarei hedyotos.* Because of the latter consideration, Rav Bivi would surely prohibit even a list high up on the wall. That objection, however, has already been solved, for the Gemara stated that writing on a wall (high or low) would not be confused with *shetarei hedyotos* (see *Rashi*).

22. That is, there are Tannaim who hold that Rabbinic decrees related to the Sabbath were formulated without exceptions [לֹא פָּלוּג]. On the other hand, there is a Tannaic view which maintains that [even] such decrees are subject to exceptions (*Rashi*).

גמ' מ"ט רב ביבי אמר גזירה שמא ימחוק אביי אמר [א] גזירה שמא יקרא בשטרי הדיוטות מאי בינייהו א"ב דכתב אכותל ומידלי למ"ד שמא ימחוק לא חיישינן ולמ"ד שמא יקרא חיישינן ולמ"ד שמא ימחוק ניחוש שמא יקרא ותו לשמא ימחוק לא חיישינן והתניא לא יקרא לאור הנר ואמר רבה אפי' גבוה שתי קומות אפי' גבוה שתי מרדעות אפי' עשרה בתים זה ע"ג זה לא יקרא אלא איכא בינייהו דכתב אכותל ומיתתי למאן דאמר שמא ימחוק חיישינן למ"ד שמא יקרא לא חיישינן גודא בשטרא לא מיחלף ולמ"ד שמא יקרא ליחוש שמא ימחוק אלא איכא בינייהו דחייק אטבלא ואפינקס למ"ד שמא ימחוק לא חיישינן למ"ד שמא יקרא חיישינן ולמ"ד שמא ימחוק ליחוש שמא יקרא וכ"ת טבלא ופינקס בשטרא לא מיחלף והתניא מונה אדם כמה מבפנים וכמה מבחוץ וכמה מנות עתיד להניח לפניהם מכתב שעל גבי הכותל אבל לא מכתב שעל גבי טבלא ופינקס היכי דמי אילימא דכתיב מיכתב מ"ש הכא ומ"ש הכא אלא לאו דחייק וקתני מכתב שעל גבי הכותל אבל לא מכתב שע"ג טבלא ופינקס אלא לעולם דכתב אכותל ומידלי ודקא קשיא לך דרבה דרבה תנאי היא דתניא מונה אדם את אורחיו ואת פרפרותיו מפיו אבל לא מן הכתב ר' אחא מתיר מכתב שעל גבי הכותל היכי דמי אילימא דכתיב מתתא ליחוש שמא ימחוק אלא לאו דכתב ומידלי וש"מ דרבה תנאי היא ש"מ והני תנאי כהני תנאי דתניא אין רואין במראה בשבת רבי מאיר מתיר במראה הקבוע בכותל מ"ש הקבוע בכותל דאדהכי והכי מדכר הכא נמי קבוע אדהכי והכי מדכר הכא במראה של מתכת עסקינן וכדרב נחמן אמר רבה בר אבוה דא"ר נחמן אמר רבה בר אבוה מפני מה אמרו מראה של מתכת אסורה מפני שאדם עשוי להשיר בה נימין המדולדלין תנו רבנן כתב המהלך תחת הצורה ותחת הדיוקנאות אסור לקרותו בשבת ודיוקנא עצמה אף בחול אסור להסתכל בה משום שנאמר אל תפנו אל האלילים מאי תלמודא אמר רבי חנין אל תפנו אל מדעתכם: מפיס אדם עם בניו וכו': עם בניו ועם בני ביתו אין ועם אחר לא מאי טעמא כדרב יהודה אמר שמואל דאמר רב יהודה אמר שמואל בני חבורה המקפידין זה על זה עוברין משום מדה ומשום משקל ומשום מנין ומשום לווין ופורעין ביו"ט וכדברי

רש"י

גמ' מ"ט. אבל לא מן הכתב: שמא ימחוק. מן האורחין שירצה שלא הכין להם כל צרכם ויתחרט שזימן יותר מן הראוי וימחוק מן הכתב כדי שלא יקראם השמש: כל הני שמא יקרא בשטרי הדיוטות של מקח וממכר קאמר (א): דכתב. מניינא אכותל בדיו: ומידלי. שאינו מגיע לשם למחוק: (אפילו גבוה שאינו מגיע לשם למחוק): אפילו גבוה. שאינו מגיע שם להטות הנר אסור דהואיל ונמוך אסור גבוה נמי אסור שלא תחלוק: ומיתתי. שנמוך ויכול להגיע שם ולמחוק: ולמ"ד שמא יקרא. היכא דליכא למיחש לשמא יקרא ליחוש לשמא ימחוק: דחייק. בסכין בתוך העץ בטבלא שאין נוחה למחוק ואדהכי מדכר וליכא למיחש למחוק: גודא. כותל: פינקס. כעין לוחות של סוחרים: כמה בפנים וכמה בחוץ. את מי ומי אושיב בפנים במקום המכובד ואת מי ומי אושיב בחוץ שאינן כל כך ספונין: אבל לא מכתב שעל גבי טבלא ופינקס. דגודא בשטרא לא מיחלף אבל טבלא ופינקס מיחלף: [דכתיב מיכתב. כתב של דיו]: אלא לעולם דכתב אכותל ומידלי. שאינו יכול למחוק ולשמא יקרא לא חיישינן דגודא בשטרא לא מיחלף ודקשיא לך לאביי דמידלי ליתסרי כדרבה דאמר גבי נר אפילו י' בתים: דרבה תנאי היא. דאיכא דחייש לשלא תחלוק באיסור שבת דרבנן ואיכא דמפליג: ליחוש לשמא ימחוק. דהא ר' אחא כותל דוקא נקט ואי מתתאי מה לי כותל מה לי אגרת: אין רואין במראה. מירוא"ר לפי שהרואה במראה אינו צריך אלא לתקן שערות ראשו וזקנו הלכך חיישי' שמא יראה נימין המדולדלות שאינן שוות עם שאר השער ויגלחן: דאדהכי והכי. שילך להביא תער או מספרים: מדכר. שהוא שבת: של מתכת. שאינו צריך להביא מספרים שהיא עצמה מגלחת השער: כתב המהלך תחת הצורה ותחת הדיוקנאות. כגון בני אדם המציירים בכותל חיות משונות או דיוקנות של בני אדם של מעשים כגון מלחמת דוד וגלית וכותבין תחתיה זו צורת חיה פלונית וזו דיוקנית פלוני ופלונית: אסור לקרותו בשבת. שמא יקרא בשטרי הדיוטות: אל מדעתכם. אל אשר אתם עושי' מדעת לבבכם והלא כולם אלילים לשון חללים: עם בניו ובני ביתו אין עם אחר לא. מלה תנא ומפיס על המנות: משום לווין ופורעין. דגזור בהו רבנן שמא יכתוב: המקפידין. שאין מוחלים ומוותרים זה לזה: וכדברי

תוספות

ולמ"ד שמא ימחוק ליחוש שמא יקרא. ולא מסיק אדעתיה גודא בשטרא לא מיחלף: בשטרי הדיוטות. פי' בקונט' של מקח וממכר ולעיל בפרק כל כתבי (דף קיז: ושם) פירש איגרות השלוחות למלוה חפץ: אלא איכא בינייהו דכתיב אכותל ומתתאי. ולא ידענא אמאי נקט מתתאי כיון דס"ד דכ"ע אית להו דרבה: אילימא דכתיב מיכתב מ"ש הכא מ"ש הכא. פירוש תרוייהו יהא אסור שמא ימחוק:

לעולם דכתב אכותל ומידלי ודקשיא לך דרבה דרבה תנאי היא. לפירוש הקונטרס נ"ל דהשתא דמוקי לה דכתיב אכותל ומידלי למ"ד שמא ימחוק איכא דאית ליה דרבה ולמ"ד שמא יקרא לית ליה דרבה והשתא מיבעיא לן למימר דבדרבה פליגי תנאי כי היכי דפליגי אמוראי דהכא וברייתא קמייתא מיתוקמא שפיר דכתיב מכתב אכותל ומידלי דכולהו אמוראי גודא בשטרא לא מיחלף וקשה לפירוש זה דהשתא לא הוה פלוגתייהו כדהוה מוקמת לה מעיקרא למאן דאמר שמא ימחוק לא חיישינן למאן דאמר שמא יקרא חיישי' וה"ר פורת פירש דאביי ורב ביבי תרוייהו לית להו דרבה דפליגי בכתב אכותל ומידלי למאן דאמר שמא ימחוק לא חיישינן כיון דמידלי ולית לן דרבה ולשמא יקרא נמי לא חייש קסבר גודא בשטרא לא מיחלף ולמ"ד שמא יקרא חייש דקסבר גודא בשטרא מיחלף ואביי לא הוה מוקי פלוגתייהו דרבי אחא ורבנן (ב) כרבה דא"כ ר' אחא ע"כ לית ליה דאביי דשרי בכותל אלמא קסבר גודא בשטרא לא מיחלף וא"כ כמאן סבירא ליה דאפילו רבנן לא פליגי עליה דר' אחא אלא משום דאית להו דרבה וגזרינן שמא ימחוק אלא הוה מפרש אביי דכ"ע לית להו דרבה ולא חיישינן לשמא ימחוק במידלי ובגודא בשטרא מיחלף פליגי והא דקאמר ש"מ דרבה תנאי היא הו"מ למימר ודאי לכ"ע לית להו דרבה כדמפרש לאביי אלא דלא מצי למוכח הא בהדיא ולהכי קאמר דתנאי היא וליכא לאקשויי לרבה והא לא מצי למימר דפליגי (ג) בחייק מיחק רבי אחא ורבנן ובגודא בשטרא מיחלף פליגי אבל כ"ע אית להו דרבה משום דסברא הוא כיון דחייק ואיתא נמי בכותל פשיטא דהא לא הוי אמרי רבנן דגודא בשטרא מיחלף וצריך לאוקמא השתא ברייתא דלעיל דחייק מיחק למאן דסבר גודא בשטרא מיחלף וקשה קצת לפירוש זה דה"ל למימר דכ"ע (ד) לית להו דרבה ואביי ורב ביבי בגודא אי מיחלף בשטרא פליגי: ודיוקני עצמה אף בחול אסור. נראה דבשויה לשם עבודת גלולים אמר אבל (ה) לנוי מותר כדמשמע מבנן של קדושים דלא הוו מסתכלי בצורתא דזוזא (ע"ז דף נ.) מכלל דאחריני הוו מסתכלי: בני חבורה המקפידין זה על זה עוברין משום משקל ומשום מדה ומשום מנין. פירוש לפי שמקפידין זה על זה עוברין אפילו על מה שאין שאר בני אדם עוברין משום מדה כדאמרינן בבילה (דף כט.) יכול אדם לומר לחבירו מלא לי כלי זה אבל לא במדה פירוש כלי שמודדין בו אסור דדמי למקח וממכר והם כיון שהם מקפידים כל כלים הוי לגבייהו מדה לפי שמקפידין לידע שיעורו לשלם להם הכלי וכן משקל ששוקלים ומכוונים זה כנגד זה ביד ואמרינן בבילה (דף כט:) אין משגיחין במאזנים ביום טוב ומשום מנין כדאמר בבילה (דף כט:) הולך אדם אצל חנוני הרגיל אצלו ואומר לו תן לי כו' ובלבד שלא יזכיר לו סכום מקח שאם היו נותנים מאה אגוזים בדינר ולקח כבר תשעים לא יאמר לו תן לי עשרים אגוזים שאתחייב לך עשרה אגוזים שנראה שעושה להשלים הדינר אבל יכול לומר לו תן לי כ' אגוזים סתם ובבני חבורה המקפידים אסור שיבא לידי איסור שיחזירו להשלים וכדברי (ו) בית הלל אף משום רבית דכשהם מחזירין זה לזה הם מקפידים מה ששוות יותר וקשה לפירוש

עין משפט נר מצוה

יד א ב ג מיי' פכ"ג מהלכות שבת הלי"ט סמג לאוין סה טור שו"ע או"ח סימן שז סעיף יג:

טו ד ה מיי' פכ"ד מהל' שבת הלכה יד סמג שם טור שו"ע או"ח סימן שז סעיף יג:

טז ו מיי' פכ"ג שם הלכה יט סמג שם טור שו"ע או"ח סימן שז סעיף טו:

יז ז מיי' פ"ג מהלכות ע"ז הלכה ב סמג לאוין יד טוש"ע יו"ד סי' קמא סעיף טו:

יח ח מיי' פ"ו מהלכות גניבה הלכה י סמג לאוין קנד ועיין בפוסקים השמיטו מטעם שכ' הב"י באו"ח סוף סי' תקיז:

רבינו חננאל

מעמידין השמועה זו כרב יוסף. חדא (דרבא) [דרבא] לגבי רב יוסף תלמיד הוא ועוד סוגיא דשמעתא רובה כרב יוסף ריהטא ועוד מדחינן רב אויא מקבל משכנתא מכלל שאם אין בידו משכון אינו יכול ליתבע. ותוב רבא בר עולא מיערם איערומי כלומר לא היה תובעו בהדיא אלא היה אומר לו הלויני וכאשר יתן לו ויבאו המעות לידו אומר לו יש לי אצלך הלואת יו"ט נשתלמתי אתם מכלל כי הלואת יו"ט כי האי גוונא יתבע אבל בהדיא לא ניתנה ליתבע וראינו תשובה לגאון ופסק כרבא. ואמר רבא בתרא הוא. וקיי"ל דהלכתא כבתראי וכן הדעת נוטה: וכן ערב פסחים בירושלים כו'. א"ר יוחנן מקדיש אדם פסחו בשבת וחגיגתו ביו"ט נימא מסייעא ליה וכן ערב פסח כו' ופשוטה היא. הא דתני ר' הושעיא. ומקדיש אוקימנא. הקדיש עליו מדרבנן ואקשינן עלה והא תנא דאמר הלכה כסתם משנה ותנן אין מקדישין ואין מעריכין ואין מחרימין ומפריקין הא דא"ר יוחנן מקדיש בשבת בחובות הקבוע להן זמן. כגון פסח שאם לא יעשנו היום אינו יכול לעשותו למחר והיא מצוה עוברת והא דתנן אין מקדישין בשבת ולא ביום טוב בחובות שאין קבוע להן זמן: מונה אדם את אורחיו ואת פרפרותיו מפיו אבל לא מן הכתב. ואמרינן מן הכתב מ"ט לא. רב ביבי אמר גזירה שמא ימחוק אביי אמר גזירה שמא יקרא בשטרי הדיוטות ופירושו כיון שיראה אדם קורא כמה אורחים צריך להביא כמה פרפריות אצלו אף הוא אומר מותר לקרוא בשטרי הדיוטות מאי בינייהו דכתיב אכותל במקום גבוה שאינו יכול למחוק דרב ביבי בכי האי גוונא שרי. ואביי אסר. ואקשינן על רב ביבי והתנן לא יקרא לאור הנר ואמר רבה אפילו גבוה ב' קומות או ב' מרדעות ואפילו עשרה בתים זה ע"ג זה לא יקרא. והא הכא דליכא למיחש אלא שמא יטה ואפי' גבוה כמה אמר (רבא) [רבה] חיישינן ואסור. ואע"ג דסלקא כתנאי הלכתא (כרבא) [כרבה] דסתם מתניתין כוותיה ולא חיישינן אמחלוקות דברייתא וחזרנו להביא

טעם אחר לומר כי אינם חלוקים אלא אם הוא הכתב בכותל נמוך שמגעת לה ויכול למחוק דלרב ביבי אסור כטעמיה ולאביי שרי דכותל בשטר לא מיחלף. ואקשינן על אביי וליחוש שמא ימחוק הואיל והכותל נמוך נדחה ואתנן לאוקמי פלוגתיה בכתב דחייק אטבלא ופנקס וגם זה נדחה. וחזרנו על הטעם הראשון דכתוב אכותל ומידלי. לרב ביבי מותר ולאביי אסור. וזה שהקשינו לרב ביבי מדברי רבה שאסר אפילו גבוה כמה. אמר לך רב ביבי דרבה תנאי היא דתניא מונה אדם את אורחיו ואת פרפרותיו מפיו אבל לא מן הכתב. ר' אחא מתיר מן הכתב שעל גבי הכותל ואוקימנא דכתוב אכותל ומידלי. ואמרינן הני תנאי כי הני תנאי כלומר ר' במחלוקת ר' אחא ות"ק דיליה דלר' אחא א) צחצוח הסיג מן המראה הוא מוחק לפיכך קתני אין רואין במראה ור' מתיר במראה הקבועה בכותל כת"ק דר' אחא ודמיא להא דאמרינן בכלל גדול (דף עה) דשף בין העמודים [חייב] משום ב) מוחק

ביתו

מסורת הש"ס

א) נ"ל והתנן, ב) לעיל יא., ג) [שם דף יב:], ד) [תוספתא פרק יח], ה) [תוספ' פי"ד], ו) [ברב אלפס איתא דבעי מתיר וכו' וכ"ה בבעל המאור ובמלחמות. אבל בהרא"ש א' ר' יהודה מתיר וכו'], ז) [ע"ז מוס' ע"ז כט. ד"ה המסתפר], ח) [תוספ' פי"ז], ט) ע"ז מג: ע"ש, י) ויגלחם במספרים כצ"ל רש"ל, כ) [וע"ע תוספות ע"ז נ. ד"ה ה"ג], ל) [דף כח.].

הגהות הב"ח

(א) רש"י ד"ה כל הני וכו' קאמר. הס"ד ואח"כ מ"ה למ"ד שמא יקרא חיישינן ואפי' גבוה: (ב) תוס' ד"ה לעולם וכו' דר' אחא ורבנן כדרבה דא"כ: (ג) בא"ד והא לא מצי למימר דפליגי ר' אחא ורבנן בחייק מיחק ובגודא בשטרא: (ד) בא"ד וקשה קצת לפירוש זה דה"ל למימר דכ"ע לית להו דרבה ואביי ורב ביבי בגודא: (ה) ד"ה ודיוקנא וכו' אבל לנוי שרי: (ו) ד"ה בני וכו' שיחזירו להשלים וכדברי הלל אף:

גליון הש"ס

גמ' אין רואין במראה בשבת. עי' ע"ז דף כט ע"א תוס' ד"ה המסתפר: שם כתב המהלך תחת הצורה. עי' לעיל דף קטז ע"ב תוס' ד"ה וכ"ש בשטרי:

תורה אור השלם

א) אַל תִּפְנוּ אֶל הָאֱלִילִם וֵאלֹהֵי מַסֵּכָה לֹא תַעֲשׂוּ לָכֶם אֲנִי יְיָ אֱלֹהֵיכֶם: [ויקרא יט, ד]

ליקוטי רש"י

בשטרי הדיוטות. כגון של חשבונות או איגרות השלוחות למלוה חפץ [לעיל קטז:, ועי' כאן ושם]. לא יקרא לאור הנר. בספר שמא יטה הנר לקרב השמן לפי הפתילה שידלק יפה ונמצא מבעיר בשבת [שם יא.]. אפילו גבוה. דליכא למיחש להטייה דכיון דגזור לא פלוג בשבילותיהו [שם יב:]. מרדעות. מלמד הבקר [שבועות מח.]. מלמד הוא לרכן, מרדע אגוילו"ן בלע"ז [שופטים ג, לא]. בני חבורה. ההולכין בדרך או יושבין בבית אחת איש ואיש. המקפידין זה על זה. שאין מוחלין על דבר מועט ומקפידין להשלים זה את זה במדה ובמשקל ובמנין. עוברין. בשבתות וימים טובים. משום לווין ופורעין. דתנן במסכת שבת (קמח:) לא ילוה כו' והתם מפרש טעמא שמא יכתוב [ב"מ עה.].

חשק שלמה על רבינו חננאל א) לכאורה לפי גי' זה צ"ל להיפך דר' אחא כרבי. ואולי דגירסתו היה להפך ומתמלה נעתק בטעות וצ"ע: ב) לעיל שם בגמ' איתא משום ממחק וצ"ע:

מוֹנֶה אָדָם אֶת אוֹרְחָיו וְאֶת פַּרְפְּרוֹתָיו מִפִּיו אֲבָל לֹא מִן הַכְּתָב – A PERSON MAY COUNT HIS GUESTS AND HIS DELICACIES ORALLY, BUT NOT FROM A WRITTEN NOTE [even if it is written on the wall]. רַבִּי אַחָא מַתִּיר מִכְּתָב שֶׁעַל גַּבֵּי הַכּוֹתֶל – R' ACHA PERMITS one to count FROM a list WRITTEN ON THE WALL. הֵיכִי דָּמֵי – Now, what are the circumstances of this list written on a wall, about which R' Acha and the Tanna Kamma disagree? אִילֵימָא דִּכְתִיב מִתַּתָּא – If you say that it was written low down on the wall, לֵיחוּשׁ שֶׁמָּא יְמְחוֹק – one should be concerned lest he erase it! Even R' Acha would surely prohibit reading such a list.[23] Hence, this cannot be the list to which the Baraisa refers. אֶלָּא לָאו דִּכְתַב וּמִידְלֵי – Rather, the Baraisa refers to a list that he wrote high up on the wall. R' Acha permits reading such a list (because it is too high to be erased easily), while the Tanna Kamma prohibits it. וּשְׁמַע מִינָּהּ דְּרַבָּה תַּנָּאֵי הִיא – Deduce from [this Baraisa] that Rabbah's ruling is the subject of a dispute between Tannaim (namely, the Tanna Kamma and Rav Acha).[24] שְׁמַע מִינָּהּ – Indeed, one can deduce this conclusion from it.

The Gemara records another Tannaic dispute in which Rabbah's principle is the point of contention:

וְהָנֵי תַּנָּאֵי כְּהָנֵי תַּנָּאֵי – And the dispute between those Tannaim [the Tanna Kamma and R' Acha] is essentially the same as the dispute between these Tannaim: דְּתַנְיָא – For it was taught in a Baraisa: אֵין רוֹאִין בְּמַרְאָה בְּשַׁבָּת – ONE MAY NOT LOOK INTO A MIRROR ON THE SABBATH, because he may come to cut his hair.[25] רַבִּי מֵאִיר מַתִּיר בְּמַרְאָה הַקָּבוּעַ בַּכּוֹתֶל – R' MEIR[26] PERMITS one to look INTO A MIRROR if it is FIXED TO THE WALL.[27] מַאי שְׁנָא הַקָּבוּעַ בַּכּוֹתֶל – Now, what is different about [a mirror] fixed to the wall? Why does R' Meir permit the use of specifically such a mirror? דְּאַדְּהָכִי וְהָכִי מִדְכַּר – The reason is presumably that in the meantime (i.e. by the time he fetches a pair of scissors with which to cut his hair), he will remember that it is the Sabbath.[28] שֶׁאֵינוֹ קָבוּעַ נָמֵי – But, if so, then using [a mirror] that is not fixed to the wall should also be permitted, אַדְּהָכִי וְהָכִי מִדְכַּר – because in the meantime (i.e. by the time he fetches scissors) he will remember that it is the Sabbath![29]

To resolve this difficulty, the Gemara limits the Baraisa to a particular case:

הָכָא בְּמַרְאָה שֶׁל מַתֶּכֶת עַסְקִינַן – We are dealing here with a metal mirror. וְכִדְרַב נַחְמָן אָמַר רַבָּה בַּר אֲבוּהָ – And the reason why it is forbidden is as Rav Nachman said in the name of Rabbah bar Avuha. דְּאָמַר רַב נַחְמָן אָמַר רַבָּה בַּר אֲבוּהָ – For Rav Nachman said in the name of Rabbah bar Avuha: מִפְּנֵי מָה אָמְרוּ מַרְאָה שֶׁל מַתֶּכֶת אֲסוּרָה – Why did they say that a metal mirror is forbidden? מִפְּנֵי שֶׁאָדָם עָשׂוּי לְהָשִׁיר בָּהּ נִימִין הַמְּדוּלְדָּלִין – Because a person is accustomed to remove straggling hairs with it; that is, he uses the sharp edge of the mirror itself to cut his hair.[30] We can now understand why R' Meir differentiates between a mirror attached to the wall and one that is unattached. If the mirror is unattached, one will use the mirror itself to cut his hair; but if it is attached, he will have to fetch a pair of scissors, by which time he will remember that it is the Sabbath. For this reason, R' Meir permits looking into a mirror if it is attached to the wall. The Tanna Kamma, however, applying Rabbah's principle, prohibits even an attached mirror.[31]

As part of its discussion of what is permitted to read on the Sabbath, the Gemara cites the following Baraisa:

תָּנוּ רַבָּנַן – The Rabbis taught in a Baraisa: כְּתָב הַמְהַלֵּךְ תַּחַת הַצּוּרָה וְתַחַת הַדְּיוֹקְנָאוֹת – WRITING (i.e. a caption) THAT RUNS UNDER A PICTURE OR UNDER TABLEAUX,[32] אָסוּר לִקְרוֹתוֹ בְּשַׁבָּת –

NOTES

23. R' Acha evidently holds that there is a decree against reading a list, because otherwise he would not have specified a wall. He would have permitted reading a list from a sheet of paper as well. Having established that Rav Acha agrees that a decree was enacted [for some reason], we can assume that it was enacted to prevent erasure [as well] (*Rashi*, as explained by *Rashash*).

24. The Tanna Kamma agrees with Rabbah's teaching that Rabbinic decrees (related to the Sabbath) are not subject to exceptions. For this reason, the Tanna Kamma holds that the decree against reading a list, which was enacted lest one erase from it, applies even where the list is beyond reach and unlikely to be erased. R' Acha, though, limits Rabbinic decrees to cases in which the Biblical transgression they were designed to prevent is likely to occur. In his view, therefore, one is allowed to read from a list written high up on a wall, since it is highly improbable that he will erase from it. [Neither Tanna is concerned in this case lest one come to read *shetarei hedyotos,* because writing on a wall would not be confused with a document (see note 11).]

The Gemara is proposing that this is also the point of contention between Rav Bivi and Abaye. Rav Bivi, who stresses that the decree against reading a list was promulgated "'lest one erase,'' agrees with the Tanna Kamma and Rabbah that this prohibition applies in all circumstances. Abaye, however, who did not say "lest he erase,'' limits the decree, as Rav Acha does, to situations in which erasure is likely (*Rashi,* as explained by *Tosafos;* see *Maharsha;* cf. *Ritva's* explanation of *Rashi;* see also *Tos. HaRosh*).

For other approaches to this passage (some based on a different text), see *Tosafos, Ramban, Rashba* et al.

25. A person looks into a mirror to groom his hair. We fear that if he sees some hairs protruding, he might trim them (*Rashi*). [Cutting hair is included in the *melachah* of גּוֹזֵז, *shearing.*]

26. Many Rishonim read here רַבִּי, *Rebbi,* instead of ר' מֵאִיר, *R' Meir* (*Rabbeinu Chananel, Rif, Ramban, Rashba* et al.). *Rosh* reads ר' יְהוּדָה, *R' Yehudah.*

27. The Tanna Kamma, however, prohibits the use of any mirror, whether or not it is attached to the wall.

28. Knowing that it is forbidden to cut hair on the Sabbath, he will not proceed.

29. [Although the interval might be shorter if the mirror is not attached, because he could take it with him to the place of the scissors, there is still sufficient time for him to remember that it is the Sabbath.]

30. The edge of a metal mirror is as sharp as a knife (*Rif*). Since he can use the mirror itself to cut his hair, he will not go to fetch a pair of scissors. Therefore, only a short time will elapse before he cuts his hair, which is not necessarily long enough for him to remember that it is the Sabbath. For this reason, one is forbidden to look into a *metal* mirror on the Sabbath. Other kinds of mirrors, however, are permitted, since by the time he fetches a pair of scissors, he will surely remember that it is the Sabbath (*Rif* et al.; see following note).

31. Thus, as in the previous dispute (regarding a list written high on the wall), these Tannaim disagree about Rabbah's principle. The Tanna Kamma accepts Rabbah's principle that Rabbinic decrees were applied without exceptions [לֹא פְּלוֹג], whereas R' Meir rejects this principle.

It should be noted, however, that although the Tanna Kamma accepts Rabbah's principle, he allows the use of non-metal mirrors [e.g. our glass mirrors]. This is because Rabbah's principle dictates only that an item belonging to a particular category is prohibited regardless of its circumstances. Items of a different category are not affected. Consequently, non-metal mirrors, which are deemed a category apart from metal mirrors, were not included in the decree (*Rif, Rosh, Ramban, Meiri* et al.; see *Aruch HaShulchan, Orach Chaim* 275:4; see *Chidushei HaRan* for a different explanation; cf. *Baal HaMaor;* see also *Beur Halachah* to 302:13 ד"ה שאין).

The Baraisa implies that using a [metal] mirror is forbidden only on the Sabbath, but is permitted on a weekday. Some Rishonim, though, maintain that a man may never look into a mirror for cosmetic purposes, because this is a feminine practice that falls under the prohibition of וְלֹא־יִלְבַּשׁ גֶּבֶר שִׂמְלַת אִשָּׁה, *and a man shall not wear a feminine garment* (*Deuteronomy* 22:5). In their opinion, this Baraisa refers only to women (see *Ritva MHK* ed., *Ran* folio 63b, *Meiri, Tosafos* to *Avodah Zarah* 29a ד"ה המסתפר). *Ran* (*Avodah Zarah* folio 9b) and *Rama* (*Yoreh Deah* 156:2) rule that this practice is prohibited to men only in locales where men generally do not use mirrors.

32. This refers to works of art drawn on walls such as pictures of various animals, or tableaux depicting famous people in scenes of their notable deeds, e.g. David and Goliath (*Rashi*), or the binding of Isaac (*Hagahos*

גמ' מ"ט רב ביבי אמר גזירה שמא ימחוק אביי אמר [א] גזירה שמא יקרא בשטרי הדיוטות מאי בינייהו א"ב דכתב אכותל ומידלי למ"ד שמא ימחוק לא חיישינן ולמ"ד שמא יקרא חיישינן ולמ"ד שמא ימחוק ניחוש שמא יקרא ותו לשמא ימחוק לא חיישינן [ב] והתניא [ג] לא יקרא לאור הנר [ג] ואמר רבה אפי' גבוה שתי קומות אפי' גבוה שתי מרדעות אפי' עשרה בתים זה ע"ג זה לא יקרא אלא איכא בינייהו דכתב אכותל ומיתתי למאן דאמר שמא ימחוק חיישינן למ"ד שמא יקרא לא חיישינן גודא בשטרא לא מיחלף ולמ"ד שמא יקרא ליחוש שמא ימחוק אלא איכא בינייהו דחייק אטבלא ואפינקס למ"ד שמא ימחוק לא חיישינן למ"ד שמא יקרא חיישינן ולמ"ד שמא ימחוק ליחוש שמא יקרא וכ"ת טבלא ופנקס בשטרא לא מיחלף והתניא [ד] מונה אדם כמה מבפנים וכמה מבחוץ וכמה מנות עתיד להניח לפניהם [ה] מכתב שעל גבי הכותל אבל לא מכתב שעל גבי טבלא ופינקס היכי דמי אילימא דכתיב מיכתב מ"ש הכא ומ"ש הכא אלא לאו דחייק וקתני מכתב שעל גבי הכותל אבל לא מכתב שע"ג טבלא ופינקס אלא לעולם דכתב אכותל ומידלי ודקא קשיא לך דרבה דרבה תנאי היא דתניא [ו] מונה אדם את אורחיו ואת פרפרותיו מפיו אבל לא מן הכתב ר' אחא מתיר מכתב שעל גבי הכותל היכי דמי אילימא דכתיב מתתא ליחוש שמא ימחוק אלא לאו דכתב ומידלי וש"מ דרבה תנאי היא ש"מ והני תנאי כהני תנאי דתניא [ז] [ח] אין רואין במראה בשבת [ז] רבי מאיר מתיר במראה הקבוע בכותל מ"ש הקבוע בכותל דאדהכי והכי מדכר דאינו קבוע נמי אדהכי והכי מדכר הכא במראה של מתכת עסקינן וכדרב נחמן אמר רבה בר אבוה דא"ר נחמן אמר רבה בר אבוה [ח] מפני מה אמרו מראה של מתכת אסורה מפני [ט] שאדם עשוי להשיר בה נימין המדולדלין תנו רבנן [ט] [י] כתב המהלך תחת הצורה ותחת הדיוקנאות אסור לקרותו בשבת [י] ודיוקנא עצמה אף בחול אסור להסתכל בה משום שנאמר [א] אל תפנו אל האלילים מאי תלמודא אמר רבי חנין אל תפנו אל מדעתכם: מפיס אדם עם בניו וכו': עם בניו ועם בני ביתו אין ועם אחר לא מאי טעמא כדרב יהודה אמר שמואל [כ] דאמר רב יהודה אמר שמואל [ח] בני חבורה המקפידין זה על זה עוברין משום מדה ומשום משקל ומשום מנין ומשום לווין ופורעין ביו"ט וכדברי

רש"י

גמ' מ"ט. אבל לא מן הכתב: שמא ימחוק. מן האורחין שירצה שלא הכין להם כל צרכם ויתחרט שזימן יותר מן הראוי וימחוק מן הכתב כדי שלא יקראם השמש: כל הני שמא יקרא בשטרי הדיוטות של מקח וממכר קאמר (א): דכתב. מגיעה אכותל בדיו: ומידלי. שאינו מגיע לשם למחוק: (אפילו גבוה שאינו מגיע לשם למחוק): אפילו גבוה. שאינו מגיע שם להטות הנר אסור דהואיל ונמוך אסור גבוה נמי אסור שלא תחלוק: ומיתתי. שנמוך ויכול להגיע שם ולמחוק: ולמ"ד שמא יקרא. היכא ליכא למיחש לשמא יקרא ליחוש לשמא ימחוק: דחייק. בסכין בתוך העץ בטבלא שאין נוחה למחוק ולהכי מדכר וליכא למיחש למחוק: גודא. כותל: פינקס. כעין לוחות של סוחרים: כמה בפנים וכמה בחוץ. את מי ומי אושיב בפנים במקום המכובד ואת מי ומי אושיב בחוץ שאינו כל כך ספון: אבל לא מכתב שעל גבי טבלא ופינקס. דגודא בשטרא לא מיחלף אבל טבלא ופינקס מיחלף: [דכתיב מיכתב. כתב של דיו]: אלא לעולם דכתב אכותל ומידלי. שאינו יכול למחוק ולשמא יקרא לא חיישינן דגודא בשטרא לא מיחלף ודקשיא לך דעל גב דמידלי ליתסרי כדרבה דאמר גבי נר אפילו י' בתים: דרבה תנאי היא. דאיכא דמחייב לשלא תחלוק באיסור שבת דרבנן ואיכא דמפליג: ליחוש לשמא ימחוק. דהא ר' אחא כותל דוקא נקט ואי מתתאי מה לי כותל מה לי אגרת: אין רואין במראה. מירוא"ה לפי שהרואה במראה אינו צריך אלא לתקן שערות ראשו חקנו הלכך חיישי' שמא יראה נימין המדולדלות שאינן שוות עם שאר השער [ט] ויגלחן: דאדהכי והכי. שילך להביא תער או מספריים: מדכר. שהוא שבת: של מתכת. שאינו צריך להביא מספרים שהיא עצמה מגלחת השער: כתב המהלך תחת הצורה ותחת הדיוקנאות. כגון בני אדם המציירים בכותל חיות משונות או דיוקנות של בני אדם של מעשים כגון מלחמת דוד וגלית וכותבין תחתיה זו צורת חיה פלונית וזו דיוקנית פלוני ופלונית: אסור לקרותו בשבת. שמא יקרא בשטרי הדיוטות: אל מדעתכם. אל תפנו אל מדעת לבבכם ואלל שלכם. אלילים לשון חללים: עם בניו ובני ביתו אין עם אחר לא. מדלא תנא ומפיס על המנות: משום לווין ופורעין. דגזור בהו רבנן שמא יכתוב: המקפידין. שאין מוחלים ומוותרין זה לזה:

תוספות

ולמ"ד שמא ימחוק ליחוש שמא יקרא. ולא מסיק אדעתיה גודא בשטרא לא מיחלף: בשטרי הדיוטות. פי' בקונט' של מקח וממכר ולעיל בפרק כל כתבי (דף קטז: ושם) פירש איגרות השלוחות למלוה חפץ: אלא איכא בינייהו דכתיב אכותל ומתתאי. ולא ידענא אמאי נקט מתתאי כיון דס"ד דכ"ע אית להו דרבה: אילימא דכתיב מיכתב מ"ש הכא מ"ש הכא. פירוש תרווייהו יהא אסור שמא ימחוק: לעולם דכתב אכותל ומידלי ודקשיא לך דרבה דרבה תנאי היא. לפירוש הקונטרס נ"ל דהשתא דמוקי לה דכתיב אכותל ומידלי למ"ד שמא ימחוק איכא דאית ליה דרבה ולמ"ד שמא יקרא לית ליה דרבה והשתא מיבעיא לן למימר דבדרבה פליגי תנאי כי היכי דפליגי אמוראי דהכא ובריית' קמייתא מיתוקמא שפיר דכתיב מכתב אכותל ומידלי דכולהו אמוראי גודא בשטרא לא מיחלף וקשה לפירוש זה דהשתא לא הוה פלוגתייהו כדהוה מוקמת לה מעיקרא למאן דאמר שמא ימחוק לא חיישינן למאן דאמר שמא יקרא חיישי' וה"ר פורת פירש דאביי ורב ביבי תרווייהו לית להו דרבה דפליגי בכתב אכותל ומידלי למאן דאמר שמא ימחוק לא חיישינן כיון דמידלי ולית לן דרבה ולשמא יקרא נמי לא חייש קסבר גודא בשטרא לא מיחלף ולמ"ד שמא יקרא חייש דקסבר גודא בשטרא מיחלף ואביי לא הוה מוקי פלוגתייהו דרבי אחא ורבנן (ב) כרבה דא"כ ר' אחא ע"כ לית ליה דאביי דשרי בכותל אלמא קסבר גודא בשטרא לא מיחלף וא"כ כמאן סבירא ליה דאפילו רבנן לא פליגי עליה דר' אחא אלא משום דאית להו דרבה וגזרינן שמא ימחוק אלא הוה מפרש אביי דכ"ע לית להו דרבה ולא חיישינן לשמא ימחוק במידלי ובגודא בשטרא מיחלף פליגי והא דקאמר ש"מ דרבה תנאי היא הו"מ למימר ודאי לכ"ע לית להו דרבה כדמפרש לאביי אלא דלא מצי למוכח הא בהדיא ולהכי קאמר דתנאי היא וליכא לאקשויי לרבה והא לא מצי למימר דפליגי (ג) בחייק מיחק רבי אחא ורבנן ובגודא בשטרא מיחלף פליגי אבל כ"ע אית להו דרבה משום דסברא הוא כיון דחייק ואיתא נמי בכותל פשיטא דבהא לא הוי אמרי רבנן דגודא בשטרא מיחלף וצריך לאוקמא השתא ברייתא דלעיל דחייק מיחק למאן דסבר גודא בשטרא מיחלף וקשה קצת לפירוש זה דה"ל למימר דכ"ע (ד) לית להו דרבה ואביי ורב ביבי בגודא אי מיחלף בשטרא פליגי: ודיוקני עצמה אף בחול אסור. נראה עבודת גלולים אמר אבל (ה) לנוי מותר כדמשמע מבנן של קדושים דלא הוו מסתכלי בצורתא דזוזא (ע"ז דף נ.) מכלל דאחריני הוו מסתכלי [ל]: בני חבורה המקפידין זה על זה עוברין משום משקל ומשום מדה ומשום מנין. פירוש לפי שמקפידין זה על זה עוברין אפילו על מה שאין שאר בני אדם עוברין משום מדה כדאמרינן בבילה (דף כט.) יכול אדם לומר לחבירו מלא לי כלי זה אבל לא במדה פירוש כלי שמודדין בו אסור דדמי למקח וממכר והם כיון שהם מקפידים כל כלים הוי לגבייהו מדה לפי שמקפידין לידע שיעורו לשלם להם הכלי וכן משקל שאסור לשקול זה כנגד זה ביד ואמרינן בבילה [ל] אין משגיחין במאזנים ביום טוב ומשום מנין דאמר בבילה (דף כט.) הולך אדם אצל חנוני הרגיל אצלו ואומר לו תן לי כו' ובלבד שלא יזכיר לו סכום מקח שאם היו נותנים מאה אגוזים בדינר ולקח כבר תשעים אגוזים שאמחשב לך עשרה אגוזים שנראה שעושה להשלים הדינר אבל יכול לומר לו תן לי כ' אגוזים סתם ובבני חבורה המקפידים אסור שיבא לידי איסור שיחזרו להשלים וכדברי (ו) בית הלל אף משום רבית דכשהם מחזירין זה לזה הם מקפידים מה שוות יותר וקשה לפירוש

עין משפט נר מצוה

יד א ב ג מיי' פכ"ג מהלכות שבת הל' יט סמג לאוין סה טור שו"ע או"ח סימן שז סעיף יג:

טו ד ה מיי' פ"ד מהל' שבת הלכה יד סמג שם טור שו"ע או"ח סימן שז סעיף יג:

טז ו מיי' פכ"ב שם הלכה יג סמג שם טור שו"ע או"ח סימן שב סעיף יג:

יז ז מיי' פ"ב מהלכות ע"ז הלכה ב סמג לאוין יד טוש"ע יו"ד סי' קמב סעיף טו:

יח ח מיי' פ"ז מהלכות גניבה הלכה י סמג לאוין עה [אבל הפוסקים השמיטו מטעם שכ' הב"י באו"ח סוף סי' תקי"ן]:

מסורת הש"ס

א) נ"ל והתנן, ב) לעיל יב., ג) [שם דף יב:], ד) [תוספתא פרק יז], ה) [תוספ' פי"ד], ו) [בכל אלפס איתא רבי מתיר וכו' וכ"ה בבעל המאור ובמלחמות. אבל בהרא"ש אי' ר' יהודה מתיר וכו'], ז) [ע' תוס' ע"ז כט. ד"ה המספרכן], ח) [תוספ' פי"ח], ט) ב"מ עה., י) ועלגש המספרים כל"ל רש"ל, כ) [וע"ע תוספות ע"ז נ. ד"ה כ"ג], ל) [דף כט.].

הגהות הב"ח

(א) רש"י ד"ה כל הני וכו' קאמר. הס"ד ואח"כ מ"ה למ"ד שמא יקרא חיישינן ואפי' גבוה: (ב) תוס' ד"ה לעולם וכו' דר' אחא ורבנן כרבה דא"כ: (ג) בא"ד והא לא מצי למימר דפליגי ר' אחא ורבנן בחייק מיחק ובגודא בשטרא: (ד) בא"ד וקשה קצת לפי' זה דה"ל למימר דכ"ע אביי ורב ביבי לית להו דרבה ובגודא: (ה) ד"ה ודיוקנא וכו' אבל לשם נוי: (ו) ד"ה בני וכו' שיחזרו להשלים וכדברי הלל אף:

גליון הש"ס

גמ' אין רואין במראה בשבת. עי' ע"ז דף כט ע"א תוס' ד"ה המספספר: רש"י ד"ה שם כתב המהלך תחת הצורה. עי' לעיל דף קטז ע"ב תוס' ד"ה וכ"ש בשטרי:

תורה אור השלם

א) אל תפנו אל האלילים ואלהי מסכה לא תעשו לכם אני יי אלהיכם: [ויקרא יט, ד]

ליקוטי רש"י

בשטרי הדיוטות. כגון של חשבונות או איגרות השלוחות למלוה חפץ [לעיל קטז:]. לא יקרא לאור הנר. בספר שמא יטה הנר בשעה שמחפש שיהא לבו טפה שילך הנר יפה ונמצא מבעיר בשבת [שם יא.]. אפילו גבוה. לטיטה [illegible] [שם יב:]. מרדעות. מלמד הבקר [שבועות מח.]. מלמד הוא דרבן. מרדע אגוויילו"ן בלע"ז [שופטים ג, לא]. בני חבורה. הולכין לדרך או יושבין בבית אחת ואוכלין יחד לסעודה. המקפידין זה על זה. שאין מוחלין על דבר מועט ומקפידין להלוות זה את זה במדה במשקל ובמנין. עוברין. בשבתות וימים טובים. משום לווין ופורעין. דתנן במסכת שבת (קמח.) ובלבד שלא יאמר לו הלויני והתם מפרש טעמא שמא יכתוב [ב"מ עה.].

רבינו חננאל

מעמידין השמועה זו כרב יוסף. חדא [דרבא] [דרבה] לגבי רב יוסף תלמיד הוא ועוד סוגיא דשמעתא רובה כרב יוסף ריהטא ועוד מדחנן רב אויא מקבל משכנא מכלל שאם אין בידו משכון אינו יכול ליתבע. ותוב רבא בר אויא מיעוט איערוזי כלומר לא היה תובע בהדיא אלא היה אומר לו הלויני וכאשר יתן לו ויבאו המעות לידו אומר לו יש לי אצלך הלואה ויש נשתלמתי אתם מכלל כי הלואה יו"ט כי האי גוונא יתבע אבל בהדיא לא ניתנה ליתבע וראינו תשובה לגאון ופסק כרבא. ואמר רבא בתרא הוא. וקיי"ל דהלכתא כבתראי. וכן הדעת נוטה: וכן ערב פסחים בירושלים כו'. א"ר יוחנן מקדיש אדם פסחו בשבת וחגיגתו ביו"ט נימא מסייעא ליה וכן ערב פסח שחל להיות בשבת כו' ושוטה היא. הא דתני ר' הושעיא ומקדישו אוקמינא. הקדיש עליו מדרבנן ואקשינן עלה והא תנא דאמר הלכה כסתם משנה ותנן אין מקדישין ואין מעריכין ואין מחרימין ומפרקינן הא דא"ר יוחנן מקדיש בשבת בחובות הקבוע להן זמן. כגון פסח שאם לא עשו היום אינו יכול לעשותו למחר והיא מצוה עוברת. והא דתנן אין מקדישין בשבת ולא ביום טוב בחובות שאין קבוע להן זמן. מונה אדם את אורחיו ואת פרפרותיו מפיו אבל לא מן הכתב. ואמרינן מאי טעמא מן הכתב לא. רב ביבי אמר גזירה שמא ימחוק אביי אמר גזירה שמא יקרא בשטרי הדיוטות ופירושו כיון שיראה אדם קורא כמה אורחים צריך להכין כמה פרפריות אצלו אף הוא אומר מותר לקרוא בשטרי הדיוטות מאי בינייהו דכתיב אכותל במקום גבוה שאינו יכול למחוק דרב ביבי בכי האי גוונא שרי. ואביי אסר. ואקשינן על רב ביבי והתנן לא יקרא לאור הנר ואמר רבה אפילו גבוה ב' קומות או ב' מרדעות ואפילו עשרה בתים זה ע"ג זה לא יקרא. והא הכא דליכא למיחש אלא שמא יטה ואפי' גבוה כמה [רבא] [רבה] חיישינן ואסור. ואע"ג דסלקא כתנאי הלכתא כ[רבא] [כרבה] דסתם מתניתין כוותיה ולא חיישינן אמחלוקות דברייתא וחזרנו להביא טעם אחר לומר כי אינם חלוקים אלא אם הוא הכתב בכותל נמוך שמגעת לה יכול למחוק דלרב ביבי אסור כטעמיה ולאביי שרי דכותל בשטר לא מיחלף. ואקשינן על אביי וליחוש שמא ימחוק הואיל והכותל נמוך נדחה ואתינן לאוקמי פלוגתייהו בכתב דחייק אטבלא ופנקס וגם זה נדחה. וחזרנו על הטעם הראשון דכתוב אכותל ומידלי. לרב ביבי מותר ולאביי אסור. וזה שהקשינו לרב ביבי מדברי רבה שאסר אפילו גבוה כמה. אמר לך רב ביבי דרבה תנאי היא. ואקשינן מתנאי דתנן מונה אדם את אורחיו ואת פרפרותיו מפיו אבל לא מן הכתב. ר' אחא מתיר מכתב שעל גבי הכותל ואוקמנא דכתוב אכותל ומידלי. ואמרינן הני תנאי כי הני תנאי כלומר ר' אחא ות"ק חולקין במחלוקת ר' ות"ק דיליה דלר' אחא א) צחצוח הסיג מן המראה הוא מוחק לפיכך קתני אין רואין במראה ור' מתיר במראה הקבועה בכותל כת"ק דר' אחא ודמיא להא דאמרינן הני תנאי כהני תנאי. ואוקמנא במראה של מתכת דקיי"ל לרב יהודה (דף עה) דשף בין העמודים [חייב] משום ממחק שדומה למוחק כתב. [illegible] ואקשינן עלה מ"ש מראה הקבועה בכותל דאדהכי והכי מדכר. ולא פירש מהו שיזכור ורמינו. יש מי שאומר כי נאסר הראיה במראה בשבת [illegible] ונדחה זה הטעם. ועמד כר"נ דאמר מפני מה מראה של מתכת אסורה מפני שאדם עשוי להשיר בה נימין המדולדלות [illegible] ת"ר כתב המהלך תחת הצורה [illegible] לקרותו בשבת ולא גרע משטרי הדיוטות דאסור בשבת. ודיוקני עצמה אסורה. אפילו בחול כטעמיה: מפיס אדם עם בניו ועם בני ביתו על השלחן [illegible] וכמה שאמר על השכר (פסחים קז) מיסרו ומפיס. בניו ובני ביתו

ONE IS FORBIDDEN TO READ IT ON THE SABBATH.[33] וּדְיוּקְנָא עַצְמָהּ – AND AS FOR THE TABLEAU ITSELF, אַף בְּחוֹל אָסוּר לְהִסְתַּכֵּל בָּהּ – EVEN ON WEEKDAYS ONE IS FORBIDDEN TO GAZE AT IT, מִשּׁוּם שֶׁנֶּאֱמַר – FOR IT IS STATED:[34] "אַל־תִּפְנוּ אֶל־הָאֱלִילִם" – *DO NOT TURN TO THE IDOLS.*

The Gemara explains how the verse teaches this point:

מַאי תַּלְמוּדָא – **What is the derivation?** אָמַר רַבִּי חָנִין – **R' Chanin said:** אַל תִּפְנוּ אֶל מִדַּעְתְּכֶם – The verse is interpreted to mean: **Do not turn to** that which comes **from your minds.**[35]

The Mishnah stated:

מֵפִיס אָדָם עִם בָּנָיו וכו' – A PERSON MAY CAST LOTS for portions of food WITH HIS CHILDREN and members of his household etc.

The Gemara draws an inference from the Mishnah:

עִם בָּנָיו וְעִם בְּנֵי בֵיתוֹ אִין – **With his children and with the members of his household – yes!** he may cast lots; וְעִם אַחֵר לֹא – **but with others – no!** he may not cast lots.[36]

The Gemara explains why it is forbidden to draw lots with people who are not members of his household:

מַאי טַעְמָא – **What is the reason?** כִּדְרַב יְהוּדָה אָמַר שְׁמוּאֵל – It is **as Rav Yehudah said in the name of Shmuel;** דְּאָמַר רַב יְהוּדָה אָמַר שְׁמוּאֵל – **for Rav Yehudah said in the name of Shmuel:** בְּנֵי חֲבוּרָה הַמַּקְפִּידִין זֶה עַל זֶה – **Members of a group**[37] **who are particular with each other**[38] עוֹבְרִין – **will come to violate** the law on account of these prohibitions regarding the Sabbath and Yom Tov; namely, מִשּׁוּם מִדָּה – **on account of** the prohibition concerning a **measure,**[39] וּמִשּׁוּם מִשְׁקָל – **and on account of** the prohibition against **weighing,**[40] וּמִשּׁוּם מִנְיָן – **and on account of** the prohibition against **counting,**[41] וּמִשּׁוּם לוֹוִין וּפוֹרְעִין – **and on account of** the prohibitions against **borrowing**[42] **and paying back.**[43] בְּיוֹם טוֹב – These violations will occur **on Yom Tov** or the Sabbath.

NOTES

Maimoniyos to *Hil. Shabbos* 23:19). Underneath the picture or tableau would appear a caption identifying the animals or persons portrayed (*Rashi*).

33. Lest one come to read *shetarei hedyotos* (*Rashi;* cf. *Meiri*). [Although it was stated above that writing on a wall is not included in this prohibition (see note 11), the Rabbis were especially stringent in this case (*Hagahos R' Simchah MiDessau*), possibly because the writing serves no Sabbath-related purpose.]

This Baraisa indicates that the prohibition against reading on the Sabbath or Yom Tov [which was enacted to prevent the reading of *shetarei hedyotos*] covers a wider range of materials than just practical items such as the guest list discussed in our Mishnah (see *Rosh*). *Rambam* (*Commentary to the Mishnah,* 148b) writes that it is forbidden to read anything, even books of secular wisdom, on the Sabbath and Yom Tov. Only the Torah and its commentaries are permitted (see *Beis Yosef* 307 ד״ה כתב הרמב״ם בפי׳ המשנה [17] and *Mishnah Berurah* ibid. §58). Some Rishonim, though, permit books of secular wisdom, because they do not resemble *shetarei hedyotos* (*Rashba* Responsa VII §288; *Ramban* cited ibid.).

As mentioned above (note 2), there is a dispute as to whether *shetarei hedyotos* signify only business documents or social letters as well. Even according to the first opinion, one may not read social letters, *lest* one come to read business documents (*Rashba, Rosh;* cf. *Tosafos* to 116b; see *Maharsha* ibid.; see also *Shulchan Aruch, Orach Chaim* 307:13,14).

34. *Leviticus* 19:4.

35. That is, do not turn to works created by man that are inspired by his own thoughts. The word אֱלִילִם (idols), which is cognate with חֲלָלִים, *recesses,* is interpreted as denoting the recesses of man's heart and mind (*Rashi;* cf. *Chidushei HaRan* and *Tos. Rid*).

Alternatively, the Gemara should be rendered: אַל תִּפְנוּ אֶל מִדַּעְתְּכֶם, *Do not remove God from your minds.* That is, do not gaze at man-made works – for when you do so, God is not present in your thoughts (*Aruch,* cited by *Ran* folio 63b; see *Meiri*).

Some Rishonim maintain that this prohibition applies only to gazing at items that have been designated for idol worship, although they have not yet been used as such (*Tosafos, Rosh*). The Torah teaches here that one should not pay any attention to matters of idolatry (*Ramban* to *Leviticus* 19:4), lest he become attracted to it (see *Rambam, Hil. Avodah Zarah* 2:2; see also *Kesef Mishneh* ibid. and *Yad David* [*Basra*]). [Once something has already been used for idol worship, one is forbidden to gaze at its beauty in any event, due to the ban against deriving benefit from idols (see *Shulchan Aruch, Yoreh Deah* 142:15 and *Shach* ibid. §33).]

Other Rishonim maintain that the prohibition is of a more general nature: One should not gaze at works of art (even if they are not idolatrous), because preoccupation with their beauty diverts a person's attention from the service of God (*Meiri; Tos. Rid; Rashi,* according to *Yad David* [*Basra*]; *Tosafos* to *Avodah Zarah* 50a; see *Aruch* cited above). Rather, it is only the beauty of God's works at which one may gaze, to gain an appreciation of His wondrous creations (*Ritva MHK* ed.)

According to both opinions, the prohibition does not apply to casual glancing (*Magen Avrohom* ibid. §21; see also *Tosafos* to *Avodah Zarah* 50a), or to gazing at insignificant items that are not alluring [e.g. a caption under a picture, as is evident from the Baraisa] (ibid. §23 with *Machatzis HaShekel*).

Magen Avraham (§21) reports that the general practice is to follow the first opinion; see also *Beur Halachah* to 307:16 ד״ה ועובר. [With regard to reading secular literature, see *Shulchan Aruch* ibid.]

36. The Gemara deduces this from the fact that the Mishnah does not simply state: מֵפִיס אָדָם עַל הַמָּנוֹת, *A person may cast lots for portions,* which would have implied that he may do so with anyone, not just his children and members of his household (*Rashi*).

37. E.g. travelers on the road or people who happen to be together under one roof. Each person, though, partakes of his own food (*Rashi* to *Bava Metzia* 75a).

38. They do not forgo even small amounts (*Rashi* ibid.). They will not share their food or drink with each other unless they receive a portion of exactly the same value in return (*Rabbeinu Chananel*).

Normally a group of people who are together on the Sabbath or Yom Tov will share their food and drink and are not at risk to transgress any law. But people who are ungenerous toward one another are likely to violate the law as regards measuring, weighing and counting, as follows (see *Tosafos*).

39. It is forbidden to measure an item on the Sabbath and Yom Tov (see Mishnah *Beitzah* 29a, *Rambam, Hil. Shabbos* 23:13, and *Shulchan Aruch, Orach Chaim* 323:1,2). These people, who are particular with each other, usually measure what they take from one another in order not to be cheated out of even a small amount. Being accustomed to this practice, they are likely to measure what they take even on the Sabbath and Yom Tov (*Tosafos;* see *Rabbeinu Chananel* and *Tosafos* to *Bava Metzia* 75a ד״ה בני).

40. Weighing is prohibited on the Sabbath and Yom Tov (see Mishnah *Beitzah* 28a, *Rambam* ibid. and *Shulchan Aruch, Orach Chaim* 500:2). Since, due to their stinginess, these people typically weigh whatever is conveyed from one to the other, they are likely to do so on the Sabbath and Yom Tov as well (*Tosafos;* see *Rabbeinu Chananel* and *Tosafos* to *Bava Metzia* 75a ד״ה בני).

41. A Baraisa (*Beitzah* 29b) teaches that one may not mention the total of one's purchases on Yom Tov. *Tosafos* understand this to mean that if, for example, a *dinar* buys 100 nuts, one who had already taken 60 nuts may not say, "Give me another 40 to complete the amount of 100." [For other interpretations, see *Tosafos* to *Bava Metzia* loc. cit. ד״ה משום and *Orach Chaim* 323:4; see also *Rambam* ibid. and *Rabbeinu Chananel.*] These stingy people typically remind the giver of the full amount to which they are entitled. They are thus liable to do so on Yom Tov (in the above manner), thereby violating the law (*Tosafos*).

42. I.e. the prohibition against borrowing mentioned in the preceding Mishnah, 148a. Actually, borrowing is permitted if one says *hashileini* (as opposed to *halveini*). Stingy people, though, will not say *hashileini* because it connotes the loan of an item that must be returned intact (see note 9 ibid.). The borrower, wishing to avoid any such demand by the lender, will say *halveini* (*Tosafos;* cf. *Tosafos* to *Bava Metzia* ibid. ד״ה ומשום).

43. One is not allowed to pay back a debt on the Sabbath or Yom Tov, because the borrower might erase the record of the loan in his ledger (*Chidushei HaRan*). It is permitted if one uses an expression of חֲזָרָה, *returning,* rather than פֵּרָעוֹן, *repayment* (*Tosafos* to *Bava Metzia* ibid.; see *Mishnah Berurah* 307:46 for the explanation). [However, these people, who tend to be overexplicit in their dealings, are likely to stress that it is a פֵּרָעוֹן, *repayment,* even on the Sabbath or Yom Tov.]

גמ' מ"ט רב ביבי אמר גזירה שמא ימחוק אביי אמר גזירה שמא יקרא בשטרי הדיוטות מאי בינייהו א"ב דכתב אכותל ומידלי למ"ד שמא ימחוק לא חיישינן ולמ"ד שמא יקרא חיישינן ולמ"ד שמא ימחוק ניחוש שמא יקרא ותו לשמא ימחוק לא חיישינן והתניא לא יקרא לאור הנר ואמר רבה אפי' גבוה שתי קומות אפי' גבוה שתי מרדעות אפי' עשרה בתים זה ע"ג זה לא יקרא אלא איכא בינייהו דכתב אכותל ומיתתי למאן דאמר שמא ימחוק חיישינן למ"ד שמא יקרא לא חיישינן גודא בשטרא לא מיחלף ולמ"ד שמא יקרא ליחוש שמא ימחוק אלא איכא בינייהו דחייק אטבלא ואפינקס למ"ד שמא ימחוק לא חיישינן למ"ד שמא יקרא חיישינן ולמ"ד שמא ימחוק ליחוש שמא יקרא וכ"ת טבלא ופינקס בשטרא לא מיחלף והתניא מונה אדם כמה מבפנים וכמה מבחוץ וכמה מנות עתיד להניח לפניהם מכתב שעל גבי הכותל אבל לא מכתב שעל גבי טבלא ופינקס היכי דמי אילימא דכתיב מיכתב מ"ש הכא ומ"ש הכא אלא לאו דחייק וקתני מכתב שעל גבי הכותל אבל לא מכתב שע"ג טבלא ופינקס אלא לעולם דכתב אכותל ומידלי ודקא קשיא לך דרבה דרבה תנאי היא דתניא מונה אדם את אורחיו ואת פרפרותיו מפיו אבל לא מן הכתב ר' אחא מתיר מכתב שעל גבי הכותל היכי דמי אילימא דכתיב מתתא ליחוש שמא ימחוק אלא לאו דכתב ומידלי וש"מ דרבה תנאי היא ש"מ והני תנאי כהני תנאי דתניא אין רואין במראה בשבת רבי מאיר מתיר במראה הקבוע בכותל מ"ש הקבוע בכותל דאדהכי והכי מדכר הכא נמי אדהכי והכי מדכר הכא במראה של מתכת עסקינן וכדרב נחמן אמר רבה בר אבוה דא"ר נחמן אמר רבה בר אבוה מפני מה אמרו מראה של מתכת אסורה מפני שאדם עשוי להשיר בה נימין המדולדלין תנו רבנן כתב המהלך תחת הצורה ותחת הדיוקנאות אסור לקרותו בשבת ודיוקנא עצמה אף בחול אסור להסתכל בה משום שנאמר אל תפנו אל האלילים מאי תלמודא אמר רבי חנין אל תפנו אל מדעתכם: מפיס אדם עם בניו וכו': עם בניו ועם בני ביתו אין ועם אחר לא מאי טעמא כדרב יהודה אמר שמואל דאמר רב יהודה אמר שמואל בני חבורה המקפידין זה על זה עוברין משום מדה ומשום משקל ומשום מנין ומשום לווין ופורעין ביו"ט וכדברי

רש"י

גמ' מ"ט. אבל לא מן הכתב: שמא ימחוק. מן האורחין שיראה שלא הכין להם כל צרכם ויתחרט שזימן יותר מן הראוי וימחוק מן הכתב כדי שלא יקראם השמש: כל הני שמא יקרא בשטרי הדיוטות של מקח וממכר קאמר (א): דכתב. מגילה אכותל לדיו: ומידלי. שאינו מגיע לשם למחוק: (אפילו גבוה שאינו מגיע לשם למחוק): אפילו גבוה. שאינו מגיע שם להטות הנר אסור דהואיל ונמוך אסור גבוה נמי אסור שלא תחלוק: ומיתתי. שנמוך ויכול להגיע שם ולמחוק: ולמ"ד שמא יקרא. היכא דליכא למיחש לשמא יקרא ליחוש לשמא ימחוק: דחייק. בסכין בתוך העץ בטבלא שאין נוחה למחוק ולאדהכי מדכר וליכא למיחש למחוק: גודא. כותל: פינקס. כעין לוחות של סוחרים: כמה בפנים וכמה בחוץ. את מי ומי מושיב בפנים במקום המכובד ואת מי ומי מושיב בחוץ שאין כל כך ספונין: אבל לא מכתב שעל גבי טבלא ופינקס. דגודא בשטרא לא מיחלף אבל טבלא ופינקס מיחלף: [דכתיב מיכתב. כתב של דיו]: אלא לעולם דכתב אכותל ומידלי. שאינו יכול למחוק ולשמא יקרא לא חיישינן דגודא בשטרא לא מיחלף ודקשיא לך דלא"ג דמידלי ליתסרי כדרבה דאמר גבי נר אפילו י' בתים: דרבה תנאי היא. דליכא דחייש לשלא תחלוק באיסור שבת דרבנן וליכא דמפליג: ליחוש לשמא ימחוק. דהא ר' אחא כותל דוקא נקט ולאי מתתי מה לי כותל מה לי אגרת: אין רואין במראה. מירו"ל לפי שהרואה במראה אינו צריך אלא לתקן שערות ראשו וזקנו הלכך חיישי' שמא יראה נימין המדולדלות שאינן שוות עם שאר השער וילגלגן: דאדהכי והכי. שילך להביא תער או מספרים: מדכר. שהוא שבת: של מתכת. שאינו צריך להביא מספרים שהיא עצמה מגלחת השער: כתב המהלך תחת הצורה ותחת הדיוקנאות. כגון בני אדם המציירים בכותל חיות משונות או דיוקנות של בני אדם של מעשים כגון מלחמת דוד וגלית וכותבין תחתיה זו צורת חיה פלונית וזו דיוקנו פלוני ופלונית: אסור לקרותו בשבת. שמא יקרא בשטרי הדיוטות: אל מדעתכם. אל אשר אתם עושי' מדעת לבכם ותלו שלכם. אלילים לשון חללים: עם בניו ובני ביתו אין עם אחר לא. מדלא תנא ומפיס על המנות: משום לווין ופורעין. דגזור בהו רבנן שמא יכתוב: המקפידין. שאין מוחלים ומוותרין זה לזה: וכדברי

תוספות

ולמ"ד שמא ימחוק ליחוש שמא יקרא. ולא מסיק אדעתיה גודא בשטרא לא מיחלף: **בשטרי** הדיוטות. פי' בקונט' של מקח וממכר ולעיל בפרק כל כתבי (דף קיו: ושם) פירש איגרות השלומות למלוה מפץ: **אלא** איכא בינייהו דכתיב אכותל ומתתאי. ולא ידענא אמאי נקט מתתאי כיון דס"ד דכ"ע אית להו דרבה: **אילימא** דכתיב מיכתב מ"ש הכא מ"ש הכא. פירוש תרוייהו יהא אסור שמא ימחוק: **לעולם** דכתב אכותל ומידלי ודקשיא לך דרבה דרבה תנאי היא. לפירוש הקונטרס ז"ל דהשתא דמוקי לה דכתיב אכותל ומידלי למ"ד שמא ימחוק איכא דאית ליה דרבה ולמ"ד שמא יקרא לית ליה דרבה והשתא מיבעיא לן למימר דבדרבה פליגי תנאי כי היכי דפליגי אמוראי דהכא ובריית' קמייתא מיתוקמא שפיר דכתיב מכתב אכותל ומידלי דכולהו אמוראי גודא בשטרא לא מיחלף וקשה לפירוש זה דהשתא לא הוה פלוגתייהו כדהוה מוקמת לה מעיקרא למאן דאמר שמא ימחוק לא חיישינן למאן דאמר שמא יקרא חיישי' וה"ר פורת פירש דאביי ורב ביבי תרוייהו לית להו דרבה דפליגי בכתב אכותל ומידלי למאן דאמר שמא ימחוק לא חיישינן כיון דמידלי ולית לן דרבה ולשמא יקרא נמי לא חיים קסבר גודא בשטרא לא מיחלף ולמ"ד שמא יקרא חיים דקסבר גודא בשטרא מיחלף ואביי לא הוה מוקי פלוגתייהו דרבי אחא ורבנן (ג) כרבה דא"כ ר' אחא ע"כ לית ליה דאביי דשרי בכותל אלמא קסבר גודא בשטרא לא מיחלף וא"כ כמאן סבירא ליה דאפילו רבנן לא פליגי עליה דר' אחא אלא משום דאית להו דרבה וגזרינן שמא ימחוק אלא הוה מפרש אביי דכ"ע לית להו דרבה ולא חיישינן לשמא ימחוק במידלי ובגודא בשטרא מיחלף פליגי והא דקאמר ש"מ דרבה תנאי היא הו"מ למימר ודאי לכ"ע לית להו דרבה כדמפרש לאביי אלא דלא מצי למוכח הא בהדיא ולהכי קאמר דתנאי היא וליכא לאקשויי לרבה והא לא מצי למימר דפליגי (ג) בחייק מיחק רבי אחא ורבנן ובגודא בשטרא מיחלף פליגי אבל כ"ע אית להו דרבה משום דסברא הוא כיון דחייק ואיתא נמי בכותל פשיטא דהא לא הוי אמרי רבנן דגודא בשטרא מיחלף וצריך לאוקמא השתא ברייתא דלעיל דחייק מיחק למאן דסבר גודא בשטרא מיחלף וקשה קצת לפירוש זה דה"ל למימר דכ"ע (ד) לית להו דרבה ואביי ורב ביבי בגודא אי מיחלף בשטרא פליגי: **ודיוקני** עצמה אף בחול אסור. נראה דבשויה לשם עבודת גלולים אמר אבל (ה) לנוי מותר כדמשמע מבנן של קדושים דלא הוו מסתכלי בצורתא דזוזא (ע"ז דף נ.) מכלל דאחריני הוו מסתכלי: **בני** חבורה המקפידין זה על זה עוברין משום משקל ומשום מדה ומשום מנין. פירוש לפי שמקפידין זה על זה עוברין אפילו על מה שאין שאר בני אדם עוברין משום מדה כדאמרינן בביצה (דף כט.) יכול אדם לומר לחבירו מלא לי כלי זה אבל לא במדה פירוש כלי שמודדין בו אסור דדמי למקח וממכר והם כיון שהם מקפידים כל כלים הוי לגבייהו מדה לפי שמקפידין לידע שיעורו לשלם להם הכלי וכן משקל ששוקלים ומכוונים זה כנגד זה ביד ואמרינן בביצה אין משגיחין במאזנים ביום טוב ומשום מנין כדאמר בביצה (דף כט:) הולך אדם אצל חנוני הרגיל אצלו ואומר לו תן לי כו' ובלבד שלא יזכיר לו סכום מקח שאם היו נותנים מאה אגוזים בדינר ולקח כבר תשעים לא יאמר לו תן לי עשרים אגוזים שאתחייב לך עשרה אגוזים שנראה שעושה להשלים הדינר אבל יכול לומר לו תן לי כ' אגוזים סתם ובבני חבורה המקפידים אסור שיבא לידי איסור שיזכירו להשלים וכדברי (ו) בית הלל אף משום רבית דכשהם מחזירין זה לזה הם מקפידים מה ששוות יותר וקשה לפירוש

עין משפט נר מצוה

יד א ב ג מיי' פכ"ג מהלכות שבת הלכה יט סמג לאוין סה טור שו"ע או"ח סימן שז סעיף יב:
טו ד ה מיי' פכ"ג מהל' שבת הלכה יג סמג שם טור שו"ע או"ח סימן שז סעיף יג:
טז ו מיי' פכ"ג שם הלכה יט סמג שם טור שו"ע או"ח סימן שז סעיף טו:
יז ז מיי' פ"ב מהלכות ע"ז הלכה ב סמג לאוין יד טוש"ע יו"ד סימן קמב סעיף טו:
יח ח מיי' פ"ו מהלכות גניבה הלכה י סמג לאוין קנה [אבל הפוסקים השמיטו מטעם שכ' הב"י באו"ח סוף סי' תקי"ז]:

מסורת הש"ס

א) ל"ל והתנן, ב) לעיל יא., ג) [שם דף יב:], ד) [תוספתא פרק יח], ה) [תוספ' פי"ד], ו) [ברב אלפס איתא רבי מתיר וכו' וכ"ה בבעל המאור ובמלחמות. אבל בהרא"ש ר' יהודה מתיר וכו'], ז) [ע' תוס' כה. ד"ה המספפר], ח) [תוספ' פי"ח], ט) ב"מ עה. י) דגלגם במספרים כל"ל רש"ל, כ) [וע' תוספות ע"ז כ. ד"ה ה"ג], ל) [דף כח.].

הגהות הב"ח

(א) רש"י ד"ה כל הני וכו' קאמר. הס"ד ואח"כ מ"ה למ"ד שמא יקרא חיישינן ואפי' גבוה: (ב) תוס' ד"ה לעולם וכו' דר' אחא ורבנן כרבה דא"כ: (ג) בא"ד והא לא מצי למימר דפליגי בחייק מיחק ובגודא בשטרא: (ד) בא"ד וקשה קצת לפי' זה דה"ל למימר דכ"ע אביי ורב ביבי לית להו דרבה ובגודא: (ה) ד"ה ודיוקנא וכו' אבל לשם נוי: (ו) ד"ה בני וכו' שיזכירו להשלים ובדברי הלל אף:

גליון הש"ס

גמ' אין רואין במראה בשבת. עי' ע"ז דף כט ע"א תוס' ד"ה המספפר: שם כתב המהלך תחת הצורה. עי' לעיל דף קטז ע"ב תוס' ד"ה כ"ש בשטרי:

תורה אור השלם

א) אַל תִּפְנוּ אֶל הָאֱלִילִם וֵאלֹהֵי מַסֵּכָה לֹא תַעֲשׂוּ לָכֶם אֲנִי יְיָ אֱלֹהֵיכֶם: [ויקרא יט, ד]

ליקוטי רש"י

בשטרי הדיוטות. כגון של חשבונות או איגרות השלומות למלוה מפץ [לעיל קטז: ועי' בתוס' כאן ושם]. לא יקרא לאור הנר. בספר שמא יטה הנר להביא השמן לפי הפתילה שידלק יפה ונמצא מבעיר בשבת [שם יא.]. אפילו גבוה. דליכא למיחש להטייה דכיון דגזור לא פלוג למילתייהו [שם יב:]. מרדעות. מרדעת. מלמד הבקר [שבועות מח.]. מלמד הוא דרבן, מרדע אגוליון בלע"ז [שופטים ג, לא]. בני חבורה. הולכין בדרך או יושבין בבית אחת איש לסעודת עצמו. המקפידין זה על זה. שאין מוחלין על דבר מועט ומקפידין להשוות זה את זה כמדה במשקל ובמנין. עוברין. בשבתות ובימים טובים. ומשום לווין ופורעין. דתנן במסכת שבת (קמח.) לא יאמר לו הלויני והכא משום לווין ופורעין שמא יכתוב [ב"מ עה.].

רבינו חננאל

מעמידין השמועה זו כרב יוסף. חדא (דרבה) [דרבא] לגבי רב יוסף תלמיד הוא ועוד סוגיא דשמעתא רובה כרב יוסף ריהטא ועוד מדחינן רב אויא מקבל משכונא מכלל שאם אין בידו משכון אינו יכול ליתבע. ותוב רבא בר עולא מיערם איערומי כלומר לא היה תובעו בהדיא אלא היה אומר לו הלויני וכאשר יתן לו ויבאו המעות לידו אומר לו יש לי אצלך הלואת יו"ט נשתלמתי אתם מכלל כי הלואת יו"ט כי האי גוונא יתכן אבל בהדיא לא ניתנה ליתבע וראינו תשובה לגאון ופסיק כרבא. ואמר רבא בתרא הוא. וקיי"ל דהלכתא כבתראי וכן הדעת נוטה: **וכן** ערב פסחים בירושלים כו'. א"ר יוחנן מקדיש אדם פסחו בשבת וחגיגתו ביו"ט נימא מסייעא ליה וכן ערב פסח כו' ופשוטה היא. הא דתני ר' הושעיא ומקדישו אוקמינא. הקדיש עלוי מדרבנן ואקשינן עלה והא תנא דאמר הלכה כסתם משנה ותנן אין מקדשין ואין מעריכין ואין מחרימין ומפרקינן הא דא"ר יוחנן מקדיש בשבת בחובות הקבוע להן זמן. כגון פסח שאם לא יעשנו היום אינו יכול לעשותו למחר והיא מצוה עוברת והא דתנן אין מקדישין בשבת ולא ביום טוב בחובות שאין קבוע להן זמן. מונה אדם את אורחיו ואת פרפריותיו מפיו אבל לא מן הכתב. ואמרינן מן הכתב מ"ט לא. רב ביבי אמר גזירה שמא ימחוק אביי אמר גזירה שמא יקרא בשטרי הדיוטות ופירושו כיון שיראה אדם קורא כמה אורחים צריך להביא כמה פרפריות אצלו אף הוא אומר מותר לקרוא בשטרי הדיוטות מאי בינייהו דכתיב אכותל במקום גבוה שאינו יכול למחוק דרב ביבי בכי האי גוונא שרי. ואביי אסר. ואקשינן על רב ביבי והתנן לא יקרא לאור הנר ואמר רבה אפילו גבוה ב' קומות או ב' מרדעות ואפילו עשרה בתים זה ע"ג זה לא יקרא. והא הכא דליכא למיחש אלא שמא יטה ואפי' גבוה כמה אמר (רבא) [רבה] חיישינן ואסור. ואע"ג דסלקא כתנאי הלכתא (כרבא) [כרבה] דסתם מתניתין כוותיה ולא חיישינן אמחלוקות דברייתא וחזרנו להביא טעם אחר לומר כי אינם חלוקים אלא אם הוא הכתב בכותל נמוך שמגעת לה ויכול למחוק דלרב ביבי אסור כטעמיה ולאביי שרי דכותל בשטר לא מיחלף. ואקשינן על אביי וליחוש שמא ימחוק הואיל והכותל נמוך הוא וגם זה הטעם נדחה ואתינן לאוקמי פלוגתיה בכתב דחייק אטבלא ופנקס וגם זה נדחה. וחזרנו על הטעם הראשון דכתוב אכותל ומידלי. לרב ביבי מותר ולאביי אסור. וזה שהקשינו לרב ביבי מדברי רבה שאסר אפילו גבוה כמה. אמר לך רב ביבי דרבה תנאי היא ואנא כתנא דשרי. דתניא מונה אדם את אורחיו ואת פרפרותיו מפיו אבל לא מן הכתב. ר' אחא מתיר מן הכתב שעל גבי הכותל ואוקימנא דכתוב אכותל ומידלי. ואמרינן הני תנאי כי הני תנאי כלומר ר' ...

עין משפט נר מצוה

יט א מיי' פכ"ג מהלכ' שבת הלכה יז סמג שם טוש"ע או"ח סימן שכב סעיף ו:
כ ב מיי' שם (ופ"ו מהל' גזילה ואבידה הל"י) סמג שם ועשין ע"ד ולאוין קנ טור שו"ע או"ח שם וטוש"ע חו"מ סימן שע סעיף ג:
כא ג ד מיי' פ"ד מהל' י"ט הלכה כ סמג לאוין עה:

גמרא

וכדברי (א) ב"ה) אף משום רבית אי הכי בניו ובני ביתו נמי בניו ובני ביתו היינו טעמא כדרב יהודה אמר רב ב) דאמר רב יהודה אמר רב מותר להלוות בניו ובני ביתו ברבית כדי להטעימן טעם רבית אי הכי מנה גדולה כנגד מנה קטנה נמי אין ה"נ וחסורי מיחסרא והכי קתני א מפים אדם עם בניו ועם בני ביתו על השלחן אפי' מנה גדולה כנגד מנה קטנה מ"ט כדרב יהודה אמר רב עם בניו ועם בני ביתו אין עם אחרים לא מ"ט כדרב יהודה אמר שמואל ב מנה גדולה כנגד מנה קטנה אף בחול לאחרים אסור מ"ט משום קוביא: ג מטילין חלשין על וכו': מאי אבל לא על המנות א"ר יעקב ג) בריה דבת יעקב אבל לא ד על המנות של חול ביו"ט פשיטא מהו דתימא הואיל וכתיב א) ועמך כמריבי כהן אפי' מנות דחול נמי קמ"ל וא"ר יעקב ד) בריה דבת יעקב ה • כל שחבירו נענש על ידו אין מכניסין אותו במחיצתו של הקב"ה מנלן אילימא משום דכתיב ב) ויאמר ה' מי יפתה את אחאב ויעל ויפול ברמות גלעד ויאמר זה בכה וזה אומר בכה ויצא הרוח ויעמוד לפני ה' ויאמר אני אפתנו וגו' ויאמר אצא והייתי רוח שקר בפי כל נביאיו ויאמר תפתה וגם תוכל צא ועשה כן ואמרינן מאי רוח ו) א"ר יוחנן זה רוחו של נבות ומאי צא אמר רב צא ממחיצתי ודילמא התם היינו טעמא דכתיב ג) דובר שקרים לא יכון לנגד עיני אלא מהכא ד) שבעת קלון מכבוד שתה גם אתה והערל וגו' שבעת קלון מכבוד זה נבוכד נצר שתה גם אתה והערל זה צדקיה חדא דכוליה קרא בנבוכד נצר כתיב ועוד צדקיה צדיקא מאי הוה ליה למיעבד ליה דא"ר יהודה אמר רב בשעה שבקש אותו רשע לעשות לאותו צדיק כך וכו' אלא מהכא ה) גם ענוש לצדיק לא טוב אין לא טוב אלא רע וכתיב ו) כי לא אל חפץ רשע אתה לא יגורך רע ז) צדיק אתה ה' ולא יגור במגורך רע מאי משמע דהאי חלשים לישנא דפורא הוא דכתיב ז) איך נפלת משמים הילל בן שחר נגדעת לארץ חולש על גוים וגו' אמר רבה בר רב הונא מלמד שהיה מטיל פור על גדולי מלכות לידע איזה בן יומו של משכב זכור וכתיב ח) כל מלכי גוים כולם וגו' אמר רבי יוחנן שנחו ממשכב זכור וא"ר יוחנן כל ימיו של אותו רשע לא נמצא שחוק בפה כל בריה שנאמר ט) נחה שקטה כל הארץ פצחו רנה מכלל דעד השתא לא הוה רנה ואמר ר' יצחק אמר ר' יוחנן אסור לעמוד בביתו של אותו רשע שנא' י) ושעירים ירקדו שם ואמר רב יהודה אמר רב בשעה שביקש אותו רשע לעשות לאותו צדיק כך נמשכה ערלתו שלש מאות אמה והיתה מחזרת על כל המסיבה כולה שנאמר שבעת קלון מכבוד שתה גם אתה והערל ערל בגימטריא שלש מאות הוי ואמר רב יהודה אמר רב בשעה שירד אותו רשע לגיהנם רעשו כל יורדי גיהנם אמרו שמא למשול עליהם הוא בא או ליחלות כמותם הוא בא שנאמר ח) גם אתה חולית כמונו אלינו נמשלת יצאתה ב"ק ואמרה כ) ממי נעמת רדה והשכבה את ערלים ל) איך שבת נוגש שבתה מדהבה א"ר יהודה אמר רב שבתה אומה זו שאמרה מדוד ומדוד

רש"י

וכדברי (בית) הלל דחיישי שמא יוקירו מיהו בהלואת ככרות אף משום רבית: בניו ובני ביתו נמי. ליחוש לרבית וכל הני: להלוות. משלו: בניו ובני ביתו. הסמוכים על שלחנו דכיון דהכל משלו אין כאן רבית: להטעימן טעם רבית. שידעו כמה קשה אלמא כיון דמשלו הוא אין כאן איסור רבית והלכך גבי מדה ומשקל ומנין נמי לאו קפידא הוא אלא להשוותם בלא קנאה: אי הכי מנה גדולה כנגד מנה קטנה נמי. דמוקמינן טעמא לקמן משום קוביא ואפי' בחול אסור וכיון דהכל משלו אמאי אסור להטעימן טעמא קוביא בעלמא הוא: מאי טעמא מותר. ולא חייש לקוביא: כדרב יהודה אמר רב. להטעימן בעלמא הוא: עם אחר לא כדרב יהודה אמר שמואל. דכיון דמקפידין עוברין משום מדה ומשקל ומנין: משום קוביא. דגזל הוא דאסמכתא לא קניא והא אסמכתא דסמיך על הגורל אם יפול גורל אמנה הגדולה לזכה בה ולפיכך תלה עצמו אף בגורל הקטנה על הספק ואילו יודע מתחלה שכן לא היה מתרצה: של חול. של קדשים של אתמול: כמריבי כהן. ככהנים אלו שהם בעלי מריבה: אפי' דחול נמי. לישתרי להו להפיס ביו"ט כי היכי דלא לינצו: זה בכה. אני אפתנו בכה: שבעת קלון. בנבוכדנצר משתעי שהיה מטיל משכב זכור על המלכים וכשהגיע יומו של צדקיהו נמשכה ערלתו ג' מאות אמה והיינו שבעת קלון: חדא דכוליה קרא בנבוכדנצר כתיב. שפיר מצית לאוקמי כוליה בנבוכדנצר וה"ק שתה גם אתה כאותם שהיית מקלה אותן והערל והתערל והתגנה: בשעה שעשה לו כו'. לקמן היא מדקאמר לאותו צדיק ש"מ אנוס היה: ענוש לצדיק לא טוב. לדיק המענים לא טוב וכיון דאינו טוב הרי הוא רע: וכתיב לא יגורך רע. אלמא אינו נכנס במחילתו: חולש על גוים. בנבוכדנצר כתיב: ושעירים ירקדו שם. ולא אנשים ובשביל הבריות מסתלקין המזיקין ונמצא מבטל גזירת המלך: המסיבה. מלכים שהיו מסובין ויושבין לפניו: גם אתה חולית כמונו אלינו וגו'. ביורדי גיהנם כתיב דכתיב לעיל מיניה שאול מתחת רגזה לך לקראת בואך וגו' (א): חולית כמונו אלינו נמשלת. לשון ממשלה: נעמת. סבור אתה להיות בנועם מן האחרים: מדוד

תוספות

לפירוש זה דאם הלל לא איירי אלא במקפידין אם כן אמאי קאמר לעיל לימא מתניתין דלא כהלל והא הלל במקפידין איירי ומתניתין דלעיל אתי שפיר כוותיה דהא רישא באין מקפידין איירי דקתני שואל דאילו למקפידין אסרינן שאלה לפי מה שפירש' להכי נראה לפרש עוברין משום מדה ומשום משקל כלומר קרובין לבא לידי כך שיעברו משום מדה שע"י שמקפידין זה ע"ז ורגילין ליקח במדה זה מזה גם ביו"ט יעשו כך וגם כל בני אדם הוי אסורין בכלי של מדה כדאמר בביצה (דף כט: ושם) אבל למקפידין נותן הוא עצה שלא ישתתפו שקרובים הן לבא לידי איסור מדה וכן לידי איסור משקל מתוך שרגילים לשקול על ידי הקפדתן גם ביו"ט לא ירגישו עד שישקלו ולידי מנין כשישאל אחד מהן ס' אגוזים יאמר לו תן לי מ' להשלים ק' כמו שרגילין לעשות ומשום לווין ופורעין ביו"ט כדאמר לעיל דלשון הלואה אסור והם מתוך שמקפידים יזכירו לשון הלואה לפי שיאמר השואל אם אזכיר לו לשון שאלה משמע דהדרא בעיניה לכך אומר לשון הלואה וכדברי הלל אף משום רבית דכשלוין זה מזה כבר באין לידי רבית לפי שפעמים שזה משלם יותר שאע"פ שמקפיד הוא בוש הוא שלא ישלם כמו שהלוהו בשביל שההנהו וכיון שאינו מוחל הוי רבית אבל שאר בני אדם מחלי ולא הוי רבית והשתא מתני' איירי במקפידין דסתם שכנים שאינם חברים מקפידין ומ"מ דרך שאלה מותר ומה שדברו כאן על מקפידין לא אמרינן אלא גבי חבורה שרגילים לישאל זה מזה תדיר ואתי לידי איסור אבל שכנים שאינן תדירין כל כך לשאול זה מזה מותרים ואין לגזור בהם שמא יבאו לידי איסור ולהכי לא משני כי אמר מתני' דלא כהלל דמתניתין איירי כשאין מקפידין משום דסתמא דמתני' איירי במקפידין כדפרישית. מ"ר:

מאי טעמא משום קוביא. היינו כרבי יהודה בשם רבי טרפון דאמר אין אחד מהן נזיר שלא נתנה נזירות אלא להפלאה וסבירא ליה דלא מחית איניש לספיקא ולית הלכתא הכי אלא כאידך דר' יהודה כדפסקינן בסנהדרין בפרק זה בורר (דף כה. ושם). מ"ר:

ס) **מטילין** חלשים על הקדשים ביו"ט. תימה דאמר בפרק ב' דקדושין (דף נג. ושם) דאין חולקין זבחים כנגד זבחים ומנחה כנגד מנחה ומפיק לה מלכל בני אהרן תהיה איש כאחיו ועוד דפריך התם מוהצנועים מושכין ידיהם והגרגרנים חולקין מאי חולקין חוטפין כו' ואומר רבי דאין מועלת בהם חלוקה וגורל שיהא ממונו לקדש בו את האשה ולהוציאו בדיינים אבל מ"מ מטילין היו חלשין לתת לכל א' חלקו פן יריבו ביחד כדכתיב (הושע ד) ועמך כמריבי כהן והא דמשני התם חולקין לאו דוקא אלא חוטפין ולא משני הכי משו' דחולקין משמע כופין לחלוק ע"כ מחמת שחוטפין אותן שאינן שלהם. מ"ר:
מה

רבינו חננאל

ביתו אין אחרים לא. משמיה דר' יהודה אמר שמואל דאמר בני חבורה המקפידין זה על זה פי' שמדקדקין זה על זה שאומר אחד לחבירו המנה שלך שלקחתה גדולה תן לי אני כמותה והוא שוקלה בידו. ואם היה דג אומר לו לקחת דג או כדומה לו שהוא ארוך יותר צריך לתת לו (שמרתן) [תמורתן] זרת דגים או קישואין או אבטיחים וכדומה להן ואם היו אגוזים ושקדים וכדומה להן אומר לקחת עשרים או אומר לו בעת (שניטלו) [נוטלו] המתן עד שאשקול המנה ועד שאמדוד אורך הדגים והקישואים ואמנה הביצים והאגוזים והשקדים שאתה נוטל שאסור גם במשקלם וכמדתם וכמנינם. וכדברי ב"ה שאומרים לא תלוה אשה מחברתה ככרות כו': ומטילין חלשים כו'. פירוש מטילין גורלות אבל לא על המנות אוקמה על המנות של חול בי"ט: נבוכדנאצר אנס צדקיהו בעבירה וכיון שנענש נ"נ ע"י צדקיהו נענש גם הוא שנאמר שבעת קלון מכבוד זה נבוכדנצר שתה גם אתה והערל זה צדקיהו ואמרינן האי קרא כוליה בנ"נ כתיב ועוד צדקיהו צדיקא מאי הוה ליה למעבד. אמר רב יהודה אמר רב בשעה שעשה אותו רשע לאותו צדיק כך נמשכה

רב נסים גאון

פרק שואל. וכדברי הלל אף משום ריבית הוא שהוקדם זכרו בראש הפרק (דף קמח) וכן היה הלל אומר לא תלוה אשה ככר לחברתה עד שתעשנו דמים שמא יוקרו חטים או יוזלו ונמצאו באות לידי ריבית ועיקר במשנה בפרק אי זהו נשך (דף עה):

ליקוטי רש"י

להטעימן. שידעו כמה מצטער ומילר הנותן ורבינו כמה עונשו גדול [ב"מ עה.]. משום קוביא. מתוכות הם על שם שמשחקין בקוביא ואמור רבנן אסמכתא לא קניא והרי הן גזלן מדרבנן דמהדורייהו אינו קרוי גזלן אלא החוטף מיד איש כדכתיב (ש"ב כג) ויגזול את החנית מיד המצרי [ר"ה כב.]. אסמכתא היינו דבר דלאו עמון לו מדעתו כעין גזילה היא אלא סומך על דבר שאינו דסבור שהוא יכול לנצח ופעמים שמנצחין אותו לא קניא והוה ליה כעין גזילה היא [סנהדרין כד:]. בריה דבת יעקב. אביו לא היה הגון לפיכך לא הזכירו [עירובין פ.]. בפי כל נביאיו. [illegible]

מסורת הש"ס

א) [נ"ל הילל], ב) ב"מ עה. [ושם מקשה הש"ס ולאו מילתא היא כו' ויש נכון על קושיא זו ביאור הט"ז באו"ח סימן שכ"ב ס"ק ד], ג) [נ"ל ברה ומשום שאביו לא היה הגון לפיכך לא הזכירו. כ"כ רש"י בעירובין פ. ד"ה בריה], ד) [נ"ל בריה], ה) סנהדרין קב. קג:, ו) [מגילה יב: סוטה מב. סנהדרין קב.], ז) פי' ליחלוש, ח) [שייך לעיל קמח: במשנה].

הגהות הב"ח

(א) רש"י ד"ה גם אתה וכו' וגו' חלית כמונו לו אלינו כל"ל והד"א:

גליון הש"ס

גמ' כל שחבירו נענש על ידו. עי' ב"ב דף כב ע"א תוס' ד"ה אבא עגמיה:

תורה אור השלם

א) אַךְ אִישׁ אַל יָרֵב וְאַל יוֹכַח אִישׁ וְעַמְּךָ כִּמְרִיבֵי כֹהֵן: [הושע ד, ד]
ב) וַיֹּאמֶר יְיָ מִי יְפַתֶּה אֶת אַחְאָב וְיַעַל וְיִפֹּל בְּרָמֹת גִּלְעָד וַיֹּאמֶר זֶה בְּכֹה וְזֶה אֹמֵר בְּכֹה: וַיֵּצֵא הָרוּחַ וַיַּעֲמֹד לִפְנֵי יְיָ וַיֹּאמֶר אֲנִי אֲפַתֶּנּוּ וַיֹּאמֶר יְיָ אֵלָיו בַּמָּה: וַיֹּאמֶר אֵצֵא וְהָיִיתִי רוּחַ שֶׁקֶר בְּפִי כָּל נְבִיאָיו וַיֹּאמֶר תְּפַתֶּה וְגַם תּוּכָל צֵא וַעֲשֵׂה כֵן: [מלכים א' כב, כ-כב]
ג) לֹא יֵשֵׁב בְּקֶרֶב בֵּיתִי עֹשֵׂה רְמִיָּה דֹּבֵר שְׁקָרִים לֹא יִכּוֹן לְנֶגֶד עֵינָי: [תהלים קא, ז]
ד) שָׂבַעְתָּ קָלוֹן מִכָּבוֹד שְׁתֵה גַם אַתָּה וְהֵעָרֵל תִּסּוֹב עָלֶיךָ כּוֹס יְמִין יְיָ וְקִיקָלוֹן עַל כְּבוֹדֶךָ: [חבקוק ב, טז]
ה) גַּם עֲנוֹשׁ לַצַּדִּיק לֹא טוֹב לְהַכּוֹת נְדִיבִים עַל יֹשֶׁר: [משלי יז, כו]
ו) כִּי לֹא אֵל חָפֵץ רֶשַׁע אָתָּה לֹא יְגֻרְךָ רָע: [תהלים ה, ה]
ז) אֵיךְ נָפַלְתָּ מִשָּׁמַיִם הֵילֵל בֶּן שָׁחַר נִגְדַּעְתָּ לָאָרֶץ חוֹלֵשׁ עַל גּוֹיִם: [ישעיה יד, יב]
ח) שְׁאוֹל מִתַּחַת רָגְזָה לְךָ לִקְרַאת בּוֹאֶךָ עוֹרֵר לְךָ רְפָאִים כָּל עַתּוּדֵי אָרֶץ הֵקִים מִכִּסְאוֹתָם כֹּל מַלְכֵי גוֹיִם: כֻּלָּם יַעֲנוּ וְיֹאמְרוּ אֵלֶיךָ גַּם אַתָּה חֻלֵּיתָ כָמוֹנוּ אֵלֵינוּ נִמְשָׁלְתָּ: [ישעיה יד, ט-י]
ט) נָחָה שָׁקְטָה כָּל הָאָרֶץ פָּצְחוּ רִנָּה: [ישעיה יד, ז]
י) וְרָבְצוּ שָׁם צִיִּים וּמָלְאוּ בָתֵּיהֶם אֹחִים וְשָׁכְנוּ שָׁם בְּנוֹת יַעֲנָה וּשְׂעִירִים יְרַקְּדוּ שָׁם: [ישעיה יג, כא]
כ) מִמִּי נָעָמְתָּ רְדָה וְהָשְׁכְּבָה אֶת עֲרֵלִים: [יחזקאל לב, יט]
ל) וְנָשָׂאתָ הַמָּשָׁל הַזֶּה עַל מֶלֶךְ בָּבֶל וְאָמַרְתָּ אֵיךְ שָׁבַת נֹגֵשׂ שָׁבְתָה מַדְהֵבָה: [ישעיה יד, ד]

וּכְדִבְרֵי הִלֵּל אַף מִשּׁוּם רִבִּית – **And according to the words of Hillel** they will **also** transgress **on account of** the law of **interest,** which is forbidden on the weekday as well.[1] To avoid these transgressions, one may not cast lots with people who are not members of his household.[2]

The Gemara asks:

אִי הָכִי – **If so,**[3] one should be forbidden to draw lots with בָּנָיו וּבְנֵי בֵיתוֹ נַמִּי – **his children and members of his household as well!**[4] – ? –

The Gemara answers:

בָּנָיו וּבְנֵי בֵיתוֹ – As far as **his children and members of his household** are concerned, הַיְינוּ טַעְמָא – **the reason** why one is allowed to cast lots with them **is** כִּדְרַב יְהוּדָה אָמַר רַב – **as Rav Yehudah stated in the name of Rav.** דְּאָמַר רַב יְהוּדָה אָמַר רַב – **For Rav Yehudah said in the name of Rav:** מוּתָּר לְהַלְווֹת בָּנָיו וּבְנֵי בֵיתוֹ בְּרִבִּית – **It is permitted for a person to lend on interest to his children and members of his household,** כְּדֵי לְהַטְעִימָן טַעַם רִבִּית – **so as to let them taste the** bitter **taste of** paying **interest.**[5]

The Gemara counters:

אִי הָכִי – **If so,**[6] then one who draws lots with his children and household members should be allowed to wager מָנָה גְדוֹלָה כְּנֶגֶד מָנָה קְטַנָּה נַמִּי – **even a large portion against a small portion.**[7] – ? –

The Gemara answers:

אִין הָכִי נַמִּי – **This is indeed so.** One *is* permitted to wager even unequal portions with his children and household members. וְחַסּוּרֵי מִיחַסְּרָא – **And [our Mishnah],** which forbids this, should be read as though it **is missing** words, וְהָכִי קָתָנֵי – **and this** is what **it** really **teaches:** מֵפִיס אָדָם עִם בָּנָיו וְעִם בְּנֵי בֵיתוֹ עַל הַשֻּׁלְחָן – **A PERSON MAY CAST LOTS WITH HIS CHILDREN AND MEMBERS OF HIS HOUSEHOLD** for portions of food **AT THE TABLE,** אֲפִילוּ מָנָה גְדוֹלָה כְּנֶגֶד מָנָה קְטַנָּה – **even** for **a large portion against a small portion.** מַאי טַעְמָא – **What is the reason?** כִּדְרַב יְהוּדָה אָמַר רַב – The reason is **as Rav Yehudah said in the name of Rav,** namely, that it is permitted for a person to lend on interest to his children etc.[8] עִם בָּנָיו וְעִם בְּנֵי בֵיתוֹ אִין – Now, the Mishnah implies that **with his children and members of his household – yes!** he may cast lots; עִם אֲחֵרִים לֹא – but **with others – no!** he may not cast lots, even for *equal* portions. מַאי טַעְמָא – **What is the reason?** כִּדְרַב יְהוּדָה אָמַר שְׁמוּאֵל – The reason is **as Rav Yehudah said in the name of Shmuel,** namely, that members of a group who are particular with each other will violate the prohibitions against measuring, weighing, etc. The Mishnah then continues: מָנָה גְדוֹלָה כְּנֶגֶד מָנָה קְטַנָּה – And with regard to waging **A LARGE PORTION AGAINST A SMALL PORTION,** אַף בְּחוֹל לַאֲחֵרִים אָסוּר – this is **forbidden with others,** who are not members of his household, **even on a weekday.** מַאי טַעְמָא – **What is the reason?** מִשּׁוּם קוּבְיָא – It is forbidden **on account of gambling.**[9]

NOTES

1. Members of a group who are particular with each other will transgress the laws of *ribbis* (interest) when they borrow food from each other and pay back the same amount. Normally, members of one group are not particular about price differences on small items such as a loaf of bread, and thus any price increase is insignificant and does not constitute interest. But in the eyes of stingy people, even this very small difference is of paramount importance. The borrower pays it only because he is too embarrassed not to return the original amount of merchandise to the person who had benefited him by granting him the loan. Since the increase in value is given only in consideration of the loan, it constitutes *ribbis* (*Tosafos*).

Repaying a loan of merchandise with the same amount of merchandise ("a *se'ah* for a *se'ah*"), even if its price increased in the interim, is forbidden only under the Rabbinic law. [There is no Biblical transgression, because in terms of the merchandise, which the parties had agreed would be the form of the loan (and repayment) there is no difference between the amount of the loan and the repayment.] According to some Tannaim though, this Rabbinic decree does not apply to trivial amounts, even if the parties involved are particular about such sums (see *Rashi* to *Bava Metzia* 75a ד״ה לוין; cf. *Tosafos* ibid. ד״ה וכדברי). The Gemara therefore specifies that the aforementioned scenario is forbidden only according to Hillel (see 148b note 21).

2. If they need to draw lots, [it is evident that] they are particular with one another and do not forgo even small amounts (*Chidushei HaRan*). [Consequently, they are likely to measure, weigh and count the portions of food, as explained above.]

3. That drawing lots is forbidden because of the above concerns (see *Shabbos Shel Mi*).

4. [The fact that they are drawing lots demonstrates that even they are particular with each other.]

5. We refer here to children and household members who rely on the father for their support. Since everything they have belongs to him, any interest they pay him comes in any case out of his own pocket and is not actual interest (*Rashi*).

The father lends them on interest as an educational exercise, so that they should feel how much paying interest distresses and pinches the borrower, and they will understand that the punishment [for transgressing the laws of *ribbis*] is great (*Rashi* to *Bava Metzia* 75a; see *Yad David* [*Basra*]).

If dependents were particular about the exact amounts of the money their father allocates to them, he would be prohibited to lend to them on interest [presumably because they would be *viewed* as independent parties]. Thus, the fact that we permit such a loan shows that they are not particular about how much of their father's money they receive, for they acknowledge that it all belongs to the father in any event. Similar reasoning applies in the case of a father who distributes portions of food to his children and members of his household. Since they are not paying for the food, they are not overly particular about the size of their respective shares. Accordingly, if a father casts lots to allocate the portions, his purpose is clearly not to avoid a serious dispute, but only to make a fair allocation without arousing jealousy. There is no concern, therefore, that they would violate the prohibitions of measuring, weighing and counting on the Sabbath and Yom Tov (see *Rashi* and *Chidushei HaRan*).

[The Gemara in *Bava Metzia* (75a) concludes that in fact one may *not* lend to his children on interest. However, the reason for this conclusion (which is stated in note 9 below) does not affect the point the Gemara seeks to make here, viz. that children and household members are not particular concerning their respective shares (*Baal HaMaor;* see also *Kesef Mishneh* to *Hil. Shabbos* 23:17 and *Taz, Orach Chaim* 322:4).]

6. I.e. if our Mishnah refers to a case in which all the food belongs to the father [and the diners are not paying for it] (*Rashi, Chidushei HaRan*).

7. The Gemara will explain below that casting lots for unequal portions is a form of gambling and is prohibited even on a weekday. Now, the reason why gambling is forbidden is that the winner is considered to be stealing from the loser (see note 9 for further explanation). This prohibition is obviously inapplicable in the case of a father and his dependents, because everything belongs to the father in any event. Therefore, he should be allowed to cast lots with them even for unequal portions so that they will know the pain of losing and refrain from gambling in the future. Why, then, does our Mishnah forbid him to wager large portions against small portions? (*Rashi*).

8. See note 5.

9. Literally: blocks; i.e. dice. This is a generic term used for all forms of gambling (*Rambam, Commentary to the Mishnah,* 148b).

Gambling is prohibited because the loser cedes his money without an absolute commitment to do so. He agreed to the bet because he expected to win. Had he known that he would lose, he would not have entered into the bet. Taking his money is therefore considered stealing [under Rabbinic law] (*Rashi; Chidushei HaRan; Shulchan Aruch, Choshen Mishpat* 370:2; *Mishnah Berurah* 322:22). Others maintain that gambling is *not* considered stealing. It is nevertheless forbidden, because (a) it is improper to take money that was not given wholeheartedly; and (b) one might make gambling his full-time pursuit and not contribute to society (*Ritva MHK* ed.; see *Meiri*). [Some authorities rule that gambling is even permitted, under certain circumstances (*Tosafos; Rama, Choshen*

עין משפט
נר מצוה

יט א מיי' פכ"ג מהלכו' שבת הלכה יז סמג שם טוש"ע או"ח סימן שכב סעיף ו:
כ ב מיי' שם (ופ"ו מהל' גזילה ואבידה הל"ו) סמג שם ועשין ריד ולאוין עג טור שו"ע או"ח שם וטוש"ע חו"מ סימן שע סעיף ג:
כא ג ד מיי' פ"ד מהל' י"ט הלכה כ סמג לאוין עה:

וכדברי (א) ב"ה) אף משום רבית אי הכי בניו ובני ביתו נמי בניו ובני ביתו היינו טעמא כדרב יהודה אמר רב ב) דאמר רב יהודה אמר רב מותר להלוות בניו ובני ביתו ברבית כדי להטעימן טעם רבית אי הכי מנה גדולה כנגד מנה קטנה נמי אין ה"נ וחסורי מיחסרא והכי קתני א מפים אדם עם בניו ועם בני ביתו על השלחן אפי' מנה גדולה כנגד מנה קטנה מ"ט כדרב יהודה אמר רב עם בניו ועם בני ביתו אין עם אחרים לא מ"ט כדרב יהודה אמר שמואל ב מנה גדולה כנגד מנה קטנה אף בחול לאחרים אסור מ"ט משום קוביא: ג מטילין חלשין על וכו': מאי אבל לא על המנות א"ר יעקב ג) בריה דבת יעקב אבל לא ד על המנות של חול ביו"ט פשיטא מהו דתימא הואיל וכתיב א) ועמך כמריבי כהן אפי' מנות דחול נמי קמ"ל וא"ר יעקב ד) בריה דבת יעקב ° כל שחבירו נענש על ידו אין מכניסין אותו במחיצתו של הקב"ה מנלן אילימא משום דכתיב ב) ויאמר ה' מי יפתה את אחאב ויעל ויפול ברמות גלעד ויאמר זה בכה וזה אומר בכה ויצא הרוח ויעמוד לפני ה' ויאמר אני אפתנו וגו' ויאמר אצא והייתי רוח שקר בפי כל נביאיו ויאמר תפתה וגם תוכל צא ועשה כן ואמרינן מאי רוח ה) א"ר יוחנן זה רוחו של נבות ומאי צא אמר רב צא ממחיצתי ודילמא התם היינו טעמא דכתיב ג) דובר שקרים לא יכון אלא מהכא ו) ד) שבעת קלון מכבוד שתה גם אתה והערל וגו' שבעת קלון מכבוד זה נבוכד נצר שתה גם אתה והערל זה צדקיה חדא דכוליה קרא בנבוכד נצר כתיב ועוד צדקיה צדיקא מאי הוה ליה למיעבד ליה דא"ר יהודה אמר רב בשעה שבקש אותו רשע לעשות לאותו צדיק כך וכו' אלא מהכא ה) גם ענוש לצדיק לא טוב אין לא טוב אלא רע וכתיב ו) כי לא אל חפץ רשע אתה לא יגורך רע ז) צדיק אתה ה' ולא יגור במגורך רע מאי משמע דהאי חלשים לישנא דפורא הוא דכתיב ז) איך נפלת משמים הילל בן שחר נגדעת לארץ חולש על גוים וגו' אמר רבה בר רב הונא מלמד שהיה מטיל פור על גדולי מלכות לידע איזה בן יומו של משכב זכור וכתיב ח) כל מלכי גוים כולם וגו' אמר רבי יוחנן שנחו ממשכב זכור וא"ר יוחנן כל ימיו של אותו רשע לא נמצא שחוק בפה כל בריה שנאמר ט) נחה שקטה כל הארץ פצחו רנה מכלל דעד השתא לא הוה רנה ואמר ר' יצחק אמר ר' יוחנן אסור לעמוד בביתו של אותו רשע שנא' י) ושעירים ירקדו שם ואמר רב יהודה אמר רב בשעה שביקש אותו רשע לעשות לאותו צדיק כך נמשכה ערלתו שלש מאות אמה והיתה מחזרת על כל המסיבה כולה שנאמר שבעת קלון מכבוד שתה גם אתה והערל ערל בגימטריא שלש מאות הוי ואמר רב יהודה אמר רב בשעה שירד אותו רשע לגיהנם רעשו כל יורדי גיהנם אמרו שמא למשול עליהם הוא בא או ט) ליחלות כמותם הוא בא שנאמר ח) גם אתה חולית כמונו אלינו נמשלת יצאתה ב"ק ואמרה כ) ממי נעמת רדה והשכבה את ערלים ל) איך שבת נוגש שבתה מדהבה א"ר יהודה אמר רב שבתה אומה זו שאמרה מדוד

וכדברי (בית) הלל דחיים שמא יוקירו חיטי בהלואת ככרות אף משום רבית: בניו ובני ביתו נמי. ליחוש לרבית וכל הני: להלוות. משלו: בניו ובני ביתו. הסמוכים על שלחנו דכיון דהכל משלו אין כאן רבית: להטעימן טעם רבית. שידעו כמה קשה אלמא כיון דמשלו הוא אין כאן איסור רבית והלכך גבי מדה ומשקל ומנין נמי לאו קפידא הוא אלא להשוותם בלא קנאה: אי הכי מנה גדולה כנגד מנה קטנה נמי. דמוקמינן טעמא לקמן משום קוביא ואפי' בחול אסור וכיון דהכל משלו אמאי אסור להטעימן טעמא קוביא בעלמא הוא: מאי טעמא מותר. ולא חייש לקוביא: כדרב יהודה אמר רב. דלהטעימן בעלמא הוא: עם אחר לא כדרב יהודה אמר שמואל. דכיון דמקפידין עוברין משום מדה ומשקל ומנין: משום קוביא. דגזל הוא דאסמכתא לא קניא והא אסמכתא דסמיך על הגורל אם יפול גורל אמנה הגדולה אזכה בה ולפיכך תלה עצמו אף לגורל הקטנה על הספק ואילו יודע מתחלה שכן לא היה מתרצה: של חול. של קדשים של אתמול: כמריבי כהן. ככהנים אלו שהם בעלי מריבה: אפי' דחול נמי. לישתרי להו להפיס ביו"ט כי היכי דלא לינצו: זה בכה. אני אפתנו בכה: שבעת קלון. בנבוכדנצר משתעי שהיה מטיל משכב זכור על המלכים וכשהגיע יומו של צדקיהו נמשכה ערלתו ג' מאות אמה והיינו שבעת קלון: חדא דכוליה קרא בנבוכדנצר כתיב. שפיר מצית לאוקמי כוליה בנבוכדנצר וה"ק שתה גם אתה כאותם שהיית מקלה אותן והערל והתערל והתגנה: בשעה שעשה לו כו'. לקמן היא מדקאמר לאותו צדיק ש"מ אנוס היה: ענוש לצדיק לא טוב. צדיק המעניש לא טוב וכיון דאינו טוב הרי הוא רע: וכתיב לא יגורך רע. אלמא אינו נכנס במחיצתו: חולש על גוים. בנבוכדנצר כתיב: ושעירים ירקדו שם. ולא אנשים ובשביל הבריות מסתלקין המזיקין ונמצא מבטל גזירת המלך: המסיבה. מלכים שהיו מסובין ויושבין לפניו: גם אתה חולית כמונו אלינו וגו'. ביורדי גיהנם כתיב דכתיב לעיל מיניה שאול מתחת רגזה לך לקראת בואך וגו' (א): חולית כמונו אלינו נמשלת. לשון ממשלה: נעמת. סבור אתה להיות בנועם מן האחרים: מדוד

לפירוש זה דאם הלל לא איירי אלא במקפידין אם כן אמאי קאמר לעיל לימא מתניתין דלא כהלל והא הלל במקפידין איירי ומתניתין דלעיל אתי שפיר כוותיה דהא רישא באין מקפידין איירי דקתני שואל דאילו למקפידין אסרינן שאלה לפי מה שפירש' להכי נראה לפרש עוברין משום מדה ומשום משקל כלומר קרובין לבא לידי כך שיעברו משום מדה שע"י שמקפידין זה ע"ז ורגילין ליקח במדה זה מזה גם ביו"ט יעשו כך וגם כל בני אדם הוי אסורין בכלי של מדה כדאמר בבילה (דף כט: ושם) אבל למקפידין נותן הוא עצה שלא ישתתפו שקרובים הן לבא לידי איסור מדה וכן לידי איסור משקל מתוך שרגילים לשקול על ידי הקפדתן גם ביו"ט לא ירגישו עד שישקלו ולידי מנין כשישאל אחד מהן ס' אגוזים יאמר לו תן לי מ' להשלים ק' כמו שרגילין לעשות ומשום לווין ופורעין ביו"ט כדאמר לעיל דלשון הלואה אסור והם מתוך שמקפידים יזכירו לשון הלואה לפי שיאמר השואל אם אזכיר לו לשון שאלה משמע דהדרא בעיניה לכך אומר לשון הלואה וכדברי הלל אף משום רבית דכשלוין זה מזה כבר באין לידי רבית לפי שפעמים שזה משלם יותר שאע"פ שמקפיד הוא בוש הוא שלא ישלם כמו שהלוהו בשביל שההנהו וכיון שאינו מוחל הוי רבית אבל שאר בני אדם מחלי ולא הוי רבית והשתא מתני' איירי במקפידין דסתם שכנים שאינם חברים מקפידין ומ"מ דרך שאלה מותר ומה שדברו כאן על מקפידין לא אמרינן אלא גבי חבורה שרגילים לישאל זה מזה תדיר ואתי לידי איסור אבל שכנים שאינן תדירין כל כך לשאול זה מזה מותרים ואין לגזור בהם שמא יבאו לידי איסור ולהכי לא משני כי אמר מתני' דלא כהלל דמתניתין איירי כשאין מקפידין משום דסתמא דמתני' איירי במקפידין כדפרישית. מ"ר: **מאי** טעמא משום קוביא. היינו כרבי יהודה בשם רבי טרפון דאמר אין אחד מהן נזיר שלא נתנה נזירות אלא להפלאה וסבירא ליה דלא מחית איניש לספיקא ולית הלכתא הכי אלא כאידך דר' יהודה כדפסקינן בסנהדרין בפרק זה בורר (דף כה. ושם). מ"ר:

ח) **מטילין** חלשים על הקדשים ביו"ט. תימה דאמר בפרק ב' דקדושין (דף נג. ושם) דאין חולקין זבחים כנגד זבחים ומנחה כנגד מנחה ומפיק לה מלכל בני אהרן תהיה איש כאחיו ועוד דפריך התם מוהצנועים מושכין ידיהם והגרגרנים חולקין מאי חולקין חוטפין כו' ואומר רבי דאין מועלת בהם חלוקה וגורל שיהא ממונו לקדש בו את האשה ולהוליאו בדיינים אבל מ"מ מטילין היו חלשין לתת לכל א' חלקו פן ירִיבו ביחד כדכתיב (הושע ד) ועמך כמריבי כהן והא דמשני התם חולקין לאו דוקא אלא חוטפין ולא משני הכי משו' דחולקין משמע כופין לחלוק ע"כ מחמת שחוטפין אותן שאינן שלהם. מ"ר: מה

רבינו חננאל

ביתו אין אחרים לא. משמיה דר' יהודה אמר שמואל דאמר בני חבורה המקפידין זה על זה פי' שמדקדקין זה על זה שאומר אחד לחבירו המנה שלך שלקחתה גדולה תן לי אני כמותה והוא שוקלה בידו. ואם היה דג אומר לו לקחת דג או כדומה לו שהוא ארוך זרת צריך לתת לו (שמדתו) [תמורתו] זרת דגים או קישואין או אבטיחים וכדומה להן ואם היו אגוזים ושקדים וכדומה להן אומר לקחת עשרים או אומר לו בעת (שניטלו) [נוטלו] המתן עד שאשקול המנה ועד שאמדוד אורך הדגים והקישואים ואמנה הביצים והאגוזים והשקדים שאתה נוטל שאטול גם במשקלם וכמדתם וכמניינם. וכדברי ב"ה שאומרים לא תלוה אשה מחברתה ככרות כו': ומטילין חלשים כו'. פירוש מטילין גורלות אבל לא על המנות אוקמוה על המנות של חול ביו"ט: נבוכדנאצר אנס צדקיהו בעבירה וכיון שנענש נ"נ ע"י צדקיהו נענש גם הוא שנאמר שבעת קלון מכבוד זה נבוכדנאצר שתה גם אתה והערל זה צדקיהו ואמרינן האי קרא כוליה בנ"נ כתיב ועוד צדקיהו צדיקא מאי הוה ליה למעבד. אמר רב יהודה אמר רב בשעה שעשה אותו רשע לאותו צדיק כן נמשכה

רב נסים גאון

פרק שואל. וכדברי הלל אף משום ריבית הוא שהוקדם וזכרו בראש הפרק (דף קמח) וכן היה הלל אומר לא תלוה אשה ככר לחברתה עד שתעשנו דמים שמא יוקרו חטים או יוזלו ונמצא באות לידי ריבית ועיקר זה במשנה בפרק איזהו נשך (דף עה).

ליקוטי רש"י

להטעימן. שידעו כמה מצטער ומיצר הנושך ויבינו כמה עונשו גדול [ב"מ עה.]. משום קוביא. מחוכת על כס שמשחקין בערבון ואמור רבנן אסמכתא לא קניא והכי הוי גזלנין מדרבנן דמדאורייתא אינו קרוי גזלן אלא החוטף מיד איש כדכתיב (ש"ב כג) ויגזל את החנית מיד המצרי [ר"ה כב.]. אסמכתא שאינו

מסורת הש"ס

א) [נ"ל הילל], ב) ב"מ עה. [ושם מסיק הש"ס ולאו מילתא היא כר' יהודה נכון על קושיא זו בילקוט הש"ס לאו"ח סימן שכ"ב ס"ק ד], ג) [נ"ל ברה ומשום שאביו לא היה הגון לפיכך לא הזכירו. כ"כ רש"י בעירובין פ. ד"ה בריה], ד) [נ"ל ברה], ה) סנהדרין קב., ו) [חגיגה יג: סוטה מב. סנהדרין קב.], ז) פ"י ליחלוש, ח) [שייך לעיל קמח: במשנה].

הגהות הב"ח

(א) רש"י ד"ה גם אתה וכו' וגו' חולית כמונו או אלינו כצ"ל והד"א:

גליון הש"ס

גמ' כל שחבירו נענש על ידו. עי' ב"ב דף כב ע"א תוס' ד"ה אגלא עגמשים:

תורה אור השלם

א) אַךְ אִישׁ אַל יָרֵב וְאַל יוֹכַח אִישׁ וְעַמְּךָ כִּמְרִיבֵי כֹהֵן: [הושע ד, ד]

ב) וַיֹּאמֶר יְיָ מִי יְפַתֶּה אֶת אַחְאָב וְיַעַל וְיִפֹּל בְּרָמֹת גִּלְעָד וַיֹּאמֶר זֶה בְּכֹה וְזֶה אֹמֵר בְּכֹה: וַיֵּצֵא הָרוּחַ וַיַּעֲמֹד לִפְנֵי יְיָ וַיֹּאמֶר אֲנִי אֲפַתֶּנּוּ וַיֹּאמֶר יְיָ אֵלָיו בַּמָּה: וַיֹּאמֶר אֵצֵא וְהָיִיתִי רוּחַ שֶׁקֶר בְּפִי כָּל נְבִיאָיו וַיֹּאמֶר תְּפַתֶּה וְגַם תּוּכָל צֵא וַעֲשֵׂה כֵן: [מלכים א' כב, כ-כב]

ג) לֹא יֵשֵׁב בְּקֶרֶב בֵּיתִי עֹשֵׂה רְמִיָּה דֹּבֵר שְׁקָרִים לֹא יִכּוֹן לְנֶגֶד עֵינָי: [תהלים קא, ז]

ד) שָׂבַעְתָּ קָלוֹן מִכָּבוֹד שְׁתֵה גַם אַתָּה וְהֵעָרֵל תִּסּוֹב עָלֶיךָ כּוֹס יְמִין יְיָ וְקִיקָלוֹן עַל כְּבוֹדֶךָ: [חבקוק ב, טז]

ה) גַּם עֲנוֹשׁ לַצַּדִּיק לֹא טוֹב לְהַכּוֹת נְדִיבִים עַל יֹשֶׁר: [משלי יז, כו]

ו) כִּי לֹא אֵל חָפֵץ רֶשַׁע אָתָּה לֹא יְגֻרְךָ רָע: [תהלים ה, ה]

ז) אֵיךְ נָפַלְתָּ מִשָּׁמַיִם הֵילֵל בֶּן שָׁחַר נִגְדַּעְתָּ לָאָרֶץ חוֹלֵשׁ עַל גּוֹיִם: [ישעיה יד, יב]

ח) שְׁאוֹל מִתַּחַת רָגְזָה לְךָ לִקְרַאת בּוֹאֶךָ עוֹרֵר לְךָ רְפָאִים כָּל עַתּוּדֵי אָרֶץ הֵקִים מִכִּסְאוֹתָם כֹּל מַלְכֵי גוֹיִם: כֻּלָּם יַעֲנוּ וְיֹאמְרוּ אֵלֶיךָ גַּם אַתָּה חֻלֵּיתָ כָמוֹנוּ אֵלֵינוּ נִמְשָׁלְתָּ: [ישעיה יד, ט-י]

ט) נָחָה שָׁקְטָה כָּל הָאָרֶץ פָּצְחוּ רִנָּה: [ישעיה יד, ז]

י) וְרָבְצוּ שָׁם צִיִּים וּמָלְאוּ בָתֵּיהֶם אֹחִים וְשָׁכְנוּ שָׁם בְּנוֹת יַעֲנָה וּשְׂעִירִים יְרַקְּדוּ שָׁם: [ישעיה יג, כא] כ) מִמִּי נָעָמְתָּ רְדָה וְהָשְׁכְּבָה אֶת עֲרֵלִים: [יחזקאל לב, יט] ל) וְנָשָׂאתָ הַמָּשָׁל הַזֶּה עַל מֶלֶךְ בָּבֶל וְאָמָרְתָּ אֵיךְ שָׁבַת נֹגֵשׂ שָׁבְתָה מַדְהֵבָה: [ישעיה יד, ד]

דבר דאינו נותן לו מדעתו אלא סומך על דבר שאינו דסבור שהוא יכול לנצח ופעמים שמנצחין אותו לא קניא והוה ליה כעין גזילה בידו [סנהדרין כד:]. בריה דבת יעקב. אביו לא היה הגון לפיכך לא הזכירו [עירובין כו:]. בפי כל נביאיו. [illegible]

The Mishnah stated:
מְטִילִין חֲלָשִׁין עַל וכו׳ – **[KOHANIM] MAY CAST LOTS FOR etc.** [sacrifices on Yom Tov,[10] but not for portions].

The Gemara explains the last point:
מַאי אֲבָל לֹא עַל הַמָּנוֹת – **What is** the meaning of: **BUT NOT FOR PORTIONS?** אָמַר רַבִּי יַעֲקֹב בְּרֵיהּ דְּבַת יַעֲקֹב – **R' Yaakov the son of Yaakov's daughter**[11] **said** that it means: אֲבָל לֹא עַל הַמָּנוֹת שֶׁל חוֹל בְּיוֹם טוֹב – **But on Yom Tov** Kohanim may **not** cast lots **for portions of** sacrifices that were offered on **the** preceding **weekday.**[12]

The Gemara asks:
פְּשִׁיטָא – **That is obvious!**[13] Why does the Mishnah have to teach this?

The Gemara answers:
מַהוּ דְּתֵימָא הוֹאִיל וּכְתִיב ,,וְעַמְּךָ כִּמְרִיבֵי כֹהֵן״ – **You might have said** that **since it is written:** ***Your people are like quarrelsome Kohanim,***[14] which indicates that Kohanim are quarrelsome by nature, אֲפִילּוּ מָנוֹת דְּחוֹל נַמִּי – Kohanim should be allowed to cast lots on Yom Tov **even** for **portions of** sacrifices that were offered on **the** preceding **weekday.**[15] קָא מַשְׁמַע לָן – **[The Mishnah] therefore teaches us** that this is not permitted.

Having cited one teaching of R' Yaakov the son of Yaakov's daughter, the Gemara presents another statement of his:
וְאָמַר רַבִּי יַעֲקֹב בְּרֵיהּ דְּבַת יַעֲקֹב – **And R' Yaakov the son of Yaakov's daughter** also **said:** כֹּל שֶׁחֲבֵירוֹ נֶעֱנָשׁ עַל יָדוֹ – **Anyone whose friend was punished on his account** אֵין מַכְנִיסִין אוֹתוֹ בִּמְחִיצָתוֹ שֶׁל הַקָּדוֹשׁ בָּרוּךְ הוּא – **is not admitted into the enclosure of the Holy One, Blessed is He.**[16] מְנָלַן – **From where do we** know this? אִילֵימָא מִשּׁוּם דִּכְתִיב – **You might say** that this is evident from Scripture, **for it is written:**[17] ,,וַיֹּאמֶר ה׳ מִי יְפַתֶּה אֶת־אַחְאָב וְיַעַל וְיִפֹּל בְּרָמֹת גִּלְעָד וַיֹּאמֶר זֶה בְּכֹה וְזֶה אֹמֵר בְּכֹה – ***And Hashem said, "Who will entice Ahab so that he shall go up and fall at Ramos Gilead?" One said thus, and another said thus.***[18] וַיֵּצֵא הָרוּחַ וַיַּעֲמֹד לִפְנֵי ה׳ וַיֹּאמֶר אֲנִי אֲפַתֶּנּוּ וגו׳ – ***And the spirit came forth and stood before Hashem and said, "I will entice him" etc.*** וַיֹּאמֶר אֵצֵא וְהָיִיתִי רוּחַ שֶׁקֶר בְּפִי כָּל־נְבִיאָיו וַיֹּאמֶר תְּפַתֶּה וְגַם־תּוּכָל צֵא וַעֲשֵׂה־כֵן״ – ***It said, "I will go forth and be a lying spirit in the mouth of all [Ahab's] prophets." [Hashem] said, "You will entice and also prevail. Go out and do so."*** וְאָמְרִינַן מַאי ,,רוּחַ״ – **And,** in explicating this passage, **we said:**[19] **What is *the spirit*** to which the verse refers? אָמַר רַבִּי יוֹחָנָן – **R' Yochanan said:** זֶה רוּחוֹ שֶׁל נָבוֹת – **This is the spirit of Navos.**[20] וּמַאי ,,צֵא״ – **And what is** the

NOTES

Mishpat 370:3). According to this opinion, our Gemara is not consistent with the halachah (*Tosafos*).]

The Gemara is not actually emending the text of the Mishnah (*Shabbos Shel Mi;* see *Tosafos* to 102a ד״ה רב אשי for another example of this). Rather, it is reinterpreting this clause by dividing it into two parts: (a) מֵפִיס אָדָם עִם בָּנָיו וְעִם בְּנֵי בֵיתוֹ עַל הַשֻּׁלְחָן, *A person may cast lots with his children and members of his household at the table.* (b) וּבִלְבַד שֶׁלֹּא יִתְכַּוֵּין לַעֲשׂוֹת מָנָה גְדוֹלָה כְּנֶגֶד מָנָה קְטַנָּה, *provided that he does not intend to wager a large portion against a small portion.* The first part, which refers to his children and household members, permits casting lots on the Sabbath in *all* cases – even for unequal portions. This implies that casting lots on the Sabbath with others (i.e. non-family members) is forbidden in all cases – even for equal portions. The second part, which differentiates between equal and unequal portions, is interpreted as referring to casting lots with non-family members on a weekday.

The Gemara in *Bava Metzia* (75a) concludes that in fact a father is *forbidden* to lend to his children on interest. The reason is that the exercise might have the opposite effect than intended. The children might realize that taking interest is easy profit and become attracted to the idea (*Rashi* ibid.). Some Rishonim argue that in the case of gambling as well, giving one's children a taste of the activity might attract them to it. Hence, in their view, the conclusion of our Gemara is not accepted in halachah. Rather, one may *not* cast lots for unequal portions (on the Sabbath or weekday) even with his children and members of his household (*Rif* and *Rosh, according to Beis Yosef, Orach Chaim* 322; *Raavad* cited by *Rashba; Chidushei HaRan*). *Rambam,* though, permits casting lots for unequal portions in the case of children and household members (*Hil. Shabbos* 23:17). In *Rambam's* opinion, the Rabbis banned lending on interest to one's children because the prohibition of *ribbis* is Biblical. Therefore, gambling, which is only a Rabbinic transgression to begin with, is permitted with one's children (*Ritva MHK* ed.; *Ran MHK* ed.; *Maggid Mishneh* ibid.; cf. *Meiri* and *Taz* 322:4).

10. We have learned that casting lots for the allocation of shares is prohibited on the Sabbath and Yom Tov, lest it lead to weighing, measuring, etc. [It is also forbidden because it resembles a business transaction (*Rambam, Hil. Shabbos* 23:17), or because it is עוּבְדָא דְחוֹל, *a weekday activity* (*Chidushei HaRan*).] Nevertheless, the Kohanim were allowed to cast lots for their sacrificial portions, because otherwise they might quarrel over them (*Chidushei HaRan;* see continuation of the Gemara). The lots thus served to facilitate the [Biblical] mitzvah of eating sacrificial foods (see *Magen Avraham, Orach Chaim* 322:9 and *Shaar HaTziyun* ibid. §24).

The Mishnah specifies Yom Tov. The commentators discuss whether Kohanim are allowed to cast lots on the Sabbath as well (see *Magen Avraham* ibid., *Shaar HaTziyun* ibid. §23, and *Shabbos Shel Mi* at length; see also *Chidushei HaRan,* cited in note 12, who mentions the Sabbath explicitly).

11. R' Yaakov's father is not named, as is customary, because he was unworthy (*Rashi* to *Eruvin* 80a ד״ה בריה; see *Hagahos Yavetz*).

12. [*Rashi;* cf. *Rambam* (*Commentary to the Mishnah* and *Hil. Shabbos* 4:20).] This is forbidden because they should have done it the day before. Alternatively, the permit to cast lots applies only to the sacrifices of that day, for which even Biblical prohibitions (e.g. slaughtering) are lifted. It does not apply to other sacrifices, whose offering does not override any Biblical prohibitions (*Chidushei HaRan*).

13. See previous note.

14. *Hosea* 4:4. [The commentaries ad loc., however, explain the verse to mean that the people quarrel *with* the Kohanim (*Targum, Rashi, Radak* et al.; see *Chasam Sofer* here).]

15. So that they will not quarrel [over the allocation of the portions] (*Rashi*).

16. One who causes punishment to befall his fellow is excluded from a certain degree of closeness to the Divine Presence [in the World to Come].

This is so even in the case of a victim whose oppressor was punished by God. Since the victim was the cause of another's suffering (albeit justifiably), he too must suffer (see *Bava Basra* 22a and *Tosafos* ibid. ד״ה אנא עגישתיה). However, this applies only where the victim actually did something to bring about the other's punishment, e.g. he prayed that God would punish his oppressor (see *Iyun Yaakov* and *Sfas Emes*). [One should pray that his suffering cease, rather than that his oppressor be punished (see *Bava Kamma* 93a).]

17. *I Kings* 22:20-22. After 400 prophets told Ahab, king of Israel, that he would prevail against Aram at Ramos Gilead, one prophet, Michayehu, informed Ahab that all the others had been deceived by "a lying spirit." Ahab did not heed Michayehu, and he was mortally wounded in battle. These verses are from Micheyahu's speech to Ahab in which he described the proceedings in Heaven.

18. Members of the Heavenly host offered suggestions as to how they would entice Ahab (see *Rashi;* cf. *Eitz Yosef,* based on *Sanhedrin* 102b).

19. In *Sanhedrin* 102b.

20. Navos owned a vineyard adjacent to Ahab's palace. Ahab wished to purchase the vineyard, but Navos refused to sell it for any price. Finally, Jezebel, Ahab's wife, hired witnesses who falsely testified that Navos had cursed God and the king, a crime punishable by death and confiscation of property. Navos was executed and the vineyard automatically became the property of the crown (*I Kings* ch. 21). [The spirit of the murdered Navos sought retribution for this crime and volunteered to bring about Ahab's death (see *Sanhedrin* 102b and *Rashi* ibid. ד״ה דפרע קיניה; see also note 16 above).]

וכדברי (א) ב"ה) אף משום רבית אי הכי בניו ובני ביתו נמי בניו ובני ביתו היינו טעמא כדרב יהודה אמר רב ב) דאמר רב יהודה אמר רב מותר להלוות בניו ובני ביתו ברבית כדי להטעימן טעם רבית אי הכי מנה גדולה כנגד מנה קטנה נמי אין ה"נ וחסורי מיחסרא והכי קתני א מפיס אדם עם בניו ועם בני ביתו על השלחן אפי' מנה גדולה כנגד מנה קטנה מ"ט כדרב יהודה אמר רב עם בניו ועם בני ביתו אין עם אחרים לא מ"ט כדרב יהודה אמר שמואל ב מנה גדולה כנגד מנה קטנה אף בחול לאחרים אסור מ"ט משום קוביא: ג מטילין חלשין על וכו': מאי אבל לא על המנות א"ר יעקב ג) בריה דבת יעקב אבל לא ד על המנות של חול ביו"ט פשיטא מהו דתימא הואיל וכתיב א) ועמך כמריבי כהן אפי' מנות דחול נמי קמ"ל וא"ר יעקב ד) בריה דבת יעקב ° כל שחבירו נענש על ידו אין מכניסין אותו במחיצתו של הקב"ה מנלן אילימא משום דכתיב ב) ויאמר ה' מי יפתה את אחאב ויעל ויפול ברמות גלעד ויאמר זה בכה וזה אמר בכה ויצא הרוח ויעמוד לפני ה' ויאמר אני אפתנו וגו' ויאמר אצא והייתי רוח שקר בפי כל נביאיו ויאמר תפתה וגם תוכל צא ועשה כן ואמרינן מאי רוח ה) א"ר יוחנן זה רוחו של נבות ומאי צא אמר רב צא ממחיצתי ודילמא התם היינו טעמא דכתיב ג) דובר שקרים לא יכון אלא מהכא ד) שבעת קלון מכבוד שתה גם אתה והערל וגו' שבעת קלון מכבוד זה נבוכד נצר שתה גם אתה והערל זה צדקיה חדא דכוליה קרא בנבוכד נצר כתיב ועוד צדקיה צדיקא מאי הוה ליה למיעבד ליה דא"ר יהודה אמר רב בשעה שבקש אותו רשע לעשות לאותו צדיק כך וכו' אלא מהכא ה) גם ענוש לצדיק לא טוב אין לא טוב אלא רע וכתיב ו) כי לא אל חפץ רשע אתה לא יגורך רע ו) צדיק אתה ה' ולא יגור במגורך רע מאי משמע דהאי חלשים לישנא דפורא הוא דכתיב ז) איך נפלת משמים הילל בן שחר נגדעת לארץ חולש על גוים וגו' אמר רבה בר רב הונא מלמד שהיה מטיל פור על גדולי מלכות לידע איזה בן יומו של משכב זכור וכתיב ח) כל מלכי גוים כולם וגו' אמר רבי יוחנן שנחו ממשכב זכור וא"ר יוחנן כל ימיו של אותו רשע לא נמצא שחוק בפה כל בריה שנאמר ט) נחה שקטה כל הארץ פצחו רנה מכלל דעד השתא לא הוה רנה ואמר ר' יצחק אמר ר' יוחנן אסור לעמוד בביתו של אותו רשע שנא' י) ושעירים ירקדו שם ואמר רב יהודה אמר רב בשעה שביקש אותו רשע לעשות לאותו צדיק כך נמשכה ערלתו שלש מאות אמה והיתה מחזרת על כל המסיבה כולה שנאמר שבעת קלון מכבוד שתה גם אתה והערל ערל בגימטריא שלש מאות הוי ואמר רב יהודה אמר רב בשעה שירד אותו רשע לגיהנם רעשו כל יורדי גיהנם אמרו שמא למשול עליהם הוא בא או ז) ליחלות כמותם הוא בא שנאמר ח) גם אתה חולית כמונו אלינו נמשלת יצאתה ב"ק ואמרה כ) ממי נעמת רדה והשכבה את ערלים ל) איך שבת נוגש שבתה מדהבה א"ר יהודה אמר רב שבתה אומה זו שאמרה

מדוד

רש"י

וכדברי (בית) הלל דחיש שמא יוקירו חיטי בהלואת ככרות אף משום רבית: בניו ובני ביתו נמי. ליחוש לרבית וכל הני: להלוות. משלו: בניו ובני ביתו. הסמוכים על שלחנו דכיון דהכל משלו אין כאן רבית: להטעימן טעם רבית. שידעו כמה קשה אלמא כיון דמשלו הוא אין כאן איסור רבית והלכך גבי מדה ומשקל ומנין נמי לאו קפידא הוא אלא להשוותם בלא קנאה: אי הכי מנה גדולה כנגד מנה קטנה נמי. דמוקמינן טעמא לקמן משום קוביא ואפי' בחול אסור וכיון דהכל משלו אמאי אסור להטעימן טעמא קוביא בעלמא הוא: מאי טעמא מותר. ולא חייש לקוביא: כדרב יהודה אמר רב. דלהטעימן בעלמא הוא: עם אחר לא כדרב יהודה אמר שמואל. דכיון דמקפידין עוברין משום מדה ומשקל ומנין: משום קוביא. דגזל הוא דאסמכתא לא קניא והא אסמכתא דסמיך על הגורל אם יפול גורל אמנה הגדולה אזכה בה ולפיכך תלה עצמו אף לגורל הקטנה על הספק ואילו יודע מתחלה שכן לא היה מתרלה: של חול. של קדשים של אתמול: כמריבי כהן. ככהנים אלו שהם בעלי מריבה: אפי' דחול נמי. לישתרי להו להפיס ביו"ט כי היכי דלא לינלו: זה בכה. אני אפתנו בכה: שבעת קלון. בנבוכדנלר משתעי שהיה מטיל משכב זכור על המלכים וכשהגיע יומו של לדקיהו נמשכה ערלתו ג' מאות אמה והיינו שבעת קלון: חדא דכוליה קרא בנבוכדנלר כתיב. שפיר מלית לאוקמי כוליה בנבוכדנלר וה"ק שתה גם אתה כלומר שהיית מקלה אותן והערל והתערל והתגנה: בשעה שעשה לו כו'. לקמן היא מדקאמר לאותו לדיק ש"מ אנוס היה: ענוש לצדיק לא טוב. לדיק המעניש לא טוב הרי הוא רע: וכתיב לא יגורך רע. אלמא אינו נכנס במחילתו: חולש על גוים. בנבוכדנלר כתיב: ושעירים ירקדו שם. ולא אנשים ובשביל הבריות מסתלקין המזיקין ונמלא מבטל גזירת המלך: המסיבה. מלכים שהיו מסובין ויושבין לפניו: גם אתה חולית כמונו אלינו וגו'. ביורדי גיהנם כתיב דכתיב לעיל מיניה שאול מתחת רגזה לך לקראת בואך וגו' (א): חולית כמונו אלינו נמשלת. לשון ממשלה: נעמת. סבור אתה להיות בנועם מן האחרים:

מדוד

תוספות

לפירוש זה דאם הלל לא איירי אלא במקפידין אם כן אמאי קאמר לעיל לימא מתניתין דלא כהלל והא הלל במקפידין איירי ומתניתין דלעיל אתי שפיר כוותיה דהא רישא באין מקפידין איירי דקתני שואל דאלו למקפידין אסרינן שאלה לפי מה שפירש' להכי נראה לפרש עוברין משום מדה ומשום משקל כלומר קרובין לבא לידי כך שיעברו משום מדה שע"י שמקפידין זה ע"ז ורגילין ליקח במדה זה מזה גם ביו"ט יעשו כך וגם כל בני אדם הוי אסורין בכלי של מדה כדאמר בבילה (דף כט: ושם) אבל למקפידין נותן הוא עלה שלא ישתתפו שקרובים הן לבא לידי איסור מדה וכן לידי איסור משקל מתוך שרגילים לשקול על ידי הקפדתן גם ביו"ט לא ירגישו עד שישקלו ולידי מנין כשישאל אחד מהן ס' אגוזים יאמר לו תן לי מ' להשלים ק' כמו שרגילין לעשות ומשום לווין ופורעין ביו"ט כדאמר לעיל דלשון הלואה אסור והם מתוך שמקפידים יזכירו לשון הלואה לפי שיאמר השואל אם אזכיר לו לשון שאלה משמע דהדרא בעייניה לכך אומר לשון הלואה וכדברי הלל אף משום רבית דכשלוין זה מזה ככר באין לידי רבית לפי שפעמים שזה משלם יותר שאע"פ שמקפיד הוא בוש הוא שלא ישלם כמו שהלוהו בשביל שההנהו וכיון שאינו מוחל הוי רבית אבל שאר בני אדם מחלי ולא הוי רבית והשתא מתני' איירי במקפידין דסתם שכנים שאינם חברים מקפידין ומ"מ דרך שאלה מותר ומה שדברו כאן על מקפידין לא אמרינן אלא גבי חבורה שרגילים לישאל זה מזה תדיר ואתי לידי איסור אבל שכנים שאין תדירין כל כך לשאול זה מזה מותרים ואין לגזור בהם שמא יבאו לידי איסור ולהכי לא משני כי אמר מתני' דלא כהלל דמתניתין איירי כשאין מקפידין משום דסתמא דמתני' איירי במקפידין כדפרישית. מ"ר:

מאי טעמא משום קוביא. היינו כרבי יהודה בשם רבי טרפון דאמר אין אחד מהן נזיר שלא נתנה נזירות אלא להפלאה וסבירא ליה דלא מחית איניש לספיקא ולית הלכתא הכי אלא כאידך דר' יהודה כדפסקינן בסנהדרין בפרק זה בורר (דף כה. ושם). מ"ר:

ט) **מטילין** חלשים על הקדשים ביו"ט. תימה דאמר בפרק ב' דקדושין (דף נג. ושם) דאין חולקין זבחים כנגד זבחים ומנחה כנגד מנחה ומפיק לה מלכל בני אהרן תהיה איש כאחיו ועוד דפריך התם מוהלנועים מושכין ידיהם והגרגרנים חולקין מאי חולקין חוטפין כו' ואומר רבי דאין מועלת בהם חלוקה וגורל שיהא ממונו לקדש בו את האשה ולהוליאו בדיינים אבל מ"מ מטילין היו חלשין לתת לכל א' חלקו פן ירינו ביחד כדכתיב (הושע ד) ועמך כמריבי כהן והא דמשני התם חולקין לאו דוקא אלא חוטפין ולא משני הכי משו' דחולקין משמע כופין לחלוק ע"כ מחמת שחוטפין אותן שאינן שלהם. מ"ר:

מה

עין משפט נר מצוה

יט א מיי' פכ"ג מהלכ' שבת הלכה יז סמג שם טוש"ע או"ח סימן שכב סעיף ו:

כ ב מיי' שם (ופ"ו מהל' גזילה ואבידה הל"ו) סמג שם ועשין ריד ולאוין עג טור שו"ע או"ח שם וטוש"ע חו"מ סימן שע סעיף ג:

כא ג ד מיי' פ"ד מהל' י"ט הלכה כ סמג לאוין עה:

רבינו חננאל

ביתו אין אחרים לא. משמיה דר' יהודה אמר שמואל דאמר בני חבורה המקפידין זה על זה פי' שמדקדקין זה על זה שאומר אחד לחבירו המנה שלך שלקחתה גדולה תן לי אני כמותה והוא שוקלה בידו. ואם היה דג אומר לו לקחת דג או כדומה לו שהוא ארוך זרת צריך לתת לו (שמדרתו) [תמורתו] זרת דגים או קישואין או אבטיחים וכדומה להן ואם היו אגוזים ושקדים וכדומה להן אומר לקחת עשרים או אומר לו בעת (שניטלו) [נוטלו] המתן עד שאשקול המנה ועד שאמדוד אורך הדגים והקישואים ואמנה הביצים והאגוזים והשקדים שאתה נוטל שאטול גם במשקלם וכמדתם וכמניינם. וכדברי ב"ה שאומרים לא תלוה אשה מחברתה ככרות כו': ומטילין חלשים כו'. פירוש מטילין גורלות אבל לא על המנות אוקמה על המנות של חול ביו"ט: נבוכדנאצר אנס צדקיהו בעבירה וכיון שנענש נ"נ ע"י צדקיהו נענש גם הוא שנאמר שבעת קלון מכבוד זה נבוכדנאצר שתה גם אתה והערל זה צדקיהו ואמרינן האי קרא כוליה בנ"נ כתיב ועוד צדקיהו צדיקא מאי הוה ליה למעבד. אמר רב יהודה אמר רב בשעה שעשה אותו רשע לאותו צדיק כן נמשכה

רב נסים גאון

פרק שואל. וכדברי הלל אף משום ריבית הוא שהוקדם זכרו בראש הפרק (דף קמח) וכן היה הלל אומר לא תלוה אשה ככר לחברתה עד שתעשנו דמים שמא יוקרו חטים או יוזלו ונמצאו באות לידי ריבית ועיקר זה במשנה בפרק אי זהו נשך (דף עה:)

ליקוטי רש"י

להטעימן. שידעו כמה מלטער ומילר הנוטנו ויבינו כמה עונשו גדול [ב"מ עה.]. משום קוביא. שחוקות של עלס שמשחקין בערבון ואמור רבנן אסמכתא לא קניא והרי הן גזלין מדרבנן דמדאורייתא אינו קרוי גזלן אלא החוטף מיד איש כדכתיב (ש"ב כג) ויגזל את החנית מיד המלרי [ר"ה כב.]. אסמכתא היינו דבר דאינו נותן לו מדעתו אלא סומך על דבר שאינו דסבור שהוא יכול לנלח ופעמים שמנלחין אותו לא קניא והוה ליה כעין גזילה בידו [סנהדרין כד:]. בריה דבת יעקב. אביו לא היה הגון לפיכך לא הזכירו [עירובין פ.]. בפי כל נביאיו. שישים דבר בפיהם לאמר עלה והצלח ויעלה ויפול מכלל שהיו נביאי אמת שלא היו מתנבאים כי אם מה שישים השם בפיהם [דה"ב יח, כ]. שאומר להם לאמר לאחאב עלה ויתן האלהים ביד המלך מכלל שהיו נביאי ה' שלא היו מתנבאים אלא דבר ה' שאם היו נביאי שקר אין הפתוי נופל עליהם שלא היו מתנבאים אלא מה שהיו בודי' מלבן ועוד שאמר יהושפט שוב האין פה נבי' לה' עוד ודאי יודע אני שהם נביאי ה' אלא מקובלני מבית אבי אבא שאין שני נביאים מתנבאים בסגנון א' ולשון א' והללו כולם מתנבאים עלה והצלח [שם, ה]. תפתה וגם תוכל. לפי שיש מפתה הבא לפתות חבירו פעמים שהמפותה מבין שזה רוצה לפתותו והוא נזהר ואינו שומע להמפתות אבל באחאב תפתה וגם תוכל [שם, כ]. רוחו של נבות. שלפי שהוא הרג נבות היה רוחו מחזר לפתותו ולהפילו [סנהדרין קב:]. כי לא אל חפץ רשע אתה. ונאה לך לאבד [illegible]

מסורת הש"ס

א) [נ"ל הילל], ב) ב"מ עה. [ושם מסיק הש"ס ולאו מילתא היא כו' ושוב נכון על קושיא זו ביאור הסמ"ע בחו"מ סימן שכ"ב ס"ק ד], ג) [נ"ל ברה ומשום שאביו לא היה הגון לפיכך לא הזכירו. כ"כ רש"י בעירובין פ. ד"ה בריה], ד) [נ"ל ברה], ה) סנהדרין פט. קב:, ו) [חגיגה יג: סוטה מב. סנהדרין קג.], ז) ס"י ליהלוש, ח) [שייך לעיל קמח: במשנה].

הגהות הב"ח

(א) רש"י ד"ה גם אתה וכו' וגו' חלית כמונו או אלינו כל"ל והד"א:

גליון הש"ס

גמ' כל שחבירו נענש על ידו. עי' ב"ב דף כב ע"א תוס' ד"ה אנא ענשתיה:

תורה אור השלם

א) אַךְ אִישׁ אַל יָרֵב וְאַל יוֹכַח אִישׁ וְעַמְּךָ כִּמְרִיבֵי כֹהֵן: [הושע ד, ד]

ב) וַיֹּאמֶר יְיָ מִי יְפַתֶּה אֶת אַחְאָב וְיַעַל וְיִפֹּל בְּרָמֹת גִּלְעָד וַיֹּאמֶר זֶה בְּכֹה וְזֶה אֹמֵר בְּכֹה: וַיֵּצֵא הָרוּחַ וַיַּעֲמֹד לִפְנֵי יְיָ וַיֹּאמֶר אֲנִי אֲפַתֶּנּוּ וַיֹּאמֶר יְיָ אֵלָיו בַּמָּה: וַיֹּאמֶר אֵצֵא וְהָיִיתִי רוּחַ שֶׁקֶר בְּפִי כָּל נְבִיאָיו וַיֹּאמֶר תְּפַתֶּה וְגַם תּוּכָל צֵא וַעֲשֵׂה כֵן: [מלכים א' כב, כ-כב]

ג) לֹא יֵשֵׁב בְּקֶרֶב בֵּיתִי עֹשֵׂה רְמִיָּה דֹּבֵר שְׁקָרִים לֹא יִכּוֹן לְנֶגֶד עֵינָי: [תהלים קא, ז]

ד) שָׂבַעְתָּ קָלוֹן מִכָּבוֹד שְׁתֵה גַם אַתָּה וְהֵעָרֵל תִּסּוֹב עָלֶיךָ כּוֹס יְמִין יְיָ וְקִיקָלוֹן עַל כְּבוֹדֶךָ: [חבקוק ב, טז]

ה) גַּם עֲנוֹשׁ לַצַּדִּיק לֹא טוֹב לְהַכּוֹת נְדִיבִים עַל יֹשֶׁר: [משלי יז, כו]

ו) כִּי לֹא אֵל חָפֵץ רֶשַׁע אָתָּה לֹא יְגֻרְךָ רָע: [תהלים ה, ה]

ז) אֵיךְ נָפַלְתָּ מִשָּׁמַיִם הֵילֵל בֶּן שָׁחַר נִגְדַּעְתָּ לָאָרֶץ חוֹלֵשׁ עַל גּוֹיִם: [ישעיה יד, יב]

ח) שְׁאוֹל מִתַּחַת רָגְזָה לְךָ לִקְרַאת בּוֹאֶךָ עוֹרֵר לְךָ רְפָאִים כָּל עַתּוּדֵי אָרֶץ הֵקִים מִכִּסְאוֹתָם כֹּל מַלְכֵי גוֹיִם: כֻּלָּם יַעֲנוּ וְיֹאמְרוּ אֵלֶיךָ גַּם אַתָּה חֻלֵּיתָ כָמוֹנוּ אֵלֵינוּ נִמְשָׁלְתָּ: [ישעיה יד, ט-י]

ט) נָחָה שָׁקְטָה כָּל הָאָרֶץ פָּצְחוּ רִנָּה: [ישעיה יד, ז]

י) וְרָבְצוּ שָׁם צִיִּים וּמָלְאוּ בָתֵּיהֶם אֹחִים וְשָׁכְנוּ שָׁם בְּנוֹת יַעֲנָה וּשְׂעִירִים יְרַקְּדוּ שָׁם: [ישעיה יג, כא]

כ) מִמִּי נָעָמְתָּ רְדָה וְהָשְׁכְּבָה אֶת עֲרֵלִים: [יחזקאל לב, יט]

ל) וְנָשָׂאתָ הַמָּשָׁל הַזֶּה עַל מֶלֶךְ בָּבֶל וְאָמָרְתָּ אֵיךְ שָׁבַת נֹגֵשׂ שָׁבְתָה מַדְהֵבָה: [ישעיה יד, ד]

meaning of *Go out?* אָמַר רַב – **Rav said:** צֵא מִמְּחִיצָתִי – God said: **"Leave My environs!"** Thus we see that the spirit of Navos was expelled from the Divine Presence because it caused the death of Ahab. This demonstrates the validity of the statement of R' Yaakov the son of Yaakov's daughter.

The Gemara questions this proof:

וְדִילְמָא הָתָם הַיְינוּ טַעְמָא – **But perhaps in that case the reason** why Navos' spirit was expelled **is** דִּכְתִיב ,,דֹּבֵר שְׁקָרִים לֹא־יִכּוֹן'' – **that it is written:** ***He who tells lies shall not be established*** *before My eyes.*[21] Perhaps the spirit of Navos was expelled from God's presence not because it caused the punishment of Ahab, but rather because it said it would become *a lying spirit.*[22] Consequently, this verse does not prove the validity of R' Yaakov's statement.

The Gemara presents a different verse to prove R' Yaakov's contention:

אֶלָּא מֵהָכָא – **Rather,** proof can be derived **from the following** verse: ,,שָׂבַעְתָּ קָלוֹן מִכָּבוֹד שְׁתֵה גַם־אַתָּה וְהֵעָרֵל וגו' '' – ***You have been sated with shame rather than honor. You, too, drink, as well as the uncircumcised one etc.***.[23] The verse is interpreted: ,,שָׂבַעְתָּ קָלוֹן מִכָּבוֹד'' זֶה נְבוּכַדְנֶצַּר – ***You have been sated with shame rather than honor*** – **this is** a reference to **Nebuchadnezzar.**[24] ,,שְׁתֵה גַם אַתָּה וְהֶעָרֵל'' זֶה צִדְקִיָּה – ***You, too, drink, as well as the uncircumcised one*** – **this is** a reference to **Zedekiah.** Since Zedekiah is called here *the uncircumcised one,* it seems that he was punished for being the cause of Nebuchadnezzar's shame.[25] This proves the statement of R' Yaakov that a person who is the cause of another's punishment is himself punished.

The Gemara rejects this interpretation of the verse for two reasons:

חֲדָא – **One** reason is דְּכוּלֵּיהּ קְרָא בִּנְבוּכַדְנֶצַּר כְּתִיב – **that the entire verse is written about Nebuchadnezzar.**[26] וְעוֹד – **Furthermore,** צִדְקִיָּה צַדִּיקָא – **Zedekiah was a righteous man.** מַאי הֲוָה לֵיהּ לְמֶיעֱבַד לֵיהּ – **What could he have done to** prevent **[Nebuchadnezzar]** from attacking him? Zedekiah was merely a helpless victim, דְּאָמַר רַב יְהוּדָה אָמַר רַב – **as** is evident from that which **Rav Yehudah said in the name of Rav:** בְּשָׁעָה שֶׁבִּקֵּשׁ אוֹתוֹ רָשָׁע לַעֲשׂוֹת לְאוֹתוֹ צַדִּיק כָּךְ וכו' – **When that wicked man** [Nebuchadnezzar] **sought to do that** disgraceful deed **to that righteous man** [Zedekiah] **etc.**[27]

The Gemara suggests a different source for R' Yaakov's teaching:

אֶלָּא מֵהָכָא – **Rather,** proof can be adduced **from the following** verse: ,,גַּם עֲנוֹשׁ לַצַּדִּיק לֹא־טוֹב'' – ***To punish is for the righteous not good.***[28] אֵין ,,לֹא־טוֹב'' אֶלָּא רַע – Now, the term ***not good* is nothing other than evil.** וּכְתִיב ,,כִּי לֹא אֵל־חָפֵץ רֶשַׁע אַתָּה לֹא יְגֻרְךָ רָע'' – **And it is written** about evil:[29] ***For You are not a God Who desires wickedness; evil does not abide with You,*** צַדִּיק אַתָּה ה' וְלֹא יָגוּר בִּמְגוּרְךָ רָע – which means: **You, Hashem, are righteous;**[30] **therefore, an evil one shall not be** allowed **in Your abode.** Since one who causes the punishment of another is defined as "evil," it follows that such a person is not allowed into God's abode. This confirms the statement of R' Yaakov to that effect.

Our Mishnah used the word *chalashim* to mean lots. In discussing this word, the Gemara links our Mishnah to the present discussion about Nebuchadnezzar:

מַאי מַשְׁמַע דְּהַאי חֲלָשִׁים לִישָּׁנָא דְּפוּרָא הוּא – **What indication** is there **that this word *chalashim* connotes lots?** דִּכְתִיב ,,אֵיךְ נָפַלְתָּ מִשָּׁמַיִם הֵילֵל בֶּן־שָׁחַר נִגְדַּעְתָּ לָאָרֶץ חוֹלֵשׁ עַל־גּוֹיִם וגו' '' – **For it is written:** ***How you have fallen from heaven, O shining one, son of dawn! You have been cut down to the ground, the one who casts lots*** *(choleish)* ***for nations etc.***[31] אָמַר רַבָּה בַּר רַב הוּנָא – **Rabbah bar Rav Huna said:** מְלַמֵּד שֶׁהָיָה מֵטִיל פּוּר עַל גְּדוֹלֵי מַלְכוּת – **[This verse] teaches that [Nebuchadnezzar] used to cast lots concerning great members of royalty** whom he had conquered, לֵידַע אֵיזֶה בֶּן יוֹמוֹ שֶׁל מִשְׁכַּב זְכוּר – **to ascertain whose day it was for sodomy.**[32]

Another teaching on this subject:

וּכְתִיב ,,כָּל־מַלְכֵי גוֹיִם כֻּלָּם וגו' '' – **And it is written:** ***All the kings of the nations, all of them, etc.*** [*lie in glory, every one in his own house*].[33] אָמַר רַבִּי יוֹחָנָן – **R' Yochanan said:** שֶׁנָּחוּ מִמִּשְׁכַּב

NOTES

21. *Psalms* 101:7. God, Who is the essence of truth, cannot tolerate falsehood in His presence.

22. Although God consented to allow the spirit to carry out its suggestion, He banished it from His presence. True, the task of being the spirit of untruth in the mouths of Ahab's prophets had to be accomplished somehow, but one should not volunteer on his own to be the instrument of any act that involves lying. The fact that Navos' spirit was eager to fulfill this mission was a character flaw (*Yad Ramah* to *Sanhedrin* 102b; see *Rif* on *Ein Yaakov*). [Alternatively,] the banishment was only a temporary one, whose purpose was to teach that God detests falsehood (*Hagahos Yavetz*).

23. *Habakkuk* 2:16. This verse is part of a prophecy concerning King Nebuchadnezzar of Babylonia.

הֵעָרֵל is actually a verb (see note 26). The Gemara homiletically interprets it as though it were vocalized הֶעָרֵל which means *the uncircumcised one.*

24. Nebuchadnezzar used to sodomize the kings who were subject to him, one of whom was King Zedekiah of Judah. When he attempted to sodomize Zedekiah, Nebuchadnezzar's foreskin grew enormously long, to his great embarrassment. This is the meaning of the prophet's words to Nebuchadnezzar: *You have been sated with shame rather than honor* (*Rashi*). [The story of the attempt to sodomize Zedekiah is told in the Gemara below.]

25. In *Ezekiel* 32:19 (quoted in the Gemara below), the word עֲרֵלִים, *uncircumcised ones,* is used to describe the inhabitants of Gehinnom. Hence, the use of this term in reference to Zedekiah indicates that he did not merit admission into God's innermost enclosure (*Rif* on *Ein Yaakov*).

The Gemara is apparently assuming that Zedekiah was not a helpless victim (based on *Rashi* ד״ה בשעה; see *Maharsha*). [Rather, he willingly allowed Nebuchadnezzar to take advantage of him, so that Nebuchadnezzar would be punished.]

26. The entire verse can aptly be interpreted as referring only to Nebuchadnezzar, and not to Zedekiah. שְׁתֵה גַם אַתָּה, *You, too, drink,* means that Nebuchadnezzar should drink like those whom he abused. [Nebuchadnezzar would have his victims come to a banquet, where he would ply them with wine until they became intoxicated, whereupon he would sodomize them (see the preceding verse with *Rashi*).] וְהֵעָרֵל is translated as a verb meaning: *and have your foreskin exposed* [just as the foreskins of your victims were exposed] (*Radak* ad loc.; see *Rashi* here).

27. (This statement appears in the Gemara below.) Rav's reference to Zedekiah as a "righteous man" indicates that Zedekiah was a helpless victim [and not a willing participant in the sodomy] (*Rashi*). Since he did not help in any way to bring about Nebuchadnezzar's humiliation, he was not deserving of punishment (see note 16).

28. *Proverbs* 17:26.

29. *Psalms* 5:5.

30. [This phrase, צַדִּיק אַתָּה ה', *You, Hashem, are righteous,* which is of Scriptural origin (*Jeremiah* 12:1), is used here for reasons of style (*Maharshal*).]

31. *Isaiah* 14:12. [The Gemara will interpret several verses from the passage, which describes the downfall of Nebuchadnezzar.]

32. Nebuchadnezzar would sodomize a different king each day. He would determine which king to sodomize by casting lots.

33. Ibid. v. 18.

וכדברי (א) ב"ה) אף משום רבית אי הכי בניו ובני ביתו נמי בניו ובני ביתו היינו טעמא כדרב יהודה אמר רב דאמר רב יהודה אמר רב מותר להלוות בניו ובני ביתו ברבית כדי להטעימן טעם רבית אי הכי מנה גדולה כנגד מנה קטנה נמי אין ה"נ וחסורי מיחסרא והכי קתני מפיס אדם עם בניו ועם בני ביתו על השלחן אפי' מנה גדולה כנגד מנה קטנה מ"ט כדרב יהודה אמר רב עם בניו ועם בני ביתו אין עם אחרים לא מ"ט כדרב יהודה אמר שמואל מנה גדולה כנגד מנה קטנה אף בחול לאחרים אסור מ"ט משום קוביא: מטילין חלשין על וכו': מאי אבל לא על המנות א"ר יעקב בריה דבת יעקב אבל לא על המנות של חול ביו"ט פשיטא מהו דתימא הואיל וכתיב ועמך כמריבי כהן אפי' מנות דחול נמי קמ"ל וא"ר יעקב בריה דבת יעקב כל שחבירו נענש על ידו אין מכניסין אותו במחיצתו של הקב"ה מנלן אילימא משום דכתיב ויאמר ה' מי יפתה את אחאב ויעל ויפול ברמות גלעד ויאמר זה בכה וזה אמר בכה ויצא הרוח ויעמוד לפני ה' ויאמר אני אפתנו וגו' ויאמר אצא והייתי רוח שקר בפי כל נביאיו ויאמר תפתה וגם תוכל צא ועשה כן ואמרינן מאי רוח א"ר יוחנן זה רוחו של נבות ומאי צא אמר רב צא ממחיצתי ודילמא התם היינו טעמא דכתיב דובר שקרים לא יכון לנגד עיני אלא מהכא שבעת קלון מכבוד שתה גם אתה והערל וגו' שבעת קלון מכבוד זה נבוכד נצר שתה גם אתה והערל זה צדקיה חדא דכוליה קרא בנבוכד נצר כתיב ועוד צדקיה צדיקא מאי הוה ליה למיעבד ליה דא"ר יהודה אמר רב בשעה שבקש אותו רשע לעשות לאותו צדיק כך וכו' אלא מהכא גם ענוש לצדיק לא טוב אין לא טוב אלא רע וכתיב כי לא אל חפץ רשע אתה לא יגורך רע צדיק אתה ה' ולא יגור במגורך רע מאי משמע דהאי חלשים לישנא דפורא הוא דכתיב איך נפלת משמים הילל בן שחר נגדעת לארץ חולש על גוים וגו' אמר רבה בר רב הונא מלמד שהיה מטיל פור על גדולי מלכות לידע איזה בן יומו של משכב זכור וכתיב כל מלכי גוים כולם וגו' אמר רבי יוחנן שנחו ממשכב זכור וא"ר יוחנן כל ימיו של אותו רשע לא נמצא שחוק בפה כל בריה שנאמר נחה שקטה כל הארץ פצחו רנה מכלל דעד השתא לא הוה רנה ואמר ר' יצחק אמר ר' יוחנן אסור לעמוד בביתו של אותו רשע שנא' ושעירים ירקדו שם ואמר רב יהודה אמר רב בשעה שביקש אותו רשע לעשות לאותו צדיק כך נמשכה ערלתו שלש מאות אמה והיתה מחזרת על כל המסיבה כולה שנאמר שבעת קלון מכבוד שתה גם אתה והערל ערל בגימטריא שלש מאות הוי ואמר רב יהודה אמר רב בשעה שירד אותו רשע לגיהנם רעשו כל יורדי גיהנם אמרו שמא למשול עליהם הוא בא או ליחלות כמותם הוא בא שנאמר גם אתה חולית כמונו אלינו נמשלת יצאתה ב"ק ואמרה ממי נעמת רדה והשכבה את ערלים איך שבת נוגש שבתה מדהבה א"ר יהודה אמר רב שבתה אומה זו שאמרה מדוד

רש"י

וכדברי (בית) הלל דחיש שמא יוקירו חיטי בהלואת ככרות אף משום רבית: בניו ובני ביתו נמי. ליחוש לרבית וכל הני: להלוות. משלו: בניו ובני ביתו. הסמוכים על שלחנו דכיון דהכל משלו אין כאן רבית: להטעימן טעם רבית. שידעו כמה קשה אלמא כיון דמשלו הוא אין כאן איסור רבית והלכך גבי מדה ומשקל ומנין נמי לאו קפידא הוא אלא להשוותם בלא קנאה: אי הכי מנה גדולה כנגד מנה קטנה נמי. דמוקמינן טעמא לקמן משום קוביא ואפי' בחול אסור וכיון דהכל משלו אמאי אסור להטעימן טעמא קוביא בעלמא הוא: מאי טעמא מותר. ולא חייש לקוביא: כדרב יהודה אמר רב. דלהטעימן בעלמא הוא: עם אחר לא כדרב יהודה אמר שמואל. דכיון דמקפידין עוברין משום מדה ומשקל ומנין: משום קוביא. דגזל הוא דאסמכתא לא קניא והא אסמכתא דסמיך על הגורל אם יפול גורל אמנה הגדולה אזכה בה ולפיכך תלה עצמו אף לגורל הקטנה על הספק ואילו יודע מתחלה שכן לא היה מתרצה: של חול. של קדשים של אתמול: כמריבי כהן. ככהנים אלו שהם בעלי מריבה: אפי' דחול נמי. לישתרי להו להפיס ביו"ט כי היכי דלא לינצו: זה בכה. אני אפתנו בכה: שבעת קלון. בנבוכדנצר משתעי שהיה מטיל משכב זכור על המלכים וכשהגיע יומו של צדקיהו נמשכה ערלתו ג' מאות אמה והיינו שבעת קלון: חדא דכוליה קרא בנבוכדנצר כתיב. שפיר מצית לאוקמי כוליה בנבוכדנצר וה"ק שתה גם אתה כאותם שהיית מקלה אותן והערל והתערל והתגנה: בשעה שעשה לו כו'. לקמן היא מדקאמר לאותו צדיק ש"מ אנוס היה: ענוש לצדיק לא טוב. צדיק המעניש לא טוב וכיון דאינו טוב הרי הוא רע: וכתיב לא יגורך רע. אלמא אינו נכנס במחילתו: חולש על גוים. בנבוכדנצר כתיב: ושעירים ירקדו שם. ולא אנשים ובשביל הבריות מסתלקין המזיקין ונמצא מבטל גזירת המלך: המסיבה. מלכים שהיו מסובין ויושבין לפניו: גם אתה חולית כמונו אלינו וגו'. ביורדי גיהנם כתיב דכתיב לעיל מיניה שאול מתחת רגזה לך לקראת בואך וגו' (א): חולית כמונו אלינו נמשלת. לשון ממשלה: נעמת. סבור אתה להיות בנועם מן האחרים: מדוד

תוספות

לפירוש זה דאם הלל לא איירי אלא במקפידין אם כן אמאי קאמר לעיל לימא מתניתין דלא כהלל והא הלל במקפידין איירי ומתניתין דלעיל אתי שפיר כוותיה דהא רישא באין מקפידין איירי דקתני שואל דאילו למקפידין אסרינן שאלה לפי מה שפירש' להכי נראה לפרש עוברין משום מדה ומשום משקל כלומר קרובין לבא לידי כך שיעברו משום מדה שע"י שמקפידין זה ע"ז ורגילין ליקח במדה זה מזה גם ביו"ט יעשו כך וגם כל בני אדם הוי אסורין בכלי של מדה כדאמר בביצה (דף כט: ושם) אבל למקפידין נותן הוא עצה שלא ישתמשו שקרובים הן לבא לידי איסור מדה וכן לידי איסור משקל מתוך שרגילים לשקול על ידי הקפדתן גם ביו"ט לא יגרעו עד שישקלו ולידי מנין כשישאל אחד מהן ק' אגוזים יאמר לו תן לי מ' להשלים ק' כמו שרגילין לעשות ומשום לווין ופורעין ביו"ט כדאמר לעיל דלשון הלואה אסור והם מתוך שמקפידים יזכירו לשון הלואה לפי שיאמר השואל אם אזכיר לו לשון שאלה משמע דהדרא בעיניה לכך אומר לשון הלואה וכדברי הלל אף משום רבית דכשלוין זה מזה ככר באין לידי רבית לפי שפעמים שזה משלם יותר שע"פ שמקפיד הוא כוש הוא שלא ישלם כמו שהלוהו בשביל שההנהו וכיון שאינו מוחל הוי רבית אבל שאר בני אדם מחלי ולא הוי רבית והשתא מתני' איירי במקפידין דאסם שכנים שאינם חברים מקפידין ומ"מ לדך שאלה מותר ומה שדכרו כאן על מקפידין לא אמרינן אלא גבי חבורה שרגילים לישאל זה מזה תדיר ואתי לידי איסור אבל שכנים שאינן מדירין כל כך לשאול זה מזה מותרים ואין לגזור בהם שמא יבאו לידי איסור ולהכי לא משני כי אמר מתני' דלא כהלל דמתמיתין איירי כשאין מקפידין משום דסתמא דמתני' איירי במקפידין כדפרישית. מ"ר: **מאי טעמא** משום קוביא. היינו כרבי יהודה בשם רבי טרפון דאמר אין אחד מהן נזיר שלא נתנה נזירות אלא להפלאה וסבירא ליה דלא ממית אינש לספיקא ולית הלכתא הכי אלא כאידך דר' יהודה דפסקינן בסנהדרין בפרק זה בורר (דף כה. ושם). מ"ר:

מטילין חלשים על הקדשים ביו"ט. תימה דאמר בפרק ב' דקדושין (דף נג. ושם) דאין חולקין זבחים כנגד זבחים ומנחה כנגד מנחה ומפיק לה מלכל בני אהרן תהיה איש כאחיו ועוד דפריך התם מהוהצנועים מושכין ידיהם והגרגרנים חולקין מאי חולקין חוטפין כו' ואומר רבי דלאו בהא מועלת בהם חלוקה וגורל שיהא ממונו לקדש בו את האשה ולהוציאו בדיינים אבל מ"מ מטילין היו חלשין לתת לכל א' חלקו פן יריבו ביחד כדכתיב (הושע ד) ועמך כמריבי כהן והא דמשני התם חולקין לאו דוקא אלא חוטפין ולא משני הכי משו' דחולקין משמע כופין לחלוק ע"כ מחמת שחוטפין אותן שאינן שלהם. מ"ר:

מה

עין משפט נר מצוה

יט א מיי' פכ"ג מהלכ' שבת הלכה יז סמג שם טוש"ע או"ח סימן שכב סעיף ו:
כ ב מיי' שם (וש"נ מהל' גזלה ואבידה הל"י) סמג שם ועשין ליד ולאוין עג טור שו"ע או"ח שם וטוש"ע או"ח סימן שע סעיף ג:
כא ג ד מיי' פ"ד מהל' י"ט הלכה כ סמג לאוין עה:

רבינו חננאל

ביתו אין אחרים לא. משמיה דר' יהודה אמר שמואל דאמר בני חבורה המקפידין זה על זה פי' שמדקדקין זה על זה שאומר אחד לחבירו המנה שלך שלקחתה גדולה תן לי אני כמותה והוא שוקלה בידו. ואם היה דג אומר לו לקחת דג או כדומה לו שהוא ארוך זרת צריך לתת לי (שמרתת) [תמורתו] זרת דגים או קישואין או אבטיחים וכדומה להן ואם היו אגודים ושקדים וכדומה להן אומר לקחת עשרים או אומר לו בעת (שניטלו) [נוטלין] המתן עד שאשקול המנה ועד שאמדוד אורך הזרת והקישואים ואמנה הביצים והאגודים והשקדים שאתה נוטל שאטול גם במשקלם ובמדתם וכמניינם. וכדברי ב"ה שאומרים לא תלוה אשה מחברתה ככרות כו': ומטילין חלשים כו'. פירוש מטילין גורלות גדולות וכו' אבל לא על המנות אוקמה על המנות של חול ביו"ט: נבוכדנצאר שנענש בצבורה וכיון שנענש ג"כ ע"י צדקיהו נענש גם הוא שנאמר שבעת קלון מכבוד זה נבוכדנאצר שתה גם אתה והערל זה צדקיהו ואמרינן חדא כוליה בנ"נ כתיב ועוד צדקיהו צדיקא מאי הוה ליה למעבד. אמר רב יהודה אמר רב בשעה שעשה אותו רשע לאותו צדיק כן נמשכה

רב נסים גאון

פרק שואל. וכדברי הלל אף משום רבית הוא שהוקדם זכרו בראש הפרק (דף קמח) הלל אומר לא תלוה אשה ככר לחברתה עד שתעשנו דמים שמא יוקרו חטים או יוזלו ונמצאו באות לידי רבית ועיקר זה במשנה בפרק איזהו נשך (דף עה):

ליקוטי רש"י

להטעימן. שידעו כמה מצטער ומילר הנותנו ויבינו כמה עונש גדול [ב"מ עה.]. משום קוביא. מחיכת של עלם שמשחקין בעכרון ולמור רבנן דאסמכתא לא קניא והכי הן גזלנין מדרבנן דמדאורייתא אינו קרוי גזלן אלא הנוטל מיד איש בזרוע [ר"ה כב.]. ...אסמכתא היינו דבר שאינו לו מדעתו אלא סומך על דבר שאינו דסבור שהוא יכול לנצח ופעמים שמנצחין אותו לא קניא והוה ליה [סנהדרין כד:]. בריה דבת יעקב. אביו לא היה הגון לפיכך לא הזכירו [עירובין פ.]. בפי כל נביאיו. ...הם לאמר עלה והצלח ויעלה ויפול מכלל שהיו נביאי אמת שלא היו מתנבאים כי אם מה שישים השם ... שאומר להם לאמר לאחאב עלה ויתן האלהים ביד המלך מכלל שהיו נביאי ה' שלא היו מתנבאים אלא דבר ה' שאם היו נביאי שקר אין הספור נופל עליהם שלא היו מתנבאים אלא מה שהיו בודי' ... ה' עוד ודאי יודע אני שהם נביאי ה' אלא מקובלני מבית אבי אבא שאין שני נביאים מתנבאים בסגנון א' ולשון א' והללו כולם מתנבאים עלה והצלח [שם, ה]. תפתה וגם תוכל. לפי שיש מפתה ... שזה רוצה לפתותו והוא נזהר ואינו שומע להתפתות אבל באחאב תפתה וגם תוכל [שם, כ]. רוחו של נבות. שלפי שהוא הרג נבות היה רוחו ממזר לפתותו ולהפילו [סנהדרין קב:]. כי לא אל חפץ רשע אתה. ... לא יגורך רע. לא יגור אצלך [תהלים ה, ה]. הילל בן שחר. כוכב הנוגה המאיר אור ככוכב הבוקר זו הקינה על סרה של בבל נאמר' שיפול משמים. נגדעת לארץ. ... מטיל גורל עליהם על המלכים [ישעיה יד, יב]. על גדולי מלכות וכו'. שהיה משקה את המלכים יין ומשכרם ושוכב עמם משכבי אשה [חבקוק ב, טו]. ושעירים. שדים [ישעיה יג, כא]. גם אתה חולית כמונו. ... למות [שם יד, י]. רדה והשכבה. אף אתה רדה לבור והשכבה אותם [יחזקאל לב, יט]. מדהבה. לשון מרבית גאוה ומשא כבד ורבותינו דרשו האומרים מדוד והבא [ישעיה שם, ד].

מסורת הש"ס

א) [ע"ל הלל], ב) ב"מ עה. [ושם מסיק הש"ס ולאו מילתא היא כו' יעוין שם נכון על קושיא זו ביאור הט"ז בא"ח סימן שכ"ב ס"ק ד], ג) [ע"ל ברה ומשום שאביו לא היה הגון לפיכך לא הזכירו. ע"י רש"י עירובין פ. ד"ה בריה], ד) [ע"ל ברה], ה) סנהדרין פט. קב:, ו) [חגיגה יב: סוטה מב. סנהדרין קב.], ז) פ"ד ליחלדים, ח) [שייך לעיל קמט: במשנה].

הגהות הב"ח

(א) רש"י ד"ה גם אתה וכו' וגו' חלית כמונו אל אלינו כצ"ל והד"א:

גליון הש"ס

גמ' כל שחבירו נענש על ידו. עי' ב"ק דף כ"ד ע"א תוס' ד"ה אלא עצמית.

תורה אור השלם

א) אַךְ אִישׁ אַל יָרֵב וְאַל יוֹכַח אִישׁ וְעַמְּךָ כִּמְרִיבֵי כֹהֵן: [הושע ד, ד]
ב) וַיֹּאמֶר יְיָ מִי יְפַתֶּה אֶת אַחְאָב וְיַעַל וְיִפֹּל בְּרָמֹת גִּלְעָד וַיֹּאמֶר זֶה בְּכֹה וְזֶה אֹמֵר בְּכֹה: וַיֵּצֵא הָרוּחַ וַיַּעֲמֹד לִפְנֵי יְיָ וַיֹּאמֶר אֲנִי אֲפַתֶּנּוּ וַיֹּאמֶר יְיָ אֵלָיו בַּמָּה: וַיֹּאמֶר אֵצֵא וְהָיִיתִי רוּחַ שֶׁקֶר בְּפִי כָּל נְבִיאָיו וַיֹּאמֶר תְּפַתֶּה וְגַם תּוּכָל צֵא וַעֲשֵׂה כֵן: [מלכים א' כב, כ-כב]
ג) לֹא יֵשֵׁב בְּקֶרֶב בֵּיתִי עֹשֵׂה רְמִיָּה דֹּבֵר שְׁקָרִים לֹא יִכּוֹן לְנֶגֶד עֵינָי: [תהלים קא, ז]
ד) שָׂבַעְתָּ קָלוֹן מִכָּבוֹד שְׁתֵה גַם אַתָּה וְהֵעָרֵל תִּסּוֹב עָלֶיךָ כּוֹס יְמִין יְיָ וְקִיקָלוֹן עַל כְּבוֹדֶךָ: [חבקוק ב, טז]
ה) גַּם עֲנוֹשׁ לַצַּדִּיק לֹא טוֹב לְהַכּוֹת נְדִיבִים עַל יֹשֶׁר: [משלי יז, כו]
ו) כִּי לֹא אֵל חָפֵץ רֶשַׁע אָתָּה לֹא יְגֻרְךָ רָע: [תהלים ה, ה]
ז) אֵיךְ נָפַלְתָּ מִשָּׁמַיִם הֵילֵל בֶּן שָׁחַר נִגְדַּעְתָּ לָאָרֶץ חוֹלֵשׁ עַל גּוֹיִם: [ישעיה יד, יב]
ח) שְׁאוֹל מִתַּחַת רָגְזָה לְךָ לִקְרַאת בּוֹאֶךָ עוֹרֵר לְךָ רְפָאִים כָּל עַתּוּדֵי אָרֶץ הֵקִים מִכִּסְאוֹתָם כֹּל מַלְכֵי גוֹיִם: כֻּלָּם יַעֲנוּ וְיֹאמְרוּ אֵלֶיךָ גַּם אַתָּה חֻלֵּיתָ כָמוֹנוּ אֵלֵינוּ נִמְשָׁלְתָּ: [ישעיה יד, ט-י]
ט) נָחָה שָׁקְטָה כָּל הָאָרֶץ פָּצְחוּ רִנָּה: [ישעיה יד, ז]
י) וְרָבְצוּ שָׁם צִיִּים וּמָלְאוּ בָתֵּיהֶם אֹחִים וְשָׁכְנוּ שָׁם בְּנוֹת יַעֲנָה וּשְׂעִירִים יְרַקְּדוּ שָׁם: [ישעיה יג, כא]
כ) מִמִּי נָעָמְתָּ רְדָה וְהָשְׁכְּבָה אֶת עֲרֵלִים: [יחזקאל לב, יט]
ל) וְנָשָׂאתָ הַמָּשָׁל הַזֶּה עַל מֶלֶךְ בָּבֶל וְאָמַרְתָּ אֵיךְ שָׁבַת נֹגֵשׂ שָׁבְתָה מַדְהֵבָה: [ישעיה יד, ד]

זְכוּר – This indicates **that** when Nebuchadnezzar died, **they** finally **rested from sodomy.**[34]

The Gemara presents another two statements of R' Yochanan concerning Nebuchadnezzar:

וְאָמַר רַבִּי יוֹחָנָן – **And R' Yochanan** also **said:** **כָּל יָמָיו שֶׁל אוֹתוֹ רָשָׁע** – **All the days of that evil man,** **לֹא נִמְצָא שְׂחוֹק בְּפֶה כָּל בְּרִיָּה** – **no laughter was found in the mouth of any creature.** **שֶׁנֶּאֱמַר ,,נָחָה שָׁקְטָה כָּל־הָאָרֶץ פָּצְחוּ רִנָּה״** – This is **as it is stated:** ***All the earth has become calm and tranquil. They burst forth in song,***[35] **מִכְּלָל דְּעַד הַשְׁתָּא לֹא הֲוָה רִנָּה** – **which implies that until now** (i.e. until the death of Nebuchadnezzar), **there was no song.**

וְאָמַר רַבִּי יִצְחָק אָמַר רַבִּי יוֹחָנָן – **And R' Yitzchak said in the name of R' Yochanan:** **אָסוּר לַעֲמוֹד בְּבֵיתוֹ שֶׁל אוֹתוֹ רָשָׁע** – **It is forbidden to stand in the house**[36] **of that wicked man,** **שֶׁנֶּאֱמַר ,,וּשְׂעִירִים יְרַקְּדוּ־שָׁם״** – **for it is stated:** ***and demons will dance there.***[37]

The Gemara records several teachings about Nebuchadnezzar reported by Rav Yehudah in the name of Rav:

וְאָמַר רַב יְהוּדָה אָמַר רַב – **And Rav Yehudah said in the name of Rav:** **בְּשָׁעָה שֶׁבִּיקֵּשׁ אוֹתוֹ רָשָׁע לַעֲשׂוֹת לְאוֹתוֹ צַדִּיק כָּךְ** – **When that wicked man** [Nebuchadnezzar] **sought to do that** disgraceful deed **to that righteous man** [Zedekiah], **נִמְשְׁכָה עָרְלָתוֹ שְׁלֹשׁ מֵאוֹת אַמָּה** – **his foreskin extended three hundred** ***amos*** **וְהָיְתָה מְחַזֶּרֶת עַל כָּל הַמְּסִיבָּה כּוּלָּהּ** – **and went around the entire gathering,** i.e. around all the kings seated before him. **שֶׁנֶּאֱמַר ,,שָׂבַעְתָּ קָלוֹן מִכָּבוֹד שְׁתֵה גַם־אַתָּה וְהֵעָרֵל״** – This is **as it is stated:** ***You have been sated with shame rather than honor. You, too, drink and have your foreskin exposed*** *(vehei'areil).*[38] **עָרֵל בְּגִימַטְרִיָּא שְׁלֹשׁ מֵאוֹת הָוֵי** – **The numerical value of** ***areil***[39] **is three hundred.**[40]

It is related that even the dead were terrified of Nebuchadnezzar:

וְאָמַר רַב יְהוּדָה אָמַר רַב – **And Rav Yehudah** also **said in the name of Rav:** **בְּשָׁעָה שֶׁיָּרַד אוֹתוֹ רָשָׁע לְגֵיהִנֹּם** – **When that wicked man descended into Gehinnom,** **רָעֲשׁוּ כָּל יוֹרְדֵי גֵיהִנֹּם** – **all those who had** already **descended into Gehinnom trembled.** **אָמְרוּ** – **They said:** **שֶׁמָּא לִמְשׁוֹל עֲלֵיהֶם הוּא בָּא** – **"Does he perhaps** come to rule over them,[41] **אוֹ לִיחָלוֹת כְּמוֹתָם הוּא בָּא** – **or does he come to be** as **weak as them?"** **שֶׁנֶּאֱמַר ,,גַּם אַתָּה חֻלֵּיתָ כָמוֹנוּ אֵלֵינוּ נִמְשָׁלְתָּ״** – This is **as it is stated:** ***Have you, too, become as weak as us? [Or] have you been made to rule over us?***[42] **יָצְאתָה בַּת קוֹל וְאָמְרָה** – **A heavenly voice went forth and proclaimed:** **,,מִמִּי נָעָמְתָּ רְדָה וְהָשְׁכְּבָה אֶת־עֲרֵלִים״** – ***Whom do you exceed in beauty? Descend and be laid to rest with the uncircumcised!***[43]

A teaching that describes the rapacity of Nebuchadnezzar's Babylonia:

,,אֵיךְ שָׁבַת נֹגֵשׂ שָׁבְתָה מַדְהֵבָה״ – ***How the oppressor has ceased, the golden one*** *(madheivah)* ***has ceased!***[44] **אָמַר רַב יְהוּדָה אָמַר רַב** – **Rav Yehudah said in the name of Rav:** **שָׁבְתָה אוּמָּה זוֹ שֶׁאָמְרָה** – The meaning of the verse is: **This nation** [Babylonia] **has ceased, which used to say,**

NOTES

34. Until then they were lying in humiliation in the house of Nebuchadnezzar (*Maharsha*).

[According to its plain meaning, this verse contrasts the dignified deaths and burials of other kings with the disgraceful end which will be suffered by Nebuchadnezzar, which is described in the next verse: *But you will be thrown out of your grave like a disgusting root.*]

35. *Isaiah* 14:7.

36. [I.e. the site of his palace.]

37. Ibid. 13:21. If people go there, the demons will leave [for demons abide in places void of human habitation (see *Bava Kamma* 21a)]. Thus, anyone who goes there interferes with God's decree (*Rashi*; see also *Chidushei HaRan*).

Maharsha understands R' Yochanan's prohibition as a measure designed to protect humans. Since this place is inhabited by demons, a person who goes there may be harmed by them.

38. See note 26.

39. [ערל is the root of וְהֵעָרֵל, *and have your foreskin exposed.*]

40. [ע=70; ר=200; ל=30.] See *Anaf Yosef* and *Ben Yehoyada* who explain the significance of the number 300 in this context.

41. They referred to themselves in the third person.

42. *Isaiah* 14:10. It is evident from the context that these words are spoken by those in Gehinnom, for the preceding verse states: *Sheol below trembles as you approach. It has awakened the giants, all the rulers of the earth, and raised all the kings of the nations from their thrones* [in Gehinnom (*Maharsha*)]. Our verse then continues: *They will all speak and say to you, "Have you, too, become as weak,* etc.*"* (*Rashi, Maharsha*). The inhabitants of Gehinnom thought that Nebuchadnezzar would rule over them there, just as he had ruled over them in this world (*Menachem Meishiv Nefesh; cf. Ben Yehoyada*).

This interpretation relates נִמְשָׁלְתָּ to מֶמְשָׁלָה, *dominion* (*Rashi*). אֵלֵינוּ נִמְשָׁלְתָּ is otherwise translated: *You have been made comparable to us* (*Metzudos*).

43. *Ezekiel* 32:19. The prophet is asking Nebuchadnezzar, "Do you think you are better than others?! Descend into Gehinnom and take your place alongside the other wicked ones who are there" (see *Rashi*).

Although this passage refers to Egypt, this particular verse is addressed to Nebuchadnezzar, asking him whether he thought he was more powerful than the Egyptians (*Maharsha; cf. Maharshal*).

44. *Isaiah* 14:4. מַדְהֵבָה is translated as *the golden one*, because דַּהֲבָא is the Aramaic equivalent of זָהָב, *gold.* It is used to describe Babylonia, which amassed great wealth through taxing the lands of its empire (*Radak* ibid.). [The Gemara will give a homiletic interpretation of מַדְהֵבָה.]

מְדוֹד וְהָבָא – **"Measure** your tribute[1] **and bring** (*medod vehavei*) it to us!"[2]

The Gemara records a different interpretation:

וְאִיכָּא דְּאָמְרִי – **But there are** those **who say** that *madheivah* should be interpreted as signifying שֶׁאָמְרָה מְאֹד מְאֹד (הביא) [הָבָא][3] בְּלֹא מִדָּה – the nation **that used to say, "Bring more and more** (*m'od havei*) **without measure!"**[4]

Another teaching about Nebuchadnezzar:

"וּרְבוּ יַתִּירָה הוּסְפַת לִי" – ***And additional greatness was given to me.***[5] אָמַר רַב יְהוּדָה אָמַר רַב יִרְמְיָה בַּר אַבָּא – **Rav Yehudah said in the name of Rav Yirmiyah bar Abba:** מְלַמֵּד שֶׁרָכַב עַל אֲרִי זָכָר – **It teaches that [Nebuchadnezzar] rode on a male lion** וְקָשַׁר תַּנִּין בְּרֹאשׁוֹ – **and tied a** great **serpent to its head,**[6] לְקַיֵּים מַה שֶּׁנֶּאֱמַר "גַּם אֶת־חַיַּת הַשָּׂדֶה נָתַתִּי לוֹ לְעָבְדוֹ" – which served **to fulfill that which is stated:** ***I am also giving him*** [Nebuchadnezzar] ***the wild beasts to serve him.***[7]

Mishnah לֹא יִשְׂכּוֹר אָדָם פּוֹעֲלִים בְּשַׁבָּת – A PERSON MAY NOT HIRE WORKERS ON THE SABBATH,[8] וְלֹא יֹאמַר אָדָם לַחֲבֵירוֹ לִשְׂכּוֹר לוֹ פּוֹעֲלִים – NOR MAY A PERSON TELL HIS FRIEND TO HIRE WORKERS FOR HIM.[9] אֵין מַחְשִׁיכִין עַל הַתְּחוּם לִשְׂכּוֹר (לוֹ) פּוֹעֲלִים וּלְהָבִיא פֵּירוֹת – ONE MAY NOT go to AWAIT NIGHTFALL AT THE Sabbath BOUNDARY FOR THE PURPOSE OF HIRING WORKERS OR BRINGING PRODUCE after the Sabbath.[10] אֲבָל מַחְשִׁיךְ הוּא לִשְׁמוֹר – BUT ONE MAY go to AWAIT NIGHTFALL at the Sabbath boundary FOR THE PURPOSE OF GUARDING his property after the Sabbath,[11] וּמֵבִיא פֵּירוֹת בְּיָדוֹ – AND HE MAY BRING back PRODUCE IN

NOTES

1. Coins of gold (*Rashi;* cf. *Maharsha*).

2. מַדְהֵבָה is interpreted as a contraction מְדוֹד וְהָבָא, *measure and bring.*

3. This emendation follows the text recorded in *Ein Yaakov* and *Maharsha,* which reads הָבָא, *bring,* instead of הֵבִיא, *he brought.*

4. This exposition renders מַדְהֵבָה as מְאֹד הָבָא, *bring more.*

Maharasha explains the difference between the two interpretations as follows: According to the first approach, the Babylonians did not want to go to the trouble of counting numerous coins, so they requested their tributaries to submit large amounts of coins by the measure. According to the second approach, the Babylonians demanded so many coins that they could not even be measured. (See also *Maharal.*)

Basing himself on a Midrash (*Eichah Rabbah* 4:15), *Ben Yehoyada* explains the first interpretation differently. This Midrash relates that when Nebuchadnezzar's general, Nebuzaradan, was besieging Jerusalem, he was initially so discouraged at his lack of progress that he sought to withdraw. Nebuzaradan was then told that as a sign of Divine displeasure with the Jews, God would cause the city's walls to sink slightly into the ground each day. Nebuzaradan measured the walls and discovered that their height decreased each day by two *tefachim.* Encouraged by this sign, he maintained his position and ultimately conquered Jerusalem. The words מְדוֹד וְהָבָא, *measure and bring,* refer to the orders of Nebuzaradan, who told his men, "*Measure* [the height of the walls] *and bring* [the army into the city]."

5. *Daniel* 4:33. In this chapter Nebuchadnezzar describes a dream he had which was interpreted by Daniel as meaning that God was displeased with Nebuchadnezzar's arrogance, and that He would humble the Babylonian king by making him live like an animal for seven years. At the end of that time Nebuchadnezzar was to be restored to his throne, suitably chastened and made aware of the overwhelming power of God. The dream came true, and after Nebuchadnezzar returned to the throne, he reported: *Over my kingdom I was established, and additional greatness was given to me.* The Gemara's seeks to define this "additional greatness" (*Rashi*).

6. The "additional greatness" mentioned in the verse was that he tied a great serpent to the lion's head, in the form of reins (*Rashi*). Alternatively, he fastened the serpent to his own head as a crown (*Maharsha*).

This metaphor means that Nebuchadnezzar subjugated Judah, whose power is represented by a lion [גּוּר אַרְיֵה יְהוּדָה, *a lion's cub is Judah* (*Genesis* 49:9)], and Egypt, whose power is symbolized by a serpent [מֶלֶךְ־מִצְרַיִם הַתַּנִּים הַגָּדוֹל, *the king of Egypt is the great sea serpent* (*Ezekiel* 29:3)] (*Anaf Yosef;* see also *Maharsha, Maharal* and *Ben Yehoyada*).

The verse alludes to this with the word יַתִּירָה, whose numerical value (625) is the same as that of כֹּחַ אֲרִי כֹּחַ נָחָשׁ, *power of a lion, power of a serpent* (*Ben Yehoyada*).

7. *Jeremiah* 27:6. This verse is from a prophetic message in which God tells Jeremiah to warn the Jews not to fight Babylonia, for God will deliver them to King Nebuchadnezzar. The message goes on to say that God will even give the Babylonian king dominion over wild beasts. It was in fulfillment of this prophecy that Nebuchadnezzar later mounted wild lions and controlled vicious snakes.

8. Hiring workers violates the injunction against pursuing one's own interests on the Sabbath, which is stated in *Isaiah* (58:13): מִמְּצוֹא חֶפְצְךָ, [refrain] *from pursuing your business* (*Rashi*). It is forbidden to hire workers on the Sabbath even for work to be done after the Sabbath (*Shulchan Aruch, Orach Chaim* 307:2), and even if one does not mention the fee (*Beur Halachah* ibid. ד"ה אסור; cf. *Meiri* and *Chidushei HaRan*).

[According to many authorities the verse מִמְּצוֹא חֶפְצְךָ, *from pursuing your business,* does not represent a Biblical obligation. It is only a Scriptural allusion to a Rabbinic law (אַסְמַכְתָּא, *asmachta*), or else it represents a law that originated with the Prophets (דִּבְרֵי קַבָּלָה, *divrei kabbalah*). See note 18 below.]

9. The Gemara will ask why the Mishnah needs to state this. It is obvious that if the law prohibits a Jew from hiring workers on the Sabbath, he may not ask another Jew to do the hiring; after all, both are subject to the same restrictions (see, however, *Sfas Emes*). Indeed, if one would ask another Jew to do so, one would violate the Torah's commandment (*Leviticus* 19:14): לִפְנֵי עִוֵּר לֹא תִתֵּן מִכְשֹׁל, *You shall not place a stumbling block before the blind* (*Rashi*), which [also] prohibits one to cause the morally blind to stumble and sin (see *Pesachim* 22b; *Rambam* in *Sefer HaMitzvos, Prohibitions* §299, and *Hil. Rotze'ach* 12:14; see also *Shabbos Shel Mi* and *Yad David* [*Basra*]).

10. As we have seen earlier in this tractate, a person may not go farther than 2,000 *amos* from the place he camps or from the edge of the city in which he resides on the Sabbath. This limit is known as תְּחוּם שַׁבָּת, *techum Shabbos* (the Sabbath boundary). The Mishnah teaches here that one may not go to the end of his 2,000-*amah* limit on the Sabbath so that he will be able to reach the people he wishes to hire as soon after the Sabbath as possible, or to reach the orchard from which he wishes to take produce as soon after the Sabbath as possible. The rule is that one may not station himself at the boundary for the purpose of performing an activity after the Sabbath if that activity is prohibited on the Sabbath itself [such as hiring workers or bringing produce] (*Rashi*).

The Mishnah's words עַל הַתְּחוּם, *at the boundary,* imply that one may not go to the boundary itself for a forbidden purpose (i..e. for the sake of performing a prohibited activity after nightfall), but one may go anywhere *within* the boundary for such a purpose. The law, however, is that even preparations within the boundary are prohibited if it is evident to onlookers that one is preparing for a forbidden activity (*Tosafos* printed on 150b; *Tos. HaRosh* here; *Ramban* to 150b ד"ה מת et al.; see *Beur Halachah* to 306:1 ד"ה שמעיין). The reason why the Mishnah specifies the boundary is that the very fact one is stationed there demonstrates one's forbidden intent to onlookers (*Maggid Mishneh* to *Hil. Shabbos* 24:2; *Shulchan Aruch, Orach Chaim* 307:9; *Mishnah Berurah* ibid. §40; *Meromei Sadeh;* cf. *Magen Avraham* ibid. §13 and *Sfas Emes;* see also *Shaar HaTziyun* ibid. §45).

[לוֹ is deleted from the text, in accordance with the version found in the text of Mishnayos.]

11. He may await nightfall at the boundary in order to reach his field soon after the Sabbath to guard its produce. Since the act of guarding produce is permitted even on the Sabbath itself (if it is within the boundary), one may await nightfall at the boundary for that purpose (*Rashi;* cf. *Chidushei HaRan*).

[It is true that he is awaiting nightfall in order to travel beyond the Sabbath boundary, which is forbidden on the Sabbath itself. This is nevertheless allowed, provided the activity for which he is traveling is permissible (see 150b note 15 for the explanation).]

מדוד והבא ואיכא דאמרי שאמרה מאד מאד הביא בלא מדה א) ורבו יתירה הוספת לי אמר רב יהודה אמר רב ירמיה בר אבא מלמד שרכב על ארי זכר וקשר תנין בראשו לקיים מה שנא' ב) וגם את חית השדה נתתי לו לעבדו:

מתני' א לא ישכור אדם פועלים בשבת ולא יאמר אדם לחבירו לשכור לו פועלים ב אין מחשיכין על התחום לשכור לו פועלים ולהביא פירות ג אבל מחשיך הוא לשמור ומביא פירות בידו כלל אמר אבא שאול כל שאני זכאי באמירתו רשאי אני להחשיך עליו:

גמ' (פשיטא) מ"ש הוא ומ"ש חבירו אמר רב פפא ס) חבר נכרי מתקיף לה רב אשי ג) ד אמירה לנכרי שבות אלא אמר רב אשי אפילו תימא חבירו ישראל הא קמ"ל לא יאמר אדם לחבירו שכור לי פועלים ה אבל אומר אדם לחבירו הנראה שתעמוד עמי לערב ומתני' מני כרבי יהושע בן קרחה היא דתניא ג) לא יאמר אדם לחבירו הנראה שתעמוד עמי לערב רבי יהושע בן קרחה אומר אומר אדם לחבירו הנראה שתעמוד עמי לערב אמר רבה בר בר חנה אמר רבי יוחנן הלכה כרבי יהושע בן קרחה ואמר רבה בר בר חנה אמר רבי יוחנן מ"ט דרבי יהושע בן קרחה דכתיב ג) ממצוא חפצך ודבר דבר ז) דיבור אסור הרהור מותר רמי ליה רב אחא בר רב הונא לרבא מי אמר ר' יוחנן דיבור אסור הרהור מותר ח) אלמא הרהור לאו כדיבור דמי ו) והאמר רבה בר בר חנה אמר רבי יוחנן בכל מקום מותר להרהר חוץ מבית המרחץ ומבית הכסא שאני התם דבעינן ד) והיה מחניך קדוש וליכא הכא נמי כתיב ה) ולא יראה בך ערות דבר ההוא מיבעי ליה לכדרב יהודה י) דאמר רב יהודה ו עכו"ם ערום אסור לקרות קרית שמע כנגדו מאי איריא עכו"ם אפי' ישראל נמי לא מיבעיא קאמר לא מיבעיא ישראל דאסור אבל עכו"ם כיון דכתיב ביה ה) אשר בשר חמורים בשרם אימא שפיר דמי קמ"ל ואימא הכי נמי אמר קרא ו) וערות אביהם לא ראו ודיבור מי אסיר ט) והא רב חסדא ורב המנונא דאמרי תרוייהו ז חשבונות של מצוה מותר לחשבן בשבת וא"ר אלעזר ח פוסקים צדקה לעניים בשבת וא"ר יעקב בר אידי אמר רבי יוחנן מפקחין פיקוח נפש ופיקוח רבים בשבת והולכין לבתי כנסיות לפקח על עסקי רבים בשבת ט וא"ר שמואל בר נחמני א"ר י) יוחנן הולכין לטרטיאות ולקרקסאות ולבסילקאות לפקח על עסקי רבים בשבת ותנא דבי מנשה כ) משדכין על התינוקות ליארס בשבת ועל התינוק ללמדו ספר וללמדו אומנות ל) אמר קרא ג) ממצוא חפצך ודבר דבר י) חפציך אסורים חפצי שמים מותרין א"ר יהודה אמר שמואל חשבונות של [נ) מלך] ושל מה בכך מותר לחשבן בשבת תנ"ה מ) חשבונות שעברו ושעתידין להיות אסור לחשבן של ס) מלך ושל

רש"י

מדוד. מעות ודינרי זהב והבא: ורבו יתירה הוספת לי. לאחר שהיה ז' שנים בהמה וחזר למלכותו היה משתבח כן ומהו התוספת שקשר תנין גדול נחש גדול בראשו של ארי כמין אפסר: **מתני' לא ישכור אדם פועלים.** דכתיב (ישעיה נח) ממצוא חפצך: **ולא יאמר לחבירו כו'.** בגמרא פריך פשיטא כיון דהוא אסור חבירו נמי אסור דהא ישראל הוא והשולחו עובר משום לפני עור לא תתן מכשול: **אין מחשיכין על התחום.** לקרב עצמו בשבת עד סוף התחום ולהחשיך שם שיהא קרוב למקום הפועלים או לפרדס להביא פירות דכל דבר שאסור לעשותו בשבת אסור להחשיך עליו: **אבל מחשיך הוא.** להיות קרוב לצאת לשמור פירותיו וזה דבר המותר בשבת לשמור פירותיו אם היו בתוך תחומו: **ומביא פירות בידו.** הואיל ועיקר מחשבתו לא היה לכך: **כלל אמר אבא שאול.** נותן היה כלל בדבר זה להוסיף דברים אחרים כיוצא בו ולקמיה מפרש לאתויי מאי: **כל שאני זכאי באמירתו.** שאני רשאי לאומרו לחבירו או לנכרי בשבת לעשות למוצאי שבת רשאי אני להחשיך עליו: **גמ' מאי שנא כו'.** ופשיטא דכיון דאמר לא ישכור ה"ה לא יאמר לחבירו דהא ישראל הוא כמותו ולא מצי לאוגריניהו: **אמירה לנכרי שבות.** וככר סתמה רבי למתני' פ) נכרי שבא לכבות אין אומרים לו כבה: **הא קמ"ל.** משנה יתירה בהדיא הוא דלא לימא ליה אבל סתמא שרי ליה למימר: **הנראה.** עכשיו נראה אם תעמוד עמי לערב אם תבא אלי לכשתחשך ושניהן יודעין שעל מנת לשוכרו לפעולתו הוא מזהירו וכיון דלא מפרש בהדיא שרי כדמפרש טעמא לקמן דבור אסור הרהור מותר: **מותר להרהר.** בדברי תורה: **והיה מחניך קדוש.** ולא כתיב ביה דבר אלא מקום חנייתך תהא בקדושה וטעמא משום דישראל מהרהרין תמיד בדברי תורה: **ערות דבר.** אלמא לא אסיר ליה אלא בשעת דבור: **ההיא כדרב יהודה.** כלומר לעולם והיה מחניך קדוש משום הרהור תורה ואפי' אין דבור ולא יראה בך ערות דבר במילתא אחריתי מיירי דלאסור בשעת הדבור ולא בשעת הרהור כגון להסתכל בערוה: **עכו"ם ערום.** כ"ש ישראל כדמפרש ואזיל: **אימא שפיר דמי.** דכבהמה בעלמא הוא: **וערות אביהם.** אלמא ערוה היא בבן נח: **ודבור מי אסור והא אמר רב חסדא כו'.** וכל הני דבור הוא: **פקוח נפש.** בדבר שיש בו סכנה פקוח דיקומבימונ"ט: **ופקוח דרבים.** כגון לרשות: **טרטייאות וקרקסאות ובסילקאות.** מיני פלטין הן שאם נאספו לבית הוועד: **ללמדו אומנות.** דהא נמי מצוה היא דכל שאינו מלמדו אומנות מלמדו לסטות ומצוה ילפינן מקרא בקדושין בהאשה ניקנית (ד' ל:): **של מלך.** של עלה שאינו שלו ואין צריך בכך כגון הרוצה לבנות בית כך וכך צריך להוציא בו ול"נ כמו מה לך מה לך ולחשבונות הללו הרי אין צורך בהן לא לך ולא לאחר כגון ההיא דפריסית:

ושל

תוספות

מה לי הוא ומה לי חבירו. ואם תאמר וניתא דחבירו היינו דאמר ליה שכור לי פועלים למחר וי"ל דא"כ מאי איריא חבירו אפי' הוא נמי לא מצי למימר אשכור פועלים למחר דעד כאן לא קאמר רב יהודה אמר שמואל מותר לאדם לומר לחבירו לכרך פלוני אני הולך למחר אלא משום דשאם יש בורגנין הולך הא לאו הכי לא:

ורבי יהושע בן קרחה היא. יש מפרש דר"ע קרוי קרחה שהיה קרח כדתניא בפרק בתרא דבכורות (דף נח. ושם) אמר בן עזאי כל חכמי ישראל דומין לפני כקליפת השום חוץ מן הקרח הזה ואומר שזה היה ר"ע והיה לו בן ששמו יהושע כדאמר בפרק קמא דשבועות ע) א"ל ר' יהושע בנו של ר"ע לר"ע ואין נראה לר"ת דמה שקראו בן עזאי לר"ע קרח בבדיחותא בעלמא אין לנו לקרותו כן כל שעה דלשון גנות הוא שנא' עלה קרח עלה קרח (מלכים ב ב) ואמרינן נמי לקמן (דף קנג.) אמר ליה ההוא צדוקי לר' יהושע בן קרחה מהכא לקרחינאה כמה הוי הרי שהיה מגנה אותו על שהיה קרח ועוד אמרי' במגילה פרק בתרא (דף כח.) שאל רבי את רבי יהושע בן קרחה במה הארכת ימים כו' א"ל רבי ברכני א"ל יהי רצון שתגיע לחצי ימי ואי ר' יהושע בן קרחה בנו של ר"ע והא קיימא לן פ) דלא נשא ר"ע בת כלבא שבוע עד שקיבל עליו לעסוק בתורה ואז היה בן מ' דתניא בסוף ספרי מ' שנה שימש ת"ח מ' שנה פירנס את ישראל וכל ימיו ק"כ שנים ואמרי' בקידושין פרק בתרא (דף עב.) עד שלא מת ר"ע נולד רבי ואפילו נולד ר' יהושע בשנה ראשונה שנשאה לא נשאר כי אם פ' שנים מר"ע ורבי יהושע בשעה שבירך את רבי היה בן ק"מ שנים לכל הפחות שבפחות מע' שנה לא היה מברכו ואז היה רבי לכל הפחות בן ס' וא"כ לא היה מברכו רק מי' שנים ועוד נראה שלא נשאה עד שעסק בי רב תרי סרי ותרי סרי שנין נמצא כשהיה רבי יהושע בן קרחה בן ק"מ היה רבי יותר מחצי ימיו לכך נראה לר"ת דלא ר"ע היה אלא איניש אחרינא היה ששמו קרחה וקרחה הוא שם אדם כמו קרח ונולד הרבה קודם ר' יהושע בנו של ר"ע: **מ"ר: אומר אדם לחבירו הנראה שתעמוד עמי לערב.** י"א דדווקא לחבירו אבל לנכרי אסור לפי שהוא (א) [עושה] לדעת אותה [אמירה] ואינו נראה דהא שרינן ליה הכא משו' דדבור אסור והרהור מותר [א"כ] ל"ש נכרי ל"ש ישראל. מ"ר: **ודיבור מי אסור.** פי' מן התורה דהא מדשרינן דיבור של מצוה מכלל דמדאורייתא שרי: **ואמר ר"א פוסקין צדקה לעניים בשבת.** וא"ת מה צריך לאתויי (ב) הא ה"ל לאתויי מילתייהו דבית הלל [כפי"ז] (בתוספתא) דתני אין פוסקים לדקה אפי' להשיא יתום ויתומה ואין משדכין על התינוקות ליארס בו דברי בית שמאי ובית הלל מתירין וי"ל דניחא ליה לאתויי מילתא דרבי אלעזר דמהתם לא הוה שמעינן פסיקת לדקה לעניים דהא לא שרי בית הלל אלא להשיא יתום ויתומה:

ואין

רבינו חננאל

נמשכה ערלתו וכו': [מתני'] **לא ישכור** פועלים בשבת ולא יאמר לחבירו שכור לי פועלים: גמ' ואקשינן עלה מ"ש הוא ומ"ש חבירו. ובא רב פפא לאוקמיה למתני' בחבירו נכרי. רב אשי אמר אפילו תימא בחבירו ישראל הא קמ"ל דלשכור פועלים הוא דלא יאמר לו אבל אומר לו הנראה שתעמוד עמי לערב כלומר אסור שיאמר לו לערב לך לשכור לי פועלים או כיוצא בו. אבל אם יאמר לו הא נראה שתעמוד עמי לערב ובדעתו שיאמר לו לערב לך לשכור לי פועלים או עשה לי מלאכה כך וכך מותר כר' יהושע בן קרחה. ואמר ר' יוחנן הלכתא כר' יהושע בן קרחה ודייק ר' יוחנן טעמיה דר' יהושע בן קרחה דיבור בפירוש אסור אבל הרהור מותר דכתיב ממצוא חפצך ודבר דבר. ואקשינן עליה והא הוא דאמר בכל מקום מותר להרהר חוץ ממרחץ ובית הכסא כו' ואמאי לא אמרינן הכא נמי הרהור מותר. ומפרקינן האי קרא מיבעי ליה לאסור אפילו ערותו של נכרי דאשכחנן קרא דאמר וערות אביהם לא ראו. ואקשי' תוב ודבור מי אסור והביאו ה' שמועות אחת שאפילו דבור אמ' מותר בשבת. ואלו הן חשבונות ופוסקין צדקה לעניים ומפקחין פיקוח רבים. והולכין לבתי כנסיות ולבתי מדרשות לפקח על עסקי רבים והולכין לבתי טאטראות ולבתי קרקסאות לפקח על עסקי רבים. ותנא משדכין על התינוקות ליארס. ועל התינוק ללמדו ספר וללמדו אומנות. ומפרקי' אלא אמר קרא ממצוא חפצך ודבר דבר חפצך אסורין כדבור חפצי שמים מותרין. ואלו כולן חפצי שמים הן: חשבונות של מלך. פירוש מילך אורחים ובא הלך לאיש העשיר כלומר מותר לאדם לחשב אורחים הקרואים להסב אצלו בסעודה וכדתנן מונה אדם את אורחיו ואת פרפרותיו פי' חשבונות של מה בכך כמו שיחשב אדם חשבון כגון חיילות המלך כך וכך אלף וכיוצא בו אומ' לו מה בכך. כלומר מה הנאה יש לך ומה צורך לך בזה כגון אלו מותר בשבת. וזה שאומרים מחשבין

חשבונות

מסורת הש"ס

א) [עי' תוס' לקמן ע"ב ד"ה ואין], ב) [עירובין מו: גיטין סו: ב"מ ס"ב], ג) ע"ג ז. [תוספ' פי"ח], ד) לעיל קיג:, ה) [ברכות כ:], ו) שם כד: לעיל מ: קידושין קב., ז) ברכות כה: זבחים קב., ח) כתובות ה., ט) [נ"ל יונתן], י) ג' רש"ל דאמר, כ) לעיל קיג., ל) מילף פי' אורחי' כדכתי' ויבא הלך כלומר מותר לאדם לחשב אורחים הקרואים. ערוך ערך הלך, מ) [תוספ' פי"ח], נ) [נ"ל מלך], ס) [דף ו:], ע) [לעיל קכג.], פ) כתובות סג., צ) [וע"ע תוס' ב"ב קיג: ד"ה ותמנו ותוס' פסחים קיב: ד"ה לוה].

הגהות הב"ח

(א) תוס' ד"ה אומר וכו' לפי שהוא עושה לדעת אותה מלאכה ואינו: (ב) ד"ה ואמר רבי אלעזר וכו' וא"ת מה צריך לאתויי מילתא דרבי אלעזר ה"ל לאתויי:

גליון הש"ס

גמ' חבר נכרי. עי' סוכה דף נו ע"א תוס' ד"ה הנוקט. ועי' מג"א סימן שז ס"ק ג:

ליקוטי רש"י

ורבו יתירה הוספת לי. וגדולה יתירה מן הראשונה נתוספה לי אמרו רבותינו שרכב על ארי וקשר תנין בראשו [דניאל ד, לג]. אמירה לנכרי שבות. רבנן גזור על אמירה לנכרי משום שבות [לעיל קכא.]. על השבת לא נצטוו בני נח ומה שאסור לישראל לומר לעובד כוכבים עשה לי כך זהו משום ממצוא חפצך ודבר דבר [ישעיה נח] דבור אסור [ע"ז טו.]. לא יאמר אדם לחבירו הנראה. עתה נראה לשון הכא נכון לו לא יאמר לו השתא הנראה אם תעמוד עמי לערב לעשות במלאכתי לערב [שם ב:]. רבי יהושע בן קרחה. הוא רבי יהושע בן קרחה שר' עקיבא קרח היה כדאמרי' בבכורות (נח.) חוץ מן הקרח הזה [שבועות ו.] והא דגרסינן בכולה הש"ס רבי יהושע בן קרחה שהיה בנו של ר"ע דגרסינן התם (שבועות ו.) אמר לו ר' יהושע בנו של ר"ע כאן [בכורות נח. ועי' תוס' כאן ושם]. ודבר דבר. שלא יהא דבורך של חול כגון מקח וממכר וחשבונות [ע"ש בתוס']. הרהור מותר. להרהר בלבו כך וכך יעשה על שדה זו [לעיל קיג:]. ולא יראה בך. [דברים כג, טו]. אשר בשר חמורים. אבר משמש [יחזקאל כג, כ]. פקוח. מוציאין לאור [כתובות ה.]. פיקוח. דשקולכרגו"ש בלע"ז לשון דבר שצריך לו לנפש כגון להעביר סכנת מות [יומא פד:]. טרטיאות. פלטי מלכים ושלטונים [כתובות שם]. ולבסילקאות. בית גבוה שעל עליה [יומא כה.] ... ללמדו אומנות. מצוה הוא דכתיב (קהלת ט) ראה חיים עם אשה אשר אהבת למוד אומנות שתחיה הימנו עם התורה ... שאביו חייב ללמדו אומנות [כתובות שם]. חיותיה הוא ואף זו מצוה על האב ללמדו דילפינן לה ... (ל:) דכתיב ראה חיים עם אשה אשר אהבת הקיש אומנות שהוא חיותו לאשה כשם שאביו ... וקחו לבניכם נשים כך חייב ללמדו אומנות [מכות ח:]. חפציך אסורים. כי ההוא דאמרינן ... אדם לסוף שדהו בשבת לידע מה היא צריכה [אחר השבת]. חפצי שמים מותרין. כגון פוסקים צדקה ומשדכין על התינוקות ליארס [לעיל שם.].

עין משפט נר מצוה

כב א מיי' פכ"ד מהל' שבת הלכה יב סמג לאוין סה טוש"ע או"ח סימן שו סעיף ג:

כג ב ג מיי' פכ"ד שם הלכה ג סמג שם טוש"ע או"ח סימן שו סעיף ח וסי' שו סעיף ה:

כד ד מיי' שם הל"א סמג שם:

כה ה מיי' שם הל"ד וסמג שם טוש"ע או"ח סימן שו סעיף ז:

כו ו מיי' פ"ג מהלכות ק"ש הלכה טז סמג עשין יח טוש"ע או"ח סימן עה סעיף ד:

כז ז ח ט י מיי' פכ"ד מהלכות שבת הל"ה סמג לאוין סה טוש"ע או"ח סימן שו סעיף ו:

כח כ מיי' פכ"ג מהל' שבת הל"יח סמג שם טוש"ע או"ח סימן שז סעיף ז:

תורה אור השלם

א) בֵּהּ זִמְנָא מַנְדְּעִי יְתוּב עֲלַי וְלִיקַר מַלְכוּתִי הַדְרִי וְזִוִי יְתוּב עֲלַי וְלִי הַדָּבְרַי וְרַבְרְבָנַי יְבַעוֹן וְעַל מַלְכוּתִי הָתְקְנַת וּרְבוּ יַתִּירָה הוּסְפַת לִי: [דניאל ד, לג]

ב) וְעַתָּה אָנֹכִי נָתַתִּי אֶת כָּל הָאֲרָצוֹת הָאֵלֶּה בְּיַד נְבוּכַדְנֶאצַּר מֶלֶךְ בָּבֶל עַבְדִּי וְגַם אֶת חַיַּת הַשָּׂדֶה נָתַתִּי לוֹ לְעָבְדוֹ: [ירמיה כז, ו]

ג) אִם תָּשִׁיב מִשַּׁבָּת רַגְלֶךָ עֲשׂוֹת חֲפָצֶךָ בְּיוֹם קָדְשִׁי וְקָרָאתָ לַשַּׁבָּת עֹנֶג לִקְדוֹשׁ יְיָ מְכֻבָּד וְכִבַּדְתּוֹ מֵעֲשׂוֹת דְּרָכֶיךָ מִמְּצוֹא חֶפְצְךָ וְדַבֵּר דָּבָר: [ישעיה נח, יג]

ד) כִּי יְיָ אֱלֹהֶיךָ מִתְהַלֵּךְ בְּקֶרֶב מַחֲנֶךָ לְהַצִּילְךָ וְלָתֵת אֹיְבֶיךָ לְפָנֶיךָ וְהָיָה מַחֲנֶיךָ קָדוֹשׁ וְלֹא יִרְאֶה בְךָ עֶרְוַת דָּבָר וְשָׁב מֵאַחֲרֶיךָ: [דברים כג, טו]

ה) וַתַּעְגְּבָה עַל פִּלַגְשֵׁיהֶם אֲשֶׁר בְּשַׂר חֲמוֹרִים בְּשָׂרָם וְזִרְמַת סוּסִים זִרְמָתָם: [יחזקאל כג, כ]

ו) וַיִּקַּח שֵׁם וָיֶפֶת אֶת הַשִּׂמְלָה וַיָּשִׂימוּ עַל שְׁכֶם שְׁנֵיהֶם וַיֵּלְכוּ אֲחֹרַנִּית וַיְכַסּוּ אֵת עֶרְוַת אֲבִיהֶם וּפְנֵיהֶם אֲחֹרַנִּית וְעֶרְוַת אֲבִיהֶם לֹא רָאוּ: [בראשית ט, כג]

HIS HAND.[12] כְּלָל אָמַר אַבָּא שָׁאוּל — ABBA SHAUL STATED A GENERAL RULE:[13] כֹּל שֶׁאֲנִי זַכַּאי בַּאֲמִירָתוֹ רַשַּׁאי אֲנִי לְהַחְשִׁיךְ עָלָיו — FOR WHATEVER I AM PERMITTED TO INSTRUCT,[14] I AM PERMITTED TO AWAIT NIGHTFALL.[15]

Gemara After ruling that one may not hire workers on the Sabbath, the Mishnah added that one may not ask his friend to do so. The Gemara asks why it was necessary to add this last point:

(פְּשִׁיטָא) — This is **obvious!** מַאי שְׁנָא הוּא וּמַאי שְׁנָא חֲבֵירוֹ — **What is the difference between him and his friend?** If he is prohibited from hiring workers, then so is his friend![16]

The Gemara answers:

אָמַר רַב פָּפָּא — **Rav Pappa said:** חָבֵר נָכְרִי — The Mishnah means **a friend** who is **a gentile.** Since a gentile is not bound by the laws of the Sabbath, one might have thought that a Jew may ask a gentile to hire workers for him on the Sabbath. It is therefore necessary for the Mishnah to state that this is prohibited.

This explanation is challenged:

מַתְקִיף לָהּ רַב אַשִׁי — **Rav Ashi objected to it:** אֲמִירָה לְנָכְרִי שְׁבוּת — But another Mishnah has already taught that **asking a gentile** to do something prohibited to Jews on the Sabbath **is** forbidden by **Rabbinic decree.**[17] Our Mishnah is not needed to teach this.[18] — ? —

In view of this difficulty, Rav Ashi offers a different explanation: אֶלָּא אָמַר רַב אַשִׁי — **Rather, said Rav Ashi,** אֲפִילּוּ תֵּימָא חֲבֵירוֹ יִשְׂרָאֵל — **you may even say that** when the Mishnah refers **to his friend,** it means **a Jew.** However, its purpose is not to teach that one is forbidden to ask a Jew to hire workers on the Sabbath; הָא קָא מַשְׁמַע לַן — rather, **this is what [the Mishnah] is teaching us:**[19] לֹא יֹאמַר אָדָם לַחֲבֵירוֹ שְׂכוֹר לִי פּוֹעֲלִים — **One may not say to his friend** on the Sabbath, **"Hire workers for me."** אֲבָל אוֹמֵר אָדָם לַחֲבֵירוֹ הֲנִרְאֶה שֶׁתַּעֲמוֹד עִמִּי לָעֶרֶב — **But one may say to his friend, "Shall we see whether you will join me in the evening** (i.e. after the Sabbath)?"[20] וּמַתְנִיתִין מַנִּי — **And,** when **our Mishnah** is interpreted in this manner, **whose** view does it follow? כְּרַבִּי יְהוֹשֻׁעַ בֶּן קָרְחָה — **It follows** the view of **R' Yehoshua ben Korchah,** דְּתַנְיָא — **for it was taught in a Baraisa:** לֹא יֹאמַר אָדָם לַחֲבֵירוֹ הֲנִרְאֶה שֶׁתַּעֲמוֹד עִמִּי לָעֶרֶב — ONE MAY NOT SAY TO HIS FRIEND, "SHALL WE SEE WHETHER YOU WILL JOIN ME IN THE EVENING?" רַבִּי יְהוֹשֻׁעַ בֶּן קָרְחָה אוֹמֵר — But R' YEHOSHUA BEN KORCHAH SAYS: אוֹמֵר אָדָם לַחֲבֵירוֹ הֲנִרְאֶה שֶׁתַּעֲמוֹד עִמִּי לָעֶרֶב — A PERSON *MAY* SAY TO HIS FRIEND, "SHALL WE SEE WHETHER YOU WILL JOIN ME IN THE EVENING?" אָמַר רַבָּה בַּר בַּר חָנָה אָמַר רַבִּי יוֹחָנָן — **Rabbah bar bar Chanah said in the name of R' Yochanan:** הֲלָכָה כְּרַבִּי יְהוֹשֻׁעַ בֶּן קָרְחָה — **The law is in accordance with R' Yehoshua ben Korchah.** וְאָמַר רַבָּה בַּר בַּר חָנָה אָמַר רַבִּי יוֹחָנָן — **And Rabbah bar bar Chanah** also **said in the name of R' Yochanan:** מַאי טַעְמָא דְּרַבִּי יְהוֹשֻׁעַ בֶּן קָרְחָה — **What is the reason of R' Yehoshua ben Korchah?** דִּכְתִיב "מִמְּצוֹא חֶפְצְךָ וְדַבֵּר דָּבָר" — It is based on **that which is written:**[21] [Refrain] *from pursuing your business and speaking words.* דִּיבּוּר אָסוּר הִרְהוּר מוּתָּר — By specifying *speaking words,* the verse implies that only **speech is forbidden; thought is permitted.**[22] From here we learn that the prohibition against using speech in

NOTES

12. One who waited at the Sabbath boundary to be able to guard his produce after nightfall may, upon returning home, bring with him some produce (which is presently attached to the ground — see 150b and *Mishnah Berurah* 307:38). This is permitted because his intent was primarily to guard his produce, not to bring it (*Rashi;* see *Sfas Emes*). [The Mishnah says "in his hand" presumably because this is the typical case, in view of the fact that the laws of הוֹצָאָה, *transferring/transporting,* prohibit him from taking a vessel with him.]

13. Abba Shaul formulated a general rule to include cases similar to those above. The Gemara (151a) will identify these additional cases (*Rashi*).

14. I.e. any activity I am permitted to tell someone, Jew or gentile, on the Sabbath to perform after the Sabbath (*Rashi;* see following note).

15. There is no question that if one is allowed to ask another to perform a certain activity *during* the Sabbath (i.e. any activity permitted on the Sabbath itself, such as guarding produce), then one is surely allowed to await nightfall at the boundary to do that activity *after* the Sabbath. Abba Shaul's point is that one may await nightfall at the boundary even for things that one may ask another to do only after the Sabbath. Specific examples are recorded in the following Mishnah (see *Rashi* to 151a ד"ה לעולם and note 4 there). [It is for this reason that *Rashi* specifies "*after* the Sabbath," as cited in the previous note.] According to the Tanna Kamma, though, one is *not* allowed to await nightfall at the boundary in preparation for activities permitted only after the Sabbath (see 151a ibid.; cf. *Meiri* here, who maintains that there is no dispute between the Tanna Kamma and Abba Shaul).

16. See note 9.

17. The Mishnah on 121a states: *One may not say to [a gentile], "Extinguish* [a flame]." Rebbi did not attribute this ruling to a specific Tanna [so it is clearly the accepted law] (*Rashi*). The rule is that one may not ask a gentile on the Sabbath to perform any act that a Jew is forbidden [even under Rabbinic law] to do on the Sabbath (*Ritva MHK* ed.; see *Chidushei HaRan* and *Meiri*).

This prohibition of אֲמִירָה לְנָכְרִי, *asking a gentile,* is also based on the verse (*Isaiah* 58:13): מִמְּצוֹא חֶפְצְךָ וְדַבֵּר דָּבָר, *from pursuing your business or speaking words* (*Rashi* to *Avodah Zarah* 15a ד"ה כיון; see 121a).

18. *Rashi;* cf. *Meiri,* who cites another approach.

The following difficulty must be addressed: The Mishnah on 121a deals with the *melachah* of כִּיבּוּי, *extinguishing.* Hence, it proves only that one may not ask a gentile to perform a Biblically forbidden act. Our Mishnah is consequently needed to teach that one not ask a gentile to commit even a Rabbinic transgression, such as hiring workers. One answer given is that the Mishnah on 121a also refers to a Rabbinic transgression, for extinguishing a flame is usually a מְלָאכָה שֶׁאֵינָהּ צְרִיכָה לְגוּפָהּ, *melachah not needed for its defined purpose* (the defined purpose of כִּיבּוּי, *extinguishing,* is making charcoal), and the Mishnah follows R' Shimon's view that such a *melachah* is prohibited only under Rabbinic law (*Meromei Sadeh; Yad David* [*Basra*]; *Shabbos Shel Mi* to 121a; see *Tos. R' Akiva Eiger's* objection to this approach; cf. *Chasam Sofer* and *Sfas Emes,* who answer that hiring workers is a Biblical violation).

It should be noted that the law even forbids one to ask another [Jew or gentile] on the Sabbath to perform a forbidden act, such as hiring workers, *after* the Sabbath (see *Tosafos* ד"ה מה and to 150b ד"ה אבל; see *Chayei Adam, Hil. Shabbos* 62:1; cf. *Tos. Rid*). The Gemara could thus have resolved its difficulty by interpreting our Mishnah as referring to such a case. The Gemara did not give this solution because it is evident from our Mishnah that it refers specifically to hiring workers *during* the Sabbath (see *Tosafos* ד"ה מה for elaboration).

19. Rav Ashi's point is that the ruling of the Mishnah is indeed superfluous. It was added only so that we should make the following inference: The Mishnah presumably refers to one who hires workers in an explicit manner. It thus implies that hiring workers explicitly is forbidden, but doing so by means of a hint is permitted [as the Gemara proceeds to explain] (*Rashi;* cf. *Tos. Rid*).

20. [Translation based on *Rashi;* see *Ran* (on *Rif*) and *Shulchan Aruch, Orach Chaim* 307:7 for another explanation of this phrase.] Both persons realize that one is hiring the other at this time to work for him after the Sabbath. However, since the hirer does not state this explicitly, it is permissible, for as the Gemara states below, it is only speech, and not thought, which is prohibited on the Sabbath (*Rashi*). Since the hirer's words do not actually convey that he wishes to hire the worker, his message is classified as thought (see *Ritva MHK* ed. and *Meiri;* cf. *Chidushei HaRan;* see also *Rama, Orach Chaim* 307:22).

If the hiring is not explicit, it is permitted regardless of whether the hiree is a Jew or a gentile (see *Tosafos;* cf. *Tos. R' Akiva Eiger*).

21. *Isaiah* 58:13.

22. One is allowed to *think* about his business affairs on the Sabbath and Yom Tov. [However, this is not the purpose for which these sacred days are intended (see the story related on 150b, and *Meiri* there).]

מדוד. מעות ודינרי זהב והבא: ורבו יתירה הוספת לי. לאחר שהיה ז' שנים בהמה וחזר למלכותו היה משתבח כן ומהו התוספת שקשר תנין גדול נחש גדול בראשו של ארי כמין אפסר: מתני' לא ישכור אדם פועלים. דכתיב (ישעיה נח) ממצוא חפצך: ולא יאמר לחבירו כו'. בגמרא פריך פשיטא כיון דהוא אסור חבירו נמי אסור דהא ישראל הוא והשולח עובר משום לפני עור לא תתן מכשול: אין מחשיכין על התחום. לקרב עצמו בשבת עד סוף התחום ולהחשיך שם שיהא קרוב למקום הפועלים או לפרדס להביא פירות דכל דבר שאסור לעשותו בשבת אסור להחשיך עליו: אבל מחשיך הוא. להיות קרוב לצאת לשמור פירותיו וזה דבר המותר בשבת לשמור פירותיו אם היו בתוך תחומו: ומביא פירות בידו. הואיל ועיקר מחשבתו לא היה לכך: כלל אמר אבא שאול. נותן היה כלל בדבר זה להוסיף דברים אחרים כיוצא בו ולקמיה מפרש לאתויי מאי: כל שאני זכאי באמירתו. שאני רשאי לאומרו לחבירו או לנכרי בשבת לעשות למוצאי שבת רשאי אני להחשיך עליו: גמ' מאי שנא כו'. ופשיטא דכיון דאמר לא ישכור ה"ה לא יאמר לחבירו דהא ישראל הוא כמותו: אמירה לנכרי שבות. וכבר סתמה רבי למתני' נכרי שבא לכבות אין אומרים לו כבה: הא קמ"ל. משנה יתירה בהדיא הוא דלא לימא ליה אבל סתמא שרי ליה למימר: הנראה. עכשיו נראה אם תעמוד עמי לערב אם תבא אלי לכשתחשך ושניהן יודעין שעל מנת לשוכרו לפעולתו הוא מזהירו וכיון דלא מפרש בהדיא שרי כדמפרש טעמא לקמן דבור אסור הרהור מותר: מותר להרהר. בדברי תורה: והיה מחניך קדוש. ולא כתיב בך יהיה דבר אלא מקום חנייתך תהא בקדושה וטעמא משום דישראל מהרהרין תמיד בדברי תורה: ערות דבר. אלמא לא אסיר ליה אלא בשעת דבור: ההיא כדרב יהודה. כלומר לעולם והיה מחניך קדוש משום הרהור תורה ואפי' אין דבור ולא יראה בך ערות דבר במילתא אחריתי מיירי דאסור בשעת הדבור ולא בשעת הרהור כגון להסתכל בערוה: עכו"ם ערום. כ"ש ישראל כדמפרש ואזיל: אימא שפיר דמי. דכבהמה בעלמא הוא: וערות אביהם. אלמא ערוה היא בבן נח: ודבור מי אסור והא אמר רב חסדא כו'. וכל הני דבור הוא: פקוח נפש. בדבר שיש בו סכנה: ופקוח דרבים. כגון לרשות: טרטיאות וקרקסאות ובסילקאות. מיני פלטין הן ששם נאספו לבית הוועד: ללמדו אומנות. דהא נמי מצוה היא דכל שאינו מלמדו אומנות מלמדו לסטות ומצוה ילפינן מקרא בקדושין בהאשה ניקנית (ד' ל:): של מלך. של עצה שאינו שלו ואין צריך בכך כגון הרוצה לבנות בית כך וכך צריך להוציא בו ולא לך ולא לאחר: ושל

מה לי הוא ומה לי חבירו. ואם תאמר ונימא דחבירו היינו דאמר ליה שכור לי פועלים למחר וי"ל דא"כ מאי איריא חבירו אפי' הוא נמי לא מצי למימר אשכור פועלים למחר דעד כאן לא קאמר רב יהודה אמר שמואל מותר לאדם לומר לחבירו לכרך פלוני אני הולך למחר אלא משום דשאם יש בורגנין הולך הא לאו הכי לא: ורבי יהושע בן קרחה היא. יש מפרש דר"ע קרוי קרחה שהיה קרח כדתניא בפרק בתרא דבכורות (דף נח. ושם) אמר בן עזאי כל חכמי ישראל דומין לפני כקליפת השום חוץ מן הקרח הזה ואומר שזה היה ר"ע והיה לו בן ששמו יהושע כדאמר בפרק קמא דשבועות (ט) א"ל ר' יהושע בנו של ר"ע לר"ע ואין נראה לר"ת דמה שקראו בן עזאי לר"ע קרח בבדיחותא בעלמא אין לנו לקרותו כן כל שעה דלשון גנות הוא שנא' עלה קרח עלה קרח (מלכים ב ב) ואמרינן נמי לקמן (דף קנב.) אמר ליה ההוא לדוקי לר' יהושע בן קרחה מהכא לקרחינאה כמה הוי הרי שהיה מגנה אותו על שהיה קרח ועוד אמרי' במגילה פרק בתרא (דף כח.) שאל רבי את רבי יהושע בן קרחה במה הארכת ימים כו' א"ל רבי ברכני א"ל יהי רצון שתגיע לחצי ימי ואי ר' יהושע בן קרחה בנו של ר"ע והא קיימא לן (פ) דלא נשא ר"ע בת כלבא שבוע עד שקיבל עליו לעסוק בתורה ואז היה בן מ' דתניא בסוף ספרי מ' שנה שימש ת"ח מ' שנה פירנס את ישראל וכל ימיו ק"כ שנים ואמרי' בקידושין פרק בתרא (דף עב.) עד שלא מת ר"ע נולד רבי ואפילו נולד ר' יהושע בשנה ראשונה שנשאה לא נשאר כי אם פ' שנים מר"ע ורבי יהושע בשעה שבירך את רבי היה בן ק"מ שנים לכל הפחות שבפחות מע' שנה לא היה מברכו ואז היה רבי לכל הפחות בן ס' וא"כ לא היה מברכו רק מי' שנים ועוד נראה שלא נשאה עד שעסק בי רב תרי סרי ותרי סרי שנין נמצא כשהיה רבי יהושע בן קרחה בן ק"מ היה רבי יותר מחצי ימיו לכך נראה לר"ת דלא ר"ע היה אלא איניש אחרינא היה ששמו קרחה וקרחה הוא שם אדם כמו קרח ונולד הרבה קודם ר' יהושע בנו של ר"ע(ל). מ"ר: אומר אדם לחבירו הנראה שתעמוד עמי לערב. י"א דדווקא לחבירו אבל לנכרי אסור לפי שהוא (א) [עושה] לדעת אותה [אמירה] ואינו נראה דהא שרינן ליה הכא משו' דדבור אסור והרהור מותר [א"כ] ל"ש נכרי ל"ש ישראל. מ"ר: ודיבור מי אסור. פי' מן התורה דהא מדשרינן דיבור של מצוה מכלל דמדאורייתא שרי: ואמר ר"א פוסקין צדקה לעניים בשבת. וא"ת מה צריך לאתויי (ב) הא ה"ל לאתויי מילתייהו דבית הלל [בפי"ז] (בתוספתא) דתני אין פוסקים לדקה אפי' להשיא יתום ויתומה ואין משדכין על התינוקות ליארס בו דברי בית שמאי ובית הלל מתירין וי"ל דניחא ליה לאתויי מילתא דרבי אלעזר דמהתם לא הוה שמעינן פסיקת לדקה לעניים דהא לא שרי בית הלל אלא להשיא יתום ויתומה:

ואין

מדוד והבא ואיכא דאמרי שאמרה מאד מאד הביא בלא מדה (א) ורבו יתירה הוספת לי אמר רב יהודה אמר רב ירמיה בר אבא מלמד שרכב על ארי זכר וקשר תנין בראשו לקיים מה שנא' (ב) וגם את חית השדה נתתי לו לעבדו:

מתני' (א) לא ישכור אדם פועלים בשבת ולא יאמר אדם לחבירו לשכור לו פועלים (א) (ב) אין מחשיכין על התחום לשכור לו פועלים ולהביא פירות (ג) אבל מחשיך הוא לשמור ומביא פירות בידו כלל אמר אבא שאול כל שאני זכאי באמירתו רשאי אני להחשיך עליו:

גמ' (פשיטא) מ"ש הוא ומ"ש חבירו אמר רב פפא (ה) חבר נכרי מתקיף לה רב אשי (ג) (ד) אמירה לנכרי שבות אלא אמר רב אשי אפילו תימא חבירו ישראל הא קמ"ל לא יאמר אדם לחבירו שכור לי פועלים (ה) אבל אומר אדם לחבירו הנראה שתעמוד עמי לערב ומתני' מני כרבי יהושע בן קרחה דתניא (ג) לא יאמר אדם לחבירו הנראה שתעמוד עמי לערב רבי יהושע בן קרחה אומר אומר אדם לחבירו הנראה שתעמוד עמי לערב אמר רבה בר בר חנה אמר רבי יוחנן הלכה כרבי יהושע בן קרחה ואמר רבה בר בר חנה אמר רבי יוחנן מ"ט דרבי יהושע בן קרחה דכתיב (ג) ממצוא חפצך ודבר דבר (ד) דיבור אסור הרהור מותר רמי ליה רב אחא בר רב הונא לרבא מי אמר ר' יוחנן דיבור אסור הרהור מותר (ה) אלמא הרהור לאו כדיבור דמי (ו) והאמר רבה בר בר חנה אמר רבי יוחנן בכל מקום מותר להרהר חוץ מבית המרחץ ומבית הכסא שאני התם דבעינן (ד) והיה מחניך קדוש וליכא הכא נמי כתיב (ד) ולא יראה בך ערות דבר ההוא מיבעי ליה לכדרב יהודה (ז) דאמר רב יהודה (ו) עכו"ם ערום אסור לקרות קרית שמע כנגדו מאי איריא עכו"ם אפי' ישראל נמי לא מיבעיא קאמר לא מיבעיא ישראל דאסור אבל עכו"ם כיון דכתיב ביה (ה) אשר בשר חמורים בשרם אימא שפיר דמי קמ"ל אימא הכי נמי אמר קרא (ו) וערות אביהם לא ראו ודיבור מי אסיר (ח) והא רב חסדא ורב המנונא דאמרי תרוייהו (ז) חשבונות של מצוה מותר לחשבן בשבת וא"ר אלעזר (ח) פוסקים צדקה לעניים בשבת וא"ר יעקב בר אידי אמר רבי יוחנן מפקחין פיקוח נפש ופיקוח רבים בשבת והולכין לבתי כנסיות לפקח על עסקי רבים בשבת (ט) וא"ר שמואל בר נחמני א"ר (ט) יוחנן הולכין לטרטיאות ולקרקסאות ולבסילקאות לפקח על עסקי רבים בשבת ותנא דבי מנשה (י) משדכין על התינוקות ליארס בשבת ועל התינוק ללמדו ספר וללמדו אומנות (י) אמר קרא (ג) ממצוא חפצך ודבר דבר (כ) חפציך אסורים חפצי שמים מותרין א"ר יהודה אמר שמואל חשבונות של [(ל) מלך] ושל מה בכך מותר לחשבן בשבת תנ"ה (מ) (כ) חשבונות שעברו ושעתידין להיו' אסור לחשבן של (נ) מלך ושל

תורה אור השלם

א) בָּה זִמְנָא מַנְדְּעִי יְתוּב עֲלַי וְלִיקַר מַלְכוּתִי הַדְרִי וְזִוִי יְתוּב עֲלַי וְלִי הַדָּבְרַי וְרַבְרְבָנַי יְבַעוֹן וְעַל מַלְכוּתִי הָתְקְנַת וּרְבוּ יַתִּירָה הוּסְפַת לִי: [דניאל ד, לג]

ב) וְעַתָּה אָנֹכִי נָתַתִּי אֶת כָּל הָאֲרָצוֹת הָאֵלֶּה בְּיַד נְבוּכַדְנֶאצַּר מֶלֶךְ בָּבֶל עַבְדִּי וְגַם אֶת חַיַּת הַשָּׂדֶה נָתַתִּי לוֹ לְעָבְדוֹ: [ירמיה כז, ו]

ג) אִם תָּשִׁיב מִשַּׁבָּת רַגְלֶךָ עֲשׂוֹת חֲפָצֶךָ בְּיוֹם קָדְשִׁי וְקָרָאתָ לַשַּׁבָּת עֹנֶג לִקְדוֹשׁ יְיָ מְכֻבָּד וְכִבַּדְתּוֹ מֵעֲשׂוֹת דְּרָכֶיךָ מִמְּצוֹא חֶפְצְךָ וְדַבֵּר דָּבָר: [ישעיה נח, יג]

ד) כִּי יְיָ אֱלֹהֶיךָ מִתְהַלֵּךְ בְּקֶרֶב מַחֲנֶךָ לְהַצִּילְךָ וְלָתֵת אֹיְבֶיךָ לְפָנֶיךָ וְהָיָה מַחֲנֶיךָ קָדוֹשׁ וְלֹא יִרְאֶה בְךָ עֶרְוַת דָּבָר וְשָׁב מֵאַחֲרֶיךָ: [דברים כג, טו]

ה) וַתַּעְגְּבָה עַל פִּלַגְשֵׁיהֶם אֲשֶׁר בְּשַׂר חֲמוֹרִים בְּשָׂרָם וְזִרְמַת סוּסִים זִרְמָתָם: [יחזקאל כג, כ]

ו) וַיִּקַּח שֵׁם וָיֶפֶת אֶת הַשִּׂמְלָה וַיָּשִׂימוּ עַל שְׁכֶם שְׁנֵיהֶם וַיֵּלְכוּ אֲחֹרַנִּית וַיְכַסּוּ אֵת עֶרְוַת אֲבִיהֶם וּפְנֵיהֶם אֲחֹרַנִּית וְעֶרְוַת אֲבִיהֶם לֹא רָאוּ: [בראשית ט, כג]

הגהות הב"ח

גליון הש"ס

ליקוטי רש"י

רבינו חננאל

pursuing one's affairs applies only to explicit statements.[23] Therefore, since the statement of "Shall we see whether you will join me in the evening?" is not explicit, it is permitted.

The preceding exposition, which was made by R' Yochanan, is based on the premise that thought is not automatically treated like speech. The Gemara questions whether this is in fact R' Yochanan's opinion:

רָמֵי לֵיהּ רַב אַחָא בַּר רַב הוּנָא לְרָבָא – **Rav Acha bar Rav Huna pointed out a contradiction to Rava:** מִי אָמַר רַבִּי יוֹחָנָן דִּיבּוּר אָסוּר הִרְהוּר מוּתָּר – **Did R' Yochanan really say** that **speech is forbidden** and **thought is permitted?** אַלְמָא הִרְהוּר לָאו כְּדִיבּוּר דָּמֵי – Such a ruling **implies that thought is not** legally **equivalent to speech.** וְהָאָמַר רַבָּה בַּר בַּר חָנָה אָמַר רַבִּי יוֹחָנָן – **But Rabbah bar bar Chanah said in the name of R' Yochanan:** בְּכָל מָקוֹם מוּתָּר לְהַרְהֵר חוּץ מִבֵּית הַמֶּרְחָץ וּמִבֵּית הַכִּסֵּא – **It is permitted to think** about Torah matters **in every place except a bathhouse and a lavatory.** This statement indicates that R' Yochanan does treat thought as stringently as speech.[24] – ? –

The Gemara answers that in general R' Yochanan does *not* treat thought like speech, and the reason why he prohibits even thought in a bathhouse and lavatory is as follows:

שָׁאנֵי הָתָם – **It is different in that case,** דִּבְעִינַן ,,וְהָיָה מַחֲנֶיךָ קָדוֹשׁ" – **because we require** observance of the commandment: ***Your camp shall be holy,***[25] וְלֵיכָּא – **and such is not** the case when a person thinks thoughts of Torah in a bathhouse or lavatory.

The Gemara objects:

הָכָא נַמִּי כְּתִיב ,,וְלֹא־יִרְאֶה בְךָ עֶרְוַת דָּבָר" – But **here too** (i.e. in that very verse) **it is written: *so that He will not see a shameful thing*** (*davar*) ***among you,*** which implies that *speech* (*davar*) is forbidden in bathhouses and lavatories.[26] – ? –

The Gemara answers by interpreting the second part of the verse as referring not to the law of a bathhouse or lavatory, but to a different situation:

הַהוּא מִיבָּעֵי לֵיהּ לִכְדְרַב יְהוּדָה – **That** part of the verse **is needed to** teach **that which** was stated by **Rav Yehudah,** דְּאָמַר רַב יְהוּדָה – **for Rav Yehudah said:** עוֹבֵד כּוֹכָבִים עָרוֹם אָסוּר לִקְרוֹת קְרִיַּת שְׁמַע כְּנֶגְדּוֹ – **It is forbidden to recite the** Shema[27] **in the presence of a naked idolater.**[28]

The Gemara wonders:

מַאי אִירְיָא עוֹבֵד כּוֹכָבִים – For **what** reason did Rav Yehudah **specify an idolater?** אֲפִילּוּ יִשְׂרָאֵל נַמִּי – This should be prohibited in the case of **a Jew as well!**

The Gemara answers:

לֹא מִיבַּעְיָא קָאָמַר – Rav Yehudah **formulates** his rule according to the principle that **there is no need** to state the more obvious case. לֹא מִיבַּעְיָא יִשְׂרָאֵל דְּאָסוּר – **There is no need** to state **that it is forbidden** to recite the Shema in the presence of a naked **Jew.** אֲבָל עוֹבֵד כּוֹכָבִים – **But** in the case of **an idolater,** כֵּיוָן דִּכְתִיב בֵּיהּ ,,אֲשֶׁר בְּשַׂר־חֲמוֹרִים בְּשָׂרָם" – **since it is written of him:**[29] ***whose flesh is the flesh of donkeys,*** אֵימָא שַׁפִּיר דָּמֵי – **one might say** that **it is all right** to recite the Shema in his presence even though he is naked. קָא מַשְׁמַע לָן – **[Rav Yehudah] therefore teaches us** that this is not true. One may not recite the Shema in the presence of anyone who is unclothed, Jew or idolater.

The Gemara asks:

אֵימָא הָכִי נַמִּי – But **say** that **this is** in fact **the case!** Perhaps, one *may* recite the Shema in the presence of a naked idolater. How does Rav Yehudah know to forbid this? The Gemara gives Rav Yehudah's source: אָמַר קְרָא ,,וְעֶרְוַת אֲבִיהֶם לֹא רָאוּ" – **Scripture states: *They did not see their father's nakedness.***[30]

Our Mishnah, which forbids hiring workers on the Sabbath, evidently holds that the prohibition against pursuing one's affairs applies even to speech,[31] and not only to activities of a more tangible nature. The Gemara questions whether this is so:

וְדִיבּוּר מִי אָסִיר – **But is** mere **speech prohibited** on the Sabbath? וְהָא רַב חִסְדָּא וְרַב הַמְנוּנָא דְּאָמְרֵי תַּרְוַיְיהוּ – **Why, Rav Chisda and**

NOTES

23. See note 20.

24. The Gemara is assuming that in reference to the ban on sacred activities in a bathhouse or lavatory, the Torah mentions only speech [see note 26] (*Chidushei HaRan*). Hence, if R' Yochanan forbids even thought, he evidently regards thought as the legal equivalent of speech.

25. *Deuteronomy* 23:15. This verse does not mention speech [in contrast to the verse: מִמְּצוֹא חֶפְצְךָ וְדַבֵּר דָּבָר, *from pursuing your business and speaking words*]. It requires only that your camp be in a state of holiness, i.e. nothing unclean should be in it. The reason for this requirement is presumably that the Jews in the camp are constantly thinking thoughts of Torah [and it is improper to think such thoughts in the presence of something unclean]. From here R' Yochanan derives that one may not even *think* matters of Torah in a bathhouse or lavatory. Thus, R' Yochanan's reason is not that he equates thought with speech, but that the Torah specifically forbids even thought in such places (*Rashi*).

26. The word דָּבָר (which is in the expression עֶרְוַת דָּבָר, *a shameful thing*) also means *speech.* The Torah thus mentions only *speech* in regard to the prohibition of sacred matters in unclean places (*Rashi*). [Thoughts of Torah should therefore be permitted, unless thought is the legal equivalent of speech.]

27. Or anything else of sanctity, such as prayer, blessings or Torah (see *Rambam, Hil. Krias Shema* 3:4,16).

28. I.e. while looking at his private parts (*Rashi, Chidushei HaRan;* see end of note). [Although Rav Yehudah mentions only an idolater, this is forbidden in the case of a Jew as well, as the Gemara proceeds to explain (*Rashi*).]

The Gemara is answering that when the verse states: וְלֹא־יִרְאֶה בְךָ עֶרְוַת דָּבָר, *so that He will not see a shameful thing among you,* which indicates a ban on speech (see note 26), it refers to one who is in the presence of an unclothed person. It is specifically in such a situation that speech is banned, while thought is permitted. Regarding other situations (such as a bathhouse or lavatory), however, the Torah does not specify speech. On the contrary, the first part of the verse, וְהָיָה מַחֲנֶיךָ קָדוֹשׁ, *your camp shall be holy,* indicates that even thought is prohibited (*Rashi*).

[*Rashi* implies that the ban against speaking sacred words in the presence of a naked man applies only while one is actually looking at his private parts. However, from *Shulchan Aruch* (*Orach Chaim* 75:4; see *Mishnah Berurah* §19) it seems that the very presence of his private parts in one's field of vision suffices to prohibit prayer or study even if one is not looking directly at them.]

29. *Ezekiel* 23:20. By comparing the flesh of an idolater to that of a donkey, the verse implies that an idolater's nakedness is treated with relative leniency. [It is permitted to look at an animal's nakedness while reciting the Shema (*Meiri*).]

30. *Genesis* 9:23. Noah became intoxicated and fell into a stupor while he was unclothed. When Noah's son, Ham, saw his father naked, he told his two bothers, Shem and Japheth, who took a garment and covered their father, taking care not to look at his nakedness.

The point is that although Noah was not a Jew, the Torah describes his nakedness as עֶרְוָה [which is also the term used in וְלֹא־יִרְאֶה בְךָ עֶרְוַת דָּבָר, *so that He will not see a shameful thing among you*] (*Meiri*). Accordingly, it is prohibited to recite the Shema even in the presence of a naked idolater.

31. *Rambam* (*Hil. Shabbos* 24:1) describes this prohibition as follows: "It is forbidden for a person to even speak about his affairs on the Sabbath. For example, he may not discuss with his partner what to buy the next day (i.e. after the Sabbath), or what to sell the next day, or how to build a certain building, or which merchandise to take to a certain place. All this and its like is forbidden . . ." (See also *Rashi* and *Tosafos* top of 113b.)

We shall learn below (150a-b) that one may not even mention the cost of a project (e.g. building a house) if that is something he currently needs to know.

מדוד והבא ואיכא דאמרי שאמרה מאד מאד הביא בלא מדה א) ורבו יתירה הוספת לי אמר רב יהודה אמר רב ירמיה בר אבא מלמד שרכב על ארי זכר וקשר תנין בראשו לקיים מה שנא' ב) וגם את חית השדה נתתי לו לעבדו:

מתני' א לא ישכור אדם פועלים בשבת ולא יאמר אדם לחבירו לשכור לו פועלים (א) ב אין מחשיכין על התחום לשכור לו פועלים ולהביא פירות ג אבל מחשיך הוא לשמור ומביא פירות בידו כלל אמר אבא שאול כל שאני זכאי באמירתו רשאי אני להחשיך עליו:

גמ' (פשיטא) מ"ש הוא ומ"ש חבירו אמר רב פפא * חבר נכרי מתקיף לה רב אשי ג) ד אמירה לנכרי שבות אלא אמר רב אשי אפילו תימא חבירו ישראל הא קמ"ל לא יאמר אדם לחבירו שכור לי פועלים ה אבל אומר אדם לחבירו הנראה שתעמוד עמי לערב ומתני' מני כרבי יהושע בן קרחה דתניא ג) לא יאמר אדם לחבירו הנראה שתעמוד עמי לערב רבי יהושע בן קרחה אומר אומר אדם לחבירו הנראה שתעמוד עמי לערב אמר רבה בר בר חנה אמר רבי יוחנן הלכה כרבי יהושע בן קרחה ואמר רבה בר בר חנה אמר רבי יוחנן מ"ט דרבי יהושע בן קרחה דכתיב ג) ו ממצוא חפצך ודבר דבר ד) ז דיבור אסור הרהור מותר רמי ליה רב אחא בר רב הונא לרבא מי אמר ר' יוחנן דיבור אסור הרהור מותר ה) אלמא הרהור לאו כדיבור דמי ו) והאמר רבה בר בר חנה אמר רבי יוחנן בכל מקום מותר להרהר חוץ מבית המרחץ ומבית הכסא שאני התם דבעינן ד) והיה מחניך קדוש וליכא הכא נמי כתיב ה) ולא יראה בך ערות דבר ההוא מיבעי ליה לכדרב יהודה ז) דאמר רב יהודה ו עכו"ם ערום אסור לקרות קרית שמע כנגדו מאי איריא עכו"ם אפי' ישראל נמי לא מיבעיא קאמר לא מיבעיא ישראל דאסור אבל עכו"ם כיון דכתיב ביה ה) אשר בשר חמורים בשרם אימא שפיר דמי קמ"ל אימא הכי נמי אמר קרא ו) וערות אביהם לא ראו ודיבור מי אסיר ח) והא רב חסדא ורב המנונא דאמרי תרוויהו ז חשבונות של מצוה מותר לחשבן בשבת וא"ר אלעזר ח פוסקים צדקה לעניים בשבת וא"ר יעקב בר אידי אמר רבי יוחנן מפקחין פיקוח נפש ופיקוח רבים בשבת והולכין לבתי כנסיות לפקח על עסקי רבים בשבת ט) וא"ר שמואל בר נחמני א"ר י) יוחנן הולכין לטרטיאות ולקרקסאות ולבסילקאות לפקח על עסקי רבים בשבת ותנא דבי מנשה ט משדכין על התינוקות ליארס בשבת ועל התינוק ללמדו ספר וללמדו אומנות י אמר קרא ג) ממצוא חפצך ודבר דבר חפציך אסורים חפצי שמים מותרין א"ר יהודה כ) אמר שמואל חשבונות של [ל) מלך] ושל מה בכך מותר לחשבן בשבת תנ"ה ל חשבונות שעברו ושעתידין להיו' אסור לחשבן של מ) מלך ושל

רש"י

מדוד. מעות ודינרי זהב והבא: ורבו יתירה הוספת לי. לאחר שהיה ז' שנים בהמה וחזר למלכותו היה משתבח כן ומהו התוספת שקשר תנין גדול נחש גדול בראשו של ארי כמין אפסר: מתני' לא ישכור אדם פועלים. דכתיב (ישעיה נח) ממצוא חפצך: ולא יאמר לחבירו כו'. בגמרא פריך פשיטא כיון דהוא אסור חבירו נמי אסור דהא ישראל הוא והשולחו עובר משום לפני עור לא תתן מכשול: אין מחשיכין על התחום. לקרב עצמו בשבת עד סוף התחום ולהחשיך שם שיהא קרוב למקום הפועלים או לפרדס להביא פירות דכל דבר שאסור לעשותו בשבת אסור להחשיך עליו: אבל מחשיך הוא. להיות קרוב לצאת לשמור פירותיו וזה דבר המותר בשבת לשמור פירותיו אם היו בתוך תחומו: ומביא פירות בידו. הואיל ועיקר מחשבתו לא היה לכך: כלל אמר אבא שאול. נותן היה כלל בדבר זה להוסיף דברים אחרים כיוצא בו ולקמיה מפרש לאתויי מאי: כל שאני זכאי באמירתו. שאני רשאי לאומרו לחבירו או לנכרי בשבת לעשות למוצאי שבת רשאי אני להחשיך עליו: גמ' מאי שנא כו'. ופשיטא דכיון דאמר לא ישכור ה"ה לא יאמר לחבירו דהא ישראל הוא כמותו ולא מצי לאוגרינהו: אמירה לנכרי שבות. וכבר סתמה רבי למתני' ס) נכרי שבא לכבות אין אומרים לו כבה: הא קמ"ל. משנה יתירה בהדיא הוא דלא לימא ליה אבל סתמא שרי ליה למימר: הנראה. עכשיו נראה אם תעמוד עמי לערב אם תבא אלי לכשתחשך ושניהן יודעין שעל מנת לשוכרו לפעולתו הוא מזהירו וכיון דלא מפרש בהדיא שרי כדמפרש טעמא לקמן דבור אסור הרהור מותר: מותר להרהר. בדברי תורה: והיה מחניך קדוש. ולא כתיב ביה דבר אלא מקום חנייתך תהא בקדושה וטעמא משום דישראל מהרהרין תמיד בדברי תורה: ערות דבר. אלמא לא אסיר ליה אלא בשעת דבור: ההיא כדרב יהודה. כלומר לעולם והיה מחניך קדוש משום הרהור תורה ואפי' אין דבור ולא יראה בך ערות דבר במילתא אחריתי מיירי לאסור בשעת הדבור ולא בשעת הרהור כגון להסתכל בערוה: עכו"ם ערום. כ"ש ישראל כדמפרש ואזיל: אימא שפיר דמי. דכבהמה בעלמא הוא: וערות אביהם. אלמא ערוה היא בבן נח: ודבור מי אסור והא אמר רב חסדא כו'. וכל הני דבור הוא: פקוח נפש. בדבר שיש בו סכנה פקוח ליקומנימונ"ט: ופקוח דרבים. כגון לרשות: טרטיאות וקרקסאות ובסילקאות. מיני פלטין הן ששם נאספו לבית הוועד: ללמדו אומנות. דהא נמי מצוה היא דכל שאינו מלמדו אומנות מלמדו לסטות ומצוה ילפינן מקרא בקדושין בהאשה נקנית (ד' ל:): של מלך. של עצה שאינו שלו ואין צריך בכך כגון הרוצה לבנות בית כך וכך צריך להוציא בו ול"נ כמו מה לך מה לך ולחשבונות הללו הרי אין צורך בהן לא לך ולא לאחר כגון ההיא דפרישית: ושל

תוספות

מה לי הוא ומה לי חבירו. ואם תאמר ונימא דחבירו היינו דאמר ליה שכור לי פועלים למחר וי"ל דא"כ מאי איריא חבירו אפי' הוא נמי לא מצי למימר אשכור פועלים למחר דעד כאן לא קאמר רב יהודה אמר שמואל מותר לאדם לומר לחבירו לכרך פלוני אני הולך למחר אלא משום דשאם יש בורגנין הולך הא לאו הכי לא:

ורבי יהושע בן קרחה היא. יש מפרש דר"ע קרוי קרחה שהיה קרח כדתניא בפרק בתרא דבכורות (דף נח. ושם) אמר בן עזאי כל חכמי ישראל דומין לפני כקליפת השום חוץ מן הקרח הזה ואומר שזה היה ר"ע והיה לו בן ששמו יהושע כדאמר בפרק קמא דשבועות (דף ו.) א"ל ר' יהושע בנו של ר"ע ואין נראה לר"ת דמה שקראו בן עזאי לר"ע קרח בבדיחותא בעלמא אין לנו לקרותו כן כל שעה דלשון גנות הוא שנא' עלה קרח עלה קרח (מלכים ב ב) ואמרינן נמי לקמן (דף קנב.) אמר ליה ההוא צדוקי לר' יהושע בן קרחה מהכא לקרחינאה כמה הוי הרי שהיה מגנה אותו על שהיה קרח ועוד אמרי' במגילה פרק בתרא (דף כז:) שאלו רבי את ר' יהושע בן קרחה במה הארכת ימים כו' א"ל רבי ברכני א"ל יהי רצון שתגיע לחצי ימי ואי ר' יהושע בן קרחה בנו של ר"ע והא קיימא לן פ) דלא נשא ר"ע בת כלבא שבוע עד שקיבל עליו לעסוק בתורה ואז היה בן מ' כדאמרינן בסוף ספרי מ' שנה שימש מ"מ מ' שנה פירנס את ישראל וכל ימיו ק"כ שנים ואמרי' בקידושין פרק בתרא (דף עב.) עד שלא מת ר"ע נולד רבי ואפילו נולד ר' יהושע בשנה ראשונה שנשאה לא נשאר כי אם פ' שנים מר"ע ורבי יהושע בשעה שבירך את רבי היה בן ק"מ שנים לכל הפחות שבפחות מע' שנה לא היה מברכו ואז היה רבי לכל הפחות בן מ' וא"כ לא היה מברכו רק מי' שנים ועוד נראה שלא נשאה עד שעסק כ"ד שנים רב תרי סרי ותרי סרי שנין נמצא כשהיה רבי יהושע בן קרחה בן ק"מ היה רבי יותר מחצי ימיו לכך נראה לר"ת דלא ר"ע היה אלא איניש אחרינא היה שמו קרחה וקרחה הוא שם אדם כמו קרח ונולד הכהנה קודם ר' יהושע בנו של ר"ע. מ"ר:

אומר אדם לחבירו הנראה שתעמוד עמי לערב. י"ל דדווקא לחבירו אבל לנכרי אסור לפי שהוא (א) [עושה] לדעת אותו [אמירה] ואינו נראה דהא שרינן ליה הכא משו' דדבור אסור והרהור מותר [א"כ] ל"ש נכרי ל"ש ישראל. מ"ר:

ודיבור מי אסור. פי' מן התורה דהא מדברין דיבור של מצוה מכלל דמדאורייתא שרי:

ואמר ר"א פוסקין צדקה לעניים בשבת. וא"ת מה צריך לאתויי (ב) הא הא לאתויי מילתיהו דבית הלל [בפי"ז] (בתוספתא) דתני אין פוסקים צדקה אפי' להשיא יתום ויתומה ואין משדכין על התינוקות ליארס בו דברי בית שמאי ובית הלל מתירין וי"ל דניחא ליה לאתויי מילתא דרבי אלעזר דמהתם לא הוה שמעינן פסיקת צדקה לעניים דהא לא שרי בית הלל אלא להשיא יתום ויתומה: ואין

מסורת הש"ס

א) [עי' תוס' לקמן ע"ב ד"ה ואין], ב) [ערובין מז: גיטין ח: ב"ק פ: ב"מ צ.], ג) ע"ז ו. [תוספ' פי"ח], ד) לעיל קיג., ה) [ברכות כ:], ו) שם כד: לעיל מ: קידושין לג. ע"ז מד: זבחים קב., ז) ברכות כה: ע"ש, ח) כתובות ה., ט) [ל"ל יונתן], י) גי' רש"ל דאמר, כ) לעיל קיג., ל) [ל"ל מילך פי' אורחי' כדכתי' ויבא הלך כלומר מותר אדם לחשב אורחיו הקרואים. ערוך ערך חשב] בס"י מה לך, מ) [תוספ' פי"ח], נ) בס"י מה לך, ס) [לעיל קכא.], ע) [דף ו.], פ) [כתובות סג. ועיין שם ובאבות דר"נ פ"ו], צ) [וע"ע תוס' בכורות נח. ד"ה חוץ ותוס' ב"ב קיג. ד"ה ומנו ותוס' פסחים קיב. ד"ה לוה].

הגהות הב"ח

(א) תוס' ד"ה אומר וכו' לפי שהוא רוצה לדעת אותה מלאכה ואינו: (ב) ד"ה ואמר רבי אלעזר וכו' וא"ת מה צריך לאתויי מילתא דרבי אלעזר ה"ל לאתויי:

גליון הש"ס

גמ' חבר נכרי. עי' סוכה דף לט ע"א תוס' ד"ה הלוקח. ועי' מג"א סימן תקי ס"ק ג:

ליקוטי רש"י

ורבו יתירה הוספת לי. וגדולה יתירה מן הראשונה נתוספת לי שאמרו רבותינו שרכב על ארי וקשר תנין בראשו [דניאל ד, לג]. אמירה לנכרי שבות. רבנן גזור על אמירה לנכרי משום שבות [לעיל קכא.]. על השבת לא נצטוו בני נח ומה שאסור לישראל לומר לעובד כוכבים עשה לי כך זהו משום ממצוא חפצך ודבר דבר (ישעיה נח) דבור אסור [ע"ז טו.]. לא יאמר אדם לחבירו הנראה. עתה נראה לשון הבאה נבוא (בראשית לז) לא יאמר לו בשבת הנראה אם תעמוד עמי לערב לעשות במלאכתי לערב [שם ז.]. רבי יהושע בן קרחה. יהושע בנו של ר' עקיבא הוא יהושע בן קרחה שר' עקיבא קרח היה כדאמרינן בבכורות (נח.) חוץ מן הקרח הזה [שבועות ו.]. הא דגרסינן בכוליה הש"ס רבי יהושע בן קרחה היינו בן של ר"ע דגרסינן התם (שבועות ו.) אמר לו ר' יהושע בנו של ר"ע לר"ע [בכורות נח. ועי' בתוס' כאן ושם]. ודבר דבר. שלא יהא דבורך של שבת כדבורך של חול כגון מקח וממכר וחשבונות [ע"ש בתוס']. הרהור מותר. להרהר בלבו כך וכך יציאות אני צריך להוציא על שדה זו [לעיל קיג:]. ולא יראה בך. הקב"ה ערות דבר [דברים כג, טו]. אשר בשר חמורים. אבר תשמיש [יחזקאל כג, כ]. מפקחין. מוציאין לאור [כתובות ה.]. פיקוח. דשקומבר"ש בלע"ז כל דבר שצריך לו לנפש להעביר סכנת מות [יומא פד:]. טרטיאות. פלטי מלכים ושלטונים [כתובות שם]. ולבסילקאות. בית גנזה שעל עלייה [יומא כה.]. פלטורין גנזוס וקורמס בסילקאות [סוכה נא:]. לשון טירה גנזוסה היא כדאמר בסדר יומא (כה.) לשכת הגזית כמין בסילקי גדולה היתה [ע"ז טז.]. ללמדו אומנות. מצוה הוא דכתיב (קהלת ט) ראה חיים עם אשה אשר אהבת הקיש אומנות לאשה מה אשה מצוה אף אומנות מצוה ואמרינן בקידושין (כט.) שאביו חייב ללמדו אומנות [כתובות שם]. חייב אדם ללמד בנו אומנות דילפינן לה מקרא בפרק קמא דקידושין (ל:) דכתיב ראה חיים עם אשה [מכות ח.]. חפצי שמים מותרין. כגון פוסקים צדקה ומשדכין על התינוקות ליארס [לעיל שם].

עין משפט נר מצוה

כב א מיי' פכ"ד מהל' שבת הלכה יב סמג לאוין סה טור שו"ע או"ח סימן שז סעיף ג:

כג ב ג מיי' פכ"ד שם הלכה ג סמג שם טור שו"ע או"ח סימן שו סעיף א וסי' שז סעיף ח:

כד ד מיי' פ"ו שם הל"א סמג שם:

כה ה מיי' פכ"ד שם הל"ד וסמג שם טור שו"ע או"ח סימן שז סעיף ז:

כו ו מיי' פ"ג מהלכות ק"ש הלכה טז סמג עשין יח טור שו"ע או"ח סימן עה סעיף ד:

כז ז ח ט י מיי' פכ"ד מהלכות שבת הל"ה סמג לאוין סה טוש"ע או"ח סימן שו סעיף ו:

כח כ מיי' פכ"ג מהל' שבת הלי"ח סמג שם טור שו"ע או"ח סימן שו סעיף ז:

תורה אור השלם

א) בה זמנא מנדעי יתוב עלי וליקר מלכותי הדרי וזוי יתוב עלי ולי הדברי ורברבני יבעון ועל מלכותי התקנת ורבו יתירה הוספת לי: [דניאל ד, לג]

ב) ועתה אנכי נתתי את כל הארצות האלה ביד נבוכדנאצר מלך בבל עבדי וגם את חית השדה נתתי לו לעבדו: [ירמיה כז, ו]

ג) אם תשיב משבת רגלך עשות חפציך ביום קדשי וקראת לשבת ענג לקדוש יי מכבד וכבדתו מעשות דרכיך ממצוא חפצך ודבר דבר: [ישעיה נח, יג]

ד) כי יי אלהיך מתהלך בקרב מחנך להצילך ולתת איביך לפניך והיה מחניך קדוש ולא יראה בך ערות דבר ושב מאחריך: [דברים כג, טו]

ה) ותעגבה על פלגשיהם אשר בשר חמורים בשרם וזרמת סוסים זרמתם: [יחזקאל כג, כ]

ו) ויקח שם ויפת את השמלה וישימו על שכם שניהם וילכו אחרנית ויכסו את ערות אביהם ופניהם אחרנית וערות אביהם לא ראו: [בראשית ט, כג]

רבינו חננאל

נמשכה ערלתו וכו': [מתני'] לא ישכור פועלים בשבת ולא יאמר לחבירו שכור לי פועלים: גמ' ואקשינן עלה מ"ש הוא ומ"ש חבירו. ובא רב פפא לאוקמיה למתני' בחבירו נכרי. רב אשי אמר אפילו תימא בחבירו ישראל הא קמ"ל דלשכור פועלים הוא דלא יאמר לו אבל אומר לו הנראה שתעמוד עמי לערב כלומר אסור שיאמר לו לערב לך לשכור לי פועלים או כיוצא בו. אבל אם אינו אומר לו הנראה שתעמוד עמי לערב ובדעתו שיאמר לו לערב לך לשכור לי פועלים או עשה לי מלאכה כל וכך מותר כר' יהושע בן קרחה. ואמר ר' יוחנן הלכתא כר' יהושע בן קרחה ודייק ר' יוחנן ואמר טעמיה דר' יהושע בן קרחה דיבור בפירוש' אסור אבל הרהור מותר דכתיב ממצוא חפצך ודבר דבר. ואקשינן עליה והא הוא דאמר בכל מקום מותר להרהר חוץ ממרחץ ובית הכסא כו' ואמאי לא אמרינן הכא נמי הרהור מותר. ומפרקינן האי קרא מיבעי ליה לאסור אפילו ערותו של נכרי דאשכחן קרא וערות אביהם לא ראו. ואקשי' תוב ודיבור מי אסור והביאו ה' שמועות אחת שאפילו דבור אמי' מותר בשבת. ואלו הן חשבונות ופוסקין צדקה לעניים ומפקחין פיקוח נפש והולכין לבתי כנסיות ולבתי מדרשות לפקח על עסקי רבים וכן הולכין לבתי טאטראות ולבתי קרקסאות לפקח על עסקי רבים. ותנא משדכין על התינוקות ליארס. ועל התינוק ללמדו ספר וללמדו אומנות. ומפרקי' אלא אמר קרא ממצוא חפצך ודבר דבר חפציך אסורין חפצי שמים מותרין. ואלו כולן חפצי שמים הן: חשבונות של מלך. פירוש מלך אורחים ובא אורח לאיש העשיר כלומר מה שאכל האורח ומה שהוצרך ומה שהוא אורחיו ואת פרפרותיו פי' חשבונות של מה בכך כמו שיחשב אדם חשבון כגון חיילות המלך כך וכך אלף וכיוצא בו או' כלומר מה הנאה יש לך ומה צורך לך בזה כגון אלו מותר בשבת. וזה שאומרים מחשבין חשבונות

Rav Hamnuna both said: חֶשְׁבּוֹנוֹת שֶׁל מִצְוָה מוּתָּר לְחַשְּׁבָן בְּשַׁבָּת – **It is permitted to make calculations** for the sake **of a mitzvah on the Sabbath.**[32] וְאָמַר רַבִּי אֶלְעָזָר – **And R' Elazar said:** פּוֹסְקִים צְדָקָה לַעֲנִיִּים בְּשַׁבָּת – **We may allocate charity to the poor on the Sabbath.**[33] וְאָמַר רַבִּי יַעֲקֹב בַּר אִידִי אָמַר רַבִּי יוֹחָנָן – **And R' Yaakov bar Idi said in the name of R' Yochanan:** מְפַקְּחִין פִּיקּוּחַ נֶפֶשׁ וּפִיקּוּחַ רַבִּים בְּשַׁבָּת – **We may attend to matters involving** danger **to life**[34] **and to matters involving the public**[35] **on the Sabbath;** וְהוֹלְכִין לְבָתֵּי כְנֵסִיּוֹת לְפַקֵּחַ עַל עִסְקֵי רַבִּים בְּשַׁבָּת – **and we may go to synagogues to attend to affairs of the public on the Sabbath.**[36] וְאָמַר רַבִּי שְׁמוּאֵל בַּר נַחְמָנִי אָמַר רַבִּי יוֹחָנָן – **And R' Shmuel bar Nachamani said in the name of R' Yochanan:** הוֹלְכִין לְטַרְטְיָאוֹת וּלְקַרְקְסָאוֹת וּלְבַסִּילְקָאוֹת לְפַקֵּחַ עַל עִסְקֵי רַבִּים בְּשַׁבָּת – **We may go to amphitheaters, circuses and basilicas**[37] **in order to attend to affairs of the public on the Sabbath.**[38] וְתָנָא דְּבֵי מְנַשֶּׁה – **And a Tanna of the academy of Menasheh taught:** מְשַׁדְּכִין עַל הַתִּינוֹקוֹת לֵיאָרֵס בְּשַׁבָּת – WE MAY ARRANGE FOR GIRLS TO BE BETROTHED ON THE SABBATH, וְעַל הַתִּינוֹק לְלַמְּדוֹ סֵפֶר וּלְלַמְּדוֹ אוּמָּנוּת – AND FOR someone TO TEACH A BOY A TEXT OR TO TEACH HIM A CRAFT.[39] In view of the fact that it is forbidden to pursue one's affairs on the Sabbath even through mere speech, why is speech permitted in the preceding cases?

The Gemara answers:

אָמַר קְרָא ,,מִמְּצוֹא חֶפְצְךָ וְדַבֵּר דָּבָר" – **Scripture states:**[40] *[Refrain] from pursuing your business and speaking words.* חֲפָצֶיךָ אֲסוּרִים – The verse implies that only *your* **wants are forbidden,** חֶפְצֵי שָׁמַיִם מוּתָּרִין – but **the business of Heaven,** i.e. matters involving a mitzvah, **are permitted.** Hence, in the above cases, since they involve the performance of a mitzvah, speech is permitted.[41]

Other types of speech permitted on the Sabbath:

אָמַר רַב יְהוּדָה אָמַר שְׁמוּאֵל – **Rav Yehudah said in the name of Shmuel:** חֶשְׁבּוֹנוֹת שֶׁל [מַלָּךְ] וְשֶׁל מַה בְּכָךְ – **Calculations of "what is it to you?"**[42] **and "what of it?"**[43] מוּתָּר לְחַשְּׁבָן בְּשַׁבָּת – **may be calculated on the Sabbath.**[44] תַּנְיָא נַמִּי הָכִי – **This was also taught in a Baraisa:** חֶשְׁבּוֹנוֹת שֶׁעָבְרוּ וְשֶׁעֲתִידִין לִהְיוֹת – CALCULATIONS of things THAT HAPPENED OR WILL HAPPEN[45] אָסוּר לְחַשְּׁבָן – MAY NOT BE CALCULATED on the Sabbath. שֶׁל מַלָּךְ – But calculations OF "WHAT IS IT TO YOU?"

NOTES

32. [E.g. one may say, "We need so-and-so much money to purchase tefillin."] The Gemara assumes that the prohibition of מִמְּצוֹא חֶפְצְךָ וְדַבֵּר דָּבָר, *from pursuing your business and speaking words,* applies even to matters that involve a mitzvah (see *Tosafos* for an explanation; see however, *Tosafos* to 121a ד״ה אין and *Shabbos Shel Mi* there). Hence, it attempts to prove from this law that the prohibition does not cover speech.

33. One may orally divide up a charity fund, allocating specific amounts to its beneficiaries (see *Meiri*). One may also pledge a specific sum of one's own money to charity (see *Shulchan Aruch Orach Chaim* 306:6 with *Rama*). Some Rishonim, though, forbid the donation of a particular *object* to charity, because this resembles the act of consecration, which is forbidden on the Sabbath (*Meiri;* see *Ran MHK* ed.; see also *Mishnah Berurah* ibid. §27 and §33).

34. *Tos. Rid* deletes the words פִּיקּוּחַ נֶפֶשׁ, *matters involving* [danger to] *life,* because even *actions* are permitted for the sake of protecting life.

35. One may speak [to the authorities] on behalf of the public if there is a matter that concerns them (*Tos. Rid*), even if it does not pertain to a mitzvah (*Rashi*). [The very fact that it is a communal need elevates it to the level of a matter involving a mitzvah (*Mishnah Berurah* 306:28).]

36. I.e. we may even hold public meetings on the Sabbath to deal with such matters (*Ran* on *Rif*).

37. This translation follows *Aruch. Rashi* explains that they are different types of palaces in which official meetings would be held. [It seems that although they were used for purposes of public entertainment (see *Rashi* to *Avodah Zarah* 18b), they were also used for civic meetings and assemblies (see *Shiltei HaGiborim* folio 64a §2).]

38. *Meiri* sees the two statements of R' Yochanan as referring to two stages of a single process: When a matter of concern to the Jewish community arises, the community (or its leaders) may assemble and hold deliberations in the synagogue in order to arrive at the proper course of action. Once a strategy is agreed upon, they may proceed to the non-Jewish court or council and intercede with the authorities.

39. Teaching one's son a trade is a mitzvah, for, as the Gemara (*Kiddushin* 29a) states: *Whoever does not teach his son a craft teaches him banditry.* [Lacking expertise in any field, the son is without a means of earning a livelihood. Ultimately, he will be forced to turn to banditry to provide for his needs.] The Gemara (ibid.) derives from Scripture that this is a mitzvah (*Rashi*).

Although it is permitted to hire a tutor on the Sabbath for these purposes, one may not specify his fee (*Shulchan Aruch* ibid. 306:6; see *Beur Halachah* there ד״ה ודווקא; cf. *Shiltei HaGiborim* §3).

40. *Isaiah* 58:13.

41. This permit applies only to *preparing* (e.g. through speech) for a transaction involving a mitzvah. One is not allowed to make actual business transactions [or violate any other Rabbinic prohibition] for the sake of a mitzvah (see *Aruch HaShulchan* 306:7).

42. מַלָּךְ means advice or deliberation (see *Maharsha*); alternatively it is a contraction of מַה לָּךְ, *what is it to you?* Either way, it is used here to signify matters that are of no practical consequence to the speaker [e.g. he says, "One who wants to build a house would have to spend this amount of money"] (*Rashi*).

43. *Rabbeinu Chananel* and *Aruch* (ע׳ חשב) interpret the word מַלָּךְ as *guests* (based on *II Samuel* 12:4). One may calculate the number of guests he will have on the Sabbath (provided he does not read from a list; see the preceding Mishnah). מַה בְּכָךְ, *what of it?*, denotes matters that affected the speaker at one time, but no longer concern him [e.g. "I spent this much money on this building"] (*Rashi,* printed on 150b).

44. Although idle chatter, which does not involve one's current finances, is permitted, it should be kept to a minimum (see *Tosafos* to 113b, *Shulchan Aruch, Orach Chaim* 307:1 and *Mishnah Berurah* ibid. §27).

45. I.e. one may not mention the cost of a past or future undertaking. This ruling seems to contradict Shmuel's permit to make calculations of מַה בְּכָךְ, *what of it?*, i.e. calculations that involve past projects (see notes 42 and 43). Moreover, the Baraisa itself proceeds to state that calculations of מַה בְּכָךְ, *what of it?* are permitted. The Gemara below (150b) deals with this problem.

מדוד והבא ואיכא דאמרי שאמרה מאד מאד הביא בלא מדה א) ורבו יתירה הוספת לי אמר רב יהודה אמר רב ירמיה בר אבא מלמד שרכב על ארי זכר וקשר תנין בראשו לקיים מה שנא' ב) וגם את חית השדה נתתי לו לעבדו: **מתני'** לא ישכור אדם פועלים בשבת ולא יאמר אדם לחבירו לשכור לו פועלים אין מחשיכין על התחום לשכור לו פועלים ולהביא פירות אבל מחשיך הוא לשמור ומביא פירות בידו כלל אמר אבא שאול כל שאני זכאי באמירתו רשאי אני להחשיך עליו: **גמ'** (פשיטא) מ"ש הוא ומ"ש חבירו אמר רב פפא חבר נכרי מתקיף לה רב אשי אמירה לנכרי שבות אלא אמר רב אשי אפילו תימא חבירו ישראל הא קמ"ל לא יאמר אדם לחבירו שכור לי פועלים אבל אומר אדם לחבירו הנראה שתעמוד עמי לערב ומתני' מני כרבי יהושע בן קרחה דתניא לא יאמר אדם לחבירו הנראה שתעמוד עמי לערב רבי יהושע בן קרחה אומר אומר אדם לחבירו הנראה שתעמוד עמי לערב אמר רבה בר בר חנה אמר רבי יוחנן הלכה כרבי יהושע בן קרחה ואמר רבה בר בר חנה אמר רבי יוחנן מ"ט דרבי יהושע בן קרחה דכתיב ממצוא חפצך ודבר דבר דיבור אסור הרהור מותר רמי ליה רב אחא בר רב הונא לרבא מי אמר ר' יוחנן דיבור אסור הרהור מותר אלמא הרהור לאו כדיבור דמי והאמר רבה בר בר חנה אמר רבי יוחנן בכל מקום מותר להרהר חוץ מבית המרחץ ומבית הכסא שאני התם דבעינן והיה מחניך קדוש וליכא הכא נמי כתיב ולא יראה בך ערות דבר ההוא מיבעי ליה לכדרב יהודה דאמר רב יהודה עכו"ם ערום אסור לקרות קריאת שמע כנגדו מאי איריא עכו"ם אפי' ישראל נמי לא מיבעיא קאמר לא מיבעיא ישראל דאסור אבל עכו"ם כיון דכתיב ביה אשר בשר חמורים בשרם אימא שפיר דמי קמ"ל איהא הכי נמי אמר קרא וערות אביהם לא ראו ודיבור מי אסיר והא רב חסדא ורב המנונא דאמרי תרוייהו חשבונות של מצוה מותר לחשבן בשבת וא"ר אלעזר פוסקים צדקה לעניים בשבת וא"ר יעקב בר אידי אמר רבי יוחנן מפקחין פיקוח נפש ופיקוח רבים בשבת והולכין לבתי כנסיות לפקח על עסקי רבים בשבת וא"ר שמואל בר נחמני א"ר יוחנן הולכין לטרטיאות ולקרקסאות ולבסילקאות לפקח על עסקי רבים בשבת ותנא דבי מנשה משדכין על התינוקות ליארס בשבת ועל התינוק ללמדו ספר וללמדו אומנות אמר קרא ממצוא חפצך ודבר דבר חפציך אסורים חפצי שמים מותרין א"ר יהודה אמר שמואל חשבונות של [מלך] ושל מה בכך מותר לחשבן בשבת תנ"ה חשבונות שעברו ושעתידין להיו' אסור לחשבן של מלך ושל

רש"י מדוד. מעות ודינרי זהב והכא: ורבו יתירה הוספת לי. לאחר שהיה ז' שנים בהמה וחזר למלכותו היה משתבח כן ומהו התוספת שקשר תנין גדול נחש גדול בראשו של ארי כמין אפסר: **מתני'** לא ישכור אדם פועלים. דכתיב (ישעיה נח) ממצוא חפצך: ולא יאמר לחבירו כו'. בגמרא פריך פשיטא כיון דהוא אסור חבירו נמי אסור דהא ישראל הוא והשולחו עובר משום לפני עור לא תתן מכשול: אין מחשיכין על התחום. לקרב עצמו בשבת עד סוף התחום ולהחשיך שם שיהא קרוב למקום הפועלים או לפרדס להביא פירות לכל דבר שאסור לעשותו בשבת אסור להחשיך עליו: אבל מחשיך הוא. להיות קרוב לצאת לשמור פירותיו וזה דבר המותר בשבת לשמור פירותיו אם היו בתוך תחומו: ומביא פירות בידו. הואיל ועיקר מחשבתו לא היה לכך: כלל אמר אבא שאול. ונתן היה כלל בדבר זה להוסיף דברים אחרים כיוצא בו ולקמיה מפרש לאתויי מאי: כל שאני זכאי באמירתו. שאני רשאי לאומרו לחבירו או לנכרי בשבת לעשות למוצאי שבת רשאי אני להחשיך עליו: **גמ'** מאי שנא כו'. ופשיטא דכיון דאמר לא ישכור ה"ה לא יאמר לחבירו דהא ישראל הוא כמותו ולא מצי לאוקמיה: אמירה לנכרי שבות. וככר סתמה רבי למתני' נכרי שבא לכבות אין אומרים לו כבה: הא קמ"ל. משנה יתירה בהדיא הוא דלא יאמר ליה אבל סתמא שרי ליה למימר: הנראה. עכשיו נראה אם תעמוד עמי לערב אם תבא אלי לכשתחשך ושניהן יודעין שעל מנת לשוכרו לפעולתו הוא מזהירו וכיון דלא מפרש בהדיא שרי כדמפרש טעמא לקמן דבור אסור הרהור מותר: מותר להרהר. בדברי תורה: והיה מחניך קדוש. ולא כתיב ביה דבר אלא מקום מניחך תהא בקדושה וטעמא משום דישראל מהרהרין תמיד בדברי תורה: ערות דבר. אלמא לא אסיר ליה אלא בשעת דבור: ההיא כדרב יהודה. כלומר לעולם והיה מחניך קדוש משום הרהור תורה ואפי' אין דבור ולא יראה בך ערות דבר במילתא אחריתי מיירי לאסור בשעת הדבור ולא בשעת הרהור כגון להסתכל בערוה: עכו"ם ערום. כ"ש ישראל כדמפרש ואזיל: אימא שפיר דמי. דכבהמה בעלמא הוא: וערות אביהם. אלמא ערוה היא דבנן נח: ודבור מי אסור והא אמר רב חסדא כו'. וכל הני דבור הוא: פקוח נפש. בדבר שיש בו סכנה פקוח דיקומדימונ"ט: ופקוח רבים. כגון לרשות: טרטיאות וקרקסאות ובסילקאות. מיני פלטין הן שאם נאספו לבית הוועד: ללמדו אומנות. דהא נמי מצוה היא דכל שאינו מלמדו אומנות מלמדו לסטות ומצוה ילפינן מקרא בקדושין בהאשה ניקנית (ד' ל:): של מלך. של עלה שאינו שלו ואין צריך בכך כגון הרוצה לבנות בית כך וכך צריך להוציא בו ול"נ כמו מה לך מה לך ולחשבונות הללו הרי אין צורך בהן לא לך ולא לאחר כגון ההיא דפריסית: ושל

תוספות מה לי הוא ומה לי חבירו. ואם תאמר ונימא דחבירו היינו דאמר ליה שכור לי פועלים למחר וי"ל דא"כ מאי איריא חבירו אפי' הוא נמי לא מצי למימר אשכור פועלים למחר דעד כאן לא קאמר רב יהודה אמר שמואל מותר לאדם לומר לחבירו לכרך פלוני אני הולך למחר אלא משום דשאם יש בורגנין הולך הא לאו הכי לא: **ורבי** יהושע בן קרחה היא. יש מפרש דר"ע קרוי קרחה שהיה קרח כדתניא בפרק בתרא דבכורות (דף נח. ושם) אמר בן עזאי כל חכמי ישראל דומין לפני כקליפת השום חוץ מן הקרח הזה ואומר שזה היה ר"ע והיה לו בן ששמו יהושע כדאמר בפרק קמא דשבועות ט) א"ל ר' יהושע בנו של ר"ע לר"ע ואין נראה לר"ת דמה שקראו בן עזאי לר"ע קרח בבדיחותא בעלמא אין לנו לקרותו כן כל שעה דלשון גנות הוא שנא' עלה קרח עלה קרח (מלכים ב ב) ואמרינן נמי לקמן (דף קנג.) אמר ליה ההוא לדוקי לר' יהושע בן קרחה מהכא לקרחינאה כמה הוי הרי שהיה מגנה אותו על שהיה קרח ועוד אמרי' במגילה פרק בתרא (דף כח.) שאל רבי את רבי יהושע בן קרחה במה הארכת ימים כו' א"ל רבי ברכני א"ל יהי רצון שתגיע לחצי ימי ואי ר' יהושע בן קרחה בנו של ר"ע והא קיימא לן ס) דלא נשא ר"ע בת כלבא שבוע עד שקיבל עליו לעסוק בתורה ואז היה בן מ' דתניא בסוף ספרי מ' שנה שימש ת"ח מ' שנה פירנס את ישראל וכל ימיו ק"כ שנים ואמרי' בקידושין פרק בתרא (דף עב.) עד שלא מת ר"ע נולד רבי ואפילו נולד ר' יהושע בשנה ראשונה שנשאה לא נשאר כי אם פ' שנים מר"ע ורבי יהושע בשעה שבירך את רבי היה בן ק"מ שנים לכל הפחות שבפחות מע' שנה לא היה מברכו ואז היה רבי לכל הפחות בן ס' וא"כ לא היה מברכו רק מי' שנים ועוד נראה שלא נשאה עד שעסק בי רב תרי סרי ותרי סרי שנין נמצא כשהיה רבי יהושע בן קרחה בן ק"מ היה רבי יותר מחצי ימיו לכך נראה לר"ת דלא ר"ע היה אלא איניש אחרינא היה ששמו קרחה וקרחה הוא שם אדם כמו קרח ונולד הרבה קודם ר' יהושע בנו של ר"ע. מ"ר: **אומר** אדם לחבירו הנראה שתעמוד עמי לערב. י"א דדווקא לחבירו אבל לנכרי אסור לפי שהוא (א) [עושה] לדעת אותה [אמירה] ואינו נראה דהא שרינן ליה הכא משו' דדבור אסור והרהור מותר [א"כ] ל"ש נכרי ל"ש ישראל. מ"ר: **ודיבור** מי אסור. פי' מן התורה דהא מדשרינן דיבור של מצוה מכלל דמדאורייתא שרי: **ואמר** ר"א פוסקין צדקה לעניים בשבת. וא"ת מה צריך לאתויי (ב) הא ה"ל לאתויי מילתייהו דבית הלל [בפי"ז] (בתוספתא) דתני אין פוסקים צדקה אפי' להשיא יתום ויתומה ואין משדכין על התינוקות ליארס בו דברי בית שמאי ובית הלל מתירין וי"ל דניחא ליה לאתויי מילתא דרבי אלעזר דמהתם לא הוה שמעינן פסיקת צדקה לעניים דהא לא שרי בית הלל אלא להשיא יתום ויתומה: ואין

רבינו חננאל משנה ערלתו וכו': [מתני'] לא ישכור פועלים בשבת ולא יאמר לחבירו שכור לי פועלים: גמ' ואקשינן עלה מ"ש הוא ומ"ש חבירו. ובא רב פפא לאוקמיה למתני' בחבירו נכרי. רב אשי אמר אפילו תימא בחבירו ישראל הא קמ"ל דלשכור פועלים הוא דלא יאמר לו אבל אומר לו הנראה שתעמוד עמי לערב כלומר אסור שיאמר לו לערב לך לשכור לי פועלים או כיוצא בו. אבל אם יאמר לו הא נראה שתעמוד עמי לערב ובדעתו שיאמר לו לערב לך לשכור לי פועלים או עשה לי מלאכה כך וכך מותר כר' יהושע בן קרחה. ואמר ר' יוחנן הלכתא כר' יהושע בן קרחה ודייק ר' יוחנן ואמר טעמיה דר' יהושע בן קרחה דיבור בפירוש' אסור אבל הרהור מותר דכתיב ממצוא חפצך ודבר דבר. ואקשינן עליה והא הוא דאמר בכל מקום מותר להרהר חוץ ממרחץ ובית הכסא כו' ואמאי לא אמרינן הכא נמי הרהור מותר. ומפרקינן האי קרא מיבעי ליה לאסור אפילו ערותו של נכרי דאשכחנן קרא דאמר וערות אביהם לא ראו. ואקשי' תוב ודבור מי אסור והביאו ה' שמועות אחת שאפילו דבור אמ' מותר בשבת. ואלו הן חשבונות ופוסקין צדקה לעניים ומפקחין פיקוח רבים. והולכין לבתי כנסיות ולבתי מדרשות לפקח על עסקי רבים והולכין לבתי טאטראות ולבתי קרקסאות לפקח על עסקי רבים. ותנא משדכין על התינוקות ליארס. ועל התינוק ללמדו ספר וללמדו אומנות. ומפרקי' אלא אמר קרא ממצוא חפצך ודבר דבר חפצך אסורין כדבור חפצי שמים מותרין. ואלו כולן חפצי שמים הן: חשבונות של מלך. פירוש מילך אורחים ובא הלך לאיש העשיר כלומר מותר לאדם לחשב אורחים הקרואים להסב אצלו בסעודה וכדתנן מונה אדם את אורחיו ואת פרפריותיו פי' חשבונות של מה בכך כמו שיחשב אדם חשבון כגון חיילות המלך כך וכך אלף וכיוצא בו אומ' לו מה בכך. כלומר מה הנאה יש לך ומה צורך לך בזה כגון אלו מותר בשבת. וזה שאומרים מחשבין חשבונות

ליקוטי רש"י ... פלטי מלכים ושלטונים [כתובות שם]. ולבסילקאות. בית גבוה שעל עלייה [יומא כה.]. פלטירין גבוהים נקראים בסילקאות [סוכה נא:]. לשון טירה גבוהה היא כדאמר בסדר יומא (כה.) לשכת הגזית כמין בסילקי גדולה היתה [ע"ז טז.]. ללמדו אומנות. מצוה הוא דכתיב (קהלת ט) ראה חיים עם אשה אשר אהבת למוד אומנות שתחיה הימנו עם התורה ואמרינן בקידושין (כט.) שאביו חייב ללמדו אומנות [כתובות שם]. חיותיה הוא ואף זו מצוה על האב ללמדו דילפינן לה מקרא בפרק קמא דקדושין (ל:) דכתיב ראה חיים עם אשה אשר אהבת הקים אומנות שהוא חיותו כאשה כשם שאביו חייב להשיאו אשה כדכתיב וקחו לבניכם נשים כך חייב ללמדו אומנות [מכות ח:]. חפציך אסורים. כי ההוא דאמרינן בעירובין (לח:) לא יטייל אדם לסוף שדהו בשבת לידע מה היא צריכה [אחר השבת]. חפצי שמים מותרין. כגון פוסקים לצדקה ומשדכין על התינוקות ליארס [לעיל שם.].

ושל מה בכך מותר לחושבן ורמינהו חושבין חשבונות שאינן צריכין ואין מחשבין חשבונות שצריכין בשבת כיצד אומר אדם לחבירו כך וכך פועלים (א) הוצאתי על שדה זו כך וכך דינרין הוצאתי על דירה זו אבל לא יאמר לו כך וכך הוצאתי וכך וכך אני עתיד להוציא ולטעמיך קשיא לך היא גופא אלא *הא דאיכא אגרא דאגירא גביה הא דליכא אגרא דאגירא גביה: אין מחשיכין: תנו רבנן מעשה בחסיד אחד שנפרצה לו פרץ בתוך שדהו ונמלך עליה לגודרה ונזכר ששבת הוא [ב] ונמנע אותו חסיד ולא גדרה ונעשה לו נס ועלתה בו צלף וממנה היתה פרנסתו ופרנסת אנשי ביתו א"ר יהודה אמר שמואל [ג] מותר לאדם לומר לחבירו לכרך פלוני אני הולך למחר שאם יש בורגנין הולך תנן אין מחשיכין על התחום לשכור פועלים ולהביא פירות בשלמא לשכור פועלים דבשבת לא מצי אגר אלא להביא פירות לימא שאם יש שם מחיצות מביא [ג] משכחת לה בפירות המחוברים והתני ר' אושעיא אין מחשיכין על התחום להביא תבן וקש בשלמא קש משכחת לה במחובר אלא תבן היכי משכחת לה בתיבנא סריא ת"ש [ד] מחשיכין על התחום לפקח על עסקי כלה ועל עסקי המת על עסקי כלה ומת אין על עסקי אחר לא בשלמא אחר דומיא דכלה משכחת לה למיגזא ליה אסא אלא מת מאי ניהו להביא לו ארון ותכריכין וקתני מת אין אבל אחר לא ואמאי לימא שאם יש שם מחיצו' מביא מת נמי משכחת לה [ה] למיגזא ליה גלימא: אבל מחשיכין: ואע"ג דלא אבדיל והאמר רבי אלעזר בן אנטיגנוס משום רבי אליעזר בן יעקב [ו] אסור לו לאדם שיעשה חפציו קודם שיבדיל וכי תימא דאבדיל בתפלה והאמר רב יהודה אמר שמואל [ז] המבדיל בתפלה צריך שיבדיל על הכוס וכי תימא דאבדיל על הכוס כוס בשדה מי איכא תרגמא רבי נתן בר אמי קמיה דרבא בין הגיתות שנו א"ל ר' אבא לרב אשי במערבא אמרינן הכי המבדיל בין קודש לחול ועבדינן צורכין אמר רב אשי כי הוינא בי רב כהנא הוה אמר המבדיל בין קודש לחול ומסלתינן סילתי: כלל אמר אבא שאול כל שאני וכו': (איבעיא להו) אבא שאול אהייא אילימא ארישא קאי אין מחשיכין על התחום לשכור פועלים להביא פירות האי

ושל מה בכך. כגון שככר היו לצורך אלא שעברו כגון כך וכך הוצאתי בבנין זה: חשבונות שעברו. לקמן מוקי לה דלא עברו לגמרי שעדיין שכר הפועלים עליו שלא נתנו להן ושל מה בכך שעברו לגמרי ואין שכר פועלים עליו: כך וכך הוצאתי. אלמא עברו מותרין: תקשי לך היא גופא. ברייתא קמייתא רישא קתני שעברו אסורין וסיפא קתני של מה בכך מותרין דהיינו עברו: צלף. אילן גדול הוא ובעל ענפים הרבה ושלשה מיני אוכל יש בפירותיו אביונות קפריסין ולולבין: שאם יש בורגנין. מע' אמה לע' אמה הולך אפי' בשבת שהכל חשוב כעיר אחת וכל העיר כד' אמות כדאמרינן בעירובין (דף כא.) וכיון דהוא דבר שיש לו היתר על ידי תקנה בשבת מותר לאומרו אפילו במקום שאין שם היתר: המחוברים. שא"א לקצצן בשבת ע"י שום תקנה: קש. זנבות השבולים אסטרל"א: בתיבנא סריא. שאפי' יש מחיצות אינו מביא משום דמוקצה הוא: על עסקי כלה ומת אין. דחפצי שמים הן אבל על עסקי אחר אפי' דומיא דכלה לא: בשלמא אחר דומיא דכלה משכחת לה. דאסור להחשיך כגון לחתוך מן המחובר: למיגז לה אסא. דעבדו לה גננא דאסא לכלתא: אלא עסקי מת מאי היא. הבאה דארון ותכריכין ואמאי לאסר לא לימא הואיל ואם יש שם מחיצות מביא: למיגז ליה גלימא. לתקן לו תכריכין דאין היתר לדבר היום כלל: ואע"ג דלא אבדיל. אסיפא דמתני' מתמה דקתני ומביא פירות בידו לקוצצן מן המחובר בלא הבדלה: בין הגיתות שנו. דאיכא כוס בשדה: המבדיל בין קודש לחול. להיכרא בעלמא ללוות את המלך: ועבדינן צורכין. ואחר כך אנו מברכין על הכוס ברכה גמורה דהבדלה וכ"ש דאי אבדיל בתפלה מותר לעשות צרכיו וחוזר ומבדיל על הכוס: ומסלתינן סילתי. חוטבין עצים: אהייא. קאי ומשוי כללא: אי נימא ארישא. דקתני ת"ק לאיסורא וקאתי אבא שאול לשויה בה כללא א"כ דכללא לאיסורא ה"ל למימר בהדיא כל שאינו זכאי באמירה כגון אלו שאינו רשאי לומר לחבירו שכור לי פועלים או הבא לי פירות למוצאי שבת אינו רשאי להחשיך מיבעי ליה: אלא

[ה] ואין מחשיכין על התחום לשכור פועלים ולהביא פירות. משמע דוקא על התחום אבל בתוך התחום מחשיכין לשכור פועלי' ולהביא פירו' וקשה לרבי דבסוף פ' בכל מערבין (עירובין דף נא:) תניא לא יהלך אדם לתוך שדהו לידע מה צריכה כיוצא בו לא יטייל אדם על פתח מדינה כדי שיכנס למרחץ מיד ואומר רבי דהתם מינכרא מילתא דאינו מטייל אלא ליכנס למרחץ מיד אחר השבת שעל פתח מדינה רגילים להיות מרחצאות כדאמרי' בפ"ק [ו] דמגילה (דף ו:) (ב) ה' מאות מעלות עשן חוץ לחומה אבל הכא אין הוכחה כ"כ בתוך התחום המחשיך לשכור פועלים ולהביא פירות וכי האי גוונא משני התם. מ"ר: אבל מחשיך הוא לשמור ומביא פירות בידו. מתוך פירוש הקונטרס משמע לשמור חוץ לתחום וכן משמע פשט המשנה וקשה לרבי מהא דאמר שמואל בגמ' מותר לאדם לומר לחבירו לכרך פלוני אני הולך למחר ופריך תנן אין מחשיכין על התחום לשכור פועלים כו' והשתא מתניתין גופיה תיקשי ליה דמוכחא מילתא כוותיה דשמואל מדקתני בסיפא כלל אמר אבא שאול כל שאני זכאי באמירתו יכול אני להחשיך עליו וקא מפרש בגמ' דמה שמותר לומר מותר להחשיך וא"כ מדשרינן להחשיך לשמור חוץ לתחום אלמא שרי למימר חוץ לתחום אני הולך למחר דהא בהא תליא והיינו כשמואל ואיני יודע מאי קשיא דאי לאו דשמואל מתני' אתיא שפיר דה"א אין לך דבר שלא יהא מותר לאדם לומר על עצמו ואפי' אשכור פועלים למחר או אבנה בנין זה יכול לומר בשבת דהוה אמינא דווקא לחבירו אסור לומר שכור לי פועלים למחר דמהני אמירתו אבל על עצמו יכול לומר כל מה שירצה דלא מהני אמירתו וכי תלי אבא שאול ההחשכה (ג) ה"מ באמירה לחבירו דיש אסורה ויש מותרת אבל אם איתא לדשמואל פריך שפיר דאסר כל אמירות אפילו על עצמו אלא דווקא לכרך פלוני אני הולך למחר משום טעמא דשאם יש שם בורגנין הולך והשתא פריך כיון דאי לאו האי טעמא הוה אסרת ליה אלא משום האי טעמא דווקא שרית ליה א"כ מתני' נמי תשתרי להביא פירות שאם יש מחיצות מביא. נ"ל:

לכרך פלוני אני הולך. תימה מאי איריא הוא אפילו לחבירו נמי יכול לומר לך לי לכרך פלוני למחר מהאי טעמא דקאמר [ז] מדשרי שמואל לקמן לומר לחבירו שמור לי פירות שבתחומך אפילו בשבת כ"ש שיכול לומר שמור לי למחר ואין לפרש דשאני התם שהן בתחומו אבל אין יכול לומר לחבירו שמור לי פירות שחוץ לתחומך דנראה הוא שאפילו זה יכול לומר מכיון שמותר להחשיך וי"ל דלא נקט שמואל דוקא לכרך פלוני אני הולך דהוא הדין לחבירו יכול לומר לך לי לכרך פלוני למחר:

בשלמא קש במחובר משכחת לה. ה"נ הו"מ למימר מטעם מוקצה דהא אינו ראוי למאכל בהמה כדאמר לעיל (דף קמא.) הקש שע"ג המטה לא ינענענו כו' אלא רבותא קאמר דאפילו במחובר משכחת לה: במחובר משכחת לה. אומר רבי דלאו משום תלישה נקט לה דאע"ג שמחובר לארץ אין בו איסור תלישה כיון שיבש אינו יונק מן הארץ כדמוכח בחולין פרק העור והרוטב (דף קכו: ושם) דאמר תאנים שלמקו באביהן מטמאין טומאת אוכלין והתולש ממנה בשבת חייב חטאת דווקא למקו אבל יבשו לא וכן משמע בכל הסוגיא דיבשו הן ועוקציהן מטמא טומאת אוכלין ואין דינו כלל כמחובר והא דקאמר הכא במחובר משכחת לה היינו משום איסור ייפוי קרקע כדאמר לעיל התולש עולשין בשבת חייב חטאת בפרק הבונה (לעיל דף קג.) והא דפריך בפרק המוכר תפילין (ערכין דף ק:) אאילן יבש הא קא נתרי פירי משמע שיש ביבש איסור תלישה אומר רבי דמיירי התם ביבשו הן ולא עוקציהן: בתיבנא סריא. והא דאמר לקמן פרק מי שהחשיך (דף קנה:) מפרכין תבן ואספסתא לפני בהמה ומוקי לה בתבנא סריא משמע דחזי לבהמה אומר רבי דמיירי כגון דלא סרי' כולי האי: אלא מת מאי ניהו להביא לו ארון ותכריכין. תימה אמאי לא קאמר למיגז ליה אסא שהיו רגילין להביא אסא למת כדאשכחן בנדה (דף לז.) דשוור אסא מערסא לערסא וי"ל ע"כ נ"ל ארון ותכריכין כדקתני במתני' בהדיא. מ"ר:

כט א טור שו"ע או"ח סימן שז סעיף ז:

ל ב ג מיי' פכ"ד מהלכו' שבת הלכה ג סמג שם טוש"ע או"ח סימן שז סעיף ח ט:

לא ד מיי' שם הלכה ה סמג שם טור שו"ע או"ח סימן שו סעיף ג:

לב ה מיי' פכ"ט מהל' שבת הלכה ה סמג עשין כט טור שו"ע או"ח סימן רצט סעיף י:

לג ו מיי' שם הלכה ו ופ"ב מהלכות תפלה הלכה יב סמג שם טוש"ע או"ח סי' רצד סעיף א:

לד ז מיי' פכ"ט מהל' שבת הל"ג סמג שם טוש"ע או"ח סימן רצט סעיף י:

רבינו חננאל

חשבונות שאין צריכין ואין מחשבין חשבונות שצריכין. כיצד אומר אדם לחבירו כך וכך פועלין כך וכך דינרין הוצאתי על שדה זו. אבל לא יאמר כך הוצאתי וכך אני עתיד להוציא. ואוקימנא אם נשאר עליו שכירות במה שעבד אסור לומר לו ואפילו כך הוצאתי שרצונו ליחשב ולידע סכום הנשאר עליו והן חשבונות שצריכין ואסור. אמר רב יהודה אמר שמואל מותר לאדם לומר לחבירו לכרך פלוני אני הולך למחר שאם יש בורגנין הולך אפילו בשבת. תנן אין מחשיכין על התחום לשכור פועלין ולהביא פירות הדא משנה היא וקשיא אקשיאו בהא. ומקשינן בשלמא לשכור פועלין היינו טעמא דאין מחשיכין על התחום ובשבת אסור לאוגורי פועלין אלא פירות נימא שאם יש מחיצות מותר להביאו ומותר להחשיך ולהביאם. ומפרקינן הא דתני אין מחשיכין להביא פירות בפירות מחוברין שאסו' לחותכן בשבת ועוד אקשינן מדתני ר' אושעיא ומפרקינן בתיבנא חריא דלא חזי וחוב אמרינן ת"ש מחשיכין על התחום לפקח על עסקי כלה ועל עסקי המת כו'. ומפרקינן לפקח על עסקי כלה למיגז לה אסא לבי גננא על עסקי המת נמי למיגר ליה גלימא לתפור לו תכריכין והללו דמשום מצוה התירו רבנן. הא אחר כגון דברים הללו אסור. אבל מחשיך הוא לשמור ומביא פירות בידו ואקשינן ואע"ג דלא אבדיל כלומר עושה מלאכה קודם הבדלה והאמר ר' אלעזר כו' אסור לעשות מלאכה קודם הבדלה. ואם יש לומר זה שמביא פירות התפלל הבדיל בתפלתו והאמר שמואל המבדיל בתפלה צריך שיבדיל על הכוס ואוקימנא מן הגיתות שנו. כלומר בשעת הגיתות מצוי בשדה בימי הבציר יין והבדיל על הכוס. וסלקא שמעתא שאסור לעשות מלאכה עד שהבדיל ואפילו לא אמר אלא המבדיל בין קודש לחול דיו. דהא רב אשי דהוא בתרא אמר כי הוינן בי רב כהנא הוה אמרינן המבדיל בין קודש לחול ואפכינן סלתי כלומר היינו מתעסקין במלאכה ולא [בא] רב אשי למעט אלא שאינו צריך לומר הבדלות. כאשר חלקו בפרק ערבי פסחים אבל צריך להזכיר ברכה גרעה מברכת הפירות וברכת המצות. וכן הלכה: כלל אמר אבא שאול. כל שאני זכאי באמירתו רשאי אני להחשיך עליו. והוצרכנו לדקדק לידע באיזה בבא דמתניתין אמר אבא שאול כלל

א) [עי' בגי' סי' ש"ו ס"ק י"ד פירוש על זה], ב) לקמן קנא., ג) ביצה ו. [ערוך גרס לאמגזר פי' לחתוך וי"ל לתפור], ד) [כרכות לג. ע"ש פסחים קה: ע"ש ודף קז.], ה) [שייך לע"א במשנה], ו) [גמ"ש ליתא אבל בעין יעקב תלאתי ע"ש], ז) ועוד מדברי כל"ל.

הגהות הב"ח

(א) גמ' כך וכך פועלים השכרתי על שדה: (ב) תוס' ד"ה ואין וכו' כדאמרינן פרק קמא דמגילה שלשה אלפים בי בני היו בו ולכל אחד וא' ה' מאות חלונות מעלות עשן: (ג) ד"ה אבל וכו' וכי תלי אבא שאול בהחשכה באמירה ה"מ:

ליקוטי רש"י

מעשה בחסיד. כל היכא דאמרינן מעשה בחסיד אחד או ר' יהודה בר בבא או ר' יהודה בר אלעאי [ב"ק קג:]. צלף. מין אילן הטוען שלשה מיני פירות אביונות וקפריסין ולולבין וכי אימיה לימיה להאי כדאמר בריש מוקף הכמים [ב"ב כח:] [לעיל ל:]. בורגנין. צריף שעושין מן ערבה וקנים לשומרי פירות או לגידי עופות ומגיל בעירובין כמילד מעברין (נה:) בורגנין מתעברין עמה מעברין (עירובין נה:) אם היו בורגנין חוץ לעיר בתוך שבעים אמה ושירים מתעברין עמה ומודדין תחום העיר משם ולהלן ומה הן בורגנין בתים שעושין שומרי העיר ואינו דבר קבוע [עירובין כא.]. תבן. הוא שעושין מן הקש המתכסך אותו כמוריגין ועושה כל זנב [השבלים] תבן [לעיל קמ.]. תיבנא סריא. נרקב ומסריח שאין ראוי למאכל בהמה [ביצה ל.]. סריא. מוסרח ויבאש (שמות טז) מתרגמינן וסרי [ב"מ צג:]. ומסלתינן סילתי. עצים דקים להבעיר אש [לעיל עד:]. לוקטין עצים בשדה מן המחובר [ביצה יט:].

וְשֶׁל מָה בְּכָךְ מוּתָּר לְחוֹשְׁבָן – AND "WHAT OF IT?" MAY BE CALCULATED on the Sabbath.

The preceding Baraisa forbids "calculations [of things] that happened." The Gemara notes that this is apparently contradicted by the following Baraisa:

וּרְמִינְהוּ – **But contrast them,** i.e. contrast the preceding Baraisa with the following one: חוֹשְׁבִין חֶשְׁבּוֹנוֹת שֶׁאֵינָן צְרִיכִין – ONE MAY MAKE CALCULATIONS THAT ARE NOT NEEDED, וְאֵין מְחַשְּׁבִין חֶשְׁבּוֹנוֹת שֶׁצְּרִיכִין – BUT ONE MAY NOT MAKE CALCULATIONS THAT ARE NEEDED,[1] בְּשַׁבָּת – ON THE SABBATH. כֵּיצַד – HOW SO? What is an illustration of these laws? אוֹמֵר אָדָם לַחֲבֵירוֹ – ONE MAY SAY TO HIS FELLOW: כָּךְ וְכָךְ פּוֹעֲלִים הוֹצֵאתִי עַל שָׂדֶה זוֹ – "I SPENT money to hire[2] SO-AND-SO many WORKERS ON THIS FIELD," כָּךְ וְכָךְ דִּינָרִין הוֹצֵאתִי עַל דִּירָה זוֹ – or "I SPENT SO-AND-SO MANY *DINARS* ON THIS RESIDENCE."[3] אֲבָל לֹא יֹאמַר לוֹ – HOWEVER, ONE MAY NOT SAY TO [HIS FELLOW]: כָּךְ וְכָךְ הוֹצֵאתִי וְכָךְ וְכָךְ אֲנִי עָתִיד לְהוֹצִיא – "I SPENT SO-AND-SO much money, AND I AM GOING TO SPEND SO-AND-SO much money."[4] This Baraisa explicitly permits one to report how much money he spent on something that already happened (e.g. "I spent so-and-so many *dinars* on this residence"). It thus contradicts the preceding Baraisa, which prohibits "calculations [of things] that happened." – ? –

The Gemara answers by examining the first Baraisa:[5]

וּלְטַעְמֵיךְ קַשְׁיָא לָךְ הִיא גּוּפָא – **But according to your premise,**[6] **you will have a difficulty with [the first Baraisa] itself.** On the one hand the first Baraisa prohibits calculations of "[things] that happened," yet on the other hand it permits calculations of "what of it?"[7] אֶלָּא הָא דְּאִיכָּא אַגְרָא דַּאֲגִירָא גַּבֵּיהּ – **Rather,** you must say that **this** term (namely, "[things] that happened") refers to a case **where he** still **has the wages of the hired workers with him,** i.e. he has not yet paid them;[8] הָא דְּלֵיכָּא אַגְרָא דַּאֲגִירָא גַּבֵּיהּ – whereas **this** term (namely, "what of it?") refers to a case **where he does not have the wages of the hired workers with him,** i.e. he has already paid them.

The Mishnah stated:

אֵין מַחְשִׁיכִין – WE MAY NOT go to AWAIT NIGHTFALL at the Sabbath boundary for the purpose of hiring workers or bringing produce after the Sabbath.

This is prohibited because it violates the injunction against *pursuing your business* on the Sabbath. The Gemara records a related narrative:

תָּנוּ רַבָּנָן – **The Rabbis taught in a Baraisa:** מַעֲשֶׂה בְּחָסִיד אֶחָד – IT HAPPENED WITH A CERTAIN PIOUS MAN שֶׁנִּפְרְצָה לוֹ פֶּרֶץ בְּתוֹךְ שָׂדֵהוּ – THAT A HOLE WAS BREACHED IN the fence OF HIS FIELD. וְנִמְלַךְ עָלֶיהָ לְגוֹדְרָהּ – HE DECIDED on the Sabbath TO FENCE IN [THE BREACH],[9] וְנִזְכַּר שֶׁשַּׁבָּת הוּא – BUT HE then REMEMBERED THAT IT WAS THE SABBATH, וְנִמְנַע אוֹתוֹ חָסִיד וְלֹא גְּדָרָהּ – AND THAT PIOUS MAN REFRAINED AND DID NOT ever FENCE IN [THE BREACH].[10] וְנַעֲשָׂה לוֹ נֵס – A MIRACLE WAS PERFORMED ON HIS BEHALF: וְעָלְתָה בּוֹ צָלָף – A CAPER TREE[11] GREW IN [THE BREACH], וּמִמֶּנָּה הָיְתָה פַּרְנָסָתוֹ וּפַרְנָסַת אַנְשֵׁי בֵיתוֹ – AND IT PROVIDED HIS LIVELIHOOD AS WELL AS THE LIVELIHOODS OF THE MEMBERS OF HIS HOUSEHOLD.

The Gemara records a discussion that involves our Mishnah:

אָמַר רַב יְהוּדָה אָמַר שְׁמוּאֵל – **Rav Yehudah said in the name of Shmuel:** מוּתָּר לְאָדָם לוֹמַר לַחֲבֵירוֹ – **It is permitted for a person to say** on the Sabbath **to his fellow,** לִכְרַךְ פְּלוֹנִי אֲנִי הוֹלֵךְ לְמָחָר – **"I am going to a certain city tomorrow,"**[12] even if the city is outside the Sabbath boundary. שֶׁאִם יֵשׁ בּוּרְגָּנִין – The reason is **that if there are huts** at prescribed intervals between his town and the city, הוֹלֵךְ – **he may go** there on the Sabbath itself.[13] Since there are conditions in which he would be allowed to go to that city on the Sabbath itself, he may say that he will travel there after the Sabbath, even if those conditions do not exist.[14]

NOTES

1. I.e. one may mention a sum of money only if he does not currently need to know the amount of that sum (see *Mishnah Berurah* 307:25, based on *Rashi* to *Kesubos* top of 5a). The Baraisa will give examples.

2. Instead of הוֹצֵאתִי, the text should read השכרתי (צ"ל שָׂכַרְתִּי), *I hired* (*Hagahos HaBach*).

3. Such statements are permitted, because they are of no current practical relevance to the speaker. He is merely telling a story about something that occurred in the past.

4. The speaker needs to know the amount of money that he still has to spend. He is consequently forbidden to mention it on the Sabbath.

5. *Rashi;* cf. *Chidushei HaRan.*

6. [Namely, that "calculations (of things) that happened" are equivalent to statements such as "I spent so-and-so many *dinars* on this residence." It was this assumption that led to your posing a contradiction between the two Baraisos.]

7. [The term *what of it?* denotes past expenditures (see 150a note 43). Hence, according to your premise that the term *[things] that happened* also signifies past expenditures, the first Baraisa contradicts itself, for it permits one, yet prohibits the other.]

8. The Gemara is answering that the term *[things] that happened* refers not to past expenditures, but to past projects. That is, it denotes projects that have already been completed, but have not yet been paid for. Since the speaker needs to know how much he must pay his workers, he may not mention this amount on the Sabbath.

Now that the term *[things] that happened* has been explained as signifying matters of current relevance, it is understandable why the first Baraisa prohibits this category, and yet allows calculations of *what of it,* which belong only to the past. By the same token, the Gemara has solved the contradiction between this Baraisa's prohibition against discussing *[things] that happened* and the second Baraisa's permit to say "I spent so-and-so many *dinars* etc.," which obviously refers to an expenditure that has already been made.

9. He forgot that it was the Sabbath (*Ritva MHK* ed.). Otherwise, he would not have even *thought* of doing [after the Sabbath] an act forbidden on the Sabbath. Although such thoughts are permitted, the pious refrain from them (*Maharshal;* see 150a note 22).

10. Although his "transgression" was inadvertent, for he thought that it was a weekday, he nevertheless punished himself by resolving never to benefit from it. In the merit of his piety, he was blessed with the caper tree (*Ritva MHK* ed.; see *Maharsha* and *Maharshal;* see also *Taz, Orach Chaim* 307:14, who suggests a different explanation).

11. A large tree with many branches. Three products of the caper tree are edible: its fruits, its flowers and its palm-like shoots (*Rashi,* from *Maasros* 4:6; see also *Tosafos* to *Beitzah* 25b ד"ה וצלף).

12. He may even ask his fellow to come with him (*Ramban, Rashba* et al.), or to go there for him (*Tosafos; Rosh*).

13. The law of *techum* mandates that a person may travel no more than 2,000 *amos* from his place of residence on the Sabbath. If he began the Sabbath in a town, the entire town is considered his place of residence, and the *techum* is measured from the edge of the town (see *Mishnah Berurah* 398:21).

A solitary house or even a hut which is situated within 70 2/3 *amos* from a town is regarded as an extension of the town and the *techum* is measured from it (see *Eruvin* 57a and *Shulchan Aruch, Orach Chaim* 398:5). A town can extend further to include also a second hut which is within 70 2/3 *amos* of the first one. Even an entire row of houses situated at intervals of less than 70 2/3 *amos* can be included within the town's boundaries, and the *techum* is measured from the outermost house (see *Eruvin* 21a and *Shulchan Aruch* ibid §6).

Thus, if two towns are linked by such a series of huts, one may walk from one town to the other on the Sabbath, regardless of the distance.

14. As a rule, one is forbidden to say that he will perform after the Sabbath an act which is prohibited [even by Rabbinic law] during the Sabbath. It is certainly forbidden to ask a Jew or gentile to perform such an act after the Sabbath (*Tosafos, Rosh;* see, however, *Ramban* and

ושל מה בכך מותר לחושבן ורמינהו חושבין חשבונות שאינן צריכין ואין מחשבין חשבונות שצריכין בשבת כיצד אומר אדם לחבירו כך וכך פועלים (א) הוצאתי על שדה זו כך וכך דינרין הוצאתי על דירה זו אבל לא יאמר לו כך וכך הוצאתי וכך וכך אני עתיד להוציא ולטעמיך קשיא לך היא גופא אלא *הא דאיכא אגרא דאגירא גביה הא דליכא אגרא דאגירא גביה: אין מחשיכין: תנו רבנן מעשה בחסיד אחד שנפרצה לו פרצה בתוך שדהו ונמלך עליה לגודרה ונזכר ששבת הוא ונמנע אותו חסיד ולא גדרה ונעשה לו נס ועלתה בו צלף וממנה היתה פרנסתו ופרנסת אנשי ביתו א"ר יהודה אמר שמואל מותר לאדם לומר לחבירו לכרך פלוני אני הולך למחר שאם יש בורגנין הולך תנן אין מחשיכין על התחום לשכור פועלים ולהביא פירות בשלמא לשכור פועלים דבשבת לא מצי אגר אלא להביא פירות לימא שאם יש שם מחיצות מביא משכחת לה בפירות המחוברים והתני ר' אושעיא אין מחשיכין על התחום להביא תבן וקש בשלמא קש משכחת לה במחובר אלא תבן היכי משכחת לה בתיבנא סריא ת"ש מחשיכין על התחום לפקח על עסקי כלה ועל עסקי המת על עסקי כלה ומת אין על עסקי אחר לא בשלמא אחר דומיא דכלה משכחת לה למיגזא ליה אסא אלא מת מאי ניהו להביא לו ארון ותכריכין וקתני מת אין אבל אחר לא ואמאי לימא שאם יש שם מחיצו' מביא מת נמי משכחת לה למיגזא ליה גלימא: אבל מחשיכין: ואע"ג דלא אבדיל והאמר רבי אלעזר בן אנטיגנוס משום רבי אליעזר בן יעקב אסור לו לאדם שיעשה חפציו קודם שיבדיל וכי תימא דאבדיל בתפלה והאמר רב יהודה אמר שמואל המבדיל בתפלה צריך שיבדיל על הכוס וכי תימא דאבדיל על הכוס כוס בשדה מי איכא תרגמא רבי נתן בר אמי קמיה דרבא בין הגיתות שנו א"ל ר' אבא לרב אשי במערבא אמרינן הכי המבדיל בין קודש לחול ועבדינן צורכין אמר רב אשי כי הוינא בי רב כהנא הוה אמר המבדיל בין קודש לחול ומסלתינן סילתי: כלל אמר אבא שאול כל שאני וכו': (איבעיא להו) אבא שאול אהייא אילימא ארישא קאי אין מחשיכין על התחום לשכור פועלים להביא פירות האי

רש"י

ושל מה בכך. כגון שכבר היו לצורך אלא שעברו כגון כך וכך הוצאתי בבנין זה: חשבונות שעברו. לקמן מוקי לה דלא עברו לגמרי שעדיין שכר הפועלים עליו שלא נתנו להן ושל מה בכך שעברו לגמרי ואין שכר פועלים עליו: כך וכך הוצאתי. אלמא עברו מותרין: תקשי לך היא גופא. בריתא קמייתא רישא קתני שעברו אסורין וסיפא קתני של מה בכך מותרין דהיינו עברו: צלף. אילן גדול הוא ובעל ענפים הרבה ושלשה מיני אוכל יש בפירותיו אביונות קפריסין ולולבין: שאם יש בורגנין. מע' אמה לע' אמה הולך אפי' בשבת שהכל חשוב כעיר אחת וכל העיר כד' אמות כדאמרינן בעירובין (דף כא.) וכיון דהוא דבר שיש לו היתר על ידי תקנה בשבת מותר לאומרו אפילו במקום שאין שם היתר: המחוברים. שא"א לקוצן בשבת ע"י שום תקנה: קש. זנבות השבולים אשטרלי"א: בתיבנא סריא. שאפי' יש מחיצות אינו מביא משום דמוקצה הוא: על עסקי כלה ומת אין. דתפלי שמים הן אבל על עסקי אחר אפי' דומיא דכלה לא: בשלמא אחר דומיא דכלה משכחת לה. דאסור להחשיך כגון לחתוך מן המחובר: למיגז לה אסא. דעבדו לה גננא דאפא לכלתא: אלא עסקי מת מאי היא. הבאה דארון ותכריכין ואמאי לאחר לא לימא הואיל ואם יש שם מחילות מביא: למיגז ליה גלימא. לתקן לו תכריכין דאין היתר לדבר היום כלל: ואע"ג דלא אבדיל. אסיפא דמתני' מתמה דקתני ומביא פירות בידו לקוצן מן המחובר בלא הבדלה: בין הגיתות שנו. דאיכא כוס בשדה: המבדיל בין קודש לחול. להיכרא בעלמא ללוות את המלך: ועבדינן צורכין. ואחר כך אנו מברכין על הכוס ברכה גמורה דהבדלה וכ"ש דאי אבדיל בתפלה מותר לעשות צרכיו ואחר ומבדיל על הכוס: ומסלתינן סילתי. חוטבין עצים: אהייא. קאי ומשוי כללא: אי נימא ארישא. דקתני ת"ק לאיסורא וקאמר אבא שאול לשויה בה כללא א"כ דכללא לאיסורא ה"ל למימר בהדיא כל שאינו זכאי באמירה כגון אלו שאינו רשאי לומר לחבירו שכור לי פועלים או הבא לי פירות למוצאי שבת אינו רשאי להחשיך מיבעי ליה: אלא

תוספות

ואין מחשיכין על התחום לשכור פועלים ולהביא פירות. השתא משמע דוקא על התחום אבל בתוך התחום מחשיכין לשכור פועלי' ולהביא פירו' וקשה לרבי דבסוף פ' בכל מערבין (עירובין דל"ח:) תניא לא יהלך אדם לתוך שדהו לידע מה צריכה כיוצא בו לא יטייל אדם על פתח מדינה כדי שיכנס למרחץ מיד ואומר רבי דהתם מיכרא מילתא דאינו מטייל אלא ליכנס למרחץ מיד אחר השבת שעל פתח מדינה רגילים להיות מרחצאות כדאמרי' בפ"ק דמגילה (דף ו:) (ג) ה' מאות מעלות עשן חוץ לחומה אבל הכא אין הוכחה כ"כ בתוך התחום הממשיך לשכור פועלים ולהביא פירות וכי האי גוונא משני התם. מ"ר: **אבל** מחשיך הוא לשמור ומביא פירות בידו. מתוך פירוש הקונטרס משמע לשמור חוץ לתחום וכן משמע פשט המשנה וקשה לרבי מהא דאמר שמואל בגמ' מותר לאדם לומר לחבירו לכרך פלוני אני הולך למחר ופריך תנן אין מחשיכין על התחום לשכור פועלים כו' והשתא מתניתין גופיה תיקשי ליה דמוכחא מילתא כוותיה דשמואל מדקתני בסיפא כלל אמר אבא שאול כל שאני זכאי באמירתו יכול אני להחשיך עליו וקא מפרש בגמ' דמה שמותר לומר מותר להחשיך וא"כ מדשרינן להחשיך לשמור חוץ לתחום אלמא שרי למימר חוץ לתחום אני הולך למחר דהא בהא תליא והיינו כשמואל ואיני יודע מאי קשיא דאי לאו דשמואל מתני' אתיא שפיר דה"א אין לך דבר שלא יהא מותר לאדם לומר על עצמו ואפי' אשכור פועלים למחר או אבנה בנין זה יכול לומר בשבת דהוה אמינא דווקא לחבירו אסור לומר שכור לי פועלים למחר דמהני אמירתו אבל על עצמו יכול לומר כל מה שירצה דלא מהני אמירתו וכי תלי אבא שאול ההחשכה (ג) ה"מ באמירה לחבירו דיש אסורה ויש מותרת אבל אם איתא לדשמואל פריך שפיר דאסר כל אמירות אפילו על עצמו אלא דווקא לכרך פלוני אני הולך למחר משום טעמא דשאם יש שם בורגנין הולך והשתא פריך כיון דלאו האי טעמא הוה אסרת ליה אלא משום האי טעמא דווקא שרית ליה א"כ מתני' נמי תשתרי להביא פירות שאם יש מחילות מביא. נ"ל: **לכרך** פלוני אני הולך. תימה מאי איריא הוא אפילו לחבירו נמי יכול לומר לך לי לכרך פלוני למחר מהאי טעמא דקאמר מדשרי שמואל לקמן לומר לחבירו שמור לי פירות שבתחומך אפילו בשבת כ"ש שיכול לומר שמור לי למחר ואין לפרש דשאני התם שהן בתחומו אבל אין יכול לומר לחבירו שמור לי פירות שחוץ לתחומך דנראה הוא שאפילו זה יכול לומר מכיון שמותר להחשיך וי"ל דלא נקט שמואל דוקא לכרך פלוני אני הולך דהוא הדין לחבירו יכול לומר לך לי לכרך פלוני למחר:

בשלמא קש במחובר משכחת לה. ה"נ הו"מ למימר מטעם מוקצה דהא אינו ראוי למאכל בהמה כדאמר לעיל (דף קמא.) הקש שע"ג המטה לא ינענענו כו' אלא רבותא קאמר דאפילו במחובר משכחת לה: **במחובר** משכחת לה. אומר רבי דלאו משום תלישה נקט לה דאע"ג שמחובר לארץ אין בו איסור תלישה כיון שיבש אינו יונק מן הארץ כדמוכח בחולין פרק העור והרוטב (דף קכח: ושם) דאמר תאנים שלמקו באביהן מטמאין טומאת אוכלין והתולש ממנה בשבת חייב חטאת דווקא למקו אבל יבשו לא וכן משמע בכל הסוגיא דיבשו הן ועוקציהן מטמא טומאת אוכלין ואין דינו כלל כמחובר והא דקאמר הכא במחובר משכחת לה היינו משום איסור ייפוי קרקע כדאמר לעיל התולש עולשין בשבת חייב חטאת בפרק הבונה (לעיל דף קג.) והא דפריך בפרק המוצא תפילין (עירובין דף ק:) אאילן יבש הא קא נתרי פירי משמע שיש ביבש איסור תלישה אומר רבי דמיירי התם דיבשו הן ולא עוקציהן: **בתיבנא** סריא. והא דאמר לקמן פרק מי שהחשיך (דף קנה:) מפרכין תבן ואספסתא לפני בהמה ומוקי לה בתבנא סריא משמע דחזי לבהמה אומר רבי דמיירי כגון דלא סרי' כולי האי: **אלא** מת מאי ניהו להביא לו ארון ותכריכין. תימה אמאי לא קאמר למיגז ליה אסא שהיו רגילין להביא אסא למת כדאשכחן בנדה (דף לז.) דשור אסא מערסא לערסא וי"ל ע"כ צ"ל ארון ותכריכין כדקתני במתני' בהדיא. מ"ר:

הא

עין משפט נר מצוה

כט א טור שו"ע או"ח סימן שז סעיף ז:

ל ב ג מיי' פכ"ד מהלכו' שבת הלכה ג סמג שם טוש"ע או"ח סימן שז סעיף ח ט:

לא ד מיי' שם הלכה ה סמג שם טור שו"ע או"ח סימן שו סעיף ג:

לב ה מיי' פכ"ט מהל' שבת הלכה ה סמג עשין כט טור שו"ע או"ח סימן רצט סעיף י:

לג ו מיי' שם הלכה ו ופ"ב מהלכות תפלה הלכה יג סמג שם טוש"ע או"ח סי' רצד סעיף א:

לד ז מיי' פכ"ט מהל' שבת הל"ג סמג שם טוש"ע או"ח סימן רצט סעיף י:

רבינו חננאל

חשבונות שאין צריכין ואין מחשבין חשבונות שצריכין. כיצד אומר אדם לחבירו כך וכך פועלין כך וכך דינרין הוצאתי על שדה זו. אבל לא יאמר כך הוצאתי וכך אני עתיד להוציא. ואוקימנא אם נשאר עליו שכירות במה שעבר אסור לומר לו ואפילו כך הוצאתי שרצונו ליחשב ולידע סכום הנשאר עליו והן חשבונות שצריכין ואסור. **אמר** רב יהודה אמר שמואל מותר לאדם לומר לחבירו לכרך פלוני אני הולך למחר שאם יש בורגנין הולך אפילו בשבת. תנן אין מחשיכין על התחום לשכור פועלין ולהביא פירות הדא משנה היא וקשיא אקשיאו בהא. ומקשינן בשלמא לשכור פועלין היינו טעמא דאין מחשיכין על התחום ובשבת אסור לאוגורי פועלין אלא פירות נימא שאם יש מחיצות מותר להביאו ומותר להחשיך ולהביאם. ומפרקינן הא דתני אין מחשיכין להביא פירות בפירות מחוברין שאסור לחותכן בשבת ועוד אקשינן מדתני ר' אושעיא ומפרקינן בתיבנא חדיא דלא חזי ותוב אמרינן ת"ש מחשיכין על התחום לפקח על עסקי כלה ועל עסקי המת כו'. ומפרקינן לפקח על עסקי כלה למיגז לה אסא לבי גננא על עסקי המת נמי למיגז ליה גלימא לחפור לו תכריכין והללו דמשום מצוה התירו רבנן. הא אחר כגון דברים הללו אבל משחיך הוא לשמור ומביא פירות בידו ואקשינן ואע"ג דלא אבדיל כלומר עושה מלאכה קודם הבדלה והאמר ר' אלעזר וכו' אסור לעשות מלאכה קודם הבדלה. ואם יש לומר זה שמביא פירות התפלל הבדיל בתפלה והאמר שמואל המבדיל בתפלה צריך שיבדיל על הכוס ואוקימנא בין הגיתות שנו. כלומר בשעת הגיתות מצוי בשדה בימי הבציר יין והבדיל על הכוס. ודלקא שמעתא שאסור לעשות מלאכה עד שהבדיל ואפילו לא אמר אלא המבדיל בין קדש לחול דיו. דהא רב אשי דהוא בתרא אמר כי הוינן בי רב כהנא הוה אמרינן המבדיל בין קודש לחול ואפכינן סלתי כלומר היינו מתעסקין במלאכה ולא [בא] רב אשי למעט אלא שאינו צריך לומר הבדלות. כאשר חלקו בפרק ערבי פסחים אבל צריך להזכיר ברכה בשם ומלכות דלית גרעה מברכת הפירות וברכת המצות. וכן הלכה: **כלל** אמר אבא שאול. כל שאני זכאי באמירתו רשאי אני להחשיך עליו. והוצרכנו לדקדק לידע באיזה בבא דמתניתין אמר אבא שאול

כלל

מסורת הש"ס

א) [עי' בע"ז סי' ש"ז ס"ק י"ד פירוש על זה], ב) לקמן קנא., ג) בילה ו. [ערוך גרס למיגד פי' לחתוך וי"א לספור], ד) [ברכות לג. ע"ש פסחים קה: ע"ש ודף קו.], ה) [שייך לע"א במשנה], ו) [בס"ם ליתא אבל בעין יעקב מלאתי ע"ש], ז) ועוד מדשרי כל"ל.

הגהות הב"ח

(א) גמ' כך וכך פועלים השכרתי על שדה: (ב) תוס' ד"ה ואין וכו' כדאמרינן פרק קמא דמגילה שלשת אלפים בי בני היה בו ולכל אחד ואחד ה' מאות חלונות מעלות עשן: (ג) ד"ה אבל וכו' וכי תלי אבא שאול ההחשכה באמירה ה"מ:

ליקוטי רש"י

מעשה בחסיד. כל היכא דאמרינן מעשה בחסיד אחד או ר' יהודה בן בבא או ר' יהודה בר' אלעאי (ב"ק קג:) [לעיל קכו:]. צלף. מין אילן הטוען שלשה מיני פירות אביונות וקפריסין ולולבין וכי איתיה ליתיה להאי כדאמר בריש חזקת הבתים (ב"ב כח:) [לעיל ל:]. בורגנין. צריף שעושין מן ערבה וקנים לשומרי פירות או לגידי עופות ומניא בעירובין בכילד מעברין (נה:) בורגנין מתעברין עמה [סוכה ג:]. דאמר בכילד מעברין (עירובין נה:) אם היו בורגנין חוץ לעיר בתוך שבעים אמה ושיריים מתעברין עמה ומודדין חוץ העיר משם ולהלן ומה הן בורגנין סוכות שעושין שומרי העיר ואינו דבר קבוע [עירובין כא.]. תבן. הוא שעושין מן הקש מחתכין אותו במורגין ועושה כל זנב [השבלים] תבן [לעיל קמ.]. תיבנא סריא. נרקב ומסריח שאין ראוי למאכל בהמה [ביצה ל.]. סריא. מוסרח ויבאש (שמות ח) מתרגמינן וסרי [ב"מ צג:]. ומסלתינן סילתי. עצים דקים להבעיר אש [לעיל עד:]. לוקטין עצים בשדה מן המחובר [ביצה יט:].

In the previous ruling, Shmuel teaches that the ban against preparing to perform a forbidden act after the Sabbath does not apply to an act that is sometimes permitted on the Sabbath itself. The Gemara challenges this premise:

תְּנַן – **We learned in** our **Mishnah:** אֵין מַחְשִׁיכִין עַל הַתְּחוּם לִשְׂכּוֹר פּוֹעֲלִים וּלְהָבִיא פֵּירוֹת – WE MAY NOT go to AWAIT NIGHTFALL AT THE Sabbath BOUNDARY FOR THE PURPOSE OF HIRING WORKERS OR BRINGING PRODUCE. בִּשְׁלָמָא לִשְׂכּוֹר פּוֹעֲלִים – **Now, it is understandable** that he may not go to the boundary **for the purpose of hiring workers,** דִּבְשַׁבָּת לֹא מָצֵי אָגַר – **for on the Sabbath** itself **he may not hire** workers under any circumstances. אֶלָּא לְהָבִיא פֵּירוֹת – **But** why does the Mishnah rule that he may not go to the boundary **for the purpose of bringing produce?** לֵימָא שֶׁאִם יֵשׁ שָׁם מְחִיצוֹת מֵבִיא – **Let us say that** he is allowed to do so, because **if there are partitions there, he may bring** produce on the Sabbath itself[15] – ? –

The Gemara answers:

מַשְׁכַּחַת לָהּ בְּפֵירוֹת הַמְחוּבָּרִים – **You can find** a case in which **this** would be prohibited, namely, **where the produce is attached** to the ground. Since there is no permissible way to detach the produce on the Sabbath itself, he may not await nightfall at the boundary for the purpose of detaching the produce after the Sabbath and bringing it back with him.

The Gemara asks:

וְהָתָנֵי רַבִּי אוֹשַׁעְיָא – **But R' Oshaya has taught** the following Baraisa: אֵין מַחְשִׁיכִין עַל הַתְּחוּם לְהָבִיא תֶּבֶן וָקַשׁ – WE MAY NOT AWAIT NIGHTFALL AT THE Sabbath BOUNDARY FOR THE PURPOSE OF BRINGING PROCESSED STRAW OR WHOLE STRAW[16] after the Sabbath. בִּשְׁלָמָא קַשׁ – **Now it is understandable** that one may not wait at the boundary in order to bring **whole straw** after the Sabbath; מַשְׁכַּחַת לָהּ בִּמְחוּבָּר – **you could find** a case in which **this** is prohibited, namely, **where** the straw is still **attached** to the ground.[17] אֶלָּא תֶּבֶן – **However,** as far as **processed straw** is concerned, which by definition is already detached from the ground,[18] הֵיכִי מַשְׁכַּחַת לָהּ – **how can you find** a case in which **it** would be forbidden to wait at the boundary to bring some back after the Sabbath?[19]

The Gemara answers:

בְּתִיבְנָא סַרְיָא – We are dealing here **with foul-smelling straw.** Such straw may not be moved on the Sabbath itself under any circumstances, because it is *muktzeh.*

The Gemara issues another challenge to Shmuel's ruling:

תָּא שְׁמַע – **Come, learn** the following proof:[20] מַחְשִׁיכִין עַל הַתְּחוּם לְפַקֵּחַ עַל עִסְקֵי כַלָּה וְעַל עִסְקֵי הַמֵּת – ONE MAY AWAIT NIGHTFALL AT THE BOUNDARY TO ATTEND TO THE AFFAIRS OF A BRIDE OR TO THE AFFAIRS OF A DECEASED PERSON. עַל עִסְקֵי כַלָּה וּמֵת אִין – This Mishnah implies: **For the affairs of a bride or a deceased person – yes!** this is permitted;[21] עַל עִסְקֵי אַחֵר לֹא – but **for the affairs of another person – no!** this is not permitted.[22] בִּשְׁלָמָא אַחֵר דּוּמְיָא דְּכַלָּה – **Now, it is fine** that the Mishnah prohibits preparations for **another person** which are **similar to** those **for a bride.** מַשְׁכַּחַת לָהּ לְמִגְזָא לֵיהּ אָסָא – **You can find** a case in which **this** would be prohibited, namely, where he awaits nightfall **to cut** down **for himself a myrtle** branch.[23] Cutting a branch is not permitted on the Sabbath under any circumstances. One is consequently forbidden to await nightfall at the boundary for the purpose of cutting a branch after the Sabbath, except for the sake of a bride. אֶלָּא מֵת מַאי נִיהוּ – **But** in the case of **a deceased person,**

NOTES

Rashba; see also *Magen Avraham* 307:11 and *Beur Halachah* to 307:8 ד״ה וכן). This prohibition is based on the verse: מִמְּצוֹא חֶפְצְךָ וְדַבֵּר דָּבָר, *from pursuing your business and speaking words* (*Shulchan Aruch* ibid. §1). However, it does not apply where the act in question is permitted on the Sabbath itself under certain circumstances. An example of such an act is traveling more than 2,000 *amos,* which, as explained above, is permitted on the Sabbath itself if there are huts at intervals of 70 2/3 *amos* along the way. Therefore one is allowed to say that he will travel more than 2,000 *amos* after the Sabbath even if there are no such huts.

Aruch HaShulchan (307:21) explains that the act of traveling more than 2,000 *amos* is essentially permitted on the Sabbath. It is only the lack of huts that forbids it. Hence, when one says, "I will travel to a certain city tomorrow," his actual words do not signify a prohibited act, for he does not verbalize the fact that there are no huts. Although he is aware of the huts' absence, that is classified as thought, which is permitted.

As stated in note 12, one may also ask a Jew or a gentile to go to a distant city for him after the Sabbath. It should be noted, though, that this permit applies only to preparing for *after* the Sabbath. One is not allowed to ask even a gentile to travel beyond the boundary for him *during* the Sabbath. In fact, the Mishnah below (151a) teaches that if a gentile brought something for a Jew from beyond the boundary on the Sabbath, even if he had not been asked to do so, one may not derive benefit from that desecration of the Sabbath [as is the case with any *melachah* done by a gentile for a Jew on the Sabbath] (see *Ramban, Rashba* et al. to 151a).

15. If the area in which he intends to carry would be enclosed by valid partitions, it would become a private domain in which carrying is permitted. Thus, carrying too is an act that can be rendered permissible through a certain adjustment. According to Shmuel, therefore, one should be allowed to say on the Sabbath, "I will carry [produce] tomorrow." One should also be allowed to await nightfall at the boundary in order to carry produce after the Sabbath, because, as Abba Shaul stated in the Mishnah, awaiting nightfall is permitted wherever speech is permitted (*Ramban, Ritva MHK* ed., *Ran MHK* ed.).

[We can now understand why our Mishnah permits one to wait at the boundary in order to guard his field after the Sabbath, although he intends to pass beyond the boundary, which is forbidden on the Sabbath itself. Since passing beyond the boundary is an act that is permitted in certain circumstances, one is allowed to prepare for it either through speech or through awaiting nightfall at the boundary (see *Tosafos* and *Maharsha*).]

16. Our translation of תֶּבֶן as *processed straw* and קַשׁ as *whole straw* follows *Rashi* to 140a ד״ה תבן and to *Zevachim* 116b ד״ה עיזא דקורקסא, where *Rashi* explains that קַשׁ is cut up to make תֶּבֶן (cf. *Tosafos* to 36b ד״ה כירה and to *Bava Metzia* 103a ד״ה המקבל).

17. [קַשׁ could signify the part of the stalk that remains attached to the ground after harvesting, i.e. stubble (see *Rashi* to 36b ד״ה קש וד״ה גבבא and *Tosafos* ibid.).] There are no circumstances in which one may uproot stubble on the Sabbath. Although uprooting stubble does not constitute קְצִירָה, *reaping,* because stubble is dead, one would nevertheless be liable for improving the land. [Any improvement of land as regards its arability falls under the *melachah* of חֲרִישָׁה, *plowing*] (*Tosafos* ד״ה במחובר, *Rashba, Ritva MHK* ed.; see *Beur Halachah* to 336:12 ד״ה חייב).

Tosafos (ד״ה בשלמא) observe that the Gemara could also have said that קַשׁ may not be brought for a different reason – namely, that it is *muktzeh* (see the Mishnah on 141a).

18. See note 16.

19. In this case, the only forbidden act is carrying the straw. Since carrying is permitted on the Sabbath itself under certain circumstances (viz. within partitions), one should be allowed to await nightfall at the boundary in order to carry after the Sabbath.

[תֶּבֶן, *processed straw,* is not *muktzeh,* because it is used as fodder.]

20. From the next Mishnah, on 151a.

21. To prepare for the wedding of a bride or the burial of a corpse, which are mitzvos, one may await nightfall at the boundary even for activities that are forbidden on the Sabbath itself. As the Gemara taught above (150a), one is allowed to prepare for חֶפְצֵי שָׁמַיִם, *business of Heaven* (*Rashi*).

22. In the case of another person, no mitzvah is involved. Hence, one may not await nightfall at the boundary in order to perform activities for his sake that would be forbidden during the Sabbath. The Gemara's point is that the very enterprise which would be permitted for the sake of a bride or deceased person is forbidden for the sake of someone else.

23. Branches of myrtle were used to adorn the wedding ceremony (*Rashi*).

ושל מה בכך מותר לחושבן ורמינהו חושבין חשבונות שאינן צריכין ואין מחשבין חשבונות שצריכין בשבת כיצד אומר אדם לחבירו כך וכך פועלים (א) הוצאתי על שדה זו וכך וכך דינרין הוצאתי על דירה זו אבל לא יאמר לו כך וכך הוצאתי וכך וכך אני עתיד להוציא ולטעמיך קשיא לך היא גופא אלא הא דאיכא אגרא דאגירא גביה הא דליכא אגרא דאגירא גביה: אין מחשיכין: תנו רבנן מעשה בחסיד אחד שנפרצה לו פרץ בתוך שדהו ונמלך עליה לגודרה ונזכר ששבת הוא ונמנע אותו חסיד ולא גדרה ונעשה לו נס ועלתה בו צלף וממנה היתה פרנסתו ופרנסת אנשי ביתו א"ר יהודה אמר שמואל מותר לאדם לומר לחבירו לכרך פלוני אני הולך למחר שאם יש בורגנין הולך תנן אין מחשיכין על התחום לשכור פועלים ולהביא פירות בשלמא לשכור פועלים דבשבת לא מצי אגר אלא להביא פירות לימא שאם יש שם מחיצות מביא משכחת לה בפירות המחוברים והתני ר' אושעיא אין מחשיכין על התחום להביא תבן וקש בשלמא קש משכחת לה במחובר אלא תבן היכי משכחת לה בתיבנא סריא ת"ש מחשיכין על התחום לפקח על עסקי כלה ועל עסקי המת על עסקי כלה ומת אין על עסקי אחר לא בשלמא אחר דומיא דכלה משכחת לה למיגזא ליה אסא אלא מת מאי ניהו להביא לו ארון ותכריכין וקתני מת אין אבל אחר לא ואמאי לימא שאם יש שם מחיצו' מביא מת נמי משכחת לה למיגזא ליה גלימא: אבל מחשיכין: ואע"ג דלא אבדיל והאמר רבי אלעזר בן אנטיגנוס משום רבי אליעזר בן יעקב אסור לו לאדם שיעשה חפציו קודם שיבדיל וכי תימא דאבדיל בתפלה והאמר רב יהודה אמר שמואל המבדיל בתפלה צריך שיבדיל על הכוס וכי תימא דאבדיל על הכוס כוס בשדה מי איכא תרגמא רבי נתן בר אמי קמיה דרבא בין הגיתות שנו א"ל ר' אבא לרב אשי במערבא אמרינן הכי המבדיל בין קודש לחול ועבדינן צורכין אמר רב אשי כי הוינא בי רב כהנא הוה אמר המבדיל בין קודש לחול ומסלתינן סילתי: כלל אמר אבא שאול כל שאני וכו': (איבעיא להו) אבא שאול אהייא אילימא ארישא קאי אין מחשיכין על התחום לשכור פועלים להביא פירות האי

רש"י

ושל מה בכך. כגון שכבר היו לצורך אלא שעברו כגון כך וכך הוצאתי בבנין זה: חשבונות שעברו. לקמן מוקי לה דלא עברו לגמרי שעדיין שכר הפועלים עליו שלא נתנו להן ושל מה בכך שעברו לגמרי ואין שכר פועלים עליו: כך וכך הוצאתי. אלמא עברו מותרין: תקשי לך היא גופא. ברייתא קמייתא רישא קתני שעברו אסורין וסיפא קתני של מה בכך מותרין דהיינו עברו: צלף. אילן גדול הוא ובעל ענפים הרבה ושלשה מיני אוכל יש בפירותיו אביונות קפריסין ולולבין: שאם יש בורגנין. מע' אמה לע' אמה הולך אפי' בשבת שהכל חשוב כעיר אחת וכל העיר כד' אמות כדאמרינן בעירובין (דף כא.) וכיון דהוא דבר שיש לו היתר על ידי תקנה בשבת מותר לאומרו אפילו במקום שאין שם היתר: המחוברים. שא"א לקצצן בשבת ע"י שום תקנה: קש. זנבות השבולים אשטרלי"א: בתיבנא סריא. שאפי' יש מחילות אינו מביא משום דמוקצה הוא: על עסקי כלה ומת אין. דחפצי שמים הן אבל על עסקי אחר אפי' דומיא דכלה לא: בשלמא אחר דומיא דכלה משכחת לה. דאסור להחשיך כגון לחתוך מן המחובר: למיגז לה אסא. דעבדו לה גננא דאסא לכלתא: אלא עסקי מת מאי היא. הבאה דארון ותכריכין ואמאי לאחר לא לימא הואיל ואם יש שם מחילות מביא: למיגז ליה גלימא. לתקן לו תכריכין דאין היתר לדבר היום כלל: ואע"ג דלא אבדיל. אסיפא דמתני' מתמה דקתני ומביא פירות בידו לקוצצן מן המחובר בלא הבדלה: בין הגיתות שנו. דאיכא כוס בשדה: המבדיל בין קודש לחול. להיכרא בעלמא ללוות את המלך: ועבדינן צורכין. ואחר כך אנו מברכין על הכוס ברכה גמורה דהבדלה וכ"ש דאי אבדיל בתפלה מותר לעשות צרכיו וחוזר ומבדיל על הכוס: ומסלתינן סילתי. חוטבין עצים: אהייא. קאי ומשוי כללא: אי נימא ארישא. דקתני ת"ק לאיסורא וקאתי אבא שאול לשוויה בה כללא א"כ דכללא לאיסורא ה"ל למימר בהדיא כל שאינו זכאי באמירה כגון אלו שאינו רשאי לומר לחבירו שכור לי פועלים או הבא לי פירות למוצאי שבת אינו רשאי להחשיך מיבעי ליה: אלא

תוספות

ואין מחשיכין על התחום לשכור פועלים ולהביא פירות. השתא משמע דוקא על התחום אבל בתוך התחום מחשיכין לשכור פועלי' ולהביא פירו' וקשה לרבי דבסוף פ' בכל מערבין (עירובין דל"ח:) תניא לא יהלך אדם לתוך שדהו לידע מה צריכה כיוצא בו לא יטייל אדם על פתח מדינה כדי שיכנס למרחץ מיד ואומר רבי דהתם מינכרא מילתא דאינו מטייל אלא ליכנס למרחץ מיד אחר השבת שעל פתח מדינה רגילים להיות מרחצאות כדאמרי' בפ"ק דמגילה (דף ו:) (ב) ה' מאות מעלות עשן חוץ לחומה אבל הכא אין הוכחה כ"כ בתוך התחום המחשיך לשכור פועלים ולהביא פירות וכי האי גוונא משני התם. מ"ר:

אבל מחשיך הוא לשמור ומביא פירות בידו. מתוך פירוש הקונטרס משמע לשמור חוץ לתחום וכן משמע פשט המשנה וקשה לרבי מהא דאמר שמואל בגמ' מותר לאדם לומר לחבירו לכרך פלוני אני הולך למחר ופריך תנן אין מחשיכין על התחום לשכור פועלים כו' והשתא מתניתין גופיה תיקשי ליה דמוכחא מילתא כוותיה דשמואל מדקתני בסיפא כלל אמר אבא שאול כל שאני זכאי באמירתו יכול אני להחשיך עליו וקא מפרש בגמ' דמה שמותר לומר מותר להחשיך וא"כ מדשרינן להחשיך לשמור חוץ לתחום אלמא שרי למימר חוץ לתחום אני הולך למחר דהא בהא תליא והיינו כשמואל ואיני יודע מאי קשיא דאי לאו דשמואל מתני' אתיא שפיר דה"א אין לך דבר שלא יהא מותר לאדם לומר על עצמו ואפי' אשכור פועלים למחר או אבנה בנין זה יכול לומר בשבת דהוה אמינא דווקא לחבירו אסור לומר שכור לי פועלים למחר דמהני אמירתו אבל על עצמו יכול לומר כל מה שירצה דלא מהני אמירתו וכי תלי אבא שאול ההחשכה (ג) ה"מ באמירה לחבירו דיש אסורה ויש מותרת אבל אם איתא לדשמואל פריך שפיר דאסר כל אמירות אפילו על עצמו אלא דווקא לכרך פלוני אני הולך למחר משום טעמא דשאם יש שם בורגנין הולך והשתא פריך כיון דאי לאו האי טעמא הוה אסרת ליה אלא משום האי טעמא דווקא שרית ליה א"כ מתני' נמי תשתרי להביא פירות שאם יש מחילות מביא. נ"ל:

לכרך פלוני אני הולך. תימה מאי איריא הוא אפילו לחבירו נמי יכול לומר לך לי לכרך פלוני למחר מהאי טעמא דקאמר ז) מדשרי שמואל לקמן לומר לחבירו שמור לי פירות שבתחומך אפילו בשבת כ"ש שיכול לומר שמור לי למחר ואין לפרש דשאני התם שהן בתחומו אבל אין יכול לומר לחבירו שמור לי פירות שחוץ לתחומך דנראה הוא שאפילו זה יכול לומר מכיון שמותר להחשיך וי"ל דלא נקט שמואל דוקא לכרך פלוני אני הולך דהוא הדין לחבירו יכול לומר לך לי לכרך פלוני למחר:

בשלמא קש במחובר משכחת לה. ה"נ הו"מ למימר מטעם מוקצה דהא אינו ראוי למאכל בהמה כדאמר לעיל (דף קמא.) הקש שע"ג המטה לא ינענענו כו' אלא רבותא קאמר דאפילו במחובר משכחת לה: במחובר משכחת לה. אומר רבי דלאו משום תלישה נקט לה דאע"ג שמחובר לארץ אין בו איסור תלישה כיון שיבש אינו יונק מן הארץ כדמוכח בחולין פרק העור והרוטב (דף קכז: ושם) דאמר תאנים שלקו באביהן מטמאין טומאת אוכלין והתולש ממנה בשבת חייב חטאת דווקא לקו אבל יבשו לא וכן משמע בכל הסוגיא דיבשו הן ועוקציהן מטמא טומאת אוכלין ואין דינו כלל כמחובר והא דקאמר הכא במחובר משכחת לה היינו משום איסור ייפוי קרקע כדאמר לעיל התולש עולשין בשבת חייב חטאת בפרק הבונה (לעיל דף קג.) והא דפריך בפרק המוצא תפילין (עירובין דף ק:) אאילן יבש הא קא נתרי פירי משמע שיש ביבש איסור תלישה אומר רבי דמיירי התם דיבשו הן ולא עוקציהן: בתיבנא סריא. והא דאמר לקמן פרק מי שהחשיך (דף קנה:) מפרכין תבן ואספסתא לפני בהמה ומוקי לה בתבנא סריא משמע דחזי לבהמה אומר רבי דמיירי כגון דלא סרי' כולי האי: אלא מת מאי ניהו להביא לו ארון ותכריכין. תימה אמאי לא קאמר למיגז ליה אסא שהיו רגילין להביא אסא למת כדאשכחן בנדה (דף לז.) דשוור אסא מערסא לערסא וי"ל ע"כ נ"ל ארון ותכריכין כדקתני במתני' בהדיא. מ"ר:

רבינו חננאל

חשבונות שאין צריכין ואין מחשבין חשבונות שצריכין. כיצד אומר אדם לחבירו כך וכך פועלין כך וכך דינרין הוצאתי על שדה זו. אבל לא יאמר כך הוצאתי וכך אני עתיד להוציא. ואוקימנא אם נשאר עליו שכירות במה שעבד אסור לומר לו ואפילו כך הוצאתי שרצונו ליחשב ולידע סכום הנשאר עליו והן חשבונות שצריכין ואסור. **אמר** רב יהודה אמר שמואל מותר לאדם לומר לחבירו לכרך פלוני אני הולך למחר שאם יש בורגנין הולך אפילו בשבת. תנן אין מחשיכין על התחום לשכור פועלין ולהביא פירות הדא משנה היא וקשיא אקשיאו בהא. ומקשינן בשלמא לשכור פועלין היינו טעמא דאין מחשיכין על התחום ובשבת אסור לאוגורי פועלין אלא פירות נימא שאם יש מחיצות מותר להביאו ומותר להחשיך ולהביאם. ומפרקינן הא דתני אין מחשיכין להביא פירות בפירות מחוברין שאסו' לחותכן בשבת ועוד אקשינן מדתני ר' אושעיא ומפרקינן בתיבנא חדיא דלא חזי ותוב אמרינן ת"ש מחשיכין על התחום לפקח על עסקי כלה ועל עסקי המת כו'. ומפרקינן לפקח על עסקי כלה למיגז לה אסא לבי גננא על עסקי המת נמי למיגר ליה גלימא לתפור לו תכריכין והללו דמשום מצוה התירו רבנן. הא אחר כגון דברים הללו אסור. אבל מחשיך הוא לשמור ומביא פירות בידו ואקשינן ואע"ג דלא אבדיל כלומר עושה מלאכה קודם הבדלה והאמר ר' אלעזר וכו' אסור לעשות מלאכה קודם הבדלה. ואם יש לומר זה שמביא פירות התפלל הבדיל בתפלתו והאמר שמואל המבדיל בתפלה צריך שיבדיל על הכוס ואוקימנא מן הגיתות שנו. כלומר בשעת הגיתות מצוי בשדה בימי הבציר יין והבדיל על הכוס. וסלקא שמעתא שאסור לעשות מלאכה עד שהבדיל ואפילו לא אמר אלא המבדיל בין קודש לחול דיו. דהא רב אשי דהוא בתרא אמר כי הוינן בי רב כהנא הוה אמרינן המבדיל בין קודש לחול ואפכינן סלתי כלומר היינו מתעסקין במלאכה ולא [בא] רב אשי למעט אלא שאינו צריך לומר הבדלות. כאשר חלקו בפרק ערבי פסחים אבל צריך להזכיר ברכה בשם ומלכות דלית גרעה מברכת הפירות וברכת המצות. וכן הלכה: **כלל** אמר אבא שאול. כל שאני זכאי באמירתו רשאי אני להחשיך עליו. והוצרכנו לדקדק לידע באיזה בבא דמתניתין אמר אבא שאול כלל

עין משפט נר מצוה

כט א טוש"ע או"ח סימן שו סעיף ו:
ל ב ג מיי' פכ"ד מהלכ' שבת הלכה ג סמג שם טוש"ע או"ח סימן שו סעיף ח ט:
לא ד מיי' שם הלכה ה סמג שם טור שו"ע או"ח סימן שו סעיף ג:
לב ה מיי' פכ"ט מהל' שבת הלכה ה סמג עשין כט טור שו"ע או"ח סימן רלט סעיף י:
לג ו מיי' שם הלכה ו ופ"ב מהלכות תפלה הלכה יב סמג שם טוש"ע או"ח סי' רצד סעיף א:
לד ז מיי' פכ"ט מהל' שבת הל"ג סמג שם טוש"ע או"ח סימן רצט סעיף י:

מסורת הש"ס

א) [עי' כתו"ז סי' ש"ו ס"ק י"ד פירוש על זה], ב) לקמן קנא., ג) ביצה ו. [ערוך גרס למיגז פי' לחתוך וע"ע לתפור], ד) [ברכות לג. ע"ש פסחים קה: ע"ש ודף קז.], ה) [שייך לע"א במשנה], ו) [בגמ"ח ליתא אבל בעין יעקב מלאתי ע"ש], ז) ועוד מדשרי כל"ל.

הגהות הב"ח

(א) גמ' כך וכך פועלים השכרתי על שדה: (ב) תוס' ד"ה ואין וכו' כדאמרינן פרק קמא דמגילה שלשה אלפים בי בני היה בו ולכל אחד ואחד ה' מאות מלוטות מעלות עשן: (ג) ד"ה אבל וכו' וכי תלי אבא שאול ההחשכה באמירה ה"מ:

ליקוטי רש"י

מעשה בחסיד. כל היכא דאמרינן מעשה בחסיד אחד או ר' יהודה בן בבא או ר' יהודה בר' אלעאי (ב"ק קג:) [לעיל קכו:]. צלף. מין אילן הטוען שלשה מיני פירות אביונות וקפריסין ולולבין וכי אלימי ליה להאי [לעיל ל:]. בורגנין. צריף שעושין מן ערבה וקנים לשומרי פירות ולגידי עופות ומנין עירובין [סוכה ג:]. המבדיל בין קודש לחול. להיכרא בעלמא [עירובין כא.]. ומסלתינן סילתי. חוטבין עצים [ביצה יט:].

what is the preparation to which the Mishnah refers? **לְהָבִיא לוֹ אָרוֹן וְתַכְרִיכִין** – It is **to bring a coffin and shrouds for him.**[24] **וְקָתָנֵי מֵת אֵין** – **And the Mishnah teaches** that for a **deceased person – yes!** one may go to the boundary to bring these items after the Sabbath; **אֲבָל אַחֵר לֹא** – **but** for **another person – no!** one may not go to the boundary to bring them after the Sabbath. **וְאַמַּאי** – **Now, why** is this forbidden? **לֵימָא שֶׁאִם יֵשׁ שָׁם מְחִיצוֹת מֵבִיא** – **Let us say that** he is allowed to do so even for another person, because **if there are partitions, he may bring** them even on the Sabbath itself. – ? –

The Gemara answers:

מֵת נַמִּי מַשְׁכַּחַת לָהּ – **You can also find** a case where one is permitted to wait at the boundary only for the sake of **a deceased person,** and not for another person, **לְמִגְזָא לֵיהּ גְּלִימָא** – namely, where one needs **to cut a cloak for him.**[25] Cutting a garment is not permitted on the Sabbath itself under any circumstance. Hence, one may not await nightfall at the boundary to cut a garment after the Sabbath except for the sake of a deceased person.

A quote from our Mishnah introduces the next discussion:

אֲבָל מַחְשִׁיכִין – **BUT ONE MAY AWAIT NIGHTFALL** at the boundary to guard his field after the Sabbath, and he may bring back produce in his hand.

The Mishnah implies that he may do the *melachah* of plucking produce even before he has recited Havdalah.[26] The Gemara therefore asks:

וְאַף עַל גַּב דְּלָא אַבְדִּיל – **And** is this permitted even **though he has not** yet **recited Havdalah!? וְהָאָמַר רַבִּי אֶלְעָזָר בֶּן אַנְטִיגְנוֹס מִשּׁוּם רַבִּי אֱלִיעֶזֶר בֶּן יַעֲקֹב** – **But R' Elazar ben Antigonos has said in the name of R' Eliezer ben Yaakov: אָסוּר לוֹ לְאָדָם שֶׁיַּעֲשֶׂה חֲפָצָיו קוֹדֶם שֶׁיַּבְדִּיל** – **It is forbidden for a person to attend to his affairs before he recites Havdalah!**[27] **וְכִי תֵּימָא דְּאַבְדִּיל בִּתְפִלָּה** – **And if you suggest that he recited Havdalah in the prayer** of Shemoneh Esrei[28] before he plucked the produce, that is inadequate, **וְהָאָמַר רַב יְהוּדָה אָמַר שְׁמוּאֵל** – **for Rav Yehudah said in the name of Shmuel: הַמַּבְדִּיל בִּתְפִלָּה צָרִיךְ שֶׁיַּבְדִּיל עַל הַכּוֹס** – **One who recites Havdalah in the prayer** of Shemoneh Esrei **must** still **recite it over a cup** of wine.[29] **וְכִי תֵּימָא דְּאַבְדִּיל עַל הַכּוֹס** – **And if you suggest that he did recite Havdalah over a cup** of wine before he plucked the produce, that is not likely, **כּוֹס בְּשָׂדֶה מִי אִיכָּא** – for **is a cup** of wine to be found **in a field?!**

The Gemara answers:

תַּרְגְּמָא רַבִּי נָתָן בַּר אַמֵּי קַמֵּיהּ דְּרָבָא – **R' Nassan bar Ami interpreted** the Mishnah **in the presence of Rava: בֵּין הַגִּיתּוֹת שָׁנוּ** – **They taught** the Mishnah in the context of **the wine-pressing season,**[30] when wine is indeed available in the fields.

The Gemara offers another explanation of the Mishnah:[31]

אָמַר לֵיהּ רַבִּי אַבָּא לְרַב אַשִׁי – **R' Abba said to Rav Ashi: בְּמַעֲרָבָא אָמְרִינַן הָכִי** – **In the West** (i.e. Eretz Yisrael) **we would recite the following words** after the Sabbath: **הַמַּבְדִּיל בֵּין קוֹדֶשׁ לְחוֹל** – **"He Who distinguishes between the sacred and the profane," וְעָבְדִינַן צוֹרְכִין** – **and** then **attend to our needs.** That is, one may perform *melachah* after reciting this formula, even before one has recited Havdalah over a cup of wine.[32] **אָמַר רַב אַשִׁי** – **Rav Ashi said: כִּי הֲוֵינָא בֵּי רַב כָּהֲנָא** – **When I was at the house of Rav Kahana, הֲוָה אָמַר הַמַּבְדִּיל בֵּין קוֹדֶשׁ לְחוֹל** – **he would recite** the words, **"He Who distinguishes between the sacred and the profane," וּמְסַלְּתִינַן סִילְתֵי** – **and** then **chop wood.**

The Gemara discusses the last part of our Mishnah:

כְּלָל אָמַר אַבָּא שָׁאוּל כֹּל שֶׁאֲנִי וכו׳ – **ABBA SHAUL STATED A GENERAL RULE: FOR WHATEVER I AM etc.** [permitted to instruct, I am permitted to await nightfall]. **(אִיבַּעְיָא לְהוּ** – **They asked:) אַבָּא שָׁאוּל אַהֵיָיא** – **To which** part of the Tanna Kamma's statement does **Abba Shaul** refer?[33] **אִילֵימָא אַרֵישָׁא קָאֵי** – **If you say** that **he refers to the first part,** which states: **אֵין מַחְשִׁיכִין עַל הַתְּחוּם לִשְׂכּוֹר פּוֹעֲלִים לְהָבִיא פֵּירוֹת** – **ONE MAY NOT** go to **AWAIT NIGHTFALL AT THE** Sabbath **BOUNDARY FOR THE PURPOSE OF HIRING WORKERS OR BRINGING PRODUCE,**

NOTES

24. As the Mishnah (151a) states explicitly (see *Tosafos* ד״ה אלא).

25. I.e. he needs to cut the shrouds from a larger garment. The coffin, too, requires some adjustment that would be forbidden on the Sabbath. When the Mishnah says that he is going "to bring a coffin and shrouds," it means that he will also form them (*Ramban*).

26. Havdalah is a formal blessing (i.e. it includes mention of God's Name and Kingship) that praises God for distinguishing between the Sabbath and the rest of the week, between the sacred and the profane, etc. It is obligatory to recite this blessing after each Sabbath and Yom Tov.

27. After the Sabbath or Yom Tov one may not eat or perform any *melachah* until he has recited Havdalah (see *Shulchan Aruch Orach Chaim* 299:1,10).

28. The Shemoneh Esrei recited on Saturday nights includes a Havdalah prayer [אַתָּה חוֹנַנְתָּנוּ] in the fourth blessing.

29. Or other important beverage (see *Shulchan Aruch* ibid. 296:2).

30. Literally: between the presses.

31. *Ritva MHK* ed.

32. Thus, our Mishnah could be referring even to one who does not have a cup of wine (*Ritva MHK* ed.).

Although it is obligatory to recite the Havdalah blessing (see note 26) over a cup of wine, one may perform *melachah* before doing so. However, he must first utter some words to mark the departure of the Sabbath, as though the Sabbath were a king from whom one must take official leave before turning to one's own affairs. A formula such as "He Who distinguishes between the sacred and the profane" suffices for this purpose. The Havdalah prayer which is inserted into the Shemoneh Esrei (see note 28) is certainly adequate (*Rashi;* see *Rashba* for a different explanation of *Rashi;* see also *Ran MHK* ed. and *Chidushei HaRan*). [It should be noted, though, that one is forbidden to *eat* until he has recited a formal Havdalah blessing over a cup of wine (*Ritva MHK* ed.; see *Shulchan Aruch* ibid. 299:11).]

According to *Rif,* R' Abba does not mean that it is sufficient to recite the words הַמַּבְדִּיל בֵּין קֹדֶשׁ לְחוֹל, *He Who distinguishes between the sacred and the profane.* Before doing *melachah,* one must recite a formal blessing, which includes mention of God's Name and Kingship. Rather, R' Abba's point is that one may abbreviate the usual blessing and say: בָּרוּךְ אַתָּה ה׳ אֱלֹהֵינוּ מֶלֶךְ הָעוֹלָם הַמַּבְדִּיל בֵּין קֹדֶשׁ לְחוֹל, *Blessed are You, Hashem, King of the universe, Who distinguishes between the sacred and the profane* (see *Rashba, Ritva MHK* ed. and *Ran MHK* ed.).

33. Abba Shaul is referring to one of the laws stated by the Tanna Kamma, and restates it in general terms (*Rashi*).

הַאי כָּל שֶׁאֲנִי זַכַּאי בַּאֲמִירָתוֹ רַשַּׁאי אֲנִי בַּחֲשֵׁיכָתוֹ – then **that** formulation: "FOR WHATEVER I AM PERMITTED TO INSTRUCT, I AM PERMITTED TO AWAIT NIGHTFALL" is inappropriate. כֹּל שֶׁאֵינִי זַכַּאי בַּאֲמִירָתוֹ אֵינִי רַשַּׁאי בַּחֲשֵׁיכָתוֹ מִיבָּעֵי לֵיהּ – **It should have been: "For whatever I am *not* permitted to instruct, I am *not* permitted to await nightfall."**[1] אֶלָּא אַסֵּיפָא קָאֵי – **Rather, [Abba Shaul] refers to the latter part** of the Tanna Kamma's statement: אֲבָל מַחְשִׁיךְ הוּא לִשְׁמוֹר וּמֵבִיא פֵּירוֹת בְּיָדוֹ – BUT ONE MAY AWAIT NIGHTFALL at the boundary FOR THE PURPOSE OF GUARDING his property after the Sabbath, AND HE MAY BRING back PRODUCE IN HIS HAND. However, that cannot be the intent of Abba Shaul's rule either, הַאי כֹּל שֶׁאֲנִי זַכַּאי בַּחֲשֵׁיכָתוֹ רַשַּׁאי אֲנִי בַּאֲמִירָתוֹ מִיבָּעֵי לֵיהּ – because then **it should have been: "For whatever I am permitted to await nightfall, I am permitted to instruct."**[2]

The Gemara explains Abba Shaul's statement:

לְעוֹלָם אַסֵּיפָא קָאֵי – **Actually, he does refer to the latter part** of the Tanna Kamma's statement. וְאַבָּא שָׁאוּל אַהָא קָאֵי – **However, Abba Shaul was referring to this** particular point, which pertains to that statement, but which the Tanna Kamma did not mention because he considered it too obvious. דְּאָמַר רַב יְהוּדָה אָמַר שְׁמוּאֵל – The point is the one **that Rav Yehudah** later **reported in the name of Shmuel:** מוּתָּר לְאָדָם לוֹמַר לַחֲבֵירוֹ – **It is permitted for a man to say to his friend** on the Sabbath, שְׁמוֹר לִי פֵּירוֹת שֶׁבִּתְחוּמְךָ וַאֲנִי אֶשְׁמוֹר לְךָ פֵּירוֹת שֶׁבִּתְחוּמִי – "**Guard for me the fruit** I own **within your boundary, and I will guard for you the fruit** you own **within my boundary.**"[3] וְקָאָמַר אַבָּא שָׁאוּל לְתַנָּא קַמָּא – **And** this is what **Abba Shaul was saying to the Tanna Kamma:** מִי לֹא מוֹדִית דְּמוּתָּר אָדָם לוֹמַר לַחֲבֵירוֹ – **Do you not agree that a person may say to his friend,** שְׁמוֹר לִי פֵּירוֹת שֶׁבִּתְחוּמְךָ וַאֲנִי אֶשְׁמוֹר לְךָ פֵּירוֹת שֶׁבִּתְחוּמִי – "**Guard for me the fruit** I own **within your boundary and I will guard for you the fruit** you own **within my boundary**"? You surely agree that this is permitted. Therefore, you should formulate a general rule, וְאֵימָא – **and say:** כֹּל שֶׁאֲנִי זַכַּאי בַּאֲמִירָתוֹ רַשַּׁאי אֲנִי לְהַחְשִׁיךְ עָלָיו – **For whatever I am permitted to instruct, I am permitted to await nightfall.**[4]

The Gemara now identifies the cases that Abba Shaul's rule serves to include:

כְּלָל לְאַתּוּיֵי מַאי – **What does the rule include?** לְאַתּוּיֵי הָא דְּתָנוּ רַבָּנָן – It serves **to include that which the Rabbis taught in a Baraisa:** אֵין מַחְשִׁיכִין עַל הַתְּחוּם לְהָבִיא בְּהֵמָה – ONE MAY NOT AWAIT NIGHTFALL AT THE Sabbath BOUNDARY FOR the purpose of BRINGING back AN ANIMAL.[5] הָיְתָה עוֹמֶדֶת חוּץ לַתְּחוּם – If [THE ANIMAL] WAS STANDING OUTSIDE THE BOUNDARY, קוֹרֵא לָהּ וְהִיא בָּאָה – HE MAY CALL TO IT SO THAT IT WILL COME to him.[6] כְּלָל אָמַר אַבָּא שָׁאוּל – ABBA SHAUL STATED A GENERAL RULE: כֹּל שֶׁאֲנִי זַכַּאי בַּאֲמִירָתוֹ רַשַּׁאי אֲנִי לְהַחְשִׁיךְ עָלָיו – FOR WHATEVER I AM PERMITTED TO INSTRUCT, I AM PERMITTED TO AWAIT NIGHTFALL. וּמַחְשִׁיכִין לְפַקֵּחַ עַל עִסְקֵי כַלָּה – AND therefore ONE MAY AWAIT NIGHTFALL at the Sabbath boundary TO ATTEND TO THE AFFAIRS OF A BRIDE, וְעַל עִסְקֵי הַמֵּת לְהָבִיא לוֹ אָרוֹן וְתַכְרִיכִין – OR TO THE

NOTES

1. If Abba Shaul stated his generalization in reference to a negative law ("We may *not* await nightfall . . . for hiring workers"), he surely would have formulated it in negative terms (see *Rashi,* bottom of 150b).

2. We have established that Abba Shaul must be referring to a positive law. However, the only positive law stated by the Tanna Kamma pertained to guarding produce, and in that context he mentioned only awaiting nightfall, and not instruction. (The Tanna Kamma only stated, "One may *await nightfall* . . . for guarding produce"; he did not also say, "One may *tell* someone to guard produce.") Thus, if Abba Shaul was generalizing about the Tanna Kamma's permit to guard produce, he would surely not have based the generalization on the law of instruction, which the Tanna Kamma had not mentioned in that context. Rather, he would have based his generalization on the law of awaiting nightfall, which the Tanna Kamma *had* mentioned (i.e. Abba Shaul would have said "For whatever I am permitted to await nightfall, I am permitted to instruct).

[*Tosafos* observe that this difficulty would not exist if we could say that Abba Shaul was referring to the first part of the Tanna Kamma's statement. There, the Tanna dealt both with awaiting nightfall ("One may not await nightfall . . . for hiring workers") *and* with instruction ("A person may not tell his friend to hire workers for him"). Hence, it would have been reasonable for Abba Shaul to begin his rule with either point. However, that approach was refuted by the Gemara for the reason that Abba Shaul's rule would then have been phrased in the negative.]

3. Since one may guard his own property on the Sabbath, one may ask another person to guard it for him on the Sabbath. This is allowed even if the property is beyond the owner's Sabbath boundary, provided that it is within the guardian's boundary.

Tosafos (cited by *Rashba* and *Ritva MHK* ed.) infer from here that one Jew may ask another to perform an act that is forbidden to the first but permitted to the second. They rule, therefore, that if a Jew has undertaken to begin observing the Sabbath before the usual time, although all the laws of the Sabbath are already incumbent upon him, he may ask another Jew to do a *melachah* for him. *Ran* (on *Rif* and *MHK* ed.), however, disagrees. [See *Shulchan Aruch, Orach Chaim* 263:17 with *Bach, Beis Yosef* and *Taz.*]

4. Abba Shaul argued with the Tanna Kamma as follows: You state that one may await nightfall at the boundary for the purpose of guarding produce. You also certainly permit one to instruct another to guard his produce [as in Shmuel's law]. These two laws are surely interrelated. That is, since one may instruct someone during the Sabbath to guard his produce [even on the Sabbath itself], he may certainly await nightfall at the boundary to guard his produce after the Sabbath. The following rule may consequently be formulated: "For *whatever* one is permitted to instruct, one is permitted to await nightfall." Why, then, did you focus on the specific case of guarding produce? You should have stated the general rule, which includes other cases as well – namely, mitzvah-related acts, such as bringing decorations for a bride or a coffin for a deceased person. Since one is permitted to instruct another to bring these items after the Sabbath [because they relate to חֶפְצֵי שָׁמַיִם, *affairs of Heaven* (see 150a)], one may also await nightfall to bring them.

The Tanna Kamma, though, avoided stating the general rule, because he holds that although one may instruct another to perform a mitzvah-related act after the Sabbath, one may *not* await nightfall at the boundary to attend to such a matter. [After all, instructing is only speech, whereas walking to the boundary is a more tangible deed.] The following Mishnah, which permits even awaiting nightfall at the boundary for purposes of a mitzvah, follows only the view of Abba Shaul (*Rashi*).

[The Tanna Kamma distinguishes between guarding produce and mitzvah-related acts. In the case of guarding produce, one is allowed to do it (or ask someone else to do it) even on the Sabbath itself; therefore, one is certainly allowed to await nightfall to do it after the Sabbath. In the case of a mitzvah-related act, however, which is forbidden on the Sabbath itself, one may only *ask* someone to attend to it (after the Sabbath); one may not *walk* to the boundary for that purpose.]

5. If one's animal strayed beyond his boundary, he is not allowed to wait at the boundary in order to retrieve it after the Sabbath. This is forbidden because he would have to carry the animal, which is *muktzeh.* The prohibitions against passing beyond the boundary and transporting in a public domain are not factors here, because in certain circumstances these activities are permitted even on the Sabbath itself (see *Tosafos;* cf. *Meiri*). [As discussed above (150b), one may prepare on the Sabbath to perform such activities after nightfall.]

The Rishonim (*Tosafos, Rashba, Ritva MHK* ed. et al.) record a different version of the text: מַחְשִׁיכִין עַל הַתְּחוּם לְהָבִיא בְּהֵמָה, *We* **may** *await nightfall at the boundary to bring an animal.* [This version apparently refers to an animal that does *not* have to be carried (see, however, *Yad David, Basra*).]

6. [Moving a *muktzeh* object is forbidden only if one manipulates it. Hence, even if calling to the animal would be deemed "speech," it would be permitted, because speech is allowed for the sake of activities permitted on the Sabbath (cf. *Tos. Rid* and *Meromei Sadeh*).]

Regarding moving beyond its new boundary an animal or object that is outside its owner's boundary, see *Ritva MHK* ed. here and *Rashi* to 53b ד״ה שהיה.

האי כל שאני זכאי באמירתו רשאי אני בחשיכתו כל שאיני זכאי באמירתו איני רשאי בחשיכתו מיבעי ליה אלא אסיפא קאי אבל מחשיך הוא לשמור ומביא פירות בידו האי כל שאני זכאי בחשיכתו רשאי אני באמירתו מיבעי ליה לעולם אסיפא קאי ואבא שאול אהא קאי דאמר רב יהודה אמר שמואל מותר לאדם לומר לחבירו שמור לי פירות שבתחומך ואני אשמור לך פירות שבתחומי וקאמר אבא שאול לת"ק מי לא מודית דמותר אדם לומר לחבירו שמור לי פירות שבתחומך ואני אשמור לך פירות שבתחומי ואימא כל שאני זכאי באמירתו רשאי אני להחשיך עליו כלל לאתויי מאי לאתויי הא דת"ר אין מחשיכין על התחום להביא בהמה היתה עומדת חוץ לתחום קורא לה והיא באה כלל אמר אבא שאול כל שאני זכאי באמירתו רשאי אני להחשיך עליו ומחשיכין לפקח על עסקי כלה ועל עסקי המת להביא לו ארון ותכריכין ואומרים לו לך למקום פלוני ואם לא מצאת במקום פלוני הבא ממקום פלוני לא מצאת במנה הבא במאתים ר' יוסי ברבי יהודה אומר ובלבד שלא יזכיר לו סכום מקח:

מתני' מחשיכין על התחום לפקח על עסקי כלה ועל עסקי המת להביא לו ארון ותכריכים נכרי שהביא חלילין בשבת לא יספוד בהן ישראל אא"כ באו ממקום קרוב עשו לו ארון וחפרו לו קבר יקבר בו ישראל ואם בשביל ישראל לא יקבר בו עולמית:

גמ' מאי ממקום קרוב רב אמר ממקום קרוב ממש ושמואל אמר חיישינן שמא (א) חוץ לחומה לנו [א] דיקא מתניתין כוותיה דשמואל דקתני עשה לו ארון וחפר לו קבר יקבר בו ישראל אלמא מספיקא שרי הכא נמי מספיקא שרי ותניא כוותיה [ב] דרב (ג) עיר שישראל ונכרים דרים בה והיתה בה מרחץ המרחצת בשבת אם רוב נכרים לערב רוחץ בה מיד אם רוב ישראל ימתין עד כדי שיחמו חמין מחצה על מחצה (אסור וימתין) עד כדי שיחמו חמין ר' יהודה אומר באמבטי קטנה אם יש בה רשות רוחץ בה מיד מאי רשות אמר רב יהודה אמר רב יצחק בריה דרב יהודה אם יש בה אדם חשוב שיש לו עשרה עבדים שמחממין לו י' קומקומין בבת אחת באמבטי קטנה מותר לרחוץ בה מיד: עשו לו ארון וחפרו לו קבר וכו': אמאי הכא נמי ימתין בכדי שיעשו אמר עולא בעומד באסרטיא תינח קבר ארון מאי איכא למימר א"ר אבהו במוטל על קברו:

מתני' עושין כל צרכי המת סכין ומדיחין אותו ובלבד שלא יזיז בו אבר שומטין את הכר מתחתיו ומטילין אותו על החול בשביל שימתין

רש"י

אלא אסיפא קאי. דקאמר ת"ק להיתרא אבל מחשיך הוא לשמור ואתא איהו ושוויה ביה כללא להביא כל כיוצא בהן: **האי כל שאני זכאי להחשיך עליו זכאי אני באמירתו מיבעי ליה.** (ג) דהיתר דחשיכה תנן והיתר דאמירה לא תנן והיכי תלי תניא בדלא תניא: **לעולם אסיפא קאי.** כדקאמרת ודקשיא לך אמירה מהיכא קאמר ליה להיתירא דתלי בה החשכה אהא קאי דאמר רב יהודה כו' אלמא זכאי אני באמירתו ואבא שאול ות"ק כולהו פשיטא להו הא דשמואל וקאמר ליה אבא שאול לת"ק מי לא מודית בהא שאתה מתיר להחשיך דמותר הוא לומר כדשמואל אלמא הואיל ומותר לומר מותר להחשיך הלכך אמאי נקטת החשכה לשמור להודות שוי כללא למילתא ואימא כל שאני זכאי באמירתו רשאי אני להחשיך עליו דש"מ הך וש"מ מת וכלה דהא נמי זכאי באמירתו הוא כדמפרש לקמן והלכך מחשיכין עליו וסיפא דמתני' דקתני מחשיכין על התחום לפקח על עסקי כלה אבא שאול היא: **כלל אמר אבא שאול כו'.** והאי נמי זכאי באמירתו כדקתני סיפא ואומר לו לך למקום פלוני: **סכום מקח.** מנה ומאתים:

מתני' נכרי שהביא חלילין בשבת. בשביל ישראל: **לא יספוד בהן ישראל.** לעולם וקנסא הוא משום דמוכחא מילתא דבשבילו הובאו דאין דרך להביא חלילין אלא בשביל מת: **ממקום קרוב.** בתוך התחום: **עשו לו ארון.** בשביל נכרי או למכור: **גמ' רב אמר ממקום קרוב ממש.** כלומר שידוע לנו בירור הדבר דממקום קרוב באו שראינום שהיו בביתו: **ושמואל אמר חיישינן שמא חוץ לחומה לנו.** אפילו הביא מחוץ לעיר אנו תולין להתיר ואומרים שמא בתוך התחום לנו ערב שבת וסופדין בהן במוצ"ש מיד וחיישינן נמי אמרינן לקולא כדאמרי' במס' חגיגה (דף טו.) גבי בתולה שעיברה חיישינן שמא באמבטי עיברה ומותרת לכהונה ולשמואל הכי קאמר מתני' לא יספוד בהן ישראל אא"כ יש לתלות שבאו ממקום קרוב ולאפוקי בידוע דממחוץ לתחום באו: ה"ג דיקא מתני' כוותיה דשמואל ותניא כוותיה דרב: **יקבר בו ישראל.** דתלינן מספיקא שמא לצורך נכרי נעשה: **תניא כוותיה דרב.** דספיקא אסור דקתני מחצה על מחצה ימתין בכדי שיחמו חמין ואי"ת בכדי שיחמו חמין מיהא שרי והכא תני לא יספוד בהן משמע לעולם הכא מוכחא מילתא אבל במרחץ לא מוכחא מילתא כולי האי הואיל ואיכא נכרים: **באמבטי קטנה.** שיש לתלות ולומר משמשיה הוחמה על ידי עבדים וקומקמין הרבה: **אם יש בה רשות.** אדם חשוב שליט: **רוחץ בה.** ישראל מיד דיש לומר משמשיה הוחמו חמין לאותו נכרי. לישנא אחרינא גרסינן תניא כוותיה דשמואל ולא גרסי' דייקא מתני' כו' עד מספיקא שרי ומייתי סייעתא לשמואל מדרבי יהודה דתלינן לקולא ורישא לא קשיא ליה כיון דמחצה על מחצה ודאי בשביל ישראל ונכרים הוחמו שהרי לא לאדם אחד לבדו הוחמו דנימא ספיקא לנכרי ספק לישראל ולשון זה נראה לי עיקר ורבותי נמי כך לא גרסי לעיל להא דקתני עשה נכרי את הארון עד מספיקא שרי ומיהו לא מפרשי לה כדפרישית: **ימתין בכדי שיעשו.** נהי דלא מוכחא מילתא מיהו י"ל שמא בשביל ישראל נעשה: **בעומד.** הקבר באיסרטיא שאין דרך ישראל ליקבר שם דודאי לא נעשה בשביל ישראל: **ארון מאי איכא למימר.** להוכיח דלא בשביל ישראל נעשה: **במוטל.** הארון: **על קברו.** של נכרי באיסרטיא דמוכחא דלשם אותו קבר נעשה הארון: **מתני' ומדיחין.** במים: **שלא יזיז בו אבר.** לא יגביה לא ידו או רגלו או ריסי עיניו:

תוספות

האי כל שאני רשאי בחשיכתו רשאי אני באמירתו מיבעי ליה. תימה הא דכי פריך לעיל האי כל שאיני רשאי באמירתו איני רשאי בחשיכתו מיבעי ליה מכלל דאי הוה תנן הכי הוה אתי שפיר אע"ג דתלי חשיכה באמירה וי"ל התם שאני דלא הוה תלי תניא בדלא תניא דאמירה נמי תניא לעיל לא יאמר אדם לחבירו שכור לי פועלים אבל השתא תלי תניא בדלא תניא דהיתר אמירה לא תניא אבל היתר החשכה תניא:

לעולם אסיפא קאי (ד) דאמר רב יהודה אמר שמואל מותר אדם לומר לחבירו שמור לי פירות שבתחומך. אע"פ שהוא אינו יכול לילך לשומרן יכול לומר לחבירו לשמרן ומתניתין הכי קאמר כל שאני זכאי באמירתו כגון לפקח על עסקי כלה ועל עסקי מת ויכול לומר לחבירו לעשות למחר רשאי אני להחשיך עליו וכ"ש מה שאני זכאי לומר לעשות היום כמו שמור לי פירות שבתחומך אע"פ שאיני רשאי לילך שם היום דמותר להחשיך עליו:

אין מחשיכין על התחום להביא בהמה. יש ספרים דגרסי מחשיכין לפי שאם יש שם בורגנים הולך ומביאה ובתוספתא גרס אין מחשיכין וי"ל דאיירי בבהמה שאינה יכולה לבא ברגליה כגון טלה קטן אא"כ ישאוהו בכתף שאפילו יש מחילות אינו רשאי להביא דאסור לטלטל בעלי חיים שהם מוקצים:

נכרי שהביא חלילים בשבת לא יספוד בהן ישראל. לא כפי' הקונטרס שפירש עולמית מדפריך בגמרא גבי עשה נכרי ארון וחפר לו קבר יקבר בו ישראל אמאי הכא נמי נימא ימתין בכדי שיעשו ואמאי קאמר נמי אי לאו דקאי אחלילים על כן נראה דלא יספוד בהן ישראל היינו עד כדי שיבואו דסתם חלילים אין מביאין אותן לשם אדם אחד אלא לשם כמה בני אדם:

אא"כ באו ממקום קרוב. תימה לרבי מה מהני שבאו ממקום קרוב הלא הביאם דרך רה"ר ומה לי ארון וקבר שנעשו בשבת ומה לי חלילים שהובאו דרך רה"ר וי"ל דהביא ממקום קרוב לא מהני כל כך הבאתו: **דיקא מתניתין כוותיה דשמואל כו' יקבר בו ישראל אלמא מספיקא שרי.** תימה היכי (ה) מוכיחנא מינה דמספיקא שרי והא מוקמ' לה בעומד באיסרטיא דודאי לצורך נכרי נעשה מיהו אומר רבי דל"ג ליה להא דקתני עשו לו ארון כו' ול"ג נמי בסמוך (ו) ת"כ גם בפי' הקונט' ל"ג אלא ה"ג דיקא נמי ממתני' עיר שישראל ונכרים דרים בה כו' ומשנה היא במסכת מכשירין (פ"ב משנה ה) ר' יהודה אומר אם יש בה רשות רוחץ בה מיד אלמא תלינן להתיר כמו כן גבי חלילין יש לתלות בהיתר ולומר חוץ לחומה לנו. מ"ר:

עד

מסורת הש"ס

א) [תוספתא פרק יז], ב) [לעיל נג:], ג) לעיל קנ:, ד) [צ"ל ותנן], ה) לעיל קכב. ע"ש מכשירין פ"ב מ"ה ע"ש, ו) צ"ל ימתין [וכ"א במשנה].

הגהות הב"ח

(א) גמ' חוץ לחומה לנו אמר רבא דיקא מתני': (ב) שם ותניא כוותיה דרב דת"ר עיר: (ג) רש"י ד"ה האי כל וכו' דהיתרא דהחשכה תנן: (ד) תוס' ד"ה לעולם אסיפא קאי ואבא שאול אהא קאי דאמר רב יהודה: (ה) ד"ה דיקא וכו' היכי מוכח מינה: (ו) בא"ד ול"ג נמי בסמוך דמנו רבנן גם בפ"ה ל"ג ליה אלא ה"ג:

הגהות הגר"א

[א] גמ' (דיקא מתני' כו' עד ה"ג מספיקא שרי). תא"מ: [ב] שם כוותיה דרב. צ"ל דשמואל:

ליקוטי רש"י

קורא לה והיא באה. דלא החסר הוא על תחום בהמתו ובלבד שלא יביאנה ממש בידיו [לעיל נג:]. **לערב.** למוצאי שבת. **עד כדי שיחמו חמין.** שלא יהנה במה שהקדימו להחם בשבת וכן בכל מעשה שבת נתנו חכמים שיעור להמתין לערב בכדי שיעשו. **אם רוב נכרים.** אדעתא דרובא מחממי ועיקר חילול שבת בשבילם [שם קכב.]. **בכדי שיעשו.** כדי שלא יהנה ממלאכת שבת [שם יח: ועי' תוס' ביצה כד:]. **אסרטיא.** רה"ר ט"ז אמה [ב"ק פא:]. מסילה שהולכין בה מעיר לעיר [לעיל ו.]. **דרך כבושה** [עירובין יז:].

עין משפט נר מצוה

לה א (מיי' פכ"ד מהל' שבת) סמג לאוין סה טוש"ע או"ח סימן שז סעיף י:

לו ב מיי' שם הלכה ג סמג שם טוש"ע או"ח סימן שו סעיף א:

לז ג מיי' שם טור שו"ע שם סעיף ב:

לח ד ה מיי' שם הל"ה טוש"ע שם סעיף ג וסימן שז סעיף ח:

לט ו ז מיי' פ"ו מהל' שבת הל"ו סמג שם טוש"ע או"ח סימן שכה סעיף טו:

מ ח מיי' שם הלכה ז טוש"ע שם סעיף טז:

מא ט י כ מיי' שם הל' ה טור שו"ע שם סעיף יד:

מב ל מיי' פכ"ו מהל' שבת הלכה כ סמג שם טוש"ע או"ח סימן שיא סעיף ז:

רבינו חננאל

כלל זה. ואמרינן אם על רישא דקתני אין מחשיכין על התחום לשכור פועלין וכו'. כל (שאני) [שאיני] זכאי בחשיכתו (אני) [איני] זכאי באמירתו היה לו לומר כי אין מחשיכין אמרה משנתנו בפירוש ומכללו נלמד האמירה כלומר מאחר שאין לי להחשיך בתחום לשכור פועלין כן אין לי לומר לחבירו השכר לי פועלין עם חשכה. אלא אסיפא. אבל מחשיך הוא לשמור וכו' כלומר כשם שמותר לו להחשיך כך מותר לו לומר לחבירו החשיך והביא לי פירות האי כל שאיני זכאי בחשיכתו זכאי אני באמירתו היה לו לומר ואוקימנא כדרב פפא דאמר מותר לאדם לומר לחבירו שמור לי פירות שבתחומך וכו' כלומר כשם שאני זכאי לומר לחברי שמור לי פירות שבתחומך כך מותר לי לשמר פירות שבתחומי. ולהחשיך עליו ואמרינן עוד ולמה ליה כלל לתנייה בהדיא ופרקינן כלל להביא הא דת"ר מחשיכין על התחום להביא בהמה היתה עומדת חוץ לתחום קורא לה והיא באה. ולפקח על עסקי כלה ועל עסקי המת להביא לו ארון ותכריכין אומרים לו לך למקום פלוני לא מצאת במקום פלוני הבא ממקום פלוני לא מצאת במאה הבא במאתים ובלבד שלא יזכור את הדמים. ר' יוסי ב"ר יהודה [אומר] ובלבד שלא יזכור לו סכום המקח: **מתני' מחשיכין** על התחום. עד אא"כ באו ממקום קרוב מאי ממקום קרוב רב אמר קרוב ממש. ושמואל אמר חיישינן שמא חוץ לחומה לנו. א) ופירוש לן מרן דברי שמואל הללו והיאך מתני' דייקא כוותיה ומה טעם חלילים שהביאם גוי בשבת שלא יספוד בהם ישראל ולמה לא ימתין בכדי שיביאו או דלמא משום דלא ידעינן מהיכן באו ועוד המותר לספוד בהן ביום ראשון ובשאר ימי החול או לאו מה פירק לו הלא אפילו אם המת מונח בדרך צריך להמתין בכדי שיחפור בקבר והדר קושיין לדוכתיה וכן בארון ליסברה לן מרן. ועוד אם הדברים הללו על עיר שרובן ישראל הם או לא. כי אם רובן גוים למה צריך להמתין והלא לענין מרחץ אמרו מותר לרחוץ בה מיד ושמואל אמר חיישינן שמא

חרץ

חשק שלמה על רבינו חננאל א) נראה דזה הוא שאלה לרבינו. וצ"ל יפרש לן מרן. (ואולי שאל מאת רב האי גאון). והתשובה חסרה כאן ובאמת שלא הפסק הוא תלי תשובה:

AFFAIRS OF A DECEASED PERSON, that is, TO BRING A COFFIN AND SHROUDS FOR HIM.[7] וְאוֹמְרִים לוֹ לֵךְ לְמָקוֹם פְּלוֹנִי – AND ONE MAY SAY TO [ANOTHER] on the Sabbath, "GO TO SUCH-AND-SUCH A PLACE after the Sabbath to get these items.[8] וְאִם לֹא מָצָאתָ בְּמָקוֹם פְּלוֹנִי – AND IF YOU DO NOT FIND them AT THAT PLACE, הָבֵא מִמָּקוֹם פְּלוֹנִי – BRING them FROM SUCH-AND-SUCH A PLACE. וְאִם לֹא מָצָאתָ בְּמָנֶה הָבֵא בְּמָאתַיִם – AND IF YOU DO NOT FIND them FOR A HUNDRED coins, BRING them FOR TWO HUNDRED." רַבִּי יוֹסֵי בְּרַבִּי יְהוּדָה אוֹמֵר – R' YOSE THE SON OF R' YEHUDAH SAYS: וּבִלְבַד שֶׁלֹּא יַזְכִּיר לוֹ סְכוּם מֶקַח – BUT this (i.e. asking someone to purchase the items) is permitted ONLY IF ONE DOES NOT MENTION TO HIM THE TOTAL cost OF THE PURCHASE.[9]

Mishnah מַחְשִׁיכִין עַל הַתְּחוּם לְפַקֵּחַ עַל עִסְקֵי כַלָּה – **One may await nightfall at the** Sabbath **boundary to attend to the affairs of a bride,**[10] וְעַל עִסְקֵי הַמֵּת לְהָבִיא לוֹ אָרוֹן וְתַכְרִיכִים – **or to the affairs of a deceased person,** that is, **to bring a coffin and shrouds for him.**[11]

Other laws that concern preparations for a funeral:[12]

נָכְרִי שֶׁהֵבִיא חֲלִילִין בְּשַׁבָּת לֹא יִסְפּוֹד בָּהֶן יִשְׂרָאֵל – **If a gentile brought flutes on the Sabbath,**[13] **a Jew may not bewail with them,**[14] אֶלָּא אִם כֵּן בָּאוּ מִמָּקוֹם קָרוֹב – **unless they came from a nearby place.**[15] עָשׂוּ לוֹ אָרוֹן וְחָפְרוּ לוֹ קֶבֶר – If **[gentiles] made a coffin for him**[16] **or dug a grave for him** on the Sabbath, יִקָּבֵר בּוֹ יִשְׂרָאֵל – **a Jew**

NOTES

7. These are the cases that Abba Shaul's rule was designed to include (see note 4; cf. *Chidushei HaRan* and *Meromei Sadeh*).

8. I.e. one may ask someone (Jew or gentile) to obtain after the Sabbath the things needed for a bride or deceased person. [As stated above (note 4), even the Tanna Kamma of our Mishnah agrees that instruction is allowed in these cases.]

[It is forbidden, however, for one to ask even a gentile to bring these things *during* the Sabbath. The next Mishnah teaches that one may not benefit from a labor done on the Sabbath by a gentile for a Jew, even if the gentile did it of his own accord (*Rambam, Rashba, Ritva MHK* ed., *Ran MHK* ed.).]

9. Disagreeing with the previous Tanna, R' Yose the son of R' Yehudah forbids one to say "one hundred coins" or "two hundred coins" (*Rashi; Ritva MHK* ed.).

Alternatively, one is forbidden to mention a total that the messenger may not exceed (*Rambam, Hil. Shabbos* 24:5, as explained by *Maggid Mishneh* [see there for the reason]; cf. *Ran's* explanation of *Rambam;* see also *Meiri*).

10. E.g. to cut myrtle branches after the Sabbath, which will be used for decorative purposes at her wedding. Although cutting branches is a *melachah,* one is allowed to prepare on the Sabbath to do it after the Sabbath since one is doing so for the sake of a mitzvah [חֶפְצֵי שָׁמַיִם, *business of Heaven*] (see 150b with notes 20-23).

11. Even if the coffin and shrouds are not yet made, so that there is *melachah* involved in their preparation, one may nevertheless await nightfall on the boundary to arrange for it, since it is a *mitzvah* matter. [If they were already made, one would be permitted to await nightfall even apart from any consideration of mitzvah, as explained on 150b.]

We have explained that this is the view of Abba Shaul. According to the Tanna Kamma of the previous Mishnah, one may not await nightfall at the boundary for an act forbidden on the Sabbath even if one is doing so for a mitzvah (see above, note 4).

12. The following laws are based on the Rabbinic prohibition against benefiting from a labor performed on the Sabbath by a gentile for a Jew. Such benefit is forbidden even after the Sabbath for the length of time it takes for that activity to be done. Once that time has elapsed, any benefit one derives from the labor is not viewed as resulting from desecration of the Sabbath, since the labor could have been done after the Sabbath (based on *Rashi* to *Beitzah* 24b ד"ה ולערב; cf. *Tosafos* ibid.; see *Mishnah Berurah* Introduction to §515). [In some situations, one may *never* benefit from the gentile's act (see notes 14 and 34).] However, if a gentile performed a labor for himself or for another gentile, a Jew is allowed to benefit from it even during the Sabbath itself (Mishnah above, 122a).

The Rishonim disagree as to whether the above prohibition applies only to the Jew for whom the activity was performed, or to all Jews (see *Rashba, Ritva MHK* ed. and *Ran MHK* ed. at length). Some rule that if the labor was a Biblical transgression, no Jew may benefit from it, but in the case of a Rabbinic transgression, it is forbidden only to the intended beneficiary (*Rashi* to *Beitzah* top of 25a; *Tosafos* above, 122a ד"ה ואם; *Shulchan Aruch, Orach Chaim* 325:8 with *Mishnah Berurah* §41).

13. He brought the flutes for a Jew [to use at a funeral] (*Rashi*).

The sound of these flutes aroused wailing and mourning (*Rambam, Commentary to the Mishnah*). It was customary to play them at a funeral procession (*Tiferes Yisrael*).

14. They may not be used even after the Sabbath because the gentile brought them for a Jew (or Jews) from outside the Sabbath boundary (see note 12).

According to *Rashi* the ban is permanent. That is, the Jew (or Jews) for whom the flutes were brought may *never* use them. This is a special penalty that the Rabbis imposed wherever it is obvious that a labor was done for the sake of a Jew. In this case, these flutes were obviously brought for Jews to use at the funeral, because flutes are not usually brought for any other purpose (see end of note 19). [Other Jews, though, may use the flutes after sufficient time to obtain new ones has passed (see *Meiri*).]

Most authorities, however, explain the ban as lasting only as long as would be required to obtain flutes after the Sabbath. After that time, one no longer benefits from the desecration of the Sabbath, since he could, in any case, have obtained new ones. There is, therefore, no reason to prohibit the use at that time of those brought on the Sabbath (*Rif, Tosafos, Ramban, Rosh, Rambam, Hil. Shabbos* 6:6, *Shulchan Aruch, Orach Chaim* 325:15 et al.).

Rashi derives that the ban is permanent from the fact that the Mishnah does not mention any limit of its duration (see ד"ה תניא). The other Rishonim argue to the contrary: Since the Mishnah states below in regard to a different case that the prohibition is permanent, but here it does not say so, it implies that this ban is *not* permanent (*Ramban, Rashba, Rosh* et al.). See *Ritva MHK* ed., who suggests a defense of *Rashi.*

15. I.e. they were brought from within the Sabbath boundary (*Rashi*). In such a case any Jew may use the flutes immediately after the Sabbath (*Rashi* ד"ה ושמואל).

The following difficulty must be addressed: Why does it make a difference that the flutes were brought from within the boundary? The gentile nevertheless performed the *melachah* of הוֹצָאָה, *transferring* with them when he carried them through the public domain! Some Rishonim answer that the flutes will not be used in any event until some time after the Sabbath, for funerals are not held immediately upon nightfall. Therefore, if the flutes were brought from somewhere within the boundary, the time needed to transport them is presumably no longer than the time that elapses between the Sabbath and the funeral. Thus, for all practical purposes, there is no need to wait in order to use the flutes (*Ramban, Ran;* cf. *Rashba* and *Tos. HaRosh*). [This approach is untenable, though, according to *Rashi's* view that the ban is permanent. Indeed, this is another one of the reasons why the Rishonim reject *Rashi's* approach.]

Tosafos answer that since the flutes were brought from nearby, one saves very little time and therefore derives very little benefit from their having been brought on the Sabbath. The Rabbis therefore did not require him to wait even that amount of time before using them after the Sabbath.

16. I.e. for another gentile or to sell (*Rashi*). The antecedent of the pronoun "him" is the gentile(s) who constructed the coffin (*Ramban;* cf. *Ritva* MHK ed.). However, the Mishnah does not necessarily mean that the gentile made the coffin for his own burial. Rather, it means that he made it for his own benefit, e.g. to profit from its sale (*Melo HaRo'im*).

The gentile did not specify for whom he made the coffin. It is assumed, therefore, that he made it for a fellow gentile, rather than for a Jew (see *Rashba* and *Ritva MHK* ed. on the Gemara below ד"ה ואמאי הכא נמי ימתין; see, however, *Chidushei HaRan* ד"ה אית ספרי).

האי כל שאני זכאי באמירתו רשאי אני בחשיכתו כל שאיני זכאי באמירתו איני רשאי בחשיכתו מיבעי ליה אלא אסיפא קאי אבל מחשיך הוא לשמור ומביא פירות בידו האי כל שאני זכאי בחשיכתו רשאי אני באמירתו מיבעי ליה לעולם אסיפא קאי ואבא שאול אהא קאי דאמר רב יהודה אמר שמואל [א] מותר לאדם לומר לחבירו שמור לי פירות שבתחומך ואני אשמור לך פירות שבתחומי וקאמר אבא שאול לת"ק מי לא מודית דמותר אדם לומר לחבירו שמור לי פירות שבתחומך ואני אשמור לך פירות שבתחומי ואימא כל שאני זכאי באמירתו רשאי אני להחשיך עליו כלל לאתויי מאי לאתויי הא דת"ר (א) אין [ב] מחשיכין על התחום להביא בהמה (ב) [ג] היתה עומדת חוץ לתחום קורא לה והיא באה כלל אמר אבא שאול [ד] כל שאני זכאי באמירתו רשאי אני להחשיך עליו ומחשיכין לפקח על עסקי כלה ועל עסקי המת להביא לו ארון ותכריכין ואומרים לו לך למקום פלוני ואם לא מצאת במקום פלוני הבא ממקום פלוני לא מצאת במנה הבא במאתים ר' יוסי ברבי יהודה אומר [ה] ובלבד שלא יזכיר לו סכום מקח:

מתני' [ו] מחשיכין על התחום לפקח על עסקי כלה ועל עסקי המת להביא לו ארון ותכריכים [י] נכרי שהביא חלילין בשבת לא יספוד בהן ישראל אא"כ באו ממקום קרוב עשו לו ארון וחפרו לו קבר יקבר בו ישראל ואם בשביל ישראל לא יקבר בו עולמית:

גמ' מאי ממקום קרוב רב אמר ממקום קרוב ממש ושמואל אמר [ז] חיישינן שמא (א) חוץ לחומה לנו [א] דיקא מתניתין כוותיה דשמואל דקתני עשה לו ארון וחפר לו קבר יקבר בו ישראל אלמא מספיקא שרי [ח] ותניא כוותיה [ב] דרב (ג) [ט] עיר שישראל ונכרים דרים בה והיתה בה מרחץ המרחצת בשבת אם רוב נכרים לערב רוחץ בה מיד אם רוב ישראל ימתין עד כדי שיחמו חמין מחצה על מחצה [י] (אסור וימתין) עד כדי שיחמו חמין ר' יהודה אומר באמבטי קטנה אם יש בה רשות רוחץ בה מיד מאי רשות אמר רב יהודה אמר רב יצחק בריה דרב יהודה אם יש בה אדם חשוב שיש לו עשרה עבדים שמחממין לו י' קומקומין בבת אחת באמבטי קטנה מותר לרחוץ בה מיד: [כ] עשו לו ארון וחפרו לו קבר וכו': אמאי הכא נמי ימתין בכדי שיעשו אמר עולא [ל] בעומד באסרטיא תינח קבר ארון מאי איכא למימר א"ר אבהו [מ] במוטל על קברו:

מתני' [נ] עושין כל צרכי המת סכין ומדיחין אותו ובלבד שלא יזיז בו אבר שומטין את הכר מתחתיו ומטילין אותו על החול בשביל שימתין

רש"י

אלא אסיפא קאי. דקאמר ת"ק להיתרא אבל מחשיך הוא לשמור ואתא איהו ושוייה ביה כללא להביא כל כיוצא בהן: האי כל שאני זכאי להחשיך עליו זכאי אני באמירתו מיבעי ליה. (ג) דהיתר דחשיכה תנן והיתר דאמירה לא תנן והיכי תלי תניא בדלא תניא: לעולם אסיפא קאי. כדקאמרת ודקשיא לך אמירה מהיכא קאמר ליה להיתירא דתלי בה החשכה אהא קאי דאמר רב יהודה כו' אלמא זכאי אני באמירתו ואבא שאול ות"ק כולהו פשיטא להו הא דשמואל וקאמר ליה אבא שאול לת"ק מי לא מודית בהא שאתה מתיר להחשיך דמותר הוא לומר כדשמואל אלמא הואיל ומותר לומר מותר להחשיך הלכך אמאי נקטת החשכה לשמור לחודא שוי כללא למילתא ואימא כל שאני זכאי באמירתו רשאי אני להחשיך עליו דש"מ הך וש"מ מת וכלה דהא נמי זכאי באמירתו הוא כדמפרש לקמן והלכך מחשיכין עליו וסיפא דמתני' דקתני מחשיכין על התחום לפקח על עסקי כלה אבא שאול היא: כלל אמר אבא שאול כו'. והאי נמי זכאי באמירתו דקתני סיפא ואומר לו לך למקום פלוני: סכום מקח. מנה ומאתים: מתני' נכרי שהביא חלילין בשבת. בשביל ישראל: לא יספוד בהן ישראל. לעולם וקנסא הוא משום דמוכחא מילתא דבשבילו הובאו דאין דרך להביא חלילין אלא בשביל מת: ממקום קרוב. בתוך התחום: עשו לו ארון. בשביל נכרי או למכור: גמ' רב אמר ממקום קרוב ממש. כלומר שידוע לנו בירור הדבר דממקום קרוב באו שראינום שהיו בביתו: ושמואל אמר חיישינן שמא חוץ לחומה לנו. אפילו הביא מחוץ לעיר אנו תולין להתיר ואומרים שמא בתוך התחום לנו ערב שבת וסופדין בהן במוצ"ש מיד וחיישינן נמי דאמרינן לקולא כדאמרי' במס' חגיגה (דף טו.) גבי בתולה שעיברה חיישינן שמא באמבטי עיברה ומותרת לכהונה ולשמואל הכי קאמר מתני' לא יספוד בהן ישראל אא"כ יש לתלות שבאו ממקום קרוב ולאפוקי בידוע דממרחק לתחום באו: ה"ג דיקא מתני' כוותיה דשמואל ותניא כוותיה דרב: יקבר בו ישראל. דתלינן מספיקא שמא לצורך נכרי נעשה: תניא כוותיה דרב. דספיקא אסור דקתני מחצה על מחצה ימתין בכדי שיחמו חמין מיהא שרי והכא תני לא יספוד בהן משמע לעולם הכא מוכחא מילתא אבל במרחץ לא מוכחא מילתא כולי האי הואיל ואיכא נכרים: באמבטי קטנה. שיש לתלות ולומר משמשיכה הוחמה על ידי עבדים וקומקמין הרבה: אם יש בה רשות. אדם חשוב שליט: רוחץ בה. ישראל מיד דיש לומר משמשיכה הוחמו חמין לאותו נכרי. לישנא אחרינא גרסינן תניא כוותיה דשמואל ולא גרסי' דייקא מתני' כו' על מספיקא שרי ומייתי סייעתא לשמואל מדברי ר' יהודה דתלינן לקולא וריש לא קשיא ליה כיון דמחצה על מחצה ודאי בשביל ישראל ונכרים הוחמו שהרי לא לאדם אחד לבדו הוחמו דנימא ספיקא לנכרי ספק לישראל ולשון זה נראה לי עיקר ורבותי נמי לא גרסי לעיל הא דקתני עשה נכרי את הארון על מספיקא שרי ומיהו לא מפרשי לה כדפרישית: ימתין בכדי שיעשו. נהי דלא מוכחא מילתא מיהו י"ל שמא בשביל ישראל נעשה: בעומד. הקבר באיסרטיא שאין דרך ישראל ליקבר שם דודאי לא נעשה בשביל ישראל: ארון מאי איכא למימר. להוכיח דלא בשביל ישראל נעשה: במוטל. הארון: על קברו. של נכרי באיסרטיא דמוכח דלשם אותו קבר נעשה הארון: מתני': ומדיחין. במים: שלא יזיז בו אבר. לא יגביה לו ידו או רגלו או ריסי עיניו: שימתין

תוספות

האי כל שאני רשאי בחשיכתו רשאי אני באמירתו מיבעי ליה. תימה הא דכי פריך לעיל האי כל שאיני רשאי באמירתו איני רשאי בחשיכתו מיבעי ליה מכלל דאי הוה תנן הכי הוה אתי שפיר אע"ג דתלי חשיכה באמירה וי"ל התם שאני דלא הוה תלי תניא בדלא תניא דאמירה נמי תנינא לעיל לא יאמר אדם לחבירו שכור לי פועלים אבל השתא תלי תניא בדלא תניא דהיתר אמירה לא תניא אבל היתר החשכה תניא:

לעולם אסיפא קאי (ד) דאמר רב יהודה אמר שמואל מותר אדם לומר לחבירו שמור לי פירות שבתחומך. אע"פ שהוא אינו יכול לילך לשומרן יכול לומר לחבירו לשמרן ומתניתין הכי קאמר כל שאני זכאי באמירתו כגון לפקח על עסקי כלה ועל עסקי מת ויכול לומר לחבירו לעשות למחר רשאי אני להחשיך עליו וכ"ש מה שאני זכאי לומר לעשות היום כמו שמור לי פירות שבתחומך אע"פ שאיני רשאי לילך שם היום דמותר להחשיך עליו:

אין מחשיכין על התחום להביא בהמה. יש ספרים דגרסי מחשיכים לפי שאם יש שם בורגנים הולך ומביאה ובתוספתא גרס אין מחשיכין וי"ל דאיירי בבהמה שאינה יכולה לבא ברגליה כגון טלה קטן אא"כ ישאוהו בכתף שאפילו יש מחילות אינו רשאי להביא דאסור לטלטל בעלי חיים שהם מוקצים:

נכרי שהביא חלילים בשבת לא יספוד בהן ישראל. לא כפי' הקונטרס שפירש עולמית מדפריך בגמרא גבי עשה נכרי ארון וחפר לו קבר יקבר בו ישראל אמאי הכא נמי נימא ימתין בכדי שיעשו ואמאי קאמר נמי אי לאו דקאי אחלילים על כן נראה דלא יספוד בהן ישראל היינו עד כדי שיבואו דסתם חלילים אין מביאין אותן לשם אדם אחד אלא לשם כמה בני אדם:

אא"כ באו ממקום קרוב. תימה לרבי מה מהני שבאו ממקום קרוב הלא הביאם דרך רה"ר ומה לי ארון וקבר שנעשו בשבת ומה לי חלילים שהובאו דרך רה"ר וי"ל דהביא ממקום קרוב לא מהני כל כך הבאתו:

דיקא מתניתין כוותיה דשמואל כו' יקבר בו ישראל אלמא מספיקא שרי. תימה היכי (ה) מוכיחנא מינה דמספיקא שרי והא מוקמ' לה בעומד באיסרטיא דודאי לצורך נכרי נעשה מיהו אומר רבי דל"ג ליה להא דקתני עשו לו ארון כו' ול"ג נמי בסמוך (ו) ת"כ גם בפי' הקונט' ל"ג אלא ה"ג דיקא נמי ממתני' עיר שישראל ונכרים דרים בה כו' ומשנה היא במסכת מכשירין (פ"ב משנה ה) ר' יהודה אומר אם יש בה רשות רוחץ בה מיד אלמא תלינן להתיר כמו כן גבי חלילין יש לתלות בהיתר ולומר חוץ לחומה לנו. מ"ר:

עד

רבינו חננאל

כלל זה. ואמרינן אם על רישא דקתני אין מחשיכין על התחום לשכור פועלין וכו'. כל (שאני) [שאיני] זכאי בחשיכתו (אני) [איני] זכאי באמירתו היה לו לומר כי אין מחשיכין אמרה משנתנו בפירוש ומכללו נלמד האמירה כלומר מאחר שאין לי להחשיך בתחום לשכור פועלין כן אין לי לומר לחבירו השכר לי פועלין עם חשכה. אלא אסיפא. אבל מחשיך הוא לשמור וכו' כלומר כשם שמותר לו להחשיך כך מותר לו לומר לחבירו החשיך והביא לי פירות האי כל שאני זכאי בחשיכתו זכאי אני באמירתו היה לו לומר ואוקימנא כדרב פפא דאמר מותר לאדם לומר לחבירו שמור לי פירות שבתחומך וכו' כלומר כשם שאני זכאי לומר לחברי שמור לי פירות שבתחומך כך מותר לי לשמור פירות שבתחומו. ולהחשיך עליו ואמרינן עוד ולמה ליה כלל לתנייה בהדיא ופרקינן כלל להביא הא דת"ר מחשיכין על התחום להביא בהמה היתה עומדת חוץ לתחום קורא לה והיא באה. ולפקח על עסקי כלה ועל עסקי המת להביא לו ארון ותכריכין אומרים לו לך למקום פלוני לא מצאת במקום פלוני הבא ממקום פלוני לא מצאת במאה הבא במאתים ובלבד שלא יזכור את הדמים. ר' יוסי ב"ר יהודה [אומר] ובלבד שלא יזכור לו סכום המקח: מתני' מחשיכין על התחום. עד אא"כ באו ממקום קרוב מאי ממקום קרוב רב אמר קרוב ממש. ושמואל אמר חיישינן שמא חוץ לחומה לנו. א) ופירוש לן מרן דברי שמואל הללו והיאך מתני' דייקא כוותיה ומה טעם חלילים שהביאם גוי בשבת שלא ידעינן בהם ישראל ולמה לא ימתין בכדי שיביאו או דלמא משום דלא ידעינן מהיכן באו ועוד המותר לספוד בהן ביום ראשון ובשאר ימי החול או לאו מה פירק לו הלא אפילו מה המת מונח בדרך צריך להמתין בכדי שיחפור בקבר והדר קושיין לדוכתיה וכן בארון ליסברה לן מרן. ועוד אם הדברים הללו על עיר שרובן ישראל הם או לא. כי אם רובן גוים למה צריך להמתין הלמא לענין מרחץ אמור מותר לרחוץ בה מיד ושמואל אמר חיישינן שמא חוץ

חשק שלמה על רבינו חננאל א) נראה דזה הוא שאלה לרבינו. וז"ל יפרש לן מרן. (ואולי שאל מאת רב האי גאון). והתשובה חסרה כאן ובאמת שאלה הכתם היא תלי משונה:

עין משפט נר מצוה

לה א (מיי' פכ"ד מהל' שבת) סמג לאוין סה טוש"ע או"ח סימן שז סעיף י:

לו ב מיי' שם הלכה ג סמג שם טוש"ע או"ח סימן שו סעיף א:

לז ג מיי' שם טור שו"ע שם סעיף ג:

לח ד ה מיי' שם הל"ה טוש"ע שם סעיף ג וסימן שז סעיף ח:

לט ו ז מיי' פ"ו מהל' שבת הל"ו סמג שם טוש"ע או"ח סימן שכה סעיף טו:

מ ח מיי' שם הלכה ז טוש"ע שם סעיף טז:

מא ט י כ מיי' שם הל' ה טור שו"ע שם סעיף יד:

מב ל מיי' פכ"ו מהל' שבת הלכה כ סמג שם טוש"ע או"ח סימן שיא סעיף ז:

מסורת הש"ס

א) [תוספתא פרק יז], ב) [לעיל נג.], ג) לעיל קנ:, ד) [ל"ל ותנן], ה) לעיל קכו. ע"ש מכשירין פ"ב מ"ה ע"ש, ו) ל"ל יבמות [וכ"א במשנה].

הגהות הב"ח

(א) גמ' חוץ לחומה לנו אמר רבא דיקא מתני': (ב) שם ותניא כוותיה דרב דת"ר עיר: (ג) רש"י ד"ה האי כל וכו' דהיתר דהחשכה תנן: (ד) תוס' ד"ה לעולם אסיפא קאי ואבא שאול אהא קאי דאמר רב יהודה: (ה) ד"ה דיקא וכו' היכי מוכח מינה: (ו) באד"ה ול"ג נמי בסמוך דמתני רבנן גם בפ"ה ל"ג ליה אלא ה"ג:

הגהות הגר"א

[א] גמ' (דיקא מתני' כו' עד ה"ג מספיקא שרי. מח"מ: [ב] שם כוותיה דרב. נ"ל דשמואל:

ליקוטי רש"י

קורא לה והיא באה. דלא החזר הוא על מחום בהמתו ובלבד שלא יוליכנה ממש בידיו [לעיל נג.]. לערב. למוצאי שבת. עד כדי שיחמו חמין. שלא יהנה במה שהקדימו להחם בשבת וכן בכל מעשה שבת נתנו חכמים שיעור להמתין לערב בכדי שיעשו. אם רוב נכרים. דלצורך רובא מחממי ועיקר חילול שבת בשבילם [שם קכב.]. בכדי שיעשו. כדי שלא יהנה ממלאכת שבת [שם יח: ועי' תוס' ביצה כד:]. אסרטיא. ה"ר [ב"ק סא.]. מסילה שהולכין בה מעיר לעיר [לעיל ו.]. דרך כבושה [עירובין יז:].

may be interred in it.[17] וְאִם בִּשְׁבִיל יִשְׂרָאֵל – **But if** they did it **for a Jew,**[18] לֹא יִקָּבֵר בּוֹ עוֹלָמִית – **he may never be interred in it.**[19]

Gemara The Gemara examines the Mishnah's statement that a Jew may use flutes that were brought for him from "a nearby place":

מַאי מִמָּקוֹם קָרוֹב – **What is** the meaning of **"from a nearby place?"** That is, when may we assume that the flutes came from a nearby place?[20] רַב אָמַר – **Rav says:** מִמָּקוֹם קָרוֹב מַמָּשׁ – We must **absolutely** know that they came **from a nearby place.**[21] וּשְׁמוּאֵל אָמַר – **But Shmuel says:** חַיְישִׁינַן שֶׁמָּא חוּץ לַחוֹמָה לָנוּ – It suffices if **we can suspect that they "spent" the night** of the Sabbath just **outside the** city **wall.**[22]

The Gemara cites our Mishnah in support of Shmuel:

דַּיְקָא מַתְנִיתִין כְּוָותֵיהּ דִּשְׁמוּאֵל – **Our Mishnah reads more precisely as** interpreted by **[Shmuel],** דְּקָתָנֵי – **for it states:** עָשָׂה לוֹ אָרוֹן וְחָפַר לוֹ קֶבֶר יִקָּבֵר בּוֹ יִשְׂרָאֵל – If [A GENTILE] MADE A COFFIN FOR HIM OR DUG A GRAVE FOR HIM, A JEW MAY BE INTERRED IN IT. אַלְמָא מִסְּפֵיקָא שָׁרֵי – **Thus** we see that even though the grave or coffin is **of questionable status,**[23] it is **permitted.** הָכָא נַמִי מִסְּפֵיקָא שָׁרֵי – So **here, too,** in the case of the flute, even if it is **of questionable status,**[24] **it is permitted**, as Shmuel asserts.

The Gemara now adduces support for Rav:

וְתַנְיָא כְּוָותֵיהּ דְּרַב – **[A Mishnah]**[25] **was taught that accords with Rav:** עִיר שֶׁיִּשְׂרָאֵל וְנָכְרִים דָּרִים בָּהּ – This is the law regarding A CITY IN WHICH both JEWS AND GENTILES RESIDE וְהָיְתָה בָּהּ מֶרְחָץ הַמַּרְחֶצֶת בְּשַׁבָּת – AND in WHICH THERE IS A BATHHOUSE THAT IS USED ON THE SABBATH: אִם רוֹב נָכְרִים – IF A MAJORITY of the bathers[26] ARE GENTILES, לָעֶרֶב רוֹחֵץ בָּהּ מִיָּד – [A JEW] MAY BATHE IN IT IN THE EVENING IMMEDIATELY after the Sabbath.[27] אִם רוֹב יִשְׂרָאֵל – IF A MAJORITY of the bathers ARE JEWS, יַמְתִּין עַד כְּדֵי שֶׁיֵּחַמּוּ חַמִּין – [A JEW] SHOULD WAIT after the Sabbath AS LONG AS IT TAKES TO HEAT the WATER. מֶחֱצָה עַל מֶחֱצָה – If HALF the bathers are gentile AND HALF are Jews, (אָסוּר וְיַמְתִּין)[28] עַד כְּדֵי שֶׁיֵּחַמּוּ חַמִּין – IT IS FORBIDDEN for a Jew to bathe there immediately after the Sabbath; RATHER, HE SHOULD WAIT AS LONG AS IT TAKES TO HEAT the WATER.[29] רַבִּי יְהוּדָה אוֹמֵר – R' YEHUDAH SAYS: בְּאַמְבַּטִּי קְטַנָּה – IN the case of A SMALL POOL,[30] אִם יֵשׁ בָּהּ רָשׁוּת רוֹחֵץ בָּהּ מִיָּד – IF THERE IS A POTENTATE IN IT, [A JEW] MAY BATHE IN IT IMMEDIATELY after the Sabbath.

The Gemara explains R' Yehudah's statement:

מַאי רָשׁוּת – **What** does R' Yehudah mean by **"a potentate"?** אָמַר רַב יְהוּדָה אָמַר רַב יִצְחָק בְּרֵיהּ דְּרַב יְהוּדָה – **Rav Yehudah said in the name of Rav Yitzchak the son of Rav Yehudah:**[31] אִם יֵשׁ בָּהּ אָדָם חָשׁוּב – R' Yehudah means that **if there is an**

NOTES

17. I.e. immediately after the Sabbath (*Chidushei HaRan; see Ritva MHK* ed.). [Although it is *possible* that the gentile made it for a Jew (see previous note), there are no restrictions on its use. The Gemara (as explained by *Rashi*) deals with this point below.]

18. I.e. if the gentiles constructed the coffin or dug the grave on the Sabbath expressly for a Jew.

19. I.e. the Jew for whom the coffin was made or for whom the grave was dug may never be buried in it. [Other Jews may be buried in it after enough time has elapsed to have dug the grave or built the coffin after the Sabbath (*Rashba, Meiri, Shulchan Aruch, Orach Chaim* 325:14).]

Why is the ban permanent? According to *Rashi,* we can answer that the Mishnah refers to a case in which it was obvious (for some reason) that the coffin was constructed or the grave dug for a Jew (see note 14). The explanation given by those who disagree with *Rashi* is stated below in note 34.

Regarding a coffin and grave the Mishnah distinguishes between one made without express intent (for either Jews or gentiles) and one made expressly for Jews. In the case of the flutes, however, the Mishnah deals with flutes brought without express intent, and states that they are forbidden for use. *Ramban* explains that flutes were used only at Jewish funerals. Hence, if a gentile brings flutes, even if he does not express his intent, it can be assumed that he is acting on behalf of Jews. On the other hand, coffins and graves were used by both Jews and gentiles. Thus, if the gentile does not express his intent to the contrary, it is assumed that he is making them for a fellow gentile.

20. It is known that "a nearby place" means within the boundary. The Gemara seeks to define the circumstances in which the flutes may be judged to have come from such a place (*Ritva MHK* ed.).

21. Rav requires evidence that the flutes were within the Sabbath boundary since the beginning of the Sabbath. For example, the flutes were seen in the gentile's house [which is within the boundary, soon after the Sabbath began] (*Rashi*). In cases of doubt, where we do not know whether the flutes came from within or beyond the boundary, Rav forbids them for use.

[*Ramban* (*Milchamos,* end of folio 65b) reconciles this view with the rule of סָפֵק דְּרַבָּנָן לְקוּלָּא, *In matters of doubt regarding Rabbinic law, we take the lenient approach.* (See also *Mishnah Berurah* 325:32,33.)]

22. Shmuel maintains that the flutes may be used immediately after the Sabbath if it is *possible* that they were within the boundary when the Sabbath began. Therefore, even if we know that the flutes had been brought from outside the city, they are still permitted, because they might have been within 2,000 *amos* of the city wall (i.e. within the boundary) when night fell. The Mishnah thus means: If a gentile brought flutes, a Jew may not bewail with them unless there is a *possibility* that they came from a nearby place. They are prohibited only if we know for sure that they were brought on the Sabbath from outside the boundary (*Rashi; see Rashba* and *Ritva MHK* ed., who elaborate on this last point).

Although the word חַיְישִׁינַן, *we suspect,* usually denotes the possibility of *prohibition,* Shmuel uses it here in the opposite sense [as in *Chagigah* 15a] (*Rashi*).

It thus emerges that in regard to this law (viz. waiting after the Sabbath to benefit from a gentile's labor), if there is a doubt as to the circumstances, Rav rules stringently and Shmuel rules leniently (*Rashi, Tosafos, Baal HaMaor, Ritva MHK* ed., *Rosh*). [Other Rishonim, though, challenge this approach. In their view, it is Rav who rules leniently and Shmuel who rules stringently (see *Rif, Ramban* and *Rashba*).]

23. The gentile did not specify for whom he was making the coffin or digging the grave (see note 16). It is possible, therefore, that he did it on behalf of a Jew.

24. [Rav will interpret this clause as referring to a case in which we have definite knowledge that the grave or coffin was made for a gentile (see Gemara below).]

25. *Machshirin* 2:5. A marginal gloss substitutes תְּנַן (which usually introduces a Mishnah) for תַּנְיָא (which typically prefaces a Baraisa).

26. I.e. those who usually use the bathhouse after the Sabbath. It is the number of these bathers, not the number of residents, that is decisive (*Mishnah Berurah* 326:38).

27. We assume that the workers in the bathhouse heated the water for the sake of the majority (Gemara above, 122a).

28. In the Mishnah as it is recorded in *Machshirin,* the parenthesized words are replaced by יַמְתִּין, *he should wait.*

29. Although we cannot tell whether the workers heated the water for Jews or for gentiles, the Mishnah rules that the bathhouse may not be used immediately after the Sabbath. This supports Rav's ruling that in cases of doubt we rule stringently (*Rashi;* cf. *Ramban,* who proposes different explanations of the proof).

However, the bathhouse is prohibited only as long as it takes to heat the water, and not permanently. A permanent prohibition is imposed only where it is obvious that the Sabbath was desecrated for a Jew (see note 14). In this case, there is no obvious desecration on behalf of a Jew, since, after all, gentiles also use the bathhouse (*Rashi*).

30. I.e. the pool of the bathhouse is relatively small.

31. A father [Rav Yehudah] is apparently quoting the words of his son [Rav Yitzchak] (see, however, *Hagahos Melo HaRo'im*).

האי כל שאני זכאי באמירתו רשאי אני בחשיכתו כל שאיני זכאי באמירתו איני רשאי בחשיכתו מיבעי ליה אלא אסיפא קאי אבל מחשיך הוא לשמור ומביא פירות בידו האי כל שאני זכאי בחשיכתו רשאי אני באמירתו מיבעי ליה לעולם אסיפא קאי ואבא שאול אהא קאי דאמר רב יהודה אמר שמואל א מותר לאדם לומר לחבירו שמור לי פירות שבתחומך ואני אשמור לך פירות שבתחומי וקאמר אבא שאול לת"ק מי לא מודית דמותר אדם לומר לחבירו שמור לי פירות שבתחומך ואני אשמור לך פירות שבתחומי ואימא כל שאני זכאי באמירתו רשאי אני להחשיך עליו כלל לאתויי מאי לאתויי הא דת"ר (א) אין ב מחשיכין על התחום להביא בהמה (ב) ג היתה עומדת חוץ לתחום קורא לה והיא באה כלל אמר אבא שאול ד כל שאני זכאי באמירתו רשאי אני להחשיך עליו ומחשיכין לפקח על עסקי כלה ועל עסקי המת להביא לו ארון ותכריכין ואומרים לו לך למקום פלוני ואם לא מצאת במקום פלוני הבא ממקום פלוני לא מצאת במנה הבא במאתים ר' יוסי ברבי יהודה אומר ה ובלבד שלא יזכיר לו סכום מקח: מתני' ג מחשיכין על התחום לפקח על עסקי כלה ועל עסקי המת להביא לו ארון ותכריכים ו נכרי שהביא חלילין בשבת לא יספוד בהן ישראל אא"כ באו ממקום קרוב עשו לו ארון וחפרו לו קבר יקבר בו ישראל ואם בשביל ישראל לא יקבר בו עולמית: גמ' מאי ממקום קרוב רב אמר ממקום קרוב ממש ושמואל אמר ז חיישינן שמא (א) חוץ לחומה לנו [א] דיקא מתניתין כוותיה דשמואל דקתני עשה לו ארון וחפר לו קבר יקבר בו ישראל אלמא מספיקא שרי הכא נמי מספיקא שרי ח ותניא כוותיה [ב] דרב (ג) עיר שישראל ונכרים דרים בה והיתה בה מרחץ המרחצת בשבת אם רוב נכרים לערב רוחץ בה מיד אם רוב ישראל ימתין עד כדי שיחמו חמין מחצה על מחצה ט (אסור וימתין) עד כדי שיחמו חמין ר' יהודה אומר באמבטי קטנה אם יש בה רשות רוחץ בה מיד מאי רשות אמר רב יהודה אמר רב יצחק בריה דרב יהודה אם יש בה אדם חשוב שיש לו עשרה עבדים שמחממין לו י' קומקומין בבת אחת באמבטי קטנה מותר לרחוץ בה מיד: ט עשו לו ארון וחפרו לו קבר וכו': אמאי הכא נמי ימתין בכדי שיעשו אמר עולא י בעומד באסרטיא תינח קבר ארון מאי איכא למימר א"ר אבהו כ במוטל על קברו: מתני' ל עושין כל צרכי המת סכין ומדיחין אותו ובלבד שלא יזיז בו אבר שומטין את הכר מתחתיו ומטילין אותו על החול בשביל שימתין

עד

רש"י

אלא אסיפא קאי. דקאמר ת"ק להיתרא אבל מחשיך הוא לשמור ואתא איהו ושוייה ביה כללא להביא כל כיוצא בהן: האי כל שאני זכאי להחשיך עליו זכאי אני באמירתו מיבעי ליה. (ג) דהיתר דחשיכה תנן והיתר דאמירה לא תנן והיכי תלי תניא בדלא תניא: לעולם אסיפא קאי. כדקאמרת ודקשיא לך אמירה מהיכא קאמר ליה להיתירא דתלי בה החשכה אהא קאי דאמר רב יהודה כו' אלמא זכאי אני באמירתו ואהא שאול ות"ק כולהו פשיטא להו הא דשמואל וקאמר ליה אבא שאול לת"ק מי לא מודית בהא שאתה מתיר להחשיך דמותר הוא לומר כדשמואל אלמא הואיל ומותר לומר מותר להחשיך הלכך אמאי נקטת החשכה לשמור לחודא שוי כללא למילתא ואימא כל שאני זכאי באמירתו רשאי אני להחשיך עליו דש"מ הך וש"מ מת וכלה דהא נמי זכאי באמירתו הוא כדמפרש לקמן והלכך מחשיכין עליו וסיפא דמתני' דקתני מחשיכין על התחום לפקח על עסקי כלה אבא שאול היא: כלל אמר אבא שאול כו'. והאי נמי זכאי באמירתו כדקתני סיפא ואומר לו לך למקום פלוני: סכום מקח. מנה ומאתים: מתני' נכרי שהביא חלילין בשבת. בשביל ישראל: לא יספוד בהן ישראל. לעולם וקנסא הוא משום דמוכחא מילתא דבשבילו הובאו דאין דרך להביא חלילין אלא בשביל מת: ממקום קרוב. בתוך התחום: עשו לו ארון. בשביל נכרי או למכור: גמ' רב אמר ממקום קרוב ממש. כלומר שידוע לנו בירור הדבר דממקום קרוב באו שראינום שהיו בביתו: ושמואל אמר חיישינן שמא חוץ לחומה לנו. אפילו הביא מחוץ לעיר אנו תולין להתיר ואומרים שמא בתוך התחום לנו ערב שבת וסופדין בהן במוצ"ש מיד וחיישינן נמי אמרינן לקולא כדאמרי' במס' חגיגה (דף טו.) גבי בתולה שעיברה חיישינן שמא באמבטי עיברה ומותרת לכהונה ולשמואל הכי קאמר מתני' לא יספוד בהן ישראל אא"כ יש לתלות שבאו ממקום קרוב ולאפוקי בידוע דמחוץ לתחום באו: ה"ג דיקא מתני' כוותיה דשמואל ותניא כוותיה דרב: יקבר בו ישראל. דתלינן מספיקא שמא לצורך נכרי נעשה: תניא כוותיה דרב. דספיקא אסור דקתני מחצה על מחצה ימתין בכדי שיחמו חמין וא"ת בכדי שיחמו חמין מיהא שרי והכא תני לא יספוד בהן משמע לעולם הכא מוכחא מילתא אבל במרחץ לא מוכחא מילתא כולי האי הואיל ואיכא נכרים: באמבטי קטנה. שיש לתלות ולומר משחשיכה הוחמה על ידי עבדים וקומקמין הרבה: אם יש בה רשות. אדם חשוב שליט: רוחץ בה. ישראל מיד דיש לומר משחשיכה הוחמו חמין לאותו נכרי. לישנא אחרינא גרסינן תניא כוותיה דשמואל ולא גרסי' דייקא מתני' כו' עד מספיקא שרי ומייתי סייעתא לשמואל מדרבי יהודה דתלינן לקולא וריש"א לא קשיא ליה כיון דמחצה על מחצה ודאי בשביל ישראל ונכרים הוחמו שהרי לא לאדם אחד לבדו הוחמו דנימא ספיקא לנכרי ספק לישראל ולשון זה נראה לי עיקר ורבותי נמי לא גרסי לעיל להא דקתני עשה נכרי את הארון עד מספיקא שרי ומיהו לא מפרשי לה כדפרישית: ימתין בכדי שיעשו. נהי דלא מוכחא מילתא מיהו י"ל שמא בשביל ישראל נעשה: בעומד. הקבר באיסרטיא שאין דרך ישראל ליקבר שם דודאי לא נעשה בשביל ישראל: ארון מאי איכא למימר. להוכיח דלא בשביל ישראל נעשה: במוטל. הארון: על קברו. של נכרי באיסרטיא דמוכח דלשם אותו קבר נעשה הארון: מתני' ומדיחין. במים: שלא יזיז בו אבר. לא יגביה לו ידו או רגלו או ריסי עיניו:

תוספות

האי כל שאני רשאי בחשיכתו רשאי אני באמירתו מיבעי ליה. תימה הא דכי פריך לעיל האי כל שאיני רשאי באמירתו איני רשאי בחשיכתו מיבעי ליה מכלל דאי הוה תנן הכי הוה אתי שפיר אע"ג דתלי חשיכה באמירה וי"ל התם שאני דלא הוה תלי תניא בדלא תניא דאמירה נמי תנינא לעיל לא יאמר אדם לחבירו שכור לי פועלים אבל השתא תלי תניא בדלא תניא דהיתר אמירה לא תניא אבל היתר החשכה תניא:

לעולם אסיפא קאי (ד) דאמר רב יהודה אמר שמואל מותר אדם לומר לחבירו שמור לי פירות שבתחומך. אע"פ שהוא אינו יכול לילך לשומרן יכול לומר לחבירו לשמרן ומתניתין הכי קאמר כל שאני זכאי באמירתו כגון לפקח על עסקי כלה ועל עסקי מת ויכול לומר לחבירו לעשות למחר רשאי אני להחשיך עליו וכ"ש מה שאני זכאי לומר לעשות היום כמו שמור לי פירות שבתחומך אע"פ שאיני רשאי לילך שם היום דמותר להחשיך עליו:

אין מחשיכין על התחום להביא בהמה. יש ספרים דגרסי מחשיכים לפי שאם יש שם בורגנים הולך ומביאה ובתוספתא גרס אין מחשיכין וי"ל דאיירי בבהמה שאינה יכולה לבא ברגליה כגון טלה קטן אא"כ ישאוהו בכתף שאפילו יש מחילות אינו רשאי להביא דאסור לטלטל בעלי חיים שהם מוקצים:

נכרי שהביא חלילים בשבת לא יספוד בהן ישראל. לא כפי' הקונטרס שפירש עולמית מדפריך בגמרא גבי עשה נכרי ארון וחפר לו קבר יקבר בו ישראל אמאי הכא נמי נימא ימתין בכדי שיעשו ואמאי קאמר נמי אי לאו דקאי אחלילים על כן נראה דלא יספוד בהן ישראל היינו עד כדי שיבואו דסתם חלילים אין מביאין אותן לשם אדם אחד אלא לשם כמה בני אדם:

אא"כ באו ממקום קרוב. תימה לרבי מה מהני שבאו ממקום קרוב הלא הביאם דרך רה"ר ומה לי ארון וקבר שנעשו בשבת ומה לי חלילים שהובאו דרך רה"ר וי"ל דהביא ממקום קרוב לא מהני כל כך הבאתו:

דיקא מתניתין כוותיה דשמואל כו' יקבר בו ישראל אלמא מספיקא שרי. תימה היכי (ה) מוכיחא מינה דמספיקא שרי והא מוקמ' לה בעומד באיסרטיא דודאי לצורך נכרי נעשה מיהו אומר רבי דל"ג ליה להא דקתני עשו לו ארון כו' ול"ג נמי בסמוך (ו) ת"כ גם כפי' הקונטר' ל"ג אלא ה"ג דיקא נמי ממתני' עיר שישראל ונכרים דרים בה כו' ומשנה היא במסכת מכשירין (פ"ב משנה ה) ר' יהודה אומר אם יש בה רשות רוחץ בה מיד אלמא תלינן להתיר כמו כן גבי חלילין יש לתלות בהיתר ולומר חוץ לחומה לנו. מ"ר:

עין משפט נר מצוה

לה א (מיי' פכ"ד מהל' שבת) סמג לאוין סה טוש"ע או"ח סימן שז סעיף י:
לו ב מיי' שם הלכה ג סמג שם טוש"ע או"ח סימן שו סעיף ח:
לז ג מיי' שם טור שו"ע שם סעיף ב:
לח ד ה מיי' שם הל"ה טוש"ע שם סעיף ג וסימן שז סעיף ט:
לט ו ז מיי' פכ"ב מהל' שבת הל"ט סמג שם טוש"ע או"ח סימן שכה סעיף טו:
מ ח מיי' שם הלכה ז טוש"ע שם סעיף טו:
מא ט י כ מיי' שם הל"ה טור שו"ע שם סעיף יד:
מב ל מיי' פכ"ו מהל' שבת הלכה כ סמג שם טוש"ע או"ח סימן שיא סעיף ז:

רבינו חננאל

כלל זה. ואמרינן אם על רישא דקתני אין מחשיכין על התחום לשכור פועלין וכו'. כל (שאני) [שאינו] זכאי בחשיכתו (אני) [איני] זכאי באמירתו היה לו לומר כי אין מחשיכין אמרה משנתנו בפירוש ומכללו נלמד האמירה כלומר מאחר שאין לי להחשיך בתחום לשכור פועלין כן אין לי לומר לחבירו השכר לי פועלין עם חשכה. אלא אסיפא. אבל מחשיך הוא לשמור וכו' כלומר כשם שמותר לו להחשיך כך מותר לו לומר לחבירו החשיך והביא לי פירות האי כל שאיני זכאי בחשיכתו זכאי אני באמירתו היה לו לומר ואוקימנא כדרב פפא דאמר מותר לאדם לומר לחבירו שמור לי פירות שבתחומך וכו' כלומר כשם שאני זכאי לומר לחבר שמור לי פירות שבתחומך כך מותר לו לשמור פירות שבתחומי. ולהחשיך עליו ואמרינן עוד ולמה ליה כלל לתגרי להדריא ופרקינן כלל להביא הא דת"ר מחשיכין על התחום להביא בהמה היתה עומדת חוץ לתחום קורא לה והיא באה. ולפקח על עסקי כלה ועל עסקי המת להביא לו ארון ותכריכין אומרים לו לך למקום פלוני ולא מצאת במקום פלוני הבא ממקום פלוני לא מצאת במאה הבא במאתים ובלבד שלא יזכור את הדמים. ר' יוסי ב"ר יהודה (אומר) ובלבד שלא יזכור לו סכום המקח: מתני' מחשיכין על התחום. עד אא"כ באו ממקום קרוב מאי ממקום קרוב רב אמר קרוב ממש. ושמואל אמר חיישינן שמא חוץ לחומה לנו. א) ופירוש לן מרן דברי שמואל הללו והיאך מתני' דייקא כוותיה ומה טעם חלילים שהביאם נכרי בשבת שלא יספוד בהם ישראל ולמה לא ימתין בכדי שיביאו או דלמא משום דלא ידעינן מהיכן באו ועוד המותר לספוד בהן ביום ראשון ובשאר ימי החול או לא אם מה פירק לו הלא אפילו אם המת מונח בדרך צריך להמתין בכדי שיחזור בקבר והדר קושיין לדוכתיה וכן בארון ליסבירה לן מרן. ועוד אם הדברים הללו על עיר שרובן ישראל הם או לא. כי אם רובן גוים למה צריך להמתין הלא לענין מרחץ אמרו מותר לרחוץ בה מיד ושמואל אמר חיישינן שמא חוץ

מסורת הש"ס

א) [תוספתא פרק יח], ב) [לעיל נג.], ג) לעיל קנ:, ד) [נ"ל ותנן], ה) לעיל קכב. ע"ש מכשירין פ"ב מ"ה ע"ש, ו) נ"ל ימתין [וכ"ה במשנה].

הגהות הב"ח

(א) גמ' חוץ לחומה לנו אמר רבא דיקא מתני': (ב) שם ותניא כוותיה דרב דס"ד עיר: (ג) רש"י ד"ה האי כל וכו' להיתר דהחשכה תנן: (ד) תוס' ד"ה לעולם אסיפא קאי ואבא שאול אהא קאי דאמר רב יהודה: (ה) ד"ה דיקא וכו' היכי מוכח מינה: (ו) באד"ה ול"ג נמי בסמוך דתנו רבנן גם כפ"ה ל"ג ליה אלא ה"ג:

הגהות הגר"א

[א] גמ' (דיקא מתני' כו' עד ה"נ מספיקא שרי). תא"מ: [ב] שם כוותיה דרב. נ"ל דשמואל:

ליקוטי רש"י

קורא לה והיא באה. דלא החסר הוא על מחוס בהמתו ובלבד שלא יבילנה ממש בידיו [לעיל נג:]. לערב. למוצאי שבת. עד כדי שיחמו חמין. שלא יהנה במה שהקדימו להחם בשבת וכן בכל מעשה שבת שנו חכמים שיעור להמתין לערב בכדי שיעשו. אם רוב נכרים. דעעמלא דרובא מחממי ועיקר מילתא שבת בשבילם [שם קכב.]. בכדי שיעשו. כדי שלא יהנה ממלאכת שבת [שם יח: ועי' תוס' ביצה כד:]. אסרטיא. כמו ר"ר ט"ז אמה [ב"ק סא.]. מסילה שהולכין בה מעיר לעיר [לעיל ו.] דרך כבושה [עירובין יז:].

חשק שלמה על רבינו חננאל א) נראה דזה הוא שאלה לרבינו. וצ"ל ימברר לן מרן. (ואולי שאל מאת רב האי גאון). והתשובה חסרה כאן וכלשמא שאלה הכתב היא אלי תשובה:

important person in [the pool], שֶׁיֵּשׁ לוֹ עֲשָׂרָה עֲבָדִים – **who has ten servants** שֶׁמְּחַמְּמִין לוֹ עֲשָׂרָה קוּמְקוּמִין בְּבַת אַחַת בְּאַמְבַּטִי קְטַנָּה – **who could heat ten kettles of water for him at the same time to fill the small pool,** מוּתָּר לִרְחוֹץ בָּהּ מִיָּד – **it is permitted** for a Jew **to bathe in it immediately** after the Sabbath.[32]

The Mishnah stated:

עָשׂוּ לוֹ אָרוֹן וְחָפְרוּ לוֹ קֶבֶר וכו׳ – If [GENTILES] MADE A COFFIN FOR HIM OR DUG A GRAVE FOR HIM on the Sabbath **etc.** [a Jew may be interred in it immediately after the Sabbath].

The Gemara questions this ruling:

אַמַּאי – **Why** is this so? הָכָא נַמִּי יַמְתִּין בִּכְדֵי שֶׁיֵּעָשׂוּ – **Here, too, one should wait** after the Sabbath **the amount of time it takes for [these items] to be made,** because they were possibly made for a Jew.[33] – ? –

The Gemara answers:

אָמַר עוּלָּא – **Ulla said:** בְּעוֹמֵד בְּאִסְרַטְיָא – The Mishnah deals **with [a grave] that is located on a main road.** Since this is not a place where Jews are buried, it is evident that the grave was dug for a gentile.

The Gemara persists:

תֵּינַח קֶבֶר – This is a **satisfactory** explanation regarding the **grave.** אָרוֹן מַאי אִיכָּא לְמֵימַר – But as for the **coffin, what is there to say?** Perhaps it was made for a Jew!

The Gemara answers:

אָמַר רַבִּי אַבָּהוּ – **R' Abahu said:** בְּמוּטָּל עַל קִבְרוֹ – The Mishnah deals **with [a coffin] that is lying on [the gentile's] grave,** i.e. it is on the grave that was dug on a highway.[34]

Mishnah The Mishnah continues discussing matters related to a deceased person: עוֹשִׂין כָּל צָרְכֵי הַמֵּת – **We may attend to all the needs of the deceased** on the Sabbath:[35] סָכִין וּמְדִיחִין אוֹתוֹ – **We may anoint**[36] **and rinse him**[37] וּבִלְבַד שֶׁלֹּא יָזִיז בּוֹ אֵבֶר – **provided we do not move any of his limbs;**[38] שׁוֹמְטִין אֶת הַכַּר מִתַּחְתָּיו – **we may pull the pillow from under him**[39] וּמַטִּילִין אוֹתוֹ עַל הַחוֹל בִּשְׁבִיל – **and lay him on the sand in order**

NOTES

32. Since this person has many servants, it would take them only a few minutes to heat the water in the small pool. It is consequently possible that this water was heated *after* the Sabbath (*Rashi;* cf. *Rav* and *Eliyahu Rabbah* to *Machshirin* ibid.). R' Yehudah holds that since this possibility exists, we allow a Jew to use the pool immediately. Unlike the Tanna Kamma who rules stringently in cases of doubt, R' Yehudah rules leniently. [The Gemara derives support for Rav's opinion from the Tanna Kamma's statement, and not from R' Yehudah's.]

When R' Yehudah says that a Jew may use the small tub "immediately," he does not mean it literally. Rather, one must wait the short time it would take for the servants to heat the water (*Rashba* and *Ran;* see *Ritva MHK* ed.; see, however, *Ramban's* objection to this approach).

Rashi records an alternative version of the text which differs from our version in two respects:

(a) It does not include the proof (for Shmuel) from our Mishnah's ruling that if a gentile made a coffin on the Sabbath, it may be used for a Jew immediately after the Sabbath. [*Tosafos* (ד״ה דיקא) point out that the proof is not valid, because the Mishnah could be speaking of a case in which we know with certainty that the coffin was made for a gentile (see Gemara below).]

(b) The Mishnah in *Machshirin* is adduced not as proof for Rav, but as proof for Shmuel. *Rashi* explains that Shmuel's ruling is supported by R' Yehudah's opinion in the Mishnah that we rule leniently in cases of doubt (see beginning of this note). Although the Tanna Kamma prohibits immediate use of the bathhouse where half the bathers are gentile and half are Jewish, that case is irrelevant because it does not involve a doubt. Rather, the workers certainly heated the water for both Jews and gentiles. It is not comparable to the cases under discussion which involve a lack of knowledge, e.g. we do not know whether or not a *melachah* was done, or we do not know whether it was done for a Jew or a gentile (see, however, *Rashi* top of 122b). According to this approach, there is no disagreement between the Tanna Kamma and R' Yehudah (*Rashba, Ritva MHK* ed., *Ran MHK* ed.).

Rashi and other Rishonim (*Rif, Tosafos, Ramban, Rosh* et al.) accept this second version as authoritative.

33. The gentile did not specify that he was working for another gentile (see note 16). It is consequently possible that he was acting on behalf of a Jew. If so, we should wait after the Sabbath as long as it takes for the labor to be completed, so as not to benefit from desecration of the Sabbath (*Rashi,* as explained by *Rashba;* see, however, *Baal HaMaor's* objection).

The Gemara's question is based on Rav's view that in cases of doubt we rule stringently (*Tos. R' Akiva Eiger* and *Korban Nesanel* §2; see *Taz, Orach Chaim* 325:12).

[For a different explanation of the Gemara's difficulty, see note 34.]

The Gemara's expression הָכָא נַמִּי, *here too,* implies that we have already encountered a case in which one is required to wait the amount of time necessary for the labor to be completed. According to *Rashi,* though, there is no such case in our Mishnah (see note 14). In view of this difficulty, *Ritva* (*MHK* ed.) suggests that the text used by *Rashi* did not include the words הָכָא נַמִּי, *here too* (see also *Tosafos* ד״ה נכרי). Some propose that the Gemara refers to the Mishnah in *Machshirin,* which requires a bather to wait as long as it takes for the bathhouse water to be heated (*Maginei Shlomo* and *Hagahos R' Simchah MiDessau*).

34. Since the coffin was evidently intended for use in that grave, and since the grave was clearly dug for a gentile, we may conclude that the coffin too was made for that gentile.

We have explained the Gemara according to *Rashi.* Other Rishonim maintain that the Gemara's difficulty was with the Mishnah's last ruling that if the grave was dug for a Jew it is prohibited forever. The Gemara asks why it is not sufficient to wait the amount of time it takes for the grave to be dug. To this, the Gemara answers that the grave was dug in a conspicuous place, such as a main road. It is a disgrace for a Jew to lie in a grave that was dug in such flagrant desecration of the Sabbath (*Rashba, Ritva, Ran, Baal HaMaor*). Some authorities rule that a permanent ban applies not only in the context of burial, but whenever the Sabbath has been flagrantly desecrated on behalf of a Jew (*Tos. Rid; Magen Avraham* 325:31 citing *Rambam*). [See *Tosafos* ד״ה נכרי for a different reason as to why the ban is permanent.]

35. [I.e. all that is necessary to retard the body's decomposition before the funeral, or to prevent its lying in an undignified state.]

36. I.e. with oil (*Meiri*).

37. I.e. with water (*Rashi*).

38. I.e. one may not lift a hand, a foot, or even an eyelid (*Rashi*), because a corpse is *muktzeh.* From here we learn that the prohibition against moving a *muktzeh* object applies to moving even a part of it (see *Ramban, Ritva MHK* ed. and *Ran*). [A corpse, as well as any other *muktzeh* object, may be touched on the Sabbath, as long as it is not moved (*Rav*).]

39. I.e. we may pull the pillow or mattress upon which the deceased is lying out from under him, thereby laying him on the cool sand or dirt near his bed. He may not be directly moved onto the sand, because, as the Mishnah just stated, not even one limb of the deceased may be moved (*Rambam, Commentary to the Mishnah*).

האי כל שאני זכאי באמירתו רשאי אני בחשיכתו כל שאיני זכאי באמירתו איני רשאי בחשיכתו מיבעי ליה אלא אסיפא קאי אבל מחשיך הוא לשמור ומביא פירות בידו האי כל שאני זכאי בחשיכתו רשאי אני באמירתו מיבעי ליה לעולם אסיפא קאי ואבא שאול אהא קאי דאמר רב יהודה אמר שמואל א מותר לאדם לומר לחבירו שמור לי פירות שבתחומך ואני אשמור לך פירות שבתחומי וקאמר אבא שאול לת״ק מי לא מודית דמותר אדם לומר לחבירו שמור לי פירות שבתחומך ואני אשמור לך פירות שבתחומי ואימא כל שאני זכאי באמירתו רשאי אני להחשיך עליו כלל לאתויי מאי לאתויי הא דת״ר א) אין ב מחשיכין על התחום להביא בהמה ג היתה עומדת חוץ לתחום קורא לה והיא באה כלל אמר אבא שאול ד כל שאני זכאי באמירתו רשאי אני להחשיך עליו ומחשיכין לפקח על עסקי כלה ועל עסקי המת להביא לו ארון ותכריכין ואומרים לו לך למקום פלוני ואם לא מצאת במקום פלוני הבא ממקום פלוני לא מצאת במנה הבא במאתים ר׳ יוסי ברבי יהודה אומר ה ובלבד שלא יזכיר לו סכום מקח:

מתני׳ ג) מחשיכין על התחום לפקח על עסקי כלה ועל עסקי המת להביא לו ארון ותכריכים ו נכרי שהביא חלילין בשבת לא יספוד בהן ישראל אא״כ באו ממקום קרוב עשו לו ארון וחפרו לו קבר יקבר בו ישראל ואם בשביל ישראל לא יקבר בו עולמית:

גמ׳ מאי ממקום קרוב רב אמר ממקום קרוב ממש ושמואל אמר ז חיישינן שמא (א) חוץ לחומה לנו [א] דיקא מתניתין כוותיה דשמואל דקתני עשה לו ארון וחפר לו קבר יקבר בו ישראל אלמא מספיקא שרי ח ותניא כוותיה [ב] דרב (ב) ט עיר שישראל ונכרים דרים בה והיתה בה מרחץ המרחצת בשבת אם רוב נכרים לערב רוחץ בה מיד אם רוב ישראל ימתין עד כדי שיחמו חמין מחצה על מחצה י (אסור וימתין) עד כדי שיחמו חמין ר׳ יהודה אומר באמבטי קטנה אם יש בה רשות רוחץ בה מיד מאי רשות אמר רב יהודה אמר רב יצחק בריה דרב יהודה אם יש בה אדם חשוב שיש לו עשרה עבדים שמחממין לו י׳ קומקומין בבת אחת באמבטי קטנה מותר לרחוץ בה מיד: כ עשו לו ארון וחפרו לו קבר וכו׳: אמאי הכא נמי ימתין בכדי שיעשו אמר עולא ל בעומד באסרטיא תינח קבר ארון מאי איכא למימר א״ר אבהו מ במוטל על קברו:

מתני׳ נ עושין כל צרכי המת סכין ומדיחין אותו ובלבד שלא יזיז בו אבר שומטין את הכר מתחתיו ומטילין אותו על החול בשביל

שימתין

רש״י

אלא אסיפא קאי. דקאמר ת״ק להיתרא אבל מחשיך הוא לשמור ואתא איהו ושוייה ליה כללא להביא כל כיוצא בהן: האי כל שאני זכאי להחשיך עליו זכאי אני באמירתו מיבעי ליה. (ג) דהיתר דהחשכה תנן והיתר דאמירה לא תנן והיכי תלי תניא בדלא תניא: לעולם אסיפא קאי. כדקאמרת ודקשיא לך אמירה מהיכא קאמר ליה להיתירא דתלי בה החשכה אהא קאי דאמר רב יהודה כו׳ אלמא זכאי אני באמירתו ואבא שאול ות״ק כולהו פשיטא להו הא דשמואל וקאמר ליה אבא שאול לת״ק מי לא מודית דהא שאתה מתיר להחשיך דמותר הוא לומר כדשמואל אלמא הואיל ומותר לומר מותר להחשיך הלכך אמאי נקטת החשכה לשמור להודא שוי כללא למילתא ואימא כל שאני זכאי באמירתו רשאי אני להחשיך עליו דש״מ הך וש״מ מת וכלה דהא נמי זכאי באמירתו הוא כדמפרש לקמן והלכך מחשיכין עליו וסיפא דמתני׳ דקתני מחשיכין על התחום לפקח על עסקי כלה אבא שאול היא: כלל אמר אבא שאול כו׳. והאי נמי זכאי באמירתו כדקתני סיפא ואומר לו לך למקום פלוני: סכום מקח. מנה ומאתים: מתני׳ נכרי שהביא חלילין בשבת. בשביל ישראל: לא יספוד בהן ישראל. לעולם וקנסא הוא משום דמוכחא מילתא דבשבילו הובאו דאין דרך להביא חלילין אלא בשביל מת: ממקום קרוב. בתוך התחום: עשו לו ארון. בשביל נכרי או למכור: גמ׳ רב אמר ממקום קרוב ממש. כלומר שידוע לנו בירור הדבר דממקום קרוב באו שראינום שהיו בביתו: ושמואל אמר חיישינן שמא חוץ לחומה לנו. אפילו הביא מחוץ לעיר אנו תולין להתיר ואומרים שמא בתוך התחום לנו ערב שבת וסופדין בהן במוצ״ש מיד וחיישינן נמי אמרינן לקולא כדאמרי׳ במס׳ חגיגה (דף טו.) גבי בתולה שעיברה חיישינן שמא באמבטי עיברה ומותרת לכהונה ולשמואל הכי קאמר מתני׳ לא יספוד בהן ישראל אא״כ יש לתלות שבאו ממקום קרוב ולאפוקי בידוע דמחוץ לתחום באו: ה״ג דיקא מתני׳ כוותיה דשמואל ותניא כוותיה דרב: יקבר בו ישראל. דתלינן מספיקא שמא לצורך נכרי נעשה: תניא כוותיה דרב. דספיקא אסור דקתני מחצה על מחצה ימתין בכדי שיחמו חמין וא״ת בכדי שיחמו חמין מיהא שרי והכא תני לא יספוד בהן משמע לעולם הכא מוכחא מילתא אבל במרחץ לא מוכחא מילתא כולי האי הואיל ואיכא נכרים: באמבטי קטנה. שיש לתלות ולומר משחשיכה הוחמה על ידי עבדים וקומקמין הרבה: אם יש בה רשות. אדם חשוב שליט: רוחץ בה. ישראל מיד דיש לומר משחשיכה הוחמו חמין לאותו נכרי. לישנא אחרינא גרסינן תניא כוותיה דשמואל ולא גרסי׳ דייקא מתני׳ כו׳ עד מספיקא שרי ומייתי סייעתא לשמואל מדרבי יהודה דתלינן לקולא וריש לא קשיא ליה כיון דמחצה על מחצה ודאי בשביל ישראל ונכרים הוחמו שהרי לא לאדם אחד לבדו הוחמו דנימא ספיקא לנכרי ספק לישראל ולשון זה נראה לי עיקר ורבותי נמי לא גרסי לעיל להא דקתני עשה נכרי את הארון עד מספיקא שרי ומיהו לא מפרשי לה כדפרישית: ימתין בכדי שיעשו. נהי דלא מוכחא מילתא מיהו י״ל שמא בשביל ישראל נעשה: בעומד. הקבר באיסרטיא שאין דרך ישראל ליקבר שם דודאי לא נעשה בשביל ישראל: ארון מאי איכא למימר. להוכיח דלא בשביל ישראל נעשה: במוטל. הארון: על קברו. של נכרי באיסרטיא דמוכח דלשם אותו קבר נעשה הארון: מתני׳ ומדיחין. במים: שלא יזיז בו אבר. לא יגביה לו ידו או רגלו או ריסי עיניו:

תוספות

האי כל שאני רשאי בחשיכתו רשאי אני באמירתו מיבעי ליה. תימה הא דמי פריך לעיל האי כל שאיני רשאי באמירתו איני רשאי בחשיכתו מיבעי ליה מכלל דאי הוה תנן הכי הוה אתי שפיר אע״ג דתלי חשיכה באמירה וי״ל התם שאני דלא הוה תלי תניא בדלא תניא דאמירה נמי תנינא לעיל לא יאמר אדם לחבירו שכור לי פועלים אבל השתא תלי תניא בדלא תניא דהיתר אמירה לא תניא אבל היתר החשכה תניא:

לעולם אסיפא קאי (ד) דאמר רב יהודה אמר שמואל מותר אדם לומר לחבירו שמור לי פירות שבתחומך. אע״פ שהוא אינו יכול לילך לשומרן יכול לומר לחבירו לשמרן ומתניתין הכי קאמר כל שאני זכאי באמירתו כגון לפקח על עסקי כלה ועל עסקי מת ויכול לומר לחבירו לעשות למחר רשאי אני להחשיך עליו וכ״ש מה שאני זכאי לומר לעשות היום כמו שמור לי פירות שבתחומך אע״פ שאיני רשאי לילך שם היום דמותר להחשיך עליו:

אין מחשיכין על התחום להביא בהמה. יש ספרים דגרסי מחשיכים לפי שאם יש שם בורגנים הולך ומביאה ובתוספתא גרס אין מחשיכין וי״ל דאיירי בבהמה שאינה יכולה לבא ברגליה כגון טלה קטן אא״כ ישאוהו בכתף שאפילו יש מחיצות אינו רשאי להביא דאסור לטלטל בעלי חיים שהם מוקצים:

נכרי שהביא חלילים בשבת לא יספוד בהן ישראל. לא כפי׳ הקונטרס שפירש עולמית מדפריך בגמרא גבי עשה נכרי ארון וחפר לו קבר יקבר בו ישראל אמאי הכא נמי נימא ימתין בכדי שיעשו ואמאי קאמר נמי אי לאו דקאי אחלילים על כן נראה דלא יספוד בהן ישראל היינו עד כדי שיבואו דסתם חלילים אין מביאין אותן לשם אדם אחד אלא לשם כמה בני אדם:

אא״כ באו ממקום קרוב. תימה לרבי מה מהני שבאו ממקום קרוב הלא הביאם דרך רה״ר ומה לי ארון וקבר שנעשו בשבת ומה לי חלילים שהובאו דרך רה״ר וי״ל דהביא ממקום קרוב לא מהני כל כך הבאתו:

דיקא מתניתין כוותיה דשמואל כו׳ יקבר בו ישראל אלמא מספיקא שרי. תימה היכי (ה) מוכיחנא מינה דמספיקא שרי והא מוקמ׳ לה בעומד באיסרטיא דודאי לצורך נכרי נעשה מיהו אומר רבי דל״ג ליה להא דקתני עשו לו ארון כו׳ ול״ג נמי בסמוך (ו) ת״כ גם בפי׳ הקונט׳ ל״ג אלא ה״ג דיקא נמי ממתני׳ עיר שישראל ונכרים דרים בה כו׳ ומשנה היא במסכת מכשירין (פ״ב משנה ה) ר׳ יהודה אומר אם יש בה רשות רוחץ בה מיד אלמא תלינן להתיר כמו כן גבי חלילין יש לתלות בהיתר ולומר חוץ לחומה לנו. מ״ר:

עד

עין משפט נר מצוה

לה א (מיי׳ פכ״ד מהל׳ שבת) סמג לאוין סה טוש״ע או״ח סימן שז סעיף י:

לו ב מיי׳ שם הלכה ג סמג שם טוש״ע או״ח סימן שו סעיף ח:

לז ג מיי׳ שם טור שו״ע שם סעיף ג:

לח ד ה מיי׳ שם הל״ה טוש״ע שם סעיף ג וסימן שז סעיף ח:

לט ו ז מיי׳ פ״ו מהל׳ שבת הל״ט סמג שם טוש״ע או״ח סימן שכה סעיף טו:

מ ח מיי׳ שם הלכה ז טוש״ע שם סעיף טו:

מא ט י כ מיי׳ שם הל׳ ט טור שו״ע שם סעיף יד:

מב ל מ מיי׳ פכ״ו מהל׳ שבת הלכה כ סמג שם טוש״ע או״ח סימן שיא סעיף ז:

רבינו חננאל

כלל זה. ואמרינן אם על רישא דקתני אין מחשיכין על התחום לשכור פועלין וכו׳. כל (שאני) [שאיני] זכאי בחשיכתו (אני) [איני] זכאי באמירתו היה לו לומר כי אין מחשיכין אמרה משנתנו בפירוש ומכללו נלמד האמירה כלומר מאחר שאין לי להחשיך בתחום לשכור פועלין כן אין לי לומר לחבירו השכר לי פועלין עם חשכה. אלא אסיפא. אבל מחשיך הוא לשמור וכו׳ כלומר כשם שמותר לו להחשיך כך מותר לו לומר לחבירו החשיך והביא לי פירות האי כל שאני זכאי בחשיכתו זכאי אני באמירתו היה לו לומר ואוקימנא כדרב פפא דאמר מותר לאדם לומר לחבירו שמור לי פירות שבתחומך וכו׳ כלומר כשם שאני זכאי לומר לחברי שמור לי פירות שבתחומך כך מותר לי לשמור פירות שבתחומו. ולהחשיך עליו ואמרינן עוד ולמה ליה כלל לתנייה בהדיא ופרקינן כלל להביא הא דת״ר מחשיכין על התחום להביא בהמה היתה עומדת חוץ לתחום קורא לה והיא באה. ולפקח על עסקי כלה ועל עסקי המת להביא לו ארון ותכריכין אומרים לו לך למקום פלוני לא מצאת במקום פלוני הבא ממקום פלוני לא מצאת במאה הבא במאתים ובלבד שלא יזכור את הדמים. ר׳ יוסי ב״ר יהודה [אומר] ובלבד שלא יזכור לו סכום המקח: מתני׳ מחשיכין על התחום. עד אא״כ באו ממקום קרוב מאי ממקום קרוב רב אמר קרוב ממש. ושמואל אמר חיישינן שמא חוץ לחומה לנו. א) ופירוש לן מרן דברי שמואל הללו והיאך מתני׳ דייקא כוותיה ומה טעם חלילים שהביאם נכרי בשבת שלא יספוד בהם ישראל ולמה לא ימתין בכדי שיביאו או דלמא משום דלא ידעינן מהיכן באו ועוד המותר לספוד בהן ביום ראשון ובשאר ימי החול או לא מה פירק לו הלא אפילו אם המת מונח בדרך צריך להמתין בכדי שיחזור בקבר והדר קושיין לדוכתיה וכן בארון ליסברה לן מרן. ועוד אם הדברים הללו על עיר שרובן ישראל הם או לא. כי אם רובן גוים למה צריך להמתין והלא לענין מרחץ אמור מותר לרחוץ בה מיד ושמואל אמר חיישינן שמא חוץ

מסורת הש״ס

א) [תוספתא פרק יז], ב) [לעיל נג:], ג) [לעיל קנ:], ד) [ל״ל ותנן], ה) לעיל קכח. ע״ש מכשירין פ״ב מ״ה ע״ש, ו) ל״ל ימתין [וכ״ה במשנה].

הגהות הב״ח

(א) גמ׳ חוץ לחומה לנו אמר רבה דיקא מתני׳: (ב) שם ותניא כוותיה דרב דתניא עיר: (ג) רש״י ד״ה האי כל וכו׳ דהיתרא דהחשכה תנן: (ד) תוס׳ ד״ה לעולם אסיפא קאי ואבא שאול אהא קאי דאמר רב יהודה: (ה) ד״ה דיקא וכו׳ היכי מוכח מינה: (ו) בא״ד ול״ג נמי בסמוך דתנו רבנן גם בפ״ה ל״ג ליה אלא ה״ג:

הגהות הגר״א

[א] גמ׳ (דיקא מתני׳ כו׳ עד ה״נ מספיקא שרי). תא״מ: [ב] שם כוותיה דרב. נ״ל דשמואל:

ליקוטי רש״י

קורא לה והיא באה. דלא החזר הוא על מנת כשתלך ובלבד שלא יוליכה ממש בידיו [לעיל נג:]. לערב. למוצאי שבת. עד כדי שיחמו חמין. שלא יהנה ממלאכת שבת [illegible] שיעור להמתין לערב בכדי שיעשו. אם רוב נכרים. דעתם דרובא ממעמי ועיקר חילול שבת בשבילם [שם קכב.]. בכדי שיעשו. כדי שלא יהנה ממלאכת שבת [שם יח: ועי׳ תוס׳ ביצה כד:]. אסרטיא. רה״ר [ב״ק סא.]. מסילה שהולכין בה מעיר לעיר [לעיל ו.]. דרך כבושה [עירובין יז:].

חשק שלמה על רבינו חננאל א) נראה דזה הוא שאלה לרבינו. ונ״ל דצ״ל ופירש לן מרן. (ואולי שאל מאת רב האי גאון). והתשובה חסרה כאן [illegible]:

עין משפט נר מצוה

מג א מיי' פכ"ו מהל' שבת הלכה כ סמג שם טוש"ע או"ח סימן שיא סעיף ז:
מד ב מיי' פ"ד מהלכות אבל הלכה ה סמג עשין ב טוש"ע יו"ד סי' שלט סעיף א:
מה ג סמג עשין עט:
מו ד מיי' פ"י מהלכות תשובה הלכה א:
מז ה מיי' פ"י מהלכות מתנות עניים הל"ג [וכה' עבדים פ"ט הל"ח] טוש"ע יו"ד סימן רמז סעיף ג:

תורה אור השלם

א) עַד אֲשֶׁר לֹא יֵרָתֵק חֶבֶל הַכֶּסֶף וְתָרֻץ גֻּלַּת הַזָּהָב וְתִשָּׁבֶר כַּד עַל הַמַּבּוּעַ וְנָרֹץ הַגַּלְגַּל אֶל הַבּוֹר: [קהלת יב, ו]
ב) הִנְנִי גֹעֵר לָכֶם אֶת הַזֶּרַע וְזֵרִיתִי פֶרֶשׁ עַל פְּנֵיכֶם פֶּרֶשׁ חַגֵּיכֶם וְנָשָׂא אֶתְכֶם אֵלָיו: [מלאכי ב, ג]
ג) בַּמֵּתִים חָפְשִׁי כְּמוֹ חֲלָלִים שֹׁכְבֵי קֶבֶר אֲשֶׁר לֹא זְכַרְתָּם עוֹד וְהֵמָּה מִיָּדְךָ נִגְזָרוּ: [תהלים פח, ו]
ד) וּמוֹרַאֲכֶם וְחִתְּכֶם יִהְיֶה עַל כָּל חַיַּת הָאָרֶץ וְעַל כָּל עוֹף הַשָּׁמָיִם בְּכֹל אֲשֶׁר תִּרְמֹשׂ הָאֲדָמָה וּבְכָל דְּגֵי הַיָּם בְּיֶדְכֶם נִתָּנוּ: [בראשית ט, ב]
ה) וְאָדָם בִּיקָר בַּל יָלִין נִמְשַׁל כַּבְּהֵמוֹת נִדְמוּ: [תהלים מט, יג]
ו) וּזְכֹר אֶת בּוֹרְאֶיךָ בִּימֵי בְּחוּרֹתֶיךָ עַד אֲשֶׁר לֹא יָבֹאוּ יְמֵי הָרָעָה וְהִגִּיעוּ שָׁנִים אֲשֶׁר תֹּאמַר אֵין לִי בָהֶם חֵפֶץ: [קהלת יב, א]
ז) כִּי לֹא יֶחְדַּל אֶבְיוֹן מִקֶּרֶב הָאָרֶץ עַל כֵּן אָנֹכִי מְצַוְּךָ לֵאמֹר פָּתֹחַ תִּפְתַּח אֶת יָדְךָ לְאָחִיךָ לַעֲנִיֶּךָ וּלְאֶבְיֹנְךָ בְּאַרְצֶךָ: [דברים טו, יא]
ח) נָתוֹן תִּתֵּן לוֹ וְלֹא יֵרַע לְבָבְךָ בְּתִתְּךָ לוֹ כִּי בִּגְלַל הַדָּבָר הַזֶּה יְבָרֶכְךָ יְיָ אֱלֹהֶיךָ בְּכָל מַעֲשֶׂךָ וּבְכֹל מִשְׁלַח יָדֶךָ: [דברים טו, י]
ט) וְלֹא יִדְבַּק בְּיָדְךָ מְאוּמָה מִן הַחֵרֶם לְמַעַן יָשׁוּב יְיָ מֵחֲרוֹן אַפּוֹ וְנָתַן לְךָ רַחֲמִים וְרִחַמְךָ וְהִרְבֶּךָ כַּאֲשֶׁר נִשְׁבַּע לַאֲבֹתֶיךָ: [דברים יג, יח]
י) עַד אֲשֶׁר לֹא תֶחְשַׁךְ הַשֶּׁמֶשׁ וְהָאוֹר וְהַיָּרֵחַ וְהַכּוֹכָבִים וְשָׁבוּ הֶעָבִים אַחַר הַגָּשֶׁם: [קהלת יב, ב]

גמרא

שימתין קושרין את הלחי לא שיעלה אלא שלא יוסיף וכן קורה שנשברה סומכין אותה בספסל או בארוכות המטה לא שתעלה אלא שלא תוסיף: גמ' והאמר רב יהודה אמר שמואל מעשה בתלמידו של רבי מאיר שנכנס אחריו לבית המרחץ ביקש להדיח קרקע אמר לו אין מדיחין לסוך קרקע אמר לו אין סכין קרקע בקרקע מחלפא מת בקרקע לא מיחלף כל לאתויי מאי לאתויי הא דת"ר מביאין כלי מיקר וכלי מתכות ומניחין על כריסו כדי שלא (א) תפוח ופוקקין את נקביו כדי שלא תיכנס בהן הרוח ואף שלמה אמר בחכמתו א) עד שלא ירתק חבל הכסף זה חוט השדרה ותרוץ גולת הזהב זה אמה ותשבר כד על המבוע זה הכרס ונרוץ הגלגל אל הבור זה פרש וכן הוא אומר ב) וזריתי פרש על פניכם פרש חגיכם אמר רב הונא ואמרי לה אמר רב חגא אלו בני אדם שמניחין דברי תורה ועושין כל ימיהם כחגים אמר רבי לוי אמר רב פפי א"ר יהושע לאחר שלשה ימים כריסו נבקעת ונופלת לו על פניו ואומרת לו טול מה שנתת בי: מתני' אין מעצמין את המת בשבת ולא בחול עם יציאת נפש והמעצים עם יציאת הנפש הרי זה שופך דמים: גמ' תנו רבנן המעצמו עם יציאת הנפש הרי זה שופך דמים משל לנר שכבה והולכת אדם מניח אצבעו עליה מיד כבתה תניא רשב"ג אומר הרוצה שיתעצמו עיניו של מת נופח לו יין בחוטמו ונותן שמן בין ריסי עיניו ואוחז בשני גודלי רגליו והן מתעצמין מאליהן תניא רשב"ג אומר תינוק בן יומו חי מחללין עליו את השבת דוד מלך ישראל מת אין מחללין עליו את השבת תינוק בן יומו חי מחללין עליו את השבת אמרה תורה חלל עליו שבת אחד כדי שישמור שבתות הרבה דוד מלך ישראל מת אין מחללין עליו כיון שמת אדם בטל מן המצות והיינו דא"ר יוחנן ג) במתים חפשי כיון שמת אדם נעשה חפשי מן המצות ותניא ר' שמעון בן אלעזר אומר תינוק בן יומו חי אין צריך לשומרו מן החולדה ומן העכברים אבל עוג מלך הבשן מת צריך לשומרו מן החולדה ומן העכברים שנאמר ד) ומוראכם וחתכם יהיה כל זמן שאדם חי אימתו מוטלת על הבריות כיון שמת בטלה אימתו אמר רב פפא נקיטינן אריה אבי תרי לא נפיל הא קא חזינן דנפיל ההוא כדרמי בר אבא דאמר רמי בר אבא אין חיה שולטת באדם עד שנדמה לו כבהמה שנאמר ה) אדם ביקר בל ילין נמשל כבהמות נדמו אמר רבי חנינא אסור לישן בבית יחידי וכל הישן בבית יחידי אחזתו לילית ותניא רשב"א אומר עשה עד שאתה מוצא ומצוי לך ועודך בידך ואף שלמה אמר בחכמתו ו) וזכור את בוראיך בימי בחורותיך עד אשר [ש]לא יבואו ימי הרעה אלו ימי הזקנה והגיעו שנים אשר תאמר אין לי בהם חפץ אלו ימי המשיח שאין בהם לא זכות ולא חובה ופליגא דשמואל דאמר שמואל אין בין העולם הזה לימות המשיח אלא שיעבוד מלכיות בלבד שנא' ז) כי לא יחדל אביון מקרב הארץ תניא ר' אלעזר הקפר אומר לעולם יבקש אדם רחמים על מדה זו שאם הוא לא בא בנו ואם בנו לא בא בן בנו בא שנאמר ח) כי בגלל הדבר הזה תנא דבי ר' ישמעאל גלגל הוא שחוזר בעולם א"ר יוסף נקיטינן האי צורבא מרבנן לא מיעני והא קא חזינן דמיעני אם איתא דמיעני אהדורי אפתחא לא מיהדר אמר לה רבי חייא לדביתהו כי אתי עניא אקדימי ליה ריפתא כי היכי דלקדמו לבנין אמרה ליה מילט קא לייטת להו אמר לה קרא קא כתיב כי בגלל הדבר הזה ותנא דבי ר' ישמעאל גלגל הוא שחוזר בעולם תניא ר' גמליאל ברבי אומר ט) ונתן לך רחמים ורחמך והרבך כל המרחם על הבריות מרחמין עליו מן השמים וכל שאינו מרחם על הבריות אין מרחמין עליו מן השמים י) עד אשר לא תחשך השמש והאור זו פדחת והחוטם והירח זו נשמה והכוכבים אלו הלסתות ושבו העבים אחר הגשם זה מאור עיניו של אדם שהולך אחר הבכי אמר שמואל האי דמעתא עד ארבעין שנין הדרא מכאן ואילך לא הדרא ואמר רב נחמן האי כוחלא עד ארבעין שנין מרווח מכאן ואילך אפילו מליא מ) כאביסנא דגירדאי אוקומי מוקים ארווחי לא מרווח מאי קא משמע לן דכמה דאלים מכוחלא טפי מעלי ר' חנינא שכיבא ליה ברתיה לא הוה קא בכי עלה אמרה ליה דביתהו תרנגולתא אפיקת מביתך אמר לה תרתי תכלא ועיורא סבר לה כי הא דאמר רבי יוחנן משום רבי יוסי בן קצרתה י) שש דמעות הן שלש יפות ושלש רעות של עשן ושל בכי ושל

רש"י

שימתין. שלא יסריח מחמת חום הסדין והכרים: קושרין את הלחי. של מת שהיה פיו הולך ונפתח קושרין את לחייו כדי שלא יפתח פיו יותר: ולא שיעלה. להסגר ממה שנפתח דהיינו מזיז אבר אלא שלא יוסיף ליפתח: סומכין אותה בספסל. שהרי תורת כלי עליו: לא שתעלה. דהוה ליה בונה: גמ' ואמר לו אין סכין. אלמא דבר האסור לטלטל אסור לסוך: קרקע בקרקע מיחלף. כלומר ההוא לאו משום טלטול הוא אלא משום אשויי גומות ואע"ג דמרחץ רצפת אבנים הוא וליכא למיחש לאשויי גומות מיחלף מיהא בקרקע אחר: כל צרכי המת לאתויי מאי. דלא תנן: כלי מיקר. שמביאים קרירות כגון זכוכית: ואף שלמה אמר בחכמתו. שכריסו של מת נופחת ונבקעת: זה חוט השדרה. שהוא כמין חבל ולבן ככסף: זו אמה. שהוא מעין של תולדה כמו גולות מים (יהושע טו): זה פרש. וגלגל לשון גלל (יחזקאל ד): אל הבור. שנופל לתוך פיו: כחגים. בתענוגים: מתני' אין מעצמין. את עיניו בשבת אפילו אחר יציאת הנפש דמזיז בו אבר: שופך דמים. כדמפרש בברייתא בגמ' שבטורח מועט מקרב מיתתו: גמ' ואוחז בשני גודלי רגליו. עוקרן באצבעותיו: וחתכם. לשון חיותכם: אריה אבי תרי לא נפיל. להורגן כדכתי' ומוראכם תרי וכתיב על כל חית הארץ ואפי' ארי: כדרמי בר אבא. דנכנסה עליו מיתה ונדמה לארי כבהמה: נמשל. מי שהיה מושלת בו בידוע שכבהמה נדמה: עשה. לדקה: עד שאתה מוצא. למי לעשות: ומצוי לך. ממון: ועודך בידך. עודך ברשותך קודם שתמות: לא זכות. לא דבר לזכות בו שכולם עשירים: ולא חובה. לאמץ לב ולקפוץ יד: על מדה זו. שלא יבא לידי עניות דדבר המזומן הוא לבא או עליו או על בנו או על בן בנו: ונתן לך רחמים. שתרחם על הבריות: זו פדחת. המצח שהוא חלק ומאהיר יותר מכל הפרצוף: זה חוטם. שהוא תואר פני אדם: זו נשמה. כדכתיב נר אלהים נשמת אדם (משלי כ): הלסתות. לחיים: ושבו העבים. חשכת עינים יבא ויכסה המאור אחר שירבה בבכיה בזקנותו מחמת תשות כח וצרות רבות עליו: מרווח. מאור עינים: אפילו מליא. כחלא בעיניו כמכחול גדול: כאביסנא של גרדאי. כובד של גרדיים אינשובל"ש בלע"ז: אוקומי. (ג) המאור מוקים שלא יחשיך יותר ממה שהוא: מאי קמ"ל. בהא דאמר אפי' כאביסנא דגרדאי: אלים. עב: מכוחלא. עץ שהוא מכניס בשפופרת ונותן בעיניו וקורין לו מכחול: תיכלא ועיורא. שיכול בנים ועיורון הדמעה: של בכי. מתוך אבל וצרה: של

מסורת הש"ס

א) לעיל מג., ב) לעיל מ:, ג) בקרא אשר לא, ד) [גירסת הערוך אין מאמצין כו' וכל המאמץ כו' פירוש סותמין עיני המת לאחר המיתה כדי שלא יהיו עיניו פתוחות כענין שנאמר ויוסף ישית ידו על עיניך ע"כ ועי' לעיל דף עז: איבעיא להו מאמצין תנן או מעמצין וכו' ואשר ע"כ ברור דטעות הוא שהקדימו בדפוס ל' קודם למ' במשנה ובברייתא דהכא וגם בפרש"י דהכא אמנם ברי"ף והרא"ש הגירסא במשנה ובברייתא על נכון המ' קודם לצ' וכ"א במשנה שבמשניות ובפי' הרב וכתב התוי"ט אין מאמצין כמו עוצם עיניו כו'], ה) בס"י איתא ר"ש בן אלעזר, ו) [יומא פה:], ז) לעיל ל. [נדה סא: ע"ש], ח) [עי' פרש"י בעירובין ה. ד"ה והאמר פירושו ע"ז], ט) [סנהדרין לח: ע"ש], י) ברכות לד: לעיל סג. פסחים סח. סנהדרין דף צא: צט., כ) [תוספתא דב"ק פ"ט], ל) [ביצה לב: ע"ש], מ) [גירסת הערוך כאבסנא], נ) [אדר"נ פמ"א].

הגהות הב"ח

(א) גמ' שלא יהא תפוח: (ב) רש"י ד"ה אוקומי. מוקים המאור שלא:

גליון הש"ס

גמ' קרקע בקרקע מיחלפא. כה"ג לעיל דף כט ע"ב ועי' בתוספות שם ד"ה גזירה:

ליקוטי רש"י

שנשברה. בשבת. בספסל. דכלי הוא ומותר לטלטלו. ארוכות המטה. לימוס"ש [לעיל מג.]. אין מדיחין. דלמא אתי לאשויי גומות [שם מ:]. משום אשויי גומות דמלאכה היא הוא בשבת דהוי כבונין [עירובין קד.]. עד אשר לא ירתק חבל הכסף. יפתחו לפקוח עצמותיו [ב"מ לח:]. זה חוט השדרה שהוא לבן ככסף ובמותו חסר מוחו ומתרוקן ויבש ומתפרק גב מתוך החליות ונעשה כשלשלת ירתק לשון (ישעיה מ, יט) ורתוקות כסף. ותרוץ גולת הזהב. זה האמה שהיא כמעין ונקבת במותו כמעין כמו (יהושע טו, יט) גולות עליות, ותרוץ לשון רצוצה. ותשבר כד על המבוע. זה הכרס שהיא עבה ונבקעת במותו [קהלת יב, ו ועי"ש עוד ובכאן במהרש"א ח"א]. מחללין עליו את השבת. פיקוח נפש נפקא לן [יומא פה:]. וחי בהם ולא שימות בהם [לעיל פה]. אמרה תורה חלל עליו שבת אחד כדי שישמור שבתות הרבה. ושמרו בני ישראל את השבת. כדי לעשות שבתות אחרות יזהרו בשבת זו בקיום שמירת שבתות הרבה [יומא פה:]. דא"ר יוחנן. קרא קא דריש במתים חפשי [לעיל שם. ע"ש בגמ' בהגרי"פ]. חפשי מן המצות. [illegible] [פסחים מ:]. וחתכם. ואימתכם כמו (איוב ו, כא) תראו חתת. ואגדה לשון חיות שכל זמן שהתינוק חי אין צריך לשומרו מן העכברים עוג מלך הבשן מת צריך לשומרו מן העכברים שנאמר ומוראכם וחתכם מוראכם על החיות כל זמן שאתם חיים [בראשית ט, ב]. נקיטינן. מסורת מאבותינו [עירובין ה.]. [נדה כד:]. ימי הרעה. ימי הזקנה והחלשות [קהלת שם, א]. ופליגא דשמואל. דאמר ימות המשיח עכשיו [פסחים סח.]. שנאמר כי לא יחדל. משמע לעולם אלמא יש עניות ועשירות שמע הנביאים ולא יהיה כנעני עוד (זכריה יד) לא לימות המשיח נתנבאו שהן מן העולם הזה דאם כן [שבת סג.]. עד אשר לא תחשך השמש. אמרו רבותינו זו פדחת שהיא מאורה ומלהבת באדם בחור קמטין ואין מלהבת. והאור. זה החוטם שהוא תואר קלסתר פנים. והירח. זו נשמה שמאירה הימנו אין לו מאור העינים. והכוכבים. אלו הלסתות רומני דאפי שקורין פומלי"ש (של) [ש] ושבו העבים אחר הגשם. תבוא כהיית המאור אחר דמעת הבכי מכמה צרות שעברו עליו [קהלת שם, ב].

רבינו חננאל

חוץ לחומה לנו ואע"ג דאיסורא הוא וקיי"ל הלכתא כרב באיסורי הכא הלכתא כשמואל דדיקא מתניתין כותיה דתנן במס' מכשירין עיר של ישראל ונכרים דרין בתוכה והיתה בה מרחץ המרחצת בשבת אם רוב נכרים מותר לרחוץ בה מיד אם רוב ישראל ימתין עד בכדי שיחמו חמין. מחצה על מחצה ימתין בכדי שיחמו חמין. ר' יהודה אומר באמבטי קטנה ואם יש רשות רוחץ בה מיד. ומפרש רב יצחק בריה דרב יהודה מאי רשות כגון אדם חשוב שיש לו עשרה עבדים שמחממין לו עשרה קומקמין בבת אחת מותר לרחוץ מיד: עשו לו ארון וחפרו לו קבר יקבר בהן ישראל ומקשינן ואמאי והא ישראל ונכרי כמחצה על מחצה דמי ימתין בכדי שיעשו ומפרק עולא כגון בנכרי מת המוטל באיסטרטא דמוכחא מלתא שזה הקבר לזה הנכרי נחפר שדומה לרוב נכרים שאין צריך להמתין בכדי שיעשו תוב אקשינן תינח קבר ארון מאי ופריק ר' אבהו בארון המוטל על הקבר שנמצא הארון בקבר א) דאילו דברי ר"מ נסבייה בדרך גררה. בפרק כירה בענין דברים של (חול) [קדש] אסור לאומרם (בלשה"ק) [בלשון חול] אלא אם הוא לאפרושי מאיסורא כגון זה שא"ר מאיר לתלמידיו אין מדיחין ואין סכין בלשה"ק אבל הרואה שסכין ומדיחין המת לא יתיר הדחה וסיכה בקרקע ולפיכך התיר ר"מ הדחת המת וסיכתו ולא גזר סיכת המת והדחתו מפני סיכת מרחץ והדחתו. כל צרכי המת כלל זה להביא הא דת"ר מביאין כלי מיקר וכלי מתכות ומניחין לו על כרסו בשבת שלא תפוח. ופוקקין נקביו בשביל שלא תכנס בהן הרוח ואף שלמה אמר בחכמתו עד אשר לא ירתק חבל הכסף וגו' ופשוטה היא: אין מאמצין את המת בשבת וכו'. פי' מאמצין סותמין את עיני המת. ת"ר המאמץ עם יציאת נפש אפילו בחול הרי זה שופך דמים משל לנר שכבה כו'. תניא ר"ש בן אלעזר אומר תינוק בן יומו חי מחללין עליו את השבת שעומד ומשמר שבתות הרבה. דוד מלך ישראל מת אין מחללין עליו את השבת

חשק שלמה על רבינו חננאל א) נראה דחסר כאן איזה תיבות ושייך להא דמקשינן כאן בגמ' והאמר ריה"ש מעשה בתלמידו של ר"מ:

שֶׁיִּמַּתִּין – **that [his body] remain moist;**[1] קוֹשְׁרִין אֶת הַלְּחִי – **we may bind up the jaw,** לֹא שֶׁיַּעֲלֶה – **not that it should rise,** אֶלָּא שֶׁלֹּא יוֹסִיף – **but that it should not continue** to drop.[2] וְכֵן קוֹרָה שֶׁנִּשְׁבְּרָה – **And so** is the law in the case of **a beam that broke:** סוֹמְכִין אוֹתָהּ בְּסַפְסָל אוֹ בַאֲרוּכוֹת הַמִּטָּה – **We may support it with a bench or with the side-pieces of a bed,**[3] לֹא שֶׁתַּעֲלֶה – **not that it should rise,** אֶלָּא שֶׁלֹּא תוֹסִיף – **but that it should not continue** to drop.[4]

Gemara The Gemara challenges the Mishnah's permit to anoint or rinse a corpse on the Sabbath:

וְהָאָמַר רַב יְהוּדָה אָמַר שְׁמוּאֵל – **But Rav Yehudah said in the name of Shmuel:** מַעֲשֶׂה בְּתַלְמִידוֹ שֶׁל רַבִּי מֵאִיר – **There was an incident involving a student**[5] **of R' Meir,** שֶׁנִּכְנַס אַחֲרָיו לְבֵית הַמֶּרְחָץ – **who followed [R' Meir] into a bathhouse.**[6] בִּיקֵּשׁ לְהָדִיחַ קַרְקַע – **He wanted to wash** the **floor** of the bathhouse for him.[7] אָמַר לוֹ אֵין מְדִיחִין – **[R' Meir] said to him: "One may not wash!"**[8] לָסוּךְ קַרְקַע – The student then wanted **to smear** the **floor** with fragrant oil,[9] אָמַר לוֹ אֵין סָכִין – whereupon **[R' Meir] said to him: "One may not smear!"** The reason why R' Meir forbade the student to smear oil[10] on the floor is presumably that its stones are *muktzeh.*[11] Our Mishnah, however, permits one to smear oil on a corpse, which also is *muktzeh.*[12] – ? –

The Gemara answers that in fact it is permitted to smear oil on a *muktzeh* object.[13] The reason for R' Meir's instruction not to smear oil on the floor is as follows:

קַרְקַע בְּקַרְקַע מִיחַלְּפָא – The law for one type of **floor will be confused**[14] **with** that of another type of **floor.** If one is allowed to smear oil on a stone floor, he might come to smear oil on a dirt floor, which is forbidden lest he level it out.[15] מֵת בְּקַרְקַע לֹא מִיחַלַּף – The law for **a corpse,** however, **will not be confused with** that of **a floor.** Even if one is allowed to smear oil on a corpse, he will not assume that the same permit applies to a floor.

Our Mishnah began, "One may attend to *all* the needs of the deceased etc." The Gemara identifies the cases included by the word "all":

כָּל לְאַתּוּיֵי מַאי – **What does** the word **"all" include** that is not stated in the Mishnah? לְאַתּוּיֵי הָא דְתָנוּ רַבָּנַן – It serves **to include that which the Rabbis taught in a Baraisa:** מְבִיאִין כְּלֵי מֵיקָר וּכְלֵי מַתָּכוֹת – **WE MAY BRING COOLING VESSELS**[16] **AND METAL VESSELS** וּמַנִּיחִין עַל כְּרֵיסוֹ – **AND PLACE** them **ON [THE CORPSE'S] STOMACH** כְּדֵי שֶׁלֹּא תִּפּוּחַ – **SO THAT IT WILL NOT SWELL.** וּפוֹקְקִין אֶת נְקָבָיו – **AND WE MAY STOP UP [THE CORPSE'S] ORIFICES** כְּדֵי שֶׁלֹּא תִּיכָּנֵס בָּהֶן הָרוּחַ – **SO THAT AIR WILL NOT ENTER THEM.**[17] וְאַף שְׁלֹמֹה אָמַר בְּחָכְמָתוֹ – **AND SOLOMON, TOO, SAID IN HIS WISDOM,** that a corpse's stomach tends to swell and burst, as it is stated:[18] "עַד [אֲשֶׁר] (ש)לֹא יֵרָתֵק חֶבֶל הַכֶּסֶף" זֶה חוּט הַשִּׁדְרָה – ***BEFORE THE SILVER ROPE SNAPS*** – **THIS** refers to **THE SPINAL CORD.**[19] "וְתָרֻץ גֻּלַּת הַזָּהָב" זֶה אַמָּה – ***AND THE GOLDEN BOWL IS SHATTERED*** – **THIS** refers to the **MEMBRUM.**[20] "וְתִשָּׁבֶר כַּד עַל־הַמַּבּוּעַ" זֶה הַכֶּרֶס – ***AND THE PITCHER IS BROKEN AT THE FOUNTAIN*** – **THIS** refers to **THE STOMACH.**[21] "וְנָרֹץ הַגַּלְגַּל אֶל־הַבּוֹר" זֶה פֶּרֶשׁ – ***AND THE WHEEL IS SMASHED AT THE PIT*** – **THIS** refers to the **EXCREMENT.**[22]

NOTES

1. [Translation based on *Aruch* (cited by *Tos. Yom Tov*) and *Tiferes Yisrael.*] A body kept in a warm place decomposes more rapidly than one in a cool place. Since the pillows and the mattress keep the body relatively warm, the body should be moved to the cooler dirt floor to retard the rate of decomposition (see *Rashi*).

2. If the mouth had begun to sag open, one may tie a strip of cloth around the head and jaw to prevent any further sagging. However, one may not bind the cloth so tightly as to push the jaw back upward, since, as stated above, one may not move any part of the corpse (*Rashi*).

3. A bench has the status of a utensil [and hence placing it under the sagging beam would not be considered *building* – see *Magen Avraham* 313:14; cf. *Eliyahu Rabbah*] (*Rashi*). The same is true of the side-pieces of a bed (*Tiferes Yisrael*).

4. The support may be introduced only at the level where it prevents the beam from sagging any lower. We may not raise the beam towards its original position because that would constitute בּוֹנֶה, *building* (*Rashi*). *Meiri* writes that it is *akin* to building. (See *Tiferes Yaakov* for another reason.)

5. Namely, R' Shimon ben Elazar (*Talmud Yerushalmi,* cited by *Yefei Einayim*).

6. On the Sabbath or Yom Tov.

7. The Rabbis issued various decrees against the use of a bathhouse on the Sabbath even if the water had been heated before the Sabbath. It is nevertheless permitted to walk through a bathhouse or to bathe there in cold water (see above, 40a).

8. It is forbidden to wash a floor on the Sabbath or Yom Tov. [The reason is stated below.]

9. It was common to do this in order to disguise unpleasant odors (*Meiri* above, 40b).

10. *Rashi* mentions only smearing oil. The following discussion, however, applies also to washing with water, as stated by *Chidushei HaRan* [as well as *Rabbeinu Chananel* and *Ritva MHK* ed.] (*Menachem Meishiv Nefesh*).

11. *Rashi, Ritva MHK* ed. and *Chidushei HaRan;* cf. *Sfas Emes.*

12. [This represents an internal contradiction in the teachings of R' Meir, because anonymous Mishnahs (such as ours) generally follow R' Meir's opinion.]

13. [Provided one does not move it.]

14. Literally: exchanged.

15. [Leveling out a floor is Biblically forbidden under the category of בּוֹנֶה, *building.*]

Although a person would level out only a dirt floor, the Rabbis nevertheless banned [washing or smearing oil on] any type of floor, because people do not differentiate between one type of floor and another (*Rashi*; see *Orach Chaim* 337:3 with commentaries).

16. Vessels that cool, e.g. glassware (*Rashi*).

17. And cause the body to swell (*Chidushei HaRan*).

18. *Ecclesiastes* 12:6. This verse belongs to a passage in which Solomon admonishes the young to repent while they are still young and in good health, before the advent of old age and death: *So remember your Creator in the days of your youth, before the evil days come, and those years arrive of which you will say, "I have no pleasure in them"* (verse 1 ibid.). In our verse, Solomon compares a person's death to the collapse of a well's machinery: עַד אֲשֶׁר לֹא־יֵרָתֵק חֶבֶל הַכֶּסֶף וְתָרֻץ גֻּלַּת הַזָּהָב וְתִשָּׁבֶר כַּד עַל־הַמַּבּוּעַ וְנָרֹץ הַגַּלְגַּל אֶל־הַבּוֹר, [Repent] *before the silver rope snaps, and the golden bowl is shattered, and the pitcher is broken at the fountain, and the wheel is smashed at the pit.* A rope is wound around the wheel of the well. At one end of the rope is a pitcher and at the other end is a bowl that serves as a counterweight. When the rope snaps (near the bowl), the bowl falls and breaks. The pitcher, having no counterweight, also descends, dragging down the wheel with it. The Baraisa interprets each part of this metaphor.

19. The spinal cord resembles a rope, and is white like silver (*Rashi*).

20. גֻּלַּת is interpreted as meaning a spring, as in גֻּלֹּת מַיִם, *springs of water* (*Joshua* 15:19). It thus signifies the membrum, which is the spring of procreation (*Rashi; see Iyun Yaakov*).

It is described as זָהָב, *golden,* which is similar to the verb זָב, *flow,* because [semen] flows from it (*Menachem Meishiv Nefesh,* based on *Rashi* to the verse; see also *Ben Yehoyada*).

21. [The stomach is likened to a pitcher, into which beverages are poured.]

Solomon thus teaches in this verse that upon a person's death, his stomach tends to swell and burst, as the Baraisa asserted above.

22. The word גַּלְגַּל, *wheel,* is interpreted as a cognate of גָּלָל, which means *excrement,* as in *Ezekiel* 4:12 (*Rashi*). בּוֹר, *pit,* alludes to the

עין משפט נר מצוה

מג א מיי' פכ"ו מהל' שבת הלכה כ סמג שם טוש"ע או"ח סימן שיא סעיף ז:

מד ב מיי' פ"ד מהלכות אבל הלכה ה סמג עשין ג טוש"ע יו"ד סי' שלט סעיף א:

מה ג סמג עשין עט:

מו ד מיי' פ"י מהלכות תשובה הלכה א:

מז ה מיי' פ"י מהלכות מתנות עניים הל"ב [וכה' עבדים פ"ט הל"ח] טוש"ע יו"ד סימן רמז סעיף ג:

תורה אור השלם

א) עַד אֲשֶׁר לֹא יֵרָתֵק חֶבֶל הַכֶּסֶף וְתָרֻץ גֻּלַּת הַזָּהָב וְתִשָּׁבֶר כַּד עַל הַמַּבּוּעַ וְנָרֹץ הַגַּלְגַּל אֶל הַבּוֹר: [קהלת יב, ו]

ב) הִנְנִי גֹעֵר לָכֶם אֶת הַזֶּרַע וְזֵרִיתִי פֶרֶשׁ עַל פְּנֵיכֶם פֶּרֶשׁ חַגֵּיכֶם וְנָשָׂא אֶתְכֶם אֵלָיו: [מלאכי ב, ג]

ג) בַּמֵּתִים חָפְשִׁי כְּמוֹ חֲלָלִים שֹׁכְבֵי קֶבֶר אֲשֶׁר לֹא זְכַרְתָּם עוֹד וְהֵמָּה מִיָּדְךָ נִגְזָרוּ: [תהלים פח, ו]

ד) וּמוֹרַאֲכֶם וְחִתְּכֶם יִהְיֶה עַל כָּל חַיַּת הָאָרֶץ וְעַל כָּל עוֹף הַשָּׁמָיִם בְּכֹל אֲשֶׁר תִּרְמֹשׂ הָאֲדָמָה וּבְכָל דְּגֵי הַיָּם בְּיֶדְכֶם נִתָּנוּ: [בראשית ט, ב]

ה) וְאָדָם בִּיקָר בַּל יָלִין נִמְשַׁל כַּבְּהֵמוֹת נִדְמוּ: [תהלים מט, יג]

ו) וּזְכֹר אֶת בּוֹרְאֶיךָ בִּימֵי בְּחוּרֹתֶיךָ עַד אֲשֶׁר לֹא יָבֹאוּ יְמֵי הָרָעָה וְהִגִּיעוּ שָׁנִים אֲשֶׁר תֹּאמַר אֵין לִי בָהֶם חֵפֶץ: [קהלת יב, א]

ז) כִּי לֹא יֶחְדַּל אֶבְיוֹן מִקֶּרֶב הָאָרֶץ עַל כֵּן אָנֹכִי מְצַוְּךָ לֵאמֹר פָּתֹחַ תִּפְתַּח אֶת יָדְךָ לְאָחִיךָ לַעֲנִיֶּךָ וּלְאֶבְיֹנְךָ בְּאַרְצֶךָ: [דברים טו, יא]

ח) נָתוֹן תִּתֵּן לוֹ וְלֹא יֵרַע לְבָבְךָ בְּתִתְּךָ לוֹ כִּי בִּגְלַל הַדָּבָר הַזֶּה יְבָרֶכְךָ יְיָ אֱלֹהֶיךָ בְּכָל מַעֲשֶׂךָ וּבְכֹל מִשְׁלַח יָדֶךָ: [דברים טו, י]

ט) וְלֹא יִדְבַּק בְּיָדְךָ מְאוּמָה מִן הַחֵרֶם לְמַעַן יָשׁוּב יְיָ מֵחֲרוֹן אַפּוֹ וְנָתַן לְךָ רַחֲמִים וְרִחַמְךָ וְהִרְבֶּךָ כַּאֲשֶׁר נִשְׁבַּע לַאֲבֹתֶיךָ: [דברים יג, יח]

י) עַד אֲשֶׁר לֹא תֶחְשַׁךְ הַשֶּׁמֶשׁ וְהָאוֹר וְהַיָּרֵחַ וְהַכּוֹכָבִים וְשָׁבוּ הֶעָבִים אַחַר הַגָּשֶׁם: [קהלת יב, ב]

גמרא

מתני' שימתין א קושרין את הלחי לא שיעלה אלא שלא יוסיף (א) וכן קורה שנשברה סומכין אותה בספסל או בארוכות המטה לא שתעלה אלא שלא תוסיף: גמ' ב) והאמר רב יהודה אמר שמואל מעשה בתלמידו של רבי מאיר שנכנס אחריו לבית המרחץ ביקש להדיח קרקע אמר לו אין מדיחין לסוך קרקע אמר לו אין סכין • קרקע בקרקע מחלפא מת בקרקע לא מיחלף כל לאתויי מאי לאתויי הא דת"ר מביאין כלי מיקר וכלי מתכות ומניחין על כריסו כדי שלא (א) תפוח ופוקקין את נקביו כדי שלא תיכנס בהן הרוח ואף שלמה אמר בחכמתו א) עד ג) שלא ירתק חבל הכסף זה חוט השדרה ותרוץ גולת הזהב זה אמה ותשבר כד על המבוע זה הכרס ונרוץ הגלגל אל הבור זה פרש וכן הוא אומר ב) וזריתי פרש על פניכם פרש חגיכם אמר רב הונא ואמרי לה אמר רב חגא אלו בני אדם שמניחין דברי תורה ועושין כל ימיהם כחגים אמר רבי לוי אמר רב פפי א"ר יהושע לאחר שלשה ימים כריסו נבקעת ונופלת לו על פניו ואומרת לו טול מה שנתת בי: מתני' אין ד) מעצמין את המת בשבת ולא בחול עם יציאת נפש ג) והמעצים עם יציאת הנפש הרי זה שופך דמים: גמ' תנו רבנן המעצמו עם יציאת הנפש הרי זה שופך דמים משל לנר שכבה והולכת אדם מניח אצבעו עליה מיד כבתה תניא ה) רשב"ג אומר הרוצה שיתעצמו עיניו של מת נופח לו יין בחוטמו ונותן שמן בין ריסי עיניו ואוחז בשני גודלי רגליו והן מתעצמין מאליהן תניא רשב"ג אומר תינוק בן יומו חי מחללין עליו את השבת דוד מלך ישראל מת אין מחללין עליו את השבת תינוק בן יומו חי מחללין עליו את השבת ו) אמרה תורה חלל עליו שבת אחד כדי שישמור שבתות הרבה דוד מלך ישראל מת אין מחללין עליו כיון שמת אדם בטל מן המצות והיינו ז) דא"ר יוחנן ג) במתים חפשי כיון שמת אדם נעשה חפשי מן המצות ותניא ר' שמעון בן אלעזר אומר תינוק בן יומו חי אין צריך לשומרו מן החולדה ומן העכברים אבל עוג מלך הבשן מת צריך לשומרו מן החולדה ומן העכברים שנאמר ד) ומוראכם וחתכם יהיה כל זמן שאדם חי אימתו מוטלת על הבריות כיון שמת בטלה אימתו אמר רב פפא ח) נקיטינן אריה אבי תרי לא נפיל הא קא חזינן דנפיל ההוא כדרמי בר אבא דאמר רמי בר אבא ט) אין חיה שולטת באדם עד שנדמה לו כבהמה שנאמר ה) אדם ביקר בל ילין נמשל כבהמות נדמו אמר רבי חנינא ג אסור לישן בבית יחידי וכל הישן בבית יחידי אחזתו לילית ותניא רשב"א אומר עשה עד שאתה מוצא ומצוי לך ועודך בידך ואף שלמה אמר בחכמתו ו) וזכור את בוראיך בימי בחורותיך עד [אשר] (ש)לא יבואו ימי הרעה ד אלו ימי הזקנה והגיעו שנים אשר תאמר אין לי בהם חפץ אלו ימי המשיח שאין בהם לא זכות ולא חובה ופליגא דשמואל י) דאמר שמואל אין בין העולם הזה לימות המשיח אלא שיעבוד מלכיות בלבד שנא' ז) כי לא יחדל אביון מקרב הארץ תניא ר' אלעזר הקפר אומר לעולם יבקש אדם רחמים על מדה זו שאם הוא לא בא בנו ואם בנו לא בא בן בנו בא שנאמר ח) כי בגלל הדבר הזה תנא דבי ר' ישמעאל גלגל הוא שחוזר בעולם א"ר יוסף נקיטינן האי צורבא מרבנן לא מיעני והא קא חזינן דמיעני אם איתא דמיעני אהדורי אפתחא לא מיהדר אמר לה רבי חייא לדביתהו כי אתי עניא אקדימי ליה ריפתא כי היכי דלקדמו לבנין אמרה ליה מילט קא לייטת להו אמר לה קרא קא כתיב כי בגלל הדבר הזה ותנא דבי ר' ישמעאל גלגל הוא שחוזר בעולם תניא כ) ר' גמליאל ברבי אומר ט) ונתן לך רחמים ורחמך והרבך ל) כל המרחם על הבריות מרחמין עליו מן השמים וכל שאינו מרחם על הבריות אין מרחמין עליו מן השמים י) עד אשר לא תחשך השמש והאור זו פדחת והחוטם והירח זו נשמה והכוכבים אלו הלסתות ושבו העבים אחר הגשם זו מאור עיניו של אדם שהולך אחר הבכי אמר שמואל האי דמעתא עד ארבעין שנין הדרא מכאן ואילך לא הדרא ואמר רב נחמן האי כוחלא עד ארבעין שנין מרווח מכאן ואילך אפילו מליא מ) כאביסנא דגירדאי אוקומי מוקים ארווחי לא מרווח מאי קא משמע לן דכמה דאלים מכוחלא טפי מעלי ר' חנינא שכיבא ליה ברתיה לא הוה קא בכי עלה אמרה ליה דביתהו תרנגולתא אפיקת מביתך אמר לה תרתי תכלא ועיורא סבר לה כי הא דאמר רבי יוחנן משום רבי יוסי בן קצרתה נ) שש דמעות הן שלש יפות ושלש רעות של עשן ושל בכי ושל

רש"י

שימתין. שלא יסריח מחמת חום הסדין והכרים: קושרין את הלחי. של מת שהיה פיו הולך ונפתח קושרין את לחייו כדי שלא יפתח פיו יותר: ולא שיעלה. להסגר ממה שנפתח דהיינו מזיז אבר אלא שלא יוסיף ליפתח: סומכין אותה בספסל. שהרי תורת כלי עליו: לא שתעלה. דהוה ליה בונה: גמ' ואמר לו אין סכין. אלמא דבר האסור לטלטל אסור לסוך: קרקע בקרקע מיחלף. כלומר ההוא לאו משום טלטול הוא אלא משום אשווי גומות ואע"ג דמרחץ רצפת אבנים הוא וליכא למיחש לאשווי גומות מיחלף בקרקע אחר: כל צרכי המת לאתויי מאי. דלא תנן: כלי מיקר. שמצילים קירות כגון זכוכית: ואף שלמה אמר בחכמתו. שכריסו של מת נופחת ונבקעת: זה חוט השדרה. שהוא כמין חבל ולבן ככסף: זו אמה. שהוא מעין של תולדה כמו גולות מים (יהושע טו): זה פרש. וגלגל לשון גלל (יחזקאל ד): אל הבור. שנופל לתוך פיו: כחגים. בתענוגים: מתני' אין מעצמין. את עיניו בשבת ואפילו אחר יציאת הנפש דמזיז בו אבר: שופך דמים. כדמפרש בברייתא בגמ' שכשורת מועט מקרב מיתתו: גמ' ואוחז בשני גודלי רגליו. עולכנן לאלעצעותיו: וחתכם. לשון מחיתתכם: אריה אבי תרי לא נפיל. להורגן כלכמי'

ומורלאכם תרי וכתיב על כל חית הארץ ואפי' ארי: כדרמי בר אבא. דנקנקסה עליו מיתה ונדמה לארי כבהמה: נמשל. מי שהיה מושלת בו בידוע שכבהמה נדמה: עשה. צדקה: עד שאתה מוצא. למי לעשות: ומצוי לך. ממון: ועודך בידך. עודך כשאתה קודם שתמות: לא זכות. לא דבר לזכות בו שכולם עשירים: ולא חובה. לאמץ לב ולקפוץ יד: על מדה זו. שלא יבא לידי עניות לדבר הממונן הוא לבא לו או על בנו או על בן בנו: ונתן לך רחמים. שתרחם על הבריות: זו פדחת. המצח שהוא חלק ומלהיר יותר מכל הפרצוף: זה חוטם. שהוא תואר פני אדם: זו נשמה. כדכתיב נר אלהים נשמת אדם (משלי כ): הלסתות. לחיים: ושבו העבים. משתח עיניים יצא ויכסה המאור אחר שירבה בבכיה בזקנותו מחמת תשות כח ולרות רבות עליו: מרווח. מאור עיניים: אפילו מליא. כחלא בעיניו כמכחול גדול: כאביסנא של גרדאי. כובד של גרדיים אינשובל"ש בלע"ז: אוקומי. (ב) המאור מוקים שלא יחשיך יותר ממה שהוא: מאי קמ"ל. בהא דאמר אפי' כאביסנא דגרדאי: אלים. עב: מכוחלא. עץ שהוא מכניס בשפופרת ונותן בעיניו וקורין לו מכחול: תיכלא ועיורא. שיכול בנים ועיורון הדמעה: של בכי. מתוך אבל וצרה: של

מסורת הש"ס

א) לעיל מג., ב) לעיל מ:, ג) בקרא אשר לא, ד) [גירסת הערוך אין מאמצין כו' וכל המאמץ כו' פירוש סותמין עיני המת לאחר המיתה כדי שלא יהיו עיניו פתוחות כענין שנאמר ויוסף ישית ידו על עיניך ע"כ ועי' לעיל דף עז: איבעיא להו מאמצין תנן או מעמצין וכו' ואשר ע"כ ברור דטעות הוא שהקדימו בדפוס ל' קודם למ' במשנה ובברייתא דהכא וגם בפרש"י דהכא אמנם ברי"ף והרא"ש הגירסא במשנה ובברייתא על נכון המ' קודם לצ' וכ"א במשנה שבמשניות ובפי' הרב וכתב התוי"ט אין מאמצין כמו עוצם עיניו כו'], ה) בס"י איתא ר"ש בן אלעזר, ו) [יומא פה.], ז) לעיל ל. [נדה סא: ע"ש], ח) [עי' פרש"י בעירובין ה. ד"ה והאמר פירושו ע"ז], ט) [סנהדרין לח: ע"ש], י) ברכות לד: לעיל סג. פסחים סח. סנהדרין דף צא: צט., כ) [תוספתא דב"ק פ"ט], ל) [ביצה לב: ע"ש], מ) [גירסת הערוך כאכסנא], נ) [אדר"נ פמ"א].

הגהות הב"ח

(א) גמ' שלא יהא תפוח: (ב) רש"י ד"ה אוקומי. מוקים המאור שלא:

גליון הש"ס

גמ' קרקע בקרקע מיחלפא. כה"ג לעיל דף כט ע"ב ועי' בתוספות שם ד"ה גזירה:

ליקוטי רש"י

שנשברה. בשבת. בספסל. דכלי הוא ומותר לטלטלו. ארוכות המטה. לימונ"ש [לעיל מג.]. אין מדיחין. דלמא אתי לאשויי גומות [שם מ:]. משום אשויי גומות דמלאכה הוא בשבת דהוי כבנין [עירובין קד.]. עד אשר לא ירתק חבל הכסף. יפתחו רתוקות עבותיה [ב"מ לח.]. זה חוט השדרה שהוא לבן ככסף ובמותו חסר מוחו ומתרוקן ויבש ומתעקם בתוך החליות ונעשה כשלשלת ירתק לשון (ישעיה מ, יט) רתוקות כסף. ותרוץ גולת הזהב. זה האמה שהיתה מקלחת מים ונובעת כמעין כמו (יהושע טו, יט) גולות עליות, ותרוץ לשון רציצה. ותשבר כד על המבוע. זה הכרס שהיא עבה ונבקעת במותו [קהלת יב, ו ע"ש עוד וכאן במהרש"א ח"א]. מחללין עליו את השבת. פיקוח נפש נפקא לן (יומא פה:) מותי בהם ולא שימות בהם [לעיל ל:]. אמרה תורה חלל עליו שבת אחד כדי שישמור שבתות הרבה. ושמרו בני ישראל את השבת. כדי לעשות שבתות אחרות יזהרו בשבת זו בקיום שמירת שבתות הרבה [יומא פה:]. דא"ר יוחנן. קרא קא דריש במתים חפשי [לעיל שם. ע"ש בגמ' בהגרי"פ]. חפשי מן המצות. מת אין מלות נוהגות בו [פסחים מ:]. וחתכם. ואימתכם כמו (איוב ו, כא) תראו חתת. ואגדה לשון חיות שכל זמן שהתינוק בן יומו חי אין אתה צריך לשומרו מן העכברים עוג מלך הבשן מת צריך לשומרו מן העכברים שנאמר ומוראכם וחתכם יהיה אימתי יהיה מוראכם על החיות כל זמן שאתם חיים [בראשית ט, ב]. נקיטינן. מסורת מאבותינו [עירובין ה.]. אחזתו לילית. שידה [נדה כד:]. ימי הרעה. ימי הזקנה והחלשות [קהלת שם, א]. ופליגא דשמואל. דאמר ימות המשיח אין משתנין משל עכשיו [פסחים סח.]. שנאמר כי לא יחדל. משמע לעולם אלמא יש עניות ועשירות שמע מינה נחמות שנתנבאו הנביאים ולא יהיה כנעני עוד (זכריה יד) לא לימות המשיח נתנבאו שהן מן העולם הזה דאם כן חדל לך אביון [לעיל סג.]. עד אשר לא תחשך השמש. אמרו רבותינו זו פדחת שהיא מאורה ומלהבת באדם בחור וכשמזקנת היא מעלת קמטין ואין מלהבת. והאור. זה החוטם שהוא תואר קלסתר פנים. והירח. זו נשמה שמאירה לאדם שכיון שניטלה הימנו אין לו מאור העינים. והכוכבים. אלו הלסתות רומני דאפי שקורין פומלי"ש (של) [שהן] לחיים שמלהיבים. ושבו העבים אחר הגשם. תבוא כהיית המאור אחר דמעת הבכי מכמה לרות שעברו עליו [קהלת שם, ב].

חשק שלמה על רבינו חננאל א) נראה דחסר כאן איזה תיבות ושייך להא דמקשינן כאן בגמ' והאמר ריא"ש מעשה בתלמידו של ר"מ:

רבינו חננאל

חוץ לחומה לנו ואע"ג דאיסורא הוא וקיי"ל הלכתא כרב באיסורי הכא הלכתא כשמואל דדיקא מתניתין כותיה דתנן במס' מכשירין עיר של ישראל ונכרים דרין בתוכה והיתה בה מרחץ המרחצת בשבת אם רוב נכרים מותר לרחוץ בה מיד אם רוב ישראל ימתין עד בכדי שיחמו חמין. מחצה על מחצה ימתין בכדי שיחמו חמין. ר' יהודה אומר באמבטי קטנה ואם יש רשות רוחץ בה מיד. ומפרש רב יצחק בריה דרב יהודה מאי רשות כגון אדם חשוב שיש לו עשרה עבדים שמחממין לו עשרה קומקמין בבת אחת מותר לרחוץ מיד: עשו לו ארון וחפרו לו קבר יקבר בהן ישראל ומקשינן אמאי והא ישראל ונכרי כמחצה על מחצה דמי ימתין בכדי שיעשו ומפרק עולא כגון בנכרי מת המוטל באיסטרטא דמוכחא מלתא שזה הקבר לזה הנכרי נחפר שדומה לרוב נכרים שאין צריך להמתין בכדי שיעשו תוב אקשינן תינח קבר ארון מאי ופריק ר' אבהו בארון המוטל על הקבר שנמצא הארון בקבר א) דאילו דברי ר"מ נסבייה בדרך גררה. בפרק כירה בענין דברים של (חול) [קדש] אסור לאומרם (בלשה"ק) [בלשון חול] אלא אם הוא לאפרושי מאיסורא כגון זה שא"ר מאיר לתלמידיו אין מדיחין ואין סכין בלשה"ק אבל הרואה שסכין ומדיחין המת לא יתיר הדחה וסיכה בקרקע ולפיכך התיר ר"מ הדחת המת וסיכתו ולא גזר סיכת המת והדחתו מפני סיכת מרחץ והדחתו. כל צרכי המת כלל זה להביא הא דת"ר מביאין כלי מיקר וכלי מתכות ומניחין לו על כרסו בשבת שלא תפוח. ופוקקין נקביו בשביל שלא תכנס בהן הרוח ואף שלמה אמר בחכמתו עד אשר לא ירתק חבל הכסף וגו' ופשוטה היא: אין מאמצין את המת בשבת וכו'. פי' מאמצין סותמין את עיני המת. ת"ר המאמץ עם יציאת נפש אפילו בחול הרי זה שופך דמים משל לנר שכבה כו'. תניא ר"ש בן אלעזר אומר תינוק בן יומו חי מחללין עליו את השבת שעומד ומשמר שבתות הרבה. דוד מלך ישראל מת אין מחללין עליו את השבת

וְכֵן הוּא אוֹמֵר ,,וְזֵרִיתִי פֶרֶשׁ עַל־פְּנֵיכֶם פֶּרֶשׁ חַגֵּיכֶם" – AND SIMILARLY IT STATES:[23] *I WILL SCATTER EXCREMENT ON YOUR FACES – THE EXCREMENT OF YOUR FESTIVALS!*

The Gemara describes the people to whom the last verse refers: אָמַר רַב הוּנָא וְאָמְרֵי לָהּ אָמַר רַב חַגָּא – **Rav Huna, and some say Rav Chaga, said:** אֵלּוּ בְּנֵי אָדָם שֶׁמַּנִּיחִין דִּבְרֵי תוֹרָה וְעוֹשִׂין כָּל יְמֵיהֶם כְּחַגִּים – **These are people who forsake the words of the Torah and turn all their days into festivals,** i.e. occasions for self-indulgence.[24]

The Gemara elaborates on the Baraisa's teaching: אָמַר רַבִּי לֵוִי אָמַר רַב פַּפִּי אָמַר רַבִּי יְהוֹשֻׁעַ – **R' Levi said in the name of Rav Pappi who said it in the name of R' Yehoshua:** לְאַחַר שְׁלֹשָׁה יָמִים – **Three days**[25] **after** a person dies, כְּרֵיסוֹ נִבְקַעַת וְנוֹפֶלֶת לוֹ עַל פָּנָיו – **his stomach bursts and** the excrement that was inside **falls on his face,** וְאוֹמֶרֶת לוֹ – **and [the stomach] says to him:** טוֹל מַה שֶּׁנָּתַתָּ בִּי – **"Take back what you put in me!"**[26]

Mishnah The next Mishnah continues the rules of handling a corpse on the Sabbath: אֵין מְעַצְּמִין אֶת הַמֵּת בְּשַׁבָּת – WE MAY NOT CLOSE THE EYES OF THE DEAD ON THE SABBATH,[27] וְלֹא בְּחוֹל עִם יְצִיאַת נֶפֶשׁ – NOR may we do so ON A WEEKDAY AT THE MOMENT OF DEATH.[28] וְהַמְעַצֵּים עִם יְצִיאַת הַנֶּפֶשׁ – WHOEVER CLOSES THE EYES of a dying person AT THE MOMENT OF DEATH הֲרֵי זֶה שׁוֹפֵךְ דָּמִים – IS A MURDERER.[29]

Gemara The Gemara explains why the Mishnah forbids closing the eyes of a person at the moment of his death:

תָּנוּ רַבָּנָן – **The Rabbis taught in a Baraisa:** הַמְעַצְּמוֹ עִם יְצִיאַת הַנֶּפֶשׁ הֲרֵי זֶה שׁוֹפֵךְ דָּמִים – WHOEVER CLOSES THE EYES [OF A DYING PERSON] AT THE MOMENT OF DEATH IS A MURDERER. מָשָׁל לְנֵר שֶׁכָּבָה וְהוֹלֶכֶת – THIS CAN BE COMPARED TO the flame of A CANDLE THAT IS flickering AND ABOUT TO GO OUT. אָדָם מַנִּיחַ אֶצְבָּעוֹ עָלֶיהָ מִיָּד כָּבְתָה – IF A PERSON PLACES HIS FINGER ON IT, IT IS IMMEDIATELY EXTINGUISHED. Similarly, touching the dying person may hasten his death.

A Baraisa describes a procedure for closing the eyes of a dead person:

תַּנְיָא – **It has been taught in a Baraisa:** רַבָּן שִׁמְעוֹן בֶּן גַּמְלִיאֵל אוֹמֵר – RABBAN SHIMON BEN GAMLIEL SAYS: הָרוֹצֶה שֶׁיִּתְעַצְּמוּ עֵינָיו שֶׁל מֵת – IF ONE DESIRES THAT THE EYES OF A DEAD PERSON SHOULD CLOSE, נוֹפֵחַ לוֹ יַיִן בְּחוֹטְמוֹ – HE SHOULD BLOW WINE INTO [THE CORPSE'S] NOSE, וְנוֹתֵן שֶׁמֶן בֵּין רִיסֵי עֵינָיו – APPLY OIL BETWEEN [THE CORPSE'S] EYELASHES, וְאוֹחֵז בִּשְׁנֵי גוּדְלֵי רַגְלָיו – AND GRAB HOLD OF and squeeze [THE CORPSE'S] TWO BIG TOES. וְהֵן מִתְעַצְּמִין מֵאֲלֵיהֶן – [THE EYES] then CLOSE OF THEIR OWN ACCORD.

The Gemara cites a Baraisa that draws a dramatic contrast between the care permitted for the living and for the dead on the Sabbath.

תַּנְיָא – **It has been taught in a Baraisa:** רַבָּן שִׁמְעוֹן בֶּן גַּמְלִיאֵל אוֹמֵר – RABBAN SHIMON BEN GAMLIEL SAYS: תִּינוֹק בֶּן יוֹמוֹ חַי מְחַלְּלִין עָלָיו אֶת הַשַּׁבָּת – To save A LIVE DAY-OLD BABY WE MAY PROFANE THE SABBATH. דָּוִד מֶלֶךְ יִשְׂרָאֵל מֵת אֵין מְחַלְּלִין עָלָיו אֶת הַשַּׁבָּת – On the other hand, for the care of DAVID KING OF ISRAEL once he is DEAD, WE MAY NOT PROFANE THE SABBATH. תִּינוֹק בֶּן יוֹמוֹ חַי מְחַלְּלִין עָלָיו אֶת הַשַּׁבָּת אָמְרָה תוֹרָה חַלֵּל עָלָיו שַׁבָּת אֶחָד כְּדֵי שֶׁיִּשְׁמוֹר שַׁבָּתוֹת הַרְבֵּה – To save A LIVE DAY-OLD BABY WE MAY PROFANE THE SABBATH. This is because THE TORAH SAID:[30] PROFANE ONE SABBATH ON HIS ACCOUNT SO THAT [THE BABY] WILL live and grow up to OBSERVE MANY SABBATHS. דָּוִד מֶלֶךְ יִשְׂרָאֵל מֵת אֵין מְחַלְּלִין עָלָיו כֵּיוָן שֶׁמֵּת אָדָם בָּטֵל מִן הַמִּצְוֹת – To attend to the body of DAVID KING OF ISRAEL once he is DEAD, WE MAY NOT PROFANE THE SABBATH; ONCE A PERSON DIES HE IS forever IDLED FROM the practice of MITZVOS. Since he will never again observe the Sabbath, we may not profane the Sabbath for his sake.[31] וְהַיְינוּ דְּאָמַר רַבִּי יוֹחָנָן – **And this is** the same idea **that R' Yochanan expressed** when he expounded: ,,בַּמֵּתִים חָפְשִׁי" – *[I am counted] among the dead who are free.*[32] In what sense is a dead person free? כֵּיוָן שֶׁמֵּת אָדָם – **Once a person dies,** נַעֲשָׂה חָפְשִׁי מִן הַמִּצְוֹת – **he becomes "free" of mitzvos.** That is, he is exempt from the observance of all commandments.

Not only does the halachah distinguish between a live and a dead body, so do animals:

וְתַנְיָא – **And it has been taught in** another **Baraisa:** רַבִּי שִׁמְעוֹן בֶּן אֶלְעָזָר אוֹמֵר – R' SHIMON BEN ELAZAR SAYS: תִּינוֹק בֶּן יוֹמוֹ חַי אֵין צָרִיךְ לְשׁוֹמְרוֹ מִן הַחוּלְדָּה וּמִן הָעַכְבָּרִים – In the case of A DAY-OLD

NOTES

mouth. The verse is thus understood to mean that when the stomach bursts, excrement oozes from it and falls into the corpse's mouth (*Rashi;* see Gemara below).

The Baraisa proceeds to quote a verse which also indicates that the excrement falls towards the face.

23. *Malachi* 2:3.

24. Since the word פֶּרֶשׁ is repeated in the verse, it is available for homiletic interpretation. Because of its resemblance to the verb פָּרַשׁ, *separate,* it is interpreted as alluding to those who separate themselves from the Torah. By stating חַגֵּיכֶם, *your festivals,* as opposed to חַגֵּי ה׳, *festivals of God,* the verse indicates a reference to festivals of a secular nature (*Maharsha;* see also *Ben Yehoyada*).

The Gemara's exposition is cited by *Rambam* (*Hil. Dei'os* 5:1) in reference to people who indulge in excessive eating and drinking.

25. See *Iyun Yaakov.*

26. [See note 22.] When a person indulges in excessive eating and drinking, his dignity is diminished. During his lifetime, however, this cannot necessarily be discerned, since food is a vital component of life. It is only when his physical life ends that the [excess] food loses its charm, and like excrement flung into his face, it destroys his dignity (see *Maharal*).

27. One normally closes the eyes of a corpse before burial (*Yoreh Deah* 352:4). However, this is not done on the Sabbath because moving an eyelid is the equivalent of moving a limb of the corpse [which is prohibited because it is *muktzeh*] (*Rashi*).

28. Literally: as the soul departs.

29. In such a state, even the slightest movement can hasten his death (*Rashi*). One should wait an appropriate length of time before closing the eyes, since the "dead" person may in fact not yet be dead but merely unconscious (*Rambam, Hil. Aveil* 4:5).

There is a difference of opinion among the legal authorities whether this statement, that one who closes the eyes at the moment of death is a murderer, actually means that he could be guilty of murder and is subject to the death penalty (*Sefer Yereim* 248), or whether the Mishnah's statement is not meant so literally (*Radvaz* II: 695, see also *Shvus Yaakov, Orach Chaim* 13).

30. This is R' Shimon ben Menasya's exposition of the verse (*Exodus* 31:16): *The Children of Israel shall observe the Sabbath in order to perform the Sabbath throughout their generations* . . . (*Yoma* 85b; see next note).

31. [This would seem to indicate that if a person is incapable of again observing the Sabbath, one may not desecrate the Sabbath in order to save him (see *Halachos Ketanos* II §38). Although this might be so according to R' Shimon ben Menasya (see previous note), the halachah does not follow his view. Instead, the halachah attaches primacy to one or more of the other expositions cited in *Yoma* 85a,b. Thus, even if is certain that an endangered infant will not live long enough to ever observe a Sabbath (or perform any other mitzvah), nevertheless one must profane the Sabbath in order to extend its life (see *Beur Halachah* 329:4 ד״ה אלא לפי שעה).]

32. *Psalms* 88:6.

שימתין [א] קושרין את הלחי לא שיעלה אלא שלא יוסיף [א] וכן קורה שנשברה סומכין אותה בספסל או בארוכות המטה לא שתעלה אלא שלא תוסיף: גמ' [ב] והאמר רב יהודה אמר שמואל מעשה בתלמידו של רבי מאיר שנכנס אחריו לבית המרחץ ביקש להדיח קרקע אמר לו אין מדיחין לסוך קרקע אמר לו אין סכין * קרקע בקרקע מחלפא מת בקרקע לא מיחלף כל לאתויי מאי לאתויי הא דת"ר מביאין כלי מיקר וכלי מתכות ומניחין על כריסו כדי שלא (א) תפוח ופוקקין את נקביו כדי שלא תיכנס בהן הרוח ואף שלמה אמר בחכמתו [א] עד [ג] שלא ירתק חבל הכסף ותרוץ גולת הזהב זה חוט השדרה ותרוץ גולת הזהב זה אמה ותשבר כד על המבוע זה הכרס ונרוץ הגלגל אל הבור זה פרש וכן הוא אומר [ב] וזריתי פרש על פניכם פרש חגיכם אמר רב הונא ואמרי לה אמר רב חגא אלו בני אדם שמניחין דברי תורה ועושין כל ימיהם כחגים אמר רבי לוי אמר רב פפי א"ר יהושע לאחר שלשה ימים כריסו נבקעת ונופלת לו על פניו ואומרת לו טול מה שנתת בי: מתני' אין [ד] מעצמין את המת בשבת ולא בחול עם יציאת נפש [ה] והמעצים עם יציאת הנפש הרי זה שופך דמים: גמ' תנו רבנן המעצמו עם יציאת הנפש הרי זה שופך דמים משל לנר שכבה והולכת אדם מניח אצבעו עליה מיד כבתה תניא [ו] רשב"ג אומר הרוצה שיתעצמו עיניו של מת נופח לו יין בחוטמו ונותן שמן בין ריסי עיניו ואוחז בשני גודלי רגליו והן מתעצמין מאליהן תניא רשב"ג אומר תינוק בן יומו חי מחללין עליו את השבת דוד מלך ישראל מת אין מחללין עליו את השבת תינוק בן יומו חי מחללין עליו את השבת [ז] אמרה תורה חלל עליו שבת אחד כדי שישמור שבתות הרבה דוד מלך ישראל מת אין מחללין עליו כיון שמת אדם בטל מן המצות והיינו [ח] דא"ר יוחנן [ג] במתים חפשי כיון שמת אדם נעשה חפשי מן המצות ותניא ר' שמעון בן אלעזר אומר תינוק בן יומו חי אין צריך לשומרו מן החולדה ומן העכברים אבל עוג מלך הבשן מת צריך לשומרו מן החולדה ומן העכברים שנאמר [ד] ומוראכם וחתכם יהיה על כל זמן שאדם חי אימתו מוטלת על הבריות כיון שמת בטלה אימתו אמר רב פפא [ט] נקיטינן אריה אבי תרי לא נפיל הא קא חזינן דנפיל ההוא כדרמי בר אבא דאמר רמי בר אבא [י] אין חיה שולטת באדם עד שנדמה לו כבהמה שנאמר [ה] אדם ביקר בל ילין נמשל כבהמות נדמו אמר רבי חנינא [כ] אסור לישן בבית יחידי וכל הישן בבית יחידי אחזתו לילית ותניא רשב"א אומר עשה עד שאתה מוצא ומצוי לך ועודך בידך ואף שלמה אמר בחכמתו [ו] וזכור את בוראיך בימי בחורותיך עד [אשר] (ש)לא יבואו ימי הרעה [ל] אלו ימי הזקנה והגיעו שנים אשר תאמר אין לי בהם חפץ אלו ימי המשיח שאין בהם לא זכות ולא חובה ופליגא דשמואל [מ] דאמר שמואל אין בין העולם הזה לימות המשיח אלא שיעבוד מלכיות בלבד שנא' [ז] כי לא יחדל אביון מקרב הארץ תניא ר' אלעזר הקפר אומר לעולם יבקש אדם רחמים על מדה זו שאם הוא לא בא בא בנו ואם בנו לא בא בן בנו בא שנאמר [ח] כי בגלל הדבר הזה תנא דבי ר' ישמעאל גלגל הוא שחוזר בעולם א"ר יוסף נקיטינן האי צורבא מרבנן לא מיעני והא קא חזינן דמיעני אם איתא דמיעני אהדורי אפתחא לא מיהדר אמר לה רבי חייא לדביתהו כי אתי עניא אקדימי ליה ריפתא כי היכי דלקדמו לבניך אמרה ליה מילט קא לייטת להו אמר לה קרא קא כתיב כי בגלל הדבר הזה ותנא דבי ר' ישמעאל גלגל הוא שחוזר בעולם תניא [נ] ר' גמליאל ברבי אומר [ט] ונתן לך רחמים ורחמך והרבך [ס] כל המרחם על הבריות מרחמין עליו מן השמים וכל שאינו מרחם על הבריות אין מרחמין עליו מן השמים [י] עד אשר לא תחשך השמש והאור זו פדחת והחוטם והירח זו נשמה והכוכבים אלו הלסתות ושבו העבים אחר הגשם זו מאור עיניו של אדם שהולך אחר הבכי אמר שמואל האי דמעתא עד ארבעין שנין הדרא מכאן ואילך לא הדרא ואמר רב נחמן האי כוחלא עד ארבעין שנין מרווח מכאן ואילך אפילו מליא [ע] כאביסנא דגירדאי אוקומי מוקים ארווחי לא מרווח מאי קא משמע לן דכמה דאלים מכוחלא טפי מעלי ר' חנינא שכיבא ליה ברתיה לא הוה קא בכי עלה אמרה ליה דביתהו תרנגולתא אפיקת מביתך אמר לה תרתי תכלא ועיורא סבר לה כי הא דאמר רבי יוחנן משום רבי יוסי בן קצרתה [פ] שש דמעות הן שלש יפות ושלש רעות של עשן ושל בכי ושל

שימתין. שלא יסריח מחמת חום הסדין והכרים: קושרין את הלחי. של מת שהיה פיו הולך ונפתח קושרין את לחיו כדי שלא יפתח פיו יותר: ולא שיעלה. להסגר ממה שנפתח דהיינו מזיז אבר אלא שלא יוסיף ליפתח: סומכין אותה בספסל. שהרי תורת כלי עליו: לא שתעלה. דהוי ליה בונה: גמ' ואמר לו אין סכין. אלמא דבר האסור לטלטל אסור לסוך: קרקע בקרקע מיחלף. כלומר הסוא לאו משום טלטול הוא אלא משום אשויי גומות ואע"ג דמרחץ רצפת אבנים הוא וליכא למיחש לאשויי גומות מיחלף מיהא בקרקע אחר: כל צרכי המת לאתויי מאי. דלא תנן: כלי מיקר. שמביאים קרירות כגון זכוכית: ואף שלמה אמר בחכמתו. שכריסו של מת נופחת ונבקעת: זה חוט השדרה. שהוא כמין חבל ולבן ככסף: זו אמה. שהוא מעין של תולדה כמו גולות מים (יהושע טו): זה פרש. וגלגל לשון גלל (יחזקאל ד): אל הבור. שנופל לתוך פיו: כחגים. במועדים: מתני' אין מעצמין. את עיניו בשבת ואפילו אחר יציאת הנפש דמזיז בו אבר: שופך דמים. כדמפרש בברייתא בגמ' שבטורתו מועטת מקרב מיתתו: גמ' ואוחז בשני גודלי רגליו. עולרן כלצבעותיו: וחתכם. לשון חיותכם: אריה אבי תרי לא נפיל. להורגן כלחד:

ומוראכם תרי וכתיב על כל חית הארץ ואפי' ארי: כדרמי בר אבא. דנכנסה עליו מיתה ונדמה לארי כבהמה: נמשל. מי שהיה מושלת בו בידוע שכבהמה נדמה: עשה. לדקה: עד שאתה מוצא. למי לעשות: ומצוי לך. ממון: ועודך בידך. עודך ברשותך קודם שתמות: לא זכות. לא דבר לזכות בו שכולם עשירים: ולא חובה. לאמץ לב ולקפוץ יד: על מדה זו. שלא יבא לידי עניות לדבר המזומן הוא לבא או עליו או על בנו או על בן בנו: ונתן לך רחמים. שתרחם על הבריות: זו פדחת. המצח שהוא חלק ומאיר יותר מכל הפרצוף: זה חוטם. שהוא תואר פני אדם: זו נשמה. כדכתיב נר אלהים נשמת אדם (משלי כ): הלסתות. לחיים: ושבו העבים. תשכח עיניו יצא ויכסה המאור אחר שירבה בבכיה בזקנותו מחמת תשות כח ולרות רבות עליו: מרווח. מאור עינים: אפילו מליא. כחלא בעיניו כמכחול גדול: כאביסנא של גרדאי. כובד של גרדיים איגוסובל"א בלע"ז: אוקומי. (ב) המאור מוקים שלא יחשיך יותר ממה שהוא: מאי קמ"ל. בהא דאמר אפי' כאביסנא דגרדאי: אלים. עב: מכוחלא. עץ שהוא מכניס בשפופרת ונותן בעיניו וקורין לו מכחול: תיכלא ועיורא. שיכול בנים ועיורון הדמעה: של בכי. מתוך אבל וצרה: של

עין משפט נר מצוה

מג א מיי' פכ"ו מהל' שבת הלכה כ סמג שם טוש"ע או"ח סימן שיא סעיף ז:
מד ב מיי' פ"ד מהלכות אבל הלכה ה סמג עשין ב טוש"ע יו"ד סי' שלט סעיף א:
מה ג סמג עשין עט:
מו ד מיי' פ"י מהלכות תשובה הלכה א:
מז ה מיי' פ"י מהלכות מתנות עניים הל"ב [וכס' עבדים פ"ט הל"ח] טוש"ע יו"ד סימן רמז סעיף ג:

תורה אור השלם

א) עַד אֲשֶׁר לֹא יֵרָתֵק חֶבֶל הַכֶּסֶף וְתָרֻץ גֻּלַּת הַזָּהָב וְתִשָּׁבֶר כַּד עַל הַמַּבּוּעַ וְנָרֹץ הַגַּלְגַּל אֶל הַבּוֹר: [קהלת יב, ו]
ב) הִנְנִי גֹעֵר לָכֶם אֶת הַזֶּרַע וְזֵרִיתִי פֶרֶשׁ עַל פְּנֵיכֶם פֶּרֶשׁ חַגֵּיכֶם וְנָשָׂא אֶתְכֶם אֵלָיו: [מלאכי ב, ג]
ג) בַּמֵּתִים חָפְשִׁי כְּמוֹ חֲלָלִים שֹׁכְבֵי קֶבֶר אֲשֶׁר לֹא זְכַרְתָּם עוֹד וְהֵמָּה מִיָּדְךָ נִגְזָרוּ: [תהלים פח, ו]
ד) וּמוֹרַאֲכֶם וְחִתְּכֶם יִהְיֶה עַל כָּל חַיַּת הָאָרֶץ וְעַל כָּל עוֹף הַשָּׁמָיִם בְּכֹל אֲשֶׁר תִּרְמֹשׂ הָאֲדָמָה וּבְכָל דְּגֵי הַיָּם בְּיֶדְכֶם נִתָּנוּ: [בראשית ט, ב]
ה) וְאָדָם בִּיקָר בַּל יָלִין נִמְשַׁל כַּבְּהֵמוֹת נִדְמוּ: [תהלים מט, יג]
ו) וּזְכֹר אֶת בּוֹרְאֶיךָ בִּימֵי בְּחוּרֹתֶיךָ עַד אֲשֶׁר לֹא יָבֹאוּ יְמֵי הָרָעָה וְהִגִּיעוּ שָׁנִים אֲשֶׁר תֹּאמַר אֵין לִי בָהֶם חֵפֶץ: [קהלת יב, א]
ז) כִּי לֹא יֶחְדַּל אֶבְיוֹן מִקֶּרֶב הָאָרֶץ עַל כֵּן אָנֹכִי מְצַוְּךָ לֵאמֹר פָּתֹחַ תִּפְתַּח אֶת יָדְךָ לְאָחִיךָ לַעֲנִיֶּךָ וּלְאֶבְיֹנְךָ בְּאַרְצֶךָ: [דברים טו, יא]
ח) נָתוֹן תִּתֵּן לוֹ וְלֹא יֵרַע לְבָבְךָ בְּתִתְּךָ לוֹ כִּי בִּגְלַל הַדָּבָר הַזֶּה יְבָרֶכְךָ יי אֱלֹהֶיךָ בְּכָל מַעֲשֶׂךָ וּבְכֹל מִשְׁלַח יָדֶךָ: [דברים טו, י]
ט) וְלֹא יִדְבַּק בְּיָדְךָ מְאוּמָה מִן הַחֵרֶם לְמַעַן יָשׁוּב יי מֵחֲרוֹן אַפּוֹ וְנָתַן לְךָ רַחֲמִים וְרִחַמְךָ וְהִרְבֶּךָ כַּאֲשֶׁר נִשְׁבַּע לַאֲבֹתֶיךָ: [דברים יג, יח]
י) עַד אֲשֶׁר לֹא תֶחְשַׁךְ הַשֶּׁמֶשׁ וְהָאוֹר וְהַיָּרֵחַ וְהַכּוֹכָבִים וְשָׁבוּ הֶעָבִים אַחַר הַגָּשֶׁם: [קהלת יב, ב]

רבינו חננאל

חרץ לחומה לנו ואע"ג דאיסורא הוא וקיי"ל הלכתא כרב באיסורי הכא הלכתא כשמואל דדיקא מתניתין כותיה דתנן במס' מכשירין עיר של ישראל ונכרים דרין בתוכה והיתה בה מרחץ המרחצת בשבת אם רוב נכרים מותר לרחוץ בה מיד אם רוב ישראל ימתין עד בכדי שיחמו חמין. מחצה על מחצה ימתין בכדי שיחמו חמין. ר' יהודה אומר באמבטי קטנה ואם יש רשות רוחץ בה מיד. ומפרש רב יצחק בריה דרב יהודה מאי רשות כגון אדם חשוב שיש לו עשרה עבדים שמחממין לו עשרה קומקמין בבת אחת מותר לרחוץ מיד: עשו לו ארון וחפרו לו קבר יקבר בהן ישראל ומקשינן אמאי והא ישראל ונכרי כמחצה על מחצה דמי ימתין בכדי שיעשו ומפרק עולא כגון בנכרי מת המוטל באיסטרטא דמוכחא מלתא שזה הקבר לזה הנכרי נחפר שדומה לרוב נכרים שאין צריך להמתין בכדי שיעשו תוב אקשינן תינח קבר ארון מאי ופריק ר' אבהו בארון המוטל על הקבר שנמצא הארון בקבר א) דאילו דברי ר"מ נסבייה בדרך גררה. בפרק כירה בענין דברים של (חול) [קדש] אסור לאומרם (בלשה"ק) [בלשון חול] אלא אם הוא לאפרושי מאיסורא כגון זה שא"ר מאיר לתלמידיו אין מדיחין ואין סכין בלשה"ק אבל הרואה שסכין ומדיחין המת לא יתיר הדחה וסיכה בקרקע ולפיכך התיר ר"מ הדחת המת וסיכתו ולא גזר סיכת המת והדחתו מפני סיכת מרחץ והדחתו. כל צרכי המת כלל זה להביא הא דת"ר מביאין כלי מיקר וכלי מתכות ומניחין לו על כרסו בשבת שלא תפוח. ופוקקין נקביו בשביל שלא תכנס בהן הרוח ואף שלמה אמר בחכמתו עד אשר לא ירתק חבל הכסף וגו' ופשוטה היא: אין מאמצין את המת בשבת וכו'. פי' מאמצין סותמין את עיני המת. ת"ר המאמץ עם יציאת נפש אפילו בחול הרי זה שופך דמים משל לנר שכבה כו'. תניא ר"ש בן אלעזר אומר תינוק בן יומו חי מחללין עליו את השבת שעומד ומשמר שבתות הרבה. דוד מלך ישראל מת אין מחללין עליו את השבת

חשק שלמה על רבינו חננאל א) נראה דחסר כאן איזה תיבות ושייך להא דמקשינן כאן בגמ' והאמר ריש"ש מעשה בתלמידו של ר"מ.

מסורת הש"ס

א) לעיל מג., ב) לעיל מ:, ג) בקרא אשר לא, ד) [גירסת הערוך אין מאמצין כו' וכל המאמץ כו' פירוש סותמין עיני המת לאחר המיתה כדי שלא יהיו עיניו פתוחות כענין שנאמר ויוסף ישית ידו על עיניך ע"כ ועי' לעיל דף עז: איבעיא להו מאמצין תנן או מעמצין וכו' ואשר ע"כ ברור דטעות הוא שהקדימו בדפוס ל' קודס למ' במשנה ובברייתא דהכא וגם בפרש"י דהכא אמנם ברי"ף והרא"ש הגירסא במשנה ובברייתא על נכון המ' קודס לצ' וכ"א במשנה שבמשניות ובפי' הרב וכתב התוי"ט אין מאמצין כמו עוצם עיניו כו'], ה) בס"י איתא ר"ש בן אלעזר, ו) [יומא פה:], ז) לעיל ל. [נדה סא: ע"ש], ח) [עי' פרש"י בעירובין ה. ד"ה והאמר פירושו ע"ז], ט) [סנהדרין לח: ע"ש], י) ברכות לד: לעיל סג. פסחים סח. סנהדרין דף לא: לט., כ) [תוספתא דב"ק פ"ט], ל) [בילה לב: ע"ש], מ) [גירסת הערוך כאבסנא], נ) [אדר"נ פמ"א].

הגהות הב"ח

(א) גמ' שלא יהא תפוח: (ב) רש"י ד"ה אוקומי. מוקים המאור שלא:

גליון הש"ס

גמ' קרקע בקרקע מיחלפא. כה"ג לעיל דף כט ע"ב ועי' בתוספות שם ד"ה גזירה:

ליקוטי רש"י

שנשברה. בשבת. בספסל. דכלי הוא ומותר לטלטלו. ארוכות המטה. לימונ"ש [לעיל מג.]. אין מדיחין. דלמא אתי לאשויי גומות [שם מ:]. משום אשויי גומות דמלאכה הוא בשבת דהוי כבנין [עירובין קד.]. עד אשר לא ירתק חבל הכסף. יפתחו רתוקות עבותיה [ב"מ לח.]. זה חוט השדרה שהוא לבן ככסף וכמותו חסר מוחו ומתרוקן ויבש ומתעקם בתוך החליות ונעשה כשלשלת ירתק לשון (ישעיה מ, יט) רתוקות כסף. ותרוץ גולת הזהב. זו האמה שהיתה מקלחת מים ונובעת כמעין כמו (יהושע טו, יט) גולות עליות, ותרוץ לשון רצילה. ותשבר כד על המבוע. זה הכרס שהיא עבה ונבקעת במותו [קהלת יב, ו ע"ש עוד וכאן במהרש"א ח"א]. מחללין עליו את השבת. פיקוח נפש נפקא לן (יומא פה:) מוחי בהם ולא שימות בהם [לעיל ל:]. אמרה תורה חלל עליו שבת אחד כדי שישמור שבתות הרבה. ושמרו בני ישראל את השבת. כדי לעשות שבתות אחרות יזהרו בשבת זו בקיום שמירת שבתות הרבה [יומא פה:]. דא"ר יוחנן. קרא קא דריש במתים חפשי [לעיל שם. ע"ש בגמ' בהגרי"פ]. חפשי מן המצות. מת אין מצות נוהגות בו [פסחים מ:]. וחתכם. ואימתכם כמו (איוב ו, כא) תראו חתת. ואגדה לשון חיות שכל זמן שהתינוק בן יומו חי אין אתה צריך לשומרו מן העכברים עוג מלך הבשן מת צריך לשומרו מן העכברים שנאמר ומוראכם וחתכם יהיה אימתי יהיה מוראכם על החיות כל זמן שאתם חיים [בראשית ט, ב]. נקיטינן. מסורת מאבותינו [עירובין ה.]. אחזתו לילית. שידה [נדה כד:]. ימי הרעה. ימי הזקנה והחלשות [קהלת שם, א]. ופליגא דשמואל. דאמר ימות המשיח אין משתנין משל עכשיו [פסחים סח.]. שנאמר כי לא יחדל. משמע לעולם אלמא יש עניות ועשירות שמע מינה נחמות שנתנבאו הנביאים ולא יהיה כנעני עוד (זכריה יד) לא לימות המשיח נתנבאו שהן מן העולם הזה דאם כן [illegible] [לעיל סג.]. עד אשר לא תחשך השמש. אמרו רבותינו זו פדחת שהיא מאירה ומלהבת באדם בחור וכשמזקין היא קמטין ואין מלהבת. והאור. זה החוטם שהוא תואר קלסתר פנים. והירח. זו נשמה שמאירה לאדם שכשהיא הימנו אין לו מאור העינים. והכוכבים. אלו הלסתות רומני דאפי שקורין פומלי"ש (של) [סכן] לחיים שמאחריהם. ושבו העבים אחר הגשם. תבוא כהיית המאור אחר דמעת הבכי מכמה צרות שעברו עליו [קהלת שם, ב].

BABY, IT IS NOT NECESSARY TO GUARD IT FROM being bitten by **A WEASEL OR** by **MICE**, for weasels and mice are afraid of living humans, no matter how tiny and helpless. **אֲבָל עוֹג מֶלֶךְ הַבָּשָׁן מֵת – BUT** if the giant **OG KING OF BASHAN DIES, צָרִיךְ לְשׁוֹמְרוֹ מִן הַחוּלְדָּה וּמִן הָעַכְבָּרִים – IT IS NECESSARY TO GUARD [HIS CORPSE] FROM WEASELS AND MICE**, for weasels and mice are not afraid of dead people, no matter how large and imposing their physique. **שֶׁנֶּאֱמַר ,,וּמוֹרַאֲכֶם וְחִתְּכֶם יִהְיֶה" – AS IT IS SAYS:**[33] ***THE FEAR OF YOU AND THE DREAD OF YOU** shall be upon every beast of the earth and upon every bird of the heavens . . .* **כָּל זְמַן שֶׁאָדָם חַי – AS LONG AS A PERSON IS ALIVE,**[34] **אֵימָתוֹ מוּטֶּלֶת עַל הַבְּרִיּוֹת – THE FEAR OF HIM LIES UPON** all **CREATURES; כֵּיוָן שֶׁמֵּת – ONCE HE DIES, בָּטְלָה אֵימָתוֹ – [THEIR] FEAR OF HIM CEASES.**

A related statement:

אָמַר רַב פָּפָּא – Rav Pappa said: נְקִיטִינַן אַרְיֵה אַבֵּי תְּרֵי לֹא נָפִיל – We have a tradition: A lion does not attack a pair of people.[35]

The Gemara asks:

הָא קָא חָזֵינַן דְּנָפִיל – But we see that [a lion] does attack two people?!

The Gemara answers:

הַהוּא כִּדְרָמֵי בַּר אַבָּא – That can be explained **in accordance with** what was taught by **Rami bar Abba, דְּאָמַר רָמֵי בַּר אַבָּא – for Rami bar Abba said: אֵין חַיָּה שׁוֹלֶטֶת בָּאָדָם עַד שֶׁנִּדְמֶה לוֹ כִּבְהֵמָה – A wild beast does not gain ascendancy over a man unless [the man] appears to it like an animal, שֶׁנֶּאֱמַר ,,וְאָדָם בִּיקָר בַּל־יָלִין נִמְשַׁל כַּבְּהֵמוֹת נִדְמוּ" – as it is said: *But as for man: In glory he shall not repose, he is ruled* [when] *he appears like animals*** to an animal.[36] Thus, Rav Pappa was correct when he stated that lions do not attack groups of people; however, this is only true when they appear to the lions as people. Lions do attack groups of people when they regard the people as animals.[37]

The Gemara presents another statement which indicates that it is safer for a person not to be alone:

אָמַר רַבִּי חֲנִינָא – R' Chanina said: אָסוּר לִישַׁן בְּבַיִת יְחִידִי – It is forbidden to sleep alone in a house,[38] **וְכָל הַיָּשֵׁן בְּבַיִת יְחִידִי אֲחָזַתּוּ לִילִית – and whoever sleeps alone in a house**[39] **will be seized by Lilith.**[40]

The Gemara presents a Tannaic statement which echoes King Solomon's admonition (cited above) to perform good deeds while one is still alive and has the chance to do so:

וְתַנְיָא – And it has been taught in another **Baraisa: רַבִּי שִׁמְעוֹן בֶּן אֶלְעָזָר אוֹמֵר – R' SHIMON BEN ELAZAR SAYS: עֲשֵׂה עַד שֶׁאַתָּה מוֹצֵא – PERFORM** charity **WHILE YOU** can still **FIND** someone to receive it from you, **וּמָצוּי לְךָ – AND** while **YOU** still **HAVE** the money to give, **וְעוֹדְךָ בְּיָדְךָ – AND** while **YOU ARE** still **IN YOUR CONTROL**, i.e. while you are still alive.[41] **וְאַף שְׁלֹמֹה אָמַר בְּחָכְמָתוֹ – AND SOLOMON, IN HIS WISDOM, SAID AS MUCH** in the Book of *Eccelesiates*:[42] **,,וּזְכֹר אֶת־בּוֹרְאֶיךָ בִּימֵי בְּחוּרֹתֶיךָ עַד אֲשֶׁר לֹא־יָבֹאוּ יְמֵי הָרָעָה" – *SO REMEMBER YOUR CREATOR IN THE DAYS OF YOUR YOUTH, BEFORE THE EVIL DAYS COME;*** **אֵלּוּ יְמֵי הַזִּקְנָה – THESE [EVIL DAYS] ARE THE DAYS OF OLD AGE. ,,וְהִגִּיעוּ שָׁנִים אֲשֶׁר תֹּאמַר אֵין־לִי בָהֶם חֵפֶץ" – *AND THOSE YEARS ARRIVE OF WHICH YOU WILL SAY, "I HAVE NO PLEASURE IN THEM";*** **אֵלּוּ יְמֵי הַמָּשִׁיחַ – THESE ARE THE** glorious **DAYS OF THE MESSIAH, שֶׁאֵין בָּהֶם לֹא זְכוּת וְלֹא חוֹבָה – WHEN THERE WILL BE NO** opportunity to acquire **MERIT OR LIABILITY.**[43]

The Gemara observes:

וּפְלִיגָא דִשְׁמוּאֵל – And this Baraisa, which indicates that poverty will be wiped out in the Messianic Era, **disagrees with Shmuel, דְּאָמַר שְׁמוּאֵל – for Shmuel said: אֵין בֵּין הָעוֹלָם הַזֶּה לִימוֹת הַמָּשִׁיחַ אֶלָּא שִׁיעְבּוּד מַלְכֻיּוֹת בִּלְבַד – There is no difference between this world and** that of **the Messianic Era except for** Jewish independence from **the dominion of** foreign **kingdoms, שֶׁנֶּאֱמַר ,,כִּי לֹא־יֶחְדַּל אֶבְיוֹן מִקֶּרֶב הָאָרֶץ" – as it is stated: *Poor people will not cease to exist within the land.***[44]

Having cited the opinion that poverty will not exist in the Messianic Era, the Gemara discusses the ubiquity of poverty in our era:

תַּנְיָא – It has been taught in a Baraisa: רַבִּי אֶלְעָזָר הַקַּפָּר אוֹמֵר – R' ELAZAR HAKAPPAR SAYS: לְעוֹלָם יְבַקֵּשׁ אָדָם רַחֲמִים עַל מִדָּה זוֹ – A PERSON SHOULD ALWAYS ASK FOR MERCY from God **REGARDING THIS FATE**, poverty. That is, one should pray that he does not become poor, **שֶׁאִם הוּא לֹא בָא – FOR** every family becomes poor sooner or later; **IF HE DOES NOT COME** to be poor, **בָּא בְנוֹ – HIS**

NOTES

33. *Genesis* 9:2. After the Flood, God told Noah that henceforth animals would fear humans.

34. This is based upon the interpretation of וְחִתְּכֶם, *the dread of you,* as חִיּוּתְכֶם, *your vitality* (*Rashi*).

35. Literally: a lion will not fall upon . . . If a lion sees two people together, he will not chase after them to kill them. This is based on the verse just cited: מוֹרַאֲכֶם, *the fear of you,* will be *upon every beast of the earth,* including lions. The word *you* here is a plural pronominal suffix, indicating the fear of two or more of you (*Rashi*).

When Rav Pappa says that a lion would not attack two people, the implication is that a lion *would* attack one person. Yet a Baraisa has just stated that the fear of even a single person is imposed upon every beast of the earth!

Ben Yehoyada reconciles the two statements in this way: A lion fears even a single person. However, from afar the lion may not be cognizant of the Divine spark within the person and thus it may pursue him until it draws near and realizes its mistake. The combined aura of two people, on the other hand, is clear to the lion from afar. Thus, he will not even attempt to pursue them (see also *Bereishis Rabbah* 34:12; cf. *Riaf* in *Ein Yaakov, Pesach Einayim*; see also *Sfas Emes*).

36. *Psalms* 49:13. [The plain reading of the end of the verse is: *He is compared, he is likened to the animals* (*Maharsha*).]

37. This occurs when a person's evil behavior earns him a Heavenly death penalty (*Rashi*). [*Maharal* states that Rami bar Abba does not mean that in the eyes of the animal the person actually appears to be another animal. Rather he means that if he acts in an unworthy manner, the animal loses its fear of attacking him.]

38. By sleeping alone in a house one risks becoming anxious, and it is forbidden to place oneself in a situation where one may be seized by anxiety. If one does find himself in such a situation, he should not succumb to fear; rather, he should trust in God and engage in the study of the Torah, which affords outstanding protection against harm (*Meiri*).

39. I.e. he sleeps at night in a room whose door is closed (*Mishnah Berurah* 239:9, see *Shaar HaTziyun;* see also *Responsa Chelkas Yaakov* III 17).

40. Lilith is the mother of demons (*Zohar, Pekudei* 276b).

41. This follows *Rashi*. According to *HaRif* in *Ein Yaakov* and *Maharsha*, it means: while you still enjoy good health and are able to perform charity, for when you become old and infirm you will be physically incapable of performing such deeds.

42. *Ecclesiastes* 12:1.

43. The Messianic Era will be a time of universal prosperity; no one will need charity. Therefore, there will be no opportunity to acquire merit through the giving of charity, nor will there be an opportunity to be hard-hearted and refuse to give (*Rashi*).

44. *Deuteronomy* 15:11. Thus, according to Shmuel, the natural laws and even the basic forms of society, including economic differentiation, will not change in the Messianic Era. There will, therefore, be plenty of opportunity to give charity or to refuse to do so.

[For an elaboration of these two views, see Schottenstein ed. of *Sanhedrin*, 99a notes 31 and 32.]

It is surprising for the Gemara to say that a Baraisa disagrees with an Amora. Normally, the Gemara would challenge Shmuel's view by saying that a Baraisa contradicts it. However, perhaps this Baraisa was not established as authoritative. Or perhaps, since the topic is Aggadic, Shmuel is empowered to challenge the Baraisa (*Rashash* to 63a).

שימתין א) קושרין את הלחי לא שיעלה אלא שלא יוסיף א) וכן קורה שנשברה סומכין אותה בספסל או בארוכות המטה לא שתעלה אלא שלא תוסיף: גמ' ג) והאמר רב יהודה אמר שמואל מעשה בתלמידו של רבי מאיר שנכנס אחריו לבית המרחץ ביקש להדיח קרקע אמר לו אין מדיחין לסוך קרקע אמר לו אין סכין קרקע בקרקע מחלפא מת בקרקע לא מיחלף כל לאתויי מאי לאתויי הא דת"ר מביאין כלי מיקר וכלי מתכות ומניחין על כריסו כדי שלא (א) תפוח ופוקקין את נקביו כדי שלא תיכנס בהן הרוח ואף שלמה אמר בחכמתו א) עד שלא ירתק חבל הכסף זה חוט השדרה ותרוץ גולת הזהב זו אמה ותשבר כד על המבוע זה הכרס ונרוץ הגלגל אל הבור זה פרש וכן הוא אומר ב) וזריתי פרש על פניכם פרש חגיכם אמר רב הונא ואמרי לה אמר רב חגא אלו בני אדם שמניחין דברי תורה ועושין כל ימיהם כחגים אמר רבי לוי אמר רב פפי א"ר יהושע לאחר שלשה ימים כריסו נבקעת ונופלת לו על פניו ואומרת לו טול מה שנתת בי: מתני' אין ד) מעצמין את המת בשבת ולא בחול עם יציאת נפש ב והמעצים עם יציאת הנפש הרי זה שופך דמים: גמ' תנו רבנן המעצמו עם יציאת הנפש הרי זה שופך דמים משל לנר שכבה והולכת אדם מניח אצבעו עליה מיד כבתה תניא ה) רשב"ג אומר הרוצה שיתעצמו עיניו של מת נופח לו יין בחוטמו ונותן שמן בין ריסי עיניו ואוחז בשני גודלי רגליו והן מתעצמין מאליהן תניא רשב"ג אומר תינוק בן יומו חי מחללין עליו את השבת דוד מלך ישראל מת אין מחללין עליו את השבת תינוק בן יומו חי מחללין עליו את השבת ו) אמרה תורה חלל עליו שבת אחד כדי שישמור שבתות הרבה דוד מלך ישראל מת אין מחללין עליו כיון שמת אדם בטל מן המצות והיינו ז) דא"ר יוחנן ג) במתים חפשי כיון שמת אדם נעשה חפשי מן המצות ותניא ר' שמעון בן אלעזר אומר תינוק בן יומו חי אין צריך לשומרו מן החולדה ומן העכברים אבל עוג מלך הבשן מת צריך לשומרו מן החולדה ומן העכברים שנאמר ד) ומוראכם וחתכם יהיה על כל חית הארץ כל זמן שאדם חי אימתו מוטלת על הבריות כיון שמת בטלה אימתו אמר רב פפא ח) נקיטינן אריה אבי תרי לא נפיל הא קא חזינן דנפיל ההוא כדרמי בר אבא דאמר רמי בר אבא ט) אין חיה שולטת באדם עד שנדמה לו כבהמה שנאמר ה) אדם ביקר בל ילין נמשל כבהמות נדמו אמר רבי חנינא ג אסור לישן בבית יחידי וכל הישן בבית יחידי אחזתו לילית ותניא רשב"א אומר עשה עד שאתה מוצא ומצוי לך ועודך בידך ואף שלמה אמר בחכמתו ו) וזכור את בוראיך בימי בחורותיך עד [אשר] (ש)לא יבואו ימי הרעה ד אלו ימי הזקנה והגיעו שנים אשר תאמר אין לי בהם חפץ אלו ימי המשיח שאין בהם לא זכות ולא חובה ופליגא דשמואל י) דאמר שמואל אין בין העולם הזה לימות המשיח אלא שיעבוד מלכיות בלבד שנא' ז) כי לא יחדל אביון מקרב הארץ תניא ר' אלעזר הקפר אומר לעולם יבקש אדם רחמים על מדה זו שאם הוא לא בא בנו ואם בנו לא בא בן בנו בא שנאמר ח) כי בגלל הדבר הזה תנא דבי ר' ישמעאל גלגל הוא שחוזר בעולם א"ר יוסף נקיטינן האי צורבא מרבנן לא מיעני והא קא חזינן דמיעני אם איתא דמיעני אהדורי אפתחא לא מיהדר אמר לה רבי חייא לדביתהו כי אתי עניא אקדימי ליה ריפתא כי היכי דלקדמו לבנין אמרה ליה מילט קא לייטת להו אמר לה קרא קא כתיב כי בגלל הדבר הזה ותנא דבי ר' ישמעאל גלגל הוא שחוזר בעולם תניא ר' גמליאל ברבי אומר ט) ונתן לך רחמים ורחמך והרבך ה כל המרחם על הבריות מרחמין עליו מן השמים וכל שאינו מרחם על הבריות אין מרחמין עליו מן השמים י) עד אשר לא תחשך השמש והאור זו פדחת והחוטם והירח זו נשמה והכוכבים אלו הלסתות ושבו העבים אחר הגשם זו מאור עיניו של אדם שהולך אחר הבכי אמר שמואל האי דמעתא עד ארבעין שנין הדרא מכאן ואילך לא הדרא ואמר רב נחמן האי כוחלא עד ארבעין שנין מרווח מכאן ואילך אפילו מליא כ) כאביסנא דגירדאי אוקומי מוקים מרווחי לא מרווח מאי קא משמע לן דכמה דאלים מכוחלא טפי מעלי ר' חנינא שכיבא ליה ברתיה לא הוה קא בכי עלה אמרה ליה דביתהו תרנגולתא אפיקת מביתך אמר לה תרתי תכלא ועיורא סבר לה כי הא דאמר רבי יוחנן משום רבי יוסי בן קצרתה י) שש דמעות הן שלש יפות ושלש רעות של עשן ושל בכי ושל

רש"י

שימתין. שלא יסריח מחמת חום הסדין והכרים: קושרין את הלחי. של מת שהיה פיו הולך ונפתח קושרין את לחייו כדי שלא יפתח פיו יותר: ולא שיעלה. להסגר ממה שנפתח דהיינו מזיז אבר אלא שלא יוסיף ליפתח: סומכין אותה בספסל. שהרי תורת כלי עליו: לא שתעלה. דהוה ליה בונה: גמ' ואמר לו אין סכין. אלמא דבר האסור לטלטל אסור לסוך. קרקע בקרקע מיחלף. כלומר ההוא לאו משום טלטול הוא אלא משום אשויי גומות ואע"ג דמרחץ רצפת אבנים הוא וליכא למיחש לאשויי גומות מיחלף מיהא בקרקע אחר: כל צרכי המת לאתויי מאי. דלא תנן: כלי מיקר. שמקבלים קרירות כגון זכוכית: ואף שלמה אמר בחכמתו. שכריסו של מת נופחת ונבקעת: זה חוט השדרה. שהוא כמין חבל ולבן ככסף: זו אמה. שהוא מעין של תולדה כמו גולות מים (יהושע טו): זה פרש. וגלגל לשון גלל (יחזקאל ד): אל הבור. שנופל לתוך פיו: כחגים. כתענוגים: מתני' אין מעצמין. את עיניו בשבת אפילו אחר יציאת הנפש דמזיז בו אבר: שופך דמים. כדמפרש בברייתא בגמ' שבטורח מועט מקרב מיתתו: גמ' ואוחז בשני גודלי רגליו. עוקמן לצלעותיו: וחתכם. לשון חיותכם: אריה אבי תרי לא נפיל. להורגן כלכתי' ומוראכם תרי וכתיב על כל חית הארץ ואפי' ארי: כדרמי בר אבא. דנכנסה עליו מיתה ונדמה לארי כבהמה: נמשל. מי שהחיה מושלת בו בידוע שכבהמה נדמה: עשה. צדקה: עד שאתה מוצא. למי לעשות: ומצוי לך. ממון: ועודך בידך. עודך ברשותך קודם שתמות: לא זכות. לא דבר לזכות בו שהכל עשירים: ולא חובה. לאמץ לב ולקפוץ יד: על מדה זו. שלא יבא לידי עניות לדבר המזומן הוא לבא או עליו או על בנו או על בן בנו: ונתן לך רחמים. שמרחם על הבריות: זו פדחת. המצח שהוא חלק ומצהיר יותר מכל הפרצוף: זה חוטם. שהוא תואר פני אדם: זו נשמה. כדכתיב נר אלהים נשמת אדם (משלי כ): הלסתות. לחיים: ושבו העבים. חשכת עינים יבא ויכסה המאור אחר שירבה בבכיה בזקנותו מחמת תשות כח וצרות רבות עליו: מרווח. מאור עינים: אפילו מליא. כחלא בעיניו כמכחול גדול: כאביסנא של גרדאי. כוכד של גרדיים אינשובל"ש בלע"ז: אוקומי. המאור מוקים שלא יחשך יותר ממה שהוא: מאי קמ"ל. בהא דאמר אפי' כאביסנא דגרדאי: אלים. עב: מכוחלא. עץ שהוא מכניס בשפופרת ונותן בעיניו וקורין לו מכחול: תיכלא ועיורא. שיכול בנים ועיורון הדמעה: של בכי. מתוך אבל וצרה: של

עין משפט נר מצוה

מג א מיי' פכ"ו מהל' שבת הלכה כ סמג שם טוש"ע א"ח סימן שיא סעיף ז:
מד ב מיי' פ"ד מהלכות אבל הלכה ה סמג עשין ב טוש"ע יו"ד סי' שלט סעיף א:
מה ג סמג עשין עט:
מו ד מיי' פ"ו מהלכות תשובה הלכה ה:
מז ה מיי' פ"י מהלכות מתנות עניים הל"ב [וכא' עבדים פ"ט הל"ח] טוש"ע יו"ד סימן רמז סעיף ג:

תורה אור השלם

א) עד אשר לא ירתק חבל הכסף ותרץ גלת הזהב ותשבר כד על המבוע ונרץ הגלגל אל הבור: [קהלת יב, ו]
ב) הנני גער לכם את הזרע וזריתי פרש על פניכם פרש חגיכם ונשא אתכם אליו: [מלאכי ב, ג]
ג) במתים חפשי כמו חללים שכבי קבר אשר לא זכרתם עוד והמה מידך נגזרו: [תהלים פח, ו]
ד) ומוראכם וחתכם יהיה על כל חית הארץ ועל כל עוף השמים בכל אשר תרמש האדמה ובכל דגי הים בידכם נתנו: [בראשית ט, ב]
ה) ואדם ביקר בל ילין נמשל כבהמות נדמו: [תהלים מט, יג]
ו) וזכר את בוראיך בימי בחורתיך עד אשר לא יבאו ימי הרעה והגיעו שנים אשר תאמר אין לי בהם חפץ: [קהלת יב, א]
ז) כי לא יחדל אביון מקרב הארץ על כן אנכי מצוך לאמר פתח תפתח את ידך לאחיך לעניך ולאבינך בארצך: [דברים טו, יא]
ח) נתון תתן לו ולא ירע לבבך בתתך לו כי בגלל הדבר הזה יברכך יי אלהיך בכל מעשך ובכל משלח ידך: [דברים טו, י]
ט) ולא ידבק בידך מאומה מן החרם למען ישוב יי מחרון אפו ונתן לך רחמים ורחמך והרבך כאשר נשבע לאבתיך: [דברים יג, יח]
י) עד אשר לא תחשך השמש והאור והירח והכוכבים ושבו העבים אחר הגשם: [קהלת יב, ב]

רבינו חננאל

חוץ לחומה לנו ואע"ג דאיסורא הוא וקיי"ל הלכתא כרב באיסורי הא הלכתא כשמואל דדיקא מתניתין כותיה דתנן במס' מכשירין עיר של ישראל ונכרים דרין בתוכה והיתה בה מרחץ המרחצת בשבת אם רוב נכרים מותר לרחוץ בה מיד אם רוב ישראל ימתין עד בכדי שיחמו חמין. מחצה על מחצה ימתין בכדי שיחמו חמין. ר' יהודה אומר באמבטי קטנה אם יש רשות רוחץ בה מיד. ומפרש רב יצחק בריה דרב יהודה מאי רשות כגון אדם חשוב שיש לו עבדים שמחממין לו עשרה קומקמין בבת אחת מותר לרחוץ מיד: עשו לו ארון וחפרו לו קבר יקבר בהן ישראל ומקשינן אמאי והא ישראל ונכרי כמחצה על מחצה דמי ימתין בכדי שיעשו ומפרק עולא כגון בנכרי מת המוטל באיסטרטא דמוכחא מלתא שזה הקבר לזה הנכרי נחפר שדומה לרוב נכרים שאין צריך להמתין בכדי שיעשו תוב אקשינן תינח קבר ארון מאי ופריק ר' אבהו בארון המוטל על הקבר שנמצא הארון בקבר א) דאילו דברי ר"מ נסבייה בדרך גררה. בפרק כירה בענין דברים של (חול) [קדש] אסור לאומרם (בלשה"ק) [בלשון חול] אלא אם הוא לאפרושי מאיסורא כגון זה שא"ר מאיר לתלמידיו אין מדיחין ואין סכין בלשה"ק אבל הרואה שסכין ומדיחין המת לא יתיר הדחה וסיכה בקרקע ולפיכך התיר ר"מ הדחה וסיכה ולא גזר סיכת המת והדחתו מפני סיכת מרחץ והדחתו. כל צרכי המת כלל זה להביא הא דת"ר מביאין כלי מיקר וכלי מתכות ומניחין לו על כרסו בשבת שלא תפוח. ופוקקין נקביו בשביל שלא תכנס בהן הרוח ואף שלמה אמר בחכמתו עד אשר לא ירתק חבל הכסף וגו' ופשוטה היא: אין מאמצין את המת בשבת וכו'. פי' מאמצין סותמין את עיני המת. ת"ר המאמץ עם יציאת נפש אפילו בחול הרי זה שופך דמים משל לנר שכבה כו'. תניא ר"ש בן אלעזר אומר תינוק בן יומו חי מחללין עליו את השבת שעומד ומשמר שבתות הרבה. דוד מלך ישראל מת אין מחללין עליו את השבת

רש"י (המשך)

הרבה. ושמרו בני ישראל את השבת. כדי לעשות שבתות אחרות יזהרו בשבת זו בקיום שמירת שבת [יומא פה:]. דא"ר יוחנן. קרא קא דריש במתים חפשי [לעיל שם. ע"ש בגמ' בהגרי"פ]. חפשי מן המצות. מת אין מצות נוהגות בו [פסחים מ:]. וחתכם. ואימתכם כמו (איוב ו, כא) תראו חתת. ואגדה לשון חיות שכל זמן שהתינוק חי אין צריך לשומרו מן העכברים עוג מלך הבשן מת צריך לשומרו מן העכברים שנאמר ומוראכם וחתכם מוראכם על החיות כל זמן שאתם חיים [בראשית ט, ב]. נקיטינן. מסורת מאבותינו [עירובין ה.]. אחותו לילית. שדה [נדה כד:]. ימי הרעה. ימי הזקנה והחלשות [קהלת שם, א]. ופליגא דשמואל. דאמר ימות המשיח [illegible] משל עכשיו [פסחים סח.]. שנאמר כי לא יחדל. משמע לעולם אלמא יש עניות ועשירות שמע מינה מה שנתנבאו הנביאים ולא יהיה כנעני עוד (זכריה יד) לא לימות המשיח נתנבאו שהן מן העולם הזה דאם כן [illegible] [לעיל סג.]. עד אשר לא תחשך השמש. אמרו רבותינו זו פדחת שהיא מאירה ומצהבת באדם [illegible] קמטין ואין מצהבת. והאור. זה החוטם שהוא תואר קלסתר פנים. והירח. זו נשמה שמאירה [illegible] הימנו אין לו מאור העינים. והכוכבים. אלו הלסתות רומני דאפי שקורין פומלי"ש (של) [illegible]. ושבו העבים אחר הגשם. תבוא כהיית המאור אחר דמעת הבכי מכמה צרות שעברו עליו [קהלת שם, ב].

חשק שלמה על רבינו חננאל א) נראה דחסר כאן איזה תיבות ושייך להא דמקשינן כאן בגמ' והאמר ריא"ש מעשה בתלמידו של ר"מ:

מסורת הש"ס

א) לעיל מג., ב) לעיל מ:, ג) בקהלת אשר לא, ד) [גירסת הערוך אין מאמצין כו' וכל המאמץ כו' פירוש סוגרין עיני המת לאחר המיתה כדי שלא יהיו עיניו פתוחות כענין שנאמר ויוסף ישית ידו על עיניך ע"כ ועיין ערך עז ...], ה) [illegible], ו) יומא פה:, ז) לעיל ל., ח) [עי' פרש"י עירובין ה. ד"ה והאמר], ט) [סנהדרין לח: ע"ש], י) ברכות לד: פסחים סח. סנהדרין צא: צט., כ) [תוספתא דב"ק פ"ט], ל) [נדה כד: ע"ש], מ) [גירסת הערוך כאבסנא], נ) [אדר"נ פמ"א].

הגהות הב"ח

(א) גמ' שלא יהא תפוח: (ב) רש"י ד"ה אוקומי. מוקים המאור שלא:

גליון הש"ס

גמ' קרקע בקרקע מיחלפא. כה"ג לעיל דף כט ע"ב ועי' בתוספות שם ד"ה גזירה:

ליקוטי רש"י

שנשברה. בשבת. בספסל. דכלי הוא ומותר לטלטלו. ארוכות המטה. לימוני"ש [לעיל מג.]. אין מדיחין. דלמא אתי לאשויי גומות [שם מ:]. משום אשויי גומות [illegible] [עירובין קד.]. עד אשר לא ירתק חבל הכסף. [illegible] [ב"מ לח.]. זה חוט השדרה שהוא לבן ככסף [illegible] כשלשלת ירתק לשון (ישעיה מ, יט) רתוקות כסף. ותרוץ גולת הזהב. זה האמה שהיא מקלחת מים ונובעת כמעין כמו (יהושע טו, יט) גולות עליות, ותרוץ לשון רציצה. ותשבר כד על המבוע. זה כרס שהיא עבה ונבקעת כמותו [קהלת יב, ו ע"ש בפרש"י ח"א]. מחללין עליו את השבת. פיקוח נפש דוחה את השבת [יומא פה:]. מותי בסם ולא שימות בסם [לעיל ל:]. אמרה תורה חלל עליו שבת אחד כדי שישמור שבתות

SON MAY COME to be poor; וְאִם בְּנוֹ לֹא בָא – AND IF HIS SON DOES NOT COME to be poor, בֶּן בְּנוֹ בָא – HIS SON'S SON MAY COME to be, שֶׁנֶּאֱמַר ,,כִּי בִּגְלַל הַדָּבָר הַזֶּה" – FOR IT IS STATED:[45] *You shall surely give [the poor person], and let your heart not feel bad when you give him,* FOR IN RETURN *(biglal)* FOR THIS MATTER, *Hashem, your God, will bless you in all your deeds and in your every undertaking.* תָּנָא דְּבֵי רַבִּי יִשְׁמָעֵאל – And, in commenting on the word *biglal*, A BARAISA WAS TAUGHT IN THE ACADEMY OF R' YISHMAEL: גַּלְגַּל הוּא שֶׁחוֹזֵר בָּעוֹלָם – [POVERTY] IS A WHEEL *(gilgal)* THAT REVOLVES IN THE WORLD, i.e. it is a cyclical phenomenon, never removed permanently from any individual. Therefore, if one is not poor now, he may one day become poor; and if it happens that he does not become poor, his descendants will become poor, for sooner or later poverty befalls every family.[46]

Torah study protects one from poverty:

אָמַר רַב יוֹסֵף נְקִיטִינַן הַאי צוּרְבָא מֵרַבָּנָן לֹא מִיעַנֵּי – **Rav Yosef said:** – **We have a tradition that a young Torah scholar does not become poor.**

The Gemara asks:

וְהָא קָא חָזֵינַן דְּמִיעַנֵּי – **But we see that they do become poor** sometimes!

The Gemara answers:

אִם אִיתָא דְּמִיעַנֵּי – **If it happens that they become poor,** אַהֲדוּרֵי אַפִּתְחָא לֹא מִיהַדַּר – **they do not go around** begging **at doors**, for if Torah students are not spared poverty, they are spared its indignities.[47]

A story related to R' Elazar HaKappar's statement:

אָמַר לָהּ רַבִּי חִיָּיא לִדְבֵיתְהוּ – **R' Chiya said to his wife:** כִּי אָתֵי עַנְיָא – **When a poor person comes** to our door, אַקְדִּימִי לֵיהּ רִיפְתָּא – **be quick to offer him bread,** כִּי הֵיכִי דְּלִקְדְּמוּ לִבְנַיִךְ – **so that** others **may be quick to offer** bread **to your children** when they are beggars. אָמְרָה לֵיהּ – **She said to him:** מֵילַט קָא לָיְיטַתְּ לְהוּ – **Are you cursing them** that they should become poor?! אָמַר לָהּ – **He said to her:** קְרָא קָא כְּתִיב ,,כִּי בִּגְלַל הַדָּבָר הַזֶּה" – It is not I but Scripture, for **it is written in a verse:** ***For in return*** *(biglal)* ***for this matter,*** וְתָנָא דְּבֵי רַבִּי יִשְׁמָעֵאל – **and a Baraisa has been taught in the academy of R' Yishmael:** גַּלְגַּל הוּא שֶׁחוֹזֵר בָּעוֹלָם – [POVERTY] IS A WHEEL THAT REVOLVES IN THE WORLD; sooner or later everyone becomes poor. Thus, it is quite possible that our children may be paupers.

A Baraisa supports R' Chiya's comment to his wife that her children would be dealt with charitably if she dealt with others charitably:

תַּנְיָא – **It has been taught in a Baraisa:** רַבָּן גַּמְלִיאֵל בְּרַבִּי אוֹמֵר – RABBAN GAMLIEL BAR REBBI SAYS: ,,וְנָתַן־לְךָ רַחֲמִים וְרִחַמְךָ וְהִרְבֶּךָ" – Scripture states:[48] ***HE WILL BESTOW UPON YOU*** the attribute ***OF COMPASSION AND SHOW COMPASSION TO YOU AND MULTIPLY YOU.*** כָּל הַמְרַחֵם עַל הַבְּרִיּוֹת מְרַחֲמִין עָלָיו מִן הַשָּׁמַיִם – From this we learn that WHOEVER IS COMPASSIONATE TOWARD [GOD'S] CREATURES[49] IS SHOWN COMPASSION BY HEAVEN. וְכָל שֶׁאֵינוֹ מְרַחֵם עַל הַבְּרִיּוֹת אֵין מְרַחֲמִין עָלָיו מִן הַשָּׁמַיִם – AND WHOEVER IS NOT COMPASSIONATE TOWARD [GOD'S] CREATURES IS NOT SHOWN COMPASSION BY HEAVEN.[50]

The Gemara above cited part of the description of the deterioration of the body in old age and death given in the twelfth chapter of *Ecclesiastes.* The Gemara now commences a sustained exposition of the rest of the passage:[51]

,,עַד אֲשֶׁר לֹא־תֶחְשַׁךְ הַשֶּׁמֶשׁ וְהָאוֹר" – ***Before the sun and the light grow dark*** – זוֹ פַּדַּחַת וְהַחוֹטֶם – **this** is a reference to the **forehead and the nose;**[52] ,,וְהַיָּרֵחַ" זוֹ נְשָׁמָה – ***and the moon*** – **this is the soul;**[53] ,,וְהַכּוֹכָבִים" אֵלּוּ הַלְּסָתוֹת – ***and the stars*** – **these are the cheeks;**[54] ,,וְשָׁבוּ הֶעָבִים אַחַר הַגָּשֶׁם" זוֹ מְאוֹר עֵינָיו שֶׁל אָדָם – ***and the clouds return after the rain*** – **this** is a reference to **a person's eyesight,** שֶׁהוֹלֵךְ אַחַר הַבֶּכִי – **which goes** (i.e. is weakened) **by weeping.**[55]

Two other statements regarding age and the eyes:

אָמַר שְׁמוּאֵל – **Shmuel said:** הַאי דִּמְעֲתָא – The rule is as follows regarding **this tear,** caused by weeping: עַד אַרְבְּעִין שְׁנִין הַדְרָא – **Until** one is **forty years** old, **it returns,** that is, the human body

NOTES

45. *Deuteronomy* 15:10.

46. Want is ordained to strike one of every three generations; however one may defeat this fate through prayer (see *Maharsha*) or through charity (*Derech Eretz Zuta* 9; see also below, 156a,b). The Gemara (*Zevachim* 113b) states that the wealth of the affluent families in Babylonia did not last three generations. *Rashi* there presents the reason: They had no compassion for their fellow men.

47. A Torah scholar has a larger network of admirers than is available to an ordinary person. If the scholar faces deprivation, these patrons will be able at least to support him to the extent that he will not be forced to go begging. Alternatively, he will avoid begging at people's doors by forcing himself to subsist on meager rations (*Maharsha*).

Some interpret this phrase homiletically: If it happens that they become poor, it is because, earlier in their lives, they would not go from door to door to solicit charity for the poor (*Siach Sarfei Kodesh* IV, p. 60; see also *Aruch HaShulchan, Yoreh Deah* 247:5).

48. *Deuteronomy* 13:18.

49. This includes kindness to animals (*Mesillas Yesharim* ch. 19).

50. Whoever is kind to the poor will be treated kindly by God. [*Rama* comments: One should consider that he is constantly beseeching God to provide him a livelihood, and just as he desires that God should listen to his prayers, so too he should accede to the entreaties of the poor (*Shulchan Aruch, Yoreh Deah* 247:3). *Beur HaGra* cites as the source the verse in *Proverbs* 21:13: *One who shuts his ear to the cry of the pauper, he too will call out and not be answered.*]

51. For the sake of convenience, the entire passage (*Ecclesiastes* 12:1-7) is presented here: *So remember your Creator in the days of your youth, before the evil days come, and those years arrive of which you will say, "I have no pleasure in them"; before the sun, the light, the moon and the stars grow dark, and the clouds return after the rain; in the day when the guards of the house will tremble, and the powerful men will stoop, and the grinders are idle because they are few, and the gazers through windows are dimmed; when the doors in the street are shut; when the sound of the grinding is low; when one rises up at the voice of the bird, and all the daughters of song grow dim; when they even fear a height and terrors in the road; and the almond tree blossoms and the grasshopper becomes a burden and the desire falls — so man goes to his eternal home, while the mourners go about the street. Before the silver cord snaps, and the golden bowl is shattered, and the pitcher is broken at the fountain, and the wheel is smashed at the pit. Thus the dust returns to the ground, as it was, and the spirit returns to God Who gave it. Futility of futilities — said Koheles — all is futile!*

52. The sun in the verse is a metaphorical allusion to the forehead of a healthy, vigorous young man, which shines with health like the sun. When the man grows old, his forehead, hitherto the smoothest and shiniest part of the visage, becomes wrinkled and loses its luster (*Rashi* here and to *Ecclesiastes;* see also *Targum*). The word אור in the verse is a reference to the nose because the nose is the defining feature (*toar*) of one's face.

53. The soul is often referred to in terms of light, as in *Man's soul is God's lamp* (*Proverbs* 20:27) (*Rashi*).

54. I.e. the cheekbones [which "shine" amidst the surrounding "night" of the dark hair of the beard] (*Rashi* to *Ecclesiastes*).

55. I.e. when a person grows old and contemplates that he is no longer as strong as he used to be, and the many troubles old age entails, he becomes depressed and weeps bitterly. This weeping has the effect of weakening his eyesight. The weakened eyesight which follows the weeping is described metaphorically as the clouds which follow the rains (*Rashi*).

שימתין קושרין את הלחי לא שיעלה אלא שלא יוסיף וכן קורה שנשברה סומכין אותה בספסל או בארוכות המטה לא שתעלה אלא שלא תוסיף: **גמ׳** והאמר רב יהודה אמר שמואל מעשה בתלמידו של רבי מאיר שנכנס אחריו לבית המרחץ ביקש להדיח קרקע אמר לו אין מדיחין לסוך קרקע אמר לו אין סכין קרקע בקרקע מיחלפא מת בקרקע לא מיחלף כל לאתויי מאי לאתויי הא דת״ר מביאין כלי מיקר וכלי מתכות ומניחין על כריסו כדי שלא תפוח ופוקקין את נקביו כדי שלא תיכנס בהן הרוח ואף שלמה אמר בחכמתו עד שלא ירתק חבל הכסף זה חוט השדרה ותרוץ גולת הזהב זה אמה ותשבר כד על המבוע זה הכרס ונרוץ הגלגל אל הבור זה פרש וכן הוא אומר וזריתי פרש על פניכם פרש חגיכם אמר רב הונא ואמרי לה אמר רב חגא אלו בני אדם שמניחין דברי תורה ועושין כל ימיהם כחגים אמר רבי לוי אמר רב פפי א״ר יהושע לאחר שלשה ימים כריסו נבקעת ונופלת לו על פניו ואומרת לו טול מה שנתת בי: **מתני׳** אין מעצמין את המת בשבת ולא בחול עם יציאת נפש והמעצים עם יציאת הנפש הרי זה שופך דמים: **גמ׳** תנו רבנן המעצמו עם יציאת הנפש הרי זה שופך דמים משל לנר שכבה והולכת אדם מניח אצבעו עליה מיד כבתה תניא רשב״ג אומר הרוצה שיתעצמו עיניו של מת נופח לו יין בחוטמו ונותן שמן בין ריסי עיניו ואוחז בשני גודלי רגליו והן מתעצמין מאליהן תניא רשב״ג אומר תינוק בן יומו חי מחללין עליו את השבת דוד מלך ישראל מת אין מחללין עליו את השבת תינוק בן יומו חי מחללין עליו את השבת אמרה תורה חלל עליו שבת אחד כדי שישמור שבתות הרבה דוד מלך ישראל מת אין מחללין עליו כיון שמת אדם בטל מן המצות והיינו דא״ר יוחנן במתים חפשי כיון שמת אדם נעשה חפשי מן המצות ותניא ר׳ שמעון בן אלעזר אומר תינוק בן יומו חי אין צריך לשומרו מן החולדה ומן העכברים אבל עוג מלך הבשן מת צריך לשומרו מן החולדה ומן העכברים שנאמר ומוראכם וחתכם יהיה כל זמן שאדם חי אימתו מוטלת על הבריות כיון שמת בטלה אימתו אמר רב פפא נקיטינן אריה אבי תרי לא נפיל הא קא חזינן דנפיל ההוא כדרמי בר אבא דאמר רמי בר אבא אין חיה שולטת באדם עד שנדמה לו כבהמה שנאמר אדם ביקר בל ילין נמשל כבהמות נדמו אמר רבי חנינא אסור לישן בבית יחידי וכל הישן בבית יחידי אחזתו לילית ותניא רשב״א אומר עשה עד שאתה מוצא ומצוי לך ועודך בידך ואף שלמה אמר בחכמתו וזכור את בוראיך בימי בחורותיך עד אשר (ש)לא יבואו ימי הרעה אלו ימי הזקנה והגיעו שנים אשר תאמר אין לי בהם חפץ אלו ימי המשיח שאין בהם לא זכות ולא חובה ופליגא דשמואל דאמר שמואל אין בין העולם הזה לימות המשיח אלא שעבוד מלכיות בלבד שנא׳ כי לא יחדל אביון מקרב הארץ תניא ר׳ אלעזר הקפר אומר לעולם יבקש אדם רחמים על מדה זו שאם הוא לא בא בא בנו ואם בנו לא בא בא בן בנו שנאמר כי בגלל הדבר הזה תנא דבי ר׳ ישמעאל גלגל הוא שחוזר בעולם א״ר יוסף נקיטינן האי צורבא מרבנן לא מיעני והא קא חזינן דמיעני אם איתא דמיעני אהדורי אפתחא לא מיהדר אמר לה רבי חייא לדביתהו כי אתי עניא אקדימי ליה ריפתא כי היכי דלקדמו לבניך אמרה ליה מילט קא לייטת להו אמר לה קרא קא כתיב כי בגלל הדבר הזה ותנא דבי ר׳ ישמעאל גלגל הוא שחוזר בעולם תניא ר׳ גמליאל ברבי אומר ונתן לך רחמים ורחמך והרבך כל המרחם על הבריות מרחמין עליו מן השמים וכל שאינו מרחם על הבריות אין מרחמין עליו מן השמים עד אשר לא תחשך השמש והאור זו פדחת והחוטם והירח זו נשמה והכוכבים אלו הלסתות ושבו העבים אחר הגשם זו מאור עיניו של אדם שהולך אחר הבכי אמר שמואל האי דמעתא עד ארבעין שנין הדרא מכאן ואילך לא הדרא ואמר רב נחמן האי כוחלא עד ארבעין שנין מרווח מכאן ואילך אפילו מליא כאביסנא דגירדאי אוקומי מוקים ארווחי לא מרווח מאי קא משמע לן דכמה דאלים מכוחלא טפי מעלי ר׳ חנינא שכיבא ליה ברתיה לא הוה קא בכי עלה אמרה ליה דביתהו תרנגולתא אפיקת מביתך אמר לה תרתי תכלא ועיורא סבר לה כי הא דאמר רבי יוחנן משום רבי יוסי בן קצרתה שש דמעות הן שלש יפות ושלש רעות של עשן ושל בכי ושל

רש״י

שימתין. שלא יסריח מחמת חום הסדין והכרים: **קושרין את הלחי.** של מת שהיה פיו הולך ונפתח קושרין את לחייו כדי שלא יפתח פיו יותר: **ולא שיעלה.** להסגר מתה שנפתח דהיינו מזיז אבר אלא שלא יוסיף ליפתח: **סומכין אותה בספסל.** שהרי תורת כלי עליו: **לא שתעלה.** דהוה ליה בונה: **גמ׳ ואמר לו אין סכין.** אלמא דבר האסור לטלטל אסור לסוך: **קרקע בקרקע מיחלף.** כלומר ההוא לאו משום טלטול הוא אלא משום אשויי גומות ואע״ג דמרחץ רצפת אבנים הוא וליכא למיחש לאשויי גומות מיחלף מיהא בקרקע אחר: **כל צרכי המת לאתויי מאי.** דלא תנן: **כלי מיקר.** שמקבלים קרירות כגון זכוכית: **ואף שלמה אמר בחכמתו.** שכריסו של מת נופחת ונבקעת: **זה חוט השדרה.** שהוא כמין חבל ולבן ככסף: **זו אמה.** שהוא מעין של תולדה כמו גולות מים (יהושע טו): **זה פרש.** וגלגל לשון גלל (יחזקאל ד): **אל הבור.** שנופל לתוך פיו: **כחגים.** בתענוגים: **מתני׳ אין מעצמין.** את עיניו בשבת אפילו אחר יציאת הנפש דמזיז בו אבר: **שופך דמים.** כדמפרש בברייתא בגמ׳ שבטורח מועט מקרב מיתתו: **גמ׳ ואוחז בשני גודלי רגליו.** עוקרן באצבעותיו: **וחתכם.** לשון חיותכם: **אריה אבי תרי לא נפיל.** להורגן כדכתי׳ ומוראכם תרי וכתיב על כל חית הארץ ואפי׳ אלי: **כדרמי בר אבא.** דנקנסה עליו מיתה ונדמה לאלי כבהמה: **נמשל.** מי שחיה מושלת בו בידוע שכבהמה נדמה: **עשה.** לדקה: **עד שאתה מוצא.** למי לעשות: **ומצוי לך.** ממון: **ועודך בידך.** עודך ברשותך קודם שתמות: **לא זכות.** לא דבר לזכות בו שכולם עשירים: **ולא חובה.** לאמץ לב ולקפוץ יד: **על מדה זו.** שלא יבא לידי עניות דדבר המזומן הוא לבא או עליו או על בנו או על בן בנו: **ונתן לך רחמים.** שתרחם על הבריות: **זו פדחת.** המצח שהוא חלק ומאיר יותר מכל הפרצוף: **זה חוטם.** שהוא תואר פני אדם: **זו נשמה.** כדכתיב נר אלהים נשמת אדם (משלי כ): **הלסתות.** לחיים: **ושבו העבים.** חשכת עיניים יבא ויכסה המאור אחר שירבה בבכיה בזקנותו מחמת תשות כח ולרות רבות עליו: **מרווח.** מאור עינים: **אפילו מליא.** כמלא בעיניו כמכחול גדול: **כאביסנא של גרדאי.** כוכד של גרדיים אינשובל״ש בלע״ז: **אוקומי.** המאור מוקים שלא יחשיך יותר ממה שהוא: **מאי קמ״ל.** בהא דאמר אפי׳ כאביסנא דגרדאי: **אלים.** עב: **מכוחלא.** עץ שהוא מכניס בשפופרת ונותן בעיניו וקורין לו מכחול: **תיכלא ועיורא.** שיכול בניו ועיורון הדמעה: **של בכי.** מתוך אבל ולרה: של

עין משפט נר מצוה

מג א מיי׳ פכ״ו מהל׳ שבת הלכה כ סמג שם טוש״ע או״ח סימן שיא סעיף ז:

מד ב מיי׳ פ״ד מהלכות אבל הלכה ה סמג עשין ב טוש״ע יו״ד סי׳ שלט סעיף א:

מה ג סמג עשין ענ:

מו ד מיי׳ פ״י מהלכות תשובה הלכה א:

מז ה מיי׳ פ״י מהלכות מתנות עניים הל״ב [וכס״ עבדים פ״ט הל״ח] טוש״ע יו״ד סימן רמז סעיף ג:

תורה אור השלם

א) עַד אֲשֶׁר לֹא יֵרָתֵק חֶבֶל הַכֶּסֶף וְתָרֻץ גֻּלַּת הַזָּהָב וְתִשָּׁבֶר כַּד עַל הַמַּבּוּעַ וְנָרֹץ הַגַּלְגַּל אֶל הַבּוֹר: [קהלת יב, ו]

ב) הִנְנִי גֹעֵר לָכֶם אֶת הַזֶּרַע וְזֵרִיתִי פֶרֶשׁ עַל פְּנֵיכֶם פֶּרֶשׁ חַגֵּיכֶם וְנָשָׂא אֶתְכֶם אֵלָיו: [מלאכי ב, ג]

ג) בַּמֵּתִים חָפְשִׁי כְּמוֹ חֲלָלִים שֹׁכְבֵי קֶבֶר אֲשֶׁר לֹא זְכַרְתָּם עוֹד וְהֵמָּה מִיָּדְךָ נִגְזָרוּ: [תהלים פח, ו]

ד) וּמוֹרַאֲכֶם וְחִתְּכֶם יִהְיֶה עַל כָּל חַיַּת הָאָרֶץ וְעַל כָּל עוֹף הַשָּׁמָיִם בְּכֹל אֲשֶׁר תִּרְמֹשׂ הָאֲדָמָה וּבְכָל דְּגֵי הַיָּם בְּיֶדְכֶם נִתָּנוּ: [בראשית ט, ב]

ה) וְאָדָם בִּיקָר בַּל יָלִין נִמְשַׁל כַּבְּהֵמוֹת נִדְמוּ: [תהלים מט, יג]

ו) וּזְכֹר אֶת בּוֹרְאֶיךָ בִּימֵי בְּחוּרֹתֶיךָ עַד אֲשֶׁר לֹא יָבֹאוּ יְמֵי הָרָעָה וְהִגִּיעוּ שָׁנִים אֲשֶׁר תֹּאמַר אֵין לִי בָהֶם חֵפֶץ: [קהלת יב, א]

ז) כִּי לֹא יֶחְדַּל אֶבְיוֹן מִקֶּרֶב הָאָרֶץ עַל כֵּן אָנֹכִי מְצַוְּךָ לֵאמֹר פָּתֹחַ תִּפְתַּח אֶת יָדְךָ לְאָחִיךָ לַעֲנִיֶּךָ וּלְאֶבְיֹנְךָ בְּאַרְצֶךָ: [דברים טו, יא]

ח) נָתוֹן תִּתֵּן לוֹ וְלֹא יֵרַע לְבָבְךָ בְּתִתְּךָ לוֹ כִּי בִּגְלַל הַדָּבָר הַזֶּה יְבָרֶכְךָ יְיָ אֱלֹהֶיךָ בְּכָל מַעֲשֶׂךָ וּבְכֹל מִשְׁלַח יָדֶךָ: [דברים טו, י]

ט) וְלֹא יִדְבַּק בְּיָדְךָ מְאוּמָה מִן הַחֵרֶם לְמַעַן יָשׁוּב יְיָ מֵחֲרוֹן אַפּוֹ וְנָתַן לְךָ רַחֲמִים וְרִחַמְךָ וְהִרְבֶּךָ כַּאֲשֶׁר נִשְׁבַּע לַאֲבֹתֶיךָ: [דברים יג, יח]

י) עַד אֲשֶׁר לֹא תֶחְשַׁךְ הַשֶּׁמֶשׁ וְהָאוֹר וְהַיָּרֵחַ וְהַכּוֹכָבִים וְשָׁבוּ הֶעָבִים אַחַר הַגָּשֶׁם: [קהלת יב, ב]

רבינו חננאל

חרץ לחומה לנו ואע״ג דאיסורא הוא וקיי״ל הלכתא כרב באיסורי הכא הלכתא כשמואל דדיקא מתניתין כותיה דתנן במס׳ מכשירין עיר של ישראל ונכרים דרין בתוכה והיתה בה מרחץ המרחצת בשבת אם רוב נכרים רוחץ בה מיד אם רוב ישראל ימתין עד בכדי שיחמו חמין. מחצה על מחצה ימתין בכדי שיחמו חמין. ר׳ יהודה אומר באמבטי קטנה ואם יש רשות רוחץ בה מיד. ומפרש רב יצחק בריה דרב יהודה מאי רשות כגון אדם חשוב שיש לו עשרה עבדים שמחממין לו עשרה קומקמין בבת אחת מותר לרחוץ מיד: **עשו** לו ארון וחפרו לו קבר יקבר בהן ישראל ומקשינן מאי שנא הכא ישראל ונכרי כמחצה על מחצה דמי ימתין בכדי שיעשו ומפרק עולא כגון בנכרי מת המוטל באיסטרטא דמוכחא מלתא שזה הקבר לזה הנכרי נחפר שדומה לרוב נכרים שאין צריך להמתין בכדי שיעשו תוב אקשינן תינח קבר ארון מאי ופריק ר׳ אבהו בארון המוטל על הקבר שנמצא הארון בקבר א) דאילו דברי ר״מ נסבייה בדרך גררה. בפרק כירה בענין דברים של (חול) [קדש] אסור לאומרם (בלשה״ק) [בלשון חול] אלא אם הוא לאפרושי מאיסורא כגון זה שא״ר מאיר לתלמידיו אין מדיחין ואין סכין בלשה״ק אבל הרואה שסכין ומדיחין המת לא יתיר הדחה וסיכה בקרקע ולפיכך התיר ר״מ הדחת המת וסיכתו ולא גזר סיכת המת והדחתו מפני סיכת מרחץ והדחתו. כל צרכי המת כלל זה להביא הא דת״ר מביאין כלי מיקר וכלי מתכות ומניחין לו על כרסו בשבת שלא תפוח. ופוקקין נקביו בשביל שלא תכנס בהן הרוח ואף שלמה אמר בחכמתו עד אשר לא ירתק חבל הכסף וגו׳ ופשוטה היא: **אין** מאמצין את המת בשבת וכו׳. פי׳ מאמצין סותמין את עיני המת. ת״ר המאמץ עם יציאת נפש אפילו בחול הרי זה שופך דמים משל לנר שכבה כו׳. תניא ר״ש בן אלעזר אומר תינוק בן יומו חי מחללין עליו את השבת שעומד ומשמר שבתות הרבה. דוד מלך ישראל מת אין מחללין עליו את השבת

מסורת הש״ס

א) לעיל מג., ב) לעיל מ:, ג) בקהלת אשר לא, ד) [גירסת הערוך אין מאמצין כו׳ וכל המאמץ כו׳ פירוש סותמין עיני המת לאחר המיתה כדי שלא יהיו עיניו פתוחות כענין שנאמר ויוסף ישית ידו על עיניך ע״כ ועי׳ לעיל דף עז: אימצא לאו מאמצין וכו׳ ואשר ע״כ ברור לדעות הוא שהקדימו בדפוס ל׳ קודם למ׳ במשנה ובברייתא דהכא אמנם בר״ף והרא״ש הגירסא במשנה ובברייתא על נכון עם קודם ל׳ וכ״ה במשנה שבמשניות ובפי׳ הר״ב וכתב התוי״ט אין מאמצין כמו עולם עיניו כו׳], ה) בכ״י איתא ר״ש בן אלעזר, ו) [יומא פה:], ז) לעיל קמ:, נדה סא., ח) [ע׳ פרש״י עירובין ה. ד״ה דאמר פירושו ע״ש], ט) [סנהדרין לח. ע״ש], י) ברכות לד: לעיל סג. פסחים סח. סנהדרין דף לא: לט., כ) [תוספתא דב״ק פ״ט], ל) [ביצה לב: ע״ש], מ) [גירסת הערוך כאבסנא], נ) [אדר״נ פמ״א].

הגהות הב״ח

(א) גמ׳ שלא יהא תפוח. (ב) רש״י ד״ה אוקומי. מוקים המאור שלא:

גליון הש״ס

גמ׳ קרקע בקרקע מיחלפא. כה״ג לעיל דף קט ע״ב ובתוספות שם ד״ה גוזרים.

ליקוטי רש״י

שנשברה. בשבת. בספסל. דכלי הוא ומותר לטלטלו. ארוכות המטה. לימנו״ש [לעיל מג.]. אין מדיחין. דלמא אתי לאשויי גומות [ב:]. משום אשויי גומות. דמלאכה הוא להשוות גומות כגון [עירובין קד.]. עד אשר לא ירתק חבל הכסף. חוט השדרה שהוא לבן ככסף ומתרוקן ויבש ומתעקם מתוך החליות ועשה כמשלשלת שלא ירתק לשון (ישעיה מ, יט) ורתוקות כסף. ותרוץ גולת הזהב. זה האמה שהיא מקלחת מים ונוטפת כמעין כמו (יהושע טו, יט) גולות עליות, ותרוץ לשון רלילה. ותשבר כד על המבוע. זה הכרס שהיא עבה ונבקעת כמותו [קהלת יב, ו; ע״ש עוד ובמהרש״א ח״א]. מחללין עליו את השבת. פיקוח נפש דוחה בין (יומא פה:) מומי שלא יהא שימות כהס [לעיל ל:]. אמרה תורה חלל עליו שבת אחד כדי שישמור שבתות הרבה. ושמרו בני ישראל את השבת. כדי לעשות שבתות אחרות יזהרו בשבת זו בקיום שמירת שבת [יומא פה:]. דא״ר יוחנן. קרא קא דריש במתים חפשי [לעיל שם. ע״ש בגמ׳ בהגרי״פ]. חפשי מן המצות. מת אין מלות עוד [פסחים מ:]. וחתכם. ואימתכם כמו (איוב ו, כא) תראו חתת. ואגדה לשון חיות שכל זמן שהתינוק חי אין צריך לשומרו מן העכברים עוג מלך הבשן מת צריך לשומרו מן העכברים שנאמר ומוראכם וחתכם יהיה מוראכם על החיות כל זמן שאתם חיים [בראשית ט, ב]. נקיטינן. מסורת מאבותינו [עירובין ה.]. אחזתו לילית. שידה [נדה כד:]. ימי הרעה. ימי הזקנה והחלשות [קהלת שם, א]. ופליגא דשמואל. דאמר ימות המשיח אין בהם לא זכות ולא חובה עכשיו [פסחים סח.]. שנאמר כי לא יחדל. משמע לעולם אלמא יש עניות ועשירות שמע מינה נחמות שנתנבאו הנביאים ולא יהיה כנעני עוד (זכריה יד) לא לימות המשיח נתנבאו שהן מן העולם הזה דאם כן [לעיל סג.]. עד אשר לא תחשך השמש. אמרו רבותינו זו פדחת שהיא מאירה ומלהבת באדם בחור קמטין ואין מלהבת. והאור. זה החוטם שהוא תואר קלסתר פנים. והירח. זו נשמה שמאירה סימנו אין לו מאור העינים. והכוכבים. אלו הלסתות רומני דאפי שקורין פומלי״ש (של) [ש]. ושבו העבים אחר הגשם. תבוא כהיית המאור אחר דמעת הבכי מכמה לרות שעברו עליו [קהלת שם, ב].

חשק שלמה על רבינו חננאל א) נראה דחסר כאן איזה תיבות ושייך להא דמקשינן כאן בגמ׳ והאמר רי״ש מעשה בתלמידו של ר״מ:

replaces the fluid lost by the weeping. מִכָּאן וְאֵילָךְ – **From then on,** לֹא הָדְרָא – **it does not return;** the body no longer replaces the fluid. וְאָמַר רַב נַחְמָן – **And Rav Nachman said:** הַאי כּוּחְלָא – This is the rule regarding **this *kochla*** (an eye salve): עַד אַרְבְּעִין שְׁנִין מַרְוַוח – **Until** one is **forty years** old, its use improves one's eyesight. מִכָּאן וְאֵילָךְ – **From then on,** אֲפִילוּ מַלְיָא כַּאֲבִיסְנָא דְגִירְדָּאֵי – **even** if you apply a large quantity of the salve, as much as can **fill a weaver's beam,** אוקוּמֵי מוּקִים – **it** merely **preserves** his eyesight against deteriorating further, אַרְווּחֵי לֹא מַרְוַוח – but **does not improve** it.

The Gemara asks:

מַאי קָא מַשְׁמַע לָן – **What is [Rav Nachman] teaching us** by referring specifically to a weaver's beam's worth of salve?[56]

The Gemara answers:

דְּכַמָּה דְאָלִים מְכוּחְלָא טָפֵי מְעַלֵּי – He informs us, in passing, **that the thicker the dabber,**[57] **the better** for the eye.

An illustration of the principle that weeping can impair one's sight:

רַבִּי חֲנִינָא שְׁכִיבָא לֵיהּ בְּרַתֵּיהּ – **R' Chanina's daughter died.** לֹא הֲוָה קָא בָּכֵי עֲלָהּ – However, **he did not cry over her.** אָמְרָה לֵיהּ דְּבֵיתְהוּ – **His wife said to him,** תַּרְנְגוֹלְתָּא אַפֵּיקַת מִבֵּיתָךְ – "How can you not cry?! **Is it** nothing more than **a chicken that you have taken out of your house?!"** אָמַר לָהּ – **He said to her,** "Of course I mourn her and of course I want to cry! but תַּרְתֵּי – shall I suffer **two** misfortunes: תִּכְלָא וְעִיוְּרָא – **Loss of children as well as blindness?!** I am an old man. If I weep I will go blind!"[58]

The Gemara observes:

סָבַר לָהּ כִּי הָא דְּאָמַר רַבִּי יוֹחָנָן מִשּׁוּם רַבִּי יוֹסֵי בֶּן קֶצַרְתָּה – **[R' Chanina] subscribed to that which R' Yochanan said in the name of R' Yose ben Ketzartah:** שֵׁשׁ דְּמָעוֹת הֵן – **There are six kinds of tears;** שָׁלֹשׁ יָפוֹת וְשָׁלֹשׁ רָעוֹת – **three are good** for the eyes, **and three are bad:** שֶׁל עָשָׁן וְשֶׁל בְּכִי – tears induces **by smoke, by crying** over one's sorrow or misfortune,

NOTES

56. A weaver's beam is very thick. If Rav Nachman made reference here to a weaver's beam, it indicates that it is appropriate to dab the eyes with such an enormous quantity of salve (*Rashi*).

57. A מִכְחוֹל is a wooden stick which was dipped into the salve and then dabbed on the eye (*Rashi*).

58. See *Ahavas Eisan* on *Ein Yaakov*.

רָעוֹת – and by stomach pains **in the lavatory** **וְשֶׁל בֵּית הַכִּסֵּא** – **are bad** for the eyes. **שֶׁל סַם וְשֶׁל שְׂחוֹק וְשֶׁל פֵּירוֹת** – Tears caused **by medicine, by laughter, and by** pungent **produce**[1] **יָפוֹת** – **are good** for the eyes.

The Gemara returns to its exposition of the passage in *Ecclesiastes* concerning man's physical decline in old age:

"בַּיּוֹם שֶׁיָּזֻעוּ שֹׁמְרֵי הַבַּיִת וְהִתְעַוְּתוּ וגו׳" – ***In the day when the guards of the house will tremble, and*** *the powerful men* ***will stoop etc.*** *and the grinders are idle because they are few, and the gazers through windows are dimmed.*[2] **"בַּיּוֹם שֶׁיָּזֻעוּ שֹׁמְרֵי הַבַּיִת"** **אֵלּוּ הַכְּסָלִים וְהַצְּלָעוֹת** – ***In the day when the guards of the house will tremble*** – **these are the flanks**[3] **and the ribs;**[4] **"וְהִתְעַוְּתוּ אַנְשֵׁי הֶחָיִל" אֵלּוּ שׁוֹקַיִם** – ***and the powerful men will stoop*** – **these are the legs;**[5] **"וּבָטְלוּ הַטֹּחֲנוֹת" אֵלּוּ שִׁינַּיִם** – ***and the grinders are idle*** *because they are few* – **these are the teeth;**[6] **"וְחָשְׁכוּ הָרֹאוֹת בָּאֲרֻבּוֹת" אֵלּוּ עֵינַיִם** – ***and the gazers through windows are dimmed*** – **these are the eyes.**

The Gemara records a dialogue bearing upon the infirmities of old age:

אָמַר לֵיהּ קֵיסָר לְרַבִּי יְהוֹשֻׁעַ בֶּן חֲנַנְיָה – **The Emperor said to R' Yehoshua ben Chananyah,** **מַאי טַעְמָא לֹא אָתֵית לְבֵי אֲבִידָן** – **"Why did you not come to Bei Avidan?"**[7] **אָמַר לֵיהּ** – **[R' Yehoshua] said to [the Emperor],** **טוּר תַּלְג** – **"The mountain is snowy;** **סַחֲרוֹנֵי גְּלִידִין** – **surrounding** it **is ice;** **כַּלְבוֹהִי לֹא נָבְחִין** – **its dogs do not bark;** **טַחֲנוֹהִי לֹא טוֹחֲנִין** – **its grinders do not grind."**[8] **בֵּי רַב אָמְרִי** – **The [students] of the academy of Rav say** R' Yehoshua ben Chananyah added: **אַדְּלָא אֲבִידְנָא בָּחִישְׁנָא** – **"For that which I have not lost, I am searching."**[9]

Adages concerning youth and old age:

תַּנְיָא – **It has been taught in a Baraisa:** **רַבִּי יוֹסֵי בַּר קִיסְמָא אוֹמֵר** – **R' YOSE BAR KISMA SAYS:** **טָבָא תְּרֵי מִתְּלָת** – **TWO ARE BETTER THAN THREE.**[10] **וַוי לָהּ לַחֲדָא דְּאָזְלָא וְלָא אַתְיָא** – **WOE TO THE ONE THAT GOES AND DOES NOT COME** back.[11] **מַאי הִיא** – **What is that** which goes and does not return? **אָמַר רַב חִסְדָּא** – **Rav Chisda said:** **יַנְקוּתָא** – **Youth.** **כִּי אֲתָא רַב דִּימִי** – **When Rav Dimi came** to Babylonia from the Land of Israel, **אָמַר** – **he said:** **יַנְקוּתָא כְּלִילָא דְּוַורְדָּא** – **Youth is a crown of roses;** **סִבוּתָא כְּלִילָא דְּחִילְפָא** – **old age is a crown of nettles.**[12]

Dietary advice for the elderly:

תָּנָא מִשְּׁמֵיהּ דְּרַבִּי מֵאִיר – **A Baraisa was taught in the name of R' Meir:** **דּוֹק בְּכַכֵּי וְתִשְׁכַּח בְּנִיגְרֵי** – **CHEW WELL WITH** your **TEETH AND YOU WILL FIND [THE FOOD] IN YOUR STEPS.**[13] **שֶׁנֶּאֱמַר "וַנִּשְׂבַּע־לֶחֶם וַנִּהְיֶה טוֹבִים וְרָעָה לֹא רָאִינוּ"** – **AS IT SAYS:** ***WE WERE SATED WITH BREAD, WE LIVED WELL AND WE SAW NO EVIL.***[14] **אָמַר לֵיהּ שְׁמוּאֵל לְרַב יְהוּדָה** – **Shmuel said to Rav Yehudah:** **שִׁינְנָא** – **Sharp-witted one!** **שְׁרֵי שַׂקִּיךְ וְעַיֵּיל לַחְמָךְ** – **Open your "sack"** (i.e. your mouth) **and let your bread enter.** **עַד אַרְבְּעִין שְׁנִין מֵיכְלָא מְעַלֵּי** – **Until** one is **forty years** old solid **foods are beneficial;** **מִכָּאן וְאֵילָךְ מִשְׁתֵּי מְעַלֵּי** – **from then on, liquids are beneficial.**

Having cited a number of aphorisms, the Gemara records an exchange of barbed aphorisms between a Tanna and a heretic:

אָמַר לֵיהּ הַהוּא גּוֹזָאָה לְרַבִּי יְהוֹשֻׁעַ בֶּן קָרְחָה – **A certain eunuch said to R' Yehoshua ben Korchah,** **מֵהָכָא לְקַרְחִינָא כַּמָּה הָוֵי** – **"How far is it from here to Karchina?"**[15] **אָמַר לֵיהּ** – **[R' Yehoshua] said to [the eunuch],** **כְּמֵהָכָא לְגוֹזְנָיָא** – "As far **as from here to Gozayna!"**[16] **אָמַר לֵיהּ צְדוּקִי** – **The heretical** eunuch **said to [R' Yehoshua],** **בַּרְחָא קַרְחָא בְּאַרְבְּעָה** – **"A bald member of the flock**[17] is sold **for four** dinars!" **אָמַר לֵיהּ** – **[R' Yehoshua] said to [the eunuch],** **עִיזָּקָא שְׁלִיפָא בִּתְמָנְיָא** – **"A castrated,**

NOTES

1. Such as the pungent aroma of mustard [or onions] (*Rashi*).

2. In this verse, Solomon, the author of *Ecclesiastes,* compares the aged human body to a house in ruins.

3. [I.e. the fleshy sides of a person between the ribs and the hip.]

4. The ribs are described as *the guards of the house* because they form a protective wall enclosing the vital internal organs of the body (*Rashi* here and to *Ecclesiastes*).

5. The legs are described as *the powerful men* because they are able to support the entire upper body (*Rashi* here and to *Ecclesiastes*).

6. Most of the teeth fall out in old age (*Rashi* to *Ecclesiastes*).

7. Bei Avidan was a place where religious debates were held between traditional Jews on one side, and deviant Jewish sectarians, such as the Sadducees and the Boethusim, on the other. The debates concerned the meaning of various Scriptural passages (*Rashi; cf. Rabbeinu Chananel*). אֲבִידָן is related to אבד, *destroy,* and בֵּי אֲבִידָן means in effect, may God destroy this house (*Rambam* in his *Commentary* to *Yadayim* 4:6). [It is possible that this institution had another similar name and "Bei Avidan" was simply a derogatory appellation used by the Sages.]

It is not surprising that the Emperor expected R' Yehoshua ben Chananyah to attend the debates at Bei Avidan: R' Yehoshua ben Chananyah was the premier defender of the faith against heretical attacks (see *Chagigah* 5b and *Rabbeinu Chananel* ad loc.; see also *Anaf Yosef* here). Indeed, he even debated a heretic in the Emperor's palace (*Chagigah* ibid.). See above, 116a with notes.

8. [R' Yehoshua explained to the Emperor that he was too old and infirm to participate in the debates at Bei Avidan: The hair on my head is snow white; *its surroundings,* my beard and moustache, have also turned white; my voice is feeble; and my teeth do not function (*Rashi*).

9. I am so old that I walk bent over and shaking and appear to be searching for money I have lost (*Rashi*). Alternatively, R' Yehoshua meant he was growing forgetful. He would search for something, thinking he lost it when in fact the item was still in his hands (*Iyei HaYam* cited in *Eitz Yosef*).

10. I.e. the two legs of youth are better than the three of old age. The third leg is the cane which an elderly person requires for support (*Rashi*).

11. That, is, a person has cause for complaint regarding this matter: He may rightfully bewail his loss (*Rashi*).

12. Youth is fragrant like the rose; old age is foul smelling like the nettle (see *Rabbeinu Chananel*). [The young lead charmed lives; the old confront constant vexations.]

Ben Yehoyada explains that it was not the physical attributes of youth that Rav Dimi was praising. Rather, he was alluding to the immense reward one earns then for resisting the temptation to sin. When one is young and in the peak of health his physical urges are intense. If in spite of this he resists the invitation of his Evil Inclination to sin, his reward is a thousand times greater than if he resists the same invitation when he is old and feeble, for then his physical desires are weaker and less difficult to control.

13. I.e. eat slowly and chew your food well. [It facilitates digestion and ensures that the food provides proper nourishment of your body.] If you do so, you will feel the beneficial effects in the "bounce" of your walk (based on *Rashi* and *Rabbeinu Chananel;* see also *Dr. J. Preuss, Biblical and Talmudic Medicine* 18:2). This advice is directed especially to the elderly, hence its inclusion here (*Maharsha*).

14. *Jeremiah* 44:17. [R' Meir's point seems to be that the verse uses the verb נִשְׂבַּע and not נֹאכַל. The latter denotes any kind of eating or consumption, whereas the former denotes satiety, which is the result of *proper* eating and good digestion. If one eats in the proper manner, the result is וַנִּהְיֶה טוֹבִים וְרָעָה לֹא רָאִינוּ, *we lived well and we saw no evil.*]

15. The eunuch was a heretic, an opponent of the Sages, and R' Yehoshua ben Korchah was bald. The eunuch's question was an insulting play on the word קֵרֵחַ, *bald man*: In effect, he was asking, "How far is it to Baldtown?" (See *Rashi; Maharshal* and *Hagahos Yavetz,* who say that there actually is a place called Karchina.)

16. The verb גוז means *to cut* or *to castrate.* R' Yehoshua retorted with a play on words that amounted to an equally disparaging allusion to the man's castration: "As far as it is from here to Eunuchville." (See *Rashi; Maharshal* and *Hagahos Yavetz* cited in the preceding note.)

17. I.e. a goat. A goat is not enveloped with wool like a sheep: It is therefore referred to as a קַרְחָא, a *baldy* (*Rashi;* see *Rashi* in *Ein Yaakov;* see above, 18b note 30). *Aruch* translates קַרְחָא as a male goat.

ושל בית הכסא רעות של סם ושל שחוק ושל פירות יפות [א] ביום שיזעו שומרי הבית והתעותו וגו' ביום שיזעו שומרי הבית אלו הכסלים והצלעות והתעותו אנשי החיל אלו שוקים ובטלו הטוחנות אלו שינים וחשכו הרואות בארובות אלו עינים א"ל קיסר לר' יהושע בן חנניה מ"ט לא אתית לבי אבידן א"ל טור תלג סחרוני גלידין כלבוהי לא נבחין טחנוהי לא טוחנין בי רב אמרי אדלא אבידנא בחישנא [א] תניא רבי יוסי בר קיסמא אומר טבא תרי מתלת ווי לה לחדא דאזלא ולא אתיא מאי היא א"ר חסדא ינקותא כי אתא רב דימי אמר ינקותא כלילא דוורדא סבותא כלילא [ב] דחילפא תנא משמיה דרבי מאיר דוק בככי ותשכח בניגרי שנאמר [ב] ונשבע לחם ונהיה טובים ורעה לא ראינו א"ל שמואל לרב יהודה [ג] שיננא שרי שקיך ועייל לחמך עד ארבעין שנין מיכלא מעלי מכאן ואילך משתי מעלי א"ל ההוא גוזאה לר' יהושע בן קרחה מהכא לקרחינא כמה הוי א"ל כמהכא לגוזניא א"ל צדוקי ברחא קרחא בארבעה אמר ליה [ד] עיקרא שליפא בתמניא חזייה דלא סיים מסאניה א"ל דעל סוס מלך דעל חמור בן חורין ודמנעלי בריגלוהי בר איניש דלא הא ולא הא דחפיר וקביר טב מיניה א"ל גוזא גוזא תלת אמרת לי תלת שמעת הדרת פנים זקן שמחת לב אשה [ג] נחלת ה' בנים ברוך המקום שמנעך מכולם א"ל קרחא מצויינא אמר ליה עיקרא שליפא תוכחה א"ל רבי לר' שמעון בן חלפתא מפני מה לא הקבלנו פניך ברגל כדרך שהקבילו אבותי לאבותיך א"ל סלעים נעשו גבוהים קרובים נעשו רחוקים משתים נעשו שלש משים שלום בבית בטל: [ד] וסגרו דלתים בשוק וגו' אלו נקביו של אדם בשפל קול הטחנה בשביל קורקבן שאינו טוחן ויקום לקול הצפור שאפילו צפור מנערתו משנתו וישחו כל בנות השיר שאפילו ([ה] קול שירים ושירות) דומות עליו כשוחה ואף ברזילי הגלעדי אמר לדוד [ה] בן שמנים שנה אנכי היום האדע בין טוב לרע מכאן שדעתן של זקנים משתנות [ה] אם יטעם עבדך את אשר אוכל ואת אשר אשתה מכאן ששפתותיהן של זקנים מתרפטות [ה] אם אשמע עוד בקול שרים ושרות מכאן שאזניהם של זקנים מתכבדות אמר רב ברזילי הגלעדי שקרא הוה דההיא אמתא דהויא בי רבי בת תשעין ותרתין שנין והות טעמא קידרא רבא אמר ברזילי הגלעדי שטוף בזמה הוה * וכל השטוף בזמה [ו] זקנה קופצת עליו תניא רבי ישמעאל ברבי יוסי אומר [ז] תלמידי חכמים כל זמן שמזקינין חכמה נתוספת בהם שנאמר [ו] בישישים חכמה ואורך ימים תבונה ועמי הארץ כל זמן שמזקינין טפשות נתוספת בהן שנאמר [ז] מסיר שפה לנאמנים וטעם זקנים יקח [ח] גם מגבוה יראו שאפילו גבשושית קטנה דומה עליו כהרי הרים וחתחתים בדרך בשעה שמהלך בדרך נעשו [א] לו [ח] תוהים וינאץ [ט] השקד זו קליבוסת ויסתבל החגב אלו עגבות ותפר האביונה זו חמדה רב כהנא הוה פסיק סידרא קמיה דרב כי מטא להאי קרא נגיד ואתנח אמר ש"מ בטל ליה חמדיה דרב אמר רב כהנא מאי דכתיב [ט] כי הוא אמר ויהי זו אשה הוא צוה ויעמוד אלו בנים תנא אשה חמת מלא צואה ופיה מלא דם והכל רצין אחריה [ח] כי הולך האדם אל בית עולמו א"ר יצחק [י] מלמד שכל צדיק וצדיק נותנין לו מדור לפי כבודו משל למלך שנכנס הוא ועבדיו לעיר כשהן נכנסין כולן בשער אחד נכנסין כשהן לנין כל אחד ואחד נותנין לו מדור לפי כבודו ואמר רבי יצחק מאי דכתיב [י] כי הילדות והשחרות הבל דברים שאדם עושה בילדותו משחירים פניו לעת זקנתו [כ] ואמר רבי יצחק קשה רימה למת כמחט בבשר החי שנאמר [כ] אך בשרו עליו יכאב ונפשו עליו תאבל אמר רב חסדא נפשו של אדם מתאבלת עליו כל שבעה שנא' [כ] ונפשו עליו תאבל וכתיב [ל] ויעש לאביו אבל שבעת ימים אמר רב יהודה [כ] מת שאין לו מנחמין הולכין י' בני אדם ויושבין במקומו ההוא דשכיב בשבבותיה דרב יהודה לא הוו לו מנחמין כל

רש"י

של בית הכסא. מתוך יסורין: של פירות. כגון ריח חרדל: הכסלים. ליפלאנק"ש: והצלעות. שהן שומרין בני המעיים וחיותו של אדם וסוגרין בעדם: אלו שוקיים. שכחו של אדם נסמך עליהם: לבי אבידן. מקום העשוי להתווכח שם לדוקים וביתוסים עם ישראל במקראות: טור תלג. ההר נעשה שלג כלומר ראשי לבן: סחרוני גלידין. סביבותיו של הר מלאו קרח כלומר שפמי וזקני הלבינו: כלבוהי לא נבחין. קולי אינו נשמע: טחנוהי. השינים: אדלא אבידנא בחישנא. אחר מה שלא אבד ממני אני מפשפש מרוב זקנה אני הולך שחוח ומנענע ונראה כמי שמבקש דינר האבד לו: תרתי טבא מתלת. טובים ב' הרגלים של ימי בחרות מג' של זקנה שצריך משענת עם רגליו: ווי לה. חבל עליה כלומר יש לו להתאונן ולצעוק ווי ההולכת ואינה חוזרת: כלילא דוורדא. נזר של וורד: חילפי. אורטיא"ש: דוק בככי ותשכח בניגרי. אכול הרבה ותמצא האכילה בפסיעותיך שיחזק כחך דוק כמו אכלה מדקה (דניאל ז) לשון כוסס: שרי שקיך. פתח פיך: גוזא. סריס ולדוקי היה: מהכא לקרחינא כמה הוי. כמה מהלך יש מכאן עד הקרח ולהקניטו על קרחתו נתכוון: כמהכא לגוזניא. כמו שמכאן עד הסריס: אמר ליה צדוקי ברחא קרחא בארבעה. שהקרח לקוח בארבע. ברחא קרחא הוא עז על שם שאינו מלובש בצמר כרחל קרוי קרחא: אמר ליה. רבי יהושע: עיקרא שליפא. זה שבליו עקורים ונתוקין לוקחין בשמנה: חזייה. לדוקי לרבי יהושע דלא סיים מסאניה: קרחא מצויינא. אתה הקרח במריבה אתה באת עמדי בתמיה: אמר לו רבי יהושע עיקרא שליפא תוכחה. אתה הסריס להקניטני ולהתווכח עמי באת: לא הקבלנו פניך. לא הקבלנו פני ודרך ענוה קאמר ליה: סלעים. קטנים נעשו גבוהים שזקני: קרובים. נדמין לי כרחוקים: שתים נעשו לי שלש. שצריך אני משענת: משים שלום בבית. אבר תשמיש: לישנא אחרינא קרובים נעשו רחוקים מרוב חלשות של אדם כשמזקין צריך להרחיק רגליו זה מזה: שאינו טוחן. שאין בני מעיו טוחנין אכילתו: קורקבן. הוא המסס שקורין ליגפי"ל: כל בנות השיר. כל קולות של שיר הויין ליה שוחה: שדעתן של זקנים משתנות. דכתיב האדע בין טוב לרע ובזקנה מרובה קאמר: מתרפטות. מתבקעות כמו מנעל המרופט (לעיל דף קמא:): מתכבדות. כמו ואזניו הכבד (ישעיה ו): שטוף. כמו סוס שוטף במלחמה (ירמיה ח) להוט אחר הדבר ורודף: וטעם זקנים יקח. וע"כ מדקשי קראי אהדדי חד מתוקם בחכמים וחד בזקני השוק: מגבוה ייראו. יראים הם הזקנים מגבשושית שבדרכים ואומרים גבוהים הם: תוהים. פחדים: וינאץ השקד. אילן של שקדים יליץ ויהיו בולטין נליס שלו: זו קליבוסת. עלם של הנק"א שהירך תקוע בו בולט ויולא מרוב תשות כחו: ויסתבל החגב. דומה עליו כסבל משא כבד: ותפר האביונה. תבטל התאוה חמדת תשמיש: פסיק סידרא. מסדר פרשיות של פסוקים: נגיד ואיתנח. רב: חמדיה. תאותו: זו אשה. אם לא על פי גזרת המלך לא היתה ראויה להתאוות לה שהיא כחמת מלאה מיאום והכל רצים אחריה: מדור לפי כבודו. מדלא כתיב אל בית העולם ש"מ כל אחד ואחד לבית המוכן לו: בשער אחד. אף כאן הכל מתים בענין אחד: שאדם עושה בילדותו. רוב תשמיש: משחירים פניו. מתיש כחו: שאין לו מנחמים. אין לו אבלים שיהו צריכין לנחמו: במקומו. במקום שמת שם: כל

מסורת הש"ס

א) מס' ד"א זוטא פ"י, ב) [פי' מיני קמשונים ערוך], ג) [לעיל נה. ברכות לו. עירובין נד. חגיגה טו: ר"ה כד: כתובות יג: יז. נג. קדושין לב. גיטין עח: ב"ק יז. טו: לו: ב"ב קלג: ע"ז מג: סנהדרין פ: כריתות יט: נדה יג. יח. כה:], ד) [נ"ל איקא ע' ערוך], ה) [נ"ל קול שרים ושירות], ו) [תענית ה:], ז) [קנים ספ"ג ע"ש ובמפרש], ח) [תרגום של ויתרד ותוה ערוך], ט) עי' מ"ר ויקרא פ' י"ח, י) [ב"מ פג:], כ) ברכות יח: לעיל יג.:

הגהות הב"ח

(א) גמ' נעשה לבו תוהים תוהים וינאץ השקד:

רב נסים גאון

אמר ליה סלעים נעשין גבוהים כמו שנאמר אח"כ שאפילו גבשושית קטנה דומה עליו כהרי הרים ושאר הענין פירשוהו במקצת ההגדה וכך אמרו רחוקים נעשו קרובים אילין עיניא דהוון חמיאן מרחוק אף מקרוב ליתנון חמאן קרובים נעשו רחוקים אילין אודניא דהוון שמעין בחד זמן כדו אף במאה זימנין ליתנון שמעין ב' נעשו ג' חוטרא ותרין ריגליא משים שלום בבית בטל זו תאוה שהיא מעלה שלום

תורה אור השלם

א) בַּיּוֹם שֶׁיָּזֻעוּ שֹׁמְרֵי הַבַּיִת וְהִתְעַוְּתוּ אַנְשֵׁי הֶחָיִל וּבָטְלוּ הַטֹּחֲנוֹת כִּי מִעֵטוּ וְחָשְׁכוּ הָרֹאוֹת בָּאֲרֻבּוֹת: [קהלת יב, ג]

ב) כִּי עָשֹׂה נַעֲשֶׂה אֶת כָּל הַדָּבָר אֲשֶׁר יָצָא מִפִּינוּ לְקַטֵּר לִמְלֶכֶת הַשָּׁמַיִם וְהַסֵּיךְ לָהּ נְסָכִים כַּאֲשֶׁר עָשִׂינוּ אֲנַחְנוּ וַאֲבֹתֵינוּ מְלָכֵינוּ וְשָׂרֵינוּ בְּעָרֵי יְהוּדָה וּבְחֻצוֹת יְרוּשָׁלִָם וַנִּשְׂבַּע לֶחֶם וַנִּהְיֶה טוֹבִים וְרָעָה לֹא רָאִינוּ: [ירמיה מד, יז]

ג) הִנֵּה נַחֲלַת יְיָ בָּנִים שָׂכָר פְּרִי הַבָּטֶן: [תהלים קכז, ג]

ד) וְסֻגְּרוּ דְלָתַיִם בַּשּׁוּק בִּשְׁפַל קוֹל הַטַּחֲנָה וְיָקוּם לְקוֹל הַצִּפּוֹר וְיִשַּׁחוּ כָּל בְּנוֹת הַשִּׁיר: [קהלת יב, ד]

ה) בֶּן שְׁמֹנִים שָׁנָה אָנֹכִי הַיּוֹם הַאֵדַע בֵּין טוֹב לְרָע אִם יִטְעַם עַבְדְּךָ אֶת אֲשֶׁר אֹכַל וְאֶת אֲשֶׁר אֶשְׁתֶּה אִם אֶשְׁמַע עוֹד בְּקוֹל שָׁרִים וְשָׁרוֹת וְלָמָּה יִהְיֶה עַבְדְּךָ עוֹד לְמַשָּׂא אֶל אֲדֹנִי הַמֶּלֶךְ: [שמואל ב יט, לו]

ו) בִּישִׁישִׁים חָכְמָה וְאֹרֶךְ יָמִים תְּבוּנָה: [איוב יב, יב] ז) מֵסִיר שָׂפָה לְנֶאֱמָנִים וְטַעַם זְקֵנִים יִקָּח: [איוב יב, כ] ח) גַּם מִגָּבֹהַּ יִרָאוּ וְחַתְחַתִּים בַּדֶּרֶךְ וְיָנֵאץ הַשָּׁקֵד וְיִסְתַּבֵּל הֶחָגָב וְתָפֵר הָאֲבִיּוֹנָה כִּי הֹלֵךְ הָאָדָם אֶל בֵּית עוֹלָמוֹ וְסָבְבוּ בַשּׁוּק הַסֹּפְדִים: [קהלת יב, ה] ט) כִּי הוּא אָמַר וַיֶּהִי הוּא צִוָּה וַיַּעֲמֹד: [תהלים לג, ט] י) וְהָסֵר כַּעַס מִלִּבֶּךָ וְהַעֲבֵר רָעָה מִבְּשָׂרֶךָ כִּי הַיַּלְדוּת וְהַשַּׁחֲרוּת הָבֶל: [קהלת יא, י] כ) אַךְ בְּשָׂרוֹ עָלָיו יִכְאָב וְנַפְשׁוֹ עָלָיו תֶּאֱבָל: [איוב יד, כב] ל) וַיָּבֹאוּ עַד גֹּרֶן הָאָטָד אֲשֶׁר בְּעֵבֶר הַיַּרְדֵּן וַיִּסְפְּדוּ שָׁם מִסְפֵּד גָּדוֹל וְכָבֵד מְאֹד וַיַּעַשׂ לְאָבִיו אֵבֶל שִׁבְעַת יָמִים: [בראשית נ, י]

עין משפט נר מצוה

מח א מיי' פ"ד מהלכות דעות הל' י"ט טור שו"ע או"ח סימן רמ סעיף יד:

מט ב מיי' פי"ג מהל' אבל הלכה ד סמג עשין ב טוש"ע יו"ד סי' שעו סעיף ג [וברב אלפס מו"ק פ"ג דרל"ז.] וברא"ש שם סימן פט:

רבינו חננאל

השבת לפי שבטל מן המצות והיינו דא"ר יוחנן מאי דכתיב במתים חפשי כיון שמת אדם נעשה חפשי מן המצות: א"ל קיסר לר' יהושע מ"ט לא אתית לבי אבידן. פי' בי אבידן בית שמתקבצין שם החכמים ונושאין ונותנין בדיני כל אומה ולשון השיבו ר' יהושע טור תלג סחרנוהי גלידין כלבוהי לא נבחין טחנוהי לא טחנן בבי רב אמרי (או לא או דן פי' בו) [אדלא אבדן בחשנא] ופירושו ההר כסהו שלג ודומה האדם להר כלומר ראשו כיסתו השיבה. וסביבותיה שהן הלחיים נעשו גלידין והוא הקרח שנקרא גליד. והגרון והלשון אינן מרימין קול. ככי שהן השניים אינן טוחנין המאכל. אדלא אבדן בחשנא. כלומר הזקן שאינו מביט מה שבפניו מתיירא שמא יכה ראשו באבן או בכיוצא בה וממשש בידו ונראה כאלו ממשש בדבר שאבד לו וזהו כמין משל ממשש הזקן מה שלא אבד. טבי תרי מתלת. פי' יותר הוא טוב המהלך על ב' רגליו מן הזקן שצריך משען כגון מקל או שבט להישען עליו והוא כמו רגל שלישי. חבל על דאזלא ולא אתיא. פי' הבחרות הולכת כשמזקין האדם ואינה חוזרת אליו. ינקותא כלילא דוורדי. הבחרות כתר של וורד ריחו נודף ושל זקנה כתר של חילף שריחו מאוס. דוק בככי ותשכח בנגרי. טחון בככי בשניים כלומר אכול כדי שיהיה לך כח להלך ברגליך. א"ל ההוא גאזא חתוך (הערוה) (הביצים) והוא סריס א"ל ר' יהושע בן קרחה מהכא לקרחינא כמה. ביקש להודיעו שהוא קרח והן ביד לו דברים כמלעיג השיבו ר' יהושע כמו הכא לגוזניא כלומר אתה גוזי. עוד אמר ליה ברחא קרחא בארבע. פי' (או) [עז] כבש גדול בד' כספים. השיבו ר' יהושע הדברים מוכיחין שגם אל דברי הסריס הם שבקשו להודיעו כי השלוף יותר מן הקרח. ילמדנו רבינו איקא שליפא בתמניא. פי' תיש נתוק ביצים בשמונה כספים. שמבקשין אותו לעשותו גזרת של שמן. חזייה דלא מסיים מסאניה. פירוש ראהו יחף. א"ל קרחה מצוי. פי' א"ל קרחה מריבה סחרחר. כדכתיב הן לריב ומצה תריבו השיבו ר' יהושע תיש נתוק תוכחה אינם דברי ריב אלא דברי תוכחה. מפני מה לא הקבלנו פניך. למה לא באת אלינו להתראות פנים: מכאן ששפתותיהן של זקנים מתרפטות. פי' מתרפטות מתבקעות והוא מתרופפות אינם מתאמצות להסתם הפה בחזקה. בגבשושית פי' גב קטן של עפר. קליבוסת פירוש מן הפקקולות ומפורש בהלכות טרפות. תרגם דאקליבוסא. ותפר האביונה. זו חמדה (כמו) [כי] בטלה ממנו תאות אשה. פי' תלוניתא כמו של שאין כח בו ממש. גשישה שם קורא דכו לשון עשה

ליקוטי רש"י

שיזעו. ירתתו. שומרי הבית. אלו הצלעות והכסלים המגינים על כל הגוף. והתעותו. אנשי החיל. אלו השוקים שנשען כל הגוף עליהם [קהלת יב, ג].

emasculated member of the flock sells **for eight!"**[18] חֲזִיָּה דְלָא סָיֵים מְסָאנֵיהּ – **[The eunuch] saw that [R' Yehoshua] was not wearing shoes.**[19] אֲמַר לֵיהּ – **[The eunuch] said to [R' Yehoshua],** דְּעַל סוּס מֶלֶךְ – **"He who** rides **on a horse is a king.** דְּעַל חֲמוֹר בֶּן חוֹרִין – **He who** rides **on a donkey is a free man,** וּדְמִנְעָלֵי בְּרִיגְלוֹהִי בַּר אִינִישׁ – **and he who has shoes on his feet is a human being.** דְּלָא הָא וְלָא הָא – But **he who has neither this nor that,** like you who have no shoes, דַּחֲפִיר וְקָבִיר טָב מִינֵּיהּ – then **one for whom a grave is dug and who is** then **buried is better off than he!"** אֲמַר לֵיהּ – **[R' Yehoshua] said to [the eunuch],** גּוֹזָא גּוֹזָא – **"Eunuch, eunuch!** תְּלַת אֲמַרְתְּ לִי – **Three** things **you have said to me;** תְּלַת שְׁמַעְתְּ – **three shall you** now **hear!** הַדְרַת פָּנִים זָקָן – **The glory of a face is** its **beard;** שִׂמְחַת לֵב אִשָּׁה – **the joy of** one's **heart is a wife;** "נַחֲלַת ה' בָּנִים" – and, as Scripture states: ***the heritage*** [bestowed by] ***God*** [upon a person] ***is children.***[20] בָּרוּךְ הַמָּקוֹם שֶׁמְּנָעֲךָ מִכּוּלָּם – **Blessed is the Omnipresent Who has denied you all of them!"** אֲמַר לֵיהּ – Stung by R' Yehoshua's allusion to his physical disabilities, **[the eunuch] said to [R' Yehoshua]:** קַרְחָא מְצוּיְינָא – "You **quarrelsome bald man!** Dare you pick a quarrel with me?!" אֲמַר לֵיהּ – **[R' Yehoshua] said to [the eunuch],** עִיקְרָא שְׁלִיפָא תּוֹכֵחָה – "You **castrated, emasculated one!** Dare you offer **provocation** to me?!"[21]

Another story of physical decline in old age:

אֲמַר לֵיהּ רַבִּי לְרַבִּי שִׁמְעוֹן בֶּן חֲלַפְתָּא – **Rebbi said to R' Shimon ben Chalafta:** מִפְּנֵי מָה לֹא הִקְבַּלְנוּ פָּנֶיךָ בָּרֶגֶל – **"Why did we not call upon you on the festival** כְּדֶרֶךְ שֶׁהִקְבִּילוּ אֲבוֹתַי לַאֲבוֹתֶיךָ – **in the same manner that my forefathers called upon your forefathers?"**[22] אֲמַר לֵיהּ – **[R' Shimon] said to [Rebbi]:** סְלָעִים נַעֲשׂוּ גְּבוֹהִים – "I am too old. **The rocks** I used to easily climb when I was young **have grown tall** in my old age, that is, they seem taller than when I was young. קְרוֹבִים נַעֲשׂוּ רְחוֹקִים – What was **near** to me when I was young **has become distant,** for it is difficult for me to travel those distances now that I am old.[23] מִשְׁתַּיִם נַעֲשׂוּ שָׁלֹשׁ – **From** a person who walks on **two** legs, **I have become** a person who walks on **three,** for I cannot walk without a cane. מֵשִׂים שָׁלוֹם בַּבַּיִת בָּטֵל – **That which promotes peace in the home has ceased."**[24]

The Gemara continues its exposition of the passage in *Ecclesiastes,* which depicts the physical decline that accompanies old age:

"וְסֻגְּרוּ דְלָתַיִם בַּשּׁוּק וגו'" – ***When the doors in the street are shut* etc.** אֵלּוּ נְקָבָיו שֶׁל אָדָם – **These are the orifices of a person**'s body;[25] they shall be stopped up. "בִּשְׁפַל קוֹל הַטַּחֲנָה" בִּשְׁבִיל קוּרְקְבָן שֶׁאֵינוֹ טוֹחֵן – ***When the sound of the grinding is low*** – **on account of the stomach, which does not grind** (i.e. digest) the food. "וְיָקוּם לְקוֹל הַצִּפּוֹר" שֶׁאֲפִילּוּ צִפּוֹר מְנַעַרְתּוֹ מִשְּׁנָתוֹ – ***When one rises at the voice of the bird*** – **even the chirping of a bird wakes [an aged person] from his sleep.**[26] "וְיִשַּׁחוּ כָּל־בְּנוֹת הַשִּׁיר" שֶׁאֲפִילּוּ קוֹל שָׁרִים וְשָׁרוֹת דּוֹמוֹת עָלָיו כְּשׁוּחָה – ***And all the voices of song grow dim*** – **even the voices of male singers and female singers sound to him like a whisper** as a result of the deterioration of his hearing in old age. וְאַף בַּרְזִילַּי הַגִּלְעָדִי אָמַר לְדָוִד "בֶּן־שְׁמֹנִים שָׁנָה אָנֹכִי הַיּוֹם הַאֵדַע בֵּין־טוֹב לְרָע" – **Barzilai the Gileadite,**[27] **too, said** as much **to David:**[28] ***I am eighty years old today. Can I distinguish between good and bad?*** מִכָּאן שֶׁדַּעְתָּן שֶׁל זְקֵנִים מִשְׁתַּנּוֹת – **From here** we infer **that the senses of the elderly undergo change** in advanced old age.[29] "אִם־יִטְעַם עַבְדְּךָ אֶת־אֲשֶׁר אֹכַל וְאֶת־אֲשֶׁר אֶשְׁתֶּה" מִכָּאן שֶׁשִּׂפְתוֹתֵיהֶן שֶׁל זְקֵנִים מִתְרַפְּטוֹת – ***Can your servant*** [i.e. can I] ***taste what I eat and what I drink?*** No! **From here** we infer **that the lips of elderly people split.**[30] "אִם־אֶשְׁמַע עוֹד בְּקוֹל שָׁרִים וְשָׁרוֹת" מִכָּאן שֶׁאָזְנֵיהֶם שֶׁל זְקֵנִים מִתְכַּבְּדוֹת – ***Can I still hear the singing of male singers and female singers?*** No! **From here** we infer **that the ears of elderly people become heavy,** that is, unable to hear properly.

NOTES

18. In our text of the Gemara, this is R' Yehoshua's retort to the eunuch. That is, the eunuch has said R' Yehoshua is nothing more than a cheap bald goat; R' Yehoshua replies with caustic humor, "Well, then, if we compare ourselves to goats *you* are indeed entitled to more prestige, for a castrated goat is renowned for its succulent flavor and is worth twice as much as a non-castrated one!" (*Maharsha*).

According to the textual versions of *Rabbeinu Chananel* and *Aruch,* both statements were made by the eunuch, who was saying that a castrated goat is more valuable than a bald one, implying that it is better to be castrated than bald.

19. It is surprising that a person of R' Yehoshua's stature was walking barefoot, something the Gemara previously indicated is inappropriate (see *Rashi* on 129a above ד"ה ויקח). [Furthermore, according to *Rashbam* (*Pesachim* 112a ד"ה ר' יהושע בן קרחה), R' Akiva commanded R' Yehoshua ben Korchah not to withhold shoes from his feet (cf. *Tosafos* ad loc. and above, 150a ד"ה ורבי יהושע בן קרחה היא who dispute the identification of this person as R' Yehoshua ben Korchah).]

Maharsha suggests that the incident here took place on Yom Kippur or Tishah B'Av, when one is not permitted to wear shoes.

20. *Psalms* 127:3.

21. This follows *Rashi* (see also the first interpretation in *Aruch* ערך שליפא). Alternatively, R' Yehoshua was saying, "I am not being contentious; I am rebuking you for your insulting behavior" (*Rabbeinu Chananel* and second interpretation in *Aruch* ibid.).

22. I.e. why did I not receive the courtesy of a visit from you on the last festival? Your family has always paid its respects to my family over the generations by paying a formal call on us on the festivals. Although Rebbe meant to ask, "Why did you not visit me?" he couched his question in polite terms, "Why did we not go to visit you?" This is an example of Rebbi's humility (*Rashi*).

23. Alternatively, I used to be able [to stand and maintain my balance when I wanted] to keep my two legs together; in old age, I am so weak that [I cannot do so unless] I distance them from each other somewhat (*Rashi;* see also *Chullin* 24b where a young healthy person is defined as someone who can stand on one foot while taking off and putting on his shoe).

24. This is a reference to the male organ [and to the cessation of marital relations in old age] (*Rashi*). If I leave my wife at home by herself in order to pay you a visit, she will become angry, and I will have no way of restoring marital harmony (*Hagahos Yavetz; see also Eitz Yosef; cf. Ben Yehoyada*).

25. The orifices of the human body normally open and close like doors (*Vayikra Rabbah* 18:1).

26. When an elderly person is asleep and hears the chirping of birds he awakes suddenly in fright because he thinks it is the sound of burglars (ibid.).

27. King David's son Absalom launched a widespread rebellion against his father. David fled Jerusalem and went to Machanaim, across the Jordan. There, Barzilai the Gileadite and a number of other individuals provided David and his famished followers with food and supplies (*II Samuel* 17:27-29). Subsequently, Absalom was killed and the rebellion collapsed. As David was making his way back to Jerusalem, Barzilai came to greet him at Gilgal, just before David crossed the Jordan. Desiring to reward Barzilai's loyalty during the rebellion, David invited Barzilai to move to Jerusalem and live there as an honored pensioner of the king. Barzilai declined, citing his old age (ibid. 19:32-35).

28. *II Samuel* 19:36.

29. I.e. the rational faculty, including the ability to distinguish between the good and the bad, the sensible and the foolish, deteriorates in advanced old age. It was to this deterioration that Barzilai referred when he bemoaned the state of his health (see *Rashi* and *Maharsha*).

30. *Rashi.* Alternatively, this term is translated as *part*; i.e. the lower lip hangs loosely down, preventing the elderly person from closing his mouth properly and enjoying his food (see *Aruch* ערך מרפט; *Biblical and Talmudic Medicine* 2:4).

ושל בית הכסא רעות של סם ושל שחוק ושל פירות יפות א) ביום שיזעו שומרי הבית והתעותו וגו' ביום שיזעו שומרי הבית אלו הכסלים והצלעות והתעותו אנשי החיל אלו שוקים ובטלו הטוחנות אלו שינים וחשכו הרואות בארובות אלו עינים א"ל קיסר לר' יהושע בן חנניה מ"ט לא אתית לבי אבידן א"ל טור תלג סחרוני גלידין כלבוהי לא נבחין טחנוהי לא טוחנין בי רב אמרי אדלא אבידנא בחישנא ט) תניא רבי יוסי בר קיסמא אומר טבא תרי מתלת ווי לה לחדא דאזלא ולא אתיא מאי היא א"ר חסדא ינקותא כי אתא רב דימי אמר ינקותא כלילא דוורדא סבותא כלילא י) דחילפא תנא משמיה דרבי מאיר דוק בכבי ותשכח בניגרי שנאמר ב) ונשבע לחם ונהיה טובים ורעה לא ראינו א"ל שמואל לרב יהודה ג) שיננא שרי שקיך ועייל לחמך עד ארבעין שנין מיכלא מעלי מכאן ואילך משתי מעלי א"ל ההוא גוזאה לר' יהושע בן קרחה מהכא לקרחינא כמה הוי א"ל כמהכא לגוזניא א"ל צדוקי ברחא קרחא בארבעה אמר ליה ד) עיקרא שליפא בתמניא חזייה דלא סיים מסאניה א"ל דעל סוס מלך דעל חמור בן חורין ודמנעלי בריגלוהי בר איניש דלא הא ולא הא דחפיר וקביר טב מיניה א"ל גוזא גוזא תלת אמרת לי תלת שמעת הדרת פנים זקן שמחת לב אשה ג) נחלת ה' בנים ברוך המקום שמנעך מכולם א"ל קרחא מצויינא אמר ליה עיקרא שליפא תוכחה א"ל רבי לר' שמעון בן חלפתא מפני מה לא הקבלנו פניך ברגל כדרך שהקבילו אבותי לאבותיך א"ל סלעים נעשו גבוהים קרובים נעשו רחוקים משתים נעשו שלש משים שלום בבית בטל: ד) וסגרו דלתים בשוק וגו' אלו נקביו של אדם בשפל קול הטחנה בשביל קורקבן שאינו טוחן ויקום לקול הצפור שאפילו צפור מנערתו משנתו וישחו כל בנות השיר שאפילו (ה) קול שירים (ושירות) דומות עליו כשוחה ואף ברזילי הגלעדי אמר לדוד ה) בן שמנים שנה אנכי היום האדע בין טוב לרע מכאן שדעתן של זקנים משתנות ה) אם יטעם עבדך את אשר אוכל ואת אשר אשתה מכאן ששפתותיהן של זקנים מתרפטות ה) אם אשמע עוד בקול שרים ושרות מכאן שאזניהם של זקנים מתכבדות אמר רב ברזילי הגלעדי שקרא הוה דההיא אמתא דהויא בי רבי בת תשעין ותרתין שנין והות טעמא קידרא רבא אמר ברזילי הגלעדי שטוף בזמה הוה *וכל השטוף בזמה י) זקנה קופצת עליו תניא רבי ישמעאל ברבי יוסי אומר ז) תלמידי חכמים כל זמן שמזקינין חכמה נתוספת בהם שנאמר ו) בישישים חכמה ואורך ימים תבונה ועמי הארץ כל זמן שמזקינין טפשות נתוספת בהן שנאמר ז) מסיר שפה לנאמנים וטעם זקנים יקח ח) גם מגבוה ייראו שאפילו גבשושית קטנה דומה עליו כהררי הרים וחתחתים בדרך בשעה שמהלך בדרך נעשו (א) לו ח) תוהים וינאץ ט) השקד זו קליבוסת ויסתבל החגב אלו עגבות ותפר האביונה זו חמדה פסיק סידרא קמיה דרב כהנא הוה פסיק סידרא קמיה דרב כי מטא להאי קרא נגיד ואתנח אמר ש"מ בטל ליה חמדיה דרב אמר רב כהנא מאי דכתיב ט) כי הוא אמר ויהי זו אשה הוא צוה ויעמוד אלו בנים תנא אשה חמת מלא צואה ופיה מלא דם והכל רצין אחריה ח) כי הולך האדם אל בית עולמו א"ר יצחק י) מלמד שכל צדיק וצדיק נותנין לו מדור לפי כבודו משל למלך שנכנס הוא ועבדיו לעיר כשהן נכנסין כולן בשער אחד נכנסין כשהן לנין כל אחד ואחד נותנין לו מדור לפי כבודו ואמר רבי יצחק מאי דכתיב י) כי הילדות והשחרות הבל דברים שאדם עושה בילדותו משחירים פניו לעת זקנתו כ) ואמר רבי יצחק קשה רימה למת כמחט בבשר החי שנאמר כ) אך בשרו עליו יכאב ונפשו עליו תאבל אמר רב חסדא נפשו של אדם מתאבלת עליו כל שבעה שנא' ל) ויעש לאביו אבל שבעת ימים אמר רב יהודה ב מת שאין לו מנחמין הולכין י' בני אדם ויושבין במקומו ההוא דשכיב בשבבותיה דרב יהודה לא הוו ליה מנחמין כל

רש"י

של בית הכסא. מתוך יסורין: של פירות. כגון ריח חרדל: הכסלים. ליפלאנק"ש: והצלעות. שהן שומרין בני המעיים וחיותו של אדם וסוגרין בעדם: אלו שוקיים. שכחו של אדם נסמך עליהם: לבי אבידן. מקום העשוי להתווכח שם לדוקים וביייתוסים עם ישראל במקראות: טור תלג. ההר נעשה שלג כלומר ראשי לבן: סחרוני גלידין. סביבותיו של הר מלאו קרח כלומר שפמי וזקני הלבינו: כלבוהי לא נבחין. קולי אינו נשמע: טחנוהי. השיניים: אדלא אבידנא בחישנא. אחר מה שלא אבד ממני אני מפשפש מרוב זקנה אני הולך שחוח ומנענע ונראה כמי שמבקש דינר שנאבד לו: תרתי טבא מתלת. טובים ב' הרגלים של ימי בחרות מג' של זקנה שצריך משענת עם רגליו: ווי לה. חבל עליה כלומר יש לו להתאונן ולצעוק ווי ההולכת ואינה חוזרת: כלילא דוורדא. נזר של וורד: חילפי. אורטיא"ש: דוק בכבי ותשכח בניגרי. אכול הרבה וממלא האכילה בפסיעותיך שיחזק כחך דוק דוק כמו אכלה מדקה (דניאל ז) לשון כוסס: שרי שקיך. פתח פיך: גוזא. סריס ולדוקי היה: מהכא לקרחינא כמה הוי. כמה מהלך יש מכאן עד הקרח ולהקניטו על קרחתו נתכוון: כמהכא לגוזניא. כמו שמכאן עד הסרים: אמר ליה צדוקי ברחא קרחא בארבעה. שהקרח לקוח בארבע. ברחא קרחא הוא עז על שם שאינו מלובש בצמר כרחל קרוי קרחא: אמר ליה. רבי יהושע: עיקרא שליפא. שה שבילוי עקורים ונתוקין לוקחין בשמנה: חזייה. לדוקי לרבי יהושע דלא סיים מסאניה: קרחא מצויינא. אתה הקרח במריבה אתה בא עמדי בתמיה: אמר לו רבי יהושע עיקרא שליפא תוכחה. אתה הסרים להקניטני ולהתווכח עמי באת: לא הקבלנו פניך. לא הקבלת פני ודרך ענוה קאמר ליה: סלעים. קטנים נעשו גבוהים שזקנתי: קרובים. נדמין לי כרחוקים: שתים נעשו לי שלש. שצריך אני משענת: משים שלום בבית. אבר תשמיש: לישנא אחרינא קרובים נעשו רחוקים מרוב חלשות של אדם כשמזקין צריך להרחיק רגליו זה מזה: שאינו טוחן. שאין בני מעיו טוחנין אכילתו: קורקבן. הוא המסס שקורין ליפי"ל: כל בנות השיר. כל קולות של שיר הוין ליה שוחה: שדעתן של זקנים משתנות. דכתיב האדע בין טוב לרע וזקנה מרובה קאמר: מתרפטות. מתבקעות כמו מנעל המרופש (לעיל דף קמא:): מתכבדות. כמו ואזניו הכבד (ישעיה ו): שטוף. כמו סוס שוטף במלחמה (ירמיה ח): וטעם זקנים יקח. וע"כ מדקשי קראי אהדדי חד מתוקם בחכמים וחד בזקני השוק: מגבוה ייראו. יראים הם הזקנים מגבשושית שבדרכים ואומרים גבוהים הם: תוהים. פחדים: וינאץ השקד. אילן של שקדים ילין ויהיו בולטין נצים שלו: זו קליבוסת. עצם של הנק"א שהירך תקוע בו בולט ויוצא מרוב תשות כחו: ויסתבל החגב. דומה עליו כסבל משא כבד: ותפר האביונה. תבטל התאוה חמדת תשמיש: פסיק סידרא. מסדר פרשיות של פסוקים: נגיד ואיתנח. רב: חמדיה. תאותו: זו אשה. אם לא על פי גזרת המלך לא היתה ראויה להתאוות לה שהיא כחמת מלאה מיאוס והכל רצים אחריה: מדור לפי כבודו. מדלא כתיב אל בית העולם ש"מ כל אחד ואחד לבית המוכן לו: בשער אחד. אף כאן כל מתים בענין אחד: שאדם עושה בילדותו. רוב תשמיש: משחירים פניו. מתיש כחו: שאין לו מנחמים. אין לו אבלים שיהו צריכין לנחמו: במקומו. במקום שמת שם: כל

עין משפט נר מצוה

מח א מיי' פ"ד מהלכות דעות הל"ט טור שו"ע או"ח סימן רמ סעיף יד:

מט ב מיי' פי"ג מהל' אבל הלכה ד סמג עשין ב טוש"ע יו"ד סי' שעו סעיף ג [וברב אלפס מו"ק פ"ג דרל"ו.] וברא"ש שם סימן פט:

רבינו חננאל

השבת לפי שבטל מן המצות והיינו דא"ר יוחנן מאי דכתיב במתים חפשי כיון שמת אדם נעשה חפשי מן המצות: א"ל קיסר לר' יהושע מ"ט לא אתית לבי אבידן. פי' בי אבידן בית שמתקבצין שם החכמים ונושאין ונותנין בדיני כל אומה ולשון השיבו ר' יהושע טור תלג סחרנוהי גלידין כלבוהי לא נבחין טחנוהי לא טחנן בבי רב אמרי (או לא או דן פי' בו) [אדלא אבדן בחשנא] ופירושו ההר כסהו שלג ודומה האדם להר כלומר ראשו כיסתו השיבה. וסביבותיה שהן הלחיים נעשו גלידין והוא הקרח שנקרא גליד. והגרון והלשון אינן מרימין קול. ככי שהן השניים אינן טוחנין המאכל. אדלא אבדן בחשנא. כלומר הזקן שאינו מביט מה שבפניו מתיירא שמא יכה ראשו באבן או בכיוצא בה וממשש בידו ונראה כאלו ממשש בדבר שאבד לו וזהו כמין משל ממשש הזקן מה שלא אבד. טבי תרי מתלת. פי' יותר הוא טוב המהלך על ב' רגליו מן הזקן שצריך משען כגון מקל או שבט להישען עליו והוא כמו רגל שלישי. חבל על דאזלא ולא אתיא. פי' הבחרות הולכת כשמזקין האדם ואינה חוזרת אליו. ינקותא כלילא דוורדי. הבחרות כתר של וורד ריחו נודף ושל זקנה כתר של חילף שריחו מאוס. דוק בככי ותשכח בנגרי. טחון בככי בשנים כלומר אכול כדי שיהיה לך כח להלך ברגליך. א"ל ההוא גאזא חתוך (הערוה) [הביצים] והוא סריס א"ל ר' יהושע בן קרחה מהכא לקרחוניא כמה. ביקש להודיעו שהוא קרח והן ביר לו דברים כמלעיג והשיבו ר' יהושע כמו הכא לגזוניא כלומר אתה גזוי. עוד אמר ליה ברחא קרחא בארבע. פי' (או) [עור] כבש גדול בד' כספים. השיבו ר' יהושע הדברים מוכיחין שגם אלו דברי הסריס הם שבקשו להודיעו כי השלוף ביוקר יותר מן הקרח. ילמדנו רבינו איקא שליפא בתמניא. פי' עור תיש נתוק ביצים בשמונה כספים. שמבקשין אותו לעשותו נודות של שמן. חזייה דלא מסיים מסאניה. פירוש ראהו יחף כו'. א"ל קרחה מצוי. פי' א"ל קרחה מריבה סחרחר. כדכתיב הן לריב ומצה וגו' השיבו ר' יהושע תיש נתוק תוכחה אינם דברי ריב אלא דברי תוכחה. מפני מה לא הקבלנו פניך. למה לא באת אלינו להתראות פנים: מיכן ששפתותיהן של זקנים מתרפטות. פי' מתרפטות משתרבבות והוא מתרפטות אינם מתאמצת להסתם הפה בחזקה. גבשושית פי' גב קטן של עפר. קליבוסת פירוש מן הפקוקלות ומפורש באלו טרפות. תרבא דאקליבוסתא. ותפר האביונה. זו חמדה (כמו) [כי] בטלה ממנו תאות אשה. פי' טלוניתא כמו על שאין בה ממש. גשייה שם ידו עליו מלשון נגששה:

מסורת הש"ס

א) מס' ד"א זוטא פ"י, ב) [פי' מיני קמשונים ערוך], ג) [לעיל נה. ברכות לו. עירובין נד. חגיגה טו: ר"ה כד: כתובות יב: יד. נג. קדושין לב. גיטין עח: ב"ק יז. טו: לו: ב"ב קלג: ע"ז מג: סנהדרין פ: כריתות יט: נדה יג. יז. כה:], ד) [נ"ל איקא ע' בערוך], ה) [נ"ל קול שרים ושרות], ו) [תענית ה:], ז) [קנים ספ"ג ע"ש ובמפרש], ח) [תרגום של ויחרד ותוה ערוך], ט) עי' מ"ר ויקרא פ' י"ח, י) [ב"מ פג:], כ) ברכות יח: לעיל יג:.

הגהות הב"ח

(א) גמ' נעשה לבו תוהים ויגאץ השקד:

רב נסים גאון

אמר ליה סלעים נעשין גבוהים כמו שנאמר אח"כ שאפילו גבשושית קטנה דומה עליו כהרי הרים ושאר הענין פירשוהו במקצת ההגדה וכך אמרו רחוקים נעשו קרובים אילין עיניא דהוון חמיאן מרחוק אף מקרוב ליתנון חמאן קרובים נעשו רחוקים אילין אודניא דהוון שמעין בחד זמן כדו אף במאה זימנין ליתנון שמעין ב' נעשו ג' חוטרא ותרין ריגליא משים שלום בבית בטל זו תאוה שהיא מעלה שלום

תורה אור השלם

א) בַּיּוֹם שֶׁיָּזֻעוּ שֹׁמְרֵי הַבַּיִת וְהִתְעַוְּתוּ אַנְשֵׁי הֶחָיִל וּבָטְלוּ הַטֹּחֲנוֹת כִּי מִעֵטוּ וְחָשְׁכוּ הָרֹאוֹת בָּאֲרֻבּוֹת: [קהלת יב, ג]

ב) כִּי עָשֹׂה נַעֲשֶׂה אֶת כָּל הַדָּבָר אֲשֶׁר יָצָא מִפִּינוּ לְקַטֵּר לִמְלֶכֶת הַשָּׁמַיִם וְהַסֵּיךְ לָהּ נְסָכִים כַּאֲשֶׁר עָשִׂינוּ אֲנַחְנוּ וַאֲבֹתֵינוּ מְלָכֵינוּ וְשָׂרֵינוּ בְּעָרֵי יְהוּדָה וּבְחֻצוֹת יְרוּשָׁלָיִם וַנִּשְׂבַּע לֶחֶם וַנִּהְיֶה טוֹבִים וְרָעָה לֹא רָאִינוּ: [ירמיה מד, יז]

ג) הִנֵּה נַחֲלַת יְיָ בָּנִים שָׂכָר פְּרִי הַבָּטֶן: [תהלים קכז, ג]

ד) וְסֻגְּרוּ דְלָתַיִם בַּשּׁוּק בִּשְׁפַל קוֹל הַטַּחֲנָה וְיָקוּם לְקוֹל הַצִּפּוֹר וְיִשַּׁחוּ כָּל בְּנוֹת הַשִּׁיר: [קהלת יב, ד]

ה) בֶּן שְׁמֹנִים שָׁנָה אָנֹכִי הַיּוֹם הַאֵדַע בֵּין טוֹב לְרָע אִם יִטְעַם עַבְדְּךָ אֶת אֲשֶׁר אֹכַל וְאֶת אֲשֶׁר אֶשְׁתֶּה אִם אֶשְׁמַע עוֹד בְּקוֹל שָׁרִים וְשָׁרוֹת וְלָמָּה יִהְיֶה עַבְדְּךָ עוֹד לְמַשָּׂא אֶל אֲדֹנִי הַמֶּלֶךְ: [שמואל ב יט, לו]

ו) בִּישִׁישִׁים חָכְמָה וְאֹרֶךְ יָמִים תְּבוּנָה: [איוב יב, יב] ז) מֵסִיר שָׂפָה לְנֶאֱמָנִים וְטַעַם זְקֵנִים יִקָּח: [איוב יב, כ] ח) גַּם מִגָּבֹהַּ יִרָאוּ וְחַתְחַתִּים בַּדֶּרֶךְ וְיָנֵאץ הַשָּׁקֵד וְיִסְתַּבֵּל הֶחָגָב וְתָפֵר הָאֲבִיּוֹנָה כִּי הֹלֵךְ הָאָדָם אֶל בֵּית עוֹלָמוֹ וְסָבְבוּ בַשּׁוּק הַסֹּפְדִים: [קהלת יב, ה] ט) כִּי הוּא אָמַר וַיֶּהִי הוּא צִוָּה וַיַּעֲמֹד: [תהלים לג, ט] י) וְהָסֵר כַּעַס מִלִּבֶּךָ וְהַעֲבֵר רָעָה מִבְּשָׂרֶךָ כִּי הַיַּלְדוּת וְהַשַּׁחֲרוּת הָבֶל: [קהלת יא, י] כ) אַךְ בְּשָׂרוֹ עָלָיו יִכְאָב וְנַפְשׁוֹ עָלָיו תֶּאֱבָל: [איוב יד, כב] ל) וַיָּבֹאוּ עַד גֹּרֶן הָאָטָד אֲשֶׁר בְּעֵבֶר הַיַּרְדֵּן וַיִּסְפְּדוּ שָׁם מִסְפֵּד גָּדוֹל וְכָבֵד מְאֹד וַיַּעַשׂ לְאָבִיו אֵבֶל שִׁבְעַת יָמִים: [בראשית נ, י]

ליקוטי רש"י

שיזועו. ירתתו. שומרי הבית. אלו הצלעות והכסלים המגינים על כל חלל הגוף. והתעותו. יאחזם עוות שקורין קרנפ"ף והתעותו אנקרופירונ"ט בלע"ז. אנשי החיל. אלו השוקים שנשען כל הגוף עליהם [קהלת יב, ג]. רבי יהושע בן קרחה. יהושע בנו של ר' עקיבא הוא יהושע בן קרחה שר' עקיבא קרח היה כדאמרי' בבכורות (נח.) חוץ מן הקרח הזה [שבועות ו.]. הא דגרסינן בכוליה הש"ס רבי יהושע בן קרחה היינו בן של ר"ע דגרסינן התם (שבועות ו.) אמר לו ר' יהושע בנו של ר"ע לר"ע [בכורות נח. ע"ש בתוס']. ברחא קרחא. עז ברחא קרוי כל צאן והעז קרי ליה קרחא על שם שאין לו צמר כל כך [סנהדרין סג:]. עז שאינה מסורבל בצמר כרחל [ע"ז כח:]. ודמנעלי בריגלוהי. שאין לך בזוי מן המהלך יחף בשוק [לעיל קכט.]. בשפל קול הטחנה. קול ריחים הטוחנים מאכל שבמעיו והוא הקורקבן והמסס. ויקום לקול הצפור. שאפילו קול צפור מנערתו משנתו משהזקין. וישחו כל בנות השיר. כל קולות של כלי השיר דומות עליו כשיחה ולפי פשוטו משמעו ישחו כמו ישפלו כל שרים ושרות יהיו שפלים בעיניו וכן ברזילי הגלעדי אמר לדוד (ש"ב יט) אם אשמע עוד בקול שרים ושרות [קהלת שם, ד]. גם מגבוה ייראו. מגבשושיות ותלוליות שבדרכים הוא דואג לבא לשוק פן יכשל בהם. וחתחתים בדרך. אימות ומחתת הרבה בדרכים יש לו. חתחתים. לשון כפול הוא בתיבה כמו גלגלים קשקשים זלזלים [עי' במהרש"א ח"א]. וינאץ השקד. לשון (שה"ש ז) הנצו הרמונים שהרי האל"ף לא נקראת בה אמרו רבותינו זו קליבוסת הנק"א בלע"ז שעגם הירך תקוע בה וכזקנותו בשרו כמוש והעגם בולט כמו נץ האילן שהוא בולט. השקד. אילן של שקדים כלומר שתקפון הזקנה עליו כשקד זה הממהר להנץ לפני כל האילנות. ויסתבל החגב. אלו העגבות שיהיו עגבותיו דומות עליו כסובל משא כבד. ויסתבל. אישדריי"ד שורפייש"ן בלע"ז. ותפר האביונה. חמדת תאות נשים שאינו נזקק לנשים לתשמיש אביונה תאוה כמו (תהלים קיט) תאבתי לישועתך [שם, ה]. קשה רימה. עקיצת הרימה [ברכות יח:].

The Gemara cites evidence that contradicts Barzilai's assertion:

אָמַר רַב – Rav said: **בַּרְזִילַּי הַגִּלְעָדִי שַׁקְרָא הֲוָה – Barzilai the Gileadite was a liar,** for it is not true that old age necessarily leads to such deterioration. **דְּהַהִיא אַמְתָא דַּהֲוָיָא בֵּי רַבִּי – For there was a certain maidservant in Rebbi's household,** **בַּת תִּשְׁעִין וְתַרְתֵּין שְׁנִין – who was ninety-two years old.** **וַהֲוַת טָעֲמָא קִידְרָא – She used to taste** the food while it was being cooked in **the pot** to see if it needed anything to enhance the flavor. Thus, we see that a woman who was much older than the eighty-year-old Barzilai still possessed an excellent sense of taste, contrary to Barzilai's assertion.

The Gemara attributes Barzilai's physical deterioration to a life-style of dissipation:

רָבָא אָמַר – Rava said: **בַּרְזִילַּי הַגִּלְעָדִי שָׁטוּף בְּזִמָּה הֲוָה – Barzilai the Gileadite was steeped in immorality,** **וְכָל הַשָּׁטוּף בְּזִמָּה זִקְנָה קוֹפֶצֶת עָלָיו – and whoever is steeped in immorality, old age comes upon him suddenly.** Thus, Barzilai's physical deterioration was not due to his advanced age but to the life of dissipation he had led.

A Baraisa contrasts the effects of old age on Torah scholars and on those who have no such knowledge:

תַּנְיָא – It has been taught in a Baraisa:[31] **רַבִּי יִשְׁמָעֵאל בְּרַבִּי יוֹסֵי אוֹמֵר – R' YISHMAEL THE SON OF R' YOSE SAYS:** **תַּלְמִידֵי חֲכָמִים כָּל זְמַן שֶׁמַּזְקִינִין חָכְמָה נִתּוֹסֶפֶת בָּהֶם – TORAH SCHOLARS – THE OLDER THEY BECOME THE MORE DOES WISDOM INCREASE WITHIN THEM,**[32] **שֶׁנֶּאֱמַר ,,בִּישִׁישִׁים חָכְמָה וְאֹרֶךְ יָמִים תְּבוּנָה" – AS IT IS STATED:**[33] ***IN THE AGED IS WISDOM AND [IN] LENGTH OF DAYS UNDERSTANDING.*** **וְעַמֵּי הָאָרֶץ – AS FOR THOSE WHO ARE BEREFT OF TORAH KNOWLEDGE,** **כָּל זְמַן שֶׁמַּזְקִינִין טִפְּשׁוּת נִתּוֹסֶפֶת בָּהֶן – THE OLDER THEY BECOME THE MORE DOES FOOLISHNESS INCREASE WITHIN THEM,** **שֶׁנֶּאֱמַר ,,מֵסִיר שָׂפָה לְנֶאֱמָנִים וְטַעַם זְקֵנִים יִקָּח" – AS IT IS STATED: *HE DISTORTS THE UTTERANCES OF THE TRUSTWORTHY, AND TAKES REASON AWAY FROM THE ELDERS.***[34]

The Gemara resumes its explication of the passage in *Ecclesiastes*:

,,גַּם מִגָּבֹהַּ יִרָאוּ" – They even fear a height – **שֶׁאֲפִילּוּ גַּבְשׁוּשִׁית קְטַנָּה דּוֹמָה עָלָיו כְּהָרֵי הָרִים – this indicates that even a small mound appears to [the elderly person] like the highest of mountains;**[35] ***,,וְחַתְחַתִּים בַּדֶּרֶךְ" – and terrors on the road –*** **בְּשָׁעָה שֶׁמְּהַלֵּךְ בַּדֶּרֶךְ נַעֲשׂוּ לוֹ תְּהָהִים – when he walks on a road he is full of anxieties;**[36] ***,,וְיָנֵאץ הַשָּׁקֵד" זוֹ קְלִיבוּסֶת – and the almond tree blossoms*** **– this is the hip;**[37] ***,,וְיִסְתַּבֵּל הֶחָגָב" אֵלּוּ עֲגָבוֹת – and the grasshopper becomes a burden*** **– these are the buttocks;**[38] ***,,וְתָפֵר הָאֲבִיּוֹנָה" זוֹ חֶמְדָּה – and the aviyonah fails*** **– this is** a reference to **desire** for women which wanes in old age.[39]

A story concerning the diminishing of desire in old age:

רַב כָּהֲנָא הֲוָה פָּסִיק סִידְרָא קַמֵּיהּ דְּרַב – Rav Kahana was reciting a section of Scripture before Rav. **כִּי מָטָא לְהַאי קְרָא – When [Rav Kahana] came to this verse,** the verse in *Ecclesiastes* that refers to the waning of desire in old age, **נָגִיד וְאִתְּנַח – [Rav] uttered a long sigh.** **אָמַר – [Rav Kahana] said:** **שְׁמַע מִינָּהּ בְּטֵל לֵיהּ חֶמְדֵּיהּ דְּרַב – You may infer from this** sigh **that Rav's desire has ceased.**[40]

Regarding man's natural desire for woman:

אָמַר רַב כָּהֲנָא – Rav Kahana said: **מַאי דִּכְתִיב ,,כִּי הוּא אָמַר וַיֶּהִי" – What is the meaning of that which is written:**[41] ***For [God] spoke, and it came to be?*** **זוֹ אִשָּׁה – This is** a reference to **woman.**[42] ***,,הוּא-צִוָּה וַיַּעֲמֹד" אֵלּוּ בָנִים – He commanded, and it took form*** **– these are** one's **children.**[43] **תָּנָא – A Baraisa has taught:** **אִשָּׁה חֵמֶת מָלֵא צוֹאָה – A woman** is like **a leather jug full of excretions,** **וּפִיהָ מָלֵא דָּם – whose opening is full of blood** (i.e. menstrual blood). **וְהַכֹּל רָצִין אַחֲרֶיהָ – Yet** in spite of this not so appealing reality, **everyone chases after her!**[44]

The Gemara resumes its exposition of *Ecclesiastes*:

,,כִּי-הֹלֵךְ הָאָדָם אֶל-בֵּית עוֹלָמוֹ" – So man goes to his eternal home. **אָמַר רַבִּי יִצְחָק – R' Yitzchak said:** **מְלַמֵּד שֶׁכָּל צַדִּיק וְצַדִּיק נוֹתְנִין לוֹ מָדוֹר לְפִי כְבוֹדוֹ – This teaches that every righteous person is given lodgings befitting his eminence.**[45]

NOTES

31. This Baraisa parallels the last Mishnah in *Kinim* (3:6). There is a view that the passage in *Kinim* is actually a Baraisa appended to the Mishnah (*R' Shlomo Algazi* יבין שמועה 322).

32. Unlike the *am haaretz*, the Torah scholar abjures a life of indulgence in the pleasures of this world, preferring to devote his time to the study of Torah, by which he gains reward in the World to Come. The less time he has to live, the better is his rate of return, for he exchanges an increasingly diminishing number of years of earthly life for a life of eternity. Thus, the older he becomes, the more profitable is his choice. Of course, the reverse is true for the *am haaretz* (*Yaaros D'vash* sermon 4; cf. *Ohr HaYashar* to *Kinim* 3:6).

33. *Job* 12:12.

34. Ibid. v. 20. The two verses contradict each other, the first stating that the old are wise, the second verse stating that the old are deprived of reason. In order to reconcile them, R' Yishmael the son of R' Yose says that the first verse refers to elderly Torah scholars while the second verse refers to elderly persons who do not possess Torah knowledge (*Rashi*).

35. He is afraid to walk to the market lest he stumble over one of these mounds (*Rashi* to *Ecclesiastes*).

36. The elderly person fears making long journeys. He asks himself, "Should I go? Should I not go? I will not go!" (*Koheles Rabbah* 12:5).

Our translation of תְּהָהִים follows *Rashi* here. *Koheles Rabbah* here interprets תְּהָהִים as *boundaries,* or *markers.* The elderly person sets limits as to how far he will go. He says, "I have the strength to go the end of the street, but I do not have the strength to go all the way to my destination."

37. Or the coccyx, the lowest end of the vertebrae (*Targum* to *Ecclesiastes* 12:5; see *Koheles Rabbah* loc. cit.; *Biblical and Talmudic Medicine* 2:2). In either case, the meaning is that in old age one's bones begin to "blossom," that is, to protrude, for the elderly person loses the body tissue that covered the bones (*Rashi* to *Ecclesiastes*).

38. The verse states that the elderly person becomes so frail that even if a grasshopper alights upon him it feels likes a heavy burden (*Rashi*). The Gemara extends this idea: Even parts of his own body become burdensome to him (*Rashi* to *Ecclesiastes*).

39. See *Rashi* to *Ecclesiastes* who explains the etymology of this word; cf. *Ben Yehoyada.*

40. Rav sighed because he no longer had a powerful aid in ensuring domestic tranquility (*Hagahos Yavetz*) or because he would no longer be able to have children. (There is a mitzvah to sire children even if one already has many and even in the twilight of one's life) (*Iyun Yaakov*).

41. *Psalms* 33:9.

42. I.e. man's carnal desire for woman. As a Baraisa proceeds to explain, a woman's body is not something that one should objectively find attractive. If man nevertheless lusts for it, it must be as a result of a Divine fiat (*Rashi*). [Rav Kahana spoke in such terms in order to provide men with a thought capable of dampening their fantasies. The satisfaction of this imagined desire is not worth the smallest moral sacrifice.]

43. [Logically, one ought not to have children, for they require much expenditure of time, energy and resources which could otherwise be devoted to one's own life. If people nevertheless want to have children, it must be something that was ordained by God.]

44. The idea of extremities awash in bodily fluids does nothing to deter men from seeking relations. Such an irrational craving must have been ordained by God (*Ben Yehoyada*).

45. The verse does not state that man goes to בֵּית הָעוֹלָם, *the eternal home.* Rather, it states that he goes to בֵּית עוֹלָמוֹ, *his eternal home.* The reference to *his* home indicates that every individual is destined to dwell in a home befitting his personal spiritual eminence (*Rashi*).

ושל בית הכסא רעות של סם ושל שחוק ושל פירות יפות א) ביום שיזועו שומרי הבית והתעותו וגו' ביום שיזועו שומרי הבית אלו הכסלים והצלעות והתעותו אנשי החיל אלו שוקים ובטלו הטוחנות אלו שינים וחשכו הרואות בארובות אלו עינים א"ל קיסר לר' יהושע בן חנניה מ"ט לא אתית לבי אבידן א"ל טור תלג סחרוני גלידין כלבוהי לא נבחין טחנוהי לא טוחנין בי רב אמרי אדלא אבידנא בחישנא ה) תניא רבי יוסי בר קיסמא אומר טבא תרי מתלת ווי לה לחדא דאזלא ולא אתיא מאי היא א"ר חסדא ינקותא כי אתא רב דימי אמר ינקותא כלילא דוורדא סבותא כלילא ו) דחילפא תנא משמיה דרבי מאיר דוק בככי ותשכח בניגרי שנאמר ב) ונשבע לחם ונהיה טובים ורעה לא ראינו א"ל שמואל לרב יהודה ג) שיננא שרי שקיך ועייל לחמך עד ארבעין שנין מיכלא מעלי מכאן ואילך משתי מעלי א"ל ההוא גוזאה לר' יהושע בן קרחה מהכא לקרחינא כמה הוי א"ל כמהכא לגוזניא א"ל צדוקי ברחא קרחא בארבעה אמר ליה ד) עיקרא שליפא בתמניא חזייה דלא סיים מסאניה א"ל דעל סוס מלך דעל חמור בן חורין ודמנעלי בריגלוהי בר איניש דלא הא ולא הא דחפיר וקביר טב מיניה א"ל גוזא גוזא תלת אמרת לי תלת שמעת הדרת פנים זקן שמחת לב אשה ג) נחלת ה' בנים ברוך המקום שמנעך מכולם א"ל קרחא מצויינא אמר ליה עיקרא שליפא תוכחה א"ל רבי לר' שמעון בן חלפתא מפני מה לא הקבלנו פניך ברגל כדרך שהקבילו אבותי לאבותיך א"ל סלעים נעשו גבוהים קרובים נעשו רחוקים משתים נעשו שלש משים שלום בבית בטל: ד) וסגרו דלתים בשוק וגו' אלו נקביו של אדם בשפל קול הטחנה בשביל קורקבן שאינו טוחן ויקום לקול הצפור שאפילו צפור מנערתו משנתו וישחו כל בנות השיר שאפילו (ס) קול שירים ושירות) דומות עליו כשוחה ואף ברזילי הגלעדי אמר לדוד ה) בן שמנים שנה אנכי היום האדע בין טוב לרע מכאן שדעתן של זקנים משתנות ה) אם יטעם עבדך את אשר אוכל ואת אשר אשתה מכאן ששפתותיהן של זקנים מתרפטות ה) אם אשמע עוד בקול שרים ושרות מכאן שאזניהם של זקנים מתכבדות אמר רב ברזילי הגלעדי שקרא הוה דההיא אמתא דהויא בי רבי בת תשעין ותרתין שנין והות טעמא קידרא רבא אמר ברזילי הגלעדי שטוף בזמה הוה *וכל השטוף בזמה ו) זקנה קופצת עליו תניא רבי ישמעאל ברבי יוסי אומר ו) תלמידי חכמים כל זמן שמזקינין חכמה נתוספת בהם שנאמר ו) בישישים חכמה ואורך ימים תבונה ועמי הארץ כל זמן שמזקינין טפשות נתוספת בהן שנאמר ז) מסיר שפה לנאמנים וטעם זקנים יקח ח) גם מגבוה ייראו שאפילו גבשושית קטנה דומה עליו כהרי הרים וחתחתים בדרך בשעה שמהלך בדרך נעשו (א) לו ט) תוהים וינאץ י) השקד זו קליבוסת ויסתבל החגב אלו עגבות ותפר האביונה זו חמדה רב כהנא הוה פסיק סידרא קמיה דרב כי מטא להאי קרא נגיד ואתנח אמר ש"מ בטל ליה חמדיה דרב אמר רב כהנא מאי דכתיב ט) כי הוא אמר ויהי זו אשה הוא צוה ויעמוד אלו בנים תנא אשה חמת מלא צואה ופיה מלא דם והכל רצין אחריה ח) כי הולך האדם אל בית עולמו א"ר יצחק י) מלמד שכל צדיק וצדיק נותנין לו מדור לפי כבודו משל למלך שנכנס הוא ועבדיו לעיר כשהן נכנסין כולן בשער אחד נכנסין כשהן לנין כל אחד ואחד נותנין לו מדור לפי כבודו ואמר רבי יצחק מאי דכתיב י) כי הילדות והשחרות הבל דברים שאדם עושה בילדותו משחירים פניו לעת זקנתו ז) ואמר רבי יצחק קשה רימה למת כמחט בבשר החי שנאמר כ) אך בשרו עליו יכאב אמר רב חסדא נפשו של אדם מתאבלת עליו כל שבעה שנא' כ) ונפשו עליו תאבל וכתיב ל) ויעש לאביו אבל שבעת ימים אמר רב יהודה מ) מת שאין לו מנחמין הולכין י' בני אדם ויושבין במקומו ההוא דשכיב בשבבותיה דרב יהודה לא הוו לו מנחמין כל

רש"י

של בית הכסא. מתוך יסורין: של פירות. כגון ריח חרדל: הכסלים. ליפלאנק"ש: והצלעות. שהן שומרין בני המעיים וחיותו של אדם וסוגרין בעדם: אלו שוקיים. שכחו של אדם נסמך עליהם: לבי אבידן. מקום העשוי להתווכח שם לדוקים וביייתוסים עם ישראל במקראות: טור תלג. ההר נעשה שלג כלומר ראשי לבן: סחרוני גלידין. סביבותיו של הר מלאו קרח כלומר שפמי וזקני הלבינו: כלבוהי לא נבחין. קולי אינו נשמע: טחנוהי. השינים: אדלא אבידנא בחישנא. אחר מה שלא אבד ממני אני מפשפש מרוב זקנה אני הולך שחוח ומנענע ונראה כמי שמבקש דינר האבד לו: תרתי טבא מתלת. טובים ב' הרגלים של ימי בחרות מג' של זקנה שצריך משענת עם רגליו: ווי לה. חבל עליה כלומר יש לו להתאונן ולצעוק ווי ההולכת ואינה חוזרת: כלילא דוורדא. נזר של וורד: חילפי. אורטיא"ש: דוק בככי ותשכח בניגרי. אכול הרבה ותמלא האכילה בפסיעותיך שיחזק כחך דוק כמו אכלה מדקה (דניאל ז) לשון כוסס: שרי שקיך. פתח פיך: גוזא. סרים ולדוקי היה: מהכא לקרחינא כמה הוי. כמה מהלך יש מכאן עד הקרח ולהקניטו על קרחתו נתכוון: כמהכא לגוזניא. כמו שמכאן עד הסרים: אמר ליה צדוקי ברחא קרחא בארבעה. שהקרח לקוח בארבע. ברחא קרחא הוא עז על שם שאינו מלובש בצמר כרחל קרוי קרחא: אמר ליה. רבי יהושע: עיקרא שליפא. שה שביציו עקורים ונתוקין לוקחין בשמנה: חזייה. לדוקי לרבי יהושע דלא סיים מסאניה: קרחא מצויינא. אתה הקרח במריבה אתה באת עמדי בתמיה: אמר לו רבי יהושע עיקרא שליפא תוכחה. אתה הסרים להקניטני ולהתווכח עמי באת: לא הקבלנו פניך. לא הקבלת פני ודרך ענוה קאמר ליה: סלעים. קטנים נעשו גבוהים שזקנתי: קרובים. נדמין לי כרחוקים: שתים נעשו לי שלש. שצריך אני משענת: משים שלום בבית. אבר תשמיש: לישנא אחרינא קרובים נעשו רחוקים מרוב חלשות של אדם כשמזקין צריך להרחיק רגליו זה מזה: שאינו טוחן. שאין בני מעיו טוחנין אכילתו: קורקבן. הוא המסס שקורין ליגפי"ל: כל בנות השיר. כל קולות של שיר הויין ליה שוחה: שדעתן של זקנים משתנות. דכתיב האדע בין טוב לרע ובזקנה מרובה קאמר: מתרפטות. מתבקעות כמו מנעל המרופט (לעיל דף קמא:): מתכבדות. כמו ואזניו הכבד (ישעיה ו): שטוף. כמו סוס שוטף במלחמה (ירמיה ח) להוט אחר הדבר ורודף: וטעם זקנים יקח. וע"כ מדקשי קראי אהדדי חד מתוקם בחכמים וחד בזקני השוק: מגבוה ייראו. יראים הם הזקנים מגבשושית שבדרכים ואומרים גבוהים הם: תוהים. פחדים: וינאץ השקד. אילן של שקדים ילין ויהיו בולטין נליס שלו: זו קליבוסת. עלס של הנק"א שהירך תקוע בו בולט ויולא מרוב תשות כחו: ויסתבל החגב. דומה עליו כסבל משא כבד: ותפר האביונה. תבטל התאוה חמדת תשמיש: פסיק סידרא. מסדר פרשיות של פסוקים: נגיד ואיתנח. רב: חמדיה. תאותו: זו אשה. אם לא על פי גזרת המלך לא היתה ראויה להתאוות לה שהיא כחמת מלאה מיאום והכל רצים אחריה: מדור לפי כבודו. מדלא כתיב אל בית העולם ש"מ כל אחד ואחד לבית המוכן לו: בשער אחד. אף כאן הכל מתים בענין אחד: שאדם עושה בילדותו. רוב תשמיש: משחירים פניו. מתיש כחו: שאין לו מנחמים. אין לו אבלים שיהו צריכין לנחמו: במקומו. במקום שמת שם:

עין משפט נר מצוה

מח א מיי' פ"ד מהלכות דעות הל"ט טוש"ע או"ח סימן רמ סעיף יד:

מט ב מיי' פי"ג מהל' אבלות הלכה ד סמג עשין ב טוש"ע יו"ד סי' שעו סעיף ג [וברב אלפס מו"ק פ"ג דרל"ז.] וברא"ש סימן פט:

רבינו חננאל

השבת לפי שבטל מן המצות והיינו דא"ר יוחנן מאי דכתיב במתים חפשי כיון שמת אדם נעשה חפשי מן המצות: א"ל קיסר לר' יהושע מ"ט לא אתית לבי אבידן. פי' בי אבידן בית שמתקבצין שם החכמים ונושאין ונותנין בדיני כל אומה ולשון השיבו ר' יהושע טור תלג סחרוני גלידין כלבוהי לא נבחין טחנוהי לא טחנן בבי רב אמרי (או לא או דן פי' בן) [אדלא אבדן בחשנא] ופירושו ההר כסהו שלג ודומה האדם להר כלומר ראשו כיסהו השיבה. וסביבותיו שהן הלחיים נעשו גלידין והוא הזקן שנקרא גליד. והגרון והלשון אינן מרימין קול. ככי שהן השניים אינן טוחנין המאכל. אדלא אבדן בחשנא. כלומר הזקן שאינו מביט מה שבפניו מתירא שמא יכה ראשו באבן או כיוצא בה וממשש בידו ונראה כאלו ממשש בדבר שאבד לו וזהו כמין משל ממשש הזקן מה שלא אבד. טבי תרי מתלת. פי' יותר הוא טוב המהלך על ב' רגליו מן הזקן שצריך משען כגון מקל או שבט להישען עליו והוא כמו רגל שלישי. חבל על דאזלא ולא אתיא. פי' הבחרות הולכת כשמזקין האדם ואינה חוזרת אליו. ינקותא כלילא דוורדי. הבחרות כתר של וורד ריחו נודף ושל זקנה כתר של חילף שריחו מאוס. דוק בככי ותשכח בנגרי. טחון בככי בשניים כלומר אכול כדי שיהיה לך כח להלך ברגליך. א"ל ההוא גאזא חתוך (הערוה) (הביצים) והוא סריס א"ל ר' יהושע בן קרחה מהכא לקרחוניא כמה. ביקש להודיעו שאתה קרח והן ביד לו דברים כמלגיע והשיבו ר' יהושע כמו הכא לגזוניא כלומר אתה גזוי. עוד אמר ליה ברחא קרחא בארבע. פי' (או) [עור] כבש גדול בד' כספים. השיבו ר' יהושע הדברים מוכיחין שגם אלו דברי הסריס הם שבקש להודיעו כי השלוף ביוקר יותר מן הקרח. ילמדנו רבינו איקא שליפא בתמניא. פי' עור תיש נתוק ביצים בשמונה כספים. שמבקשין אותו לעשותו נודות של שמן. חזייה דלא מסיים מסאניה. פירוש ראהו יחף כו'. א"ל קרחה מצוי. פי' א"ל קרחה מריבה סחרחר. כדכתיב הן לריב ומצה וגו' השיבו ר' יהושע תיש נתוק תוכחה

מסורת הש"ס

א) מס' ד"א זוטא פ"י, ב) [פי' מיני קמשונים ערוך], ג) [לעיל נה. ברכות לו. עירובין נד. חגיגה טו: ר"ה כד: כתובות טו: יד: יג. קדושין לג. גיטין עח: ב"ק ז. טו: ב"ב קנג: ע"ז מג: סנהדרין פ: כריתות יב. נדה יב. יז. כה:], ד) [נ"ל איקא ע' בערוך], ה) [נ"ל קול שרים ושרות], ו) [תענית ה:], ז) [קנים ספ"ג ע"ש ובמפרש], ח) [תרגום של ויפרד ומוה ערוך], ט) ע' מ"ר ויקרא פ' י"ח, י) [ב"מ פג:], כ) ברכות יח: לעיל יג.

הגהות הב"ח

(א) גמ' נעשה לבו תוהים תוהים ויגאץ השקד:

רב נסים גאון

אמר ליה סלעים נעשו גבוהים כמו שנאמר אח"כ שאפילו גבשושית קטנה דומה עליו כהרי הרים ושאר הענין פירשנוה במקצת ההגדה וכך אמרו רחוקים נעשו קרובים אילין עיניא דהוון חמיין מרחוק אף מקרוב ליתנון חמאן קרובים נעשו רחוקים אילין אודניא דהוון שמעין בחד זמן כדו אף במאה זמנין ליתנון שמעין שתים נעשו ג' חוטרא ותרין ריגליא משים שלום בבית בטל זו תאוה שהיא מעלה שלום

תורה אור השלם

א) ביום שיזעו שמרי הבית והתעותו אנשי החיל ובטלו הטחנות כי מעטו וחשכו הראות בארבות: [קהלת יב, ג]

ב) כי עשה נעשה את כל הדבר אשר יצא מפינו לקטר למלכת השמים והסיך לה נסכים כאשר עשינו אנחנו ואבתינו מלכינו ושרינו בערי יהודה ובחצות ירושלים ונשבע לחם ונהיה טובים ורעה לא ראינו: [ירמיה מד, יז]

ג) הנה נחלת יי בנים שכר פרי הבטן: [תהלים קכז, ג]

ד) וסגרו דלתים בשוק בשפל קול הטחנה ויקום לקול הצפור וישחו כל בנות השיר: [קהלת יב, ד]

ה) בן שמנים שנה אנכי היום האדע בין טוב לרע אם יטעם עבדך את אשר אכל ואת אשר אשתה אם אשמע עוד בקול שרים ושרות ולמה יהיה עבדך עוד למשא אל אדני המלך: [שמואל ב יט, לו]

ו) בישישים חכמה וארך ימים תבונה: [איוב יב, יב] ז) מסיר שפה לנאמנים וטעם זקנים יקח: [איוב יב, כ] ח) גם מגבה יראו וחתחתים בדרך וינאץ השקד ויסתבל החגב ותפר האביונה כי הלך האדם אל בית עולמו וסבבו בשוק הספדים: [קהלת יב, ה] ט) כי הוא אמר ויהי הוא צוה ויעמד: [תהלים לג, ט] י) והסר כעס מלבך והעבר רעה מבשרך כי הילדות והשחרות הבל: [קהלת יא, י] כ) אך בשרו עליו יכאב ונפשו עליו תאבל: [איוב יד, כב] ל) ויבאו עד גרן האטד אשר בעבר הירדן ויספדו שם מספד גדול וכבד מאד ויעש לאביו אבל שבעת ימים: [בראשית נ, י]

אינם דברי ריב אלא דברי תוכחה. מפני מה לא הקבלנו פניך. למה לא באת אלינו להתראות פנים: מיכן ששפתותיהן של זקנים מתרפטות. פי' שפתותיהן משתרבבות והוא תרגום של מתרפטות אינם מתאמצות להחזיק הפה בחזקה. גבשושית פי' גב קטן של עפר. קליבוסת פירוש מן הפקודות ומפורש באלו טרפות. חרבא דאקליבוסתא. ותפר האביונה. זו חמדה (כמו) [כי] בטלה ממנו תאות אשה. פי' טלוניתא כמו על שאין בה ממש. גשיה שהן ידו עליו מלשון נגששה:

ליקוטי רש"י

שיזועו. ירתתו. שומרי הבית. אלו הצלעות והכסלים המגינים על כל חלל הגוף. והתעותו. יתעקמו כמו עוות ואונקרופיו"ט בלע"ז. אנשי החיל. אלו השוקים שנושאן כל הגוף עליהם [קהלת יב, ג]. רבי יהושע בן קרחה. היה כדאמרי' בבכורות (נח.) חוץ מן הקרח הזה [שבועות ו.]. בשפל קול הטחנה. קול ריחים הטוחנים מאכל שבמעיו והוא הקורקבן והמסס. ויקום לקול הצפור. שאפילו קול צפור מנערתו משנתו. וישחו כל בנות השיר. כל קולות של שירים ושרות. גם מגבוה ייראו. מגבשושית ומתלוליות. וחתחתים בדרך. אימות ופחדים. וינאץ השקד. זו קליבוסת. ויסתבל החגב. אלו עגבות. ותפר האביונה. חמדת תאות תשמיש. קשה רימה. לגוף המת.

מָשָׁל לְמֶלֶךְ שֶׁנִּכְנַס הוּא וַעֲבָדָיו לְעִיר – **This may be compared to a king who, together with his servants, entered a city.** כְּשֶׁהֵן נִכְנָסִין – **When they enter,** כּוּלָּן בְּשַׁעַר אֶחָד נִכְנָסִין – **all of them enter through the same gate;** כְּשֶׁהֵן לָנִין – however, **when they spend the night,** כָּל אֶחָד וְאֶחָד נוֹתְנִין לוֹ מָדוֹר לְפִי כְּבוֹדוֹ – **each one is given lodgings in accordance with his eminence.**[46]

Two other statements by R' Yitzchak concerning the consequences of sin one feels in old age and death:

וְאָמַר רַבִּי יִצְחָק – And **R' Yitzchak also said:** מַאי דִּכְתִיב ,,כִּי־הַיַּלְדוּת וְהַשַּׁחֲרוּת הָבֶל״ – **What is the meaning of that which is written:**[47] ***for childhood and youth (shacharus) are vanity?*** דְּבָרִים שֶׁאָדָם עוֹשֶׂה בְּיַלְדוּתוֹ מַשְׁחִירִים פָּנָיו לְעֵת זִקְנָתוֹ – **The things a man does in his youth blacken** (*mashchirim*) **his countenance in his old age.**[48] וְאָמַר רַבִּי יִצְחָק – And **R' Yitzchak also said:** קָשָׁה רִימָּה לַמֵּת כְּמַחַט בִּבְשַׂר הַחַי – **Worms are as painful to the dead as pins are to the flesh of the living.**[49] שֶׁנֶּאֱמַר ,,אַךְ־בְּשָׂרוֹ עָלָיו יִכְאָב״ – **For it is stated: *But his flesh will be pained over itself.***[50] אָמַר רַב חִסְדָּא – **Rav Chisda said:** נַפְשׁוֹ שֶׁל אָדָם מִתְאַבֶּלֶת עָלָיו כָּל שִׁבְעָה – **A person's soul mourns over him all of the seven** days that follow his death. שֶׁנֶּאֱמַר ,,וְנַפְשׁוֹ עָלָיו תֶּאֱבָל״ – This is evident from the second half of the aforementioned verse, **for it says: *and his soul will mourn over itself,*** וּכְתִיב ,,וַיַּעַשׂ לְאָבִיו אֵבֶל שִׁבְעַת יָמִים״ – **and it is written:**[51] ***and he ordained a mourning for his father, seven days.*** Thus, we see that the term "mourning" in Scripture denotes a seven-day period, so when the verse states that the soul mourns over itself, it indicates a seven-day mourning period, as Rav Chisda stated.

A story illustrates Rav Chisda's assertion that the soul mourns the person for seven days following the death:

אָמַר רַב יְהוּדָה – **Rav Yehudah said:** מֵת שֶׁאֵין לוֹ מְנַחֲמִין – **If a deceased person has no mourners,**[52] הוֹלְכִין עֲשָׂרָה בְּנֵי אָדָם וְיוֹשְׁבִין בִּמְקוֹמוֹ – **ten men should go and sit** in mourning **in his place** (i.e. the place where the person died) for the seven days following the burial. הַהוּא דְּשָׁכֵיב בִּשְׁבָבוּתֵיהּ דְּרַב יְהוּדָה – **There was [a person] who died in the neighborhood of Rav Yehudah.** לֹא הָיוּ לוֹ מְנַחֲמִין – **[The person] had no mourners.**

NOTES

46. Similarly, every person departs life in the same manner; all souls enter the next world "through the same gate." However, they do not all retire to the same home. Rather, each soul occupies a different level [one suited to the good or bad deeds performed by the person when he was alive] (see *Rashi*).

47. *Ecclesiastes* 11:10.

48. That is, the deeds of his youth weaken him in his old age. This is a reference to excessive marital relations (*Rashi*). The debilitative effects of such activity on a person's physical condition are not evident when he is young, but those effects do become evident when he reaches old age (*Torah Temimah* to the verse). Another interpretation is that the sins one performs when he is young cause him to cringe with shame when he recalls them in his old age (*HaRif* in *Ein Yaakov*).

49. This is not to be taken literally in the sense that the dead body feels pain. Rather, R' Yitzchak means that the soul of the dead person suffers pain when it contemplates how the body, its former abode, is now ingloriously consumed like a piece of meat (*Sefer Chasidim* §1163). See also *Teshuvos Rashba* §369, who also maintains that the dead body does not feel pain.

50. *Job* 14:22.

51. *Genesis* 50:10.

52. Literally: *no comforters,* that is, he left no relatives or other mourners for visitors to comfort (*Rashi*; see *Maharsha*).

ושל בית הכסא רעות של סם ושל שחוק ושל פירות יפות א) ביום שיזועו שומרי הבית והתעותו וגו' ביום שיזועו שומרי הבית אלו הכסלים והצלעות והתעותו אנשי החיל אלו שוקים ובטלו הטוחנות אלו שינים וחשכו הרואות בארובות אלו עינים א"ל קיסר לר' יהושע בן חנניה מ"ט לא אתית לבי אבידן א"ל טור תלג סחרוני גלידין כלבוהי לא נבחין טחנוהי לא טוחנין בי רב אמרי אדלא אבידנא בחישנא תניא רבי יוסי בר קיסמא אומר טבא תרי מתלת ווי לה לחדא דאזלא ולא אתיא מאי היא א"ר חסדא ינקותא כי אתא רב דימי אמר ינקותא כלילא דוורדא סבותא כלילא דחילפא תנא משמיה דרבי מאיר דוק בככי ותשכח בניגרי שנאמר ב) ונשבע לחם ונהיה טובים ורעה לא ראינו א"ל שמואל לרב יהודה שיננא שרי שקך ועייל לחמך עד ארבעין שנין מיכלא מעלי מכאן ואילך משתי מעלי א"ל ההוא גוזאה לר' יהושע בן קרחה מהכא לקרחינא כמה הוי א"ל כמהכא לגוזניא א"ל צדוקי ברחא קרחא בארבעה אמר ליה עיקרא שליפא בתמניא חזייה דלא סיים מסאניה א"ל דעל סוס מלך דעל חמור בן חורין ודמנעלי בריגלוהי בר איניש דלא הא ולא הא דחפיר וקביר טב מיניה א"ל גוזא גוזא תלת אמרת לי תלת שמעת הדרת פנים זקן שמחת לב אשה ג) נחלת ה' בנים ברוך המקום שמנעך מכולם א"ל קרחא מצויינא אמר ליה עיקרא שליפא תוכחה א"ל רבי לר' שמעון בן חלפתא מפני מה לא הקבלנו פניך ברגל כדרך שהקבילו אבותי לאבותיך א"ל סלעים נעשו גבוהים קרובים נעשו רחוקים משתים נעשו שלש משים שלום בבית בטל: ד) וסגרו דלתים בשוק וגו' אלו נקביו של אדם בשפל קול הטחנה בשביל קורקבן שאינו טוחן ויקום לקול הצפור שאפילו צפור מנערתו משנתו וישחו כל בנות השיר שאפילו (קול שירים ושירות) דומות עליו כשוחה ואף ברזילי הגלעדי אמר לדוד ה) בן שמנים שנה אנכי היום האדע בין טוב לרע מכאן שדעתן של זקנים משתנות אם יטעם עבדך את אשר אוכל ואת אשר אשתה מכאן ששפתותיהן של זקנים מתרפטות אם אשמע עוד בקול שרים ושרות מכאן שאזניהם של זקנים מתכבדות אמר רב ברזילי הגלעדי שקרא הוה דההיא אמתא דהויא בי רבי בת תשעין ותרתין שנין והות טעמא קידרא רבא אמר ברזילי הגלעדי שטוף בזמה הוה וכל השטוף בזמה זקנה קופצת עליו תניא רבי ישמעאל ברבי יוסי אומר תלמידי חכמים כל זמן שמזקינין חכמה נתוספת בהם שנאמר ו) בישישים חכמה ואורך ימים תבונה ועמי הארץ כל זמן שמזקינין טפשות נתוספת בהן שנאמר ז) מסיר שפה לנאמנים וטעם זקנים יקח ח) גם מגבוה ייראו שאפילו גבשושית קטנה דומה עליו כהרי הרים וחתחתים בדרך בשעה שמהלך בדרך נעשו (א) לו תוהים וינאץ השקד זו קליבוסת ויסתבל החגב אלו עגבות ותפר האביונה זו חמדה רב כהנא הוה פסיק סידרא קמיה דרב כי מטא להאי קרא נגיד ואתנח אמר ש"מ בטל ליה חמדיה דרב אמר רב כהנא מאי דכתיב ט) כי הוא אמר ויהי זו אשה הוא צוה ויעמוד אלו בנים תנא אשה חמת מלא צואה ופיה מלא דם והכל רצין אחריה ח) כי הולך האדם אל בית עולמו א"ר יצחק מלמד שכל צדיק וצדיק נותנין לו מדור לפי כבודו משל למלך שנכנס הוא ועבדיו לעיר כשהן נכנסין כולן בשער אחד נכנסין כשהן לנין כל אחד ואחד נותנין לו מדור לפי כבודו ואמר רבי יצחק מאי דכתיב י) כי הילדות והשחרות הבל דברים שאדם עושה בילדותו משחירים פניו לעת זקנתו ואמר רבי יצחק קשה רימה למת כמחט בבשר החי שנאמר כ) אך בשרו עליו יכאב אמר רב חסדא נפשו של אדם מתאבלת עליו כל שבעה שנא' ונפשו עליו תאבל וכתיב ל) ויעש לאביו אבל שבעת ימים אמר רב יהודה מת שאין לו מנחמין הולכין י' בני אדם ויושבין במקומו ההוא דשכיב בשבבותיה דרב יהודה לא היו לו מנחמין כל

רש"י

של בית הכסא. מתוך יסורין: של פירות. כגון ריח חרדל: הכסלים. ליפלאנק"ש: והצלעות. שהן שומרין בני המעיים וחיותו של אדם וסוגרין בעדם: אלו שוקיים. שכחו של אדם נסמך עליהם: לבי אבידן. מקום העשוי להתווכח שם לצדוקים וביייתוסים עם ישראל במקראות: טור תלג. ההר נעשה שלג כלומר ראשי לבן: סחרוני גלידין. סביבותיו של הר מלאו קרח כלומר שפמי וזקני הלבינו: כלבוהי לא נבחין. קולי אינו נשמע: טחנוהי. השינים: אדלא אבידנא בחישנא. אחר מה שלא אבד ממני אני מפשפש מרוב זקנה אני הולך שחוח ומנענע ונראה כמי שמבקש דינר האבד לו: תרתי טבא מתלת. טובים ב' הרגלים של ימי בחרות מג' של זקנה שצריך משענת עם רגליו: ווי לה. אבל עליה כלומר יש לו להתאונן ולצעוק ווי ההולכת ואינה חוזרת: כלילא דוורדא. נזר של וורד: חילפי. אורטיא"ש: דוק בככי ותשכח בניגרי. אכול הרבה ותמצא האכילה בפסיעותיך שיחזק כחך דוק כמו אכלה מדקה (דניאל ז) לשון כוסס: שרי שקיך. פתח פיך: גוזא. סריס ולדוקי היה: מהכא לקרחינא כמה הוי. כמה מהלך יש מכאן עד הקרח ולהקניטו על קרחתו נתכוון: כמהכא לגוזניא. כמו שמכאן עד הסריס: אמר ליה צדוקי ברחא קרחא בארבעה. שהקרח לקוח בארבע. ברחא קרחא הוא עז על שם שאינו מלובש בצמר כרחל קרוי קרחא: אמר ליה. רבי יהושע: עיקרא שליפא. שה שביציו עקורים ונתוקין לוקחין בשמנה: חזייה. צדוקי לרבי יהושע דלא סיים מסאניה: קרחא מצויינא. אתה הקרח במריבה אתה בא עמדי בתמיה: אמר לו רבי יהושע עיקרא שליפא תוכחה. אתה הסרים להקניטני ולהתווכח עמי באת: לא הקבלנו פניך. לא הקבלת פני ודרך ענוה קאמר ליה: סלעים. קטנים נעשו גבוהים שזקנתי: קרובים. נדמין לי כרחוקים: שתים נעשו לי שלש. שצריך אני משענת: משים שלום בבית. אבר תשמיש: לישנא אחרינא קרובים נעשו רחוקים מרוב חלשות של אדם כשמזקין צריך להרחיק רגליו זה מזה: שאינו טוחן. שאין בני מעיו טוחנין אכילתו: קורקבן. הוא המסס שקורין ליגפי"ל: כל בנות השיר. כל קולות של שיר הויין ליה שוחה: שדעתן של זקנים משתנות. דכתיב האדע בין טוב לרע ובזקנה מרובה קאמר: מתרפטות. מתבקעות כמו מנעל המרופט (לעיל דף קמא:): מתכבדות. כמו ואזניו הכבד (ישעיה ו): שטוף. כמו סוס שוטף במלחמה (ירמיה ח) להוט אחר הדבר ורודף: וטעם זקנים יקח. וע"כ מדקשי קראי אהדדי חד מתוקם בחכמים וחד בזקני השוק: מגבוה ייראו. יראים הם הזקנים מגבשושית שבדרכים ואומרים גבוהים הם: תוהים. פחדים: וינאץ השקד. אילן של שקדים יציץ ויהיו בולטין נצים שלו: זו קליבוסת. עצם של הנק"א שהירך תקוע בו בולט ויוצא מרוב תשות כחו: ויסתבל החגב. דומה עליו כסבל משא כבד: ותפר האביונה. תבטל התאוה חמדת תשמיש: פסיק סידרא. מסדר פרשיות של פסוקים: נגיד ואיתנח. רב: חמדיה. תאותו: זו אשה. אם לא על פי גזרת המלך לא היתה ראויה להתאוות לה שהיא כחמת מלאה מיאוס והכל רצים אחריה: מדור לפי כבודו. מדלא כתיב אל בית העולם ש"מ כל אחד ואחד לבית המוכן לו: בשער אחד. אף כאן הכל מתים בענין אחד: שאדם עושה בילדותו. רוב תשמיש: משחירים פניו. מתיש כחו: שאין לו מנחמים. אין לו אבלים שיהו צריכין לנחמו: במקומו. במקום שמת שם: כל

עין משפט נר מצוה

מח א מיי' פ"ד מהלכות דעות הל' יג טור שו"ע או"ח סימן רמ סעיף יד:

מט ב מיי' פי"ג מהל' אבל הלכה ד סמג עשין ב טוש"ע יו"ד סי' שעו סעיף ג [וברב אלפס מו"ק דף יז.] ועי' ש"ך שם סימן פט:

רבינו חננאל

השבת לפני שבטל מן המצות והיינו דא"ר יוחנן מאי דכתיב במתים חפשי כיון שמת אדם נעשה חפשי מן המצות: א"ל קיסר לר' יהושע מ"ט לא אתית לבי אבידן. פי' בי אבידן בית שמקבצין שם החכמים ונושאין ונותנין בדיני כל אומה ולשון השיבו ר' יהושע טור תלג סחרנוהי גלידין כלבוהי לא נבחין טחנוהי לא טחנן בבי רב אמרי (או לא או דן פי' בי) [אדלא אבדן בחשנא] ופירושו ההר כסהו שלג ודומה האדם להר לומר ראשו כיסהו השיבה. וסביבותיו שהן הלחיים נעשו גלידין והוא הקרח שנקרא גליד. והגרון והלשון אינן מרימין קול. ככי שהן השניים אינן טוחנין המאכל. אדלא אבדן בחשנא. כלומר הזקן שאינו מביט מה שבפניו מתירא שמא יכה ראשו באבן או בכיוצא בה וממשש בידו ונראה כאלו ממשש בדבר שאבד לו וזהו כמין משל ממשש הזקן מה שלא אבד. טבי תרי מתלת. פי' יותר הוא טוב המהלך על ב' רגליו מן הזקן שצריך משען כגון מקל או שבט להישען עליו והוא כמו רגל שלישי. חבל על דאזלא ולא אתיא. פי' הבחרות הולכת כשמזקין האדם ואינה חוזרת אליו. ינקותא כלילא דוורדי. הבחרות כתר של וורד ריחו נודף ושל זקנה כתר של חילף שריחו מאוס. דוק בככי ותשכח בנגרי. טחון בככי בשניים כלומר אכול כדי שיהיה לך כח להלך ברגליך. א"ל ההוא גאזא חתוך (הערוה) [הביצים] והוא סריס א"ל ר' יהושע בן קרחה מהכא לקרחוניא כמה. ביקש להודיעו שהוא קרח הן ביד לו כמלעיג והשיבו ר' יהושע כמו הכא לגוזניא כלומר אתה גזוי. עוד אמר ליה ברחא קרחא בארבע. פי' (או) [עוד] כבש גדול בד' כספים. השיבו ר' יהושע הדברים מוכיחין שגם אלו דברי הסרים הם שבקשו להודיעו כי השלוף בזיקור יותר מן הקרח. ולמדנו רבינו איקא שליפא בתמניא. פי' עוד תיש נתוק ביצים בשמונה כספים. שמבקשין אותו לעשותו נודות של שמן. חזייה דלא מסיים מסאניה. פירוש ראהו יחף כו'. א"ל קרחה מצר. פי' א"ל קרחה מריבה סחרחר. כדכתיב בן לריב ומצה וגו' והשיבו ר' יהושע תיש נתוק תוכחה

מסורת הש"ס

א) מס' ד"א זוטא פ"י, ב) [פי' מיני תמשוטים ערוך], ג) [לעיל נד. ברכות לו. עירובין כח: חגיגה טו: ר"ה כו: כתובות קיא: קידושין לב: גיטין עג: ב"ק יז. סנהדרין פ: כריתות יט: נדה יג. לו:], ד) [ג"ע איקא ערכין], ה) [ג"ע קול שרים ושרות], ו) [תענית ה.], ז) [קנים ספ"ג ע"ש ובמפרש], ח) [תרגום של ויקרא וגו' ערוך], ט) [ג"מ פג:], י) עי' ברכות יח. לעיל נג.

הגהות הב"ח

[illegible]

רב נסים גאון

אמר ליה סלעים נעשין גבוהים כמו שנאמר אח"כ שאפילו גבשושית קטנה דומה עליו כהרי הרים ושאר הענין פירושו במקצת ההגדה וכך אמרו רחוקים נעשו קרובים אילין עיניא דהוון חמיין מרחוק אף מקריב ליתנון חמאן קרובים נעשו רחוקים אילין אודניא דהוון שמעין בחד זימנין במאה זמנין ליתנון שמעין ב' נעשו ג' חוטרא ותרין ריגליא משים שלום בבית בטל זו תאוה שהיא מעלה שלום

תורה אור השלם

א) בַּיּוֹם שֶׁיָּזֻעוּ שֹׁמְרֵי הַבַּיִת וְהִתְעַוְּתוּ אַנְשֵׁי הֶחָיִל וּבָטְלוּ הַטֹּחֲנוֹת כִּי מִעֵטוּ וְחָשְׁכוּ הָרֹאוֹת בָּאֲרֻבּוֹת: [קהלת יב, ג]

ב) כִּי עָשֹׂה נַעֲשֶׂה אֶת כָּל הַדָּבָר אֲשֶׁר יָצָא מִפִּינוּ לְקַטֵּר לִמְלֶכֶת הַשָּׁמַיִם וְהַסֵּיךְ לָהּ נְסָכִים כַּאֲשֶׁר עָשִׂינוּ אֲנַחְנוּ וַאֲבֹתֵינוּ מְלָכֵינוּ וְשָׂרֵינוּ בְּעָרֵי יְהוּדָה וּבְחֻצוֹת יְרוּשָׁלָיִם וַנִּשְׂבַּע לֶחֶם וַנִּהְיֶה טוֹבִים וְרָעָה לֹא רָאִינוּ: [ירמיה מד, יז]

ג) הִנֵּה נַחֲלַת יְיָ בָּנִים שָׂכָר פְּרִי הַבָּטֶן: [תהלים קכז, ג]

ד) וְסֻגְּרוּ דְלָתַיִם בַּשּׁוּק בִּשְׁפַל קוֹל הַטַּחֲנָה וְיָקוּם לְקוֹל הַצִּפּוֹר וְיִשַּׁחוּ כָּל בְּנוֹת הַשִּׁיר: [קהלת יב, ד]

ה) בֶּן שְׁמֹנִים שָׁנָה אָנֹכִי הַיּוֹם הַאֵדַע בֵּין טוֹב לְרָע אִם יִטְעַם עַבְדְּךָ אֶת אֲשֶׁר אֹכַל וְאֶת אֲשֶׁר אֶשְׁתֶּה אִם אֶשְׁמַע עוֹד בְּקוֹל שָׁרִים וְשָׁרוֹת וְלָמָּה יִהְיֶה עַבְדְּךָ עוֹד לְמַשָּׂא אֶל אֲדֹנִי הַמֶּלֶךְ: [שמואל ב' יט, לו]

ו) בִּישִׁישִׁים חָכְמָה וְאֹרֶךְ יָמִים תְּבוּנָה: [איוב יב, יב]

ז) מֵסִיר שָׂפָה לְנֶאֱמָנִים וְטַעַם זְקֵנִים יִקָּח: [איוב יב, כ]

ח) גַּם מִגָּבֹהַּ יִרָאוּ וְחַתְחַתִּים בַּדֶּרֶךְ וְיָנֵאץ הַשָּׁקֵד וְיִסְתַּבֵּל הֶחָגָב וְתָפֵר הָאֲבִיּוֹנָה כִּי הֹלֵךְ הָאָדָם אֶל בֵּית עוֹלָמוֹ וְסָבְבוּ בַשּׁוּק הַסֹּפְדִים: [קהלת יב, ה]

ט) כִּי הוּא אָמַר וַיֶּהִי הוּא צִוָּה וַיַּעֲמֹד: [תהלים לג, ט]

י) וְהָסֵר כַּעַס מִלִּבֶּךָ וְהַעֲבֵר רָעָה מִבְּשָׂרֶךָ כִּי הַיַּלְדוּת וְהַשַּׁחֲרוּת הָבֶל: [קהלת יא, י]

כ) אַךְ בְּשָׂרוֹ עָלָיו יִכְאָב וְנַפְשׁוֹ עָלָיו תֶּאֱבָל: [איוב יד, כב]

ל) וַיָּבֹאוּ עַד גֹּרֶן הָאָטָד אֲשֶׁר בְּעֵבֶר הַיַּרְדֵּן וַיִּסְפְּדוּ שָׁם מִסְפֵּד גָּדוֹל וְכָבֵד מְאֹד וַיַּעַשׂ לְאָבִיו אֵבֶל שִׁבְעַת יָמִים: [בראשית נ, י]

ליקוטי רש"י

שיזועו. ירתתו. שומרי הבית. אלו הצלעות והכסלים המגינים על כל הגוף. והתעותו. [illegible] אנשי החיל. [illegible]

[illegible]

כל יומא הוה דבר רב יהודה בי עשרה ויתבי בדוכתיה לאחר שבעה ימים איתחזי ליה בחילמיה דרב יהודה ואמר ליה תנוח דעתך שהנחת את דעתי א"ר אבהו כל שאומרים בפני המת יודע עד שיסתם הגולל פליגי בה רבי חייא ור"ש ברבי חד אמר עד שיסתם הגולל וחד אמר עד שיתעכל הבשר מאן דאמר עד שיתעכל הבשר דכתיב (א) אך בשרו עליו יכאב ונפשו עליו תאבל מאן דאמר עד שיסתם הגולל דכתיב (ב) וישוב העפר על הארץ כשהיה וגו' ת"ר (ב) והרוח תשוב אל האלהים אשר נתנה תנה לו כמו שנתנה לך בטהרה אף אתה בטהרה משל למלך ב"ו שחלק בגדי מלכות לעבדיו פקחין שבהן קיפלום והניחום בקופסא טפשים שבהן הלכו ועשו בהן מלאכה לימים ביקש המלך את כליו פקחין שבהן החזירום לו כשהן מגוהצין טפשין שבהן החזירום לו כשהן מלוכלכין שמח המלך לקראת פקחין וכעס לקראת טפשין על פקחין אמר ינתנו כלי לאוצר והם ילכו לבתיהם לשלום ועל טפשין אמר כלי ינתנו לכובס והן יתחבשו בבית האסורים אף הקב"ה על גופן של צדיקים אומר (ג) יבא שלום ינוחו על משכבותם ועל נשמתן הוא אומר (ד) והיתה נפש אדוני צרורה בצרור החיים על גופן של רשעים הוא אומר (ה) אין שלום אמר ה' לרשעים ועל נשמתן הוא אומר (ד) ואת נפש אויביך יקלענה בתוך כף הקלע תניא ר' אליעזר אומר נשמתן של צדיקים גנוזות תחת כסא הכבוד שנאמר והיתה נפש אדני צרורה בצרור החיים ושל רשעים זוממות והולכות [ומלאך אחד עומד בסוף העולם ומלאך אחר עומד בסוף העולם ומקלעין נשמתן זה לזה] שנא' ואת נפש אויביך יקלענה בתוך כף הקלע א"ל רבה לר"נ של בינונים מאי א"ל איכא שכיבנא לא אמרי לכו האי מילתא הכי אמר שמואל אלו ואלו לדומה נמסרין הללו יש להן מנוח והללו אין להן מנוח אמר (ליה) רב מרי עתידים צדיקים דהוו עפרא דכתיב (ב) וישוב העפר על הארץ כשהיה הנהו קפולאי דהוו קפלי בארעא דרב נחמן נחר בהו רב אחאי בר יאשיה אתו ואמרו ליה לרב נחמן נחר בן גברא אתא ואמר ליה מאן ניהו מר אמר ליה אנא אחאי בר יאשיה א"ל ולאו אמר רב מרי עתידי צדיקי דהוו עפרא א"ל ומני מרי דלא ידענא ליה א"ל והא קרא כתיב וישוב העפר על הארץ כשהיה אמר ליה דאקרייך קהלת לא אקרייך משלי דכתיב (ו) ורקב עצמות קנאה כל מי שיש לו קנאה בלבו עצמותיו מרקיבים כל שאין לו קנאה בלבו אין עצמותיו מרקיבים גששיה חזייה דאית ביה מששא אמר ליה ליקום מר לגוויה דביתא אמר ליה גלית אדעתך דאפילו נביאי לא קרית דכתיב (ז) וידעתם כי אני ה' בפתחי את קברותיכם א"ל והכתיב (ח) כי עפר אתה ואל עפר תשוב א"ל ההוא שעה אחת קודם תחיית המתים א"ל ההוא צדוקי לר' אבהו אמריתו נשמתן של צדיקים גנוזות תחת כסא הכבוד אובא טמיא היכא אסקיה לשמואל בנגידא א"ל התם בתוך שנים עשר חדש הוה דתניא כל י"ב חדש גופו קיים ונשמתו עולה ויורדת לאחר י"ב חדש הגוף בטל ונשמתו

ונשמתו

רש"י

כל יומא. ז' ימי אבילות: גולל. הוא כיסוי ארונו: ונפשו עליו תאבל. כל זמן שיש לו בשר יש לו לנפש לב חיות להבין: וישוב העפר. גופו קרוי עפר ומשנשב אל הארץ כשהיה מיד והרוח תשוב שאין בו רוח עוד: אשר נתנה. קרא יתירה הוא לדרש הוי זהיר שתשיבנה אליו כמה שנתנה לך נקייה בלי עון: כלי ינתנו לאוצר. להכניס אף זו תינתן תחת כסא הכבוד: לכובס. ללבנן אף זו לגיהנם ללורפם שם: בבית האסורים. בחשך בלא אורה ושלוה: כף הקלע. רחב הקלועה שנותן האבן לתוכה לקלע עשויה כעין כף: בצרור החיים וגו'. את ה' אלהיך עמו בכסאו: זוממות. כמו בזוממת דפחלא (לעיל דף נח:) מכושות בבית הסוהר: אלו ואלו. רשעים ובינונים: לדומה. מלאך הממונה על הרוחות: דהוו עפרא. אפילו צדיקים נרקבים ונעשים אפר: קפולאי. חופרים: נחר בהו (ב) רבי אחאי. שהיה נקבר שם: דלא ידענא ליה. ואיני חש לדבריו: מי שיש לו קנאה. ותחרות על חברו: עצמותיו מרקיבים. ועליו נאמר וישוב אל העפר: ליקום מר לגוויה. (ג) יבא אדוני לבית: בפתחי. בהעלותי עד שיעלנו הקדוש ברוך הוא מקברותינו אין לנו רשות לעלות: והא כתיב ואל עפר תשוב. והאי ליכא למימר ברשעים למודייהו דכל קללותיו של אדה"ר כל דורותיו שוין בהן: אובא טמיא. בעלת אוב שמשמשת בעצמות טמיא בלשון ארמי עצמות וכן פירש רב האי בפירושו של טהרות בית שהוא מלא טמיא מלא עצמות: בנגידא. כן קורין למכשפות של אוב בלשון ארמי: אם

תוספות

עד שיסתם הגולל. בכל מקום מפרש רש"י דגולל הוא כיסוי ארונו של מת ודופק דף שנתון מלידו ונקרא דופק על שם שהמת דופק שם כמו תחיכה גופה תיהוי סימן אי דאדפקא אי דאטמא בפרק אלו מציאות (ב"מ דף כג:) שנקרא דופק לפי שהנשימה דופקת ואין נראה לר"ת מדאמר בברכות פרק מי שמתו (דף יט: ושם) מדלגים היינו ע"ג ארונות לקראת מלכי אומות העולם ואי ארון היינו גולל ודופק היאך היו מדלגין עליו והלא גולל ודופק מטמאין באהל כדאמר בחולין בפרק העור והרוטב (דף קכו:) גולל ודופק מטמא במגע ובאהל ואינו מטמא במשא ועוד דאמר בעירובין (דף טו:) כל דבר שיש בו רוח חיים אין עושין אותו לא גולל לקבר ולא דופן לסוכה ולא לחי למבוי ואי כפי' הקונט' וכי דרך לעשות כיסוי ארון מבעלי חיים ועוד בפרק בהמה המקשה (חולין עב.) מרבינן (ד) דופק דמטמא מדכתיב על פני השדה ולפי' הקונטרס הוא מונח בקרקע דהיינו ארון ולא על פני השדה ועוד דתנן במס' אהלות בפ"ב (משנה ד) דופק דופקים טהור ואי כפירוש הקונטרס וכי דרך להניח שני קרשים מימין המת ופירש ר"ת דגולל היינו אבן גדולה שעל ארונו של מת שקורין מצבה וגוללין אותה שם הקרובי' לסימן ולשון גולל נופל באבן כדכתיב (בראשית כט) וגללו את האבן וגולל אבן אליו תשוב (משלי כו) ודופק הם שתי אבני' שנותנין (ה) אחת לראשו ואחת לרגליו לציון ופעמים שעדיין האבן אינה מוכנת לשום שם נותנין שם בהמה או שום דבר לסימן עד שימצאו אבן והיינו דתנן בעירובין (דף טו.) דבר שיש בו רוח חיים אין עושין כו' וההיא דמדלגין היינו ע"ג ארונות שלא היה שם לא גולל ולא דופק ומחמת המת לא היינו מיטמאים כדמפרש התם שהיה ברוב ארונות (ו) חלל טפח ומרבי נמי שפיר גולל ודופק מעל פני השדה והא דקאמר דופק דופקים פעמים שמניחים הגולל ע"ג שתי אבנים ועוד מניחין לראש הגולל אבן אחת ולסופו אבן אחרת ולא תקשה לר' יהושע דאמר בפרק קמא דכתובות (דף ד: ושם) מאימתי חל אבילות משיסתם הגולל במקום שאין גולל מתי חל די"ל מכי אהדרי אפייהו מקברא כדאמר במו"ק (ד' כג.) בהנהו דלא אזלי בתר שכבא מנו מכי אהדרי אפייהו ויש דוחין ראיה של ר"ת דמאי דמייתי ראיה מדמדלגין היינו אף על פי שהגולל מטמא באהל מ"מ יכולין היינו לדלג ולטמא עצמנו בגולל דהא תניא כל טומאה שאין הנזיר מגלח עליה אין כהן מוזהר עליו וגולל ודופק אין הנזיר מגלח עלייהו כדתנן במסכת נזיר פרק כ"ג (דף נד.) ואמר ר"ת דמשבשתא היא דמסכת שמחות דהא הש"ס ערוך דרביעית דם אין הנזיר מגלח עליו כדתנן התם בנזיר וכהן מוזהר ואם הברייתא בהש"ס הוה פריך עלה ומשבש לה כדאשכחינן בכמה דוכתין דמשבש להו ואפילו הויא מתרצתא אכתי היאך מדלגין הלא מחמת המת היו מיטמאים והגולל ודופק לא היו חוללין ומה שהביא ראיה מעירובין יש דוחין דאע"פ שאין רגילות לעשות כסוי ארון מבעלי חיים כמה דברים אשכחן דלא שכיחי ומיירי בהו הש"ס להראות לנו הדין ודרוש וקבל שכר כדאמרי' בבהמה המקשה (חולין דף ע.) בלעתו חולדה והוציאתו והכניסתו והקיאתו ויצא מאליו מהו הדביק שני רחמים ויצא מזה ונכנס לזה מהו ואף על פי שזה לא יהיה לעולם ועוד מקשין לפירוש ר"ת מדתני בהדיא בתוספתא דאהלות בפרק אמר רבי יהודה שתי אבנים גדולות שעשאן גולל לקבר המאהיל על גבי שתיהן טמא ניטלה אחת מהן המאהיל על גבי שנייה טהור מפני שיש לטומאה דרך שתצא ומה דרך שתצא שייך לפירוש ר"ת ובערוך פירש בענין אחר בערך גלל וכפירושו יתכן מה שבתוספתא (ז):

ונשמתו

עין משפט נר מצוה

נ א סמג עשין דרבנן ב:

רב נסים גאון

שלום בין איש לאשתו: אלו ואלו נמסרין לדומה הללו יש להן מנוח והללו אין להן מנוח. בפרק כל ישראל יש להם חלק (סנהדרין דף צד) גרסינן א"ר יוחנן אותו מלאך שהוא ממונה על הרוחות דומה שמו וכבר הזכרנו אותו בברכות:

סליק שואל אדם

תורה אור השלם

א) אַךְ בְּשָׂרוֹ עָלָיו יִכְאָב וְנַפְשׁוֹ עָלָיו תֶּאֱבָל: [איוב יד, כב]

ב) וְיָשֹׁב הֶעָפָר עַל הָאָרֶץ כְּשֶׁהָיָה וְהָרוּחַ תָּשׁוּב אֶל הָאֱלֹהִים אֲשֶׁר נְתָנָהּ: [קהלת יב, ז]

ג) יָבוֹא שָׁלוֹם יָנוּחוּ עַל מִשְׁכְּבוֹתָם הֹלֵךְ נְכֹחוֹ: [ישעיה נז, ב]

ד) וַיָּקָם אָדָם לִרְדָפְךָ וּלְבַקֵּשׁ אֶת נַפְשֶׁךָ וְהָיְתָה נֶפֶשׁ אֲדֹנִי צְרוּרָה בִּצְרוֹר הַחַיִּים אֵת יְיָ אֱלֹהֶיךָ וְאֵת נֶפֶשׁ אֹיְבֶיךָ יְקַלְּעֶנָּה בְּתוֹךְ כַּף הַקָּלַע: [שמואל א' כה, כט]

ה) אֵין שָׁלוֹם אָמַר יְיָ לָרְשָׁעִים: [ישעיה מח, כב]

ו) חַיֵּי בְשָׂרִים לֵב מַרְפֵּא וּרְקַב עֲצָמוֹת קִנְאָה: [משלי יד, ל]

ז) וִידַעְתֶּם כִּי אֲנִי יְיָ בְּפִתְחִי אֶת קִבְרוֹתֵיכֶם וּבְהַעֲלוֹתִי אֶתְכֶם מִקִּבְרוֹתֵיכֶם עַמִּי: [יחזקאל לז, יג]

ח) בְּזֵעַת אַפֶּיךָ תֹּאכַל לֶחֶם עַד שׁוּבְךָ אֶל הָאֲדָמָה כִּי מִמֶּנָּה לֻקָּחְתָּ כִּי עָפָר אַתָּה וְאֶל עָפָר תָּשׁוּב: [בראשית ג, יט]

ליקוטי רש"י

גולל. זה כסוי העליון דף שנותנין על המת [חולין קכו.]. זה כסוי של ארון המת [כתובות ד:]. יבוא שלום. יבא הצדיק הזה אל אבותיו בשלום [ישעיה נז, ב]. כף הקלע. מקיפות עור רחבה עשויה כמין כף באמצע הקלע שנותן בה האבן [ש"א כה, כט]. דומה. מלאך שהוא ממונה על המתים [ברכות יח:]. שומר המתים שמו דומה [חגיגה ה.]. אובא טמיא. בעל אוב של עצמות שעושה כשוף בעצמות המת וטמיא עצמות ודומה לו במסכת כלים בית שהוא מלא טמיא ופירש רב האי מלא טמיא בית שהוא מלא עצמות והביא ראיה על זה מברייתא רבה דקתני בדברים ספק טמאה ואין לפרש טמא שאין זה הלשון [ברכות נט.].

מסורת הש"ס

א) [פסחים לב: יומא פו: סנהדרין לז: מנחות מה. ק.], ב) [צ"ל את ה' אלהיך על כו'], ג) זוממות והולכות שנאמר ואת נפש כו' פי' דדייק מדלא אמרה יקלענה בכף הקלע ואמר בתוך כף הקלע וכו', ד) [ערוך ערך כנגידא פי' כשוף], ה) ר"ה יז. ד"ה ... , ו) [עי' תוס' סוכה כג. ד"ה ולא], ז) [עי' תוספות ברכות יט: ד"ה מדלגין ותוס' כתובות ד: ד"ה ותוס' סנהדרין מז: ד"ה משיסתם].

הגהות הב"ח

(א) גמ' איכא שכיבנא. נ"ב כלומר אי שכיבנא: (ב) רש"י ד"ה נחר בהו רבי אחאי: (ג) ד"ה ליקום מר לגויה דביתא יבא: (ד) תוס' ד"ה עד שיסתם וכו' מרבינן גולל ודופק דמטמא: (ה) בא"ד שנותנין אחת לראשו ואחת לרגליו וכן הוא בתוספות לכתובות דף ד' וע"ש בפרק מי שמתו בדף יט: (ו) בא"ד ברוב ארונות שלהם חלל טפח.

גליון הש"ס

גמ' על גופן של רשעים הוא אומר אין שלום אמר אלהי. עי' שם: כל מי שיש לו קנאה בלבו. עי' ב"ב דף יז ע"א תוס' ד"ה שבעה:

כָּל יוֹמָא הֲוָה דָּבַר רַב יְהוּדָה בֵּי עַשְׂרָה – So **every day** following the burial, **Rav Yehudah would bring a group of ten** men, וְיָתְבִי בְּדוּכְתֵּיהּ – **and they would sit** in mourning **in his place.** לְאַחַר שִׁבְעָה יָמִים – **After seven days,** אִיתְחֲזֵי לֵיהּ בְּחֶילְמֵיהּ דְּרַב יְהוּדָה – **[the dead man] appeared in Rav Yehudah's dream** וְאָמַר לֵיהּ – **and said to [Rav Yehudah]:** תָּנוּחַ דַּעְתְּךָ שֶׁהֵנַחְתָּ אֶת דַּעְתִּי – **Let your mind be at ease, for you have set my mind at ease.** Evidently, then, it is for a period of a week following death that the soul mourns its passing.

The Gemara explores further aspects of the soul's experience after death.

אָמַר רַבִּי אַבָּהוּ – **R' Abahu said:** כֹּל שֶׁאוֹמְרִים בִּפְנֵי הַמֵּת – **Everything that [people] say in the presence of a corpse** יוֹדֵעַ – **is known** by that person's soul עַד שֶׁיִּסָּתֵם הַגּוֹלֵל – **until the top of the casket is closed** over the body prior to burial.[1] Once this occurs, the soul no longer perceives what is said by the living.

A dispute is presented concerning this point:

פְּלִיגֵי בָּהּ רַבִּי חִיָּיא וְרַבִּי שִׁמְעוֹן בְּרַבִּי – **R' Chiya and R' Shimon the son of Rebbi disagree concerning this.** חַד אָמַר עַד שֶׁיִּסָּתֵם הַגּוֹלֵל – **One says** that **until the top of the casket is closed,** the deceased is aware of what is said in the presence of his corpse. וְחַד אָמַר עַד שֶׁיִּתְעַכֵּל הַבָּשָׂר – **And** the other **one says** that the deceased remains aware of these things **until the flesh** of his corpse **decomposes** in the grave.

The Gemara finds a Scriptural allusion to each of these views:

מַאן דְּאָמַר עַד שֶׁיִּתְעַכֵּל הַבָּשָׂר – **The one who says until the flesh decomposes** can claim the support of Scripture, דִּכְתִיב – **for it is written:** ,,אַךְ־בְּשָׂרוֹ עָלָיו יִכְאָב וְנַפְשׁוֹ עָלָיו תֶּאֱבָל'' – ***But his flesh will be pained over its [demise], and his soul shall mourn itself.***[2] מַאן דְּאָמַר עַד שֶׁיִּסָּתֵם הַגּוֹלֵל – And **the one who says until the top of the casket is closed** can likewise adduce Scriptural support, דִּכְתִיב – **for it is written:** ,,וְיָשֹׁב הֶעָפָר עַל־הָאָרֶץ כְּשֶׁהָיָה וגו' '' – ***The dust shall return to the earth as it was* etc.,** *and the spirit returns to God, Who gave it.*[3]

The second part of this verse is expounded:

תָּנוּ רַבָּנַן – **The Rabbis taught in a Baraisa:** ,,וְהָרוּחַ תָּשׁוּב אֶל־הָאֱלֹהִים אֲשֶׁר נְתָנָהּ'' – Scripture states:[4] ***AND THE SPIRIT RETURNS TO GOD, WHO GAVE IT.*** From the seemingly superfluous phrase "Who gave it," we expound: תְּנָה לוֹ כְּמוֹ שֶׁנְּתָנָהּ לְךָ – Be careful to **GIVE IT** [the soul], back **TO HIM** [God] **LIKE HE GAVE IT TO YOU.** בְּטָהֳרָה – Just as when God gives a soul to a person at birth, it is in a pristine state **OF PURITY,** אַף אַתָּה בְּטָהֳרָה – **SO TOO, YOU** must see to it that when you return this soul at the time of death, it is likewise in a state of **PURITY,** unsullied by sin.

The Baraisa elaborates:

מָשָׁל לְמֶלֶךְ בָּשָׂר וָדָם – **IT IS ANALOGOUS TO** a situation where **A KING OF FLESH AND BLOOD** שֶׁחִלֵּק בִּגְדֵי מַלְכוּת לַעֲבָדָיו – **DISTRIBUTED ROYAL APPAREL TO HIS SERVANTS.** פִּקְחִין שֶׁבָּהֶן קִיפְּלוּם וְהִנִּיחוּם בְּקוּפְסָא – **THOSE AMONG [THE SERVANTS] WHO WERE WISE FOLDED** the clothes **AND PLACED THEM IN A BOX** for safekeeping.[5] טִפְּשִׁים שֶׁבָּהֶן הָלְכוּ וְעָשׂוּ בָּהֶן מְלָאכָה – And **THOSE AMONG THEM WHO WERE FOOLISH** donned these garments and **WENT AND PERFORMED LABOR WITH THEM.** לְיָמִים – **SOMETIME LATER,** בִּיקֵּשׁ הַמֶּלֶךְ אֶת כֵּלָיו – **THE KING REQUESTED** that **HIS GARMENTS** be returned to him. פִּקְחִין שֶׁבָּהֶן הֶחֱזִירוּם לוֹ כְּשֶׁהֵן מְגוֹהָצִין – **THOSE** servants **WHO HAD BEEN WISE RETURNED THEM TO [THE KING]** clean and **NEATLY PRESSED,** for they had properly safeguarded these garments and had seen to it that they remained pristine. טִפְּשִׁין שֶׁבָּהֶן הֶחֱזִירוּם לוֹ כְּשֶׁהֵן מְלוּכְלָכִין – **THOSE WHO HAD BEEN FOOLISH,** however, **RETURNED THEM TO [THE KING] SOILED,** for the garments had become dirty while they labored in them. שָׂמַח הַמֶּלֶךְ לִקְרַאת פִּקְחִין – **THE KING GREETED THE WISE** servants **WITH HAPPINESS,** וְכָעַס לִקְרַאת טִפְּשִׁין – **AND GREETED THE FOOLISH** servants **WITH ANGER.** עַל פִּקְחִין אָמַר – **CONCERNING THE WISE** servants **HE SAID:** יִנָּתְנוּ כֵּלַי לָאוֹצָר – **LET MY GARMENTS** that I entrusted to these people **BE PLACED** directly **IN** my **CHEST,** for their royal stature is undiminished;[6] וְהֵם יֵלְכוּ לְבָתֵּיהֶם לְשָׁלוֹם – **AND** as for the wise servants themselves, **LET THEM GO** back **TO THEIR HOMES IN PEACE.** וְעַל טִפְּשִׁין אָמַר – **BUT CONCERNING THE FOOLISH** servants **HE SAID:** כֵּלַי יִנָּתְנוּ לְכוֹבֵס – **LET MY GARMENTS** that I entrusted to these fools **BE GIVEN TO A LAUNDERER,** for in their present state they are unbefitting royalty.[7] וְהֵן יִתְחַבְּשׁוּ בְּבֵית הָאֲסוּרִים – And as for these servants themselves, **LET THEM BE CONFINED IN PRISON** for their irresponsible behavior.

The Baraisa concludes:

אַף הַקָּדוֹשׁ בָּרוּךְ הוּא – **SO IT IS WITH THE HOLY ONE, BLESSED IS HE:** עַל גּוּפָן שֶׁל צַדִּיקִים אוֹמֵר – **CONCERNING THE BODIES OF THE RIGHTEOUS,** He is pleased with the way they safeguarded their souls, and **HE SAYS:**[8] ,,יָבוֹא שָׁלוֹם יָנוּחוּ עַל־מִשְׁכְּבוֹתָם'' – ***LET HIM COME IN PEACE; LET THEM REST UPON THEIR COUCHES;*** i.e. their bodies shall rest peacefully in the grave. וְעַל נִשְׁמָתָן הוּא אוֹמֵר – **AND CONCERNING THE SOULS [OF THE RIGHTEOUS], HE SAYS:** ,,וְהָיְתָה נֶפֶשׁ אֲדֹנִי צְרוּרָה בִּצְרוֹר הַחַיִּים'' – ***MAY THE SOUL OF MY MASTER BE BUNDLED IN THE BUNDLE OF LIFE.***[9] עַל גּוּפָן שֶׁל רְשָׁעִים הוּא אוֹמֵר – However, **CONCERNING THE BODIES OF THE WICKED, HE SAYS:**[10] ,,אֵין שָׁלוֹם אָמַר ה' לָרְשָׁעִים'' – ***THERE SHALL***

NOTES

1. I.e. in the immediate aftermath of death, the soul remains connected in some way to the body, and in this state, it retains an awareness of the earthly proceedings surrounding his body.

After the casket is closed, this awareness ceases. Nevertheless, commentators state that at certain times the soul of a deceased person can be made aware of earthly events long after his death and burial. See *Berachos* 18b and *Nishmas Chaim,* vol. II ch. 22.

Our translation of גולל as a casket cover follows *Rashi* here and throughout the Talmud. *Tosafos,* however, defines גולל as a tombstone.

2. *Job,* 14:22. The verse implies that as long as flesh remains on a corpse, the soul of the deceased continues to mourn its death. This indicates that until the corpse actually decomposes, the soul retains some sort of connection with the body, and consequently, it maintains a residual cognizance of its condition and surroundings (see *Rashi*).

3. *Ecclesiastes* 12:7. The phrase "the dust" refers to the human body, for Adam's body was formed out of dust (see *Genesis* 2:7; *Maharsha*). Thus, the phrase alludes to the idea that when the body is lowered into the ground [*returns to the earth*], it is then that the soul departs the body and returns to God, becoming oblivious of its previous physical existence (see *Rashi*).

4. *Ecclesiastes* 12:7.

5. That is, the wise servants were careful to wear the clothes only when there was no danger of their becoming soiled. Thus, whenever those servants performed a task which might dirty their clothes, they first made sure to remove the royal apparel and neatly fold and store them. Similarly, the righteous make sure that the souls with which they have been endowed do not become soiled by sin (*Maharsha;* cf. *Iyun Yaakov*).

6. [God's "royal chest" is a metaphor for the Heavenly "place" where the souls of the righteous repose.]

7. The "launderer" is a metaphor for Gehinnom, *purgatory,* where souls sullied by sin must be purged before they can be admitted to Paradise (*Rashi*).

8. *Isaiah* 57:2.

9. *I Samuel* 25:29. With these words, Avigail, wife of Naval, prophesied that David's soul would reside in Paradise (*Maharsha*). The end of the verse, which speaks of the Heavenly fate awaiting David's enemies, is cited at the end of this Baraisa.

10. *Isaiah* 48:22.

עין משפט נר מצוה

נ א סמג עשין דרבנן ב:

רב נסים גאון

שלום בין איש לאשתו: **אלו** ואלו נמסרין לדומה הללו יש להן מנוח והללו אין להן מנוח. בפרק כל ישראל יש להם חלק (סנהדרין דף צד) גרסינן א"ר יוחנן אותו מלאך שהוא ממונה על הרוחות דומה שמו וכבר הזכרנו אותו בברכות:

סליק שואל אדם

תורה אור השלם

א) אַךְ בְּשָׂרוֹ עָלָיו יִכְאָב וְנַפְשׁוֹ עָלָיו תֶּאֱבָל: [איוב יד, כב]

ב) וְיָשֹׁב הֶעָפָר עַל הָאָרֶץ כְּשֶׁהָיָה וְהָרוּחַ תָּשׁוּב אֶל הָאֱלֹהִים אֲשֶׁר נְתָנָהּ: [קהלת יב, ז]

ג) יָבוֹא שָׁלוֹם יָנוּחוּ עַל מִשְׁכְּבוֹתָם הֹלֵךְ נְכֹחוֹ: [ישעיה נז, ב]

ד) וַיָּקָם אָדָם לִרְדָפְךָ וּלְבַקֵּשׁ אֶת נַפְשֶׁךָ וְהָיְתָה נֶפֶשׁ אֲדֹנִי צְרוּרָה בִּצְרוֹר הַחַיִּים אֵת יְיָ אֱלֹהֶיךָ וְאֵת נֶפֶשׁ אֹיְבֶיךָ יְקַלְּעֶנָּה בְּתוֹךְ כַּף הַקָּלַע: [שמואל א' כה, כט]

ה) אֵין שָׁלוֹם אָמַר יְיָ לָרְשָׁעִים: [ישעיה מח, כב]

ו) חַיֵּי בְשָׂרִים לֵב מַרְפֵּא וּרְקַב עֲצָמוֹת קִנְאָה: [משלי יד, ל]

ז) וִידַעְתֶּם כִּי אֲנִי יְיָ בְּפִתְחִי אֶת קִבְרוֹתֵיכֶם וּבְהַעֲלוֹתִי אֶתְכֶם מִקִּבְרוֹתֵיכֶם עַמִּי: [יחזקאל לז, יג]

ח) בְּזֵעַת אַפֶּיךָ תֹּאכַל לֶחֶם עַד שׁוּבְךָ אֶל הָאֲדָמָה כִּי מִמֶּנָּה לֻקָּחְתָּ כִּי עָפָר אַתָּה וְאֶל עָפָר תָּשׁוּב: [בראשית ג, יט]

ליקוטי רש"י

גולל. זה כסוי העליון דף שנותנין על המת [חולין קכו:]. זה כסוי של ארון המת [כתובות ד:]. יבא שלום. יבא הצדיק הזה אל אבותיו בשלום [ישעיה נז, ב]. כף הקלע. עור למטה שעושה כמין כף באמצע הקלע שנותן בה האבן [ש"א כה, כט]. דומה. מלאך שהוא ממונה על המתים [ברכות יח:]. שומר המתים ששמו דומה [חגיגה ה.]. אובא טמיא. בעל אוב של עצמות שעושה כשוף בעצמות המת ודומה לו במסכת כלים בית מלא עצמות טמיא ופירש רב האי בית שהוא מלא עצמות והביא ראיה על זה מברייתא דקתני אדריינוס שחיק טמיא דהיינו שחיק עצמות ואין לפרש אוב טמא שאין זה הלשון [ברכות נט.].

כל יומא הוה דבר רב יהודה בי עשרה ויתבי בדוכתיה לאחר שבעה ימים איתחזי ליה בחילמיה דרב יהודה ואמר ליה א) תנוח דעתך שהנחת את דעתי א"ר אבהו א)כל שאומרים בפני המת יודע עד שיסתם הגולל פליגי בה רבי חייא ור"ש ברבי חד אמר עד שיסתם הגולל וחד אמר עד שיתעכל הבשר מאן דאמר עד שיתעכל הבשר דכתיב א) אך בשרו עליו יכאב ונפשו עליו תאבל מאן דאמר עד שיסתם הגולל דכתיב ב) וישוב העפר על הארץ כשהיה וגו' ת"ר ב) והרוח תשוב אל האלהים אשר נתנה תנה לו כמו שנתנה לך בטהרה אף אתה בטהרה משל למלך ב"ו שחלק בגדי מלכות לעבדיו פקחין שבהן קיפלום והניחום בקופסא טפשים שבהן הלכו ועשו בהן מלאכה לימים ביקש המלך את כליו פקחין שבהן החזירום לו כשהן מגוהצין טפשין שבהן החזירום לו כשהן מלוכלכין שמח המלך לקראת פקחין וכעס לקראת טפשין על פקחין אמר ינתנו כלי לאוצר והם ילכו לבתיהם לשלום ועל טפשין אמר כלי ינתנו לכובס והן יתחבשו בבית האסורים אף הקב"ה על גופן של צדיקים אומר ג) יבא שלום ינוחו על משכבותם ועל נשמתן הוא אומר ד) והיתה נפש אדוני צרורה בצרור החיים ב) על גופן של רשעים הוא אומר ה) אין שלום אמר ה' לרשעים ועל נשמתן הוא אומר ד) ואת נפש אויביך יקלענה בתוך כף הקלע תניא ר' אליעזר אומר נשמתן של צדיקים גנוזות תחת כסא הכבוד שנאמר והיתה נפש אדני צרורה בצרור החיים ושל רשעים ג) זוממות והולכות [ד) ומלאך אחד עומד בסוף העולם ומלאך אחר עומד בסוף העולם ומקלעין נשמתן זה לזה] שנא' ואת נפש אויביך יקלענה בתוך כף הקלע א"ל רבה לר"נ של בינונים מאי א"ל ה) איכא (א) שכיבנא לא אמרי לכו האי מילתא הכי אמר שמואל אלו ואלו לדומה נמסרין הללו יש להן מנוח והללו אין להן מנוח אמר (ליה) רב מרי עתידים צדיקים דהוו עפרא דכתיב ב) וישוב העפר על הארץ כשהיה הנהו קפולאי דהוו קפלי בארעא דרב נחמן ו) נחר בהו רב אחאי בר יאשיה אתו ואמרו ליה לרב נחמן נחר בן גברא אתא ואמר ליה מאן ניהו מר אמר ליה אנא אחאי בר יאשיה א"ל ולאו אמר רב מרי עתידי צדיקי דהוו עפרא א"ל ומני מרי דלא ידענא ליה א"ל והא קרא כתיב וישוב העפר על הארץ כשהיה א"ל מאן דאקריך קהלת לא אקריך משלי דכתיב ו) ורקב עצמות קנאה • כל מי שיש לו קנאה בלבו עצמותיו מרקיבים כל שאין לו קנאה בלבו אין עצמותיו מרקיבים גששיה חזייה דאית ביה מששא אמר ליה ליקום מר לגווה דביתא אמר ליה גלית אדעתך דאפילו נביאי לא קרית דכתיב ז) וידעתם כי אני ה' בפתחי את קברותיכם א"ל והכתיב ח) כי עפר אתה ואל עפר תשוב א"ל ההוא שעה אחת קודם תחיית המתים א"ל ההוא צדוקי לר' אבהו אמריתו נשמתן של צדיקים גנוזות תחת כסא הכבוד אובא טמיא היכא אסקיה לשמואל ט) בנגידא א"ל התם בתוך שנים עשר חדש הוה דתניא כל י"ב חדש גופו קיים ונשמתו עולה ויורדת לאחר י"ב חדש הגוף בטל ונשמתו

רש"י

כל יומא. ז' ימי אבילות: גולל. הוא כיסוי שנותנים על ארונו: ונפשו עליו תאבל. כל זמן שיש לו בשר יש לו לנפש לב חיות להבין: וישוב העפר. גופו קרוי עפר ומשגב אל הארץ כשהיה מיד והרוח תשוב שאין בו רוח עוד: אשר נתנה. קרא יתירה הוא לידרש הוי זהיר שתשיבנה אליו כמה שנתנה לך נקייה בלי עון: כלי ינתנו לאוצר. להצניען אף זו תינתן תחת כסא הכבוד: לכובס. ללבן אף זו לגיהנם לצורפם שם: בבית האסורים. בחשך בלא אורה ושלוה: כף הקלע. רחב הרצועה שנותן האבן לתוכה לקלע עשויה כעין כף: בצרור החיים וגו'. את ה' אלהיך עמו בכסאו: זוממות. כמו בזוממא דפרזלא (לעיל דף נא:) חבושות בבית הסוהר: אלו ואלו. רשעים ובינונים: לדומה. מלאך הממונה על הרוחות: דהוו עפרא. אפילו צדיקים נרקבים ונעשים אפר: קפולאי. חופרים: נחר בהו (ב) רבי אחאי. שהיה נקבר שם: דלא ידענא ליה. ואיני חש לדבריו: מי שיש לו קנאה. ותחרות על חברו: עצמותיו מרקיבים. ועליו נאמר וישוב אל העפר: ליקום מר לגווה. (ג) יבא אדוני לבית: בפתחי. בהעלותי עד שיעלנו הקדוש ברוך הוא מקברותינו אין לנו רשות לעלות: והא כתיב ואל עפר תשוב. והאי ליכא למימר ברשעים לחודייהו דכל קללותיו של אדה"ר כל דורותיו שוין בהן: אובא טמיא. בעלת אוב שמשתמש בעצמות טמיא בלשון ארמי עצמות וכן פירש רב האי בפירושו של טהרות בית שהוא מלא טמיא מלא עצמות ט): בנגידא. כן קורין למכשפות של אוב בלשון ארמי: אם

תוספות

עד שיסתם הגולל. בכל מקום מפרש רש"י דגולל הוא כיסוי ארונו של מת ודופק דף שנתון מלידו ונקרא דופק על שם שהמת דופק שם כמו חתיכה גופה תיהוי סימן אי דלדפקא אי לאטמא בפרק אלו מציאות (ב"מ דף כג:) שנקרא דופק לפי שהנשימה דופקת ואין נראה לר"ת מדאמר בברכות פרק מי שמתו (דף יט: ושם) מדלגים היינו ע"ג ארונות לקראת מלכי אומות העולם ואי ארון היינו גולל ודופק היאך היו מדלגין עליו והלא גולל ודופק מטמאין באהל כדאמר בחולין בפרק העור והרוטב (דף קכו:) גולל ודופק מטמא במגע ובאהל ואינו מטמא במשא ועוד דאמר בעירובין (דף טו:) כל דבר שיש בו רוח חיים אין עושין אותו לא גולל לקבר ולא דופן לסוכה ולא לחי למבוי ואי כפי' הקונט' וכי דרך לעשות כיסוי ארון מבעלי חיים ועוד בפרק בהמה המקשה (חולין עב.) מרבינן (ד) דופק דמטמא מדכתיב על פני השדה ולפי' הקונטרס הוא מונח בקרקע דהיינו ארון ולא על פני השדה ועוד דתנן במס' אהלות בפ"ב (משנה ד) דופק דופקים טהור ואי כפירוש הקונטרס וכי דרך להניח שני קרשים מימין המת ופירש ר"ת דגולל היינו אבן גדולה שעל ארונו של מת שקורין מצבה וגוללין אותה שם הקברות' לסימן ולשון גולל נופל באבן כדכתיב (בראשית כט) וגללו את האבן וגולל אבן אליו תשוב (משלי כו) ודופק הם שתי אבני' שנותנין (ה) אחת לראשו ואחת לרגליו לציון ופעמים שעדיין האבן אינה מוכנת לשום שם נותנין שם בהמה או שום דבר לסימן עד שימצאו אבן והיינו דתנן בעירובין (דף טו.) לדבר שיש בו רוח חיים אין עושין כו' ובההיא דמדלגין היינו ע"ג ארונות שלא היה שם לא גולל ולא דופק ומחמת המת לא היינו מיטמאים כדמפרש התם שהיה ברוב ארונות (ו) חלל טפח ומרבי נמי שפיר גולל ודופק מעל פני השדה והא דקאמר דופק דופקים פעמים שמניחים הגולל ע"ג שתי אבנים ועוד מניחין לראש הגולל אבן אחת ולסופו אבן אחרת ולא תקשה לר' יהושע דאמר בפרק קמא דכתובות (דף ד: ושם) מאימתי חל אבילות משיסתם הגולל במקום שאין גולל מתי חל די"ל מכי אהדרי אפייהו מקברא כדאמר במו"ק (ד' כב.) בהנהו דלא אזלי בתר שכבא מנו מכי אהדרי אפייהו ויש דוחין ראיה של ר"ת דמאי דמייתי ראיה מדמדלגין היינו אף על פי שהגולל מטמא באהל מ"מ יכולין היינו לדלג ולטמא עצמנו בגולל דהא תניא י) כל טומאה שאין הנזיר מגלח עליה אין כהן מוזהר עליו וגולל ודופק אין הנזיר מגלח עלייהו כדתנן במסכת נזיר פרק כ"ג (דף נד.) ואמר ר"ת דמשבשתא היא דמסכת שמחות דהא הש"ס ערוך דרביעית דם אין הנזיר מגלח עליו כדתנן התם בנזיר ט) וכהן מוחר ואם הברייתא בהש"ם הוה פריך עלה ומשני לה כדאשכחינן בכמה דוכתין דמשבש להו ואפילו הויא מתרלתא מכתי היאך מדלגין הלא מחמת המת היו מיטמאים והגולל והדופק לא היו מוחלין ומה שהביא ראיה מעירובין יש דוחין דאע"פ שאין רגילות לעשות כסוי ארון מבעלי חיים כמה דברים אשכחן דלא שכיחי ומיירי בהו הש"ס להראות לנו הדין ודרוש וקבל שכר כדאמרי' בבהמה המקשה (חולין דף ע.) בלעתו חולדה והוליאתו והכניסתו והקיאתו ויצא מאליו מהו הדביק שני רחמים ויצא מזה ונכנס לזה מהו ואף על פי שזה לא יהיה לעולם ועוד מקשין לפירוש ר"ת מדתני בהדיא בתוספתא דאהלות בפרק אמר רבי יהודה שתי אבנים גדולות שעשאן גולל לקבר המאהיל על גבי שתיהן טמא ניטלה אחת מהן המאהיל על גבי שנייה טהור מפני שיש לטומאה דרך שתצא ומה דרך שתצא שייך לפירוש ר"ת ובערוך פירש בענין אחר בערך גלל וכפירושו יתכן מה שבתוספתא ל):

ונשמתו

מסורת הש"ס

א) [פסחים לב: יומא סו: סנהדרין ל: מנחות מה. ק.], ב) [צ"ל **את ה' אלהיך** על כו'], ג) **זוממת והולכת שנאמר ואת נפש** כו' פי' דדייק מדלא אמרה יקלענה בכף הקלע ואמר בתוך כף הקלע משמע שהיא חבושה וכבושה בתוך כף הקלע ואינה יוצאה ממנו ומלאך ממלאכי חבלה מקלע אותה רצועה לכאן ולכאן וזהו לשון זוממות, ד) גי' רש"ל לא משמע כן מפי' רש"י שפי' שהן חבושין ולגי' זו אינן חבושי' ואולי מלא גי' כו אבל גי' רש"י אינו כן מ"כ, ה) [ע"ז נה.], ו) [עי' פירושו ברש"י גיטין סח. ד"ה נחר], ז) [צ"ל **את קברותיכם ובהעלותי אתכם מקברותיכם** עמי וכ"א בע"י וזהו תבין פרש"י ד"ה בפתחי בהעלותי עד שיעלנו וכו'], ח) [ערוך ערך בנגידא פי' בכישוף], ט) ראה רש"י ברכות נט. ד"ה אובא, י) [במס' שמחות פ"ד הל' כ"א ע"ש], כ) [דף נד.], ל) [וע"ע תוספות ברכות יט: ד"ה מדלגין ותוס' סוכה כג. ד"ה ולא ותוס' כתובות ד: ד"ה עד ותוס' סנהדרין מז: ד"ה משיסתום].

הגהות הב"ח

(א) גמ' איכא שכיבנא. נ"ב כלומר אי שכיבנא: (ב) רש"י ד"ה נחר בהו גער בהו רבי אחא: (ג) ד"ה ליקום מר לגויה דביתא יבא: (ד) תוס' ד"ה עד שיסתום וכו' מרבינן גולל ודופק דמטמא: (ה) בא"ד שנותנין אחת לראשו. נ"ב פי' לראשו ולרגליו של גולל וכן הוא בתוספות פ"ק דכתובות דף ד' וע"ש בפרק מי שמתו בדף יט: (ו) בא"ד ברוב ארונות שלהם חלל טפח:

גליון הש"ס

גמ' על גופן של רשעים הוא אומר אין שלום אמר אלהי. כל"ל: שם כל מי שיש לו קנאה בלבו. עי' ב"ב דף יז ע"א תוס' ד"ה שבעה:

BE NO PEACE, SAYS GOD, FOR THE WICKED. וְעַל נִשְׁמָתָן הוּא אוֹמֵר – AND CONCERNING THEIR SOUL HE SAYS:[11] ,,וְאֵת נֶפֶשׁ אֹיְבֶיךָ יְקַלְּעֶנָּה בְּתוֹךְ כַּף הַקָּלַע" – *AND AS FOR THE SOUL OF YOUR ENEMY, MAY [GOD] SLING IT AS FROM THE HOLLOW OF A SLING!*

A Baraisa further expounds this last verse:

תַּנְיָא – It was taught in a Baraisa: רַבִּי אֱלִיעֶזֶר אוֹמֵר – R' ELIEZER SAYS: נִשְׁמָתָן שֶׁל צַדִּיקִים גְּנוּזוֹת תַּחַת כִּסֵּא הַכָּבוֹד – THE SOULS OF THE RIGHTEOUS ARE ENSCONCED BENEATH THE HEAVENLY THRONE, שֶׁנֶּאֱמַר ,,וְהָיְתָה נֶפֶשׁ אֲדֹנִי צְרוּרָה בִּצְרוֹר הַחַיִּים" – AS IT IS WRITTEN: *MAY THE SOUL OF MY MASTER BE BUNDLED IN THE BUNDLE OF LIFE with Hashem your God.*[12] וְשֶׁל רְשָׁעִים זוֹמְמוֹת וְהוֹלְכוֹת – BUT as for [THE SOULS] OF THE WICKED, THEY ARE PERPETUALLY CONFINED,[13] וּמַלְאָךְ אֶחָד עוֹמֵד בְּסוֹף הָעוֹלָם – AND AN ANGEL STANDS AT one END OF THE UNIVERSE וּמַלְאָךְ אַחֵר עוֹמֵד בְּסוֹף הָעוֹלָם – AND ANOTHER ANGEL STANDS AT the other END OF THE UNIVERSE; וּמְקַלְּעִין נִשְׁמָתָן זֶה לָזֶה – AND THEY SLING THE SOULS [OF THE WICKED] back and forth TO ONE ANOTHER,[14] שֶׁנֶּאֱמַר ,,וְאֵת נֶפֶשׁ אֹיְבֶיךָ יְקַלְּעֶנָּה בְּתוֹךְ כַּף הַקָּלַע" – AS IT IS WRITTEN in the end of that verse: *AND AS FOR THE SOUL OF YOUR ENEMY, MAY [GOD] SLING IT AS FROM THE HOLLOW OF A SLING.*

The Gemara discusses the fate of those who were of intermediate merit, neither completely righteous nor completely wicked:

אָמַר לֵיהּ רַבָּה לְרַב נַחְמָן – **Rabbah said to Rav Nachman:** שֶׁל בֵּינוֹנִים מַאי – And **what of the intermediate** persons? What is the fate of their souls after death? אָמַר לֵיהּ – **[Rav Nachman] replied to him:** אִיכָּא שְׁכִיבְנָא לָא אָמְרִי לְכוּ הַאי מִילְּתָא – **Had I died, I would not** have been able to **tell you** about **this matter.**[15] הָכִי אָמַר שְׁמוּאֵל – But **so said Shmuel** on this issue: אֵלּוּ וָאֵלּוּ לְדוּמָה נִמְסָרִין – Both **these and those,** i.e. the souls of the wicked as well as the souls of the intermediate, **are handed over to** the angel **Dumah.**[16] הַלָּלוּ יֵשׁ לָהֶן מְנוּחָה – However, **these** souls of persons who led intermediate lives **have rest** in the Heavenly sphere; הַלָּלוּ אֵין לָהֶן מְנוּחָה – whereas **those** souls who led wicked lives **have no rest.**[17]

The Gemara further expounds a verse cited above:

אָמַר (לֵיהּ) רַב מָרִי – **Rav Mari said:** עֲתִידִים צַדִּיקִים דְּהָווּ עַפְרָא – Even the bodies of **the righteous are destined to become dust** in the grave;[18] דִּכְתִיב ,,וְיָשֹׁב הֶעָפָר עַל־הָאָרֶץ כְּשֶׁהָיָה" – this is the universal fate of man, **as it is written:** ***And the dust shall return to the earth as it was.***[19]

A related incident:

הָנְהוּ קַפּוּלָאֵי דְּהָווּ קָפְלֵי בְּאַרְעָא דְּרַב נַחְמָן – **There were** once **some diggers who were digging on the land of Rav Nachman.** They unwittingly came upon a corpse, that of Rav Achai bar Yoshiyah, a sage who had died generations earlier; נְחַר בְּהוּ רַב אַחַאי בַּר יֹאשִׁיָּה – and, having been disturbed in the grave, the body of **Rav Achai bar Yoshiyah snorted at them.** אָתוּ וְאָמְרוּ לֵיהּ לְרַב נַחְמָן – Frightened, those who had been digging **came** back **and said to Rav Nachman:** נְחַר בָּן גַּבְרָא – A dead **man snorted at us!** אָתָא וְאָמַר לֵיהּ – [Rav Nachman] then **came** to the grave site **and said to [the corpse]:** מַאן נִיהוּ מַר – **Who are you?**[20] אָמַר לֵיהּ – **[The corpse] replied to [Rav Nachman]:** אֲנָא אַחַאי בַּר יֹאשִׁיָּה – **I am** the body of **Achai bar Yoshiyah.**

The Gemara relates an ensuing discussion between Rav Nachman and the body:

אָמַר לֵיהּ – **[Rav Nachman] said to [the corpse]:** How is it that your body has not decomposed? וְלָאו אָמַר רַב מָרִי – **But did not Rav Mari say:** עֲתִידֵי צַדִּיקֵי דְּהָווּ עַפְרָא – Even the bodies of **the righteous are destined to become dust** in the grave?[21] אָמַר לֵיהּ – **[The corpse] replied to him:** וּמַנִּי מָרִי – **And** just **who is** this **Mari** whom you quote? דְּלָא יָדַעְנָא לֵיהּ – **I do not know him,** and I pay no mind to his words. אָמַר לֵיהּ – **[Rav Nachman] replied to [the corpse]:** וְהָא קְרָא כְּתִיב – **But** it is not just Rav Mari who has said this; it is **a verse written** in **Scripture** that declares the very same: ,,וְיָשֹׁב הֶעָפָר עַל־הָאָרֶץ כְּשֶׁהָיָה" – ***And the dust shall return to the earth as it was.*** Clearly, then, it is the way of things that a corpse turns to dust in the grave; why has your body not done so?[22]

The corpse retorts:

אָמַר לֵיהּ – **[The body]** of Rav Achai then **said to [Rav Nachman]:**

NOTES

11. *I Samuel* 25:29.

12. Anthropomorphically speaking, the souls will be in close proximity to God, under the throne upon which He sits (see *Rashi*).

Explicating the words צְרוֹר הַחַיִּים, *bundle of life, Rambam* (*Hil. Teshuvah* 8:3) states that the phrase denotes eternal life. *Rambam* characterizes this state of immortality, in which the soul delights in the presence of its Creator, as a condition of unimagined bliss, being the very greatest reward attainable.

13. The souls of the wicked are pictured as being trapped in *the hollow of a sling* [בְּתוֹךְ כַּף הַקָּלַע; see below], implying that they are confined as a stone is in the pocket of a sling (marginal gloss to the Vilna edition).

14. *Maharal* interprets our Gemara in the following vein: To live a righteous life is to live a life carefully balanced between extremes of behavior. The wicked, on the other hand, lead lives that incline dangerously towards one extreme or another, lacking the discipline to achieve balance. Such lives are characterized by instability and violent shifts from one pole to another – thus, fittingly, the same applies after their death. Their souls are portrayed as hurled "from one end of the universe to another," as even in the grave they will be unable to find stability or lasting repose.

Maharsha adopts a different interpretation, seeing our Gemara as alluding to the doctrine of גִּלְגּוּל, *transmigration of the soul.* The soul of one who led a wicked life is not permitted to find rest after the person's death; rather, it must return to earth as the soul of another person. If that second person lives a righteous life, the soul is permitted to rest after that person's death; however, should that person, too, lead a sinful life, the soul repeats the process yet again. Thus, the soul of a wicked person is "hurled" from person to person, and lifetime to lifetime.

For other intepretations of the Gemara, see *Nishmas Chaim* 1:7.

15. Rav Nachman was one of the few who had heard Shmuel's teaching concerning this mystery. Had he died without relating it to anyone, knowledge of the teaching would have been lost to the world (*Ben Yehoyada*).

16. Dumah [literally: silence] is the name of the angel who oversees the spirits of the dead (*Rashi*). The capacity of speech is what distinguishes man when he is alive; thus, his death is associated with *silence* (*Maharal*).

17. Rather, they are "flung from place to place," as mentioned earlier (see above, note 14).

18. I.e. the bodies of the righteous will eventually rot and become dust, just like the bodies of other persons (see *Rashi*).

19. *Ecclesiastes* 12:7; see above, note 3.

20. Literally: Who is the master?

21. *Maharal* explains the entire discussion between Rav Nachman and the corpse allegorically. In *Maharal's* interpretation, for example, Rav Nachman realized that R' Achai's soul had been spiritually pained in some way by the disturbance of its corpse by the diggers. Rav Nachman was puzzled by this, however, for he had been under the impression that eventually, as a corpse decomposes, the last residual bonds between the soul and the body in which it used to reside are broken. This, indeed, is how Rav Nachman understood the import of Rav Mari's teaching that "the bodies of the righteous become dust"; i.e. eventually, as the body ceases to exist as a physical entity, the soul ceases to care about its fate. R' Achai's pain at the disturbance of his grave many generations after his death, however, seemed to contradict this notion.

For a completely different explanation of this narrative, see *Maharsha*.

22. [I.e. why is it that you, the soul, still ascribe significance to your body so many years after its death? (see *Maharal*).]

כל יומא הוה דבר רב יהודה בי עשרה ויתבי בדוכתיה לאחר שבעה ימים איתחזי ליה בחילמיה דרב יהודה ואמר ליה ^ט תנוח דעתך שהנחת את דעתי א"ר אבהו ^א כל שאומרים בפני המת יודע עד שיסתם הגולל פליגי בה רבי חייא ור"ש ברבי חד אמר עד שיסתם הגולל וחד אמר עד שיתעכל הבשר מאן דאמר עד שיתעכל הבשר דכתיב ^א אך בשרו עליו יכאב ונפשו עליו תאבל מאן דאמר עד שיסתם הגולל דכתיב ^ב וישוב העפר על הארץ כשהיה וגו' ת"ר ^ב והרוח תשוב אל האלהים אשר נתנה תנה לו כמו שנתנה לך בטהרה אף אתה בטהרה משל למלך ב"ו שחלק בגדי מלכות לעבדיו פקחין שבהן קיפלום והניחום בקופסא טפשים שבהן הלכו ועשו בהן מלאכה לימים ביקש המלך את כליו פקחין שבהן החזירום לו כשהן מגוהצין טפשין שבהן החזירום לו כשהן מלוכלכין שמח המלך לקראת פקחין וכעס לקראת טפשין על פקחין אמר ינתנו כלי לאוצר והם ילכו לבתיהם לשלום ועל טפשין אמר כלי ינתנו לכובס והן יתחבשו בבית האסורים אף הקב"ה על גופן של צדיקים אומר ^ג יבא שלום ינוחו על משכבותם ועל נשמתן הוא אומר ^ד והיתה נפש אדוני צרורה בצרור החיים ^י על גופן של רשעים הוא אומר ^ה אין שלום אמר ה' לרשעים ועל נשמתן הוא אומר ^ד ואת נפש אויביך יקלענה בתוך כף הקלע תניא ר' אליעזר אומר נשמתן של צדיקים גנוזות תחת כסא הכבוד שנאמר והיתה נפש אדני צרורה בצרור החיים ושל רשעים ^ג זוממות והולכות [^ד ומלאך אחד עומד בסוף העולם ומלאך אחר עומד בסוף העולם ומקלעין נשמתן זה לזה] שנא' ואת נפש אויביך יקלענה בתוך כף הקלע א"ל רבה לר"נ של בינונים מאי א"ל ^ה איכא (א) שכיבנא לא אמרי לכו האי מילתא הכי אמר שמואל אלו ואלו לדומה נמסרין הללו יש להן מנוח והללו אין להן מנוח אמר (ליה) רב מרי עתידים צדיקים דהוו עפרא דכתיב ^ב וישוב העפר על הארץ כשהיה הנהו קפולאי דהוו קפלי בארעא דרב נחמן ^ו נחר בהו רב אחאי בר יאשיה אתו ואמרו ליה לרב נחמן נחר בן גברא אתא ואמר ליה מאן ניהו מר אמר ליה אנא אחאי בר יאשיה א"ל ולאו אמר רב מרי עתידי צדיקי דהוו עפרא א"ל ומני מרי דלא ידענא ליה א"ל והא קרא כתיב וישוב העפר על הארץ כשהיה אמר ליה דאקרייך קהלת לא אקרייך משלי דכתיב ^ו ורקב עצמות קנאה ^ל כל מי שיש לו קנאה בלבו עצמותיו מרקיבים כל שאין לו קנאה בלבו אין עצמותיו מרקיבים גששיה חזייה דאית ביה מששא אמר ליה ליקום מר לגווה דביתא אמר ליה גלית אדעתך דאפילו נביאי לא קרית דכתיב ^ז וידעתם כי אני ה' בפתחי ^ז את קברותיכם א"ל והכתיב ^ח כי עפר אתה ואל עפר תשוב א"ל ההוא שעה אחת קודם תחיית המתים א"ל ההוא צדוקי לר' אבהו אמריתו נשמתן של צדיקים גנוזות תחת כסא הכבוד אובא טמיא היכא אסקיה לשמואל ^מ בנגידא א"ל התם בתוך שנים עשר חדש הוה דתניא כל י"ב חדש גופו קיים ונשמתו עולה ויורדת לאחר י"ב חדש הגוף בטל ונשמתו

כל יומא. ז' ימי אבילות: גולל. הוא כיסוי ארונו של מת ודופק דף שנותנים על ארונו: ונפשו עליו תאבל. כל זמן שיש לו בשר יש לו לנפש לב חיות להבין: וישוב העפר. גופו קרוי עפר ומשבא אל הארץ כשהיה מיד והרוח תשוב שאין בו רוח עוד: אשר נתנה. קרא יתירה הוא לדרש הוי זהיר שתשיבנה אליו כמה שנתנה לך נקייה בלי עון: כלי ינתנו לאוצר. להכניסן אף זו תינתן תחת כסא הכבוד: לכובס. ללבנן אף זו לגיהנם לצורפס שם: בבית האסורים. במשך בלא אורה ושלוה: כף הקלע. רחב הקלועה שנותן האבן לתוכה לקלע עשויה כעין כף: בצרור החיים וגו'. את ה' אלהיך עמו בכסאו: זוממות. כמו בזוממת דפרזלא (לעיל דף נא:) חבושות כבית הסוהר: אלו ואלו. רשעים ובינונים: לדומה. מלאך הממונה על הרוחות: דהוו עפרא. אפילו צדיקים נרקבים ונעשים עפר: קפולאי. חופרים: נחר בהו (ג) רבי אחאי. שהיה נקבר שם: דלא ידענא ליה. ואינו חש לדבריו: מי שיש לו קנאה. ותחרות על חברו: עצמותיו מרקיבים. ועליו נאמר וישוב אל העפר: ליקום מר לגוויה. (ג) יבא לדורי לבית: בפתחי. בהעלותי עד שיעלנו הקדוש ברוך הוא מקברותינו אין לנו רשות לעלות: והא כתיב ואל עפר תשוב. והאי ליכא למימר ברשעים דהוה מודיעו לכל קללותיו של אדה"ר כל דורותיו שוין בהן: אובא טמיא. בעלת אוב שמשתמש בעצמות טמאה בלשון ארמי עצמות וכן פירש רב האי בפירושו של טהרות בית שהוא מלא טמיא מלא עצמות ^ט: בנגידא. כן קורין למכשפות של אוב בלשון ארמי: אם

עד שיסתם הגולל. בכל מקום מפרש רש"י דגולל הוא כיסוי ארונו של מת ודופק דף שנותן מלידו ונקרא דופק על שם שהמת דופק שם כמו חתיכה גופה תיהוי סימן מי לאדפקא אי לאטמאה בפרק אלו מגילות (כ"מ דף כג:) שנקרא דופק לפי שהנשמה דופקת ואין נראה לר"ת מדאמר בברכות פרק מי שמתו (דף יט: ושם) מדלגים היינו ע"ג ארונות לקראת מלכי אומות העולם ואי ארון היינו גולל ודופק היאך היו מדלגין עליו והלא גולל ודופק מטמאין באהל כדאמר בחולין בפרק העור והרוטב (דף קכו:) גולל ודופק מטמא במגע ובאהל ואינו מטמא במשא ועוד דאמר בעירובין (דף טו:) כל דבר שיש בו רוח חיים אין עושין אותו לא גולל לקבר ולא דופק לסוכה ולא לחי למבוי ואי כפי' הקונט' וכי דרך לעשות כיסוי ארון מבעלי חיים ועוד בפרק בהמה המקשה (חולין עב.) מרבינן (ד) דופק לטמאה מדכתיב על פני השדה ולפי' הקונטרס הוא מונח בקרקע דהיינו ארון ולא על פני השדה ועוד דתנן במס' אהלות בפ"ב (משנה ד) דופק דופקים טהור ואי כפירוש הקונטרס וכי דרך להביא שני קרשים מימין המת ומשמאלו ופירש ר"ת דגולל היינו אבן גדולה שעל ארונו של מת שקורין מצבה וגוללין אותה שם הקברוי' לסימן ולשון גולל נופל באבן כדכתיב (בראשית כט) וגללו את האבן וגולל אבן עליו תשוב (משלי כו) ודופק הם שתי אבני' שנותנין (ה) אחת לראשו ואחת לרגליו לציון ופעמים שעדיין האבן אינה מוכנת לשום שם נותנין שם בהמה או שום דבר לסימן עד שימצאו אבן והיינו דתנן בעירובין (דף טו.) לדבר שיש בו רוח חיים אין עושין כו' והביא דמדלגין היינו ע"ג ארונות שלא היה שם לא גולל ולא דופק ומחמת המת לא היינו מיטמאים כדמפרש התם שהיה ברוב ארונות (ו) חלל טפח ומרבי נמי שפיר גולל ודופק מעל פני השדה והא דקאמר דופק דופקים פעמים שמניחים הגולל ע"ג שתי אבנים ועוד מניחין לראש הגולל אבן אחת ולסופו אבן אחרת ולא מקשה לר' יהושע דאמר בפרק קמא דכתובות (דף ד: ושם) מאימתי חל אבילות משיסתם הגולל במקום שאין גולל מאי הוה לי"ל מכי אהדרי אפייהו מקברא כדאמר במו"ק (דף כג:) בההוא דלא אזלי בתר ערסא מנו מכי אהדרי אפייהו ויש דוחין ראיה של ר"ת מדאמרי ראיה מדמדלגין היינו אף על פי שהגולל מטמא באהל מ"מ יכולין היינו לדלג ולטמא עצמנו בגולל דהא תניא ^י כל טומאה שאין הנזיר מגלח עליה אין כהן מוזהר עליו וגולל ודופק אין הנזיר מגלח עלייהו כדתנן במסכת נזיר פרק כ"ג (דף מ.) ואמר ר"ת דמשבשתא היא דמסכת שמחות דהא הש"ס ערוך דרביעית דם אין הנזיר מגלח עליו כדתנן התם בנזיר ^כ וכהן מוזהר ואם הברייתא בהש"ס הוה פריך עלה ומשבש לה כדאשכחינן בכמה דוכתין דמשבש להו ואפילו הויא מתרצתא אכתי היאך מדלגין הלא מחמת המת היו מיטמאים והגולל ודופק לא היו חוללין ומה שהביא ראיה מעירובין יש דוחין דאע"פ שאין רגילות לעשות כסוי ארון מבעלי חיים כמה דברים אשכחן דלא שכיחי ומיירי בהו הש"ס להראות לנו הדין ודרוש וקבל שכר כדאמרי' בבהמה המקשה (חולין דף ע.) בלעתו חולדה והוליאתו והכניסתו והקיאתו ויצא מאליו מהו הדביק שני רחמים ויצא מזה ונכנס לזה מהו ואף על פי שזה לא יהיה לעולם ועוד מקשין לפירוש ר"ת מדתני בהדיא בתוספתא דאהלות בפרק אמר רבי יהודה שתי אבנים גדולות שעשאן גולל לקבר המאהיל על גבי שתיהן טמא ניטלה אחת מהן המאהיל על גבי שנייה טהור מפני שיש לטומאה דרך שתצא ומה דרך שתצא שייך לפירוש ר"ת ובערוך פירש בענין אחר בערך גלל וכפירושו יתכן מה שבתוספתא ^ל:

ונשמתו

עין משפט נר מצוה

נ א סמג עשין דרבנן ב:

רב נסים גאון

שלום בין איש לאשתו: **אלו** ואלו נמסרין לדומה הללו יש להן מנוח והללו אין להן מנוח. בפרק כל ישראל יש להם חלק (סנהדרין דף צד) גרסינן א"ר יוחנן אותו מלאך שהוא ממונה על הרוחות דומה שמו וכבר הזכרנו אותו בברכות:

סליק שואל אדם

תורה אור השלם

א) אַךְ בְּשָׂרוֹ עָלָיו יִכְאָב וְנַפְשׁוֹ עָלָיו תֶּאֱבָל: [איוב יד, כב]

ב) וְיָשֹׁב הֶעָפָר עַל הָאָרֶץ כְּשֶׁהָיָה וְהָרוּחַ תָּשׁוּב אֶל הָאֱלֹהִים אֲשֶׁר נְתָנָהּ: [קהלת יב, ז]

ג) יָבוֹא שָׁלוֹם יָנוּחוּ עַל מִשְׁכְּבוֹתָם הֹלֵךְ נְכֹחוֹ: [ישעיה נז, ב]

ד) וַיָּקָם אָדָם לִרְדָפְךָ וּלְבַקֵּשׁ אֶת נַפְשֶׁךָ וְהָיְתָה נֶפֶשׁ אֲדֹנִי צְרוּרָה בִּצְרוֹר הַחַיִּים אֵת יְיָ אֱלֹהֶיךָ וְאֵת נֶפֶשׁ אֹיְבֶיךָ יְקַלְּעֶנָּה בְּתוֹךְ כַּף הַקָּלַע: [שמואל א' כה, כט]

ה) אֵין שָׁלוֹם אָמַר יְיָ לָרְשָׁעִים: [ישעיה מח, כב]

ו) חַיֵּי בְשָׂרִים לֵב מַרְפֵּא וּרְקַב עֲצָמוֹת קִנְאָה: [משלי יד, ל]

ז) וִידַעְתֶּם כִּי אֲנִי יְיָ בְּפִתְחִי אֶת קִבְרוֹתֵיכֶם וּבְהַעֲלוֹתִי אֶתְכֶם מִקִּבְרוֹתֵיכֶם עַמִּי: [יחזקאל לז, יג]

ח) בְּזֵעַת אַפֶּיךָ תֹּאכַל לֶחֶם עַד שׁוּבְךָ אֶל הָאֲדָמָה כִּי מִמֶּנָּה לֻקָּחְתָּ כִּי עָפָר אַתָּה וְאֶל עָפָר תָּשׁוּב: [בראשית ג, יט]

ליקוטי רש"י

גולל. זה כסוי העליון דף שנותנין על המת [חולין קכו:]. זה כסוי של ארון המת [כתובות ד:]. **יבא שלום.** יבא הצדיק הזה אל אבותיו בשלום [ישעיה נז, ב]. **כף הקלע.** חתיכת עור רחבה עשויה כמין כף באמצע הקלע שנותן בה האבן [ש"א כה, כט]. **דומה.** מלאך שהוא ממונה על המתים [ברכות יח:]. שומר המתים ששמו דומה [חגיגה ה.]. **אובא טמיא.** בעל אוב של עצמות שעושה כשוף בעצמות המת טמיא עצמות ודומה לו במסכת כלים בית מלא טמיא ופירש רב האי מלא טמיא בית שהוא מלא עצמות והביא ראיה על זה מברא'שית רבה דקתני אדריינוס שחיק טמיא ...

מסורת הש"ס

א) [פסחים לג: יומא סו: סנהדרין ל: מנחות מה. ק.], ב) [נ"ל את ה' אלהיך על כו'], ג) זוממות והולכות שנאמר ואת נפש כו' פי' דדייק מדלא אמרה יקלענה בכף הקלע ואמר בתוך כף הקלע משמע שהיא מכוסה וכבושה בתוך כף הקלע ואינה יוצאת ממנו ומלאך ממלאכי חבלה מקלע אותה רלועה לכאן ולכאן וזהו לשון זוממות, ד) גי' רש"ל לא משמע כן מפי' רש"י שפי' שהן חבושין וגי' זו אינן חבושי' ואולי מלא גי' כו אבל גי' רש"י אינו כן מ"כ, ה) [ע"ז נה.], ו) [עי' פירושו ברש"י גיטין סח. ד"ה נחר], ז) [נ"ל את קברותיכם ובהעלותי אתכם מקברותיכם עמי וכו"א בע"י וכזה מבין פרש"י ד"ה בפתחי בהעלותי עד שיעלנו וכו'], ח) [ערוך ערך בנגידא פי' בכישוף], ט) ראה רש"י ברכות נט. ד"ה אובא, י) [במס' שמחות פ"ד הל' כ"א ע"ש], כ) [דף נד.], ל) [וע"ע תוספות ברכות יט: ד"ה מדלגין ותוס' סוכה כג. ד"ה ולא ותוס' כתובות ד: ד"ה עד ותוס' סנהדרין מז: ד"ה משיסתם].

הגהות הב"ח

(א) גמ' איכא שכיבנא. נ"ב כלומר אי שכיבנא: (ב) רש"י ד"ה נחר בהו גער בהו רבי אחאי: (ג) ד"ה ליקום מר לגויה דביתא יבא: (ד) תוס' ד"ה עד שיסתם וכו' מרבינן גולל ודופק למטמא: (ה) בא"ד שנותנין אחת לראשו. נ"ב פי' לראשו ולרגליו של גולל וכן הוא בתוספות פ"ק דכתובות דף ד' וע"ש בפרק מי שמתו בדף יט: (ו) בא"ד ברוב ארונות שלהם חלל טפח:

גליון הש"ס

גמ' על גופן של רשעים הוא אומר אין שלום אמר אלהי. כנ"ל: שם כל מי שיש לו קנאה בלבו. ע' ב"ב דף יו ע"א תוס' ד"ה שבעה:

דְּאַקְרְיָיךְ קֹהֶלֶת לֹא אַקְרְיָיךְ מִשְׁלֵי – He who taught you the Book of ***Ecclesiastes*** evidently **did not teach you** the Book of ***Proverbs,*** **דִּכְתִיב ,,וּרְקַב עֲצָמוֹת קִנְאָה" – for** you appear to be ignorant of **the verse** that **states:**[23] ***The rotting of bones is [caused by] envy.*** **כָּל מִי שֶׁיֵּשׁ לוֹ קִנְאָה בְּלִבּוֹ** – This implies: **Whoever has envy in his heart** while he is alive **עֲצָמוֹתָיו מַרְקִיבִים** – will have **his bones rot** in the grave after he dies; **כָּל שֶׁאֵין לוֹ קִנְאָה בְּלִבּוֹ** – and **whoever does not have envy in his heart** while alive **אֵין עֲצָמוֹתָיו מַרְקִיבִים** – will **not** have **his bones rot** after he dies.[24] Now, I was not guilty of envy while I was alive; hence, my body still retains its significance even many years after my death.

The Gemara continues its narrative:

גַּשְׁשֵׁיהּ – **[Rav Nachman]** then reached out and **felt [Rav Achai's corpse]. חַזְיֵיהּ דְּאִית בֵּיהּ מַמָּשָׁא – He perceived that there was,** indeed, **substance to it;** i.e. the flesh on the bones was real, not just a mirage. **אָמַר לֵיהּ** – So **[Rav Nachman] said to [the corpse]:** As your body is evidently intact, **לֵיקוּם מַר לְגַוֵּיהּ דְּבֵיתָא – let master arise** and come **into** my **house.**[25] **אָמַר לֵיהּ – [The corpse] replied to [Rav Nachman]: גַּלִּית אַדַּעְתָּךְ דַּאֲפִילּוּ נְבִיאֵי לֹא קְרֵית** – Now **you have demonstrated that** you are not only ignorant of portions of ***Proverbs*** [a book in the third part of the Bible], but **you have not even read Prophets** [the second third of the Bible]! **דִּכְתִיב – For** in Prophets **it is written:** **,,וִידַעְתֶּם כִּי־אֲנִי ה' בְּפִתְחִי אֶת־קִבְרוֹתֵיכֶם" –** ***And you will recognize that I am Hashem, when I open your graves.***[26] This indicates that it is only God Who may bring forth the dead; unless He grants us permission, we may not do so on our own.

Rav Nachman returns to question why the corpse of R' Achai has not decomposed:

אָמַר לֵיהּ – [Rav Nachman] said to [the body of Rav Achai]: וְהָכְתִיב ,,כִּי־עָפָר אַתָּה וְאֶל־עָפָר תָּשׁוּב" – But it is written: ***For you are dust, and to dust shall you return.***[27] This seems to indicate that *all* persons, regardless of whether they may have been envious in their lifetimes, turn to dust after death;[28] why, then, has your body remained intact? **אָמַר לֵיהּ – [The corpse] replied to [Rav Nachman]: הַהוּא שָׁעָה אַחַת קוֹדֶם תְּחִיַּית הַמֵּתִים – That** verse speaks of what will take place in the Messianic Era, **a moment before the resurrection of the dead.**[29] Until then, the bodies of persons who were worthy will remain preserved in their graves.

A related narrative:

אָמַר לֵיהּ הַהוּא צְדוּקִי לְרַבִּי אַבָּהוּ – A certain Sadducee once **said to R' Abahu: אֲמְרִיתוּ נִשְׁמָתָן שֶׁל צַדִּיקִים גְּנוּזוֹת תַּחַת כִּסֵּא הַכָּבוֹד – You have said** that **the souls of the righteous are ensconced beneath the Heavenly Throne** of God. **אוֹבָא טְמְיָא הֵיכָא אַסְקֵיהּ לִשְׁמוּאֵל בִּנְגִידָא** – But if so, how did **that bone-necromancer**[30] **raise** the dead prophet Samuel **through necromancy?**[31]

The Gemara recounts R' Abahu's reply:

אָמַר לֵיהּ – [R' Abahu] said to him: הָתָם בְּתוֹךְ שְׁנֵים עָשָׂר חֹדֶשׁ הֲוָה – There, in the case of Saul and the sorceress, **it was within twelve months** of Samuel's death that they summoned his soul; thus, his soul had not yet reached its final resting place. **דְּתַנְיָא – For it was taught in a Baraisa: כָּל שְׁנֵים עָשָׂר חֹדֶשׁ גּוּפוֹ קַיָּים** – For **ALL** of **TWELVE MONTHS** after one dies, **HIS BODY REMAINS INTACT וְנִשְׁמָתוֹ עוֹלָה וְיוֹרֶדֶת – AND HIS SOUL RISES** into the next world **AND DESCENDS** back towards his body in this world. **לְאַחַר שְׁנֵים עָשָׂר חֹדֶשׁ – AFTER TWELVE MONTHS** elapse, **הַגּוּף בָּטֵל – THE BODY CEASES TO EXIST,**

NOTES

23. *Proverbs* 14:30.

24. I.e. when the verse in *Ecclesiastes* states that the body returns to dust, it refers only to the bodies of those who experienced envy. Other bodies are indeed preserved (see *Rashi* ד"ה והא כתיב ואל עפר תשוב).

Maharal indicates that the corpse did not actually speak to Rav Nachman; rather, the Gemara speaks allegorically of an inner dialogue Rav Nachman had with himself. R' Achai's evident pain at the disturbance of his grave indicated to Rav Nachman that Rav Mari's teaching was problematic, and forced him to formulate an alternative reading of the verse Rav Mari had cited. Rav Nachman mentally chastised himself for not recalling the verse in *Proverbs* that links the demise of the body to envy, and, on the basis of that verse, he finally concluded that the body recedes into insignificance only for those persons who had experienced envy in their lifetimes (see *Maharal*).

[The emotion of envy indicates a fundamental lack in the person who experiences it. Were it not for his lacking something, he would not feel envious of someone else who possesses it. This "lack" during one's life is expressed in death by the deterioration of the body (*Maharal*).]

25. I.e. separate yourself from the grave, for the grave is the mechanism which returns the body to the earth and allows for its demise [and in your case this is evidently not applicable] (*Maharal*).

26. *Ezekiel* 37:13. I.e. God will bring forth the dead during the Messianic Era; until then, we are not granted permission to arise (*Rashi*).

27. *Genesis* 3:19.

28. The verse was stated as God's punishment to the first man for sinning in the Garden of Eden. This punishment, then, clearly applies to *all* of Adam's descendants [i.e. all mankind], righteous and wicked alike (*Rashi*).

29. I.e. the bodies of the righteous will not decompose until just before the Resurrection; at that moment, they will return to dust so that their bodies may be resurrected like all others (*Iyun Yaakov* ד"ה א"ל רב מרי; cf. *Maharal*).

30. An אוב is a necromancer, i.e. one who communicates with the dead by means of sorcery. Necromancy is prohibited by the Torah (*Deuteronomy* 18:11) and is indeed punishable by death (*Leviticus* 20:27). *Rashi*, following *Rav Hai Gaon,* interprets טְמְיָא as *a bone.* Thus, the Sadducee was referring to a necromancer who raised the dead through some act of sorcery involving bones (cf. *Aruch*).

31. The Book of *Samuel* (*I Samuel* ch. 28) records that King Saul, about to face the Philistines in battle at Gilboa, became frightened and desperately wished to know the fate that awaited him. He tried to inquire this of God, but received no answer. In an act of desperation, he disguised himself and went to consult a necromancer at Ein Dor, in violation of Torah law. The sorceress succeeded in raising the soul of the recently deceased Samuel, and Saul posed his question to the prophet.

The Sadducee challenged R' Abahu on grounds that if the souls of the righteous really resided with God, it would seem inconceivable that their souls could be summoned on demand by a sorceress (*Maharsha*)

וְשׁוּב וְנִשְׁמָתוֹ עוֹלָה – AND HIS SOUL ARISES into the next world, אֵינָהּ יוֹרֶדֶת – AND THEN IT NO LONGER DESCENDS.[1] Now, the incident involving Saul and the sorceress took place within twelve months of Samuel's death. Hence, the soul could still be summoned with necromancy, since it had not yet come to its final repose beneath the Heavenly Throne.

The Gemara begins a related discussion:

אָמַר רַב יְהוּדָה בְּרֵיהּ דְּרַב שְׁמוּאֵל בַּר שִׁילַת מִשְּׁמֵיהּ דְּרַב – **Rav Yehudah the son of Rav Shmuel bar Shilas said in the name of Rav:** מֵהֶסְפֵּדוֹ שֶׁל אָדָם – **From a person's eulogy** and the affect it has on those assembled at his funeral, נִיכָּר אִם בֶּן הָעוֹלָם הַבָּא הוּא אִם לָאו – **it can be discerned whether or not [the deceased] is destined to** enter **the World to Come.**[2]

This statement is challenged:

אִינִי – Now, **is this really so?** וְהָאָמַר לֵיהּ רַב לְרַב שְׁמוּאֵל בַּר שִׁילַת – **But Rav** himself once **said to Rav Shmuel bar Shilas:** אַחִים בְּהֶסְפֵּידָא – "Take care to **deliver a moving eulogy**[3] at my funeral, דְּהָתָם קָאֵימְנָא – **for I shall be standing there** in spirit watching you!" Now, if it is so that the eulogy of a truly righteous person invariably evokes tears from the audience, why did Rav, who was certainly a righteous person, find it necessary to admonish Rav Shmuel to deliver a stirring eulogy for him? Invariably, the eulogy ought to have the desired effect! —?—

The Gemara resolves the problem:

לָא קַשְׁיָא – Actually, **there is no difficulty,** for in any case, an audience will be moved only if an appropriately stirring eulogy is delivered. הָא דְּמִחַמּוּ לֵיהּ וְאַחִים – But **here,** where the deceased was truly righteous, **when [the eulogizer]** attempts to **stir [the audience],** he succeeds; **[the audience] is** indeed **stirred** by his words. הָא דְּמִחַמּוּ לֵיהּ וְלָא אַחִים – **And there,** in the case of a deceased person who was less virtuous, **when [the eulogizer]** attempts **to stir [the audience], they are not stirred.**[4]

A conversation on this theme between Abaye and Rabbah, his teacher:

אָמַר לֵיהּ אַבַּיֵי לְרַבָּה – **Abaye said to Rabbah:** כְּגוֹן מָר דְּסָנוּ לֵיהּ כּוּלְּהוּ פּוּמְבְּדִיתָאֵי – In the case of someone **such as master** [i.e. such as yourself], **who is hated by all the citizens of Pumbedisa,**[5] מַאן אַחִים הֶסְפֵּידָא – **who will deliver a** suitably **moving eulogy** over you when you pass away?[6] אָמַר לֵיהּ – **[Rabbah] replied to [Abaye]:** מִיסְתַּיָּא אַתְּ וְרַבָּה בַּר רַב חָנָן – **It would be sufficient if you and Rabbah bar Rav Chanan** deliver eulogies at my funeral.

Rav sets forth another arbiter of whether one has merited entrance into the World to Come:

בְּעָא מִינֵּיהּ רַבִּי אֶלְעָזָר מֵרַב – **R' Elazar inquired of Rav:** אֵיזֶהוּ בֶּן הָעוֹלָם הַבָּא – **Who is** a person **destined for the World to Come?** אָמַר לֵיהּ – **[Rav] replied to him** by citing the following verse: "וְאָזְנֶיךָ תִּשְׁמַעְנָה דָבָר מֵאַחֲרֶיךָ לֵאמֹר זֶה הַדֶּרֶךְ לְכוּ בוֹ כִּי תַאֲמִינוּ וְכִי תַשְׂמְאִילוּ" – ***And your ears shall hear something from behind you; [someone] saying,*** ***"This is the way; walk in it, whether you turn right or left."***[7]

Another opinion on the matter:

רַבִּי חֲנִינָא אָמַר – **R' Chanina said:** כֹּל שֶׁדַּעַת (רבותינו) [רַבּוֹתָיו] נוֹחָה הֵימֶנּוּ – **Anyone whose [conduct] pleases his teachers** is destined for the World to Come.[8]

Earlier (152a), the Gemara expounded a verse in *Ecclesiastes* 12:5 [*so man goes to his eternal home*]. The Gemara now returns to expound the next section of this verse:

"וְסָבְבוּ בַשּׁוּק הַסּוֹפְדִים" – Scripture states: *So man goes to his eternal home* ***while the eulogizers go about the streets.*** בְּנֵי גָלִילָא אָמְרֵי – Citing this verse, **the people of Galilee say:** עֲשֵׂה דְּבָרִים לִפְנֵי מִטָּתְךָ – **Perform** good **deeds before your coffin.**[9] בְּנֵי יְהוּדָה אָמְרֵי – Whereas **the people of Judah,** citing the same verse, **say:** עֲשֵׂה דְּבָרִים לְאַחַר מִטָּתְךָ – **Perform** good **deeds behind your coffin.**

NOTES

1. I.e. it no longer can be forcibly summoned. Should the soul wish to descend, though, it may (*Tosafos*).

2. If the crowd is moved to tears when the speaker recounts the virtues of the deceased, it is likely that the deceased was truly righteous and will enter the World to Come. If the audience remains unmoved by the eulogy, it is because the deceased was not truly virtuous. Thus, the audience's reaction to the eulogy is a reliable indicator of whether the deceased has merited entrance to the World to Come (*Rashi;* cf. *Maharal*).

3. Literally: "Warm [them] up in [your] eulogy."

4. Thus, Rav needed to exhort Rav Shmuel bar Shilas to deliver a stirring eulogy. For if the speaker failed to movingly evoke Rav's greatness, the audience might well remain unmoved [since Rav lived to a ripe old age and his death was not otherwise tragic] (*Rashi*).

Others interpret the intent of Rav's demand differently. They explain that Rav exhorted his colleague to deliver a moving eulogy so that others would be inspired by his example to emulate his righteous ways. These positive acts performed by his followers would then serve as a continuing source of merit for Rav in the Next World. This was particularly important, because once one leaves the earthly sphere, he no longer has the opportunity to perform meritorious deeds; in the Next World, he merely "stands" in place, reaping the rewards for deeds he performed earlier. Thus, Rav stated that if people continued to emulate his example after his death, then even while "standing in the Next World" [דְּהָתָם קָאֵימְנָא], he would continually achieve new spiritual heights (*Eitz Yosef;* see also *Yaaros Devash* § 11; cf. *Binah LeIttim* §72).

Shelah (to *Taanis* 66b) offers another interpretation: *Be warm in your eulogy, but let your words reflect my actual standing;* that is, be sure not to exaggerate my virtues.

5. Rabbah was disliked by the local residents because he, their spiritual leader, outspokenly rebuked them to improve their ways. A constant state of friction existed between him and the community, certain elements of which were notorious for their unethical practices (*Rashi;* see *Chulin* 127a, *Bava Basra* 46a and *Avodah Zarah* 70a).

[On a related note, Abaye — Rabbah's nephew and student at Pumbedisa — once stated that any Rabbinic leader who is well liked in his community can attribute his popularity to his failure to properly admonish the populace (see *Kesubos* 105b).]

6. Rabbah was evidently so unpopular in Pumbedisa that Abaye feared no one would do justice to his greatness in a eulogy. Some find difficulty with this notion, and suggest an alternative interpretation: Rabbah's utter fearlessness in reproving the populace set such a remarkable standard of righteousness and adherence to principle that Abaye feared it was beyond anyone's ability to properly eulogize him (see *Binah LeIttim* §72).

7. *Isaiah* 30:21. Rav homiletically interprets the verse as referring to the funeral of a truly righteous person. Addressing the soul of the deceased, the verse states: If at your funeral you hear people invoking the example of your life as something to emulate [*saying, "This is the way [to live your life]; walk in it"*], then you can be certain you are destined for the World to Come (*Rashi*).

8. One's parents and friends may be predisposed to judge one favorably. But if one succeeds in impressing his teachers with his conduct, he can be sure that he has acted righteously (*Maharal*).

9. I.e. see to it that you perform good deeds during your lifetime, so that when the time comes for you to be eulogized, the speaker — who addresses the crowd standing before your coffin — will have positive things to say about you (see *Rashi*). [The phrase *while the eulogizers go about the streets* conveys the sense of eulogizers interviewing people after a death to inquire about the life of the deceased so as to be able to properly eulogize him.]

ונשמתו עולה ושוב אינה יורדת אמר רב יהודה בריה דרב שמואל בר שילת משמיה דרב מהספדו של אדם ניכר אם בן העוה"ב הוא אם לאו איני והאמר ליה רב לרב שמואל בר שילת אחים בהספידא דהתם קאימנא לא קשיא הא דמחמו ליה ואחים הא דמחמו ליה ולא אחים א"ל אביי לרבה כגון מר דסנו ליה כולהו פומבדיתאי מאן אחים הספידא א"ל מיסתיא את ורבה בר רב חנן בעא מניה רבי אלעזר מרב איזהו בן העוה"ב א"ל ואזניך תשמענה דבר מאחריך לאמר זה הדרך לכו בו כי תאמינו וכי תשמאילו ר' חנינא אמר כל שדעת רבותינו נוחה הימנו וסבבו בשוק הסופדים בני גלילא אמרי עשה דברים לפני מטתך בני יהודה אמרי עשה דברים לאחר מטתך ולא פליגי מר כי אתריה ומר כי אתריה תנן התם רבי אליעזר אומר שוב יום אחד לפני מיתתך שאלו תלמידיו את ר"א וכי אדם יודע איזהו יום ימות אמר להן וכל שכן ישוב היום שמא ימות למחר ונמצא כל ימיו בתשובה ואף שלמה אמר בחכמתו בכל עת יהיו בגדיך לבנים ושמן על ראשך אל יחסר א"ר יוחנן בן זכאי משל למלך שזימן את עבדיו לסעודה ולא קבע להם זמן פיקחין שבהן קישטו את עצמן וישבו על פתח בית המלך אמרו כלום חסר לבית המלך טיפשין שבהן הלכו למלאכתן אמרו כלום יש סעודה בלא טורח בפתאום ביקש המלך את עבדיו פיקחין שבהן נכנסו לפניו כשהן מקושטין והטיפשים נכנסו לפניו כשהן מלוכלכין שמח המלך לקראת פיקחים וכעס לקראת טיפשים אמר הללו שקישטו את עצמן לסעודה ישבו ויאכלו וישתו הללו שלא קישטו עצמן לסעודה יעמדו ויראו חתנו של ר"מ משום ר"מ אמר אף הן נראין כמשמשין אלא אלו ואלו יושבין הללו אוכלין והללו רעבין הללו שותין והללו צמאים שנאמר (א) כה אמר ה' הנה עבדי יאכלו ואתם תרעבו הנה עבדי ישתו ואתם תצמאו הנה עבדי ירונו מטוב לב ואתם תצעקו מכאב לב ד"א בכל עת יהיו בגדיך לבנים אלו ציצית ושמן על ראשך אל יחסר אלו תפילין:

הדרן עלך שואל

מי שהחשיך (ה) בדרך נותן כיסו לנכרי ואם אין עמו נכרי מניחו על החמור הגיע לחצר החיצונה נוטל את הכלים הניטלין בשבת ושאינן ניטלין בשבת מתיר החבלים והשקין נופלין מאיליהם: **גמ'** מאי טעמא שרו ליה רבנן למיתב כיסיה לנכרי קים להו לרבנן דאין אדם מעמיד עצמו על ממונו אי לא שרית ליה אתי לאיתויי ד' אמות ברה"ר אמר רבא דוקא כיסו אבל מציאה לא פשיטא כיסו תנן מהו דתימא הוא הדין אפילו מציאה והאי דקתני כיסו אורחא דמילתא קתני קמ"ל ולא אמרן אלא דלא אתי לידיה אבל אתי לידיה ככיסיה דמי איכא דאמרי בעי רבא מציאה הבאה לידו מהו כיון דאתא לידיה ככיסיה דמי או דילמא כיון דלא טרח בה לאו ככיסיה דמי תיקו: אין עמו נכרי: טעמא דאין עמו נכרי הא יש עמו נכרי לנכרי יהיב ליה מאי טעמא חמור אתה מצווה על שביתתו נכרי אי אתה מצווה על שביתתו חמור וחרש שוטה וקטן אחמור מנח ליה לחרש שוטה וקטן לא יהיב ליה מ"ט הני אדם האי לאו אדם חרש ושוטה לשוטה שוטה וקטן לשוטה איבעיא להו חרש וקטן מאי אליבא דר"א לא תיבעי לך דתניא ר' יצחק אומר משום ר' אליעזר תרומת חרש לא

רש"י

אם בן עוה"ב הוא. שאם כשר היה הכל בוכין עליו ומורידין דמעות ומספרים שבחו: אחים בהספידא דהתם קאימנא. בשעת מיתתי התאמץ בהספד שלי שיתחממו ויכמרו רחמי העומדים ויבכו: דהתם קאימנא. בשעת הספד ואשמע איך מתחממם אלמא איצטריך לרב לאזהוריה אהספדא וכיון דרב גברא רבה ובן העולם הבא למה ליה לאזהוריה הא אמר מהספדו ניכר: הא דמחממין ליה. להספידא ואחים כו' לעולם חמומי בעי שאין בני אדם נכמרים כל כך על זקן ומיהו לאדם חסיד כי מחממו בהספידא מחממי ובכו כולהו ולמי שאינו חסיד כל כך מחממו ליה ולא מחממו: דסנו ליה כולהו פומבדיתאי. משום דמוכח להו במילי דשמיא (ב) וכני פומבדיתאי רמאין הן כדאמרינן בשחיטת חולין (חולין קכז.) פומבדיתאי לוייך שני אושפיזך: ואזניך תשמענה דבר מאחריך לאמר זה הדרך לכו (ג) בה. מאחרי מטתך כשתמות תשמע כשיאמרו זה הדרך שהלך בה זה לכו בה מובטח שהוא בן העוה"ב: נוחה הימנו. דעתם נוחה עליהם ממה ששומעין עליו ורואין בו: עשה דברים. שיאמרו לפני מטתך בהספדך: לאחר מטתך. היא היא אלא שבגליל היו הספדנין לפני המטה וביהודה לאחר המטה: וכ"ש. שמפני שאינו יודע איזה יום ימות (ד) וטובה תשובה יום אחד לפני מיתתו נמצא כל ימיו בתשובה יהיו: בגדיך לבנים. נשמתך טהורה ונקיה: כלום חסר בית המלך. בתמיה הכל מוכן ושמא יבהילנו לבא פתאום ואנו צריכין ליכנס לסעודה מקושטין: כלום יש סעודה בלא טורח. עדיין יצטרכו לטרוח לצורכי סעודה של בית המלך ויש לנו שהות הרבה להתקשט: יעמדו ויראו. ואף לעוה"ב צדיקים יושבים ואוכלים ורשעים עומדים ורואים: ר"מ אומר. אין עומדין ורואין שא"כ אף הם היו נראים מן הקרואים ולשמש שכן דרך המשרתים עומדים ואין כאן בושה: זה ציצית. שמלובן הבגד: אלו תפילין. שהם שם משמן טוב דכתיב וראו כל עמי הארץ כי שם וגו' ותנא ר"א הגדול אומר אלו תפילין שבראש (ברכות דף ו.):

הדרן עלך שואל

מי שהחשיך (ו) נותן כיסו לנכרי. מבעוד יום: ואם אין עמו. הא יש עמו לנכרי עדיף כדמפרש בגמרא: לחצר החיצונה. של עיר שהוא מקום המשתמר ראשון ובא לפרק מן החמור: נוטל. בידו מעליו כלים הניטלין בשבת ושאין ניטלין מתיר החבלים של אוכף שהן קשורים בהן והשקין נופלין: גמ' מאי טעמא שרי ליה למיתב לנכרי. והרי הוא שלוחו ליטלו בשבת: מעמיד עצמו. מלהציל ממונו: דוקא כיסו. דכיון דטרח בה שע"י טורח הוא משתכר חייס עלה ואי לא שרית ליה הא אתי לאיתויי: ולא אמרן. דמציאה לא אלא דלא אתיא לידיה קודם שתחשך ולא הגביהה ולא זכה בה: האי אדם. ויש במינו שחייב במצות ואתי לאיחלופי: לשוטה. יהיב דלית ליה דעת כלל אבל חרש דעתא קלישתא אית ליה כדאמרי' ביבמות (דף קיג.):

תוספות

ונשמתו עולה ושוב אינה יורדת. אף על פי כן כשהיא רוצה היא יורדת כי ההיא דלעיל דרבי אמי בר יאשיה וכההיא מעשה דר' בנאה דחזקת הבתים (ב"ב דף נח. ושם) דהוה מציין מערתא כי מטא למערתא דאברהם אשכחיה לאליעזר עבד אברהם דקאי אבבא אמר ליה מאי קא עביד אברהם כו' אמר ליה ניעול וניתי כו' אע"פ שנשמתו היתה גנוזה מתחת כסא הכבוד. מ"ר:

הדרן עלך שואל

מי שהחשיך כו' חרש שוטה וקטן. אע"ג דאמר לעיל בפרק כל כתבי (דף קכא.) גבי קטן שבא לכבות דקטן העושה לדעת אביו אסור מיהו הכא לא איירי כגון דעביד הקטן עקירה והנחה אלא כדאמרינן לקמן גבי חמור כשהיא מהלכת מניחו עליה וכשהיא עומדת נוטלו הימנה. מ"ר:

מסורת הש"ס

א) נ"א שילא וכן לקמן, ב) [ל"ל רבותיו וכ"א בכריך והרא"ש], ג) [פסחים ג. וש"נ], ד) [אבות פ"ב מ"י], ה) [לעיל יז:], ו) [יבמות קיג.], ז) [שם איתא אלעזר].

גליון הש"ס

גמרא בני גלילא אמרי עשה דברים לפני מטתך. מסכת שמחות פ"ג ה"ו:

תורה אור השלם

א) וְאָזְנֶיךָ תִּשְׁמַעְנָה דָבָר מֵאַחֲרֶיךָ לֵאמֹר זֶה הַדֶּרֶךְ לְכוּ בוֹ כִּי תַאֲמִינוּ וְכִי תַשְׂמְאִילוּ: [ישעיה ל, כא]

ב) גַּם מִגָּבֹהַּ יִרָאוּ וְחַתְחַתִּים בַּדֶּרֶךְ וְיָנֵאץ הַשָּׁקֵד וְיִסְתַּבֵּל הֶחָגָב וְתָפֵר הָאֲבִיּוֹנָה כִּי הֹלֵךְ הָאָדָם אֶל בֵּית עוֹלָמוֹ וְסָבְבוּ בַשּׁוּק הַסֹּפְדִים: [קהלת יב, ה]

ג) בְּכָל עֵת יִהְיוּ בְגָדֶיךָ לְבָנִים וְשֶׁמֶן עַל רֹאשְׁךָ אַל יֶחְסָר: [קהלת ט, ח]

ד) לָכֵן כֹּה אָמַר אֲדֹנָי אֱלֹהִים הִנֵּה עֲבָדַי יֹאכֵלוּ וְאַתֶּם תִּרְעָבוּ הִנֵּה עֲבָדַי יִשְׁתּוּ וְאַתֶּם תִּצְמָאוּ הִנֵּה עֲבָדַי יִשְׂמָחוּ וְאַתֶּם תֵּבֹשׁוּ: [ישעיה סה, יג]

ה) הִנֵּה עֲבָדַי יָרֹנּוּ מִטּוּב לֵב וְאַתֶּם תִּצְעֲקוּ מִכְּאֵב לֵב וּמִשֵּׁבֶר רוּחַ תְּיֵלִילוּ: [ישעיה סה, יד]

ליקוטי רש"י

בכל עת יהיו בגדיך לבנים. הזהר עצמך בכל שעה במעשה טוב שאם תמות היום תכנס בשלום ומשל שלמה המכנס את הדבר לאדם שהזמינו המלך ליום סעודה ולא קבע לו זמן אם חכם הוא לא פקח מיד מכבס כסותו ורוחץ וסך עד עת שמא יקרא אל הסעודה יהיה כל שעה בגדיו לבנים וכו' רחוץ וסך כך לשוטו דרכשו רבותינו במסכת שבת [קהלת ט, ח]. עבדי. הצדיקים (של ישראל). ואתם. הרשעים [ישעיה סה, יג]. נותן כיסו לנכרי. ולא יטלטלנו פחות פחות מארבע אמות [לעיל יז:]. חרש שוטה וקטן. חרש שדברו בו חכמים בכל מקום שאינו שומע ואינו מדבר הכי קים להו לרבנן דמי שאינו שומע ואינו מדבר אינו בר דעה [חגיגה ב:]. חרש. אינו מועטת שאין מחודד להבין כשאר בני אדם [יבמות קיג.].

עין משפט נר מצוה

נא א מיי' פ"ז מהלכות תשובה הלכה ג:

א ב מיי' פ"ו מהלכות שבת הלכה כב סמג לאוין סה טוש"ע א"ח סי' רסו סעיף א וסעיף ח וסימן שמט סעיף ה:

ב ג מיי' פ"כ שם הלכה ו סמג שם טוש"ע א"ח סי' רסו סעיף ב:

ג ד מיי' פכ"א שם הל' י סמג שם טוש"ע שם סעיף ב:

ד ה מיי' שם הלכה כב סמג שם:

ה ו ז מיי' פ"כ שם הלכה ז סמג שם טוש"ע שם סעיף א:

ו ח מיי' פ"כ שם הלכה ו סמג שם טוש"ע שם סעיף א:

ז ט מיי' שם הלכה ז טוש"ע שם סעיף ג:

ח י מיי' שם טוש"ע שם סעיף ד:

ט כ מיי' שם טוש"ע שם סעיף ה:

הגהות הב"ח

(א) גמ' שנאמר לכן כה אמר: (ב) רש"י ד"ה דסנו וכו' דבני פומבדיתא: (ג) ד"ה אזנך וכו' לכו בו מאחרי: (ד) ד"ה וכ"ש שמפני וכו' יום מות שישוב בתשובה: (ה) במשנה מי שהחשיך לו בדרך: (ו) רש"י ד"ה מי שהחשיך לו נותן:

רבינו חננאל

איזה בן עולם הבא כל שדעת רבותיו נוחה הימנו כך שמעתא דא סלקא: הדרן עלך שואל אדם

פרק כד מי שהחשיך בדרך נותן כיסו לנכרי וכו' ואוקי' למתניתין דאין מעמיד עצמו על ממונו ואם התירו לו לתת כיסו לנכרי בשביל שלא ישאנו הוא בעצמו. ובא רבא ודקדק ואמר דוקא כיסו אבל מציאה דלא אתא לידיה לא התירו לו לתתו לנכרי ובמציאה דאתאי לידיה ללישנא בתרא עלתה בתיקו. וכל תיקו דאיסורא לחומרא והלכתא כרבא דאוקמא (לידיה) [למתני'] בכיסו ממש. אין עמו נכרי מניחו על חמור דייקינן מינה בעת שמצויין ביחד נכרי וחמור לנכרי יהיב ליה מפני שאינו מצווה על שביתתו של נכרי ולכן לא התירו לו לתת כיסו על החמור אלא אם אין שם נכרי אלא חמור. וישראל חרש או שוטה או קטן אינו נותן כיסו לאחד מהן אלא גונתן כיסו על החמור ולעולם לגרוע שבהן נותן כגון חרש ושוטה לשוטה וקטן נותן והשוטה גרוע בבני אדם שאין הפרש בין אדם לבהמה אלא הדעת והתבונה וזה כיון שאין לו דעת כבהמה חשוב:

The Gemara adds:

וְלָא פְּלִיגֵי – And [these] two statements **are not contradictory.** מַר כִּי אַתְרֵיהּ – One **master's** statement **reflects** the custom of **his locale,** וּמַר כִּי אַתְרֵיהּ – and the other **master's** statement **reflects** the custom of **his locale.**[10]

The Gemara expounds on the virtue of repentance before one's death:

תְּנַן הָתָם – **We learned there, in a Mishnah:**[11] רַבִּי אֱלִיעֶזֶר אוֹמֵר – R' ELIEZER SAYS: שׁוּב יוֹם אֶחָד לִפְנֵי מִיתָתְךָ – REPENT ONE DAY BEFORE YOUR DEATH.[12] שָׁאֲלוּ תַּלְמִידָיו אֶת רַבִּי אֱלִיעֶזֶר – Hearing this teaching from their mentor, **R' Eliezer's students asked him:** וְכִי אָדָם יוֹדֵעַ אֵיזֶהוּ יוֹם יָמוּת – **But does a person know** on **which day he will die?** Certainly not. How, then, can he fulfill your maxim to repent just before his death?

R' Eliezer responds:

אָמַר לָהֶן – **He said to them:** וְכָל שֶׁכֵּן – On the contrary; my teaching applies **all the more so:** יָשׁוּב הַיּוֹם שֶׁמָּא יָמוּת לְמָחָר – **Let [a person]** always say to himself that he must **repent today** because **he may die tomorrow,** וְנִמְצָא כָּל יָמָיו בִּתְשׁוּבָה – **and** in this way **he will find** himself living **all his days in** a state of **penitence,** something to which we surely all aspire!

The Gemara brings home a similar point:

וְאַף שְׁלֹמֹה אָמַר בְּחָכְמָתוֹ – **And Solomon, as well, said** the same **in his wisdom;** for in *Ecclesiastes* he wrote: ,,בְּכָל־עֵת יִהְיוּ בְגָדֶיךָ לְבָנִים – *At all times let your garments be white,* וְשֶׁמֶן עַל־רֹאשְׁךָ אַל־יֶחְסָר״ – *and your head never lack oil.*[13]

The Gemara explicates the verse with a parable:

אָמַר רַבָּן יוֹחָנָן בֶּן זַכַּאי – **Rabban Yochanan ben Zakkai said:** What is King Solomon teaching in this verse? מָשָׁל לְמֶלֶךְ שֶׁזִּימֵּן אֶת עֲבָדָיו לִסְעוּדָה – **It may be compared to a king who invited his servants to a banquet,** וְלֹא קָבַע לָהֶם זְמַן – **but he did not set an exact time for them** to arrive. פִּיקְחִין שֶׁבָּהֶן קִישְּׁטוּ אֶת עַצְמָן – Now, **the wise [servants] among them** promptly **adorned themselves** in clothes appropriate for a royal affair, וְיָשְׁבוּ עַל פֶּתַח בֵּית הַמֶּלֶךְ – **and sat** waiting **at the door of the palace.** אָמְרוּ – For **they said** to themselves: כְּלוּם חָסֵר לְבֵית הַמֶּלֶךְ – **Does the king's palace lack for anything?**[14] Certainly not; the banquet may be ready at any moment, and we must be properly attired if we are suddenly summoned! טִיפְּשִׁין שֶׁבָּהֶן הָלְכוּ לִמְלַאכְתָּן – **The foolish [servants] among them,** however, **went about their work** and neglected to dress for the banquet. אָמְרוּ – **They said** to themselves: כְּלוּם יֵשׁ סְעוּדָה בְּלֹא טוֹרַח – **Is there any** such thing as a **banquet** prepared **without toil?** It will surely take the palace much time to ready the feast, and meanwhile, let us go about our business.

The Gemara continues its parable:

בְּפִתְאוֹם בִּיקֵּשׁ הַמֶּלֶךְ אֶת עֲבָדָיו – **Suddenly** and without warning, **the king summoned his servants** to the banquet. פִּיקְחִין שֶׁבָּהֶן נִכְנְסוּ לְפָנָיו כְּשֶׁהֵן מְקוּשָּׁטִין – **The wise [servants] among them entered before [the king]** properly **adorned,** וְהַטִּיפְּשִׁים נִכְנְסוּ לְפָנָיו כְּשֶׁהֵן מְלוּכְלָכִין – **while the foolish [servants] entered before him** with clothes all **soiled** from the work with which they had just been engaged. שָׂמַח הַמֶּלֶךְ לִקְרַאת פִּיקְחִים – Now, **the king was happy to greet the wise** servants, for they had made certain to appear at the palace appropriately dressed. וְכָעַס לִקְרַאת טִיפְּשִׁים – **But he was angry** when **he greeted the foolish** servants.

אָמַר – Addressing the wise ones, **[the king] said:** הַלָּלוּ שֶׁקִּישְּׁטוּ אֶת עַצְמָן לִסְעוּדָה – **These** servants **who adorned themselves for the banquet,** יֵשְׁבוּ וְיֹאכְלוּ וְיִשְׁתּוּ – let them **sit, eat and drink** at the affair, for they prepared themselves appropriately for this. הַלָּלוּ שֶׁלֹּא קִישְּׁטוּ עַצְמָן לִסְעוּדָה – But **those who failed to adorn themselves for the banquet,** יַעַמְדוּ וְיִרְאוּ – **they may** merely **stand and watch** the others partake.[15]

Another Tanna takes issue with the last part of this parable:

חַתְנוֹ שֶׁל רַבִּי מֵאִיר מִשּׁוּם רַבִּי מֵאִיר אָמַר – **The son-in-law of R' Meir said in the name of R' Meir:** אַף הֵן נִרְאִין כִּמְשַׁמְּשִׁין – In the parable as given above, **even** the foolish servants **appear** at least **to be attendants** serving the other guests, and thus do not seem entirely out of place at the affair. This, then, conveys a wrong impression about the state of the wicked in the Next World.[16] אֶלָּא אֵלּוּ וָאֵלּוּ יוֹשְׁבִין – **Rather,** a more apt analogy would be the following: Both **these and those** [i.e. the wise servants as well as the foolish ones] **are seated** at the banquet. הַלָּלוּ אוֹכְלִין – But **these** [the wise ones] are privileged to **eat** there, וְהַלָּלוּ רְעֵבִין – **while these** [the foolish ones] **must go hungry.** הַלָּלוּ שׁוֹתִין – **These** [the wise servants] **drink** at the banquet, וְהַלָּלוּ צְמֵאִים – **while these** [the foolish servants] **thirst** there, שֶׁנֶּאֱמַר – **as it is written:**[17] ,,כֹּה־אָמַר ה׳ – *Thus says Hashem:* הִנֵּה עֲבָדַי יֹאכֵלוּ וְאַתֶּם תִּרְעָבוּ – *Behold, My servants will eat, but you will hunger;* הִנֵּה עֲבָדַי יִשְׁתּוּ וְאַתֶּם תִּצְמָאוּ . . . – *My servants will drink, but you will thirst;* הִנֵּה עֲבָדַי יָרֹנּוּ מִטּוּב לֵב – *My servants will sing for gladness of heart,* וְאַתֶּם תִּצְעֲקוּ מִכְּאֵב לֵב״ – *and you will cry out from heartache.*

In the preceding discussion, the Gemara construed the Scriptural charge *let your garments be white* as an exhortation to maintain the purity of one's soul. The Gemara now concludes by citing an alternative interpretation of this passage:

דָּבָר אַחֵר – **Another interpretation:** When Scripture states:

NOTES

10. Both the Galileans and the Judeans were saying the same thing, and they merely alluded to different burial practices. In Galilee the person delivering a eulogy would stand in front of the coffin, and in Judah he would stand behind the coffin (*Rashi*).

11. *Avos* 2:10.

12. I.e. even if one has committed many sins during his lifetime and lived a far from exemplary life, still, the path of repentance continually remains open to him. If even in the last moments of life he repents with sincerity, God will accept him (*Eitz Yosef*).

13. *Ecclesiastes* 9:8. The "garment" is a metaphor for the soul: See to it that at all times, you keep your soul "white" and pure through continuous, daily repentance (*Rashi*).

Ben Yehoyada sees a connection between the "white garments" mentioned in the verse and burial shrouds, which are traditionally white. When one contemplates that he may soon be dressed in these shrouds, he shies away from sin.

14. [I.e. the king's palace is always well stocked with everything needed; they are thus able to prepare a banquet on very short notice.]

15. So it is with the righteous and wicked. The righteous, who, through continual repentance, perpetually readied themselves for entrance into the Next World, are privileged to enjoy the "banquet" for which they prepared themselves. The wicked, however, neglected to prepare properly for this experience. Hence, they are condemned to merely stand and watch the righteous; they themselves may not partake in the delights of the World to Come (*Rashi*).

16. Even serving as an attendant at a royal banquet is an honor of sorts. The souls of the wicked, though, would not be accorded such dignity in the World to Come. On the contrary, upon entering the "palace" of the Next World, they would be deeply shamed by their lack of readiness for the experience (see *Rashi*).

17. *Isaiah* 65:13-14.

ונשמתו עולה ושוב אינה יורדת אמר רב יהודה בריה דרב שמואל בר [א] שילת משמיה דרב מהספדו של אדם ניכר אם בן העוה"ב הוא אם לאו איני והאמר ליה רב לרב שמואל בר שילת אחים בהספידא דהתם קאימנא לא קשיא הא דמחמו ליה ואחים הא דמחמו ליה ולא אחים א"ל אביי לרבה כגון מר דסנו ליה כולהו פומבדיתאי מאן אחים הספידא א"ל מיסתיא את ורבה בר רב חנן בעא מניה רבי אלעזר מרב איזהו בן העוה"ב א"ל [א] ואזניך תשמענה דבר מאחריך לאמר זה הדרך לכו בו כי תאמינו וכי תשמאילו ר' חנינא אמר כל שדעת [ג] רבותינו נוחה הימנו [ב] וסבבו בשוק הסופדים [ה] בני גלילא אמרי עשה דברים לפני מטתך בני יהודה אמרי עשה דברים לאחר מטתך ולא פליגי [ו] מר כי אתריה ומר כי אתריה תנן התם רבי אליעזר אומר [ז] א שוב יום אחד לפני מיתתך שאלו תלמידיו את ר"א וכי אדם יודע איזהו יום ימות אמר להן וכל שכן ישוב היום שמא ימות למחר ונמצא כל ימיו בתשובה ואף שלמה אמר בחכמתו [ג] בכל עת יהיו בגדיך לבנים ושמן על ראשך אל יחסר א"ר יוחנן בן זכאי משל למלך שזימן את עבדיו לסעודה ולא קבע להם זמן פיקחין שבהן קישטו את עצמן וישבו על פתח בית המלך אמרו כלום חסר לבית המלך טיפשין שבהן הלכו למלאכתן אמרו כלום יש סעודה בלא טורח בפתאום ביקש המלך את עבדיו פיקחין שבהן נכנסו לפניו כשהן מקושטין והטיפשים נכנסו לפניו כשהן מלוכלכין שמח המלך לקראת פיקחים וכעס לקראת טיפשים אמר הללו שקישטו את עצמן לסעודה ישבו ויאכלו וישתו הללו שלא קישטו עצמן לסעודה יעמדו ויראו חתנו של ר"מ משום ר"מ אמר אף הן נראין כמשמשין אלא אלו ואלו יושבין הללו אוכלין והללו רעבין הללו שותין והללו צמאים שנאמר (א) [ד] כה אמר ה' הנה עבדי יאכלו ואתם תרעבו הנה עבדי ישתו ואתם תצמאו [ה] הנה עבדי ירונו מטוב לב ואתם תצעקו מכאב לב ד"א בכל עת יהיו בגדיך לבנים אלו ציצית ושמן על ראשך אל יחסר אלו תפילין:

הדרן עלך שואל

מי ב שהחשיך (ה) בדרך נותן כיסו לנכרי ג ואם אין עמו נכרי מניחו על החמור ד הגיע לחצר החיצונה נוטל את הכלים הניטלין בשבת ושאינן ניטלין בשבת מתיר החבלים והשקין נופלין מאליהם: גמ' מאי טעמא שרו ליה רבנן למיתב כיסיה לנכרי קים להו לרבנן ה דאין אדם מעמיד עצמו על ממונו אי לא שרית ליה אתי לאיתויי ד' אמות ברה"ר אמר רבא ו דוקא כיסו אבל מציאה לא פשיטא כיסו תנן מהו דתימא הוא הדין אפילו מציאה והאי דקתני כיסו אורחא דמילתא קתני קמ"ל ולא אמרן אלא ז דלא אתי לידיה אבל אתי לידיה ככיסיה דמי איכא דאמרי בעי רבא מציאה הבאה לידו מהו כיון דאתא לידיה ככיסיה דמי או דילמא כיון דלא טרח בה לאו ככיסיה דמי תיקו: אין עמו נכרי: טעמא דאין עמו נכרי הא יש עמו נכרי לנכרי יהיב ליה מאי טעמא ח חמור אתה מצווה על שביתתו נכרי אי אתה מצווה על שביתתו חמור וחרש שוטה וקטן ט אחמור מנח ליה לחרש שוטה וקטן לא יהיב ליה מ"ט הני אדם האי לאו אדם י חרש ושוטה לשוטה כ שוטה וקטן לשוטה איבעיא להו ל חרש וקטן מאי אליבא דר"א לא תיבעי לך דתניא [ח] ר' יצחק אומר משום ר' [ז] אליעזר תרומת חרש לא

רש"י

אם בן עוה"ב הוא. שאם כשר היה הכל בוכין עליו ומורידין דמעות ומספרים שבחו: אחים בהספידא דהתם קאימנא. בשעת מיתתי התאמץ בהספד שלי שיתחממו ויכמרו רחמי העומדים ויבכו: דהתם קאימנא. בשעת הספד ואשמע איך מתחמם אלמא איצטריך לרב לאזהוריה אהספדא וכיון דרב גברא רבה ובן העולם הבא הוא למה ליה לאזהוריה הא אמר מהספדו ניכר: הא דמחממין ליה. להספידא ואחים כו' לעולם תמוהי בעי שאין בני אדם נכמרים כל כך על זקן ומיהו לאדם חסיד כי מחממו בהספידא מחממי ובכו כולהו ולמי שאינו חסיד כל כך מחממו ליה ולא מחממו: דסנו ליה כולהו פומבדיתאי. משום דמוכח להו במילי דשמיא (ב) ובני פומבדיתא רמאין הן כדאמרינן בשחיטת חולין (חולין קכז.) פומבדיתאי לוייך שני אושפיזך: ואזניך תשמענה דבר מאחריך לאמר זה הדרך לכו (ג) בה. מאחרי מטתך כששמות תשמע כשיאמרו זה הדרך שהלך בה זה לכו בה מובטח שהוא בן העוה"ב: נוחה הימנו. דעתם נוחה עליהם ממה ששומעין עליו ורואין בו: עשה דברים. שיאמרו לפני מטתך בהספדך: לאחר מטתך. היא היא אלא שבגליל היו הספדנין לפני המטה וביהודה לאחר המטה: וכ"ש. שמפני שאינו יודע איזה יום ימות (ד) וטובה תשובה יום אחד לפני מיתתו נמצא כל ימיו בתשובה יהיו: בגדיך לבנים. נשמתך טהורה ונקיה: כלום חסר בית המלך. בתמיה הכל מוכן ושמא יבהילנו לבא פתאום ואנו צריכין ליכנס לסעודה מקושטין: כלום יש סעודה בלא טורח. עדיין יצטרכו לטרוח לצורכי סעודה של בית המלך ויש לנו שהות הרבה להתקשט: יעמדו ויראו. ואף לעוה"ב צדיקים יושבים ואוכלים ורשעים עומדים ורואים: ר"מ אומר. אין עומדין ורואין שא"כ אף הם היו נראים מן הקרואים ולשמש שכן דרך המשרתים עומדים ואין כאן בושה: זה ציצית. שמלובן הבגד: אלו תפילין. שהם שם משמן טוב דכתיב וראו כל עמי הארץ כי שם וגו' ותנא ר"א הגדול אומר אלו תפילין שבראש (ברכות דף ו.):

הדרן עלך שואל

מי שהחשיך (ו) נותן כיסו לנכרי. מבעוד יום: ואם אין עמו. הא יש עמו לנכרי עדיף כדמפרש בגמרא: לחצר החיצונה. של עיר שהוא מקום המשתמר ראשון ובא לפרק מן החמור: נוטל. בידו מעליו כלים הניטלין בשבת ושאין ניטלין מתיר החבלים של אוכף שהן קשורים בהן והשקין נופלין: גמ' מאי טעמא שרי ליה למיתב לנכרי. והרי הוא שלוחו לישאנו בשבת: מעמיד עצמו. מלהציל ממונו: דוקא כיסו. דכיון דטרח בה שע"י טורח הוא משתכר חיים עלה ואי לא שרית ליה הא אתי לאיתויי: ולא אמרן. דמציאה לא אלא דלא אתיא לידיה קודם שחשך ולא הגביהה ולא זכה בה: האי אדם. ויש במינו שחייב במצות ואתי לאיחלופי: לשוטה. יהיב דלית ליה דעת כלל אבל חרש דעתא קלישתא אית ליה כדאמרי' ביבמות (דף קיג.): לא

תוספות

ונשמתו עולה ושוב אינה יורדת. אף על פי כן כשהיא רוצה היא יורדת כי ההיא דלעיל דרבי אחי בר יאשיה וכההיא מעשה דר' בנאה דחזקת הבתים (ב"ב דף נח. ושם) דהוה מציין מערתא כי מטא למערתא דאברהם אבינו אשכחיה לאליעזר עבד אברהם דקאי אבבא אמר ליה מאי קא עביד אברהם כו' אמר ליה ניעול וניתי כו' אע"פ שנשמתו היתה גנוזה מתחת כסא הכבוד. מ"ר:

הדרן עלך שואל

מי שהחשיך כו' חרש שוטה וקטן. אע"ג דאמר לעיל בפרק כל כתבי (דף קכא.) גבי קטן שבא לכבות דקטן העושה לדעת אביו אסור מיהו הכא לא איירי כגון דעביד הקטן עקירה והנחה אלא כדאמרינן לקמן גבי חמור כשהיא מהלכת מניחו עליה וכשהיא עומדת נוטלו הימנה. מ"ר: כי

מסורת הש"ס

א) נ"א שילא וכן לקמן, ב) [נ"ל רבותיו וכ"ה בכי"ף והרא"ש], ג) [פסחים נ. וש"נ], ד) [אבות פ"ב מ"י], ה) [לעיל יז:], ו) [יבמות קיג.], ז) [שם איתא אלעזר].

גליון הש"ס

גמרא בני גלילא אמרי עשה דברים לפני מטתך. מסכת שמחות פ"ג ה"ז:

תורה אור השלם

א) וְאָזְנֶיךָ תִּשְׁמַעְנָה דָבָר מֵאַחֲרֶיךָ לֵאמֹר זֶה הַדֶּרֶךְ לְכוּ בוֹ כִּי תַאֲמִינוּ וְכִי תַשְׂמְאִילוּ: [ישעיה ל, כא]

ב) גַּם מִגָּבֹהַּ יִרָאוּ וְחַתְחַתִּים בַּדֶּרֶךְ וְיָנֵאץ הַשָּׁקֵד וְיִסְתַּבֵּל הֶחָגָב וְתָפֵר הָאֲבִיּוֹנָה כִּי הֹלֵךְ הָאָדָם אֶל בֵּית עוֹלָמוֹ וְסָבְבוּ בַשּׁוּק הַסֹּפְדִים: [קהלת יב, ה]

ג) בְּכָל עֵת יִהְיוּ בְגָדֶיךָ לְבָנִים וְשֶׁמֶן עַל רֹאשְׁךָ אַל יֶחְסָר: [קהלת ט, ח]

ד) לָכֵן כֹּה אָמַר אֲדֹנָי אֱלֹהִים הִנֵּה עֲבָדַי יֹאכֵלוּ וְאַתֶּם תִּרְעָבוּ הִנֵּה עֲבָדַי יִשְׁתּוּ וְאַתֶּם תִּצְמָאוּ הִנֵּה עֲבָדַי יִשְׂמָחוּ וְאַתֶּם תֵּבֹשׁוּ: [ישעיה סה, יג]

ה) הִנֵּה עֲבָדַי יָרֹנּוּ מִטּוּב לֵב וְאַתֶּם תִּצְעֲקוּ מִכְּאֵב לֵב וּמִשֵּׁבֶר רוּחַ תְּיֵלִילוּ: [ישעיה סה, יד]

ליקוטי רש"י

בכל עת יהיו בגדיך לבנים. התקן עצמך בכל שעה במעשה טוב שאם תמות היום תכנס בשלום ומשל שלמה החכם את הדבר לאדם שזימנו המלך ליום סעודה ולא קבע לו זמן אם חכם הוא לא מקח מיד מכבס כסותו ורוחץ וסך עד עת יקרא אל הסעודה יהיו כל שעה בגדיו לבנים והוא רוחץ וסך כך לרשותו רעותיו במסכת שבת [קהלת ט, ח]. עבדי. הצדיקים (של ישראל). ואתם. הפושעים כי [ישעיה סה, יג]. נותן כיסו לנכרי. ולא יטלטלנו פחות פחות מארבע אמות [לעיל יז:]. חרש שוטה וקטן. חרש האמור בו בחכמים בכל מקום שהשוו אותו לשוטה לפוטרו לא דברו אלא במי שאינו שומע ואינו מדבר הכי קים להו לרבנן דמי שאינו שומע ואינו מדבר דלאו בני דעה נינהו [חגיגה ב:]. חרש. דעתו מועטת שאין מחודד להבין כשאר בני אדם [יבמות קיג.].

עין משפט נר מצוה

נא א מיי' פ"ז מהלכות תשובה הלכה ב:

א ב מיי' פ"ו מהלכות שבת הלכה כב סמג לאוין סה טוש"ע א"ח סי' רסו סעיף א וסעיף ח וסימן שמט סעיף ה:

ב ג מיי' פ"כ שם הלכה ו סמג שם טוש"ע א"ח סי' רסו סעיף ג:

ג ד מיי' פ"כ שם הל' ה סמג שם טוש"ע שם סעיף ט:

ד ה מיי' שם הלכה כב סמג שם:

ה ו ז מיי' שם ופ"כ שם הלכה ז סמג שם טוש"ע שם סעיף ה:

ו ח מיי' פ"כ שם הלכה ו סמג שם טוש"ע שם סעיף ה:

ז ט מיי' שם הלכה ז טוש"ע שם סעיף ג:

ח י מיי' שם טוש"ע שם סעיף ד:

ט כ ל מיי' שם טוש"ע שם סעיף ה:

הגהות הב"ח

(א) גמ' שנאמר לכן כה אמר: (ב) רש"י ד"ה דסנו וכו' דבני פומבדיתא: (ג) ד"ה אזניך וכו' לכו בו מאחרי: (ד) ד"ה וכ"ש שמפני וכו' יום ימות בתשובה:

פרק כד

(ה) במשנה מי שהחשיך לו בדרך: (ו) רש"י ד"ה מי שהחשיך לו נותן:

רבינו חננאל

איזה בן עולם הבא כל שדעת רבותינו נוחה הימנו כך שמעתא דא סלקא:

הדרן עלך שואל אדם

פרק כד מי שהחשיך בדרך נותן כיסו לנכרי וכו' ואוקי' למתניתין דאין אדם מעמיד עצמו על ממונו והתירו לו לתת כיסו לנכרי בשביל שלא ישאנו הוא בעצמו. ובא רבא ודקדק ואמר דוקא כיסו אבל מציאה דלא אתא לידיה לא התירו לו לתתו לנכרי ובמציאה דאתאי לידיה ללישנא בתרא עלתה בתיקו. וכל תיקו דאיסורא לחומרא והלכתא כרבא דאוקמא (לידיה) [למתני'] בכיסו ממש. אין עמו נכרי מניחו על חמור דייקינן מינה בעת שמצויין ביחד נכרי וחמור לנכרי יהיב ליה מפני שאינו מצווה על שביתתו של נכרי ולכן לא התירו לו לתת כיסו על החמור שהוא מצווה על שביתתו אלא אם אין שם נכרי אלא חמור. וישראל חרש או שוטה או קטן אינו נותן כיסו לאחד מהן אלא נותן כיסו על החמור ולעולם לגרוע שבהן נותן כגון חרש ושוטה לשוטה נותן חרש ושוטה וקטן לשוטה נותן והשוטה גרוע בבני אדם שאין הפרש בין אדם לבהמה אלא הדעת והתבונה וזה כיון שאין לו דעת כבהמה חשוב:

,,בְּכָל־עֵת יִהְיוּ בְגָדֶיךָ לְבָנִים" – ***At all times let your garments be white,*** אֵלּוּ צִיצִית – **this** refers to one's *tzitzis.*[18] And when it states: ,,וְשֶׁמֶן עַל־רֹאשְׁךָ אַל־יֶחְסָר" – ***and your head never lack oil,*** אֵלּוּ תְּפִילִּין – **this** refers to one's tefillin.[19]

הדרן עלך שואל

WE SHALL RETURN TO YOU, SHO'EIL

NOTES

18. The *tzitzis* – the fringes that by Torah law (*Numbers* 15:37-41) must be placed on a four-cornered garment – are comprised of blue [*techeiles*] and white threads. Yet even when the blue strands are unavailable to you [as has been the case for centuries, since the method for producing *techeiles* has been lost], still see to it that you wear at least the white threads [*at all times let your garments be white*] (*Maharsha*).

Sfas Emes (*Parshas Shelach* p. 109) suggests the following homiletical interpretation. In *Ecclesiastes* (ch. 3), King Solomon delineates twenty-eight different "times" [עתים] of life, each with a response uniquely appropriate [e.g. *there is a time to love and a time to hate; a time to make war and a time to make peace*]. Corresponding to this, there are also twenty-eight [white] strands in the *tzitzis* that adorn one's clothes. The composite allusion is thus: "In every one of life's [twenty-eight] *times*" – no matter what joys or troubles one experiences in the course of life, "let his clothes always remain clean" – let him never compromise his spiritual purity.

19. Oil, שֶׁמֶן, is related to the word שֵׁם, *name* (see *Ecclesiastes* 7:1), a term that is in turn associated with tefillin [see *Berachos* 6a, which expounds the word "Name" found in *Deuteronomy* 28:10: *Then all the peoples of the world will see that God's Name* (שֵׁם) *is called upon you*, as a reference to tefillin] (*Rashi*). [Indeed, kings of Israel are anointed with oil on the same spot on the head where tefillin are placed (*Kad HaKemach* p. 440; see also *Maharal*).]

According to *Maharsha*, the Gemara expounds the verse to say that one should always wear head-tefillin [*may your head never lack oil*] even if he does not have hand-tefillin available to him.

מסורת הש"ס

א) נ"א שילא וכן לקמן, ב) [נ"ל רבותיו וכ"א ברי"ף והרא"ש], ג) [פסחים נ. וש"נ], ד) [אבות פ"ב מ"י], ה) [לעיל יז.], ו) [יבמות קיג.], ז) [שם איתא אלעזר].

ונשמתו עולה ושוב אינה יורדת אמר רב יהודה בריה דרב שמואל בר שילת משמיה דרב מהספדו של אדם ניכר אם בן העוה"ב הוא אם לאו איני והאמר ליה רב לרב שמואל בר שילת אחים בהספידא דהתם קאימנא לא קשיא הא דמחמו ליה ואחים הא דמחמו ליה ולא אחים א"ל אביי לרבה כגון מר דסנו ליה כולהו פומבדיתאי מאן אחים הספידא א"ל מיסתיא את ורבה בר רב חנן בעא מניה רבי אלעזר מרב איזהו בן העוה"ב א"ל ואזניך תשמענה דבר מאחריך לאמר זה הדרך לכו בו כי תאמינו וכי תשמאילו ר' חנינא אמר כל שדעת רבותינו נוחה הימנו וסבבו בשוק הסופדים בני גלילא אמרי עשה דברים לפני מטתך בני יהודה אמרי עשה דברים לאחר מטתך ולא פליגי מר כי אתריה ומר כי אתריה תנן התם רבי אליעזר אומר שוב יום אחד לפני מיתתך שאלו תלמידיו את ר"א וכי אדם יודע איזהו יום ימות אמר להן וכל שכן ישוב היום שמא ימות למחר ונמצא כל ימיו בתשובה ואף שלמה אמר בחכמתו בכל עת יהיו בגדיך לבנים ושמן על ראשך אל יחסר א"ר יוחנן בן זכאי משל למלך שזימן את עבדיו לסעודה ולא קבע להם זמן פיקחין שבהן קישטו את עצמן וישבו על פתח בית המלך אמרו כלום חסר לבית המלך טיפשין שבהן הלכו למלאכתן אמרו כלום יש סעודה בלא טורח בפתאום ביקש המלך את עבדיו פיקחין שבהן נכנסו לפניו כשהן מקושטין והטיפשים נכנסו לפניו כשהן מלוכלכין שמח המלך לקראת פיקחים וכעס לקראת טיפשים אמר הללו שקישטו את עצמן לסעודה ישבו ויאכלו וישתו הללו שלא קישטו עצמן לסעודה יעמדו ויראו חתנו של ר"מ משום ר"מ אמר אף הן נראין כמשמשין אלא אלו ואלו יושבין הללו אוכלין והללו רעבין הללו שותין והללו צמאים שנאמר (א) כה אמר ה' הנה עבדי יאכלו ואתם תרעבו הנה עבדי ישתו ואתם תצמאו הנה עבדי ירונו מטוב לב ואתם תצעקו מכאב לב ד"א בכל עת יהיו בגדיך לבנים אלו ציצית ושמן על ראשך אל יחסר אלו תפילין:

הדרן עלך שואל

מי שהחשיך (ה) בדרך נותן כיסו לנכרי ואם אין עמו נכרי מניחו על החמור הגיע לחצר החיצונה נוטל את הכלים הניטלין בשבת ושאינן ניטלין בשבת מתיר החבלים והשקין נופלין מאיליהם: **גמ'** מאי טעמא שרו ליה רבנן למיתב כיסיה לנכרי קים להו לרבנן דאין אדם מעמיד עצמו על ממונו אי לא שרית ליה אתי לאיתויי ד' אמות ברה"ר אמר רבא דוקא כיסו אבל מציאה לא פשיטא כיסו תנן מהו דתימא הוא הדין אפילו מציאה והאי דקתני כיסו אורחא דמילתא קתני קמ"ל ולא אמרן אלא דלא אתי לידיה אבל אתי לידיה ככיסיה דמי איכא דאמרי בעי רבא מציאה הבאה לידו מהו כיון דאתא לידיה ככיסיה דמי או דילמא כיון דלא טרח בה לאו ככיסיה דמי תיקו: אין עמו נכרי: טעמא דאין עמו נכרי הא יש עמו נכרי לנכרי יהיב ליה מאי טעמא חמור אתה מצווה על שביתתו נכרי אי אתה מצווה על שביתתו חמור וחרש שוטה וקטן אחמור מנח ליה לחרש שוטה וקטן לא יהיב ליה מ"ט הני אדם האי לאו אדם חרש ושוטה לשוטה שוטה וקטן לשוטה איבעיא להו חרש וקטן מאי אליבא דר"א לא תיבעי לך דתניא ר' יצחק אומר משום ר' אליעזר תרומת חרש לא

רש"י

אם בן עוה"ב הוא. שאם כשר היה הכל בוכין עליו ומורידין דמעות ומספרים שבחו: **אחים בהספידא דהתם קאימנא.** בשעת מיתתי התאמץ בהספד שלי שיתחממו ויכמרו רחמי העומדים ויבכו: **דהתם קאימנא.** בשעת הספד ואשמע איך מתחממים אלמא איצטריך לרב לאזהוריה אהספדא וכיון דרב גברא רבה וכן העולם הבא למה ליה לאזהוריה הא אמר מהספדו ניכר: **הא דמחמו ליה.** להספידא ואחים כו' לעולם חמומי בעי שאין בני אדם נכמרים כל כך על זקן ומיהו לאדם חסיד כי מחממו בהספידא מחממי ובכו כולהו ולמי שאינו חסיד כל כך מחממו ליה ולא מחממו: **דסנו ליה כולהו פומבדיתאי.** משום דמוכח להו במילי דשמיא (ב) ובני פומבדיתאי רמאין הן כדאמרינן בשחיטת חולין (חולין קכז.) פומבדיתאי לוייך שני אושפיזך: **ואזניך תשמענה דבר מאחריך לאמר זה הדרך לכו** (ג) **בה.** מאחרי מטתך כשתמות תשמע כשיאמרו זה הדרך שהלך בה זה לכו בה מובטח שהוא בן העוה"ב: **נוחה הימנו.** דעתם נוחה עליהם ממה ששומעין עליו ורואין בו: **עשה דברים.** שיאמרו לפני מטתך בהספדך: **לאחר מטתך.** היא היא אלא שבגליל היו הספדנין לפני המטה וביהודה לאחר המטה: **וכ"ש.** שמפני שאינו יודע איזה יום ימות (ד) וטובה תשובה יום אחד לפני מיתתו נמצא כל ימיו בתשובה יהיו: **בגדיך לבנים.** נשמתך טהורה ונקיה: **כלום חסר בית המלך.** במה הכל מוכן ושמא יבהילונו לבא פתאום ואנו צריכין ליכנס לסעודה מקושטין: **כלום יש סעודה בלא טורח.** עדיין יצטרכו לטרוח לצורכי סעודה של בית המלך ויש לנו שהות הרבה להתקשט: **יעמדו ויראו.** ואף לעוה"ב לצדיקים יושבים ואוכלים ורשעים עומדים ורואים: **ר"מ אומר.** אין עומדין ורואין שא"כ אף הם היו נראים מן הקרואים ולשמש שכן דרך המשרתים עומדים ואין כאן בושה: **זה ציצית.** שמלובן הבגד: **אלו תפילין.** שהם שם משמן טוב דכתיב וראו כל עמי הארץ כי שם וגו' ותניא ר"א הגדול אומר אלו תפילין שבראש (ברכות דף ו.):

הדרן עלך שואל

מי שהחשיך (ו) **נותן כיסו לנכרי.** מבעוד יום: **ואם אין עמו.** הא יש עמו לנכרי עדיף כדמפרש בגמרא: **לחצר החיצונה.** של עיר שהוא מקום המשתמר ראשון ובא לפרק מן החמור: **נוטל.** בידו מעליו כלים הניטלין בשבת ושאין ניטלין מתיר החבלים של אוכף שהן קשורים בהן והשקין נופלין: **גמ' מאי טעמא** שרי ליה למיתב לנכרי. והרי הוא שלוחו לישאנו בשבת: **מעמיד עצמו.** מלהציל ממונו: **דוקא כיסו.** דכיון דטרח בה שע"י טורח הוא משתכר חייס עלה ואי לא שרית ליה הא אתי לאיתויי: **ולא אמרן.** דמציאה לא אלא דלא אתיא לידיה קודם שתחשך ולא הגביהה ולא זכה בה: **האי אדם.** ויש במינו שחייב במצות ואתי לאיחלופי: **לשוטה.** יהיב דלית ליה דעת כלל אבל חרש דעתא קלישתא אית ליה כדאמרי' ביבמות (דף קיג.):

תוספות

ונשמתו עולה ושוב אינה יורדת. אף על פי כן כשהיא רוצה היא יורדת כי ההיא דלעיל דרבי אחי בר יאשיה וכההיא מעשה דר' בנאה דחזקת הבתים (ב"ב דף נח. ושם) דהוה מציין מערתא כי מטא למערתא דאברהם אבינו אשכחיה לאליעזר עבד אברהם דקאי אבבא אמר ליה מאי קא עביד אברהם כו' אמר ליה ניעול וניתי כו' אע"פ שנשמתו היתה גנוזה מתחת כסא הכבוד. מ"ר:

הדרן עלך שואל

מי שהחשיך כו' חרש שוטה וקטן. אע"ג דאמר לעיל בפרק כל כתבי (דף קכא.) גבי קטן שבא לכבות דקטן העושה לדעת אביו אסור מיהו הכא לא איירי כגון דעביד הקטן עקירה והנחה אלא כדאמרינן לקמן גבי חמור כשהיא מהלכת מניחו עליה וכשהיא עומדת נוטלו הימנה. מ"ר:

כי

עין משפט נר מצוה

נא א מיי' פ"ו מהלכות תשובה הלכה ג:
א ב מיי' פ"ו מהלכות שבת הלכה כב סמג לאוין סה טוש"ע א"ח סי' רסו סעיף א וסעיף ח וסימן שמט סעיף ה:
ב ג מיי' פ"כ שם הלכה ו סמג שם טוש"ע א"ח סי' רסו סעיף ג:
ג ד מיי' פכ"א שם הל' י סמג שם טוש"ע שם סעיף ט:
ד ה מיי' שם הלכה כב סמג שם:
ה ו ז מיי' שם ופ"כ שם הלכה ז סמג שם טוש"ע שם סעיף ה:
ו ח מיי' פ"כ שם הלכה ו סמג שם טוש"ע שם סעיף א:
ז ט מיי' שם הלכה ז טוש"ע שם סעיף ג:
ח י מיי' שם טוש"ע שם סעיף ד:
ט כ ל מיי' שם טוש"ע שם סעיף ה:

הגהות הב"ח

(א) גמ' שנאמר לכן כה אמר: (ב) רש"י ד"ה דסנו וכו' דבני פומבדיתאי: (ג) ד"ה ואזנך וכו' לכו בו מאחרי: (ד) ד"ה וכ"ש שמפני וכו' ימות ישוב בתשובה:

פרק כד

(ה) במשנה מי שהחשיך לו בדרך: (ו) רש"י ד"ה מי שהחשיך לו נותן:

רבינו חננאל

איזה בן עולם הבא כל שדעת רבותיו נוחה הימנו כך שמעתא דא סלקא:

הדרן עלך שואל אדם

פרק כד מי שהחשיך בדרך נותן כיסו לנכרי וכו' ואוקי' למתניתין דאין מעמיד עצמו על ממונו והתירו לו לתת כיסו לנכרי בשביל שלא ישאנו הוא בעצמו. ובא רבא ודקדק ואמר דוקא כיסו אבל מציאה דלא אתא לידיה לא התירו לו לתתו לנכרי ובמציאה דאתאי לידיה ללישנא בתרא עלתה בתיקו. וכל תיקו דאיסורא לחומרא והלכתא כרבא דאוקמא (לידיה) [למתני'] בכיסו ממש. אין עמו נכרי מניחו על חמור דייקינן מינה בעת שמצויין ביחד נכרי וחמור לנכרי יהיב ליה מפני שאינו מצווה על שביתתו של נכרי ולכן לא התירו לו לתת כיסו על החמור שהוא מצווה על שביתתו אלא אם אין שם נכרי אלא חמור. וישראל חרש או שוטה או קטן אינו נותן כיסו לאחד מהן אלא נותן כיסו על החמור ולעולם לגרוע שבהן נותן כגון חרש ושוטה לשוטה נותן קטן לשוטה נותן והשוטה גרוע בבני אדם שאין הפרש בין אדם לבהמה אלא הדעת והתבונה וזה כיון שאין לו דעת כבהמה חשוב:

גליון הש"ס

גמרא בני גלילא אמרי עשה דברים לפני מטתך. מסכת שמחות פ"ג ה"ז:

תורה אור השלם

א) וְאָזְנֶיךָ תִּשְׁמַעְנָה דָבָר מֵאַחֲרֶיךָ לֵאמֹר זֶה הַדֶּרֶךְ לְכוּ בוֹ כִּי תַאֲמִינוּ וְכִי תַשְׂמְאִילוּ: [ישעיה ל, כא]

ב) גַּם מִגָּבֹהַּ יִרָאוּ וְחַתְחַתִּים בַּדֶּרֶךְ וְיָנֵאץ הַשָּׁקֵד וְיִסְתַּבֵּל הֶחָגָב וְתָפֵר הָאֲבִיּוֹנָה כִּי הֹלֵךְ הָאָדָם אֶל בֵּית עוֹלָמוֹ וְסָבְבוּ בַשּׁוּק הַסֹּפְדִים: [קהלת יב, ה]

ג) בְּכָל עֵת יִהְיוּ בְגָדֶיךָ לְבָנִים וְשֶׁמֶן עַל רֹאשְׁךָ אַל יֶחְסָר: [קהלת ט, ח]

ד) לָכֵן כֹּה אָמַר אֲדֹנָי אֱלֹהִים הִנֵּה עֲבָדַי יֹאכֵלוּ וְאַתֶּם תִּרְעָבוּ הִנֵּה עֲבָדַי יִשְׁתּוּ וְאַתֶּם תִּצְמָאוּ הִנֵּה עֲבָדַי יִשְׂמָחוּ וְאַתֶּם תֵּבֹשׁוּ: [ישעיה סה, יג]

ה) הִנֵּה עֲבָדַי יָרֹנּוּ מִטּוּב לֵב וְאַתֶּם תִּצְעֲקוּ מִכְּאֵב לֵב וּמִשֵּׁבֶר רוּחַ תְּיֵלִילוּ: [ישעיה סה, יד]

ליקוטי רש"י

בכל עת יהיו בגדיך לבנים. התקן עצמך כל שעה במעשים טובים שאם תמות היום תכנס בשלום ומשל שלמה המכסה את הדבר לאדם שהזמינו המלך ליום סעודה ולא קבע לו זמן אם חכם הוא מיד מכבס ורוחץ וסך וכן עם חמר עד עת יקרא אל הסעודה יהיו כל שעה בגדיו לבנים והוא רוחץ וסך כך לדבוקו רבותינו במסכת שבת [קהלת ט, ח]. **עבדי.** הצדיקים [של ישראל]. **ואתם.** הפושעים בי [ישעיה סה, יג]. **נותן כיסו לנכרי.** ולא יטלטלנו פחות פחות מארבע אמות [לעיל יז:]. **חרש** שדברו בו חכמים בכל מקום שהוא אינו שומע ואינו מדבר אלא כמי שאינו שומע ואינו מדבר הכי קים להו לרבנן דמי שאינו שומע ואינו מדבר דלאו בני דעה נינהו [חגיגה ב:]. **חרש.** דעתו מעוטת שאין ממודד להבין כשאר בני אדם [יבמות קיג.].

Chapter Twenty-Four

Mishnah מִי שֶׁהֶחְשִׁיךְ בַּדֶּרֶךְ – ONE WHO WAS ON THE ROAD AS DUSK APPROACHED on Friday נוֹתֵן כִּיסוֹ לְנָכְרִי – SHOULD GIVE HIS PURSE TO A GENTILE while it is still daytime.[1] וְאִם אֵין עִמּוֹ נָכְרִי – IF THERE IS NO GENTILE WITH HIM, מַנִּיחוֹ עַל הַחֲמוֹר – HE SHOULD PLACE [THE PURSE] ON [HIS] DONKEY.[2] הִגִּיעַ לֶחָצֵר הַחִיצוֹנָה – WHEN HE REACHES THE OUTERMOST COURTYARD of the city[3] and commences to unload the donkey, נוֹטֵל אֶת הַכֵּלִים הַנִּיטָּלִין בְּשַׁבָּת – HE MAY TAKE off ANY UTENSILS THAT MAY normally BE MOVED ON THE SABBATH. וְשֶׁאֵינָן נִיטָּלִין בְּשַׁבָּת – HOWEVER, THOSE utensils THAT MAY NOT BE MOVED ON THE SABBATH, because they are *muktzeh*, he may not take himself; מַתִּיר הַחֲבָלִים וְהַשַּׂקִּין נוֹפְלִין מֵאֵילֵיהֶם – instead HE UNDOES THE ROPES that hold them fastened to the saddle, AND THE SACKS FALL down ON THEIR OWN.[4]

Gemara The Gemara questions the Mishnah's first ruling: מַאי טַעְמָא שָׁרוּ לֵיהּ רַבָּנָן לְמֵיתַב כִּיסֵיהּ לְנָכְרִי – **Why did the Rabbis permit him to give his purse to a gentile** to carry for him? Normally one is not allowed to ask a gentile to perform a forbidden labor on the Sabbath![5] – ? –

The Gemara answers:

קִים לְהוּ לְרַבָּנָן דְּאֵין אָדָם מַעֲמִיד עַצְמוֹ עַל מָמוֹנוֹ – **The Rabbis determined that a person cannot** generally **restrain himself** from saving **his property;** אִי לָא שָׁרֵית לֵיהּ – therefore, **if you do not permit him** to ask a gentile to transport his purse for him, אָתֵי לְאֵיתוּיֵי אַרְבַּע אַמּוֹת בִּרְשׁוּת הָרַבִּים – **he may come to carry it** himself **four** ***amos*** **in the public domain,** thereby commiting a capital violation of the Sabbath.[6]

The Gemara presents a related ruling:

אָמַר רָבָא – **Rava said:** דַּוְקָא כִּיסוֹ – He may ask the gentile to carry **his purse only,** אֲבָל מְצִיאָה לֹא – **but** he may **not** ask him to carry **a found object.**[7]

The Gemara questions the necessity for this ruling:

פְּשִׁיטָא – **That is obvious!** כִּיסוֹ תְּנַן – **We learned in our Mishnah** that he may give **HIS PURSE** to a gentile; clearly a found object is not in that category. – ? –

The Gemara explains:

מַהוּ דְּתֵימָא – **You might have said** הוּא הַדִּין אֲפִילוּ מְצִיאָה – **that the same law applies even to a found object,** וְהַאי דְּקָתָנֵי כִּיסוֹ – **and when [the Mishnah] teaches** HIS PURSE אוֹרְחָא דְּמִילְּתָא קָתָנֵי – **it is** merely **teaching the typical case.** קָא מַשְׁמַע לָן – **[Rava's ruling]** therefore **informs us** that this is not so; one's purse may be given to a gentile but not a found object.

The Gemara qualifies this ruling:

וְלָא אֲמָרַן אֶלָּא דְּלָא אָתֵי לִידֵיהּ – **And we say this** distinction (between a purse and a found object) **only where [the found object] had not come into his hands** before the Sabbath.[8] אֲבָל אָתֵי לִידֵיהּ – **If, however, [the found object]** already **came into his hands** before the Sabbath began כְּכִיסֵיהּ דָּמֵי – then **it is comparable to his own purse** and may be given to the gentile.[9]

The Gemara quotes a different tradition regarding this last point:

אִיכָּא דְּאָמְרֵי – **Some say:** בָּעֵי רָבָא – **Rava inquired:** מְצִיאָה

NOTES

1. Although a Jew is forbidden to carry in a public domain on the Sabbath, he need not abandon his purse on the road; rather, before the Sabbath begins he hands his purse (and other valuables) to a gentile and asks him to carry it into town for him. The gentile returns the purse to him after the Sabbath (see *Tosefta* 18:12, quoted by *Rashba* here; *Shulchan Aruch, Orach Chaim* 266:1). Although under normal circumstances it is forbidden to ask a gentile to perform a *melachah* on one's behalf on the Sabbath, this is only a Rabbinic injunction and is waived in this case. The reason for this, and the parameters for this leniency, will be explained more fully in the Gemara.

[If possible, he should hand the purse over to the gentile before the Sabbath commences, so as to avoid handling it on the Sabbath, when it is *muktzeh* (*Shiltei HaGiborim*, explaining *Rashi*; see also *Beur HaGra* to *Orach Chaim* 266:1; cf. *Ritva MHK* ed. ד"ה מאי טעמא).]

2. [As the Gemara will explain, this too would be forbidden under normal circumstances, but is allowed here as a special dispensation.]

The Mishnah's language indicates that one uses a donkey only if there is no gentile available. The Gemara will explain why this is so (*Rashi*).

3. I.e. the first secure area within the city (*Rashi*). Once he has reached a secure area, he can no longer make use of the above dispensation and cannot allow the donkey to carry his valuables any further through the streets of the town (cf. *Rambam's Commentary* and *Meiri*).

4. He cannot simply leave them on the donkey, for this would cause unwarranted suffering to the animal (see Gemara below, 154b; *Mishnah Berurah* 266:24).

5. It is Rabbinically prohibited for a Jew to ask a gentile to perform a *melachah* on the Sabbath for him. This is termed אֲמִירָה לְעַכּוּ"ם, *instructing a gentile* [to violate the Sabbath]. Even where, as in our Mishnah, he spoke to the gentile before the Sabbath began, this prohibition still applies, since when the gentile carries out his instructions on the Sabbath he acts as the Jew's agent (*Rashi*, as explained by *Beis Meir, Even HaEzer* 5:4 and *Teshuvos Chasam Sofer, Orach Chaim* §84; see also *Rashi* to *Avodah Zarah* 15a ד"ה כיון דזבנה; *Hagahos Maimoniyos, Hil. Shabbos* 6:2; *Sfas Emes* here; *Teshuvos Avnei Nezer, Orach Chaim* §43; *Shulchan Aruch HaRav, Orach Chaim* 243:1; ibid., *Kuntres Acharon* 263:8).

[It should be noted that the prohibition of *instructing a gentile* applies not only to Sabbath prohibitions. In general, it is forbidden for a Jew to ask a gentile to perform, on his behalf, any action that would be forbidden for the Jew to do himself. See *Bava Metzia* 90a; *Rama, Yoreh Deah* 297(II):4; *Shach*, ad loc.; *Magen Avraham* and *Hagahos R' Akiva Eiger* to *Orach Chaim* 307:21.]

6. The Rabbis feared that if he is not afforded a lawful way to transport his purse to town, the desperate traveler may be unable to restrain himself and will carry the purse himself, which would be a Biblical violation of the Sabbath. They therefore relaxed the Rabbinic prohibition of instructing a gentile in this instance, and allowed him to ask a gentile to carry his purse.

[It emerges that the Rabbis waived the prohibition of instructing a gentile not in order to save the purse, but in order to save the traveler from a more severe violation. We have also learned above (117b) that in the case of a fire the Rabbis acted in the reverse manner, *limiting* the amount a person may save for fear that allowing him to save more will lead him to perform a *melachah*. See *Ramban* and *Rashba* here for a discussion of this point; cf. *Sefer HaTerumah* 226; see further in *Aruch HaShulchan, Orach Chaim* 334:13-22.]

7. The difference is this: The money in his purse was earned through his own exertion; a person finds difficulty giving this up and may be unable to restrain himself from carrying it home himself. In contrast, the found object became his without any exertion at all, and this a person can forgo. The Rabbis therefore did not see any reason to relax the prohibition of instructing a gentile in this case (*Rashi*; cf. *Meiri*; see also *Melo HaRo'im*; *Levushei Serad* to *Taz, Orach Chaim* 266:1).

8. I.e. he had not yet picked it up and gained possession of it when the Sabbath began. In such a case he is not allowed to ask the gentile to pick it up and carry it for him (see *Rashi*; *Ritva MHK* ed.).

9. Once the found object came into his hands he is less able to bring himself to abandon it as the Sabbath approaches; it is therefore comparable to his own purse, and may be given to a gentile to carry (see *Ran*).

ונשמתו עולה ושוב אינה יורדת אמר רב יהודה בריה דרב שמואל בר (א) שילת משמיה דרב מהספדו של אדם ניכר אם בן העוה"ב הוא אם לאו איני והאמר ליה רב לרב שמואל בר שילת אחים בהספידא דהתם קאימנא לא קשיא הא דמחמו ליה ואחים הא דמחמו ליה ולא אחים א"ל אביי לרבה כגון מר דסנו ליה כולהו פומבדיתאי מאן אחים הספידא א"ל מיסתיא את ורבה בר רב חנן בעא מניה רבי אלעזר מרב איזהו בן העוה"ב א"ל (א) ואזניך תשמענה דבר מאחריך לאמר זה הדרך לכו בו כי תאמינו וכי תשמאילו ר' חנינא אמר כל שדעת רבותינו נוחה הימנו (ב) וסבבו בשוק הסופדים בני גלילא אמרי עשה דברים לפני מטתך בני יהודה אמרי עשה דברים לאחר מטתך ולא פליגי מר כי אתריה ומר כי אתריה תנן התם רבי אליעזר אומר א שוב יום אחד לפני מיתתך שאלו תלמידיו את ר"א וכי אדם יודע איזהו יום ימות אמר להן וכל שכן ישוב היום שמא ימות למחר ונמצא כל ימיו בתשובה ואף שלמה אמר בחכמתו (ג) בכל עת יהיו בגדיך לבנים ושמן על ראשך אל יחסר א"ר יוחנן בן זכאי משל למלך שזימן את עבדיו לסעודה ולא קבע להם זמן פיקחין שבהן קישטו את עצמן וישבו על פתח בית המלך אמרו כלום חסר לבית המלך טיפשין שבהן הלכו למלאכתן אמרו כלום יש סעודה בלא טורח בפתאום ביקש המלך את עבדיו פיקחין שבהן נכנסו לפניו כשהן מקושטין והטיפשים נכנסו לפניו כשהן מלוכלכין שמח המלך לקראת פיקחים וכעס לקראת טיפשים אמר הללו שקישטו את עצמן לסעודה ישבו ויאכלו וישתו הללו שלא קישטו עצמן לסעודה יעמדו ויראו חתנו של ר"מ משום ר"מ אמר אף הן נראין כמשמשין אלא אלו ואלו יושבין הללו אוכלין והללו רעבין הללו שותין והללו צמאים שנאמר (א) (ד) כה אמר ה' הנה עבדי יאכלו ואתם תרעבו הנה עבדי ישתו ואתם תצמאו (ה) הנה עבדי ירונו מטוב לב ואתם תצעקו מכאב לב ד"א בכל עת יהיו בגדיך לבנים אלו ציצית ושמן על ראשך אל יחסר אלו תפילין:

הדרן עלך שואל

מי שהחשיך (ה) בדרך נותן כיסו לנכרי ואם אין עמו נכרי מניחו על החמור הגיע לחצר החיצונה נוטל את הכלים הניטלין בשבת ושאינן ניטלין בשבת מתיר החבלים והשקין נופלין מאיליהם: גמ' מאי טעמא שרו ליה רבנן למיתב כיסיה לנכרי קים להו לרבנן דאין אדם מעמיד עצמו על ממונו אי לא שרית ליה אתי לאיתויי ד' אמות ברה"ר אמר רבא דוקא כיסו אבל מציאה לא פשיטא כיסו תנן מהו דתימא הוא הדין אפילו מציאה והאי דקתני כיסו אורחא דמילתא קתני קמ"ל ולא אמרן אלא דלא אתי לידיה אבל אתי לידיה ככיסיה דמי איכא דאמרי בעי רבא מציאה הבאה לידו מהו כיון דאתא לידיה ככיסיה דמי או דילמא כיון דלא טרח בה לאו ככיסיה דמי תיקו: אין עמו נכרי: טעמא דאין עמו נכרי הא יש עמו נכרי לנכרי יהיב ליה מאי טעמא חמור אתה מצווה על שביתתו נכרי אי אתה מצווה על שביתתו חמור וחרש שוטה וקטן אחמור מנח ליה לחרש שוטה וקטן לא יהיב ליה מ"ט הני אדם האי לאו אדם חרש ושוטה לשוטה שוטה וקטן לשוטה איבעיא להו חרש וקטן מאי אליבא דר"א לא תיבעי לך דתניא ר' יצחק אומר משום ר' אליעזר תרומת חרש לא

רש"י

אם בן עוה"ב הוא. שאם כשר היה הכל בוכין עליו ומורידין דמעות ומספרים שבחו: אחים בהספידא דהתם קאימנא. בשעת מיתתי התאמץ בהספד שלי שיתחממו ויכמרו רחמי העומדים ויבכו: דהתם קאימנא. בשעת הספד ואשמע איך מתחממים אלמא אילטריך לרב לאזהוריה אהספדא וכיון דרב גברא רבה ובן העולם הבא הוא למה ליה לאזהוריה הא אמר מהספדו ניכר: הא דמחממין ליה. להספידא ואחים כו' לעולם תמומי בעי שאין בני אדם נכמרים כל כך על זקן ומיהו לאדם חסיד כי מחממו בהספידא מחממי ובכו כולהו ולמי שאינו חסיד כל כך מחממו ליה ולא מחממו: דסנו ליה כולהו פומבדיתאי. משום דמוכח להו במילי דשמיא (ג) ובני פומבדיתאי רמאין הן כדאמרינן בשחיטת חולין (חולין קכז.) פומבדיתאי לוייך שני אושפיזך: ואזניך תשמענה דבר מאחריך לאמר זה הדרך לכו (ג) בה. מאחרי מטתך כשתמות תשמע כשיאמרו זה הדרך שהלך בה זה לכו בה מובטח שהוא בן העוה"ב: נוחה הימנו. דעתם נוחה עליהם ממה ששומעין עליו ורואין בו: עשה דברים. שיאמרו לפני מטתך בהספדך: לאחר מטתך. היא היא אלא שבגליל היו הספדנין לפני המטה וביהודה לאחר המטה: וכ"ש. שמפני שאינו יודע איזה יום ימות (ד) וטובה תשובה יום אחד לפני מיתתו נמצא כל ימיו בתשובה יהיו: בגדיך לבנים. נשמתך טהורה ונקיה: כלום חסר בית המלך. בתמיה הכל מוכן ושמא יבהילנו לבא פתאום ואנו צריכין ליכנס לסעודה מקושטין: כלום יש סעודה בלא טורח. עדיין יטרחו לטרוח לצורכי סעודה של בית המלך ויש לנו שהות הרבה להתקשט: יעמדו ויראו. ואף לעוה"ב צדיקים יושבים ואוכלים ורשעים עומדים ורואים: ר"מ אומר. אין עומדין ורואין שא"כ אף הם היו נראים מן הקרואים ולשמש שכן דרך המשרתים עומדים ואין כאן בושה: זה ציצית. שמלובן הבגד: אלו תפילין. שהם שם משמן טוב דכתיב וראו כל עמי הארץ כי שם וגו' ותנא ר"א הגדול אומר אלו תפילין שבראש (ברכות דף ו.):

הדרן עלך שואל

מי שהחשיך (ו) נותן כיסו לנכרי. מבעוד יום: ואם אין עמו. הא יש עמו לנכרי עדיף כדמפרש בגמרא: לחצר החיצונה. של עיר שהוא מקום המשתמר ראשון ובא לפרק מן החמור: נוטל. בידו מעליו כלים הניטלין בשבת ושאין ניטלין מתיר החבלים של אוכף שהן קשורים בהן והשקין נופלין: גמ' מאי טעמא שרי ליה למיתב לנכרי. והרי הוא שלוחו לישאנו בשבת: מעמיד עצמו. מלהציל ממונו: דוקא כיסו. דכיון דטרח בה שע"י טורח הוא משתכר חיים עלה ואי לא שרית ליה הא אתי לאיתויי: ולא אמרן. דמציאה לא אלא דלא אתיא לידיה קודם שחשך ולא הגביהה ולא זכה בה: האי אדם. ויש במינו שחייב במצות ואתי לאיחלופי: לשוטה. יהיב דלית ליה דעת כלל אבל חרש דעתא קלישתא אית ליה כדאמרי' ביבמות (דף קיג.): לא

תוספות

ונשמתו עולה ושוב אינה יורדת. אף על פי כן כשהיא רוצה היא יורדת כי ההיא דלעיל דרבי אחי בר יאשיה וכההיא מעשה דר' בנאה דחזקת הבתים (ב"ב דף נח. ושם) דהוה מציין מערתא כי מטא למערתא דאברהם אשכחיה לאליעזר עבד אברהם דקאי אבבא אמר ליה מאי קא עביד אברהם כו' אמר ליה ניעול וניחזי כו' אע"פ שנשמתו היתה גנוזה מתחת כסא הכבוד. מ"ר:

הדרן עלך שואל

מי שהחשיך כו' חרש שוטה וקטן. אע"ג דאמר לעיל בפרק כל כתבי (דף קכא.) גבי קטן שבא לכבות דקטן העושה לדעת אביו אסור מיהו הכא לא איירי כגון דעביד הקטן עקירה והנחה אלא כדאמרינן לקמן גבי חמור כשהיא מהלכת מניחו עליה וכשהיא עומדת נוטלו הימנה. מ"ר:

כי

מסורת הש"ס

א) נ"א שילא וכן לקמן, ב) [נ"ל רבותיו וכ"א ברי"ף והרא"ש], ג) [פסחים ג. וש"נ], ד) [אבות פ"ב מ"י], ה) [לעיל יז:], ו) [יבמות קיג.], ז) [שם איתא אלעזר].

גליון הש"ס

גמרא בני גלילא אמרי עשה דברים לפני מטתך. מסכת שמחות פ"ג ה"ז:

תורה אור השלם

א) וְאָזְנֶיךָ תִּשְׁמַעְנָה דָבָר מֵאַחֲרֶיךָ לֵאמֹר זֶה הַדֶּרֶךְ לְכוּ בוֹ כִּי תַאֲמִינוּ וְכִי תַשְׂמְאִילוּ: [ישעיה ל, כא]

ב) גַּם מִגָּבֹהַּ יִרָאוּ וְחַתְחַתִּים בַּדֶּרֶךְ וְיָנֵאץ הַשָּׁקֵד וְיִסְתַּבֵּל הֶחָגָב וְתָפֵר הָאֲבִיּוֹנָה כִּי הֹלֵךְ הָאָדָם אֶל בֵּית עוֹלָמוֹ וְסָבְבוּ בַשּׁוּק הַסֹּפְדִים: [קהלת יב, ה]

ג) בְּכָל עֵת יִהְיוּ בְגָדֶיךָ לְבָנִים וְשֶׁמֶן עַל רֹאשְׁךָ אַל יֶחְסָר: [קהלת ט, ח]

ד) לָכֵן כֹּה אָמַר אֲדֹנָי אֱלֹהִים הִנֵּה עֲבָדַי יֹאכֵלוּ וְאַתֶּם תִּרְעָבוּ הִנֵּה עֲבָדַי יִשְׁתּוּ וְאַתֶּם תִּצְמָאוּ הִנֵּה עֲבָדַי יִשְׂמָחוּ וְאַתֶּם תֵּבֹשׁוּ: [ישעיה סה, יג]

ה) הִנֵּה עֲבָדַי יָרֹנּוּ מִטּוּב לֵב וְאַתֶּם תִּצְעֲקוּ מִכְּאֵב לֵב וּמִשֵּׁבֶר רוּחַ תְּיֵלִילוּ: [ישעיה סה, יד]

ליקוטי רש"י

בכל עת יהיו בגדיך לבנים. התקן עצמך בכל שעה במעשה טוב שאם תמות היום תכנס בשלום ומשל שלמה החכם את הדבר לאדם שהזמינו המלך ליום סעודה ולא קבע לו זמן אם חכם הוא לא פקח מיד מכבס כסותו ורוחץ וסך וכן עם מחר עד עת יקרא אל הסעודה יהיו כל שעה בגדיו לבנים והוא רחוץ וסך כך דרשוהו רבותינו במסכת שבת [קהלת ט, ח]. עבדי. הצדיקים (של ישראל). ואתם. הפושעים בי [ישעיה סה, יג]. נותן כיסו לנכרי. ולא יטלטלנו פחות פחות מארבע אמות [לעיל יז:]. חרש שוטה וקטן. חרש שדברו בו חכמים בכל מקום שהשוו אותו לשוטה לפוטרו לא דברו אלא במי שאינו שומע ואינו מדבר הכי קים להו לרבנן דמי שאינו שומע ואינו מדבר דלאו בני דעה נינהו [חגיגה ב:]. חרש. דעתו מועטת שאין מחודד להבין כשאר בני אדם [יבמות קיג.].

עין משפט נר מצוה

נא א מיי' פ"ז מהלכות תשובה הלכה ב:
א ב מיי' פ"ו מהלכות שבת הלכה כב סמג לאוין סה טוש"ע א"ח סי' רסו סעיף א וסעיף ח וסימן שמט סעיף ה:
ב ג מיי' פ"כ שם הלכה ו סמג שם טוש"ע א"ח סי' רסו סעיף ב:
ג ד מיי' פכ"א שם הל' י סמג שם טוש"ע שם סעיף ט:
ד ה מיי' פ"ו שם הלכה כב סמג שם:
ה ו ז מיי' שם ופ"כ שם הלכה ז סמג שם טוש"ע שם סעיף א:
ו ח מיי' פ"כ שם הלכה ו סמג שם טוש"ע שם סעיף א:
ז ט מיי' שם הלכה ז טוש"ע שם סעיף ג:
ח י מיי' שם טוש"ע שם סעיף ד:
ט כ ל מיי' שם טוש"ע שם סעיף ה:

הגהות הב"ח

(א) גמ' שנאמר לכן כה אמר: (ב) רש"י ד"ה דסנו וכו' דבני פומבדיתא: (ג) ד"ה אזניך וכו' לכו בו מאחרי: (ד) ד"ה וכ"ש שמפני וכו' יומת ישוב בתשובה: פרק כד (ה) במשנה מי שהחשיך לו בדרך: (ו) רש"י ד"ה מי שהחשיך לו נותן:

רבינו חננאל

איזה בן עולם הבא כל שדעת רבותיו נוחה הימנו כך שמעתא דא סלקא:
הדרן עלך שואל אדם
פרק כד מי שהחשיך בדרך נותן כיסו לנכרי וכו' ואוקי' למתניתין דאין אדם מעמיד עצמו על ממונו והתירו לו לתת כיסו לנכרי בשביל שלא ישאנו הוא בעצמו. ובא רבא ודקדק ואמר דוקא כיסו אבל מציאה דלא אתא לידיה לא התירו לו לתתו לנכרי ובמציאה דאתאי לידיה ללישנא בתרא עלתה בתיקו. וכל תיקו דאיסורא לחומרא והלכתא כרבא דאוקמא (לידיה) [למתני'] בכיסו ממש. אין עמו נכרי מניחו על חמור דייקינן מינה בעת שמצויין ביחד נכרי וחמור לנכרי יהיב ליה מפני שאינו מצווה על שביתתו של נכרי ולכן לא התירו לו לתת כיסו על החמור שהוא מצווה על שביתתו אלא אם אין שם נכרי אלא חמור. וישראל חרש או שוטה או קטן אינו נותן כיסו לאחד מהן אלא נותן כיסו על החמור ולעולם לגרוע שבהן נותן כגון חרש ושוטה לשוטה נותן שוטה וקטן לשוטה נותן והשוטה גרוע בבני אדם שאין הפרש בין אדם לבהמה אלא הדעת והתבונה וזה כיון שאין לו דעת כבהמה חשוב:

הַבָּאָה לְיָדוֹ מַהוּ – **What is the status of a found object that came into his hands** before the Sabbath commenced? כֵּיוָן דְּאָתָא לִידֵיהּ כְּכִיסֵיהּ דָּמֵי – Do we say that **since it has** already **come into his hands, it** should be **comparable to his purse;** אוֹ דִילְמָא – **or perhaps,** כֵּיוָן דְּלֹא טָרַח בָּהּ לָאו כְּכִיסֵיהּ דָּמֵי – **since he expended no effort in** acquiring **it, it is not comparable to his purse?**

This version concludes:

תֵּיקוּ – **Let it stand** unresolved.[10]

The Mishnah said:

אֵין עִמּוֹ נָכְרִי – IF THERE IS NO GENTILE WITH HIM, he should place the purse on his donkey.

The Gemara infers:

טַעְמָא דְּאֵין עִמּוֹ נָכְרִי – **The reason** he may place it on his donkey to have it transported **is because there is no gentile with him;** הָא יֵשׁ עִמּוֹ נָכְרִי – **if, however, there was a gentile with him,** לְנָכְרִי יָהֵיב לֵיהּ – **he should** rather **give** the purse **to the gentile.** מַאי טַעְמָא – **What is the reason** he cannot have his donkey transport it in the first place?

The Gemara answers:

חֲמוֹר אַתָּה מְצוּוֶּה עַל שְׁבִיתָתוֹ – **You are commanded regarding the repose of** your **donkey,** נָכְרִי אִי אַתָּה מְצוּוֶּה עַל שְׁבִיתָתוֹ – but **you are not commanded regarding the repose of a gentile.**[11]

The Gemara states the law in some other cases:

חֲמוֹר וְחֵרֵשׁ שׁוֹטֶה וְקָטָן – If he has with him **a donkey, a deaf-mute,**[12] **a deranged person and a minor,** אַחֲמוֹר מַנַּח לֵיהּ – **he should place [the purse] on the donkey;** לְחֵרֵשׁ שׁוֹטֶה וְקָטָן לֹא יָהֵיב לֵיהּ – **he should not give it to the deaf-mute, the deranged person or the minor.** מַאי טַעְמָא – **What is the reason?** הָנֵי אָדָם – **These** last three **are human,**[13] הַאי לָאו אָדָם – whereas **this** one [the donkey] **is not human.** חֵרֵשׁ וְשׁוֹטֶה – If he has with him only **a deaf-mute and a deranged person,** לְשׁוֹטֶה – he should give the purse **to the deranged person.**[14] שׁוֹטֶה וְקָטָן – Likewise, if he has with him **a deranged person and a minor,** לְשׁוֹטֶה – he should give the purse **to the deranged person.**[15]

A query:

אִיבַּעְיָא לְהוּ – **They inquired:** חֵרֵשׁ וְקָטָן מַאי – What if he has with him **a deaf-mute and a minor, what** is the law; to whom should he give the wallet?

The Gemara notes that the question is easily resolved according to one Tanna:

אַלִּיבָּא דְּרַבִּי אֱלִיעֶזֶר לֹא תִּיבָּעֵי לָךְ – **According to R' Eliezer you need not be in doubt,** דְּתַנְיָא – **as it was taught in a Baraisa:** רַבִּי יִצְחָק אוֹמֵר מִשּׁוּם רַבִּי אֱלִיעֶזֶר – R' YITZCHAK SAYS IN THE NAME OF R' ELIEZER: תְּרוּמַת חֵרֵשׁ – The *TERUMAH* separated BY A DEAF-MUTE

NOTES

10. [*Shulchan Aruch* decides this issue leniently: If he took possession of the found object before the Sabbath, it has the same status as his purse (*Orach Chaim* 266:1).]

11. The Torah obligates a Jew to insure that his animal desist from *melachah* on the Sabbath, i.e. that no *melachah* be done with his animal (see *Avodah Zarah* 15a). This is a negative Biblical commandment, and derives from the verse (*Deuteronomy* 5:14; see also *Exodus* 20:10): *Do not do any melachah, you . . . and your animal.* This prohibition will be discussed at length in the Gemara below (see *Rashi* to *Avodah Zarah* ibid. ד״ה גזרה משום; *Eglei Tal, Choresh* 13:9; cf. *Rambam, Hil. Shabbos* 20:1,2 with *Maggid Mishneh*; *Ramban* below, 153b ד״ה והלא מחמר, and gloss to *Sefer HaMitzvos, Shoresh* 14; see also Introduction to Chapter 5, above).

Since there is no such Biblical prohibition regarding asking a gentile to perform a *melachah* on the Sabbath, it is preferable to have a gentile carry the purse, rather than place it on his donkey.

A question: If having his donkey transport the wallet involves a Biblical prohibition, how can our Mishnah allow this even where no gentile is available? The Gemara below (153b) will address this issue.

12. [A deaf-mute is deemed to lack a lucid understanding and is not legally competent (see *Terumos* 1:2; *Yevamos* 113a).]

13. Although they are not legally competent and are not themselves obligated to observe the Sabbath, one might confuse them with other (competent) humans who must do so (*Rashi*).

14. A deranged person has no understanding at all; a deaf-mute, on the other hand, has at least a limited understanding (*Rashi,* from *Yevamos* 113a) and, therefore, may more easily be confused with a competent person (*Shulchan Aruch HaRav* ibid:9).

15. A deranged person is preferable to a minor, since the minor will, in the natural course of events, become a fully competent person (*Shulchan Aruch* 266:5); alternatively, a minor, although not legally competent, has at least more understanding than a deranged person (*Hagahos R' Akiva Eiger* ad loc.).

ונשמתו עולה ושוב אינה יורדת אמר רב יהודה בריה דרב שמואל בר [א] שילת משמיה דרב מהספדו של אדם ניכר אם בן העוה"ב הוא אם לאו איני והאמר ליה רב לרב שמואל בר שילת אחים בהספידא דהתם קאימנא לא קשיא הא דמחמו ליה ואחים הא דמחמו ליה ולא אחים א"ל אביי לרבה כגון מר דסנו ליה כולהו פומבדיתאי מאן אחים הספידא א"ל מיסתיא את ורבה בר רב חנן בעא מניה רבי אלעזר מרב איזהו בן העוה"ב א"ל [א] ואזניך תשמענה דבר מאחריך לאמר זה הדרך לכו בו כי תאמינו וכי תשמאילו ר' חנינא אמר כל שדעת [ג] רבותינו נוחה הימנו [ב] וסבבו בשוק הסופדים ◦ בני גלילא אמרי עשה דברים לפני מטתך בני יהודה אמרי עשה דברים לאחר מטתך ולא פליגי [ד] מר כי אתריה ומר כי אתריה תנן התם רבי אליעזר אומר [ז] א שוב יום אחד לפני מיתתך שאלו תלמידיו את ר"א וכי אדם יודע איזהו יום ימות אמר להן וכל שכן ישוב היום שמא ימות למחר ונמצא כל ימיו בתשובה ואף שלמה אמר בחכמתו [ג] בכל עת יהיו בגדיך לבנים ושמן על ראשך אל יחסר א"ר יוחנן בן זכאי משל למלך שזימן את עבדיו לסעודה ולא קבע להם זמן פיקחין שבהן קישטו את עצמן וישבו על פתח בית המלך אמרו כלום חסר לבית המלך טיפשין שבהן הלכו למלאכתן אמרו כלום יש סעודה בלא טורח בפתאום ביקש המלך את עבדיו פיקחין שבהן נכנסו לפניו כשהן מקושטין והטיפשים נכנסו לפניו כשהן מלוכלכין שמח המלך לקראת פיקחים וכעס לקראת טיפשים אמר הללו שקישטו את עצמן לסעודה ישבו ויאכלו וישתו הללו שלא קישטו עצמן לסעודה יעמדו ויראו חתנו של ר"מ משום ר"מ אמר אף הן נראין כמשמשין אלא אלו ואלו יושבין הללו אוכלין והללו רעבין הללו שותין והללו צמאים שנאמר (א) [ד] כה אמר ה' הנה עבדי יאכלו ואתם תרעבו הנה עבדי ישתו ואתם תצמאו [ה] הנה עבדי ירונו מטוב לב ואתם תצעקו מכאב לב ד"א בכל עת יהיו בגדיך לבנים אלו ציצית ושמן על ראשך אל יחסר אלו תפילין:

הדרן עלך שואל

[ה] מי [ב] שהחשיך (ה) בדרך נותן כיסו לנכרי [ג] ואם אין עמו נכרי מניחו על החמור [ד] הגיע לחצר החיצונה נוטל את הכלים הניטלין בשבת ושאינן ניטלין בשבת מתיר החבלים והשקין נופלין מאיליהם: גמ' מאי טעמא שרו ליה רבנן למיתב כיסיה לנכרי קים להו לרבנן [ה] דאין אדם מעמיד עצמו על ממונו אי לא שרית ליה אתי לאיתויי ד' אמות ברה"ר אמר רבא [ו] דוקא כיסו אבל מציאה לא פשיטא כיסו תנן מהו דתימא הוא הדין אפילו מציאה והאי דקתני כיסו אורחא דמילתא קתני קמ"ל ולא אמרן אלא [ז] דלא אתי לידיה אבל אתי לידיה ככיסיה דמי איכא דאמרי בעי רבא מציאה הבאה לידו מהו כיון דאתא לידיה ככיסיה דמי או דילמא כיון דלא טרח בה לאו ככיסיה דמי תיקו: אין עמו נכרי: טעמא דאין עמו נכרי הא יש עמו נכרי לנכרי יהיב ליה מאי טעמא [ח] חמור אתה מצווה על שביתתו נכרי אי אתה מצווה על שביתתו חמור וחרש שוטה וקטן [ט] חמור מנח ליה לחרש שוטה וקטן לא יהיב ליה מ"ט הני אדם האי לאו אדם [י] חרש ושוטה לשוטה [כ] שוטה וקטן לשוטה איבעיא להו [ל] חרש וקטן מאי אליבא דר"א לא תיבעי לך דתניא [י] ר' יצחק אומר משום ר' [י] אליעזר תרומת חרש לא

רש"י

אם בן עוה"ב הוא. שאם כשר היה הכל בוכין עליו ומורידין דמעות ומספרים שבחו: אחים בהספידא דהתם קאימנא. בשעת מיתתי התאמץ בהספד שלי שיתחממו ויכמרו רחמי העומדים ויבכו: דהתם קאימנא. בשעת הספד ואשמע איך תתחמם אלמא איצטריך לרב לאזהוריה אהספדא וכיון דרב גברא רבה ובן העולם הבא למה ליה לאזהוריה הא אמר מהספידו ניכר: הא דמחממין ליה. להספידא ואחים כו' לעולם חמומי בעי שאין בני אדם נכמרים כל כך על זקן ומיהו לאדם חסיד כי מחממו בהספידא מחממי ובכו כולהו ולמי שאינו חסיד כל כך מחממו ליה ולא מחממו: דסנו ליה כולהו פומבדיתאי. משום דמוכח להו במילי דשמיא (ב) ובני פומבדיתאי רמאין הן כדאמרינן בשחיטת חולין (חולין קכז.) פומבדיתאי לוייך שני אושפיזך: ואזניך תשמענה דבר מאחריך לאמר זה הדרך לכו (ג) בה. מאחרי מטתך כשתמות תשמע כשיאמרו זה הדרך שהלך בה זה לכו בה מובטח שהוא בן העוה"ב: נוחה הימנו. דעתם נוחה עליהם ממה ששומעין עליו ורואין בו: עשה דברים. שיאמרו לפני מטתך בהספדך: לאחר מטתך. היא היא אלא שבגליל היו הספדנין לפני המטה וביהודה לאחר המטה: וכ"ש. שמפני שאינו יודע איזה יום ימות (ד) וטובה תשובה יום אחד לפני מיתתו נמצא כל ימיו בתשובה יהיו: בגדיך לבנים. נשמתך טהורה ונקיה: כלום חסר בית המלך. בתמיה הכל מוכן ושמא יבהילנו לבא פתאום ואנו צריכין ליכנס לסעודה מקושטין: כלום יש סעודה בלא טורח. עדיין יצטרכו לטרוח לצורכי סעודה של בית המלך ויש לנו שהות הרבה להתקשט: יעמדו ויראו. ואף לעוה"ב צדיקים יושבים ואוכלים ורשעים עומדים ורואים: ר"מ אומר. אין עומדין ורואין שא"כ אף הם היו נראים מן הקרואים ולשמש שכן דרך המשרתים עומדים ואין כאן בושה: זה ציצית. שמלובן הבגד: אלו תפילין. שהם שם משמן טוב דכתיב וראו כל עמי הארץ כי שם וגו' ותנא ר"א הגדול אומר אלו תפילין שבראש (ברכות דף ו.):

הדרן עלך שואל

מי שהחשיך (ו) נותן כיסו לנכרי. מבעוד יום: ואם אין עמו. הא יש עמו לנכרי עדיף כדמפרש בגמרא: לחצר החיצונה. של עיר שהוא מקום המשתמר ראשון ובא לפרק מן החמור: נוטל. בידו מעליו כלים הניטלין בשבת ושאין ניטלין מתיר החבלים של אוכף שהן קשורים בהן והשקין נופלין: גמ' מאי טעמא שרי ליה למיתב לנכרי. והרי הוא שלוחו לישאנו בשבת: מעמיד עצמו. מלהפליג ממונו: דוקא כיסו. דכיון דטרח בה שע"י טורח הוא משתכר חיים עלה ואי לא שרית ליה הא אתי לאיתויי: ולא אמרן. דמציאה לא אלא דלא אתיא לידיה קודם שתחשך ולא הגביהה ולא זכה בה: האי אדם. ויש במינו שחייב במצות ואתי לאיחלופי: לשוטה. יהיב דלית ליה דעת כלל אבל חרש דעתא קלישתא אית ליה כדאמרי' ביבמות (דף קיג.): לא

תוספות

ונשמתו עולה ושוב אינה יורדת. אף על פי כן כשהיא רוצה היא יורדת כי ההיא דלעיל דרבי אחי בר יאשיה וכההיא מעשה דר' בנאה דחזקת הבתים (ב"ב דף נח. ושם) דהוה מציין מערתא כי מטא למערתא דאברהם אבינו אשכחיה לאליעזר עבד אברהם דקאי אבבא אמר ליה מאי קא עביד אברהם כו' אמר ליה ניעול וניתי כו' אע"פ שנשמתו היתה גנוזה מתחת כסא הכבוד. מ"ר:

הדרן עלך שואל

מי שהחשיך כו' חרש שוטה וקטן. אע"ג דאמר לעיל בפרק כל כתבי (דף קכא.) גבי קטן שבא לכבות דקטן העושה לדעת אביו אסור מיהו הכא לא איירי כגון דעביד הקטן עקירה והנחה אלא כדאמרינן לקמן גבי חמור כשהיא מהלכת מניחו עליה וכשהיא עומדת נוטלו הימנה. מ"ר:

כי

עין משפט נר מצוה

נא א מיי' פ"ז מהלכות תשובה הלכה ב:

א ב מיי' פ"ו מהלכות שבת הלכה כב סמג לאוין סה טוש"ע א"ח סי' רסו סעיף א וסעיף ח וסימן שמט סעיף ה:

ב ג מיי' פ"כ שם הלכה ו סמג שם טוש"ע א"ח סי' רסו סעיף ב:

ג ד מיי' פכ"א שם הל' י סמג שם טוש"ע שם סעיף ט:

ד ה מיי' פ"ו שם הלכה כב סמג שם:

ה ו ז מיי' שם ופ"כ שם הלכה ז סמג שם טוש"ע שם סעיף א:

ו ח מיי' פ"כ שם הלכה ו סמג שם טוש"ע שם סעיף א:

ז ט מיי' שם הלכה ז טוש"ע שם סעיף ג:

ח י מיי' שם טוש"ע שם סעיף ד:

ט כ ל מיי' שם טוש"ע שם סעיף ה:

הגהות הב"ח

(א) גמ' שנאמר לכן כה אמר: (ב) רש"י ד"ה דסנו וכו' דבני פומבדיתא: (ג) ד"ה אזניך וכו' לכו בו מאחרי: (ד) ד"ה וכ"ש שמפני וכו' ימות שישוב בתשובה:

פרק כד

(ה) במשנה מי שהחשיך לו בדרך: (ו) רש"י ד"ה מי שהחשיך לו נותן:

רבינו חננאל

איזה בן עולם הבא כל שדעת רבותיו נוחה הימנו כך שמעתא דא סלקא:

הדרן עלך שואל אדם

פרק כד מי שהחשיך בדרך נותן כיסו לנכרי וכו' ואוקי' למתניתין דאין אדם מעמיד עצמו על ממונו והתירו לו לתת כיסו לנכרי בשביל שלא ישאנו הוא בעצמו. ובא רבא ודקדק ואמר דוקא כיסו אבל מציאה דלא אתא לידיה לא התירו לו לתתו לנכרי ובמציאה דאתאי לידיה ללישנא בתרא עלתה בתיקו. וכל תיקו דאיסורא לחומרא והלכתא כרבא דאוקמא (לידיה) [למתני'] בכיסו ממש. אין עמו נכרי מניחו על חמור דייקינן מינה בעת שמצויין ביחד נכרי וחמור לנכרי יהיב ליה מפני שאינו מצווה על שביתתו של נכרי ולכן לא התירו לו לתת כיסו על החמור שהוא מצווה על שביתתו אלא אם אין שם נכרי אלא חמור. וישראל חרש או שוטה או קטן אינו נותן כיסו לאחד מהן אלא נותן כיסו על החמור ולעולם לגרוע שבהן נותן כגון חרש ושוטה לשוטה נותן שוטה וקטן לשוטה נותן והשוטה גרוע בבני אדם שאין הפרש בין אדם לבהמה אלא הדעת והתבונה וזה כיון שאין לו דעת כבהמה חשוב:

מסורת הש"ס

א) נ"א שילא וכן לקמן, ב) [נ"ל רבותיו וכ"א ברי"ף והרא"ש], ג) [פסחים ג. וש"נ], ד) [אבות פ"ב מ"י], ה) [לעיל יז:], ו) [יבמות קיג.], ז) [שם איתא אלעזר].

גליון הש"ס

גמרא בני גלילא אמרי עשה דברים לפני מטתך. מסכת שמחות פ"ג ה"ז:

תורה אור השלם

א) וְאָזְנֶיךָ תִּשְׁמַעְנָה דָבָר מֵאַחֲרֶיךָ לֵאמֹר זֶה הַדֶּרֶךְ לְכוּ בוֹ כִּי תַאֲמִינוּ וְכִי תַשְׂמְאִילוּ: [ישעיה ל, כא]

ב) גַּם מִגָּבֹהַּ יִרָאוּ וְחַתְחַתִּים בַּדֶּרֶךְ וְיָנֵאץ הַשָּׁקֵד וְיִסְתַּבֵּל הֶחָגָב וְתָפֵר הָאֲבִיּוֹנָה כִּי הֹלֵךְ הָאָדָם אֶל בֵּית עוֹלָמוֹ וְסָבְבוּ בַשּׁוּק הַסֹּפְדִים: [קהלת יב, ה]

ג) בְּכָל עֵת יִהְיוּ בְגָדֶיךָ לְבָנִים וְשֶׁמֶן עַל רֹאשְׁךָ אַל יֶחְסָר: [קהלת ט, ח]

ד) לָכֵן כֹּה אָמַר אֲדֹנָי אֱלֹהִים הִנֵּה עֲבָדַי יֹאכֵלוּ וְאַתֶּם תִּרְעָבוּ הִנֵּה עֲבָדַי יִשְׁתּוּ וְאַתֶּם תִּצְמָאוּ הִנֵּה עֲבָדַי יִשְׂמָחוּ וְאַתֶּם תֵּבֹשׁוּ: [ישעיה סה, יג]

ה) הִנֵּה עֲבָדַי יָרֹנּוּ מִטּוּב לֵב וְאַתֶּם תִּצְעֲקוּ מִכְּאֵב לֵב וּמִשֵּׁבֶר רוּחַ תְּיֵלִילוּ: [ישעיה סה, יד]

ליקוטי רש"י

בכל עת יהיו בגדיך לבנים. התקן עצמך בכל שעה במעשה טוב שאם תמות היום תכנס בשלום ומשל שלמה החכם את הדבר לאדם שהזמינו המלך ליום סעודה ולא קבע לו זמן אם חכם הוא או פקח מיד מכבס כסותו ורוחץ וסך וכן עד מחר עד עת יקרא אל הסעודה יהיו כל שעה בגדיו לבנים והוא רחוץ וסך כך דרשוהו רבותינו במסכת שבת [קהלת ט, ח]. עבדי. הצדיקים (של ישראל). ואתם. הפושעים בי [ישעיה סה, יג]. נותן כיסו לנכרי. ולא יטלטלנו פחות פחות מארבע אמות [לעיל יז:]. חרש שוטה וקטן. חרש שדברו בו חכמים בכל מקום שהשוטה אותו לשוטה לפוטרו לא דברו אלא במי שאינו שומע ואינו מדבר הכי קים להו לרבנן דמי שאינו שומע ואינו מדבר דלאו בר דעת הוא [חגיגה ב:]. חרש. דעתו מועטת שאין מתוקן להבין כשאר בני אדם [יבמות קיג.].

לא תצא לחולין מפני שהוא ספק כי תיבעי לך אליבא דרבנן דתנן חמשה לא יתרומו ואם תרמו אין תרומתן תרומה אלו הן חרש שוטה וקטן והתורם את שאינו שלו ונכרי שתרם את של ישראל אפילו ברשותו אין תרומתו תרומה מאי לחרש יהיב ליה דקטן אתי לכלל דעת או דילמא לקטן יהיב ליה דחרש אתי לאחלופי בגדול פיקח איכא דאמרי לחרש יהיב ליה איכא דאמרי לקטן יהיב ליה אין שם לא נכרי ולא חמור ולא חרש ולא שוטה ולא קטן מאי אמר רבי יצחק עוד אחרת היתה ולא רצו חכמים לגלותה מאי עוד אחרת היתה מוליכו פחות פחות מד' אמות אמאי לא רצו חכמים לגלותה משום כבוד אלהים הסתר דבר וכבוד מלכים חקור דבר והכא מאי כבוד אלהים איכא דילמא אתי לאתויי ד' אמות ברה"ר תניא ר"א אומר בו ביום גדשו סאה ר' יהושע אומר בו ביום מחקו סאה תניא משל דר"א למה הדבר דומה לקופה מלאה קישואין ודילועין אדם נותן לתוכה חרדל והיא מחזקת משל דר' יהושע למה הדבר דומה לעריבה מלאה דבש נותן לתוכה רימונים ואגוזים והיא מקיאה אמר מר אין עמו נכרי מניחו על החמור והלא מחמר ורחמנא אמר לא תעשה כל מלאכה א"ר אדא בר אהבה מניחו עליה כשהיא מהלכת והא אי אפשר דלא קיימא להשתין מים ולהטיל גללים ואיכא עקירה והנחה כשהיא מהלכת מניחו עליה כשהיא עומדת נוטלו הימנה אי הכי אפילו חברו נמי אמר רב פפא כל שבגופו חייב חטאת בחברו פטור אבל אסור כל שחברו פטור אבל אסור בחמורו מותר לכתחלה א"ר אדא בר אהבה היתה חבילתו מונחת לו על כתיפו רץ תחתיה עד שמגיע לביתו דוקא רץ אבל קלי קלי לא מאי טעמא כיון דלית ליה היכירא אתי למיעבד עקירה והנחה סוף סוף כי מטא לביתיה אי אפשר דלא קאי פורתא וקמעייל מרשות הרבים לרה"י דזריק ליה כלאחר יד אמר רמי בר חמא המחמר אחר בהמתו בשבת בשוגג חייב חטאת במזיד חייב סקילה מאי טעמא אמר רבא דאמר קרא לא תעשה כל מלאכה אתה ובהמתך דומיא דידיה מה הוא בשוגג חייב חטאת במזיד חייב סקילה אף בהמתו נמי בשוגג חייב חטאת במזיד חייב סקילה אמר רבא שתי תשובות בדבר חדא דכתיב תורה אחת יהיה לכם לעושה בשגגה והנפש אשר תעשה ביד רמה הוקשה כל התורה כולה לע"ז מה ע"ז דעביד מעשה בגופיה ה"נ עד דעביד מעשה בגופיה ועוד תנן המחלל את השבת בדבר שחייבין על שגגתו חטאת ועל זדונו סקילה מכלל דאיכא מידי דאין חייבין על שגגתו חטאת ולא על זדונו סקילה ומאי ניהו לאו דמחמר לא תחומין ואליבא דר"ע והבערה אליבא דר' יוסי רב

כי תבעי לך אליבא דרבנן. הכא משמע דהלכה כרבנן ובמסכת יבמות פרק חרש (דף קיג.) משמע דהלכה כר"א דסבירא ליה לרב חייא בר אשי (ומר) שמואל כוותיה. מ"ר: **דחרש** אתי לאיחלופי בגדול פקח. תימה דלעיל נמי אמאי קאמר שוטה וקטן לשוטה הא אמרינן דאתי לאיחלופי בגדול פקח: **בו** ביום גדשו סאה כו' נותן לתוכה חרדל והיא מחזקת. ה"נ כשגזרו י"ח דבר היתה חסרה גזירה זו של נותן כיסו לנכרי עד שגזרו עליה ולאו הסאה לגמרי כמו שנמנו חרדל לתוכה: ר' יהושע אומר בו ביום מחקו סאה כו' נותן לתוכה אגוזים ורמונים והיא מקיאה. כמו כן קודם שגזרו על נתינת כיס לנכרי היו מותרין להוליכו פחות פחות מד' אמות מתוך כך אתי לאיתויי ד' אמות כעריבה שהיתה מקיאה על שספרו האגוזים והרמונים ולאחר שספרו האגוזים והרמונים שוב לא הקיאה יותר כך כשגזרו ליתן כיסו לנכרי אסרו נמי להוליך פחות פחות מד' אמות והשתא ר"א ורבי יהושע שניהם לשבח ולא כפירוש הקונטרס דפירש דרבי יהושע לאמר שלא עשו היטב שהרבו לגזור יותר מדאי דלא משמע הכי בירושלמי בפ"ק דמכילתין דאמר התם אמר ליה ר"א אלו היתה חסרה ומלאה יאות תבית שהיא מלאה אגוזים כל מה שאתה נותן לתוכה שומשמין היא מחזקת א"ל ר' יהושע אלו היתה מלאה וחסרוה יאות תבית שהיא מלאה שמן כל מה שאתה נותן לתוכה מים היא מפזרת השמן. מ"ר: ולגרסה נ"ל שסירו' קשה לו דלא שייך למימר גבי מים כמו שמפר"י גבי נותן לתוכה אגוזים ורמונים: **סוף** סוף כי מטי לביתיה א"א דלא קאי וקא מעייל מרשות הרבים לרשות היחיד. תימה כדפרכינן להוליכו פחות פחות מד' אמות תקשי ליה נמי הכי: ואמרי

לא תצא לחולין. והוא תרומה לאסור לזרים ויחזור ויתרום הפקח אחרת: **שהוא ספק.** אי דעת גדלות היא אי לא ולר' יצחק ודלי לקטן יהיב ליה דלאו בר מצות הוא ולא לחרש דספק חייב במצות הוא: **אליבא דרבנן.** דאמרי לאו דעתא גדלותא היא ולענין מצות הרי הוא כקטן: **ותורם את שאינו שלו.** בלא רשות דכתיב (דברים יד) תבואת זרעך וחרש שוטה וקטן דכתיב אשר ידענו לנו שיש לו לב להתכוין בהם ירושלמי: **אפילו ברשות.** דשליחות מהיכא אתרבי מכן תרימו גם אתם גם לרבות שלוחכם ומה אתם בני ברית אף שלוחכם בני ברית: **עוד אחרת היתה.** תקנה לכיס להצילו: **ואמאי לא רצו לגלותה.** להעלים דברי תורה: **כבוד אלהים הסתר דבר.** מותר להסתיר דברי תורה לכבוד שמים: **וכבוד מלכים חקור דבר.** אין להסתיר לכבוד עושר אדם ושיכותו אלא שב ותחקרהו: **בו ביום גדשו סאה.** ביום שעלו לעליית חנניה בן חזקיה וגזרו י"ח דבר והיו אותה מכה היתה כדאמרינן בפ"ק (דף יז:) נותן כיסו לנכרי בו ביום גזרו שלא יוליכו פחות פחות מד"א אם יש שם נכרי אותו יום הרבו סייג לתורה במדה גדושה ויפה מדדו להרבות גדר לישראל: **מחקו סאה.** במדה מחוקה מדדו בו ביום שהרבו לגזור יותר מדאי ואין יכולין לעמוד בגזירתם ומתוך כך עוברין על דברי תורה נמצאת מדתם מחוקה מטופפתה וטוב היה להם להיות מדתם טפופה ולא תבא לידי מחק מרוב גודשה: **והיא מחזקת.** את החרדל שנופל החרדל בין הקישואין אף כאן יפה תקנו והוסיפו דבר המתקיים: **והיא מקיאה.** את הדבש שהיה בה לאשון אף אלו ע"י גזירתם גרמו לעבור דשמא לא יאמין את הנכרי והם לא התירו להוליכו פחות פחות מארבע ואדם אינו מעמיד עצמו על ממונו ואתי לאיתויי ד' אמות: **והלא מחמר.** מנהיג חמור טעונה קרוי מחמר: **ורחמנא אמר לא תעשה כל מלאכה אתה ובהמתך.** ואיזוהי סתם מלאכה העשויה על ידי שניהם זו היא שהיא טעונה והוא מחמר: **מניחו עליה כשהיא מהלכת.** לאחר שנעקרה ללכת דלאו עקירה היא כדאמר בפ"ק (דף ג.) גבי הטעינו חברו אוכלין ומשקין וכיון דאדם לא מיחייב בה חטאת כי האי גוונא כאן מותר דהכא נמי מלאכה כתיב והא לאו מלאכה היא: **וקאתי למיעבד עקירה והנחה.** כשחוזרת ונעקרת ללכת אחר הטלת מים או גללים: **נוטלו הימנה.** ולאחר שתחזור ותעקור רגל יניחנו: **אי הכי אפילו על חברו.** יכול לעשות כן כיון דלאו איסורא דאורייתא היא גבי כיס שרי: **כל שבגופו חייב חטאת.** כי עביד ליה איהו כוליה כגון מעביר ד' אמות ברה"ר אפי' עקרו מן הארץ דרך הליכתו חייב דהא איכא עקירת חפץ בידים ולא בעינן עמידה אלא בטעון ועומד מבעוד יום או כשהטעינו חבירו דלא עקר ליה להאי חפץ אבל הכא הא עקר ליה הלכך כי עביד ליה חבריה הוי ליה שנים שעשאוה ואסור מדרבנן ולא שריוה גבי כיס: **מונחת לו על כתיפו.** מבעו"י וקדש עליו היום: **רץ תחתיה.** וכל כמה דלא עמד לפוש אין כאן עקירה לאיסור: **קלי קלי.** מעט מעט כלומר בנחת: **למיעבד עקירה והנחה.** כלומר לזימנין דקאי ולאו אדעתיה אבל רץ היכרא איכא: **כלאחר יד.** שלא כדרך זריקה כגון מכתיפיו ולאחוריו: **בשוגג.** במלאכה שהוא עושה לבדו: **אף בהמתו.** אף מלאכה שעושה על ידי בהמתו דהיינו מחמר אחר חמור טעונה: **חדא דכתיב תורה אחת יהיה לכם וגו'** עד דעביד מעשה בגופיה. כדכתיב לעושה בשגגה והכא לא קא עביד מלאכה אלא דבור בעלמא שמנהיג בקול הרי דבשוגג אינו חייב קרבן: **ועוד.** דקאמרת נמי במזיד חייב סקילה קשיא דתנן בסנהדרין (דף נג.) גבי נסקלים המחלל את השבת נסקל אם חללו בדבר שחייבים על שגגתו חטאת ועל זדונו סקילה: **מכלל דאיכא.** חילול דאין חייבין על שגגתו חטאת ולא על זדונו סקילה: **ואליבא דר"ע.** דאמר דאורייתא ניהו והוי מחלל ומיהו אין חייבין לא על שגגתו חטאת כו': **אליבא דר' יוסי.** דאמר בפרק כלל גדול (לעיל דף ע.) הבערה ללאו יצאת:

רב

עין משפט נר מצוה

י א מיי' פ"ד מהלכות תרומות הלכה ב סמג עשין קלג טוש"ע י"ד סימן שלא סעיף לג:
יא ב מיי' פ"ו מהלכות שבת הלכה ז סמג לאוין סה טוש"ע א"ח סי' רסו סעיף ז:
יב ג מיי' שם הלכה ו טוש"ע שם סעיף ב:
יג ד מיי' פ"ג שם הלכה יב:
יד ה ו מיי' פ"כ מהל' שבת הלכה א סמג לאוין סה טוש"ע א"ח סי' רסו סעיף יא:
טו ז מיי' פ"א שם הלכה א ב:

רבינו חננאל

בזמן שאין עמו נכרי ולא חמור ולא חרש וקטן לאיזה מהן יתן כיסו יש מהן שאומר לחרש יש מהן שאומר לקטן ואם אין עמו נכרי ולא חמור ולא חרש ולא שוטה ולא קטן. א"ר יצחק יש שם דרך להתיר לו להביאו למקום הראוי לשמירה והוא הבאתו פחות פחות מד' אמות ולא רצו חכמים לגלותה ואמרי אמאי לא רצו חכמים לגלותה ואמרו גזירה דילמא אתי לאתויי ד' אמות ברה"ר. תניא ר' אליעזר אומר בו ביום גדשו סאה ...

מסורת הש"ס

א) תרומות פ"א מ"א יבמות קיג., ב) גיטין נג:, ג) [ע"ז ע. ועיין תוספ' עירובין לו: ד"ה רבי שמעון], ד) [תוספתא פ"א], ה) [ע"ז דף טו.], ו) [צ"ל רבה], ז) [מכות טו. ע"ש, ע"ל סנהדרין סו.], ח) סנהדרין נג. ...

רב נסים גאון

פרק מי שהחשיך תניא ר' אליעזר אומר בו ביום גדשו סאה ר' יהושע אומר בו ביום מחקו סאה ...

תורה אור השלם

א) כְּבֹד אֱלֹהִים הַסְתֵּר דָּבָר וּכְבֹד מְלָכִים חֲקֹר דָּבָר: [משלי כה, ב]

ב) וְיוֹם הַשְּׁבִיעִי שַׁבָּת לַיְיָ אֱלֹהֶיךָ לֹא תַעֲשֶׂה כָל מְלָאכָה אַתָּה וּבִנְךָ וּבִתֶּךָ עַבְדְּךָ וַאֲמָתֶךָ וּבְהֶמְתֶּךָ וְגֵרְךָ אֲשֶׁר בִּשְׁעָרֶיךָ: [שמות כ, י]

ג) הָאֶזְרָח בִּבְנֵי יִשְׂרָאֵל וְלַגֵּר הַגָּר בְּתוֹכָם תּוֹרָה אַחַת יִהְיֶה לָכֶם לָעֹשֶׂה בִּשְׁגָגָה: וְהַנֶּפֶשׁ אֲשֶׁר תַּעֲשֶׂה בְּיָד רָמָה מִן הָאֶזְרָח וּמִן הַגֵּר אֶת יְיָ הוּא מְגַדֵּף וְנִכְרְתָה הַנֶּפֶשׁ הַהִוא מִקֶּרֶב עַמָּהּ: [במדבר טו, כט-ל]

ליקוטי רש"י

לא תצא לחולין מפני שהוא ספק. אי דעתא גדלותא היא ...

לֹא תֵצֵא לְחוּלִּין – SHOULD NOT BE ALLOWED UNCONSECRATED STATUS, i.e. it must be treated with the stringencies of *terumah,*[1] מִפְּנֵי שֶׁהוּא סָפֵק – BECAUSE the status of a deaf-mute IS QUESTIONABLE: Perhaps he is competent; perhaps not.[2] There is no question, then, that according to R' Eliezer the purse should be transported by a minor and not by a deaf-mute.[3] כִּי תִּיבָּעֵי לָךְ – **When** (i.e. according to whom) **do you have a** valid **query?** אַלִּיבָּא דְּרַבָּנָן – **According to the Rabbis** who differ with R' Eliezer and consider it certain that a deaf-mute is not legally competent, דִּתְנַן – **as we learned in the following Mishnah:**[4] חֲמִשָּׁה לֹא יִתְרוֹמוּ – THERE ARE FIVE individuals WHO SHOULD NOT SEPARATE *TERUMAH,* וְאִם תָּרְמוּ אֵין תְּרוּמָתָן תְּרוּמָה – AND IF THEY DID SEPARATE *TERUMAH,* THEIR *TERUMAH* IS NO *TERUMAH* at all. אֵלּוּ הֵן – And THESE ARE THE ONES: חֵרֵשׁ שׁוֹטֶה וְקָטָן – (1) A DEAF-MUTE; (2) A DERANGED PERSON; (3) A MINOR;[5] וְהַתּוֹרֵם אֶת שֶׁאֵינוֹ שֶׁלּוֹ – (4) ONE WHO SEPARATES *TERUMAH* FROM produce THAT IS NOT HIS;[6] וְנָכְרִי שֶׁתָּרַם אֶת שֶׁל יִשְׂרָאֵל אֲפִילּוּ בִּרְשׁוּתוֹ – (5) AND so too A GENTILE WHO SEPARATES *TERUMAH* FROM the produce OF A JEW, EVEN WITH HIS CONSENT, אֵין תְּרוּמָתוֹ תְּרוּמָה – HIS *TERUMAH* IS NO *TERUMAH.*[7] According to the Rabbis a deaf-mute is no more obligated to observe the commandments than a minor. מַאי – Therefore we inquired: **What** is the law regarding the purse? לְחֵרֵשׁ יָהִיב לֵיהּ – **Should he give it to the deaf-mute,** דְּקָטָן אָתֵי לִכְלַל דַּעַת – **since the minor** at least **will** one day **reach** the age of **understanding,** whereas the deaf-mute will presumably always be deaf and mute; אוֹ דִילְמָא לְקָטָן יָהִיב לֵיהּ – **or perhaps he should give it to the minor,** דְּחֵרֵשׁ אָתֵי לְאַחְלוּפֵי בְּגָדוֹל פִּיקֵּחַ – **since a deaf-mute,** being an adult, **may** more easily **be confused with a competent adult?**

The Gemara records two opinions:

אִיכָּא דְּאָמְרֵי לְחֵרֵשׁ יָהִיב לֵיהּ – **Some say he should give it to the deaf-mute;** אִיכָּא דְּאָמְרֵי לְקָטָן יָהִיב לֵיהּ – **and some say he should give it to the minor.**[8]

From the preceding Gemara it emerges that the traveler has at his disposal several means of transporting his purse on the Sabbath. These are, in order of preference: a gentile; the person's donkey; a deranged person; a deaf-mute or a minor. The Gemara now inquires:

אֵין שָׁם לֹא נָכְרִי וְלֹא חֲמוֹר וְלֹא חֵרֵשׁ וְלֹא שׁוֹטֶה וְלֹא קָטָן מַאי – **If there is neither a gentile, nor a donkey, nor a deaf-mute, nor a deranged person, nor a minor** there with him, **what** should he do?

The Gemara answers:

אָמַר רַבִּי יִצְחָק – **R' Yitzchak said:** עוֹד אַחֶרֶת הָיְתָה – **There was yet another** method allowed in this case, וְלֹא רָצוּ חֲכָמִים לְגַלּוֹתָהּ – **but the Sages did not wish to reveal it.**

The Gemara explains:

מַאי עוֹד אַחֶרֶת הָיְתָה – To **what** does **"there was yet another** method" refer? מוֹלִיכוֹ פָּחוֹת פָּחוֹת מֵאַרְבַּע אַמּוֹת – To the fact that, if he has no other choice, **he may carry it** himself in increments of **less than four** *amos.*[9]

The Gemara asks:

אַמַּאי לֹא רָצוּ חֲכָמִים לְגַלּוֹתָהּ – And **why did the Sages not want to reveal [this method]?**[10]

The Gemara replies:

מִשּׁוּם "כְּבֹד אֱלֹהִים הַסְתֵּר דָּבָר וּכְבֹד מְלָכִים חֲקֹר דָּבָר" – **Because** they applied the verse: ***[Regarding]* the honor of God, you should conceal a matter; but *[regarding]* the honor of kings you should investigate a matter.**[11] Because publicizing this method would compromise *the honor of God,* the Sages did not want to reveal it.

The Gemara asks:

וְהָכָא מַאי "כְּבֹד אֱלֹהִים" אִיכָּא – **And here what** threat to ***the honor of God* is there** in publicizing this method?

The Gemara answers:

דִּילְמָא אָתֵי לְאַתּוּיֵי אַרְבַּע אַמּוֹת בִּרְשׁוּת הָרַבִּים – Because **one** who uses this method **might come to carry [the purse]** a full **four**

NOTES

1. I.e. it is prohibited to non-Kohanim [since the *terumah* separation may have taken effect; however, it cannot be eaten by a Kohen either, since the *terumah* separation may not have taken effect, in which case all the produce is forbidden to Kohen and non-Kohen alike, until *terumah* is separated properly] (*Rashi*).

2. [A deaf-mute has a certain limited understanding.] R' Eliezer is uncertain whether or not, within those limits, he can reason lucidly and should, on that account, be considered competent (*Rashi* from *Yevamos* 113a). Since only a mentally competent person can separate *terumah* (see note 5 below), R' Eliezer considers the *terumah* separated by a deaf-mute of questionable status. Therefore, a legally competent person should separate *terumah* again (*Rashi*).

3. A minor is certainly not obligated to observe the commandments of the Torah; according to R' Eliezer, a deaf person may indeed be obligated. Thus, one should clearly give the purse to a minor to carry and not to a deaf-mute (*Rashi*). [See *Sfas Emes* and *Ishei Yisrael,* who discuss whether one may have a deaf-mute transport the wallet according to R' Eliezer, when no other method is available.]

4. *Terumos* 1:1.

5. These three are excluded on the basis of the verse (*Exodus* 25:2): *Speak to the Children of Israel and let them take for Me terumah, from every man whose heart motivates him you shall take My terumah.* Only a person who has a heart [i.e. a mind] that could motivate him may separate *terumah*; someone who, legally, has no mind, cannot separate *terumah* effectively (*Rashi,* from *Yerushalmi Terumos* 1:1; see *Rav, Terumos* ibid.; cf. *Tosafos* to *Chulin* 13a ד״ה תיבעי).

From the fact that the Rabbis (whose view this Mishnah reflects) include a deaf-mute in this category, it emerges that they differ with R' Eliezer, and consider a deaf-mute to be definitely incompetent.

6. This is derived from the verse (*Deuteronomy* 14:22): עַשֵּׂר תְּעַשֵּׂר אֵת כָּל־תְּבוּאַת זַרְעֶךָ – *You shall tithe the entire crop of* ***your*** *planting,* which indicates that only the owner can tithe his crops (*Rashi*; cf. *Yerushalmi Terumos* 1:1; *Rashi* to *Yevamos* 113a ד״ה התורם את שאינו שלו; see also *Bava Metzia* 88b; Rashi to *Niddah* 47a ד״ה ולא נתחייבו). [The owner may, however, authorize someone else to tithe on his behalf; see next note.]

7. This is derived from the verse (*Numbers* 18:28): כֵּן תָּרִימוּ גַם־אַתֶּם תְּרוּמַת ה׳, *... thus, you shall also separate terumah.* The word "also" seems superfluous, and the Gemara in *Kiddushin* expounds it to teach that not only *you* [the owner] may tithe but *also* your agent may do so. The phrasing of the verse also indicates that the agent must resemble the owner in one important respect: Just as *you* [the owner] are a Jew [who is obligated to tithe] so the agent *also* must be a Jew (*Rashi,* from *Kiddushin* 41b; see also *Bava Metzia* 71b; see also the sources cited above, 153a note 4, for when the agency of a gentile *may* be valid).

8. [See *Teshuvos Chasam Sofer, Orach Chaim* §83, who discusses the reasons for each of these views.]

Since the Gemara does not reach a definitive ruling on this issue, the halachah is that he may choose to have either the minor or the deaf-mute transport his purse (*Shulchan Aruch, Orach Chaim* 266:5; see there *Beur Halachah* ד״ה יתננו).

9. From a Biblical standpoint, one is permitted to carry an object even several miles in a public domain so long as he does so in increments of less than four *amos*; i.e. as long as he stops so often that he never traverses four *amos* at one time. [See *Mishnah Berurah* 266:18 regarding what would constitute a stop in this context.] Although Rabbinically this is forbidden, the Rabbis allowed a traveler to use this method to transport his purse when none of the other methods outlined earlier are available.

10. Why would they want to conceal halachic teachings? (*Rashi*).

11. *Proverbs* 25:2. One should exercise discretion when a particular revelation impinges on the honor of God. [Thus, if publicizing a certain leniency will lead to Torah violations, one should not do so.] However, when the honor compromised is that of a wealthy or powerful person, this should not deter one from a thorough investigation [where such an investigation is warranted] (*Rashi*).

לא תצא לחולין מפני שהוא ספק כי תיבעי לך אליבא דרבנן דתנן[א] חמשה לא יתרומו ואם תרמו אין תרומתן תרומה אלו הן חרש שוטה וקטן והתורם את שאינו שלו ונכרי שתרם את של ישראל אפילו ברשותו אין תרומתו תרומה מאי לחרש יהיב ליה דקטן אתי לכלל דעת או דילמא לקטן יהיב ליה דחרש אתי לאחלופי בגדול פיקח איכא דאמרי לחרש יהיב ליה איכא דאמרי לקטן יהיב ליה אין שם לא נכרי ולא חמור ולא חרש ולא שוטה ולא קטן מאי אמר רבי יצחק עוד אחרת היתה ולא רצו חכמים לגלותה מאי עוד אחרת היתה מוליכו פחות פחות מד' אמות אמאי לא רצו חכמים לגלותה משום[א] כבוד אלהים הסתר דבר וכבוד מלכים חקור דבר והכא מאי כבוד אלהים איכא דילמא אתי לאתויי ד' אמות ברה"ר תניא ר"א אומר בו ביום גדשו סאה ר' יהושע אומר בו ביום מחקו סאה תניא משל דר"א למה הדבר דומה לקופה מלאה קישואין ודילועין אדם נותן לתוכה חרדל והיא מחזקת משל דר' יהושע למה הדבר דומה לעריבה מלאה דבש נותן לתוכה רימונים ואגוזים והיא מקיאה אמר מר אין עמו נכרי מניחו על החמור והלא מחמר ורחמנא אמר[ב] לא תעשה כל מלאכה א"ר אדא בר אהבה מניחו עליה כשהיא מהלכת והא אי אפשר דלא קיימא להשתין מים ולהטיל גללים ואיכא עקירה והנחה כשהיא מהלכת מניחו עליה כשהיא עומדת נוטלו הימנה אי הכי אפילו חברו נמי אמר רב פפא כל שבגופו חייב חטאת בחברו פטור אבל אסור כל שבחברו פטור אבל אסור בחמורו מותר לכתחלה א"ר אדא בר אהבה היתה חבילתו מונחת לו על כתיפו רץ תחתיה עד שמגיע לביתו דוקא רץ אבל קלי קלי לא מאי טעמא כיון דלית ליה היכירא אתי למיעבר עקירה והנחה סוף סוף כי מטא לביתיה אי אפשר דלא קאי פורתא וקמעייל מרשות הרבים לרה"י דזריק ליה כלאחר יד אמר רמי בר חמא המחמר אחר בהמתו בשבת בשוגג חייב חטאת במזיד חייב סקילה מאי טעמא אמר רבא דאמר קרא לא תעשה כל מלאכה אתה ובהמתך דומיא דידיה מה הוא בשוגג חייב חטאת במזיד חייב סקילה אף בהמתו נמי בשוגג חייב חטאת במזיד חייב סקילה אמר רבא שתי תשובות בדבר חדא דכתיב[ג] תורה אחת יהיה לכם לעושה בשגגה והנפש אשר תעשה ביד רמה הוקשה כל התורה כולה לע"ז מה ע"ז דעביד מעשה בגופיה ה"נ עד דעביד מעשה בגופיה ועוד תנן המחלל את השבת בדבר שחייבין על שגגתו חטאת ועל זדונו סקילה מכלל דאיכא מידי דאין חייבין על שגגתו חטאת ולא על זדונו סקילה ומאי ניהו לאו דמחמר לא תחומין ואליבא דר"ע והבערה אליבא דר' יוסי רב

תוספות

כי תבעי לך אליבא דרבנן. הכא משמע דהלכה כרבנן ובמסכת יבמות פרק חרש (דף קיג.) משמע דהלכה כר"א דסבירא ליה לרב חייא בר אשי (ומר) שמואל כוותיה. מ"ר: **דחרש** אתי לאיחלופי בגדול פקח. תימה א"כ לעיל נמי אמאי קאמר שוטה וקטן לשוטה הא אמרינן אתא לאיחלופי בגדול פקח: **בו** ביום גדשו סאה כו' נותן לתוכה חרדל והיא מחזקת. ה"נ כשגזרו י"ח דבר היתה חסרה גזירה זו של נותן כיסו לנכרי עד שגזרו עליה ומלאו הסאה לגמרי כמו שנתנו חרדל לתוכה: ר' יהושע אומר בו ביום מחקו סאה כו' נותן לתוכה אגוזים ורמונים והיא מקיאה. כמו כן קודם שגזרו על נתינת כיס לנכרי היו מותרין להוליכו פחות פחות מד' אמות מתוך כך אתי לאיתויי ד' אמות כעריבה שהיתה מקיאה עד שהסירו האגוזים והרמונים ואחר שהסירו האגוזים והרמונים שוב לא הקיאה יותר כך כשגזרו ליתן כיסו לנכרי אסרו נמי להוליך פחות פחות מד' אמות והשתא ר"א ורבי יהושע שניהם לשבח ולא כפירוש הקונטרס דפירש דרבי יהושע דאמר שלא עשו היטב שהרבו לגזור יותר מדאי דלא משמע הכי בירושלמי בפ"ק דמכילתין דאמר התם אמר ליה ר"א אלו היתה חסרה ומלאה יאות חבית שהיא מלאה אגוזים כל מה שאתה נותן לתוכה שומשמין היא מחזקת א"ל ר' יהושע אלו היתה מליאה וחסרוה יאות חבית שהיא מלאה שמן כל מה שאתה נותן לתוכה מים היא מפזרת השמן. מ"ר: ואדרבה נ"ל שהירו' קשה לו דלא שייך למימר גבי מים כמו שמפרש"י גבי נותן לתוכה אגוזים ורמונים: **סוף** סוף כי מטי לביתיה א"א דלא קאי וקא מעייל מרשות הרבים לרשות היחיד. תימה כדשרינן להוליכו פחות פחות מד' אמות תקשי ליה נמי הכי: ולמרי

רש"י

לא תצא לחולין. והויא תרומה לאסור לזרים ויחזור ויתרום הפקא אחרת: **שהוא ספק.** אי דעת צלולה היא אי לא ולר' יצחק ודאי לקטן יהיב ליה דלאו בר מצות הוא ולא לחרש דספק חייב במצות הוא: **אליבא דרבנן.** דאמרי לאו דעתא צלולה היא ולענין מצות הרי הוא כקטן: **ותורם את שאינו שלו.** בלא רשות דכתיב (דברים יד) תבואת זרעך וחרש שוטה וקטן דכתיב אשר ידבנו לבו שיש לו לב להתנדב בהש"ס ירושלמי: **אפילו ברשות.** דשליחות מהיכא אתרבי מכן תרימו גם אתם גם לרבות שלוחכם ומה אתם בני ברית אף שלוחכם בני ברית: **עוד אחרת היתה.** תקנה לכיס להצילו: **ואמאי לא רצו לגלותה.** להעלים דברי תורה: **כבוד אלהים הסתר דבר.** מותר להסתיר דברי תורה לכבוד שמים: **וכבוד מלכים חקור דבר.** אין להסתיר לכבוד עושר אדם וחשיבותו אלא שב ותחקרהו: **בו ביום גדשו סאה.** ביום שעלו לעליית חנניה בן חזקיה וגזרו י"ח דבר וזו אחת מהן היתה כדאמרינן בפ"ק (דף יז:) נותן כיסו לנכרי בו ביום גזרו שלא יוליכנו פחות פחות מד"א אם יש שם נכרי אותו יום הרבו סייג לתורה במדה גדושה ויפה מדדו להרבות גדר בישראל: **מחקו סאה.** במדה מחוקה מדדו בו ביום שהרבו לגזור יותר מדאי ואין יכולין לעמוד בגזירתם ומתוך כך עוברין על דברי תורה נמצאת מדתם מחוקה מטפיפתה וטוב היה להם להיות מדתם טפופה ולא תבא לידי מחק מרוב גודשה: **והיא מחזקת.** את החרדל שנופל החרדל בין הקישואין אף כאן יפה תקנו והוסיפו דבר המתקיים: **והיא מקיאה.** את הדבש שהיה בה ראשון אף אלו ע"י גזירתם גרמו לעבור דשמא לא יאמין את הנכרי והם לא התירו להוליכו פחות פחות מארבע ואדם אינו מעמיד עצמו על ממונו ואתי לאיתויי ד' אמות: **והלא מחמר.** מנהיג חמור טעונה קרוי מחמר: **ורחמנא אמר לא תעשה כל מלאכה אתה ובהמתך.** ואיזוהי סתם מלאכה העשויה על ידי שניהם זו היא שהיא טעונה והוא מחמר: **מניחו עליה כשהיא מהלכת.** לאחר שנעקרה ללכת דלאו עקירה היא כדאמר בפ"ק (דף ג.) גבי הטעינו חברו אוכלין ומשקין וכיון דאדם לא מיחייב בה חטאת כי האי גוונא כאן מותר דהכא נמי מלאכה כתיב והא לאו מלאכה היא: **וקאתי למיעבד עקירה והנחה.** כשחוזרת ונעקרת ללכת אחר הטלת מים או גללים: **נוטלו הימנה.** ולאחר שתחזור ותעקור רגל ימינו: **אי הכי אפילו על חברו.** יכול לעשות כן כיון דלאו איסורא דאורייתא היא גבי כיס שרי: **כל שבגופו חייב חטאת.** כי עביד ליה איהו כוליה כגון מעביר ד' אמות ברה"ר אפי' עקרו מן הארץ דרך הליכתו חייב דהא איכא עקירת חפץ בידים ולא בעינן עמידה אלא בטעון ועומד מבעוד יום או כשהטעינו חבירו דלא עקר ליה להאי חפץ אבל הכא הא עקר ליה הלכך כי עביד ליה חבריה הוי ליה שנים שעשאוה ואסור מדרבנן ולא שריוה גבי כיס: **מונחת לו על כתיפו.** ועקרו עליו היום: **רץ תחתיה.** וכל כמה דלא עמד לא פוש אין כאן עקירה לאיסור: **קלי קלי.** מעט מעט כלומר בנחת: **למיעבד עקירה והנחה.** כלומר דזימנין דקאי ולאו אדעתיה אבל רץ היכרא איכא: **כלאחר יד.** שלא כדרך זריקה כגון מכתפיה ולאחוריו: **בשוגג.** במלאכה שהוא עושה לבדו: **אף בהמתו.** אף מלאכה עשויה על ידי בהמתו דהיינו מחמר אחר חמור טעונה: **חדא דכתיב תורה אחת יהיה לכם וגו' עד דעביד מעשה בגופיה.** דכתיב לעושה בשגגה והכא לא קא עביד מלאכה אלא אמר דבור בעלמא שמנהיג בקול הרי דבשגגה אינו חייב קרבן: **ועוד.** דקאמרת נמי במזיד חייב סקילה קשיא דתנן בסנהדרין (דף ס.) גבי נסקלים המחלל את השבת בדבר שחייבים על שגגתו חטאת ועל זדונו סקילה: **מכלל דאיכא.** חילול דאין חייבין על שגגתו חטאת ולא על זדונו סקילה: **ואליבא דר"ע.** דאמר (לעיל דף ע.) דאורייתא ניהו והוי מחלל ומיהו אין חייבין לא על שגגתו חטאת ולא על זדונו כו': **אליבא דר' יוסי.** דאמר בפרק כלל גדול (לעיל דף ע.) הבערה ללאו יצאת:

רב

עין משפט נר מצוה

י א מיי' פ"ד מהלכות תרומות הלכה ב סמג עשין קלד טוש"ע י"ד סימן שלא סעיף לג:
יא ב מיי' פ"ו מהלכות שבת הלכה ג סמג לאוין סה טוש"ע א"ח סי' רסו סעיף ז:
יב ג מיי' שם הלכה ו טוש"ע שם סעיף ב:
יג ד מיי' פ"ו שם הלכה יב:
יד ה ו מיי' פ"כ מהל' שבת הלכה ט סמג לאוין סה טוש"ע א"ח סי' רסו סעיף יא:
טו ז מיי' פ"א שם הלכה א ב:

רבינו חננאל

בזמן שאין עמו נכרי ולא חמור אלא חרש וקטן לאיזה מהן יתן כיסו יש מהן שאומר לחרש יש מהן שאומר לקטן ואם עשה כאחד מהן עשה. ואם אין עמו נכרי ולא חמור ולא חרש ולא שוטה ולא קטן. א"ר יצחק יש שם דרך להתיר לו להביאו במקום הראוי לשמירה והוא הבאתו פחות פחות מד' אמות ולא רצו חכמים לגלותה ואמרי' אמאי לא רצו חכמים לגלותה ואמרו גזירה דלמא אתו לאתויי ד' אמות ברה"ר. תניא ר' אליעזר אומר בו ביום גדשו סאה פי' בו ביום שהושיבו את רבי אלעזר בן עזריה בראש גדשו סאה. מדת הסאה ששת קבין והיא מחוקה הוסיפו רבותינו כמה דברים מדבריהם כגון הגדישה שהיא יתירה על העיקר והדברים שהוסיפו מהן להיתר ומהן לאיסור והכל להיות העיקר שמור ומוזהר והוא כמו זה ששנינו נותן כיסו התירו לו לתתו לנכרי שלא יביאהו בעצמו ויחלל את השבת. זה וכיוצא בו. ולאיסור כל גזירות שגזרו מקצת מן היתר המותר לעשות גדר לנשאר שהוא אסור מן התורה. ורבי יהושע אומר בו ביום מחקו סאה פי' העמידו כל דבר על עיקרו לא פחתו ולא הוסיפו. אלא התירו העיקר המותר מן התורה. שאלו באו להוסיף מדבריהן חוששין שמא יפסדו גם דברי תורה שהן העיקר שיבוא אדם להתיר ולומר כשם שזה אינו מן התורה אלא מדרבנן גם זולתי זה יש מן המצות האחרות מדרבנן כמותן ובאו לגדור ונמצאו פורצים: **אמר מר** [אין] עמו נכרי מניחו על החמור והקשינן עלה והלא מחמר הוא ורחמנא אמר לא תעשה כל מלאכה. ואוקימנא כדתנא כשהיא מהלכת מניחו עליה. כשהיא עומדת נוטלו הימנה. אי הכי חבירו נמי שרי ולמה חמור ולא אמר חבירו ופריק רב פפא כל שבגופו חייב חטאת בחבירו פטור אבל אסור פי' כל מלאכה שהעושה חייב חטאת כגון טעונת משוי ד' אמות ברה"ר אם יטענו חבירו פטור אבל אסור ואם יטענו בהמתו מותר לכתחלה ובלבד שלא תהא עקירה והנחה וזה שאמר רב אדא בר אהבה היתה חבילה מונחת לו על כתיפו רץ תחתיה עד שמגיע לביתו דייקינן למימרא דוקא רץ ומפרקינן לטעמי' ש"מ

מסורת הש"ס

א) תרומות פ"א מ"א יבמות קיג., ב) גיטין נג., ג) [ע"ז ע. ועיין תוספ' עירובין לו: ד"ה רבי שמעון], ד) [תוספתא פ"א], ה) [ע"ז דף טו.], ו) [נ"ל רבה], ז) [מכות ט.], ח) [לעיל סט.], ט) סנהדרין סו. ע"ש, י) סנהדרין סו. כרת, כ) [לעיל סט. וש"נ], ל) ס"א מעשה, מ) [נ"ל אמר].

רב נסים גאון

פרק מי שהחשיך תניא ר' אליעזר אומר בו ביום גדשו סאה ר' יהושע אומר בו ביום מחקו סאה זה היום הוא היום שנכנס בו ר' אלעזר בן עזריה בישיבה כמו שאמרו בברכות בפרק תפלת השחר (דף כח) תנא עדיות בו ביום נשנית וכל בו ביום דאמרינן ההוא יומא הוה ואיתמר י"ח דבר שגזרו בו ביום באותו היום נאמרו אחת מהן מי שהחשיך לו בדרך חבסק מא א) שדחו ביציאות השבת (דף יז) ולפיכך אמר בכאן בו ביום גדשו סאה נתכוונו בדבר זה למה שהוסיפו מן הגזירות שהזכירום: תחומין ואליבא דר' עקיבא. עיקר דברי ר' עקיבא במסכת סוטה (פרק כשם דף כז:) וכבר פירשנו דבר זה במה שעבר. הבערה ואליבא דר'

חשק שלמה על רב נסים גאון

א) פירושו לפי מה:

תורה אור השלם

א) כְּבֹד אֱלֹהִים הַסְתֵּר דָּבָר וּכְבֹד מְלָכִים חֲקֹר דָּבָר: [משלי כה, ב]
ב) וְיוֹם הַשְּׁבִיעִי שַׁבָּת לַיי אֱלֹהֶיךָ לֹא תַעֲשֶׂה כָל מְלָאכָה אַתָּה וּבִנְךָ וּבִתֶּךָ עַבְדְּךָ וַאֲמָתְךָ וּבְהֶמְתֶּךָ וְגֵרְךָ אֲשֶׁר בִּשְׁעָרֶיךָ: [שמות כ, י]
ג) הָאֶזְרָח בִּבְנֵי יִשְׂרָאֵל וְלַגֵּר הַגָּר בְּתוֹכָם תּוֹרָה אַחַת יִהְיֶה לָכֶם לָעֹשֶׂה בִּשְׁגָגָה: וְהַנֶּפֶשׁ אֲשֶׁר תַּעֲשֶׂה בְּיָד רָמָה מִן הָאֶזְרָח וּמִן הַגֵּר אֶת יי הוּא מְגַדֵּף וְנִכְרְתָה הַנֶּפֶשׁ הַהִוא מִקֶּרֶב עַמָּהּ: [במדבר טו, כט-ל]

ליקוטי רש"י

לא תצא לחולין מפני שהוא ספק. אי דעתא צלולה היא אותה הדעת שיש לו או לגלגלה היא [עירובין שם]. **התורם את שאינו שלו.** שלוחות נפקא לן [קידושין מא:] מאתם גם אתם לרבות שלוחכם הלכך מה אתם בני ברית אף שלוחכם בני ברית. **ונכרי שתרם את של ישראל אפי' ברשותו.** אין תרומתו תרומה.

***amos* in the public domain** without stopping. The Sages therefore did not wish to reveal it.

The Gemara cites a Baraisa:

תַּנְיָא – **It was taught in a Baraisa:** רַבִּי אֱלִיעֶזֶר אוֹמֵר – R' ELIEZER SAYS: בּוֹ בַּיּוֹם גָּדְשׁוּ סְאָה – ON THAT DAY that the law stated in our Mishnah was enacted[12] THEY HEAPED UP THE *SE'AH* measure.[13] רַבִּי יְהוֹשֻׁעַ אוֹמֵר – R' YEHOSHUA SAYS: בּוֹ בַּיּוֹם מָחֲקוּ סְאָה – ON THAT DAY THEY LEVELED THE *SE'AH*[14] measure.

A related Baraisa:

תַּנְיָא – **It was taught in a Baraisa:** מָשָׁל דְּרַבִּי אֱלִיעֶזֶר – THE following PARABLE illustrates R' ELIEZER'S opinion: לְמָה הַדָּבָר דּוֹמֶה – TO WHAT IS THE MATTER COMPARABLE? לְקוּפָּה מְלֵאָה קִישׁוּאִין וְדִילוּעִין – TO A BOX FULL OF MELONS AND GOURDS. אָדָם נוֹתֵן לְתוֹכָהּ חַרְדָּל וְהִיא מַחֲזֶקֶת – If A PERSON POURS MUSTARD SEED INTO IT, all the gaps will be filled in AND [THE BOX] WILL HOLD its contents.[15] מָשָׁל דְּרַבִּי יְהוֹשֻׁעַ – THE following PARABLE illustrates R' YEHOSHUA'S opinion: לְמָה הַדָּבָר דּוֹמֶה – TO WHAT IS THE MATTER COMPARABLE? לַעֲרֵיבָה מְלֵאָה דְּבַשׁ – TO A BASIN FULL OF HONEY. נוֹתֵן לְתוֹכָהּ רִימּוֹנִים וֶאֱגוֹזִים וְהִיא מְקִיאָה – If A PERSON PLACES POMEGRANATES AND NUTS INTO IT, some of the honey will be displaced AND [THE BASIN] WILL DISGORGE the honey that was there first.[16]

The Gemara returns to the Mishnah and questions it:

אָמַר מַר – **The master said:** אֵין עִמּוֹ נָכְרִי מַנִּיחוֹ עַל הַחֲמוֹר – IF THERE IS NO GENTILE WITH HIM, HE SHOULD PLACE [THE PURSE] ON [HIS] DONKEY. וְהָא מְחַמֵּר – **But** in doing so, **he is leading a [loaded] animal** on the Sabbath, i.e. causing an animal to perform a *melachah,* וְרַחֲמָנָא אָמַר ,,לֹא־תַעֲשֶׂה כָל־מְלָאכָה" – **whereas the Merciful One said:** ***Do not do any melachah,*** *you . . . and your animal*![17] – ? –

The Gemara answers:

אָמַר רַב אַדָּא בַּר אַהֲבָה – **Rav Adda bar Ahavah said:** In the Mishnah's case מַנִּיחוֹ עָלֶיהָ כְּשֶׁהִיא מְהַלֶּכֶת – **he places [the purse] on [the donkey] when it is** already **walking,** so that the donkey does not perform a complete *melachah.* The prohibition would be violated in this case only if the loaded animal were made to walk from a standing position.[18]

The Gemara raises an objection:

וְהָא אִי אֶפְשָׁר דְּלָא קָיְימָא לְהַשְׁתִּין מַיִם וּלְהַטִּיל גְּלָלִים – **But it is impossible that [the donkey] will not stand still** at some point in order **to urinate or defecate,** וְאִיכָּא עֲקִירָה וְהַנָּחָה – and when it then starts walking again **there is a lifting up, and** when it stops again, **a placing down** as well. Thus, one will violate the prohibition of leading an animal to perform a *melachah*! – ? –

The Gemara explains how to avoid this problem:

כְּשֶׁהִיא מְהַלֶּכֶת מַנִּיחוֹ עָלֶיהָ – **When [the donkey] is** already **walking, he should place [the purse] on it,** כְּשֶׁהִיא עוֹמֶדֶת נוֹטְלוֹ הֵימֶנָּה – **and when it stops** to urinate or defecate **he removes it** until after the donkey begins walking again.[19]

NOTES

12. The implied ruling of our Mishnah, that the stranded traveler should not transport the purse himself (even in increments of less than four *amos*) if there is a gentile available, was one of eighteen decrees enacted in the attic of Chananyah ben Chizkiyah (*Rashi;* see above, 17b; cf. *Baal HaMaor* above, 13b; see also *Chidushei Chasam Sofer* at the beginning of our chapter). As related in the Gemara (above, 13b), Chananyah isolated himself in an attic to write a commentary on the Book of *Ezekiel.* On one occasion a large contingent of disciples of both Shammai and Hillel came to visit him, and all the great scholars of the time were present. They then took the opportunity to enact various laws (*Rambam* and *Rav* in commentaries to the Mishnah, ibid.). [*Rav Nissim Gaon* states that this was the same day R' Elazar ben Azaryah was appointed *Nasi* (see *Berachos* 27b-28a; cf. *Yad Malachi* 116; cf. *Tosafos* to *Pesachim* 19b ד"ה ונימא).]

13. I.e. they enacted, appropriately, a great many fences around Biblical law. They added to Biblical law in good measure, similar to a *se'ah* measure that is filled with flour and carefully heaped up so that it holds considerably more than a *se'ah* (*Rashi*).

14. I.e. they decreed too much [more than the masses could tolerate], thereby causing some individuals to violate Torah law. It is as if they took a *se'ah* measure and heaped it up so much that they ultimately wiped off everything above the fill line. It would have been preferable that [they would not have enacted all these decrees and] they would have been left at least with a liberal measure of flour (*Rashi;* cf. *Tosafos*).

15. Similarly, the Sages of that era decreed well and constructed a lasting legal edifice (*Rashi*).

16. Similarly, because of their decree, they forced some individuals into a situation where they are likely to desecrate the Sabbath on a Biblical level. For perhaps the traveler will not be willing to trust an available gentile with his purse; by not sanctioning his carrying it himself in segments of less than four *amos* we may drive him, in his desperation, to carry it directly without stopping at all (*Rashi;* cf. *Sfas Emes*; *Tosefta* 18:12).

17. *Exodus* 20:10.

There is a negative Biblical commandment that prohibits an animal performing a *melachah* in conjunction with a person on the Sabbath. This prohibition is derived from the verse quoted in our Gemara (*Exodus* 20:10): *Do not do any melachah, you, your son, your daughter and your animal.* The language of the verse (*you . . . and your animal*) implies that the person and the animal together accomplish the *melachah.* The classic example of such a case is where a person leads a loaded donkey – even by means of his voice – to walk a distance of four *amos* or more in a *reshus harabim,* thereby performing the *melachah* of מַעֲבִיר, *transporting.* This prohibition also includes leading an animal in the performance of other *melachos,* but it is generally referred to as מְחַמֵּר, *leading a [loaded] animal* (see *Minchas Chinuch,* Mitzvah 32 – *Mosach HaShabbos* מחמר).

[The Rishonim ask why the Gemara does not also question this procedure on the grounds that it violates the commandment to allow one's animals to rest on the Sabbath (see 153a note 11). See *Ramban, Rashba, Ran,* et al. for resolutions to this question. See also *Ran* to *Avodah Zarah,* page 4b; and *Teshuvos Meishiv Davar* I:23.]

[It should be noted that the verse quoted above also makes reference to a son and daughter; in fact, it is Biblically prohibited to have a child perform a *melachah* on one's behalf on the Sabbath. There is also a more general injunction against causing a minor to transgress any Torah prohibition. See *Yevamos* 114a; *Tosafos* and *Ramban* above, 153a; *Rashba* here; *Teshuvos Chasam Sofer, Orach Chaim* §83; *Teshuvos She'ailas David, Yoreh Deah* §12; *Teshuvos Achiezer,* vol. 3, 81:25.]

18. The prohibition of leading an animal to perform a *melachah* is violated, on a Biblical level, only when the animal does an action that would be deemed a Biblical *melachah* if done by a person. [This is because the word *melachah* is written in connection with this prohibition: *Do not do any melachah, you . . . and your animal.*] Thus, a *lifting* (עֲקִירָה, *akirah*), a conveyance of four *amos,* and a *setting down* (הֲנָחָה, *hanachah*) would be required. Since the animal first starts walking and only then is loaded, there is no *akirah* (*Rashi*).

[If the purse were placed on the donkey's back while it was standing still, then when the donkey commenced walking that itself would be considered an *akirah* of the purse, on the principle that *lifting one's body is like lifting the object from its place* (see above, 3a). But if the donkey is already walking when the purse is placed on it, then the donkey is not deemed to have performed an *akirah* of the purse at all (see *Rashi*).]

19. Since the purse is never placed on the animal except while it is in motion, no *akirah* of the purse takes place. Thus, no *melachah* will ever be done (see *Rashi*).

[According to *Rambam* (*Hil. Shabbos* 20:6), the traveler must take care that the animal perform neither an *akirah* nor a *hanachah.* Accordingly, not only must the traveler place the purse on the animal *after* it commences walking, he must also remove the purse from the animal *before* it comes to a full stop. *Rashba,* however, disputes the necessity for this. In his view, it is sufficient that the animal does not perform an *akirah.*]

[The Rishonim dispute whether this same procedure must be adopted when having the purse transported by a deaf-mute, a deranged person, or a minor. See *Tosafos* 153a, *Ramban* and *Rashba* here; *Rambam, Hil. Shabbos* 20:7; *Teshuvos Chasam Sofer, Orach Chaim* §83.]

לא תצא לחולין מפני שהוא ספק כי תיבעי לך אליבא דרבנן דתנן א) חמשה לא יתרומו ואם תרמו אין תרומתן תרומה אלו הן חרש שוטה וקטן והתורם את שאינו שלו ונכרי שתרם את של ישראל אפילו ברשותו אין תרומתו תרומה מאי לחרש יהיב ליה דקטן אתי לכלל דעת או דילמא לקטן יהיב ליה דחרש אתי לאחלופי בגדול פיקח איכא דאמרי לחרש יהיב ליה איכא דאמרי לקטן יהיב ליה אין שם לא נכרי ולא חמור ולא חרש ולא שוטה ולא קטן מאי אמר רבי יצחק עוד אחרת היתה ולא רצו חכמים לגלותה מאי עוד אחרת היתה ב) מוליכו פחות פחות מד' אמות אמאי לא רצו חכמים לגלותה משום א) כבוד אלהים הסתר דבר וכבוד מלכים חקור דבר והכא מאי כבוד אלהים איכא דילמא אתי לאתויי ד' אמות ברה"ר תניא ר"א אומר בו ביום גדשו סאה ר' יהושע אומר בו ביום מחקו סאה תניא משל דר"א למה הדבר דומה לקופה מלאה קישואין ודילועין אדם נותן לתוכה חרדל והיא מחזקת משל דר' יהושע למה הדבר דומה לעריבה מלאה דבש נותן לתוכה רימונים ואגוזים והיא מקיאה אמר מר אין עמו נכרי מניחו על החמור והלא מחמר ורחמנא אמר ב) לא תעשה כל מלאכה א"ר אדא בר אהבה מניחו עליה כשהיא מהלכת והא אי אפשר דלא קיימא להשתין מים ולהטיל גללים ואיכא עקירה והנחה ג) כשהיא מהלכת מניחו עליה כשהיא עומדת נוטלו הימנה אי הכי אפילו חברו נמי אמר רב פפא ד) כל שבגופו חייב חטאת בחברו פטור אבל אסור כל שחברו פטור אבל אסור בחמורו מותר לכתחלה א"ר אדא בר אהבה ה) היתה חבילתו מונחת לו על כתיפו רץ תחתיה עד שמגיע לביתו דוקא רץ אבל קלי קלי לא מאי טעמא כיון דלית ליה היכירא אתי למיעבד עקירה והנחה סוף סוף כי מטא לביתיה אי אפשר דלא קאי פורתא וקמעייל מרשות הרבים לרה"י ו) דזריק ליה כלאחר יד אמר רמי בר חמא ז) המחמר אחר בהמתו בשבת בשוגג חייב חטאת במזיד חייב סקילה מאי טעמא אמר ח) רבא דאמר קרא ב) לא תעשה כל מלאכה אתה ובהמתך בהמתו דומיא דידיה מה הוא בשוגג חייב חטאת במזיד חייב סקילה אף בהמתו נמי בשוגג חייב חטאת במזיד חייב סקילה אמר רבא שתי תשובות בדבר חדא דכתיב ג) תורה אחת יהיה לכם לעושה בשגגה והנפש אשר תעשה ביד רמה ט) הוקשה כל התורה כולה לע"ז מה ע"ז דעביד מעשה בגופיה ה"נ עד דעביד מעשה בגופיה ועוד תנן י) המחלל את השבת בדבר שחייבין על שגגתו חטאת ועל זדונו כ) סקילה מכלל דאיכא מידי דאין חייבין על שגגתו חטאת ולא על זדונו סקילה ומאי ניהו לאו דמחמר לא ל) תחומין ואליבא דר"ע והבערה אליבא דר' יוסי רב

רש"י

לא תצא לחולין. והוא תרומה לאסור לזרים ויחזור ויתרום הפקת אחרת: **שהוא ספק.** אי דעת גלולתא היא אי לא ולר' יצחק ודאי לקטן יהיב ליה דלאו בר מלות הוא ולא לחרש דספק חייב במלות הוא: **אליבא דרבנן.** דאמרי לאו דעתא גלולתא היא ולענין מלות הרי הוא כקטן: **ותורם את שאינו שלו.** בלא רשות דכתיב (דברים יד) תבואת זרעך וחרש שוטה וקטן דכתיב אשר ידבנו לבו שיש לו לב להתנדב בהש"ס ירושלמי: **אפילו ברשות.** דשליחות מהיכא אתרבי מכן תרימו גם אתם לרבות שלוחכם ומה אתם בני ברית אף שלוחכם בני ברית: **עוד אחרת היתה.** תקנה לכיס להלילו: **ואמאי לא רצו לגלותה.** להעלים דברי תורה: **כבוד אלהים הסתר דבר.** מותר להסתיר דברי תורה לכבוד שמים: **וכבוד מלכים חקור דבר.** אין להסתיר לכבוד עושר אדם ושישבותו אלא שב ותמקרהו: **בו ביום גדשו סאה.** ביום שעלו לעליית חנניה בן חזקיה וגזרו י"ח דבר וזו אחת מהן היתה כדאמרינן בפ"ק (דף יז.) נותן כיסו לנכרי בו ביום גזרו שלא יוליכנו פחות פחות מד"א אם יש שם נכרי אותו יום הרבו סייג לתורה במדה גדושה ויפה עשו להרבות גדר בישראל: **מחקו סאה.** במדה מחוקה מדדו בו ביום שהרבו לגזור יותר מדאי ואין יכולין לעמוד בגזירתם וממתוך כך עוברין על דברי תורה נמלאת מדתם מחוקה מטפיפתה וטוב היה להם להיות מדתם טפופה ולא תבא לידי מחק מרוב גודשה: **והיא מחזקת.** את החרדל שנופל החרדל בין הקישואין אף כאן יפה תקנו והוסיפו דבר המתקיים: **והיא מקיאה.** את הדבש שהיה בה ראשון אף כאן על ע"י גזירתם גרמו לעבור דשמא לא יאמין את הנכרי והם לא התירו להוליכו פחות פחות מארבע ואדם אינו מעמיד עלמו על ממונו ואתי לאתויי ד' אמות: **והלא מחמר.** מנהיג חמור טעונה קרוי מחמר: **ורחמנא אמר לא תעשה כל מלאכה אתה ובהמתך.** ואיזוהי מלאכה העשויה על ידי שניהם זו היא שהיא טעונה והוא מחמר: **מניחו עליה כשהיא מהלכת.** דלאחר שנעקרה ללכת הניחו עליה דלאו עקירה היא כדאמר בפ"ק (דף ג.) גבי הטעינו חבירו אוכלין ומשקין וכיון דלאדם לא מיחייב בה חטאת לא כי האי גוונא לא מותר דהכא נמי מלאכה כתיב והא לאו מלאכה היא: **וקאתי למיעבד עקירה והנחה.** כשחוזרת ונעקרת ללכת אחר הטלת מים או גללים: **נוטלו הימנה.** ולאחר שתחזור ותעקור רגל יניחנו: **אי הכי אפילו על חברו.** דלאו איסורא דאורייתא היא גבי כים שרי: **כל שבגופו חייב חטאת.** כי עביד ליה איהו כוליה כגון מעביר ד' אמות ברה"ר אפי' עקרו מן הארץ דרך הליכתו חייב דהא איכא עקירת חפץ בידים ולא בעינן עמידה אלא בטעון ועומד מבעוד יום או כשהטעינו חבירו דלא עקר ליה להאי חפץ אבל הכא הא עקר ליה הלכך כי עביד ליה חבריה הוי ליה שנים שעשאוה ואסור מדרבנן ולא שריוה גבי כים: **מונחת לו על כתיפו.** מבעו"י וקדם עליו היום: **רץ תחתיה.** וכל כמה דלא עמד לא פוש אין כאן עקירה לאיסור: **קלי קלי.** מעט מעט כלומר בנחת: **למיעבד עקירה והנחה.** כלומר דזימנין דקאי ולאו אדעתיה אבל רץ היכרא איכא: **כלאחר יד.** שלא כדרך זריקה כגון מכתיפיו ולאחוריו: **בשוגג.** במלאכה שהוא עושה לבדו: **אף בהמתו.** אף מלאכה שעושה על ידי בהמתו דהיינו מחמר אחר בהמתו טעונה: **חדא דכתיב תורה אחת יהיה לכם וגו' עד דעביד מעשה בגופיה.** כדכתיב לעושה בשגגה והכא לא קא עביד מלאכה אלא דבור בעלמא שמנהיג בקול הרי דבשוגג אינו חייב קרבן: **ועוד.** דקאמרת נמי במזיד חייב סקילה קשיא דתנן בסנהדרין (דף סג.) גבי נסקלים המחלל את השבת בדבר שחייבין על זדונו סקילה ועל שגגתו חטאת: **מכלל דאיכא.** מילי דלאו חייבין על שגגתו חטאת ולא על זדונו סקילה ומאי ניהו לאו דמחמר: **ואליבא דר"ע.** דאמר בפרק כלל גדול (לעיל דף ע.) הבערה ללאו יצאת: **אליבא דר' יוסי.** דאמר בפרק כלל גדול (לעיל דף ע.) הבערה ללאו יצאת:

תוספות

כי תבעי לך אליבא דרבנן. הכא משמע דהלכה כרבנן ובמסכת יבמות פרק חרש (דף קיג.) משמע דהלכה כר"א דסבירא ליה לרב חייא בר אשי (ומר) שמואל כוותיה. מ"ר: **דחרש** אתי לאיחלופי בגדול פקח. תימה א"כ לעיל נמי אמאי קאמר שוטה וקטן לשוטה הא אמרינן אתא לאיחלופי בגדול פקח: **בו** ביום גדשו סאה כו' נותן לתוכה חרדל והיא מחזקת. ה"נ כשגזרו י"ח דבר היתה חסרה גזירה זו של נותן כיסו לנכרי עד שגזרו עליה ונמלא הסאה לגמרי כמו שנתנו חרדל לתוכה: ר' יהושע אומר בו ביום מחקו סאה כו' נותן לתוכה אגוזים ורמונים והיא מקיאה. כמו כן קודם שגזרו על נתינת כיס לנכרי היו מותרין להוליכו פחות פחות מד' אמות ומתוך כך לא אתי לאיתויי ד' אמות כעריבה שהיתה מקיאה עד שהסירו האגוזים והרמונים ואחר שהסירו האגוזים והרמונים שוב לא הקיאה יותר כך כשגזרו ליתן כיסו לנכרי אסרו נמי להוליך פחות פחות מד' אמות והשתא ר"א ורבי יהושע שניהם לשבח ולא כפירוש הקונטרס דפירש דרבי יהושע לאמר שלא עשו היטב שהרבו לגזור יותר מדאי דלא משמע הכי בירושלמי בפ"ק דמפלגתין דאמר התם אמר ליה ר"א אלו היתה חסרה ומלאוה יאות חבית שהיא מלאה אגוזים כל מה שאתה נותן לתוכה שומשמין היא מחזקת א"ל ר' יהושע אלו היתה מליאה וחסרוה יאות חבית שהיא מלאה שמן כל מה שאתה נותן לתוכה מים היא מפזרת השמן. מ"ר: ולהדרבה נ"ל שהירו' קשה לו דלא שייך למימר גבי מים כמו שמפר"י גבי נותן לתוכה אגוזים ורמונים: **סוף** סוף כי מטי לביתיה א"א דלא קאי וקא מעייל מרשות הרבים לרשות היחיד. תימה לדשרינן להוליכו פחות פחות מד' אמות תקשי ליה נמי הכי: ואמרי

עין משפט נר מצוה

י א מיי' פ"ד מהלכות תרומות הלכה ג סמג עשין קלד טוש"ע יו"ד סימן שלא סעיף ג:
יא ב מיי' פ"כ מהלכות שבת הלכה ב סמג לאוין סה טוש"ע א"ח סי' רסו סעיף ז:
יב ג מיי' שם הלכה ו טוש"ע שם סעיף ט:
יג ד מיי' פ"ג שם הלכה יב:
יד ה ו מיי' פי"ג מהל' שבת הלכה ט סמג לאוין סה טוש"ע א"ח סי' רמו סעיף יח:
טו ז מיי' פ"א שם הלכה א ב:

רבינו חננאל

בזמן שאין עמו נכרי ולא חמור אלא חרש וקטן לאיזה מהן יתן כיסו יש מהן שאומר לקטן יש מהן שאומר לחרש ואם עשה כאחד מהן עשה. ואם אין עמו נכרי ולא חמור ולא חרש ולא שוטה ולא קטן. א"ר יצחק יש שם דרך להתיר לו להביאו במקום הראוי לשמירה והוא הבאתו פחות פחות מד' אמות ולא רצו חכמים לגלותה ואמרי' אמאי לא רצו חכמים לגלותה ואמרו גזירה דלמא אתו לאתויי ד' אמות ברה"ר. תניא ר"א אומר בו ביום גדשו סאה פי' בו ביום שהושיבו את רבי אלעזר בן עזריה בראש גדשו סאה. מדת הסאה ששת קבין והיא מחוקה הוסיפו רבותינו כמה דברים מדבריהם כגון הגדישה שהיא יתירה על העיקר והדברים שהוסיפו מהן להיתר ומהן לאיסור והכל להיות העיקר שמור ומוזהר והוא כמו זה ששנינו נותן כיסו התירו לו לתתו לנכרי שלא יביאהו בעצמו ויחלל את השבת. זה וכיוצא בו. ולאיסור כל גזירות שגזרו מקצת מן היתר המותר לעשות גדר לנשאר שהוא אסור מן התורה. ורבי יהושע אומר בו ביום מחקו סאה פי' העמידו כל דבר על עיקרו לא פחתו ולא הוסיפו. ולא התירו העיקר המותר מן התורה. שאלו באו להוסיף מדבריהן חוששין שמא יוסיפו גם דברי תורה שהן העיקר שיבוא אדם להרהר ולומר כשם שזה אינו מן התורה אלא מדרבנן גם זולתי זה יש מן המצות האחרות מדרבנן כמותן ובאו לגדור נמצאו פורצים: אמר מר [אין] עמו נכרי מניחו על החמור ואקשינן עלה והלא מחמר הוא ורחמנא אמר לא תעשה כל מלאכה. ואוקימנא כדרבא כשהיא מהלכת מניחו עליה. כשהיא עומדת נוטלו הימנה. אי הכי חבירו נמי שרי ולמה חמור ולא אמר חבירו ופירק רב פפא כל שבגופו חייב חטאת בחבירו פטור אבל אסור כל שבגופו פטור אבל אסור פי' כל מלאכה שהעושה חייב חטאת כגון טעונת משוי בר"ה ד' אמות ברה"ר אם יטעון חבירו פטור אבל אסור ואם יטעון בהמתו מותר לכתחלה ובלבד שלא תהא עקירה והנחה עליו והוא שאמר רב אדא בר אהבה היתה חבילתו מונחת בין כתיפו רץ תחתיה עד שמגיע לביתו ... שמגיע לביתו מדריכין למימרא ... ומפרקינן לטעמי' ש"מ

הלכתא כוותיה ותו דליכא מאן דפליג עליה ופירוש' דזריק לה כלאחר יד לאו שמכניסה ומפרקה אלא מהלך בריצה וכשמגיע לפתחו מחזיר אחוריו כלפי פתח החצר וזורק החבילה מעל כתיפו בחצר דרך הפתח ע"י ריצה בלא עמידה וזה פי' דזריק לה כלאחר יד שזורקה שלא כדרכו ... אמר רמי בר חמא המחמר אחר בהמתו בשבת בשוגג חייב חטאת. במזיד חייב סקילה. פי' המחמר המנהיג בהמתו ועליה משוי ... תורה אחת יהיה לכם לעושה בשגגה. והנפש אשר תעשה ביד רמה הוקשה כל התורה לע"ז מה ע"ז דעביד מעשה בגופה ... ועוד תנן המחלל את השבת בדבר שחייבין על שגגתו חטאת ועל זדונו סקילה מכלל דאיכא מידי דאין חייבין לא על שגגתו חטאת ולא על זדונו סקילה ומאי ניהו לאו מחמר ופריק ליה דלמא בתחומין

מסורת הש"ס

א) תרומות פ"א מ"ב יבמות קיג., ב) גיטין נג:, ג) [ע"ז ע. ועיין תוספ' עירובין לז: ד"ה רבי שמעון], ד) [תוספתא פ"א], ה) [ע"ז לו.], ו) [צ"ל רבה], ז) [מכות יג: לעיל סט.], ח) סנהדרין סו. ע"ש, ט) סנהדרין סג: כרת, י) [לעיל סט. וש"נ], כ) פ"א מעשה, ל) סוטה כו:, מ) [צ"ל אמר].

רב נסים גאון

פרק מי שהחשיך תניא ר' אליעזר אומר בו ביום גדשו סאה ר' יהושע אומר בו ביום מחקו סאה זה היום הוא היום שנסמך בו ר' אלעזר בן עזריה בישיבה כמו שאמרו בברכות בפרק תפלת השחר (דף כח) תנא עדיות בו ביום נשנית וכל בו ביום דאמרינן ההוא יומא הוא. ואיתמר י"ח דבר שגזרו בו ביום באותו היום שנאמר אחת מהן מי שהחשיך (א) שדחו ביציאות השבת (דף יז) ולפיכך אמר בכאן בו ביום גדשו סאה נתכוונו בדבר זה למה שהוסיפו מן הגזירות שהזכירום: **תחומין** ואליבא דר' עקיבא. עיקר דברי ר' עקיבא במסכת סוטה (פרק כשם דף כז) וכבר פירשנו דבר זה במה שעבר. הבערה ואליבא דר'

חשק שלמה על רב נסים גאון

א) פירושו לפי מה:

תורה אור השלם

א) כְּבֹד אֱלֹהִים הַסְתֵּר דָּבָר וּכְבֹד מְלָכִים חֲקֹר דָּבָר: [משלי כה, ב]

ב) וְיוֹם הַשְּׁבִיעִי שַׁבָּת לַיְיָ אֱלֹהֶיךָ לֹא תַעֲשֶׂה כָל מְלָאכָה אַתָּה וּבִנְךָ וּבִתֶּךָ עַבְדְּךָ וַאֲמָתְךָ וּבְהֶמְתֶּךָ וְגֵרְךָ אֲשֶׁר בִּשְׁעָרֶיךָ: [שמות כ, י]

ג) הָאֶזְרָח בִּבְנֵי יִשְׂרָאֵל וְלַגֵּר הַגָּר בְּתוֹכָם תּוֹרָה אַחַת יִהְיֶה לָכֶם לָעֹשֶׂה בִּשְׁגָגָה: וְהַנֶּפֶשׁ אֲשֶׁר תַּעֲשֶׂה בְּיָד רָמָה מִן הָאֶזְרָח וּמִן הַגֵּר אֶת יְיָ הוּא מְגַדֵּף וְנִכְרְתָה הַנֶּפֶשׁ הַהִוא מִקֶּרֶב עַמָּהּ: [במדבר טו, כט-ל]

ליקוטי רש"י

לא תצא לחולין מפני שהוא ספק. אי דעתא צלולתא היא ... **התורם את שאינו שלו.** ... **ונכרי שתרם את של ישראל אפי' ברשות** אין תרומתו תרומה ומותרת לזר [יבמות קיג.]. משום דשליחות לתרומה דכתיב כן תרימו גם אתם ודרשינן מדמלי למכתב אתם גם אתם לרבות שלוחכם ... מה אתם בני ברית אף שלוחכם בני ברית ... אפילו ברשותו של ישראל דעשאו שליח אין תרומתו תרומה [גיטין כג:]. **פחות פחות מארבע אמות.** ... **מחמר.** ... **אי אפשר דלא קאי פורתא.** ...

The Gemara asks:

אִי הָכִי – **If so,** if that is the procedure that he follows, אֲפִילּוּ חֲבֵרוֹ נַמִּי – then he should **also** be permitted to place the wallet on **even his** Jewish **friend** in that fashion.[20] – ? –

The Gemara resolves this question:

אָמַר רַב פָּפָּא – **Rav Pappa said:** כֹּל שֶׁבְּגוּפוֹ חַיָּיב חַטָּאת – Regarding **any** *melachah* **that** if he performs it **by himself he is liable to a** *chatas,* בַּחֲבֵירוֹ פָּטוּר אֲבָל אָסוּר – if he completes it jointly **with a friend he is exempt** from a *chatas* **but is** nonetheless **prohibited** to do so, even in the case of a traveler.[21] כֹּל שֶׁחֲבֵירוֹ פָּטוּר אֲבָל אָסוּר – In turn, regarding **any** *melachah* **that** if he completes it jointly **with a friend he is exempt but prohibited** to do so: בַּחֲמוֹרוֹ מוּתָּר לְכַתְּחִלָּה – if he completes it jointly **with his donkey it is permitted outright,** in order to transport his purse.[22]

The Gemara provides another option for a person caught on the road close to the Sabbath:

אָמַר רַב אַדָּא בַּר אַהֲבָה – **Rav Adda bar Ahavah said:** הָיְתָה חֲבִילָתוֹ מוּנַּחַת לוֹ עַל כְּתֵיפוֹ – **If he had a pack resting on his shoulder** as the Sabbath approached, רָץ תַּחְתֶּיהָ עַד שֶׁמַּגִּיעַ לְבֵיתוֹ – **he may run beneath it** without stopping **until he reaches his house.**[23]

The Gemara qualifies this ruling:

דַּוְקָא רָץ – This is permitted **only if he runs,** אֲבָל קַלֵּי קַלֵּי לֹא – **but if** he walks **leisurely**[24] it is **not** permitted. מַאי טַעְמָא – **Why** not? כֵּיוָן דְּלֵית לֵיהּ הֶיכֵּירָא – **Since,** when he walks, **he has no reminder** that he may not stop, אָתֵי לְמֶיעְבַּד עֲקִירָה וְהַנָּחָה – **he may** easily forget himself and **come to perform a lifting up and a setting down.**[25]

The Gemara challenges this leniency:

סוֹף סוֹף כִּי מָטָא לְבֵיתֵיהּ – **Inevitably, when he reaches his house,** אִי אֶפְשָׁר דְּלֹא קָאֵי פּוּרְתָּא – **it is impossible that he will not stand for a moment** before going inside, וְקָמְעַיֵּיל מֵרְשׁוּת הָרַבִּים לִרְשׁוּת הַיָּחִיד – **and,** at that point, **he will bring** his pack **in from a public domain into a private domain.** For, having stopped outside his house, when he then enters the house he has "lifted" the pack from the street and set it down in his house. – ? –

The Gemara answers:

דְּזָרִיק לֵיהּ כִּלְאַחַר יָד – That is not an issue, **because he** then **throws [his pack]** into the house ***backhandedly,*** i.e. in an unusual manner.[26] Thus, no *melachah* is violated.

The Gemara discusses the punishments due for leading a loaded animal:

אָמַר רָמִי בַּר חָמָא – **Rami bar Chama said:** הַמְחַמֵּר אַחַר בְּהֶמְתּוֹ בְּשַׁבָּת – Regarding **one who leads his loaded animal on the Sabbath** by goading it with his voice: בְּשׁוֹגֵג חַיָּיב חַטָּאת – **If** he does so **inadvertently he is liable to a** ***chatas***; בְּמֵזִיד חַיָּיב סְקִילָה – **if** he does so **intentionally he is liable to** death by **stoning.**

The Gemara asks:

מַאי טַעְמָא – **What is the reason?** He is not performing any *melachah* himself! – ? –

The Gemara answers:

אָמַר רַבָּה – **Rabbah said:** דְּאָמַר קְרָא – It is **because the verse states:** ,,לֹא־תַעֲשֶׂה כָל־מְלָאכָה אַתָּה . . . וּבְהֶמְתֶּךָ" – ***Do not do any melachah, you ... and your animal*** (*Exodus* 20:10). בְּהֶמְתּוֹ דּוּמְיָא דִּידֵיהּ – The language of the verse implies that a *melachah* performed by means of **his animal is analogous to a** *melachah* done by **himself:** מָה הוּא – **Just as** when **he** does a *melachah,* בְּשׁוֹגֵג חַיָּיב חַטָּאת בְּמֵזִיד חַיָּיב סְקִילָה – if it was done **inadvertently he is liable to a** ***chatas*** and if it was done **intentionally he is liable to stoning,** אַף בְּהֶמְתּוֹ נַמִּי – **so too** when he causes an animal to perform a *melachah,* בְּשׁוֹגֵג חַיָּיב חַטָּאת בְּמֵזִיד חַיָּיב סְקִילָה – if it was done **inadvertently he is liable to a** ***chatas*** and if it was done **intentionally he is liable to stoning.**[27]

The Gemara challenges this:

אָמַר רָבָא – **Rava said:** שְׁתֵּי תְשׁוּבוֹת בַּדָּבָר – **There are two** possible **rebuttals to this.** חֲדָא דִּכְתִיב – **First, because it is written:**[28] ,,תּוֹרָה אַחַת יִהְיֶה לָכֶם לָעֹשֶׂה בִּשְׁגָגָה וְהַנֶּפֶשׁ אֲשֶׁר־תַּעֲשֶׂה בְּיָד רָמָה" – ***There shall be a single law for you, for one who acts with inadvertence. But a person who shall act high-handedly ...*** This passage discusses someone who commits idolatry. Thus, when the verse says that there shall be a single law,

NOTES

20. [That is, he should give the purse to his friend while he is in midstride, and take it from him whenever he stops. If the purse is transported in this manner, no Biblical prohibition will be violated either; why then does the Mishnah insist that he have his donkey, and not his friend, transport the purse? (see *Rashi, Rabbeinu Chananel*).]

21. On a Biblical level, if a *melachah* is completed jointly by two people, neither one is considered liable (see above, 92b-93b). Rabbinically, however, it is prohibited for two people to jointly complete a *melachah.*

Now, in our case, if one person were to combine all the actions done here – picking up an object in midstride, carrying it four *amos,* and then placing it down – he would be liable for performing a complete *melachah.* [As *Rashi* points out, one performs a valid *akirah* by taking an object from its resting place even if the person is walking while doing so.] It therefore follows that the traveler and his friend will have violated the Rabbinic prohibition for two people to jointly complete an entire *melachah.* The Rabbis did not waive this prohibition, even for the sake of a traveler (*Rashi*).

22. The Rabbinic prohibition of jointly completing a *melachah* applies only to two people; it does not apply to a person and a donkey. Thus, in the case of the donkey we need concern ourselves only with the donkey's actions; and, so long as the purse is placed on it while the donkey is in motion, the donkey transports it without an *akirah*; thus, the Biblical prohibition of leading an animal to perform a *melachah* does not apply.

Although a conveyance alone, without an *akirah,* is prohibited Rabbinically, and although it is forbidden to cause an animal to perform even a Rabbinically prohibited activity on the Sabbath (see *Pesachim* 66b), the Rabbis waived this Rabbinic prohibition for a stranded traveler, lest he be driven to carry the purse himself, as explained earlier in the Gemara (see *Teshuvos Meishiv Davar,* ibid.).

23. As long as he never stops to rest, there will not be a forbidden *akirah* (*Rashi*), since he began moving before the Sabbath.

24. Literally: little by little.

25. He may stop absent-mindedly [and then start and stop again]. However, if he runs, he constantly reminds himself [that he may not stop] (*Rashi*).

The Rishonim differ over whether this device is permitted for a purse as well: According to some, it is only permitted with a pack, since it is unusual to run while carrying a pack and this serves to remind him not to stop. The Rishonim also dispute whether this method should be utilized only when the method of stopping every several *amos* is not feasible (see *Ramban* here, et al.; see also *Rambam, Hil. Shabbos* 13:9 with *Lechem Mishneh,* and *Magen Avraham* 266:18).

26. For example, he faces away from the door and throws the pack from his shoulders backwards (*Rashi*); thus, the transfer is done in an unusual manner, for which there is no Biblical violation (see *Maharsha*; see also *Beur Halachah* to *Orach Chaim* 266:11 ד"ה כי היכי).

27. One might ask: According to this opinion, why is *leading a loaded animal* not mentioned among the *av melachos* listed above in the Mishnah (73a)? *Ramban* dismisses the question: Leading a loaded animal is not a new type of *melachah*; rather, it teaches that just as a person is liable if he performs a *melachah* (such as *transporting*) himself, so too is he liable if he performs it with his animal.

28. *Numbers* 15:29-30.

עין משפט נר מצוה

י א מיי' פ"ד מהלכות תרומות הלכה ב סמג עשין קלג טוש"ע י"ד סימן של"א סעיף ג:
יא ב מיי' פ"כ מהלכות שבת הלכה ז סמג לאוין סה טוש"ע א"ח סי' רסו סעיף ז:
יב ג מיי' שם הלכה ו טוש"ע שם סעיף יב:
יג ד מיי' פ"ג שם הלכה יב:
יד ה ו מיי' פי"ג מהל' שבת הלכה ט סמג לאוין סה טוש"ע א"ח סי' רסו סעיף יב:
טו ז מיי' פ"א שם הלכה א ב:

רבינו חננאל

בזמן שאין עמו נכרי ולא חמור אלא חרש וקטן לאיזה מהן יתן כיסו יש מהן שאומר לחרש יש מהן שאומר לקטן ואם עשה כאחד מהן עשה. ואם אין עמו נכרי ולא חמור ולא חרש ולא שוטה ולא קטן. א"ר יצחק יש שם דרך להתיר לו להביאו במקום הראוי לשמירה והוא הבאתו פחות פחות מד' אמות ולא רצו חכמים לגלותה ואמרי' אמאי לא רצו לגלותה ומפרקינן גזירה דלמא אתו לאתויי ד' אמות ברה"ר. תניא ר' אליעזר אומר בו ביום גדשו סאה פי' בו ביום שהושיבו את רבי אלעזר בן עזריה בראש גדשו סאה. מדת הסאה ששת קבין והיא מחוקה הוסיפו רבותינו כמה דברים מדבריהם כגון הגדישה שהיא יתירה על העיקר והדברים שהוסיפו מהן להיתר ומהן לאיסור והכל להיות העיקר שמור ומוזהר והוא כמו זה ששנינו נותן כיסו התירו לו לתתו לנכרי שלא יביאנו בעצמו ויחלל את השבת. זה וכיוצא בו. ולאיסור כל גזירות שגזרו לעשות גדר לגשאר שהוא אסור מן התורה. ורבי יהושע אומר בו ביום מחקו סאה פי' העמידו כל דבר על עיקרו לא פחתו ולא הותירו. אלא התירו העיקר המותר מן התורה. שאלו באו להוסיף מדבריהן חוששין שמא יפסדו גם דברי תורה שהן העיקר שיבוא אדם להרהר ולומר כשם שזה אינו מן התורה אלא מדרבנן גם זולתי זה יש מן המצות האחרות מדרבנן כמותן ובאו לגדור נמצאו פורצים: אמר מר [אין] עמו נכרי מניחו על החמור ואקשינן עלה והלא מחמר הוא ורחמנא אמר לא תעשה כל מלאכה. ואוקימנא כדתנא כשהיא מהלכת מניחו עליה. כשהיא עומדת נוטלו הימנה. אי הכי חבירו נמי שרי ולמה חמור ולא אמר חבירו ופירק רב פפא כל שבגופו חייב חטאת בחבירו פטור אבל אסור פי' כל מלאכה שהעושה חייב חטאת כגון טעונת משוי ד' אמות ברה"ר אם יטעון חבירו פטור אבל אסור ואם יטעון בהמתו מותר לכתחלה ובלבד שלא תהא עקירה והנחה וזה שאמר רב אדא בר אהבה היתה חבילה מונחת לו בין כתיפו רץ תחתיה עד שמגיע לביתו מדייקינן למימרא דוקא רץ ומפרקינן לטעמי' ש"מ

מסורת הש"ס

א) תרומות פ"א מ"א יבמות קיג., ב) גיטין נג:, ג) [ע"ז ע. ועיין תוספ' עירובין לז: ד"ה רבי שמעון], ד) [תוספתא פ"א], ה) [ע"ז דף עו.], ו) [צ"ל רבה], ז) [מכות יג: לעיל סט.], ח) סנהדרין סו. ע"ש, ט) סנהדרין הגי' כרת, י) [לעיל סט. וש"נ], כ) לעיל מעשה, ל) סוטה כו:, מ) [צ"ל אמר].

רב נסים גאון

פרק מי שהחשיך תניא ר' אליעזר אומר בו ביום גדשו סאה ר' יהושע אומר בו ביום מחקו סאה היום הוא היום שנסמך בו ר' אלעזר בן עזריה בישיבה כמו שאמרו בברכות בפרק תפלת השחר (דף כח) תנא עדיות בו ביום תיקנום וכל בו ביום דאמרינן ההוא יומא איתמר וי"ח דבר שגזרו בו ביום באותו היום נאמרו אחת מהן מי שהחשיך בדרך חסב מא א) שדחו ביציאות השבת (דף יז) ולפיכך אמר כבאן בו ביום גדשו סאה נתכוונו בדבר זה למה שהוכירום מן הגזירות תחומין ואליבא דר' עקיבא. עיקר דבריו ר' עקיבא במסכת סוטה (פרק כשם דף כז) וכבר פירשנו דבר זה במה שעבר. הבערה ואליבא דר'

חשק שלמה על רב נסים גאון

א) פירושו לפי מה:

תורה אור השלם

א) כְּבֹד אֱלֹהִים הַסְתֵּר דָּבָר וּכְבֹד מְלָכִים חֲקֹר דָּבָר: [משלי כה, ב]

ב) וְיוֹם הַשְּׁבִיעִי שַׁבָּת לַייָ אֱלֹהֶיךָ לֹא תַעֲשֶׂה כָל מְלָאכָה אַתָּה וּבִנְךָ וּבִתֶּךָ עַבְדְּךָ וַאֲמָתֶךָ וּבְהֶמְתֶּךָ וְגֵרְךָ אֲשֶׁר בִּשְׁעָרֶיךָ: [שמות כ, י]

ג) הָאֶזְרָח בִּבְנֵי יִשְׂרָאֵל וְלַגֵּר הַגָּר בְּתוֹכָם תּוֹרָה אַחַת יִהְיֶה לָכֶם לָעֹשֶׂה בִּשְׁגָגָה: וְהַנֶּפֶשׁ אֲשֶׁר תַּעֲשֶׂה בְּיָד רָמָה מִן הָאֶזְרָח וּמִן הַגֵּר אֶת יְיָ הוּא מְגַדֵּף וְנִכְרְתָה הַנֶּפֶשׁ הַהִוא מִקֶּרֶב עַמָּהּ: [במדבר טו, כט-ל]

ליקוטי רש"י

לא תצא לחולין מפני שהוא ספק. אי דעתו צלולה היא אוקם תלמוד היא ובמה שהוא נותן דעתו ועושה דבר ודאי צלולה היא [עירובין עד.]. התורם את שאינו שלו. שלא מדעת בעל הבית נפקא לן (קדושין מא:) אתם גם אתם לרבות שלוחכם מה אתם לדעתכם אף שלוחכם לדעתכם. ונכרי שתרם את של ישראל אפי' ברשותו אין תרומתו תרומה. דבעינן מה אתם בני ברית וכו' [פסחים...]

[Gemara]

לא תצא לחולין מפני שהוא ספק כי תיבעי לך אליבא דרבנן דתנן א חמשה לא יתרומו ואם תרמו אין תרומתן תרומה אלו הן חרש שוטה וקטן והתורם את שאינו שלו ג ונכרי שתרם את של ישראל אפילו ברשותו אין תרומתו תרומה מאי לחרש יהיב ליה דקטן אתי לכלל דעת או דילמא לקטן יהיב ליה דחרש אתי לאחלופי בגדול פיקח איכא דאמרי לחרש יהיב ליה איכא דאמרי לקטן יהיב ליה אין שם לא נכרי ולא חמור ולא חרש ולא שוטה ולא קטן מאי אמר רבי יצחק עוד אחרת היתה ולא רצו חכמים לגלותה מאי עוד אחרת היתה ב מוליכו פחות פחות מד' אמות ואמאי לא רצו חכמים לגלותה משום א כבוד אלהים הסתר דבר וכבוד מלכים חקור דבר והכא מאי כבוד אלהים איכא דילמא אתי לאתויי ד' אמות ברה"ר תניא ד ר"א אומר בו ביום גדשו סאה ר' יהושע אומר בו ביום מחקו סאה תניא משל דר"א למה הדבר דומה לקופה מלאה קישואין ודילועין אדם נותן לתוכה חרדל והיא מחזקת משל דר' יהושע למה הדבר דומה לעריבה מלאה דבש נותן לתוכה רימונים ואגוזים והיא מקיאה אמר מר אין עמו נכרי מניחו על החמור והלא מחמר ורחמנא אמר ב לא תעשה כל מלאכה א"ר אדא בר אהבה מניחו עליה כשהיא מהלכת והא אי אפשר דלא קיימא להשתין מים ולהטיל גללים ואיכא עקירה והנחה ג כשהיא מהלכת מניחו עליה כשהיא עומדת נוטלו הימנה אי הכי אפילו חברו נמי אמר רב פפא ד כל שבגופו חייב חטאת בחברו פטור אבל אסור כל שחברו פטור אבל אסור בחמורו מותר לכתחלה א"ר אדא בר אהבה ה היתה חבילתו מונחת לו על כתיפו רץ תחתיה עד שמגיע לביתו דוקא רץ אבל קלי קלי לא מאי טעמא כיון דלית ליה היכירא אתי למיעבד עקירה והנחה סוף סוף כי מטא לביתיה אי אפשר דלא קאי פורתא וקמעייל מרשות הרבים לרה"י ו דזריק ליה כלאחר יד אמר רמי בר חמא ז המחמר אחר בהמתו בשבת בשוגג חייב חטאת במזיד חייב סקילה מאי טעמא אמר ח רבא דאמר קרא ב לא תעשה כל מלאכה אתה ובהמתך דומיא דידיה מה הוא בשוגג חייב חטאת במזיד חייב סקילה אף בהמתו נמי בשוגג חייב חטאת במזיד חייב סקילה אמר רבא שתי תשובות בדבר חדא דכתיב ג תורה אחת יהיה לכם לעושה בשגגה והנפש אשר תעשה ביד רמה ט הוקשה כל התורה כולה לע"ז מה ע"ז דעביד מעשה בגופיה ה"נ עד דעביד מעשה בגופיה ועוד כ תנן י המחלל את השבת בדבר שחייבין על שגגתו חטאת ועל זדונו ט סקילה מכלל דאיכא מידי דאין חייבין על שגגתו חטאת ולא על זדונו סקילה ומאי ניהו לאו דמחמר לא ל תחומין ואליבא דר"ע והבערה אליבא דר' יוסי

רב

[Rashi]

לא תצא לחולין. והויא תרומה לאסור לזרים ויחזור ויתרום הפקח אחרת: שהוא ספק. אי דעת צלולה היא אי לא ולר' יצחק ודאי לקטן יהיב ליה דלאו בר מצות הוא ולא לחרש דספק חייב במצות הוא: אליבא דרבנן. דאמרי לאו דעתא צלולתא היא ולענין מצות הרי הוא כקטן: ותורם את שאינו שלו. בלא רשות דכתיב (דברים יד) תבואת זרעך וחרש שוטה וקטן דכתיב אשר ידבנו לבו שיש לו לב להתנדב בהש"ס ירושלמי: אפילו ברשות. דשליחות מהיכא אתרבי מכן תרימו גם אתם גם לרבות שלוחכם ומה אתם בני ברית אף שלוחכם בני ברית: עוד אחרת היתה. תקנה לכיס להצילו: ואמאי לא רצו לגלותה. להעלים דברי תורה: כבוד אלהים הסתר דבר. מותר להסתיר דברי תורה לכבוד שמים: וכבוד מלכים חקור דבר. אין להסתיר לכבוד עושר אדם וחשיבותו אלא שב ותחקרהו: בו ביום גדשו סאה. ביום שעלו לעליית חנניה בן חזקיה וגזרו י"ח דבר וזו אחת מהן היתה כדאמרינן בפ"ק (דף יז:) נותן כיסו לנכרי בו ביום גזרו שלא יוליכנו פחות פחות מד"א אם יש שם נכרי אותו יום הרבו סייג לתורה במדה גדושה ויפה מדדו להרבות גדר בישראל: מחקו סאה. במדה מחוקה מדדו בו ביום שהרבו לגזור יותר מדאי ואין יכולין לעמוד בגזירתם ומתוך כך עוברין על דברי תורה נמצאת מדתם מחוקה מטפיפתה וטוב היה להם להיות מדתם טפופה ולא תבא לידי מחק מרוב גודשה: והיא מחזקת. את החרדל שנופל החרדל בין הקישואין אף כאן יפה תקנו והוסיפו דבר המתקיים: והיא מקיאה. את הדבש שהיה בה ראשון אף אלו ע"י גזירתם גרמו לעבור דשמא לא יאמין את הנכרי והם לא התירו להוליכו פחות פחות מארבע ואדם אינו מעמיד עצמו על ממונו ואתי לאיתויי ד' אמות: והלא מחמר. מנהיג חמור טעונה קרוי מחמר: ורחמנא אמר לא תעשה כל מלאכה אתה ובהמתך. ואיזוהי סתם מלאכה העשויה על ידי שניהם זו היא שהיא טעונה והוא מחמר: מניחו עליה כשהיא מהלכת. לאחר שנעקרה ללכת דלאו עקירה היא כדאמר בפ"ק (דף ג.) גבי הטעינו חברו אוכלין ומשקין וכיון דאדם לא מיחייב בה חטאת כי האי גוונא כאן מותר דהכא נמי מלאכה כתיב והא לאו מלאכה היא: וקאתי למיעבד עקירה והנחה. כשחוזרת ונעקרת ללכת אחר הטלת מים או גללים: נוטלו הימנה. ולאחר שתחזור ותעקור רגל יניחנו: אי הכי אפילו על חברו. יכול לעשות כן כיון דלאו איסורא דאורייתא היא גבי כיס שרי: כל שבגופו חייב חטאת. כי עביד ליה איהו כוליה כגון מעביר ד' אמות ברה"ר אפי' עקרו מן הארץ דרך הליכתו חייב דהא איכא עקירת חפץ בידים ולא בעינן עמידה אלא בטעון ועומד מבעוד יום או כשהטעינו חבירו דלא עקר ליה להאי חפץ אבל הכא הא עקר ליה הלכך כי עביד ליה חבריה הוי ליה שנים שעשאוה ואסור מדרבנן ולא שריוה גבי כיס: מונחת לו על כתיפו. מבעו"י וקדש עליו היום: רץ תחתיה. וכל כמה דלא עמד לפוש אין כאן עקירה לאיסור: קלי קלי. מעט מעט כלומר בנחת: למיעבד עקירה והנחה. כלומר דזימנין דקאי ולאו אדעתיה אבל רץ היכרא איכא: כלאחר יד. שלא כדרך זריקה כגון מכתיפיו ולאחוריו: בשוגג. במלאכה שהוא עושה לבדו: אף בהמתו. אף מלאכה שעושה על ידי בהמתו דהיינו מחמר אחר חמור טעונה: חדא דכתיב תורה אחת יהיה לכם וגו' עד דעביד מעשה בגופיה. [illegible] קרבן: ועוד. דקאמרת נמי במזיד חייב סקילה קשיא דתנן בסנהדרין (דף סו.) גבי נסקלים המחלל את השבת נסקל אם חללו בדבר שחייבים על שגגתו חטאת ועל זדונו סקילה: מכלל דאיכא. [illegible] ואליבא דר"ע. [illegible] אליבא דר' יוסי. דאמר בפרק כלל גדול (לעיל דף ע.) הבערה ללאו יצאת:

[Tosafot]

כי תבעי לך אליבא דרבנן. הכא משמע דהלכה כרבנן ובמסכת יבמות פרק חרש (דף קיג.) משמע דהלכה כר"א דסבירא ליה לרב חייא בר אשי (מ) ומר) שמואל כוותיה. מ"ר: דחרש אתי לאיחלופי בגדול פקח. תימה א"כ לעיל נמי מאי קאמר שוטה וקטן לשוטה הא אמרינן אתא לאיחלופי בגדול פקח: בו ביום גדשו סאה כו' נותן לתוכה חרדל והיא מחזקת. ה"נ כשגזרו י"ח דבר היתה חסרה גזירה זו של נותן כיסו לנכרי עד שגזרו עליה ומלאו הסאה לגמרי כמו שנתנו חרדל לתוכה: ר' יהושע אומר בו ביום מחקו סאה כו' נותן לתוכה אגוזים ורמונים והיא מקיאה. כמו כן קודם שגזרו על נתינת כיס לנכרי היו מותרין להוליכו פחות פחות מד' אמות מתוך כך אתי לאיתויי ד' אמות כעריבה שהיתה מקיאה עד שהסירו האגוזים והרמונים ואחר שהסירו האגוזים והרמונים שוב לא הקיאה יותר כך כשגזרו ליתן כיסו לנכרי אסרו נמי להוליך פחות פחות מד' אמות והשתא ר"א ורבי יהושע שניהם לשבח ולא כפירוש הקונטרס דפירש דרבי יהושע דאמר שלא עשו היטב שהרבו לגזור יותר מדאי דלא משמע הכי בירושלמי בפ"ק דמכילתין דאמר התם אמר ליה ר"א אלו היתה חסרה ומלאה יאות תבית שהיא מלאה אגוזים כל מה שאתה נותן לתוכה שומשמין היא מחזקת א"ל ר' יהושע אלו היתה מליאה וחסרוה יאות תבית שהיא מלאה שמן כל מה שאתה נותן לתוכה מים היא מפזרת השמן. מ"ר: ואדרבה נ"ל שהירו' קשה לו דלא שייך למימר גבי מים כמו שמפר"י גבי נותן לתוכה אגוזים ורמונים: סוף סוף כי מטי לביתיה א"א דלא קאי וקא מעייל מרשות הרבים לרשות היחיד. תימה כדשרינן להוליכו פחות פחות מד' אמות תקשי ליה נמי הכי: ואמרי

[illegible]

הוּקְשָׁה כָּל הַתּוֹרָה כּוּלָּהּ לַעֲבוֹדָה זָרָה – it means that **all the** prohibitions of the **Torah are compared to** the performance of **idolatry.**[29] **מָה עֲבוֹדָה זָרָה דְּעָבִיד מַעֲשֶׂה בְּגוּפֵיהּ** – Therefore, **just as idolatry** requires a *chatas* only **when he performs an action himself, הָכָא נַמִּי עַד דְּעָבִיד מַעֲשֶׂה בְּגוּפֵיהּ** – **so here also,** a Sabbath violation incurs a *chatas* **only if he performs an action himself.** This would exclude leading a loaded animal.[30] This is the first criticism of Rami bar Chama's ruling. **וְעוֹד תְּנַן** – **And furthermore, we learned in a Mishnah** that discusses one of the persons who is subject to death by stoning:[31] **הַמְחַלֵּל אֶת הַשַּׁבָּת** – ONE WHO DESECRATES THE SABBATH **בְּדָבָר שֶׁחַיָּיבִין עַל שִׁגְגָתוֹ חַטָּאת וְעַל זְדוֹנוֹ סְקִילָה** – BY DOING SOMETHING THAT IS SUBJECT TO A *CHATAS* WHEN DONE INADVERTENTLY, IS SUBJECT TO STONING WHEN HE DOES IT DELIBERATELY.[32] **מִכְּלָל דְּאִיכָּא מִידֵי** – **This** rule **implies that there is something** that is considered desecration of the Sabbath **דְּאֵין חַיָּיבִין עַל שִׁגְגָתוֹ חַטָּאת** – **for which one is not liable to a *chatas* when done inadvertently וְלֹא עַל זְדוֹנוֹ סְקִילָה** – **and,** consequently, for which one is **not** liable to death by **stoning when done deliberately. וּמַאי נִיהוּ** – **What** transgression **is this? לָאו דִּמְחַמֵּר** – Presumably, **the prohibition of leading a** loaded **animal.**

The Gemara provides two possible answers to Rava's second question:

לֹא תְּחוּמִין וְאַלִּיבָּא דְּרַבִּי עֲקִיבָא – **No,** the reference is either to the ***techum*** laws, **and** this **according to R' Akiva,** who holds this prohibition to be Biblical,[33] **וְהַבְעָרָה אַלִּיבָּא דְּרַבִּי יוֹסֵי** – **or** the prohibition of **kindling** a flame **according to R' Yose,** who holds this not to be subject to stoning.[34]

NOTES

29. The Gemara's derivation is understood as follows: The subject of this passage is idolatry (see *Sifrei* ad loc.). When the verse states: *There shall be a single law for you, for one who acts with inadvertence,* this means that, regarding inadvertent transgression, there shall be a single rule regarding idolatry *and other commandments* (see *Rashi* 69a ד״ה וכי תשגו). What is this rule? If a person transgresses any commandment unintentionally, he offers a *chatas* only if he performs an *action* in transgressing. If his transgression consisted of a thought, a statement or some other form of what is legally considered a non-action, he does not offer a *chatas.* And this is derived from the words לָעֹשֶׂה בִּשְׁגָגָה, *for one who **acts** with inadvertence* (*Rashi,* as explained by *Yad David, Mahadura Kamma*).

30. Merely leading an animal by calling to it does not qualify as a *melachah* [that the person is doing himself] (*Rashi,* as found in our texts). [Even where the person actually took hold of the animal and led it, the *person* is not doing a *melachah* (see above, note 27, and *Ishei Yisrael*). See also *Ramban,* gloss to *Sefer HaMitzvos, Shoresh* 14; *Sefer HaChinuch* §32; *Kli Chemdah, Parshas Yisro* 6:2.]

31. *Sanhedrin* 66a.

32. [Translation follows *Rashash.*] This is actually a paraphrase of the Mishnah in *Sanhedrin.*

33. One may not walk beyond a boundary of two thousand *amos* from his place of residence (as defined in *Eruvin,* chs. 4 and 5) on the Sabbath. This boundary is known as the *techum Shabbos.* The opinion of most of the Sages is that this prohibition is of Rabbinic origin. R' Akiva, however, maintains that it is a Biblical prohibition (see *Sotah* 27b). Nevertheless, R' Akiva agrees that it is not subject to *kares* or a *chatas* offering, nor to stoning [because walking beyond the *techum* boundary is not considered a *melachah* (*Yad Ramah* to *Sanhedrin* 66a)]. This is evidenced by the fact that when a Mishnah (above, 73a) lists all the types of *melachah* that are subject to *kares* and a *chatas* offering – and omits the transgression of *techum* – R' Akiva does not voice dissent (*Rashi* to *Sanhedrin,* ibid.). Thus, this Mishnah, which indicates the existence of a type of Sabbath desecration that is Biblically forbidden yet exempt from stoning, *kares* or *chatas,* might be referring to the *techum* prohibition, and it would thus follow the opinion of R' Akiva.

34. The Torah (*Exodus* 35:3) sets down a specific prohibition on kindling a flame on the Sabbath. This prohibition is superfluous, since there is a prohibition on performing any *melachah* on the Sabbath (*Exodus* 20:10) and kindling is a form of *melachah.* R' Yose therefore interprets the specific prohibition on kindling as teaching that, unlike other types of *melachah,* which are subject to stoning, *kares* and a *chatas* offering (depending on the circumstances of transgression), the act of kindling is merely the subject of a negative commandment – if one kindles a flame (having been forewarned) he merely receives lashes. There is a dissenting Tannaic opinion, according to which one who kindles a flame (having been forewarned) is liable for either stoning, *kares* or a *chatas* offering (see above, 70a). This Mishnah, which indicates that there is a type of Sabbath desecration that is not subject to stoning, *kares* or a *chatas* offering, might be alluding to the prohibition of kindling, and it would thus follow the opinion of R' Yose.

The Gemara records a different version of Rami bar Chama's ruling:

רַב זְבִיד מַתְנֵי הָכִי – **Rav Zevid taught** the ruling **this way:** אָמַר רָמִי בַּר חָמָא – **Rami bar Chama said:** הַמְחַמֵּר אַחַר בְּהֶמָה בְּשַׁבָּת – **One who leads a** laden **animal on the Sabbath:** בְּשׁוֹגֵג אֵינוֹ חַיָּיב חַטָּאת בְּמֵזִיד חַיָּיב סְקִילָה – **If** he does so **inadvertently, he is not liable to a** ***chatas,***[1] but **if** he does so **intentionally, he is liable to** death by **stoning.**[2]

Rava challenges this version of Rami bar Chama's ruling, from the same Mishnah:[3]

מָתִיב רָבָא – **Rava challenged this:** הַמְחַלֵּל אֶת הַשַּׁבָּת בְּדָבָר שֶׁחַיָּיבִין עַל שִׁגְגָתוֹ חַטָּאת – ONE WHO DESECRATES THE SABBATH BY DOING SOMETHING FOR WHICH ONE IS SUBJECT TO A *CHATAS* WHEN DONE INADVERTENTLY חַיָּיבִין עַל זְדוֹנוֹ סְקִילָה – IS SUBJECT TO STONING WHEN HE DOES IT INTENTIONALLY. הָא אֵין חַיָּיבִין עַל שִׁגְגָתוֹ חַטָּאת – **But,** this implies, **if one is not subject to a** ***chatas*** **when** this act is done **inadvertently,** אֵין חַיָּיבִין עַל זְדוֹנוֹ סְקִילָה – then **he is not subject to stoning when** it is done **intentionally.** Thus, if inadvertently leading an animal to perform a *melachah* does not require a *chatas,* intentionally doing so cannot require stoning. – ? –

The Gemara rejects Rava's inference:

מִי קָתָנֵי – **Did the Mishnah state** explicitly: הָא אֵין חַיָּיבִין כו׳ – BUT IF ONE IS NOT SUBJECT to a *chatas,* **etc.?** No! הָכִי קָאָמַר – Perhaps then **this is what [the Mishnah]** means to **say:** דָּבָר שֶׁחַיָּיבִין עַל שִׁגְגָתוֹ חַטָּאת – **Something for which one is subject to a** ***chatas*** **when it is done inadvertently,** חַיָּיבִין עַל זְדוֹנוֹ סְקִילָה – **one is** always **subject to stoning when it is done intentionally.** וְיֵשׁ דָּבָר שֶׁאֵין חַיָּיבִין עַל שִׁגְגָתוֹ חַטָּאת – **But there is** also **something for which one is not subject to a** ***chatas*** **when it is done inadvertently,** וְחַיָּיבִין עַל זְדוֹנוֹ סְקִילָה – **but for which he is** nonetheless **subject to stoning when it is done intentionally.** וּמַאי נִיהוּ – **And what is that?** מְחַמֵּר – **Leading** a laden **animal.**

The Gemara cites a third formulation of the ruling regarding leading a laden animal. There are two versions as to who stated this ruling:

רָבָא אֲחוּהַ דְּרַב מָרִי בַּר רָחֵל – **Rava the brother of Rav Mari bar Rachel,** וְאָמְרִי לָהּ אֲבוּהַ דְּרַב מָרִי בַּר רָחֵל – **and some say** that Rava was **the father of Rav Mari bar Rachel.**

The Gemara interrupts itself before it gets to the actual ruling and expresses surprise at the second version:

לְלִישָּׁנָא בַּתְרָא – **According to the latter version,** קַשְׁיָא הָא דְּרַב אַכְשְׁרֵיהּ לְרַב מָרִי בַּר רָחֵל – **it is difficult** to understand **that** incident **in which Rav declared Rav Mari bar Rachel**[4] **fit** וּמַנְיֵיהּ בְּפוּרְסֵיהּ דְּבָבֶל – **and appointed him among the officers of Babylon.** If his father was an Israelite, why was Rav's declaration necessary?[5]

The Gemara suggests an explanation:

דִּילְמָא תְּרֵי מָרִי בַּר רָחֵל הֲווּ – **Perhaps there were two** separate men named **Mari bar Rachel.**[6]

The Gemara resumes where it left off:

הֲוָה מַתְנֵי לָהּ לְהָא שְׁמַעְתֵּיהּ מִשְּׁמֵיהּ דְּרַבִּי יוֹחָנָן לִפְטוֹר – **He would teach this ruling in the name of R' Yochanan** and to the effect that the transgressor is always **exempt,** as follows: אָמַר רַבִּי יוֹחָנָן – **R' Yochanan said:** הַמְחַמֵּר אַחַר בְּהֶמְתּוֹ בְּשַׁבָּת פָּטוּר מִכְּלוּם – **One who leads his** laden **animal on the Sabbath is entirely exempt:** בְּשׁוֹגֵג לֹא מִחַיֵּיב חַטָּאת – **If** he does so **inadvertently, he is not liable to a** ***chatas,*** דְּהוּקְשָׁה כָּל הַתּוֹרָה כּוּלָּהּ לַעֲבוֹדָה זָרָה – **because all** the prohibitions of **the Torah** for which one brings a *chatas* **must be analogous to** the performance of **idolatry.** בְּמֵזִיד נַמִּי לָא מִיחַיֵּיב – **Also,** if he leads a laden animal **intentionally, he is not liable** to death by stoning, דִּתְנַן – **as we learned in the Mishnah:** הַמְחַלֵּל אֶת הַשַּׁבָּת בְּדָבָר שֶׁחַיָּיבִין עַל שִׁגְגָתוֹ חַטָּאת – ONE WHO DESECRATES THE SABBATH BY DOING SOMETHING THAT IS SUBJECT TO A *CHATAS* WHEN IT IS DONE INADVERTENTLY וְעַל זְדוֹנוֹ סְקִילָה – IS SUBJECT TO STONING WHEN HE DOES IT INTENTIONALLY.[7] הָא אֵין חַיָּיבִין עַל שִׁגְגָתוֹ חַטָּאת – **But if one is not subject to a** ***chatas*** **when** the act is done **inadvertently,** אֵין חַיָּיבִין עַל זְדוֹנוֹ סְקִילָה – then **he is not subject to stoning when** it is done **intentionally.** בְּלָאו נַמִּי לֹא מִיחַיֵּיב – **Furthermore, he is not** even **liable** to the penalty of lashes **for** having transgressed **a negative commandment,** דַּהֲוָה לֵיהּ לָאו שֶׁנִּיתָּן לְאַזְהָרַת מִיתַת בֵּין דִּין – because this **prohibition,** *do not do any melachah,* **serves as a warning** not to do any *melachah* on pain of liability **to court-imposed execution,**[8]

NOTES

1. In this version, Rami bar Chama accepts Rava's first point, that the violation of a prohibition can warrant a *chatas* only if the violator himself performs the forbidden act. Since leading an animal to perform a *melachah* does not involve such an act, a *chatas* is not brought. (This is derived above from the passage of the idolatry *chatas;* see 153b note 29.)

2. As we derived above from the juxtaposition of the words *you . . . and your animal*: [Just as a *melachah* done by yourself is punished with stoning, so too a *melachah* done by you and your animal is punished with stoning] (*Rashi*).

3. [See *Rashash,* 153b; cf. marginal note here.]

4. Throughout the Talmud, Rav Mari is known not by his father's name but rather by his mother's (*bar Rachel,* son of Rachel). His mother, Rachel, was Shmuel's daughter. She was taken captive, and one of her captors, Issur, cohabited with her, and she conceived Mari. Later, Issur converted and was known as Issur the Convert.

Issur was thus biologically Rav Mari's father [but not legally, since the Torah does not recognize any legal connection between a Jewish child, born of a Jewish mother, and his non-Jewish father]. Out of respect to Rav Mari, therefore, Rav Mari is not known by his father's name but rather by his mother's (*Rashbam* to *Bava Basra* 149a; *Rashi* to *Bava Metzia* 73b; see also *Tosafos* here).

[Many Rishonim delete the second version entirely because, besides the question cited in the Gemara here, how can we say that his father's name was Rava when we know it to have been Issur (see *Rashi* and *Tosafos;* cf. *Rabbeinu Chananel*).

5. A convert, or the son of two converts, may not be appointed to a position of authority over Israelite Jews (i.e. Jews descended from Abraham, Isaac and Jacob). The source for this law is cited in *Kiddushin* 76b [see also *Yevamos* 45b]: The verse states (*Deuteronomy* 17:15): *You must appoint [som tasim] over you a king . . . who is from the midst of your brothers.* The double expression *som tasim* (literally: appoint, you shall appoint) teaches us that any appointment made, even a minor one, should be conferred only on someone of native Israelite descent. Thus, it would seem that Rav Mari bar Rachel could not legally serve as an officer. However, Rav ruled that he could because, even though his father was not an Israelite, his mother was and this is sufficient to render him *from the midst of your brothers.*

Now, if Rav Mari bar Rachel's father was someone named Rava [a native Israelite – see *Tosafos*] then it is obvious that Rav Mari is fit to serve as minister: He is descended from two native Israelites!

6. [As to why Rav Mari the son of Rava was called after his mother, see *Tosafos Bava Basra* 149a ד״ה רב מרי.]

As mentioned, *Rashi* and *Tosafos* prefer a variant reading of our Gemara in which this entire passage, from *and some say* etc., does not appear. In this version, the Gemara simply cites Rava, the brother of Rav Mari bar Rachel.

7. [The translation reflects the emendation of the *Bach*; see also *Rashash* to 153b.]

8. Every punishable transgression requires two Scriptural sources – one that sets forth the basic prohibition [אַזְהָרָה, *Scriptural warning*] and a second that describes the punishment incurred. The prohibition contained in the verse: *Do not do any melachah you . . . and your animal,* serves as the Scriptural warning not only for the non-capital

רב זביד מתני הכי אמר רמי בר חמא המחמר אחר בהמה בשבת בשוגג אינו חייב חטאת במזיד חייב סקילה מתיב רבא [א]המחלל את השבת בדבר שחייבין על שגגתו חטאת חייבין על זדונו סקילה הא אין חייבין על שגגתו חטאת אין חייבין על זדונו סקילה מי קתני הא אין חייבין כו' הכי קאמר דבר שחייבין על שגגתו חטאת חייבין על זדונו סקילה ויש דבר שאין חייבין על שגגתו חטאת וחייבין על זדונו סקילה ומאי ניהו מחמר רבא אחוה דרב מרי בר רחל (א) ואמרי לה אבוה דרב מרי בר רחל ללישנא בתרא קשיא הא דרב [ב]אכשריה לרב מרי בר רחל ומנייה בפורסיה דבבל דילמא תרי מרי בר רחל הוו הוה מתני לה להא שמעתיה משמיה דרבי יוחנן לפטור אמר רבי יוחנן [א]המחמר אחר בהמתו בשבת פטור מכלום בשוגג לא מחייב חטאת דהוקשה כל התורה כולה לע"ז במזיד נמי לא מחייב דתנן [ג]המחלל את השבת בדבר שחייבין על שגגתו חטאת (ג) ועל זדונו סקילה הא אין חייבין על שגגתו חטאת אין חייבין על זדונו סקילה בלאו נמי לא מיחייב דהוה ליה לאו שניתן לאזהרת מיתת ב"ד וכל [ד] [א]לאו שניתן לאזהרת מיתת ב"ד אין לוקין עליו ואפילו

רש"י

רב זביד מתני. להא דרמי בר חמא הכי: **אינו חייב חטאת.** דילפינן מע"ז דעד דעביד מעשה בגופיה: **אבל במזיד חייב סקילה.** מהיקישא דאתה ובהמתך דלעיל: **מי קתני.** הך דיוקא דדייקינן הא אין חייב כו' דילמא הכי קאמר המחלל בדבר שחייבין על שגגתו חטאת [חייבים על זדונו סקילה] הא דבר שאין חייבים על שגגתו חטאת יש מהן שחייבין על זדונו סקילה ויש שאין חייבין ומאי ניהו דחייבין [על זדונו] סקילה ואין חייבין על שגגתו חטאת מחמר: **ואמרי לה אבוה דרב מרי בר רחל** ל"ג דאבוה דרב מרי איסור גיורא שמיה ומאן דגרס ליה גרס בתריה הכי להך לישנא בתרא קשיא הך דרב אכשריה לרב מרי בר רחל ומניה בפורסי דבבל והך מילתא במסכת יבמות היא (דף מה:) בפורסי בלע"ז מנסטר"ל הן שוטרים ואף על גב דאמר מר כל משימות שאתה משים לא יהו אלא מקרב אחיך האי כיון דאמו מישראל מקרב אחיך קרינן ביה: **לאזהרת מיתת בית דין.** דשאר מלאכות דשבת נמי מהאי קרא נפקא להו אזהרה הלכך לאזהרת מיתת בית דין ניתן דלא ענש מיתה אלא אם כן הזהיר הלכך עיקר אזהרתו למקום שיש בו מיתה אתאי ולא למלקות:

תוספות

ואמרי לה רבא אבוה דרב מרי בר רחל. לא גרסינן ליה דהא מוכח ביבמות דאבוה דרב מרי גר הוה דאמר בהחולץ (יבמות מה: ושם) רב אכשריה לרב מרי בר רחל ומנייה אפורסיה דבבל וקאמר כיון דאמו מישראל מקרב אחיך קרינן ביה וליכא למימר דרבא אבוה דרב מרי נמי גר הוה דאם כן הוה ליה למימר רבא גיורא כדאמר הש"ס בעלמא איסור גיורא ועוד דאביו של רב מרי בר רחל משמע בבבא בתרא פרק מי שמת (דף קמט. ושם) דהיינו איסור גיורא דאמרינן איסור גיורא הוה ליה תריסר אלפי זוזי בי רבא ורב מרי בריה הורתו שלא בקדושה ולידתו בקדושה הוה אע"ג דהתם לא גרסינן רב מרי בר רחל בריה דומה הוא שאותו היה מיהו אי אמרינן שהוא היה רב מרי בר רחל צריכא למימר דאיסור גיורא בא על רחל בת מר שמואל קודם שנתגייר דהא קאמר התם דהורתו שלא בקדושה הוה ורחל בת מר שמואל היתה כדאמר בכמה דוכתין רב מרי בר רחל בת מר שמואל ואמרינן בכתובות (דף כג.) דבנתיה דמר שמואל אישתביין ושמא אז בא עליה ואף על גב דאתו לקמיה דר"ח ואמרו נשביתי וטהורה אני לאו כולהו אמרו הכי מיהו תימה אי רב מרי בריה דאיסור גיורא היינו ההוא דיבמות איך חי איסור כל כך מימות רב עד רבא והא רב יהודה תלמידו של רב ואמרינן בקדושין (דף עב:) יום שמת רב יהודה נולד רבא ואפילו רב מרי בנו כבר היה גדול בתורה הרבה בימי רב מדמנייה אפורסיה דבבל ורב מרי נמי איך יתכן שחי כ"כ ונראה כפירוש ר"ח דגרסינן ביבמות דרב אשי אכשריה לרב מרי בר רחל ואע"ג דביום שמת רבא נולד רב אשי יכול להיות שהיה רב מרי קטן בימי רבא ובימי רב אשי כבר היה גדול בתורה חקן ומינהו אפורסיה דבבל וכן ודאי נראה דיש בספרים רבים שכתוב בהם בשמעתא (ג) לאמרי לה והקשה דרב אשי אכשריה לרב מרי בר רחל ומשני תרי רב מרי הוו ופירוש הוא שנכתב בספרים. מ"ר [ה]:

בלאו נמי לא מיחייב דה"ל לאו שניתן לאזהרת מיתת ב"ד. תימה לר"י מה בכך מ"מ ילקה על לאו דלא תעשה כל מלאכה דכיון שבא להזהיר על מחמר ובמחמר ליכא מיתה אע"פ שבא להזהיר נמי על שאר מלאכות דשייך בהו מיתה מכל מקום יש לו ללקות כדאשכחן בבבא קמא (דף עד: ושם) דפליגי ר' יוחנן ור"א התם בעדים שהוכחשו בנפש ולבסוף הוזמו דחד אמר נהרגין וחד אמר אין נהרגין ואמרינן נמי תסתיים דר' אלעזר דאמר אין נהרגין דאמר ר"א עדים שהוכחשו בנפש לוקין ואי ס"ד ר"א דאמר נהרגין אמאי לוקין הוה ליה לאו שניתן לאזהרת מיתת ב"ד אלא ש"מ ר"א דאמר אין נהרגין תסתיים אלמא משום דלאין נהרגין כשהוכחשו בתחילה לוקין ואע"ג דבעלמא ניתן לאו דלא תענה לאזהרת מיתת ב"ד היכא דהוזמו תחילה ועוד תימה לר"י דכל לאוין שבעולם שניתנו לאזהרת מיתת ב"ד יהיו לוקין עליהם כשלא התרו בהם למיתה אלא למלקות מההוא טעמא דלא ניתנו באותה שעה לאזהרת מיתת ב"ד ונראה לר"י דשאני לאו דלא תענה דגלי ביה קרא דניתן למלקות כדאשכחן גבי עדות בן גרושה כדמפקינן בריש מסכת מכות (דף ב: ושם) (ד) מוהרשיעו את הרשע והיה אם בן הכות הרשע וכיון דכתב בלא תענה מלקות בהדיא אע"ג דניתן לאזהרת מיתת ב"ד אית לן לאוקמי בכל מילי דלא מצי אתי לידי מיתה ומהאי טעמא נמי אתי שפיר הא דאמר במכות בגמרא מעידין אנו את איש פלוני שהוא חייב לחבירו מאתים זוז ונמצאו זוממים לוקין ומשלמין דברי ר' מאיר וחכמים אומרים כל המשלם אינו לוקה דקאמר בשלמא לרבנן כדי רשעתו משום רשעה אחת אתה מחייבו כו' וקשה לר"י ל"ל למימר טעמא דרבנן משום כדי רשעתו תיפוק ליה דרבנן מוקמי לא תענה לאזהרה לעדים זוממין ולא למלקות כדמוכח התם על משנת מעידים אנו את איש פלוני שחייב מלקות ארבעים וקשה לר"י נמי היכי מצי למימר לרבנן דלאזהרה דעדים זוממים הוא דאתא ולא למלקות הא בהזמה דגלות ובן גרושה מודו רבנן דאיכא מלקות ולמאי דפרישית אתי שפיר דכי היכי דלא אתי לידי מיתה או לידי מלקות ע"י כאשר זמם לוקה משום לא תענה כיון דהתם לא צריך קרא דלא תענה לאזהרה לכאשר זמם משום הכי לקי במעידים אנו בפלוני שהוא בן גרושה או שחייב גלות ואתי נמי שפיר הא דתלי טעמא דרבנן התם משום כדי רשעתו דאי לאו משום כדי רשעתו היו לוקין משום לא תענה אפי' לרבנן דלאע"ג דסבירא להו דלא תענה אזהרה לכאשר זמם הוא דאתא דלא ענש כאשר זמם אלא אם כן הזהיר והוי כלאו שניתן לאזהרת מיתת ב"ד שלא נכתב למלקות אלא לאזהרת מיתה ה"מ דוקא כשחייב מלקות מכאשר זמם כגון מעידים אנו באיש פלוני שחייב מלקות אבל כשאין חייבים מכאשר זמם אלא ממון לא מבעי התם לא תענה לאזהרה דכאשר זמם הוו מודו רבנן דלוקין משום לא תענה כמו בבן גרושה וגלות אי לאו משום כדי רשעתו וא"ת למאי דפירש דאי לאו דגלי קרא בהדיא מלקות בלא תענה מוהלדיקו את הלדיק לא הוה מחייבינן ביה משום דניתן לאזהרת מיתת ב"ד אם כן הא דמפיק עולא דעדים זוממים לוקין מוהלדיקו את הלדיק בריש מכות ופריך עלה תיפוק ליה מלא תענה ומשני משום דהוה ליה לאו שאין בו מעשה אמאי לא משני משום דהוה ליה לאו שניתן לאזהרת מיתת ב"ד ותירץ דההוא סוגיא לא הוה אתי אלא לרבנן דלר' מאיר איכא תרי לאוי חד לאזהרה כאשר זמם היכא דזמם מיתה או מלקות וחד למילקי עליה ולהכי ניחא טפי למימר טעמא דלאו שאין בו מעשה לאוקמא מילתא בין לרבנן בין לרבי מאיר דמתניתין דמכות אע"ג דטעמא דלאו שאין בו מעשה נמי לא אתי לר"י ולמאי דפי' איצטריך והלדיקו למלקות אפי' למאן דמחייב בלאו שאין בו מעשה ועוד היה רגיל לתרץ כיון דלא תענה סתם כתיב אכל מילי קאי ולהכי מיחייב מלקות כאילו נכתב אבן גרושה ואגלות וכאילו נכתב לא תענה שקר בממון ולבן גרושה וגלות שאז לא היה הנכתב לממון ניתן לאזהרה כאשר זמם ולכך היה ראוי ללקות עליו והכי נמי השתא אע"פ שזה לא היה ראוי ללקות על אותו הניתן לאזהרת מיתה אפי' כשאינו יכול לבא לידי מיתה עכשיו יש ללקות עליו כל זמן שלא יוכל לבא לידי מיתה הואיל ונכתב על מיתה וממון ביחד סתם וניתן להלקות עליו בהזמת מיתה נמי ניתן ללקות כל זמן שלא יוכל לבא לידי מיתה ולפי טעם זה לא היה יכול לתרץ בריש מכות משום דהוה ליה לאו שניתן לאזהרת מיתת ב"ד כי פריך ותיפוק ליה משום לא תענה דלאע"פ שניתן לאזהרת מיתה יש ללקות עליו הואיל ונכתב סתם על מיתה ודברים אחרים כדפרישית ולפי לשון זה לא אתי דרשה דהלדיקו אלא למאן דלית ליה לאו שאין בו מעשה אין לוקין עליו למיפרך בריש מכות אבל קשה דבכל הש"ס חשיב לאו דשבת ניתן לאזהרת מיתת ב"ד ואמאי הא קאי אלאו דמחמר והאזהרה דאיסור (לעיל דף ו:) דליכא מיתה ור"י כיון דכתיב כל העושה בו מלאכה יומת משמע סתם מלאכה דשבת היינו בשמיה והכי קאמר לא תעשה כל מלאכה אתה ובהמתך משמע חיובי שבת טפי ממחמר משמע שאר דברים שאין בהן מיתה ומלקות וכן לאו דמחמר לא תעשה כל מלאכה אתה מדכתיב הכא לא"ג מדכתיב לא תעשה והוצאה לא כתיב לא תעשו והוא ולא ע"ג דנפקא מלא ילא (עירובין יז:) בהדי תחומין דמלקות אין לוקין עליו אפי' לא התרו בו למיתה דכל סתם הוצאה דשבת איתא בקרא דויכלא העם מהביא ותירוץ ראשון * נראה לר"י עיקר. מ"ר:

והא

מסורת הש"ס

א) [בריתא היא ועי' תוס' לעיל ו: ד"ה הא קמ"ל], ב) [יבמות מה: ע"ש], ג) [סנהדרין סו. ע"ש], ד) [ערובין יז: ע"ש] סנהדרין סג: מכות יג: שבועות ד., ה) [עי' תוספות ב"מ עג: ד"ה רב].

הגהות הב"ח

(א) גמ' רבא אחוה דרב מרי בר רחל (ואמרי לה רבא אבוה דרב וכו' מרי רב מרי בר רחל הוו) תא"מ, ונ"ב ס"א ל"ג אין זה. וכן רש"י ותוס' לא גרסי ליה: (ב) שם על שגגתו חטאת חייבים על זדונו סקילה: (ג) תוס' ד"ה ואמרי לה וכו' בשמעתא לאמרי לה וקשיא הא דרב וכו': (ד) ד"ה בלאו וכו' כריש מס' מכות מוהלדיקו את הלדיק והרשיעו את:

ליקוטי רש"י

בעבודת כוכבים משמעי קרא דגנאי בספרי ר"ש אומר בעבודת כוכבים הכתוב מדבר שנא' כי דבר ה' בזה שכה על דיבור ראשון שנאמר בו אנכי ה' אלהיך ולא יהיה לך אלהים אחרים על פני [הוריות ח.]. הוקשה כל התורה כולה לע"ז. כלן הוקשו כל עבירות שבתורה בשגגתן לעבודת כוכבים לענין קרבן [מכות יג:]. המחלל את השבת. משביש ליה תנא במקלקלין כגון שמללו במלאכה גמורה. בדבר שחייבין. כגון דבר שיש בו מעשה ומלאכת מחשבת ולא המתעסק [סנהדרין סו.]. ואליבא דר' עקיבא. דאמר במסכת סוטה תחומין דאורייתא נינהו דתנן בו ביום דרש ר' עקיבא ומקומו ממקום [לעיל כו']. דיליף להו מקרא במסכת סוטה [כז:]. ור' עקיבא מודה דהנך נמי במחומין דאין חייבים עליהם כרת דתנן [כריתות ב.], לבד מכל הכריתות סקר אמת ולא פליג ר' עקיבא. והבערה אליבא דר' יוסי. שאין חייבין עליה כרת וסקילה כשאר מלאכות אלא מה שאמר בה [לעיל ע.] ללאו יצאת מכלל שאר המלאכות לומר לך שאין בה כרת וסקילה אלא לאו בעלמא [סנהדרין לה:]. דתניא [שבת ע.] הבערה ללאו יצאת שהיתה בכלל כל לא תעשה כל מלאכה חזר והוציאה מכללו ופרט בה לא תבערו לומר לך שאינה במיתה כשאר מלאכות שבת אלא בלאו בלבד [יבמות לג:]. דר' יוסי אומר לא כל המלאכות שבת אלא בלאו [פסחים ה:]. הבערה שיצאה מכלל לא תעשה כל מלאכה (שמות כ) דכתבה ותעשה בה לאו להוציאה מכלל מחוייבי סקילה ולאמר עליה שאינה לא בכרת ולא בסקילה אלא בלאו [סנהדרין סב.]. [ע"כ שייך לדף קנג:]

אכשריה לרב מרי בר רחל. בת שמואל הוה ונשבית ואתא לא נכרי ונתגייר גיורא ושמיה איסור גיורא ורב מרי הורתו שלא בקדושה ולידתו בקדושה ונסמכת בשלטונו של עם הארץ [ב"מ עג: ע"ש בתוס']. איסור גיורא שבא על רחל בת מר שמואל קודם שנתגייר ונתעברה הימנו בגיות ואח"כ נתגייר וכשנולד רב מרי בר רחל ונסמך על כן נקרא על שם אמו שהיתה בישראל שהורתו שלא בקדושה ולידתו בקדושה.

עין משפט נר מצוה

טז א מיי' פ"ג מהלכות שבת הלכה ט: [טז] [א] [מיי' פ"ח מהלכות סנהדרין הלכה ב]:

רבינו חננאל

ואליבא דרבי עקיבא דסבר תחומין דאורייתא ועיקרו בסוטה פרק כשם שהמים בודקין אותו וחייב לאו כדכתיב אל יצא איש ממקומו ביום השביעי והבערה אליבא דר' יוסי דתניא הבערה ללאו יצאת דברי ר' יוסי ר' נתן אומר לחלק יצאת רב זביד מתני הכי אמר רמי בר חמא המחמר אחר בהמתו בשבת בשוגג פטור במזיד חייב סקילה ואקשי עליה רבא המחלל את השבת בדבר שחייבין על שגגתו חטאת חייבין על זדונו סקילה הא אין חייבין על שגגתו חטאת אין חייבין על זדונו סקילה ופריק ופשוטה היא. רבא אחוה דרב מרי בר רחל (או) [ואמרי לה] כי רבא הוא אבוה דרב מרי בר רחל והוא מישראל קשיא ליה הא דרב אשי דאכשריה דכיון דאימיה מישראל מקרב אחיך קרינא ביה מכלל שלא היה אביו מישראל אלא אמו. ומפרש בפרק החולץ ליבמתו. ומפרקי דלמא תרי רב מרי בר רחל הוו אביו מישראל וכן תירוץ שמועה זו רבא אבוה דרב מרי בר רחל: א"ר יוחנן המחמר אחר בהמתו בשבת פטור מכלום בשוגג לא מחייב חטאת. [דהוקשה] כל התורה כולה לע"ז במזיד נמי לא מחייב (חטאת) [סקילה]. דתנן בפרק ארבע מיתות נמסרו לבית דין [המחלל את השבת בדבר כו'] ואוקימנא התם בתחומין ואליבא דר"ע בהבערה אליבא דר' יוסי א) דתנן המחלל את השבת בדבר שחייבין על זדונו סקילה הא אין חייבין על שגגתו חטאת אין חייבין על זדונו סקילה. לאו נמי לא מיחייב דהוה ליה לאו שניתן לאזהרת מיתת ב"ד וכל לאו שניתן לאזהרת מיתת ב"ד אין לוקין עליו:

חשק שלמה על רבינו חננאל

א) נראה דנתחלפו השורות בכאן וכן צ"ל דתנן בפרק ד' מיתות נמסרו לב"ד המחלל את השבת בדבר שחייבין על שגגתו חטאת חייבין על זדונו סקילה. הא אין חייבין על שגגתו חטאת אין חייבין על זדונו סקילה. ואוקימנא התם בתחומין ואליבא דר"ע בהבערה אליבא דר"י לאו נמי וכו':

גליון הש"ס

תוס' ד"ה בלאו נמי וכו' וכו' כמש"ל נראה לר"י עיקר. עיין סנהדרין דף סג ע"א בתוספות ד"ה משום לאו:

רב נסים גאון

דרבי יוסי גרסי לה בפרק כלל גדול (דף ע) הבערה ללאו יצאת דברי רבי יוסי:

ולפי שבת לרב מרי הוה רב אשי בתחלתו יתכן שבבלנו עליו אבל אם היה שכן שבטבון גבי רבא אחוה דרב מרי והוא אחיו מן האם ולא מן האב כלאותו דאמר רב הונא כל האכשריה לרב מרי בר רחל ומנייה בפורסיה דבבל (כ) [רשב"ם ב"ב קמט. ע"ש בתוס']. מעוכד כוכבים הבא על ישראלית הוה. ומנייה בפורסיה דבבל. גבאים ממונים על ישראל ואע"ג דגר בעלמא אסור למנותו פרנס על ישראל דאמר מר שום תשים עליך מלך מקרב אחיך תשים עליך מלך כל משימות שאתה משים לא יהיו אלא מקרב אחיך הא כיון דאמו מישראל מקרב אחיך קרינא ביה (יבמות מה:). וכל לאו שניתן לאזהרת מיתת ב"ד. שלא יעשה דבר שחייבין עליו מיתה [מכות יג:]. שלא ענש קרא אלא א"כ הזהיר. אין לוקין עליו. אפילו לא התרו בו למיתה דהא לא קא לקי אלאזהרה דהאי לאו ניתן למלקות [עירובין יז:]. לא ניתן לעונש מלקות דלא משום מלקות אתא בב"ד [שבועות ד.]. דמיתת ב"ד הוא עונשו על לאו [ב"ק שם]. ואפילו יפטרנו מן המיתה שהרי לא התרו בו למיתה אין לוקין עליו דלא מיתה ולא מלקות דלא דמי לשאר הלאוין שאין בהם אלא לאו מלקות כתיב בהו מלקות ולא דמי לשאר לאוין שאינו יכול למיתה כשאר לאוין שאינו יכול למיתה לפיכך מלקות אין בו [מכות שם].

וְכָל לָאו שֶׁנִּיתַּן לְאַזְהָרַת מִיתַת בֵּית דִּין – and any prohibition that serves as a warning for a court-imposed execution **אֵין לוֹקִין עָלָיו – does not carry the penalty of lashes.**[9]

NOTES

offense of leading a laden animal, but also for the capital offense of committing a *melachah* himself (*Rashi*).

9. A prohibition that serves as the Scriptural warning for a death penalty cannot also serve as the warning for incurring lashes. Therefore, if a prohibition can be violated in a way that would incur the death penalty, there are no lashes administered for its violation even when it is violated in such a way that the death penalty is not incurred. Thus, since the verse prohibiting leading an animal to perform a *melachah* can be violated in a way that incurs the death penalty (i.e. by performing a *melachah* himself), then even if it is violated in a lesser way (i.e. by leading an animal to perform a *melachah*) no lashes are incurred.

רב זביד מתני הכי אמר רמי בר חמא המחמר אחר בהמה בשבת בשוגג אינו חייב חטאת במזיד חייב סקילה מתיב רבא [א] המחלל את השבת בדבר שחייבין על שגגתו חטאת חייבין על זדונו סקילה הא אין חייבין על שגגתו חטאת אין חייבין על זדונו סקילה מי קתני הא אין חייבין כו' הכי קאמר דבר שחייבין על שגגתו חטאת חייבין על זדונו סקילה ויש דבר שאין חייבין על שגגתו חטאת וחייבין על זדונו סקילה ומאי ניהו מחמר רבא אחוה דרב מרי בר רחל (א) ואמרי לה אבוה דרב מרי בר רחל ללישנא בתרא קשיא הא דרב [ב] אכשריה לרב מרי בר רחל ומנייה בפורסיה דבבל דילמא תרי מרי בר רחל הוו הוה מתני לה להא שמעתיה משמיה דרבי יוחנן לפטור אמר רבי יוחנן [א] המחמר אחר בהמתו בשבת פטור מכלום בשוגג לא מחייב חטאת דהוקשה כל התורה כולה לע"ז במזיד נמי לא מיחייב דתנן [ג] המחלל את השבת בדבר שחייבין על שגגתו חטאת (ב) ועל זדונו סקילה הא אין חייבין על שגגתו חטאת אין חייבין על זדונו סקילה בלאו נמי לא מיחייב דהוה ליה לאו שניתן לאזהרת מיתת ב"ד וכל [ד] [א] לאו שניתן לאזהרת מיתת ב"ד אין לוקין עליו ואפילו

רש"י

רב זביד מתני. להא דרמי בר חמא הכי: **אינו חייב חטאת.** דילפינן מע"ז דעד דעביד מעשה בגופיה: **אבל במזיד חייב סקילה.** מהיקישא דאתה ובהמתך דלעיל: **מי קתני.** הך דיוקא דדייקינן הא אין חייב כו' דילמא הכי קאמר המחלל בדבר שחייבין על שגגתו חטאת [חייבים על זדונו סקילה] הא דבר שאין חייבים על שגגתו חטאת יש מהן שחייבין על זדונו סקילה ויש שאין חייבין ומאי ניהו דחייבין [על זדונו] סקילה ואין חייבין על שגגתו חטאת מחמר: **ואמרי לה אבוה דרב מרי בר רחל** ל"ג דאבוה דרב מרי איסור גיורא שמיה ומאן דגרס ליה גרס בתריה הכי להך לישנא בתרא קשיא הך דרב אכשריה לרב מרי בר רחל ומניה בפורסי דבבל והך מילתא במסכת יבמות היא (דף מה:) בפורסי בלע"ז מנשטר"ל הן שוטרים ואף על גב דאמר מר כל משימות שאתה משים לא יהו אלא מקרב אחיך האי כיון דאמו מישראל מקרב אחיך קרינן ביה: **לאזהרת מיתת בית דין.** דשאר מלאכות דשבת נמי מהאי קרא נפקא להו אזהרה הלכך לאזהרת מיתת בית דין ניתן דלא ענש מיתה אלא אם כן הזהיר הלכך עיקר אזהרתו למקום שיש בו מיתה אתאי ולא למלקות:

תוספות

ואמרי לה רבא אבוה דרב מרי בר רחל. לא גרסינן ליה דהא מוכח ביבמות דאבוה דרב מרי גר הוה דאמר בהחולץ (יבמות מה: ושם) רב אכשריה לרב מרי בר רחל ומנייה אפורסיה דבבל וקאמר כיון דאמו מישראל מקרב אחיך קרינן ביה וליכא למימר דרבא אבוה דרב מרי נמי גר הוה דאם כן הוה ליה למימר רבא גיורא כדאמר הש"ס בעלמא איסור גיורא ועוד דאביו של רב מרי בר רחל משמע בבבא בתרא פרק מי שמת (דף קמט. ושם) דהיינו איסור גיורא דאמרינן איסור גיורא הוה ליה תריסר אלפי זוזי בי רבא ורב מרי בריה הורתו שלא בקדושה ולידתו בקדושה הוה אע"ג דהתם לא גרסינן רב מרי בר רחל בריה דומה הוא שאותו היה מיהו אי אמרינן שהוא היה רב מרי בר רחל צריכא למימר דאיסור גיורא בא על רחל בת מר שמואל קודם שנתגייר דהא קאמר התם דהורתו שלא בקדושה הוה ורחל בת מר שמואל היתה כדאמר בכמה דוכתין רב מרי בר רחל בת מר שמואל ואמרינן בכתובות (דף כג.) דבנתיה דמר שמואל אישתביין ושמא אז בא עליה ואף על גב דאתו לקמיה דר"ח ואמרו נשביתי וטהורה אני לאו כולהו אמרו הכי מיהו תימה אי רב מרי בריה דאיסור גיורא היינו ההוא דיבמות איך חי איסור כל כך מימות רב עד רבא והא רב יהודה תלמידו של רב ואמרינן בקדושין (דף עב:) יום שמת רב יהודה נולד רבא ואפילו רב מרי בנו כבר היה גדול בתורה הרבה בימי רב מדמנייה אפורסיה דבבל ורב מרי נמי איך יתכן שחי כ"כ ונראה כפירוש ר"ח דגרסינן ביבמות דרב אשי אכשריה לרב מרי בר רחל ואע"ג דביום שמת רבא נולד רב אשי יכול להיות שהיה רב מרי קטן בימי רבא ובימי רב אשי כבר היה גדול בתורה וזקן ומינהו אפורסייה דבבל וכן ודאי נראה דיש בספרים רבים שכתוב בהם בשמעתא (ג) לאמרי לה והקשה דרב אשי אכשריה לרב מרי בר רחל ומשני תרי רב מרי הוו ופירוש הוא שנכתב בספרים. מ"ר [ה]:

בלאו נמי לא מיחייב דהד"ל לאו שניתן לאזהרת מיתת ב"ד. תימה לר"י מה בכך מ"מ ילקה על לאו דלא תעשה כל מלאכה דכיון שבא להזהיר על מחמר ובמחמר ליכא מיתה אע"פ שבא להזהיר נמי על שאר מלאכות דשייך בהו מיתה מכל מקום יש לו ללקות כדאשכחן בבבא קמא (דף עד: ושם) דפליגי ר' יוחנן ור"א התם בעדים שהוכחשו בנפש ולבסוף הוזמו דחד אמר נהרגין וחד אמר אין נהרגין ואמרינן נמי תסתיים דר' אלעזר דאמר אין נהרגין דאמר ר"א עדים שהוכחשו בנפש לוקין ואי ס"ד ר"א דאמר נהרגין אמאי לוקין הוה ליה לאו שניתן לאזהרת מיתת ב"ד אלא ש"מ ר"א דאמר אין נהרגין תסתיים אלמא משום דאין נהרגין כשהוכחשו בתחילה לוקין ואע"ג דבעלמא ניתן לאו דלא תענה לאזהרת מיתת ב"ד היכא דהוזמו תחילה ועוד תימה לר"י דכל לאוין שבעולם שניתנו לאזהרת מיתת ב"ד יהיו לוקין עליהם כשלא התרו בהם למיתה אלא למלקות מההוא טעמא דלא ניתנו באותה שעה לאזהרת מיתת ב"ד ונראה לר"י דשאני לאו דלא תענה דגלי ביה קרא דניתן למלקות כדאשכחן גבי עדות בן גרושה כדמפקינן בריש מסכת מכות (דף ב: ושם) (ד) מוהרשיעו את הרשע והיה אם בן הכות הרשע וכיון דכתב בלא תענה מלקות בהדיא אע"ג דניתן לאזהרת מיתת ב"ד אית לן לאוקמי בכל מילי דלא מצי אתי לידי מיתה ומהאי טעמא נמי אתי שפיר הא דאמר בגמרא במכות מעידין אנו את איש פלוני שהוא חייב לחבירו מאתים זוז ונמצאו זוממים לוקין ומשלמין דברי ר' מאיר וחכמים אומרים כל המשלם אינו לוקה דקאמר בשלמא לרבנן כדי רשעתו משום רשעה אחת אתה מחייבו כו' וקשה לר"י ל"ל למימר טעמא דרבנן משום כדי רשעתו תיפוק ליה דרבנן מוקמי לא תענה לאזהרה לעדים זוממין ולא למלקות כדמוכח התם על משנת מעידים אנו את איש פלוני שחייב מלקות ארבעים וקשה לר"י נמי היכי מצי למימר לרבנן דלאזהרה דעדים זוממים הוא דאתא ולא למלקות הא בהזמה דגלות ובן גרושה מודו רבנן דאיכא מלקות ולמאי דפרישית אתי שפיר דכי היכי דלא אתי לידי מיתה או לידי מלקות ע"י כאשר זמם לוקה משום לא תענה כיון דהתם לא צריך קרא דלא תענה לאזהרה לכאשר זמם משום הכי לקי במעידים אנו בפלוני שהוא בן גרושה או שחייב גלות ואתי נמי שפיר הא דתלי טעמא דרבנן התם משום כדי רשעתו דאי לאו משום כדי רשעתו היו לוקין משום לא תענה אפי' לרבנן דאע"ג דסבירא להו דלא תענה אזהרה לכאשר זמם הוא דאתא דלא ענש כאשר זמם אלא אם כן הזהיר והוי כלאו שניתן לאזהרת מיתת ב"ד שלא נכתב למלקות אלא לאזהרת מיתה ה"מ דוקא כשחייב מלקות מכאשר זמם כגון מעידים אנו באיש פלוני שחייב מלקות אבל כשאין חייבים מכאשר זמם אלא ממון לא מבעי התם לא תענה לאזהרה דכאשר זמם הוו מודו רבנן דלוקין משום לא תענה כמו בבן גרושה וגלות אי לאו משום כדי רשעתו וא"ת למאי דפירש דאי לאו דגלי קרא בהדיא מלקות בלא תענה מוהצדיקו את הצדיק לא הוה מחייבינן ביה משום דניתן לאזהרת מיתת ב"ד אם כן הא דמפיק עולא דעדים זוממים לוקין מוהצדיקו את הצדיק בריש מכות ופריך עלה תיפוק ליה מלא תענה ומשני משום דהוה ליה לאו שאין בו מעשה אמאי לא משני משום דהוה ליה לאו שניתן לאזהרת מיתת ב"ד ותירץ דההוא שנויא לא הוה אתי אלא לרבנן דלר' מאיר איכא תרי לאוי חד לאזהרה כאשר זמם היכא דזמם מיתה או מלקות וחד למילקי עליה ולהכי ניחא טפי למימר טעמא דלאו שאין בו מעשה לאוקמא מילתא בין לרבנן בין לרבי מאיר דמתניתין דמכות אע"ג דטעמא דלאו שאין בו מעשה נמי לא אתי לר"י ולמאי דפי' איצטריך והצדיקו למלקות אפי' למאן דמחייב בלאו שאין בו מעשה ועוד היה רגיל לתרץ כיון דלא תענה סתם כתיב אכל מילי קאי ולהכי מיחייב מלקות כאילו נכתב אבן גרושה ואגלות וכאילו נכתב לא תענה שקר בממון ולבן גרושה וגלות שאז לא היה הנכתב לממון ניתן לאזהרה כאשר זמם ולכך היה ראוי ללקות עליו והכי נמי השתא אע"פ שזה לא היה ראוי ללקות על אותו הניתן לאזהרת מיתה אפי' כשאינו יכול לבא לידי מיתה עכשיו יש ללקות עליו כל זמן שלא יוכל לבא לידי מיתה הואיל ונכתב על מיתה וממון ביחד סתם וניתן להלקות עליו בהזמת מיתה נמי ניתן ללקות כל זמן שלא יוכל לבא לידי מיתה ולפי טעם זה לא היה יכול לתרץ בריש מכות משום דהוה ליה לאו שניתן לאזהרת מיתת ב"ד כי פריך ותיפוק ליה משום לא תענה דאע"פ שניתן לאזהרת מיתה יש ללקות עליו הואיל ונכתב סתם על מיתה ודברים אחרים כדפרישית ולפי לשון זה לא אתי דרשה דוהצדיקו אלא למאן דאית ליה לאו שאין בו מעשה אין לוקין עליו כדמשני בריש מכות אבל קשה דבכל הש"ס חשיב לאו דשבת ניתן לאזהרת מיתת ב"ד ואמאי הא קאי נמי אלאו דמחמר ואהבערה דאיסי (לעיל דף ו:) דליכא מיתה וי"ל כיון דכתיב כל העושה בו מלאכה יומת משמע סתם מלאכה דשבת היינו שבמיתה ולהכי לא משמע לאו דמלאכה דאיסי אבל לאו דלא תענה משמע שאר דברים שאין בהן מיתה ומלקות וכן לאו דמחמר דלא תעשה כל מלאכה אתה ובהמתך משמע אשאר חיובי שבת טפי ממחמר מדכתיב אתה כדקאמר הכא א"נ מדכתיב לא תעשה ולא כתיב לא תעשו והוצאה נמי אע"ג דנפקא מאל יצא (עירובין יז:) בהדי תחומין דבמלקות אין לוקין עליו אפי' לא התרו בו למיתה דכל סתם הוצאה דשבת איתא בקרא דויכלא העם מהביא ותירוץ ראשון ° נראה לר"י עיקר. מ"ר: והא

עין משפט נר מצוה

טז א מיי' פ"כ מהלכות שבת הלכה א:

[טז] [א] [מיי' פ"ח מהלכות סנהדרין הלכה ב]:

מסורת הש"ס

א) [ברייתא היא ועי' תוס' לעיל ו: סד"ה הא קמ"ל], ב) [יבמות מה: ע"ש], ג) [סנהדרין סו. ע"ש], ד) [עירובין יז: ב"ק עד: סנהדרין פו: מכות יג: שבועות ד.], ה) [עי' תוספות ב"מ עג: ד"ה רב].

הגהות הב"ח

(א) גמ' רבא אחוה דרב מרי בר רחל (ואמרי לה רבא אבוה דרב וכו' מרי רב מרי בר רחל הוו) תא"מ. ונ"ב ס"א אין זה. וכן רש"י ותוס' לא גרסי ליה: (ב) שם על שגגתו חטאת חייבים על זדונו סקילה: (ג) תוס' ד"ה ואמרי לה וכו' בשמעתא לאמרי לה וקשיא הא דרב אשי: (ד) ד"ה בלאו וכו' בריש מס' מכות מוהצדיקו את הצדיק והרשיעו את:

ליקוטי רש"י

בעבודת כוכבים משמעי קרא דתניא בסיפרי ר"ש אומר בעבודת כוכבים הכתוב מדבר שנא' כי דבר ה' בזה שבזה על דיבור ראשון שנאמר בו אנכי ה' אלהיך ולא יהיה לך אלהים אחרים על פני [הוריות ח.]. **הוקשה כל התורה כולה לע"ז.** כאן הוקשו כל עבירות שבתורה כשגגתן לעבודת כוכבים לענין קרבן [מכות יג:]. **המחלל את השבת.** דחשיב ליה תנא בנסקלין כגון שחללו במלאכה גמורה. **בדבר שחייבין.** כגון דבר שיש בו מעשה ומלאכת מחשבת ולא המתעסק [סנהדרין סו.]. **ואליבא דר' עקיבא.** דאמר במסכת סוטה תחומין דאורייתא ניהו דתנן בו ביום דרש רבי עקיבא ומדותם מחוץ לעיר כו' [לעיל סט.]. דיליף להו מקראי במסכת סוטה (ס:). ור' עקיבא מודה נמי בתחומים דאין חייבים עליהם כרת דתנן (שבת עג.) אבות מלאכות ארבעים חסר אחת ולא פליג ר' עקיבא [סנהדרין שם]. **והבערה אליבא דר' יוסי.** שאין חייבין עליה כרת וסקילה כשאר מלאכות אלא מה שאמור בה [לעיל ע.]. ללאו יצאת מכלל שאר המלאכות לומר לך שאין בה כרת וסקילה אלא לאו בעלמא [סנהדרין לה:]. דתניא (שבת ע.) הבערה ללאו יצאת שהיתה בכלל לא תעשה כל מלאכה חזר והוציאה מכללו ופרט בה לאו לעצמה לומר לך שאינה במיתת בית דין כשאר מלאכות אלא בלאו זה לבדו וכו' אלמא לר' יוסי לאו אב מלאכה היא [פסחים ה:]. הבערה שיצאה מכלל לא תעשה כל מלאכה (שמות כ) לשבת ללאו יצאה להוציאה מחומרי שאר מלאכות וללמד עליה שאינה לא בכרת ולא במיתה אלא בלאו [סנהדרין סב.]. [ע"כ שייך לדף קנג:].

אכשריה לרב מרי בר רחל. בת שמואל הוה ונשבית ונשאה נכרי ונתגייר ושמיה איסור גיורא ורב מרי הורתו שלא בקדושה ולידתו בקדושה ומחמת כבודו תלאוהו על שם אמו [ב"מ עג: ע"ש בתוס']. איסור גיורא שבא על רחל בת מר שמואל קודם שנתגייר ונתעברה הימנו בגיות את רב מרי בר רחל ובתוך כך נתגייר ואח"כ נולד רב מרי והוה ליה הורתו שלא בקדושה ולידתו בקדושה והיא מבנות שמואל שנשבו כדאיתא בכתובות (כג.) [רשב"ם ב"ב קמט. ע"ש בתוס']. מעובד כוכבים הבא על ישראלית הוה. **ומנייה בפורסיה דבבל.** גבאים ממונים על ישראל ואע"ג דגר בעלמא אסור למנותו פרנס על ישראל דאמר מר כו' האי כיון דאמו מישראל מקרב אחיך קרינן ביה [יבמות מה:]. **וכל לאו שניתן לאזהרת מיתת ב"ד.** לאזהרת דבר שחייבין עליו מיתת ב"ד [מכות יג:]. שלא יעשה כך שלא ימיתוהו ב"ד [ב"ק עד:]. שלא יעשה כן שמתחייב עליו מיתת בית דין. **אין לוקין עליו.** אפילו לא התרו בו למיתה והתרו בו למלקות דהשתא לא מיקטיל אפילו הכי לא לקי דלאזהרת מיתה ניתן ולא למלקות [עירובין יז:]. לא ניתן לעונש מלקות אלא שאם יעבור עליו יתרה בו המתרה שהוא בסקילה ויסקל ואם לא התרה בו סקילה והתרה בו מלקות אין דינו ללקות שלא לעונש מלקות כתבו מתחלה [שבועות ד.]. דמיתת ב"ד הוא עונשו של לאו [ב"ק שם]. ואפילו יפטרו מן המיתה שהרי לא לאזהרת מלקות ניתן [סנהדרין פו:]. כשהתרו בו מלקות בלא מיתה לפי שלא לאו זה לאזהרת עונש מלקות כשאר לאוין שהרי הוצרך להזהירו שאם לא כן לא היה יכול לחייבו מיתה [מכות שם].

רבינו חננאל

ואליבא דרבי עקיבא דסבר תחומין דאורייתא ועיקרו בסוטה פרק כשם שהמים בודקין אותו וחייב לאו כדכתי' אל יצא איש ממקומו ביום השביעי והבערה אליבא דר' יוסי דתניא הבערה ללאו יצאת דברי ר' יוסי ר' נתן אומר לחלק יצאת רב זביד מתני הכי אמר רמי בר חמא המחמר אחר בהמתו בשבת בשוגג פטור במזיד חייב סקילה ואקשי עליה רבא המחלל את השבת בדבר שחייבין על שגגתו חטאת חייבין על זדונו סקילה הא אין חייבין על שגגתו חטאת אין חייבין על זדונו סקילה ופריק ופשוטה היא. רבא אחוה דרב מרי בר רחל (אר') [ואמרי לה] כי רבא הוא אבוה דרב מרי בר רחל והוא מישראל קשיא ליה הא דרב אשי דאכשריה דכיון דאימיה מישראל מקרב אחיך קרינא ביה מכלל שלא היה אביו מישראל אלא אמו. ומפורש בפרק החולץ ליבמתו. ומפרקי' דלמא תרי רב מרי בר רחל הוו אביו מישראל וכן תירץ שמועה זו רבא אבוה דרב מרי בר רחל: **א"ר** יוחנן המחמר אחר בהמתו בשבת פטור מכלום בשוגג לא מחייב חטאת. (והוקשה) [דהוקשה] כל התורה כולה לע"ז במזיד נמי לא מחייב (חטאת) [סקילה]. דתנן בפרק ארבע מיתות נמסרו לבית דין [המחלל את השבת וכו'] ואוקימנא התם בתחומין ואליבא דר"ע בהבערה ואליבא דר' יוסי א) דתנן המחלל את השבת בדבר שחייבין על שגגתו חטאת חייבין על זדונו סקילה הא אין חייבין על שגגתו חטאת אין חייבין על זדונו סקילה לאו נמי לא מיחייב דהוי לאו שניתן לאזהרת מיתת ב"ד וכל לאו שניתן לאזהרת מיתת ב"ד אין לוקין

חשק שלמה על רבינו חננאל

א) נראה דנתחלפו השורות כאן וכן צ"ל. דתנן בפרק ד' מיתות נמסרו לב"ד המחלל את השבת בדבר שחייבין על שגגתו חטאת חייבין על זדונו סקילה. הא אין חייבין על שגגתו חטאת אין חייבין על זדונו סקילה. ואוקימנא התם בתחומין ואליבא דר"ע בהבערה אליבא דר"י לאו נמי וכו':

גליון הש"ס

תוס' ד"ה בלאו נמי וכו' בסה"ד נראה לר"י עיקר. עיין סנהדרין דף סג ע"א בתוספות ד"ה משום דהוי:

רב נסים גאון

דרבי יוסי גרסי לה בפרק כלל גדול (דף ע) הבערה ללאו יצאת דברי רבי יוסי:

קנד: מי שהחשיך פרק עשרים וארבע שבת

ואפי' למ"ד לוקין ליכתוב רחמנא לא תעשה כל מלאכה ובהמתך אתה למה לי הוא ניהו דמיחייב בהמתו לא מיחייב: הגיע לחצר החיצונה: אמר רב הונא היתה בהמתו טעונה כלי זכוכית מביא כרים וכסתות ומניח תחתיה ומתיר החבלים והשקין נופלים והאנן תנן נוטל את הכלים הניטלין בשבת כי קאמר רב הונא בקרני דאומנא דלא חזיא ליה והא קא מבטל כלי מהיכנו בשליפי זוטרי מיתיבי היתה בהמתו טעונה טבל ועששיות מתיר את החבלים והשקין נופלין ואע"פ שמשתברין התם בבולסא דיקא נמי דקתני דומיא דטבל מה טבל דלא חזי ליה אף הכא נמי לא חזי ליה ומאי אע"פ שמשתברין מהו דתימא להפסד מועט נמי חששו קמ"ל תניא ר"ש בן יוחי אומר היתה בהמתו טעונה שליף של תבואה מניח ראשו תחתיה ומסלקו לצד אחר והוא נופל מאליו חמורו של רבן גמליאל היתה טעונה דבש ולא רצה לפורקה עד מוצאי שבת למחר מתה והאנן תנן נוטל כלים הניטלין כשהדביש הדביש למאי חזי לכתיתא דגמלי ויתיר חבלים ויפלו שקין מיצטרו זיקי ויביא כרים וכסתות ויניח תחתיהן מטנפי וקמבטל כלי מהיכנו והאיכא צער בעלי חיים קסבר צער בעלי חיים דרבנן אביי אשכחיה לרבה דקא משפשף ליה לבריה אגבא דחמרא א"ל קא משתמש מר בבעלי חיים א"ל צדדין הן וצדדין לא גזרו בהו רבנן מנא תימרא דתנן מתיר (א) חבלים והשקין נופלין מאי לאו בחבר גוולקי דהוו להו צדדין וצדדין לא גזרו בהו רבנן לא בחבר אגלווקי דלא הוו צדדין אי נמי בלכתא איתיביה שתים בידי אדם ואחת באילן כשרה ואין עולין לה ביו"ט מאי לאו דחק ביה באילן דהוו להו צדדין וצדדין אסורין לא דכפייה לאילן ואנח סיכוך עילויה (ב) דקמשמש באילן א"ה אימא סיפא שלש בידי אדם ואחת באילן כשרה ועולין לה ביו"ט ואי דכפייה לאילן אמאי עולין לה ביו"ט ואלא מאי צדדין אסורין סוף סוף אמאי עולין לה בי"ט אלא התם בגוואזא פרסכנא דאילן גופיה דופן בעלמא הוא דשוויה דיקא נמי דקתני זה הכלל כל (ג) אילו שינטל האילן ויכולה לעמוד עולין לה ביו"ט ש"מ לימא כתנאי אין עולין לה ביו"ט רשב"א אומר משום ר"מ עולין לה ביו"ט מאי לאו בהא קמיפלגי דמ"ס צדדין אסורין ומר סבר מותרין אמר אביי לא דכ"ע צדדין אסורין והכא בצדי צדדין קמיפלגי מ"ס צדי צדדין אסורין ומ"ס צדי צדדין מותרין רבא אמר מאן דאסר בצדדין אסר נמי בצדי צדדין מאן דשרי בצדי צדדין שרי נמי בצדדין איתיביה רב משרשיא לרבא נעץ יתד

רש"י

ואפי' למ"ד לוקין. במסכת מכות (דף יג:) הכא אפי' לאו ליכא דאי לאזהורי אמלאכה שעל ידו וע"י בהמתו אתא כגון מחמר ליכתוב לא תעשה כל מלאכה ובהמתך מאי אתה משמע אתה לבדך ובהמתך לבדה: בהמתו. במלאכה הנעשית ע"י בהמתו לא מיחייב לאו גמור ללקות עליו: טעונה כלי זכוכית. שאין ניטלין בידו להניחן לארץ: והאנן תנן נוטל את הכלים הניטלין. וכלי זכוכית ניטלין הן ולמה לי מתיר את החבלים: דאומני. מקיז דם שאין ראויין בשבת לכלום לפי שמאוסים: והא (ד) מבטל כלי. כרים וכסתות כשמניחן תחת דבר שאין ניטל מבטלן מהיכנן דשוב לא יטלם משם ודמי לסותר: בשליפי זוטרי. משואות קטנים ששומט הכר מתחתיהם ונופלין על הכר השני וכן עד שמגיען לארץ: עששיות של זכוכית. מש"ש בלע"ז ואע"פ שהעששיות משתברין אלמא אסור להניח כרים וכסתות תחתיהן: בבולסא. חתיכות רחבות של זכוכית שאינם כלים ועושין מהן חלונות וכיון דליכא פסידא בשבירתן וסופן להחתך בחתיכות קטנות לא שרו להביא כרים ולהניח תחתיהן: [טבל לא חזי ליה. דמוקצה הוא ואפילו לכהנים לא חזי]: ומאי אף על פי שמשתברין. הא ליכא פסידא: מהו דתימא להפסד מועט נמי חששו. ויביא כרים ויניח תחתיהם דהא ודאי אי אפשר בלא הפסד מועט שנילונות ניתזין בשבירתן שאינם ראוין לכלום: שליף. משוי של תבואה של טבל: והא אנן תנן כו'. ודבש ניטל בשבת ואמאי לא רצה לפורקה: כשהדביש. החמיץ: למאי חזי. ואמאי אייתי רבן גמליאל: לכתיתא דגמלי. לכתית של גמלים לדוישדוד"א: ויתיר החבלים ויפלו שקים. דהכי תנן במתניתין בדבר שאינו ניטל ומשני מצטרו זיקי נבקעים הנודות בנפילתן לארץ: מטנפי. בדבר הנשפך עליהם וקא מבטל כלי מהיכנו דשוב אין ראוין לבו ביום לכלום: והא איכא צער בעלי חיים. וליתי לאורייתא ולידחי דרבנן ביטול כלי מהיכנו: קסבר. ר"ג צער בעלי חיים דרבנן ופלוגתא היא באלו מציאות (ב"מ לג.): דמשפשף לבריה אגבא דחמרא. בשבת לשעשע התינוק: קא משתמש מר בבעלי חיים. ותנן (ביצה דף לו:) לא רוכבין על גבי בהמה וה"ה לכל תשמיש: צדדין. שאינו מרכיבו עליו אלא משפשפו על צדי גבו ואין זה דרך תשמישו ורבנן לא גזרו בה: מאי לאו בחבר גוולקי. דהוו להו צדדין גוואלקי עשקי"ם חבר גוואלקי שתים מחוברות יחד ברצועות ומרכיבין על החמור זו מכאן וזו מכאן וצריך לסלקן יחד וליקרב אצל החמור ומשפשף עצמו ונשען גופו בצדי החמור: בחבר אגלווקי. שתים שאין מחוברות יחד אלא על ידי טבעת מתכת שבראש הרצועה וכו מסמר קטן כעין שעושין לחבק שקורין ליגגל"א שאינו צריך אלא למשוך מעט והמסמר יוצא והן מתנתקות זו מזו: אי נמי בלכתא. כעין שעושין לדרדור יין שיש בהן טבעות של חבל לכל אחד ואחד ומכניס טבעת בטבעת ונוטל עץ כפוף קטן ומכניסו בפנימי ושוב אינו יוצא מחברו וכשבא לסלקו מושך העץ אליו והן מתנתקין זה מזה ונופלין: שתים בידי אדם ואחת באילן. גבי סוכה תנן שכשירה בג' דפנות ואם עשה שתים כהלכתן והשלישי עשה באילן כשירה. דפנות לא איכפת לן אם מחוברות הם וה"ה אם כולן נקבעות באילן והא דנקט שתים בידי אדם רבותא אשמועינן דאפילו הכי אין עולין לה לאכול ולישן באותה סוכה בי"ט מפני שסככה קשור בדופניה ונשען עליה והוא משתמש על סככה ונותן כליו ונמצא משתמש באילן. כל כניסה דסוכה נקיט בלשון עלייה במסכת סוכה לפי שרובן עושין סוכותיהן בראש גגן דבכמה דוכתין תנן בה הכי אין מטריחין אותו לעלות אמר להם העלוס לסוכה אבל מוריד הוא את הכלים וכן הרבה: מאי לאו דחק ביה באילן. ואותיב ביה קנים של דפנות בנקבים שנקב הרבה בגופו של אילן וסיכך שוב על אותן דפנות ומ"מ אין כאן תשמיש אלא בצדי אילן: דכפייה לאילן. לענפיו העליונים הטה לצד אילן אחר וכן של זה לזה וקשרן אלו עם אלו ומהן נעשה הדופן: אמאי עולין לה בי"ט. הרי הסכך נשען עליו והוא משתמש בו: ה"ג אלא מאי צדדין אסורין סוף סוף אמאי עולין לה בי"ט אלא התם בגוואזא פרסכנא שאילן גופיה דופן בעלמא שווייה. גוואזא פרסכנא אילן שענפיו הרבה יוצאין מלדדין ומתפשטין לכאן ולכאן ושוינהו דופן בעלמא לסוכה ולא סמך הסכך עליהן ולהכי נקט גוואזא פרסכנא ולא שבקיה כדקא ס"ד בדכפייה וליתני כגון דלא סמך הסכך עליה משום דכיון דדופן רביעי הוא שאינו צריך לסוכה דהא בג' כשירה כשסמך נמי לא סמך עליה לא טרח למעבד לו דופן להכי אוקמא בגוואזא פרסכנא וממילא הוא בלא טרחא: מאי לאו בהא קמיפלגי כו'. וכגון דחק באילן ומותיב קנים בצדדין וסיכך עליהן דהוה ליה משתמש בצדדין כשמשתמשין על ידי סככה דלאו כ"ע פליגי במאי מוקמא פלוגתייהו דהא כולי עלמא סברי אסור להשתמש באילן: אמר אביי. א"נ בהכי פליגי ליכא למימר דסבירא ליה (לת"ק) לצדדין מותרין הכי לאו לצדדין ניהו אלא לצדי צדדים שהקנים התחובים בנקבים לצדדין והסיכוך הנתון על גבן לצדי צדדים פליגי: יתד

תוספות

והא מבטל כלי מהיכנו. פירשנו למעלה בפרק כירה (דף מג.): שתים בידי אדם ואחת באילן. בסוכה בפ"ב (דף כב:) (ושם) תנן העושה סוכתו בראש האילן יש לפרש בשני ענינים העושה סוכתו בראש האילן כגון שהסכך של סוכה על גבי האילן והאילן סומך אותה שאין יכול לעלות על אותו סכך אלא אם כן ישתמש באילן שרגילין היו לתת כליהן על הסכך א"נ יש לפרש שהתקרה סמוכה באילן שבנאה בגובה ותחתיה על האילן להשתא כל שעה שהוא מהלך בסוכה משתמש באילן: בחיבור גוולקי. שני שקין אחד בימין החמור ואחד משמאלו ובראש כל אחד מן השקין רצועה אחת וקושרין אותן שתי הרצועות יחד ועכשיו מונח הקשר כנגד גבו של החמור והשקין מכבידין לכאן ולכאן ואי אפשר להתיר הקשר אם לא יגביהו השקין מעט ונסמכין שתי השקין בכריסו של החמור והוו להו כלדדים: למטה

עין משפט נר מצוה

יז א ב ג מיי' פכ"א מהלכות שבת הלכה י סמג לאוין סה טוש"ע א"ח סי' רסו סעיף ט:
יח ד ה מיי' שם טוש"ע שם וסימן שה סעיף יח:
יט ו מיי' פ"ד מהלכות סוכה הלכה ה טוש"ע א"ח סי' תרכח סעיף ג:

תורה אור השלם

א) וְיוֹם הַשְּׁבִיעִי שַׁבָּת לַייָ אֱלֹהֶיךָ לֹא תַעֲשֶׂה כָל מְלָאכָה אַתָּה וּבִנְךָ וּבִתֶּךָ עַבְדְּךָ וַאֲמָתְךָ וּבְהֶמְתֶּךָ וְגֵרְךָ אֲשֶׁר בִּשְׁעָרֶיךָ: [שמות כ, י]

רבינו חננאל

עליו ואפי' למאן דאמר לוקין א"כ לכתוב קרא לא תעשה כל מלאכה ובהמתך אתה למה לי אלא לומר לך כל מלאכה ניהו דכי עביד מיחייב בבהמתו לא מיחייב. והלכתא כר' יוחנן דהא דרמי ליתא דרבא אהדר עליה ופריך לטעמיה. ואע"ג דפריק לנפשיה לא שבקינן דברי רבא וסמכינן אשנוייה: הגיע לחצר החיצונה כו'. אמר רב הונא היתה בהמתו טעונה כלי זכוכית מביא כרים וכסתות ומניח תחתיה ומתיר הכלים והשקין נופלים ואקשינן עלה והתנן נוטל את הכלים הניטלין בשבת וכלי זכוכית ניטלין בשבת ולמה אין ניטלין בפני עצמן. ופריק רב הונא מי סברת הא דאמרי' היתה [בהמתו] טעונה כלי זכוכי' בכוסות ואשישות קאמינא דשרי לטלטלן בשבת קאמר בקרני (דאוני) [דאומנא] קאמינא שמוצצין בהן הדם שאסור לטלטלן ולמה אסור לטלטלן והא קיי"ל דדבר שמלאכתו לאיסור אפי' לצורך גופו ומקומו שרי. תוב אקשי' עליה הא אמרת מביא כרים וכסתות ומניח תחת משאוי הבהמה כדי שיפלו כלי זכוכית הללו על דבר רך שלא ישברו והלא אסור להשתמש באותן הכרים והכסתות כל זמן שאלו כלי זכוכית עליהן ואינו יכול ליטול בהם והנה מבטל כלי מהיכנו ופריק רב אשי בשליפי זוטרי. פי' שמנער את הכר או את הכסת מעט מעט והן נופלות כי הא דתנן מנער את הכר והן נופלות. ואקשינן עליה היתה בהמתו טעונה עששיות מתיר חבלים והשקין נופלים. ואע"פ שמשתברין ופריק רב הונא אלו העששיות אינן כלי זכוכית עשוין אלא פולסא פי' חתיכות גדולות כדכתיב ברזל עשות ורוצה להכניסם לכור לעשות מהן כלי זכוכית והלכתא כרב הונא דאע"ג דאיתותב הא שני לה ושנוייא שינויין אינון דהא מתרץ לה מאן דמוקמה ואמרינן דיקא נמי דקתני דומיא דטבל מה טבל לא חזי ליה אף הכא אלא אחר שיתקן אף האי נמי לא חזי ליה. והא דתניא רבי שמעון בן יוחי אומר היתה בהמתו טעונה שליף של תבואה מכניס ראשו תחתיו ומסלקו לצד אחר הלכתא כוותיה שאינו מפרק אלא מכבידו לצד אחר ונופל מעצמו:

מסורת הש"ס

א) [עמ"ש תוס' לעיל מג: ד"ה כבר], ב) [עי' תוס' ב"ק טו. ד"ה טבלא], ג) [פסחים טו: כ: נה. ביצה לו. ב"ק קז. ב"מ לב:], ד) [עי' רש"י ב"מ לב. ד"ה הדביק ופרש"י סנהדרין קח. ד"ה מדבים], ה) [לעיל מג. וש"נ], ו) [ב"מ לב: וש"נ], ז) [פי' שקים ערוך ופי' בערך חבר פי' בארוכות], ח) סוכה כב:, ט) [עירובין לג.], י) [תוספתא סוכה פ"א], כ) [ברייתא סוכה כב.], ל) [שם כו:], מ) [סוכה מה.], נ) [צ"ל כר' מאיר וכ"ה גורסין לדדים והקנים הנתונים בנקבים לדדי לדדים וגי' שלפנינו עיקר רש"ל], ס) [עי' שייך אחר ד"ה כתבתי].

הגהות הב"ח

(א) גמ' ומנא תימרא דתנן מתיר החבלים: (ב) שם דקמשתמש באילן: (ג) שם זה הכלל כל שאילו יטול: (ד) רש"י ד"ה והא קא מבטל כלי מהיכנו כרים:

רב נסים גאון

ואפי' למאן דאמר לוקין. כלו' שר' יוחנן סבר כי לאו שניתן לאזהרת [מיתת] ב"ד לוקין עליו ור"ל סבר לאו שניתן לאזהרת [מיתת] ב"ד אין לוקין עליו: והא קא מבטל כלי מהיכנו. כבר פירשנו בפ' מפנין שעיקרו בפרק

ליקוטי רש"י

בקרני דאומנא. מקיז דם בקרן כמלנא [מכות טז:]. והא קא מבטל כלי מהיכנו. שהיה מוכן מתחלה לטלטלו ועכשיו עושהו מוקצה [לעיל מג.]. עששיות. חתיכות עבות [יומא לד:]. שליף. [illegible]

וַאֲפִילּוּ לְמַאן דְּאָמַר לוֹקִין – **And even according to the one who says** that such a prohibition **does carry the penalty of lashes,**[1] leading a loaded animal does not. לִיכְתּוֹב רַחֲמָנָא – For were the Torah's intent in this prohibition simply to forbid leading a loaded animal (or, in general, causing an animal to perform a *melachah*) then **the Merciful One should have written,** לֹא תַעֲשֶׂה כָל מְלָאכָה וּבְהֶמְתֶּךָ – **Do not do any *melachah,* and your animal,** which we would understand to mean: *with* your animal. ,,אַתָּה" לָמָּה לִי – **Why** then **do I need** the word ***you,*** as the verse says: *you and your animal*? This extra word serves to divide the verse and teach the following: הוּא נִיהוּ דְּמִיחַיֵּיב – **It is he who,** if he performs a *melachah,* **is liable** on that account; בְּהֶמְתּוֹ לֹא מִיחַיֵּיב – but as for the actions of **his animal,** although he is responsible for them, **he is not liable** for them.[2]

The Gemara cites the next line of the Mishnah:

הִגִּיעַ לֶחָצֵר הַחִיצוֹנָה – **WHEN HE REACHES THE OUTERMOST COURTYARD** of the city, and commences to unload the donkey, he may take off any utensils that may normally be moved on the Sabbath. However, those utensils that may not be moved on the Sabbath, because they are *muktzeh,* he may not move himself; instead he undoes the ropes that hold them fastened to the saddle, and the sacks fall down on their own.

The Gemara cites a ruling that elaborates on the proper procedure in unloading *muktzeh* utensils from an animal on the Sabbath:

אָמַר רַב הוּנָא – **Rav Huna said:** הָיְתָה בְּהֶמְתּוֹ טְעוּנָה כְּלֵי זְכוּכִית – **If his animal was loaded with glass utensils,** מֵבִיא כָּרִים וּכְסָתוֹת וּמַנִּיחַ תַּחְתֶּיהָ – **he may bring pillows and cushions, place them underneath [the animal]** וּמַתִּיר הַחֲבָלִים וְהַשַּׂקִּין נוֹפְלִים – **and** then **loosen the ropes so that the sacks fall** upon them.[3]

The Gemara questions the need for this procedure:

וְהָאֲנַן תְּנַן – **But we learned in the Mishnah:** נוֹטֵל אֶת הַכֵּלִים הַנִּיטָּלִין בְּשַׁבָּת – **HE MAY TAKE** off **ANY UTENSILS THAT MAY** normally **BE MOVED ON THE SABBATH.** Now, glass utensils are typically not *muktzeh;* why then does Rav Huna require that they be removed by loosening the ropes?

The Gemara explains:

כִּי קָאָמַר רַב הוּנָא בְּקַרְנֵי דְּאוּמָּנָא – **Rav Huna stated** his ruling **in reference to** used glass **pipettes of a bloodletter,**[4] דְּלָא חֲזוּ לֵיהּ – **which are useless** on the Sabbath and therefore *muktzeh.*[5] These types of utensils may not be handled directly and may be unloaded only by loosening the ropes and allowing them to drop by themselves.

The Gemara objects to Rav Huna's ruling that he may cushion the fall of these *muktzeh* utensils:

וְהָא קָא מְבַטֵּל כְּלִי מֵהֵיכָנוֹ – **But** by allowing the pipettes to fall on pillows and cushions **he** will be **nullifying the preparedness of a utensil!**[6] – ? –

The Gemara resolves the difficulty:

בִּשְׁלִיפֵי זוּטְרֵי – Rav Huna is referring **to small sacks** of pipettes. Because of their small size, these sacks can be rolled off the pillows and cushions on the Sabbath without being handled directly.[7] Thus, the pillows and cushions need not be immobilized for the entire Sabbath, and the prohibition against *nullifying the preparedness of a utensil* does not apply.[8]

The Gemara cites a Baraisa that seems to be at odds with Rav Huna's ruling:

מֵיתִיבֵי – **They challenged it** from the following Baraisa: הָיְתָה בְּהֶמְתּוֹ טְעוּנָה טֶבֶל וְעֶשְׁשִׁיּוֹת – **IF HIS ANIMAL WAS LOADED WITH** sacks of **UNTITHED PRODUCE AND GLASS BARS,** מַתִּיר אֶת הַחֲבָלִים וְהַשַּׂקִּין נוֹפְלִין – **HE MUST LOOSEN THE ROPES AND LET THE SACKS FALL** to the ground, וְאַף עַל פִּי שֶׁמִּשְׁתַּבְּרִין – **EVEN THOUGH [THE GLASS BARS] WILL BREAK** by his doing so.[9] But according to Rav

NOTES

1. [The Gemara in *Makkos* (13b) records a view that one can incur the penalty of lashes even for a prohibition that serves as a warning for a court-imposed execution.]

2. Had the Torah simply intended to prohibit leading an animal to perform a *melachah* it would have sufficed to state: *Do not do a melachah, and your animal.* The seemingly superfluous word *"you"* indicates that the verse is actually referring to two separate cases: *"You"* refers to a person performing a *melachah* himself, while *"your animal"* refers to an animal that is led to perform a *melachah.* By distinguishing between these two cases, the Torah implies that there is a difference between them: Performing *melachah* oneself is a full-fledged prohibition which carries the normal penalty of lashes; having an animal perform a *melachah* is a lesser prohibition, for which there is no corporal punishment (see *Rashi*; *Ritva MHK* ed.).

Ramban (154a and in a gloss to *Sefer HaMitzvos, Shoresh* 14) explains further that the Torah, by distinguishing between a *melachah* that one performs oneself and a *melachah* that an animal is led to perform, is indicating that the essential forbidden act in the latter case is not the action of the person leading the animal but, rather, the animal performing the *melachah* (for which the Torah holds the person responsible, being that he led the animal to do it). And it is axiomatic that one can incur lashes only for an act that one performs oneself.

3. [As the Gemara will soon make clear,] Rav Huna is speaking of glass utensils that are *muktzeh* (*Rashi*; see *Ramban*). [As to what Rav Huna might be teaching us by this, see above, 43b *Tosafos* ד״ה כבר, and *Milchamos* here.]

4. [It was the custom in earlier times to visit a bloodletter periodically (for reasons of health). The bloodletter made an incision in his client and collected the blood with a glass pipette.]

5. Once the pipettes are used for bloodletting they are too repulsive to use for any other purpose [and are therefore *muktzeh*] (*Rashi*).

[Apparently Rav Huna subscribes to the view that accepts the concept of *muktzeh by dint of repulsiveness* (see below, 157a note 19). Alternatively, these pipettes are so completely repulsive that they are deemed *muktzeh* according to all views (*Ramban*; see also *Rashba* and *Ran MHK* ed.; see *Ritva MHK* ed. for an alternative explanation).]

6. Once the pipettes fall, the pillows and cushions will be immobilized for the remainder of the Sabbath, since one will be not be able to move them with the *muktzeh* pipettes lying on them, nor will one be able to take the pipettes off until after the Sabbath. Immobilizing a utensil in this fashion is called בִּטּוּל כְּלִי מֵהֵיכָנוֹ, *nullifying the preparedness of a utensil,* i.e. nullifying its non-*muktzeh* state and making it unavailable for movement and use. The Rabbis considered this similar to destroying a vessel [which is itself similar to a violation of the *melachah* of סותר, *destroying*] and they therefore prohibited it (*Rashi* here and to 128b ד״ה והא קמבטל כלי מהיכנו). [*Tosafos* (43a ד״ה דמבטל) point out that *Rashi* elsewhere (42b ד״ה כלי תחת הנר) compares immobilizing a utensil to cementing a utensil in place, which is a violation of the *melachah* of בונה, *building.* For a resolution of this apparent contradiction, see *Pnei Yehoshua* to *Tosafos* (loc. cit.); *Chasam Sofer,* Introduction to *Beitzah* ד״ה בימי; *Toras Refael, Hil. Shabbos* §19. See also *Mishbetzos Zahav* 265:1.]

7. This can be done by having the sacks fall on a pile of cushions: After a sack falls on the top cushion, the cushion is slid out from beneath it and the sack falls onto the next cushion. This continues until the sack falls gently on the ground (*Rashi*). Since the sacks are not handled directly, this is permissible.

[Regarding whether the pillows and cushions should be considered a *base to muktzeh* and, if so, how they can be pulled out from under the sacks, see *Ran and Ritva MHK* eds.; *Magen Avraham* 265:2; *Hagahos R' Akiva Eiger* ad loc. and to our Mishnah §179. See also *Rashi* to 51a ד״ה הרי זה נוטל ומחזיר.]

8. This prohibition applies only where the utensil will be immobilized for the entire Sabbath (see *Rashi* ד״ה מטנפי; *Rashi* to 47b ד״ה והא קא מבטל כלי מהיכנו; see *Tosafos* above, 43b ד״ה כבר; cf. *Ramban, Rashba* et al, here).

9. [He cannot unload the sacks directly, since they contain untithed produce, which is *muktzeh* (see *Rashi* below ד״ה טבל לא חזי ליה; *Tosafos* 43a ד״ה טבל). Nor can he simply leave them on the animal for the duration of the Sabbath, since it is forbidden to cause an animal suffering, as

יז א ב ג מיי' פכ"א מהלכות שבת הלכה י סמג לאוין סה טוש"ע א"ח סי' רסו סעיף ט:
יח ד ה מיי' שם טוש"ע שם וסימן שה סעיף יח:
יט ו מיי' פ"ד מהלכות סוכה הלכה ו טוש"ע א"ח סי' תרכח סעיף ג:

תורה אור השלם

א) וְיוֹם הַשְּׁבִיעִי שַׁבָּת לַיי אֱלֹהֶיךָ לֹא תַעֲשֶׂה כָל מְלָאכָה אַתָּה וּבִנְךָ וּבִתֶּךָ עַבְדְּךָ וַאֲמָתְךָ וּבְהֶמְתֶּךָ וְגֵרְךָ אֲשֶׁר בִּשְׁעָרֶיךָ: [שמות כ, י]

רבינו חננאל

עליו ואפי' למאן דאמר לוקין א"כ לכתוב קרא לא תעשה כל מלאכה ובהמתך אתה למה לי אלא לומר לך כל מלאכה ניהו דכי עביד מיחייב בבהמתו לא מיחייב. והלכתא כר' יוחנן דהא דרמי ליתא דרבא אהדר עליה ופריק לטעמיה. ואע"ג דפריק לנפשיה לא שבקינן דברי רבא וסמכינן אשנוייה: הגיע לחצר החיצונה נוטל הכלים וכו'. אמר רב הונא היתה בהמתו טעונה כלי זכוכית מביא כרים וכסתות ומתיר הכלים והשקין נופלים ואקשינן עלה והתנן נוטל את הכלים הניטלין בשבת וכלי זכוכית ניטלין בשבת ולמה אין ניטלין בפני עצמן. ופריק רב הונא מי סברת הא דאמרי' היתה [בהמתו] טעונה כלי זכוכי' בכוסות ואשישות קאמינא דשרי לטלטלן בשבת קאמר קרני [דאוני] [דאומנא] קאמינא שמוצצין בהן הדם שאסור לטלטלן ולמה אסור לטלטלו והא קיי"ל דבר שמלאכתו לאיסור אפי' לצורך גופו ומקומו שרי. תוב אקשי' עליה הא אמרת מביא כרים וכסתות ומניח תחת הבהמה כדי שיפלו כלי זכוכית עליהן על דבר רך שלא ישברו והלא אסור להשתמש באותן הכרים והכסתות כל זמן שאלו כלי זכוכית עליהן ואינו יכול לישן בהם והנה מבטל כלי מהיכנו ופריק רב אשי בשליפי זוטרי. פי' שמנער את הכר או את הכסת מעט והן נופלות כי הא דתנן מצות שעל הכר מנער את הכר והן נופלות. ואקשינן עליה היתה בהמתו טעונה עששיות מתיר חבלים והשקין נופלים. ואע"פ שמשתברין ופריק רב הונא אלו העששיות אינן כלי זכוכית עשוין אלא פולסא פי' חתיכות גדולות כדכתיב ברזל עשות ורוצה להכניסם לכור לעשות מהן כלי זכוכית והלכתא כרב הונא דאע"ג דאיתותב הא שני לה ושנוייא שינויין אינון דהא מתרץ לה מאן דמותבה ואמרינן דיקא נמי דקתני דומיא דטבל מה טבל דלא חזו ליה פי' אלא אחר שיתקנן אף האי נמי לא חזי ליה. והא דתניא רבי שמעון בן יוחי אומר היתה בהמתו טעונה שליף של תבואה מכניס ראשו תחתיו ומסלקו לצד אחר הלכתא כוותיה שאינו מפרק אלא מכבידו

א) [עמ"ש תוס' לעיל מג: ד"ה ככר], ב) [עי' תוס' שם. ד"ה טלטל], ג) [פסחים עו: ג: נה. ביצה לו. ב"ק קיז. ב"מ לב:], ד) [עי' רש"י ב"מ לח. ד"ה הדביש ובפרש"י סנהדרין קח. ד"ה מדביש], ה) [לעיל מג. וש"נ], ו) [ב"מ לב: וש"נ], ז) [פי' שקים ערוך ועי' בערוך סבר פי' באריכות], ח) סוכה כב:, ט) [עירובין לג:], י) [תוספתא סוכה פ"א], כ) [כריתות סוכה כב.], ל) [שם טו:], מ) [סוכה מג.], נ) [צ"ל ר' מאיר] וכן גורסין ברי"ף ורא"ש, ס) מ"ש מסגוע בנקבים והקנים הנתונים בנקבים לצדי צדדים וגו' שלפנינו עיקר רש"ל, ע) שייך אחר ד"ה כחיכו.

הגהות הב"ח

(א) גמ' ומנא תימרא דתנן מתיר החבלים: (ב) שם דקמשתמש באילן: (ג) שם זה הכלל כל שאילו יטול האילן: (ד) רש"י ד"ה והא קא מבטל כלי מהיכנו כרים.

רב נסים גאון

ואפי' למאן דאמר לוקין. כלו' ר' ישמעאל סבר כי לאו שניתן לאזהרת [מיתת] ב"ד לוקין עליו ור"ע סבר לאו שניתן לאזהרת [מיתת] ב"ד אין לוקין עליו: והא קא מבטל כלי מהיכנו. כבר פירשנו בפ' מפנין שעיקרו בפרק

ליקוטי רש"י

בקרני דאומנא. מקיזי דם שקרן כמלוגה [מכות טז:]. והא קא מבטל כלי מהיכנו. שהיה מוכן מתחלה לטלטלו ועכשיו עושהו מוקצה [לעיל מג. ע"ש בתוס' ובפנ"י]. דדומה לסותר בנין מלרכנן [שם קכח:]. אסור לבטל כלי מהיכנו להושיב כלי במקום שלא יוכל עוד ליטלו

ואפי' למ"ד לוקין ליכתוב רחמנא לא תעשה כל מלאכה ובהמתך א אתה למה לי הוא ניהו דמיחייב בהמתו לא מיחייב: הגיע לחצר החיצונה: אמר א רב הונא היתה בהמתו טעונה כלי זכוכית מביא כרים וכסתות ומניח תחתיה ומתיר החבלים והשקין נופלים והאנן תנן נוטל את הכלים הניטלין בשבת ב כי קאמר רב הונא בקרני דאומנא דלא חזיא ליה והא קא מבטל כלי מהיכנו ב בשליפי זוטרי מיתיבי היתה בהמתו טעונה ג טבל ועששיות מתיר את החבלים והשקין נופלין ואע"פ שמשתברין התם בכולסא דיקא נמי דקתני דומיא דטבל מה טבל דלא חזי ליה אף הכא נמי לא חזי ליה ומאי אע"פ שמשתברין ג מהו דתימא ג להפסד מועט נמי חששו קמ"ל תניא ר"ש בן יוחי אומר ד היתה בהמתו טעונה שליף של תבואה מניח ראשו תחתיה ומסלקו לצד אחר והוא נופל מאליו חמורו של רבן גמליאל היתה טעונה דבש ולא רצה לפורקה עד מוצאי שבת למוצאי שבת מתה והאנן תנן נוטל כלים הניטלין כשהדביש ד הדביש למאי חזי לכתיתא דגמלי ויתיר חבלים ויפלו שקין מיצטרו זיקי ויביא כרים וכסתות ויניח תחתיהן מטנפי ו וקמבטל כלי מהיכנו ה והאיכא צער בעלי חיים קסבר י צער בעלי חיים דרבנן אביי אשכחיה לרבה דקא משפשף ליה לבריה אגבא דחמרא א"ל קא משתמש מר בבעלי חיים א"ל צדדין הן וצדדין לא גזרו בהו רבנן מנא תימרא דתנן מתיר (א) חבלים והשקין נופלין מאי לאו בחבר ז גוולקי דהוו להו צדדין וצדדין לא גזרו בהו רבנן לא בחבר אגלווקי דלא הוו צדדין אי נמי בלכתא איתיביה ח שתים בידי אדם ואחת באילן כשרה ואין עולין לה ביו"ט מאי לאו דחק ביה באילן דהוו להו צדדין ט וצדדין אסורין לא דכפייה לאילן ואנח סיכוך עילויה (ב) דקמשמש באילן א"ה אימא סיפא שלש בידי אדם ואחת באילן כשרה ועולין לה ביו"ט ואי דכפייה לאילן אמאי עולין לה ביו"ט ואלא מאי צדדין אסורין סוף סוף אמאי עולין לה בי"ט אלא התם בגוואזא פרסכנא דאילן גופיה דופן בעלמא הוא דשוויה דיקא נמי דקתני זה הכלל כל (ג) אילו שינטל האילן ויכולה לעמוד עולין לה ביו"ט ש"מ לימא כתנאי אין עולין לה ביו"ט י רשב"א אומר משום ר"מ עולין לה ביו"ט מאי לאו בהא קמיפלגי דמ"ס צדדין אסורין ומר סבר מותרין אמר אביי לא דכ"ע צדדין אסורין והכא בצדי צדדין קמיפלגי מ"ס צדי צדדין אסורין ומ"ס צדי צדדין מותרין רבא אמר מאן דאסר בצדדין אסר נמי בצדי צדדין מאן דשרי בצדי צדדין שרי נמי בצדדין איתיביה רב משרשיא לרבא נעץ יתד

והא מבטל כלי מהיכנו. פירשנו למעלה בפרק כירה (דף מג.): **שתים** בידי אדם ואחת באילן. בסוכה בפ"ב (דף כב: ושם) תנן העושה סוכתו בראש האילן יש לפרש בשני עניינים העושה סוכתו בראש האילן כגון שהסכך של סוכה על גבי האילן והאילן סומך אותה שאין יכול לעלות על אותו סכך אלא אם כן ישתמש באילן שרגילין היו לתת כליהן על הסכך א"נ יש לפרש שהסוכה סמוכה באילן שבנויה בגובה ומתחיה על האילן דהשתא כל שעה שהוא מהלך בסוכה משתמש באילן: **בחיבור** גוולקי. שני שקין אחד בימין החמור ואחד משמאלו ובראש כל אחד מן השקין רצועה אחת וקושרין אותן שתי הרצועות יחד ועכשיו מונח הקשר כנגד גבו של החמור והשקין מכבידין לכאן ולכאן ולא אפשר להתיר הקשר אם לא יגביהו השקין מעט ונסמכין שתי השקין בכרים של החמור והוו להו כצדדים: למטה

ואפי' למ"ד דלוקין (דף יג:) הכא אפי' לאו ליכא דלאו להזהיר אמלאכה שעל ידו וע"י בהמתו אתא כגון מחמר דלכתוב לא תעשה כל מלאכה והמתך מאי אתה משמע אתה לבדך ובהמתך לבדה: בהמתו. במלאכה הנעשית ע"י בהמתו לא מיחייב לאו גמור ללקות עליו: **טעונה כלי זכוכית.** שאין ניטלין בידו להניחן לארץ: **והאנן תנן נוטל את הכלים הניטלין.** וכלי זכוכית ניטלין הן ולמה לי מתיר את החבלים: **דאומני.** מקיז דם שאין ראוין בשבת לכלום לפי שמאוסים: **והא** (ד) **מבטל כלי.** כרים וכסתות כשמניחן תחת דבר שאין ניטל מבטלן מהיכנו דשוב לא יטלם משם ודמי לסותר: **בשליפי זוטרי.** משפופות קטנים שסותם הכר מתמחים ונופלין על הכר השני וכן עד שמגיען לארץ: **עששיות של זכוכית.** מס"ס בלע"ז ואע"פ שהעששיות משתברין אלמא אסור להניח כרים וכסתות תחתיהן: **בכולסא.** חתיכות רחבות של זכוכית שאינם כלים ועושין מהן חלונות וכיון דליכא פסידא בשבירתן וסופן להחתך בחתיכות קטנות לא שרו להביא כרים ולהניח תחתיהן: [**טבל לא חזי ליה.** דמוקצה הוא ואפילו לכהנים לא חזי]: **ומאי אף על פי שמשתברין.** הא ליכא פסידא: **מהו דתימא להפסד מועט נמי חששו.** ויביא כרים ויניח תחתיהם דהא ודאי אי אפשר בלא הפסד מועט שנילולות ניתזין בשבירתן שאינם ראוין לכלום: **שליף.** משוי של תבואה של טבל: **והא אנן תנן כו'.** ודבש ניטל בשבת ואמאי לא רצה לפורקה: **כשהדביש.** החמיץ: **למאי חזי.** ואמאי אייתי רבן גמליאל: **לכתיתא דגמלי.** לכתית של גמלים רדויישדוד"א: **ויתיר החבלים ויפלו שקים.** דהכי תנן במתניתין בדבר שאינו ניטל ומשני מנטרו זיקי נבקעים הנודות בנפילתן לארץ: **מטנפי.** בדבר הנשפך עליהם וקא מבטל כלי מהיכנו דשוב אין ראוין לבו ביום לכלום: **והא איכא צער בעלי חיים.** וליתי דאורייתא ולידחי דרבנן ביטול כלי מהיכנו: **קסבר.** ר"ג צער בעלי חיים דרבנן ופלוגתא היא באלו מציאות (ב"מ לב:): **דמשפשף לבריה אגבא דחמרא.** בשבת לשעשע התינוק: **קא משתמש מר בבעלי חיים.** ותנן (ביצה דף לו:) לא רוכבין על גבי בהמה וה"ה לכל תשמיש: **צדדין.** שאינו מרכיבו עליו אלא משפשפו על צדי גבו ואין זה דרך תשמישו ורבנן לא גזרו בה: **מאי לאו בחבר גוולקי.** דהוו להו צדדין גוואלקי עשקנ"ם חבר גוואלקי שתים מחוברות יחד ברצועות ומרכיבין על החמור זו מכאן וזו מכאן וצריך לסלקן יחד וליקרב אצל החמור ומשפשף עצמו ונשען גופו בצדי החמור: **בחבר אגלווקי.** שתים שאין מחוברות יחד אלא על ידי טבעת מתכת שבראש הרצועה ובו מסמר קטן כעין שעושין לחבק שקורין ציגגל"א וא"צ אלא למשוך מעט והמסמר יוצא והן מתנתקות זו מזו: **אי נמי בלכתא.** כעין שעושין לדרדור יין שיש בהן טבעות של מתכת לכל אחד ואחד ומכניס טבעת בטבעת ונוטל עץ כפוף קטן ומכניסו בפנימי ושוב אינו יוצא מחברו וכשבא לסלקו מושך העץ אליו והן מתנתקין זה מזה ונופלין: **שתים בידי אדם ואחת באילן.** גבי סוכה תנן שכשירה בג' דפנות ואם עשה שתים כהלכתן והשלישי עשה באילן כשירה. דפנות לא איכפת לן אם מחוברות הם וה"ה אם כולן נקבעות באילן והא דנקט שתים בידי אדם רבותא אשמועינן דאפילו הכי אין עולין לה לאכול ולישן באותה סוכה בי"ט מפני שסככה קשור בדופניה ונשען עליה והוא משתמש על סככה ונותן כליו ונמצא משתמש באילן. כל כניסה דסוכה נקיט בלשון עלייה במסכת סוכה לפי שרובן עושין סוכותיהן בראש גגן דבחמה דוכתין תנן בה הכי כ אין מטריחין אותו לעלות ל אמר להם העלוס לסוכה מ אבל מוריד הוא את הכלים וכן הרבה: **מאי לאו דחק ביה באילן.** ואותיב ביה קנים של דפנות בנקבים שנקב הרבה בגופו של אילן וסיכך שוב על אותן דפנות ומ"מ אין כאן תשמיש אלא בצדדי אילן: **דכפייה לאילן.** לענפי העליונים הטה לצד אילן אחר וכן של זה לזה וקשרן אלו עם אלו ומהן נעשה הדופן: **אמאי עולין לה בי"ט.** הרי הסכך נשען עליו והוא משתמש בו: **ה"ג אלא מאי צדדין אסורין סוף סוף אמאי עולין לה בי"ט אלא התם בגוואזא פרסכנא שאילן גופיה דופן בעלמא שוויה.** גוואזא פרסכנא אילן שענפים הרבה יוצאין מלדדין ומתפשטין לכאן ולכאן ושויהו דופן בעלמא לסוכה ולא סמך הסכך עליהן ולהכי נקט גוואזא פרסכנא ולא שבקיה דקדק מ"ד דכפייה ולישני כגון דלא סמך הסכך עליה משום דכיון דדופן רביעי הוא שאינו צריך לסוכה דהא בג' כשירה והסכך נמי לא סמך עליה לא טרח למעבד לו דופן להכי אוקמא בגוואזא פרסכנא וממילא הוא בלא טרחא: **מאי לאו בהא קמיפלגי כו'.** וכגון דחק באילן ומותיב קנים בצדדין וסיכך עליהן דהוה ליה משתמש בצדדין כשמשתמשין על ידי סככה דאי לאו בהא פליגי במאי מוקמא פלוגתייהו דהא כולי עלמא סברי אסור להשתמש באילן: **אמר אביי.** א"נ בהכי פליגי ליכא למימר דסבירא ליה (לת"ק) לצדדין מותרין דהכי לאו לצדדין ניתנו אלא לצדי צדדין ס שהקנים הנתונים בנקבים צדדין והסיכוך הנתון על גבן צדי צדדים ולצדי צדדים פליגי: יתד

צער בעלי חיים. לער בעלי חיים דאורייתא שנאמר עזוב תעזוב עמו ואיכא מאן דאמר לאו דאורייתא

ובאנו להקשות ממשנתנו דאדרבן גמליאל שהיתה חמורו טעונה דבש דלא רצה לפרק חמורו. והא אנן תנן נוטל את הכלים הניטלין בשבת וזה הדבש הוא ראוי לאכילה היה לו לנוטלו ומפרקינן דבש זה הדביש כדמפרש בפרק המפקיד. ותוב אקשינן עליה היה לו להתיר החבלים ומעצמן יפלו השקין. ופרקי' חיישי דלמא כשיפלו השקין בקרקע מצטרו זיקי דפי' מתבקעין הנודות. ותוב אקשינן עליה היה לו להביא כרים וכסתות ויניח תחתיהן ויפלו השקין עליהן ולא יתבקעו כרב הונא ופרקי' אם יפלו זיקי אילין על הכסתות נמצא מבטל כלי מהיכנו ויטנפו הכסתות. ותוב אקשינן והא איכא צער בעלי חיים ופריק רשב"ג צער בעלי חיים דרבנן. אביי אשכחיה לרבה דקא משפשף לבריה אגבא דחמרא. פי' שפשוף כלומר שהיה מרכיבו ע"ג החמור בצדו ומשתמש בו. אמר ליה אביי משתמש מר בבעלי חיים. כלומר המשתמש בבעלי חיים עובר משום דתנן לא רוכבין על גבי בהמה

Huna he should be allowed to prevent their breaking by cushioning the fall with pillows and cushions! – ? –

The Gemara answers:

הָתָם בְּכוּלְסָא – **There,** in the Baraisa, "glass bars" refers **to slabs of glass.** These are *muktzeh,*[10] and too large to be rolled off the pillows and cushions.[11] Therefore, they may not be allowed to fall onto pillows and cushions, since doing so would immobilize them for the entire Sabbath.

The Gemara brings support to this interpretation of the Baraisa: דַּיְקָא נַמִּי דְּקָתָנֵי – **This is also** indicated by **a precise** reading of the wording of the Baraisa itself, **for** by juxtaposing untithed produce and glass bars **the Baraisa implies** דּוּמְיָא דְּטֶבֶל – that it refers to *bars* that are **similar to untithed produce:** מַה טֶּבֶל דְּלֹא חֲזֵי לֵיהּ – **Just as untithed produce is** something that is **useless to him** on the Sabbath, אַף הָכָא נַמִּי לֹא חֲזֵי לֵיהּ – **so too here** when the Baraisa refers to *glass bars* it means the kind of glass bars **that are useless to him** on the Sabbath, namely: glass slabs, which are thus *muktzeh.*

The Gemara raises an objection to this interpretation:

וּמַאי אַף עַל פִּי שֶׁמִּשְׁתַּבְּרִין – **But** then **what** is the point of the Baraisa's emphasizing that one must allow the glass items to fall EVEN THOUGH THEY MAY BREAK? Apparently, one might have thought that the loss of the glass is a mitigating factor and should warrant cushioning the fall with pillows and cushions, and the Baraisa wishes to dispel this notion. But if the Baraisa is referring to glass slabs, then there is no loss involved in their breaking and no reason for anyone to think that we should allow cushioning their fall.[12] – ? –

The Gemara replies:

מַהוּ דְּתֵימָא לְהֶפְסֵד מוּעָט נַמִּי חָשְׁשׁוּ – **You might have thought that [the Rabbis] were concerned with a minimal financial loss as well** as with a substantial loss, and would therefore waive the prohibition of *nullifying the preparedness of a utensil* and permit cushioning the fall of these glass slabs.[13] קָא מַשְׁמַע לָן – **[The Baraisa]** therefore **informs us** that this is not so: The Rabbis did not waive this prohibition for the sake of the minimal loss involved in the fall of large glass slabs, and did not allow cushioning their fall.[14]

The Gemara continues to discuss methods of unloading *muktzeh* from an animal on the Sabbath:

תַּנְיָא – **It was taught in a Baraisa:** רַבִּי שִׁמְעוֹן בֶּן יוֹחַי אוֹמֵר – R' SHIMON BEN YOCHAI SAYS: הָיְתָה בְּהֶמְתּוֹ טְעוּנָה שְׁלִיף שֶׁל תְּבוּאָה – IF HIS ANIMAL WAS LOADED WITH A SACK OF untithed PRODUCE, מַנִּיחַ רֹאשׁוֹ תַּחְתֶּיהָ – HE SHOULD POSITION HIS HEAD UNDER one end of IT וּמְסַלְּקוֹ לְצַד אַחֵר – AND PUSH IT UP and over TO THE OTHER SIDE וְהוּא נוֹפֵל מֵאֵלָיו – AND [THE SACK] WILL FALL BY ITSELF.[15]

The Baraisa continues:

חֲמוֹרוֹ שֶׁל רַבָּן גַּמְלִיאֵל הָיְתָה טְעוּנָה דְּבַשׁ – THE DONKEY OF RABBAN GAMLIEL WAS once LOADED WITH HONEY as the Sabbath began. וְלֹא רָצָה לְפוֹרְקָהּ עַד מוֹצָאֵי שַׁבָּת – BUT [RABBAN GAMLIEL] DID NOT WANT TO UNLOAD [THE DONKEY] UNTIL SATURDAY NIGHT. לְמוֹצָאֵי שַׁבָּת מֵתָה – ON SATURDAY NIGHT, [THE DONKEY] DIED.

The Gemara wonders why Rabban Gamliel did not want to unload the honey on the Sabbath:

וְהָאֲנַן תְּנַן – **But we have learned in the Mishnah:** נוֹטֵל כֵּלִים הַנִּיטָּלִין – HE MAY TAKE off ANY UTENSILS THAT MAY normally BE MOVED on the Sabbath. Now since honey is edible, it is not *muktzeh* and may be taken off the donkey. Why did Rabban Gamliel not do so?

The Gemara explains:

כְּשֶׁהִדְבִּישׁ – The case was **where the honey had soured**[16] and was thus *muktzeh.*

The Gemara questions this:

הַדְּבִישׁ לְמַאי חֲזֵי – **Of what use is spoiled honey?** Why was Rabban Gamliel transporting it?

The Gemara answers:

לִכְתִּיתָא דְּגַמְלֵי – It can be applied as a salve **to the abrasions on a camel's** back.[17]

The Gemara continues to question Rabban Gamliel's behavior:

וְיַתִּיר חֲבָלִים וְיִפְּלוּ שַׂקִּין – **But he should have loosened the ropes and allowed the sacks** containing the honey **to fall** to the ground, as we learned in our Mishnah! – ? –

The Gemara answers:

מִיצְטְרוּ זִיקֵי – **The sacks would have split open,** and the honey would have been ruined.

The Gemara asks:

וְיָבִיא כָּרִים וּכְסָתוֹת וְיַנִּיחַ תַּחְתֵּיהֶן – **But he should have brought pillows and cushions and placed them beneath [the containers].** – ? –

The Gemara answers:

מִטַּנְּפֵי – **The [pillows and cushions] would have become soiled** from spillage, וְקָמְבַטֵּל כְּלִי מֵהֵיכָנוֹ – **and he would** thereby **nullify the preparedness of a vessel.**[18]

The Gemara asks:

וְהָאִיכָּא צַעַר בַּעֲלֵי חַיִּים – **But** how could he leave the donkey burdened with such a heavy load for the entire Sabbath? **There is** the issue of causing the **suffering of a living creature,** which is Biblically prohibited![19] – ? –

NOTES

the Gemara will explain later. He therefore has no choice but to let the sacks fall, even though the glass inside will break.]

10. [They are muktzeh because] they are not [finished] utensils; rather, they are to be cut into smaller sections for use as window panes (*Rashi*).

11. [*Sfas Emes,* explaining *Rashi*; see also *Lechem Mishneh* to *Rambam, Hil. Shabbos* 21:10; *Magen Avraham* 266:14; cf. *Ramban*; *Rashba.*]

12. Since these slabs are made to be cut up into window panes anyway, their value is not significantly reduced if they fall and break into smaller pieces (*Rashi*).

13. When the slabs fall to the ground, small chips of glass will inevitably fly off. These tiny chips represent a slight loss, as they cannot be used for anything (*Rashi*).

14. Where, however, a substantial loss is involved, the Rabbis did waive the prohibition of *nullifying the preparedness of a utensil,* and allowed placing pillows and cushions under the falling sacks (*Magen Avraham* 266:14 from *Rashi* ד״ה והא איכא צער בעלי חיים; see also *Dagul MeiRevavah,* ad loc.; *Maggid Mishneh* to *Rambam, Hil. Shabbos* ibid; cf. *Ramban*; *Rashba*).

[As for why the Gemara earlier forbade cushioning the fall of large sacks of glass pipettes, despite the financial loss involved, see note 20 below.]

15. Although the untithed produce is *muktzeh,* he may push it off the animal with his head. The Rabbis never forbade the movement of *muktzeh* with one's body (*Ramban,* in his last explanation, citing the Mishnah on 141a and the Gemara above, 127a; cf. *Ran*; see *Magen Avraham* 305:9).

16. *Rashi* (see *Rashi* to *Bava Metzia* 38a ד״ה והדביש).

17. [See *Rashi* above 76b ד״ה כתית.]

However, the sour honey is *muktzeh* because one is not permitted to apply salves to animals on the Sabbath (*Ritva MHK* ed., citing 53b).

18. Once the honey spills upon the cushions, they will not be usable for the remainder of the day (*Rashi*).

19. Rabban Gamliel should have allowed the honey to fall onto pillows and cushions, thus violating the merely Rabbinic prohibition of *nullifying the preparedness of a utensil,* rather than leave the donkey loaded the entire Sabbath and violating the Biblical prohibition of causing pain to a living creature (*Rashi*; cf. *Ramban*).

Actually Rabban Gamliel had a third option: He could have allowed the honey to fall on the floor and break, thus avoiding both prohibitions. The Gemara does not suggest this course of action because it knows that

והא מבטל כלי מהיכנו. פירשנו למעלה בפרק כירה (דף מג.): **שתים** בידי אדם ואחת באילן. בסוכה בפ"ב (דף כג: ושם) תנן העושה סוכתו בראש האילן יש לפרש בשני ענינים העושה סוכתו בראש האילן כגון שהסכך של סוכה על גבי האילן והאילן סומך אותה שאין יכול לעלות על אותו סכך אלא אם כן ישתמש באילן שרגילין היו לתת כליהן על הסכך א"נ יש לפרש שהתקרה סמוכה באילן שגבוהה בגובה ומחמיה על האילן להשתמש כל שעה שהוא מהלך בסוכה משתמש באילן: **בחיבור** גוולקי. שני שקין אחד בימין החמור ואחד משמאלו ובראש כל אחד מן השקין רצועה אחת וקושרין אותן שתי הרצועות יחד ועכשיו מונח הקשר כנגד גבו של חמור והשקין מכבידין לכאן ולכאן ואי אפשר להתיר הקשר אם לא יגביהו השקין מעט ונסמכין שתי השקין בכריסו של החמור והוו להו כלדדים: למטה

ואפי' למ"ד דלוקין. במסכת מכות (דף יג:) הכלא אפי' לאו ליכא דלאו לאזהורי אמלאכה שעל ידו וע"י בהמתו אתא כגון מחמר ליכתוב לא תעשה כל מלאכה והמחמר מאי אתה משמע אתה לבדך והמחמר לבדה: בהמתו. במלאכה הנעשית ע"י בהמתו לא מיחייב דלאו גמור ללקות עליו: **טעונה כלי זכוכית.** שאין ניטלין בידו להניחן לארץ: והאנן תנן נוטל את הכלים הניטלין. וכלי זכוכית ניטלין הן ולמה לי מתיר את החבלים: **דאוממי.** מקיז דם שאין ראוין בשבת לכלום לפי שמאוסים: **והא** (ד) **מבטל כלי.** כרים וכסתות כשמניחן תחת דבר שאין ניטל מבטלן מהיכנו דשוב לא יטלם משם ודמי לסותר: **בשליפי זוטרי.** משאות קטנים שעושה הסכר מתחתיהם ונופלין על הסכר השני וכן עד שמגיען לארץ: **עששיות** של זכוכית. מס"ש בלע"ז ואע"פ שהעששיות משתברין אלמא אסור להניח כרים וכסתות תחתיהן: **בכולסא.** חתיכות רחבות של זכוכית שאינם כלים ועושין מהן חלונות וכיון דליכא פסידא בשבירתן וסופן להחתך בחתיכות קטנות לא שרו להביא כרים ולהניח תחתיהן: [טבל לא חזי ליה. דמוקלה הוא ואפילו לכהנים לא חזי]: ומאי אף על פי שמשתברין. הא ליכא פסידא: מהו דתימא להפסד מועט נמי חששו. ויביא כרים ויניח תחתיהם דהא ודאי אי אפשר בלא הפסד מועט שנילולות ניתזין בשבירתן שאינם ראוין לכלום: שליף. משוי של תבואה של טבל: והא אנן תנן כו'. ודבש ניטל בשבת ואמאי לא רצה לפורקה: כשהדביש. החמיץ: למאי חזי. ואמאי אייתי רבן גמליאל: לכתיתא דגמלי. לכתית של גמלים רדויישדוד"א: ויתיר החבלים ויפלו שקים. דהכי תנן במתניתין בדבר שאינו ניטל ומשני מלטרו זיקי נבקעים הנודות בנפילתן לארץ: מטנפי. בדבר הנשפך עליהם וקא מבטל כלי מהיכנו דשוב אין ראויין לבו ביום לכלום: והא איכא צער בעלי חיים. וליתי דאורייתא ולידחי דרבנן ביטול כלי מהיכנו: קסבר. ר"ג צער בעלי חיים דרבנן ופלוגתא היא באלו מציאות (ב"מ לב:): דמשפשף לבריה אגבא דחמרא. בשבת לשעשע התינוק: קא משתמש מר בבעלי חיים. ותנן (ביצה דף לו.) לא רוכבין על גבי בהמה וה"ה לכל תשמיש: צדדין. שאינו מרכיבו עליו אלא משפשפו על צדי גבו ואין זה דרך תשמישו ורבנן לא גזרו בה: מאי לאו בחבר גוולקי. דהוו להו לצדדין גוואלקי עשקנ"ש חבר גוואלקי שתים מחוברות יחד ברצועות ומרכיבין על החמור זו מכאן וזו מכאן וצריך לסלקן יחד וליקרב אצל החמור ומשפשף עצמו ונשען גופו בצדי החמור: בחבר אנגלוקי. שתים שאין מחוברות יחד אלא על ידי טבעת מתכת שבראש הרצועה וכו מסמר קטן כעין שעושין לחבק שקורין ליינגל"א שאינו צריך אלא למשוך מעט והמסמר יוצא והן מתנתקות זו מזו: אי נמי בלכתא. כעין שעושין לדרדור יין שיש בהן טבעות של חבל לכל אחד ואחד ומכניס טבעת בטבעת ונוטל עץ כפוף קטן ומכניסו בפנימי ושוב אינו יוצא מחברו וכשבא לסלקו מושך העץ אליו והן מתנתקין זה מזה ונופלין: שתים בידי אדם ואחת באילן. גבי סוכה תנן שכשירה בג' דפנות ואם עשה שתים כהלכתן והשלישי עשה באילן כשירה. דפנות לא איכפת לן אם מחוברות הם וה"ה אם כולן נקבעות באילן והא דנקט שתים בידי אדם רבותא אשמועינן דאפילו הכי אין עולין לה לאכול ולישן באותה סוכה בי"ט מפני שסככה קשור בדופניה ונשען עליה והוא משתמש על סככה ונותן כליו ונמצא משתמש באילן. כל כניסה דסוכה נקיט בלשון עלייה במסכת סוכה לפי שרובן עושין סוכותיהן בראש גגן דבכמה דוכתין תנן בה הכי [ו] אין מטריחין אותו לעלות [ז] אמר להם העלוס לסוכה [ח] אבל מוריד הוא את הכלים וכן הרבה: מאי לאו דחק ביה באילן. והותיב ביה קנים של דפנות בנקבים שנקב הרבה בגופו של אילן וסיכך שוב על אותן דפנות ומ"מ אין כאן תשמיש אלא בצדי אילן: דכפייה לאילן. לענפיו העליונים הטה לצד אילן אחר וכן של זה לזה וקשרן אלו עם אלו ומהן נעשה הדופן: אמאי עולין לה בי"ט. הרי הסכך נשען עליו והוא משתמש בו: ה"ג אלא מאי צדדין אסורין סוף סוף אמאי עולין לה בי"ט אלא התם בגוואזא פרסכנא שאילן גופיה דופן בעלמא שוויה. גוואזא פרסכנא אילן שענפים הרבה יוצאין מלדדין ומתפשטין לכאן ולכאן ושויהו דופן בעלמא לסוכה ולא סמך הסכך עליהן ולהכי נקט גוואזא פרסכנא ולא שבקיה כדקא ס"ד בדכפייה ולישני כגון דלא סמך הסכך עליה משום דכיון דדופן רביעי הוא שאינו צריך לסוכה דהא בג' כשירה והסכך נמי לא סמך עליה לא טרח למעבד לו דופן להכי אוקמא בגוואזא פרסכנא וממילא הוא בלא טרחא: מאי לאו בהא קמיפלגי כו'. וכגון דדחק באילן ומותיב קנים בצדדין וסיכך עליהן דהוה ליה משתמש בצדדין כשמשתמשין על ידי סככה דאי לא בהא פליגי במאי מוקמא פלוגתייהו דהא כולי עלמא סברי אסור להשתמש באילן: אמר אביי. א"נ בהכי פליגי ליכא למימר דסבירא ליה (לת"ק [י]) לצדדין מותרין דהכי לאו לצדדין ניהו אלא לצדי צדדים [ט] שהקנים הנתונים בנקבים לצדדין והסיכוך הנתון על גבן לצדי צדדים פליגי: יתד

והא מבטל כלי מהיכנו.

ואפי' למ"ד לוקין ליכתוב רחמנא לא תעשה כל מלאכה ובהמתך [א] אתה למה לי הוא ניהו דמיחייב בהמתו לא מיחייב: הגיע לחצר החיצונה: אמר [ב] רב הונא היתה בהמתו טעונה כלי זכוכית מביא כרים וכסתות ומניח תחתיה ומתיר החבלים והשקין נופלים והאנן תנן נוטל את הכלים הניטלין בשבת [א] כי קאמר רב הונא בקרני דאוממא דלא חזיא ליה והא קא מבטל כלי מהיכנו [ג] בשליפי זוטרי מיתיבי היתה בהמתו טעונה [ד] טבל ועששיות מתיר את החבלים והשקין נופלין ואע"פ שמשתברין התם בכולסא דיקא נמי דקתני דומיא דטבל מה טבל דלא חזי ליה אף הכא נמי לא חזי ליה ומאי אע"פ שמשתברין [ה] מהו דתימא להפסד מועט [ו] נמי חששו קמ"ל תניא ר"ש בן יוחי אומר [ז] היתה בהמתו טעונה שליף של תבואה מניח ראשו תחתיה ומסלקו לצד אחר והוא נופל מאליו חמורו של רבן גמליאל היתה טעונה דבש ולא רצה לפורקה עד מוצאי שבת למוצאי שבת מתה והאנן תנן נוטל כלים הניטלין כשהדביש [ח] הדביש למאי חזי לכתיתא דגמלי ויתיר חבלים ויפלו שקין מיצטרו זיקי ויביא כרים וכסתות ויניח תחתיהן מטנפי [ט] וקמבטל כלי מהיכנו [י] והאיכא צער בעלי חיים קסבר [כ] צער בעלי חיים דרבנן אביי אשכחיה לרבה דקא משפשף ליה לבריה אגבא דחמרא א"ל קא משתמש מר בבעלי חיים א"ל צדדין הן וצדדין לא גזרו בהו רבנן מנא תימרא דתנן מתיר (א) חבלים והשקין נופלין מאי לאו בחבר [ל] גוולקי דהוו להו צדדין וצדדין לא גזרו בהו רבנן לא בחבר אנגלוקי דלא הוו צדדין אי נמי בלכתא איתיביה [מ] שתים בידי אדם ואחת באילן כשרה ואין עולין לה ביו"ט מאי לאו דחק ביה באילן דהוו להו צדדין [נ] וצדדין אסורין לא דכפייה לאילן ואנח סיכוך עילויה (ג) דקמשתמש באילן א"ה אימא סיפא שלש בידי אדם ואחת באילן כשרה ועולין לה ביו"ט ואי דכפייה לאילן אמאי עולין לה ביו"ט ואלא מאי צדדין אסורין סוף סוף אמאי עולין לה בי"ט אלא התם בגוואזא פרסכנא דאילן גופיה דופן בעלמא הוא דשוויה דיקא נמי דקתני זה הכלל [ס] כל (ג) אילו שינטל האילן ויכולה לעמוד עולין לה ביו"ט ש"מ לימא כתנאי אין עולין לה ביו"ט [ע] רשב"א אומר משום ר"מ עולין לה ביו"ט מאי לאו בהא קמיפלגי דמ"ס צדדין אסורין ומר סבר מותרין אמר אביי לא דכ"ע צדדין אסורין והכא בצדי צדדין קמיפלגי מ"ס צדי צדדין אסורין ומ"ס צדי צדדין מותרין רבא אמר מאן דאסר בצדדין אסר נמי בצדי צדדין מאן דשרי בצדי צדדין שרי נמי בצדדין איתיביה רב משרשיא לרבא נעץ יתד

ואבנו להקשות ממשנתנו אדרבן גמליאל שהיתה חמורו טעונה דבש דלא רצה לפרק חמורו. והא אנן תנן נוטל את הכלים הניטלין בשבת והדבש הוא ראוי לאכילה היה לו לנטלו ומפרקינן דבש זה הדביש פי' הופסד כדמפרש בפרק המפקיד. ותוב אקשינן עליה היה לו להתיר החבלים ויפלו השקין. ופרקי' חייש דלמא כשיפלו השקין בקרקע מצטרו זיקי ופי' מתבקעין הנודות שהדבש בהן כדכתיב וילכו ויצטיירו. ותוב אקשינן עליה היה לו להביא כרים וכסתות ויניח תחתיהן ויפלו השקין בהן ולא יתבקעו דהכי שרי למעבד כרב הונא ופרקי' אם יפלו זיקי אילין על הכסתות נמצא מבטל כלי מהיכנו שהן מתלכלכין ואם תאמר יצערו ויבטל הכסתות כמו שאמרנו למעלה אע"פ שינצערו אינן ראוין להשתמש בהן היום דקא מטנפי. עוד אקשינן עליה ולמה הניח חמורו טעונה הא איכא צער ב"ח ופריק רשב"ג צער בעלי חיים דרבנן. אביי אשכחיה לרבה דקא משפשף לבריה אגבא דחמרא. פי' שפשוף כדאמרינן ומגבב ישפשף כלומר הוליך ויביא ידו על גופו שיושב מעל"ה מושיבו ע"ג החמור כמו שפשוף ע"ג החמור מן הצד לא על שדרו של חמור כדרך רכיבה אלא היה מושיבו ע"ג החמור והתינוק מתגדר ונחות ואביו מחזיק בו ומחזיקו שלא יפול לארץ. א"ל אביי משתמש מר בבעלי חיים. כלומר המשתמש בבה"ח עובר משום הא דתנן ולא רוכבין על גבי בהמה השיבו רבה אינו שדרו של

צער בעלי חיים. צער בעלי חיים דאורייתא שנאמר עזוב תעזוב עמו ואיכא מאן דלית ליה דקרא משום דקרא משום צער בעלי חיים בעלי מליאות (ב"מ לג ב'). לכתא. עץ קטן שכפול ראשו ומכניסין אותו בלולאה ומעברין ומקשרין שתי לולאות שהדרדורים עקלים שהדרדורים מלוין בהן (לעיל קכח.) ...

יז א ב ג מיי' פכ"ב מהלכות שבת הלכה י סמג לאוין סה טוש"ע א"ח סי' רסו סעיף ט:
יח ד ה מיי' שם טוש"ע שם וסימן שה סעיף יח:
יט ו מיי' פ"ד מהלכות סוכה הלכה ו טוש"ע א"ח סי' תרכח סעיף ג:

תורה אור השלם

א) וְיוֹם הַשְּׁבִיעִי שַׁבָּת לַיי אֱלֹהֶיךָ לֹא תַעֲשֶׂה כָל מְלָאכָה אַתָּה וּבִנְךָ וּבִתֶּךָ עַבְדְּךָ וַאֲמָתְךָ וּבְהֶמְתֶּךָ וְגֵרְךָ אֲשֶׁר בִּשְׁעָרֶיךָ: [שמות כ, י]

רבינו חננאל

עליו ואפי' למאן דאמר לוקין א"כ לכתוב קרא לא תעשה כל מלאכה ובהמתך אתה למה לי אלא לומר לך כל מלאכה ניהו דכי עביד מיחייב בבהמתו לא מיחייב. והלכתא כר' יוחנן דהא דרמי ליתא דרבא אהדר עליה ופריך לטעמיה. ורא"ש דפריך לנפשיה לא שבקינן דברי רבא וסמכינן אשנוייה: הגיע לחצר החיצונה נוטל הכלים וכו'. אמר רב הונא היתה בהמתו טעונה כלי זכוכית מביא כרים וכסתות ומניח תחתיה ומתיר החבלים והשקין נופלים ואקשינן עלה והתנן נוטל את הכלים הניטלין בשבת וכלי זכוכית ניטלין בשבת ולמה אין ניטלין בפני עצמן. ופריק רב הונא מי סברת הא דאמרי' היתה [בהמתו] טעונה כלי זכוכי' בכוסות ואשישות קאמינא דשרי לטלטלן קאמינא קאמר בקרני (דאוני) [דאומנא] קאמינא שמוצצין בהן הדם שאסור לטלטלן ולמה אסור לטלטלן והא קיי"ל דבר שמלאכתו לאיסור אפי' לצורך גופו ומקומו שרי. תוב אקשי' עליה הא אמרת מביא כרים וכסתות ומניח תחת הבהמה כדי שיפלו כלי זכוכית הללו על דבר רך שלא ישברו והלא אסור להשתמש באותן הכרים והכסתות כל זמן שאלו כלי זכוכית עליהן ואינו יכול לישן בהם והנה מבטל כלי מהיכנו ופריק רב אשי בשליפי זוטרי. פי' שמנער את הכר או את הכסת מעט והן נופלות כו' הא דתנן מעות שעל הכר מנער את הכר והן נופלות. ואקשינן עליה היתה בהמתו טעונה עששיות מתיר חבלים והשקין נופלים. ואע"פ שמשתברין ופריק רב הונא אלו העששיות אינן כלי זכוכית עשוין אלא פולסא פי' חתיכות גדולות כדכתיב ברזל עשות ורוצה להכניסם לבור לעשות מהן כלי זכוכית והלכתא כרב הונא דאע"ג דאיתותב הא שני לה ושנויא שינויין אינון דהא מתרץ לה מאן דמותבה ואמרינן דיקא נמי דקתני דומיא דטבל מה טבל דלא חזו ליה פי' אלא אחר שיתקנן אף הכא נמי לא חזו ליה. והא דתניא רבי שמעון בן יוחי אומר היתה בהמתו טעונה שליף של תבואה מכניס ראשו תחתיו ומסלקו לצד אחר ונופל מעצמו פי' שליף כמו שק שאינו מפרק אלא מכבידו לצד אחר ונופל מעצמו והוא הדין בכל אחר הלכתא כוותיה

מסורת הש"ס

א) [עמ"ש תוס' לעיל לה. ד"ה ככר], ב) [עי' תוס' שם. ד"ה טלטל], ג) [פסחים טו: כ: נה: ביצה לו. ב"ק קח. ב"מ לב:], ד) [עי' רש"י ב"מ לב. ד"ה הדביש ובפרש"י סנהדרין קא. ד"ה מדביש], ה) [לעיל מג. וש"נ], ו) [ב"מ לב: וש"נ], ז) [פי' שקים ערוך ועי' בערך חבר פי' באריכות], ח) [סוכה כב:], ט) [עירובין לג.], י) [תוספתא סוכה פ"ב], כ) [כריתות סוכה כב.], ל) [שם כו:], מ) [סוכה מא.], נ) [ע"ל לר' מאיר וע"ש גורסין לרשב"א], ס) מ"א שהגוע לדדים הקנים הנתונים בנקבים לצדי לצדדים וגו' שלפנינו עיקר רש"י, ע) שייך אחר ד"ה כחיבור.

הגהות הב"ח

(א) גמ' ומנא תימרא דתנן מתיר החבלים: (ב) שם דקמשתמש באילן: (ג) שם זה הכלל כל שאילו ינטל האילן: (ד) רש"י ד"ה והא קא מבטל כלי מהיכנו כרים:

רב נסים גאון

ואפי' למאן דאמר לוקין. כלו' שר' ישמעאל סבר כי לאו שאין בו מעשה [מיתת] ב"ד לוקין עליו ור"ע סבר לאו שניתן לאזהרת [מיתת] ב"ד אין לוקין עליו: **והא** קא מבטל כלי מהיכנו. כבר פירשנו בפ' מפנין שיעקרו בפרק

ליקוטי רש"י

בקרני דאוממא. מקיזי דם שקרן משמש בה [מכות טז:]. **והא קא מבטל כלי מהיכנו.** שהיה מוכן ממתלה לטלטלו ועכשיו עושהו מוקצה [לעיל מג. ע"ש בתוס' ובפרש"י]. דדומה לסותר בנין מדרבנן [שם קכח:]. אסור לבטל כלי מהיכנו שאינו יכול עוד ליטלו [משם] דהוי כקובע לו מקום ומחברו בטיט ודמי למלאכה וכלי זה משיהא בו מוקצה יהא אסור לטלטלו. עששיות. חתיכות עבות כמו עשת שן (שה"ש ה) ולף לשון חלמים מנורה כאלה כן העששת (מנחות כח.) משי"ה בלע"ז [יומא לד:]. שליף. משאוי שבאמתחת ...(טעם דובשו והחמיץ) אשמלי"ר בלע"ז [כמו] (איוב לא) ובכל תבואתי תשרש תעקר שרשיה וכמו עד לא ירחק חבל הכסף (קהלת יב) יפתחו רתוקות עבותיה [ב"מ לח.]. מתקלקל ונעשה גלול מחמת חמימות [סנהדרין קא.]. **לכתיתא דגמלא.** לכתישה שעל הגמל שגבו כתוש ומסוקר מחמת משאוי אייסר"א בלע"ז [ב"מ שם:]. חטוטר' אלדרוב"א בלע"ז יש לו לגמל במקום טעינת המשא וע"ש שמתרקבת תמיד וסכין שם דבש לרפואה קרויה דבשת דלמלאכא...

The Gemara answers:

קָסָבַר – **[Rabban Gamliel] contends** that the prohibition of צַעַר בַּעֲלֵי חַיִּים דְּרַבָּנָן – causing **suffering to a living creature is** merely **Rabbinic** and does not supersede another Rabbinic prohibition.[20]

The Gemara takes up another issue that relates to our Mishnah:

דְּקָא אַבָּיֵי אַשְׁכְּחֵיהּ לֵיהּ לְרַבָּה – **Abaye once discovered Rabbah** מְשַׁפְשֵׁף לֵיהּ לִבְרֵיהּ אַגַּבָּא דַּחֲמָרָא – **as he was sliding his son down** from **the back of a donkey** on the Sabbath.[21] אָמַר לֵיהּ – **[Abaye]** thereupon **said to him:** קָא מִשְׁתַּמֵּשׁ מָר בְּבַעֲלֵי חַיִּים – The **master is making use of a living creature** and it is prohibited to do so on the Sabbath.[22] אָמַר לֵיהּ – **[Rabbah] replied to him:** צְדָדִין הֵן – **These are** merely the **sides** of the donkey that I am using, וּצְדָדִין לֹא גָּזְרוּ בְּהוּ רַבָּנָן – **and the Rabbis never decreed** a prohibition **regarding** the **sides** of an animal.[23]

The Gemara brings support for Rabbah's view:

מְנָא תֵּימְרָא – **From where can you infer** that this is so? דִּתְנַן – **For we learned in our Mishnah:** מַתִּיר חֲבָלִים וְהַשַּׂקִּין נוֹפְלִין – HE UNDOES THE ROPES that hold the *muktzeh* items fastened to the saddle, AND THE SACKS FALL down ON THEIR OWN. מַאי לָאו בְּחֶבֶר גּוּוּלְקֵי – Now to what type of sacks is the Mishnah referring? **Is it not** referring to **tied saddlebags?**[24] In such a case, he would need to lean on the donkey as he removes the saddlebags,[25] דַּהֲווּ לְהוּ צְדָדִין – **which would be** a use of its **sides.** Since the Mishnah permits this, we see וּצְדָדִין לֹא גָּזְרוּ בְּהוּ רַבָּנָן – **that the Rabbis never decreed** a prohibition regarding the **sides** of an animal.

The Gemara refutes this proof:

לֹא בְּחֶבֶר (אגלוקי) [אַגּוּוּלְקֵי] – **No,** that is not the case of our Mishnah; rather, our Mishnah speaks of **untied saddlebags** that are merely held together by a clasp.[26] One merely needs to free this clasp in order for the saddlebags to fall on their own, דְּלָא הָווּ צְדָדִין – **which does not entail** leaning on the **sides** of the donkey at all. אִי נַמִּי – **Alternatively,** the saddlebags are joined with rope chains fastened together בְּלַכְתָּא – **with a clip.**[27] Here too, one need only remove the wooden clip in order to release the sacks, which does not require leaning on the donkey.

Abaye attempts to refute Rabbah's view that it is permitted to make use of the sides of an animal:

אֵיתִיבֵיהּ – **[Abaye] challenged [Rabbah]** from the following Mishnah:[28] שְׁתַּיִם בִּידֵי אָדָם וְאַחַת בָּאִילָן – IF TWO walls of a *succah* ARE MAN-MADE AND ONE IS formed BY A TREE, כְּשֵׁרָה וְאֵין עוֹלִין לָהּ בְּיוֹם טוֹב – IT IS VALID, BUT ONE MAY NOT GO UP INTO IT ON THE FESTIVAL.[29] מַאי לָאו דָּחַק בֵּיהּ בָּאִילָן – Now how are the walls formed by a tree?[30] **Is it not that he carved** holes **into the tree,** inserted planks into these holes to form a wall and then

NOTES

the Rabbis waived the Rabbinic prohibition of *nullifying the preparedness of a utensil* in cases of substantial financial loss such as this (see above, note 14, and the sources cited there; cf. *Rashash*).

20. This dispute is discussed in *Bava Metzia* 32b.

The halachah follows the view that it is Biblically prohibited to cause pain to a living creature. Thus, it emerges that when faced with a choice between: (a) allowing the sacks to remain on the animal for the duration of the Sabbath (and violating a Biblical prohibition), (b) having them fall on the floor and break (and suffering a substantial financial loss), and (c) having them fall on pillows and cushions (and violating the Rabbinic prohibition of *nullifying the preparedness of a utensil*), one should choose the last option and have them fall on pillows and cushions (*Magen Avraham* ibid., according to *Rashi*; see there for another view).

[The Rishonim point out the following difficulty: The Gemara earlier ruled that one may *not* allow large sacks of bloodletter's pipettes to fall on pillows and cushions, since this would involve *nullifying the preparedness of a utensil.* But according to the Gemara here, the prohibition against causing pain to an animal should take precedence over the prohibition of *nullifying the preparedness of a utensil*! See *Ran MHK* ed., who explains that the Gemara earlier was referring to a case where the sacks of pipettes are not heavy enough to cause the animal distress even if left on it for the entire Sabbath; in such a case there is no warrant to violate the prohibition of *nullifying the preparedness of a utensil,* and one must leave the sacks on the animal until after the Sabbath. (See also *Magen Avraham* ibid.; *Hagahos R' Akiva Eiger* to *Magen Avraham* 335:4; *Leshon HaZahav* here; for a different approach to our entire passage see *Ramban*; *Rashba.*)]

21. Literally: rubbing his son on the donkey's back. Rabbah was playing with the child (*Rashi*; see also *Rabbeinu Chananel,* who explains that he was sliding the child down the sides of the donkey while holding him).

22. It is prohibited by Rabbinic decree to ride an animal on the Sabbath or festival, lest one forgetfully tear a branch off a tree to use as a whip, in violation of the *melachah* of קוֹצֵר, *reaping.* [A similar injunction prohibits ascending a tree, lest one forgetfully tear a branch off it (see *Beitzah* 36b; see also above, 45a note 1).] These injunctions also prohibit any other use of an animal that is similar to riding or sitting on it, e.g. putting something down on it (*Rashi*; cf. *Teshuvos Chasam Sofer* vol. 6, *Likkutim* §97; *Eglei Tal, Kotzer,* §44).

23. Rabbah did not sit his son astride the donkey; rather, he merely slid him down the donkey's sides. This is not the part of the donkey that is usually used and the Rabbis did not include it in the injunction (see *Rashi* here and to *Chagigah* 16b ד״ה שמע מינה).

24. I.e. two saddlebags connected by ropes that pass over the donkey's back, where they are knotted together (*Rashi*; cf. *Rabbeinu Chananel*).

25. Since the bags are tied together he needs to lean on the animal in order to loosen the bags (*Rashi;* cf. *Tosafos*; see also *Rabbeinu Chananel*).

26. I.e. the saddlebag ropes are connected to each other with a metal ring and pin. The pin requires only a small tug to separate it from the ring (*Rashi*; cf. *Rabbeinu Chananel*). [Emendation follows *Dikdukei Soferim.*]

27. Each rope chain is a series of rope links joined together. The rope chains are held together by a wooden clip which is inserted into a link from each chain (*Rashi*). [*Rashi* adds that flasks of wine in his time were bound together in just such a manner. See also *Rashi* above, 102a ד״ה אתאן ללכתא ומיתנא]

28. [*Succah* 22b. Although the Mishnah discusses the use of a tree, this is analogous to the use of an animal; see note 22 above.]

This Mishnah discusses the construction of a *succah.* If a *succah* has only three walls, it is valid. If one of the walls is formed by a tree or even if all three walls are formed by trees, it is still valid. [Although the roofing of a *succah,* the *s'chach,* may not be comprised of plants or trees still attached to the earth,] there are no such restrictions concerning the walls (*Rashi*).

29. Because one may come to make use of the *s'chach* which is supported by a tree. In earlier times, it was customary to place utensils on, and remove them from, the *s'chach.* When the *s'chach* is held up by a tree, use of the *s'chach* constitutes prohibited use of the tree. As a precautionary measure, the Sages forbade the use of such a *succah* on Yom Tov (*Rashi;* see also *Mishnah Berurah* 628:17; but see *Rashi* to *Succah* 22b where he gives a very different explanation of this Mishnah, in which it is the *floor* of the *succah,* not its *s'chach,* that is held up by the tree; see also *Tosafos* here who cites both explanations; for attempts at a resolution of the apparent contradiction in *Rashi* see *Chidushei Chasam Sofer* here; *Aruch LaNer* to *Succah* ibid.).

[Although a *succah* is valid even if all three of its walls are formed by trees, the Mishnah chose to teach a case where only one wall is formed by a tree to teach us a novel law: Even in this case, one may not enter the *succah* on Yom Tov (*Rashi*).]

[The phrase אֵין עוֹלִין לָהּ בְּיוֹם טוֹב, *One may not enter it on the festival,* literally means: *One may not ascend it on the festival.* In Mishnaic times, most people built their *succahs* on their roofs. Thus, the Mishnah uses such phrasing in many places. See, for example, *Succah* 26b, 29a and 48a (*Rashi*).]

30. [The Gemara assumes at this point that the tree is not wide enough to be used itself as a wall.]

עין משפט נר מצוה

יז א ב ג מיי' פכ"א מהלכות שבת הלכה י סמג לאוין סה טוש"ע א"ח סי' רסו סעיף ט:
יח ד ה מיי' שם טוש"ע שם וסימן שה סעיף יח:
יט ו מיי' פ"ד מהלכות סוכה הלכה ו טוש"ע א"ח סי' תרכח סעיף ג:

תורה אור השלם

א) וְיוֹם הַשְּׁבִיעִי שַׁבָּת לַייָ אֱלֹהֶיךָ לֹא תַעֲשֶׂה כָל מְלָאכָה אַתָּה וּבִנְךָ וּבִתֶּךָ עַבְדְּךָ וַאֲמָתְךָ וּבְהֶמְתֶּךָ וְגֵרְךָ אֲשֶׁר בִּשְׁעָרֶיךָ: [שמות כ, י]

גמרא

ואפי' למ"ד לוקין ליכתוב רחמנא לא תעשה כל מלאכה ובהמתך [א] אתה למה לי הוא ניהו דמיחייב בהמתו לא מיחייב: הגיע לחצר החיצונה: אמר [ה] רב הונא היתה בהמתו טעונה כלי זכוכית מביא כרים וכסתות ומניח תחתיה ומתיר החבלים והשקין נופלים והאנן תנן נוטל את הכלים הניטלין בשבת [א]כי קאמר רב הונא בקרני דאומנא דלא חזיא ליה והא קא מבטל כלי מהיכנו [ב]בשליפי זוטרי מיתיבי היתה בהמתו טעונה [ג]טבל ועששיות מתיר את החבלים והשקין נופלין ואע"פ שמשתברין התם בכולסא דיקא נמי דקתני דומיא דטבל מה טבל דלא חזי ליה אף הכא נמי לא חזי ליה ומאי אע"פ שמשתברין [ג]מהו דתימא [ג]להפסד מועט נמי חששו קמ"ל תניא ר"ש בן יוחי אומר [ד]היתה בהמתו טעונה שליף של תבואה מניח ראשו תחתיה ומסלקו לצד אחר והוא נופל מאליו חמורו של רבן גמליאל היתה טעונה דבש ולא רצה לפורקה עד מוצאי שבת למוצאי שבת מתה והאנן תנן נוטל כלים הניטלים בשבת [ו]כשהדביש למאי חזי לכתיתא דגמלי ויתיר חבלים ויפלו שקין מיצטרו זיקי ויביא כרים וכסתות ויניח תחתיהן מטנפי וקמבטל כלי מהיכנו [ה]והאיכא צער בעלי חיים קסבר [ו]צער בעלי חיים דרבנן אביי אשכחיה לרבה דקא משפשף ליה לבריה אגבא דחמרא א"ל קא משתמש מר בבעלי חיים א"ל צדדין הן וצדדין לא גזרו בהו רבנן מנא תימרא דתנן מתיר (א) חבלים והשקין נופלין מאי לאו בחבר [ז]גוולקי דהוו להו צדדין וצדדין לא גזרו בהו רבנן לא בחבר אגלווקי דלא הוו צדדין אי נמי בלכתא איתיביה [ח]שתים בידי אדם ואחת באילן כשרה ואין עולין לה ביו"ט מאי לאו דחק ביה באילן דהוו להו צדדין [ט]וצדדין אסורין לא דכפייה לאילן ואנח סיכוך עילויה (ב) דקמשתמש באילן א"ה אימא סיפא שלש בידי אדם ואחת באילן כשרה ועולין לה ביו"ט ואי דכפייה לאילן אמאי עולין לה ביו"ט ואלא מאי צדדין אסורין סוף סוף אמאי עולין לה בי"ט אלא התם בגוואזא פרסכנא דאילן גופיה דופן בעלמא הוא דשוויה דיקא נמי דקתני זה הכלל [י]כל (ג) אילו שינטל האילן ויכולה לעמוד עולין לה ביו"ט ש"מ לימא כתנאי אין עולין לה ביו"ט [כ] רשב"א אומר משום ר"מ עולין לה ביו"ט מאי לאו בהא קמיפלגי דמ"ס צדדין אסורין ומר סבר מותרין אמר אביי לא דכ"ע צדדין אסורין והכא בצדי צדדין קמיפלגי מ"ס צדי צדדין אסורין ומ"ס צדי צדדין מותרין רבא אמר מאן דאסר בצדדין אסר נמי בצדי צדדין מאן דשרי בצדי צדדין שרי נמי בצדדין איתיביה רב משרשיא לרבא נעץ
יתד

רש"י

ואפי' למ"ד לוקין. במסכת מכות (דף יג:) הכא אפי' לאו ליכא דלאו לאזהורי אמלאכה שעל ידו וע"י בהמתו אתא כגון מחמר ליכתוב לא תעשה כל מלאכה והמתך מאי אתה משמע אתה לבדך ובהמתך לבדה: **בהמתו.** במלאכה הנעשית ע"י בהמתו לא מיחייב לאו גמור ללקות עליו: **טעונה כלי זכוכית.** שאין ניטלין בידו להניחן לארץ: **והאנן תנן נוטל את הכלים הניטלין.** וכלי זכוכית ניטלין הן ולמה לי מתיר את החבלים: **דאומני.** מקיז דם שאין ראויין בשבת לכלום לפי שמאוסים: **והא** (ד) **מבטל כלי.** כרים וכסתות כשמניחן תחת דבר שאין ניטל מבטלן מהיכנו דשוב לא יטלם משם ודמי לסותר: **בשליפי זוטרי.** משפופות קטנים ששומט הכר מתחתיהם ונופלין על הכר השני וכן עד שמגיען לארץ: **עששיות** של זכוכית. מת"ש בלע"ז ואע"פ שהעששיות משתברין אלמא אסור להניח כרים וכסתות תחתיהן: **בכולסא.** חתיכות רחבות של זכוכית שאינם כלים ועושין מהן חלונות וכיון דליכא פסידא בשבירתן וסופן להתתך בחתיכות קטנות לא טרו להביא כרים ולהניח תחתיהן: [טבל **לא חזי ליה.** דמוקצה הוא ואפילו להכניס לא חזי]: **ומאי אף על פי שמשתברין.** הא ליכא פסידא: **מהו דתימא להפסד מועט נמי חששו.** ויביא כרים ויניח תחתיהם דהא ודאי אי אפשר בלא הפסד מועט שילוות ניתזין בשבירתן שאינם ראוין לכלום: **שליף.** משוי של תבואה של טבל: **והא אנן תנן כו'.** ודבש ניטל בשבת ואמאי לא רצה לפורקה: **כשהדביש.** החמיץ: **למאי חזי.** ולמאי אימא רבן גמליאל: **לכתיתא דגמלי.** לכתית של גמלים לדורסוד"א: **ויתיר החבלים ויפלו שקים.** דהכי תנן במתניתין בדבר שאינו ניטל ומשני מצטרו זיקי נבקעים הנודות בנפילתן לארץ: **מטנפי.** בדבר הנשפך עליהם וקא מבטל כלי מהיכנו דשוב אין ראוין לבו ביום לכלום: **והא איכא צער בעלי חיים.** וליתי דאורייתא ולידחי דרבנן ביטול כלי מהיכנו: **קסבר.** ר"ג צער בעלי חיים דרבנן ופלוגתא היא באלו מציאות (ב"מ לב:): **דמשפשף לבריה אגבא דחמרא.** בשבת לשעשע התינוק: **קא משתמש מר בבעלי חיים.** ותנן (ביצה דף לו.) לא רוכבין על גבי בהמה וה"ה לכל תשמיש: **צדדין.** שאינו מרכיבו עליו אלא משפשפו על צדי גבו ואין זה דרך תשמישו ורבנן לא גזרו בה: **מאי לאו בחבר גוולקי.** דהוו להו צדדין גוואלקי עשקי"ם חבר גוואלקי שתים מחוברות יחד ברצועות ומרכיבין על החמור זו מכאן וזו מכאן וצריך לסלקן יחד וליקרב אצל החמור ומשפשף עצמו ונשען גופו בצדי החמור: **בחבר אגלווקי.** שתים שאין מחוברות יחד אלא על ידי טבעת מתכת שבראש הרצועה ובו מסמר קטן כעין שעושין לאבק שקורין ליגגל"א שאינו צריך אלא למשוך מעט והמסמר יוצא והן מתנתקות זו מזו: **אי נמי בלכתא.** כעין שעושין לדרדור יין שיש בהן טבעות של חבל לכל אחד ואחד ומכניס טבעת בטבעת ונוטל עץ כפוף קטן ומכניסו בפנימי ושוב אינו יוצא מחברו וכשבא לסלקו מושך העץ אליו והן מתנתקין זה מזה ונופלין: **שתים בידי אדם ואחת באילן.** גבי סוכה תנן שכשירה בג' דפנות ואם עשה שתים כהלכתן והשלישי עשה באילן כשירה. דפנות לא איכפת לן אם מחוברות הם וה"ה אם כולן נקבעות באילן והא דנקט שתים בידי אדם רבותא אשמועינן דאפילו הכי אין עולין לה לאכול ולישן באותה סוכה בי"ט מפני שסככה קשור בדופניה ונשען עליה והוא משתמש על סככה ונותן כליו ונמצא משתמש באילן. כל כניסה דסוכה נקיט בלשון עלייה במסכת סוכה לפי שרובן עושין סוכותיהן בראש גגן דבכמה דוכתין תנן בה הכי [כ] אין מטריחין אותו לעלות [ל] אמר להם העלום לסוכה [מ] אבל מוריד הוא את הכלים וכן הרבה: **מאי לאו דחק ביה באילן.** ואותיב ביה קנים של דפנות בנקבים שנקב הרבה בגופו של אילן וסיכך שוב על אותן דפנות ומ"מ אין כאן תשמיש אלא בצדי אילן: **דכפייה לאילן.** לענפיו העליונים הטה לצד אילן אחר וכן של זה לזה וקשרן אלו עם אלו ומהן נעשה הדופן: **אמאי עולין לה בי"ט.** הרי הסכך נשען עליו והוא משתמש בו: ה"ג **אלא מאי צדדין אסורין** סוף סוף **אמאי עולין לה בי"ט אלא התם בגוואזא פרסכנא** שאילן גופיה דופן בעלמא שווייה. גוואזא פרסכנא אילן שענפים הרבה יוצאין מצדדין ומתפשטין לכאן ולכאן ושויהו דופן בעלמא לסוכה ולא סמך הסכך עליהן ולהכי נקט גוואזא פרסכנא ולא שבקיה כדקא ס"ד בדכפייה ולישני כגון דלא סמך הסכך עליה משום דכיון דדופן רביעי הוא שאינו צריך לסוכה דהא בג' כשירה והסכך נמי לא סמך עליה לא טרח למעבד לו דופן להכי אוקמא בגוואזא פרסכנא וממילא הוא בלא טרחא: **מאי לאו בהא קמיפלגי כו'.** וכגון דחק באילן ומותיב קנים בצדדין וסיכך עליהן דהוה ליה משתמש בצדדין כשמשתמשין על ידי סככה דאי לא בהא פליגי במאי מוקמא פלוגתייהו דהא כולי עלמא סברי אסור להשתמש באילן: **אמר אביי.** א"נ בהכי פליגי ליכא למימר דסבירא ליה (לת"ק [ס]) צדדין מותרין דהכי לאו צדדין ניהו אלא צדי צדדים [פ] שהקנים הנתונים בנקבים צדדין והסיכוך הנתון על גבן צדי צדדים ובצדי צדדים פליגי:

תוספות

והא מבטל כלי מהיכנו. פירשנו למעלה בפרק כירה (דף מג.): [ע] **שתים** בידי אדם ואחת באילן. בסוכה בפ"ב (דף כב: ושם) תנן העושה סוכתו בראש האילן יש לפרש בשני ענינים העושה סוכתו בראש האילן כגון שהסכך של סוכה על גבי האילן והאילן סומך אותה שאין יכול לעלות על אותו סכך אלא אם כן ישתמש באילן שרגילין היו לתת כליהן על הסכך א"נ יש לפרש שהתקרה סמוכה באילן שבנאה בגובה ותחתיה על האילן דהשתא כל שעה שהוא מהלך בסוכה משתמש באילן: **בחיבור** גוולקי. שני שקין אחד בימין החמור ואחד משמאלו ובראש כל אחד מן השקין רצועה אחת וקושרין אותן שתי הרצועות יחד ועכשיו מונח הקשר כנגד גבו של החמור והשקין מכבידין לכאן ולכאן ואי אפשר להתיר הקשר אם לא יגביהו השקין מעט ונסמכין שתי השקין בכריסו של החמור והוו להו כצדדים:
למטה

רבינו חננאל

עליו ואפי' למאן דאמר לוקין א"כ לכתוב קרא לא תעשה כל מלאכה ובהמתך אתה למה לי אלא לומר לך כל מלאכה ניהו דכי עביד מיחייב בבהמתו לא מיחייב. והלכתא כר' יוחנן דהא דרמי ליתא דרבא אהדר עליה ופריך לטעמיה. ואע"ג דפריק לנפשיה לא שבקינן דברי רבא וסמכינן אשנוייה: **הגיע** לחצר החיצונה נוטל הכלים וכו'. אמר רב הונא היתה בהמתו טעונה כלי זכוכית מביא כרים וכסתות ומניח תחתיה ומתיר הכלים והשקין נופלים ואקשינן עלה והתנן נוטל את הכלים הניטלין בשבת וכלי זכוכית ניטלין בשבת ולמה אין ניטלין בפני עצמן. ופריק רב הונא מי סבירת הא דאמרי' היתה [בהמתו] טעונה כלי זכוכי' בכוסות ואשישות קאמינא דשרי לטלטלן בשבת קאמר בקרני (דאוני) [דאומנא] קאמינא שמוצצין בהן הדם שאסור לטלטלן ולמה אסור לטלטלן והא קיי"ל דדבר שמלאכתו לאיסור מותר לצורך גופו ומקומו שרי. תוב אקשי' עליה הא אמרת מביא כרים וכסתות ומניח תחת משאוי הבהמה כדי שיפלו כלי זכוכית הללו על דבר רך שלא ישברו והלא אסור להשתמש באותן הכרים והכסתות כל זמן שאלו כלי זכוכית עליהן ואינו יכול לישן בהם והנה מבטל כלי מהיכנו ופריק רב אשי בשליפי זוטרי. פי' שמנער את הכר או את הכסת מעט והן נופלות כי הא דתנן מעות שעל הכר מנער את הכר והן נופלות. ואקשינן עליה היתה בהמתו טעונה עששיות מתיר חבלים והשקין נופלים. ואע"פ שמשתברין ופריק רב הונא אלו העששיות אינן כלי זכוכית עשוין אלא פולסא פי' חתיכות גדולות כדכתיב ברזל עשות ורוצה להכניסם לבור לעשות מהן כלי זכוכית והלכתא כרב הונא דאע"ג דאיתותב הא שני לה ושנויא שינויין אינון דהא מתרץ לה מאן דמותבה ואמרינן דיקא נמי דקתני דומיא דטבל מה טבל דלא חזו ליה פי' אלא אחר שיתקנן אף האי נמי לא חזי ליה. והא דתניא רבי שמעון בן יוחי אומר היתה בהמתו טעונה שליף של תבואה מכניס ראשו תחתיו ומסלקו לצד אחר הלכתא כוותיה שאינו מפרק אלא מכבידו לצד אחר ונופל מעצמו ובאנו להקשות ממשנתנו אדרבן גמליאל שהיתה חמורו טעונה דבש דלא רצה לפרק חמורו. והא אנן תנן נוטל את הכלים הניטלין בשבת וזה הדבש הוא ראוי לאכילה היה לו לנוטלו ומפרקינן דבש זה הדביש פי' הופסד כדמפרש בפרק המפקיד. ותוב אקשינן עליה היה לו להתיר החבלים ומעצמו יפלו השקין. ופרקי' חייש דלמא כשיפלו השקין בקרקע מצטרו זיקי ופי' מתבקעין הנודות שהדבש בהן כדכתיב ויבקעו ויצטררו. ותוב אקשינן עליה היה לו להביא כרים וכסתות ויניח תחתיהן ויפלו השקין בהן ולא יתבקעו דהכי שרי למעבד כרב הונא ופרקי' אם יפלו זיקי אילין על הכסתות ויטול הכסתות כמו שאמרנו למעלה אע"פ שינערם אינן ראוין להשתמש בהן היום דקא מיטנפי. עוד אקשינן עליה ולמה הניח חמורו טעונה הא איכא צער ב"ח ופריק רשב"ג צער בעלי חיים דרבנן. אביי אשכחיה לרבה דקא משפשף לבריה אגבא דחמרא. פי' שפשוף כדאמרינן ואם מבערב ישפשף כלומר יוליך ויביא ידו על גופו שיוסר מעליו טינוף הקרי כן רבא היה מעלה ומוריד בנו כעין שפשוף ע"ג החמור מן הצד לא על שדרו של חמור כדרך רכיבה אלא היה מושיבו ע"ג החמור והתינוק מתגדר ונחית ואבוי מחזיק בו ומחזיקו שלא יפול לארץ. א"ל אביי משתמש מר בבעלי חיים. כלומר המשתמש בב"ח עובר משום הא דתנן ולא רוכבין על גבי בהמה השיבו רבה אינו שדרו של

מסורת הש"ס

א) [עמ"ש תוס' לעיל מג: ד"ה כבר], ב) [עי' תוס' שם. ד"ה טבלא], ג) [פסחים טו: כ: נה: ביצה לו. ב"ק קיז. ב"מ לח:], ד) [עי' רש"י ב"מ לח. ד"ה הדביש ובפרש"י סנהדרין קא. ד"ה מדביש], ה) [לעיל מג. וש"נ], ו) [ב"מ לב: וש"נ], ז) [פי' שקים ערוך ועי' בערך חבר פי' באריכות], ח) סוכה כב:, ט) [עירובין לג.], י) [תוספתא סוכה פ"א], כ) [ברייתא סוכה כט.], ל) [שם כו:], מ) [סוכה מח.], נ) [צ"ל לר' מאיר] ויש גורסין לרשב"א, ס) פ"א שהגזע לצדדים והקנים הנתונים בנקבים לצדי צדדים וגי' שלפנינו עיקר רש"ל, ע) שייך אחר ד"ה בחיבור.

הגהות הב"ח

(א) גמ' ומנא תימרא דתנן מתיר החבלים: (ב) שם דקמשתמש באילן: (ג) שם זה הכלל כל שאילו ינטל האילן: (ד) רש"י ד"ה והא קא מבטל כלי מהיכנו כרים:

רב נסים גאון

ואפי' למאן דאמר לוקין. כלו' שר' ישמעאל סבר כי לאו שניתן לאזהרת [מיתת] ב"ד לוקין עליו ור"ע סבר לאו שניתן לאזהרת [מיתת] ב"ד אין לוקין עליו: **והא** קא מבטל כלי מהיכנו. כבר פירשנו בפ' מפנין שעיקרו בפרק

ליקוטי רש"י

בקרני דאומנא. מקיזי דם בקרן במציצה [מכות טז:]. **והא קא מבטל כלי מהיכנו.** שהיה מוכן מתחלה לטלטלו ועכשיו עושהו מוקצה [לעיל מג. ע"ש בתוס' ובפנ"י]. דדומה לסותר בנין מדרבנן [שם קכח:]. אסור לבטל כלי מהיכנו להושיבו במקום שלא יוכל עוד ליטלו [משם] דהוי כקובע לו מקום ומחברו בטיט ודמי למלאכה וכלי זה שמיטלו בו המוקצה יהא אסור לטלטלו [לעיל מג.]. **עששיות.** חתיכות עבות כמו עשת מן העשת ואף לשון חכמים מנורה באה מן העשת [מנחות כח.]. מת"ש בלע"ז [יומא לד:]. **שליף.** משאוי שבאמתחת [ב"ק יז:]. **הדביש.** לא נעשה דובש והמחמץ אשמלי"ר בלע"ז [כמון] (איוב לא) וכל תבואתי תשרש תעקר שרשיה וכמו עד לא ירתק חבל הכסף (קהלת יב) יפתחו רתוקות עבותיה [ב"מ לח.]. מתקלקל ונעשה כלול מחמת חמימות [סנהדרין קא.]. **לכתיתא דגמלא.** לכתישה שעל הגמל שגבו כתוש ומסוכך מחמת משאוי אישר"א בלע"ז [ב"מ שם]. סטוטר' אלדרוש"א בלע"ז יש לו לגמל במקום טעינת המשא וע"ש שמתרקבת תמיד וסכין שם דבש לרפואה קרויה דבשת כדאמרינן בב"מ דבש והדביש חזי לכתישא דגמלי [ישעיה ל, ו]. **והאיכא צער בעלי חיים.** צער בעלי חיים דאורייתא שנאמר עזוב תעזוב עמו ואיכא מאן דדריש טעמא דקרא משום צער בעלי חיים באלו מציאות (ב"מ לב:) [לעיל קכח:]. **לכתא.** עץ קטן שכפול ראשו וצריך למחורים נושאים לדרדורים של יין שתוחבין אותו בשני עקלים שהדרדורים תלוין בהן משני צידי החמור ומחברים בו הדרדורים שיחזיק זה את זה [שם קב.]. **כשרה.** לאוכלו של מועד ואף ביום טוב אם עבר ועלה לה יצא ידי חובתו. **ואין עולין לה ביום טוב.** דגזור בה רבנן דאין עולין באילן ואין משתמשין בו שמא יתלוש [סוכה כב:].

rested the roof of the succah upon these plank walls, דְּהָווּ לְהוּ צִדְדִין – so that the *s'chach* is supported by the plank walls, **which are** considered the **"sides"** of the tree? Now the Mishnah forbids entering this succah on the festival lest he make use of the *s'chach*[31] which, it emerges, is supported by the "sides" of the tree. We see, then, וְצִדְדִין אֲסוּרִין – **that** making use of the **sides** of a tree **is forbidden.** And, by the same token, making use of the sides of an animal ought to be forbidden.

The Gemara deflects Abaye's refutation of Rabbah by offering an alternative explanation of this Mishnah:

לֹא דִּכְפָיֵיהּ לְאִילָן וְאַנַּח סִיכּוּךְ עִילָוֵיהּ – **No,** the case is **where he bent the tree over** to form the tree itself into a wall,[32] **and rested the *s'chach*** directly **upon it.** One should certainly be prohibited to enter such a *succah* on the festival, דְּקָמִשְׁתַּמֵּשׁ בְּאִילָן – **because** in this case if he makes use of the *s'chach,* which rests on the tree itself, **he will be making use of the tree** proper, and not merely of its "sides."[33]

It emerges that, according to Rabbah, the Mishnah must be dealing with a case where the *s'chach* rests directly on a tree, which he has bent over to form a wall. The Gemara challenges this explanation:

אִי הָכִי – **If so,** that the *s'chach* roof rests directly on the tree, אֵימָא סֵיפָא – **consider the end** of the Mishnah: שָׁלֹשׁ בִּידֵי אָדָם וְאַחַת בְּאִילָן – IF THREE walls ARE MAN-MADE AND ONE IS formed BY A TREE, כְּשֵׁרָה וְעוֹלִין לָהּ בְּיוֹם טוֹב – IT IS VALID, AND ONE MAY GO UP INTO IT ON THE FESTIVAL. וְאִי דִּכְפָיֵיהּ לְאִילָן – **Now, if** Mishnah refers to where **he bent the tree over** and rested the *s'chach* directly on it, אַמַּאי עוֹלִין לָהּ בְּיוֹם טוֹב – then **why,** where there are three man-made walls, **is one allowed to go up into [the succah] on the festival?** After all, the fourth side of the *s'chach* still rests on a tree, and if he makes use of the *s'chach* he will be making use of the tree! – ? –

The Gemara points out this part of the Mishnah is just as difficult for Abaye as it is for Rabbah:

וְאֶלָּא מַאי צִדְדִין אֲסוּרִין – **But what then** is the correct explanation? – That Abaye is correct that making use of the **sides** of a tree **is prohibited,** and the Mishnah speaks of where the *s'chach* rests on plank walls which are supported by the tree? סוֹף סוֹף אַמַּאי עוֹלִין לָהּ בְּיוֹם טוֹב – But the problem remains: **Still, why** in the last case of the Mishnah (where there are three man-made walls) **is he allowed to go up into [the *succah*] on the festival?** This should be forbidden, since the fourth wall is supported by the plank wall which is supported by the tree (and which is considered a "side" of the tree) and, according to Abaye, it is prohibited to make use of the sides of a tree! – ? –

The Gemara resolves the difficulty:

אֶלָּא הָתָם בְּגַוְואזָא פַּרְסְכְנָא – In fact, the fourth wall was formed from the tree itself. However, it was not formed by bending the tree over; **rather,** the Mishnah **there** in its last case **refers to a branch with thick foliage,** which can be used as a wall just as it stands. Furthermore, the *s'chach* rested solely on the three man-made walls, and did not rest on the tree at all; דְּאִילָן גּוּפֵיהּ דּוֹפֶן בְּעָלְמָא הוּא דְּשַׁוְיֵיהּ – rather, **he had the tree serve as a mere wall** and not as a support for the *s'chach.*[34] Therefore, when he makes use of the *s'chach* he will not be making use of the tree, and for this reason he is permitted to enter the *succah.*[35]

The Gemara adds:

דַּיְקָא נַמִּי דְּקָתָנֵי – **This** explanation **is also** indicated by **a precise reading** of the wording of the Mishnah, **for the Mishnah states** in its conclusion: זֶה הַכְּלָל – THIS IS THE GENERAL RULE: כָּל אִילּוּ שֶׁיִּנָּטֵל הָאִילָן וִיכוֹלָה לַעֲמוֹד – WHEREVER THE TREE CAN BE REMOVED AND [THE *S'CHACH*] CAN STAND by itself, עוֹלִין לָהּ בְּיוֹם טוֹב – it is valid and ONE MAY GO UP INTO IT ON THE FESTIVAL. שְׁמַע מִינָּהּ – **Learn from this** that the last case of the Mishnah, where he is allowed to enter the *succah,* is a case where the tree is not supporting the *succah's* roof at all.

Thus, it emerges that when the Mishnah refers to a wall formed by a tree it means that the tree itself formed a wall. Therefore, it cannot be used to refute Rabbah's view that one may make use of the sides of a tree.

The Gemara now suggests that this issue may be in dispute elsewhere:

לֵימָא כְּתַנָּאֵי – **Shall we say** that the dispute between Rabbah and Abaye **is** the subject of a dispute between **Tannaim,** as we see in the following Baraisa: אֵין עוֹלִין לָהּ בְּיוֹם טוֹב – ONE MAY NOT GO UP INTO [THE *SUCCAH*] ON THE FESTIVAL; רַבִּי שִׁמְעוֹן בֶּן אֶלְעָזָר אוֹמֵר מִשּׁוּם רַבִּי מֵאִיר – R' SHIMON BEN ELAZAR SAYS IN THE NAME OF R' MEIR: עוֹלִין לָהּ בְּיוֹם טוֹב – ONE MAY GO UP INTO IT ON THE FESTIVAL.[36] מַאי לָאו בְּהָא קָמִיפַּלְגֵי – Now what issue is being argued here? **Is it not that they dispute this:** The succah's roof rests in part on a plank wall supported by a tree; דְּמַר סָבַר צִדְדִין אֲסוּרִין – **thus, one master** (The Tanna Kamma) **contends that the sides** of a tree **are prohibited** for use וּמַר סָבַר מוּתָּרִין – **and** the other **master** (R' Meir) **contends that they are permitted.**[37]

Abaye responds that the matter being disputed is something else:

אָמַר אַבָּיֵי לֹא – **Abaye said: No,** this is based on a mistaken

NOTES

31. [See note 29 above.]

32. Two trees stand near each other: The upper branches of each are bent down towards the other and then the two sets of branches are tied together, and the trees now form a wall (*Rashi*).

33. The Gemara here, in its defense of Rabbah, assumes that since the *s'chach* rests *on top* of the tree's branches, use of the *s'chach* is considered a use of the tree itself, and not of its "sides." [Abaye, however, may not share this assumption; see below, note 38.]

34. Since the *s'chach* already had sufficient support from the three man-made walls, he did not need to use the tree to support the *s'chach* at all (see *Maharsha*).

35. In contrast, in the Mishnah's first case where there are only two man-made walls, these two walls were not sufficient to support the *s'chach,* and he used the tree not only as a third wall but also to support the *s'chach.* Therefore, when he makes use of the *s'chach* he will be making use of the tree, and for that reason he may not enter it on the festival (ibid.)

Rashi anticipates the following question: The crux of the Gemara's answer is that the *s'chach* does not rest on the fourth wall. Why, then, did the Gemara need to introduce the element of a tree with thick foliage? Why couldn't the Gemara continue to maintain that he bent the trees over to form a wall, and simply answer that he avoided resting the *s'chach* on this wall?

Rashi explains that this is an improbable scenario: Since the tree is not needed to validate the *succah* (since there are already three man-made walls) or to support the *s'chach,* it is unlikely someone would go to the trouble of bending trees over to form a wall. If, however, a thick-leafed tree happened to be standing in the right spot, he might very well use it as a fourth wall. (See *Chidushei HaRan* for another answer.)

36. This opinion is cited in *Tosefta Succah* 1:9. The case there is of a *succah* comprised of two man-made walls and one wall formed by a tree.

37. I.e. the Tanna Kamma holds one may not enter the *succah,* since he might place his utensils on the *s'chach,* thereby making use of the "sides" of the tree (i.e. the plank walls which support the *s'chach*). R' Shimon ben Elazar does not share this concern since he maintains that one may make use of the sides of a tree.

We are compelled to say that the dispute centers around use of the sides of a tree [and presume the existence of plank walls], since everyone agrees that use of the tree proper is prohibited (*Rashi*).

ואפי' למ"ד לוקין ליכתוב רחמנא לא תעשה כל מלאכה ובהמתך א) אתה למה לי הוא ניהו דמיחייב בהמתו לא מיחייב: הגיע לחצר החיצונה: אמר רב הונא היתה בהמתו טעונה כלי זכוכית מביא כרים וכסתות ומניח תחתיה ומתיר החבלים והשקין נופלים והאנן תנן נוטל את הכלים הניטלין בשבת כי קאמר רב הונא בקרני דאומנא דלא חזיא ליה והא קא מבטל כלי מהיכנו בשליפי זוטרי מיתיבי היתה בהמתו טעונה טבל ועששיות מתיר את החבלים והשקין נופלין ואע"פ שמשתברין התם בכולסא דיקא נמי דקתני דומיא דטבל מה טבל דלא חזי ליה אף הכא נמי לא חזי ליה ומאי אע"פ שמשתברין מהו דתימא להפסד מועט נמי חיישו קמ"ל תניא ר"ש בן יוחי אומר היתה בהמתו טעונה שליף של תבואה מניח ראשו תחתיה ומסלקו לצד אחר והוא נופל מאליו חמורו של רבן גמליאל היתה טעונה דבש ולא רצה לפורקה עד מוצאי שבת למוצאי שבת מתה והאנן תנן נוטל כלים הניטלין כשהדביש הדביש למאי חזי לכתיתא דגמלי ויתיר חבלים ויפלו שקין מיצטרו זיקי ויביא כרים וכסתות ויניח תחתיהן מטנפי וקמבטל כלי מהיכנו והאיכא צער בעלי חיים קסבר צער בעלי חיים דרבנן אביי אשכחיה לרבה דקא משפשף ליה לבריה אגבא דחמרא א"ל קא משתמש מר בבעלי חיים א"ל צדדין הן וצדדין לא גזרו בהו רבנן מנא תימרא דתנן מתיר (א) חבלים והשקין נופלין מאי לאו בחבר גוולקי דהוו להו צדדין וצדדין לא גזרו בהו רבנן לא בחבר אגלוקי דלא הוו צדדין אי נמי בלכתא איתיביה שתים בידי אדם ואחת באילן כשרה ואין עולין לה ביו"ט מאי לאו דחק ביה באילן דהוו להו צדדין וצדדין אסורין לא דכפייה לאילן ואנח סיכוך עילויה (ב) דקמשמש באילן א"ה אימא סיפא שלש בידי אדם ואחת באילן כשרה ועולין לה ביו"ט ואי דכפייה לאילן אמאי עולין לה ביו"ט ואלא מאי צדדין אסורין סוף סוף אמאי עולין לה בי"ט אלא התם בגוואזא פרסכנא דאילן גופיה דופן בעלמא הוא דשוויה דיקא נמי דקתני זה הכלל כל (ג) אילו שינטל האילן ויכולה לעמוד עולין לה ביו"ט ש"מ לימא כתנאי אין עולין לה ביו"ט רשב"א אומר משום ר"מ עולין לה ביו"ט מאי לאו בהא קמיפלגי דמ"ס צדדין אסורין ומר סבר מותרין אמר אביי לא דכ"ע צדדין אסורין והכא בצדי צדדין קמיפלגי מ"ס צדי צדדין אסורין ומ"ס צדי צדדין מותרין רבא אמר מאן דאסר בצדדין אסר נמי בצדי צדדין מאן דשרי בצדי צדדין שרי נמי בצדדין איתיביה רב משרשיא לרבא נעץ
יתד

רש"י

טעונה כלי זכוכית. שאין ניטלין בידו להניחן לארץ: והאנן תנן נוטל את הכלים הניטלין. וכלי זכוכית ניטלין הן ולמה לי מתיר את החבלים: דאומני. מקיזי דם שאין ראוין בשבת לכלום לפי שמאוסים: והא (ד) מבטל כלי. כרים וכסתות כשמניחן תחת דבר שאין ניטל מבטלן מהיכנן דשוב לא יטלם משם ודמי לסותר: בשליפי זוטרי. משואות קטנים ששומט הכר מתחתיהם ונופלין על הכר השני וכן עד שמגיען לארץ: עששיות של זכוכית. מש"ש בלע"ז ואע"פ שהעששיות משתברין אלמא אסור להניח כרים וכסתות תחתיהן: בכולסא. חתיכות רחבות של זכוכית שאינם כלים ועושין מהן חלונות וכיון דליכא פסידא בשבירתן וסופן להחתך בחתיכות קטנות לא שרו להביא כרים ולהניח תחתיהן: [טבל לא חזי ליה. דמוקצה הוא ואפילו לכהנים לא חזין]: ומאי אף על פי שמשתברין. הא ליכא פסידא: מהו דתימא להפסד מועט נמי חיישו. ויביא כרים ויניח תחתיהם דהא ודאי אי אפשר בלא הפסד מועט שנילוזות ניתזין בשבירתן שאינם ראוין לכלום: שליף. משוי של תבואה של טבל: והא אנן תנן כו'. ודבש ניטל בשבת ואמאי לא רצה לפורקה: כשהדביש. החמיץ: למאי חזי. ואמאי אייתי רבן גמליאל: לכתיתא דגמלי. לכתית של גמלים רדוישדו"א: ויתיר החבלים ויפלו שקים. דהכי תנן במתניתין בדבר שאינו ניטל ומשני מיצטרו זיקי נבקעים הנודות בנפילתן לארץ: מטנפי. בדבר הנשפך עליהם וקא מבטל כלי מהיכנו דשוב אין ראוין לבו ביום לכלום: והא איכא צער בעלי חיים. וליתי דאורייתא ולידחי דרבנן ביטול כלי מהיכנו: קסבר. ר"ג צער בעלי חיים דרבנן ופלוגתא היא באלו מציאות (ב"מ לב:): דמשפשף לבריה אגבא דחמרא. בשבת לשעשע התינוק: קא משתמש מר בבעלי חיים. ותנן (ביצה דף לו.) לא רוכבין על גבי בהמה וה"ה לכל תשמיש: צדדין. שאינו מרכיבו עליו אלא משפשפו על צדי גבו ואין זה דרך תשמישו ורבנן לא גזרו בה: מאי לאו בחבר גוולקי. דהוו להו צדדין גוואלקי עשקנ"ם חבר גוואלקי שתים מחוברות יחד ברצועות ומרכיבין על החמור זו מכאן וזו מכאן וצריך לסלקן יחד וליקרב אצל החמור ומשפשף עצמו ונשען גופו בצדי החמור: בחבר אגלוקי. שתים שאין מחוברות יחד אלא על ידי טבעת מתכת שבראש הרצועה וכו מסמר קטן כעין שעושין לחבק שקורין לינגל"א שאינו צריך אלא למשוך מעט והמסמר יוצא והן מתנתקות זו מזו: אי נמי בלכתא. כעין שעושין לדרדור יין שיש בהן טבעות של לכל אחד ואחד ומכניס טבעת בטבעת ונוטל עץ כפוף קטן ומכניסו בפנימי ושוב אינו יוצא מחברו וכשבא לסלקו מושך העץ והן מתנתקין זה מזה ונופלין: שתים בידי אדם ואחת באילן. גבי סוכה תנן שכשירה בג' דפנות ואם עשה שתים כהלכתן והשלישי עשה באילן כשירה. דפנות לא איכפת לן אם מחוברות הם וה"ה אם כולן נקבעות באילן והא דנקט שתים בידי אדם אשמועינן דאפילו הכי אין עולין לה לאכול ולישן באותה סוכה בי"ט מפני שסככה קשור בדופניה ונשען עליה והוא משתמש על סככה ונותן כליו ונמצא משתמש באילן. כל כניסה דסוכה נקיט בלשון עלייה במסכת סוכה לפי שרובן עושין סוכותיהן בראש גגן דכמה דוכתין תנן בה הכי אין מטריחין אותו לעלות אמר להם העלום לסוכה אבל מוריד הוא את הכלים וכן הרבה: מאי לאו דחק ביה באילן. ואותיב ביה קנים של דפנות בנקבים שנקב הרבה בגופו של אילן וסיכך שוב על אותן דפנות ומ"מ אין כאן תשמיש אלא בצדי אילן: דכפייה לאילן. לענפיו העליונים הטה לצד אילן אחר וכן של זה לזה וקשרן אלו עם אלו ומהן נעשה הדופן: אמאי עולין לה בי"ט. הרי הסכך נשען עליו והוא משתמש בו: ה"ג אלא מאי צדדין אסורין סוף סוף אמאי עולין לה בי"ט אלא התם בגוואזא פרסכנא שאילן גופיה דופן בעלמא שווייה. גואזא פרסכנא אילן שענפים הרבה יוצאין מצדדין ומתפשטין לכאן ולכאן ושויהו דופן בעלמא לסוכה ולא סמך הסכך עליהן והכי נקט גואזא פרסכנא ולא שבקיה כדקא ס"ד בדכפייה ולישני כגון דלא סמך הסכך עליה משום דכיון דדופן רביעי הוא שאינו צריך לסוכה דהא בג' כשירה והסכך נמי לא סמך עליה לא טרח למעבד לו דופן להכי אוקמא בגוואזא פרסכנא וממילא הוא בלא טרחא: מאי לאו בהא קמיפלגי כו'. וכגון דחק באילן ומותיב קנים בצדדין וסיכך עליהן דהוה ליה משתמש בצדדין כשמשתמשין על ידי סככה דאי לא בהא פליגי במאי מוקמא פלוגתייהו דהא כולי עלמא סברי אסור להשתמש באילן: אמר אביי. א"נ בהכי פליגי ליכא למימר דסבירא ליה (לת"ק) צדדין מותרין דהכי לאו צדדין ניהו אלא צדי צדדים שהקנים הנתונים בנקבים צדדין והסיכוך הנתון על גבן צדי צדדים ובצדי צדדים פליגי:

תוספות

והא מבטל כלי מהיכנו. פירשנו למעלה בפרק כירה (דף מג.):

שתים בידי אדם ואחת באילן. בסוכה בפ"ב (דף כב:) [ושם] תנן העושה סוכתו בראש האילן יש לפרש בשני ענינים העושה סוכתו בראש האילן כגון שהסכך של סוכה על גבי האילן והאילן סומך אותה שאין יכול לעלות על אותו סכך אלא אם כן ישתמש באילן שרגילין היו לתת כליהן על הסכך א"נ יש לפרש שהתקרה סמוכה באילן שבנאה בגובה ותחתיה על האילן להשתמש כל שעה שהוא מהלך בסוכה משתמש באילן:

בחיבור גוולקי. שני שקין אחד בימין החמור ואחד משמאלו ובראש כל אחד מן השקין רצועה אחת וקושרין אותן שתי הרצועות יחד ועכשיו מונח הקשר כנגד גבו של החמור והשקין מצדדין לכאן ולכאן ואי אפשר להתיר הקשר אם לא יגביהו השקין מעט ונסמכין שתי השקין בכריסו של החמור והוו להו צדדים למטה:

ואפי' למ"ד דלוקין. במסכת מכות (דף יג:) הכא אפי' לאו ליכא דלאי לאזהורי אמלאכה שעל ידו וע"י בהמתו אתא כגון מחמר ליכתוב לא תעשה כל מלאכה והמתך מאי אתה משמע אתה לבדך ובהמתך לבדה: בהמתו. במלאכה הנעשית ע"י בהמתו לא מיחייב לאו גמור ללקות עליו:

עין משפט נר מצוה

יז א ב ג מיי' פכ"א מהלכות שבת הלכה י סמג לאוין סה טוש"ע א"ח סי' רסו סעיף ט:
יח ד ה מיי' פ"ד שם ופוסקין שם סעיף יג:
יט ו מיי' פ"ד מהלכות סוכה הלכה ו טוש"ע א"ח סי' תרכח סעיף ג:

תורה אור השלם

א) וְיוֹם הַשְּׁבִיעִי שַׁבָּת לַיְיָ אֱלֹהֶיךָ לֹא תַעֲשֶׂה כָל מְלָאכָה אַתָּה וּבִנְךָ וּבִתֶּךָ עַבְדְּךָ וַאֲמָתֶךָ וּבְהֶמְתֶּךָ וְגֵרְךָ אֲשֶׁר בִּשְׁעָרֶיךָ: [שמות כ, י]

רבינו חננאל

עליו ואפי' למאן דאמר לוקין א"כ לכתוב קרא לא תעשה כל מלאכה והמתך אתה למה לי אלא לומר לך כל מלאכה ניהו דכי עביד מיחייב בבהמתו לא מיחייב. והלכתא כר' יוחנן דהא דרמי ליתא דרבא אהדדר ופריך לטעמיה. ואע"ג דפריק לנפשיה לא שבקינן דברי רבא וסמכינן אשנויה: הגיע לחצר החיצונה נוטל הכלים וכו'. אמר רב הונא היתה בהמתו טעונה כלי זכוכית מביא כרים וכסתות ומתיר החבלים והשקין נופלים ואקשינן עלה והתנן נוטל את הכלים הניטלים בשבת ולי זכוכית ניטלין בשבת ולמה אין ניטלין בפני עצמן. ופריק רב הונא מי סברת הא דאמרי' [בהמתו] טעונה כלי זכוכי' בכוסות ואשישות קאמינא דשרי לטלטלן בשבת קאמר בקרני (דאוני) [דאומנא] קאמינא שמוצצין בהן הדם שאסור לטלטלן ולמה אסור לטלטלן והא קי"ל דבר שמלאכתו לאיסור אפי' לצורך גופו ומקומו שרי. תוב אקשי' עליה הא אמרת מביא כרים וכסתות ומניח תחת הבהמה כדי שיפלו כלי זכוכית הללו על דבר רך שלא ישברו והלא אסור להשתמש באותן הכרים והכסתות כל זמן שאלו כלי זכוכית עליהן ואינו כלי לישן בהם והנה מבטל כלי מהיכנו ופריק רב אשי בשליפי זוטרי. פי' שמנער את הכר או את הכסת מעט והן נופלות כי הא דתנן מעות שעל הכר מנער את הכר והן נופלות. ואקשינן עליה היתה בהמתו טעונה עששיות מתיר החבלים והשקין נופלים. ואע"פ שמשתברין ופריק רב הונא אלו העששיות אינן של זכוכית עשוין אלא פולסא פי' חתיכות גדולות כדכתרי ברזל עשות ורוצה להכניסם לבור לעשות מהן כלי זכוכית והלכתא כרב הונא דאע"ג דאיתותב הא שני לה ושנוייא שינויין אינון הן כדאי הוא ואמרינן דיקא נמי דקתני דומיא דטבל מה טבל דלא חזי ליה אף האי נמי לא חזי ליה. והא דתניא רבי שמעון בן יוחי אומר היתה בהמתו טעונה שליף של תבואה מכניס ראשו תחתיו ומסלקו לצד אחר הלכתא כוותיה שאינו מפרק אלא מכבידו לצד אחר ונופל מעצמו ובאנו להקשות ממשנתנו אדרבן גמליאל שהיתה חמורו טעונה דבש דלא רצה לפרק חמורו. והא אנן תנן נוטל את הכלים הניטלין בשבת וזה הדבש הוא ראוי לאכילה היה לו לנוטלו ומפרקינן דבש זה הדביש פי' הופסד כדמפרש בפרק המפקיד. ותוב אקשינן עליה היה לו להתיר החבלים ומעצמו יפלו השקין. ופרקי' חייש דלמא כשיפלו השקין בקרקע מצטרו זיקו ופי' מתבקעין הנודות שהדבש בהן כדכתיב וילכו ויצטיירו. ותוב אקשינן עליה היה לו להביא כרים וכסתות ויניח תחתיהן ויפלו השקין בהן ולא יתבקעו דהכי שרי למעבד כרב הונא ופרקי' אם יפלו זיקי אילין על הכסתות נמצא מבטל כלי מהיכנו ואם תאמר ינערם ויטול הכסתות כמו שאמרנו למעלה אע"פ שינערם אינן ראוין להשתמש בהן היום דקא מיטנפי. עוד אקשינן עליה ולמה הניח חמורו טעונה הא איכא צער ב"ח ופריק רשב"ג צער בעלי חיים דרבנן. אביי אשכחיה לרבה דקא משפשף דחמרא. פי' שפשוף כדאמרינן ואם מבערב ישפשף כלומר יוליך ויביא ידו על גופו שיוסר מעליו טינוף הקרי כן רבא היה מעלה ומוריד בנו כעין שפשוף ע"ג החמור מן הצד לא על שדרו של חמור כדרך רכיבה אלא היה מושיבו ע"ג החמור והתינוק ומתגדר ונחית ואביו מחזיק בו ומחזיקו שלא יפול לארץ. א"ל אביי משתמש מר בבעלי חיים. כלומר המשתמש בב"ח עובר משום הא דתנן ולא רוכבין על גבי בהמה השיבו רבה אינו שדרו של

מסורת הש"ס

א) [עמ"ש תוס' לעיל מג. ד"ה ככר], ב) [עי' תוס' שם. ד"ה טלטל], ג) [פסחים טו: כו: נה: ביצה לו. ב"ק קיז. ב"מ לח:], ד) [עי' רש"י ב"מ לח. ד"ה הדבש ובפרש"י סנהדרין קא. ד"ה מדבש], ה) [לעיל מג. וש"נ], ו) [ב"מ לב: וש"נ], ז) [פי' שקים ערוך ועי' בערך סבר פי' בארוכות], ח) סוכה כב:, ט) [עירובין לג.], י) [תוספתא סוכה פ"א], כ) [בריתא סוכה כט.], ל) [שם טו.], מ) [סוכה מא.], נ) [נ"ל לר' מאיר וכן גירסת לרשב"א], ס) פי' שהגוף לצדדין והקנים הנתונים בנקבים לצדי לצדדים וגי' שלפנינו עיקר רש"ל, ע) שייך אחר ד"ה כמיכור.

הגהות הב"ח

(א) גמ' ומנא תימרא דתנן מתיר החבלים: (ב) שם דקמשתמש באילן: (ג) שם זה הכלל כל שאילו ינטל האילן: (ד) רש"י ד"ה והא קא מבטל כלי מהיכנו כרים:

רב נסים גאון

ואפי' למאן דאמר לוקין. כלו' שרי ישמעאל סבר כי לאו שניתן לאזהרת [מיתת] ב"ד לוקין עליו ור"ש סבר לאו שניתן לאזהרות [מיתת] ב"ד אין לוקין עליו: והא קא מבטל כלי מהיכנו. כבר פירשנו בפ' מפנין שעיקרו בפרק

ליקוטי רש"י

בקרני דאומנא. מקיזי דם שקרן במלאכה [מכות טז:]. והא קא מבטל כלי מהיכנו. שהיה מוכן מתחלה לטלטלו ועכשיו עושהו מוקצה [לעיל מג. ע"ש בתוס' ובפסי']. דדומה לסותר בנין מדרבנן [ביצה לו:]. אסור לבטל כלי מהיכנו להושיב כלי במקום שלא יוכל עוד לטלטלו דהוי כקובע לו מקום ומתכוין בטיט ודמי למלאכה ולא זה מיהו כו המוקצה יהא אסור לטלטלו [שם מב:]. עששיות. מדוכות עששית כמו עשת כן ואף לשון חכמים מנורה באה מן עששית (מנחות כח.) משי"ש בלע"ז [יומא לד:]. שליף. משאוי. הדביש. צער בעלי חיים. צער בעלי חיים דאורייתא שנאמר עזוב תעזוב עמו ואיכא מאן דדריש טעמא דקרא משום צער בעלי חיים באלו מציאות (ב"מ לב:) [לעיל קכח:]. לכתא. עץ קטן שכפול ראשו וצריך לחמורים נושאים דרדורים של יין שמותן עקלים שהדרדורים תלוין בהן משני צידי החמור ומחברים בו הדרדורים שיחזיק זה את זה [שם קב.]. כשרה. ואף ביום טוב אם עבר ועלה בה יצא ידי חובתו. ואין עולין לה ביום טוב. דגזור בה רבנן דאין עולין באילן שמא יתלוש [סוכה כב:].

assumption. For even though, as you say, the case being argued is where the *s'chach* rests on plank walls supported by the tree, the issue between them is not that of using the sides of a tree, דְּכוּלֵּי עָלְמָא צְדָדִין אֲסוּרִין – **for everyone,** including R' Meir, **agrees** with me **that** the **sides** of a tree **are prohibited** for use. וְהָכָא בְּצִדֵּי צְדָדִין קָמִיפְלְגֵי – Rather, **here they dispute using** the **"sides of the sides"** of a tree:[38] מַר סָבַר צִדֵּי צְדָדִין אֲסוּרִין – **One master** (the Tanna Kamma) **contends that the "sides of the sides"** of a tree **are prohibited** for use, וּמַר סָבַר צִדֵּי צְדָדִין מוּתָּרִין – **and one master** (R' Meir) **contends that the "sides of the sides"** of a tree **are permitted** for use.

An opposing view:

רָבָא אָמַר – **Rava said:** מַאן דְּאָסַר בִּצְדָדִין – **Whoever prohibits** using the **sides** of a tree אָסַר נַמִּי בְּצִדֵּי צְדָדִין – **prohibits** using the **"sides of the sides"** of a tree **as well.** מַאן דְּשָׁרֵי בְּצִדֵּי צְדָדִין – And **whoever permits** using the **"sides of the sides"** of a tree שָׁרֵי נַמִּי בִּצְדָדִין – **permits** using **the sides** of a tree **as well.** Thus, the Tannaim in the above Baraisa who disagree regarding the use of the "sides of the sides" of a tree would likewise disagree regarding the use of the sides of a tree.

Rava is challenged:

אֵיתִיבֵיהּ רַב מְשַׁרְשִׁיָּא לְרָבָא – **Rav Mesharshiya challenged Rava** from the following Baraisa: נָעַץ – IF ONE STUCK

NOTES

38. If one were to make use of the [tops of] the plank walls themselves, that would be deemed a use of the sides of a tree, since the plank walls are considered a "side" of the tree. But making use of the *s'chach,* [which extends beyond the planks] is equivalent to using the sides *of the planks*; thus, it is a use of the "sides of the sides" of a tree. According to Abaye, using the sides of a tree is clearly prohibited; using the "sides of the sides" of a tree is a matter of Tannaic dispute (*Rashi*; cf. *Ran MHK* ed.).

[It would seem that since Abaye maintains that where the *s'chach* rests on the plank walls, use of the *s'chach* is considered use of a "side of the sides" of the tree, it ought to follow that where the *s'chach* rests directly on the tree, use of the *s'chach* should be considered use of the "side" of the tree. Thus, Abaye would take issue with the Gemara earlier that assumed that use of the *s'chach* in such a case is considered use of the tree itself (see above, note 33). See *Shaar HaTziyun* 628:24, who seems to be in doubt about this point as regards the halachah.]

יָתֵד בְּאִילָן – A STAKE INTO A TREE, וְתָלָה בָּהּ כַּלְכָּלָה – HUNG A BASKET ON [THE STAKE], and put his *eruv* into this basket, the law is as follows:[1] לְמַעְלָה מֵעֲשָׂרָה טְפָחִים – If this basket hangs HIGHER THAN TEN *TEFACHIM*, אֵין עֵירוּבוֹ עֵירוּב – HIS *ERUV* IS NOT A valid *ERUV*, because he is forbidden to take the *eruv* out of the basket on the Sabbath.[2] לְמַטָּה מֵעֲשָׂרָה טְפָחִים – If, however, the basket hangs LOWER THAN TEN *TEFACHIM*, עֵירוּבוֹ עֵירוּב – HIS *ERUV* IS A valid *ERUV*, since he may take it out of the basket on the Sabbath.[3] טַעְמָא דְנָעַץ יָתֵד בְּאִילָן – Now by its choice of case the Baraisa implies that **the reason** that he may remove the *eruv* when it is beneath ten *tefachim* **is that he drove a stake into the tree** first, so that the basket did not hang directly from the tree; הָא לֹא נָעַץ – **but had he not driven** a stake into the tree, but simply hung the basket from the tree, אֲפִילוּ לְמַטָּה מֵעֲשָׂרָה טְפָחִים אֵין עֵירוּבוֹ עֵירוּב – **his *eruv* would not be a** valid ***eruv*** **even** if it hung **lower than ten *tefachim*.**[4] וְהָא הַאי תַּנָּא דְּקָאָסַר בְּצִדְדִין – **Now, here** we see that **this Tanna prohibits** using the **"sides"** of a tree, i.e. a basket hung directly from the tree, וְקָשָׁרֵי בְּצִדֵּי צְדָדִין – **but permits** using the **"sides of sides."** How then could Rava say that no Tanna makes such a distinction?

The Gemara answers:

אָמַר רַב פָּפָּא – **Rav Pappa said:** הָכָא בְּכַלְכָּלָה דְחוּקָה עָסְקִינַן – **Here,** in this Baraisa, **we are dealing with a narrow-mouthed basket** into which he must force his hand, דְּבַהֲדֵי דְּשָׁקִיל לֵיהּ לְעֵירוּב – so **that,** had it hung from the tree itself, **when he would have taken the *eruv*** קָמְנִיד לֵיהּ לְאִילָן – **he would** perforce **have moved the tree.** וְקָמִשְׁתַּמֵּשׁ בְּאִילָן גּוּפֵיהּ – **And** by doing so, **he would be "using" the tree itself,** something that is prohibited according to all opinions.[5] The Tanna therefore requires that the basket not hang directly from the tree but, rather, be suspended from a stake.[6]

The Gemara concludes:

וְהִלְכְתָא – **And the halachah is** צְדָדִין אֲסוּרִין צִדֵּי צְדָדִין מוּתָּרִין – that **the sides** of a tree **are forbidden** for use on the Sabbath, but the **"sides of sides" are permitted.**

The Gemara points out a practical application of this ruling: אָמַר רַב אַשִׁי – **Rav Ashi said:** הַשְׁתָּא דְּאָמַרְתְּ צְדָדִין אֲסוּרִין – **Now that you have said that the sides** of a tree **are forbidden** for use, this bears upon הַאי דַּרְגָּא דְמַדְלָא – the case of an **elevated ladder,**[7] in the following way: לֹא לִינַּחֵיהּ אִינִישׁ אַדִּיקְלָא – **A person should not lean** a ladder **on the palm** next to a watchtower, דְּהָווּ לְהוּ צְדָדִין – **since** the ladder **would** then **have the status of the "sides"** of the tree and thus be forbidden.[8] אֶלָּא לִינַּחֵיהּ אַגְוָואזֵי לְבַר מִדִּיקְלָא – **Rather, he should rest [the ladder] on stakes** coming **out of the palm.** In this way, the ladder will be considered a "side of a side" of the tree and he will be permitted to climb it.[9] וְכִי סָלִיק – **Also, as he ascends** לֹא לִינַּח כַּרְעֵיהּ אַגְוָואזֵי – **he should not rest his foot on the stakes,** since that would be a use of the stakes themselves, which are a "side" of the tree. אֶלָּא לִיתְנַהּ אַקָּנִין – **Rather, he should rest his foot on the rungs** of the ladder,[10] which is merely the "side of the sides" of the tree.

Mishnah The Mishnah discusses the preparation of animal feed on the Sabbath:[11] מַתִּירִין פְּקִיעֵי עָמִיר לִפְנֵי בְהֵמָה – ONE MAY UNTIE BUNDLES (*pekiin*) OF STRAW BEFORE AN ANIMAL,[12] וּמְפַסְפְּסִין אֶת הַכִּיפִּין – AND ONE MAY SCATTER *KIPIN* for it,[13] אֲבָל לֹא אֶת הַזִּירִין – BUT NOT *ZIRIN*. אֵין מְרַסְּקִין לֹא אֶת הַשַּׁחַת וְלֹא אֶת הֶחָרוּבִין לִפְנֵי בְהֵמָה – ONE MAY NOT SHRED EITHER FODDER[14] OR CAROBS BEFORE AN ANIMAL,[15] בֵּין דַּקָּה וּבֵין גַּסָּה – WHETHER IT IS A SMALL [ANIMAL] OR A LARGE [ANIMAL].[16] רַבִּי יְהוּדָה מַתִּיר בְּחָרוּבִין לְדַקָּה – R' YEHUDAH PERMITS the shredding of CAROBS FOR A SMALL ANIMAL.[17]

NOTES

1. [An *eruv* is food placed in a specific location in order to establish a person's Sabbath residence there. A person is forbidden to go more than two thousand *amos* from this legally defined residence on the Sabbath.] In the Baraisa's case, the person intended to establish his Sabbath residence beneath the tree (*Rashi*).

2. [In Talmudic times] baskets were typically at least four *tefachim* wide. When such a basket is suspended ten *tefachim* or more above the ground, it is deemed a *reshus hayachid* (see *Menachem Meishiv Nefesh* and *Ishei Yisrael*). A person standing in a *reshus harabim* is prohibited to remove anything from it. Since he intended to establish his Sabbath residence in the *reshus harabim* and he cannot remove his *eruv* from the basket and eat it there, the *eruv* fails to establish a residence for him (*Rashi*).

3. Below ten *tefachim*, the basket is deemed to be part of the surrounding *reshus harabim*. Since both he and his *eruv* are in the same domain, the *eruv* can establish a Sabbath residence for him there (*Rashi;* see *Tosafos* ד״ה למטה).

4. The distinction is as follows: Were the basket hung directly from the tree, then the basket would have the status of a "side" of the tree, and removing the *eruv* from the basket would be considered a use of the side of the tree which this Tanna, apparently, does not allow (see *Rashi*; see *Mishnah Berurah* 336:12). But where he first drove a stake into the tree and then hung a basket from that stake, the basket — which hangs below the stake — is merely a "side of a side," whose use this Tanna does allow (see *Magen Avraham* 336:15).

5. Since he cannot use the basket without shaking the tree, he is using the tree itself, which is forbidden. See *Orach Chaim* §336 with *Mishnah Berurah*, end of §63, and *Beur Halachah* there ד״ה ומותר.

6. [Apparently, when the basket hangs from a stake one can remove the *eruv* without shaking the tree (see *Rashi; Magen Avraham* ibid.).]

7. Such as a ladder that leads to a watchtower. Such watchtowers were built atop tall poles and positioned near palm trees, and one reached them by means of ladders (*Rashi*).

8. Since the ladder rests on the tree itself, the ladder is considered a "side" of the tree, whose use is forbidden.

9. [However, the act of setting up the ladder is a use of the stakes themselves, which are considered "sides" of the tree. Accordingly, he must be careful to set the ladder up before the Sabbath commences (see *Mishnah Berurah* 366:60).

10. Or, if he wishes, on the sticks coming out of the poles that support the watchtower (*Rashi*; see also *Rashi* to *Rif*).

11. [The Gemara will cite two widely divergent interpretations of our Mishnah. Following *Rashi's* lead (see *Rashi* ד״ה שחת), we will explain the Mishnah according to the view of the Amora, Rav Yehudah.]

12. *Pekiin* denotes [a type of] bundle of straw (*Rashi*); a more precise definition of this term, as well as of the terms *kipin* and *zirin* which follow in the Mishnah, will be given in the Gemara.

One may untie these bundles on the Sabbath so that the animal may easily eat them (*Rashi*).

13. Normally, when one gives these bundles to an animal, one scatters them first in order to render them more appetizing; if they are packed together, they become warm and fail to release much of a scent. As a result, the animal finds them unpalatable (*Rashi*).

14. Fodder is stubble of a type of fast-growing grain, and corresponds to the Aramaic *aspasta* (see *Rashi* here and to *Bava Basra* 28b ד״ה אספסתא).

15. Shredding these items is prohibited as excessive exertion (*Rashi*). [Since the fodder and carobs are readily edible as is, any effort expended on their improvement is superfluous and thus proscribed on the Sabbath.] With regard to the question of *grinding*, see *Orach Chaim* 324:7 with commentaries and *Rambam, Hil. Shabbos* 21:18 with commentaries.

16. Livestock are divided into two general categories: *large animals* (*beheimah gasah*), which includes cattle, horses, donkeys and mules, and *small animals* (*beheimah dakah*), which includes sheep and goats (see *Meiri* to *Kiddushin* 25b).

17. A small animal's teeth are themselves small. It would be difficult for such an animal to chew through [tough carobs] unless these are first shredded (*Rashi*).

יתד באילן ותלה בה כלכלה למעלה מעשרה טפחים אין עירובו עירוב למטה מי' טפחים עירובו עירוב טעמא דנעץ יתד באילן הא לא נעץ אפילו למטה מי' טפחים אין עירובו עירוב והא האי תנא דקאסר בצדדין וקשרי בצדי צדדין אמר רב פפא הכא בכלכלה דחוקה עסקינן דבהדי דשקיל ליה לעירוב קמניד ליה לאילן וקמשמש באילן גופיה ° א והלכתא (א) צדדין אסורין צדי צדדין מותרין אמר רב אשי השתא דאמרת צדדין אסורין האי דרגא דמדלא לא לינחיה איניש אדיקלא דהוו להו צדדין אלא לינחיה אגוואזי לבר מדיקלא וכי סליק לא לינח כרעיה אגוואזי אלא ליתנח אקנין: **מתני'** מתירין פקיעי עמיר לפני בהמה ומפספסין את הכיפין אבל לא את (א) הזירין אין מרסקין לא את השחת ולא את החרובין לפני בהמה בין דקה ובין גסה רבי יהודה מתיר בחרובין לדקה: **גמ'** אמר רב הונא הן הן פקיעין הן הן כיפין תרי פקיעין תרי כיפין תלתא (ב) זירין דארזי וה"ק מתירין פקיעי עמיר לפני בהמה ומפספסין והוא הדין לכיפין אבל לא את הזירין לא לפספס ולא להתיר אמר רב חסדא מאי טעמא דרב הונא קא סבר למטרח באוכלא טרחינן לשווי אוכלא לא משוינן רב יהודה אמר הן הן פקיעין הן הן זירין תרי פקיעין תרי זירין תלתא כיפין דארזי וה"ק ב מתירין פקיעי עמיר לפני בהמה אבל פספוסי לא וכיפין פספוסי נמי מפספסינן אבל לא הזירין לפספס [א] אלא להתיר אמר רבא מאי טעמא דרב יהודה קסבר ג שווי אוכלא משוינן מטרח באוכלא לא טרחינן תנן ד אין מרסקין את השחת ואת החרובין לפני בהמה בין דקה ובין גסה מאי לאו חרובין דומיא דשחת מה שחת דרכיכי אף חרובין דרכיכי אלמא לא טרחינן באוכלא ותיובתיה דרב הונא אמר לך רב הונא לא שחת דומיא דחרובין מה חרובין דאקושי אף שחת דאקושי היכי משכחת לה בעילי זוטרי ת"ש רבי יהודה מתיר בחרובין לדקה לדקה אין לגסה לא אי אמרת בשלמא ת"ק סבר מיטרח באוכלא לא טרחינן שווי משוינן היינו דקא אמר ר' יהודה (ג) החרובין לדקה נמי שווי אוכלא הוא אלא אי אמרת ת"ק סבר שווי אוכלא לא משוינן מיטרח באוכלא מטרחינן רבי יהודה (ד) דמתיר בחרובין לדקה כל שכן לגסה מי סברת דקה דקה ממש מאי דקה גסה (ה) ומאי קרי לה דקה דדייקא באוכלא הא מדקתני רישא בין דקה ובין גסה מכלל דרבי יהודה דקה דקה ממש קאמר קשיא תא שמע ו מחתכין את

רש"י

יתד. נגר: ותלה בה כלכלה. ונתן בה עירובו והוא נתכוון לשבות למטה תחת האילן: למטה מי' טפחים. אם הכלכלה בתוך י' לארץ עירובו עירוב דהוא ועירובו ברה"ר אבל למעלה מי' וסתם כלכלה רחבה ארבעה הויא לה כלכלה רשות היחיד והוא נתכוון לשבות ברשות הרבים ואינו יכול ליטלו שם ולאכלו וכיון דאינה סעודה הראויה לו אינו קונה שביתה על ידה: טעמא דנעץ יתד. דכי שקיל לעירובו משתמש בצדי לצדדין אבל לא נעץ יתד אלא קשרה בצדי אילן לא: הכא בכלכלה דחוקה. שפיה צר וקצרה היא ומכניס ידו לתוכה בדוחק הלכך אי ממש הוה קטר לה בצדי אילן כי שקיל ליה לעירוביה מניד ליה לאילן הלכך כי איכא יתד הוא דשרי ואי לא לא: האי דרגא דמדלא. סולם שעולין בו לסוכת נוצרים שעושין ע"ג קונדיסין גבוהין והיא סמוכה לאילן: לא לינחיה. ראש הסולם אדיקלא לא יסמוך ראש הסולם לצד דקל דכי סליק משתמש בצדדין: אלא לינחיה אגוואזי לבר מדיקלא. יתקע יתד בצדי האילן ויסמוך הסולם עליו דהוה ליה יתד לצדים וסולם צדי לצדין: וכי סליק לא לינח כרעיה על היתד אלא אקניא. על שליבות הסולם או קנים היוצאים מהקונדיסין: **מתני'** פקיעי עמיר. קשין של שבלים (שאותם) שאוגדים מתירין אותם שיהו נוחין לבהמה לאוכלה: מפספסין. שכן דרך שמפזרים לבהמה העשבים ויפין לה לאוכלן שכשהן דחוקין מתחממין ואינה מריחה ריחה כל כך וקצה בהן: את הכיפין. מפרש בגמרא וכן זירין: אין מרסקין. אין מחתכין: שחת. עשב של תבואה והוא אספסתא ומשום דטירחא דלא צריך הוא: רבי יהודה מתיר בחרובין לדקה. ששיניה דקות וקשין לה: **גמ'** הן הן פקיעין הן הן כיפין. כולן קשין של שבלין הן מיהו פקיעין תרי שאינן קשורין אלא בשני ראשים: כיפין תלת. קשורין ג' [אגודים]: זירין דארזא. ענפים לחין של ארז שמזרדין אותם ובעודם לחין ראויין לבהמה ורוב בני אדם מניחין אותם לעצים: וה"ק מתירין פקיעי עמיר ומפספסין. דכיון דמעיקרא אוכלא נינהו מותר לטרוח בהן להכשירם למתקן לה ואת הכיפין אף הן מתירין ומפספסין ואע"ג דנפיש טרחייהו אבל לא הזירין לא לפספס ולא להתיר דכיון דמעיקרא סתמייהו לאו אוכלא והשתא הוא דמשוי להו אוכלא ה"ל אולודי אוכלא בשבת: מיטרח באוכלא. בדבר שתחילתו אוכל קודם תיקון זה טרחינן ומכשרינן לייפותן לה: הן הן פקיעין הן הן זירין. שניהן בקשים של שבלים ומה שהתיר בזה התיר בזה ודקתני אבל לא הזירין אפספוס קאי: וה"ק מתירין פקיעי עמיר. דכל זמן שהוא קשור לאו אוכלא הוא ומתירו לשווי אוכלא ומשום צער בהמה שרי אבל פספוס לא דסגי ליה בהתרה ואיתעביד אוכלא ופספוסיה לתענוג בעלמא הוא ומטרח באוכל בדבר שהוא כבר אוכל בלא תיקון זה לא טרחינן ומפספסין את הכיפין דארזא דבלאו פספוס לא הוי אוכלא אבל לא את הזירין לפספס אלא להתיר שלשה אוגדיהן בפקיעין דהתרת אוגדיהן שווי אוכלא הוא: אין מרסקין. סיפא דמתניתין היא וחד טעמא: דרכיכי. כגון חרובין לחין דראויין למאכל בהמה בלא ריסוק וריסוק דידהו לתענוג בעלמא: דאקושי. קשין כגון שיבשו: בעילי זוטרי. עיירים קטנים שאף השחת קשה להם וצריכה ריסוק לשווי אוכלא: לדקה אין. דהוה ליה שווי אוכלא: לגסה לא. דהוה ליה מטרח באוכלא: אי אמרת בשלמא. שמע רבי יהודה לת"ק דאמר מיטרח באוכלין אסור ואין מרסקין ברכיכי קאמר אבל שווי אוכלא שרי היינו דקאמר ליה רבי יהודה חרובין לדקה לית לן למיסר דשווי אוכלא הוא ואע"ג דרכיכי אלא אי אמרת קסבר ת"ק מיטרח באוכלא שרי שווי אוכלא אסור ואין מרסקין דקאמר בדאקושי קאמר דשווי אוכלא הוי: רבי יהודה מתיר בחרובין לדקה. בתמיה הא כל שכן דלגסה למיטרח באוכלא הוא ושרי הכי ה"ל למיתני ור' יהודה מתיר בחרובין לגסה דהוה ליה מיטרח באוכלא והא ליכא למימר דר' יהודה מפיך דשווי אוכלא שרי מיטרח באוכלא אסיר דהא ת"ק בדאקושי קאמר וגבי גסה נמי שווי אוכלא הוא וה"ל למיתני ורבי יהודה מתיר סתמא בין דקה בין גסה ועוד הוה ליה למישרי נמי זירין להתיר ולפספס דשווי אוכלא נמי הוא: דדייקא. כוססת יפה ומדקת אוכלין בפיה: והא מדקתני רישא בין דקה בין גסה שמע מינה דקה ממש. ורבי יהודה את"ק קאי:

תוספות

למטה מי' טפחים עירובו עירוב. קשה אמאי עירובו עירוב והא כרמלית הוא כיון שרחבה ארבעה ואסור לטלטל לרה"ר וי"ל אין כרמלית בכלים כדפירש בקונטרס בפ"ק דמכילתין (דף ח.) גבי היתה קופתו מונחת כו' ° אי נמי כרבי דאמר ג כל דבר שהוא משום שבות לא גזרו עליו בין השמשות: **אמר** רב פפא הכא בכלכלה דחוקה עסקינן. מדמשני רב פפא הכי משמע דסבירא ליה לצדדין מותרין ורב אשי משמע בסמוך דסבר דאסורין מדאמר רב אשי בסמוך השתא דאמרת לצדדין אסורין וקשה לי הא איפכא שמעינן להו במסכת חגיגה בפ"ב (דף יז. ושם) דאמר רב פפא שמע מינה לצדדין אסורין דאי סלקא דעתך לצדדין מותרים נסמוך אריסא דלצדדין נינהו רב אשי אמר אפילו תימא לצדדין מותרין כל דלהדי גבה כגבה דמי ד: **והלכתא** צדדין אסורין צדי צדדין מותרין. ותימה לרבי אמאי לא חשיב הני בהדי יע"ל קג"ס דהלכה כאביי (בבבא מציעא דף כב:) דאמר רבא מאן דאסר בצדדין אסר נמי בצדי צדדין ואביי אמר בצדדין כולי עלמא לא פליגי [דאסור] ובצדי צדדין פליגי: **רב** יהודה אמר הן הן פקיעין כו' וה"ק מתירים פקיעי עמיר כו'. פירש בקונטרס דהתרת פקיעים הויא שווי אוכלא וצריך לפרש (ו) נמי בהא דרב יהודה חשיב התרת פקיעין שווי אוכלא ורב הונא לא חשיב לה שווי אוכלא מדשרי לה ואין נראה לרבינו תם לאפלוגינהו בהכי אלא לתרוייהו לא הויא התרת פקיעי עמיר לא שווי אוכלא ולא מיטרח באוכלא דלא שייך טורח בהתרה ולהכי שריא לתרוייהו. מ"ר:

עין משפט נר מצוה

כ א מיי' פכ"ו מהל' שבת הלכה ט סמג לאוין סה טוש"ע א"ח סימן שצ סעיף יח:

כא ב ג מיי' פכ"א מהל' שבת הל' יח טוש"ע א"ח סי' שכד סעיף ד:

כב ד מיי' שם טוש"ע שם סעיף ה:

הגהות הגר"א

[א] גמ' לפספס אלא להתיר. נ"ב גירסת הרי"ף ולא להתיר וכן מלד:

רבינו חננאל

חמור אלא בצידי החמור אני משפשף (ויגדלן) [וצדדין] לא גזרו בהו רבנן מדתנן מתיר החבלים והשקין נופלין מאי לאו בחבר גואלקי ולא גזרו בהו רבנן פי' חבר גואלקי כשטוענין הבהמה מביאין שק וטוענין אותו מצד אחד ושק האחר מצד השני ומביא חבל וקושרן ומחברן (ומשרכבן) [ומשכיבן] בצדי הבהמה וכשמבקשין לפרק משאוי מגביה השקין לפרוק קשר החבל להיות נוח להתיר ומתיר ומניח השקין והן יורדין מצדי הבהמה ויורדין לארץ נמצא מגביה ומוריד השקין בצידי החמור כאשר אני מגביה ע"ג החמור והוא יורד בדרך שפשוף אמר לך אביי אינו אומר מתיר החבלים בחבר גואלקי אלא באבר גואלקי כדתנן כיצד מאברין את העדים ומפרשינן ליה מלשון אבר כן מוסיף כמין אבר בגואלקי והוא למעלה כדאמרי' בפ' לא יחפור (ב"ב כה:) באברורי הוו יתבי פי' אברורי למעלה מן המשאוי כגון שהיה צד המשאוי האחד כבד והשני קל ורצונו להשוות המשאוי שלא יהיה (א) מטרטן ומוסיף על הצד הקל דבר להשוות המשקל שלא יהיה אחד מהן מכריע ועליו אמרה משנתנו מתיר החבלים והשקין נופלים שקשר למעלה הוא. ואין צריך להגביה שק ולא להוריד אלא כשמתיר החבר נופלין אבר גואלקי נמצאו גואלקי על צידי הבהמה ואם זה על צידי גואלקי נמצא אבר זה צדי צדדין אי נמי בגואלקי דגואלקי עצמו אינן קשורין בחבלים אלא כמנהג שהי' לאורחים המהלכים בדרכים שעושין בראש השקין כמין קרסים ולולאות מן החבלים ומכניס הלולאות בקרסים אי נמי לולאות בלבד ומכניס בהן עץ ומחברן וכשרוצה לפרקן מושך העץ ההוא והן נופלים ונקרא עץ ההוא לכתא ואינו מגיע לצדדין ואותו האבר נמי שמוסיפין על המשאוי הוא צדי צדדין והוא מותר אבל הצדדין אסורין. ועוד אקשי ליה אביי לרבה הא ב' בידי אדם ואחת באילן כו' ופריק רבה התם דכפייה לאילן וסיכך על גביו שנמצא משתמש באילן עצמו. תוב אקשינן עליה מסיפא דקתני ג' בידי אדם ואחת באילן כשרה ועולין לה ביו"ט ואי כפייה לאילן וסיכך ע"ג אמאי עולין לה ביו"ט הא משתמש באילן ואסור ופריק ליה התם ופרסי כאנא פי' גיחא ופרסיכנא תרתב מאבקא ב) ועלה דייקינן זה הכלל כל שינטל האילן ויכולה לעמוד עולין לה ביו"ט לימא כתנאי אין עולין לה ביו"ט כו' סברי לה כגון דחק באילן ונתן הנסרין שהן הסכך באותה החקיקה והן הצדדין זה אוסר להשתמש בצדדין וזה מתיר אמר אביי כולי עלמא צדדין אסורין והכא בצידי צדדין פליגי פי' כגון דחק באילן ונתן באותה החקיקה עץ חזק כמין קורה ושם ראשי הנסרים על העץ הנתון כמין קורה שנמצא העץ ההוא צדדי האילן והנסרים הנתונין על גביו צדדי צדדין רבא א' צדדין וצדדי צדדין דינם אחד האוסר בצדדין אוסר גם בצידי צדדין והמתיר צדדי צדדין גם בצדדין מתיר ובא אביי לרבה דאמר המתיר בצידי צדדין גם בצדדין מתיר הא דתניא נעץ יתד באילן ותלה בו כלכלה למטה מעשרה עירובו עירוב למטה מי' טפחים אין עירובו עירוב. ודייקינן מינה טעמא דנעץ יתד באילן ותלה בו כלכלה בה יתד צידי האילן והכלכלה צידי צדדין ולפיכך למטה מעשרה טפחים עירובו עירוב אבל אם לא נעץ יתד ותלה בו אלא תלה באמירי האילן אפילו למטה מעשרה אין עירובו עירוב דהוה לי' צדדין הדר נתברר כי זה

מסורת הש"ס

א) [חגיגה טז:], ב) לקמן קנו:, ג) [לעיל ח:], ד) [וע' תוספות חגיגה יז. ד"ה רב אשי דלא מקשה אלא לרב אשי מדרב אשי וכתבו מירוץ לזה].

הגהות הב"ח

(א) במשנה את הכיפין אבל לא את הזרדין אין: (ב) גמ' כיפין תלתא זרדין דארזי וכו' אבל לא את הזרדין וכו' למטרח באוכלא טרחינן לשווי אוכלא לא משוינן וכו' הן הן זרדין תרי זרדין תלתא כיפין וכו' אבל לא הזרדין לפספסא: (ג) שם היינו דקא אמר ר' יהודה חרובין לדקה נמי שווי אוכלא: (ד) שם ר' יהודה מתיר בכ"ל ואות ד' נמחק: (ה) שם מאי דקה גסה ומאי קרי: (ו) תוס' ד"ה ר' יהודה וכו' וצריך לפרש דפליגי נמי בהא:

גליון הש"ס

גמ' והלכתא צדדים אסורין. עיין עירובין דף לג ע"א: תוס' ד"ה למטה מי' וכו' א"נ כרבי וכו'. ותמוה דא"כ אפי' לא נעץ יתד נמי דשימוש באילן הוי רק שבות ולי"ג בה"ש. אח"כ ראיתי שתמה כן בתשובת מעיל צדקה סימן ט'. ולענ"ד י"ל דנ"מ בע"ש שחל להיות ביו"ט והניח עירוב בערב יו"ט בכלכלה זו שיהיה עירוב ליו"ט ושבת. ולפי דב' קדושות הן לריך שיהיה עירובו קיים ביה"ש דקודם שבת וכזה אם לא נעץ יתד לא מהני עירובו דביה"ש דשבת אינו יכול ליטול עירובו דהוי יום טוב ...

רב נסים גאון

בפרק כירה (דף מב) ופירשנו כי החלוקה בצער בעלי חיים דאורייתא או דרבנן תמצא בפרק אלו מציאות (דף לב:)

ליקוטי רש"י

למעלה מעשרה טפחים אין עירובו עירוב. המערב עירובי תחומין עירובו קונה לו שביתה שם שיוכל לילך משם לכל רוח אלפים כאילו שבת שם וצריך שיהיה יכול לקנות שביתתו במקום שיוכל לאכול שם עירובו אם היה רוצה לאוכלו שמתוך כך מועיל לו עירובו לקנות שביתה במקום שהוא גורם להיות שם שייך אליו ... ליום [לעיל ח.] הלכך למעלה מעשרה אין עירובו עירוב דמקום שנתכוון לשבות שם היה שביתתו וכיון דלאו הוה בעי למשקל עירוביה ומיכליה בשעה שהעירוב זוכה לו דהיינו בין השמשות לא מצי שקיל דמיימי מרשות ... לא הוה עירובו עירוב וכו' [עירובין לב:]. והא האי תנא דקאסר בצדדין. כגון הכא דאינו משתמש ... שקיל לעירובו אפילו בשבת בכלכלה הוא דמשתמש שהוא לצדי אילן [שם לג.]. שחת. תבואת חיטין ושעורין קודם שתמלא בזירין ובלע"ז פירי"א [ע"ז כ:].

חשק שלמה על רבינו חננאל א) עיין ערוך ערך אברורי: ב) פה הדברים משובשים בכ"י ומלוה לתקנם. ועי' בערוך ערך גז האחרון:

Gemara The Gemara presents the first of two explanations of the Mishnah:

אָמַר רַב הוּנָא – **Rav Huna said:** הֵן הֵן פְּקִיעִין הֵן הֵן כִּיפִּין – ***Pekiin* are identical to *kipin,*** i.e. both terms denote bundles of straw, פְּקִיעִין תְּרֵי כִּיפִּין – except that ***pekiin* are** bundles tied **twice** – תְּלָתָא – and ***kipin* are** bundles tied **three times.**[18] זִירִין דְּאַרְזֵי – ***Zirin,*** on the other hand, refers to **cedar boughs.**[19] וְהָכִי קָאָמַר – **And this is what [the Mishnah] means:** מַתִּירִין פְּקִיעֵי עָמִיר לִפְנֵי בְהֵמָה וּמְפַסְפְּסִין – ONE MAY UNTIE *PEKIIN* (i.e. doubly bound bundles) OF STRAW BEFORE AN ANIMAL, AND ONE MAY even SCATTER the straw afterwards, וְהוּא הַדִּין לְכִיפִּין – **and the same applies to *KIPIN*** (i.e. triply bound bundles of straw);[20] אֲבָל לֹא אֶת הַזִּירִין – BUT this is NOT permitted for *ZIRIN* (i.e. cedar boughs), לֹא לְפַסְפֵּס וְלֹא לְהַתִּיר – **neither in regard to scattering nor in regard to untying.**

Thus, according to Rav Huna one may untie and scatter both kinds of bundles of straw, but one may do neither with bundles of cedar boughs.[21]

Rav Huna's position is explained:

אָמַר רַב חִסְדָּא – **Rav Chisda said:** מַאי טַעְמָא דְּרַב הוּנָא – **What is Rav Huna's reasoning?** קָא סָבַר לְמִטְרַח בְּאוּכְלָא טָרְחִינַן – **He contends that one may exert himself** to improve an existing **food,**[22] לְשַׁוּו[יֵי] אוּכְלָא לֹא מְשַׁוִּינַן – **but one may not make food,** i.e. make a non-food item into food, on the Sabbath.[23]

The Gemara presents an alternative interpretation of the Mishnah:

רַב יְהוּדָה אָמַר – **Rav Yehudah said:** הֵן הֵן פְּקִיעִין הֵן הֵן זִירִין – ***Pekiin* are identical to *zirin:*** They are both bundles of straw, פְּקִיעִין תְּרֵי – except that ***pekiin* are** bound **twice,** זִירִין תְּלָתָא – whereas ***zirin* are** bound **three times.** כִּיפִּין דְּאַרְזֵי – ***Kipin* are cedar boughs.** וְהָכִי קָאָמַר – **And this is what [the Mishnah] means:** מַתִּירִין פְּקִיעֵי עָמִיר לִפְנֵי בְהֵמָה אֲבָל פַּסְפּוּסֵי לֹא – ONE MAY UNTIE *PEKIIN* (i.e.doubly bound bundles) OF STRAW BEFORE AN ANIMAL, **but one may not scatter them.** וְכִיפִּין פַּסְפּוּסֵי נַמֵּי מְפַסְפְּסִינַן – AND *KIPIN* (i.e. cedar boughs) ONE MAY even SCATTER, as well as untie. אֲבָל לֹא הַזִּירִין לְפַסְפֵּס אֶלָּא לְהַתִּיר – BUT this leniency does NOT apply to *ZIRIN* (i.e. triply bound bundles of straw) **in regard to scattering; rather** it applies to them only **in regard to untying.**

Thus, according to Rav Yehudah one may untie both kinds of bundles of straw, but scatter neither; but one may both untie and scatter bundles of cedar boughs.

Rav Yehudah's position is explained:

אָמַר רָבָא – **Rava said:** מַאי טַעְמָא דְּרַב יְהוּדָה – **What is Rav Yehudah's reasoning?** קָסָבַר שַׁוּוּ[יֵי] אוּכְלָא מְשַׁוִּינַן – **[Rav Yehudah] maintains that one may make food,** i.e. one may make food edible for an animal on the Sabbath, מִטְרַח בְּאוּכְלָא לֹא טָרְחִינַן – **but one may not exert oneself for** the mere enhancement of animal **food.**[24]

The Gemara challenges Rav Huna's view:

תְּנַן – **We learned in our Mishnah:** אֵין מְרַסְּקִין אֶת הַשַּׁחַת וְאֶת הֶחָרוּבִין לִפְנֵי בְהֵמָה – ONE MAY NOT SHRED EITHER FODDER OR CAROBS BEFORE AN ANIMAL, בֵּין דַּקָּה וּבֵין גַּסָּה – WHETHER IT IS A SMALL [ANIMAL] OR A LARGE [ANIMAL]. מַאי לָאו חָרוּבִין דּוּמְיָא דְשַׁחַת – **What** is the Mishnah's case? Are we **not** speaking of **carobs** that are **analogous to fodder?** מַה שַּׁחַת דְּרַכִּיכֵי – **Just as fodder is** normally **tender,** אַף חָרוּבִין דְּרַכִּיכֵי – **so too the carobs** referred to here **are tender** and moist and are therefore already suitable for animal food. Yet the Mishnah teaches that one may not shred them. אַלְמָא לֹא טָרְחִינַן בְּאוּכְלָא – **Apparently, one may not exert oneself to** merely enhance animal **food,** וְתְיוּבְתֵּיהּ דְּרַב הוּנָא – **and this is a refutation of Rav Huna! – ? –**

The Gemara answers:

אָמַר לָךְ רַב הוּנָא לֹא – **Rav Huna could tell you** that this is **not** the case of our Mishnah; rather, שַׁחַת דּוּמְיָא דְחָרוּבִין – **we are** speaking of **fodder** that is **analogous to carobs:** מַה חָרוּבִין דְּאַקּוּשֵׁי – **Just as carobs are** commonly **hard,**[25] אַף שַׁחַת דְּאַקּוּשֵׁי – **so too the fodder** mentioned here **is hard** for the animal to eat and requires some softening. הֵיכִי מַשְׁכַּחַת לָהּ – **And where do you find a case** of fodder that is too hard for a (large) animal's consumption? בְּעִילֵי זוּטְרֵי – **Regarding young donkeys,** for which even regular fodder is too hard.[26]

NOTES

18. *Pekiin* are tied at each end; *kipin* have a third tie [in the middle] as well (*Rashi*).

19. These are moist branches pruned from a cedar tree. As long as they retain their moistness, they are fit for animal food; most people, however, leave them to dry for fuel (*Rashi*).

[Regarding whether these cedar boughs are *muktzeh* on the Sabbath, since they are earmarked for fuel, and, if so, how they can be handled to feed an animal, see *Rashba; Shiltei HaGiborim; Beur Halachah* to 324:5 (ד״ה בעודם לחים).]

20. [One may both untie the three knots and scatter the straw.]

21. The Gemara will immediately explain the rationale for these rulings.

22. Rav Huna holds that one may take something that is already considered food and enhance it for an animal, despite the exertion involved. Thus, one may not only untie the two knots of *pekiin,* but even the three knots of *kipin,* and he may scatter both as well (*Rashi*).

23. As noted before, cedar boughs are usually left for fuel and are not normally considered animal feed. When one unties and scatters a bunch of cedar boughs for an animal, he is thereby converting it into food. Rav Huna holds that one may not make a non-food substance into food on the Sabbath; he may only enhance something already considered food (*Rashi;* cf. *Meiri;* see also above, 50b note 9; *Teshuvos Minchas Shlomo* §6).

[Emendation of לְשַׁוּוּיֵי here and below follows *Dikdukei Soferim.*]

24. The animal cannot eat the bundles of straw while they are tied up; untying these bundles is therefore necessary to make these items edible and is permitted, lest the animal go hungry. Scattering these bundles to make them more palatable is a mere enhancement of the food, and is regarded as an unnecessary effort on behalf of the animal (*Rashi;* cf. *Tosafos*; see *Ramban*).

On the other hand, the animal will not eat cedar boughs at all unless they are scattered; scattering them, therefore, is considered making a food, i.e. making it edible, and is permitted.

It emerges that Rav Huna's and Rav Yehudah's views are diametrically opposed: Rav Huna forbids making food, but permits exerting oneself to enhance a food, whereas Rav Yehudah permits making food, but forbids exerting oneself to merely enhance a food.

[However, it should be noted that the meaning of the term *making food* is not the same for Rav Huna as it is for Rav Yehudah. For Rav Huna, making food means taking a non-food item, e.g. cedar boughs (which are normally used as fuel), and giving it the status of food, e.g. by untying it and scattering it in front of an animal. For Rav Yehudah, however, making food refers to any basic preparation that is necessary to make the food *edible* for the animal (as opposed to mere enhancement of the food). Thus, by Rav Yehudah's definition, untying bundles of straw qualifies as making food, since the straw cannot be eaten until it is untied; but it is not making food by Rav Huna's definition, since the straw had the status of animal food even before it was untied (and, indeed, before it was tied in the first place). Therefore, although Rav Huna forbids making food and Rav Yehudah permits it, they both agree that one may untie bundles of straw (*Meromei Sadeh* in explanation of *Rashi;* see also *Leshon HaZahav;* cf. *Tosafos*).]

25. Viz. when dry (*Rashi*).

26. Thus, the fodder requires shredding in order to transform it into food (*Rashi*); making an item into food, according to Rav Huna, is forbidden.

יתד באילן ותלה בה כלכלה למעלה מעשרה טפחים אין עירובו עירוב למטה מי' טפחים עירובו עירוב טעמא דנעץ יתד באילן הא לא נעץ אפילו למטה מי' טפחים אין עירובו עירוב והא האי תנא דקאסר בצדדין וקשרי בצדי צדדין אמר רב פפא הכא בכלכלה דחוקה עסקינן דבהדי דשקיל ליה לעירוב קמניד ליה לאילן וקמשמש באילן גופיה * והלכתא צדדין אסורין צדי צדדין מותרין אמר רב אשי השתא דאמרת צדדין אסורין האי דרגא דמדלא לא לינחיה איניש אדיקלא דהוו להו צדדין אלא לינחיה אגוואזי לבר מדיקלא וכי סליק לא לינח כרעיה אגוואזי אלא ליתנח אקנין: **מתני'** מתירין פקיעי עמיר לפני בהמה ומפספסין את הכיפין אבל לא את (א) הזירין אין מרסקין לא את השחת ולא את החרובין לפני בהמה בין דקה ובין גסה רבי יהודה מתיר בחרובין לדקה: **גמ'** אמר רב הונא הן הן פקיעין הן הן כיפין פקיעין תרי כיפין תלתא (ב) זירין דארזי וה"ק מתירין פקיעי עמיר לפני בהמה ומפספסין והוא הדין לכיפין אבל לא את הזירין לא לפספס ולא להתיר אמר רב חסדא מאי טעמא דרב הונא קא סבר למטרח באוכלא טרחינן לשווי אוכלא לא משוינן רב יהודה אמר הן הן פקיעין הן הן זירין תרי זירין תלתא כיפין דארזי וה"ק ב מתירין פקיעי עמיר לפני בהמה אבל פספוסי לא וכיפין פספוסי נמי מפספסינן אבל לא הזירין לפספס [א] אלא להתיר אמר רבא מאי טעמא דרב יהודה קסבר ג שווי אוכלא משוינן מטרח באוכלא לא טרחינן תנן ד אין מרסקין את השחת ואת החרובין לפני בהמה בין דקה ובין גסה מאי לאו חרובין דומיא דשחת מה שחת דרכיכי אף חרובין דרכיכי אלמא לא טרחינן באוכלא ותיובתיה דרב הונא אמר לך רב הונא לא שחת דומיא דחרובין מה חרובין דאקושי אף שחת דאקושי היכי משכחת לה בעילי זוטרי ת"ש רבי יהודה מתיר בחרובין לדקה לדקה אין לגסה לא אי אמרת בשלמא ת"ק סבר מיטרח באוכלא לא טרחינן שווי משוינן היינו דקא אמר ר' יהודה (ג) החרובין לדקה נמי שווי אוכלא הוא אלא אי אמרת ת"ק סבר שווי אוכלא לא משוינן מיטרח באוכלא מטרחינן רבי יהודה (ד) דמתיר בחרובין לדקה כל שכן לגסה מי סברת דקה דקה ממש מאי דקה גסה (ה) ומאי קרי לה דקה דדייקא באוכלא הא מדקתני רישא בין דקה ובין גסה מכלל דרבי יהודה דקה דקה ממש קאמר קשיא תא שמע ה מחתכין את

יתד. נגר: **ותלה בה כלכלה.** ונתן בה עירובו והוא נתכוון לשבות למטה תחת האילן: **למטה מי' טפחים.** אם הכלכלה בתוך י' לארץ עירובו עירוב דהוא ועירובו ברה"ר אבל למעלה מי' ושתם כלכלה רחבה ארבעה הויא לה כלכלה רשות היחיד והוא נתכוון לשבות ברשות הרבים ואינו יכול ליטלו שם ולאכלו וכיון דאינה סעודה הראויה לו אינו קונה שביתה על ידה: **טעמא דנעץ יתד.** דכי שקיל לעירובו משתמש בצדי צדדין אבל לא נעץ יתד אלא קשרה בצדי אילן לא: **הכא בכלכלה דחוקה.** שפיה צר וקצרה היא ומכניס ידו לתוכה בדוחק הלכך אי ממש הוה קטר לה בצדי אילן כי שקיל ליה לעירוביה מניד ליה לאילן הלכך כי איכא יתד הוא דשרי ואי לא לא: **האי דרגא דמדלא.** סולם שעולין בו לסוכת נוטרים שעושין ע"ג קונדיסין גבוהין והיא סמוכה לאילן: **לא לינחיה.** ראש הסולם אדיקלא לא יסמוך ראש הסולם לצד דקל דכי סליק משתמש בצדדין: **אלא לינחיה אגוואזי לבר מדיקלא.** יתקע יתד בצדי האילן ויסמוך הסולם עליו דהוה ליה יתד צדדים וסולם צדי צדדין: **וכי סליק לא לינח כרעיה על היתד אלא אקניא.** על שליבות הסולם או קנים היוצאים מהקונדיסין: **מתני' פקיעי עמיר.** קשין של שבלים (שאוסם) שאוגדים ומתירין אותם שיהו נותנין לבהמה לאוכלה: **מפספסין.** שכן דרך שמפזרים לבהמה העשבים ויפין לה לאוכלן שכשהן דחוקין מתחממין ואינה מריחה ריחה כל כך וקצה בהן: **את הכיפין.** מפרש בגמרא וכן זירין: **אין מרסקין.** אין מחתכין: **שחת.** עשב של תבואה והוא אספסתא ומשום דטירחא דלא צריך הוא: **רבי יהודה מתיר בחרובין לדקה.** שפיה דקות וקשין לה: **גמ' הן הן פקיעין הן הן כיפין.** כולן קשין של שבלין הן אימתי פקיעין תרי שאינן קשורין אלא בשני ראשים: **כיפין תלת.** קשורין ג' [אגודים]: **זירין דארזא.** ענפים לחין של ארז שמגדלין אותם ועושים לאין ראוין לבהמה ורוב בני אדם מניחין אותם לעצים: **וה"ק מתירין פקיעי עמיר ומפספסין.** דכיון דמעיקרא אוכלא נינהו מותר לטרוח בהן להכשירם למתקן לה ואת הכיפין אף הן מתירין ומפספסין ואע"ג דנפיש טרחייהו אבל לא הזירין לא לפספס ולא להתיר דכיון דמעיקרא סתמייהו לאו אוכלא והשתא הוא דמשוי להו אוכלא ה"ל אולודי אוכלא בשבת: **מיטרח באוכלא.** בדבר שתחילתו אוכל קודם תיקון זה טרחינן ומכשרינן לייפותן לה: **הן הן פקיעין הן הן זירין.** שניהן בקשים של שבלים ומה שהתיר בזה התיר בזה ודקתני אבל לא הזירין אפספוס קאי: **וה"ק מתירין פקיעי עמיר.** דכל זמן שהוא קשור לאו אוכלא הוא ומתירו לשווי אוכלא ומשום צער בהמה שרי אבל פספוס לא דסגי ליה בהתרה ואיתעביד אוכלא ופספוסיה לתענוג בעלמא הוא ומטרח באוכל בדבר שהוא כבר אוכל בלא תיקון זה לא טרחינן ומפספסין את הכיפין דארזא דבלאו פספוס לא הוי אוכלא אבל לא את הזירין לפספס אלא להתיר שלשה אוגדיהן בפקיעין דהתרת אוגדיהן שווי אוכלא הוא: **אין מרסקין.** סיפא דמתניתין היא וחד טעמא: **דרכיכי.** כגון חרובין לחין דראויין למאכל בהמה בלא ריסוק וריסוק דידהו לתענוג בעלמא: **דאקושי.** קשין כגון שיבשו: **בעילי זוטרי.** עיירים קטנים שאף השחת קשה להם וצריכה ריסוק לשווי אוכלא: **לדקה אין.** דהוה ליה שווי אוכלא: **לגסה לא.** דהוה ליה מטרח באוכלא: **אי אמרת בשלמא.** שמע רבי יהודה לת"ק דאמר מיטרח באוכלין אסור ואין מרסקין ברכיכי קאמר אבל שווי אוכלא שרי היינו דקאמר ליה רבי יהודה חרובין לדקה לית לן למיסר דשווי אוכלא הוא ואע"ג דרכיכי אלא אי אמרת קסבר ת"ק מיטרח באוכלא שרי שווי אוכלא אסור ואין מרסקין דקאמר בדאקושי קאמר דשווי אוכלא הוי: **רבי יהודה מתיר בחרובין לדקה.** בתמיה הא כל שכן דלגסה למיטרח באוכלא הוא ושרי הכי ה"ל למיתני ור' יהודה מתיר בחרובין לגסה דהוה ליה מיטרח באוכלא והא ליכא למימר דר' יהודה מפיך דשווי אוכלא שרי מיטרח באוכלא אסיר דהא ת"ק בדאקושי קאמר וגבי גסה נמי שווי אוכלא הוא וה"ל למיתני ורבי יהודה מתיר סתמא בין דקה בין גסה ועוד הוה ליה למישרי נמי זירין להתיר ולפספס דשווי אוכלא נמי הוא: **דדייקא.** כוססת יפה ומדקת אוכלין בפיה: **והא מדקתני רישא בין גסה בין דקה שמע מינה דקה ממש.** ורבי יהודה את"ק קאי:

למטה מי' טפחים עירובו עירוב. קשה אמאי עירובו עירוב והא כרמלית הוא כיון שרחבה ארבעה ואסור לטלטל לרה"ר וי"ל אין כרמלית בכלים כדפירש בקונטרס בפ"ק דמכילתין (דף ח.) גבי היתה קופתו מונחת כו' ° אי נמי כרבי דאמר ג) כל דבר שהוא משום שבות לא גזרו עליו בין השמשות: **אמר רב פפא הכא בכלכלה דחוקה עסקינן.** מדמשני רב פפא הכי משמע דסבירא ליה צדדין מותרין ורב אשי משמע בסמוך דסבר דאסורין מדאמר רב אשי בסמוך השתא דאמרת צדדין אסורין וקשה לי הא איפכא שמעינן להו במסכת חגיגה בפ"ב (דף יז. ושם) דאמר רב פפא שמע מינה צדדין אסורין דאי סלקא דעתך צדדין מותרים נסמוך ארישא דצדדין נינהו רב אשי אמר אפילו תימא צדדין מותרין כל דלהדי גבה כגבה דמי ד): **והלכתא צדדין אסורין צדי צדדין מותרין.** ותימה לרבי אמאי לא חשיב הני בהדי יע"ל קג"ס דהלכה כאביי (בבבא מציעא דף כב:) דאמר רבא מאן דאסר בצדדין אסר נמי בצדי צדדין ואביי אמר בצדדין כולי עלמא לא פליגי [דאסור] ובצדי צדדין פליגי: **רב יהודה אמר הן הן פקיעין כו' וה"ק מתירים פקיעי עמיר כו'.** פירש בקונטרס דהתרת פקיעים הויא שווי אוכלא וצריך לפרש (ו) נמי בהא דרב יהודה חשיב התרת פקיעין שווי אוכלא ורב הונא לא חשיב לה שווי אוכלא מדשרי לה ואין נראה לרבינו תם לאפלוגינהו בהכי אלא לתרוייהו לא הויא התרת פקיעי עמיר לא שויא אוכלא ולא מיטרח באוכלא דלא שייך טורח בהתרה ולהכי שריא לתרוייהו. מ"ר:

ה בעי למשקל עירוביה ומיכליה בשעה שהעירוב זוכה לו דהיינו בין השמשות לא מצי שקיל דמייתי מרשות ... לא הוה עירובו עירוב וכו' [עירובין לב:]. **והא האי תנא דקאסר בצדדין.** כגון הכא דלאו משתמש ... שקיל לעירובו אפילו בשבת בכלכלה הוא דמשתמש שהוא לידי אילן [שם לג.]. **שחת.** תבואת חיטין ושעורין קודם שתמלא בזירין ובלע"ז פירינ"א [ע"ז כ:].

עין משפט נר מצוה

כ א מיי' פכ"ו מהל' שבת הלכה ט סמג לאוין סה טוש"ע א"ח סימן שה סעיף יח:

כא ב ג מיי' פכ"א מהל' שבת הל' יא טוש"ע א"ח סי' שכד סעיף ד:

כב ד מיי' שם טוש"ע שם סעיף ח:

הגהות הגר"א

[א] גמ' לפספס אלא להתיר. נ"ב גירסת הרי"ף ולא להתיר וכן עיקר מאד:

רבינו חננאל

חמור אלא בצידי החמור אני משפשף (ויגדלן) [וצדדין] לא גזרו בהו רבנן מדתנן מתיר החבלים והשקין נופלין מאי לאו בחבר גואלקי ולא גזרו בהו רבנן פי' חבר גואלקי כשטוענין הבהמה מביאין שק וטוענין אותו מצד אחד ושק האחר מצד השני ומביא חבל וקושרן ומחברן (ומשרכבן) [ומשכיבן] בצדי הבהמה וכשמבקשין לפרק משאוי מגביה השקין לרפרף קשר החבל להיות נוח להתיר ומתיר ומניח השקין והן יורדין מצדי הבהמה ויורדין לארץ נמצא מגביה ומוריד השקין בצידי החמור כאשר אני מגביה ע"ג החמור והוא יורד בדרך שפשוף אמר לך אביי אינו אומר מתיר החבלים בחבר גואלקי אלא באבר גואלקי כדתנן כיצד מאברין את העדים ומפרשינן ליה מלשון אבר כן מוסיף כמין אבר בגואלקי והוא למעלה כדאמרי' בפ' לא יחפור (ב"ב כד:) באברורי הוו יתבי פי' אברורי למעלה מן המשאוי כגון שהיה צד המשאוי האחד כבד והשני קל ורצינו להשוות המשאוי שלא יהיה א) מטרטן ומוסיף על הצד הקל דבר להשוות המשקל שלא יהיה אחד מהן מכריע ועליו אמרה משנתנו מתיר החבלים והשקין נופלים שהקשר למעלה הוא. ואין צריך להגביה שק ולא להוריד אלא כשמתיר החבר נופלין אבר גואלקי נמצאו גואלקי על צידי בהמה ואם זה על גואלקי נמצא אבר זה צדי צדדין אי נמי בגואלקי דגואלקי עצמו אינן קשורין בחבלים אלא כמנהג שהי' לאורחים המהלכים בדרכים שעושין בראש השקין כמין קרסים ולולאות מן החבלים ומכניס הלולאות בקרסים אי נמי לולאות לבלבד ומכניס בהן עץ ומחברן וכשרוצה לפרקן מושך העץ ההוא והן נופלים ונקרא עץ ההוא לכתא ואינו מגיע לצדדין ואותו האבר נמי שמוסיפין על המשאוי הוא צדי צדדין והוא מותר אבל הצדדין אסורין. ועוד אקשי ליה אביי לרבה הא ב' בידי אדם ואחת באילן כו' ופריק רבה התם דכפייה לאילן וסיכך על גביו שנמצא משתמש באילן עצמו. תוב אקשינן עליה מסיפא דקתני ג' בידי אדם ואחת באילן כשרה ועולין לה ביו"ט ואי כפייה לאילן וסיכך ע"ג אמאי עולין לה ביו"ט הא משתמש באילן ואסור ופריק ליה התם ופרסי כאנא פי' גיחא ופרסיכנא תרתב מאבקא ב) ועלה דייקינן זה הכלל כל שינטל האילן ויכולה לעמוד עולין לה ביו"ט לימא כתנאי אין עולין לה ביו"ט כו' סברי לה הנסרין שהן הסכך באותה החקיקה והן הצדדין זה אוסר להשתמש בצדדין וזה מתיר אמר אביי כולי עלמא צדדין אסורין והכא בצידי צדדין פליגי פי' כגון דחק באילן ונתן באותה החקיקה עץ חזק כמין קורה ושם ראשי הנסרים על אותו העץ הנתון כמין קורה שנמצא העץ ההוא צדדי האילן והנסרים הנתונין על גביו צדדי צדדין רבא א' צדדין וצדדי צדדין דינם אחד האוסר בצדדין אוסר גם בצידי צדדין והמתיר צדדי צדדין גם בצדדין מתיר ובא רב משרשיא לאותובי לרבה דאמר המתיר בצידי צדדין גם בצדדין מתיר הא דתניא נעץ יתד באילן ותלה בו כלכלה למטה מעשרה עירובו עירוב למטה מי' טפחים אין עירובו עירוב. ודייקינן מינה טעמא דנעץ יתד באילן ותלה בו כלכלה יתד צידי האילן והכלכלה צידי צדדין ולפיכך למטה מעשרה טפחים עירובו עירוב אבל אם לא נעץ יתד ותלה בו אלא תלה בו באמירי האילן אפילו למטה מעשרה אין עירובו עירוב דהוה לי' צדדין הדר נתברר כי זה

חשק שלמה על רבינו חננאל א) עיין ערוך ערך אטרטן: ב) פה הדברים משובשים בכ"י ומלוה לתקנם. ועי' בערוך ערך גז המחרון:

מסורת הש"ס

א) [חגיגה טז:], ב) [לקמן קנו.], ג) [לעיל מ:], ד) [וע"ע תוספות חגיגה יז. ד"ה רב אשי דלא מקשה אלא לרב אשי אדרב אשי וכתבו תירוץ לזה].

הגהות הב"ח

(א) במשנה את הכיפין אבל לא את הזירין: (ב) גמ' כיפין תלתא וזירין דארזי וכו' אבל לא את הזירין לא לפספס וכו' אבל לא הזירין לפספס: (ג) שם היינו דקא אמר ר' יהודה חרובין לדקה נמי שווי אוכלא: (ד) שם ר' יהודה מתיר כל"ל והא ד' נמחק: (ה) שם מאי דקה גסה ומאי קרי: (ו) תוס' ד"ה רב יהודה וכו' וצריך לפרש דפליגי נמי בהא:

גליון הש"ס

גמ' והלכתא צדדים אסורין. עיין עירובין דף לג ע"א תוס' ד"ה למטה מי' ובר' א"נ כרבי וכו'. ותמוה לה"ל אפי' לא נעץ יתד נמי דשימוש באילן הוי רק שבות ול"ג בה"ש ... שלא לסית ביו"ט והניח עירוב בערב יו"ט בכלכלה זו שיהיה עירוב ליו"ט ושבת ... דבה"ש אינו יכול ליטול עירובו ... משום שבות לא גזרינן בה"ש ... איסור הואה:

רב נסים גאון

בפרק כירה (דף מב) ופירשנו כי החלוקה בצער בעלי חיים דאורייתא או דרבנן תמצא בפרק אלו מציאות (דף לב):

ליקוטי רש"י

למעלה מעשרה טפחים אין עירובו עירוב. המערב עירובי תחומין עירובו קונה לו שביתתו שם שיכול לילך משם לכל רוח אלפים כאילו שבת שם וצריך שיתכוון לקנות שביתתו במקום עירובו שיוכל לאוכלו שם אם היה רוצה לאכלו ... לפיכך למעלה מעשרה אין עירובו עירוב שהוא נתכוון לשבות שם ...

The Gemara mounts another challenge to Rav Huna's view: תָּא שְׁמַע – **Come, learn** a refutation of Rav Huna's position from the continuation of the Mishnah: רַבִּי יְהוּדָה מַתִּיר בְּחָרוּבִין לְדַקָּה – R' YEHUDAH PERMITS the shredding of CAROBS FOR A SMALL ANIMAL, implying: לְדַקָּה אִין – **for a small animal – yes,**[27] לְגַסָּה לֹא – **for a large animal – no.**[28] אִי אָמְרַתְּ בִּשְׁלָמָא – **Now, this is fine if you maintain,** as does (the Amora) Rav Yehudah, that תַּנָּא קַמָּא סָבַר מִיטְרַח בְּאוּכְלָא לֹא טָרְחִינַן – **the Tanna Kamma holds we may not exert** ourselves **to** enhance **food** [שְׁוּוֵי] מְשַׁוִּינַן – **but we may make** food edible: הַיְינוּ דְּקָא אָמַר רַבִּי יְהוּדָה – **That** explains **what R' Yehudah** (the Tanna) **said:** [הֶחָרוּבִין לְדַקָּה נַמִּי שְׁוּוֵי[י – The shredding of **carobs for a small animal** should **also** be considered **making food** edible.[29] אֶלָּא אִי אָמְרַתְּ – **However, if you will say,** as Rav Huna explains, that we are dealing with hard carobs and תַּנָּא קַמָּא סָבַר [שְׁוּוֵי[י] אוּכְלָא לֹא מְשַׁוִּינַן מִיטְרַח בְּאוּכְלָא (מ)טָרְחִינַן – **the Tanna Kamma holds we may not make food** (but **we may exert** ourselves improving **food),** רַבִּי יְהוּדָה דְּמַתִּיר בְּחָרוּבִין לְדַקָּה – then how do you account for the fact **that R' Yehudah,** in the conclusion of the Mishnah, who **permits** the shredding of hard **carobs for a small animal,** is implying: a small animal – yes, but a large animal – no? But if R' Yehudah's point is that the shredding of hard carobs is merely an enhancement, כָּל שֶׁכֵּן לְגַסָּה – then this should **certainly** be true **for a large animal.** Yet R' Yehudah specifically excludes large animals![30] – ? –

The Gemara answers:

מִי סָבְרַתְּ דַּקָּה – **Do you think** that when R' Yehudah says *DAKAH* דַּקָּה מַמָּשׁ – he means **a** ***dakah*** (small animal) **literally?** No! מַאי דַּקָּה – **What** does he mean by *DAKAH?* גַּסָּה – **A large [animal].** [וְ[אַ]מַּאי קָרֵי לָהּ דַּקָּה – **And why does he call [a large animal] a** ***dakah*?** דְּדָיְקָא בְּאוּכְלָא – **Because [a large animal] chews** (*dayka*) its **food** very well.[31]

The Gemara rejoins:

הָא מִדְּקָתָנֵי רֵישָׁא – **But since we learned the first part** of the Mishnah, i.e. the Tanna Kamma's words, as follows, בֵּין דַּקָּה וּבֵין גַּסָּה – WHETHER IT IS A SMALL [ANIMAL] (*dakah*) OR WHETHER IT IS A LARGE [ANIMAL] (*gasah*), מִכְּלָל דְּרַבִּי יְהוּדָה דַּקָּה – **we may conclude that** when **R' Yehudah** speaks of a *DAKAH,* דַּקָּה מַמָּשׁ קָאָמַר – **he is referring to a** ***dakah*** **literally.**[32]

The Gemara concedes:

קַשְׁיָא – This is indeed **a difficulty:**[33]

The Gemara challenges Rav Yehudah's opinion:

תָּא שְׁמַע – **Come, learn** a proof from this Mishnah:[34] מְחַתְּכִין – ONE MAY CUT UP

NOTES

27. For a small animal, shredding is the creation of food (*Rashi*), which R' Yehudah, apparently, permits.

28. For a large animal, shredding is merely [the enhancement of food and is prohibited because it is excessive] exertion (*Rashi*).

29. According to this approach, R' Yehudah heard the Tanna Kamma say the following: "It is prohibited to enhance existing food; thus, it is prohibited to shred soft carobs. It is permitted, though, to make food [edible]." To which R' Yehudah responded: "There is no reason then to prohibit the shredding of carobs for a small animal, even though they are soft, for this too merely makes the food [edible]" (*Rashi*).

30. According to this approach, the Tanna Kamma says, "It is prohibited to make [a non-food into] food; thus, it is prohibited to shred hard carobs. It is permitted, though, to enhance existing food." R' Yehudah's reply is puzzling: "There is no reason to prohibit the shredding of hard carobs for a small animal, since this is only an enhancement." But if shredding is only an enhancement for a small animal [with delicate teeth] it is certainly no more than a enhancement for a large animal [with stronger teeth] and should be permitted! Why then does the Mishnah imply that R' Yehudah permits this only for small animals?! We might have expected the Mishnah to rather say, "R' Yehudah permits the shredding of carobs [*even* for a small animal]," and certainly for a large animal (*Rashi,* as explained by *Maharsha*).

[One cannot explain that R' Yehudah's opinions are completely opposite those of the Tanna Kamma. That is, the Tanna Kamma prohibits making food and permits enhancement whereas R' Yehudah permits making food and prohibits enhancement. This is because the Tanna Kamma is discussing hard carobs and rules that their shredding is considered making them into food even for large animals. If R' Yehudah allows making something into food, the Mishnah should simply end, "R' Yehudah permits," which would connote leniency for both small and large animals. Also, if R' Yehudah permits making something into food, he should also permit the untying and scattering of cedar boughs earlier in the Mishnah, since these actions constitute the making of a non-food into food (*Rashi; see Maharsha, Nimukei R' Yehudah Bachrach;* cf. *Chidushei HaRan*).]

31. [Thus, R' Yehudah's response is cogent: He does permit the shredding of carobs for a large animal, since he considers this to be merely an enhancement.]

[Emendation follows *Hagahos HaBach.*]

32. [Since the Tanna Kamma refers to a *dakah* in contradistinction to a *gasah,* and a *gasah* undoubtedly means a large animal, there can be no question that the Tanna Kamma is using the term *dakah* in the conventional sense of a small animal.] And since R' Yehudah is responding to the Tanna Kamma, [he is not going to use one of the Tanna Kamma's terms in a radically different way than the Tanna Kamma did]! (*Rashi*).

33. See *Shabbos Shel Mi.*

34. Below, 156b.

יתד באילן ותלה בה כלכלה למעלה מעשרה טפחים אין עירובו עירוב למטה מי' טפחים עירובו עירוב טעמא דנעץ יתד באילן הא לא נעץ אפילו למטה מי' טפחים אין עירובו עירוב והא האי תנא דקאסר בצדדין וקשרי בצדי צדדין אמר רב פפא הכא בכלכלה דחוקה עסקינן דבהדי דשקיל ליה לעירוב קמניד ליה לאילן וקמשתמש באילן גופיה * א והלכתא (א) צדדין אסורין צדי צדדין מותרין אמר רב אשי השתא דאמרת צדדין אסורין האי דרגא דמדלא לא לינחיה איניש אדיקלא דהוו להו צדדין אלא לינחיה אגוואזי לבר מדיקלא וכי סליק לא לינח כרעיה אגוואזי אלא ליתנח אקנין: **מתני'** מתירין פקיעי עמיר לפני בהמה ומפספסין את הכיפין אבל לא את (א) הזירין אין מרסקין לא את השחת ולא את החרובין לפני בהמה בין דקה ובין גסה רבי יהודה מתיר בחרובין לדקה: **גמ'** אמר רב הונא הן הן פקיעין הן הן כיפין פקיען תרי כיפין תלתא (ב) זירין דארזי וה"ק מתירין פקיעי עמיר לפני בהמה ומפספסין והוא הדין לכיפין אבל לא את הזירין לא לפספס ולא להתיר אמר רב חסדא מאי טעמא דרב הונא קא סבר למטרח באוכלא טרחינן לשווי אוכלא לא משוינן רב יהודה אמר הן הן פקיעין הן הן זירין תרי זירין תלתא כיפין דארזי וה"ק ב מתירין פקיעי עמיר לפני בהמה אבל פספוסי לא וכיפין פספוסי נמי מפספסינן אבל לא הזירין לפספס [א] אלא להתיר אמר רבא מאי טעמא דרב יהודה קסבר ג שווי אוכלא משוינן מטרח באוכלא לא טרחינן תנן ד אין מרסקין את השחת ואת החרובין לפני בהמה בין דקה ובין גסה מאי לאו חרובין דומיא דשחת מה שחת דרכיכי אף חרובין דרכיכי אלמא לא טרחינן באוכלא ותיובתיה דרב הונא אמר לך רב הונא לא שחת דומיא דחרובין מה חרובין דאקושי אף שחת דאקושי היכי משכחת לה בעילי זוטרי ת"ש רבי יהודה מתיר בחרובין לדקה לדקה אין לגסה לא אי אמרת בשלמא ת"ק סבר מיטרח באוכלא לא טרחינן שווי משוינן היינו דקא אמר ר' יהודה (ג) החרובין לדקה נמי שווי אוכלא הוא אלא אי אמרת ת"ק סבר שווי אוכלא לא משוינן מיטרח באוכלא מטרחינן רבי יהודה (ד) דמתיר בחרובין לדקה כל שכן לגסה מי סברת דקה דקה ממש מאי דקה גסה (ה) ומאי קרי לה דקה דדייקא באוכלא הא מדקתני רישא בין דקה ובין גסה מכלל דרבי יהודה דקה דקה ממש קאמר קשיא תא שמע ה מחתכין את

רש"י

יתד. נגר: ותלה בה כלכלה. ונתן בה עירובו והוא נתכוון לשבות למטה תחת האילן: למטה מי' טפחים. אם הכלכלה בתוך י' לארץ עירובו עירוב דהוא ועירובו ברה"ר אבל למעלה מי' וסתם כלכלה רחבה ארבעה היא לה כלכלה רשות היחיד והוא נתכוון לשבות ברשות הרבים ואינו יכול ליטלו משם ולאכלו וכיון דאינו קונה שביתה על ידה: טעמא דנעץ יתד. דכי שקיל לעירובו משתמש בצדי צדדין אבל לא נעץ יתד אלא קשרה בבדי אילן לא: הכא בכלכלה דחוקה. שפיה צר וקצרה היא ומכניס ידו לתוכה בדוחק הלכך אי ממש הוא קטר לה בבדי אילן כי שקיל ליה לעירוביה מניד ליה לאילן הלכך כי איכא יתד הוא דשרי ואי לא לא: האי דרגא דמדלא. סולם שעולין בו לסוכת נוטרים שעושין ע"ג קונדיסין גבוהין והיא סמוכה לאילן: לא לינחיה. ראש הסולם אדיקלא לא יסמוך ראש הסולם לצד דקל דכי סליק משתמש בדקלא: אלא לינחיה אגוואזי לבר מדיקלא. יתקע יתד בצדי האילן ויסמוך הסולם עליו דהוה ליה יתד לדדים וסולם לדי לדדין: וכי סליק לא לינח כרעיה על היתד אלא אקניא. על שליבות הסולם או קנים היוצאים מהקונדיסין: מתני' פקיעי עמיר. קשין של שבלים (שאותם) שאוגדים מתירין אותם שיהו נותנין לבהמה לאוכלה: מפספסין. שכן דרך שמפזרים לבהמה העשבים ויפין לה לאוכלן שכשהן דחוקין מתממסמין ואינה מריחה ריחה כל כך וקצה בהן: את הכיפין. מפרש בגמרא וכן זירין: אין מרסקין. אין מחתכין: שחת. עשב של תבואה והוא אספסתא ומשום דטירחא דלא צריך הוא: רבי יהודה מתיר בחרובין לדקה. ששיניה דקות וקשין לה: גמ' הן הן פקיעין הן הן כיפין. כולן קשין של שבלין הן מיהו פקיען תרי שאינן קשורין אלא בשני ראשים: כיפין תלת. קשורין ג' [אגודים]: זירין דארזא. ענפים לחין של ארז שמזרדין אותם ובעודם לחין ראויין לבהמה ורוב בני אדם מניחין אותם לעצים: וה"ק מתירין פקיעי עמיר ומפספסין. דכיון דמעיקרא אוכלא נינהו מותר לטרוח בהן להכשירם למתקן לה ואת הכיפין אף הן מתירין ומפספסין ואע"ג דנפיש טרחייהו אבל לא הזירין לא לפספס ולא להתיר דכיון דמעיקרא סתמייהו לאו אוכלא והשתא הוא דמשוי להו אוכלא ה"ל אולודי אוכלא בשבת: מיטרח באוכלא. בדבר שתחילתו אוכל קודם תיקון זה טרחינן ומכשרינן לייפותן לה: הן הן פקיעין הן הן זירין. שניהן בקשים של שבלים ומה שהתיר בזה התיר בזה ודקתני אבל לא הזירין אפספום קאי: וה"ק מתירין פקיעי עמיר. דכל זמן שהוא קשור לאו אוכלא הוא ומתירו לשווי אוכלא ומשום צער בהמה שרי אבל פספוס לא דסגי ליה בהתרה ואיתעביד אוכלא ופספוסיה לתענוג בעלמא הוא ומטרח באוכל בדבר שהוא כבר אוכל בלא תיקון זה לא טרחינן ומפספסין את הכיפין דארזא דבלאו פספוס לא הוי אוכלא אבל לא את הזירין לפספס אלא להתיר שלשה אוגדיהן בפקיעין דהתרת אוגדיהן שווי אוכלא הוא: אין מרסקין. סיפא דמתניתין היא וחד טעמא: דרכיכי. כגון חרובין לחין דראויין למאכל בהמה בלא ריסוק וריסוק דידהו לתענוג בעלמא: דאקושי. קשין כגון שיבשו: בעילי זוטרי. עיירים קטנים שאף השחת קשה להם וצריכה ריסוק לשווי אוכלא: לדקה אין. דהוה ליה שווי אוכלא: לגסה לא. דהוה ליה מטרח באוכלא: אי אמרת בשלמא. שמע רבי יהודה לת"ק דאמר מיטרח באוכלין אסור ואין מרסקין ברכיכי קאמר אבל שווי אוכלא שרי היינו דקאמר ליה רבי יהודה חרובין לדקה לית לן למיסר דשווי אוכלא הוא ואע"ג דרכיכי אלא אי אמרת קסבר ת"ק מיטרח באוכלא שרי שווי אוכלא אסור ואין מרסקין דקאמר בדאקושי קאמר דשווי אוכלא הוי: רבי יהודה מתיר בחרובין לדקה. בתמיה הא כל שכן דלגסה למיטרח באוכלא הוא ושרי הכי ה"ל למיתני ור' יהודה מתיר בחרובין לגסה דהוה ליה מיטרח באוכלא והא ליכא למימר דר' יהודה מפיך דשווי אוכלא שרי מיטרח באוכלא אסיר דהא ת"ק בדאקושי קאמר וגבי גסה נמי שווי אוכלא הוא וה"ל למיתני ורבי יהודה מתיר סתמא בין דקה בין גסה ועוד הוה ליה למישרי נמי זירין להתיר ולפספס דשווי אוכלא נמי הוא: דדייקא. כוססת יפה ומדקת אוכלין בפיה: והא מדקתני רישא בין גסה בין דקה שמע מינה דקה ממש. ורבי יהודה את"ק קאי:

תוספות

למטה מי' טפחים עירובו עירוב. קשה אמאי עירובו עירוב והא כרמלית הוא כיון שרחבה ארבעה ואסור לטלטל לרה"ר וי"ל אין כרמלית בכלים כדפירש בקונטרס בפ"ק דמכילתין (דף ח.) גבי היתה קופתו מונחת כו' * אי נמי כרבי דאמר ג) כל דבר שהוא משום שבות לא גזרו עליו בין השמשות: **אמר** רב פפא הכא בכלכלה דחוקה עסקינן. מדמשני רב פפא הכי משמע דסבירא ליה לדדין מותרין ורב אשי משמע בסמוך דסבר דאסורין מדאמר רב אשי בסמוך השתא דאמרת לדדין אסורין וקשה לי הא איפכא שמעינן להו במסכת חגיגה בפ"ב (דף יז. ושם) דאמר רב פפא שמע מינה לדדין אסורין דאי סלקא דעתך לדדין מותרים נסמוך ארישא דלדדין נינהו רב אשי אמר אפילו תימא לדדין מותרין כל דלהדי גבה כגבה דמי ד): **והלכתא** צדדין אסורין צדי צדדין מותרין. ותימה לרבי אמאי לא חשיב הני בהדי יע"ל קג"ס דהלכה כאביי (בבבא מציעא דף כב:) דאמר רבא מאן דאסר בלדדין אסר נמי בלדי לדדין ואביי אמר בלדדין כולי עלמא לא פליגי [דאסור] ובלדי לדדין פליגי: **רב** יהודה אמר הן הן פקיעין כו' וה"ק מתירים פקיעי עמיר כו'. פירש בקונטרס דהתרת פקיעים הויא שווי אוכלא ולריך לפרש (ו) נמי בהא דרב יהודה חשיב התרת פקיעין שווי אוכלא ורב הונא לא חשיב לה שווי אוכלא מדשרי לה ואין נראה לרבינו תם לאפלוגינהו בהכי אלא לתרוייהו לא הויא התרת פקיעי עמיר לא שויא אוכלא ולא מיטרח באוכלא דלא שייך טורח בהתרה ולהכי שריא לתרוייהו. מ"ר:

מסורת הש"ס

א) [חגיגה טז:], ב) לקמן קנו:, ג) [לעיל מ:], ד) [וע' תוספות חגיגה יז. ד"ה רב אשי דלא מקשה אלא לרב אשי דלרב אשי וכתבו תירוץ לזה].

הגהות הב"ח

(א) במשנה את הכיפין את הזירין אין: (ב) גמ' כיפין תלתא וזירין דארזי וכו' אבל לא את הזירין לא ליפספס וכו' למטרח באוכלא טרחינן לשווי אוכלא לא משוינן וכו' הן הן זירין פקיעין תרי זירין תלתא וכו' אבל לא את הזירין לפספס: (ג) שם היינו דקא אמר ר' יהודה חרובין לדקה נמי שווי אוכלא: (ד) שם ר' יהודה מתיר כ"ל ואות ד' נמחק: (ה) שם מאי דקה גסה ומאי קרי: (ו) תוס' ד"ה ר' יהודה וכו' ולריך לפרש דפליגי נמי בהא:

גליון הש"ס

גמ' והלכתא צדדים אסורין. עיין עירובין דף לג ע"א: תוס' ד"ה למטה מי' וכו' א"נ כרבי וכו'. [illegible]

רב נסים גאון

בפרק כירה (דף מב) ופירשנו כי החלוקה בצער בעלי חיים דאורייתא או דרבנן תמצא בפרק אלו מציאות (דף לב):

ליקוטי רש"י

למעלה מעשרה טפחים אין עירובו עירוב. המערב עירובי תחומין עירובו קונה לו שביתתו [illegible]

עין משפט נר מצוה

כ א מיי' פכ"ו מהל' שבת הלכה כ סמג לאוין סה טוש"ע א"ח סימן שה סעיף יח:
כא ב ג מיי' פכ"א מהל' שבת הל' יט טוש"ע א"ח סי' שכד סעיף ד:
כב ד מיי' שם טוש"ע שם סעיף ח:

הגהות הגר"א

[א] גמ' לפספס אלא להתיר. נ"ב גירסת הרי"ף ולא להתיר וכמון מלד:

רבינו חננאל

חמור אלא בצידי החמור אני משפשף (ורגלין) [וצדדין] לא גזרו בהו רבנן מדתנן מתיר החבלים והשקין נופלין מאי לאו בחבר גואלקי ולא גזרו בהו רבנן פי' חבר גואלקי כשטוענין הבהמה מביאין שק וטוענין אותו מצד אחד ושק האחר מצד השני ומביא חבל וקושרן ומחברן (ומשרכבן) [ומשכיבן] בצדי הבהמה וכשמבקשין לפרוק משאוי מגביה השקין לרפוף קשר החבל להיות נוח להתיר ומתיר ומניח השקין והן יורדין מצדי הבהמה ויורדין לארץ נמצא מגביה ומוריד השקין בצידי החמור כאשר אני מגביה ע"ג החמור והוא יורד בדרך שפשוף אמר לך אביי אינו אומר מתיר החבלים בחבר גואלקי אלא באבר גואלקי כדתנן כיצד מאברין את העדים ומפרשינן ליה מלשון אבר כן מוסיף כמין אבר בגואלקי והוא למעלה כדאמרי' בפ' לא יחפור (ב"ב כד:) באברורי הוו יתבי פי' אברוורי למעלה מן המשאוי כגון שהיה צד המשאוי האחד כבד והשני קל ורצינו להשוות המשאוי שלא יהיה א) מטרטן ומוסיף על הצד הקל דבר להשוות המשקל שלא יהיה אחד מהן מכריע ועליו אמרה משנתנו מתיר החבלים והשקין נופלים שהקשר למעלה הוא. ואין צריך להגביה שק ולא להוריד אלא כשמתיר החבר נופלין אבר גואלקי נמצאו גואלקי על צידי הבהמה ואם זה על גואלקי נמצא אבר זה צדי צדדין אי נמי בגואלקי דגואלקי עצמו אינן קשורין בחבלים אלא כמנהג שהי' לאורחים המהלכים בדרכים שעושין בראש השקין כמין קרסים ולולאות מן החבלים ומכניס הלולאות בקרסים [illegible] ומכניס בהן עץ ומחבר וכשרוצה לפרקן מושך העץ ההוא והן נופלים ונקרא עץ ההוא לכתא ואינו מגיע לצדדין ואותו האבר נמי שמוסיפין על המשאוי הוא צדי צדדין והוא מותר אבל הצדדין אסורין. ועוד אקשי ליה אביי לרבה הא ב' בידי אדם ואחת באילן כו' ופריק רבה התם דכפייה לאילן וסיכך על גביו שנמצא משתמש באילן עצמו. תוב אקשינן עליה [illegible]

[illegible]

חשק שלמה על רבינו חננאל א) עיין ערוך ערך אגוזי: [illegible]

את הדלועין. התלושין ולא אמרינן מוקצין הן לבהמה דמאכל אדם הן: אשוני. קשין: א"נ. כלבים דקאמר בגורייתא זוטרי דכל נבלה קשה להן: ומערבין. התבן והאספסתא יחד והבהמה אוכלת התבן בשביל האספסתא: תבן בתיבנא סריא. דלא חזיא והשתא משוי לה אוכלא והאי סריא לאו סריא לגמרי דהסיא לטינא קיימא ואסורה לטלטל: מתני' אין אובסין. מאכילין אותו הרבה על כרחו ותוחבין לו בגרונו ובגמרא מפרש לשון אובסין עושין לו כמין אבוס בתוך מעיה: ולא דורסין. שדורס לה בתוך גרונה את השעורין ומיהו לא הוי כל כך כמו אובסין: אבל מלעיטין. מפרש בגמרא: אין מאמירין. מפרש בגמרא: מהלקטין. מפרש בגמרא: אין נותנין מים לפני דבורים. מפרש טעמא בגמרא אי משום דאין מזונותיהן עליו שיולאין ואוכלין בשדה אי משום דמיא באגמא שכיח להו: הרדיסאות. על שם מקומן וניזונין בתוך הבית: גמ' כי האי גוונא. שיאכילנה כל כך שירחיבו מעיה כאבוס: אטענה כורא. על גבה למזונות לדרך לבד שאר משאות: למקום שאינה יכולה להחזיר. שתוחבו לה לפנים מבית הבליעה: בכלי. בתרווד: דספי בידים. תוחבו לתוך פיו: אלא יוני שובך וכו'. בתמיה ולמאי לא מאי טרחא איכא: אלא לאו כו'. ומדמהלקטין דמתניתין למקום שאינה יכולה להחזיר נמי שרי שמע מינה מלעיטין דעגלים וגמלים למקום שאינה יכולה להחזיר ושרי אלא דגבי בהמה קרי ליה הלעטה וגבי עופות קרי ליה הילקוט ועל כרחך אין מאמירין דקאסר בכלי הוא: לעולם מהלקטין דספי ליה בידים. ולמקום שיכולה להחזיר: אין מזונותן עליך. דשכיחי להו בדברא: חזיר אין מזונותן עליך. דאסור יהודי שיגדל חזירים: מתני' נמי דיקא. דאפילו שדי קמייהו נמי לא: דשכיחי באגמא. אבל מזונות לא שכיחי להו: שמזונותיו מועטין. שאין אדם חס עליו לתת לו מזונות הרבה: כמה תשהה במעיו. דהכלב שאכל בשר מת ומת הכלב בבית תוך ג' ימים מטמא באהל אבל בחייו לא מטמא דטומאה בלועה בבעלי חיים לא מיטמא כדאמר בבהמה המקשה (חולין דף עא:): שמע מינה. מדקאמר שהקפיד הקדוש ברוך הוא על מזונותיו: משח אודניה. מעט כמות אזנו וחוטרא בתריה יכהו במקל מיד שלא יהא מרגילו אצלו: אבל במתא לא. ליתיב ליה מידי אי לאו דידיה הוא: משום דאתי למסרך. בתריה ויפסידו: לית דעתיר מחזירא. שכל מאכל ראוי לו ומוצא לאכול ואף מאכילין לו הרבה: כוותיה דרב יהודה. שהמראה למקום שאינו יכול להחזיר: פוקס את פיה. נותן הכה לתוך פיה שלא תוכל לסגור פיה: ומאכילה כרשינין ומים בבת אחת. והמים מבליעין הכרשינין לתוך בית בליעתה על כרחה: מאכילה מעומד. נותן לתוך פיה וכל זמן שאינו מרביצה אינו יכול לתחוב כל כך ויכול להחזירה: מתניתין מני. דקתני נותן מים לתוך המורסן דנתינת מים לא זהו גיבולו: אפי' רבי יוסי מודה. דזהו גיבולו: קלי. קמח של תבואה שנתייבשה כשהן קלויות בתנור ואותו קמח לעולם מתוק והוא קמחא דאבשונא ועושין ממנו שתיתא משמן ומים ומלח שמערבין בו: רבי

אין אובסין את הגמל וכו'. והא דאמרינן בעירובין פרק עושין פסין (דף כ: ושם) גמל שראשו ורובו מבפנים אובסין אותו מבפנים הך אביסה לאו היינו אביסה ממש דהא אמרינן הכא אין אובסין כו' והתם אביסה היינו הלעטה וכן פירש רבינו שמואל: **אלא** קמח דבר גיבול הוא. פירשתי לעיל בפ"ק (דף יח. ושם) (ס): מהו

את הדלועין לפני הבהמה ואת הנבלה לפני הכלבים מאי לאו דלועין דומיא דנבלה מה נבלה דרכיכא אף דלועין דרכיכי אלמא טרחינן באוכלא ותיובתא דרב יהודה אמר לך רב יהודה לא נבלה דומיא דדלועין מה דלועין דאשוני אף נבלה דאשונא והיכי משכחת לה בבשר פילי א"נ בגורייתא זוטרי תא שמע דתני רב חנן מנהרדעא מפרכינן תבן ואספסתא ומערבין אלמא טרחינן באוכלא תבן בתיבנא סריא אספסתא בעילי זוטרי: **מתני'** אין אובסין את הגמל ולא דורסין אבל מלעיטין ואין מאמירין את העגלים אבל מלעיטין ומהלקטין לתרנגולין ונותנין מים למורסן אבל לא גובלין ואין נותנין מים לפני דבורים ולפני יונים שבשובך אבל נותנין לפני אווזין ותרנגולין ולפני יוני הרדיסיות: **גמ'** מאי אין אובסין אמר רב יהודה אין עושין לה אבוס בתוך מעיה וכדאמר רב ירמיה מדיפתי לדידי חזי לי ההוא טייעא דאכלא כורא ואטעינא כורא: אין מאמירין: איזו היא המראה ואיזו היא הלעטה אמר רב יהודה המראה למקום שאינה יכולה להחזיר הלעטה למקום שיכולה להחזיר רב חסדא אמר אידי ואידי למקום שאינה יכולה להחזיר והמראה בכלי הלעטה ביד מתיב רב יוסף מהלקטין לתרנגולין ואין צריך לומר שמלקטין ואין מלקטין ליוני שובך וליוני עלייה ואין צריך לומר שאין מהלקטין מאי מהלקטין ומאי מלקטין אילימא מהלקטין דספי ליה בידים מלקטין דשדי ליה (א) קמייהו מכלל דיוני שובך ויוני עלייה מישדא קמייהו נמי לא אלא לאו מהלקטין למקום שאינה יכולה להחזיר מלקטין למקום שיכולה להחזיר מכלל דהמראה בכלי ותיובתא דרב יהודה אמר לך רב יהודה לעולם מהלקטין דספי ליה בידים מלקטין דשדי ליה קמייהו ודקא קשיא לך יוני שובך ויוני עלייה למישדא קמייהו נמי לא הני מזונותן עליך והני אין מזונותן עליך כדתניא נותנין מזונות לפני כלב ואין נותנין מזונות לפני חזיר ומה הפרש בין זה לזה זה מזונותיו עליך וזה אין מזונותיו עליך אמר רב אשי מתניתין נמי דיקא אין נותנין מים לפני דבורים ולפני יונים שבשובך אבל נותנין לפני אווזין ולפני תרנגולין ולפני יוני הרדיסיות מ"ט לאו משום דהני מזונותן עליך והני אין מזונותן עליך ולטעמיך מאי איריא מיא אפילו חיטי ושערי נמי לא אלא שאני מיא דשכיחי באגמא דרש רבי יונה אפיתחא דבי נשיאה מאי דכתיב (א) יודע צדיק דין דלים יודע הקב"ה בכלב שמזונותיו מועטין לפיכך שוהה אכילתו במעיו ג' ימים כדתנן כמה תשהה אכילתו במעיו ויהא טמא בכלב ג' ימים מעת לעת ובעופות ובדגים כדי שתפול לאור ותשרף אמר רב המנונא שמע מינה אורח ארעא למשדא אומצא לכלבא וכמה אמר רב מרי משח אודניה וחוטרא אבתריה הני מילי בדברא אבל במתא לא דאתא למסרך אמר רב פפא לית דעניא מכלבא ולית דעתיר מחזירא תניא כוותיה דרב יהודה איזו היא המראה ואיזו היא הלעטה המראה מרביצה ופוקס את פיה ומאכילה כרשינין ומים בבת אחת הלעטה מאכילה מעומד ומשקה מעומד ונותנין כרשינין בפני עצמן ומים בפני עצמן: מהלקטין לתרנגולין כו': אמר אביי אמריתה קמיה דמר מתניתין מני ואמר לי ר' יוסי בר יהודה היא דתניא אחד נותן את הקמח ואחד נותן לתוכו מים האחרון חייב דברי רבי ר' יוסי בר יהודה אומר אינו חייב עד שיגבל דילמא עד כאן לא קאמר רבי יוסי בר יהודה התם אלא קמח דבר גיבול הוא אבל מורסן דלאו בר גיבול הוא אפילו רבי יוסי בר יהודה מודה לא סלקא דעתך דתניא בהדיא אין נותנין מים למורסן דברי רבי ר' יוסי בר יהודה אומר נותנין מים למורסן ת"ר אין גובלין את הקלי וי"א גובלין מאן י"א א"ר חסדא רבי

עין משפט נר מצוה

כג א מיי' פכ"א מהל' שבת הלכה יח סמג לאוין סה טוש"ע א"ח סימן שכד סעיף ו:
כד ב ג מיי' שם טוש"ע שם סעיף ז:
כה ד ה מיי' שם הלכה לה טוש"ע שם סע"ט:
כו ו מיי' שם והלכה לו טוש"ע שם סעיף י:
כז ז ח ט מיי' שם טוש"ע שם סעיף יא:
כח י מיי' פ"כ מהלכות טומאת מת הלכה ד:
כט כ מיי' פכ"א מהל' שבת הלכה לה:
ל ל מיי' פכ"א מהלכות שבת הלכה לד טוש"ע א"ח סי' שכד סע"ג:

רבינו חננאל

זה התנא אוסר בצדדין ומתיר בצידי צדדין. ופריק רב פפא אליבא דרבא הכא בכלכלה דחוקה וכו'. ודברי רב פפא פשוטין הן ומפקינן בה והלכתא צדדין אסורין צדדי צדדין מותרין: **דרגא** דמדלא סולם העשוי לעלות בו בערסל והוא (שכתוב) [שת"י] כמלונה במקשה [כערסל]. והוא מלונה לשומרי פירות ודקדק רב אשי מזו ההלכה שאסור להניח סולם על הדקל ולעלות בו שנמצא משתמש בצידי האילן ואסור. ופירוש שאם יחקוק באילן ויניח באותה חקיקה גואזי שהן עצים ויניח באותו העצים הסולם נמצא הסולם נתון בעצים כמין הכלכלה ביתד ושרי וגם אסור להניח רגלי העולה באותה סולם בעצים הנעוצין באילן מפני שהן צדדין והצדדין אסורין. וכי אינו מותר לו להשתמש ולעלות אלא בקנים שהן מעלות הסולם והן שליבותיו שהן ודאי צדדי צדדין: [מתני'] **מתירין** פקיעי עמיר כו'. פי' פקיעי אגודות כדתנן פקעת גמי בא רב הונא לפרש משנתנו ואמר הפקיעין והכיפין שניהם אגודות קשורות הן. אלא הפקיעין ב' אגודות כפקיע והכפין ג' אגודות בכף זירין דארדי כשמתגזאין ומתקשין נקראין דארדי והן אחד אחד ואינן נאגדין באגודה. ואם אגדן בחזקתן עומדין ותרצה רב הונא למתניתין הכי מתירין פקיעי עמיר לפני בהמה ומפספסין פי' מפספסין מפרכין כעין פיתות (לרכנן לייתות) [לרכנן] לאכלה ומצינו בתלמוד א"י שאמרו בענין (תינוק פתילה) מפספסין ופי' מחרכין כדכתיב ושער ראשיהון לא התחרך ונראין הדברים שהחריכה מרככת כעין הפתיתה דהוא מעין פסיסה. כדאמרינן בידות האוכלין שכססן לגורן וכשם שמתירין ומפספסין הפקיעין הוא הדין לכפין אבל הזירין לא יפספס ולא להתיר אם נקשרו ובא רב חסדא ופי' טעמא דרב הונא ואמר שהעמידו למשנתנו שמתירין

ומפספסין הפקיעין והכפין שהן מקודם אוכל ויכולין להיאכל כמות שהן התהרה והפספוס לא להוסיף להם אלא הכשר לאכילה בלבד מדברין הללו דקסבר מותר למטרח באוכל ומוסיף לו הכשר אבל אם אין יכול להיאכל כגון הזירין שהן דארדי אלא אחרי התר ופספוס אסור וזהו לשורי אוכלא לא משוינן [illegible] [והזירין שניהן אגודות מפספס [illegible] טרחינן ואם יש לומר מניין לנו ראיה [illegible] באים בתוכו לפיכך אינן חוצצין [illegible] ופשוטה היא. ופריק רב הונא לא [illegible] יכולין להיאכל אף שחת כמותן [illegible] קטנים. ותוב אקשינן על רב הונא [illegible] רב יהודה לת"ק החינח לגסה [illegible] אוכלא לדקה ולגסה הוא ואסור [illegible] רב יהודה דתנן מחתכין את הדלועין [illegible] כרב הונא ריחשא הא איתותב [illegible] באוכלא מכלל דרב הונא לא הוה [illegible] כדכתיב וברבורים אבוסים והוא [illegible] מלעיטין איזו היא המראה ואיזו היא [illegible] להמרות. אבל להלעוטי כדכתיב [illegible] ואין

מסורת הש"ס

א) [נ"ל מפרכין וכן העתיקו תוס' לעיל קנ: וכן בתוס' ב"ב יט: ד"ה בתיבנא], ב) [עי' תוס' ב"מ פ: ד"ה פתם], ג) [תוספתא פרק יח], ד) [בקרא כתיב ידע חסר וי"ו], ה) אהלות פי"א מ"ז, ו) [תוספת' פי"ח], ז) לעיל יח., ח) [לעיל יח. אימ' רבי יוסי], ט) [עי' מ"ש תוס' ב"ב לג: ד"ה מאן], י) [סוטה מט:], כ) [פסחים לט:], ל) בד"ה אבל.

הגהות הב"ח

(א) גמ' דשדי ליה קמיה אלא ליוני שוכך:

גליון הש"ס

גמרא מאי לאו דלועין. כעין זה בב"מ דף קט ע"ב. ועיין שיטה מקובצת שם ד"ה ה"נ:

תורה אור השלם

א) יֹדֵעַ צַדִּיק דִּין דַּלִּים רָשָׁע לֹא יָבִין דָּעַת: [משלי כט, ז]

ליקוטי רש"י

את הדלועין. תלושין לפני הבהמה ולא אמרינן טרחא דלאו צורך הוא [ביצה ב.]. התלושין ומיהו סתמן לאו למאכל בהמה קיימי אלא לאדם [לקמן קנו:]. ואת הנבלה לפני הכלבים. ואע"פ שנתנבלה בשבת דבין השמשות לא היתה עומדת לאכילת כלבים אפילו הכי שרי דלית לן מוקצה בשבת [ביצה שם]. וכשנתנבלה בשבת קאמר מדפליג רבי יהודה עלה ואמר אם לא היתה נבלה מערב שבת אסורה לפי שאינה מן המוכן [שם כז:]. שנתנבלה היום ובין השמשות היתה עומדת לאדם ואפילו הכי מחתכין [לקמן שם]. אין אובסין. שתוחב לה מספוא הרבה על כרחה בבית הבליעה יותר מכדי אכילתה עד שנעשה כאיבוס במעיה כשיוצא למדבר ומתיירא שלא תמצא מאכל [עירובין כ:]. מורסן. היא הקליפה העליונה שמוציאין מחטין הכתושין במכתשת [רשב"ם ב"ב צג:]. קליפה היוצאת כשכותשים במכתשת [חולין פח:]. יוני הרדיסיות. שדרכם ליגדל עם בני אדם [שם קלח:]. הרדיסאות על שם מקומם ויש אומרים על שם הורדוס והן הגדלים בבתים [ביצה כד.]. טייעא. ישמעאל [לעיל פב.]. סוחר ישמעאלים [מו"ק כה:]. ערבי [ב"ק נה.]. סוחר ערבי [ברכות ו:]. יוני שובך. שמבקשים מזונותיהן בשדה וקיניהן בשובך ואין אלו יוני הרדסיאות הגדלים בבתים [ב"מ קב.]. ליוני שובך וליוני עליה. יוני הבר הן ושטין ואוכלין בחוץ [ביצה שם]. דין דלים. ייסורי דלים ומה הם צריכים ונותן להם לב [משלי כט, ז]. האחרון חייב. משום לש שהוא אב מלאכה [לעיל יח.]. קלי. אבשונא, שנתייבשו החטים בתנור בעודן כרמל וקמח שלהן מתוק לעולם [מגילה ז:].

וְאֶת הַדְּלוּעִין לִפְנֵי הַבְּהֵמָה – GOURDS BEFORE AN ANIMAL[1] הַנְּבֵלָה לִפְנֵי הַכְּלָבִים – OR A CARCASS BEFORE DOGS.[2] מַאי לָאו דְּלוּעִין דּוּמְיָא דִּנְבֵלָה מַה נְּבֵלָה דְּרַכִּיכָא אַף דְּלוּעִין דְּרַכִּיכֵי – What is the case of this Mishnah? **Is it not** speaking of **gourds** that are **similar to** the meat of **a carcass?** That is, **just as carcass** meat **is soft, so too the gourds** mentioned here **are soft.** Yet the Mishnah rules that we may cut up these gourds for animal consumption. אַלְמָא טַרְחִינַן בְּאוּכְלָא – **Thus,** we see that **one may exert** himself **to** improve **something that is** already **edible.** וּתְיוּבְתָּא דְּרַב יְהוּדָה – Accordingly, this Mishnah is **a refutation of R' Yehudah,** who maintains that one may not expend such efforts! – ? –

The Gemara responds on behalf of Rav Yehudah:

אָמַר לָךְ רַב יְהוּדָה לֹא – **Rav Yehudah would say to you** that this is **not** the correct understanding of the Mishnah. נְבֵלָה דּוּמְיָא דִּדְלוּעִין – Rather, we are speaking of **a carcass that is similar to gourds:** מַה דְּלוּעִין דְּאַשּׁוּנֵי אַף נְבֵלָה דְּאַשּׁוּנָא – **Just as gourds are** generally **tough,** and need to be cut up, **so too the carcass** referred to here **is tough,** and must be cut up to be eaten. וְהֵיכִי מַשְׁכַּחַת לַהּ – **And where do you find such** a case? בִּבְשַׂר פִּילֵי – **In** the case of **elephant meat,** which is tough for any dog; אִי נַמִּי בְּגוּרְיָיאתָא זוּטְרֵי – **or, alternatively,** in the case of regular meat that is being fed **to small puppies,** who cannot eat it without it being cut up.

The Gemara raises a final challenge to Rav Yehudah:

תָּא שְׁמַע – **Come, learn** this proof: דְּתָנֵי רַב חָנָן מִנְּהַרְדְּעָא – **For Rav Chanan of Nehardea taught the following Baraisa:** מְפַרְכִינַן תֶּבֶן וְאַסְפַּסְתָּא – ONE MAY CRUMBLE STRAW AND FODDER,[3] וּמְעָרְבִין – AND one may MIX them together.[4] Now, both the straw and the fodder are edible without crumbling, yet the Baraisa permits one to further enhance them by crumbling. אַלְמָא טַרְחִינַן בְּאוּכְלָא – **Apparently, one may exert** himself **to** merely improve an already edible animal **food! – ? –**

The Gemara answers:

תֶּבֶן בְּתִיבְנָא סַרְיָא – **The straw** we are speaking of is somewhat **spoiled straw.**[5] It is therefore not edible unless he mixes it with the fodder. אַסְפַּסְתָּא בְּעִילֵי זוּטְרֵי – And **the fodder** requires crumbling because, in the Baraisa's case, the fodder is being fed **to young donkeys,** who cannot eat it without crumbling. And since the fodder is crumbled, the straw will not mix with it unless it is crumbled as well.[6] Thus, both the straw and the fodder must be crumbled in order to be edible.

Mishnah

The Mishnah discusses the feeding of animals:[7]

אֵין אוֹבְסִין אֶת הַגָּמָל – ONE MAY NOT STUFF A CAMEL,[8] וְלֹא דּוֹרְסִין – NOR MAY HE CRAM IT,[9] אֲבָל מַלְעִיטִין – BUT HE MAY PUT FOOD DOWN ITS THROAT.[10] וְאֵין מַאֲמִירִין אֶת הָעֲגָלִים – ALSO, ONE MAY NOT FATTEN[10] CALVES, אֲבָל מַלְעִיטִין – BUT ONE MAY PUT FOOD DOWN THEIR THROATS. וּמְהַלְקְטִין לַתַּרְנְגוֹלִין – ONE MAY FORCE-FEED CHICKENS,[11] וְנוֹתְנִין מַיִם לַמּוּרְסָן – AND ONE MAY PUT WATER INTO their BRAN, אֲבָל לֹא גּוֹבְלִין – BUT ONE MAY NOT KNEAD the bran and water together.[12] וְאֵין נוֹתְנִין מַיִם לִפְנֵי דְבוֹרִים וְלִפְנֵי יוֹנִים שֶׁבְּשׁוֹבָךְ – ONE MAY NOT PLACE WATER BEFORE BEES OR BEFORE DOVES IN A DOVECOTE,[13] אֲבָל נוֹתְנִין לִפְנֵי אַוָּזִין וְתַרְנְגוֹלִין וְלִפְנֵי יוֹנֵי הַרְדֵּסִיּוֹת – BUT ONE MAY PLACE WATER BEFORE GEESE, CHICKENS AND HERODIAN[14] PIGEONS.[15]

Gemara

The Gemara examines the Mishnah's first statement:

מַאי אֵין אוֹבְסִין – **What is** the meaning of: ONE MAY NOT STUFF (*ovsin*) a camel?

The Gemara explains:

אָמַר רַב יְהוּדָה – **Rav Yehudah said:** אֵין עוֹשִׂין לָהּ אֵבוּס בְּתוֹךְ

NOTES

1. I.e. gourds that have already been harvested. [Those still attached to the ground may, of course, not be cut on the Sabbath.] The principle behind this law is this: Although gourds are usually set aside for human consumption, this does not render them *muktzeh* in regard to animals (*Rashi*); see below, 156b note 14.

2. The carcass is not considered *muktzeh,* as will be explained below (ibid.).

3. [See above, 155a note 13.]

4. The straw is mixed with the fodder so that the animal will consume the straw on account of the fodder (*Rashi*).

5. [The straw is only somewhat spoiled; completely spoiled straw is used for construction purposes and is *muktzeh* (*Rashi;* see above, 155a note 18).]

6. [*Melo HaRo'im;* see also *Meiri; Mishnah Berurah* 518:36.]

7. [The Mishnah will distinguish between methods of feeding that are permissible on the Sabbath and methods that are not. The terms used for these methods are not readily able to be translated into English. Moreover, the Gemara will cite a dispute as to the meanings of some of these terms. The translations offered are therefore only approximations.]

8. One may not force-feed it a huge quantity of food. The Gemara traces the word אוֹבְסִין to אֵבוּס, *a trough;* i.e. we may not stuff the camel with so much food that we create a veritable trough in its belly (*Rashi*). Before setting out on a journey through the desert, it was customary for camel drivers to stuff their camels with enough food to last two or three days as there were few opportunities to obtain camel feed in the desert (*Meiri*).

9. He force-feeds the barley down its throat. [This is essentially similar to *stuffing,*] save that the amount crammed here is smaller (*Rashi*).

These methods of feeding are prohibited on the Sabbath because they entail excessive and unnecessary exertion (*Meiri;* see also *Shaar HaTziyun* 324:23). Alternatively, we fear that one may come to crush beans or knead flour for this purpose (*Rambam, Hil. Shabbos* 21:35).

10. This term will be [more clearly] defined in the Gemara (*Rashi*).

11. The Gemara will make clear that this term corresponds to the term מַלְעִיטִין, *to put food down the throat,* which the Mishnah uses in respect to camels; whereas מַלְעִיטִין is the term of choice for camels, מְהַלְקְטִין is the term of choice for birds (see *Rashi* below ד"ה אלא לאו).

12. [This too involves preparation of food for livestock.] The Mishnah teaches that merely adding water to bran does not constitute "kneading," one of the thirty-nine *melachos.* However, *kneading* bran and water together, i.e. stirring them, is forbidden, either because it violates the *melachah* of "kneading" (at least on a Rabbinic level; see below, note 50), or because it is an unnecessarily exertion, since the chickens tend to stir the mixture themselves as they peck at it and do not need to have it mixed for them (*Ramban* below, 156a).

13. The Gemara offers two alternative reasons why this is forbidden: (a) These creatures are not dependent on their keeper for their food, since they forage on their own; [since the keeper is not responsible for feeding them, he is prohibited to do so because it is unnecessary exertion]. (b) [Even if they cannot find food on their own quite so readily,] they can certainly find water on their own, so that for their keeper to provide them with water is a completely needless exertion (*Rashi*).

14. Or, Hydrosian pigeons (*Rashi* printed with *Rif;* see *Chullin* 139b). If the proper term is "Herodian," they are called so after Herod, who first began breeding them. If "Hydrosian," they are named after their locale (*Chullin* loc. cit., with *Rashi*). Note that *Rashi* here writes that these pigeons are named after their locale – apparently, his text of the Mishnah read: Hydrosian pigeons (*Rashash*). In any event, these are a type of domesticated pigeon (*Rashi*).

15. These birds are fed at home (*Rashi*); since they do not forage for themselves, their keeper may provide them with food and water, even on the Sabbath.

עין משפט נר מצוה

כג א מיי' פכ"א מהל' שבת הלכה יח סמג לאוין סה טוש"ע א"ח סימן שכד סעיף ז:
כד ב ג מיי' שם טוש"ע שם סעיף ז:
כה ד ה מיי' שם הלכה לה טוש"ע שם סעי' יג:
כו ו מיי' שם הלכה ט טוש"ע שם סעיף יא:
כז ז ח ט מיי' שם טוש"ע שם סעיף יא:
כח י מיי' פ"ב מהלכות טומאת מת הלכה ה:
כט כ מיי' פכ"א מהל' שבת הלכה לה:
ל ל מיי' פכ"א מהלכות שבת הלכה לג טוש"ע א"ח סי' שכד סעי' ג:

את הדלועין לפני הבהמה ואת הנבלה לפני הכלבים מאי לאו דלועין דומיא דנבלה מה נבלה דרכיכא אף דלועין דרכיכי אלמא טרחינן באוכלא ותיובתא דרב יהודה אמר לך רב יהודה לא נבלה דומיא דדלועין מה דלועין דאשוני אף נבלה דאשונא והיכי משכחת לה בבשר פילי א"נ בגורייתא זוטרי תא שמע דתני רב חנן מנהרדעא מפרכינן תבן ואספסתא ומערבין אלמא טרחינן באוכלא תבן בתיבנא סריא אספסתא בעילי זוטרי: **מתני'** אין אובסין את הגמל ולא דורסין אבל מלעיטין ואין ממרים את העגלים אבל מלעיטין ומהלקטין לתרנגולין ונותנין מים למורסן אבל לא גובלין ואין נותנין מים לפני דבורים ולפני יונים שבשובך אבל נותנין לפני אווזין ותרנגולין ולפני יוני הרדסיות: **גמ'** מאי אין אובסין אמר רב יהודה [ד] אין עושין לה אבוס בתוך מעיה מי איכא כי האי גוונא אין וכדאמר רב ירמיה מדיפתי לדידי חזי לי ההוא טייעא דאכלא כורא ואטעינא כורא: אין מאמירין: איזו היא המראה ואיזו היא הלעטה אמר רב יהודה [ה] המראה למקום שאינה יכולה להחזיר הלעטה למקום שיכולה להחזיר רב חסדא אמר אידי ואידי למקום שאינה יכולה להחזיר והמראה בכלי והלעטה ביד מתיב רב יוסף [ו] מהלקטין לתרנגולין ואין צריך לומר שמלקטין ואין מלקטין ליוני שובך וליוני עלייה ואין צריך לומר שאין מהלקטין מאי מהלקטין ומאי מלקטין אילימא מהלקטין דספי ליה בידים מלקטין דשדי ליה (א) קמייהו מכלל דיוני שובך ויוני עלייה מישדא קמייהו נמי לא אלא לאו מהלקטין למקום שאינה יכולה להחזיר מלקטין למקום שיכולה להחזיר מכלל דהמראה בכלי ותיובתא דרב יהודה אמר לך רב יהודה לעולם מהלקטין דספי ליה בידים מלקטין דשדי ליה קמייהו ודקא קשיא לך יוני שובך ויוני עלייה למישדא קמייהו נמי לא הני מזונותן עליך והני אין מזונותן עליך כדתניא [ז] נותנין מזונות לפני כלב ואין נותנין מזונות לפני חזיר ומה הפרש בין זה לזה זה מזונותיו עליך וזה אין מזונותיו עליך אמר רב אשי מתניתין נמי דיקא [ח] אין נותנין מים לפני דבורים ולפני יונים שבשובך אבל נותנין לפני אווזין ולפני תרנגולין ולפני יוני הרדסיות מ"ט לאו [ט] משום דהני מזונותן עליך והני אין מזונותן עליך ולטעמיך מאי איריא מיא אפילו חיטי ושערי נמי לא אלא שאני מיא דשכיחי באגמא דרש רבי יונה אפיתחא דבי נשיאה מאי דכתיב (א) (ד) יודע צדיק דין דלים יודע הקב"ה בכלב שמזונותיו מועטין לפיכך שוהה אכילתו במעיו ג' ימים [י] כדתנן כמה תשהה אכילתו במעיו ויהא טמא בכלב ג' ימים מעת לעת ובעופות ובדגים כדי שתפול לאור ותשרף אמר רב המנונא שמע מינה אורח ארעא למשדא אומצא לכלבא וכמה אמר רב מרי משח אודניה וחוטרא אבתריה הני מילי בדברא אבל במתא לא דאתא למסרך אמר רב פפא לית דעניא מכלבא ולית דעתיר מחזירא תניא כוותיה דרב יהודה איזו היא המראה ואיזו היא הלעטה המראה מרביצה ופוקם את פיה ומאכילה כרשינין ומים בבת אחת הלעטה מאכילה מעומד ומשקה מעומד ונותנין כרשינין בפני עצמן ומים בפני עצמן: מהלקטין לתרנגולין: אמר אביי אמריתה קמיה דמר מתניתין מני ואמר לי ר' יוסי בר יהודה היא דתניא אחד נותן את הקמח ואחד נותן לתוכו מים האחרון חייב דברי רבי [כ] ר' יוסי בר יהודה אומר אינו חייב עד שיגבל ודילמא עד כאן לא קאמר רבי יוסי בר יהודה התם אלא קמח דבר גיבול הוא אבל מורסן דלאו בר גיבול הוא אפילו רבי יוסי בר יהודה מודה לא סלקא דעתך דתניא בהדיא [ל] נותנין מים למורסן ת"ר אין גובלין את הקלי וי"א גובלין מאן י"א א"ר חסדא רבי

תוספות

אין אובסין את הגמל וכו'. והא דאמרינן בעירובין פרק עושין פסין (דף כ: ושם) גמל שראשו ורובו מבפנים אובסין אותו מבפנים הך אביסה לאו היינו אביסה ממש דהא אמרינן הכא אין אובסין כו' והתם אביסה היינו הלעטה וכן פירש רבינו שמואל: **אלא** קמח דבר גיבול הוא. פירשתי לעיל בפ"ק (דף יח. ושם):

מהו

רש"י

את הדלועין. התלושין ולא אמרינן מוקצין הן לבהמה דמאכל אדם הן: **אשוני.** קשין: **א"נ.** כלבים דקאמר בגורייתא זוטרי דכל נבלה קשה להן: **ומערבין.** התבן והאספסתא יחד והבהמה אוכלת התבן בשביל האספסתא: **תבן בתיבנא סריא.** דלא חזיא והשתא משוי לה אוכלא והאי סריא לאו סריא לגמרי דהשתא לטינא קיימא ואסורה לטלטל: **מתני' אין אובסין.** מאכילין אותו הרבה על כרחו ותוחבין לו בגרונו ובגמרא מפרש לשון אובסין עושין לה כמין אבוס בתוך מעיה: **ולא דורסין.** שדורס לה בתוך גרונה את השעורין ומיהו לא הוי כל כך כמו אובסין: **אבל מלעיטין.** מפרש בגמרא: **אין מאמירין.** מפרש בגמרא: **מהלקטין.** מפרש בגמרא: **אין נותנין מים לפני דבורים.** מפרש טעמא בגמרא לאו משום דלאין מזונותיהן עליו שיוצאין ואוכלין בשדה לאו משום דמיא באגמא שכיחי להו: **הרדסיות.** על שם מקומן ונזונין בתוך הבית: **גמ' כי האי גוונא.** שיאכילנה כל כך שירחיבו מעיה כאבוס: **אטעינא כורא.** על גבה למזונות לדרך לבד שאר משאות: **למקום שאינה יכולה להחזיר.** שתוחבו לה לפנים מבית הבליעה: **בכלי.** במרווד: **דספי בידים.** תוחבו לתוך פיו: **אלא יוני שובך וכו'.** בתמיה ואמאי לא מאי טרחא איכא: **אלא לאו כו'.** ומדמהלקטין דמתניתין למקום שאינה יכולה להחזיר נמי שרי שמע מינה מלעיטין דעגלים וגמלים למקום שאינה יכולה להחזיר ושרי אלא דגבי בהמה קרי ליה הלעטה וגבי עופות קרי ליה הילקוט ועל כרחך אין מאמירין דקאסר בכלי הוא: **לעולם מהלקטין דספי ליה בידים.** ולמקום שיכולה להחזיר: **אין מזונותן עליך.** דשכיחי להו בדברא: **חזיר אין מזונותו עליך.** דאסור ליהודי לגדל חזירים: **מתני' נמי דיקא.** דאפילו שדי קמייהו נמי לא: **דשכיחי באגמא.** אבל מזונות לא שכיחי להו: **שמזונותיו מועטין.** שאין אדם חס עליו לתת לו מזונות הרבה: **כמה תשהה במעיו.** הכלב שאכל בשר מת ומת הכלב בבית תוך ג' ימים מטמא באהל אבל בחייו לא מטמא דטומאה בלועה בבעלי חיים לא מיטמיא כדאמר בבהמה המקשה (חולין דף עא:): **שמע מינה.** מדקאמר שהקפיד הקדוש ברוך הוא על מזונותיו: **משח אודניה.** מעט כמות אורך אזנו וחוטרא בתריה יכהו במקל מיד שלא יהא מרגילו אצלו: **אבל במתא לא.** ליתיב ליה מידי אי לאו דידיה הוא: **משום דאתי למסרך.** בתריה ויפסידו: **לית דעתיר מחזירא.** שכל מאכל ראוי לו ומוצא לאכול ואף מאכילין לו הרבה: **כוותיה דרב יהודה.** שהמראה למקום שאינו יכול להחזיר: **פוקם את פיה.** פותח נותן חכה לתוך פיה שלא תוכל לסגור פיה: **ומאכילה כרשינין ומים בבת אחת.** והמים מבליעין הכרשינין לתוך בית בליעתה על כרחה: **מאכילה מעומד.** נותן לתוך פיה וכל זמן שאינו מרביצה אינו יכול לתחוב כל כך ויכול להחזירה: **מתניתין מני.** דקתני נותן מים לתוך המורסן דנתינת מים לא זהו גיבולו: **אפי' רבי יוסי מודה.** דזהו גיבולו: **קלי.** קמח של תבואה שנתייבשה כשהן קליות בתנור ואותו קמח לעולם מתוק והוא (כ) קמחא דאבשונא ועושין ממנו שתיתא משמן ומים ומלח שמערבין בו:

רבי

רבינו חננאל

זה התנא אוסר בצדדין ומתיר בצידי צדדין. ופריק רב פפא אליבא דרבא הכא בכלכלה רחוקה וכו'. ודברי רב פפא פשוטין הן ומפקינן בה והלכתא צדדין אסורין צדדי צדדין מותרין: **דרגא** דמדלא סולם העשוי לעלות בו בערסל והוא (שכתוב) [שת"ין] כמלונה במקשה [כערסל]. והוא מלונה לשומרי פירות ודקדק רב אשי מזו ההלכה שאסור להניח סולם על הדקל ולעלות בו שנמצא משתמש בצידי האילן ואסור. ופירוש שאם יחקוק באילן ויניח באותה חקיקה גואזי שהן עצים ויניח באותו העצים הסולם נמצא הסולם נתון בעצים כמין הכלכלה ביתד ושרי וגם אסור להניח רגלי העולה באותה סולם בעצים הנעוצין באילן מפני שהן צדדין והצדדין אסורין. וכי אינו מותר לו להשתמש ולעלות אלא בקנים שהן מעלות הסולם והן שליבותיו שהן ודאי צדדי צדדין: [מתני'] **מתירין** פקיעי עמיר כו'. פי' פקיעי אגודות כדתנן פקעת גמי בא רב הונא לפרש משנתנו ואמר הפקיעין והכיפין שניהם אגודות קשורות הן. אלא הפקיעין ב' אגודות כפקיע והכפין ג' אגודות בכף זירין דארדי כשמתגזאין ומתקשין נקראין דארדי והן אחד אחד ואינן נאגדין באגודה. ואם אגדן בחזקתן עומדין ותרצה רב הונא למתניתין הכי מתירין פקיעי עמיר לפני בהמה ומפספסין פי' מפספסין מפרכין כעין פיתות (לרכנן לייתות) [לרככן] לאכלה ומצינו בתלמוד א"י שאמרו בענין (תינוק פתילה) מפספסין ופי' מחרכין כדכתיב ושער ראשיהן לא התחרך ונראין הדברים שהחריכה מרככת כעין הפתיתה דהוא מעין פסיסה. כדאמרינן בידות האוכלין שכססן לגורן וכשם שמתירין ומפספסין הפקיעין הוא הדין לכפין אבל הזירין לא יפספס ולא להתיר אם נקשרו ובא רב חסדא ופי' טעמא דרב הונא ואמר שהעמידו למשנתנו שמתירין ומפספסין הפקיעין והכפין שהן מקודם אוכל ויכולין להיאכל כמות שהן וכן ההתרה והפספוס לא להוסיף להם אלא הכשר לאכילה בלבד דייקינן מדבריו הללו דקסבר מותר למיטרח באוכל ומוסיף לו הכשר אבל אם אין יכול להיאכל כגון הזירין שהן דארדי אלא אחרי התר ופספוס אסור וזהו לשוויי אוכלי לא משוינן ורב יהודה חלק על רב הונא לדברי רבה דאוקמינהו לדברי רב יהודה שוויה אוכלא לא משוינן ואמר רבה מדתרצה למתניתין שהפקיעין [והזירין שניהן אגודות מפספס למה הן מיהו הפקיעין שתים באגודה והעמירן ג' מותר להתיר הפקיעין שקשרן מתירן] ואם לא יתירם אינן נאכלין בטוב ושלש אין קשרן אמיץ ונאכלין וכיון שיכולים להיאכל קסבר אטרוחי באכילה טרחינן ואם יש לומר מניין לנו ראיה שיש הפרש בין ב' לג' שאלו קישרם אמיץ יתר מאלו מצאנו לדבריהן שאומרים נימה אחת קשורה חוצצת ג' אין חוצצת ב' איני יודע פי' ג' אינן חוצצת שאין קשרן מתחזק ומרפרף הוא והמים באים בתוכו לפיכך אינן חוצצין אבל הכפים שהן דידי והן קשין כמו שאמרנו למעלה מפספסין כדי לשוותם אוכל וכ"ש שמתירין ובאנו להקשות לרב הונא מסיפא דהא מתניתין דקתני אין מרסקין לא את השחת ולא את החרובין ופשוטה היא. ופריק רב הונא לא שהחרובין רכין הן כמות שהן (שהדות) [שהדתאה] שהן רכין ויכולין להיאכל אין מרסקין אותן אלמא לא מטרחינן באוכלא אלא שחת דומיא דחרובין מה חרובין דאשיני פירוש יבישין וקשין ואין יכולין להיאכל אף שחת כמותן שנתייבש ונתקשה ואינו אוכל והריסוק משוייהו אוכל ומתניתין כותי דאמרי שוויי אוכלא לא משוינן ואזו היא בהמה שאינה יכולה לאכול השחת אלא אחרי ריסוק ואמרנו בעילי זוטרי פי' עיירים קטנים. ותוב אקשינן על רב הונא מדרב יהודה נשמע לרבנן לאו ר' יהודה מתיר בחרובין לדקה. לדקה [אין] לגסה לא מכלל דרבנן סברי כיון שיכולין להיאכל כמות שהן לא טרחינן לדחוקינהו להו דמטרח באוכלא לא טרחינן. וא"ל רב יהודה לת"ק התינח לגסה שיכולה לאכול כמות שהיא בלא ריסוק אלא לדקה שאינה יכולה לאוכלה כמות שהיא בלא ריסוק שוויי אוכלא הוא ושוי דאם נאמר כי ת"ק סבר מטרח טרחינן שוויי אוכלא לא משוינן וריסוק זה שוויי אוכלא לדקה ולגסה הוא ואסור וא"ל ר' יהודה לדקה אוכלא הוא ומיטרח באוכל שרי ואם הוא אוכל לדקה כ"ש לגסה ולא היה צריך לומר אלא ר' יהודה מתיר סתם בין לדקה בין לגסה. ועלתה בקשיא לרב הונא וחזרנו להקשות על רב יהודה דתנן מחתכין את הדלועין לפני הבהמה ואת הנבלה לפני הכלבים ופריק ליה ופשוטה היא וכן הא דתני רב חנן מנהרדעא מפריכין תבן ואספסתא ומערבין אלמא טרחינן באוכלא ופריק גם זו ואע"ג דרוב סוגיא דשמעתא כרב הונא ריחשא הא איתותב ולא אשכח לה פירוקא ועלתה בה קושיא ותוב רב יהודה ורבה רישי מתיבתא הוו דאמרינן האי שיפורא מעיקרא בי רב יהודה ולבסוף בי רבה והלכתא כוותיה ומשוינן אוכלא ולא קא טרחינן באוכלא מכלל דרב הונא לא הוה ריש מתיבתא והא אמרינן כי הוו מפטרי רבנן מבי רב הונא הוו פיישי כו' ואמרינן ואמרי במערבא קמא לה מתיבתא דהונא בבלאה: [מתני'] **אין אובסין** את הגמל כו'. פי' אובסין מפטמין כדכתיב וברבורים אבוסים והוא מאכילין את הגמל הרבה כרב ירמיה דאמר אנא חזיתיה לההוא טייעא דאכלא כו' כורא ואטענה כורא וכן הלכה דאסור לפטם בהמה בשבת ולא אפילו עופות. אין ממרים את העגלים אבל מלעיטין איזו היא המראה ואיזו הלעטה. אמר רב יהודה המראה למקום שאינה יכולה להחזיר. פי' המראה שמוריד בידו המאכל בבלעו של עגלים במקום שאינו יכול להחזירו מתוך בלעו אבל חשוב הוא כבלוע כגון זה אסור להמרות. אבל להלעוטי כדכתיב הלעיטני וגו' לתת המאכל בחך שלו מותר וזה וזה ביד. ורב חסדא אמר אידי ואידי למקום שאין יכול להחזיר והמראה בכלי והלעטה ביד ואותביה רב יוסף לרב יהודה מהלקטין לתרנגולין

ואין

מסורת הש"ס

א) [נ"ל מפרכין וכן העתיקו תוס' לעיל קנ: וכן בתוס' ב"ב יט: ד"ה במיכנא], ב) [עי' תוס' ב"מ פ: ד"ה סמס], ג) [תוספתא פרק יח], ד) [בקרא כתיב ידע חסר ו"ו], ה) אהלות פי"א מ"ז, ו) [תוספתא פי"ח], ז) לעיל יח. ע"ש, ח) [עי' תוס' ב"ב לג: ד"ה מאן], ט) [סוטה מט:], י) [פסחים לט:], כ) בד"ה אבל.

הגהות הב"ח

(א) גמ' דשדי ליה קמיה אלא דיוני שובך:

גליון הש"ס

גמרא מאי לאו דלועין. כעין זה בב"מ דף קט ע"ב. ועיין שיטה מקובצת שם ד"ה ה"נ:

תורה אור השלם

א) יֹדֵעַ צַדִּיק דִּין דַּלִּים רָשָׁע לֹא יָבִין דָּעַת: [משלי כט, ז]

ליקוטי רש"י

את הדלועין. תלושין לפני הבהמה ולא אמרינן טרחא דלאו לורך הוא [ביצה ב.]. התלושין ומיהו סתמן לאו למאכל בהמה קיימי אלא לאדם [לקמן קנו:]. **ואת הנבלה לפני הכלבים.** ואע"פ שנתנבלה בשבת דבין השמשות לא היתה עומדת לאכילת כלבים אפילו הכי שרי דלית לן מוקצה בשבת [ביצה שם]. וכשנתנבלה בשבת קאמר מדפליג רבי יהודה עלה ואמר אם לא היתה נבלה מערב שבת אסורה לפי שאינה מן המוכן [שם כז:]. שנתנבלה היום וכיון השמשות היתה עומדת לאדם ואפילו הכי מחתכין [לקמן שם]. **אין אובסין.** שתוחב לה מאכל הרבה על כרחה בבית הבליעה יותר מכדי אכילתה עד שנעשה כאיבוס במעיה כשיוצא למדבר ומפרשה שלא תמצא מאכל [עירובין כ:]. **מורסן.** היא הקליפה העליונה שמוציאין מחטין הכתושין במכתשת [רשב"ם ב"ב צג.]. קליפה שיוצאה כשכותשין במכתשת [חולין פח:]. **יוני הרדסיות.** שדרכם לגדל עם בני אדם בבית [ביצה כד.]. הרדסיות על שם הורדוס שהיה מגדלן בבית, ויש אומרים על שם מקומם, והן הגדלים בבתים [ביצה כד.]. **טייעא.** ישמעאל [לעיל כב.]. סוחר ישמעאלי [מו"ק כה.]. ערבי [ב"ק נה.]. סוחר ערבי [ברכות ו:]. **יוני שובך.** שמקננים בשובך מזונותיהן בשדה וקוניהן בשובך ואין לאו יוני הרדסיות הגדלים בבתים [ב"מ קב.]. **וליוני עליה.** יוני הבר הן וקנין ואוכלין מחוץ [ביצה שם]. **דין דלים.** יודע דלים ומה הם לרכים ונותן להם לב [משלי כט, ז]. **האחרון חייב.** משום לש שהוא מלאכה [לעיל יח.]. **קלי.** לאבשונא, שנתייבשו החטים בעודן כרמל ובתנור, שלהן מתוק לעולם [מגילה ז:].

מֵעֶיהָ – **One may not make a** veritable **trough** (*eivus*) **in its belly.**[16]

The Gemara asks:

מִי אִיכָּא כִּי הַאי גַּוְונָא – How could that be the Mishnah's meaning? **Is it possible** to stuff an animal **to such an extent?!**[17]

The Gemara answers:

אִין וְכִדְאָמַר רַב יִרְמְיָה מִדִּיפְתִּי – **Yes, as Rav Yirmiyah of Difti** once **recounted:** לְדִידִי חֲזֵי לִי הַהוּא טַיָּיעָא – **"I once saw a certain Arab merchant** דְּאוֹכְלָא כּוֹרָא וְאַטְעֵינָא כּוֹרָא – **who fed**[18] **[his camel]** an entire ***kor***[19] of food **and** then **loaded it with an** additional ***kor*** of provisions for the way."[20] Thus, we see that it is possible to stuff an animal to such an extreme.

The Gemara cites a later section of the Mishnah:

אֵין מַאֲמִירִין – ONE MAY NOT FATTEN [calves, but one may put food down their throats].

The Gemara asks:

אֵיזוֹ הִיא הַמְרָאָה וְאֵיזוֹ הִיא הַלְעָטָה – **Which** actions **are** termed ***fattening*** **and which are** termed ***putting food down their throats?***

The Gemara defines these terms:

אָמַר רַב יְהוּדָה – **Rav Yehudah said:** הַמְרָאָה לְמָקוֹם שֶׁאֵינָהּ יְכוֹלָה לְהַחֲזִיר – ***Fattening*** (which the Mishnah forbids) denotes putting the food **into an area** of the animal's throat **that** is so far back **[the animal] cannot bring the food back up.**[21] הַלְעָטָה לְמָקוֹם שֶׁיְּכוֹלָה לְהַחֲזִיר – ***Putting food down their throats*** (which the Mishnah permits) denotes placement **in an area where [the animal] can** still **bring** the food **back up.**

The Gemara records a dissenting view:

רַב חִסְדָּא אָמַר – **Rav Chisda said:** אִידֵי וְאִידֵי לְמָקוֹם שֶׁאֵינָהּ יְכוֹלָה לְהַחֲזִיר – **Both of these** terms denote placing the food far back, **where [the animal] can no longer bring** the food **back up.** וְהַמְרָאָה בִּכְלִי – However, ***fattening*** refers to where this is done **with an implement,**[22] and this is what the Mishnah forbids; הַלְעָטָה בְּיָד – whereas ***putting food down their throats*** refers to where this is done **by hand,** and the Mishnah permits this.

It emerges that according to Rav Yehudah one may not feed an animal on the Sabbath by placing food in its throat so far back that it cannot bring it back up. According to Rav Chisda, however, this is permitted so long as it is not done with an implement.

Rav Yosef challenges Rav Yehudah's view:

מָתִיב רַב יוֹסֵף – **Rav Yosef challenged this from a Baraisa:** מְהַלְקְטִין לְתַרְנְגוֹלִין – ONE MAY FORCE-FEED CHICKENS, וְאֵין צָרִיךְ לוֹמַר שֶׁמַּלְקִיטִין – AND CERTAINLY ONE MAY FEED THEM.[23] וְאֵין מַלְקִיטִין לְיוֹנֵי שׁוֹבָךְ וּלְיוֹנֵי עֲלִיָּיה – HOWEVER, ONE MAY NOT FEED DOVECOTE DOVES OR ATTIC DOVES, וְאֵין צָרִיךְ לוֹמַר שֶׁאֵין מְהַלְקְטִין – AND CERTAINLY ONE MAY NOT FORCE-FEED THEM. מַאי מְהַלְקְטִין וּמַאי מַלְקִיטִין – Now, **what is** meant here by ***force-feeding*** **and what is meant** by ***feeding?*** אִילֵימָא – **If you say** that מְהַלְקְטִין דְּסָפֵי לֵיהּ בְּיָדַיִם – ***force-feeding*** refers to **when he feeds** the birds by placing food down their throats **by hand,** מַלְקִיטִין דְּשָׁדֵי לֵיהּ קַמַּיְיהוּ – **and *feeding*** refers to **when he** simply **throws [the food] in front of them,** מִכְּלָל דְּיוֹנֵי שׁוֹבָךְ וְיוֹנֵי עֲלִיָּיה מִישְׁדָא קַמַּיְיהוּ נַמִּי לֹא – then **that implies that,** when it comes to **dovecote doves and attic doves, even throwing** food **in front of them is not** allowed. But that certainly cannot be![24] אֶלָּא לָאו – **Rather,** then, these are **not** the correct definitions. Instead, we must say that מְהַלְקְטִין לְמָקוֹם שֶׁאֵינָהּ יְכוֹלָה לְהַחֲזִיר – ***force-feeding*** entails putting the food, by hand, **in an area** of the chicken's throat **where it can no longer bring** the food **back up,** מַלְקִיטִין לְמָקוֹם שֶׁיְּכוֹלָה לְהַחֲזִיר – while ***feeding*** entails putting the food, by hand, **in an area** of the chicken's throat **where it can bring the food back up.** Thus, it emerges that the Baraisa permits force-feeding a chicken by hand, even if the food is placed so far back that the chicken cannot bring it back up. מִכְּלָל דְּהַמְרָאָה בִּכְלִי – But **that implies that *fattening,*** which our Mishnah forbids, must refer to something even more forceful, namely, force-feeding the animal **with an implement.**[25] וּתְיוּבְתָּא דְּרַב יְהוּדָה – This Baraisa, then, is **a refutation of** the view of **Rav Yehudah! – ? –**

The Gemara deflects the challenge:

אָמַר לָךְ רַב יְהוּדָה – **Rav Yehuda could tell you:** לְעוֹלָם מְהַלְקְטִין דְּסָפֵי לֵיהּ בְּיָדַיִים – **Really, *force-feeding*** **is** when he places food down their throats **by hand,**[26] מַלְקִיטִין דְּשָׁדֵי לֵיהּ קַמַּיְיהוּ – **and *feeding* is when he throws it in front of [the birds].** וְדְקָא קַשְׁיָא לָךְ – **And as to that which was difficult for you** to understand, יוֹנֵי שׁוֹבָךְ וְיוֹנֵי עֲלִיָּיה לְמִישְׁדָא קַמַּיְיהוּ נַמִּי לֹא – namely, why is it that in regard to **dovecote doves and attic doves even the throwing** of food **in front of them is not** allowed, the reasoning is as follows: הָנֵי מְזוֹנוֹתָן עָלֶיךָ – **These** creatures that one is permitted to feed, viz. chickens, **depend upon you for their food;** וְהָנֵי אֵין מְזוֹנוֹתָן עָלֶיךָ – **but these** doves, which you are forbidden to feed, **do not depend upon you for their food.**[27]

It follows from Rav Yehudah's interpretation of this Baraisa that a person may not place food on the Sabbath in front of an animal for whose feeding he is not responsible. The Gemara adduces support for this principle:

כִּדְתַנְיָא – **As it was taught in a Baraisa:** נוֹתְנִין מְזוֹנוֹת לִפְנֵי כֶּלֶב – ONE MAY PLACE FOOD BEFORE A DOG, וְאֵין נוֹתְנִין מְזוֹנוֹת לִפְנֵי חֲזִיר – BUT ONE MAY NOT PLACE FOOD BEFORE A PIG. וּמָה הֶפְרֵשׁ בֵּין זֶה לָזֶה – NOW WHAT DIFFERENCE IS THERE BETWEEN THIS ONE

NOTES

16. See note 8.

17. Can one feed a camel so much that its belly will grow to the size of a trough? (*Rashi*).

18. [See *Rashash.*]

19. [A *kor* is a measure of volume consisting of 30 *se'ah;* a *se'ah* is equal to the volume of 144 eggs.]

20. I.e. he loaded on its back a *kor* of provisions above and beyond its normal burdens (*Rashi*). [See *Tosafos* to *Bava Metzia* 80b ד״ה סתם, who explain why *Rashi* comments here that there were other burdens.]

21. The food is thrust past the point where the calf swallows (*Rashi*). [It is therefore impossible for the calf to spit it out.]

22. E.g. with a spoon (*Rashi*).

23. Both the terms מְהַלְקְטִין and מַלְקִיטִין have the sense of feeding. The former, however, is a more intense form and denotes greater forcefulness. We have therefore rendered the former *to force-feed,* and the latter simply *to feed.*

[Note that the root לָקַט also means *gathered.* Similarly, the Aramaic word סְפָא can mean both *gathered* (see *Bava Metzia* 114b), and *fed* (see below, 156a).]

24. Why should this be forbidden? What effort is involved? (*Rashi*).

25. The laws governing the feeding of camels, calves or poultry are identical; only the terms vary from species to species. Thus, if we know that it is permitted to stuff food far down a chicken's throat by hand, it is permitted to do so for other animals as well. Regarding a chicken, this is called מְהַלְקְטִין, *force-feeding;* regarding calves and camels, we must conclude that this is called הַלְעָטָה, *putting food down their throats,* since this is the only method permitted by our Mishnah. It follows that הַמְרָאָה, *fattening,* which the Mishnah forbids, must denote [something even more forceful and laborious, viz.] force-feeding the animal with an implement (*Rashi*).

26. And only to a point where the animal can still spit it out (*Rashi*).

27. They can easily find food in the outdoors (*Rashi*). Since they can forage for food on their own, it is not their keeper's responsibility to feed them and he may not even place food in front of them (see *Ramban;* see also *Rashi* above, 106b ד״ה ואין נותנין לפניהם מזונות; *Ramban* ad loc.; see also *Beitzah* 24a).

את הדלועין לפני הבהמה ואת הנבלה לפני הכלבים מאי לאו דלועין דומיא דנבלה מה נבלה דרכיכא אף דלועין דרכיכי אלמא טרחינן באוכלא ותיובתא דרב יהודה אמר לך רב יהודה לא נבלה דומיא דדלועין מה דלועין דאשוני אף נבלה דאשונא והיכי משכחת לה בבשר פילי א"נ בגורייאתא זוטרי תא שמע דתני רב חנן מנהרדעא מפרכינן תבן ואספסתא ומערבין אלמא טרחינן באוכלא תבן בתיבנא סריא אספסתא בעילי זוטרי: **מתני'** אין אובסין את הגמל ולא דורסין אבל מלעיטין ואין מאמירין את העגלים אבל מלעיטין ומהלקטין לתרנגולין ונותנין מים למורסן אבל לא גובלין ואין נותנין מים לפני דבורים ולפני יונים שבשובך אבל נותנין לפני אווזין ותרנגולין ולפני יוני הרדיסיות: **גמ'** מאי אין אובסין אמר רב יהודה אין עושין לה אבוס בתוך מעיה אין מי איכא כי האי גוונא אין וכדאמר רב ירמיה מדיפתי לדידי חזי לי ההוא טייעא דאכלא כורא ואטעינא כורא: אין מאמירין: איזו היא המראה ואיזו היא הלעטה אמר רב יהודה המראה למקום שאינה יכולה להחזיר הלעטה למקום שיכולה להחזיר רב חסדא אמר אידי ואידי למקום שאינה יכולה להחזיר והמראה בכלי הלעטה ביד מתיב רב יוסף מהלקטין לתרנגולין ואין צריך לומר שמלקטין ליוני שובך וליוני עלייה ואין צריך לומר שאין מהלקטין מאי מהלקטין ומאי מלקיטין אילימא מהלקטין דספי ליה בידים מלקיטין דשדי ליה (א) קמייהו מכלל דיוני שובך ויוני עלייה מישדא קמייהו נמי לא אלא לאו מהלקטין למקום שאינה יכולה להחזיר מלקיטין למקום שיכולה להחזיר מכלל דהמראה בכלי ותיובתא דרב יהודה אמר לך רב יהודה לעולם מהלקטין דספי ליה בידים מלקיטין דשדי ליה קמייהו ודקא קשיא לך יוני שובך ויוני עלייה למישדא קמייהו נמי לא הני מזונותן עליך והני אין מזונותן עליך כדתניא נותנין מזונות לפני כלב ואין נותנין מזונות לפני חזיר ומה הפרש בין זה לזה זה מזונותיו עליך וזה אין מזונותיו עליך אמר רב אשי מתניתין נמי דיקא אין נותנין מים לפני דבורים ולפני יונים שבשובך אבל נותנין לפני אווזין ולפני תרנגולין ולפני יוני הרדיסיות מ"ט לאו משום דהני מזונותן עליך והני אין מזונותן עליך ולטעמיך מאי איריא מיא אפילו חיטי ושערי נמי לא אלא שאני מיא דשכיחי באגמא דרש רבי יונה אפיתחא דבי נשיאה מאי דכתיב א) יודע צדיק דין דלים יודע הקב"ה בכלב שמזונותיו מועטין לפיכך שוהה אכילתו במעיו ג' ימים כדתנן כמה תשהה אכילתו במעיו ויהא טמא בכלב ג' ימים מעת לעת ובעופות ובדגים כדי שתפול לאור ותשרף אמר רב המנונא שמע מינה אורח ארעא למשדא אומצא לכלבא וכמה אמר רב מרי משח אודניה וחוטרא אבתריה הני מילי בדברא אבל במתא לא דאתא למסרך אמר רב פפא לית דעניא מכלבא ולית דעתיר מחזירא תניא כוותיה דרב יהודה איזו היא המראה ואיזו היא הלעטה המראה מרביצה ופוקס את פיה ומאכילה כרשינין ומים בבת אחת הלעטה מאכילה מעומד ומשקה מעומד ונותנין כרשינין בפני עצמן ומים בפני עצמן: מהלקטין לתרנגולין כו': אמר אביי אמריתה קמיה דמר מתניתין מני ואמר לי ר' יוסי בר יהודה היא דתניא אחד נותן את הקמח ואחד נותן לתוכו מים האחרון חייב דברי רבי ר' יוסי בר יהודה אומר אינו חייב עד שיגבל דילמא עד כאן לא קאמר רבי יוסי בר יהודה התם אלא קמח דבר גיבול הוא אבל מורסן דלאו בר גיבול הוא אפילו רבי יוסי בר יהודה מודה לא סלקא דעתך דתניא בהדיא אין נותנין מים למורסן דברי רבי ר' יוסי בר יהודה אומר נותנין מים למורסן ת"ר אין גובלין את הקלי וי"א גובלין מאן י"א א"ר חסדא רבי

רש"י

את הדלועין. התלושין ולא אמרינן מוקצין הן לבהמה דמאכל אדם הן: אשוני. קשין: א"נ. כלבים דקאמר בגורייתא זוטרי דכל נבלה קשה להן: ומערבין. התבן והאספסתא יחד והבהמה אוכלת התבן בשביל האספסתא: תבן בתיבנא סריא. דלא חזיא והשתא משוי לה אוכלא והאי סריא לאו סריא לגמרי דהויא לטינא קיימא ואסורה לטלטל: מתני' אין אובסין. מאכילין אותו הרבה על כרחו ותוחבין לו בגרונו ובגמרא מפרש לשון אובסין עושין לה כמין אבוס בתוך מעיה: ולא דורסין. שדורס לה בתוך גרונה את השעורין ומיהו לא הוי כל כך כמו אובסין: אבל מלעיטין. מפרש בגמרא: אין מאמירין. מפרש בגמרא: מהלקטין. מפרש בגמרא: אין נותנין מים לפני דבורים. מפרש טעמא בגמרא אי משום דאין מזונותיהן עליו שיוצאין ואוכלין בשדה אי משום דמיא באגמא שכיח להו: הרדיסאות. על שם מקומן וניזונין בתוך הבית: גמ' כי האי גוונא. שיאכילנה כל כך שירחיבו מעיה כאבוס: אטענה כורא. על גבה למזונות לדרך לבד שאר משאות: למקום שאינה יכולה להחזיר. שתוחבו לה לפנים מבית הבליעה: בכלי. בתרווד: דספי בידים. תוחבו לתוך פיו: אלא יוני שובך וכו'. בתמיה ואמאי לא מאי טרחא איכא: אלא לאו כו'. ומדמהלקטין דמתניתין למקום שאינה יכולה להחזיר נמי שרי שמע מינה מלעיטין דעגלים וגמלים למקום שאינה יכולה להחזיר ושרי אלא דגבי בהמה קרי ליה הלעטה וגבי עופות קרי ליה הילקוט ועל כרחך אין מאמירין דקאסר בכלי הוא: לעולם מהלקטין דספי ליה בידים. ולמקום שיכולה להחזיר: אין מזונותן עליך. דשכיחי להו בדברא: חזיר אין מזונותן עליך. דאסור ליהודי שיגדל חזירים: מתני' נמי דיקא. דאפילו שדי קמייהו נמי לא: דשכיחי באגמא. אבל מזונות לא שכיחי להו: שמזונותיו מועטין. שאין אדם חס עליו לתת לו מזונות הרבה: כמה תשהה במעיו. דהכלב שאכל בשר מת ומת הכלב בבית תוך ג' ימים מטמא באהל אבל בחייו לא מטמא דטומאה בלועה בבעלי חיים לא מיטמא כדאמר בבהמה המקשה (חולין דף ע:): שמע מינה. מדקאמר שהקפיד הקדוש ברוך הוא על מזונותיו: משח אודניה. מעט כמות אזנו וחוטרא בתריה יכהו במקל מיד שלא יהא מרגילו אצלו: אבל במתא לא. ליתיב ליה מידי אי לאו דידיה הוא: משום דאתי למסרך. בתריה ויפסידו: לית דעתיר מחזירא. שכל מאכל ראוי לו ומוצא לאכול ואף מאכילין לו הרבה: כוותיה דרב יהודה. שהמראה למקום שאינו יכול להחזיר: פוקס את פיה. נותן חכה לתוך פיה שלא תוכל לסגור פיה: ומאכילה כרשינין ומים בבת אחת. והמים מבליעין הכרשינין לתוך בית בליעתה על כרחה: מאכילה מעומד. נותן לתוך פיה וכל זמן שאינו מרביצה אינו יכול לתחוב כל כך ויכול להחזירה: מתניתין מני. דקתני נותן מים לתוך המורסן דנתינת מים לא זהו גיבולו: אפי' רבי יוסי מודה. דזהו גיבולו: קלי. קמח של תבואה שנתייבשה כשהן קליות בתנור ואותו קמח לעולם מתוק והוא קמחא דאבשונא ועושין ממנו שתיתא משמן ומים ומלח שמערבין בו:

תוספות

אין אובסין את הגמל וכו'. והא דאמרינן בעירובין פרק עושין פסין (דף כ: ושם) גמל שראשו ורובו מבפנים אובסין אותו מבפנים הך אביסה לאו היינו אביסה ממש דהא אמרינן הכא אין אובסין כו' וההיא אביסה היינו הלעטה וכן פירש רבינו שמואל: אלא קמח דבר גיבול הוא. פירשתי לעיל בפ"ק (דף יח. ושם):

עין משפט נר מצוה

כג א מיי' פכ"א מהל' שבת הלכה יח סמג לאוין סה טוש"ע א"ח סימן שכד סעיף ו:
כד ב ג מיי' שם טוש"ע שם סעיף ז:
כה ד ה מיי' שם הלכה לה טוש"ע שם סעי' ט:
כו ו מיי' שם והלכה לו טוש"ע שם סעיף י:
כז ז ח ט מיי' שם טוש"ע שם סעיף יא:
כח י מיי' פ"ב מהלכות טומאת מת הלכה ד:
כט כ מיי' פכ"א מהל' שבת הלכה לה:
ל ל מיי' פכ"א מהלכות שבת הלכה כב טוש"ע א"ח סי' שכד סע' ג:

רבינו חננאל

זה התנא אוסר בצדדין ומתיר בצידי צדדין. ופריק רב פפא אליבא דרבא הכא בכלכלה חדוקה וכו'. ובדרב פפא פשוטין הן ומפקינן בה והלכתא צדדין אסורין צידי צדדין מותרין: דרגא דמדלא סולם העשוי לעלות בו בערסל [שח"ו] והוא (שכתוב) כמלונה במקשה [כערסל]. והוא מלונה לשומרי פירות והדקדק רב אשי מזו הלכה שאסור להניח סולם על הדקל ולעלות בו שנמצא משתמש בצידי האילן ואסור. ופירש שאם יחקוק באילן ויניח באותה חקיקה גואי שהן עצים ויניח באותו העצים הסולם נמצא הסולם נתון בעצים כמין הכלכלה ביתר ושרי וגם אסור להניח רגלי הערלה באותה סולם בעצים הנעוצין באילן מפני שהן צדדין הצדדין אסורין. וכי אין צדדין אסור מותר לו להשתמש ולעלות אלא בקנים שהן מעלות הסולם והן שליביהו שהן ודאי צדדי צדדין: [מתני'] מתירין פקיעי עמיר כו'. פי' פקיעי אגודות כדתנן פקעת גמי בא רב הונא לפרש משנתנו ואמר אינו בתוכו לפקיעין שניהם אגודות קשורות הן. אלא הפקיעין ב' אגודות כפקיע והכפין ג' אגודות בכף זירין דארזי כשמתגואזין ומתקשין נקראין דארזי הן זהו אחד ואינן נאגדין באגודה. ואם אגדן בזוקין עומדין ותרצה רב הונא למתניתין הכי מתירין פקיעי עמיר לפני הבהמה ומפספסין פי' מפספסין מפרכין כעין פיתות [לרכבן ליותנ] [לרככן] לאכלה ומצינו בתלמוד א"י שאמרו בענין (תנוק פתילה) מפספסין ופי' מחרכין כדכתיב שער ראשיהון לא התחרך ותנאין הדברים שהחריכה מרכבת כעין הפתיחה דהוא מעין פסיסה. כדאמרינן בידות האוכלין שכססן לגורן וכשם שמתירין ומפספסין הפקיעין הוא הדין לכפין אבל הזירין לא יפספס ולא להתיר אם נקשרו ובא רב חסדא ופי' טעמא דרב הונא ואמר שהעמידו למשנתנו שמתירין ומפספסין הפקיעין והכפין שהן מקודם אוכל ויכולין להיאכל כמות שהן וכן ההתרה והפספוס לא להוסיף להם אלא הכשר לאכילה בלבד דייקינן מדבריו הללו דקסבר מותר למיטרח באוכל ומוסיף לו הכשר אבל אם אין יכול להיאכל כגון הזירין שהן דארזי אלא אחרי התר ופספוס אסור וזהו לשויי אוכלי לא משוינן ורב יהודה חלק על רב הונא לדברי רבה דאוקמינהו לדברי רב יהודה שוויה אוכלא לא משוינן ואמר רבה מדתרצה למתניתין שהפקיעין [והזירין שניהן אגודות מפספס למה הן מיהו הפקיעין שתים באגודה והעמירין ג' מותר להתיר הפקיעין שקשרן מתירן] ואם לא יתירם אינן נאכלין בטוב ושלש אין קשרן אמיץ ונאכלין וכיון שיכולים להיאכל קסבר אטרוחי באכילה טרחינן ואם יש לומר מניין לנו ראיה שיש הפרש בין ב' לג' שאלו קישרם אמיץ יתר מאלו מצאנו לדבריהן שאומרים נימה אחת קשורה חוצצת ג' אין חוצצת ב' איני ידע פי' ג' אינן חוצצת שאין קשרן מתחזק ומרפרף הוא והמים באים בתוכו לפיכך אינן חוצצין אבל הכפים שהן דידי והן קשין כמו שאמרנו למעלה מפספסין כדי לשוותם אוכל וכ"ש שמתירין ובאנו להקשות לרב הונא מסיפא דהא מתניתין דקתני אין מרסקין לא את השחת ולא את החרובין ופשוטה היא. ופריק רב הונא לא שהחרובין רכין הן כמות שהן (שהדות) [שהדתאה] שהן רכין ויכולין להיאכל אין מרסקין אותן אלמא לא מטרחינן באוכלא אלא שחת דומיא דחרובין מה חרובין דאשיני פירוש יבישין וקשין ואין יכולין להיאכל אף שחת כמותן שנתייבש ונתקשה ואינו אוכל והריסוק משוויהו אוכל ומתניתין כותי דאמרי שוויי אוכלא לא משוינן ואזו היא בהמה שאינה יכולה לאכול השחת אלא אחרי ריסוק ואמרנו בעילי זוטרי פי' עיירים קטנים. ותוב אקשינן על רב הונא מדרב יהודה נשמע לרבנן לאו ר' יהודה מתיר בחרובין לדקה. לדקה [אין] לגסה לא מכלל דרבנן סברי כיון שיכולין להיאכל כמות שהן לא טרחינן לדחוקינהו להו דמטרח באוכלא לא טרחינן. וא"ל רב יהודה לת"ק התינח לגסה שיכולה לאכול כמות שהיא בלא ריסוק אלא לדקה שאינה יכולה לאוכלה כמות שהיא בלא ריסוק שוויי אוכלא הוא ושרי דאם נאמר כי ת"ק סבר מטרח טרחינן שוויי אוכלא לא משוינן וריסוק זה שוויי אוכלא לדקה ולגסה הוא ואסור וא"ל ר' יהודה לדקה אוכלא הוא ומיטרח באוכל שרי ואם הוא אוכל לדקה כ"ש לגסה ולא היה צריך לומר אלא ר' יהודה מתיר סתם בין לדקה בין לגסה. ועלתה בקשיא לרב הונא וחזרנו להקשות על רב יהודה דתנן מחתכין את הדלועין לפני הבהמה ואת הנבלה לפני הכלבים ופריק ליה ופשוטה היא וכן הא דתני רב חנן מנהרדעא מפריכין תבן ואספסתא ומערבין אלמא טרחינן באוכלא ופריק גם זו ואע"ג דרוב סוגיא דשמעתא כרב הונא ריחשא הא איתותב ולא אשכח לה פירוקא ועלתה בה קושיא ותוב רב יהודה ורבה רישי מתיבתא הוו דאמרינן האי שיפורא מעיקרא בי רב יהודה ולבסוף בי רבה והלכתא כוותיה ומשוינן אוכלא ולא קא טרחינן באוכלא מכלל דרב הונא לא הוה ריש מתיבתא והא אמרינן כי הוו מפטרי רבנן מבי רב הונא הוו פיישי כו' ואמרינן ואמרי במערבא קמא לה מתיבתא דהונא בבלאה: [מתני'] **אין אובסין** את הגמל כו'. פי' אובסין מפטמין כדכתיב וברבורים אבוסים והוא מאכילין את הגמל הרבה כרב ירמיה דאמר אנא חזיתיה לההוא טייעא דאכלא כו' כורא ואטענה כורא וכן הלכה דאסור לפטם בהמה בשבת ולא אפילו עופות. אין ממרים את העגלים אבל מלעיטין איזו היא המראה ואיזו הלעטה. אמר רב יהודה המראה למקום שאינה יכולה להחזיר. פי' המראה שמוריד בידו המאכל בבלועו של עגלים במקום שאינו יכול להחזירו מתוך בלעו אבל חשוב הוא כבלוע כגון זה אסור להמרות. אבל להלעוטי כדכתיב הלעיטני וגו' לתת המאכל בחך שלו מותר וזה וזה ביד. ורב חסדא אמר אידי ואידי למקום שאין יכול להחזיר והמראה בכלי והלעטה ביד ואותביה רב יוסף לרב יהודה מהלקטין לתרנגולין ואין

מסורת הש"ס

א) [נ"א מפרכין וכן הערוך גורס] לעיל קנ: וכן בתוס' ב"ב יע: ד"ה בתיבנא], ב) [עי' תוס' ב"מ פ: ד"ה פסס], ג) [תוספתא פרק יח], ד) [בקהלת כתיב יודע צדיק דין דלים], ה) אהלות פ"א מ"ג, ו) [תוספ' פי"ח], ז) לעיל יח. ח) [עי' תוס' ב"ב צ: ד"ה מלן], ט) [סוטה מט:], י) [פסחים לט:], כ) בד"ה אבל.

הגהות הב"ח

(א) גמ' דשדי ליה קמיה אלא דיוני שובך:

גליון הש"ס

גמרא מאי לאו דלועין. כעין זה בב"מ דף קט ע"ב. ועיין שיטה מקובצת שם ד"ה הכי.

תורה אור השלם

א) יֹדֵעַ צַדִּיק דִּין דַּלִּים רָשָׁע לֹא יָבִין דָּעַת: [משלי כט, ז]

ליקוטי רש"י

את הדלועין. תלושין לפני הבהמה ולא אמרינן טרחא דלאו צורך הוא [ביצה כ:]. התלושין ומיהו שמתן לאו מאכל בהמה קיימי אלא לאדם [לקמן קנו:]. ואת הנבלה לפני הכלבים. ולא"ש שנתנבלה בשבת דבין השמשות לא היתה עומדת לאכילת כלבים ואפ"ה שרי דלית לן מוקצה בשבת [ביצה שם]. וכשנתנבלה בשבת קאמר מדפליג רבי יהודה בין נבלה מאתמול אם לא היתה נבלה מערב שבת אסורה לפי שאינה מן המוכן [שם כז:]. שנתנבלה היום וכן בהמות היתה עומדת לאדם ואפילו הכי מחתכין [לקמן שם]. אין אובסין. מפטמין לה שמאכילה על כרחה בבית הבליעה יותר מכדי אכילתה עד שנעשה בית בליעתה כאבוס [עירובין כ:]. יוני הרדיסיות. על שם מקומם [ביצה שם]. ליוני שובך וליוני עלייה. [illegible] [ב"מ קב.]. דין דלים. [illegible] [משלי כט, ז]. האחרון חייב. [illegible] [לעיל יח.]. קלי. אבשונא [illegible] מתוק לעולם [מגילה ז:].

AND THAT ONE? זֶה מְזוֹנוֹתָיו עָלֶיךָ – THIS ONE (the dog) DEPENDS UPON YOU FOR ITS FOOD, וְזֶה אֵין מְזוֹנוֹתָיו עָלֶיךָ – WHEREAS THAT ONE (the pig) DOES NOT DEPEND UPON YOU FOR ITS FOOD.[28]

It emerges from Rav Yehudah's interpretation of the above Baraisa that one may not place food in front of dovecote doves and attic doves, since they can forage for food on their own. The Gemara brings support for this conclusion from our Mishnah:

אָמַר רַב אַשִׁי – **Rav Ashi said:** מַתְנִיתִין נַמִּי דַּיְקָא – **Our Mishnah indicates this as well,** for we learned: אֵין נוֹתְנִין מַיִם לִפְנֵי דְבוֹרִים וְלִפְנֵי יוֹנִים שֶׁבַּשּׁוֹבָךְ – ONE MAY NOT PLACE WATER BEFORE BEES OR BEFORE DOVES IN A DOVECOTE, אֲבָל נוֹתְנִין לִפְנֵי אַוָּזִין וְלִפְנֵי תַרְנְגוֹלִין וְלִפְנֵי יוֹנֵי הַרְדְּסִיּוֹת – BUT ONE MAY PLACE WATER BEFORE GEESE, CHICKENS AND HERODIAN DOVES. מַאי טַעְמָא – **What is the reason** to differentiate? לָאו מִשּׁוּם דְּהָנֵי מְזוֹנוֹתָן עָלֶיךָ וְהָנֵי אֵין מְזוֹנוֹתָן עָלֶיךָ – **Is it not because these,** viz. the geese, chickens and Herodian doves, **depend upon you for their food whereas those,** viz. bees and dovecote doves, **do not depend upon you for their food?**

The Gemara counters:

וְלִיטַעְמִיךְ – **And according to your reasoning,** מַאי אִירְיָא מַיָּא – **for what reason** does our Mishnah refer only to **water?** If your view is correct, אֲפִילּוּ חִיטֵּי וְשַׂעֲרֵי נַמִּי לֹא – **even wheat and barley** should **not** be given to dovecote doves, since they can forage on their own! אֶלָּא שָׁאנֵי מַיָּא דִּשְׁכִיחֵי בְּאַגְמָא – **Rather,** it is possible that our Mishnah does not subscribe to this view and **water is different,** i.e. only water is forbidden to be given to bees and dovecote doves, **since [water]** is readily **available in a pond.**[29]

The Gemara digresses:

דָּרַשׁ רַבִּי יוֹנָה אַפִּיתְחָא דְּבֵי נְשִׂיאָה – **R' Yonah expounded at the entrance to the Exilarch's palace:** מַאי דִּכְתִיב – **What is** the meaning of **that which is written:**[30] "יֹדֵעַ צַדִּיק דִּין דַּלִּים" – ***The Righteous One knows the suffering of the poor?*** יוֹדֵעַ הַקָּדוֹשׁ בָּרוּךְ הוּא בְּכֶלֶב שֶׁמְּזוֹנוֹתָיו מוּעָטִין – **The Holy One, Blessed is He, knows that a dog's food is** typically **meager;**[31] לְפִיכָךְ שׁוֹהֶה אֲכִילָתוֹ בְּמֵעָיו שְׁלֹשָׁה יָמִים – **He therefore** decreed that **[a dog's] food should linger in its belly for three days,** כִּדְתְנַן – **as we learned in a Mishnah:**[32] כַּמָּה תִּשְׁהֶה אֲכִילָתוֹ בְּמֵעָיו וִיהֵא טָמֵא – HOW LONG MAY [A LIVING CREATURE'S] FOOD LINGER in its stomach AND still BE CONSIDERED *TAMEI?* בְּכֶלֶב – REGARDING A DOG the time limit is שְׁלֹשָׁה יָמִים מֵעֵת לְעֵת – THREE TWENTY-FOUR-HOUR PERIODS. וּבְעוֹפוֹת וּבְדָגִים – REGARDING BIRDS OR FISH the time limit is כְּדֵי שֶׁתִּפּוֹל לָאוּר וְתִשָּׂרֵף – AS LONG AS IT WOULD TAKE [THE FOOD] TO FALL INTO A FIRE AND BECOME CONSUMED.[33]

A related teaching:

אָמַר רַב הַמְנוּנָא – **Rav Hamnuna said:** שְׁמַע מִינָּהּ – **Learn from this** that we have said, that the Holy One was particular regarding a dog's meals, אוֹרַח אַרְעָא לְמִשְׁדָּא אוּמְצָא לְכַלְבָּא – that **it is proper to throw** a chunk of **meat to a** stray **dog.**[34]

The Gemara asks:

וְכַמָּה – **And how much?** How large should the chunk be?

The Gemara answers:

אָמַר רַב מָרִי – **Rav Mari said:** מְשַׁח אוּדְנֵיהּ וְחוּטְרָא אַבַּתְרֵיהּ – Throw it a chunk **the size of its ear, followed immediately by** the rap of **a stick.**[35]

The Gemara qualifies this:

הָנֵי מִילֵּי בְּדַבְרָא – But **this is so only in the desert,** i.e. an unpopulated area; אֲבָל בְּמָתָא לֹא – **however, in the city** one should **not** throw it any meat,[36] דְּאָתָא לְמִסְרַךְ – **because it will tend to tag along after him.**[37]

A final teaching on this subject:

אָמַר רַב פָּפָּא – **Rav Pappa said:** לֵית דְּעַנְיָא מִכַּלְבָּא – **There is no** creature **poorer than a dog** וְלֵית דַּעֲתִיר מֵחֲזִירָא – **and no** creature **wealthier than a pig.**[38]

The Gemara returns to the Amoraic dispute concerning our Mishnah:

תַּנְיָא כְּוָותֵיהּ דְּרַב יְהוּדָה – **A Baraisa has been taught in accordance with** the view of **Rav Yehudah:**[39] אֵיזוֹ הִיא הַמְרָאָה וְאֵיזוֹ הִיא הַלְעָטָה – WHICH actions ARE termed *FATTENING* AND WHICH ARE termed *PUTTING FOOD DOWN THEIR THROATS?* הַמְרָאָה מַרְבִּיצָהּ וּפוֹקֵס אֶת פִּיהָ – *FATTENING* denotes that ONE BRINGS [THE ANIMAL] TO ITS KNEES, PROPS OPEN ITS MOUTH so that the animal cannot close it, וּמַאֲכִילָהּ כַּרְשִׁינִין וּמַיִם בְּבַת אַחַת – AND FEEDS IT VETCH[40] AND WATER AT THE SAME TIME.[41]

NOTES

28. The Sages pronounced a curse upon any Jew who raises a pig (*Rashi;* see *Sotah* 49b for the background of this pronouncement). [Since one is forbidden to raise pigs, the feeding of a pig can never be considered a Jew's responsibility (see *Ramban;* see also *Mishnah Berurah* 234:30).]

A dog, on the other hand, may be raised if it is kept chained (*Bava Kamma* 79b) or, perhaps, even unchained if it is not a vicious dog (*Rama, Choshen Mishpat* 409:3; see also *Maharsha, Chidushei Aggados* here).

29. But food is not [similarly] available to them (*Rashi*).

Although the Gemara has rejected the proof from our Mishnah, the halachah nonetheless follows Rav Yehudah that a person may not give food on the Sabbath to dovecote doves and attic doves nor to any animal that can forage for itself (*Shulchan Aruch, Orach Chaim* 324:11; see *Beis Yosef,* ad loc.; *Shiltei HaGiborim* here, §2).

[For this reason many authorities object to the popular custom of putting out wheat or bread crumbs for the birds on *Shabbos Shirah,* the Sabbath on which the Torah portion dealing with the splitting of the Red Sea is read. See *Ramban, Magen Avraham* and *Mishnah Berurah* to *Orach Chaim* 324:11.]

30. *Proverbs* 29:7.

31. No one pities it enough to provide it with ample meals (*Rashi*).

32. *Oholos* 11:7. [The Mishnah discusses the digestive cycle of a dog in connection with the law of corpse contamination. If an animal consumes flesh from a human corpse, the flesh no longer transmits *tumah* since it is swallowed up within a living creature (see *Chullin* 71b). If the animal subsequently dies, the flesh resumes its properties of contamination (e.g. it transmits *tumah* to people or vessels under the same roof). If, however, the flesh is already digested by the time the animal dies, it can no longer contaminate (*Rashi*).]

33. [Thus, we see that a dog's digestive cycle is significantly longer than that of other creatures.]

34. [See *Maharsha.*]

[*Magen Avraham* (324:7) deduces from this Gemara that the feeding of even a stray dog is considered one's responsibility and one may do so even on the Sabbath. See also *Machatzis HaShekel* ad loc.; cf. *Levush;* see *Aruch HaShulchan* 324:2.]

35. The chunk should be a small one, as large as its ear, and one should immediately drive it away with a stick so that it should not begin to tag after its benefactor (*Rashi*).

36. Unless he is the dog's owner (*Rashi*).

37. And be a financial drain on him (*Rashi*).

38. Any kind of food is suitable for a pig, so it comes by its meals easily. Furthermore, people are accustomed to feed it abundantly (*Rashi*).

See *Ben Yehoyada* for several allegoric interpretations of this passage.

39. I.e. that *fattening* (which the Mishnah forbids) refers to force-feeding the animal [by hand] so far down its throat that it cannot spit the food back up, [while *putting food down its throat* (which the Mishnah permits) refers to placing the food in an area where the animal can still bring the food back up] (*Rashi*).

40. A type of bean that is customarily soaked in water and then used for fodder (see *Rashi* and *Rav* to the Mishnah on 17b above).

41. In this way, the food is forcibly washed down the animal's throat so that it cannot spit it out (*Rashi*).

עין משפט
נר מצוה

כג א מיי' פכ"א מהל' שבת הלכה יח סמג לאוין סה טוש"ע א"ח סימן שכד סעיף ו:
כד ב ג מיי' שם טוש"ע שם סעיף ז:
כה ד ה מיי' שם הלכה לה טוש"ע שם סע"ט:
כו ו מיי' שם והלכה לו טוש"ע שם סעיף י:
כז ז ח ט מיי' שם טוש"ע שם סעיף יא:
כח י מיי' פ"כ מהלכות טומאת מת הלכה ד:
כט כ מיי' פכ"א מהל' שבת הלכה לה:
ל ל מיי' פכ"א מהלכות שבת הלכה לד טוש"ע א"ח סי' שכד סע"ג:

רבינו חננאל

זה התנא אוסר בצדדין ומתיר בצידי צדדין. ופריק רב פפא אליבא דרבא הכא בכלכלה דחוקה וכו'. ודברי רב פפא פשוטין הן ומפקינן בה והלכתא צדדין אסורין צדדי צדדין מותרין: **דרגא** דמדלא סולם העשוי לעלות בו בערסל והוא (שכתוב) [שת"י] כמלונה במקשה [כערסל]. והוא מלונה לשומרי פירות ודקדק רב אשי מזו ההלכה שאסור להניח סולם על הדקל ולעלות בו שנמצא משתמש בצידי האילן ואסור. ופירוש שאם יחקוק באילן ויניח באותה חקיקה גואזי שהן עצים ויניח באותו העצים הסולם נמצא הסולם נתון בעצים כמין הכלכלה ביתד ושרי וגם אסור להניח רגלי העולה באותה סולם בעצים הנעוצין באילן מפני שהן צדדין והצדדין אסורין. וכי אינו מותר לו להשתמש ולעלות אלא בקנים שהן מעלות הסולם והן שליבותיו שהן ודאי צדדי צדדין: [מתני'] **מתירין** פקיעי עמיר כו'. פי' פקיעי אגודות כדתנן פקעת גמי בא רב הונא לפרש משנתנו ואמר הפקיעין והכיפין שניהם אגודות קשורות הן. אלא הפקיעין ב' אגודות כפקיע והכפין ג' אגודות בכף זירין דארזי כשמתגזאין ומתקשין נקראין דארזי והן אחד אחד ואינן נאגדין באגודה. ואם אגדן בחזקתן עומדין ותרצה רב הונא למתניתין הכי מתירין פקיעי עמיר לפני בהמה ומפספסין פי' מפספסין מפרכין כעין פיתות (לרכנן לייתות) [לרככן] לאכלה ומצינו בתלמוד א"י שאמרו בענין (תינוק פתילה) מפספסין ופי' מחרכין כדכתיב ושער ראשיהון לא התחרך ונראין הדברים שהחריכה מרככת כעין הפתיתה דהוא מעין פסיסה. כדאמרינן בידות האוכלין שכססן לגורן וכשם שמתירין ומפספסין הפקיעין הוא הדין לכפין אבל הזירין לא יפספס ולא להתיר אם נקשרו ובא רב חסדא ופי' טעמא דרב הונא ואמר שהעמידו למשנתנו שמתירין

אין אובסין את הגמל וכו'. והא דאמרינן בעירובין פרק עושין פסין (דף כ: ושם) גמל שראשו ורובו מבפנים אובסין אותו מבפנים הך אביסה לאו היינו אביסה ממש דהא אמרינן הכא אין אובסין כו' וההיא אביסה היינו הלעטה וכן פירש רבינו שמואל: **אלא** קמח דבר גיבול הוא. פירשתי לעיל בפ"ק (דף יח. ושם ל): מהו

את הדלועין. המלושין ולא אמרינן מוקצין הן לבהמה דמאכל אדם הן: אשוני. קשין: א"נ. כלבים דקאמר בגורייתא זוטרי דכל נבלה קשה להן: ומערבין. התבן והאספסתא יחד והבהמה אוכלת התבן בשביל האספסתא: תבן בתיבנא סריא. דלא חזיא והשתא משוי לה אוכלא והאי סריא לאו סריא לגמרי דההיא לטינא קיימא ואסורה לטלטל: **מתני' אין אובסין.** מאכילין אותו הרבה על כרחו ותוחבין לו בגרונו ובגמרא מפרש לשון אובסין עושין לה כמין אבוס בתוך מעיה: **ולא דורסין.** שדורס לה בתוך גרונה את השעורין ומיהו לא הוי כל כך כמו אובסין: **אבל מלעיטין.** מפרש בגמרא: **אין מאמירין.** מפרש בגמרא: **מהלקטין.** מפרש בגמרא: **אין נותנין מים לפני דבורים.** מפרש טעמא בגמרא אי משום דלאו מזונותיהן עליו שיוצאין ואוכלין בשדה אי משום דמיא באגמא שכיח להו: **הרדיסאות.** על שם מקומן וניזונין בתוך הבית: **גמ' כי האי גוונא.** שימלאנה כל כך שירכינו מעיה כאבוס: **אטענה כורא.** על גבה למזונות לדרך לבד שאר משאות: **למקום שאינה יכולה להחזיר.** שתוחבו לה לפנים מבית הבליעה: **בכלי.** במרוד: **דספי בידים.** תוחבו לתוך פיו: **אלא יוני שובך וכו'.** בתמיה ומאי לא מאי טרחא איכא: **אלא לאו כו'.** ומדמהלקטין דמתניתין למקום שאינה יכולה להחזיר נמי שרי שמע מינה מלעיטין דעגלים ומלגים למקום שאינה יכולה להחזיר ושרי אלא דגבי בהמה קרי ליה הלעטה וגבי עופות קרי ליה הילקוט ועל כרחך אין מאמירין דקאמר בכלי הוא: **לעולם מהלקטין דספי ליה בידים.** ולמקום שיכולה להחזיר: **אין מזונותן עליך.** דשכיחי להו בדברא: **חזיר אין מזונותן עליך.** דאמור יהודי לגדל חזירים: **מתני' נמי דיקא.** דאפילו שדי קמייהו נמי לא: **דשכיחי באגמא.** אבל מזונות לא שכיחי להו: **שמזונותיו מועטין.** שאין אדם חס עליו לתת לו מזונות הרבה: **כמה תשהה במעיו.** הכלב שאכל בשר מת ומת הכלב בבית תוך ג' ימים מטמא באהל אבל בחיים לא מטמא דטומאה בלועה בבעלי חיים לא מיטמא כדאמר בבהמה המקשה (חולין דף עא:): **שמע מינה.** מדקאמר שהקפיד הקדוש ברוך הוא על מזונותיו: **משח אודניה.** מעט כמות אחנו וחוטרא בתריה יכהו במקל מיד שלא יהא מרגילו אצלו: **אבל במתא לא.** ליתיב ליה מידי אי לאו דידיה הוא: **משום דאתי למסרך.** בתריה ויפסדו: **לית דעתיר מחזירא.** שכל מאכל ראוי לו ומוצא לאכול ואף מאכילין לו הרבה: **כוותיה דרב יהודה.** שהמראה למקום שאינו יכול להחזיר: **פוקס את פיה.** נותן מכה לתוך פיה שלא תוכל לסגור פיה: **ומאכילה כרשינין ומים בבת אחת.** והמים מבליעין הכרשינין לתוך בית בליעתה על כרחה: **מאכילה מעומד.** נותן לתוך פיה וכל זמן שאינו מרביצה אינו יכול לחזור כל כך ויכול להחזירה: **מתניתין מני.** דקתני נותן מים לתוך המורסן דנתינת מים לא זהו גיבולו: **אפי' רבי יוסי מודה.** דזהו גיבולו: **קלי.** קמח של תבואה שנתייבשה כשהן קליות בתנור ואותו קמח לעולם מתוק והוא קמחא דלאבשונא ועושין ממנו שתיתא משמן ומים ומלח שמערבין בו:

את הדלועין לפני הבהמה ואת הנבלה לפני הכלבים מאי לאו דלועין דומיא דנבלה מה נבלה דרכיכא אף דלועין דרכיכי אלמא טרחינן באוכלא ותיובתא דרב יהודה אמר לך רב יהודה לא נבלה דומיא דדלועין מה דלועין דאשוני אף נבלה דאשונא והיכי משכחת לה בבשר פילי א"נ בגורייאתא זוטרי תא שמע דתני רב חנן מנהרדעא מפרכינן תבן ואספסתא ומערבין אלמא טרחינן באוכלא תבן בתיבנא סריא אספסתא בעילי זוטרי: **מתני'** אין אובסין את הגמל ולא דורסין אבל מלעיטין ואין מאמירין את העגלים אבל מלעיטין ומהלקטין לתרנגולין ונותנין מים למורסן אבל לא גובלין ואין נותנין מים לפני דבורים ולפני יונים שבשובך אבל נותנין לפני אווזין ותרנגולין ולפני יוני הרדיסיות: **גמ'** מאי אין אובסין אמר רב יהודה אין עושין לה אבוס בתוך מעיה מי איכא כי האי גוונא אין וכדאמר רב ירמיה מדיפתי לדידי חזי לי ההוא טייעא דאכלא כורא ואטעינא כורא: אין מאמירין: איזו היא המראה ואיזו היא הלעטה אמר רב יהודה המראה למקום שאינה יכולה להחזיר הלעטה למקום שיכולה להחזיר רב חסדא אמר אידי ואידי למקום שאינה יכולה להחזיר והמראה בכלי הלעטה ביד מתיב רב יוסף מהלקטין לתרנגולין ואין צריך לומר שמלקטין ואין מלקיטין ליוני שובך וליוני עלייה ואין צריך לומר שאין מהלקטין מאי מהלקטין ומאי מלקיטין אילימא מהלקטין דספי ליה בידים מלקיטין דשדי ליה (א) קמייהו מכלל דיוני שובך ויוני עלייה מישדא קמייהו נמי לא אלא לאו מהלקטין למקום שאינה יכולה להחזיר מלקיטין למקום שיכולה להחזיר מכלל דהמראה בכלי ותיובתא דרב יהודה אמר לך רב יהודה לעולם מהלקטין דספי ליה בידים מלקיטין דשדי ליה קמייהו ודקא קשיא לך יוני שובך ויוני עלייה למישדא קמייהו נמי לא הני מזונותן עליך והני אין מזונותן עליך כדתניא נותנין מזונות לפני כלב ואין נותנין מזונות לפני חזיר ומה הפרש בין זה לזה זה מזונותיו עליך וזה אין מזונותיו עליך אמר רב אשי מתניתין נמי דיקא אין נותנין מים לפני דבורים ולפני יונים שבשובך אבל נותנין לפני אווזין ולפני תרנגולין ולפני יוני הרדיסיות מ"ט לאו משום דהני מזונותן עליך והני אין מזונותן עליך וליטעמיך מאי איריא מיא אפילו חיטי ושערי נמי לא אלא שאני מיא דשכיחי באגמא דרש רבי יונה אפיתחא דבי נשיאה מאי דכתיב א (יודע) צדיק דין דלים יודע הקב"ה בכלב שמזונותיו מועטין לפיכך שוהה אכילתו במעיו ג' ימים כדתנן כמה תשהה אכילתו במעיו ויהא טמא בכלב ג' ימים מעת לעת ובעופות ובדגים כדי שתפול לאור ותשרף אמר רב המנונא שמע מינה אורח ארעא למשדא אומצא לכלבא וכמה אמר רב מרי משח אודניה וחוטרא אבתריה הני מילי בדברא אבל במתא לא דאתא למסרך אמר רב פפא לית דעניא מכלבא ולית דעתיר מחזירא תניא כוותיה דרב יהודה איזו היא המראה ואיזו היא הלעטה המראה מרביצה ופוקס את פיה ומאכילה כרשינין ומים בבת אחת הלעטה מאכילה מעומד ומשקה מעומד ונותנין כרשינין בפני עצמן ומים בפני עצמן: מהלקטין לתרנגולין כו': אמר אביי אמריתה קמיה דמר מתניתין מני ואמר לי ר' יוסי בר יהודה היא דתניא אחד נותן את הקמח ואחד נותן לתוכו מים האחרון חייב דברי רבי ר' יוסי בר יהודה אומר אינו חייב עד שיגבל דילמא עד כאן לא קאמר רבי יוסי בר יהודה התם אלא קמח דבר גיבול הוא אבל מורסן דלאו בר גיבול הוא אפילו רבי יוסי בר יהודה מודה לא סלקא דעתך דתניא בהדיא אין נותנין מים למורסן דברי רבי ר' יוסי בר יהודה אומר נותנין מים למורסן ת"ר אין גובלין את הקלי וי"א גובלין מאן י"א א"ר חסדא רבי

ומפספסין הפקיעין והכפין שהן מקודם אוכל יכולין להיאכל כמות שהן וכן ההתרה והפספוס לא להוסיף להם אלא הכשר לאכילה בלבד דייקינן מדבריו הללו דקסבר מותר למיטרח באוכל ומוסיף לו הכשר אבל אם אין יכול להיאכל כגון הזירין שהן דארזי אלא אחרי התר ופספוס אסור וזהו לשווי אוכלי לא משוינן ורב יהודה חלק על רב הונא [illegible] [והזירין שניהן אגודות מפספס למה הן מיהו הפקיעין שתים באגודה [illegible]] [illegible] טרחינן [illegible] ופשוטה היא. ופריק רב הונא [illegible] קטנים. ותוב אקשינן על רב הונא [illegible] רב יהודה לת"ק [illegible] אוכלא לדקה ולגסה הוא ואסור [illegible] רב יהודה דתנן מחתכין את הדלועין [illegible] כרב הונא ריחשא הא איתותב [illegible] באוכלא מכלל דרב הונא לא [illegible] כדכתיב וברבורים אבוסים והוא [illegible] מלעיטין איזו היא המראה ואיזו [illegible] להמרות. אבל להלעוטי כדכתיב [illegible] ואין

מסורת הש"ס

א) [נ"ל מפרכין וכן העתיקו תוס' לעיל קנ: וכן בתוס' ב"ב יט: ד"ה במיבנא], ב) [עי' תוס' ב"מ פ: ד"ה ססם], ג) [תוספתא פרק יח], ד) [בקרא כתיב ידע חסר וי"ו], ה) אהלות פי"א מ"ז, ו) [תוספת' פי"ח], ז) לעיל יח., ח) [לעיל יח. אית' רבי יוסי], ט) [עי' מ"ש תוס' ב"ב לג: ד"ה מאן], י) [סוטה מט:], כ) [פסחים לט:], ל) בד"ה אבל.

הגהות הב"ח

(א) גמ' דשדי ליה קמיה אלא דיוני שובך:

גליון הש"ס

גמרא מאי לאו דלועין. כעין זה בב"מ דף קט ע"ב. ועיין שיטה מקובצת שם ד"ה ה"ג:

תורה אור השלם

א) יֹדֵעַ צַדִּיק דִּין דַּלִּים רָשָׁע לֹא יָבִין דָּעַת: [משלי כט, ז]

ליקוטי רש"י

את הדלועין. מלושין לפני הבהמה ולא אמרינן טרחא דלאו צורך הוא [ביצה ב.]. המלושין ומיהו סתמן לאו למאכל בהמה קיימי אלא לאדם [לקמן קנו:]. **ואת הנבלה לפני הכלבים.** ואע"פ שנתנבלה בשבת דבין השמשות לא היתה עומדת לאכילת כלבים אפילו הכי שרי דלית לן מוקצה בשבת [ביצה שם]. וכשנתנבלה בשבת קאמר מדפליג רבי יהודה עלה ואמר אם לא היתה נבלה מערב שבת אסורה לפי שאינה מן המוכן [שם כז:]. שנתנבלה היום ובין השמשות היתה עומדת לאדם ואפילו הכי מחתכין [לקמן שם]. **אין אובסין.** שמוסך לה מספוא הרבה על כרחה בבית הבליעה יותר מכדי אכילתה עד שנעשה כאיבוס במעיה כשיוציא למדבר וממיירא שלא תמצא מאכל [עירובין כ:]. **מורסן.** היא הקליפה העליונה שמוציאין מחטין הכתושין במכתשת [רשב"ם ב"ב צג:]. קליפה היוצאת כשכותשים במכתשת [חולין פח:]. **יוני הרדיסיות.** שדרכם ליגדל עם בני אדם [שם קלח:]. הרדיסאות על שם מקומם ויש אומרים על שם הורדוס והן הגדלים בבתים [ביצה כד.]. **טייעא.** ישמעאל [לעיל פב.]. סוחר ישמעאלים [מו"ק כה:]. ערבי [ב"ק נה.]. סוחר ערבי [ברכות ו:]. **יוני שובך.** שמבקשים מזונותיהן בשדה וקניהן בשובך ואין אלו יוני הרדסיאות הגדילים בבתים [ב"מ קב.]. **ליוני שובך וליוני עליה.** יוני הבר הן ושטין ואוכלין בחוץ [ביצה שם]. **דין דלים.** יסורי דלים ומה הם לריקים ונותן להם לב [משלי כט, ז]. **האחרון חייב.** משום לש שהוא אב מלאכה [לעיל יח.]. **קלי.** אבשונה, שנתייבשו החטים בתנור בעודן כרמל וקמח שלהן מתוק לעולם [מגילה ז:].

הַלְעָטָה מַאֲכִילָהּ מְעוּמָּד וּמַשְׁקָהּ מְעוּמָּד – *PUTTING FOOD DOWN ITS THROAT* denotes that ONE FEEDS IT STANDING AND WATERS IT STANDING, without forcing its mouth open, וְנוֹתְנִין כַּרְשִׁינִין בִּפְנֵי עַצְמָן וּמַיִם בִּפְנֵי עַצְמָן – AND GIVES IT VETCH SEPARATELY AND WATER SEPARATELY.[42]

The Gemara cites the Mishnah:

מְהַלְקְטִין לַתַּרְנְגוֹלִין כו׳ – ONE MAY PUT FOOD DOWN THE THROATS OF CHICKENS etc., and one may put water into their bran, but one may not knead the bran and water together.

The Gemara comments:

אָמַר אַבַּיֵי – **Abaye said:** אֲמַרִיתָהּ קַמֵּיהּ דְּמַר – **I said [the following] before the master:**[43] מַתְנִיתִין מַנִּי – **Who is the Tanna of our Mishnah,** who apparently maintains that pouring water into bran is not a violation of the *melachah* of "kneading"? Which Tanna holds this view? וְאָמַר לִי – **And he said to me:** רַבִּי יוֹסֵי בַּר יְהוּדָה הִיא – **It is R' Yose bar Yehudah,** דְּתַנְיָא – **as it was taught in a Baraisa:** אֶחָד נוֹתֵן אֶת הַקֶּמַח – IF ONE person CONTRIBUTES THE FLOUR וְאֶחָד נוֹתֵן לְתוֹכוֹ מַיִם – AND ANOTHER person CONTRIBUTES THE WATER, הָאַחֲרוֹן חַיָּיב – THE LAST ONE IS LIABLE for violating the *melachah* of "kneading."[44] דִּבְרֵי רַבִּי – THESE ARE THE WORDS OF REBBI. רַבִּי יוֹסֵי בַּר יְהוּדָה אוֹמֵר – R' YOSE BAR YEHUDAH SAYS: אֵינוֹ חַיָּיב עַד שֶׁיְּגַבֵּל – HE IS NOT LIABLE for "kneading" UNTIL HE actually KNEADS the mixture manually, i.e. until he kneads it into a dough.[45]

The Gemara[46] questions this association:

דִּילְמָא – **Perhaps** our Mishnah does not accord with R' Yose bar Yehudah's view either: עַד כָּאן לֹא קָאָמַר רַבִּי יוֹסֵי בַּר יְהוּדָה הָתָם אֶלָּא קֶמַח – **Thus far, R' Yose bar Yehudah,** who disputes Rebbi, **says there** that the mere addition of water does not constitute "kneading" **only in regard to flour,** דְּבַר גִּיבּוּל הוּא – **which is kneadable** and can be formed into a dough.[47] אֲבָל מוּרְסָן – **However,** in regard to **bran** דְּלָאו בַּר גִּיבּוּל הוּא – **which is not kneadable,**[48] אֲפִילוּ רַבִּי יוֹסֵי בַּר יְהוּדָה מוֹדֶה – perhaps **even R' Yose bar Yehudah would agree** that simply adding water to the bran is forbidden as an act of "kneading."[49] – ? –

The Gemara refutes this possibility:

לֹא סָלְקָא דַעְתָּךְ – **It should not enter your mind** to make such a distinction. דְּתַנְיָא בְּהֶדְיָא – **For it was taught in a Baraisa explicitly:** אֵין נוֹתְנִין מַיִם לְמוּרְסָן – ONE MAY NOT PUT WATER INTO BRAN; דִּבְרֵי רַבִּי – THESE ARE THE WORDS OF REBBI. רַבִּי יוֹסֵי בַּר יְהוּדָה אוֹמֵר – R' YOSE BAR YEHUDAH SAYS: נוֹתְנִין מַיִם לְמוּרְסָן – ONE MAY PUT WATER INTO BRAN.[50]

A related Baraisa:

תָּנוּ רַבָּנַן – **The Rabbis taught in a Baraisa:** אֵין גּוֹבְלִין אֶת הַקָּלִי – ONE MAY NOT KNEAD TOASTED GRAIN flour[51] with water on the Sabbath; וְיֵשׁ אוֹמְרִים גּוֹבְלִין – AND SOME SAY ONE MAY KNEAD it.

The Gemara asks:

מַאן יֵשׁ אוֹמְרִים – **Who is** the Tanna meant by **"and some say"?**

The Gemara answers:

אָמַר רַב חִסְדָּא – **Rav Chisda said:**

NOTES

42. As long as the animal is not kneeling, one cannot stuff the food in very deeply, and the animal can still spit it out (*Rashi*).

43. I.e. Rav Yosef (see above, 18a, and *Ritva MHK* ed. here).

44. Whoever introduced the second ingredient – whether flour or water – is liable for "kneading," since he is the one who caused the ingredients to mix together, even though no manual kneading has been done.

45. Apparently, R' Yose bar Yehudah holds that the *melachah* of "kneading" requires actually kneading the ingredients into a doughlike mass.

Thus, our Mishnah, which permits the pouring of water into bran if one does not knead them together, must reflect the opinion of R' Yose bar Yehudah, who does not consider this a violation of the *melachah* of "kneading."

46. [Or, perhaps, Abaye himself (*Chazon Ish, Orach Chaim* 58:3).]

47. I.e. the particles of flour adhere to each other and form a dough. In such a case R' Yose bar Yehudah maintains that the *melachah* of "kneading" requires that one knead the particles together manually so that they form a dough (see ibid.).

48. I.e. its particles do not adhere to form a doughlike mass.

49. The Gemara suggests that R' Yose bar Yehudah may define the *melachah* of "kneading" differently for substances that adhere to form a doughlike mass ("kneadable" substances) than he does for substances that do not adhere in that way ("non-kneadable" substances). Regarding kneadable substances, R' Yose bar Yehudah defines the *melachah* as kneading them manually into a dough; consequently, he maintains that one is not liable unless one actually kneads them together manually. In regard to non-kneadable substances, R' Yose bar Yehudah defines the *melachah* as simply mixing the two substances together; consequently, he would agree with Rebbi that one is liable for simply adding water to the mixture (see ibid.).

[See *Melo HaRo'im* and *Leshon HaZahav,* who discuss which view is reflected in our Mishnah.]

50. Thus, the Baraisa proves conclusively that even in regard to bran, which cannot be kneaded into a doughlike mass, R' Yose bar Yehudah does not consider adding water to a mixture to be an act of "kneading."

According to most Rishonim, the halachah follows R' Yose bar Yehudah (see *Mishnah Berurah* 321:50).

[It would seem that according to the Gemara's conclusion the definition of "kneading" is no different in respect to kneadable substances than it is in respect to substances that are not kneadable. In either case, R' Yose bar Yehudah maintains that the *melachah* is not violated unless one kneads the mixture into a dough. It would then follow that in the case of non-kneadable substances (such as bran), where this is impossible, one cannot possibly violate the *melachah* of "kneading" on a Biblical level with these substances. It further follows that although our Mishnah forbids kneading bran and water, this is a merely Rabbinic prohibition. This, in fact, is the view of *Rambam* (*Hil. Shabbos* 8:16 and 21:34), and seems to be that of *Rashi* as well (see *Rashi* to *Beitzah* 32b ד״ה וקיטמא שרי; *Terumas HaDeshen* §53; *Eglei Tal, Lash* §9; *Beur Halachah* to *Orach Chaim* 324:3; cf. *Chazon Ish,* loc. cit.). For other approaches see *Tosafos* to 18a ד״ה אבל דיו; *Ramban* here, et al.; see also *Eglei Tal* and *Beur Halachah,* loc. cit., at length.]

51. A type of flour produced from moist grain kernels that have been oven dried. This flour retains its sweetness indefinitely. When oil, water and salt are mixed into this flour, the result is a food called שְׁתִיתָא, *shasis* (*Rashi;* cf. *Rambam, Hil. Shabbos* 21:33, with *Maggid Mishneh*).

רַבִּי יוֹסֵי בְּרַבִּי יְהוּדָה הִיא – **It is R' Yose the son of R' Yehudah,** who maintains that merely adding water to flour is not considered "kneading"; one is liable only for kneading the ingredients manually into a doughlike mass. And in this case, he permits even manual kneading. וְהָנֵי מִילֵּי הוּא דִּמְשַׁנֵּי – **However, this is** permitted only **provided he deviates** from the normal manner of kneading.[1]

The Gemara asks:

הֵיכִי מְשַׁנֵּי – **How should he deviate?**

The Gemara explains:

אָמַר רַב חִסְדָּא – **Rav Chisda said:** עַל יָד עַל יָד – He should knead only **a small amount at a time.**[2]

The Gemara cites the end of the Baraisa:

וְשָׁוִין שֶׁבּוֹחֲשִׁין אֶת הַשְּׁתִית בַּשַּׁבָּת – AND both [THE TANNA KAMMA AND R' YOSE THE SON OF R' YEHUDAH] AGREE THAT ONE MAY STIR *SHASIS* ON THE SABBATH.[3] וְשׁוֹתִים זִיתוֹם הַמִּצְרִי – FURTHERMORE, they agree that ONE MAY DRINK EGYPTIAN *ZISOM*[4] on the Sabbath, even though it is frequently used for medicinal purposes.[5]

The Baraisa has stated that one may stir *shasis* even according to the Tanna Kamma, to which the Gemara raises the obvious objection:

וְהָאָמְרַתְּ אֵין גּוֹבְלִין – **But you have** just **said** that according to the Tanna Kamma **one may *not* knead** toasted-grain flour! How then could the Tanna Kamma permit the stirring of *shasis,* which is made from toasted-grain flour?

The Gemara resolves the contradiction:

לָא קַשְׁיָא – **This is not difficult:** הָא בְּעָבָה – **This** first ruling of the Tanna Kamma, which prohibits kneading toasted-grain flour, **regards thick** *shasis.* הָא בְּרַכָּה – **This** second ruling, which permits stirring, **regards thin** *shasis.*[6]

The Gemara adds a restriction to the stirring of thin *shasis*:

וְהָנֵי מִילֵּי הוּא דִּמְשַׁנֵּי – **But this** leniency **is** granted **only if he deviates** from the normal manner of stirring.

The Gemara asks:

הֵיכִי מְשַׁנֵּי – **How should he deviate?**

The Gemara answers:

אָמַר רַב יוֹסֵף – **Rav Yosef said:** בְּחוֹל נוֹתֵן אֶת הַחוֹמֶץ וְאַחַר כָּךְ נוֹתֵן אֶת הַשְּׁתִית – **During the week, one** normally **pours in the vinegar**[7] first **and** only **afterwards pours in the *shasis,*** i.e. the flour. בְּשַׁבָּת נוֹתֵן אֶת הַשְּׁתִית וְאַחַר כָּךְ נוֹתֵן אֶת הַחוֹמֶץ – Therefore, **on the Sabbath, he should** first **pour in the *shasis* and** only **afterward pour in the vinegar.**[8]

The Gemara relates:

לֵוִי בְּרֵיהּ דְּרַב הוּנָא בַּר חִיָּיא אַשְׁכְּחֵיהּ לְגַבְּלָא דְּבֵי נְשִׁיהּ – **Levi the son of Rav Huna bar Chiya once discovered the mixer of fodder of his father's estate**[9] דְּקָא גָּבֵיל וְסָפֵי לֵיהּ לְתוֹרֵיהּ – **as he was kneading** some bran and water on the Sabbath **and feeding it to his ox,** i.e. to an ox in his charge.[10] בְּטַשׁ בֵּיהּ – **[Levi] kicked him** in disapproval, since the Mishnah states that one may not knead bran and there is no dissenting view. אֲתָא אֲבוּהַ אַשְׁכְּחֵיהּ – **His father,** Rav Huna bar Chiya, **came and found him.** אֲמַר לֵיהּ – **He told [his son]:** הָכִי אָמַר אֲבוּהַ דְּאִמָּךְ מִשְּׁמֵיהּ דְּרַב – **This is what the father of your mother said in the name of Rav:**

The Gemara interjects:

וּמַנּוּ – **And who was this?** רַבִּי יִרְמְיָה בַּר אַבָּא – **R' Yirmiyah bar Abba.**

The Gemara returns to Rav's ruling:

גּוֹבְלִין וְלֹא מַסְפִּין – **One may knead** bran for cattle on the

NOTES

1. [As we have seen, R' Yose the son of R' Yehudah maintains that the *melachah* of "kneading" requires kneading the mixture into a doughlike mass. [According to him, substances that cannot be kneaded into a dough, such as toasted-grain flour, are not subject to this prohibition at all, on a Biblical level (see above, 155b note 50). Although it is Rabbinically prohibited to knead even such a substance,] the Rabbis waived this prohibition where the kneading was performed in an unusual manner.

In contrast, Rebbi's view is that the *melachah* of "kneading" does not require the ingredients to be kneaded manually at all. According to him, merely adding water, even to a non-kneadable substance [such as toasted-grain flour], constitutes a Biblical violation. [Therefore it is of no avail to knead the dough in an unusual manner, since one will already have violated the prohibition by merely adding liquid to the toasted-grain flour] (*Rashi;* see *Ramban;* see also *Hagahos R' Simchah of Dessau;* cf. *Maharshal*).

[Nor does it avail, according to Rebbi, to add the liquid in an unusual manner since, in fact, there is no significantly unusual method of adding liquid to form such a mixture (see *Eglai Tal, Lisha* 1:3, see also *Ramban*).]

2. [The translation follows *Rif, Rabbeinu Chananel, Ramban* and *Aruch.* See also *Eglei Tal, Lisha* §19; *Beur Halachah* to 321:14, ד"ה שמא יבוא; cf. *Nishmas Adam, Hil. Shabbos* 19:1.]

This is a deviation from the normal procedure in which much is prepared at one time (see *Rashi* ד"ה רבי יוסי בר יהודה היא; *Ramban,* Machon HaTalmud HaYisraeli ed.; *Eglei Tal* and *Beur Halachah,* loc. cit.).

It emerges that according to R' Yose the son of R' Yehudah it is permitted to knead a non-kneadable substance with water, as long as one does so in an unusual fashion, viz. a little at a time. But this leads to the following difficulty: We learned in our Mishnah that one may pour water into bran for chicken feed, but one may not knead the mixture. Now, the Gemara has already established that our Mishnah follows the view of R' Yose the son of R' Yehudah; accordingly, he ought to be allowed to knead the bran and water together, as long as he mixes only a little at a time! See below, note 14.

3. I.e. with a spoon, which is equivalent to kneading (*Rashi;* cf. *Ritva MHK* ed.).

[As noted before (155b note 51), *shasis* is made from toasted-grain flour mixed with water and oil. Thus, this statement directly contradicts the Tanna Kamma's statement above that one may *not* knead toasted-grain flour. The Gemara will immediately reconcile this contradiction.]

4. A type of beer with medicinal properties; see above, 110a.

5. [Generally speaking, medicine may not be taken on the Sabbath for minor ailments. However,] if a particular beverage is normally consumed on its own merits, it may be consumed by a sick person for its medical benefit (*Rashi,* citing 109b; see *Tosafos* 110a ד"ה רבי יוסי, and *Maginei Shlomo* ad loc.).

6. [The *melachah* of "kneading" applies only to thick mixtures; it does not apply to thin, pourable mixtures, such as batter.] Thus, although Rebbi forbids mixing a thick *shasis,* he concedes that one may stir a thin *shasis,* since that is not included in the Biblical prohibition of "kneading" (*Rashi*). Nevertheless, this mixing must be done in a manner that deviates from normal, as the Gemara will immediately explain.

7. [Although *Rashi* earlier (see above, 155b note 51) described *shasis* as being made from toasted-grain flour mixed with water and oil, it appears from the Gemara here that it was sometimes mixed with vinegar.]

8. By adopting this deviation it is permitted to mix even large quantities of thin *shasis* (*Ramban*).

The Gemara did not suggest this method earlier when it discussed mixing a thick *shasis* according to R' Yose the son of R' Yehudah, because since on a Biblical level the *melachah* of kneading applies specifically to thick mixtures (see note 6), the mixing of thick *shasis* requires a substantial deviation, viz. mixing only a little at a time. Adding the vinegar last is a minor deviation, and is effective only for thin *shasis* (*Ramban;* see also *Chidushei HaRan.* See *Eglai Tal, Lisha* 30:14 and *Chazon Ish* 58:2).

9. [See *Rabbeinu Bachya* to *Genesis* 41:51 regarding the phrase דְּבֵי נָשָׂא.]

10. He was kneading bran using some form of deviation (*Rashi*).

רבי יוסי בר יהודה היא. (דאי רבי לא מהני ליה שינוי דמנתינת מים מיחייב אפילו במידי דלאו בר גיבול כדאמרינן גבי מורסן אבל לרבי יוסי בר יהודה) דאמר עד שיגבל הכא גובלין כלאחר יד כדמפרש ואזיל והנ"מ הוא דקא משני: שבוחשין. בתרווד דהיינו גובלין: ושותים זיתום המצרי. דבלאו רפואה נמי משקה הוא דתנן כל המשקין שותה אדם לרפואה (לעיל דף קט:): בעבה. אין גובלין ברכה בוחשין שאין זו לישה: בחול נותן החומץ כו'. כלומר כן דרכו בחול: לגבלא דבי נשיה. שומר בהמות אביו ומגבל מאכלן: דקא גביל. מורסן ע"י שינוי: בטש ביה. דהא לכולי עלמא אבל לא גובלין תנן: גובלין. מורסן ע"י שינוי כדמפרש ואזיל והוא דקא משני: ולא מספין. לתורי אין מאמירין אותן: ודלא לקיט בלישניה. עגל קטן שעדיין לא לומד לאכול: והני מילי. דאמרן דמותר לגבל מורסן: שתי וערב. פעם אחת מוליך המקל שתי ופעם אחת ערב: מנערו לכלי. והוא מתערב מאליו: אפינקסיה. לוחות קשורות זו עם זו כאותן של סוחרים: מהו לפרק. ליתן מתוך כלי שלפני בהמה זו וליתן לפני חברתה: חדא קמי חדא. מילתא באפי נפשה היא אלא מדה שרגילין ליתן לפני בהמה מותר ליתן לפניה בשבת וכן תרתי קמי תרתי האוכלות באבוס אחד: אבל תלתא קמי תרתי. הואיל ובחול לא יהיב להו כי האי הוי טרחא דלא צריך וכ"ש תרתי קמי חדא: אמרית קמיה רבי. רבי לוי משתעי דהוא אמר קדם רבי על הנך אינשי דגבלין שתיתא: מדר' יוסי בר יהודה. בר פלוגתיה דהוה שרי לעיל אף בעבה ועל ידי שינוי והיו נוהגין כמותו: האי מאן דבחד בשבא. הנולד באחד בשבת: יהא גבר ולא חדא ביה. יהא אדם שלם במדה אחת יהא ולא אחת בו ממדה אחרת ולקמן מפרש לה ואזיל: והוא ריש גנבי. דמאן דבחד בשבא יהא ראש כמו שהיום ראש למעשה בראשית מיהו שמע מינה דנולדים בו לדיקים ורשעים: דאיפליגו מיא. כך הוא יבדל מכל אדם: זנאי. נואף: דאיברו ביה עשבים. דכתי' (בראשית א) תדשא הארץ והוא דבר שפרה ורבה מאד וממהר לגדל ולצמוח דהוא ענין פריצות אשווי"א בלע"ז [ל"א] דלא כתיב למינהו בעשבים כלוויים (ועוד) שיוצאין בערבוביא ויונקין זו מזו: ונהיר. זיותן: דאיתלו ביה מאורות. וכתיב ותורה אור: דאיברו ביה דגים ועופות. שאין טורחין לאוכלין אלא ניזונים בחסדו של הקב"ה: חזרן. מחזר אחר מלות: חזרן במצות. שכן דרך ע"ש לחזר אחר מלות שבת: וקדישא רבה יתקרי. שיהא פרוש וקדוש דכתיב (שמות כ) ויקדשהו: אמר להו רבי חנינא. לתלמידים שקראו פנקסו של ר' יהושע: מזל שעה. ז' מזלות הן המשמשין את השעות חנכ"ל שצ"ם חמה היינו חמה ממש והוא אחד מן המזלות וכן לבנה והשאר הויין כוכבים: זיותן. כשמש המאיר: אכיל מדיליה. כשמש שאינו מסיג גבול רעהו למשול בלילה: ורזוהי גליין. אין לו רשות לכסות סודו ונסתרותיו אלא כשמש הזה שהוא פומבי לכל: דתלי ביה נורא. אש תלוי באותו מזל יצר של תשמיש בוער כתנור: מזל כוכב. הוא סופר של מזל חמה לכתוב דרך הילוכו ותקופותיו ומלוי אללו תמיד: סביל מרעין. כלבנה זו (ג) שמתוונה והולכת: בנאי וסתיר. כלבנה זו שגדילה ומתמעטת: אכיל לא דיליה. ° כלבנה המסגת גבול החמה למשול אף ביום: ורזוהי כסיין. כלבנה שאינה מאירה: דבשבתאי. מזל כוכב ששמו שבתאי: בטלין. כמו לא ישבותו (בראשית ח): צדקן במצות. לדקה לעניים דקרי ליה מלוה (בכל לשון אגדה): גנבא. ליסטים ההורג נפשות: אומנא. מקיז דם: עניש. בני אדם העוברין על דבריו: מזל מחכים. לפי המזל היא החכמה כדאמר דבחמה נהיר וחכים: ויש מזל לישראל. שאין תפלה ולדקה משנה את המזל: אין מזל לישראל. דעל ידי תפלה וזכות משתנה מזלו לטובה: איצטגנינות. חכמת המזלות: צא מאיצטגנינותך. היינו דכתיב ויוצא אותו החוצה חוץ מאילטגנינותו: דקאי

רבי יוסי בר' יהודה היא והנ"מ הוא דמשני היכי משני א"ר חסדא על יד על יד ושוין שבוחשין את השתית בשבת ושותים זיתום המצרי והאמרת אין גובלין ל"ק הא בעבה הא ברכה והני מילי הוא דמשני היכי משני אמר רב יוסף בחול נותן את החומץ ואח"כ נותן את השתית בשבת נותן את השתית ואח"כ נותן את החומץ לוי בריה דרב הונא בר חייא אשכחיה לגבלא דבי נשיה דקא גביל וספי ליה לתוריה בטש ביה אתא אבוה אשכחיה א"ל הכי אמר אבוה דאמך משמיה דרב ומנו רבי ירמיה בר אבא גובלין ולא מספין ודלא לקיט בלישניה מהלקיטין ליה וה"מ הוא דמשני היכי משני אמר רב יימר בר שלמיא משמיה דאביי שתי וערב והא לא מערב שפיר אמר רב יהודה מנערו לכלי כתיב אפינקסיה דזעירי אמרית קדם רבי ומנו רבי חייא מהו לגבל אמר אסור מהו לפרק אמר מותר אמר רב [מנשיא] חד קמי חד תרי קמי תרי שפיר דמי תלתא קמי תרי אסור רב יוסף אמר קב ואפילו קביים עולא אמר כור ואפילו כוריים כתיב אפינקסיה דלוי אמרית קדם רבי ומנו רבינו הקדוש על דהוו גבלין שתיתא בבבל והוה צווח רבי ומנו רבינו הקדוש על דהוו גבלין שתיתא ליה ולית דשמיע ליה ולית חילא בידיה למיסר מדרבי יוסי בר' יהודה כתיב אפינקסיה דרבי יהושע בן לוי האי מאן דבחד בשבא יהי גבר ולא חדא ביה מאי [ולא חדא ביה] אילימא ולא חד לטיבו והאמר רב אשי אנא בחד בשבא הואי אלא לאו חדא לבישו והאמר רב אשי אנא ודימי בר קקוזתא הויין בחד בשבא אנא מלך והוא הוה ריש גנבי אלא אי כולי לטיבו אי כולי לבישו (מאי טעמא דאיברו ביה אור וחושך) האי מאן דבתרי בשבא יהי גבר רגזן מ"ט משום דאיפליגו ביה מיא האי מאן דבתלתא בשבא יהי גבר עתיר וזנאי יהא מ"ט משום דאיברו ביה עשבים האי מאן דבארבעה בשבא יהי גבר חכים ונהיר מ"ט משום דאיתלו ביה מאורות האי מאן דבחמשה בשבא יהי גבר גומל חסדים מ"ט משום דאיברו ביה דגים ועופות האי מאן דבמעלי שבתא יהי גבר חזרן אמר ר"נ בר יצחק חזרן במצות האי מאן דבשבתא יהי בשבתא ימות על דאחילו עלוהי יומא רבא דשבתא אמר רבא בר רב שילא וקדישא רבא יתקרי אמר להו רבי חנינא פוקו אמרו ליה לבר ליואי לא מזל יום גורם אלא מזל שעה גורם האי מאן דבחמה יהי גבר זיותן יהי אכיל מדיליה ושתי מדיליה ורזוהי גליין אם גניב לא מצלח האי מאן דבכוכב נוגה יהי גבר עתיר וזנאי יהי מ"ט משום דאיתיליד ביה נורא האי מאן דבכוכב יהי גבר נהיר וחכים משום דספרא דחמה הוא האי מאן דבלבנה יהי גבר סביל מרעין בנאי וסתיר סתיר ובנאי אכיל דלא דיליה ושתי דלא דיליה ורזוהי כסיין אם גנב מצלח האי מאן דבשבתאי יהי גבר מחשבתיה בטלין ואית דאמרי כל דמחשבין עליה בטלין האי מאן דבצדק יהי גבר צדקן אמר ר"נ בר יצחק וצדקן במצות האי מאן דבמאדים יהי גבר אשיד דמא א"ר אשי אי אומנא אי גנבא אי טבחא אי מוהלא אמר רבה אנא במאדים הואי אמר אביי מר נמי עניש וקטיל איתמר רבי חנינא אומר מזל מחכים מזל מעשיר ויש מזל לישראל רבי יוחנן אמר אין מזל לישראל ואזדא רבי יוחנן לטעמיה דא"ר יוחנן מניין שאין מזל לישראל שנאמר כה אמר ה' אל דרך הגוים אל תלמדו ומאותות השמים אל תחתו כי יחתו הגוים מהמה הם יחתו ולא ישראל ואף רב סבר אין מזל לישראל דאמר רב יהודה אמר רב מניין שאין מזל לישראל שנאמר ויוצא אותו החוצה אמר אברהם לפני הקב"ה רבש"ע בן ביתי יורש אותי אמר לו לאו כי אם אשר יצא ממעיך אמר לפניו רבש"ע נסתכלתי באיצטגנינות שלי ואיני ראוי להוליד בן אמר ליה צא מאיצטגנינות שלך שאין מזל לישראל מאי דעתיך דקאי

מהו לפרק. פירש בקונטרס לפרק מלפני בהמה זו וליתן לפני אחרת וכן פירש בערוך בערך פרק וקשה לר"י דהיינו מתניתין גבי בהמה (לעיל דף קמ:) ונראה לר"י לפרק היינו להריק המים וגם המורסן מכלי אל כלי שתגבל היטב ובערוך פירש כמה לשונות:

אין מזל לישראל. והא דאמר רבא בשילהי מו"ק (דף כח. ושם) בני חיי ומזוני לאו בזכותא תליא מילתא אלא במזלא תליא מילתא מכל מקום על ידי זכות גדול משתנה אבל פעמים שאין המזל משתנה כדאמר ביבמות פרק החולץ (דף נ. ושם) זכה מוסיפין לו לא זכה פוחתין לו (דלאין מזל לישראל): כלדאי

עין משפט נר מצוה

לא א ב ג ד מיי' שם הלכה לג סמג שם טוש"ע א"ח סימן שכא סעיף יד:

גליון הש"ס

גמרא אתא אבוה אשכחיה. עי' לעיל דף כג ע"ב תוס' ד"ה דבי נשא: רש"י ד"ה אכיל דלא דיליה כלבנה המסגת. עיין דבר נחמד בזה בכתנות אור לבעל פמ"א בפ' בראשית:

רבינו חננאל

ואין צ"ל שמלקטין כו' ופריק רב יהודה הכי לעולם פי' מתניתא דאמר כך היא מהלקטין דספו ליה בידיה והיא פחותה מהלעטה שאמרנו ומלקטין שמשליך לפניה שעורים וכיוצא בהן דברים שהן מאכל לעופות. ואין משליכין מאכל לפני יוני שובך ויוני [עליה] לפי שאינן [בני] תרבות ואין מזונותן עליך וכי [הא] דתניא נותנין מזונות לפני הכלב ואין נותנין מזונות לפני חזיר ומה הפרש בין זה לזה כלב מזונותיו עליך חזיר אין מזונותיו עליך ובא רב אשי לסייע דברי רב יהודה ולומר שנויא דשני שינויא היא מדוקיא דמתניתין דקתני אין נותנין מים לפני דבורים ולפני יונים שבשובך אבל נותנים לפני אווזים ותרנגולים ולפני יונים הרדוסיית מ"ט לאו משו' דהני מזונותיו עליך והני אין מזונותיו עליך ולא עמדו דברי רב אשי והלכה כרב יהודה דתניא כוותיה דתניא איזו היא המראה ואיזו היא הלעטה המראה מרביצה ופוקס את פיה ומאכילה כרשינין ומים בבת אחת. הלעטה מאכילה מעומד ומשקה מעומד ונותן לה כרשינין בפ"ע ומים בפ"ע: מהלקטין לתרנגולים ונותנין מים למורסן אבל לא גובלין אוקימנא לר' יוסי ב"ר יהודה דתניא אחד נותן את הקמח ואחד נותן לתוכו מים האחרון חייב דברי ר' ור' יוסי בר יהודה אומר עד שיגבל אלמא אמרינן [דנתינת מים זהו גיבולו] ממאי דלמא עד כאן לא קאמר ר' יוסי ב"ר יהודה עד שיגבל אלא בקמח דבר גיבול הוא. אבל מורסן דלאו בר גיבול הוא אפי' ר' יוסי ב"ר יהודה מודי שנתינת מים למורסן אסור שזהו גיבולו ואשכחנן תניא בהדיא אין נותנין מים למורסן דברי ר' [ר'] יוסי ב"ר יהודה אומר נותנים מים למורסן ואע"ג דבכל מקום הלכתא כרבי מחבירו הכא הלכה כר' יוסי דתנינן מתניתין סתמא כוותיה. ותוב מהא דכתוב אפינקסיה דלוי אמרית קדם רבינו הקדוש והוא רבי עד דהוו גבלין שתיתא בבבל והוא צווח רבי דלית דשמע ליה ולית חילא בידיה למיסר מדר' יוסי ב"ר יהודה מהא נמי שמעינן דהלכתא כר' יוסי ב"ר יהודה דהוא בר פלוגתיה לא אסר ונפק עובדא כוותיה: ת"ר אין גובלין את הקליא וי"א גובלין ואמרינן מאן י"א ואמר רב חסדא ר' יוסי ב"ר יהודה היא והוא דמשני היכי משני אמר רב חסדא על יד על יד פי' מעט מעט מדמתרץ רב חסדא אליבא דר' יוסי ב"ר יהודה הלכתא

מסורת הש"ס

א) ברכות לח., ב) [צ"ל נשא ועמ"ש תוספו' לעיל כג: ד"ה דבי], ג) [עי' תוספות חולין ז. ד"ה מכניס וכו' דגרסי רב מנשה], ד) רש"ל מ"ז, ה) [פי' זכרן ערוך], ו) (סוכה כט.), ז) [סוכה כט.], ח) [נדרים לב.], ט) רש"ל מ"ז, י) ר"מ מוחק זה.

הגהות הב"ח

(א) גמ' מאן דבחמה יהא כו'. נ"ב תחלת סדר הליכתן שצ"ם חנכ"ל [וכאן נקט חנכ"ל שצ"ם] לפי סדר סימני הימים חל"ס כלנ"ש נקט חמה ברישא והדר נקט נוגה וכו' לפי סדר [השעות והמזלות כשמתחיל ממזל חמה שהוא משמש בתחלת יום א' נמלא סדר השעות] חנכ"ל שצ"ם וחזר בלילה כדאיתא ברש"י ס"פ מפנין וע"ש: (ב) רש"י ד"ה סביל וכו' זו שמתמעטת והולכת:

תורה אור השלם

א) כֹּה אָמַר יְיָ אֶל דֶּרֶךְ הַגּוֹיִם אַל תִּלְמָדוּ וּמֵאֹתוֹת הַשָּׁמַיִם אַל תֵּחָתּוּ כִּי יֵחַתּוּ הַגּוֹיִם מֵהֵמָּה: [ירמיה י, ב]

ב) וַיּוֹצֵא אֹתוֹ הַחוּצָה וַיֹּאמֶר הַבֶּט נָא הַשָּׁמַיְמָה וּסְפֹר הַכּוֹכָבִים אִם תּוּכַל לִסְפֹּר אֹתָם וַיֹּאמֶר לוֹ כֹּה יִהְיֶה זַרְעֶךָ: [בראשית טו, ה]

ג) וַיֹּאמֶר אַבְרָם הֵן לִי לֹא נָתַתָּה זָרַע וְהִנֵּה בֶן בֵּיתִי יוֹרֵשׁ אֹתִי: [בראשית טו, ג]

ד) וְהִנֵּה דְבַר יְיָ אֵלָיו לֵאמֹר לֹא יִירָשְׁךָ זֶה כִּי אִם אֲשֶׁר יֵצֵא מִמֵּעֶיךָ הוּא יִירָשֶׁךָ: [בראשית טו, ד]

ליקוטי רש"י

על יד על יד. מעט מעט [ביצה יב:]. שתית. מאכל העשוי מקמח קליות שנתייבשו בתנור בעוד שהשבלים לחים [ברכות לח.]. מאכל שעושין מקמח קלי שנתייבש בתנור ונותנין דבש לתוך התבשיל [עירובין כט:]. תבשיל העשוי מקמח של קליות שייבשן בתנור ויש שעושין אותו מקמח עדשים ולפי שהן מתוקין יותר מדאי טומן שם חומץ [ע"ז לח:]. שבוחשין. מגיסין בכף לערבו יפה במימיו [ברכות שם]. זיתום המצרי. הוא מי דקרים ועל שם שדוקרים את החולי [לעיל קי.]. מפורש במסכת פסחים (דף מ"ב:) [ברכות שם]. בטש. בעט [שבועות לו.]. מזל שעה. שצ"ם חנכ"ל סדר השעות כשנתלו המאורות והמזלות שעה ראשונה של רביעי בשבת שימש שבתאי ובשניה צדק ולאחריו מאדים ולאחריו חמה ולאחריו נוגה ולאחריו כוכב ולאחריו לבנה נמצאו שבע המזלות לשבע השעות וחוזרים חלילה לעולם נמצא כסדר זה לעולם סימני מזלות המשמשין בתחלת לילי השבוע כלנ"ש חל"ס מזלו שבת שעה ראשונה של ליל שבת כוכב תחלת ליל שני צדק וכן כסדר הזה והדר תחלת סימני...

לראשונה של לאחד באחד בשבת חמה ושל שני בשבת לבנה וכן כולם [לעיל קכט:]. אל דרך הגוים אל תלמדו. ולא מאותות השמים אל תחתו [ירמיהו י, ב]. לעשות כמעשיהם ומשפטם לרצות לאותות השמים אל תחתו [סוכה כט.]. איצטגנינות. להיות בקי בהליכות המזלות ומהלכות השעות לכל אילטגנינות גדולה היתה בלבו ... [יומא כח:]. אילטגנינות דכל הש"ס לשון כוכבים [סנהדרין סה:]. צא מאיצטגנינות שלך. ממשפט חכמת מזלות שלך והיינו דכתיב (בראשית טו) ויוצא אותו החוצה [ר"ן נדרים לב.].

Sabbath,[11] **but one may not gorge** them.[12] **וּדְלָא לָקִיט בְּלִישָׁנֵיהּ – And in regard to** a young calf **that is not yet accustomed to feed itself with its own tongue, מְהַלְקִיטִין לֵיהּ – one may force-feed it.**[13] **וְהָנֵי מִילֵּי הוּא דִּמְשַׁנֵּי –** But **this** permit to knead bran for cattle **is** only given **provided that he deviates** from the normal manner of kneading.

The Gemara asks:

הֵיכִי מְשַׁנֵּי – How should he deviate?

The Gemara answers:

אָמַר רַב יֵימַר בַּר שְׁלַמְיָא מִשְּׁמֵיהּ דְּאַבַּיֵי – Rav Yeimar bar Shelamya said in the name of Abaye: שְׁתִי וָעֵרֶב – He should place his stirring stick in the mixture and move it **crosswise.**[14]

The Gemara protests:

וְהָא לָא מְעָרֵב שַׁפִּיר – But such a method **is not effective in mixing** the bran and water! – ? –

The Gemara offers an additional method:

אָמַר רַב יְהוּדָה – Rav Yehudah said: מְנַעֲרוֹ לַכְּלִי – He should shake the vessel which contains the mixture.[15]

The Gemara cites a written record pertinent to our discussion:

כְּתִיב אַפִּינְקְסֵיהּ דִּזְעֵירִי – It was written in Zeiri's ledger.[16] **אֲמַרִית קֳדָם רַבִּי – I said before my teacher . . .**

The Gemara interjects:

וּמַנּוּ רַבִּי חִיָּיא – And who was this? R' Chiya.

The Gemara returns to the notebook record:

מַהוּ לְגַבֵּל – . . . what is the law in regard to kneading a thick mixture [17] on the Sabbath? **אָמַר אָסוּר – He said: It is prohibited.**[18] **מַהוּ לְפָרֵק –** I said: **What is the law in regard to transferring** food from one animal's pail to another's?[19] **אָמַר מוּתָּר – He said: It is permitted.**

The Gemara introduces a new law concerning the feeding of animals:

אָמַר רַב מְנַשְׁיָא – Rav Menashya said: חַד קַמֵּי חַד – If one wishes to set **one** portion **before one** animal on the Sabbath, **תְּרֵי קַמֵּי תְּרֵי –** or **two** portions **before two** animals sharing a trough,[20] **שַׁפִּיר דָּמֵי – that is fine;** it is permissible. **תְּלָתָא קַמֵּי תְּרֵי אָסוּר –** However, if he wishes to set **three** portions **before two** animals, **that is prohibited,** since it is an excessive exertion.[21]

A dissenting opinion:

רַב יוֹסֵף אָמַר – Rav Yosef said: קַב וַאֲפִילּוּ קַבַּיִים – One may feed the animals **a *kav*, or even two *kavs*. עוּלָּא אָמַר – Ulla said: כּוֹר וַאֲפִילּוּ כּוֹרַיִים –** One may feed them **a *kor* or even two *kors*!**[22]

Another ledger record pertaining to kneading:

כְּתִיב אַפִּינְקְסֵיהּ דְּלֵוִי – It was written in Levi's notebook: אֲמַרִית קֳדָם רַבִּי – I stated before my teacher . . .

The Gemara interjects:

וּמַנּוּ רַבֵּינוּ הַקָּדוֹשׁ – And who is this? Our holy teacher, Rebbi.[23]

The ledger record continues:

עַל דַּהֲווּ גָּבְלִין שְׁתִיתָא בְּבָבֶל – . . . concerning the fact that people were kneading *shasis* in Babylonia on the Sabbath. **וַהֲוָה צָוַח רַבִּי – And my teacher protested vehemently . . .**

The Gemara interjects:

וּמַנּוּ רַבֵּינוּ הַקָּדוֹשׁ – And who is this? Our holy teacher, Rebbi.

The ledger record continues:

עַל דַּהֲווּ גָּבְלִין שְׁתִיתָא – . . . to their practice of kneading *shasis*, וְלֵית דִּשְׁמִיעַ לֵיהּ – but no one listened to him. וְלֵית חֵילָא בִּידֵיהּ לְמֵיסַר – And he did not have the power to prohibit it, מִדְּרַבִּי יוֹסֵי בְּרַבִּי יְהוּדָה – because of the lenient ruling of **R' Yose the son of R' Yehudah.**[24]

Another ledger record:

כְּתִיב אַפִּינְקְסֵיהּ דְּרַבִּי יְהוֹשֻׁעַ בֶּן לֵוִי – It was written in R' Yehoshua ben Levi's ledger: הַאי מַאן דִּבְחַד בְּשַׁבָּא – He who is born **on a Sunday יְהֵי גְּבַר וְלָא חֲדָא בֵּיהּ – will be a man** of one nature, **without one** trace of any other nature **in him.**[25]

The Gemara explains this statement:

מַאי [וְלָא חֲדָא בֵּיהּ] – What does "without one trace of any other nature **in him"** mean? **אִילֵימָא וְלָא חַד לְטִיבוּ – If you say** it

NOTES

11. Provided one deviates from the normal manner of kneading; the Gemara will shortly prescribe how this should be done.

12. I.e. one may not "fatten" them (*Rashi*); i.e. one may not place food so far down their throats that they cannot bring it back up (*Ritva MHK* ed.) [This accords with Rav Yehudah's view in the Gemara earlier (155b); see next note.]

13. As defined by Rav Yehudah earlier in the Gemara (ibid.), to "force-feed" means to place food down the animal's throat, but not so deeply that it cannot bring the food back up. Although our Mishnah has already stated that this is permitted, the novelty of Rav's ruling here is that one may place food down the throat of a young calf to the same depth as one would down the throat of an adult cow, even though the calf, which is not used to eating, cannot bring the food back up even from so shallow a depth (*Chidushei HaRan*; for other approaches see *Maharshal; Teshuvos Rama* §79).

14. I.e. once vertically and once horizontally (*Rashi;* cf. *Beis Yosef, Orach Chaim* 324; *Beur Halachah* to 324:3 ד"ה ומעביר).

He may not mix it any more than this very rudimentary stirring.

In this case we do not allow him to mix the bran thoroughly a little bit at a time, as we did in the case of *shasis.* This is so because the Sages allowed the exertion of mixing thoroughly only when preparing food for people, but not when preparing food for animals. Furthermore, bran and water are edible for animals with only a rudimentary mixing, whereas people would not consume *shasis* if it were not mixed well (*Ramban;* see *Beur Halachah* ibid. ד"ה מורסן; cf. *Ritva MHK* ed.).

Even this permit to stir the bran and water crosswise is given only for cattle; chicken feed may not be stirred at all, for the chickens themselves tend to stir the mixture as they peck at it. Alternatively, chickens do not need their bran and water mixed for them at all, and therefore doing so is a totally needless exertion. (*Ramban; Rashba;* note however that *Shulchan Aruch* 324:3 does not mention this distinction).

15. *Ritva MHK* ed. and *Beis Yosef, Orach Chaim* 324 read: מְנַעֲרוֹ לִכְלִי אַחֵר, *he should pour it into another vessel;* i.e. after stirring the mixture once vertically and once horizontally he should pour it into another vessel, thereby mixing it more thoroughly.

16. This "ledger" consisted of tablets bound together, similar to those used by merchants (*Rashi;* see above, 104b note 5; see also *Chidushei Maharatz Chayes*).

17. [See next note.]

18. R' Chiya does not permit kneading [a thick mixture] on the Sabbath at all. Apparently he follows the view of Rebbi who absolutely forbids mixing thick *shasis* (*Ramban;* see also *Baal HaMaor, Milchamos* et. al for alternative explanations of R' Chiya's statement).

19. [*Rashi;* see the Mishnah above, 140b; cf. *Tosafos,* et al.]

20. [*Rashi;* cf. *Chidushei HaRan.*]

21. And it is certainly prohibited to place two portions before one animal. In both cases, he is providing the animals with more feed than he gives them during the week; such efforts are excessive and forbidden (*Rashi*).

22. Two *kors* is an enormous quantity of food (see above 155b note 19). Ulla's point is that no consideration of excessive exertion applies to the quantity fed an animal.

23. [R' Yehudah HaNasi.]

24. R' Yose the son of R' Yehudah, as we have learned, was Rebbi's disputant above in the Baraisa regarding *shasis.* R' Yose the son of R' Yehudah permitted the kneading of *shasis,* even as a thick mixture, as long as a deviation was employed. The people in Babylonia followed his ruling (*Rashi*).

25. The Gemara proceeds to explain this record, statement by statement.

רבי יוסי בר' יהודה היא והנ"מ הוא [א]דמשני היכי משני א"ר חסדא [ב]על יד על יד [ה] ושוין שבוחשין את השתית בשבת ושותים זיתום המצרי והאמרת אין גובלין ל"ק הא [ג]בעבה הא ברכה והני מילי הוא דמשני היכי משני אמר רב יוסף בחול נותן את החומץ ואח"כ נותן את השתית [ד]בשבת נותן את השתית ואח"כ נותן את החומץ לוי בריה דרב הונא בר חייא אשכחיה לגבלא דבי [ו] נשיה דקא גביל וספי ליה לתוריה בטש ביה • אתא אבוה אשכחיה א"ל הכי אמר אבוה דאמך משמיה דרב ומנו רבי ירמיה בר אבא גובלין ולא מספין ודלא לקיט בלישניה מהלקיטין ליה וה"מ הוא דמשני היכי משני אמר רב יימר בר שלמיא משמיה דאביי שתי וערב והא לא מערב שפיר אמר רב יהודה מנערו לכלי כתיב אפינקסיה דזעירי אמרית קדם רבי ומנו רבי חייא מהו לגבל אמר אסור מהו לפרק אמר מותר אמר רב [ג]מנשיא] חד קמי חד תרי קמי תרי שפיר דמי תלתא קמי תרי אסור רב יוסף אמר קב ואפילו קביים עולא אמר כור ואפילו כוריים כתיב אפינקסיה דלוי אמרית קדם רבי ומנו רבינו הקדוש על דהוו גבלין שתיתא בבבל והוה צוח רבי ומנו רבינו הקדוש על דהוו גבלין שתיתא ולית דשמע ליה ולית חילא בידיה למיסר מדרבי יוסי בר' יהודה כתיב אפינקסיה דרבי יהושע בן לוי האי מאן דבחד בשבא יהי גבר ולא חדא ביה מאי [ולא חדא ביה] אילימא ולא חד לטיבו והאמר רב אשי אנא בחד בשבא הואי אלא לאו חדא לבישו והאמר רב אשי אנא ודימי בר קקוזתא הוויין בחד בשבא אנא מלך והוא הוה ריש גנבי אלא אי כולי לטיבו אי כולי לבישו [ז](מאי טעמא דאיברו ביה אור וחושך) האי מאן דבתרי בשבא יהי גבר רגזן מ"ט משום דאיפליגו ביה מיא האי מאן דבתלתא בשבא יהי גבר עתיר וזנאי יהא מ"ט משום דאיברו ביה עשבים האי מאן דבארבעה בשבא יהי גבר חכים [ח] ונהיר מ"ט משום דאיתלו ביה מאורות האי מאן דבחמשה בשבא יהי גבר גומל חסדים מ"ט משום דאיברו ביה דגים ועופות האי מאן דבמעלי שבתא יהי גבר חזרן אמר ר"נ בר יצחק חזרן במצות האי מאן דבשבתא יהי בשבתא ימות על דאחילו עלוהי יומא רבא דשבתא אמר רבא בר רב שילא וקדישא רבא יתקרי אמר להו רבי חנינא פוקו אמרו ליה לבר ליואי לא מזל יום גורם אלא מזל שעה גורם האי מאן דבחמה (א) יהי גבר זיותן יהי אכיל מדיליה ושתי מדיליה ורזוהי גליין אם גניב לא מצלח האי מאן דבכוכב נוגה יהי גבר עתיר וזנאי יהי מ"ט משום דאיתיליד ביה נורא האי מאן דבכוכב יהי גבר נהיר וחכים משום דספרא דחמה הוא האי מאן דבלבנה יהי גבר סביל מרעין בנאי וסתיר סתיר ובנאי אכיל דלא דיליה ושתי דלא דיליה ורזוהי כסיין אם גנב מצלח האי מאן דבשבתאי יהי גבר מחשבתיה בטלין ואית דאמרי כל דמחשבין עליה בטלין האי מאן דבצדק יהי גבר צדקן אמר ר"נ בר יצחק וצדקן במצות האי מאן דבמאדים יהי גבר אשיד דמא א"ר אשי אי אומנא אי גנבא אי טבחא אי מוהלא אמר רבה אנא במאדים הואי אמר אביי מר נמי עניש וקטיל איתמר רבי חנינא אומר מזל מחכים מזל מעשיר ויש מזל לישראל רבי יוחנן אמר אין מזל לישראל ואזדא רבי יוחנן לטעמיה [י]דא"ר יוחנן מניין שאין מזל לישראל שנאמר [א]כה אמר ה' אל דרך הגוים אל תלמדו ומאותות השמים אל תחתו כי יחתו הגוים מהמה [י]הם יחתו ולא ישראל ואף רב סבר אין מזל לישראל דאמר רב יהודה אמר רב מניין שאין מזל לישראל שנאמר [ס] [ב]ויוצא אותו החוצה אמר אברהם לפני הקב"ה רבש"ע [ג]בן ביתי יורש אותי אמר לו לאו [ד]כי אם אשר יצא ממעיך אמר לפניו רבש"ע נסתכלתי באיצטגנינות שלי ואיני ראוי להוליד בן אמר ליה צא מאיצטגנינות שלך שאין מזל לישראל מאי דעתיך דקאי

רש"י

רבי יוסי בר יהודה היא. [ט](דאי רבי לא מהני ליה שינוי דמנתינת מים מיחייב אפילו במידי דלאו בר גיבול כדאמרינן גבי מורסן אבל לרבי יוסי בר יהודה) דאמר עד שיגבל הכא גובלין כלאחר יד כדמפרש ואזיל והכ"מ הוא דקא משני: שבוחשין. בתרווד דהיינו גובלין: ושותים זיתום המצרי. דבלאו רפואה נמי משקה הוא דתנן כל המשקין שותה אדם לרפואה (לעיל דף קט:): בעבה. אין גובלין ברכה בוחשין שאין זו לישה: בחול נותן החומץ כו'. כלומר כן דרכו בחול: לגבלא דבי נשיה. שומר בהמות אביו ומגבל מאכלן: דקא גביל. מורסן ע"י שינוי: בטש ביה. דהא לכולי עלמא אבל לא גובלין תנן: גובלין. מורסן ע"י שינוי כדמפרש ואזיל והוא דקא משני: ולא מספין. לתורי אין מאמירין אותן: ודלא לקיט בלישניה. עגל קטן שעדיין לא לומד לאכול: והני מילי. דאמרן דמותר לגבל מורסן: שתי וערב. פעם אחת מוליך המקל שתי ופעם אחת ערב: מנערו לכלי. והוא מתערב מאליו: אפינקסיה. לוחות קשורות זו עם זו כאותן של סוחרים: מהו לפרק. לתת מתוך כלי שלפני בהמה זו ולתת לפני חברתה: חדא קמי חדא. מילתא באפי נפשה היא אלא מדה שרגילין לתת לפני בהמה מותר לתת לפניה בשבת וכן תרתי קמי תרתי האוכלות באבוס אחד: אבל תלתא קמי תרתי. הואיל ובחול לא יהיב להו כי האי הוי טרחא דלא צריך וכ"ש תרתי קמי חדא: אמרית קמיה רבי. רבי לוי משתעי דהוא אמר קדם רבי על הנך אינשי דגבלין שתיתא: מדר' יוסי בר יהודה. בר פלוגתיה דהוה שרי לעיל אף בעבה ועל ידי שינוי והיו נוהגין כמותו: האי מאן דבחד בשבא. הנולד באחד בשבת: יהא גבר ולא חדא ביה. יהא אדם שלם במדה אחת יהא ולא אחת בו ממדה אחרת ולקמן מפרש לה ואזיל: והוא ריש גנבי. דמאן דבחד בשבא יהא ראש כמו שהיום ראש למעשה בראשית מיהו שמע מינה דנולדים בו צדיקים ורשעים: דאיפליגו מיא. כך הוא יבדל מכל אדם: זנאי. נואף: דאיברו ביה עשבים. דכתי' (בראשית א) תדשא הארץ והוא דבר שפרה ורבה מאד וממהר לגדל ולצמוח דהוא ענין פריצות אשוו"א בלע"ז [ל"א] דלא כתיב למינהו בעשבים כלווים (ועוד) שיואין בערבוביא ויונקין זו מזו: ונהיר. זיותן: דאיתלו ביה מאורות. וכתיב ותורה אור: דאיברו ביה דגים ועופות. שאין טורחין לאוכלין אלא ניזונים בחסדו של הקב"ה: חזרן. מחזר אחר מצות: חזרן במצות. שכן דרך ע"ש לחזר אחר מצות שבת: וקדישא רבה יתקרי. שיהא פרוש וקדוש דכתיב (שמות כ) ויקדשהו: אמר להו רבי חנינא. לתלמידים שקראו פנקסו של ר' יהושע: מזל שעה. ז' מזלות הן המשמשין את השעות שנכ"ל שצ"ם חמה היינו חמה ממש והוא אחד מן המזלות וכן לבנה והשאר הויין כוכבים: זיותן. כשמש המאיר: אכיל מדיליה. כשמש שאינו מסיג גבול רעהו למשול בלילה: ורזוהי גליין. אין לו רשות לכסות סודו ונסתרותיו אלא כשמש הזה שהוא פומבי לכל: דתלי ביה נורא. אש תלוי באותו מזל יקר של תשמיש בוער כתנור: מזל כוכב. הוא סופר של מזל חמה לכתוב דרך הילוכו ותקופותיו ומצוי אצלו תמיד: סביל מרעין. כלבנה זו (ג) שמתנוונה והולכת: בנאי וסתיר. כלבנה זו שגדילה ומתמעטת: אכיל לא דיליה. • כלבנה המסגת גבול החמה למשול אף ביום: ורזוהי כסיין. כלבנה שאינה מאירה: דבשבתאי. מזל כוכב ששמו שבתאי: בטלין. כמו לא ישבותו (בראשית ח): צדקן במצות. לדקה לעניים דקרי ליה מצוה (בכל לשון אגדה): גנבא. ליסטים ההורג נפשות: אומנא. מקיז דם: עניש. בני אדם העוברין על דבריו: מזל מחכים. לפי המזל היא החכמה כדאמר דבחמה נהיר וחכים: ויש מזל לישראל. שאין תפלה ולדקה משנה את המזל: אין מזל לישראל. דעל ידי תפלה וזכות משתנה מזלו לטובה: איצטגנינות. חכמת המזלות: צא מאיצטגנינותך. היינו דכתיב ויוצא אותו החוצה חוץ מאיצטגנינותו:

תוספות

מהו לפרק. פירש בקונטרס לפרק מלפני בהמה זו וליתן לפני אחרת וכן פירש בערוך בערך פרק וקשה לר"י דהיינו מתניתין גבי בהמה (לעיל דף קמ:) ונראה לר"י לפרק היינו להריק המים וגם המורסן מכלי אל כלי שתגבל היטב ובערוך פירש כמה לשונות:

אין מזל לישראל. והא דאמר רבא בשילהי מו"ק (דף כח. ושם) בני חיי ומזוני לאו בזכותא תליא מילתא אלא במזלא תליא מילתא מכל מקום על ידי זכות גדול משתנה אבל פעמים שאין המזל משתנה כדאמר ביבמות פרק החולץ (דף נ. ושם) זכה מוסיפין לו לא זכה פוחתין לו [י](דאין מזל לישראל): כלדאי

עין משפט נר מצוה

לא א ב ג ד מיי' שם הלכה לג סמג שם טוש"ע א"ח סימן שכא סעיף יד:

גליון הש"ס

גמרא אתא אבוה אשכחיה. עי' לעיל דף כג ע"ב תוס' ד"ה דבי נשא: רש"י ד"ה אכיל דלא דיליה כלבנה המסגת. עיין דבר נחמד בזה בכתנות אור לבעל פמ"א בפ' בראשית:

רבינו חננאל

ואין צ"ל שמלקטין כו' ופריק רב יהודה הכי לעולם פי' מתניתא דאמר כך היא מהלקטין דספו ליה בידיה והיא פחותה מהלעטה שאמרנו ומלקטין שמשליך לפניה שעורים וכיוצא בהן דברים שהן מאכל לעופות. ואין משליכין מאכל לפני יוני שובך ויוני [עליה] לפי שאינן [בני] תרבות ואין מזונותן עליך וכי [הא] דתניא נותנין מזונות לפני הכלב ואין נותנין מזונות לפני חזיר ומה הפרש בין זה לזה כלב מזונותיו עליך חזיר אין מזונותיו עליך ובא רב אשי לסייע דברי רב יהודה ולומר שנויא דשני שינויא היא מדוקיא דמתניתין דקתני אין נותנין מים לפני דבורים ולפני יונים שבשובך אבל נותנים לפני אווזים ותרנגולים ולפני יוני הרדוסיית מ"ט לאו משו' דהני מזונותיו עליך והני אין מזונותיו עליך ולא עמדו דברי רב אשי והלכה כרב יהודה דתניא כוותיה דתניא איזו היא המראה ואיזו היא הלעטה המראה מרביצה ופוקס את פיה ומאכילה כרשינין ומים בבת אחת. הלעטה מאכילה מעומד ומשקה מעומד ונותן לה כרשינין בפ"ע ומים בפ"ע: מהלקטין לתרנגולים ונותנין מים למורסן אבל לא גובלין אוקימנא לר' יוסי ב"ר יהודה דתניא אחד נותן את הקמח ואחד נותן לתוכו מים האחרון חייב דברי ר' ור' יוסי בר יהודה אומר עד שיגבל אלמא אמרינן [דנתינת מים זהו גיבולו] ממאי דלמא עד כאן לא קאמר ר' יוסי ב"ר יהודה עד שיגבל אלא בקמח דבר גיבול הוא. אבל מורסן דלאו בר גיבול הוא אפי' ר' יוסי ב"ר יהודה מודי שנתינת מים למורסן אסור שזהו גיבולו ואשכחנן תניא בהדיא אין נותנין מים למורסן דברי ר' [ר'] יוסי ב"ר יהודה אומר נותנים מים למורסן ואע"ג דבכל מקום הלכתא כרבי מחבירו הכא הלכה כר' יוסי דתנינן מתניתין סתמא כוותיה. ותוב מהא דכתוב אפינקסיה דלוי אמרית קדם רבינו הקדוש והוא רבי עד דהוו גבלין שתיתא בבבל והוא צווח רבי דלית דשמע ליה ולית חילא בידיה למיסר מדר' יוסי ב"ר יהודה מהא נמי שמעינן דהלכתא כר' יוסי ב"ר יהודה דהוא בר פלוגתיה לא אסר ונפק עובדא כוותיה: ת"ר אין גובלין את הקליא וי"א גובלין ואמרינן מאן י"א ואמר רב חסדא ר' יוסי ב"ר יהודה היא והוא דמשני היכי משני אמר רב חסדא על יד על יד פי' מעט מעט מדמתרץ רב חסדא אליבא דר' יוסי ב"ר יהודה הלכתא

מסורת הש"ס

א) כריתות לח., ב) [ל"ל נשא ועמ"ש תוספות לעיל כג: ד"ה דבי], ג) [ע' תוספות חולין ד. ד"ה מכניס וכו' דגרסי רב מנשה], ד) רש"ל מ"ז, ה) [פי' זכרון ערוך], ו) [סוכה כט.], ח) [מדרש לב.], ט) רש"ל מ"ז, י) ר"מ מוחק זה.

הגהות הב"ח

(א) גמ' מאן דבחמה יהא כו'. נ"ב ...

תורה אור השלם

א) כֹּה אָמַר יְיָ אֶל דֶּרֶךְ הַגּוֹיִם אַל תִּלְמָדוּ וּמֵאֹתוֹת הַשָּׁמַיִם אַל תֵּחָתּוּ כִּי יֵחַתּוּ הַגּוֹיִם מֵהֵמָּה: [ירמיה י, ב]

ב) וַיּוֹצֵא אֹתוֹ הַחוּצָה וַיֹּאמֶר הַבֶּט נָא הַשָּׁמַיְמָה וּסְפֹר הַכּוֹכָבִים אִם תּוּכַל לִסְפֹּר אֹתָם וַיֹּאמֶר לוֹ כֹּה יִהְיֶה זַרְעֶךָ: [בראשית טו, ה]

ג) וַיֹּאמֶר אַבְרָם הֵן לִי לֹא נָתַתָּה זָרַע וְהִנֵּה בֶן בֵּיתִי יוֹרֵשׁ אֹתִי: [בראשית טו, ג]

ד) וְהִנֵּה דְבַר יְיָ אֵלָיו לֵאמֹר לֹא יִירָשְׁךָ זֶה כִּי אִם אֲשֶׁר יֵצֵא מִמֵּעֶיךָ הוּא יִירָשֶׁךָ: [בראשית טו, ד]

ליקוטי רש"י

על יד על יד. מעט מעט [ביצה יב:]. שתית. מאכל שעושין מקמח קליות ...

לאחד של אחד בשבת חמה ושל שני בשבת לבנה ושל שלישי בשבת מאדים [לעיל קכט:]. אל דרך הגוים אל תלמדו. ולא מאותות השמים אל תחתו מחמה לוקה ומהמזלות לוקין [ירמיהו י, ב]. לעשות כמעשיהם ומשמעו לענין מאותות השמים אל תחתו [סוכה כט.]. איצטגנינות. לפיות בקי בהליכות המזלות ותחילת השעות דהכי תניא בבבא בתרא (טז:) ה' בירך את אברהם בכל איצטגנינות גדולה היתה בלבו וכל מלכי מזרח ומערב משכימין לפתחו לשאול במזלות [יומא כח:]. איצטגנינות לשון מזלות וחוזים בכוכבים [סנהדרין סה:]. צא מאיצטגנינות שלך. ממפשט חכמת מזלות שלך והיינו דכתיב (בראשית טו) ויוצא אותו החוצה [ר"ן נדרים לב.].

means he will be **without one** trace **of goodness,** that cannot be, וְהָאָמַר רַב אַשִׁי – **for Rav Ashi has said:** אֲנָא בְּחַד בְּשַׁבָּא הֲוַאי – **I was born on a Sunday.** Obviously, Rav Ashi had more than a trace of goodness! אֶלָּא לָאו – **Is it not,** then, that he will be without חֲדָא לְבִישׁוּ – **one** trace **of badness?** But this cannot be either, וְהָאָמַר רַב אַשִׁי – **for Rav Ashi has** also **said:** אֲנָא וְדִימִי בַּר קַקּוּזְתָא הֲוֵויַן בְּחַד בְּשַׁבָּא – **I and Dimi bar Kakuzta were** both **born on a Sunday:** אֲנָא מֶלֶךְ וְהוּא הֲוָה רֵישׁ גַּנָּבֵי – **I became a king,** i.e. the head of a Torah academy, **and he became a leader** of a gang of **thieves.**[26] אֶלָּא – **Rather,** it must really mean this: אִי כּוּלֵּי לְטִיבוּ אִי כּוּלֵּי לְבִישׁוּ – **Either** the person's nature will be **all good** without a trace of bad **or all bad** without a trace of good.[27]

The Gemara explains:

(מַאי טַעְמָא – **What is the reason** a person born on a Sunday will tend to extremes? דְּאִיבְּרוּ בֵּיהּ אוֹר וְחוֹשֶׁךְ – **Because on [Sunday],** the first day of Creation, **light and darkness were created.**)

The ledger record continues:

הַאי מַאן דְּבִתְרֵי בְּשַׁבָּא – **He who is** born **on a Monday** יְהֵי גְּבַר רַגְזָן – **will be an angry man.** מַאי טַעְמָא – **What is the reason?** מִשּׁוּם דְּאִיפְּלִיגוּ בֵּיהּ מַיָּא – **Because on [Monday]** of Creation **the waters were divided.**[28] הַאי מַאן דִּבְתְלָתָא בְּשַׁבָּא – **He who is** born **on a Tuesday** יְהֵי גְּבַר עָתִיר – **will be a wealthy man,** וְזַנַּאי יְהֵא – **and he will be a promiscuous man.**[29] מַאי טַעְמָא – **What is the reason?** מִשּׁוּם דְּאִיבְּרוּ בֵּיהּ עֲשָׂבִים – **Because on** [Tuesday] of Creation **herbage was created.**[30] הַאי מַאן דְּבְאַרְבָּעָה בְּשַׁבָּא – **He who is** born **on a Wednesday** יְהֵי גְּבַר חַכִּים וְנָהִיר – **will be a wise and radiant**[31] **man.** מַאי טַעְמָא – **What is the reason?** מִשּׁוּם דְּאִיתְּלוּ בֵּיהּ מְאוֹרוֹת – **Because on** [Wednesday] of Creation **the luminaries were set in place.**[32] הַאי מַאן דִּבְחַמְשָׁא בְּשַׁבָּא – **He who is** born **on a Thursday** יְהֵי גְּבַר גּוֹמֵל חֲסָדִים – **will be a man who performs deeds of kindness.** מַאי טַעְמָא – **What is the reason?** מִשּׁוּם דְּאִיבְּרוּ בֵּיהּ דָּגִים וְעוֹפוֹת – **Because on [Thursday]** of Creation **fish and fowl were created.**[33] הַאי מַאן דִּבְמַעֲלֵי שַׁבְּתָא – **He who is** born **on a Friday** יְהֵי גְּבַר חַזְרָן – **will be an assiduous man.**

The Gemara explains:

אָמַר רַב נַחְמָן בַּר יִצְחָק – **R' Nachman bar Yitzchak said:** חַזְרָן בְּמִצְוֹת – **Assiduous in** the pursuit of **mitzvos.**[34]

The ledger record continues:

הַאי מַאן דְּבְשַׁבְּתָא – **He who is** born **on a Sabbath** יְהֵי בְּשַׁבְּתָא יָמוּת – **will** be destined to **die on a Sabbath,** עַל דְּאַחִילוּ עֲלוֹהִי יוֹמָא רַבָּא דְשַׁבְּתָא – **since they had to desecrate the great day of Sabbath on his behalf.**[35]

The Gemara adds:

אָמַר רָבָא בַּר רַב שִׁילָא – **Rava bar Rav Shila said:** וְקַדִּישָׁא רַבָּא יִתְקְרֵי – **And he shall be called a great and holy [man].**[36]

The Gemara cites an opinion dissenting from the one reflected in R' Yehoshua ben Levi's ledger:

אָמַר לְהוּ רַבִּי חֲנִינָא – **R' Chanina said to [the students who read the ledger]:** פּוּקוּ אֱמַרוּ לֵיהּ לְבַר לֵיוָאִי – **Go out and tell the son of Leva'i** [R' Yehoshua ben Levi]: לֹא מַזָּל יוֹם גּוֹרֵם – **It is not** the celestial **sign of the day that influences** a man's nature; אֶלָּא מַזָּל שָׁעָה גּוֹרֵם – **rather it is the** celestial **sign** that dominates at **the hour** of one's birth[37] **that influences** a man's nature, as follows: הַאי מַאן דִּבְחַמָּה – **He who is** born **during** the hour of **the sun** יְהֵי גְּבַר זִיוְתָן – **will be a person of lustrous appearance.** יְהֵי אָכִיל מִדִּילֵיהּ וְשָׁתֵי מִדִּילֵיהּ – **He will eat of his own** food **and drink of his own** beverages, וְרָזוֹהִי גַּלְיָין – **but his secrets will be revealed** to all. אִם גָּנִיב לֹא מַצְלַח – **If he** attempts to **steal, he will not be successful.**[38] הַאי מַאן דְּבְכוֹכָב נוֹגַהּ – **He who is** born **during** the hour of **the planet Venus** יְהֵי גְּבַר עָתִיר וְזַנַּאי יְהֵי – **will be a wealthy man and will be a promiscuous man.** מַאי טַעְמָא – **What is the reason?** מִשּׁוּם דְּאִיתְיְלִיד בֵּיהּ נוּרָא – **Because the fire** of passion **burns in it.**[39] הַאי מַאן דְּבְכוֹכָב – **He who is** born **during** the hour of **Mercury** יְהֵי גְּבַר נָהִיר וְחַכִּים – **will be a radiant and wise man.** מִשּׁוּם דְּסַפְרָא דְחַמָּה הוּא – **Because [Mercury] is the secretary,** i.e. the constant companion, **of the sun.**[40] הַאי מַאן דִּבְלְבָנָה – **He who** is born **during** the hour of **the moon** יְהֵי גְּבַר סָבִיל מַרְעִין – **will be a man who suffers afflictions.** בָּנֵאי וְסָתִיר – **He will build and raze,** סָתִיר וּבָנֵאי – **raze and build.** אָכִיל דְּלָא דִילֵיהּ וְשָׁתֵי דְּלָא דִילֵיהּ – **He will** have to **eat** food **that is not his own and drink** beverages **that are not his own,** וְרָזוֹהִי כַּסְיָין – **but his secrets will remain concealed.** אִם גָּנַב מַצְלַח – **If he** attempts **to steal, he will succeed.**[41] הַאי מַאן דְּבְשַׁבְּתַאי – **He who is**

NOTES

26. Rav Ashi's point is that a person born on Sunday will be a leader of something, just as Sunday leads off the rest of the week. However, we see that both righteous and wicked people are born that day (*Rashi*).

27. Rav Ashi was all virtue; Dimi, all vice (see *Maharshal; Hagahos Chochmas Manoach*).

28. *Genesis* 1:6,7. Similarly, division will exist between him and all others (*Rashi*).

29. I.e. an adulterer (*Rashi*).

30. As it says: *Let the earth fill up with herbage* (*Genesis* 1:11). *Rashi* presents two explanations: (a) Herbage sprouts and grows very quickly; this is related to the idea of promiscuity and wealth; (b) [Unlike trees,] the command creating herbage did not specify that each herb should stay within its species. As a result, different varieties of herbs would grow together, deriving nourishment from one another (but see *Chulin* 60a). [This parallels a man who consorts with the wives of other men.]

31. I.e. lustrous in appearance (*Rashi;* cf. *Rashash*).

32. *Genesis* 1:16,17. [Accordingly, he will be wise in Torah,] as it says: *And Torah is light* (*Proverbs* 6:23) (*Rashi*).

33. *Genesis* 1:21. Fish and birds do not expend much effort in acquiring their food; rather, they are supported by God, Who, in His kindness, [makes the food easily available to them].

34. Typically, one spends part of Friday pursuing preparations for the mitzvos of the Sabbath (*Rashi;* cf. *Maharsha*).

35. Childbirth on the Sabbath inevitably entails certain Sabbath violations. Since the Sabbath had to be desecrated for him, it is fitting that his demise occur on the Sabbath.

See *Teshuvos Maharil* (§203) who notes that many people who are born on the Sabbath do not die on the Sabbath; the Gemara means only that he ought to die on the Sabbath, but other factors, merits and demerits, may intervene to cause him to die on a different day.

36. I.e. he will be a pious and holy man, as it says (*Exodus* 20:11): *Therefore God blessed the seventh day and sanctified it* (*Rashi;* see *Maharsha*).

37. There are seven celestial bodies each of whose influence holds sway during successive hours of the day and night: The sun, the moon and five planets, viz. Venus, Mercury, Saturn, Jupiter and Mars. This cycle of seven hours repeats itself endlessly (see above, 129b, note 11 and chart there; see also *Pirkei DeR' Eliezer* ch. 5).

38. He will be luminous like the shining sun; he will not consume the property of others just as the sun does not encroach upon its colleague's territory (i.e. the sun does not shine during the night); he will be unable to cover up his private matters from others, similar to the sun which is in full view of all (*Rashi*).

39. This planet is associated with fire, i.e. lust (see *Maharsha*), which burns in the heart like a furnace (*Rashi;* see also *Rashash*).

40. Mercury appears as a scribe following his master around in order to write [whatever is dictated him]. Thus, Mercury follows the sun in its path through the heavens and in all seasons (*Rashi*).

41. He will build and raze, then build again, just as the moon waxes, wanes and waxes again. He will need to nourish himself from the food of others like the moon which infringes on the sun's territory and appears during the day. He will succeed in being discreet similar to the moon which does not give off [a full] light (*Rashi;* see *Rashash*).

רבי יוסי בר יהודה היא. [ט] (דאי רבי לא מהני ליה שינוי דמנתינת מים מחייב אפילו במידי דלאו בר גיבול כדאמרינן גבי מורסן אבל לרבי יוסי בר יהודה) דאמר עד שיגבל הכא גובלין כלאחר יד כדמפרש ואזיל והנ"מ הוא דקא משני: שבוחשין. בתרווד דהיינו גובלין: ושותים זיתום המצרי. דבלאו רפואה נמי משקה הוא דתנן כל המשקין שותה אדם לרפואה (לעיל דף קט:): בעבה. אין גובלין ברכה. בוחשין שאין זו לישה: בחול נותן החומץ כו'. כלומר כן דרכו בחול: לגבלא דבי נשיה. שומר בהמות אביו ומגבל מאכלן: דקא גביל. מורסן ע"י שינוי: בטש ביה. דהא לכולי עלמא אבל לא גובלין תנן: גובלין. מורסן ע"י שינוי כדמפרש ואזיל והוא דקא משני: ולא מספין. לתורי אין מאמירין אותן: ודלא לקיט בלישניה. עגל קטן שעדיין לא לומד לאכול: והני מילי. דאמרן דמותר לגבל מורסן: שתי וערב. פעם אחת מוליך המקל שתי ופעם אחת ערב: מנערו לכלי. והוא מתערב מאליו: אפינקסיה. לוחות קשורות זו עם זו כאותן של סוחרים: מהו לפרק. לתת מתוך כלי שלפני בהמה זו ולתת לפני חברתה: חדא קמי חדא. מילתא באפי נפשה היא חדא מדה שרגילין לתת לפני בהמה מותר לתת לפניה בשבת וכן תרתי קמי תרתי האוכלות באבוס אחד: אבל תלתא קמי תרתי. ואזיל ובחול לא יהיב להו כי האי הוי טרחא דלא צריך וכ"ש תרתי קמי חדא: אמרית קמיה רבי. רבי לוי משתעי דהוא אמר קדם רבי על הנך איניש דגבלין שתיתא: מדר' יוסי בר יהודה. בר פלוגתיה דהוה שרי לעיל אף בעבה ועל ידי שינוי והיו נוהגין כמותו: האי מאן דבחד בשבא. הנולד באחד בשבת: יהא גבר ולא חדא ביה. יהא אדם שלם במדה אחת יהא ולא אחת בו ממדה אחרת ולקמן מפרש לה ואזיל: והוא ריש גנבי. דמאן דבחד בשבא יהא ראש כמו שהיום ראש למעשה בראשית מיהו שמע מינה דנולדים בו צדיקים ורשעים: דאיפליגו מיא. כך הוא יבדל מכל אדם: זנאי. נואף: דאיברו ביה עשבים. דכתי' (בראשית א) תדשא הארץ והוא דבר שפרה ורבה מאד וממהר לגדל ולצמוח והוא ענין פריצות אשו"א בלע"ז [נ"א] דלא כתיב למינהו בעשבים כוויים (ועוד) שיונקין בערבוביא ויונקין זו מזו: ונהיר. זיותן: דאיתלו ביה מאורות. וכתיב ותורה אור: דאיברו ביה דגים ועופות. שאין טורחין לאוכלין אלא ניזונים בחסדו של הקב"ה: חזרן. מחזר אחר מצות: חזרן במצות. שכן דרך ע"ש לחזר אחר מצות שבת: וקדישא רבה יתקרי. שיהא פרוש וקדוש דכתיב (שמות כ) ויקדשהו: אמר להו רבי חנינא. לתלמידים שקראו פנקסו של ר' יהושע: מזל שעה. ז' מזלות הן המשמשין את השעות סנכ"ל שצ"ם חמה היינו חמה ממש והוא אחד מן המזלות וכן לבנה והשאר הויין כוכבים: זיותן. כשמש המאיר: אכיל מדיליה. כשמש שאינו מסיג גבול רעהו למשול בלילה: ורזוהי גליין. אין לו רשות לכסות סודו ונסתרותיו אלא כשמש הזה שהוא פומבי לכל: דתלי ביה נורא. אם תלוי באותו מזל יצר של תשמיש בוער כתנור: מזל כוכב. הוא סופר של מזל חמה לכתוב דרך הילוכו ותקופותיו ומלוי אצלו תמיד: סביל מרעין. כלבנה זו (ג) שמתנונה והולכת: בנאי וסתיר. כלבנה זו שגדילה ומתמעטת: אכיל לא דיליה. ° כלבנה המסגת גבול החמה למשול אף ביום: ורזוהי כסיין. כלבנה שאינה מאירה: דבשבתאי. מזל כוכב ששמו שבתאי: בטלין. כמו לא ישבותו (בראשית ח): צדקן במצות. צדקה לעניים דקרי ליה מצוה (בכל לשון אגדה): גנבא. ליסטים ההורג נפשות: אומנא. מקיז דם: עניש. בני אדם העוברין על דבריו: מזל מחכים. לפי המזל היא החכמה כדאמר דבחמה נהיר וחכים: ויש מזל לישראל. שאין תפלה וצדקה משנה את המזל: אין מזל לישראל. דעל ידי תפלה וזכות משתנה מזלו לטובה: איצטגנינות. חכמת המזלות: צא מאיצטגנינותך. היינו דכתיב ויוצא אותו החוצה חוץ מאיצטגנינותו:

דקאי

רבי יוסי בר' יהודה היא והנ"מ הוא [א] דמשני היכי משני א"ר חסדא [ב] על יד על יד [ה] ושוין שבוחשין את השתית בשבת ושותים זיתום המצרי והאמרת אין גובלין ל"ק הא [ג] בעבה הא ברכה והני מילי הוא דמשני היכי משני אמר רב יוסף בחול נותן את החומץ ואח"כ נותן את השתית [ד] בשבת נותן את השתית ואח"כ נותן את החומץ לוי בריה דרב הונא בר חייא אשכחיה לגבלא דבי [ו] נשיה דקא גביל וספי ליה לתוריה בטש ביה [ה] אתא אבוה אשכחיה א"ל הכי אמר אבוה דאמך משמיה דרב ומנו רבי ירמיה בר אבא גובלין ולא מספין ודלא לקיט בלישניה מהלקיטין ליה וה"מ הוא דמשני היכי משני אמר רב ימר בר שלמיא משמיה דאביי שתי וערב והא לא מערב שפיר אמר רב יהודה מנערו לכלי כתיב אפינקסיה דזעירי אמרית קדם רבי ומנו רבי חייא מהו לגבל אמר אסור מהו לפרק אמר מותר אמר רב [[ג] מנשיא] חד קמי חד תרי קמי תרי שפיר דמי תלתא קמי תרי אסור רב יוסף אמר קב ואפילו קביים עולא אמר כור ואפילו כוריים כתיב אפינקסיה דלוי אמרית קדם רבי ומנו רבינו הקדוש על דהוו גבלין שתיתא בבבל והוה צוח רבי ומנו רבינו הקדוש על דהוו גבלין שתיתא ולית דשמיע ליה ולית חילא בידיה למיסר מדרבי יוסי בר' יהודה כתיב אפינקסיה דרבי יהושע בן לוי האי מאן דבחד בשבא יהי גבר ולא חדא ביה מאי [ולא חדא ביה] אילימא ולא חד לטיבו והאמר רב אשי אנא בחד בשבא הואי אלא לאו חדא לבישו והאמר רב אשי אנא ודימי בר קקוזתא הוויין בחד בשבא אנא מלך והוא הוה ריש גנבי אלא אי כולי לטיבו אי כולי לבישו [ז] (מאי טעמא דאיברו ביה אור וחושך) האי מאן דבתרי בשבא יהי גבר רגזן מ"ט משום דאיפליגו ביה מיא האי מאן דבתלתא בשבא יהי גבר עתיר וזנאי יהא מ"ט משום דאיברו ביה עשבים האי מאן דבארבעה בשבא יהי גבר חכים [ח] ונהיר מ"ט משום דאיתלו ביה מאורות האי מאן דבחמשה בשבא יהי גבר גומל חסדים מ"ט משום דאיברו ביה דגים ועופות האי מאן דבמעלי שבתא יהי גבר חזרן אמר ר"נ בר יצחק חזרן במצות האי מאן דבשבתא יהי בשבתא ימות על דאחילו עלוהי יומא רבא דשבתא אמר רבא בר רב שילא וקדישא רבא יתקרי אמר להו רבי חנינא פוקו אמרו ליה לבר ליואי לא מזל יום גורם אלא מזל שעה גורם האי מאן דבחמה (א) יהי גבר זיותן יהי אכיל מדיליה ושתי מדיליה ורזוהי גליין אם גניב לא מצלח האי מאן דבכוכב נוגה יהי גבר עתיר וזנאי יהי מ"ט משום דאיתיליד ביה נורא האי מאן דבכוכב יהי גבר נהיר וחכים משום דספרא דחמה הוא האי מאן דבלבנה יהי גבר סביל מרעין בנאי וסתיר וסתיר ובנאי אכיל דלא דיליה ושתי דלא דיליה ורזוהי כסיין אם גנב מצלח האי מאן דבשבתאי יהי גבר מחשבתיה בטלין ואית דאמרי כל דמחשבין עליה בטלין האי מאן דבצדק יהי גבר צדקן אמר ר"נ בר יצחק וצדקן במצות האי מאן דבמאדים יהי גבר אשיד דמא א"ר אשי אי אומנא אי גנבא אי טבחא אי מוהלא אמר רבה אנא במאדים הואי אמר אביי מר נמי עניש וקטיל איתמר רבי חנינא אומר מזל מחכים מזל מעשיר ויש מזל לישראל רבי יוחנן אמר אין מזל לישראל ואזדא רבי יוחנן לטעמיה [ט] דא"ר יוחנן מניין שאין מזל לישראל שנאמר [א] כה אמר ה' אל דרך הגוים אל תלמדו ומאותות השמים אל תחתו כי יחתו הגוים מהמה [י] הם יחתו ולא ישראל ואף רב סבר אין מזל לישראל דאמר רב יהודה אמר רב מניין שאין מזל לישראל שנאמר [כ] [ב] ויוצא אותו החוצה אמר אברהם לפני הקב"ה רבש"ע [ג] בן ביתי יורש אותי אמר לו לאו [ד] כי אם אשר יצא ממעיך אמר לפניו רבש"ע נסתכלתי באיצטגנינות שלי ואיני ראוי להוליד בן אמר ליה צא מאיצטגנינות שלך שאין מזל לישראל מאי דעתיך

דקאי

מהו לפרק. פירש בקונטרס לפרק מלפני בהמה זו וליתן לפני אחרת וכן פירש בערוך בערך פרק וקשה לר"י דהיינו מתניתין גבי בהמה (לעיל דף קמ:) ונראה לר"י לפרק היינו להריק המים וגם המורסן מכלי אל כלי שתגבל היטב ובערוך פירש כמה לשונות:

אין מזל לישראל. והא דאמר רבא בשילהי מו"ק (דף כח. ושם) בני חיי ומזוני לאו בזכותא תליא מילתא אלא במזלא תליא מילתא מכל מקום על ידי זכות גדול משתנה אבל פעמים שאין המזל משתנה כדאמר ביבמות פרק החולץ (דף נ. ושם) זכה מוסיפין לו לא זכה פוחתין לו [י] (דאין מזל לישראל):

כלדאי

עין משפט נר מצוה

לא א ב ג ד מיי' שם הלכה לג סמג שם טוש"ע א"ח סימן שכד סעיף יד:

גליון הש"ס

גמרא אתא אבוה אשכחיה. עי' לעיל דף כג ע"ב תוס' ד"ה דכי נסו: רש"י ד"ה אכיל דלא דיליה כלבנה המסגת. עיין דבר נחמד בזה בכתונת אור לגול פמ"א בפ' בראשית:

מסורת הש"ס

א) ברכות לח. ב) [נ"ל בשא ועמ"ש תוספות לעיל כב. ד"ה דכי], ג) [ער' תוספות חולין ד. ד"ה מכניס וכו' דגרסי רב מנשה], ד) רש"ל מ"ז, ה) [ער' ערוך ערך זכר], ו) [סוכה כט.], ז) [סוכה כט.], ח) [נדרים לב.], ט) רש"ל מ"ז, י) רש"ל מוחק זה.

הגהות הב"ח

(א) גמ' מאן דבחמה יהא גבר. נ"ב תחלת סדר הליכתן שצ"ם חנכ"ל (וכאן נקט מנכ"ל שצ"ם) לפי סדר סימני הימים חל"ם לכ"ש נקט חמה ברישא והדר נקט נוגה וכו' לפי סדר [השעות וכמבואר בשמשות מזל] חמה שהוא משמש בתחלת יום א' נמצא סדר השעות כסדר שצ"ם ואחר סלילה כלומר כסדר חל"ם מפנין ע"ש: (ב) רש"י ד"ה סביל וכו' זו שמתמעטת והולכת:

תורה אור השלם

א) כֹּה אָמַר יְיָ אֶל דֶּרֶךְ הַגּוֹיִם אַל תִּלְמָדוּ וּמֵאֹתוֹת הַשָּׁמַיִם אַל תֵּחָתּוּ כִּי יֵחַתּוּ הַגּוֹיִם מֵהֵמָּה: [ירמיה י, ב]

ב) וַיּוֹצֵא אֹתוֹ הַחוּצָה וַיֹּאמֶר הַבֶּט נָא הַשָּׁמַיְמָה וּסְפֹר הַכּוֹכָבִים אִם תּוּכַל לִסְפֹּר אֹתָם וַיֹּאמֶר לוֹ כֹּה יִהְיֶה זַרְעֶךָ: [בראשית טו, ה]

ג) וַיֹּאמֶר אַבְרָם הֵן לִי לֹא נָתַתָּה זָרַע וְהִנֵּה בֶן בֵּיתִי יוֹרֵשׁ אֹתִי: [בראשית טו, ג]

ד) וְהִנֵּה דְבַר יְיָ אֵלָיו לֵאמֹר לֹא יִירָשְׁךָ זֶה כִּי אִם אֲשֶׁר יֵצֵא מִמֵּעֶיךָ הוּא יִירָשֶׁךָ: [בראשית טו, ד]

ליקוטי רש"י

על יד על יד. מעט מעט [ביצה יב:]. ... ראשונה שלו כוכב תחלת ליל שני לדק וכן בסדר הזה וסדר תחלת סימני הימים חל"ם כלנ"ש שעה ראשונה של אחד בשבת חמה ושל שני בשבת לבנה ושל שלישי בשבת מאדים [לעיל קכט:]. אל דרך הגוים אל תלמדו. ולא מאותות השמים אל תחתו ממאה לוקה וממאורות לוקין [ירמיהו י, ב]. לעשות כמעשיהם ומשמעו רצונו מאותות השמים אל תחתו [סוכה כט.]. איצטגנינות. להיות בקי בהליכות המזלות ותחילות השעות דהכי מגיא בבבא בתרא (טז:) וה' ברך את אברהם בכל איצטגנינות גדולה היתה בלבו וכל מלכי מזרח ומערב משכימין לפתחו לשאול במזלות [יומא כח:]. איצטגנינות דכל הש"ס לשון מזלות ומחשב כוכבים [סנהדרין מט.]. צא מאיצטגנינות שלך. ממשפט חכמת מזלות שלך והיינו דכתיב (בראשית טו) ויוצא אותו החוצה [ר"ן נדרים לב.].

רבינו חננאל

... יוסי ב"ר יהודה מהא נמי שמעינן דהלכתא כר' יוסי ב"ר יהודה דהוא בר פלוגתיה לא אסר ונפק עובדא כוותיה: ת"ר אין גובלין את הקליא וי"א גובלין ואמרינן מאן י"א ואמר רב חסדא ר' יוסי ב"ר יהודה היא והוא דמשני היכי משני אמר רב חסדא על יד על יד פי' מעט מעט מדמתרץ רב חסדא אליבא דר' יוסי ב"ר יהודה הלכתא

born **during** the hour of **Saturn** יְהֵי גְּבַר מַחְשְׁבָתֵיהּ בְּטֵלִין **– will be a man whose every plan comes to naught.**[42] וְאִית דְּאָמְרִי **– But some say:** כֹּל דְּמַחְשְׁבִין עֲלֵיהּ בְּטֵילִין **– Every plan that is plotted against him will come to naught.** הָאי מַאן דִּבְצֶדֶק **– He who is** born **during** the hour of **Jupiter** יְהֵי גְּבַר צַדְקָן **– will be a man of rectitude.**

The Gemara explains:

אָמַר רַב נַחְמָן בַּר יִצְחָק **– R' Nachman bar Yitzchak said:** וְצַדְקָן בְּמִצְוֹת **– That** means he will be **a man of rectitude regarding mitzvos,** i.e. he will be charitable.[43]

R' Chanina concludes:

הָאי מַאן דִּבְמַאְדִים **– He who is** born **during** the hour of **Mars** יְהֵי גְּבַר אָשֵׁיד דְּמָא **– will be a man who spills blood.**[44]

The Gemara explains:

אָמַר רַבִּי אַשִׁי **– R' Ashi said:** He is destined to be a spiller of blood in some way, אִי אוּמָּנָא אִי גַּנָּבָא אִי טַבָּחָא אִי מוֹהֲלָא **– whether** he becomes **a bloodletter or a thief**[45] **or a** ***shochet*** **or a** ***mohel.***

The Gemara objects to R' Chanina's opinion:

אָמַר רַבָּה **– Rabbah said:** אֲנָא בְּמַאְדִים הֲוַאי **– I was born during** the hour of **Mars,** and yet I am not a spiller of blood!

The Gemara responds:

אָמַר אַבַּיֵי **– Abaye said to him:** מַר נַמִּי עָנִישׁ וְקָטֵיל **– The master has also punished and killed** those who violate his rulings. Thus, in this sense, you are also a spiller of blood.[46]

A fundamental dispute:

אִיתְּמַר **– It was stated:** רַבִּי חֲנִינָא אוֹמֵר **– R' Chanina says:** מַזָּל מַחְכִּים **– The** celestial **sign** of one's birth **determines intelligence;**[47] מַזָּל מַעֲשִׁיר **– the** celestial **sign** of one's birth **determines wealth;** וְיֵשׁ מַזָּל לְיִשְׂרָאֵל **– and the** celestial **signs hold sway** even **over Israel,** i.e. no one can escape the fate foretold by the celestial signs.[48] רַבִּי יוֹחָנָן אָמַר **– R' Yochanan says:** אֵין מַזָּל לְיִשְׂרָאֵל **– The** celestial **signs hold no sway over Israel,** i.e. prayer and merits can prevail over the fate they foretell.[49] וְאָזְדָא רַבִּי יוֹחָנָן לְטַעְמֵיהּ **– And R' Yochanan follows his own reasoning** expressed elsewhere, דְּאָמַר רַבִּי יוֹחָנָן **– for R' Yochanan said:** מִנַּיִין שֶׁאֵין מַזָּל לְיִשְׂרָאֵל **– From where do we know that the** celestial **signs hold no sway over Israel?** שֶׁנֶּאֱמַר **– As it says:**[50] "כֹּה אָמַר ה׳ אֶל־דֶּרֶךְ הַגּוֹיִם אַל־תִּלְמָדוּ וּמֵאֹתוֹת הַשָּׁמַיִם אַל־תֵּחָתּוּ כִּי־יֵחַתּוּ הַגּוֹיִם מֵהֵמָּה" **–** ***So says Hashem: Do not adopt the way of the nations and do not fear the signs of the heavens, for the nations fear them.*** הֵם יֵחַתּוּ וְלֹא יִשְׂרָאֵל **– They,** the nations, **should fear** them, **but not Israel.**

The Gemara adds:

וְאַף רַב סָבַר אֵין מַזָּל לְיִשְׂרָאֵל **– And Rav too holds that the** celestial **signs hold no sway over Israel.** דְּאָמַר רַב יְהוּדָה אָמַר רַב **– For Rav Yehudah said in the name of Rav:** מִנַּיִין שֶׁאֵין מַזָּל לְיִשְׂרָאֵל **– From where do we know that the** celestial **signs hold no sway over Israel?** שֶׁנֶּאֱמַר **– As it says:**[51] "וַיּוֹצֵא אֹתוֹ הַחוּצָה" **–** ***And He took him outside,*** *and said: Gaze toward the Heavens . . .* אָמַר אַבְרָהָם לִפְנֵי הַקָּדוֹשׁ בָּרוּךְ הוּא **– Abraham said before the Holy One, Blessed is He:** רִבּוֹנוֹ שֶׁל עוֹלָם **– Master of the Universe,** "בֶּן־בֵּיתִי יוֹרֵשׁ אֹתִי" **–** ***my steward inherits me . . .***[52] אָמַר לוֹ לָאו **– [The Holy One] replied to him: No,** *that one will not inherit you;* "כִּי־אִם אֲשֶׁר יֵצֵא מִמֵּעֶיךָ" **–** ***only he that shall come forth from within you*** *shall inherit you.*[53] אָמַר לְפָנָיו רִבּוֹנוֹ שֶׁל עוֹלָם **– [Abraham] then said before him: Master of the Universe!** נִסְתַּכַּלְתִּי בְּאִיצְטַגְנִינוּת שֶׁלִּי **– I have already consulted my astrology,** וְאֵינִי רָאוּי לְהוֹלִיד בֵּן **– and I** see that **I am not fit to bear a son!** אָמַר לֵיהּ **– [The Holy One] said to him:** צֵא מֵאִיצְטַגְנִינוּת שֶׁלְּךָ **– Go outside of your astrology,**[54] שֶׁאֵין מַזָּל לְיִשְׂרָאֵל **– for the celestial signs hold no sway over Israel!** מַאי דַּעְתֵּיךְ **– What do you suppose,**

NOTES

42. שַׁבְּתַאי, the name for Saturn, is cognate to שְׁבָת, *cessation,* as in the verse (*Genesis* 8:22): לֹא יִשְׁבֹּתוּ, *they shall never cease.*

43. In general the unqualified word mitzvah refers, in the Aggadic literature, to charity (*Rashi;* see also *Toras Chaim* to *Avodah Zarah* 4a; *Likkutei Amarim* p. 48b).

44. [Presumably this reflects Mars' red color, as well as its Hebrew name: מַאְדִים, from אָדוֹם, *red.*]

45. I.e. a highway robber who kills (*Rashi*).

46. [*Ohr HaYashar* suggests that Abaye offers two responses: First, that Rabbah punishes those who violate his rulings; second, that Rabbah killed R' Zeira (and then, through his prayers, brought him back to life) in a celebrated incident recorded in *Megillah* 7b; cf. *Teshuvos Chasam Sofer, Orach Chaim* §185, §196.]

47. As the Gemara stated earlier, that someone born during the hour of the sun's influence will be radiant and wise (*Rashi;* see *Rashash* who points out that this was actually stated in regard to someone born during the hour of Mercury's influence).

48. No prayer or act of charity can counteract it (*Rashi*).

49. Both R' Chanina and R' Yochanan agree that the celestial bodies influence events in this world. However, R' Chanina views their influence as inescapable whereas R' Yochanan maintains that prayer or good deeds can improve one's fortunes (*Rashi*). Furthermore, their dispute revolves only around individuals; R' Chanina concedes that the celestial signs hold no sway over the Jewish people collectively. Otherwise, what would be the meaning of all the Torah's many promises of physical blessings if we observe the commandments? (*Teshuvos Rashba* I:148,409; *Maharsha* here.)

Ran writes that the disagreement between R' Chanina and R' Yochanan concerns only such matters as wealth and intelligence. In regard to character and virtue, however, all agree that no man is compelled to sin or to do good, nor to be a person of base or noble character. Although the raw material of one's nature may be inclined in a certain direction, a person's spirit is free to overcome and to direct this inclination. Thus, for example, if a person is born under the influence of Mars and has a martial spirit, he can overcome his blood lust in two ways: First, he can strive to better his nature. He can exercise his free will and use the Torah's commandments to control his impulses and choose another path. Second, he can channel the drive to shed blood into acting as a *mohel* or surgeon. The same applies to all base drives (*Derashos HaRan* §8; see also *Meiri* here in a similar vein; cf. *Abarbanel, Commentary* to *Deuteronomy* 4:15 ד״ה היסוד הא׳ ff.).

[For other views on this Gemara and on this subject generally see *Rambam, Hil. Avodah Zarah* 11:16; ibid., *Letter to the Sages of Montpellier;* ibid., *Iggeres Teiman; Abarbanel, Commentary* to *Deuteronomy* 4:15, at length; *Rabbeinu Bachya, Commentary* to *Deuteronomy* 8:18 and 31:14; see also *Megadim Chadashim* here. See also: *Tosafos* here and to *Moed Katan* 28a ד״ה אלא במולא תליא מילתא and *Kiddushin* 82a ד״ה אלא הכל לפי זכותו; *Ramban, Commentary* to *Deuteronomy* 18:9; *Teshuvos Meyuchasos LeRamban* §283; *Teshuvos Rashba* V:48; *Kuzari* 4:9; *Asarah Maamaros* 1:2:30; *Tiferes Yisrael* (*Boaz*) to *Kiddushin* 4:14; *Michtav MeEliyahu* v. 4 p. 98.]

50. *Jeremiah* 10:2.

51. *Genesis* 15:5.

52. Ibid. v. 3.

53. Ibid. v. 4.

54. This is the meaning of *and He took him outside . . .:* i.e. He took him outside of his astrologically based conceptions (*Rashi;* see also *Asarah Maamaros,* cited in note 49).

רבי יוסי בר' יהודה היא והנ"מ הוא [א] דמשני היכי משני א"ר חסדא [ב] על יד על יד [ו] ושוין שבוחשין את השתית בשבת ושותים זיתום המצרי והאמרת אין גובלין ל"ק הא [ג] בעבה הא ברכה והני מילי הוא דמשני היכי משני אמר רב יוסף בחול נותן את החומץ ואח"כ נותן את השתית [ד] בשבת נותן את השתית ואח"כ נותן את החומץ לוי בריה דרב הונא בר חייא אשכחיה לגבלא דבי [ט] נשיה דקא גביל וספי ליה לתוריה במש ביה [ט] אתא אבוה אשכחיה א"ל הכי אמר אבוך דאמך משמיה דרב ומנו רבי ירמיה בר אבא גובלין ולא מספין ודלא לקיט בלישניה מהלקיטין ליה וה"מ הוא דמשני היכי משני אמר רב ייבר בר שלמיא משמיה דאביי שתי וערב והא לא מערב שפיר אמר רב יהודה מנערו לכלי

כתיב אפינקסיה דזעירי אמרית קדם רבי ומנו רבי חייא מהו לגבל אמר אסור מהו לפרק אמר מותר אמר רב [[ג] מנשיא] חד קמי חד תרי קמי תרי שפיר דמי תלתא קמי תרי אסור רב יוסף אמר קב ואפילו קביים עולא אמר כור ואפילו כוריים כתיב אפינקסיה דלוי אמרית קדם רבי ומנו רבינו הקדוש על דהוו גבלין שתיתא בבבל והוה צוח רבי ומנו רבינו הקדוש על דהוו גבלין שתיתא ולית דשמיע ליה ולית חילא בידיה למיסר מדרבי יוסי בר' יהודה כתיב אפינקסיה דרבי יהושע בן לוי האי מאן דבחד בשבא יהי גבר ולא חדא ביה מאי [ולא חדא ביה] אילימא ולא חד לטיבו והאמר רב אשי אנא בחד בשבא הואי אלא לאו חדא לבישו והאמר רב אשי אנא ודימי בר קקוזתא הווין בחד בשבא אנא מלך והוא הוה ריש גנבי אלא אי כולי לטיבו אי כולי לבישו [י] (מאי טעמא דאיברו ביה אור וחושך) האי מאן דבתרי בשבא יהי גבר רגזן מ"ט משום דאיפליגו ביה מיא האי מאן דבתלתא בשבא יהי גבר עתיר וזנאי יהא מ"ט משום דאיברו ביה עשבים האי מאן דבארבעה בשבא יהי גבר חכים [ח] ונהיר מ"ט משום דאיתלו ביה מאורות האי מאן דבחמשה בשבא יהי גבר גומל חסדים מ"ט משום דאיברו ביה דגים ועופות האי מאן דבמעלי שבתא יהי גבר חזרן אמר ר"נ בר יצחק חזרן במצות האי מאן דבשבתא בשבתא יהי ימות על דאחילו עלוהי יומא רבא דשבתא אמר רבא בר רב שילא וקדישא רבא יתקרי אמר להו רבי חנינא פוקו אמרו ליה לבר ליואי לא מזל יום גורם אלא מזל שעה גורם האי מאן דבחמה (א) יהי גבר זיותן יהי אכיל מדיליה ושתי מדיליה ורזוהי גליין אם גניב לא מצלח האי מאן דבכוכב נוגה יהי גבר עתיר וזנאי יהי מ"ט משום דאיתיליד ביה נורא האי מאן דבכוכב יהי גבר נהיר וחכים משום דספרא דחמה הוא האי מאן דבלבנה יהי גבר סביל מרעין בנאי וסתיר סתיר ובנאי אכיל דלא דיליה ושתי דלא דיליה ורזוהי כסיין אם גנב מצלח האי מאן דבשבתאי יהי גבר מחשבתיה בטלין ואית דאמרי כל דמחשבין עליה בטלין האי מאן דבצדק יהי גבר צדקן אמר ר"נ בר יצחק וצדקן במצות האי מאן דבמאדים יהי גבר אשיד דמא א"ר אשי אי אומנא אי גנבא אי טבחא אי מוהלא אמר רבה אנא במאדים הואי אמר אביי מר נמי עניש וקטיל איתמר רבי חנינא אומר מזל מחכים מזל מעשיר ויש מזל לישראל רבי יוחנן אמר אין מזל לישראל ואזדא רבי יוחנן לטעמיה [י] דא"ר יוחנן מניין שאין מזל לישראל שנאמר [א] כה אמר ה' אל דרך הגוים אל תלמדו ומאותות השמים אל תחתו כי יחתו הגוים מהמה [ז] הם יחתו ולא ישראל ואף רב סבר אין מזל לישראל דאמר רב יהודה אמר רב מניין שאין מזל לישראל שנאמר [ט] [ב] ויוצא אותו החוצה אמר אברהם לפני הקב"ה רבש"ע [ג] בן ביתי יורש אותי אמר לו לאו [ד] כי אם אשר יצא ממעיך אמר לפניו רבש"ע נסתכלתי באיצטגנינות שלי ואיני ראוי להוליד בן אמר ליה צא מאיצטגנינות שלך שאין מזל לישראל מאי דעתיך
דקאי

רש"י

רבי יוסי בר יהודה היא. [י] (דלא רבי לא מהני ליה שינוי דמנתינת מים מיחייב אפילו במידי דלאו בר גיבול כדאמרינן גבי מורסן אבל לרבי יוסי בר יהודה) דאמר עד שיגבל הכא גובלין כלאחר יד דמפרש ואזיל והנ"מ הוא דקא משני: שבוחשין. בתרווד דהיינו גובלין: ושותים זיתום המצרי. דבלאו רפואה נמי משקה הוא דתנן כל המשקין שותה אדם לרפואה (לעיל דף קט:): בעבה. אין גובלין ברכה בוחשין שאין זו לישה: בחול נותן החומץ כו'. כלומר כן דרכו בחול: לגבלא דבי נשיה. שומר בהמות אביו ומגבל מאכלן: דקא גביל. מורסן ע"י שינוי: במש ביה. דהא לכולי עלמא אבל לא גובלין תנן: גובלין. מורסן ע"י שינוי כדמפרש ואזיל והוא דקא משני: ולא מספין. לתורי אין מאמירין אותן: ודלא לקיט בלישניה. עגל קטן שעדיין לא לומד לאכול: והני מילי. דאמרן דמותר לגבל מורסן: שתי וערב. פעם אחת מוליך המקל שתי ופעם אחת ערב: מנערו לכלי. והוא מתערב מאליו: אפינקסיה. לוחות קשורות זו עם זו כאותן של סוחרים: מהו לפרק. לתת מתוך כלי שלפני בהמה זו ולתת לפני חברתה: חדא קמי חדא. מילתא באפי נפשה היא אלא מדה שרגילין לתת לפני בהמה מותר לתת לפניה בשבת וכן תרתי קמי תרתי האוכלות באבוס אחד: אבל תלתא קמי תרתי. הואיל ובחול לא יהיב להו כי האי הוי טרחא דלא לצורך וכ"ש תרתי קמי חדא: אמרית קמיה רבי. רבי לוי משתעי דהוה אמר קדם רבי על הנך אינשי דגבלין שתיתא: מדר' יוסי בר' יהודה. בר פלוגתיה דהוה שרי לעיל אף בעבה ועל ידי שינוי והיו נוהגין כמותו: האי מאן דבחד בשבא. הנולד באחד בשבת: יהא גבר ולא חדא ביה. יהא אדם שלם במדה אחת יהא ולא אחת בו ממדה אחרת ולקמן מפרש לה ואזיל: והוא ריש גנבי. דמאן דנולד בשבת יהא ראש כמו שהיום ראש למעשה בראשית מיהו שמע מינה דנולדים בו לצדיקים ולרשעים: דאיפליגו ביה מיא. כך הוא יבדל מכל אדם: זנאי. נואף: דאיברו ביה עשבים. דכתי' (בראשית א) תדשא הארץ והוא דבר שפרה ורבה מאד וממהר לגדל ולצמוח דהוא ענין פריצות אשו"ה בלע"ז [ל"א] דלא כתיב למינהו בעשבים כבויים (ועוד) שיוצאין בערבוביא ויונקין זו מזו: ונהיר. זוהר: דאיתלו ביה מאורות. וכתיב ותורה אור: דאיברו ביה דגים ועופות. שאין טורחין לאוכלין אלא ניזונים בחסדו של הקב"ה: חזרן. מחזר אחר מצות: חזרן במצות. שכן דרך ע"ש לחזור אחר מצות שבת: וקדישא רבא יתקרי. שיהא פרוש וקדוש דכתיב (שמות כ) ויקדשהו: אמר להו רבי חנינא. לתלמידים שקראו פנקסו של ר' יהושע: מזל שעה. ז' מזלות הן המשמשין את השעות תנכ"ל שצ"ם חמה היינו חמה ממש והוא אחד מן המזלות וכן לבנה והשאר הווין כוכבים: זיותן. כשמש המאיר: אכיל מדיליה. כשמש שאינו מסיג גבול רעהו למשול בלילה: ורזוהי גליין. אין לו רשות לכסות סודו ונסתרותיו אלא כשמש הזה שהוא פומבי לכל: דתלי ביה נורא. אש תלוי באותו מזל יקר של תשמיש בוער כתנור: מזל כוכב. הוא סופר של מזל חמה לכתוב דרך הילוכו ותקופותיו ומצוי אצלו תמיד: סביל מרעין. כלבנה זו (ג) שמתנונה והולכת: בנאי וסתיר. כלבנה זו שגדילה ומתמעטת: אכיל לא דיליה. ° כלבנה המסגת גבול החמה למשול אף ביום: ורזוהי כסיין. כלבנה שאינה מאירה: דבשבתאי. מזל כוכב ששמו שבתאי: בטלין. כמו לא ישבותו (בראשית ח): צדקן במצות. צדקה לעניים דקרי ליה מצוה (בכל לשון אגדה): גנבא. ליסטים ההורג נפשות: אומנא. מקיז דם: עניש. בני אדם העוברין על דבריו: מזל מחכים. לפי המזל היא החכמה כדאמר דבחמה נהיר וחכים: ויש מזל לישראל. שאין תפלה וצדקה משנה את המזל: אין מזל לישראל. דעל ידי תפלה וזכות משתנה מזלו לטובה: איצטגנינות. חכמת המזלות: צא מאיצטגנינותך. היינו דכתיב ויוצא אותו החוצה חוץ מאיצטגנינותו:
דקאי

תוספות

מהו לפרק. פירש בקונטרס לפרק מלפני בהמה זו וליתן לפני אחרת וכן פירש בערוך בערך פרק וקשה לר"י דהיינו מתניתין גבי בהמה (לעיל דף קמ:) ונראה לר"י לפרק היינו להריק המים וגם המורסן מכלי אל כלי שתגבל היטב ובערוך פירש כמה לשונות:

אין מזל לישראל. והא דאמר רבא בשילהי מו"ק (דף כח. ושם) בני חיי ומזוני לאו בזכותא תליא מילתא אלא במזלא תליא מילתא מכל מקום על ידי זכות גדול משתנה אבל פעמים שאין המזל משתנה כדאמר ביבמות פרק החולץ (דף נ. ושם) זכה מוסיפין לו לא זכה פוחתין לו [י] (דאין מזל לישראל): כלדאי

עין משפט נר מצוה

לא א ב ג ד מיי' שם הלכה לג סמג שם טוש"ע א"ח סימן שכד סעיף יד:

גליון הש"ס

גמרא אתא אבוה אשכחיה. ע"י לעיל דף כג ע"ב תוס' ד"ה דבי נשא: רש"י ד"ה אכיל דלא דיליה כלבנה המסגת. עיין דבר נחמד בזה בכמנות אור לנעל פמ"א בפ' בראשית:

רבינו חננאל

ואין צ"ל שמלקטין כו' ופריק רב יהודה הכי לעולם פי' מתניתא דאמר כך היא מהלקטין דספו ליה בידיה והיא פתוחה מהלעטה שאמרנו ומלקטין שמשליך לפניה שעורים וכיוצא בהן דברים שהן מאכל לעופות. ואין משליכין מאכל לפני יוני שובך ויוני [עליה] לפי שאינן [בני] תרבות ואין מזונותן עליך וכו' [אן] דתניא נותנין מזונות לפני הכלב ואין נותנין מזונות לפני חזיר ומה הפרש בין זה לזה כלב מזונותיו עליך חזיר אין מזונותיו עליך ובא רב אשי לסייע דברי רב יהודה ולומר שנויא דשני שינויא היא מדוקיא דמתניתין דקתני אין נותנין מים לפני דבורים ולפני יונים שבשובך אבל נותנין לפני אווזים ותרנגולים ולפני יוני הרדסיות מ"ט לאו משום דהני מזונותיו עליך והני אין מזונותיו עליך ולא עמדו דברי רב אשי והלכה כרב יהודה דתניא כוותיה דתניא איזו היא המראה ואיזו היא הלעטה המראה מרביצה ופוקס את פיה ומאכילה כרשינן ומים בבו"א. הלעטה מאכילה מעומד ומשקה מעומד ונותן לה כרשינין בפ"ע ומים בפ"ע: מלקטין לתרנגולים ונותנין מים למורסן אבל לא גובלין אוקימנא לר' יוסי ב"ר יהודה דתניא אחד נותן את הקמח ואחד נותן לתוכו מים האחרון חייב דברי רבי ר' יוסי בר יהודה אומר עד שיגבל אלמא אמרינן [דנתינת מים זהו גיבולו] ממאי דלמא עד כאן לא קאמר ר' יוסי ב"ר יהודה עד שיגבל אלא בקמח דבר גיבול הוא. אבל מורסן דלאו בר גיבול הוא אפי' ר' יוסי ב"ר יהודה מודי שנתינת מים למורסן אסור שזהו גיבולו ואשכחנן תניא בהדיא אין נותנין מים למורסן דברי [ר'] יוסי ב"ר יהודה אומר נותנים מים למורסן ואע"ג דבכל מקום הלכתא כרבי מחבירו הכא הלכה כר' יוסי דתנינן מתניתין סתמא כוותיה. ותוב מהא דכתוב אפינקסיה דלוי אמרית קדם רבינו הקדוש והוא רבי על דהוו גבלין שתיתא בבבל והוא צווח רבי ולית דשמע ליה ולית חילא בידיה למיסר מדר' יוסי ב"ר יהודה מהא נמי שמעינן דהלכתא כר' יוסי ב"ר יהודה דהוא בר פלוגתיה לא אסר תנפק עובדא כוותיה: ת"ר אין גובלין את הקליא וי"א גובלין ואמרינן מאן י"א ר' יוסי ב"ר יהודה היא והוא דמשני היכי משני אמר רב חסדא על יד על יד פי' מעט מעט מדמזדק רב חסדא אליבא דר' יוסי ב"ר יהודה הלכתא

מסורת הש"ס

א) ברכות לח., ב) [נ"ל נשא ועמ"ש תוספות לעיל כג: ד"ה דבי], ג) [ע' תוספות חולין ד. ד"ה מכניס וכו' דגרסי רב מנשה], ד) רש"ל מ"ז, ה) [פי' זכן ערוך], ו) (סוכה כט.), ז) [סוכה כט.], ח) [נדרים לב.], ט) רש"ל מ"ז, י) ר"מ מוחק זה.

הגהות הב"ח

(א) גמ' מאן דבחמה יהא בר. נ"ב תחלת סדר הליכתן שצ"ם חנכ"ל [ולמאן נקט חנכ"ל שצ"ם] לפי סדר סימני הימים חנכ"ל כלנ"ש וכו' לקט מחה בריש והדר נקט נוגה וכו' לפי סדר [השעות והמזלות בתחלתן מזל שמשמש בתחלת יום א' נמצא סדר השעות חנכ"ל שצ"ם וחוזר חלילה כדאיתא בר"ה פ"ק] מפרנק וע"ש: (ב) רש"י ד"ה סביל וכו' זו שמתמעטת והולכת:

תורה אור השלם

א) כֹּה אָמַר יְיָ אֶל דֶּרֶךְ הַגּוֹיִם אַל תִּלְמָדוּ וּמֵאֹתוֹת הַשָּׁמַיִם אַל תֵּחָתּוּ כִּי יֵחַתּוּ הַגּוֹיִם מֵהֵמָּה: [ירמיה י, ב]

ב) וַיּוֹצֵא אֹתוֹ הַחוּצָה וַיֹּאמֶר הַבֶּט נָא הַשָּׁמַיְמָה וּסְפֹר הַכּוֹכָבִים אִם תּוּכַל לִסְפֹּר אֹתָם וַיֹּאמֶר לוֹ כֹּה יִהְיֶה זַרְעֶךָ: [בראשית טו, ה]

ג) וַיֹּאמֶר אַבְרָם הֵן לִי לֹא נָתַתָּה זָרַע וְהִנֵּה בֶן בֵּיתִי יוֹרֵשׁ אֹתִי: [בראשית טו, ג]

ד) וְהִנֵּה דְבַר יְיָ אֵלָיו לֵאמֹר לֹא יִירָשְׁךָ זֶה כִּי אִם אֲשֶׁר יֵצֵא מִמֵּעֶיךָ הוּא יִירָשֶׁךָ: [בראשית טו, ד]

ליקוטי רש"י

על יד על יד. מעט מעט [ביצה כב:]. שתית. מאכל העשוי מקמח קליות שנותנים בתנור בעוד שמבשלים לחים [ברכות לח.]. מאכל שעושין מקמח קלי שמתייבש בתנור ומערבין דבש לתוך מתבשיל [עירובין כט:]. מאכל העשוי מקמח של קליות שייבשן בתנור ויש שעושין אותו מקמח עדשים ולפי שהן מתוקין יותר [ע"ז לח:]. שבוחשין. מגיסין בכף לערבו יפה במימיו [ברכות שם]. זיתום המצרי. הוא של קדירים ועל שם שזוקרים את החולי [לעיל קי.]. מפורש במסכת פסחים (דף מ"ב:) [ברכות שם]. במש. בעט [שבועות לג:]. מזל שעה. שצ"ם חנכ"ל סדר השעות המזלות ...

...חמה ושל שני בשבת לבנה ושל שלישי בשבת מאדים [לעיל קכט:]. אל דרך הגוים אל תלמדו. ולא מאותות השמים אל תחתו מחמה לוקה ומהמאורות לוקין [ירמיהו י, ב]. לעשות כמעשיהם ומשמעטו לרעה מאותות השמים אל תחתו [סוכה כט.]. איצטגנינות. להיות בקי בהליכות המזלות ותחילות השעות דהכי תניא בבבא בתרא (טז:) וה' ברך את אברהם בכל איצטגנינות גדולה היתה בלבו וכל מלכי מזרח ומערב משכימין לפתחו לשאול במזלות [יומא כח:]. איצטגנינות כלל הש"ס לשון מזלות וחוזה בכוכבים [סנהדרין סה:]. צא מאיצטגנינות שלך. ממשפט חכמת מזלות שלך וזהו דכתיב (בראשית טו) ויוצא אותו החוצה [ר"ן נדרים לב.].

עין משפט נר מצוה

לב א טוש"ע י"ד סימן רמו סעיף ד:
לג ב טוש"ע א"ח סימן ג סעיף ו:
לד ג ד מיי' פכ"א מהלכות שבת הל' יח סמג שם טוש"ע א"ח סימן שכד סעיף ו ז:
לה ה מיי' פ"ב מהלכות י"ט הלכה טז סמג לאוין עה:

דקאי צדק במערב מהדרנא ומוקמינא ליה במזרח והיינו דכתיב (א) מי העיר ממזרח צדק יקראהו לרגלו ומדשמואל נמי אין מזל לישראל דשמואל ואבלט הוו יתבי והוו קאזלי הנך אינשי לאגמא א"ל אבלט לשמואל האי גברא אזיל ולא אתי טריק ליה חוויא ומיית א"ל שמואל אי בר ישראל הוא אזיל ואתי אדיתבי אזיל ואתי קם אבלט שדיה לטוניה אשכח ביה חוויא דפסיק ושדי בתרתי גובי א"ל שמואל מאי עבדת א"ל כל יומא הוה מרמינן ריפתא בהדי הדדי ואכלינן האידנא הוה איכא חד מינן דלא הוה ליה ריפתא הוה קא מיכסף אמינא להו אנא קאימנא וארמינא כי מטאי לגביה שואי נפשאי כמאן דשקילי מיניה כי היכי דלא ליכסיף א"ל מצוה עבדת א נפק שמואל ודרש (ב) וצדקה תציל ממות ולא ממיתה משונה אלא ממיתה עצמה ומדר"ע נמי אין מזל לישראל דר"ע הויא ליה ברתא אמרי ליה כלדאי ההוא יומא דעיילה לבי גננא טריק לה חויא ומיתא הוה דאיגא אמילתא טובא ההוא יומא שקלתה למכבנתא דצתא בגודא איתרמי איתיב בעיניה דחוויא לצפרא כי קא שקלה לה הוה קא סריך ואתי חוויא בתרה אמר לה אבוה מאי עבדת אמרה ליה בפניא אתא עניא קרא אבבא והוו טרידי כולי עלמא בסעודתא וליכא דשמעיה קאימנא שקלתי (א) לריסתנאי דיהבית לי יהבתיה ניהליה אמר לה מצוה עבדת נפק ר"ע ודרש וצדקה תציל ממות ולא ממיתה משונה אלא ממיתה עצמה ומדר"נ בר יצחק נמי אין מזל לישראל דאימיה דר"נ בר יצחק אמרי לה כלדאי בריך גנבא הוה לא שבקתיה גלויי רישיה אמרה ליה ג כסי רישיך כי היכי דתיהוו עלך אימתא דשמיא ובעי רחמי לא הוה ידע אמאי קאמרה ליה יומא חד יתיב קא גרים תותי דיקלא נפל גלימא מעילויה רישיה דלי עיניה חזא לדיקלא אלמיה יצריה סליק פסקיה לקיבורא בשיניה: **מתני'** ג מחתכין את הדלועין לפני הבהמה ד ואת הנבלה לפני הכלבים רבי יהודה אומר אם לא היתה נבלה מערב שבת אסורה לפי שאינה מן המוכן: **גמ'** איתמר (ער"ל שח"ז סימן) אמר עולא הלכה כרבי יהודה (ג) ושמואל אמר הלכה כר"ש ואף רב סבר הלכה כרבי יהודה מדרכבי דוזי ד דרב אסר ושמואל שרי ואף לוי סבר הלכה כרבי יהודה כי הא דלוי כי הוו מייתי טריפתא לקמיה ביומא טבא לא הוה חזי לה אלא כי יתיב ה אקילקליתא דאמר דילמא לא מתכשרא ואפילו לכלבים לא חזיא ושמואל אמר הלכה כרבי שמעון ואף זעירי סבר הלכה כר"ש דתנן ו בהמה שמתה לא יזיזנה ממקומה ותרגמא זעירי ה בבהמת קדשים אבל בחולין שפיר דמי ואף רבי יוחנן אמר הלכה כר"ש ומי א"ר יוחנן הכי ז והא א"ר יוחנן הלכה כסתם משנה ותנן אין

רש"י

דקאי צדק. שהוא מזל שלך: במערב. שהוא מקום מגונן ואין ראוי להוליד בך מלאתי בהש"ם רבינו הלוי: במזרחו. שהוא מקום חום: צדק. הקב"ה קראו להביאו למזרח: לרגלו. בשבילו: אבלט. שם חכם נכרי היה וחוזה בכוכבים: אזיל ואתי. דאין מזל לישראל ויועיל לו תפלה: בתרתי גובי. בשתי חתיכות שקצצו עם הקנים בלא ידע: מרמינן בהדדי. מטילין פת [לסל] לכל החבורה כאחד ואוכלין יחד והאחד גובה מכולן: אנא קאימנא ומרמינא. אגבה ואשים בסל: שוואי נפשאי כמאן דשקלי מיניה. עשיתי עצמי כגובה ממנו ונתתי משלי חלקו: לא ממיתה משונה. ומיהו מיתה הגונה ימות אלא ממיתה עצמה מצלת ונותנת חיים: כלדאי. חוזים בכוכבים: דצתא. תחבתה: למכבנתא. [אישפינגלי"ז בלע"ז] נושקא של זהב שיש כמו טס בראשה: ריסתנאי. אמנשטריישו"ן: ובעי רחמי. בקש רחמים שלא ישלוט בך יצר הרע: קיבורא. אשכול תמרים והדקל לא שלו היה: מתני' את הדלועין. התלושין ומיהו סתמן לאו למאכל בהמה קיימי אלא לאדם: ואת הנבלה. שנתנבלה היום ובין השמשות היתה עומדת לאדם ואפ"ה מחתכין: גמ' כר"ש. דלית ליה מוקצה: מדכרכי דוזי. מחצלות העשויות לספינות לכסות פרקמטיא שבתוכן. זוזי ספינות בלשון ארמי כך מצאתי בתשובת הגאונים: כי הוו מייתי טריפתא לקמיה. בהמה שנולד בה ספק טרפות וצריכה להוראת חכם: אקילקלתא. ° על האשפה שאם יראנה טריפה יניחה שם: ואפילו לכלבים לא חזיא. דנשחטה היום ולא יוכלו לטלטל כרבי יהודה: תרגמא זעירי. במסכת ביצה בבהמת קדשים דאסורה בהנאה ולא חזיא לכלבים הא דחולין שפיר דמי להאכילה לכלבים:

תוספות

כלדאי. בכולה סוגיא משמע דהיינו חוזים בכוכבים ולא כמו שפירש"י בערבי פסחים (דף קיג:) מניין שאין שואלין בכלדאים שנאמר תמים תהיה וגו' ופירש דהיינו אוב וגו' וקשה דבהדיא כתיב אל תפנו וגו' ובספרי דרש מנין שאין שואלין בגורלות שנאמר תמים תהיה וגורל וחוזה בכוכבים חדא מילתא היא:

רבי יהודה אומר אם לא היתה נבלה מע"ש כו'. תימה היכי מוכח בפסחים פרק מקום שנהגו בסופו (דף נו: ושם) ובפ"ק דביצה (דף ו: ושם) מהך מתניתין דמוכן לאדם לא הוי מוכן לכלבים לעולם מוכן לאדם הוי מוכן לכלבים והכא היינו טעמא דאסירא לכלבים משום דהואי מוקצה מחמת איסור שלא היתה ראויה חיה (ח לא) לאדם (ח ולא לכלבים) ותירץ ר"י דיש דברים ראויים ליתן לפני הכלבים חיים כגון עופות וכיוצא בהן הלכך אי לאו דמוכן לאדם לא הוי מוכן לכלבים הוה שריא ליתן לכלבים וה"ר יצחק בן הר"ר מאיר גריס במתני' אם לא היתה נבלה מעיו"ט אסורה השתא אתי שפיר בפשיטות דמוכן שפיר לאדם ואינו מוקצה מחמת איסור ולא נהירא לי דבריש ביצה (דף ב.) דייק מינה דגבי שבת סתם לה תנא כר"ש אלמא גבי שבת מיתניא וה"ר פורת מפרש דממשנה יתירה דייק דה"ל למתני אם לא היתה נבלה מע"ש אסורה ותו לא דמאי נ"ל לפי שאינה מן המוכן אלא להכי תני לה דאפילו הוי מוכן לאדם לגמרי שלא היה מוקצה מחמת איסור לא הוי מוכן לכלבים. מ"ר:

ושמואל אמר הלכה כר"ש. תימה לר"י תרתי דשמואל למה לי דתיפוק ליה מההיא דכרכי דזוזי ועז לחלבה ורחל לגיזתה דשילהי פ"ק (דף יט: ושם) ותירץ ר"י דמוקצה דהתם קיל ממוקצה דהכא:

תרגמא זעירי בבהמת קדשים. תימה לר"י היכי מוכח מהכא דס"ל לזעירי כר"ש ע"כ אליבא דר"י מוקמה בבהמת קדשים כדמוכח פרק אין צדין (ביצה דף כז:) משום דמתני' נמי דיקא דקתני עלה ולא החלה שנטמאת מה חלה דקדשים אף בהמה דקדשים ומכח האי דיוקא פריך התם למר בר אמימר דאמר מודה היה ר"ש בבעלי חיים שמתו שאסורין ודחיק ר"י לתרץ ° דהכי קים ליה להש"ס שלא פירש זעירי כן אלא משום דבעי לאוקמה כר"ש. מ"ר:

והא א"ר יוחנן הלכה כסתם משנה ותנן אין מבקעין כו'. תימה לר"י היכי מוכח מהכא דלא ס"ל כר"ש דההיא ודאי כרבי יהודה דשמא אית ליה לרבי יוחנן מיגו דאיתקצאי לבין השמשות איתקצאי לכולי יומא וקורה שנשברה אפילו לר"ש איתקצאי בין השמשות קודם שבירתה דהואי מוקצה מחמת חסרון כיס דמודה ביה ר"ש אבל במתניתין לא איתקצאי בין השמשות דלית ליה ההיא מוקצה מה שהיא עומדת לאדם והיה רוצה רבי לתרץ דאי אית ליה לר' יוחנן מיגו דאיתקצאי היה אוסר ודאי לטלטל בהמה שנתנבלה בשבת שהרי נהי שהיתה ראויה לכלבים (ג) בלא שחיטה כדפירשית לעיל מיהו לטלטל היתה אסורה דכולי עלמא מודו דבעלי חיים הם מוקצים הוה לן למימר מיגו דאיתקצאי ודנתי לפני רבי כיון שהיא ראויה לכלבים משום שהיא מוקצה לטלטל אין לנו לאוסרה לטלטל נבלה בשבת מידי דהוה אפירות הנושרין דתלינן טעמא בריש ביצה (דף ג.) שמא יעלה ויתלוש ומשום מוקצה לא אסירי לטלטל כיון דחזו לעורבים בעודן מחוברין אע"פ (ג) שבעת חבורן היו אסורין לטלטל ותירץ רבי דמסתמא מתניתין בכל ענין איירי בין אותן שראוין לכלבים בעודן חיים בין שאינן ראוין [illegible]

והא אמר רבי יוחנן הלכה כסתם משנה. בריש ביצה (דף ב.) אמרינן גבי שבת דסתם לן תנא כר"ש משמע דחשיב [illegible] רבי לאו משום סתמא קאמר [illegible] מ"ר:

רבינו חננאל

הלכתא כוותיה ונתברר שהלכה כר' יוסי ב"ר יהודה שנותנין מים למורסן וגובלין את הקליא מעט מעט. ושורין שבחשתין את השתית בשבת. [illegible]

מסורת הש"ס

א) [גיטין נז.] [illegible]

הגהות הב"ח

(א) גמרא שקלתיה לריסתנאי. נ"ב פירוש חלק סעודה שלי. ועי' בברכות דף מב: (ב) תום' ד"ה אלא ר' יוחנן וכו' ראויה לכלבים בע"ש כדפי' לעיל: (ג) באד"ה בזמן שבעת חבורן:

גליון הש"ס

רש"י ד"ה אקלקלתא על האשפה. [illegible]

תורה אור השלם

א) מִי הֵעִיר מִמִּזְרָח צֶדֶק יִקְרָאֵהוּ לְרַגְלוֹ יִתֵּן לְפָנָיו גּוֹיִם וּמְלָכִים יַרְדְּ יִתֵּן כֶּעָפָר חַרְבּוֹ כְּקַשׁ נִדָּף קַשְׁתּוֹ: [ישעיה מא, ב]
ב) לֹא יוֹעִילוּ אוֹצְרוֹת רֶשַׁע וּצְדָקָה תַּצִּיל מִמָּוֶת: [משלי י, ב]

ליקוטי רש"י

[illegible]

דְּקָאֵי צֶדֶק בְּמַעֲרָב – **that Jupiter,** in whose hour you were born, **is situated in the west,** and you are therefore infertile?[1] מְהַדַּרְנָא וּמוֹקְמִינָא לֵיהּ בְּמִזְרָח – **I will** simply **move it around and situate it in the east.**[2] וְהַיְינוּ דִּכְתִיב – **And that is** the meaning of that **which is written:**[3] ,,מִי הֵעִיר מִמִּזְרָח צֶדֶק יִקְרָאֵהוּ לְרַגְלוֹ" – ***Who awoke Tzedek** [Jupiter] **from the east, He summoned it because of him** [Abraham].*[4]

Several incidents are cited that corroborate this principle:

וּמִדִּשְׁמוּאֵל נַמִּי אֵין מַזָּל לְיִשְׂרָאֵל – **And so too from** an incident **that** once occurred **with Shmuel,** we may conclude that **the** celestial **signs hold no sway over Israel.** דִּשְׁמוּאֵל וְאַבְלֵט הֲווּ יָתְבֵי – **For Shmuel and Avleit**[5] **were once sitting** together וַהֲווּ קָאָזְלֵי הָנָךְ אִינְשֵׁי לְאַגְמָא – **as some men were going to a swamp** to cut reeds. אָמַר לֵיהּ אַבְלֵט לִשְׁמוּאֵל – **Avleit said to Shmuel:** הַאי גַּבְרָא אָזִיל וְלָא אָתֵי – **This man will go but he will not come back;** טָרִיק לֵיהּ חִוְיָא וּמָיֵית – **a snake will bite him and he will die.**[6] אָמַר לֵיהּ שְׁמוּאֵל – **Shmuel said to [Avleit]:** אִי בַּר יִשְׂרָאֵל הוּא – **If he is a Jew,** אָזִיל וְאָתֵי – **he will go and come.**[7] אַדְּיָתְבֵי אָזִיל וְאָתֵי – **While [Shmuel and Avleit] were sitting** there, **[the man] went and came back.** קָם אַבְלֵט שַׁדְיֵהּ לְטוּנֵיהּ – **Avleit stood up and threw off [the man's] pack** of reeds. אַשְׁכַּח בֵּיהּ חִוְיָא דִּפְסִיק וּשְׁדֵי בִּתְרָתֵי גּוּבֵי – **He found amid** the reeds **a snake that had been cut into two pieces.**[8] אָמַר לֵיהּ שְׁמוּאֵל – **Shmuel said to [the man]:** מַאי עֲבַדְתְּ – **What have you done** that might have made you worthy of escaping death? אָמַר לֵיהּ – **He said to [Shmuel]:** כָּל יוֹמָא הֲוָה מַרְמִינַן רִיפְתָּא בַּהֲדֵי הֲדָדֵי וְאָכְלִינַן – **Every day we all throw our bread together** in one basket **and eat it.**[9] הָאִידְנָא הֲוָה אִיכָּא חַד מִינַן דְּלָא הֲוָה לֵיהּ רִיפְתָּא – **Today** I realized **there was one of us who did not have any bread** to throw in, הֲוָה קָא מִיכְסִיף – **and he was growing embarrassed.** אָמֵינָא לְהוּ – **I told them** all: אֲנָא קָאֵימְנָא וְאַרְמֵינָא – **I am going to get up and collect** the bread today. כִּי מְטַאי לְגַבֵּיהּ – **When I reached that person,** שַׁוַּאי נַפְשַׁאי כְּמַאן דִּשְׁקִילִי מִינֵּיהּ – **I pretended to take** something **from him,** and made up the difference with my own bread, כִּי הֵיכִי דְּלָא לִיכַּסִּיף – **so that he should not become embarrassed.** אָמַר לֵיהּ – **[Shmuel]** then **told him:** מִצְוָה עֲבַדְתְּ – **You have done a good deed,** i.e. an act of true charity.[10] נְפַק שְׁמוּאֵל וְדָרַשׁ – **Shmuel went out and expounded:** ,,וּצְדָקָה תַּצִּיל מִמָּוֶת" – ***And charity saves from death;***[11] וְלָא מִמִּיתָה מְשׁוּנָּה – **and not** just **from an unusual death,** אֶלָּא מִמִּיתָה עַצְמָהּ – **but** even **from death itself.**[12]

וּמִדְּרַבִּי עֲקִיבָא נַמִּי אֵין מַזָּל לְיִשְׂרָאֵל – **And so too from** an incident **that** once occurred **with R' Akiva** we may conclude that **the** celestial **signs hold no sway over Israel.** דְּרַבִּי עֲקִיבָא הֲוָיָא לֵיהּ בְּרַתָּא – **For R' Akiva had a daughter** about whom אָמְרֵי לֵיהּ כַּלְדָּאֵי – **the astrologers**[13] **told him:** הַהוּא יוֹמָא דְּעָיְילָה לְבֵי גְּנָנָא – **The day she enters her bridal chamber** טָרִיק לָהּ חִוְיָא וּמֵיתָא – **a snake will bite her and she will die.** הֲוָה דְּאִיגָא אַמִּילְּתָא טוּבָא – **[R' Akiva] was extremely worried over this matter.** הַהוּא יוֹמָא שְׁקַלְתָּא לְמַכְבַּנְתָּא – **On that day** (of her wedding) **she took her brooch** דַּצְתָּא בְּגוּדָא – **and stuck it in the wall.** אִיתְרַמֵּי אִיתִיב בְּעֵינֵיהּ דְּחִוְיָא – **It happened that** when she did so, **[the needle] lodged in the eye of a snake,** killing it. לְצַפְרָא כִּי קָא שָׁקְלָה לָהּ – **In the morning, when she took [the brooch]** out of the wall, הֲוָה קָא סָרִיךְ וְאָתֵי חִוְיָא בַּתְרַהּ – **the dead snake followed, stuck fast to [the brooch];** אָמַר לָהּ אֲבוּהָ – upon which **her father said to her:** מַאי עֲבַדְתְּ – **What have you done** to be worthy of such a close escape? אָמְרָה לֵיהּ – **She said to him:** בְּפַנְיָא אָתָא עַנְיָא קָרָא אַבָּבָא – **In the afternoon, a pauper came and called out from the doorway,** וַהֲווּ טְרִידֵי כּוּלֵּי עָלְמָא בִּסְעוּדְתָּא – **but everyone was busy at the** wedding **banquet** וְלֵיכָּא דְּשַׁמְעֵיהּ – **and no one heard him.** קָאֵימְנָא שְׁקַלְתִּי לְרִיסְתְּנַאי דִּיהָבִית לִי – **I stood up and took my portion that had been given me** וִיהַבְתֵּיהּ נִיהֲלֵיהּ – **and I gave it to him.** אָמַר לָהּ – **[R' Akiva] said to her:** מִצְוָה עֲבַדְתְּ – **You have done a good deed,** an act of true charity. נְפַק רַבִּי עֲקִיבָא וְדָרַשׁ – **R' Akiva went out and expounded:** ,,וּצְדָקָה תַּצִּיל מִמָּוֶת" – ***And charity saves from death;*** וְלָא מִמִּיתָה מְשׁוּנָּה – **and not** just **from an unusual death,** אֶלָּא מִמִּיתָה עַצְמָהּ – **but** even **from death itself.**

Another incident:

וּמִדְּרַבִּי נַחְמָן בַּר יִצְחָק נַמִּי אֵין מַזָּל לְיִשְׂרָאֵל – **And so too from** the incident **that** occurred **with R' Nachman bar Yitzchak** we may conclude that **the** celestial **signs hold no sway over Israel.** דְּאִימֵּיהּ דְּרַבִּי נַחְמָן בַּר יִצְחָק אָמְרֵי לָהּ כַּלְדָּאֵי – **For the astrologers once told R' Nachman bar Yitzchak's mother:** בְּרִיךְ גַּנָּבָא הֲוָה – **Your son will be a thief.** לָא שְׁבַקְתֵּיהּ גַּלּוּיֵי רֵישֵׁיהּ – **She never allowed him to uncover his head.** אָמְרָה לֵיהּ – **She told him:** כַּסִּי רֵישָׁיךְ כִּי הֵיכִי דְּתֶיהֱוֵי עֲלָךְ אֵימְתָא דִשְׁמַיָּא – **Cover your head so that the fear of Heaven should be upon you,**[14]

NOTES

1. The west is a "cold" region: The influence of a western sign is not conducive towards having children (*Rashi,* citing [a marginal note in] the Talmud of *Rabbeinu HaLevi*).

[That Abraham was born under the sign of Jupiter may be inferred from the Gemara's teaching on the previous *amud,* that someone who is born under the sign of Jupiter will be charitable; Abraham was the epitome of charity (*Maharsha*).]

2. [See previous note.] The east is a "warm" region (*Rashi*). This demonstrates that according to Rav the celestial signs hold no sway over the Jewish people. That is, although Abraham's ability to sire children is still controlled by his sign, nevertheless, the sign itself may be changed by Divine intervention (see 156a note 49; cf. *Abarbanel,* cited there).

3. *Isaiah* 41:2.

4. In its simple meaning the verse also refers to Abraham, and should be rendered: *Who* [but God] *inspired* [Abraham to come] *from* [Aram in] *the east,* [Abraham whose every] *step was accompanied by righteousness* . . . (see *Rashi, Radak* ad loc.).

5. A non-Jewish wise man and astrologer (*Rashi*). [He is also mentioned together with Shmuel above, 129a; *Avodah Zarah* 30a; see also *Yerushalmi Shabbos* 3:3.]

6. [Perhaps Avleit was familiar with this person and knew under what signs he was born (*Hagahos R' Yaakov Emden*).]

7. Because the celestial signs hold no sway over the Jewish people, prayer will be able to save him (*Rashi*).

8. As the man was cutting reeds, he unwittingly chopped the snake in two (*Rashi*).

9. Every member of the group throws his bread into a communal basket and then they eat its contents together. One person would do the collecting (*Rashi*).

10. [See above, 156a note 43.]

11. *Proverbs* 10:2.

12. Do not say that if a person is supposed to die, the merit of his charity will ensure he dies a normal death. Rather, charity spares him from death itself and gives him life (*Rashi*). [The Gemara in *Bava Basra* (10a) seems to differ: There the Gemara *does* interpret this verse to say that charity saves one from an unusual death. *Maharsha* reconciles the two passages in this way: If a person has lived out his allotted time and he must die, the merit of charity will prevent him from dying an abnormal death. However, if his time is not yet up [but his life is still threatened], charity will rescue him from death and grant him life.]

13. Literally: Chaldeans. The Chaldean nation was famed for its stargazers (see *Teshuvos Meyuchasos LeRamban* §283; cf. *Rashi* to *Pesachim* 113b ד"ה כלדיים).

14. [This is one source for the practice of wearing a yarmulka; see *Orach Chaim* 2:6.]

It was not uncommon for adults in the Talmudic era to wear a head-covering. However, it was unusual for children to do so (see

דקאי צדק במערב מהדרנא ומוקמינא ליה במזרח והיינו דכתיב (א) מי העיר ממזרח צדק יקראהו לרגלו ומדשמואל נמי אין מזל לישראל דשמואל ואבלט הוו יתבי והוו קאזלי הנך אינשי לאגמא א"ל אבלט לשמואל האי גברא אזיל ולא אתי טריק ליה חיויא ומיית א"ל שמואל אי בר ישראל הוא אזיל ואתי אדיתבי אזיל ואתי קם אבלט שדיה לטוניה אשכח ביה חיויא דפסיק ושדי בתרתי גובי א"ל שמואל מאי עבדת א"ל כל יומא הוה מרמינן ריפתא בהדי הדדי ואכלינן האידנא הוה איכא חד מינן דלא הוה ליה ריפתא הוה קא מיכסף אמינא להו אנא קאימנא וארמינא כי מטאי לגביה שואי נפשאי כמאן דשקילי מיניה כי היכי דלא ליכסוף א"ל מצוה עבדת נפק שמואל ודרש (ב) וצדקה תציל ממות ולא ממיתה משונה אלא ממיתה עצמה ומדר"ע נמי אין מזל לישראל דר"ע הויא ליה ברתא אמרי ליה כלדאי ההוא יומא דעיילה לבי גננא טריק לה חיויא ומיתה הוה דאיגא אמילתא טובא ההוא יומא שקלתה למכבנתא דצתא בגודא איתרמי איתיב בעיניה דחיויא לצפרא כי קא שקלה לה הוה קא סריך ואתי חיויא בתרה אמר לה אבוה מאי עבדת אמרה ליה בפניא אתא עניא קרא אבבא והוו טרידי כולי עלמא בסעודתא וליכא דשמעיה קאימנא שקלתי (א) לריסתנאי דיהבית לי יהבתיה ניהליה אמר לה מצוה עבדת נפק ר"ע ודרש וצדקה תציל ממות ולא ממיתה משונה אלא ממיתה עצמה ומדר"נ בר יצחק נמי אין מזל לישראל דאימיה דר"נ בר יצחק אמרי לה כלדאי בריך גנבא הוה לא שבקתיה גלויי רישיה אמרה ליה כסי רישך כי היכי דתיהוי עלך אימתא דשמיא ובעי רחמי לא הוה ידע אמאי קאמרה ליה יומא חד יתיב קא גריס תותי דיקלא נפל גלימא מעילויה רישיה דלי עיניה חזא לדיקלא אלמיה יצריה סליק פסקיה לקיבורא בשיניה: **מתני'** מחתכין את הדלועין לפני הבהמה ואת הנבלה לפני הכלבים רבי יהודה אומר אם לא היתה נבלה מערב שבת אסורה לפי שאינה מן המוכן: **גמ'** איתמר (ער"ל שח"ז סימן) אמר עולא הלכה כרבי יהודה ושמואל אמר הלכה כר"ש ואף רב סבר הלכה כרבי יהודה מדכרכי דזוזי דרב אסר ושמואל שרי ואף לוי סבר הלכה כרבי יהודה כי הא דלוי כי הוו מייתי טריפתא לקמיה ביומא טבא לא הוה חזי לה אלא כי יתיב אקילקליתא דאמר דילמא לא מתכשרא ואפילו לכלבים לא חזיא ושמואל אמר הלכה כרבי שמעון ואף זעירי סבר הלכה כר"ש דתנן בהמה שמתה לא יזיזנה ממקומה ותרגמא זעירי בבהמת קדשים אבל בחולין שפיר דמי ואף רבי יוחנן סבר הלכה כר"ש ומי א"ר יוחנן הכי והא א"ר יוחנן הלכה כסתם משנה ותנן אין

רש"י

דקאי צדק. שהוא מזל שלך: במערב. שהוא מקום מלונן ואין ראוי להוליד כך מלאתי בהש"ם רבינו הלוי: במזרחו. שהוא מקום חום: צדק. הקב"ה קראו להביאו למזרח: לרגלו. בשבילו: אבלט. שם חכם נכרי היה וחוזה בכוכבים: אזיל ואתי. דאין מזל לישראל ויועיל לו תפלה: בתרתי גובי. בשתי חתיכות שקללו עם הקנים בלא יודע: מרמינן בהדדי. מטילין פת [לסל] לכל החבורה כאחד ואוכלין יחד והאחד גובה מכולן: אנא קאימנא ומרמינא. אגבה ואשים בסל: שוואי נפשאי כמאן דשקלי מיניה. עשיתי עצמי כגובה ממנו ונתתי משלי חלקו: לא ממיתה משונה. ומיהו מיתה הגונה ימות אלא ממיתה עצמה מצלת ונותנת חיים: כלדאי. חוזים בכוכבים: דצתא. מחבתה: למכבנתא. [איספינגלי"ז בלע"ז] נושקא של זהב שיש כמו טס בראשה: ריסתנאי. אמנסטריישו"ן: ובעי רחמי. בקש רחמים שלא ישלוט בך יצר הרע: קיבורא. אשכול תמרים והדקל לא שלו היה: **מתני'** את הדלועין. התלושין ומיהו סתמן לאו למאכל בהמה קיימי אלא לאדם: ואת הנבלה. שנתנבלה היום ובין השמשות היתה עומדת לאדם ואפ"ה מחתכין: **גמ'** כר"ש. דלית ליה מוקצה: מדכרכי דזוזי. מחצלות העשויות לספינות לכסות פרקמטיא שבתוכן. זוזי ספינות בלשון ארמי כך מצאתי בתשובת הגאונים: כי הוו מייתי טריפתא לקמיה. בהמה שנולד בה ספק טרפות וצריכה להוראת חכם: אקלקילתא. ° על האשפה שאם יראנה טריפה יניחה שם: ואפילו לכלבים לא חזיא. דנשחטה היום ולא יוכלו לטלטל כרבי יהודה: תרגמא זעירי. במסכת ביצה בבהמת קדשים דאסורה בהנאה ולא חזיא לכלבים הא דחולין שפיר דמי להאכילה לכלבים: אין

לטלטולי משום מוקצה דרב סבר כר' יהודה במוקצה ושמואל סבר כר' שמעון דלית ליה מוקצה שהשמיך [לעיל יט:]. בבהמת קדשים. שאסורה בהנאה וטעונה קבורה ואינה נפדית דבעיא העמדה והערכה ואין פודין קדשים להאכיל לכלבים ואפילו למאן דאמר פודין ביום טוב לא פרקי לה הלכך לא חזיא. הלכה כסתם משנה. רבי הוא סדר המשנה וכשראה דברי חכם וישרו בעיניו שנאן סתם ולא הזכיר שם אומרו עליהן כדי שיהו שנויה מפי יחיד ונראין כאלו נשנו מפי המרובים ויעשו כמותן [שם ב:].

תוספות

כלדאי. בכולה סוגיא משמע דהיינו חוזים בכוכבים ולא כמו שפירש"י בערבי פסחים (דף קיג:) מניין שאין שואלין בכלדאים שנאמר תמים תהיה וגו' ופירש דהיינו אוב ועוד קשה דבהדיא כתיב אל תפנו וגו' ובספרי דרש מנין שאין שואלין בגורלות שנאמר תמים תהיה וגורל וחוזה בכוכבים חדא מילתא היא:

רבי יהודה אומר אם לא היתה נבלה מע"ש כו'. תימה היכי מוכח בפסחים פרק מקום שנהגו בסופו (דף נו: ושם) ובפ"ק דביצה (דף ו: ושם) מהך מתניתין דמוכן לאדם לא הוי מוכן לכלבים לעולם מוכן לאדם הוי מוכן לכלבים והכא היינו טעמא דאסירא לכלבים משום דהואי מוקצה מחמת איסור שלא היתה ראויה חיה (ה) לא לאדם (ה) ולא לכלבים) ותירץ ר"י דיש דברים ראויים ליתן לפני הכלבים חיים כגון עופות וכיוצא בהן הלכך אי לאו דמוכן לאדם לא הוי מוכן לכלבים הוה שריא ליתן לכלבים וה"ר יצחק בן הר"ר מאיר גרים במתני' אם לא היתה נבלה מעיו"ט אסורה השתא אתי שפיר בפשיטות דמוכן שפיר לאדם ואינו מוקצה מחמת איסור ולא נהירא לי דבריש ביצה (דף ב.) דייק מינה דגבי שבת סתם לה תנא כר"ש אלמא גבי שבת מיתניא וה"ר פורת מפרש דממשנה יתירה דייק דה"ל למתני אם לא היתה נבלה מע"ש אסורה ותו לא דמאי נ"ל לפי שאינה מן המוכן אלא להכי תני לה דאפילו הוי מוכן לאדם לגמרי שלא היה מוקצה מחמת איסור לא הוי מוכן לכלבים. מ"ר:

ושמואל אמר הלכה כר"ש. תימה לר"י תרתי דשמואל למה לי דתיפוק ליה מההיא דכרכי דזוזי ועז לחלבה ורחל לגיזתה דשילהי פ"ק (דף יט: ושם) ותירץ ר"י דמוקצה דהתם קיל ממוקצה דהכא:

תרגמא זעירי בבהמת קדשים. תימה לר"י היכי מוכח מהכא דס"ל כר"ש ע"כ איצטריך לאוקמה בבהמת קדשים כדמוכח פרק אין צדין (ביצה דף כז:) משום דמתני' נמי דיקא דקתני עלה ולא החלה שנטמאת מה חלה דקדשים אף בהמה דקדשים ומכח האי דיוקא פריך התם למר בר אמימר דאמר מודה היה ר"ש בבעלי חיים שמתו שאסורין ודחיק ר"י לתרץ ° דהכי קים ליה להש"ס שלא פירש זעירי כן אלא משום דבעי לאוקמה כר"ש. מ"ר:

והא א"ר יוחנן הלכה כסתם משנה ותנן אין מבקעין כו'. תימה לר"י היכי מוכח מהכא דלא ס"ל כר"ש דהכא כרבי יהודה דשמא אית ליה לרבי יוחנן מיגו דאיתקצאי לבין השמשות איתקצאי לכולי יומא וקורה שנשברה אפילו לר"ש איתקצאי בין השמשות קודם שבירתה דהואי מוקצה מחמת חסרון כיס דמודה ביה ר"ש אבל במתניתין לא איתקצאי בין השמשות דלית ליה ההיא מוקצה מה שהיא עומדת לאדם והיה רוצה רבי לתרץ דאי אית ליה לר' יוחנן מיגו דאיתקצאי היה אוסר ודאי לטלטל בהמה שנתנבלה בשבת שהרי נהי שהיתה ראויה לכלבים (ג) בלא שחיטה כדפירשית לעיל מיהו לטלטל היתה אסורה דכולי עלמא מודו דבעלי חיים הם מוקצים הוה לן למימר מיגו דאיתקצאי ודחי לפני רבי כיון שהיא ראויה לכלבים משום שהיא מוקצה לטלטל אין לנו לאוסרה לטלטל נבלה בשבת מידי דהוה אפירות הנושרין דתלינן טעמא בריש ביצה (דף ג.) שמא יעלה ויתלוש ומשום מוקצה לא אסירי לטלטל כיון דחזו לעורבים בעודן מחוברין אע"פ (ג) שבעת חבורן היו אסורין לטלטל ותירץ רבי דמסתמא מתניתין בכל ענין איירי בין אותן שראויין לכלבים בעודן חיים בין שאין ראויין לכלבים דבכולהו שרי ר"ש ואכולהו קאי רבי יוחנן דאמר הלכה כרבי שמעון דמתניתין ולא למחצה אלמא לית ליה מיגו דאיתקצאי. מ"ר:

והא אמר רבי יוחנן הלכה כסתם משנה. בריש ביצה (דף ג.) אמרינן גבי שבת דסתם לן תנא כר"ש משמע דחשיב לסתמא דמתני' סתמא. אמר רבי לאו משום סתמא קאמר דודאי לא חשיב כסתמא כיון דבמתניתין נמי פליג רבי יהודה וסתמא לאו דוקא אלא חשיב כרבים. מ"ר (ט):

עין משפט נר מצוה

לב א טוש"ע י"ד סימן רמו סעיף ד:
לג ב טוש"ע א"ח סימן ג סעיף ו:
לד ג ד מיי' פכ"ה מהלכות שבת הל' יח סמג שם טוש"ע א"ח סימן שכד סעיף ז ו:
לה ה מיי' פ"ב מהלכות י"ט הלכה טז סמג לאוין עה:

רבינו חננאל

הלכתא כוותיה ונתברר שהלכה כר' יוסי ב"ר יהודה שנותנין מים למורסן וגובלין את הקליא מעט מעט. ושוין שבוחשין את השתית בשבת. פי' השתית היא שתיתא דאמור רבנן בכיצד מברכין (דף ל"ח ע"א) ודברי הכל מותר לבחוש בשבת והוא נתינת השתית שהוא הקליא בכלי ואחר כך יתן בו חומץ ויערבנו שתי וערב בתרווד או כיוצא בו כלי הניטל בשבת וינער אח"כ את הכלי לכלי אחר אבל לא יערבנו כדרך מריסה שמריץ התרווד סביבות כל הכלי שבתוכו השתית אלא שתי וערב בלבד. והני מילי דבחיש בה רכה אבל לבוחשה עבה גיבול הוא ואסור. ואקשינן עלה היכי אמרת דשוין שבוחשין את השתית ומי שרי והא אמרת רישא אין גובלין את הקליא. כלומר ת"ק וי"א (אסור) [מתיר] גיבול הקליא וקתני סיפא דשוין שבוחשין את הקליא מכלל דאפי' [ת"ק] שרי ומפרקי' ל"ק הא דתני אין גובלין בעבה וסיפא דקתני ושוין שבוחשין ברכה והוא דמשני ממעשה דחול שדרכו בחול נותן החומץ ואחר כך הקמח ובשבת ישנה יתן השתית ואחר כך יתן החומץ ואפילו נתינת מים למורסן כעין גיבול בשנוי שרי כדאמרי משמיה דרב ירמיה בר אבא גובלין ולא מספין ודלא לקיט בלשניה מלקיטין והני מילי גיבול בשנוי והוא עירוב שתי וערב וניעור מכלי אל כלי אחר אבל מירוס כעין טוחן ברחים של יד שמסבב ומוליך ומביא אסור. אמרו לו לרבי חנינא מה לבבל אמר להו אסור לפרק מאי אמר [להן] מות' ולמה לא פירשו מהו לפרק ומהו חד קמי חדא ותרי קמי תרתי כר' שראיתי בין הגאונים חילוקים בפירושם הלכתא כוולא דאמר אפילו כור אפילו כוריים שרי ואפילו לשלשה ועוד ובלבד ע"י שינוי כאשר פירשנו למעלה ושאר השמועה פשוטה היא: אבלט שהיה חבר לשמואל אומר גוי הוא דאמרינן בפרק אין מעמידין בהמה בפונדקאות של גוים שמואל ואבלט הוו יתבי כו': מתני' מחתכין את הדלועין לפני הבהמה ואת הנבלה לפני הכלבים. רבי יהודה אומר אם לא היתה נבלה מע"ש אסורה: איתמר עי"ל אמר הלכה כר' יהודה. פי' עי"ל סימן שמות החכמים דאמרו דהלכה כר' יהודה והם עולא ורב ולוי אילו שלשתן אמרו הלכה כר' יהודה עולא בפירוש אמר הלכה כר' יהודה רב מכלל חלוקתו על שמואל בכראכי דזוגי פי' מחצלאות הכרוכות זוגות זוגות העומדות לתפירה דרב אסר להתירן שמעינן מינה כיון שהן לסחורה מוקצות הן מכלל דסבר הלכתא כר' יהודה לוי נמי מכללא דכי הוו מייתי טרפה לקמיה דלוי ביו"ט לא הוה חזי ליה אלא אקיקלתא סבר דלמא לא מכשרא ואפילו לכלבים לא חזי שמעינן מינה דכר' יהודה סבירא ליה דאמר לפי שאינה מן המוכן: ש'ז'ח' סימן והן שמואל זעירי ור' יוחנן: שמואל ור' יוחנן בהדיא אמרי הלכתא כר' שמעון וזעירי מכללא מדחזינן ליה לזעירי דמתרגם להא דתנן בהמה שמתה לא יזיזנה ממקומה

מסורת הש"ס

א) [גירסת הערוך לדרשתנא פי' מלבן], ב) ביצה ב. ו: פסחים נו: חולין יד., ג) רש"ל מ"ז, ד) [לעיל יט: ע"ש], ה) [ע' פרש"י ב"ק כה. ובע"ז כה. ד"ה ניקרא], ו) ביצה כז., ז) [לעיל מו. וש"נ], ח) רש"ל מ"ז, ט) [וע' תוספות ביצה ג: ד"ה גבי שבת].

הגהות הב"ח

(א) גמרא שקלתיה לריסתנאי. נ"ב פירוש חלק סעודה שלי. וע' בברכות דף מב: (ב) תוס' ד"ה והא א"ר יוחנן וכו' ראויה לכלבים בע"ש כדפי' לעיל: (ג) בא"ד אע"פ שבשעת חבורן:

גליון הש"ס

רש"י ד"ה אקלקילתא על האשפה. מאשפות ירים אביון (תהלים קיג) תרגום מקלקלתא מרים משוה. רש"י ע"פ דף כח ע"ב ד"ה ויקרא: תוס' ד"ה תרגמא וכו' דהכי פריך ליה. עיין לעיל דף ט ע"ב תוס' ד"ה הא לן וש"נ:

תורה אור השלם

א) מִי הֵעִיר מִמִּזְרָח צֶדֶק יִקְרָאֵהוּ לְרַגְלוֹ יִתֵּן לְפָנָיו גּוֹיִם וּמְלָכִים יַרְדְּ יִתֵּן כֶּעָפָר חַרְבּוֹ כְּקַשׁ נִדָּף קַשְׁתּוֹ: [ישעיה מא, ב]
ב) לֹא יוֹעִילוּ אוֹצְרוֹת רֶשַׁע וּצְדָקָה תַּצִּיל מִמָּוֶת: [משלי י, ב]

ליקוטי רש"י

טוניה. משאו [ע"פ ב"מ קז.]. גננא. חופה [גיטין נז.]. דצתא. דוך. מקום כדאמר דלא מלאפה [שבת נג.]. לשון ארמית והכוונה עצמה שם [שבת נג.]. דך ביה מידי [חולין נג.]. דלא כמו דעשה ... לשון [בראשית ל, לח]. גודא. כותל [לעיל קמ.]. מחתכין את הדלועין. תלושין לפני הבהמה ולא אמרינן טרחא דלאו לצורך הוא [ביצה ב.]. התלושין דלא חזו אלא לאדם להאכיל לבהמה [לעיל קנה.]. ואת הנבלה לפני הכלבים. ולע"פ שנתנבלה בשבת דבין השמשות עומדת לאדם היתה עומדת לאכילת כלבים אפילו הכי שרי דלית ליה מוקצה בשבת [ביצה שם]. ונתנבלה בשבת קאמר מדלפני רבי יהודה עלה ואמר אם לא היתה נבלה מערב שבת אסורה לפי שאינה מן המוכן [שם ב.]. שאינה מן המוכן. אלמא לא היתה עומדת למאכל כלבים בשבת שהיא עומדת לאכילת אדם כשחייתה [חולין יד.]. כרכי דזוזי. זוג של מחצלאות שעושין כהן מפרגמטיא של ספינה חוזי לשון זוג ושלא מלאכי ונחשבות הגאונים מלאתי כרכי דזוזי ומפרש משום לשון ספינה בלשון ארמי [ע"ש בב"ח]. דרב אסר.

וּבְעֵי רַחֲמֵי – and pray for God's **mercies** that the evil inclination should not dominate you. לֹא הֲוָה יָדַע אַמַּאי קָאָמְרָה לֵיהּ – **He never knew why she told him this.** יוֹמָא חַד – **One day,** יָתִיב קָא גָּרִיס תּוּתֵי דִּיקְלָא – **he sat studying under a palm tree,** נְפַל גְּלִימָא מֵעִילָּוֵיהּ רֵישֵׁיהּ – **and the cloak fell off his head.** דָּלֵי עֵינֵיהּ חֲזָא לְדִיקְלָא – **He lifted his eyes and saw the palm.** אַלְמֵיהּ יִצְרֵיהּ – **His evil inclination overpowered him,** סְלִיק פַּסְקֵיהּ לְקִיבּוּרָא בְּשִׁינֵּיהּ – **and he went up and chopped off a cluster of dates with his teeth.**[15]

Mishnah The next Mishnah continues the laws of feeding animals on the Sabbath. The Mishnah reflects a recurring disagreement between R' Yehudah and R' Shimon: whether or not an item must be "prepared" for Sabbath use at the onset of the Sabbath.[16] מְחַתְּכִין אֶת הַדְּלוּעִין לִפְנֵי הַבְּהֵמָה – WE MAY CUT UP GOURDS BEFORE AN ANIMAL on the Sabbath for it to eat,[17] וְאֶת הַנְּבֵלָה לִפְנֵי הַכְּלָבִים – AND we may cut up A CARCASS BEFORE DOGS for them to eat.[18] רַבִּי יְהוּדָה אוֹמֵר – R' YEHUDAH SAYS: אִם לֹא הָיְתָה נְבֵלָה מֵעֶרֶב שַׁבָּת אֲסוּרָה – IF IT WAS NOT already A CARCASS BEFORE the onset of THE SABBATH IT IS PROHIBITED to cut it up on the Sabbath, לְפִי שֶׁאֵינָהּ מִן הַמּוּכָן – SINCE IT IS NOT SOMETHING THAT WAS PREPARED for the dogs' use.[19]

Gemara The Gemara cites three Amoraim who decided the law in accordance with R' Yehudah and three who decided in accordance with R' Shimon:

אִיתְּמַר – **It has been stated:**

The Gemara interrupts to offer a mnemonic:

(עֲרִ"ל שַׁחַ"ז סִימָן – **A mnemonic:UReL SHaCHaZ.**)[20]

The Gemara continues, citing the first of the three Amoraim who decided in favor of R' Yehudah:

אָמַר עוּלָּא – **Ulla said:** הֲלָכָה כְּרַבִּי יְהוּדָה – **The halachah follows R' Yehudah.** (וּשְׁמוּאֵל אָמַר הֲלָכָה כְּרַבִּי שִׁמְעוֹן – **And Shmuel said: The halachah follows R' Shimon.**)[21]

The second Amora:

וְאַף רַב סָבַר הֲלָכָה כְּרַבִּי יְהוּדָה – **And Rav also held that the halachah follows R' Yehudah,** מִדִּכְרָכֵי דְּזוּוֵי – as we see **from** his decision concerning **ships' mats,** i.e. mats used for covering a ship's cargo,[22] דְּרַב אָסַר וּשְׁמוּאֵל שָׁרֵי – **for Rav prohibited** their movement **while Shmuel permitted** it.

The third Amora:

וְאַף לֵוִי סָבַר הֲלָכָה כְּרַבִּי יְהוּדָה – **And Levi too held that the halachah follows R' Yehudah,** כִּי הָא דְּלֵוִי – as we see from **this** practice **of Levi:** כִּי הֲווּ מַיְיתֵי טְרֵיפְתָּא לְקַמֵּיהּ בְּיוֹמָא טָבָא – **Whenever they would bring a** potential ***treifah***[23] **before him on Yom Tov,** לֹא הֲוָה חָזֵי לָהּ אֶלָּא כִּי יָתִיב אַקִּילְקְלִיתָא – **he would not inspect it unless he was sitting by a garbage dump** on which he could lay the animal. דְּאָמַר דִּילְמָא לֹא מִתַּכְשְׁרָא – **For he said: Perhaps it will not be found kosher,** וַאֲפִילּוּ לִכְלָבִים לֹא חַזְיָא – **and then it will not even be fit for dogs,** since it will be *muktzeh.*[24] Since the carcass lay already on a dump, it could simply be left there.

NOTES

Nedarim 30b; *Magen Avraham* 2:6; *Beur HaGra* to *Orach Chaim* 8:2; cf. *Maharsha* here).

15. The palm tree was not his [and thus he stole the dates] (*Rashi*). Therefore we see that R' Nachman bar Yitzchak was destined to be a thief, yet prayer and a reverent mode of dress altered his destiny.

[*Megadim Chadashim* suggests that this episode happened in R' Nachman bar Yitzchak's childhood, before he had a chance to overcome his inborn nature; see above, 156a note 49.]

16. As we have seen many times in this tractate, R' Yehudah and R' Shimon dispute the scope of the *muktzeh* prohibition. This dispute finds expression in many areas of the laws of *muktzeh*. It stems from a disagreement over how to interpret the basic rule that whatever was set aside from being used on the Sabbath is *muktzeh*. According to R' Yehudah, this includes any object that in the normal course of events does not stand to be used on the Sabbath. Since the owner did not intend or expect to use the object, it lacks "preparation" for Sabbath use and is *muktzeh*. R' Shimon, on the other hand, holds that the mere fact that an object does not stand to be used is not a consideration. Rather, as long as something is fit for use, it is not rendered *muktzeh* unless the owner sets it aside (see above, 43b note 5, and the sources cited there).

17. The Mishnah refers to gourds that are not attached to the ground (*Rashi*), having been harvested before the Sabbath (*Tosafos* to *Chullin* 14a ד"ה מחתכין, second explanation). [If they were presently attached, detaching them would involve the *melachah* of קוֹצֵר, *reaping.*] Gourds are usually not designated for animal consumption but, rather, for human consumption. The Mishnah thus teaches that a food "prepared" for human consumption is not *muktzeh* in regard to animals [see next note] (*Rashi* here and above, 155b ד"ה את הדלועין; cf. *Rashi* to *Beitzah* 2a).

18. The Mishnah speaks of a case in which the animal was alive when the Sabbath began, so that at the onset of the Sabbath (during *bein hashemashos*) it stood to be used for human consumption (*Rashi*).

In general we consider that something that stands to be used for human consumption does not stand to be used for animal consumption. Thus in our case, at the onset of the Sabbath when the animal was alive and stood to be slaughtered and eaten by people, it did not stand to be fed to animals. Now, however, the animal is dead and must be used as dog food. Thus, the animal was not prepared at the onset of the Sabbath for its present use. According to R' Yehudah, therefore, it lacks the requisite preparation and is *muktzeh*. Nonetheless, the Tanna of our Mishnah allows it to be cut up and fed to dogs, because he follows the view of R' Shimon who does not require an item to be prepared at the onset of the Sabbath (see *Beitzah* 2a).

19. R' Yehudah here follows his view that an item must be prepared at the onset of the Sabbath in order for it to be used on the Sabbath. Since in this case the animal was prepared at the beginning of the Sabbath only for human consumption and not for its ultimate fate as dog food, it must be considered *muktzeh* (see *Pesachim* 56b, and *Beitzah* 6b).

[*Tosafos* question the need for this explanation. Why not say simply that R' Yehudah views the animal as *muktzeh* because of the prohibition to slaughter it on the Sabbath, since R' Yehudah is known to subscribe to the concept of *muktzeh by dint of a prohibition*? (see below 157a note 16) *Tosafos* suggest various solutions to this difficulty; for still other solutions see *Rashba* to *Chullin* 15a).]

[According to R' Yehudah the gourds mentioned in the first clause of the Mishnah are *muktzeh* as well; since they stand to be eaten by people, they are not considered prepared for animals (*Ritva MHK* ed., explaining *Rashi; Tosafos R' Akiva Eiger* to this Mishnah §180; cf. *Ritva MHK* ed.; *Rashash*).]

20. Urel (ערל) is an acronym for the three Amoraim who side with R' Yehudah: **U** (ע) = **U**lla; **R** (ר) = **R**av; **L** (ל) = **L**evi. SHaCHaZ (שח"ז) denotes the three Amoraim who follow R' Shimon: **SH** (ש) = **Sh**muel; **CH** (ח) = R' Yo**ch**anan; **Z** (ז) = **Z**eiri. [In the ensuing Gemara, Zeiri is mentioned before R' Yochanan. This accords with *Rabbeinu Chananel's* version of the mnemonic: ער"ל שז"ח.]

21. [*Maharshal* omits these words, presumably because the Gemara repeats these exact words below.]

22. These were mats reserved for the commercial purpose of covering a ship's cargo (*Rashi;* cf. *Rashi* to 19b ד"ה כרכי). Since they are set aside for this purpose, they are not prepared for Sabbath use and are *muktzeh* according to R' Yehudah (*Ritva MHK* ed. to 19b; cf. *Tosafos* there, ד"ה הני).

23. I.e. a slaughtered animal that had been found to bear a physical defect that might render it a *treifah*. The animal thus called for a rabbinic decision (*Rashi*).

24. Levi follows R' Yehudah's view. Since at the onset of Yom Tov (before it was known to be *treifah*) the animal stood to be eaten by people, it was not prepared for animal consumption and cannot now be fed to dogs; hence it is *muktzeh*.

דקאי צדק במערב מהדרנא ומוקמינא ליה במזרח והיינו דכתיב א) מי העיר ממזרח צדק יקראהו לרגלו ומדשמואל נמי אין מזל לישראל דשמואל ואבלט הוו יתבי והוו קאזלי הנך אינשי לאגמא א"ל אבלט לשמואל האי גברא אזיל ולא אתי טריק ליה חיויא ומיית א"ל שמואל אי בר ישראל הוא אזיל ואתי אדיתבי אזיל ואתי קם אבלט שדיה לטוניה אשכח ביה חיויא דפסיק ושדי בתרתי גובי א"ל שמואל מאי עבדת א"ל כל יומא הוה מרמינן ריפתא בהדי הדדי ואכלינן האידנא הוה איכא חד מינן דלא הוה ליה ריפתא הוה קא מיכסף אמינא להו אנא קאימנא וארמינא כי מטאי לגביה שואי נפשאי כמאן דשקילי מיניה היכי דלא ליכסיף א"ל מצוה עבדת א נפק שמואל ודרש ב) וצדקה תציל ממות ולא ממיתה משונה אלא ממיתה עצמה ומדר"ע נמי אין מזל לישראל דר"ע הויא ליה ברתא אמרי ליה כלדאי ההוא יומא דעיילה לבי גננא טריק לה חיויא ומיתא הוה דאיגא אמילתא טובא ההוא יומא שקלתה למכבנתא דצתא בגודא איתרמי איתיב בעיניה דחיויא לצפרא כי קא שקלה לה הוה קא סריך ואתי חיויא בתרה אמר לה אבוה מאי עבדת אמרה ליה בפניא אתא עניא קרא אבבא והוו טרידי כולי עלמא בסעודתא וליכא דשמעיה קאימנא שקלתי (א) לריסתנאי דיהבית לי יהבתיה ניהליה אמר לה מצוה עבדת נפק ר"ע ודרש וצדקה תציל ממות ולא ממיתה משונה אלא ממיתה עצמה ומדר"נ בר יצחק נמי אין מזל לישראל דאימיה דר"נ בר יצחק אמרי לה כלדאי בריך גנבא הוה לא שבקתיה גלויי רישיה אמרה ליה ג כסי רישיך כי היכי דתיהוי עלך אימתא דשמיא ובעי רחמי לא הוה ידע אמאי קאמרה ליה יומא חד יתיב קא גריס תותי דיקלא נפל גלימא מעילויה רישיה דלי עיניה חזא לדיקלא אלמיה יצריה סליק פסקיה לקיבורא בשיניה: **מתני'** ג מחתכין את הדלועין לפני הבהמה ד ואת הנבלה לפני הכלבים רבי יהודה אומר אם לא היתה נבלה מערב שבת אסורה לפי שאינה מן המוכן: **גמ'** איתמר (עי' שח"ז סימן) אמר עולא הלכה כרבי יהודה (ג ושמואל אמר הלכה כר"ש) ואף רב סבר הלכה כרבי יהודה מדכרכי דוזזי ה דרב אסר ושמואל שרי ואף לוי סבר הלכה כרבי יהודה כי הא דלוי כי הוו מייתי טריפתא לקמיה ביומא טבא לא הוה חזי לה אלא כי יתיב ו אקילקליתא דאמר דילמא לא מתכשרא ואפילו לכלבים לא חזיא ושמואל אמר הלכה כרבי שמעון ואף זעירי סבר הלכה כר"ש דתנן ז בהמה שמתה לא יזיזנה ממקומה ותרגמא זעירי ח בבהמת קדשים אבל בחולין שפיר דמי ואף רבי יוחנן אמר הלכה כר"ש ומי א"ר יוחנן הכי ט והא א"ר יוחנן הלכה כסתם משנה ותנן

אין

רש"י

דקאי צדק. שהוא מזל שלך: במערב. שהוא מקום מלונו ואין ראוי להוליד כך מלאתי בהס"ם רבינו הלוי: במזרחו. שהוא מקום חום: צדק. הקב"ה קראו להביאו למזרח: לרגלו. בשבילו: אבלט. שם חכם נכרי היה וחוזה בכוכבים: אזיל ואתי. דאין מזל לישראל ויועיל לו תפלה: בתרתי גובי. בשתי חתיכות שקצצו עם הקנים בלא יודע: מרמינן בהדדי. מטילין פת [לסל] לכל החבורה כאחד ואוכלין יחד והאחד גובה מכולן: אנא קאימנא ומרמינא. אגבה ואשים בסל: שוואי נפשאי כמאן דשקלי מיניה. עשיתי עצמי כגובה ממנו ונתתי משלי חלקו: לא ממיתה משונה. ומיהו מיתה הגונה ימות אלא ממיתה עצמה מצלת ונותנת חיים: כלדאי. חוזים בכוכבים: דצתא. תחבתה: למכבנתא. [אישפינגלי"ז בלע"ז] נוסקא של זהב שיש כמו עם בראשה: ריסתנאי. אמנסטרייסו"ן: ובעי רחמי. בקש רחמים שלא ישלוט בך יצר הרע: קיבורא. אשכול תמרים והדקל לא שלו היה: **מתני'** את הדלועין. התלושין ומיהו סתמן לאו למאכל בהמה קיימי אלא לאדם: ואת הנבלה. שנתנבלה היום ובין השמשות היתה עומדת לאדם ואפ"ה מחתכין: **גמ'** כר"ש. דלית ליה מוקצה: מדכרכי דוזזי. מחצלות העשויות לספינות לכסות פרקמטיא שבתוכן. דוזי ספינות בלשון ארמי כך מצאתי בתשובת הגאונים: כי הוו מייתי טריפתא לקמיה. בהמה שנולד בה ספק טרפות וצריכה להוראת חכם: אקלקילתא. ° על האשפה שאם יראנה טריפה יניחה שם: ואפילו לכלבים לא חזיא. דנשחטה היום ולא יוכלו לטלטל כרבי יהודה: תרגמא זעירי. במסכת ביצה בבהמת קדשים דאסורה בהנאה ולא חזיא לכלבים הא דחולין שפיר דמי להאכילה לכלבים:

תוספות

כלדאי. בכולה סוגיא משמע דהיינו חוזים בכוכבים ולא כמו שפירש"י בערבי פסחים (דף קיג:) מניין שאין שואלין בכלדאים שנאמר תמים תהיה וגו' ופירש דהיינו אוב ועוד קשה דבהדיא כתיב אל תפנו וגו' ובספרי דרש מנין שאין שואלין בגורלות שנאמר תמים תהיה וגורל וחוזה בכוכבים חדא מילתא היא:

רבי יהודה אומר אם לא היתה נבלה מע"ש כו'. תימה היכי מוכח בפסחים פרק מקום שנהגו בסופו (דף נו. וכו) ובפ"ק דביצה (דף ו: וכו) מהך מתניתין דמוכן לאדם לא הוי מוכן לכלבים לעולם מוכן לאדם הוי מוכן לכלבים והכא היינו טעמא דאסירה לכלבים משום דהואי מוקצה מחמת איסור שלא היתה ראויה היא (ב) לא לאדם (ב) ולא לכלבים) ותירץ ר"י דיש דברים ראויים ליתן לפני הכלבים חיים כגון עופות וכיוצא בהן הלכך אי לאו דמוכן לאדם לא הוי מוכן לכלבים הוה שריא ליתן לכלבים וה"ר יצחק בן הר"ר מאיר גרים במתני' אם לא היתה נבלה מעי"ט אסורה השתא אתי שפיר בפשיטות דמוכן לאדם ואינו מוקצה מחמת איסור ולא נהירא לי דבריש ביצה (דף ב.) דייק מינה דגבי שבת סתם לה תנא כר"ש אלמא גבי שבת מיתניא וה"ר פורת מפרש דממשנה יתירה דייק דה"ל למתני אם לא היתה נבלה מע"ש אסורה ותו לא דמאי נ"ל לפי שאינה מן המוכן אלא להכי תני לה דאפילו הוי מוכן לאדם לגמרי שלא היה מוקצה מחמת איסור לא הוי מוכן לכלבים. מ"ר:

ושמואל אמר הלכה כר"ש. תימה לר"י תרתי דשמואל למה לי דתיפוק ליה מההיא דכרכי דוזי ועז לחלבה ורחל לגיזתה דשילהי פ"ק (דף יט: וכו) ותירץ ר"י דמוקצה דהתם קיל ממוקצה דהכא:

תרגמא זעירי בבהמת קדשים. תימה לר"י היכי מוכח מהכא דס"ל כר"ש ע"כ איצטריך לאוקמה בבהמת קדשים כדמוכח פרק אין צדין (ביצה דף מ:) משום דמתני' נמי דיקא דקתני עלה ולא החלה שנטמאת מה חלה דקדשים אף בהמה דקדשים ומכח האי דיוקא פריך התם למר בר אמימר דאמר מודה היה ר"ש בבעלי חיים שמתו שאסורין ודחיק ר"י לתרץ ° דהכי קים ליה להש"ס שלא פירש זעירי כן אלא משום דבעי לאוקמה כר"ש. מ"ר:

והא א"ר יוחנן הלכה כסתם משנה ותנן אין מבקעין כו'. תימה לר"י היכי מוכח מהכא דלא ס"ל כר"ש דההיא ודאי כרבי יהודה דשמא אית ליה לרבי יוחנן מיגו דאיתקצאי לבין השמשות איתקצאי לכולי יומא וקורה שנשברה אפילו לר"ש איתקצאי בין השמשות קודם שבירתה דהואי מוקצה מחמת חסרון כיס דמודה ביה ר"ש אבל במתניתין לא איתקצאי בין השמשות דלית ליה ההיא מוקצה מה שהיא עומדת לאדם והיה רוצה רבי לתרץ דאי אית ליה לר' יוחנן מיגו דאיתקצאי היה אוסר ודאי לטלטל בהמה שנתנבלה בשבת שהרי נהי שהיתה ראויה לכלבים (ג) בלא שחיטה כדפירשית לעיל מיהו לטלטל היתה אסורה דכולי עלמא מודו דבעלי חיים הם מוקצים הוה לן למימר מיגו דאיתקצאי ודנתי לפני רבי כיון שהיא ראויה לכלבים משום שהיא מוקצה לטלטל אין לנו לאוסרה לטלטל נבלה בשבת מידי דהוה אפירות הנושרין דתלינן טעמא בריש ביצה (דף ג.) שמא יעלה ויתלוש ומשום מוקצה לא אסירי לטלטל כיון דחזו לעורבים בעודן מחוברין אע"פ (ג) שבעת חבורן היו אסורין לטלטל ותירץ רבי דמסתמא מתניתין בכל ענין איירי בין אותן שראויין לכלבים בעודן חיים בין שאינן ראויין לכלבים דבכולהו שרי ר"ש ואכולהו קאי רבי יוחנן דאמר הלכה כרבי שמעון דמתניתין ולא למחצה אלמא לית ליה מיגו דאיתקצאי. מ"ר:

והא אמר רבי יוחנן הלכה כסתם משנה. בריש ביצה (דף ג.) אמרינן גבי שבת דסתם לן תנא כר"ש משמע דחשיב לסתמא דמתני' סתמא. אמר רבי לאו משום סתמא קאמר דודאי לא חשיב כסתמא כיון דבמתניתין נמי פליג רבי יהודה וסתמא לאו דוקא אלא חשיב כרבים. מ"ר (ט):

אין

עין משפט נר מצוה

לב א טוש"ע י"ד סימן רמו סעיף ד:
לג ב טוש"ע א"ח סימן ג סעיף ו:
לד ג ד מיי' פכ"ה מהלכות שבת הל' יח סמג שם טוש"ע א"ח סימן שכד סעיף ו ז:
לה ה מיי' פ"ב מהלכות יו"ט הלכה טז סמג לאוין עה:

רבינו חננאל

הלכתא כוותיה ונתברר שהלכה כר' יוסי ב"ר יהודה שנותנין מים למורסן וגובלין את הקליא מעט מעט. ושורין שבחשין את השתית בשבת. פי' השתית היא שתיתא דאמור רבנן בכיצד מברכין (דף לח ע"א) ודברי הכל מותר לבחוש בשבת והוא נתינת השתית שהוא הקליא בכלי ואחר כך יתן בו חומץ ויערבנו שתי וערב בתרווד או כיוצא בו כלי הניטל בשבת וינער אח"כ את הכלי לכלי אחר אבל לא יערבנו כדרך מרישה שמריץ התרווד סביבות כל הכלי שבתוכו השתית אלא שתי וערב בלבד. והני מילי דבחיש בה רכה אבל לבוחשה עבה גיבול הוא ואסור. ואקשינן עלה היכי אמרת דשרין שבוחשין את השתית ומי שרי והא אמרת רישא אין גובלין את הקליא. כלומר ת"ק ר"א (אסור) [מתיר] גיבול הקליא וקתני סיפא דשרין שבוחשין את הקליא מכלל דאפי' (ת"ק) שרי ומפרקי' ל"ק הא דתני אין גובלין בעבה וסיפא דקתני ושרין שבוחשין ברכה והוא דמשני ממעשה דחול שדרכו בחול נותן החומץ ואחר כך הקמח ובשבת ישנה יתן השתית ואחר כך יתן החומץ ואפילו נתינת מים למורסן כעין גיבול בשנוי שרי כדאמרי משמיה דרב ירמיה בר אבא גובלין ולא מספין ודלא לקיט בלשניה מלקיטין והני מילי גיבול בשנוי והוא עירוב שתי וערב ונינער מכלי אל כלי אחר אבל מירוס כעין טוחן ברחים של יד שמסבב ומוליך ומביא אסור. אמרו לו לרבי חנינא מהו לגבל אמר להו אסור לפרק מאי אמר [להו] מותר ולמה לא פירש מהו לפרק ומהו חד קמי חדא ותרי קמי תרתי שראיתי בין הגאונים חילוק בפירושם הלכתא כעולא דאמר אפילו כור אפילו כוריים שרי ואפילו לשלשה ועוד ולבלבד ע"י שינוי כאשר פירשנו למעלה ושאר השמועה פשוטה היא: אבלט שהיה רבן שמואל אומר גוי הוא דאמרינן בפרק אין מעמידין בהמה בפונדקאות של גוים שמואל ואבלט הוו יתבי כו': מתני' מחתכין את הדלועין לפני הבהמה ואת הנבלה לפני הכלבים. רבי יהודה אומר אם לא היתה נבלה מע"ש אסורה: איתמר ע"ר"ל אמר הלכה כר' יהודה. פי' ע"ר"ל סימן שמות החכמים דאמרו דהלכה כר' יהודה והם עולא ורב ולוי אילו שלשתן כר' יהודה עולא בפירוש אמר הלכה כר' יהודה רב מכלל חלוקתו על שמואל בכרכי דוזי פי' מחצלאות הכרוכות זוגות זוגות העומדות לתפירה דרב אסר להתירן ולישב בהן שמעינן מינה כיון שהן לסחורה מוקצות הן מכלל דסבר הלכתא כר' יהודה לוי נמי מכללא דכי הוו מייתי טרפה לקמיה דלוי ביו"ט לא הוה חזי ליה אלא אקילקלתא סבר דלמא לא מכשרא ואפילו לכלבים לא חזי שמעינן מינה דסבר כר' יהודה סבירא ליה דאמר לפי שאינה מן המוכן: שז"ח סימן והן שמואל זעירי ור' יוחנן: שמואל ור' יוחנן בהדיא אמרי הלכתא כר' שמעון וזעירי דמתרגם להא דתנן בהמה שמתה לא יזיזנה ממקומה

מסורת הש"ס

א) [גירסת הערוך לדפשתנא פי' חלוק], ב) ביצה ו. ג) מ: פסחים נו: חולין יא. ד) רש"ל מ"ז, ה) [ע"ל יט:], ו) [פ' פרש"י ב"ק פה. וכעי"ז כת' ד"ה ניקולין], ז) ביצה מ:, ח) [לעיל מו. וש"נ], ט) רש"ל מ"ז, י) [ע' תוספות ביצה ב: ד"ה גבי שבת].

הגהות הב"ח

(א) גמרא שקלתינהו לריסתנאי. נ"ב פירוש חלק סעודה שלי. ועי' בברכות דף מב: (ב) תוס' ד"ה והא א"ר יוחנן וכו' ראויה לכלבים בע"ש כדפי' לעיל: (ג) באד"ה מ"ש שבשעת חבורן:

גליון הש"ס

רש"י ד"ה אקלקילתא. על האשפה. מאשפות ירים אביון (תהלים קיג) תרגום מקלקלתא מרים חשוכא. רש"י ע"ג דף קל ע"ב ד"ה ויקפלו. תוס' ד"ה קיים ליה. עיין לעיל דף ט ע"ב תוס' ד"ה הא לן וש"נ:

תורה אור השלם

א) מִי הֵעִיר מִמִּזְרָח צֶדֶק יִקְרָאֵהוּ לְרַגְלוֹ יִתֵּן לְפָנָיו גּוֹיִם וּמְלָכִים יַרְדְּ יִתֵּן כֶּעָפָר חַרְבּוֹ כְּקַשׁ נִדָּף קַשְׁתּוֹ: [ישעיה מא, ב]
ב) לֹא יוֹעִילוּ אוֹצְרוֹת רֶשַׁע וּצְדָקָה תַּצִּיל מִמָּוֶת: [משלי י, ב]

ליקוטי רש"י

טוניה. משאו [ע"פ ב"מ קז.]. גננא. חופה [גיטין נז.]. דצתא. דוך. לשון מיקום כלומר לא שלפה [שבת נ:] [יבמות קטו:]. לשון תחיבה ונעיצה הוא בלשון ארמית והרבה יש בגמ' דלא ושלפה [שבת נ:]. דץ ביה מידי [חולין נ:]. דצה לא כמו דעלה אלא שמקום לשון [בראשית ל, לח]. גודא. כותל [לעיל קמט.]. מחתכין את הדלועין. תלושין לפני הבהמה ולא אמרינן כיון דסתמן עומדין לאדם לאו מוכן לבהמה [ביצה ב.]. התלושין וגו' אמרינן מוקצין הן לבהמה דמאכל אדם הן [שם קנה:]. ואת הנבלה לפני הכלבים. ואע"פ שנתנבלה היום ובין השמשות לא היתה עומדת למאכל כלבים אפילו הכי שרי דלית ליה לר"ש מוקצה [ביצה שם]. והכי שנתנבלה בשבת קאמר מדפליג רבי יהודה עלה ואמר אם לא היתה נבלה מערב שבת אסורה לפי שאינה מן המוכן [שם כו:]. שאינה מן המוכן. שבין השמשות לא היתה עומדת למאכל כלבים [חולין יד.]. כרכי דוזי. זוג של מחצלות מוכרות כגון אלו פרגמטיא של ספינה חבור שלא היו מוכנין שכן שום ועשויות להחליף ובתשובות הגאונים מצאתי כרכי דוזי ממכרות דוזי לשון ספינה בלשון ארמי [ע"ש בב"ח]. דרב אסר.

לטלטולי משום מוקצה דרב סבר כר' יהודה למוקצה ושמואל סבר כר' שמעון דלית ליה מוקצה כמו שהסביר [לעיל יט:]. בבהמת קדשים. שאסורה בהנאה וטעונה קבורה ואינה נפדית דבעינן העמדה והערכה לא חזי אין פודין קדשים להאכילן לכלבים ואפילו למאן דאמר פודין היכא דלא פרקי לה הלכך לא חזיא [ביצה שם]. הלכה כסתם משנה. רבי הוא סדר המשנה ושנה דברי חכם ויש יחידים שנה סתם ולא הזכיר שם האומרו עליהן כדי שלא יהו שנויה מפי יחיד ונראין כאלו נשנו מפי המרובים ויעשו כמותן [שם ב:].

The Gemara cites the three Amoraim who decide with R' Shimon that an object does not have to be prepared for Sabbath use:

וּשְׁמוּאֵל אָמַר הֲלָכָה כְּרַבִּי שִׁמְעוֹן – And Shmuel said: The halachah follows R' Shimon. **וְאַף זְעִירִי סָבַר הֲלָכָה כְּרַבִּי שִׁמְעוֹן – And Zeiri too held that the halachah follows R' Shimon,** **דִּתְנַן – for we learned in a Mishnah:**[25] **בְּהֵמָה שֶׁמֵּתָה** – IF AN ANIMAL DIED on Yom Tov, **לֹא יְזִיזֶנָּה מִמְּקוֹמָהּ** – ONE MAY NOT MOVE IT FROM ITS PLACE. **וְתַרְגְּמָא זְעִירִי – Now Zeiri interpreted** this Mishnah **בִּבְהֱמַת קָדָשִׁים – to refer to a consecrated animal** that died. Benefit may not be derived from its carcass because of its consecrated status; it is therefore *muktzeh,* even according to R' Shimon.[26] **אֲבָל בְּחוּלִּין שַׁפִּיר דָּמֵי** – Apparently, **however, regarding an ordinary animal, this would be fine,** i.e. one could move it and feed it to dogs.[27]

The third Amora:

וְאַף רַבִּי יוֹחָנָן אָמַר הֲלָכָה כְּרַבִּי שִׁמְעוֹן – And R' Yochanan also said: The halachah follows R' Shimon.

The Gemara challenges this:

וּמִי אָמַר רַבִּי יוֹחָנָן הָכִי – Now, did R' Yochanan really **say this?** **וְהָא אָמַר רַבִּי יוֹחָנָן – But R' Yochanan has said:** **הֲלָכָה כִּסְתָם מִשְׁנָה – The halachah** always **follows an anonymous Mishnah!** **וּתְנַן – And we learned in a Mishnah:**[28]

NOTES

25. *Beitzah* 27b.

26. An animal that has been designated as a sacrifice is prohibited for any other purpose, even if it dies. This type of dead animal is completely useless, and is consequently *muktzeh,* even according to R' Shimon (see *Rashi* to *Beitzah* 27b ד״ה בבהמת קדשים).

27. Obviously, then, Zeiri holds with R' Shimon that an ordinary animal that died on the Sabbath or on Yom Tov is not *muktzeh,* despite its not having been prepared for its present use as dog food.

28. *Beitzah* 31a.

אֵין מְבַקְּעִין עֵצִים מִן הַקּוֹרוֹת – WE MAY NOT SPLIT WOOD FROM BEAMS for firewood on Yom Tov,[1] וְלֹא מִן הַקּוֹרָה שֶׁנִּשְׁבְּרָה בְּיוֹם טוֹב – NOR FROM A BEAM THAT BROKE ON YOM TOV.[2] Now, this anonymous Mishnah clearly supports R' Yehudah's opinion, so how could R' Yochanan have said that the law follows R' Shimon?

The Gemara answers:

רַבִּי יוֹחָנָן הַהוּא כְּרַבִּי יוֹסֵי בַּר יְהוּדָה מַתְנֵי לָהּ – **R' Yochanan** does not consider that Mishnah to be anonymous; rather he **taught that it reflects** the opinion of **R' Yose bar Yehudah.**[3]

The Gemara cites another anonymous Mishnah that seems to conflict with R' Shimon, and thus poses a difficulty for R' Yochanan:

תָּא שְׁמַע מַתְחִילִין בַּעֲרֵימַת הַתֶּבֶן – **Come, learn** a proof to this from the following Mishnah:[4] WE MAY BEGIN using A STACK OF STRAW as fuel for a fire on Yom Tov,[5] אֲבָל לֹא בְּעֵצִים שֶׁבַּמּוּקְצֶה – BUT NOT WOOD that is IN A BACKYARD.[6] This Mishnah seems to follow the view of R' Yehudah. – ? –

The Gemara answers:

הָתָם בְּאַרְזֵי וְאַשּׁוּחֵי – The wood **referred to there** in that Mishnah is expensive wood, namely the wood of [male] **cedars and** ***ashuchei***[7] דְּמוּקְצֶה מֵחֲמַת חֶסְרוֹן כִּיס – **which,** because it is ***muktzeh for fear of monetary loss,***[8] אֲפִילוּ רַבִּי שִׁמְעוֹן מוֹדֶה – **even R' Shimon admits** is *muktzeh.* Thus, this anonymous Mishnah does not run counter to R' Shimon's view.[9]

The Gemara cites another anonymous Mishnah that conflicts with R' Shimon, again posing a difficulty for R' Yochanan:

תָּא שְׁמַע – **Come, learn** the following Mishnah:[10] אֵין מַשְׁקִין וְשׁוֹחֲטִין אֶת הַמִּדְבָּרִיּוֹת – WE MAY NOT WATER AND SLAUGHTER RANGE ANIMALS, since they are not prepared for consumption on Yom Tov, אֲבָל מַשְׁקִין וְשׁוֹחֲטִין אֶת הַבַּיְיתוֹת – BUT WE MAY WATER AND SLAUGHTER DOMESTIC ANIMALS.[11] This anonymous Mishnah seems to follow the view of R' Yehudah, who requires an item to be prepared for Yom Tov use. – ? –

The Gemara answers:

רַבִּי יוֹחָנָן סְתָמָא אַחֲרִינָא אַשְׁכַּח – **R' Yochanan found another anonymous Mishnah**[12] which supports R' Shimon's view, as follows: בֵּית שַׁמַּאי אוֹמְרִים – BEIS SHAMMAI SAY: מַגְבִּיהִין מֵעַל הַשֻּׁלְחָן עֲצָמוֹת וּקְלִיפִּין – WE MAY REMOVE BONES AND HUSKS FROM THE TABLE on the Sabbath by hand.[13] וּבֵית הִלֵּל אוֹמְרִים – BUT BEIS HILLEL SAY: מְסַלֵּק אֶת הַטַּבְלָה כּוּלָּהּ וּמְנַעֲרָהּ – ONE MUST TAKE UP THE ENTIRE TABLE BOARD AND SHAKE IT clean, and not handle the bones and husks directly.[14] וְאָמַר רַב נַחְמָן – **And Rav Nachman said** regarding this Mishnah: אָנוּ אֵין לָנוּ אֶלָּא – **We have no** reliance on this version of the Mishnah, for it

NOTES

1. The Mishnah here refers to a stack of wood that has been set aside for later use in construction (*Rashi;* see *Beitzah* 31b).

2. Since a broken beam is unfit for use in construction, it would normally be used for firewood. However, since this particular beam was whole at the onset of Yom Tov, it could not be prepared at that time for its present Yom Tov use (as firewood). [Consequently, it is *muktzeh* according to R' Yehudah, whose view this Mishnah follows] (*Rashi*).

[As to whether the first case of this Mishnah must also reflect the view of R' Yehudah, or might R' Shimon concede that a stack of wood that has been set aside for construction is *muktzeh,* see *Tosafos* to *Beitzah* 2b ד״ה אין; but see above, 125b; see also *Hagahos R' Akiva Eiger* to *Orach Chaim* 308:1.]

3. R' Yochanan had a different version of that Mishnah: In R' Yochanan's version, the Mishnah ended: These are the words of R' Yose bar Yehudah. Thus, he did not view that Mishnah as anonymous (*Maharshal;* see also *Hagahos R' Yaakov Emden*).

4. *Beitzah* 29b-30a.

5. [I.e. we may take some straw from a stack that had earlier been stockpiled for future use as animal food.]

The Gemara assumes at this point that the Mishnah is referring to straw that had become decayed and unfit for animal food. Because it can no longer be used for animal food – [the purpose for which it was stockpiled] – it stands to be used immediately as fuel [and is therefore considered prepared for Yom Tov use, even according to R' Yehudah] (*Rashi;* see *Tosafos* to *Beitzah* 30a ד״ה התם).

[Furthermore, the Gemara must assume that the straw cannot be used for construction purposes, because it is full of thorns; had it been fit for construction purposes, it would not stand to be used as fuel and would, therefore, be *muktzeh* according to R' Yehudah (see *Beitzah* 30a, and above, 155b note 5).]

6. [The infrequently used space behind houses was called a מוּקְצֶה, *muktzeh,* because it was seldom entered; it is therefore "set out" of one's mind.] It was used as long-term storage for wood and other items not in current use. The Gemara assumes at this point that the reason one may not use this wood is because it has been put away for storage and does not stand to be used on Yom Tov. Apparently, then, this Mishnah follows the view of R' Yehudah.

7. *Ashuchei* are the female cedar trees. The lumber of cedar trees is expensive and is used exclusively for construction, not as fuel (*Rashi*). Thus, even R' Shimon would consider it to be *muktzeh,* as the Gemara proceeds to explain.

8. I.e. an object which is not merely unprepared for Sabbath or Yom Tov use, but which is mentally set aside not to be used on the Sabbath or Yom Tov because it is valuable, and using it for anything except its usual purpose might damage it, causing a monetary loss (see Introduction to Chapter Three).

9. Since the Gemara has now established that this Mishnah may indeed conform with R' Shimon's view, it becomes possible that the beginning of the Mishnah does not refer to decayed straw at all (see note 5). Even though the straw was stored away for animal food, and is not prepared for Yom Tov use, R' Shimon does not require any such preparation (see *Beitzah* 30a).

10. *Beitzah* 40a.

11. Range animals are animals that pasture freely and are not seen for an extended period of time. [Since they are not accessible at the onset of Yom Tov, they do not stand to be used on Yom Tov and are therefore *muktzeh* according to R' Yehudah, whose view this Mishnah follows.] Domestic animals, on the other hand, pasture beyond the *techum* of a settled area but come back to spend the night within the *techum.* [Thus, they stand to be used on Yom Tov] (*Rashi,* as emended by *Hagahos HaBach;* see also *Tosafos* and *Ramban* ד״ה אין; see also *Beitzah* loc. cit. and above, 45b).

The Mishnah mentions "watering" in conjunction with slaughtering [only] because it was common practice to water animals before slaughtering them in order to facilitate their skinning (*Rashi;* see *Beitzah* 40a). Watering them, in and of itself, is not prohibited at all, since they fall under the category of animals for whose feeding one is responsible (*Ran* to *Beitzah* fol. 21b, as explained by *Magen Avraham* 497:2; see there for a different view).

12. Above, 143a.

Actually, this Mishnah is not anonymous at all, but rather records a dispute between Beis Shammai and Beis Hillel. However, a ruling of Beis Hillel has the force of an anonymous Mishnah (*Rashi*).

13. *Tosafos* (above, 143a) and other Rishonim explain that the Mishnah speaks of bones and nutshells that are unfit for human consumption, but which are still fit to be used as animal food. Although at the onset of the Sabbath they were part of a food that stood to be eaten by people and, consequently, were not prepared as animal food, Beis Shammai apparently follow the view of R' Shimon, who does not require an item to be prepared for Sabbath use.

However, *Rashi* (above, 143a) writes that the bones and shells are not suitable even for animals. But this seems difficult for, if so, they resemble wood and stones, which according to all opinions are *muktzeh*! For an explanation of *Rashi's* view, see above, 143a note 5.

14. Since the bones and shells were not prepared as animal food at the onset of the Sabbath, Beis Hillel consider them *muktzeh* and they may not, therefore, be handled directly. However, since the table board qualifies as a utensil, it may be removed and shaken (*Rashi* above, 143a, and to *Beitzah* 2a). Apparently Beis Hillel follow the view of R' Yehudah who requires an item to be prepared for Sabbath use.

אין מבקעין עצים מן הקורות ולא מן הקורה שנשברה ביו"ט רבי יוחנן ההוא כרבי יוסי בר יהודה מתני לה תא שמע מתחילין בערימת התבן אבל לא בעצים שבמוקצה התם בארזי ואשוחי דמוקצה מחמת חסרון כיס אפילו רבי שמעון מודה ת"ש אין משקין ושוחטין את המדבריות אבל משקין ושוחטין את הבייתות ר' יוחנן סתמא אחרינא אשכח ב"ש אומרים מגביהין מעל השלחן עצמות וקליפין וב"ה אומרים מסלק את הטבלה כולה ומנערה וא"ר נחמן אנו אין לנו אלא ב"ש כרבי יהודה וב"ה כר"ש פליגי בה רב אחא ורבינא חד אמר בכל השבת כולה הלכה כר"ש לבר ממוקצה מחמת מיאוס ומאי ניהו נר ישן וחד אמר במוקצה מחמת מיאוס נמי הלכה כר"ש לבר ממוקצה מחמת איסור ומאי ניהו נר שהדליקו בה באותה שבת אבל מוקצה מחמת חסרון כיס אפילו ר"ש מודה דתנן כל הכלים ניטלין בשבת חוץ ממסר הגדול ויתד של מחרישה:

מתני' מפירין נדרים בשבת ונשאלין לנדרים שהן לצורך השבת ופוקקין את המאור ומודדין את המטלית ואת המקוה ומעשה בימי אביו של רבי צדוק ובימי אבא שאול בן בטנית שפקקו את המאור בטפיח [ה] וקשרו את המקידה בגמי לידע אם יש בגיגית פותח טפח אם לאו ומדבריהם למדנו שפוקקין ומודדין וקושרין בשבת:

גמ' איבעיא להו הפרה בין לצורך ובין שלא לצורך ושאלה לצורך אין שלא לצורך לא ומשום הכי קפלגינהו מהדדי או דילמא הפרה נמי לצורך אין שלא לצורך לא והא דקא פליג להו מהדדי משום דהפרה אין צריך ב"ד ושאלה צריכה ב"ד ת"ש דתני זוטי דבי רב פפא מפירין נדרים בשבת לצורך השבת לצורך השבת אין שלא לצורך השבת לא לישנא אחרינא איבעיא להו לצורך אתרווייהו קתני ושלא לצורך לא אלמא הפרת נדרים מעת לעת או דילמא כי קתני לצורך אשאלה הוא דקתני אבל הפרת נדרים אפילו שלא לצורך אלמא הפרת נדרים כל היום תא שמע דתני רב זוטי דבי רב פפי מפירין נדרים בשבת לצורך השבת לצורך השבת אין שלא לצורך השבת לא אלמא הפרת נדרים מעת לעת א"ר אשי והאנן תנן הפרת נדרים כל היום ויש בדבר להקל ולהחמיר כיצד נדרה לילי שבת מיפר לילי שבת ויום השבת עד שתחשך נדרה עם חשכה מיפר עד שלא תחשך שאם לא הפר משחשכה אינו יכול להפר תנאי היא דתניא הפרת נדרים כל היום ר' יוסי בר יהודה ורבי אלעזר ברבי שמעון אמרו מעת לעת: ונשאלים לנדרים: איבעיא להו כשלא היה לו פנאי או דלמא אפילו היה לו פנאי תא שמע דאזדקיקו ליה רבנן לרב זוטרא בריה דרב זירא ושרו ליה נדריה ואף על גב דהוה ליה פנאי: שפקקו את המאור בטפיח וקשרו את המקידה בגמי: אמר רב יהודה אמר רב הילקטי קטנה היתה בין שני בתים [וטומאה היתה שם]

וגיגית

רש"י

אין מבקעין עצים מן הקורות. סואר של הקורות המוקצות וסדורות לבנין: **ולא מן קורה.** הישנה שנשברה היום ומהשתא להסקה קיימא ואפ"ה אסור הואיל ובין השמשות לא איתכן להכי: **מתחילין.** להסיק בערימת התבן קא סלקא דעתך בתיבנא סריא דסתמיה להסקה: **אבל לא בעצים שבמוקצה.** שהכניס ברחבה שאחורי ביתו והקצם לימות הגשמים. מוקצה רחבה שאחורי בתים שהקצה אחורי ביתו להכניס שם דבר לאוצר: **בארזי ואשוחי.** ארז זכר וארז נקבה שעומדין לבנין: **משקין.** אורחא דמילתא נקט משום סירכא דמשכא שתהא נוחה להפשיט: **מדבריות.** (א) הרועות באפר תמיד ולנות בתוך התחום: **סתמא אחרינא.** בית הלל חשיב כסתמא: **כל הכלים ניטלין.** ואפי' מלאכתן לאיסור ורבי שמעון היא: **חוץ מן המסר הגדול.** מגירה שהיא לאומנין לקוץ בה עצים ומוקצה מחמת חסרון כיס הוא שלא ישתברו חריצים שהוא עשוי כסכין מלא פגימות: **ויתד של מחרישה.** החופר את הקרקע קולטר"א בלע"ז: **מתני' מפירין.** בעל לאשתו: **ונשאלין.** לחכם: **שהן לצורך השבת.** כגון שנדר שלא לאכול [היום]: **ופוקקין את המאור.** כרבנן דאמרי (לעיל דף קכה:) פוקקין פקק החלון: **ומודדין את המקוה.** במדה שיהא שם עמוק שלש אמות מים ברוחב אמה על אמה: **ואת המטלית.** (ב) שתהא שלש על שלש אצבעות כגון אם היתה טמאה ונגעה בטהרות: **בטפיח.** פך של חרס (ג) וחבירו בפי"ז (דף קכה:) זמורה שהיא קשורה בטפיח ממלאין בה בשבת: **מקידה.** כלי חרס: **לידע אם יש בגיגית פותח טפח.** בגמרא מפרש לה: **וקושרין.** קשר שאינו של קיימא אפילו לכתחילה: **ומודדין.** להתלמד על דבר הוראה: **גמ' איבעיא להו הפרה.** דמתניתין בין לצורך [בין שלא לצורך] השבת דגבי הפרה ביום שמעו כתיב (במדבר ל) ואם לא מיפר האידנא שוב אינו מיפר: **ושאלה לצורך אין שלא לצורך לא.** דיכול לישאל למחר ומשום הכי מפליג להו מהדדי ולא קתני מפירין ונשאלין לנדרים שהן לצורך השבת דלא קאי לצורך אלא אשאלה: **בית דין.** חכם: **הכי גרסי' ל"א איבעיא להו** (במסכת נדרים דף עז.) **לצורך** אתרווייהו קאי. אהפרה ואשאלה אבל הפרה שלא לצורך לא אלמא הפרת נדרים מעת לעת הא שמע בשבת יכול להפר משתחשך בתוך מעת לעת של שמיעה הלכך שלא לצורך לא שרינן בשבת: **כל היום.** עד שתחשך ותו לא ואפילו שמע סמוך לחשיכה הלכך אפי' שלא לצורך (ע) שאם לא יפר עכשיו לא יפר עוד: **לצורך השבת.** אלמא הפרת נדרים מעת לעת של שמיעה הלכך שלא לצורך (ד) לא מדלא שרי אלא לצורך: **להקל ולהחמיר.** כלומר פעמים שיש שהות גדול ופעמים שאינו אלא מעט: **איבעיא להו.** הא דקתני נשאלין לנדרים שהן לצורך: **כשלא היה לו פנאי.** לשאל מערב שבת קאמר או אפילו כשהיה לו פנאי: **הילקטי קטנה.** שביל קטן בין שני בתים:

וגיגית

תוספות

אין משקין ושוחטין את המדבריות. הוה מצי למימר דהני כגרוגרות וצמוקין דמיין כדאמר בפרק כירה (לעיל דף מה:): **לבר** ממוקצה מחמת איסור. וכגון איסור דדחייה בידים כגון נר שהדליקו באותו שבת כדפירשתי בפ"ק בסופו:

והלכתא מעת לעת. לא גרס בפירוש ר"ח דבנדרים משמע דלית הלכתא הכי דאמר בפרק נערה המאורסה (כתובות דף עו:) אין הלכה כאותו הזוג. מ"ר:

הלקטי קטנה. מפרש בקונטרס שביל קטן היתה בין שני בתים והגיגית סדוקה מונחת על גבן והמת מוטל בהלקטי תחת הגיגית נגד הסדק וקשרו המקידה לידע אם יש בסדק פותח טפח ולהאי פירושא קשה לר"י דאפי' אין בסדק פותח טפח כיון שהמת נגדו לא חשבינן לה כמאהיל על המת כיון שאין [זהו] דרך מאהיל (ה) כדמוכח במסכת אהלות (פי"ד מ"ה) ומייתי לה בסוף פרק קמא דסוכה (דף יח. ושם) אין בארובה פותח טפח והמת בבית מה שבבית כנגד ארובה טהור המת כנגד ארובה מה שבבית טהור וכיון שהמת היה נגד הסדק מה היה להם לקשור המקידה ועוד פירש שלפני מות המת פקקו המאור בטפיח ולא הבין רבי לפירושו הלא אותו מת לא היה מת שלם שהרי לא ידעו אם למעלה הימנו היה פותח טפח והמת היה כולו תחת הסדק אלא ודאי כזית מן המת היה וא"כ לא היה לו לומר לפני מות המת אלא לפני שבא כזית מן המת לשם ומיהו יתכן לומר שהמת היה כולו מוטל תחת הגיגית שלא כנגד הסדק והגיגית היתה סדוקה באמצע מראשה לסופה ואילו היה באותו סדק על פני כולו פותח טפח לא היתה טומאה עוברת דלא חשיב כאהל אחד אבל אין בו פותח טפח כאלו אין כאן סדק וחשיב כאהל אחד ומביא את הטומאה לבית וקושיא ראשונה מכל מקום במקומה עומדת ונראה כפירוש ר"ח דמפרש דהלקטי היינו תל המתלקט ואותה הלקטי היתה בין שני בתים והמת היה בבית אחד ואותה הגיגית היתה למעלה מן התל עד לתקרה ואותה הגיגית לא היתה טמאה שהרי בטלה שם ואם לא היתה סדוקה לא היה הבית אחר טמא אלא הגיגית היתה סדוקה מגלה והשתא אתי שפיר דקתני סדוקה לפי שהיא מגלה אבל לפירוש הקונטרס לא אתי שפיר דכיון דפירש שהסדק למעלה מן הגיגית היה לו לומר פתוחה ולא סדוקה אבל לפר"ח אתי שפיר שהסדק היה מן הצד וקשרו את המקידה לידע אם יש בו פותח טפח ויש לנו לומר שאותו חור היה עשוי לתשמיש לחור העשוי לתשמיש שיעורו בפותח טפח ואם היה פותח טפח הבית אחר טמא ואם לאו טהור ומיהו קשה לר"י לפירוש ר"ח דלא הוה ליה למימר על גבן אלא על גבה. מ"ר:

באוגנה

עין משפט נר מצוה

לו א מיי' פ"ב מהלכות יו"ט הלכה יב סמג לאוין עה טוש"ע א"ח סימן תקז סעיף א:

לז ב ג מיי' שם הלכה יא וסמג שם טוש"ע א"ח סי' תקיט סעיף ג:

לח ד מיי' שם הלכה י סמג שם טוש"ע א"ח סימן תצח סעיף ב:

לט ה מיי' שם הלכה ב וסמג שם טוש"ע א"ח סי' תצ סעיף ג:

[ה] [טוש"ע א"ח סימן שח סעיף מז]:

מ ו מיי' פכ"ד מהלכות שבת הלכה ו ופי"ג מהלכות נדרים הלכה ח וסמג לאוין רמב טוש"ע א"ח סימן שמא סעיף א וטוש"ע י"ד סימן רלד סעיף כד:

מא ז מיי' פ"ו מהל' שבת הלכה ו וסמג שם ומיי' פ"ו מהלכות שבועות הלכה ו סמג לאוין רמב טוש"ע שם וטוש"ע י"ד סי' רכח סעיף ג:

מב ח מיי' פי"ג מהל' נדרים הלכה טו סמג לאוין רמב טוש"ע י"ד סימן רלד סעיף כה:

מג ט מיי' פכ"ד מהל' שבת הלכה ו ופ"ו מהלכות שבועות הלכה ו סמג שם לאוין רמב טוש"ע א"ח סימן שמא סעיף א וטוש"ע י"ד סימן רכח סעיף ג:

רבינו חננאל

ממוקצה בדבהמות קדשים [מיירי] מכלל דהוו שרי כר' [שמעון] דלית ליה מוקצה. ומקשינן על ר' יוחנן וכי סבר ר' יוחנן הלכה כרבי שמעון והא אמר ר' יוחנן הלכה כסתם משנה ותנן אין מבקעין עצים מן הקורות ולא מן הקורה שנשברה ומפרקינן האי כר' יוסי בר' יהודה מתני לה ר' יוחנן ולית סתמא. ואמרינן תוב ת"ש מתחילין בערימת התבן אבל לא בעצים שבמוקצה ומפרקינן התם בארזי [ואשוחי] דמוקצה מחמת חסרון כיס. דאפילו ר' שמעון מודה. פי' ארזי ואשוחי עצי ארזים וברושים העשויין לקורות שאין דעתו של אדם עליהן להסיקן תחת תבשילו וגמור הקצה אותן. ואמרינן ת"ש אין משקין ושוחטין את המדבריות אבל משקין ושוחטין הבייתות וסתם משנה כר' יהודה ורבי יוחנן סבירא ליה הלכתא כסתם משנה קשיא הלכתא אהלכתא ומפרקינן ר' יוחנן סתמא אחרינא אשכח בה"א מגביהין מעל השלחן עצמות וקליפין וב"ש אומרים מסלק את הטבלא כולה ומנערה. ואמר רב נחמן אנו אין לנו אלא ב"ש כר' יהודה וב"ה כר' שמעון והלכתא כר' שמעון וכדפסק ר' יוחנן פליגי בה רב אחא ורבינא חד אמר בכולה שבת הלכתא כר' שמעון בר ממוקצה מחמת מיאוס. וחד אמר במוקצה [מחמת] מיאוס נמי הלכתא כוותיה לבר ממוקצה מחמת איסורו כגון הנר שהדליקו בו באותה שבת ובערב אבל

רב נסים גאון

מפירין נדרים בשבת. אמרו [בתוספתא פ' י"ח] מפני מה נדרי שבת מפירין אותן בשבת שאם חשיכה ולא הפר אינו

הגהות הב"ח

(א) רש"י ד"ה מדבריות וכו' תמיד באפר ולנות באפר הל"ל מה"ד בייתות שרועות חוץ לתחום ובאות ולנות בתוך התחום: (ב) ד"ה ואת המטלית לידע אם יש בה שלש על שלש: (ג) ד"ה בטפיח פך של חרס וחבירו וכו' בשבת קמ"ו. וכ"ב הג"ה היא: (ד) ד"ה לצורך השבת וכו' שלא לצורך הס"ד ואח"כ מה"ד והלכך וכו' כמס' נדרים הס"ד: (ה) תוס' ד"ה הלקטי וכו' שאין דרך מאהיל בכך כדמוכח:

סליק מסכת שבת בס"ד

ליקוטי רש"י

אין מבקעין עצים. ביום טוב אין מבקעין מן הקורות הסדורות זו על גב זו בקרקע ועומדות לבנין. **ולא מן הקורה** שנשברה ביום טוב. ואף על פי שעומדת להסקה ובין השמשות לא הוי קיימא לבנין [ביצה ב:]. **אבל לא בעצים שבמוקצה.** קרויה מוקצה על שהיא מוקצה לאסור ואין נכנסים ויוצאים בה תמיד ושם נותנין עצים וכל דבר שאין דעתו ליטול עד זמן מרובה. **ארזי ואשוחי.** אין אדם מסיק אותן דעומדין לבנין. **מחמת חסרון כיס.** **אין משקין ושוחטין את המדבריות.** משום מוקצה. **משקין.** משום סרכא דמשכא שתהא נוחה להפשיט. **המדבריות.** **מגביהין.** **עצמות.** **מסלק הטבלה.** **וקליפין** של אגוזים ולא מייחדי למוקצה. **ובית הלל אומרים.** אין מטלטלין אותן בידים דמוקצה הן. **מסלק הטבלה.** ואמר רב נחמן אנו אין לנו. **נר ישן.**

reverses the opinions, but **rather,** on the following version, which I heard from my masters:[15] בֵּית שַׁמַּאי כְּרַבִּי יְהוּדָה – **Beis Shammai** rule **like R' Yehudah,** and prohibit the direct handling of bones and shells, וּבֵית הִלֵּל כְּרַבִּי שִׁמְעוֹן – **while Beis Hillel** rule **like R' Shimon,** and permit this. Since, in this version, Beis Hillel accord with R' Shimon, R' Yochanan decided in R' Shimon's favor, despite the existence of a contrary anonymous Mishnah.

Besides their dispute whether or not an object must be prepared for Sabbath (and Yom Tov) use, R' Yehudah and R' Shimon dispute several other areas of Sabbath law.[16] The Gemara records an Amoraic dispute regarding the final halachah in these matters: פְּלִיגֵי בָּהּ רַב אַחָא וְרָבִינָא – **Rav Acha and Ravina disputed [the halachah]:** חַד אָמַר – **One said:** בְּכָל הַשַּׁבָּת כּוּלָּהּ הֲלָכָה כְּרַבִּי שִׁמְעוֹן – **Regarding** all the laws of **the Sabbath, the law follows R' Shimon,** לְבַר מִמּוּקְצֶה מֵחֲמַת מִיאוּס – **except in regard to** the issue of ***muktzeh by dint of repugnance,*** where the law follows R' Yehudah.[17] וּמַאי נִיהוּ – **And what is** an example of **this?** נֵר יָשָׁן – **An old** (i.e. used) clay **lamp.**[18] וְחַד אָמַר – **And one said:** בְּמוּקְצֶה מֵחֲמַת מִיאוּס נַמִי הֲלָכָה כְּרַבִּי שִׁמְעוֹן – **Even in regard to** the issue of ***muktzeh by dint of repugnance*** **the law follows R' Shimon.** Thus, the law always follows R' Shimon, לְבַר מִמּוּקְצֶה מֵחֲמַת אִיסּוּר – **except in regard to** the issue of ***muktzeh by dint of a prohibition.***[19] וּמַאי נִיהוּ – **And what is** an example of **this?** נֵר שֶׁהִדְלִיקוּ בָּהּ בְּאוֹתָהּ שַׁבָּת – **A lamp in which** a flame **had been lit for the Sabbath,** and which was burning at the onset of the Sabbath. Even though the fire has since gone out, it is considered *muktzeh by dint of a prohibition.*[20] אֲבָל מוּקְצֶה מֵחֲמַת חֶסְרוֹן כִּיס – **However, in regard to** something that is ***muktzeh for fear of monetary loss,***[21] אֲפִילּוּ רַבִּי שִׁמְעוֹן מוֹדֶה – **even R' Shimon concedes** that it should be treated stringently, דִּתְנַן – **for we learned in a Mishnah:**[22] כָּל הַכֵּלִים נִיטָּלִין בְּשַׁבָּת – ALL UTENSILS MAY BE TAKEN ON THE SABBATH[23] חוּץ מִמַּסָּר הַגָּדוֹל – EXCEPT FOR A LARGE SAW[24] וְיָתֵד שֶׁל מַחֲרֵישָׁה – AND A COLTER,[25] which are not used for other purposes lest they become damaged.[26]

Mishnah מְפִירִין נְדָרִים בְּשַׁבָּת – **We may annul vows on the Sabbath,**[27] וְנִשְׁאָלִין לִנְדָרִים שֶׁהֵן לְצוֹרֶךְ הַשַּׁבָּת – **and we may seek release from vows** made to abstain from things **that are necessary for the Sabbath.**[28] וּפוֹקְקִין אֶת הַמָּאוֹר – **And we may** temporarily **shutter a window** on the

NOTES

15. *Rashi* to *Beitzah* 2a.

16. The ensuing Gemara will make particular reference to two other areas of *muktzeh* law about which R' Yehudah and R' Shimon disagree:

(a) *Muktzeh by dint of repugnance:* This type of *muktzeh* includes items that do not stand to be used on the Sabbath due to their repugnance (see below, note 18, for an example). R' Yehudah accepts this category of *muktzeh,* but R' Shimon does not (see above, 44a).

(b) *Muktzeh by dint of a prohibition:* This category of *muktzeh* consists of items that one was unable to use at the onset of the Sabbath without violating a prohibition (see below, note 20, for an example). According to R' Yehudah, items in this category are *muktzeh* even after the underlying prohibition ceases to be applicable. R' Shimon, however, disagrees (see ibid.).

[According to some Amoraim, R' Yehudah and R' Shimon also dispute the category of *nolad,* an object that first achieves its useful state on the Sabbath or on Yom Tov; see *Rosh,* end of *Beitzah.*]

17. According to this view, the halachah follows R' Shimon that an item need not be prepared for Sabbath use. However, the halachah follows R' Yehudah in accepting the category of *muktzeh by dint of repugnance.* And certainly, according to this view, the halachah follows R' Yehudah in accepting the category of *muktzeh by dint of a prohibition* as well, since this category is even more stringent than that of *muktzeh by dint of repugnance* (see *Ramban, Rashba, Rosh;* see also *Tosafos* to 19b ד״ה הני כרכי דזוזי; cf. *Tos. Yeshanim* above, 46a; see also *Sfas Emes*).

[According to some Rishonim, the Gemara's statement that the halachah follows R' Shimon "regarding all the laws of the Sabbath" is not limited to *muktzeh* issues, but states a general rule that the halachah follows R' Shimon in all matters of Sabbath law; e.g. in regard to his well-known positions that *an unintentional act* is permitted on the Sabbath and that there is no liability for *a labor not needed for its defined purpose* (see the General Introduction to this tractate) (*Ramban; Rashba;* see also *Ritva MHK* ed.; cf. *Meiri; Rambam, Hil. Shabbos* 1:7).]

18. A used clay oil lamp cannot be used for its primary function of lighting, since that is prohibited on the Sabbath, and it is not commonly used for any other purpose (e.g. storing trinkets) because of its oily deposits.

19. According to this view the halachah follows R' Shimon's lenient view even in rejecting the category of *muktzeh by dint of repugnance;* the halachah follows R' Yehudah only in recognizing the category of *muktzeh by dint of a prohibition.*

The halachah regarding the Sabbath follows this view. Thus, like R' Yehudah, the halachah recognizes the category of *muktzeh by dint of a prohibition,* but it follows R' Shimon in not accepting the category of *muktzeh by dint of repugnance;* nor does the halachah require, as R' Yehudah does, that an item be "prepared" for use at the onset of the Sabbath (see *Rosh,* et al.).

[The Rishonim dispute whether the halachah is equally lenient on Yom Tov; see *Rosh* here and at the end of *Beitzah; Shulchan Aruch, Orach Chaim* 495:4, with *Mishnah Berurah.*]

20. At the onset of the Sabbath when the flame was burning it was forbidden to move the lamp, since the lamp served as a *base to muktzeh,* i.e. as a base to the flame (see above, 47a). Accordingly, even after the flame goes out the lamp remains *muktzeh by dint of a prohibition,* i.e. by dint of the prohibition which was attached to moving the lamp at the onset of the Sabbath (see *Tosafos* here with *Maharshal*).

21. See above, note 8.

22. Above, 123b.

23. Even those used primarily for work prohibited on the Sabbath [and, therefore, not prepared for Sabbath use]; (thus, this Mishnah must accord with the view of R' Shimon) (*Rashi;* see *Ishei Yisrael* here; cf. *Tosafos* above, 36a ד״ה הא ר׳ יהודה and ד״ה הא ר׳ שמעון; see also note 4 there).

24. I.e. a professional saw used to cut down trees. It is *muktzeh for fear of monetary loss* because its teeth might be damaged if used indiscriminately (*Rashi*).

25. An agricultural tool; specifically, the large, knife-like part of a plow that cuts into the ground to make furrows (see *Rashi* to 123b).

26. And are therefore *muktzeh for fear of monetary loss;* since this Mishnah follows the view of R' Shimon (see note 23) it demonstrates that R' Shimon accepts this category of *muktzeh.*

27. This refers to a husband annulling the vows of his wife (*Rashi*), or a father annulling the vows of his daughter (*Rambam, Commentary to the Mishnah; Rav*).

[If a person takes a vow (known as a *neder*), he is legally bound to fulfill it. However, a husband can annul his wife's vows on the day that he learns of them (see Gemara below), as can a father the vows of his daughter (if she is between the ages of eleven and twelve and a half, and has sprouted at least two pubic hairs) (see *Numbers* 30:2-17). The Mishnah teaches that such annulment (called הֲפָרָה) may be performed on the Sabbath (but see *Yoreh Deah* 234:24 for the language that must be employed when performing a Sabbath annulment).]

28. I.e. we may apply to a sage [or to a court of three laymen – see *Nedarim* 77a] to release us from a vow by finding a basis to declare it erroneous, but only if the release [called הַתָּרָה] is necessary for the Sabbath itself, e.g. if one vowed not to eat on the Sabbath (*Rashi;* see *Nedarim* 21b-23a and throughout ch. 9 for the guidelines for declaring a vow erroneous).

The reason release cannot be granted on the Sabbath unless it is necessary for the Sabbath is because of the Rabbinic prohibition against unnecessary טִירְחָא, *effort,* on the Sabbath. Since release can be deferred

א) ביצה כ:, ב) [שם לה.], ג) [פי' ערוך אריזים וברושים, ערוך], ד) [ביצה מ. לעיל מה:], ה) [לעיל קמב. ביצה כ:], ו) [לעיל מד:], ז) [ביצה לב:], ח) [לעיל קכג. עירובין לה.], ט) לעיל מו: נדרים עז., י) לעיל דף קכה., כ) עירובין עז:, ל) נדרים עז., מ) [נדרים עו:], נ) שם עז., ס) גי' רש"ל, ע) [שבת זו נמי רש"ל].

הגהות הב"ח

(א) רש"י ד"ה מדבריות וכו' תמיד בס"ד ואח"כ מה"ד בייתות שרועות תוך התחום ובאות ולנות בתוך התחום: (ב) ד"ה ואת המטלית לידע אם יש בה שלש על שלש: (ג) ד"ה בטפיח פך של חרס (ותבירו וכו' בשבת) תא"מ. ונ"ב הג"ה היא: (ד) ד"ה לצורך השבת וכו' שלא לצורך הס"ד ואח"כ מה"ד והאנן תנן במס' נדרים הס"ד: (ה) תוס' ד"ה הלקטי וכו' שאין דרך מאהיל בכך כדמוכח:

סליק מסכת שבת בס"ד

ליקוטי רש"י

אין מבקעין עצים. ביום טוב לא מן הקורות הסדורות זו על גב זו בקרקע ועומדות לבנין. ולא מן הקורה שנשברה ביום טוב. ואף על פי שעומדת מעכשיו להסיק הואיל ובין השמשות לאו להכי קיימא [ביצה ל:]. אבל לא בעצים שבמוקצה. רחבה שאחורי הבתים קרויה מוקצה על שם שהיא מוקצה לאסור ואין מכניסים לשם אלא דבר שאין צריך לו וכל דבר שאין דעתו ליטול עד זמן מרובה. ארזי ואשוחי. אין אדם מסיק אותן שעומדין לבנין. אשוחי. ארז נקבה. דמוקצה מחמת חסרון כיס. אין משקין ושוחטין את המדבריות. משום סרכא דמשכא שתהא נוחה להפשיט. הבייתות. מגביהין. מעל השלחן. עצמות. וקליפין. כ"ה. ובית הלל אומרים. מסלק הטבלא כולה ומנערה. שמאי אומרים. ואמר רב נחמן אנו אין לנו [ביצה שם].

אין משקין ושוחטין את המדבריות. הוה מצי למימר דהני כגרוגרות וצמוקין דמיין כדאמר בפרק כירה (לעיל דף מה:): **לבר** ממוקצה מחמת איסור. וכגון איסור דדחייה בידים כגון נר שהדליקו באותו שבת כדפירשתי בפ"ק בסופו: **והלכתא** מעת לעת. לא גרס בפירוש ר"ח דבנדרים משמע דלית הלכתא הכי דאמר בפרק נערה המאורסה (כתובות דף עו:) אין הלכה כאותו הזוג. מ"ר: **הלקטי** קטנה. מפרש בקונטרס שביל קטן היתה בין שני בתים והגיגית סדוקה מונחת על גבן והמת מוטל בהלקטי תחת הגיגית נגד הסדק וקשרו המקידה לידע אם יש בסדק פותח טפח ולהאי פירושא קשה לר"י דאפי' אין בסדק פותח טפח כיון שהמת נגדו לא חשבינן לה כמאהיל על המת כיון שאין [זה] דרך מאהיל (ה) כדמוכח במסכת אהלות (פי"ג מ"ה) ומייתי לה בסוף פרק קמא דסוכה (דף יח. ושם) אין בארובה פותח טפח והמת בבית מה שבבית כנגד ארובה טהור המת כנגד ארובה מה שבבית טהור וכיון שהמת היה נגד הסדק מה היה להם לקשור המקידה ועוד פירש שלפני מות המת פקקו המאור בטפיח ולא הבין רבי לפירושו הלא אותו מת לא היה מת שלם שהרי לא ידעו אם למעלה הימנו היה פותח טפח והמת היה כולו תחת הסדק אלא ודאי כזית מן המת היה וא"כ לא היה לו לומר לפני מות המת אלא לפני שבא כזית מן המת לשם ומיהו יתכן לומר שהמת היה כולו מוטל תחת הגיגית שלא כנגד הסדק והגיגית היתה סדוקה באמצע מראשה לסופה ואילו היה באותו סדק על פני כולו פותח טפח לא היתה טומאה עוברת דלא חשיב כאהל אחד אבל אין בו פותח טפח כאלו אין כאן סדק וחשיב כאהל אחד ומביא את הטומאה לבית וקושיא ראשונה מכל מקום במקומה עומדת ונראה כפירוש ר"ח דמפרש דהלקטי היינו תל המתלקט ואותה הלקטי היתה בין שני בתים והמת והגיגית היתה למעלה מן התל עד לתקרה ואותה הגיגית לא היתה טמאה שהרי בטלה שם ואם לא היתה סדוקה לא היה הבית אחר טמא אלא הגיגית היתה סדוקה מלמטה והשתא אתי שפיר דקתני סדוקה לפי שהיא מלמטה אבל לפירוש הקונטרס לא אתי שפיר דכיון דפירש שהסדק למעלה מן הגיגית היה לו לומר פתוחה ולא סדוקה אבל לפר"ח אתי שפיר שהסדק היה מן הצד וקשרו את המקידה לידע אם יש בו פותח טפח ויש לנו לומר שאותו חור היה עשוי לתשמיש דחור העשוי לתשמיש שיעורו בפותח טפח ואם היה פותח טפח הבית אחר טמא ואם לאו טהור ומיהו קשה לר"י לפירוש ר"ח דלא הוה ליה למימר על גבן אלא על גבה. מ"ר: באוונא

אין מבקעין עצים מן הקורות. סואר וסדורות לבנין: ולא מן קורה. הישנה שנשברה היום ומתמלת להסקה קיימא ואפ"ה אסור הואיל ובין השמשות לא איתכן להסקי: מתחילין. להסיק בערימת התבן קא סלקא דעתך במיגנא סריא דסתמיה להסקה: אבל לא בעצים שבמוקצה. שהניחם ברחבה שאחורי ביתו והקצם לימות הגשמים. מוקצה רחבה שאחורי בתים שהקצה אחורי ביתו להכניס שם דבר לאוצר: בארזי ואשוחי. ארז זכר וארז נקבה שעומדין לבנין: משקין. אורחא דמילתא נקט משום סירכא דמשכא שהוא נוחה להפשיט: מדבריות. (א) שרועות באפר תמיד ולנות בתוך התחום: סתמא אחרינא. בית הלל חשיב כסתמא: כל הכלים ניטלין. ואפי' מלאכתן לאיסור ורבי שמעון היא: חוץ מן המסר הגדול. מגירה שהיא לאומנין לקוץ בה עצים ומוקצה מחמת חסרון כיס הוא שלא ישתברו חריצים שהוא עשוי כסכין מלא פגימות: ויתד של מחרישה. החופר את הקרקע קולטר"א בלע"ז: מתני' מפירין. בעל לאשתו: ונשאלין. לחכם: שהן לצורך השבת. כגון שנדר שלא לאכול [היום]: ופוקקין את המאור. כרבנן דאמרי (לעיל דף קכה:) פוקקין פקק החלון: ומודדין את המקוה. במדה שיהא שם עמוק שלש אמות מים ורוחב אמה על אמה: ואת המטלית. (ב) שתהא שלש על שלש אצבעות כגון אם היתה טמאה ונגעה בטהרות: בטפיח. פך של חרס (ג) ותבירו בפי"ז (דף קכה:) זמורה שהיא קשורה בטפיח ממלאין בה בשבת: מקידה. כלי חרס: לידע אם יש בגיגית פותח טפח. בגמרא מפרש לה: וקושרין. קשר שאינו של קיימא אפילו לכתחילה: ומודדין. להתלמד על דבר הוראה: גמ' איבעיא להו הפרה. דמתניתין בין לצורך [בין שלא לצורך] השבת דגבי הפרה ביום שמעו כתיב (במדבר ל) ואם לא מיפר האידנא שוב אינו מיפר: ושאלה לצורך אין שלא לצורך לא. דיכול לישאל למחר ומשום הכי מפליג להו מהדדי ולא קתני מפירין ונשאלין לנדרים שהן לצורך השבת דלא קאי לצורך אלא אשאלה: בית דין. חכם: הכי גרסי' ל"א איבעיא להו (במסכת נדרים דף עז.) לצורך אתרוייהו קאי. אהפרה ואשאלה אבל הפרה שלא לצורך לא אלמא הפרת נדרים מעת לעת וזה ששמע בשבת יכול להפר משתחשך בתוך מעת לעת של שמיעה הלכך שלא לצורך לא שרינן בשבת: כל היום. עד שתחשך ותו לא ואפילו שמע סמוך לחשיכה הלכך אפי' שלא לצורך (ט) שאם לא יפר עכשיו לא יפר עוד: לצורך השבת. אלמא הפרת נדרים מעת לעת של שמיעה הלכך שלא לצורך (ד) לא מדלא שרי אלא לצורך: להקל ולהחמיר. כלומר פעמים שיש שהות גדול ופעמים שאינו אלא מעט: איבעיא להו. הא דקתני נשאלין לנדרים שהן לצורך: כשלא היה לו פנאי. לשאל מערב שבת קאמר או אפילו כשהיה לו פנאי: הילקטי קטנה. שביל קטן בין שני בתים: וגיגית

א **אין** מבקעין עצים מן הקורות ולא מן הקורה שנשברה ביו"ט רבי יוחנן ההוא כרבי יוסי בר יהודה מתני לה תא שמע ב מתחילין בערימת התבן אבל לא בעצים שבמוקצה התם ג בארזי ואשוחי דמוקצה מחמת חסרון כיס אפילו רבי שמעון מודה ת"ש ד אין משקין ה ושוחטין את המדבריות אבל משקין ושוחטין את הבייתות ר' יוחנן סתמא אחרינא אשכח ו ב"ש אומרים מגביהין מעל השלחן עצמות וקליפין וב"ה אומרים מסלק את הטבלה כולה ומנערה וא"ר נחמן אנו אין לנו אלא ב"ש כרבי יהודה וב"ה כר"ש פליגי בה רב אחא ורבינא חד אמר בכל השבת כולה הלכה כר"ש לבר ממוקצה מחמת מיאוס ומאי ניהו ז נר ישן וחד אמר במוקצה מחמת מיאוס נמי הלכה כר"ש לבר ממוקצה מחמת איסור ומאי ניהו נר שהדליקו בה באותה שבת אבל ח מוקצה מחמת חסרון כיס אפילו ר"ש מודה דתנן ט כל הכלים ניטלין בשבת חוץ ממסר הגדול ויתד של מחרישה:

מתני' י מפירין נדרים בשבת ונשאלין לנדרים שהן לצורך השבת ופוקקין את המאור ומודדין את המטלית ואת המקוה ומעשה בימי אביו של רבי צדוק ובימי אבא שאול בן בטנית שפקקו את המאור בטפיח [ה] וקשרו את המקידה בגמי לידע אם יש בגיגית פותח טפח אם לאו כ ומדבריהם למדנו שפוקקין ומודדין וקושרין בשבת: **גמ'** ל איבעיא להו הפרה בין לצורך ובין שלא לצורך ושאלה לצורך אין שלא לצורך לא ומשום הכי קפלגינהו מהדדי או דילמא הפרה נמי לצורך אין שלא לצורך לא והא דקא פליג להו מהדדי משום דהפרה אין צריך ב"ד ושאלה צריכה ב"ד ת"ש דתני זוטי דבי רב פפא מפירין נדרים בשבת לצורך השבת לצורך השבת אין שלא לצורך השבת לא לישנא אחרינא איבעיא להו לצורך אתרוייהו קתני ושלא לצורך לא אלמא הפרת נדרים מעת לעת או דילמא כי קתני לצורך אשאלה הוא דקתני אבל הפרת נדרים אפילו שלא לצורך אלמא הפרת נדרים כל היום תא שמע דתני רב זוטי דבי רב פפי מפירין נדרים בשבת לצורך השבת אין שלא לצורך השבת לא אלמא הפרת נדרים מעת לעת א"ר אשי והאנן מ תנן נ הפרת נדרים כל היום ויש בדבר להקל ולהחמיר כיצד נדרה לילי שבת מיפר לילי שבת ויום השבת עד שתחשך נדרה עם חשכה מיפר עד שלא תחשך שאם לא הפר משחשכה אינו יכול להפר תנאי היא דתניא ס הפרת נדרים כל היום ר' יוסי בר יהודה ורבי אלעזר ברבי שמעון אמרו מעת לעת: ונשאלים לנדרים: ע איבעיא להו כשלא היה לו פנאי או דלמא אפילו היה לו פנאי תא שמע דאזדקיקו ליה רבנן לרב זוטרא בריה דרב זירא פ ושרו ליה נדריה ואף על גב דהוה ליה פנאי: שפקקו את המאור בטפיח וקשרו את המקידה בגמי: אמר רב יהודה אמר רב הילקטי קטנה היתה בין שני בתים צ [וטומאה היתה שם] וגגית

עין משפט נר מצוה

לו א מיי' פ"ב מהלכות יו"ט הלכה יג סמג לאוין עה טוש"ע א"ח סימן תקח סעיף א:
לז ב ג מיי' שם הלכה יא וסמג שם טוש"ע א"ח סי' תקיז סעיף ו:
לח ד מיי' שם הלכה ט סמג שם טוש"ע א"ח סימן תצח סעיף ג:
לט ה מיי' שם הלכה ב וסמג שם טוש"ע א"ח סי' תנ סעיף ג:
[ה] [טוש"ע א"ח סימן שח סעיף מ]:
מ ו מיי' פכ"ד מהלכות שבת הלכה ו ופי"ג מהלכות נדרים הלכה ט וסמג לאוין שמב טוש"ע א"ח סימן שמא סעיף א וטוש"ע י"ד סימן רלד סעיף כה:
מא ז מיי' פכ"ד מהל' שבת הלכה ו וסמג שם ומיי' פ"ו מהלכות שבועות הלכה ו סמג לאוין רמב טוש"ע א"ח סי' שמא וטוש"ע י"ד סי' רכח סעיף [illegible]:
מב ח מיי' פי"ג מהל' נדרים הלכה כג סמג לאוין רמב טוש"ע י"ד סימן רלד סעיף כג:
מג ט מיי' פכ"ד מהל' שבת הלכה ו ומיי' פ"ו מהלכות שבועות הלכה ו סמג לאוין שם ולאוין רמב טוש"ע א"ח סימן שמא סעיף א וטוש"ע י"ד סימן רכח סעיף ג:

רבינו חננאל

ממקומה דבבהמת קדשים [מיירי] מכלל דהולך קדשים כר' [שמעון] דלית ליה מוקצה. ומקשינן על ר' יוחנן וכי סבר רבי יוחנן הלכה כרבי שמעון והא אמר ר' יוחנן הלכה כסתם משנה ותנן אין מבקעים עצים מן הקורות ולא מן הקורה שנשברה ומפרקינן האי כר' יוסי ב"ר יהודה מתני לה דהוא רבי יוחנן ולית סתמא. ואמרינן תוב ת"ש מתחילין בערימת התבן אבל לא בעצים שבמוקצה ומפרקינן התם בארזי ואשוחי דמוקצה מחמת חסרון כיס. דאפילו ר' שמעון מודה. פי' ארזי ואשוחי עצי ארזים וברושים העשויין לקורות שאין דעתו של אדם עליהן להסיקן תחת תבשילו וגמר והקצה אותן. ואמרינן תוב אין משקין ושוחטין את המדבריות אבל משקין ושוחטין הבייתות והנה סתמא כר' יהודה ורבי יוחנן סבירא ליה הלכתא כסתם משנה קשיא הלכתא אהלכתא ומפרקינן ר' יוחנן סתמא אחרינא אשכח כב"ה דב"א מגביהין מעל השלחן עצמות וקליפין וב"ש אומרים מסלק את הטבלא כולה ומנערה. ואמר רב נחמן אנו אין לנו אלא ב"ש כר' יהודה וב"ה כר' שמעון והלכתא כב"ה ולא עוד וכדפסק ר' יוחנן פליגי בה רב אחא ורבינא חד אמר בכולה שבת הלכתא כר' שמעון בר ממוקצה מחמת מיאוס. וחד אמר במוקצה [מחמת] מיאוס נמי הלכתא כר' שמעון בר ממוקצה מחמת איסורו כגון הנר שהדליקו בה באותה שבת וכיוצא בו אבל

רב נסים גאון

מפירין נדרים בשבת. אמרו [בתוספתא פ' י"ח] מפני מה נדרי שבת מפירין אותן בשבת שאם חשיכה ולא הפר אינו

מות שהיה שניה אלא מוחלפת שיטתה וב"ש כרבי יהודה וכו' [לעיל שם]. נר ישן. דמוקצה מחמת מיאוס הוא [חולין יד:]. נר שהדליקו בה באותה שבת. שהיה נר דולק בו בין השמשות דמוקצה מחמת איסור וכיון שהוקצה לבין השמשות הוקצה לכל היום [שם מד.]. מסר הגדול. מגירה גדולה [לעיל קכג:]. מפירין נדרים בשבת. בעל לאשתו ואב לבתו [לעיל מו:]. ונשאלין לנדרים. לחכם להתיר [נדרים עז.]. [המשך בע"ב]

יכול להפר ורבי יוסי ב"ר יהודה ורבי אלעזר ברבי שמעון שאמרו הפרת נדרים מעת לעת אין הלכה כמותם כדגרסינן בנדרים בפרק נערה המאורסה (דף עו) אלא אמר רבי שמעון בן פזי אין הלכה כאותו הזוג לוי סבר למיעבד עובדא כי האי זוגא אמר ליה רב הכי אמר רבי אין הלכה כאותו הזוג ואע"פ שהתירו הפרת נדרים בשבת בדבר זה תנאי מאליו א"ר יוחנן וצריך שיבטל בלבו תניא בית שמאי אומרים מבטל בלבו ובערב [illegible] אחד זה ואחד זה מבטל בלבו ואינו צריך להוציא בשפתיו תמצאנו עוד בפרק נערה המאורסה (דף עז)

אם

Sabbath,[29] וּמוֹדְדִין אֶת הַמַּטְלִית – **and we may measure a rag** to determine whether it is able to generate *tumah,* וּמוֹדְדִין אֶת הַמִּקְוֶה – **and we may measure a *mikveh*** to determine whether it measures three cubic *amos.*[30] וּמַעֲשֶׂה בִּימֵי אָבִיו שֶׁל רַבִּי צָדוֹק וּבִימֵי אַבָּא שָׁאוּל בֶּן בָּטְנִית – There was **an incident in the days of R' Tzadok's father and in the days of Abba Shaul ben Batnis,** שֶׁפָּקְקוּ אֶת הַמָּאוֹר בְּטָפִיחַ – **in which they shuttered the window with an earthenware flask,** וְקָשְׁרוּ אֶת הַמְּקִידָה בְּגֶמִי – **and they tied an earthenware vessel with a** strand of **reed-grass** לֵידַע אִם יֵשׁ בְּגִיגִית פּוֹתֵחַ טֶפַח אִם לָאו – in order **to determine whether or not there was a handbreadth-sized opening in a** certain **barrel.**[31] וּמִדִּבְרֵיהֶם לָמַדְנוּ שֶׁפּוֹקְקִין וּמוֹדְדִין וְקוֹשְׁרִין בְּשַׁבָּת – **And from their words we learned that we may shutter, measure and tie on the Sabbath.**[32]

Gemara The Gemara sets forth an inquiry regarding the Mishnah's ruling concerning annulment:

אִיבַּעְיָא לְהוּ – **They inquired:** הֲפָרָה בֵּין לְצוֹרֶךְ וּבֵין שֶׁלֹּא לְצוֹרֶךְ – Do we say that when the Mishnah permits **annulment** of vows on the Sabbath, it allows **both** annulment **that is necessary** for the Sabbath **and** that **which is not necessary** for the Sabbath, וּשְׁאֵלָה לְצוֹרֶךְ אִין שֶׁלֹּא לְצוֹרֶךְ לֹא – **but** when it permits **seeking release** from vows, then if the release **is necessary** for the Sabbath – **yes,** it is permitted, but if it **is not necessary** for the Sabbath – **no,** it is not permitted,[33] וּמִשּׁוּם הָכִי קַפַּלְגִינְהוּ מֵהֲדָדֵי – **and it is because of this** distinction that **[the Mishnah] separated these** methods of abrogating vows **from one another?**[34] אוֹ דִילְמָא – **Or perhaps** we say הֲפָרָה נַמִּי לְצוֹרֶךְ אִין שֶׁלֹּא לְצוֹרֶךְ לֹא – that with regard to **annulment** of vows **too,** if the annulment **is necessary** for the Sabbath – **yes,** it is permitted, but if it **is not necessary** for the Sabbath – then **no,** it is not permitted;[35] וְהָא דְּקָא פָּלֵיג לְהוּ מֵהֲדָדֵי – **and [the reason] [the Mishnah] separated these** methods **from one another** is not because of any difference between them with respect to vows whose abrogation is not necessary for the Sabbath, מִשּׁוּם דַּהֲפָרָה אֵין צָרִיךְ בֵּית דִּין – but **because annulment does not require a court,** וּשְׁאֵלָה צְרִיכָה בֵּית דִּין – **while seeking release does require a court!**[36]

The Gemara cites a Baraisa as proof:

תָּא שְׁמַע – **Come, learn** a proof. דְּתָנֵי זוּטֵי דְּבֵי רַב פַּפָּא – **For Zutei of the academy of Rav Pappa taught** a Baraisa: מְפִירִין נְדָרִים בְּשַׁבָּת לְצוֹרֶךְ הַשַּׁבָּת – ONE MAY ANNUL VOWS ON THE

NOTES

until after the Sabbath, its performance on the Sabbath is reckoned unnecessary effort (*Mishnah Berurah* 341:1 from *Ran* and *Levush*). Alternatively, the reason is because of a Scriptural verse [מִמְּצוֹא חֶפְצְךָ] (*Isaiah* 58:13) that enjoins one from attending to his weekday needs on the Sabbath (see above, 113a). Since this vow does not affect the Sabbath, being released from it is deemed a weekday need (*Levush, Yoreh Deah* 228:3; see *Rambam, Hil. Shabbos* 24:6; see also *Chasam Sofer*). [For whether release can be granted on the Sabbath in order to allow performance of a mitzvah, see *Mishnah Berurah* ibid. with *Shaar HaTzion* ad loc.]

29. This ruling refers to a dispute cited in a Mishnah above (125b). The dispute concerns shuttering a window on the Sabbath with a board that is not attached to it. R' Eliezer rules that since one who inserts this shutter appears to be adding to the structure, its placement is prohibited by Rabbinic law, as it resembles the *melachah* of בּוֹנֶה, *building.* The Sages, however, permit placing the shutter into the window, for since it is only a *temporary* addition to the structure, its insertion does not resemble building (see 125b notes 4,5,33). Our Mishnah rules in accordance with the Sages, and therefore permits one to shutter a window on the Sabbath (*Rashi*).

30. The act of measuring (e.g. determining size, volume, weight) is prohibited on the Sabbath by Rabbinic decree because it resembles a weekday activity [עוּבְדָּא דְחוֹל] (*Tosafos* to 126b ד״ה ומדבריהן; see General Introduction). This sort of decree, however, is more lenient than most Rabbinical injunctions in that it is waived when performed for the purpose of a mitzvah (*Tosafos* ibid.; *Mishnah Berurah* 306:34). One is accordingly permitted to measure a rag to determine whether it can generate *tumah,* and a *mikveh* to determine whether it measures three cubic *amos,* as these are halachic inquiries, and their resolution is deemed a mitzvah (*Rashi;* see *Orach Chaim* 306:7 with *Mishnah Berurah*).

The case of measuring a rag concerns a [wool or linen] rag of more than three by three fingerbreadths that came into contact with a contaminant, was reduced in size, and after being reduced came into contact with *tohoros* (i.e. food that must be kept *tahor*). [Now, the rule is that a cloth of wool or linen will neither become *tamei* nor generate *tumah* unless it measures three by three fingerbreadths, as this is the minimum size necessary for it to be legally regarded as a "garment" [*beged*] (see above, 26b).] The rag must therefore be measured to determine whether it still measured three by three fingerbreadths after it was reduced, in which case it contaminated the *tohoros,* or whether its reduction left it with less than these critical dimensions (*Rashi; Rav,* as explained by *Tos. Yom Tov*). In the case of measuring a *mikveh,* we wish to ascertain whether it will contain forty *se'ah* of water, the minimum amount necessary for a valid *mikveh.* Forty *se'ah* requires a cubic measure of at least three *amos* [i.e. 1×1×3 *amos*] (*Rashi*). Since these two acts of measuring are meant to resolve a halachic question, they are mitzvos, and are therefore permitted on the Sabbath.

31. The Gemara will elaborate regarding this incident.

32. The incident concerned an act of shuttering, and measuring and tying. We thus see that it is permissible on the Sabbath to temporarily shutter a window, to measure an article in order to resolve a halachic question [or perform some other mitzvah], and to tie temporary knots [for the purpose of performing a mitzvah even though tying such knots is normally forbidden by Rabbinic decree – see 111b,112a] (*Rashi,* as explained by *Beis Yosef, Orach Chaim* §317; *Rambam, Commentary to the Mishnah;* see *Mishnah Berurah* 317:12,13). See also *Tos. Yom Tov* here.

33. This side of the question assumes that annulment must be performed on the day the vow becomes known to the husband. Since there will thus be no opportunity to annul the vow after the Sabbath, its annulment can be termed neither unnecessary effort nor weekday activity. One may therefore annul the vow whether or not it affects the Sabbath. Release, by contrast, can be sought at any time; granting it on the Sabbath is thus prohibited unless it is necessary for the Sabbath (*Rashi;* cf. *Ramban*). [For why the woman cannot wait until after the Sabbath and then seek release from a court, see *Chidushei HaRan;* see *Meiri; Ishei Yisrael; Leshon HaZahav.*]

The source to limit annulment to the day the vow becomes known is the verse in *Numbers* (30:13) that sets out a husband's ability to annul vows. The verse begins with this phrase: וְאִם־הָפֵר יָפֵר אֹתָם אִישָׁהּ בְּיוֹם שָׁמְעוֹ, *And if her husband will annul them on the day of his hearing* [of them]. The words *on the day of his hearing* seemingly limit his power to annul her vows to the day upon which he learns of them (*Rashi,* from *Nedarim* 76b).

34. The Mishnah could have combined the clauses concerning annulment and release as follows: מְפִירִין וְנִשְׁאָלִין לִנְדָרִים שֶׁהֵן לְצוֹרֶךְ הַשַּׁבָּת, *We may annul and seek release from vows made to abstain from things necessary for the Sabbath.* This would have indicated that both annulment and release are limited to vows that affect the Sabbath. The Gemara wonders whether the Mishnah separated between these two methods of abrogation to imply that *annulment* may be performed even if not necessary for the Sabbath (*Rashi*).

35. [This side of the question assumes that annulment may be performed for a full twenty-four hours after the husband first learns of the vow (see below, note 38). Since even a vow taken on the Sabbath can accordingly be annulled after the Sabbath, its annulment on the Sabbath is forbidden, for the reasons given above [note 28] (see *Ritva MHK* ed.; cf. *Leshon HaZahav;* see also *Chasam Sofer*).]

36. Composed of [either] a sage [or three laymen] (*Rashi;* see *Lashon HaZahav*).

א אין מבקעין עצים מן הקורות ולא מן הקורה שנשברה ביו"ט רבי יוחנן ההוא כרבי יוסי בר יהודה מתני לה תא שמע מתחילין בערימת התבן אבל לא בעצים שבמוקצה התם בארזי ואשוחי דמוקצה מחמת חסרון כיס אפילו רבי שמעון מודה ת"ש אין משקין ושוחטין את המדבריות אבל משקין ושוחטין את הבייתות ר' יוחנן סתמא אחרינא אשכח ב"ש אומרים מגביהין מעל השלחן עצמות וקליפין וב"ה אומרים מסלק את הטבלה כולה ומנערה וא"ר נחמן אנו אין לנו אלא ב"ש כרבי יהודה וב"ה כר"ש פליגי בה רב אחא ורבינא חד אמר בכל השבת כולה הלכה כר"ש לבר ממוקצה מחמת מיאוס ומאי ניהו נר ישן וחד אמר במוקצה מחמת מיאוס נמי הלכה כר"ש לבר ממוקצה מחמת איסור ומאי ניהו נר שהדליקו בה באותה שבת אבל מוקצה מחמת חסרון כיס אפילו ר"ש מודה דתנן כל הכלים ניטלין בשבת חוץ ממסר הגדול ויתד של מחרישה: **מתני'** מפירין נדרים בשבת ונשאלין לנדרים שהן לצורך השבת ופוקקין את המאור ומודדין את המטלית ומודדין את המקוה ומעשה בימי אביו של רבי צדוק ובימי אבא שאול בן בטנית שפקקו את המאור בטפיח וקשרו את המקידה בגמי לידע אם יש בגיגית פותח טפח אם לאו ומדבריהם למדנו שפוקקין ומודדין וקושרין בשבת: **גמ'** איבעיא להו הפרה בין לצורך ובין שלא לצורך ושאלה לצורך אין שלא לצורך לא ומשום הכי קפלגינהו מהדדי או דילמא הפרה נמי לצורך אין שלא לצורך לא והא דקא פליג להו מהדדי משום דהפרה אין צריך ב"ד ושאלה צריכה ב"ד ת"ש דתני זוטי דבי רב פפא מפירין נדרים בשבת לצורך השבת לצורך השבת אין שלא לצורך השבת לא לישנא אחרינא איבעיא להו לצורך אתרוייהו קתני ושלא לצורך לא אלמא הפרת נדרים מעת לעת או דילמא כי קתני לצורך אשאלה הוא דקתני אבל הפרת נדרים אפילו שלא לצורך אלמא הפרת נדרים כל היום תא שמע דתני רב זוטי דבי רב פפי מפירין נדרים בשבת לצורך השבת לצורך השבת אין שלא לצורך השבת לא אלמא הפרת נדרים מעת לעת א"ר אשי והאנן תנן הפרת נדרים כל היום ויש בדבר להקל ולהחמיר כיצד נדרה לילי שבת מיפר לילי שבת ויום השבת עד שתחשך נדרה עם חשכה מיפר עד שלא תחשך שאם לא הפר משחשכה אינו יכול להפר תנאי היא דתניא הפרת נדרים כל היום ר' יוסי בר יהודה ורבי אלעזר ברבי שמעון אמרו מעת לעת: ונשאלים לנדרים: איבעיא להו כשלא היה לו פנאי או דלמא אפילו היה לו פנאי תא שמע דאזדקיקו ליה רבנן לרב זוטרא בריה דרב זירא ושרו ליה נדריה ואף על גב דהוה ליה פנאי: שפקקו את המאור בטפיח וקשרו את המקידה בגמי: אמר רב יהודה אמר רב הילקטי קטנה היתה בין שני בתים [וטומאה היתה שם] וגגית

רש"י

אין מבקעין עצים מן הקורות. סואר של הקורות המוקצות וסדורות לבנין: **ולא מן קורה.** הישנה שנשברה היום ומהשתא להסקה קיימא ואפ"ה אסור הואיל ובין השמשות לא איתכן להכי: **מתחילין.** להסיק בערימת התבן קא סלקא דעתך בתיבנא דסתמיה להסקה: **אבל לא בעצים שבמוקצה.** שהכניס ברחבה שאחורי ביתו והקצם לימות הגשמים. מוקצה רחבה שאחורי בתים שהקצה אחורי ביתו להכניס שם דבר לאוצר: **בארזי ואשוחי.** ארז זכר וארז נקבה שעומדין לבנין: **משקין.** אורחא דמילתא נקט משום סירכא דמשכא שתהא נוחה להפשיט: **מדבריות.** (א) שרועות באפר תמיד ולנות בתוך התחום: **סתמא אחרינא.** בית הלל חשיב כסתמא: **כל הכלים ניטלין.** ואפי' מלאכתן לאיסור ורבי שמעון היא: **חוץ מן המסר הגדול.** מגירה שהיא לאומנין לקוץ בה עצים ומוקצה מחמת חסרון כיס הוא שלא ישתברו חריציה שהוא עשוי כסכין מלא פגימות: **ויתד של מחרישה.** החופר את הקרקע קולטר"א בלע"ז: **מתני' מפירין.** בעל לאשתו: **ונשאלין.** לחכם: **שהן לצורך השבת.** כגון שנדר שלא לאכול [היום]: **ופוקקין את המאור.** כרבנן דאמרי (לעיל דף קכה:) פוקקין פקק החלון: **ומודדין את המקוה.** במדה שיהא שם עמוק שלש אמות מים ורוחב אמה על אמה: **ואת המטלית.** (ב) שתהא שלש על שלש אצבעות כגון אם היתה טמאה ונגעה בטהרות: **בטפיח.** פך של חרס (ג) וחבירו בפי"ז (דף קכה:) זמורה שהיא קשורה בטפיח ממלאין בה בשבת: **מקידה.** כלי חרס: **לידע אם יש בגיגית פותח טפח.** בגמרא מפרש לה: **וקושרין.** קשר שאינו של קיימא אפילו לכתחילה: **ומודדין.** להתלמד על דבר הוראה: **גמ' איבעיא להו הפרה.** דמתניתין בין לצורך [בין שלא לצורך] השבת דגבי הפרה ביום שמעו כתיב (במדבר ל) ואם לא מיפר האידנא שוב אינו מיפר: **ושאלה לצורך אין שלא לצורך לא.** דיכול לישאל למחר ומשום הכי מפליג להו מהדדי ולא קתני מפירין ונשאלין לנדרים שהן לצורך השבת דלא קאי לצורך אלא אשאלה: **בית דין.** חכם: הכי גרסי' ל"א **איבעיא להו** (במסכת נדרים דף עז.) **לצורך אתרוייהו קאי.** אהפרה ואשאלה אבל הפרה שלא לצורך לא אלמא הפרת נדרים מעת לעת וזה ששמע בשבת יכול להפר משתחשך בתוך מעת לעת של שמיעה הלכך שלא לצורך לא שרינן בשבת: **כל היום.** עד שתחשך ותו לא ואפילו שמע סמוך לחשיכה הלכך אפי' שלא לצורך (ט) שאם לא יפר עכשיו לא יפר עוד: **לצורך השבת.** אלמא הפרת נדרים מעת לעת של שמיעה הלכך שלא לצורך (ד) לא מדלא שרי אלא לצורך: **להקל ולהחמיר.** כלומר פעמים שיש שהות גדול ופעמים שאינו אלא מעט: **איבעיא להו.** הא דקתני נשאלין לנדרים שהן לצורך: **כשלא היה לו פנאי.** לשאל מערב שבת קאמר או אפילו כשהיה לו פנאי: **הילקטי קטנה.** שביל קטן בין שני בתים: וגגית

תוספות

אין משקין ושוחטין את המדבריות. הוה מצי למימר דהני כגרוגרות ולצימוקין דמיין כדאמר בפרק כירה (לעיל דף מה:): **לבר** ממוקצה מחמת איסור. וכגון איסור דדחייה בידים כגון נר שהדליקו באותו שבת כדפירשתי בפ"ק בסופו: **והלכתא** מעת לעת. לא גרס בפירוש ר"ח דבנדרים משמע דלית הלכתא הכי דאמר בפרק נערה המאורסה (כתובות דף עו:) אין הלכה כאותו הזוג. מ"ר: **הלקטי** קטנה. מפרש בקונטרס שביל קטן היתה בין שני בתים והגיגית סדוקה מונחת על גבן והמת מוטל בהלקטי תחת הגיגית נגד הסדק וקשרו המקידה לידע אם יש בסדק פותח טפח ולהאי פירושא קשה לר"י דאפי' אין בסדק פותח טפח כיון שהמת נגדו לא חשבינן לה כמאהיל על המת כיון שאין [זה] דרך מאהיל (ה) כדמוכח במסכת אהלות (פ"י מ"ה) ומייתי לה בסוף פרק קמא דסוכה (דף יח. ושם) אין בארובה פותח טפח והמת בבית מה שבבית כנגד ארובה טהור המת כנגד ארובה מה שבבית טהור וכיון שהמת היה נגד הסדק מה היה להם לקשור המקידה ועוד פירש שלפני מות המת פקקו המאור בטפיח ולא הבין רבי לפירושו הלא אותו מת לא היה מת שלם שהרי לא ידעו אם למעלה הימנו היה פותח טפח והמת היה כולו תחת הסדק אלא ודאי כזית מן המת היה וא"כ לא היה לו לומר לפני מות המת אלא לפני שבא כזית מן המת לשם ומיהו יתכן לומר שהמת היה כולו מוטל תחת הגיגית שלא כנגד הסדק והגיגית היתה סדוקה באמצע מראשה לסופה ואילו היה באותו סדק על פני כולו פותח טפח לא היתה טומאה עוברת דלא חשיב כאהל אחד אבל אין בו פותח טפח כאלו אין כאן סדק וחשיב כאהל אחד ומביא את הטומאה לבית וקושיא ראשונה מכל מקום במקומה עומדת ונראה כפירוש ר"ח דמפרש דהלקטי היינו תל המתלקט ואותה הלקטי היתה בין שני בתים והמת היה בבית אחד ואותה הגיגית היתה למעלה מן התל עד לתקרה ואותה הגיגית לא היתה טמאה שהרי בטלה שם ואם לא היתה סדוקה לא היה הבית אחר טמא אלא הגיגית היתה סדוקה מלדה והשתא אתי שפיר דקתני סדוקה לפי שהיא מלדה אבל לפירוש הקונטרס לא אתי שפיר דכיון דפירש שהסדק למעלה מן הגיגית היה לו לומר פתוחה ולא סדוקה אבל לפר"ח אתי שפיר שהסדק היה מן הצד וקשרו את המקידה לידע אם יש פותח טפח ויש לנו לומר שאותו חור היה עשוי לתשמיש דחור העשוי לתשמיש שיעורו בפותח טפח ואם היה פותח טפח הבית אחר טמא ואם לאו טהור ומיהו קשה לר"י לפירוש ר"ח דלא הוה ליה למימר על גבן אלא על גגה. מ"ר:

באוונא

מסורת הש"ס

א) ביצה ב: לא., ב) [שם לג.], ג) [פי' ערי ארזים וברושים. ערוך], ד) [ביצה ה. לעיל מה:], ה) [לעיל קמג. ביצה ב.], ו) [לעיל קכג:], ז) [לעיל קכה:], ח) [לעיל קנה. עירובין לה.], ט) לעיל מו: נדרים עו., י) לעיל דף קכה:, כ) [נדרים דף עז. ע"ש], ל) נדרים עו., מ) [נדרים עו.], נ) שם עז., ס) גי' רש"ל, ע) [שבת זו נמי רש"ל].

הגהות הב"ח

(א) רש"י ד"ה מדבריות וכו' תמיד הס"ד ואח"כ מה"ד ביימות שרועות תוך התחום ובאות ולנות בתוך התחום: (ב) ד"ה ואת המטלית לידע אם יש בה שלש על שלש: (ג) ד"ה בטפיח פך של חרס וחבירו וכו' בשבת ואח"כ וכו' בה"ג הוא: (ד) ד"ה לצורך השבת וכו' שלא לצורך הס"ד ואח"כ מה"ד והאנן תנן כמו נדרים הס"ד: (ה) תוס' ד"ה הלקטי וכו' שאין דרך מאהיל בכך כדמוכח:

סליק מסכת שבת בס"ד

ליקוטי רש"י

אין מבקעין עצים. ביום טוב לא מן הקורות הסדורות זו על גב זו בקרקע ועומדות לבנין. **ולא מן הקורה שנשברה ביום טוב.** ואף על פי שעומדת מעכשיו להיסק הואיל ובין השמשות לאו להכי קיימא לבין השמשות אתקצאי לכולי יומא [ביצה ב:]. **אבל לא בעצים שבמוקצה.** רחבה שאחורי הבתים קרויה מוקצה על שם שהיא מוקצה לאוצר ואין נכנסים ויוצאין בה תדיר ושם נותנין עצים וכל דבר שאין דעתו ליטול עד זמן מרובה. **ארזי ואשוחי.** אין אדם מסיק אותן שעומדין לבנין. **אשוחי.** ארז נקבה. **דמוקצה מחמת חסרון כיס ניגהו.** שדמיה יקרין [שם ל.]. **אין משקין ושוחטין את המדבריות.** משום מוקצה. **משקין.** משום סרכא דמשכא שתהא נדבק יותר מדאי בבשר [שם מ.]. דרך להשקות הבהמה לפני שחיטה שתהא נוחה להפשיט. **המדבריות.** **מגביהין.** בשבת מעל השלחן [ביצה ב.]. בידים מעל השלחן [לעיל קמג.]. **עצמות.** שאינן ראוין לאכילה וקליפי אגוזים ולא חיישינן למוקצה [ביצה שם]. קשין שאינן ראוין לכלב וקליפין של אגוזים דליכא להו לבית הלל שלי מוקצה [לעיל שם]. **ובית הלל אומרים.** אין מטלטלין אותן בידים דמוקצה הן. **מסלק הטבלה.** שיש תורת כלי עליה ומנערה [ביצה שם]. שיש תורת כלי עליה אבל לא יטלטל הקליפין בידים כר' יהודה [לעיל שם]. **ואמר רב נחמן אנו אין לנו.** בשיטת משנה זו לפי שמחלוקת שיטתה דבית שמאי כך שמעתי מרבותינו כר' יהודה וממתרי ובית הלל כרבי שמעון [ביצה שם]. אין לנו

עין משפט נר מצוה

לו א מיי' פ"ב מהלכות יו"ט הלכה יג סמג לאוין עה טוש"ע א"ח סימן תקא סעיף ו:

לז ב ג מיי' שם הלכה יא וסמג שם טוש"ע א"ח סי' תקיח סעיף ו:

לח ד מיי' שם הלכה ח סמג שם טוש"ע א"ח סימן תצח סעיף ג:

לט ה מיי' שם הלכה ב וסמג שם טוש"ע א"ח סי' של סעיף ג:

[ה] [טוש"ע א"ח סימן שח סעיף לא]:

מ ו מיי' פכ"ד מהלכות שבת הלכה ו ופי"ג מהלכות נדרים הלכה ח וסמג לאוין עה טוש"ע א"ח סימן שמא סעיף א וטוש"ע י"ד סימן רלד סעיף כד:

מא ז מיי' פכ"ד מהל' שבת הלכה ו וסמג שם ומיי' פי"ג מהלכות שבועות הלכה ו סמג לאוין רמב טוש"ע א"ח סי' שמא וטוש"ע י"ד סי' רכח סעיף:

מב ח מיי' פי"ב מהל' נדרים הלכה טו סמג לאוין רמב טוש"ע י"ד סימן רלד סעיף כג:

מג ט מיי' פכ"ד מהל' שבת הלכה ו ופ"ו מהלכות שבועות הלכה ו סמג לאוין שם ולאוין רמב טוש"ע א"ח סימן שמא סעיף א וטוש"ע י"ד סימן רכח סעיף ג:

רבינו חננאל

ממקומה דבבהמת קדשים [מיירי] מכלל דחולין שרי כר' [שמעון] דלית ליה מוקצה. ומקשינן על ר' יוחנן וכי סבר רבי יוחנן הלכה כרבי שמעון והא אמר ר' יוחנן הלכה כסתם משנה ותנן אין מבקעים עצים מן הקורות ולא מן הקורה שנשברה ומפרקינן האי כר' יוסי ב"ר יהודה מתני לה דהוי ר' יוחנן ולית סתמא. ואמרינן תוב ת"ש מתחילין בערימת התבן אבל לא בעצים שבמוקצה ומפרקינן התם בארזי ואשוחי [ואשוחי] דמוקצה מחמת חסרון כיס. דאפילו ר' שמעון מודה. פי' ארזי ואשוחי עצי ארזים וברושים העשויין לקורות שאין דעתו של אדם עליהן להסיקן תחת הבשילו וגמר הקצה אותן. ואמרינן תוב אין משקין ושוחטין את המדבריות אבל משקין ושוחטין הבייתות והנה סתמא כר' יהודה ורבי יוחנן סבירא ליה הלכתא כסתם משנה קשיא הלכתא אהלכתא ומפרקינן ר' יוחנן סתמא אחרינא אשכח בה"א מגביהין מעל השלחן עצמות וקליפין בש"א מסלק את הטבלה כולה ומנערה. ואמר רב נחמן אנו אין לנו אלא ב"ש כר' יהודה וב"ה כר' שמעון והלכתא כר' יוחנן פליגי בה וכדפסק רב אחא ורבינא חד אמר בכולה שבת הלכתא כר' שמעון בר ממוקצה מחמת מיאוס. וחד אמר במוקצה [מחמת] מיאוס נמי הלכתא כוותיה לבר ממוקצה מחמת איסורו כגון הנר שהדליקו בה באותה שבת וכיוצא בה אבל

רב נסים גאון

מפירין נדרים בשבת. אמרו [בתוספתא פ' י"ח] מפני מה נדרי שבת מפירין אותן בשבת שאם חשיכה ולא הפר אינו

סומכין על משניות כמות שהיא שנויה אלא מוחלפת שיטתה וב"ש כרבי יהודה וכו' [לעיל שם]. **נר ישן.** דמוקצה מחמת מיאוס הוא [חולין קג:]. **נר שהדליקו בה באותה שבת.** שהיה נר דולק בו בין השמשות הוקצה לכל היום [שם טו.]. **מסר הגדול.** מגירה גדולה. הואיל כלי גדול הוא מקפיד עליו שלא ישתבר. **ויתד של מחרישה.** קולטר"א בלע"ז [לעיל קכב:]. **מפירין נדרים בשבת.** בעל לאשתו ואב לבתו [נדרים עז.]. **ונשאלין לנדרים.** לחכם להתירן [לעיל מו:]. [המשך בע"ב]

יכול להפר ורבי יוסי ב"ר יהודה ורבי אלעזר ברבי שמעון שאמרו הפרת נדרים מעת לעת אין הלכה כמותם כדגרסינן בנדרים בפרק נערה המאורסה (דף עו) אלא אמר רבי שמעון בן פזי אין הלכה כאותו הזוג לוי סבר למיעבד עובדא כי האי זוגא א"ל רב הכי אמר רבי אין הלכה כאותו הזוג ואע"פ שהתירו הפרת נדרים בשבת בדבר זה תנאי מאליא א"ר יוחנן וצריך שיבטל בלבו ויאמר לה טול ואכלי טול ושתי ולא יאמר כדרך שאומר בחול מוצא שפתיך ובה"א אומרים אחד זה ואחד זה מבטל בלבו ואינו צריך להוציא בשפתיו תמצאנו שם בפרק נערה המאורסה (דף עו)

אם

SABBATH IF their annulment is NECESSARY FOR THE SABBATH.

The Gemara concludes:

לְצוֹרֶךְ הַשַּׁבָּת אֵין – We see from this Baraisa that if an annulment is **necessary for the Sabbath – yes,** it may be performed on the Sabbath, שֶׁלֹּא לְצוֹרֶךְ הַשַּׁבָּת לֹא – but if it is **not necessary** for the **Sabbath – no,** it may not be performed! Thus, the inquiry is resolved.

The Gemara presents a second version of the inquiry, in which the two sides of the question are elucidated:[37]

לִישָּׁנָא אַחֲרִינָא – **Another version** of this inquiry: אִיבַּעְיָא לְהוּ – **They inquired:** לְצוֹרֶךְ אַתַּרְוַיְיהוּ קָתָנֵי – Do we say that the Mishnah's limiting clause of "THAT ARE NECESSARY for the Sabbath" **refers to both** annulment and seeking release, וְשֶׁלֹּא לְצוֹרֶךְ לֹא – **and** that therefore, if the annulment of the vow is **not necessary** for the Sabbath – then **no,** it is not permitted, אַלְמָא הֲפָרַת נְדָרִים מֵעֵת לְעֵת – **according to which** we must conclude that **annulment of vows** may be performed **from the moment** one knows of the vows **until the** same **moment** a full twenty-four hours later?[38] אוֹ דִילְמָא – **Or perhaps** we say כִּי קָתָנֵי לְצוֹרֶךְ – that **when did the Mishnah teach** the clause of "THAT ARE NECESSARY for the Sabbath"? – אַשְּׁאֵלָה הוּא דְקָתָנֵי – **It taught it** only **with regard to** the law of **seeking release** on the Sabbath.[39] אֲבָל הֲפָרַת נְדָרִים – **But with regard to the annulment of vows** on the Sabbath – אֲפִילוּ שֶׁלֹּא לְצוֹרֶךְ – it may be performed **even if it is not necessary** for the Sabbath! אַלְמָא הֲפָרַת נְדָרִים כָּל הַיּוֹם – We **thus** would conclude that **the annulment of vows** may be performed only for **the entire** calendar **day** upon which the vows become known,[40] but not for a full twenty-four-hour period from that moment! Thus, the question of whether vows that do not affect the Sabbath may be annulled on the Sabbath is directly dependent upon whether one's ability to annul a vow is limited to the calendar day upon which he learns of it, or whether it extends for a full twenty-four-hour period from that time. If annulment is limited to the calendar day, then one may annul even vows that have no bearing upon the Sabbath, for once the Sabbath passes there will be no further opportunity to annul them. However, if the period given for annulment is twenty-four hours, then one may annul only vows that affect the Sabbath, since there will be opportunity to annul other sorts of vows after the Sabbath ends.

In this version too, the Gemara brings proof from the Baraisa cited above:

תָּא שְׁמַע – **Come, learn** a proof. דְּתָנֵי רַב זוּטֵי דְּבֵי רַב פַּפִּי – **For Rav Zutei of the academy of Rav Pappi taught a Baraisa:** מְפִירִין נְדָרִים בְּשַׁבָּת לְצוֹרֶךְ הַשַּׁבָּת – ONE MAY ANNUL VOWS ON THE SABBATH IF their annulment is NECESSARY FOR THE SABBATH.

The Gemara concludes:

לְצוֹרֶךְ הַשַּׁבָּת אֵין – We see from this Baraisa that if an annulment is **necessary for the Sabbath – yes,** it may be performed on the Sabbath, שֶׁלֹּא לְצוֹרֶךְ הַשַּׁבָּת לֹא – but if it is **not necessary** for the Sabbath – **no,** it may not be performed! אַלְמָא הֲפָרַת נְדָרִים מֵעֵת לְעֵת – We **thus** see that **the annulment of vows** may be performed **from the moment** the vows become known **until the** same **moment** a full twenty-four hours later.

The Gemara contrasts the implication of this Baraisa to the words of a Mishnah:

אָמַר רַב אַשִׁי – **Rav Ashi said:** וְהָאֲנַן תְּנַן – **But we have learned in a Mishnah** elsewhere:[41] הֲפָרַת נְדָרִים כָּל הַיּוֹם – ANNULMENT OF VOWS may be performed for no more than THE ENTIRE calendar DAY upon which the vows become known. וְיֵשׁ בַּדָּבָר לְהָקֵל וּלְהַחְמִיר – AND IN THIS FACT THERE IS both CAUSE FOR LENIENCY AND CAUSE FOR STRINGENCY in the time allowed for annulment.[42] כֵּיצַד – HOW SO? נָדְרָה לֵילֵי שַׁבָּת – IF SHE MADE A VOW ON THE SABBATH EVE,[43] מֵיפֵר לֵילֵי שַׁבָּת וְיוֹם הַשַּׁבָּת עַד שֶׁתֶּחְשַׁךְ – HE CAN ANNUL it all THE NIGHT OF THE SABBATH AND all THE SABBATH DAY, UNTIL DARK. נָדְרָה עִם חֲשֵׁכָה – But IF SHE MADE THE VOW WITH the onset of DARK, i.e. on the Sabbath day just before nightfall, מֵיפֵר עַד שֶׁלֹּא תֶּחְשַׁךְ – HE MUST ANNUL it BEFORE DARK, שֶׁאִם לֹא הֵפֵר – FOR IF HE HAS NOT ANNULLED it by dark, מִשֶּׁחָשְׁכָה אֵינוֹ יָכוֹל לְהָפֵר – ONCE IT IS already DARK HE IS UNABLE TO ANNUL it any more. This Mishnah states explicitly that one may annul a vow only on the calendar day upon which he learns of it. It thus contradicts the implication of the aforecited Baraisa!

The Gemara answers:

תַּנָּאֵי הִיא – **This** issue **is** the subject of **a Tannaic dispute.** דְּתַנְיָא – **For it has been taught in a Baraisa:** הֲפָרַת נְדָרִים כָּל הַיּוֹם – ANNULMENT OF VOWS may be performed for no more than THE ENTIRE calendar DAY upon which the vows become known. רַבִּי יוֹסֵי בַּר יְהוּדָה וְרַבִּי אֶלְעָזָר בְּרַבִּי שִׁמְעוֹן אָמְרוּ – R' YOSE BAR YEHUDAH AND R' ELAZAR THE SON OF R' SHIMON SAID: מֵעֵת לְעֵת – It may be performed FROM THE MOMENT the vows become known UNTIL THE same MOMENT twenty-four hours later.[44] The Mishnah cited follows the opinion of the Tanna Kamma of this Baraisa, while the Baraisa cited earlier is in accordance with R' Yose bar Yehudah and R' Elazar the son of R' Shimon.[45]

NOTES

37. *Ritva MHK* ed.; see *Rashi* with *Chasam Sofer;* cf. *Ramban.*

38. For the reason one is prohibited to annul vows that do not affect the Sabbath is because there will be opportunity to annul them after the Sabbath. Thus, if the Mishnah is in fact prohibiting annulment of such vows, it must hold that annulment is permitted for a full twenty-four hours after hearing of the vow. Opportunity is thus provided to annul the vow after the Sabbath (*Rashi*). The source for allowing a full twenty-four hours for annulment is the verse (*Numbers* ibid. v. 15) that speaks of a husband who affirms his wife's vow by remaining silent after learning of it. The verse states (*Numbers* 30:15): וְאִם־הַחֲרֵשׁ יַחֲרִישׁ לָהּ אִישָׁהּ מִיּוֹם אֶל־יוֹם, *And if her husband is silent regarding her [vow] from one day to the next day,* thus implying that he enjoys a full twenty-four period in which to register his disapproval (*Nedarim* 76b; see *Ran* there).

39. [Which, since it can be performed after the Sabbath, may not be performed on the Sabbath.]

40. I.e. on the Sabbath day until nightfall, but not longer, even if the vow was taken a moment before dark. Since there is thus no opportunity to annul the vow after the Sabbath, one may annul it even on the Sabbath [as was explained above, note 33] (*Rashi*). [In Jewish law, a day begins and ends at nightfall.]

41. *Nedarim* 76b.

42. For since annulment must be performed by day's end, one will sometimes have more time to perform it and sometimes less [depending upon when the vow was made] (*Rashi*). [This Mishnah does not mean to say that this ruling is both lenient and stringent in comparison to the opinion allowing annulment for a full twenty-four hours, for, in fact, since this ruling never allows more time for annulment than is allowed according to that opinion, it is *never* more lenient than it! Rather, these terms simply denote the sometimes greater, sometimes lesser amounts of time available for annulment according to *this* ruling (see *Ran, Nedarim* ibid. ד״ה להקל ולהחמיר; but see also *Rashash, Nedarim* ibid.).]

43. [I.e. on Friday night.] These laws apply equally to one who made a vow on a weekday; see *Ran* ibid. ד״ה נדרה בלילי שבת for why the Mishnah discusses one who takes a vow on the Sabbath.

44. See above, notes 33 and 38 for the Scriptural proofs to each of these opinions. For how each opinion deals with the proof-text of its disputant, see *Nedarim* ibid.

45. [However, the halachah follows the view that annulment may only be performed on the day the vow became known (*Yoreh Deah* 234:21), and, accordingly, that even vows that do not affect the Sabbath may be annulled on the Sabbath (*Orach Chaim* 341:1).]

אין מבקעין עצים מן הקורות ולא מן הקורה שנשברה ביו"ט רבי יוחנן ההוא כרבי יוסי בר יהודה מתני לה תא שמע מתחילין בערימת התבן אבל לא בעצים שבמוקצה התם בארזי ואשוחי דמוקצה מחמת חסרון כיס אפילו רבי שמעון מודה ת"ש אין משקין ושוחטין את המדבריות אבל משקין ושוחטין את הבייתות ר' יוחנן סתמא אחרינא אשכח ב"ש אומרים מגביהין מעל השלחן עצמות וקליפין וב"ה אומרים מסלק את הטבלה כולה ומנערה וא"ר נחמן אנו אין לנו אלא ב"ש כרבי יהודה וב"ה כר"ש פליגי בה רב אחא ורבינא חד אמר בכל השבת כולה הלכה כר"ש לבר ממוקצה מחמת מיאוס ומאי ניהו נר ישן וחד אמר במוקצה מחמת מיאוס נמי הלכה כר"ש לבר ממוקצה מחמת איסור ומאי ניהו נר שהדליקו בה באותה שבת אבל מוקצה מחמת חסרון כיס אפילו ר"ש מודה דתנן כל הכלים ניטלין בשבת חוץ ממסר הגדול ויתד של מחרישה:

מתני' מפירין נדרים בשבת ונשאלין לנדרים שהן לצורך השבת ופוקקין את המאור ומודדין את המטלית ומודדין את המקוה ומעשה בימי אביו של רבי צדוק ובימי אבא שאול בן בטנית שפקקו את המאור בטפיח וקשרו את המקידה בגמי לידע אם יש בגיגית פותח טפח אם לאו ומדבריהם למדנו שפוקקין ומודדין וקושרין בשבת:

גמ' איבעיא להו הפרה בין לצורך ובין שלא לצורך ושאלה לצורך אין שלא לצורך לא ומשום הכי קפלגינהו מהדדי או דילמא הפרה נמי לצורך אין שלא לצורך לא והא דקא פליג להו מהדדי משום דהפרה אין צריך ב"ד ושאלה צריכה ב"ד ת"ש דתני זוטי דבי רב פפא מפירין נדרים בשבת לצורך השבת לצורך השבת אין שלא לצורך השבת לא לישנא אחרינא איבעיא להו לצורך אתרוייהו קתני ושלא לצורך לא אלמא הפרת נדרים מעת לעת או דילמא כי קתני לצורך אשאלה הוא דקתני אבל הפרת נדרים אפילו שלא לצורך אלמא הפרת נדרים כל היום תא שמע דתני רב זוטי דבי רב פפי מפירין נדרים בשבת לצורך השבת לצורך השבת אין שלא לצורך השבת לא אלמא הפרת נדרים מעת לעת א"ר אשי והאנן תנן הפרת נדרים כל היום ויש בדבר להקל ולהחמיר כיצד נדרה לילי שבת מיפר לילי שבת ויום השבת עד שתחשך נדרה עם חשכה מיפר עד שלא תחשך שאם לא הפר משחשכה אינו יכול להפר תנאי היא דתניא הפרת נדרים כל היום ר' יוסי בר יהודה ורבי אלעזר ברבי שמעון אמרו מעת לעת: ונשאלים לנדרים: איבעיא להו כשלא היה לו פנאי או דלמא אפילו היה לו פנאי תא שמע דאזדקיקו ליה רבנן לרב זוטרא בריה דרב זירא ושרו ליה נדריה ואף על גב דהוה ליה פנאי: שפקקו את המאור בטפיח וקשרו את המקידה בגמי: אמר רב יהודה אמר רב הילקטי קטנה היתה בין שני בתים [וטומאה היתה שם] וגיגית

רש"י

אין מבקעין עצים מן הקורות. סותר של הקורות המוקצות וסדורות לבנין: **ולא מן קורה.** הישנה שנשברה היום והשתא להסקה קיימא ואפ"ה אסור הואיל ובין השמשות לא איתכן להכי: **מתחילין.** להסיק בערימת התבן קא סלקא דעתך במתניתא קריא דסתמיה להסקה: **אבל לא בעצים שבמוקצה.** שהכניס ברחבה שאחורי ביתו והקצם לימות הגשמים. מוקצה רחבה שאחורי בתים שהקצה אחורי ביתו להכניס שם דבר לאוצר: **בארזי ואשוחי.** ארז זכר וארז נקבה שעומדין לבנין: **משקין.** אורחא דמילתא נקט משום סירכא דמשכא שתהא נוחה להפשיט: **מדבריות.** (א) שרועות באפר תמיד ולנות בתוך התחום: **סתמא אחרינא.** בית הלל חשיב כסתמא: **כל הכלים ניטלין.** ואפי' מלאכתן לאיסור ורבי שמעון היא: **חוץ מן המסר הגדול.** מגירה שהיא לאומנין לקוץ בה עצים ומוקצה מחמת חסרון כיס הוא שלא ישתברו חריצים שהוא עשוי כסכין מלא פגימות: **ויתד של מחרישה.** החופר את הקרקע קולטר"א בלע"ז: **מתני' מפירין.** בעל לאשתו: **ונשאלין.** לחכם: **שהן לצורך השבת.** כגון שנדר שלא לאכול [היום]: **ופוקקין את המאור.** כרבנן דאמרי (לעיל דף קכה:) פוקקין פקק החלון: **ומודדין את המקוה.** במדה שיהא שם עמוק שלש אמות מים ורוחב אמה על אמה: **ואת המטלית.** (ב) שתהא שלש על שלש אצבעות כגון אם היתה טמאה ונגעה בטהרות: **בטפיח.** פך של חרס (ג) ותבירו בפי"ז (דף קכה:) זמורה שהיא קשורה בטפיח ממלאין בה בשבת: **מקידה.** כלי חרס: **לידע אם יש בגיגית פותח טפח.** בגמרא מפרש לה: **וקושרין.** קשר שאינו של קיימא אפילו לכתחילה: **ומודדין.** להתלמד על דבר הוראה: **גמ' איבעיא להו הפרה.** דמתניתין בין לצורך [בין שלא לצורך] השבת דגבי הפרה ביום שמעו כתיב (במדבר ל) ואם לא מיפר האידנא שוב אינו מיפר: **ושאלה לצורך אין שלא לצורך לא.** דיכול לישאל למחר ומשום הכי מפליג להו מהדדי ולא קתני מפירין ונשאלין לנדרים שהן לצורך השבת דלא קאי לצורך אלא אשאלה: **בית דין.** חכם: הכי גרסי' ל"א איבעיא להו (במסכת נדרים דף עז.) **לצורך אתרוייהו קאי.** אהפרה ואשאלה אבל הפרה שלא לצורך לא אלמא הפרת נדרים מעת לעת וזה ששמע בשבת יכול להפר משתחשך בתוך מעת לעת של שמיעה הלכך שלא לצורך לא שרינן בשבת: **כל היום.** עד שתחשך ותו לא ואפילו שמע סמוך לחשיכה הלכך אפי' שלא לצורך שאם לא יפר עכשיו לא יפר עוד: **לצורך השבת.** אלמא הפרת נדרים מעת לעת של שמיעה הלכך שלא לצורך (ד) לא מדלא שרי אלא לצורך: **להקל ולהחמיר.** כלומר פעמים שיש שהות גדול ופעמים שאינו אלא מעט: **איבעיא להו.** הא דקתני נשאלין לנדרים שהן לצורך: **כשלא היה לו פנאי.** לשאל מערב שבת קאמר או אפילו כשהיה לו פנאי: **הילקטי קטנה.** שביל קטן בין שני בתים: וגיגית

תוספות

אין משקין ושוחטין את המדבריות. הוה מצי למימר דהכי כגרוגרות וצמוקין דמיין כדאמר בפרק כירה (לעיל דף מה:): **לבר** ממוקצה מחמת איסור. וכגון איסור דדחייה בידים כגון נר שהדליקו באותו שבת כדפירשתי בפ"ק בסופו:

והלכתא מעת לעת. לא גרס בפירוש ר"ח דבנדרים משמע דלית הלכתא הכי דאמר בפרק נערה המאורסה (כתובות דף עו:) אין הלכה כאותו הזוג. מ"ר:

הלקטי קטנה. מפרש בקונטרס שביל קטן היתה בין שני בתים והגיגית סדוקה מונחת על גבן והמת מוטל בהלקטי תחת הגיגית נגד הסדק וקשרו המקידה לידע אם יש בסדק פותח טפח ולהאי פירושא קשה לר"י דאפי' אין בסדק פותח טפח כיון שהמת נגדו לא חשבינן לה כמאהיל על המת כיון שאין [זהו] דרך מאהיל (ה) כדמוכח במסכת אהלות (פי"ו מ"ה) ומייתי לה בסוף פרק קמא דסוכה (דף יח. ושם) אין בארובה פותח טפח והמת בבית מה שבבית כנגד ארובה טהור המת כנגד ארובה מה שבבית טהור וכיון שהמת היה נגד הסדק מה היה להם לקשור המקידה ועוד פירש שלפני מות המת פקקו המאור בטפיח ולא הבין רבי לפירושו הלא אותו מת לא היה מת שלם שהרי לא ידעו אם למעלה הימנו היה פותח טפח והמת היה כולו תחת הסדק אלא ודאי כזית מן המת היה וא"כ לא היה לו לומר לפני מות המת אלא לפני שבא כזית מן המת לשם ומיהו יתכן לומר שהמת היה כולו מוטל תחת הגיגית שלא כנגד הסדק והגיגית היתה סדוקה באמצע מראשה לסופה ואילו היה באותו סדק על פני כולו פותח טפח לא היתה טומאה עוברת דלא חשיב כאהל אחד אבל אין בו פותח טפח כאלו אין כאן סדק וחשיב כאהל אחד ומביא את הטומאה לבית וקושיא ראשונה מכל מקום במקומה עומדת ונראה כפירוש ר"ח דמפרש דהלקטי היינו תל המתלקט ואותה הלקטי היתה בין שני בתים והמת היה בבית אחד ואותה הגיגית היתה למעלה מן התל עד לתקרה ואותה הגיגית לא היתה טמאה שהרי בטלה שם ואם לא היתה סדוקה לא היה הבית אחר טמא אלא הגיגית היתה סדוקה מלדה והשתא אתי שפיר דקתני סדוקה לפי שהיא מלדה אבל לפירוש הקונטרס לא אתי שפיר דכיון דפירש שהסדק למעלה מן הגיגית היה לו לומר פתוחה ולא סדוקה אבל לפר"ח אתי שפיר שהסדק היה מן הצד וקשרו את המקידה לידע אם יש פותח טפח ויש לנו לומר שאותו חור היה עשוי לתשמיש דחור העשוי לתשמיש שיעורו בפותח טפח ואם היה פותח טפח הבית אחר טמא ואם לאו טהור ומיהו קשה לר"י לפירוש ר"ח דלא הוה ליה למימר על גבן אלא על גבה. מ"ר:

באוונא

עין משפט נר מצוה

לז א מיי' פ"ב מהלכות יו"ט הלכה יג סמג לאוין עה טוש"ע א"ח סימן תקיח סעיף א:

לח ב ג מיי' שם הלכה יא וסמג שם טוש"ע א"ח סי' תקיח סעיף ו:

לט ד מיי' שם הלכה י סמג שם טוש"ע א"ח סימן תצה סעיף ג:

מ ה מיי' שם הלכה ב וסמג שם טוש"ע א"ח סי' תצ סעיף ג:

[הגה] [טוש"ע א"ח סימן שיח סעיף ח]:

מא ו מיי' פכ"ד מהלכות שבת הלכה ו ופי"ג מהלכות נדרים הלכה ח וסמג לאוין סה טוש"ע א"ח סימן שמא סעיף א וטוש"ע יו"ד סימן רלד סעיף כד:

מב ז מיי' פכ"ד מהל' שבת הלכה ו וסמג שם ומיי' פ"ו מהלכות שבועות הלכה ו סמג לאוין רמא טוש"ע א"ח שם וטוש"ע יו"ד סי' רכח סעיף [illegible]:

מג ח מיי' פי"ג מהל' נדרים הלכה כה סמג לאוין רמב טוש"ע יו"ד סימן רלד סעיף כב:

מד ט מיי' פכ"ד מהל' שבת הלכה ו ופ"ו מהלכות שבועות הלכה ו סמג לאוין רמב טוש"ע א"ח סימן שמא סעיף א וטוש"ע יו"ד סי' רכח סעיף ג:

רבינו חננאל

ממקומה דבבהמת קדשים [מיירי] מכלל דהוליך שרי כר' [שמעון] דלית ליה מוקצה. ומקשינן על ר' יוחנן וכי סבר רבי יוחנן הלכה כרבי שמעון והא אמר ר' יוחנן הלכה כסתם משנה ותנן אין מבקעים עצים מן הקורות ולא מן הקורה שנשברה ביו"ט ופרקינן האי כר' יוסי ב"ר יהודה מתני לה דרבי יוחנן ולית סתמא. ואמרינן תוב ת"ש מתחילין בערימת התבן אבל לא בעצים שבמוקצה ומפרקינן התם בארזי ואשוחי [ואשוחי] דמוקצה מחמת חסרון כיס. דאפילו ר' שמעון מודה. פי' ארזי ואשוחי עצי ארזים וברושים העשויין לקורות שאין דעתו של אדם עליהן להסיקן תחת תבשילו וגמר הקצה אותן. ואמרינן תוב אין משקין ושוחטין את המדבריות אבל משקין ושוחטין הבייתות והנה סתמא כר' יהודה ורבי יוחנן סבירא ליה הלכתא כסתם משנה קשיא הלכתא אהלכתא ומפרקינן ר' יוחנן סתמא אחרינא אשכח בה"א מגביהין מעל השלחן עצמות וקליפין בש"א מסלק את הטבלה כולה ומנערה. ואמר רב נחמן אנו אין לנו אלא ב"ש כר' יהודה וב"ה כר' שמעון והלכתא כר' שמעון וכדפסק ר' יוחנן פליגי בה רב אחא ורבינא חד אמר בכולה שבת הלכתא כר' שמעון בר ממוקצה מחמת מיאוס. וחד אמר במוקצה [מחמת] מיאוס נמי הלכתא כוותיה לבר ממוקצה מחמת איסורו כגון הנר שהדליקו בה באותה שבת וכיוצא בו אבל

רב נסים גאון

מפירין נדרים בשבת. אמרו [בתוספתא פ' י"ח] מפני מה נדרי שבת מפירין אותן בשבת שאם חשיכה ולא הפר אינו יכול להפר ורבי יוסי ב"ר יהודה ורבי אלעזר ברבי שמעון שאמרו הפרת נדרים מעת לעת אין הלכה כמותם [illegible]

מסורת הש"ס

א) ביצה ב: לג., ב) [שם כו.], ג) [פי' עלי אלהים וברושים. ערוך], ד) [ביצה מ. לעיל מה:], ה) [לעיל קמב. ביצה ב:], ו) [ביצה לג:], ז) [לעיל קכג.], ח) לעיל מז: נדרים עז., ט) לעיל דף קכו:, י) [נדרים דף עז:], כ) נדרים עו:, ל) [נדרים עז.], מ) שם עז., נ) ג"י רש"ל, ס) [שבת זו גמי רש"ל].

הגהות הב"ח

(א) רש"י ד"ה מדבריות וכו' תמיד הס"ד ואח"כ מה"ד בימות הגשמים חוץ לתחום ובאות ולנות בתוך התחום: (ב) ד"ה ואת המטלית לידע אם יש בה שלש על שלש: (ג) ד"ה בטפיח פך של חרס (ותבירו וכו' בשבת) תא"מ. ונ"ב הג"ה היא: (ד) ד"ה לצורך השבת וכו' שלא לצורך השבת ואח"כ מה"ד והלכך שלא לצורך לא: (ה) תוס' ד"ה הלקטי וכו' שאין דרך מאהיל בכך כדמוכח:

סליק מסכת שבת בס"ד

ליקוטי רש"י

אין מבקעין עצים. ביום טוב לא מן הקורות הסדורות זו על גב זו בקרקע ועומדות לבנין. ולא מן הקורה שנשברה ביום טוב. ואף על פי שעומדת מעכשיו להסקה הואיל ובין השמשות לאו להכי קיימא [ביצה ב:]. אבל לא בעצים שבמוקצה. רחבה שאחורי הבתים קרויה מוקצה לפי שהיא מוקצה לאוצר ואין נכנסים ויוצאים בה תדיר ושם טומנין עצים או כל דבר שאין צריך לו עד זמן מרובה. ארזי ואשוחי. אין אדם מסיק אותן דעומדין לבנין. אשוחי. ארז נקבה. דמוקצה מחמת חסרון כיס ניגהו. שדמיה יקרין [שם ל.]. אין משקין ושוחטין את המדבריות. משום מוקצה. משקין. משום סרכא דמשכא [illegible] [שם מ.]. המדבריות. [illegible] [לעיל מה:]. מגביהין. בשבת מעל השלחן [ביצה ב.]. בידים מעל השלחן [לעיל קמג.]. עצמות. שאינן ראוין לאכילה [illegible] [ביצה שם]. [illegible] [לעיל שם]. ובית הלל אומרים. אין מטלטלין אותן בידים דמוקצה [ביצה שם]. מסלק הטבלה. שיש תורת כלי עליה ומנערה [illegible] [לעיל שם]. ואמר רב נחמן אנו אין לנו. [illegible]

[illegible] נר ישן. [illegible] מפירין נדרים בשבת. בעל לאשתו ולא בעל [illegible] ונשאלין לנדרים. לחכם להתירם [נדרים עז.] [המשך בע"ב]

The Mishnah stated:

וְנִשְׁאָלִים לִנְדָרִים – AND WE MAY SEEK RELEASE FROM VOWS.

The Gemara presents an inquiry regarding a detail of this law: **אִיבַּעְיָא לְהוּ** – **They inquired:** **כְּשֶׁלֹּא הָיָה לוֹ פְּנַאי** – When the Mishnah permits one to seek release from vows on the Sabbath, does it refer only to a case **in which he had no opportunity** to do so before the Sabbath,[46] **אוֹ דִלְמָא אֲפִילוּ הָיָה לוֹ פְּנַאי** – **or** does it **perhaps** refer **even** to a case **in which he did have an opportunity** to do so before the Sabbath?

The Gemara answers:

תָּא שְׁמַע – **Come, learn** a proof to this: **דְּאִיזְדַּקִּיקוּ לֵיהּ רַבָּנָן לְרַב זוּטְרָא בְּרֵיהּ דְּרַב זֵירָא** – **For the Rabbis** once **involved themselves with Rav Zutra the son of Rav Zeira,** **וְשָׁרוּ לֵיהּ נִדְרֵיהּ** – **and released him** from **his vow** on the Sabbath **וְאַף עַל גַּב דַּהֲוָה לֵיהּ פְּנַאי** – **even though he had had the opportunity** to seek release before the Sabbath. We see that one may seek release on the Sabbath even from vows that could have been dealt with before the Sabbath.[47]

The Mishnah states further:

שֶׁפָּקְקוּ אֶת הַמָּאוֹר בְּטָפִיחַ וְקָשְׁרוּ אֶת הַמְּקֵידָה בְּגֶמִי – [There was an incident ...] IN WHICH THEY SHUTTERED THE WINDOW WITH AN EARTHENWARE FLASK, AND THEY TIED AN EARTHENWARE VESSEL WITH A strand of REED-GRASS.

The Gemara gives the particulars of this incident:

אָמַר רַב יְהוּדָה אָמַר רַב – **Rav Yehudah said in the name of Rav:** **הִילְקְטִי קְטַנָּה הָיְתָה בֵּין שְׁנֵי בָּתִּים** – **There was a narrow alley**[48] **between two houses,** **[וְטוּמְאָה הָיְתָה שָׁם]** – **and *tumah*** in the form of a corpse **was there** in the alley.

NOTES

46. Such as one who took a vow just as the Sabbath came in or who could not find a sage to grant him release before the Sabbath arrived (*Ran* ibid. 77a ד״ה אתבעי).

47. However, it is certainly *preferable* for one to seek release *before* the Sabbath; but if he did not do so, we do not penalize him, but allow him to do so on the Sabbath (*Beur Halachah* to 341:1 ד״ה אע״פ).

48. *Rashi;* cf. *Tosafos;* see *Maginei Shlomo.*

אין מבקעין עצים מן הקורות ולא מן הקורה שנשברה ביו"ט רבי יוחנן ההוא כרבי יוסי בר יהודה מתני לה תא שמע מתחילין בערימת התבן אבל לא בעצים שבמוקצה התם בארזי ואשוחי דמוקצה מחמת חסרון כיס אפילו רבי שמעון מודה ת"ש אין משקין ושוחטין את המדבריות אבל משקין ושוחטין את הבייתות ר' יוחנן סתמא אחרינא אשכח ב"ש אומרים מגביהין מעל השלחן עצמות וקליפין וב"ה אומרים מסלק את הטבלה כולה ומנערה וא"ר נחמן אנו אין לנו אלא ב"ש כרבי יהודה וב"ה כר"ש פליגי בה רב אחא ורבינא חד אמר בכל השבת כולה הלכה כר"ש לבר ממוקצה מחמת מיאוס ומאי ניהו נר ישן וחד אמר במוקצה מחמת מיאוס נמי הלכה כר"ש לבר ממוקצה מחמת איסור ומאי ניהו נר שהדליקו בה באותה שבת אבל מוקצה מחמת חסרון כיס אפילו ר"ש מודה דתנן כל הכלים ניטלין בשבת חוץ ממסר הגדול ויתד של מחרישה:

מתני' מפירין נדרים בשבת ונשאלין לנדרים שהן לצורך השבת ופוקקין את המאור ומודדין את המטלית ואת המקוה ומעשה בימי אביו של רבי צדוק ובימי אבא שאול בן בטנית שפקקו את המאור בטפיח [ה] וקשרו את המקידה בגמי לידע אם יש בגיגית פותח טפח אם לאו ומדבריהם למדנו שפוקקין ומודדין וקושרין בשבת:

גמ' איבעיא להו הפרה בין לצורך ובין שלא לצורך ושאלה לצורך אין שלא לצורך לא ומשום הכי קפלגינהו מהדדי או דילמא הפרה נמי לצורך אין שלא לצורך לא והא דקא פליג להו מהדדי משום דהפרה אין צריך ב"ד ושאלה צריכה ב"ד ת"ש דתני זוטי דבי רב פפא מפירין נדרים בשבת לצורך השבת ונשאלין לנדרים לצורך השבת אין שלא לצורך השבת לא לישנא אחרינא איבעיא להו לצורך אתרווייהו קתני ושלא לצורך לא אלמא הפרת נדרים מעת לעת או דילמא כי קתני לצורך אשאלה הוא דקתני אבל הפרת נדרים אפילו שלא לצורך אלמא הפרת נדרים כל היום תא שמע דתני רב זוטי דבי רב פפי מפירין נדרים בשבת לצורך השבת אין שלא לצורך השבת לא אלמא הפרת נדרים מעת לעת א"ר אשי והאנן תנן הפרת נדרים כל היום ויש בדבר להקל ולהחמיר כיצד נדרה לילי שבת מיפר לילי שבת ויום השבת עד שתחשך נדרה עם חשכה מיפר עד שלא תחשך שאם לא הפר משחשכה אינו יכול להפר תנאי היא דתניא הפרת נדרים כל היום ר' יוסי בר יהודה ורבי אלעזר ברבי שמעון אמרו מעת לעת: ונשאלים לנדרים: איבעיא להו כשלא היה לו פנאי או דלמא אפילו היה לו פנאי תא שמע דאזדקיקו ליה רבנן לרב זוטרא בריה דרב זירא ושרו ליה נדריה ואף על גב דהוה ליה פנאי: שפקקו את המאור בטפיח וקשרו את המקידה בגמי: אמר רב יהודה אמר רב הילקטי קטנה היתה בין שני בתים [וטומאה היתה שם] וגיגית

רש"י

אין מבקעין עצים מן הקורות. סותר של הקורות המוקצות וסדורות לבנין: **ולא מן קורה.** הישנה שנשברה היום ומהשתא להסקה קיימא ואפ"ה אסור הואיל ובין השמשות לא איתכן להכי: **מתחילין.** להסיק בערימת התבן קא סלקא דעתך בתבנא סריא דסתמייה להסקה: **אבל לא בעצים שבמוקצה.** שכונס ברחבה שאחורי ביתו והקצה לימות הסתיו. מוקצה רחבה שאחורי בתים שהקצה אחורי ביתו להכניס שם דבר לאוצר: **בארזי ואשוחי.** ארז זכר וארז נקבה שעומדין לבנין: **משקין.** אורחא דמילתא נקט משום סירכא דמשכא שתהא נוחה להפשיט: **מדבריות.** (א) שרועות באפר תמיד ולנות בתוך התחום: **סתמא אחרינא.** בית הלל חשיב כסתמא: **כל הכלים ניטלין.** ואפי' מלאכתן לאיסור ורבי שמעון היא: **חוץ מן המסר הגדול.** מגירה שהיא אומנין לקוץ בה עצים ומוקצה מחמת חסרון כיס הוא שלא ישתברו חריצים שהוא עשוי כסכין שלא תהא פגימות: **ויתד של מחרישה.** החופר את הקרקע קולטר"א בלע"ז: **מתני' מפירין.** בעל לאשתו: **ונשאלין.** לחכם: **שהן לצורך השבת.** כגון שנדר שלא לאכול [היום]: **ופוקקין את המאור.** כרבנן דאמרי (לעיל דף קכה:) פוקקין פקק החלון: **ומודדין את המקוה.** במדה שיהא שם עמוק שלש אמות מים ורוחב אמה על אמה: **ואת המטלית.** (ב) שתהא שלש על שלש אצבעות כגון אם היתה טמאה ונגעה בטהרות: **בטפיח.** פך של חרס (ג) וחבירו כפי' (דף קכה:) זמורה שהיא קשורה בטפיח ממלאין בה בשבת: **מקידה.** כלי חרס: **לידע אם יש בגיגית פותח טפח.** בגמרא מפרש לה: **וקושרין.** קשר שאינו של קיימא אפילו לכתחילה: **ומודדין.** להתלמד על דבר הוראה: **גמ' איבעיא להו הפרה.** דמתניתין בין לצורך [בין שלא לצורך] השבת דגבי הפרה ביום שמעו כתיב (במדבר ל) ואם לא מיפר האידנא שוב אינו מיפר: **ושאלה לצורך אין שלא לצורך לא.** דיכול לישאל למחר ומשום הכי מפליג להו מהדדי ולא קתני מפירין ונשאלין לנדרים שהן לצורך השבת דלא קאי לצורך אלא אשאלה: **בית דין.** חכם: הכי גרסי' **ל"א איבעיא להו** (במסכת נדרים דף עז.) **לצורך אתרווייהו קאי.** אהפרה ואשאלה אבל הפרה שלא לצורך לא אלמא הפרת נדרים מעת לעת וזה ששמע בשבת יכול להפר משתחשך בתוך מעת לעת של שמיעה הלכך שלא לצורך לא שרינן בשבת: **כל היום.** עד שתחשך ותו לא ואפילו שמע סמוך לחשיכה הלכך אפי' שלא לצורך (ע) שאם לא יפר עכשיו לא יפר עוד: **לצורך השבת.** אלמא הפרת נדרים מעת לעת של שמיעה הלכך שלא לצורך (ד) לא מדלא שרי אלא לצורך: **להקל ולהחמיר.** כלומר פעמים שיש שהות גדול ופעמים שאינו אלא מעט: **איבעיא להו.** הא דקתני נשאלין לנדרים שהן לצורך: **כשלא היה לו פנאי.** לשאול מערב שבת קאמר או אפילו כשהיה לו פנאי: **הילקטי קטנה.** שביל קטן בין שני בתים: וגיגית

תוספות

אין משקין ושוחטין את המדבריות. הוה מצי למימר דהני כגרוגרות ולצמוקין דמיין כדאמר בפרק כירה (לעיל דף מה:): **לבר** ממוקצה מחמת איסור. וכגון איסור דדחייה בידים כגון נר שהדליקו באותו שבת כדפירשתי בפ"ק בסופו: **והלכתא** מעת לעת. לא גרס בפירוש ר"ח דבנדרים משמע דלית הלכתא הכי דאמר בפרק נערה המאורסה (כתובות דף עו:) אין הלכה כאותו הזוג. מ"ר: **הלקטי** קטנה. מפרש בקונטרס שביל קטן היתה בין שני בתים והגיגית סדוקה מונחת על גבן והמת מוטל בהלקטי תחת הגיגית נגד הסדק וקשרו המקידה לידע אם יש בסדק פותח טפח ולהאי פירושא קשה לר"י דאפי' אין בסדק פותח טפח כיון שהמת נגדו לא חשבינן לה כמאהיל על המת כיון שאין [זה] דרך מאהיל (ה) כדמוכח במסכת אהלות (פי"ג מ"ה) ומייתי לה בסוף פרק קמא דסוכה (דף יח. ושם) אין בארובה פותח טפח והמת בבית מה שבבית כנגד ארובה טהור המת כנגד ארובה מה שבבית טהור וכיון שהמת היה נגד הסדק מה היה להם לקשור המקידה ועוד פירש שלפני מות המת פקקו המאור בטפיח ולא הבין רבי לפירושו הלא אותו מת לא היה מת שלם שהרי לא ידעו אם למעלה הימנו היה פותח טפח והמת היה כולו תחת הסדק אלא ודאי כזית מן המת היה וא"כ לא היה לו לומר לפני מות המת אלא לפני שבא כזית מן המת לשם ומיהו יתכן לומר שהמת היה כולו מוטל תחת הגיגית שלא כנגד הסדק והגיגית היתה סדוקה באמצע מראשה לסופה ואילו היה באותו סדק על פני כולו פותח טפח לא היתה טומאה עוברת דלא חשיב כאהל אחד אבל אין בו פותח טפח כאלו אין כאן סדק וחשיב כאהל אחד ומביא את הטומאה לבית וקושיא ראשונה מכל מקום במקומה עומדת ונראה כפירוש ר"ח דמפרש דהלקטי היינו תל המתלקט ואותה הלקטי היתה בין שני בתים והמת היה בבית אחד ואותה הגיגית היתה למעלה מן התל עד לתקרה ואותה הגיגית לא היתה טמאה שהרי בטלה שם ואם לא היתה סדוקה לא היה הבית אחר טמא אלא הגיגית היתה סדוקה מלדה והשתא אתי שפיר דקתני סדוקה לפי שהיא מלדה אבל לפירוש הקונטרס לא אתי שפיר דכיון דפירש שהסדק למעלה מן הגיגית היה לו לומר פתוחה ולא סדוקה אבל לפר"ח אתי שפיר שהסדק היה מן הצד וקשרו את המקידה לידע אם יש פותח טפח ויש לנו לומר שאותו חור היה עשוי לתשמיש דחור העשוי לתשמיש שיעורו בפותח טפח ואם היה פותח טפח הבית אחר טמא ואם לאו טהור ומיהו קשה לר"י לפירוש ר"ח דלא הוה ליה למימר על גבן אלא על גגה. מ"ר: באותה

עין משפט נר מצוה

לז א מיי' פ"ב מהלכות יו"ט הלכה יב סמג לאוין עה טוש"ע א"ח סימן תקז סעיף א:
לז ב ג מיי' שם הלכה יא וסמג שם טוש"ע א"ח סי' תקיז סעיף ב:
לח ד מיי' שם הלכה י סמג שם טוש"ע א"ח סימן תצח סעיף ה:
לט ה מיי' שם הלכה ג וסמג שם טוש"ע א"ח סי' תקא סעיף ג:
[ה] [טוש"ע א"ח סימן שח סעיף לח]:
מ ו מיי' פכ"ד מהלכות שבת הלכה יא ופי"ג מהלכות נדרים הלכה ט סמג לאוין רמב טוש"ע א"ח סימן שמא סעיף א וטוש"ע י"ד סימן רלד סעיף כו:
מא ז מיי' פכ"ג מהל' שבת הלכה ו וסמג שם ומיי' פ"ו מהלכות שבועות הלכה ו סמג לאוין רמא טוש"ע א"ח סימן שמא וטוש"ע י"ד סימן רכח סעיף ג:
מב ח מיי' פי"ג מהל' נדרים הלכה טו סמג לאוין רמב טוש"ע י"ד סימן רלד סעיף כו:
מג ט מיי' פכ"ד מהל' שבת הלכה ו ופ"ו מהלכות שבועות הלכה ו סמג לאוין רמא טוש"ע א"ח סימן שמא סעיף א וטוש"ע י"ד סימן רכח סעיף ג:

רבינו חננאל

ממקומה דבבהמות קדשים [מיירי] מכלל דהולכין שרי כר' [שמעון] דלית ליה מוקצה. ומקשינן על ר' יוחנן וכי סבר רבי יוחנן הלכה כרבי שמעון והא אמר ר' יוחנן הלכה כסתם משנה ותנן אין מבקעים עצים מן הקורות ולא מן הקורה שנשברה ומפרקינן האי כר' יוסי בר יהודה מתני לה רבי יוחנן ולית סתמא. ואמרינן תוב ת"ש מתחילין בערימת התבן אבל לא בעצים שבמוקצה ומפרקינן התם בארזי [ואשוחי] דמוקצה מחמת חסרון כיס. דאפילו ר' שמעון מודה. פי' ארזי ואשוחי עצי ארזים וברושים העשויין לקורות שאין דעתו של אדם עליהן להסיקן תחת תבשילו וגמר והקצה אותן. ואמרינן תוב אין משקין ושוחטין את המדבריות אבל משקין ושוחטין הבייתות וזהו סתמא כר' יהודה ורבי יוחנן סבירא ליה הלכתא כסתם משנה קשיא הלכתא אהלכתא ומפרקינן ר' יוחנן סתמא אחרינא אשכח בה"א מגביהין מעל השלחן עצמות וקליפין ובש"א מסלק את הטבלה כולה ומנערה. ואמר רב נחמן אנו אין לנו אלא ב"ש כר' יהודה וב"ה כר' שמעון והלכתא כר' שמעון וכדפסק ר' יוחנן פליגי בה רב אחא ורבינא חד אמר בכולה שבת הלכה כר' שמעון בר ממוקצה מחמת מיאוס. וחד אמר במוקצה [מחמת] מיאוס נמי הלכתא כוותיה לבר ממוקצה מחמת איסורא כגון הנר שהדליקו בה באותה שבת וכיוצא בו אבל

רב נסים גאון

מפירין נדרים בשבת. אמרו [בתוספתא פ' י"ח] מפני מה נדרי שבת מפירין אותן בשבת שאם חשיכה ולא הפר אינו [illegible]

מסורת הש"ס

א) ביצה ב: לג., ב) [שם כו.], ג) [פי' עלי ארזים וברושים. ערוך], ד) [ביצה מ. לעיל מה:], ה) [לעיל קמג. ביצה ב.], ו) [לעיל מד.], ז) [ביצה לג:], ח) [לעיל קכב. עירובין לה.], ט) לעיל מו: נדרים עז., י) לעיל דף קכו:, כ) [נדרים עז:], ל) נדרים עז:, מ) [נדרים עו: עז.], נ) שם עז., ס) גי' רש"ל, ע) [שבת זו גמי רש"ל].

הגהות הב"ח

(א) רש"י ד"ה מדבריות וכו' תמיד הס"ד ואח"כ מה"ד בימות הגשמים שרועות חוץ לתחום ובאות ולנות בתוך התחום: (ב) ד"ה ואת המטלית לידע אם יש בה שלש על שלש: (ג) ד"ה בטפיח פך של חרס (וחבירו וכו' בשבת) תא"מ. ונ"ב ס"א בה"ג היא: (ד) ד"ה לצורך השבת וכו' שלא לצורך השבת ואח"כ מה"ד והאנן תנן כמ"ש הס"ד נדרים הס"ד: (ה) תוס' ד"ה הלקטי וכו' שאין דרך מאהיל בכך כדמוכח:

סליק מסכת שבת בס"ד

ליקוטי רש"י

אין מבקעין עצים. ביום טוב לא מן הקורות הסדורות זו על גב זו בקרקע ועומדות לבנין. ולא מן הקורה שנשברה ביום טוב. ואף על פי שעומדת מעכשיו להסקה הואיל ובין השמשות לאו להכי קיימא [illegible] ולכולי יומא [ביצה ב:]. אבל לא בעצים שבמוקצה. רחבה שאחורי הבתים קרויה מוקצה [illegible] [ביצה שם]. ארזי ואשוחי. אין אדם מסיק אותן שעומדין לבנין. אשוחי. ארז נקבה. דמוקצה מחמת חסרון כיס. ניגהו. שדמיו יקרין [שם ל.]. אין משקין ושוחטין את המדבריות. משום מוקצה. משקין. [illegible] להשקות בהמה לפני שחיטה שתהא נוחה להפשיט. המדבריות. [illegible] [לעיל מה:]. מגביהין. בשבת מעל השלחן [ביצה ב.]. כלים מעל השלחן [לעיל קמג.]. עצמות. הראוין לכלב וקליפי אגוזים [illegible] למוקצה [ביצה שם]. [illegible] ובית הלל אומרים. [illegible] אמר רב נחמן אנו אין לנו. [illegible] כרבי יהודה [illegible] שמעון [ביצה שם]. אין לנו [illegible]

מילוס הוא שהדעת קלה בו [חולין יד:]. נר שהדליקו בה באותה שבת. שהיה בו דולק בין השמשות דמוקצה מחמת איסור שאסור לטלטל וכיון שהוקצה לבין השמשות הוקצה לכל היום [שם טו.]. מסר הגדול. [illegible] מחרישה. [illegible] נדרים בשבת. בעל לאשתו ולא לנכרו [נדרים עז.]. ונשאלין לנדרים. לחכם להתירן [לעיל מו:]. [המשך בע"ב]

יכול להפר ורבי יוסי ב"ר יהודה ורבי אלעזר ברבי שמעון שאמרו הפרת נדרים מעת לעת אין הלכה כמותם כדגרסינן בנדרים בפרק נערה המאורסה (דף עו) אלא אמר רבי שמעון בן פזי אין הלכה כאותו הזוג [illegible] אחד זה ואחד זה מבטל בלבו ואינו צריך להוציא בשפתיו [illegible] בפרק נערה המאורסה (דף עז)

אם

וגיגית סדוקה מונחת על גביו. והמת מוטל בהילקטי תחת הגיגית [כנגד] הסדק ולפני מות המת פקקו בשבת המאור בטפיח שמא אין בסדק הגיגית פותח טפח ונמצא המת מוטל באהל שאין לו מקום לצאת דרך מעלה וחור שבין שני בתים מכניס את הטומאה לצד שני במלא אגרוף לפיכך סתמוהו בכלי חרס וגבו כנגד ההילקט וכלי חרס אינו מטמא מגבו וחוצך: וקשרו מקידה. שהיא רחבה טפח: בגמי לידע. אם תכנס בסדק הגיגית ובמסכת אהלות (פ"י) שנינו (דאין) חילוק בארובה שבתוך הבית וטומאה מקלחה כנגד ארובה ומקלחה בתוך הבית בין יש בארובה פותח טפח לאין בארובה פותח טפח ואני לא יכולתי להבין בו ולהכי נקט גמי שראוי למאכל בהמה ולא מיבטל ליה להיות קשר של קיימא דמנתק כשיבש: באוונא. בגיגית מלאה מים: מתעסק. שלא לצורך אלא לאיעסוקי בעלמא:

הדרן עלך מי שהחשיך וסליקא לה מסכת שבת

וגיגית סדוקה מונחת על גבן ופקקו את המאור בטפיח [א]וקשרו את המקידה בגמי לידע אם יש שם בגיגית פותח טפח אם לאו: ומדבריהם למדנו שפוקקין ומודדין וקושרין בשבת: עולא איקלע לבי ריש גלותא חזייה לרבה בר רב הונא דיתיב [א] באוונא דמיא וקא משח ליה אמר ליה [ב]אימר דאמרי רבנן מדידה דמצוה דלאו מצוה מי אמור אמר ליה מתעסק בעלמא אנא:

באוונא דמיא. אמבטי של מים וכך פירש בערוך: **מדידה** דמצוה דלאו דמצוה מי אמור כו'. בפקיקה לא בעינן של מצוה כדפירש' לעיל בשילהי כל הכלים (דף קכו:) אלא דווקא במדידה בעינן של מצוה:

הדרן עלך מי שהחשיך וסליקא לה מסכת שבת

הדרן עלך מי שהחשיך וסליקא לה מסכת שבת

עין משפט נר מצוה

מד א מיי' פ"י מהל' שבת הלכה ו סמג לאוין סה טוש"ע א"ח סימן שח סעיף א:

מה ב מיי' פכ"ד מהל' שבת הלכה ה סמג שם טוש"ע א"ח סימן שו סעיף ו:

רבינו חננאל

אבל מוקצה [מחמת] חסרון כיס אפילו ר"ש מודה דתנן כל הכלים ניטלין בשבת חוץ ממסר הגדול ויתד של מחרישה וקיי"ל דכל היכא דפליגי רב אחא ורבינא הלכתא כדברי המיקל ואסקינן בה הלכה למעשה. שהלכה כרבי שמעון בהלכות שבת כולן ואין הלכה כרבי יהודה אלא במוקצה מחמת איסורו ואשכחנן ר' יוחנן דאמר מודה ר' שמעון בזה. דגרסינן בפרק כירה א"ר חייא בר אבא א"ר יוחנן אין מוקצה לר' שמעון אלא כעין שמן שבנר בשעה שדולק הואיל והוקצה לאיסורו והוקצה למצוותו ומוקצה מחמת חסרון כיס דברי הכל מוקצה הוא ואסור וקשיא לן הדא הלכתא דאמרינן בפ' כירה [ד' מ"ה] כי אתא ר' יצחק בר יוסף אמר הלכה כר' יהודה. וריב"ל אמר הלכה כר"ש וכו' וצריכא עיונא. (ואם) [ואכן] יש לומר הא ר' יצחק בר יוסף א"ר יוחנן הלכה כר' יהודה. הא ריב"ל פליג עליה ואמר הלכתא כר"ש ואע"ג [דאמר] רב יוסף [התם] היינו דאמר רבה בר בר חנה א"ר יוחנן אמרו הלכה כר' שמעון וליה לא ס"ל (דא"ל) [וא"ל] אביי לרב יוסף ואת לא תסברא דר' יוחנן כר' יהודה סבירא ליה הני כולהו שמעתתא לא דייקינן: **מתני' מפירין נדרים** בשבת ונשאלין לנדרים שהן לצורך השבת ומבעיא לן האי דקתני מפירין נדרים בשבת לצורך הוא אבל שלא לצורך השבת לא אלמא הפרת נדרים מעת לעת או דלמא כי קתני לצורך אשאלה בלבד. אבל הפרת נדרים אפילו שלא לצורך השבת מפירין. אלמא הפרת נדרים כל אותו היום בלבד וסלקא כתנאי דתניא הפרת נדרים כל היום. ר' יוסי בר יהודה ורבי אלעזר בר שמעון אומרים מעת לעת והלכתא הפרת נדרים כל היום בלבד וגרסינן בפ' נערה המאורסה אביה ובעלה מפירין נדריה פי' שמועה זו והכי פסקה לה [התם] ר"ש בן פזי אריב"ל אין הלכה כאותו הזוג. ונשאלין לנדרים לצורך השבת. ומיבעיא לן בשלא היה לו פנאי מערב שבת או דלמא אפילו היה לו פנאי ופשטנא אפילו היה לו פנאי מערב (יום) [שבת] והוה אפשר להו לשאל נשאלין בשבת ושפיר דמי. מפירין נדרים שמפר הבעל לאשתו ונשאלין לנדרים שאילה לחכמים ומפרשינן בפרק נערה המאורסה סבר רב יוסף למימר נשאלין נדרים ביחיד מומחה בשבת ביחיד מומחה אין [בשלשה הדיוטות] לא דמורה בי דינא א"ל אביי כיון דסבירא לן אפילו מעומד ואפילו בקרובין ואפילו בלילה לא מחזי בי דינא. אמר רבא אמר רב נחמן הלכתא נשאלין נדרים מעומד יחידי ובלילה ובשבת ובקרובין ואפילו אפשר להן מבע"י: **פוקקין** את המאור. פירוש מניחין בגג מקום פתוח כגון זרת הן חסר הן יתיר ליכנס ממנו אור ותקרא מאור ותנן [אהלות פרק י"ג] העושה לו מאור בתחלה שיעורו מלא מקדח גדול של לשכה שירי המאור רום אצבעיים על רוחב גודל. ואם רוצה בשבת לסותמו מותר ועל זה שנינו פוקקין את המאור ופירושו סותמין את המאור כאשר פירשנו ומודדין את המטלית ואת המקוה אם הוא אמה על אמה ברום שלש ראוי לטבול בו: **פקקו** את המאור בטפיח. פי' טפיח כלי חרס קטן והוא כגון פתיא [וברבים] נקראין פתותא כדגרסינן בע"ז בגמרא אלו דברים של נכרים אוסרין ואיסורן איסור הנאה [ד' ל"ג ע"ב] וכדתנן זמורה שהיא קשורה בטפיח ממלאין בה בשבת וקושרין את המקידה בגמי פי' מקידה כלי חרס כגון זה ששנינו בפ' היה מביא את מנחתה פיילי של (חדשה) [חרס] ונותן בתוכה חצי לוג מים מן הכיור [א]. וזו שאמר רב יהודה אמר רב הילקטי קטנה היתה בין ב' בתים וגיגית סרוקה מנחת על גבן ופקקו את המאור בטפיח וקשרו את המקידה בגמי לידע אם יש בגיגית פותח טפח אם לאו מדבריהם למדנו שפוקקין ומודדין וקושרין בשבת וכך פירושו היה שם ב' בתים. והילקטי מלשון תל המתלקט והוא כמין קיר חוצצין ביניהן: וגיגית כלי כמין פתיא סדוק או כמין כפושא מפולשת והיה קבוע בכותל (חלול) [חלון] פתוח ובאותה שבת היה המת מוטל בבית אחד ובבית האחר היו רוצים להכנס בו כהנים ולא היו יודעים בבירור אם יש בגיגית פותח טפח ומביא את הטומאה אם לאו שכך שנו במשנתנו. טפח על טפח על רום טפח מביא את הטומאה. ועוד שנינו פרק העושה מאור [פי"ג משנה ד'] לזון את עיניו ולדבר עם חבירו ולתשמיש בפותח טפח וסתמו את המאור בטפיח הוא כמין כלי לכסות את המאור הפתוח שלא יאהילו העומדים על הגג באותו המאור ויטמאו מן הטומאה המוטלת בתוך הבית כנגד המאור שהיה נפתח המאור יתר ממלא מקדח גדול של לשכה שזה שיעורו ומפורש במשנתנו פרק [הנזכר] לפיכך הוצרכו לסותמו. ואותה הגיגית היתה בכותל גבוהה מקומת אדם ופישוט זרועותיו ולמטה מן הגג מכדי תליית אדם ופישוט זרועותיו ולקחו מקידה שהיא כלי חרס ויש בה בכולה טפח וקשרוה בגמי ושלשלוה והעמידה כנגד פי הגיגית לראות אם פי הגיגית נתמלאה הנה יש בה טפח ומביאה הטומאה מבית לבית ואם היא פחותה ממלא הגיגית נתברר שאין בגיגית פותח טפח ואינה מביאה הטומאה. ויש אומרים קשרו המקידה בגמי בראש הקנה ושיעור פתחה של גיגית אם יש בה פותח טפח ואם לאו. עולא איקלע לבי ריש גלותא חזייה לרבה בר רב הונא דיתיב באדנא דמיא והיה מודד המים גובה במים ורוחבו. אמר לו אימר דאמרינן שהתירו חכמים מדידה דמצוה כגון מדידה של מקוה שצריך לטבילת מקוה מדידה דלאו מצוה מי אמור א"ל מתעסק בעלמא אנא כלומר אני מודד ולא מתכוון למדידה אני:

הדרן עלך מי שהחשיך בדרך. תהלה לעל במתי עב דורך:

מסורת הש"ס

א) [ברי"ף וברי"ן איתא באגנא וכן הוא ברש"י שם וע' בערוך ערך אודנא וכן בברכות כב. ר' זירא הוה יתיב באגנא דמיא פרש"י באגנא גיגית].

רב נסים גאון

אם יש בגיגית. עיקר דיליה במס' אהלות (פרק ג משנה ו) כזית מן המת פתחו בטפח והמת פתחו בד' טפחים להציל את הטומאה על הפתחים אבל להוציא את הטומאה בפותח טפח. **אמר ליה** אנא מתעסק בעלמא אנא. עיקר שלו כבר פירשנו בפרק כלל גדול שהמתעסק פטור לענין שבת כמו שאמרו בכריתות בפרק אכל חלב (דף יט) אמר רב נחמן אמר שמואל מתעסק בחלבים ובעריות חייב שכבר נהנה מתעסק בשבת פטור מלאכת מחשבת אסרה תורה ובגמרא דהזורק דבני מערבא (סוף פירקא) גרסי המתעסק בשבת פטור היך עבידה אמר הריני קוצר חצי גרוגרת וקצר כגרוגרת פטור:

סליק מי שהחשיך וסליקא לה מסכתא דשבת בסייעתא דשמיא

ליקוטי רש"י

[שייך לע"א] **שפוקקין**. את המאור בדבר שאינו קשור ותלוי. **ומודדין**. מקוה ומטלניות [לעיל קכו:]. **איבעיא להו הפרה בין לצורך ובין שלא לצורך**. שבת דלא קאי אלא אשאלה משום דכיון דלריך חכם או שלשה הדיוטות מיחזי כדינא א"נ שאין שעה עוברת לשאלה [ר"ן נדרים שם]. **לצורך**. שהן לצורך השבת כגון שנדרה מאכילה או מתכשיטין [נדרים שם]. **או דילמא הפרה נמי לצורך**. הא דקתני לצורך השבת אכולה מתניתין קאי דאפי' הפרה דוקא לצורך השבת [ר"ן שם]. **לצורך אתרוייהו קתני ושלא לצורך לא**. שלא לצורך השבת אין מפירין כשנדרה בשבת מפני שיכול להפר אחר השבת. **אלמא הפרת נדרים כל היום**. הלכך אפי' שלא לצורך השבת מפר שאם אינו מפר עכשיו בשבת שוב אין יכול להפר [רש"י שם]. דכיון שהזמן עובר הקילו להפר שלא לצורך משא"כ בשאלה דאפשר בחול [ר"ן שם]. **הפרת נדרים כל היום**. יום השמיעה. **להקל ולהחמיר**. לאו דוקא להקל ולהחמיר דהא לא שייכא קולא וחומרא הכא אלא ה"ק פעמים שזמנו מרובה פעמים שזמנו מועט לאפוקי מעת לעת דלעולם זמנו שוה [ר"ן שם עו:]. **נדרה לילי שבת**. יכול להפר לה כל אותו ליל שבת ויום שבת [רש"י שם]. כבכניסתו מפר בלילי שבת וביום השבת עד שתחשך והיינו להקל [ר"ן שם]. **לילי שבת**. והוא הדין נמי כי נדרה במ"ש שיפר כל אותו היום בה' בשבת אלא הא דנקיט לילי שבת משום דלאשמועי' כמה שאמרו הפרת נדרים כל היום כלילי שבת ויומו שהלילה הולך אחר היום כדכתיב ויהי ערב ויהי בקר יום אחד אבל לא ליום ולילה שאם נדרה ביום ולא הפר לה שוב אינו יכול להפר לה משתחשך שאין הפרת נדרים אלא אותו יום שנדרה ומשכה כבר נכנס יום אחר [רש"י שם]. ה"ה בחול והאי דנקט שבת מילתא אגב אורחיה קמ"ל דמפירין נדרים בשבת ואע"פ שאינן לצורך השבת וכדדייקינן בגמרא. **נדרה עם חשכה**. שנדרה בשבת סמוך לחשכה מפר עד שלא תחשך והיינו להחמיר ובדין הוא דליתני אינו מפר אלא (לכשתחשך) [עד שתחשך] כיון דלהחמיר קתני אלא להכי תנא האי לישנא משום דשייך ביה טפי מאי דמסיים מלתיה שאם קודם חשכה לא הפר אינו יכול להפר דלאשמועינן בהאי לישנא דמפירין נדרים בשבת אפילו שלא לצורך השבת לפי שזמנם עובר שאם קודם חשכה לא הפר שוב אינו יכול להפר [ר"ן שם]. **תנאי היא**. ולא קשו מתניתין וברייתא דתני רב זוטי אהדדי דפלוגתא דתנאי היא [ר"ן שם עז.]. **כשלא היה לו פנאי**. לישאל עליהן מבעוד יום הוא דקאמר דנשאלין עליהן בשבת [רש"י שם]. כשלא היה אפשר להן מבעוד יום כגון שנדרה ערב שבת עם חשכה א"נ דלא אזקיק לה חכם מבעוד יום ואסיקנא דאפי' בנדרים שהיה להן אפשר מבעוד יום נשאלין לצורך השבת [ר"ן שם]. **דאזדקיקו ליה רבנן**. שנטפלו חכמים כולן להתיר לו בשבת ואפילו בנדרים שהיה לו אפשר לישאל עליהן מבעוד יום [רש"י שם].

גירסא ירושלמי בר"ה פרק אם אין מכירין בתחלתו. אמר עד אחד נולד לאיש פלוני בשבת מלין אותו על פיו חשכה מוצאי שבת מטלטלין אותו על פיו. ר' חייא אמר מטלטלין אפומא (דימלותא) [דמליתא]. רבי מתניאה מטלטל על אברתיה דיזירא. ר' (ממל) [אמי מל] על פי נשים דאמרי שמשא הות בסוסיתא:

סליקא לה מסכת שבת. משירי אהודנו צח דודי. כי כביר מצאה ידי.

מי שזיכני להתחיל והוא יזכני לסיים. חזק ונתחזק הכותב לעד לא יזוק.

חשק שלמה על רבינו חננאל א) כמדומה שחסר כאן לאין בסוטה דף ע' דאיתא שם לפיכך הכהן משקה אותה במקידה של חרס. וכ"ה ג"כ שם דף ל"ב. וכן מלין הערוך ערך קד:

וְגִיגִית סְדוּקָה מוּנַּחַת עַל גַּבָּן – **And a cracked barrel rested upon [the two houses],** sheltering over the corpse. וּפָקְקוּ אֶת הַמָּאוֹר בְּטָפִיחַ – Before the person died, **they** had **shuttered the window** of the house **with an earthenware flask,** to ensure that when he would die no *tumah* would enter the house. וְקָשְׁרוּ אֶת הַמְּקֵידָה בְּגֶמִי – **They then tied an earthenware vessel** measuring a handbreadth wide **with a** strand of **reed-grass** and attempted to pass it through the crack in the barrel לֵידַע אִם יֵשׁ שָׁם בַּגִּיגִית פּוֹתֵחַ טֶפַח אִם לָאו – **to determine whether or not there was a handbreadth-sized opening in the barrel** that would allow the *tumah* to escape.[1]

The Mishnah stated:

וּמִדִּבְרֵיהֶם לָמַדְנוּ שֶׁפּוֹקְקִין וּמוֹדְדִין וְקוֹשְׁרִין בְּשַׁבָּת – **AND FROM THEIR WORDS WE LEARNED THAT WE MAY SHUTTER, MEASURE AND TIE ON THE SABBATH.**

The Gemara recounts an incident that bears upon the law of measuring on the Sabbath:

עוּלָּא אִיקְלַע לְבֵי רֵישׁ גָּלוּתָא – **Ulla happened to go to the house of the Exilarch.** חַזְיֵיהּ לְרַבָּה בַּר רַב הוּנָא – **He saw Rabbah bar Rav Huna,** דְּיָתִיב בְּאַוְונָא דְמַיָּא וְקָא מָשַׁח לֵיהּ – **who was sitting in a tub of water** on the Sabbath **and was measuring it.** אָמַר לֵיהּ – **[Ulla] said to him:** אֵימַר דְּאָמְרֵי רַבָּנָן – **When did the Rabbis say** that one is allowed to measure on the Sabbath – מְדִידָה דְּמִצְוָה – only if it is **measuring** performed for the purpose **of a mitzvah;**[2] דְּלָאו מִצְוָה – **but if it is not** for the purpose of **a mitzvah,** מִי אָמוּר – **did they** then **say** that it is permitted? No! Why, then, do you measure the tub?[3]

Rabbah bar Rav Huna answers:

אָמַר לֵיהּ – **He said to him:** מִתְעַסֵּק בְּעָלְמָא אֲנָא – **I am merely busying** myself, but am not measuring for any purpose.[4]

הדרן עלך מי שהחשיך

WE SHALL RETURN TO YOU, MI SHEHECHSHICH

וסליקא לה מסכת שבת

AND TRACTATE SHABBOS IS CONCLUDED.

NOTES

1. [The law is that a roof (*ohel*) that shelters a corpse will transmit the corpse's *tumah* to people or utensils that share it with the corpse. The *tumah* is not confined to the room in which the corpse is found, but can travel to adjoining rooms through openings in the walls (provided that the roof is not interrupted before reaching the wall, and that the adjoining room is also roofed; see *Oholos* ch. 13 for the requisite measurements of these openings).] However, if there is a one-by-one-handbreadth hole in the roof directly opposite any part of the corpse, the *tumah* will escape through the hole, and will not spread through the room. In the incident recounted by our Mishnah, a man lay dying in an alley between two houses, under a barrel that, reaching from one house to the other, served as a "roof" over him. In a wall below the barrel was a fist-sized hole (see *Oholos* 13:1,3; *Keilim* 17:12) that opened into one of the houses. The barrel itself had a crack in it, whose dimensions were in doubt; the dying man was lying partially opposite the crack. Now, if the crack measured one-by-one handbreadths, then when the man died his *tumah* would escape by means of the crack. If the dimensions of the crack were less than this measure, the *tumah* would not escape, but would spread throughout the area under the barrel, and into the adjoining house through the hole in the wall. To keep *tumah* from entering the house, its residents immediately plugged the hole with an earthenware vessel. They faced the bottom of the vessel toward the alley; the vessel was thus able to interpose before the *tumah,* since the outside of an earthenware vessel is impervious to *tumah.* Having ensured that the *tumah* would not enter the house, they attempted to check the size of the crack [to see if the hole could safely be unplugged] by suspending an earthenware vessel a handbreadth wide from a strand of reed-grass and attempting to pass it through the crack. They used reed-grass for two reasons. Firstly, because since it is fit for consumption by animals, one who uses it for tying will not intend it to remain tied indefinitely; the knot is therefore not deemed a permanent one, and may be tied on the Sabbath (at least on the Biblical level). Secondly, because since it will eventually dry out, causing the knot to become untied, any knot tied with it can *only* be temporary, and thus [Biblically] permissible to tie on the Sabbath (*Rashi; Meiri; Chidushei HaRan;* see *Maharsha; Rashash;* cf. *Tosafos* to 157a; see *Maginei Shlomo;* see also *Tosafos, Bava Basra* 20a ד״ה היא גופא תיחוץ and *Meiri, Megillah* 26b ד״ה כל בית). [In the course of this incident they permitted acts of tying and measuring were performed for the purpose of a mitzvah – i.e. determining the legal status of the crack in the barrel (see *Mishnah Berurah* 306:35). We thus see that these acts are permitted for this purpose on the Sabbath. They also allowed an act of temporary shuttering, thus teaching that this act too may be performed on the Sabbath (although it need not be for a mitzvah-related purpose; see *Tosafos* here and to 126b ד״ה ומדבריהן למדנו for the reason why).]

[*Meiri* (and *Rashi,* according to *Maharsha*) question the law apparently assumed by our Gemara on the basis of the Mishnahs in *Oholos* (10:1-3) which seem to say that even if a corpse is partially opposite a one-by-one-handbreadth hole in the roof, its *tumah* will nonetheless spread throughout the room. See *Maginei Shlomo* and *Rashash;* cf. *Maharshal* and *Shabbos Shel Mi.*

2. See 157a note 26.

3. Ulla knew that Rabbah bar Rav Huna was certainly not measuring the tub to determine whether it was of requisite *mikveh* size, since, as a vessel [כְּלִי], it was not valid for *mikveh* use! (*Ritva MHK* ed.).

4. *Rashi.* [In such a case the Rabbis did not impose their decree against measuring (see *Shulchan Aruch HaRav, Orach Chaim* 306:19; see *Shabbos Shel Mi* for a homiletical interpretation of the exchange between these two Amoraim).]

Hadran – הַדְרָן

Upon the סיום, *completion*, of the study of an entire tractate, a festive meal (which has the status of a *seudas mitzvah*) should be eaten – preferably with a *minyan* in attendance. The following prayers of thanksgiving are recited by those who have completed the learning. [The words in brackets are inserted according to some customs.]

The first paragraph is recited three times.

הַדְרָן עֲלָךְ מַסֶּכֶת שַׁבָּת וְהַדְרָךְ עֲלָן. דַּעְתָּן עֲלָךְ מַסֶּכֶת שַׁבָּת וְדַעְתָּךְ עֲלָן. לָא נִתְנְשֵׁי מִנָּךְ מַסֶּכֶת שַׁבָּת וְלָא תִתְנְשֵׁי מִנָּן – לָא בְּעָלְמָא הָדֵין וְלָא בְּעָלְמָא דְּאָתֵי.

הַדְרָן *We shall return*[1] *to you, Tractate Shabbos, and you shall return to us. Our thoughts are on you, Tractate Shabbos, and your thoughts are on us. We will not forget you, Tractate Shabbos, and you will not forget us – neither in This World, nor in the World to Come.*

יְהִי רָצוֹן מִלְּפָנֶיךָ יי אֱלֹהֵינוּ וֵאלֹהֵי אֲבוֹתֵינוּ, שֶׁתְּהֵא תוֹרָתְךָ אֻמָּנוּתֵנוּ בָּעוֹלָם הַזֶּה וּתְהֵא עִמָּנוּ לָעוֹלָם הַבָּא. חֲנִינָא בַּר פָּפָּא, רָמִי בַּר פָּפָּא, נַחְמָן בַּר פָּפָּא, אַחָאי בַּר פָּפָּא, אַבָּא מָרִי בַּר פָּפָּא, רַפְרָם בַּר פָּפָּא, רָכִישׁ בַּר פָּפָּא, סוּרְחָב בַּר פָּפָּא, אַדָּא בַּר פָּפָּא, דָּרוּ בַּר פָּפָּא.

יְהִי רָצוֹן *May it be Your will,* Hashem, *our God, and the God of our forefathers, that Your Torah be our preoccupation in This World, and may it remain with us in the World to Come. Chanina bar Pappa,*[2] *Rami bar Pappa, Nachman bar Pappa, Achai bar Pappa, Abba Mari bar Pappa, Rafram bar Pappa, Rachish bar Pappa, Surchav bar Pappa, Adda bar Pappa, Daru bar Pappa.*

הַעֲרֶב נָא יי אֱלֹהֵינוּ אֶת דִּבְרֵי תוֹרָתְךָ בְּפִינוּ וּבְפִיפִיּוֹת עַמְּךָ בֵּית יִשְׂרָאֵל. וְנִהְיֶה [כֻּלָּנוּ,] אֲנַחְנוּ וְצֶאֱצָאֵינוּ [וְצֶאֱצָאֵי צֶאֱצָאֵינוּ] וְצֶאֱצָאֵי עַמְּךָ בֵּית יִשְׂרָאֵל, כֻּלָּנוּ יוֹדְעֵי שְׁמֶךָ וְלוֹמְדֵי תוֹרָתֶךָ [לִשְׁמָהּ]. מֵאֹיְבַי תְּחַכְּמֵנִי מִצְוֹתֶךָ, כִּי לְעוֹלָם הִיא לִי. יְהִי לִבִּי תָמִים בְּחֻקֶּיךָ, לְמַעַן לֹא אֵבוֹשׁ. לְעוֹלָם לֹא אֶשְׁכַּח פִּקּוּדֶיךָ, כִּי בָם חִיִּיתָנִי. בָּרוּךְ אַתָּה יי, לַמְּדֵנִי חֻקֶּיךָ. אָמֵן אָמֵן אָמֵן, סֶלָה וָעֶד.

הַעֲרֶב נָא *Please,* Hashem, *our God, sweeten the words of Your Torah in our mouth and in the mouths of Your people, the House of Israel, and may [we all –] we, our offspring, [the offspring of our offspring,] and the offspring of Your people, the House of Israel, all of us – know Your Name and study Your Torah. Your commandment makes me wiser than my enemies, for it is forever with me.*[3] *May my heart be perfect in Your statutes, so that I not be shamed.*[4] *I will never forget Your precepts, for through them You have preserved me.*[5] *Blessed are You,* Hashem, *teach me Your statutes.*[6] *Amen. Amen. Amen. Selah! Forever!*

מוֹדִים אֲנַחְנוּ לְפָנֶיךָ יי אֱלֹהֵינוּ וֵאלֹהֵי אֲבוֹתֵינוּ, שֶׁשַּׂמְתָּ חֶלְקֵנוּ מִיּוֹשְׁבֵי בֵּית הַמִּדְרָשׁ, וְלֹא שַׂמְתָּ חֶלְקֵנוּ מִיּוֹשְׁבֵי קְרָנוֹת. שֶׁאָנוּ מַשְׁכִּימִים וְהֵם מַשְׁכִּימִים, אָנוּ מַשְׁכִּימִים לְדִבְרֵי תוֹרָה, וְהֵם מַשְׁכִּימִים לִדְבָרִים בְּטֵלִים. אָנוּ עֲמֵלִים וְהֵם עֲמֵלִים, אָנוּ עֲמֵלִים וּמְקַבְּלִים שָׂכָר, וְהֵם עֲמֵלִים וְאֵינָם מְקַבְּלִים שָׂכָר. אָנוּ רָצִים וְהֵם רָצִים, אָנוּ רָצִים לְחַיֵּי הָעוֹלָם הַבָּא, וְהֵם רָצִים לִבְאֵר שַׁחַת, שֶׁנֶּאֱמַר: וְאַתָּה אֱלֹהִים, תּוֹרִדֵם לִבְאֵר שַׁחַת, אַנְשֵׁי דָמִים וּמִרְמָה לֹא יֶחֱצוּ יְמֵיהֶם, וַאֲנִי אֶבְטַח בָּךְ.

מוֹדִים *We express gratitude before You,* Hashem, *our God, and the God of our forefathers, that You have established our portion with those who dwell in the study hall, and have not established our portion with idlers. For we arise early and they arise early; we arise early for the words of Torah, while they arise early for idle words. We toil and they toil; we toil and receive reward, while they toil and do not receive reward. We run and they run; we run to the life of the World to Come, while they run to the well of destruction, as it is said: But You, O God, You will lower them into the well of destruction, men of bloodshed and deceit shall not live out half their days; and I will trust in You.*[7]

---

1. הַדְרָן עֲלָךְ – *We shall return to you* ... We express the hope that we will review constantly what we have learned and that, in the merit of our desire to learn, the Torah itself will long to return to us, as it were. Thus, the word is derived from הָדַר, *to return*. This is in the spirit of the Talmudic dictum that תּוֹרָה מְחַזֶּרֶת עַל אַכְסַנְיָא שֶׁלָּהּ, *the Torah returns to its inn*, i.e., the place or people where it was made welcome (*Bava Metzia* 88a).

According to *Sefer HaChaim*, the term is derived from the word הָדָר, *glory*. Thus, whatever glory we have attained is due to the Torah, and we pray that the Torah shed its glory upon us.

2. חֲנִינָא בַּר פָּפָּא – *Chanina bar Pappa* ... In the simple sense, Rav Pappa was a very wealthy man who, whenever he completed a tractate, used to make great celebrations to which he invited his ten sons, as well as many others. As a result, he brought glory to the Torah, which was reflected in the scholarly attainments of his sons. The nation, therefore, honors Rav Pappa and his family by mentioning them at every *siyum*. Furthermore, esoterically, Rav Pappa symbolizes Moses and the names of his sons symbolize the Ten Commandments (*Teshuvos HaRema; Yam Shel Shelomo, Bava Kamma,* end of ch. 7).

3. *Psalms* 119:98. 4. 119:80. 5. 119:93. 6. 119:12. 7. 55:24.

יְהִי רָצוֹן לְפָנֶיךָ יי אֱלֹהַי, כְּשֵׁם שֶׁעֲזַרְתַּנִי לְסַיֵּים מַסֶּכֶת שַׁבָּת כֵּן תְּעַזְרֵנִי לְהַתְחִיל מַסֶּכְתּוֹת וּסְפָרִים אֲחֵרִים וּלְסַיְּמָם, לִלְמוֹד וּלְלַמֵּד לִשְׁמוֹר וְלַעֲשׂוֹת וּלְקַיֵּם אֶת כָּל דִּבְרֵי תַלְמוּד תּוֹרָתֶךָ בְּאַהֲבָה. וּזְכוּת כָּל הַתַּנָּאִים וַאֲמוֹרָאִים וְתַלְמִידֵי חֲכָמִים יַעֲמוֹד לִי וּלְזַרְעִי, שֶׁלֹּא תָמוּשׁ הַתּוֹרָה מִפִּי וּמִפִּי זַרְעִי וְזֶרַע זַרְעִי עַד עוֹלָם. וְתִתְקַיֶּם בִּי: בְּהִתְהַלֶּכְךָ תַּנְחֶה אֹתָךְ, בְּשָׁכְבְּךָ תִּשְׁמֹר עָלֶיךָ, וַהֲקִיצוֹתָ הִיא תְשִׂיחֶךָ. כִּי בִי יִרְבּוּ יָמֶיךָ, וְיוֹסִיפוּ לְךָ שְׁנוֹת חַיִּים. אֹרֶךְ יָמִים בִּימִינָהּ, בִּשְׂמֹאלָהּ עֹשֶׁר וְכָבוֹד. יי עֹז לְעַמּוֹ יִתֵּן, יי יְבָרֵךְ אֶת עַמּוֹ בַשָּׁלוֹם.

יְהִי רָצוֹן *May it be Your will, HASHEM, my God, that just as You have helped me complete Tractate Shabbos, so may You help me to begin other tractates and books, and to complete them; to learn and to teach, to safeguard and to perform, and to fulfill all the words of Your Torah's teachings with love. May the merit of all the Tannaim, Amoraim, and Torah scholars stand by me and my children, that the Torah shall not depart from my mouth and from the mouth of my children and my children's children forever. May there be fulfilled for me the verse: When you walk, it (i.e., the Torah) will guide you; when you lie down, it will watch over you; and when you wake up, it will converse with you.*[8] *For because of me (i.e., the Torah), your days will increase, and years of life will be added to you.*[9] *Long days are in its right hand, and in its left hand are wealth and honor.*[10] *HASHEM will give might to His people, HASHEM will bless His people with peace.*[11]

If a *minyan* is present, the following version of the Rabbis' *Kaddish* is recited by one or more of those present. It may be recited even by one whose parents are still living.

יִתְגַּדַּל וְיִתְקַדַּשׁ שְׁמֵהּ רַבָּא. (Cong. – אָמֵן.) בְּעָלְמָא דִּי הוּא עָתִיד לְאִתְחַדָּתָא, וּלְאַחֲיָאָה מֵתַיָּא, וּלְאַסָּקָא יָתְהוֹן לְחַיֵּי עָלְמָא, וּלְמִבְנֵא קַרְתָּא דִירוּשְׁלֵם, וּלְשַׁכְלְלָא הֵיכְלֵהּ בְּגַוַּהּ, וּלְמֶעְקַר פָּלְחָנָא נֻכְרָאָה מִן אַרְעָא, וְלַאֲתָבָא פָּלְחָנָא דִי שְׁמַיָּא לְאַתְרֵהּ, וְיַמְלִיךְ קֻדְשָׁא בְּרִיךְ הוּא בְּמַלְכוּתֵהּ וִיקָרֵהּ, [וְיַצְמַח פֻּרְקָנֵהּ וִיקָרֵב מְשִׁיחֵהּ (Cong. – אָמֵן)] בְּחַיֵּיכוֹן וּבְיוֹמֵיכוֹן וּבְחַיֵּי דְכָל בֵּית יִשְׂרָאֵל, בַּעֲגָלָא וּבִזְמַן קָרִיב. וְאִמְרוּ: אָמֵן.

(Cong. – אָמֵן. יְהֵא שְׁמֵהּ רַבָּא מְבָרַךְ לְעָלַם וּלְעָלְמֵי עָלְמַיָּא.)

יְהֵא שְׁמֵהּ רַבָּא מְבָרַךְ לְעָלַם וּלְעָלְמֵי עָלְמַיָּא.

יִתְבָּרַךְ וְיִשְׁתַּבַּח וְיִתְפָּאַר וְיִתְרוֹמַם וְיִתְנַשֵּׂא וְיִתְהַדָּר וְיִתְעַלֶּה וְיִתְהַלָּל שְׁמֵהּ דְּקֻדְשָׁא בְּרִיךְ הוּא (Cong. – בְּרִיךְ הוּא) °לְעֵלָּא מִן כָּל (From Rosh Hashanah to Yom Kippur substitute – °לְעֵלָּא וּלְעֵלָּא מִכָּל) בִּרְכָתָא וְשִׁירָתָא תֻּשְׁבְּחָתָא וְנֶחֱמָתָא, דַּאֲמִירָן בְּעָלְמָא. וְאִמְרוּ: אָמֵן. (Cong. – אָמֵן.)

עַל יִשְׂרָאֵל וְעַל רַבָּנָן, וְעַל תַּלְמִידֵיהוֹן וְעַל כָּל תַּלְמִידֵי תַלְמִידֵיהוֹן, וְעַל כָּל מָאן דְּעָסְקִין בְּאוֹרַיְתָא, דִּי בְאַתְרָא הָדֵין וְדִי בְכָל אֲתַר וַאֲתַר. יְהֵא לְהוֹן וּלְכוֹן שְׁלָמָא רַבָּא, חִנָּא וְחִסְדָּא וְרַחֲמִין, וְחַיִּין אֲרִיכִין, וּמְזוֹנֵי רְוִיחֵי, וּפֻרְקָנָא מִן קֳדָם אֲבוּהוֹן דִּי בִשְׁמַיָּא [וְאַרְעָא]. וְאִמְרוּ: אָמֵן. (Cong. – אָמֵן.)

יְהֵא שְׁלָמָא רַבָּא מִן שְׁמַיָּא, וְחַיִּים [טוֹבִים] עָלֵינוּ וְעַל כָּל יִשְׂרָאֵל. וְאִמְרוּ: אָמֵן. (Cong. – אָמֵן.)

Take three steps back. Bow left and say . . . עֹשֶׂה; bow right and say . . . הוּא; bow forward and say . . . וְעַל כָּל . . . אָמֵן. Remain standing in place for a few moments, then take three steps forward.

עֹשֶׂה שָׁלוֹם בִּמְרוֹמָיו, הוּא בְּרַחֲמָיו יַעֲשֶׂה שָׁלוֹם עָלֵינוּ, וְעַל כָּל יִשְׂרָאֵל. וְאִמְרוּ: אָמֵן. (Cong. – אָמֵן.)

יִתְגַּדַּל *May His great Name grow exalted and sanctified* (Cong. – *Amen*) *in the world that will be renewed and where He will resuscitate the dead and raise them up to eternal life, and rebuild the city of Jerusalem and complete His Temple within it, and uproot alien worship from the earth, and return the service of Heaven to its place, and may the Holy One, Blessed is He, reign in His sovereignty and splendor [and cause salvation to sprout and bring near His Messiah* (Cong. – *Amen*)*] in your lifetimes and in your days, and in the lifetimes of the entire House of Israel, swiftly and soon. Now respond: Amen.*

(Cong. – *Amen. May His great Name be blessed forever and ever.*)

May His great Name be blessed forever and ever.

Blessed, praised, glorified, exalted, extolled, mighty, upraised, and lauded be the Name of the Holy One, Blessed is He (Cong. – *Blessed is He*), (From Rosh Hashanah to Yom Kippur add: *exceedingly*) *beyond any blessing and song, praise, and consolation that are uttered in the world. Now respond: Amen.* (Cong. – *Amen.*)

Upon Israel, upon the teachers, upon their disciples and upon all of their disciples' disciples and upon all those who engage in the study of Torah, who are here or anywhere else; may they and you have abundant peace, grace, kindness, and mercy, long life, ample nourishment, and salvation, from before their Father Who is in Heaven [and on earth]. Now respond: Amen. (Cong. – *Amen.*)

May there be abundant peace from Heaven, and [good] life upon us and upon all Israel. Now respond: Amen. (Cong. – *Amen.*)

Take three steps back. Bow left and say, *'He Who makes peace . . .'*; bow right and say, *'may He . . .'*; bow forward and say, *'and upon all Israel . . . Amen.'* Remain standing in place for a few moments, then take three steps forward.

He Who makes peace in His heights, may He, in His compassion, make peace upon us, and upon all Israel. Now respond: Amen. (Cong. – *Amen.*)

---

8. *Proverbs* 6:22. 9. 9:11. 10. 3:16. 11. *Psalms* 29:11.

◆§ Glossary

◆§ Scriptural Index

Glossary

Adar – twelfth month of the Hebrew calendar.

agav – see **kinyan agav.**

agency – the principle that an agent may act as a proxy of a principal and have his actions legally accepted on behalf of the principal.

Aggadah, aggadata – the homiletical teachings of the Sages and all non-halachic Rabbinic literature found in the Talmud.

akirah – the **melachah** of transferring involves the moving of an article from one domain to another. To be Biblically liable one must perform both *akirah,* the *lifting* of the article from its domain of origin, and *hanachah,* the *setting down* of the article in its new domain.

akum – idolater.

Altar – the great *Altar*, which stands in the Courtyard of the **Beis HaMikdash.** Certain portions of every offering are burnt on the *Altar*. The blood of most offerings is applied to the walls of the *Altar*.

amah [pl. **amos**] – cubit; a linear measure equaling six **tefachim.** Opinions regarding its modern equivalent range between 18 and 22.9 inches.

am haaretz [pl. **amei haaretz**] – a common, ignorant person who, possibly, is not meticulous in his observance of **halachah.**

Amora [pl. **Amoraim**] – sage of the **Gemara;** cf. **Tanna.**

amud – one side of the **daf** in the **Gemara.**

Anshei Knesses HaGedolah – see **Men of the Great Assembly.**

arayos – see **ervah.**

arus [f. **arusah**] – one who is betrothed and thereby entered the **erusin** stage of marriage. See **erusin.**

asham [pl. **ashamos**] – guilt offering, an offering brought to atone for one of several specific sins; in addition, a part of certain purification offerings. It is one of the **kodshei kodashim.**

asheirah – a tree either designated for worship or under which an idol is placed.

asmachta – lit. reliance. (a) a conditional commitment made by a party who does not really expect to have to honor it; (b) a verse cited by the **Gemara** not as a Scriptural basis for the law but rather as an allusion to a Rabbinic law.

Av – (a) fifth month of the Hebrew calendar; (b) l.c. [pl. avos] see **melachah.**

av [pl. **avos**] **hatumah** – lit. father of **tumah.** See **tumah.**

avi avos hatumah – lit. father of fathers of **tumah.** See **tumah.**

avodah [pl. **avodos**] – the sacrificial service, or any facet of it. There are four critical *avodos* to the sacrificial service. They are **shechitah, kabbalah, holachah** and **zerikah.**

avodah zarah – idol worship, idolatry.

aylonis [pl. **aylonios**] – an adult woman who never developed the physical signs of female maturity. She is therefore assumed to be incapable of bearing children.

azharah – (a) Scriptural warning; the basic prohibition stated in the Torah, which serves to warn the potential sinner against incurring the punishment prescribed for a particular action; (b) term Gemara uses to refer to a negative commandment, the transgression of which is punishable by **kares.**

baal keri [pl. **baalei keri**] – one who experienced a seminal emission. He is **tamei** (ritually impure) and must immerse himself in a **mikveh.**

bagrus – the age when a girl becomes a *bogeress* (a full adult), the final legal state of a girl's physical development. A girl automatically becomes a *bogeress* six months after she becomes a **naarah.**

bamah [pl. **bamos**] – lit. high place; altar. This refers to any altar other than the **Altar** of the **Tabernacle** or **Temple.** During certain brief periods of Jewish history, it was permitted to offer sacrifices on a *bamah*. There are two types of *bamah.* The *communal* (or: *major*) *bamah* was the altar of the public and was the only *bamah* on which communal offerings could be sacrificed. Private voluntary offerings could be brought even on a *private* (or *minor*) *bamah* which was an altar erected anywhere by an individual for private use.

Baraisa [pl. **Baraisos**] – the statements of **Tannaim** not included by **Rebbi** in the **Mishnah.** R' Chiya and R' Oshaya, the students of Rebbi, researched and reviewed the *Baraisa* and compiled an authoritative collection of them.

bechor – (a) firstborn male child; (b) a firstborn male kosher animal. Such an animal is born with sacrificial sanctity, and must be given to a **Kohen** who then offers it (if unblemished) as a *bechor* sacrifice in the **Temple** and eats its sacred meat. Unlike other sacrifices, the *bechor* is automatically sacred from birth even without designation.

bedek habayis – **Temple** treasury.

bedi'avad – after the fact. See **lechatchilah.**

beheimah – domesticated species, livestock. In regard to various laws, the Torah distinguishes between *beheimah:* domestic species, e.g. cattle, sheep, goats; and, **chayah,** wild species, e.g. deer, antelope.

bein ha'arbayaim – lit. between the darkenings. It refers to the hours between the "darkening of the day" and the "darkening of the night." The darkening of the day starts at midday, when the shadows begin to lengthen. The darkening of the night is simply the beginning of the night, after sunset. Thus *bein ha'arbayim* connotes the afternoon.

bein hashemashos – the twilight period preceding night. The legal status of *bein hashemashos* as day or night is uncertain.

beis din – court; Rabbinical court comprised minimally of three members. Such a court is empowered to rule on civil matters. See also **Sanhedrin.**

beis hamidrash – a **Torah** study hall.

Beis HaMikdash – Holy **Temple** in Jerusalem. The **Temple** edifice comprised (a) the Antechamber or **Ulam;** (b) the **Holy** or **Heichal;** and (c) the **Holy of Holies.** See **Sanctuary.**

beis kor – 75,000 square **amos** – fifteen times the size of two **beis se'ah.**

beis se'ah – an area 50 **amos** by 50 *amos.*

bereirah – retroactive clarification. This principle allows for the assignment of a legal status to a person or object whose identity is as yet undetermined, but which will be retroactively clarified by a subsequent choice.

bikkurim – the first-ripening fruits of any of the seven species (wheat, barley, grapes, figs, pomegranates, olives, dates), with which the Torah praises Eretz Yisrael. They are brought to the **Temple** where certain rites are performed, and given to the **Kohanim.**

binyan av – one of the thirteen principles of Biblical hermeneutics. This is exegetical derivation based on a logical analogy between different areas of law. Whenever a commonality of law or essence is found in different areas of **Torah** law, an analogy is drawn between them, and the laws that apply to one can therefore be assumed to apply to the others as well.

Bircas HaMazon – the blessings recited after a meal.

Bircas Kohanim – see **Priestly Blessing.**

bitul (or **bitul b'rov**) – the principle of nullification in a majority. Under certain circumstances, a mixture of items of differing legal status assumes the status of its majority component.

bitul reshus – renunciation of [one's] rights [in his domain]. This is a Rabbinical device whereby the owners of the various houses in a courtyard "renounce" their "ownership" in the courtyard in favor of one of their colleagues. The courtyard now "belongs" to that owner, and he may carry from his house to the courtyard without the benefit of an *eruv chatzeiros*.

bosis – an item that is a base for a **muktzeh** item and which becomes **muktzeh** itself.

Bris Milah – ritual circumcision.

chalifin – see **kinyan chalifin.**

challah – portion removed from a dough of the **five grains,** given to a **Kohen;** if *challah* is not taken, the dough is **tevel** and may not be eaten. The minimum amount of dough from which *challah* must be separated is the volume-equivalent of 43.2 eggs, which is one **issaron.** Nowadays the *challah* is removed and burned.

chametz – leavened products of the five species of grain. *Chametz* is forbidden on **Pesach.**

Chanukah – Festival of Lights. The holiday that commemorates the Maccabean victory over the Greeks. It begins on the 25th of **Kislev** and lasts for eight days.

chatas [pl. **chataos**] – sin offering; an offering generally brought in atonement for the inadvertent transgression of a prohibition punishable by **kares** when transgressed deliberately. A *chatas* is also brought as one of various purification offerings. It is one of the **kodshei kodashim.**

chatzeir [pl. **chatzeiros**] – courtyard(s).

chaver [pl. **chaverim**] – (a) one who observes the laws of ritual purity even regarding non-consecrated foodstuffs; (b) a Torah scholar, scrupulous in his observance of **mitzvos.** Regarding tithes, **tumah** and other matters, such as the necessity for **hasraah,** he is accorded a special status.

chayah – see **beheimah.**

chazakah – (a) legal presumption that conditions remain unchanged unless proven otherwise; (b) one of the methods of acquiring real estate; it consists of performing an act of improving the property, such as enclosing it with a fence or plowing it in preparation for planting; (c) "established rights"; uncontested usage of another's property establishes the right to such usage; since the owner registered no protest, acquiescence is assumed; (d) uncontested holding of real property for three years as a basis for claiming acquisition of title from the prior owner.

chazarah – returning to the **kirah** a pot of cooked food that had been left there before the Sabbath and was later removed. Also replacing an already cooked item into a pot on the fire.

cheilev – The Torah forbids certain fats of cattle, sheep and goats for human consumption. These are primarily the hind fats (suet) placed on the **Altar.** See **shuman.**

cherem – (a) a vow in which one uses the expression "*cherem*" to consecrate property, placing it under jurisdiction of the Temple; (b) land or property upon which a ban has been declared, forbidding its use to anyone, e.g. the city of Jericho.

Cheshvan – see **Marcheshvan.**

chilazon – an aquatic creature from whose blood the blue *techeiles* dye was produced.

chilul Hashem – lit. profanation of God's Name. (a) behavior which casts Jews in a negative light; (b) violation of a Torah prohibition done in the presence of ten male Jews.

Chol HaMoed – the Intermediate Days of the Festivals of **Pesach** and **Succos**; these enjoy a quasi-**Yom Tov** status.

chullin – lit. profane things; any substance that is not sanctified. See **kodesh.**

chupah – (a) the bridal canopy; (b) a procedure for effecting **nisuin,** the final stage of marriage.

closed mavoi – a dead-end alley enclosed on three sides and open to the public domain on the fourth side.

common characteristic – see **tzad hashaveh.**

Cutheans – a non-Jewish tribe brought by the Assyrians to settle the part of **Eretz Yisrael** left vacant by the exile of the Ten Tribes. Their subsequent conversion to Judaism was considered questionable and their observance of many laws was lax.

daf [pl. **dafim**] – folio (two sides) in the **Gemara.**

dayyo – lit. it is sufficient. Principle which limits the application of a **kal vachomer** argument, for it states: When a law is derived from case A to case B, its application to B cannot exceed its application to A.

death penalty – This refers to a court-imposed death penalty, in contrast to one imposed by Heaven.

dinar – a coin. The silver content of the coin was equivalent to ninety-six grains of barley. Its value was 1/25 of a gold *dinar*.

donated offering – There is a difference between a נֶדֶר, *neder* (vowed offering), and a נְדָבָה, *nedavah* (donated offering). In the case of a *neder,* the vower declares הֲרֵי עָלַי קָרְבָּן, "It is hereby incumbent upon me to bring a sacrifice." He fulfills his vow by later designating a specific animal as the sacrifice and offering it. In the case of a *nedavah,* the vower declares הֲרֵי זוּ קָרְבָּן, "This [animal] is a sacrifice," designating from the very start the particular animal he wishes to bring as an offering. In the case of a *neder,* if the designated animal is lost or dies, the vower must bring another in its place, since he has not yet fulfilled his vow "to bring a sacrifice." In the case of a *nedavah,* however, if anything happens to the designated animal the vower need not replace it since his vow was only to bring "*this* animal."

double payment – a punitive fine. A person convicted of theft is required to return both the stolen object (or its monetary equivalent) and pay the owner a fine equal to its value. If he stole a sheep or goat and slaughtered or sold it, he pays four times the value of the animal. If he stole an ox and slaughtered or sold it, he pays five times its value.

Elohim – (a) a Name of God; (b) [l.c.] sometimes used to refer to a mortal power or the authority of an ordained judge.

Elul – sixth month of the Hebrew calendar.

emurin – the portions of an animal offering burnt on the **Altar.**

ephah [pl. **ephos**] – a measure of volume equal to three **se'ah.**

Eretz Yisrael – Land of Israel.

erusin – betrothal, the first stage of marriage. This is effected by the man giving the woman an object of value, in the presence of witnesses, to betroth her. At this point the couple is not yet permitted to have conjugal relations, but is nonetheless considered legally married in most respects and the woman requires a divorce before she can marry again; see **nisuin.**

eruv – popular contraction of **eruvei chatzeiros, eruvei tavshilin,** or **eruvei techumin.**

eruvei chatzeiros – a legal device which merges several separate ownerships **(reshus hayachid)** into a single joint ownership. Each resident family of a **chatzeir** contributes food to the *eruv,* which is then placed in one of the dwellings of the *chatzeir.* This procedure allows us to view all the houses opening into the courtyard as the property of a single consortium (composed of all the residents of the courtyard). This permits all the contributing residents of the **chatzeir** to carry items during the Sabbath from the houses into the *chatzeir* and from one house to another.

eruvei tavshilin – the prepared food set aside prior to a **Yom Tov** that falls on Friday to serve as token food for the Sabbath that follows. Once this token food has been set aside, the person is allowed to complete his preparations for Sabbath on **Yom Tov.** Such preparation is generally forbidden otherwise.

eruvei techumin – merging of boundaries; a legal device that allows a person to shift his Sabbath residence from which the 2,000-**amah techum** is measured. This is accomplished by placing a specific amount of food at the desired location before the start of the Sabbath. The place where the food has been placed is then viewed as his Sabbath residence, and his *techum*-limit is measured from there. This does not extend his **techum** Shabbos, but merely shifts the point from which it is measured.

ervah [pl. **arayos**] – (a) matters pertaining to sexual relationships forbidden under penalty of **kares** or death, as enumerated in *Leviticus* ch. 18; (b) a woman forbidden to a man under pain of one of these penalties.

fines – punitive payments that do not bear a strict relation to actual damages.

forbidden labors of the Sabbath – see **avos melachah.**

forty lashes – see **malkus**.

Gaon [pl. **Geonim**] – (a) title accorded the heads of the academies in Sura and Pumbedisa, the two Babylonian seats of Jewish learning, from the late 6th to mid-11th centuries C.E. They served as the link in the chain of Torah tradition that joined the **Amoraim** to the **Rishonim;** (b) subsequently used to describe any brilliant Torah scholar.

Gemara – portion of the Talmud which discusses the **Mishnah;** also, loosely, a synonym for the Talmud as a whole.

gematria – the numeric valuation of the Hebrew alphabet.

get [pl. **gittin**] – bill of divorce; the document that, when it is placed in the wife's possession, effects the dissolution of a marriage.

gezeirah shavah – one of the thirteen principles of Biblical hermeneutics. If a similar word or phrase occurs in two otherwise unrelated passages in the **Torah,** the principle of *gezeirah shavah* teaches that these passages are linked to one another, and the laws of one passage are applied to the other. Only those words which are designated by the **Oral Sinaitic Law** for this purpose may serve as a basis for a *gezeirah shavah.*

Golden Altar – see **Inner Altar**.

Great Court – see **Sanhedrin**.

hachnasah – transferring an object from a public domain to a private domain.

hafarah – revocation of a woman's vow by her husband on the grounds that her vow impinges on their marital relationship or that it causes her deprivation.

hagbahah – lifting; one of the methods of acquisition used for movable objects.

halachah [pl. **halachos**] – (a) a **Torah** law; (b) [u.c.] the body of Torah law; (c) in cases of dispute, the position accepted as definitive by the later authorities and followed in practice; (d) a **Halachah LeMoshe MiSinai.**

Halachah LeMoshe MiSinai – laws taught orally to Moses at Sinai, which cannot be derived from the Written Torah.

half-shekel – While the Temple stood, every Jew was required to donate a half-*shekel* annually to fund the purchase of the various communal offerings (including among others, the daily **tamid** offerings and the holiday **mussaf** offerings).

hanachah – the *setting down* of a transferred article in its new domain; see ***akirah.***

Hashem – lit. the Name; a designation used to refer to God without pronouncing His Ineffable Name.

hasraah – warning. One does not incur the death penalty or lashes unless he was warned, immediately prior to commission, of the forbidden nature of the crime and the punishment to which he would be liable.

hatarah – annulment of a vow by an expert sage or a group of three competent laymen.

Havdalah – lit. distinction; the blessing recited at the conclusion of the Sabbath.

Hebrew maidservant – a Jewish girl between the age of six and twelve sold by her father into servitude.

Hebrew servant – a Jewish man who is sold as an indentured servant, generally for a six-year period. Either he is sold by the court because he was convicted of stealing and lacks the funds to make restitution, or he sells himself for reasons of poverty.

hechsher l'tumah – rendering a food susceptible to **tumah** contamination by contact with one of seven liquids – water, dew, milk, bee honey, oil, wine or blood.

hefker – ownerless.

hefker beis din hefker – principle which establishes the power of Rabbinic courts to declare property ownerless.

Heichal – See **Beis HaMikdash.**

hekdesh – (a) items consecrated to the **Temple** treasury or as offerings. *Hekdesh* can have two levels of sanctity: **monetary sanctity** and **physical sanctity.** Property owned by the Temple treasury is said to have monetary sanctity. Such property can be redeemed or can be sold by the *hekdesh* treasurers, and the proceeds of the redemption or sale become *hekdesh* in its place. Consecrated items that are fit for the Temple service (e.g. unblemished animals or sacred vessels) are deemed to have physical sanctity; (b) the state of consecration; (c) the **Temple** treasury.

hekeish – an exegetical derivation based on a connection that Scripture makes (often through juxtaposition) between different areas of law. By making this connection, Scripture teaches that the laws that apply to one area can be applied to the other area as well.

heset – see **tumas heset.**

hin – liquid measure equal to twelve **lugin.**

holachah – one of the four essential blood **avodos.** It involves conveying the blood of the offering to the **Altar.**

Holy – anterior chamber of the **Temple** edifice (**Heichal**) containing the **Shulchan, Inner Altar** and **Menorah.**

Holy Ark – the Ark containing the Tablets of the Ten Commandments and the Torah Scroll written by Moses. It stood in the **Holy of Holies.**

Holy of Holies – interior chamber of the **Temple** edifice **(Heichal).** During most of the First Temple era, it contained the **Holy Ark;** later it was empty of any utensil. Even the **Kohen Gadol** is prohibited from entering there except on **Yom Kippur.**

hotzaah – transferring an object from a private domain to a public domain.

Inner Altar – the gold-plated Altar which stood in the **Sanctuary.** It was used for the daily incense service and for the blood applications of inner **chataos.**

issaron – a dry measure equal to one tenth of an **ephah** or approximately (depending on the conversion factor) as little as eleven or as much as twenty-one cups.

Iyar – second month of the Hebrew calendar.

Jubilee – see **Yovel.**

kabbalah – (a) term used throughout the Talmud to refer to the books of the *Prophets.* It derives from the Aramaic root – to complain or cry out. It thus refers primarily to the admonitory passages of these books; (b) receiving in a **kli shareis** the blood of a sacrificial animal that is slaughtered; one of the four blood **avodos.**

kal vachomer – lit. light and heavy, or lenient and stringent; an *a fortiori* argument. One of the thirteen principles of Biblical hermeneutics. It involves the following reasoning: If a particular stringency applies in a usually lenient case, it must certainly apply in a more serious case; the converse of this argument is also a *kal vachomer.*

kares – excision; Divinely imposed premature death decreed by the **Torah** for certain classes of transgression.

karmelis – any area at least four **tefachim** square which cannot be classified as either a **reshus harabim,** *public domain* (because it is not set aside for public use) or a **reshus hayachid,** *private domain* (because it does not have the required partitions), e.g. a field, empty lot, or a four-*tefach* square elevation between three and ten **tefachim** above the ground level of a public domain.

karpaf – Mishnaic term for a large open area enclosed by a fence or wall. As a properly enclosed area, a *karpaf* is a **reshus hayachid** in every respect as long it does not exceed two **beis se'ah** (an area 50 *amos* x 100 *amos,* or 5,000 square *amos.* A *karpaf* larger than this, however, is subject to a special rule: Carrying in it is permitted only if the *karpaf* was enclosed for residential use. If it was not, then carrying in it is forbidden as in a **karmelis.**

kav [pl. **kabim]** – a measure equal to four **lugin.**

kebeitzah – an egg's volume.

Kehunah – priesthood; the state of being a **Kohen.**

keifel – see **double payment.**

kelutah – contained. Although an object thrown across a public domain does not *physically* come to rest in that domain, it does so *legally,* by way of the principle that an object "contained" in the airspace of a domain is viewed as if it had come to rest there.

kessef – (a) money; (b) Tyrian currency which is comprised solely of pure silver coins.

kesubah – (a) marriage contract; the legal commitments of a husband to his wife upon their marriage, the foremost feature of which is the payment awarded her in the event of their divorce or his death; (b) document in which this agreement is recorded.

Kesuvim – Hagiographa – Holy Writings. It consists of eleven volumes: *Psalms, Proverbs, Job, Song of Songs, Ruth, Lamentations, Ecclesiastes, Esther, Daniel, Ezra-Nehemiah, Chronicles.*

kezayis – the volume of an olive; minimum amount of food whose consumption is considered "eating."

kiddush – (a) the benediction recited over wine before the evening and morning meals on the **Sabbath** and **Yom Tov**; (b) sanctification of **mei chatas.**

kiddushin [betrothal] – Jewish marriage consists of two stages: **erusin** and **nisuin.** *Kiddushin* is the procedure which establishes the first stage of marriage [*erusin*].

kilayim – various forbidden mixtures, including: **shaatnez** (cloth made from a blend of wool and linen); cross-breeding of animals; cross-breeding (or side-by-side planting) of certain food crops; working with different species of animals yoked together; and mixtures of the vineyard.

kilei hakerem – forbidden mixtures of the vineyard; see **kilayim.**

kinyan [pl. **kinyanim]** – formal act of acquisition; an action that causes an agreement or exchange to be legally binding.

kinyan agav – lit. acquisition by dint of; the term for the acquisition of movable property by means of the acquisition of land. The **kinyan** used for the land serves for the movable property.

kinyan chalifin – lit. acquisition by exchange. (a) Even exchange: an exchange of two items of comparable value, in which each item serves as payment for the other. The acquisition of any one of the items automatically effects the acquisition of the other. (b) Uneven exchange: An item of relatively negligible value is given in order to effect the acquisition of the other item. A kerchief or the like is traditionally used.

kinyan chatzeir – the acquisition of movable property by virtue of it being in the premises of the person acquiring it.

kinyan chazakah – see **chazakah (b).**

kinyan sudar – see **kinyan chalifin (b).**

kirah – a rectangular stove that is open on top and is large enough to accommodate two pots. The pots may be placed inside the *kirah,* either directly on the coals or suspended above them, or on the rim or cover of the *kirah.*

Kislev – ninth month of the Hebrew calendar.

kli shareis [pl. **klei shareis]** – service vessel(s); a vessel sanctified for use in the sacrificial service.

kodashim kalim – offerings of lesser holiness (one of the two classifications of sacrificial offerings). They may be eaten anywhere in Jerusalem by any **tahor** person. They include the **todah,** regular **shelamim, bechor, nazir's ram, maaser** and **pesach offerings.** This category of offerings is not subject to the stringencies applied to **kodshei kodashim.**

kodesh – (a) any consecrated object; (b) the anterior chamber of the **Temple** – the **Holy;** (c) portions of sacrificial offerings.

kodshei kodashim – most-holy offerings (one of the two classifications of sacrificial offerings). They may be eaten only in the Temple courtyard and only by male **Kohanim.** They include the **olah** (which may not be eaten at all), **chatas, asham** and communal **shelamim.** These are subject to greater stringencies than **kodashim kalim.**

Kohen [pl. **Kohanim]** – member of the priestly family descended in the male line from Aaron. The Kohen is accorded the special priestly duties and privileges associated with the **Temple** service and is bound by special laws of sanctity.

Kohen Gadol – High Priest.

kor – large dry measure; a measure of volume consisting of thirty **se'ah.**

korah – a crossbeam, at least one **tefach** wide, reaching across a **mavoi** to serve as a rudimentary partition or a reminder of the *mavoi's* halachic status.

korban – a sacrificial offering brought in the **Beis HaMikdash.**

kri u'ksiv – a word in Scripture written one way but read differently by special directive to Moses at Sinai.

kupach – a cubical stove which accommodates only one pot. It retains more heat than a **kirah.**

lashes – see **malkus** and **makkas mardus.**

lavud – principle which states that whatever is within three **tefachim** of a surface is viewed as an extension of that surface; by the same token, a gap of less than three *tefachim* is legally viewed as closed.

leaning – see **semichah.**

lechatchilah – (a) before the fact; (b) performance of a **mitzvah** or procedure in the proper manner.

lechi – (a) a sidepost, at least ten **tefachim** high, placed at the side of a **mavoi** entrance to serve as a rudimentary partition or reminder of the *mavoi's* halachic status; (b) the sidepost of a **tzuras hapesach.**

Levi [pl. **Leviim**] – male descendant of the tribe of *Levi* in the male line, who is sanctified for auxiliary services in the **Beis HaMikdash.** The *Leviim* were the recipients of **maaser rishon.**

libation – see **nesachim.**

litra – (a) a liquid measure equal to the volume of six eggs; (b) a unit of weight.

log [pl. **lugin**] – a liquid measure equal to the volume of six eggs, between 16 and 21 ounces in contemporary measure.

maah [pl. **maos**]– the smallest silver unit in Talmudic coinage. Thirty-two copper **perutos** equal one *maah* and six *maos* equal a silver **dinar.**

Maariv – the evening prayer service.

maaser [pl. **maasros**] – tithe. It is a Biblical obligation to give two tithes, each known as *maaser,* from the produce of the Land of Israel. The first tithe (**maaser rishon**) is given to a **Levi.** The second tithe (**maaser sheni**) is taken to Jerusalem and eaten there or else is redeemed with coins which are then taken to Jerusalem for the purchase of food to be eaten there. In the third and sixth years of the seven year **shemittah** cycle, the *maaser sheni* obligation is replaced with **maaser ani,** the tithe for the poor.

maaser ani – see **maaser.**

maaser beheimah – the animal tithe. The newborn kosher animals born to one's herds and flocks are gathered into a pen and made to pass through an opening one at a time. Every tenth animal is designated as **maaser.** It is brought as an offering in the Temple and is eaten by the owner.

maaser of animals – see **maaser beheimah.**

maaser rishon – see **maaser.**

maaser sheni – see **maaser.**

mah matzinu – lit. just as we find; a **binyan av** from one verse. Just as one particular law possesses aspect A and aspect B, so any other law that possesses aspect A should also possess aspect B.

makkas mardus – lashes for rebelliousness. This is the term used for lashes incurred by Rabbinic – rather than Biblical – law.

malkus – the thirty-nine lashes (forty minus one) imposed by the court for violations of Biblical prohibitions, where a more severe punishment is not indicated.

mamzer [pl. **mamzerim**] [f. **mamzeress**] – (a) offspring of most illicit relationships punishable by **kares** or capital punishment; (b) offspring of a *mamzer* or *mamzeress.*

mamzerus – state of being a **mamzer.**

maneh – (a) equivalent to 100 **zuz;** (b) a measure of weight, equal to aproximately 17 ounces.

Marcheshvan – eighth month of the Hebrew calendar

matzah – unleavened bread; any loaf made from dough that has not been allowed to ferment or rise. One is Biblically obligated to eat *matzah* on the night of the 15th of Nissan.

mavoi – alley; specifically an alley into which **chatzeiros** (courtyards) open. See **shitufei mevo'os.**

mayim chayim – living water. Springwater generally has the status of *mayim chayim*. It is so designated because it issues out of the ground with a natural force which makes it "alive" and moving. It is fit to be used for three purposes for which the Torah specifies *mayim chayim*: (a) the immersion of **zavim,** (b) the sprinkling for **metzoraim,** (c) to consecrate therefrom **mei chatas.**

mayim sheuvin – drawn water; water that flows out of a vessel is designated as *sheuvin* and is unfit for use to constitute the forty **se'ah** of a **mikveh.**

mechussar kapparah [pl. **mechussar kippurim**] – lit. lacking atonement; the status accorded to a **tevul yom** in the interim between sunset of the day of his immersion and the time he brings his offerings. During that interval, he retains a vestige of his earlier **tumah** and is thus forbidden to enter the Temple Courtyard or partake of the offerings.

mei chatas – springwater consecrated by the addition of ashes of a **parah adumah.** This was used to purify individuals or objects of **tumas meis.**

me'ilah – unlawfully benefiting from **Temple** property or removing such property from the Temple ownership. As a penalty one must pay the value of the misappropriated item plus an additional one fifth of the value. He must also bring an **asham** offering.

meis mitzvah – see **abandoned corpse.**

mekom petur – exempt area; an area within – but distinct from – a public domain, which lacks the dimensions necessary to qualify as a **karmelis** (its width or length is less than four **tefachim**). One may carry from the exempt area into either a **reshus hayachid** or a **reshus harabim** or the reverse. Biblically a *karmelis* is a *mekom petur.*

melachah [pl. **melachos**] – labor; specifically, one of the thirty-nine labor categories whose performance is forbidden by the Torah on the Sabbath and **Yom Tov.** These prohibited categories are known as *avos melachah.* Activities whose prohibition is derived from one of these thirty-nine categories are known as *tolados* (s. *toladah*) – secondary labor.

melikah – the unique manner in which bird offerings were slaughtered. *Melikah* differs from **shechitah** in two respects: (a) The cut is made with the **Kohen's** thumbnail rather than with a knife; (b) the neck is cut from the back rather than from the throat. Only birds for sacrificial purposes may be slaughtered by *melikah;* all others require *shechitah.* See **shechitah.**

melog – a married woman's property in which she retains ownership of the property itself, but her husband enjoys the right of usufruct, i.e. he owns the yield of that property.

menachos – see **minchah.**

Men of the Great Assembly – a group of 120 sages active at the end of the Babylonian exile and during the early years of the Second Temple. They were responsible for the formulation of our prayers and many other enactments.

Menorah – the seven-branched gold candelabrum which stood in the **Holy.**

meshichah – pulling, or otherwise causing an object to move; one of the methods of acquisition used for movable property.

mesirah – handing over; transferring the animal to a buyer by handing him its reins or mane; a means of acquisition used for articles too heavy to be acquired via **meshichah** or **hagbahah.**

metzora – A *metzora* is a person who has contracted **tzaraas** (erroneously described as leprosy), an affliction mentioned in *Leviticus* (chs. 13,14). *Tzaraas* manifests itself (on people) as white or light-colored spots on the body.

mezuzah [pl. **mezuzos**] – a small scroll, containing the passages of *Deuteronomy* 6:4-9 and 11:13-21, that is affixed to the right doorpost.

midras – If someone who is **tamei** as a result of a bodily emission (e.g. a **zav, zavah, niddah,** woman who has given birth) sits or leans on a bed, couch, or chair, it acquires the same level of **tumah** as the person from whom the *tumah* emanates (i.e. **av hatumah**). This form of *tumah* transmission is called *midras.*

midras tumah – see **midras.**

migo – lit. since; a rule of procedure. If one makes a claim that on its own merits the court would reject, it nonetheless will be accepted "since" had he wished to tell an untruth he would have chosen a claim that certainly is acceptable to the court.

mikveh – ritualarium; a body of standing water containing at least forty **se'ah.** It is used to purify (by immersion) people and utensils of their **tumah**-contamination. A *mikveh* consists of waters naturally collected, without direct human intervention. Water drawn in a vessel is not valid for a *mikveh.*

mil – 2,000 **amos;** a measure of distance between 3,000 and 4,000 feet.

minchah – (a) [u.c.] the afternoon prayer service; (b) [pl. **menachos**] a flour offering, generally consisting of fine wheat flour, oil and frankincense, part of which is burnt on the **Altar.** See **kemitzah.**

minyan – quorum of ten adult Jewish males necessary for the communal prayer service and other matters.

Mishkan – predecessor of the **Temple.** See **Tabernacle.**

mishmar [pl. **mishmaros**] – lit. watch; one of the twenty-four watches of **Kohanim** and **Leviim** who served in the Temple for a week at a time on a rotating basis. These watches were subdivided into family groups each of which served on one day of the week.

Mishnah [pl. **Mishnahs**] – (a) the organized teachings of the **Tannaim** compiled by **R' Yehudah HaNasi;** (b) a paragraph of that work.

mitzvah [pl. **mitzvos**] – a **Torah** command whether of Biblical or Rabbinic origin.

mi'un – By Rabbinic enactment, an underaged orphan girl may be given in marriage by her mother or brothers. She may annul the marriage anytime before reaching majority by declaring, before a **beis din** of three judges, her unwillingness to continue in the marriage. This declaration and process is called *mi'un.*

mixtures of the vineyard – see **kilayim.**

monetary sanctity – see **hekdesh.**

movables, movable property – property that is transportable; in contrast to real estate.

muad – lit. warned one. A bull that gores three times and whose owner was duly warned after each incident to take precautions is considered a *muad* bull. The owner must pay full damage for the fourth and all subsequent incidents. See **tam.**

muchzak – one who has physical possession of an object and who is therefore assumed to be in legal possession of it.

muktzeh – lit. set aside; (a) a class of objects which, in the normal course of events, do not stand to be used on the Sabbath or **Yom Tov.** The Rabbis prohibited moving such objects on the Sabbath or Yom Tov; (b) an animal set aside to be sacrificed for idolatry.

mum [pl. mumim] – physical defects that render a **Kohen** or sacrifice unfit.

mussaf – (a) additional sacrifices offered on the Sabbath, **Rosh Chodesh,** or **Yom Tov;** (b) [u.c.] the prayer service which is recited in lieu of these sacrifices.

naarah – a girl at least 12 years old who has sprouted a minimum of two pubic hairs. This marks her coming of age to be considered an adult. She is deemed a *naarah* for six months; after that she becomes a **bogeres.**

naarus – the state of being a **naarah.**

Nasi [pl. **Nesiim**] – the Prince. He serves as the head of the **Sanhedrin** and de facto as the spiritual leader of the people.

nazir [f. **nezirah**] – a person who takes the vow of **nezirus,** which prohibits him to drink wine, eat grapes, cut his hair or contaminate himself with the **tumah** of a corpse.

nedavah – see **donated offering.**

neder – a vow which renders objects, in contradistinction to actions, prohibited. There are two basic categories of vows; (a) restrictive vows; (b) vows to donate to **hekdesh.** See **hekdesh;** see also **donated offering.**

negaim – spots that appear on the skin of a **metzora.**

nesachim – a libation, generally of wine, which is poured upon the **Altar.** It accompanies certain offerings; and can be donated separately as well.

neveilah [pl. **neveilos**] – the carcass of an animal that was not slaughtered according to procedure prescribed by the Torah. A *neveilah* may not be eaten. It is an **av hatumah.**

Neviim – Prophets; it consists of the following Books: *Joshua, Judges, Samuel, Kings, Jeremiah, Ezekiel, Isaiah,* **Twelve Prophets.**

nezirus – the state of being a **nazir.**

niddah – a woman who has menstruated but has not yet completed her purification process, which concludes with immersion in a **mikveh.**

Nissan – first month of the Hebrew calendar.

nisuin – second stage of marriage. It is effected by a procedure called **chuppah.** See **kiddushin.**

Noahide laws – the seven commandments given to Noah and his sons, which are binding upon all gentiles. These laws include the obligation to have a body of civil law, and the prohibitions against idolatry, immorality, bloodshed, blasphemy, stealing and robbing, and eating limbs from a live animal.

nolad – lit. newborn. This is a category of **muktzeh.** It refers to objects that came into their present state of being (they previously did not exist or were not usable) on Sabbath or **Yom Tov.** Since their very existence was unanticipated before Sabbath or Yom Tov, they are *muktzeh.*

nossar – part of a **korban** left over after the time to eat it has passed.

olah [pl. **olos**] – burnt or elevation offering; an offering which is consumed in its entirety by the **Altar** fire. It is one of the **kodshei kodashim.**

omer – an obligatory **minchah** offering brought on the sixteenth of **Nissan.** It was forbidden to eat from the new grain crop (**chadash**) before this offering was brought.

onein [f. **onenes;** pl. **onenim**] – see **aninus.**

Oral Sinaitic Law – see **Halachah LeMoshe MiSinai.**

orlah – lit. sealed; fruit that grows on a tree during the first three years after it has been planted (or transplanted). The Torah prohibits any benefit from such fruit.

Outer Altar – the **Altar** that stood the Courtyard of the **Beis HaMikdash,** to which the blood of most offerings is applied, and on which the offerings are burned.

parah adumah – lit. red cow. The ashes of the *parah adumah* are mixed with springwater. The resulting mixture is known as **mei chatas** and is used in the purification process of people or objects who have contracted **tumah** from a human corpse.

Paroches – curtain: specifically, the curtain that divided the **Holy** from the **Holy of Holies.**

parsah [pl. **parsaos**] – measure of length equal to eight thousand **amos.**

pasul – lit. invalid; (a) any *tamei* object that cannot convey its **tumah;** (b) something invalid.

peace offering – see **shelamim.**

perutah [pl. **perutos**] – smallest coin used in Talmudic times. In most cases its value is the minimum that is legally significant.

Pesach – Passover; the **Yom Tov** that celebrates the Exodus of the Jewish nation from Egypt.

pesach offering – sacrifice offered on the afternoon of the fourteenth day of **Nissan** and eaten after nightfall. It is one of the **kodashim kalim.**

Pesach Sheni – lit. Second **Pesach;** (a) the fourteenth of **Iyar.** This day fell one month after the **Yom Tov** of Pesach. Any individual who is **tamei** at the time designated for the **pesach offering** must wait till *Pesach Sheni* to bring his offering; (b) a *pesach* offering brought on the fourteenth of Iyar.

physical sanctity – see **hekdesh.**

pikuach nefesh – lit. saving a life; a life-threatening situation. All prohibitions (except for murder, immorality and idolatry) are waived, if necessary, in such situations.

positive commandment – a Torah commandment expressed as a requirement *to do.*

poskim – authoritative decisors of Torah law.

Priestly Blessing – the blessing the **Kohanim** are obligated to confer upon the congregation. It consists of the verses designated for this purpose by the Torah (*Numbers* 6:24-26). It is recited aloud by the **Kohanim**, toward the conclusion of the **Shemoneh Esrei.**

prohibition – a negative commandment, which the Torah expresses as a command *not to do.*

Prophets – see **Neviim.**

prozbul – The Torah requires all loans to be canceled by **shemittah.** The Rabbis enacted a law allowing for loans to be collected after the Sabbatical year through a process whereby the lender authorizes the court to collect all his debts. The document which authroizes the court to assume responsibility for the collection of those debts is called a *prozbul.*

p'sik reisha – This is "the rule of inevitable consequence." It states that if the performance of a permissible act will *inevitably* result in the occurrence of a prohibited act, that the otherwise permissible act is forbidden.

purification waters – see **mei chatas.**

rasha – (a) a wicked person; (b) a person disqualified from serving as a witness by his commission of certain transgressions.

R' – Rabbi; specifically a **Tanna,** or **Amora** of **Eretz Yisrael.**

Rebbi – R' Yehudah HaNasi; the redactor of the **Mishnah.**

regel – any of the three pilgrimage festivals – **Pesach, Shavuos** and **Succos.**

Reish Gelusa – Exilarch, head of the Babylonian Jewish community; parallels the **Nasi** in **Eretz Yisrael.**

reshus harabim – lit. public domain; any unroofed, commonly used street, public area or highway at least sixteen **amos** wide and open at both ends. According to some, it must be used by at least 600,000 people.

reshus hayachid – lit. private domain; any area measuring at least four **tefachim** by four *tefachim* and enclosed by partitions at least ten *tefachim* high. According to most opinions, it needs to be enclosed only on three sides to qualify as a *reshus hayachid*. Private ownership is not a prerequisite.

revii l'tumah – see **tumah.**

reviis – a quarter of a **log.**

ribbis – a Talmudic term for interest.

Rishon [pl. **Rishonim**] – a **Torah** authority of the period following the **Geonim** (approx. 1000-1500 C.E.).

rishon l'tumah – first degree of acquired **tumah.** See **tumah.**

Rosh Chodesh – (a) festival celebrating the new month; (b) the first of the month.

Rosh Hashanah – the **Yom Tov** that celebrates the new year. It falls on the first and second days of **Tishrei.**

rov – majority; a principle used in halachah to determine the origin or status of a particular object. An object of undetermined origin or status is assumed to partake of the same origin or status as do that of the majority. See also **bitul b'rov.**

rova – a quarter-**kav** (one twenty-fourth of a **se'ah**).

Sabbath residence – (a) one's halachic place of dwelling (for the Sabbath); (b) wherever one happens to be at the beginning of the Sabbath, i.e. an area of four **amos,** if one is in a completely open space, or the building or city in which he is located.

Sadducees – heretical sect active during the Second **Temple** era named after Tzaddok, a disciple of Antigonas of Socho. They denied the Divine origin of the **Oral Law** and refused to accept the Sages' interpretation of the **Torah.**

Sages – (a) the collective body of Torah authorities in the Mishnaic era; (b) the anonymous majority opinion in a **Mishnah** or **Baraisa;** (c) [l.c.] Torah scholar and authority.

Sanctuary – a term applied to the Temple building that housed the **Holy** and the **Holy of Holies.**

Sanhedrin – (a) the High Court of Israel; the Supreme Court consisting of seventy-one judges whose decisions on questions of Torah law are definitive and binding on all courts; (b) [l.c.] a court of twenty-three judges authorized to adjudicate capital and corporal cases.

se'ah – a Mishnaic measure of volume; six **kav.**

Seder [pl. **Sedarim**] – lit. order. (a) The Mishnah is divided into six *sedarim*: *Zeraim* (Plants), *Moed* (Festivals), *Nashim* (Women), *Nezikim* (Damages), *Kodashim* (Sacred Things) and *Taharos* (Ritual Purities); (b) [l.c.] ritual festive meal on **Pesach.**

sekilah – lit. stoning; one of the four forms of death penalty imposed by the court.

sela [pl. **selaim**] – a silver coin having the weight of 384 barleycorns. This is the equivalent of four **dinars.**

semichah – (a) Rabbinical ordination empowering one to serve as a judge. This ordination stretches back in an unbroken chain to Moses; (b) a rite performed with almost all personal sacrificial offerings. The owner of the offering places both his hands on the top of the animal's head and presses down with all his might. In the case of a **chatas,** or an **asham,** he makes his confession during *semichah*. In the case of a **shelamim** or **todah** offering, he praises and thanks God.

semuchin [pl. **semuchim**] – Scriptural juxtaposition. This principle states that two consecutive verses or passages may be compared for purposes of inferring law from one to the other. It is one of the rules of exegesis employed by the Sages.

seven species – see **bikkurim.**

shaatnez – see **kilayim.**

Shabbos – (a) the Sabbath; (b) the Talmudic tractate that deals with the laws of the Sabbath.

Shacharis – the morning prayer service.

Shavuos – Pentecost; the festival that celebrates the giving of the **Torah** to the Jewish nation at Mount Sinai.

Shechinah – Divine Presence.

shechitah – (a) ritual slaughter; the method prescribed by the **Torah** for slaughtering a kosher animal to make it fit for consumption. It consists of cutting through most of the esophagus and windpipe from the front of the neck with a specially sharpened knife that is free of nicks; (b) one of the four essential blood **avodos.**

shehiyah – This refers to the act of leaving a pot of cooked food on a **kirah** before the Sabbath so that it will continue to stew on the Sabbath.

shekel [pl. **shekalim, shekels**] – Scriptural coin equivalent to the Aramaic **sela** or four **dinars.** In Mishnaic terminology, the Scriptural half-*shekel* is called a **shekel,** and the Scriptural **shekel** is called by its Aramaic name, **sela.**

shelamim – peace offering; generally brought by an individual on a voluntary basis; part is burnt on the **Altar,** part is eaten by a **Kohen** (and the members of his household) and part is eaten by the owner. It is one of the **kodashim kalim.**

shelichus – see **agency.**

shelishi l'tumah – see **tumah.**

Shemini Atzeres – the eighth and concluding day of the **Succos** celebration. In many respects, it is a **Yom Tov** in its own right.

shemittah – the Sabbatical year, occurring every seventh year, during which the land of **Eretz Yisrael** may not be cultivated.

Shemoneh Esrei – also called *Amidah*; the silent, standing prayer, which is one of the main features of the daily prayer services.

sheni l'tumah – see **tumah.**

sheretz [pl. **sheratzim**] – one of eight rodents or reptiles, listed by the Torah, whose carcasses transmit **tumah.** A sheretz is an *av hatumah.* See **tumah.**

Shevat – eleventh month of the Hebrew calendar.

sheviis – see **shemittah.**

shitufei mevo'os – incorporation of the alleys; a provision similar to **eruvei chatzeiros,** instituted to permit carrying from a courtyard into an alley on the Sabbath. It merges the different courtyards that are in common ownership of a **mavoi.**

shofar – trumpet formed from the horn of a ram or certain other animals. It is a Biblical obligation to hear the blowing of a *shofar* on **Rosh Hashanah.**

shomer [pl. **shomrim**] – one who has assumed custodial responsibility for another's property.

shtar [pl. **shtaros**] – legal document.

Shulchan – lit. table; the golden Table for the **lechem hapanim,** located in the **Holy.**

shuman – animal fats that are permitted for consumption. See **cheilev.**

Sifra – lit. the book; the primary collection of Tannaic exegesis, mainly halachic in nature, on the Book of *Leviticus.* It is also known as *Toras Kohanim.*

Sifri (or Sifrei) – lit. the books; the counterpart of the **Sifra;** it expounds on the Books of *Numbers* and *Deuteronomy.*

Sivan – third month of the Hebrew calendar.

sotah – an adulteress or a woman whose suspicious behavior has made her suspected of adultery. The Torah prescribes, under specific circumstances, that her guilt or innocence be established by having her drink specially prepared water.

sprinkling – see **hazaah.**

stoning – see **sekilah.**

succah – (a) the temporary dwelling in which one must live during the festival of **Succos;** (b) [u.c.] the Talmudic tractate that deals with the laws that pertain to the festival of Succos.

Succos – one of the three **pilgrimage festivals,** during which one must dwell in a **succah.**

Tabernacle – a portable **Sanctuary** for the sacrificial service used during the forty years of national wandering in the Wilderness and the first fourteen years after entry into **Eretz Yisrael.**

taharah – a halachically defined state of ritual purity; the absence of **tumah**-contamination.

tahor – person or object in a state of **taharah.**

tam – lit. ordinary; a bull the first three times it gores another animal. See **muad.**

tamei – person or object that has been contaminated by **tumah** and that can convey *tumah* to another object of its genre.

tamid [pl. **temidin**] – communal **olah,** offered twice daily.

Tammuz – fourth month of the Hebrew calendar.

Tanna [pl. **Tannaim**] – Sage of the Mishnaic period whose view is recorded in a **Mishnah** or **Baraisa.**

Tanna Kamma – the anonymous first opinion of a **Mishnah** or **Baraisa.**

tanur – a trapezoidal oven that is open on top. Its shape causes it to retain more heat than a **kirah.**

tarkav – half a **se'ah.**

Targum – lit. translation; the Aramaic interpretive translation of Scripture.

techum [pl. **techumim**] – Sabbath boundary; the distance of 2,000 **amos** from a person's Sabbath residence which he is permitted to travel on the Sabbath or **Yom Tov.**

tefach [pl. **tefachim**] – handbreadth; a measure of length equal to the width of four thumbs.

tefillah – (a) prayer; (b) in Talmudic usage, **tefillah** invariably refers to **Shemoneh Esrei.**

tefillin – phylacteries; two black leather casings, each of which contains Torah passages written on parchment. It is a **mitzvah** for adult males to wear one on the head and one on the arm.

temei'ah – female for **tamei.**

Temple – see **Beis HaMikdash.**

Temple Mount – the site of the Holy **Temple.** See **Beis HaMikdash.**

tereifah [pl. tereifos] – (a) a person, animal or bird that possesses one of a well-defined group of eighteen defects which will certainly cause its death. Any of these defects renders the animal or bird prohibited for consumption even if it was ritually slaughtered; (b) a generic term for all non-kosher food.

terumah [pl. **terumos**] – the first portion of the crop separated and given to a **Kohen,** usually between 1/40 and 1/60 of the total crop. It is separated prior to **maaser,** and upon separation attains a state of sanctity which prohibits it from being eaten by a non-**Kohen,** or by a **Kohen** in a state of **tumah.**

terumah gedolah – see **terumah.**

terumas maaser – the tithe portion separated by the **Levi** from the **maaser rishon** he receives and given to a **Kohen.**

tevel – produce of **Eretz Yisrael** that has become subject to the obligation of **terumah** and **tithes;** it is forbidden for consumption until *terumah* and all tithes have been designated.

Teves – tenth month of the Hebrew calendar.

tevilah – immersion in a **mikveh** for the purpose of purification from **tumah**-contamination.

tevul yom [pl. **tevulei yom**] lit. one who has immersed that day. This is a person who had been rendered ritually impure with a Biblical **tumah** from which he purified himself with immersion in a **mikveh.** A residue of the *tumah* lingers until nightfall of the day of his immersion, leaving him *tamei* in regard to sacrifices, **terumah** and entering the **Temple** Courtyard. A person in this reduced state of *tumah* is known as a *tevul yom.*

Tishah B'Av – lit. the Ninth of Av; the fast day that commemorates the destruction of the First **Beis HaMikdash** and the Second one as well as other national tragedies.

Tishrei – seventh month of the Hebrew calendar.

todah [pl. **todos**] – thanksgiving offering brought when a person survives a potentially life-threatening situation. It is unique in that forty loaves of bread accompany it.

toladah [pl. **tolados**] – lit. offspring; subcategory of an **av** (pl. **avos**). See **melachah.**

Torah – the five books of Moses; the Chumash or Pentateuch.

Tosefta – a written collection of **Baraisos**.

tumah [pl. **tumos**] – legally defined state of ritual impurity affecting certain people or objects. The strictest level of *tumah,* **avi avos hatumah** [literally: father of fathers of *tumah*], is limited to a human corpse. The next, and far more common level, is known as *av hatumah,* primary [literally: father] *tumah.* This category includes: one who touched a human corpse; **sheretz,** the carcass of one of the eight species of creeping creatures listed in *Leviticus* 11:29-30; the carcass of a **neveilah,** an animal that died by some means other than a valid ritual slaughter; or one who is a **zav, zavah, niddah** or **metzora.**

An object that is contaminated by an **av hatumah** [primary *tumah*] becomes a **rishon l'tumah** (first degree of [acquired] *tumah*). This degree of contamination is also called **v'lad hatumah,** (secondary *tumah*) [literally: child (as opposed to *av,* father) of *tumah*]. An object contracting *tumah* from a *rishon* becomes a **sheni l'tumah,** (second degree *of* [acquired] *tumah*) – or **v'lad v'lad hatumah,** (child of child of *tumah*). In the case of *chullin,* unsanctified food, contamination can go no further than a *sheni;* thus, if a *sheni* touches unsanctified food, that food acquires no degree of contamination whatsoever.

Commensurate with the respectively greater degrees of stringency associated with **terumah** and sacrifices, their levels of contamination can go beyond that of *sheni.* Thus, if a *sheni* touches *terumah,* it becomes a **shelishi l'tumah** (third degree of [acquired] *tumah*) but the *tumah* of *terumah* goes no further than this degree. Sacrificial items can go a step further, to **revii l'tumah** (fourth degree of [acquired] *tumah*).

As a general rule, the word **tamei,** contaminated, is applied to an object that can convey its *tumah* to another object of its genre. An object that cannot convey its *tumah* in this way is called **pasul** invalid rather than *tamei.*

tumas heset – lit. moving; a form of **tumas masa** (carrying *tumah*) that is generated by a **zav, zavah, niddah** or a woman who has given birth, by moving people, utensils, foods, or liquids, or by a **tahor** person moving the **zav,** etc.

tumas meis – the **tumah** of a human corpse.

tumas midras – see **midras**

tumas ohel – lit. roof **tumah;** the *tumah* conveyed to objects or persons when they are under the same roof as certain *tumah* conveyors, generally a human corpse.

Twelve Prophets – the final Book of the Prophets which consists of twelve short prophetic works: *Hosea, Joel, Amos, Obadiah, Jonah, Micah, Nahum, Habakkuk, Zephaniah, Haggai, Zechariah, Malachi.*

twofold payment – see double payment.

tzad hashaveh – an exegetical derivation based on the pre- sumption that a law found in two contexts results from characteristics common to both rather than from characteristics unique to each. Any other context possessing these common characteristics is also subject to the common law, even if the third context differs from the first two in regard to their *unique* features.

tzaraas – see **metzora.**

tzitzis – the fringes that by **Torah** law must be placed on a four-cornered garment.

tzuras hapesach – a structure shaped in the form of a doorway and effective as a partition; it consists of two posts topped by a connecting bar. This halachic device is widely used to convert an open area into a private domain.

variable [chatas] offering – a special type of **chatas** offering whose quality varies in accordance with the sinners financial resources. He is liable to a regular *chatas* offering of a female lamb or kid only if he is a person of means. Should he be poor, he is required to bring only two turtledoves or two young pigeons, one as a *chatas* and the other as an **olah.** If he is very poor, he brings a tenth of an **ephah** of fine flour for a **minchah.**

v'lad hatumah – see **tumah.**

v'lad v'lad hatumah – see **tumah.**

Women's Courtyard – the Courtyard of the **Temple** that faced the eastern wall of the main Courtyard.

yad soledes bo – heating to a degree that one's hand recoils when it comes into contact with it.

yavam – see **yibum.**

yetzer hara – Evil Inclination.

ye'ush – abandonment. This refers to an owner's despairing of recovering his lost or stolen property.

yevamah – see **yibum.**

yibum – levirate marriage. When a man dies childless, the **Torah** provides for one of his brothers to marry the widow. This marriage is called *yibum*. Pending this, the widow is forbidden to marry anyone else. The surviving brother, upon whom the obligation to perform the **mitzvah** of *yibum* falls, is called the *yavam.* The widow is called the *yevamah. Yibum* is effected only through cohabitation. If the brother should refuse to perform *yibum*, he must release her from her *yibum*-bond by performing the alternate rite of *chalitzah,* in which she removes his shoe before the court and spits before him and declares: *So should be done to the man who will not build his brother's house* (*Deuteronomy* 25:5-10).

Yisrael [pl. **Yisraelim**] – (a) Jew; (b) Israelite (in contradistinction to **Kohen** or **Levi**).

Yom Kippur – Day of Atonement; a day of prayer, penitence, fasting and abstention from **melachah.**

Yom Tov [pl. **Yamim Tovim**] – holiday; the festival days on which the Torah prohibits **melachah.** Specifically, it refers to the first and last days of **Pesach,** the first day of **Succos, Shemini Atzeres, Shavuos, Yom Kippur** and the two days of **Rosh Hashanah.** Outside of Eretz Yisrael, an additional day of **Yom Tov** is added to each of these festivals, except **Yom Kippur** and **Rosh Hashanah.**

Yovel – fiftieth year [Jubilee]; the year following the conclusion of a set of seven **shemittah** cycles. On **Yom Kippur** of that year, the **shofar** is sounded to proclaim freedom for the Jewish servants, and to signal the return to the original owner of fields sold in **Eretz Yisrael** during the previous forty-nine years.

zav [pl. **zavim**] – a man who has become **tamei** because of a specific type of seminal emission. If three emissions were experienced during a three-day period, the man must bring offerings upon his purification.

zavah [pl. **zavos**] – After a woman concludes her seven days of **niddah,** there is an eleven-day period during which any menseslike bleeding renders her a *minor zavah.* If the menstruation lasts for three consecutive days, she is a *major zavah* and must bring offerings upon her purification.

zerikah [pl. **zerikos**] – throwing; applying the blood of an offering to the Outer **Altar** in the prescribed manner. It is one of the four essential blood **avodos.**

zivah – lit. seepage or flow; the type of discharge which if repeated renders one to be a **zav** or **zavah.**

zuz [pl. **zuzim**] – (a) monetary unit equal to a **dinar;** (b) a coin of that value; (c) the weight of a *zuz* coin.

Scriptural Index